THE ALL ENGLAND LAW REPORTS

Consolidated Tables and Index
1936–2022

Volume 3
Subject Index

Sections I–Z

Index Editor
WENDY HERRING MA (Oxon)
of Lincoln's Inn, Barrister

Index Manager
JACEY SIVADASAM LLB, Dip LP

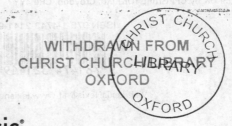
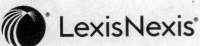 LexisNexis

LexisNexis® UK & Worldwide

United Kingdom	RELX (UK) Limited trading as LexisNexis®, 1–3 Strand, London WC2N 5JR
LNUK Global Partners	LexisNexis® encompasses authoritative legal publishing brands dating back to the 19th century including: Butterworths® in the United Kingdom, Canada and the Asia-Pacific region; Les Editions du Juris Classeur® in France; and Matthew Bender® worldwide. Details of LexisNexis® locations worldwide can be found at www.lexisnexis.com

First published in 2022
© 2022 RELX (UK) Ltd.

Published by LexisNexis®

This is a Butterworths® title

ISBN for this volume
ISBN 9781474321419

ISBN for complete set of volumes
ISBN 9781474321426

Typeset in the UK by Letterpart Ltd, Caterham on the Hill, Surrey CR3 5XL

Printed in the UK by CPI Group (UK) Ltd, Croydon, CR0 4YY

ISBN 978-1-4743-2141-9

9 781474 321419

Visit LexisNexis® at www.lexisnexis.co.uk

THE
ALL ENGLAND
LAW REPORTS

Consolidated
Tables and Index
1936–2022

Volume 3

THE
ALL ENGLAND
LAW REPORTS

Consolidated
Tables and Index
1936–2022

Volume 3

Introduction

The purpose of the subject index is to enable the reader to obtain the names and references of cases on a particular topic. The arrangement of the index follows the conventional pattern of legal indexes, being based on an alphabetical sequence of main headings each of which is subdivided into further sub-headings, also arranged in alphabetical sequence, covering topics which fall within the generality of the main heading. For every entry, other than cross-reference entries, the process of subdivision has been taken two stages further. Thus each entry has been classified under a main index heading and three further sub-headings in descending order of generality. If superior headings have not already done so, the third level of sub-heading should identify with sufficient particularity the entries relevant to the particular topic on which the reader is seeking authority.

For example, a reader who is searching for cases on the duty of disclosure under a contract of marine insurance should refer to the general heading 'MARINE INSURANCE'. He will there find over 100 entries listed under that heading. Almost all of those cases will clearly be irrelevant to the point on which the reader is seeking authority. The next step, therefore, is to turn to the sub-heading 'Contract of marine insurance' under the general heading 'MARINE INSURANCE'. He will there find ten entries listed under that sub-heading. The search may however be taken two stages further by turning to the sub-sub-heading 'Disclosure', which covers seven entries, and the further sub-heading 'Duty to disclose' which will reveal six entries expressly on the topic on which authority is being sought.

The different levels of heading and sub-heading are indicated typographically thus:

> **MARINE INSURANCE**
> Contract of marine insurance—
> Disclosure—
> Duty to disclose—

The main heading and first two levels of sub-headings are not repeated for every entry to which they relate but only for the first relevant entry and, for convenience, at the top of each new page, followed by '(cont)—' to indicate the continuation.

It will not usually be necessary to proceed to the third level of sub-heading to identify relevant cases with sufficient particularity. Thus, a reference to the sub-heading 'Deviation' under the main heading 'MARINE INSURANCE' will reveal that there is only one case on that topic.

In most cases main entries, ie entries other than cross-reference entries, do not conclude with the third level of sub-heading but continue with sufficient 'catchphrases' to indicate the salient facts of the case referred to and/or the point of law on which the case is authority. Main entries conclude with the name of the case which is being referred to and its citation.

In searching for entries on a particular topic, the reader will not always choose the same words or phrase, or start with the same generality of heading, as that used in the index. For this reason the index has been fully cross-referenced. Thus, a reader searching for cases on mutual wills who looks up the main heading '**MUTUAL WILLS**' will find a cross-reference stating: 'Generally. *See* **Will** (Mutual Wills)', indicating that he should refer to the sub-heading 'Mutual Wills' under the main heading '**WILL**'.

Cross-reference entries fall into two categories: (i) cross-references from one main heading to another main heading (external cross-references) and (ii) cross-references within the limits of a particular main heading (internal cross-references). All cross-references of either variety begin with the word '*See*' in italic type.

(i) In external cross-references the word '*See*' is followed by a word or phrase in bold type followed, where appropriate, by further words or phrases within brackets. The word or phrase in bold type denotes the main heading which is being referred to and the words in brackets the sub-headings under that main heading to which reference should be made in order to locate the entries on the topic in question. The following are examples: '*See* **Auctioneer**' means that the reader should refer to all the entries under the heading '**AUCTIONEER**'; '*See* **Landlord and tenant** (Forfeiture of lease—Arrears of rent)' means that the reader should refer to the sub-sub-heading 'Arrears of rent' under the sub-heading 'Forfeiture of lease' under the main heading '**LANDLORD AND TENANT**'.

(ii) In internal cross-references there are no words in bold type or in brackets. The word '*See*' is followed by words or phrases in ordinary Roman type which are in turn followed by the word '*above*' or '*below*' in italic type. These indicate the sub-heading and, where appropriate, further sub-headings which appear under the same main heading as the cross-reference itself. Thus under the main heading '**PATENT**' there is a sub-heading 'Certiorari' followed by a sub-sub-heading 'Patent appeal tribunal'. This is followed by the cross-reference '*See* Appeal tribunal—Certiorari to quash decision of tribunal, *above*'. This indicates that to locate the relevant entries, the reader should refer to the sub-sub-heading 'Certiorari to quash decision of tribunal' under the sub-heading 'Appeal tribunal' under the same main heading '**PATENT**'. Internal cross-references always start with the principal sub-heading under the relevant main heading, even though the cross-reference entry itself may also appear under that sub-heading. Thus following the entry:

ROAD TRAFFIC
Breath test—
Suspicion of alcohol

there is a cross-reference '*See* Breath test—Person driving or attempting to drive—Suspicion of alcohol, *above*'. This refers to the entry under the sub-sub-heading 'Person driving or attempting to drive' under the same principal sub-heading 'Breath test'.

LexisNexis
December 2022

I

ICE
    Highway—
        Obstruction—
            Civil liability for failure to remove obstruction. *See* **Highway** (Obstruction—Removal—Civil liability for failure to remove obstruction—Snow and ice on highway).

ICE CREAM VAN
    Chimes in street—
        Advertisement. *See* **Advertisement** (Trade or business—Use of loudspeaker for advertising purposes—Prohibition against loudspeaker being operated in street for purpose of advertising any trade or business).

IDENTIFICATION PARADE
    Criminal proceedings. *See* **Criminal evidence** (Identity—Identification parade).

IDENTITY
    Defamation cases—
        Identification of plaintiff as person defamed. *See* **Libel and slander** (Identification of plaintiff as person defamed).
        Persons to whom publication made—
            Innuendo—Persons having knowledge of facts rendering published words defamatory—Duty to plead particulars identifying those persons. *See* **Libel and slander** (Innuendo—Particulars—Duty of plaintiff to plead facts on which he relies for his claim—Identity of persons to whom publication made and who have knowledge of facts which render published words defamatory).
    Evidence in criminal proceedings—
        Generally. *See* **Criminal evidence** (Identity).
        Jamaica. *See* **Jamaica** (Criminal evidence—Identity).
    False identity documents—
        Criminal law. *See* **Criminal law** (False identity documents).
    Maintainer—
        Maintenance of action. *See* **Maintenance of action** (Identity of maintainer).
    Mistake—
        Contract. *See* **Contract** (Mistake—Identity of party).
        Lessee's identity. *See* **Landlord and tenant** (Lease—Avoidance—Mistake as to identity of lessee).
    Witness—
        Disclosure of identity in breach of court ruling—
            Contempt of court. *See* **Contempt of court** (Witness—Disclosure of identity).
        Order against disclosure of witness's identity—
            Criminal proceedings. *See* **Criminal law** (Trial—Witnesses—Identity).

IDENTITY CARD
    Student travel scheme—
        Sale of card for purpose of scheme—
            Value added tax—Zero-rating—Transport of passengers. *See* **Value added tax** (Zero-rating—Transport of passengers—Supply of travel concession voucher—Student travel scheme—Sale of identity card for purpose of scheme).

ILL-TREATMENT
    Child—
        Proceedings in juvenile court. *See* **Children and young persons** (Care proceedings in juvenile court—Conditions to be satisfied before making order—Neglect or ill-treatment of child or young person).

ILLEGAL DISTRESS
    Damages. *See* **Distress** (Distress for rent—Illegal distress—Damages).

ILLEGAL ENTRANT
    Detention. *See* **Immigration** (Detention—Illegal entrant).

ILLEGAL PREMIUM
    Lease. *See* **Rent restriction** (Premium).

ILLEGAL SALE
    Aiding and abetting. *See* **Criminal law** (Aiding and abetting—Illegal sale).

ILLEGAL USER
    Premises. *See* **Landlord and tenant** (Lease—Illegal purpose—Illegal user of premises).

ILLEGALITY
    Bill of exchange. *See* **Bill of exchange** (Illegality).
    Building contract. *See* **Building contract** (Illegality).
    Commission—
        Estate agent. *See* **Estate agent** (Commission—Illegal commission).
    Contract. *See* **Contract** (Illegality).
    Conversion—
        Defence. *See* **Conversion** (Defence—Illegality).

ILLEGALITY (cont)—
Defence to civil claim—
Fraud—
Claimant purchasing property with assistance of mortgage advance procured by fraud—Solicitors failing to register transfer—Claim against solicitors for breach of duty—Solicitors admitting breach of duty—Whether claim barred by illegality—Proper balance of policy considerations. **Grondona v Stoffel & Co** [2021] **1 Comm** 1139, SC; [2021] **2** 239, SC.
Manslaughter—
Patient killing mother during psychotic episode—Plea of manslaughter by reason of diminished responsibility accepted—Claim against NHS trust for breach of duty—NHS trust admitting breach of duty—Whether claim barred by illegality—Proper balance of policy considerations. **Henderson (a protected party, by her litigation friend the Official Solicitor) v Dorset Healthcare University NHS Foundation Trust** [2021] **2** 257, SC.
Fraud—
Defence. *See* **Tort** (Fraud—Defence of illegality).
Hire-purchase—
Generally. *See* **Hire-purchase** (Illegality).
Passing of property under illegal agreement. *See* **Contract** (Illegality—Passing of property—Hire-purchase agreement).
Insurance. *See* **Insurance** (Illegality).
Lease—
Agreement for lease. *See* **Landlord and tenant** (Agreement for lease—Illegality).
Covenant—
Exclusion of jurisdiction of court. *See* **Contract** (Illegality—Public policy—Jurisdiction of court—Exclusion—Lease).
Reinsurance business. *See* **Insurance** (Reinsurance—Reinsurance business—Illegality).

ILLEGALLY OBTAINED EVIDENCE
Criminal proceedings. *See* **Criminal evidence** (Illegally obtained evidence).

ILLEGITIMATE CHILD
Access—
Child in care of local authority—
Access by putative father. *See* **Child** (Welfare—Child in care of local authority—Access by putative father).
Jurisdiction of court to entertain application by putative father. *See* **Child** (Care—Local authority—Illegitimate children—Putative father applying for interim access and custody).
Adoption—
Consent. *See* **Adoption** (Consent—Parent or guardian—Parent—Parent of illegitimate child).
Custody and—
Conflicting applications. *See* **Adoption** (Custody—Illegitimate child—Conflicting applications).
Generally. *See* **Adoption** (Illegitimate child).
Affiliation proceedings. *See* **Affiliation**.
Care of local authority—
Generally. *See* **Child** (Care—Local authority—Illegitimate child).
Child of family—
Divorce. *See* **Divorce** (Infant—Child of the family).
Custody—
Child in care. *See* **Child** (Care—Local authority—Assumption by authority of parental rights—Illegitimate child—Custody).
Custody and adoption—
Conflicting applications. *See* **Adoption** (Custody—Illegitimate child—Conflicting applications).
Financial relief—
Generally. *See* **Child** (Illegitimate child—Financial relief).
Legitimation—
Conflict of laws. *See* **Conflict of laws** (Legitimation).
Generally. *See* **Legitimation**.
Local authority—
Assumption of parental rights. *See* **Child** (Care—Local authority—Assumption by authority of parental rights—Illegitimate child).
Maintenance. *See* **Minor** (Maintenance—Illegitimate child).
Mental patient's child—
Settlement. *See* **Mental health** (Patient's property—Settlement—Illegitimate son).
Parental rights and duties. *See* **Child** (Illegitimate child—Parental rights and duties).
Succession to personal property in England. *See* **Will** (Legitimacy—Succession to personal property in England).
Will—
Generally. *See* **Will** (Children—Illegitimate child).

ILLNESS
Absence from work—
Frustration of contract of employment—
Short-term periodic contract. *See* **Employment** (Contract of service—Frustration—Short-term periodic contract—Absence from work because of illness).
Mental. *See* **Mental health**.

IMMIGRATION
Adoption—
Leave to enter. *See* Leave to enter—Adoption, *below*.
Adoption application and immigration control—
Factors to be considered. *See* **Adoption** (Order—Discretion—Nationality—Immigration control).
Appeal—
Appeal to adjudicator. *See* Leave to enter—Refusal of leave—Appeal—Appeal to adjudicator, *below*.

Asylum and Immigration Tribunal—
Assessment of risk—Relationship between lack of credibility and assessment of risk—Impact of asylum claimant's lies—Approach of Court of Appeal to interference with assessment of facts made by tribunal on grounds of error of law. **MA (Somalia) v Secretary of State for the Home Dept** [2011] **2** 65, SC.
Matters to be considered on appeal—Appeal against refusal of entry clearance tribunal to consider only circumstances appertaining at time of decision to refuse—Right to respect for private and family life—Whether exclusion of evidence concerning matters arising after date of decision to refuse incompatible with right to respect for private and family life—Human Rights Act 1998, Sch 1, Pt I, art 8—Nationality, Immigration and Asylum Act 2002, s 85(4), (5). **AS (Somalia) v Secretary of State for the Home Dept** [2009] **4** 711, HL.
Matters to be considered on appeal—Requirement to state additional grounds for application—Jurisdiction of tribunal—Nationality, Immigration and Asylum Act 2002, ss 82, 84, 85, 96, 120. **AS (Afghanistan) v Secretary of State for the Home Dept** [2010] **2** 21, CA.
Reconsideration of decision—Scope of reconsideration—Procedure—Guidance—Nationality, Immigration and Asylum Act 2002, s 103A—Asylum and Immigration Tribunal (Procedure) Rules 2005, SI 2005/230, rr 30(2), 32(2). **DK (Serbia) v Secretary of State for the Home Dept** [2007] **2** 483, CA.
Reconsideration of decision—Transfer of proceedings to immigration judge to enable additional facts to be found—Whether new judge should receive original decision—Nationality, Immigration and Asylum Act 2002—Asylum and Immigration (Treatment of Claimants, etc) Act 2004. **Swash v Secretary of State for the Home Dept** [2007] **1** 1033, CA.
Reconsideration of decision—Whether High Court having power to set aside decision made by it on application for order requiring tribunal to reconsider appeal decision—Nationality, Immigration and Asylum Act 2002, s 103A. **R (on the application of AM (Cameroon)) v Asylum and Immigration Tribunal** [2008] **4** 1159, CA.
Asylum seeker. See Asylum seeker—Appeal, *below.*
Commonwealth citizen. See **Commonwealth immigrant** (Appeal).
Conditions on which leave to enter granted—
Appeal after entry against conditions imposed on entry—Procedure—Rules regulating appeal—Applicant wishing to appeal after entry against conditions imposed on entry—Whether applicant required to leave United Kingdom and apply for fresh entry—Immigration Act 1971, ss 13, 14—Statement of Immigration Rules for Control on Entry: Commonwealth Citizens (1972-73), para 70. **R v Immigration Appeal Tribunal, ex p Coomasaru** [1983] **1** 208, CA.
Court of appeal—
Practice. See **Court of Appeal** (Practice—Civil Division—Asylum and immigration cases).
Decision relating to person's entitlement to enter or remain in United Kingdom—
Approach to appeal in which proportionality in issue—Immigration and Asylum Act 1999, s 65. **Edore v Secretary of State for the Home Dept** [2003] **3** 1265, CA.
Decision-making role and function of appellate immigration authorities. See Leave to enter—Refusal of leave—Appeal, *below.*
Deportation—
Appeal against deportation on grounds of national security—Secretary of State concluding that Pakistani national supporting terrorist organisation abroad and deciding to deport him on grounds of national security—Appeals commission not being satisfied of truth of factual allegations on high civil balance of probabilities—Whether activities capable of being threat to national security if not targeted at United Kingdom or its citizens—Whether appeals commission applying correct approach to standard of proof. **Secretary of State for the Home Dept v Rehman** [2002] **1** 122, HL.
Appeal against deportation on grounds of national security—Special Immigration Appeals Commission—Fairness of proceedings—Right to respect for private and family life—Whether right to respect for private and family life giving rise to irreducible minimum of procedural fairness—Human Rights Act 1998, Sch 1, Pt I, art 8—Special Immigration Appeals Commission (Procedure) Rules 2003, SI 2003/1034. **IR (Sri Lanka) v Secretary of State for the Home Dept** [2011] **4** 908, CA.
Appeal against deportation on grounds of national security—Special Immigration Appeals Commission—Prohibition of torture—Fairness of proceedings—Secretary of State deciding to deport Algerian nationals on grounds of national security—Algerian nationals appealing to Special Immigration Appeals Commission—Both 'closed' and 'open' material before Commission—Whether proceedings fair—Human Rights Act 1998, Sch 1, Pt I, art 3. **RB (Algeria) v Secretary of State for the Home Dept** [2008] **2** 786, CA.
Appeal against deportation on grounds of national security—Special Immigration Appeals Commission—Prohibition of torture—Fairness of proceedings—Secretary of State deciding to deport foreign nationals on grounds of national security—Foreign nationals appealing to Special Immigration Appeals Commission—Commission using 'closed material'—Commission dismissing appeals—Grounds for challenging commission's decisions—Whether appeal confined to error of law—Whether use of 'closed material' breaching right to fair trial—Whether United Kingdom authorities entitled to rely on assurances from receiving states—Whether detention for 50 days without charge flagrant breach of right to liberty—Whether military court in receiving state or risk of use of evidence obtained by torture flagrant breaches of right to fair hearing—Special Immigration Appeals Commission Act 1997, s 7—Human Rights Act 1998, Sch 1, Pt I, arts 3, 5, 6. **RB (Algeria) v Secretary of State for the Home Dept** [2009] **4** 1045, HL.
Appeal against deportation on grounds of national security—Special Immigration Appeals Commission—Secretary of State concluding that Pakistani national supporting terrorist organisation abroad and deciding to deport him on grounds of national security—Appeal commission not being satisfied of truth of allegations on high civil balance of probabilities standard—Whether activities not targeted against United Kingdom capable of being threat to national security—Whether appeal commission applying correct approach to standard of proof. **Secretary of State for the Home Dept v Rehman** [2000] **3** 778, CA.

IMMIGRATION (cont)—
  Appeal (cont)—
    Deportation (cont)—
      Appeal against deportation on grounds of national security—Special Immigration Appeals Commission—Secretary of State deciding to deport appellant Algerian nationals on grounds of national security—Appellants seeking to adduce evidence from witness on appeal of risk of ill-treatment of appellants if returned to Algeria—Witness fearing persecution from Algerian authorities if evidence given by and identity of witness communicated by Secretary of State to Algerian authorities—Whether open to Special Immigration Appeals Commission to make order for absolute and irreversible guarantee of total confidentiality in respect of witness's identity and evidence before that identity and evidence disclosed to Secretary of State. **W (Algeria) v Secretary of State for the Home Dept** [2012] **2** 699, SC.
      Appeal to tribunal from adjudicator—When leave must be granted—Direction that person is to be removed to country where he fears persecution—Is to be removed—Iraqi citizen required to leave United Kingdom—Applicant fearing persecution if he returned to Iraq—Whether applicant to be treated as a person 'to be removed' to Iraq—Whether applicant having right of appeal from adjudicator to tribunal—Immigration Act 1971, s 14(1)—Immigration Appeals (Procedure) Rules 1972, r 14(2)(b). **R v Immigration Appeal Tribunal, ex p Enwia** [1983] **2** 1045, CA.
      Deportation pending appeal—Illegal entrant—Entrant claiming refugee status—Whether illegal entrant claiming refugee status entitled to remain in United Kingdom pending appeal—Whether removal of entrant prior to appeal contrary to United Kingdom's obligations under 1951 Geneva Convention on Refugees—Immigration Act 1971, s 13(3)—Convention and Protocol relating to the Status of Refugees 1951, art 35. **Bugdaycay v Secretary of State for the Home Dept** [1987] **1** 940, HL.
      Deportation pending appeal—Statutory provision requiring Secretary of State to issue certificate in respect of certain asylum claims unless satisfied that asylum or human rights claims 'not clearly unfounded'—Whether procedure for dealing with such claims fair—Approach to be adopted in determining whether claims 'not clearly unfounded'—Nationality, Immigration and Asylum Act 2002, s 115. **R (on the application of L) v Secretary of State for the Home Dept** [2003] **1** 1062, CA.
      Detention pending deportation—Statutory power to detain non-nationals suspected of terrorism—Whether power constituting lawful derogation from right to liberty—Human Rights Act 1998, Sch 1, Pt I, arts 5, 14—Anti-terrorism, Crime and Security Act 2001, s 23—Human Rights Act 1998 (Designated Derogation) Order 2001, SI 2001/3644. **A v Secretary of State for the Home Dept** [2003] **1** 816, CA; [2005] **3** 169, HL.
      Earlier right of appeal—Appeal against immigration decision not to be brought if claim or application to which decision relates relying on matter that could have been raised in appeal against previous decision—Meaning of 'matter'—Nationality, Immigration and Asylum Act 2002, s 96(1)(b). **R (on the application of Khan) v Secretary of State for the Home Dept** [2013] **3** 499, QBD; [2014] **2** 973, CA.
      Function of immigration adjudicator—Power to inquire into decision to deport—Whether adjudicator entitled to inquire whether person making decision to deport had power to do so—Whether adjudicator entitled to inquire whether decision to deport invalid—Immigration Act 1988, s 5(1). **Oladehinde v Secretary of State for the Home Dept** [1990] **3** 393, HL.
      Matters to be considered on appeal against deportation—Relevant factors and circumstances—Compassionate circumstances—Appellant illegally overstaying leave to enter—Appellant becoming valued member of Sikh community in United Kingdom—Whether effect of deportation on third party interests a relevant factor or circumstance—Whether effect of appellant's deportation on Sikh community relevant—Statement of Changes in Immigration Rules (HC Paper (1982-83) no 66), paras 154, 156, 158. **Singh v Immigration Appeal Tribunal** [1986] **2** 721, HL.
      Right of appeal—Appeal against immigration decision—Appeal while appellant in United Kingdom—Statute providing right of appeal while appellant in United Kingdom where appellant has made asylum claim or human rights claim while in United Kingdom—Appellants subject of deportation orders—Appellants unsuccessfully appealing against orders on human rights and/or Refugee Convention grounds—Secretary of State declining to revoke deportation orders—Whether expression 'an asylum claim, or a human rights claim' limited to first asylum or human rights claim or second or subsequent claim accepted as a 'fresh claim'—Nationality, Immigration and Asylum Act 2002, ss 82(2)(k), 92(4)(a), 94(2), 96, 113(1)—Statement of Changes in the Immigration Rules 1994 (HC 395), r 353. **R (on the application of BA (Nigeria)) v Secretary of State for the Home Dept** [2010] **2** 95, SC.
      Right of appeal—Appeal against immigration decision—Appeal while appellant in United Kingdom—Statute providing right of appeal while appellant in United Kingdom where appellant has made asylum claim or human rights claim while in United Kingdom—Meaning of 'has made a claim', 'an asylum claim, or a human rights claim'—Nationality, Immigration and Asylum Act 2002, ss 82, 92(4)(a). **R (on the application of Etame) v Secretary of State for the Home Dept** [2008] **4** 798, QBD.
      Right of appeal—Appeal against immigration decision—Human rights claim—Foreign national's human rights claims against deportation rejected and rights of appeal exhausted—Foreign national making further representations on human rights to Secretary of State—Secretary of State concluding that further representations not 'fresh claim'—Whether right of appeal existing in respect of human rights claims not accepted as 'fresh claims' by Secretary of State—Nationality, Immigration and Asylum Act 2002, ss 82, 92, 94—Immigration Rules 1994 (HC 395), r 353. **R (on the application of Robinson (formerly JR (Jamaica))) v Secretary of State for the Home Dept** [2019] **3** 741, SC.
      Right of appeal—Limited right of appeal—Applicant entering United Kingdom and becoming liable to deportation before 1 August 1988—Notice of decision to deport given after 1 August 1988—No right of appeal on merits after 1 August 1988 against Home Secretary's discretion to deport—Whether provision limiting right of appeal validly brought into force—Whether legislation having retrospective effect—Whether persons entering United Kingdom and becoming liable to deportation before 1 August 1988 having right of appeal on merits against Home Secretary's discretion to deport—Immigration Act 1971, s 3(5)(a), 19(1)—Immigration Act 1988, ss 5(1), (5), 12(4). **R v Secretary of State for the Home Dept, ex p Mundowa** [1992] **3** 606, CA.

4

IMMIGRATION (cont)—
Appeal (cont)—
Dismissal of appeal in absence of immigrant—
Remedy available to immigrant—Reference of case to adjudicator by Secretary of State for further consideration—Procedure—Duty of adjudicator—Immigration Act 1971, s 21. **Al-Mehdawi v Secretary of State for the Home Dept** [1989] **3** 843, HL.
Secretary of State's power to refer case to adjudicator for further consideration—Whether reason for failure of appeal relevant factor in determining whether to exercise power of referral—Immigration Act 1971, s 21. **R v Secretary of State for the Home Dept, ex p Yousaf** [2000] **3** 649, CA.
Evidence—
Appellant arriving at port of entry with expired United Kingdom passport and claiming right of abode—Immigration officer refusing appellant leave to enter—Statutory provision confining appeal on grounds of right of abode to those producing United Kingdom passport or certificate of entitlement—Whether passport having to be current—Whether right of abode provable on appeal by means other than those prescribed—Immigration Act 1971, ss 3, 13, 33. **Akewushola v Secretary of State for the Home Dept** [2000] **2** 148, CA.
Evidence of facts coming into existence after Secretary of State's decision—Whether adjudicator or appeal tribunal can admit evidence of facts occurring after Secretary of State's decision—Immigration Act 1971, s 14. **R v Immigration Appeal Tribunal, ex p Bastiampillai** [1983] **2** 844, QBD.
Evidence of facts coming into existence after entry clearance officer's decision—Whether adjudicator or appeal tribunal can admit evidence of facts occurring after entry officer's decision—Immigration Act 1971, s 19(2)—Immigration Appeals (Procedure) Rules 1972, rr 18(1), 29(1). **R v Immigration Appeal Tribunal, ex p Kotecha** [1983] **2** 289, CA.
Evidence of facts existing at time of Secretary of State's decision—Secretary of State deciding to deport applicant—Secretary of State unaware of facts when decision to deport made—Whether adjudicator or tribunal can admit evidence of facts not considered by Secretary of State—Immigration Act 1971, s 19. **R v Immigration Appeal Tribunal, ex p Hassanin** [1987] **1** 74, CA.
Explanatory statement by Home Office of facts relating to Secretary of State's decision or action—Evidence of facts coming into existence after Secretary of State's decision—Whether Home Office statement a pleading or evidence in appeal—Whether adjudicator can admit evidence of facts occurring after Secretary of State's decision—Immigration Act 1971, s 19(1)—Immigration Appeals (Procedure) Rules 1972, r 8(1). **R v Immigration Appeal Tribunal, ex p Weerasuriya** [1983] **1** 195, QBD.
Extension of time. *See* Practice—Asylum and Immigration Tribunal granting permission to appeal to Court of Appeal, *below.*
Immigration adjudicator—
Duty to hear parties. *See* **Natural justice** (Hearing—Duty to hear parties etc—Immigration adjudicator).
Jurisdiction to dispense with oral hearing—Conditions to be satisfied—No party to appeal requesting hearing—Applicants instructing Immigrants Advisory Service to lodge appeal and request oral hearing—Advisory service failing to record applicants' change of address and unable to notify them of hearing date—Advisory service inviting adjudicator to dispense with oral hearing—Adjudicator dismissing appeal without hearing—Whether adjudicator entitled to dismiss appeal without hearing—Immigration Appeals (Procedure) Rules 1972, r 12. **Rahmani v Diggines** [1986] **1** 921, HL.
Immigration Appeal Tribunal—
Appeal from special adjudicator—Source and nature of tribunal's power to remit appeal to special adjudicator—Whether full tribunal having power to set aside or vary order of chairman of tribunal sitting alone—Immigration Act 1971, ss 19, 20, 22—Immigration Appeals (Procedure) Rules 1984, rr 21, 38—Asylum Appeals (Procedure) Rules 1996, r 17(2). **R (on the application of the Secretary of State for the Home Dept) v Immigration Appeal Tribunal** [2001] **4** 430, QBD.
Approach to be taken by tribunal in considering political and legal situation in foreign country in recurrent classes of applications for asylum. **Shirazi v Secretary of State for the Home Dept** [2004] **2** 602, CA.
Hearing of appeal—Hearing—Jurisdiction to dispense with oral hearing—Power to dispose of appeal without hearing if leave to appeal granted and hearing not warranted—Whether power to dispose of appeal without hearing intra vires—Immigration Act 1971, s 22(1), (5)—Immigration Appeals (Procedure) Rules 1984, r 20(c). **R v Immigration Appeal Tribunal, ex p Jones** [1988] **2** 65, CA.
Judicial review—Failed asylum seekers unsuccessfully applying for statutory review of Immigration Appeal Tribunal's refusal of permission to appeal—Asylum seekers applying for judicial review—Whether availability of judicial review ousted by provision of statutory review—Whether refusal of judicial review discriminatory—Human Rights Act 1998, Sch 1, Pt I, art 14—Nationality, Immigration and Asylum Act 2002, s 101. **R (on the application of G) v Immigration Appeal Tribunal** [2004] **3** 286, QBD; [2005] **2** 165, CA.
Jurisdiction—Claimant entering United Kingdom and applying for asylum—Claimant residing in Scotland—Adjudicator in England dismissing appeal against refusal of asylum—Tribunal in England refusing leave to appeal from adjudicator's decision—Claimant applying to Court of Session for judicial review of decisions of tribunal and adjudicator—Whether Court of Session having jurisdiction. **Tehrani v Secretary of State for the Home Dept (Scotland)** [2007] **1** 559, HL.
Leave to appeal—
Generally. *See* Leave to appeal, *below.*
Non-compliance with procedural requirement—Secretary of State applying for leave to appeal against decisions to grant asylum—Secretary of State not using prescribed form in making application—Whether failure to use prescribed form rending appeal a nullity—Immigration Appeals (Procedure) Rules 1984, r 38—Asylum Appeals (Procedure) Rules 1993, r 13(3). **R v Immigration Appeal Tribunal, ex p Jeyeanthan** [1999] **3** 231, CA.
Leave to appeal. *See* Leave to remain—Appeal , *below.*
Leave to remain. *See* Leave to remain—Appeal , *below.*

5

IMMIGRATION (cont)—

Appeal (cont)—

Notice of appealable decision—

Giving of notice—Notice sent by recorded delivery to person's last known place of abode—Whether notice 'given' to person—Immigration Appeals (Notices) Regulations 1972, reg 6. **R v Secretary of State for the Home Dept, ex p Yeboah** [1987] **3** 999, CA.

Giving of notice—Special adjudicator dismissing appeal against refusal of asylum—Notice of determination being sent to asylum seeker's old address—Rule of procedure providing that application for leave to appeal could not be made later than five days after receipt of determination—Further rule deeming that determination received on certain date 'regardless of when or whether it was received'—Whether deeming provision ultra vires for purposes of application for leave to appeal—Immigration Act 1971, ss 20(1), 22—Asylum Appeals (Procedure) Rules 1996, rr 13(2), 42(1)(a). **R v Secretary of State for the Home Dept, ex p Saleem** [2000] **4** 814, CA.

Whereabouts of person entitled to appeal unknown to authorities—Notice of decision to deport not required to be given to persons whose whereabouts are unknown—Secretary of State sending notice by recorded delivery to person's last known address—Notice returned undelivered—Whether return of notice sufficient evidence that person's whereabouts unknown—Immigration Appeals (Notices) Regulations 1972, reg 3(4). **R v Secretary of State for the Home Dept, ex p Yeboah** [1987] **3** 999, CA.

Whereabouts of person entitled to appeal unknown to authorities—Regulations providing that written notice need not be given to persons whose whereabouts are unknown—Whether regulations ultra vires—Immigration Act 1971, s 18(1)(a)—Immigration Appeals (Notices) Regulations 1972 (SI 1972 No 1683), r 3(4). **R v Immigration Appeal Tribunal, ex p Mehmet** [1977] **2** 602, QBD.

Whereabouts of person entitled to appeal unknown to authorities—Regulations providing that written notice need not be given to persons whose whereabouts are unknown—Whether regulations ultra vires—Whether unreasonable to send notice to last known address when person known not to be abiding there—Immigration Act 1971, s 18(1)—Immigration Appeals (Notices) Regulations 1984, regs 3, 6. **Pargan Singh v Secretary of State for the Home Dept** [1992] **4** 673, HL.

Procedure for challenging appeal decision—

Administrative Court. *See* **Practice** (Administrative Court—Procedure for challenging decisions of Immigration Appeal Tribunal).

Public interest considerations—

Precarious immigration status—Financial independence—Secretary of State making determination to remove appellant Tanzanian national from UK—Appellant contending that determination unlawful for violation of right to respect for private life—Statute providing that little weight to be given to private life established when immigration status precarious—Whether appellant's immigration status 'precarious'—Whether appellant 'financially independent'—Human Rights Act 1998, Sch 1, Pt 1, art 8—Nationality, Immigration and Asylum Act 2002, ss 117A, 117B. **Rhuppiah v Secretary of State for the Home Dept** [2019] **1** 1007, SC.

Reasons for decision—

Immigration Appeal Tribunal—Appeal against deportation order made on ground that applicant had entered into marriage of convenience—Tribunal dismissing appeal—Reasons for decision not making it apparent, directly or by inference, that tribunal had considered all the elements constituting marriage of convenience—Whether failure to give adequate reasons an error of law. **R v Immigration Appeal Tribunal, ex p Khan (Mahmud)** [1983] **2** 420, CA.

Rehearing—

Asylum claimant from Iraq claiming asylum in United Kingdom in 2000—Adjudicator finding claimant to be a refugee—Immigration Appeal Tribunal allowing appeal against adjudicator's decision—Claimant appealing—Circumstances in Iraq changing—Court of Session allowing appeal and remitting case for rehearing by new adjudicator—Whether court correct to remit case for rehearing. **Saber v Secretary of State for the Home Dept** [2008] **3** 97, HL.

Right of appeal—

Asylum claim—Grant of leave to remain for period exceeding one year—Application for variation of leave to remain as refugee—Secretary of State rejecting asylum claim—Period of leave remaining at time of refusal less than one year—Whether right of appeal—Nationality, Immigration and Asylum Act 2002, s 83. **MS (Uganda) v Secretary of State for the Home Dept** [2017] **3** 709, SC.

Directions for removal—Whether right of appeal against immigration decision on ground that 'country' or 'territory' of destination stated in notice of decision not one that would satisfy statutory requirements should removal directions to that country or territory be given—Meaning of 'immigration decision'—Immigration Act 1971, Sch 2, para 8(1)(c) - Nationality, Immigration and Asylum Act 2002, s 82(2)(h). **MS (Palestinian Territories) v Secretary of State for the Home Dept** [2010] **4** 866, SC.

Special Immigration Appeals Commission, from—

Jurisdiction. *See* **Court of Appeal** (Jurisdiction—Appeal from Special Immigration Appeals Commission).

Time limit for appealing—

Appeal to tribunal from adjudicator—Appeal to tribunal within prescribed period—Leave to appeal granted by adjudicator on oral application—Notice of appeal to be served as soon as practicable thereafter—Whether time limit applicable where leave given on oral application—Whether notice of appeal to be served as soon as practicable and in any event within prescribed period—Immigration Appeals (Procedure) Rules 1970 (SI 1970 No 794), rr 13(1), (2), 14(1), (2). **R v Immigration Appeal Tribunal, ex p Samaraweera** [1974] **2** 171, QBD.

Notice not given within limitation period—Discretion of adjudicator or tribunal to allow appeal to proceed—Discretion where by reason of special circumstances just and right to do so—Matters constituting 'special circumstances'—Merits of case—Mistake on part of appellant's legal advisers—Immigration Appeals (Procedure) Rules 1972, (SI 1972 No 1684), r 11(4). **Mehta v Secretary of State for the Home Dept** [1975] **2** 1084, CA.

IMMIGRATION (cont)—
Appeal (cont)—
  Tribunal—
    Immigration and Asylum Chamber—Fast track rules ('FTR')—FTR governing asylum and immigration appeals against refusal of asylum applications—Whether rules ultra vires—Effect of declaration that rules ultra vires—Application to quash or set aside appeal decision—Asylum and Immigration Tribunal (Fast Track Procedure) Rules 2005, SI 2005/560—Tribunal Procedure (First-tier Tribunal) (Immigration and Asylum Chamber) Rules 2014, SI 2014/2604. **R (on the application of TN (Vietnam)) v Secretary of State for the Home Dept** [2017] **4** 399, QBD; [2019] **3** 433, CA; [2022] **1** 1005, SC.
    Immigration and Asylum Chamber—Jurisdiction—First-tier Tribunal—Whether First-tier Tribunal having jurisdiction to set aside earlier appeal decision—Tribunals, Courts and Enforcement Act 2007, s 9, Sch 5, para 15—Asylum and Immigration Tribunal (Fast Track Procedure) Rules 2005, SI 2005/560—Tribunal Procedure (First-tier Tribunal) (Immigration and Asylum Chamber) Rules 2014, SI 2014/2604, rr 32, 35, 36, 46. **R (on the application of TN (Vietnam)) v First-tier Tribunal (Immigration and Asylum Chamber)** [2019] **3** 460, DC.
    Immigration and Asylum Chamber—Matters to be considered on appeal—Requirement to state additional grounds for application—New evidence—Nationality, Immigration and Asylum Act 2002, ss 85, 120—Immigration, Asylum and Nationality Act 2006, s 47. **Patel v Secretary of State for the Home Dept** [2014] **1** 1157, SC.
Assisting illegal entry into United Kingdom—
  Assisting entry—
    Knowingly carrying out arrangements for facilitating entry of anyone known or believed to be illegal entrant—Arrangements carried out after entrant having entered United Kingdom—Whether an offence—Immigration Act 1971, s 25(1). **R v Singh (Amar Jit)** [1973] **1** 122, CA.
    Knowingly carrying out arrangements for facilitating entry of persons known or believed to be illegal entrants or asylum claimants—Whether actual entry essential ingredient of offences—Immigration Act 1971, s 25(1). **R v Eyck** [2000] **3** 569, CA.
  Illegal entry—
    Asylum seeker—Asylum seeker using false documents to leave country of origin—Asylum claimed immediately on disembarkation in United Kingdom—False documents not used to gain entry into United Kingdom—Whether asylum seeker 'illegal entrant'—Whether person assisting asylum seeker to enter United Kingdom facilitating illegal entry—Immigration Act 1971, ss 3, 11, 25. **R v Naillie** [1993] **2** 782, HL.
Asylum—
  Persecution, fear of. *See* Leave to enter—Refugee—Asylum—Fear of persecution by applicant for refugee status, *below.*
  Refugee—
    Decision of United Nations High Commission granting refugee status—Effect of grant of refugee status—Weight to be given to decision granting refugee status in domestic asylum claim. **IA v Secretary of State for the Home Dept** [2014] **1** 1015, SC.
    Qualification for subsidiary protection—Serious harm—Appellant presenting suicide risk—Whether appellant being a 'person eligible for subsidiary protection'—Whether real risk of serious harm to physical or psychological health if returned to country of origin—Human Rights Act 1998, Sch 1, Pt I, art 3—Council Directive 2004/83/EC, arts 2, 15. **MP (Sri Lanka) v Secretary of State for the Home Dept** [2017] **2** 155n, SC.
    Temporary admission—Removal—Eritrean national formerly resident in Ethiopia claiming asylum in United Kingdom—Well-founded fear of persecution if returned to Eritrea—Secretary of State proposing removal to Ethiopia—Whether person recognised to be refugee and having temporary admission for the purpose of the determination of a claim for asylum 'lawfully' in United Kingdom—Meaning of 'lawfully'—United Nations Convention relating to the Status of Refugees 1951, art 32. **R (on the application of ST (Eritrea)) v Secretary of State for the Home Dept** [2012] **3** 1037, SC.
Asylum and Immigration Tribunal—
  Appeal. *See* Appeal, *above.*
Asylum seeker—
  Appeal—
    Abandonment of appeal—Deemed abandonment of pending appeal—Asylum-seeker leaving United Kingdom while appeal to Court of Appeal pending—Whether appeal to Court of Appeal deemed abandoned—Immigration and Asylum Act 1999, s 58(8). **Shirazi v Secretary of State for the Home Dept** [2004] **2** 602, CA.
    Appellants' claims for asylum in United Kingdom dismissed—Appellants granted discretionary leave to remain for less than 12 months as unaccompanied minors disallowing immediate right to statutory appeal—Secretary of State breaching duty to trace families of appellants—Whether breach vitiating refusal of claims to asylum—Whether corrective justice requiring court to grant asylum—Whether lack of statutory right to appeal depriving appellants of 'effective remedy'—Nationality, Immigration and Asylum Act 2002, ss 82, 83—Council Directive 2005/85/EC, art 39—Asylum Seekers (Reception Conditions) Regulations 2005, SI 2005/7, reg 6. **TN (Afghanistan) v Secretary of State for the Home Dept** [2015] **4** 34, SC.
    Certification of claims as 'clearly unfounded'—Fresh claim—Further submissions made following certification—Secretary of State not considering immigration rule relating to fresh claims in affirming certification—Whether immigration rule relating to fresh claims applying—Whether test for certification and test under immigration rule differing—Approach by court in respect of challenge to either certification or rejection of fresh claim—Nationality, Immigration and Asylum Act 2002, s 94—Statement of Changes in the Immigration Rules 1994 (HC 395), r 353. **ZT (Kosovo) v Secretary of State for the Home Dept** [2009] **3** 976, HL.
    Certification of claims as 'clearly unfounded'—Fresh claim—Test of 'realistic prospect of success'—Whether test for certification and test under immigration rule differing—Guidance—Approach by court in respect of challenge to either certification or rejection of fresh claim—Nationality, Immigration and Asylum Act 2002, s 94(2) - Statement of Changes in the Immigration Rules 1994 (HC 395), r 353. **R (on the application of YH) v Secretary of State for the Home Dept** [2010] **4** 448, CA.

IMMIGRATION (cont)—
   Asylum seeker (cont)—
      Decision (cont)—
         Delay in reaching decision—Right to respect for private and family life—Right to request permission to take up employment—Asylum applicant having right to apply for permission to take up employment if decision not taken on asylum application within one year—Failed asylum seeker making fresh claim—Policy delaying consideration of fresh claim for several years—Failed asylum seeker applying for permission to take up employment—Failed asylum seeker not 'asylum applicant' until fresh claim considered—Whether breach of right to respect for private and family life—Human Rights Act 1998, Sch 1, Pt I, art 8. **Tekle v Secretary of State for the Home Dept** [2009] **2** 193, QBD.

      Deportation—
         Inhuman or degrading treatment—Asylum seeker from Uganda suffering from HIV/AIDS—Asylum seeker receiving anti-retroviral drugs in United Kingdom—Asylum seeker likely to die within two years without drugs—Ability to obtain necessary medication problematic if asylum seeker returned to Uganda—Whether return of asylum seeker with HIV/AIDS incompatible with convention right not to be subjected to inhuman or degrading treatment—Human Rights Act 1998, Sch 1, Pt I, art 3. **N v Secretary of State for the Home Dept** [2005] **4** 1017, HL.

         Right to respect for private and family life—Foreign national with criminal record in United Kingdom claiming asylum—Secretary of State refusing asylum and ordering deportation—Circumstances in which deportation of foreign criminal contrary to right to respect for private and family life—Whether interference with family life proportionate—Proper interpretation of new immigration rules—Human Rights Act 1998, Sch 1, Pt I, art 8—Statement of Changes in Immigration Rules (HC Paper 395) paras 398-399A. **MF (Nigeria) v Secretary of State for the Home Dept** [2014] **2** 543, CA.

         Right to respect for private and family life—Prohibition of discrimination—Father in Lebanon awarded custody of son with mother awarded physical custody of son until age of seven—Father entitled to require transfer of physical custody of son at age of seven—Father having seen son only on day of his birth—Mother leaving Lebanon with son and claiming asylum—Whether removal of mother and son breach of right to respect for private and family life—Whether breach of prohibition of discrimination—Human Rights Act 1998, Sch 1, Pt I, arts 8, 14. **EM (Lebanon) v Secretary of State for the Home Dept** [2009] **1** 559, HL.

      Destitute asylum seeker with disabled children—
         Duty to provide adequate accommodation—Meaning of 'adequate'—Whether duty of providing adequate accommodation for destitute asylum seeker with disabled children falling on central government or local authority—Immigration and Asylum Act 1999, ss 95, 122. **R (on the application of A) v National Asylum Support Service** [2004] **1** 15, CA.

      Detention—
         Detention for purpose of transfer to European member state responsible for asylum application—Whether detention lawful—Whether assessment of risk of absconding based on objective criteria—Whether damages recoverable—Immigration Act 1971, Sch 2, para 16(2)—European Parliament and Council Regulation 604/2013/EU, arts 2(n), 28. **R (on the application of Hemmati) v Secretary of State for the Home Dept** [2020] **1** 669, SC.

         Detention pending decision on claim—Claimant asylum-seekers being detained at reception centre for short periods pending decisions on their claims—Whether detention infringing claimants' right to liberty—Human Rights Act 1998, Sch 1, Pt I, art 5(1). **R (on the application of Saadi) v Secretary of State for the Home Dept** [2002] **4** 785, HL.

         Generally. *See* Detention—Asylum seeker, *below.*

      Evidence—
         Evidence of torture—Sri Lankan national alleging torture by government forces—Claim for asylum and appeals against refusal of asylum dismissed—Medical expert concluding that clinical findings 'highly consistent' with claimant's account of torture—Whether medical expert exceeding proper limit of role—Whether tribunal erring. **KV (Sri Lanka) v Secretary of State for the Home Dept** [2019] **3** 727, SC.

      Family amnesty—
         Secretary of State announcing policy giving certain asylum seeking families indefinite leave to remain—Appellants arriving in United Kingdom as minors and claiming asylum—Appellants not falling within terms of family amnesty—Whether family amnesty discriminating unlawfully against appellants—Human Rights Act 1998, Sch 1, Pt I, art 14. **AL (Serbia) v Secretary of State for the Home Dept** [2008] **4** 1127, HL.

      Fresh claim. *See* Asylum seeker—Appeal—Certification of claims as 'clearly unfounded'—Fresh claim, *above.*

      Illegal entry. *See* Assisting illegal entry into United Kingdom—Illegal entry—Asylum seeker, *above.*

      Income support. *See* **Social security** (Income support—Urgent cases payments—Asylum seekers).

      Infirm destitute asylum-seeker—
         Whether local authority or central government having to provide accommodation for infirm destitute asylum-seeker—National Assistance Act 1948, s 21—Immigration and Asylum Act 1999, s 95(1)—Asylum Support Regulations 2000, reg 6(4). **R (on the application of Westminster City Council) v National Asylum Support Service** [2002] **4** 654, HL.

      Member state responsible for examining application for international protection—
         'Take charge' requests—Syrian nationals in France requesting entry to United Kingdom—Requests by unaccompanied minors and vulnerable adult—Whether process for determining member state responsible could be bypassed by reason of convention rights—European Parliament and Council Regulation 604/2013/EU—Human Rights Act 1998, Sch 1, Pt I, art 8. **R (on the application of ZT (Syria)) v Secretary of State for the Home Dept (United Nations High Commissioner for Refugees intervening)** [2017] **2** 1024, CA.

      Persecution, fear of. *See* Leave to enter—Refugee—Asylum—Fear of persecution by applicant for refugee status, *below.*

IMMIGRATION (cont)—
  Asylum seeker (cont)—
    Refugee—
      Removal from United Kingdom to state of which person not national or citizen—Prohibition of torture, inhuman or degrading treatment or punishment—Asylum seekers arriving in United Kingdom having previously claimed asylum in Italy—Asylum seekers arriving in United Kingdom having previously been granted refugee status in Italy—Secretary of State issuing removal directions—Secretary of State certifying claims as clearly unfounded—Appropriate test—Human Rights Act 1998, Sch 1, Pt I, art 3—Council Regulation (EC) 343/2003. **R (on the application of EM (Eritrea)) v Secretary of State for the Home Dept** [2014] **2** 192, SC.
    Removal from United Kingdom to state of which person not national or citizen—
      Prohibition of torture, inhuman or degrading treatment or punishment—Legislation deeming specified states to be safe—Whether deeming provision compatible with prohibition of torture, inhuman or degrading treatment or punishment—Human Rights Act 1998, Sch 1, Pt I, art 3—Asylum and Immigration (Treatment of Claimants, etc) Act 2004, Sch 3, para 3. **R (on the application of Nasseri) v Secretary of State for the Home Dept** [2008] **1** 411, QBD; [2009] **1** 116, CA; [2009] **3** 774, HL.
      Vulnerable persons—Removal of beneficiary of international protection and asylum seeker to Italy—Provision of accommodation, healthcare and support—Whether removals breaching prohibition of torture—Human Rights Act 1998, Sch 1, Pt I, art 3—Asylum and Immigration (Treatment of Claimants etc) Act 2004, Sch 3, para 5(4). **NA (Sudan) v Secretary of State for the Home Dept** [2017] **3** 885, CA.
    Unaccompanied asylum seeker claiming to be under 18 years old—
      Initial age assessment—Detention—Secretary of State's guidance for detention where asylum seeker's physical appearance/demeanour very strongly suggesting significantly over 18—Whether guidance lawful. **R (on the application of BF (Eritrea)) v Secretary of State for the Home Dept (Equality and Human Rights Commission intervening)** [2020] **1** 396, CA; [2022] **1** 213, SC.
      Local authority assessing whether asylum seeker child in need—Determination of age—Guidance—Children Act 1989. **R (on the application of B) v Merton London BC** [2003] **4** 280, QBD.
      Local authority assessment—Local authority concluding claimant presenting physically and in demeanour as aged 20-25 years—Whether abbreviated assessment of age based on physical appearance and demeanour lawful—Whether abbreviated assessment properly identifying margin of error. **R (on the application of AB) v Kent CC** [2020] **4** 235, QBD.
  British citizen—
    Right of abode—
      Right to live in United Kingdom with spouse—British citizen marrying Bangladeshi wife in Bangladesh—Wife having no right of entry into United Kingdom—Wife arriving in United Kingdom from Bangladesh without entry certificate—Wife refused entry and having to return to Bangladesh to obtain entry certificate—Whether British citizen's right to live in United Kingdom 'without let or hindrance' including right to bring forthwith into United Kingdom wife who requires entry certificate—Whether delay in granting entry certificate to wife infringing husband's right of abode—Immigration Act 1971, s 1(1). **R v Secretary of State for the Home Dept, ex p Ullah** [1988] **3** 1, CA.
      Right to live in United Kingdom 'without let or hindrance'—Right to live in United Kingdom with spouse—British citizen marrying Bangladeshi wife in Bangladesh—Wife having no right of entry into United Kingdom—Wife arriving in United Kingdom from Bangladesh without entry certificate—Wife refused entry and having to return to Bangladesh to obtain entry certificate—Whether right to live in United Kingdom 'without let or hindrance' including right to bring forthwith into United Kingdom wife who required entry certificate—Whether delay in granting entry certificate to wife infringing husband's right of abode—Whether requirement that wife return to Bangladesh to obtain entry certificate unreasonable—Immigration Act 1971, s 1(1). **R v Secretary of State for the Home Dept, ex p Ullah** [1987] **1** 1025, QBD.
  Change of circumstances in relevant citizen country—
    Appeal. *See* Appeal—Rehearing —Asylum claimant from Iraq claiming asylum in United Kingdom in 2000, *above*.
  Child subject to immigration legislation—
    Wardship jurisdiction of court. *See* **Ward of court** (Jurisdiction—Child subject to immigration legislation).
  Children of failed asylum seekers. *See* Asylum seeker—Children of failed asylum seekers, *above*.
  Circumvention of immigration control—
    Adoption of minor—
      Whether true purpose of application for adoption order circumvention of immigration control. *See* **Adoption** (Order—Discretion—Nationality—Immigration control).
  Citizenship. *See* **Citizenship**.
  Commonwealth citizen. *See* **Commonwealth immigrant**.
  Conspiracy to evade controls. *See* **Criminal law** (Conspiracy—Act injurious to public interest—Immigration controls—Evasion).
  Contravention of order prohibiting entry—
    Mens rea. *See* **Singapore** (Criminal law—Mens rea—Immigration).
  Criminals—
    Deportation. *See* Deportation—Deportation of criminals, *below*.
  Data protection. *See* **Data protection** (Processing of information—Personal data—Exemptions from legislative regime—Immigration exemption).
  Dependent parents—
    Indefinite stay—
      Leave. *See* Leave for indefinite stay—Dependent parents, *below*.
    Leave to enter. *See* Leave to enter—Dependent parents, *below*.
  Deportation—
    Alien. *See* **Alien** (Deportation).
    Appeal. *See* Appeal—Deportation, *above*.
    Asylum seeker. *See* Asylum seeker—Deportation, *above*.

IMMIGRATION (cont)—
Deportation (cont)—
Bail—

National Security—Decision being taken to deport claimant on grounds of national security—Claimant being released from detention on bail—Bail conditions amounting to deprivation of liberty—Bail conditions being varied—Whether bail proceedings determining claimant's civil rights and obligations—Whether right to respect for private life requiring disclosure of gist of allegations—Human Rights Act 1998, Sch 1, arts 5(4), 6(1), 8. **R (on the application of BB) v Special Immigration Appeals Commission (Secretary of State for the Home Dept, interested party)** [2013] 2 419, CA.

National Security—Decision being taken to deport claimant on grounds of national security—Claimant being released from detention on bail—Bail conditions amounting to deprivation of liberty—Bail conditions being varied—Whether varied bail conditions amounting to deprivation of liberty—Whether bail proceedings determining claimant's civil rights and obligations—Human Rights Act 1998, Sch 1, arts 5(4), 6(1). **R (on the application of BB) v Special Immigration Appeals Commission (Secretary of State for the Home Dept, interested party)** [2012] 1 229, DC.

Tribunal deciding to grant bail within 14 days of removal date under removal directions—Secretary of State withholding consent to release on bail—Whether Secretary of State having power to withhold consent on basis of disagreement with tribunal's decision—Immigration Act 1971, Sch 2, para 22(4). **R (on the application of Roszkowski) v Secretary of State for the Home Dept** [2018] 2 878, CA.

Co-operation with Secretary of State's requests—

Deportation of Zimbabwean national—Zimbabwean government requiring consent of nationals before issuing Extraordinary Travel Document ('ETD')—Secretary of State issuing notice requiring detainee to consent to return if asked by Zimbabwean officials—Whether Secretary of State able to lawfully require such specified action—Asylum and Immigration (Treatment of Claimants) Act 2004, s 35. **R (on the application of JM (Zimbabwe)) v Secretary of State for the Home Dept** [2018] 2 1015, CA.

Decision to deport—

Delegation of power to make decision—Secretary of State authorising immigration inspectors to act on his behalf in reaching decision whether to deport person—Whether Secretary of State having power to authorise immigration inspector to act on his behalf in deciding whether to deport—Whether Secretary of State entitled to devolve exercise of power to issue notices of intention to deport—Immigration Act 1971, s 3(5)(a). **Oladehinde v Secretary of State for the Home Dept** [1990] 2 367, QBD and CA.

Deportation of parent—Best interests of child—Congolese citizen and wife entering United Kingdom illegally—Children born in United Kingdom—Secretary of State refusing asylum or humanitarian protection—Whether interference with right to private and family life proportionate to legitimate need to control immigration—Whether Secretary of State failing to have regard to best interests of children—Human Rights Act 1998, Sch 1, Pt I, art 8. **Zoumbas v Secretary of State for the Home Dept** [2014] 1 638, SC.

Deportation of parent—Best interests of child—Views of child—Mother coming to United Kingdom from Tanzania—Mother forming relationship with British citizen and having children whilst immigration status precarious—Mother's immigration and human rights claims being dismissed—Tribunal finding that mother's removal from United Kingdom would not disproportionately interfere with family life—Court of Appeal upholding finding on basis that children could follow mother to Tanzania—Consideration of weight to be given to best interests of child affected by decision to remove parent from United Kingdom—Consideration of ways in which child's best interests to be discovered—Whether disproportionate to deport mother—Human Rights Act 1998, Sch 1, Pt I, art 8—United Nations Convention on the Rights of the Child, arts 3(1), 7, 8. **ZH (Tanzania) v Secretary of State for the Home Dept** [2011] 2 783, SC.

Procedural impropriety in decision to deport. *See* Deportation—Order—Power to make deportation order—Decision to deport, *below.*

Deportation of criminals—

Automatic deportation—Exceptions—Right to respect for private and family life—Appeal against revocation of refugee status and order for deportation—Whether refusal to adjourn pending service of Offender Assessment System report procedurally unfair—Whether appellant 'socially and culturally integrated in the United Kingdom'—Nationality, Immigration and Asylum Act 2002, s 117C(4)—Immigration Rules, para 399A(b). **AM (Somalia) v Secretary of State for the Home Dept** [2019] 4 714, CA.

Automatic deportation—Exceptions—Right to respect for private and family life—Certification allowing removal of foreign criminal pending determination of appeal or substantive claim against deportation—Whether removal pending outcome of appeal breaching substantive rights—Whether out of country appeals guaranteed requirements of procedural fairness—Human Rights Act 1998, Sch 1, Pt I, art 8—Nationality, Immigration and Asylum Act 2002, s 94B. **R (on the application of Kiarie) v Secretary of State for the Home Dept** [2016] 3 741, CA.

Automatic deportation—Exceptions—Right to respect for private and family life—Certification allowing removal of foreign criminal pending determination of appeal or substantive claim against deportation—Whether removal pending outcome of appeal breaching substantive rights—Whether out of country appeals guaranteeing requirements of procedural fairness—Human Rights Act 1998, s 6, Sch 1, Pt I, art 8—Nationality, Immigration and Asylum Act 2002, s 94B. **R (on the application of Kiarie) v Secretary of State for the Home Dept** [2017] 4 811, SC.

Automatic deportation—Exceptions—Right to respect for private and family life—Circumstances in which deportation of foreign criminal contrary to right to respect for private and family life—Human Rights Act 1998, Sch 1, Pt I, art 8—UK Borders Act 2007, ss 32, 33—Statement of Changes in Immigration Rules (HC Paper 395) paras 398-399A. **R (on the application of Akpinar) v Upper Tribunal (Immigration and Asylum Chamber)** [2015] 2 870, CA.

IMMIGRATION (cont)—
  Deportation (cont)—
    Deportation of criminals (cont)—
      Automatic deportation—Exceptions—Right to respect for private and family life—Prohibition of discrimination—Appellant born to Jamaican mother and British father who never married—Appellant never applying for British citizenship—Appellant convicted of serious criminal offences—Whether appellant liable to automatic deportation as foreign criminal—Whether denial of British citizenship infringing human rights—British Nationality Act 1981, ss 3, 41A—Human Rights Act 1998, Sch 1, Pt I, arts 8, 14—UK Borders Act 2007, ss 32, 33. **R (on the application of Johnson) v Secretary of State for the Home Dept** [2017] **4** 91, SC.
      Bail—Appellants released on bail by First-tier Tribunal pending deportation—Appellants required to report to immigration officer—Appellants re-detained in order to attend interview for purposes of obtaining emergency travel documentation—Whether re-detention lawful—Immigration Act 1971, Sch 3, para 2(3). **R (on the application of Lucas) v Secretary of State for the Home Dept** [2019] **2** 43, CA.
      Derivative right of residence—Zambrano carer—Jamaican national convicted of serious criminal offence—Dependent child European Union citizen—Whether third-country national, otherwise benefiting from derivative right to reside within EU, enjoying enhanced protection against deportation—Whether additional requirement to show 'exceptional circumstances'. **Robinson (Jamaica) v Secretary of State for the Home Dept** [2021] **2** 429, SC.
      Human rights considerations—Inhuman or degrading treatment—Serious medical condition—Appellant HIV positive—Appellant seeking to make human rights argument on basis appropriate medical treatment not available in receiving country—Test to be applied in considering whether inhuman and degrading treatment—Human Rights Act 1998, Sch 1, Pt I, art 3. **AM (Zimbabwe) v Secretary of State for the Home Dept** [2020] **3** 1003, SC.
      Public interest considerations—Right to respect for private and family life—Interests of qualifying children—Member of armed forces convicted of dishonesty offence and sentenced to two years' imprisonment—Secretary of State making deportation order—Whether effect of deportation would be 'unduly harsh' on qualifying children—Weight to be given to armed forces covenant—Nationality, Immigration and Asylum Act 2002, s 117C. **LE (St Vincent and the Grenadines) v Secretary of State for the Home Dept** [2020] **4** 699, CA.
      Public interest considerations—Right to respect for private and family life—Presumption deportation in public interest—Exceptions—Effect of deportation unduly harsh to partner or child—Guidance—Human Rights Act 1998, Sch 1, Pt I, art 8—Nationality, Immigration and Asylum Act 2002, s 117C—UK Borders Act 2007, s 32—Immigration Rules, para 399. **HA (Iraq) v Secretary of State for the Home Dept** [2021] **2** 898, CA.
      Right to respect for private and family life—Appellant sentenced to four years' imprisonment while in United Kingdom unlawfully—Secretary of State ordering deportation as foreign criminal—Recognition of public interest in deporting foreign criminals—Whether deportation disproportionate interference with right to respect for private and family life—Effect of changes to Immigration Rules—Human Rights Act 1998, Sch 1, Pt I, art 8—UK Borders Act 2007, ss 32, 33—Immigration Rules, rr 398, 399, 399A. **Ali v Secretary of State for the Home Dept** [2017] **3** 20, SC.
      Right to respect for private and family life—Settled migrant—Offences committed as child—Proper approach in deportation cases consequent upon criminal offending by those lawfully settled in United Kingdom as children—Whether 'very serious reasons' required to justify deportation—Meaning of 'very significant obstacles to ... integration' in receiving state—Human Rights Act 1998, Sch 1, Pt I, art 8—Nationality, Immigration and Asylum Act 2002, s 117C(4). **Sanambar v Secretary of State for the Home Dept** [2021] **4** 873, SC.
      Right to respect for private and family life—Whether respondent Secretary of State having duty to investigate impact of appellant's deportation on appellant's children—Whether duty discharged—Human Rights Act 1998, Sch 1, Pt I, art 8. **Makhlouf v Secretary of State for the Home Dept (Northern Ireland)** [2017] **3** 1, SC.
    Deportation order—
      Leave to remain. *See* Leave to remain—Indefinite leave to remain—Indefinite leave to remain invalidated by subsequent deportation order, *below*.
    Detention pending deportation—
      Deportation following completion of sentence of person having permanent right of residence in United Kingdom as family member of EEA national—Whether power to detain discriminatory—Whether power to detain disproportionate—Whether power to detain lawful—Immigration (European Economic Area) Regulations 2006, SI 2006/1003, regs 21, 24—European Parliament and Council Directive 2004/38/EC, arts 27, 28—Article 18 TFEU. **R (on the application of Nouazli) v Secretary of State for the Home Dept** [2016] **4** 720, SC.
      Deportation in interests of national security—Right to liberty and security—Lawfulness of detention—Bail—Closed material—Standard of disclosure—Detained person making bail application after closed judgment finding detained person a danger to national security—Approach to requirements of disclosure of closed material in bail application—Special Immigration Appeals Commission Act 1997—Human Rights Act 1998, Sch 1, Pt I, art 5(4). **R (on the application of BB) v Special Immigration Appeals Commission** [2011] **4** 210, DC.
      Detention following completion of sentence of foreign national prisoners—Statutory warrant for detention issued after recommendation for deportation by sentencing court—Statutory warrant continuing after deportation order made—Unpublished policy of detaining foreign national prisoners—Whether unlawful policy undermining statutory warrant—Whether detention unlawful—Immigration Act 1971, Sch 3, para 2(1), (3). **R (on the application of Francis) v Secretary of State for the Home Dept** [2014] **1** 68, QBD.
      Detention following completion of sentence of foreign national prisoners—Unpublished policy of Secretary of State containing presumption in favour of detention—Whether operation of policy unlawful—Whether lawful for Secretary of State to operate policy in relation to foreign national prisoners pending deportation containing presumption in favour of detention—Immigration Act 1971, Sch 3, para 2. **R (on the application of Lumba) v Secretary of State for the Home Dept** [2011] **4** 1, SC; **R (on the application of WL (Congo)) v Secretary of State for the Home Dept** [2010] **4** 489, CA.

IMMIGRATION (cont)—
  Deportation (cont)—
    Detention pending deportation (cont)—
      Detention following completion of sentence of foreign national prisoners—Whether unlawful decision to deport having bearing on decision to detain—Immigration Act 1971, Sch 3, para 2(3)—Nationality, Immigration and Asylum Act 2002, s 72. **DN (Rwanda) v Secretary of State for the Home Dept** [2018] **3** 772, CA; **R (on the application of DN (Rwanda)) v Secretary of State for the Home Dept** [2020] **3** 353, SC.

      Executive detention of Lithuanian national following completion of sentence—Grounds for challenging detention—Whether power to detain on basis of conviction without individualised information—Whether detention unlawful—Whether substantial or nominal damages to be awarded—Whether reasonable prospect of deportation within reasonable time—Immigration (European Economic Area) Regulations 2006, SI 2006/1003, reg 24(1)—European Parliament and Council Directive 2004/38/EC, art 27(2). **R (on the application of Lauzikas) v Secretary of State for the Home Dept** [2018] **4** 141, QBD; [2020] **2** 462, CA.

      Extent of Secretary of State's power to detain person subject to a deportation order—Immigration Act 1971, Sch 3, para 2(3). **R v Governor of Durham Prison, ex p Singh** [1984] **1** 983, QBD.

      Extent of Secretary of State's power to detain person subject to a deportation order—Right to liberty and security—Secretary of State failing to conduct reviews of continued lawfulness of detention of person subject to deportation order as required by delegated legislation and policy—Whether detention of person subject to deportation order lawful—Whether compliance with rules and policy condition precedent to lawfulness of detention—Whether breach of right to liberty and security—Immigration Act 1971, Sch 3, para 2(2)—Human Rights Act 1998, Sch 1, Pt I, art 5(1)—Detention Centre Rules 2001, SI 2001/238. **R (on the application of SK) v Secretary of State for the Home Dept** [2009] **2** 365, CA.

      Extent of Secretary of State's power to detain person subject to deportation order—Secretary of State's published policy requiring reviews of detention to be held at specified intervals—Whether failure to conduct reviews material, in public law terms, to legality of detention—Whether appellant entitled to damages for false imprisonment—Immigration Act 1971, Sch 3, para 2. **R (on the application of Kambadzi) v Secretary of State for the Home Dept (sub nom R (on the application of SK) v Secretary of State for the Home Dept)** [2011] **4** 975, SC.

      Illegal entrant—Generally. *See* Detention—Illegal entrant—Detention pending deportation, *below*.

      Mental illness. *See* Detention—Unlawful detention—Claimant being released from prison into administrative detention pending deportation, *below*.

    European Economic Area (EEA) national—
      Right to reside in United Kingdom—Deportation of EEA national with right to reside in United Kingdom—Continuity of residence—Custodial sentence—Whether detention in young offenders' institution 'imprisonment' breaking continuity of residence for purposes of enhanced protection—Immigration (European Economic Area) Regulations 2016, SI 2016/1052, reg 3(3). **Viscu v Secretary of State for the Home Dept (Advice on Individual Rights in Europe (AIRE) Centre intervening)** [2020] **1** 988, CA.

      Right to reside in United Kingdom—Deportation of EEA national with right to reside in United Kingdom—Deportation of EEA national with permanent right of residence for entering or attempting to enter into marriage of convenience with non-EEA national—Duty to facilitate entry into United Kingdom of partners of EEA nationals with 'durable relationship'—Whether burden of proof on Secretary of State to establish marriage of convenience and absence of durable relationship—Immigration (European Economic Area) Regulations 2006, SI 2006/1003, regs 19(3)(c), 21B(1)—European Parliament and Council Directive 2004/38/EC, arts 3(2), 35. **Sadovska v Secretary of State for the Home Dept** [2018] **1** 757, SC.

      Right to reside in United Kingdom—Deportation of EEA national with right to reside in United Kingdom—Deportation of EEA national with permanent right of residence requiring serious grounds of public policy or public security—Deportation of EEA national residing in United Kingdom for continuous period of ten years requiring imperative grounds of public security—Nature of permanent residence—Meaning of 'imperative grounds ground of public security'—Immigration (European Economic Area) Regulations 2006, SI 2006/1003, reg 21(3), (4)(a)—EP and Council Directive (EC) 2004/38, art 28. **FV (Italy) v Secretary of State for the Home Dept** [2013] **1** 1180, CA.

      Right to reside in United Kingdom—Deportation of EEA national with right to reside in United Kingdom—Deportation of EEA national with permanent right of residence requiring serious grounds of public policy or public security—Deportation of EEA national residing in United Kingdom for continuous period of ten years requiring imperative grounds of public security—Secretary of State deciding to deport EEA national present in United Kingdom for ten years on serious grounds of public policy—Whether period of 'residence' including period of imprisonment—Immigration (European Economic Area) Regulations 2006, SI 2006/1003, reg 21(3), (4)(a)—EP and Council Directive (EC) 2004/38, art 28(2), (3). **HR (Portugal) v Secretary of State for the Home Dept** [2010] **1** 144, CA.

      Right to reside in United Kingdom—Deportation of EEA national with right to reside in United Kingdom—Deportation of EEA national with permanent right of residence requiring serious grounds of public policy or public security—Italian national living in UK for 16 years before serving sentence of imprisonment—Secretary of State deciding to deport—Whether acquiring permanent right of residence for enhanced protection—Immigration (European Economic Area) Regulations 2006, SI 2006/1003, reg 21—European Parliament and Council Directive 2004/38/EC, arts 16, 28. **Vomero v Secretary of State for the Home Dept** [2020] **1** 287, SC.

      Right to reside in United Kingdom—Deportation of EEA national with right to reside in United Kingdom—Exclusion and removal from United Kingdom—Free movement of persons—Whether administrative detention of EEA national pending deportation permissible—Immigration (European Economic Area) Regulations 2006, SI 2006/1003, regs 19, 24—EP and Council Directive (EC) 2004/38, arts 24, 27. **R (on the application of Nouazli) v Secretary of State for the Home Dept** [2014] **1** 1144, CA.

IMMIGRATION (cont)—
  Deportation (cont)—
    European Economic Area (EEA) national (cont)—
      Right to reside in United Kingdom—Respondent Italian national living in United Kingdom for 16 years before serving sentence of imprisonment for manslaughter by reason of provocation—Appellant Secretary of State deciding to deport respondent—Secretary of State maintaining respondent not having acquired permanent right of residence so not having enhanced protection—Court of Appeal finding respondent having unbroken prior integrative link with UK—Whether enhanced protection depending upon possession of right of permanent residence—European Parliament and Council Directive 2004/38/EC, arts 16, 28. **FV (Italy) v Secretary of State for the Home Dept** [2017] **1** 999n, SC.
    Exclusion of immigrant deemed to be conducive to public good—
      Immigrant having obtained original leave to enter and settlement visa by deception—Immigrant subsequently refused leave to re-enter on ground that exclusion conducive for public good having regard to deception in obtaining original leave to enter—Power of Secretary of State to deem deportation to be conducive to public good where original entry obtained by deception—Immigration Act 1971, s 3(5)(b). **Patel v Immigration Appeal Tribunal** [1988] **2** 378, HL.
    Expiration of leave to remain in United Kingdom—
      Decision to deport—Interview of overstayer before making deportation order—Whether persons overstaying leave to enter having right or legitimate expectation of interview before deportation order made. **R v Secretary of State for the Home Dept, ex p Malhi** [1990] **2** 357, CA.
      Variation of leave—Refusal of application to vary leave—Appeal pending—Applicant not to be deported so long as appeal pending—Applicant who has a limited leave to enter or remain in the United Kingdom—Applicant's leave having expired before application made for further period of leave—Whether applicant immune from deportation until application determined and appeal procedure exhausted—Immigration Act 1971, ss 3(5)(a), 14(1). **Suthendran v Immigration Appeal Tribunal** [1976] **3** 611, HL.
    Judicial review applications against removal directions—
      Principles—Guidance. **R (on the application of Madan) v Secretary of State for the Home Dept** [2008] **1** 973, CA.
    Order—
      Power to make deportation order—Decision to deport—Procedural impropriety in decision—Function of immigration adjudicator—Whether adjudicator entitled to inquire whether alleged procedural impropriety rendering decision to deport a nullity—Whether power to make deportation order if decision flawed by procedural impropriety—Immigration Act 1988, s 5(1). **R v Secretary of State for the Home Dept, ex p Malhi** [1990] **2** 357, CA.
    Public interest considerations—
      Additional considerations in cases involving foreign criminals—Secretary of State making deportation order against Nigerian national born in United Kingdom—Whether public concern about private and family life considerations tending to preclude deportation of foreign national criminal additional factor to public interest—Human Rights Act 1998, Sch 1, Pt I, art 8—Nationality, Immigration and Asylum Act 2002, s 117C. **Akinyemi v Secretary of State for the Home Dept (No 2)** [2020] **3** 857, CA.
      Right to respect for private and family life—Deportee having parental relationship with qualifying child—Whether, in determining whether reasonable to expect child to leave United Kingdom with parent or whether effect of deportation of parent on child unduly harsh, tribunal concerned only with position of child—Meaning of 'unduly harsh'—Nationality, Immigration and Asylum Act 2002, ss 117B, 117C—Immigration Rules, para 276ADE(1). **KO (Nigeria) v Secretary of State for the Home Dept (Equality and Human Rights Commission intervening)** [2019] **1** 675, SC.
    Recommendation. *See* **Sentence** (Deportation).
    Refugee—
      Asylum—Deportation back to third country—Provision of international convention protecting those with well-founded fear of persecution—Asylum seekers fearing persecution from non-state agents and arriving in United Kingdom via third countries—Third countries interpreting convention provision as applying only to persecution by state—Secretary of State certifying return of asylum seekers to third countries—Whether convention provision open to range of permissible interpretations—Asylum and Immigration Act 1996, s 2(2)(c)—Geneva Convention relating to the Status of Refugees 1951, art 1A(2). **R v Secretary of State for the Home Dept, ex p Adan** [2001] **1** 593, HL.
      Asylum—Deportation of asylum seeker not leading to torture or inhuman or degrading treatment or punishment—Whether asylum seeker's right to respect for private and family life capable of being engaged—Human Rights Act 1998, Sch 1, Pt I, art 8. **R (on the application of Razgar) v Secretary of State for the Home Dept** [2004] **3** 821, HL.
      Asylum—Deportation of asylum seekers not leading to torture or inhuman or degrading treatment or punishment—Whether other rights and freedoms of asylum seekers therefore excluded from consideration—Human Rights Act 1998, Sch 1, Pt I, arts 2, 3, 4, 5, 6, 7, 8, 9. **R (on the application of Ullah) v Special Adjudicator** [2003] **3** 1174, CA; [2004] **3** 785, HL.
      Asylum—Deportation to third country—Third country not recognising persecution by non-state agents where state not complicit—Whether third country 'safe'—Asylum and Immigration Act 1996, s 2(2)(c)—Convention relating to the Status of Refugees 1951. **R v Secretary of State for the Home Dept, ex p Adan** [1999] **4** 774, CA.
      Asylum—Expulsion—Refugee lawfully in territory of contracting state not to be expelled save on grounds of national security or public order—Whether refugee without leave to enter or remain lawfully within United Kingdom—Convention and Protocol relating to the Status of Refugees 1951, arts 32, 33. **R (on the application of T) v Secretary of State for the Home Dept** [2010] **4** 314, CA.
      Asylum—Person served with deportation notice seeking asylum—Secretary of State deciding deportation conducive to public good—Whether Secretary of State required to balance risk to national security against risk to applicant for refugee status—Whether decision to deport perverse—Statement of Changes in Immigration Rules (HC Paper (1989-90) No 251) paras 162, 164, 167—Geneva Convention on Refugees, arts 32, 33. **R v Secretary of State for the Home Dept, ex p Chahal** [1995] **1** 658, CA.

14

IMMIGRATION (cont)—
  Deportation (cont)—
    Refugee (cont)—
      Asylum—Well-founded fear of persecution—Asylum claimants outside country of nationality having left with well-founded fear of persecution—Change in circumstances of country of nationality ending fear of persecution—Claimants alleging presence of compelling reasons preventing their return—Whether claimants entitled to refugee status—Convention and Protocol relating to the Status of Refugees, arts 1A, 1C(5). **R (on the application of Hoxha) v Special Adjudicator** [2005] **4** 580, HL.

      Asylum—Well-founded fear of persecution—Whether person having well-founded fear of persecution where he could voluntarily return to his country in safety despite risk of persecution on involuntary return—Nationality Immigration and Asylum Act 2002, s 84(1)(g)—Convention and Protocol relating to the Status of Refugees 1951, arts 1A(2), 33. **AA v Secretary of State for the Home Dept** [2007] **2** 160, CA.

      Subsidiary protection status. *See* Deportation—Subsidiary protection status, *below.*

    Specified safe states, to. *See* Asylum seeker—Removal from United Kingdom to state of which person not national or citizen, *above.*

    Subsidiary protection status—
      Serious and individual threat to life by reason of indiscriminate violence in situations of armed conflict—Real risk of suffering harm if returned to country of origin—Determination of qualification for subsidiary protection status—Council Directive (EC) 2004/83, arts 2(e), 15(c). **QD (Iraq) v Secretary of State for the Home Dept** [2010] **2** 971, CA.

  Detention—
    Application for leave to apply for judicial review—
      Bail—Detention pending hearing of application for leave to apply for judicial review—Grant of bail pending hearing of application—Immigration Act 1971, Sch 2, para 16. **R v Secretary of State for the Home Dept, ex p Swati** [1986] **1** 717, CA.

    Asylum seeker—
      Generally. *See* Asylum seeker—Detention, *above.*

      Secretary of State implementing new policy on detention of asylum seekers whose claims could be decided quickly—Policy providing for short period of detention in reception centre pending decision—Claimants being detained under new policy and challenging lawfulness of detention—Whether detention infringing claimants' right to liberty under human rights convention—Immigration Act 1971, Sch 2, para 16(1)—Human Rights Act 1998, Sch 1, Pt I, art 5(1). **R (on the application of Saadi) v Secretary of State for the Home Dept** [2001] **4** 961, QBD and CA.

    Bail—
      Application for judicial review. *See* Detention—Application for leave to apply for judicial review—Bail, *above.*

      Whether statutory power existing to grant immigration bail to person who could no longer be lawfully detained—Immigration Act 1971, Sch 2, paras 22, 29, Sch 3, para 2(2). **B (Algeria) v Secretary of State for the Home Dept** [2018] **2** 759, SC.

      Whether statutory power existing to impose immigration bail on person who could no longer be lawfully detained—Meaning of 'liable to detention'—Human Rights Act 1998, Sch 1, Pt I, art 5—Nationality, Immigration and Asylum Act 2002, s 67—Immigration Act 2016, Sch 10, para 1(2), (5). **R (on the application of Kaitey) v Secretary of State for the Home Dept (Bail for Immigration Detainees intervening)** [2022] **3** 835, CA.

      Whether statutory power existing to impose immigration bail on person who could no longer be lawfully detained—Meaning of 'liable to detention'—Immigration Act 2016, s 61(3), Sch 10, para 1(2), (5). **R (on the application of Kaitey) v Secretary of State for the Home Dept (Bail for Immigration Detainees intervening)** [2021] **2** 719, QBD.

    Detention centre—
      Police liability for riot damage. *See* **Riot** (Damage—Compensation—Police authority).

    Detention pending deportation—
      Extent of Secretary of State's power to detain person subject to deportation order—Tribunal order for immigration bail—Order defective—Whether government could lawfully act in manner inconsistent with defective order without applying for and obtaining variation or setting aside of order—Immigration Act 1971, Sch 2, para 22, Sch 3, para 2. **R (on the application of Majera (formerly SM (Rwanda))) v Secretary of State for the Home Dept** [2022] **2** 305, SC.

    Detention pending deportation. *See* Deportation—Detention pending deportation, *above.*

    Illegal entrant—
      Burden of proof that entry illegal—Entrant obtaining indefinite leave to enter and remain in United Kingdom—Leave obtained in consequence of fraud—Illegal entrant returning to United Kingdom with new passport after short visit abroad—Immigration officer accepting false explanation for passport—Officer granting indefinite leave to stay and stamping passport accordingly—Entrant subsequently detained as illegal entrant—Whether grant of indefinite leave on face of passport proof that entrant in United Kingdom legally—Whether sufficient for Secretary of State to show that on evidence as a whole he had reasonable grounds for concluding entry illegal—Immigration Act 1971, Sch 2, para 16(2). **R v Secretary of State for the Home Dept, ex p Hussain** [1978] **2** 423, QBD and CA.

      Burden of proof that entry illegal—Immigration officials refusing entry certificate because not accepting identity of applicant—Applicant successfully appealing to adjudicator—Applicant obtaining indefinite leave to enter United Kingdom—Secretary of State obtaining further evidence casting doubt on applicant's identity—Whether burden of proof on Secretary of State to show that on balance of probalities applicant an illegal entrant—Whether further evidence obtained after adjudicator's decision showing that fraud practised on adjudicator. **Ali v Secretary of State for the Home Dept** [1984] **1** 1009, CA.

      Detention pending deportation—Applicants not having leave to enter or remain in the United Kingdom—Applicants applying for political asylum after arrival—Applicants detained pending directions for removal—Whether detention lawful pending determination of applications for asylum—Immigration Act 1971, Sch 2, para 16—Asylum and Immigration Appeals Act 1993, s 6. **R v Secretary of State for the Home Dept, ex p Khan** [1995] **2** 540, CA.

IMMIGRATION (cont)—
  Detention (cont)—
    Illegal entrant (cont)—
      Detention pending deportation—Habeas corpus—Evidence—Hearsay—Whether court entitled to take into account hearsay evidence relied on by Secretary of State on application for habeas corpus. **R v Secretary of State for the Home Dept, ex p Rahman** [1997] **1** 796, CA.

      Detention pending deportation—Rights of entrant—Temporary release—Right to marry—Right to temporary release to get married—Whether illegal entrant entitled to release for purpose of getting married—Immigration Act 1971, Sch 2, para 21(1)—Convention for the Protection of Human Rights and Fundamental Freedoms 1950, art 12. **R v Secretary of State for Home Affairs, ex p Bhajan Singh** [1975] **2** 1081, CA.

      Detention pending deportation—Unauthorised migrants from Vietnam detained in Hong Kong pending removal—Repatriation to Vietnam constituting sole means of removal—Vietnamese authorities not accepting repatriation of non-nationals—Whether statutory power of detention limited—Whether court having jurisdiction to determine reasonableness of duration of detention—Whether non-Vietnamese nationals being detained 'pending removal'—Immigration Ordinance (Hong Kong), s 13D. **Tan Te Lam v Superintendent of Tai A Chau Detention Centre** [1996] **4** 256, PC.

      Entry in breach of immigration laws—Entrant not knowingly in breach of immigration laws—Leave to enter given on basis of false passport—Passport obtained for entrant by husband—Passport that of husband's second wife—Entrant, his third wife, illiterate and believing passport her own—Whether entrant an illegal entrant where ignorant that document on which leave based was false—Whether illegal entrant if leave to enter in fact given—Immigration Act 1971, ss 3(1)(a), 33(1). **Khan v Secretary of State for the Home Dept** [1977] **3** 538, CA.

      Entry in breach of immigration laws—Entrant not knowingly in breach of immigration laws—Leave to enter given on basis of invalid work permit—Work permit obtained for entrant by third party—Entrant unaware work permit invalid—Whether entrant entering 'in accordance with' immigration legislation—Whether entrant an 'illegal entrant'—Immigration Act 1971, ss 3(1), 33(1). **R v Immigration Officer, ex p Chan** [1992] **2** 738, CA.

      Entry in breach of immigration laws—Entrant remaining in United Kingdom as illegal entrant after expiry of visitor's permit—Entrant obtaining new passport and going on visit abroad—Entrant returning to United Kingdom and convincing immigration officer that he was settled in United Kingdom—Officer stamping passport with indefinite leave to stay—Entrant subsequently detained as illegal entrant—Whether entrant entitled to rely on stamp in passport—Whether court entitled to interfere in Secretary of State's exercise of discretion to detain entrant—Immigration Act 1971, ss 3(1), 33(1). **R v Secretary of State for the Home Dept, ex p Choudhary** [1978] **3** 790, CA.

      Entry in breach of immigration laws—Immigration officer mistakenly giving entrant leave to enter and stay indefinitely—Passport so stamped—Entrant not obtaining leave by fraud or misrepresentation—Entrant subsequently detained as illegal entrant—Whether entrant entitled to rely on stamp in passport—Whether immigration officer acting within his authority in giving indefinite leave to person not entitled to such leave—Immigration Act 1971, s 4. **R v Secretary of State for the Home Dept, ex p Ram** [1979] **1** 687, QBD.

      Illegal entrant not given leave to enter or remain in United Kingdom—Detention pending directions for removal—Persons entering United Kingdom and present there in breach of immigration laws—Commonwealth immigrant—Immigrant entering United Kingdom clandestinely in breach of laws relating to Commonwealth immigrants previously in force—Immigrant no longer liable to prosecution under previous laws—Whether immigrant 'settled' in United Kingdom and deemed to have indefinite leave to remain—Whether immigrant 'illegal entrant' liable to detention and removal—Commonwealth Immigrants Act 1962, ss 4, 4A (as added by the Commonwealth Immigrants Act 1968, s 3)—Immigration Act 1971, ss 1(2), 4(2), 33(1),(2), 34(1)(a), Sch 2, paras 9, 16(2). **Azam v Secretary of State for the Home Dept** [1973] **2** 765, HL.

  Minor—
    Minor given leave to enter United Kingdom—Minor registered as United Kingdom citizen on application made on his behalf by his alleged father—Evidence subsequently obtained that minor not son of alleged father—Detention of minor pending removal from United Kingdom as illegal immigrant—Whether minor immune from order directing his removal by virtue of registration as United Kingdom citizen—Whether registration as United Kingdom citizen effective—Whether detention lawful—British Nationality Act 1948, ss 7, 20. **R v Secretary of State for the Home Dept, ex p Akhtar** [1980] **2** 735, CA.

  Unlawful detention—
    Claimant being released from prison into administrative detention pending deportation—Claimant suffering from mental illness—Claimant unsuccessfully bringing judicial review proceedings challenging lawfulness and detention—Whether claimant's detention unlawful—Whether Secretary of State in breach of policy relating to detention of mentally ill claimants pending deportation—Meaning of 'satisfactory management'—Immigration Act 1971, Sch 3, para 2. **R (on the application of O) v Secretary of State for the Home Dept** [2016] **4** 1003, SC.

    False imprisonment—Damages—Whether immigration officers immune to claims for damages for false imprisonment—Immigration Act 1971, Sch 2. **D v Home Office** [2006] **1** 183, CA.

    False imprisonment—Detention pending fast track determination of asylum claim—Whether policy on screening for fast track determination complied with. **R (on the application of JB (Jamaica)) v Secretary of State for the Home Dept** [2014] **2** 91, CA.

    False imprisonment—Removal while claim for asylum pending—Secretary of State directing removal of claimant unaccompanied minor to safe third country—Claimant detained pending removal—Subsequent judgment establishing claim to be determined by member state in which claimant present—Whether Secretary of State having 'reasonable grounds for suspecting' claimant could lawfully be removed to safe third country—Whether mistake of law amounting to 'reasonable grounds for suspecting' person liable to removal—Whether detention unlawful as removal not within reasonable time—Immigration Act 1971, Sch 2, para 16(2)—Council Regulation 343/2003/EC. **R (on the application of Mohammed) v Secretary of State for the Home Dept** [2016] **3** 419, QBD.

IMMIGRATION (cont)—
Detention (cont)—
Unlawful detention (cont)—
Remedy—Habeas corpus—Appeal—Detainee making out a prima facie case that he is not an illegal entrant—Whether entitled as of right to writ of habeas corpus—Whether bound to rely on statutory appeal procedure—Immigration Act 1971, s 16. **Azam v Secretary of State for the Home Dept** [1973] **2** 741, CA.
Victims of torture—
Whether defendant Secretary of State's guidance unlawfully altering definition of torture—Whether guidance containing exhaustive list of indicators of particular vulnerability—Whether guidance unlawful—Whether public sector equality duty fulfilled—Equality Act 2010, s 149—Immigration Act 2016, s 59—Detention Centre Rules 2001, SI 2001/238, r 35—United Nations Convention against Torture and Other Cruel, Inhuman or Degrading Treatment or Punishment. **R (on the application of Medical Justice) v Secretary of State for the Home Dept (Equality and Human Rights Commission intervening)** [2018] **1** 400, QBD.
Work done whilst in detention—
Work paid at flat-rate set by Secretary of State—Whether rate unlawful—Whether regime discriminatory—Whether prisoners appropriate comparators—Whether regime justified—Human Rights Act 1998, Sch 1, Pt I, arts 4, 8, 14, Pt II, art 1—Immigration and Asylum Act 1999, s 153—Detention Centre Rules 2001, SI 2001/238, rr 3(1), 7. **R (on the application of Badmus) v Secretary of State for the Home Dept** [2021] **1** 1193, CA.
Discrimination—
Family amnesty for asylum seekers. *See* Asylum seeker—Family amnesty, *above*.
Right to marry and. *See* **Marriage** (Right to marry—Immigration—Discrimination).
Education—
Migrant programme schemes—
Medical training. *See* **National Health Service** (Hospital—Staff—Post-graduate training positions—International medical graduates).
European Economic Area nationals—
Right of admission—
Family members—Extended family members—EEA nationals becoming guardians of child under Islamic kefalah system pursuant to Algerian law—Entry clearance officer deciding that child not family member or extended family member of EEA national and refusing entry clearance—Whether statutory right of appeal—Whether child 'extended family member' or 'direct descendant' of EEA national—Whether reference to Court of Justice of the European Union required—Meaning of 'EEA decision'—Immigration (European Economic Area) Regulations 2006, SI 2006/1003, regs 2, 8, 12, 26—European Parliament and Council Directive 2004/38/EC, arts 2(2)(c), 3(2)(a). **SM (Algeria) v Entry Clearance Officer, UK Visa Section** [2018] **3** 177, SC.
Right of residence—
Family members—Conditions—Condition of comprehensive sickness insurance cover—Whether condition satisfied by right to use National Health Service—Immigration (European Economic Area) Regulations 2006, SI 2006/1003—EP and Council Directive 2004/38/EC, art 7. **Ahmad v Secretary of State for the Home Dept** [2015] **1** 933, CA.
Family members—Extended family members—Appellant seeking EEA residence card on basis of relationship with mother's partner—Mother and partner not being married or in civil partnership—Whether child of person in relationship with EU citizen 'direct descendant' of citizen—Whether appellant dependant of EU citizen before arriving in UK—Immigration (European Economic Area) Regulations 2006, SI 2006/1003, regs 7, 8—European Parliament and Council Directive 2004/38/EC, arts 2, 3. **Latayan v Secretary of State for the Home Dept** [2020] **4** 685, CA.
Family members—Extended family members—Right to respect for private and family life—Delay in issuing European Economic Area residence card to extended family member—Whether breach of statutory duty—Human Rights Act 1998, Sch 1, Pt I, art 6—Immigration (European Economic Area) Regulations 2006, SI 2006/1003—Treaty on the Functioning of the European Union, arts 20, 21—Parliament and Council Directive (EC) 2004/38. **B v Home Office** [2012] **4** 276, QBD.
Systematic verification—Immigration enforcement operation to determine whether detained foreign national lawfully in UK—Questioning of detained foreign nationals—Whether operation infringing prohibition on systematic verification—Whether police questioning outside police functions—Immigration (European Economic Area) Regulations 2006, SI 2006/1003, reg 20B—European Parliament and Council Directive 2004/38/EC, art 14(2). **R (on the application of the Centre for Advice on Individual Rights in Europe) v Secretary of State for the Home Dept** [2019] **4** 246, CA.
European Union. *See* **European Union** (Immigration).
Evidence in application—
Exclusion of evidence in criminal proceedings. *See* **Criminal evidence** (Exclusion of evidence—Adverse effect on fairness of proceedings—Evidence in asylum application).
False statement—
Statement to person lawfully acting in execution of statute—
Investigation of allegation that accused an illegal immigrant—Statement made by accused to constable investigating allegation—Whether constable 'acting in the execution of' statute—Immigration Act 1971, s 26(1)(c). **R v Gill** [1976] **2** 893, CA.
Police officer, in the course of investigating another matter, having cause to suspect that accused was an illegal immigrant—Police officer questioning accused and accused making false statement to police officer—Whether police officer 'acting in the execution of' statute—Immigration Act 1971, s 26(1)(c). **R v Clarke** [1985] **2** 777, HL.
Fast Track Rules (FTR). *See* Appeal—Tribunal—Immigration and Asylum Chamber, *above*.
Housing—
Homeless person—
Whether local authority duty to provide housing extending to illegal immigrant. *See* **Housing** (Homeless person—Duty of housing authority to provide accommodation—Immigrant applicant for housing).
Humanitarian protection policy—
Leave to remain. *See* Leave to remain—Indefinite leave to remain, *below*.

IMMIGRATION (cont)—

Humanitarium protection—

Appeal. *See* Asylum seeker—Appeal—Humanitarian protection, *above.*

Illegal entrant—

Application for exceptional leave to remain—

Judicial review—Illegal entrant alleging real risk of being subjected to torture or inhuman or degrading treatment or punishment on return to country of origin—Secretary of State rejecting contention and refusing to grant exceptional leave to remain—Illegal entrant challenging Secretary of State's decision in judicial review proceedings on grounds of irrationality—Whether judicial review court having primary fact-finding roleon such a challenge—European Convention for the Protection of Human Rights and Fundamental Freedoms 1950, art 3. **R v Secretary of State for the Home Dept, ex p Turgut** [2001] **1** 719, CA.

Assisting illegal entrance. *See* Offence—Assisting unlawful immigration to member state, *below.*

Detention. *See* Detention—Illegal entrant, *above.*

Entry in breach of immigration laws—

Entrants not knowingly in breach of immigration laws—Work permit—Work permits obtained for entrants in good faith by third party—Work permits improperly issued by government official—Whether work permits valid—Whether entrants 'illegal entrants'—Immigration Act 1971, s 33(1). **R v Secretary of State for the Home Dept, ex p Ku** [1995] **2** 891, CA.

Husband obtaining British passport fraudulently—

Appellant obtaining naturalisation as wife of British citizen—Appellant declared illegal immigrant after returning from trip abroad and not applying for leave for entry—Whether appellant's naturalisation as British citizen a nullity—Whether appellant remaining British citizen unless and until deprived of such status—British Nationality Act 1981, ss 6, 40, 42(5). **R v Secretary of State for the Home Dept, ex p Ejaz** [1994] **2** 436, CA.

Illegal entrant or overstayer—

Persons in need of care and attention—

Illegal overstayers applying for assistance from local authorities as persons needing care and attention—Whether person subject to immigration control qualifying for assistance only if not destitute—Whether illegal entrant or overstayer precluded from obtaining assistance—National Assistance Act 1948, s 21. **R v Wandsworth London BC, ex p O** [2000] **4** 590, CA.

Illegal entry and other offences—

Time limit for prosecution—

Continuing offences—Remaining in United Kingdom beyond time limit for leave—Failure to observe condition of leave—Entrant given leave to enter limited to one month—Entrant taking up employment during month in breach of condition of leave—Entrant remaining in employment in United Kingdom for four years—Whether entrant committing offences four years later—Immigration Act 1971, ss 24(1)(b), (3), 28(1). **Singh (Gurdev) v R** [1974] **1** 26, QBD.

Continuing offences—Remaining in United Kingdom beyond time limit for leave—Immigrant applying for further leave to remain—Leave to remain expiring while application being considered—Immigrant refused further leave to remain and then making further application to Home Office—Application subsequently refused—Whether immigrant 'knowingly' committing offence when leave expiring or when further application refused—Immigration Act 1971, s 24(1)(b)(i). **Grant v Borg** [1982] **2** 257, HL.

Immigration adjudicator—

Deportation appeal—

Function of adjudicator. *See* Appeal—Deportation—Function of immigration adjudicator, *above.*

Duty to hear parties. *See* **Natural justice** (Hearing—Duty to hear parties etc—Immigration adjudicator).

Jurisdiction to dispense with oral hearing. *See* Appeal—Immigration adjudicator—Jurisdiction to dispense with oral hearing, *above.*

Immigration Appeal Tribunal. *See* Appeal, *above.*

Immigration authority—

Hong Kong—

Natural justice—Duty to hear parties. *See* **Natural justice** (Hearing—Duty to hear parties etc—Hong Kong Immigration Authority).

Immigration document—

Offences—

Failure to provide immigration document within three days of leave or asylum interview—Reasonable excuse—Defendant unable to obtain immigration document—Defendant entering United Kingdom on false immigration document—Defendant disposing of false immigration document—Defendant not providing immigration document within three days of interview—Whether defendant having reasonable excuse for failure to provide immigration document—Asylum and Immigration (Treatment of Claimants, etc) Act 2004, s 2(1), (3), (6)(b), (12). **Thet v DPP** [2007] **2** 425, DC.

Immigration officer—

Authority—

Stamping passport—Entrant mistakenly given leave to enter and stay indefinitely—No fraud or misrepresentation by entrant—Entrant subsequently detained as illegal entrant. *See* Detention—Illegal entrant—Entry in breach of immigration laws—Immigration officer mistakenly giving entrant leave to enter and stay indefinitely—Passport so stamped—Entrant not obtaining leave by fraud or misrepresentation—Entrant subsequently detained as illegal entrant—Whether entrant entitled to rely on stamp in passport—Whether immigration officer acting within his authority in giving indefinite leave to person not entitled to such leave, *above.*

Examination of entrant—

Examination away from place of entry—Whether immigration officer entitled to conduct examination of immigrant away from place of entry—Whether immigration officer entitled to conduct examination of immigrant at a later date after entry—Immigration Act 1971, Sch 2, para 2. **Baljinder Singh v Hammond** [1987] **1** 829, QBD.

Natural justice—Duty of officer to act fairly—Duty to allow entrant to give explanation of why he should be given leave to enter—Whether duty to give entrant an opportunity to explain evidence tending to contradict statements made by entrant. **R v Secretary of State for the Home Dept, ex p Mughal** [1973] **3** 796, CA.

18

IMMIGRATION (cont)—
Immigration ordinance—
  Fiji—
    Repugnancy to British Nationality Act 1948. *See* **Fiji** (Deportation—Immigration ordinance—Repugnancy).
Immigration rules. *See* Rules, *below.*
Immigration status—
  Discrimination on grounds of. *See* **Employment** (Discrimination—Nationality, on grounds of—Immigration status).
Indefinite leave to remain. *See* Leave to remain—Indefinite leave to remain, *below.*
Infirm destitute asylum-seeker. *See* Asylum seeker—Infirm destitute asylum-seeker, *above.*
Iraq—
  Appeal. *See* Appeal—Rehearing —Asylum claimant from Iraq claiming asylum in United Kingdom in 2000, *above.*
Judicial review—
  Removal. *See* Removal—Decision to remove, *below.*
Leave for indefinite stay—
  Dependent parents—
    Other relatives in their own country to turn to—Applicants' children all settled in United Kingdom—Applicants living with daughter rent and board free—Applicants applying for conditions of stay to be removed on ground that they were dependent on children settled in United Kingdom and had no 'other close relatives in their own country to turn to'—Other close relatives in their own country to turn to—Statement of Changes in Immigration Rules (HC Paper (1979-80) no 394), para 48. **R v Immigration Appeal Tribunal, ex p Bastiampillai** [1983] **2** 844, QBD.
    Wholly or mainly dependent—Applicants' children all settled in United Kingdom—Applicants living with daughter rent and board free—Whether applicants 'wholly or mainly dependent' on child settled in United Kingdom—Whether dependence limited to financial dependence—Whether emotional dependence to be taken into account in determining dependence—Statement of Changes in Immigration Rules (HC Paper (1979-80) no 394), para 48. **R v Immigration Appeal Tribunal, ex p Bastiampillai** [1983] **2** 844, QBD.
  Exemption from immigration control—
    Member of diplomatic mission—Whether member of mission exempt from immigration control from moment of entry or from moment appointment notified to Foreign and Commonwealth Office—Immigration Act 1971, s 8(3). **R v Secretary of State for the Home Dept, ex p Bagga** [1991] **1** 777, CA.
Leave to appeal—
  Indefinite leave—
    Person having indefinite leave to enter and remain in United Kingdom at coming into force of Immigration Act 1973 and settled there—In the United kingdom—Physical presence at relevant date—Non-patrial settled in United Kingdom before relevant date—Non-patrial on visit abroad on relevant date—Whether to be treated as being in the United Kingdom on that date—Immigration Act 1971, s 1(2). **R v Secretary of State for the Home Dept, ex p Mughal** [1973] **3** 796, CA.
  Non-patrial—
    Right of entry—Expellee—Obligation of country under international law to receive back its nationals expelled from other countries—British protected person—Non-patrial expelled from normal country of residence—Expellee claiming to be British protected person—Right of British protected person to enter United Kingdom—Expellee refused leave to enter United Kingdom as of right for purpose of settling there permanently—Immigration Act 1971, s 3(1). **Thakrar v Secretary of State for the Home Dept** [1974] **2** 261, CA.
    Right of entry—Onus of satisfying immigration officer of right to enter—Non-patrial treated as having indefinite leave to enter and remain in United Kingdom—Non-patrial returning to United Kingdom after visit abroad—Whether entitled to entry as of right—Whether onus on non-patrial to satisfy immigration officer of right to enter—Immigration Act 1971, ss 1(2), (5), 3(2)—Immigration Rules (1973), r 51. **R v Secretary of State for the Home Dept, ex p Mughal** [1973] **3** 796, CA.
Leave to enter—
  Adoption—
    De facto adoption—Child seeking entry to United Kingdom as de facto adopted child of sponsor previously granted asylum as refugee—Meaning of 'adoption'—Immigration Rules (HC Paper 251) paras 6, 309A, 352D. **AA (Somalia) v Entry Clearance Officer (Addis Ababa)** [2012] **3** 893, CA; [2014] **1** 774, SC.
    Entry of child for purposes of adoption—Secretary of State issuing circular setting out criteria and procedure for entry of children for purposes of adoption—Whether circular creating legitimate expectation that Secretary of State would apply criteria and procedure set out in it—Whether Secretary of State entitled to apply different criteria and procedure. **R v Secretary of State for the Home Dept, ex p Khan** [1985] **1** 40, CA.
    Order. *See* **Adoption** (Order—Discretion—Nationality).
  Asylum—
    Deportation back to third country—Human rights—Secretary of State certifying as manifestly unfounded human rights challenge by claimant to decision to remove him to safe third country—Approach to be adopted by Secretary of State when issuing such a certificate—Human Rights Act 1998, Sch 1, Pt I, art 3—Immigration and Asylum Act 1999, s 72(2)(a). **R (on the application of Yogathas) v Secretary of State for the Home Dept** [2002] **4** 800, HL.
    Deportation back to third country—Requirement that Secretary of State be satisfied that third country would not send asylum-seeker back to another country otherwise than in accordance with international refugee convention—Whether Secretary of State entitled to be so satisfied if third country providing protection for asylum-seeker under its domestic legislation rather than under convention—Asylum and Immigration Act 1996, s 2(2)(c). **R (on the application of Yogathas) v Secretary of State for the Home Dept** [2002] **4** 800, HL.

IMMIGRATION (cont)—
  Leave to enter (cont)—
    Asylum (cont)—
      Fear of persecution by applicant for refugee status—Right not to be subjected to torture or to
      inhuman or degrading treatment or punishment—Applicant fearing persecution by non-state
      agents—Secretary of State refusing application—Risk of serious harm by non-state agents on
      return to receiving state—Receiving state providing reasonable level of protection—Whether
      breach of right not to be subjected to torture or to inhuman or degrading treatment or
      punishment—Human Rights Act 1998, Sch 1, Pt I, art 3. **R (on the application of Bagdanavicius) v
      Secretary of State for the Home Dept** [2005] **4** 263, HL.

  Dependent parents—
    Other close relatives in their own country to turn to—Needs for which an elderly parent may turn to
    close relative—Whether needs of elderly parent restricted to provision of home or financial
    support—Whether parents' needs extending to any sort of need which may afflict elderly
    person—Statement of Changes in Immigration Rules (HC Paper (1982-83) no 169), para 52. **R v
    Immigration Appeal Tribunal, ex p Swaran Singh** [1987] **3** 690, CA.

  Dependent relatives. *See* Leave to enter—Indefinite leave—Spouses, children and other dependent
  relatives, *below*.

  Indefinite leave—
    Entrant deemed to have indefinite leave of notice giving or refusing leave not given within
    prescribed period—Leave given which ought not to have been given—Leave to enter given on
    basis that passport valid—Passport stamped as valid—Immigration authority subsequently
    discovering passport false—Whether leave to enter given when passport stamped as
    valid—Whether leave a nullity—Whether notice giving or refusing leave not given—Whether
    entrant deemed to have indefinite leave to enter—Immigration Act 1971, Sch 2, para 6(1). **Khan v
    Secretary of State for the Home Dept** [1977] **3** 538, CA.

    Open date stamp placed on passport in mistaken belief that entrant a member of diplomatic
    mission—Whether open date stamp consitituting notice in writing that entrant has been granted
    indefinite leave to enter—Whether entrant deemed to have been granted indefinite leave to
    enter—Immigration Act 1971, s 4(1), Sch 2, para 6(1). **R v Secretary of State for the Home Dept,
    ex p Bagga** [1991] **1** 777, CA.

    Parent, grandparent or other dependent relative of person settled in United Kingdom—Living in
    most exceptional compassionate circumstances and mainly dependent financially on relatives
    settled in United Kingdom—Meaning of 'most exceptional compassionate circumstances'—
    Statement of Changes in Immigration Rules 1994 (HC Paper 395), para 317(i)(e). **Mohamed v
    Secretary of State for the Home Dept** [2012] **3** 420, CA.

    Person who is settled in United Kingdom—Person ordinarily resident without restriction on period
    for which he can remain—Restriction—Immigrant's passport containing entry 'employed with Sri
    Lanka High Commission'—Passport stamped with unrestricted entry stamp—Whether immigrant
    having unrestricted right of entry—Whether period of entry restricted to period of employment
    with high commission—Whether immigrant given right of entry as a diplomat—Immigration Act
    1971, ss 2(3)(d), 8(5). **R v Immigration Appeal Tribunal, ex p Coomasaru** [1983] **1** 208, CA.

    Spouses, children and other dependent relatives—Requirement for maintenance of family
    members seeking leave to enter United Kingdom without recourse to public funds—Whether
    third party support permitted in considering whether family members would be maintained
    without recourse to public funds—Statement of Changes in Immigration Rules 1994 (HC 395),
    rr 281, 297, 317. **Mahad v Entry Clearance Officer** [2010] **2** 535, SC.

  Leave obtained by deception—
    Entry as a child using passport issued in third party's name—Entrant aware of passport
    deception—Entrant subsequently obtaining passports in false name and using passports to
    re-enter United Kingdom—Whether entrant entitled to be treated as being settled in United
    Kingdom—Whether deceptions practised on re-entry constituting entrant an 'illegal
    immigrant'—Immigration Act 1971, ss 26(1)(c), 33(1)—Statement of Changes in Immigration
    Rules (HC Paper (1982-83) no 169), paras 56, 76. **R v Secretary of State for the Home Dept, ex p
    Miah** [1990] **2** 523, CA.

    Entry as a child using passport issued in third party's name—Entrant not aware of passport
    deception—Entrant subsequently obtaining passports in false name and using passports to
    re-enter United Kingdom—Whether entrant entitled to be treated as being settled in United
    Kingdom—Whether deceptions practised on re-entry constituting entrant an 'illegal
    entrant'—Immigration Act 1971, ss 26(1)(c), 33(1)—Statement of Changes in Immigration Rules
    (HC Paper (1982-83) no 169), para 56. **R v Secretary of State for the Home Dept, ex p Khan**
    [1990] **2** 531, CA.

  Leave to remain—
    Right to respect for private and family life—Right to marry—Forced marriage—Legislative policy of
    reducing forced marriages—Rules permitting spouses of United Kingdom citizens to enter or
    remain in United Kingdom—Rules not permitting spouses of United Kingdom citizens to enter or
    remain in United Kingdom where either spouse aged under 21 years—Foreign national aged
    under 21 marrying citizen of United Kingdom aged under 21—Whether legislative objective
    justifying limitation on fundamental right—Whether rule rationally connected to legislative
    objective—Whether rule proportionate—Human Rights Act 1998, Sch 1, Pt I, arts 8 ,
    12—Statement of Changes in Immigration Rules (HC Paper 1113) r 277. **R (on the application of
    Aguilar Quila) v Secretary of State for the Home Dept (Aguilar, interested party)** [2011] **3** 81,
    CA; [2012] **1** 1011, SC.

    Right to respect for private and family life—Rule precluding in-country application to change visa
    status to remain in United Kingdom—Foreign national separating from husband to return abroad
    to make entry clearance application in compliance with rule—Whether rule proportionate—
    Human Rights Act 1998, Sch 1, Pt I, art 8—Statement of Changes in Immigration Rules (HC Paper
    395) para 391C(h)(i). **R (on the application of Zhang) v Secretary of State for the Home Dept**
    [2014] **2** 560, QBD.

IMMIGRATION (cont)—
  Leave to enter (cont)—
    Non-patrial—

Leave to enter obtained by deception—Entrant subsequently applying for variation of leave—Leave extended pending determination of application—Whether extension of leave untainted by original deception—Whether applicant entitled to remain in United Kingdom until application formally determined and right of appeal exhausted—Immigration (Variation of Leave) Order 1976, art 3(1). **R v Secretary of State for the Home Dept, ex p Lapinid** [1984] **3** 257, CA.

Leave to enter obtained by deception—Entrant subsequently found to be illegal entrant—Whether leave given when it was not known that entry was illegal a relevant consideration when deciding whether to give directions for summary removal of entrant—Immigration Act 1971, Sch 2, para 9. **R v Secretary of State for the Home Dept, ex p Lapinid** [1984] **3** 257, CA.

Right of entry—Change of circumstances removing basis on which entry certificate granted—Applicant born in Pakistan and applying for entry certificate—Applicant eligible for entry certificate at time of application—Entry certificate granted two years later by which time applicant ineligible—Whether applicant under obligation when entering to disclose change of circumstances affecting his right to enter—Immigration Rules for Control on Entry: EEC and Other Non-Commonwealth Nationals (1972-73), paras 10, 39. **Zamir v Secretary of State for the Home Dept** [1980] **2** 768, HL.

Right of entry—Change of circumstances removing basis on which entry certificate granted—Applicant eligible for entry as unmarried dependant at time application made—Applicant married after application made but before entry certificate granted—Whether applicant under obligation when entering to disclose change of circumstances—Whether non-disclosure amounting to fraud or deception—Whether applicant obtaining leave to enter by fraud or deception an illegal entrant—Whether court entitled to examine evidence relied on by immigration officer—Whether court limited to enquiring whether immigration officer had reasonable grounds to conclude that applicant was illegal entrant. **Khawaja v Secretary of State for the Home Dept** [1983] **1** 765, HL.

Right of entry—Change of circumstances since entry certificate granted—Applicant born in Pakistan and applying for entry certificate—Applicant eligible for entry certificate at time of application—Entry certificate granted four years later by which time applicant ineligible—Applicant granted indefinite leave to enter and not asked about change of circumstances—Whether officer who granted entry certificate or immigration officer who granted leave to enter waiving requirements of immigration rules—Whether basis of original application still continuing at time of grant of entry certificate—Whether applicant under obligation when entering to disclose change of circumstances affecting his right to enter—Immigration Rules for Control on Entry: EEC and Other Non-Commonwealth Nationals (1972-73), para 39. **R v Secretary of State for the Home Dept, ex p Khan** [1980] **2** 337, CA.

Right of entry—Date at which applicant's eligibility for entry certificate to be determined—Change of circumstances removing basis on which entry certificate granted—Applicant born in Pakistan and applying for entry certificate—Applicant eligible for entry certificate at time of application—Entry certificate granted two years later by which time applicant ineligible—Whether applicant's eligibility for entry certificate to be determined at date of application or date of grant of certificate—Whether applicant under obligation when entering to disclose change of circumstances affecting his right to enter—Immigration Rules for Control on Entry: EEC and Other Nationals (1972-73), paras 10,39. **Zamir v Secretary of State for the Home Dept** [1979] **2** 849, QBD.

Right of entry—Duty to disclose facts—Applicant failed to disclose all material facts to immigration officer—Whether failure to disclose coupled with conduct amounting to fraud or deception—Whether applicant obtaining leave to enter by fraud or deception an illegal entrant—Whether court entitled to examine evidence relied on by immigration officer—Whether court limited to enquiring whether immigration officer had reasonable grounds to conclude that applicant was illegal entrant. **Khawaja v Secretary of State for the Home Dept** [1983] **1** 765, HL.

Right of entry—Duty to disclose facts—Material facts—Failure to disclose intention to claim refugee status and asylum—Disclosure of intention might have caused leave to be granted—Whether failure to disclose intention to seek asylum a non-disclosure of a 'material' fact—Whether leave to enter vitiated by non-disclosure of material fact. **Bugdaycay v Secretary of State for the Home Dept** [1987] **1** 940, HL.

Right of entry—Duty to disclose facts—Vitiation of leave to enter by non-disclosure—Immigrant seeking entry only required to disclose material facts decisively affecting grant of leave to enter—Failure to disclose immaterial facts not vitiating leave to enter. **R v Secretary of State for the Home Dept, ex p Jayakody** [1982] **1** 461, CA.

Right of entry—Duty to disclose facts—Vitiation of leave to enter by non-disclosure—Immigrant seeking entry required to disclose material facts decisively affecting grant of leave to enter—Failure to disclose material facts vitiating leave to enter. **Khawaja v Secretary of State for the Home Dept** [1982] **2** 523, CA.

Student—Applicant required to produce to immigration officer proof of acceptance for course of study at school or university—Officer required to refuse entry if not satisfied that applicant would leave United Kingdom on completion of full-time course of study—Full-time course of study—Proof by schoolboy applicant that he was accepted by school for three-year 'O' level course of study—Officer not satisfied that applicant would leave on completion of three-year course because applicant stated that he expected to stay until completion of university study—Refusal by officer to grant applicant leave to enter as a student—Whether officer had interpreted rules correctly—Statement of Changes in Immigration Rules (HC Paper (1979-80) no 394) paras 21, 22. **R v Chief Immigration Officer, Gatwick Airport, ex p Kashayar Kharrazi** [1980] **3** 373, CA.

IMMIGRATION (cont)—
　Leave to enter (cont)—
　　Non-patrial (cont)—
　　　Student—Requirements for entry—Applicant producing evidence of genuine intention to study in United Kingdom—Applicant unable to satisfy immigration officer of intention to leave United Kingdom on completion of course—Immigration officer refusing leave to enter—Whether necessity to satisfy immigration officer of intention to leave country on completion of course a 'requirement' for entry—Whether applicant not satisfying 'requirements' for entry—Whether immigration officer having discretion to admit student for short period despite failure to show intention to leave country on completion of course—Statement of Immigration Rules for Control on Entry: Commonwealth Citizens (HC Paper (1972-73) no 79), paras 19, 21. **Alexander v Immigration Appeal Tribunal** [1982] **2** 766, HL.

　　　Student—Variation of leave for purpose of study—Intention to leave at end of studies—Whether applicant must prove intention to leave at end of studies when he applies for variation of his leave to enter—Whether applicant must prove merely that he wishes to remain as bona fide student—Whether applicant's wish to remain after end of studies if permitted disentitling him to apply for variation of leave to enter in order to complete studies—Whether applicant must prove requisite intention at time of application for variation or at time of hearing of appeal from refusal to grant variation—Immigration Rules for Control on Entry: EEC and Other Non-Commonwealth Nationals (1972-73), para 17—Immigration Rules for Control after Entry: EEC and Other Non-Commonwealth Nationals (1972-73), para 12. **R v Immigration Appeal Tribunal, ex p Shaikh** [1981] **3** 29, QBD.

　　Refugee—
　　　Asylum—Applicant for asylum entering country illegally on false documents—Applicant fearing threat to life or freedom in home country—Applicant a member of illegal political organisation carrying out terrorist activities in home country—Application for asylum refused on grounds of applicant's involvement in 'serious non-political crimes'—Circumstances in which crimes to be characterised as 'political'—Convention relating to the Status of Refugees 1951, art 1F. **T v Secretary of State for the Home Dept** [1996] **2** 865, HL.

　　　Asylum—Application for asylum refused without consideration of claim—Detention pending removal to safe third country—Applicant obtaining writ of habeas corpus—Whether writ of habeas corpus appropriate remedy—Whether prior administrative decision refusing leave to enter open to investigation on application for writ of habeas corpus—Whether appropriate remedy judicial review of administrative decision—Whether application for leave to move for judicial review should be granted. **R v Secretary of State for the Home Dept, ex p Muboyayi** [1991] **4** 72, CA.

　　　Asylum—Asylum seeker's application for asylum rejected—Asylum seeker making further submissions to Secretary of State—Asylum seeker claiming further submissions constituting fresh claim—Asylum seeker applying for permission to work pending determination of fresh claim—Secretary of State dismissing application—Directive providing for access to the labour market pending application for asylum—Whether application for asylum including only first application for asylum—Council Directive (EC) 2003/9, arts 2, 11. **R (on the application of ZO (Somalia)) v Secretary of State for the Home Dept** [2010] **4** 649, SC.

　　　Asylum—Child—Asylum seeker claiming to be under 18—Local authority assessing age as over 18—Secretary of State detaining asylum seeker on basis of age assessment—Asylum seeker released from detention—Subsequent age assessment carried out finding asylum seeker to be under 18—Whether detention unlawful—Immigration Act 1971, Sch 2, para 16—Children Act 1989, s 20—Borders, Citizenship and Immigration Act 2009, s 55. **R (on the application of AA) v Secretary of State for the Home Dept** [2013] **4** 140, SC.

　　　Asylum—Child—Claimant assessed as adult and detained pending removal—Claimant subsequently found to be under 18—Whether assessment as 'child' objective—Whether detention lawful—Immigration Act 1971, Sch 2, paras 16(2A), 18B. **R (on the application of Ali) v Secretary of State for the Home Dept** [2017] **4** 964, CA.

　　　Asylum—Deportation back to third country—Home Secretary issuing certificate that applicant's claim that removal from United Kingdom would breach 1951 Geneva Convention on Refugees was without foundation—Applicant appealing to special adjudicator—Whether Home Secretary obliged to make available to adjudicator material on which he based certificate—Whether sufficient evidence before adjudicators to decide appeals—Asylum Appeals (Procedure) Rules 1993, r 5(6)—Statement of Changes in Immigration Rules (HC Paper (1993) No 725), para 180K. **Abdi v Secretary of State for the Home Dept** [1996] **1** 641, HL.

　　　Asylum—Deportation back to third country—Home Secretary's certificate that applicant's claim that removal from United Kingdom would breach the 1951 Convention on Refugees was without foundation—Whether claim for asylum without foundation if it was unnecessary for Home Secretary to decide whether claimant a refugee because he could be removed to safe third country—Function of special adjudicators on appeal against Home Secretary's certificate—Asylum and Immigration Appeals Act 1993, Sch 2, para 5(3)(a)—Statement of changes in Immigration Rules (HC Paper (1993) No 725), para 180K. **R v Secretary of State for the Home Dept, ex p Mehari** [1994] **2** 494, QBD.

　　　Asylum—Deportation back to third country—Requirement that Secretary of State be satisfied that government of third country would not send asylum seeker back to another country otherwise than in accordance with Convention relating to the Status of Refugees 1951—Test to be applied—Sufficient if no real risk—Asylum and Immigration Act 1996, s 2(2). **R v Secretary of State for the Home Dept, ex p Canbolat** [1998] **1** 161, CA.

　　　Asylum—Deportation to country which would send applicant back to country where he would be persecuted—Ugandan national entering United Kingdom from Kenya—Applicant seeking asylum because of fear of persecution in Uganda—Secretary of State proposing to remove applicant to Kenya—Secretary of State not taking into account Kenyan repatriation of Ugandan nationals—Whether Secretary of State's decision should be quashed—Convention and Protocol relating to the Status of Refugees 1951, art 33. **Bugdaycay v Secretary of State for the Home Dept** [1987] **1** 940, HL.

IMMIGRATION (cont)—
　　Leave to enter (cont)—
　　　Refugee (cont)—
　　　　Asylum—Exclusion from provisions of Refugee Convention—Acts contrary to purpose and principles of United Nations—Principles of liability to be applied for purpose of exclusion—Application of exclusion to person giving nursing and medical assistance to terrorist organisation—Immigration, Asylum and Nationality Act 2006, s 54—Convention relating to the Status of Refugees, art 1F(c). **MH (Syria) v Secretary of State for the Home Dept** [2009] 3 564, CA.

　　　　Asylum—Exclusion from provisions of Refugee Convention—Acts contrary to purpose and principles of United Nations—Principles of liability to be applied for purposes of exclusion—Serious reasons for considering applicants to be guilty of acts contrary to purposes and principles of United Nations—Whether all acts falling within domestic definition of terrorism constituting acts contrary to purposes and principles of United Nations—Whether participation in armed insurrection against United Nations-mandated force contrary to purposes and principles of United Nations—Meaning of 'serious reasons for considering'—Immigration, Asylum and Nationality Act 2006, s 54—Council Directive (EC) 2004/83, art 12(2)(c)—United Nations Convention relating to the Status of Refugees 1951, art 1F(c). **Al-Sirri v Secretary of State for the Home Dept** [2013] 1 1267, SC.

　　　　Asylum—Exclusion from provisions of Refugee Convention—Commission of crime against peace, war crime or crime against humanity—Principles of liability to be applied for purpose of exclusion—Joint criminal enterprise liability—Convention relating to the Status of Refugees, art 1F(a). **R (on the application of JS (Sri Lanka)) v Secretary of State for the Home Dept** [2009] 3 588, CA; [2010] 3 881, SC.

　　　　Asylum—Exclusion from provisions of Refugee Convention—Commission of crime against peace, war crime or crime against humanity—Raids on farms in Zimbabwe—Whether acts of similar character to list of specified crimes against humanity—Whether acts intentionally causing 'great suffering, or serious injury to body or to mental or physical health'—Whether acts of sufficient seriousness to amount to crime against humanity—United Nations Convention relating to the Status of Refugees 1951, art 1F(a)—Rome Statute of the International Criminal Court 1998, art 7.1. **SK (Zimbabwe) v Secretary of State for the Home Dept** [2012] 4 1205, CA.

　　　　Asylum—Exclusion from provisions of Refugee Convention—Commission of serious non-political crime outside country of refuge prior to admission—Expiation—Whether facts arising since commission of offence to be taken into account—Meaning of 'serious'—United Nations Convention relating to the Status of Refugees 1951, art 1F(b)—Council Directive 2004/83/EC, art 12. **AH (Algeria) v Secretary of State for the Home Dept** [2016] 3 453, CA.

　　　　Asylum—Fear of persecution by applicant for refugee status—Social group—Homosexuals—Applicant seeking asylum on basis of fear of persecution in home country due to homosexuality—Assessment made as to asylum seeker's likelihood of behaving discreetly and ability to tolerate restrictions on homosexual activity thereby reducing threat of persecution in home country—Whether test appropriate—Test to be applied when determining whether homosexual applicant having well-founded fear of persecution—Convention and Protocol relating to the Status of Refugees 1951, art 1A(2). **HJ (Iran) v Secretary of State for the Home Dept** [2011] 2 591, SC.

　　　　Asylum—Fear of persecution by applicant for refugee status—Conscientious objection to military service—Whether international law recognising right of conscientious objection to military service for purpose of establishing refugee status—Convention and Protocol relating to the Status of Refugees 1951, art 1A(2). **Sepet v Secretary of State for the Home Dept** [2003] 3 304, HL.

　　　　Asylum—Fear of persecution by applicant for refugee status—Political opinion—Fear of persecution on basis of imputed political opinion—Protection of persons holding no political opinions—Convention and Protocol relating to the Status of Refugees 1951. **RT (Zimbabwe) v Secretary of State for the Home Dept** [2012] 4 843, SC.

　　　　Asylum—Fear of persecution by applicant for refugee status—Social group—Homosexuals—Designation of home country as one where in general no serious risk of persecution existing—Homosexuals in home country routinely reviled and attacked with no protection from state—Whether designation of home country unlawful—Nationality, Immigration and Asylum Act, s 94. **R (on the application of JB (Jamaica)) v Secretary of State for the Home Dept** [2014] 2 91, CA; [2015] 3 317, SC.

　　　　Asylum—Fear of persecution held by applicant for refugee status—Allegation of persecution by non-state agents—Whether failure of state to provide protection prerequisite of 'persecution'—Convention relating to the Status of Refugees 1951, art 1A(2). **Horvath v Secretary of State for the Home Dept** [2000] 3 577, HL.

　　　　Asylum—Fear of persecution held by applicant for refugee status—Applicant making fraudulent and baseless application for asylum—Home Secretary refusing application—Appeal—Applicant claiming risk of persecution as a failed asylum seeker—Whether fraudulent application an automatic barrier to grant of asylum—Convention relating to the Status of Refugees, art 1A(2). **M v Secretary of State for the Home Dept** [1996] 1 870, CA.

　　　　Asylum—Fear of persecution held by applicant for refugee status—Applicant unjustly suspected of terrorist activity—Whether applicant entitled to protection—Convention and Protocol Relating to the Status of Refugees, art 1A. **R (on the application of Sivakumar) v Secretary of State for the Home Dept** [2003] 2 1097, HL.

　　　　Asylum—Fear of persecution held by applicant for refugee status—Civil war in country of origin—Home Office refusing to grant refugee status—Applicant not having current well-founded fear of persecution if returned to country of origin—Whether sufficient that applicant originally fled country or remained abroad for well-founded fear of persecution—Meaning of 'refugee' in context of civil war—Convention and Protocol relating to the Status of Refugees, art 1A(2). **Adan v Secretary of State for the Home Dept** [1998] 2 453, HL.

　　　　Asylum—Fear of persecution held by applicant for refugee status—Non-state persecution—Well-founded fear of persecution by reason of membership of 'a particular social group'—Whether person seeking asylum from non-state persecution could establish membership of such a group merely by proving that someone had marked it out for special attention—Convention and Protocol relating to the Status of Refugees 1951, art 1A. **Skenderaj v Secretary of State for the Home Dept** [2002] 4 555, CA.

IMMIGRATION (cont)—
  Leave to enter (cont)—
    Refugee (cont)—
      Scheme enabling immigration rules to be operated extra-territorially—Pre-entry clearance system at Prague airport—Claimants Czech Roma refused entry—Whether system contrary to international refugee convention—Whether system contrary to customary international law—Whether operation of system racially discriminatory—Race Relations Act 1976, s 1(1)(a)—Convention relating to the Status of Refugees 1951, art 33. **European Roma Rights Centre v Immigration Officer at Prague Airport (United Nations High Comr for Refugees intervening)** [2003] **4** 247, CA.

      Sovereign Base Area (SBA)—Respondent refugees living in Cyprus SBA—Whether Refugee Convention applying—Whether convention entitling respondents to be resettled in United Kingdom—United Nations Convention and Protocol Relating to the Status of Refugees 1951, art 40. **R (on the application of Bashir) v Secretary of State for the Home Dept (AIRE Centre intervening)** [2018] **4** 911, SC.

  Refusal of leave—
    Appeal—Appeal to adjudicator—Right to respect for private and family life—Decision-making role and function of appellate immigration authorities—Guidance—Human Rights Act 1998, Sch 1, Pt I, art 8. **AG (Eritrea) v Secretary of State for the Home Dept** [2008] **2** 28, CA.

    Appeal—Appeal to adjudicator—Right to respect for private and family life—Decision-making role and function of appellate immigration authorities—Guidance—Human Rights Act 1998, Sch 1, Pt I, art 8—Immigration and Asylum Act 1999, s 65, Sch 4, paras 21, 22. **Huang v Secretary of State for the Home Dept** [2005] **3** 435, CA; [2007] **4** 15, HL.

    Delay—Right to respect for private and family life—Asylum seeker claiming removal amounting to unlawful interference with right to respect for private and family life—Whether delay by Secretary of State affecting substantive claim for right to private and family life—Human Rights Act 1998, Sch 1, Pt I, art 8. **EB (Kosovo) v Secretary of State for the Home Dept** [2008] **4** 28, HL.

    Leader of American religious, social and political movement wishing to enter United Kingdom to address British followers—Secretary of State excluding claimant on grounds that visit would constitute threat to public order—Whether exclusion engaging convention right to freedom of expression—Human Rights Act 1998, Sch 1, Pt I, art 10. **R (on the application of Farrakhan) v Secretary of State for the Home Dept** [2002] **4** 289, CA.

    Reasons for decision—Adequacy of reasons—Entrant seeking leave to enter for one week—Immigration officer refusing leave because she was 'not satisfied that [entrant] genuinely seeking entry only for ... limited period'—Whether immigration officer's statement constituting sufficient 'reasons for the decision'—Immigration Appeals (Notices) Regulations 1984, reg 4(1)(a). **R v Secretary of State for the Home Dept, ex p Swati** [1986] **1** 717, CA.

    Removal of immigrant—Direction to airline to remove immigrant—Validity—Locus standi of immigrant to challenge validity of direction—Direction to remove immigrant when his application to enter finally resolved—Whether direction valid if it merely indicates immigrant might be required to be removed—Whether direction must indicate immediate requirement to remove immigrant—Immigration Act 1971, Sch 2, para 8(1)(b). **R v Immigration Officer, ex p Shah** [1982] **2** 264, QBD.

    Right to respect for private and family life—Foreign national seeking leave to enter to visit elderly relatives—Whether refusal infringing convention right to private life—Human Rights Act 1998, Sch 1, Pt I, art 8. **Secretary of State for the Home Dept v Abbas** [2018] **2** 156, CA.

  Spouse or civil partner—
    Rule imposing pre-entry English language test for foreign spouses and partners of British citizens or persons settled in United Kingdom—Whether rule breaching human rights of spouses and families—Human Rights Act 1998, Sch 1, Pt I, art 8—Immigration Rules, App FM, paras E-ECP 4.1, E-ECP 4.2. **R (on the application of Bibi) v Secretary of State for the Home Dept (Liberty and Joint Council for the Welfare of Immigrants, intervening)** [2016] **2** 193, SC.

    Rule imposing pre-entry English language test for foreign spouses and partners of British citizens or persons settled in United Kingdom—Whether rule breaching human rights of spouses and families—Human Rights Act 1998, Sch 1, Pt I, arts 8, 12, 14—Immigration Rules (HC 395), para 281. **R (on the application of Bibi) v Secretary of State for the Home Dept (Liberty and Joint Council for the Welfare of Immigrants, intervening)** [2013] **3** 778, CA; **R (on the application of Chapti) v Secretary of State for the Home Dept (Liberty and Joint Council for the Welfare of Immigrants, intervening)** [2012] **2** 653, QBD.

  Spouses, children and other dependent relatives—
    Immigration rules—Minimum income requirements—Evidential requirements—Cases falling outside requirements under immigration rules—Right to respect for private and family life—Guidance—Human Rights Act 1998, Sch 1, Pt I, art 8—Nationality, Immigration and Asylum Act 2002, ss 85, 85A(2)—Immigration Rules, Apps FM, FM-SE. **SS (Congo) v Secretary of State for the Home Dept** [2016] **1** 706, CA.

    Indefinite leave. *See* Leave to enter—Indefinite leave—Parent, grandparent or other dependent relative of person settled in United Kingdom, *above*.

    Requirement for maintenance of family members seeking leave to enter United Kingdom without recourse to public funds—Sponsor having been granted indefinite leave to remain—Sponsor having obtained British citizenship—Whether requirement for maintenance of family members applying to spouse and children seeking leave to enter—Statement of Changes in the Immigration Rules 1994 (HC Paper 395), paras 352A, 352D. **ZN (Afghanistan) v Entry Clearance Officer (Karachi)** [2010] **4** 77, SC.

  Successive applications—
    Application on more than one ground—Applicant refused to enter as visitor—Applicant then applying for asylum while still in United Kingdom—Whether adjudicator having jurisdiction to entertain appeal from refusal of leave to enter as visitor—Whether applicant can make successive applications for leave to enter—Immigration Act 1971, s 13. **R v Immigration Appeal Tribunal, ex p Secretary of State for the Home Dept** [1990] **3** 652, CA.

IMMIGRATION (cont)—
Leave to remain—
Appeal —
Removal of certain persons unlawfully in the United Kingdom—Statutory appeal—Appeal to tribunal—Judicial review—Whether judicial review available remedy—Immigration and Asylum Act 1999, s 10. **R (on the application of Khan) v Secretary of State for the Home Dept** [2015] **1** 1057, QBD.

Removal: persons with statutorily extended leave—Persons granted leave to enter applying for further leave to remain—Secretary of State refusing application but not considering making removal direction—Whether refusal of application lawful—Whether Secretary of State bound to consider making removal direction at same time as making decision to refuse application—Immigration, Asylum and Nationality Act 2006, s 47. **Patel v Secretary of State for the Home Dept** [2012] **4** 94, CA; [2014] **1** 1157, SC.

Right to respect for private and family life—Appellants forming relationships with British citizens during unlawful residence and subsequently applying for leave to remain as partners—Secretary of State applying Immigration Rules and refusing leave to remain on ground that no 'insurmountable obstacles' to family life continuing outside UK—Secretary of State further applying Immigration Directorate Instructions that 'exceptional circumstances' required for leave to be granted outside Rules—Whether refusals lawful—Human Rights Act 1998, Sch 1, Pt I, art 8—Immigration Rules, App FM, para EX.1(b)—Immigration Directorate Instructions. **R (on the application of Agyarko) v Secretary of State for the Home Dept** [2017] **4** 575, SC.

Right to respect for private and family life—Proportionality—Public interest—Whether value of person to community in United Kingdom capable of being relevant factor in assessing public interest—Human Rights Act 1998, Sch 1, Pt I, art 8. **UE (Nigeria) v Secretary of State for the Home Dept** [2011] **2** 352, CA.

Right to respect for private and family life—Whether immigration appellate authorities should take account of impact of appellant's proposed removal on all members of family—Immigration and Asylum Act 1999, s 65—Nationality, Immigration and Asylum Act 2002, s 84. **Beoku-Betts v Secretary of State for the Home Dept** [2008] **4** 1146, HL.

Evidence—
Burden of proof—English language proficiency—Secretary of State cancelling leave to remain on basis of allegations of dishonesty in English language proficiency tests (ETS)—Whether Secretary of State discharging legal burden of proof. **Majumder v Secretary of State for the Home Dept** [2017] **3** 756n, CA.

Indefinite leave to remain—
Cancellation—Secretary of State cancelling claimant's indefinite leave to remain after claimant travelled outside UK—Claimant detained as illegal entrant upon re-entry—Whether Secretary of State having power to cancel indefinite leave to remain—Immigration Act 1971, ss 3, 3B—Immigration (Leave to Enter and Remain) Order 2000, SI 2000/1161, art 13(7). **R (on the application of C1) v Secretary of State for the Home Dept** [2021] **4** 292, QBD; [2022] **3** 1082, CA.

Claimant foreign nationals convicted of serious offences in United Kingdom—Claimants each being sentenced to more than 12 months' imprisonment—Claimants seeking indefinite leave to remain—Claimants being refused indefinite leave in accordance with policy of Secretary of State—Policy requiring certain persons, including those convicted of serious crimes, to complete ten years' continuous discretionary leave to remain in United Kingdom before being considered for settlement—Whether exclusion of persons sentenced to more than 12 months' imprisonment from humanitarian protection policy contrary to principle—Whether policy unlawfully fettered discretion of Secretary of State—Immigration Act 1971, s 3. **R (on the application of Mayaya) v Secretary of State for the Home Dept** [2012] **1** 1491, Admin Ct.

Fees—Windrush scandal—Claimant victim of Windrush scandal entitled to indefinite leave to remain—Claimant seeking permission for her family to join her in UK—Remainder of family not victims of Windrush scandal and liable to full fees—Whether requirement to pay full fees breach of right to private and family life—Whether discriminatory—Human Rights Act 1998, Sch 1, Pt I, arts 8, 14. **R (on the application of Mahabir) v Secretary of State for the Home Dept** [2022] **1** 895, QBD.

Indefinite leave to remain invalidated by subsequent deportation order—Deportation order revoked—Whether indefinite leave to remain revived by revocation of deportation order—Immigration Act 1971, s 5—Nationality, Immigration and Asylum Act 2002, s 76. **R (on the application of George) v Secretary of State for the Home Dept** [2014] **3** 365, SC.

Long residence—Secretary of State refusing application for indefinite leave to remain based on '10 years continuous lawful residence'—Whether short 'gaps' in lawful residence could be disregarded—Immigration Rules, para 276B. **R (on the application of Ahmed) v Secretary of State for the Home Dept** [2020] **2** 73, CA.

Refusal—Earnings discrepancy cases—Discrepancy between earnings claimed in applications for indefinite leave to remain and in tax returns—Secretary of State refusing claims on basis of conduct—Whether procedurally fair—Whether convention rights engaged—Human Rights Act 1998, Sch 1, Pt I, art 8—Immigration Rules, para 322(5). **R (on the application of Balajigari) v Secretary of State for the Home Dept** [2019] **4** 998, CA.

Natural justice—
Procedural fairness—Application for leave to remain sponsored by employer—Employer's sponsor licence revoked while application outstanding—Secretary of State failing to inform applicant of revocation—Application subsequently rejected—Whether duty to promptly notify of revocation—Whether duty to allow reasonable period for alternative application. **R (on the application of Pathan) v Secretary of State for the Home Dept** [2021] **2** 761, SC.

Points-based system for entrepreneurs—
Documents submitted with application—Errors in documents—Secretary of State's guidance on evidential flexibility—Whether guidance creating general duty to allow correction of minor errors beyond terms of Immigration Rules—Meaning of 'specified documents' for purposes of rules—Immigration Rules, Pt 6A, para 245AA. **Mudiyanselage v Secretary of State for the Home Dept** [2018] **4** 35, CA.

IMMIGRATION (cont)—
  Leave to remain (cont)—
    Points-based system for entrepreneurs (cont)—
      Procedural fairness—Claimant refused leave to remain—Secretary of State finding certain inconsistencies and inaccuracies in claimant's application—Whether Secretary of State under duty to put claimant on notice of concerns about application—Whether decision irrational—Immigration Rules, para 245DD. **R (on the application of Taj) v Secretary of State for the Home Dept** [2021] **4** 1159, CA.
    Points-based system for skilled workers—
      Post-study work—Requirement for applicant to make application within 12 months of obtaining relevant qualification—Applicants making application before obtaining qualifications—Applicants obtaining qualifications before Secretary of State con-sidering applications—Whether applicants making applications within 12 months of obtaining qualifications—Statement of Changes in Immigration Rules (HC Paper 395), paras 34G, 245FD, App A, Table 10. **Raju v Secretary of State for the Home Dept** [2013] **4** 1043, CA.
    Points-based system for students—
      Documents not submitted with applications—Documents submitted after application—Sequence of documents with some documents in sequence omitted—Requirement for specified documents demonstrating required level of maintenance funds—Applicant submitting one page bank statement showing required level of maintenance fund covering only last part of specified period—Whether preceding bank statement part of sequence of documents—Statement of Changes in Immigration Rules 1994 (HC 395), para 245AA. **R (on the application of Gu) v Secretary of State for the Home Dept** [2015] **1** 363, QBD.
      Documents submitted with application—Applicant required to demonstrate he held at least £5,400 for a consecutive period of 28 days—Applicant submitting statement with application demonstrating he held relevant funds for 22-day period—Border agency refusing application without asking applicant for additional information to demonstrate he held relevant funds—Whether agency acting unlawfully in refusing application without first inviting applicant to supply evidence showing he held relevant funds for all of 28-day period. **Mandalia v Secretary of State for the Home Dept** [2016] **4** 189, SC.
    Student loans. See **Education** (Higher education—Student loans—Immigration status).
    Variation—
      Applicant applying for extension of leave to remain as student—Licence of educational sponsor subsequently revoked—Variation of application to specify new educational sponsor—Whether maintenance requirements to be fulfilled at time of original or varied application—Immigration Act 1971, s 3C—Immigration Rules, para 34E, Appendix C, para 1A(a). **Secretary of State for the Home Dept v Khan** [2017] **2** 831, CA.
      Continuation of leave pending variation decision—Appellants applying to extend leave to remain before original leave expiring—Applications being deemed invalid for failure to comply with immigration rules—Further applications for leave to remain being made after original leave expiring—Whether further applications engaging statutory extension of leave to remain pending determination of applications—Immigration Act 1971, s 3C. **R (on the application of Iqbal) v Secretary of State for the Home Dept** [2017] **3** 824, SC.
      Continuation of leave pending variation decision—Appellants applying to extend leave to remain before original leave expiring—Applications being deemed invalid for failure to comply with rules—Further applications for leave to remain being made after original leave expiring—Whether further applications engaging statutory extension of leave to remain in the United Kingdom pending determination of applications—Whether Secretary of State unreasonably delaying processing of application—Meaning of 'application'—Immigration Act 1971, s 3C. **R (on the application of Iqbal) v Secretary of State for the Home Dept** [2016] **2** 469, CA.
      Removal: persons with statutorily extended leave—Secretary of State refusing variation of leave to remain and deciding that claimant should be removed from United Kingdom in same decision—Whether practice of issuing combined decision on variation and removal lawful—Whether decision to remove valid—Immigration Act 1971, ss 3C, 4—Nationality, Asylum and Immigration Act 2002, s 82—Immigration (Continuance of Leave) (Notices) Regulations 2006, SI 2006/2170, reg 2. **R (on the application of Ahmadi) v Secretary of State for the Home Dept** [2013] **4** 442, CA.
  Marriage—
    Right to marry—
      Discrimination. See **Marriage** (Right to marry—Immigration).
  National security—
    Appeal against deportation on grounds of. See Appeal—Deportation—Appeal against deportation on grounds of national security, *above*.
  Non-patrial—
    Deportation. See Deportation, *above*.
    Leave to enter. See Leave to enter—Non-patrial, *above*.
  Non-residents—
    National Health Service charges. See **National Health Service** (England—Charges—Charges in respect of non-residents).
  Notice—
    Removal. See Removal—Decision to remove—Notice of removal, *below*.
  Offence—
    Assisting unlawful immigration to member state—
      Act facilitating commission of breach of immigration law—Meaning of 'immigration law'—Offence of entering United Kingdom without passport, etc—Whether 'immigration law'—Immigration Act 1971, s 25(2)—Asylum and Immigration (Treatment of Claimants, etc) Act 2004, s 2. **R v Kapoor** [2012] **2** 1205, CA.

IMMIGRATION (cont)—

Patrial—

Right of abode—

Wife of patrial—Proof of patriality—Certificate of patriality—Right of wife to certificate—Grant of certificate not to be refused arbitrarily or delayed without good reason—Wife of patrial arriving in United Kingdom without certificate—Application to Home Office for certificate—Home Office rejecting application on ground that it could be dealt with more satisfactorily in wife's country of origin—Long delay in country of origin because of large number of applicants—Most applicants seeking leave to enter—Whether Home Office bound to consider wife's application on merits—Immigration Act 1971, ss 2(1)(a)(2), 3(9)—Immigration Rules (1973), r 4. **R v Secretary of State for the Home Dept, ex p Phansopkar** [1975] **3** 497, QBD and CA.

Wife of patrial—Wife an alien—Wife entitled to be registered as United Kingdom citizen—Husband a patrial having a right of abode in United Kingdom—Wife arriving in United Kingdom—Whether wife having a right to enter—British Nationality Act 1948, s 6(2). **R v Secretary of State for the Home Dept, ex p Akhtar** [1975] **3** 1087, QBD.

Points-based system—

Student—

Leave to remain. *See* Leave to remain—Points-based system for students, *above*.

Port and border controls—

Terrorism, prevention of. *See* **Terrorism** (Prevention of—Port and border controls).

Practice—

Appeal. *See* Appeal, *above*.

Application to Divisional Court—

Simplification of presentation of application—Forms—Immigration Act 1971. **Practice Direction** [1979] **2** 880, QBD.

Asylum and Immigration Tribunal granting permission to appeal to Court of Appeal—

Solicitors failing to serve notice of appeal in time—Whether Court of Appeal to extend time—Guidance—CPR PD 52, para 21.7(3). **BR (Iran) v Secretary of State for the Home Dept** [2007] **3** 318, CA.

Legal representation—

Duty to court. *See* **Solicitor** (Duty—Duty to court—Solicitors Regulation Authority—Referral—Immigration and asylum).

Refugee—

Asylum. *See* Asylum—Refugee, *above*.

Change of circumstance in refugee country of origin—

European Union. *See* **European Union** (Reference to European Court—Request for preliminary ruling concerning interpretation of Community law—Interpretation of directive—Refugee status).

Deportation. *See* Deportation—Refugee, *above*.

European Union. *See* **European Union** (Reference to European Court—Request for preliminary ruling concerning interpretation of European Union law—Interpretation of regulation—Refugee status).

Exclusion from provisions of Refugee Convention. *See* Leave to enter—Refugee—Asylum—Exclusion from provisions of Refugee Convention, *above*.

Illegal entry or presence—

Provision of international convention protecting refugees from penalties for illegal entry or presence—Domestic statute providing defence for refugees charged with listed offences—Refugee flying to United Kingdom and entering under false passport—Refugee immediately seeking to fly to United States to seek asylum using second false passport—Refugee charged with two offences arising out of same facts in relation to use of second false passport—Refugee relying on statutory defence for first offence and seeking to rely on provision of international convention in relation to second offence—Refugee convicted of second offence—Whether provision of international convention applying to offences committed in course of leaving United Kingdom—Whether prosecution of second offence amounting to abuse of process—Immigration and Asylum Act 1999, s 31—United Nations Convention relating to the Status of Refugees 1951, art 31(1). **R v Asfaw** [2008] **3** 775, HL.

Provision of international convention protecting refugees from penalties for illegal entry or presence—Domestic statute providing defence for refugees charged with listed offences—Refugees pleading guilty to entering United Kingdom in possession of false identity documents—Refugees not advised on availability of defence in case of short-term stopovers en route to intended country of refuge—Whether guilty pleas in absence of accurate legal advice null—Whether defences would quite probably have succeeded—United Nations Convention relating to the Status of Refugees 1951, art 31(1)—Immigration and Asylum Act 1999, s 31. **R v Mateta** [2014] **1** 152, CA.

Provision of international convention protecting refugees from penalties for illegal entry or presence—Scope and effect of provision—UN Convention relating to the Status of Refugees 1951, art 31(1). **R v Uxbridge Magistrates' Court, ex p Adimi** [1999] **4** 520, QBD.

Leave to enter. *See* Leave to enter—Refugee, *above*.

Relocation in country of nationality. *See* Leave to enter—Refugee—Asylum—Fear of persecution held by applicants for refugee status—Place of relocation in country of nationality, *above*.

Removal—

Decision to remove—

Appeal—Victim of human trafficking—National Referral Mechanism (NRM) concluding appellant not victim of human trafficking—Whether tribunal bound by decision of NRM—Relevance of finding of trafficking to human rights considerations—Human Rights Act 1998, Sch 1, Pt I, art 4. **MS (Pakistan) v Secretary of State for the Home Dept (Equality and Human Rights Commission and others intervening)** [2020] **3** 733, SC.

IMMIGRATION (cont)—
Removal (cont)—
Decision to remove (cont)—
Defendant Secretary of State issuing decisions to remove claimants and to refuse variation of pre-existing leave to remain in the United Kingdom—Claimants seeking judicial review—Applications failing and claimants appealing—Whether, when removal decision being made, relevant statutory provision invalidating automatically extended leave—Whether sequence of notices of decision invalidating leave and refusing variation of leave rendering right of appeal in-country—Circumstances in which, notwithstanding right to statutory out-of-country appeal, appropriate for matter to be dealt with by judicial review—Immigration Act 1971, ss 3, 3C—Immigration and Asylum Act 1999, s 10—Nationality, Immigration and Asylum Act 2002, ss 82(2), 92. **R (on the application of Mehmood) v Secretary of State for the Home Dept** [2016] **3** 398, CA.

Notice of removal—Persons without leave to enter or remain—Policy for removal of irregular migrants—Policy involving short period in which no risk of removal followed by removal window during which migrant might be removed without further notice—Whether requirement to serve further notice—Whether policy affording adequate access to justice—Whether policy unlawful—Immigration and Asylum Act 1999, s 10. **R (on the application of FB (Afghanistan)) v Secretary of State for the Home Department (Equality and Human Rights Commission intervening)** [2021] **3** 424, CA.

Direction—
Refusal of application for leave to remain. *See* Leave to remain—Appeal —Removal: persons with statutorily extended leave, *above*.

Escorts and duty—
Police, complaint against. *See* **Police** (Complaint against police—Investigation—Independent Police Complaints Commission—Removal centres and detained persons).

Variation of leave to remain. *See* Leave to remain—Variation, *above*.

Residence—
Derivative right of residence—
Applicants applying for derivative residence cards on basis that primary carers of a British citizen—Whether dependent citizen under compulsion to leave European Union if derivative claim refused—Criteria and considerations for grant of derivative right of residence—Whether Zambrano principle altered by recent CJEU decision—Immigration (European Economic Area) Regulations 2006, SI 2006/1003, reg 15A. **Patel v Secretary of State for the Home Dept** [2018] **2** 1093, CA; [2020] **2** 557, SC.

Residence. *See* European Economic Area nationals—Right of residence, *above*.

Rules—
Commonwealth citizens, wives and children settled in United Kingdom at coming into force of statute—
Rules not to make Commonwealth citizens less free to enter or leave United Kingdom than if statute had not been passed—Amendment of rules—Amendment following withdrawal of Pakistan from Commonwealth—Wife of Pakistani citizen settled in United Kingdom treated as non-Commonwealth citizen and required to obtain visa to enter United Kingdom—Wives of Commonwealth citizens required to obtain entry clearance—Whether amendment to rules affecting wife of Pakistani citizen valid—Immigration Act 1971, s 1(5)—Immigration Rules for Control on Entry: EEC and Non-Commonwealth Nationals (1973), para 13. **R v Chief Immigration Officer, Heathrow Airport, ex p Salamat Bibi** [1976] **3** 843, CA.

Rules not to make Commonwealth citizens less free to enter or leave United Kingdom than if statute had not been passed—Amendment of rules—Rule made in 1980 requiring children over 18 of Commonwealth citizens settled in United Kingdom to qualify for entry in their own right—Pre-1971 rules giving immigration officers discretion to give adult sons over 18 leave to enter—Whether 1980 rule rendering adult sons over 18 less free to come into United Kingdom than if Act had not been passed—Immigration Act 1971, ss 1(5), 3(2)—Statement of Changes in Immigration Rules (HC Paper (1979-80) no 394), para 47. **R v Immigration Appeal Tribunal, ex p Ruhul** [1987] **3** 705, CA.

Statement of changes in immigration rules—
Presumption against retrospectivity—Overseas medical doctor applying for leave to remain as postgraduate doctor—Immigration rules changing after date of application—New rules excluding doctors with non-United Kingdom medical degrees—Secretary of State refusing doctor's application—Whether doctor's application to be considered under former rules—Whether presumption against retrospectivity applying—Statement of Changes in Immigration Rules 2006 (HC 1016). **Odelola v Secretary of State for the Home Dept** [2009] **3** 1061, HL.

Right to respect for private and family life—Statements of rules or changes in rules to be laid before Parliament—Changes in rules requiring post-study work migrants applying for leave to remain to have £800 and produce specified documents—Changes laid before Parliament—Policy guidance specifying documents as bank statements showing balance of £800 held continuously for three months before date of application—Whether three month requirement enforceable—Whether right to respect for private and family life applicable to policy—Immigration Act 1971, s 3(2)—Human Rights Act 1998, Sch 1, Pt I, art 8—Statement of Changes in Immigration Rules 1994 (HC Paper 395)—Statement of Changes in Immigration Rules 2008 (HC Paper 607). **Pankina v Secretary of State for the Home Dept** [2011] **1** 1043, CA.

Statements of rules or changes in rules to be laid before Parliament—Deportation policy—Secretary of State introducing deportation policy applying to cases where children had long residence—Secretary of State withdrawing policy—Whether withdrawal of policy a statement of changes in immigration rules—Whether withdrawal of policy requiring to be laid before Parliament—Whether power to make immigration rules an exercise of prerogative power—Immigration Act 1971, s 3(2). **R (on the application of Munir) v Secretary of State for the Home Dept** [2012] **4** 1025, SC.

Statements of rules or changes in rules to be laid before Parliament—Points-based system for skilled workers—Extent of requirement of Parliamentary scrutiny—Whether list of skilled occupations required to be laid before Parliament—Immigration Act 1971, s 3(2)—Statement of Changes in Immigration Rules (HC Paper 395), App A, para 82(a)(i). **R (on the application of Alvi) v Secretary of State for the Home Dept** [2012] **4** 1041, SC.

IMMIGRATION (cont)—
Rules (cont)—
Statement of changes in immigration rules (cont)—
Statements of rules or changes in rules to be laid before Parliament—Sponsor guidance—Tier 4 (General) Sponsors—Highly trusted sponsor status—Whether sponsor licensing scheme unlawful—Whether sponsor guidance requiring to be laid before Parliament—Whether Secretary of State unlawfully delegating powers—Immigration Act 1971, ss 1(4), 3(2)—Statement of Changes in Immigration Rules (HC Paper 395) paras 245ZV, 245ZX. **R (on the application of New London College Ltd) v Secretary of State for the Home Dept** [2013] **4** 195, SC.
Special Immigration Appeals Commission—
Admissibility of evidence. *See* **Evidence** (Admissibility—Special Immigration Appeals Commission).
Appeal against deportation on grounds of national security. *See* Appeal—Deportation—Appeal against deportation on grounds of national security—Special Immigration Appeals Commission, *above*.
Disclosure—
Closed material procedure—Secretary of State directing exclusion of non-EEA national and refusing applications for naturalisation—Parties applying to SIAC for review—SIAC requiring disclosure of closed material to special advocates appointed—Extent of disclosure required—Special Immigration Appeal Commission Act 1997, ss 2C, 2D—Special Immigration Appeals Commission (Procedure) Rules 2003, SI 2003/1034, r 4(3). **Secretary of State for the Home Dept v Special Immigration Appeals Commission** [2016] **2** 620, DC.
Judicial review. *See* **Judicial review** (Special Immigration Appeals Commission).
Sponsorship—
Statement of changes in immigration rules. *See* Rules—Statement of changes in immigration rules—Statements of rules or changes in rules to be laid before Parliament—Sponsor guidance, *above*.
Spouse or civil partner. *See* Leave to enter—Spouse or civil partner, *above*.
Spouses, children and other dependent relatives. *See* Leave to enter—Spouses, children and other dependent relatives, *above*.
Statute controlling immigration—
Retrospective operation—
Penal provisions—Illegal entry—Possession of false passport—Acts performed before statute creating offences came into force—Statute applied to persons entering United Kingdom before it came into force—Acts done under former immigration laws having effect as if done under statute—Whether statute creating offences in respect of acts performed before it came into force—Immigration Act 1971, ss 24(1)(a), 26(1)(d), 34(1). **Waddington v Miah** [1974] **2** 377, HL.
Student—
Leave to remain—
Points-based system. *See* Leave to remain—Points-based system for students, *above*.
Student loans. *See* **Education** (Higher education—Student loans—Immigration status).
Terrorism, prevention of—
Port and border controls. *See* **Terrorism** (Prevention of—Port and border controls).
Trafficking people for exploitation—
Criminal law. *See* **Criminal law** (Trafficking people for exploitation).
Removal. *See* Removal—Decision to remove—Appeal, *above*.
Treatment of claimants—
Asylum. *See* Leave to enter—Refugee—Asylum—Treatment of claimants, *above*.
United Nations—
United Nations Convention relating to the Status of Refugees 1951. *See* Refugee—Illegal entry or presence—Provision of international convention protecting refugees from penalties for illegal entry or presence, *above*.
Workers—
Freedom of movement—
Nationals of member states of European Community—Restrictions imposed by member states on freedom of movement—Public policy—Measures imposing restrictions to be based exclusively on personal conduct of individual concerned—Personal conduct—Meaning—Membership of socially harmful organisation—Voluntary act of individual in associating with organisation—Organisation not unlawful—Church of Scientology—Dutch Scientologist wishing to enter United Kingdom to take up employment with Church—Church regarded by United Kingdom government as socially harmful—Whether act of associating with Church 'personal conduct'—Whether government permitted to refuse Scientologist leave to enter United Kingdom—EEC Directive 64/221, art 3(1). **Van Duyn v Home Office (No 2) (Case 41/74)** [1975] **3** 190, ECJ.

IMMORAL EARNINGS
Prostitution. *See* **Criminal law** (Prostitution—Living on earnings of prostitution).

IMMORAL PURPOSES
Soliciting for immoral purposes. *See* **Criminal law** (Soliciting for immoral purposes).

IMMORAL USER
Premises—
Forfeiture of lease—
Court's discretion to grant relief. *See* **Landlord and tenant** (Relief against forfeiture—Immoral user of premises—Court's discretion to grant relief).

IMMUNITY
Arbitration—
Foreign sovereign state. *See* **Constitutional law** (Foreign sovereign state—Immunity from suit—Exceptions—Arbitration).
Barrister—
Negligence. *See* **Counsel** (Negligence—Immunity).
Diplomatic immunity from legal process. *See* **Constitutional law** (Diplomatic privilege—Immunity from legal process).

IMMUNITY (cont)—
Extradition—
Immunity from extradition. *See* **Extradition** (Immunity from extradition).
Foreign sovereign state—
Immunity from suit. *See* **Constitutional law** (Foreign sovereign state—Immunity from suit).
Immunity from taxation. *See* **Constitutional law** (Foreign sovereign state—Immunity from taxation).
Heads of foreign states. *See* **Constitutional law** (Heads of foreign states—Immunity from suit).
Public interest immunity—
Privilege. *See* **Privilege** (Public interest immunity).
Public interest immunity. *See* **Constitutional law** (Heads of foreign states—Immunity from suit).
Solicitor—
Negligence. *See* **Solicitor** (Negligence—Immunity).
State immunity—
Heads of foreign states. *See* **Constitutional law** (Heads of foreign states—Immunity from suit).
Suit, from—
Act of State. *See* **Constitutional law** (Act of State—Immunity from suit).
Arbitrator—
Negligence. *See* **Negligence** (Immunity from suit—Arbitrator).
Crown, proceedings against. *See* **Crown** (Proceedings against—Liability of Crown—Immunity from suit
in respect of claim in tort by serviceman for personal injury sustained during service).
Expert witness. *See* **Action** (Immunity from suit—Witness—Expert witness).
Foreign sovereign state. *See* **Constitutional law** (Foreign sovereign state—Immunity from suit).
Generally. *See* **Action** (Immunity from suit).
International organisations—
Wife applying for financial relief following break down of marriage—Husband claiming immunity
from suit as Permanent Representative of St Lucia to International Maritime Organisation—
Whether husband entitled to immunity in principle—Whether husband permanently resident in
UK—Whether proceedings relating to discharge of official functions—Human Rights Act 1998,
Sch 1, Pt I, art 6—International Maritime Organisation (Immunities and Privileges) Order 2002, SI
2002/1826, art 15—Vienna Convention on Diplomatic Relations, art 39. **Estrada v Al-Juffali
(Secretary of State for Foreign and Commonwealth Affairs intervening)** [2017] **1** 790, CA.
Judge. *See* **Judge** (Immunity from suit).
Medical practitioner—
Disciplinary panel—Immunity from suit. *See* **Medical practitioner** (Disciplinary panel—Immunity
from suit).
Sequestrator—
Negligence. *See* **Negligence** (Immunity from suit—Sequestrator).
Solicitor—
Negligence. *See* **Solicitor** (Negligence—Immunity).
Surveyor—
Negligence. *See* **Negligence** (Immunity from suit—Surveyor).
Trade dispute—
Acts done in contemplation or furtherance of trade dispute—
Immunity from civil action. *See* **Trade dispute** (Acts done in contemplation or furtherance of trade
dispute—Immunity from civil action).
Vicarious—
Tort. *See* **Tort** (Vicarious immunity).
Witness—
Immunity from suit. *See* **Action** (Immunity from suit—Witness).

IMPEACHING CREDIT OF WITNESS
Criminal proceedings—
Generally. *See* **Criminal evidence** (Impeaching credit of witness).

IMPECUNIOSITY
Damages—
Mitigation of loss. *See* **Damages** (Mitigation of loss—Impecuniosity).

IMPERFECT TRUST PROVISION
Validation by statute. *See* **Charity** (Validation by statute—Imperfect trust provision).

IMPERSONATION
Police officer. *See* **Police** (Impersonation).

IMPLEMENTS OF FORGERY
See **Criminal law** (Forgery—Implements of forgery).

IMPLIED CONDITION
Contract. *See* **Contract** (Implied term).
Sale of land. *See* **Sale of land** (Condition—Implied condition).

IMPLIED COVENANT
Landlord and tenant—
Generally. *See* **Landlord and tenant** (Covenant—Implied covenant).
Repair. *See* **Landlord and tenant** (Implied covenant to repair).

IMPLIED GRANT
Easement. *See* **Easement** (Implied grant).

IMPLIED INDEMNITY
See **Indemnity** (Implied indemnity).

IMPLIED TERM
Charterparty—
  Arrival of ship under port charterparty—
    Commencement of lay days. *See* **Shipping** (Commencement of lay days—Arrived ship under port charterparty—Implied term).
Contract—
  Building contract. *See* **Building contract** (Construction—Implied term).
  Employment—
    Equality of treatment of men and women. *See* **Employment** (Equality of treatment of men and women—Equality clause).
    Generally. *See* **Employment** (Contract of service—Implied term).
  Generally. *See* **Contract** (Implied term).
  Sale of goods. *See* **Sale of goods**.
Insurance—
  Reinsurance. *See* **Insurance** (Reinsurance—Non-proportional reinsurance—Terms—Implied terms).
Option—
  Option to purchase. *See* **Option** (Option to purchase—Implied term).
Sale of goods—
  Feeding stuffs. *See* **Agriculture** (Feeding stuffs—Sale for use as food for cattle or poultry—Implied warranty suitable for use as such).
  Fitness. *See* **Sale of goods** (Implied condition as to fitness).
  Merchantable quality. *See* **Sale of goods** (Implied condition as to merchantable quality).
  Quiet possession. *See* **Sale of goods** (Implied warranty—Quiet possession).

IMPORT DUTY
Commonwealth preference. *See* **Customs and excise** (Duties—Commonwealth preference).
Interest. *See* **Customs and excise** (Imported goods—Delivery on giving security for duty—Interest on security).

IMPORTATION
Animal. *See* **Animal** (Importation of animal).
Drugs—
  Assisting in importation of drugs into foreign country. *See* **Drugs** (Dangerous drugs—Assisting in or inducing commission of offences outside United Kingdom).
EC restrictions. *See* **European Union** (Imports).
Food—
  Marks of origin. *See* **Food and drugs** (Marks of origin—Imported food).
Goods—
  Customs duty. *See* **Customs and excise**.
  European Community. *See* **European Union** (Imports).
  Prohibited goods. *See* **Customs and excise** (Importation of prohibited goods).
  Trade description. *See* **Trade description** (Indication of origin on imported goods).
Import licence—
  Duty to obtain. *See* **Licence** (Import licence—Duty to obtain).
Medicinal product—
  European rules on competition. *See* **European Union** (Rules on competition—Abuse of dominant position—Undertaking importing, warehousing and distributing medicinal products).
  Product licence. *See* **Medicine** (Product licence).
Prohibition on imports—
  Application of EEC Treaty—
    Coins. *See* **European Union** (Freedom of movement—Goods—Coins).
    Direct application in member states—Municipal law no longer applicable. *See* **European Union** (Treaty provisions—Direct application in member states—Municipal law no longer applicable—Prohibition on imports).
    Generally. *See* **European Union** (Imports—Prohibition on imports).
  Importation of prohibited goods—
    Generally. *See* **Customs and excise** (Importation of prohibited goods).
Sound recordings—
  Importation for resale in United Kingdom—
    Infringement of copyright—Right of action of person having limited interest in copyright. *See* **Copyright** (Conflict of laws—Right of action—Person having limited interest in copyright—Exclusive licensee—Importation into United Kingdom of article lawfully made abroad).

IMPORTUNING
Immoral purposes. *See* **Criminal law** (Soliciting for immoral purposes).

IMPOSSIBLE OFFENCE
Attempt. *See* **Criminal law** (Attempt—Impossible offence).

IMPOTENCE
Damages—
  Disability resulting from brain injury. *See* **Damages** (Personal injury—Brain damage—Disabilities resulting from brain injury—Loss of sense of taste and smell—Sexual impotence).

IMPOTENT PERSON
Relief—
  Charitable purpose. *See* **Charity** (Benefit to community—Impotent person).

IMPRISONMENT
Contempt of court—
  Criminal contempt—
    Power to commit instantly to prison. *See* **Contempt of court** (Criminal contempt—Power to commit instantly to prison).

IMPRISONMENT (cont)—
Contempt of court (cont)—
  Release from custody—
    Factors to be taken into account. *See* **Contempt of court** (Committal—Breach of undertaking—Period of custody).
Dangerousness—
  Public protection. *See* **Sentence** (Custodial sentence—Dangerous offenders—Specified offence—Serious offence—Assessment of dangerousness—Imprisonment for public protection for serious offences).
Employee—
  Frustration of contract of employment. *See* **Employment** (Contract of service—Frustration—Imprisonment of employee).
Extended term. *See* **Sentence** (Extended term of imprisonment).
False imprisonment. *See* **False imprisonment**.
Generally. *See* **Sentence** (Imprisonment).
Immigrant—
  False imprisonment. *See* **Immigration** (Detention—Unlawful detention—False imprisonment).
Life imprisonment—
  Generally. *See* **Sentence** (Life imprisonment).
  Mandatory sentence. *See* **Sentence** (Mandatory life sentence).
Life sentence—
  Release of prisoner on licence. *See* **Prison** (Release on licence).
Murder. *See* **Sentence** (Murder).
Non-payment of fine—
  Magistrates. *See* **Magistrates** (Fine—Committal to prison in default of payment).
Non-payment of rates—
  Imprisonment in default of distress. *See* **Rates** (Distress for rates—Imprisonment in default of distress).
Prisons. *See* **Prison**.
Youthful offender. *See* **Sentence** (Youthful offender—Imprisonment).

IMPROVEMENT
Business premises—
  Generally. *See* **Landlord and tenant** (Improvements—Business premises).
  Tenancy—
    Compensation. *See* **Landlord and tenant** (Improvements—Business premises—Compensation).
Dwelling—
  Grant. *See* **Housing** (Improvement grant).
  Leasehold enfranchisement—
    Reduction in rateable value. *See* **Landlord and tenant** (Leasehold enfranchisement—House—Rateable value—Reduction—Improvement by execution of works amounting to structural alteration, extension or addition).
  Notice. *See* **Housing** (Improvement notice).
  Protected tenancy—
    Application for determination of new fair rent. *See* **Rent restriction** (Rent—Determination of fair rent—Application—Change in condition of dwelling-house).
Income tax—
  Capital or revenue expenditure. *See* **Income tax** (Deduction in computing profits—Capital or revenue expenditure—Improvements).
Matrimonial home. *See* **Husband and wife** (Matrimonial home—Improvement).
Rent review—
  Reasonable rent—
    Improvements made to demised premises. *See* **Landlord and tenant** (Rent—Review—Reasonable rent—Improvements made to demised premises).
Trunk roads. *See* **Highway** (Trunk roads—Improvement).
Valuation—
  Leasehold enfranchisement. *See* **Landlord and tenant** (Leasehold enfranchisement—Valuation—Improvement).

INACTIVITY
Criminal offence—
  Inactivity on part of defendant—
    Gross indecency with child. *See* **Criminal law** (Gross indecency—Child—Inactivity on part of defendant).
Estoppel by conduct. *See* **Estoppel** (Conduct—Silence or inactivity).

INCAPACITY
Adult—
  Practice—
    Family Division. *See* **Practice** (Family Division—Incapacitated adults).
Consummation of marriage. *See* **Nullity** (Incapacity to consummate marriage).
Mental health. *See* **Mental health**.
Partner—
  Dissolution of partnership. *See* **Partnership** (Dissolution—Incapacity of partner).

INCEST
See **Criminal law** (Incest).

INCHOATE OFFENCES
Attempt—
  Crime. *See* **Criminal law** (Attempt).

INCITEMENT

Child—
   Inciting child under 14 to commit act of gross indecency. See **Criminal law** (Gross indecency—Child—Inciting child under 14 to commit act of gross indecency).
Disaffection, to—
   Indictment—
      Duplicity. See **Indictment** (Duplicity—Incitement to disaffection).
Generally. See **Criminal law** (Incitement).
Infringement of copyright—
   Right of action. See **Copyright** (Conflict of laws—Right of action—Authorisation of infringement).
Murder. See **Criminal law** (Incitement—Commission of crime—Murder).
Racial discrimination. See **Race relations** (Incitement).
Racial hatred. See **Criminal law** (Public order—Incitement to racial hatred).

INCOME

Accumulation. See **Accumulation**.
Capital distinguished—
   Administration of estates. See **Administration of estates** (Capital or income).
Discretionary trust—
   Payment or application of income. See **Trust and trustee** (Discretionary trust—Payment or application of income).
Husband and wife—
   Divorce proceedings—
      Periodical payments order—Assessment of joint income. See **Divorce** (Financial provision—Periodical payments—Assessment of joint income of husband and wife).
Income protection insurance. See **Insurance** (Income protection insurance).
Legal aid cases—
   Assessment of resources of income. See **Legal aid** (Entitlement—Assessment of resources).
Resources—
   Legal aid cases—
      Assessment of income. See **Legal aid** (Entitlement—Assessment of resources).
   Supplementary benefit—
      Calculation of benefit. See **Social security** (Supplementary benefit—Calculation of benefit—Deduction of resources from requirements—Income resources).
Settlement—
   Capital or income. See **Settlement** (Capital or income).
   Capital transfer tax—
      Beneficiary entitled to income. See **Capital transfer tax** (Settlement—Interest in possession—Beneficiary entitled under settlement to income of property subject to trustees' power to accumulate).
Taxation—
   Generally. See **Income tax**.
Will—
   Gift of income. See **Will** (Gift—Income).
   Residue—
      Intermediate income. See **Will** (Residue—Intermediate income).

INCOME SUPPORT

European Community—
   Freedom of movement of workers. See **European Union** (Workers—Freedom of movement—Social security—Income support).
Generally. See **Social security** (Income support).

INCOME TAX

Accommodation—
   Perquisites or profits from employment—
      Occupation of house. See **Emoluments** from office or employment—Perquisites or profits—Occupation of house, below.
   Provision to employee by body corporate—
      Benefit in kind. See **Emoluments** from office or employment—Benefits in kind—Expense incurred by body corporate—Accommodation, below.
   Residence provided by employers—
      Rent in part paid by employers. See **Emoluments** from office or employment—Expenses wholly, exclusively and necessarily incurred—Residence provided by employers to employee, below.
Accountancy principles—
   Computation of profits. See Computation of profits—Accountancy principles, below.
Accounting period—
   Company—
      Alteration of period—Effect—Alteration of period of account of company—Decision and direction of Commissioners of Inland Revenue fixing periods of account—Appeal to Special Commissioners—Hardship—Power of Special Commissioners to grant such relief as just—Effects of alteration in accounting period—Double use of nine month period of profits in assessment to tax—Increase in liability to corporation tax—Income Tax Act 1952, s 127(2)(b)(3) as amended by Income Tax Management Act 1964, Sch 4. **IRC v Helical Bar Ltd** [1972] **1** 1205, HL.
Accrued expenses—
   Deduction in computing profits. See Deduction in computing profits—Expenses wholly and exclusively laid out for purposes of trade—Accrued expenses, below.
Additional assessment—
   Disclosure—
      Facts known to commissioners adequate to support assessment—Assessment made on basis of erroneous belief that facts otherwise—Competency of assessments—Income Tax Act 1918, s 125(1). **Beatty (Earl) v IRC** [1953] **2** 758, Ch D.

INCOME TAX (cont)—
    Additional assessment (cont)—
        Disclosure (cont)—
            Mistake—Mistake in general law—Discovery that a person chargeable has been undercharged—'Discovers'—Discovery that mistake made in applying law to facts—Income Tax Act 1918, s 125(1). **Commercial Structures Ltd v Briggs (Inspector of Taxes)** [1948] **2** 1041, CA.
            Mistake—Mistake in general law—No new facts discovered—Income Tax Act 1952, s 41(1). **Cenlon Finance Co Ltd v Ellwood (Inspector of Taxes)** [1962] **1** 854, HL.
            Mistake—Mistaken view of law applicable to facts—Finality of determination—Appeal against original assessment determined by agreement—Subsequent additional assessment—Discovery being inspector's change of mind on treatment of dividends—Validity of assessments—Income Tax Act 1952, ss 41(1), 50(2), 510(1). **Cenlon Finance Co Ltd v Ellwood (Inspector of Taxes)** [1962] **1** 854, HL.
            Onus on inspector—No onus to show prima facie case—Income Tax Act 1952, s 41, Sch D, Case III, Case V. **Hume (Inspector of Taxes) v Asquith** [1969] **1** 868, Ch D.
        Discovery—
            Assessment made on grounds self-assessment insufficient—Deliberateness—Taxpayer participating in scheme to generate employment-related loss to set off against income for previous year—Taxpayer claiming loss on partnership page in tax return with explanation—Whether discovery of insufficiency of tax—Whether insufficiency brought about deliberately by taxpayer—Meaning of 'deliberate inaccuracy'—Taxes Management Act 1970, ss 29, 118(7). **Tooth v Revenue and Customs Comrs** [2021] **3** 711, SC.
        Fraud or wilful default—
            Default committed on behalf of any person—False returns by taxpayer's accountant—Taxpayer not personally in default—Power to make additional assessment at any time—Income Tax Act 1952, s 47(1). **Clixby v Pountney (Inspector of Taxes)** [1968] **1** 802, Ch D.
        Neglect—
            Normal year—Time limit—Assessment for 'normal year' made before statute enabling Crown to go back beyond six-year period enacted—Validity—Income Tax Act 1952, s 47(1)—Finance Act 1960, s 51. **Thurgood v Slarke (Inspector of Taxes)** [1971] **3** 606, Ch D.
            Procedure—Application for leave to make assessment for six years immediately preceding normal year—Taxpayer given no opportunity to be heard—Finance Act 1960, s 51—Income Tax Management Act 1964, s 6. **Pearlberg v Varty (Inspector of Taxes)** [1972] **2** 6, HL.
        Time limit—
            Normal year. *See* Additional assessment—Neglect—Normal year—Time limit, *above*.
            Partnership—Additional assessment on partnership—One partner dead more than three years—Years of assessment more than six years before his death—Validity of assessment—Liability of executors and of surviving partner—Income Tax Act 1952, ss 47(2), 144(1)—Finance Act 1960, ss 53, 63(3). **Harrison (Inspector of Taxes) v Willis Bros** [1965] **3** 753, CA.
        Validity—
            Appeal against discovery assessment—Assessment made on discovery of insufficiency—Taxpayer making claim for loss relief—HMRC issuing discovery assessment disallowing claim—Whether discovery assessment validly made—Taxes Management Act 1970, s 29. **Anderson v Revenue and Customs Comrs** [2018] **4** 338, UT.
            Appeal against discovery assessment—Assessment made on discovery of insufficiency—Whether assessment valid on facts found by tribunal—Whether statutory requirements satisfied—Taxes Management Act 1970, s 29(1), (5). **Sanderson v Revenue and Customs Comrs** [2016] **3** 203, CA.
        Valuation of property—
            Preparatory year and year of revaluation—Income Tax Act 1918, s 125—Finance Act 1930, ss 28, 31, 32, Sch I, Part I. **Kliman (Inspector of Taxes) v Stone** [1936] **1** 859, KBD.
            When annual value determined for purposes of tax under Schedule A—Income Tax Act 1952, ss 35, 53. **BP Refinery (Kent) Ltd v Kent River Board** [1956] **2** 834, QBD.
    Advance corporation tax. *See* Corporation tax—Advance corporation tax, *below*.
    Advantage. *See* Tax advantage, *below*.
    Adventure in the nature of trade. *See* Trade—Adventure in nature of trade, *below*.
    Allowances—
        Annual value of land. *See* Land—Annual value—Allowances, *below*.
        Apportionment of undistributed income. *See* Undistributed income—Computation of income for apportionment—Allowances, *below*.
        Capital allowances. *See* **Capital allowances**.
        Child. *See* Child relief, *below*.
        Depreciation allowance—
            Canada. *See* **Canada** (Income tax—Allowances—Depreciation).
            Deduction in computing profits. *See* Deduction in computing profits—Depreciation allowance, *below*.
        Expenses allowances—
            Emoluments from office or employment. *See* Emoluments from office or employment—Expenses allowances, *below*.
        Investment grant. *See* **Investment grant**.
        Married person's allowance. *See* Husband and wife—Married person's allowance, *below*.
        Widow's bereavement allowance—
            Allowance not available to widowers—Statutory provision discriminating against widowers—Taxes Management Act 1970, s 1—Income and Corporation Taxes Act 1988, s 262—Human Rights Act 1998, ss 6(2)(b), 8, Sch 1, Pt I, art 14, Pt II, art 1. **R (on the application of Wilkinson) v IRC** [2003] **3** 719, CA; [2006] **1** 529, HL.
    Amortisation of capital—
        Capital or income receipts. *See* Capital or income receipts, *below*.
    Annual income—
        Interest. *See* Interest—Interest, annuities and other annual income, *below*.

INCOME TAX (cont)—
  Annual payment—
    Annuity—
      Monthly loans by insurance company—Life assurance—Loans to assured—Recovery out of amount payable at death—Payments not in nature of annuities—Income Tax Act 1918, Sch D, Case III, All Schedules Rules, r 21. **IRC v Wesleyan & General Assurance Society** [1948] **1** 555, HL.
    Appropriation to taxed profits—
      Interest—Attribution by taxpayer of part to capital—Effect—Part of annual payments (mortgage interest) attributed in company's accounts to capital—Amount available for dividend thereby increased—Profits available to meet the annual payments—Whether attribution of part of annual payments to capital was binding for income tax purposes—Income Tax Act 1952, ss 169, 170. **Chancery Lane Safe Deposit and Offices Co Ltd v IRC** [1966] **1** 1, HL.
      Payment out of profits—Profits already largely absorbed by dividends—No other fund from which to pay dividends—Annual payments in fact set in special ledger account against capital instalments received—Whether the annual payments could be treated as between company and Revenue as paid out of taxed profits—Whether company must account to Revenue for income tax deducted from annual payments—Income Tax Act 1952, ss 169, 170. **Nobes (BW) & Co Ltd v IRC** [1966] **1** 30, HL.
    Capital or income—
      Annuity—Deficiency—Will—Direction in will to make up deficiency of income out of capital—Payments made prior to ascertainment of residue—'Residuary estate'—Payments 'in respect of income'—Irrelevant that payments made out of capital—Recurrent payments—'Annual payment'—Whether payment 'in respect of' a limited interest in residue—Income Tax Act 1918, Sch D, Case III, r 1(a), All Schedules Rules, r 21—Finance Act 1927, s 26—Finance Act 1938, ss 30(1), (2), 35(3). **Cunard's Trustees v IRC** [1946] **1** 159, CA.
      Consideration for transfer of capital asset—Rentcharges. *See* Capital or income receipts—Transfer of capital asset—Cash payments of fixed amounts over fixed period as consideration for transfer—Rentcharges, *below.*
      Debt—Payment by instalments—Instalments to continue during life of creditor—Whether instalments payments of capital from which tax not deductible—Income Tax Act 1918, All Schedules Rules, r 19. **Dott v Brown** [1936] **1** 543, CA.
      Purchase price—Interest element—Price payable by instalments—Total price exceeding current value of property sold—Price computed having regard to interest factor—Dissection of annual payment into capital and interest for tax purposes. **Vestey v IRC** [1961] **3** 978, Ch D.
    Compensation for nationalisation—
      Interim income payment—Payments in respect of compensation on nationalisation of coal industry—Recurrence—Payment by the Crown—Income Tax Act 1918, Sch D, Case III, r 1(a)—Coal Industry Nationalisation Act 1946, s 22(1), (2), (3), (4)—Coal Industry (No 2) Act 1949, s 1(1), (2), (3). **Whitworth Park Coal Co Ltd (in liq) v IRC** [1959] **3** 703, HL.
    Contingent and variable in amount—
      Guarantee of fixed dividend—Taxpayer company undertaking to make up dividends of another company to fixed amount—Dividends paid in each of five years—Different amounts paid in each year—Whether annual payments liable to tax—Income Tax Act 1918, Sch D, Case III, r 1(a), All Schedules Rules, r 21—Finance Act 1927, s 26. **Moss' Empires Ltd v IRC** [1937] **3** 381, HL.
    Covenanted payments to charity—
      Benefit in return for payments—Club accepted as charity—Club providing benefits and facilities to members—Members paying subscriptions under seven year covenant—Whether club entitled to recover tax deducted from payments—Income Tax Act 1952, s 447(1)(b). **IRC v National Book League** [1957] **2** 644, CA.
      Benefit in return for payments—Common intention that covenanted payments should be used by charity to buy business of covenantor's educational establishment—Plan to covert tutorial establishment to educational trust—Whether covenanted payments income in hands of charity and thus annual payments—Income Tax Act 1952, ss 169(1), 447(1)(b). **Campbell and anor (Trustees of Davies's Educational Trust) v IRC** [1968] **3** 588, HL.
      Benefit in return for payments—Covenantor obtaining benefit of counter-obligations by charity—Obligations not importing absence of bounty—Payments not income in the hands of charity trustees—Educational trust intended to provide means of purchasing goodwill of covenantor's tutorial business—Application of moneys received by trustees on application for charitable purposes, but no tax relief as covenanted sums not annual payments—Income Tax Act 1952, ss 169, 447(1)(b). **Campbell and anor (Trustees of Davies's Educational Trust) v IRC** [1966] **2** 736, Ch D.
    Deduction from total income. *See* Total income—Deduction of annual payments, *below.*
    Deduction of tax—
      Failure to deduct—Rent on long lease—Liability of recipient to be assessed—Income Tax Act 1952, ss 1, 122, 148, 170(1), (2), (3), 177(2), Sch D. **Grosvenor Place Estates Ltd v Roberts (Inspector of Taxes)** [1961] **1** 341, CA.
      Insufficient deduction—Recovery of money overpaid—Payment under mistake of fact—Rent under long lease—Payment without deduction of tax at standard rate—Lessee's erroneous belief that lease for short term—Income Tax Act 1918, General Rules Applicable to All Schedules, r 19(2)—Finance Act 1940, s 17(1)(a), (2). **Turvey v Dentons (1923) Ltd** [1952] **2** 1025, QBD.
      Local authority—Retention of tax deducted from interest payment—Separate undertakings—Whether excess of taxed income in one account can be set off against excess of interest payments in another account—Income Tax Act 1918, All Schedules Rules, rr 19, 21—Local Government Act 1933, ss 185, 194—South Shields Corporation Act 1935, ss 112-115. **Allchin v Coulthard** [1943] **2** 352, HL.
      Notification to payee of tax deducted—Allowance to wife under separation deed—Necessity for calculation and notification of deduction—Income Tax Act 1918, All Schedules Rules, r 19(1). **Hemsworth v Hemsworth** [1946] **2** 117, KBD.
      Past income—Arrears—Weekly payments under maintenance agreement between husband and wife—Right of husband to deduct tax on making payment of arrears—Income Tax Act 1918, All Schedules Rules, r 19. **Taylor v Taylor** [1937] **3** 571, CA.
      Payments not out of profits etc already taxed. *See* Annual payment—Payment not out of profits already taxed, *below.*

INCOME TAX (cont)—
Annual payment (cont)—
Deduction of tax (cont)—
Street works—Cost payable to local authority in annual instalments—Instalments including sum for interest—Whether payments subject to deduction of tax on whole amount. **Goole Corp v Aire and Calder Navigation Trustees** [1942] **2** 276, KBD.
Insurance premiums—
Payments—Liability to tax—Contracts with mutual society providing for weekly payments in event of disability—Premiums to society to continue during receipt of benefit payments—Liability of payments to tax—Income Tax Act 1918, Sch D, Case III, r 1. **Forsyth v Thompson** [1940] **3** 465, KBD.
Manufactured overseas dividends—
Pension fund—Fund trustees entering into stock lending transactions—Transactions involving both UK shares and overseas shares—Manufactured overseas dividends in respect of overseas shares subject to withholding tax—Whether manufactured overseas dividend regime involving restriction on movement of capital—Whether, if so, restriction justified—Whether, if not, conforming interpretation of legislation possible—Income and Corporation Taxes Act 1988, s 796, Sch 23A, para 4—Finance Act 2004, s 186—Article 63 TFEU. **Coal Staff Superannuation Scheme Trustees Ltd v Revenue and Customs Comrs** [2020] **2** 756, CA.
Pension fund—Fund trustees entering into stock lending transactions—Transactions involving both UK shares and overseas shares—Manufactured overseas dividends in respect of overseas shares subject to withholding tax—Whether manufactured overseas dividend regime involving restriction on movement of capital—Appropriate remedy for infringement—Income and Corporation Taxes Act 1988, s 796, Sch 23A, para 4—Article 63 TFEU. **Coal Staff Superannuation Scheme Trustees Ltd v Revenue and Customs Comrs** [2022] **3** 335, SC.
Meaning—
Dividend distinguished—Agreement between two companies for sharing of profits and losses—Payment of share of profits under agreement by one company to other—Whether dividend or annual payment—Whether distributed—Income Tax Act 1918, Sch D, Case III, All Schedules Rules, rr 20, 21—Finance Act 1931, s 7(1). **Utol Ltd v IRC** [1944] **1** 190, KBD.
Order of court—
Maintenance order—Maintenance to be paid free of tax—Certificate given for deduction of tax—Maintenance payments allowed as deduction against income—Right of divorced woman to repayment. **Spilsbury (Inspector of Taxes) v Spofforth** [1937] **4** 487, KBD.
Maintenance order—Order to pay 'free of tax'—Effect—Income Tax Act 1952, s 170. **J v J** [1955] **2** 617, CA.
Payment free of tax—
Annuity—Settlement giving annuities free of tax—Effect—Right of annuitant to receive a net amount calculated after deduction of tax thereon—Income Tax Act 1918, All Schedules Rules, r 23. **Goodson's Settlement, Re** [1943] **1** 201, Ch D.
Payment not out of profits already taxed—
Attribution by taxpayer to capital—Company incurring interest charges for purpose of its business—Interest payments charged to profit and loss account—Interest payments capitalised by transfer of equivalent sums to cost of land and buildings shown in balance sheet—Whether interest paid out of profits or gains brought into charge—Whether company liable to account for tax deducted from interest—Income Tax Act 1952, s 170. **Fitzleet Estates Ltd v Cherry (Inspector of Taxes)** [1977] **3** 996, HL.
Payment out of profits etc already taxed—
Annual payments due under deed of covenant—Fees for training course—Requirement by course organisers that students be sponsored by local authorities—Local authority sponsoring taxpayer's son as student provided taxpayer entered into agreement to repay fees paid by it—Taxpayer entering into deed of covenant to cover payment of fees—Payments made under covenant net of tax—Whether covenanted payments made in return for services—Whether local authority entitled to refund of tax already paid—Income and Corporation Taxes Act 1970, s 52(1). **Essex CC v Ellam (Inspector of Taxes)** [1989] **2** 494, CA.
Deduction of tax—Deduction by person through whom payment paid—Dividends—Payment of dividends by company guaranteed by associated company—Guarantor authorising payment by company—Payment debited to guarantor—Company person through whom payment made—Effect of transaction payment of gross amount by guarantor—Payments income in shareholders' hands—Company liable to be charged for tax. **Aeolian Co Ltd v IRC** [1936] **2** 219, KBD.
Individual taxpayer—Onus of showing payment made out of taxed profits—Normally sufficient to show that in relevant year sufficient taxed profits in taxpayer's hands to entitle him to make deduction—Claim debarred only if possible to show an election by taxpayer that payments to be notionally attributed to capital rather than income—Income and Corporation Taxes Act 1970, s 52(1). **IRC v Plummer** [1977] **3** 1009, Ch D.
Inference that payment made net of tax—Royalties—Assignment of performance rights to American company—Royalties payable under assignment agreement—Taxability in hands of payee—No inference that payment made out of taxed profits by American company—Income Tax Act 1952, Sch D, Case III. **Hume (Inspector of Taxes) v Asquith** [1969] **1** 868, Ch D.
Remuneration—Trustees—Court order that annual sum be paid to trustees as 'remuneration for services'—Whether annual payment wholly out of profits or gains brought into charge—Whether trustees liable to assessment in respect thereof—Income Tax Act 1918, All Schedules Rules, r 19. **Hearn (Inspector of Taxes) v Morgan** [1945] **2** 480, KBD.
Tax avoidance scheme—Manufactured overseas dividends—Arrangements for transfer of loan notes—Taxpayer claiming deduction in respect of payments made in relation to certain loan notes on basis that payments constituting manufactured overseas dividends—Whether payments 'manufactured overseas dividends' and therefore annual payments deductible in computing income tax—Whether tax relief available even though transaction forming part of scheme designed solely for purpose of obtaining tax relief and having no wider or other commercial justification—Income and Corporation Taxes Act 1988, Sch 23A, para 4—Income Tax (Manufactured Overseas Dividends) Regulations 1993, SI 1993/2004, reg 2B. **Chappell v Revenue and Customs Comrs** [2017] **1** 550, CA.

37

INCOME TAX (cont)—
  Annual payment (cont)—
    Payment out of profits etc already taxed (cont)—
      Tax avoidance scheme—Sale of annuity by surtax payer to charitable company in return for capital—Capital sum invested by payer in promissory notes and payments met out of proceeds of notes—Self-cancelling scheme—Whether 'annuity or other annual payment'—Income and Corporation Taxes Act 1970, s 52(1). **Moodie v IRC** [1993] **2** 49, HL.
      Tax avoidance scheme—Sale of annuity by surtax payer to charitable company in return for capital—Capital sum invested by payer in promissory notes and payments met out of proceeds of notes—Whether 'annuity or other annual payment'—Whether payment in reality repayments of capital—Whether payment out of profits or gains already taxed—Income and Corporation Taxes Act 1970, s 52(1). **IRC v Plummer** [1979] **3** 775, HL.
  Personal debt or obligation by virtue of contract—
    Consideration for cancellation of service agreement—Payments made under contract—Right of payer to deduct tax at source—Payments pure income profit—Income Tax Act 1970, Sch D, Case III, r 1—All Schedules Rules, rr 19, 21. **Asher v London Film Productions Ltd** [1944] **1** 77, CA.
    Receipts payable as a personal debt or obligation—Medical practitioners—Agreement with Minister of Health—Payments by Minister towards maintenance of assurance policy—Whether payments assessable as annual payments. **Hawkins (Inspector of Taxes) v Leahy (et contra)** [1952] **2** 759, Ch D.
    Trust—Beneficiaries children of settlor's employees—Payments to trustees—Consideration for payments—Covenant to pay sum to trustees for seven years—Trust as part of scheme for overseas employees of company—Provision for education of employees' children—Trustees' discretion to make payments to employees' children—No consideration from employee or child—Whether income tax deducted from payments recoverable. **Barclays Bank Ltd v Naylor (Inspector of Taxes)** [1960] **3** 173, Ch D.
  Settlement—
    Payments out of capital—Trustees directed to make up deficiency of income out of capital—Protective trust for benefit of settlor—Payments made to settlor out of capital—Capital or income payments—Treatment of sums paid as gross or net—Income Tax Act 1918, All Schedules Rules, r 21 (as amended by Finance Act 1927, s 26(1). **Morant Settlement (Trustees) v IRC, IRC v Morant Settlement (Trustees)** [1948] **1** 732, CA.
  Special services—
    Periodical payments—Payments in consideration of services rendered to company by taxpayer—Death of taxpayer—Periodical payments under contract received by trustees of will—Liability to tax—Income Tax Act 1918, Sch D, Case III—Income Tax Act 1952, Sch D, Case III. **Westminster Bank Ltd v Barford (Inspector of Taxes)** [1958] **1** 829, Ch D.
  Statutory liability—
    Payment to taxpayer under statutory liability—Payments to conservators of forest—Statutory liability to contribute to upkeep of forest—Amount of contribution ascertained by reference to excess of conservators' expenditure over other income—Right of contributor to deduct tax and of conservators to recover it—Income Tax Act 1918, Sch D, Case III, r 1(a). **IRC v City of London Corp (as the Conservators of Epping Forest)** [1953] **1** 1075, HL.
  Ultra vires payment—
    Interest—Payments termed 'interest' on debentures—Finding that not in the nature of interest—Creation of debentures on requirement of controlling company—Not in furtherance of objects of company creating—Payments a nullity—Disallowance of repayment claim—Income Tax Act 1952, s 169. **Ridge Securities Ltd v IRC** [1964] **1** 275, Ch D.
  Annual profits or gains. *See* Profits, *below.*
  Annual value—
    Land—
      Generally. *See* Land—Annual value, *below.*
    Valuation of property—
      Additional assessment. *See* Additional assessment—Valuation of property, *above.*
  Annuity—
    Annual payment—
      Generally. *See* Annual payment—Annuity, *above.*
      Payment free of tax. *See* Annual payment—Payment free of tax—Annuity, *above.*
    Capital or income. *See* Annual payment—Capital or income—Annuity, *above.*
  Anti-nationalisation campaign—
    Deduction of expenses in computing profits. *See* Deduction in computing profits—Expenses wholly and exclusively laid out for purposes of trade—Prevention of seizure of business by state—Anti-nationalisation campaign, *below.*
  Anticipated profits—
    Discounting bills of exchange. *See* Computation of profits—Discounting bills of exchange—Anticipated profits, *below.*
  Appeal—
    Allowing—
      Consent—Allowing appeal by consent—Appeal from Income Tax Commissioners—Dismissal or withdrawal on agreed terms giving effect to appellant's contention—Income Tax Act 1952, s 64(6). **Slaney (Inspector of Taxes) v Kean** [1970] **1** 434, Ch D.
    Apportionment of income—
      Investment company. *See* Investment company—Apportionment of income—Appeal, *below.*
    Assessment, against. *See* Assessment—Appeal, *below.*
    Case stated. *See* Case stated, *below.*
    Commissioners—
      Adjournment of appeal—Taxpayer appealing to commissioners against assessments—Crown alleging fraud, wilful default or neglect by taxpayer—Taxpayer asking for adjournment of appeal—Commissioners refusing to adjourn appeal and hearing appeal in taxpayer's absence—Commissioners finding that taxpayer had been fraudulent—Whether commissioners should have adjourned appeal—Whether injustice caused to taxpayer. **Ottley v Morris (Inspector of Taxes)** [1979] **1** 65, Ch D.

INCOME TAX (cont)—
Appeal (cont)—
  Decision of commissioners—
    Finality—Commissioners' clerk advising commissioners that they had no power to reopen determination—Taxpayer alleging that clerk gave advice maliciously—Relevance of maliciousness if advice correct—Taxes Management Act 1970, s 46(2). **R v Epping and Harlow General Comrs, ex p Goldstraw** [1983] **3** 257, QBD and CA.
    Finality—Property tax—Deduction by occupier from rent—Relief under sched A in respect of unlet tenements—Disagreement between landlord and tenant as to deduction—Reference to General Commissioners—Income Tax Act 1918, All Schedules Rules, r 22—Finance Act 1930, s 21. **Ecclesiastical Comrs for England v Sackville Estates Ltd** [1937] **2** 720, KBD.
  Dismissal—
    Consent—Appeal from Income Tax Commissioners—Dismissal of appeal by consent—Practice. **Practice Note** [1956] **1** 880, Ch D.
  Failure to appeal—
    Effect—Assessments made on taxpayer—Taxpayer failing to appeal within time limit—Proceedings by Crown to recover tax assessed—Denial of liability by taxpayer—No defence to proceedings by Crown—Income Tax Act 1918 s 169—Finance Act 1941, Sch I, para 5. **IRC v Pearlberg** [1953] **1** 388, CA.
  Findings of fact—
    Appellate court—Jurisdiction to review findings—Findings of fact by commissioners—Power of appellate court to review. **Edwards (Inspector of Taxes) v Bairstow** [1955] **3** 48, HL.
  Hearing—
    Adjournment—Unjustified refusal of adjournment—Effect—Whether ground for rehearing or for discharge of assessment—Assessment under Sch E made in respect of unexplained increase in taxpayer's wealth—Increase alleged by Crown to represent payments from undisclosed profits of private company controlled by taxpayer—Claim by taxpayer that increase arose from betting winnings—Taxpayer too ill to attend hearing and give evidence—Subsequent recovery in health would have enabled him to give evidence at adjourned hearing—Hearing in absence—Assessments affirmed by commissioners—Appeal to High Court—Order for rehearing—Decline in health of taxpayer following High Court decision—Taxpayer's ill-health precluding him from ever giving evidence—Effect of refusal of adjournment to deprive taxpayer of opportunity of ever giving evidence—Whether refusal justifying discharge of assessment. **Rose v Humbles (Inspector of Taxes)** [1972] **1** 314, CA.
    Natural justice—Duty to hear parties—Appeal to Special Commissioners—Taxpayer in person—Taxpayer not attending hearing—Taxpayer seeking to conduct hearing by presenting written argument—Taxpayer sending documents to commissioners—Commissioners refusing to read or admit documents—Whether breach of rules of natural justice—Whether commissioners exercising discretion to admit documents properly—Whether privilege to plead before commissioners by writing extending to litigants in person—Taxes Management Act 1970, s 50(5). **Banin v MacKinlay (Inspector of Taxes)** [1985] **1** 842, CA.
    Separate appeals—Hearing of separate but connected appeals by different taxpayers simultaneously—Admission by one taxpayer accepted as evidence against other—Appeal by company against additional assessment to profits tax and excess profits tax in relation to alleged undisclosed profits—Appeal by taxpayer controlling company against additional assessments in relation to alleged remuneration from undisclosed profits of company—Application for separate hearings—Imperfectly stated refusal—Counsel for taxpayer and company reasonably understanding that application accepted—Counsel forbearing to submit that figures, calculations etc accepted by taxpayer and evidence by Crown not accepted by or evidence against company—No evidence against company—Discharge of assessment against company. **Rose v Humbles (Inspector of Taxes)** [1972] **1** 314, CA.
  High Court—
    Appeal by way of case stated. See Case stated, below.
  House of Lords—
    Leave to appeal—Terms imposed as condition of granting leave—Surtax. **IRC v Wood Bros (Birkenhead) Ltd (in liq)** [1959] **1** 53, HL.
  Jamaica. See **Jamaica** (Income tax—Appeal).
  Penalty—
    Summary award. See Penalty—Summary award of penalty—Appeal, below.
  Pending appeal—
    Production of documents—Notice. See Information—Production of documents—Documents relevant to taxpayer's liability to tax—Pending appeal, below.
  Point of law—
    Point not raised before commissioners—Point arising on facts found to raise on appeal. **Try (W S) Ltd v Johnson (Inspector of Taxes)** [1946] **1** 532, CA.
  Settlement—
    Agreement—Inspector agreeing settlement in principle—Apportionment of sum between capital gains tax and income tax—Taxpayer bringing actions for damages for breach of agreement to purchase shareholding and for compensation for loss of office—Actions settled by payment to taxpayer of single sum—Taxpayer proposing apportionment of sum between claims—Inspector of taxes agreeing apportionment—No figures agreed—Inspector subsequently assessing entire sum to capital gains tax as award in respect of shares—Taxpayer claiming inspector bound by agreement in principle—Whether inspector and taxpayer having 'come to an agreement'—Taxes Management Act 1970, s 54(1). **Delbourgo v Field (Inspector of Taxes)** [1978] **2** 193, CA.
    Agreement—Settlement by agreement—Onus of proof on appeal—Whether point of substance settled previously by agreement—Income Tax Act 1952, s 510. **Skinner (Inspector of Taxes) v Berry Head Lands Ltd** [1971] **1** 222, Ch D.
    Further assessment after settlement—Whether further assessment precluded. See Assessment—Appeal—Settlement by agreement—Further assessment after settlement, below.
  Special commissioners—
    Competence to hear appeal—Hearing by two commissioners—Unnecessary that all commissioners should be summoned—Income Tax Act 1918, ss 62(5), 137(1)(4), 230(2). **Hood-Barrs v IRC** [1946] **2** 768, CA; **R v Hood-Barrs** [1943] **1** 665, CCA.

39

Appeal (cont)—
Special commissioners (cont)—
Duty to hear parties. *See* Appeal—Hearing—Natural justice—Duty to hear parties—Appeal to Special Commissioners, *above.*
Valuation of land—
Valuation by person of skill—Valuation not on face bad in law—Examination of valuer—Whether valuer may be required to justify valuation—Income Tax Act 1918, s 138—Finance Act 1923, s 26. **Lyons v Collins (Inspector of Taxes)** [1936] **3** 788, CA.
Apportionment of income—
Income arising under settlement. *See* Settlement—Income arising under a settlement—Apportioned income, *below.*
Investment company. *See* Investment company—Apportionment of income, *below.*
Undistributed income. *See* Undistributed income—Apportionment, *below.*
Appropriate year—
Deduction in computing profits. *See* Deduction in computing profits—Appropriate year, *below.*
Arrangement—
Arrangement having purpose or effect of avoiding liability. *See* Avoidance—Arrangement having purpose or effect of avoiding liability, *below.*
Settlement for tax purposes. *See* Settlement—Meaning—Arrangement, *below.*
Assessment—
Additional assessment. *See* Additional assessment, *above.*
Appeal—
Assessment following appeal—Commissioners deciding appeal by stating amount of income assessable to tax—Whether commissioners required to state amount of tax payable—Whether commissioners had 'determined' appeal—Taxes Management Act 1970, ss 50(6)(7), 55(2)(b). **Hallamshire Industrial Finance Trust Ltd v IRC** [1979] **2** 433, Ch D.
Settlement by agreement—Further assessment after settlement—Loss relief—Further assessment disallowing deduction of losses—Details of losses not appearing in company's accounts or specifically brought to inspector's attention on making of original assessment—Whether further assessment precluded—Income Tax Act 1952, s 510. **Scorer (Inspector of Taxes) v Olin Energy Systems Ltd** [1985] **2** 375, HL.
Appropriate year—
Bonus salary—Years to which attributable—Bonus paid in one year attributable to services rendered over several years—Income Tax Act 1918, Sch E, rr 1, 5. **Heasman v Jordan (Inspector of Taxes)** [1954] **3** 101, Ch D.
Compensation—Date when right to compensation arose rather than date payable or date of receipt—Trade receipt—Company engaged in ribbon development—Compensation paid to company for refusal of permission to build houses—Appropriate year of assessment—Income Tax Act 1918, Sch D, Case I—Restriction of Ribbon Development Act 1935, ss 1, 2, 7, 9. **Try (W S) Ltd v Johnson (Inspector of Taxes)** [1946] **1** 532, CA.
Dividends—Declaration and payment—Dividends of foreign corporation—Dividend payable four years after declaration—Whether shareholders assessable in year of declaration or in year of payment. **Associated Insulation Products Ltd v Golder (Inspector of Taxes)** [1944] **2** 203, CA.
Option to purchase shares—Exercise of option—Option to purchase its shares sold to company's employee—Subsequent exercise of right of purchase—Increase in value of shares since date of option—In what year value of option assessable—Income Tax Act 1952, s 156, Sch E, Case I, r 1. **Abbott v Philbin (Inspector of Taxes)** [1960] **2** 763, HL.
Assessment out of time—
Leave to issue assessment out of time—Leave to apply for judicial review of commissioner's decision to grant leave to issue assessment out of time. *See* **Judicial review** (Leave to apply for judicial review—Circumstances in which leave may be granted—Decision of income tax commissioner—Decision to grant Revenue leave to issue assessment out of time).
New Zealand—Making assessment—Whether assessment only made where process of determination produces taxable income on which tax payable—Whether determination that no tax payable constituting an 'assessment'—Whether further assessment may be made more than four years after determination made that no tax was payable—Income Tax Act 1976 (NZ), ss 19, 25. **Lloyds Bank Export Finance Ltd v IRC** [1991] **4** 303, PC.
Balancing charge—
Wear and tear. *See* Balancing charge—Wear and tear—Assessment, *below.*
Emoluments from office or employment. *See* Emoluments from office or employment—Assessment, *below.*
Estoppel. *See* **Estoppel** (Crown—Assessment to income tax).
Excessive assessment—
Relief—Error or mistake—Whether statutory provision for relief for tax paid under mistake excluding all other common law and equitable claims—Whether statutory provision capable of construction so as to give claimants effective remedy to recover unlawful tax paid for relief compliant with Community law principle of effectiveness—Taxes Management Act 1970, s 33. **Test Claimants in the Franked Investment Income Group Litigation v Revenue and Customs Comrs** [2012] **3** 909, SC.
Judicial review—
Availability of remedy. *See* **Judicial review** (Availability of remedy—Alternative remedy available—Discretion of court to grant relief—Appeal against assessments to income tax).
Mistake, defect or omission not invalidating assessment—
Mistake—Assessment based on mistaken assumptions common to Crown and taxpayer—No mistake in form of assessment—Assessment charging taxpayer under wrong case of schedule—Form setting out assessment inspector intended to make on basis of information supplied to him—Whether mistake in assessment—Whether assessment capable of being treated as unaffected by mistake—Income Tax Act 1952, s 514(2). **Bath and West Counties Property Trust Ltd v Thomas (Inspector of Taxes)** [1978] **1** 305, Ch D.

INCOME TAX (cont)—

Assessment (cont)—

Mistake, defect or omission not invalidating assessment (cont)—

Mistake—Error in computation of tax due—Further assessment to recover tax lost—Further assessment stated to be made pursuant to statutory provision inapplicable in circumstances—Validity of assessment—Whether 'assessment to tax' including error in computation tax—Taxes Management Act 1970, s 29(3)(b), (c). **Vickerman (Inspector of Taxes) v Mason's Personal Representatives** [1984] **2** 1, Ch D.

Person or property charged designated according to common intent and understanding—Common intent and understanding—Whether subjective intent and understanding of parties or objective intent and understanding of tax specialists—Income Tax Act 1952, s 514(2). **Bath and West Counties Property Trust Ltd v Thomas (Inspector of Taxes)** [1978] **1** 305, Ch D.

Partnership—

Assessment in partnership name. *See* Partnership—Assessment in partnership name, *below*.

Perquisite of office or employment—

Basis of assessment. *See* Emoluments from office or employment—Basis of assessment—Perquisite, *below*.

Res judicata—

Previous decision of board of review that trust income exempt as charitable—Whether estopped from alleging that income of future years was not held for charitable purposes—Ceylon Income Tax Ordinance, s 7(1)(c). **Caffoor (Trustees of the Abdul Gaffoor Trust) v Income Tax Comr, Colombo** [1961] **2** 436, PC.

Time limit—

Notice requiring wife to pay the tax she would have had to pay if separately assessed—Tax assessed on husband and attributable to wife's income. *See* Husband and wife—Collection from wife of tax assessed on husband and attributable to wife's income—Notice requiring wife to pay the tax she would have had to pay if separately assessed—Time limit, *below*.

Year of assessment—

Emoluments. *See* Emoluments from office or employment—Year of assessment, *below*.

Assets—

Transfer abroad. *See* Avoidance—Transfer of assets abroad, *below*.

Australia. *See* **Australia** (Income tax).

Author. *See* Profits—Profession or vocation—Author, *below*.

Avoidance—

Accelerated payment notices—

HMRC opening enquiry into taxpayer's self-assessment return and subsequently issuing accelerated payment notice against taxpayer without making an assessment—Whether issuance of payment notice lawful in circumstances—Finance Act 2014, s 219. **R (on the application of Walapu) v Revenue and Customs Comrs** [2016] **4** 955, QBD.

Partner payment notices (PPNs)—HMRC issuing taxpayer with PPN—Taxpayer issued with penalty for late payment of PPN—Taxpayer seeking to challenge validity of PPN on appeal against penalty notice—Whether First-tier Tribunal having jurisdiction to entertain challenges to underlying PPN—Whether alleged invalidity of PPN could be considered in context of reasonable excuse defence to penalties for non-compliance with PPNs—Finance Act 2014, Pt 4, Ch 3, Sch 32. **Beadle v Revenue and Customs Comrs** [2021] **1** 237, CA.

Representations about a notice—Judicial review challenge to notice—Costs—Whether recipient of notice obliged to utilise statutory representation procedure before issuing judicial review proceedings—Whether taxpayer entitled to costs of discontinued judicial review claim—Finance Act 2014, s 222. **R (on the application of Archer) v Revenue and Customs Comrs** [2020] **1** 716, CA.

Agreement or arrangement having purpose or effect of avoiding liability—

Medical partnership—Australia. *See* **Australia** (Income tax—Avoidance—Agreement or arrangement having purpose or effect of avoiding liability).

Annual payment—

Payment out of profits etc already taxed. *See* Annual payment—Payment out of profits etc already taxed, *above*.

Arrangement having purpose or effect of altering incidence of tax—

New Zealand. *See* **New Zealand** (Income tax—Avoidance—Arrangement having purpose or effect of altering incidence of tax).

Arrangement having purpose or effect of avoiding liability—

Arrangement—Meaning—Overt acts showing scheme to avoid tax—Undistributed profits of company—Dealings in company's shares having effect of avoiding liability under provisions relating to undistributed profits—Commonwealth Income Tax and Social Services Contribution Assessment Act 1936-61 (Australia), s 260. **Newton v Comr of Taxation of Commonwealth of Australia** [1958] **2** 759, PC.

Maintenance and advancement of taxpayer's family—Whether arrangement for the maintenance and advancement of taxpayer's family. **Mangin v IRC** [1971] **1** 179, PC.

Artificial transactions in land—

Acquisition of land with sole or main object of realising gain from disposal thereof—Person directly or indirectly providing opportunity of realising gain liable to tax on gain—Land owned by company controlled by English taxpayer—Land sold at full market value to Guernsey company—Land subsequently sold to another company at a profit—Purchase price payable by instalments subject to contingencies—Whether a 'gain' if land sold at full market value—Whether opportunity of realising gain provided 'directly or indirectly' by taxpayer—Whether gain taxable if person realising it not effectively able to enjoy or dispose of it—Income and Corporation Taxes Act 1970, ss 488(2), (3), (8), 489(13). **Yuill v Wilson (Inspector of Taxes)** [1980] **3** 7, HL.

INCOME TAX (cont)—
  Avoidance (cont)—
    Artificial transactions in land (cont)—
      Acquisition of land with sole or main purpose of realising gain from disposal thereof—Person who is a party to, or concerned in, the transaction—Majority shareholder of group of companies acquiring land with the object of realising gains from its disposal—Taxpayers minority shareholders—Majority shareholder declaring himself a trustee of a share of his interest in land for taxpayers—Sale of land to group at full market value by series of transactions to defer liability to tax on proceeds of sale—Payment to taxpayers of their share of proceeds in 1970-71 and 1971-72—Whether artificial transactions in land—Whether taxpayers 'parties to' or 'concerned in' the transactions—Whether taxpayers assessable on shares of gains realised in 1970-71 but not received in that year—Income and Corporation Taxes Act 1970, s 488(2). **Winterton v Edwards (Inspector of Taxes)** [1980] **2** 56, Ch D.
  Burden of proof—
    Valid assessment on loan interest—Alteration of company's loan arrangements—Continuation of assessment—Necessity for authorities to show rearrangement not a real transaction. **Income Tax Comr, Bombay Presidency and Aden v Bombay Trust Corp Ltd** [1936] **2** 1679, PC.
  Deduction of tax from dividends. *See* Dividends—Deduction of tax—Tax avoidance transactions, *below*.
  Follower notice—
    Relevant judicial ruling—Asserted tax advantage—Interest relief—Claim for relief for interest paid on loans used to provide money to partnership involved in acquisition of film rights—HMRC issuing follower notices relying on judicial ruling said to involve similar arrangements—Nature of asserted tax advantage—Whether HMRC entitled to form opinion that principles or reasoning in previous litigation would deny asserted tax advantage—Income and Corporation Taxes Act 1988, ss 353, 362(1)—Finance Act 2014, s 204. **R (on the application of Locke) v Revenue and Customs Comrs** [2020] **1** 459, CA.
    Relevant judicial ruling—Principles laid down or reasoning given—HMRC forming opinion earlier ruling applying so as to deny taxpayer tax advantage—HMRC issuing taxpayer with follower notice—Degree of certainty required from HMRC that principles or reasoning in earlier ruling applying—Whether HMRC misdirecting themselves as to what was decided in earlier ruling—Whether decision in earlier ruling as to place of effective management of trust a finding of fact only and could not be relied on by HMRC—Whether failure to give adequate reasoning in notice rendering it invalid—Finance Act 2014, ss 204-206. **R (on the application of Haworth) v Revenue and Customs Comrs** [2019] **4** 506, CA; [2021] **3** 997, SC.
  Jamaica. *See* **Jamaica** (Income tax—Avoidance).
  Medical partnership—
    Australia. *See* **Australia** (Income tax—Avoidance—Agreement or arrangement having purpose or effect of avoiding liability—Partnership of medical practitioners dissolved).
  Settlement—
    Element of bounty—Bona fide commercial transaction—Tax avoidance scheme. *See* Settlement—Meaning—Element of bounty—Bona fide commercial transaction—Tax avoidance scheme, *below*.
  Surtax—
    Sales cum dividend—Apportionment—'Exceptional and not systematic' avoidance—Single act of avoidance 'exceptional' even though planned and carried out by a number of sales—Finance Act 1927, s 33(3), (4). **Bilsland v IRC** [1936] **2** 616, KBD.
  Tax advantage. *See* Tax advantage, *below*.
  Transfer of assets abroad—
    Associated operation—Acquisition of rights by means of operation—Rights—Transfer of assets to company in Republic of Ireland—Whether transfer gave rise to right whereby there is power to enjoy income—'Right'—Income Tax Act 1952, s 412(1), (3)(a), (4). **IRC v Herdman** [1969] **1** 495, HL, NICA.
    Associated operation—Connection between operations—Lapse of time between operations—Transfer of assets to English company—Purpose of transfer to release trustees of family estate—Subsequent decision to transfer assets to Canadian company—Whether transfer to Canadian company 'associated' with transfer to English company—Finance Act 1936, s 18. **Corbett's Executrices v IRC** [1943] **2** 218, CA.
    Associated operation—Settlement of interest in remainder—Transfer of assets to company in Canada in consideration of shares etc—Settlement of shares by transferor on taxpayer—Interest in remainder following transferor's life interest—Right to income required by virtue of settlement—Finance Act 1936, s 18(1), (2). **Bambridge v IRC** [1955] **3** 812, HL.
    Associated operation—Transfer by company the greater part of the share capital in which is held by taxpayer—Transfer to company resident in United Kingdom which subsequently moves abroad—Finance Act 1936, s 18, Sch II, para 6—Finance Act 1938, s 28. **Congreve v IRC** [1948] **1** 948, HL.
    Associated operation—Transfer of assets to company in Republic of Ireland—Company charging assets to bank—Subsequent unsecured loan of cash by transferor to company—Payment into company's banking account—Whether loan an 'associated operation'—Whether income of company to be deemed that of transferor—Income Tax Act 1952, s 412(2), (4). **Fynn v IRC** [1958] **1** 270, Ch D.
    Burden of proof of intention—Transfer of income of persons abroad—Operation part of transaction also necessary for protection of settlor—Burden of proof of avoidance—Death of taxpayer before passing of legislation—Liability of executors—Finance Act 1936, s 18. **Cottingham's Exors v IRC** [1938] **4** 663, CA.
    Income payable to persons abroad by virtue of a transfer of assets—Lease of foreign assets to company—Rent payable to trustees abroad—Trust deed executed by lessors directing trustees to hold rent for benefit of widows and issue of lessors as the lessors should appoint—Lessors retaining power to direct and vary investments—Whether power to direct investments an 'interest'—Whether power to determine lease rendered lessors 'entitled to property comprised in the settlement'—Whether benefit to a widow a benefit to a wife—'Power to enjoy income of a person resident out of the United Kingdom'—'Property payable to the settlor'—Income Tax Act 1918, All Schedules Rules, r 18—Finance Act 1936, s 18(1), (3), (5)(a)—Finance Act 1938, s 38(1), (2), (3), (4). **Vestey's (Lord) Exors v IRC** [1949] **1** 1108, HL.

INCOME TAX (cont)—
   Avoidance (cont)—
      Transfer of assets abroad (cont)—
         Income payable to persons resident or domiciled out of the United Kingdom—Income—Taxpayer transferring shares to non-resident trustee of settlement of which taxpayer beneficiary—Taxpayer ordinarily resident in United Kingdom—Assignment by non-resident trustee of right to dividend for consideration paid out of dividend—Whether trustee receiving capital or income—Income and Corporation Taxes Act 1970, s 478. **IRC v McGuckian** [1997] **3** 817, HL.

         Income payable to persons resident or domiciled out of the United Kingdom—Persons resident out of United Kingdom—Settlement—Trustees—Transfer of assets to trustees resident out of United Kingdom to hold on discretionary trusts—Proper law of settlement law of Northern Ireland—Whether trustees 'persons resident out of United Kingdom'—Whether statutory provisions regarding tax avoidance applicable—Income Tax Act 1952, s 412, preamble. **Vestey v IRC** [1977] **3** 1073, Ch D.

         Income payable to persons resident or domiciled out of the United Kingdom—Statutory provision deeming income of foreign transferee to be that of transferor—Whether provision relieving foreign transferee of normal liability to pay tax on its income—Income and Corporation Taxes Act 1988, s 739(2). **R v Dimsey (No 2)** [2001] **4** 786, HL.

         Income payable to persons resident or domiciled outside the United Kingdom—Investment in offshore premium bonds—Holder having ability to choose underlying investments—Offshore bonds subject to separate tax regime—Whether purpose of transfer being avoidance of liability to taxation—Income and Corporation Taxes Act 1988, s 741. **IRC v Willoughby** [1997] **4** 65, HL.

         Income payable to persons resident or domiciled outside the United Kingdom—Residence of transferor—Whether transferor required to be ordinarily resident in United Kingdom for charge to income tax—Income and Corporation Taxes Act 1988, s 739. **IRC v Willoughby** [1997] **4** 65, HL.

      Information—Power of commissioners by notice to require information—Power to require such information as commissioners think necessary for specified purposes—Commissioners not entitled to have regard to irrelevant considerations or to act unreasonably—Information as to introduction of customers to bank with view to carrying out specified transactions—Information as to advice given to customer resulting in carrying out transactions—Plaintiff London representative of bank incorporated in Bermuda—Bank providing facilities for and advice in relation to transfer of money to Bermuda—Commissioners serving notice on plaintiff requiring particulars of customers and transactions or operations—Validity of notice—Income and Corporation Taxes Act 1970, s 481(1)(2). **Clinch v IRC** [1973] **1** 977, QBD.

      Information—Power of commissioners by notice to require information—Power to require such particulars as commissioners think necessary for specified purposes—Ordinary banking transactions between bank and customer—Sales of gilt-edged stocks by bank on behalf of company incorporated abroad—Notice by commissioners to bank requiring particulars of transactions and of persons representing or interested in company—Whether particulars that may be required confined to particulars of transaction in which addressee of notice engaged—Whether sales of stock 'ordinary banking transactions'—Income Tax Act 1952, s 414(1)(3)(5). **Royal Bank of Canada v IRC** [1972] **1** 225, Ch D.

      Persons liable to tax—Individuals ordinarily resident in United Kingdom—Discretionary trust—Beneficiaries—Power to enjoy income of person resident or domiciled overseas—Receipt by United Kingdom resident of capital sum payment of which connected with transfer of assets abroad—Transfer of assets to trustees abroad—Trustees holding assets on discretionary trusts—Trustees accumulating income and paying sums to selected appointees from class of beneficiaries—Beneficiaries 'ordinarily resident in United Kingdom'—Whether liability limited to person ordinarily resident in United Kingdom who transferred assets—Whether appointees liable to tax—Income Tax Act 1952, s 412. **Vestey v IRC (Nos 1 and 2)** [1979] **3** 976, HL.

      Power to enjoy income of person resident or domiciled overseas—Partnership interest—Sale by taxpayer's wife to Rhodesian company in consideration of issue of shares and interest bearing debentures—Profits of company applied in redeeming debentures—Share of partnership profits becoming 'payable' to company—Wife having power to enjoy income—Finance Act 1936, s 18. **Latilla v IRC** [1943] **1** 265, HL.

      Power to enjoy income of person resident or domiciled overseas—Transfer of assets to company in Canada—Income operative to increase the value of taxpayer's assets—Finance Act 1936, s 18(3). **Howard de Walden (Lord) v IRC** [1942] **1** 287, CA.

      Prevention of avoidance of liability to tax—Income of transferee deemed to be income of transferor—Gains accruing from acquisition and disposal of chargeable assets—Short-term capital gains tax—Taxpayer transferring assets to investment company resident outside United Kingdom—Company selling certain assets and making gain—Abolition of short-term capital gains tax on companies—Whether company's gain deemed to be income pof taxpayer—Whether gain to be computed in the same way as profits—Income Tax Act 1952, s 412(1)—Finance Act 1962, s 16(8), Sch 10—Finance Act 1968, s 82(2). **Chetwode (Lord) v IRC** [1976] **1** 641, CA.

      Prevention of avoidance of liability to tax—Income of transferee deemed to be income of transferor—Meaning of 'income'—Computation of income—Taxpayer resident in United Kingdom—Taxpayer transferring assets to investment company resident outside United Kingdom—Investment company incurring expenses of a revenue nature in managing portfolio—Whether management expenses deductible in computing income of company—Income Tax Act 1952, s 412(1). **Chetwode (Lord) v IRC** [1976] **1** 641, CA; [1977] **1** 638, HL.

      Purpose of transfer—Avoidance of liability to taxation not one of purposes—Onus of proof—Onus on taxpayer to show that avoidance of tax not one of purposes—Transfer of assets by taxpayer's father having effect of avoiding tax—Failure to adduce evidence of transferor's purpose—Transferor resident in Republic of Ireland—Transfer of securities in United Kingdom companies to Irish residents prior to transferor changing own residence to Switzerland—Transferor's advice to son in relation to subsequent transaction effected for purpose of tax saving—Inference to be drawn as to transferor's purpose—Income Tax Act 1952, s 412(3)(a). **Philippi v IRC** [1971] **3** 61, Ch D and CA.

INCOME TAX (cont)—
    Avoidance (cont)—
        Transfer of assets abroad (cont)—
            Receipt by United Kingdom resident of capital sum payment whereof connected with transfer or associated operation—Any income which by reason of transfer or associated operation income of transferee deemed to be income of recipient of capital sum—Any income—Settlement—Transfer of property to trustees abroad to hold on discretionary trusts—Investment of income from property to form capital fund—Income produced by investment of capital fund divided equally between two other funds—Accumulation and investment of income of each of those funds—Appointment of capital to beneficiary of one of those funds—Whether beneficiary chargeable to tax in respect of whole of income of settlement which had become payable to trustees thereafter—Income Tax Act 1952, s 412(2). **Vestey v IRC** [1977] **3** 1073, Ch D.
            Receipt by United Kingdom resident of capital sum payment whereof connected with transfer or associated operation—Any income which by reason of transfer or associated operation income of transferee deemed to be income of recipient of capital sum—Associated operation—Operation in relation to income arising from transferred assets or to assets representing the accumulations of income arising from such assets—Sub-accumulations—Capital sum paid out of accumulations of income of accumulations—Whether 'accumulations' including sub—accumulations of income—Whether payment 'connected with ... associated operation'—Income Tax Act 1952, s 412(2)(4). **Vestey v IRC** [1977] **3** 1073, Ch D.
    Balancing charge—
        Wear and tear—
            Assessment—Charge to be made by means of an additional assessment—No effect on amount of profit chargeable—Income Tax Act 1945, s 55(3). **Townsend (Inspector of Taxes) v Electrical Yarns Ltd** [1952] **1** 918, Ch D.
            Event occurring before trade is permanently discontinued—Sale of business as going concern—Business continued by purchaser—Balancing charge in respect of plant and fittings—Income Tax Act 1945, s 17(1). **IRC v Barr (t/a Henry & Galt)** [1954] **2** 218, HL.
            Sale of undertaking to the Crown—Undertaking carried on by Crown—'Person [who] succeeds to any trade'—Inclusion of Crown—Assessment as if trade 'discontinued'—Balancing charge properly made—Income Tax Act 1918, sched D, Rules Applicable to Cases I and II, r 11(2), as substituted by Finance Act 1926, s 32(1)—Income Tax Act 1945, s 17(1). **Madras Electric Supply Corp Ltd (in liq) v Boarland (Inspector of Taxes)** [1955] **1** 753, HL.
            Vehicles of road haulage company—Compulsory acquisition by British Transport Commission—'Sale' of machinery or plant—'Before the trade is discontinued—' ... a person succeeds to any trade'—Treatment of machinery or plant as if sold—Income Tax Act 1918, Sch D, Rules Applicable to Cases I and II, r 11(2), as substituted by Finance Act 1926, s 32(1)—Income Tax Act 1945, ss 17(1), 60(1). **Bramford's Road Transport Ltd v Evans (Inspector of Taxes)** [1953] **2** 1308, Ch D.
            Wagons of coal merchants—Vesting in Bristish Transport Commission—Whether a 'sale'—Income Tax Act 1945, s 17(1)—Transport Act 1947, ss 29, 30(1). **Kirkness (Inspector of Taxes) v John Hudson & Co Ltd** [1955] **2** 345, HL.
    Bank interest—
        Relief. *See* Relief—Bank interest, *below*.
    Benefit in kind—
        Emoluments from office or employment. *See* Emoluments from office or employment—Benefits in kind, *below*.
    Bets—
        Winnings—
            Incident of profession. *See* Profits—Profession or vocation—Profits arising from profession—Winnings from bets, *below*.
    Bills of exchange—
        Discounting—
            Computation of profits. *See* Computation of profits—Discounting bills of exchange, *below*.
    Bonus—
        Debentures. *See* Profits, *below*.
        Employee's bonus. *See* Emoluments from office or employment—Personal gifts distinguished from emoluments—Bonuses, *below*.
        Salary—
            Appropriate year of assessment. *See* Assessment—Appropriate year—Bonus salary, *above*.
    Book debt—
        Profit on collection. *See* Profits—Trading receipts—Book debt, *below*.
    Building society—
        Interest and dividends paid to depositors—
            Transitional provision in respect of payments of interest and dividends in 1985-86—Transitional provision made by regulations made pursuant to income tax legislation—Regulations charging tax on interest and dividends paid by building societies between end of accounting period ending in 1985-86 and 1 March 1986—Whether regulations ultra vires—Income and Corporation Taxes Act 1970, s 343(1A)—Finance Act 1986, s 47(1)—Income Tax (Building Societies) Regulations 1986, regs 3, 11. **Woolwich Equitable Building Society v IRC** [1991] **4** 92, HL.
    Business expansion scheme—
        Loan-linked investments—
            Enterprise investment scheme relief. *See* Enterprise investment scheme relief—Loan-linked investments—Business expansion scheme, *below*.
    Business expenses—
        Deduction in computing profits. *See* Deduction in computing profits, *below*.
    Canada. *See* **Canada** (Income tax).
    Capital allowances. *See* **Capital allowances**.
    Capital gains. *See* **Capital gains tax**.
    Capital or income expenditure—
        Deduction in computing profits. *See* Deduction in computing profits, *below*.
        Disposition of income for short period. *See* Disposition of income for short period—Capital or income payment, *below*.

INCOME TAX (cont)—

Capital or income receipts—

Amortisation of capital—

Electricity undertakers—Centralisation of supply—Sterilisation of undertakings—Annual sums paid by central authority to undertakers—Sums for operating generating stations as agents of authority—Annual sums including sum required by undertakers for amortisation of capital expenditure—Whether sum capital receipt—Income Tax Act 1918, Sch D, Cases I and II, rr 3, 5(1). **Cattermole v Reigate Corp** [1941] **2** 765, CA.

Annuity—

Payment out of capital. *See* Annual payment—Capital or income—Annuity—Deficiency, *above*.

Capital distribution by company—

Dividends paid in debentures—Debentures redeemable at any time on notice—Debentures paid to another company which subsequently paid dividends in cash—Cash dividends representing value of debentures—Whether payments in respect of debentures capital or income—Finance Act 1936, Sch II, para 3. **Aykroyd v IRC** [1942] **2** 665, KBD.

Compulsory acquisition of land—

Assessment of compensation for disturbance. *See* **Compulsory purchase** (Compensation—Assessment—Compensation for disturbance—Deduction in respect of income tax).

Copyright—

Assignment—Lump sum consideration—Assignor not engaged in trade or profession of dealing in copyright—Assignment of film rights—Whether proceeds capital or income—Income Tax Act 1918, Sch D, Case VI. **Withers (Inspector of Taxes) v Nethersole** [1948] **1** 400, HL.

Assignment—Sale of film rights of book—Sale by authoress of book—Whether consideration income or capital receipt—Whether profit from profession or vocation—Income Tax Act 1918, Sch D, Case II. **Howson (Inspector of Taxes) v Monsell** [1950] **2** 1239, Ch D.

Damages—

Breach of contract—Right of pre-emption—Loss of profit from right of pre-emption—Breach of contract to give pre-emption over surplus stocks—Whether taxable as a revenue receipt—Income Tax Act 1952, Sch D, Case I. **Sommerfields Ltd v Freeman (Inspector of Taxes)** [1967] **2** 143, Ch D.

Capital loss or loss of profit—Loss of profitable use of asset—Damage to jetty—Payment by shipowners responsible—Apportionment in negotiations with jetty owner's underwriters—Part attributed to loss of use of jetty—Income Tax Act 1952, s 137. **London and Thames Haven Oil Wharves Ltd v Attwooll (Inspector of Taxes)** [1967] **2** 124, CA.

Loss of profit in respect of property—Damages awarded to landlord against tenant unlawfully remaining in occupation of property—Damages representing difference between rent paid by tenant and rent obtainable in open market—Whether damages liable to income tax as 'income'—Income Tax Act (Singapore), s 10(1). **Raja's Commercial College v Gian Singh & Co Ltd** [1976] **2** 801, PC.

Disposal of capital asset—

Asset constituting whole structure of taxpayers' trade—Taxpayer company's exclusive agency—Major part of company's distributive trade—Grant of concurrent sub-agency to other company—Payments of lump sum consideration constituting income of taxpayer company—Income Tax Act 1952, Sch D. **Fleming (Inspector of Taxes) v Bellow Machine Co Ltd** [1965] **2** 513, Ch D.

Royalty agreement—Finding that initially it was stock-in-trade—Conversion by company as fixed capital asset—Inference of appropriation as such—Income Tax Act 1952, Sch D. **British-Borneo Petroleum Syndicate Ltd v Cropper (Inspector of Taxes)** [1969] **1** 104, Ch D.

Dividends—

Dividend paid out of capital profits of company—Whether dividend 'income' in hands of recipient—British Guiana Income Tax Ordinance, s 5(c). **Bicber Ltd v Comr of Income Tax** [1962] **3** 294, PC.

Emoluments from office or employment—

Capital distribution—Trust fund for benefit of employees—Trust determined—Proceeds of realisation of trust fund divided between employees in accordance with trust deed—Money paid to employee capital in hands of trustees—Whether liable to income tax as an emolument in hands of employee—Income and Corporation Taxes Act 1970, s 181(1)(Sch E). **Brumby (Inspector of Taxes) v Milner** [1975] **2** 773, Ch D.

Extrinsic evidence—

Admissibility—Rentcharge—Evidence to show whether rentcharge representing capital or income—Sale of reversion by long leaseholder to lessee in exchange for rentcharge—Lessee company deducting tax in paying rentcharges—Lessor charity seeking to recover tax deducted—Revenue claiming rentcharge representing partly income and partly capital and charity only entitled to recover tax on income element—Revenue seeking to adduce evidence relating to negotiations between parties prior to contract of sale—Whether evidence admissible—Income Tax Act 1952, ss 177, 447(1)(a). **IRC v Church Comrs for England** [1974] **3** 529, Ch D.

Foreign possessions—

Instalments of capital of estate—Will of testatrix domiciled in the United States—Beneficiary in England entitled to annual instalments of capital of estate—Capital payments according to state law of the United States—Character in the hands of the beneficiary determined by English law—Income in beneficiary's hands by English law—Income Tax Act 1952, s 122, Sch D, s 123(1). **Inchyra (Baron) v Jennings (Inspector of Taxes)** [1965] **2** 714, Ch D.

Government grant—

Ploughing grant made by government for ploughing up pasture land—Agricultural Development Act 1939—Agriculture (Miscellaneous War Provisions) Act 1940. **Higgs v Wrightson (Inspector of Taxes)** [1944] **1** 488, KBD.

Income from foreign possessions. *See* Foreign possessions—Income arising from possessions out of United Kingdom—Capital or income, *below*.

Insurance—

Payment under policy—Lump sum received by employer in respect of death of employee—Whether capital or trade receipt—Income Tax Act 1918, Sch D, Case I. **Murphy v Thomas E Gray & Co Ltd** [1940] **3** 214, KBD.

INCOME TAX (cont)—
  Capital or income receipts (cont)—
    Insurance (cont)—
      Payment under policy—Purchase of capital assets—Insurance against late delivery—Ship-building contract—Insurances against late delivery of ships to be built—Whether payments under policies revenue or capital receipts—Income Tax Act 1952, Sch D. **Crabb (Inspector of Taxes) v Blue Star Line Ltd** [1961] **2** 424, Ch D.

      Premiums—Return of excess premiums—Mutual insurance company—Sole income premiums from members—Members trading companies—Liquidation of insurance company—Rules requiring surplus assets to be distributed to members in proportion to premiums paid—Whether returned premiums capital or taxable as trading receipts—Companies Act 1948, ss 20, 302—Income Tax Act 1952, Sch D, Case I. **Stafford Coal and Iron Co Ltd v Brogan (Inspector of Taxes)** [1963] **3** 277, HL.

      Proceeds of policy. *See* Capital or income receipts—Proceeds of insurance policy, *below*.

    Know-how—
      Consideration for imparting technical knowledge—Shares issued in return—Company manufacturing tools—Substantial Indian trade—Setting up of new Indian controlled company—Indian government pressure—Transfer of Indian business and techniques to new company—Consideration in form of shares in new company—Income or capital nature. **Wolf Electric Tools Ltd v Wilson (Inspector of Taxes)** [1969] **2** 724, Ch D.

      Lump sum—Payment of lump sum for imparting of secret processes and for furnishing plans, etc, for erecting factory—Whether income or capital receipt—Income Tax Act 1952, Sch D, Case I. **Moriarty (Inspector of Taxes) v Evans Medical Supplies Ltd** [1957] **3** 718, HL.

      Lump sum—Payment of lump sum for imparting technical knowledge—Whether income or capital receipt—Income Tax Act 1952, Sch D, Case I. **Rolls Royce Ltd v Jeffrey (Inspector of Taxes)** [1962] **1** 801, HL.

    Licence—
      Consideration—Lump sum payment for grant of exclusive licence—Licence to use patent—Lump sum payable in instalments and further sum payable each year during continuance of licence—Whether capital receipt or royalty payment from which tax deductible—Income Tax Act 1918, All Schedules Rules, r 21. **British Salmson Aero Engines Ltd v IRC** [1938] **3** 283, CA.

      Patent—Payment in advance for licence to use patent—Lump sum payable in instalments—Whether capital payment or royalty payment from which tax deductible. **Desoutter Bros Ltd v Hanger & Co Limited and Artificial Limb Makers Ltd** [1936] **1** 535, KBD.

    Proceeds of insurance policy—
      Insurance of member of company—Insurance for benefit of company—Whether proceeds of policy capital or income receipt. **Williams v IRC** [1944] **1** 381, HL.

    Professional sportsman—
      Payment for relinquishing amateur status—Football player—Signing-on fee—Lump sum payment—Whether capital or income—Income Tax Act 1952, s 156, Sch E. **Jarrold (Inspector of Taxes) v Boustead** [1964] **3** 76, CA.

      Signing-on fee—Footballer—Fee paid in consideration of footballer agreeing to serve—Proportionate part recoverable if footballer unable to play—No mention of relinquishment of amateur status—Whether fee taxable as an income profit from the employment—Income Tax Act 1952, s 156, Sch E, r 1, as amended by Finance Act 1956, s 44(9), Sch 5, Pt 1. **Riley (Inspector of Taxes) v Coglan** [1968] **1** 314, Ch D.

    Profit on investment—
      Once and for all profit—Absence of possibility of recurrence—Subscription to mining venture—Allotment of shares in development company—Difference between subscription and nominal value of shares allotted—Whether a trading or capital profit. **Lowry (Inspector of Taxes) v Field** [1936] **2** 735, KBD.

    Restrictive covenant—
      Lump sum consideration—Licence—Covenant by licensor—Licences for manufacture of Terylene in foreign countries—Covenants of licensor not to manufacture or licence manufacture there—Lump sum payments for covenants—Whether capital or income—Income Tax Act 1952, Sch D, Case II. **Murray (Inspector of Taxes) v Imperial Chemical Industries Ltd** [1967] **2** 980, CA.

    Royalties—
      Commutation for lump sum—Authoress entitled to royalties under agreement—Grant of licence to publish in return for lump sum—Whether income or capital receipt—Whether profit from profession or vocation—Income Tax Act 1918, Sch D, Case II. **Glasson (Inspector of Taxes) v Rougier** [1944] **1** 535, KBD.

    Sale of property—
      Land—Building contractors—Receipts from sale of land—Land bought in order to enable builders to acquire adjoining house—House alone required for conversion to flats—House constituting stock-in-trade—Land not used or let—Whether profit from land on subsequent sale taxable as income. **Snell (Inspector of Taxes) v Rosser, Thomas & Co Ltd** [1968] **1** 600, Ch D.

      Land—Turf—Sale of turf from land—Agreement that purchaser should remove turves from specified area of land—Whether taxpayer making partial realisation of freehold—Whether profits or gains arising from payment for right to use land—Finance Act 1963, ss 15(1)(c), 28(3), Sch D, Case VIII. **Lowe (Inspector of Taxes) v JW Ashmore Ltd** [1971] **1** 1057, Ch D.

      Price payable in instalments—Instalments calculated as percentage of profits derived from property—Railway siding—Construction of private siding by railway company—Purchase of siding by taxpayer and resale to railway company—Consideration on resale paid in annual instalments out of railway company's share of freight—Whether instalments capital payments. **Legge v Flettons Ltd** [1939] **3** 220, KBD.

      Profits or gains arising from property in United Kingdom—Payment for provision of information—Contract made between newspaper and agent for taxpayer—Contract requiring taxpayer to provide information about her life with her convict husband—Taxpayer resident abroad—Contract governed by English law and payment to be made to agent on behalf of taxpayer—Whether payment 'profits or gains arising ... from property ... in the United Kingdom'—Whether payment received as capital or income—Whether payment arising from the contract or from the services performed by taxpayer—Income and Corporation Taxes Act 1970, s 108, para 1 (a)(iii). **Alloway v Phillips (Inspector of Taxes)** [1980] **3** 138, CA.

INCOME TAX (cont)—
    Capital or income receipts (cont)—
        Sale of property (cont)—
            Racehorse—Acquisition of right to send mares to stallion free of charge—No trading—Sale of right—Whether receipt in nature of income—Income Tax 1918, Sch D, Case VI. **Leader v Counsell (Inspector of Taxes)** [1942] **1** 435, KBD.
        Surrender of lease—
            Lump sum payment to lessee—Payment in respect of future rents—Whether payment to be treated as capital or income. **Greyhound Racing Association (Liverpool) Ltd v Cooper** [1936] **2** 742, KBD.
        Transfer of capital asset—
            Cash payments of fixed amounts over fixed period as consideration for transfer—Rentcharges—Sale of land—Sale of reversions on long leaseholds to lessee—Consideration for sale rentcharges payable annually for a period of ten years—Amount of rentcharges calculated to maintain income equivalent to previous rental income of vendor during ten year period and to accumulate fund to maintain income after ten year period—Whether rentcharge payments partly of a capital nature—Income Tax Act 1952, s 177. **IRC v Church Comrs for England** [1976] **2** 1037, HL.
            Purchase price—Instalments including interest element. *See* Annual payment—Capital or income—Purchase price—Interest element, *above*.
    Capital or revenue expenditure. *See* Deduction in computing profits—Capital or revenue expenditure, *below*.
    Carry-forward of losses. *See* Loss relief—Carry forward of losses, *below*.
    Case stated—
        Decision of commissioners—
            Further evidence—Affidavit—Admissibility—Affidavit supplementing or contradicting decision as expressed in case stated. **Cannon Industries Ltd v Edwards (Inspector of Taxes)** [1966] **1** 456, Ch D.
        Determination of appeal by commissioners—
            Declaration of dissatisfaction—Declaration immediately after determination—Immediately—Crown declaring dissatisfaction and requiring case to be stated for opinion of the High Court—Commissioners' determination communicated by post—Delay of 13 days before Crown declaring dissatisfaction—Alternative assessments—Commissioners upholding one assessment and discharging alternative assessment at Crown's invitation—Taxpayer expressing dissatisfaction and requiring case to be stated in respect of first assessment—Whether Crown precluded by reason of invitation from expressing dissatisfaction with discharge of alternative assessment—Whether dissatisfaction declared immediately—Whether failure to declare dissatisfaction immediately precluding commissioners from stating case—Income Tax Act 1952, s 64(1)(2). **R v HM Inspector of Taxes, ex p Clarke** [1972] **1** 545, CA.
            Declaration of dissatisfaction—Dissatisfaction expressed by taxpayer with decision against him—Taxpayer successful on one only of two points—No dissatisfaction expressed by Crown—Whether Crown entitled, after notice, to raise on appeal contention on which taxpayer had succeeded—Income Tax Act 1952, s 64C1). **Muir v IRC** [1966] **3** 38, CA.
            Request for case stated—Jurisdiction of commissioners to state case—Appeal—Partnership—Whether one partner entitled to appeal against commissioners' determination without consent of other partners—Whether that partner 'the appellant' for the purposes of appeal to High Court by way of case stated—Taxes Management Act 1970, s 56. **Sutherland v Gustar (Inspector of Taxes)** [1994] **4** 1, CA.
            Request for case stated—Time limit—Supplemental case—Original case remitted to commissioners—Issue raised in court involving new facts—Appeal dismissed—Case remitted to commissioners to determine new issue raised—Order remitting case intended to mean, and so understood by parties, that either side might ask for special Case Stated if point of law emerged—Decision of commissioners adverse to taxpayer—Decision communicated by post—Taxpayer requiring commissioners to state special Case after lapse of ten months—Commissioners complying with request—Whether supplemental case part of original Case Stated and request to state supplemental case covered by original request made within time limit prescribed—Income Tax Act 1918, s 149—Finance Act 1927, s 42(7)—Finance Act 1938, s 38. **Burston v IRC (No 1)** [1945] **2** 61, KBD.
        Form—
            Practice. **Cole Bros Ltd v Phillips (Inspector of Taxes)** [1982] **2** 247, HL.
        High Court—
            Appeal by way of case stated—Whether court having jurisdiction to strike out case stated on grounds that it disclosed no reasonable cause of action or was scandalous or vexatious—RSC Ord 18, r 19. **Petch v Gurney (Inspector of Taxes)** [1994] **3** 731, CA.
        Jurisdiction of court to hear and determine questions of law and make appropriate order—
            Assessment under wrong case—Discretion of court to deal with assessment on basis of case under which it ought to have been made—Crown assessing taxpayer to tax under Sch D, Cases III to VIII, on basis of information supplied by taxpayer—Taxpayer unwittingly supplying misleading information—Revenue subsequently discovering assessment should have been made under Sch D, Case I—Statutory period for making assessment expired—Whether court should exercise discretion in favour of allowing Crown to change assessment to proper case—Taxes Management Act 1970, s 56(6). **Bath and West Counties Property Trust Ltd v Thomas (Inspector of Taxes)** [1978] **1** 305, Ch D.
        Notification to respondent—
            Notification at or before time of transmission of case to High Court—Crown failing to notify taxpayer until six days after transmission of case to High Court—Whether requirement of notification mandatory or merely directory—Whether court having jurisdiction to hear appeal—Taxes Management Act 1970, s 56(5). **Hughes (Inspector of Taxes) v Viner** [1985] **3** 40, Ch D.
        Order for rehearing—
            Competence—Order by High Court for rehearing—Order in respect of assessments not in case stated—Assessments dealt with by commissioners but not appealed—Income Tax Act 1952, s 64(6). **Rose v Humbles (Inspector of Taxes)** [1972] **1** 314, CA.

INCOME TAX (cont)—
Case stated (cont)—
Reference back—
Doubt as to commissioners' findings—Matters not found with sufficient clarity—Statutory power to refer cases back to commissioners where clear doubt as to what finding means. **Neild v IRC** [1947] **1** 480, CA.
Relief in respect of error or mistake—
Point of law—Decision of Special Commissioners—Decision on appeal from Board of Inland Revenue—Right to require case to be stated by Special Commissioners—Point of law arising in connection with computation of profits or income—Returns—Income from hereditament taxable under sched A included in return under sched D, Case I—Application for relief—Case stated by commissioners for the opinion of the court—Whether 'point of law arising in connection with the computation of profits or income'—Limitation of jurisdiction of court—Income Tax Act 1918, s 149—Finance Act 1923, s 24(3)(5). **Carrimore Six Wheelers Ltd v IRC** [1944] **2** 503, CA.
Remission to commissioners—
Findings—Further findings—Circumstances in which case will be remitted for further findings. **Collins v Fraser (Inspector of Taxes)** [1969] **3** 524, Ch D.
Findings—Further findings—Circumstances in which case will be remitted for further findings—Taxes Management Act 1970, s 56(7). **Consolidated Goldfields plc v IRC** [1990] **2** 398, Ch D.
Further evidence—Failure to call evidence—Inference made by judge on evidence available—Whether assumptions made by judge justified—Whether case should have been remitted for further evidence. **Pyrah (Inspector of Taxes) v Annis & Co Ltd** [1957] **1** 196, CA.
Rehearing—Further evidence—Deception of commissioners—Commissioners giving decision in favour of taxpayer—Evidence adduced before commissioners concealing material facts to knowledge of taxpayer—Evidence which would have affected commissioners' decision becoming available subsequently—Case stated disclosing error of law on part of commissioners—Power of court to remit case to commissioners with direction to hear further evidence. **Brady (Inspector of Taxes) v Group Lotus Cars Cos plc** [1987] **3** 1050, CA.
Separate cases—
Procedure—One appeal only in each case. **Rushden Heel Co Ltd v Keene (Inspector of Taxes)** [1946] **2** 141, KBD.
Transmission of case to High Court—
Time limit—Jurisdiction of court to hear appeal—Taxpayer requiring commissioners to state case for opinion of court—Taxpayer transmitting case to court outside 30-day statutory time limit—Whether statutory provision prescribing time limit mandatory—Whether court having jurisdiction to hear appeal—Taxes Management Act 1970, s 56(4). **Petch v Gurney (Inspector of Taxes)** [1994] **3** 731, CA.
Validity—
Signature of commissioners—Omission of signature—Appeal against assessment heard by two Special Commissioners—Case stated signed by one commissioner only owing to death of the other—Whether appeal competent. **Norman v Golder (Inspector of Taxes)** [1945] **1** 352, CA.
Casual profit. *See* Profits—Profits not otherwise charged—Casual profit, *below*.
Cessation of employment. *See* Emoluments from office or employment—Assessment—Cessation of office or employment, *below*.
Ceylon. *See* **Ceylon** (Income tax).
Charge on income—
Deduction in computing profits—
Corporation tax. *See* Deduction in computing profits—Corporation tax—Charge on income, *below*.
Charge to tax—
Liability—
Determination of liability—Procedure—Whether matter may be determined otherwise than by statutory procedure. **Vandervell Trustees Ltd v White** [1969] **3** 496, CA.
Persons chargeable. *See* Persons chargeable, *below*.
Validity—
International convention—Proceeds of tax—Application of proceeds in part for purposes allegedly contrary to convention ratified by the United Kingdom government—Whether assessment to tax invalidated—Allocation of proceeds of taxes to construction of nuclear weapon—Geneva Conventions Act 1957, preamble. **Cheney v Conn (Inspector of Taxes)** [1968] **1** 779, Ch D.
Charity—
Charitable purposes—
Aesthetic education—Advancement of choral singing—Royal Choral Society—Whether established for 'charitable purposes'—Income Tax Act 1918, s 37(b), Sch D—Finance Act 1921, s 30. **Royal Choral Society v IRC** [1943] **2** 101, CA.
Agricultural society—Society to promote interests of foxhound breeding—Income Tax Act 1918, s 37—Finance Act 1921, s 30—Finance Act 1923, s 11—Finance Act 1924, s 23—Finance Act 1927, s 24. **Peterborough Royal Foxhound Show Society v IRC** [1936] **1** 813, KBD.
Artistic and dramatic work—Company incorporated to present such works as well as classical, cultural and educational dramatic works—A further object being to do all such things as might be thought conducive to the attainment of its objects—Whether entitled to exemption from income tax—Income Tax Act 1952, s 448(1)(c)(3). **Associated Artists Ltd v IRC** [1956] **2** 583, Ch D.
Body or trust established for charitable purposes only—Evidence as to detrimental effect of body's object—Admissibility—Anti-Vivisection Society—Whether established for charitable purposes only—Income Tax Act 1918, ss 37(b), 40. **National Anti-Vivisection Society v IRC** [1947] **2** 217, HL.
Company—Objects clause—Trade carried on by charity—Statement in memorandum—Relevance of motives of formation and subsequent acts—Main and subsidiary objects—Whether company established for charitable purposes only—Finance Act 1921, s 30(1)(c)(as substituted by Finance Act 1927, s 24(3)). **Tennant Plays Ltd v IRC** [1948] **1** 506, CA.

INCOME TAX (cont)—
  Charity (cont)—
    Charitable purposes (cont)—
      Overriding trust 'for charitable purposes'—Proviso for educational purposes not in law charitable, invalid as infringing rule against perpetuities—Whether trust established for charitable purposes only—Income applied to charity, but doubtful whether the charity was an object of the trust—Whether a ground of objection to exemption from income tax—Educational trust—Surplus income—Company directors' power to direct special application for purpose not in law charitable—Need for evidence that application of funds was for purpose in fact charitable where that depended on poverty of recipient—Income Tax Act 1952, s 447(1)(b). **George Drexler Ofrex Foundation Trustees v IRC** [1965] **3** 529, Ch D.
      Protection of interests of holders in the United Kingdom of foreign bonds—Whether established for 'charitable purposes'—Income Tax Act 1918, s 37(b), Sch D. **Corp of Foreign Bondholders v IRC** [1944] **1** 420, CA.
      Recreation ground for employees of limited company—Land conveyed to trustees as recreation ground—Money expended on recreational facilities—Whether expended for charitable purposes—Income Tax Act 1918, s 37(b). **Wernher's (Sir Harold A) Charitable Trust (Trustees) v IRC** [1937] **2** 488, KBD.
      Religion—Oxford Group—'Advancement of Christian religion'—Support and development of group movement 'in every way'—Whether power too wide to be regarded as charitable—Income Tax Act 1918, s 37(a)(b)—Finance Act 1921, s 30(1)(a). **Oxford Group v IRC** [1949] **2** 537, CA.
      Scotland—Law to be applied in Scotland—Trust not for exclusively charitable purposes according to English law—Police athletic association. **IRC v City of Glasgow Police Athletic Association** [1953] **1** 747, HL.
      Social objects—Institute for Welsh people—Objects party social—Trust to maintain institute in London to give social, educational and other amenities to Welsh people or people connected with Wales—Trust property comprising houses—Direction to trustees to apply rents and profits from settled properties to carrying on institute and maintaining properties—Rents and profits so applied—Whether trust for charitable purposes—Whether moneys applied for charitable purposes only—Income Tax Act 1918, s 37(a), Sch A. **Williams' (Sir Howell Jones) Trustees v IRC** [1947] **1** 513, HL.
    Covenanted donations to charity—
      Annual payment. *See* Annual payment—Covenanted payments to charity, *above*.
      Deduction in computing profits—Investment company. *See* Investment company—Actual income from all sources—Deduction, *below*.
    Donations from one charity to another—
      Donations accumulated by recipient charity—Whether donations 'applied to charitable purposes'—Income and Corporation Taxes Act 1970, s 360(1). **IRC v Helen Slater Charitable Trust Ltd** [1981] **3** 98, CA.
    Established in United Kingdom—
      Original trustees resident in United Kingdom—One trustee still so resident. **IRC v Gull** [1937] **4** 290, KBD.
    Income of charity—
      Income under void trust—Discretionary trust to pay income among unascertainable class—Certain members, including charities, ascertainable—Payments of income made to charities—Trust invalid but payments deemed to be authorised by settlor—Whether payments exempt as income of charity—Income Tax Act 1918, s 37(b). **IRC v Broadway Cottages Trust** [1954] **3** 120, CA.
    India. *See* **India** (Income tax—Charity).
    Overseas charity—
      Charity established abroad—Activities exclusively abroad—Tax on income arising in United Kingdom—Liability—Income Tax Act 1918, s 37(b). **Camille and Henry Dreyfus Foundation Inc v IRC** [1955] **3** 97, HL.
    Payments to charity—
      Deduction in computing profits. *See* Deduction in computing profits—Payments to charity, *below*.
    Scheme sanctioned by court—
      Estoppel against Crown—Attorney General party to order sanctioning scheme—Whether Crown estopped from denying trusts charitable—Income Tax Act 1952, ss 447, 448. **Vernon (Trustees of the Employees Fund of William Vernon & Sons Ltd) v IRC** [1956] **3** 14, Ch D.
    Selection of beneficiaries—
      Preferential application of income for private class—Company established for charitable educational purposes—Main income from another company by way of covenanted payments—Major part of income applied towards education of children associated with covenantor company—Public benefit essential to charitable purpose—Whether income applied to charitable purposes only—Income Tax Act 1952, s 447(1)(b). **IRC v Educational Grants Association Ltd** [1967] **2** 893, CA.
    Void trust—
      Income applied for benefit of charity—Discretionary trust including charitable institutions—Whole class of beneficiaries not ascertainable—Trust invalid—Payments made to charitable institutions—Whether payments exempt from tax—Income Tax Act 1918, s 37(b). **IRC v Broadway Cottages Trust** [1954] **3** 120, CA.
  Child relief—
    Child over age of 16 receiving full-time instruction—
      Instruction at any university, college, school or other educational establishment—Other educational establishment—Meaning of education—Training of mind in contradistinction to training in manual skills—Taxpayer's son attending a training unit for the mentally subnormal—Training predominantly in factory work—Academic training every day or every alternate day—Whether unit educational establishment—Income and Corporation Taxes Act 1970, s 10(2). **Barry v Hughes (Inspector of Taxes)** [1973] **1** 537, Ch D.
  Entitlement—
    Advice—Racial discrimination. *See* **Race relations** (Unlawful discrimination—Provision of goods, facilities or services—Services—Advice to taxpayer enabling him to claim tax relief to which he is entitled).

INCOME TAX (cont)—
  Child relief (cont)—
    Entitlement (cont)—
      Custody of child—Person other than parent having custody—Legal or factual custody—Wife leaving husband to live with another man—Children of marriage living with wife and man in man's house as a family—Man assuming responsibility for family and contributing to maintenance of children—Legal custody of children in wife—Husband also contributing to children's maintenance—Whether man had 'custody' of children—Whether entitled to claim child relief—Income and Corporation Taxes Act 1970, s 10(1)(b) (as amended by the Finance Act 1971, s 37, Sch 6, para 6(a). **Robertson v Walton** [1977] **1** 465, Ch D.
    Income of child—
      Daughter—Marriage during year of assessment—Post-nuptial income of daughter—Income deemed for income tax purposes to be husband's income and not to be her income—Whether daughter entitled to post-nuptial income in her own right—Whether post-nuptial income to be disregarded for purposes of child relief—Income Tax Act 1952, ss 212(4)(as substituted by the Finance Act 1963, s 13), 354(1). **Murphy v Ingram (Inspector of Taxes)** [1974] **2** 187, CA.
      Earnings—Earnings of child—Whether earnings 'income' to which child 'entitled in his own right'—Income Tax Act 1952, s 212(4)(as substituted by the Finance Act 1963, s 13). **Murphy v Ingram (Inspector of Taxes)** [1974] **2** 187, CA.
      Foreign income—Earning by undergraduate abroad—No money remitted to United Kingdom—Effect on father's child allowance—Income Tax Act 1952, s 212(4). **Mapp (Inspector of Taxes) v Oram** [1968] **1** 643, Ch D.
      Maintenance—Income to which child entitled in own right—Maintenance order in divorce proceedings against husband—Order to pay sums to wife for maintenance of children—Whether children entitled to sums in their own right—Finance Act 1920, s 21. **Stevens v Tirard** [1939] **4** 186, CA.
      Wages—Child living with parent earning wages—Whether wages 'income'—Finance Act 1920, s 21(1)(3)—Finance (No 2) Act 1939, s 9(3). **Williams v Doulton (Inspector of Taxes)** [1948] **1** 603, KBD.
    Reduction or disallowance of relief—
      Income of child. *See* Child relief—Income of child, *above*.
  Children—
    Child relief. *See* Child relief, *above*.
    Settlement. *See* Settlement—Children, *below*.
  Christmas gift—
    Customary gift. *See* Emoluments from office or employment—Voluntary payment—Customary gift—Huntsman—Christmas gifts, *below*.
    Receipt from employment. *See* Emoluments from office or employment—Receipt 'from' employment—Gift to employee—Christmas gifts, *below*.
  Close company—
    Apportionment of income—
      Addition to income to be apportioned—Amounts of annual payments to be deducted in arriving at company's distributable income—Covenanted donations to charity—Trading company—Prohibition on apportionment in absence of shortfall assessment—Whether prohibition applying to amounts of annual payments deducted in arriving at company's distributable income—Whether covenanted donations to charity may be apportioned even though no shortfall assessment—Finance Act 1965, s 78(2)(4)(as amended by the Finance Act 1966, s 27, Sch 5, para 10(1)). **Clark (C & J) Ltd v IRC** [1975] **1** 801, CA.
      Apportionment for surtax—Undistributed income—Manner of apportionment—Apportionment of income on basis of interest in winding-up—Special Commissioners' jurisdiction to review the decision—Income and Corporation Taxes Act 1970, s 296(5)(10). **Lothbury Investment Corp Ltd v IRC** [1979] **3** 860, Ch D.
      Relevant income—Maintenance and development of business—Business—Taxpayer company carrying on business as manufacturers of chalkboards—Decline in demand for chalkboards—Taxpayer company planning to acquire motor-dealership to improve its trading position—Acquisition of dealership within taxpayer company's objects—Whether acquisition of dealership a 'development' of taxpayer company's business—Whether planned expenditure on acquisition of dealership a 'requirement' of taxpayer company's business—Finance Act 1972, Sch 16, para 8(2). **Wilson & Garden Ltd v IRC** [1982] **3** 219, HL.
    Loan to close company—
      Interest on loan applied in lending money to close company—Relief. *See* Interest—Relief—Interest on loan applied in lending money to close company, *below*.
    Shortfall in distributions—
      Articles of association restricting distribution of profits. *See* **Company** (Articles of association—Restriction imposed on company—Restriction imposed by articles of association—Restriction imposed by law—Close company—Shortfall in distributions).
      Calculation of shortfall—Restriction imposed by law as regards making of distributions—Imposed by law—Taxpayer company acquiring two companies by issuing its own shares in exchange for the shares of the two companies—Payment of gross dividends by acquired companies out of their pre-acquisition profits—Whether taxpayer company obliged to create share premium account in respect of excess value of shares acquired over the nominal value of its shares issued in exchange therefor—Whether taxpayer company subject to restrictions imposed by law as regards making of distribution—Companies Act 1948, s 56—Income and Corporation Taxes Act 1970, s 290(4). **Shearer (Inspector of Taxes) v Bercain Ltd** [1980] **3** 295, Ch D.
  Closure notice—
    Validity—
      Judicial review—Rectification of defects—HMRC issuing closure notices without stating amounts of tax payable—Taxpayer challenging by way of judicial review—Whether requirement to state amount of tax due—Whether closure notices capable of rectification—Whether effective statutory right of appeal—Whether judicial review proceedings abuse of process—Taxes Management Act 1970, ss 28A, 31(1)(b), 59B(5), 114(1). **R (on the application of Archer) v Revenue and Customs Comrs** [2017] **3** 524, QBD.

INCOME TAX (cont)—
Club—
    Members' club—
        Mutuality principle. *See* Profits—Mutuality principle—Members' club, *below.*
Commissioners—
    Case stated by commissioners. *See* Case stated, *above.*
    Direction as to undistributed income. *See* Undistributed income—Direction by commissioners, *below.*
    Finality of decision. *See* Appeal—Decision of commissioners—Finality, *above.*
    General Commissioners. *See* General Commissioners, *below.*
    Generally. *See* Commissioners of Inland Revenue, *below.*
    Power to require information—
        Transfer of assets abroad. *See* Avoidance—Transfer of assets abroad—Information, *above.*
    Special Commissioners—
        Appeal. *See* Appeal—Special commissioners, *above.*
        Judicial review of decision of commissioner—Availability of remedy. *See* **Judicial review** (Availability of remedy—Special Commissioner).
        Perjury. *See* **Criminal law** (Perjury—Judicial proceeding—Special Commissioners of Income Tax).
Commissioners of Inland Revenue—
    Administration and management of taxation system—
        Advice and guidance to taxpayers—Advance tax clearance—Withdrawal—Inspector of taxes giving applicant unqualified clearance—Full and accurate disclosure not given by applicant when seeking clearance—Revenue Financial Institutions Division subsequently withdrawing clearance—Whether Revenue bound by inspector's clearance—Whether withdrawal of clearance unfair and amounting to abuse of power by Revenue. **Matrix-Securities Ltd v IRC** [1994] **1** 769, HL.
        Advice and guidance to taxpayers—Reliance on ruling by commissioners—Legitimate expectation—Index-linked bonds—Assurance that index-linked element would be taxed as capital gain and not income—Banks proposing to issue index-linked US or Canadian dollar securities for Lloyd's market—Investors relying on indication from Revenue that index-linked element would not be taxed as income—Revenue subsequently deciding to tax index-linked element as income—Whether Revenue's decision amounting to abuse of power. **R v Board of Inland Revenue, ex p MFK Underwriting Agencies Ltd** [1990] **1** 91, QBD.
        Tax credits—Legitimate expectation—Authorisation given to company to pay dividend gross—Authorisation revoked before dividend paid—Whether Revenue entitled to revoke authorisation previously given—Whether company having legitimate expectation that authorisation would not be revoked—Who may invoke doctrine of legitimate expectation in regard to termination of Revenue practice operating to benefit class of taxpayer—Income and Corporation Taxes Act 1988, s 232(3). **R v IRC, ex p Camacq Corp** [1990] **1** 173, QBD and CA.
    Judicial review of commissioners' exercise of discretion—
        Availability of remedy. *See* **Judicial review** (Availability of remedy—Exercise of discretion on behalf of Crown—Inland Revenue Commissioners).
    Party to civil proceedings. *See* **Practice** (Parties—Adding persons as parties—Necessary party—Inland Revenue Commissioners).
Company—
    Close company—
        Generally. *See* Close company, *above.*
    Corporation tax—
        Generally. *See* Corporation tax, *below.*
    Deduction in computing profits. *See* Deduction in computing profits, *below.*
Director—
    Emoluments from office or employment. *See* Emoluments from office or employment, *below.*
Group relief—
    Appropriation of assets to trading stock—Transfer between members of group—Company dealing in shares and securities acquiring shares and debts from parent at small market value—Parent company having acquired assets for large sum—Acquiring company electing to have assets brought into its trading account at value equal to cost of assets to parent company—Whether assets acquired as trading stock—Finance Act 1965, Sch 7, para 1(1)(3)—Income and Corporation Taxes Act 1970, ss 137(4), 274(1). **Reed (Inspector of Taxes) v Nova Securities Ltd** [1985] **1** 686, HL.
    Appropriation of assets to trading stock—Transfer between members of group—Property dealing company acquiring lease at slightly less than market value from development company in same group—Lease not part of trading stock of development company—Market value of lease at acquisition substantially less than costs incurred by development company on lease—Property dealing company disposing of lease to another member of group for market value—Property dealing company electing to have lease brought into its trading account—Whether property dealing company acquired lease as trading stock—Finance Act 1965, Sch 7, para 1(3)—Income and Corporation Taxes Act 1970, s 274(1). **Coates (Inspector of Taxes) v Arndale Properties Ltd** [1985] **1** 15, HL.
    Claim—Validity—Sufficiency of claim—Claim made in notice of appeal against assessment and in accounts submitted to inspector—Surrendering companies not identified—Amount of reliefs to be surrendered not identified—Inspector rejecting claim as informal and not made within two-year time limit for making claims—Whether valid claim made within time limit—Taxes Management Act 1970, s 42(5)—Income and Corporation Taxes Act 1970, ss 258, 264(1)(c). **Gallic Leasing Ltd v Coburn (Inspector of Taxes)** [1992] **1** 336, HL.
    Determination of surrendering company's profits—Profits for accounting period to be determined without regard to any deduction in respect of losses or allowances of any other period—Profits including realised chargeable gain—Whether realised chargeable gain reduced by allowable losses from previous accounting period—Whether deduction of allowable losses from previous accounting period from realised chargeable gain a deduction of losses or allowances of any other period—Income and Corporation Taxes Act 1988, s 403(7), (8). **Taylor (Inspector of Taxes) v MEPC Holdings Ltd** [2004] **1** 536, HL.

INCOME TAX (cont)—
  Company (cont)—
    Group relief (cont)—
      Entitlement—Arrangements for transfer of company to another group—Arrangement—Scheme for taxpayer to offset its profits against capital allowances of another company—Scheme involving wholly-owned subsidiaries—Taxpayer and other company acquiring equal shareholding in former subsidiary of other company—Former subsidiary not under control of taxpayer—Former subsidiary entitled to claim capital allowance—Taxpayer purchasing claim to capital allowance at discount—Whether taxpayer entitled to group relief by setting its profits against claim to capital allowances—Finance Act 1973, s 20(1)(b)(ii). **Pilkington Bros Ltd v IRC** [1982] **1** 715, HL.
    Undistributed income. *See* Undistributed income, *below.*
  Compensation—
    Appropriate year of assessment. *See* Assessment—Appropriate year—Compensation, *above.*
    Compulsory acquisition of land—
      Assessment of compensation for disturbance. *See* **Compulsory purchase** (Compensation—Assessment—Compensation for disturbance—Deduction in respect of income tax).
    Emolument from office or employment. *See* Emoluments from office or employment—Compensation, *below.*
    Loss of employment. *See* Pension—Compensation—Loss of employment, *below.*
    Loss of office—
      Deduction in computing profits. *See* Deduction in computing profits—Expenses wholly and exclusively laid out for purposes of trade—Compensation for loss of office, *below.*
      Emoluments from office or employment. *See* Emoluments from office or employment—Compensation—Loss of office, *below.*
  Compulsory acquisition of land—
    Assessment of compensation for disturbance—
      Deduction in respect of income tax. *See* **Compulsory purchase** (Compensation—Assessment—Compensation for disturbance—Deduction in respect of income tax).
  Computation of profits—
    Accountancy principles—
      Earnings or cash basis—Accountants' fees determinable after year end—Cash basis adopted for twenty years—Revenue's change to earnings basis—Reversion to cash basis four years later. **Wetton, Page & Co v Attwooll (Inspector of Taxes)** [1963] **1** 166, Ch D.
      Evidence—Application of principles of commercial accountancy—Evidence—Evidence of experts on principles adopted in practice by commercial accountants—Evidence not conclusive of correct principles—Duty of court to determine correct principles of commercial accountancy. **Odeon Associated Theatres Ltd v Jones (Inspector of Taxes)** [1971] **2** 407, Ch D.
      Evidence—Weight of evidence—Issue whether expenditure of a capital or revenue nature—Issue a question of law for court to determine—Weight to be given to evidence as to practice of commercial accountants—Evidence not binding on court. **Heather (Inspector of Taxes) v P-E Consulting Group Ltd** [1973] **1** 8, CA.
      Stock—Valuation—Last in first out method—Whether suitable for tax purposes—Excess profits tax in Canada. **Minister of National Revenue v Anaconda American Brass Ltd** [1956] **1** 20, PC.
      Stock—Valuation—Valuation of stock at end of year—Original cost or market value—Meaning of market value—Replacement value or retail sale value. **BSC Footwear Ltd (formerly Freeman, Hardy & Willis Ltd) v Ridgway (Inspector of Taxes)** [1971] **2** 534, HL.
      Work in progress—Valuation—'Direct cost' or 'oncost' method—Motor vehicle body building company. **Ostime (Inspector of Taxes) v Duple Motor Bodies Ltd** [1961] **2** 167, HL.
    Contingent liability—
      Accountancy provision for contingent liability—Provision for retirement benefits for employees—Statutory scheme—Future payments of lump sums calculated by reference to length of service and salary in closing year—Proper method of reflecting effect of scheme in accounts. **Southern Rly of Peru Ltd v Owen (Inspector of Taxes)** [1956] **2** 728, HL.
    Deductions. *See* Deduction in computing profits, *below.*
    Discounting bills of exchange—
      Anticipated profits—Increase in value of bills as maturity approaches—Apportioned part of increase for each year preceding maturity treated as profit attributable to that year—Bank discounting or purchasing bills of exchange—Bills sold or held to maturity—Provision made in annual accounts including proportion of anticipated profits—Profits realised on sale or maturity—Whether proportion of profits anticipated on sale or maturity to be included in bank's taxable profits for accounting years preceding sale or maturity. **Willingale (Inspector of Taxes) v International Commercial Bank Ltd** [1976] **2** 468, Ch D; [1978] **1** 754, HL.
      Generally. *See* Discounts—Bill of exchange or promissory note, *below.*
    Disposal of stock-in-trade—
      Disposal by taxpayer for own use—Notional receipt—Market value or cost—Racehorse—Transfer of horses from stud farm to racing stable in same ownership—Credit figure in farm accounts—Cost of breeding or market value—Income Tax Act 1918, Sch D, Case I. **Sharkey (Inspector of Taxes) v Wernher** [1955] **3** 493, HL.
      Disposal by taxpayer for own use—Notional receipt—Taxpayer owning two businesses—Transfer of stock-in-trade from one business to the other—Hatchery business and poultry farm—Transfer from hatchery of day old chicks—Whether profits based on market price or cost of production. **Watson Bros v Hornby (Inspector of Taxes)** [1942] **2** 506, KBD.
      Sale at undervalue—Associated companies—Transactions between associated companies—Company dealing in securities, stocks and shares—Sales to associated company at under-value—Transactions not in the course of trade—Seller credited with market value for tax purposes—Transaction of purchase and sale eliminated from company's accounts. **Petrotim Securities Ltd (formerly Gresham Trust Ltd) v Ayres (Inspector of Taxes)** [1964] **1** 269, CA.
    Exchange transaction—
      Assets received—Valuation—Shares received as consideration for transfer of property—Company dealing in gold mining concessions—Transfer of concessions to associate company for fully paid-up shares—Valuation of shares for purpose of computing profits—Valuation at end of accounting period in which received—Income Tax Act 1918, Sch D, Case I. **Gold Coast Selection Trust Ltd v Humphrey (Inspector of Taxes)** [1948] **2** 379, HL.

INCOME TAX (cont)—
　Computation of profits (cont)—
　　Opening stock—
　　　Valuation—Company commencing trading—Stock and other assets acquired in consideration of cash and the issue of fully-paid shares—Apportionment of price paid for stock. **Osborne v Steel Barrel Co Ltd** [1942] **1** 634, CA.
　　　Valuation—Speculative shares taken over on reconstruction of company—Investment company—Cost of shares. **Craddock v Zevo Finance Co Ltd** [1946] **1** 523, HL.
　　Stock-in-trade—
　　　Disposal. See Computation of profits—Disposal of stock-in-trade, above.
　　　Opening stock. See Computation of profits—Opening stock, above.
　　　Right of pre-emption—Value of right of pre-emption immediately before exercise—Purchase and sale of asset—Purchase in exercise of right of pre-emption—Whether right of pre-emption part of trading stock—Whether value of right of pre-emption immediately before exercise to be deducted in computing profits as part of cost of acquisition of asset. **Bath and West Counties Property Trust Ltd v Thomas (Inspector of Taxes)** [1978] **1** 305, Ch D.
　　　Valuation—Base stock method—Fixed process stock on machines not in trading account—Spare process stock awaiting process at arbitrary valuation. **Patrick (Inspector of Taxes) v Broadstone Mills Ltd** [1954] **1** 163, CA.
　　　Valuation—Cost or market value—Need to value all items on same basis—Valuation of each item at lower cost or market value. **IRC v Cock, Russell & Co Ltd** [1949] **2** 889, KBD.
　　　Valuation—Land—Taxpayer carrying on business of building houses for sale—Taxpayer accepting customers' existing properties in satisfaction or part-satisfaction of purchase price of houses—Taxpayer selling properties in their existing condition—Whether properties 'land'—Whether properties can be included in taxpayer's stock-in-trade—Whether taxpayer entitled to stock relief in respect of any increase in value of properties—Finance Act 1976, Sch 5, para 29(2)(b)(3). **Payne (Inspector of Taxes) v Barratt Developments (Luton) Ltd** [1985] **1** 257, HL.
　　Trade debts—
　　　Valuation—Speculative builder—Part of purchase price not advanced by building society advanced by builder on security—Sums agreed to be paid to builder not assessable in year of contract as profits of trade—Assessment on value of debts in that year—Income Tax Act 1918, Sch D, Cases I and II, r 3(i). **Absalom v Talbot (Inspector of Taxes)** [1944] **1** 642, HL.
　　Year in which profit arising—
　　　Change in method of valuation of work in progress showing surplus representing anticipated profits of earlier years—Change from on-cost basis to accrued profit basis of valuation—Change in valuation resulting in surplus profit—Revaluation of work in progress at beginning of first accounting period in which accrued profit method applied—Whether resulting surplus chargeable to tax as profits arising in that accounting period—Income and Corporation Taxes Act 1970, s 247(1). **Pearce (Inspector of Taxes) v Woodall-Duckham Ltd** [1978] **2** 793, CA.
　Construction industry scheme—
　　Registration for gross payment—
　　　Cancellation—Scope of power to cancel registration—Material factors—Whether HMRC obliged to take account of effect of cancelling registration on taxpayer's business—Whether decision to cancel violating taxpayer's right to enjoyment of its possessions—Human Rights Act 1998, Sch 1, Pt II, art 1—Finance Act 2004, s 66. **JP Whitter (Water Well Engineers) Ltd v Revenue and Customs Comrs** [2018] **4** 95, SC.
　Contingent liability—
　　Computation of profits. See Computation of profits—Contingent liability, above.
　Copyright—
　　Assignment—
　　　Capital or income receipts. See Capital or income receipts—Copyright—Assignment, above.
　　　Royalties. See Profits—Profession or vocation—Author—Royalties—Death of author—Assignment of copyright, below.
　　Sale—
　　　Adventure in the nature of trade. See Trade—Adventure in nature of trade—Isolated transaction—Sale of copyright, below.
　　　Payment for services. See Profits—Mutuality principle, below.
　Corporation tax—
　　Advance corporation tax—
　　　Company ceasing to trade and transferring assets to associated company—Purchase price left outstanding with no provision for payment of interest—Company paying dividend to parent subject to payment of advance corporation tax—Company claiming to carry back surplus advance corporation tax—Whether company having accounting period when dividend paid—Whether company having ceased to be within charge to corporation tax—Income and Corporation Taxes Act 1988, ss 12(2), 239(3), 832(1). **Walker (Inspector of Taxes) v Centaur Clothes Group Ltd** [2000] **2** 589, HL.
　　　Company liable to pay sum of advance corporation tax—Company not paying advance corporation tax—Company later ascertaining that it was liable to pay lesser sum of corporation tax—Company paying lesser sum—Whether company liable to pay interest on sum of advance corporation tax while outstanding—Whether company having 'paid' an amount of advance corporation tax—Whether payment effected by set off—Taxes Management Act 1970, s 87—Income and Corporation Taxes Act 1988, s 246N(2). **Burton (Collector of Taxes) v Mellham Ltd** [2006] **2** 917, HL.
　　　Transitional provisions—Rights or obligations created before 6th April 1973 expressed by reference to dividend at gross rate or of gross amount—Reference in relation to dividends payable after 6th April to take effect as reference to dividend of amount which with addition of advance corporation tax equals gross rate or amount—Calculation to be made by reference to rate of advance corporation tax ruling 'on that date'—Meaning of 'on that date'—Whether 6th April 1973 or date on which dividend payable—Finance Act 1972, Sch 23, para 18(1). **Sime Darby London Ltd v Sime Darby Holdings Ltd** [1975] **3** 691, Ch D.

INCOME TAX (cont)—
  Corporation tax (cont)—
    Advance corporation tax (cont)—
      United Kingdom law allowing groups of companies resident in United Kingdom to make group income election such that subsidiary company could pay dividends to parent company free of advance corporation tax—Group income election not available where parent company resident outside United Kingdom—Double taxation agreements between United Kingdom and United States and United Kingdom and Japan containing non-discrimination provisions—Whether restriction of group income election to United Kingdom resident groups discriminatory—Income and Corporation Taxes Act 1988, s 247—Double Taxation Relief (Taxes on Income) (Japan) Order 1970, SI 1970/1948, art 25(3)—Double Taxation Relief (Taxes on Income) (The United States of America) Order 1980, SI 1980/568, art 24(5). **Boake Allen Ltd v Revenue and Customs Comrs** [2007] **3** 605, HL.
    Closure notice. *See* **Tax** (Closure notice).
    Computation of profits. *See* Computation of profits, *above.*
    Debt contracts—
      Company entering into tax avoidance scheme creating debt contracts under which options granted and premiums paid in relation to gilts so as to create loss—Whether single composite transaction—Finance Act 1994, ss 147A, 150A(1). **IRC v Scottish Provident Institution** [2005] **1** 325, HL.
    Deduction in computing profits. *See* Deduction in computing profits—Corporation tax, *below.*
    Double taxation relief. *See* Double taxation relief—Corporation tax, *below.*
    European Union—
      Freedom of establishment. *See* **European Union** (Freedom of establishment—Principle of non-discrimination—Direct internal taxation—Corporation tax).
      Freedom of movement. *See* **European Union** (Freedom of movement—Capital—Principle of non-discrimination—Corporation tax).
    Generally. *See* **Corporation tax**.
    Group relief. *See* Company—Group relief, *above.*
    Loan relationship—
      Credits and debits to be brought into account—Parent company assigning right to interest on loan stock issued by subsidiary to another subsidiary in consideration of issue of preference shares—Whether receipts of interest arising from loan relationship between subsidiaries—Finance Act 1996, ss 81, 84, 85(1)(a). **Greene King plc v Revenue and Customs Comrs** [2017] **2** 947, CA.
      Credits and debits to be brought into account—Sale and repurchase transactions—Interest received on underlying securities treated as interest on loan relationship—Deemed manufactured interest treated as interest on loan relationship—Company entering into net-paying repurchase transactions over gilts with bank—Repurchase price reduced to reflect receipt of interest on gilts—Repurchase price deemed to be increased by interest—Company chargeable on difference between sale and repurchase price as interest on loan relationship—Company deemed to make payment of manufactured interest to bank—Company claiming debit for deemed manufactured interest payment—Whether credits and debits fairly representing interest under company's loan relationships—Income and Corporation Taxes Act 1988, ss 730A, 737A, 737C—Finance Act 1996, ss 84, 97. **DCC Holdings (UK) Ltd v Revenue and Customs Comrs** [2011] **1** 537, SC.
      Unallowable purpose—Exclusion of debits or credits attributable to unallowable purpose—Taxpayer company operating tax avoidance scheme with object of creating loss available for group relief throughout group of companies of which taxpayer forming part—Whether terms of relevant closure notice precluding HMRC from arguing that legislation applying so as to deny taxpayer benefit of loss claimed—Whether Upper Tribunal erring in finding debit in issue being wholly attributable to unallowable purpose—Finance Act 1996, Sch 9, paras 13, 19A. **Fidex Ltd v Revenue and Customs Comrs** [2016] **4** 1063, CA.
    Migration etc of companies—
      Treasury consent—Consent for body corporate resident in the United Kingdom to cease to be so resident or to transfer trade or business to person not so resident—Whether requirement of Treasury consent restricting freedom of establishment guaranteed to nationals of member states of European Economic Community—Income and Corporation Taxes Act 1970, s 482(1)—EEC Treaty, arts 52, 58—EC Council Directive 73/148. **R v HM Treasury, ex p Daily Mail and General Trust plc** [1989] **1** 328, ECJ.
    Profits. *See* **Corporation tax** (Profits).
    Right to appeal assessment—
      Company property. *See* **Company** (Winding up—Liquidator—Powers—Property).
    Small companies' relief—
      Associated company—Control—Attributions—Whether Revenue having to make statutory attributions if requisite conditions satisfied—Identification of requisite conditions—Income and Corporation Taxes Act 1988, ss 13, 416. **R v IRC, ex p Newfields Developments Ltd** [2001] **4** 400, HL.
    Transitional provisions—
      Liability for excess over standard amount—Excessive dividends in 1965—66—Treatment as paid on 6th April 1966—Certificate of exemption—Whether a main purpose to avoid or reduce tax liability—Directors' knowledge of effect of provisions—Finance Act 1965, s 83(1), (11). **Bromilow & Edwards Ltd v IRC** [1970] **1** 174, CA.
      Transitional relief—Company with overseas trading income—Foreign company becoming United Kingdom resident in 1965—United Kingdom resident company not liable for 1965-66 corporation tax—Transitional relief not available—Finance Act 1965, s 84 and Sch 20, paras 1, 2. **Shell Petroleum Co Ltd v Carr (Inspector of Taxes)** [1971] **3** 350, CA.
    Voluntary winding up—
      Corporation tax on chargeable gains. *See* **Company** (Voluntary winding up—Corporation tax on chargeable gains).
  Covenant—
    Payments to charity. *See* Annual payment—Covenanted payments to charity, *above.*
    Seven year covenant to pay annual sums. *See* Disposition of income for short period, *below.*

INCOME TAX (cont)—
Crown—
    Exemption. *See* Exemption—Crown, *below*.
Damages—
    Breach of contract—
        Wrongful dismissal. *See* **Contract** (Damages for breach—Wrongful dismissal—Income tax).
    Capital or income. *See* Capital or income receipts—Damages, *above*.
    Interest. *See* Interest—Damages, *below*.
    Loss of capital asset or profit—
        Agency agreement—Wrongful determination—Settlement of action—Claim for arrears of commission abandoned—Whether sum assessable as profits or gains of trade—Income Tax Act 1918, Sch D, para 1(a)(iii). **Wiseburgh v Domville (Inspector of Taxes)** [1956] **1** 754, CA.
    Loss of earnings—
        Loss of future earnings—Allowance for deduction of tax. *See* **Damages** (Personal injury—Loss of future earnings—Income tax).
        Tax rebate. *See* **Damages** (Personal injury—Loss of earnings—Income tax).
    Measure of damages. *See* **Damages** (Measure of damages—Income tax).
    Underwriting losses. *See* **Damages** (Underwriting losses—Income tax).
    Wrongful dismssal—
        Contract. *See* **Contract** (Damages for breach—Wrongful dismissal—Income tax).
Dealing in securities—
    Trading receipts. *See* Profits—Trading receipts—Dealing in securities, *below*.
Death of taxpayer—
    Profession or vocation. *See* Profits—Profession or vocation—Death of taxpayer, *below*.
Deduction in computing profits—
    Annual value of land—
        Abolition of Sch A—Repeal of provision permitting deduction—Repeal applicable to 1963-64—Income for 1963-64 based on profits for 1962-63—Deductibility of annual value for Sch A from 1962-63 profits used as basis of Sch D assessment for 1963-64—Income Tax Act 1952, s 136(1), (3)—Finance Act 1963, s 29(1), Sch 13, Part 1, proviso. **Provan (Inspector of Taxes) v Scott** [1965] **3** 326, Ch D.
        Amount of deductions—Exception for mills, factories or similar premises—Cold stores owned by company carrying on cold storage business—Whether 'mills, factories, or other similar premises'—Income Tax Act 1918, Sch D, Cases I and II, r 5(2). **Ellerker v Union Cold Storage Co Ltd** [1939] **1** 23, KBD.
    Appropriate year—
        Attribution of outgoings to period of acount—Secretarial service charge—Charge by service comapny wholly owned by taxpayer firm—Arrangement that service company should make only nominal profit—Debit of large charge in excess of normal rate in first year of partnership business—Arrangement for adjustment in future years—Charge in first year affecting firm's liability for three years—Whether part of charge in excess of normal rate allowable as deduction in computing profits of firm. **Stephenson (Inspector of Taxes) v Payne, Stone, Fraser & Co (a firm)** [1968] **1** 524, Ch D.
    Calculation of profits or gains—
        Relevant emoluments—Potential emoluments—Amounts or benefits reserved in accounts of employer or held by intermediary with a view to their becoming relevant emoluments—Companies making contributions to employee benefit trust—Whether contributions to employee benefit trust potential emoluments—Whether contributions held by intermediary with a view to their becoming potential emoluments—Finance Act 1989, s 43(11)(a). **MacDonald (Inspector of Taxes) v Dextra Accessories Ltd** [2005] **4** 107, HL.
    Capital or revenue expenditure—
        Accountancy principles—Application of principles of commercial accountancy—Evidence—Trust to enable employees to purchase shares in company—Agreement between taxpayer company and trustees that taxpayer company should make annual payment out of profits to trustees—Trust funds to be used to purchase shares in company holding issued shares of taxpayer company—Employees entitled to acquire shares from trustees on payment of fair value—Expert evidence that cost of securing and retaining services of employees usually treated by accountants as revenue expenditure—Impossibility of evaluating employee goodwill—Whether payments to trustees of a capital nature for tax purposes. **Heather (Inspector of Taxes) v P-E Consulting Group Ltd** [1972] **2** 107, Ch D.
        Acquisition of capital asset—Acquisition by taxpayer of means of supplying himself with stock-in-trade—Timber merchant—Purchase of standing timber. **Hood-Barrs v IRC** [1957] **1** 832, HL.
        Acquisition of capital asset—Advantage of enduring nature properly treated as capital—Expenditure for price-maintenance—Trade association—Expenditure to secure acquisition of business for its winding-up to prevent it being acquired by persons outside association—Expenditure to secure acquisition of business that it would become an active member of the association. **Collins (Inspector of Taxes) v Adamson (Joseph) & Co** [1937] **4** 236, KBD.
        Acquisition of capital asset—Cost of acquiring right to excavate deposits of sand and gravel—Gravel merchants—Rights a capital asset providing merchants with means of obtaining stock-in-trade—Income Tax Act 1918, Sch D, Case I. **Stow Bardolph Gravel Co Ltd v Poole (Inspector of Taxes)** [1954] **3** 637, CA.
        Acquisition of capital asset—Exclusive right to custom—Petrol supply—Premium on grant of leases—Acquisition of interest in land and exclusive right to tenants custom—Oil company—Tied service stations—Lease of premises to oil company for premium—Sub-lease back to proprietor at nominal rent—Covenants binding proprietor to use company's oil—Deductibility of premium in computing company's profits—Income Tax Act 1952, s 137(f). **Regent Oil Co Ltd v Strick (Inspector of Taxes)** [1965] **3** 174, HL.
        Acquisition of capital asset—Exclusive right to custom—Petrol supply—Tied filling station—Lump sum and other payments to retailers—Whether allowable as deduction from assessable income—Income Tax and Social Services Contribution Assessment Act 1936—1953, s 187. **BP Australia Ltd v Comr of Taxation of the Commonwealth of Australia** [1965] **3** 209, PC; **Mobil Oil Australia Ltd v Comr of Taxation of the Commonwealth of Australia** [1965] **3** 225, PC.

Deduction in computing profits (cont)—
Capital or revenue expenditure (cont)—
Acquisition of capital asset—Expenditure for purposes of taxpayer's trade—Acquisition of new asset in place of asset disposed of—Access to taxpayer's premises for heavy lorries—Access via residential road—Complaints by residents of disturbance—Taxpayer entering agreement with local authority—Taxpayer disposing of narrow strip of land between premises and residential road so as to shut off access—Authority licensing taxpayer to construct new road over authority's land—Taxpayer acquiring permanent easement of way over land—Whether expenditure by taxpayer on constructing new road of capital or revenue nature. **Pitt (Inspector of Taxes) v Castle Hill Warehousing Co Ltd** [1974] **3** 146, Ch D.

Acquisition of capital asset—Fruit crop—Purchase of freehold land and cherry orchard including year's fruit crop—Admissibility of deduction of apportioned cost of cherries—Income Tax Act 1918, Sch D, Cases I and II, r 3(f). **Saunders (Inspector of Taxes) v Pilcher** [1949] **2** 1097, CA.

Acquisition of capital asset—Rent—Acquisition by payment of rent—Company holding 88 year lease of premises—Scheme to acquire freehold—Subsidiary becoming freeholder—Freeholder becoming lessee for 22 years—Company becoming sublessee—Company's higher rent for shorter period—No deduction of increase of rent—Payment for acquisition of capital asset (freehold)—Income Tax Act 1952, s 137(a), (f). **Littlewoods Mail Order Stores Ltd v McGregor (Inspector of Taxes)** [1969] **3** 855, CA.

Acquisition of capital asset—Road haulage licence—Taxpayers haulage contractors—Expenditure on abortive application for variation in road haulage licence—Income Tax Act 1952, Sch D, Case I. **Pyrah (Inspector of Taxes) v Annis & Co Ltd** [1957] **1** 196, CA.

Acquisition of stock-in-trade rather than capital asset—Raw materials for business—Cigarette manufacturers—Contract giving manufacturers right to go on land to collect and remove leaves from forests—Right given in consideration of sum payable in instalments—Indian Income Tax Act 1922, s 10(2), para xii. **Mohanlal Hargovind of Jubbulpore v Comr of Income Tax, Central Provinces and Berar, Nagpur** [1949] **2** 652, PC.

Alteration to asset—Expenditure for purpose of making a permanent alteration to asset owned by taxpayer—Alteration permanently enhancing value of asset for purpose of taxpayer's trade—Land—Planning permission—Quarry—Taxpayer engaged in business of operating quarries—Taxpayer applying for planning permission to quarry on land which it owned—Application unsuccessful—Expenses incurred in pursuing application—Whether expenses of a capital or revenue nature. **ECC Quarries Ltd v Watkis (Inspector of Taxes)** [1975] **3** 843, Ch D.

Brewers—New licences—Expense of obtaining—Premises compulsorily acquired in redevelopment—Scheme for holding licences in 'bank'—Delayed transfer to new premises—Brewers' anticipated ultimate reduction in premises—Maintenance of barrelage—Expenditure in obtaining replacement licences capital—Income Tax Act 1952, s 137(f). **Pendleton (Inspector of Taxes) v Mitchells & Butlers Ltd** [1969] **2** 928, Ch D.

Capital asset or stock-in-trade—Cost of maintaining kennel of greyhounds—Kennel maintained by company operating racing track—Greyhounds purchased only to make up requisite numbers of entries at race meetings—Company not trading in greyhounds—Cost of replacements only chargeable against income—Income Tax Act 1918, Sch D, Case I, Rules Applicable to Cases I and II, r 3(f). **Abbott (Inspector of Taxes) v Albion Greyhounds (Salford) Ltd** [1945] **1** 308, KBD.

Compensation paid to another company of group for abandoning production for one year—Compensation paid by company to maintain own level of production during year. **Comr of Taxes v Nchanga Consolidated Copper Mines Ltd** [1964] **1** 208, PC.

Covenants in restraint of trade—Payments in consideration of covenants—Company directors retiring from office—Covenants by directors in restraint of trade—Payments made by company to retiring directors in consideration of covenants—payments not deductible from company's trading profits as revenue expenditure—Income Tax Act 1918, Sch D, Case I. **Associated Portland Cement Manufacturers Ltd v IRC** [1946] **1** 68, CA.

Expenditure for purpose of earning profits rather than seeming advantage of enduring benefit—Brewery company—Procuring Sunday opening of licensed premises—Local option in Wales and Monmouthshire—Whether company's contribution to cost of stimulating interest in polls in favour of Sunday opening—Capital or revenue expenditure. **Cooper (Inspector of Taxes) v Rhymney Breweries Ltd** [1965] **3** 416, Ch D.

Improvements—Statutory appropriations towards installations at racecourses—Whether capital expenditure. **Racecourse Betting Control Board v Young (Inspector of Taxes)** [1959] **3** 215, HL.

Initiation or extension of business—Expenditure for purpose of initiating or extending a business—Expenditure abortive—Taxpayer a farmer—Visit to Australia with a view to buying a farm and emigrating—Taxpayer deciding not to emigrate—Expenses of visit—Whether capital or revenue in nature. **Sargent (Inspector of Taxes) v Eayrs** [1973] **1** 277, Ch D.

Licence to use buildings—Annual payment for licence—Part applied constituting instalments of capital value of cost of construction—Whether whole payment of revenue nature. **Racecourse Betting Control Board v Wild** [1938] **4** 487, KBD.

Licensed premises—Monopoly value—Licensee lessee of premises—Payment of monopoly value to landlord by instalments—Whether amount of instalments deductible—Licensing (Consolidation) Act 1910, s 14. **Henriksen v Grafton Hotels Ltd** [1942] **1** 678, CA.

Licensed premises—Monopoly value—Sum paid as monopoly value—Whether capital expenditure—Licensing (Consolidation) Act 1910, s 14. **Kneeshaw v Abertolli** [1940] **3** 500, KBD.

Maintenance of existing trading structure—Payment to maintain structure—Payment for release of option—Payment for purpose of retaining important customer—Customer limited company—Taxpayer owning shares in customer—Managing director of customer having option to purchase taxpayer's shares—Taxpayer paying substantial sum to managing director for release of option—Payment made for purpose of retaining trading relationship with customer—Whether payment capital or revenue expenditure—Income Tax Act 1952, s 137(f). **Walker (Inspector of Taxes) v Cater Securities Ltd** [1974] **3** 63, Ch D.

Payment to preserve existing trade—Risk of insolvency of taxpayer company and subsidiary—Purchase of subsidiary by Bank of England subject to injection of £50m into subsidiary by taxpayer company—Whether payment capital or revenue—Whether expenditure incurred wholly and exclusively for purposes of taxpayer company's trade. **Lawson (Inspector of Taxes) v Johnson Matthey plc** [1992] **2** 647, HL.

INCOME TAX (cont)—
 Deduction in computing profits (cont)—
  Capital or revenue expenditure (cont)—
   Payment to secure improvement in asset—Payment to secure modification of rent obligation in lease—Modification necessary to enable taxpayer to trade profitably—Modification resulting in reduction of revenue expenses—Whether capital or revenue expenditure. **Tucker (Inspector of Taxes) v Granada Motorway Services Ltd** [1979] **2** 801, HL.

   Release from statutory obligation—Coal mine—Statutory obligation to remedy damage to district drainage system resulting from subsidence—Contribution to scheme releasing mine owner from statutory obligation—Contribution payable by instalments—Whether capital or revenue expense. **Doncaster Amalgamated Collieries Ltd v Bean (Inspector of Taxes)** [1946] **1** 642, HL.

   Repairs—Deferred repairs—Acquisition of cinema in poor repair—Cinema fully capable of commercial use—Vendor's failure to repair before acquisition—Vendor precluded by war time restrictions from carrying out repairs—No diminution in price in respect of disrepair—Deferred repairs begun two years after acquisition—Repairs spread over several years—No indication of extra cost over and above cost of ordinary repairs—Expenditure on deferred repairs charged to revenue account as separate item from expenditure on current repairs—Expert evidence on accountancy practice—Finding that charging to revenue according with accountancy practice—No conflict with statute—Conclusiveness of finding—Whether expenditure deferred repairs capital or revenue expenditure for income purposes—Whether deductible in computing profits—Income Tax Act 1952, s 137. **Odeon Associated Theatres Ltd v Jones (Inspector of Taxes)** [1972] **1** 681, CA.

   Repairs—Expenditure on accumulated repairs to hereditament—Lease of old premises in disrepair—Lessees' covenant to reinstate—Compensating rent reduction in earlier years—Whether expenditure on repairs deductible—Income Tax Act 1952, Sch D. **Jackson (Inspector of Taxes) v Laskers Home Furnishers Ltd** [1956] **3** 891, Ch D.

   Repairs—Increased cost—Increased cost attributable to need to preserve trade—Premises kept open for business during rehabilitation work—Work extended and cost increased in consequence—Whether extra cost deductible. **Mann, Crossman & Paulin Ltd v Compton (Inspector of Taxes), Same v IRC** [1947] **1** 742, KBD.

   Repairs—Stand for spectators in football stadium replaced with new stand—Whether replacement of stand constituting 'repairs'—Income and Corporation Taxes Act 1970, s 130(d). **Brown (Inspector of Taxes) v Burnley Football and Athletic Co Ltd** [1980] **3** 244, Ch D.

   Trust to enable employees to purchase shares in taxpayer company—Payments to trust fund—Taxpayer company's business dependent on highly qualified staff promoting business free from outside control—Annual payments to trust fund related to taxpayer company's profits—Aggregate amount of payments unpredictable—Object of scheme to enable employees to acquire stake in taxpayer company and to remove possibility of outside interference in business—Whether payments to trust fund capital or revenue expenditure. **Heather (Inspector of Taxes) v P-E Consulting Group Ltd** [1973] **1** 8, CA.

   Trust to provide benefits for employees receiving inadequate pensions—Payments by company to fund for purchase of shares in itself—Shares to be held for benefit of employees—Whether payment capital or revenue expenditure. **Jeffs (Inspector of Taxes) v Ringtons Ltd** [1986] **1** 144, Ch D.

 Ceylon. *See* **Ceylon** (Income tax—Deduction in computing profits).

 Corporation tax—
   Charge on income—Annuities—Liability incurred for valuable and sufficient consideration—Disposition for more than six years—Seven year covenant—Bank's overseas branches—Education of European staff's children—Difficulty in obtaining education abroad—Scheme to meet costs of education in United Kingdom—Bank making monthly payments to trustees—Benefit accruing to bank from scheme—Bank able to retain and recruit European staff—Whether liability to make payments incurred for 'valuable and sufficient consideration'—Finance Act 1965, s 52(4)(b). **Ball (Inspector of Taxes) v National and Grindlays Bank Ltd** [1971] **3** 485, Ch D and CA.

   Charge on income—Charge on income not being a distribution of the company—Meaning of distribution—Close company—Interest paid to person who is an associate of a director who is not a whole-time service director—Director a participator in company—Meaning of associate—Person interested in shares or obligations of company in which participator interested—Meaning of interested in—Executors of unadministered estate—Estate owning shares in company registered in deceased's name—Company indebted to estate—One of executors a director of and participator in company—Interest paid by company to executors—Executors 'interested in' deceased's shares—Executors 'associates' of director in his capacity as participator—Payment of interest a 'distribution' of company—Company not entitled to deduct interest payment as a 'charge on income' in computing profits—Finance Act 1965, s 52(1), (2), (3)(a), Sch 11, para 9(1), Sch 18, para 5(c). **Willingale (Inspector of Taxes) v Islington Green Investment Co** [1972] **3** 849, CA.

   Charge on income—Interest payments—Statutory provision entitling companies to deduct from taxable profits any yearly interest 'paid'—Taxpayer company owing large arrears of interest to its owner and having no money to pay debt—Owner lending taxpayer money to pay the debt with a view to creating tax loss in taxpayer's favour—Taxpayer using the loan to discharge the interest debt—Whether taxpayer having 'paid' interest—Income and Corporation Taxes Act 1988, s 338. **MacNiven (Inspector of Taxes) v Westmoreland Investments Ltd** [2001] **1** 865, HL.

   Depreciation—No deduction in computing profits in respect of sum employed as capital in trade—Company calculating accounting profit by deducting only depreciation in fixed assets relating to production of goods sold during year—Whether company required for tax purposes to add back total depreciation—Companies Act 1985, Sch 4, para 1(1)(b)—Income and Corporation Taxes Act 1988, s 74(1)(f). **Revenue and Customs Comrs v William Grant & Sons Distillers Ltd** [2007] **2** 440, HL.

INCOME TAX (cont)—
    Deduction in computing profits (cont)—
        Debt—
            Subsequent release—Estimate of probable loss—Debt—No entry made in accounts in respect of debt—Greater part of debt subsequently released—Accounts re-opened—Whether debt to be entered at the figure remaining payable after release or at the estimate of probable loss which would have been made at the time of preparation of the accounts which were being reopened. **Simpson v Jones (Inspector of Taxes)** [1968] **2** 929, Ch D.
            Subsequent release—Indebtedness set off against profits and subsequently released—Construction of enactment—Finance Act 1960, s 36. **Simpson v Jones (Inspector of Taxes)** [1968] **2** 929, Ch D.
        Deficiency in rent—
            Computation—Brewery company—Leasehold premises let to tied tenant—Premium paid by brewers on grant of purchase of lease—Sum expended by brewers on alterations under covenant—Amount of debt forgone on assignment of lease to brewers in satisfaction of debt—Rackrent. **Collyer (Inspector of Taxes) v Hoare & Co Ltd** [1937] **3** 491, KBD.
            Computation—Brewery company—Tied houses—Premises held under long leases—Premises sub-let at rents lower than those obtainable without tie—Deduction of rent forgone—Income Tax Act 1918, Sch D, Cases I and II, r 3(a)—Finance Act 1940, s 17(2). **Nash (Inspector of Taxes) v Tamplin & Sons Brewery (Brighton) Ltd** [1951] **2** 869, HL.
        Depreciation allowance—
            Lessee—Entitlement to allowance—Burden falling on lessee—Depreciation of buildings—Full repairing covenant by lessee—Whether 'whole of the burden of any depreciation' falls on lessee—Finance Act 1937, s 15(1), (5). **Boarland (Inspector of Taxes) v Pirie Appleton & Co Ltd** [1940] **3** 306, CA.
        Domestic or private expenses—
            Farming—Farmhouse used for purpose of managing farming operations for one hour each day—Taxpayer living in farmhouse—Whether rates, repairs, maintenance and insurance of farmhouse deductible—Whether all expenses incurred in running farmhouse deductible—'Farmhouse'—Income Tax Act 1952, ss 137(b), 526(1). **IRC v Korner** [1969] **1** 679, HL.
        Expenditure incurred solely for purpose of making or earning profits or gains—
            Agreement to pay half net profits to another company in consideration of operation and control of that company's business—Whether payments deductible—Indian Income Tax Act 1922 (No 11 of 1922), s 12(2). **Indian Radio & Cable Communications Co Ltd v Income Tax Comrs, Bombay** [1937] **3** 709, PC.
        Expenditure wholly and exclusively laid out or expended for purposes of trade. *See* Deduction in computing profits—Expenses wholly and exclusively laid out for purposes of trade, *below*.
        Expense or disbursement—
            Notional expense—Issue of shares to employees at nominal value—Loss of premium obtainable by sale on open market—Whether notional loss an expense or disbursement. **Lowry v Consolidated African Selection Trust Ltd** [1940] **2** 545, HL.
        Expenses wholly and exclusively laid out for purposes of trade—
            Accrued expenses—Expenses accruing prior to carrying on trade—Meaning of 'accrued'. **Odeon Associated Theatres Ltd v Jones (Inspector of Taxes)** [1972] **1** 681, CA.
            Broadcasting corporation—Subscription to news agency—Necessary to maintain news service—Keeping agency in existence—Income Tax Act 1952, s 137(a). **BBC v Johns (Inspector of Taxes)** [1964] **1** 923, CA.
            Compensation for loss of office—Directors—Agreement between directors in personal negotiations—Subsequent adoption in company's resolution—Commissioners' finding right to deduction not established—Sufficiency of evidence to support—Income Tax Act 1952, s 137(a). **Smith (George J) & Co Ltd v Furlong (Inspector of Taxes)** [1969] **2** 760, Ch D.
            Conference expenses—Accountant—Expenses of attending accountancy conference—Sole reason for trip to New York—Income Tax Act 1952, s 137(a). **Edwards (Inspector of Taxes) v Warmsley Henshall & Co** [1968] **1** 1089, Ch D.
            Conference expenses—Solicitor—Expenses of attending law conferences—Trip combining holiday—Income Tax Act 1952, s 137(a)(b). **Bowden (Inspector of Taxes) v Russell and Russell** [1965] **2** 258, Ch D.
            Cost of acquiring stock-in-trade—Computation of cost—Price or value at date of acquisition—Hotel bought by property developer—Negotiated price £72,000—Value at time £150,000—Conveyance direct to own company at £72,000—Finding of commercial acquisition by company—Not a gift by developer to company—Price not value deductible—Income Tax Act 1952, s 137. **Jacgilden (Weston Hall) Ltd v Castle (Inspector of Taxes)** [1969] **3** 1110, Ch D.
            Employee's tax—Failure to deduct—Taxpayer paying employee's tax to revenue authorities under PAYE regulations—Taxpayer failing to deduct sum paid from employee's salary—Whether payment of tax wholly and exclusively for purposes of taxpayer's trade—Income Tax Act 1952, s 137(e). **Bamford (Inspector of Taxes) v ATA Advertising Ltd** [1972] **3** 535, Ch D.
            Entertaining expenses—Expenses incurred in provision by person of anything in his trade to provide—Newspaper printers and publishers—Provision of hospitality to informants and contributors—Finance Act 1965, s 15(9). **Associated Newspapers Group Ltd v Fleming (Inspector of Taxes)** [1972] **2** 574, HL.
            Entertaining expenses—Sole object of expenditure promotion of business—Solicitors entertaining clients to lunch—Whether cost of lunch deductible—Income Tax Act 1918, Sch D, Cases I and II, r 3(a). **Bentleys Stokes and Lowless v Beeson (Inspector of Taxes)** [1952] **2** 82, CA.
            Guarantee—Payment under guarantee—Solicitors temporarily guaranteeing client's overdraft—Ordinary activity of practice of solicitors to give such guarantees—Income Tax Act 1952, ss 137(a), 123, Sch D, Case II. **Jennings (Inspector of Taxes) v Barfield & Barfield** [1962] **2** 957, Ch D.
            Legal costs. *See* Deduction in computing profits—Legal costs, *above*.
            Meals—Taxpayer working away from home—Cost of lunch when working away from home exceeding cost of lunch at home—Whether difference in cost deductible as money wholly and exclusively expended for purposes of taxpayer's trade—Income and Corporation Taxes Act 1970, s 130(a). **Caillebotte (Inspector of Taxes) v Quinn** [1975] **2** 412, Ch D.

Deduction in computing profits (cont)—
Expenses wholly and exclusively laid out for purposes of trade (cont)—
Medical expenses—Cost of operation—Draftsman—Part-time guitarist—Played guitar partly as hobby and partly professionally—Whether expense not exclusively expended for purposes of profession—Income Tax Act 1952, s 137(a)(b). **Prince v Mapp (Inspector of Taxes)** [1970] **1** 519, Ch D.

Medical expenses—Illness due to poor working conditions—Professional shorthand writer—Medical expenses incurred due to illness caused by working in unfavourable conditions—Expenses not laid out for the purpose of profession—Income Tax Act 1918, Sch D, Cases I and II, r 3(a)(b). **Norman v Golder (Inspector of Taxes)** [1945] **1** 352, CA.

Medical expenses—Nursing home charges—Expenses not being money 'wholly and exclusively expended for the purpose of the profession'—Trade mark agent—Charges for treatment in private nursing home—Need of office facilities to maintain business—Charges not exclusively expended for purposes of profession—Income Tax Act 1952, s 137(a)(b). **Murgatroyd (Inspector of Taxes) v Evans-Jackson** [1967] **1** 881, Ch D.

Prevention of seizure of business by state—Anti-nationalisation campaign—Expenditure on campaign against proposal to nationalise industry—Income Tax Act 1918, Sch D, Cases I and II, r 3(a). **Morgan (Inspector of Taxes) v Tate & Lyle Ltd** [1954] **2** 413, HL.

Purpose of expenditure—Barrister's clothing—Woman barrister's court clothes—Whether expenditure incurred in replacing, cleaning and laundering clothes deductible—Income and Corporation Taxes Act 1970, s 130(a). **Mallalieu v Drummond (Inspector of Taxes)** [1983] **2** 1095, HL.

Purpose of expenditure—Dual purpose—Expenditure incurred in part for non-trading purposes—Expenditure incurred by company for purpose of acquiring right to develop land—Expenditure greatly in excess of commercial value of development rights—Expenditure also incurred for purpose of facilitating tax avoidance scheme devised by and for benefit of controlling shareholder—Whether expenditure incurred wholly and exclusively for purposes of company's trade—Income Tax Act 1952, s 137(a). **Ransom (Inspector of Taxes) v Higgs** [1974] **3** 949, HL.

Purpose of expenditure—Dual purpose—Partnership—Relocation expenses of partners met by firm—Whether private interests of partners incidental to business interests of partnership—Whether expenses deductible in computing partnership profits—Income and Corporation Taxes Act 1970, s 130(a). **MacKinlay (Inspector of Taxes) v Arthur Young McClelland Moores & Co (a firm)** [1990] **1** 45, HL.

Purpose of expenditure—Political objects—Publication of pamphlet attacking government—Pamphlet containing company chairman's 'supplementary remarks' at annual meeting—Whether expenditure on publication deductible—Income Tax Act 1918, Sch D, Rules Applicable to Cases I and II, r 3(a). **Boarland (Inspector of Taxes) v Kramat Pulai Ltd** [1953] **2** 1122, Ch D.

Purpose of expenditure—Subsidiary company—Parent company incurring expenditure in respect of its employee seconded to manage its subsidiary—Expenditure incurred for sole benefit of parent company—Whether expenditure incurred wholly and exclusively for purposes of parent company's trade—Whether payment in nature of capital expenditure—Income and Corporation Taxes Act 1970, s 130(a)(b). **Robinson (Inspector of Taxes) v Scott Bader Co Ltd** [1981] **2** 1116, CA.

Purpose of expenditure—Subsidiary company—Trading account between principal and subsidiary company—Loss of subsidiary company written off trading account—Whether money laid out for trade of principal company—Income Tax Act 1918, Sch D, Cases I and II, r 3(a), (e), (f), (i). **Odhams Press Ltd v Cook (Inspector of Taxes)** [1940] **3** 15, HL.

Purpose of expenditure—Surrender of lease—Consideration for surrender—Lease of land on which warehouse erected—Lessees finding they had sufficient storage elsewhere agreeing to surrender lease for £6,000—Whether sum expenditure for purpose of trade or for purpose protanto of putting an end to trade—Income Tax Act 1918, Sch D, Cases I and II, r 3. **Union Cold Storage Co Ltd v Ellerker** [1938] **4** 692, KBD.

Rent—Difference between rent paid for buildings and rent received from sub-tenants—Control of buildings essential to trade—Printers of newspaper—Distribution of newspapers—Income Tax Act 1918, Sch D, Cases I and II, r 3(a). **Allied Newspapers Ltd v Hindsley (Inspector of Taxes)** [1937] **4** 677, CA.

Rent—Difference between rent paid for shop premises and rent received from sub-tenant—Shop one of number of chain stores closed owing to loss of profits—Business carried on at remaining stores—Income Tax Act 1918, Sch D, Cases I and II, r 3(a). **Hyett v Lennard** [1940] **3** 133, KBD.

Statutory body—Distribution pursuant to statute from funds after deduction of working expenses—Distribution benefiting body's trading activity—Whether deductible as expense for income tax purposes—Racecourse Betting Act 1928, s 3(6)—Income Tax Act 1952, s 137(a). **Racecourse Betting Control Board v Young (Inspector of Taxes)** [1959] **3** 215, HL.

Subscriptions to charity on behalf of employees—Subscriptions to pension fund of charity—Employees thereby obtaining right to vote in election of pensioners and becoming eligible for pension or other benefit—Whether subscriptions expenditure wholly and exclusively for purpose of employers' trade—Income Tax Act 1918, Sch D, Cases I and II, r 3(a). **Hutchinson & Co (Publishers) Ltd v Turner (Inspector of Taxes)** [1950] **2** 633, Ch D.

Technical and financial knowledge and advice—Company agreeing to pay percentage of net profits to another company in consideration of giving benefit of experience. **British Sugar Manufacturers Ltd v Harris (Inspector of Taxes)** [1938] **1** 149, CA.

Travelling expenses. *See* Deduction in computing profits—Travelling expenses, *above*.

Trust fund for employees—Payments to trust fund—Trust to enable employees to purchase shares in taxpayer company—Taxpayer company's business dependent on highly qualified staff promoting business free from outside control—Object of scheme to enable employees to acquire stake in taxpayer company and to remove possibility of outside interference in business—Whether payments to trust fund wholly and exclusively for purposes of trade—Income Tax Act 1952, s 137(a). **Heather (Inspector of Taxes) v P-E Consulting Group Ltd** [1973] **1** 8, CA.

Investment company. *See* Investment company—Actual income from all sources—Deduction, *below*.

Legal costs—
Appeal against assessment to excess profits tax—Appeal vital to retain services of valuable employee—Income Tax Act 1918, Sch D, Cases I and II, r 3(a)—Finance Act 1940, s 32—Finance Act 1941, s 34. **Smith's Potato Estates Ltd v Bolland (Inspector of Taxes)** [1948] **2** 367, HL.

INCOME TAX (cont)—
    Deduction in computing profits (cont)—
        Legal costs (cont)—
            Appeal in respect of incidence of excess profits tax—Income Tax Act 1918, Sch D, Rules Applicable to Cases I and II, r 3(a)—Finance (No 2) Act 1939, s 18(1). **Rushden Heel Co Ltd v Keene (Inspector of Taxes)** [1948] **2** 378, HL.
            Compromise of action—Payments made under compromise and costs of settling deed—Income Tax Act 1918, Sch D, Cases 1 and 11, r 3. **Scammell (G) & Nephew Ltd v Rowles** [1939] **1** 337, CA.
            Criminal proceedings—Partnership—Chartered accountants—Legal costs incurred in connection with criminal proceedings against one of the partners—Not moneys wholly and exclusively laid out or expended for the purposes of the profession—Income Tax Act 1918, Sch D, Case II, r 3(a). **Spofforth v Golder (Inspector of Taxes)** [1945] **1** 363, KBD.
            Damages awarded in litigation. *See* Deduction in computing profits—Loss connected with or arising out of trade—Litigation, *above*.
            Defending action relating to business transaction—Defence necessary for protection of business interest as creditor. **Income Tax Comr, Bihar and Orissa v Singh** [1942] **1** 362, PC.
            Defending title to property—Expenditure incurred in litigation concerning validity of title to property—Expense of maintaining company's property. **Southern v Borax Consolidated Ltd** [1940] **4** 412, KBD.
            Payment to avoid costs of defending action—Sum paid to settle action for fraud in conduct of trade—Fraud not proved or admitted—Income Tax Act 1918, Sch D, Cases I and II, r 3(a). **Golder (Inspector of Taxes) v Great Boulder Pty Gold Mines Ltd** [1952] **1** 360, Ch D.
        Loans—
            Loan relationship debit—Companies participating in scheme designed to achieve loan relationship debit in shareholding company—Use of total return swap in relation to shares in subsidiary to create deemed creditor loan relationship—Value of shares depressed by novating liability for large loan to subsidiary—Whether debits and interest charges allowable—Whether loan relationship debits and interest charges having unallowable purposes—Finance Act 1996, s 91B, Sch 9, para 13. **Travel Document Service v Revenue and Customs Comrs** [2018] **3** 60, CA.
        Local authority—
            Interest on loans on security of general rate fund—Deduction of tax suffered on profits of trading concern—Electricity undertaking—Loan to electricity undertaking of corporation—Electricity undertaking separate entity—Loan used by undertaking for financing sale of electrical appliances and installations—Proportion of loan, recovered by consumers, repaid by undertaking to corporation—Annual profits of undertaking assessable to income tax—Annual profits available in aid of local rate—Amount so applied limited to 'one and a half per cent of the outstanding debt of the undertaking'—Whether difference between original amount of loan and sums already recovered 'outstanding debt of the undertaking' at end of financial year—Electric Lighting (Clauses) Act 1899, s 7—Income Tax Act 1918, Sch D, Miscellaneous Rules, r 6—Electricity (Supply) Act 1926, Sch V. **Boucher (Treasurer of Wallasey County Borough) v Hood (Inspector of Taxes)** [1945] **1** 691, KBD.
        Loss connected with or arising out of trade—
            Fraudulent appropriation of funds—Company director—Appropriation of substantial sum out of company's funds—Director authorised to draw cheques on company's account—Misappropriation of funds unknown to other directors—Whether a loss arising out of or in connection with company's trade—Income Tax Act 1952, s 137(e). **Bamford (Inspector of Taxes) v ATA Advertising Ltd** [1972] **3** 535, Ch D.
            Litigation—Libel action—Libel by sugar broker against chairman of rival company—Damages and costs awarded against sugar broker—Whether a loss 'connected with or arising out of' his trade—Income Tax Act 1918, Sch D, Cases I and II, r 3(a) (e). **Fairrie (JL) v Hall (JM) (Inspector of Taxes)** [1947] **2** 141, KBD.
            Transaction outside normal business—Loss on transaction—Property dealing and development company—of all shares in property company—Aim to develop parent company's leasehold land—property in fact developed by parent company—Winding-up of property company—Payments in liquidation to development company and parent company—Difference between price of shares and liquidation payments—Deductibility of difference in computing development company's profits—Income Tax Act 1952, Sch D, Case I. **Fundfarms Developments Ltd (in liq) v Parsons (Inspector of Taxes)** [1969] **3** 1161, Ch D.
        Meals—
            Accommodation—Solicitors holding lunch-time and evening meetings of partners and annual conference—Whether cost of meals provided at meetings and conference expenditure wholly and exclusively for purpose of profession—Whether cost of overnight accommodation expenditure wholly and exclusively for purposes of profession—Income and Corporation Taxes Act 1970, s 130(a)(b). **Watkis (Inspector of Taxes) v Ashford Sparkes & Harward (a firm)** [1985] **2** 916, Ch D.
        New Zealand. *See* **New Zealand** (Income tax—Assessable income—Deductions in computing income).
        Payments to charity—
            Understanding but no written agreement—Taxpayers publishing journals on behalf of charity—Profits from journals paid to charity—Publication undertaken on 'distinct understanding' that profits were to be paid to charity—Whether forming part of taxpayer's profits—Whether deductible in computing profits. **Hutchinson & Co (Publishers) Ltd v Turner (Inspector of Taxes)** [1950] **2** 633, Ch D.
        Reimbursement of profits tax—
            Amount deductible—Subsidiary company's reimbursement of profits tax paid by principal—Principal company's notice that subsidiary's profits be treated as principal's—Whether amount payable 'by virtue of the notice' was whole profits tax paid by principal—Finance Act 1947, s 38(3). **Chloride Batteries Ltd v Gahan (Inspector of Taxes)** [1956] **1** 828, HL.
        Subvention payments—
            Payments to meet deficits of associated company—Associated company no longer trading—Whether trading expenses of payor company—Finance Act 1953, s 20(1) (9) (10). **Davies Jenkins & Co Ltd v Davies (Inspector of Taxes)** [1967] **1** 913, HL.

INCOME TAX (cont)—
　Deduction in computing profits (cont)—
　　Technical education payments—
　　　Education of particular individuals—Fees paid by taxpayer farmer for employees to attend agricultural college—Employees sons of taxpayer—Whether fees payments 'to be used for purposes of techinal education'—Income Tax Act 1952, s 140(1). **Wickwar (Inspector of Taxes) v Berry** [1963] **2** 1058, CA.
　　Travelling expenses—
　　　Medical practitioner—Emergency cases—General medical practitioner practising at his residence and also holding part-time appointments at hospital 15 miles away—Hospital work as obstetrician and anaesthetist—Expenses of travel by car to and from hospital for emergency cases—Whether expenses deductible—Income Tax Act 1952, s 156, Sch E, Case I, (as substituted by Finance Act 1956, s 10(1)), Sch 9, r 7. **Owen v Pook (Inspector of Taxes)** [1969] **2** 1, HL.
　　　Sub-contracting bricklayer—Working for main contractor on different building sites—Home base for carrying on business—Contracts made, tools and books kept there—Expenditure on travelling between home and building sites—Expenditure wholly and exclusively for purposes of his trade—Income Tax Act 1952, s 137(a). **Horton v Young (Inspector of Taxes)** [1971] **3** 412, CA.
　　　Travel between home and place of work—Barrister travelling between chambers and home where he did part of his professional work—Income Tax Act 1918, Sch D, Rules Applicable to Cases I and II, r 3(a). **Newsom v Robertson (Inspector of Taxes)** [1952] **2** 728, CA.
　　　Travel between home and place of work—Dental surgeon maintaining a laboratory to repair, alter and manufacture dentures—Laboratory between taxpayer's home and surgery—Taxpayer calling at his laboratory on his journey to and from his home to the surgery—Whether expense of travelling between laboratory and surgery wholly and exclusively laid out for purpose of taxpayer's practice—Income and Corporation Taxes Act 1970, s 130 (a). **Sargent (Inspector of Taxes) v Barnes** [1978] **2** 737, Ch D.
　　Wear and tear of machinery or plant—
　　　Carry forward of allowances—Amalgamation of companies—Right of new company to accrued deductions of constituent companies—Income Tax Act 1918, Sch D, Cases I and II, rr 6, 11—Finance Act 1926, ss 32, 33. **United Steel Companies Ltd v Cullington (Inspector of Taxes)** [1940] **2** 170, HL.
　　　Items—Separate consideration—Each item of plant and machinery to be considered separately—Surplus on one item not to be set off against deficiency on another item—Income Tax Act 1918, Sch D, Cases I and II, rr 6, 7. **Charente Steamship Co Ltd v Wilmot** [1942] **1** 85, CA.
　　　Lessor and lessee—Repairing covenant by lessee—Full repairing covenant—Lessee bearing expenses of renewals of revenue nature—Whether machinery and plant declared to belong to lessee for tax purposes—Whether lessee entitled to wear and tear allowance—Income Tax Act 1918, Sch D Cases 1 and 11 r 6(2)(6). **Union Cold Storage Co Ltd v Simpson** [1939] **2** 94, CA.
　　　Sale by person having control over buyer—Sale at market price—Restriction of wear and tear allowances by reference to 'limit of re-charge'—Application of restriction to sale taking place before Income Tax Act 1945, received Royal Assent—Income Tax Act 1945, s 59(3)(b). **Prior (Inspector of Taxes) v Martin (George) (Fulham) Ltd** [1953] **1** 16, Ch D.
　　　Sale by person having control over buyer—Sale at open market price—Application of limit of recharge—Income Tax Act 1945, ss 59(2) (3)(b). **IRC v Wilsons (Dunblane) Ltd** [1954] **1** 301, HL.
　Deduction of tax—
　　Annual payment. *See* Annual payment—Deduction of tax, *above*.
　　Dividends. *See* Dividends—Deduction of tax, *below*.
　　Earned income relief—
　　　Income taxed by deduction.　*See* Earned income relief—Earned income—Income taxed by deduction, *below*.
　　Interest. *See* Interest—Deduction of tax by payer, *below*.
　　Pay as you earn. *See* Pay as you earn system—Deduction of tax by employer, *below*.
　　Royalties. *See* Royalties—Deduction of tax, *below*.
　　Under-deduction. *See* Under-deduction of tax, *below*.
　Director of company—
　　Emoluments from office or employment. *See* Emoluments from office or employment, *below*.
　Disciplinary proceedings arising out of conduct of business—
　　Stockbroker being found guilty of misconduct by regulatory body—
　　　Stockbroker incurring legal costs in defending proceedings and seeking to deduct them in calculating profits—Whether legal expenses incurred in defending disciplinary proceedings expenditure incurred for purposes of trade—Income and Corporation Taxes Act 1970, s 130(a). **McKnight (Inspector of Taxes) v Sheppard** [1999] **3** 491, HL.
　Disclosure—
　　Additional assessment. *See* Additional assessment—Disclosure, *above*.
　Discontinuance of trade—
　　Company—
　　　Company ceasing to carry on principal object for which it was formed and commencing business under subsidiary object—Company ceasing tobacco trading and letting out warehouse for rent—Company authorised by memorandum of association to grant licences and deal generally with land and other property—Whether company 'carrying on a business'—Whether rents received were 'gains or profits from a business'—Whether company entitled to carry forward or set off losses incurred in tobacco trading against income from rents—Income Tax Act 1967 (Malaysia), ss 4, 43. **American Leaf Blending Co Sdn Bhd v Director-General of Inland Revenue** [1978] **3** 1185, PC.
　　　Sale of business to partnership—Partnership consisting of individuals—Resale of business by individuals to same company and one individual—First sale before 6th April 1966—Second sale after that date—No permanent discontinuance of trade after first sale—Statutory provision saving 'subsequent change' from effect of permanent discontinuance ceasing to have effect as respects any relevant change occurring before 6th April 1966—Whether permanent discontinuance of trade after second sale—Finance Act 1954, s 17(1), (2)—Finance Act 1965, s 61(9). **Crisp Malting Ltd v Bourne (Inspector of Taxes)** [1972] **1** 700, Ch D.

INCOME TAX (cont)—
Disposition of income for short period—
Capital or income payment—
Covenant to pay annual sums over seven year period—Pre-existing obligation to pay a sum equal to total amount of annual sums—Whether a disposition of 'income'—Finance Act 1922, s 20(1)(b). **IRC v Sir Harry Mallaby-Deeley (Personal Representative of)** [1938] **4** 818, CA.
Period exceeding six years—
Constant element in payments—Covenant to pay specific amount for first year and three-quarters of actual income for each of eight subsequent years—Necessary elements in annual payments—Whether annual payment diminishing income—Income Tax Act 1918, s 27(1)(b)—Finance Act 1922, s 20(1)(b). **D'Ambrumenil v IRC** [1940] **2** 71, KBD.
Share transaction—Covenant with company—Taxpayer principal shareholder in company—Finance Act 1922, s 20(1)(b). **IRC v Morgan-Grenville-Gavin** [1936] **1** 895, KBD.
Period which cannot exceed six years—
Any income—Income for tax purposes—Person resident abroad—Disposition for daughter resident in England—Inapplicability of provision—Income Tax Act 1952, s 392. **Becker (Inspector of Taxes) v Wright** [1966] **1** 565, Ch D.
Dividends—Preference shares—Right to dividend—Dividend of 50 per cent for five years—5 per cent thereafter—Settlement of shares—Payment of dividend in excess of 50 per cent—Whether to be treated as income of settler—Finance Act 1922, s 20(1)(b). **IRC v Prince-Smith** [1943] **1** 434, KBD.
Payment made in less than six years—Covenant to pay difference between annual letting value of and income actually received from certain properties—Sums due in fact paid within 2 years—Finance Act 1922, s 20(1)(b). **IRC v Black** [1940] **4** 445, CA.
Distribution—
Undistributed income. *See* Undistributed income—Distribution, *below*.
Dividends—
Advance corporation tax. *See* Corporation tax—Advance corporation tax, *above*.
Annual payment distinguished. *See* Annual payment—Meaning—Dividend distinguished, *above*.
Appropriate year of assessment. *See* Assessment—Appropriate year—Dividends, *above*.
Capital or income receipts. *See* Capital or income receipts—Dividends, *above*.
Deduction of tax—
Appropriate rate—Standard rate when dividend declared—Cumulative dividend—Underpayment—Distribution of aggregate sum in respect of underpayment—Rate of tax deductible. **Phillips (Godfrey) Ltd v Investment Trust Corp Ltd** [1953] **1** 7, Ch D.
Net dividend—Declaration of dividend of net amount of footing that the dividend was subject to deduction of income tax—Net amount exhausting whole available profits of company—Shareholder's loss repayment claim—No profits from which tax deduction possible—Claim unmaintainable—Income Tax Act 1952, ss 184(1)(2) 186(1). **Johns (Inspector of Taxes) v Wirsal Securities Ltd** [1966] **1** 865, Ch D.
Public revenue dividends. *See* Public revenue dividends—Deduction of tax, *below*.
Tax avoidance transactions—No profit available on adjustment of tax avoidance transaction—Dividend paid on preference shares consequently not subject to deduction of tax. **Ridge Securities Ltd v IRC** [1964] **1** 275, Ch D.
Loss relief—
Repayment claim. *See* Loss relief—Claim—Repayment claim—Tax deducted from dividends on shares, *below*.
Relief from surtax—
Income attributable to period exceeding a year—Dividends—Exclusion of relief—Exclusion in respect of dividends treated as income of year 1965-66—Deduction of tax from dividends—Deduction of tax from full amount of profits or gains of company—Dividend forming part of income for year by reference to which standard rate tax deductible—Year in which amount payable 'became due'—Interim dividends declared in March 1965 and payable in May 1965—Whether dividends 'became due' when declared or when paid—Income Tax Act 1952, ss 184(1), 238—Finance Act 1966, s 24. **Potel v IRC** [1971] **2** 504, Ch D.
Total income. *See* Total income—Dividends, *below*.
Trading receipts—
Dividends subject to deduction of tax. *See* Profits—Trading receipts—Dividends subject to deduction of tax, *below*.
Whether transaction in securities. *See* Tax advantage—Transaction in securities—Distribution of profits of company, *below*.
Divorce—
Financial provision—
Effect of order sought. *See* **Divorce** (Financial provision—Evidence—Effect of order sought—Tax).
Tax implications. *See* **Divorce** (Financial provision—Tax implications).
Domicile—
Acquisition of domicile of choice in England—
Intention to make permanent home in England—Intention to return to domicile of origin on happening of future uncertain event—Taxpayer having a Canadian domicile of origin—Taxpayer joining Royal Air Force—Taxpayer intending to return to Canada on completion of service—Taxpayer marrying an Englishwoman—Wife unwilling to live in Canada—Taxpayer and wife establishing permanent matrimonial home in England—Taxpayer intending to return to Canada in the event of his wife's predeceasing him—Taxpayer retaining his Canadian citizenship—Taxpayer's declaration in his will that his domicile was Nova Scotia—Whether taxpayer had acquired domicile of choice in England. **IRC v Bullock** [1976] **3** 353, CA.
Change of domicile—
Onus of proof—Taxpayer having South African domicile of origin—Taxpayer coming to United Kingdom and obtaining employment—Statement by taxpayer in answer to Revenue questionnaire that he intended to remain permanently in United Kingdom—Whether sufficient to establish taxpayer's acquisition of English domicile of choice—Income Tax Act 1952, s 132(2)(a). **Buswell v IRC** [1974] **2** 520, CA.
Generally. *See* **Domicile**.

INCOME TAX (cont)—
  Double taxation relief—
    Conflict between taxing Act and agreement for relief—
      Ceylon and United Kingdom. *See* **Ceylon** (Income tax—Double taxation relief—Agreement with United Kingdom for relief—Subsequent).
    Corporation tax—
      Transitional provisions—Dividends paid by company resident in United Kingdom to shareholder resident abroad—Introduction of corporation tax for United Kingdom companies—Transitional provisions relating to double taxation relief—Amount of income tax chargeable in respect of dividends subject to such limitation as would apply under relevant agreement in the converse case—Shareholder resident in South Africa—Shareholder not liable to South African tax on dividends—United Kingdom shareholders liable to tax on dividends from South African companies—Shareholder would be liable to United Kingdom tax 'in the converse case'—Shareholder entitled to relief in respect of income tax under transitional provisions—Whether 'income tax' including surtax—Whether shareholder entitled to relief in respect of surtax—Finance Act 1966, s 31(2). **Hewitt v IRC** [1972] **2** 453, Ch D.
    Credit of foreign tax against income tax—
      Allowance of overseas tax as credit against United Kingdom tax payable 'in respect of' overseas income—New Zealand income—Change in basis of assessment of overseas tax—Alteration in New Zealand from previous year's to current year's basis—Tax in New Zealand not chargeable on income for last year of old basis—Assessment to United Kingdom tax based on previous year's income being the income of the year on which tax not chargeable in New Zealand—Allowance 'in respect of' income referring to income of year of assessment and not to income of year used as measure of liability—Income Tax Act 1952, s 347, Sch 16, para 2(1)(2)—Double Taxation Relief (Taxes on Income)(New Zealand) Order 1947 (SR & O 1947 No 1776), art XIV(1). **Duckering (Inspector of Taxes) v Gollan** [1965] **2** 115, HL.
      Computation—Tax borne by the body corporate—Attributable to proportion of 'relevant profits' represented by dividends—Meaning of relevant profits—Profits in accounts of foreign body corporate or as assessed for foreign tax purposes—Income Tax Act 1952, s 347, Sch 16, para 9. **Bowater Paper Corp Ltd v Murgatroyd (Inspector of Taxes)** [1969] **3** 111, HL.
    Dividends and interest paid by United States corporation to United Kingdom resident—
      Recipient a United States citizen and a citizen of the United Kingdom and Colonies—Double taxation convention with United States—No relief granted to 'citizen of that other Contracting Party'—Meaning—Whether limited to citizen of United States—Whether including citizen of the United Kingdom and Colonies—Double Taxation Relief (Taxes on Income)(USA) Order 1946 (SR & O 1946 No 1327), Sch, art XV (as substituted by Double Taxation Relief (Taxes on Income)(USA) Order 1966 (SI 1966 No 1188), art 11). **Avery Jones v IRC** [1976] **2** 898, Ch D.
    Dividends paid to British shareholders—
      Deduction of tax—Shares in British companies held by Canadian company—Dividends of British companies suffering tax—Dividends of Canadian company paid to British shareholders less tax by company's London agents—Relief claimed by Canadian company in respect of tax so deducted—Income Tax Act 1918, s 147, Sch D, Case V—Miscellaneous Rules, r 7, All Schedules Rules, r 20. **Selection Trust Ltd v Devitt (Inspector of Taxes)** [1945] **2** 499, HL.
    Dominion tax—
      Allowances and deductions—Tax on debenture interest paid by company but recoverable from debenture holders—Finance Act 1920, s 27—Finance Act 1927, s 46, Sch V, Part II, para 2(1). **IRC v National Mortgage and Agency Co of New Zealand Ltd** [1938] **2** 88, HL.
    Double super-tax—
      Payment of income tax and super-tax in both United Kingdom and Irish Free State—Admissibility of claim for relief in respect of double super-tax—Finance Act 1920, s 27—Relief in respect of Double Taxation (Irish Free State) Declaration 1923. **McCalmont v IRC** [1938] **3** 174, CA.
    Effect on dividends—
      Ceiling on repayment—Tax deducted from dividends—Dividends subject to double taxation relief—Calculation of repayment—Based on tax paid or rate of tax paid by dividend-paying company—Income Tax Act 1952, s 350(1). **Shell Petroleum Co Ltd v Jones (Inspector of Taxes)** [1971] **2** 569, HL.
    Foreign shareholders—
      Shares in English company held by Indian company—Dividends of English company suffering tax—Relief to preference shareholder in Indian company. **Barnes (Inspector of Taxes) v Hely Hutchinson** [1939] **3** 803, HL.
    Foreign wife—
      Dividends and interest paid by American corporations to taxpayer's wife—Taxpayer a citizen of and resident in United Kingdom—Taxpayer's wife American citizen resident in United Kingdom—Double taxation convention with United States—Whether taxpayer's wife a resident of the United Kingdom within meaning of convention—Whether taxpayer entitled to relief in respect of wife's American income—Double Taxation Relief (Taxes on Income)(USA) Order 1946 (SR & O 1946 No 1327), Schedule, arts II(1)(g), (3), XV, as amended by the Double Taxation Relief (Taxes on Income)(USA) Order 1966. **Strathalmond (Lord) v IRC** [1972] **3** 715, Ch D.
    Income from employment—
      Diver carrying out engagements in UK continental shelf waters—Whether income from employment or business profits—Meaning of 'employment'—Income Tax (Trading and Other Income) Act 2005, s 15—Double Taxation Relief (Taxes on Income) (South Africa) Order 2002, SI 2002/3138, arts 3(2), 7, 14. **Fowler v Revenue and Customs Comrs** [2019] **1** 717, CA; [2021] **1** 97, SC.
    Mutual life assurance society—
      Resident abroad—Australian company with branch office in the United Kingdom—Assessments to income tax on income of society's life assurance fund—Whether assessments competent—Income Tax Act 1918, Sch 1, Sch D, Rules applicable to Case III, r 3—Finance (No 2) Act 1945, s 51(1)—Income Tax Act 1952, ss 347(1), 430, 437(1)—Double Taxation Relief (Taxes on Income)(Australia) Order 1947 (SR & O 1947 No 806). Schedule, art II(1)(i), art III(2), (3). **Ostime (Inspector of Taxes) v Australian Mutual Provident Society** [1959] **3** 245, HL.

INCOME TAX (cont)—
   Double taxation relief (cont)—
      Nationality—
         Remuneration and pensions payable out of public funds of one of contracting parties—Taxpayer
         required to be national of both contracting parties to qualify for relief—Federal Republic of
         Germany—Taxpayer British subject and German national by birth—Taxpayer a Jew—Taxpayer
         having emigrated to England before second world war—Taxpayer deprived of German nationality
         by German government decree during war—Basic Law of Federal Republic enacted on basis that
         wartime decree void—Basic Law requiring person deprived of nationality by wartime decree to
         apply for renaturalisation—Taxpayer not having applied—Whether taxpayer a German national
         for purpose of tax relief under double taxation convention—Double Taxation Relief (Taxes on
         Income)(Federal Republic of Germany) Order 1967 (SI 1967 No 25) Schedule, art IX(2).
         Oppenheimer v Cattermole (Inspector of Taxes) [1975] **1** 538, HL.
      Profits of trade—
         Foreign company carrying on business in United Kingdom—Reinsurance business—Profits from
         underwriting—Dutch company resident in Netherlands carrying on business of reinsurance—
         Permanent branch in London—Accumulation by company of surplus sums from underwriting—
         Separate London portfolio of investments including dollar investments—Dollar investments
         vested in American trustees and earmarked for American claims—Whether realised profits on
         London portfolio and dividends and interest from dollar investments should be included in
         company's profits under Sch D, Case I—Whether excluded from computation by reason of double
         taxation agreement with Netherlands—Income Tax Act 1952, s 123 (Sch D, Case I)—Double
         Taxation Relief (Taxes on Income)(Netherlands Order 1950 (SI 1950 No 1195), art III, para (3).
         General Reinsurance Co Ltd v Tomlinson (Inspector of Taxes) [1970] **2** 436, Ch D.
         Taxpayer's share of profits of US limited liability company taxed in US on basis company was
         partnership—Balance of profits remitted to UK—Amount remitted subject to UK income
         tax—Taxpayer seeking double taxation relief—Whether UK and US tax charged on same profits
         or income—Whether taxpayer entitled to relief—Double Taxation Relief (Taxes on Income) (The
         United States of America) Order 1980, SI 1980/568, art 23(2)(a). **Revenue and Customs Comrs v
         Anson** [2015] **4** 288, SC.
      Rate of exchange—
         Alteration—Effect—USA tax allowable against UK tax—Alteration in rate of exchange between
         initial payment and refund of USA tax—Effect on UK tax liability—Income Tax Act 1952, s 347,
         Sch XVI, para 2(1)—Double Taxation Relief (Taxes on Income)(USA) Order 1946 (SR & O 1946
         No 1327), Sch, art XIII(2). **Greig (Inspector of Taxes) v Ashton** [1956] **3** 123, Ch D.
      Removal of exemption by statute—
         Person entitled to exemption under any enactment—Resident of Republic of Ireland—Whether
         exempt under enactment or under double taxation agreement—Removal of exemption—A
         person entitled under any enactment to an exemption—Application to resident in the Republic of
         Ireland—Dividend stripping—Finance (No 2) Act 1955, s 4(2). **Collco Dealings Ltd v IRC**
         [1961] **1** 762, HL.
      Shares in foreign company—
         British company holding shares in American company which held shares in five British
         companies—Dividends received by American company from British companies and by British
         company from American company suffering tax—Relief claimed by British company—Income
         Tax Act 1918, Sch D, Case I. **Selection Trust Ltd v Devitt (Inspector of Taxes)** [1945] **2** 499, HL.
         Company acquiring foreign shares—Shares constituting new source or addition to source of
         income—Case V assessment of dividends—Based on initial year's income in that and ensuing
         year—Claim for allowance of foreign tax in initial year against both assessments—Income Tax Act
         1952, s 347, Sch 16, para 13—Double Taxation Relief (Taxes on Income)(Australia) Order 1947 (SR
         & O 1947 No 806), Schedule, art XII(1). **Imperial Chemical Industries Ltd v Caro (Inspector of
         Taxes)** [1961] **1** 658, CA.
   Duties performed abroad. *See* Foreign employment—Duties performed abroad, *below*.
   Earned income relief—
      Computation of earned income—
         Deduction from actual earned income of charges allowable against income—Deduction of
         payments of mortgage and building society and bank loan interest from income earned—Finance
         Act 1925, s 15(1), as amended by Finance Act 1948, s 27(2)—Income Tax Act 1918, s 17. **Lewin v
         Aller (Inspector of Taxes)** [1954] **2** 703, CA.
      Dissolution of partnership—
         Payments under dissolution agreement—Retiring partner in firm of solicitors agreeing to give
         advice and render assistance to continuing partner—Covenanted payments to retiring partner not
         solely referable to obligation to give advice and render assistance—Consideration not
         apportionable to that obligation. **Hale v Shea (Inspector of Taxes)** [1965] **1** 155, Ch D.
   Earned income—
      Computation. *See* Earned income relief—Computation of earned income, *above*.
      Income from shares of company—Shares settled on taxpayer as inducement to remain a director of
      company—Taxpayer entitled to income so long as he should be engaged in the management of
      the company—Whether dividends from the shares were earned income—Income Tax Act 1952,
      s 525(1)(a). **White (Inspector of Taxes) v Franklin** [1965] **1** 692, CA.
      Income immediately derived from carrying on or exercise of trade, profession or
      vocation—Immediately derived—Interest—Solicitor—Clients' deposit account—Account opened
      by solicitor in course of exercising profession—Solicitor placing money held on behalf of clients
      in deposit account in accordance with rules of profession—Solicitor entitled to retain portion of
      interest—Whether interest retained 'immediately derived' from carrying on of profession—
      Income Tax Act 1952, s 525(1)(c). **Northend (Inspector of Taxes) v White & Leonard and Corbin
      Greener (a firm)** [1975] **2** 481, Ch D.
      Income immediately derived from carrying on or exercise of trade, profession or
      vocation—Immediately derived—Partnership—Accountants—Retirement of partner—Agreement
      with continuing partners—Payment of 'retirement allowance'—Allowance computed as a
      percentage of the profits of the firm—Whether the allowance 'immediately derived' by retired
      partner from carrying on of his profession as a partner—Income Tax Act 1952, s 525(1)(c). **Pegler
      v Abell (Inspector of Taxes)** [1973] **1** 53, Ch D.

INCOME TAX (cont)—
  Earned income relief (cont)—
    Earned income (cont)—
      Income taxed by deduction—Partnership—Partner's share of investment income taxed by deduction—Firm of merchant bankers—Taxpayer a partner—Loss on firm's trading—Greater sum received by firm by way of income taxed by deduction—Credit balance divisible between partners—Whether taxpayer's share of interest charged under Case III and of interest and dividends charged under Case IV or V of Sch D 'earned income' of taxpayer—Apportionment between partners of income qualifying for earned income relief (if any)—Income Tax Act 1952, s 525(1). **Bucks v Bowers (Inspector of Taxes)** [1970] **2** 202, Ch D.
    Interest—
      Property of taxpayer—Solicitor—Interest on clients' money—Money in hands of Scottish advocate placed in firm name with words 'for clients' added on deposit receipt—Interest treated by him as professional income in accordance with opinion of Council of Law Society of Scotland—Clients' money loaned by him to other clients—Difference in interest charged to borrowing clients and that allowed to lender clients similarly treated as professional income—Claim by advocate to earned income relief in respect of interest—Whether interest property of the solicitor—Income Tax Act 1952, s 211. **Brown v IRC** [1964] **3** 119, HL.
  Remuneration in respect of office of profit—
    Trustee—Annuity payable to trustee conditional on his acting as such—Whether investment or earned income. **Dale v IRC** [1953] **2** 671, HL.
  Earnings from employment—
    Earnings of workers supplied by service companies etc—
      Managed service companies—Managed service company provider—Third party company setting up taxpayer companies for provision of services by individuals to end clients—Whether taxpayer companies 'managed service companies'—Whether third party company 'managed service company provider'—Income Tax (Earnings and Pensions) Act 2003, s 61B. **Christianuyi Ltd v Revenue and Customs Comrs** [2019] **3** 178, CA.
      Provision of services through intermediary—Individual establishing personal service company—Company contracting with client for provision of services of individual—Whether sufficient control of individual existing under hypothetical contract to establish employment relationship between individual and client—Whether other provisions of hypothetical contract inconsistent with contract of service—Test to be applied—Income Tax (Earnings and Pensions) Act 2003, s 49—Social Security Contributions (Intermediaries) Regulations 2000, SI 2000/727. **Revenue and Customs Comrs v Atholl House Productions Ltd** [2022] **4** 461, CA.
      Provision of services through intermediary—Individual establishing personal service company—Company contracting with client for provision of services of individual—Whether sufficient mutuality of obligation and control of individual existing under hypothetical contract to establish employment relationship between individual and client—Income Tax (Earnings and Pensions) Act 2003, s 49—Social Security Contributions (Intermediaries) Regulations 2000, SI 2000/727. **Revenue and Customs Comrs v Kickabout Productions Ltd** [2022] **4** 500, CA.
    Employment—
      Meaning—Contract of employment or contract for services—Taxpayer engaging referees to officiate football matches—Whether contracts between taxpayer and referees contracts of employment or contracts for services. **Professional Game Match Officials Ltd v Revenue and Customs Comrs** [2022] **1** 971, CA.
    Income and exemptions relating to securities—
      Securities acquired in connection with employment—Restricted securities—Taxpayer company embarking on scheme to pay bonuses to employees—Bonus sums paid into scheme used to purchase interests in shares—Whether sums paid into scheme earnings of employees—Whether shares purchased as part of scheme restricted securities—Whether scheme falling within exemption in relevant legislative provision—Income Tax (Earnings and Pensions) Act 2003, ss 423, 425, 429. **UBS AG v Revenue and Customs Comrs** [2016] **3** 1, SC.
      Securities acquired in connection with employment—Securities disposed of for more than market value—Taxpayer company's managing director allotted shares in parent company—Entire share capital of parent company acquired by third party purchaser—Managing director becoming entitled to disproportionately large part of consideration paid by purchaser—Whether managing director's shares disposed of for more than market value—Income Tax (Earnings and Pensions) Act 2003, ss 446X, 446Y. **Grays Timber Products Ltd v Revenue and Customs Comrs** [2010] **2** 1, SC.
    Remuneration trusts—
      Employer making contributions to employee remuneration trust—Sub-trusts established in names of individual employees—Loan facility made available to employees—Whether payments taxable as emoluments or earnings when paid to third party and employee having no prior entitlement to receipt—Income and Corporation Taxes Act 1988, ss 19, 131—Income Tax (Earnings and Pensions) Act 2003, s 62(2)—Income Tax (Employments) Regulations 1993, SI 1993/744, reg 6—Income Tax (Pay As You Earn) Regulations 2003, SI 2003/2682, reg 21. **RFC 2012 plc (in liq) (formerly Rangers Football Club plc) v Advocate General for Scotland** [2017] **4** 654, SC.
    Taxable benefits—
      Cars, vans and related benefits—Taxpayer group of companies leasing vehicles to employees—Whether arrangements amounting to taxable benefits—Income Tax (Earnings and Pensions) Act 2003, ss 114, 120. **Revenue and Customs Comrs v Apollo Fuels Ltd** [2016] **4** 464, CA.
  East Africa. *See* **East Africa** (Income tax).
  Education—
    Child allowance—
      Child over age of 16 receiving full-time instruction. *See* Child relief—Child over age of 16 receiving full-time instruction, *above*.
    Technical education payments—
      Deduction in computing profits. *See* Deduction in computing profits—Technical education payments, *above*.

INCOME TAX (cont)—
  Emoluments from office or employment—
    Advantage convertible into money—
      Allotment of shares to employees—Allotment of bonus shares at par value to senior company officials—Shares saleable only with permission of directors—Whether difference between market value and par price paid a profit or gain arising from office—Value of shares—Income Tax Act 1918, Sch E, r 1. **Ede (Inspector of Taxes) v Wilson and Cornwall** [1945] **1** 367, KBD.
    Assessment—
      Basis of. *See* Emoluments from office or employment—Basis of assessment, *below.*
      Cessation of office or employment—Additional assessment—Deputy town clerk becoming town clerk of another borough during year of assessment—Additional assessment in respect of increased remuneration—Whether a cessation of employment—Finance Act 1927, s 45(5). **Hathaway v Turner** [1942] **1** 16, KBD.
    Basis of assessment—
      Emoluments received in respect of earlier years—Teacher suspended from duty on half salary—Salary withheld but subsequently paid on reinstatement—Whether income paid on reinstatement assessable by reference to year of receipt or year in which it was earned—Income Tax Ordinance (Trinidad and Tobago), ss 5(1)(e), 6. **Board of Inland Revenue v Suite** [1986] **2** 577, PC.
      Perquisite—Value of perquisite—Employer's gift of suit of clothes—Computation of value—Cost to employer or second-hand value to taxpayer—Income Tax Act 1952, Sch 9, r 1 (Rules applicable to Sch E). **Wilkins (Inspector of Taxes) v Rogerson** [1961] **1** 358, CA.
      Perquisite—Value of perquisite—Litigation expenses—Company incurring expense on defence of director on criminal charge—'Payment made primarily for company's benefit'—Payment in excess of what director would have paid if defending out of his own resources—Whether whole expense to be treated as taxable perquisite—Income Tax Act 1952, ss 160(1), 161(1). **Rendell v Went (Inspector of Taxes)** [1964] **2** 464, HL.
  Benefits derived by directors and higher paid employees from employment—
    Cash equivalent of benefit—Cost of providing benefit—Concessionary fees scheme operated by school for sons of teaching staff—Whether cost of benefit limited to additional costs directly incurred by school in providing benefit—Finance Act 1976, ss 61(1), 63(1)(2). **Pepper (Inspector of Taxes) v Hart** [1993] **1** 42, HL.
    Scholarship awarded to employee's child by employer—Whether award emolument from parent's employment—Income and Corporation Taxes Act 1970, s 375(1)—Finance Act 1976, ss 61(1), 72(3). **Wicks v Firth (Inspector of Taxes)** [1982] **2** 9, CA.
  Benefits in kind—
    Car loan scheme—Employees participating in scheme receiving lower wages—Whether gross wages affected by acceptance of lower wages and use of car. **Heaton (Inspector of Taxes) v Bell** [1969] **2** 70, HL.
    Expense incurred by body corporate—Accommodation—Accommodation and benefits provided to directors and others—Expenses incurred by body corporate—Treatment as income of directors etc—Director renting house from company—Company paying all current expenses—Director entertaining company's customers—Need for apportionment of total sum—Reflection of use for business purposes—Absence of severance of accommodation—Income Tax Act 1952, ss 161(1)(6), 162(1), Sch 9, para 7. **Westcott (Inspector of Taxes) v Bryan** [1969] **3** 564, CA.
    Expense incurred by body corporate—Accommodation—Company providing accommodation for employee—Employee charged only part of rent—Whether difference income of employee—Income Tax Act 1952, s 161(1). **McKie (Inspector of Taxes) v Warner** [1961] **3** 348, Ch D.
    Expense incurred by body corporate—Accommodation—Provision of accommodation for directors or other employees—Director renting house from company—Genuine transaction at arm's length—Company paying sums for owner's rates, insurance to fabric, landlord's repairs and renewals—Expenses on house exceeded rent—Whether excess of such expenses over rent chargeable as notional expense of director refunded to him by company and thus as his income—Income Tax Act 1952, ss 160(1), 161(1), 162(4). **Luke v IRC** [1963] **1** 655, HL.
    Expense incurred by body corporate—Accommodation—Service occupation—Service house of mill manager—Company's payments for coal, electricity and garden—Emoluments of manager—Income Tax Act 1952, s 161(1)(3). **Butter (Inspector of Taxes) v Bennett** [1962] **3** 204, CA.
    Expense incurred by body corporate—Provision of benefits for directors or other employees—Christmas gifts to employees—£10 vouchers—Assessability to tax—Income Tax Act 1952, s 161. **Laidler v Perry (Inspector of Taxes)** [1965] **2** 121, HL.
    Premises available to occupier by reason of holding an office or employment—Beneficial or representative occupation—Obligation to occupy as condition of employment—Occupation enabling taxpayer to perform duties of employment more effectively—Taxpayer a police officer—Taxpayer required to live in accommodation approved by chief constable—Police authority providing rent-free houses for police officers—Houses allocated by order—Taxpayer having no right to choose house in which to live—Whether taxpayer's occupation in beneficial or representative capacity—Whether value of premises part of emoluments of taxpayer—Finance Act 1963, s 47(1). **Langley v Appleby (Inspector of Taxes)** [1976] **3** 391, Ch D.
  Capital or income receipt. *See* Capital or income receipts—Emoluments from office or employment, *above.*
  Causal nexus between employment and benefit received—
    Preferential right to apply for shares—Parent company offering shares for sale—Shares tendered to public—Ten per cent of shares reserved at preferential price for group employees—Purpose of offering shares to employees to encourage them to become shareholders and bring them into closer relationship with parent company—Taxpayer employed by subsidiary company—Taxpayer buying 5,000 shares at preferential price—Shares increasing in value after allotment—Whether taxpayer's profit deriving from his employment—Whether benefit an emolument from his employment—Finance Act 1956, Sch 2, para 1(1). **Tyrer v Smart (Inspector of Taxes)** [1979] **1** 321, HL.
  Compensation—
    Loss of office—Abrogation of service agreement—Separate agreement for payment of compensation—Payment not under service contract—Whether a profit from employment—Income Tax Act 1918, Sch E, r 1. **Henley v Murray (Inspector of Taxes)** [1950] **1** 908, CA.

INCOME TAX (cont)—
Emoluments from office or employment (cont)—
Compensation (cont)—
Loss of office—Exemption from tax—Contract not requiring holder of office to perform any duties in United Kingdom—Contract of employment with foreign company—Contract not stipulating where duties to be performed—Implication of term that duties not required to be performed in United Kingdom—Appointment as managing director of company carrying on business abroad—Performance of some duties in United Kingdom within three years of termination of contract—Whether exempt from tax only if express provision in contract that duties need not be performed in United Kingdom—Income and Corporation Taxes Act 1970, s 188(2)(b). **Wienand v Anderton (Inspector of Taxes)** [1977] **1** 384, Ch D.

Loss of office—Payment in consideration or in consequence of termination of office—Payment not otherwise chargeable to tax—Registrarship of limited company—Registrarship held by firm of advocates incidentally to their business—Firm ceasing to be registrars—Terminal payment—Whether payment chargeable to tax as trading receipt of firm—Income Tax Act 1952, Sch E—Finance Act 1960, ss 37(1), (2), 38(3). **IRC v Brander & Cruickshank** [1971] **1** 36, HL.

Loss of office—Payment of lump sum—Accountant—Auditor to group of companies—Fees taxed under Sch E—Payment on relinquishing office—Office as an asset of accountant's business and a subject of taxation under Sch D—Inconsistency of findings of Special Commissioners with view that the auditorships were such an asset—No ground for holding findings unreasonable—No factual basis in findings for establishing that auditorships were such an asset—Finance Act 1960, s 38(3). **Ellis (Inspector of Taxes) v Lucas** [1966] **2** 935, Ch D.

Loss of office—Payment of lump sum—Solatium—Accountants—Auditors to group of companies—Fees taxed under Sch E—Payment on relinquishing office—Payment made to persons carrying on profession—Persons assessable under Sch D—Whether payment emolument from office or receipt of trade or business. **Walker (Inspector of Taxes) v Carnaby, Harrower, Barham & Pykett** [1970] **1** 502, Ch D.

Loss of office—Term in service agreement for payment on termination of service agreement—Whether compensation arising from employment—Income Tax Act 1918, Sch E, r 1. **Dale v de Soissons** [1950] **2** 460, CA.

Reduction of salary—Company director—Payment of lump sum in consideration of acceptance of reduced salary—Whether profit arising from office. **Wilson (Inspector of Taxes) v Nicholson Sons and Daniels Ltd** [1943] **2** 732, KBD.

Reduction of salary—Company director—Payment of lump sum to company director in consideration of acceptance of reduced salary and alteration of director's tenure of office—Compensation not in nature of a capital receipt—Income Tax Act 1918, Sch E. **Leeland v Boarland (Inspector of Taxes)** [1946] **1** 13, KBD.

Relinquishment of rights under service agreement—Lump sum—Compensation for loss of pension rights and reduced salary—Whether whole or part of lump sum taxable as emoluments—Income Tax Act 1918, Sch E. **Tilley v Wales (Inspector of Taxes)** [1943] **1** 280, HL.

Relinquishment of rights under service agreement—Lump sum—Taxpayer refuse collector in employment of local authority—Taxpayer originally entitled under salvage agreement to sell salvage and retain proceeds of sale—Termination of salvage agreement by local authority—Acceptance by taxpayer of £450 in place of former rights as to salvage—Whether payment emolument from employment—Income Tax Act 1952, s 156, as amended by Finance Act 1956, s 10. **Holland (Inspector of Taxes) v Geoghegan** [1972] **3** 333, Ch D.

Restrictive covenant—Payment of lump sum in consideration of acceptance of covenant—Company director—Whether profit arising from office—Income Tax Act 1918, Sch E, r 1. **Beak (Inspector of Taxes) v Robson** [1943] **1** 46, HL.

Deduction from emoluments—
Expenses necessarily incurred in performance of duties of office of employment—Medical professional—Training expenses—Whether expenses incurred in association with training wholly, exclusively and necessarily incurred in performance of taxpayer's duties of employment—Income and Corporation Taxes Act 1988, s 198. **Revenue and Customs Comrs v Banerjee** [2009] **3** 915, Ch D; [2011] **1** 985, CA.

Deduction of tax—
Agreement to pay remuneration without deduction of tax—Effect of agreement—Income Tax Act 1918, All Schedules Rules, r 23(2). **Jaworski v Institution of Polish Engineers in GB Ltd** [1950] **2** 1191, CA.

Failure to deduct tax—Appointment by parent company of taxpayer as executive director of subsidiary—Terms of appointment enabling taxpayer to acquire shares in subsidiary—Shares resold to parent company for consideration in excess of then market value—Whether consideration 'emoluments'—Whether parent company an 'employer'—Whether parent company liable to account for tax—Income and Corporation Taxes Act 1970, s 204—Finance Act 1972, s 79—Finance Act 1976, s 67—Income Tax (Employments) Regulations 1973, reg 2. **IRC v Herd** [1993] **3** 56, HL.

Emoluments received in United Kingdom—
Sums derived from emoluments paid overseas—Loans—Emoluments paid to taxpayer overseas—Emoluments invested by subscribing for shares in overseas company controlled by taxpayer—Interest free loans by company to second company not controlled by taxpayer—Second company granting taxpayer similar loans in United Kingdom—Whether loans received by taxpayer emoluments—Income Tax Act 1952, s 156 (as amended by the Finance Act 1956, s 10(1)(Sch E, para 1, Case III). **Harmel v Wright (Inspector of Taxes)** [1974] **1** 945, Ch D.

Employment—
Contract of employment—What amounts to contract of employment—Payment of lump sum for cancellation of contract—Contract for exclusive services—Operative for twelve to sixteen consecutive weeks of each of three successive years—Option to acquire film rights in novels—Not a contract of employment—Income Tax Act 1918, Sch E, r 1, Sch D, Case II. **Household v Grimshaw (Inspector of Taxes)** [1953] **2** 12, Ch D.

INCOME TAX (cont)—

Emoluments from office or employment (cont)—

Employment (cont)—

Contract of service—Contract an incident in carrying on of profession—Professional dancer—Dancer entering into engagements in the carrying on of his profession—Engagement with theatrical company under standard form contract—Contract amounting to contract of service—Whether earnings from contract constituting emoluments from 'employment'—Income and Corporation Taxes Act 1970, s 181(1)(Sch E). **Fall (Inspector of Taxes) v Hitchen** [1973] **1** 368, Ch D.

Expenses allowances—

Body corporate—Sums paid in respect of expenses by body corporate to director or employee—Director—Expenses in respect of activity outside normal duties—Director given special assignment—Director paid travelling expenses—Expenses relating only to special assignment and not to directorship—Whether expenses chargeable as emoluments from office of director—Income Tax Act 1952, ss 156(Sch E), 160(1). **Taylor v Provan (Inspector of Taxes)** [1974] **1** 1201, HL.

Expenses payments. *See* Emoluments from office or employment—Perquisites or profits—Expenses payments, *below.*

Expenses wholly, exclusively and necessarily incurred—

Army officer—Annual mess subscription—Income Tax Act 1918, Rules Applicable to Sch E, r 9. **Griffiths (Inspector of Taxes) v Mockler** [1953] **2** 805, Ch D.

Army officer—Territorial Army officer—Subscription. *See* Emoluments from office or employment—Expenses wholly, exclusively and necessarily incurred—Subscription—Territorial Army officer, *below.*

Conference expenses—County surveyor—Attendance at conference—By-pass scheme proposed by county council—Surveyor attending international conference abroad in hope of obtaining first class opinion on merits of scheme—Attendance during period of annual leave and without obtaining authority of county council—Whether expense of attending conference necessarily incurred in performance of his duties—Income Tax Act 1952, Sch 9, r 7. **Owen v Burden (Inspector of Taxes)** [1972] **1** 356, CA.

Employment agency—Fee paid to agency—Employment obtained through employment agency on payment of fee—Fee calculated on a percentage of one year's earnings—Whether fee so paid 'money wholly, exclusively, and necessarily' expended in the performance of the employment—Income Tax Act 1918, Sch E, r 9. **Henderson Shortt v McIlgorm (Inspector of Taxes)** [1945] **1** 391, KBD.

Examination fees—Solicitor's articled clerk—Fee for Law Society's examination—Income Tax Act 1952, Sch 9, r 7. **Hind v Hind** [1969] **1** 1083, Div.

Meals—Allowance for meals—Local government officer required to attend evening council meeting—Allowance paid to officer for meals in connection with evening work—Excess cost of meals not deductible—Income Tax Act 1952, Sch IX, Rules Applicable to Sch E, r 7. **Durbidge v Sanderson (Inspector of Taxes)** [1955] **3** 154, Ch D.

Newspaper allowance—Journalists receiving newspaper allowance as reimbursement towards expenses incurred in purchasing newspapers and periodicals—Whether reading of other newspapers and periodicals to be regarded as means of maintaining general qualifications and fitness of journalists to carry out employment or as part of daily performance of journalists' duties—Whether expenses wholly, exclusively and necessarily incurred in performance of journalists' duties—Income and Corporation Taxes Act 1970, s 189(1). **Smith (Inspector of Taxes) v Abbott** [1994] **1** 673, HL.

Parsonage house—Rector required to live in house—House held by rector as corporation sole—Expenses incurred by rector in opposing Bill in Parliament for compulsory acquisition of parsonage house. **Mitchell (Inspector of Taxes) v Child** [1942] **2** 504, KBD.

Residence provided by employers to employee—Employee required to live in flat and to entertain customers—Part of rent paid by employers—Whether sum paid by employers deduction from employee's emoluments as notionally increased by that sum—Income Tax Act 1952, Sch 9, Rules applicable to Sch E, r 7. **McKie (Inspector of Taxes) v Warner** [1961] **3** 348, Ch D.

Subscription—Club—Bank manager—Membership of club practically requisite for employment as manager—Income Tax Act 1952, Rules applicable to Sch E, Sch 9, r 7. **Brown v Bullock (Inspector of Taxes)** [1961] **3** 129, CA.

Subscription—Territorial Army officer—Mess subscription and expenses, camp expenses, cost of necessary attendance at dances—Excess cost over allowance for hotel expenses at conferences and exercises—Income Tax Act 1918, Rules Applicable to Sch E, r 9. **London Corp v Cusack-Smith** [1953] **2** 80, QBD.

Travelling expenses—Attendance at evening classes condition of employment—Expenses so incurred not in performance of duties of office—Income Tax Act 1918, Sch E, r 9. **Blackwell (Inspector of Taxes) v Mills** [1945] **2** 655, KBD.

Travelling expenses—Evidence that expenses necessarily incurred—Company directors—Man and wife sole shareholders and directors—Visit to Australia in connection with company's business—No evidence as to functions wife to perform in Australia—Income Tax Act 1952, ss 161(1), 162(1), Sch IX, r 7. **Maclean (Inspector of Taxes) v Trembath** [1956] **2** 113, Ch D.

Travelling expenses—Taxpayer resident abroad—Taxpayer director of English company—Sole function to expand company by mergers etc—Arrangement with company contemplating duties would be performed mainly outside United Kingdom—Taxpayer flying to United Kingdom periodically in connection with duties—Taxpayer reimbursed by company for money expended on air fares—Sums reimbursed constituting emoluments of office—Whether cost of air fares necessarily incurred by taxpayer in performance of duties of his office of director—Income Tax Act 1952, s 156(Sch E), Sch 9, para 7. **Taylor v Provan (Inspector of Taxes)** [1974] **1** 1201, HL.

Travelling expenses—Travelling expenses which office holder is 'necessarily obliged to incur'—Employee's use of own car—Use encouraged but not a condition of employment—Mileage allowance made—Claim to deduct balance of cost involved—Income Tax Act 1952, Sch 9, r 7. **Marsden v IRC** [1965] **2** 364, Ch D.

69

INCOME TAX (cont)—
    Emoluments from office or employment (cont)—
        Expenses wholly, exclusively and necessarily incurred (cont)—
            Travelling expenses—War work—Weekly wage earner—Change to place of work through circumstances connected with war—Additional travelling expenses—Housewife directed to work in factory—Whether claim for deduction admissible—Income Tax Act 1918, sched E, r 9—Finance Act 1941, s 23. **Phillips (Inspector of Taxes) v Emery** [1946] **1** 144, KBD.
        Foreign employment. *See* Foreign employment, *below*.
        Future employment—
            Undertaking by taxpayer to serve company—Transfer of shares in company to taxpayer in consideration of undertaking—Tripartite agreement between taxpayer, company and controlling shareholder in company—Taxpayer to take up employment with company not later than specified date six months after agreement—Shares to be transferred to taxpayer by controlling shareholder—Transfer of shares taking place before taxpayer starting work for the company—Whether transferred shares taxable emoluments of taxpayer from office or employment—Income Tax Act 1952, s 156(Sch E), as amended by Finance Act 1956, s 10(1). **Pritchard (Inspector of Taxes) v Arundale** [1971] **3** 1011, Ch D.
        Gifts distinguished from emoluments—
            Personal gifts. *See* Emoluments from office or employment—Personal gifts distinguished from emoluments, *below*.
            Voluntary payment. *See* Emoluments from office or employment—Voluntary payment, *below*.
        Living accommodation—
            Benefits in kind—Director—Shadow director—Whether shadow director having same liability to tax as director in respect of provision of living accommodation and benefits in kind—Income and Corporation Taxes Act 1988, s 168(8). **R v Allen (No 2)** [2001] **4** 768, HL.
        Moneys improperly obtained—
            Liability to account—Moneys alleged to have been improperly paid to taxpayer out of undisclosed profits of company of which taxpayer director—Additional assessment under Sch E on taxpayer—Whether, if moneys improperly paid, taxpayer held moneys as trustee for company—Whether taxpayer could in law have received moneys as emoluments. **Rose v Humbles (Inspector of Taxes)** [1970] **2** 519, Ch D.
        Office—
            Barrister's clerk—Taxpayer employed as barristers' senior clerk—Taxpayer entering into new contractual arrangement with members of chambers—Taxpayer agreeing to provide full clerking services to chambers in return for percentage of barristers' fees—Taxpayer assessed to income tax on emoluments from office or employment—Whether taxpayer holding 'office' of barristers' head clerk—Income and Corporation Taxes Act 1970, s 181(1) (Sch E). **McMenamin (Inspector of Taxes) v Diggles** [1991] **4** 370, Ch D.
            Inspector appointed to hold public local inquiry—Whether inspector holding an 'office'—Whether inspector's remuneration taxable under Sch E, Case I—Income and Corporation Taxes Act 1970, s 181(1). **Edwards (Inspector of Taxes) v Clinch** [1981] **3** 543, HL.
            Part-time appointment—Profits from office and from profession—Deduction of expenses—Exclusivity of schedules—Expenses of office not deductible from profits of profession—Medical specialist—Part-time consultant at national health service hospital—Income Tax Act 1952, ss 122 (Sch D, para 1, proviso), 156 (Sch E, para 2). **Mitchell (Inspector of Taxes) v Ross** [1961] **3** 49, HL.
        Pay as you earn. *See* Pay as you earn system, *below*.
        Payable out of the public revenue. *See* Office or employment under the Crown—Emoluments payable out the public revenue of the United Kingdom, *below*.
        Payment—
            Bonus—Bonus credited to director's account in taxpayer company's books—Whether crediting of bonus a 'payment' to director—Income and Corporation Taxes Act 1970, s 204(1). **Garforth (Inspector of Taxes) v Newsmith Stainless Ltd** [1979] **2** 73, Ch D.
            Continuance in office in consideration for payment—Company director—Agreement to continue in office in return for payment of lump sum—Whether a profit from office—Income Tax Act 1918, Sch E, r 1. **Cameron v Prendergast (Inspector of Taxes)** [1940] **2** 35, HL.
            Voluntary payment. *See* Emoluments from office or employment—Voluntary payment, *below*.
        Perquisites or profits—
            Basis of assessment—Perquisite. *See* Emoluments from office or employment—Basis of assessment—Perquisite, *above*.
            Benefits in kind. *See* Emoluments from office or employment—Benefits in kind, *above*.
            Car loan scheme for employees—Adjustment of employee's wage to meet costs—Scheme terminable by 14 days' notice—Whether car loan a taxable perquisite of employment—Income Tax Act 1952, s 156 (Sch E), amended—Finance Act 1956, s 10, Sch 2, Para 1. **Heaton (Inspector of Taxes) v Bell** [1969] **2** 70, HL.
            Expenses payments—Body corporate—Payments to director or employee. *See* Emoluments from office or employment—Expenses allowances, *above*.
            Expenses payments—Travelling expenses—Medical practitioner practising at residence and also holding part-time appointments at hospital 15 miles away as obstetrician and anaesthetist—Emergency cases—Payment of allowance for travel by car to hospital—Payment irrespective of the method of travel—Whether emoluments from office—Finance Act 1956, Sch 2, para 1(1). **Owen v Pook (Inspector of Taxes)** [1969] **2** 1, HL.
            Gold sovereigns—Taxpayer's wages paid in gold sovereigns—Open market value of each sovereign substantially more than its nominal value—Whether the value of the sovereigns for tax purposes was their nominal value or open market value—Income and Corporation Taxes Act 1970, s 183(1)—Coinage Act 1971, s 2. **Jenkins v Horn (Inspector of Taxes)** [1979] **2** 1141, Ch D.
            Occupation of house—Rates and property tax paid by employers—Minister of religion—Manse—Minister required to live in house—Occupation representative and not beneficial—Whether amount of rates and property tax emoluments from office. **Reed v Cattermole (Inspector of Taxes)** [1937] **1** 541, CA.
            Value of perquisite. *See* Emoluments from office or employment—Basis of assessment—Perquisite, *above*.

INCOME TAX (cont)—
Emoluments from office or employment (cont)—
Personal gifts distinguished from emoluments—
Bonuses—Bonuses paid to employees after 25 years' service—Whether gifts or remuneration—Income Tax Act 1918, Sch E, r 1. **Weston v Hearn (Inspector of Taxes)** [1943] **2** 421, KBD.
Christmas gifts. *See* Emoluments from office or employment—Receipt 'from' employment—Gift to employee—Christmas gifts, *below*.
Place of performance of duties—
Duties treated as performed in United Kingdom—Duties of office or employment under the Crown of a public nature—Emoluments payable out of public revenue—Taxpayer permanent civil servant employed outside United Kingdom—Taxpayer without professional or technical qualifications—Implementing instructions handed down by superior officers—Subordinate position with limited duties—Whether employment 'of a public nature'—Finance Act 1956, para Sch 2, para 6. **Graham v White (Inspector of Taxes)** [1972] **1** 1159, Ch D.
Public office in United Kingdom—
Director of English company—Director of private company permanently resident abroad—Remuneration fixed by company's articles—Remuneration subject to income tax—Income Tax Act 1918, Sch E, rr 1, 6. **McMillan v Guest** [1942] **1** 606, HL.
Receipt 'from' employment—
Gift to employee—Christmas gifts—£10 vouchers—Whether perquisites or profits of employment—Income Tax Act 1952, Sch E (s 156)—Finance Act 1956, s 10(1) Sch 2 para 1(1). **Laidler v Perry (Inspector of Taxes)** [1965] **2** 121, HL.
Payment for services—Indemnity scheme for employees—Indemnity against loss on house purchase—Employers' housing assistance scheme—Reimbursement of loss on transfer to new place of employment—Whether indemnity a payment for services—Income Tax Act 1952, Sch 9, Rules applicable to Sch E, r 1. **Hochstrasser (Inspector of Taxes) v Mayes** [1959] **3** 817, HL.
Payment in return for variation of service contract—Lump sum payment—Payment made to compensate employee for loss of commission—Whether payment emolument from employment—Income and Corporation Taxes Act 1970, ss 181, 183. **McGregor (Inspector of Taxes) v Randall** [1984] **1** 1092, Ch D.
Payment made as inducement to enter employment—Ex gratia payment to employee in consideration of employee giving up contingent right to non-statutory redundancy payment—Whether payment emolument from employment—Income and Corporation Taxes Act 1988, s 19(1). **Mairs (Inspector of Taxes) v Haughey** [1993] **3** 801, HL.
Payment made in return for acting as or being an employee and for no other reason—Payment made in return for continuing in employment with loss of rights under employment protection legislation—Whether payment 'emolument' from employment—Income and Corporation Taxes Act 1970, ss 181, 183(1). **Hamblett v Godfrey (Inspector of Taxes)** [1987] **1** 916, CA.
Payment made in return for acting as or being an employee and for no other reason—Profit-sharing scheme for employees of company—Termination of scheme—Division of trust fund between employees—Trustees holding shares in company to provide income for division between employees—Scheme terminated on merger of company with another company—Proceeds of realisation of trust fund divided between employees in accordance with trust deed—Whether sum received by employee an emolument from employment—Income and Corporation Taxes Act 1970, ss 181(1) (Sch E), 183(1). **Brumby (Inspector of Taxes) v Milner** [1976] **3** 636, HL.
Payment on retirement or removal from office—Inducement to enter into employment—Transfer fee paid to football player—Taxpayer paid sum by old club for agreement to play for new club—Whether payment an emolument 'from' employment by new club—Whether relevant that payment made by person other than employer—Whether sum taxable in hands of taxpayer—Income and Corporation Taxes Act 1970, s 181(1). **Shilton v Wilmshurst (Inspector of Taxes)** [1991] **3** 148, HL.
Purpose of employer in making payment—Inducement to give up professional status and to become and continue as employee—Company making lump sum payment to chartered accountant on taking up employment with company—Whether payment emolument from employment—Income and Corporation Taxes Act 1970, ss 181(1), 183(1). **Glantre Engineering Ltd v Goodhand (Inspector of Taxes)** [1983] **1** 542, Ch D.
Receipts after employment has ceased—Distribution of assets of trusts for benefit of employees—Employing company taken over—Employment transferred to parent company—Trusts wound up and assets distributed among all employees after transfer of employment to parent company—Whether receipts attributable to any year or years of employment—Income and Corporation Taxes Act 1970, s 181. **Bray (Inspector of Taxes) v Best** [1989] **1** 969, HL.
Testimonial—Payment by way of testimonial to mark exceptional achievement in performance of services—Professional footballers—Outstanding performance in World Cup championships—Special payment of bonus by football association—Whether sum taxable as emolument—Income Tax Act 1952, s 156 (Sch E), as amended by Finance Act 1956, s 10(1). **Moore v Griffiths (Inspector of Taxes)** [1972] **3** 399, Ch D.
Reward for services—
Loan scheme for course of training—Employee granted loan by employer to undergo course of training—Employment ceasing whilst employee on course—Loan ceasing to be repayable if employee resuming employment for period of 18 months from end of course—Loan equivalent to amount of salary employee would have received during period of course—Employee duly fulfilling conditions of loan—Loan turned into absolute payment—Payment taxable as reward for past services—Income Tax Act 1952, s 156 (Sch E)—Finance Act 1956, Sch 2. **Clayton (Inspector of Taxes) v Gothorp** [1971] **2** 1311, Ch D.
Securities, exemptions relating to. *See* Earnings from employment—Income and exemptions relating to securities, *above*.
Voluntary payment—
Bonus. *See* Emoluments from office or employment—Personal gifts distinguished from emoluments—Bonuses, *above*.
Customary gift—Huntsman—Christmas gifts—Huntsman engaged by master and under his orders—Custom for gifts to be given to huntsman at Christmas—Income Tax Act 1952, s 156, Sch E, para 1, para 2, Sch 9, Rules applicable to Sch E, r 1. **Wright v Boyce (Inspector of Taxes)** [1958] **2** 703, CA.

INCOME TAX (cont)—

Emoluments from office or employment (cont)—

Voluntary payment (cont)—

Gift of shares in company—Recognition of work of directors—Covenant to transfer shares—Consideration expressed as undertaking by directors to continue engagements with company—Whether personal gifts or remuneration for services—Income Tax Act 1952, Sch IX, Rules applicable to Sch E, r 1. **Bridges (Inspector of Taxes) v Hewitt** [1957] **2** 281, CA.

Payment arising in ordinary course of taxpayer's employment—Professional cricketer—Collections made for meritorious performances—Occasions for collection arising repeatedly—Income Tax Act 1918, Rules applicable to Sch E, r 1. **Moorhouse (Inspector of Taxes) v Dooland** [1955] **1** 93, CA.

Payment arising in ordinary course of taxpayer's employment—Professional football players—Proceeds of benefit matches or payments in lieu thereof. **Corbett v Duff** [1941] **1** 512, KBD.

Payment arising in ordinary course of taxpayers employment—Taxi-cab driver—Tips—Whether tips paid to driver taxable as profits arising from employment—Income Tax Act 1918, Sch E, r 1. **Calvert (Inspector of Taxes) v Wainwright** [1947] **1** 282, KBD.

Personal gifts distinguished from emoluments. *See* Emoluments from office or employment—Personal gifts distinguished from emoluments, *above*.

Year of assessment—

Option to purchase shares—Grant of option to purchase shares—Exercise of option—Option to purchase its shares sold to company's employee—Subsequent exercise of right of purchase—Increase in value of shares since date of option—Whether increase taxable at date of exercise of option—Income Tax Act 1952, s 156, Sch E, Case I, r 1. **Abbott v Philbin (Inspector of Taxes)** [1960] **2** 763, HL.

Employment—

Emoluments from office or employment. *See* Emoluments from office or employment, *above*.

Foreign employment. *See* Foreign employment, *below*.

Payments or benefits on termination of employment etc—

Any payment made in consideration or in consequence of, or otherwise in connection with, termination of employment—Exemption for payment made on account of injury—Compromise of employment tribunal claim for unfair dismissal and unlawful age discrimination—Whether settlement payment received in consideration or in consequence of, or otherwise in connection with, termination of employment—Whether 'injury' encompassing injury to feelings—Whether part of payment representing age discrimination claim exempt from charge to income tax—Income Tax (Earnings and Pensions) Act 2003, ss 401, 406. **Moorthy v Revenue and Customs Comrs** [2018] **3** 1062, CA.

Enemy property—

Liability of custodian for income tax. *See* **Trading with the enemy** (Custody of enemy property—Vesting of property in custodian of enemy property—Liability of custodian for income tax on proceeds of property vested in him).

Enquiry into return. *See* Return—Self-assessment—Enquiry, *below*.

Enterprise investment scheme relief—

Loan-linked investments—

Business expansion scheme—Subscription for eligible shares in qualifying companies—Issue of shares—Meaning of 'issue'—Whether shares 'issued' as soon as company contractually bound to enter name of nominee in register of members and applicant contractually bound to accept such entry of nominee for him—Income and Corporation Taxes Act 1988, ss 289, 299A. **National Westminster Bank plc v IRC** [1994] **3** 1, HL.

Entertaining expenses—

Deduction in computing profits. *See* Deduction in computing profits—Expenses wholly and exclusively laid out for purposes of trade—Entertaining expenses, *above*.

Error or mistake—

Relief—

Case stated. *See* Case stated—Relief in respect of error or mistake, *above*.

European Community—

Free movement of capital. *See* **European Union** (External relations—Agreements with third countries—Switzerland —Scope of agreement—Free movement of capital).

Principle of non-discrimination—

Freedom of establishment. *See* **European Union** (Freedom of establishment—Principle of non-discrimination—Income tax).

Freedom of movement. *See* **European Union** (Freedom of movement—Principle of non-discrimination—Income tax).

Evidence—

Nature of transaction for purpose of ascertaining tax liability—

Extrinsic evidence—Whether extrinsic evidence admissible for purpose of determining nature of transaction—Whether court restricted to considering terms of transaction. **IRC v Church Comrs for England** [1976] **2** 1037, HL.

Excess rent. *See* Profits—Excess rent, *below*.

Exchange transaction—

Computation of profits. *See* Computation of profits—Exchange transaction, *above*.

Executor—

Liability. *See* Persons chargeable—Executors, *below*.

Exemption—

Charity. *See* Charity, *above*.

Co-operative society—

Sums representing discount, rebate, dividend or bonus to members—Member—Division or return in proportion to purchase—Trader member receiving sum as 'division or return' on purchases—Whether trader exempt from income tax on sum—Finance Act 1933, s 31(1)(3). **Pope v Beaumont** [1941] **3** 9, KBD.

Compensation for loss of office. *See* Emoluments from office or employment—Compensation—Loss of office—Exemption from tax, *above*.

INCOME TAX (cont)—
  Exemption (cont)—
    Crown—
      Custodian of enemy property—Proceeds of property vested in him—Liability for tax on proceeds—Income Tax Act 1918, Sch D, Miscellaneous Rules, r 1. **Bank Voor Handel en Scheepvaart NV v Administrator of Hungarian Property** [1954] **1** 969, HL.
      Person—Whether Crown a 'person' within income tax legislation—Income Tax Act 1918, Sch D, case III, r 1(a) All Schedules Rules r 19, r 21. **Whitworth Park Coal Co Ltd (in liq) v IRC** [1959] **3** 703, HL.
      Public corporation—Broadcasting—British Broadcasting Corporation—Whether entitled to Crown immunity from taxation. **BBC v Johns (Inspector of Taxes)** [1964] **1** 923, CA.
    Gratuities etc to members of armed forces—
      Bounty—Sums payable by way of bounty out of public revenue—Public revenue—Bounty paid to members of Civil Defence Corps out of local authority funds—Local authority being partly reimbursed from central government funds—Whether bounty paid out of public revenue and thus exempt from tax—Income Tax Act 1952, s 457(4). **Mohan v R** [1967] **2** 58, PC.
    New Zealand. *See* **New Zealand** (Income tax—Exemption).
    Newfoundland. *See* **Canada** (Income tax—Exemption—Newfoundland).
    Non-resident trader—
      Interest on Government securities—Interest on securities of foreign and colonial companies—Expenses of earning profits exempt from tax—Income Tax Act 1918, s 46, Sch C, r 2(d), Sch D, Cases I and II, rr 3, 5, Miscellaneous Rules, r 7(2). **Hughes (Inspector of Taxes) v Bank of New Zealand** [1938] **1** 778, HL.
    Scholarship income—
      Loan agreement—Loan by employer to employee to undergo course of training—Loan equivalent to salary employee would have received if continuing in employment—Loan ceasing to be repayable if employee resuming employment for period of 18 months after completion of course—Whether loan agreement a scholarship—Income Tax Act 1952, s 458. **Clayton (Inspector of Taxes) v Gothorp** [1971] **2** 1311, Ch D.
    Statute—
      Generality of words—Local Act—Exemption from payment of any taxes—Whether including income tax as well as local taxes—Ancholme Drainage Act 1767. **Ancholme Drainage and Navigation Comrs v Wedhen (Inspector of Taxes)** [1936] **1** 759, KBD.
    Superannuation contribution—
      Ordinary annual contribution—Payment of back contributions by annual instalments—Finance Act 1921, s 32(1)—Regulations dated 10th November 1921 (SR & O 1921 No 1699), reg 5. **Kneen (Inspector of Taxes) v Ashton** [1950] **1** 982, Ch D.
    Trade union—
      Provident benefits—Payments by way of legal assistance—Exemption under Sch C and Sch D—Sums paid out of general fund, not special fund, of union—Whether provision of legal assistance a provident benefit—Income Tax Act 1952, s 440(2). **R v Special Comrs of Income Tax, ex p National Union of Railwaymen** [1966] **2** 759, QBD.
  Expenses—
    Deduction from emoluments from office or employment. *See* Emoluments from office or employment—Expenses wholly, exclusively and necessarily incurred, *above.*
    Deduction in computing profits. *See* Deduction in computing profits, *above.*
    Management expenses. *See* Management expenses, *below.*
    Training expenses. *See* Emoluments from office or employment—Deduction from emoluments—Expenses necessarily incurred in performance of duties of office of employment—Medical professional—Training expenses, *above.*
  Farming—
    Annual profits or gains. *See* Profits—Annual profits or gains—Farming, *below.*
    Farm—
      Land wholly or mainly occupied for the purpose of husbandry—Holding comprising eighty per cent farm land—Separate assessment of farm land—Finance Act 1941, ss 10, 11. **De Poix v Chapman (Inspector of Taxes)** [1947] **2** 649, KBD.
      Market gardens—Garden—Watercress beds—Whether a 'garden'—Income Tax Act 1918, Sch B, rr 1, 8. **Inspector of Taxes v Barter** [1944] **2** 154, KBD.
    Mixed farm—
      Assessment—Apportionment—Nurseries and market-gardens—Worked as a single unit—Income Tax Act 1918, Sch B, r 1, r 8. **Bomford v Osborne** [1941] **2** 426, HL.
      Partnership—Division of profits—Brood mare sole partnership asset—Mare kept on stud farm of which one partner tenant—Some progeny sold as yearlings—Some sold after racing—Share of profits from mare as brood mare chargeable on tenant partner under Sch B—Income Tax Act 1918, s 20(1), Sch B. **Dawson v Counsell (Inspector of Taxes)** [1938] **3** 5, CA.
    One trade—
      All farming to be treated as one trade—Farming operations outside United Kingdom—Taxpayer farming in United Kingdom—Visit to Australia with a view to buying a farm and emigrating—Expenses of visit—Expenses attributable to taxpayer's farming activities—Whether incurred for the purpose of trade within United Kingdom—Income Tax Act 1952, ss 124(1), 152. **Sargent (Inspector of Taxes) v Eayrs** [1973] **1** 277, Ch D.
      Separate farms—Losses brought forward—Two farms carried on by one company for three months—Sale of original farm—Allowance of losses and capital allowances for original farm brought forward—Income Tax Act 1952, s 152. **Bispham (Inspector of Taxes) v Eardiston Farming Co (1919) Ltd** [1962] **2** 376, Ch D.
    Trading receipts. *See* Profits—Trading receipts—Farming, *below.*
  Foreign company—
    Agents of foreign company—
      Liability of agents—British company using French company's ship in business during war—Purporting to act as agents of French company—Acts ratified by French company after war—Whether British company taxable—Income Tax Act 1918, Sch D, para 1(a)(iii), All Schedules Rules, rr 5, 6, 10. **Boston Deep Sea Fishing & Ice Co Ltd v Farnham (Inspector of Taxes)** [1957] **3** 204, Ch D.

INCOME TAX (cont)—
    Foreign company (cont)—
        Branch in United Kingdom—
            Head office abroad—Profits—Income from investments of life assurance fund—Inclusion of income from investments exempted from United Kingdom tax—Income Tax Act 1918, Sch D, Case III, r 3(1). **IRC v Australian Mutual Provident Society** [1947] **1** 600, HL.
        Shares—
            Double taxation relief. *See* Double taxation relief—Shares in foreign company, *above*.
        Subsidiary in United Kingdom—
            Contracts with foreign distributors—Subsidiary accepting and discharging orders—Whether agents of foreign company—Whether foreign company carrying on trade within United Kingdom—Income Tax Act 1918, Sch D, para 1, All Schedules Rules, rr 5, 10. **Firestone Tyre and Rubber Co Ltd v Lewellin (Inspector of Taxes)** [1957] **1** 561, HL.
    Foreign employment—
        Duties performed abroad—
            Residence in United Kingdom—Earnings arising wholly from employment abroad—Whether earnings chargeable to income tax—Income Tax Act 1918, s 1, Sch D, Case II, Sch E, r 6—Finance Act 1922, s 18. **Eaton-Turner v McKenna** [1936] **3** 215, HL.
        Duties performed in United Kingdom—
            Employers resident abroad—Contract of employment made abroad—Employee's work and residence in United Kingdom—Income Tax Act 1918, Sch D, Case V, r 2. **Bray (Inspector of Taxes) v Colenbrander** [1953] **1** 1090, HL.
        Duties performed partly in United Kingdom—
            Place of employment abroad—Residence in United Kingdom—Income Tax Act 1918, Sch D, Case V, r 2. **Bennett v Marshall** [1938] **1** 93, CA.
    Foreign possessions—
        Dominion trust—
            Life tenant resident in United Kingdom—Residuary estate subject to annuity—Dominion 'securities'—Dominion 'stocks, shares and rents'—Dominion 'possessions'—Whether life tenant assessable on whole income or amount received in United Kingdom—Income Tax Act 1918, Sch D, Case IV, r 1, Case V, rr1, 2. **Nelson v Adamson** [1941] **2** 44, KBD.
    Income arising from possessions out of United Kingdom—
        Capital or income—Law applicable—Will of United States testator—Beneficiary resident and domiciled in England entitled to life interest under trusts of Californian will—Trust fund—Holdings in United States companies—Bonus shares—Pennsylvania rule—Bonus shares transferred by trustee to beneficiary in the United States—Not remitted to United Kingdom—Character in hands of beneficiary determined by English law—Capital in beneficiary's hands by English law—Income Tax Act 1952, ss 122 (Sch D), 123(1). **Lawson v Rolfe (Inspector of Taxes)** [1970] **1** 761, Ch D.
        Debts incurred in London and discharged in Ceylon—Income Tax Act 1918, Sch D, Case V, r 2. **IRC v Gordon** [1952] **1** 866, HL.
        Dividend paid out of capital profits of South African company—Income Tax Act 1918, Sch D, Case V. **IRC v Reid's Trustees** [1949] **1** 354, HL.
        Income arising from securities out of United Kingdom—Taxpayer's life interest in American estates—Income credited in New York bank account—Cheques drawn by taxpayer in dollars on account—Cheques purchased by English banks—Proceeds credited to taxpayer's English bank account—Whether sums received by taxpayer in United Kingdom—Income Tax Act 1918, Sch D, Case IV, r 2, Case V, r 2. **Thomson (Inspector of Taxes) v Moyse** [1960] **3** 684, HL.
        Partnership between taxpayer and Bahamian company—Partnership activities carried on outside United Kingdom—Taxpayer's motive for entering into partnership to avoid tax on overseas earnings—Object of partnership to exploit taxpayer's talents as television personality—Objects of company including 'all kinds of financial commercial trading or other operations'—Partnership carrying on genuine commercial trade of exploiting taxpayer's talents—Taxpayer entitled to 95 per cent of partnership profits—No part of profits remitted to United Kingdom—Whether income arising from foreign possessions—Whether motive for entering into partnership overriding genuine commercial nature of partnership—Partnership Act 1890, s 1—Income and Corporation Taxes Act 1970, ss 109(2), 122(2)(3). **Newstead (Inspector of Taxes) v Frost** [1980] **1** 363, HL.
        Return of foreign company's capital—Distribution of sum from share premium reserve—Income Tax Act 1952, Sch D, Case V. **Courtaulds Investments Ltd v Fleming (Inspector of Taxes)** [1969] **3** 1281, Ch D.
        Trustee—Liability—Discretionary settlement—Principal beneficiaries not resident in United Kingdom—No beneficiary entitled to income as it accrued—Trust assets and income administered outside United Kingdom—No income remitted to United Kingdom—Three trustees of whom only one resident in United Kingdom—Whether United Kingdom resident trustee liable for assessment to income tax on income derived from trust assets—Income and Corporation Taxes Act 1970, s 108, Sch D, para 1(a), s 114(1). **Dawson v IRC** [1989] **2** 289, HL.
    Income or capital receipts. *See* Capital or income receipts—Foreign possessions, *above*.
    New source of income—
        New source in year of assessment—Shares in foreign company—Acquired prior to 1942-43—Income first received in 1942-43—Liability to tax in that year—New source of income 'in any year of assessment'—Finance Act 1926, s 30, proviso (ii). **Goodlass Wall & Lead Industries Ltd v Atkinson (Inspector of Taxes)** [1950] **2** 314, HL.
        Source—Will of textatrix domiciled in the United States—Daughter's rights in estate—One-fourth income, instalments of capital—Accrual subsequently of remaining three-fourths of income—Single source of income only, viz, the testatrix' estate—No new source on accrual of three-fourths of income of trust estate—Income Tax Act 1952, s 134(3). **Inchyra (Baron) v Jennings (Inspector of Taxes)** [1965] **2** 714, Ch D.
    Receipt of income in United Kingdom—
        Gift—Foreign trust—Income transmitted to England—Life tenant resident in England—Revocable mandate to transmit part of income to named persons in England—Income of life tenant—Income Tax Act 1918, Sch D, Case V, r 2, Miscellaneous Rules applicable to Sch D, r 1—Finance Act 1922, s 18. **Timpson's Exors v Yerbury** [1936] **1** 186, CA.

INCOME TAX (cont)—
  Foreign possessions (cont)—
    Receipt of income in United Kingdom (cont)—
      Gift—Gift complete in foreign country—Purchase of banker's draft in foreign country—Draft posted to drawer in United Kingdom—Whether liable to tax—Income Tax Act 1918, Sch D, Case V, r 2, Miscellaneous Rules Applicable to Sch D, Case 1. **Carter (Inspector of Taxes) v Sharon** [1936] **1** 720, KBD.
    Remittances from foreign possessions—
      Method of computations—Change in method—Applicability to remittances from foreign possessions—Finance Act 1926, ss 29(1), 36(2)—FinanceAct 1927, s 43, Sch VI, Part I. **Gibson v Mitchell (Inspector of Taxes)** [1942] **2** 51, CA.
    Residence in United Kingdom—
      Acquisition of residence in year of assessment—Sums received in United Kingdom in previous year—Assessment in respect of sums received in previous year—New resident—Income from same source in previous year—Finance Act 1926, s 29(1)(b)(iv). **Carter (Inspector of Taxes) v Sharon** [1936] **1** 720, KBD.
  Foreign securities—
    Income arising from securities out of United Kingdom—
      Income arising from—Payment by guarantor—Foreign bonds secured on foreign property—Principal debtor dissolved, assets frozen, and moratorium declared by foreign government—Guarantor dissolved and successor relieved by foreign government from succession to guarantee—Successor liable under English law—Whether payments by successor in England represented income arising from securities out of the United Kingdom—Income Tax Act 1952, ss 123, 170, Sch D, Case III. **Westminster Bank Exor and Trustee Co (Channel Islands) Ltd v National Bank of Greece SA** [1971] **1** 233, HL.
      Interest—Interest arising from securities—Foreign bonds—Interest coupons—Coupons issued to bondholders in lieu of interest—Sale of interest coupons—Liability of proceeds to tax. **Paget v IRC** [1938] **1** 392, CA.
      Interest—Interest arising from securities—Foreign bonds—Payment of interest suspended—Issue of funding bonds in place of interest—Sale of funding bonds—Liability to tax on proceeds of sale. **Cross v London & Provincial Trust Ltd** [1938] **1** 428, CA.
      Sale of cheques for dollars—Income credited to taxpayer's foreign account—Cheques drawn on account sold to English banks—Whether proceeds of sale income arising from securities out of United Kingdom. **Thomson (Inspector of Taxes) v Moyse** [1960] **3** 684, HL.
  Foreign tax—
    Credit against income tax. *See* Double taxation relief—Credit of foreign tax against income tax, *above*.
  Fraud—
    Fraud or wilful default—
      Additional assessment. *See* Additional assessment—Fraud or wilful default, *above*.
    Offence. *See* Offence—Fraud, *below*.
  Gambling transactions. *See* Profits—Trading receipts—Gambling transactions, *below*.
  General Commissioners—
    Jurisdiction—
      Penalty proceedings. *See* Penalty—Proceedings—Jurisdiction of General Commissioners, *below*.
      Sub-contractors in the construction industry—Taxpayer company making payment to uncertified sub-contractors without deduction on account of income tax—Collector not exempting taxpayer company from liability to pay the amount that ought to have been deducted—Assessment made on taxpayer company in respect of the amount—Commissioners discharging assessment on ground that failure to deduct had arisen through an error made in good faith—Whether commissioners had jurisdiction to discharge assessment—Finance Act 1971, ss 29,30—Taxes Management Act 1970, s 50(6)—Income Tax (Payments to Sub-Contractors in the Construction Industry) Regulations 1971 (SI 1971 No 1779), regs 6(3), 11(1). **Slater (Inspector of Taxes) v Richardson & Bottoms Ltd** [1979] **3** 439, Ch D.
    Power to summon witnesses—
      Subpoena duces tecum—Issue out of Crown Office—Whether issued as of course—Whether necessary to obtain leave of judge or master of Queen's Bench Division—Income Tax Act 1952, s 59(1)—RSC, Ord 37, r 30. **Soul v IRC** [1963] **1** 68, CA.
  Gift—
    Charitable body, gift to—
      European Community. *See* **European Union** (Freedom of movement—Capital—Principle of non-discrimination—Income tax—Deduction of gifts to bodies recognised as charitable).
    Foreign trust—
      Receipt in United Kingdom. *See* Foreign possessions—Receipt of income in United Kingdom—Gift—Foreign trust, *above*.
    Personal gift to employee. *See* Emoluments from office or employment—Personal gifts distinguished from emoluments, *above*.
    Trading receipt. *See* Profits—Trading receipts—Voluntary payment, *below*.
    Voluntary payment to employee. *See* Emoluments from office or employment—Voluntary payment, *above*.
  Government grant—
    Capital or income. *See* Capital or income receipts—Government grant, *above*.
  Government subsidy—
    Trading receipt. *See* Profits—Trading receipts—Government subsidy, *below*.
  Housekeeper—
    Relief. *See* Relief—Housekeeper, *below*.

INCOME TAX (cont)—
   Husband and wife—
      Collection from wife of tax assessed on husband and attributable to wife's income—
         Notice requiring wife to pay the tax she would have had to pay if separately assessed—Time limit—Assessment on husband in time—Non-payment by husband of surtax—Assessments to surtax for years 1961-62 and 1965-66—Notice served on wife in 1974 requiring her to pay that part of unpaid tax which would have been payable by her if she had been separately assessed—Whether time limit for making assessments applicable to notice—Whether notice effective—Taxes Management Act 1970, s 34—Income and Corporation Taxes Act 1970, s 40(2). **Johnson v IRC** [1978] **2** 65, CA.
      Divorce—
         Financial provision—Tax implications. See **Divorce** (Financial provision—Tax implications).
      Husband's liability—
         Wife's pre-nuptial income—Wife's income preceeding year of assessment acquired before marriage—Inclusion in husband's assessment—Income Tax Act 1918, Sch D, Cases IV and V, All Schedules Rules, r 16. **Elmhirst v IRC** [1937] **2** 349, KBD.
      Income of wife deemed income of husband—
         Annual payments to minors by wife under deed of covenant—Whether wife's annual payments deductible in computing husband's chargeable income—Income Tax Ordinance (Trinidad and Tobago) 1938, ss 10(1)(f), 18, 34(2). **Reynolds v Comr of Income Tax for Trinidad and Tobago** [1965] **3** 901, PC.
      Married person's allowance—
         Nullity decree—Effect—Additional assessment for years before decree—Assessment on basis nullity decree retrospective and husband only entitled to single person's allowance—Whether Revenue authorities entitled to make additional assessment—Income Tax Act 1918, s 125(1). **Dodworth v Dale** [1936] **2** 440, KBD.
      Non-resident husband—
         Place of assessment—Wife resident in United Kingdom—War loan interest and bank interest receivable by wife—Husband in United Kingdom part of each year—Wife treated as living with husband for income tax purposes—Husband liable to assessment when in United Kingdom—Income Tax Act 1918, s 102(3), Sch D, Miscellaneous Rules, r 4(5). **Duckworth v Lowe (Inspector of Taxes)** [1937] **2** 418, KBD.
      Relief—
         Wife's entitlement to benefit of repayment claims made in respect of her income assessed to tax on her husband—Income Tax Act 1952, ss 314, 341, 354(1)(2). **Cameron (decd), Re, Kingsley v IRC** [1965] **3** 474, Ch D.
      Wife's liability—
         Living separate from husband—Income from property abroad—Husband on military service overseas—Income Tax Act 1918, All Schedules Rules, r 16, proviso (2). **Nugent-Head v Jacob (Inspector of Taxes)** [1948] **1** 414, HL.
   Income—
      Capital or income receipts. See Capital or income receipts, above.
      Earned income relief. See Earned income relief, above.
      Emoluments from office or employment. See Emoluments from office or employment, above.
      Profits of trade, profession or vocation. See Profits, below.
      Undistributed income. See Undistributed income, below.
   Indemnity scheme for employees. See Emoluments from office or employment—Receipt 'from' employment—Payment for services—Indemnity scheme for employees, above.
   Industrial building or structure—
      Capital allowances. See **Capital allowances** (Industrial building or structure).
   Information—
      Failure to furnish information to commissioners—
         Penalty. See Penalty—Failure to furnish information to commissioners, below.
      Power to obtain information and documents—
         Informal investigation—Right of access to court—HMRC conducting informal investigation into claimants' tax affairs—Whether HMRC having power to conduct informal investigation—Whether judicial review of informal investigations only available in exceptional circumstances—Taxes Management Act 1970, s 9A—Commissioners for Revenue and Customs Act 2005, ss 5, 9(1)—Finance Act 2008, Sch 36. **R (on the application of JJ Management Consulting LLP) v Revenue and Customs Comrs** [2020] **4** 212, CA.
         Information notices—Validity—Issuing of third party notices for information relating to investigation of taxpayers by overseas tax authorities—Authorised officer of HMRC operating procedure for issuing third party notices to UK residents—Whether right to make representations or appear at application for authorisation of third party notices—Whether procedures breaching right to fair trial—Human Rights Act 1998, Sch 1, Pt I, arts 6, 8—Finance Act 2008, Sch 36, paras 2, 3. **R (on the application of Derrin Brother Properties Ltd) v Revenue and Customs Comrs (HSBC Bank plc and anor, interested parties)** [2016] **4** 203, CA.
      Production of documents—
         Documents relevant to taxpayer's liability to tax—Pending appeal—Notice by Board to taxpayer to produce wide range of documents—Taxpayer a solicitor—Documents including details of clients' affairs—Whether notice valid—Whether notice should have been served by the Board or by commissioners hearing appeal—Whether taxpayer able to challenge notice—Taxes Management Act 1970, ss 20(2), 51. **R v IRC, ex p Taylor (No 2)** [1990] **2** 409, CA.
         Documents relevant to taxpayer's or another's tax liability—Notice to produce documents—Duty of inspector—Duty to place before commissioner all relevant information—Judicial review of notice—Affidavit in support of application for judicial review—Whether challenge should be made to notice or to consent to notice—Taxes Management Act 1970, s 20. **Coombs (T C) & Co (a firm) v IRC** [1991] **3** 623, HL.

INCOME TAX (cont)—
  Information (cont)—
    Production of documents (cont)—
      Documents relevant to taxpayer's or another's tax liability—Notice to produce documents—Inspector requiring stockbrokers to deliver documents relating to tax liability of clients and former employee—Inspector's notice given with consent of commissioner—Stockbrokers challenging notice—Revenue refusing on grounds of confidentiality to reveal to court information placed by inspector before commissioner when seeking consent to notice—Whether commissioner presumed to have been satisfied that inspector had reasonable grounds for giving notice—Whether silence of Revenue justified—Whether notice valid—Taxes Management Act 1970, s 20. **Coombs (T C) & Co (a firm) v IRC** [1991] **3** 623, HL.
    Settlement. *See* Settlement—Information—Power of commissioners by notice to require information for specified purposes, *below*.
    Transfer of assets abroad—
      Power of commissioners to require information. *See* Avoidance—Transfer of assets abroad—Information, *above*.
  Inspector holding public local inquiry—
    Remuneration. *See* Emoluments from office or employment—Office—Inspector appointed to hold public local inquiry, *above*.
  Inspector of taxes—
    Discovery—
      Onus on inspector. *See* Additional assessment—Disclosure—Onus on inspector, *above*.
  Instalments—
    Purchase price payable in instalments—
      Capital or income receipts. *See* Capital or income receipts—Sale of property—Price payable in instalments, *above*.
  Insurance—
    Payment under policy—
      Capital or income. *See* Capital or income receipts—Insurance—Payment under policy, *above*.
    Premiums—
      Capital or income. *See* Capital or income receipts—Insurance—Premiums, *above*.
  Interest—
    Annual interest—
      Short loan interest—Computation of total income—Income tax not deductible from payments of interest—whether any right to deduct 'short' interest in compiling total income—Income Tax Act 1952, ss 221, 524(1), (2), Sch 6, paras 1, 2, Sch 24. **IRC v Frere** [1964] **3** 796, HL.
    Building society—
      Interest paid to depositors. *See* Building society—Interest and dividends paid to depositors, *above*.
    Circumstances in which payment constitutes interest—
      Necessity for sum of money by reference to which interest is to be ascertained—Requirement that sum should be due to person entitled to interest—Payments made by bank towards expenditure incurred in development of land—Payments made under agreement with developer—Agreement providing that 'interest' should be paid quarterly by developer to bank when total payments exceeded certain figure—Interest to be paid at an agreed rate by reference to total sums paid by bank—Sums paid by bank not in any sense 'due' to bank—Whether payments made to bank by developer under the agreement 'interest of the agreement money'—Income and Corporation Taxes Act 1970, ss 54(1), 109(2) (Sch D, Case III). **Euro Hotel (Belgravia) Ltd, Re** [1975] **3** 1075, Ch D.
    Damages—
      Claim for account—Award including certain sums as interest—Claim against trustees—No allegation of fraud or breach of trust—Whether interest element liable to tax as interest payable under contract. **IRC v Barnato** [1936] **2** 1176, CA.
      Interest on damages included in total award—Award of damages in Admiralty Court—Right to deduct income tax on interest—Whether interest element in damages 'interest of money'—Income Tax Act 1952, ss 169, 170. **Norseman, The** [1957] **2** 660, Admin Ct.
    Deduction of tax by payer—
      Adjustment between local authorities—Transfer of functions—Balance including sum called 'interest'—Whether interest or an element in calculation of capital sum. **Southport Corp v Lancashire CC** [1937] **2** 626, KBD.
      Annual sum not having genuinely the character of interest—Payments described and undertaken as being interest on debentures—Creation of debentures at requirement of controlling company—Annual interest payment of an amount exceeding debenture capital—Payment made soon after creation of debentures—Repayment claim—Income Tax Act 1952, s 341. **Ridge Securities Ltd v IRC** [1964] **1** 275, Ch D.
      Damages—Shipping—Collision cases. *See* **Shipping** (Damages in collision cases—Interest—Right to deduct income tax on interest).
      Failure to deduct tax—Effect—Interest on payments in advance of calls on shares—Rate of interest fixed by articles—Payment of full rate without deduction for tax—Presumption of agreement for payment at higher rate. **Noel v Trust and Agency Co of Australasia Ltd** [1937] **2** 673, Ch D.
      Foreign currency—Interest on debentures—Payable in foreign currency at fixed rate of exchange—Deduction of income tax—Income Tax Act 1918, All Schedules Rules, r 21—Finance Act 1924, s 33(1)—Finance Act 1927, s 26. **Rhokana Corp Ltd v IRC** [1938] **2** 51, HL.
      Mortgage interest—Interest on mortgage retained out of proceeds of sale—Mortgagee also solicitor acting in sale for mortgagor—Whether receipt as agent for mortgagor or as mortgagee—Person by or through whom payment made—Income Tax Act 1918, All Schedules Rules, r 21. **Howells v IRC** [1939] **3** 144, KBD.
      Mortgage interest—Mortgage of reversionary interest—Interest added to principal—Capitalisation of interest—Interest ultimately received as part of purchase price on sale of mortgaged property—Liability to tax. **IRC v Lawrence, Graham & Co** [1937] **2** 1, CA.
      Retention—Retention where interest payable wholly out of profits and gains brought into charge—Debenture stock charged to capital account under private Act—Interest—Right of railway company to retain income tax deducted from interest—Income Tax Act 1918, All Schedules Rules, rr 19, 21. **Central London Rly Co v IRC** [1936] **2** 375, HL.

INCOME TAX (cont)—
  Interest (cont)—
    Deduction of tax by payer (cont)—
      Retention—Retention where interest payable wholly out of profits and gains brought into charge—Losses brought forward greater than net profits for year—Whether brought into charge—Income Tax Act 1918, All Schedules Rules, r 19—Finance Act 1926, s 33. **Trinidad Petroleum Development Co Ltd v IRC** [1936] **3** 801, CA.
    Discounts—
      Refunding of debt. *See* Discounts—Refunding of debt, *above*.
    Earned income relief. *See* Earned income relief—Earned income, *above*.
    Foreign securities. *See* Foreign securities—Income arising from securities out of United Kingdom—Interest, *above*.
    Interest, annuities and other annual income—
      Profit income of recurring character—Compensation payments—Nationalisation of coal industry—Interim income payments in respect of compensation on nationalisation of coal industry—Payments in respect of specified periods—Whether income of those periods or of years of receipt—Income Tax Act 1918, Sch D, Case VI, r 2. **Whitworth Park Coal Co Ltd (in liq) v IRC** [1959] **3** 703, HL.
    Judgment debt—
      Interest included in total sum for which judgment given—Whether amount of award for interest constituting 'interest of money'—Income Tax Act 1918, Sch D, para 1(b), All Schedules Rules, r 21—Law Reform (Miscellaneous Provisions) Act 1934, s 3(1). **Riches v Westminster Bank Ltd** [1947] **1** 469, HL.
    Mortgage interest—
      Capitalisation of interest—Mortgage of reversionary interest—Addition of interest to capital not amounting to payment of interest—Reversion falling into possession—Funds handed over to trustees of mortgagee—Funds available in part for payment of interest—Income tax deducted by mortgagor at date of actual payment—Income Tax Act 1918, All Schedules Rules, r 21. **IRC v Oswald** [1945] **1** 641, HL.
      Deduction of tax by payer. *See* Interest—Deduction of tax by payer—Mortgage interest, *above*.
    Overdue tax—
      Tax recovered for purpose of making good loss of tax due to taxpayer's fault—Loss of tax—Meaning—Delay in payment—Payment ultimately secured—Delay because of taxpayer's failure to make return in reasonable time—Whether a loss of tax—Taxes Management Act 1970, s 88(1). **R v HM Inspector of Taxes, ex p Frank Rind Settlement Trustees** [1975] **1** 30, QBD.
    Payment to debenture holders—
      Interest charged to capital account under private Act—Whether 'payable wholly out of profits or gains brought into charge'—Right of company to retain income tax deducted from interest—All Schedules Rules, rr 19, 21. **Central London Rly Co v IRC** [1936] **2** 375, HL.
    Persons chargeable. *See* Persons chargeable—Profits and interest of money, *below*.
    Premiums on redemption—
      Premiums calculated according to annual rate—Company issuing registered convertible notes repayable with premiums at specified date—Notes not carrying interest—Premiums paid on redemption of notes—Premiums not intended to be accretion of capital—Income Tax Act 1918, Sch D, Case III, r 1. **Davies (Inspector of Taxes) v Premier Investment Co Ltd** [1945] **2** 681, KBD.
    Public revenue dividends—
      Deduction of tax. *See* Public revenue dividends—Deduction of tax—Interest, *below*.
    Receipt—
      Charge to tax. *See* Persons chargeable—Receipt of income—Person receiving income chargeable—Interest on money, *below*.
    Relief—
      Bank interest. *See* Relief—Bank interest, *below*.
      Interest on loan applied in lending money to close company—Close company incurring debt by overdrawing bank account—Debt guaranteed by taxpayer—Taxpayer required to implement guarantee—Payment of debt and interest thereon by taxpayer—Whether taxpayer entitled to relief on interest paid under guarantee—Finance Act 1974, Sch 1, para 9. **Hendy (Inspector of Taxes) v Hadley** [1980] **2** 554, Ch D.
      Loan for purchase or improvement of land—Bridging loan for house purchase—Taxpayer purchasing house intending to use it as his main residence—Purchase financed partly by bank loan—Taxpayer selling house without ever having used it as his main residence—Whether taxpayer entitled to relief for interest payments made on bank loan—Finance Act 1972, Sch 9, Pt I—Finance Act 1974, Sch 1, paras 4(1), 6(1). **Hughes (Inspector of Taxes) v Viner** [1985] **3** 40, Ch D.
      Pre-1970 loans—Debt incurred on or before 15th April 1969—Incurred—Contract to advance money for purchase of shares—Contract concluded before 15th April—Shares acquired by borrower's stockbroker before 15th April—Lenders instructing their bankers to settle with borrower's stockbroker after 15th April—Whether debt incurred by borrower before 15th April—Income and Corporation Taxes Act 1970, s 62(1). **Law v Coburn (Inspector of Taxes)** [1972] **3** 1115, Ch D.
    Right to deduct income tax on interest—
      Damages in collision cases. *See* **Shipping** (Damages in collision cases—Interest—Right to deduct income tax on interest).
    Tax reserve certificates—
      Interest on certificates—Distribution to shareholders—Certificates surrendered in payment of tax interest being credited—Sums equal to interest earned distributed to shareholders—Whether tax payable on sums distributed—Finance Act 1942, s 29(1). **Hutton v IRC** [1953] **2** 93, Ch D.
    Value payments under war damage legislation—
      Interest on value payments—Whether 'interest ... payable out of any public revenue by any public office or department of the Crown'—Whether chargeable under Sch C or Sch D—Income Tax Act 1918, Sch C and fourth r 1 Sch D r 1(b)—Finance Act 1939, s 14(8)—War Damage Act 1943, s 3. **IRC v Bew Estates Ltd** [1956] **2** 210, Ch D.

INCOME TAX (cont)—
  Interest (cont)—
    Yearly interest of money—
      Company in administration—Payment of statutory interest in administration—Whether payment of statutory interest amounting to yearly interest—Income Tax Act 2007, s 874—Insolvency (England and Wales) Rules 2016, SI 2016/1024, r 14.23(7). **Revenue and Customs Comrs v Joint Administrators of Lehman Brothers International** [2019] 2 559, SC.
      Loan repayable on demand—Interest on loan—Loan secured by mortgage of dwelling-house—Loan in nature of investment—Whether 'yearly interest of money'—Income Tax Act 1952, s 169. **Corinthian Securities Ltd v Cato** [1969] 3 1168, CA.
  Investment company—
    Actual income from all sources—
      Deduction—Covenanted donation to charity—Payments under seven year covenant—If payments made by individual this would fall to be treated as income of individual for purpose of computing total income—Whether payments an allowable deduction from income liable to apportionment—Income Tax Act 1952, ss 262(2), proviso (a), 415(1). **Coathew Investments Ltd v IRC** [1966] 1 1032, HL.
      Estate or trading income excluded—Income in part consisting of estate or trading income—Capital allowances and loss reliefs—Apportionment—Whether allowances and reliefs 'outgoings'—Whether allowances and reliefs should be allocated rateably between estate or trading income and other income—Income Tax Act 1952, s 262(4). **Leconfield Estate Co (now Egremont Estate Co) v IRC** [1970] 3 273, Ch D.
    Apportionment of income—
      Appeal—Right of appeal—Member—Whole income apportioned to member—No appeal by company against either directions or apportionments—Appeal by member—Aggrieved person—Right of appeal confined to company only—Finance Act 1922, s 21, Sch I, paras 1, 2, 3, 10—Finance Act 1936, s 19(5)—Finance Act 1939, ss 14, 15. **Burston v IRC (No 2)** [1945] 1 687, KBD.
      Apportionment according to members' interests in assets of company—Apportionment in proportion to dividend rights—Redeemable preference shares—Whether additional interest from contributions to redemption fund—Finance Act 1922, s 21(1), (8), Sch I, para 8. **Wigram Family Settled Estates Ltd (in liq) v IRC** [1958] 1 338, HL.
      Apportionment according to members' interests in assets of company—Apportionment to members on register of company—Shares registered in names of trustees—Apportionment made to trustees—Assessment on beneficiaries—Finance Act 1922, s 21—Finance Act 1937, s 14(2), (3)—Finance Act 1938, s 38(2), (3), s 41(4)(a)(ii)—Finance Act 1939, s 38. **Penang and General Investment Trust Ltd v IRC** [1943] 1 514, HL.
      Apportionment according to members' interests in assets of company—Interest 'corresponding to' interest in assets of company—Assets available for distribution among members in event of a winding up—Method of apportionment of income to be adopted—Finance Act 1937, s 14(3). **IRC v Fred's Securities Co** [1939] 3 241, KBD.
      Facts on which apportionment based—Facts existing at any time during year—Apportionment to one member—All income apportioned by Special Commissioners to one member—Whether facts to be considered in apportioning income are those existing at the end of the year—Whether commissioners having jurisdiction to direct that income of company is deemed to be income of member—Finance Act 1922, s 21, Sch I, paras 4, 9—Finance Act 1936, s 20(1)—Finance Act 1939, ss 14(1), 15(2), (3). **Fendoch Investment Trust Co v IRC** [1945] 2 140, HL.
      Non-member—Apportionment of whole income to non-member—Controlling interest in company held by another company of which apportionee in control—Apportionee governing director of both companies—Settlement by apportionee for benefit of wife and children—Power of apportionee to remove any trustee at will and to appoint new trustees—Whether apportionee to be treated as a member of the first company—Finance Act 1922, s 21—Finance Act 1939, ss 15(1), (6), 16. **Chamberlain v IRC** [1945] 2 351, CA.
      Part of income—Apportionment of 'such part' as appears appropriate—Whether power to apportion whole income to one person—Finance Act 1922, s 21—Finance Act 1939, s 15. **Chamberlain v IRC** [1945] 2 351, CA.
    Direction and apportionment—
      Compellability of direction—Profits tax, if payable, exceeding actual income from all sources—Appeal against profits tax—Meaning of 'payable'—When profits tax 'falls to be computed'—Right of election relieving from profits tax—Power dependent on issue of surtax direction—Whether mandamus to commissioners to issue direction should be granted—Income Tax Act 1952, s 245, s 262(1)—Finance Act 1952, s 68(1)—Finance Act 1947, s 31(3). **Special Comrs of Income Tax v Linsleys (Established 1894) Ltd** [1958] 1 343, HL.
      Discretion of commissioners—Matters to be taken into consideration—Relief—Power to give such relief as appears just—Effect of direction that taxpayer charged to surtax on income twice over—Finance Act 1922, s 21(1)—Finance Act 1927, s 34—Finance Act 1939, s 14. **Gollin v IRC** [1943] 1 346, CA.
    Income available for distribution—
      Loan creditor—Sums available for repayment or redemption of loan—Apportionment of income—Loan repayable by stated instalments—Option to redeem larger sum on notice—Whether commissioners entitled to apportion to loan creditors greater sum than that actually paid to redeem debt—Finance Act 1922, s 21, Sch I—Finance Act 1936, s 20. **IRC v Kered Ltd** [1939] 1 45, CA.
    Income consisting mainly of investment income—
      Investment income—Company carrying on business as dealer in stocks and shares—Dividend stripping operation—Whether dividends obtained from dividend stripping operation trading income or investment income—Whether company an 'investment company'—Income Tax Act 1952, ss 257(2), 525(1). **IRC v F S Securities Ltd** [1964] 2 691, HL.
      Investment income—Income from granting of copyright licences—Licences for representation of a fictional character by dolls, toys, etc—Whether company carrying on a trade, although having no separate office and its manager being remunerated by another company—Income Tax Act 1952, ss 257, 525, 526. **Noddy Subsidiary Rights Co Ltd v IRC** [1966] 3 459, Ch D.

INCOME TAX (cont)—
Investment company (cont)—
Income consisting mainly of investment income (cont)—
Test to be applied—Company incurring losses but still receiving investment income—Whether an investment company—Finance Act 1936, s 20(1). **FPH Finance Trust Ltd (in liq) v IRC** [1944] **1** 653, HL.
Management expenses. See Management expenses—Investment company, below.
Person treated as member of company—
Power of person to secure that income applied for his benefit—Power to secure—Lawful means—Taxpayer trustee of shares in company—Consent of beneficiaries necessary before taxpayer could secure that assets or income applied for his benefit—Finance Act 1922, s 21—Finance Act 1937, s 14(2)—Finance Act 1939, ss 14, 15. **IRC v LB (Holdings) Ltd** [1946] **1** 598, HL.
Power of person to secure that income applied for his benefit—Trust—Taxpayer trustee—Trust fund of shares for maintenance of taxpayer's children—Trustees' discretion subject to taxpayer's approval—Taxpayer having controlling interest in company—Whether open to commissioners to find that taxpayer having power to secure that income would be applied directly or indirectly for his benefit—Finance Act 1939, ss 14(4), 15(3). **Hulme Estate Co Ltd (in liq) v IRC** [1946] **2** 516, CA.
Trading receipts. See Profits—Trading receipts—Investment company, below.
Investment income—
Special charge. See Special charge—Investment income, below.
Surcharge—
Payments made by covenantor out of earned income. See Settlement—Income arising under a settlement—Covenant—Payments made by covenantor out of earned income, below.
Irrevocable settlement—
Children. See Settlement—Children—Irrevocable settlement, below.
Isolated transaction—
Profits. See Profits—Isolated transaction, below.
Trading. See Trade—Adventure in nature of trade, below.
Jamaica. See **Jamaica** (Income tax).
Know-how—
Consideration for imparting know-how—
Capital or income receipt. See Capital or income receipts—Know-how, above.
Land—
Adventure in the nature of trade. See Trade—Adventure in nature of trade—Land, below.
Annual value—
Allowances—Maintenance—Depreciation of value of lease—Premiums on insurance policy to produce sum equivalent to purchase price—Income Tax Act 1918, Sch A, No 1(1), No V, r 8(1). **Pearce v Doulton (Inspector of Taxes)** [1947] **1** 378, KBD.
Allowances—Private road—Cost of local authority making up private road—Frontager not owning private road—Not part of maintenance and repair of frontager's dwelling-house—Income Tax Act 1952, s 101(1). **Davidson v Deeks (Inspector of Taxes)** [1956] **3** 612, Ch D.
Allowances—Repairs—Repair of lift—Block of offices—Assessment on landlord—One entire house or tenement—Gross annual value—Allowance made in ascertaining gross annual value although the authorised deductions for repairs granted—Income Tax Act 1918, Sch A, No V, rr 7, 8, No VII, r 8(c)—Finance Act 1936, s 22. **Pearl Assurance Co Ltd v O'Callaghan (Inspector of Taxes)** [1943] **1** 624, CA.
Deduction in computing profits. See Deduction in computing profits—Annual value of land, above.
Profits from ancillary activities—Aerodrome—Occupiers deriving profits from activities ancillary to main purpose of aerodrome—Whether covered by Sch A assessment—Income Tax Act 1918, Schs A, B, C. **Croft v Sywell Aerodrome Ltd** [1942] **1** 110, CA.
Relief—Air raid protection works—Rent or other consideration for lease greater than would otherwise have been—Rent or other consideration—Air-raid shelter constructed by landlord—Tenant to pay 8 per cent of cost each year for 12 years—Whether payments constituting rent or other consideration for lease—Finance Act 1938, s 17(1)(a), proviso. **Associated London Properties Ltd v Williams (Inspector of Taxes)** [1948] **1** 442, CA.
Rent—Deductions by occupier from rent—Sub-tenants paying rents to Inland Revenue—Whether landlord is an 'occupier' entitled to deduct from rent due to superior landlord—Income Tax Act 1918, Sch A, No VII, r 8, No VIII, r 9—Finance Act 1941, s 12, Sch I, Parts II, III. **Thorley v Payne** [1943] **1** 354, KBD.
Rent—Insurance premium—Additional sum, being insurance premium, made payable as rent—Whether commissioners entitled to take premiums into account in assessing annual value—Income Tax Act 1918, sched A, No IV, r 1(a), (b). **House Property and Investment Trust Ltd v Kneen (Inspector of Taxes)** [1938] **2** 514, KBD.
Rules for estimating value—Sand pit—Assessment—Amount of rackrent or preceding years profits—Farmer permitting various contractors to remove sand from land for payment per ton—Whether whole farm to be assessed on rackrent basis—Income Tax Act 1918, Sch A, No III, r 3. **Russell (Inspector of Taxes) v Scott** [1948] **2** 1, HL.
Valuation of property—'New property'—Part of farm sold for development—Use as gravel pit—Whether separate valuation or apportioned part of farm value—Income Tax Act 1952, s 82, para 2 ss 84(3), 108. **Welford Gravels Ltd v De Voil (Inspector of Taxes)** [1963] **2** 1039, HL.
Artificial transactions—
Tax avoidance. See Avoidance—Artificial transactions in land, above.
Compulsory acquisition—
Assessment of compensation for disturbance. See **Compulsory purchase** (Compensation—Assessment—Compensation for disturbance—Deduction in respect of income tax).
Excess rent. See Profits—Excess rent, below.
Maintenance, repairs, insurance management—
Allowance for costs of maintenance etc—Loss due to dishonesty—Misappropriations by agent collecting rents—Whether a cost of management—Income Tax Act 1952, ss 101(1), 175(3). **Pyne (Inspector of Taxes) v Stallard-Penoyre (Exor of S B Stallard-Penoyre (decd))** [1965] **1** 487, Ch D.

INCOME TAX (cont)—
  Land (cont)—
    Occupation of land—
      Occupier—Bankruptcy of taxpayer—Trustee in bankruptcy going into possession of land—Only
      creditor paid off and trustee going out of possession—Whether taxpayer 'occupier' of land during
      bankruptcy. **Joly v Pinhoe Nurseries Ltd** [1936] **1** 841, KBD.
      Occupier—Trustees of golf course on common—Any member of public entitled to play upon
      payment of fee—Whether trustees in occupation of golf course—Income Tax Act 1918, Sch B.
      Mitcham Golf Course Trustees v Ereaut (Inspector of Taxes) [1937] **3** 450, KBD.
      Unoccupied land—Person having use of land—Grounds of mansion house—House and grounds
      vacated—Owner of house entitled to use of grounds—Whether owner 'having the use of'
      grounds—Whether owner chargeable as occupier of grounds—Income Tax Act 1918, Sch A,
      No VII, rr 1, 2, 4. **Bertram v Wightman (Inspector of Taxes)** [1936] **2** 487, KBD.
      Widow—Widow continuing to live in husband's house after his death and before residue of estate
      ascertained—Whether occupation in own right or as representative of executors—Income Tax Act
      1918, Sch A. **IRC v Lady Wolverton** [1940] **2** 327, KBD.
    Person chargeable—
      Landlord—House or building let in different apartments or tenements—House containing separate
      flats—Landlord responsible for common staircase—Whether tenant chargeable on ground house
      'divided into distinct properties'—Whether landlord chargeable on ground house a 'house or
      building let in different apartments or tenements'—Income Tax Act 1918, Sch A, No VII, rr 8(c), 12.
      Gatehouse v Vise (Inspector of Taxes) [1957] **2** 183, CA.
      Landlord—Property let for less than year—Rent including sum calculated to cover capital cost of
      property after 30 years—Right to terminate tenancy on giving seven days' notice—Tenant entitled
      to conveyance of property at expiration of 30 years—Instalments sufficient to cover capital cost of
      property reserved as rent—Relationship of landlord and tenant—Owner-occupier—Whether
      vendor chargeable as landlord—Income Tax Act 1918, Sch A, No VII, r 8(b). **Ellis & Sons Third**
      Amalgamated Properties Ltd v Jackson [1940] **4** 409, KBD.
    Rents and other receipts—
      Premium—Deduction from premiums and rent received—Premium treated as rent—Deduction
      from excess rents received by lessee from sub-lessees—Premium payable to lessor as
      consideration for the variation or waiver of the terms of a lease—Lessee committing breaches of
      covenant—Lessee thereby forfeiting option to renew lease—Lessor agreeing to accept payment
      of sum by lessee as consideration for restoration of lessee's right to exercise option—Clause
      providing for forfeiture of option not thereby modified in respect of any future or unascertained
      breaches of covenant—Whether sum payable as consideration for the waiver of terms of the
      lease—Whether lessee entitled to deduct from rents received by him sum paid to lessor—Finance
      Act 1963, s 22(4), Sch 4, paras 8, 9. **Banning v Wright (Inspector of Taxes)** [1972] **2** 987, HL.
    Sale—
      Capital or income receipt. *See* Capital or income receipts—Sale of property—Land, *above*.
      Trading receipts. *See* Profits—Trading receipts—Land, *below*.
  Law reports—
    Citation in revenue cases. *See* **Practice** (Citation of cases—Reports—Revenue cases).
  Legal costs—
    Deduction in computing profits. *See* Deduction in computing profits—Legal costs, *above*.
  Liability—
    Documents relevant to taxpayer's liability to tax—
      Production. *See* Information—Production of documents—Documents relevant to taxpayer's liability
      to tax, *above*.
    Generally. *See* Charge to tax, *above*.
    Statutory agent of foreign company—
      Trinidad and Tobago. *See* **Trinidad and Tobago** (Income tax—Dividend paid by cancellation of credit
      due to company from foreign company—Liability of company to tax as statutory agent of foreign
      company).
    Tax return, as to. *See* Return—Liability to make return, *below*.
  Life assurance companies—
    Management expenses. *See* Management expenses—Life assurance company, *below*.
    Profits—
      Computation—Receipts to be brought into account—Long-term business fund—Decrease in market
      value of assets—Sums brought into account during relevant accounting periods where losses
      sustained—Whether sums brought into account having to be taken into account—Whether sums
      brought into account constituting increase in value or reflecting allowable loss—Meaning of
      'increase in value [of] assets'—Finance Act 1989, s 83(2)(b). **Scottish Widows plc v Revenue and**
      Customs Comrs [2012] **1** 379, SC.
  Liquidation of company—
    Transaction in securities—
      Tax advantage in consequence of transaction. *See* Tax advantage—Transaction in securities—Tax
      advantage in consequence of transaction—Combined effect of transaction and liquidation of
      company, *below*.
    Undistributed income. *See* Undistributed income—Liquidation of company, *below*.
  Loan—
    Employee, to—
      Loan scheme for course of training. *See* Emoluments from office or employment—Reward for
      services—Loan scheme for course of training, *above*.
    Repayment in kind—
      Profits. *See* Profits—Profit in kind—Loan for building development—Loan repaid by conveyance of
      ground rents, *below*.
    Scholarship—
      Exemption from tax. *See* Exemption—Scholarship income—Loan agreement, *above*.
  Loss—
    Deduction in computing profits. *See* Deduction in computing profits—Loss connected with or arising
    out of trade, *above*.
    Relief. *See* Loss relief, *below*.

INCOME TAX (cont)—

Loss of office—

Compensation—

Emoluments from office or employment. *See* Emoluments from office or employment—Compensation—Loss of office, *above*.

Loss of tax—

Tax recovered for purpose of making good loss of tax—

Interest. *See* Interest—Overdue tax—Tax recovered for purpose of making good loss of tax due to taxpayer's fault, *above*.

Loss relief—

Carry forward of losses—

Loss for initial accounting period—Profits in subsequent years—Assessment for second and third years based on same period, viz first year's trading—Part of profits of second accounting period apportioned to first year's trading period—Apportioned amount taken into account in reduction of initial loss for each of the second and third years of assessment—Scottish authority followed—Income Tax Act 1952, ss 155, 342. **Westward Television Ltd v Hart (Inspector of Taxes)** [1968] **3** 91, CA.

Six following years of assessment—Meaning—Finance Act 1926, s 33(1). **Harling v Celynen Collieries Workmen's Institute** [1940] **3** 446, CA.

Claim—

Enforcement—Procedure—Originating summons—Court asked to determine company's entitlement on assumption company a dealer in stocks and shares—Summons struck out—Company required to pursue claim by means prescribed by statute—Commissioners to determine initial question whether transactions in question trading transactions—Income Tax Act 1952, s 341. **Argosam Finance Co Ltd v Oxby (Inspector of Taxes)** [1964] **3** 561, CA.

Repayment claim—Tax deducted from dividends on shares—Ownership of shares—Acquisition without receiver's authority—Ratification bv successor receiver—Validity—Income Tax Act 1952, s 341. **Lawson (Inspector of Taxes) v Hosemaster Machine Co Ltd** [1966] **2** 944, CA.

Repayment claim—Tax deducted from dividends on shares—Title to shares—Need to show benefical title to shares—Absence of actual or ostensible authority to acquire the shares on taxpayer company's behalf—Receiver already appointed by debenture-holders—Purchase subsequently ratified by subsequent receiver appointed by new debenture-holders—Whether purported ratification valid—Income Tax Act 1952, s 341. **Lawson (Inspector of Taxes) v Hosemaster Machine Co Ltd** [1966] **2** 944, CA.

Validity—Limited partnerships claiming relief for trading losses—Individual partners seeking relief for their share of the partnership losses—HMRC opening enquiry into partnerships' returns—Allowable losses in partnerships' returns reduced by compromise agreement—HMRC notifying partners that carry-back claims in their partnership returns would be amended in line with lower figures in partnership compromise agreement—Partners arguing HMRC were obliged to open enquiries into their returns and were time-barred from so doing—Whether HMRC entitled to amend partners' individual returns—Taxes Management Act 1970, ss 8, 9, 9A, 42, Schs 1A, 1B. **R (on the application of De Silva) v Revenue and Customs Comrs** [2018] **1** 280, SC.

Validity—Share loss relief—Claim made in tax return for year prior to year in which loss occurred—Whether claim valid—Taxes Management Act 1970, Sch 1B—Income Tax Act 2007, ss 23, 132. **R (on the application of Derry) v Revenue and Customs Comrs** [2019] **4** 127, SC.

Validity—Taxpayers seeking to carry back losses—Taxpayers appealing against striking out of proceedings—Whether HMRC obliged to give effect to carry-back claims—Whether proceedings to be struck out—Taxes Management Act 1970, s 9A, Schs 1A, 1B. **Knibbs v Revenue and Customs Comrs** [2020] **3** 116, CA.

Trade—

Share-dealing—Company dealing in shares and securities—Purchase of shares in other companies—Profit to be made by recovery of income tax on loss claims—Companies' dividends depreciating value of shares—Dividends to accrue over period of years—Not an adventure or concern in the nature of trade—Shares not to be regarded as stock-in-trade—Income Tax Act 1952, s 341. **Bishop (Inspector of Taxes) v Finsbury Securities Ltd** [1966] **3** 105, HL.

Share-dealing—Company dealing in shares and securities—Taxpayer company purchased shares in F Ltd, which had a short lease of property at a low rent during the first three years—Dividends paid by F Ltd on its shares from rent received under sub-lease of property—Taxpayer company wrote down value of shares in F Ltd correspondingly—Resulting loss was basis of repayment claim—Complicated transaction which involved no profit unless tax repayment claim succeeded, and involved holding F Ltd's shares for several years—Whether purchase of shares was a transaction in the trade of dealing in shares—Income Tax Act 1952, s 341. **Cooper (Inspector of Taxes) v Sandiford Investments Ltd** [1967] **3** 835, Ch D.

Share-dealing—Company dealing in shares—Group's property companies' unrealised profits—Properties worth more than book values—Scheme to reduce income tax on profits as realised—Forward dividend strip—Transfer of properties to four-year life company—Sale in second year of life—Purchase of four-year company's shares by taxpayer company—Declaration of dividends by four-year company—Diminution in value of its shares—Taxpayer company dealer in shares—Loss claim on basis of diminished value—Whether transaction in course of trade or venture in nature of trade—Income Tax Act 1952, s 341. **Thomson (Inspector of Taxes) v Gurneville Securities Ltd** [1971] **3** 1071, HL.

Share-dealing—Company dealing in shares—Purchase of shares of other companies—Profit to be made by recovery of income tax on loss claim—Other company's dividend depreciating value of shares—Transaction dividend-stripping—Tax recovery device not in the nature of trade—Loss claim rejected—Income Tax Act 1952, s 341. **F A & A B Ltd v Lupton (Inspector of Taxes)** [1971] **3** 948, HL.

INCOME TAX (cont)—
  Loss relief (cont)—
    Trade (cont)—
      Share-dealing—Purpose of transaction to obtain loss relief—Merchant company having incurred losses changed to finance company trading in shares—Single purchase of shares in another company in year of assessment—Dividend then declared and received by finance company—Shares sold at loss after dividend declared—Dividend stripping operation—Purpose of transaction to set off losses (including losses on merchant trading) against divident so received—Whether transaction of purchase and sale of shares 'trading'—Other financial share dealings in next year of assessment—Income Tax Act 1952, s 341. **Griffiths (Inspector of Taxes) v Harrison (JP) (Watford) Ltd** [1962] **1** 909, HL.
      Share-dealing—Trade and stock-in-trade—Company dealing in shares and securities—Purchase of shares in associated company—Receipt of dividends on shares—Writing down of value of shares correspondingly—Resultant loss founding repayment claim—Activities constituting trading—Income Tax Act 1952, s 341. **Johns (Inspector of Taxes) v Wirsal Securities Ltd** [1966] **1** 865, Ch D.
      Share-dealing—Transactions in the course of trade—Company a dealer in shares—Transactions with subsidiary companies—Dividend stripping operations—Sale of depreciated shares at an undervalue—Device to secure repayment of tax from Inland Revenue—Whether transactions as a whole could be treated as being in the course of trade—Income Tax Act 1952, s 341. **Ridge Securities Ltd v IRC** [1964] **1** 275, Ch D.
      Sideways loss relief—Taxpayer claiming loss relief in respect of investment in soccer academy—HMRC disallowing claim—Whether investment activities forming part of trade—Whether assumed trade carried on on commercial basis—Income Tax Act 2007, ss 64, 66, 74. **Anderson v Revenue and Customs Comrs** [2018] **4** 338, UT.
  Lump sum payment—
    Trading receipt. *See* Profits—Trading receipts—Lump sum payment, *below.*
  Machinery—
    Capital allowances. *See* **Capital allowances** (Machinery or plant).
    Profits from letting. *See* Profits—Profits not otherwise charged—Profits from letting machinery and plant, *below.*
    Wear and tear—
      Deduction in computing profits. *See* Deduction in computing profits—Wear and tear of machinery or plant, *above.*
  Maintenance—
    Arrears—
      Deduction of tax. *See* Annual payment—Deduction of tax—Past income—Arrears—Weekly payments under maintenance agreement between husband and wife, *above.*
    Education or training—
      Maintenance order including element in respect of school fees—Tax relief. *See* **Minor** (Maintenance—Education or training—Maintenance order including element in respect of school fees).
    Maintenance order. *See* Annual payment—Order of court—Maintenance order, *above.*
  Malaysia. *See* **Malaysia** (Income tax).
  Management expenses—
    Expenses allowable under schedule for repairs, maintenance etc—
      Investment company—Business making investments in real property—Payments to surveyors—Expenses for which relief might be claimed or allowed under Sch A, No V, rr 7, 8—Whether claim for relief as management expenses permissible—Income Tax Act 1918, s 33. **London and Northern Estates Co Ltd v Harris (Inspector of Taxes)** [1937] **3** 252, KBD.
    Investment company—
      Directors' fees—Company's surplus for year distributed among directors as fees—Finding by Special Commissioners that only a proportion of fees management expenses—Finding conclusive—Income Tax Act 1952, s 425(1)(2). **Berry (L G) Investments Ltd v Attwooll (Inspector of Taxes)** [1964] **2** 126, Ch D.
      Dividends subject to double taxation relief—Income bearing tax at different rates—Amount of tax repayable—Income Tax Act 1952, s 425(1). **Shell Petroleum Co Ltd v Jones (Inspector of Taxes)** [1971] **2** 569, HL.
      Expenses of changing investments—Brokerage and stamp duty—Whether 'expenses of management'—Income Tax Act 1918, s 33(1). **Capital and National Trust Ltd v Golder (Inspector of Taxes)** [1949] **2** 956, CA.
      Expenses of raising or re-arranging loan capital—Income Tax Act 1918, s 33(1). **London County Freehold and Leasehold Properties Ltd v Sweet (Inspector of Taxes)** [1942] **2** 212, KBD.
    Life assurance company—
      Expenses of changing investments—Brokerage and stamp duties—Whether 'expenses of management'—Income Tax Act 1918, s 33(1). **Sun Life Assurance Society v Davidson (Inspector of Taxes)** [1957] **2** 760, HL.
  Married person's allowance. *See* Husband and wife—Married person's allowance, *above.*
  Married woman—
    Tax advantage. *See* Tax advantage—Married woman, *below.*
  Meals—
    Deduction of cost of meals in computing profits. *See* Deduction in computing profits—Expenses wholly and exclusively laid out for purposes of trade—Meals, *above.*
    Deduction of expenses of meals—
      Emoluments from office or employment. *See* Emoluments from office or employment—Expenses wholly, exclusively and necessarily incurred—Meals, *above.*
  Meaning of 'income tax'—
    Surtax—
      Partnership agreement—Covenant by partners to discharge outgoing partner's liability for 'income tax'—Whether including surtax. **Conway v Wingate** [1952] **1** 782, CA.
  Medical expenses—
    Deduction in computing profits. *See* Deduction in computing profits—Expenses wholly and exclusively laid out for purposes of trade—Medical expenses, *above.*

INCOME TAX (cont)—
    Mining rents—
        Easement—
            Occupied in connection with concern—Rent payable in respect of easement—Licence to extract gravel on making tonnage payments—Contractors needing gravel to construct runways at aerodrome—Agreement with landowner whereby contractors granted right to take surface gravel—Whether licence an 'easement'—Whether gravel pit a 'concern'—Whether tax deductible from payments by contractors to landowner—Income Tax Act 1918, s 237, All Schedules Rules, r 19, Sch A, No III, rr 1, 2, 3, Sch D, Case I—Finance Act 1934, s 21. **Mosley v Wimpey (George) & Co Ltd** [1945] **1** 674, CA.
        Mines—
            Dumps of waste material—Minerals recovered from dumps—Whether dumps had become part of the land—Whether dumps a 'mine'—payments at a rate per ton worked—Whether rent or payment in respect of an easement—Income Tax Act 1952, ss 180(1)(2)(3), 82, Sch A, para 1(b). **Rogers (Inspector of Taxes) v Longsdon** [1966] **2** 49, Ch D.
        Right to let down surface—
            Payments in respect of right—Acreage payment as liquidated damages—Whether right an 'easement'—Whether payments 'rent'—Finance Act 1934, s 21(4)(b)(c). **Fitzwilliam's (Earl) Collieries Co v Phillips (Inspector of Taxes)** [1943] **2** 346, HL.
            Payments in respect of right—Minimum yearly payments—Payment for benefit over or derived from land—Not deductible in computing profits or gains—Finance Act 1934, s 21. **IRC v New Sharlston Collieries Co Ltd** [1937] **1** 86, CA.
    Mistake—
        Additonal assessment. *See* Additional assessment—Disclosure—Mistake, *above*.
    Mutual life insurance company—
        New Zealand. *See* **New Zealand** (Income tax—Mutual life insurance company).
    Mutuality principle. *See* Profits—Mutuality principle, *below*.
    Neglect—
        Additional assessment. *See* Additional assessment—Neglect, *above*.
    New Zealand—
        Assessment out of time. *See* Assessment—Assessment out of time—New Zealand, *above*.
        Generally. *See* **New Zealand** (Income tax).
    Non-resident—
        Assessment in name of agent—
            Exemption—Broker—General commission agent—Meaning of 'general commission agent'—Company virtually sole agent of non-resident—Lack of generality of custom—Many non-broker like activities—Income Tax Act 1952, ss 370, 373(1) proviso. **Fleming (Inspector of Taxes) v London Produce Co Ltd** [1968] **2** 975, Ch D.
        Calculation of relief—
            British subject on service abroad—Computation of proportionate allowances—Income consisting of army pay, colonial allowance, and income from New Zealand sources—Income Tax Act 1918, Sch D, Case V, r 2—Finance Act 1920, s 24. **MacKillop v IRC** [1943] **2** 215, CA.
    Notional expense. *See* Deduction in computing profits—Expense or disbursement—Notional expense, *above*.
    Offence—
        Fraud—
            Suspected offence—Warrant to enter and seize documents—Validity—Warrant not specifying offence suspected but drawn in general terms of provision empowering issue of warrant—Proceedings for judicial review of warrant and seizure—Whether warrant ought to specify nature of suspected offence—Whether Revenue sole arbiter that reasonable belief documents required as evidence of an offence existed—Whether Revenue entitled to withhold grounds for seizure—Whether in proceedings for judicial review court entitled to make final declaration that seizure unlawful where action claiming damages for unlawful seizure pending—Taxes Management Act 1970, s 200(1)(3) (as inserted by the Finance Act 1976, s 57(1), Sch 6)—RSC Ord 53. **IRC v Rossminster Ltd** [1979] **3** 385, QBD and CA; [1980] **1** 80, HL.
    Office—
        Compensation for loss of office—
            Emolument from office. *See* Emoluments from office or employment—Compensation—Loss of office, *above*.
        Office or employment under the Crown. *See* Office or employment under the Crown, *below*.
        What constitutes an office—
            Emoluments from office or employment. *See* Emoluments from office or employment—Office, *above*.
    Office or employment under the Crown—
        Emoluments payable out the public revenue of the United Kingdom—
            Taxpayer appointed to corps of specialists by government department—Taxpayer assigned to advise Fiji government—Taxpayer's salary paid by government department—United Kingdom government recovering contribution from Fiji government equal to Fiji rate for taxpayer's office—Whether taxpayer holding office or employment under the Crown—Whether taxpayer's salary payable out of the public revenue of the United Kingdom—Income and Corporation Taxes Act 1970, s 184(3)(a). **Caldicott v Varty (Inspector of Taxes)** [1976] **3** 329, Ch D.
    Option—
        Profit on exercise of option—
            Investment company—Option to acquire shares at par. *See* Profits—Trading receipts—Investment company—Option to acquire shares at par, *below*.
        Year of assessment—
            Grant of option to employee. *See* Emoluments from office or employment—Year of assessment—Option to purchase shares, *above*.
    Overdue tax—
        Interest. *See* Interest—Overdue tax, *above*.

INCOME TAX (cont)—
Partnership—
  Assessment in partnership name—
    Effect—Additional assessment following death of one of partners—Whether assessment effective against surviving partner—Whether effective against deceased partner's executors—Income Tax Act 1952, s 144—Finance Act 1960, s 63(3). **Harrison (Inspector of Taxes) v Willis Bros** [1965] **3** 753, CA.
  Change in partnership—
    Admission of new partner—Assessment of profits—'Succession'—Continuance of business—Power of commissioners to adjust assessment—Income Tax Act 1918, Sch D, Cases I and II, rr 8, 9, 10, 11—Finance Act 1926, s 32. **Income Tax Comrs v Gibbs** [1942] **1** 415, HL.
    Discontinuance of trade—Election to treat old trade as discontinued—Limits of right of continuing partner to relief in respect of losses in old trade—Finance Act 1926, ss 32(1), 33. **Batty v Schroder (Baron)** [1939] **3** 299, KBD.
Pay as you earn system—
  Deduction of tax by employer—
    Failure to deduct tax—Employee receiving emoluments knowing that employer has wilfully failed to deduct tax—Knowing—Wilfully—Director receiving emoluments over a number of years without deduction of tax—Whether material on which commissioners could reasonably form opinion that employee had received emoluments knowing that employer had wilfully failed to deduct tax—Income Tax (Employments) Regulations 1973 (SI 1973 No 334), reg 26(4). **R v IRC, ex p Chisholm** [1981] **2** 602, QBD.
    Failure to deduct tax—Foreign employer—Employees employed in United Kingdom sector of North Sea—Employees paid in US dollars by cheques sent from abroad—Employees liable to Sch E tax—Employer having branch or agency in United Kingdom and liable to corporation tax—Whether employer to be required to deduct PAYE tax from employees working in United Kingdom sector of North Sea—Whether legislation requiring collection of PAYE tax having extra-territorial effect—Whether employer having sufficient 'tax presence' in United Kingdom to require it to collect PAYE tax—Income and Corporation Taxes Act 1970, s 204—Finance Act 1973, s 38(4)(6). **Clark (Inspector of Taxes) v Oceanic Contractors Inc** [1983] **1** 133, HL.
    Failure to deduct tax—Recovery—Employers' failure to deduct tax from gross salary—Tax claimed from, but not paid by, employers—Tax not recoverable by employers from employee as money paid to the use of employer or from employee as trustee for employers—Income Tax (Employments) Act 1943, ss 1(1)(2) (as extended by Income Tax (Offices and Employments) Act 1944, ss 1(1)), 2—Income Tax (Employments) Regulations 1950 (SI 1950 No 453), reg 52(2). **Bernard & Shaw Ltd v Shaw (Rubin third party)** [1951] **2** 267, KBD.
    Money paid by one person under compulsion of law—Employer accounting for tax and national insurance under PAYE system on exercise of share options by former employee—Employer seeking reimbursement from former employee—Whether amount of tax and national insurance paid recoverable in quasi contract. **McCarthy v McCarthy & Stone plc** [2006] **4** 1127, Ch D.
    Money paid by one person under compulsion of law—Employer accounting for tax and national insurance under PAYE system on exercise of share options by former employee—Employer seeking reimbursement from former employee—Whether amount of tax and national insurance recoverable from employee—Taxes Management Act 1970, ss 59A, 59B—Income Tax (Earnings and Pensions) Act 2003, s 710(4), (6). **McCarthy v McCarthy & Stone plc** [2008] **1** 221, CA.
    Theft of tax deducted—Liability—Deduction of tax from wages—Money deducted by employer set aside and stolen—Liability of employer—Income Tax (Employments) Act 1943, s 2(1)(a)—Income Tax (Employments) Regulations 1944 (SR & O 1944 No 251), reg 27(1). **A-G v Antoine** [1949] **2** 1000, KBD.
Payment—
  Emoluments from office or employment. *See* Emoluments from office or employment—Payment, *above*.
  Unlawful demand for tax—
    Recovery of money paid and interest. *See* **Restitution** (Money paid to Crown—Payment of unlawful demand for tax).
Penalty—
  Bankruptcy—
    Whether penalty for income tax offence 'debt provable in bankruptcy'. *See* **Bankruptcy** (Debts provable in bankruptcy—Penalty—Penalties in respect of income tax offences).
  Failure to furnish information to commissioners—
    Daily penalty—Validity—Summary award of penalty—Award of daily penalty for continuing failure thereafter—Appeals against assessments to corporation tax—Adjournment of hearing and subsequent hearings—Precept issued requiring delivery of accounts within 90 days—Penalty summarily awarded for non-compliance with precept—Further meeting of commissioners—Non-compliance with precept continuing—Imposition of penalty calculated on daily rate since date of original penalty—Whether failure to comply with precept declared by commissioners before whom 'proceedings' had been commenced so as to justify further daily penalty—Taxes Management Act 1970, ss 51(1), 53(1), 98(1), 100(1). **Script & Play Productions Ltd v Comrs for the General Purposes of the Income Tax for the Division of St George's, Hanover Square, London** [1972] **1** 577, Ch D.
    Making documents available—Notice requiring taxpayer to 'make available' certain documents for inspection by commissioners—Meaning of 'make available'—Whether positive obligation on taxpayer to supply documents—Taxes Management Act 1970, s 51. **Campbell v Rochdale General Comrs** [1975] **2** 385, Ch D.
  False returns—
    Liability—Taxpayer entitled to same relief even if he had made true returns—Whether penalties applicable—Income Tax Act 1918, s 30. **A-G v Lloyds Bank Ltd (Exor of Lillicrap)** [1944] **2** 157, KBD.
  Fraudulent return—
    Deceased taxpayer—proceedings not prosecuted until after deceased's death—Widow sole beneficiary in his estate—Widow not party to fraud—Whether widow's financial position to be taken into account in awarding penalty against deceased's estate—Finance Act 1960, s 56(5)(6)(b). **Dawes v Income Tax General Comrs** [1965] **1** 258, Ch D.

INCOME TAX (cont)—
  Penalty (cont)—
    Incorrect return—
      Amount of penalty—Treble the tax which he ought to be charged—Whether treble the total amount of tax payable for year of assessment or only treble amount of tax evaded—Income Tax Act 1952, s 25(3)(a). **IRC v Hinchy** [1960] **1** 505, HL.
      Executors—Death of person liable to pay penalty—Liability of estate—Income Tax Act 1918, s 30(1). **A-G v Canter** [1939] **1** 13, CA.
  Proceedings—
      Compromise—Power of Revenue to compromise proceedings to recover penalty—Bankruptcy—Compromise by trustee in bankruptcy of penalties in proceedings pending before General Commissioners—Whether trustees may agree or compromise penalties—Whether prior consent of bankrupt required—Taxes Management Act 1970, ss 93, 95. **Hurren (a bankrupt), Re, ex p the Trustee v IRC** [1982] **3** 982, Ch D.
      Jurisdiction of General Commissioners—Proceedings relating to trade—Appropriate division—Place where trade is carried on—Place where taxpayer ordinarily resident—Taxpayer carrying on trade at place outside division in which ordinarily resident—Taxpayer submitting incorrect accounts in respect of trade for particular years of assessment—Penalty summons on ground taxpayer fraudulent or negligent in submitting accounts—Taxpayer having ceased to carry on trade at date summons issued—Whether relevant years of assessment or date of summons appropriate date for determining where 'trade...is carried on'—Whether penalty summons 'proceedings relating to a trade'—Taxes Management Act 1970, Sch 3, rr 2, 6. **R v IRC, ex p Knight** [1973] **3** 721, CA.
  Recovery—
      Time limit—Premature proceedings—Recovery in connection with tax covered by assessment—Fraud or wilful default—Commencement within three years of final determination—'Within three years' meaning not later than three years—Assessments to income tax and surtax—Proceedings commenced before surtax assessment finally determined—Whether proceedings premature—Taxes Management Act 1970, s 103(2). **R v IRC, ex p Knight** [1973] **3** 721, CA.
  Summary award of penalty—
      Appeal—Jurisdiction of court on appeal—Power to confirm or reverse decision or reduce or increase penalty—Contention by appellant that no proper hearing because no notice of hearing issued—Whether Court of Appeal having jurisdiction to decide that there had been no proper hearing—Taxes Management Act 1970, s 53(2). **Campbell v Rochdale General Comrs** [1975] **2** 385, Ch D.
  Pension—
    Approved occupational pension scheme—
      Individual with no written contract of service executive director of company—Individual retiring from company but continuing as unpaid non-executive director—Individual receiving payments from pension scheme—Whether payments chargeable to tax—Whether payments authorised by rules of scheme—Whether individual retired from service—Income and Corporation Taxes Act 1988, s 600. **Venables v Hornby (Inspector of Taxes)** [2004] **1** 627, HL.
    Approved scheme—
      Withdrawal of approval—HMRC notifying administrators of withdrawal of approval of scheme—Administrators assessed to tax in respect of year in which notice given—Whether year of assessment year in which notice given or year when scheme ceased to be eligible—Income and Corporation Taxes Act 1988, ss 591B(1), 591C, 591D. **John Mander Pension Trustees Ltd v Revenue and Customs Comrs** [2015] **4** 896, SC.
    Compensation—
      Loss of employment—Periodical payments by way of compensation—Local government officer—Termination of employment—Long-term compensation payable under statutory regulations—Compensation payable for loss of employment or loss or diminution of emoluments—Compensation payable until date officer qualifying for pension—Payments payable at intervals equivalent to those at which emoluments of employment previously paid—Whether payment liable to assessment as 'pension' under Sch E or as 'annual payments' under Sch D, Case III—Income Tax Act 1952, ss 122 (Sch D, para 1, proviso), 123 (Sch D, Case III), 156 (Sch E, para 2). **McMann (Inspector of Taxes) v Shaw** [1972] **3** 732, Ch D.
    Relief—
      Conspiracy to defraud—Conspiracy to cheat—'Pension schemes' securing payment of income tax relief at source (RAS)—Whether RAS obtained unlawfully—Whether pension schemes sham—Whether fraud on HMRC or clients—Meaning of 'active member'—Finance Act 2004, ss 151(2), 188(1). **R v Quillan** [2016] **2** 653, CA.
    Return of contributions—
      Excessive contributions returnable on taxpayer's death—Personal representatives entitled to receive after taxpayer's death difference between amount of sums paid as pension and amount of contributions made by taxpayer—Whether taxpayer's right to pension in part a right to return of contributions and so not assessable—Income Tax Act 1918, Sch D, Case V, r 2. **Bridges (Inspector of Taxes) v Watterson** [1952] **2** 910, Ch D.
  Perquisites or profits. *See* Emoluments from office or employment—Perquisites or profits, *above*.
  Persons chargeable—
    Executors—
      Emolument from deceased's employment—Sum payable on termination of office—Death—Assessment on executors—Income Tax Act 1918, All Schedules Rules, r 18—Finance Act 1927, s 45(5), (6). **Allen v Trehearne (Inspector of Taxes)** [1938] **2** 698, CA.
      Years preceding year of death—Untaxed income of deceased not returned by him—Assessment including deceased wife's income—Assessment in respect of years preceding year of death—Apportionment—Income Tax Act 1918, All Schedules Rules, rr 16, 18. **Palmer v Cattermole (Inspector of Taxes)** [1937] **2** 667, KBD.
  Land. *See* Land—Person chargeable, *above*.
  Life tenant—
      Advancement to life tenant's son—Life tenant absolutely entitled to income—Trustees applying income under purported advancement to life tenant's son—Whether life tenant liable to surtax. **Spens v IRC** [1970] **3** 295, Ch D.

Persons chargeable (cont)—
  Profits and interest of money—
    Person entitled to income chargeable—Commissions on insurance premiums—Taxpayer agent for insurers—Taxpayer entitled to deduct amount of commission from premiums paid by insured—Taxpayer re-imbursing insured amount of commissions—Whether taxpayer 'entitled to' or having 'received' commissions—Income Tax Act 1952, s 148. **Way v Underdown (Inspector of Taxes) (No 2)** [1975] **2** 1064, CA.
    Person receiving income chargeable—Interest of money—Agent receiving interests belonging to principal—Estate agent collecting rents on behalf of clients—Agent depositing clients' money in bank deposit account in own name—Interest arising on deposit account—Whether interest to be charged on taxpayer as interest of money received by him—Income Tax Act 1952, ss 123(1) (Sch D, Case III), 148. **Aplin v White (Inspector of Taxes)** [1973] **2** 637, Ch D.
  Receipt of income—
    Person receiving income chargeable—Interest on money—Deposit account in bank's name retained to satisfy taxpayer's liability to bank under guarantee—Interest paid into account—Guarantee discharged—Deposit and interest transferred to taxpayer—Whether taxpayer received interest on deposit when credited—Income Tax Act 1952, s 148. **Dunmore v McGowan (Inspector of Taxes)** [1978] **2** 85, CA.
Plant—
  Capital allowances. *See* **Capital allowances** (Plant).
  Profits from letting. *See* Profits—Profits not otherwise charged—Profits from letting machinery and plant, *below.*
  Wear and tear—
    Deduction in computing profits. *See* Deduction in computing profits—Wear and tear of machinery or plant, *above.*
Production of documents. *See* Information—Production of documents, *above.*
Profession—
  Profits. *See* Profits—Profession or vocation, *below.*
Profits—
  Annual payment—
    Payment not out of profits etc already taxed. *See* Annual payment—Payment not out of profits already taxed, *above.*
    Payment out of profits already taxed. *See* Annual payment—Payment out of profits etc already taxed, *above.*
  Annual profits or gains—
    Farming—Sale of turf from farm—Taxpayer not trading in turf or producing turf for resale—Taxpayer carrying on trade of farming—Land from which turf taken ploughed and drilled for corn after removal of turf—Turf removed by purchasers themselves over period of months—Whether receipts from sale 'annual profits'—Income Tax Act 1952, s 122. **Lowe (Inspector of Taxes) v JW Ashmore Ltd** [1971] **1** 1057, Ch D.
  Capital or income receipts. *See* Capital or income receipts, *above.*
  Cattle dealer—
    Lands insufficient for the keep of the cattle—Meaning of 'cattle'—Inclusion of pigs—Income Tax Act 1918, Sch D, Case III, r 4. **Phillips (Inspector of Taxes) v Bourne** [1947] **1** 374, KBD.
  Computation. *See* Computation of profits, *above.*
  Deduction in computing profits. *See* Deduction in computing profits, *above.*
  Double taxation relief. *See* Double taxation relief—Profits of trade, *above.*
  Emoluments from office or employment. *See* Emoluments from office or employment, *above.*
  Excess rent—
    Compensation for requisitioning—Requisition of hotel—Compensation deemed to be rent—Assessment of excess over Sch A valuation—Compensation (Defence) Act 1939, s 2—Finance Act 1940, s 15. **Mellows (HM Inspector of Taxes) v Buxton Palace Hotel Ltd** [1944] **1** 223, CA.
    Licensed houses—Rent received by lessors in excess of Sch A assessment—Liability to tax under Sch D on surplus—Liability in respect of use of good will, use of trade marks and other property not being corporeal hereditaments—Income Tax Act 1918, Schs A, D. **Loughnan v Marston's Dolphin Brewery Ltd (in liq)** [1936] **1** 468, HL.
    Relief in respect of losses—Set-off against profits—Excess rent of immediate lessor—Leasehold properties sub-let at rents exceeding head rents and net annual values—Other properties sub-let at rents below head rents or not sub-let—Whether excess rents 'profits' from which taxpayer entitled to deduct 'losses' on other properties—Finance Act 1927, s 27(1)—Finance Act 1940, s 15(1). **Barron (Inspector of Taxes) v Littman** [1952] **2** 548, HL.
    Rent including sum for right to use furniture—Furnished cinema—Rent received by lessors in excess of Sch A assessment—Apportionment of rent in respect of premises and furniture—Income Tax Act 1918, Schs A, D. **Shop Investments Ltd v Sweet** [1940] **1** 533, KBD.
    Rent payable under lease—Licence to extract sand and gravel—Taxpayer company granting licence to lessee—Lease and licence separate documents but executed on same date—Licence providing for payment of royalty for sand and gravel extracted—Licence not containing right of re-entry for non-payment of royalties—Whether royalties 'rent' payable under a lease—Whether right to distrain essential ingredient of rent—Whether absence of right of re-entry precluding exercise of right to distrain—Income Tax Act 1952, s 175. **T & E Homes Ltd v Robinson (Inspector of Taxes)** [1979] **2** 522, CA.
    Sand pit—Rent and royalty for sand taken—Rent received by lessors in excess of Sch A assessment—Computation of excess rent—Income Tax Act 1952, s 82, s 175(1)(a), Sch A, para 2. **Tollemache Settled Estates (Trustees) v Coughtrie (Inspector of Taxes)** [1961] **1** 593, HL.
  Foreign entertainers and sportsmen—
    Whether foreign entertainers and sportsmen having liability for income tax on payments received in connection with their commercial activities in United Kingdom from foreign entities with no residence or trading presence in United Kingdom—Income and Corporation Taxes Act 1988, ss 555, 556. **Agassi v Robinson (Inspector of Taxes)** [2006] **3** 97, HL.

INCOME TAX (cont)—
   Profits (cont)—
      Isolated transaction—
         Loan of money—Loan by solicitor to builder to purchase property—Sum payable to solicitor on re-sale—Income Tax Act 1918, Sch D, Case VI. **Wilson (Inspector of Taxes) v Mannooch** [1937] **3** 120, KBD.
         Payment for services—Reminiscences of taxpayer's life—Newspaper articles—Taxpayer providing reminiscences and documents—Newspaper's 'ghost' writer producing articles—Whether payment for services—Income Tax Act 1952, Sch D, Case VI. **Housden (Inspector of Taxes) v Marshall** [1958] **3** 639, Ch D.
         Payment for services—Sale of copyright—Taxpayer writing reminiscences for newspaper—Contract involving sale of copyright—Whether revenue payment—Income Tax Act 1918, Sch D, Case VI. **Hobbs v Hussey (Inspector of Taxes)** [1942] **1** 445, KBD.
      Mutuality principle—
         Members' club—Surplus—Whether club's activity a trade giving rise to a profit or mutual arrangement giving rise to a surplus—Bathing club—Ordinary members and 'hotel' members—Local hotels joining club as members and paying same subscription as ordinary members—Hotel members also paying additional sum calculated in accordance with number of guests—Hotel guests having right to use club but not themselves paying anything to club—Hotels previously having trading relationship with club—Hotel members having one vote each—Number of hotel members very small in comparison with number of ordinary members—Ordinary members having overwhelmingly greater interest in surplus than hotel members—Whether relationship of ordinary members with hotels becoming one of mutuality or remaining of trading character. **Fletcher v Income Tax Comr** [1971] **3** 1185, PC.
         Mutual insurance association—Surplus funds—Surplus arising from transactions with members—Whether assessable—Finance Act 1933, s 31(1). **IRC v Ayrshire Employers Mutual Insurance Association Ltd** [1946] **1** 637, HL.
         Public corporation—Broadcasting—Surplus revenue from broadcasting—Nature of surplus revenue—British Broadcasting Corporation—Receipts derived from Postmaster General—Surplus ultimately at his disposition—Whether surplus of receipts taxable as profits or gains—Income Tax Act 1952, s 122, s 123, Sch D, Case I, Case VI. **BBC v Johns (Inspector of Taxes)** [1964] **1** 923, CA.
         Society—Sale of produce to members—No common fund to which members contributed and in which they participated—Co-operative society—Loans to society by members—Produce sold exclusively to members at market prices—Whether profits on sales taxable—Assam Agricultural Income Tax Act (No IX of 1939), s 3. **English and Scottish Joint Co-op Wholesale Society Ltd v Assam Agricultural Income Tax Comrs** [1948] **2** 395, PC.
   Persons chargeable. *See* Persons chargeable—Profits and interest of money, *above*.
   Profession or vocation—
      Asset of profession—Loss of asset—Accountant—Office of auditor—Asset alleged to constitute whole structure of taxpayer's business—Auditorships constituting 17 per cent of taxpayer's fees as accountant—Whether payment for loss of office profit arising from profession. **Ellis (Inspector of Taxes) v Lucas** [1966] **2** 935, Ch D.
      Author—Disposal of rights in unpublished book—Gift of rights in unpublished book to father—Whether author taxable on value of rights—Income Tax Act 1952, Sch D. **Mason (Inspector of Taxes) v Innes** [1967] **2** 926, CA.
      Author—Royalties—Death of author—Assignment of copyright—Assignment by beneficiary under will—Liability of assignee to tax—Income Tax Act 1952, Sch D. **Hume (Inspector of Taxes) v Asquith** [1969] **1** 868, Ch D.
      Death of taxpayer—Film director/actor—Agreement to produce film—Renumeration including lump sum to be paid in instalments two and a half years after first showing of film—Death of taxpayer before payments made—Payments made to executors—Payments not liable to tax as taxpayer had ceased to carry on profession—Income Tax Act 1918, Sch I, Sch D, Cases II, III, IV. **Gospel v Purchase (Inspector of Taxes)** [1951] **2** 1071, HL.
      Death of taxpayer—Royalties—Deceased author—Periodical payments under deceased's contracts received by executor—Liability of payments to tax—Income Tax Act 1918, Sch 1, Sch D, Cases II, III, VI—Income Tax Act 1952, Sch D, Cases II, III, VI. **Carson (Inspector of Taxes) v Peter Cheyney's Exor** [1958] **3** 573, HL.
      Employment—Contract of service or contract for services—Matters to be considered—Duration of particular engagement—Number of people by whom taxpayer engaged—Vision mixer—Taxpayer working as freelance vision mixer for various television production companies—Taxpayer working at production company studios and using studio equipment—Taxpayer providing no equipment of his own—Taxpayer not contributing to production costs or sharing in profits or losses—Taxpayer receiving fees for services rendered under short-term contracts with production companies—Whether taxpayer's contracts with production companies contracts of service or contracts for services—Income and Corporation Taxes Act 1988, s 19, Sch E. **Hall (Inspector of Taxes) v Lorimer** [1994] **1** 250, CA.
      Profits arising from profession—Payments under agreement—Medical practitioner—Payments made by Minister of Health towards maintenance of policy of assurance—Whether payments profits of profession or taxable as annual payments—Income Tax Act 1918, Sch D, para 1a(ii), Case II—Sch D, Rules applicable to Case III, r 1(a)—National Health Service (Superannuation) Regulations 1947 (S R & O 1947 No 1755), reg 38(3)(m). **Hawkins (Inspector of Taxes) v Leahy (et contra)** [1952] **2** 759, Ch D.
      Profits arising from profession—Winnings from bets—Professional golfer—Bets on private games—Balance of gains over losses arising from bets—Whether taxable as profit arising from profession or vocation—Income Tax Act 1918, Sch D, Case II. **Down (Inspector of Taxes) v Compston** [1937] **2** 475, KBD.
   Profit in kind—
      Loan for building development—Loan repaid by conveyance of ground rents—Ground rents greater in value than loan—Whether difference in market value between value of ground rent and sum advanced taxable as income profit—Income Tax Act 1918, Sch D, Cases III, VI. **Ruskin Investments Ltd v Copeman (Inspector of Taxes)** [1943] **1** 378, CA.

INCOME TAX (cont)—
  Profits (cont)—
    Profits not otherwise charged—
      Casual profit—Estate agent—Gratuitous payment for consenting to a deal between a company and a society, the client of the estate agent—Compensation for withdrawal of any claim that the estate agent might have—No legal basis for any claim—Company taking over land under negotiation—Estate agent's intended acquisition of an interest in the land as an investment—Whether compensation taxable as a casual profit—Income Tax Act 1952, Sch D, Case VI. **Scott (Inspector of Taxes) v Ricketts** [1967] 2 1009, CA.
      Profits from letting machinery and plant—Machinery and plant the value of which not taken into account for tax under Sch A—Railway wagons—Whether profits from letting wagons chargeable under Case I or Case VI of Sch D—Finance Act 1936, s 22(2). **North Central Wagon and Finance Co Ltd v Fifield (Inspector of Taxes)** [1953] 1 1009, CA.
      Sums payable under contract—Lease of racehorse—Sums equivalent to one-half winnings from racehorse leased to be paid under lease to lessor—Contractual entitlement to sums—Sums not income arising from a merely recreational activity—Sums not having character of race winnings—Income Tax Act 1952, s 123 (Sch D, Case VI). **Norman (Inspector of Taxes) v Evans** [1965] 1 372, Ch D.
      Voluntary payment—Unenforceable contract—Payment under—Purchase of land—Taxpayer's contract with owners and prospective purchaser—Purchaser's promise of £10,000 if offer accepted—No stipulation as to services by taxpayer—Taxpayer's word to owners favouring acceptance—Absence of consideration for promise—Whether taxable as a payment for services rendered—Income Tax Act 1952, Sch D, Case VI. **Dickinson (Inspector of Taxes) v Abel** [1969] 1 484, Ch D.
    Profits or gains arising from land—
      Rents and other receipts—Rentcharges—Consideration for transfer of capital asset—Capital or income receipt. See Capital or income receipts—Transfer of capital asset—Cash payments of fixed amounts over fixed period as consideration for transfer—Rentcharges, *above.*
    Sale of property—
      New Zealand. See **New Zealand** (Income tax—Profits or gains derived from sale of property).
    Shareholders—
      Bonus debentures—Redemption—Capitalisation of profits by company—Distribution of accumulated profits—Issue of debentures subsequently redeemed—Whether shareholders having received taxable income. **Income Tax Comr Bengal v Mercantile Bank of India Ltd** [1936] 2 857, .
    Stock-in-trade—
      Valuation—Cost of metals used during year—Closing inventory of metals—Last-in-first-out method or first-in-first-out method—Canada—Excess Profits Tax Act 1940 (SC 1940), s 3—Income War Tax Act (RSC 1927). **Minister of National Revenue v Anaconda American Brass Ltd** [1956] 1 20, PC.
    Trading receipts—
      Bad debts—Recovery—Part recovery of debts previously written off as bad—Amounts so received to be included in computation of profits—Amounts taxable in year of receipt—Income Tax Act 1918, Sch D, Cases I and II, r 3(1). **Bristow (Inspector of Taxes) v Dickinson (William) & Co Ltd** [1946] 1 448, CA.
      Book debt—Profit on collection—Book debt included among assets acquired from predecessor—Purchase of debt at discount—Election to be treated as having set up new trade—Ultimate payment of debt in full—Income Tax Act 1918, Sch D, Case I. **Crompton (Inspector of Taxes) v Reynolds & Gibson** [1952] 1 888, HL.
      Brewery—Tied houses—Premiums paid by tenant—Brewery acquiring tied houses from another company—Whether premiums payable by tenants to be taken into account—Income Tax Act 1918, Sch D, Case I. **Lucas (Inspector of Taxes) v Charles Hammerton & Co Ltd** [1944] 2 133, KBD.
      Dealing in securities—Associated company—Business of acquiring and holding securities—Transfer of certain securities of company to associated company in consideration of shares in associated company—Whether transferor company dealing company—Whether securities trading stock of transferor company—Whether profits of associated company on realisation of securities acquired from transferor company taxable income—Income Tax Act 1952, s 143(4)(a)—Finance Act 1960, ss 25(1)(a), 43(4)(d). **General Reinsurance Co Ltd v Tomlinson (Inspector of Taxes)** [1970] 2 436, Ch D.
      Dividends subject to deduction of tax—Share speculations by company—Contango transactions—Dividends declared during currency of 'contango' transaction—Practice of Stock Exchange—Broker crediting dividends, less tax, to company—Actual dividends not collected—Whether dividends income already taxed at source or trading receipts of company—'Discovery'—Income Tax Act 1918, s 125(1), Sch D, Case I. **Multipar Syndicate Ltd v Devitt** [1945] 1 298, KBD.
      Farming—Profits or gains from carrying on trade of farming—Sale of turf from farm—Taxpayer not trading in turf or producing turf for resale—Land from which turf taken ploughed and drilled for corn after removal of turf—Turf removed by purchasers themselves over period of months—Whether turf sold as part of trade of farming—Income Tax Act 1952, ss 123(1), 124(1), Sch D, Case I. **Lowe (Inspector of Taxes) v JW Ashmore Ltd** [1971] 1 1057, Ch D.
      Gambling transactions—Winnings at cards—Proprietary club—Proprietor taking part in members' card games—Taxability of winnings. **Burdge v Pyne (Inspector of Taxes)** [1969] 1 467, Ch D.
      Government subsidy—Subsidy received by sugar manufacturers from government—Whether amount of subsidy liable to income tax—British Sugar (Subsidy) Act 1925,—British Sugar Industry (Assistance) Act 1931. **Lincolnshire Sugar Co Ltd v Smart (Inspector of Taxes)** [1937] 1 413, HL.
      Investment company—Option to acquire shares at par—Appreciation in value of shares—Exercise of option at enhanced value—Option part of stock-in-trade—Loan to company whose shares acquired reduced by amount subscribed for shares—Whether realisation of profit for tax purposes by exercise of option—Income Tax Act 1952, s 122 (Sch D, Case I). **British South Africa Co v Varty (Inspector of Taxes)** [1965] 2 395, HL.
      Land—Disposal—Taxpayer acquiring land for development—Acquisition for building up a port folio of investments sufficient for the flotation of a public company—Sale of land in view of deterioration of business prospects—Whether surplus on sale taxable as taxpayer's trading receipts. **Simmons (as liquidator of Lionel Simmons Properties Ltd) v IRC** [1980] 2 798, HL.

INCOME TAX (cont)—
  Profits (cont)—
    Trading receipts (cont)—

Land—Profits from use of land—Apportionment—Municipal corporation—Town hall used for activities in the nature of trade—No apportionment of profits between trade and ownership of land—Income Tax Act 1918, Schs A, D, Rules applicable to Cases I and II, r 5. **Jennings (Inspector of Taxes) v Middlesbrough Corp** [1953] **2** 207, Ch D.

Lump sum payment—Cancellation of contract—Consideration—Contract in ordinary course of trade—Cancellation not excluding company from part of business. **Bush, Beach & Gent Ltd v Road** [1939] **3** 302, KBD.

Lump sum payment—Relinquishment of contract—Consideration—Payment for relinquishing contract of services—Payment by third party—Simultaneous relinquishing of contract and of control in contracting company—Inflated sum paid in respect of contract—Sale of shares part of taxpayer's trade—Whether sum taxable—Income Tax Act 1918, Sch D, Case I. **Anglo-French Exploration Co Ltd v Clayson (Inspector of Taxes)** [1956] **1** 762, CA.

Payment to make good losses—Payments made under deed of covenant—Commercial undertaking—Payments made to reimburse loss on national newsfilm operations of company—Profit not intended to be made by undertaking—Whether trade receipt by taxpayer company or payment of pure income profit by payer—Whether taxpayer company entitled to reclaim tax deducted by payer from payment—Income Tax Act 1952, s 341—Finance Act 1953, s 15(3). **British Commonwealth International Newsfilm Agency Ltd v Mahany (Inspector of Taxes)** [1963] **1** 88, HL.

Profits arising from trade—Compulsory sale of foreign exchange—Sale at profit—Company having purchased foreign exchange for importing goods for purposes of trade—Company required to stop imports and to sell surplus foreign exchange to Treasury—Whether profit on sale a profit arising from trade—Income Tax Act 1918, Sch D, Case I. **Imperial Tobacco Co (of GB and Ireland) Ltd v Kelly** [1943] **2** 119, CA.

Transactions in course of trade—Associated companies—Transactions between associated companies—Company dealing in land—Sale to parent company at under-value—Transaction not in the course of trade. **Skinner (Inspector of Taxes) v Berry Head Lands Ltd** [1971] **1** 222, Ch D.

Unclaimed balances—Balances owing to clients—Partnership holding funds on behalf of clients—Unclaimed balances transferred to partners' current accounts—Whether trading receipts. **Morley (Inspector of Taxes) v Tattersall** [1938] **3** 296, CA.

Unclaimed balances—Deposits on purchases—Taxpayers carrying on business as tailors—Deposits on made-to-measure garments ordered—Deposit part payment of purchase price—Deposits refunded to purchasers who declined to take garments—Garments on occasions not taken and deposits not reclaimed—Whether deposits taxable as income of year of receipt—Income Tax Act 1952, Sch D, Case I. **Elson (Inspector of Taxes) v Prices Tailors Ltd** [1963] **1** 231, Ch D.

Voluntary payment—Client terminating trading connection with taxpayer—Client making voluntary payment to taxpayer in recognition of past services—Services provided by way of trade—Whether payment chargeable to tax as a trading receipt—Income Tax Act 1952, ss 122, 123 (Sch D, Case I). **Simpson (Inspector of Taxes) v John Reynolds & Co (Insurances) Ltd** [1975] **2** 88, CA.

Voluntary payment—Compulsory acquisition of wool by government—Price paid on appraisement—Subsequent voluntary additional payment—Whether a trading receipt. **Australia (Commonwealth) Comr of Taxation v Squatting Investment Co Ltd** [1954] **1** 349, PC.

Voluntary payment—Medical practitioner—Surrender value of life insurance policies—Policies taken out by board of voluntary hospital in recognition of professional services given voluntarily—Whether surrender value of policies assigned to medical practitioner taxable—Income Tax Act 1918, Sch D. **Temperley (Inspector of Taxes) v Smith** [1956] **3** 92, Ch D.

Voluntary payment—Motive of payer in making payment—Relevance—Unsolicited payment to trader—Motive of payer to acknowledge long and friendly relationship with trader and to maintain goodwill and image in industry—Trading relationship between payer and trader continuing but payment not linked to future relationship—No disclosure by payer of basis on which payment calculated—No bargaining or negotiation between parties over amount—Taxpayer holding public houses on tied tenancies from payer—Termination of tied tenancies by payer—Ex gratia payments made to taxpayer in consequence of termination—Whether payments chargeable to tax as profits arising or accruing from taxpayer's trade. **Murray (Inspector of Taxes) v Goodhews** [1978] **2** 40, CA.

Voluntary payment—Payment attributable to specific work—Payment by third party—Third party under no legal or moral obligation to make payment—Taxpayer estate agent—Taxpayer retained by client to negotiate purchase of site for development—Taxpayer inadequately remunerated for work done in acquiring site for client—Custom whereby estate agents who had negotiated purchase of site retained to do more remunerative work of selling and letting property built on site—Site sold by client to third party before taxpayer having opportunity to do more remunerative work—Third party refusing to appoint taxpayer as selling agent—Ex gratia payment by third party as compensation for loss of opportunity to obtain additional remuneration—Whether payment chargeable to tax as trading receipt. **McGowan (Inspector of Taxes) v Brown and Cousins (t/a Stuart Edwards)** [1977] **3** 844, Ch D.

Voluntary payment—Payment made gratuitously and not under legal claim—Government grant paid as 'remuneration'—Payment made after discontinuance of trade—Whether trading payments having been finally settled—Whether government payment to be taken into account in computing profits—Income Tax Act 1918, Sch D. **Severne (Inspector of Taxes) v Dadswell** [1954] **3** 243, Ch D.

Voluntary payment—Unsolicited payment to trader—Motive of payer to acknowledge long and friendly relationship with trader and to maintain goodwill and image in industry—Trading relationship between payer and trader continuing but payment not linked to future relationship—Taxpayer holding public houses on tied tenancies from W—Termination of tied tenancies by W—Ex gratia payments by W to taxpayer in connection with loss of tenancies—Whether payments chargeable to tax as profits arising or accruing from taxpayer's trade. **Murray (Inspector of Taxes) v Goodhews** [1976] **2** 296, Ch D.

INCOME TAX (cont)—
  Profits (cont)—
    Trading receipts (cont)—
      War damage value payments—Property dealing company—Damage to properties comprising
      stock-in-trade—Whether value payments part of trading receipts—War Damage Act 1943,
      s 66(1)—Income Tax Act 1918, Sch D, Case I—War Damage (Public Utility Undertakings, etc) Act
      1949, s 28. **London Investment and Mortgage Co Ltd v Worthington (Inspector of Taxes)**
      [1958] **2** 230, HL.
  Profits tax. *See* **Profits tax**.
  Public revenue dividends—
    Deduction of tax—
      Interest—Damages and interest thereon payable by Crown—Whether interest on damages profit
      arising from public revenue dividends—Income and Corporation Taxes Act 1970, s 93, Sch C,
      s 107, Sch 5, para 5. **Esso Petroleum Co Ltd v Ministry of Defence** [1990] **1** 163, Ch D.
  Racehorse—
    Lease of horse. *See* Profits—Profits not otherwise charged—Sums payable under contract—Lease of
    racehorse, *above*.
  Rate—
    Surcharge on surtax rate for previous year—
      Retrospective operation of statute. *See* Statute—Retrospective operation—Surcharge on surtax rate
      for previous year, *below*.
  Receipt of income—
    Charge to tax. *See* Persons chargeable—Receipt of income, *above*.
  Receipts of trade. *See* Profits—Trading receipts, *above*.
  Receiver—
    Company—
      Liability of receiver to tax—Receiver appointed by debenture holders—Assessment in respect of
      income of company—Income Tax Act 1918, Sch D, Miscellaneous Rules, r 1. **Meeruppe**
      Sumanatissa Terunnanse v Warakapitiye Pangnananda Terunnanse [1936] **2** 651, PC.
  Recovery of sums not due—
    Restitution. *See* **Restitution** (Common law claims—Recovery of sums not due).
  Reduction of salary—
    Compensation for reduction. *See* Emoluments from office or employment—Compensation—Reduction
    of salary, *above*.
  Relief—
    Annual value of land. *See* Land—Annual value—Relief, *above*.
    Bank interest—
      Interest payable in United Kingdom—Interest on bank overdraft on account kept at
      Guernsey—Interest paid to Guernsey branch of bank having its head office in London—Whether
      interest payable in United Kingdom—Income Tax Act 1918, s 36(1). **Maude v IRC** [1940] **1** 464,
      KBD.
      Loan for purchase or improvement of land. *See* Interest—Relief—Loan for purchase or
      improvement of land, *above*.
      Payment of interest—Loan account—Interest added to loan each half-year—Whether interest
      'paid'—Income Tax Act 1918, s 36, All Schedules Rules, rr 19, 21. **Paton (Fenton's Trustee) v IRC**
      [1938] **1** 786, HL.
    Capital allowances. *See* **Capital allowances**.
    Child. *See* Child relief, *above*.
    Dividends—
      Relief from surtax. *See* Dividends—Relief from surtax, *above*.
    Double taxation. *See* Double taxation relief, *above*.
    Earned income. *See* Earned income relief, *above*.
    Housekeeper—
      Non-resident housekeeper—Woman employed by taxpayer as housekeeper—Married woman
      attending daily—Whether taxpayer entitled to relief for non-resident housekeeper—Finance Act
      1924, s 22. **Brown v Adamson (Inspector of Taxes)** [1937] **2** 792, KBD.
      Non-resident housekeeper—Woman employed to look after taxpayer's children during
      day—Whether taxpayer entitled to relief for non-resident housekeeper—Income Tax Act 1952,
      s 214(1). **Barentz (Inspector of Taxes) v Whiting** [1965] **1** 685, CA.
    Interest. *See* Interest—Relief, *above*.
    Loss relief. *See* Loss relief, *above*.
    Losses—
      Excess rent. *See* Profits—Excess rent—Relief in respect of losses, *above*.
    Non-resident. *See* Non-resident, *above*.
    School fees—
      Maintenance order including element in respect of fees. *See* **Minor** (Maintenance—Education or
      training—Maintenance order including element in respect of school fees).
    Special contribution. *See* **Special contribution** (Relief).
    Undistributed income—
      Apportionment. *See* Undistributed income—Relief, *below*.
  Remuneration—
    Office or employment. *See* Emoluments from office or employment, *above*.
  Rent—
    Capital or revenue expenditure. *See* Deduction in computing profits—Capital or revenue
    expenditure—Acquisition of capital asset—Rent, *above*.
    Deduction in computing profits. *See* Deduction in computing profits—Expenses wholly and exclusively
    laid out for purposes of trade—Rent, *above*.
    Deficiency—
      Deduction in computing profits. *See* Deduction in computing profits—Deficiency in rent, *above*.
    Excess rent. *See* Profits—Excess rent, *above*.
    Land—
      Rents and other receipts. *See* Land—Rents and other receipts, *above*.

Rentcharges—
  Capital or income receipts. *See* Capital or income receipts—Transfer of capital asset—Cash payments of fixed amounts over fixed period as consideration for transfer—Rentcharges, *above*.
Repairs—
  Capital or revenue expenditure. *See* Deduction in computing profits—Capital or revenue expenditure—Repairs, *above*.
Repayment—
  Increase in standard rate—
    Transfer of stock—Deficiency payment—Income derived from investments of superannuation funds—Claims for repayment of tax deducted at source—Two Finance Acts in respect of same financial year—Second Act increasing standard rate of tax imposed by first Act—Increased rate payable in respect of whole financial year—Sale of investments by trustees before increase of standard rate—Deduction made at original rate—Deficiency in tax deduction to be made up by adding to deduction due on next payment—Purchase of investments by trustees after increase of standard rate—Income received on new investments not only less tax at increased rate but also less deficiency in tax arising through transferors having suffered tax only at former standard rate—Deficiency payment to be 'accounted for and assessed in the same manner as the tax deducted from original payment'—Payments of tax in fact made by transferees—Transferors not to be treated as persons who made payments—Income Tax Act 1918, s 27—Finance Act 1921, s 32—Finance (No 2) Act 1939, s 7, Sch VI, paras 1, 2—Finance (No 2) Act 1940, s 6, Sch V, paras 1, 2. **Shadbolt (Inspector of Taxes) v The Rt Hon Lord Pender and Admiral Henry William Grant** [1946] **1** 16, KBD.
  Repayment claim—
    Loss relief. *See* Loss relief—Claim—Repayment claim, *above*.
  Unlawful demand for tax. *See* **Restitution** (Money paid to Crown—Payment of unlawful demand for tax).
Reports of cases—
  Citation. *See* **Practice** (Citation of cases—Reports—Revenue cases).
Residence—
  Company—
    Dual residence—Residence in countries where sufficient part of 'superior and directing authority' is found. **Union Corp Ltd v IRC** [1953] **1** 729, HL.
    Place where management and control is exercised—Subsidiary company in East Africa—Parent company in fact exercising central management and control in London—Management by parent company contrary to articles of subsidiary company—Whether subsidiary company resident in United Kingdom—Finance Act 1953, s 20(9). **Unit Construction Co Ltd v Bullock (Inspector of Taxes)** [1959] **3** 831, HL.
  Foreign employment—
    Residence in United Kingdom. *See* Foreign employment—Duties performed abroad—Residence in United Kingdom, *above*.
  Foreign possessions—
    Residence in United Kingdom. *See* Foreign possessions—Residence in United Kingdom, *above*.
  Husband and wife—
    Non-resident husband. *See* Husband and wife—Non-resident husband, *above*.
  Individual—
    Residence and ordinary residence—Revenue guidance—Revenue rejecting taxpayers' claims not to be resident or ordinarily resident in United Kingdom—Construction of guidance—Whether ordinary practice of Revenue giving rise to a legitimate expectation that taxpayers neither resident nor ordinarily resident in United Kingdom. **R (on the application of Davies) v Revenue and Customs Comrs** [2012] **1** 1048, SC.
  Non-resident—
    Generally. *See* Non-resident, *above*.
    Husband and wife. *See* Husband and wife—Non-resident husband, *above*.
  Payment of rent by employers—
    Deduction from emoluments. *See* Emoluments from office or employment—Expenses wholly, exclusively and necessarily incurred—Residence provided by employers to employee, *above*.
  Persons working abroad—
    Place of abode in United Kingdom to be disregarded—Duties of office or employment in substance performed outside United Kingdom—Duties performed in United Kingdom 'merely incidental to' other duties performed outside United Kingdom—Taxpayer a pilot with Dutch airline—Taxpayer's home in England—Taxpayer commuting between home and Amsterdam—Duties always commencing in Amsterdam—On certain services taxpayer landing in and taking off from United Kingdom as part of scheduled flight—Taxpayer's duties in substance performed abroad—Whether landings and take-offs from United Kingdom 'merely incidental to' duties performed abroad—Finance Act 1956, s 11. **Robson v Dixon (Inspector of Taxes)** [1972] **3** 671, Ch D.
  Six month's residence—
    Month—Meaning—Calendar or lunar months—Fractions of days to be counted in hours—Income Tax Act 1918, Sch D, Miscellaneous Rules, r 2. **Wilkie v IRC** [1952] **1** 92, Ch D.
Return—
  Currency—
    Income derived from British funded stock—Return made in Australia—Currency in which return must be expressed. **Payne v Deputy Federal Comr of Taxation** [1936] **2** 793, PC.
  False return—
    Penalty. *See* Penalty—False return, *above*.
  Fraudulent return—
    Penalty. *See* Penalty—Fraudulent return, *above*.
  Incorrect return—
    Penalty. *See* Penalty—Incorrect return, *above*.

INCOME TAX (cont)—
Return (cont)—
Liability to make return—
Notice by inspector—Notice requiring person to give return of income which is not his but in respect of which he is chargeable—Notice only requiring return of certain sources of income—Validity—Whether notice must require return of all sources of income—Taxes Management Act 1970, s 8(2). **R v HM Inspector of Taxes, ex p Frank Rind Settlement Trustees** [1975] **1** 30, QBD.
Self-assessment—
Enquiry—Notice of intention to enquire into return—Validity of notice—Taxpayer appointing tax agent to act in his tax affairs—Taxpayer signing Form 64-8 granting tax agent authority to act—HMRC sending notice of enquiry into return both to taxpayer and to tax agent—Notice received by agent but not by taxpayer—Whether tax agent having actual or apparent authority to receive notice of enquiry on taxpayer's behalf—Whether valid notice of enquiry given—Whether taxpayer estopped by convention from denying that valid notice of enquiry given—Taxes Management Act 1970, s 9A. **Tinkler v Revenue and Customs Comrs** [2020] **1** 61, CA.
Enquiry—Notice of intention to enquire into return—Validity of notice—Taxpayer appointing tax agent to act in his tax affairs—Taxpayer signing Form 64-8 granting tax agent authority to act—HMRC sending notice of enquiry to taxpayer's old address—HMRC sending copy of notice to taxpayer's agent—Agent responding and entering into correspondence—HMRC issuing closure notice—During appeal taxpayer raising issue notice not validly served—Whether taxpayer estopped by convention from denying that valid notice of enquiry given—Principles to be applied—Taxes Management Act 1970, s 9A. **Tinkler v Revenue and Customs Comrs** [2022] **1** 1028, SC.
Enquiry—Taxpayer filing tax return for 2007-08 and leaving Revenue to calculate tax due—Revenue producing tax calculation—Taxpayer amending 2007-08 tax return to include loss relief claim for 2008-09—Taxpayer averring effect of claim that no further taxes due for 2007-08—Revenue producing second tax calculation in same amount as first calculation—Revenue opening enquiry into loss relief claim—Revenue commencing enforcement proceedings in county court—Whether Revenue entitled to open enquiry—Taxes Management Act 1970, ss 9A, 42, Sch 1A. **Revenue and Customs Comrs v Cotter** [2014] **1** 1, SC.
Revocable settlement. *See* Settlement—Revocable settlement, *below.*
Royalties—
Assignment of copyright. *See* Profits—Profession or vocation—Author—Royalties—Death of author—Assignment of copyright, *above.*
Commutation for lump sum—
Capital or income. *See* Capital or income receipts—Royalties—Commutation for lump sum, *above.*
Deceased taxpayer. *See* Profits—Profession or vocation—Death of taxpayer—Royalties, *above.*
Deduction of tax—
Payment net of tax. *See* Annual payment—Payment out of profits etc already taxed—Inference that payment made net of tax—Royalties, *above.*
Sand pit—Devise of land for fixed rent—Right to take away sand—Royalties payable on amount taken—Rent to merge in royalties payable—Tax deducted by tenant—Landowner accepting deduction under mistake of law—Estoppel—Accord and satisfaction—Later objection to deduction—Jurisdiction of court—Whether landowner entitled to recover tax deducted—Excess rent under short lease—Income Tax Act 1918, All Schedules Rules, r 22(1)(a)—Finance Act 1934, s 21(1)(a)—Finance Act 1940, s 15(1). **Gwyther v Boslymon Quarries Ltd** [1950] **1** 384, KBD.
Under-deduction of tax. *See* Under-deduction of tax—Royalties, *below.*
Salary—
Office or employment. *See* Emoluments from office or employment, *above.*
Sale of land—
Adventure in the nature of trade. *See* Trade—Adventure in nature of trade—Isolated transaction—Sale of land, *below.*
Sale of property—
Capital or income receipt. *See* Capital or income receipts—Sale of property, *above.*
Scholarship income—
Exemption from tax. *See* Exemption—Scholarship income, *above.*
Securities—
Dealing in securities—
Trading receipts. *See* Profits—Trading receipts—Dealing in securities, *above.*
Self-assessment. *See* Return—Self-assessment, *above.*
Settlement—
Accumulation of income—
Beneficiary absolutely entitled—Beneficiary leaving fund to accumulate in hands of trustees—Liability to tax. **IRC v Hamilton-Russell Exors** [1943] **1** 474, .
Children—
Deed of separation—Father covenanting to make monthly payments for his children—Payments duly made after deduction of income tax—Claim on behalf of children for repayment of deducted tax—Whether payments made under a settlement—Whether payments to be treated as income of father—Income and Corporation Taxes Act 1970, ss 437, 444. **Harvey (Inspector of Taxes) v Sivyer** [1985] **2** 1054, Ch D.
Irrevocable settlement—Income payable to settlor in any circumstances whatsoever—Trust fund invested in companies controlled by settlor—Winding-up by settlor destroying trust fund—Terms of settlement not providing for payment to settlor—Irrelevant settlor in position to put an end to trust fund by liquidation of companies—Finance Act 1936, s 21(8). **Jenkins v IRC** [1944] **2** 491, CA.
Irrevocable settlement—Settlement before specified date—Irrevocable on that date—Settlement not revocable in circumstances existing at that date but possibly revocable later—Finance Act 1936, s 21(10). **IRC v Lord Glenconner** [1941] **3** 265, KBD.
Irrevocable settlement—Settlement before specified date—Settlement not deemed to be irrevocable—Full discretionary trust to pay income for benefit of daughter or to wife or for benefit of other children or to charitable institutions—No power of revocation—Revocable settlement—Finance Act 1936, s 21. **Eastwood v IRC** [1943] **1** 350, CA.

INCOME TAX (cont)—
   Settlement (cont)—
      Children (cont)—
         Irrevocable settlement—Settlement before specified date—Settlement not deemed to be irrevocable—Full discretionary trust to pay income to father, any wife of his, and his issue—No power of revocation—Revocable settlement—Finance Act 1936, s 21(8)(10). **IRC v Lord Delamere** [1939] **3** 386, KBD.

         Life of child—Income payable for period less than life of child—Interest liable to be dimished by the birth of further children who shall survive the settlor or by exercise of power of appointment—Whether interest for a period less than life of child—Finance Act 1922, s 20(1)(c). **Mauray v IRC** [1944] **1** 472, CA.

         Life of child—Income payable for period less than life of child—Trusts to determine if child ceased to be British subject—Whether disposition 'for some period less than the life of the child'—Finance Act 1922, s 20(1)(c). **Whigham v IRC** [1941] **2** 524, KBD.

         Payment of income for benefit of child of settlor—Payment—Undistributed income of company—Notional distribution—Distribution on order by commissioner—Infant shareholders whose shares had been transferred to them by their father—Whether notional distribution a 'payment'—Whether sums notionally distributed to infants deemed to be father's income for tax purposes—East African Income Tax (Management) Act 1952 (No 8 of 1952), ss 22(1), 24(1). **Houry v Income Tax Comr** [1959] **3** 781, PC.

   Discretionary power for benefit of settlor or spouse—
      Adjustment to exclude power—Settlor's wife included in specified class of beneficiaries—Power of appointment in favour of one or more of specified class other than wife in settlor's lifetime—Power to appoint any person other than settlor member of specified class with written consent of settlor—Purported exercise of power of appointment in favour of members of specified class—Appointment resetting capital 'upon the like trusts' subject to the omission of wife or widow from specified class—Validity of appointment—Effect—Whether power remaining to appoint wife to specified class—Whether power remaining to pay or apply for benefit of wife any part of income or property—Finance Act 1958, s 22(1)(5). **Blausten v IRC** [1972] **1** 41, CA.

   Discretionary trust—
      Accumulation of income as part of capital fund. *See* **Settlement** (Power of appointment—Transfer of assets to trustees to hold on discretionary trusts—Trustees directed to accumulate income as part of capital fund).

      Income arising from possessions out of United Kingdom. *See* Foreign possessions—Income arising from possessions out of United Kingdom—Trustee—Liability—Discretionary settlement, *above*.

      Income—Additional rate of tax—Expenses properly chargeable to income—Premiums paid by trustees to effect and maintain policies of life assurance—Fees paid to investment advisers—Trustees having power to pay premiums and fees out of income—Trustees making payments out of income—Whether premiums and fees 'expenses of the trustees ... properly chargeable to income'—Whether premiums and fees deductible in ascertaining amount of income chargeable at additional rate—Finance Act 1973, s 16(2). **Carver v Duncan (Inspector of Taxes)** [1985] **2** 645, HL.

      Income—Additional rate of tax—Expenses properly chargeable to income—Trust incurring expenses in administering trust—Whether expenses properly chargeable to income of trust—Whether trustees' fees properly chargeable to income or capital—Income and Corporation Taxes Act 1988, s 686(2AA). **Revenue and Customs Comrs v Trustees of the Peter Clay Discretionary Trust** [2008] **2** 283, Ch D; [2009] **2** 683, CA.

      Income—Additional rate of tax—Income chargeable at additional rate in addition to being chargeable at basic rate—Protective trust for beneficiary with power in trustees to accumulate—Whether trustees liable to tax at additional rate on accumulated income—Finance Act 1973, s 16(2). **IRC v Berrill** [1982] **1** 867, Ch D.

      Payment under discretionary trust—Payment pursuant to power of appointment of capital—Sums appointed applied in paying medical and nursing home expenses for beneficiary—Whether sums appointed income in the hands of beneficiary—Finance Act 1973, s 17. **Stevenson (Inspector of Taxes) v Wishart** [1987] **2** 428, CA.

   Disposition of income for short period. *See* Disposition of income for short period, *above*.
   Income arising under a settlement—
      Apportioned income—Undistributed income of foreign company—Apportionment and sub-apportionment—Taxpayer controlling chain of foreign companies—Whether undistributed income from foreign companies 'actual income' and therefore liable to apportionment—Finance Act 1922, s 21—Finance Act 1938, s 41(4)(a)(ii)—Finance Act 1939, s 13(3). **Howard de Walden (Lord) v IRC** [1948] **2** 825, HL.

      Covenant—Payments made by covenantor out of earned income—Whether sums paid 'income arising under a settlement' liabile to investment income surcharge—Income and Corporation Taxes Act 1970, ss 454, 457—Finance Act 1971, s 32. **Ang v Parrish (Inspector of Taxes)** [1980] **2** 790, Ch D.

      Income of property of which settlor has divested himself absolutely—Income which may become payable to him or applicable for his benefit—Resulting trust—Gift of shares to college, they granting a purchase option to trustee company—Dividends to provide funds for chair in pharmacology—Intent—Beneficial trusts of option not defined—Whether resulting trust inferred from primary facts or established in law on the evidence—Income Tax Act 1952, s 145(1)(d), (2). **Vandervell v IRC** [1967] **1** 1, HL.

   Information—
      Power of commissioners by notice to require information for specified purposes—Power to require such information as commissioners think necessary—Burden on taxpayer of proving that no reasonable commissioner could have thought information necessary—Grounds for thinking that settlement falls within statutory provisions—Commissioners having no or insufficient particulars to determine whether settlement falls within provisions—Whether commissioners entitled to require information where no grounds for thinking settlement falls within provisions—Income and Corporation Taxes Act 1970, s 453. **Wilover Nominees Ltd v IRC** [1974] **3** 496, CA.

INCOME TAX (cont)—
  Settlement (cont)—
    Meaning—

      Any trust—Children—Maintenance order—Husband—Maintenance order in divorce proceedings against husband—Order providing for payment of annual sum to be held in trust for children—Whether order a settlement—Whether husband settlor—Whether husband entitled to claim children's allowance in respect of sums paid—Finance Act 1936, s 21(1), (9)(b), (c). **Yates (Inspector of Taxes) v Starkey** [1951] **1** 732, CA.

      Arrangement—Company exploiting taxpayer's services—Taxpayer a director—Shares issued to trustees for benefit of taxpayer's children—Taxpayer aware of but not a party to transaction—Dividend paid from company's receipts from exploitation of taxpayer's services—Whether an arrangement—Income Tax 1952, ss 397, 403. **Crossland (Inspector of Taxes) v Hawkins** [1961] **2** 812, CA.

      Arrangement—Formation of company—Investment of trust funds in purchase of shares in company—Alteration in capital structure of company—Funds held on trust for settlor's wife and children—Further settlements of shares on children—Sale by settlor of shares to company—Whether formation and structure of company with settlements and sale an 'arrangement'—Finance Act 1938, ss 38(2), 41(4)(b). **Chamberlain v IRC** [1943] **2** 200, HL.

      Arrangement—Investment of trusts funds in ordinary shares of company—Conversion of shares into preference shares—Variation of rights—50 per cent dividend in first five years and 5 per cent—Whether an arrangement—Finance Act 1922, s 20(1)(b). **IRC v Prince-Smith** [1943] **1** 434, KBD.

      Disposition—Allotment of shares in company—Taxpayer and wife owners of all shares in company—Allotment of shares by company to children—Nominal consideration for allotment—Whether allotment of shares a 'disposition'—Finance Act 1936, s 21(9)(b). **Copeman v Coleman** [1939] **3** 224, KBD.

      Disposition—Surrender of reversionary life interest—Surrenderor's children becoming entitled as if she were dead—Surrender a 'disposition'—Subsequent surrender of prior life interest—Income of children applicable for their benefit in consequence of surrender of reversionary life interest—Finance Act 1936, s 21(9)—Finance Act 1943, s 20, Sch 6, Part 2. **IRC v Buchanan** [1957] **2** 400, CA.

      Element of bounty—Bona fide commercial transaction—No element of bounty—Transfer of shares to a finance company—Design to forestall take-over bid—Option to repurchase—Treatment of income as income of settlor—Income Tax Act 1952, ss 404(2), 405(1). **Bulmer v IRC** [1966] **3** 801, Ch D.

      Element of bounty—Bona fide commercial transaction—Tax avoidance scheme—Transaction part of scheme—Disposition for valuable and sufficient consideration—Sale of annuity by surtax payer to charitable company in return for capital sum—Transaction involving no element of bounty on either side—Whether 'disposition' or 'settlement'—Income and Corporation Taxes Act 1970, ss 434(1), 454(3), 457(1). **IRC v Plummer** [1979] **3** 775, HL.

      Element of bounty—Company owned by husband and wife earning profits by exploiting husband's personal services—Company profits distributed as dividends equally to husband and wife—Whether dividend income paid to wife income arising under settlement to be treated as husband's income—Whether corporate structure a settlement—Whether element of bounty in arrangement—Whether outright gift by one spouse to the other of property from which income arises—Whether property given wholly or substantially right to income—Income and Corporation Taxes Act 1988, ss 660A(1), (6), 660G(1). **Jones v Garnett (Inspector of Taxes)** [2006] **2** 381, CA; [2007] **4** 857, HL.

      Transfer of assets—Absolute gift—Deposits to child's account in Post Office Savings Bank and purchases of Defence Bonds for child—Whether gifts 'settlements'—Finance Act 1936, s 21(9)(b). **Thomas v Marshall (Inspector of Taxes)** [1953] **1** 1102, HL.

      Transfer of assets—Transfer of shares to daughters as an absolute gift—Dividends declared after transfer—Assessment of settlor in respect of amount of dividends—Recovery from children of amount of tax—Finance Act 1922, s 20(2)—Finance Act 1936, s 21(1), (9)(b), (c). **Hood-Barrs v IRC** [1946] **2** 768, CA.

  Revocable settlement—

      Irrevocable covenant for limited period—Period of less than six years—Extension of period—Effect—Covenant to pay annual sum to son—Covenant irrevocable for period of less than six years—Extension of period of restriction on power of revocation for full six years by subsequent deed—Extension of period made while original covenant still irrevocable—Payments made under covenant irrevocable for period of less than six years to be treated as settlor's income—Income Tax Act 1918, All Schedules Rules, r 23(2)—Finance Act 1938, s 38, Sch III, Part II, para 1(c). **Taylor v IRC** [1946] **1** 488, CA.

      Irrevocable covenant for limited period—Period of less than six years—Settlement revocable after seven years—Cesser of liability to make annual payments—Further deed postponing operation of power of revocation for further three years—Finance Act 1938, s 38(1). **IRC v Nicholson** [1953] **2** 123, Ch D.

      More than one settlor—Assessment on settlor who would not have been entitled to income of settled property if no settlement—Settlement by tenant for life and remainderman—Remainderman not entitled to income in absence of settlement—Whether remainderman properly assessed—Finance Act 1938, s 38(2). **Herbert v IRC** [1943] **1** 336, KBD.

      Power of settlor to appoint future income to himself—Construction of deed—Trust for persons who were employees of company whom settlor might appoint—Possibility that settlor might become employee—Possibility that settlor could become sole beneficiary and terminate liability for annual payments—Whether deed should be construed as impliedly excluding settlor—Finance Act 1938, s 38(1). **IRC v Fitte** [1943] **2** 228, CA.

      Power to revoke or otherwise determine settlement—Determination by act of any person—Terms providing for determination—Special power of appointment—Whether appointment of whole settled fund to one beneficiary sui juris would be a determination of the settlement—Income Tax Act 1952, s 399(b), proviso (ii). **IRC v Jamieson** [1963] **2** 1030, HL.

INCOME TAX (cont)—
    Settlement (cont)—
        Revocable settlement (cont)—
            Power to revoke or otherwise determine settlement—Foreign settlement—Settlor and trustees resident abroad—Trust funds in United Kingdom—Trusts for settlor's issue subject to her life interest—Trustee's power to declare sums held on trust for settlor absolutely—Amounts might ultimately exhaust fund—Whether terms of settlement such that trustees might have power to determine it—Finance Act 1938, s 38(2). **Kenmare (Countess) v IRC** [1957] **3** 33, HL.

            Power to revoke or otherwise determine settlement—Power to dispose of nearly whole capital subject to settlement—Whether power to determine settlement or any provision thereof—Finance Act 1938, s 38(1)(a), (2)(a). **Saunders v IRC** [1957] **3** 43, HL.

            Power to revoke or otherwise determine settlement—Terms of settlement—Power not found in terms of settlement—Settlement of dividends from shares in company controlled by settlor—Power of settlor to prevent declaration of dividend or to wind up company—Whether a revocable settlement—Finance Act 1938, s 38(1)(a). **IRC v Wolfson** [1949] **1** 865, HL.

            Power to revoke—Release of power—Implied release. See **Power** (Implied release—Settlement—Power to revoke settlement).

        Settlor—
            Person providing or undertaking to provide funds for purpose of settlement—Indirect provision of funds—Bank loan to trustees to purchase shares—Nominal interest—Loan conditional on taxpayer making interest free deposit of equivalent amount with bank—Income Tax Act 1952, s 411(2). **IRC v Wachtel** [1971] **1** 271, Ch D.

            Person providing or undertaking to provide funds for purpose of settlement—Indirect provision of funds—Company exploiting taxpayer's services—Taxpayer a director—Shares issued to trustees for taxpayer's children—Taxpayer aware of but not a party to transaction—Dividend paid from company's receipts from exploitation of taxpayer's services—Whether taxpayer provided funds for the settlement—Income Tax Act 1952, ss 397, 403. **Crossland (Inspector of Taxes) v Hawkins** [1961] **2** 812, CA.

            Person providing or undertaking to provide funds for purpose of settlement—Indirect provision of funds—Provision through interposition of company—Allotment of shares to taxpayer's children—Nominal consideration—Taxpayer and wife owning all shares in company—Whether taxpayer having indirectly provided funds—Finance Act 1936, s 21(9)(c). **Copeman v Coleman** [1939] **3** 224, KBD.

            Person providing or undertaking to provide funds for purpose of settlement—Infant—Capacity to provide funds for purpose of settlement—Taxpayer a child film actress—Company incorporated by taxpayer's father—Settlement by father of shares in company for benefit of taxpayer—Taxpayer entering service agreement with company for small salary—Company making large profits by exploiting taxpayer's services—Dividends declared out of profits paid to trustees of settlement and not distributed—Whether taxpayer a settlor in relation to settlement—Whether taxpayer having an interest in income arising under settlement—Whether dividends paid to trustees assessable to surtax as income of taxpayer—Income Tax Act 1952, ss 405, 409(2)(6), 411(2). **IRC v Mills** [1972] **3** 977, CA; [1974] **1** 722, HL.

            Retaining interest—Application of income for settlor's benefit—Income—Wide powers to borrow money—Trust fund in companies controlled by settlor—Loan by settlor to trustees—Loan repaid out of income under settlement—Whether money applied in discharge of loan 'income'—Whether money had become applicable for benefit of settlor—Finance Act 1938, s 38(3)(4). **Jenkins v IRC** [1944] **2** 491, CA.

            Retaining interest—Application of income for settlor's benefit—Payment direct or indirect to settlor—Bank overdraft arranged by trustees of settlement to purchase investment—Separate deposit by settlor with bank as collateral—Overdraft reduced by trust income—Settlor's deposit reduced pro tanto—Income Tax Act 1962, ss 405 411(2). **IRC v Wachtel** [1971] **1** 271, Ch D.

            Retaining interest—Application of income for settlor's benefit—Settlor deemed to have an interest if any income might become applicable for his benefit—Possibility of invalidity and resulting trust—Trustees' power to capitalise income—Income could be thus applied in payment of premiums on policy under another settlement—Settlor's possible interest in policy under imaginary other settlement—Income Tax Act 1952, s 405(1)(2). **Muir v IRC** [1966] **3** 38, CA.

            Retaining interest—Benefit for settlor or wife—Wife—Meaning—Whether including 'widow'—Finance Act 1938, s 38(4). **Gaunt v IRC** [1941] **2** 662, CA.

            Retaining interest—Resulting trust—Ultimate trust for settlor—Ultimate resulting trust for settlor's estate—Whether resulting trust an 'interest' of settlor—Finance Act 1938, s 38(3)(4). **Gaunt v IRC** [1941] **2** 82, KBD.

            Retaining interest—Statutory power of advancement—Effect—Expression of contrary intention—Direction for accumulation—Accumulation of income during settlor's lifetime—Trusts in favour of settlor's wife and unborn children—Beneficiaries benefiting on settlor's death—Power of advancement negatived by trust for accumulation—Income Tax Act 1952, s 405(1), (2)—Trustee Act 1925, ss 32(1), 69(2). **IRC v Bernstein** [1961] **1** 320, CA.

            Retaining interest—Undistributed income—Power of appointment—Investments to be held on such trusts as settlor and son might appoint—Trustees to accumulate income with power to transfer accumulations to son on happening of certain events—No appointment made and no event bringing accumulation to an end having occurred—Whether settlor to be deemed to have an interest in income from investments—Finance Act 1938, s 38(3)(4). **Glyn v IRC** [1948] **2** 419, KBD.

        Sums paid to settlor otherwise than as income—
            Body corporate connected with a settlement—Loans to settlor by body corporate—Amount of a loan paid direct to settlor deemed to be income paid to him by trustees of settlement—Available income—Deduction of past capital payments—Method of computation—Income Tax Act 1952, ss 408(1)(2)(7), 411(4). **Bates v IRC** [1967] **1** 84, HL.

            Body corporate connected with a settlement—Loans to settlor by body corporate—Payments made by company on behalf of settlor—Obligation of settlor to repay—Whether sums paid by company capital paid indirectly to settlor—Finance Act 1938, s 40(3)(5)(a). **Potts' Exors v IRC** [1951] **1** 76, HL.

INCOME TAX (cont)—
 Settlement (cont)—
  Sums paid to settlor otherwise than as income (cont)—
   Capital sum—Repayment of loan—Settlor's wife making loan to trustees of settlement of whom
    she was one—Loan repaid out of trust fund—Amount of repayment treated as income of
    settlor—Settlor assessed to surtax on amount grossed up—Income Tax Act 1952, s 408(1), (7). **De
    Vigier v IRC** [1964] **2** 907, HL.
 Settlement of appeal by agreement. *See* Appeal—Settlement—Agreement, *above.*
 Seven year covenant. *See* Disposition of income for short period, *above.*
 Share dealing—
  Trade—
   Loss relief. *See* Loss relief—Trade—Share-dealing, *above.*
 Share loss relief. *See* Loss relief—Claim—Validity, *above.*
 Short-term capital gains. *See* **Capital gains tax** (Short-term gains).
 Small maintenance order—
  Divorce. *See* **Divorce** (Maintenance—Income tax—Small maintenance payments).
 Source of income—
  Profits or income chargeable under Sch D, Case III—
   Acquisition of new 'source' of income—Sum paid by taxpayer to credit of deposit account with
    bank—Deposit account already in existence for several years—Whether interest on sum
    deposited arising from 'new source'—Income Tax Act 1918, Sch D, Case III, r 2(1), as substituted
    by Finance Act 1922, s 17—Finance Act 1926, s 30—Finance Act 1951, s 21. **Hart (Inspector of
    Taxes) v Sangster** [1957] **2** 208, CA.
 South Africa—
  Assessment on capital appreciation of mining claims in Southern Rhodesia. *See* **South Africa** (Income
   tax—Assessment—Capital appreciation).
 Special charge—
  Investment income—
   Investment income for 1967-68 exceeding £3,000 plus amount of surtax personal allowances—
    Income under a trust—Foreign trust—Relief from charge—Taxpayer not absolutely entitled as
    against trustees to capital of trust—Taxpayer becoming absolutely entitled as from 14th
    December 1967—Whether entitled to claim relief in respect of income received prior to 14th
    December 1967—Finance Act 1968, s 41, Sch 15, para 9(1)(b). **Franklin v IRC** [1971] **2** 1411, Ch D.
   Investment income for 1967-68 exceeding £3,000 plus amount of surtax personal allowance—
    Taxpayer holding £7,000 ordinary stock in investment company—Accounts of company made up
    to 31st January in each year—Final dividend normally paid at the end of March or the beginning
    of April before end of fiscal year—Final dividend for year ended 31st January 1968 declared at
    annual general meeting on 3rd April 1968—Dividend resolved to be paid on 18th April
    1968—Whether dividend to be included in taxpayer's aggregate investment income for
    1967-68—Finance Act 1968, ss 41, 42, 50(1), (2)(b). **IRC v Greaves** [1971] **3** 1271, Ch D.
 Special commissioners—
  Appeal. *See* Appeal—Special commissioners, *above.*
  Judicial review of decision of commissioner—
   Availability of remedy. *See* **Judicial review** (Availability of remedy—Special Commissioner).
  Perjury. *See* **Criminal law** (Perjury—Judicial proceeding—Special Commissioners of Income Tax).
 Special contribution—
  Assessment on executor of taxpayer. *See* **Special contribution** (Additional assessment—Limitation on
   time for making).
  Investment income. *See* **Special contribution** (Investment income).
 Statute—
  Retrospective operation—
   Surcharge on surtax rate for previous year—Surcharge on assessment imposed retrospectively—
    Validity of surcharge—Finance Act 1974, s 8(2). **James v IRC** [1977] **2** 897, Ch D.
 Stock-in-trade—
  Cost of acquisition—
   Acquisition of capital asset distinguished. *See* Deduction in computing profits—Capital or revenue
    expenditure—Capital asset or stock-in-trade, *above.*
   Deduction in computing profits. *See* Deduction in computing profits—Expenses wholly and
    exclusively laid out for purposes of trade—Cost of acquiring stock-in-trade, *above.*
  Valuation—
   Computation of profits. *See* Computation of profits—Stock-in-trade, *above.*
   Discontinuance of trade. *See* Discontinuance of trade—Trading stock—Valuation, *above.*
 Subvention payments—
  Deduction in computing profits. *See* Deduction in computing profits—Subvention payments, *above.*
 Succession to trade—
  Merger—
   Company and subsidiaries—Division of manufacture—One process carried on by subsidiary
    companies—Remaining process carried on by parent company—Sales effected by another
    subsidiary company—Merger of manufacturing companies but not of selling company—Whether
    company assessable as successor to part of trade carried on by subsidiaries—Income Tax Act
    1918, Sch D, Cases I and II, r 11(2)—Finance Act 1926, s 32(2). **Briton Ferry Steel Co Ltd v Barry**
    [1939] **4** 541, CA.
  Subsidiary companies—
   Wholesale trade—Wholesale manufacturing trade carried on by subsidiary company—Taken over
    by retail company—Whether retail company succeeding to wholesale trade—Income Tax Act
    1918, Sch D, Cases I and II, r 11(2). **Laycock (Inspector of Taxes) v Freeman, Hardy & Willis Ltd**
    [1938] **4** 609, .
 Superannuation contribution—
  Exemption. *See* Exemption—Superannuation contribution, *above.*
 Surcharge on surtax rate for previous year—
  Retrospective operation of statute. *See* Statute—Retrospective operation—Surcharge on surtax rate for
   previous year, *above.*

INCOME TAX (cont)—

Surtax—

Restrictive covenant—

Consideration for restrictive covenant—Future employment—Undertaking in connection with the employment—Undertaking restricting employee's conduct or activities—Barrister undertaking to cease practice to take up employment—Employer paying him lump sum as an inducement for undertaking to cease practice—Whether payment in respect of 'an undertaking...the tenor or effect of which is to restrict him as to his conduct or activities'—Income and Corporation Taxes Act 1970, s 34. **Vaughan-Neil v IRC** [1979] **3** 481, Ch D.

Tax advantage—

Consideration representing assets available for distribution by way of dividend—

Available—Meaning—Legally available—Company's current liabilities exceeding current assets—Company in which taxpayer had controlling interest—Sale to company of taxpayer's shares in five other companies—Bank loan to pay for shares—Whether bona fide commercial transaction—Whether sum 'available for distribution by way of dividend'—Finance Act 1960, s 28(1), (2)(c), (d). **IRC v Brown** [1971] **3** 502, CA.

Counteracting—

Appeal against notice—Statutory grounds of appeal—Taxpayer wishing to question notice on other grounds—Claim for declaratory relief—Notification by commissioners specifying transactions in question—Decision of tribunal that prima facie case for proceeding—Taxpayer claiming declarations in High Court that notification and decision void on ground commissioners' reasons for questioning transactions not disclosed to him—Whether taxpayer entitled to claim declarations—Whether taxpayer limited to statutory appeal procedure—Income and Corporation Taxes Act 1970, s 462(1). **Balen v IRC** [1977] **2** 406, Ch D.

Commissioner's counter-statement—Validity—Counter-statement containing detailed analysis of events leading up to transactions in question and laying foundation of commissioners' case—Counter-statement not shown to taxpayer—Whether tribunal entitled to take counter-statement into consideration—Whether tribunal in breach of natural justice—Whether commissioners required to make known their case to taxpayer—Income and Corporation Taxes Act 1970, s 460(7)(a). **Balen v IRC** [1977] **2** 406, Ch D; [1978] **2** 1033, CA.

Notice—Validity—Notification by commissioners specifying transactions in question—Reasons for questioning transactions not stated in notification—Whether commissioners required to make known their case to taxpayer—Whether commissioners in breach of natural justice—Whether notification void—Income and Corporation Taxes Act 1970, s 460(6). **Balen v IRC** [1978] **2** 1033, CA.

Transaction in securities—Consideration received in connection with distribution of profits of company—Receipt of shares—Property transactions resulting in substantial profit to company wholly owned by taxpayer—Taxpayer exchanging his shares in that company for those in second company, also wholly owned by him, at a premium—First company paying dividend to second company without deduction of tax—Third company unconnected with taxpayer making loans to taxpayer—Second company acquiring all the issued shares in third company—Whether loans by third company transaction in securities—Whether by receiving loans from third company taxpayer obtaining tax advantage—Income and Corporation Taxes Act 1970, ss 460, 461, 466, 467. **Williams v IRC** [1980] **3** 321, HL.

Transaction in securities—Transaction carried out for bona fide commercial reasons—Commercial reasons—Transactions carried out for purpose of perpetuating family control of business—Family company—Bonus issue of redeemable preference shares—Issue to provide funds for estate duty purposes and thereby avoid loss of family control of company on death of major shareholders—Redemption of shares resulting in tax advantage—Whether issue and redemption of shares 'carried out for bona fide commercial reasons'—Finance Act 1960, s 28(1). **IRC v Goodwin** [1976] **1** 481, HL.

Transactions carried out before 5th April 1960—Agreements for sales of shares made in 1958—Payments in pursuance thereof extending beyond 5th April 1960—Validity of notice applying provisions—Whether agreement for sale of shares only relevant transaction—Whether transaction 'carried out' before 5th April 1960—Finance Act 1960, s 28(1), (3). **Greenberg v IRC** [1971] **3** 136, HL.

Tribunal—Determination whether there is a prima facie case—Participation by members of tribunal in determination—Absence of member—Effect—Member not participating in determination owing to absence abroad—Whether determination valid—Finance Act 1960, s 28(7). **Howard v Borneman (No 2)** [1975] **2** 418, HL.

Tribunal—Determination whether there is a prima facie case—Procedure—Determination on documents—Whether taxpayer had right to be heard at that stage—Finance Act 1960, s 28(5). **Wiseman v Borneman** [1969] **3** 275, HL.

Married woman—

Not separately assessed—Capacity to obtain tax advantage—Capitalisation of profits as redeemable preference shares—Shares issued to taxpayer—Taxpayer married woman living with husband and not separately assessed—Subsequent redemption of shares—Notice served on married woman—Whether she obtained tax advantage although not assessable to tax—Validity of notice—Finance Act 1960, ss 28(1), (2), (3), 43(4)(g). **IRC v Brook** [1967] **3** 620, Ch D.

Not separately assessed—Liability of woman—Return of capital and capitalisation of profits—Notice served on married woman—Whether she obtained tax advantage—Whether notice valid—Finance Act 1960, ss 28(1), (3), 43(4)(g). **IRC v Hague** [1968] **2** 1252, .

Meaning of 'tax advantage'—

Avoidance of a possible assessment—Transaction in connection with the distribution of profits—Phrase including transfer of assets of company—Accrual of receipts so as not to attract tax—Necessity of comparing like with like—Shareholder's sale of shares in one company to another—Shareholders still controlling all shares in both companies—Receipt of purchase price not comparable to gratuitous payment by way of dividend—Whether tax advantage obtained—Finance Act 1960, ss 28(1), (2)(d), 43(4)(g). **Cleary v IRC** [1967] **2** 48, HL.

INCOME TAX (cont)—
Tax advantage (cont)—
Transaction in securities—
Consideration received in connection with distribution of profits of company—Company acquiring valuable chattel—Taxpayer holding all issued shares in company—Sale of shares in company for a consideration representing the value of the chattel—Whether by selling shares taxpayer obtaining tax advantage—Whether consideration representing value of company's trading stock—Income and Corporation Taxes Act 1970, ss 461, 466, 467. **IRC v Wiggins** [1979] **2** 245, Ch D.

Distribution of profits of company—Abnormal amount by way of dividend—Whether payment of dividend transaction in securities—Income and Corporation Taxes Act 1988, ss 703(1), 709(2). **IRC v Laird Group plc** [2003] **4** 669, HL.

Distribution of profits of company—Consideration received in connection with distribution of profits accruing on realisation of company's assets—Taxpayers receiving interest-free loans from company in consequence of another company making non-taxable profit on sale of property and declaring abnormal dividend—Whether taxpayers obtaining a tax advantage—Whether tax advantage limited to amount remaining in taxpayers' hands after repaying loan—Income and Corporation Taxes Act 1970, ss 460(3), 466. **Bird v IRC** [1988] **2** 670, HL.

Main object—Finding of commissioners as to main object—Conclusiveness—Return of capital and capitalisation of profits—Bona fide commercial transaction—One of main objects found to be tax advantages to stockholders generally—Not a finding which no reasonable man could reach—What fraction of payment to stockholder quantified to counteract tax advantage—Finance Act 1960, s 28(1)(3). **IRC v Hague** [1968] **2** 1252, .

Main object—Intention to obtain tax advantage—Subjective question—Two methods of carrying out commercial transactions, one involving more and the other less tax liability—Not a necessary consequence of adopting latter course that main object was to obtain tax advantage—Defeating take-over bid—Company's cash resource made available by way of return of capital, not as income—Finance Act 1960, s 28. **IRC v Brebner** [1967] **1** 779, HL.

Main object—Taking advantage of statutory rights—Dealer in securities—Purchase of debenture stock—Calculation of price—No distinction made between capital and interest—Right to exclude interest (tax deducted) from accounts—Resulting loss shown on transaction—Recouping through lower tax assessment—Not proof that tax advantage a main object—Finance Act 1960, s 28(2), (3). **IRC v Kleinwort Benson Ltd** [1969] **2** 737, Ch D.

Tax advantage in consequence of transaction—Combined effect of transaction and liquidation of company—Agreement to liquidate company—Agreement between shareholders providing for method of appropriating surplus assets between shareholders on liquidation—Taxpayer principal shareholder—Object and effect of agreement to ensure that assets of company representing undistributed profits were received by taxpayer in tax-free form—Whether liquidation agreement a 'transaction in securities'—Whether tax advantage obtained by taxpayer 'in consequence of ... the combined effect of the transaction ... and of the liquidation of a company'—Income and Corporation Taxes Act 1970, ss 460(1), (2), 467(1). **IRC v Joiner** [1975] **3** 1050, HL.

Tax advantage in consequence of transaction—Company—Reduction of capital—Return of part of sums paid by subscribers—Capital increased by capitalisation of profits—Single or divisible transaction—Successive resolutions—Immateriality—Main object tax advantages to shareholders—Finance Act 1960, s 28(1), (2). **IRC v Horrocks** [1968] **3** 296, Ch D.

Tax advantage in consequence of transaction—Redemption of debentures—Capitalisation of profits as debentures—Subsequent redemption of debentures—Whether redemption a transaction in securities—Whether tax advantage a consequence of capitalisation or of redemption—Finance Act 1960, ss 28(1), (2), (3), 43(4)(f), (g), (i). **IRC v Parker** [1966] **1** 399, HL.

Transaction carried out for bona fide commercial reasons—Commercial reasons—Meaning—Transactions carried out for purpose of perpetuating family control of business—Family company—Bonus issue of redeemable preference shares—Issue to provide funds for estate duty purposes and thereby avoid loss of family control of company on death of major shareholders—Redemption of shares resulting in tax advantage—Whether issue and redemption of shares 'carried out ... for bona fide commercial reasons'—Finance Act 1960, s 28(1). **IRC v Goodwin** [1975] **1** 708, CA.

Transaction carried out for bona fide commercial reasons—Commercial reasons—Taxpayer and his brother selling all the issued share capital in H Ltd to a family company to perpetuate family control of another company—Taxpayer selling his shares in H Ltd for the purpose of raising money to purchase neighbouring farm to improve his farming business—Sale of shares resulting in tax advantage—Whether sale of shares carried out for 'bona fide commercial reasons'—Income and Corporation Taxes Act 1970, s 460(1). **Clark v IRC** [1979] **1** 385, Ch D.

Tax avoidance—
Generally. *See* Avoidance, *above*.
Medical partnership—
Australia. *See* **Australia** (Income tax—Avoidance—Agreement or arrangement having purpose or effect of avoiding liability—Partnership of medical practitioners dissolved).

Tax credits—
Powers of Inland Revenue Commissioners. *See* Commissioners of Inland Revenue—Administration and management of taxation system, *above*.

Tax evasion—
Offence in connection with tax evasion—
Decision to prosecute—Judicial review of decision—Availability of remedy. *See* **Judicial review** (Availability of remedy—Decision to prosecute—Offence in connection with tax evasion).

Tax reserve certificate—
Interest. *See* Interest—Tax reserve certificates, *above*.

Technical education payments—
Deduction in computing profits. *See* Deduction in computing profits—Technical education payments, *above*.

Testimonial—
Payment to employee to mark exceptional achievement. *See* Emoluments from office or employment—Receipt 'from' employment—Testimonial, *above*.

INCOME TAX (cont)—
Time—
Time limit—
Assessment—Notice requiring wife to pay the tax she would have had to pay if separately assessed—Tax assessed on husband and attributable to wife's income. *See* Husband and wife—Collection from wife of tax assessed on husband and attributable to wife's income—Notice requiring wife to pay the tax she would have had to pay if separately assessed, *above*.
Total income—
Computation—
Apportioned sum out of income of company—Deed assigning part of income to trustees—Income defined as income of settlor as computed for purpose of Income Tax Acts—Income of company deemed to be income of taxpayer—Whether such income subject to deed. **IRC v Payton** [1940] **4** 419, CA.
Deduction of annual payments—
Annual sum payable by deed—Effective payment—Sum paid returned to payer—Sum to be held or applied for benefit of payer—Whether an effective payment under a disposition. **Russell v IRC** [1944] **2** 192, CA.
Annuity—Will—Appropriation of fund by executors—Fund insufficient—Fund made up by advance charged on residue—Whether residuary legatee entitled to deduct as annual payment share of amounts borrowed to make up deficiency—Income Tax Act 1918, s 27(1)(b), All Schedules Rules, r 19. **Bowen (Sir Edward C) v IRC** [1937] **1** 607, CA.
Capital or income payments—Purchase money—Payment of sums on account—Partnership—Purchase of deceased's partner's share—Capital or annual payment. **IRC v Ledgard** [1937] **2** 492, KBD.
Covenant for payments—When payment due—Payments to be made on 1st May in each year—Termination of covenant on expiration of eight years from 5th May 1953—Whether 'year' meant calendar year or year commencing with 5th May. **IRC v Hobhouse** [1956] **3** 594, Ch D.
Covenant—Annuity—Covenants to pay annuities for more than 6 years—Contemporaneous agreements for repayment—Smaller sums repaid—What deductions allowable. **Lee v IRC** [1943] **2** 672, KBD.
Foreign decree—Alimony paid to former wife under foreign decree—Former wife resident abroad—Tax not deductible from payment—Payment not deductible from total income—Income Tax Act 1918, All Schedules Rules, r 19—Finance Act 1927, s 39(3). **Bingham v IRC** [1955] **3** 321, Ch D.
Husband and wife—Separation—Allowance by husband to wife—Voluntary allowance under oral agreement—Whether deductible in assessing total income. **Peters (Exors) v IRC** [1941] **2** 620, CA.
Maintenance of wife of unsound mind—Undertaking by husband on appointment as wife's receiver—Undertaking embodied in order of matter in lunacy—Payments to make up deficiency between patient's income and sum required for maintenance—Whether payments deductible in computing total income—Income Tax Act 1918, s 27. **Watkins v IRC** [1939] **3** 165, KBD.
Dividends—
Dividend paid without deduction of tax—Nil assessment for income tax on company—Whether shareholder should be taxed on amount of dividend received or on grossed-up amount—Finance Act 1931, s 7. **Cull v IRC** [1939] **3** 761, HL.
Dividend paid without deduction of tax—Payment out of profits assessed to tax—Whether dividends to be grossed up for purposes of surtax—Finance Act 1931, s 7(2). **IRC v Pearson** [1936] **2** 731, KBD.
Payment out of profits—Profits or gains assessed at nil—Repayments by as company of tax deducted on assessment being overruled—Sums paid to taxpayer equalling tax recovered by company—Whether payment assessable to surtax—Income Tax Act 1918, All Schedules Rules, r 20—Finance Act 1927, s 39(1)—Finance Act 1931, s 7. **Benn v IRC** [1937] **3** 852, KBD.
Income from residue under will—
Date beneficiary entitled to income—Beneficiary having no title to residue until residue ascertained in due course of administration—Sums credited to residuary life tenant during period of administration—Whether income of life tenant. **Corbett v IRC** [1937] **4** 700, CA.
Income received by taxpayer on behalf of third party—
Assessment to tax at standard rate—Taxpayer assessed as person 'receiving' income—Assessment final and conclusive for purposes of tax at standard rate—Assessment also final and conclusive in estimating total income—Whether income to be included in total income of taxpayer although not belonging to taxpayer beneficially—Income Tax Act 1952, ss 148, 524(4). **Aplin v White (Inspector of Taxes)** [1973] **2** 637, Ch D.
Share of profits—
Partnership—Bequest of share—Widow of deceased partner entitled under his will to share of profits—Widow's share of profits in year of assessment amounting to considerable sum—Continuing partners unable to pay share of profits during year of assessment—Whether widow liable to assessment on sum representing her share—Income Tax Act 1918, Sch D, Case III, r 1(a), All Schedules Rules, r 19. **IRC v Lebus** [1946] **1** 476, KBD and CA.
Trust income—
Accumulation—Infant life tenant—Vested life interest—Accumulation of income during minority—Whether income of infant and subject to tax—Trustee Act 1925, s 31(2). **Stanley v IRC** [1944] **1** 230, CA.
Trade—
Adventure in nature of trade—
Casual profit on hedge against devaluation—Purchase of silver bullion—Profit on re-sale—Finding that other considerations influenced purchase unsupported by evidence—Whether adventure in the nature of trade—Income Tax Act 1952, Sch D, Case I. **Wisdom v Chamberlain (Inspector of Taxes)** [1969] **1** 332, CA.
Isolated transaction—Acquisition of houses—Acquisition by timber company possessing building powers—Purchase of houses from subsidiary building company—Object to assist managing director to re-start business—Company receiving rents and not taking steps to sell houses—Following offers houses sold at profit—Whether acquisition of houses an investment or adventure in nature of trade—Income Tax Act 1952, Sch D, Case I, ss 123, 526. **Lucy & Sunderland Ltd v Hunt (Inspector of Taxes)** [1961] **3** 1062, Ch D.

INCOME TAX (cont)—
Trade (cont)—
Adventure in nature of trade (cont)—
Isolated transaction—Sale of copyright—Actor—Acquisition of film rights in book—Acquisition as an investment—Subsequent sale of film rights at a profit—Actor having carried out no other similar transaction—Whether trading profit—Income Tax Act 1952, s 123(1), Sch D, Case I. **Shiner v Lindblom (Inspector of Taxes)** [1960] **3** 832, Ch D.

Isolated transaction—Sale of land—Building company approached by council for acquisition of fields zoned for school site—Agreement to negotiate—Formation of associated company as investment company—Sale of fields by building company to associated company—Subsequent sale by associated company to council at large profit—Whether adventure in the nature of trade and taxable under Case 1 of Sch D—Income Tax Act 1952, ss 122, 123(1), 526(1). **Eames (Inspector of Taxes) v Stepnell Properties Ltd** [1967] **1** 785, CA.

Isolated transaction—Sale of land—Contract to sell before contract to purchase—Income Tax Act 1952, s 526(1), Sch D, Case I. **Johnston (Inspector of Taxes) v Heath** [1970] **3** 915, Ch D.

Isolated transaction—Sale of land—Husband purchasing building site and making unconditional gift of it to wife—Re-sale of site at profit by wife to husband's nominees—Transaction repeated two years later—Trading negatived by commissioners—Income Tax Act 1918, s 237, Sch D, rr 1(a)(ii), 2, Cases I, VI, All Schedules Rules, r 16(1). **Williams (Inspector of Taxes) v Davies** [1945] **1** 304, KBD.

Land—Transaction in land—Steps taken to enhance value of land for purpose of sale—Taxpayer not otherwise engaged in trade of dealing in land—Taxpayer purchasing property for possible use as a residence—Property subsequently found not to be suitable for residential purposes—Taxpayer thereafter taking steps to obtain permission to develop property—Resale of property with planning permission at substantial profit—Purchase not a trading activity—Whether activities of taxpayer subsequent to purchase constituting adventure in the nature of trade—Income Tax Act 1952, ss 123(1) (Sch D Case 1) 526(1). **Taylor v Good (Inspector of Taxes)** [1974] **1** 1137, CA.

Transactions in endowment policies—Purchase of endowment policies on other oeople's lives—Purchase made with intention of providing ascertained annual sums—No intention to sell policies—Realisation of policies—Whether transactions represented 'adventure or concern in the nature of trade'—Income Tax Act 1918, s 237, Sch D, Case I. **Barry v Cordy (Inspector of Taxes)** [1946] **2** 396, CA.

Debts—
Valuation. See Computation of profits—Trade debts—Valuation, *above.*
Discontinuance. See Discontinuance of trade, *above.*
Executors—
Partnership business—Dealing in land—Death of partner—Realisation of estate—Postponement of account until particular development completed—Whether executors having agreed to carry on business. **Marshall's Exors, Hood's Exors and Rogers v Joly** [1936] **1** 851, KBD.

Farming. See Farming, *above.*
Isolated transaction—
Adventure in the nature of trade. See Trade—Adventure in nature of trade—Isolated transaction, *above.*
Profits. See Profits—Isolated transaction, *above.*
Liquidator—
Sale in course of liquidation. See Trade—Sale in course of liquidation, *below.*
Trade carried on on behalf of liquidator—Company in liquidation—Contracts entered into by company before liquidation performed by agreement by another company—Part of profits arising from performance of contracts paid to company in liquidation—Whether trade carried on by other company on behalf of liquidator—Whether liquidator liable to be taxed on profits made. **Baker v Cook (Inspector of Taxes)** [1937] **3** 509, KBD.

Loss relief. See Loss relief—Trade, *above.*
Meaning—
Operations of commercial character involving dealings with other people—Taxpayer receiving or entitled to profits arising from trade—Profits from dealings in or developing land—Tax avoidance scheme—Taxpayer not himself dealing in or developing land—Taxpayer receiving benefit of tax saving—Taxpayer implementing scheme through medium of companies under his control—Development of land by companies—Effect of scheme to divert companies' prospective profits from development into hands of trustees of taxpayer's family settlement as a tax-free capital sum—Whether sum received by trustees a profit arising from an adventure in nature of trade carried out by taxpayer—Income Tax Act 1952, ss 122, 123(1)(Sch D, Case I), 526(1). **Ransom (Inspector of Taxes) v Higgs** [1974] **3** 949, HL.

Meaning of 'trade'—
View to profit—LLPs established as part of marketed tax avoidance scheme—Individual members making capital contributions—Commissioning distributor also funding—Whether carrying on 'trade'—Whether carrying on 'with a view to profit'—Income Tax (Trading and Other Income) Act 2005, s 863—Income Tax Act 2007, s 64. **Ingenious Games LLP v Revenue and Customs Comrs** [2022] **2** 338, CA.

Mutuality principle. See Profits—Mutuality principle, *above.*
Profits of trade. See Profits, *above.*
Receipts. See Trade receipts, *below.*
Sale in course of liquidation—
Sale of asset by liquidator—Parent rights—Agreement by company to sell parent rights—Company going into liquidation—Proceeds of sale distributed to shareholders—Whether sale carried out by liquidator in course of carrying on company's trade. **Wilson Box (Foreign Rights) Ltd (in liq) v Brice (inspector of Taxes)** [1936] **3** 728, CA.

Separate traders—
New trade or extension of old—Company manufacturing gas appliances and chemical plant—Commencing buying, selling and assembling electrical food mixers. **Cannon Industries Ltd v Edwards (Inspector of Taxes)** [1966] **1** 456, Ch D.

Succession to trade. See Succession to trade, *above.*

INCOME TAX (cont)—
  Trade (cont)—
    Trade association—
      Stock exchange—Stock exchange providing premises for transaction of members' business—Stock exchange's income consisting of founders' contributions, members' entrance fees and monthly subscriptions—Whether stock exchange a club or a trading association—Whether founders' contributions and members' entrance fees qualifying as 'subscriptions'—Inland Revenue Ordinance (Hong Kong), s 24(1)(2). **Kowloon Stock Exchange Ltd v IRC** [1985] **1** 205, PC.
    Trading receipts. *See* Profits—Trading receipts, *above*.
    Woodlands. *See* Woodlands—Trading activities, *below*.
  Trade receipts—
    Profit—
      Profit from sale of land—Capital or income—Tenants in common under gift in will—Purchase by one tenant of other tenant's share—Sale of portion of land in order to raise money for purchase of share—Profit made from sale—Whether land acquired for purpose of profit-making by sale—Whether profit from carrying out of profit-making undertaking or scheme—Whether transaction adventure in the nature of trade—Income Tax and Social Services Contribution Assessment Act 1936-1963, s 26(a). **McClelland v Comr of Taxation of the Commonwealth of Australia** [1971] **1** 969, PC.
  Trade union—
    Exemption. *See* Exemption—Trade union, *above*.
  Trading receipts. *See* Profits—Trading receipts, *above*.
  Transaction in securities—
    Counteracting tax advantage. *See* Tax advantage—Counteracting—Transaction in securities, *above*.
    Generally. *See* Tax advantage—Transaction in securities, *above*.
  Transfer of assets—
    Settlement. *See* Settlement—Meaning—Transfer of assets, *above*.
  Transfer of trade—
    Discontinuance. *See* Discontinuance of trade—Transfer of trade, *above*.
  Travelling expenses—
    Deduction from emoluments. *See* Emoluments from office or employment—Expenses wholly, exclusively and necessarily incurred—Travelling expenses, *above*.
    Deduction in computing profits. *See* Deduction in computing profits—Travelling expenses, *above*.
  Tribunal—
    Duty to hear parties etc. *See* **Natural justice** (Income tax tribunal—Duty to hear parties etc).
  Under-deduction of tax—
    Royalties—
      Omission to deduct tax—Recovery—Payment of royalties not brought into charge—Payment made before passage of annual Finance Act—Whether payers entitled to recover tax—Provisional Collection of Taxes Act 1913—Income Tax Act 1918, s 211(2), All Schedules Rules, r 21. **Nesta Ltd v Wyatt** [1940] **4** 217, KBD.
  Undistributed income—
    Actual income from all sources—
      Balancing charge—Voluntary liquidation—Balancing charge equal to excess of sale price of plant and machinery over written down value for income tax purposes—Whether balancing charge should be included in actual income—Income Tax Act 1952, ss 245, 248(1), 255(3), 292(1)(3), 323(4). **IRC v Wood Bros (Birkenhead) Ltd (in liq)** [1959] **1** 53, HL.
    Adequacy of distribution—
      Repayment of capital—Capital issued otherwise than for adequate consideration—Surplus applied by revaluation of capital by paying up in full new ordinary shares—Shares issued by way of capitalisation to holders of existing ordinary shares—Finance Act 1922, s 21(1), as amended by Finance Act 1927, s 31(1), and Finance Act 1936, s 19(4). **IRC v Thornton, Kelley & Co Ltd** [1957] **1** 650, Ch D.
    Apportionment—
      Apportionment of actual income of relevant year—Actual income meaning income actually received—Sub-apportionment of excess of apportioned sum over 'actual income from all sources' of company—Dividend received in relevant year, but appropriated in accounts of prior year to other purposes, not deductible in computing excess—Income tax Act 1952, ss 245, 254(1). **Princes Investments Ltd v IRC** [1967] **2** 238, CA.
      Computation of income for apportionment. *See* Undistributed income—Computation of income for apportionment, *below*.
      Exemption. *See* Undistributed income—Exemption from apportionment provisions, *below*.
      Interests of members in actual income—Apportionment in accordance with the respective 'interests' of the members—Shareholders selling all their shares before end of accounting period to a company not subject to apportionment provisions—Whether original shareholders had any interest after end of accounting period for purposes of apportionment provisions—Whether apportionment valid—Income Tax Act 1952, ss 245, 248(1). **CHW (Huddersfield) Ltd v IRC** [1963] **2** 952, HL.
      Members who would not have received income in event of distribution—Preference shareholders entitled to surplus assets on winding-up—Direction and apportionment by commissioners—Basis of apportionment—Interests of the members—Interest in capital assets—Limitation of time for direction—Finance Act 1922, s 21(1), (7), Sch I, paras 4, 8, 9—Finance Act 1928, s 18—Finance Act 1937, ss 14(3), 31(4). **FPH Finance Trust Ltd (in liq) v IRC** [1945] **1** 492, HL.
      Sub-apportionments—Notice—Failure to give notice of sub-apportionments to company given surtax direction—Effect—Income Tax Act 1952, ss 248(1)-(3), 254(3)-(5). **Princes Investments Ltd v IRC** [1967] **2** 238, CA.
    Close company. *See* Close company, *above*.
    Company under control of not more than five persons—
      Person—Principal and nominee—Treatment of principal and nominee as single person—Income Tax Act 1952, s 256(1)(3). **Morrisons Holdings Ltd v IRC** [1966] **1** 789, Ch D.

INCOME TAX (cont)—
Undistributed income (cont)—
Computation of income for apportionment—
Allowances—Maintenance, repairs, insurance and management—Deduction on five years' average cost or relevant year's expenditures—Income Tax Act 1952, ss 101(1), 245, 248, 255(3). **Cadogan Settled Estates Co (in liq) v IRC** [1969] 2 878, Ch D.
Recomputation—Claim for refund of profits tax—Resulting increase of income—Power to issue further apportionment—Income Tax Act 1952, ss 245, 248(1)(2), 255(3)—Finance Act 1952, s 68(2)—Finance Act 1947, s 31(2). **Cadogan Settled Estates Co (in liq) v IRC** [1969] 2 878, Ch D.
Direction by commissioners—
Condition precedent—Intimation by commissioners to company—Whether intimation a condition precedent to direction—Finance Act 1928, s 18(3). **Star Entertainments Ltd v IRC** [1942] 2 33, CA.
Distribution—
Reasonable time after end of accounting period—Company becoming subsidiary company towards end of accounting period—Apportionment on time basis—Shareholders ceasing to be members before end of accounting period—Dividend declared after previous decision not to declare dividend—Whether distribution within reasonable time after the accounting period—Income Tax Act 1952, s 245, s 256(4). **CHW (Huddersfield) Ltd v IRC** [1963] 2 952, HL.
What constitutes distribution—Dividend—Dividend paid by cheque on condition that sum paid be lent to payer—No genuine distribution of income. **IRC v Marbob Ltd** [1939] 3 309, KBD.
Exemption from apportionment provisions—
Company in which public substantially interested—Public—Exclusion of relatives, nominees etc of persons having control, when determining whether public substantially interested—Choice of shareholdings by Revenue—Settlements—Relatives—Whether trustees or executors as shareholders persons interested in shares—Income Tax Act 1952, s 256(1), (3), (5). **IRC v Park Investments Ltd** [1966] 2 785, .
Company in which public substantially interested—Public—Meaning—Members of company not in control—Controlling interest in company—Percentage of voting power—Taxpayer holding 74 per cent of voting shares—Taxpayer's brother holding almost all balance—Whether brother member of public—Income Tax Ordinance 1940 (Ordinance No 8 of 1940 of the Uganda Proctectorate), s 21(2). **Income Tax Comr v Bjordal** [1955] 1 401, PC.
Company in which public substantially interested—Quotation in official list of stock exchange—Shares held by relative of person controlling company—Shares not quoted among official quotations of stock exchange—Subject of dealings thereon and mentioned in list of business done—Whether relative a member of public—Whether shares 'quoted in the official list' of stock exchange—Finance Act 1922, s 21—Finance Act 1927, s 31—Finance Act 1936, s 19(2)(a). **Tatem Steam Navigation Co Ltd v IRC** [1941] 2 616, CA.
Company in which public substantially interested—Relatives—Exclusion from 'public'—Beneficiaries under settlements of shares—Beneficiaries including relatives and non-relatives—Whether settled shares held beneficially for the 'public'—Income Tax Act 1952, s 256(1), (5). **Morrisons Holdings Ltd v IRC** [1966] 1 789, Ch D.
Subsidiary company—Control—Control by reference to beneficial ownership of shares and control not by reference thereto contrasted—Joint ownership of share with controlling voting power—Voting rights in company whose name stands first on share register—Finance Act 1922, s 21(6)—Finance Act 1936, s 19(1)—Finance Act 1937, s 14(1). **IRC v Harton Coal Co Ltd (in liq)** [1960] 3 48, Ch D.
Subsidiary company—Subsidiary of foreign company—Whether a 'subsidiary company'—Finance Act 1922, s 21(6)—Finance Act 1927, s 31(3). **Barrowford Holdings Ltd v IRC** [1939] 4 380, CA.
Income available for distribution—
Current requirements of business—Income not applied or applicable to current requirements of company's business—Sum applied out of income in or towards payment for first business, undertaking or property acquired by company—Meaning of 'income'—Profits or gross receipts—Property dealing company—Sum expended on first acquisition of property—Property resold at a profit exceeding amount of purchase price—Whether purchase price paid 'out of the income' of the company—Income Tax Act 1952, s 246(2). **Hanstead Investments Ltd v IRC** [1975] 2 1066, CA.
Liquidation of company. *See* Undistributed income—Liquidation of company—Income available for distribution, *below*.
Liquidation of company—
Accounts not made up—Sale of business—Voluntary liquidation—Accounts not made up until after sale—Liquidation having effect that retention of profits no longer reasonable—Finance Act 1922, s 21—Finance Act 1927, s 31. **Austins of East Ham Ltd v IRC** [1937] 4 275, KBD.
Income available for distribution—Income for broken period before winding-up resolution—Whether income necessarily income unreasonably withheld from distribution—Finance Act 1927, s 31(4)—Finance Act 1922, s 21(1), proviso. **Mucklow (A & J) Ltd v IRC** [1954] 2 508, CA.
Member of company—
Husband of member—Liability of husband to apportionment—Apportionment to members—Member a married woman living with her husband—Whether husband liable to apportionment—Income Tax Act 1918, All Schedules Rules, r 16, proviso (1)—Finance Act 1922, s 21(1), (2), (3), (7) (as amended by Finance Act 1927, s 31(2))—Finance Act 1927, s 42(7)—Finance Act 1936, s 19(5). **IRC v Barclays Bank Ltd** [1951] 1 1, HL.
Person having share or interest in capital or profits or income—Debenture stockholders—Whether debenture stockholders members—Income Tax Act 1952, ss 245, 255(1), (2), 256(2). **IRC v R Woolf & Co (Rubber) Ltd** [1961] 2 651, CA.
Person having share or interest in capital or profits or income—Permanent director with option to take up shares—Whether a member—Finance Act 1922, s 21(7)—Finance Act 1937, s 14(3). **IRC v Tring Investments Ltd** [1939] 2 105, CA.
Reasonable part of income not distributed—
Shares charged to bank—Covenant to pay all dividends received from shares to bank—Company having no other income—Whether directors acted unreasonable in not distributing income—Finance Act 1922, s 21(1). **Fattorini Ltd v IRC** [1942] 1 619, HL.

INCOME TAX (cont)—
    Undistributed income (cont)—
        Relief—
            Double assessment—Apportionment—Relief on subsequent distribution—Extent of relief—
            Direction by commissioners—Subsequent distribution exceeding profits available for distribution
            in relevant years—Income Tax Act 1952, ss 245, 249(5). **IRC v Hudspeth** [1959] **2** 752, Ch D.
    Valuation of property—
        Additional assessment. *See* Additional assessment—Valuation of property, *above*.
    Value added tax. *See* **Value added tax**.
    Vehicles—
        Capital allowances. *See* **Capital allowances** (Vehicles).
    Victoria. *See* **Victoria** (Income tax).
    Vocation—
        Profits of vocation. *See* Profits—Profession or vocation, *above*.
    Voluntary payment—
        Employee. *See* Emoluments from office or employment—Voluntary payment, *above*.
        Profit not otherwise charged to tax. *See* Profits—Profits not otherwise charged—Voluntary payment,
        above.
        Trading receipt. *See* Profits—Trading receipts—Voluntary payment, *above*.
    Wages. *See* Emoluments from office or employment, *above*.
    Wear and tear—
        Balancing charge. *See* Balancing charge—Wear and tear, *above*.
        Machinery or plant—
            Capital allowances. *See* **Capital allowances** (Machinery or plant—Wear and tear).
            Deduction in computing profits. *See* Deduction in computing profits—Wear and tear of machinery
            or plant, *above*.
    Wilful default—
        Additional assessment. *See* Additional assessment—Fraud or wilful default, *above*.
    Woodlands—
        Trading activities—
            Sawmill—Preparation of timber for market—Respects in which work extending beyond such
            preparation—Taxpayer also trading as timber merchant—Whether operation assessable under
            Sch D—Income Tax Act 1952, Schs B, D. **Collins v Fraser (Inspector of Taxes)** [1969] **3** 524, Ch D.
            Sawmill—Timber worked up before sale—Timber grown on estate and timber bought outside
            worked up and sold—Whether treating and sale of timber grown on estate carrying on of a
            trade—Income Tax Act 1918, Schs A, B and D. **Christie v Davies** [1945] **1** 370, KBD.
    Work in progress—
        Change in method of valuation—
            Change showing surplus representing anticipated profits of earlier year—Year in which profit
            arising. *See* Computation of profits—Year in which profit arising—Change in method of valuation
            of work in progress showing surplus representing anticipated profits of earlier years, *above*.
    Year—
        Appropriate year of assessment. *See* Assessment—Appropriate year, *above*.
        Attribution of outgoings. *See* Deduction in computing profits—Appropriate year, *above*.
        Emoluments—
            Year of assessment. *See* Emoluments from office or employment—Year of assessment, *above*.
        Profits—
            Year in which profit arising—Computation of profits. *See* Computation of profits—Year in which
            profit arising, *above*.
    Yearly interest of money. *See* Interest—Yearly interest of money, *above*.

INCOMPLETE GIFT
    Generally. *See* **Gift** (Incomplete gift).

INCORRIGIBLE ROGUE
    See **Criminal law** (Incorrigible rogue).

INCRIMINATION
    Co-accused—
        Statement by co-accused incriminating accused. *See* **Criminal evidence** (Co-accused—Statement
        incriminating accused).
    Inspection of property—
        Property subject-matter of action or in respect of which question arising—
            Privilege against self-incrimination. *See* **Practice** (Pre-trial or post-judgment relief—Search
            order—Privilege against self-incrimination).
    Privilege against self-incrimination—
        Anton Piller order. *See* **Practice** (Pre-trial or post-judgment relief—Search order—Privilege against
        self-incrimination).
        Contempt of court proceedings. *See* **Contempt of court** (Defence—Self-incrimination).
    Spouse—
        Privilege against self-incrimination. *See* **Evidence** (Privilege—Incrimination of witness or spouse).
    Witness—
        Privilege against self-incrimination. *See* **Evidence** (Privilege—Incrimination of witness or spouse).

INCUMBENT
    See **Ecclesiastical law** (Incumbent).

INCURABLES
    Home for incurables—
        Whether hospital. *See* **National Health Service** (Hospital—Institution for the reception and treatment of
        persons—Treatment—Home for incurables).

INDECENCY

Act outraging public decency. *See* **Criminal law** (Public decency—Act outraging public decency).

Article or electronic communication of indecent or grossly offensive nature—
Sending letters etc with intent to cause distress or anxiety. *See* **Criminal law** (Sending letters etc with intent to cause distress or anxiety—Article or electronic communication of indecent or grossly offensive nature—Freedom of thought, conscience and religion).

Evidence of similar offences. *See* **Criminal evidence** (Improper conduct of accused on other occasions—Similar offences—Indecency).

Gross indecency. *See* **Criminal law** (Gross indecency).

Indecent assault. *See* **Criminal law** (Indecent assault).

Mental disorder—
Restriction order. *See* **Sentence** (Hospital order—Restriction order).

Performances and exhibitions. *See* **Criminal law** (Disorderly house—Indecent performances and exhibitions).

Photographs of children—
Fraudulent evasion of prohibition or restriction. *See* **Criminal law** (Indecent photographs of persons under 16—Fraudulent evasion of prohibition or restriction).

Making indecent photographs of children. *See* **Criminal law** (Indecent photographs or pseudo-photographs of children—Making indecent photographs of children).

Obscene publications. *See* **Criminal law** (Obscene publications—Indecent photographs of children).

Possessing indecent photographs of children. *See* **Criminal law** (Indecent photographs or pseudo-photographs of children—Possessing indecent photographs of children).

Publications—
Indecent or obscene. *See* **Criminal law** (Obscene publications—Indecent or obscene).

Unsolicited publications describing sexual techniques. *See* **Criminal law** (Unsolicited publications—Publications describing or illustrating human sexual techniques).

Time limit for bringing prosecution—
Indecent offences between males. *See* **Criminal law** (Time—Time limit for bringing prosecution—Indecent offences between males).

INDECENT ASSAULT

Indecent assault. *See* **Criminal law** (Indecent assault).

INDECENT BEHAVIOUR

Church. *See* **Ecclesiastical law** (Church—Indecent behaviour).

INDECENT EXPOSURE

See **Criminal law** (Indecent exposure).

INDEMNITY

Agent—
Termination of agency. *See* **Agent** (Termination of agency—Indemnity).

Breach of statutory duty—
Contract—
Factory building contract—Indemnity against every 'claim ... under any statute or at common law ... arising ... from any cause other than negligence'—Whether 'negligence' included breach of statutory duty. **Murfin v United Steel Companies Ltd (Power Gas Corp Ltd, third party)** [1957] **1** 23, CA.

Broker—
Commodities market. *See* **Commodities market** (Broker—Indemnity).

Building contract—
Negligence. *See* Negligence—Building contract, *below*.

Charterparty—
Implied term. *See* **Shipping** (Charterparty—Implied term—Indemnity).

Company—
Indemnity between former directors. *See* **Company** (Winding up—Misfeasance—Indemnity claim against one respondent by other respondents).

Construction of indemnity clause—
Agreement for sale and purchase of share capital of insurance broker—
Agreement indemnifying purchaser against loss 'following and arising out of claims or complaints' to regulatory authorities pertaining to mis-selling—Company making reference to regulator and agreeing remediation scheme—Whether clause requiring indemnity where no claim or complaint made by customer. **Wood v Capita Insurance Services Ltd** [2017] **4** 615, SC; [2018] **1 Comm** 51, SC.

Indemnity against consequence of own negligence—
Concurrent causes of accident—Accident caused by negligence and breach of statutory duty of party seeking indemnity—Absence of express words covering consequences of negligence of party seeking indemnity—Rules of construction where indemnity clause not including consequences of negligence of party seeking indemnity—Whether negligent party entitled to indemnity. **EE Caledonia Ltd v Orbit Valve plc** [1995] **1** 174, CA.

Express provision exempting proferens from liability for own or servants' negligence—Need to include word 'negligence' or some synonym expressly—Clause indemnifying proferens against 'any liability, loss, claim or proceedings whatsoever'—Whether words constituting an express provision exempting proferens from liability for own negligence. **Smith v South Wales Switchgear Ltd** [1978] **1** 18, HL.

Indemnity against claims and liabilities arising in respect of injury—Sub-contract made on back-to-back basis with main contract—Injury suffered by claimant employee of sub-contractor—No causal nexus between injury and sub-contract work—Main contractor accepting liability and seeking indemnity under sub-contract—Whether indemnity engaged by negligence unconnected with sub-contract work—Whether indemnity extending to claim for contractual indemnity of main contractor. **Campbell v Conoco (UK) Ltd** [2003] **1 Comm** 35, CA.

INDEMNITY (cont)—
  Construction of indemnity clause (cont)—
    Indemnity against consequence of own negligence (cont)—
      Words wide enough in ordinary meaning to cover negligence of proferens—Construction of clause
      contra proferentem where any doubt—Supplier of services under-taking to indemnify purchaser
      against 'any liability, loss, claim or proceedings whatsoever' in respect of personal injury to any
      person—Indemnity applying only where order for services involving carrying out of work by
      supplier and only in respect of injuries 'arising out of or in the course of...the execution of the
      order'—Supplier's employee engaged on work for purchaser injured in consequence of
      purchaser's negligence—Whether clause to be construed as applying only to liability of
      purchaser for acts and omissions of supplier in carrying out work—Whether purchaser entitled to
      be indemnified for liability for own negligence. **Smith v South Wales Switchgear Ltd** [1978] **1** 18,
      HL.
    Insurers settling personal injury claims made against oil platform operator—
      Sums paid in settlement exceeding values of claims in domestic courts—Operators seeking to
      recover indemnity from contractors—Whether operator entitled to indemnity under indemnity
      clause—Whether recovery of sums in excess of those available under domestic law possible.
      Caledonia North Sea Ltd v Norton (No 2) Ltd (in liq) [2002] **1 Comm** 321, HL.
    Provision of dry-docking services—
      Contract containing reciprocal indemnity provisions in respect of damage to property or personal
      injury—Vessel damaged by fire whilst in dry dock—Whether shipyard liable to indemnify
      shipowner in respect of damage to vessel. **Acergy Shipping Ltd v Société Bretonne de
      Reparation Navale SAS** [2012] **1 Comm** 369, QBD.
    Recovery of sums paid—
      Parties each holding 50% interest in licence of petroleum exploration areas in Uganda—Parties
      entering into sale and purchase agreement (SPA) in respect of defendant's share in licence—SPA
      providing for 'non-transfer taxes' to be responsibility of defendant—Government of Uganda /
      Ugandan Revenue Authority serving notices on claimant seeking payment of tax—Claimant
      subsequently seeking recovery of sums paid in respect of non-transfer tax by way of indemnity
      pursuant to SPA—Whether claimant knowing or believing notices not valid. **Tullow Uganda Ltd v
      Heritage Oil and Gas Ltd** [2014] **1 Comm** 22, QBD.
    Whether a penalty clause. *See* **Contract** (Penalty—Indemnity clause).
  Contract between builders and scaffolding contractors—
    Personal injuries—
      Indemnity against liability—Contractors indemnifying builders against liability in respect of
      personal injuries arising out of execution of work by reason of any act, default or omission of
      contractors—Whether liability or injuries had to be causally connected with act, default or
      omission. **Smith v Vange Scaffolding and Engineering Co Ltd** [1970] **1** 249, QBD.
  Contract of carriage—
    Negligence. *See* Negligence—Contract of carriage, *below*.
  Contractor and sub-contractor—
    Workmen's compensation. *See* **Workmen's compensation** (Indemnity—Contractor and sub-contractor).
  Costs—
    Generally. *See* **Costs** (Order for costs—Indemnity costs).
    Legal aid cases. *See* **Legal aid** (Costs—Indemnity costs).
    Minority shareholder—
      Action by minority shareholder—Generally. *See* **Company** (Minority shareholder—Action by
      minority shareholder—Costs—Indemnity).
      Representative action. *See* **Company** (Minority shareholder—Representative action—Costs—
      Indemnity).
    Personal representative—
      Action against personal representative. *See* **Executor and administrator** (Action against—Costs of
      litigation).
    Taxation of costs on 'indemnity' basis. *See* **Costs** (Taxation—'Indemnity' basis).
  Court order for indemnity—
    Appeal—
      Judgment against two defendants—Order against one defendant to indemnify other
      defendant—Successful appeal by that defendant against judgment only—Effect on order for
      indemnity. **Woods v W H Rhodes & Son Ltd** [1953] **2** 658, CA.
  Employment and indemnity clause—
    Time charterparty. *See* **Shipping** (Time charterparty—Employment and indemnity clause).
  Estoppel. *See* **Estoppel** (Indemnity).
  Extent of liability under indemnity—
    Settlement of proceedings against principal—
      Indemnity clause in asset purchase agreement covering all outstanding liabilities and all
      proceedings, claims and demands in respect thereof—Proceedings for breach of contract and
      negligence against principal determined by consent judgment—Whether indemnity covering
      obligations under consent judgment. **Rust Consulting Ltd (in liquidation) v PB Ltd** [2012] **1
      Comm** 455, CA.
      Indemnity clause in asset purchase agreement covering all outstanding liabilities and all
      proceedings, claims and demands in respect thereof—Proceedings for breach of contract and
      negligence against principal determined by consent judgment—Whether indemnity covering
      obligations under consent judgment—Whether principal having to establish its liability to creditor
      in order to rely on indemnity—Whether party giving indemnity estopped from denying obligation
      under consent judgment. **Rust Consulting Ltd (in liquidation) v PB Ltd** [2011] **1 Comm** 951, QBD.
  Guarantee distinguished—
    Hire-purchase agreement by infant in respect of motor car—
      Agreement void—Document signed by third party undertaking to indemnify hire-purchase finance
      company against any loss arising out of hire-purchase agreement—Whether valid as a contract of
      indemnity or void as a guarantee of a void contract. **Yeoman Credit Ltd v Latter** [1961] **2** 294, CA.

INDEMNITY (cont)—
Guarantee distinguished (cont)—
Oral promise by majority shareholder to purchase minority shareholdings if not bought by prospective purchaser of majority shareholding—
Whether enforceable—Whether indemnity or guarantee—Statute of Frauds (1677), s 4. **Pitts v Jones** [2008] **1 Comm** 548, CA; [2008] **1** 941, CA.
Guarantor—
Rights against debtor. *See* **Guarantee** (Surety—Rights against debtor).
Hire-purchase. *See* **Hire-purchase** (Indemnity).
Hiring—
Loss howsoever caused—
Loss arising out of hiring—Indemnity of crane owners against all damage injury or loss 'howsoever caused' arising directly or indirectly out of or in connexion with the hiring or use of a crane—Hirers' employee injured when wagon that he was loading was negligently moved forward by crane owners' servant—No negligence by hirers, their employee, or the crane driver—Whether crane owners entitled to indemnity from hirers. **Wright v Tyne Improvement Comrs (Osbeck & Co Ltd, third party)** [1968] **1** 807, CA.
Implied indemnity—
Act done at request of another—
Request by stockbroker to company to register transfer of shares in favour of client—Name of transferor on deed forged unknown to company or stockbroker—Whether stockbroker liable to indemnify company. **Yeung v Hong Kong and Shanghai Banking Corp** [1980] **2** 599, PC.
Promissory note—
Act done at request of another injuring third party—Government promissory note—Renewal—No express indemnity against claims under the note exacted by the government—Implied common law indemnity—Indian Securities Act 1920, ss 12, 13, 16, 21. **Secretary of State for India v Bank of India Ltd** [1938] **2** 797, PC.
Insurance—
Fire insurance—
Measure of indemnity. *See* **Insurance** (Fire insurance—Measure of indemnity).
Generally. *See* **Insurance** (Indemnity insurance).
Life insurance and indemnity insurance. *See* **Insurance** (Life insurance—Indemnity insurance).
Marine insurance—
Loss. *See* **Marine insurance** (Loss—Indemnity).
Measure of indemnity. *See* **Marine insurance** (Measure of indemnity).
Motor insurance—
Person driving with consent of insured. *See* **Motor insurance** (Compulsory insurance against third party risks—Persons driving with consent of insured—Indemnity of authorised driver).
Professional indemnity insurance. *See* **Insurance** (Liability insurance—Professional indemnity insurance).
Lease—
Indemnity clause. *See* **Landlord and tenant** (Lease—Indemnity clause).
Limitation of action. *See* **Limitation of action** (Indemnity).
Marine insurance—
Loss. *See* **Marine insurance** (Loss—Indemnity).
Misrepresentation—
Duty of disclosure—
Plaintiff guaranteeing subsidiary company's performance obligations and confirming that company would remain its subsidiary—Plaintiff selling company and wishing to transfer guarantee obligations to defendant—Defendant seeking to obtain consent of beneficiaries to transfer and indemnifying plaintiff—Defendant promising to provide security for indemnity—Beneficiaries not giving consent to transfer and defendant failing to make security payment—Plaintiff seeking specific performance and defendant raising non-disclosure defence—Whether plaintiff under duty to disclose all material facts in respect of indemnity agreement. **Geest plc v Fyffes plc** [1999] **1 Comm** 672, QBD.
Negligence—
Building contract—
Liability to specialist contractor—Building owner negligent as well as building contractor, and both liable to specialist contractor for damage to his property on the site—Whether indemnity clause in building contract should be construed so as not to extend to building owner's liability for negligence. **AMF International Ltd v Magnet Bowling Ltd** [1968] **2** 789, QBD; **Walters v Whessoe Ltd and Shell Refining Co Ltd** [1968] **2** 816, CA.
Contract of carriage—
Contract between trader and carrier—Trader to keep carrier indemnified against 'all claims or demands whatsoever—Van and driver hired to trader by carrier—Trader having exclusive use of van and driver—Loss of goods belonging to trader's customer whilst in van—Loss due to driver's negligence—Customer recovering damages from carrier—Whether indemnity extending to claims which succeed on ground of carrier's negligence—Road Haulage Association Conditions of Carriage (1967 revision), cl 3(4). **Gillespie Bros & Co Ltd v Roy Bowles Transport Ltd** [1973] **1** 193, CA.
Contract to discharge ship—
Agreement by shipowners to indemnify stevedores against claims for personal injury by employees—Stipulation against use of 'improper or inadequate gear'—'Gear'—'Ship's gear'—Use by stevedore's foreman of defective ship lampholder for unsuitable purpose—Liability of shipowners to injured employee of stevedores. **Maltby (TF) Ltd v Pelton Steamship Co Ltd** [1951] **2** 954, KBD.
Licensor—
Licence to occupy railway premises—Indemnity by licensee against liability for personal injury, except when caused solely by licensor's negligence, and 'which, but for the permission hereby granted, would not have arisen'—Accident to servant of licensees—Accident due partly to negligence of licensor's servants and partly to negligence of licensee's servant—Whether licensor entitled to indemnity. **Warrellow v Chandler & Braddick (GF Lester & Co (Birmingham) Ltd, third party)** [1956] **3** 305, Assizes.

INDEMNITY (cont)—
    Negligence (cont)—
        Railway company—
            Railway company granting privilege to employee of wagon repairing company to enter on railway company's property—Repairing company undertaking to indemnify railway company against damages, etc, for injury to repairing company's employees—Requisition of railways and wagons by government during war—Whether indemnity undertaking still effective. **Henson v London and North Eastern Rly Co** [1946] **1** 653, CA.
    Partner—
        Indemnity of outgoing partner. *See* **Partnership** (Dissolution—Indemnity of outgoing partner).
    Professional indemnity—
        Insurance. *See* **Insurance** (Liability insurance—Professional indemnity insurance).
    Receiver—
        Jurisdiction of Companies Court to enforce indemnity. *See* **Company** (Companies Court—Jurisdiction—Receiver—Contract of indemnity).
    Rectification of land register—
        Loss suffered by reason of rectification. *See* **Land registration** (Rectification of register—Loss suffered by reason of rectification—Indemnity).
    Sale of business—
        Indemnity in respect of tax on sale—
            Liabilities in relation to business—Purchaser agreeing to discharge all the liabilities of the vendor 'in relation to' the business—Vendor continuing business as agent for the purchaser and entitled to be indemnified accordingly—Vendor asessable to income tax and surtax by reason of profits made on sale to purchaser, and by reason of profits while carrying on business as purchaser's agent—Whether vendor entitled to be indemnified in respect of such tax. **Hollebone's Agreement, Re** [1959] **2** 152, CA.
    Sale of land—
        Indemnification of vendor against tenant's claim. *See* **Sale of land** (Condition—Indemnification of vendor against tenant's claim).
    Sale of ship—
        Seller's indemnity. *See* **Shipping** (Sale of ship).
    Subrogation—
        Contract of indemnity—
            Right of indemnifier to be subrogated to rights of indemnified—Nature of right—Right as an incident to all contracts of indemnity—Exclusion of right—Implied exclusion—Circumstances in which right will be excluded—Contract between firm of cleaners and factory owner to clean factory—Contract containing indemnity by cleaners to indemnify owner against loss or damages caused by negligence of factory owner's servants—Cleaners' servant injured at factory by negligence of factory owner's servant—Indemnity sought by factory owner against cleaners for liability to cleaners' servant—Cleaners seeking to be subrogated to owner's right of action against his own negligent servant. **Morris v Ford Motor Co Ltd** [1973] **2** 1084, CA.
        Counter-indemnity—
            Letter of credit—Claimant providing counter-indemnity for guarantor by irrevocable letter of credit—Letter of credit payable on certification that 'amount demanded represents and covers the unpaid sums due'—Guarantor discharging principal debtor's liability and making demand on letter of credit—Whether claimant entitled to be subrogated to guarantor—Whether debtor's liability to creditor discharged if creditor recovers equivalent amount to debt from bank under letter of credit. **Ibrahim v Barclays Bank plc** [2012] **2 Comm** 1167, CA; [2012] **4** 160, CA.
    Tenancy agreement—
        Indemnity by tenant—
            Indemnity for unpaid rent. *See* **Landlord and tenant** (Assignment of lease—Implied covenant—Indemnity for unpaid rent).
            Loss arising from tenancy—Loss 'which but for the tenancy...would not have arisen'—Premises adjacent to railway—Fire caused by locomotive—Damage to goods—Applicability of indemnity clause. **Lee (John) & Son (Grantham) Ltd v Railway Executive** [1949] **2** 581, CA.
    Time charterparty. *See* **Shipping** (Time charterparty—Indemnity).
    Vicarious liability—
        Indemnity of master for servant's negligence. *See* **Vicarious liability** (Employer and employee—Indemnity of master for servant's negligence).

INDEMNITY CLAUSE
    Lease. *See* **Landlord and tenant** (Lease—Indemnity clause).

INDEMNITY INSURANCE
    Generally. *See* **Insurance** (Indemnity insurance).

INDEPENDENT BROADCASTING AUTHORITY
    Government control over broadcasting. *See* **Broadcasting** (Government control over broadcasting).
    Statutory duty. *See* **Broadcasting** (Television—Authority—Statutory duty—Content of programmes—Independent Broadcasting Authority).

INDEPENDENT CONTRACTOR
    Building—
        Application of building regulations. *See* **Building** (Building regulations—Application—Independent contractor).
    Building contract—
        Limitation of action—
            Concealment of right of action by fraud—Concealment by agent. *See* **Limitation of action** (Concealment of right of action by fraud—Concealment by agent).
    Occupier's liability—
        Duty to independent contractor. *See* **Occupier's liability** (Duty to independent contractor).
        Liability for independent contractor. *See* **Occupier's liability** (Liability for independent contractor).
    Vicarious liability. *See* **Vicarious liability** (Independent contractor).

INDEPENDENT SCHOOL
Generally. *See* **Education** (School—Independent school).

INDEPENDENT TRADE UNION
Certification. *See* **Trade union** (Certification as independent trade union).

INDIA
Criminal evidence—
  Admissions and confessions—
    Murder—Statement made to police by accused while in custody—Admissibility in evidence—Code of Criminal Procedure, s 162(1)—Code of Criminal Procedure Amendment Act (India) 1923, s 34. **Swami (Pakala Narayana) v King-Emperor** [1939] **1** 396, PC.
Criminal law—
  Conspiracy to murder—
    Appeal to court of judicial commissioner North West Frontier Province—Appeal heard by judge sitting alone—Evidence of conspiracy—Statement by fellow-conspirator after conspiracy ended—Indian Penal Code, s 302/120B—North West Frontier Province Courts Regulation 1931, s 7—Indian Evidence Act, s 10. **Mirza Akbar v King-Emperor** [1940] **3** 585, PC.
Extradition—
  Surrender of prisoner to native state—
    Exclusion of writ of habeas corpus—India Extradition Act 1903 (No 15 of 1903) s 7—Code of Criminal Procedure 1898 (No 5 of 1898), ss 75, 491, 561A—Government of India Act 1935, s 223—Appellate Side Rules of the Madras High Court, rr 2, 2A. **Matthen v Trivandrum District Magistrate** [1939] **3** 356, PC.
Income tax—
  Charity—
    Object of general public utility—Policy of newspaper—Duty of commissioner—Indian Income Tax Act 1922 (No 11 of 1922), s 4(3)(i). **Tribune Press, Lahore (Trustee) v Income Tax Comrs Punjab, Lahore** [1939] **3** 469, PC.
Jurisdiction—
  Appeals from High Court of India—
    Case involving interpretation of Government of India Act 1935 or order made thereunder—Certificate that case involves such interpretation—Question not considered by High Court—Government of India Act 1935, ss 205, 293—Government of India (Adaptation of Indian Laws) Order in Council 1937 (SR & O 1937 No 269). **Mackay v Forbes** [1939] **4** 368, PC.
    Case not involving interpretation of Government of India Act 1935—Whether High Court should make order withholding certificate that case does not involve such interpretation—Government of India Act 1935, s 205. **Punjab Co-op Bank Ltd, Amritsar v Income Tax Comr, Lahore** [1940] **4** 87, PC.
Mortgage by deposit of deeds—
  Accompanying memorandum—
    Memorandum referring to money hereby secured and containing power of sale—Whether memorandum or operative security—Registration—Transfer of Property Act 1882 (No 4 of 1882), s 59—Indian Registration Act 1908 (No 16 of 1908), ss 17(1)(b), 49(c). **Paul (Sir Hari Sankar) v Dassa (Srimati Jogemaya)** [1939] **2** 737, PC.
North-West Frontier Province—
  Compulsory purchase—
    Resumption of possession of cantonment—Appurtenances—Compensation—Land Acquisition Act (No 1 of 1894), ss 4, 6, 9, 11, 18. **Hari Chand v Secretary of State** [1939] **3** 707, PC.
Public authorities—
  Acts of State—
    Cession of territory—Title to land—Right of government to refuse to recognise prior title—Recourse to municipal courts. **Secretary of State for India v Sardar Rustam Khan** [1941] **2** 606, .
Rangoon—
  Conflict of laws—
    Succession—Buddhist—Chinese Buddhist domiciled in Burma—Burma Laws Act (xiii of 1898), s 13. **Tan Ma Shwe Zin v Khoo Soo Chong** [1939] **4** 43, PC.
State of emergency—
  Governor-General sole judge as to state of emergency—
    Ordinance setting up special criminal courts—Applicability to province left to discretion of Provincial Government—Validity of Ordinance—Ordinance intra vires the Governor-General—Government of India Act 1935, ss 102, 223, 317, Sch 9, para 72—India and Burma (Emergency Provisions) Act 1940, s 1(3)—Ordinance No 11, 1942. **King-Emperor v Benoari Lal Sarma** [1945] **1** 210, PC.

INDICTABLE OFFENCE
Committal of young person for trial. *See* **Children and young persons** (Trial of persons under 17—Committal for trial).
Compensation order. *See* **Sentence** (Compensation—Order—Indictable offence).
Legal aid—
  Representation by counsel. *See* **Legal aid** (Criminal cases—Representation by counsel—Indictable offence).
Summary trial for indictable offence—
  Committal for sentence. *See* **Magistrates** (Committal for sentence—Sentence for indictable offence tried summarily).
  Costs. *See* **Criminal law** (Costs—Magistrates' court—Indictable offences—Summary trial or inquiry as examining justices).
  Generally. *See* **Magistrates** (Summary trial for indictable offence).
Verdict—
  Alternative offence—
    Summary offence. *See* **Criminal law** (Verdict—Alternative offence—Summary and indictable offences).

INDICTMENT

Addition of new counts—
Committal for non-existent offence—
Validity of added charges—Committal for trial on charge of shooting with intent to resist lawful arrest—Indictment containing in addition counts of shooting with intent to cause grievous bodily harm and of using firearm to resist lawful apprehension—Committal charge a nullity—Validity of conviction of added offence—Administration of Justice (Miscellaneous Provisions) Act 1933, s 2(2), proviso (i). **R v Lamb (Thomas)** [1969] **1** 45, CA.

Copy to accused. *See* Copy of indictment—Supply to accused—Addition of counts, *below*.

Count founded on facts or evidence before examining justices—
Co-accused committed in separate committal proceeding—Co-accused included in indictment against appellant—Separate counts against co-accused and appellant—Counts against co-accused not based on evidence disclosed in committal proceedings against appellant—Whether indictment valid—Administration of Justice (Miscellaneous Provisions) Act 1933, s 2(2)(as amended by the Criminal Appeal Act 1964, s 5, Sch 2). **R v Groom** [1976] **2** 321, CA.

Count based on evidence before examining justices but in respect of which defendant not committed—Whether permissible to add or substitute count based on evidence before examining justices but not founded on same facts or forming part of series of same or similar offences as counts in existing indictment—Administration of Justice (Miscellaneous Provisions) Act 1933, s 2(2) proviso—Indictment Rules 1971, r 9. **R v Lombardi** [1989] **1** 992, CA.

Similarity to committal charge—
Graver offences added—Offence charged triable summarily or on indictment—Election by accused for trial by jury—Ill-treatment of child—Charges of causing and inflicting grievous bodily harm added on indictment—Whether additional counts valid—Administration of Justice (Miscellaneous Provisions) Act 1933, s 2(2), proviso (i). **R v Roe** [1967] **1** 492, CA.

Substitution—
Summary offence charged—Election by offender for trial by jury—Committal for trial for summary offence—Substitution in indictment of different offence—Whether substitution permissible—Summary Jurisdiction Act 1879, s 17(1)—Administration of Justice (Miscellaneous Provisions) Act 1933, s 2(2)(a)(i). **R v Phillips** [1953] **1** 968, CCA.

Summary offence—
Election by accused to be tried by jury—New counts added on indictment in respect of offences not triable on indictment except by election of accused—New counts founded on evidence disclosed in examination before justices—Addition of counts permissible so long as not unfair or oppressive—Administration of Justice (Miscellaneous Provisions) Act 1933, s 2(2), proviso (i). **R v Nisbet** [1971] **3** 307, CA.

Transfer of case—
Addition after transfer—Validity—Committal to quarter sessions for trial—No indictment preferred before quarter sessions—Remitted to assizes for trial—Indictment preferred at assizes containing charge not before quarter sessions—Accused lawfully indicted—Administration of Justice (Miscellaneous Provisions) Act 1933, s 2(1). **R v Wilson** [1967] **2** 1088, CA.

Alternative counts—
Larceny or receiving. *See* **Criminal law** (Larceny—Indictment—Alternative counts).

Ambiguity. *See* Uncertainty or ambiguity, *below*.

Amendment—
Amendment after arraignment—
Circumstances in which permissible—Prejudice to defendant—Addition of new counts charging defendants individually with offences with which they had been charged jointly—Indictments Act 1915, s 5(1). **R v Johal** [1972] **2** 449, CA.

Effect of amendment—New offence or correction of misdescription—Charge of obtaining money by false pretences—Evidence that cheques, not money, obtained—Amendment to one count substituting 'obtaining valuable security'—Amendment to one count substituting 'procuring delivery of valuable security' to a third party—Whether amendments correcting misdescription of original offence or charging new offence—Indictments Act 1915, s 5(1). **R v Harden** [1962] **1** 286, CCA.

New counts added to indictment based on evidence obtained after committal proceedings and plea and case management hearing—Whether court having power to add new counts—Indictments Act 1915, s 5—Administration of Justice (Miscellaneous Provisions) Act 1933, s 2(2). **R v Thompson** [2011] **4** 408, CA.

Amendment before arraignment—
Injustice to defendant—New count added before arraignment—No injustice—Validity. **R v Hall** [1968] **2** 1009, CCA.

New count charging correct offence shown by depositions—No injustice caused to prisoner—Whether amendment properly allowed—Indictments Act 1915, s 5(1). **R v Martin** [1961] **2** 747, CCA.

Receiving stolen goods—Amendment of count by substituting receiving eight pictures for three pictures—Plea of guilty by accused to amended count—No injustice caused to accused—Whether amendment valid—Indictments Act 1915, s 5(1). **R v Hall** [1968] **2** 1009, CCA.

False pretences—
Charge of obtaining money by false pretences—Evidence that cheques, not money, obtained—Amendment to meet evidence. **R v Smith** [1950] **2** 679, CCA.

Handling stolen goods. *See* **Criminal law** (Handling stolen goods—Indictment—Amendment).

Indictment not bad on its face—
Application—Duty of counsel—Amendment of matter of description—Charge of obtaining money by false pretences—Evidence that cheques, not money, obtained—Amendment to meet evidence—Responsibility of counsel for accuracy of indictment—Time to apply for amendment—Indictments Act 1915, s 5(1). **R v Smith** [1950] **2** 679, CCA.

New offence—
Amendment alleging new offence—No application to quash at hearing—Appeal—Administration of Justice (Miscellaneous Provisions) Act 1933, s 2. **R v Cleghorn** [1938] **3** 398, CCA.

INDICTMENT (cont)—
  Amendment (cont)—
    Retrial—
      Amendment of fresh indictment on retrial—Court of Appeal ordering retrial and preferring fresh
      indictment—Trial judge amending fresh indictment with consent of parties—Amendment
      resulting in defendants being tried for offences for which no retrial could have been
      ordered—Whether judge having power to amend indictment in such circumstances—Indictments
      Act 1915, s 5(1)—Criminal Appeal Act 1968, s 7(2). **R v Hemmings** [2000] **2** 155, CA.
      Amendment of fresh indictment on retrial—Indictment amended on retrial to add further
      defendant—Evidence of added defendant adversely affecting defence of original defendant—
      Whether amendment of indictment on retrial permissible where defendant put in worse position
      than at original trial—Indictments Act 1915, s 5(1)—Criminal Appeal Act 1968, s 7(2). **R v Booker**
      [2011] **3** 905, CA.
  Assault. See **Criminal law** (Assault—Indictment or information).
  Assisting offender. See **Criminal law** (Assisting offender—Indictment).
  Bankruptcy offence—
    Form. See **Bankruptcy** (Offences—Undischarged bankrupt obtaining credit—Obtaining credit to extent
    of £10 or upwards—Indictment—Form).
  Bill of indictment—
    Generally. See **Criminal law** (Bill of indictment).
    Jamaica. See **Jamaica** (Criminal law—Bill of indictment).
  Capital murder. See **Criminal law** (Murder—Capital murder—Indictment).
  Causing death by dangerous driving. See **Road traffic** (Dangerous driving—Causing death by dangerous
    driving—Indictment).
  Committal supporting indictment—
    Indictment quashed following committal—
      Effect—Second indictment—Committal capable of supporting only one indictment—Direction of
      Court of Appeal or High Court judge necessary for second indictment—Leave of circuit judge
      insufficient—Administration of Justice (Miscellaneous Provisions) Act 1933, s 2(2)(b). **R v**
      Thompson [1975] **2** 1028, CA.
  Company—
    Fraudulent trading—
      Duplicity. See Duplicity—Fraudulent trading, *below*.
    Written order—
      Leave to prefer against company—Necessity for written order—Duty of clerk of assize before
      signing bill—Duty to ensure proper order made by magistrate. **R v Sherman (H) Ltd** [1949] **2** 207,
      CCA.
  Consent certificate—
    Discharge of juror—
      Discharge during trial—Consent certificate to be attached to indictment. **R v Browne** [1962] **2** 621,
      CCA.
  Conspiracy—
    Auction—
      Illegal bidding agreement—Competency of proceedings on indictment. See **Auction** (Illegal bidding
      agreement—Conspiracy—Indictment).
    Duplicity. See Duplicity—Conspiracy, *below*.
    Generally. See **Criminal law** (Conspiracy—Indictment).
    Inclusion of charge—
      Specific offences also charge—Desirability of including conspiracy charge—Verdict—Guilty of
      conspiracy, but Not Guilty on specific charges—Unreasonable verdict—Criminal Appeal Act 1907,
      s 4. **R v Cooper and Compton** [1947] **2** 701, CCA.
  Conviction of lesser offence—
    Assault with intent to prevent apprehension—
      Evidence disclosing proposed apprehension unlawful—Whether open to jury to convict of common
      assault—Offences against the Person Act 1861, s 38. **R v Wilson** [1955] **1** 744, CCA.
    Causing grievous bodily harm with intent—
      Particulars of way grievous bodily harm caused not specified—Whether open to court to accept
      plea to and verdict of unlawful wounding—Whether indictment amounting to or including
      expressly or by implication allegation of unlawful wounding—Criminal Law Act 1967, s 6(3). **R v**
      McCready [1978] **3** 967, CA.
    Inflicting grievous bodily harm—
      Charge of burglary by entering a building as a trespasser and inflicting grievous bodily
      harm—Whether open to jury to convict of lesser offence of assault occasioning actual bodily
      harm—Criminal Law Act 1967, s 6(3). **R v Wilson (Clarence), R v Jenkins (Edward John)**
      [1983] **3** 448, HL.
      Particulars of way grievous bodily harm caused not specified—Whether open to jury to convict of
      lesser offence of assault occasioning actual bodily harm—Criminal Law Act 1967, s 6(3). **R v**
      Wilson (Clarence), R v Jenkins (Edward John) [1983] **3** 448, HL.
  Copy of indictment—
    Supply to accused—
      Addition of counts—Notice—Counts based on fresh facts included in indictment after
      committal—Duty of police to inform accused of fresh counts as soon as it is decided to formulate
      them—Duty of defence to obtain copy of indictment as soon as possible from clerk of
      assize—Convictions quashed where accused had only six days' notice of additional counts in
      indictment and was unable to call alibi witness—Indictments Act 1915, Sch 1, r 13. **R v Dickson**
      [1969] **1** 729, CA.
  Count—
    Addition. See Addition of new counts, *above*.
    Several counts—
      Joinder of charges. See Joinder of charges—Several counts, *below*.
    Severance of counts—
      Shortening of trial. See **Criminal law** (Trial—Shortening of trial—Severance of counts).

INDICTMENT (cont)—
  Count (cont)—
    Severance of counts (cont)—
      Similar facts—Counts founded on similar facts—Course to be taken by trial judge—Submission by accused that evidence on each count inadmissible in relation to other counts—Submission before arraignment that counts should be severed. **R v Scarrott** [1978] **1** 672, CA.
  Crown Court—
    Costs. *See* **Crown Court** (Costs—Trial on indictment).
    Supervisory jurisdiction of High Court. *See* **Crown Court** (Supervisory jurisdiction of High Court—Trial on indictment).
  Demurrer—
    Writing—
      Insufficient evidence to support charge—Demurrer not in writing—Plea improperly upheld—Whether plea should continue to be used in criminal cases. **R v Deputy Chairman of Inner London Quarter Sessions, ex p Metropolitan Police Comr** [1969] **3** 1537, QBD.
  Departure from form of charge before examining justices—
    Different offence—
      Conspiracy—Charge of conspiring with named person and others unknown—Count of indictment omitting 'and with others unknown'—Whether departure justifying quashing count—Administration of Justice (Miscellaneous Provisions) Act 1933, s 2(2)(a). **R v McDonnell** [1966] **1** 193, Assizes.
  Duplicity—
    Causing death by dangerous driving. *See* **Road traffic** (Dangerous driving—Causing death by dangerous driving—Indictment—Duplicity).
    Conjunctive form—
      Offence expressed disjunctively—Charge in conjunctive form—Driving vehicle recklessly or in manner dangerous to public—Charge alleging driving recklessly and in dangerous manner—Whether count bad for duplicity or uncertainty. **R v Clow** [1963] **2** 216, CCA.
      Offence expressed disjunctively—Charge in conjunctive form—Sending indecent or obscene print etc—Charge of sending indecent and obscene article—Whether indictment in proper form—Whether charge could be expressed disjunctively. **R v Stanley** [1965] **1** 1035, CCA.
    Conspiracy—
      Single or separate conspiracies—Count charging conspiracy—Allegation that conspiracy extending over several years—Evidence adduced by prosecution consistent with several conspiracies—Whether count bad for duplicity. **R v Greenfield** [1973] **3** 1050, CA.
    Found in public place about to commit offence—
      Two places alleged—Accused with previous convictions charged in one count with being found in two separate places waiting for an opportunity to commit an offence—Whether indictment bad for duplicity—Prevention of Crimes Act 1871, s 7. **R v Johnson** [1945] **2** 105, CCA.
    Fraudulent trading—
      Statute creating two offences—Fraudulent trading with intent and fraudulent trading for purpose of achieving certain objectives—Particulars of methods of carrying out one category of offence not rendering count bad for duplicity—Companies Act 1948, s 332(1), (3). **R v Inman** [1966] **3** 414, CCA.
    Incitement to disaffection—
      Endeavouring to seduce member of armed forces from his duty or allegiance to Crown—Count alleging defendant had endeavoured to seduce member of forces from 'duty or allegiance'—Whether count bad for duplicity—Incitement to Disaffection Act 1934, s 1—Indictment Rules 1971 (SI 1971 No 1253), r 7. **R v Arrowsmith** [1975] **1** 463, CA.
    Information in criminal proceedings before magistrates. *See* **Magistrates** (Information—Duplicity).
    Larceny—
      Aggregate of sums charged in other counts—Count charging larceny of aggregated—Count bad aggregate for duplicity. **R v Williams** [1953] **1** 1068, CCA.
    Separate acts—
      Single offence charged—Inducement to enter into agreement to invest money—Indictment charging in one count two statements and two promises as the inducement—Whether count bad for duplicity—Nature of offence—Prevention of Fraud (Investments) Act 1958, s 13(1)(a). **R v Linnell** [1969] **3** 849, CA.
    Separate offences in single count—
      Charge of warehouse-breaking—Sections of statute creating separate offences—Breaking and entering and committing felony—Breaking and entering with intent—Count referring to both sections—Count bad for duplicity—Larceny Act 1916, s 26(1), s 27(2). **R v Nicholls** [1960] **2** 449, CCA.
  Embezzlement. *See* **Criminal law** (Embezzlement—Indictment).
  False pretences. *See* **Criminal law** (False pretences—Indictment).
  Form—
    Common law offence—
      Offence covered by words of modern statute—Indictment should be framed contra formam statuti. **R v Pollock and Divers** [1966] **2** 97, CCA.
    Evasion of prohibition on importation of prohibited goods. *See* **Customs and excise** (Importation of prohibited goods—Evasion of prohibition—Indictment).
    Making or possession of explosive under suspicious circumstances. *See* **Explosives** (Offence—Knowingly possessing explosive substance under suspicious circumstances—Indictment—Form of indictment).
  Fraudulent conversion. *See* **Criminal law** (Fraudulent conversion—Indictment).
  Handling stolen goods. *See* **Criminal law** (Handling stolen goods—Indictment).
  Joinder of accused—
    Separate committals—
      Indictment in respect of one committal already signed—Whether permissible to join counts founded on separate committals in one indictment. **Practice Note** [1976] **2** 326, CA.

INDICTMENT (cont)—
  Joinder of charges—
    Charges founded on same facts—
      False pretences and obtaining credit by false pretences—Whether joinder justified—Direction to jury—Debtors Act 1869, s 13(1)—Larceny Act 1916, s 32(1). **R v Torr** [1966] **1** 178, CCA.
      Manslaughter and offences against property—A and B charged on one indictment with manslaughter—A, B, C, D and E charged in second indictment with offences against property—Bill indictment comprising all charges granted. **R v Smith** [1958] **1** 475, CCC.
      Mutually contradictory counts—Defendant charged with obtaining property by deception or conspiracy to import controlled drugs illegally—Counts mutually contradictory and mutually destructive—Whether judge entitled to leave both counts to jury—Whether prosecution required to elect on which count it intends to proceed. **R v Bellman** [1989] **1** 22, HL.
      Practice—Charges which may be joined under rules should in general be joined—No rule of practice that count of murder should not be joined with other counts—Power of court to prevent abuse of process—Indictments Act 1915, Sch 1, r 1. **Connelly v DPP** [1964] **2** 401, HL.
      Sedition and effecting public mischief—Charges founded on same speech—Charges of making seditious speech and of effecting a public mischief contrary to common law in respect of same speech—Undesirability of charging both offences. **Joshua v R** [1955] **1** 22, PC.
    Conspiracy count and substantive counts—
      Duty of prosecution to justify joinder of conspiracy count with substantive counts—Election to proceed with substantive or conspiracy counts required if joinder not justified. **Practice Note** [1977] **2** 540, Ch D.
    Dissimilar offences—
      Offences not founded on same facts—Indictment charging accused with drug offences and assault offences—Judge ordering separate trial of each set of offences—Whether order proper—Whether indictment defective—Whether trial valid—Whether retrial appropriate—Indictments Act 1915, s 5(1)(3)—Criminal Appeal Act 1968, s 2(1)—Indictment Rules 1971, r 9. **R v Newland** [1988] **2** 891, CA.
      Prejudice to accused—Dissimilar offences charged in one indictment—Whether prejudicial to accused—Whether separate trials should be ordered. **R v Muir** [1938] **2** 516, CCA.
    Motor vehicle offences—
      Different offences—Prejudice to accused—Driving while disqualified for holding licence—Joinder with a different offence relating to a motor vehicle, or to driving it, permissible—If prejudicial, counsel may to apply before arraignment for separate trials. **R v Andrews** [1967] **1** 170, CA.
    Murder—
      Murder or manslaughter counts may be joined with other counts—Prosecution to frame indictment as appropriate—Discretion of trial judge to direct that prisoner be tried separately on any one or more counts—Indictments Act 1915, s 5(3). **Practice Direction** [1964] **3** 509, CCA.
      Two counts of murder—Undesirability—Whether invalidating conviction. **R v Davis** [1937] **3** 537, CCA.
    Offences of same or similar character—
      Gibraltar. *See* **Gibraltar** (Criminal law—Indictment—Joinder of counts).
      Nexus between offences—Relevance of considerations of law and fact—Attempted larceny and robbery with violence—Offences committed within short period of time in neighbouring public houses—Whether of 'similar' character—Indictments Act 1915, Sch 1, r 3. **Ludlow v Metropolitan Police Comr** [1970] **1** 567, HL.
      Similar features establishing prima facie case that offences may be properly and conveniently tried together—Indictments Act 1915, Sch 1, r 3. **R v Kray** [1969] **3** 941, CA.
    Road traffic offences—
      Dangerous driving—Causing death by dangerous driving—Drunk in charge—Road Traffic Act 1960, ss 1, 2, 6. **R v McBride** [1961] **3** 6, CCA.
      Motor vehicle offences. *See* Joinder of charges—Motor vehicle offences, *above*.
    Same incident—
      Undesirability of one and the same incident being made subject-matter of distinct charges. **R v Harris** [1969] **2** 599, CA.
    Series of offences—
      Different transactions—Nexus—Fraud on insurers—Charges of arson, arson with intent to defraud insurers and attempting to obtain money from insurers by false pretences—Nexus of defrauding insurers present throughout—Indictments Act 1915, Sch 1, r 3. **R v Clayton-Wright** [1948] **2** 763, CCA.
      Series—Meaning—Whether two offences constitute series—Indictments Act 1915, Sch 1, r 3. **R v Kray** [1969] **3** 941, CA.
    Several counts—
      Each count a separate indictment. **R v Plain** [1967] **1** 614, CA.
    Single accused—
      Statutory rule governing joinder—Whether rule confined to joinder of charges against one accused—Indictments Act 1915, Sch 1, r 3. **R v Assim** [1966] **2** 881, CCA.
  Joinder of two or more accused—
    Individual offences—
      Circumstances in which joinder permissible—Circumstances in which several offenders charged with committing individual offences may be tried together. **R v Assim** [1966] **2** 881, CCA.
    Joint charge—
      Acquittal of one accused—Effect—Joint charge of assault occasioning actual bodily harm—One accused acquitted for want of sufficient evidence—Jury told acquittal of one accused no bar to conviction of other accused—Other accused convicted—No evidence of joint action between two accused—Whether evidence of joint action necessary—Whether open to convict second accused as if charged with independent offence. **R v Rowlands** [1972] **1** 306, CA.
      Conviction of committing offence independently—Validity—Charges of assault and malicious damage—Two persons convicted of joint offences—Offences committed by both independently—Whether convictions can stand. **R v Scaramanga** [1963] **2** 852, CCA.

INDICTMENT (cont)—

Joinder of two or more accused (cont)—

Joint charge (cont)—

Conviction of committing offence independently—Validity—Joint charge of wounding with intent—First accused pleaded guilty—Trial of second accused—Jury directed that no need to go into question of common purpose—Conviction of second accused on evidence of victim that second accused stabbed him—Whether open to jury to convict second accused of committing independently the offence which was the subject matter of the joint charge. **DPP v Merriman** [1972] **3** 42, HL.

Conviction of committing offence independently—Validity—Theft charged jointly of two garments—One accused pleaded guilty and convicted—Other accused found guilty of independent theft of one garment—Conviction quashed. **R v Parker** [1969] **2** 15, CA.

Need for charge of joint offence—Perjury—Counts for two several charges of perjury against different defendants cannot be joined in one indictment in the absence of a charge of a joint offence. **R v Leigh and Harrison** [1966] **1** 687, Assizes.

Receiving stolen property—

Independent receivings—Property severally received stolen by same thief at same time—Whether joinder permissible—Accessories and Abettors Act 1861, s 6—Larceny Act 1916, s 40(3), s 44(5). **R v Tizard** [1962] **1** 209, CCA.

Same offence—

Seperate counts. *See* **Criminal evidence** (Character of accused—Evidence against co-accused—Same offence—Evidence against other person charged with same offence—Accused and co-accused charged in separate counts of same indictment with causing death by dangerous driving).

Joint charge—

Separate trials. *See* **Criminal law** (Separate trials—Joint charge).

Joint indictment—

Offensive weapons. *See* **Criminal law** (Offensive weapons—Article intended for use for causing injury—Joint indictment).

Larceny. *See* **Criminal law** (Larceny—Indictment).

Motion to quash—

Time for making application—

Before plea. **R v Maywhort** [1955] **2** 752, Assizes.

Murder—

Generally. *See* **Criminal law** (Murder—Indictment).

Joinder of charges. *See* Joinder of charges—Murder, *above*.

Offence triable summarily or on indictment—

Summary trial. *See* **Magistrates** (Summary trial—Offence triable summarily or on indictment).

Particulars—

Accuracy—

Bankruptcy offence. *See* **Bankruptcy** (Offences—Undischarged bankrupt obtaining credit—Obtaining credit to extent of £10 or upwards—Indictment).

Conspiracy. *See* **Criminal law** (Conspiracy—Indictment—Particulars of offence).

Defect—

Particulars of offence not amended at trial—No embarrassment caused to accused—Applicability of proviso to Criminal Appeal Act 1907, s 4(1). **R v Yule** [1963] **2** 780, CCA.

Handling stolen goods. *See* **Criminal law** (Handling stolen goods—Indictment—Particulars of offence).

Omission—

Possession of explosives—Knowledge of accused—Knowingly omitted from particulars of offence—Arraignment of accused by reading particulars, but not statement, of offence—Knowledge admitted by accused at trial—No substantial miscarriage of justice—Whether indictment defective or bad—Explosive Substances Act 1883, s 4(1)—Indictments Act 1915, s 3, Sch 1, r 4. **R v McVitie** [1960] **2** 498, CCA.

Place of trial—

Transfer to convenient court. *See* **Criminal law** (Trial—Place of trial—Transfer to convenient court—Indictment).

Power to quash—

Evidence disclosed by depositions—

Depositions disclosing no evidence to support conviction—Whether trial court having power to quash indictment. **R v County of London Quarter Sessions Chairman, ex p Downes** [1953] **2** 750, KBD.

Previous conviction—

Averment of previous convictions—

Corrective training or preventive detention—Liability of accused—Need to include averment in indictment. **R v Allen** [1949] **2** 808, CCA.

Quashing—

Motion to quash. *See* Motion to quash, *above*.

Power to quash. *See* Power to quash, *above*.

Riot. *See* **Criminal law** (Riot—Indictment).

Second indictment—

Pendency of earlier indictment—

Same offence—Second indictment or information not inherently bad by reason of the pendency of an earlier one for the same offence. **Poole v R** [1960] **3** 398, PC.

Second indictment preferred to cure earlier defective indictment—

Earlier indictment charging defendant and others with disparate offences not arising out of same facts—Judge giving leave to prefer three further bills of indictment—Original indictment stayed—Fresh indictment containing two counts against accused—One count same as in original indictment—Second count based on evidence given at committal proceedings—Whether new indictment valid—Indictment Rules 1971, r 9. **R v Follett** [1989] **1** 995, CA.

Settling of indictment—

Alterations and additions—

Notification of alterations and additions—Inspection by prosecution and accused. **Practice Note** [1956] **3** 704, CCA.

INDICTMENT (cont)—
Statute—
Duplicity—
Whether enactment creating one or several offences. See **Statute** (Offence—Duplicity—One or more offences).
Summary offence—
Addition of new counts. See Addition of new counts—Summary offence, *above*.
Supervisory jurisdiction of High Court. See **Crown Court** (Supervisory jurisdiction of High Court—Trial on indictment).
Theft-related offences—
Framing of indictment where theft or attempted theft of specific objects not alleged—
Necessity to give accused adequate details of alleged offence. **R v Walkington** [1979] **3** 143, HL.
Two indictments—
Indictments for same offence against same person—
Validity of indictments—Duty of prosecution to elect the one on which trial to proceed. **Practice Note** [1976] **2** 326, CA.
Joint trial—
Indictments tried together—Nullity. **R v Olivo** [1942] **2** 494, CCA.
Uncertainty or ambiguity—
Unlawful killing—
Assisting offender—Principal offender charged with murder—Possibility of conviction of manslaughter—Charge against assistant alleging principal offender guilty of 'unlawful killing'—Irregularity of no practical importance—Conviction of principal offender of murder making gravity of assistant's offence—No miscarriage of justice—Criminal Law Act 1967, ss 4(1)(3), 6(3). **R v Morgan** [1972] **1** 348, CA.
Validity—
Signature of proper officer—
Bill of indictment required to be 'signed' by proper officer of the court—Indictment only signed by proper officer after amendment at end of trial—Defendants convicted—Whether indictment valid—Whether trial valid—Administration of Justice (Miscellaneous Provisions) Act 1933, s 2(1). **R v Clarke** [2008] **2** 665, HL.
Bill of indictment required to be 'signed' by proper officer of the court—Whether requirement directory or mandatory—Whether initialling of bill by judge sufficient—Administration of Justice (Miscellaneous Provisions) Act 1933, s 2(1). **R v Morais** [1988] **3** 161, CA.
Witnesses listed on back of indictment. See **Criminal law** (Trial—Prosecution).

INDIVIDUAL RIGHTS
International law—
Enforcement of rights in English courts. See **International law** (Municipal law—Relationship—Right of individual under international law—Enforcement of right in English courts).

INDORSEMENT
Bill of exchange. See **Bill of exchange** (Indorsement).
Cheque. See **Bank** (Cheque—Endorsement).
Irish warrant. See **Magistrates** (Indorsement of Irish warrant—Irish warrant indorsed for execution in England).
Judgment—
Default of defence. See **Judgment** (Default of defence—Indorsement of court copy of judgment).
Warrant of magistrates. See **Magistrates** (Warrant).
Writ—
Claim for possession—
Protected tenancy. See **Rent restriction** (Possession—Procedure—Indorsement on writ of summons).
Generally. See **Writ** (Indorsement).

INDUCEMENT
Admission or confession obtained by inducement—
Admissibility in criminal proceedings. See **Criminal evidence** (Admissions and confessions—Inducement).
Breach of contract—
Tort. See **Tort** (Inducement to commit breach of contract).
Investment of money—
Criminal liability. See **Criminal law** (Inducement to invest money).

INDUSTRIAL ACTION
Dismissal in connection with industrial action—
Unfair dismissal. See **Unfair dismissal** (Dismissal in connection with strike or other industrial action).
Remuneration of employee. See **Employment** (Remuneration—Industrial action).
Strike—
Prison officers, by—
Prisoner's action for false imprisonment. See **False imprisonment** (Prisoner serving sentence—Strike by prison officers in breach of contract).

INDUSTRIAL AND PROVIDENT SOCIETIES
Conversion of registered society into company—
Effect on liabilities of society incurred before conversion—
Trust deeds establishing pension fund for benefit of employees of society—Whether trust deeds affected by conversion—Industrial and Provident Societies Act 1893, s 54. **London Housing Society Ltd's Trust Deeds, Re** [1940] **3** 665, Ch D.

INDUSTRIAL AND PROVIDENT SOCIETIES (cont)—
Determination of disputes—
Arbitration—
Arbitration in disputes between society and member—Expulsion of member—Non-compliance with rules—Member seeking declaration expulsion invalid—Whether jurisdiction of court ousted—Industrial and Provident Societies Act 1893, s 49(1). **Judson v Ellesmere Port Ex-Servicemen's Club Ltd** [1948] **1** 844, CA.
Award—Extent to which member bound by award—Dispute submitted to arbitration while defendant was a member of the society—Award made in final amended form after defendant's membership had ceased—Whether term implied that member no longer bound by rule after membership ceased. **Birtley District Co-op Society Ltd v Windy Nook and District Industrial Co-op Society Ltd** [1959] **1** 623, QBD.
Award—Extent to which member bound by award—Dispute submitted to arbitration while respondents a member of society—Withdrawal of respondents from membership of society after award—Whether respondents continued to be bound by award. **Bellshill & Mossend Co-op Society Ltd v Dalziel Co-op Society Ltd** [1960] **1** 673, HL.
Insolvency—
Appointment of receiver. See Receiver —Appointment , below.
Receiver —
Appointment —
Floating charge holder not to appoint administrative receiver of company—Whether society a company—Whether receiver an administrative receiver—Whether provisions on liability for contracts entered into by receivers appointed out of court applying to receiver—Industrial and Provident Societies Act 1965, s 55—Insolvency Act 1986, ss 29(2), 37, 72A(1). **Dairy Farmers of Britain Ltd, Re** [2009] **4** 241, Ch D.
Rules—
Member's debts to society to be liquidated by reduction of capital—
Winding-up of society—Position of liquidator where rule ignored. **Lloyd v Francis** [1937] **4** 489, CA.
Mode of application of profits of society—
Allocation of part of profits to political fund—Validity—Industrial and Provident Societies Act 1896, s 10(6). **Cahill v London Co-op Society Ltd** [1937] **1** 631, Ch D.
Trade union—
Definition. See **Trade union** (Definition of trade union).
Winding up—
Compulsory winding up—
Society carrying on speculative dealings in shares—Undertaking to register under Companies Act—Prevention of Fraud (Investments) Act 1939, s 10. **First Mortgage Co-op Investment Trust Ltd, Re** [1941] **2** 529, Ch D.
Voluntary winding up—
Payment of preferential creditors—Receivers appointed under debenture creating floating charge—Whether receivers obliged to pay preferential creditors before handing surplus assets to liquidator—Whether society a 'company'—Companies Act 1985, s 735(1)(4)—Insolvency Act 1986, ss 40, 251. **Devon and Somerset Farmers Ltd, Re** [1994] **1** 717, Ch D.
Winding up under the Companies Act—
Petition by shareholders—Just and equitable ground—Petitions by members of two societies solely in order to remove obstacles in way of sale of smallholdings at inflated prices—Abuse of winding-up procedure—Petitions opposed by other members of the two societies—Societies still performing useful function—Whether just and equitable that societies should be wound up—Degree of relevance of Prevention of Fraud (Investments) Act 1958, s 10(2)—Companies Act 1948, s 222(f). **Surrey Garden Village Trust Ltd, Re** [1964] **3** 962, Ch D.

INDUSTRIAL BUILDING
Classes of use. See **Town and country planning** (Development—Use classes—Industrial building).
Income tax—
Capital allowances. See **Capital allowances** (Industrial building or structure).
Town planning scheme. See **Town and country planning** (Town planning scheme—Industrial building).

INDUSTRIAL COURT
National Industrial Relations Court. See **Industrial relations** (National Industrial Relations Court).
Reference by Minister—
Failure to hear and determine reference—
Industrial Court acting as arbitral tribunal—Whether mandamus lay. **R v Industrial Court, ex p ASSET** [1964] **3** 130, QBD.
Jurisdiction—
Reference of question of observance of Fair Wages Resolution incorporated in government supply contract. **R v Industrial Court, ex p ASSET** [1964] **3** 130, QBD.
Trade dispute. See **Trade dispute** (Reference—Fair Wages Resolution).

INDUSTRIAL DERMATITIS
Damages. See **Damages** (Personal injury—Dermatitis—Industrial dermatitis).

INDUSTRIAL DEVELOPMENT
Certificate of—
Whether grant assumed in assessing compensation for compulsory acquisition of land. See **Compulsory purchase** (Compensation—Town development—Assumption of planning permission).

INDUSTRIAL DISEASE
Generally. See **Workmen's compensation** (Industrial disease).

INDUSTRIAL DISPUTE
Industrial relations. See **Industrial relations** (Industrial dispute).
Trade dispute. See **Trade dispute**.

INDUSTRIAL DISPUTES TRIBUNAL
    Certiorari to quash decision. *See* **Certiorari** (Jurisdiction—Industrial Disputes Tribunal).
    Costs—
        Motion for prohibition—
            Unnecessary parties. *See* **Costs** (Prohibition—Motion for prohibition to Industrial Disputes Tribunal—Unnecessary for both Minister and trade union to be represented).

INDUSTRIAL INJURY
    Appeal to industrial injuries commissioner—
        Oral hearing—
            Assessor—Whether assessor should sit at hearing—Functions of assessor—Courses open to industrial injuries commissioner requiring medical assistance—National Insurance (Industrial Injuries) (Determination of Claims and Questions) Regulations 1948, (SI 1948 No 1299), regs 22(6), 26(1). **R v Deputy Industrial Injuries Comr, ex p Jones** [1962] **2** 430, QBD.
            Evidence—Admissibility—Medical opinions in previous cases put to expert witnesses—Incorporation of previous medical opinions in decision of industrial injuries commissioner—National Insurance (Industrial Injuries) (Determination of Claims and Questions) Regulations 1948, (SI 1948 No 1299), reg 26(1)(b). **R v Deputy Industrial Injuries Comr, ex p Moore** [1965] **1** 81, CA.
    Contribution—
        National insurance. *See* **Social security—Contribution**.
    Damages for personal injuries—
        Deduction of industrial injury benefit etc. *See* **Damages** (Personal injury—Loss of earnings—Deduction of industrial injury, disablement, sickness or invalidity benefit accruing to injured person).
    Determination of claims—
        Powers of Minister or insurance tribunal—
            Power to refer to medical practitioner for examination and report—Medical appeal tribunal requesting opinion of consultant—Medical officer from Ministry transmitting papers etc to consultant—Whether essential reference made by tribunal—National Insurance (Industrial Injuries) (Determination of Claims and Questions) (No 2) Regulations 1967 (SI 1967 No 1571), reg 19(2). **R v National Insurance Comr, ex p Viscusi** [1974] **2** 724, CA.
    Disablement benefit—
        Generally. *See* **Social security** (Disablement benefit).
        Medical appeal tribunal's jurisdiction. *See* Medical appeal tribunal—Claim for disablement benefit, *below*.
    Employed person. *See* **Social security** (Employed person—Contract of service—Employments to be treated as employment under contract of service).
    Industrial injuries benefit—
        Personal injury caused by accident arising out of and in the course of employment—
            Fire officer developing post-traumatic stress disorder after attending fatal accidents and claiming benefit for injury caused 'by accident'—Whether claimant having to establish causative event separate from injury—Social Security Contributions and Benefits Act 1992, s 94(1). **Chief Adjudication Officer v Faulds** [2000] **2** 961, HL.
    Insurable employment—
        Employment under contract of service—
            Trade union—Sick steward—Spare-time duties—Contract of membership of union providing for obligatory employment—Rules defining duties, payment, penalties, in considerable detail—Whether employment under a contract of service—Whether sick steward entitled to industrial injury benefit—National Insurance (Industrial Injuries) Act 1946, Sch 1, Part 1, Part 2—National Insurance (Industrial Injuries) (Insurable and Excepted Employments) Regulations 1948 (SI 1948 No 1456), Sch 2, Part 2. **Amalgamated Engineering Union v Minister of Pensions and National Insurance** [1963] **1** 864, QBD.
            Trapeze artiste in circus—Required to carry out usherette duties and assist at moves—Whether employment under a contract of service—Whether entitled to industrial injury benefit—National Insurance (Industrial Injuries) Act 1946, Sch 1, Pt 1, para 1. **Whittaker v Minister of Pensions and National Insurance** [1966] **3** 531, QBD.
    Medical appeal tribunal—
        Claim for disablement benefit—
            Scope of jurisdiction—Appeal by claimant against final assessment of disability as too small—Tribunal's right and duty to use their own expert knowledge—Whether tribunal had jurisdiction to set aside assessment on the ground that there was then no loss of faculty resulting from the industrial injury—National Insurance (Industrial Injuries) Act 1946, s 39(2). **R v Medical Appeal Tribunal (North Midland Region), ex p Hubble** [1959] **3** 40, CA.
            Scope of jurisdiction—Previous finding by statutory authority (another medical appeal tribunal) on claim for benefit that injured workman suffered serious disablement as result of accident—Decision of statutory authority on claim 'final'—Statutory authority making provisional assessment for specific period—Medical appeal tribunal discharging assessment made in respect of subsequent period—Whether medical appeal tribunal bound to accept finding of earlier tribunal—National Insurance (Industrial Injuries) Act 1965, s 50(1). **R v National Insurance Comr, ex p Viscusi** [1974] **2** 724, CA.
            Scope of jurisdiction—Previous finding by statutory authority (deputy commissioner) on claim for injury benefit that insured workman suffered personal injury caused by accident—Subsequent application by workman for disablement benefit—Whether Medical Appeal Tribunal bound to accept finding of statutory authority that injury was caused by accident—Whether tribunal's jurisdiction confined to question of loss of faculty as result of injury—National Insurance (Industrial Injuries) Act 1946, s 7(1), s 36 (as amended), s 49(4). **Minister of Social Security v Amalgamated Engineering Union** [1967] **1** 210, .
            Scope of jurisdiction—Previous finding by statutory authority (local appeal tribunal) in claim for injury benefit—Finding that workman suffered injuries including heart condition caused by accident—Decision of statutory authority on claim 'final'—Subsequent claim by workman for disablement benefit—Whether medical appeal tribunal bound to accept finding that heart condition caused by accident—National Insurance (Industrial Injuries) Act 1965, ss 5(1), 37, 50(1). **Jones v Secretary of State for Social Services** [1972] **1** 145, HL.

INDUSTRIAL INJURY (cont)—

Medical appeal tribunal (cont)—

Nature of proceedings. *See* **Social security** (Disablement benefit—Claim—Nature of proceedings—Medical appeal tribunal).

Record and notice of decision—

Contents—Statement of reasons and findings on all questions of fact—Detail required—National Insurance (Industrial Injuries) (Determination of Claims and Questions) (No 2) Regulations 1967 (SI 1967 No 1571), reg 12(1). **R v National Insurance Comr, ex p Viscusi** [1974] **2** 724, CA.

Review of decision—

Fresh evidence—Medical appeal tribunal's determination setting aside an assessment of loss of faculty—Whether grounds for setting aside assessment—National Insurance (Industrial Injuries) Act 1946, s 40(1). **R v Medical Appeal Tribunal (North Midland Region), ex p Hubble** [1959] **3** 40, CA.

Medical board—

Evidence of member of board in subsequent proceedings—

Admissibility—Evidence as to condition of claimant for disablement benefit—Evidence as to conclusions of board—National Insurance (Industrial Injuries) Act 1946, s 39(1). **Ward v Shell-Mex and BP Ltd** [1951] **2** 904, KBD.

Tribunal—

Natural justice—

Evidence. *See* **Natural justice** (Industrial injuries tribunal—Evidence).

Workmen's compensation—

Right to compensation—

Statute abolishing right—Sawing—Exception—Prescribed disease—Right not arising before appointed day—Insurance under statute—Dermatitis—Attack before 5th July 1948—Recurrence after that date—Right of workman to workmen's compensation—National Insurance (Industrial Injuries) Act 1946, s 89(1), proviso (a). **Hales v Bolton Leathers Ltd** [1951] **1** 643, HL.

INDUSTRIAL PURPOSES

Permitted development—

Town and country planning. *See* **Town and country planning** (Development—Permitted development—Development for industrial purposes).

INDUSTRIAL RELATIONS

Advisory, Conciliation and Arbitration Service—

Duty to improve industrial relations—

Recognition of trade union. *See* **Trade union** (Recognition—Reference of recognition issue to Advisory, Conciliation and Arbitration Service—Duty of Service to improve industrial relations and encourage extension of collective bargaining).

Code of Practice—

Unfair dismissal—

Determination whether dismissal fair or unfair. *See* **Unfair dismissal** (Determination whether dismissal fair or unfair—Code of Practice).

Collective agreement—

Proper law. *See* **Conflict of laws** (Contract—Proper law of contract—Collective agreement).

Collective bargaining—

Remedial action where procedure agreement non-existent or defective—

Application to Industrial Court relating to procedural provisions—Application with respect to unit of employment—Unit of employment—Meaning—Unit of employment only where an employer and employees or workers—Worker—Person who has entered into contract for work or services—Broadcasting authority—Authors of scripts for sound broadcasting—Contracts between authors and authority giving authority right to broadcast—Contracts not requiring authors to do anything—Whether authors 'workers'—Whether broadcasting authority an employer in relation to authors—Industrial Relations Act 1971, ss 37(1)(2), 167(1). **Writers' Guild of GB v BBC** [1974] **1** 574, NIRC.

Sole bargaining agent—

Recognition—Application to Industrial Court—Organisation of workers seeking negotiating rights—Application by employer—Application for reference to Commission on Industrial Relations of question whether trade union should be recognised as sole bargaining agent—Trade union not seeking recognition—Whether court having power to refer question to commission—Industrial Relations Act 1971, ss 45, 46(1). **Car Collection Co Ltd, The v The Transport and General Workers Union** [1972] **2** 97, NIRC.

Recognition—Application to Industrial Court—Organisation of workers seeking negotiating rights—Trade union—Refusal by employer to recognise union—Embargoes against employer organised by union—Application to court by employer—Denial by union that seeking recognition any longer—Embargoes continuing 1n force—Whether embargoes constituting a request for recognition—Industrial Relations Act 1971, ss 45, 46(1). **Car Collection Co Ltd, The v The Transport and General Workers Union** [1972] **2** 97, NIRC.

Conciliation officers—

Communications made to conciliation officers—

Admissibility in evidence—Proceedings before Industrial Court and tribunals—Communications to conciliation officers in connection with performance of their functions—Circumstances in which communications admissible—Industrial Relations Act 1971, s 146(6). **Grazebrook (M & W) Ltd v Wallens** [1973] **2** 868, NIRC.

Employment tribunal. *See* **Employment tribunal**.

Industrial action—

Deduction from wages. *See* **Employment** (Remuneration—Deduction from wages—Deduction in respect of industrial action).

INDUSTRIAL RELATIONS (cont)—

Industrial action (cont)—

Emergency procedure—

Application to Industrial Court for order for ballot—Statutory conditions to be satisfied before grant of order—Irregular industrial action short of a strike begun or likely to begin—Breach of contract—Concerted course of conduct in furtherance of an industrial dispute—Conduct involving breach of contract in one respect only—Conduct lawful in other respects—Whether necessary that concerted course of conduct in its entirety should involve a breach of contract to constitute irregular industrial action—Industrial Relations Act 1971, ss 33(4), 141(1)(a). **Secretary of State for Employment v Associated Society of Locomotive Engineers and Firemen (No 2)** [1972] **2** 949, NIRC, CA.

Application to Industrial Court for order for ballot—Statutory conditions to be satisfied before grant of order—Minister's declaration that 'it appears to' him that requisites for order exist—Jurisdiction of court to interfere with Minister's decision—Jurisdiction to interfere only where bad faith or material misdirection on facts or law established—Not sufficient that Minister's application disclosing mistake on particular fact—Unneccessary for Minister to specify reasons for doubting whether workers wanting to take part in industrial action—Industrial Relations Act 1971, s 141(1)(a), (c). **Secretary of State for Employment v Associated Society of Locomotive Engineers and Firemen (No 2)** [1972] **2** 949, NIRC, CA.

Application to Industrial Court with view to discontinuing or deferring industrial action—Statutory conditions to be satisfied before grant of order—Condition that it appears to Secretary of State that irregular industrial action short of a strike has begun—Railway union executives instructing railway union members to 'work to rule'—Union members working to rule—Work to rule constituting irregular industrial action short of a strike—Appropriate order—Effect of order—Industrial Relations Act 1971, ss 33(4), 138, 139. **Secretary of State for Employment v Associated Society of Locomotive Engineers and Firemen** [1972] **2** 853, NIRC.

Organisation of workers—

Meaning—Principal objects including regulation of relations between workers and employers—Employers' complaint of unfair industrial practice—Picketing of complainants' premises—Picketing organised by committee of shop stewards—Function of committee to recommend and organise industrial action in docks—Committee unconnected with complainants and unrecognised as bargaining agent—Whether committee 'organisation of workers'—Industrial Relations Act 1971, s 61(1). **Midland Cold Storage Ltd v Turner** [1972] **3** 773, NIRC.

Industrial Court. See National Industrial Relations Court, *below.*

Industrial dispute—

Act done in contemplation or furtherance of an industrial dispute—

Act not actionable in tort on specified grounds—Act not actionable if consisting of inducement or threat of breach of contract—Act also constituting unfair industrial practice—Whether fact that act an unfair practice capable of rendering it actionable in tort—Industrial Relations Act 1971, s 132. **Cory Lighterage Ltd v Transport and General Workers Union** [1973] **2** 558, CA.

Act not actionable in tort on specified grounds—Dispute between workmen and workmen—Workman allowing membership of trade union to lapse—Fellow workers refusing to work with him—Union threatening employers with strike action if workman not withdrawn—Employers supporting union's membership policy—Employers unable to dismiss workman without consent of statutory board—Consent refused—Worker suspended on full pay—Whether a dispute between employers and union—Whether union's threats made in contemplation or furtherance of industrial dispute—Industrial Relations Act 1971, ss 132(1)(2), 167(1). **Cory Lighterage Ltd v Transport and General Workers Union** [1973] **2** 558, CA.

Meaning—

Dispute between employers and workers—Dispute between worker and worker—Worker resigning from union—Union members objecting to resignation—Union threatening employers with industrial action if employee allowed to work—Employee suspended from work in consequence of threat—Whether dispute between employer and one or more workers—Industrial Relations Act 1971, ss 96(1), 167(1). **Langston v Amalgamated Union of Engineering Workers** [1974] **1** 980, CA.

Dispute between employers and workers—Dispute relating wholly or mainly to specified matters—Terms and conditions of employment—Suspension of employment—Dispute between workmen and workmen not an industrial dispute—Whether 'terms and conditions of employment' confined to contractual terms and conditions—Whether 'suspension of employment' including suspension on full pay—Industrial Relations Act 1971, s 167(1). **Cory Lighterage Ltd v Transport and General Workers Union** [1973] **2** 558, CA.

Unfair industrial practice—

Action in contemplation or furtherance of dispute. See Unfair industrial practice—Action in contemplation or furtherance of industrial dispute, *below.*

Industrial tribunal. See **Employment tribunal.**

National Industrial Relations Court—

Contempt of court—

Breach of injunction—Evidence of contempt. See **Contempt of court** (Committal—Breach of injunction—Evidence of contempt—National Industrial Relations Court).

Jurisdiction—

Appeals from industrial tribunals—Court's jurisdiction limited to appeals on question of law—Possibility of order for costs against appellant if appeal not involving question of law—Industrial Relations Act 1971, s 114—Industrial Court Rules 1971 (SI 1971 No 1777), r 69. **Practice Direction** [1973] **2** 1264, NIRC.

Unfair industrial practice—

Relief—Order restraining respondent from continuing action—Discretion. See Unfair industrial practice—Relief—Order restraining respondent from continuing action—Discretion of court to grant order, *below.*

INDUSTRIAL RELATIONS (cont)—
  Organisation of workers—
    Breach of rules—
      Complaint by member against organisation—Complaint that action by organisation constituted a breach of its rules—Rules—Meaning—Rules conferring individual rights on members against organisation—Employee making unsuccessful application to employers for senior post—Employee's union refusing to make representations on employee's behalf to employers—Union rules stating object of union 'to...protect the interests of its members'—Complaint to industrial tribunal by employee against union alleging breach of union rules—Whether clause stating overall aim of union a 'rule'—Industrial Relations Act 1971, s 107(3)(b). **Oddy v Transport Salaried Staffs Association** [1973] **3** 610, NIRC.

    Industrial action. See Industrial action—Organisation of workers, above.
  Picketing. See **Trade dispute** (Picketing).
  Practice—
    Claim for redundancy payment or compensation for unfair dismissal—
      Position where doubt whether employee's dismissal on account of redundancy or an unfair dismissal. **Chapman v Goonvean & Rostowrack China Clay Co Ltd** [1973] **1** 218, NIRC.
  Proceedings—
    Duplication—
      Avoidance—Proceedings in courts other than National Industrial Relations Court—Proceedings in tort—Discretion to stay proceedings arising out of acts in respect of which proceedings have been, or could be, brought in the Industrial Court—Principles governing exercise of discretion—Industrial Relations Act 1971, ss 131, 132(4). **Midland Cold Storage Ltd v Steer** [1972] **3** 941, Ch D.
  Trade dispute. See **Trade dispute**.
  Trade union—
    Generally. See **Trade union**.
    Membership and activities. See Trade union membership and activities, below.
  Trade union membership and activities—
    Rights of worker as against employer—
      Dismissal for exercising rights—Unfair dismissal—Dismissal for taking part in trade union activities—Trade union—Unregistered union—Employee dismissed for taking part in activities of unregistered union—Employee member of union entered on provisional register at date of his engagement by employers—Union ceasing to be registered shortly thereafter—Employee organising union meeting two months later—Employee dismissed immediately after for organising meeting—Whether 'trade union' including unregistered or de-registered union—Whether employee unfairly dismissed—Industrial Relations Act 1971, ss 5(1), 22(1), 28, 29(1). **Kenyon v Fred Miller Ltd** [1972] **3** 686, NIRC.
      Dismissal for exercising rights—Unfair dismissal—Generally. See **Unfair dismissal** (Trade union membership and activities).
      Dismissal for exercising rights—Unfair dismissal—Right of worker to be member of trade union—Employee summarily dismissed after one year's service—Reason for dismissal the employee's indication of intention to join a union—Employee not decided which union to join or whether chosen union to be one registered or unregistered—Whether an exercise of employee's statutory right to become a member of a trade union—Whether competent for employee to claim unfair dismissal—Industrial Relations Act 1971, ss 5(1)(a), 29(1). **Cotter v Lynch Bros** [1972] **3** 809, NIRC.
      Right to take part in union activities at appropriate time—Activities on employer's premises—Activities outside working hours—Activities not requiring provision of facilities by employer—Whether workers entitled to carry out such activities on employer's premises without employer's consent—Industrial Relations Act 1971, s 5(1)(c). **Post Office v Union of Post Office Workers** [1974] **1** 229, HL.
      Right to time off for carrying out trade union activities—Attendance at union meeting—Meeting to discuss industrial relations strategy—Discussion not wholly confined to topics for which union recognised by employer—Whether officials entitled to time off with pay to attend meeting—Employment Protection (Consolidation) Act 1978, s 27(1)(a). **Beal v Beecham Group Ltd** [1982] **3** 280, CA.
      Unfair industrial practice by employer—Action short of dismissal—Action taken against employee as an individual—Derecognition of union—Payment of salary differential to employees who switched from collective bargaining to individual contracts of employment—Whether omission to offer employee a benefit conferred on another employee amounting to 'action taken against' employee from whom benefit was withheld—Whether employer's purpose in paying a salary differential was to prevent or deter union membership—Employment Protection (Consolidation) Act 1978, ss 23(1), 153(1). **Associated Newspapers Ltd v Wilson** [1995] **2** 100, HL.
      Unfair industrial practice by employer—Action short of dismissal—Action taken against employee as an individual—Employer paying wage increase to members of one union but not to members of another union doing same job—Whether failure to pay wage increase to members of other union 'action short of dismissal'—Whether employer's action taken against employees as 'individuals'—Whether action to prevent employees joining a particular union permissible—Employment Protection (Consolidation) Act 1978, ss 23(1)(a), 153(1). **National Coal Board v Ridgway** [1987] **3** 582, CA.
      Unfair industrial practice by employer—Discrimination by employer against worker by reason of exercise of such rights—Discrimination—Discrimination against members of unrecognised union—Discrimination in respect of negotiating rights permitted—Meaning of 'negotiating rights'—Negotiation for purpose of collective bargaining—Right of employee to be accompanied by union representative at interview to negotiate increase in individual salary—Right accorded to members of recognised unions but denied to members of unrecognised unions—Whether discrimination in respect of negotiating rights—Whether discrimination against member of unrecognised union an unfair industrial practice—Industrial Relations Act 1971, ss 5(2)(b), 44(b). **Howle v GEC Power Engineering Ltd** [1974] **1** 275, NIRC.

INDUSTRIAL RELATIONS (cont)—
  Trade union membership and activities (cont)—
    Rights of worker as against employer (cont)—
      Unfair industrial practice by employer—Discrimination by employer against worker by reason of exercise of such rights—Discrimination—Discrimination against union—Discrimination against union members—Facilities for union activities—Employees of same employer belonging to different unions—Only one union recognised by employer for negotiating purposes—Recognised union granted facilities for carrying out activities on employer's premises—Unrecognised union refused any such facilities—Refusal amounting to discrimination against members of unrecognised union—Discrimination against members by reason of the exercise of right to join one union rather than another—Discrimination unfair industrial practice except in relation to facilities for negotiating purposes—Industrial Relations Act 1971, s 5(2)(b). **Post Office v Union of Post Office Workers** [1972] **3** 485, NIRC; [1974] **1** 229, HL.
      Unfair industrial practice by employer—Discrimination by employer against worker by reason of exercise of such rights—Discrimination—Employers recognising four unions for negotiating and other purposes—Agreement for setting up of works committee—Committee consisting of representatives of management and of workers who were members of one of recognised unions—Two workers not being members of a recognised union seeking nomination for membership of works committee—Nomination papers rejected by employers because workers not members of a recognised union—Whether discrimination by employers against workers—Distinction in discriminating against workers and discriminating between workers—Industrial Relations Act 1971, s 5(2)(b), (4). **Central Electricity Generating Board v Coleman** [1973] **2** 709, NIRC.
      Worker—Meaning—Person working under contract whereby he undertakes to perform personally any work or services for other party—Test whether contract for personal work or services—Contract not permitting delegation of work or services—Football pools promoters—Scheme for collecting bets from punters—Main collector responsible to area concessionaire for appointing collectors to call on punters—Main collector required to work in accordance with instructions of area concessionaire—Whether main collector a 'worker'—Industrial Relations Act 1971, ss 5(2), 167(1). **Broadbent v Crisp** [1974] **1** 1052, NIRC.
  Unfair dismissal. *See* **Unfair dismissal**.
  Unfair industrial practice—
    Action in contemplation or furtherance of industrial dispute—
      Industrial dispute—Dispute between employers and workers—Employer's complaint of unfair industrial practice by workers not employed by them—Whether 'industrial dispute' if no nexus between employers and respondent workers—Industrial Relations Act 1971, ss 96, 97, 98, 167(1). **Midland Cold Storage Ltd v Turner** [1972] **3** 773, NIRC.
    Complaint—
      Pressure on employer to infringe rights of workers—Who may make complaint—Person against whom action taken—Action deemed to be taken against employer not worker—Threat by union against employers to take industrial action if employee allowed to work—Employee suspended by employers in consequence of threat—Complaint of unfair industrial practice by employee against union—Whether competent for employee to make complaint against union—Industrial Relations Act 1971, ss 33(3)(a), 101(1)(c), 105(1). **Langston v Amalgamated Union of Engineering Workers** [1974] **1** 980, CA.
      Time limit—Complaint to be presented before end of period of four weeks—Unfair dismissal—Period of four weeks beginning with the effective date of termination of contract—Meaning of 'presented'—Calculation of four week period—Industrial Tribunals (Industrial Relations, etc) Regulations 1972 (SI 1972 No 38), Sch, para 2(1). **Hammond v Haigh Castle & Co Ltd** [1973] **2** 289, NIRC.
      Time limit—Discretion to entertain complaint made out of time—Principles on which discretion to be exercised—Industrial Tribunals (Industrial Relations, etc) Regulations 1972 (SI 1972 No 38), Sch, r 2(1). **Westward Circuits Ltd v Read** [1973] **2** 1013, NIRC.
      Time limit—Jurisdiction to hear—Complaint made out of time—Industrial Relations Act 1971, Sch 6, para 5(1). **Westward Circuits Ltd v Read** [1973] **2** 1013, NIRC.
      Time limit—Not practicable in circumstances for complaint to be presented before end of limitation period—Circumstances to be taken into account in determining whether practicable—Complaint of unfair dismissal—Negotiation over severance terms—Agreement by employee at request of employer not to present complaint while negotiations proceeding—Validity of agreement—Relevance of question of validity—Presentation of complaint within prescribed period likely to jeopardise negotiations—Whether agreement to be disregarded as an agreement precluding presentation of complaint or excluding operation of statute and therefore void—Whether agreement rendering it not 'practicable' to present complaint within prescribed period—Industrial Relations Act 1971, s 161(1)—Industrial Tribunals (Industrial Relations, etc) Regulations 1972 (SI 1972 No 38), Sch, r 2(1). **Owen v Crown House Engineering Ltd** [1973] **3** 618, NIRC.
      Time limit—Not practicable in circumstances for complaint to be presented before end of limitation period—Complaint by employee of unfair dismissal—Circumstances in which employee's ignorance of legal right will be regarded as rendering it 'not practicable' for him to present complaint within period—Employee knowing that he had certain statutory rights—Employee ignorant of time limit—Employee seeking legal advice within limitation period—Legal advisers at fault in failing to present complaint within period—Whether practicable for employee to present complaint within period—Industrial Tribunals (Industrial Relations, etc) Regulations 1972 (SI 917 1972 No 38), Sch, r 2(1). **Dedman v British Building and Engineering Appliances Ltd** [1974] **1** 520, CA.
      Time limit—Not practicable in circumstances for complaint to be presented before end of limitation period—Employee unaware of right to make complaint to industrial tribunal until after expiry of time limit—Whether 'practicable' for employee to have made complaint within limitation period—Industrial Tribunals (Industrial Relations, etc) Regulations 1972 (SI 1972 No 38), Sch, r 2(1). **Westward Circuits Ltd v Read** [1973] **2** 1013, NIRC.
      Time limit—Not practicable in circumstances for complaint to be presented before end of limitation period—Meaning of 'practicable'—Industrial Tribunals (Industrial Relations, etc) Regulations 1972 (SI 1972 No 38), Sch, para 2(1). **Hammond v Haigh Castle & Co Ltd** [1973] **2** 289, NIRC.

INDUSTRIAL RELATIONS (cont)—
    Unfair industrial practice (cont)—
        Inducement or threat to induce breach of contract—
            Breach of contract—Contractual right to work—Suspension on full pay—Employee suspended on full pay by employers in consequence of threat by union to withdraw labour if employee allowed to work—Whether suspension on full pay a breach of contract—Whether union having induced breach of contract—Industrial Relations Act 1971, s 96(1). **Langston v Amalgamated Union of Engineering Workers** [1974] **1** 980, CA.
        Peaceful picketing—
            Peaceful picketing permissible under general law—Employers' complaint that respondent workers guilty of unfair industrial practice—Practice consisting of peaceful picketing—Whether peaceful picketing capable of constituting an unfair industrial practice—Industrial Relations Act 1971, ss 33(3), 96, 97, 98, 134. **Midland Cold Storage Ltd v Turner** [1972] **3** 773, NIRC.
        Relief—
            Order restraining respondent from continuing action—Discretion of court to grant order—Just and equitable to grant order—Exercise of discretion—Practice—Industrial action—Order restraining industrial action not to be made before enquiry into causes of underlying dispute—Industrial Relations Act 1971, s 101(2), (3). **Shipside (Ruthin) Ltd v Transport and General Workers Union** [1973] **3** 514, NIRC.
        Rights of worker as against employer. *See* Trade union membership and activities—Rights of worker as against employer—Unfair industrial practice by employer, *above.*
        Trade union—
            Liability of unregistered union—Act of shops stewards—Scope of authority. *See* **Trade union** (Official—Wrongful acts—Liability of union).

INDUSTRIAL TRAINING
    Board. *See* Training board, *below.*
    Levy—
        Activities of industry—
            Engineering industry—Erection of steam generating plant at thermal power station—Whether activity fell within engineering or construction—'Civil engineering work'—'Installation'—'Structures forming part of a building'—Industrial Training (Engineering Board) Order 1968 (SI 1968 No 1333 as amended by SI 1969 No 1376), Sch, paras 1(h), 2(d), 3. **Engineering Industry Training Board v Foster Wheeler John Brown Boilers Ltd** [1970] **2** 616, CA.
            Hotel and catering industry—Meals supplied to airlines for passengers' consumption—Whether supply to persons for immediate consumption—Industrial Training (Hotel and Catering Board) Order 1966 (SI 1966 No 1347), Sch 1, para 1(a). **NAS Airport Services Ltd v Hotel and Catering Industry Training Board** [1970] **3** 928, CA.
        Assessment—
            Appeal—Jurisdiction of appeal tribunal—Grounds on which liability to pay levy may be disputed—Exclusive jurisdiction of appeal tribunal to determine validity of grounds on which liability disputed—Action in High Court by Road Transport Industry Training Board against employers for recovery of sum assessed by way of levy—Employers disputing liability to pay levy—Whether court having jurisdiction to determine validity of grounds on which liability disputed—Industrial Training Act 1964, ss 4(3), 12(2)—Industrial Training Levy (Road Transport) Order 1968 (SI 1968 No 1835), art 7. **Road Transport Industry Training Board v J Wyatt Junior (Haulage) Ltd** [1972] **3** 913, QBD.
            Company providing self-employed operatives to construction industry clients—Clients contracting with company not operatives—Whether company 'employer in the construction industry'—Whether company 'construction establishment' from which principal construction industry activities taking place—Industrial Training Act 1982, ss 1(2), 11(2)—Industrial Training Levy (Construction Industry Training Board) Order 2015, SI 2015/701, arts 3(1), 5(2), (4). **Hudson Contract Services Ltd v Construction Industry Training Board** [2020] **4** 1007, CA.
            Notice—Form—Address for service of notice of appeal—Whether general address of board sufficient—Industrial Training Levy (Agricultural, Horticultural and Forestry) Order 1967 (SI 1967 No 1747), art 4(3). **Agricultural, Horticultural and Forestry Industry Training Board v Kent** [1970] **1** 304, CA.
    Training board—
        Establishment—
            Activities of industry or commerce—Hotel and catering industry—Whether members' clubs subject to levy—Whether order in part ultra vires—Industrial Training (Hotel and Catering Board) Order 1966 (SI 1966 No 1347), Sch 1, para 3(c)(ii)—Industrial Training Act 1964, s 1(1), s 4. **Hotel and Catering Industry Training Board v Automobile Pty Ltd** [1969] **2** 582, HL.
            Consultation—Duty of Minister to consult with specified organisations appearing to him to be representative of those engaged in industry—Failure to consult—Effect—Failure to consult association—Association a specialist branch of parent body—Consultation with parent body—Appropriate invitation for comments on draft order sent by Minister to association—Invitation not received by association—Association having no knowledge of order until after it was made—Whether Minister under duty to consult association—Whether consultation with parent body and sending of invitation for comments constituting consultation—Whether order applicable to members of association—Industrial Training Act 1964, s 1(4)—Industrial Training (Agricultural, Horticultural and Forestry Board) Order 1966 (SI 1966 No 969). **Agricultural, Horticultural and Forestry Industry Training Board v Aylesbury Mushrooms Ltd** [1972] **1** 280, QBD.
        Registration as a charity—
            Control by court. *See* **Charity** (Registration—Control by the court—Control by court in exercise of its charitable jurisdiction—Statutory corporation—Industrial training board).

INDUSTRIAL TRIBUNAL
    See **Employment tribunal**.

INDUSTRY

Development council—
    Power to set up—
        Necessity of showing council desired by a substantial number of persons engaged in the industry—Need to ascertain wishes of employers and employed—Industrial Organisation and Development Act 1947, s 1(4). **Thorneloe & Clarkson Ltd v Board of Trade** [1950] **2** 245, KBD.

INEQUALITY OF BARGAINING POWER

See **Equity** (Undue influence—Inequality of bargaining power).

INFANT

Access—
    Adoption. *See* **Adoption** (Access).
Accumulation of income under a trust. *See* **Accumulation** (Surplus income—Accumulation during minority).
Adoption. *See* **Adoption**.
Advancement—
    Powers of trustee. *See* **Trust and trustee** (Powers of trustee—Advancement).
Affiliation. *See* **Affiliation**.
Appointing person to convey property. *See* **Trust and trustee** (Appointing person to convey property).
Appointment of new trustee by infant. *See* **Trust and trustee** (Appointment of new trustee—By infant).
Blood test to determine paternity. *See* **Paternity** (Blood test).
Care—
    Local authority. *See* **Child** (Care—Local authority).
Care and control—
    Ward of court. *See* **Ward of court** (Care and control).
Contract—
    Apprenticeship—
        Benefit of infant. *See* **Employment** (Apprenticeship—Benefit of infant).
Custody—
    Conflict of laws—
        Wardship proceedings. *See* **Ward of court** (Jurisdiction).
    Divorce. *See* **Divorce** (Custody).
    Wardship jurisdiction. *See* **Ward of court** (Custody).
Damages recovered by infant—
    Jurisdiction of court to postpone entitlement until after attainment of majority. *See* **Variation of trusts** (Jurisdiction—Damages recovered by infant).
Death of mother—
    Fatal accident—
        Damages for loss of services as mother. *See* **Fatal accident** (Damages—Death of mother—Loss of services as mother).
Designation—
    Designation of persons of less than full age in Chancery proceedings—
        Use of term 'minor'. *See* **Practice** (Chancery Division—Designation of persons of less than full age).
Disentailing deed—
    Appointing person to convey property. *See* **Trust and trustee** (Appointing person to convey property—Infant beneficially interested—Disentailing deed).
Evidence—
    Criminal proceedings. *See* **Criminal evidence** (Child).
Generally. *See* **Minor**.
Gross indecency with infant. *See* **Criminal law** (Gross indecency—Child).
Guardian ad litem—
    Variation of trusts. *See* **Variation of trusts** (Infant—Guardian ad litem).
Guardianship—
    Guardian's allowance. *See* **Social security** (Guardian's allowance).
    Jurisdiction—
        Magistrates' court order—Wardship proceedings. *See* **Ward of court** (Previous custody order of magistrates made under jurisdiction conferred by guardianship legislation—Circumstances in which High Court will make different order under wardship jurisdiction).
    Originating summons—
        Form. *See* **Originating summons** (Guardianship of infant—Form).
Intoxicating liquor—
    Sale to. *See* **Licensing** (Knowingly selling liquor to person under age).
Kidnapping—
    Foreign child—
        Removal by parents from foreign jurisdiction—Wardship proceedings. *See* **Ward of court** (Jurisdiction—Kidnapping).
Legitimacy. *See* **Legitimacy**.
Limitation of action—
    Extension of time from which limitation period begins to run—
        Custody of parent. *See* **Limitation of action** (Persons under disability—Custody of parent).
Local authority—
    Care. *See* **Child** (Care—Local authority).
Maintenance—
    Generally. *See* **Minor** (Maintenance).
Minor—
    Use of word 'minor' in Chancery proceedings. *See* **Practice** (Chancery Division—Designation of persons of less than full age).
Parens patriae jurisdiction. *See* **Statute** (Crown—Parens patriae jurisdiction).
Paternity. *See* **Paternity**.

INFANT (cont)—
    Removal outside jurisdiction—
        Foreign court—
            Whether English court will return infant to foreign jurisdiction. *See* **Ward of court** (Jurisdiction—Alien—Alien children).
    Trespasser—
        Duty of occupier to child trespasser. *See* **Occupier's liability** (Child trespasser).
    Trust—
        Relative advantages between infant and adult beneficiaries—
            Variation of trusts by the court. *See* **Variation of trusts** (Benefit—Infant beneficially interested).
        Resettlement. *See* **Variation of trusts** (Jurisdiction—Infant's resettlement).
    Variation of trusts. *See* **Variation of trusts** (Variation by the court—Infant's interests).
    Ward of court. *See* **Ward of court**.
    Welfare of infant—
        Adoption proceedings. *See* **Adoption** (Welfare of infant).
    Workman—
        Compensation—
            Review. *See* **Workmen's compensation** (Review of compensation—Infant workman).

INFECTED WATER
    Water supply—
        Supply of water for domestic purposes. *See* **Water supply** (Supply of water for domestic purposes—Duty of undertakers as respects sufficiency and purity—Infected water).

INFERIOR COURT
    Contempt of court—
        Generally. *See* **Contempt of court** (Court—Inferior court).
        Publications concerning legal proceedings. *See* **Contempt of court** (Publications concerning legal proceedings—Court—Inferior court).
    Injunction—
        Jurisdiction of High Court. *See* **Injunction** (Inferior court—Jurisdiction of High Court over inferior court).

INFIRM DESTITUTE ASYLUM-SEEKER
    See **Immigration** (Asylum seeker—Infirm destitute asylum-seeker).

INFIRM PERSON
    Manslaughter—
        Assumption of duty of care for infirm person—
            Breach of duty amounting to recklessness. *See* **Criminal law** (Manslaughter—Recklessness or gross negligence—Assumption of duty of care for infirm person—Breach of duty amounting to recklessness).

INFLATION
    Damages—
        Personal injury—
            Damages increased for inflation. *See* **Interest** (Damages—Personal injury—Damages increased for inflation).
    Relevance to assessment—
        Fatal accident. *See* **Fatal accident** (Damages—Inflation).
        Personal injury. *See* **Damages** (Personal injury—Amount of damages—Post-trial financial loss—Inflation).
    Retirement pension—
        Uprating. *See* **Social security** (Retirement pension—Inflation uprating).
    Solicitor's remuneration—
        Legal aid taxation—
            Fees and expenses—Criminal proceedings—Certificate that owing to exceptional circumstances sums payable under regulations not fair remuneration—Inflation as an exceptional circumstance. *See* **Legal aid** (Taxation of costs—Solicitor's fees and expenses—Criminal proceedings—Fair remuneration—Power of taxing authority to certify that owing to exceptional circumstances sums payable under regulations would not provide fair remuneration—Exceptional circumstances—Inflation).
    State retirement pension—
        Uprating. *See* **Social security** (Retirement pension—Inflation uprating).

INFORMATION (CRIMINAL PROCEDURE)
    Amendment—
        Jurisdiction of Crown Court to allow amendment. *See* **Crown Court** (Appeal to Crown Court—Power of court on appeal—Appeal against conviction by magistrates—Jurisdiction to allow amendment).
    Dangerous dog, as to. *See* **Animal** (Dog—Dangerous dog—Information).
    Dangerous driving. *See* **Road traffic** (Dangerous driving—Information).
    Food and drugs offence—
        Proceedings against third party. *See* **Food and drugs** (Proceedings against third party—Information).
    Generally. *See* **Magistrates** (Information).
    Handling stolen goods. *See* **Criminal law** (Handling stolen goods—Information—Magistrates' court—Information in general terms).
    Jurisdiction. *See* **Magistrates** (Jurisdiction—Trial of information).
    Obtaining pecuniary advantage. *See* **Criminal law** (Obtaining pecuniary advantage by deception—Information).
    Road traffic offence—
        Failure to provide specimen for analysis or laboratory test. *See* **Road traffic** (Failure to provide specimen for analysis or laboratory test—Offence—Information).
        Summons or information. *See* **Road traffic** (Offence—Summons or information).

INFORMATION (CRIMINAL PROCEDURE) (cont)—
  Statutory nuisance—
    Right of any person aggrieved by statutory nuisance to lay information. *See* **Nuisance** (Statutory nuisance—Abatement notice—Failure to comply—Complaint to justices—Procedure—Initiation of proceedings—Complaint by individual—Information laid by person aggrieved by nuisance).
  Summons or information—
    Road traffic offence. *See* **Road traffic** (Offence—Summons or information).

INFORMATION (KNOWLEDGE)
  Access to—
    European Union institutions. *See* **European Union** (EU Institutions—Access to information).
  Collateral use of information—
    Disclosure. *See* **Disclosure and inspection of documents** (Collateral use of information obtained).
  Confidential information—
    Breach of confidence. *See* **Equity** (Breach of confidence—Confidential information).
    Generally. *See* **Confidential information**.
  Court proceedings in relation to child—
    Proceedings in private—
      Publication of information. *See* **Child** (Court proceedings in relation to child—Proceedings in private—Publication of information).
  Data protection. *See* **Data protection**.
  Disclosure—
    Care proceedings. *See* **Family proceedings** (Confidential information in care proceedings).
    Complaint of maladministration—
      Local government—Complaint to local commissioner. *See* **Local government** (Maladministration—Complaint to local commissioner—Production of documents or information to commissioner for purpose of investigating complaint).
    Confidential information—
      Disclosure of documents—Privilege. *See* **Disclosure and inspection of documents** (Privilege—Confidential documents).
      Generally. *See* **Confidential information**.
      Journalist—Refusal to divulge source of information—Contempt of court. *See* **Contempt of court** (Refusal to disclose source of information—Journalist).
    Contempt of court—
      Refusal by journalist to disclose source of information. *See* **Contempt of court** (Refusal to disclose source of information—Journalist).
    Police, by. *See* **Police** (Disclosure of information).
    Power of court to withhold information from parties. *See* **Natural justice** (Disclosure to parties of information before court—Court empowered to seek information—Power to withhold information from parties).
    Press—
      Privilege—Evidence. *See* **Evidence** (Privilege—Press).
    Public interest in disclosure of information—
      Confidence—Implied undertaking—Disclosure of documents. *See* **Disclosure and inspection of documents** (Production of documents—Confidence—Implied undertaking—Public interest in disclosure of information).
  Employer's duty to provide. *See* **Safe system of working** (Duty to give information or advice).
  Freedom of information. *See* **Freedom of information**.
  Furnishing false information. *See* **Criminal law** (Furnishing false information).
  Income tax purposes, for. *See* **Income tax** (Information).
  Insurance—
    Sharing of information by insurance companies—
      European community rules on competition, contrary to. *See* **European Union** (Rules on competition—Agreements preventing, restricting or distorting competition—Insurance companies entering information sharing agreements).
  Journalist—
    Refusal to divulge source of information—
      Contempt of court. *See* **Contempt of court** (Refusal to disclose source of information—Journalist).
  National insurance inspector—
    Power to require. *See* **Social security** (Inspector—Power to require information for the purpose of ascertaining whether contributions payable).
  Negligence—
    Generally. *See* **Negligence** (Information or advice).
    Knowledge third party might rely on information. *See* **Negligence** (Information or advice).
  Police—
    Disclosure by. *See* **Police** (Disclosure of information).
  Road traffic offence—
    Duty to give information. *See* **Road traffic** (Offence—Duty to give information).

INFORMATION TECHNOLOGY
  Disclosure and inspection of documents—
    Computer database. *See* **Disclosure and inspection of documents** (Legal professional privilege—Computer database).

INFORMER
  Criminal proceedings—
    Evidence for prosecution. *See* **Criminal evidence** (Prosecution evidence—Informer).

INHERITANCE
  Expectation of inheriting estate—
    Estoppel. *See* **Estoppel** (Proprietary estoppel—Expectation of inheriting estate).
  Family provision. *See* **Family provision**.
  Inheritance tax. *See* **Inheritance tax**.

INHERITANCE (cont)—
Loss of prospect of inheritance—
Damages—
Fatal accident cases. *See* **Fatal accident** (Damages—Loss of prospect of inheritance).
Widow. *See* **Family provision** (Widow).
Will. *See* **Will**.

INHERITANCE TAX
Exemptions and relief—
Agricultural property relief—
Deceased's estate including property comprising farmhouse and assortment of outbuildings—
Whether an 'agricultural property' entitled to relief from inheritance tax—Whether 'agricultural
land or pasture' including 'buildings and other structures'—Inheritance Tax Act 1984,
s 115—Interpretation Act 1978, s 5, Sch 1. **Starke and anor (executors of Brown (decd)) v IRC**
[1996] **1** 622, CA.
Gifts to charities—
Trust subject to Jersey law having United Kingdom law charitable purposes—Inheritance tax relief
limited to legacies and gifts to UK charities subject to jurisdiction of UK courts—Whether Jersey
to be treated as part of UK for purposes of free movement of capital—Whether refusal of
inheritance tax relief justifiable under EU law—Inheritance Tax Act 1984, s 23—Article 63 TFEU.
Routier v Revenue and Custom Comrs [2020] **1** 191, SC.
Mistake of fact. *See* **Mistake** (Mistake of fact—Equity—Transferor making transfers potentially exempt
from charge to inheritance tax if transferor surviving seven years).
Purchase exemption—
Associated operations—Transfer of pension plan—Deceased transferring funds out of one
registered pension scheme into another—Whether transfer of funds constituting transfer of value
for purposes of inheritance tax—Whether deceased's omission to take lifetime pension benefits
to be treated as disposition and transfer of value—Whether combination of transfer and omission
to take benefits an 'associated operation'—Inheritance Tax Act 1984, ss 3(1), (3), 10, 268. **Revenue
and Customs Comrs v Parry** [2019] **2** 288, CA; [2021] **1** 365, SC.
Lifetime transfer—
Gift of property subject to a reservation—
Transfer of freehold interest subject to leases in favour of donor—Whether property enjoyed to
exclusion of donor—Whether property subject to a reservation of benefit—Finance Act 1986,
s 102. **Ingram and anor (exors of the estate of Lady Ingram (decd)) v IRC** [1997] **4** 395,
CA; [1999] **1** 297, HL.
Nil-rate band—
Gift in will. *See* **Will** (Gift—Amount equal to unused-nil rate band).
Probate. *See* **Probate** (Inheritance tax).
Settled property—
Charge at ten year anniversary—
Relevant property—Scrip dividend shares—Whether scrip dividend proceeds income or
capital—Whether scrip dividend proceeds liable to ten-yearly charge—Inheritance Tax Act 1984,
s 64—Income and Corporation Taxes Act 1988, s 249(6). **Gilchrist (as trustee of the JP Gilchrist
1993 Settlement) v Revenue and Customs Comrs** [2014] **4** 943, UT.

INJUNCTION
Abortion—
Husband applying for injunction to stop wife having abortion—
Wife obtaining necessary medical certificates for legal abortion. *See* **Abortion** (Legal
abortion—Power of husband to prevent wife having abortion—Wife obtaining necessary medical
certificates for legal abortion—Wife wanting abortion—Husband applying for injunction to stop
her having abortion).
Adoption—
Adoption order—
Injunction restraining natural parents from making contact with child and adoptive family as term
of order. *See* **Adoption** (Order—Terms and conditions which may be imposed—Injunction
restraining natural parents from making contact with child and adoptive family).
Alternative remedies—
Alternative remedies not exhausted—
Power of court to grant relief. **Leigh v National Union of Railwaymen** [1969] **3** 1249, Ch D.
Power of court to grant relief—Breach of statute—Statutory remedy for breach—Statutory remedy
by way of prosecution in magistrates' court—Failure to comply with statutory notice—Appeal to
magistrates' court against issue of notice—Appeal not yet determined—Defendant continuing to
flout statutory notice—Proceedings in High Court for injunction—Whether interlocutory
injunction should be granted—Control of Pollution Act 1974, s 58(8). **Hammersmith London
Borough v Magnum Automated Forecourts Ltd** [1978] **1** 401, CA.
Power of court to grant relief—Breach of statute—Statutory remedy for breach—Statutory remedy
by way of prosecution in magistrates' court—Fines payable under statute relatively
small—Defendant unlawfully holding Sunday market—Defendant prosecuted once by local
authority—Defendant instituting appeal against conviction but appeal not yet determined—
Defendant continuing to flout statutory provision against Sunday trading—Profits arising from
market making it worthwhile for defendant to contravene statute and pay the fines—Whether
injunction should be granted. **Stafford BC v Elkenford Ltd** [1977] **2** 519, Ch D.
Relator action—Administrative discretion of Attorney General where doubtful whether other
remedies exhausted. **A-G (ex rel Hornchurch UDC) v Bastow** [1957] **1** 497, QBD.
Procedure provided by statute misused for delay—
Penalty provided by statute. **A-G (ex rel Egham UDC) v Smith** [1958] **2** 557, QBD.

INJUNCTION (cont)—

Alternative remedies (cont)—

Statutory remedy in magistrates' court—

Remedy not immediately available—Defendants allegedly in breach of statutory requirement not to occupy premises until fire certificate issued by council—Criminal proceedings pending—Hearing not for several weeks—Magistrates powerless to make order prohibiting occupation until after conviction—Relator action—Power of High Court to grant injunction—London Building Acts (Amendment) Act 1939, s 34(4), (5). **A-G v Chaudry** [1971] 3 938, Ch D and CA.

Anti-suit injunction—

Anti-arbitration injunction. *See* **Arbitration** (Injunction—Power of court—Anti-arbitration injunction).

Arbitration. *See* **Arbitration** (Injunction—Power of court—Anti-suit injunction).

Charterparties containing English law and arbitration clauses—

Owners entering into charterparties with nominee company of guarantor—Guarantor providing guarantees for chartering obligations of nominee company—Owners instituting arbitration in England following failure of nominee company to make hire payments—Guarantor bringing proceedings in Russia—Owners bringing proceedings in England and obtaining anti-suit injunction against defendant—Whether guarantor's conduct unconscionable—Whether anti-suit injunction should be continued. **Star Reefers Pool Inc v JFC Group Co Ltd** [2012] 2 Comm 225, CA.

Conflict of laws—

Arbitration. *See* **Conflict of laws** (Foreign proceedings—Restraint of foreign proceedings—Jurisdiction—Arbitration).

Arbitration—Contract for sale of cotton—Contract incorporating rules and bylaws of international trade association—Rules containing requirement for dispute resolution by arbitration—Contract containing arbitration clause—Bangladeshi buyer refusing to complete—Seller submitting dispute to arbitration in accordance with trade association rules—Buyer obtaining interim injunction in Bangladesh—Buyer contending contract not binding—Buyer contending dispute not covered by arbitration clause—Whether Bangladeshi proceedings breach of arbitration clause—Whether strong reasons not to grant injunction. **Ecom Agroindustrial Corp Ltd v Mosharaf Composite Textile Mill Ltd** [2013] 2 Comm 983, QBD.

Challenge to jurisdiction. *See* **Conflict of laws** (Jurisdiction—Challenge to jurisdiction—Claimant commencing proceedings in England—Defendants obtaining anti-suit injunction in Guernsey).

Restraint of foreign proceedings. *See* **Conflict of laws** (Foreign proceedings—Restraint of foreign proceedings).

Construction contract governed by English law and containing arbitration agreement—

Arbitral tribunal seated in London finding contract lawfully terminated by Jordanian company—French company commencing proceedings in Jordan for annulment of contract based on alleged unconstitutionality of Jordanian law provision establishing Jordanian company—Jordanian company seeking permanent anti-suit injunction—Whether claim to invalidate contract falling within language of arbitration agreement—Whether absence of strong reasons for not granting injunction—Whether just to grant injunction. **Aqaba Container Terminal (PVT) Co v Soletanche Bachy France SAS** [2020] 1 Comm 86, QBD.

Statements of case—

Claimants applying for continuation of interim anti-suit injunctions restraining defendant's third party proceedings against them in Singapore—General principles on anti-suit injunctions—Whether, by anti-suit injunction, one contracting party able to enforce exclusive jurisdiction clause against other contracting party, so as to prevent tort proceedings against third party—Whether grounds to continue interim anti-suit injunctions—Whether claimants to be granted permission to amend respective statements of case—CPR 6B PD 3.1. **Clearlake Shipping Pte Ltd v Xiang Da Marine Pte Ltd** [2020] 1 Comm 61, QBD.

Appeal—

Act which might deprive appellant of fruits of appeal—

Order to restrain. **Orion Property Trust Ltd v Du Cane Court Ltd** [1962] 3 466, Ch D.

Application—

Premature application. *See* Premature application for order, *below*.

Arbitration—

Generally. *See* **Arbitration** (Injunction).

Want of prosecution—

Injunction restraining claimant from proceeding with arbitration. *See* **Arbitration** (Practice—Want of prosecution—Injunction restraining claimant from proceeding with arbitration).

Assault—

Injunction restraining commission of assault—

Jurisdiction to grant. **Egan v Egan** [1975] 2 167, Ch D.

Availability of remedy. *See* **Judicial review** (Availability of remedy).

Balance of convenience—

Interlocutory injunction. *See* Interlocutory—Balance of convenience, *below*.

Breach of confidence. *See* **Equity** (Breach of confidence—Injunction).

Breach of contract—

Breach of implied negative term—

Need for certainty—Need to be clear exactly what it is that defendant may not do—Agreement between plaintiff vendor and company—Agreement that company should form new company and that plaintiff should sell plots of land to new company in return for shares and cash—Company formed for purpose of developing land as marina—New company subsequently advertising one of plots of land for sale—Plaintiff seeking injunction restraining company and new company from disposing of any of land—Contract at most requiring company to use best endeavours to procure if practicable development of property as marina—Obligation not sufficiently certain to found claim for injunction to restrain company or new company from disposing of land. **Bower v Bantam Investments Ltd** [1972] 3 349, Ch D.

INJUNCTION (cont)—

Breach of contract (cont)—

Breach of restrictive covenant —

Negotiating damages—Undisputed breaches of covenant that vessel sold for demolition purposes only—Whether seller entitled to injunction enforcing terms of covenant—Whether negotiating damages available to seller—Whether declaration that seller entitled only to nominal damages for past breaches and any future breaches appropriate. **Priyanka Shipping Ltd v Glory Bulk Carriers PTE Ltd** [2020] **1 Comm** 1040, QBD.

Contract for personal services—

Breach of restrictive covenant—Whether necessary to prove that damage will result from breach—Enforcement of contract for personal services. **Marco Productions Ltd v Pagola** [1945] **1** 155, KBD.

Injunction restraining third party from inducing breach of contract. *See* **Employment** (Contract of service—Injunction—Injunction restraining third party from inducing breach of contract).

Management agreement between group of musicians and manager—Professional careers of group to be advanced—Personal and fiduciary character of services to be rendered by manager—Repudiation of agreement by group for alleged breaches—Injunction sought by manager to restrain group until trial from engaging new manager—Grant of interlocutory injunction would compel group to continue to employ manager and thus enforce rendering of personal services by manager—Whether injunction should be refused as tantamount to specific performance of a contract for personal service. **Page One Records Ltd v Britton and ors (t/a 'The Troggs')** [1967] **3** 822, Ch D.

Foreign corporation—

Submission to English jurisdiction—No evidence of assets within jurisdiction—Whether remedy by injunction available to restrain its agents from further breaches of contract. **Hospital for Sick Children (Board of Governors) v Walt Disney Productions Inc** [1967] **1** 1005, CA.

Interlocutory injunction to protect payment made under contract pending hearing—

Jurisdiction—Plaintiffs purchasing business stock from defendants by means of postdated cheque—Cheque presented pursuant to solicitors' undertaking—Plaintiffs bringing action against defendants to recover alleged overpayment—Plaintiffs also applying for injunction to restrain defendants from presenting postdated cheque for payment prior to trial—Whether injunction should be granted—Whether plaintiffs' action amounting to personal claim for money had and received or proprietary claim. **Eldan Services Ltd v Chandag Motors Ltd** [1990] **3** 459, Ch D.

Irrevocable licence—

Grant of irrevocable licence to use theatre—Negative covenant by licensor not to revoke implied in grant—Right of licensees to injunction to restrain licensor from acting on purported revocation. **Winter Garden Theatre (London) Ltd v Millenium Productions Ltd** [1947] **2** 331, HL.

Procuring breach of contract—

Plaintiffs' contracts with third parties terminable by proper notice—Plaintiffs having agreements with tenants of public houses to supply and maintain coin-operated amusement machines—Agreements terminable on two weeks' notice—Defendants taking over management of public houses and requiring tenants to deal with nominated suppliers of amusement machines—Plaintiffs not included in defendants' list of nominated suppliers—Defendants requiring tenants to cease doing business with plaintiffs—Whether plaintiffs entitled to injunction restraining defendants from procuring breach of contracts between plaintiffs and tenants. **Cutsforth v Mansfield Inns Ltd** [1986] **1** 577, QBD.

Breach of covenant—

Breach of undertaking—

Contract of service—Undertaking expressed to be perpetual and worldwide—Employee employed in royal household on terms that he would not disclose information about his employment without authority to unauthorised persons or in a book—Employee planning to publish book about his employment in royal household—Attorney General bringing action against employee and Canadian publisher controlled by employee for worldwide restraint against publication—Whether Attorney General entitled to worldwide interlocutory injunction against employee and publisher restraining publication of book—Whether injunction should be limited to United Kingdom. **A-G v Barker** [1990] **3** 257, CA.

Breach of injunction—

Aiding and abetting breach—

Unlawful interference with trade or business—Unlawful interference by compliance with another's unlawful directions—Directions unlawful as given in breach of injunction—Defendant foreign company refusing to continue supplying plaintiffs with an essential part of equipment—Equipment manufactured and sold by plaintiffs under licence from another foreign company—Licence agreement stated to be subject to English law—Injunction granted to plaintiffs against licensors restraining them from impeding plaintiffs in manufacture and sale of equipment—Licensors, in breach of injunction, instructing defendants not to supply essential part of equipment to the plaintiffs—No contract between plaintiffs and defendants—Whether remedy by way of injunction available against defendants. **Acrow (Automation) Ltd v R Chainbelt Inc** [1971] **3** 1175, CA.

Committal for contempt of court. *See* **Contempt of court** (Committal—Breach of injunction).

Company—

Compulsory winding up. *See* **Company** (Compulsory winding up—Restraining presentation of petition—Injunction).

Contempt of court—Generally. *See* **Contempt of court** (Company—Breach of injunction).

Effect of breach—

Wilful disobedience or disregard of injunction—Resolution changing union rules passed in defiance of injunction—Effect on rules—Whether resolution and changes in rules illegal and invalid. **Clarke v Chadburn** [1985] **1** 211, Ch D.

Sentence. *See* **Contempt of court** (Committal—Breach of injunction—Maximum sentence).

INJUNCTION (cont)—
  Breach of statutory duty—
    Breach by public authority—
      Failure of local education authority to make schools available for full-time education—Statute
      providing remedy of complaint to Secretary of State—Whether existance of remedy in statute
      excluding remedies of injunction or damages on application of parent suffering damage—
      Education Act 1944, ss 8, 99(1). **Meade v Haringey London Borough** [1979] **2** 1016, CA.
  Breach of undertaking given to court—
    Aiding and abetting breach—
      Respondents to motion for injunction not parties to the action—Whether injunction was the
      appropriate remedy. **Elliot v Klinger** [1967] **3** 141, Ch D.
  Cause of action—
    Necessity to have cause of action to support injunction—
      Plaintiff claiming defendant's acts harmful and unfair and it would be just and convenient to grant
      injunction—Defendant's acts not otherwise unlawful—Whether plaintiff having good cause of
      action—Whether injunction would be granted to restrain defendant's acts—Supreme Court Act
      1981, s 37(1). **Associated Newspapers Group plc v Insert Media Ltd** [1988] **2** 420, Ch D.
  Children—
    Child of the dissolved marriage—
      Child at school in Scotland—Injunction restraining divorced wife from allowing letter sent to child's
      school to be handed to him—Supreme Court of Judicature (Consolidation) Act 1925, s 45(1). **R v
      R and I** [1961] **3** 461, Div.
    Injunction against child—
      Parent's house—Injunction restraining child from entering house. **Egan v Egan** [1975] **2** 167, Ch D.
    Molestation. See Husband and wife—Molestation—Molestation of child, *below*.
    Removal from jurisdiction—
      Divorce. See Husband and wife—Removing children from jurisdiction—Petition for divorce
      presented in England by husband, *below*.
      Generally. See **Minor** (Removal outside jurisdiction—Injunction).
      Husband and wife. See Husband and wife—Removing children from jurisdiction, *below*.
  Company—
    Breach of injunction—
      Contempt of court—Generally. See **Contempt of court** (Company—Breach of injunction).
    Compulsory winding up—
      Injunction restraining presentation of petition. See **Company** (Compulsory winding up—Restraining
      presentation of petition—Injunction).
  Compliance outside defendant's control—
    Local authority—
      Authority unable to comply with injunction without financial grant—Grant obtainable only on
      authority of Minister—Whether ground for refusing injunction. **Pride of Derby and Derbyshire
      Angling Association Ltd v British Celanese Ltd** [1952] **1** 1326, Ch D.
  Confidential information—
    Employment. See Interlocutory—Barring-out relief—Employee acquiring confidential information
      during course of employment, *below*.
    Interlocutory injunction. See Interlocutory—Confidential information, *below*.
    Power of court to restrain disclosure—
      Breach of confidence. See **Equity** (Breach of confidence—Injunction).
      Cabinet proceedings. See **Constitutional law** (Cabinet—Proceedings—Disclosure of documents or
        information—Confidential information—Public interest in non-disclosure—Disclosure of informa-
        tion by Cabinet Minister).
      Generally. See **Confidential information** (Injunction against disclosure of information).
      Trade secrets. See **Employment** (Duty of servant—Confidential information—Injunction restraining
        disclosure).
  Contract of service—
    Breach of undertaking. See Breach of covenant—Breach of undertaking—Contract of service, *above*.
    Generally. See **Employment** (Contract of service—Breach of contract—Injunction).
  County court—
    Breach of injunction—
      Committal for contempt of court—Jurisdiction. See **Contempt of court** (Committal—Breach of
        injunction—Jurisdiction—County court).
    Jurisdiction—
      Attachment of power of arrest to injunction—Domestic violence. See Husband and wife—Domestic
        violence—Attachment of power of arrest to injunction—Jurisdiction of county court, *below*.
      Divorce Court—Wife's petition for divorce pending—Application by wife to restrain proceedings
        against daughters of full age for eviction from matrimonial home. **Murcutt v Murcutt**
        [1952] **2** 427, Div.
      Exclusion of party from matrimonial home. See Exclusion of party from matrimonial
        home—County court—Jurisdiction, *below*.
      Generally. See **County court** (Jurisdiction—Injunction).
      Local authority seeking injunctions against individuals in terms typical of anti-social behaviour
        orders—Whether court having jurisdiction to grant injunctions—Standard of proof to be
        applied—Local Government Act 1972, s 222. **Birmingham City Council v Shafi** [2009] **3** 127, CA.
  Court of Appeal—
    Jurisdiction. See **Court of Appeal** (Jurisdiction—Injunction).
  Criminal law—
    Injunction to restrain breach of criminal law—
      Relator action by Attorney General. See **Attorney General** (Relator action—Injunction—Breach of
        criminal law).

INJUNCTION (cont)—
  Criminal proceedings—
    Civil proceedings instituted previously—
      Issues of law in both sets of proceedings substantially the same—Originating summons to determine whether plaintiff company subject to Pilotage Act 1913, ss 11, 43—Informations laid by defendants' employee against plaintiff company's employee alleging offences under ss 11, 43—Whether injunction granted to restrain criminal proceedings while civil proceedings pending. **Thames Launches Ltd v Corp of the Trinity House of Deptford Strond** [1961] **1** 26, Ch D.
  Cross-undertaking in damages—
    Public authority—
      Financial Services Authority. *See* **Financial services** (Financial Services Authority (FSA)—Regulation of financial services—Law enforcement).
  Damages in lieu of injunction—
    Breach of confidence. *See* **Equity** (Breach of confidence—Damages).
    Breach of restrictive covenant affecting land—
      Conduct of parties—Restrictive covenant against use of land otherwise than for horse-racing—Tort of inducing breach of contract by entering into agreement for sale and purchase of land for housing—Vendor contending that horse-racing on land no longer profitable—Vendor deciding to cease operating racecourse, with consequence that land would probably be acquired compulsorily for housing—Whether damages should be granted in lieu of injunction. **Tophams Ltd v Earl of Sefton** [1966] **1** 1039, HL.
      Measure of damages—Breach not diminishing value of retained land—Defendant making profit from breach—Plaintiff not limited to nominal damages—Damages representing a percentage of profit anticipated from activity constituting breach—Calculation of percentage. **Wrotham Park Estate Co v Parkside Homes Ltd** [1974] **2** 321, Ch D.
      Trespass—Defendants owning house in private road—Defendants building new house behind their own property with access to roadway over their garden—Defendants thus causing acts of trespass on plaintiff's section of roadway and breaching covenant not to use land other than for garden—Plaintiff applying for injunction when building well under way—Judge refusing injunction and granting damages in lieu—Whether injunction should have been granted—Whether judge's assessment of damages correct. **Jaggard v Sawyer** [1995] **2** 189, CA.
    Judicial discretion. *See* **Nuisance** (Noise—Motor racing—Remedies—Damages in lieu of injunction).
    Measure of damages—
      Defendant expropriating property belonging to claimant and incorporating it into own property—Court declining to order recovery of property—Whether determination of damages to be on basis of value of lost land or value of land to defendant. **Ramzan v Brookwide Ltd** [2011] **2** 38, Ch D; [2012] **1** 903, CA; [2012] **1 Comm** 979, CA.
    Nuisance. *See* **Nuisance** (Noise—Motor racing—Remedies—Damages in lieu of injunction).
    Positive or negative obligation—
      Solus agreement in relation to petrol filling station—Consequence of injunction that proprietor obliged to keep garage open. **Esso Petroleum Co Ltd v Harper's Garage (Stourport) Ltd** [1966] **1** 725, CA.
  Danger that defendant may transfer assets out of jurisdiction—
    Practice—
      Generally. *See* **Practice** (Pre-trial or post-judgment relief—Freezing order).
  Defamation cases. *See* **Libel and slander** (Injunction).
  Defence—
    Undertaking—
      Offer of undertaking with denial of liability—Right of plaintiff to disregard undertaking. **Oliver v Dickin** [1936] **2** 1004, Ch D.
  Discharge—
    Interlocutory injunction. *See* Interlocutory—Discharge, *below*.
  Disciplinary power—
    Whether court will interfere with exercise. *See* **Fire brigade** (Discipline—Exercise of disciplinary power—Interference by court—Injunction).
  Disclosure in aid of injunction—
    Freezing order. *See* **Practice** (Pre-trial or post-judgment relief—Freezing order—Disclosure in aid of injunction).
    Generally. *See* **Practice** (Pre-trial or post-judgment relief—Disclosure in aid of injunction).
  Discretion—
    Acquiescence by plaintiff in activities constituting breach of plaintiff's rights—
      Restrictive covenant affecting land—Plaintiff initially uncertain whether activities of defendant constituting breach of covenant—Defendant's activities gradually increasing so as to constitute clear breach of covenant—Plaintiff's failure to protest at early date giving defendant false sense of security—Defendant continuing to expand activities and to invest large sums of money—Whether appropriate case for grant of injunction. **Shaw v Applegate** [1978] **1** 123, CA.
    Interlocutory injunction—
      Trade dispute. *See* Interlocutory—Trade dispute—Claim by party against whom injunction sought that he had acted in contemplation or furtherance of trade dispute—Judicial discretion, *below*.
    Mandatory injunction. *See* Mandatory injunction—Discretion over grant of remedy, *below*.
    Natural justice—
      Injunction to restrain breach of rules of natural justice—Failure to give party opportunity to be heard—University—Suspension of student—Student not denying commission of offence—Student suffering no injustice by reason of breach of rules—Refusal of injunction. **Glynn v Keele University** [1971] **2** 89, Ch D.
  Domestic violence—
    Attachment of power of arrest to injunction. *See* Husband and wife—Domestic violence—Attachment of power of arrest to injunction, *below*.
    Exclusion of party from matrimonial home. *See* Exclusion of party from matrimonial home, *below*.
    Molestation. *See* Molestation—Domestic violence, *below*.
  Duty not to mislead court—
    Freezing order. *See* **Practice** (Pre-trial or post-judgment relief—Freezing order—Discharge of injunction for breach of duty not to mislead court).

130

INJUNCTION (cont)—
Ex parte injunction—
Appeal—
Appeal against ex parte injunction granted by Chancery Division of High Court—Injunction discharged. **Harper v Secretary of State for the Home Dept** [1955] **1** 331, CA.
Application—
Costs. *See* **Costs** (Order for costs—Ex parte proceedings—Motion for injunction).
Discharge—
Application by one defendant—Other defendants not having applied for discharge—Court satisfied at hearing of application that injunctions against all defendants should be discharged—Whether court having jurisdiction to discharge injunctions against defendants who had not applied for discharge. **Harbottle (RD) (Mercantile) Ltd v National Westminster Bank Ltd** [1977] **2** 862, QBD.
Husband and wife. *See* Husband and wife—Ex parte applications, *below.*
Jurisdiction to make—
Court's inability to hear full application—No fault of plaintiff or defendant—Prima facie case showing irreparable damage likely to plaintiff. **Beese (Managers of Kimpton Church of England Primary School) v Woodhouse** [1970] **1** 769, CA.
Grant prior to issue of originating process—Custody of children—Inherent jurisdiction in cases of urgency—Divorce proceedings to be issued in county court—Exercise of High Court jurisdiction—Supreme Court of Judicature (Consolidation) Act 1925, s 45—RSC Ord 29, r 1(3). **L v L** [1969] **1** 852, Div.
Pending appeal—Application made when appeal pending against refusal of interlocutory injunction—Ex parte motion for injunction—Motion dismissed—Jurisdiction of judge to grant ex parte application pending appeal against dismissal of motion. **Erinford Properties Ltd v Cheshire CC** [1974] **2** 448, Ch D.
Matrimonial proceedings—
When court should grant ex parte injunction—Grant of injunction only in an emergency where interests of justice or protection of applicant or a child require immediate intervention—Duration of ex parte injunction—Date of expiry to be specified—Injunction to be limited to the period required to arrange a hearing inter partes—Longer period may be fixed if difficulty in serving other party anticipated but order should then provide that other party can apply to court on 24 hours' notice to discharge injunction—Interim injunction granted on husband's ex parte application restraining wife from entering matrimonial home or molesting husband—Validity. **Ansah v Ansah** [1977] **2** 638, CA.
Matters to be considered before granting injunction—
Injunction prohibiting payment of irrevocable letter of credit etc—Injunction not normally to be granted in absence of substantial challenge to validity of letter of credit etc—Uncorroborated statement of bank's customer not normally sufficient evidence. **Bolivinter Oil SA v Chase Manhattan Bank (note)** [1984] **1** 351, CA.
Exclusion of party from matrimonial home—
County court—
Children's interests paramount—Home needed to accommodate children—Man and woman living together with children in house of which they were joint tenants—Relationship breaking down—No violence or molestation by man towards woman or children—Woman leaving home with children and refusing to return—Woman and children living with friends in congested conditions—Whether jurisdiction to exclude man from house if he had not been violent—Domestic Violence and Matrimonial Proceedings Act 1976, s 1(1)(c). **Spindlow v Spindlow** [1979] **1** 169, CA.
Children's interests paramount—Home needed to accommodate children—Need for wife to be with children—Husband violent towards wife—Parties married with five children aged from four to 11—Wife leaving with children and going to live at mother's house—Wife and children living in cramped conditions at mother's house—Husband occupying matrimonial home—Matrimonial home large enough to accommodate children—Whether order should be made excluding husband from matrimonial home—Domestic Violence and Matrimonial Proceedings Act 1976, s 1(1)(c). **Rennick v Rennick** [1978] **1** 817, CA.
Jurisdiction—Application for injunction made after decree absolute but during pendency of proceedings for ancillary relief—Parties continuing to live in matrimonial home after decree absolute but wife living in extension to home without any amenities—Wife applying for injunction to exclude husband from home—Whether court having jurisdiction under statute or at common law—Whether if jurisdiction proper exercise of discretion to grant injunction—Domestic Violence and Matrimonial Proceedings Act 1976, s 1(1)(c). **O'Malley v O'Malley** [1982] **2** 112, CA.
Jurisdiction—Application for injunction made in course of custody proceedings—Power to grant interlocutory injunction excluding father of child from property—Mother and father joint tenants of property but not married to each other—Parties not living in property as husband and wife—Mother marrying someone else and wishing to bring husband to live in property with her and child—Whether court having jurisdiction to grant injunction sought—Whether mother having legal right to exclude father of child from property—Guardianship of Minors Act 1971—Supreme Court Act 1981, s 37—County Courts Act 1984, s 38. **Ainsbury v Millington** [1986] **1** 73, CA.
Man and woman who are living with each other in the same household as husband and wife—Parties living in small flat—Parties' relationship breaking down but parties continuing to live in flat in separate rooms, without speaking to each other—Whether court having jurisdiction to entertain application for injunction—Whether parties living 'in the same household as husband and wife'—Domestic Violence and Matrimonial Proceedings Act 1976, s 1(2). **Adeoso (orse Ametepe) v Adeoso** [1981] **1** 107, CA.
Man and woman who are living with each other in the same household as husband and wife—Relevant date for purpose of determining whether parties 'are living' together—Acts of violence by man against woman—Woman leaving home and subsequently applying for injunction containing provision excluding man from home—Whether necessary to show that man and woman 'are living with each other' at date application made—Whether sufficient if parties living together when relevant acts of violence occurred—Domestic Violence and Matrimonial Proceedings Act 1976, s 1(2). **B v B** [1978] **1** 821, CA.

INJUNCTION (cont)—
    Exclusion of party from matrimonial home (cont)—
        County court (cont)—
            Respondent having proprietary interest in home—Applicant having no proprietary interest—Man and woman living together as husband and wife—Man entitled to occupy home by virtue of tenancy—Woman having no proprietary interest—Violence shown to woman by man—Application by woman for injunction containing provision excluding man from home—Whether county court having jurisdiction to exclude from home party who has proprietary interest—Domestic Violence and Matrimonial Proceedings Act 1976, s 1(1). **B v B** [1978] **1** 821, CA.
            Respondent having proprietary interest in home—Joint tenancy—Home needed to accommodate children. *See* Exclusion of party from matrimonial home—County court—Children's interests paramount—Home needed to accommodate children—Man and woman living together with children in house of which they were joint tenants, *above*.
            Respondent having proprietary interest in home—Joint tenancy—Man and woman living together as husband and wife in house of which they were joint tenants—Violence shown to woman by man—Application by woman for injunction containing provision excluding man from house—Whether county court having jurisdiction to exclude from house party who is joint tenant—Domestic Violence and Matrimonial Proceedings Act 1976, s 1(1). **Cantliff v Jenkins** [1978] **1** 836, CA; **Davis v Johnson** [1978] **1** 1132, HL.
            Time limit on operation of injunction—Application by respondent to discharge injunction—Application by applicant to extend injunction—Domestic Violence and Matrimonial Proceedings Act 1976, s 1(1)(c). **Practice Note** [1978] **2** 1056, Fam D.
            Time limit on operation of injunction—Remedy essentially short term pending other arrangements for accommodation being made by applicant or steps being taken to clarify matrimonial status—Remedy not to operate as permanent substitute for property adjustment order if applicant has no intention of proceeding to divorce or judicial separation—Domestic Violence and Matrimonial Proceedings Act 1976, s 1. **Hopper v Hopper** [1979] **1** 181, CA.
            Time limit on operation of injunction—Time limit not to exceed three months in normal cases—Where danger to applicant still possible at end of three months application may be made to extend duration of injunction—Domestic Violence and Matrimonial Proceedings Act 1976, s 1(1)(c). **Practice Note** [1981] **1** 224, Fam D.
            Unmarried parties living together as joint tenants of council flat—Ouster order in respect of one of the parties—Appropriateness of order. *See* Exclusion of party from matrimonial home—Unmarried parties living together as joint tenants of council flat, *below*.
        Decree nisi granted—
            Applicant having no proprietary interest in home—Council dwelling—Tenancy in husband's name—Wife granted decree in consequence of husband's behaviour—Parties living together in home with grown-up children—Husband and wife not on speaking terms—Application by wife for injunction to exclude husband from home—Whether court having jurisdiction to grant injunction. **Brent v Brent** [1974] **2** 1211, Fam D.
            Jurisdiction—Injunction requiring husband to leave matrimonial home and restraining him from molesting wife. **Cook v Cook** [1961] **2** 791, Div.
            Restraint on husband's continuing in residence—Wife's rights in matrimonial home of which husband statutory tenant—Wife's entitlement to jurisdiction to prevent trespass after decree absolute—Injunction to restrain assaulting and molesting—Jurisdiction of court to restrain husband from continuing in residence—Matrimonial Homes Act 1967, ss 1, 7—Supreme Court of Judicature (Consolidation) Act 1925, s 45(3). **Maynard v Maynard** [1969] **1** 1, Div.
            Wife's application to exclude husband—Factors to be considered—Wife granted decree nisi on ground of husband's behaviour—Wife having custody of children and looking after them—Serious friction between parties and between them and children—Non-molestation order against husband—Whether fair, just and reasonable in all the circumstances to exclude husband from matrimonial home. **Walker v Walker** [1978] **3** 141, CA.
        Divorce proceedings pending—
            Balance of hardship—Circumstances making it impossible or intolerable for wife to live in same house as husband—Wife looking after child of family—Need to provide home for wife and child—No suitable alternative accommodation for wife and child—Marriage relationship having broken down completely—Hostility between parties—Matrimonial home too small to allow parties to live there separately—No evidence that husband would have difficulty in finding alternative accommodation—Whether wife entitled to injunction excluding husband from home. **Bassett v Bassett** [1975] **1** 513, CA.
            Husband owner of home—Wife leaving home prior to institution of proceedings—Husband installing mistress in home shortly after wife's departure—Power of court to order husband to leave home—No apprehension of cruelty by husband or of pressure on wife to abandon petition—Injunctions ordering husband and mistress to leave home and restraining husband from preventing wife's return. **Jones v Jones** [1971] **2** 737, CA.
            Mistress living in home—Three-roomed home—Husband occupying small separate bedroom—Husband moved into sitting-room, and admitted mistress and their baby to live there with him—Injunction on husband to remove mistress and restraining him from continuing to occupy sitting-room—Injunction that husband should leave matrimonial home not granted. **Pinckney v Pinckney** [1966] **1** 121, Div.
            Unpleasantness, inconvenience or tension pending divorce proceedings—Insufficient grounds for excluding spouse—Protection of spouse and interests of the children relevant considerations—Petition by wife for judicial separation on ground of cruelty—Whether exclusion of husband from matrimonial home justifiable—Whether impossible for both parties to live together—Parties living in large house belonging to husband—Husband away at work all day—No evidence that order necessary for wife's protection or in children's interests. **Hall v Hall** [1971] **1** 762, CA.
            Wife having moved out of matrimonial home with children of marriage and living in unsuitable accommodation—Wife applying for order excluding husband from matrimonial home—Wife not having reasonable grounds for refusing to live in matrimonial home with husband but refusing to return while husband living there—Whether grounds for court to exclude husband from matrimonial home—Whether needs of children rather than justice between husband and wife proper test of whether husband should be excluded—Matrimonial Homes Act 1967, s 1—Guardianship of Minors Act 1971, s 1. **Richards v Richards** [1983] **2** 807, HL.

INJUNCTION (cont)—
Exclusion of party from matrimonial home (cont)—
Divorce proceedings pending (cont)—
Wife owner of home—Jurisdiction to make order excluding spouse exercised cautiously. **Boyt v Boyt** [1948] **2** 436, CA.
Wife owner of home—Whether entitled to exclude husband—Married Women's Property Act 1882, s 12, as amended by Law Reform (Married Women and Tortfeasors) Act 1935, s 5, Sch 1. **Gorulnick v Gorulnick** [1958] **1** 146, CA.
Judicial separation—
Parties continuing to live in same premises after decree—Tenancy of premises in husband's name—Jurisdiction to restrain husband by injunction from molesting wife—No jurisdiction to compel husband to leave premises. **Montgomery v Montgomery** [1964] **2** 22, Div.
Proceedings pending. **Silverstone v Silverstone** [1953] **1** 556, PDA.
Maintenance proceedings pending—
Relief sought by husband not sufficiently related to wife's claim for maintenance—RSC Ord 29, r 1(1)—Supreme Court of Judicature (Consolidation) Act 1925, s 45(1). **Des Salles d'Epinoix v Des Salles d'Epinoix** [1967] **2** 539, CA.
Marriage dissolved—
Parties joint tenants of former matrimonial home—Parties continuing to live in home—Circumstances in which injunction will be granted—Injunction against husband—Conditions making it tolerable for wife and child to continue sharing accommodation with husband—Husband's behaviour endangering mental health of wife and child—No evidence of physical assault or apprehension of violence. **Phillips v Phillips** [1973] **2** 423, CA.
Unmarried parties living together as joint tenants of council flat—
Breakdown of relationship—Woman excluding man from premises and seeking ouster order—Man seeking order allowing him to return to flat—Judge finding man not violent to woman or child but making order excluding him on ground that no longer practicable for parties to live together in flat—Whether in all circumstances ouster order appropriate—Domestic Violence and Matrimonial Proceedings Act 1976, s 1—Matrimonial Homes Act 1983, s 1(3). **Wiseman v Simpson** [1988] **1** 245, CA.
Wife legal owner of home—
Right to exclude husband from home—Discretion of court. **Boyt v Boyt** [1948] **2** 436, CA.
Right to exclude husband from home—Divorce proceedings pending. See Exclusion of party from matrimonial home—Divorce proceedings pending—Wife owner of home, *above*.
Wife's application to exclude husband—
Factors to be considered—Wife leaving matrimonial home with young child—Wife and child living in overcrowded conditions—Wife applying for order to exclude husband from matrimonial home so that she and child could return—Wife genuinely feeling that she could never live with husband again—Whether sufficient grounds for court to exclude husband from matrimonial home. **Myers v Myers** [1982] **1** 776, CA.
Factors to be considered—Wife leaving matrimonial home with young children—Wife and children living in overcrowded conditions—Wife applying for order to exclude husband from matrimonial home so that she and children could return—Wife refusing to return while husband in occupation—Whether there were sufficient grounds for court to exclude him. **Samson v Samson** [1982] **1** 780, CA.
Family proceedings—
Interim care order or emergency protection order—
Attachment of power of arrest to exclusion requirement—Procedure—Announcement of terms of order in open court—Arrest for breach of order—Procedure following arrest—Children Act 1989, ss 38A(5), 44A(5). **Practice Direction** [1998] **2** 928, Fam D.
Fire brigade—
Disciplinary power—
Whether court will interfere with exercise. See **Fire brigade** (Discipline—Exercise of disciplinary power—Interference by court—Injunction).
Foreign proceedings—
Divorce petition by wife—
Injunction to restrain respondent from proceeding with suit in France—Burden of proof. **Orr-Lewis v Orr-Lewis** [1949] **1** 504, Div.
Form of order—
Breach of confidence—
Restraining manufacture of goods 'merely colourably differing' from goods of certain styles. **Peter Pan Manufacturing Corp v Corsets Silhouette Ltd** [1963] **3** 402, Ch D.
Interlocutory injunction—
Nuisance—Use of adjoining premises for prostitution. **Thompson-Schwab v Costaki** [1956] **1** 652, CA.
Mandatory injunction—
Order in general terms not specifying details of work to be done—Injunction requiring defendants to take all necessary steps to restore the support to the plaintiffs' land. **Redland Bricks Ltd v Morris** [1969] **2** 576, HL.
Nuisance—
Local authority—Licence needed for work necessary for compliance with injunction. **Pride of Derby and Derbyshire Angling Association Ltd v British Celanese Ltd** [1953] **1** 179, CA.
Passing off—
Action against limited company—Order against 'defendants by their servants workmen agents or otherwise', not against 'the defendants their staff servants and agents'. **Marengo v Daily Sketch and Sunday Graphic Ltd** [1948] **1** 406, HL.
Qualified injunction—Defendant selling alcoholic drink made of vodka and fermented alcohol of 22% alcohol by volume in similar get-up to vodka of 37·5% alcohol by volume under brand name similar to word 'vodka'—Claimant bringing passing off action—Judge granting qualified injunction—Whether judge erring. **Diageo North America Inc v InterContinental Brands (ICB) Ltd** [2011] **1** 242, CA.
Sale of goods—
Selling car as new. **Morris Motors Ltd v Phelan** [1960] **2** 208, Ch D.

INJUNCTION (cont)—
Form of order (cont)—
Two defendants—
Injunction restraining the defendants from obstructing roadway—Acts of obstruction done by second defendant alone—Whether acts by one defendant alone constituted breach of injunction. **Lenton v Tregoning** [1960] **1** 717, CA.
Freezing order—
County court. *See* **County court** (Practice—Freezing order).
Generally. *See* **Practice** (Pre-trial or post-judgment relief—Freezing order).
Service out of the jurisdiction. *See* **Practice** (Service out of the jurisdiction—Pre-trial or post-judgment relief—Freezing order).
Third parties—
Freezing order granted in respect of defendants' assets—Intervening third party having benefit of debenture given by second defendant over assets covered by injunction—Third party applying for amendment to freezing order to effect that nothing in order should prevent or restrict it from enforcing its rights—Whether freezing order an obstacle to third party's enforcement of security—Whether third party required to apply to court for variation of freezing order before enforcing rights as secured creditor. **Taylor v Van Dutch Marine Holding Ltd (TCA Global Credit Master Fund LP, third party)** [2017] **4** 627, Ch D; [2018] **1 Comm** 250, Ch D.
Grant of injunction before issue of originating process—
Title of proceedings. *See* **Practice** (Title of proceedings—Application for injunction—Grant of injunction before issue of originating process).
Grant of injunction in advance of plaintiff's claim—
Danger that defendant may transfer assets out of jurisdiction. *See* **Practice** (Pre-trial or post-judgment relief—Freezing order).
Harassment—
Tort. *See* **Tort** (Harassment—Injunction).
High Court—
Applications in matrimonial proceedings—
Procedure. **Practice Direction** [1974] **2** 1119, Fam D.
Injunction to protect integrity of administration of justice—
Attorney General seeking injunction barring vexatious litigant from entering Royal Courts of Justice without permission—Whether injunction appropriate. **A-G v Ebert** [2002] **2** 789, QBD DC.
Restraint of proceedings pending in High Court—
Garnishee proceedings—Supreme Court of Judicature (Consolidation) Act 1925, s 41. **Llewellyn v Carrickford** [1970] **2** 24, Ch D.
Housing—
Duty of housing authority to provide accommodation for homeless person—
Injunction as a remedy for breach of duty. *See* **Housing** (Homeless person—Duty of housing authority to provide accommodation—Remedy for breach of duty).
Local authority housing—
Enforcement of tenant's right to buy. *See* **Housing** (Local authority houses—Tenant's right to buy—Enforcement of right—Injunction).
Husband and wife—
Decree absolute—
Grant of injunction after decree absolute—Jurisdiction. *See* **Divorce** (Injunction—Jurisdiction—Grant of injunction extending beyond decree absolute).
Decree for restitution of conjugal rights—
Injunction after—Jurisdiction to grant. *See* **Divorce** (Injunction—Jurisdiction—Grant of injunction after decree of restitution of conjugal rights).
Domestic violence—
Attachment of power of arrest to injunction—Application to be made by party to marriage—Former wife applying for power of arrest to be attached to injunction excluding former husband from former matrimonial home—Whether 'party to a marriage' including party to a former marriage—Domestic Violence and Matrimonial Proceedings Act 1976, s 2(1)(2). **White v White** [1983] **2** 51, CA.
Attachment of power of arrest to injunction—Committal to custody for breach of protection order—Whether 'committal to custody' the same as imprisonment—Whether magistrates having power to order consecutive periods of custody for separate breaches of protection order—Domestic Proceedings and Magistrates' Courts Act 1978, ss 16(6), 18—Magistrates' Courts Act 1980, ss 63(3), 133(1). **Head v Head** [1982] **3** 14, Fam D.
Attachment of power of arrest to injunction—Ex parte application for injunction—Announcement of grant of injunction in open court—Arrest for breach of injunction—Procedure following arrest—Procedure where arrested person cannot conveniently be brought to courtroom—Domestic Violence and Matrimonial Proceedings Act 1976, s 2. **Practice Direction** [1991] **2** 9, Fam D.
Attachment of power of arrest to injunction—Husband not violent for nine months but continuing to harass wife—Wife entitled to injunction in county court restraining husband from assaulting, molesting or interfering with her—Whether power of arrest should be attached to injunction—Domestic Violence and Matrimonial Proceedings Act 1976, s 2(1). **Horner v Horner** [1982] **2** 495, CA.
Attachment of power of arrest to injunction—Jurisdiction of county court—Divorce proceedings—Application by petitioner for power of arrest to be attached to injunction—Whether county court having jurisdiction to attach power of arrest to injunction granted in divorce proceedings—Domestic Violence and Matrimonial Proceedings Act 1976, s 2. **Lewis (A H) v R W F Lewis** [1978] **1** 729, CA.
Attachment of power of arrest to injunction—Practice—Application—Need for applicant to give respondent notice of intention to apply for power of arrest to be attached to injunction. **Lewis (A H) v R W F Lewis** [1978] **1** 729, CA.
Attachment of power of arrest to occupation or non-molestation order—Procedure—Announcement of terms of order in open court—Arrest for breach of order—Procedure following arrest—Family Law Act 1996, Pt IV. **Practice Direction** [1998] **2** 927, Fam D.

INJUNCTION (cont)—
  Husband and wife (cont)—
    Ex parte applications—
      Cases of urgency—Applications at Royal Courts of Justice—Applications to be made only where immediate danger of serious injury or irreparable damage—Selection of early hearing date—CCR Ord 13, rr 1(1) (b), 8(2)(3)—Matrimonial Causes Rules 1971 (SI 1971 No 953), r 114(2). **Practice Note** [1978] **2** 919, Fam D.
      Cases of urgency—Applications at Royal Courts of Justice—Procedure—Form of injunction—High Court—County courts—Divorce Registry—CCR Ord 13, rr 1(1)(b), 8(2), (3)—Matrimonial Causes Rules 1971 (SI 1971 No 953), r 114(2). **Practice Direction** [1972] **2** 1360, Fam D.
    Ex parte injunction. *See* Ex parte injunction—Matrimonial proceedings, *above*.
    Exclusion from matrimonial home. *See* Exclusion of party from matrimonial home, *above*.
    Maintenance proceedings—
      Dealing with assets—Injunction to prevent husband dealing with property pending hearing of applications to vary secured and unsecured maintenance. **Wright v Wright** [1954] **1** 707, Div.
      Removal of assets abroad—Injunction to prevent husband removing assets outside jurisdiction pending hearing of application for maintenance—Law Reform (Miscellaneous Provisions) Act 1949, s 5(1). **Scott v Scott** [1950] **2** 1154, CA.
    Matrimonial home—
      Exclusion of party from matrimonial home. *See* Exclusion of party from matrimonial home, *above*.
      Restraining wife dealing with her interest. **Bedson v Bedson** [1965] **3** 307, QBD.
    Molestation—
      Meaning—Harassment by husband—Jurisdiction of county court—Wife obtaining order in magistrates' court restraining husband from using violence—Husband refraining from violence but continuing to harass wife—Whether magistrates' court order extending to husband's harassment—Whether wife entitled to obtain county court order restraining husband from molesting her—Domestic Violence and Matrimonial Proceedings Act 1976, s 1(1)(a)—Domestic Proceedings and Magistrates' Courts Act 1978, s 16. **Horner v Horner** [1982] **2** 495, CA.
      Meaning—Pestering—Absence of violence—Relevance of past conduct—Injunction restraining husband from molesting wife—Husband having inflicted violence on wife on earlier occasions—Husband previously committed several times for breaches of similar injunction—Husband calling on wife at home and place of work—Husband pestering wife to go out with him—Husband not committing violence against wife—Wife frightened of husband and pestering affecting health—Whether husband guilty of molestation. **Vaughan v Vaughan** [1973] **3** 449, CA.
      Molestation of child—Injunction not granted except where purpose was protection of child. **D v D** [1970] **3** 893, Div.
    Wife's application for leave to present petition for divorce within three years of marriage—Wife's application for injunction—Jurisdiction of court to entertain. **Winstone v Winstone** [1959] **3** 580, Vacation Ct.
    Wife's application for leave to present petition for divorce within three years of marriage—Wife's application for injunction—Jurisdiction of court to entertain—Whether sufficient nexus between injunction sought and application for leave to present petition—Supreme Court of Judicature (Consolidation) Act 1925, s 225—Matrimonial Causes Act 1965, s 2—Matrimonial Causes Act 1967, s 10(1)—RSC Ord 29, r 1. **McGibbon v McGibbon** [1973] **2** 836, Fam D.
    Wife's petition for judicial separation—Husband's application for injunction to restrain molestation—Husband of sufficient means to live elsewhere than in matrimonial home, but choosing to remain there—Injunction not granted. **Freedman v Freedman** [1967] **2** 680, Div.
  Removing children from jurisdiction—
    Petition for divorce presented in England by husband—Preliminary issue as to domicile—Children living with husband but no order for their custody—Removal of children out of jurisdiction by wife—Order against wife to bring children within jurisdiction within specified time. **Fabbri v Fabbri** [1962] **1** 35, Div.
  Settlement of property—
    Interlocutory injunction to restrain dealings with property constituting alleged settlements—Jurisdiction. **Hindley v Hindley** [1957] **2** 653, Div.
  Illegal act of statutory body—
    Injunction to restrain—
      Suspension of dock workers. **Barnard v National Dock Labour Board** [1952] **2** 424, QBD.
  Inferior court—
    Jurisdiction of High Court over inferior court—
      Inferior court exceeding jurisdiction—Jurisdiction to grant injunction to restrain party from executing order of inferior court—Prohibition appropriate remedy—Leave required for application for prohibition—Jurisdiction to grant injunction restraining party from enforcing order of inferior court alleged to be a nullity—RSC Ord 53, r 1. **Johns v Chatalos** [1973] **3** 410, Ch D.
  Interim—
    Arbitration, pending. *See* **Arbitration** (Injunction—Interim injunction—Power of court).
    Damages not appropriate remedy—
      Adequate remedy—Contract containing provision limiting recoverable damages—Party to contract seeking interim injunction requiring other party to perform obligations under contract and restraining other party from terminating contract—Whether injunction to be granted—Whether damages adequate remedy. **AB v CD** [2014] **2 Comm** 242, CA; [2014] **3** 667, CA.
    Injunction against disclosure of confidential information. *See* **Confidential information** (Injunction against disclosure of information—Interim injunction).
    Injunction prohibiting enforcement of guarantee—
      Football transfer fee—Claimant alleging fraud—Whether seriously arguable case of fraud shown. **Sunderland Association Football Club Ltd v Uruguay Montevideo FC** [2001] **2 Comm** 828, QBD.
    Injunction to restrain call on performance bond—
      Claimant seeking to restrain beneficiary under bond—Beneficiary of bond party to underlying contract—Applicable test. **TTI Team Telecom International Ltd v Hutchison 3G UK Ltd** [2003] **1 Comm** 914, QBD.

INJUNCTION (cont)—
 Interim (cont)—
  Proprietary injunction—
   Crypto currencies—Insurer making ex parte applications including for interim injunctive relief arising from hacking of customer's computer systems by unknown persons—'Ransom' payment of $US950,000 in Bitcoins made—Whether crypto currencies such as Bitcoins constituting property for purposes of obtaining proprietary injunction—Whether requirements for proprietary injunction met—Whether ancillary relief to be granted—Whether permission to be granted for amending claim form, service out of jurisdiction and alternative service—Whether Bankers Trust/Norwich Pharmacal relief to be granted—Whether hearing to be in private—Human Rights Act 1998, s 12—Civil Jurisdiction and Judgments Act 1982, s 25(1)—CPR 6.15, 39.2(3), PD 6B—UK Jurisdiction Task Force legal statement on Crypto assets and Smart contracts. **AA v Persons Unknown** [2020] **2 Comm** 704, QBD.
  Specific performance—
   Freedom of expression—Real prospect of obtaining order for specific performance or final injunction—Exercise of defendant's right to freedom of expression—Artistic expression—Human Rights Act 1998, s 12(1), (4), Sch 1, Pt I, art 10. **Ashworth v Royal National Theatre** [2014] **4** 238, QBD.
   Interim relief against company not resident within jurisdiction—First defendant incorporated in India—First defendant manufacturing condoms in India—First defendant refusing to supply condoms to claimants allegedly in breach of contract—Claimants issuing proceedings and seeking interim injunctive relief in England—Whether appropriate for English court to grant interim injunctive relief. **SSL International plc v TTK LIG Ltd** [2012] **1 Comm** 429, CA.
 Interlocutory—
  Action by member of public to enforce public right—
   Refusal of Attorney General to consent to relator action—Claim for declaration or injunction—Enforcement of criminal law. *See* **Attorney General** (Relator action—Refusal of consent to relator action—Right of member of public to sue in own name—Claim for declaration or injunction—Enforcement of public rights).
  Action for declaration—
   Plaintiff Welsh football clubs joining English football association to take part in English competitions—Welsh football association refusing to allow plaintiffs to play home matches in Wales—Welsh association's decisions resulting in loss of revenue and sponsorship—Plaintiffs seeking declaration that Welsh association's decisions void as being in unreasonable restraint of trade—Plaintiffs also seeking interlocutory injunction to allow them to play home matches in Wales for following season—Whether court having jurisdiction to grant interlocutory injunction where only claim was for a declaration. **Newport Association Football Club Ltd v Football Association of Wales Ltd** [1995] **2** 87, Ch D.
  Affidavit in support of interlocutory injunction—
   Admissibility. *See* **Affidavit** (Admissibility in evidence—Affidavit in support of interlocutory injunction).
  Arbitration agreement—
   Power of court. *See* **Arbitration** (Injunction—Interlocutory injunction—Power of court).
  Balance of convenience—
   Bank—Confidential information between bank and customer—Bank seeking to comply with foreign subpoena to produce in foreign court documents belonging to customer—Disclosure of documents likely to harm customer beyond adequate compensation—Bank fearing that it would be liable to proceedings in foreign court for contempt of court if documents not produced—Whether court should grant injunction restraining bank from complying with subpoena. **X AG v A bank** [1983] **2** 464, QBD.
   Breach of contractual negative stipulation—Strong prima facie case of breach—Interlocutory injunction not available as matter of course—Maintenance of status quo—Protection of plaintiff's interests—Damages inadequate remedy. **Texaco Ltd v Mulberry Filling Station Ltd** [1972] **1** 513, Ch D.
   Breach of covenant not to solicit clients of former employer—Court granting general injunction in favour of employer—Injunction not enforceable in respect of particular breach—Whether appropriate to make such order. **John Michael Design plc v Cooke** [1987] **2** 332, CA.
   Irrelevance where relief sought to prevent clear breach of covenant. **Hampstead and Suburban Properties Ltd v Diomedous** [1968] **3** 545, Vacation Ct Ch D.
   Likelihood of loss to plaintiff if interlocutory relief refused—No evidence that defendant would suffer greater hardship—Plaintiff corporation claiming statutory monopoly of right to hold markets within area of city—Defendant holding unlicensed market within city—Plaintiff establishing clear prima facie right—Potential loss to plaintiff from fall in revenue from licensed markets—No greater loss to defendant from grant of injunction—Defendant's business not involving much capital outlay. **Birmingham Corp v Perry Barr Stadium Ltd** [1972] **1** 725, Ch D.
   Matters to be considered by court in determining whether balance of convenience lies in favour of granting or refusing relief. **American Cyanamid Co v Ethicon Ltd** [1975] **1** 504, HL.
   Prima facie entitlement to relief—Serious question to be tried—Unnecessary for applicant to establish prima facie case—Open to court to consider whether on balance of convenience interlocutory relief should be granted provided claim not frivolous or vexatious. **American Cyanamid Co v Ethicon Ltd** [1975] **1** 504, HL; **Fellowes v Fisher** [1975] **2** 829, CA.
   Procuring breach of service contract—Servant not party to proceedings—Alternative remedy dismissal of servant. **Hivac Ltd v Park Royal Scientific Instruments Ltd** [1946] **1** 350, CA.
   Prospect that defendants' activities would interfere with plaintiffs' business—Defendants picketing plaintiffs' offices in support of campaign—Injunction forbidding picketing not preventing defendants from pursuing campaign. **Hubbard v Pitt** [1975] **3** 1, CA.
   Relative strength of each party's case—Circumstances in which relative strength should be taken into account—Action for breach of covenant in restraint of trade—Allegation that covenant invalid as being too wide. **Fellowes v Fisher** [1975] **2** 829, CA.
   Relative strength of each party's case—Circumstances in which relative strength should be taken into account—Action not able to be tried before period of restraint has expired or almost expired—Grant of interlocutory injunction effectively disposing of action. **David (Lawrence) Ltd v Ashton** [1991] **1** 385, CA; **Lansing Linde Ltd v Kerr** [1991] **1** 418, CA.

INJUNCTION (cont)—
  Interlocutory (cont)—
    Barring-out relief—
      Employee acquiring confidential information during course of employment—Employee leaving first
      employer and entering employment with competitor—First employer applying for injunctive
      relief to prevent employee undertaking tasks in relation to first employer's commercial
      relationship with competitor—Whether barring-out relief capable of being granted in employee
      and employer relationship—Whether employee fiduciary of first employer. **Caterpillar Logistics**
      Services (UK) Limited v Huesca de Crean [2012] **3** 129, CA.
    Breach of contract—
      Interlocutory injunction to protect payment made under contract pending hearing. *See* Breach of
      contract—Interlocutory injunction to protect payment made under contract pending hearing,
      above.
    Breach of EEC Treaty provisions. *See* **European Union** (Treaty provisions—Breach of treaty
      provisions—Injunction to restrain breach).
    Company—
      Resolution to remove director—Whether director entitled to interlocutory injunction to restrain
      company acting on resolution. *See* **Company** (Director—Removal—Resolution to remove
      director—Interlocutory injunction to restrain company acting on resolution).
    Condition of relief—
      Security for fulfilment of cross-undertaking—Foreign company as plaintiffs. **Harman Pictures NV v**
      Osborne [1967] **2** 324, Ch D.
    Confidential information—
      Trade secrets—Plaintiffs unable to define with precision confidential information or trade secrets
      requiring protection—Whether injunction should be granted. **David (Lawrence) Ltd v Ashton**
      [1991] **1** 385, CA.
    Conspiracy—
      Defendants alleging that plaintiffs financially unsound and dishonest—Plaintiffs seeking injunction
      restraining publication of further communications of that kind—Plaintiffs alleging words
      published in pursuance of conspiracy having sole or dominant purpose of injuring
      them—Whether injunction restraining further publication should be granted. **Femis-Bank**
      (Anguilla) Ltd v Lazar [1991] **2** 865, Ch D.
    Copyright—
      Defence of fair dealing—Newspaper reporting current events—No interlocutory injunction if fair
      dealing pleaded. **Fraser v Evans** [1969] **1** 8, CA.
      Defence of fair dealing—Plaintiff having arguable case not sufficient to justify grant where defence
      of fair dealing raised. **Hubbard v Vosper** [1972] **1** 1023, CA.
      Delay—Entitlement to interlocutory relief. *See* Interlocutory—Delay—Entitlement to interlocutory
      relief—Copyright, *below.*
      Musical work. *See* **Practice** (Pre-trial or post-judgment relief—Search order—Interlocutory
      motion—Ex parte application—Jurisdiction to make order—Writ claiming injunctions to restrain
      defendant from producing and selling unauthorised recordings of live performances of musical
      works).
      Plaintiff entitled to call for an assignment of copyright—Plaintiff owner in equity of
      copyright—Whether plaintiff entitled to move for interlocutory injunction as 'owner' of
      copyright—Copyright Act 1956, s 17. **Merchant Adventurers Ltd v M Grew & Co Ltd (t/a Emess**
      Lighting) [1971] **2** 657, Ch D.
      Prima facie entitlement—Preservation of status quo governing consideration after establishing
      prima facie case. **Donmar Productions Ltd v Bart (1964)** [1967] **2** 338, Ch D.
      Screenplay alleged to infringe plaintiff's film copyright in book—Historical subject—Common
      sources of material—Plaintiffs' book supplied with others to author of screenplay—Similarities of
      incidents and situations—Differences in detail—Absence of explanation by author of screenplay
      of manner and extent of use of plaintiffs' book and of how he worked and for how long—Whether
      interlocutory injunction should be granted and whether limited in scope. **Harman Pictures NV v**
      Osborne [1967] **2** 324, Ch D.
    Crown officer, against—
      Jurisdiction to grant injunction. *See* **Crown** (Relief against the Crown—Interlocutory
      relief—Jurisdiction—Injunction against officer of the Crown).
    Damages not appropriate remedy—
      Occupation of dwelling by employee under terms of employment—Termination of employment—
      Retaking of possession by employer without court proceedings—Whether employee entitled to
      interlocutory injunction designed to secure access to dwelling—Rent Act 1965, s 32(1), (2).
      Warder v Cooper [1970] **1** 1112, Ch D.
    Danger that defendant may transfer assets out of jurisdiction—
      Generally. *See* **Practice** (Pre-trial or post-judgment relief—Freezing order).
      Writ of ne exeat regno in support of injunction—Jurisdiction to issue writ. *See* **Equity** (Ne exeat
      regno—Writ—Application for writ and freezing order).
    Defamation cases. *See* **Libel and slander** (Injunction—Interlocutory).
    Delay—
      Entitlement to interlocutory relief—Copyright—Infringement—Plaintiff writing to defendant seeking
      undertaking that defendant would cease infringing plaintiff's copyright—Plaintiff not seeking
      interlocutory relief immediately—Whether delay disentitling plaintiff to interlocutory injunction.
      Express Newspapers plc v Liverpool Daily Post and Echo plc [1985] **3** 680, Ch D.
    Discharge—
      Injunction granted on ex parte application—Ex parte application to discharge or vary—Whether
      order will be made. **London City Agency (JCD) Ltd v Lee** [1969] **3** 1376, Ch D.
      Subsequent decisions of Court of Appeal reversing decisions subsisting when injunction granted.
      Regent Oil Co Ltd v Leavesley (JT) (Lichfield) Ltd [1966] **2** 454, Ch D.

INJUNCTION (cont)—
  Interlocutory (cont)—
    Disclosure—
      Disclosure before statement of claim—Jurisdiction of court to order discovery in aid of interlocutory relief—Whether discovery relating to any 'matters in question in the action' if in aid of interlocutory relief—Whether discovery necessary 'for disposing fairly of the cause or matter'—Whether discovery ought to be ordered in aid of interlocutory relief before pleadings—RSC Ord 24, rr 1, 7, 8. **RHM Foods Ltd v Bovril Ltd** [1982] **1** 673, CA.
    Form of order. *See* Form of order—Interlocutory injunction, *above*.
    Freezing order—
      Generally. *See* **Practice** (Pre-trial or post-judgment relief—Freezing order).
      Service out of the jurisdiction. *See* **Practice** (Service out of the jurisdiction—Pre-trial or post-judgment relief—Freezing order).
    Grant or refusal effectively ending action—
      Monetary compensation irrelevant to both parties—Transmission of broadcast or publication of article—Impact and value depending on timing of transmission or publication—Whether interlocutory injunction should be granted if plaintiff able to show good arguable case and that balance of convenience lay in granting injunction—Whether court should assess relative strength of parties' cases before deciding whether injunction should be granted. **Cambridge Nutrition Ltd v BBC** [1990] **3** 523, CA.
    Injunction having effect of granting sole relief claimed in action—
      Petition to wind up company on just and equitable grounds—Injunction restraining petitioner moving court to wind up company—Whether interlocutory relief appropriate. **Bryanston Finance Ltd v de Vries (No 2)** [1976] **1** 25, CA.
      Unincorporated association—Membership in dispute—Relief sought for members deprived of rights—Whether proper case for granting injunction. **Woodford v Smith** [1970] **1** 1091, Ch D.
    Injunction prohibiting enforcement of guarantee—
      Jurisdiction—Share sale agreement under which purchase price payable in instalments—Payment of third instalment secured by performance guarantee under which guarantors entitled to indemnity from buyers—Buyers refusing to pay third instalment on grounds of sellers' fraud and bringing action for rescission and damages—Sellers denying fraud and seeking to enforce guarantee—Buyers applying for interlocutory injunction to restrain sellers from giving notice under guarantee—Whether court having jurisdiction to grant injunction to prevent operation of guarantee—Whether evidence sufficient to establish arguable case of fraud—Whether injunction unnecessary or excessive relief. **Themehelp Ltd v West** [1995] **4** 215, CA.
    Injunction restraining defendant from leaving jurisdiction—
      Bankrupt—Trustee having suspicion of undisclosed assets—Trustee having power to enforce bankrupt's statutory duties—Trustee applying for bankrupt's committal for contempt of court and injunction restraining him from leaving jurisdiction until after hearing—Whether court having jurisdiction to grant injunction—Whether pre-existing cause of action required—Insolvency Act 1986, ss 333, 366. **Morris v Murjani** [1996] **2** 384, CA.
      Director of company—Company in creditors' voluntary liquidation—Director ignoring attempts to communicate with him—Director returning to jurisdiction for short time—Liquidators applying for order for private examination of director and injunction restraining him from leaving jurisdiction until after examination—Whether court having jurisdiction to grant injunction—Supreme Court Act 1981, s 37(1)—Companies Act 1985, s 561. **Oriental Credit Ltd, Re** [1988] **1** 892, Ch D.
      Plaintiffs obtaining relief in Mareva and Anton Piller forms pending hearing of action in respect of distribution and sale of counterfeit goods—Real risk of defendant evading execution of orders unless restrained from leaving jurisdiction—Whether jurisdiction to order that defendant be restrained from leaving jurisdiction—Whether appropriate in circumstances to make order—Supreme Court Act 1981, s 37(1). **Bayer AG v Winter** [1986] **1** 733, CA.
    Irrevocable letters of credit—
      Injunction restraining bank from paying on presentation of draft. *See* **Bank** (Documentary credit—Irrevocable credit—Circumstances in which court may restrain bank from paying on presentation of draft—Interlocutory injunction).
    Judicial review proceedings—
      Interim injunction against officer of Crown—Jurisdiction to grant injunction. *See* **Crown** (Relief against the Crown—Interlocutory relief—Jurisdiction—Injunction against officer of the Crown).
    Jurisdiction—
      County court—Power to grant interlocutory injunction in support of custody order. *See* **County court** (Jurisdiction—Application for custody order—Power to grant interlocutory injunction).
      Injunction restraining enforcement of legislation pending reference to European Court—Applicants seeking injunction restraining Secretary of State from enforcing legislation against applicants pending reference to European Court—Legislation not requiring assistance from court for its enforcement—Legislation unambiguous—Whether court having jurisdiction to disapply legislation pending reference to European Court—Merchant Shipping Act 1988, Pt II, s 14(1)—Merchant Shipping (Registration of Fishing Vessels) Regulations 1988. **Factortame Ltd v Secretary of State for Transport** [1989] **2** 692, HL.
    Libel action—
      Generally. *See* **Libel and slander** (Injunction—Interlocutory).
    Mandatory injunction—
      Circumstances in which mandatory injunction may be granted in interlocutory proceedings—Test of whether injustice to defendant if plaintiff granted injunction but failing at trial outweighing injustice to plaintiff if injunction refused but plaintiff succeeding at trial. **Films Rover International Ltd v Cannon Film Sales Ltd** [1986] **3** 772, Ch D.
      Circumstances in which mandatory injunction may be granted in interlocutory proceedings—Test to be applied. **Locabail International Finance Ltd v Agroexport** [1986] **1** 901, CA.
      Enforcement of housing authority's duty to provide accommodation for homeless person pending enquiries. *See* **Housing** (Homeless person—Preliminary duty to house pending inquiries—Enforcement of duty by interim mandatory injunction).

INJUNCTION (cont)—
  Interlocutory (cont)—
    Mandatory injunction (cont)—
      Injunction mandatory in substance—Injunction to restrain unlawful withholding of supplies under Resale Prices Act 1964—Injunction in substance mandatory—Scheme of the Act taking injunction out of normal sphere of operation of injunctions. **Comet Radiovision Services Ltd v Farnell-Tandberg Ltd** [1971] 3 230, Ch D.
      Local authority in breach of obligations to tenants—Obligation to provide heating—Industrial dispute between local authority and its employees resulting in failure to maintain tenants' heating system—Whether appropriate for court to grant injunction requiring local authority to restore heating. **Parker v Camden London BC** [1985] 2 141, CA.
      Probability of success at trial—Reluctance of court to grant mandatory injunction except when success at trial probable. **Hounslow London Borough v Twickenham Garden Developments Ltd** [1970] 3 326, Ch D.
    Mareva injunction—
      Generally. *See* **Practice** (Pre-trial or post-judgment relief—Freezing order).
      Service out of the jurisdiction. *See* **Practice** (Service out of the jurisdiction—Pre-trial or post-judgment relief—Freezing order).
    Nuisance. *See* Nuisance—Interlocutory injunction, *below.*
    Pending proceedings—
      Judicial review—Application for judicial review of grant of approval for herbicide—Application for stay of approval pending determination of proceedings and decision of European Court—Principles to be applied—Whether interim relief should be granted. **R v Ministry of Agriculture Fisheries and Food, ex p Monsanto plc (Clayton Plant Protection Ltd intervening)** [1998] 4 321, QBD.
      Judicial review—Interlocutory injunction sought to restrain publication of public authority's decision pending outcome of judicial review proceedings—Self regulatory public authority supervising advertising standards upholding complaint relating to misleading advertisement published by applicants—Applicants applying for judicial review of authority's decision and injunction to prevent publication of decision pending outcome of judicial review proceedings—Whether potential damage to applicants by publication of decision amounting to pressing ground for restraining publication—Whether publication of decision should be restrained. **R v Advertising Standards Authority Ltd, ex p Vernons Organisation Ltd** [1993] 2 202, QBD.
  Practice—
    Chancery Division—Ex parte injunction—Grant of injunction prior to issue of writ or originating summons—Undertaking to be given to issue writ forthwith—Consequence of failure to implement undertaking—Duty of intended plaintiff's solicitor—RSC Ord 29, r 1(3). **Refson (P S) & Co Ltd v Saggers** [1984] 3 111, Ch D.
  Preservation of position pending trial—
    Prevention of disclosure of confidential information—Protection of security service—Former security service officer proposing to publish memoirs—Attorney General obtaining interlocutory injunction against defendant newspapers restraining publication of material derived from officer's memoirs—Subsequent publication of memoirs outside jurisdiction—Whether protection of security service a ground for granting interlocutory injunction—Whether interlocutory injunction should be continued. **A-G v Guardian Newspapers Ltd** [1987] 3 316, Ch D, CA and HL.
  Preservation of proceeds of crime—
    Appointment of receiver—Extent of court's powers to grant injunction in favour of police—Accused obtaining mortgage advances by deception—Accused using advances to buy houses—Houses sold leaving substantial profit—Whether police entitled to injunction restraining dealings with surplus proceeds made from sale of houses pending criminal proceedings. **Chief Constable of Leicestershire v M** [1988] 3 1015, Ch D.
    Extent of court's powers to grant injunction in favour of police—Money in bank account—Accused obtaining money by deception on forged instruments—Accused paying that money into his own bank account—Police seeking injunction to freeze money in bank account—Whether court having power to grant injunction sought—Supreme Court Act 1981, s 37(1). **Chief Constable of Kent v V** [1982] 3 36, CA.
    Extent of court's powers to grant injunction in favour of police—Money in bank account—Money obtained through fraudulent trading—Money mixed with legitimately obtained money in bank account—Moneys incapable of separation into legitimate and illegitimate elements—Whether police entitled to injunction restraining dealings with bank account—Supreme Court Act 1981, s 37(1). **Chief Constable of Hampshire v A** [1984] 2 385, CA.
    Extent of court's powers to grant injunction in favour of the Crown—Defendant benefiting from criminal offence but unlikely that he would be brought to trial—Proceedings instituted by Attorney General, as guardian of public interest, in civil courts in aid of criminal law—Whether court's jurisdiction extended to enforcing and upholding public policy of ensuring that a criminal did not retain profit directly derived from commission of his crime. **A-G v Blake (Jonathan Cape Ltd, third party)** [1998] 1 833, CA.
    Proceeds held in bank account—Police applying for injunction to freeze account—Identifiable sums resulting from alleged crime paid into bank account—Whether High Court having power to grant police injunction restraining dealing with bank account to ensure proceeds of crime would be restored to rightful owner after affender's trial—RSC Ord 29, r 2(1). **West Mercia Constabulary v Wagener** [1981] 3 378, QBD.
  Preservation of status quo—
    Prospect of obtaining permanent injunction at trial—Failure to show strong or at least reasonable prospect not a factor precluding grant of interlocutory injunction—Factor weighing against grant. **Evans Marshall & Co Ltd v Bertola SA** [1973] 1 992, CA.
  Preservation of subject matter of cause—
    Injunction restraining removal of assets out of jurisdiction—Application to vary injunction to enable defendant to pay debts and legal expenses and meet reasonable living expenses—Whether injunction should be maintained to preserve trust fund and plaintiff's tracing rights if successful in action. **PCW (Underwriting Agencies) Ltd v Dixon** [1983] 2 697, CA.

INJUNCTION (cont)—
Interlocutory (cont)—
Principle governing grant—
Anticipated litigation—Abuse of process of court—Injunction to restrain anticipated litigation on ground it would constitute an abuse of process—Action for injunction restraining presentation of petition to wind up company on specified grounds—Motion for interlocutory injunction— Whether company having to establish prima facie case that petition abuse of process. **Bryanston Finance Ltd v de Vries (No 2)** [1976] **1** 25, CA.

Defendant's case not unarguable—Defendant nonetheless openly flouting statute—Sunday trading in breach of statute—Defendant claiming to be entitled as Jewish shopkeeper to exemption from restrictions on Sunday trading—Defendant in breach of planning leglisation in holding market—Whether injunction should be refused if defendant's case not wholly unarguable— Whether open flouting of statute a reason for granting an injunction. **Thanet DC v Ninedrive Ltd** [1978] **1** 703, Ch D.

Grant or refusal effectively ending action—Court's approach to grant or refusal—Avoidance of injustice—Grant of injunction having effect of giving judgment for plaintiff and denying defendant right to trial. **Cayne v Global Natural Resources plc** [1984] **1** 225, CA.

Judgment for costs to be taxed—Danger of defendant disposing of assets before taxation—Defendant indicating by conduct that he intended to dispose of assets and become bankrupt to defeat order for costs—Whether plaintiff entitled to injunction before taxation restraining defendant from disposing of assets—Supreme Court of Judicature (Consolidation) Act 1925, s 45(1). **Faith Panton Property Plan Ltd v Hodgetts** [1981] **2** 877, CA.

Right to freedom of expression—Application for interim injunction which might affect convention right to freedom of expression—Approach to be adopted—Human Rights Act 1998, s 12(3), Sch 1, Pt I, art 10. **Cream Holdings Ltd v Banerjee** [2003] **2** 318, CA; [2004] **4** 617, HL.

Right to freedom of expression—Approach to be adopted on application for interim injunction engaging convention right to freedom of expression—Human Rights Act 1998, s 12, Sch 1, Pt I, art 10. **Imutran Ltd v Uncaged Campaigns Ltd** [2001] **2** 385, Ch D.

Strength of parties' cases—Company seeking injunction to restrain use of commercial information and company equipment by ex-employees—Factors relevant to court's discretion—Weight to be accorded to apparent strength or weakness of plaintiff's case as disclosed by affidavit evidence. **Series 5 Software Ltd v Clarke** [1996] **1** 853, Ch D.

Trial issue—Serious question to be tried of which outcome uncertain—Not necessary for parties firmly to establish outcome of case—Whether defendant's deposed positive case necessarily to be preferred to plaintiff's case relying solely on inference. **Cayne v Global Natural Resources plc** [1984] **1** 225, CA.

Public authority—
Public authority seeking to enforce law—Party against whom law sought to be enforced impugning validity of law—Grant of injunction to restrain enforcement of impugned law—Factors to be considered—Balance of convenience—Public interest in upholding law—Whether party impugning law having strong prima facie case that law invalid. **Factortame Ltd v Secretary of State for Transport (No 2) (Case C-213/89)** [1991] **1** 70, HL and ECJ.

Public authority performing statutory duties as defendant—
Balance of convenience—Matters to be considered by court in determining whether balance of convenience lies in favour of granting or refusing relief—Position where defendant a public authority performing duties to the public—Local education authority. **Smith v Inner London Education Authority** [1978] **1** 411, CA.

Prospect of obtaining permanent injunction against authority at trial—Injunction to restrain public authority from exercising statutory powers—Local education authority—Necessary for applicant to establish real prospect of obtaining permanent injunction at trial of action—Where defendant a public authority unnecessary to establish prima facie case—Interlocutory injunction sought by parents of boys at grammar school to restrain education authority from implementing proposals to cease to maintain school—Allegation that proposals unlawful as abuse of authority's powers under Education Act 1944—Whether parents establishing real prospect of obtaining permanent injunction—Whether proposals unlawful. **Smith v Inner London Education Authority** [1978] **1** 411, CA.

Reference to European Court—
Directive banning advertising and sponsorship of tobacco products within European Community—United Kingdom government proposing to implement directive by secondary legislation—Tobacco companies challenging validity of directive and seeking injunction restraining implementation pending judgment on validity—Judge granting injunction but Court of Appeal reversing decision—Tobacco companies appealing to House of Lords—European Court of Justice holding directive invalid before determination of appeal—Whether House of Lords entitled to give ruling on questions of law raised by appeal—Council Directive (EC) 98/43. **R v Secretary of State for Health, ex p Imperial Tobacco Ltd** [2000] **1** 572, CA; [2001] **1** 850, HL.

Injunction restraining enforcement of legislation pending reference to European Court—Discretion of English Court to suspend operation of legislation temporarily—Grant of interim injunction suspending operation of legislation to protect rights claimed by party under directly enforceable provisions of Community law. **Factortame Ltd v Secretary of State for Transport (No 2) (Case C-213/89)** [1991] **1** 70, HL and ECJ.

Restraint of trade—
Applicability of established principles relating to grant of interlocutory injunctions—Whether established principles relating to grant of interlocutory injunctions applicable to interlocutory injunctions to enforce covenants in restraint of trade. **David (Lawrence) Ltd v Ashton** [1991] **1** 385, CA.

Covenant by employee not to enter into trade similar to that carried on by employer for two years from termination of employment—Employer dismissing employee and seeking to enforce covenant—Speedy trial of action possible—Whether employer showing serious issue to be tried—Whether damages would be adequate remedy—Whether balance of convenience in favour of granting injunction because speedy trial possible—Whether injunction should be granted. **David (Lawrence) Ltd v Ashton** [1991] **1** 385, CA.

INJUNCTION (cont)—
  Interlocutory (cont)—
    Restraint of trade (cont)—
      Delay in trial of action—Covenant by employee not to enter trade similar to that carried on by employer for 12 months from termination of employment—Employee resigning and employer seeking to enforce covenant—Trial of action likely to be delayed until period of restraint almost expired—Whether employer showing serious issue to be tried—Whether damages would be adequate remedy—Whether balance of convenience in favour of refusing injunction because of delay in trial of action. **Lansing Linde Ltd v Kerr** [1991] **1** 418, CA.
    Specific performance—
      Mandatory injunction compelling execution of contractual obligation. *See* **Execution** (Instrument—Execution by person nominated by High Court—Jurisdiction—Contract).
    Trade dispute—
      Claim by party against whom injunction sought that he had acted in contemplation or furtherance of trade dispute—Judicial discretion—Likelihood of party against whom injunction sought succeeding at trial of action in establishing matters which would afford defence to action—Union in dispute with British Steel Corporation deciding to extend strike action to private steel sector—Private steel companies seeking injunction restraining union—Judge deciding that union's defence that acting in contemplation or furtherance of trade dispute likely to succeed at trial—Judge refusing injunction—Court of Appeal substituting own exercise of discretion and granting injunction—Whether judge exercising discretion wrongly—Whether Court of Appeal entitled to substitute own exercise of discretion—Trade Union and Labour Relations Act 1974, s 17(2) (as amended by the Employment Protection Act 1975, Sch 16, Part III, para 6). **Duport Steels Ltd v Sirs** [1980] **1** 529, HL, QBD CA.
      Claim by party against whom injunction sought that he had acted in contemplation or furtherance of trade dispute—Likelihood of that party's succeeding at trial of action in establishing defence to action—Matters to be considered by court before granting injunction—Weight to be given by court to likelihood of defendants establishing at trial that action in contemplation or furtherance of dispute connected with terms and conditions of employment—Trade Union and Labour Relations Act 1974, ss 13(1) (as amended by the Trade Union and Labour Relations (Amendment) Act 1976, s 3(2)), 17(2) (as amended by the Employment Protection Act 1975, s 125, Sch 16, Part III, para 6). **NWL Ltd v Woods** [1979] **3** 614, HL.
      Claim by party against whom injunction sought that he had acted in contemplation or furtherance of trade dispute—Likelihood of that party's succeeding at trial of action in establishing matters which would afford defence to action—Likelihood of establishing claim that dispute connected with terms and conditions of employment—Claim by employers for injunction against officers of employees' union—Broadcasting corporation—Threat by employees of corporation to stop transmission of television programme to South Africa—Employees' union disapproving of South African government's racial policy—Application by corporation for interlocutory injunction against union officers—Whether likelihood of defendants establishing at trial that action in contemplation or furtherance of dispute connected with terms and conditions of employment—Trade Union and Labour Relations Act 1974, ss 13 (as amended by the Trade Union and Labour Relations (Amendment) Act 1976, s 3(2)), 17(2) (as added by the Employment Protection Act 1975, Sch 16, Part III, para 6), 29(1). **BBC v Hearn** [1978] **1** 111, CA.
      Claim by party against whom injunction sought that he had acted in furtherance of trade dispute—Likelihood of that party's succeeding at trial in establishing matters which would afford defence to action—Employees of national newspaper company instructed by union to black copy from Press Association—Genuine belief of union that blacking of copy would advance cause of its members on provincial newspapers involved in pay dispute with provincial newspaper proprietors—Application by national newspaper company for interlocutory injunction against union officers—Whether likelihood of union officers establishing at trial that they had acted 'in furtherance of' trade dispute—Trade Union and Labour Relations Act 1974, s 13(1) (as amended by Trade Union and Labour Relations (Amendment) Act 1976, s 3(2)). **Express Newspapers Ltd v MacShane** [1979] **2** 360, CA.
      Legality of proposed strike action—Rail services—Whether proposed strike unlawful interference with right of establishment—Whether proposed strike unlawful interference with right to provide and receive services -Articles 49, 56 TFEU. **Govia GTR Railway Ltd v Associated Society of Locomotive Engineers and Firemen** [2017] **4** 982, CA.
    Trespass—
      Air space. *See* **Trespass to land** (Air space—Invasion of air space of another—Injunction).
      No defence on facts—Whether interlocutory remedy available for substantial relief before final judgment. **Manchester Corp v Connolly** [1970] **1** 961, CA.
      Revocation of licence—Defendant's licence to be on premises revoked—Forcible re-entry. **Thompson v Park** [1944] **2** 477, CA.
      Trespass to land—Defendant's trespass not causing harm to plaintiff—Principles on which interlocutory injunction to restrain trespass to land will be granted—No evidence that defendant had any right to do what he did—Whether interlocutory injunction should be granted. **Patel v W H Smith (Eziot) Ltd** [1987] **2** 569, CA.
    Undertaking as to damages—
      Attorney General—Charity proceedings—Proceedings by Attorney General against trustee of charity—Attorney General seeking interlocutory injunction—Whether Attorney General required to give cross-undertaking as to damages as condition of grant of injunction. **A-G v Wright** [1987] **3** 579, Ch D.
      Cross-undertaking as to damages—Enforcement of undertaking—By whom and for whose benefit undertaking enforceable—Restitution—Claim in restitution by members of group not subjects of interim undertaking—Whether claim in restitution existing. **SmithKline Beecham plc v Apotex Europe Ltd** [2006] **2** 53, Ch D; [2006] **4** 1078, CA.
      Cross-undertaking as to damages—Liquidator of Russian bank giving cross-undertaking limited in amount on obtaining freezing order—Continuation of freezing order conditional on provision of cross-undertaking unlimited in amount and fortified by payment of sum—Whether judge erring in requiring cross-undertaking unlimited in amount. **JSC Mezhdunarodniy Promyshlenniy Bank v Pugachev** [2015] **2** Comm 816, CA.

INJUNCTION (cont)—
  Interlocutory (cont)—
    Undertaking as to damages (cont)—
      Cross-undertaking as to damages—Whether insurance policy satisfactory fortification of cross-undertaking in damages—Whether fortification 'in a form reasonably satisfactory to the [defendants]' importing subjective or objective test—Whether judge wrong to hold no objectively reasonable apprehension of risk of avoidance by insurers. **Holyoake v Candy** [2017] **2 Comm** 513, CA.

      Discharge of injunction—Inquiry as to damages—Freezing orders improperly obtained—Whether defendants suffering loss as consequence of freezing orders—Whether defendants entitled to damages for loss of opportunity to invest frozen funds. **Fiona Trust & Holding Corp v Privalov (No 2)** [2017] **2 Comm** 57, QBD; [2017] **2** 570, QBD.

      Discharge of injunction—Inquiry as to damages—Mareva injunction—Whether inquiry as to damages should be ordered before trial. **Cheltenham and Gloucester Building Society v Ricketts** [1993] **4** 276, CA.

      Discharge of injunction—Inquiry as to damages—Search and seizure order—Freezing order—Whether general, aggravated and exemplary damages recoverable under cross-undertakings in damages in such orders. **Al-Rawas v Pegasus Energy Ltd** [2009] **1** 346, QBD; [2009] **1 Comm** 393, QBD.

      Discharge of injunction—Inquiry as to damages—Whether enquiry would be ordered prior to trial. **Ushers Brewery Ltd v PS King & Co (Finance) Ltd** [1971] **2** 468, Ch D.

      Local authority seeking to restrain Sunday trading—Local authority having power to enforce statute by prosecution or action for injunction—Whether local authority required to give cross-undertaking in damages in proceedings for injunction—Whether Crown immunity from giving cross-undertaking in damages extending to local authority acting in law enforcement capacity—Whether cross-undertaking in damages required under European law to protect retroactive effect of Community law rights—Shops Act 1950, ss 47, 71(1)—Local Government Act 1972, s 222—EEC Treaty, art 30. **Kirklees Metropolitan BC v Wickes Building Supplies Ltd** [1991] **4** 240, CA; [1992] **3** 717, HL.

      Matrimonial and children's matters concerning personal conduct—High Court—County court—Undertaking not to be incorporated in order except in certain circumstances. **Practice Direction** [1974] **2** 400, Fam D.

      Undertaking by Crown—Proceedings against companies for injunction to enforce compliance with statutory order—Order made by Secretary of State regulating prices at which companies permitted to sell drugs—Companies alleging order invalid and ultra vires—Secretary of State applying for interlocutory injunction—Whether companies entitled to undertaking as to damages as condition of submitting to interlocutory injunction—Monopolies and Restrictive Practices (Inquiry and Control) Act 1948, ss 10(1) (as amended by the Monopolies and Mergers Act 1965, ss 3(2), 11(5), Sch 3), 11(2)—Monopolies and Mergers Act 1965, s 3(1)(4). **Hoffmann-La Roche (F) & Co AG v Secretary of State for Trade and Industry** [1974] **2** 1128, HL.

      Undertaking by Director General of Fair Trading—Injunction sought in attempt to enforce law—Control of misleading advertisements—Director General seeking interlocutory injunction to restrain publication of misleading advertisements—Whether Director General should be required to give cross-undertaking in damages. **Director General of Fair Trading v Tobyward Ltd** [1989] **2** 266, Ch D.

      Undertaking by local authority—Proceedings to enforce compliance with statute—Local authority having power to enforce statute by prosecution or action for injunction—Whether local authority may be required to give cross-undertaking in damages where it commences proceedings for injunction—Shops Act 1950. **Rochdale BC v Anders** [1988] **3** 490, QBD; [1993] **1** 520, ECJ.

  Jurisdiction—
    Consumer contract. *See* **Contract** (Consumer contract—Unfair terms—General challenge—Relief—Power of court to grant injunctive relief).

    Declaration. *See* **Declaration** (Jurisdiction—Injunction).

    Injunction against Minister. *See* **Crown** (Relief against the Crown—Injunction against Minister—Jurisdiction).

  Landlord and tenant—
    Covenant—
      Breach—Claim for injunction joined with claim for possession on forfeiture of lease. *See* **Landlord and tenant** (Forfeiture of lease—Action for possession by lessor—Injunctions to restrain breaches of covenant also claimed, without prejudice to claim for possession).

    Generally. *See* **Landlord and tenant** (Injunction).

  Legal right—
    Injunction in aid of legal right—
      No other means of enforcing right unused for over a century. **Wyld v Silver** [1962] **3** 309, CA.

      Triviality of injury. **Armstrong v Sheppard & Short Ltd** [1959] **2** 651, CA.

  Libel and slander actions. *See* **Libel and slander** (Injunction).

  Locus standi—
    Criminal offence created by statute—
      No legal right conferred on individual—Enforcement under the control of the Attorney General—Incitement to racial hatred—Alleged anti-German propaganda by broadcast and television—No cause of action by individual without consent of Attorney General—Race Relations Act 1965, ss 3, 6. **Thorne v BBC** [1967] **2** 1225, CA.

    Enforcement of public right—
      Refusal of Attorney General to consent to relator action—Right of member of public to sue in own name. *See* **Attorney General** (Relator action—Refusal of consent to relator action—Right of member of public to sue in own name—Claim for declaration or injunction).

    Exclusion of director from board of company—
      Sufficiency of interest to obtain relief. **Hayes v Bristol Plant Hire Ltd** [1957] **1** 685, Ch D.

INJUNCTION (cont)—
Locus standi (cont)—
  Injunction to support performance of statutory duties by statutory body—
    Patient in special hospital seeking to publish book justifying manslaughter for which he had been convicted and referring to other patients—Hospital authority seeking injunction restraining patient from publishing book to prevent detrimental effect on his health and assaults by other patients—Whether authority having standing to claim injunction. **Broadmoor Hospital Authority v R** [2000] **2** 727, CA.
  Landlord—
    Sufficiency of interest—Covenant restraining annoyance by music from restaurant—Breach of covenant—Interlocutory application—Whether landlord had sufficient interest in relief sought—Balance of convenience irrelevant in instance of clear breach of covenant. **Hampstead and Suburban Properties Ltd v Diomedous** [1968] **3** 545, Vacation Ct Ch D.
Mandatory injunction—
  Covenant not to transfer land without procuring purchaser to enter into similar restrictive covenant—
    Transferor company owning petrol station subject to solus agreement with plaintiffs—Holding company acquiring control of transferor company—Holding company procuring company to transfer petrol station to another subsidiary company free of solus agreement—Whether court having power to compel retransfer of petrol station to transferor company. **Esso Petroleum Co Ltd v Kingswood Motors (Addlestone) Ltd** [1973] **3** 1057, QBD.
  Discretion over grant of remedy—
    Breach of covenant in conveyance—Suspension of injunction to allow defendant to ameliorate breach—Propriety. **Charrington v Simons & Co Ltd** [1971] **2** 588, CA.
    Effect of order to sanction continuation of unlawful acts—Order not capable of enforcement. **Stephen (Harold) & Co Ltd v Post Office** [1978] **1** 939, CA.
    Franchise ferry—Owner sustaining loss—Injunction to maintain and operate ferry refused. **A-G (ex rel Allen) v Colchester Corp** [1955] **2** 124, QBD.
    Franchise ferry—Owner sustaining loss—Order sought requiring ferry owner to maintain current hours of operation of ferry—Whether order should be granted. **Gravesham BC v British Railways Board** [1978] **3** 853, Ch D.
    Houses built in breach of restrictive covenant—No interlocutory relief claimed—Whether plaintiff entitled to injunction requiring demolition of houses. **Wrotham Park Estate Co v Parkside Homes Ltd** [1974] **2** 321, Ch D.
    Interlocutory motion—Criteria for exercise of discretion. **Shepherd Homes Ltd v Sandham** [1970] **3** 402, Ch D.
    Order sought requiring supervision over period of years—Negative injunction mandatory in form—Covenant by local authority to maintain airfield as municipal aerodrome—Injunction to enforce covenant refused—Remedy in damages. **Dowty Boulton Paul Ltd v Wolverhampton Corp** [1971] **2** 277, Ch D.
    Unreasonable expense—Loss of support of plaintiffs' land by reason of defendants' excavation on neighbouring land—Order requiring expenditure of £30,000 for benefit of land, etc, worth not more than £12,000. **Redland Bricks Ltd v Morris** [1969] **2** 576, HL.
  Form of order. *See* Form of order—Mandatory injunction, *above.*
  Interference with contract—
    Performance of predecessor's covenants—Interference with remedies for breach of contract—Sale of shares by party to contract—Transferor bound by contractual covenants including covenant not to transfer shares without procuring transferee to enter into similar covenants—Transferor selling shares to transferee without procuring transferee to enter into similar covenants—Transferee failing to perform covenants—Whether transferee bound in equity to perform covenants—Whether court having power to compel retransfer of shares. **Law Debenture Trust Corp plc v Ural Caspian Oil Corp Ltd** [1993] **2** 355, Ch D.
  Interlocutory. *See* Interlocutory—Mandatory injunction, *above.*
  Quia timet action—
    Jurisdiction—Loss of support of plaintiff's house by reason of defendant's excavation—Excavation causing loss of support of land near house—Real probability that in time loss of support would cause actual damage to house—Jurisdiction to grant injunction. **Hooper v Rogers** [1974] **3** 417, CA.
    Jurisdiction—Pt 20 claimant seeking quia timet injunction in event that freezing order not granted—Principles to be applied in determining whether quia timet jurisdiction to be exercised—Whether quia timet injunction should be granted. **Papamichael v National Westminster Bank plc** [2002] **2 Comm** 60, QBD.
  Trespass—
    Advertising sign projecting eight inches into air space above shop premises. **Kelsen v Imperial Tobacco Co (of GB and Ireland) Ltd** [1957] **2** 343, QBD.
Mareva injunction—
  Generally. *See* **Practice** (Pre-trial or post-judgment relief—Freezing order).
  Service out of the jurisdiction. *See* **Practice** (Service out of the jurisdiction—Pre-trial or post-judgment relief—Freezing order).
Matrimonial home—
  Exclusion of party from home. *See* Exclusion of party from matrimonial home, *above.*
Matrimonial injunction. *See* Husband and wife, *above.*
Minister, against—
  Jurisdiction. *See* **Crown** (Relief against the Crown—Injunction against Minister—Jurisdiction).
Misleading advertisement—
  Injunction to restrain publication of advertisement—
    Terms of injunction. *See* **Advertisement** (Control—Misleading advertisements—Advertisement in similar terms—Injunction—Terms of injunction).

INJUNCTION (cont)—
  Molestation—
    Domestic violence—
      Attachment of power of arrest to injunction—Acts of violence committed while unmarried couple living together as husband and wife—Parties later ceasing to cohabit—Woman obtaining non-molestation injunction against former cohabitee—Former cohabitee committing non-violent breaches of injunction—Judge imposing three months' suspended sentence on contemnor for contempt of court—Whether sentence excessive—Whether power to attach power of arrest to fresh injunction—Domestic Violence and Matrimonial Proceedings Act 1976, s 2. **McCann v Wright** [1996] **1** 204, CA.
      County court—Jurisdiction—Wife obtaining order in magistrates' court restraining husband from using violence—Jurisdiction of county court to restrain husband from molesting wife—Domestic Violence and Matrimonial Proceedings Act 1976, s 1(1)(a)—Domestic Proceedings and Magistrates' Courts Act 1978, s 16. **Horner v Horner** [1982] **2** 495, CA.
      County court—Man and woman living together with children in same household—Relationship breaking down—No violence or molestation by man towards woman or children—Woman leaving home with children and refusing to return—Whether jurisdiction to grant injunction restraining man from molesting woman or children—Domestic Violence and Matrimonial Proceedings Act 1976, s 1(1)(a)(b). **Spindlow v Spindlow** [1979] **1** 169, CA.
    Husband and wife. *See* Husband and wife—Molestation, *above*.
    Non-molestation order—
      Power to order exclusion zone—Defendant harassing plaintiff at her home—District judge granting injunction restraining defendant from harassing, molesting or communicating with plaintiff or from coming within 250 yards of home—Whether county court having power to impose exclusion zone when making non-molestation order—Supreme Court Act 1981, s 37(1)—County Courts Act 1984, s 38. **Burris v Azadani** [1995] **4** 802, CA.
  Noise nuisance—
    Interlocutory injunction. *See* Nuisance—Interlocutory injunction—Noise nuisance, *below*.
  Nuisance—
    Continuing damage—
      Roots of trees causing damage to adjoining premises. **McCombe v Read** [1955] **2** 458, QBD.
    Continuing threat of damage—
      Balance of conflicting interests—Interest of public at large conflicting with interest of private individual—Cricket played on village cricket ground for 70 years—House then built on edge of ground—Cricket balls landing on householder's property and causing damage—Precautionary measures taken by cricket club incapable of affording complete protection against continuing threat of damage—Householder applying for injunction to prevent use of ground for cricket—Nuisance established—Whether public interest of inhabitants of village in preserving ground for recreation should prevail over private interest of householder—Whether injunction should be granted. **Miller v Jackson** [1977] **3** 338, CA.
      Balance of conflicting interests—Interest of public at large conflicting with interest of private individual—Right of private interest to be protected despite interest of public at large—Grant of damages in lieu of injunction—Power boat club causing noise nuisance to adjoining house owner—Race meetings organised by club attracting large public attendances—Whether private interest of house owner should prevail over public interest of spectators at club's race meetings—Whether damages should be awarded in lieu of injunction—Chancery Amendment Act 1858 (Lord Cairns's Act). **Kennaway v Thompson** [1980] **3** 329, CA.
      Only effective remedy—Suspension. **Lotus Ltd v British Soda Co Ltd** [1971] **1** 265, Ch D.
    Damages in lieu of injunction. *See* **Nuisance** (Noise—Motor racing—Remedies—Damages in lieu of injunction).
    Form of order—
      Generally. *See* Form of order—Nuisance, *above*.
      Interlocutory injunction. *See* Form of order—Interlocutory injunction—Nuisance, *above*.
    Interlocutory injunction—
      Form of order. *See* Form of order—Interlocutory injunction—Nuisance, *above*.
      Noise nuisance—Grant of injunction to prevent infringement of criminal law—Defendants managing construction site adjacent to housing estate—Noise from site causing nuisance to residents on estate—Council serving notice requiring defendants to restrict noisy operations at night and on weekends—Defendants contravening notice by carrying out operations at night and on weekends—Council seeking injunction to restrain defendants from contravening notice—Whether necessary for council to prove defendants deliberately and flagrantly flouting law—Whether injunction should be granted—Local Government Act 1972, s 222—Control of Pollution Act 1974, s 60. **City of London Corp v Bovis Construction Ltd (1988)** [1992] **3** 697, CA.
      Sex shop—Defendant opening sex shop in predominantly residential area—Residents contending that sex shop would attract undesirable customers who would threaten ordinary family life of area—Residents also fearing adverse effect of shop on property values—Whether appropriate case for grant of interlocutory injunction. **Laws v Florinplace Ltd** [1981] **1** 659, Ch D.
    Public nuisance—
      Dust and vibration from quarry affecting adjoining householders—Remedial measures taken since action begun—Relevance of defendants' attitude to complaints—Whether injunction should be granted—Whether isolated acts would amount to a public nuisance and thus constitute a breach of an injunction against committing one. **A-G (ex rel Glamorgan CC and Pontardawe RDC) v PYA Quarries Ltd** [1957] **1** 894, CA.
  Parliamentary affairs—
    Opposition to private Bill—
      Jurisdiction of court. **Bilston Corp v Wolverhampton Corp** [1942] **2** 447, Ch D.
  Passing off—
    Form of order. *See* Form of order—Passing off, *above*.
  Patent—
    Generally. *See* **Patent** (Injunction).
    Infringement. *See* **Patent** (Infringement—Injunction).

INJUNCTION (cont)—
Person under disability—
    Injunction not able to be enforced effectively by court—
        Proceedings for injunctions issued against mentally ill person and child under 17—Whether fact of disability a bar to granting injunction—Whether appropriate to grant injunction if not able to be enforced effectively by court by reason of disability of person against whom injunction sought. **Wookey v Wookey** [1991] **3** 365, CA.
Persons unknown, against. *See* **Practice** (Parties—Unnamed defendant—Injunction).
Planning control, enforcement of. *See* **Town and country planning** (Enforcement of planning control—Civil remedy).
Possession action—
    Anti-social behaviour—
        Anti-social behaviour injunctions made on without notice application with power of arrest—Possession order made with immediate effect—Anti-social behaviour orders made for four years—Orders made taking hearsay evidence into account—Whether orders appropriate—Guidance—Civil Evidence Act 1995, s 4(2)—Housing Act 1996, ss 153A, 153D—Crime and Disorder Act 1998, s 1. **Moat Housing Group South Ltd v Harris** [2005] **4** 1051, CA.
Post-judgment—
    Injunction restraining defendant from leaving jurisdiction—
        Consent order disposing of action brought by husband and providing for husband to pay wife's costs—Husband failing to pay wife's costs—Husband foreign national on visit to England—Whether court having power to restrain husband from leaving jurisdiction until he paid wife's costs—Supreme Court Act 1981, s 37(1). **B v B (injunction: restraint on leaving jurisdiction)** [1997] **3** 258, Fam D.
Practice—
    Parties. *See* **Practice** (Parties—Unnamed defendant—Injunction).
Premature application for order—
    Disciplinary rules—
        Alleged breach—Member invited to attend meeting—Proceedings commenced by member before meeting held. **Draper v British Optical Association** [1938] **1** 115, Ch D.
Proprietary injunction—
    Crypto currencies. *See* Interim—Proprietary injunction—Crypto currencies, *above*.
    Interim. *See* Interim—Proprietary injunction, *above*.
Public authority—
    Statutory powers. *See* **Local authority** (Statutory powers—Injunction).
Public nuisance. *See* Nuisance—Public nuisance, *above*.
Public right—
    Relator action—
        Refusal of Attorney General of consent to relator action—Right of member of public to sue in own name. *See* **Attorney General** (Relator action—Refusal of consent to relator action—Right of member of public to sue in own name—Claim for declaration or injunction).
        Scope of court's discretion in relator action. **A-G (ex rel Hornchurch UDC) v Bastow** [1957] **1** 497, QBD; **A-G (ex rel Manchester Corp) v Harris** [1960] **3** 207, CA.
Quia timet action—
    Defamation case—
        Particularity of pleadings. *See* **Libel and slander** (Particulars—Quia timet injunction).
    Local authority seeking injunction prohibiting encampment in relation to all accessible public spaces—
        Injunction sought against Gypsy and Traveller community—Whether injunction breaching convention rights—Whether injunction proportionate—Guidance—Human Rights Act 1998, Sch 1, Pt I, arts 6, 8—Equality Act 2010, s 149. **Bromley London BC v Persons unknown (London Gypsies and Travellers intervening)** [2020] **4** 114, CA.
    Mandatory injunction. *See* Mandatory injunction—Quia timet action, *above*.
Relator action—
    Circumstances in which relator procedure may be dispensed with. *See* **Attorney General** (Relator action—Dispensing with relator procedure—Circumstances in which procedure may be dispensed with—Claim for injunction or declaration).
    Generally. *See* Public right—Relator action, *above*.
Restraint of foreign proceedings—
    Conflict of laws. *See* **Conflict of laws** (Foreign proceedings—Restraint of foreign proceedings).
Sale of goods—
    Form of order. *See* Form of order—Sale of goods, *above*.
    Motor car—
        Sale of car as new—Injunction at instance of manufacturers against retail purchaser re-selling car as new. **Morris Motors Ltd v Lilley (t/a G & L Motors)** [1959] **3** 737, Ch D.
Secretary of State, against—
    Jurisdiction. *See* **Crown** (Relief against the Crown—Injunction against Secretary of State—Jurisdiction).
Service out of the jurisdiction—
    Action in which injunction sought. *See* **Practice** (Service out of the jurisdiction—Action in which injunction sought).
    Freezing order. *See* **Practice** (Service out of the jurisdiction—Pre-trial or post-judgment relief—Freezing order).
Solus agreement—
    Supplier and buyer—
        Injunction to restrain breach of tie. *See* **Restraint of trade by agreement** (Supplier and buyer—Solus agreement—Enforcement of agreement—Injunction to restrain breach of tie).
Summary procedure—
    Practice—
        Summary judgment for injunction—Master not having power to grant injunction—Application direct to judge—RSC Ord 14. **Shell-Mex and BP Ltd v Manchester Garages Ltd** [1971] **1** 841, CA.

INJUNCTION (cont)—

Sunday—
    Dies non juridicus—
        Judicial acts not to be done on Sunday—Interim injunction granted as emergency measure on a Sunday to prevent father abducting children on terms that summons to make them wards of court be issued on the next day—Whether granting of injunction was excepted from judicial acts not to be done on a Sunday—Title of order for injunction—RSC Ord 29, r 1. **N (infants), Re** [1967] **1** 161, Ch D.

Time limit on operation—
    Exclusion of party from matrimonial home—
        County court. *See* Exclusion of party from matrimonial home—County court—Time limit on operation of injunction, *above*.

Title of proceedings—
    Grant of injunction before issue of originating process. *See* **Practice** (Title of proceedings—Application for injunction—Grant of injunction before issue of originating process).

Transfer of assets abroad by defendant—
    Interlocutory injunction. *See* **Practice** (Pre-trial or post-judgment relief—Freezing order).

Tree preservation—
    Local authority's injunction. *See* **Practice** (Parties—Local authority—Promotion or protection of interests of inhabitants of their area—Local authority obtaining injunction to restrain breaches by defendant of tree preservation order).

Undertaking—
    Construction—
        Judge granting injunction with undertaking that company will not dispose of, deal with or diminish value of any funds belonging to it or held to its order other than in ordinary and proper course of its business—Declaration made that 'ICSID expenditure' would not be in 'ordinary and proper course of company's business'—Declaration made that proposed payments of legal fees in connection with proceedings for extradition of company's director would not be in 'ordinary and proper course of company's business'—Whether expenditure and payments in 'ordinary and proper course of company's business'—Whether declarations properly made. **Koza Ltd v Akcil** [2020] **1 Comm** 301, CA.

    Discharge—
        Undertaking in lieu of injunction—Defendant giving undertaking on hearing of interlocutory motion—Undertaking given until trial or further order—Defendant indicating that subsequently he might apply to discharge undertaking—Motion adjourned generally—Defendant subsequently applying to have undertaking discharged—Judge refusing to discharge undertaking—Whether undertaking binding until trial—Whether matter could be reopened before trial. **Butt v Butt** [1987] **3** 657, CA.

    Undertaking as to damages—
        Interlocutory injunction. *See* Interlocutory—Undertaking as to damages, *above*.

    Variation—
        Form—Release and substitution of new undertaking—Undertaking in lieu of injunction to admit bookmaker to greyhound racing track until further order—Dissolution of injunction granted on similar terms in another action against the same defendants by Court of Appeal—Application for variation of undertaking—Application wrong in form—Betting and Lotteries Act 1934, s 11(2)(a). **Cutler v Wandsworth Stadium Ltd** [1945] **1** 103, CA.

    'Without prejudice' offer to give undertaking before hearing. *See* **Compromise** (Offer made before hearing—Injunction).

Unlawful occupation of land—
    Possession proceedings. *See* **Land** (Summary proceedings for possession—Extent of court's jurisdiction—Persons unlawfully occupying woodland).

Unnamed defendant—
    Practice. *See* **Practice** (Parties—Unnamed defendant—Injunction).

Variation—
    Interlocutory injunction restraining removal of assets out of jurisdiction. *See* **Practice** (Pre-trial or post-judgment relief—Freezing order—Injunction restraining removal of assets out of the jurisdiction—Variation of injunction).

Variation or discharge—
    Jurisdiction—
        High Court judge granting interim injunction—High Court judge allowing application for judgment in default and making interim injunction permanent—Master setting aside default judgment and varying or discharging injunction—Whether master having jurisdiction—CPR PD 2B, para 2.2. **Richmond v Burch** [2007] **1** 658, Ch D.

Wardship proceedings—
    Whether inherent jurisdiction to grant injunction before issue of originating process. *See* **Ward of court** (Jurisdiction—Injunction—Interim injunction—Originating process not yet issued).

'Without prejudice' offer to submit to injunction. *See* **Compromise** (Offer made before hearing—Injunction).

Worldwide injunction—
    Breach of covenant in contract of service. *See* Breach of covenant—Breach of undertaking—Contract of service—Undertaking expressed to be perpetual and worldwide, *above*.

    Mareva injunction. *See* **Practice** (Pre-trial or post-judgment relief—Freezing order—Worldwide freezing order).

INJURIOUS AFFECTION

Compensation. *See* **Compensation** (Injurious affection).

Compulsory purchase of land—
    Compensation. *See* **Compulsory purchase** (Compensation—Injurious affection).

INJURIOUS FALSEHOOD

See **Malicious falsehood**.

INJURIOUS FOOD

Offences in connection with preparation and sale of. *See* **Food and drugs**.

INJURY

Accident arising out of and in the course of employment—
Workman—
    Compensation. *See* **Workmen's compensation** (Injury by accident arising out of and in the course of employment).
Aggravation of injury by war service. *See* **War pension** (Aggravation of injury by war service).
Animal—
  Protection from injury and unnecessary suffering—
    Carriage by sea, air, road or rail. *See* **Animal** (Carriage by sea, air, road or rail—Protection from injury and unnecessary suffering).
Compensation—
  Criminal injuries. *See* **Compensation** (Criminal injuries).
  War injury. *See* **War injury** (Compensation).
  Workman. *See* **Workmen's compensation**.
Damages—
  Apportionment. *See* **Damages** (Apportionment—Indivisible injury).
  Fatal accident. *See* **Fatal accident** (Damages).
  Generally. *See* **Damages** (Personal injury).
Disablement benefit. *See* **Social security** (Disablement benefit).
Industrial—
  Benefit. *See* **Social security** (Disablement benefit).
  Generally. *See* **Industrial injury**.
Limitation of action—
  Court's power to override time limit. *See* **Limitation of action** (Court's power to override time limit in personal injury or fatal accident claim).
Occupier's liability. *See* **Occupier's liability**.
War—
  Generally. *See* **War injury**.
  War pension. *See* **War pension** (Attributability of injury to war service).

INLAND REVENUE COMMISSIONERS

Appeal. *See* **Income tax** (Appeal).
Case stated. *See* **Income tax** (Case stated).
Generally. *See* **Income tax** (Commissioners of Inland Revenue).
Judicial review of commissioners' exercise of discretion—
  Availability of remedy. *See* **Judicial review** (Availability of remedy—Exercise of discretion on behalf of Crown—Inland Revenue Commissioners).

INLAND WATER

Boundary. *See* **Boundary** (Inland water).

INN

Damage to guest's property—
  Liability of innkeeper at common law—
    Extent of hospitium—Permission by innkeeper to park motor coach at petrol station—Petrol station owned by inn, but separated by public road—Garages and car park at inn—Coach damaged. **Watson v People's Refreshment House Association Ltd** [1952] **1** 289, KBD.
    Guest's car left in garage of inn—Garage destroyed by fire and car ruined—No negligence on part of innkeeper. **Williams v Owen** [1956] **1** 104, Assizes.
Duty to supply refreshment and lodging to traveller—
  Refusal—
    Action by traveller—No special damage—Right to general damages. **Constantine v Imperial London Hotels Ltd** [1944] **2** 171, KBD.
    Reasonableness of refusal—Question of fact for jury—Extent of duty at common law—Right to reserve tables. **R v Higgins** [1947] **2** 619, CCA.
Lien—
  Luggage—
    Ring handed to innkeeper as security for bill—Bill unpaid—Right of innkeeper to exercise lien on ring. **Marsh v Police Comr and McGee** [1944] **2** 392, CA.
Loss of guest's property—
  Liability of innkeeper—
    Bedroom door without lock—Fur cape left by guest in bedroom—Theft of cape. **Brewster v Drennan** [1945] **2** 705, CA.
    Failure of guest to take reasonable care of property—Locking bedroom—Failure to deliver jewellery to innkeeper for safe custody—Innkeepers' Liability Act 1863, ss 1, 3. **Shacklock v Ethorpe Ltd** [1939] **3** 372, HL.
    Residential hotel—Theft of resident's clothing from room—Key left on board in office during absence—No proper system of control. **Olley v Marlborough Court Ltd** [1949] **1** 127, CA.
    Theft of luggage from motor car—Car parked in inn garage three hundred yards from inn—Hospitium of inn—Notices excluding liability—Guest's own negligence. **Gresham v Lyon** [1954] **2** 786, QBD.
    Theft of motor car from car park of inn—Need to prove guest a traveller—Traveller—Resident in neighbourhood—Car park within hospitium of inn—Notice relieving innkeeper of liability. **Williams v Linnitt** [1951] **1** 278, CA.
Safety of premises—
  Hotel drive—
    Duty to take reasonable care to see reasonably safe—Slipperiness. **Bell v Travco Hotels Ltd** [1953] **1** 638, CA.
  Lighting of passages—
    Duty to light passages—Reasonable hours—Doorway leading immediately to steep flight of steps. **Campbell v Shelbourne Hotel Ltd** [1939] **2** 351, KBD.

INNOCENT DISSEMINATION
    Libel. *See* **Libel and slander** (Publication—Innocent dissemination).

INNOCENT MISREPRESENTATION
    Damages. *See* **Misrepresentation** (Damages—Innocent misrepresentation).
    Generally. *See* **Misrepresentation** (Innocent misrepresentation).

INNS OF COURT
    Judges as visitors of Inns of Court—
        Disciplinary jurisdiction. *See* **Counsel** (Disciplinary jurisdiction—Judges as visitors of Inns of Court).
    Senate of the Four Inns of Court—
        Disciplinary jurisdiction. *See* **Counsel** (Disciplinary jurisdiction—Senate of the Four Inns of Court).

INNUENDO
    Defamation. *See* **Libel and slander** (Innuendo).

INPUT TAX
    Value added tax. *See* **Value added tax** (Input tax).

INQUEST
    Coroner—
        Generally. *See* **Coroner** (Inquest).
        Jurisdiction. *See* **Coroner** (Jurisdiction—Inquest).
    Practice and procedure. *See* **Coroner** (Inquest—Practice and procedure).

INQUIRY
    Appeal against enforcement notice. *See* **Town and country planning** (Enforcement notice—Appeal against notice—Inquiry by inspector appointed by minister).
    Appeal against refusal of permission for development. *See* **Town and country planning** (Appeal to Minister against refusal of permission for development—Local inquiry).
    Commission of inquiry—
        Bahamas. *See* **Bahamas** (Commission of inquiry).
        Contempt of court. *See* **Contempt of court** (Court—Commission of inquiry).
        Procedure—
            Freedom to obtain information its own way where no procedure prescribed—Requirements of natural justice. **University of Ceylon v Fernando** [1960] **1** 631, PC.
    Inspector appointed to hold public local inquiry—
        Remuneration—
            Income tax. *See* **Income tax** (Emoluments from office or employment—Office—Inspector appointed to hold public local inquiry).
    Natural justice—
        Duty to hear parties—
            Opportunity to consider reasons for decision—Housing—Compulsory purchase order. *See* **Natural justice** (Public inquiry—Duty to hear parties—Opportunity to consider reasons for decision—Reasons not put forward at hearing—Housing—Compulsory purchase order—Inquiry by inspector).
        Public inquiry. *See* **Natural justice** (Public inquiry).
    Next-of-kin, for. *See* **Practice** (Chancery Division—Inquiries for next-of-kin).
    Report of proceedings—
        Qualified privilege. *See* **Libel and slander** (Qualified privilege—Report of proceedings of public inquiry).
    Tribunal of inquiry. *See* **Tribunal** (Tribunal of inquiry).

INSANITY
    Automatism distinguished. *See* **Criminal law** (Automatism—Insanity distinguished).
    Contract—
        Capacity of person of unsound mind to enter into contract. *See* **Contract** (Parties—Capacity—Insanity).
    Criminal cases—
        Appeal. *See* **Criminal law** (Appeal—Insanity).
        Defence in. *See* **Criminal law** (Insanity).
    Divorce—
        Ground for. *See* **Divorce** (Insanity).
    Generally. *See* **Mental health**.
    Inquest—
        Unlawful killing. *See* **Coroner** (Inquest—Verdict—Unlawful killing—Standard of proof—Insanity).
    Nullity of marriage—
        Grounds for nullity. *See* **Nullity** (Insanity).

INSCRIPTION
    Gravestone, on—
        Charge for—
            Burial board, by. *See* **Burial** (Burial ground—Charge for monumental inscription—Right of burial board to charge for permission to cut inscriptions on gravestone).

INSENSATE PATIENT
    Medical treatment—
        Withdrawal of treatment. *See* **Medical treatment** (Withdrawal of treatment—Insensate patient).

INSIDER DEALING
    See **Company** (Insider dealing).

INSOLVENCY

Administration order—

    Administration order made in respect of equipment leasing company—

        Equipment owned by finance companies and supplied to company under hire-purchase and lease agreements—Whether finance companies having absolute entitlement to periodical payments due under hire-purchase agreements and headleases during company's administration—Whether payments falling due under hire-purchase agreements and headleases to be treated as expense of administration payable by administrators—Whether finance companies requiring leave to enforce proprietary rights in respect of equipment—Whether leave should be granted if leave required—Insolvency Act 1986, ss 8(3)(d), 11(3)(c). **Atlantic Computer Systems plc, Re** [1992] **1** 476, CA.

    Company—

        Generally. *See* **Company** (Administration order).

    Debtor owning property as joint tenant—

        Debtor dying before order made—Whether order relating back to date of debtor's death—Whether order severing joint tenancy—Insolvency Act 1986, s 283—Administration of Insolvent Estates of Deceased Persons Order 1986, Sch 1. **Palmer (decd) (a debtor), Re** [1994] **3** 835, CA.

    Independent report on company's affairs—

        Content of report—Concise statement of company's situation and prospects of administration order achieving purpose—Availability of finance required during administration—Disproportionate investigation and expense to be avoided in preparing report—Oral evidence to supplement report—Supplemental report covering matters in oral evidence for court file—Appointment of administrator to report on whether administration should continue—Court may require administrator to hold meeting of creditors before reporting back to court—Insolvency Act 1986, Pt II—Insolvency Rules 1986, r 2.2. **Practice Note** [1994] **1** 324, Ch D.

Agent, of—

    Termination of agency. *See* **Agent** (Commercial agent—Termination of agency—Insolvency).

Anti-deprivation rule—

    Property available for distribution. *See* Property available for distribution—Anti-deprivation rule, *below*.

Appeal—

    Appeal from district judge—

        Hearing outside London by circuit judge—Lodging of notice of appeal—Insolvency Act 1986, s 375(2)—Insolvency Rules 1986, rr 7.47(2), 7.49(2), 13.2(3). **Practice Direction** [1992] **3** 921, Ch D.

        Hearing outside London by circuit judge—Lodging of notice of appeal—Insolvency Act 1986, s 375(2)—Insolvency Rules 1986, rr 7.48(2), 7.49(1), (2). **Practice Note** [1995] **4** 129, Ch D.

    Appeal from registrar—

        Appeal to judge—Debtor appealing against bankruptcy order made by registrar—Whether appeal amounting to true appeal or rehearing—Insolvency Rules 1986, r 7.48(2). **Gilmartin (a bankrupt), Re, ex p the bankrupt v International Agency and Supply Ltd** [1989] **2** 835, Ch D.

        Appeal to judge—Leave—Whether leave required to appeal from registrar to single judge. **Busytoday Ltd, Re** [1992] **4** 61, Ch D.

    Appeals etc from courts exercising insolvency jurisdiction—

        Jurisdiction of appellate court—Insolvency Act 1986, s 375. **Sands v Layne** [2015] **2** 332, Ch D.

        Whether power to review extending to appellate orders—Insolvency Act 1986, s 375. **National Asset Loan Management Ltd v Cahillane** [2015] **4** 380, Ch D; [2016] **1** Comm 310, Ch D.

    Hearing on Northern or North Eastern Circuit—

        Chancery Division practice. *See* **Practice** (Chancery Division—Northern Area—Appeals—Insolvency and revenue appeals).

    Locus standi—

        Appeal by bankrupt personally—Bankruptcy petition founded on unsatisfied judgment—Bankrupt wishing to appeal from judgment on which petition founded—Whether bankrupt having locus standi to pursue appeal in own name—Whether leave to appeal should be granted to bankrupt—Insolvency Act 1986, s 285(3). **Heath v Tang** [1993] **4** 694, CA.

    Notice of appeal—

        Chancery Division. *See* **Practice** (Chancery Division—Bankruptcy—Lists—Appeals).

Application—

    Ordinary application—

        Striking out—Jurisdiction—Application in pending bankruptcy brought by applicant seeking declarations against trustee in bankruptcy—Whether court having power under rules of court or inherent jurisdiction to strike out notwithstanding interlocutory nature of application—Insolvency Rules 1986, r 7.2—RSC Ord 18, r 19. **Port v Auger** [1994] **3** 200, Ch D.

Arbitration—

    Jurisdiction. *See* **Arbitration** (Jurisdiction—Insolvency).

Assignment of fruits of litigation—

    Champerty. *See* **Maintenance of action** (Champerty—Statutory exemption—Assignment of fruits of litigation to third party by liquidator of insolvent company).

Bankruptcy—

    Administration by trustee—

        Acquisition, control and realisation of bankrupt's estate—Income payments orders—Income of bankrupt—Payment in the nature of income from time to time made to bankrupt or to which he from time to time becomes entitled—Bankrupt of pensionable age having entitlement to elect to draw pension—Bankrupt not having elected—Whether income payments order could be made—Whether income of bankrupt—Insolvency Act 1986, s 310(7). **Raithatha (as trustee in bankruptcy for Williamson) v Williamson** [2012] **3** 1028, Ch D.

        Acquisition, control and realisation of bankrupt's estate—Income payments orders—Income payments agreement—Jurisdiction of court to make income payments orders—Whether income payments order could be made if income payments agreement made previously—Insolvency Act 1986, ss 310, 310A. **Thomas v Edmondson** [2014] **3** 976, Ch D.

INSOLVENCY (cont)—
  Bankruptcy (cont)—
    Administration by trustee (cont)—
      Acquisition, control and realisation of bankrupt's estate—Income payments orders—Payment in nature of income from time to time made to bankrupt or to which he from time to time becomes entitled—Pension rights—Right to elect to draw down payment not yet exercised—Meaning of 'income'—Whether pension rights forming part of income 'to which he from time to time becomes entitled'—Insolvency Act 1986, ss 310(7), 333—Welfare Reform and Pensions Act 1999, s 11. **Henry (a bankrupt), Re** [2017] **3** 735, CA.
    Bankrupt's estate—
      Matrimonial home—Transaction at undervalue—Trustee in bankruptcy seeking declaration more than three years after bankruptcy order that transfer of matrimonial home to bankrupt's spouse was transfer at undervalue—Limitation period running three years from trustee's knowledge or awareness of bankrupt's interest—Whether claim time-barred by trustee's awareness of possible claim at time of bankruptcy order—Whether bankrupt's interests including possible claims—Insolvency Act 1986, ss 283A(5), 339. **Stonham (trustee in bankruptcy of Ramrattan) v Ramrattan** [2011] **4** 392, CA.
      Matrimonial home—Trustee in bankruptcy assigning beneficial interest in bankrupt's estate to creditor—Contingent sale agreement providing for deferred consideration—Married claimants challenging realisation of interest in matrimonial home—Meaning of 'realises'—Whether realisation occurring at time of assignment or at time of conversion of interest into cash or money—Insolvency Act 1986, s 283A(3)(a). **Lewis v Metropolitan Property Realisations Ltd** [2009] **4** 141, CA.
      Vesting in trustee. *See* Bankrupt's estate—Vesting in trustee, *above*.
    Conflict of laws. *See* **Conflict of laws** (Bankruptcy).
    Discharge—
      Release of bankruptcy debts by discharge—Contingent liability—Whether liability to repay overpaid benefit because of misrepresentation constituting bankruptcy debt if determination of recoverability of overpayment made subsequent to commencement of bankruptcy—Insolvency Act 1986, s 382—Social Security Administration Act 1992, s 71(1). **R (on the application of Steele) v Birmingham City Council** [2007] **1** 73, CA.
      Release of bankruptcy debts by discharge—Fraud exception—Whether undue influence constituting 'fraud' for purposes of fraud exception to release of bankruptcy debts by discharge—Insolvency Act 1986, s 281(3). **Mander v Evans** [2001] **3** 811, Ch D.
      Release of bankruptcy debts by discharge—Fraudulent breach of trust—Whether dishonesty essential ingredient of 'fraudulent breach of trust' for purposes of exception to release of bankruptcy debts by discharge—Insolvency Act 1986, s 281(3). **Woodland-Ferrari v UCL Group Retirement Benefits Scheme** [2002] **3** 670, Ch D.
      Release of bankruptcy debts by discharge—Overpayment of benefit—Recovery—Secretary of State determining that recipient of benefits liable to repay overpaid benefits—Recipient of benefits declared bankrupt—Secretary of State seeking to recover overpayment by deduction from prescribed benefits—Whether discharge from bankruptcy releasing recipient of benefits from liability to repay overpayment—Insolvency Act 1986, ss 281, 382—Social Security Administration Act 1992, s 71. **R (on the application of Balding) v Secretary of State for Work and Pensions** [2007] **4** 422, DC; [2008] **3** 217, CA.
    Generally. *See* **Bankruptcy**.
    Proceedings against a bankrupt. *See* Jurisdiction—Leave to commence proceedings, *below*.
    Restriction on proceedings and remedies—
      Assured tenancy—Arrears of rent—Landlord bringing possession proceedings against assured tenant—Assured tenant adjudged bankrupt—Prohibition against remedy in respect of debt provable in bankruptcy—Whether possession order could be made against tenant—Insolvency Act 1986, s 285. **Sharples v Places for People Homes Ltd, Godfrey v A2 Dominion Homes Ltd** [2012] **1** 582, CA.
    Bankrupt's estate—
    Vesting in trustee—
      Annuity income under occupational pension scheme—Whether annuity income vesting in trustee in bankruptcy as part of bankrupt's estate—Whether statutory provisions compatible with right to peaceful enjoyment of possessions—Insolvency Act 1986, ss 306, 310, 436—Human Rights Act 1998, Sch 1, Pt II, art 1. **Rowe v Sanders (note)** [2002] **2** 800, CA.
      Assurance policy—Permanent disablement benefit—Appellant taking out life assurance policies containing provision for earlier payment on receipt of proof of permanent disability—Appellant suffering permanent disablement and making claims under policies—Appellant being made bankrupt—Policy provider accepting claims—Appellant's trustee in bankruptcy claiming policy moneys—Whether policy moneys belonging to bankrupt if contractual claim to them relying on bankrupt's pain and suffering. **Cork (as trustee in bankruptcy for Rawlins) v Rawlins** [2001] **4** 50, CA.
      Bankrupts having rights to annuities and benefits under annuity contracts and pension schemes—Policies prohibiting surrender or assignment—Whether restrictions on alienation preventing policies from vesting in trustee in bankruptcy—Whether moneys due under policies only becoming available to creditors on making of income payments order—Insolvency Act 1986, ss 283(1), 310—Convention for the Protection of Human Rights and Fundamental Freedoms, First Protocol, art 1. **Krasner v Dennison** [2000] **3** 234, CA.
      Cause of action—Bankrupt bringing proceedings for negligence against professional advisers for failure to prevent making of bankruptcy order—Trustee in bankruptcy claiming right of action vesting in him—County court holding that trustee had no interest in right of action—Whether open to professional advisers to contend that right of action vested in trustee. **Mulkerrins v PricewaterhouseCoopers (a firm)** [2003] **4** 1, HL.
      Cause of action—Discharged bankrupt bringing proceedings for medical negligence suffered before bankruptcy—Claimant seeking recovery of damages for loss of earnings and pain and suffering—Whether cause of action vesting in trustee in bankruptcy—Insolvency Act 1986, s 436. **Ord v Upton (as trustee to the property of Ord)** [2000] **1** 193, CA.

INSOLVENCY (cont)—

Bankrupt's estate (cont)—

Vesting in trustee (cont)—

Cause of action—Harassment—Claim for damages for anxiety and financial loss—Alleged harassment and losses occurring both before and after bankruptcy—Whether harassment claim purely personal in all circumstances—Whether entirety of cause of action vesting in trustee—Protection from Harassment Act 1997, s 1. **Hayes v Butters** [2015] **3** 702, Ch D.

Distributions of royalties for musical works—Royalties payable to bankrupt after commencement of bankruptcy in respect of pre-bankruptcy works—Whether right to distributions vesting in trustee—Whether right to distributions a mere expectancy—Insolvency Act 1986, s 306. **Performing Right Society Ltd v Rowland** [1997] **3** 336, Ch D.

Personal correspondence—Former government minister being made bankrupt—Trustee in bankruptcy wishing to sell bankrupt's personal correspondence to media—Whether personal correspondence forming part of bankrupt's estate—Whether trustee in bankruptcy entitled to sell bankrupt's personal correspondence—Insolvency Act 1986, ss 306, 311(1)—Insolvency Regulations 1994, reg 30. **Haig v Aitken** [2000] **3** 80, Ch D.

Retirement annuity policy effected by bankrupt prior to bankruptcy—Policy providing that annuity could not be assigned and that annuitant could commute part of annuity for a lump sum—Annuity becoming payable after bankrupt's discharge from bankruptcy—Trustee in bankruptcy claiming to be entitled to payments and to commute part of annuity for a lump sum—Whether trustee so entitled—Whether policy had vested in trustee on his appointment—Whether payments after-acquired property—Whether payments income of bankrupt—Insolvency Act 1986, ss 306, 307, 310(7). **Landau (a bankrupt), Re** [1997] **3** 322, Ch D.

Bankrupt's estate—

Exceptions—

Equipment necessary for use personally in employment, business or vocation—Whether trustee having reasonable belief entitled to seize property—Effect of trustee's release on liability—Guidance—Insolvency Act 1986, ss 283, 299, 304. **Birdi v Price** [2019] **3** 250, Ch D.

Company—

Administration order. *See* **Company** (Administration order).

Charity. *See* **Charity** (Company—Insolvency).

Compulsory winding up. *See* **Company** (Compulsory winding up).

Cross-border insolvency. *See* Cross-border insolvency, *below*.

Generally. *See* **Company** (Insolvency).

Inability to pay debts—

Company unable to pay its debts as they fall due—Company unable to pay debts if value of assets is less than amount of liabilities, taking into account contingent and prospective liabilities—Whether company reaching point of no return because of incurable deficiency in assets—Whether company unable to meet future or contingent liabilities because failure was inevitable—Effect of post-enforcement call option—Insolvency Act 1986, s 123(2). **BNY Corporate Trustee Services Ltd v Eurosail-UK 2007-3BL plc** [2011] **3** 470, Ch D and CA; [2013] **2 Comm** 531, SC; [2013] **3** 271, SC.

Winding up. *See* **Company** (Winding up).

Conflict of laws—

Enforcement of foreign judgment. *See* **Conflict of laws** (Foreign judgment—Enforcement—Insolvency proceedings).

Creditor's petition—

Proceedings on. *See* Proceedings on creditor's petition, *below*.

Cross-border insolvency—

Company—

Winding up. *See* **Company** (Winding up—Cross-border insolvency).

EEA insolvency measure. *See* **Company** (Winding up—Cross-border insolvency—EEA insolvency measure).

Letter of request—

Jurisdiction—Letter of request from Royal Court of Jersey to English High Court for assistance by appointment of administrators—No insolvency proceedings or intended proceedings in Jersey—Whether appointment of administrators would 'assist' Jersey court in its functions as an insolvency court—Whether High Court having jurisdiction to accede to request—Insolvency Act 1986, s 426(4). **HSBC Bank plc v Tambrook Jersey Ltd** [2013] **3** 850, Ch D and CA.

Recognition of foreign proceeding—

Bankruptcy. *See* **Conflict of laws** (Bankruptcy—Order of foreign bankruptcy court—Recognition and enforcement).

Company wound up in Bermuda on just and equitable ground—Liquidators seeking recognition in Great Britain of liquidation as foreign main proceeding—Whether 'foreign proceeding' in respect of solvent company entitled to recognition—Whether Bermudan liquidation pursuant to law relating to insolvency -Companies Act 1981 (Bermuda), s 161(g)—Cross-Border Insolvency Regulations 2006, SI 2006/1030, Sch 1. **Sturgeon Central Asia Balanced Fund Ltd (in liq), Re** [2020] **1 Comm** 701, Ch D.

Relief—Azeri court approving plan to restructure debts of Azeri bank—Respondents' debts governed by English law—Application for order to continue moratorium to prevent respondents from enforcing debts—Whether respondents' claims against bank discharged by restructure—Whether jurisdiction to extend moratorium beyond termination of foreign proceeding—Whether rule that debt governed by English law could not be discharged by foreign insolvency proceeding applying—Cross-Border Insolvency Regulations 2006, SI 2006/1030, Sch 1, arts 20, 21(1). **OJSC International Bank of Azerbaijan, Re** [2018] **4** 964, Ch D; [2019] **1 Comm** 597, CA; [2019] **2** 713, CA.

Debt relief order—

Discharge—

Overpayment of benefit—Debtor owing repayments from social fund loan—Debtor owing social security benefit overpayment—Secretary of State attempting to recover social fund loan and overpayment by deductions from benefits—Whether power to deduct benefits remedy in respect of debt—Whether Secretary of State entitled to make deductions during moratorium—Insolvency Act 1986, s 251G(2)—Social Security Administration Act 1992, ss 71, 78(2). **R (on the application of Payne) v Secretary of State for Work and Pensions** [2012] **2** 46, SC.

INSOLVENCY (cont)—
    Debt relief order (cont)—
        Moratorium from qualifying debts—
            Assured tenancy—Arrears of rent—Landlord bringing possession proceedings against assured tenant—Assured tenant becoming subject to debt relief order—Prohibition during moratorium against remedy in respect of qualifying debt—Whether possession order could be made against tenant—Insolvency Act 1986, s 251G. **Sharples v Places for People Homes Ltd, Godfrey v A2 Dominion Homes Ltd** [2012] **1** 582, CA.
    Discharge—
        Generally. See **Bankruptcy** (Discharge).
        Discharge. See Bankruptcy—Discharge, *above*.
    Electronic money—
        Electronic money institutions required to safeguard funds received in exchange for electronic money—
            Electronic money institution placed into administration—Administrators unable to determine whether funds safeguarded—Administrators applying for directions as to distribution of funds—Whether funds held on implied statutory trust—Whether statutory protection extending to funds not safeguarded as required—Electronic Money Regulations 2011, SI 2011/99, regs 20-22, 24—European Parliament and Council Directive 2009/110/EC, art 7—European Parliament and Council Directive 2015/2366/EU, art 10. **ipagoo LLP (in admin), Re** [2022] **2 Comm** 813, CA.
    Employer—
        Protection of employees on employer's insolvency—
            European Union. See **European Union** (Employment—Protection of employees on employer's insolvency).
    European Economic Area (EEA)—
        Cross-border insolvency. See **Company** (Winding up—Cross-border insolvency).
    Evidence—
        Criminal proceedings—
            Admissibility at trial of bankrupt of incriminating statements made at public examination in bankruptcy. See **Criminal evidence** (Bankruptcy proceedings).
    Fraudulent trading—
        Bank knowingly participating in company's fraud—
            Court ordering bank to make contribution to company's assets—Jurisdiction of court to award interest as part of order—Insolvency Act 1986, s 213. **Bank of Credit and Commerce International SA (in liq), Re** [2005] **1 Comm** 209, QBD.
        Knowledge—
            Attribution—Company entering into arrangement with bank to deposit moneys with bank for fixed term to be used by bank to grant loan to another company nominated by company for same period—Bank entering into six transactions with company—Company entering into transactions with intent to defraud creditors—Chief manager of bank having approved transactions—Whether bank knowingly participated in fraud—Whether bank liable to contribute to losses to creditors of company—Insolvency Act 1986, s 213(2). **Bank of Credit and Commerce International SA (in liq), Re** [2005] **1 Comm** 209, QBD.
    Income payments orders—
        Jurisdiction of court. See Bankruptcy—Administration by trustee—Acquisition, control and realisation of bankrupt's estate—Income payments orders, *above*.
    Individual voluntary arrangement—
        Approval by creditors. See Voluntary arrangement—Approval by creditors—Creditors' meeting called to approve an individual voluntary agreement, *below*.
        Child support. See **Child** (Maintenance—Child support—Non-resident parent—Individual voluntary arrangement).
    Industrial and Provident Societies—
        Appointment of receiver. See **Industrial and provident societies** (Receiver).
    Inquiry as to bankrupt's dealings and property—
        Summons to persons capable of giving information—
            Solicitors acting for associate companies and wife of bankrupt subject to orders for oral examination in relation to bankrupt's affairs—Orders made ex parte by reference to confidential evidence not disclosed to solicitors—Solicitors applying for rescission or variation of orders—Availability of legal professional privilege—Whether solicitors entitled to disclosure of evidence—Whether trustee justified in proceeding ex parte—Insolvency Act 1986, s 366. **Murjani (a bankrupt), Re** [1996] **1** 65, Ch D.
    Insurance company—
        Liability of Motor Insurers' Bureau to compensate following insurer's insolvency. See **Motor insurance** (Motor Insurers' Bureau—Liability of bureau to compensate following insurer's insolvency).
    Judicial assistance—
        Cross-border insolvency. See Cross-border insolvency—Letter of request, *above*.
    Jurisdiction—
        Leave to commence proceedings—
            Proceedings against bankrupt begun issued after making of bankruptcy order—Leave of court not obtained to commencement of proceedings in accordance with statutory requirement—Whether court having jurisdiction to give retrospective leave—Insolvency Act 1986, s 285(3). **Saunders (a bankrupt), Re** [1997] **3** 992, Ch D.
            Proceedings against bankrupt begun issued after making of bankruptcy order—Leave of court not obtained to commencement of proceedings in accordance with statutory requirement—Whether proceedings a nullity—Insolvency Act 1986, s 285(3). **Taylor (a bankrupt), Re** [2007] **3** 638, Ch D.
        Stay of proceedings—
            Non-payment of rates—Committal order postponing issue of warrant on conditions—Debtor failing to comply with conditions—Debtor adjudicated bankrupt—Debtor obtaining order for stay of committal proceedings from bankruptcy court—Whether committal order intended to be punitive—Whether bankruptcy court having jurisdiction to stay committal proceedings—General Rate Act 1967, ss 102, 103(1)—Insolvency Act 1986, s 285(1). **Smith v Braintree DC** [1989] **3** 897, HL.
    Limitation of action—
        Bankruptcy proceedings. See **Limitation of action** (Bankruptcy proceedings).

INSOLVENCY (cont)—
  Liquidator—
    Power of liquidator—
      Inquiry into company's dealings—Statutory provision giving court power to require certain persons to produce books, papers or other company records—Liquidator applying for production order against respondent, identified as company's former bookkeeper—Respondent resident abroad in Republic of Ireland—Questions arising on jurisdiction of English court—Whether relevant provision having extraterritorial effect—Whether order sought to be granted—Civil Jurisdiction and Judgments Act 1982—Insolvency Act 1986, s 236—CPR 6.33(1)—Insolvency Rules 2016, SI 2016/1024—Council Regulation 1346/2000/EC, arts 3(1), 16—Lugano Convention 1988. **Wallace (as liquidator of Carna Meats (UK) Ltd) v Wallace** [2020] **1 Comm** 429, Ch D.
      Inquiry into company's dealings—Statutory provision giving court power to require certain persons to produce books, papers or other company records—Whether power having extra-territorial effect—Insolvency Act 1986, s 236(3)—Council Regulation 1346/2000/EC, art 3(1). **Akkurate Ltd (in liq), Re** [2021] **1 Comm** 1339, Ch D.
    Validity of appointment—
      Non-compliance with deemed consent procedure for creditors' nomination of liquidators—Notices not sent to purported creditor—Whether procedural irregularity on appointment of liquidator invalidating appointment—Insolvency Act 1986, ss 100, 246ZF—Insolvency (England and Wales) Rules 2016, SI 2016/1024. **Cash Generator Ltd v Fortune** [2018] **4** 325, Ch D.
  Lists—
    Practice. See **Practice** (Chancery Division—Bankruptcy—Lists).
  Matrimonial home—
    Generally. See **Bankruptcy** (Property available for distribution—Matrimonial home).
    Sale under trust for sale. See Property available for distribution—Matrimonial home—Sale under trust for sale, *below*.
  Order—
    Rescission—
      Jurisdiction of court—Discretion—Principles on which discretion should be exercised—Insolvency Act 1986, s 375(1). **Papanicola (as trustee in bankruptcy for Mak) v Humphreys** [2005] **2** 418, Ch D.
  Orders without attendance—
    Consent orders on inter partes applications—
      Applications to set aside statutory demand—Petitions—Other applications—Documents to be lodged with application—Adjournment—Time for lodging application—Correspondence not alternative to application—Insolvency Act 1986, Pt VIII (ss 252-263)—Insolvency Rules 1986, Sch 4, Form 6.21. **Practice Note** [1992] **2** 300, Ch D.
  Partnership—
    Insolvent partnership—
      Debtors only partners in business—Official Receiver making conjoined application in separate bankruptcies of two debtors—Partnership not wound up—Whether court having power to grant relief sought to wind up affairs of partnership and administer its property as if debtors had presented joint bankruptcy petition—Insolvency Act 1986, s 303(2A), (2B), (2C). **Official Receiver v Hollens** [2007] **3** 767, Ch D.
      Statutory demand—Service on individual as member of partnership—Amendment of prescribed form of statutory demand—Insolvent Partnerships Order 1986, Sch 3, Form 3. **Practice Direction** [1988] **2** 127, Ch D.
    Partnership members—
      Winding-up order made against partnership—Partners paying debt in respect of which petitions presented—Whether court required to make bankruptcy orders against individual partners because winding-up order has been made against partnership—Whether court can make bankruptcy order if debt has been paid—Insolvency Act 1986, s 271(1)(2A)—Insolvent Partnerships Order 1986. **Marr and anor (bankrupts), Re** [1990] **2** 880, CA.
  Petition—
    Compulsory winding up petition by Revenue—
      Disputed debt—Proposal by taxpayer company to pay tax as it fell due and arrears of tax in instalments—Collector of taxes stating that he would seek approval for the proposal from his superiors and would revert to taxpayer company if it was unacceptable—Whether Revenue's silence constituting acceptance—Whether collector having actual or ostensible authority to enter into agreement—Whether agreement supported by consideration—Whether Revenue estopped from presenting winding-up petition. **Selectmove Ltd, Re** [1995] **2** 531, CA.
    Conditions for presentation—
      Debtor carrying on business in England and Wales—Debtor selling business as going concern—Debts of business or liability for taxation remaining—Whether debtor continuing to carry on business even though business sold—Insolvency Act 1986, s 265(1)(c)(ii). **Debtor (No 784 of 1991), Re a, ex p the Debtor v IRC** [1992] **3** 376, Ch D.
      Debtor's petition—Order requiring payment of deposit as security for official receiver's fees prior to issue of petition—Applicant unable to afford deposit—Whether order ultra vires legislation conferring powers on Lord Chancellor to provide payment of deposit—Whether order abrogating applicant's constitutional right of access to courts or violating right to fair hearing—Insolvency Act 1986, s 415—Insolvency Fees Order 1986, arts 8(1), 9(b)—Convention for the Protection of Human Rights and Fundamental Freedoms, arts 6, 14. **R v Lord Chancellor, ex p Lightfoot** [1998] **4** 764, QBD; [1999] **4** 583, CA.
      Expedited bankruptcy petition—Statutory demand—Debtor applying to set aside statutory demand—Creditors presenting expedited bankruptcy petition on ground of serious possibility of jeopardy to debtor's property—Petition presented within three weeks of statutory demand—Whether petition valid—Insolvency Act 1986, ss 267(2)(c)(d), 268(1), 270—Insolvency Rules 1986, rr 6.8(2)(b)(ii), 7.55. **Debtor (No 22 of 1993), Re a** [1994] **2** 105, Ch D.
      Proof of debtor's inability to pay—Summary judgment for amount of debt—Attempted execution of writ of fi fa—Sheriff failing to gain access to debtor's premises—Whether execution properly returned as unsatisfied—Whether defect curable as procedural irregularity—Insolvency Act 1986, s 268(1)(b)—Insolvency Rules 1986, r 7.55. **Debtor (No 340 of 1992), Re a, ex p the Debtor v First National Commercial Bank plc** [1996] **2** 211, CA.

INSOLVENCY (cont)—
  Petition (cont)—
    Creditor's petition—
      Compulsory winding up of company. *See* **Company** (Compulsory winding up—Petition by creditor).

      Debt claimed—Only debt claimed may be included in petition. **Practice Direction** [1987] **3** 640, Fam D.

      Debts provable in bankruptcy—Whether order for costs in family proceedings a provable debt in bankruptcy—Circumstances in which bankruptcy order can be made on basis of non-provable debt—Insolvency Act 1986—Insolvency Rules 1986, rr 6.5(4)(d), 12.3(2)(a). **Levy v Legal Services Commission** [2001] **1** 895, CA.

      Dismissal. *See* Proceedings on creditor's petition—Dismissal of petition, *below*.

      Issue estoppel—Debtor applying to set aside statutory demand—Application dismissed because no substantial grounds on which debt could be disputed—Debtor appealing out of time—Judge adjourning hearing of petition to enable debtor to adduce further evidence—Whether dismissal of application to set aside creating estoppel on issue of debtor's liability—Whether court entitled to go behind issue estoppel and exercise discretion to adjourn petition—Insolvency Rules 1986, rr 6.5(4)(b), 6.25(1). **Eberhardt & Co Ltd v Mair** [1995] **3** 963, Ch D.

      New form of petition—Acceptance for filing—Insolvency Rules 1986, Sch 4, Forms 6.7, 6.8, 6.9. **Practice Direction** [1988] **2** 127, Ch D.

      New form of petition—Completion of form—Title—Debt claimed—Date of service of statutory demand—Certificate at end of petition—Deposit on petition—Insolvency Act 1986, ss 267-269—RSC Ord 65, r 7—Insolvency Rules 1986, rr 6.1(4), 6.3, 6.6-6.12, Sch 4, Forms 6.7-6.9. **Practice Direction** [1987] **1** 602, RPC.

      Petitioner seeking leave to withdraw petition—Change of carriage of petition—Insolvency Rules 1986, rr 6.31, 6.32. **Purvis, Re** [1997] **3** 663, Ch D.

      Proceedings on. *See* Proceedings on creditor's petition, *below*.

     Dismissal. *See* Proceedings on creditor's petition—Dismissal of petition, *below*.

     Extension of time for hearing—

      Failure to attend listed hearing—Costs—Relisting—Dismissal on relisted hearing—Statement to accompany application for extension of time—Attendance of petitioning creditor—Insolvency Rules 1986, r 6.28(3). **Practice Direction** [1992] **1** 704, Ch D.

    Partnership—

      Joint bankruptcy petition. *See* Partnership—Insolvent partnership—Debtors only partners in business, *above*.

    Service—

      Substituted service—Evidence required to justify order for substituted service—Deemed time of service where substituted service by post—Insolvency Rules 1986, rr 6.14, 6.15. **Practice Direction** [1987] **1** 604, Ch D.

  Practice—
    Individual insolvency—

      Applications—Applications to judge—Applications to registrar—Matters to be heard in open court—Listing of petitions—Applications to Chief Clerk—Bankruptcy Act 1914, ss 26(1), 108(1), 109(3), 129, Sch 1, para 1—Insolvency Act 1976, s 8(3)—Insolvency Act 1986, ss 268, 280, 293, 376—Regulations as to the Conduct of Business in Bankruptcy in the High Court (dated 1 January 1884)—Bankruptcy Rules 1952, rr 8, 21, 172(1), 188, 193, 218—Insolvency Rules 1986, rr 6.35, 6.50, 6.172, 6.216(2), 6.217(2), 7.13, 13.2(2). **Practice Direction** [1988] **3** 984, Ch D.

      Applications—Applications to judge—Applications to registrar—Matters to registrar—Matters to be heard in open court—Listing of petitions—Appeals and applications to Divisional Court—Bankruptcy judge—Ex parte applications—Urgent matters—Insolvency Act 1986, ss 268, 375(2)—Bankruptcy Rules 1952, r 8. **Practice Direction** [1987] **2** 1000, Ch D.

    Petition—

      Generally. *See* Petition, *above*.

  Proceedings on creditor's petition—
    Dismissal of petition—

      Creditor petitioning for debtor's bankruptcy—Supporting creditors being eligible to apply for change of carriage order—Debtor tendering payment of petition debt in full subject to petition being dismissed—Creditor refusing tender and court making bankruptcy order—Whether payment of petition debt from debtor's property precluding court from making bankruptcy order—Insolvency Act 1986, ss 271, 284—Insolvency Rules 1986, rr 6.30, 6.31. **Smith v Ian Simpson & Co (a firm)** [2000] **3** 434, CA.

      Voluntary arrangement proposed by debtor—Unreasonable refusal of offer—Debtor offering legal charges as security for payment to Revenue and Customs Commissioners as petitioning creditors—Revenue refusing offer of security—Whether unreasonable refusal—Insolvency Act 1986, s 271(3). **Ross v Revenue and Customs Comrs** [2010] **2** 126, Ch D.

      Voluntary arrangement proposed by debtor—Unreasonable refusal of offer—Whether offer to pay sole petitioning creditor less than half of debt constituted 'an offer to ... compound for a debt in respect of which the petition is presented'—Whether court having jurisdiction to dismiss petition on ground that petitioning creditor has unreasonably refused debtor's offer to compound for debt—Insolvency Act 1986, s 271(1)(3). **Debtor (No 32 of 1993), Re a** [1995] **1** 628, Ch D.

      Voluntary arrangement proposed by debtor—Unreasonable refusal of offer—Whether proposed voluntary arrangement 'an offer to secure or compound for a debt in respect of which the petition is presented'—Whether proposed voluntary arrangement to be treated as offer to each creditor capable of being accepted or refused by petitioning creditor—Whether court having jurisdiction to dismiss petition on ground that petitioning creditor has unreasonably refused proposal if he votes against it or fails to vote—Insolvency Act 1986, s 271(3). **Debtor (No 2389 of 1989), Re a, ex p Travel and General Insurance Co plc v The Debtor** [1990] **3** 984, Ch D.

INSOLVENCY (cont)—
Property available for distribution—
  Anti-deprivation rule—
    Pari passu principle—Interest rate swap transactions subject to master agreement—Condition precedent to payment obligations that no event of default with respect to other party—Payment obligation of non-defaulting party suspended indefinitely during period of event of default—Event of default triggered by insolvency—Whether suspension of payment obligation infringing anti-deprivation rule and pari passu principle—ISDA Master Agreement (Multicurrency—Cross Border) (1992 edn). **Lomas and ors (joint administrators of Lehman Brothers International (Europe)) v JFB Firth Rixson Inc (International Swaps and Derivatives Association Inc intervening)** [2012] **2 Comm** 1076, CA.
  Bankrupt receiving award from Criminal Injuries Compensation Board—
    Application for award made before bankruptcy order—Action by trustee in bankruptcy claiming award—Whether award part of bankrupt's estate at time of bankruptcy order—Whether award representing a future or contingent interest in 'property'—Insolvency Act 1986, ss 283, 436. **Campbell (a bankrupt), Re** [1996] **2** 537, Ch D.
  Matrimonial home—
    Sale under trust for sale—Equitable accounting between trustee in bankruptcy and co-owner left in occupation—Joint tenants—Husband leaving wife in sole occupation—Wife thereafter paying mortgage instalments and repairs and improvements—Husband made bankrupt and joint tenancy severed as a result—Trustee in bankruptcy obtaining orders for possession and sale—Date for commencement of equitable accounting between trustee and wife—Whether equitable accounting should include increased value resulting from wife's payments prior to bankruptcy—Whether occupation rent payable by wife should be set off against mortgage interest payments. **Pavlou (a bankrupt), Re** [1993] **3** 955, Ch D.
  Whether liquidators of insolvent insurance companies participating in pool behind front company entitled to claim percentage share of proceeds from reinsurance agreement. **North Atlantic Insurance Co Ltd v Nationwide General Insurance Co** [2004] **2 Comm** 351, CA.
Redundancy—
  Employer's duty to consult appropriate trade union—
    Insolvency as a circumstance rendering it not reasonably practicable to comply with duty. *See* **Redundancy** (Employer's duty to consult appropriate trade union—Special circumstances rendering it not reasonably practicable to comply with duty—Insolvency).
Service—
  Service out of jurisdiction—
    Company in compulsory liquidation—Public examination of officer of company—British person resident abroad—Whether court having jurisdiction to direct public examination of officer resident abroad and order service of process out of jurisdiction—Whether power to order public examination limited to persons in England at relevant time—Insolvency Act 1986, s 133. **Seagull Manufacturing Co Ltd (in liq), Re** [1993] **2** 980, CA.
    Statutory demand. *See* Statutory demand—Service—Service out of jurisdiction, *below*.
    Transaction at an undervalue—Claim by creditor against defendants with foreign domicile—Defendants owning vessel being held by creditor—Creditor seeking to set aside purported transaction made by defendants for sale of vessel—Creditor applying to serve proceedings out of jurisdiction—Whether court having power to order service out of jurisdiction of claim to set aside transaction at an undervalue—Insolvency Act 1986, s 423—CPR 6.36, 6.37—CPR PD 6B, paras 3.1(3), (20). **Orexim Trading Ltd v Mahavir Port and Terminal Private Ltd** [2019] **1 Comm** 15, CA.
    Transaction at undervalue—Office-holder of company seeking reversal of transaction entered into by company at undervalue—Whether court having jurisdiction to entertain application against foreign person resident abroad and order service of process out of jurisdiction—Insolvency Act 1986, s 238—Insolvency Rules 1986, r 12.12. **Paramount Airways Ltd, Re** [1992] **3** 1, CA.
    Whether leave to serve out of jurisdiction required—Whether method of service out of jurisdiction required to be in accordance with law of country where service to be effected. **Busytoday Ltd, Re** [1992] **4** 61, Ch D.
  Statutory demand. *See* Statutory demand—Service, *below*.
Set-off—
  Mutual dealings—
    Bankrupt's right of action against creditor—Creditor having counterclaim against bankrupt—Assignment by trustee in bankruptcy of right of action before taking of account—Whether trustee entitled to assign right of action to plaintiff bankrupt before account taken of mutual dealings with creditor—Insolvency Act 1986, s 323. **Stein v Blake** [1995] **2** 961, HL.
Statutory demand—
  Debt—
    Costs—Order for costs made in favour of assisted person—Whether court order creating judgment debt. **Debtor (No 68/5D/97), Re a** [1998] **4** 779, Ch D.
    Costs—Plaintiff appealing against decision to strike out proceedings against defendant—Defendant being made bankrupt before appeal heard but discharged before judgment in appeal—Court allowing plaintiff's appeal and making costs order against defendant in respect of pre-bankruptcy period—Plaintiff serving statutory demand for sum covered by costs order—Whether order for costs a contingent liability at commencement of bankruptcy—Insolvency Act 1986, s 382. **Glenister v Rowe** [1999] **3** 452, CA.
    Sum claimed expressed in foreign currency—Demand claiming higher sum than amount due and omitting claim for interest and costs—Whether statement of sterling equivalent required in demand—Whether demand causing injustice to debtor—Insolvency Act 1986, s 268(1)(a). **Debtor (No 51/SD/91), Re a, ex p Ritchie Bros Auctioneers v The Debtor** [1993] **2** 40, Ch D.
  Form of demand—
    Insolvent partnership. *See* Partnership—Insolvent partnership—Statutory demand, *above*.
    Local authority serving statutory demand bearing name of authority's chief legal officer—Officer not signing demand personally but his name entered by person authorised by him to do so—Whether creditor's agent having to sign statutory demand personally—Insolvency Rules 1986, r 6.1(1). **Horne, Re (a bankrupt)** [2000] **4** 550, CA.
    Prescribed form—Insolvency (Amendment) Rules 1987, Sch, Pt 5, s 1, Forms 6.1, 6.2, 6.3. **Practice Direction** [1988] **2** 127, Ch D.

INSOLVENCY (cont)—
 Statutory demand (cont)—
  Insolvent partnership. *See* Partnership—Insolvent partnership—Statutory demand, *above.*
  Service—
   Proof of service—Insolvency Rules 1986, r 6.11(3)(4)(5), Sch 4, Forms 6.11, 6.12. **Practice Direction** [1987] **1** 606, Ch D.
   Service out of jurisdiction—RSC Ord 11, rr 5, 6, 8—Insolvency Rules 1986, r 6.3(2). **Practice Direction** [1988] **2** 126, Ch D.
   Substituted service—Circumstances in which substituted service permissible—Methods of substituted service—Substituted service by post—Substituted service by advertisement—Form of advertisement—Deemed time of service where substituted service by post—Insolvency Rules 1986, rr 6.3, 6.11. **Practice Direction** [1987] **1** 604, Ch D.
  Setting aside statutory demand—
   Affidavit in support—Copies of documents to be lodged—Effect of not lodging required copies of documents—Circumstances in which statutory demand will be set aside—Extension of time to apply to set aside statutory demand—Insolvency Rules 1986, rr 6.4, 6.5, 7.4(1), Sch 4, Forms 6.4, 6.5. **Practice Direction** [1987] **1** 607, Ch D.
   Debt disputed on substantial grounds—Security in respect of debt—Debtor's claim against third party assigned to creditor—Whether security in respect of debt restricted to debts secured over debtor's property—Whether security in respect of debt including claim against third party assigned to creditor—Insolvency Act 1986, s 383(2)—Insolvency Rules 1986, rr 6.1(5), 6.5(4)(c). **Debtor (No 310 of 1988), Re a, ex p the Debtor v Arab Bank Ltd** [1989] **2** 42, Ch D.
   Dismissal of application to set aside statutory demand—Jurisdiction to review, rescind or vary order dismissing application to set aside statutory demand—Nature and extent of court's jurisdiction—Admissibility of fresh evidence—Whether court having jurisdiction to review, rescind or vary order dismissing application to set aside statutory demand—Whether fresh evidence admissible on application—Nature of fresh evidence which is admissible—Insolvency Act 1986, ss 267(2), 375(1). **Debtor (No 32/SD/91), Re a** [1993] **2** 991, Ch D.
   Dismissal of application to set aside statutory demand—Orders dismissing applications not containing statement that creditor having right to apply to have orders set aside, varied or stayed—Whether outstanding application to set aside statutory demand—Whether subsequent presentation of bankruptcy petition invalid—Insolvency Act 1986, s 267(2)(d)—Insolvency Rules 1986, SI 1986/1925, rr 6.5(1), 7.51A(2)—CPR 3.3(5). **Clarke v Cognita Schools Ltd (t/a Hydesville Tower School)** [2015] **2 Comm** 663, Ch D; [2016] **1** 477, Ch D.
   Grounds on which statutory demand may be set aside—Debt disputed on substantial grounds—Demand overstating amount of debt—Whether court having power to set aside demand if part of debt demanded is disputed—Insolvency Rules 1986, r 6.5(4)(b). **Debtor (No 490/SD/91), Re a, ex p the Debtor v Printline (Offset) Ltd** [1992] **2** 664, Ch D.
   Grounds on which statutory demand may be set aside—Debt disputed on substantial grounds—Whether court having power to set aside demand if part of debt demanded is disputed—Insolvency Rules 1986, r 6.5(4)(b). **Debtor (No 10 of 1988, Aylesbury), Re a, ex p Lovell Construction (Southern) Ltd v The debtor** [1989] **2** 39, Ch D.
   Grounds on which statutory demand may be set aside—Debt for liquidated sum—Whether statutory demand which did not specify figures used to calculate liquidated sum valid—Insolvency Act 1986, s 267—Insolvency Rules 1986, r 6.1(5). **Debtor (No 64 of 1992), Re a** [1994] **2** 177, Ch D.
   Grounds on which statutory demand may be set aside—Other grounds—Applicant being guarantor for company of which he was executive director and shareholder—Company being principal debtor to creditor in respect of rent—Company presenting claim against creditor equalling or exceeding amount of debt—Common ground that company likely to succeed in setting aside statutory demand for arrears of rent because of cross-claim exceeding amount of debt—Creditor serving statutory demand on applicant instead—Judge finding applicant able to pay—Judge refusing to set aside statutory demand—Whether judge in error—Insolvency Rules 1986, SI 1986/1925, r 6.5(4)(a), (d). **Remblance v Octagon Assets Ltd** [2010] **2** 688, CA.
   Grounds on which statutory demand may be set aside—Other grounds—Creditor refusing debtor's offer to secure or compound for debt—Debtor contending creditor's refusal unreasonable—Whether debtor entitled to have statutory demand set aside—Whether court will consider reasonableness of creditor's refusal of offer—Whether court will not consider reasonableness of creditor's refusal of offer until it comes to consider bankruptcy petition—Insolvency Act 1986, s 271(3)(c)—Insolvency Rules 1986, r 6.5(4)(d). **Debtor (No 415/SD/93), Re a, ex p the Debtor v IRC** [1994] **2** 168, Ch D.
   Grounds on which statutory demand may be set aside—Other grounds—Statutory demand deficient—Whether debtor prejudiced by deficiencies—Whether statutory demand containing deficiencies should be set aside—Insolvency Rules 1986, r 6.5(4)(d). **Debtor (No 1 of 1987, Lancaster), Re a, ex p the Debtor v Royal Bank of Scotland plc** [1989] **2** 46, CA.
 Stay of proceedings—
  Committal proceedings for non-payment of rates—
   Jurisdiction of bankruptcy court to stay committal proceedings. *See* Jurisdiction—Stay of proceedings—Non-payment of rates, *above.*
  Generally. *See* **Practice** (Stay of proceedings—Bankruptcy).
 Transaction at undervalue—
  Dividend—
   Wholly owned subsidiary paying dividend to holding company by way of set off for inter-company debt—Whether dividend 'transaction entered into at an undervalue'—Whether dividend paid for purpose of putting assets beyond reach of claimant or otherwise prejudicing its interests—Insolvency Act 1986, s 423(1), (3). **BTI 2014 LLC v Sequana SA** [2019] **2 Comm** 13, CA; [2019] **2** 784, CA.

INSOLVENCY (cont)—
Transaction at undervalue (cont)—
Linked transactions—
Company's assets including computer equipment held on lease—Purchaser wishing to buy company's business—Company transferring business to subsidiary and agreeing to transfer its shares in subsidiary to purchaser—Purchaser's parent company covenanting to pay rent to company for use of computer equipment—Whether parent company's covenant to be taken into account in determining whether shares sold at an undervalue—Whether covenant having any value—Insolvency Act 1986, s 238(4). **Phillips v Brewin Dolphin Bell Lawrie Ltd** [1999] **2** 844, CA; [2001] **1** 673, HL.
Property adjustment order in ancillary relief proceedings—
Whether transaction at undervalue—Whether receiving party giving consideration—Whether consideration in money or money's worth—Insolvency Act 1986, s 339(3)(a), (c). **Hill v Haines** [2008] **2** 901, CA.
Service out of jurisdiction. *See* Service—Service out of jurisdiction—Transaction at an undervalue, *above*.
Transaction for prohibited purpose—
Debtors' land and assets charged to bank—Debtors assigning tenancy of leased land for consideration of £1 to members of family—Debtors leasing freehold land to family members for annual rent payable in arrears—Whether transactions entered into at undervalue—Whether purpose of transactions to prejudice bank's interests—Insolvency Act 1986, s 423. **Barclays Bank plc v Eustice** [1995] **4** 511, CA.
Victim of transaction—Purpose of putting assets beyond reach of person making claim or otherwise prejudicing interests of such person—Nature of purpose—Whether 'victim' necessary—Insolvency Act 1986, s 423(1), (2), (3), (5). **Hill v Spread Trustee Co Ltd** [2007] **1** 1106, CA.
Transfer of matrimonial home to wife prior to divorce proceedings—
Wife assuming sole liability for mortgage—Husband made bankrupt—Whether transfer of husband's interest in matrimonial home to wife at undervalue—Whether wife's assumption of sole liability for mortgage sufficient consideration—Whether consideration provided by wife significantly less than value of husband's interest in matrimonial home—Insolvency Act 1986, s 339. **Kumar (a bankrupt), Re, ex p Lewis v Kumar** [1993] **2** 700, Ch D.
Trustee in bankruptcy. *See* **Bankruptcy** (Trustee in bankruptcy).
Voluntary arrangement—
Approval by creditors—
Creditor having claims against debtor for past and future rent under lease—Chairman of creditor's meeting putting minimum estimated value on future rent without creditor's agreement—Whether creditor bound by arrangement in respect of future rent—Whether material irregularity at meeting—Whether unfair prejudice to creditor's interests—Insolvency Act 1986, s 262—Insolvency Rules 1986, r 5.17. **Doorbar v Alltime Securities Ltd** [1996] **2** 948, CA.
Creditors' meeting called to approve an individual voluntary agreement—Part of debt assigned by associate of debtor to another creditor—Whether assignor or assignee entitled to vote at creditors' meeting—Whether 'material irregularity' arising at creditors' meeting if vote of creditor, who has taken an assignment from associate of debtor on uncommercial terms and for sole purpose of enabling assignee to vote in favour of individual voluntary arrangement, is taken into account—Whether principle of good faith between debtors and creditors applicable—Insolvency Act 1986, s 262(1)(b)—Insolvency Rules 1986, SI 1986/1925, rr 5.21(2)(a), 5.23(4). **Kapoor v National Westminster Bank plc** [2012] **1** 1201, CA.
Notice of creditors' meeting sent but not received by creditor—Whether creditor deemed to have received constructive notice of meeting—Whether creditor bound by voluntary arrangement—Insolvency Act 1986, ss 257, 260(2)—Insolvency Rules 1986, r 12.16. **Debtor (No 64 of 1992), Re a** [1994] **2** 177, Ch D.
Company—
Future or contingently payable debt—Landlord creditor having claims against company for accrued rent and future rent payable on unexpired term of lease—Proposals for voluntary arrangement providing that future rent claimable only under its terms—Landlord given indication as to likely valuation of claim—Landlord voting against proposals by proxy at creditors' meeting—Voluntary arrangment approved—Whether creditor bound by voluntary arrangement in respect of future or contingently payable debt—Meaning of 'creditor'—Whether value of unliquidated debt required to be agreed with creditor—Insolvency Act 1986, s 5—Insolvency Rules 1986, rr 1.17, 5.17. **Cancol Ltd, Re** [1996] **1** 37, Ch D.
Whether liquidation terminating trusts created by voluntary arrangement—Insolvency Act 1986, Pt I. **Gallagher (NT) & Son Ltd (in liq), Re** [2002] **3** 474, CA.
Interim order—
Continuation—Creditor's meeting serving no useful purpose—Whether court having discretion to refuse to continue interim order if creditors' meeting would serve no useful purpose or further extension of time would unduly prejudice creditors—Whether court having discretion to discharge directions for convening creditors' meeting—Insolvency Act 1986, ss 252, 257(1), 262(7). **Cove (a debtor), Re** [1990] **1** 949, Ch D.
Creditors' meeting—Voting in respect of voluntary arrangements—Proxies sent by fax—Creditor transmitting to chairman's office by fax completed form of proxy—Chairman declining to act on faxed voting instructions—Whether faxed document a form of proxy 'signed by the principal'—Whether faxed proxy valid—Insolvency Rules 1986, r 8.2(3). **Debtor (No 2021 of 1995), Re a, ex p IRC v The Debtor** [1996] **2** 345, Ch D.
Order without attendance—
Cases suitable for making orders without attendance of either party—14-day interim order—Order on consideration of nominee's report—'Concertina' order—Final order on consideration of chairman's report—Attendance or representation not normally required at adjourned hearing for consideration of nominee's or chairman's report—Sealed copy of order to be posted to applicant or solicitor and nominee—New procedure not intended to dicourage attendance—Filing of documents—Insolvency Act 1986, Pt VIII, s 256(1)—Insolvency Rules 1986, rr 5.10(2)(3), 5.22(2). **Practice Direction** [1992] **1** 678, Ch D.

INSOLVENCY (cont)—

Voluntary arrangement (cont)—

Solvent co-debtors—

Effect of arrangement on solvent co-debtors—Plaintiff shareholders sureties under lease taken by company—Plaintiffs selling shares and purchasers agreeing to indemnify them against claims under lease—Plaintiffs meeting claims under lease and seeking indemnity from purchasers—Individual purchaser entering into voluntary arrangement with creditors—Plaintiffs given notice of creditors' meeting—Whether arrangement extinguishing liability of solvent co-debtors to plaintiffs—Whether arrangement releasing co-debtors from debt by operation of law. **Johnson v Davies** [1998] **2** 649, CA.

Subsequent bankruptcy order—

Individual voluntary arrangement proposed by debtor—Arrangement approved by creditors including bankrupts former wife—Bankruptcy order based on petition for debt incurred after approval of arrangement subsequently made against debtor—Whether bankruptcy order bringing voluntary arrangement to an end—Whether supervisor holding funds on trust for creditors under arrangement or whether funds forming part of estate in bankruptcy—Whether bankrupts former wife bound by and party to arrangement—Whether former wifes claims under orders for financial ancillary relief in divorce proceedings ranking for dividend in voluntary arrangement—Insolvency Act 1986, ss 260(2)(b), 382(1)(b)—Insolvency Rules 1986, r 5.17(3). **Bradley-Hole (a bankrupt), Re** [1995] **4** 865, Ch D.

Unfair prejudice to creditor's interests—

Creditor having potential rights against debtor's insurers—Approval of voluntary arrangement by other creditors—Arrangement impairing rights of creditor—Whether arrangement causing unfair prejudice to creditor's interests—Meaning of 'creditor'—Insolvency Act 1986, s 262. **Sea Voyager Maritime Inc v Bielecki (t/a Hughes Hooker & Co)** [1999] **1** 628, Ch D.

Creditor in same position as other creditors—Creditor challenging validity of debts voted in favour of voluntary arrangement—Whether arrangement causing unfair prejudice to creditor's interests—Insolvency Act 1986, s 262. **Debtor (No 259 of 1990), Re a** [1992] **1** 641, Ch D.

Unreasonable refusal of offer. *See* Proceedings on creditor's petition—Dismissal of petition—Voluntary arrangement proposed by debtor, *above*.

Variation—

Individual voluntary arrangement containing no power to vary terms—Applicant creditor waiving right to dividend in voluntary arrangement—Other creditors agreeing to variation of voluntary arrangement—Applicant challenging variation—Whether voluntary arrangement could be varied without express power of variation—Insolvency Act 1986, s 263(3). **Raja v Rubin** [1999] **3** 73, CA.

INSPECTOR

Appointment—

Board of Trade investigation into affairs of company. *See* **Company** (Investigation by Board of Trade—Appointment of inspectors).

Evidence before—

Board of Trade investigation into affairs of company. *See* **Company** (Investigation by Board of Trade—Evidence before inspectors).

Health and safety inspector—

Negligence—

Duty to take care. *See* **Negligence** (Duty to take care—Existence of duty—Health and safety inspector).

Remuneration—

Income tax. *See* **Income tax** (Emoluments from office or employment—Office—Inspector appointed to hold public local inquiry).

INSULTING BEHAVIOUR

Generally. *See* **Criminal law** (Insulting behaviour).

Offensive conduct conducive to breaches of peace. *See* **Public order** (Offensive conduct conducive to breaches of peace—Threatening, abusive or insulting words or behaviour).

INSURANCE

Accident insurance—

Condition—

Notice of proceedings—Notification to insurers—Policy requiring immediate notification to insurers of proceedings against insured—Failure to give notification of proceedings—Plaintiff obtaining judgment in default against insured—Whether insurers liable to pay adjudged sum notwithstanding insured's failure to give notification of proceedings before judgment—Whether insurers required to show prejudice in order to rely on breach of notification condition—Third Parties (Rights Against Insurers) Act 1930, s 1. **Pioneer Concrete (UK) Ltd v National Employers Mutual General Insurance Association Ltd** [1985] **2** 395, QBD.

Exception clause—

Age limit for personal injuries—Exclusion of personal injuries sustained by insured if over the age of sixty-five years—Personal injuries—Insured aged sixty-five years, seven months. **Lloyds Bank Ltd v Eagle Star Insurance Co Ltd** [1951] **1** 914, KBD.

Exclusion of liability if it resulted from deliberate exposure to exceptional danger—Exclusion of liability if it resulted from insured's own criminal act—Voluntary consumption of alcohol before driving motor car—Alcohol impairing insured's judgment—Insured driving car negligently at excessive speed and crashing into railings—Immediate cause of crash negligent driving—Predisposing cause consumption of alcohol—Whether death resulting from 'deliberate' exposure to risk of crash—Whether death resulting from insured's 'criminal act'—Whether criminal act limited to crime of moral turpitude—Whether insured's road traffic offences 'criminal act'. **Marcel Beller Ltd v Hayden** [1978] **3** 111, QBD.

Exclusion of liability if it resulted from wilful exposure to needless peril—Deceased jumping onto bumper of stationary or barely moving car—Driver driving off in zig-zag fashion at 15 to 20 mph—Deceased thrown off car and sustaining fatal injuries—Whether deceased wilfully exposing himself to needless peril—Whether exclusion clause applying to exclude liability. **Morley v United Friendly Insurance plc** [1993] **3** 47, CA.

INSURANCE (cont)—
  Accident insurance (cont)—
    Exception clause (cont)—
      Influence of intoxicating liquor—Exclusion of liability if injury sustained 'whilst under the influence of intoxicating liquor'—Whether the word 'whilst' connoted a casual connexion—What state was predicated by the words 'under the influence of intoxicating liquor'. **Louden v British Merchants Insurance Co Ltd** [1961] **1** 705, QBD.
    Perils insured against—
      Accidental injury resulting in death—Causation—Voluntary consumption of alcohol before driving motor car—Alcohol impairing insured's judgment—Insured driving car negligently at excessive speed and crashing into railings—Immediate cause of accident negligent driving—Predisposing cause consumption of alcohol—Whether death resulting from 'accidental'injury—Whether immediate cause of death to be regarded in isolation from predisposing cause. **Marcel Beller Ltd v Hayden** [1978] **3** 111, QBD.
      Accidental injury resulting in death—Causation—Whether asphyxia caused by inhalation of vomit following deliberate excessive drinking amounting to bodily injury—Whether resulting death caused by accidental means. **Dhak v Insurance Co of North America (UK) Ltd** [1996] **2** 609, CA.
      Accident—Public policy—Hearth and home policy—Liability to third parties—Extent of cover—Public policy precluding claim—Death resulting from insured threatening violence with loaded gun—No intention to cause death or injury—First shot deliberately fired into ceiling to frighten deceased—Second shot resulting in death involuntarily fired when insured fell down staircase while grappling with deceased—Whether death caused by 'accident'—Public policy precluding claim for accident arising from threatening violence with gun—Insured not entitled to indemnity in respect of damages claimed by deceased's dependants. **Gray v Barr (Prudential Assurance Co Ltd, third party)** [1971] **2** 949, CA.
      Causation—Accident whilst riding in, mounting into, or dismounting from car—Car accident causing concussion—Insured walking into river while in such state—Independency of accident and death. **Smith v Cornhill Insurance Co Ltd** [1938] **3** 145, KBD.
      Company insured under personal injury accident policy in respect of death of director—Insured event being accident occurring during journey undertaken on insured's behalf—Claim under policy in respect of deaths of two directors—Whether directors' journey had been on insured's behalf—Whether necessary to show that one of two purposes for journey predominated over the other. **Killick v Rendall** [2000] **2 Comm** 57, CA.
      Demolition—Liability to third parties—Use of explosives—Warranty—Change of risk. **Beauchamp v National Mutual Indemnity Insurance Co Ltd** [1937] **3** 19, KBD.
      Subsidence or collapse of building—Construction of policy—Meaning of 'subsidence' and 'collapse'. **Allen (David) & Sons Billposting Ltd v Drysdale** [1939] **4** 113, KBD.
  Policy of insurance effected by any man on his own life—
    Moneys payable on disablement or death—Married Women's Property Act 1882, s 11. **Gladitz, Re** [1937] **3** 173, Ch D.
  Admiralty proceedings—
    Arrested property. *See* **Admiralty** (Practice—Insurance—Arrested property).
  After-the-event (ATE) insurance premium—
    Costs—
      Jurisdiction. *See* **Costs** (Order for costs—Jurisdiction—After-the-event (ATE) insurance premium).
  All risks insurance—
    Consequential loss policy—
      Construction—Policy covering loss of anticipated rent arising from damage to property used by insured property developers for purposes of business—Policy containing material damage proviso requiring insurance of insured's interest in the property—Fire destroying site office and architects' drawings—Resulting delay in completion of project and loss of rental income—Whether loss arising from damage to property used by insured for purposes of its business—Whether insured having an insurable interest in drawings—Whether proviso operating to exclude indemnity. **Glengate-KG Properties Ltd v Norwich Union Fire Insurance Society Ltd** [1996] **2** 487, CA.
    Contractors' all risks policy—
      Construction—Contract between contractor and principal assured providing for scope of cover to be effected in respect of contractor—Whether contractor entitled to co-extensive cover. **BP Exploration Operating Co Ltd v Kvaerner Oilfield Products Ltd (Cooper Cameron (UK) Ltd, Pt 20 defendant)** [2004] **2 Comm** 266, QBD.
      Construction—Insurers seeking to exercise right of subrogation against third and fourth parties—Whether assured could sue co-assured for loss where co-assured was entitled to benefit of same insurance. **Co-operative Retail Services Ltd v Taylor Young Partnership Ltd (Tarmac Construction (Contracts) Ltd (formerly Wimpey Construction UK Ltd), third parties)(Genergy plc (formerly Dale Power Systems plc), fourth party)(Flue-Stox Engineering Ltd, fifth party)** [2000] **1 Comm** 721, QBD.
      Construction—Policy to indemnify insured including contractors and sub-contractors—Insurance policy taken out by head contractors to cover risk to all contractors and sub-contractors—Loss resulting from negligence of defendants engaged by sub-contractors of head contractor—Insurers seeking to exercise right of subrogation against defendants—Whether defendants acting as sub-contractors—Whether sub-contractors insured in respect of whole contract works or only in respect of own property—Whether nature of interest insured insurance of property or only insurance against liability in respect of other parties on site. **Petrofina (UK) Ltd v Magnaload Ltd** [1983] **3** 35, QBD.
  Marince insurance. *See* **Marine insurance** (Perils insured against—All risks).
  Policy covering property whilst in bank—
    Prior advice of removal—Extension of cover given for period when property not in bank subject to prior advice to broker of intention to remove from bank custody—Policy covering jewellery—Broker knowing jewellery not in bank at inception of policy—Loss of jewellery—Underwriters' liability—Whether necessary for jewellery first to be placed in bank before underwriters on risk—Whether prior advice deemed to have been given to broker. **Jaglom v Excess Insurance Co Ltd** [1972] **1** 267, QBD.
  Property insurance. *See* Property insurance—Perils insured against—All risks, *below*.

INSURANCE (cont)—
  Arbitration clause—
    Conflict of laws. *See* **Conflict of laws** (Contract—Arbitration clause—Claim on insurance policy made on Bermuda form).
  Assessor—
    Appointment—
      Appointment by broker at request of insurer. **Anglo-African Merchants Ltd v Bayley** [1969] **2** 421, QBD; **North and South Trust Co v Berkeley** [1971] **1** 980, QBD.
  Aviation insurance—
    Condition—
      Breach of condition—Onus of proof. **Bond Air Services Ltd v Hill** [1955] **2** 476, QBD.
    Contract of insurance—
      Construction of contract—Claimant losing aircraft and spare parts in Iraqi invasion—Claimant subsequently recovering some aircraft and spare parts—Claimant claiming loss from insurers—Whether claimant entitled to retain recoveries sufficient to indemnify losses on an overall basis—Whether claimant's recoveries to be valued in accordance with market value or value listed in policy. **Kuwait Airways Corp v Kuwait Insurance Co SAK** [2000] **1 Comm** 182, QBD.
    War risks—
      Plaintiff airline insuring against war risks and seizure—Spare parts cover extending to seizure risk but not war risk—Policy providing for recovery of sue and labour costs—Foreign invader taking aircraft and spare parts belonging to plaintiff airline—Whether plaintiff could recover for lost spare parts—Whether plaintiff could recover sue and labour costs. **Kuwait Airways Corp v Kuwait Insurance Co SAK** [1999] **1 Comm** 481, HL.
  Bankers' policy—
    Policy protecting against theft on bank premises—
      Scope of policy—Chairman of company committing theft of security documents deposited by company with bank as security for credit line—Chairman persuading bank to release documents in return for alternative security to be delivered to bank later—Documents delivered to junior employee of company on bank's premises—Alternative security never delivered to bank—Bank's securities subject of theft—Whether theft occurring on bank's premises—Whether loss caused by theft recoverable under bankers' policy. **Deutsche Genossenschaftsbank v Burnhope** [1995] **4** 717, HL.
  Broker—
    Appointment of assessors by broker at request of insurer—
      Non-disclosure to assured—Breach of duty by broker. **Anglo-African Merchants Ltd v Bayley** [1969] **2** 421, QBD; **North and South Trust Co v Berkeley** [1971] **1** 980, QBD.
    Commission. *See* **Agent** (Commission—Effective cause—Insurance).
    Duty—
      Bank obtaining through brokers composite insurance with owner of charged property—Insurers repudiating liability on grounds of non-disclosure by owner—Whether brokers in breach of duty of care to bank in failing to ensure inclusion of mortgagee protection clause in policy. **FNCB Ltd v Barnet Devanney & Co Ltd** [1999] **2 Comm** 233, CA.
      Commercial combined policy of insurance—Policy grossly undervaluing stock, machinery and business of insured company—Whether broker failing to properly advise insured as to type and scope of cover needed—Whether broker under duty to read documents sent by insured after inception and identify potential coverage issues. **Eurokey Recycling Ltd v Giles Insurance Brokers Ltd** [2015] **2 Comm** 55, QBD.
      Completion of proposal form—Broker completing form on basis of information supplied by client—Duty of broker to record accurately answers to questions given by client—Mis-statement in form due to slip or misunderstanding—Client invited to check completed form before signing it—Client glancing through form and failing to notice mis-statement—Consequent repudiation of liability by insurers on claim made under policy—Whether broker in breach of duty to complete form accurately—Whether failure of client to notice error sole and effective cause of loss. **O'Connor v BDB Kirby & Co (a firm)** [1971] **2** 1415, CA.
      Delay in forwarding cover note to insured—No cover obtained against loss sustained before cover note received. **United Mills Agencies Ltd v Harvey (RE) Bray & Co** [1952] **1** 225, KBD.
      Duty to assignee of insurance policy—Policy insuring bank against non-payment of letters of credit confirmed by bank for customer—Brokers placing insurance with underwriters—Bank claiming under policies—Underwriters denying liability—Bank claiming against brokers—Whether contractual relationship between bank and brokers—Whether brokers owing bank duty of care. **Punjab National Bank v de Boinville** [1992] **3** 104, CA.
      Duty to principal—Effect of custom. *See* **Agent** (Duty to principal—Effect of custom—Acts inconsistent with duty to principal—Acts in accordance with long standing practice—Insurance brokers).
      Failure to insure clients against employers' liability—Accident through employers' negligence and breach of statutory duty—Employers held liable for damages—Action by employers against brokers—Defence that no damage suffered because insurers could have set up breach of condition in projected policy—Condition that employer should take reasonable precautions to prevent accidents—Need for breach of condition to be reckless to afford defence—Need to show that insurers would have repudiated liability on policy. **Fraser v B N Furman (Productions) Ltd** [1967] **3** 57, CA.
      Plaintiff instructing defendant brokers to obtain fire insurance for nightclub premises—Defendant instructing Lloyd's brokers to obtain quotation from underwriters—Lloyd's brokers providing quotation including auditorium warranty—Lloyd's brokers placing insurance on terms of quotation—Fire damaging plaintiff's premises—Underwriters disclaiming liability because of breach of auditorium warranty—Plaintiff suing defendant for allegedly failing to explain auditorium warranty—Defendant contending that Lloyd's brokers had duty to advise plaintiff about warranty—Whether Lloyd's brokers having duty to advise plaintiff. **Pangood Ltd v Barclay Brown & Co Ltd (Bradstock Blunt & Thompson Ltd, third party)** [1999] **1 Comm** 460, CA.
      Policy wording not permitting aggregation of related claims by separate claimants—Whether broker in breach of duty in proffering to insured. **Standard Life Assurance Ltd v Oak Dedicated Ltd** [2008] **2 Comm** 916, QBD.

INSURANCE (cont)—
    Broker (cont)—
        Duty (cont)—
            Post-placement duty—Broker placing risk with insurer and then placing back-to-back reinsurance with reinsurers on behalf of insurer—Whether broker under duty after placement of risk to draw insurer's attention to information having a material and potentially deleterious effect on insurance cover. **HIH Casualty and General Insurance Ltd v JLT Risk Solutions Ltd** [2007] **2 Comm** 1106, CA.
        Negligence—
            Limitation of action. *See* **Limitation of action** (Accrual of cause of action—Negligence—Brokers).
        Registration—
            Application for registration—Application on ground that applicant has 'carried on' business as an insurance broker for prescribed period—Whether applicant required to have adequate practical experience in work of insurance broking—Insurance Brokers (Registration) Act 1977, s 3(1)(c)-(g). **Pickles v Insurance Brokers Registration Council** [1984] **1** 1073, QBD.
            Application for registration—Refusal of application—Powers of court—RSC Ord 55, r 3(1). **Pickles v Insurance Brokers Registration Council** [1984] **1** 1073, QBD.
        Slip tendered to underwriters by broker—
            Underwriters' liability—Effect of amendments made to slip by subsequent underwriters—Basis on which underwriters agreeing to take a line. **Jaglom v Excess Insurance Co Ltd** [1972] **1** 267, QBD.
        Underwriting agency agreement—
            Agreement placing obligation on broker to manage run-off—Broker terminating agreement—Underwriter asserting right to manage run-off—Whether broker having right to manage run-off contrary to underwriter's wishes. **Temple Legal Protection Ltd v QBE Insurance (Europe) Ltd** [2010] **1 Comm** 703, CA.
    Burglary—
        Intruder alarm condition—
            Construction of contract terms. *See* Contract of insurance—Construction of terms—Retail and wholesale policy—Intruder alarm condition, *below*.
    Burglary insurance—
        Claim—
            Repudiation of claim without repudiation of policy by insurance company. **West v National Motor and Accident Insurance Union Ltd** [1955] **1** 800, CA.
        Risk—
            Description of risk—Clause relating to theft while van in garage—Meaning of garage. **Barnett and Block v National Parcels Insurance Co Ltd** [1942] **2** 55, CA.
    C i f contract. *See* **Sale of goods** (C i f contract—Insurance).
    Capital gains tax—
        Rights of insured under policy of insurance. *See* **Capital gains tax** (Insurance policies—Rights of insured under policy of insurance).
    Church property—
        Movables. *See* **Ecclesiastical law** (Insurance—Property of parish church—Movables).
    Civil and environmental engineer—
        Professional indemnity insurance. *See* Liability insurance—Professional indemnity insurance—Civil and environmental engineer, *below*.
    Claim—
        Compromise of—
            Mistake as to validity of claim. *See* **Mistake** (Agreement to compromise—Mistake as to validity of claim).
        Conflict of laws. *See* **Conflict of laws** (Damages—Assessment—Direct claim against insurer).
        Fraud—
            Effect of fraud on moneys paid under policy prior to perpetration of fraud—Insurance policy containing clause forfeiting benefit under policy if claim made fraudulently—Claimant insurance company and defendant agreeing to compromise of defendant's insurance claim—Settlement moneys to be paid in interim and final payments—Final payment subject to satisfaction of condition precedent—Defendant asserting falsely that condition satisfied—Whether all benefit under policy forfeited. **Direct Line Insurance plc v Fox** [2009] **1 Comm** 1017, QBD.
            Effect of fraud on moneys paid under policy prior to perpetration of fraud—Whether whole of claim to which fraud related forfeit—Whether different claims not subject to fraud under same policy forfeit. **Axa General Insurance Ltd v Gottlieb** [2005] **1 Comm** 445, CA.
        Liability—
            Contract providing payment of premiums as a condition precedent to any liability—Contract entitling insurer to retain premium and terminate all liability following breach of condition precedent—Insured breaching policy and insurers serving notice terminating agreement—Whether insured could recover on claim made after service of notice—Whether insurers could recover money paid in satisfaction of claim made before breach. **Kazakstan Wool Processors (Europe) Ltd v Nederlandsche Credietverzekering Maatschappij NV** [2000] **1 Comm** 708, CA.
            Policy containing condition limiting time period for claims—Insured claiming under policy—Insurer alleging fraud by insured—Whether allegation of fraud precluding insurer from relying on limitation condition—Whether negotiations over claim between insurer and insured continuing beyond time period consituting waiver of condition by insurer or estoppel. **Super Chem Products Ltd v American Life and General Insurance Co Ltd** [2004] **1 Comm** 713, PC; [2004] **2** 358, PC.
            Policy containing condition precedent requiring insured to give notice in writing to insurer 'as soon as possible after the occurrence of any event likely to give rise to a claim'—Insured claiming under policy—Insurer declining cover on ground that insured failing to comply with condition precedent—Whether insurer entitled to rely upon condition as ground for denying liability. **Zurich Insurance plc v Maccaferri Ltd** [2018] **1 Comm** 112, CA.
        Notice—
            Condition—Employer's liability. *See* Employer's liability insurance—Condition—Notice of claim, *below*.
        Particulars—
            Fire insurance. *See* Fire insurance—Condition—Particulars of claim, *below*.

INSURANCE (cont)—
  Claim (cont)—
    Repudiation—
      Burglary insurance. *See* Burglary insurance—Claim—Repudiation of claim without repudiation of
        policy by insurance company, *above*.
  Claim by insurer—
    Conflict of laws. *See* **Conflict of laws** (Jurisdiction—Challenge to jurisdiction—Claim by insurer).
  Commission—
    Professional indemnity insurance—
      Trust. *See* **Trust and trustee** (Profit from trust—Account of profits—Commission—Professional
        indemnity insurance).
  Company—
    Information sharing—
      European community rules on competition, contrary to. *See* **European Union** (Rules on
        competition—Agreements preventing, restricting or distorting competition—Insurance com-
        panies entering information sharing agreements).
    Loans by—
      Annual payments for income tax purposes. *See* **Income tax** (Annual payment—Annuity—Monthly
        loans by insurance company).
    Winding up. *See* **Company** (Insurance company—Winding up).
  Compromise of claim—
    Mistake as to validity of claim. *See* **Mistake** (Agreement to compromise—Mistake as to validity of
      claim).
  Compulsory insurance—
    Third party risks, against—
      Motor insurance. *See* **Motor insurance** (Compulsory insurance against third party risks).
  Conflict of laws—
    Jurisdiction. *See* **Conflict of laws** (Jurisdiction—Challenge to jurisdiction—Insurance proceedings).
  Contingency insurance—
    Risk—
      Description of risk—Cover against non-receipt of money within a given time—Money received after
        time expired—Right to subrogation. **Meacock v Bryant & Co** [1942] **2** 661, KBD.
  Contract of insurance—
    Challenge to jurisdiction. *See* **Conflict of laws** (Jurisdiction—Challenge to jurisdiction—Insurance
      contract).
    Commercial inclusive policy—
      Insurance policy containing separate sections providing different types of cover—Plaintiff selecting
        fire and theft sections—Theft section including burglar alarm warranty—Plaintiff breaching
        burglar alarm warranty—Plaintiff making claim under fire section—Whether breach of burglar
        alarm warranty discharged insurers' liability under fire section. **Printpak (a firm) v AGF Insurance
        Ltd** [1999] **1 Comm** 466, CA.
    Construction—
      Marine insurance. *See* **Marine insurance** (Policy—Construction).
    Construction of terms—
      Aviation insurance. *See* Aviation insurance—Contract of insurance—Construction of contract,
        above.
      Business interruption insurance—Cover including losses resulting from policy list of infectious
        diseases—COVID-19 not appearing on list—Claim made for losses resulting from COVID-19—
        Insurer applying to strike out claim on basis infectious disease list closed and
        exhaustive—Whether COVID-19 included within scope of specific diseases listed—Whether policy
        intended to cover highly infectious or contagious diseases even if not listed—CPR 3.4, 24.2.
        Rockliffe Hall Ltd v Travelers Insurance Co Ltd [2022] **1 Comm** 723, Comm Ct.
      Business loss insurance—Disease clauses—Prevention of access clauses—Hybrid clauses—Trends
        clauses—Causation—Claims made as result of COVID-19 pandemic and resulting public health
        measures—Test case—Proper approach to construction of various clauses—Proper approach to
        establishing proximate cause of loss. **Financial Conduct Authority v Arch Insurance (UK) Ltd**
        [2021] **2 Comm** 779, SC; [2021] **3** 1077, SC.
      Claims co-operation conditions—Provision of information and documents—Conditions imposing
        no express time limit—Whether reasonable time requirement to be implied into terms—Whether
        prejudice caused to insurer relevant to question of fact as to reasonableness of time taken to
        comply with condition. **Shinedean Ltd v Alldown Demolition (London) Ltd (in liq)** [2006] **1
        Comm** 224, QBD; [2006] **2 Comm** 982, CA.
      Combined contract works and third party liability insurance—Damage to property—Damage to
        punched windows installed by sub-contractor—Whether sub-contractor entitled to an indemnity.
        Seele Austria GmbH & Co KG v Tokio Marine Europe Insurance Ltd [2009] **1 Comm** 171, CA.
      Combined contract works and third party liability insurance—Perils insured against—Flood and
        bursting of pipes—Very significant quantity of water escaping on building site—Whether escape
        of water amounting to flood and/or bursting of pipe. **Board of Trustees of the Tate Gallery v Duffy
        Construction Ltd** [2007] **1 Comm** 1004, TCC.
      Condition precedent—Condition in liability insurance imposing notification requirements of
        occurrence that could give rise to indemnity—Policy providing that insurers' liability conditional
        on insured observing terms and conditions of insurance—Whether notification requirements
        being condition precedent—Whether defendant complying with condition precedent. **Aspen
        Insurance UK Ltd v Pectel Ltd** [2009] **2 Comm** 873, QBD.
      Condition precedent—Condition stating that no claim to be payable unless condition complied with
        not described in policy as condition precedent—Other condition of policy described as condition
        precedent—Whether condition was a condition precedent. **George Hunt Cranes Ltd v Scottish
        Boiler & General Insurance Co Ltd** [2002] **1 Comm** 366, CA.

INSURANCE (cont)—
  Contract of insurance (cont)—
    Construction of terms (cont)—

      Condition precedent—Jewellers claiming under policy for alleged theft of valuable ring—Condition precedent that insured provide such information as insurers 'may reasonably require and may be in the insured's power'—Insured, on police advice, retaining footage from only one CCTV camera—Whether condition precedent requiring insured to ask insurers if they required all CCTV footage—Whether insured in breach of condition precedent in not retaining footage and providing it to insurers. **Widefree Ltd (t/a Abrahams & Ballard) v Brit Insurance Ltd** [2010] **2 Comm** 477, QBD.

      Contract of insurance providing that failure to comply with any warranty shall invalidate claim for loss 'wholly or partly due to or affected by such failure to comply'—Contract further providing that policies not invalidated by act or omission unknown to assured or beyond his control—Whether assured could claim for loss not wholly or partly due to breach of warranty if some loss caused by breach—Whether non-invalidation clause applicable to breach of warranty—Whether non-invalidation clause applicable to misrepresentation. **Seashell of Lisson Grove Ltd v Aviva Insurance Ltd** [2012] **1 Comm** 754, QBD.

      Contractors all risks policy—Improvement works planned for building—Claim made in respect of fire damage to building—Judge finding works insured but not building—Court of Appeal reversing judge's decision—Whether building insured. **Sun Alliance (Bahamas) Ltd v Scandi Enterprises Ltd (Bahamas)** [2017] **2 Comm** 1019, PC.

      Credit default insurance—Assured providing finance to sub-prime customers to purchase motor vehicles—Customer having option to purchase add-on insurance—Assured giving customer credit for insurance premiums—Credit default insurance containing underwriting criterion of maximum advance—Whether customer insurance premiums to be taken into account in calculating maximum advance. **College Credit Ltd v The National Guarantee Corp Ltd** [2004] **2 Comm** 409, QBD.

      Credit indemnity insurance—Bank insured in event of 'bankruptcy' event including counterparty bankruptcy—Debtor seeking to open 'procédure de sauvegarde' in French court—Bank seeking to terminate credit agreement—French court opening 'procédure de sauvegarde'—Whether counterparty bankruptcy occurring—Whether bank entitled to terminate and validly terminating credit agreement—Whether counterparty bankupcty having to follow counterparty failure to pay in order to qualify as bankruptcy trigger event. **Merrill Lynch International Bank Ltd v Winterthur Swiss Insurance Co** [2007] **2 Comm** 846, QBD.

      Declaration relating to prior insolvency—Question requiring disclosure of insolvency of any company of which insured previously directors—Claimant arguing that question ambiguous—Approach to construction—Whether necessary for court to determine true construction of question or rely on claimant's reasonable interpretation where ambiguity alleged. **R & R Developments Ltd v Axa Insurance UK plc** [2010] **2 Comm** 527, Ch D.

      Declaration relating to prior insolvency—Whether declaration requiring disclosure of insolvency of any company where insured previously directors. **Doheny v New India Assurance Co Ltd** [2005] **1 Comm** 382, CA.

      Exclusion clause—Contract of insurance excluding liability for 'any wilful or malicious act' by insured—Fire started by insured—Insured suffering from persistent delusional disorder and intoxicated with alcohol—Whether insured insane at time of fire—Whether claim excluded by public policy, general insurance law or exclusion clause. **Porter v Zurich Insurance Co** [2009] **2 Comm** 658, QBD.

      Exclusion clause—Contract of insurance excluding liability for 'wilful, malicious or criminal acts' causing accidental damage—Meaning of 'wilful act'—Whether requiring deliberate act and intention to cause damage leading to subject of claim. **Ronson International Ltd v Patrick (Royal London Mutual Insurance Society Ltd, Pt 20 defendant)** [2005] **2 Comm** 453, QBD; [2006] **2 Comm** 344, CA.

      Fine art insurance—Work of art damaged in fire—Claimant and defendant disputing sum recoverable—Interpretation of partial loss clause—Whether policy a valued policy. **Quorum A/S v Schramm** [2002] **2 Comm** 147, QBD.

      Guarantee risks insurance—Claim made in respect of yacht—Building of yacht commencing before policy in place—Policy in place at time of delivery—Whether guarantee clause liability covered by policy. **Heesens Yacht Builders BV v Cox Syndicate Management Ltd** [2006] **2 Comm** 173, CA.

      Insured's stores damaged by riots over two days—Contract providing for limit 'per occurrence'—Meaning of expression 'per occurrence'—Whether riots constituting single occurrence. **Mann v Lexington Insurance Co** [2000] **2 Comm** 163, QBD; [2001] **1 Comm** 28, CA.

      Legal expenses risks insurance—Claims notification clause—Whether assured failing to give notice of cause, event or circumstance 'likely' to give rise to a construction claim. **Laker Vent Engineering Ltd v Templeton Insurance Ltd** [2009] **2 Comm** 755, CA.

      Liability insurance. *See* Liability insurance—Construction of terms, *below*.

      Liability insurance. *See* Liability insurance—Professional indemnity insurance—Construction of terms, *below*.

      Lloyd's jewellers' block policy—Special conditions—Hold-up or robbery limit clause—Director of assured being kidnapped—Kidnappers holding director's family and ordering him to go to assured's office to take jewellery—Director taking jewellery from office—Whether circumstances of incident falling within hold-up or robbery limit clause. **Canelhas Comercio Importacao e Exportacao Ltd v Wooldridge (as representative of Lloyd's Property Consortium Syndicate 9091)** [2005] **1 Comm** 43, CA.

      Primary policy of insurance covering promoter of concert tour against losses should tour be cancelled, rescheduled, abandoned or curtailed—Primary policy coverage subject to one show deductible—Deductible buy-back policy indemnifying promoter for losses which would have been recoverable under primary policy but for one show deductible—Concert being cancelled and rescheduled because of performer's illness—Second concert having to be cancelled because of rescheduling—Whether losses occasioned by cancellation of second concert recoverable under deductible buy-back policy. **Quinta Communications SA v Warrington (Odyssey Re (London) Ltd intervening)** [1999] **2 Comm** 123, CA.

163

INSURANCE (cont)—
  Contract of insurance (cont)—
    Construction of terms (cont)—
      Public liability insurance —Disturbance occurring at immigration detention facility causing damage to property within area of local police authority—Police having statutory liability to pay compensation in respect of damage to property caused by rioting persons—Whether such liability amounting to 'liability to pay as damages' within meaning of policy—Riot (Damages) Act 1886. **Bedfordshire Police Authority v Constable** [2009] **2 Comm** 200, CA.

      Retail and wholesale policy—Intruder alarm condition—Burglary—Condition of policy requiring attendance of keyholder at premises or working alarm system at all times—Burglary taking place while requirements not met—Term not applicable where theft involving violence or threat of violence—Meaning of threat of violence—Whether appropriate to imply term that condition not applying where personal danger to keyholder involved. **Anders & Kern UK Ltd (t/a Anders & Kern Presentation Systems) v CGU Insurance plc (t/a Norwich Union Insurance)** [2007] **2 Comm** 1160, QBD; [2008] **2 Comm** 1185, CA.

      Warranty—Burglary from insured's warehouse—Insurance policy containing promissory warranties as to protections for safety of goods and alarm systems—Defects in alarm system and protections—Whether warranties limited to protections and alarm system in place at time of inception of insurance—Whether breach of warranty only if insured knew or ought to have known of defects. **AC Ward & Son Ltd v Catlin (Five) Ltd** [2010] **2 Comm** 683, QBD.

  Exclusion clause—
    All risks policy—Loss of source code by operation of computer virus and burglary—Exclusion of loss deliberately caused by malicious persons—Exclusion of other loss—Insured seeking indemnity in respect of business interruption—Whether loss excluded from cover. **Tektrol Ltd (formerly Atto Power Controls Ltd) v International Insurance Co of Hanover Ltd** [2005] **1 Comm** 132, QBD; **Tektrol Ltd (Formerly Atto Power Controls Ltd) v International Insurance Co of Hanover Ltd** [2006] **1 Comm** 780, CA.

    Exclusion of claim arising from failure of 'any fire or intruder alarm switch gear control panel or machinery to perform its intended function'—Fire protection system installed by claimant in client's premises failing to operate—Whether liability to claimant excluded by virtue of exclusion clause. **Reilly v National Insurance and Guarantee Corp Ltd** [2008] **2 Comm** 612, QBD; [2009] **1 Comm** 1166, CA.

    Exclusion of liability for deliberate acts—Pursuer's husband killed in altercation with door stewards—Steward's employers having indemnity insurance—Policy excluding 'liability arising out of deliberate acts'—Whether death brought about by 'deliberate acts'—Whether 'deliberate acts' including recklessness. **Burnett or Grant v International Insurance Co of Hanover Ltd** [2021] **3 503,** SC.

    Exclusion of loss caused by deliberate act or omission of insured—Liability insurance in respect of operator of children's homes—Claimants suffering physical and/or sexual abuse whilst in home—Acts of abuse carried out by managing director and other managerial employees—Whether loss for such acts excluded. **KR v Royal & Sun Alliance plc** [2007] **1 Comm** 161, CA.

    Incorporation in contract—Repugnancy—Insurance against material damage and business interruption—Insured renewing policy by request for quotation—Request for quotation purporting to amend exclusion clause—Whether request for quotation overriding existing exclusion clause—Whether existing exclusion clause repugnant to policy. **Great North Eastern Rly Ltd v Avon Insurance plc** [2001] **2 Comm** 526, CA.

    Policy excluding asbestosis-related claims—Whether policy excluding all claims relating to exposure to asbestos. **T&N Ltd (in administration) v Royal & Sun Alliance plc (Curzon Insurance Ltd, Pt 20 defendant)** [2003] **2 Comm** 939, Ch D.

  Follow settlements clause—
    Reinsurance. *See* Reinsurance—Contract for excess of loss reinsurance—Follow settlements clause, *below*.

  Jurisdiction—
    Conflict of laws. *See* **Conflict of laws** (Jurisdiction—Exclusive jurisdiction—Contracts of insurance).

  Jurisdiction challenge. *See* **Conflict of laws** (Jurisdiction—Challenge to jurisdiction—Insurance contract).

  Nature of contract—
    Capital investment bond—Policy benefits on surrender or on death of life insured—Whether policy an 'insurance on the life of any person'—Whether contract a policy of life insurance—Life Assurance Act 1774, s 1. **Fuji Finance Inc v Aetna Life Insurance Co Ltd** [1996] **4** 608, CA.

    Contract for a benefit other than money or money's worth—Medical Defence Union—Contract for proper consideration by Medical Defence Union of application for help by medical or dental practitioner against whom claim is made—No right to require union to conduct legal proceedings on behalf of or indemnify practioner—Whether contract of insurance—Whether Medical Defence Union carrying on insurance business within Insurance Companies Act 1974. **Medical Defence Union Ltd v Dept of Trade** [1979] **2** 421, Ch D.

    Contract for the payment of a sum of money on happening of specified event—Contract for the provision of services on happening of event—Whether contracts of insurance limited to contracts for payment of sum of money. **Dept of Trade and Industry v St Christopher Motorists Association Ltd** [1974] **1** 395, Ch D.

    Service providers offering extended warranty contracts providing for repair or replacement of electrical equipment—Regulatory body alleging that contracts being contracts of general insurance—Service providers not being authorised under relevant legislation to carry out insurance business — Regulatory body seeking winding-up orders against service providers for unlawfully carrying out regulated activities — Whether contracts providing for repair or replacement of equipment being contracts of general insurance — Financial Services and Markets Act 2000 (Regulated Activities) Order 2001, SI 2001/544, art 3(1), Sch 1, Pt 1, para 16(b). **Digital Satellite Warranty Cover Ltd, Re** [2012] **2 Comm** 38, CA.

INSURANCE (cont)—
  Contract of insurance (cont)—
    Nature of contract (cont)—
      Service providers offering extended warranty contracts providing for repair or replacement of electrical equipment—Regulatory body alleging that contracts being contracts of general insurance—Service providers not being authorised under relevant legislation to carry out insurance business—Regulatory body seeking winding-up orders against service providers for unlawfully carrying out regulated activities—Whether contracts providing for repair or replacement of equipment being contracts of general insurance—Financial Services and Markets Act 2000 (Regulated Activities) Order 2001, SI 2001/544, Sch 1, Pt 1, para 16(b)—Council Directive (EEC) 73/239—Council Directive (EEC) 84/641—Council Directive (EEC) 92/49. **Digital Satellite Warranty Cover Ltd, Re** [2013] **1 Comm** 625, SC; [2013] **2** 202, SC.
    Public contract—
      Public procurement exemption. *See* **Public procurement** (Public contracts—Public services contracts—Public procurement exemption—Mutual insurer).
  Contract to insure—
    Carriage of goods—
      Generally. *See* **Carriers** (Contract—Carriage of goods—Contract to insure).
  Contractors all-risks policy of insurance—
    Insurance clause providing for exclusion of liability where property insured in defective condition—
      Claimant earthworks sub-contractor employed in construction of motorway section—Damage occurring to layers of road surface due to bad weather and despite temporary drainage measures—Insurer seeking to exclude liability—Whether temporary drainage being part of 'property insured'. **CA Blackwell (Contractors) Ltd v Gerling Allegemeine Verischerungs AG** [2008] **1 Comm** 885, CA.
  Contribution between insurers of same risk—
    Liability insurance. *See* Liability insurance—Contribution between insurers of same risk, *below*.
  Cover note—
    Delay in forwarding note—
      Breach of duty by broker. *See* Broker—Duty—Delay in forwarding cover note to insured, *above*.
  Credit default insurance—
    Construction of contract. *See* Contract of insurance—Construction of terms—Credit default insurance, *above*.
  Credit indemnity insurance—
    Construction. *See* Contract of insurance—Construction of terms—Credit indemnity insurance, *above*.
  Credit insurance—
    Exclusion clause—
      Plaintiff taking out insurance for bad debts—Policy excluding liability for losses arising from delivery of goods whose export from or import into the insured's place of business was prohibited—Insured delivering beef to customer—Customer failing to pay for beef due to ban on British beef exports—Plaintiff claiming under policy—Insurer contending that loss excluded under policy—Whether exclusion clause applied to domestic transactions. **Hewitt (G & G B) Ltd v SA Namur-Assurances du Credit** [1999] **1 Comm** 851, CA.
  Damages—
    Personal injury. *See* **Damages** (Personal injury—Insurance).
  Demolition—
    Accident insurance. *See* Accident insurance—Perils insured against—Demolition, *above*.
  Disclosure—
    Duty to disclose—
      Duty of utmost good faith—Assured making claim under policy for legal expenses risks—Insurer repudiating liability on basis assured failing to disclose material circumstance, namely existence of dispute, prior to renewal of policy—Whether assured failing to disclose material circumstance. **Laker Vent Engineering Ltd v Templeton Insurance Ltd** [2009] **2 Comm** 755, CA.
      Duty of utmost good faith—Breach of duty—Assured producing knowingly false document to insurers' solicitors to assist in jurisdictional dispute—Whether production of knowingly false document for interlocutory matter breach of duty of utmost good faith. **K/S Merc-Scandia XXXXII v Certain Lloyd's Underwriters** [2000] **2 Comm** 731, QBD.
      Duty of utmost good faith—Breach of duty—Damages for breach—Breach by insurer—Whether doctrine of contributory negligence applicable to breach of duty of utmost good faith. **Banque Financière de la Cité SA v Westgate Insurance Co Ltd** [1987] **2** 923, QBD.
      Duty of utmost good faith—Breach of duty—Damages for breach—Breach by insurer—Whether insured entitled to damages or merely avoidance of contract of insurance and return of premium. **Banque Financière de la Cité SA v Westgate Insurance Co Ltd** [1987] **2** 923, QBD; [1989] **2** 952, CA.
      Duty of utmost good faith—Breach of duty—Damages for breach—Contracts for and of insurance—Contract including statement of truth clause—Insurers repudiating liability on ground of misrepresentation and non-disclosure of agent—Whether statement excluding right of insurer to avoid or rescind contract—Whether insurer entitled to damages for non-disclosure or misrepresentation. **HIH Casualty and General Insurance Ltd v Chase Manhattan Bank** [2001] **1 Comm** 719, QBD; **HIH Casualty and General Insurance Ltd v Chase Manhattan Bank (conjoined appeals)** [2003] **1 Comm** 349, HL.
      Duty of utmost good faith—Reciprocal nature of duty—Failure to disclose material facts—Banks making loans to companies guaranteed by credit insurance policies arranged by broker—Broker's employee dishonestly issuing cover notes when part of cover missing—Banks lending large sums in reliance on cover notes—Insurers aware of broker's employee's deception—Insurers not informing banks of deception—Companies defaulting on loans—Whether duty of utmost good faith reciprocal—Whether insurers in breach of duty of utmost good faith. **Banque Financière de la Cité SA v Westgate Insurance Co Ltd** [1987] **2** 923, QBD.

INSURANCE (cont)—
  Disclosure (cont)—
    Duty to disclose (cont)—
      Duty of utmost good faith—Reciprocal nature of duty—Failure to disclose material facts—Insurer's duty of disclosure—Banks making loans to companies guaranteed by credit insurance policies arranged by broker—Broker's employee dishonestly issuing cover notes when part of cover missing—Banks lending large sums in reliance on cover notes—Insurers aware of broker's employee's deception—Insurers not informing banks of deception—Companies defaulting on loans—Whether duty of utmost good faith reciprocal—Whether insurers in breach of duty of utmost good faith. **Banque Financière de la Cité SA v Westgate Insurance Co Ltd** [1987] **2** 923, QBD; [1989] **2** 952, CA.

      Duty of utmost good faith—Respondent guaranteeing liabilities of Lloyd's names under plans marketed to them—Names taking out endowment/life policies as part of plans and assigning them to respondent as security—Names suffering losses and respondent making payments under guarantees—Names contending that respondent dishonestly concealed from them its knowledge of impending losses when entering agreements—Whether concealment of such information breaching insurer's common law duty of disclosure—Whether breach of statutory prohibition on dishonest concealment giving rise to action for damages—Financial Services Act 1986, s 47. **Norwich Union Life Insurance Co Ltd v Qureshi** [1999] **2 Comm** 707, CA.

      Duty to warn principal of agents' past misconduct—Insurer's duty of disclosure—Banks making loans to companies guaranteed by credit insurance policies arranged by broker—Broker's employee dishonestly issuing cover notes when part of cover missing—Insurer's aware of broker's employee's deception in an earlier transaction—Insurers not informing banks of deception—Companies defaulting on loans—Whether insurers owing duty to banks to warn of broker's employee's deception—Whether broker's employee's deception cause of banks' loss. **Banque Financière de la Cité SA v Westgate Insurance Co Ltd** [1990] **2** 947, HL.

      Marine insurance. *See* **Marine insurance** (Contract of marine insurance—Disclosure—Duty to disclose).

      Property insurance. *See* Property insurance—Non-disclosure—Duty of assured to disclose material facts, *below*.

    Duty to disclose such facts as a reasonable or prudent insurer might treat as material—

      Moral character of insured—Criminal convictions—Property insurance—No proposal form—Purchase of dwelling-house by means of building society mortgage—Insurance of house effected by society on behalf of insured under society's block policy with insurers—Society's application form containing no questions expressly relating to insured's moral character—Insured failing to disclose previous convictions for offences including robbery—Whether criminal convictions a material fact—Whether absence of proposal form modifying duty to disclose convictions—Whether insurers entitled to avoid policy for non-disclosure of material fact. **Woolcott v Sun Alliance and London Insurance Ltd** [1978] **1** 1253, QBD.

    Marine insurance. *See* **Marine insurance** (Contract of marine insurance—Disclosure).

    Non-disclosure—

      Avoidance of policy—Driver failing to disclose conviction—Insurer purporting to avoid policy—Whether avoidance valid—Burden of proof. **Drake Insurance plc v Provident Insurance plc** [2004] **2 Comm** 65, CA.

      Material non-disclosure—Buildings insurance—Insurers seeking to avoid policy on basis of non-disclosure—Whether non-disclosure material. **Meisels v Norwich Union Insurance Ltd** [2007] **1 Comm** 1138, QBD.

      Material non-disclosure—Commercial property owners policy of insurance—Assured declaring on policy proposal that premises protected by automatic sprinkler system—Sprinkler system being turned off—Premises damaged by fire—Whether turning off of sprinkler system amounting to material change in the facts stated in the proposal form—Whether insurer entitled to cancel policy. **Ansari v New India Assurance Ltd** [2009] **2 Comm** 926, CA.

      Material non-disclosure—Marine insurance—Avoidance of policy—Hull and Machinery—Claimant assured bringing action against defendant insurers for damaged yacht—Insurers seeking to avoid policy on grounds of material non-disclosure and/or misrepresentation regarding value of yacht—Whether non-disclosure material—Whether insurers waiving right to avoid—Whether misrepresentation inducing insurers to enter into policy—Whether sub-broker owing duty of care to insured. **Involnert Management Inc v Aprilgrange Ltd (AIS Insurance Services Ltd and anor, third parties)** [2016] **1 Comm** 913, QBD.

      Material non-disclosure—Marine insurance—War risks policy—Marine and non-marine insurance—Claimant assured bringing action against defendant insurers for loss of vessel—Defendant insurers alleging claimant's owner involved in suspicious loss of other vessels—Whether claimant under duty to disclose owner's involvement in loss of other vessels—Burden and standard of proof in allegations of dishonest involvement by owner in loss of vessels other than insured vessel. **Strive Shipping Corp v Hellenic Mutual War Risks Association (Bermuda) Ltd** [2002] **2 Comm** 213, QBD.

      Material non-disclosure—Marine insurance—War risks policy—Marine and non-marine insurance—Test of material non-disclosure—Construction project—Building foundations differing from proposed design disclosed to underwriters prior to acceptance of risk—Subsidence damage occurring during construction—Whether underwriters entitled to avoid policy for non-disclosure of material facts or misrepresentation—Whether test of materiality requiring that undisclosed or misrepresented facts would have led a prudent insurer to appreciate an increased risk—Whether underwriters induced by non-disclosure or misrepresentation to enter into contract—Marine Insurance Act 1906, s 18(2)(3). **St Paul Fire and Marine Insurance Co (UK) Ltd v McConnell Dowell Constructors Ltd** [1996] **1** 96, CA.

INSURANCE (cont)—
 Disclosure (cont)—
  Non-disclosure (cont)—
   Material non-disclosure—Marine insurance—War risks policy—Marine and non-marine insurance—
    Test of material non-disclosure—Whether contract of insurance can only be avoided if full and
    accurate disclosure would have had decisive influence on prudent insurer's decision to accept
    risk—Whether any circumstance having effect on mind of prudent insurer in weighing up risk a
    relevant circumstance—Whether misrepresentation or non-disclosure must have induced making
    of policy—Whether underwriter who was not induced by misrepresentation or non-disclosure of
    material fact entitled to rely on misrepresentation or non-disclosure to avoid contract—Marine
    Insurance Act 1906, s 18(2). **Pan Atlantic Insurance Co Ltd v Pine Top Insurance Co Ltd**
    [1994] **3** 581, HL.
   Material non-disclosure—Marine insurance—War risks policy—Marine insurance—War risks
    policy—Non-disclosure of allegations of dishonesty unproven at time of placing—Insurers
    seeking to avoid policy—Whether non-disclosure material. **North Star Shipping Ltd v Sphere
    Drake Insurance plc (No 2)** [2006] **2 Comm** 65, CA.
   Material non-disclosure—Marine insurance—War risks policy—Motor insurance—Double
    insurance—Claimant insurer claiming contribution in equity from defendant insurer—Defendant
    insurer avoiding policy for non-disclosure—Assured erroneously informing defendant insurer of
    previous 'fault' accident—Assured failing to disclose material fact of speeding conviction—
    Defendant's underwriting criteria providing for increased premium when 'fault' accident and
    speeding conviction combined—Whether non-disclosure inducing defendant to renew policy on
    terms more favourable than it would otherwise have agreed—Whether defendant entitled to
    avoid for material non-disclosure—Whether decision to avoid breach of duty of utmost good
    faith. **Drake Insurance plc v Provident Insurance plc** [2003] **1 Comm** 759, QBD.
   Material non-disclosure—Reinsurance. See Reinsurance—Disclosure—Material non-disclosure,
    below.
  Reinsurance. See Reinsurance—Disclosure, below.
 Duty of broker. See Broker—Duty, above.
 Election. See Liability insurance—Notification requirements—Failure to comply with notification
  requirements—Election, below.
 Employer's liability insurance—
  Accident at work—
   Statutory duty on employer to insure against liability for injury sustained by employees in course of
    employment—Failure to insure being a criminal offence—Company director or secretary also
    guilty of offence if failure to insure occurring with his consent or connivance or facilitated by his
    neglect—Whether plaintiff entitled to bring civil claim for damages against directors and
    secretary—Employers' Liability (Compulsory Insurance) Act 1969, ss 1, 5. **Richardson v
    Pitt-Stanley** [1995] **1** 460, CA.
  Broker—
   Failure to insure client. See Broker—Duty—Failure to insure clients against employers' liability,
    above.
  Condition—
   Condition as to prevention of accidents—Employer to take reasonable precautions to prevent
    accidents—Need for failure to be reckless not merely negligent—Failure to fence machinery in
    breach of statutory duty—Alteration of machine nullifying former precaution against
    accident—Employers not appreciating danger. **Fraser v B N Furman (Productions) Ltd** [1967] **3** 57,
    CA.
   Condition as to prevention of accidents—Employer to take reasonable precautions to prevent
    accidents—Question as to safety of works and plant—Whether directed to present or to future
    state of works and plant. **Woolfall & Rimmer Ltd v Moyle** [1941] **3** 304, CA.
   Notice of claim—Subrogation—Receiver and manager appointed for employers—Employee
    obtaining judgment in default of appearance against employers—Action by employee against
    insurers for damages and costs—Condition of policy—Every writ served on employers to be
    notified to insurers immediately on receipt—Failure of employee to notify insurers until judgment
    obtained—Whether breach of condition relieving insurers of liability—Third Parties (Rights
    against Insurers) Act 1930, s 1(1)(b). **Farrell v Federated Employers Insurance Association Ltd**
    [1970] **3** 632, CA.
  Costs—
   Employers seeking indemnity for defence costs from Financial Services Compensation
    Scheme—Whether Scheme required to pay such costs—Construction of words 'in respect
    of'—Policyholders Protection Act 1975, s 6(5). **R (on the application of Geologistics Ltd) v
    Financial Services Compensation Scheme** [2004] **1 Comm** 943, CA; [2004] **3** 39, CA.
  Description of risk—
   Contract of service—Whether servant under 'contract of service' with assured—Loan of servant to
    assured—Unskilled labourer. **Denham v Midland Employers' Mutual Assurance Ltd** [1955] **2** 561,
    CA.
   Injury arising out of and in the course of employment—Loan of car by employers to employee on
    condition that fellow employee given lifts to work—Fellow employee injured by negligent driving
    of employee—Whether employers entitled to indemnity under policy. **Vandyke v Fender (Sun
    Insurance Office Ltd, third party)** [1970] **2** 335, CA.
  Indemnity insurance. See Indemnity insurance—Employers' liability, below.
  Mesothelioma. See Indemnity insurance—Employers' liability—Mesothelioma, below.
  Third party's rights against insurers—
   Action by third party against insurers—Employee contracting respiratory disease through
    inhalation of cotton dust in course of employment—Employee alleging disease caused by
    negligence of employer company—Company insured against liability for personal injuries to
    employees—Company dissolved twelve years before action brought—Amount or existence of
    liability of company to employee not established before company dissolved—Whether employee
    entitled to indemnity from insurers in respect of company's liability—Third Parties (Rights against
    Insurers) Act 1930, s 1(1)(b). **Bradley v Eagle Star Insurance Co Ltd** [1989] **1** 961, HL.

INSURANCE (cont)—
  Employer's liability insurance (cont)—
    Third party's rights against insurers (cont)—
      Claimant companies in administration—Claimants insured by Lloyd's syndicate—Condition of
        insurance that claimants bear cost of employers' liability claims based on asbestosis or
        mesothelioma—Captive insurance company indemnifying claimants against liability to
        syndicate—Whether claimants' rights against insurer vesting in syndicate—Third Parties (Rights
        Against Insurers) Act 1930, s 1(1). **T&N Ltd (in administration) v Royal & Sun Alliance plc (Curzon
        Insurance Ltd, Pt 20 defendant)** [2003] **2 Comm** 939, Ch D.
      Set-off by insurers—Third party's claim—Judgment against employer in action for personal
        injuries—Bankruptcy of employer—Premiums owing by employer to insurers—Whether statutory
        transferred rights enjoyed by third party against insurers were subject to set-off in respect of
        premiums owing—Third Parties (Rights against Insurers) Act 1930, s 1. **Murray v Legal and
        General Assurance Society Ltd** [1969] **3** 794, QBD.
      Undisclosed principal—Shipping agents—Shipowners instructing agents to obtain employers'
        liability insurance—Insurers issuing employers' liability policy to agents—Crew members
        drowned when ship capsized—Personal representatives awarded damages against shipowners in
        respect of deaths—Shipowners wound up before judgment satisfied—Personal representatives
        claiming payment from insurers in respect of award—Whether insurers liable to shipowners as
        undisclosed principal—Third Parties (Rights Against Insurers) Ordinance (Hong Kong), s 2. **Siu
        Yin Kwan v Eastern Insurance Co Ltd** [1994] **1** 213, PC.
  Employer's liability insurance—
    Accident at work—
      Statutory duty on employer to insure against liability for injury sustained by employees in course of
        employment—Appellant employee being injured at work and injury not covered by
        insurance—Company going into liquidation—Whether director of company liable in damages for
        company's failure to comply with statutory obligations—Employers' Liability (Compulsory
        Insurance) Act 1969, ss 1, 5. **Campbell v Peter Gordon Joiners Ltd** [2017] **2** 161, SC.
  Equal treatment of men and women—
    European Union. *See* **European Union** (Equality of treatment of men and women—Access to and
      supply of goods and services—Derogation from principle of equal treatment—Insurance premiums
      and benefits).
  European Union. *See* **European Union** (Insurance).
  Exclusion clause—
    Accident—
      Insurance. *See* Accident insurance, *above*.
    Construction. *See* Contract of insurance—Construction of terms—Exclusion clause, *above*.
    Credit insurance. *See* Credit insurance—Exclusion clause, *above*.
    Insurance contract. *See* Contract of insurance—Construction of terms—Exclusion clause, *above*.
  Explosion—
    Fire insurance—
      Explosion of boiler. *See* Fire insurance—Perils insured against—Explosion of boiler, *below*.
  Fatal accident—
    Liability admitted by insurance company—
      Writ issued more than 12 months after death. *See* **Limitation of action** (Fatal accident—Application
        of statutory limitation period—Third-party insurance).
  Fidelity insurance—
    Accrual of cause of action. *See* **Limitation of action** (Indemnity—Accrual of cause of action—Policy of
      fidelity insurance).
    Proposal form—
      Answers to questions as to duties of person proposed—Whether warranties. **Hearts of Oak
        Building Society v Law Union and Rock Insurance Co Ltd** [1936] **2** 619, KBD.
  Financial services, regulation of—
    Generally. *See* **Financial services** (Insurance—Financial Conduct Authority (FCA)—Regulation of
      financial services).
    Warranty. *See* Contract of insurance—Nature of contract—Service providers offering extended
      warranty contracts providing for repair or replacement of electrical equipment, *above*.
  Fine art insurance—
    Contract of insurance. *See* Contract of insurance—Construction of terms—Fine art insurance, *above*.
    Work of art damaged in fire—
      Whether sub-molecular damage 'direct physical damage'—Whether diminution in value because of
        damage by insured peril separate element of stigma—Approach to valuation of work of art.
        Quorum A/S v Schramm [2002] **2 Comm** 147, QBD.
  Fire insurance—
    Amount payable by insurer—
      Where insured's interest limited—Goods held in trust or on commission—Extent of
        insurance—Profits—Right of bailee to deduct from insurance moneys in respect of commission
        and charges not earned. **Maurice v Goldsbrough Mort & Co Ltd** [1939] **3** 63, PC.
    Condition—
      Burden of proof—Loss by reason of specified occurrences—Abnormal conditions—Whether
        insurers liable. **Levy v Assicurazioni Generali** [1940] **3** 427, PC.
      Construction—Breach of condition requiring precautions to be taken when burning and welding
        equipment used—Precautions not taken and fire caused—Defendant not having actual
        knowledge of such equipment being used—Whether actual knowledge of use of equipment
        required for condition to apply—Whether defendants entitled to be indemnified by insurers.
        Bonner-Williams v Peter Lindsay Leisure Ltd [2001] **1 Comm** 1140, QBD.
      Insurer resisting claim under policy in respect of thefts from property after fire on basis that
        co-operation condition not complied with—Co-operation clause not condition precedent—
        Whether consequences of breach of condition cancelling out any claim under policy. **Porter v
        Zurich Insurance Co** [2009] **2 Comm** 658, QBD.

INSURANCE (cont)—
  Fire insurance (cont)—
    Condition (cont)—
      Insurers resisting claim under policy on basis that condition relating to notification of loss not complied with—Insured alleging repudiation by insurer of liability with consequential release of obligation to comply with procedural conditions of policy—Whether alleged repudiation capable of releasing insured from further procedural obligations. **Diab (Nasser) v Regent Insurance Co Ltd** [2006] **2 Comm** 704, PC.
      Particulars of claim—Conditions precedent—Compliance within a reasonable time—Banking accounts only disclosed on cross-examination. **Welch v Royal Exchange Assurance** [1938] **4** 289, CA.
    Covenant in lease. See **Landlord and tenant** (Covenant—Insurance—Fire).
    Insurable interest—
      Agricultural holding—Tenant's insurance—Crops—Crops destroyed by fire after tenant quitted holding pursuant to notice to quit—Whether tenant had insurable interest in crops after quitting holding. **Thomas v National Farmers Union Mutual Insurance Society Ltd** [1961] **1** 363, QBD.
      Landlord and tenant—Landlord covenanting to insure premises up to full reinstatement value against all specified risks including fire—Tenant covenanting to pay additional rent to cover premiums—Landlord covenanting in case of destruction or damage to premises to apply insurance money in reinstating premises—Contract for sale for property—Premises destroyed by fire between date of contract for sale and completion date—Sale completed without regard to fire damage—Landlord receiving full purchase price without abatement for fire damage—Insurers refusing to reinstate premises at tenant's request—Whether landlord's liability limited to injury to reversion—Whether insurers liable for cost of full reinstatement of premises. **Lonsdale & Thompson Ltd v Black Arrow Group plc** [1993] **3** 648, Ch D.
      Landlord and tenant—Landlord letting part of premises to tenant—Landlord covenanting to insure premises and tenant covenanting to pay portion of premiums—Landlord agreeing to apply insurance moneys received in reinstating premises—Premises destroyed by fire caused by tenant's negligence—Landlord receiving insurance moneys for cost of rebuilding premises—Whether landlord precluded from recovering damages for negligence from tenant—Whether landlord's insurers entitled by subrogation to recover damages from tenant. **Rowlands (Mark) Ltd v Berni Inns Ltd** [1985] **3** 473, CA.
    Landlord and tenant—
      Estoppel. See **Estoppel** (Landlord and tenant—Fire insurance).
      Insurable interest. See Fire insurance—Insurable interest—Landlord and tenant, *above*.
    Market value—
      Reinstatement or market value. See Fire insurance—Measure of indemnity—Basis of calculation—Cost of reinstatement or market value, *below*.
    Measure of indemnity—
      Basis of calculation—Cost of reinstatement or market value—Empty cottage placed on market for sale—Cottage insured for not less than 'full value'—Full value defined in policy as amount it would cost to replace cottage in its existing form were it totally destroyed—Policy stating that insurer would at its option, by payment, reinstatement or repair indemnify plaintiff for loss by fire—Fire totally destroying cottage—Whether plaintiff entitled to reinstatement cost or market value at date of fire. **Leppard v Excess Insurance Co Ltd** [1979] **2** 668, CA.
      Basis of calculation—Mansion partly destroyed by fire—Agreed value in excess of actual value. **Elcock v Thomson** [1949] **2** 381, KBD.
    Mortgage—
      Mortgagor's covenant to insure mortgaged property against loss or damage by fire—Insurance to be effected in name of mortgagee—Mortgagor effecting insurance in own name—Mortgagee's interest noted by insurer as party interested in insurance—Property destroyed by fire—Whether mortgagee entitled to proceeds of insurance policy—Whether mortgagee having interest by way of charge in proceeds—Property Law Act 1952 (NZ), s 78, Sch 4, cl (2). **Colonial Mutual General Insurance Co Ltd v ANZ Banking Group (New Zealand) Ltd** [1995] **3** 987, PC.
    Payment of loss—
      Mistake—Policy indorsed in favour of three named parties 'for their respective rights and interests'—Claim made by one and payment by cheque in favour of all three—Cheques indorsed by all and paid to credit of claimant—Action to recover amount paid on ground of arson by claimant's employee—Whether money recoverable from parties other than claimant as paid under mistake of fact. **General Accident, Fire and Life Assurance Corp Ltd v Midland Bank Ltd** [1940] **3** 252, CA.
    Perils insured against—
      Explosion of boiler—Use for domestic purposes—Insurance against damage by explosion of boilers used for domestic purposes only—Boiler used for heating building—Certain rooms in building used for business purposes—Whether boiler used for domestic purposes only. **Willesden Corp and Municipal Mutual Insurance Ltd's Application, Re** [1945] **1** 444, CA.
      Ignition—Goods placed in grate for safety—Fire lit forgetting goods placed there—Whether insurers liable. **Harris v Poland** [1941] **1** 204, KBD.
    Reinstatement—
      Approach to claim for reinstatement—Options open to insured—Duty of insured to notify insurer of improvements or changes—Whether insureds complying with duty. **Tonkin v UK Insurance Ltd** [2006] **2 Comm** 550, QBD.
      Double insurance clause—Insurance of premises by lessor and lessee—Equitable interest—Ratification of insurance—Reinstatement of premises—Fires Prevention (Metropolis) Act 1774, s 83. **Portavon Cinema Co Ltd v Price and Century Insurance Co Ltd** [1939] **4** 601, KBD.
      Fire risk—Claimant company's premises, plant and machinery insured for fire—Policy providing for indemnity to be calculated by reference to reinstatement—Claimant claiming under policy—Defendant insurer submitting claimant failing to show intention to reinstate—Whether claimant entitled to indemnity to be calculated on reinstatement basis—Whether principle of betterment applying. **Sartex Quilts & Textiles Ltd v Endurance Corporate Capital Ltd** [2020] **1 Comm** 229, Comm Ct; [2020] **2 Comm** 1050, CA.
      Reinstatement or market value. See Fire insurance—Measure of indemnity—Basis of calculation—Cost of reinstatement or market value, *above*.

INSURANCE (cont)—
  Flood—
    Householder's policy. *See* Householder—Storm, tempest or flood, *below*.
  Fraudulent insurance claim—
    Jurisdiction. *See* **Conflict of laws** (Jurisdiction—Challenge to jurisdiction—Matters relating to tort—Place where harmful event occurring).
    Marine insurance. *See* **Marine insurance** (Claim—Fraud).
  Group litigation—
    Costs liability for uninsured claimants. *See* **Costs** (Order for costs—Payment of costs by non-party—Product liability group litigation).
  Guarantee insurance—
    Bonds—
      Guarantee of payment of bonds—Bonds containing gold clause—Guarantee of redemption at par—Whether insurance of payment on a gold basis. **Sturge (A L) & Co v Excess Insurance Co Ltd** [1938] **4** 424, KBD.
    Contract of insurance. *See* Contract of insurance—Construction of terms—Guarantee risks insurance, *above*.
    Subrogation. *See* Subrogation—Guarantee insurance, *below*.
  Hearth and home policy—
    Accident. *See* Accident insurance—Perils insured against—Accident—Public policy—Hearth and home policy, *above*.
  Householder—
    Householder's contents policy—
      Liability insurance. *See* Liability insurance—Householder's contents policy, *below*.
    Storm, tempest or flood—
      Flood—Gradual ingress of water from natural source—Policy covering loss, destruction or damage to property from 'storm, tempest or flood'—Seepage of water into plaintiff's lavatory caused by natural source beneath—Water on lavatory floor standing three inches deep—Whether a 'flood'. **Young v Sun Alliance and London Insurance Ltd** [1976] **3** 561, CA.
  Ignition—
    Fire insurance. *See* Fire insurance—Perils insured against—Ignition, *above*.
  Illegality—
    Enforcement of policy contrary to public policy—
      Uncustomed goods—Insurance against theft—Policy not tainted by illegality—Goods sent to West Germany with false invoice to enable recipient to avoid West German customs duty—Whether implied term that transaction to be carried out lawfully—Whether insurance claim tainted with foreign illegality unenforceable—Marine Insurance Act 1906, s 41. **Euro-Diam Ltd v Bathurst** [1987] **2** 113, QBD; [1988] **2** 23, CA.
      Uncustomed goods—Insurance against theft—Policy not tainted by illegality—Subject-matter of insurance including goods imported by insured without being declared to the customs authorities and on which customs duty payable—Goods liable to forfeiture—Goods stolen—Whether contrary to public policy for court to assist insured by enforcing claim to indemnity in respect of goods. **Geismar v Sun Alliance and London Insurance Ltd** [1977] **3** 570, QBD.
    Restriction on carrying on insurance business—
      Insurance business carried on without authority of Secretary of State—Defendant purporting to sell debt collecting and debt indemnity services on behalf of a limited company—Neither defendant nor company authorised to sell such insurance—Defendant convicted of carrying on insurance business without authorisation—Circumstances in which an individual could be guilty of offence charged—Whether necessary to have concluded contract to be 'carrying on insurance business'—Insurance Companies Act 1982, ss 2, 14. **R v Wilson** [1997] **1** 119, CA.
      Insurance business carried on without authority of Secretary of State—Effect of illegality on reinsurance—Plaintiff insurance company carrying on marine insurance without authorisation—Plaintiff reinsuring risks with defendant—Whether illegality of original contracts affecting reinsurance contract—Whether original contracts void—Insurance Companies Act 1974, ss 2(1), 11(1), 83(4). **Bedford Insurance Co Ltd v Instituto de Resseguros do Brasil** [1984] **3** 766, QBD.
      Insurance business carried on without authority of Secretary of State—Effect of illegality on reinsurance—Plaintiff reinsuring risks with foreign insurance company—Foreign insurance company not authorised to carry on insurance in Great Britain—Whether illegality of reinsurers' business affecting reinsurance contract—Whether reinsurance contract void—Insurance Companies Act 1974, ss 2(1), 11(1), 83(4). **Stewart v Oriental Fire and Marine Insurance Co Ltd** [1984] **3** 777, QBD.
      Insurance business carried on without authority of Secretary of State—Effect of reclassification of classes of insurance business—Plaintiffs carrying on aviation contingency business as part of marine, aviation and transport business—Effect of transitional provisions—Whether aviation contingency business which was previously authorised ceasing to be authorised on reclassification—Whether such business continuing to be authorised business by virtue of transitional provisions—Whether prohibition of unauthorised insurance business rendering contracts of insurance entered into by unauthorised insurer void for illegality—Insurance Companies Act 1974, ss 2(1), 11(1), 83(4)—Insurance Companies (Classes of General Business) Regulations 1977, Sch 1, class 16, Sch 4, para 2. **Phoenix General Insurance Co of Greece SA v Administratia Asigurarilor de Stat** [1987] **2** 152, CA.
      Insurance company restricted to business of insurance—Benefits under capital investment bond payable on surrender or on death of life assured—Whether insurance company prohibited from issuing policy—Whether policy unenforceable—Insurance Companies Act 1982, s 16. **Fuji Finance Inc v Aetna Life Insurance Co Ltd** [1994] **4** 1025, Ch D.
    Reinsurance business. *See* Reinsurance—Reinsurance business—Illegality, *below*.
  Income protection insurance—
    Policy—
      Claimant suffering injury—Claimant having genuine belief of disability—Whether genuine belief part of disability for purposes of recovery. **Haghiran v Allied Dunbar Insurance** [2001] **1 Comm** 97, CA.

INSURANCE (cont)—
  Income tax—
    Payment under policy—
      Capital or income. *See* **Income tax** (Capital or income receipts—Insurance—Payment under policy).
  Indemnity insurance—
    Credit card protection plan offering cardholders indemnification and other forms of assistance on loss or theft of card—
      Plan operator instructing insurance broker to arrange insurance for cardholders under block policy—Whether plan constituting one whole or several individual supplies of services—Value Added Tax Act 1983, s 17, Sch 6, Group 2—Council Directive (EEC) 77/388, art 13(B). **Card Protection Plan Ltd v Customs and Excise Comrs** [2001] **1 Comm** 438, HL; [2001] **2** 143, HL.
    Employers' liability—
      Mesothelioma—Employers' liability policies covering sustaining of injury or contracting of disease—Employees inhaling asbestos fibres in course of employment and developing mesothelioma many years later—Whether employees suffering injury when asbestos fibres inhaled—Whether policies covering period when asbestos fibres inhaled. **Durham v BAI (Run Off) Ltd (in scheme of arrangement)** [2009] **1 Comm** 805, QBD; [2009] **2** 26, QBD; [2011] **1** 605, CA; [2011] **1 Comm** 811, CA; [2012] **2 Comm** 1187, SC; [2012] **3** 1161, SC.
      Mesothelioma—Employers' liability policies—Employer liable to employee for exposure to asbestos during whole of employee's period of employment—Insurer providing employers' liability policies to employer for part of employee's period of employment—Employer seeking indemnity from insurer—Whether employer's right of indemnity limited to amount proportionate to period insured—Whether provision of indemnity for full period of employee's employment where premium paid only during part of period unfair. **International Energy Group Ltd v Zurich Insurance plc UK Branch** [2013] **2 Comm** 336, CA; [2013] **3** 395, CA.
      Notification clause—Failure to give details of claim—Whether insurers entitled to repudiate insurance. **Alfred McAlpine plc v BAI (Run-Off) Ltd** [2000] **1 Comm** 545, CA.
    Employers' liability—
      Mesothelioma—Employers' liability policies—Employer liable to employee for exposure to asbestos—Insurer providing employers' liability policies to employer for part of employee's period of employment—Employer seeking indemnity from insurer—Whether employer's right of indemnity limited to amount proportionate to period insured—Whether insurer entitled to seek contributions from other insurers or employer. **International Energy Group Ltd v Zurich Insurance plc UK Branch** [2015] **4** 813, SC; [2016] **1 Comm** 114, SC.
  Life insurance. *See* Life insurance—Indemnity insurance, *below*.
  Marine insurance—
    Company trading in agricultural commodities—Company being victim of fraud in relation to contracts under which certain cargoes purchased—Company having insurance under marine cargo open policy and seeking indemnity in respect of cargoes—Policy underwriters contending no loss of physical property and purely financial loss uninsured—Whether company entitled to indemnity—Whether company having insurable interest—Whether breach of implied term to pay sums due within reasonable time—Insurance Act 2015, s 13A. **Quadra Commodities SA v XI Insurance Company SE** [2022] **2 Comm** 334, QBD.
  Pecuniary loss indemnity insurance—
    Reinsurance—Warranty—Reinsurers claiming warranty incorporated into insurance and reinsurance contracts—Insurers claiming clause requiring payment on both insurance and reinsurance contracts—Whether warranty incorporated into contracts—Whether clause precluding insurers and reinsurers from rejecting claim. **HIH Casualty & General Insurance Ltd v New Hampshire Insurance Co** [2001] **2 Comm** 39, CA.
  Personal contract of insurance—
    Employers' liability insurance—Whether indemnity insurance a personal contract—Whether indemnity insurance an exception to general rule that undisclosed principal can sue on contract made by agent—Whether rights of undisclosed principal excluded. **Siu Yin Kwan v Eastern Insurance Co Ltd** [1994] **1** 213, PC.
  Professional indemnity insurance. *See* Liability insurance—Professional indemnity insurance, *below*.
  Industrial injuries—
    Social security. *See* **Social security** (Disablement benefit).
  Insurable interest—
    Fire insurance. *See* Fire insurance—Insurable interest, *above*.
  Insurance company—
    Information sharing—
      European community rules on competition, contrary to. *See* **European Union** (Rules on competition—Agreements preventing, restricting or distorting competition—Insurance companies entering information sharing agreements).
    Loans by—
      Annual payments for income tax purposes. *See* **Income tax** (Annual payment—Annuity—Monthly loans by insurance company).
    Winding up. *See* **Company** (Insurance company—Winding up).
  Insurance premium tax—
    State aid—
      European Community. *See* **European Union** (State aids—Concept of state aid—Insurance premium tax).
    Value added tax—
      European Community. *See* **European Union** (Value added tax—Supply of goods or services—Insurance premium tax).
  Insurance transactions—
    Value added tax—
      Exemption—European Community. *See* **European Union** (Value added tax—Exemptions—Insurance transactions).
  Insurer—
    Agent—
      Duty to account to insurer. *See* **Agent** (Duty to principal—Duty to account).
    Duty to disclose. *See* Disclosure—Duty to disclose, *above*.

INSURANCE (cont)—
  Insurer (cont)—
    Negligence—
      Duty of care. *See* **Negligence** (Duty to take care—Insurer).
  Jurisdiction—
    Conflict of laws. *See* **Conflict of laws** (Jurisdiction—Challenge to jurisdiction—Claim by insurer).
  Lease—
    Covenant. *See* **Landlord and tenant** (Covenant—Insurance).
  Legal expenses insurance—
    Before-the-event (BTE) insurance—
      Right of insured person to choose lawyer—Assessment of costs payable under terms of contract—Costs reasonably incurred and reasonable in amount—Insured persons choosing solicitors not from insurer's panel—Fees charged by solicitors higher than fees chargeable under insurer's non-panel solicitors terms—Whether solicitors appointed to act under policy—Whether solicitors' fees to be assessed by reference to non-panel terms—Insurance Companies (Legal Expenses Insurance) Regulations 1990, SI 1990/1159, reg 6—CPR 48.3. **Brown-Quinn v Equity Syndicate Management Ltd** [2012] **1** 778, Comm Ct.
      Right of insured person to choose lawyer—Assessment of costs payable under terms of contract—Costs reasonably incurred and reasonable in amount—Insured persons choosing solicitors not from insurer's panel—Fees charged by solicitors higher than fees chargeable under insurer's non-panel solicitors terms—Whether solicitors appointed to act under policy—Whether solicitors' fees to be assessed by reference to non-panel terms—Insurance Companies (Legal Expenses Insurance) Regulations 1990, SI 1990/1159, reg 6—Council Directive (EEC) 87/344, art 4. **Brown-Quinn v Equity Syndicate Management Ltd** [2013] **3** 505, CA.
    Claimant solicitors acting for insured having policy of legal expenses insurance—
      Insured becoming insolvent—Claimant bringing action against insurers—Whether rights under policy transferring to claimant solicitors—Third Parties (Rights Against Insurers) Act 1930, s 1. **Tarbuck v Avon Insurance plc** [2001] **1 Comm** 422, QBD; [2001] **2** 503, QBD.
    European Community—
      Right of insured person to choose lawyer—Conditions of policy allowing insurer to select the legal representative of all insured persons concerned where large number of insured persons suffering loss as result of the same event—Whether Community law permitting insurer to select legal representative in such circumstances—Council Directive (EEC) 87/344, art 4(1). **Eschig v UNIQA Sachversicherung AG** (Case C-199/08) [2010] **1 Comm** 576, ECJ.
    Order for costs. *See* **Costs** (Order for costs—Legal expenses insurance).
  Liability insurance—
    Ascertainment—
      Assured bringing proceedings for sums allegedly owing under building contract—Defendant to action making counterclaim—Proceedings compromised in global sum—Assured seeking indemnity under liability policies—Whether assured entitled to indemnity—Whether requirement of ascertainment satisfied. **Lumbermens Mutual Casualty Co v Bovis Lend Lease Ltd** [2005] **2 Comm** 669, QBD.
    Construction of terms—
      Combined liability insurance—Medical negligence—Limitation of liability—Policy providing for £10m limit of indemnity for 'any one claim'—Separate clause providing for £10m limit of indemnity payable for claims 'consequent on or attributable to one source or original cause'—Multiple claims brought against assured—Whether policy aggregating linked claims. **Spire Healthcare Ltd v Royal & Sun Alliance Insurance plc** [2019] **1 Comm** 294, CA.
      Damage—Installation of glass panels into building, a small number of which fracturing—No damage to fabric of building other than to panels themselves—Whether 'damage' within terms of cover. **Pilkington United Kingdom Ltd v CGU Insurance plc** [2005] **1 Comm** 283, CA.
      Policy of liability insurance issued to pharmaceutical group—Policy on form usually governed by New York law—Form amended to be governed by English law—Insured settling personal injury claims—Insurer providing indemnity in respect of sums paid by way of settlement and associated defence costs—Insurer seeking indemnity from reinsurers—Whether insured entitled to indemnity—Whether construction of terms under New York law relevant—Whether underlying policy covering settlements where no actual legal liability established—Whether policy covering defence costs where no actual legal liability established. **AstraZeneca Insurance Co Ltd v XL Insurance (Bermuda) Ltd** [2013] **2 Comm** 97, QBD.
    Contribution between insurers of same risk—
      Liability to contribute—Co-insurers statutorily liable for third party risk—Whether contribution between co-insurers to be determined in accordance with extent of respective liabilities to person insured for loss under separate contracts of insurance—Whether contribution to be determined in accordance with respective statutory liabilities—Road Traffic Act (Bahamas), s 12. **Eagle Star Insurance Co Ltd v Provincial Insurance plc** [1993] **3** 1, PC.
      Liability to contribute—Insurer settling claim under policy in full and claiming 50% contribution from co-insurer—Co-insurer denying liability on ground that insured had not given notice of claim within time specified in policy issued by co-insurer—Whether insurer entitled to contribution from co-insurer—Whether right to contribution excluded by insured's failure to notify co-insurer of potential claim within specified time—Whether right to contribution excluded where insurer's policy providing for liability only in respect of rateable proportion of loss—Road Traffic Act 1972, s 149. **Legal and General Assurance Society Ltd v Drake Insurance Co Ltd** [1989] **3** 923, QBD; [1992] **1** 283, CA.
      Rateable proportion clause—Assessment of rateable proportion—Basis—Independent liability basis—Liability of each insurer ascertained as if he were the sole insurer—Total liability to assured divided in proportion to independent liabilities. **Commercial Union Assurance Co Ltd v Hayden** [1977] **1** 441, CA.

INSURANCE (cont)—
  Liability insurance (cont)—
    Determination of proximate cause—
      Claimants providing personal pension plans—Defendants insuring claimants against negligent advice—Claimants failing properly to train representatives selling pension plans—Representatives providing negligent advice—Claimants liable to investors—Whether individual policyholders' claims falling within aggregation clause—Whether series of claims constituting 'related series of acts or omissions'. **Lloyds TSB General Insurance Holdings Ltd v Lloyds Bank Group Insurance Co Ltd** [2001] **1 Comm** 13, QBD; [2002] **1 Comm** 42, CA; [2003] **2 Comm** 665, HL; [2003] **4** 43, HL.
    Forged documents—
      Bank—Indemnity against loss due to advance on invalid documents—Payment to be for excess of named sum lost 'by each and every loss or occurrence'—Daily advances on security of invoices—Fictitious invoices—Whether series of losses or one large loss. **Philadelphia National Bank v Price** [1938] **2** 199, CA.
    Householder's comprehensive policy—
      Damage to premises by settlement caused by tree roots—Whether damage caused 'by accident'—Whether insurers liable. **Mills v Smith (Sinclair, third party)** [1963] **2** 1078, QBD.
      Policy covering sums for which assured liable as occupier of flat—Damage to premises by fire negligently lit by assured in order to destroy birds' nest under cornice of building—Whether insurers liable. **Sturge v Hackett** [1962] **3** 166, CA.
    Householder's contents policy—
      Insurance cover based on insured's assessment of full contents value—Obligation on insured when renewing his policy—Whether insured representing to insurer that valuation based on objectively reasonable grounds—Whether honest belief that valuation correct sufficient—Extent of duty of disclosure as to contents. **Economides v Commercial Union Assurance Co plc** [1997] **3** 636, CA.
    Notification requirements—
      Failure to comply with notification requirements—Election—Whether room for doctrine of election—Whether insurers electing to accept claim. **Kosmar Villa Holidays plc v Trustees of Syndicate 1243** [2007] **2 Comm** 217, QBD; [2008] **2 Comm** 14, CA.
    Professional indemnity insurance—
      Accountant—Accountant in firm giving advice to client but also dealing with client in personal capacity—Client bringing unsuccessful action against firm—Firm claiming costs of successful defence from insurers—Whether insurance policy covering costs of successful defence—Whether consent to costs given by insurers under policy—Whether insurer estopped from denying consent—Whether separate policy formed by correspondence—Whether claims relating to personal capacity of individual employed by assured or assured in its professional capacity. **Thornton Springer v NEM Insurance Co Ltd** [2000] **1 Comm** 486, QBD; [2000] **2** 489, QBD.
      Accountant—Indemnity against claims in respect of neglect, default or error—Q C clause—Accountants' clerk converting client's money to own use—Action by client against accountants—Whether client's claim covered by policy—Meaning of 'claim' in policy. **West Wake Price & Co v Ching** [1956] **3** 821, QBD.
      Accountant—Policy providing cover for defence costs—Court proceedings being issued against insured and insurer funding defence costs—Insurer referring cover dispute to arbitration—Awards holding insurer entitled to reimbursement of defence and arbitration costs—Insured claiming serious irregularity in making of arbitration cost orders—Insured delaying bringing challenges—Whether appropriate to grant extension of time—Whether entitlement to recover defence costs on proper construction of relevant documents—Whether arbitrator in breach of general duty—Arbitration Act 1996, ss 33, 68, 69. **Oldham v QBE Insurance (Europe) Ltd** [2018] **1 Comm** 1064, QBD.
      All losses—Loss due to embezzlement by employee. **Goddard and Smith v Frew** [1939] **4** 358, CA.
      Apportionment—Claimant mis-selling investment fund giving rise to potential third party claims—Claimant seeking to reduce brand damage by making cash injection to restore fund—Claimant seeking indemnity from defendant insurer under professional indemnity insurance policy—Policy providing for indemnity for 'mitigation costs'—Defendant submitting dominant purpose of cash injection being to reduce brand damage and not falling within mitigation costs—Judge finding cash injection made in order to avoid or reduce third party claims and recoverable—Whether judge erring. **Standard Life Assurance Ltd v Ace European Group** [2013] **1 Comm** 1371, CA.
      Civil and environmental engineer—Claim brought against insured for negligent design—Whether claim falling within scope of policy. **Encia Remediation Ltd v Canopius Managing Agents Ltd** [2007] **2 Comm** 947, QBD.
      Construction of policy—Second defendant umbrella corporation insured against claims where member company incurring liability in providing professional services for other member company or for negligence in relation to the conduct of professional services—Insurers seeking to avoid second defendant's claim on basis of member company's non-disclosure or breach of warranty—Whether member company insured by policy. **Brit Syndicates Ltd v Italaudit SpA** [2007] **1 Comm** 785, CA; [2008] **2 Comm** 1, HL; [2008] **2 Comm** 1140, HL.
      Construction of terms—Excess—Excess of £25m 'each and every claim and/or claimant'—Whether permissible to have regard to wording of slip in construing policy—Whether policy permitting aggregation of related claims by separate claimants. **Standard Life Assurance Ltd v Oak Dedicated Ltd** [2008] **2 Comm** 916, QBD.
      Construction of terms—Firm of architects and engineers insured through layers of personal indemnity insurance policies providing worldwide cover—Insurer associated company providing three layers of excess of loss insurance and final additional cover reinsured by defendant reinsurer—Final additional cover excluding claims from United States and Canada and providing for liability to arise only where intermediate insurers becoming liable—Insurer arguing that claims capable of being addressed to different layers of insurance with effect of leaving claims emanating from United States and Canada to be dealt with under final additional cover and consequently by reinsurer—Whether necessary for claims to be addressed to insurance policies in any particular order. **Teal Assurance Co Ltd v WR Berkley Insurance (Europe) Ltd** [2012] **1 Comm** 969, CA; [2013] **2 Comm** 1009, SC; [2013] **4** 643, SC.

173

INSURANCE (cont)—
    Liability insurance (cont)—
        Professional indemnity insurance (cont)—
            Construction of terms—Insured selling group of insurance companies and entering into contracts of insurance in relation to liabilities arising under deed of indemnity relating to sale—Group of companies having sold insurance containing unsuitable policy excess definition clause to savings and investments company prior to sale—Same insurance continuing to be provided by buyer—Savings and investment company suffering losses due to inadequacy of insurance and bringing claim in negligence against buyer—Buyer bringing claim under deed—Insured claiming under contracts of insurance—Insurers disputing insured's liability to buyer—Whether insured liable under deed—Whether insured's claim within scope of contracts of insurance. **Beazley Underwriting Ltd v Travelers Companies Inc** [2012] **1 Comm** 1241, QBD.

            Excess layer—Terms—Claims notification clause—Whether term a condition precedent to excess insurers' liability—Whether term an innominate term—Whether breach freeing excess insurers of liability. **Friends Provident Life and Pensions Ltd v Sirius International Insurance Corp** [2005] **2 Comm** 145, CA.

            Financial advisor—Cover in form of primary layer policy and excess layer policy—Policies written on a 'claims made' basis—Notification of circumstances which might give rise to a claim—Whether excess policies covering claims arising out of circumstances notified to underwriters during policy period—Whether notice to primary layer underwriters sufficient to bring claim within excess layer policies. **Friends Provident Life and Pensions Ltd v Sirius International Insurance Corp** [2004] **2 Comm** 707, QBD.

            Policy containing claims made clause—Accountants—Assured seeking indemnity on basis that notification of claim made within policy period—Insurers denying liability—Whether notification given as soon as practicable after awareness of circumstances leading to potential claims—Meaning of 'as soon as practicable'. **HLB Kidsons (a firm) v Lloyd's Underwriters subscribing to Lloyd's Policy No 621/PKID00101** [2008] **1 Comm** 769, QBD; [2009] **2 Comm** 81, CA.

            Policy containing claims made clause—Building company notifying insurers of certain defects in building and of proposed investigation—Other defects and damage subsequently coming to light—Insured entering into settlement agreement—Whether defects and damage emerging in period after notification and expiry of the cover effectively subject matter of what was notified. **Kajima UK Engineering Ltd v Underwriter Insurance Co Ltd** [2008] **1 Comm** 855, QBD.

            Policy containing claims made clause—Notification requirements—Indemnity insurance claim involving successive policies—Claimant incurring costs to mitigate potential third party claims arising from circumstances notified to insurer—Whether circumstances notified under first policy or under second policy. **Euro Pools plc (in admin) v Royal & Sun Alliance Insurance plc** [2020] **2 Comm** 40, CA.

            Policy providing for excess to apply on each and every basis to claims arising out of pensions transfer activities—Policy defining any claim or any loss as one occurrence or series of occurrences—Whether pensions misselling claims to be treated as one claim for the purposes of applying indemnity limit. **Countrywide Assured Group plc v Marshall (AIG Europe (UK) Ltd and ors, intervening)** [2003] **1 Comm** 237, QBD.

            Professional indemnity insurance policy indemnifying insured for claims alleging neglect or omission—Policy providing that insured not indemnified for claim arising from dishonest act of employee perpetrated after it could have been reasonably discovered—Third party bringing claim against insured for damages for breach of contract but not alleging fraud—Insured settling claim and claiming indemnity under neglect provision—Insurers alleging that true cause of loss was event falling within exception—Whether insured required to prove that neglect was proximate cause of loss. **MDIS Ltd (formerly McDonnell Information Systems Ltd) v Swinbank** [1999] **2 Comm** 722, CA.

            Solicitor—Claimant successfully suing defendant solicitors' firm in liquidation for breach of disbursements funding agreement—Claimant bringing proceedings against defendant's insurer—Judge finding insurer not liable on basis of exclusion clause in insurance policy—Whether professional indemnity insurers obliged to indemnify solicitors liable to reimburse loans made to their clients—Third Parties (Rights Against Insurers) Act 1930. **Impact Funding Solutions Ltd v Barrington Support Services Ltd (formerly Lawyers at Work Ltd) (AIG Europe Insurance UK Ltd, third party)** [2015] **4** 319, CA; [2017] **2 Comm** 863, SC; [2017] **4** 169, SC.

            Solicitor—Indemnity in respect of loss arising from neglect, omission, or error committed by solicitors or their employees—Fraud on clients by employee—Resulting loss by solicitors—Whether covered by policy. **Davies v Hosken** [1937] **3** 192, KBD.

            Solicitor—Law Society's group scheme—Law Society authorised to 'take out and maintain insurance with authorised insurer's' against loss arising from claims against solicitors and their employees etc in respect of liability for professional negligence or breach of duty—Law Society arranging master policy with specified insurers—Law Society requiring all solicitors to participate in group scheme and pay premiums set under master policy—Law Society sharing commission with brokers—Whether Law Society accountable to individual solicitors for commission received—Whether Law Society placing itself in fiduciary position in relation to premium payers—Whether Law Society in exercising its powers performing public or private duty—Whether necessary to imply trust to secure commercial viability of scheme—Solicitors Act 1974, s 37. **Swain v Law Society** [1982] **2** 827, HL.

            Solicitor—Law Society's group scheme—Plaintiff partner in firm of solicitors insured under Solicitors' Indemnity Fund for £1m—Partner signing top-up insurance policy for £1m with defendant insurers—Policy providing that defendants would not seek to avoid, repudiate or rescind insurance on any ground whatsoever—Partner failing to disclose circumstances relating to potential claim against firm—Judgment entered against firm in sum of £2m and plaintiff seeking indemnity from defendants—Defendants denying liability on ground of breach of warranty—Whether plaintiff entitled to indemnity. **Kumar v AGF Insurance Ltd** [1998] **4** 788, QBD.

            Solicitor—Limitation of liability—Aggregation clause—Senior partner carrying out numerous thefts of clients' money over many years—Whether thefts arising out of series of related acts or omissions—Whether aggregation clause applying. **Bishop of Leeds v Dixon Coles & Gill (Solicitors Regulation Authority Ltd intervening) (No 2)** [2022] **1 Comm** 1167, CA; [2022] **2** 1032, CA.

INSURANCE (cont)—
Liability insurance (cont)—
Professional indemnity insurance (cont)—
Solicitor—Limitation of liability—Liability limited to £3,000 in respect of each occurrence—Advice to several persons injured in same accident—Widow advised to become administratrix of estate against which claim to be made—Claims allowed to become statute barred—Whether one occurrence—Repudiation by insurers of liability in excess of £3,000—Whether solicitor entitled to recover own costs in contesting claims. **Forney v Dominion Insurance Co Ltd** [1969] **3** 831, QBD.
Solicitor—Limitation of liability—Multiple, individual claims brought against firm of solicitors responsible for overseeing investment mechanism—Aggregation clause in policy of insurance providing claims treated as 'one claim' where transactions 'a series of related matters or transactions'—Whether claims constituted 'one claim'—Whether relevant transactions had to be dependent on one another—Whether relevant transactions had to have intrinsic relationship with each other. **AIG Europe Ltd v OC320301 LLP (formerly The International Law Partnership LLP)** [2016] **2 Comm** 1058, CA; [2017] **1** 143, CA; [2018] **1** 936, SC; [2018] **1 Comm** 1097, SC.
Public liability insurance—
Construction of contract. *See* Contract of insurance—Construction of terms—Public liability insurance , *above*.
Construction of policy—Claimant hydrocarbon manufacturer acquiring insurance policy containing public liability indemnity—Fire at claimant's factory leading to pollution of adjoining watercourse—Environment Agency executing necessary works and seeking expenses from claimant—Claimant making claim under insurance policy—Insurers resisting claim on basis that policy only providing indemnity in relation to liability to damages—Whether liability to Environment Agency being liability to damages. **Bartoline Ltd v Royal & Sun Alliance Insurance plc** [2007] **1 Comm** 1043, QBD.
Construction of policy—Policy indemnifying local authority for liability for compensation arising out of actions of employees and police officers—Extent of indemnity for exemplary damages—Whether 'compensation' including exemplary damages—Whether public policy precluding indemnity for exemplary damages awarded against insured for conduct of employee or police officer for which insured vicariously liable. **Lancashire CC v Municipal Mutual Insurance Ltd** [1996] **3** 545, CA.
Exception clause—Cause of damage—Exception in respect of damage attributable to specified cause—Damage resulting from more than one cause—Cover against legal liability to pay damages consequent on damage to property as a result of accident—Exception in respect of damage caused by nature of goods supplied by insured—Insured held liable for damage to factory from fire—Two causes of fire—Nature of goods supplied by insured and negligent conduct of insured's employee—Whether nature of goods supplied dominant and effective cause—Whether, if both causes equally effective, damage within exception clause. **Wayne Tank and Pump Co Ltd v The Employers' Liability Assurance Corp Ltd** [1973] **3** 825, CA.
Third party's rights against insurers—Action by third person against insurers—Damage to Post Office cable in street by insured company digging for water main—Liability denied by company—Company went into liquidation—Post Office sued insurers direct—Liability of company not yet established and its amount not yet ascertained—Whether action maintainable—Third Parties (Rights against Insurers) Act 1930, s 1(1). **Post Office v Norwich Union Fire Insurance Society Ltd** [1967] **1** 577, CA.
Third party's rights against insurers—Damage to premises caused by fire—Fire said to have been caused by sub-contractor carrying out building works—Letter of claim sent to sub-contractor—Sub-contractor's insurer refusing to provide an indemnity—Judgment entered against sub-contractor and sub-contractor being wound-up—Sub-contractor's rights against insurer vesting in claimants—Claimants bringing proceedings against insurer—Insurer contending claims time-barred by reference to conditions of policy—Whether claims time-barred. **William McIlroy (Swindon) Ltd v Quinn Insurance Ltd** [2012] **1 Comm** 241, CA.
Third party's rights against insurers—
Contractual liability—Duty to give information reasonably required—Company insured against liabilities arising under extended warranty contracts—Application to administrators of assured for disclosure of information—Whether statutory scheme applying to insurance against liability generally or only to tortious liability and liability akin to tortious liability—Whether third party entitled to receive information on event of insolvency or only on establishment of liability—Third Parties (Rights Against Insurers) Act 1930, ss 1, 2. **OT Computers Ltd (in administration), Re** [2004] **1 Comm** 320, Ch D; [2004] **2 Comm** 331, CA.
Negligent performance of dredging contract with port authority—Whether policy covering failure to fulfill contractual obligations—Whether cost of removing silt deposited in public waterway constituting financial loss resulting from property damage. **Jan de Nul (UK) Ltd v AXA Royale Belge SA (formerly NV Royale Belge)** [2002] **1 Comm** 767, CA.
Life assurance—
European Community. *See* **European Union** (Insurance—Life assurance).
Generally. *See* Life insurance, *below*.
Life insurance—
Accident and illness insurance. *See* Life insurance—Personal accident and illness insurance, *below*.
Assignment—
Stamp duty—Sufficiency of stamp—Amount recoverable by assignee—Interest. **Waterhouse's Policy, Re** [1937] **2** 91, Ch D.
Capital investment bond—
Whether contract a policy of life insurance. *See* Contract of insurance—Nature of contract—Capital investment bond, *above*.
Death of assured resulting from criminal act of beneficiary under policy—
Public policy—Defendant and deceased purchasing house together by means of endowment mortgage—Defendant murdering deceased—Mortgagee claiming under insurance policy and using proceeds of policy to pay off mortgage—House sold—Whether defendant entitled to his share of proceeds of sale of house—Whether proceeds belonging to personal representatives of deceased. **Davitt v Titcumb** [1989] **3** 417, Ch D.

INSURANCE (cont)—
  Life insurance (cont)—
    Death of assured resulting from suicide—
      Suicide aided and abetted by beneficiary under policy who survived suicide pact with
        assured—Forfeiture rule—Modification of rule—Whether beneficiary precluded by forfeiture rule
        from benefiting under life insurance policy—Whether court should modify effect of forfeiture
        rule—Suicide Act 1961, s 2(1)—Forfeiture Act 1982, s 2. **Dunbar (administrator of Dunbar (decd))
        v Plant** [1997] **4** 289, CA.
    Estate duty—
      Gift inter vivos. See **Estate duty** (Gift inter vivos—Settlement—Property taken—Proposal for
        assurance on life of settlor made by trustee).
      Property in which deceased had an interest. See **Estate duty** (Aggregation—Property in which
        deceased had an interest—Insurance policy).
    Exception—
      Suicide—Suicide 'within one year from commencement of insurance'—Suicide nine years after
        issue—Public policy. **Beresford v Royal Insurance Co Ltd** [1938] **2** 602, HL.
    Indemnity insurance—
      Personal accident and illness insurance. See Life insurance—Personal accident and illness
        insurance—Indemnity insurance, below.
      Persons interested or for whose benefit policy made—Whether indemnity insurance void because
        policy not stating persons interested or for whom policy made—Life Assurance Act 1774, s 2.
        Rowlands (Mark) Ltd v Berni Inns Ltd [1985] **3** 473, CA.
      Persons interested or for whose benefit policy made—Whether indemnity insurance void because
        policy not stating persons interested or for whose benefit policy made—Whether statutory
        requirement that persons interested or for whose benefit policy made be named in policy
        applying to indemnity insurance—Life Assurance Act 1774, s 2. **Siu Yin Kwan v Eastern Insurance
        Co Ltd** [1994] **1** 213, PC.
    Joint policy—
      Family provision. See **Family provision** (Reasonable provision—Property available for financial
        provision—Property held on joint tenancy).
    Life assurance company—
      Income tax. See **Income tax** (Life assurance companies).
    Personal accident and illness insurance—
      Indemnity insurance—Master lineslip policy—P&I club insured for losses in respect of injury to any
        person on board members' vessels—Insurers paying club fixed benefits in respect of
        claims—Insurers reinsuring risks with defendant reinsurers—Whether club having insurable
        interest at inception—Life Assurance Act 1774, s 1. **Feasey v Sun Life Assurance Co of Canada**
        [2002] **2 Comm** 492, QBD; [2003] **2 Comm** 587, CA.
    Policy—
      Beneficiary—Entitlement—Policy moneys—Trust—Policy taken out by father on the life and for the
        benefit of his daughter—Premiums paid by father up to his death and thereafter by executors of
        his will until benefit of policy assigned to daughter—Policy moneys not payable until after the
        anniversary of commencement of insurance next before attainment by daughter of twenty-five
        years—Whether policy gave rise to a trust for the daughter of the policy moneys. **Foster's Policy,
        Re** [1966] **1** 432, Ch D.
      Policy benefits on surrender or on death of life insured—Whether contract a policy of life insurance.
        See Contract of insurance—Nature of contract—Capital investment bond—Policy benefits on
        surrender or on death of life insured, above.
      Policy effected for benefit of widow or children—'Post-nuptial settlement'. **Lort-Williams v
        Lort-Williams** [1951] **2** 241, CA.
      Policy moneys. See Life insurance—Policy moneys, below.
      Rectification—Illustration stating terms of insurance issued with proposal form—Policy
        subsequently issued in different terms—Whether rectification should be granted. **Sun Life
        Assurance Co of Canada v Jervis** [1943] **2** 425, CA.
    Policy moneys—
      Child's endowment policy—Godchild of assured—Right of assured's estate—Law of Property Act
        1925, s 56. **Sinclair's Life Policy, Re** [1938] **3** 124, Ch D.
      Lien on policy moneys—Policy taken out by father on life of son—Proceeds held to belong to
        father's estate—Premiums after death of father paid by or on behalf of son—Premiums paid
        under common mistake as to right to policy moneys. **Foster Re, (No 2)** [1938] **3** 610, Ch D.
      Lien on policy moneys—Policy taken out by husband for benefit of wife—Death of wife—Husband
        continuing to pay premiums—Married Women's Property Act 1882, s 11. **Smith, Re** [1937] **3** 472,
        Ch D.
      Policy taken out by father on life of son—Powers exercisable on behalf of son—Father's interest to
        cease on son attaining 21 years—Policy held in trust for son. **Webb, Re** [1941] **1** 321, Ch D.
      Policy taken out by father on life of son—Whether father's estate or son's estate entitled—Law of
        Property Act 1925, s 56. **Foster, Re** [1938] **3** 357, Ch D.
      Trust—Benefit of wife and named daughter—Named person an adopted child. **Clay's Policy of
        Assurance, Re** [1937] **2** 548, Ch D.
    Premium—
      Payment—Assignment of policy—Offer by assignee to pay premium—Refusal by insurance
        company—Post-dated cheque given by assured in respect of premium—Death of assured before
        date of cheque—Tender. **Farquharson v Pearl Assurance Co Ltd** [1937] **3** 124, KBD.
  Limitation of liability—
    Professional indemnity assurance. See Liability insurance—Professional indemnity insurance—
      Solicitor—Limitation of liability, above.
  Lloyd's. See Society of Lloyd's, below.
  Loans by insurance company—
    Annual payments for income tax purposes. See **Income tax** (Annual payment—Annuity—Monthly
      loans by insurance company).
  Local authority houses, of. See **Housing** (Local authority houses—Management—Insurance).
  Long-term insurance business—
    Transfer of. See Transfer of long-term insurance business, below.

INSURANCE (cont)—
Marine insurance—
Generally. *See* **Marine insurance**.
Policy moneys—
Lien. *See* **Marine insurance** (Proceeds of policy—Lien).
Material non-disclosure. *See* Disclosure—Non-disclosure—Material non-disclosure, *above*.
Misrepresentation—
Marine insurance. *See* **Marine insurance** (Contract of marine insurance—Disclosure—Misrepresentation).
Materiality—
Inducement—Insurers varying contract and removing endorsement in insurance policy after misrepresentations by insured—Whether misrepresentations as to material fact—Whether insurers induced to vary contract by misrepresentations—Whether insurers entitled to rescind variation and rely on endorsement. **AC Ward & Son Ltd v Catlin (Five) Ltd [2010] 2 Comm 683,** QBD.
Mistake—
Payment of loss—
Fire insurance. *See* Fire insurance—Payment of loss—Mistake, *above*.
Moral character—
Disclosure—
Duty to disclose such facts as a reasonable or prudent insurer might treat as material. *See* Disclosure—Duty to disclose such facts as a reasonable or prudent insurer might treat as material—Moral character of insured, *above*.
Motor insurance—
Ceylon. *See* **Ceylon** (Motor insurance).
European Community provisions. *See* **European Union** (Insurance—Compulsory insurance of motor vehicles).
Generally. *See* **Motor insurance**.
Motor Insurers' Bureau—
Generally. *See* **Motor insurance** (Motor Insurers' Bureau).
Rights of third parties against insurers. *See* **Motor insurance** (Rights of third parties against insurers—Motor Insurers' Bureau).
Mutual insurance association—
Income tax. *See* **Income tax** (Profits—Mutuality principle—Mutual insurance association).
National health insurance. *See* **National health insurance**.
National insurance. *See* **Social security**.
Negligence—
Contract—
Concurrent remedies. *See* **Negligence** (Contract—Concurrent remedies—Duty of care—Insurance).
Duty to take care. *See* **Negligence** (Duty to take care—Insurance).
Insurer—
Duty of care. *See* **Negligence** (Duty to take care—Insurer).
Lloyd's underwriting agent—
Duty to take care. *See* **Negligence** (Duty to take care—Insurance—Lloyd's underwriting agent).
Non-disclosure—
Generally. *See* Disclosure, *above*.
Property insurance. *See* Property insurance—Non-disclosure, *below*.
Notice of claim—
Condition—
Employer's liability insurance. *See* Employer's liability insurance—Condition—Notice of claim, *above*.
Notification requirements—
Liability insurance. *See* Liability insurance—Professional indemnity insurance—Policy containing claims made clause, *above*.
Notification requirements. *See* Liability insurance—Notification requirements, *above*.
Occupational pension insurance—
European Community—
Freedom of movement. *See* **European Union** (Freedom of movement—Services—Occupational pension insurance).
Payment protection insurance—
Policy. *See* Policy—Payment protection insurance, *below*.
Payments under policy—
Capital or income—
Administration of estates. *See* **Administration of estates** (Capital or income—Payments under insurance policy).
Personal accident—
Damages. *See* **Damages** (Personal injury—Insurance).
School—
Sport—Whether school under duty to insure pupils against injuries received while playing sport. *See* **Negligence** (School—Duty of care—Sport—Injury to pupil).
Travel insurance—
Construction of policy. *See* Policy—Construction—Travel insurance, *below*.
Personal accident and illness insurance—
Life insurance. *See* Life insurance—Personal accident and illness insurance, *above*.
Personal injury—
Damages. *See* **Damages** (Personal injury—Insurance).
Policy—
Compromise—
Fraud. *See* Claim—Fraud—Effect of fraud on moneys paid under policy prior to perpetration of fraud—Insurance policy containing clause forfeiting benefit under policy if claim made fraudulently—Claimant insurance company and defendant, *above*.
Construction—
Deletions. *See* **Contract** (Construction—Deletions—Reinsurance contract).

INSURANCE (cont)—
  Policy (cont)—
    Construction (cont)—
      Excess. *See* Liability insurance—Professional indemnity insurance—Construction of terms—Excess, *above.*
      Follow the settlements clause. *See* **Marine insurance** (Policy—Construction—Follow the settlements clause).
      Marine insurance. *See* **Marine insurance** (Policy—Construction).
      Travel insurance—Personal accident. **McGeown v Direct Travel Insurance** [2004] **1 Comm** 609, CA.
    Jurisdiction—
      Challenge to jurisdiction. *See* **Conflict of laws** (Jurisdiction—Challenge to jurisdiction—Insurance policy).
    Life insurance. *See* Life insurance—Policy, *above.*
    Payment protection insurance—
      Claimants obtaining loan and payment protection insurance (PPI) from lender—Claimants not informed in telephone conversation that PPI being purchased by further loan to finance advance payment to insurance company—Subsequent documents setting out full cost of PPI—Whether conversation and documents constituting single process during which full and clear breakdown of cost of PPI given—Whether claimants misled. **Figurasin v Central Capital Ltd** [2014] **2 Comm** 257, CA.
    Proper law. *See* **Conflict of laws** (Contract—Proper law of contract—Insurance policy).
    Protection of policyholders. *See* Protection of policyholders, *below.*
    Solicitor—
      Negligence—Action on motor insurance policy—Solicitor giving effect to pooling arrangement among insurance companies. *See* **Solicitor** (Negligence—Action on motor insurance policy—Solicitor giving effect to pooling arrangement among insurance companies).
    Stamp duty. *See* **Stamp duty** (Insurance policy).
    Variation of settlement—
      Sum payable on death of husband. *See* **Variation of Settlement (Matrimonial Causes)** (Insurance policy—Sum payable on death of husband).
    Waiver. *See* Reinsurance—Claims co-operation clause—Reinsurers alleging breach of claims co-operation clause but continuing to communicate with insurers in relation to claim, *below.*
  Policy moneys—
    Estate duty. *See* **Estate duty** (Property deemed to pass on death—Insurance policy).
    Life insurance. *See* Life insurance—Policy moneys, *above.*
    Trust—
      Discretionary power under endowment assurances for pension. *See* **Trust and trustee** (Discretionary trust—Uncertainty—Power of selection).
  Policyholder—
    Protection of. *See* Protection of policyholders, *below.*
  Premium—
    After-the-event insurance premium—
      Order for costs. *See* **Costs** (Order for costs—Jurisdiction—After-the-event (ATE) insurance premium).
    Before-the-event insurance premium—
      Order for costs. *See* **Costs** (Order for costs—Legal expenses insurance—Before-the-event (BTE) insurance).
    Income tax—
      Annual payment. *See* **Income tax** (Annual payment—Insurance premiums).
      Capital or income. *See* **Income tax** (Capital or income receipts—Insurance—Premiums).
    Life insurance. *See* Life insurance—Premium, *above.*
    Refund—
      Construction all risks policy—Work ceasing before completion of building project—Cedant claiming entitlement to refund of reinsurance premium—Whether cedant entitled to refund. **Swiss Reinsurance Co v United India Insurance Co Ltd** [2005] **2 Comm** 367, QBD.
  Proceedings—
    Jurisdiction—
      Conflict of laws. *See* **Conflict of laws** (Jurisdiction—Challenge to jurisdiction—Insurance proceedings).
  Product liability insurance—
    Third party's rights against insurer. *See* Third party's rights against insurer—Application of statutory scheme—Product liability insurance, *below.*
  Professional indemnity insurance. *See* Liability insurance—Professional indemnity insurance, *above.*
  Property insurance—
    All risks. *See* All risks insurance, *above.*
    Goods in transit—
      Duration of risk—Carriers insured goods against all risks of loss 'whilst temporarily housed during the course of transit'—Goods delivered by customer to carriers—Goods stolen while awaiting loading—Whether lost during the course of transit. **Crows Transport Ltd v Phoenix Assurance Co Ltd** [1965] **1** 596, CA.
      Duration of risk—Policy describing goods as property of I, in transit, and including loading and unloading—Insurance pursuant to agreement by carrier with I to effect full comprehensive insurance—Goods stolen after carrier's vehicle arrived at I's premises but before unloading—No negligence by carrier—Whether goods still on risk—Whether carrier could recover in respect of owner's proprietary interest. **Hepburn v A Tomlinson (Hauliers) Ltd** [1966] **1** 418, HL.
      Employee's reference—Carrier's insurance under goods in transit policy—Clause providing that insured shall take all reasonable precautions for the protection and safeguarding of goods—Lorry driver employed without reference being checked—Lorry and load stolen—Whether clause referred to selection of staff or only to protection of physical safety of goods—Need for failure to take precautions to be reckless not merely negligent. **Lane (W & J) v Spratt** [1970] **1** 162, QBD.

INSURANCE (cont)—
  Property insurance (cont)—
    Goods in transit (cont)—
      Insurance of haulage contractors against liability for loss of goods in transit carried by
      sub-contractors—Goods delivered by the contractors' order to vehicle apparently that of
      sub-contractors—Theft of goods—Whether goods held by contractors 'in trust' within policy.
      Rigby (John) (Haulage) Ltd v Reliance Marine Insurance Co Ltd [1956] **3** 1, CA.
    Non-disclosure—
      Duty of assured to disclose material facts—Lloyd's jewellers' block policy—Foreign jurisdiction
      clause—Policy covering stock-in-trade of diamond merchants against loss—Diamonds and pearls
      lost by theft in Italy—Alleged discovery by underwriters of practice of assured to smuggle
      diamonds into Italy—Repudiation of liability by underwriters on ground of non-disclosure and
      illegality—Whether such dispute was within foreign jurisdiction clause. **Mackender v Feldia AG**
      [1966] **3** 847, CA.
      Duty of assured to disclose material facts—Nature and age of goods material—'New men's clothes
      in bales for export'—Government surplus goods described in trade as new—Nature and age of
      goods not brought to attention of insurer—Insurer not put on enquiry by description of goods.
      Anglo-African Merchants Ltd v Bayley [1969] **2** 421, QBD.
    Perils insured against—
      All risks—Goods sent to Germany for treatment—Insolvency of German firm—Accident or
      fortuitous casualty. **London and Provincial Leather Processes Ltd v Hudson** [1939] **3** 857, KBD.
      All risks—Insurance covering goods held by the insured 'in trust for which the insured is
      responsible'—Whether those words restricting insurer's liability to goods damaged in way which
      imposed liability on bailee. **Ramco (UK) Ltd v International Insurance Co of Hanover** [2004] **2
      Comm** 866, CA.
      Escape of water from mains—Escape occurring before policy taken out—Loss or damage to
      property resulting from escape occurring during period of policy—Insurers agreeing in policy to
      indemnify insured in respect of 'events' occurring during period of insurance—Whether 'events'
      referring to occurrence of perils insured against or to loss or damage resulting from insured
      peril—Whether policy protecting insured against damage occurring during period of policy but
      resulting from peril occurring before policy came into effect. **Kelly v Norwich Union Fire
      Insurance Society Ltd** [1989] **2** 888, CA.
      Theft—Business interruption losses—Cover extended to include theft not involving 'forcible and
      violent' means of entry and exit and business interruption losses caused by theft or attempted
      theft—Parties not selecting 'theft by employees' section of insurer's standard wording—Business
      interruption losses caused by dishonesty of employee excluded—Whether policy covering theft
      by employees not involving forcible and violent means of entry and exit—Whether policy
      covering business interruption losses caused by theft by employees not involving forcible and
      violent means of entry and exit. **Ted Baker plc v AXA Insurance UK plc** [2013] **1 Comm** 129, QBD.
      Theft—Loss or damage from theft involving 'forcible and violent' means of entry to
      premises—'Violent' means of entry—Thieves stealing keys to premises and entering premises by
      normal use of keys to unlock doors—No physical damage caused to locks or doors—Whether
      entry by 'violent' means. **Dino Services Ltd v Prudential Assurance Co Ltd** [1989] **1** 422, CA.
      Theft—Property belonging to another—Sale of goods—Passing of property—Plaintiff and rogue
      discussing purchase of watch and ring from plaintiff over telephone—Rogue later paying for
      articles with stolen building society cheque and taking delivery of articles—Whether contract for
      sale of articles made on telephone or when cheque handed over—Whether articles property of
      another at time of delivery—Whether rogue committing theft—Theft Act 1968, s 1(1). **Dobson v
      General Accident Fire and Life Assurance Corp plc** [1989] **3** 927, CA.
    Risk—
      Description of risk—Goods insured while 'in store'—Goods packed in lift vans and placed in
      enclosed yard at depository—Whether goods 'in store'. **Wulfson v Switzerland General Insurance
      Co Ltd** [1940] **3** 221, KBD.
  Proposal—
    Form—
      Fidelity insurance. *See* Fidelity insurance—Proposal form, *above*.
  Protection of policyholders—
    Liquidation of insurance company—
      Interim payments to policyholders—Indemnity to liquidator—Power of board to give liquidator
      indemnity covering such payments—Extent of power—Indemnity against personal liability of
      liquidator in event of deficiency of assets—Whether power including a power to give company an
      undertaking to make good shortfall of assets resulting from payments—Policyholders Protection
      Act 1975, s 15(3)(b). **Policyholders Protection Board v Official Receiver** [1976] **2** 58, Ch D.
    Liquidation of insurer—
      Conditions for claiming statutory protection—Employers' liability insurance—Policy including cover
      for legal costs—Claimant left to bear legal costs after liquidation of insurer—Whether costs
      arising 'in respect of' liability subject to compulsory insurance—Whether Financial Services
      Compensation Scheme obliged to compensate claimant for costs—Policyholders Protection
      Act 1975, s 6(5). **R (on the application of Geologistics Ltd) v Financial Services Compensation
      Scheme** [2003] **2 Comm** 165, QBD; [2004] **1** 198, QBD.
      Conditions for claiming statutory protection—Policyholder—Person having contingent interest
      under policy at beginning of liquidation—Partnership having corporate partners—Person who
      stands to benefit under policy—Person having derivative interest under policy—Whether person
      having contingent or derivative interest under policy or who stands to benefit from policy can be
      'policyholder'—Whether partner in partnership having corporate partners can be 'policyholder'—
      Policyholders Protection Act 1975, ss 4(2), 6(7), 8(2)—Insurance Companies Act 1982, s 96(1).
      Scher v Policyholders Protection Board (Nos 1 and 2) [1994] **2** 37, HL.
      Requirement that insurers establish sufficient technical provisions and adequate solvency margin
      for entire business—Payment of claims from assets held in guarantee fund to represent technical
      provisions—Greek legislation establishing priority for payment of claims arising from
      employment relationships over payment of insurance claims—Whether legislation compatible
      with Community law—Council Directive (EEC) 73/239, arts 15, 16—Council Directive (EEC) 79/267,
      arts 17, 18. **Epikouriko Kefalaio v Ipourgos Anaptixis (Case C-28/03)** [2006] **EC** 112, ECJ.

INSURANCE (cont)—
  Protection of policyholders (cont)—
    United Kingdom policy—
      Liquidation of insurer—Payment of claims overseas—Plaintiffs taking out professional liability policies in United States and Canada with authorised United Kingdom insurers—Insurers going into liquidation and unable to meet plaintiffs' claims—Plaintiffs claiming indemnity from Policyholders Protection Board—Whether policies issued to plaintiffs United Kingdom policies—Whether plaintiffs entitled to indemnity from board—Policyholders Protection Act 1975, ss 4, 8(2). **Scher v Policyholders Protection Board (Nos 1 and 2)** [1994] **2** 37, HL.
  Public liability insurance. See Liability insurance—Public liability insurance, *above.*
  Reinsurance—
    Arbitration clause—
      Validity—Separability. *See* **Arbitration** (Agreement—Arbitration clause—Validity of arbitration clause—Separability—Reinsurance contracts containing arbitration clause).
    Breach of warranty—
      Defendant insurance company agreeing to indemnify shipping company in respect of liability for loss of or damage to cargo—Claimants reinsuring defendant—Reinsurance contract containing typhoon warranty clause—Captain of vessel being given typhoon warning—Captain sailing from port—Vessel capsizing in typhoon—Whether breach of typhoon warranty clause and reinsurance contract avoided. **Amlin Corporate Member Ltd v Oriental Assurance Corp** [2014] **1 Comm** 415, QBD.
      Pecuniary loss indemnity insurance providing collateral for financing of film projects—Warranties specifying number of films to be made—Defendants receiving monthly reports indicating shortfall—Defendants raising no objections—Whether breach of warranty waived—Waiver by estoppel—Whether clear and unequivocal representation of waiver of rights. **HIH Casualty & General Insurance Ltd v Axa Corporate Solutions** [2002] **2 Comm** 1053, CA.
    Brokers—
      Negligence—Limitation of action—Accrual of cause of action. *See* **Limitation of action** (Accrual of cause of action—Negligence—Brokers—Reinsurance).
    Claims co-operation clause—
      Construction—Reinsurance of directors and officers policy of insurance—Knowledge of loss or losses—Meaning of loss or losses—Whether insurer complying with requirements of claims co-operation clause. **AIG Europe (Ireland) Ltd v Faraday Capital Ltd** [2007] **1 Comm** 527, QBD.
      Construction—Reinsurance of directors' errors and omissions policy of insurance—Knowledge of loss or losses—Meaning of loss or losses—Whether insurer complying with requirements of claims co-operation clause. **AIG Europe (Ireland) Ltd v Faraday Capital Ltd** [2008] **2 Comm** 362, CA.
      Follow the settlements policy—Policy providing that underwriters 'shall control the negotiations and settlements of any claims'—Reassured seeking indemnity in respect of claim settled not under reinsurers' control—Whether reinsurers bound to indemnify reassured in respect of settlement. **Eagle Star Insurance Co Ltd v J N Cresswell** [2004] **1 Comm** 508, QBD; [2004] **2 Comm** 244, CA.
      Policy requiring approval of reinsurer to settlement/compromise and admission of liability—Insurer entering into settlement/compromise—Reinsurer seeking declaration of non-liability—Whether breach of clause established only by settlement/compromise agreed with admission of liability—Whether approval of settlement not to be reasonably withheld—Whether insurer able to recover from reinsurer following breach of condition precedent although liable to insured. **Gan Insurance Co Ltd v Tai Ping Insurance Co Ltd (No 2)** [2001] **2 Comm** 299, CA.
      Reinsurers alleging breach of claims co-operation clause but continuing to communicate with insurers in relation to claim—Reinsurers subsequently alleging and relying on second breach of claims co-operation clause as discharging them from liability—Whether reinsurers waiving right to rely on claims co-operation clause by alleging breach—Whether as matter of construction claims co-operation clause ceasing to operate following first allegation of breach. **Lexington Insurance Co v Multinacional de Seguros SA** [2009] **1 Comm** 35, QBD.
    Conflict of laws—
      Jurisdiction. *See* **Conflict of laws** (Jurisdiction—Challenge to jurisdiction—Reinsurance contract).
    Construction of terms—
      Brokerage—Brokerage related to premium—Whether brokerage clause to follow same pattern as premium clause. **Absalom (on behalf of Lloyd's Syndicate 957) v TCRU Ltd** [2006] **1 Comm** 375, QBD and CA.
    Contract for excess of loss reinsurance—
      Follow settlements clause—Effect of clause where insured also reinsurer—Settlements made by insured binding on reinsurers providing settlements were within terms and conditions of original policies and 'within the terms and conditions of this reinsurance'—Loss of reinsured aircraft—Effect of settlements made by insured—Whether reinsurers entitled to dispute basis of settlement. **Hill v Mercantile and General Reinsurance Co plc** [1996] **3** 865, HL.
      Follow settlements clause—Effect of clause—Insurance settlements binding on reinsurers providing settlement within terms and conditions of insurance policy—Insured's claim in respect of property damage and business interruption—Effect of insurance settlement—Whether retrocession reinsurers entitled to dispute basis of settlement. **Tokio Marine Europe Insurance Ltd v Novae Corporate Underwriting Ltd** [2015] **1 Comm** 168, QBD.
      Follow settlements clause—Joint Excess Loss Committee Excess Loss Clauses—Settlements made by insured binding on reinsurers only if within terms and conditions of original policies—Loss of reinsured aircraft and oil spill—Losses entering London Market Excess of Loss spiral—Losses erroneously aggregated and irrecoverable claims wrongly included—Claimant seeking to prove recoverable losses by use of appropriate discounts to strip out wrongly aggregated or irrecoverable elements—Claimant seeking to rely on actuarial models to assess recoverable losses—Whether contracts requiring claimant to prove loss at each level of spiral—Whether use of actuarial models permitted. **Equitas Ltd v R&Q Reinsurance Co (UK) Ltd** [2010] **2 Comm** 855, QBD.
      Liability under contracts of reinsurance—Insurers settling claim by original insured—Whether insurers entitled to claim indemnity in respect of settlement under reinsurance policies. **Commercial Union Assurance Co plc v NRG Victory Reinsurance Ltd** [1998] **2** 434, CA.

INSURANCE (cont)—
  Reinsurance (cont)—
    Contract for excess of loss reinsurance (cont)—
      Losses 'arising from one event'—9/11 terrorists hijacking two planes and crashing them into Twin Towers of World Trade Center—Arbitral tribunal finding terrorist acts arising out of two events and not one—Whether tribunal erring. **Aioi Nissay Dowa Insurance Co Ltd v Heraldglen Ltd** [2013] **2 Comm** 231, QBD.
      Losses 'arising from one event'—Aggregation of losses—First airline's aircraft seized by invading army—Second airline's aircraft destroyed by bombing in subsequent war—Correct approach to aggregation—Whether first and second airline's losses arising out of same event. **Scott v Copenhagen Reinsurance Co (UK) Ltd** [2003] **2 Comm** 190, CA.
      Losses 'arising out of one event'—Losses arising 'from one originating cause'—Aggregation of losses—Lloyd's names successfully suing underwriters—Underwriters claiming from liability insurers under errors and omissions policy—Liability insurers claiming from reinsurers under excess of loss policy—Errors and omissions policy providing for aggregation of claims for losses arising out of one event for purposes of limitation of liability—Excess of loss policy providing for aggregation of claims for losses arising from one originating cause for purposes of limitation of liability—Whether losses arising from one originating cause for purpose of errors and omissions policy also arising out of one event for purpose of excess of loss policy. **Axa Reinsurance (UK) plc v Field** [1996] **3** 517, HL.
      Premium review clause—Triggering event—Construction of clause—Waiver or estoppel—Whether review clause validly invoked. **Charman v New Cap Reinsurance Corp Ltd (in liq)** [2004] **1 Comm** 114, CA.
      Reinsurers liable to indemnify insurers in respect of 'sum actually paid' by insurers in settlement of losses or liability—Insurers in provisional liquidation and unable to pay claims under policies which they had reinsured—Whether reinsurers liable to indemnify insurers in respect of sums not yet paid but where amount of loss had been agreed—Whether 'sum actually paid' denoting requirement of prior disbursement. **Charter Reinsurance Co Ltd v Fagan** [1996] **3** 46, HL.
  Disclosure—
    Material non-disclosure—Marine and non-marine insurance—Contracts of reinsurance covering losses caused by dishonest or fraudulent acts of bank employees—Media reports of serious impropriety on part of bank employees—Defendant insurers not disclosing reports and denying truth of allegations—Whether claimants entitled to avoid contracts—Whether allegations immaterial if shown to be untrue at trial—Whether materiality of circumstances to be assessed only at time of placement. **Brotherton v Aseguradora Colseguros SA** [2003] **1 Comm** 774, QBD; [2003] **2 Comm** 298, CA.
    Material non-disclosure—Marine and non-marine insurance—Fair presentation—Inducement—Reinsurer given unfair presentation of risk—Judge finding reinsurer failing to establish its broker would have declined risk if fair presentation made—Whether judge applying wrong test—Whether proper basis for judge's hypothetical broke. **Axa Versicherung AG v Arab Insurance Group** [2017] **1 Comm** 929, CA.
    Material non-disclosure—Marine and non-marine insurance—Non-disclosure by insurers' agent to proposed reinsurers of dishonest conduct amounting to fraud on principal—Agent effecting reinsurances through brokers—Whether duty on agent to disclose to reinsurers its own dishonest conduct—Whether agent's dishonesty being a circumstance which in the ordinary course of business ought to be known to assured—Whether agent being an agent to insure—Marine Insurance Act 1906, ss 18(1), 19(a). **PCW Syndicates v PCW Reinsurers** [1996] **1** 774, CA.
    Material non-disclosure—Marine and non-marine insurance—Reinsurers concluding reinsurance contracts with reinsured companies through agency of underwriters—Underwriters not disclosing to reinsurers intention of individual members to retain commission amounting to fraud on principal reinsured—Whether reinsurers entitled to avoid for material non-disclosure—Whether fraud being a circumstance which in the ordinary course of business ought to be known to reinsured—Marine Insurance Act 1906, s 18. **Deutsche Ruckversicherung AG v Walbrook Insurance Co Ltd** [1996] **1** 791, CA.
    Non-disclosure—Material non-disclosure—Waiver—Affirmation—Slip presentation referring to clocks—Cargo containing high-value branded watches—Reinsurers purporting to avoid contract on basis of non-disclosure—Whether reinsurers waiving disclosure—Whether reinsurers affirming contract by issuing notice of cancellation. **WISE Underwriting Agency Ltd v Grupo Nacional Provincial SA** [2004] **1 Comm** 495, QBD; [2004] **2 Comm** 613, CA.
  Employer's liability policies—
    Employer liable to employees for exposure to asbestos causing mesothelioma—Insurer settling insurance claims made by employees in view of current state of law—Insurer claiming under its reinsurances—Dispute arising as to method of presentation of reinsurer's liability—Arbitrator making findings in favour of insurer—Appeal on questions of law—Arbitration Act 1996, s 69. **Equitas Insurance Ltd v Municipal Mutual Insurance Ltd** [2019] **2 Comm** 843, CA; [2020] **1** 16, CA.
  Facility quota share treaties—
    Disclosure—Claimant insurers entering into facility quota share treaties with defendant reinsurer—Claimants protecting casualty account by excess of loss insurance—Claimants obliged to return 50% of risks—Defendant subsequently seeking to avoid treaties on grounds of misrepresentation and non-disclosure—Whether defendant entitled to avoid treaties. **Kingscroft Insurance Co Ltd v Nissan Fire and Marine Insurance Co Ltd** [2000] **1 Comm** 272, QBD.
  Jurisdiction—
    Conflict of laws. *See* **Conflict of laws** (Jurisdiction—Challenge to jurisdiction—Reinsurance contract).
  Liability under contract of reinsurance—
    Back-to-back reinsurance—Reassured settling claims of underlying insured in light of judgment of United States court—Settlement including losses occurring outside period of cover—Whether reinsurers liable to indemnify reassured for settlement. **Wasa International Insurance Co Ltd v Lexington Insurance Co** [2008] **1 Comm** 286, QBD; [2008] **1 Comm** 1085, CA; [2009] **4** 909, HL; [2010] **2 Comm** 324, HL.

INSURANCE (cont)—
  Reinsurance (cont)—
    Liability under contract of reinsurance (cont)—
      Claimant insurers participation in hull and machinery insurance including a 'follow the leader' clause—Change in class of vessel accepted by lead insurers—Vessel subsequently running aground and declared total loss—Whether 'follow the leader' clause incorporated into reinsurance policy. **American International Marine Agency of New York Inc v Dandridge** [2005] **2 Comm** 496, QBD.
      'Follow the settlements' clause—Insurer settling claim under original policy—Whether claim covered by policy of reinsurance—Whether reinsurer entitled to require insurer to show claim as recognised by insurer falling within risks covered by reinsurance. **Assicurazioni Generali SpA v CGU International Insurance plc** [2003] **2 Comm** 425, QBD; [2004] **2 Comm** 114, CA.
      'Follow the settlements' clause—Insurer settling insurance claim—Whether claim recognised by insurer fell within retrocession as matter of law—Whether the correct test to determine whether claim fell within retrocession was balance of probabilities or arguability. **Tokio Marine Europe Insurance Ltd v Novae Corporate Underwriting Ltd** [2015] **1 Comm** 168, QBD.
    Misrepresentation—
      Reinsured renewing reinsurance for warehouse—Reinsured's brokers telling reinsurer they had been informed that warehouse had hydrants—Warehouse only having dry risers—Fire destroying warehouse and reinsurer seeking to avoid for misrepresentation—Whether reinsured's statement a representation of fact or belief. **Sirius International Insurance Corp v Oriental Assurance Corp** [1999] **1 Comm** 699, QBD.
      Retrocession. *See* Reinsurance—Retrocession—Misrepresentation, *below*.
    Negligence—
      Measure of damages. *See* **Damages** (Measure of damages—Negligence—Reinsurance).
    Non-proportional reinsurance—
      Terms—Implied terms—Implied terms—Whether implied term that reinsureds would conduct business involved in risks declared to the cover prudently, reasonably carefully and in accordance with ordinary practice of the market—Whether any other implied terms. **Bonner v Cox** [2006] **1 Comm** 565, CA.
    Premium—
      Payment of premium by broker—Policy providing 'premium payable on cash basis to London Underwriters within 90 days of attachment'—Reassured failing to pay premium to broker—Broker bringing claim for premium—When broker's cause of action accruing—Marine Insurance Act 1906, s 53(1). **Heath Lambert Ltd v Sociedad de Corretaje de Seguros** [2004] **2 Comm** 656, CA; [2005] **1** 225, CA.
    Proper law of contract. *See* **Conflict of laws** (Contract—Proper law of contract—Insurance and reinsurance policies).
    Proportional reinsurance—
      Costs incurred in investigating, settling or defending claims by insured—Whether insurer able to recover proportion of such costs from reinsurer—Whether term to that effect to be implied into contract of reinsurance. **Baker v Black Sea and Baltic General Insurance Co Ltd (Equitas Reinsurance Ltd intervening)** [1998] **2** 833, HL.
    Reinsurance business—
      Illegality—Restrictions on carrying on insurance business—Reinsurers concluding reinsurance contracts with reinsured companies through agency of underwriters—Reinsurers not authorised to conduct insurance business—Reinsured seeking to draw down on letters of credit provided by reinsurers—Reinsurers seeking injunction to prevent draw down in reliance on illegality of reinsurance contracts—Whether reinsurance contracts illegal, unenforceable and void—Whether letters of credit tainted by illegality of contracts—Insurance Companies Act 1982, s 2—Financial Services Act 1986, s 132. **Deutsche Ruckversicherung AG v Walbrook Insurance Co Ltd** [1996] **1** 791, CA.
      Retrocession—Whether reinsurance business constituting 'insurance business'—Whether long term reinsurance business constituting 'long term business'—Whether retrocession arrangements also 'insurance business' and 'long term business'—Insurance Companies Act 1982. **NRG Victory Reinsurance Ltd, Re** [1995] **1** 533, Ch D.
    Retention clause—
      Full reinsurance clause—Reinsurance contract including standard 'full reinsurance clause' into which percentage of risk retained by insurer to be inserted—Space for percentage left blank—Effect of retention clause in reinsurance contract—Whether failure to retain part of risk by insurer absolving reinsurer from liability. **Phoenix General Insurance Co of Greece SA v Administratia Asigurarilor de Stat** [1987] **2** 152, CA.
    Retrocession—
      Misrepresentation—Alleged misrepresentation of third party reinsurer's participation—Disclosure—Reserving policy—Claim that reserving policy imprudent and unusual. **Assicurazioni Generali SpA v Arab Insurance Group (BSC)** [2003] **1 Comm** 140, CA.
    Risks insured—
      Breach of condition—Livestock insurance for Norwegian fish farm—Original insurance policy governed by Norwegian law—Reinsurance policy made in England covering 90 per cent of liability—Both policies containing condition that 24-hour watch be kept on fish farm—Breach of 24-hour watch condition not rendering original policy null and void under Norwegian law if breach irrelevant to loss—Breach of condition rendering reinsurance policy null and void under English law irrespective of whether breach relevant to loss—Fish stock destroyed by storm—Insured in breach of 24-hour watch condition but breach irrelevant to loss—Norwegian insurers paying loss—Whether reinsurer liable to make good loss under resinsurance policy. **Forsikringsaktieselskapet Vesta v Butcher (No 1)** [1989] **1** 402, HL.
      Breach of warranty—Defendant insuring vessels under policy governed by Venezuelan law—Policy containing class maintenance guarantee—Claimants providing reinsurance cover 'as original'—Reinsurance policy containing class maintenance warranty—Shipowners making claim under insurance policy under Venezuelan law—Claimants contending that breach of class warranty in reinsurance contracts discharging liability—Whether reinsurance cover 'free-standing' from warranties in original cover. **Groupama Navigation et Transports v Catatumbo CA Seguros** [1999] **2 Comm** 970, QBD; [2000] **2 Comm** 193, CA.

INSURANCE (cont)—
  Reinsurance (cont)—
    Risks insured (cont)—
      Copper-mining company constructing new furnace and acid plant—Construction contracts providing for period of testing to full design capacity following commissioning—Company's operational insurance policy providing that policy not covering object 'before it had been installed and completely tested'—Policy defining 'completely tested' as operating 'in the capacity for which it was designed as part of the normal process'—Insurer reinsuring risk on same terms as original—Lead reinsurer putting down scratch that reinsurance subject to exclusion of testing and commissioning—Furnace and acid plant suffering damage after start-up but before testing—Whether furnace and acid plant attaching to reinsurance policy. **Kennecott Utah Copper Corp v Cornhill Insurance plc** [1999] **2 Comm** 801, QBD.
      Meaning of 'removal of debris'—Whether words including expense of cleaning-up pollution caused by oil spillage. **King v Brandywine Reinsurance Co (UK) Ltd (formerly known as Cigna RE Co (UK) Ltd)** [2004] **2 Comm** 443, QBD; **King v Brandywine Reinsurance Company** [2005] **2 Comm** 1, CA.
      Plaintiffs becoming members of insurance pool managed by agent—Members of pool agreeing to apportion loss in event of insolvency of pool member—Defendant reinsuring plaintiffs for loss arising out of risks written by agent—Whether reinsurance agreement covered loss arising out of apportionment agreement. **Württembergische AG Versicherungsbeteiligungsgesellschaft v Home Insurance Co** [1999] **1 Comm** 535, CA.
      Underlying policy providing for annual aggregate deduction—Reinsurance policy applying to losses in excess of original annual aggregate deductible and original underlying deductibles—Whether reinsurance back-to-back in respect of risks insured. **Goshawk Syndicate Management Ltd v XL Speciality Insurance Co** [2004] **2 Comm** 512, QBD.
    Transfer of long-term business—
      Insurer reinsuring policies with subsidiary—Parties proposing to 'transfer' the subsidiary's reinsurance business to insurer—Whether proposed arrangement was a 'transfer'—Insurance Companies Act 1982, Sch 2C, Pt 1, para 1. **Friends' Provident Life Office, Re** [1999] **2 Comm** 437, CA.
      Sanction of court—Whether applicant entitled to assign benefit of reinsurance contracts without consent of reinsurers—Financial Services and Markets Act 2000, s 112(2)(a). **WASA International (UK) Insurance Co Ltd v WASA International Insurance Co Ltd (a Swedish company)** [2003] **1 Comm** 696, Ch D.
  Repudiation of claim—
    Burglary insurance. See Burglary insurance—Claim—Repudiation of claim without repudiation of policy by insurance company, *above*.
  Risk—
    Description of risk—
      Burglary insurance. See Burglary insurance—Risk—Description of risk, *above*.
      Contingency insurance. See Contingency insurance—Risk—Description of risk, *above*.
      Property insurance. See Property insurance—Risk—Description of risk, *above*.
    Duration of risk—
      Goods in transit. See Property insurance—Goods in transit—Duration of risk, *above*.
    Motor insurance. See **Motor insurance** (Risk).
    Re-insurance. See Reinsurance—Risks insured, *above*.
  Safe port—
    Charterparty. See **Shipping** (Charterparty—Safe port—Insurance).
  Settlement—
    Reinsurers, liability of. See Reinsurance—Liability under contract of reinsurance—Back-to-back reinsurance, *above*.
  Shipbuilders' all risks policy—
    Shipyard—
      Shipyard not expressly named as assured on slip—Vessel sustaining damage during completion work—Whether shipyard an assured—Whether shipyard entitled to enforce contract as undisclosed principal. **Talbot Underwriting Ltd v Nausch, Hogan & Murray Inc** [2006] **2 Comm** 751, CA.
  Sickness insurance—
    European Community—
      Equality of treatment of men and women. See **European Union** (Equality of treatment of men and women—Social security—Sickness insurance).
  Society of Lloyd's—
    Documents—
      Disclosure of documents by broker to underwriter—Underwriter seeking access to placing, claims and premium accounting documents—Lloyd's Terms of Business Agreement—Whether implied contract between underwriters and insureds permitting underwriters to inspect documents—Whether similar right against brokers to inspect documents in their possession. **Goshawk Dedicated Ltd v Tyser & Co Ltd** [2005] **2 Comm** 115, QBD; [2006] **1 Comm** 501, CA.
    Premium trust deed—
      Lloyd's requiring names to execute trust deed—Trust fund including premiums and other monies belonging or becoming payable to names in connection with underwriting—Trust deed containing power of amendment—Lloyd's exercising power to bring litigation recoveries within trust—Whether litigation recoveries covered by unamended deed—Whether power of amendment properly exercised. **Society of Lloyd's v Robinson** [1999] **1 Comm** 545, HL.
  Solicitor—
    Conditional fee agreement. See **Solicitor** (Costs—Conditional fee agreement—Success fee uplift).
    Professional indemnity insurance. See Liability insurance—Professional indemnity insurance—Solicitor, *above*.
  Subrogation—
    Guarantee insurance—
      Export contract—Policy insuring exporting company against percentage of loss from buyer's inability to transfer currency owing to foreign exchange control restrictions—Claim under policy satisfied by insurer—Insurer's right against liquidator of company—Assignment of rights to sums recovered from buyer. **Miller, Gibb & Co Ltd, Re** [1957] **2 266**, Ch D.

INSURANCE (cont)—
   Subrogation (cont)—
      Guarantee insurance (cont)—
         Export contract—Right of insurer to sums recovered—Relevance of principle of subrogation—Express terms of policy—Insurers entitled to 90 per cent of sums recovered 'in respect of a loss to which policy applies'—Insurance relating to export contract between merchant and foreign buyer—Risks covered including delay in payment by foreign buyer—Insurers undertaking to pay 90 per cent of loss—Amount of loss—Payment under contract in foreign currency—Rate of exchange—Loss to be calculated according to rate of exchange at date of export—Delay in payment caused by exchange control restrictions imposed by buyer's country—Payment by insurers in respect of loss—Subsequent payment by buyers—Sterling proceeds of payment exceeding loss calculated under policy because of devaluation of sterling—Whether insurers entitled to recover sum in excess of amount paid in respect of loss. **Lucas (L) Ltd v Export Credits Guarantee Dept** [1973] **2** 984, CA.

         Express terms of policy—Right of insurers to sums recovered in respect of loss—Principle of subrogation—Principle to be applied only when doubt or ambiguity as to express terms of policy. **Lucas (L) Ltd v Export Credits Guarantee Dept** [1973] **2** 984, CA.
      Recoupment from insured—
         Insured claiming on insurance policy for damage allegedly caused by third parties—Insurers repudiating liability and insured bringing actions against insurers and third parties—One of third parties making payment into court—Insurers settling action by paying sum equal to amount paid into court by third party—Third party being found liable for amount in excess of payment into court—Whether insurers entitled to lien over sum paid into court by third party—Whether insured entitled to deduct irrecoverable costs from sum recouped by insurers. **England v Guardian Insurance Ltd** [1999] **2 Comm** 481, QBD.
      Stop-loss insurance—
         Assured insured by stop-loss insurers against underwriting losses—Assured sustaining losses through negligence of underwriter's agent—Stop-loss insurers paying assured under policies—Assured bringing action against agent in respect of losses and recovering damages in settlement of claim—Whether stop-loss insurers having equitable proprietary right in settlement moneys—Policy providing excess to be borne by assured—Whether assured entitled to deduct from settlement moneys loss occurring below excess before reimbursing insurers by way of subrogation—Whether stop-loss insurers entitled to injunction restraining payment of settlement moneys to assured before stop-loss insurers reimbursed. **Napier and Ettrick (Lord) v Hunter** [1993] **1** 385, HL.
   Suicide—
      Exception of life policy. *See* Life insurance—Exception—Suicide, *above*.
   Theft, against—
      Property insurance. *See* Property insurance—Perils insured against—Theft, *above*.
   Third party's rights—
      Employer's liability insurance. *See* Employer's liability insurance—Third party's rights against insurers, *above*.
      Marine insurance. *See* **Marine insurance** (Third parties' rights against insurers).
      Motor insurance. *See* **Motor insurance** (Rights of third parties against insurers).
      Public liability insurance. *See* Liability insurance—Public liability insurance—Third party's rights against insurers, *above*.
   Third party's rights against insurer—
      Application of statutory scheme—
         Policy containing retained limit—Policy containing contractual definition of insolvency event—Terms affecting rights of third parties on occurrence of statutory insolvency event—Terms purporting to alter rights on occurrence of contractual insolvency event—Whether transfer of rights to third party where retained limit not reached—Whether transfer of claims handling rights affecting rights of third parties—Whether occurrence of contractual insolvency event capable of triggering operation of statutory scheme—Third Party (Rights Against Insurers) Act 1930, s 1. **Centre Reinsurance International Co v Curzon Insurance Ltd** [2004] **2 Comm** 28, Ch D; **Centre Reinsurance International Co v Freakley** [2005] **2 Comm** 65, CA.
         Policy providing for transfer of claims handling rights on occurrence of insolvency event—Claims handling expenses—Claims handling expenses incurred by insurer—Whether provisions transferring claims handling rights surviving operation of statutory scheme—Whether costs and expenses incurred by reinsurers in handling claims part of ultimate net loss—Whether costs and expenses incurred by reinsurers to be treated as costs of administration—Third Parties (Rights Against Insurers) Act 1930, s 1(3)—Insolvency Act 1986, s 19. **Centre Reinsurance International Co v Freakley** [2005] **2 Comm** 65, CA.
         Product liability insurance—Policy containing clause excluding liability in contract 'unless liability would have attached in the absence of such contract or agreement'—Claimant obtaining judgment against assured based on liability in contract—Assured going into liquidation—Claimant seeking declaration of liability in respect of insurer—Whether liability would have arisen in absence of contract between claimant and assured—Whether insurer liable to indemnify claimant. **Omega Proteins Ltd v Aspen Insurance UK Ltd** [2011] **1 Comm** 313, QBD.
      Liability insurance. *See* Liability insurance—Public liability insurance—Third party's rights against insurers, *above*.
   Transfer of long-term insurance business—
      Sanction by court of scheme for transfer of long-term insurance business—
         Principles to be applied in exercise of court's discretion—Exchange of rights in inherited estate for incentive payment—Whether court should sanction scheme—Insurance Companies Act 1982, s 49, Pt I, Sch 2C. **Axa Equity & Law Life Assurance Society plc and Axa Sun Life plc, Re** [2001] **1 Comm** 1010, Ch D.
         Principles to be applied in exercise of court's discretion—Factors to be considered—Financial Services and Markets Act 2000, s 111(3). **Prudential Assurance Co Ltd and Rothesay Life plc, Re** [2020] **2** 393n, Ch D.
         Principles to be applied in exercise of court's discretion—Insurance Companies Act 1982, Sch 2C. **Hill Samuel Life Assurance Ltd, Re** [1998] **3** 176, Ch D.
      Reinsurance. *See* Reinsurance—Transfer of long-term business, *above*.

INSURANCE (cont)—
Travel insurance—
    Construction of policy. *See* Policy—Construction—Travel insurance, *above*.
Underwriter—
    Liability—
        Amendments to slip. *See* Broker—Slip tendered to underwriters by broker—Underwriters' liability, *above*.
        Lloyd's underwriting agent—Negligence. *See* **Negligence** (Duty to take care—Insurance—Lloyd's underwriting agent).
        Lloyd's underwriting agent—Written agreement required by Lloyd's byelaw—No written agreement existing between managing agent and name—Whether agreement void for illegality—Lloyd's Byelaw No 8 of 1988—Lloyd's Act 1982. **P & B (Run-Off) Ltd v Woolley** [2001] **1 Comm** 1120, QBD; [2002] **1 Comm** 577, CA.
Unemployment insurance—
    Equality of treatment of men and women—
        European Community. *See* **European Union** (Equality of treatment of men and women—Social security—Pension and unemployment insurance).
    Generally. *See* **Unemployment insurance**.
Value added tax—
    Exemption—
        Generally. *See* **Value added tax** (Exemptions—Insurance).
        Insurance transactions—European Community. *See* **European Union** (Value added tax—Exemptions—Insurance transactions).
Variation of trust—
    Protection against possible shortfall in consequence of capital transfer tax. *See* **Variation of trusts** (Protection against possible shortfall in consequence of capital transfer tax—Insurance).
War damage—
    Insurance of goods against war damage. *See* **War damage** (Insurance of goods against war damage).
War risks—
    Aviation insurance. *See* Aviation insurance—War risks, *above*.
    Marine insurance. *See* **Marine insurance** (War risks policy).
Warranty, breach of—
    Reinsurance. *See* Reinsurance—Breach of warranty, *above*.

INSURANCE COMPANY
Loans by—
    Annual payments for income tax purposes. *See* **Income tax** (Annual payment—Annuity—Monthly loans by insurance company).
Winding up. *See* **Company** (Insurance company—Winding up).

INTELLECTUAL PROPERTY
Confidential information. *See* **Confidential information**.
Copyright—
    Conflict of laws. *See* **Conflict of laws** (Jurisdiction—Challenge to jurisdiction—Copyright).
    Copyright Tribunal—
        Costs. *See* **Costs** (Copyright Tribunal).
    European Union. *See* **European Union** (Copyright).
    Generally. *See* **Copyright**.
Copyright and related rights in the information society—
    European Union. *See* **European Union** (Intellectual property rights—Copyright—Related rights in the information society).
Data protection. *See* **Data protection**.
Databases, legal protection of—
    European Union. *See* **European Union** (Intellectual property rights—Copyright—Legal protection of databases).
Design. *See* **Design**.
European Union. *See* **European Union** (Intellectual property rights).
Image rights—
    Representation agreement—
        Restraint of trade. *See* **Restraint of trade by agreement** (Exclusive agent and principal—Image rights representation agreement).
Legal protection of databases. *See* **European Union** (Intellectual property rights—Copyright—Legal protection of databases).
Passing off—
    Generally. *See* **Passing off**.
Patent—
    Conflict of laws. *See* **Conflict of laws** (Jurisdiction—Challenge to jurisdiction—Patent).
    European Union. *See* **European Union** (Patent).
    Generally. *See* **Patent**.
Trade mark—
    European Union. *See* **European Union** (Trade marks).
    Generally. *See* **Trade mark**.

INTELLIGENCE SERVICES
Scrutiny of investigatory powers and functions of intelligence services—
    Tribunal established by statute—
        Proceedings against intelligence services—Statutory tribunal only appropriate tribunal for proceedings claiming intelligence services acting in way incompatible with convention right—Former member of intelligence services bringing claim including convention claim against refusal of intelligence service to consent to publication of book describing his work—Whether court's jurisdiction ousted—Human Rights Act 1998, s 7(1)—Regulation of Investigatory Powers Act 2000, s 65(2). **A v B (Investigatory Powers Tribunal: jurisdiction)** [2008] **4** 511, QBD; [2009] **3** 416, CA; [2010] **1** 1149, SC.

INTENTION

Corporate body. *See* **Landlord and tenant** (Opposition to grant of new tenancy of business premises—Intention of landlord to demolish or reconstruct premises comprised in holding—Local authority landlord).

Creation of legal relations. *See* **Contract** (Intention to create legal relationship).

Criminal liability. *See* **Criminal law** (Intention).

Cruelty—
    Divorce. *See* **Divorce** (Cruelty—Elements of offence—Intention).

Deed not giving effect to parties' common intention—
    Rectification—
        Deed of release. *See* **Deed** (Rectification—Deed of release—Deed not giving effect to parties' common intention).

Desertion—
    Divorce. *See* **Divorce** (Desertion—Intention).

Domicile—
    Abandonment of domicile of choice. *See* **Domicile** (Abandonment of domicile of choice—Intention).

Intoxication negativing intention—
    Defence to criminal proceedings. *See* **Criminal law** (Intoxication as a defence—Capacity to form intent).

Lease—
    Exclusion from protection of Rent Acts—
        Holiday letting. *See* **Rent restriction** (Protected tenancy—Excluded tenancies—Holiday letting—Intention of parties).

INTER VIVOS GIFT

Generally. *See* **Gift** (Inter vivos gift).

Negligence—
    Solicitor. *See* **Solicitor** (Negligence—Inter vivos gift).

INTER-STATE TRADE

Freedom of—
    Australia. *See* **Australia** (Freedom of inter-state trade).

INTERCEPTION OF COMMUNICATIONS

Evidence—
    Criminal proceedings—
        Generally. *See* **Criminal evidence** (Interception of communications).
    Extradition proceedings. *See* **Extradition** (Committal—Evidence—Telephone intercept).

Police powers—
    Interception of telephone conversation. *See* **Police** (Powers—Telephone tapping).

INTEREST

Arbitration award. *See* **Arbitration** (Award—Interest).

Bank account. *See* **Bank** (Account—Interest).

Building society—
    Interest paid to depositors—
        Income tax. *See* **Income tax** (Building society—Interest and dividends paid to depositors).

Charging order. *See* **Execution** (Charging order—Interest on order).

Compensation—
    Compulsory purchase—
        Reinstatement basis. *See* **Compulsory purchase** (Compensation—Reinstatement basis—Interest).

Compound interest—
    Bank—
        Entitlement of bankers to capitalise interest—Usage of bankers—Debt owed to bank—Capitalisation of interest until debt paid—Relationship of banker and customer—Mortgage—Mortgage securing bank's guarantee of payment of instalments of purchase price of vessel—No express provision in mortgage entitling bank to charge compound interest—Bank issuing written demand for repayment under mortgage—Whether relationship of banker and customer terminated following demand for repayment—Whether bank entitled to charge compound interest following demand for repayment—Whether entitlement to compound interest restricted to mercantile accounts current for mutual transactions. **National Bank of Greece SA v Pinios Shipping Co No 1** [1989] **1** 213, CA; [1990] **1** 78, HL.
        Entitlement of bankers to capitalise interest—Usage of bankers—Debt owed to bank—Construction of clause in loan agreement. **Kitchen v HSBC Bank plc** [2000] **1 Comm** 787, CA.

Simple or compound interest—
    Damages—Breach of fiduciary duty. *See* Damages—Award of interest—Equitable jurisdiction—Simple or compound interest—Fiduciary duty—Breach, *below*.

Value added tax, refund of. *See* **Value added tax** (Overpayment of tax—Interest on repayment of overpaid tax—Compound interest).

Conflict of interest—
    Solicitor's duty. *See* **Solicitor** (Duty—Conflict of interest).

Costs—
    Criminal cases—
        Jurisdiction to award interest on costs paid out of central funds. *See* **Criminal law** (Costs—Award out of central funds—Interest).
    Divorce. *See* **Divorce** (Costs—Interest on costs).
    Generally. *See* **Costs** (Interest on costs).
    Solicitor—
        Non-contentious business. *See* **Solicitor** (Costs—Non-contentious business—Interest).

Customs duty—
    Deposit by way of security for unpaid duty. *See* **Customs and excise** (Imported goods—Delivery on giving security for duty—Interest on security).

Damages—
    Arbitration award. *See* **Arbitration** (Award—Interest—Damages).

INTEREST (cont)—
  Damages (cont)—
    Award in foreign currency—
      Rate of interest—Contract governed by foreign law—Entitlement to interest determined by foreign law—Interest to be assessed in accordance with English law as lex fori—Appropriate rate that at which person could reasonably have borrowed in foreign currency—Law Reform (Miscellaneous Provisions) Act 1934, s 3(1)(a). **Miliangos v George Frank (Textiles) Ltd (No 2)** [1976] **3** 599, QBD.
  Award of interest—
    Common law jurisdiction—Simple or compound interest—Damages for late payment of debt—Whether interest payable—Whether compound interest payable. **Sempra Metals Ltd (formerly Metallgesellschaft Ltd) v IRC** [2007] **4** 657, HL.
    Damages for inconvenience and disappointment—Whether interest should be awarded. **Saunders v Edwards** [1987] **2** 651, CA.
    Date from which interest payable—Complex insurance claim—Whether interest to run immediately from occurrence of loss—Whether insurers to have reasonable time to consider claim. **Quorum A/S v Schramm (No 2)** [2002] **2 Comm** 179, QBD.
    Enhanced interest—Defendant rejecting claimant's Pt 36 offer—Claimant achieving greater award at trial—Judge finding defendant's conduct unreasonable—Claimant awarded enhanced rate of interest on damages—Whether provisions for enhanced interest entirely compensatory—Whether maximum level of enhanced interest appropriate—CPR 36.14(3)(a). **OMV Petrom SA v Glencore International AG (No 2)** [2018] **1 Comm** 210, CA; [2018] **1** 703, CA.
    Enhanced interest—Power to award enhanced interest on damages and costs where defendant failing to beat claimant's Pt 36 offer—Principles governing exercise of power—CPR 36.21. **Petrotrade Inc v Texaco Ltd** [2001] **4** 853, CA.
    Enhanced interest—Power to award enhanced interest on damages and costs where defendant failing to beat claimant's Pt 36 offer—Whether power to be exercised in relation to jury awards in defamation cases—CPR 36.21(2). **McPhilemy v Times Newspapers Ltd (No 2)** [2001] **4** 861, CA.
    Equitable jurisdiction—Simple or compound interest—Fiduciary duty—Breach—Funds used in joint venture—Funds partly used for plaintiff's benefit—Whether compound or simple interest should be awarded on sums due to plaintiff. **O'Sullivan v Management Agency and Music Ltd** [1985] **3** 351, CA.
    Equitable jurisdiction—Simple or compound interest—Fiduciary duty—Breach—Misappropriation of funds by person in fiduciary position—Company director—Funds used for purpose of commercial transaction—Presumption that profit made by wrongdoer out of use of funds—Rate of interest—Loans obtained from company by director to purchase shares in company—Judgment against director in respect of transaction—Court entitled to award compound interest with yearly rests—Rate of interest one per cent above bank rate or minimum lending rate. **Wallersteiner v Moir (No 2)** [1975] **1** 849, CA.
    Jurisdiction to include interest—Generally. *See* Damages—Jurisdiction to include interest in award of damages, *below*.
    Purpose of award of interest—Compensation for being kept out of money and having to borrow in meantime—Simple interest only awardable—Supreme Court Act 1981, s 35A(1). **Wentworth v Wiltshire CC** [1993] **2** 256, CA.
  Breach of contract—
    Pleading. *See* **Practice** (Interest—Pleading).
    Receipts from insurers—Whether receipts from insurers to be taken into account in awarding interest. **Harbutt's Plasticine Ltd v Wayne Tank and Pump Co Ltd** [1970] **1** 225, CA.
    Remoteness—Causation—Mitigation—Ship's managers arresting ship in breach of contract with owners—Owners arranging bank guarantee to secure release of ship—Amount of guarantee added to owners' overdraft and owners charged interest thereon—Owners claiming interest from managers—Whether interest too remote—Whether interest caused by arrest—Whether interest expended by owners in mitigation of managers' breach. **Cia Financiera Soleada SA v Hamoor Tanker Corp Inc** [1981] **1** 856, CA.
  Carriage of goods by air—
    International carriage—Limitation of carrier's liability. *See* **Carriage by air** (Carriage of goods—International carriage—Limitation of carrier's liability—Interest on damages).
  Claim to—
    Prejudice to client's claim by delay in service of writ—Liability of solicitor. *See* **Solicitor** (Litigation—Delay in issuing and serving writ).
  Collision at sea—
    Collision during war between British ship and ship belonging to enemy alien—Damages awarded to alien at end of hostilities—Time from which interest accrues—Date of collision. **Berwickshire, The** [1950] **1** 699, Admin Ct.
    Interest included in award of Admiralty Court—Income tax deductible—Whether notification to be given on payment into court. **Norseman, The** [1957] **2** 660, Admin Ct.
  Commercial cases—
    Appropriate rate of interest on damages—Case involving foreign currency. **Braspetro Oil Services Co v FPSO Construction Inc** [2007] **2 Comm** 924n, QBD.
    Appropriate rate of interest on damages—Commercial court practice—Practice of Commercial Court to award interest at base rate plus 1%—Practice no more than mere presumption—Whether court can depart from usual rate where it would be substantially unfair to either party. **Shearson Lehman Hutton Inc v Maclaine Watson & Co Ltd (No 2)** [1990] **3** 723, QBD.
    Appropriate rate of interest on damages—Insurers claiming by subrogation—Insurers borrowing at commercial rates or applying own funds and losing investment value—Whether interest on damages should be at commercial rate. **Metal Box Ltd v Currys Ltd** [1988] **1** 341, QBD.
    Appropriate rate of interest on damages—Method of assessing appropriate rate. **Cremer v General Carriers SA** [1974] **1** 1, QBD.

INTEREST (cont)—
  Damages (cont)—
    Commercial cases (cont)—
      Appropriate rate of interest on damages—Method of assessing appropriate rate—Period over
        which interest allowed—Damages awarded to plaintiff for dredging costs incurred when
        defendant wrongfully failed to dredge away siltation in river bed—Dredging costs incurred in 7
        out of 14 years after negligence occurring—Plaintiff deducting dredging costs from gross income
        for purposes of corporation tax—Whether plaintiff entitled to commercial rate of interest or rate
        of interest on short-term investment account awarded in personal injury claims—Whether tax
        saving made by plaintiff deductible from damages in awarding interest. **Tate & Lyle Food and
        Distribution Ltd v Greater London Council** [1981] 3 716, QBD; [1982] 2 854, CA.
    Deduction of tax—
      Public revenue dividends. *See* **Income tax** (Public revenue dividends—Deduction of tax—Interest).
    Judgment on admission of facts—
      Payment into court—Admission of negligence but denial of damage—Interlocutory judgment. *See*
        Judgment (Judgment on admission of facts—Negligence—Admission of negligence but denial of
        damage—Payment into court—Interlocutory judgment—Interest on damages).
    Jurisdiction to include interest in award of damages—
      Court not authorised to give interest upon interest—Meaning of 'interest upon interest'—Damages
        for breach of contract—Plaintiffs entitled under contract to pay purchase price in instalments over
        two year period—In consequence of defendants' breach plaintiffs having to pay whole purchase
        price immediately—Claim for damages representing loss of interest incurred in consequence of
        having to pay whole purchase price immediately—Claim for interest on damages—Whether a
        claim for 'interest upon interest'—Law Reform (Miscellaneous Provisions) Act 1934, s 3(1).
        Bushwall Properties Ltd v Vortex Properties Ltd [1975] 2 214, Ch D.
      Damages awarded in respect of non-income-producing chattel—Plaintiff's goods destroyed by fire
        as result of defendant's negligence—Plaintiff reimbursed by insurers for loss—Plaintiff obtaining
        judgment for amount of destroyed goods—Whether plaintiff entitled to interest on judgment sum
        notwithstanding that chattel not income-producing and that interest would go to
        insurers—Supreme Court Act 1981, s 35A. **Metal Box Ltd v Currys Ltd** [1988] 1 341, QBD.
      Equitable jurisdiction—Generally. *See* Damages—Award of interest—Equitable jurisdiction, *above*.
      Lands Tribunal—Coal mining subsidence cases. *See* **Coal mining** (Subsidence—Compensation for
        subsidence damage—Determination of disputes—Interest).
      New Zealand—Rate of interest—Fluctuation in rate of interest between date of cause of action and
        date of judgment—Reckoning of rate of interest on award of damages—Judicature Act 1908 (NZ),
        s 87. **Rowling v Takaro Properties Ltd** [1988] 1 163, PC.
      Part payment of damages by third party prior to commencement of proceedings—Whether court
        having jurisdiction to award interest on such part payment—Whether court having jurisdiction to
        award interest on any sum other than sum for which judgment entered—Supreme Court Act
        1981, s 35A(1). **I M Properties plc v Cape & Dalgleish (a firm)** [1998] 3 203, CA.
      Payment of damages prior to hearing—Plaintiff claiming damages and interest—Defendants paying
        sum due in respect of claim for damages but refusing to pay interest—Plaintiff appropriating
        payment to principal only and seeking summary judgment for interest—Whether court having
        jurisdiction to award interest if damages paid prior to hearing—Supreme Court Act 1981, s 35A.
        Edmunds v Lloyd Italico e L'Ancora Cia di Assicurazioni e Riassicurazioni SpA [1986] 2 249, CA.
      Privy Council. *See* **Privy Council** (Jurisdiction—Interest—Interest on award of damages).
      Summary judgment—Whether court having discretion to enter judgment in form which does not
        attract interest—RSC Ord 14, r 3(1). **Putty v Hopkinson** [1990] 1 1057, QBD.
      Summary judgment—Whether proceedings concluded by summary judgment 'tried' in
        court—Whether court having jurisdiction to award interest on summary judgment—Law Reform
        (Miscellaneous Provisions) Act 1934, s 3(1)—RSC Ord 14. **Gardner Steel Ltd v Sheffield Bros
        (Profiles) Ltd** [1978] 3 399, CA.
  Negligence—
    Valuer—Valuer negligently valuing properties for loans made by bank—Properties substantially
      overvalued—Valuer liable for bank's losses flowing from overvaluation—Date when cause of
      action arose—Date from which interest to run—Whether interest payable on damages ordered to
      be repaid. **Nykredit Mortgage Bank plc v Edward Erdman Group Ltd (No 2)** [1998] 1 305, HL.
  Personal injury—
    Amount of damages increased on appeal—Interest on increase to run from date of trial—Rate of
      interest. **Cook v JL Kier & Co Ltd** [1970] 2 513, CA.
    Damages increased for inflation—Whether interest can be awarded if damages have been
      increased for inflation. **Pickett v British Rail Engineering Ltd** [1979] 1 774, HL.
    Fatal accident—Guidelines to be applied in awarding interest—Two years' interest deducted for
      unjustifiable delay in prosecuting case—Interest deducted in respect of its investment return
      element and not at full short term investment account rate—Whether analysis of investment
      return and inflation elements of interest constituting special reason for departing from
      guidelines. **Spittle v Bunney** [1988] 3 1031, CA.
    Fatal accident—Infant plaintiff—Delay of 11 1/2 years from mother's death in commencing
      proceedings and bringing action to trial—Judge disallowing four years' interest on pre-trial
      damages because of excessive delay—Whether proper exercise of discretion. **Corbett v Barking
      Havering and Brentwood Health Authority** [1991] 1 498, CA.
    Fatal accident—Pleading. *See* **Practice** (Interest—Pleading).
    Fatal accident—Pre-trial loss and post-trial loss—Interest on award for pre-trial loss at half-rate—No
      interest for post-trial loss. **Cookson v Knowles** [1978] 2 604, HL; **Fletcher (Executrix of the estate
      of Carl Fletcher (deceased)) v A Train & Sons Ltd** [2008] 4 699, CA.
    Fatal accident—Principles to be applied in awarding interest—Special damages and general
      damages—Law Reform (Miscellaneous Provisions) Act 1934, s 3, as amended by the
      Administration of Justice Act 1969, s 22. **Jefford v Gee** [1970] 1 1202, CA.

INTEREST (cont)—
  Damages (cont)—
    Personal injury (cont)—
      General damages—Date from which interest payable—Notice of claim—Service of writ by plaintiff on first defendant—Third party notice served by first defendant on second defendant—Second defendant subsequently added as defendant to plaintiff's action—Liability apportioned between first and second defendants—Date from which interest on general damages payable by second defendant—Law Reform (Miscellaneous Provisions) Act 1934, s 3, as amended by the Administration of Justice Act 1969, s 22. **Slater v Hughes (Jones, third party)** [1971] **3** 1287, CA.
      Loss of earning capacity—Damages awarded to cover risk that plaintiff might have to take less well paid employment or be without employment—Whether interest payable on award. **Joyce v Yeomans** [1981] **2** 21, CA.
      Pain, suffering and loss of amenities—No interest to be awarded on sum awarded for pain, suffering and loss of amenities. **Cookson v Knowles** [1977] **2** 820, CA.
      Pain, suffering and loss of amenities—Rate of interest—Interest to be awarded at rate of 2 per cent from date of writ to date of judgment—Law Reform (Miscellaneous Provisions) Act 1934, s 3. **Wright v British Railways Board** [1983] **2** 698, HL.
      Pain, suffering and loss of amenities—Rate of interest—Interest to be awarded at rate of 2 per cent from date of writ to date of trial—Interest to be awarded for lesser period if plaintiff unjustifiably delays trial. **Birkett v Hayes** [1982] **2** 710, CA.
      Payment into court—Order for payment out to plaintiff—RSC Ord 22, r 5—Law Reform (Miscellaneous Provisions) Act 1934, s 3(1A) (added by Administration of Justice Act 1969, s 22). **Waite v Redpath Dorman Long Ltd** [1971] **1** 513, QBD.
      Payment into court—RSC Ord 22, r 5—Law Reform (Miscellaneous Provisions) Act 1934, s 3(1A) (added by Administration of Justice Act 1969, s 22). **Newall v Tunstall** [1970] **3** 465, Assizes.
      Rate of interest—Special damage—Loss of wages—Plaintiff injured in course of his employment—Plaintiff off work for two periods as a result of accident and losing wages—Loss quantified at end of each period—Trial not taking place until four years later—Principles to be applied—Whether interest should be awarded at full or half rate—Whether interest may be awarded at other than half rate when special circumstances exist. **Dexter v Courtaulds Ltd** [1984] **1** 70, CA.
      Rate of interest—Special damage—Special damage incurred substantially at date of accident—Special damage not of continuing nature—Whether interest should be awarded at half-rate. **Ichard v Frangoulis** [1977] **2** 461, QBD.
      Special damages—Claimants receiving state benefits—Whether benefits received to be deducted when calculating interest on special damages—Social Security (Recovery of Benefits) Act 1997, s 17. **Wadey v Surrey CC** [2000] **2** 545, HL.
      Split trial—Whether interest runs from date of judgment on damages or date of judgment on liability—Judgments Act 1838, s 17. **Thomas v Bunn** [1991] **1** 193, HL.
    Unliquidated damages—
      Award of interest on damages during period of assessment—Law Reform (Miscellaneous Provisions) Act 1934. **Carr v Boxall** [1960] **1** 495, Ch D.
    Wrongful dismissal—
      Rate of interest—Date from which interest to run. **Bold v Brough, Nicholson & Hall Ltd** [1963] **3** 849, QBD.
  Debt—
    Action for recovery of debt or damages—
      Award of interest in 'proceedings (whenever instituted)' for recovery of 'debt'—Claimant residing in nursing home—Defendant health boards denying responsibility for funding of claimant's health care at nursing home—Claimant seeking judicial review of decision and claiming restitution of sums already paid by him for his care—Review panel agreeing to reimburse claimant before permission stage of judicial review proceedings—Whether court having jurisdiction to award interest on sum to be reimbursed—Supreme Court Act 1981, s 35A. **R (on the application of Kemp) v Denbighshire Local Health Board** [2006] **3** 141, QBD.
      Meaning of 'debt or damages'—Law Reform (Miscellaneous Provisions) Act 1934, s 3(1). **BP Exploration Co (Libya) Ltd v Hunt (No 2)** [1982] **1** 925, HL, QBD and CA.
  Company—
    Winding up—Application of bankruptcy rules. See **Company** (Winding up—Application of bankruptcy rules—Interest on debts).
    Winding up—Proof. See **Company** (Winding up—Proof of debts—Interest on debt).
  Default interest—
    Agreements providing for payment of additional 1% interest while borrower in default—Whether increase in rate of interest unenforceable as a penalty. **Lordsvale Finance plc v Bank of Zambia** [1996] **3** 156, QBD.
  Jurisdiction to include interest in default judgment—
    Judgment in default of appearance—Whether proceedings ending with entry of judgment in default 'tried' in court—Whether court having jurisdiction to award interest up to the entry of judgment—Law Reform (Miscellaneous Provisions) Act 1934, s 3(1). **Lawrie (Alex) Factors Ltd v Modern Injection Moulds Ltd** [1981] **3** 658, QBD.
  Late payment of debt—
    Commercial debt—Point from which interest begins to run—Claimant issuing interim invoices for 65% of fees said to be due—Dispute as to rate for calculating fees—Issue as to applicable rate determined against claimant at trial of preliminary issues—Claimant subsequently claiming interest on whole of debt from date of interim invoices—Whether interim invoices amounting to notice of amount of fees found to be due following trial of preliminary issues—Late Payment of Commercial Debts (Interest) Act 1998, s 4(5). **Ruttle Plant Ltd v Secretary of State for the Environment, Food and Rural Affairs (No 2)** [2009] **1 Comm** 73, QBD; [2010] **1 Comm** 444, CA.
    Contractual term providing for interest on late payment at 0·5 per cent above base rate—Whether clause providing for a substantial remedy for late payment—Whether statutory rate should be substituted for rate specified in contract—Late Payment of Commercial Debts (Interest) Act 1998, ss 8(1), 9. **Yuanda (UK) Co Ltd v WW Gear Construction Ltd** [2011] **1 Comm** 550, QBD.

INTEREST (cont)—
  Debt (cont)—
    Late payment of debt (cont)—
      Power to award interest by way of general damages—Debt paid late but before proceedings for
        recovery commenced—Whether court having power to award interest by way of general
        damages—Law Reform (Miscellaneous Provisions) Act 1934, s 3(1)—Supreme Court Act 1981,
        s 35A. **President of India v La Pintada Cia Navegacion SA** [1984] **2** 773, HL.
      Merger of right to interest in judgment for principal sum and interest—
        Application of doctrine of merger—Local authority making improvement grant to defendants—
        Grant repayable by instalments—Authority having statutory right to interest on instalments until
        paid—Authority obtaining judgment for repayment of outstanding instalments and interest down
        to judgment—Judgment debt payable by monthly payments—Whether authority's right to
        interest merged in judgment or whether authority having continuing right to interest after date of
        judgment until instalments actually repaid—Whether interest payable on county court
        judgment—Housing Act 1969, s 6(4). **Ealing London Borough v El Isaac** [1980] **2** 548, CA.
  Deposit—
    Sale of land—
      Deposit held by estate agent. *See* **Estate agent** (Deposit—Interest).
  Discretion of court to award—
    Generally. *See* **Practice** (Interest—Discretion of court to award).
  Foreign currency—
    Damages. *See* Damages—Commercial cases—Appropriate rate of interest on damages, *above*.
  Income tax—
    Annual payments—
      Appropriation to taxed profits. *See* **Income tax** (Annual payment—Appropriation to taxed
        profits—Interest).
    Generally. *See* **Income tax** (Interest).
    Person chargeable—
      Receipt of interest. *See* **Income tax** (Persons chargeable—Receipt of income—Person receiving
        income chargeable—Interest on money).
    Ultra vires payment. *See* **Income tax** (Annual payment—Ultra vires payment—Interest).
  Interest rate swap agreement—
    Restitution. *See* **Contract** (Restitution—Interest rate swap agreement).
    Whether contract a wagering contract. *See* **Gaming** (Contract by way of gaming or wagering—Interest
      rate swap agreement).
  Interim payment—
    Practice. *See* **Practice** (Pre-trial or post-judgment relief—Interim payment—Interest).
    Repayment of interim payment. *See* **Practice** (Pre-trial or post-judgment relief—Interim payment—
      Repayment of interim payment—Interest).
  Legacy—
    Date from which legacy carrying interest—
      Legacy to infant—Legacy payable at 21—Trustees empowered to use legacy or any part thereof for
        education of legatee until he shall attain age of 21—Payment of interest from date of testator's
        death. **Selby-Walker (decd), Re** [1949] **2** 178, Ch D.
  Limitation fund—
    Admiralty—
      Jurisdiction. *See* **Shipping** (Limitation of liability—Limitation fund—Interest).
      Practice—Rate of interest. *See* **Admiralty** (Practice—Interest—Rate of interest on limitation fund).
  Moneylender—
    Rate of interest—
      Generally. *See* **Moneylender** (Interest—Rate).
      Memorandum. *See* **Moneylender** (Memorandum—Rate of interest charged on loan).
  Mortgage—
    Entitlement of mortgagee in redemption action to arrears of interest. *See* **Mortgage** (Redemption—
      Mortgagee's entitlement to arrears of interest).
    Generally. *See* **Mortgage** (Interest).
    Matrimonial home—
      Interest payments. *See* **Husband and wife** (Matrimonial home—Mortgage repayments—Interest
        payments).
    Notice by mortgagor to pay off—
      Failure to pay on date named—Sum due not set aside and available on date of expiry of
        notice—Right to interest after date of expiry. **Barratt v Gough-Thomas** [1951] **2** 48, Ch D.
    Notice by mortgagor to redeem—
      Right to interest after date of expiry of notice. *See* **Mortgage** (Interest—Notice by mortgagor to pay
        off).
  Payment into court. *See* **Practice** (Payment into court—Interest).
  Payment out of court. *See* **Practice** (Payment out of court—Interest).
  Pleading. *See* **Practice** (Interest—Pleading).
  Proceeds of sale—
    Jurisdiction of court to award interest—
      Interest on proceeds of sale of gold bars and bank balances belonging to Dutch bank and sold by
        Administrator of Hungarian Property—Owners entitled to recover property, or proceeds of sale,
        from Administrator 'but not to any other remedy'—Treaty of Peace (Hungary) Order 1948 (SI 1948
        No 116), art 1(5)(g). **Bank Voor Handel en Scheepvaart v Slatford (sued as Custodian of Enemy
        Property)** [1951] **2** 779, KBD.
  Rate of interest—
    Damages—
      Personal injury cases. *See* Damages—Personal injury—Rate of interest, *above*.
    Debt—
      Company—Winding up—Application of bankruptcy rules. *See* **Company** (Winding up—Application
        of bankruptcy rules—Interest on debts—Rate of interest).
      Moneylender. *See* **Moneylender** (Interest—Rate).

INTEREST (cont)—
  Sale of land—
    Interest on unpaid purchase money. *See* **Sale of land** (Interest on unpaid purchase money).
  Sale of pawned articles—
    Surplus proceeds—
      Unredeemed articles sold by pawnbroker—Surplus proceeds withheld by pawnbroker pending third party claim to ownership of articles—Surplus proceeds paid to pawnor without interest—Pawnor claiming interest in equity on surplus proceeds for period between sale and payment—Whether pawnbroker liable for interest—Whether fiduciary relationship between parties. **Mathew v T M Sutton Ltd** [1994] 4 793, Ch D.
  Sale of shares—
    Interest on unpaid purchase money—
      Vendor not entitled to interest if 'delay on our part'—Vendor prevented by third party's injunction from completing—Whether purchaser liable to interest during period of delay. **Harvela Investments Ltd v Royal Trust Co of Canada (CI) Ltd** [1985] 2 966, HL.
  Stamp duty—
    Repayment. *See* **Stamp duty** (Repayment—Interest on overpaid duty).
  Trust—
    Breach of trust—
      Rate of interest chargeable against trustee. *See* **Trust and trustee** (Breach of trust—Interest chargeable against trustee).
  Will—
    Apportionment—
      Interest accruing after death of tenants for life. *See* **Will** (Apportionment—Interest accruing after death of tenant for life).

INTERFERENCE WITH BUSINESS INTEREST
  Tort. *See* **Tort** (Interference with trade or business).

INTERFERENCE WITH CONTRACTUAL RELATIONS
  Tort. *See* **Tort** (Interference with contractual relations).

INTERFERENCE WITH DUE ADMINISTRATION OF JUSTICE
  Contempt of court. *See* **Contempt of court**.

INTERFERENCE WITH GOODS
  Conversion. *See* **Conversion**.

INTERFERENCE WITH PARENTAL RIGHTS
  Right of action in tort. *See* **Parent** (Rights in respect of child—Unlawful interference with parental rights—Tort).

INTERFERENCE WITH TRADE OR BUSINESS
  Tort. *See* **Tort** (Interference with trade or business).

INTERIM ANTI-SOCIAL BEHAVIOUR ORDER
  Magistrates' court. *See* **Magistrates** (Proceedings—Anti-social behaviour order—Interim anti-social behaviour order).

INTERIM CARE ORDER
  Family proceedings. *See* **Family proceedings** (Orders in family proceedings—Interim care order).

INTERIM CERTIFICATE
  Architect—
    Building contract. *See* **Building contract** (Architect—Interim certificate).

INTERIM PAYMENTS ORDER
  Generally. *See* **Practice** (Pre-trial or post-judgment relief—Interim payment).
  Landlord and tenant—
    Action for forfeiture of lease. *See* **Landlord and tenant** (Forfeiture of lease—Interim payments order).

INTERIM RENT
  Business premises. *See* **Landlord and tenant** (Rent—Business premises—Interim rent).

INTERLOCUTORY APPEAL
  County court—
    Leave—
      Appeal from county court on point of law. *See* **County court** (Appeal—Right of appeal—Point of law—Interlocutory appeal).
    Criminal cases. *See* **Criminal law** (Court of Appeal—Jurisdiction—Interlocutory appeal).
  Divorce—
    Financial provision order—
      County court. *See* **Divorce** (Financial provision—Practice and procedure—County court—Interlocutory appeal in matrimonial proceedings).
  Generally. *See* **Court of Appeal** (Interlocutory appeal).

INTERLOCUTORY APPLICATION
  Bankruptcy—
    Chancery Division—
      Divisional Court—Appeal from county court. *See* **Bankruptcy** (Appeal—Appeal from county court—Appeal to Divisional Court of Chancery Division—Practice—List of appeals to be heard during term—Addition of appeals to list—Interlocutory applications to be made to Divisional Court if sitting).

INTERLOCUTORY APPLICATION (cont)—
Costs—
Order for costs. *See* **Costs** (Order for costs—Interlocutory application).
Practice—
Generally. *See* **Practice** (Interlocutory proceedings).

INTERLOCUTORY INJUNCTION
Affidavit in support of interlocutory injunction—
Admissibility. *See* **Affidavit** (Admissibility in evidence—Affidavit in support of interlocutory injunction).
Arbitration agreement—
Generally. *See* **Arbitration** (Injunction—Interlocutory injunction).
Power of court. *See* **Arbitration** (Injunction—Interim injunction—Power of court).
Crown officer, against—
Jurisdiction to grant injunction. *See* **Crown** (Relief against the Crown—Interlocutory relief—Jurisdiction—Injunction against officer of the Crown).
Defamation cases. *See* **Libel and slander** (Injunction—Interlocutory).
Freezing order. *See* **Practice** (Pre-trial or post-judgment relief—Freezing order).
Generally. *See* **Injunction** (Interlocutory).
Mareva injunction. *See* **Practice** (Pre-trial or post-judgment relief—Freezing order).

INTERLOCUTORY MOTION
Disclosure—
Application for. *See* **Disclosure and inspection of documents** (Interlocutory motion).
Preservation of subject-matter of cause of action. *See* **Practice** (Pre-trial or post-judgment relief—Search order—Interlocutory motion).
Rectification of land register. *See* **Land registration** (Rectification of register—Interlocutory motion).
Vacation of entry in land charges register—
Jurisdiction to order vaction on motion. *See* **Land charge** (Vacation of entry in register—Interlocutory motion—Jurisdiction to order vacation on motion).

INTERLOCUTORY ORDER
Consent order. *See* **Judgment** (Order—Consent order—Interlocutory order).
Costs—
Form of order for costs. *See* **Costs** (Order for costs—Interlocutory application).
Drawing-up—
Order made without personal attendance. *See* **Practice** (Order—Drawing-up—Interlocutory order made without personal attendance).
Wrongful interference with goods—
Order for delivery up of goods. *See* **Tort** (Wrongful interference with goods—Interlocutory relief—Delivery up of goods).

INTERLOCUTORY PROCEEDINGS
Affidavit—
Application to strike out. *See* **Affidavit** (Striking out—Hearsay—Exception—Interlocutory proceedings).
Chancery Division—
Practice. *See* **Practice** (Chancery Division).
Commercial Court—
Practice. *See* **Commercial Court** (Practice—Interlocutory proceedings).
Declaration—
Jurisdiction to make final declaration affecting party's rights. *See* **Declaration** (Jurisdiction—Interlocutory proceedings).
Evidence—
Hearsay. *See* **Evidence** (Hearsay—Interlocutory proceedings).
Injunction. *See* **Injunction** (Interlocutory).
Practice—
Generally. *See* **Practice** (Interlocutory proceedings).

INTERNATIONAL AIR TRANSPORT ASSOCIATION
Clearing house—
Members—
Agreement to settle mutual debits and credits through clearing house only—Members in liquidation—Whether agreement binding on liquidation. *See* **Company** (Voluntary winding up—Distribution of company property—Application in satisfaction of liabilities—Contract having effect of varying statutory rules—Validity—Public policy—Contract entered into for good business reasons and not for purpose of circumventing insolvency legislation—International Air Transport Association clearing house).

INTERNATIONAL ATHLETICS ASSOCIATION
Rules—
Construction. *See* **Unincorporated association** (Rules—Construction—International athletics association).

INTERNATIONAL CARRIAGE BY AIR
Air traffic. *See* **Air traffic**.
Goods. *See* **Carriage by air** (Carriage of goods—International carriage).
Passengers. *See* **Carriage by air** (Carriage of passengers—International carriage).

INTERNATIONAL CARRIAGE BY ROAD
Goods. *See* **Carriers**.
Private international law. *See* **Conflict of laws**.

INTERNATIONAL CIVIL AVIATION
Generally. *See* **Air traffic** (International civil aviation).

INTERNATIONAL CONVENTION

Generally. *See* **International law** (Convention).

Ratification—

Conflict with statute law. *See* **Conflict of laws** (International convention—Ratified by executive— Implemented by statute—Conflict between convention and statute).

Statute giving effect to—

Construction of statute. *See* **Statute** (Construction—Convention given effect by legislation).

INTERNATIONAL LAW

Act of State. *See* **Constitutional law** (Act of State).

Armed forces of foreign state. *See* **Constitutional law** (Foreign sovereign state—Armed forces of foreign state).

Convention—

Enforcement by English courts—

Provisions of convention not given force by Act of Parliament—Rights of individuals under convention—Human rights and fundamental freedoms—Whether convention part of English law—Whether convention conferring enforceable rights on individuals—Convention for the Protection of Human Rights and Fundamental Freedoms, art 8(1). **R v Chief Immigration Officer, Heathrow Airport, ex p Salamat Bibi** [1976] **3** 843, CA.

Generally. *See* **Conflict of laws** (International convention).

Statute giving effect to international convention—

Construction of statute. *See* **Statute** (Construction—Convention given effect by legislation).

Criminal jurisdiction. *See* **Criminal law** (Jurisdiction).

Customary law—

Regional customary law—

Death penalty—Whether freestanding principle existing of regional customary international law of non-refoulement by member states of Council of Europe to third countries where death penalty available. **R (on the application of Al-Saadoon) v Secretary of State for Defence** [2010] **1** 271, CA.

Enforcement by English courts—

Rules of international law which form part of English law—

Doctrine of stare decicis—Change in rule of international law—Earlier rule recognised by decision of English court—Effect of doctrine of stare decisis—Rule recognised by decision of English court no longer prevailing rule of international law—Change in rules of international law relating to sovereign immunity—Whether rule recognised by decision of English court or prevailing rule of international law forming part of English law—Whether English court bound to follow earlier decision or free to recognise new rule of international law. **Trendtex Trading Corp v Central Bank of Nigeria** [1977] **1** 881, CA.

European Community. *See* **European Union**.

Foreign sovereign state—

Immunity from suit. *See* **Constitutional law** (Foreign sovereign state—Immunity from suit).

Municipal law—

Relationship—

Right of individual under international law—Enforcement of right in English courts—Necessity of showing rule of international law has been adopted by English law—Duty of country to receive back nationals expelled by foreign state—British protected person—Whether British protected person having right to enter United Kingdom on being expelled from country of residence—Whether right enforceable by individual English courts. **Thakrar v Secretary of State for the Home Dept** [1974] **2** 261, CA.

Private international law. *See* **Conflict of laws**.

Recognition of foreign government—

Law as declared by foreign government—

Conflict of laws. *See* **Conflict of laws** (Foreign government—Recognition—Law as declared by foreign government).

Retroactive effect—

Offer of compensation by former government—Payment of compensation to officers and men of Polish merchant navy on their leaving their ships—Offer made in London on 5th July 1945, by Minister of old Polish government, on behalf of Polish shipping company—Recognition by British government of new Polish government from midnight on 5th/6th July 1945—Offer accepted and acted on, in England, after recognition of new Polish government. **Gdynia Ameryka Linie Zeglugowe Spolka Akcyjna v Boguslawski** [1952] **2** 470, HL.

Ownership of aircraft in Hong Kong—Property of Chinese nationalist government—Sale before recognition by British government of communist government as de jure government of China—Effect of decrees of communist government before recognition. **Civil Air Transport Inc v Central Air Transport Corp** [1952] **2** 733, PC.

Validity of laws. *See* **Conflict of laws** (Foreign government—Recognition—Law as declared by courts of foreign country).

United Nations Organisation. *See* **United Nations**.

INTERNATIONAL MARITIME TRANSPORT

EC competition rules—

Abuse of dominant position. *See* **European Union** (Rules on competition—Abuse of dominant position—Collective dominant position—International maritime transport).

INTERNATIONAL ORGANISATION

Immunity from suit. *See* **Constitutional law** (Foreign sovereign state—Immunity from suit—International organisation).

Recognition—

Conflict of laws. *See* **Conflict of laws** (Foreign organisation—Recognition).

United Nations. *See* **United Nations**.

Winding up by court. *See* **Company** (Compulsory winding up—Unregistered company—International organisation).

INTERNATIONAL TIN COUNCIL

Immunity from suit. *See* **Constitutional law** (Foreign sovereign state—Immunity from suit—International organisation).

Judgment debt—

Appointment of receiver to enforce judgment against council. *See* **Execution** (Equitable execution—Receiver—Appointment of receiver to enforce judgment against debtor—International organisation set up by treaty).

Winding up by court. *See* **Company** (Compulsory winding up—Unregistered company—International organisation—International Tin Council).

INTERNATIONAL TREATY

European Community. *See* **European Union** (International treaties).

INTERNET

Copyright and related rights in the information society. *See* **European Union** (Intellectual property rights—Copyright—Related rights in the information society).

Copyright infringement. *See* **Copyright** (Infringement—Internet).

Data protection—

European Union. *See* **European Union** (Data protection—Internet).

Defamation—

Anonymous publication. *See* **Judgment** (Default of acknowledgment of service—Power of court to proceed in absence of party—Anonymous defendants).

Fair comment. *See* **Libel and slander** (Fair comment).

Publication. *See* **Libel and slander** (Publication—Internet posting).

Domain name—

Dispute resolution—

Contract. *See* **Contract** (Dispute resolution—Internet domain name).

European Union—

Intellectual property rights—

Copyright and related rights in the information society. *See* **European Union** (Intellectual property rights—Copyright—Related rights in the information society).

File sharing website. *See* **European Union** (Intellectual property rights—Internet file sharing website).

Internet domain name—

Passing off—

Trade name. *See* **Passing off** (Trade name—Internet domain names).

Registration as trade mark. *See* **Trade mark** (Infringement—Name—Internet domain names—Registration of company trade marks as Internet domain names).

Internet service provider—

Injunction—

Trade mark infringement. *See* **Trade mark** (Infringement—Internet—Injunction against internet service providers (ISPs)).

Jury, use by. *See* **Criminal law** (Trial—Direction to jury—Collective responsibility—Deliberations—Use of internet).

Public electronic communications network—

Criminal law. *See* **Criminal law** (Public electronic communications network).

Publishing or distributing written material—

Jurisdiction. *See* **Criminal law** (Jurisdiction—Racial hatred—Publishing or distributing written material).

Racial hatred. *See* **Criminal law** (Racial hatred—Publishing or distributing written material).

Rules on competition—

European Community. *See* **European Union** (Rules on competition—Abuse of dominant position—Undertaking—Market for services in high-speed internet access).

Trade mark infringement—

European Union. *See* **European Union** (Trade marks—Infringement—Internet).

Generally. *See* **Trade mark** (Infringement—Internet).

INTERPLEADER

Appeal—

Appeal from county court—

Leave—Necessity for leave—Value of goods less than £20—Claim for damages for illegal distress—Whether claim for damages part of interpleader proceedings—Whether leave necessary—County Courts Act 1934, s 105(c)—County Court Rules 1936, Ord 28, r 11. **Crocker v Hadley** [1941] 3 286, CA.

Appeal from registrar—

Order for costs against petitioner in divorce suit—Execution on motor car—Appeal against registrar's order—Whether appeal lies to judge in chambers or Divisional Court—Matrimonial Causes Rules 1950 (SI 1950 no 1940), r 59. **Waight v Waight and Walker** [1952] 2 290, Div.

Application—

Time—

When entitled to relief—Must be real foundation for expectation of being sued by rival claimant. **Watson v Park Royal (Caterers) Ltd** [1961] 2 346, QBD.

Issue of interpleader summons—

Circumstances in which district judge required to issue interpleader summons—

County Courts Act 1984, s 101. **Newman (t/a Mantella Publishing) v Modern Bookbinders Ltd** [2000] 2 814, CA.

Claimant a company in compulsory liquidation—

Leave of Companies Court required for issue of interpleader summons to which company a respondent—Companies Act 1948, s 231. **Eastern Holdings Establishment of Vaduz v Singer & Friedlander Ltd (Able Securities Ltd, in liq, First Claimant; Sempah (Holdings) Ltd, Second Claimant)** [1967] 2 1192, Ch D.

INTERPLEADER (cont)—
Jurisdiction—
    Order barring claim—
        Power of master to bar—Signature to claim by director of company in wrong capacity—Validity of claim—Competence of action by claimants against execution creditors—RSC Ord 57, rr 10, 16(1). **JRP Plastics Ltd v Gordon Rossall Plastics Ltd (Hexa Pen Co Ltd, claimants)** [1950] **1** 241, KBD.
    Order directing trial of issue between claimants—
        Husband and wife—Property stored by wife—Claim by husband against warehouseman—Right of warehouseman to interplead—Order directing issue between husband and wife—Jurisdiction to make such order—Married Women's Property Act 1882, ss 12, 17—RSC Ord 57, r 7. **De La Rue v Hernu, Peron and Stockwell Ltd, De La Rue, claimant** [1936] **2** 411, CA.
    Reference of interpleader issues to arbitration. *See* **Arbitration** (Interpleader proceedings).
    Sheriff's interpleader—
        Claimant the wife of the debtor—
            Claim to all furniture and goods seized in the matrimonial home—Application by execution creditor for wife to give evidence on oath and be cross-examined—Adjournment refused and wife's claim allowed—Order set aside—Proper practice on such claims—Meaning of words, may 'summarily determine the question at issue', in RSC Ord 17, r 5(2). **Davis (P B J) Manufacturing Co Ltd v Fahn (Fahn claimant)** [1967] **2** 1274, CA.
        Position of sheriff—
            Position analogous to that of officer of court—Neutrality in dispute between parties—Inventory—Claim covering all goods—Copy not to one party only—Production at earliest practicable moment to court. **Fredericks and Pelhams Timber Buildings v Wilkins (Read, claimant)** [1971] **3** 545, CA.
    Summary determination—
        Consent of claimants—Regard to be had to nature of dispute and value of property—Claim to chattels of considerable overall value—Prospect of difficult point of law—Whether summary determination of claim appropriate—RSC Ord 17, r 5(2). **Fredericks and Pelhams Timber Buildings v Wilkins (Read, claimant)** [1971] **3** 545, CA.
        Dispensing with precise formulation of issue and pleadings—Need for normal trial of issue—Allegations of fraud—Need for clear formulation in advance—RSC Ord 17, r 5(2). **Fredericks and Pelhams Timber Buildings v Wilkins (Read, claimant)** [1971] **3** 545, CA.
    Writ of fi fa. *See* **Execution** (Writ of fi fa—Interpleader proceedings).

INTERPRETER
Costs—
    Criminal cases—
        Award of costs out of central funds. *See* **Criminal law** (Costs—Power to award costs—Award out of central funds).
Evidence—
    Practice. *See* **Practice** (Interpreter—Evidence).

INTERROGATION
Suspected criminal—
    Admissibility of answers. *See* **Criminal evidence** (Admissions and confessions—Answers and statements to police—Judges' Rules—Interrogation).

INTERROGATORY
Acknowledgment of debt—
    Interrogatory answer amounting to acknowledgment. *See* **Limitation of action—Acknowledgment**.
Defamation actions. *See* **Libel and slander** (Interrogatory).
Divorce. *See* **Divorce** (Practice—Interrogatories).
Generally. *See* **Disclosure and inspection of documents** (Interrogatory).
Joint tortfeasors. *See* **Tort** (Joint tortfeasors—Interrogatories).
Mareva injunction—
    Interrogatory in aid of injunction. *See* **Practice** (Pre-trial or post-judgment relief—Freezing order—Disclosure or interrogatory in aid of injunction).

INTERVENTION
Admiralty action in rem. *See* **Admiralty** (Practice—Action in rem—Intervention).
Attorney General, by. *See* **Practice** (Parties—Intervention by persons not parties—Attorney General).
Divorce proceedings, in. *See* **Divorce** (Intervention).

INTESTACY
Administration pendente lite—
    Number of administrators—
        Power to appoint one administrator—Supreme Court of Judicature (Consolidation) Act 1925, ss 160(1), 163(1). **Haslip (decd), Re** [1958] **2** 275, Prob; **Lindley (decd), In the Estate of** [1953] **2** 319, Prob.
    Practice—
        Probate Division—Follows practice of Chancery Division in appointing receivers. **Bevan (decd), Re** [1948] **1** 271, CA.
Appropriation by personal representatives—
    Surviving spouse—
        Matrimonial home—Right of surviving spouse to require appropriation of matrimonial home in or towards satisfaction of spouse's interest in intestate's estate—In or towards satisfaction of interest—Value of home greater than surviving spouse's absolute interest in estate—Whether right to require appropriation 'in or towards satisfaction of interest giving right to require appropriation of home of greater value than interest—Administration of Estates Act 1925, s 41—Intestates' Estates Act 1952, Sch 2, paras 1(1), 5(2). **Phelps (decd), Re** [1979] **3** 373, CA.

INTESTACY (cont)—
    Appropriation by personal representatives (cont)—
        Surviving spouse (cont)—
            Matrimonial home—Valuation—Date of valuation—Right of surviving spouse of intestate to require
                appropriation of matrimonial home in or towards satisfaction of spouse's interest in intestate's
                estate—Valuation of home for purpose of appropriation—Whether home to be valued at date of
                intestate's death or date of appropriation—Administration of Estates Act 1925, s 41—Intestates'
                Estates Act 1952, Sch 2, para 1(1). **Robinson v Collins** [1975] **1** 321, Ch D.
            Spouse as sole personal representative appropriating deceased's shares in unquoted company in
                satisfaction of her statutory legacy—Appropriation without consent of beneficiaries or
                authorisation by court—Whether appropriation valid—Administration of Estates Act 1925, s 41.
                Kane v Radley-Kane [1998] **3** 753, Ch D.
    Beneficial interest. See **Administration of estates** (Beneficial interest).
    Conflict of laws—
        Succession. See **Conflict of laws** (Succession—Intestacy).
    Crown rights. See **Crown** (Rights on intestacy).
    Distribution of intestate's estate—
        Generally. See **Administration of estates** (Distribution).
        Right of widow—
            Wife leaving husband and living in adultery at the time of his death—Onus of proof—Alberta
                Intestate Succession Act 1928, s 19(1). **Burns v Burns** [1938] **4** 173, PC.
    Domicile—
        Deceased domiciled abroad—
            Grant of administration. See Grant of administration—Grant where deceased domiciled abroad,
                below.
    Evidence—
        Admissibility of evidence to prove testator had not died intestate. See **Will** (Evidence—Executor dying
            without taking out probate—Admissibility of evidence to prove that testator had not died intestate).
    Exclusion from benefit. See Succession—Exclusion from benefit, below.
    Family provision—
        Generally. See **Family provision**.
    Foreign adoption—
        Devolution of property. See **Adoption** (Foreign adoption—Death—Devolution of property—Intestacy).
    Grant of administration—
        Application—
            Practice—Applicant's right dependent on a person's legitimation. **Practice Direction** [1965] **2** 560,
                Prob.
            Presumption of death—Declaration of death by competent foreign court—Independent evidence.
                Schulhof, In the Goods of [1947] **2** 841, Prob.
        Estate of enemy alien—
            Discretionary grant—Enemy national dying in England—Persons entitled enemies resident in
                enemy country—Supreme Court of Judicature (Consolidation) Act 1925, s 162—Administration of
                Justice Act 1928, s 9. **Fischer, Re** [1940] **2** 252, Prob.
            Grant ad colligenda bona—Grant to Public Trustee—Special powers—Motion in court when
                necessary—Supreme Court of Judicature (Consolidation) Act 1925, s 162—Administration of
                Justice Act 1928, s 9(b). **Sanpietro, In the Estate of** [1940] **4** 482, Prob.
        Ghana. See **Ghana** (Intestacy—Grant of administration).
        Grant for purpose of representation of deceased in action—
            Grant to Official Solicitor—Whether general grant or one limited to defending particular
                action—Supreme Court of Judicature (Consolidation) Act 1925, s 162—Administration of Justice
                Act 1928, s 9—Law Reform (Miscellaneous Provisions) Act 1934, s 1(1). **Knight, In the Goods of**
                [1939] **3** 928, Prob.
        Grant to sole administrator—
            Possible life interest—Jurisdiction of court—Supreme Court of Judicature (Consolidation) Act 1925,
                s 160(1), s 162(1) (as amended by Administration of Justice Act 1928, s 9). **Hall (decd), Re**
                [1950] **1** 718, Prob.
        Grant to trust corporation—
            Consent of persons interested in estate—Grant stating that named individuals only persons entitled
                to share in estate—Named persons alone known to be interested at time of grant—Subsequent
                appearance of other persons equally interested—Whether necessary to revoke or amend letters
                of administration to enable other persons to participate. **Ward (decd), Re** [1971] **2** 1249, Ch D.
        Grant to widow—
            Divorce proceedings pending—Wife's notice of application for decree nisi to be made absolute
                received and filed on day of husband's death—Death of husband prior to receipt of notice by
                registrar—Whether wife entitled to grant of letters of administration as widow. **Seaford (decd), Re**
                [1968] **1** 482, CA.
        Grant where deceased domiciled abroad—
            Grant to person entitled to administer under law of domicile—Discretion of court—Court of Probate
                Act 1857, s 73—Supreme Court of Judicature (Consolidation) Act 1925, s 162(1) (as amended by
                Administration of Justice Act 1928, s 9). **Kaufman, In the Estate of** [1952] **2** 261, Prob.
            Procedure—Non-Contentious Probate Rules 1954 (SI 1954 No 796), r 29. **Practice Direction**
                [1957] **1** 576, Prob.
        Oath of administrator. See Grant of administration—Practice—Oath of administrator, below.
        Partial intestacy—
            Residue undisposed of—Claim by Crown of administration—Persons to be cited—Administration of
                Estates Act 1925, s 46(1)(vi)—Non-Contentious Probate Rules, r 119. **Hanley, In the Estate of**
                [1941] **3** 301, CA.
        Person incapable of managing his own affairs—
            Applicant not authorised by Court of Protection—Application for use and benefit of person not
                resident in institution—Evidence of incapacity of such person. **Practice Direction** [1969] **1** 494,
                Prob.
            Applicant not authorised by Court of Protection—Evidence of incapacity of person for whose
                benefit grant required. **Practice Note** [1958] **2** 600, Prob; [1962] **2** 613, Prob.

INTESTACY (cont)—
  Grant of administration (cont)—
    Practice—
      Oath of administrator—Clearing of prior classes—Relationship of proposed grantee to deceased—Illegitimate child—Family Law Reform Act 1969. **Practice Direction** [1969] **3** 1343, Prob.
    Revocation of grant—
      Discovery of will—Effect of laches. **Coghlan, Re** [1948] **2** 68, CA.
    Solicitor's estate—
      Grant of Law Society's nominee—Grant to nominees where solicitor practising on his own at his death—Procedure. **Practice Direction** [1965] **1** 923, Prob.
  Interest on intestacy—
    Disclaimer—
      Effect—Bona vacantia—Disclaimer of interest arising on partial intestacy by sole members of class—Whether Crown entitled to interest as bona vacantia—Whether interest passing to members of class next entitled on intestacy—Administration of Estates Act 1925, s 46(1) (as amended by the Intestates Estates Act 1952, s 1). **Scott (decd), Re** [1975] **2** 1033, Ch D.
  Legitimacy. *See* Succession—Legitimacy, *below.*
  Notice to quit—
    Service. *See* **Landlord and tenant** (Notice to quit—Service—Intestacy).
  Palestine. *See* **Palestine** (Intestacy).
  Partial intestacy—
    Grant of administration. *See* Grant of administration—Partial intestacy, *above.*
    Hotchpot. *See* **Administration of estates** (Partial intestacy—Hotchpot).
  Person of unsound mind—
    Succession. *See* Succession—Person of unsound mind, *below.*
  Revocation of grant of administration. *See* Grant of administration—Revocation of grant, *above.*
  Rights of surviving spouse—
    Personal chattels—
      Herd of shorthorn cattle—Administration of Estates Act 1925, ss 46(1), 55(1)(x). **Ogilby, Re** [1942] **1** 524, Ch D.
      Horses used for racing—Administration of Estates Act 1925, ss 46(1)(i), 55(1)(x). **Hutchinson (decd), Re** [1955] **1** 689, Ch D.
    Rights as respects matrimonial home—
      Right to appropriate interest in home to interest in estate—Nature of right—Occupation of matrimonial home by widow—Registered proprietor sought possession—Application to have defence struck out—Defendant widow had no interest recognisable by law in the house—No locus standi to defend action—Proceedings launched to join Official Solicitor as defendant to defend rights of estate—Intestates' Estates Act 1952, s 5, Sch 2, para 1. **Lall v Lall** [1965] **3** 330, Ch D.
  Statutory trusts—
    Advancement—
      Property held on statutory trusts for issue divisible into shares—Presumption of advancement—Contrary intention—Contrary intention appearing from circumstances of case—Test for determining whether contrary intention appearing—Transfer of shares in family company to son and daughter—Son and daughter employed in company's business—Transfer to exclusion of daughter not employed in business—Clear intention to prefer son and daughter so far as business concerned—Whether intention to prefer them with regard to whole of expected inheritance—Administration of Estates Act 1925, s 47(1)(iii). **Hardy v Shaw** [1975] **2** 1052, Ch D.
      Property held on statutory trusts for issue divisible into shares—Presumption of advancement—Meaning of 'advancement'—Gift whereby permanent provision made for donee—Transfer of shares in family company to son and daughter—Son and daughter employed in company's business—Transfers to exclusion of daughter not employed in business—Whether transfers by way of advancement—Administration of Estates Act 1925, s 47(1)(iii). **Hardy v Shaw** [1975] **2** 1052, Ch D.
  Succession—
    Conflict of laws. *See* **Conflict of laws** (Succession—Intestacy).
    Death after 1952—
      Nearest surviving relatives being issue of uncles and aunts of the whole blood who had predeceased intestate—Whether entitled to take—Administration of Estates Act 1925, ss 46(1)(v), 47(1)(i)(3)(5), as added by Intestates' Estates Act 1952, ss 1, 4, Sch 1. **Lockwood, Re** [1957] **3** 520, Ch D.
    Exclusion from benefit—
      Public policy—Felonious killing of deceased—Exclusion of killer from class entitled on intestacy—Interest of Crown—Bona vacantia—Administration of Estates Act 1925, s 46(1). **Callaway (decd), Re** [1956] **2** 451, Ch D.
      Public policy—Felonious killing of deceased—Insanity—Onus of proof—Sufficiency of proof. **Pollock, Re** [1941] **1** 360, Ch D.
      Public policy—Manslaughter. *See* **Will** (Benefit—Exclusion from benefit—Public policy—Manslaughter).
      Public policy—Murder of deceased—Plaintiff's father murdering his parents and being disqualified from succession on intestacy—Plaintiff claiming succession to grandparents' estates—Plaintiff capable of taking only if father predeceasing grandparents—Executors of grandfather's sister claiming succession to his estate on failure of trusts in favour of his issue—Whether disqualified child of intestate to be treated as having predeceased intestate—Whether sister taking even though intestate leaving disqualified son—Administration of Estates Act 1925, ss 46, 47. **DWS (decd), Re** [2000] **2** 83, Ch D; [2001] **1** 97, CA.
    Legitimacy—
      Children of polygamous marriage legitimate according to law of domicile—Succession to intestate's estate—Whether English laws of succession apply only to children of monogamous marriage—Marriage Ordinance of the Colony of Lagos (No 14 of 1884), s 41. **Bamgbose v Daniel** [1954] **3** 263, PC.

INTESTACY (cont)—
  Succession (cont)—
    Person of unsound mind—
      Gavelkind land—Lunatic surviving 1925 and dying without recovering testamentary capacity—Whether descent according to custom or to common-law heir. **Higham, Re** [1937] **2** 17, Ch D.
      Lunatic entitled as sole next-of-kin to estate of intestate brother—Brother entitled at his death to freehold property—Nature of lunatic's beneficial interest in brother's estate—'Beneficial interest in real estate'—Administration of Estates Act 1925, ss 33(1), (4), 52(2). **Donkin, Re** [1947] **2** 690, Ch D.
      Lunatic entitled on father's death in 1906 to undivided share in freehold estates—Freeholds unsold and held by trustees on statutory trusts—Nature of lunatic's interest—'Beneficial interest in real estate'—Administration of Estates Act 1925, s 51(2). **Bradshaw (decd), Re** [1950] **1** 643, CA.
      Real estate—Beneficial interest in proceeds of sale of land formerly copyhold—Deceased incapable of making a will and not recovering capacity before death—Whether technical term 'real estate' included copyhold lands—Whether beneficial interest in proceeds of sale devolved according to the general law applicable to freehold land before 1926—Administration of Estates Act 1925, s 51(2). **Sirett (decd), Re** [1968] **3** 186, Ch D.
    Surviving spouse—
      Polygamous spouses—Whether surviving polygamous spouses are 'surviving spouse' for purposes of intestate succession—Whether there is single statutory legacy for surviving polygamous spouses—Whether polygamous spouse's share of life interest in residuary estate accruing on her death to other widows or vesting in her children—Administration of Estates Act 1925, s 46(2). **Official Solicitor v Yemoh** [2011] **4** 200, Ch D.
  Surviving spouse—
    Appropriation by personal representatives. *See* Appropriation by personal representatives—Surviving spouse, *above*.
    Rights of spouse. *See* Rights of surviving spouse, *above*.
  Will—
    Construction. *See* **Will** (Construction—Intestacy).

INTIMIDATION
  Jury. *See* **Jury** (Intimidating or threatening jury).
  Threat to break contract. *See* **Tort** (Intimidation—Unlawful act—Threat to break contract).
  Trade dispute—
    Picketing. *See* **Trade dispute** (Picketing—Intimidation).
  Witness—
    Generally. *See* **Criminal law** (Witness—Intimidating a witness).
    Obstructing course of justice. *See* **Criminal law** (Obstructing course of justice—Witness—Intimidation).

INTOXICATING LIQUOR
  Accident insurance—
    Exception clause. *See* **Insurance** (Accident insurance—Exception clause—Influence of intoxicating liquor).
  Addiction—
    Negligence—
      Contributory negligence. *See* **Negligence** (Contributory negligence—Causation—Proximate cause of injury—Prisoner addicted to drugs and alcohol allocated top bunk bed).
  Consumption after permitted hours. *See* **Licensing** (Consumption of intoxicating liquor after permitted hours).
  Driving offences in connection with. *See* **Road traffic**.
  Intoxication as a defence—
    Sexual assault. *See* **Criminal law** (Intoxication as a defence—Capacity to form intent—Sexual assault).
  Licensed premises—
    Constable—
      Right of entry—Constable's right to enter premises for purpose of preventing or detecting commission of offence—Whether reasonable suspicion of commission of offence necessary prerequisite to exercise of constable's right—Licensing Act 1964, s 186(1). **Valentine v Jackson** [1972] **1** 90, QBD.
    Generally. *See* **Licensing**.
  Licensing. *See* **Licensing**.
  Manslaughter—
    Intoxication. *See* **Criminal law** (Manslaughter—Mens rea—Causing death by unlawful act—Intoxication).
  Murder—
    Diminished responsibility. *See* **Criminal law** (Murder—Diminished responsibility—Abnormality of mind—Effect of alcohol).
  Offences—
    Drunk and disorderly in a public place—
      Repeal of enactment creating offence—Whether enactment creating the offence was repealed before the replacing enactment in s 91 of the Criminal Justice Act 1967 was brought into operation—Licensing Act 1872, s 12(1)—Criminal Justice Act 1967, ss 91(5), 103(2), Sch 7, Pt 1—Criminal Justice Act 1967 (Commencement No 1) Order 1967 (SI 1967 No 1234), art 1, Sch 1, App. **Osgerby v Rushton** [1968] **2** 1196, QBD.
    Drunk in possession of a loaded firearm—
      Firearm—Whether 'firearm' includes an air rifle—Licensing Act 1872, s 12. **Seamark v Prouse** [1980] **3** 26, QBD.
  Road traffic legislation, under. *See* **Road traffic**.
  Tied house covenants. *See* **Restraint of trade by agreement** (Public house).
  Weights and measures. *See* **Weights and measures**.

INTOXICATION
  Criminal proceedings—
    Defence. *See* **Criminal law** (Intoxication as a defence).

INTOXICATION (cont)—
Criminal proceedings (cont)—
Rape—
Complainant's voluntary intoxication. *See* **Criminal law** (Rape—Consent—Complainant's voluntary intoxication).

INTRODUCTORY TENANCY
Possession. *See* **Housing** (Local authority houses—Possession—Introductory tenancy).

INVALID CARE ALLOWANCE
Equality of treatment of men and women—
European Community. *See* **European Union** (Equality of treatment of men and women—Social security—Severe disablement allowance—Invalid care allowance).
Generally. *See* **Social security** (Invalid care allowance).

INVALIDITY BENEFIT
Damages for personal injuries—
Deduction of invalidity benefit. *See* **Damages** (Personal injury—Loss of earnings—Deduction of industrial injury, disablement, sickness or invalidity benefit accruing to injured person).
European Community—
Workers—
Freedom of movement. *See* **European Union** (Workers—Freedom of movement—Social security—Invalidity benefits).

INVALIDITY PENSION
Non-contributory invalidity pension. *See* **Social security** (Non-contributory invalidity pension).

INVENTION
Confidence—
Breach of confidence—
Use of information given by inventor in confidence. *See* **Equity** (Breach of confidence—Damages—Use of information obtained in confidence—Springboard for activities detrimental to informant—Unpatented device disclosed by inventor as alternative in course of negotiation for marketing his patented device).
Invention of servant. *See* **Employment** (Invention of servant).
Patent. *See* **Patent** (Invention).

INVESTIGATORY POWERS
Freedom of expression. *See* **Human rights** (Freedom of expression—Investigatory powers).
Investigation of electronic data protected by encryption—
Power to require disclosure—
Protected information—Self-incrimination—Privilege against self-incrimination—Notices requiring disclosure of protected information—Whether notices infringing privilege against self-incrimination—Regulation of Investigatory Powers Act 2000, s 49. **R v S** [2009] **1** 716, CA.
Investigatory Powers Tribunal—
Exercise of tribunal's jurisdiction—
Statute providing decisions of tribunal '... shall not be subject to appeal or be liable to be questioned in any court'—Whether decision of tribunal amenable to judicial review—Regulation of Investigatory Powers Act 2000, s 67(8). **R (on the application of Privacy International) v Investigatory Powers Tribunal** [2018] **3** 95, CA.
Statute providing decisions of tribunal '... shall not be subject to appeal or be liable to be questioned in any court'—Whether decision of tribunal amenable to judicial review—Regulation of Investigatory Powers Act 2000, ss 65, 67(8). **R (on the application of Privacy International) v Investigatory Powers Tribunal** [2017] **3** 1127, DC.
Regulation of investigatory powers—
Interception of private communications—
National security. *See* **Telecommunications** (Interception of communications—Directions in the interests of national security).
Non-governmental organisations alleging unrestrained interception and retention of private data of UK citizens—Data allegedly obtained by information sharing with US intelligence services and by surveillance by UK intelligence services—Whether statutory regime providing sufficient safeguards against arbitrary abuse—Whether distinction between internal and external communications giving rise to indirect discrimination against non-UK nationals—Whether statutory regime in accordance with the law for purposes of right to respect for private and family life—Whether statutory regime sufficiently foreseeable and proportionate to justify interference with convention rights—Regulation of Investigatory Powers Act 2000, ss 8, 16—Human Rights Act 1998, Sch 1, Pt I, arts 8, 10, 14. **Liberty (National Council of Civil Liberties) v Government Communications Headquarters** [2015] **3** 142, IPT.
Non-governmental organisations criticising communications interception regime employed by UK intelligence services—Intelligence services making further disclosures concerning procedures during hearing before Investigatory Powers Tribunal—Tribunal finding regime in accordance with requirements of European Convention rights for foreseeability and proportionality—Whether regime in accordance with Convention rights prior to disclosures during hearing—Whether safeguards for use of intercepted material sufficient—Human Rights Act 1998, Sch 1, Pt I, art 8—Regulation of Investigatory Powers Act 2000, ss 8(4), 15, 16. **Liberty (National Council of Civil Liberties) v Government Communications Headquarters (No 2)** [2015] **3** 212, IPT.
Phone tapping—Members of Parliament—Status, meaning and effect of Wilson Doctrine restricting interception of parliamentarian communications—Whether doctrine applying to warrants—Whether doctrine enforceable at law—Regulation of Investigatory Powers Act 2000, s 8(1), (4). **Lucas MP v Security Service** [2017] **1** 283, IPT.

INVESTIGATORY POWERS (cont)—
Regulation of investigatory powers (cont)—
Surveillance and covert human intelligence sources—
Authorisation of surveillance and human intelligence sources—Lawful surveillance—Authorisation of directed surveillance—Legal professional privilege—Right to respect for private and family life—Person in custody consulting with legal or medical adviser—Whether directed surveillance lawful—Whether breach of right to respect for private and family life—Human Rights Act 1998, Sch 1, Pt I, art 8—Regulation of Investigatory Powers Act 2000, ss 27, 28. **McE, Re** [2009] **4** 335, HL.
Authorisation of surveillance and human intelligence sources—Right to respect for private and family life—Voluntary declared interview—Covert making of recording of voluntary declared interview—Whether 'surveillance'—Human Rights Act 1998, Sch 1, Pt I, art 8—Regulation of Investigatory Powers Act 2000, Pt II. **Complaint of Surveillance, Re a** [2014] **2** 576, UT.
Personal or other relationship—Tribunal established by statute—Tribunal only appropriate tribunal for proceedings relating to taking place in any challengeable circumstances of any conduct and use of covert human intelligence sources—Person being a covert human intelligence source if he establish or maintain a personal or other relationship with a person for a covert purpose—Whether 'personal or other relationship' including intimate sexual relationship—Human Rights Act 1998, s 7(1)—Regulation of Investigatory Powers Act 2000, ss 26(8)(a), 65. **AJA v Metropolitan Police Comr** [2014] **1** 882, CA.
Tax. See **Income tax** (Information—Power to obtain information and documents).

INVESTIGATORY POWERS TRIBUNAL
Exercise of tribunal's jurisdiction—
Statute providing decisions of tribunal '... shall not be subject to appeal or be liable to be questioned in any court'—
Whether decision of tribunal amenable to judicial review—Regulation of Investigatory Powers Act 2000, s 67(8). **R (on the application of Privacy International) v Investigatory Powers Tribunal** [2019] **4** 1, SC.

INVESTMENT
Enterprise investment scheme—
Tax relief. See **Income tax** (Enterprise investment scheme relief).
Friendly society funds. See **Friendly society** (Investment of funds).
Funds in court—
Admiralty action. See **Admiralty** (Practice—Directions—Application of Admiralty Registrar's practice directions).
Generally. See **Practice** (Funds in court).
Public Trustee. See **Public Trustee** (Funds in court—Investment of).
Income—
Capital allowances. See **Capital allowances**.
Inclusion in computation of profits for purposes of excess profits tax. See **Excess profits tax** (Computation of profits—Inclusion of income received from investments).
Special charge to tax. See **Income tax** (Special charge—Investment income).
Inducement to invest money—
Criminal liability. See **Criminal law** (Inducement to invest money).
Investment business. See **Investment business**.
Investment grant. See **Investment grant**.
Investors Compensation Scheme. See **Investment business** (Investors Compensation Scheme).
Profit—
Unjust enrichment—
Restitution. See **Restitution** (Unjust enrichment—Investment profit).
Settlement. See **Settlement** (Investment).
Trust—
Charity—
Trustee's powers. See **Charity** (Trustee—Investment policy).
Discretion of trustees. See **Variation of trusts** (Extension of powers of investment—Discretion).
Evidence of stockbroker or expert. See **Variation of trusts** (Evidence—Investment).
Powers of investment—
Duty of trustee to beneficiary. See **Trust and trustee** (Duty of trustee—Duty towards beneficiary—Investments).
Extension—Generally. See **Variation of trusts** (Extension of powers of investment).
Extension—Jurisdiction of court to extend powers. See **Variation of trusts** (Variation by the court—Investment clause—Extension of powers of investment).
Trustee's. See **Trust and trustee** (Investments).

INVESTMENT ALLOWANCE
Income tax. See **Capital allowances**.

INVESTMENT BUSINESS
Authorisation—
Authorisation in other member state—
Danish company lawfully authorised under Danish legislation to carry on investment business in Denmark pending determination of application for authorisation—Managing director of company mistakenly believing that Danish authority entitled company to carry on investment business in United Kingdom—Whether managing director of company person knowingly concerned in contravening Act—Financial Services Act 1986, ss 3, 6(2). **Securities and Investments Board v Scandex Capital Management A/S** [1998] **1** 514, CA.

INVESTMENT BUSINESS (cont)—
  Collective investment scheme—
    Regulation—
      Land banking—Companies selling plots of land to individual investors—Representations that permission would be obtained for residential development, that land would be sold and investors would receive share of proceeds—Contracts for sale of plots entered into after investors had paid in full—Whether arrangements in respect of land constituted collective investment scheme—Meaning of 'arrangements'—Whether investors had to have shared understanding of arrangements—Whether purpose of arrangements to enable participants to receive profits from disposal of sites with residential planning permission—Whether investors had day-to-day control over management of property—Whether property managed as a whole by or on behalf of scheme operators—Financial Services and Markets Act 2000, s 235. **Financial Conduct Authority v Asset LI Inc** [2015] **1** 1, CA; [2015] **1 Comm** 116, CA; [2016] **2 Comm** 189, SC; [2016] **3** 93, SC.
  Company—
    Investigation by Department of Trade and Industry. *See* **Company** (Investigation by Department of Trade and Industry—Affairs of company—Investment business).
  Contract for differences—
    Stock market index movements—
      Contract to secure profit by reference to fluctuations in index—Whether wager on movement of stock market index enforceable—Whether wager amounting to 'contract for differences'—Gaming Act 1845, s 18—Financial Services Act 1986, s 63, Sch 1, para 9. **City Index Ltd v Leslie** [1991] **3** 180, CA.
  Investment management agreements—
    Dealing in securities—
      Appellants making investment management agreements with respondent—Respondent's unlicensed representative making and signing agreements—Whether agreements void because of lack of licence—Prevention of Fraud (Investments) Act 1958, s 1. **Hughes v Asset Managers plc** [1995] **3** 669, CA.
  Investors Compensation Scheme—
    Assignment of action to scheme—
      Interpretation of contractual document—Matrix of fact—Badly drafted document—Document to be interpreted to reflect parties' intention. **Investors Compensation Scheme Ltd v West Bromwich Building Society** [1998] **1** 98, HL.
    Compensation—
      Compensation to extent 'essential to provide fair compensation'—Nature of compensation—Whether scheme required to provide compensation equal to amount of defaulting broker's liability—Whether board administering scheme having discretion as to amount of compensation payable—Whether board's decision to limit claims in respect of cost of professional advice or to refuse claims in respect of illness, distress etc irrational—Financial Services (Compensation of Investors) Rules 1990, rr 2.02.2(a), 2.04.1. **R v Investors Compensation Scheme Ltd, ex p Bowden** [1995] **3** 605, HL.
      Home income plans—Elderly couples raising money by mortgaging jointly-owned homes to provide income—Homes liable to repossession because of falling house values, rising interest rates and declining investment performance—Brokers worthless and in default—One spouse dying before brokers declared in default—Whether surviving spouse entitled to claim compensation. **R v Investors Compensation Scheme Ltd, ex p Weyell** [1994] **1** 601, QBD.
      Home income plans—Elderly people mortgaging homes to provide income—Homes liable to repossession because of market conditions and declining investment performance—Whether investors entitled to claim compensation from the Investors Compensation Scheme equal to amount of defaulting brokers' liability. **R v Investors Compensation Scheme Ltd, ex p Bowden** [1995] **3** 605, HL.
      Liability incurred by authorised persons in connection with investment business—Applicant making original investment in April 1986 prior to commencement of scheme—Broker persuading applicant to reinvest in 1991—Broker misappropriating funds and ceasing trading—Applicant claiming under compensation scheme—Whether claim in respect of 1991 reinvestment based on liability incurred prior to December 1986 threshold date for valid claims—Financial Services Act 1986, s 54—Financial Services (Compensation of Investors) Rules 1990, r 1.02.3. **R v Investors Compensation Scheme Ltd, ex p Taylor** [1998] **1** 711, CA.
      Scheme business claims—Compensation arising out of investment business conducted by defaulting broker on or after date scheme set up—Investors negligently advised by insurance brokers to enter into home income plans before compensation scheme set up—Brokers under duty to manage investor's portfolio in accordance with FIMBRA rules and with reasonable skill and care—Brokers in breach of rules and obligations after scheme set up—Whether investors entitled to compensation—Financial Services (Compensation of Investors) Rules 1990, r 2.03.1. **R v Investors Compensation Scheme Ltd, ex p Weyell** [1994] **1** 601, QBD.
    Legal proceedings concerning operation of scheme—
      Procedure—Whether questions should be determined by originating summons or by application for judicial review—Financial Services Act 1986, s 54. **R v Investors Compensation Scheme Ltd, ex p Weyell** [1994] **1** 601, QBD.
    Liability incurred by authorised persons in connection with investment business—
      Claims against authorised persons unable to satisfy liabilities—Scheme coming into operation on 27 August 1988—Provisions defining 'investment' and 'investment business' coming into force on 18 December 1986—Whether compensation payable in respect of liabilities incurred before compensation scheme became effective—Whether compensation payable in respect of liabilities incurred after 18 December 1986—Financial Services Act 1986, ss 1, 3, 54. **Securities and Investments Board v Financial Intermediaries Managers and Brokers Regulatory Association Ltd** [1991] **4** 398, Ch D.

INVESTMENT BUSINESS (cont)—
>Regulation—
>>Client account—
>>>SFA ordering company to cease investment business and transfer client accounts—Company opening new client account to segregate potential surpluses on existing client accounts from general corporate funds—Company intending that any actual surplus should go into its general funds—Company going into liquidation with deficit on client accounts—Whether new account held on trust for clients—Whether creation of such a trust a voidable preference—Whether post-liquidation payment from account an unlawful disposition of company property—Insolvency Act 1986, ss 127, 239—Securities and Futures Authority Rules, r 4-67. **Branston & Gothard Ltd, Re** [1999] **1 Comm** 289, Ch D.
>>Information given to regulatory body—
>>>Privilege—Financial services regulatory body conducting inquiry into firm of stockbrokers managed by claimants—Defendants providing regulatory body with information by letter—Claimants bringing proceedings for libel against defendants—Whether letter attracting absolute privilege. **Mahon v Rahn (No 2)** [1999] **2 Comm** 789, QBD.
>Restitution—
>>Interim payment—
>>>Person found to have been knowingly concerned in carrying on investment business in United Kingdom in contravention of Act—Whether court having jurisdiction to order interim payment into court—Financial Services Act 1986, s 6(2). **Securities and Investments Board v Scandex Capital Management A/S** [1998] **1** 514, CA.
>>Restitution order—
>>>Liability to make restitution—Person contravening Act—Carrying on investment business in contravention of Act—Person 'knowingly concerned' in contravention of Act—Solicitors acting for client allegedly carrying on unauthorised investment business—Swiss companies carrying on investment business in United Kingdom without authority—English solicitors alleged to be knowingly concerned in companies' breaches of Act—Whether person knowingly concerned in contravention of Act can be ordered to repay to investors moneys lost—Whether solicitors could be ordered to repay to investors sums paid to companies—Financial Services Act 1986, ss 6(2), 61(1). **Securities and Investments Board v Pantell SA (No 2)** [1993] **1** 134, CA.
>Restricted information—
>>Disclosure—
>>>Statutory prohibition on disclosure of information relating to person's business or other affairs without consent of that person or of informant—Securities and Investments Board allegedly disclosing restricted information—Whether disclosure of restricted information actionable at suit of persons whose consent was required for disclosure—Whether Securities and Investments Board was acting in bad faith—Whether restricted information disclosed—Financial Services Act 1986, ss 179, 187(3). **Melton Medes Ltd v Securities and Investments Board** [1995] **3** 880, Ch D.
>Self-regulating organisation—
>>LAUTRO—
>>>Intervention in member's business—Duty to hear representations before making decision to intervene—Whether regulatory body under duty to invite or hear representations before making decision to intervene in member's business and if so from whom. **R v Life Assurance and Unit Trust Regulatory Organisation Ltd, ex p Ross** [1993] **1** 545, CA.
>>>Intervention in member's business—Intervention affecting appointed representative of member—Right of appeal—Whether appointed representative having right of appeal to Lautro's appeal tribunal—Financial Services Act 1986, s 8—Lautro Rules 1988, rr 2.12(1), 7.3(11), 7.23. **R v Life Assurance and Unit Trust Regulatory Organisation Ltd, ex p Ross** [1993] **1** 545, CA.

INVESTMENT COMPANY
>Income tax. See **Income tax** (Investment company).

INVESTMENT GRANT
>Discretion to grant—
>>Exercise of discretion—
>>>No obligation to make grant in respect of each eligible product—Industrial Development Act 1966, s 1(1). **British Oxygen Co Ltd v Minister of Technology** [1970] **3** 165, HL.
>>Limit of cost—
>>>Application of rule applying limit of cost below which no grant to be made—Whether proper exercise of discretion—Industrial Development Act 1966, s 1(1). **British Oxygen Co Ltd v Minister of Technology** [1970] **3** 165, HL.
>Machinery and plant—
>>Dual purpose plant—
>>>One purpose to which plant used eligible—Other purpose not eligible—Whether competent for Minister to approve grant in respect of expenditure referable to eligible purpose. **British Oxygen Co Ltd v Minister of Technology** [1970] **3** 165, HL.
>>Vehicle—
>>>Articulated vehicle with tank and tanker lorry—Tanks integral part of vehicle—Industrial Development Act 1966, s 13(1). **British Oxygen Co Ltd v Minister of Technology** [1970] **3** 165, HL.
>>>Trailer with battery of detachable cylinders—Cylinders in practice not detached—Primary use of cylinders for delivery rather than storage—Cylinders integral part of vehicle—Industrial Development Act 1966, s 13(1). **British Oxygen Co Ltd v Minister of Technology** [1970] **3** 165, HL.
>Qualifying industrial process—
>>Storage—
>>>Storage ceasing when cylinders used for storage despatched for delivery of product to customer—Industrial Development Act 1966, s 1(3). **British Oxygen Co Ltd v Minister of Technology** [1970] **3** 165, HL.

INVITATION TO TENDER
>See **Contract** (Invitation to tender).

INVITEE
Occupier's liability—
  Duty to invitee. *See* **Occupier's liability** (Duty to invitee).
  Invitee or licensee—
    Distinction. *See* **Occupier's liability** (Invitee or licensee).

INVOLUNTARY MANSLAUGHTER
Accessory before the fact. *See* **Criminal law** (Accessory before the fact—Involuntary manslaughter).

IRELAND
Northern Ireland. *See* **Northern Ireland**.
Republic of Ireland—
  Extradition. *See* **Magistrates** (Indorsement of Irish warrant).

IRISH WARRANT
Indorsement. *See* **Magistrates** (Indorsement of Irish warrant).

IRON AND STEEL INDUSTRY
Compensation—
  Denationalisation—
    Loss of employment—Sale of subsidiary company by Iron and Steel Holding and Realisation Agency to consortium under statutory duty—Resale of company by consortium to two members—Closure of company shortly after resale—Novus actus interveniens—Whether employee's loss of employment was 'in consequence of' sale by Agency—Iron and Steel Act 1953, s 24(1)(b)—Iron and Steel (Compensation to Officers and Servants) (No 2) Regulations 1953 (SI 1953 No 1849), reg 3(1)(d). **Iron and Steel Holding and Realisation Agency v Compensation Appeal Tribunal** [1966] **1** 769, QBD.

IRREGULARITY
Civil proceedings—
  Correction of irregularity—
    Practice. *See* **Practice** (Irregularity).
Criminal trial—
  Appeal. *See* **Criminal law** (Appeal).
  Right of appeal. *See* **Criminal law** (Appeal—Right of appeal—Irregularity at trial).

IRRETRIEVABLE BREAKDOWN OF MARRIAGE
Divorce. *See* **Divorce** (Irretrievable breakdown of marriage).

IRREVOCABLE SETTLEMENT
Children—
  Income tax. *See* **Income tax** (Settlement—Children—Irrevocable settlement).

ISLE OF MAN
Criminal law—
  Proceeds of crime—
    Criminal conduct—Criminal property—Money laundering—Arrangement facilitating acquisition, retention, use or control of criminal property by or on behalf of another person—Knowing or suspecting arrangement facilitating use of criminal property—Requirement of knowledge or suspicion—Proceeds of Crime Act (Isle of Man) 2008, s 140(1). **Holt v A-G** [2014] **2** 397, PC.
Disclosure of trust documents. *See* **Trust and trustee** (Disclosure of trust documents—Isle of Man).
Discretionary trust—
  Powers of trustee. *See* **Powers of trustee** (Discretionary trusts—Isle of Man).
Divorce —
  Financial provision—
    Maintenance agreement—Financial arrangements—Alteration of agreements by court—Husband and wife making separation agreement—Whether contrary to public policy—Matters to be considered by court when making order for ancillary relief—Matrimonal Causes Act 1973, ss 34, 35—Matrimonial Proceedings Act (Isle of Man) 2003, ss 49, 50. **MacLeod v MacLeod** [2009] **1** 851, PC.
Evidence by person from—
  Whether necessary for evidence to be given in person—
    Whether Isle of Man 'beyond the seas'—Whether document statement by person admissible. *See* **Document** (Admissibility in evidence—Admission of documentary statement without calling maker—Person beyond the seas:).
Mines and minerals—
  Crown rights to minerals, flagg, slate and stone—
    Shale—Whether included in the rights reserved—Act of Settlement 1703-4. **A-G for Isle of Man v Moore** [1938] **3** 263, PC.
Negligence—
  Duty to take care—
    Existence of duty—Statutory powers—Isle of Man's Treasurer's duty to depositors in respect of licensing of banks. *See* **Negligence** (Duty to take care—Existence of duty—Matters to be considered in determining whether duty existing—Statutory powers—Regulatory powers—Isle of Man).

ISLE OF MAN (cont)—
    Practice—
        Service out of the jurisdiction—
            Appropriate forum—Challenge to jurisdiction—Principles to be applied—Krygyz company seeking to enforce Krygyz judgment against Manx companies in Isle of Man—Manx companies counterclaiming and applying to add defendant companies as defendants to counterclaim—Counterclaim governed by Krygyz law—Manx appellate court adding defendants to counterclaim—Defendants appealing—Whether counterclaim being pursued in appropriate jurisdiction. **AK Investment CJSC v Kyrgyz Mobil Tel Ltd** [2011] **4** 1027, PC; [2012] **1 Comm** 319, PC.

ISSUE
    Will—
        Children. *See* **Will** (Gift—Specific donees—Heirs and surviving issue).
        Specific donees—
            Heirs and surviving issue. *See* **Will** (Gift—Specific donees—Heirs and surviving issue).
            Issue of our marriage. *See* **Will** (Gift—Specific donees—Issue of our marriage).

ISSUE ESTOPPEL
    Arbitration—
        Interim award. *See* **Arbitration** (Award—Interim award—Estoppel—Issue estoppel).
    Bankruptcy petition—
        Proceedings under Insolvency Act 1986. *See* **Insolvency** (Petition—Creditor's petition—Issue estoppel).
    Care proceedings. *See* **Family proceedings** (Orders in family proceedings—Care order—Evidence—Issue estoppel).
    Generally. *See* **Estoppel** (Issue estoppel).
    Res judicata. *See* **Estoppel** (Res judicata—Issue estoppel).
    Town and country planning appeal. *See* **Town and country planning** (Appeal—Issue estoppel).

ISSUING HOUSE
    Moneylender—
        Whether exempt from Moneylenders Acts. *See* **Moneylender** (Exception from definition of moneylender).

J

JACK RUSSELL TERRIERS
Attack on child—
> Liability of owner in negligence. *See* **Animal** (Negligence—Domestic animal—Liability of owner or keeper—Liability in negligence for personal injuries caused by animal—Dog—Dog not known to have propensity to attack humans—Defendant breeder of Jack Russell terriers).

JAMAICA
Civil proceedings—
> Proceedings for leave to apply for certiorari to quash minister's allocation of imported motor vehicles—Whether 'civil proceedings'—Whether proceedings should be brought against Attorney General rather than minister—Crown Proceedings Act (Jamaica), s 18(2). **Minister of Foreign Affairs Trade and Industry v Vehicles and Supplies Ltd** [1991] **4** 65, PC.

Constitutional law—
Entrenched provisions of Constitution—
> Trial by jury—Grave crimes tried by judge with jury when Constitution came into force—Statute enacting that certain crimes to be tried by judge without a jury—Statute not enacted by special procedure for amending entrenched provisions—Whether trial by jury entrenched in Constitution—Whether statute required to be passed by special procedure—Jamaica (Constitution) Order in Council 1962 (SI 1962/1550), art 13(1), Sch 2, s 97(1). **Stone v R** [1980] **3** 148, PC.

Fundamental rights and freedoms—
> Constitution prohibiting inhuman or degrading punishment—Death penalty—Delay in carrying out death penalty—Whether prolonged delay in carrying out death penalty an inhuman or degrading punishment—Constitution of Jamaica, ss 17(1), 25, 90, 91. **Pratt v A-G for Jamaica** [1993] **4** 769, PC.

> Constitution prohibiting inhuman or degrading punishment—Prohibition not extending to punishment which was lawful immediately prior to constitution coming into force—Sentences of death for murder passed under pre-existing law—Long delays in execution of sentences—Whether execution of sentences after such delays constituting inhuman or degrading punishment—Whether exception for punishment under pre-existing law applicable—Jamaica (Constitution) Order in Council 1962 (SI 1962/1550), Sch 2, s 17. **Riley v A-G of Jamaica** [1982] **3** 469, PC.

> Criminal proceedings to be in public—Presumption that proceedings in camera reasonably required in interests of public safety, public order or protection of private lives of persons concerned in proceedings—Special court established to deal with firearms offences—Provision that court should sit in camera—Whether provision unconstitutional—Jamaica (Constitution) Order 1962 (SI 1962/1550), Sch 2, s 20(3)(4)—Gun Court Act 1974 (Jamaica), s 13(1). **Hinds v R** [1976] **1** 353, PC.

> Review of capital offence. *See* Criminal law—Review of capital offence—Protection of fundamental rights and freedoms, *below*.

> Right of defendant in criminal proceedings to be permitted to defend himself by legal representative of his choice—Permitted—Defendant charged with capital offence of murder—Defendant not seeking legal aid—Defendant's counsel withdrawing from case without consent of trial judge because they had not been put in funds—Judge ordering trial to continue with defendant unrepresented—Whether defendant's constitutional rights infringed—Jamaica (Constitution) Order in Council 1962 (SI 1962/1550), Sch 2, s 20(6)(c). **Robinson v R** [1985] **2** 594, PC.

> Right to 'fair hearing within a reasonable time'—Reasonable time—Delay—Factors to be considered in determining whether delay unreasonable—Accused ordered to be retried in March 1979—Accused discharged in November 1981—Accused rearrested in February 1982 and new trial set for May 1982—Whether unreasonable delay in bringing accused to trial—Whether accused required to show prejudice—Jamaica (Constitution) Order in Council 1962, Sch 2, s 20(1). **Bell v DPP of Jamaica** [1985] **2** 585, PC.

Judicature—
> Higher judiciary—Jurisdiction—Constitution impliedly prohibiting transfer of jurisdiction to courts consisting of members of lower judiciary—Constitution containing special provisions for appointment and tenure of office of members of higher judiciary—Statute establishing special court to deal with firearm offences—Division of court consisting of members of lower judiciary—Division having jurisdiction over offences previously cognisable only by higher judiciary—Whether statutory provisions establishing provision void as being inconsistent with Constitution—Jamaica (Constitution) Order 1962 (SI 1962/1550), Sch 2, ss 2, 97(1)—Gun Court Act 1974 (Jamaica), ss 4(b), 5(2). **Hinds v R** [1976] **1** 353, PC.

Separation of powers—
> Judicature—Punishment of offences—Transfer of power to executive body—Validity—Firearms offences—Statute establishing mandatory sentence—Detention at hard labour during Governor-General's pleasure—Convicted person only to be discharged at direction of Governor-General acting in accordance with recommendation of review board—Majority of members of review board not members of judiciary—Whether provision for mandatory sentence void—Jamaica (Constitution) Order 1962 (SI 1962/1550), Sch 2, s 2—Gun Court Act 1974 (Jamaica), ss 8(2), 22(1). **Hinds v R** [1976] **1** 353, PC.

Criminal evidence—
Identity—
> Identification evidence—Direction to jury—Judge failing to give appropriate direction to jury—Whether appellate court entitled to dismiss appeal if evidence of visual identification of exceptionally good quality—Judicature (Appellate Jurisdiction) Act (Jamaica), s 14(1) proviso. **Freemantle v R** [1994] **3** 225, PC.

JAMAICA (cont)—

Criminal evidence (cont)—

Prosecution evidence—

Written statements made to police by prosecution witnesses not disclosed before or at trial—Evidence of witnesses at trial based on statements not foreshadowed in depositions—Discrepancies between witnesses' evidence and statements—Whether non-disclosure constituting a material irregularity. **Berry v R** [1992] **3** 881, PC.

Statement by accused—

Unsworn statement by accused from dock—Statement raising alibi defence—Whether judge required to direct jury about possible impact of rejection of alibi on identification evidence. **Mills v R** [1995] **3** 865, PC.

Criminal law—

Appeal—

Allowing appeal—New trial—Venire de novo—Court quashing conviction on ground that trial was a nullity—Majority verdict returned prematurely—Whether jurisdiction to order new trial—Whether 'new trial' including venire de novo—Judicature (Appellate Jurisdiction) Act (Jamaica), s 14(2). **DPP of Jamaica v White** [1977] **3** 1003, PC.

Appeal against conviction—Prescribed grounds of appeal—Wrong decision of a question of law—Miscarriage of justice—Error on face of record—Record showing majority verdict returned prematurely—Appeal court allowing appeal and quashing conviction on ground that trial was a nullity—Whether error on face of record constituting wrong decision of a question of law or a miscarriage of justice—Judicature (Appellate Jurisdiction) Act (Jamaica), s 14(1). **DPP of Jamaica v White** [1977] **3** 1003, PC.

Bill of indictment—

Information charging defendant dismissed by resident magistrate on ground of no case to answer—DPP applying to judge for voluntary bill of indictment against defendant for same offence—Defendant not given notice of DPP's application—Warrant issued before indictment preferred—DPP having power to prefer bill of indictment without applying to judge—Whether judge having jurisdiction to prefer indictment—Whether defendant entitled to notice of application—Whether abuse of process for bill of indictment to be preferred where defendant discharged after preliminary inquiry in absence of fresh evidence—Whether warrant for arrest valid—Constitution of Jamaica, s 94(6)—Criminal Justice (Administration) Act (Jamaica), s 2(2). **Brooks v DPP of Jamaica** [1994] **2** 231, PC.

Evidence. *See* Criminal evidence, *above.*

Review of capital offence—

Protection of fundamental rights and freedoms—Appellant convicted in 1983 of murder committed during robbery and sentenced to death—Statutory provision enacted in 1992 providing for murder to be classified into capital and non-capital murder—Cases of prisoners awaiting death sentence to be reviewed and classified by Court of Appeal judge—Prisoner entitled to have judge's classification reviewed by panel of three Court of Appeal judges—Whether prisoner entitled to legal representation and to make submissions when case reviewed by single judge—Whether review procedure unconstitutional—Offences against the Person (Amendment) Act 1992 (Jamaica), s 7—Constitution of Jamaica, s 20. **Huntley v A-G for Jamaica** [1995] **1** 308, PC.

Sentence—

Age of offender. *See* **Sentence** (Age of offender).

Trial—

Counsel—Withdrawal of counsel from trial—Judge's duty—Counsel's withdrawal causing defendant significant prejudice—Whether defendant in murder trial having absolute right to legal representation throughout trial—Judge under duty to persuade counsel to remain or to adjourn trial to allow defendant opportunity to obtain alternative representation—Constitution of Jamaica, s 20(6)(c)—International Covenant on Civil and Political Rights, art 14(3)(d). **Dunkley v R** [1995] **1** 279, PC.

Direction by judge to jury—Request by jury for direction—Duty of judge to direct jury on facts as well as law if requested to do so by jury. **Berry v R** [1992] **3** 881, PC.

No case to answer—Submission of no case to answer—Whether submission of no case to answer should be heard and determined in absence of jury. **Crosdale v R** [1995] **2** 500, PC.

Retirement of jury—Judge asking jury whether they wished to retire to consider verdict—Whether judge applying pressure on jury to reach verdict. **Crosdale v R** [1995] **2** 500, PC.

Evidence—

Criminal proceedings. *See* Criminal evidence, *above.*

Income tax—

Appeal—

Right of any person who objects to the amount of any repayment by commissioner to appeal—Meaning of amount—Whether including a nil amount—Whether person to whom no repayment made having right of appeal—Income Tax Law (No 59 of 1954), s 63(3). **Seramco Ltd Superannuation Fund Trustees v Income Tax Comr** [1976] **2** 28, PC.

Avoidance—

Artificial or fictitious transaction reducing amount of tax payable—Right of commissioner to disregard artificial transaction—Sale of shares in company to trustees of exempt superannuation fund—Purchase price payable by instalments—Trustees having no moneys to invest in purchase of shares—Trustees paying instalments from dividends declared by company—Dividends paid after deduction of tax—Whether transaction 'artificial or fictitious'—Whether commissioner entitled to disregard transaction and refuse to repay tax—Income Tax Law (No 59 of 1954), s 10(1). **Seramco Ltd Superannuation Fund Trustees v Income Tax Comr** [1976] **2** 28, PC.

Wear and tear allowance—

Business—Carrying on business—Acquisition and letting of premises—Whether acquisition and letting of premises was a business—Whether building let was used by owner for the purpose of acquiring income from a business carried on by him—Income Tax Law (No 59 of 1954), s 8(o). **Comr of Income Tax v Hanover Agencies Ltd** [1967] **1** 954, PC.

JAMAICA (cont)—
  Local authority—
    Action against authority—
      Notice—Action improperly constituted in absence of notice—Action against corporation and not individual officer—Whether notice required—Public Health Law 1925 (Jamaica), ss 22(2)(a), 89(1), (2)—Kingston and St Andrew Corporation Law 1931, s 223. **Hall v Kingston and St Andrew Corp** [1941] **2** 1, PC.
  Moneylending—
    Mortgage—
      Variation of contract—Interest—Rate of interest raised—Increase accepted by mortgagor by letter—No provision in mortgage for raising rate of interest but principal repayable on demand—No written memorandum of variation complying with Moneylending Law—No memorandum in writing of original mortgage necessary—Whether mortgage enforceable without the variation in rate of interest—Moneylending Law of Jamaica, s 8. **United Dominions Corp (Jamaica) Ltd v Shoucair** [1968] **2** 904, PC.
  Patent—
    Validity—
      Invention by importation—Application for patent for invention not previously known in jurisdiction—Status of applicant—Expiration of patent for same invention in another country—Application for and subsequent grant of patent in Jamaica relating to amlodipine besylate—Applicant assigning patent to P for nominal sum—Expiration of P's patent for same invention in Egypt—Whether applicant acting as attorney for P—Whether patent invalid upon expiration of Egyptian patent irrespective of capacity of applicant—Meaning of 'attorney'—Meaning of 'absentee'—Meaning of 'applicant'—Patent Act 1857 (Jamaica), ss 3, 29, 31—Patent Law Amendment Act 1852, s 25. **Pfizer Ltd v Medimpex Jamaica Ltd** [2014] **4** 431, PC.

JERSEY
  Désastre proceedings—
    Order in aid. *See* **Bankruptcy** (Order in aid of British court—Scope of orders in aid—British court having jurisdiction in matters of bankruptcy—Désastre proceedings in Royal Court of Jersey against insolvent debtor).

JET SKI
  Shipping offence—
    Act of master of ship causing death or serious injury—
      Rider of jet ski causing serious injury. *See* **Shipping** (Offence—Act of master of ship causing death or serious injury—Rider of jet ski causing serious injury).

JEWELLER
  Ear-piercing operation—
    Duty to exercise reasonable skill and care. *See* **Negligence** (Professional person—Duty to exercise reasonable skill and care—Minor surgical operation—Jeweller undertaking minor surgical operation often done by jewellers).

JEWELLERY
  Will—
    Gift—
      Specific bequests. *See* **Will** (Gift—Specific bequests—Jewellery).

JEWISH LAW
  Arbitration—
    Appeal. *See* **Arbitration** (Award—Leave to appeal against award—Question of law—Serious irregularity—Arbitral proceedings governed by Jewish law before Beth Din).

JEWISH SHOP
  Sunday closing—
    Exemption. *See* **Shop** (Sunday closing—Exemption—Jewish shop).

JOB EVALUATION STUDY
  Equality of treatment between men and women. *See* **Employment** (Equality of treatment of men and women).

JOBSEEKER'S ALLOWANCE
  European Community—
    Freedom of movement of workers. *See* **European Union** (Workers—Freedom of movement—Social security).
  Generally. *See* **Social security** (Jobseeker's allowance).
  Income support and. *See* **Social security** (Income support—Jobseeker's allowance).

JOCKEY CLUB
  Judicial review of club's decision—
    Availability of remedy. *See* **Judicial review** (Availability of remedy—Jockey Club).
  Trainer's licence—
    Withdrawal—
      Natural justice. *See* **Natural justice** (Domestic tribunal—Jockey club—Withdrawal of trainer's licence).

JOINDER
  Accused—
    Committal proceedings before justices. *See* **Criminal law** (Committal—Preliminary hearing before justices—Joinder of two or more accused).
    Indictment. *See* **Indictment** (Joinder of two or more accused).
  Causes of action. *See* **Practice** (Joinder of causes of action).

JOINDER (cont)—
   Charges—
      Indictment. *See* **Indictment** (Joinder of charges).
   Originating summons—
      Joinder of Crown as party. *See* **Originating summons** (Parties—Joinder of Crown as party).
   Parties—
      Bankruptcy—
         Proceedings for declaration of fraudulent preference—Joinder of surety. *See* **Bankruptcy** (Fraudulent preference—Joinder of parties—Bankrupt's account guaranteed by surety).
      Generally. *See* **Practice** (Parties—Joinder of parties).
      Originating summons. *See* **Originating summons** (Parties).
      Wardship and custody proceedings—
         Joinder of child as party. *See* **Minor** (Practice—Wardship and custody proceedings—Joinder of child as party).

JOINT ACCOUNT
   Bank. *See* **Bank** (Account—Joint account).
   Husband and wife. *See* **Husband and wife** (Property—Joint account).

JOINT CUSTODY ORDER
   Divorce. *See* **Divorce** (Custody—Joint custody order).

JOINT ENTERPRISE
   Criminal liability—
      Concerted action. *See* **Criminal law** (Concerted action).
      Conspiracy. *See* **Criminal law** (Conspiracy).
      Murder. *See* **Criminal law** (Murder—Concerted action).

JOINT TENANCY
   Bankruptcy—
      Property available for distribution. *See* **Bankruptcy** (Property available for distribution—Joint tenancy).
   Bankruptcy of one of joint tenants—
      Death of bankrupt's joint tenant after commission of act of bankruptcy but before adjudication—Whether adjudication restrospectively severing joint tenancy. *See* **Bankruptcy** (Property available for distribution—Joint tenancy—Severance—Death of joint tenant before adjudication).
      Husband and wife—
         Matrimonial home. *See* **Bankruptcy** (Property available for distribution—Matrimonial home—Husband and wife joint tenants).
      Joint tenancy of property charged to secure loan. *See* **Bankruptcy** (Proof—Secured creditor—Joint tenancy of property charged to secure loan).
   Business premises—
      New tenancy—
         Application. *See* **Landlord and tenant** (Business premises—Application for new tenancy—Joint tenants).
   Charging order. *See* **Execution** (Charging order—Land—Interest in land—Joint tenancy).
   Constructive trust. *See* **Trust and trustee** (Constructive trust—Joint tenants).
   Death of one of two joint tenants—
      Rent—
         Liability of executors. *See* **Landlord and tenant** (Rent—Joint tenancy—Death of one of two joint tenants—Tenancy of committee rooms—Liability of executors).
   Determination—
      Generally. *See* **Landlord and tenant** (Tenancy—Joint tenancy—Determination).
   Equitable charge—
      Creation of charge. *See* **Equity** (Charge—Creation of equitable charge—Joint tenancy).
   Land held on trust for sale—
      Joint tenants legally and beneficially entitled—
         Whether tenants' interest an interest in land. *See* **Execution** (Charging order—Land—Interest in land—Property held legally and beneficially by joint tenants).
   Matrimonial home—
      Deserted wife in occupation—
         Bankruptcy of husband. *See* **Bankruptcy** (Property available for distribution—Matrimonial home—Deserted wife).
      Injunction—
         Exclusion of party from matrimonial home—Respondent having proprietary interest in home. *See* **Injunction** (Exclusion of party from matrimonial home—County court—Respondent having proprietary interest in home—Joint tenancy).
      Property available for financial provision. *See* **Family provision** (Property available for financial provision—Property held on joint tenancy).
   Means of effecting severance—
      Agreement or conduct—
         Agreement—Unenforceable agreement—Agreement indicating parties no longer intended tenancy to operate as joint tenancy—Agreement subsequently repudiated by one party—Whether agreement effecting severance of joint tenancy. **Burgess v Rawnsley** [1975] **3** 142, CA.
        Conduct falling short of agreement—Conduct indicating common intention that joint tenancy should be regarded as severed—Whether conduct effecting severance. **Burgess v Rawnsley** [1975] **3** 142, CA.
        Inference of agreement—Conduct giving rise to inference of agreement to sever—Letter and subsequent transfer of share. **Hawksley v May** [1955] **3** 353, QBD.
        Inference of agreement—Conduct giving rise to inference of agreement to sever—Two joint tenants negotiating agreement to sever joint tenancy—Death of one joint tenant before agreement concluded—Whether conduct of joint tenants supporting an inference of agreement to sever. **Nielson-Jones v Fedden** [1974] **3** 38, Ch D.

JOINT TENANCY (cont)—
Means of effecting severance (cont)—
  Agreement or conduct (cont)—
    Intention of parties—Partnership accounts—Parties living together as man and wife—Parties purchasing farm in joint names as beneficial joint tenants—One party providing most of purchase money—Farm run as guest house on partnership basis—Farm included in partnership accounts as partnership asset—One party dying intestate—Whether intention of parties that property be held on joint tenancy—Whether joint tenancy severed before death of deceased. **Barton v Morris** [1985] **2** 1032, Ch D.
  Application to determine interests in matrimonial property—
    Service of summons and supporting affidavit—Land—Dwelling-house conveyed to husband and wife in fee simple as joint tenants at law and in equity—Wife subsequently obtained decree nisi and applied under s 17 of the Married Women's Property Act 1882, for sale and distribution of the proceeds of sale—Husband remained in possession until shortly before his death—Whether beneficial joint tenancy severed in lifetime of husband—Law of Property Act 1925, s 36(2). **Draper's Conveyance, Re** [1967] **3** 853, Ch D.
  Notice in writing of desire to sever joint tenancy in equity—
    Prayer in divorce petition—Prayer for transfer of or settlement or variation of settlement of former matrimonial home—Whether effective to constitute severance of joint tenancy in equity—Law of Property Act 1925, s 36(2). **Harris v Goddard** [1983] **3** 242, CA.
  Notice of severance—
    Notice in writing of desire to sever joint tenancy in equity—Daughter of joint tenant applying to Court of Protection for financial order—Other joint tenant applying to Court of Protection for authority to sell jointly owned property—Daughter subsequently appointed as deputy—First joint tenant dying—Whether second application written notice capable of effecting severance of joint tenancy—Whether notice validly served—Law of Property Act 1925, s 36(2). **Quigley v Masterson** [2012] **1** 1224, Ch D.
  Unilateral declaration—
    Unequivocal declaration by one of two joint tenants that he wishes to sever joint tenancy—Whether unilateral declaration capable of severing joint tenancy. **Nielson-Jones v Fedden** [1974] **3** 38, Ch D.
Notice of severance—
  Form of notice—
    Irrevocable notice—Originating summons supported by affidavit—Power of plaintiff to withdraw proceedings—Whether originating summons capable of constituting effective notice of severance—Law of Property Act 1925, s 36(2). **Nielson-Jones v Fedden** [1974] **3** 38, Ch D.
  Notice in writing of desire to sever joint tenancy in equity. *See* Means of effecting severance—Notice of severance—Notice in writing of desire to sever joint tenancy in equity, *above.*
  Personalty—
    Written notice of desire to sever joint tenancy communicated by one joint tenant to the other—Whether written notice capable of effecting severance of joint tenancy of personalty. **Burgess v Rawnsley** [1975] **3** 142, CA.
  Service—
    Joint tenant sending notice of severance to address of joint tenant—Notice delivered by ordinary first class post at address of joint tenant—Sender no longer desiring to sever tenancy and destroying notice—Whether joint tenancy severed—Whether notice validly served—Law of Property Act 1925, ss 36(2), 196(3). **Kinch v Bullard** [1998] **4** 650, Ch D.
    Registered post—Recorded delivery—Law of Property Act 1925, ss 36(2), 196(4). **Berkeley Road (88), London NW9, Re** [1971] **1** 254, Ch D.
Settlement—
  Disagreement as to exercise of power of sale. *See* **Settlement** (Powers of tenant for life—Joint tenants).
Severance—
  Land held as joint tenancy at law—
    Purchase price paid in unequal shares—Lease of business premises—Two companies sharing leased accommodation for separate commercial interests—Parties dividing floor space unequally and paying all costs pro rata—Whether parties holding beneficial interest as joint tenants or as tenants in common in unequal shares. **Malayan Credit Ltd v Jack Chia-MPH Ltd** [1986] **1** 711, PC.
  Land held on trust for sale—
    Severance of joint tenancy—Beneficial interests—Conveyance to plaintiff and defendant as joint tenants—Declaration of trust that plaintiff and defendant to hold on trust for themselves as joint tenants—Whether terms of declaration conclusive of parties' beneficial interests. **Goodman v Gallant** [1986] **1** 311, CA.
    Severance of joint tenancy—Creation of charge by joint tenant on property held jointly—Charge effectual to create charge of 'interest ... in ... property'—Whether beneficial interest of joint tenant under statutory trust for sale an 'interest ... in ... property'—Whether joint tenancy severed—Law of Property Act 1925, s 63. **Cedar Holdings Ltd v Green** [1979] **3** 117, CA.
  Means of effecting severance. *See* Means of effecting severance, *above.*
  Notice of. *See* Notice of severance, *above.*
Statutory tenancy—
  Termination of protected tenancy—
    One only of two joint tenants in occupation on termination of protected tenancy. *See* **Rent restriction** (Statutory tenancy—Protected tenant in occupation on termination of protected tenancy—Joint tenancy).
Statutory trust for sale—
  Application to court for order for sale—
    Contract not to sell without unanimous consent—Overriding trust—Law of Property Act 1925, ss 30, 35, 36. **Buchanan-Wollaston's Conveyance, Re** [1939] **2** 302, CA.
  Continuance of trust—
    Whole property accruing to survivor. *See* **Trust and trustee** (Joint tenants—Statutory trust for sale—Whole property accruing to survivor).

JOINT TENANCY (cont)—
  Surrender—
    Surrender by one tenant of rights held jointly—
      Absence of express authority from other tenant—Whether joint tenancy terminated. **Leek & Moorlands Building Society v Clark** [1952] **2** 492, CA.
  Tenants in common. *See* **Tenants in common**.

JOINT TORTFEASORS
  Acts within course of employment—
    Vicarious liability. *See* **Vicarious liability** (Employer and employee—Act within course of employment—Joint tortfeasors).
  Contribution between joint tortfeasors. *See* **Tort** (Contribution between joint tortfeasors).
  Costs. *See* **Costs** (Joint tortfeasors).
  Generally. *See* **Tort** (Joint tortfeasors).
  Limitation of action—
    When time begins to run. *See* **Limitation of action** (When time begins to run—Joint tortfeasors).
  Negligence—
    Generally. *See* **Negligence** (Joint tortfeasors).
  Practice—
    Generally. *See* **Practice** (Joint tortfeasors).

JOINT VENTURE AGREEMENT
  Construction. *See* **Contract** (Construction—Joint venture agreement).

JOINT WILL
  Probate. *See* **Probate** (Grant—Joint will).

JOINTURE RENTCHARGE
  Settlement. *See* **Settlement** (Jointure rentcharge).

JOURNAL
  Passing off—
    Alteration of copies without authority. *See* **Passing off** (Journal).

JOURNALIST
  Contempt of court—
    Publications concerning legal proceedings. *See* **Contempt of court** (Publications concerning legal proceedings).
    Refusal to disclose source of information. *See* **Contempt of court** (Refusal to disclose source of information—Journalist).
  Income tax—
    Newspaper allowance. *See* **Income tax** (Emoluments from office or employment—Expenses wholly, exclusively and necessarily incurred—Newspaper allowance).
  Prison visits. *See* **Prison** (Visits—Visits by journalists).
  Privilege—
    Evidence. *See* **Evidence** (Privilege—Press—Newspaper reporter).
    Libel and slander. *See* **Libel and slander** (Privilege—Qualified privilege—Common law privilege—Responsible journalism).
  Refusal to disclose source of information—
    Contempt of court. *See* **Contempt of court** (Refusal to disclose source of information—Journalist).
  Responsible journalism—
    Libel and slander. *See* **Libel and slander** (Privilege—Qualified privilege—Common law privilege—Responsible journalism).

JUDGE
  Adjournment to judge—
    Chambers proceedings. *See* **Practice** (Chambers proceedings—Adjournment to judge).
  Appeal—
    Presence of judge in court—
      Presence at time of judgment—Dismissal of appeal in Fiji on reading of reserved written judgments of judges who had come to Fiji to hear appeal but were not present when judgments were read—Validity. **Bharat, Son of Dorsamy v R** [1959] **3** 292, PC.
  Bias—
    Criminal trial. *See* **Criminal law** (Trial—Judge—Bias).
    Natural justice. *See* **Natural justice** (Judge—Bias).
  Characteristics of office. *See* **Court** (Judicial office—Characteristics).
  Circuit judge—
    Circuit judges sitting as judges of High Court—
      Hearing of 'short' High Court matrimonial causes. *See* **Practice** (Hearing—Matrimonial causes—Royal Courts of Justice—Circuit judges sitting as judges of High Court).
    Deputy circuit judge—
      Mode of address—Style of reference in court list. **Practice Direction** [1982] **1** 320, CA.
      Recorder—Mode of address—Style of reference in court list. **Practice Note** [1978] **1** 64, CA.
    Immunity from suit. *See* Immunity from suit—Circuit judge, *below*.
  Colonial judge—
    Appointment—
      Trinidad and Tobago. *See* **Trinidad and Tobago** (Colonial courts—Judges—Appointment as acting judge of Supreme Court).
    Tenure of office—
      Tenure during pleasure—Appointment by letter from Secretary of State—Letter stating retiring age 62—Appointment terminated when judge 61—Whether contract to employ judge until 62. **Terrell v Secretary of State for the Colonies** [1953] **2** 490, QBD.

JUDGE (cont)—
County court—
  Notes of evidence—
    Appeal. *See* **County court** (Appeal—Evidence—Judge's notes of evidence).
    Generally. *See* **County court** (Judge—Judge's notes of evidence).
Criminal trial—
  Conduct of judge—
    Appeal. *See* **Criminal law** (Appeal—Conduct of trial judge).
    Generally. *See* **Criminal law** (Trial—Judge).
Crown Court—
  Circuit judge—
    Immunity from suit. *See* Immunity from suit—Circuit judge—Crown Court, *below*.
  Justices. *See* **Crown Court** (Justices as judges).
Deployment of judges—
  Judicial review of Lord Chancellor's decision. *See* **Judicial review** (Lord Chancellor—Deployment of judges).
Direction to jury—
  Criminal trial. *See* **Criminal law** (Trial—Direction to jury).
  Generally. *See* **Jury** (Direction to jury).
Discretion—
  Reasons for exercise of discretion. *See* Reasons—Exercise of discretion, *below*.
  Reference to European Court. *See* **European Union** (Reference to European Court—Request for preliminary ruling concerning interpretation of treaty—Power of national court to refer question it considers necessary to enable it to give judgment—Discretionary power of trial judge).
  Review of exercise of discretion on appeal. *See* **Court of Appeal** (Discretion of judge—Review of exercise of discretion).
District judge—
  Fast track procedure—
    Jurisdiction. *See* **Practice** (Fast track—District judge—Jurisdiction).
Function of judge—
  Civil action—
    Intervention on examination of witnesses. **Jones v National Coal Board** [1957] **2** 155, CA.
    Negligence—Latent defect—System of maintenance—Decision on evidence before judge—Whether he should pursue enquiries on his own. **Henderson v Henry E Jenkins & Sons** [1969] **1** 401, CA.
High Court—
  Hearings of longer applications in county court matrimonial causes. *See* **Practice** (Hearing—Matrimonial causes—Royal Courts of Justice).
  Jurisdiction to set aside order of another High Court judge on ground fresh evidence obtained. *See* **Evidence** (Fresh evidence—Application to High Court for order for new trial—Original trial by High Court judge).
Immunity from suit—
  Circuit judge—
    Crown Court—Appeal from magistrate—Appeal against recommendation for deportation—Order by magistrate that appellant be not detained pending decision on recommendation—Appeal dismissed—Magistrate's order remaining in force—Crown Court having jurisdiction to amend so as to authorise detention—Jurisdiction not exercised—Judge mistakenly believing appellant liable to detention—Judge ordering detention—Whether Crown Court exercising appellate jurisdiction superior or inferior court—Whether judge immune from action for assault and false imprisonment. **Sirros v Moore** [1974] **3** 776, CA.
  Scope of immunity—
    Acts done in judicial capacity—Acts outside jurisdiction—Act done in honest but mistaken belief that within jurisdiction—Distinction between immunity of judges of superior and inferior courts—Liability of judge of inferior court for acts outside jurisdiction—Whether immune provided he is acting bona fide. **Sirros v Moore** [1974] **3** 776, CA.
Inspection by. *See* **Practice** (Inspection by judge).
Judge in fact—
  De facto doctrine—
    Meaning of doctrine—Whether de facto judge 'a tribunal established by law'—Human Rights Act 1998, Sch 1, Pt I, art 6(1). **Coppard v Customs and Excise Comrs** [2003] **3** 351, CA.
    Recorder eligible for authorisation to act as High Court judge but not so authorised—Recorder adjudicating on High Court action believing action to be in County Court—Whether order to be set aside—Whether recorder acting as de facto High Court judge. **Baldock v Webster** [2005] **3** 655, CA.
Judicial visits—
  Medical treatment. *See* **Medical treatment** (Withdrawal of treatment—Judicial visits).
Jurisdiction—
  Criminal contempt—
    Summary committal. *See* **Contempt of court** (Criminal contempt—Jurisdiction—Summary committal—Power of judge on own motion to commit summarily for contempt).
Jury—
  Criminal proceedings—
    Communication between judge and jury after retirement of jury. *See* **Criminal law** (Trial—Retirement of jury—Communication with judge).
    Direction to jury—Generally. *See* **Criminal law** (Trial—Direction to jury).
Mode of address—
  Recorder—
    Recorder of Cardiff. **Practice Direction** [1999] **2** 352, Sup Ct.
  Style of reference in court list. **Practice Direction** [1982] **1** 320, CA.
Natural justice. *See* **Natural justice** (Judge).
Notes—
  Appeal. *See* **Court of Appeal** (Judge's note).
  County court. *See* **County court** (Appeal—Evidence—Judge's notes of evidence).

JUDGE (cont)—
Notorious facts—
Judicial notice. *See* **Judicial notice** (Notorious facts).
Reasons—
Appeal on ground reasons inadequate—
Appeal court allowing appeal and ordering remittal to judge to state reasons for decision—Whether order valid. **BMC Software Ltd v Shaikh** [2019] **2** 748n, CA.
Exercise of discretion—
Duty of judge to give reasons for exercise of discretion. **Eagil Trust Co Ltd v Piggott-Brown** [1985] **3** 119, CA.
Failure by judge to give reasons for conclusion essential to judgment—
Appeals on ground of inadequacy of reasons—Guidance. **English v Emery Reimbold & Strick Ltd** [2002] **3** 385, CA.
Plaintiffs bringing action against defendant for negligent valuation—Case depending on expert evidence—Judge preferring defendant's expert evidence but not giving reasons—Whether failure to give reasons for conclusion essential to decision constituting ground of appeal. **Flannery v Halifax Estate Agencies Ltd** [2000] **1** 373, CA.
Removal from office—
Trinidad and Tobago. *See* **Trinidad and Tobago** (Judge—Removal from office).
Retirement—
Evidence taken before his retirement. *See* **Admiralty** (Practice—Evidence—New trial—Retirement of trial judge during original trial).
Single judge—
Refusal of leave to appeal—
Criminal proceedings. *See* **Criminal law** (Appeal—Leave to appeal—Refusal—Single judge).
Visitor of Inns of Court—
Disciplinary jurisdiction. *See* **Counsel** (Disciplinary jurisdiction—Judges as visitors of Inns of Court).
Witness—
Compellability of judge as witness. *See* **Evidence** (Witness—Judge).

JUDGE ADVOCATE
See **Court-martial** (Judge-advocate).

JUDGES' RULES
Court-martial—
Application of Judges' Rules to. *See* **Court-martial** (Evidence—Admissibility—Judges' Rules).
Generally. *See* **Criminal evidence** (Admissions and confessions—Answers and statements to police).

JUDGMENT
Action on—
Limitation period. *See* **Limitation of action** (Action—Action on judgment).
Admission of facts. *See* Judgment on admission of facts, *below.*
Alteration—
Court of Appeal—
Criminal appeal. *See* **Criminal law** (Court of Appeal—Order of court—Alteration).
Variation of decision after judgment delivered—
Application by party for court to reconsider order pronounced but not yet sealed—Proper considerations for court. **AIC Ltd v Federal Airports Authority of Nigeria** [2021] **4** 163, CA.
Application by party for court to reconsider order pronounced but not yet sealed—Proper considerations for court—CPR 1.1. **AIC Ltd v Federal Airports Authority of Nigeria** [2022] **4** 777, SC.
Judge's power to recall and change judgment. **Paulin v Paulin** [2009] **3** 88n, CA.
Judge's power to recall and change judgment—Judge in care proceedings exonerating mother and finding father responsible for injuries to child—Judgment not perfected—Judge later distributing revised judgment holding that perpetrator could not be identified—Whether judge having jurisdiction to change decision—Whether exercise of power dependent on existence of exceptional circumstances. **L and B (children) (care proceedings: power to revise judgment), Re** [2013] **2** 294, SC.
Judge's power to recall and change judgment—Judgment dismissing application—Order not drawn up or perfected—Judge changing mind and deciding to grant application—Whether judge entitled to recall judgment and change decision. **Pittalis v Sherefettin** [1986] **2** 227, CA.
Judge's power to recall and change judgment—Whether exercise of power dependent on existence of exceptional circumstances. **Cie Noga D'Importation et D'Exportation SA v Abacha** [2001] **3** 513, QBD.
Variation of decision prior to issue—
Application to reopen judgment after drafted and circulated to legal representatives but prior to issue—Proper considerations for court. **Barclay-Watt v Alpha Panareti Public Ltd** [2021] **3** 804n, Comm Ct.
Amendment—
Correction of clerical mistakes or accidental slips or omissions. *See* Order—Correction—Accidental slip or omission, *below.*
Restrictive Practices Court. *See* **Restrictive trade practices** (Appeal to Court of Appeal by way of case stated—Application after judgment for judgment to be amplified or amended).
Tribunal decision. *See* **Tribunal** (Decision—Amendment of decision).
Anonymisation—
Handed down judgments. *See* Handed down judgments—Judgments in advance of hearing, *below.*
Appeal—
Additional findings of lower court pending appeal. *See* **Court of Appeal** (Jurisdiction—Pending appeal—Matters requiring additional findings of fact if ground of appeal substantiated).
Prior reading of judgment or decision and cases cited therein. *See* **Court of Appeal** (Practice—Prior reading of judgment or decision and cases cited therein).
Arbitrator's award. *See* **Arbitration** (Award).

JUDGMENT (cont)—
  Assignment—
    Recovery of possession—
      Judgment for recovery of land—Whether judgment passes with land on conveyance thereof.
      Chung Kwok Hotel Co Ltd v Field [1960] **3** 143, CA.
  Bankruptcy notice—
    Notice requiring debtor to pay in accordance with judgment or order—
      Defect in notice. *See* **Bankruptcy** (Bankruptcy notice—Validity—Prescribed form—Formal defect or
      irregularity—Jurisdiction of court to cure defect—Judgment or order).
  Chambers proceedings—
    Chancery Division—
      Status of judgment. *See* **Practice** (Chancery Division—Chambers proceedings—Judgment).
  Charging order. *See* **Execution** (Charging order).
  Compromise of action—
    Approval of court. *See* **Practice** (Compromise of action—Approval of court).
  Consent—
    Amendment of title of action after judgment. *See* **Practice** (Parties—Substitution—Substitution after
    judgment).
    Order. *See* Order—Consent order, *below*.
    Res judicata—
      Whether judgment by consent giving rise to plea of res judicata in subsequent proceedings. *See*
      Estoppel (Res judicata—Consent judgment).
  Consumer credit—
    Default—
      Recovery of amount outstanding. *See* **Consumer credit** (Default—Recovery of amount
      outstanding—Judgment).
  County court—
    Appeal—
      Provision of note of county court judgment. *See* **County court** (Appeal—Note of county court
      judgment—Provision of note).
    Generally. *See* **County court** (Judgment or order).
  Court of Appeal—
    Civil proceedings. *See* **Court of Appeal** (Judgment).
  Damages—
    Contract and tort—
      Power of court to enter judgment for damages for breach of contract and tort. *See* **Damages**
      (Contract and tort—Power of court to enter judgment for damages for breach of contract and
      tort).
  Debtor—
    Costs—
      Unsuccessful garnishee proceedings. *See* **Costs** (Garnishee proceedings—Discretion of
      court—Unsuccessful garnishee proceedings—Power of court to award costs against judgment
      debtor).
  Declaratory judgment—
    Agent's right to commission. *See* **Agent** (Commission—Right to commission—Declaratory judgment).
    Generally. *See* **Declaration**.
  Default judgment—
    Effect of default judgment—
      Proceedings for personal injury—Claim brought against two defendants—Judgment in default
      entered against one defendant—Whether entry of default judgment bar to subsequent finding of
      liability against other defendant. **Balgobin v South West Regional Health Authority** [2012] **4** 655,
      PC.
    Enforcement of foreign default judgment. *See* **Conflict of laws** (Foreign judgment—Enforcement—
    Default judgment).
    Setting aside judgment—
      Claimant obtaining default judgment against defendant—Defendant's successor applying to have
      judgment set aside after seven years—Judge concluding that there was defence on merits and
      setting aside judgment—Claimant appealing and contending that defendant had taken tactical
      decision not to challenge judgment—Whether judgment should have been set aside. **Rayner (JH)**
      (Mincing Lane) Ltd v Cafénorte SA Importadora [1999] **1 Comm** 120, QBD; [1999] **2 Comm** 577,
      CA.
      Default of defence. *See* Default of defence—Setting aside judgment, *below*.
      Defendant foreign state—Claimant granted permission to serve proceedings out of the jurisdiction
      on foreign state—Default judgment subsequently entered—Foreign state applying after
      considerable delay to set aside service out of jurisdiction and default judgment—Whether order
      permitting service out of jurisdiction to be set aside—Whether default judgment to be set aside.
      Mid-East Sales Ltd v United Engineering and Trading Company (Pvt) Ltd [2014] **2 Comm** 623,
      QBD.
  Default judgment. *See* Default of defence, *below*.
  Default of acknowledgment of service—
    Power of court to proceed in absence of party—
      Anonymous defendants—Claim for damages for libel—Time for filing acknowledgement of service
      and defence by defendants expiring—Whether defendants having proper notice of
      proceedings—Whether appropriate to proceed on basis of claimant's unchallenged pleaded
      case—Whether defendants' right to freedom of expression engaged—Human Rights Act 1998,
      s 12—CPR 12.3(1), 12.4(2), 12.11(1), 23.11. **Brett Wilson LLP v Person(s) Unknown, responsible for**
      the operation and publication of the website www.solicitorsfromhelluk.com [2016] **1** 1006, QBD.
  Default of appearance—
    Application for leave to enter judgment—
      Dismissal—Application dismissed as to part of sum claimed on ground that it might be a
      penalty—Whether RSC Ord 13, r 19, ultra vires—Alternative procedures for obtaining
      judgment—RSC Ord 13, rr 12, 19, Ord 27, r 11. **Lombank Ltd v Cook** [1962] **3** 491, QBD.

JUDGMENT (cont)—
  Default of appearance (cont)—
    Application for leave to enter judgment (cont)—
      Jurisdiction—Writ containing or including claim other than for liquidated demand etc—Writ containing claim for liquidated demand and for injunction to restrain defendant from removing assets out of jurisdiction—Plaintiff granted injunction—Whether claim for injunction in writ precluding plaintiff from entering judgment in claim for liquidated demand in default of appearance by defendant—RSC Ord 13, r 6. **Stewart Chartering Ltd v C & O Managements SA** [1980] **1** 718, QBD.
    Costs—
      New practice and procedure. *See* **Practice** (Queen's Bench Division and Chancery Division—New practice and procedure).
    Discovery of mistake—
      Motion to set aside order—Inherent jurisdiction of court not to be invoked where alternative remedy available. **Perry v St Helens Land and Construction Co Ltd** [1939] **3** 113, CA.
    Discrepancy between writ and statement of claim—
      Discretion of court—Amendment of writ—RSC Ord 28, r 1. **Mann v Phillips** [1948] **1** 138, Ch D.
    Interest—
      Jurisdiction to include interest in default judgment. *See* **Interest** (Debt—Jurisdiction to include interest in default judgment).
    Interlocutory judgment—
      Liquidated demand—Writ claiming price of goods and damages for breach of contract—Value of goods and damages claimed in statement of claim—RSC Ord 13, r 7. **Abbey Panel and Sheet Metal Co Ltd v Barson Products** [1947] **2** 809, CA.
    Liquidated demand—
      Claim for specific sum fraudulently converted—RSC Ord 13, r 3. **Baker (GL) Ltd v Barclays Bank Ltd** [1956] **3** 519, CA.
    Possession—
      Rent controlled premises. *See* **Rent restriction** (Possession—Procedure—Court—Judgment for possession signed in High Court by landlord in default of appearance).
    Postal delay. *See* **Practice** (Post—Postal delay—Time limited for entry of appearance—Entry of judgment in default of appearance).
    Setting aside judgment—
      Discretion of judge—Power of Court of Appeal to interfere with discretion exercised by judge in chambers—RSC Ord 13, r 10—RSC Ord 27, r 15. **Evans v Bartlam** [1937] **2** 646, HL.
      Excessive amount to plaintiffs' knowledge—Acceptance by plaintiffs, entitled to enter judgment in default of appearance, of cheque for part of sum claimed—Judgment entered for full amount after cheque taken—Cheque subsequently met—Defendants' right to have judgment set aside and to have order as to costs. **Bolt & Nut Co (Tipton) Ltd v Rowlands, Nicholls & Co Ltd** [1964] **1** 137, CA.
      Summary judgment—Specific performance—Purchaser's action—Appearance not entered by vendor—Judgment obtained under RSC Ord 14A—Judgment not carried into effect—Action commenced to have judgment set aside on ground of vendor's contractual incapacity and of undue influence—Application by purchaser to have statement of claim struck out—Whether second action appropriate procedure—Whether judgment under RSC Ord 14A was a judgment by default within RSC Ord 27, r 15. **Dsane v Hagan** [1961] **3** 380, Ch D.
    Writ not received. *See* **Writ** (Service on company—Service by post—Writ not received by company—Judgment in default of appearance).
  Default of defence—
    Defence struck out for failure to comply with order for discovery—
      Judgment in default of defence entered against defendant as personal representative—Amendment of defence at trial or hearing. *See* **Pleading** (Amendment—Amendment at trial or hearing—Defence—Defence struck out for failure to comply with order for discovery—Judgment in default of defence entered against defendant as personal representative).
    Duty of court—
      Court to give such judgment as plaintiff entitled to—Requirement directory not mandatory—Allegations of fraud—Open to defendant to show he has good defence—Defendant only to be shut out from defending charge of fraud if admissions or evidence showing no defence—RSC Ord 19, r 7(1). **Wallersteiner v Moir** [1974] **3** 217, CA.
      Court to give such judgment as plaintiff entitled to—Statement of claim alleging infringement of copyright and seeking injunctive relief—Whether court retaining any discretion—Whether court entitled to set time limit to injunction—Whether court entitled to attach conditions to injunction—RSC Ord 19, r 7(1). **Phonographic Performance Ltd v Maitra (Performing Right Society Ltd intervening)** [1998] **2** 638, CA.
    Elapse of one year or more since last proceeding in action—
      Notice of intention to proceed—Notice to proceed served shortly before expiry of one year from last proceeding—Judgment in default of defence entered after expiry of one year from last proceeding—Whether notice to proceed can be served only after expiry of one year from last proceeding—Whether judgment would be set aside as irregular—RSC Ord 3, r 6. **Suedeclub Co Ltd v Occasions Textiles Ltd** [1981] **3** 671, Ch D.
    Form of order—
      Declaratory relief—Declaration only appropriate where justice to plaintiff requires it—In general declaratory relief to be granted only after trial. **Wallersteiner v Moir** [1974] **3** 217, CA.
    Indorsement of court copy of judgment—
      RSC Ord 19. **Practice Direction** [1979] **2** 1062, QBD.
    Liquidated demand—
      Plaintiff issuing writ against defendant in respect of claim for debts owed and obtaining judgment in default of defence—Defendant applying to set aside judgment on grounds that it contained irregularities, alternatively, that there was a set-off defence to the claim—Whether judgment should be set aside ex debito justitiae—Whether sufficient merits in defendant's defence justifying setting aside judgment—RSC Ord 13, r 9. **Bank of Credit and Commerce International (Overseas) Ltd (in liq) v Habib Bank Ltd** [1998] **4** 753, Ch D.

JUDGMENT (cont)—
   Default of defence (cont)—
      Regularity—
         Defence served after expiry of time limit and without leave to serve out of time—Judgment in
         default entered after late service of defence—Whether judgment regular—RSC Ord 19, r 2. **Anson**
         (Lady Elizabeth) (t/a Party Planners) v Trump [1998] **3** 331, CA.
      Setting aside judgment—
         Conditions to be satisfied for obtaining default judgment—Whether court having jurisdiction to
         enter judgment in default where defence filed prior to judgment but without extension
         application having been determined—Whether judgment to be set aside as of right—CPR 3.9,
         3.10, 12.3, 13.2. **Clements Smith v Berrymans Lace Mawer Service Co** [2020] **3** 71, QBD.
         Judgment in default of defence obtained against defendant for failure to serve defence within time
         stipulated—Application by defendant to set aside judgment—Test to be applied—Whether
         necessary for court to be satisfied there was a real likelihood that defendant would
         succeed—Whether judgment should be set aside. **Day v RAC Motoring Services Ltd**
         [1999] **1** 1007, CA.
      Specific performance. *See* **Specific performance** (Judgment in default of defence).
   Delay—
      Counterclaims dismissed in judgment given almost 22 months after conclusion of trial—
         Whether delay rendering judgment unsafe. **Bank St Petersburg PJSC v Arkhangelsky** [2021] **1** 119,
         CA; **Bank St Petersburg PJSC v Arkhangelsky** [2020] **2 Comm** 756, CA.
   Detinue. *See* **Detinue** (Judgment).
   Divorce—
      Reading judgment in previous suit between same parties—
         Discretion case. **Sharma v Sharma and Davis** [1959] **3** 321, CA.
   Draft judgment—
      Anonymisation. *See* Handed down judgments—Judgments in advance of hearing, *below.*
      Purpose of. *See* Handed down judgments—Judgments in advance of hearing, *below.*
   Drawing-up. *See* **Practice** (Order—Drawing-up).
   Effect—
      Order made but irregular in form—
         Want of jurisdiction to make order in that form. *See* Order—Form of order—Irregularity, *below.*
      Retrospective or prospective effect. *See* **Motor insurance** (Extent of cover—Indemnity—'Owner driver
      only' insurance policy).
   Employment tribunal—
      Reasons for decision. *See* **Employment tribunal** (Procedure—Decision—Reasons for decision).
   Enforcement—
      Costs—
         Costs of previous attempts to enforce judgment—Procedure—Ex parte application—Affidavit in
         support—Exhibits—Indorsement of recoverable costs on affidavit by master or district
         judge—Directions as to taxation where amount indorsed is less than amount claimed—
         Enforcement of any further costs to which judgment creditor entitled—Interest—Courts and Legal
         Services Act 1990, s 15(3)(4). **Practice Direction** [1991] **4** 762, QBD.
      County court judgment. *See* **County court** (Judgment or order—Enforcement).
      European Community. *See* **European Union** (Enforcement of judgment).
      Foreign judgment. *See* **Constitutional law** (Foreign sovereign state—Immunity from suit—Enforcement
      proceedings—Enforcement of foreign judgment against foreign state).
      Foreign state, against. *See* **Constitutional law** (Foreign sovereign state—Immunity from
      suit—Enforcement proceedings).
      Leave. *See* **Emergency legislation** (Leave to enforce judgment or order).
      Stay of execution. *See* **Execution** (Stay).
   Estoppel by. *See* **Estoppel** (Res judicata).
   European Union—
      Enforcement of judgment. *See* **European Union** (Enforcement of judgment).
   European Court of Justice—
      General Court. *See* **European Union** (European Court of Justice—General Court—Judgment).
   Execution—
      Anton Piller order in aid of execution. *See* **Practice** (Pre-trial or post-judgment relief—Search order—Ex
      parte application for search order—Application after judgment).
      Generally. *See* **Execution**.
   Final or interlocutory order—
      Legal aid. *See* **Legal aid** (Unassisted person's costs out of legal aid fund—Order—Order by judge in
      chambers—Final or interlocutory order).
      Test to be applied—
         Leave granted to enter final judgment—Judge not certifying that he required further argument—No
         leave obtained from Federal Court of Malaysia or judge of High Court to bring appeal—Whether
         appeal competently brought—Courts of Judicature Act 1964 (Malaysia), s 68(2). **Haron bin Mohd**
         Zaid v Central Securities (Holdings) Bhd [1982] **2** 481, PC.
   Foreign currency—
      Award of arbitrator. *See* **Arbitration** (Award—Foreign currency).
      Jurisdiction to order payment of sum expressed in foreign currency—
         Contract—Currency of contract foreign currency—European Economic Community—Creditor of
         member state entitled against debtor of another member state to payment in own
         currency—Circumstances in which judgment should be given for payment of a sum expressed in
         foreign currency—EEC Treaty, art 106. **Schorsch Meier GmbH v Hennin** [1975] **1** 152, CA.
         Contract—Law of foreign country proper law of contract—Money of account and payment
         expressed in currency of that country—Action in English court for price of goods sold and
         delivered under contract—Whether court having jurisdiction to give judgment for sum expressed
         in foreign currency. **Miliangos v George Frank (Textiles) Ltd** [1975] **3** 801, HL.
         Contract—Proper law of contract English—Currency of account and payment foreign—Whether
         court having jurisdiction to order payment of sum expressed in foreign currency. **Barclays Bank**
         International Ltd v Levin Bros (Bradford) Ltd [1976] **3** 900, QBD.

JUDGMENT (cont)—
  Foreign currency (cont)—
    Jurisdiction to order payment of sum expressed in foreign currency (cont)—
      Damages for breach of contract—Currency in which damages to be awarded—Award of arbitrator.
        See **Arbitration** (Award—Foreign currency—Damages—Breach of contract—Currency in which
        damages to be awarded).
      Damages for breach of contract—Currency in which damages to be awarded—Charterparty
        governed by English law—Currency of contract US dollars—Damage discovered when cargo
        unloaded in France—French cargo receivers dealing in cargo as a dollar commodity—Whether
        judgment for damages should be expressed in dollars or francs. **Société Française Bunge SA v
        Belcan NV** [1985] **3** 378, QBD.
      Damages for breach of contract—Law of foreign country proper law of contract—Money of account
        and payment expressed in currency of that country—Action in English court for damages for
        non-acceptance of goods—Whether court having jurisdiction to give judgment for sum expressed
        in foreign currency. **Kraut (Jean) AG v Albany Fabrics Ltd** [1977] **2** 116, QBD.
      Damages for tort—Currency in which judgment to be given—Loss and expenditure incurred in
        several foreign currencies in consequence of tort—Whether court having jurisdiction to give
        judgment for sum expressed in currency other than sterling—Whether damages to be awarded in
        plaintiff's own currency or currencies in which expenditure or loss directly and immediately
        incurred. **Despina R, The** [1979] **1** 421, HL.
      Proper law of contract English—Currency of contract foreign—Charterparty—Demurrage—
        Demurrage expressed to be payable in dollars—Charterparty governed by English law—Whether
        jurisdiction to award demurrage in dollars. **Federal Commerce and Navigation Co Ltd v Tradax
        Export SA** [1977] **2** 41, CA.
    Payment of sum of money in. *See* Payment of sum of money—Foreign currency, *below*.
    Pleading claims in foreign currency—
      Statement in writ—Pleading of facts relied on to support claim. **Practice Direction** [1977] **1** 544,
      SC Taxing Office.
  Foreign judgment—
    Conflict of laws. *See* **Conflict of laws** (Foreign judgment).
    Enforcement of default judgment. *See* **Conflict of laws** (Foreign judgment—Enforcement—Default
    judgment).
    Generally. *See* **Conflict of laws** (Foreign judgment).
    Registration in England. *See* **Conflict of laws** (Foreign judgment—Registration in England).
  Form of judgment—
    Claim for possession by mortgagee—
      Irregular procedure—RSC Ord 55, r 8A. **Redditch Benefit Building Society v Roberts** [1940] **1** 342,
      CA.
    Contributory negligence—
      Both parties to blame—Claim and counterclaim—Equal share of blame—Judge dismissing claim
      and counterclaim—Proper form of order judgment for both parties for half damages proved by
      each—Law Reform (Contributory Negligence) Act 1945, s 1(1). **Smith v W H Smith & Sons Ltd**
      [1952] **1** 528, CA.
    Defendants joined on different causes of action—
      Causes of action in respect of same subject-matter—Supreme Court of Judicature (Consolidation)
      Act 1925, s 41—RSC Ord 16, r 4. **Morris (B O) Ltd v Perrott and Bolton** [1945] **1** 567, CA.
    Detinue. *See* **Detinue** (Judgment—Forms of judgment).
  Handed down judgments—
    Availability—
      Judgments in advance of hearing—Approved versions—Uncorrected copies—Approved
      judgments—Restrictions on disclosure or reporting—Approved versions of ex tempore
      judgments—Citation of authorities. **Practice Statement** [1998] **2** 667, Sup Ct.
    Judgments in advance of hearing—
      Approved judgments. **Practice Note** [1999] **1** 125, Sup Ct.
      Correction of minor errors. **Perotti v Collyer-Bristow (a firm) (No 2)** [2004] **4** 72, CA.
      Draft judgments—Anonymisation—General principles—Tax appeals. **Revenue and Customs Comrs
      v Banerjee (No 2)** [2009] **3** 930n, Ch D.
      Draft judgments—Confidentiality—CPR 40 PD E. **DPP v P (No 2) (Note)** [2007] **4** 648, DC.
      Draft judgments—Confidentiality—Guidance—CPR PD 40E. **R (on the application of Counsel
      General for Wales) v Secretary of State for Business, Energy and Industrial Strategy** [2022] **4** 599,
      CA.
      Draft judgments—Request for clarification—Family Court—Guidance. **I (children) (clarification of
      judgments), Re** [2019] **3** 818n, CA.
      Judge sending draft judgment to parties' lawyers—Parties compromising dispute before judgment
      formally handed down—Whether judge having discretion to hand down judgment
      notwithstanding settlement agreement. **Prudential Assurance Co Ltd v McBains Cooper (a firm)**
      [2001] **3** 1014, CA.
      Purpose of providing draft judgments—Reconsidering points of substance. **Egan v Motor Services
      (Bath) Ltd** [2008] **1** 1156n, CA.
  Indorsement—
    Default of defence. *See* Default of defence—Indorsement of court copy of judgment, *above*.
  Industrial tribunal—
    Decision—
      Reasons for decision. *See* **Employment tribunal** (Procedure—Decision—Reasons for decision).
  Interest—
    Damages. *See* **Interest** (Damages).
    Judgment debt. *See* **Practice** (Payment out of court—Interest—Payment to plaintiff in satisfaction of
    judgment debt).
    Proceeds of sale. *See* **Interest** (Proceeds of sale).
  Judgment on admission of facts—
    Availability of defence—
      Tort—Criminal conviction of defendant. *See* **Tort** (Availability of defence—Criminal conviction of
      defendant—Judgment on admission of facts).

JUDGMENT (cont)—
  Judgment on admission of facts (cont)—
    Discretion of court—
      Specially indorsed writ—Unconditional leave to defend granted although claim partially admitted—Defence partially admitting claim—Payment into court—RSC Ord 32, r 6. **Lancashire Welders Ltd v Harland & Wolff Ltd** [1950] **2** 1096, CA.
    Interlocutory or final judgment—
      Appeal—Whether appeal against judgment ranking as an interlocutory or final appeal—RSC Ord 27, r 3. **Technistudy Ltd v Kelland** [1976] **3** 632, CA.
    Negligence—
      Admission of negligence but denial of damage—Payment into court—Interlocutory judgment—Interest on damages—Plaintiff not entitled to judgment on admission of negligence only—Proof of damage necessary to establish liability—Failure to obtain judgment disentitling plaintiff to claim interest on money paid into court—RSC Ord 27, r 3. **Blundell v Rimmer** [1971] **1** 1072, QBD.
      Admission of negligence by defendant—Right of plaintiff to judgment—Plaintiff not entitled to judgment on admission of negligence only—Proof required that plaintiff suffered damage as result of negligence—RSC Ord 27, r 3. **Rankine v Garton Sons and Co Ltd** [1979] **2** 1185, CA.
  Judgments, orders and other documents for use abroad. *See* **Practice** (Document—Document for use abroad).
  Judicial decision as authority. *See* **Precedent**.
  Merger of cause of action in judgment—
    Effect on recovery of interest. *See* **Interest** (Debt—Merger of right to interest in judgment for principal sum and interest).
  Multiple defendants—
    Judgment against one of more defendants—
      Effect on remaining defendants. *See* Default judgment—Effect of default judgment, *above*.
  Note of judgment—
    Appeal from Chancery Division or Queen's Bench Division—
      Practice. *See* **Practice** (Note of judgment—Appeal from Chancery Division or Queen's Bench Division).
    Counsel's fees for taking note of judgment. *See* **Counsel** (Fees—Note of judgment).
  Judge's note—
    Court of Appeal. *See* **Court of Appeal** (Judge's note).
  Numbering of judgments—
    Neutral citation—
      Extension of neutral citation to all parts of High Court. **Practice Direction** [2002] **1** 351, Sup Ct.
Order—
  Amendment—
    Correction of accidental slip or omission. *See* Order—Correction—Accidental slip or omission, *below*.
    Interlocutory appeal—Costs—RSC Ord 20, r 11. **Adam & Harvey Ltd v International Maritime Supplies Co Ltd** [1967] **1** 533, CA.
  Ante-dating of order—
    Death of party after judgment reserved—RSC Ord 41, r 3. **Bonsor v Musicians' Union** [1954] **1** 822, CA.
  Compensation—
    Criminal proceedings. *See* **Sentence** (Compensation—Order).
  Compromise of action—
    Approval of court. *See* **Practice** (Compromise of action—Approval of court).
  Consent order—
    Amendment—Addition of 'liberty to apply'—Order for forfeiture. **Chandless-Chandless v Nicholson** [1942] **2** 315, CA.
    Appeal—Order made by registrar—Appeal without registrar's leave—Supreme Court of Judicature (Consolidation) Act 1925, s 31(1)(h). **Purcell v FC Trigell Ltd (t/a Southern Window and General Cleaning Co)** [1970] **3** 671, CA.
    Compromise of action. *See* **Practice** (Compromise of action—Consent order).
    Construction—Evidence of surrounding circumstances—Consent order on appeal construed having regard to limits of order at first instance. **General Accident, Fire and Life Assurance Corp Ltd v IRC** [1963] **3** 259, CA.
    Counsel entering compromise agreement without authority. *See* **Counsel** (Authority—Limitation—Compromise—Consent order based on compromise—Power to set aside order).
    Drawing-up in Chancery Division. **Practice Direction** [1960] **3** 415, Ch D.
    Financial provision—Divorce. *See* **Divorce** (Financial provision—Consent order).
    Interlocutory order—Setting aside—Contractual effect of order—Grounds for setting aside order. **Purcell v FC Trigell Ltd (t/a Southern Window and General Cleaning Co)** [1970] **3** 671, CA.
    Interlocutory order—Setting aside—Grounds for setting aside interlocutory order—Defendants giving undertaking on hearing of interlocutory motion—Undertaking embodied in consent order until trial or further order—Point at issue subsequently decided by Court of Appeal in another case—Defendants applying to have undertaking discharged—Judge refusing to discharge undertaking and refusing leave to appeal—Whether defendants entitled to leave to appeal—Whether contractual effect of undertaking making it binding until trial—Whether defendants required to adduce grounds sufficient to set aside a contract—Whether acquisition of subsequent evidence and Court of Appeal decision justifying discharge of undertaking and rehearing of interlocutory motion. **Chanel Ltd v F W Woolworth & Co Ltd** [1981] **1** 745, Ch D and CA.
    Maintenance—Divorce—Effect of order. *See* **Divorce** (Maintenance—Order by consent).
    Maintenance—Divorce—Variation of order. *See* **Divorce** (Maintenance—Variation of order—Consent order).
    Misrepresentation. **Thorne v Smith** [1947] **1** 39, CA.
    Procedure for obtaining. *See* **Practice** (Consent order—Summons issued and indorsed with consent—Procedure for obtaining order).

JUDGMENT (cont)—
  Order (cont)—
    Construction—
      Unambiguous judgment—Pleadings and history of action not regarded for purpose of construing judgment. **Gordon v Gonda** [1955] **2** 762, CA.
    Correction—
      Accidental slip or omission—Damages awarded against two defendants—Judgment entered as 'each defendant liable for half judgment'—Whether error can be corrected under slip rule. **Smith v Harris** [1939] **3** 960, CA.
      Accidental slip or omission—Discretion to refuse correction—No intervening rights of third parties in ignorance of error—Discretion wherever something intervened since date of order rendering correction inexpedient or inequitable—Stay of execution pending appeal omitted from order as drawn up—Appeal prosecuted to House of Lords—Subsequent application to insert stay of execution in judgment refused—RSC Ord 20, r 8, r 11. **Moore v Buchanan** [1967] **3** 273, CA.
      Accidental slip or omission—Divorce decree—Application to amend to refer to prior marriage—Matrimonial Causes Rules 1950 (SI 1950 No 1940), r 80—RSC Ord 28, r 11. **Thynne (Marchioness of Bath) v Thynne (Marquess of Bath)** [1955] **3** 129, CA.
      Accidental slip or omission—Divorce—Ancillary proceedings—Wife consenting to dismissal of claim for periodical payments if husband's half share in home transferred to her—Judge making order transferring half share to her subject to a charge in husband's favour for half the value of his share—Judge making 'no order' for periodical payments—Subsequently judge purporting to vary order under slip rule by substituting 'application ... dismissed' instead of 'no order'—Whether variation of order permitted under slip rule—CCR Ord 15, r 12. **Carter v Carter** [1980] **1** 827, CA.
      Accidental slip or omission—Election court for local election—Correction of order for costs—Whether correction permissible—RSC Ord 20, r 11. **R v Cripps, ex p Muldoon** [1984] **2** 705, CA.
      Accidental slip or omission—Final charging order—Amendment to include 'all sums' owed to claimant in respect of judgment debt and costs—Whether final charging order could differ from interim charging order—Whether use of 'slip rule' permitted—Whether further application to vary terms of final charging order could only be made by way of appeal—CPR 40.12. **Santos-Albert v Ochi** [2018] **4** 265, Ch D.
      Accidental slip or omission—Judgment awarding damages—Accidental omission of award of interest—Application by summons inter partes for award of interest—Summons dismissed for want of jurisdiction—Subsequent application under slip rule for amendment of judgment by inclusion of award of interest—Whether court precluded from amending judgment by reason of dismissal of earlier summons. **Tak Ming Co Ltd v Yee Sang Metal Supplies Co** [1973] **1** 569, PC.
      Accidental slip or omission—Omission of counsel to apply for certain costs—Costs incurred before issue of summons—RSC Ord 28, r 11. **Inchcape, Re** [1942] **2** 157, Ch D.
      Accidental slip or omission—Right to apply for correction—RSC Ord 28, r 11. **Marly Laboratory Ltd, Re an application by** [1952] **1** 1057, CA.
      Omission of remuneration of trustees of debenture trust deed—Matter not in mind of court when order made—Fund from which remuneration to be paid still in hand—Correction of date—RSC Ord 55, r 71. **City Housing Trust Ltd, Re** [1942] **1** 369, Ch D.
    Costs. *See* **Costs** (Order for costs).
    County court. *See* **County court** (Judgment or order).
    Court of Appeal—
      Criminal appeal. *See* **Criminal law** (Court of Appeal—Order of court).
    Discharge—
      Motion to discharge district registrar's order—Action in Chancery Division of High Court in London—Action in warned list at date of application to district registrar to alter venue. **Fullerton v Ryman** [1956] **2** 232, Ch D.
      Motion to discharge order made in chambers—Time for. **Eastcheap Alimentary Products Ltd, Re** [1936] **3** 276, Ch D.
    Drawing-up—
      Chancery Division. *See* **Practice** (Chancery Division—Order—Order on motion—Drawing up of order).
      Generally. *See* **Practice** (Order—Drawing-up).
    Enforcement—
      Leave. *See* **Emergency legislation** (Leave to enforce judgment or order).
    Ex parte order—
      Setting aside—General rule—Exclusion by statute. *See* **Limitation of action** (Extension of time limit—Order for extension).
    Form of order—
      Irregularity—Effectiveness of order until varied—Order for family provision for widow of deceased—Made in form in which there was not jurisdiction to make it. **Gale (decd), In the Estate of** [1966] **1** 945, CA.
      Judgment requiring execution of deed—Judgment in default of appearance. *See* **Practice** (Chancery Division—Order—Order requiring execution of deed—Judgment in default of appearance—Form of order).
      Order dismissing action unless fixed for trial within six years from 'date of alleged loss'—Order inoperative as uncertain. **Abalian v Innous** [1936] **2** 834, CA.
    Four-day order—
      Whether available to enforce order for payment out of testator's estate. *See* **Family provision** (Order—Order for payment to dependant of sum out of capital of testator's estate—Enforcement—No payment made under order—Application for four day order for payment).
    Interlocutory order—
      Leave to appeal against order. *See* **Court of Appeal** (Interlocutory appeal—Leave to appeal).
    Minutes of order drawn by counsel—
      Chancery Division. **Practice Direction** [1960] **3** 415, Ch D.
    Procedural orders made in chambers—
      Drawing up in Chancery Division. **Practice Direction** [1960] **3** 415, Ch D.

JUDGMENT (cont)—
Order (cont)—
Recall by judge—
Chancery Division. **Harrison's Share under a Settlement, Re** [1955] **1** 185, CA.
Setting aside order—
Consent order—Interlocutory order. *See* Order—Consent order—Interlocutory order—Setting aside, *above*.
Order of court of unlimited jurisdiction. *See* **Court** (Order—Court of unlimited jurisdiction).
Supplemental order—
Jurisdiction to make supplemental order—New facts—Plaintiffs obtaining order for specific performance—Subsequent application by plaintiffs for supplemental order for enquiry into damages—Supplemental order limited to damage arising after date of order for specific performance. **Ford-Hunt v Raghbir Singh** [1973] **2** 700, Ch D.
Payment of sum of money—
Foreign currency—
Claims in foreign currency—Applications for transfer of claims to county court—Payment of foreign currency into court—Interest—Enforcement of judgment debt in foreign currency—Forms. **Practice Direction** [1976] **1** 669, SC Taxing Office.
Conversion date—Bill of exchange—Bills payable in foreign currency—Bills accepted but dishonoured on presentment—Appropriate date for conversion—Whether judgment sum to be calculated in accordance with rate of exchange in force on days bills payable or on date of payment or enforcement of judgment—Bills of Exchange Act 1882, s 72(4). **Barclays Bank International Ltd v Levin Bros (Bradford) Ltd** [1976] **3** 900, QBD.
Enforcement of judgment—Judgment for payment of sum of money expressed in foreign currency—Conversion of sum into sterling—Appropriate date for conversion—Whether sum to be converted in accordance with rate of exchange prevailing on date leave given to enforce judgment. **Miliangos v George Frank (Textiles) Ltd** [1975] **3** 801, HL.
Jurisdiction to order payment of sum expressed in foreign currency. *See* Foreign currency—Jurisdiction to order payment of sum expressed in foreign currency, *above*.
Precedent. *See* **Precedent**.
Preparation of judgments—
Numbering of approved judgments—
Paragraph numbering—Neutral citation. **Practice Note** [2001] **1** 193, CA.
Publication restrictions—
Public security. *See* **Privilege** (Public interest immunity—Production contrary to public interest—Risk of serious harm to public security—Judgment).
Reasons. *See* **Judge** (Reasons).
Reserved judgment—
Court of Appeal, Civil Division—
Practice. *See* **Court of Appeal** (Practice—Civil Division—Reserved judgments).
Revision—
Variation of decision after judgment delivered. *See* Alteration—Variation of decision after judgment delivered, *above*.
Secret proceedings—
Practice—
Chancery Division. *See* **Practice** (Chancery Division—Secret proceedings—Judgment).
Setting aside—
Default judgment. *See* Default judgment—Setting aside judgment, *above*.
Judgment after trial in absence of party—
Application by party who failed to attend trial for judgment or order to be set aside—Relationship of application and appeal—Guidance—CPR 39.3. **Bank of Scotland v Pereira** [2011] **3** 392, CA.
Factors to be considered in setting aside judgment after trial—Whether reason for party's absence a material factor—Whether conduct of parties to be considered—Whether successful party prejudiced if judgment set aside—Whether different principles applying to application to set aside judgment after trial and judgment in default—RSC Ord 35, r 2(1). **Shocked v Goldschmidt** [1998] **1** 372, CA.
Rule of procedure dealing with applications to set aside judgments made against party who had failed to attend trial—Rule empowering court to set aside judgment only if defendant had reasonable prospects of success at trial—Whether rule applying where defendant not served with proceedings and having no knowledge of them—CPR 39.3(5). **Nelson v Clearsprings (Management) Ltd** [2007] **2** 407, CA.
Judgment in default of appearance. *See* Default of appearance—Setting aside judgment, *above*.
Judgment in default of defence. *See* Default of defence—Setting aside judgment, *above*.
Judgment obtained by fraud—
Claim to set aside default judgment entered in favour of finance company on ground of fraud—Whether alleged fraud by finance company operative cause of decision to enter default judgment—Whether fraud claim an abuse of court's process. **Park v CNH Industrial Capital Europe Ltd (t/a CNH Capital)** [2022] **2** Comm 415, CA; [2022] **3** 867, CA.
Power of court to impose terms—RSC Ord 27, r 15—RSC Ord 36, r 33. **Kennedy v Dandrick** [1943] **2** 606, Ch D.
Whether requirement of reasonable diligence on party seeking to set judgment aside—Whether claim to set aside earlier judgment abuse of process. **Takhar v Gracefield Developments Ltd** [2019] **3** 283, SC.
Judgment without jurisdiction—
Applicant in contempt—Applicant failing to comply with order for discovery and having defence struck out—Applicant taking no further part in action—Judgment entered against applicant but proceedings not finalised—Applicant applying to set aside judgment on ground that statement of claim not able in law to support plaintiffs' claim—Applicant not offering to purge contempt—Whether application to set aside judgment should be granted where applicant in contempt—RSC Ord 35, r 2(1). **Midland Bank Trust Co Ltd v Green (No 3)** [1979] **2** 193, Ch D.
Inherent power of court to set aside. **Kofi Forfie (Chief) v Barima Kwabena Seifah** [1958] **1** 289, PC.

JUDGMENT (cont)—
Setting aside (cont)—
Mistaken admission—
Irregular judgment—Jurisdiction to set aside judgment—CPR 3.1(2)(m). **Northern Rock (Asset Management) plc v Chancellors Associates Ltd** [2012] **2** 501n, QBD.
Order for extension of time limit. *See* **Limitation of action** (Extension of time limit—Order for extension).
Supreme Court—
Application to set aside previous judgment on basis of unfair procedure—House of Lords judgment upholding decision of Secretary of State to prevent right of abode or access to British Indian Ocean Territory—Secretary of State failing to disclose potentially relevant documents—Whether previous judgment to be set aside in light of undisclosed documents. **R (on the application of Bancoult) v Secretary of State for Foreign and Commonwealth Affairs** [2017] **1** 403, SC.
Setting aside. *See* Default of defence—Setting aside judgment, *above*.
Specific performance—
Judgment in default of defence. *See* **Specific performance** (Judgment in default of defence).
Summary judgment—
Generally. *See* **Practice** (Summary judgment).
Injunction. *See* **Injunction** (Summary procedure—Practice—Summary judgment for injunction).
Interest—
Award of interest on summary judgment. *See* **Interest** (Damages—Jurisdiction to include interest in award of damages—Summary judgment).
Set-off—
Right of set-off. *See* **Set-off** (Right of set-off—Summary judgment).
Tender—
Claim for £149—
£106 paid into court—£136 awarded to plaintiff—Amount for which judgment should be given—Costs—County Courts Act 1934, s 47. **Read's Trustee in Bankruptcy v Smith (Portman Building Society, third party)** [1951] **1** 406, Ch D.
Title—
Infant plaintiff having attained full age—
Action started by next friend—Adoption of action by infant on attaining full age—Proper title of proceedings. **Carberry v Davies** [1968] **2** 817, CA.
Transcript—
Correction and alteration by judge—
Appeal—Whether original version admissible to be looked at on appeal. **Bromley v Bromley** [1964] **3** 226, CA.
Variation or revocation—
Judgment on admission of liability. *See* **Practice** (Order—Final order—Power to vary or revoke orders—Judgment on admissions).
West Africa—
Judgment without jurisdiction. *See* **West Africa** (Judgment—Judgment without jurisdiction).
Writ—
Amendment of writ after judgment—
Jurisdiction. *See* **Writ** (Amendment—Amendment to correct party's name—Amendment after judgment).

JUDGMENT DEBT
Deceased's estate. *See* **Administration of estates** (Order of application of assets—Judgment debt).
Discovery in aid of execution—
Examination of judgment debtor. *See* **Execution** (Disclosure in aid of execution—Examination of judgment debtor).
Examination of judgment debtor—
Practice. *See* **Execution** (Disclosure in aid of execution—Examination of judgment debtor—Practice).
Interest—
Generally. *See* **Practice** (Payment out of court—Interest—Payment to plaintiff in satisfaction of judgment debt).
Income tax. *See* **Income tax** (Interest—Judgment debt).
Non-payment of—
Committal. *See* **Debt** (Non-payment of judgment debt—Committal).
Secured debt—
Bankruptcy petition by creditor. *See* **Bankruptcy** (Petition—Creditor's petition—Secured creditor—Judgment debt).

JUDICATURE
Constitutional position—
Jamaica. *See* **Jamaica** (Constitutional law—Judicature).

JUDICIAL COMMITTEE
See **Privy Council.**

JUDICIAL FEES
House of Lords. *See* **House of Lords** (Judicial fees).

JUDICIAL IMMUNITY
See **Judge** (Immunity from suit).

JUDICIAL NOTICE
Dangerous article. *See* **Criminal evidence** (Judicial notice—Dangerous article).

JUDICIAL NOTICE (cont)—
Notorious facts—
Judge's local knowledge—
Defendant council failing to honour undertaking to repair property—Plaintiff bringing proceedings to enforce undertaking—Judge taking judicial notice of defendant's failure to honour previous undertakings in similar cases in considering appropriate penalty—Whether judge right to do so. **Mullen v Hackney London BC** [1997] 2 906, CA.
Offensive weapons. *See* **Criminal evidence** (Judicial notice—Offensive weapons).

JUDICIAL OFFICE
Characteristics. *See* **Court** (Judicial office—Characteristics).

JUDICIAL PRECEDENT
See **Precedent**.

JUDICIAL PROCEEDINGS
Absolute privilege—
Libel and slander. *See* **Libel and slander** (Privilege—Absolute privilege—Judicial proceedings).

JUDICIAL REVIEW
Abuse of process—
Actionable abuse of process. *See* **Tort** (Abuse of process—Actionable abuse of process—Judicial review proceedings).
Acts done in pursuance of statute—
Protection in respect of acts done in pursuance of statute—
Extent of protection—Mental health. *See* **Mental health** (Protection in respect of acts done in pursuance of statute—Extent of protection—Judicial review).
Alternative remedy available. *See* Availability of remedy—Alternative remedy available, *below*.
Appeal—
County court. *See* **County court** (Appeal—Judicial review).
Court of Appeal—
Jurisdiction. *See* **Court of Appeal** (Jurisdiction—Appeal from Divisional Court—Application for judicial review).
House of Lords—
Jurisdiction. *See* **House of Lords** (Appeal from Court of Appeal, Civil Division—Jurisdiction—Judicial review).
Application for judicial review—
Amenability to judicial review—
Local authority refusing to renew solicitor's lease for office premises—Whether decision amenable to judicial review—Whether authority acting unlawfully—Local Government Act 1972, s 123. **R (on the application of Trafford) v Blackpool BC** [2014] 2 947, QBD.
Application for leave to apply for judicial review—
Crown Office list. *See* **Practice** (Crown Office list—Judicial review).
Ex parte application. *See* Leave to apply for judicial review—Ex parte applications, *below*.
Grant of leave—Applicant seeking to challenge executive decision authorising action by third party—Court granting leave to apply for judicial review, but refusing to grant stay of decision pending hearing of substantive application—Grant of stay would adversely affect third party's operations—Principles to be applied by court in deciding whether to grant stay. **R v Inspectorate of Pollution, ex p Greenpeace Ltd** [1994] 4 321, CA.
Leave granted on some grounds but not on others—Whether necessary to seek additional leave to pursue further grounds—Whether applicant granted leave on some grounds entitled to rely on other grounds at substantive hearing of application. **R v Bow Street Stipendiary Magistrate, ex p Roberts** [1990] 3 487, QBD.
Leave to apply for order of prohibition or certiorari—Stay of proceedings—Grant of leave operating as stay of proceedings—Whether grant of leave operating as injunction—Whether stay having any effect on executive decision already made. **Minister of Foreign Affairs Trade and Industry v Vehicles and Supplies Ltd** [1991] 4 65, PC.
Renewal of application. *See* Leave to apply for judicial review—Renewal of application, *below*.
Requirement that 'application be made promptly and in any event within three months'—Whether 'application' referring to application for leave or substantive application—RSC Ord 53, r 4(1). **R v Stratford-on-Avon DC, ex p Jackson** [1985] 3 769, CA.
Stay of proceedings—Grant of leave operating as stay of 'proceedings to which application relates'—Decision of Secretary of State approving proposals for acquisition of grant-maintained status by school—Whether Secretary of State's decision 'proceedings'—Whether court having jurisdiction to grant stay of implementation of Secretary of State's decision when granting leave—RSC Ord 53, r 3(10)(a). **R v Secretary of State for Education and Science, ex p Avon CC** [1991] 1 282, CA.
Vexatious litigant—Whether application for leave constituting institution of proceedings. *See* **Vexatious proceedings** (Instituting proceedings—Institute—Application for leave to apply for judicial review).
Application for permission to apply for judicial review—
Applicant seeking to challenge decisions of committee of Lloyd's of London—Whether decisions amenable to judicial review—Whether Lloyd's exercising public function—Human Rights Act 1998, s 6. **R (on the application of West) v Lloyd's of London** [2004] 2 **Comm** 1, CA; [2004] 3 251, CA.
Locus standi of applicant—Sufficient interest—Environment Agency carrying out public consultation exercise before permitting company to make trial use of alternative source of fuel—Applicant taking no part in consultation exercise—Other objectors ineligible for public funding—Applicant applying for judicial review—Applicant obtaining legal funding certificate—Whether applicant having sufficient interest to apply for judicial review—Whether claim abuse of process. **R (on the application of Edwards) v Environment Agency (Rugby Ltd, interested party)** [2004] 3 21, QBD.

JUDICIAL REVIEW (cont)—
  Application for judicial review (cont)—
    Application for permission to apply for judicial review (cont)—
      Requirement that application be made within three months 'from the date when grounds for the
      application first arose'—Whether three-month time limit for challenging grant of planning
      permission running from actual grant of permission or from preliminary resolution authorising
      conditional grant of permission—RSC Ord 53, r 4(1)—CPR 54.5(1). **R (on the application of
      Burkett) v Hammersmith and Fulham London BC** [2002] **3** 97, HL.

      Standing of claimant—Sufficient interest—Ten-year-old boys murdering claimant's infant
      son—Lord Chief Justice setting tariff for boys—Claimant seeking to challenge tariff in judicial
      review proceedings—Whether member of victim's family having standing to apply for judicial
      review of Lord Chief Justice's decision on appropriate tariff for juvenile detainees. **R (on the
      application of Bulger) v Secretary of State for the Home Dept** [2001] **3** 449, QBD DC.

      Whether High Court having jurisdiction to hear fresh application for permission to apply for judicial
      review if permission refused at previous oral hearing —Approach to be adopted to exercise of
      jurisdiction—CPR 52.15. **R (on the application of Opoku) v Principal of Southwark College**
      [2003] **1** 272, QBD.

    Costs. *See* Costs of application, *below.*
    Locus standi of applicant—
      Alternative remedy available—Discrimination against women in field of employment—Part-time
      worker made redundant after working for employer for less than five years—Part-time worker
      alleging that United Kingdom redundancy legislation discriminatory against women—Part-time
      worker seeking judicial review of Secretary of State's refusal to introduce amending
      legislation—Whether appropriate forum for claim an industrial tribunal—Whether part-time
      worker having locus standi to apply for judicial review. **Equal Opportunities Commission v
      Secretary of State for Employment** [1994] **1** 910, HL.

      Equal Opportunities Commission—Discrimination against women in field of employment—
      Commission alleging that United Kingdom employment legislation discriminatory against
      women—Secretary of State expressing view that United Kingdom not in breach of European
      Community law—Commission seeking judicial review of Secretary of State's refusal to introduce
      amending legislation—Whether commission having locus standi to apply for judicial
      review—Whether Secretary of State's view on state of law amounting to decision susceptible to
      judicial review. **Equal Opportunities Commission v Secretary of State for Employment**
      [1994] **1** 910, HL.

      Northern Ireland Human Rights Commission—Proceedings relating to protection of human
      rights—Challenge to statutory prohibition on abortion in Northern Ireland—Whether Commission
      competent to institute abstract proceedings—Human Rights Act 1998, ss 6, 7—Northern Ireland
      Act 1998, ss 69, 71. **Northern Ireland Human Rights Commission's application for judicial review
      (reference by the Court of Appeal (Northern Ireland)), Re** [2019] **1** 173, SC.

      Sufficient interest—Company authorised to discharge radioactive waste from premises—Company
      granted variation of authorisations to test new plant—Environmental protection organisation
      concerned at extent of radioactive discharge—Organisation having international profile and 2,500
      supporters in area of new plant—Whether organisation having sufficient interest to apply for
      judicial review of executive decision to vary authorisations—Supreme Court Act 1981,
      s 31(3)—RSC Ord 53, r 3(7). **R v Inspectorate of Pollution, ex p Greenpeace Ltd (No 2)**
      [1994] **4** 329, QBD.

      Sufficient interest—Grant of overseas aid—Application for judicial review by non-partisan pressure
      group having expertise and interest in promoting and protecting British aid to underdeveloped
      nations—Whether applicant having locus standi to bring application. **R v Secretary of State for
      Foreign Affairs, ex p World Development Movement Ltd** [1995] **1** 611, QBD.

      Sufficient interest—Review of taxation of costs in legally-aided case—Decision of Legal Aid Board
      refusing authority for review of taxation of legally-aided party's solicitor's costs—Applicant
      legally-aided plaintiff—Legal Aid Board refusing application by applicant's solicitors for authority
      for review of taxation—Applicant applying for judicial review—Whether applicant having
      sufficient interest to apply for judicial review—Supreme Court Act 1981, s 31(3)—Civil Legal Aid
      (General) Regulations 1989, reg 114. **R v Legal Aid Board, ex p Bateman** [1992] **3** 490, QBD.

    Undue delay—
      Court satisfied good reason existing for delay—Court extending time limit and granting leave to
      apply—Whether on hearing of substantive application court can refuse relief on ground of such
      delay—Supreme Court Act 1981, s 31(6)(7)—RSC Ord 53, r 4(1). **R v Stratford-on-Avon DC, ex p
      Jackson** [1985] **3** 769, CA.

  Availability of remedy—
    Alternative remedy available—
      Alternative remedy by way of appeal—Consumer protection—Local authority issuing suspension
      notice in respect of unsafe product—Manufacturer having statutory right of appeal—
      Manufacturer applying for judicial review of notice—Whether judicial review appropriate when
      alternative statutory remedy available—Consumer Protection Act 1987, ss 14, 15. **R v Birmingham
      City Council, ex p Ferrero Ltd** [1993] **1** 530, CA.

      Alternative remedy by way of appeal—Guidance. **R v Falmouth and Truro Port Health Authority, ex
      p South West Water Ltd** [2000] **3** 306, CA.

      Alternative remedy by way of appeal—Whether availability of alternative remedy precluding
      application for judicial review. **R v IRC, ex p Opman International UK** [1986] **1** 328, QBD.

      Alternative remedy not pursued—Immigration officer refusing applicant leave to enter United
      Kingdom—Applicant not pursuing statutory right of appeal—Whether appropriate to grant leave
      to apply for judicial review—Immigration Act 1971, s 13. **R v Secretary of State for the Home
      Dept, ex p Swati** [1986] **1** 717, CA.

      Alternative remedy not pursued—Whether appropriate to grant leave to apply for judicial review. **R
      v Epping and Harlow General Comrs, ex p Goldstraw** [1983] **3** 257, QBD and CA.

JUDICIAL REVIEW (cont)—
  Availability of remedy (cont)—
    Alternative remedy available (cont)—

      Clandestine entrants—Penalty for carrying clandestine entrants—Secretary of State issuing claimant with penalty notice as person responsible for clandestine entrants—Secretary of State upholding notice despite service of notice of objection—Claimant applying for judicial review—Whether judicial review appropriate remedy—Immigration and Asylum Act 1999, ss 32, 34, 35, 37. **R (on the application of Balbo B & C Auto Transporti Internazionali) v Secretary of State for the Home Dept** [2001] **4** 423, QBD DC.

      Discretion of court to grant relief—Appeal against assessments to income tax—Benefit to applicants—Transaction involving acquisition and disposal of land—Inspector making assessments on grounds that applicants had directly or indirectly provided opportunity for another person to realise a gain—No evidence that applicants beneficially entitled to land or gain—Whether inspector acting improperly in exercising his power to raise assessments—Whether applicants' inability to recover costs if successful in appeal before Special Commissioners a ground for granting leave to apply for judicial review. **R v Inspector of Taxes, ex p Kissane** [1986] **2** 37, QBD.

      Discretion of court to grant relief—Complaint to Secretary of State—Secretary of State's default power where local authority fails to carry out duty comprising a social services function—Whether duty to consult a 'social services function'—Whether judicial review appropriate remedy—Local Authority Social Services Act 1970, s 7D. **R v Devon CC, ex p Baker** [1995] **1** 73, CA.

      Discretion of court to grant relief—Disciplinary proceedings—Complaint against police officer—Police regulations requiring notification of complaints to officer 'as soon as practicable'—Officer not notified until two years after complaints made—Chief constable determining charge arising out of complaint despite delay in giving notice—Officer not pursuing internal appeal—Officer applying for judicial review of chief constable's determination—Whether judicial review should be granted despite availability of internal appeal—Police (Discipline) Regulations 1977, reg 7. **R v Chief Constable of Merseyside Police, ex p Calveley** [1986] **1** 257, CA.

      Discretion of court to grant relief—Factors to be taken into account. **R v Huntingdon DC, ex p Cowan** [1984] **1** 58, QBD.

      Discretion of court to grant relief—Whether failure to exhaust alternative remedies bar to judicial review application—Statement of Changes in Immigration Rules (HC Paper 395) paras 2, 391C(h)(i). **R (on the application of Zhang) v Secretary of State for the Home Dept** [2014] **2** 560, QBD.

      National Trust taking decision to ban deer-hunting with hounds on its land—Plaintiffs seeking to challenge decision by way of judicial review—Whether alternative remedy available—Whether plaintiffs should be granted leave to move for judicial review. **Scott v National Trust for Places of Historic Interest or Natural Beauty** [1998] **2** 705, Ch D.

  Case stated—

    Challenge to case stated—Applicant appealing against decision of Special Commissioner—Commissioner determining taxpayer's liability and stating case for opinion of High Court—Taxpayer complaining that case stated not setting out certain matters in dispute—Taxpayer alleging that commissioner refusing him opportunity to make a case or reply—Whether taxpayer entitled to judicial review of commissioner's determination. **R v Comr for the Special Purposes of the Income Tax Acts, ex p Napier** [1988] **3** 166, CA.

  Certiorari—

    Declaration or injunction—Dismissal of employee—Disciplinary procedure for dismissal forming part of contract of employment—Whether relief by way of judicial review of dismissal available—Supreme Court Act 1981, s 31(1)—RSC Ord 53, r 1(1)(a)(2). **R v BBC, ex p Lavelle** [1983] **1** 241, QBD.

  Chief Rabbi—

    Disciplinary proceedings against rabbi—Chief Rabbi deciding that rabbi morally and religiously unfit to hold rabbinical office—Rabbi dismissed from congregation—Whether Chief Rabbi's decisions susceptible to judicial review—Whether Chief Rabbi's decisions within sphere of public law. **R v Chief Rabbi of the United Hebrew Congregations of GB and the Commonwealth, ex p Wachmann** [1993] **2** 249, QBD.

  Child abuse register—

    Register maintained by local authority—Registration of alleged abuser—Child making allegations of abuse against applicant—Local authority convening case conference to consider allegations—Applicant given opportunity to make written submissions but not allowed to attend case conference—Case conference deciding to place applicant's name on register—Whether case conference's decision part of authority's internal administrative procedures—Whether case conference's decision subject to judicial review. **R v Harrow London BC, ex p D** [1990] **3** 12, CA.

    Register maintained by local authority—Registration of alleged abuser—Child making allegations of sexual abuse against applicant—Local authority convening case conference to consider allegations—Case conference deciding to place applicant's name on register and secretly inform his employers—Applicant given no opportunity to rebut allegations—Whether case conference's decision part of authority's internal administrative procedures—Whether case conference's decision subject to judicial review. **R v Norfolk CC, ex p M** [1989] **2** 359, QBD.

  Companies registrar—

    Decision to register charge—Charge registered despite defects in application for registration—Whether registrar's decision to register charge open to judicial review—Whether fact that certificate of registration conclusive precluding judicial review of decision—Companies Act 1948, s 98(2)—Tribunals and Inquiries Act 1971, s 14(1). **R v Registrar of Companies, ex p Central Bank of India** [1986] **1** 105, CA.

  Correction of mistakes of law—

    Distinction between courts of law and administrative tribunals exercising quasi-judicial functions. **Racal Communications Ltd, Re** [1980] **2** 634, HL.

223

JUDICIAL REVIEW (cont)—
Availability of remedy (cont)—
Criminal investigation into fraud outside the jurisdiction—

Australian authorities submitting letter of request to Secretary of State to arrange for evidence to be obtained from persons in England—Secretary of State nominating magistrates' court—Claimants learning they would be referred to in replies to questions posed by Australian authorities—Claimants seeking to challenge decisions of Secretary of State—Whether decisions of Secretary of State susceptible to judicial review—Crime (International Co-operation) Act 2003, ss 13(1), 14(1), 15(1). **R (on the application of Hafner) v Secretary of State for the Home Dept** [2006] **3** 382, DC.

Decision not to discontinue prosecution—

Whether Crown Prosecution Service decision not to discontinue prosecution of adult amenable to judicial review. See **Criminal law** (Proceedings—Prosecution of adult—Decision not to discontinue prosecution).

Decision to prosecute—

Juvenile—Offence committed by juvenile—Discretion to continue or to discontinue criminal proceedings—Policy of cautioning juveniles—Police recommending prosecution rather than caution—Crown Prosecution Service deciding not to discontinue prosecution—Whether Crown Prosecution Service's decision amenable to judicial review—Prosecution of Offences Act 1985, s 10(1). **R v Chief Constable of Kent County Constabulary, ex p L (a minor)** [1993] **1** 756, QBD.

Offence in connection with tax evasion—Commissioners' policy of selective prosecution—Commissioners deciding to prosecute applicants but not other taxpayers alleged to be guilty of similar offences—Whether decision amenable to judicial review—Whether availability of alternative remedies precluding application for judicial review—Whether decision unlawful and ultra vires. **R v Chief Constable of Kent County Constabulary, ex p L (a minor)** [1993] **1** 756, QBD.

Declaration—

Grant of declaratory judgment when prerogative order cannot be made—Whether court having jurisdiction to grant declaration. **Equal Opportunities Commission v Secretary of State for Employment** [1994] **1** 910, HL.

Inunction or. See Availability of remedy—Declaration or injunction, *below*.

Declaration or injunction—

Relief sought in action begun by originating motion seeking declaration, injunction or damages—Damages—Prisoner complaining of inadequate medical treatment in prison—Prisoner's originating motion disclosing no public law claim—Whether motion should be dismissed as abuse of process—Whether proceedings should be ordered to continue as if begun by writ—Supreme Court Act 1981, s 31(4)—RSC Ord 53, r 9(5). **R v Secretary of State for the Home Dept, ex p Dew** [1987] **2** 1049, QBD.

Relief sought in action begun by originating summons claiming declaration or injunction—Suspension of greyhound trainer by stewards controlling greyhound racing—Disciplinary procedure derived from contract between trainer and domestic body which controlled greyhound racing—Whether relief by way of judicial review of trainer's suspension available—Supreme Court Act 1981, s 31(1)(2)—RSC Ord 53. **Law v National Greyhound Racing Club Ltd** [1983] **3** 300, CA.

Relief sought in action begun by writ claiming declaration or injunction—Dismissal of employee—Disciplinary procedure for dismissal forming part of contract of employment—Criminal proceedings for theft pending against employee—Whether jurisdiction to interfere with dismissal by injunctive or declaratory relief—Whether pending criminal proceedings requiring proceedings under disciplinary procedure to be postponed until conclusion of criminal proceedings—Supreme Court Act 1981, s 31(2)—RSC Ord 53, r 9(5). **R v BBC, ex p Lavelle** [1983] **1** 241, QBD.

Disciplinary proceedings—

Jockey Club. See Availability of remedy—Jockey Club—Disciplinary proceedings against local steward, *below*.

Judges as visitors of Inns of Court—Judicial review of decision of judges sitting as visitors of Inns of Court in disciplinary matters. See **Counsel** (Disciplinary jurisdiction—Judges as visitors of Inns of Court—Judicial review).

Professional Conduct Committee of Bar Council—Decision of committee to bring charges against barrister—Head of chambers lodging complaint that member of chambers guilty of professional misconduct—Committee deciding to prefer lesser charge of breach of proper professional standards against barrister—Head of chambers applying for judicial review of committee's decision—Whether head of chambers having locus standi to apply for judicial review of committee's decision—Whether court having jurisdiction to hear and determine application—Whether prosecuting authority's decision to prosecute reviewable—Whether public policy preventing court considering application—Whether committee's decision unreasonable or tainted by procedural irregularity—Code of Conduct for the Bar of England and Wales (3rd edn), paras 6, 7, 8. **R v General Council of the Bar, ex p Percival** [1990] **3** 137, QBD.

Discretion of court to grant relief—

Statutory authorisation—Company authorised to discharge radioactive waste from premises—Government departments granting variation of authorisations to enable testing of new plant—Environmental protection organisation concerned at increasing levels of radioactive discharge applying for judicial review of executive decision—Whether judicial review should be granted—Whether variation of authorisations valid or justified—Whether new authorisations required for testing process—Radioactive Substances Act 1960, ss 6(1), 8(1), (4), (7)—Council Directive (Euratom) 80/836, art 6. **R v Inspectorate of Pollution, ex p Greenpeace Ltd (No 2)** [1994] **4** 329, QBD.

JUDICIAL REVIEW (cont)—
    Availability of remedy (cont)—
        Discretion of court to grant relief (cont)—
            Statutory authorisation—Company obtaining authorisations to operate thermal oxide reprocessing plant—Environmental protection organisation and local authority seeking judicial review of decision to grant authorisations and Secretary of State's further decision not to call in applications or hold public inquiry—Whether judicial review should be granted—Whether justification for authorisations in terms of overall benefit a legal requirement—Whether legislation to be construed to accord with relevant Community directive—Whether decision not to hold inquiry flawed—Whether environmental impact assessment a legal requirement—Radioactive Substances Act 1993, ss 13, 16, 24(2)—Council Directive (Euratom) 80/836, arts 6, 13—Council Directive (EEC) 85/337. **R v Secretary of State for the Environment, ex p Greenpeace Ltd** [1994] 4 352, QBD.

    Employment by public authority—

        Dismissal of employee—Conditions of employment approved by Secretary of State and required by statutory instrument to be incorporated in contract of employment—Whether employee having public law rights—Whether employee entitled to judicial review of dismissal—RSC Ord 53. **R v East Berkshire Health Authority, ex p Walsh** [1984] 3 425, CA.

        Dismissal of employee—Dismissal of prison officer—Prison officer's employment governed by code of discipline deriving authority from statute—Application by prison officer for judicial review of dismissal—Whether prison officer's dismissal having public law element—Whether prison officer entitled to judicial review of dismissal—Prison Act 1952, s 47(1)—Prison Rules 1964, r 84. **R v Secretary of State for the Home Dept, ex p Benwell** [1984] 3 854, QBD.

        Dismissal of employee—Employment by Crown—Dismissal of civil servant—Appeal to Civil Service Appeal Board—Board giving no reasons for decision that dismissal fair—Whether board's decision susceptible to judicial review. **R v Civil Service Appeal Board, ex p Bruce (A-G intervening)** [1988] 3 686, QBD.

        Employment by Crown—Internal disciplinary proceedings—Whether civil servant employed under contract of employment—Whether conduct of internal disciplinary proceedings in civil service subject to judicial review. **R v Lord Chancellor's Dept, ex p Nangle** [1992] 1 897, QBD.

    Exclusion by statute—

        Public right of way order—Validity of order not to be 'questioned in any legal proceedings whatsoever' until order confirmed—Order not confirmed—Applicants applying for judicial review to quash order—Whether court having jurisdiction to grant judicial review before order confirmed—Wildlife and Countryside Act 1981, Sch 15, para 12(3). **R v Cornwall CC, ex p Huntington** [1994] 1 694, CA.

    Exercise of discretion on behalf of Crown—

        Inland Revenue Commissioners—Powers to initiate machinery for cancellation of tax advantage—Assurance given to taxpayer by Revenue in 1978 that no further investigation would be made into sale of certain shares—Taxpayer forgoing claims for tax relief in reliance on assurance—Revenue deciding in 1982 to reopen investigation into sale of shares—Whether court could review decision to reopen investigation—Whether decision to reopen investigation an abuse of power—Income and Corporation Taxes Act 1970, ss 460, 465. **Preston v IRC** [1985] 2 327, HL.

    Football Association—

        Decision to set up new football league—Football Association deciding to set up Premier League run by Football Association and not by Football League—Football League seeking judicial review of Football Association's decision to set up and run new Premier League—Whether Football Association's decisions susceptible to judicial review. **R v Football Association Ltd, ex p Football League Ltd** [1993] 2 833, Ch D and QBD.

    Immigration Appeal Tribunal. *See* **Immigration** (Appeal—Immigration Appeal Tribunal—Judicial review).

    Investigatory Powers Tribunal. *See* **Investigatory Powers** (Investigatory Powers Tribunal—Exercise of tribunal's jurisdiction).

    Jockey Club—

        Disciplinary proceedings against local steward—Jockey Club withdrawing applicant's name from list of persons approved to act as chairmen of stewards at race meetings—Whether Jockey Club's decisions susceptible to judicial review—Whether Jockey Club's decisions within sphere of public law. **R v Disciplinary Committee of the Jockey Club, ex p Massingberd-Mundy** [1993] 2 207, QBD.

        Disqualification of racehorse found to be doped—Owner and trainer not found to be at fault—Owner seeking judicial review of decision to disqualify horse—Whether Jockey Club's decisions susceptible to judicial review—Whether Jockey Club's decisions within sphere of public law. **R v Disciplinary Committee of the Jockey Club, ex p Aga Khan** [1993] 2 853, CA.

        Licensing of racecourses—Legitimate expectation—Jockey Club carrying out policy review of fixture list—Jockey Club accepting report that additional 60 fixtures ought to be allocated in 1990 and 1991 seasons—Applicant wishing to establish new racecourse and applying for additional fixtures to be allocated to new course—Jockey Club refusing to allocate fixtures to new course—Whether report raising legitimate expectation that Jockey Club would grant fixtures for applicant's new racecourse—Whether Jockey Club's decisions susceptible to judicial review. **R v Jockey Club, ex p RAM Racecourses Ltd** [1993] 2 225, QBD.

    Justiciable issue—

        Legal Aid Board—Solicitors' tender to legal aid committee to act for generic plaintiffs—Committee refusing tender—Whether committee's decision justiciable—Whether decision within domain of private or public law—If so, whether decision-making process flawed. **R v Legal Aid Board, ex p Donn & Co (a firm)** [1996] 3 1, QBD.

JUDICIAL REVIEW (cont)—
  Availability of remedy (cont)—
    Legitimate expectation—
      Change of government policy—Policy permitting transfer of fishing licences between vessels—Trawler holding miscellaneous licence with no track record of North Sea beam trawling—Applicant hoping to transfer aggregation of beam trawl licence entitlements to trawler—Ministry of Agriculture changing policy to licensing by track record—Applicant in process of aggregating beam trawl licence entitlements for transfer to trawler—Whether applicant's expectation that government policy would not frustrate its plans legitimate—Whether pipe-line provisions should have been included in policy to protect transaction already in progress—Approach of decision-maker to making exceptions to policy. **R v Ministry of Agriculture Fisheries and Food, ex p Hamble (Offshore) Fisheries Ltd** [1995] **2** 714, QBD.
      Denial of legitimate expectation—Minister exercising prerogative power to deprive civil servants of benefits of trade union membership—Minister not consulting civil servants before acting—Whether civil servants having legitimate expectation that they would be consulted—Whether denial of legitimate expectation grounds for judicial review. **Council of Civil Service Unions v Minister for the Civil Service** [1984] **3** 935, HL.
      Denial of legitimate expectation—Severely disabled patient moving to new facility after receiving health authority assurance that she could live there for as long as she chose—Authority deciding to close new facility—Whether breach of assurance constituting abuse of power—European Convention on Human Rights and Fundamental Freedoms, art 8. **R v North and East Devon Health Authority, ex p Coughlan (Secretary of State for Health intervening)** [2000] **3** 850, CA.
      Expectation of consultation—Minister directing Greater London Council to make grant to London Regional Transport—Direction stipulating maximum grant permitted under statute—Council not given opportunity to make representations that less than maximum grant should be directed—Whether council having legitimate expectation that it would be consulted before direction made—London Regional Transport Act 1984, s 49. **R v Secretary of State for Transport, ex p Greater London Council** [1985] **3** 300, QBD.
      Interception of telephone calls—Warrant to intercept telephone calls issued by Secretary of State—Criteria governing issue of warrants—Whether criteria giving rise to legitimate expectation—Whether doctrine of legitimate expectation confined to cases where there is a right to be consulted or opportunity to make representations—Whether warrant issued in breach of criteria—Whether Secretary of State guilty of misfeasance in a public office. **R v Secretary of State for the Home Dept, ex p Ruddock** [1987] **2** 518, QBD.
    Magistrate declining jurisdiction to hear information—
      Whether appropriate remedy application for judicial review or appeal by way of case stated. **R v Clerkenwell Metropolitan Stipendiary Magistrate, ex p DPP** [1984] **2** 193, QBD.
    Mandamus—
      Wrongful dismissal of police constable—Rules of natural justice not observed in dismissal procedure—Impractical to order reinstatement—Whether mandamus should be issued requiring constable to be reinstated—Whether constable merely entitled to declaration that he was entitled to rights and remedies not including reinstatement. **Chief Constable of North Wales Police v Evans** [1982] **3** 141, HL.
    Ministerial Code—
      Declaration sought as regards whether Prime Minister correctly interpreting part of code dealing with bullying—Whether issue justiciable—Whether Prime Minister wrongly interpreting code. **R (on the application of the FDA) v Prime Minister and Minister for the Civil Service** [2022] **3** 675, DC.
    National security—
      Exclusion order—Northern Ireland politician linked to acts of terrorism in Northern Ireland—Secretary of State prohibiting entry of politician into United Kingdom—Secretary of State omitting to provide reasons for his decision to make exclusion order—Whether decision amenable to judicial review—Whether Secretary of State required to give reasons for decision and thereby disclose sensitive intelligence information—Prevention of Terrorism (Temporary Provisions) Act 1989, s 5. **R v Secretary of State for the Home Dept, ex p Adams** [1995] **EC** 177, QBD.
      Exercise of prerogative on grounds of national security—Whether national security preventing judicial review of exercise of prerogative. **Council of Civil Service Unions v Minister for the Civil Service** [1984] **3** 935, HL.
      Exercise of prerogative on grounds of national security—Applicant and family in danger of attack by members of terrorist organisations while living in Northern Ireland—Secretary of State suspecting applicant of involvement in terrorist activities—Secretary of State making exclusion order preventing applicant from entering Great Britain—Applicant seeking judicial review—Whether court entitled to consider Secretary of State's reasons for making order—Prevention of Terrorism (Temporary Provisions) Act 1989, s 5. **R v Secretary of State for the Home Dept, ex p McQuillan** [1995] **4** 400, QBD.
      Warrant to intercept telephone calls issued by Secretary of State—No admission made as to existence of warrant by Secretary of State on grounds of national security—Whether national security preventing judicial review of exercise of power to issue warrant. **R v Secretary of State for the Home Dept, ex p Ruddock** [1987] **2** 518, QBD.
    Overseas aid—
      Ministerial decision to grant overseas aid—Foreign Secretary deciding to approve grant of aid to Pergau dam scheme in Malaysia—Foreign Secretary having regard to political implications when deciding to approve grant of aid—Scheme economically unsound—Whether grant of aid for scheme lawful—Overseas Development and Co-operation Act 1980, s 1. **R v Secretary of State for Foreign Affairs, ex p World Development Movement Ltd** [1995] **1** 611, QBD.
    Parliamentary Commissioner for Standards—
      Relationship between Parliament and courts—Complainant dissatisfied with conclusion of the commissioner's investigation into complaint—Commissioner an independent person appointed by Parliament to exercise an investigative function—Whether commissioner's activities susceptible to judicial review—Bill of Rights (1688), s 1, art 9. **R v Parliamentary Comr for Standards, ex p Al Fayed** [1998] **1** 93, CA.

JUDICIAL REVIEW (cont)—

Availability of remedy (cont)—

Policy documents and statements of practice—

Grounds for review—Test to be applied. **R (on the application of A) v Secretary of State for the Home Dept** [2022] **1** 177, SC; **R (on the application of BF (Eritrea)) v Secretary of State for the Home Dept (Equality and Human Rights Commission intervening)** [2022] **1** 213, SC.

Public authority—

Dismissal of employee—Whether employee entitled to judicial review of dismissal. *See* Availability of remedy—Employment by public authority, *above.*

Operation of air and sea ports—Ban on lawful trade in livestock in response to unlawful protest by animal rights campaigners—Whether public authorities operating air and sea ports entitled to ban lawful trade. **R v Coventry City Council, ex p Phoenix Aviation** [1995] **3** 37, QBD.

Quashing of committal proceedings—

Misreception of evidence—Defendant suffering real injustice—Whether certiorari lying to quash committal. **Neill v North Antrim Magistrates' Court** [1992] **4** 846, HL.

Misreception of inadmissible evidence—No other evidence supporting committal—Witness statements served after committal—Whether certiorari lying to quash committal—Whether flaw in committal proceedings cured by subsequent service of witness statements—Magistrates' Courts Act 1980, s 6(1). **Williams v Bedwellty Justices** [1996] **3** 737, HL.

Royal prerogative—

Prerogative of mercy—Home Secretary's decision not to grant posthumous conditional pardon—Whether Home Secretary's decision susceptible to judicial review—Whether grant of pardon dependent on moral and technical innocence of crime committed. **R v Secretary of State for the Home Dept, ex p Bentley** [1993] **4** 442, QBD.

Scheduling of ancient monument—

Secretary of State's refusal to schedule site containing remains of Elizabethan theatre as a national monument—Applicant seeking judicial review of the Secretary of State's decision—Whether applicant having locus standi to apply for judicial review—Whether applicant having sufficient interest to apply for judicial review—Whether Secretary of State having broad discretion not to schedule monument once it was shown to be of national importance—Whether Secretary of State taking into account irrelevant factors in deciding not to schedule site—Ancient Monuments and Archaeological Areas Act 1979, s 1(1), (3)—Supreme Court Act 1981, s 31(3). **R v Secretary of State for the Environment, ex p Rose Theatre Trust Co** [1990] **1** 754, QBD.

Special Commissioner—

Special Commissioner in London postponing tax assessment raised in Scotland—Postponement application heard in London a request of taxpayer's advisers—Taxpayer applying to English court for judicial review of commissioner's decision—Whether English court having jurisdiction to review commissioner's decision—Whether application for judicial review should be stayed. **R v Comr for the Special Purposes of the Income Tax Acts, ex p R W Forsyth Ltd** [1987] **1** 1035, QBD.

Statutory appeal—

Immigration. *See* **Immigration** (Leave to remain—Appeal —Removal of certain persons unlawfully in the United Kingdom).

Take-over Panel—

Panel on Take-overs and Mergers a self-regulating unincorporated association operating City Code on Take-overs and Mergers—Whether panel performing public duty—Whether panel amenable to public law remedies—Whether panel's decisions subject to judicial review. **R v Panel on Take-overs and Mergers, ex p Datafin plc (Norton Opax plc intervening)** [1987] **1** 564, CA.

Panel refusing to adjourn hearing held to determine whether company's take-over affected by operation of concert party in breach of Take-over Code—Company applying for judicial review of panel's decision to refuse adjournment—Company not exercising right of appeal to panel's appeal committee—Whether panel's refusal to grant adjournment causing injustice—Whether panel's decision subject to judicial review. **R v Panel on Take-overs and Mergers, ex p Guinness plc** [1989] **1** 509, CA.

Upper Tribunal—

Amenability of Upper Tribunal to judicial review—Jurisdiction of High Court—Whether decisions of Upper Tribunal amenable to judicial review by High Court—Scope of High Court's power judicially to review decisions of Upper Tribunal—Tribunals, Courts and Enforcement Act 2007, ss 3(5), 25(1)(a). **R (on the application of Cart) v Upper Tribunal (Secretary of State for Justice and anor, interested parties) (Public Law Project, intervening)** [2010] **4** 714, CA; [2011] **4** 127, SC.

Bail—

Jurisdiction to grant bail in connection with judicial review proceedings. *See* **Bail** (Jurisdiction to grant bail—Judicial review proceedings).

Certiorari—

Generally. *See* **Certiorari**.

Challenge to validity of public authority's decision—

Circumvention of judicial review procedure—

Commissioners demanding payment of excise duty on hydrocarbon oil delivered to plaintiff—Plaintiff claiming entitlement to relief from payment on grounds that use of oil a 'qualifying use'—Commissioners refusing relief—Plaintiff bringing action for restitution claiming repayment of duty paid—Whether private law remedy available—Whether decision of commissioners amenable to judicial review—Hydrocarbon Oil Duties Act 1979, ss 6, 9. **British Steel plc v Customs and Excise Comrs** [1997] **2** 366, CA.

Decision of public authority challenged in defence to action brought by it—Defendant occupying council flat—Local authority resolving to increase rent of flat—Defendant refusing to pay increase—Local authority bringing claim for arrears of rent—Whether defendant entitled to challenge validity of resolution increasing rent by way of defence to claim for arrears of rent—Whether defendant only entitled to challenge validity of resolution by way of application for judicial review—RSC Ord 53. **Wandsworth London BC v Winder** [1984] **3** 976, HL.

JUDICIAL REVIEW (cont)—
  Challenge to validity of public authority's decision (cont)—
    Circumvention of judicial review procedure (cont)—
      Telecommunications companies asking Director General of Telecommunications to resolve dispute as to construction of terms of licence to run telecommunications system—Plaintiff company challenging Director's determination and issuing originating summons seeking declaration as to proper construction of terms of licence—Whether private law remedy available—Whether Director's determination amenable to judicial review—Whether action to be struck out as abuse of process of court—RSC Ord 53. **Mercury Communications Ltd v Director General of Telecommunications** [1996] **1** 575, HL.
    Decision to institute proceedings—
      Challenge by defendant to proceedings—Whether defendant should challenge decision by way of judicial review or defence in action. **Waverley BC v Hilden** [1988] **1** 807, Ch D.
    Local authority approving reduction in youth services budget—
      Claimant seeking judicial review of decision—Claim dismissed—Court of Appeal finding in favour of claimant on substantive issues but refusing to make quashing order—Court of Appeal refusing to grant alternative relief—Whether Court of Appeal should have made declaration that authority failing in its statutory obligations—Whether Court of Appeal erring in failing to make order for costs in claimant's favour. **R (on the application of Hunt) v North Somerset Council** [2016] **1** 95, SC.
  Chief Rabbi's decision—
    Whether Chief Rabbi's decisions susceptible to judicial review. *See* Availability of remedy—Chief Rabbi, *above*.
  Circumvention of judicial review procedure—
    Challenge to validity of public authority's decision. *See* Challenge to validity of public authority's decision—Circumvention of judicial review procedure, *above*.
    Declaration. *See* Declaration—Circumvention of judicial review procedure, *below*.
  Closed material procedure—
    Proceedings in a criminal cause or matter. *See* Jurisdiction—Proceedings in a criminal cause or matter, *below*.
  Commissioner for Local Administration—
    Report of commissioner on complaint of maladministration by local authority—
      Whether report susceptible to judicial review. *See* **Local government** (Maladministration—Complaint to local commissioner—Commissioner's report).
  Community Legal Service Funding. *See* **Community legal service funding** (Criteria—Judicial review).
  Coroner's inquest—
    Generally. *See* **Coroner** (Inquest—Judicial review).
    Whether coroner's decision indicating appearance of bias. *See* **Coroner** (Inquest—Bias—Judicial review).
  Costs—
    Compromise of action. *See* Costs (Order for costs—Compromise—Consent order—Judicial review).
    Costs of application. *See* Costs of application, *below*.
    Costs orders for or against inferior courts or tribunals. *See* **Costs** (Order for costs—Discretion—Costs orders for or against inferior courts or tribunals appearing in public law proceedings).
    Discretion. *See* **Costs** (Order for costs—Discretion).
    Divisional Court—
      Jurisdiction—Generally. *See* **Divisional Court** (Function—Review of decisions of courts or bodies exercising public law functions—Court of Appeal or court of first instance—Judicial review—Costs).
      Set-off—Separate proceedings. *See* **Costs** (Set-off—Separate proceedings—Costs of judicial review proceedings).
    Payment by justices. *See* **Magistrates** (Costs—Payment by justices—Appeal by way of case stated—Judicial review proceedings).
  Costs of application—
    Application abandoned—
      Revenue delaying determination on company's liability to tax—Company granted leave to apply for judicial review—No warning of proceedings given to Revenue—Revenue making determination in company's favour after granting of leave—Company abandoning application—Whether company entitled to costs of application for judicial review. **R v IRC, ex p Opman International UK** [1986] **1** 328, QBD.
    Application for permission for judicial review—
      Costs incurred prior to grant of permission—Costs awarded to defendant after full judicial review proceedings—Award of pre-permission costs—Guidance. **Davey v Aylesbury Vale DC** [2008] **2** 178, CA.
    Pre-emptive order for costs—
      Protective costs order—Governing principles—Requirements of general public interest and exceptionality—Procedure in Court of Appeal—Guidance. **R (on the application of Compton) v Wiltshire Primary Care Trust** [2009] **1** 978, CA.
      Protective costs order—Guidance. **R (on the application of Corner House Research) v Secretary of State for Trade and Industry** [2005] **4** 1, CA.
      Protective costs order—Principles—Proceedings to be not prohibitively expensive—Nature of test—Council Directive (EEC) 85/337—Council Directive (EC) 96/61. **R (on the application of Garner) v Elmbridge BC** [2011] **3** 418, CA.
      Protective costs order—Principles—Proceedings to be not prohibitively expensive—Nature of test—Jurisdiction of Supreme Court costs officers—Supreme Court Rules 2009, SI 2009/1603—Council Directive (EEC) 85/337—Council Directive (EC) 96/61. **R (on the application of Edwards) v Environment Agency (No 2)** [2014] **1** 760, SC.
      Protective costs order—Principles—Proceedings to be not prohibitively expensive—Nature of test—Jurisdiction of Supreme Court costs officers—Supreme Court Rules 2009, SI 2009/1603—Council Directive (EEC) 85/337—Council Directive (EC) 96/61. **R (on the application of Edwards) v Environment Agency** [2011] **1** 785n, SC.

JUDICIAL REVIEW (cont)—
Costs of application (cont)—
Pre-emptive order for costs (cont)—
Protective costs order—Whether and in what circumstances court could make such an order in favour of defendant in public law proceedings. **R (on the application of Ministry of Defence) v Wiltshire and Swindon Coroner (Craik and ors, interested parties)** [2005] **4** 40, QBD.
Public interest challenge—Applicants applying for order that no order for costs be made against them whatever outcome of application—Principles to be applied in exercise of court's discretion—Whether pre-emptive orders should be made—RSC Ord 62, r 3(3). **R v Lord Chancellor, ex p Child Poverty Action Group** [1998] **2** 755, QBD.
Crown Court order—
Order preventing publication of details calculated to lead to identification of child or young person—Whether 'a matter relating to trial on indictment'—Whether order subject to judicial review. *See* **Crown Court** (Supervisory jurisdiction of High Court—Trial on indictment—High Court having no supervisory jurisdiction in matters relating to trial on indictment—Order preventing publication of details calculated to lead to identification of child or young person).
Crown prerogative. *See* **Crown** (Prerogative—Review of exercise of prerogative power by court).
Declaration—
Circumvention of judicial review procedure—
Action for declaration circumventing procedure for judicial review—Plaintiffs found guilty of disciplinary offences and penalties imposed by board of prison visitors—Plaintiffs commencing action by writ and originating summons for declaration that board's findings and awards null and void by reason of breach of natural justice—Application by board to strike out actions as abuse of court's process—Whether judicial review the only remedy to impugn adjudications by prison visitors—RSC Ord 53. **O'Reilly v Mackman** [1982] **3** 680, QBD and CA; [1982] **3** 1124, HL.
Landowner applying to Chancery Division for declaration entitling him to have land removed from commons register—Whether landowner required to apply to Queen's Bench Division for judicial review. **Tillmire Common, Heslington, Re** [1982] **2** 615, Ch D.
Plaintiff bringing action for damages in negligence against local authority for advice given in respect of enforcement notice—Local authority seeking to strike out statement of claim on ground that abuse of the process of the court—Whether claim in negligence involving public or private rights—Whether plaintiff entitled to protection of public law and therefore unable to defend right by way of ordinary action. **Davy v Spelthorne BC** [1983] **3** 278, HL.
Plaintiff found guilty of disciplinary offences by board of prison visitors—Plaintiff issuing writ in Chancery Division claiming declaration that adjudication of board null and void—Application by board for order to stop plaintiff proceeding except by way of application for judicial review in Queen's Bench Division—Whether proceedings in Chancery Division should be allowed to continue—RSC Ord 53. **Heywood v Hull Prison Board of Visitors** [1980] **3** 594, Ch D.
Locus standi—
Sufficient interest—Revenue introducing special arrangement to prevent tax evasion by certain casual workers in future—Revenue agreeing not to assess and collect tax due from workers in respect of years prior to April 1977—Taxpayers' association applying for judicial review in form of declaration that Revenue acting unlawfully in agreeing not to assess and collect tax due from workers—Whether applicants having 'sufficient interest' to apply for judicial review—RSC Ord 53, r 3(5). **IRC v National Federation of Self-Employed and Small Businesses Ltd** [1981] **2** 93, HL.
Sufficient interest—United Kingdom undertaking to finance supplementary budget of European Community from Consolidated Fund—Undertaking purporting to be a treaty 'ancillary' to Community treaties—United Kingdom taxpayer seeking judicial review of determination that undertaking is ancillary to Community treaties—Whether taxpayer having sufficient locus standi. **R v HM Treasury, ex p Smedley** [1985] **1** 589, CA.
Delay—
Point at which time starts to run—
Challenge to rate paid to immigration detainees for work done while in detention—Whether time running from point at which rate set or when claimant first becoming affected by it. **R (on the application of Badmus) v Secretary of State for the Home Dept** [2021] **1** 1193, CA.
Reasons for delay—
Application to set out reasons for delay—Extension of time—Consent of proposed respondent—Application by proposed respondent to set aside leave or direction given—RSC Ord 53, r 4. **Practice Note** [1983] **2** 1020, QBD.
Refusal of relief—
Application for judicial review of decision of Criminal Injuries Compensation Board—Undue delay—Court satisfied good reason existing for delay—Court extending time limit and granting leave to apply—Whether on hearing of substantive application in absence of hardship, prejudice or detriment, undue delay in itself sufficient basis for refusing relief—Whether failure of police to give accurate evidence capable of rendering board's decision unfair—Supreme Court Act 1981, s 31(6)—RSC Ord 53, r 4(1). **R v Criminal Injuries Compensation Board, ex p A** [1997] **3** 745, CA.
Grant of relief likely substantially to prejudice rights of another person—Application to review decision of Secretary of State—Applicants applying for judicial review more than six months after Secretary of State's decision—Applicants guilty of undue delay—Whether court should refuse relief—Whether grant of relief likely substantially to prejudice rights of respondent—Whether causal connection required between prejudice and delay—Supreme Court Act 1981, s 31(6)—RSC Ord 53, r 4(1). **R v Secretary of State for Health, ex p Furneaux** [1994] **2** 652, CA.
Grant of relief likely to be detrimental to good administration—Application to review decision of Dairy Produce Quota Tribunal fixing quota for dairy farm—Tribunal misconstruing regulations—Applicants applying for leave to apply for judicial review more than two years after tribunal's decision—Whether undue delay in applying for leave—Whether grant of relief likely to be detrimental to good administration—Supreme Court Act 1981, s 31(6)—RSC Ord 53, r 4(1). **Caswell v Dairy Produce Quota Tribunal for England and Wales** [1990] **2** 434, HL.
Disciplinary proceedings—
Judicial review of decision in disciplinary proceedings—
Availability of remedy—Alternative remedy available. *See* Availability of remedy—Alternative remedy available—Discretion of court to grant relief—Disciplinary proceedings, *above*.
Generally. *See* Availability of remedy—Disciplinary proceedings, *above*.

Disciplinary proceedings (cont)—
    Police disciplinary proceedings. *See* **Police** (Discipline—Disciplinary proceedings—Judicial review of decision in disciplinary proceedings).
Disclosure of documents. *See* **Disclosure and inspection of documents** (Judicial review proceedings).
Duty to give reasons—
    Civil Service Appeal Board—
        Board deciding unfair dismissal claims by Crown servants—Whether board under duty to give reasons when deciding whether dismissal of Crown servant fair or unfair and, if unfair, when assessing amount of compensation—Employment Protection (Consolidation) Act 1978, s 146. **R v Civil Service Appeal Board, ex p Cunningham** [1991] **4** 310, CA.
    Higher Education Funding Council—
        Council assessing quality of institutional research of university and other institutions to determine research grants—Council deciding to lower applicant institute's rating for grant purposes—Whether council under duty to give reasons for decision. **R v Higher Education Funding Council, ex p Institute of Dental Surgery** [1994] **1** 651, QBD.
    Local authority—
        Local authority refusing discretionary grant for university education—Local authority stating merely that it considered circumstances of case—Whether local authority must disclose reasons—Education Act 1962, s 1(6). **R v Lancashire CC, ex p Huddleston** [1986] **2** 941, CA.
Equal Opportunities Commission—
    Locus standi of commission to apply for judicial review. *See* Application for judicial review—Locus standi of applicant—Equal Opportunities Commission, *above*.
Estoppel—
    Issue estoppel. *See* **Estoppel** (Issue estoppel—Judicial review).
European Union—
    European structural and investment funds. *See* **European Union** (European Structural and Investment Funds).
Evidence—
    Evidence in support of claim for relief—
        Record of proceedings in Parliament—Admissibility—Applicant claiming relief in respect of something done outside Parliament—Applicant relying on statements made in Parliament and recorded in Hansard to support his claim—Whether Hansard can be used to support claim for judicial review. **R v Secretary of State for Trade, ex p Anderson Strathclyde plc** [1983] **2** 233, QBD.
    Expert evidence—
        Decision challenged on basis of technical error—Whether expert evidence admissible—Procedure to be followed—CPR Pt 35. **R (on the application of the Law Society) v Lord Chancellor** [2019] **1** 638, DC.
    Fresh evidence—
        Categories of fresh evidence admissible on judicial review—Expert evidence in truly technical field. **R (on the application of Lynch) v General Dental Council** [2004] **1** 1159, QBD.
    Certiorari. *See* **Certiorari** (Evidence—Fresh evidence—Judicial review).
Exhaustion of alternative remedies. *See* Availability of remedy—Alternative remedy available, *above*.
Exhumation licence. *See* **Burial** (Exhumation licence).
Extradition order. *See* **Extradition** (Extradition order—Judicial review).
Football Association—
    Judicial review of Football Association's decision—
        Availability of remedy. *See* Availability of remedy—Football Association, *above*.
Higher Education Funding Council—
    Duty to give reasons. *See* Duty to give reasons—Higher Education Funding Council, *above*.
House of Lords—
    Jurisdiction—
        Appeal from Court of Appeal, Civil Division. *See* **House of Lords** (Appeal from Court of Appeal, Civil Division—Jurisdiction—Judicial review).
Housing authority's decision in respect of homeless person—
    Decision adverse to applicant—
        Whether applicant's only remedy application for judicial review. *See* **Housing** (Homeless person—Duty of housing authority to provide accommodation—Remedy for breach of duty).
Human rights proceedings—
    Procedure. *See* **Human rights** (Infringement of human rights—Judicial acts—Procedure).
Immigration—
    Removal directions. *See* **Immigration** (Deportation—Judicial review applications against removal directions).
Information—
    Power to require information—
        Production of documents—Inspector issuing notice to claimants to produce documents relevant to tax avoidance scheme—Documents including communications between claimants and accountants advising on tax law—Claimants objecting on grounds that documents covered by legal professional privilege—Whether legal professional privilege extending to legal advice on tax given by accountants. **R (on the application of Prudential plc) v Special Comr of Income Tax** [2010] **1** 1113, QBD.
        Production of documents—Inspector issuing notice to claimants to produce documents relevant to tax avoidance scheme—Documents including communications between claimants and accountants advising on tax law—Claimants objecting on grounds that documents covered by legal professional privilege—Whether legal professional privilege extending to legal advice on tax given by accountants—Human Rights Act 1998, Sch 1, Pt I, art 8. **R (on the application of Prudential plc) v Special Comr of Income Tax** [2011] **1** 316, CA.
        Production of documents—Inspector issuing notice to claimants to produce documents relevant to tax avoidance scheme—Documents including communications between claimants and accountants advising on tax law—Claimants objecting on grounds that documents covered by legal professional privilege—Whether legal professional privilege extending to legal advice on tax given by accountants. **R (on the application of Prudential plc) v Special Comr of Income Tax** [2013] **2** 247, SC.

JUDICIAL REVIEW (cont)—
  Injunction—
    Interim injunction against officer of Crown—
      Jurisdiction to grant injunction against officer of Crown in judicial review proceedings. *See* **Crown**
      (Relief against the Crown—Interlocutory relief—Jurisdiction—Injunction against officer of the
      Crown—Interim injunction—Judicial review proceedings).
    Interlocutory injunction to restrain publication of public authority's decision pending outcome of
    judicial review proceedings. *See* **Injunction** (Interlocutory—Pending proceedings—Judicial review).
  Jockey Club decision—
    Whether Jockey Club's decisions susceptible to judicial review. *See* Availability of remedy—Jockey
    Club, *above*.
  Jurisdiction—
    Crown Court order—
      Extent of High Court's supervisory jurisdiction. *See* **Crown Court** (Supervisory jurisdiction of High
      Court).
    Jurisdiction of Divisional Court—
      Jurisdiction of English court over execution of Scottish warrant in England—Act of
      Union—Applicant committing offences in Scotland—Warrant for arrest issued in Scotland—
      Applicant forcibly returned to England from South Africa without recourse to lawful extradition
      procedures—Applicant seeking injunction restraining police from executing Scottish warrant in
      England—Whether execution of warrant an abuse of process of English court—Whether English
      court having power to prevent execution of Scottish warrant in England—Union with Scotland
      Act 1706, art XIX. **R v Comr of Police of the Metropolis, ex p Bennett** [1995] **3** 248, QBD.
    Proceedings in a criminal cause or matter—
      Judicial review of decision not to bring criminal prosecution—Application for closed material
      procedure—Whether judicial review 'proceedings in a criminal cause or matter'—Justice and
      Security Act 2013, s 6. **R (on the application of Belhaj) v DPP** [2018] **4** 561, SC.
    Review of order of local election court—
      Direction as to costs. *See* **Elections** (Election court—Election court for local election—Election court
      making ultra vires direction as to costs—Application for judicial review—Jurisdiction of High
      Court to grant judicial review).
  Jurisdiction of High Court—
    Trial on indictment, matters relating to. *See* **Crown Court** (Supervisory jurisdiction of High Court—Trial
    on indictment).
  Justiciable issue—
    Crown prerogative. *See* **Crown** (Prerogative—Review of exercise of prerogative power by court).
  Landlord and tenant—
    Registered social landlord. *See* **Human rights** (Public authority—Private person performing functions of
    public nature—Registered social landlord bringing action against tenant for possession on
    mandatory grounds).
  Leave to apply for judicial review—
    Affidavit in reply—
      Time for filing affidavit—Increase in time for filing—Extension of time only to be granted in
      exceptional circumstances—Hearing applications for extension of time—Abridgment of time
      where expedited hearing ordered—RSC Ord 3, r 5, Ord 53, r 6(1), (4)—RSC (Amendment) 1989.
      Practice Note [1989] **1** 1024, QBD.
    Application. *See* Application for judicial review—Application for leave to apply for judicial review,
    above.
    Circumstances in which leave may be granted—
      Decision of income tax commissioner—Decision to grant Revenue leave to issue assessment out of
      time—No provision for appeal of grant of leave to issue assessment—Provision for appeal
      against assessment precluding question of discharge of grant of leave to issue
      assessment—Taxpayer contending there was no evidence to justify grant of leave to issue
      assessment—Whether taxpayer should be granted leave to apply for judicial review of
      commissioner's decision—Taxes Management Act 1970, s 41—Income and Corporation Taxes Act
      1970, s 247(3). **R v Comr for the Special Purposes of the Income Tax Acts, ex p Stipplechoice Ltd**
      [1985] **2** 465, CA.
    Ex parte applications—
      Listing of applications—Time allowed for applications—Counsel to provide written estimate and
      special fixture to be arranged where application requiring more than 20 minutes. **Practice Note**
      [1991] **1** 1055, QBD.
    Matrimonial and family matters—
      Practice—Applications to contain request that matter be dealt with by judge of Family Division. **R v**
      Dover Magistrates' Court, ex p Kidner [1983] **1** 475, QBD.
    Point of law of general public importance—
      Application to Divisional Court for permission to bring judicial review proceedings where applicant
      seeking to overturn previous decision of Supreme Court—Proper approach of court. **R (on the**
      application of Al Rabbat) v City of Westminster Magistrates' Court [2017] **4** 1084, QBD.
    Procedure for challenging grant of leave—
      Applicant granted discovery pending hearing of application for judicial review—Respondents
      appealing against order for discovery—Respondents seeking on appeal to challenge grant of
      leave to apply for judicial review—Whether court having urisdiction on discovery appeal to set
      aside grant of leave to apply for judicial review—Supreme Court Act 1981, s 16(1)—RSC Ord 53,
      r 3. **R v Secretary of State for the Home Dept, ex p Herbage (No 2)** [1987] **1** 324, CA.
    Promptness—
      Whether application for judicial review launched sufficiently promptly. **Mauritius Shipping**
      Corporation Ltd v Employment Relations Tribunal [2020] **1** 844, PC.
    Refusal—
      Appeal—Grant of leave by Court of Appeal—Hearing of substantive application—Practice—
      Substantive application normally to be heard by single judge. **Practice Note** [1990] **1** 128, CA.
      Appeal—Grant of leave by Court of Appeal—Hearing of substantive application—Practice—
      Substantive application normally to be made to Divisional Court. **Practice Direction** [1982] **3** 800,
      CA.

JUDICIAL REVIEW (cont)—
Leave to apply for judicial review (cont)—
  Renewal of application—
    Application for leave made to and refused by Court of Appeal—Further application for leave to be made to Court of Appeal. **M v Home Office** [1992] **4** 97, QBD and CA.
  Sufficient interest—
    Application to challenge decision to cancel listing of shares by stock exchange—Applicant overcoming restrictions on tardy applications—Whether application should fail on ground that applicant lacked sufficient interest in decision challenged—Supreme Court Act 1981, s 31(3)(6). **R v International Stock Exchange of the UK and the Republic of Ireland Ltd, ex p Else (1982) Ltd** [1993] **1** 420, CA.
  Undue delay—
    Delay due to difficulties in obtaining legal aid—Applicant not at fault—Whether delay in obtaining legal aid good reason for extending time limit—Whether leave to apply should be granted—RSC Ord 53, r 4(1). **R v Stratford-on-Avon DC, ex p Jackson** [1985] **3** 769, CA.
Legal aid—
  Civil legal services. *See* **Legal aid** (Civil legal services—Judicial review).
  Entitlement. *See* **Legal aid** (Entitlement—Judicial review).
Legal Aid Board—
  Judicial review of decision—
    Availability of remedy. *See* Availability of remedy—Justiciable issue—Legal Aid Board, *above*.
Legitimate expectation—
  HMRC guidance—
    Taxpayer company receiving interest payments on loans made to US subsidiary—US imposing withholding tax on interest received—Taxpayer claiming double taxation relief in respect of US withholding tax—HMRC refusing claim on basis that legislation operating to prevent availability of relief—Whether HMRC manual containing representation giving rise to legitimate expectation—Whether taxpayer relying on relevant representation—Income and Corporation Taxes Act 1988, ss 790, 793A—Double Taxation Relief (Taxes on Income) (The United States of America) Order 2002, SI 2002/2848, art 23. **R (on the application of Aozora GMAC Investment Ltd) v Revenue and Customs Comrs** [2020] **1** 803, CA.
Local authority—
  Consultation. *See* **Natural justice** (Duty to act fairly—Consultation).
Locus standi of applicant. *See* Application for judicial review—Locus standi of applicant, *above*.
Lord Chancellor—
  Deployment of judges—
    High Court judge appointed to preside over fraud trial and ordering severance of counts in indictment at preparatory hearing—Trial proceeding in respect of two counts—Trial judge promoted to Court of Appeal during trial but continuing to sit as Crown Court judge until conclusion of trial at Lord Chancellor's request—Whether judge's refusal to deal with remaining counts in the absence of further request from Lord Chancellor unlawful—Whether trial of remaining counts 'ancillary matter relating to' first trial or 'proceedings arising out of' that trial—Whether Lord Chancellor's refusal to make request irrational—Supreme Court Act 1981, ss 8,9(1)(4)(7)—Criminal Justice Act 1987, s 7. **R v Lord Chancellor, ex p Maxwell** [1996] **4** 751, QBD.
Magistrates' proceedings. *See* **Magistrates** (Proceedings—Control by judicial review).
Matrimonial and family matters—
  Leave to apply for judicial review. *See* Leave to apply for judicial review—Matrimonial and family matters, *above*.
Mental health—
  Protection in respect of acts done in pursuance of statute—
    Extent of protection. *See* **Mental health** (Protection in respect of acts done in pursuance of statute—Extent of protection—Judicial review).
Panel on Take-overs and Mergers—
  Judicial review of panel's decision—
    Availability of remedy. *See* Availability of remedy—Take-over Panel, *above*.
Parliamentary Commissioner for Administration—
  Judicial review of commissioner's decision and report—
    Complainant dissatisfied with result of commissioner's investigation into her complaints—Whether court having jurisdiction to review commissioner's exercise of discretion—Whether court's power of review restricted to exceptional cases of abuse of discretion—Whether commissioner required to investigate all complaints made by complainant—Whether commissioner required to show draft report to complainant—Whether commissioner having power to reopen investigation without further referral by member of Parliament—Parliamentary Commissioner Act 1967, ss 5, 7, 10. **R v Parliamentary Comr for Administration, ex p Dyer** [1994] **1** 375, QBD.
Parliamentary Commissioner for Standards—
  Whether commissioner's activities susceptible to judicial review. *See* Availability of remedy—Parliamentary Commissioner for Standards, *above*.
Parties—
  Persons directly affected—
    Notice of motion required to be served on persons directly affected—Respondents bringing judicial review proceedings against local authority for refusal or failure to determine claims to housing benefit—Secretary of State applying to be joined as party as person directly affected by proceedings because of payment by him of subsidy to reimburse large proportion of housing benefit paid by local authorities—Whether Secretary of State directly affected by proceedings—Whether Secretary of State entitled to be joined as party to judicial review proceedings brought by respondents against local authority—RSC Ord 53, r 5(3). **R v Rent Officer Service, ex p Muldoon** [1996] **3** 498, HL.
Permission to bring judicial review proceedings. *See* Leave to apply for judicial review, *above*.
Practice—
  Concurrent wardship and judicial review proceedings. *See* **Ward of court** (Practice—Judicial review—Concurrent wardship and judicial review proceedings).

JUDICIAL REVIEW (cont)—
  Practice (cont)—
    Crown Office list—
      Uncontested proceedings. *See* **Practice** (Uncontested proceedings—Crown Office list—Civil proceedings—Judicial review, cases stated, statutory appeals etc).
    Leave to apply for judicial review. *See* Leave to apply for judicial review, *above*.
  Privy Council—
    Decision to recommend grant of Royal Charter. *See* **Privy Council** (Grant of Royal Charter—Decision of committee to recommend grant of charter to professional body).
  Proportionality, principle of—
    EU state aids. *See* **European Union** (State aids—Structural funds).
  Protection in respect of acts done in pursuance of statute—
    Mental health. *See* **Mental health** (Protection in respect of acts done in pursuance of statute—Extent of protection—Judicial review).
  Protective costs order. *See* Costs of application—Pre-emptive order for costs—Protective costs order, *above*.
  Radio Authority—
    Ban on political advertising—
      Advertising by Amnesty—Radio Authority deciding that Amnesty's objects political and banning advertising by Amnesty—Whether Radio Authority correctly interpreting statutory provisions—Whether Radio Authority's decision unreasonable—Broadcasting Act 1990, s 92(2)(a)(i). **R v Radio Authority, ex p Bull** [1997] 2 561, CA.
  Refusal of relief—
    Delay in applying for judicial review. *See* Delay—Refusal of relief, *above*.
    Dismissal of civil servant—
      Appeal to Civil Service Appeal Board—Complaint also made to industrial tribunal—High Court action commenced to enforce alleged compromise of industrial tribunal proceedings—Civil Service Appeal Board concluding that dismissal fair—Board giving no reasons for its decision—Application for judicial review of board's decision—Divisional Court dismissing application in view of other remedies being pursued—Whether Divisional Court properly exercising its jurisdiction in dismissing application. **R v Civil Service Appeal Board, ex p Bruce (A-G intervening)** [1989] 2 907, CA.
  Royal prerogative of mercy—
    Judicial review of Home Secretary's decision—
      Availability of remedy. *See* Availability of remedy—Royal prerogative—Prerogative of mercy, *above*.
  Search warrant—
    Income tax—
      Suspected offence. *See* **Income tax** (Offence—Fraud—Suspected offence—Warrant to enter and seize documents—Validity—Warrant not specifying offence suspected but drawn in general terms of provision empowering issue of warrant—Proceedings for judicial review of warrant and seizure).
  Social security commissioner's decision—
    Decision to refuse leave to appeal—
      Onus on applicant for judicial review. *See* **Social security** (Appeal—Decision of social security commissioner—Decision to refuse leave to appeal—No reasons given for decision—Judicial review of decision).
  Special Immigration Appeals Commission—
    Amenability of Special Immigration Appeals Commission to judicial review—
      Jurisdiction of High Court —Whether decisions of Special Immigration Appeals Commission amenable to judicial review by High Court—Special Immigration Appeals Commission Act 1997, s 1(3). **R (on the application of Cart) v Upper Tribunal (Secretary of State for Justice and anor, interested parties) (Public Law Project, intervening) and related claims** [2010] 1 908, DC.
    Disclosure of sensitive material—
      Review of certain naturalisation and citizenship decisions—Power of Secretary of State to certify decision to refuse naturalisation made in reliance on information which should not be made public in interests of national security—Secretary of State refusing applications for naturalisation—Claims for judicial review by naturalisation applicants dismissed—Appeals in judicial review proceedings stayed—Secretary of State certifying decisions—Entitlement of naturalisation applicants following certification to apply to Special Immigration Appeals Commission—Whether judicial review proceedings to continue—Special Immigration Appeals Commission Act 1997. **R (on the application of AHK) v Secretary of State for the Home Dept** [2014] 3 437, CA.
    Jurisdiction of High Court—
      Disclosure of sensitive material—Review of certain exclusion decisions—Power of Secretary of State to certify direction to exclude made in reliance on information which should not be made public in interests of national security—Certificate terminating judicial review proceedings relating to direction or decision to which certificate relating—Secretary of State deciding to exclude non-European Economic Area (EEA) national from United Kingdom on grounds conducive to public good—Non-EEA national commencing proceedings for judicial review—Secretary of State certifying direction—Whether certificate terminating proceedings for judicial review—Special Immigration Appeals Commission Act 1997, s 2C—Justice and Security Act 2013, ss 15, 19, Sch 3, para 4—Justice and Security Act (Commencement, Transitional and Savings Provisions) Order 2013, SI 2013/1482, art 4. **R (on the application of Ignaoua) v Secretary of State for the Home Dept** [2014] 1 649, QBD and CA.
  Stay of proceedings—
    Concurrent complaint to adjudicator. *See* University—Stay of proceedings—Concurrent complaint to Office of the Independent Adjudicator, *below*.
  Suitability of remedy—
    Challenge to validity of byelaw—
      Defendant in summary proceedings challenging validity of byelaw under which he has been charged—Whether judicial review appropriate means of challenging validity of byelaw. **R v Crown Court at Reading, ex p Hutchinson** [1988] 1 333, QBD.

JUDICIAL REVIEW (cont)—

Suitability of remedy (cont)—
Challenge to validity of stop notice under town and country planning legislation—
Whether judicial review appropriate means of challenging validity of stop notice. **R v Jenner** [1983] **2** 46, CA.

Tax—
Closure notice. *See* **Income tax** (Closure notice—Validity—Judicial review).

Terrorism—
Arrest—
Detention—Extension of detention—Police arresting terrorism suspects—Search warrant granting police authority to enter specified premises 'on one occasion'—District judge granting police applications for warrant of further detention and extension of warrant of further detention—Warrant of further detention granted partly on basis of information produced at closed hearing—Judicial review proceedings brought challenging legality of arrest and detention, width of search warrants and decisions to extend detention—Whether judicial review appropriate—Whether process of granting warrant of further detention lawful—Human Rights Act 1998, Sch 1, Pt I, art 5(4)—Terrorism Act 2000, s 41, Sch 8. **Sher v Chief Constable of Greater Manchester Police** [2011] **2** 364, DC.

University—
Stay of proceedings—
Concurrent complaint to Office of the Independent Adjudicator—Former students seeking judicial review of higher education providers' decisions terminating their courses of study—Judge ordering stay of judicial review proceedings pending conclusion of complaints to Office of the Independent Adjudicator—Whether judge erring in failing to take into account or give due weight to status of judicial review as remedy of last resort—Whether judge erring in guidance on timings and procedure. **R (on the application of Rafique-Aldawery) v St George's, University of London (Office of the Independent Adjudicator, interested party)** [2019] **2** 703, CA.

Upper Tribunal—
Amenability of Upper Tribunal to judicial review—
Jurisdiction of High Court —Whether decisions of Upper Tribunal amenable to judicial review by High Court—Tribunals, Courts and Enforcement Act 2007, s 3(5). **R (on the application of Cart) v Upper Tribunal (Secretary of State for Justice and anor, interested parties) (Public Law Project, intervening) and related claims** [2010] **1** 908, DC.

JUDICIAL SEPARATION

Generally. *See* **Husband and wife** (Judicial separation).

JUDICIAL TRUSTEE

See **Trust and trustee** (Judicial trustee).

JUDICIARY

Constitutional position. *See* **Constitutional law** (Constitution—Separation of powers).
Police, co-operation with—
European Community. *See* **European Union** (Police and judicial co-operation in criminal matters).

JURISDICTION

Adjudication—
Building contract. *See* **Building contract** (Adjudication—Jurisdiction).
Arbitration—
Appointment of arbitrator. *See* **Arbitration** (Arbitrator—Appointment—Jurisdiction of court).
Conflict of laws. *See* **Conflict of laws** (Foreign proceedings—Restraint of foreign proceedings—Jurisdiction—Arbitration).
Generally. *See* **Arbitration** (Jurisdiction).
Reference to arbitration. *See* **Arbitration** (Jurisdiction of court—Reference to arbitration).
Setting aside award. *See* **Arbitration** (Award—Setting aside award—Jurisdiction).
Asylum and Immigration Tribunal—
Appeal. *See* **Immigration** (Appeal—Asylum and Immigration Tribunal).
Company—
Scheme of arrangement. *See* **Company** (Scheme of arrangement—Jurisdiction).
Concurrent proceedings—
Assumption of jurisdiction—
Concurrent proceedings in same matter pending in courts of co-ordinate jurisdiction—Civil and criminal proceedings—Declaration sought whether conduct giving rise to criminal proceedings an offence—Issue in both proceedings a point of law—Whether civil court should assume jurisdiction notwithstanding criminal proceedings pending. **Imperial Tobacco Ltd v A-G** [1979] **2** 592, CA.
Conflict of laws—
Challenge to jurisdiction. *See* **Conflict of laws** (Jurisdiction—Challenge to jurisdiction).
Foreign proceedings. *See* **Conflict of laws** (Foreign proceedings—Restraint of foreign proceedings—Jurisdiction).
Generally. *See* **Conflict of laws** (Jurisdiction).
Prorogation of jurisdiction by agreement. *See* **Conflict of laws** (Jurisdiction—Prorogation of jurisdiction by agreement).
Conflict of laws. *See* **Conflict of laws** (Jurisdiction).
Court-martial—
Civil offence. *See* **Court-martial** (Civil offence—Jurisdiction).
Divorce. *See* **Divorce** (Jurisdiction).
Employment tribunal. *See* **Employment tribunal** (Jurisdiction).
European Union. *See* **European Union** (Jurisdiction).
Exclusive jurisdiction—
Conflict of laws. *See* **Conflict of laws** (Jurisdiction—Exclusive jurisdiction).
Family proceedings. *See* **Family proceedings** (Jurisdiction).

JURISDICTION (cont)—
Freezing order—
  Generally. *See* **Practice** (Pre-trial or post-judgment relief—Freezing order—Jurisdiction).
  Worldwide freezing order. *See* **Practice** (Pre-trial or post-judgment relief—Freezing order—Worldwide freezing order).
Governmental jurisdiction—
  Human rights. *See* **Human rights** (Jurisdiction).
High court—
  Judicial review—
    Special Immigration Appeals Commission. *See* **Judicial review** (Special Immigration Appeals Commission—Jurisdiction of High Court).
  Protective jurisdiction—
    Vulnerable persons—Capacity—Local authority seeking injunction to protect elderly parents of adult child—Parents not lacking mental capacity—Whether High Court having inherent jurisdiction to grant protective injunction in respect of vulnerable adults who did not lack mental capacity—Whether court's inherent jurisdiction to protect adults surviving inception of statutory scheme—Whether exercise of inherent jurisdiction compatible with European Convention for the Protection of Human Rights and Fundamental Freedoms—Mental Capacity Act 2005, s 2(1)—Human Rights Act 1998, Sch 1, art 8. **Local Authority (A) v DL** [2012] **3** 1064, CA.
  Tax. *See* **High Court** (Jurisdiction—Tax).
Jurisdiction clause—
  Construction. *See* **Contract** (Construction—Jurisdiction clause).
Publication on internet—
  Racial hatred. *See* **Criminal law** (Jurisdiction—Racial hatred—Publishing or distributing written material).
Relief from forfeiture. *See* **Equity** (Forfeiture—Relief).
Right to life—
  Armed forces serving overseas. *See* **Human rights** (Right to life—Jurisdiction—Armed forces serving overseas).
Supreme Court of the United Kingdom. *See* **Supreme court** (Supreme Court of the United Kingdom—Practice—Jurisdiction).
Tax—
  High Court. *See* **High Court** (Jurisdiction—Tax).
Variation of settlement (matrimonial causes). *See* **Variation of Settlement (Matrimonial Causes)** (Jurisdiction).

JURY
Answers—
  Finality—
    Civil proceedings—Jury answering questions in civil action and being discharged by judge—Jury remaining in court while judge clarifying outcome of case for benefit of claimant—Jury foreman realising jury had misunderstood question—Judge permitting jury to alter answer—Whether judge in civil proceedings having discretion to allow discharged jury to alter answer given by them—Guidance on exercise of discretion. **Igwemma v Chief Constable of Greater Manchester Police** [2001] **4** 751, CA.
    Defamation—Questions put to jury and their answers returned in presence of all jurors—Judgment subsequently given on those answers—Jurors wishing to change answers, as they were dissatisfied with result—Application for new trial—Affidavit by jurors that the answers were given under misapprehension not admissible. **Boston v WS Bagshaw & Sons Ltd** [1967] **2** 87, CA.
Civil action—
  Practice. *See* **Practice** (Trial—Trial by jury).
Communication with judge after retirement. *See* **Criminal law** (Trial—Retirement of jury—Communication with judge).
Composition—
  Multiracial jury—
    Black defendant requesting multiracial jury—Trial judge refusing request—Whether defendant entitled to multiracial jury—Whether trial judge having discretion to empanel multiracial jury. **R v Ford** [1989] **3** 445, CA.
  Talesmen—
    Twelve jurors secured by praying a tales—Whether jury can be entirely composed of talesmen. **R v Solomon** [1957] **3** 497, CCA.
Coroner's jury. *See* **Coroner** (Inquest—Jury).
Defamation case—
  Answers to questions—
    Finality. *See* Answers—Finality—Defamation, *above*.
  Perverse verdict. *See* **Libel and slander** (Justification—Jury).
  Trial by jury. *See* Trial by jury—Defamation, *below*.
Direction to jury—
  Accessory after the fact. *See* **Criminal law** (Accessory after the fact—Direction to jury).
  Admissions and confessions—
    Admissibility in criminal proceedings. *See* **Criminal evidence** (Admissions and confessions—Direction to jury).
  Alibi—
    Comment on defence not being disclosed before trial. **R v Hoare** [1966] **2** 846, CCA.
  Another offence covered by indictment—
    Whether verdict on other offence should be left to jury—Discretion of judge—Criminal Law Act 1967, s 6(3). **R v McCormack** [1969] **3** 371, CA.
  Burden of proof—
    Criminal proceedings—Generally. *See* **Criminal evidence** (Burden of proof—Direction to jury).
    Criminal proceedings—Prosecution case based on circumstantial evidence—Proof beyond reasonable doubt—Whether judge required to give further direction that facts proved must be inconsistent with any reasonable conclusion other than guilt of accused. **McGreevy v DPP** [1973] **1** 503, HL.

JURY (cont)—
    Direction to jury (cont)—
        Burden of proof (cont)—
            Criminal proceedings—Prosecution evidence calling for explanation by accused—Direction that presumption of guilt raised if explanation rejected by jury—Whether misdirection. **R v Bradbury** [1969] **2** 758, CA.
        Character of accused—
            Good character—Primarily a matter which goes to credibility. **R v Bellis** [1966] **1** 552, CCA.
        Comment by judge—
            Adverse comment. *See* **Criminal law** (Trial—Summing up—Adverse comment).
        Confession—
            Voluntariness—Jury should not be directed that, unless satisfied of the voluntary character of an admission, they should disregard it. **R v Ovenell** [1968] **1** 933, CA.
            Voluntariness—Ruling by judge on admissibility—Whether in summing-up to jury subsequently judge should direct them that they must be satisfied that statement was voluntarily made before attaching any weight to it. **R v Burgess** [1968] **2** 54, CA.
        Conviction. *See* **Criminal law** (Trial—Direction to jury—Direction to convict).
        Corroboration—
            Abortion. *See* **Criminal law** (Abortion—Corroboration—Direction to jury).
            Accomplice—Duress by one accused alleged as defence by other accused—Appropriate direction to jury. **R v Bone** [1968] **2** 644, CA.
            Generally. *See* **Criminal evidence** (Corroboration—Direction to jury).
        Damages—
            Breach of contract—Remoteness of damage. *See* **Contract** (Damages for breach—Remoteness of damage—Functions of judge and jury—Direction by judge).
        Defendant's lies. *See* **Criminal law** (Trial—Direction to jury—Lies).
        Diminished responsibility—
            Murder charge. *See* **Criminal law** (Murder—Diminished responsibility—Direction to jury).
        Failure of motorist to provide specimen for laboratory test—
            Reasonable excuse. *See* **Road traffic** (Failure to provide specimen for laboratory test—Reasonable excuse).
        Fitness to plead—
            Appeal. *See* **Criminal law** (Appeal—Fitness to plead—Direction to jury).
            Generally. *See* **Criminal law** (Trial—Direction to jury).
        Identification—
            Visual identification—Possibility of mistaken identification. *See* **Criminal evidence** (Identity—Visual identification—Possibility of mistaken identification—Direction to jury).
        Inability to agree—
            Direction that jury should have regard to arguments of other jurors in attempting to reach verdict—Appropriate direction to be given—Discretion whether and when to give direction. **R v Watson** [1988] **1** 897, CA.
            Direction that jury should have regard to arguments of other jurors in attempting to reach verdict—Circumstances in which such direction may be given. **R v Ashley** [1987] **2** 605, CA.
            Majority verdict direction given—Proper direction when jury still unable to agree. **R v Isequilla** [1975] **1** 77, CA.
        Inquest. *See* **Coroner** (Inquest—Directions to jury).
        Internet, use of. *See* **Criminal law** (Trial—Direction to jury—Collective responsibility).
        Intoxication—
            Murder charge. *See* **Criminal law** (Murder—Intent—Drunkenness—Effect—Proper direction to jury).
        Majority verdict. *See* Majority verdict—Direction to jury, *below*.
        Murder—
            Provocation. *See* **Criminal law** (Murder—Provocation—Direction to jury).
            Reduction to manslaughter. *See* **Criminal law** (Murder—Manslaughter—Reduction to manslaughter—Direction to jury).
        Pressure on jury to agree—
            Trial a retrial—Judge exhorting jury to reach unanimous verdict to save public inconvenience and expense of third trial—Whether direction an irregularity. **R v Mansfield** [1978] **1** 134, CA.
        Provocation—
            Murder charge. *See* **Criminal law** (Murder—Provocation—Direction to jury).
        Requirement of unanimity in decision—
            Form of direction. **R v Davey** [1960] **3** 533, CCA.
            Such direction not normally necessary. **R v Kalinski** [1967] **2** 398, CA.
        Robbery—
            Accused's honest belief of entitlement to property left to jury—Whether proper direction. **Ludlow v Metropolitan Police Comr** [1969] **3** 701, CA.
        Self-defence—
            Burden of proof—Mistake—Correction. **R v Moon** [1969] **3** 803, CA.
            Burden of proof—Plea of self-defence a plea of not guilty—Duty to direct jury that onus on prosecution to prove accused not acting in self-defence. **R v Abraham** [1973] **3** 694, CA.
        Standard of proof—
            Criminal proceedings. **R v Allan** [1969] **1** 91, CA.
        Summing up—
            Generally. *See* **Criminal law** (Trial—Summing up).
        Written material for jurors. *See* **Criminal law** (Trial—Direction to jury—Written material for jurors).
    Disagreement—
        Acquiescence of minority—
            Propriety—Improper for minority to acquiesce in verdict of majority for any reason other than conviction majority view right. **R v Mills** [1939] **2** 299, CCA.
        Return of jury into court—
            Judge's direction as to duty to agree. **Wright, In the Estate of** [1936] **1** 877, CA.
    Discharge of juror—
        Generally. *See* Juror—Discharge during trial, *below*.

JURY (cont)—
  Discharge of juror (cont)—
    Indictment—
      Consent certificate. *See* **Indictment** (Consent certificate—Discharge of juror).
  Discharge of jury—
    Discharge without returning a verdict—
      Discharge of jury before two hour's deliberation—Jury at deadlock—No majority verdict—Re-trial and conviction by a majority verdict—Whether discharge of jury at first trial bar to accused being tried by another jury—Whether conviction at re-trial should stand—Criminal Justice Act 1967, s 13. **R v Elia** [1968] 2 587, CA.
    Judge's discretion—
      Whether judge's discretion to discharge jury reviewable by Court of Appeal. **R v Gorman** [1987] 2 435, CA.
    Tampering, danger of. *See* Trial by jury—Trials on indictment without a jury, *below*.
  Disqualification of juror—
    Juror's knowledge of accused's criminal record. *See* Juror—Disqualification, *below*.
  Dissension among jury—
    Procedure to be adopted by trial judge when dissension among jury apparent—
      Whether judge should question jurors individually or as a whole. **R v Orgles** [1993] 4 533, CA.
  Evidence in absence of jury. *See* **Criminal law** (Trial—Evidence in absence of jury).
  Inquest. *See* **Coroner** (Inquest—Jury).
  Intervention by jury—
    Right to intervene—
      Request by jury to stop case during defendants' case—No direction to jury by judge—Libel action—Plea of justification—Plaintiff not having given evidence but contemplating giving evidence in rebuttal—Invitation to jury on behalf of defence to stop case and award a farthing damages. **Beevis v Dawson** [1956] 3 837, CA.
  Intimidating or threatening jury—
    What constitutes intimidation or threat—
      Judge giving jury time limit in which to reach verdict—Whether conviction should be quashed. **R v Rose** [1982] 2 536, CA.
      Jury in West Indies told by judge to remember their oath—Direction to put aside extraneous matters, to make up their minds one way or the other and to accept reason one from the other—Not told that they were at liberty to disagree—Whether such coercion as to invalidate jury's verdict. **Shoukatallie v R** [1961] 3 996, PC.
      Jury recalled by judge and told that they would be kept for the night if they did not reach a verdict in ten minutes—Freedom of jury to take time—Convictions quashed. **R v McKenna** [1960] 1 326, CCA.
  Juror—
    Bias—
      Connection between juror and member of defendant's family—Discovery of connection after verdict given—Whether defendant receiving fair trial—Test of bias—Whether real danger that accused might not have had fair trial. **R v Gough** [1993] 2 724, HL.
      Persons concerned with administration of justice—Right to a fair trial—Serving police officer sitting on jury—Crown Prosecution Service employee sitting on jury—Prison officer sitting on jury—Whether actual or apparent bias—Whether independent and impartial tribunal—Juries Act 1974, Sch 1, Pt I—Human Rights Act 1998, Sch 1, Pt I, art 6. **R v Khan** [2008] 3 502, CA.
      Persons concerned with administration of justice—Serving police officer sitting on jury—Crown Prosecution Service solicitor sitting on jury—Whether actual or apparent bias—Juries Act 1974, Sch 1, Pt I. **R v Abdroikov** [2005] 4 869, CA; [2008] 1 315, HL.
      Prosecution witness known to juror. *See* **Natural justice** (Juror —Bias—Prosecution witness known to juror).
      Test for apparent bias. *See* **Natural justice** (Juror —Bias—Prosecution witness known to juror).
    Challenge—
      Failure to inform accused of right to challenge—Accused represented by both counsel and solicitor—Jurors not challenged—Accused not prejudiced—Conviction—Whether miscarriage of justice. **R v Berkeley** [1969] 3 6, CA.
      Jury same as one which had previously tried and convicted person whom accused called as witness—Accused and witness had been together in car on occasion out of which charges against them arose—Court declined to empanel a new jury and intimated challenge for cause would be disallowed—Venire de novo not sought—Whether conviction should be quashed. **R v Gash** [1967] 1 811, CA.
      Right to stand by jurors—Whether an accused has a legal right to stand by jurors. **R v Chandler** [1964] 1 761, CCA.
    Discharge during trial—
      Discharge for good reason—Direction to jury—Whether judge required to direct jury to ignore views expressed by discharged juror. **R v Carter** [2010] 4 285, CA.
      Discretion to discharge juror—Exercise of discretion—Discharge of juror by judge otherwise than in open court—Trial continuing with only 11 jurors—Defendant and counsel unaware of discharge of juror—Whether discharge of juror can take place only in open court—Whether discharge of juror by judge before coming into court a material irregularity in the trial—Juries Act 1974, s 16(1). **R v Richardson** [1979] 3 247, CA.
      Discretion to discharge juror—Exercise of discretion—Juror's wife having same occupation as defendants—Juror making known anti-defence views—Juror discharged—Whether entire jury should be discharged—Test to be applied. **R v Spencer, R v Smails** [1985] 1 673, CA.
      Discretion to discharge juror—Exercise of discretion—Review of exercise of discretion—Discharge of juror to go on holiday—Judge entitled to infer that important to juror to commence holiday on date arranged—Jury continuing as a properly constituted jury after discharge of juror—Whether appellate court having jurisdiction to review exercise of discretion—Whether discretion properly exercised—Juries Act 1974, s 16(1). **R v Hambery** [1977] 3 561, CA.
      Necessity for consent of prisoner—Consent certificate to be attached to indictment—Criminal Justice Act 1925, s 15. **R v Browne** [1962] 2 621, CCA.

JURY (cont)—
  Juror (cont)—
    Disqualification—
      Juror knowing prisoner or knowing from hearsay of his bad character—Whether juror should sit on jury. **R v Box** [1963] **3** 240, CCA.
      Juror recognising accused's wife when she appeared as witness and knowing from hearsay that accused had criminal record—Juror's knowledge not disclosed at trial to any other juror—Affidavit of juror read, as dealing only with extrinsic matters—Whether jury should be discharged. **R v Hood** [1968] **2** 56, CA.
      Person attainted of felony—Attainted—Conviction of receiving—Whether juror disqualified—Whether juror liable to serve if name in jurors book, although entitled to exemption. **R v Kelly** [1950] **1** 806, CCA.
    Excusal from jury service—
      Consolidation of practice directions etc. See **Practice** (Criminal proceedings—Consolidation of existing practice directions, practice statements and practice notes).
    Excuse—
      Application to be excused—Procedure on hearing of application—Chief clerk to determine application on merits—Discretion to permit legal representation—Discretion to be exercised carefully and sympathetically—Juries Act 1974, s 9(2). **R v Crown Court at Guildford, ex p Siderfin** [1989] **3** 7, QBD.
      Grounds on which juror may be excused. **Practice Note** [1973] **1** 240, QBD.
      Grounds on which juror may be excused—Good reason for being excused jury service—Membership of religious sect—Adherence to particular religious belief—Whether membership of religious sect or adherence to particular religious belief capable of being good reason for excusal from jury service—Juries Act 1974, s 9(2). **R v Crown Court at Guildford, ex p Siderfin** [1989] **3** 7, QBD.
      Grounds on which juror may be excused—Juries Act 1974, Sch 1, Pt III. **Practice Note** [1988] **3** 177, QBD.
    Oath—
      Form of oath—Trial of criminal charge. **Practice Note** [1957] **1** 290, Div; [1984] **3** 528, CA.
    Qualification—
      Householder—Rateable value—Aggregation of properties—Juries Act 1825, s 1. **Perrins v Pye** [1947] **1** 872, KBD.
    Right to stand by jurors—
      Crown's right to stand by jurors—Exercise of right. **Practice Note** [1988] **3** 1086, .
      Crown's right to stand by jurors—Exercise of right following abolition of defendants' right of peremptory challenge—Criminal Justice Act 1988, s 118. **Practice Note** [1988] **3** 1086, .
      Crown's right to stand by jurors—Right exercisable without provable valid objection until panel exhausted—Thereafter Crown required to show valid objection. **R v Mason** [1980] **3** 777, CA.
    Stand by—
      Right to stand by jurors. See Juror—Right to stand by jurors, above.
      Vetting. See Jury vetting, below.
  Jury vetting—
    Antecedents of members of panel—
      Legality of jury vetting. **R v Crown Court at Sheffield, ex p Brownlow** [1980] **2** 444, QBD and CA; **R v Mason** [1980] **3** 777, CA.
    Attorney General's guidelines. **Practice Note** [1988] **3** 1086, .
    Crown Court ordering jury panel to be investigated for previous convictions—
      Whether Divisional Court having jurisdiction to hear application for certiorari to quash order. See **Crown Court** (Supervisory jurisdiction of High Court—Trial on indictment—High Court having no supervisory jurisdiction in matters relating to trial on indictment—Matters relating to trial on indictment—Jury vetting).
  Majority verdict—
    Direction to jury—
      Practice to be followed—Criminal Justice Act 1967, s 13. **Practice Direction** [1967] **3** 137, CA.
    Statement of number of assenting and dissenting jurors—
      Number of dissenting jurors—Failure to comply with requirement that number of dissenting jurors be stated by foreman in open court—Foreman stating number of assenting jurors in open court—Judge accepting majority verdict and convicting defendant—Whether mandatory to state number of dissenting jurors—Whether failure to comply with requirement rendering verdict nugatory—Juries Act 1974, s 17(3). **R v Reynolds** [1981] **3** 849, CA.
      Number of dissenting jurors—Failure to comply with requirement that number of dissenting jurors be stated by foreman in open court—Validity of verdict—Whether mandatory to state number of dissenting jurors—Whether failure to comply with requirement rendering verdict nugatory—Juries Act 1974, s 17(3). **R v Pigg** [1983] **1** 56, HL.
      Verdict not to be accepted until statement made by foreman in open court—Failure to comply with requirement—Whether requirement mandatory—Whether failure to comply rendering verdict invalid—Juries Act 1974, s 17(2). **R v Barry (Christopher)** [1975] **2** 760, CA.
    Time to elapse before majority verdict accepted—
      Not less than two hours for deliberation—Computation of time—Period in excess of two hours—Criminal Justice Act 1967, s 13(3). **R v Bateson** [1969] **3** 1372, CA.
      Not less than two hours for deliberation—Computation of time—Return to court to ask question—Interval after arriving at verdict before returning to court—Inclusion in computing period of time—Criminal Justice Act 1967, s 13(3). **R v Adams** [1968] **3** 437, CA.
      Practice to be followed—Criminal Justice Act 1967, s 13. **Practice Note** [1970] **2** 215, CA.
  Multiracial jury. See Composition—Multiracial jury, above.
  Practice—
    Communication from jury—
      Desirability of recording communication on judge's note or shorthand note. **Naismith v London Film Productions Ltd** [1939] **1** 794, CA.

JURY (cont)—
  Protection of jury—
    Judge's discretion—
      Prosecution applying for jury protection without giving reasons or calling evidence—Judge
      granting application and ordering that jurors should be known by numbers instead of having
      their names read out—Whether judge right to do so—Whether defendant's conviction
      unsafe—Juries Act 1974, s 12(3). **R v Comerford** [1998] **1** 823, CA.
  Question of fact for jury—
    Game of skill—
      Fact to be determined by jury—Whether game is game of skill a question for jury. **R v Tompson**
      [1943] **2** 130, CCA.
  Questions to jury after verdict—
    General verdict—
      Questions as to reasons for verdict. *See* Verdict—General verdict—Questions as to reasons for
      verdict, *below*.
    Questions directed to knowledge of prisoner where offence was an absolute offence—
      Application for leave to appeal against sentence in view of questions put to jury. **Warner v**
      Metropolitan Police Comr [1967] **3** 93, CA.
  Recommendation to mercy. *See* **Criminal law** (Trial—Recommendation to mercy).
  Retirement—
    Generally. *See* **Criminal law** (Trial—Retirement of jury).
    Jamaica. *See* **Jamaica** (Criminal law—Trial—Retirement of jury).
    Power to enquire into what happens in juryroom—
      Power of Court of Criminal Appeal. **R v Thompson** [1962] **1** 65, CCA.
    Separation after being given in charge of bailiff—
      Juror leaving juryroom—Discharge of juror—Verdict given by remaining jurors—Accused
      convicted—Discharge of juror depriving accused of one potential supporter—Whether whole jury
      should have been discharged—Whether verdict should be quashed. **R v Goodson** [1975] **1** 760,
      CA.
      Juror returning to courtroom to collect exhibit—No communication or attempted communication
      with juror—Irregularity infringing fundamental principle—Irregularity not so grave as to justify
      quashing conviction. **R v Alexander** [1974] **1** 539, CA.
      Permission by recorder to leave court and take luncheon together—Power to order new trial. **R v**
      Neal [1949] **2** 438, CCA.
  Right to trial by jury—
    Bahamas. *See* **Bahamas** (Constitution—Right to trial by jury).
    Brothel keeping. *See* **Criminal law** (Brothel—Keeping a brothel—Right to trial by jury).
    Summary offence, for. *See* **Magistrates** (Right of accused to claim trial by jury for summary offence).
  Separation of jurors after retirement. *See* Retirement—Separation after being given in charge of bailiff,
  above.
  Special jury—
    Right to. *See* Trial by jury—Special jury, *below*.
  Stand by—
    Exercise of Crown's right of stand by. *See* Juror—Right to stand by jurors, *above*.
    Jury vetting. *See* Jury vetting, *above*.
  Tampering—
    Discharge of jury—
      Juror receiving social media friend request from person related to defendant—Judge discharging
      jury and ordering trial to proceed without jury—Whether judge in error—Whether tampering
      established—Whether involvement of defendant necessary—Whether proceeding without jury in
      interests of justice—Whether proceeding without jury fair to defendant—Criminal Justice Act
      2003, s 46. **R v McManaman** [2016] **4** 608, CA.
    Discharge of jury. *See* Trial by jury—Trials on indictment without a jury, *below*.
  Trial by jury—
    Action for damages for personal injuries—
      Discretion of judge to order trial by jury—Nature of discretion—Judge's discretion absolute—RSC
      Ord 36, r 1(3). **Pease v George** [1960] **1** 709, CA.
      Exceptional circumstances—Running down action—No special circumstances—Trial by judge
      alone—Administration of Justice (Miscellaneous Provisions) Act 1933, s 6(1)—RSC Ord 36, r 1(3).
      Hennell v Ranaboldo [1963] **3** 684, CA.
      Exceptional circumstances—Severe injuries—Factories Act case—No exceptional circumstances—
      Trial by judge alone—RSC Ord 36, r 1(3). **Sims v Howard (William) & Son Ltd** [1964] **1** 918, CA.
      Exceptional circumstances—Severe injuries—Inability of plaintiff to have sexual intercourse—
      Concurrent action by plaintiff's husband discontinued—No special circumstances—Trial by judge
      alone—Administration of Justice (Miscellaneous Provisions) Act 1933, s 6(1)—RSC Ord 36, r 1(3).
      Watts v Manning [1964] **2** 267, CA.
      Exceptional circumstances—Severe injuries—Trial by jury ordered—Exercise of discretion by judge
      upheld. **Hodges v Harland & Wolff Ltd** [1965] **1** 1086, CA.
      Exceptional circumstances—Severe injuries—Trial with a jury should not be ordered in personal
      injury cases except in exceptional circumstances. **Ward v James** [1965] **1** 563, CA.
    Action involving allegation of fraud—
      Discretion of judge to order trial by jury—Exercise of discretion. **Cecil-Wright v McCulloch**
      [1936] **3** 518, CA.
    Application for trial by jury—
      Time—Second defendant added at trial and applying—Whether entitled to trial by jury. **Salvalene**
      Lubricants Ltd v Darby [1938] **1** 224, CA.
    Cases where party entitled to trial by jury—
      Queen's Bench Division—Libel, slander, malicious prosecution and false imprisonment—Case
      management—Application for claim to be tried with jury to be made within 28 days of service of
      defence—Meaning of 'defence'—Senior Courts Act 1981, s 69—CPR 26.11(1). **Gregory v**
      Metropolitan Police Comr [2015] **1** 1029, QBD.

JURY (cont)—

Trial by jury (cont)—

Cases where party entitled to trial by jury (cont)—

Queen's Bench Division—Libel, slander, malicious prosecution and false imprisonment—Whether entitlement to jury trial applying to action for misfeasance in public office—Supreme Court Act 1981, s 69. **Racz v Home Office** [1994] **1** 97, HL.

Civil action—

Estimate of length of trial. *See* **Practice** (Trial—Estimate of length of trial—Jury trial—Civil actions).

Constitutional right—

Jamaica. *See* **Jamaica** (Constitutional law—Entrenched provisions of Constitution—Trial by jury).

County court. *See* **County court** (Trial by jury).

Defamation—

Libel—Generally. *See* Trial by jury—Libel, *below*.

Proper roles of judge and jury in respect of issues of fact—Supreme Court Act 1981, s 69—CPR Pt 24. **Alexander v Arts Council of Wales** [2001] **4** 205, CA.

Summary judgment—Claimant bringing proceedings for libel against defendant—Judge concluding that words complained of were defamatory and giving summary judgment for claimant—Whether judge usurping role of jury—Supreme Court Act 1981, s 69(1)—Civil Procedure Act 1997, ss 1(3), 4—CPR 24.2. **Safeway Stores plc v Tate** [2001] **4** 193, CA.

Libel—

Claim in respect of libel—Action on covenant in deed—Covenant to be void if plaintiff libelled defendant—Defence that covenant avoided by such libel—No counterclaim—Administration of Justice (Miscellaneous Provisions) Act 1933, s 6(1)(b). **Shordiche-Churchward v Cordle** [1959] **1** 599, CA.

Default in delivery of defence—Plaintiff's right to trial by jury—RSC Ord 27, r 11—RSC, Ord 30, r 1(a). **Nagy v Co-op Press Ltd** [1949] **1** 1019, CA.

Trial of action requiring prolonged examination of documents and accounts—Practice. *See* **Practice** (Trial—Trial by jury—Libel).

Trial of action requiring prolonged examination of documents—Discretion of court to order trial by judge alone—Exercise of discretion—Circumstances in which proper to order trial by jury although trial requiring prolonged examination of documents—Importance of case to party's reputation and honour—Action raising issues of national importance—Party entitled to trial by jury if he desires it—Administration of Justice (Miscellaneous Provisions) Act 1933, s 6(1). **Rothermere v Times Newspapers Ltd** [1973] **1** 1013, CA.

Practice—

Opening of pleadings by junior counsel for plaintiff or petitioner—Practice to be discontinued. **Practice Direction** [1960] **2** 390, QBD and PDA.

Right to trial by jury—

Bahamas. *See* **Bahamas** (Constitution—Right to trial by jury).

Right of accused to claim trial by jury for summary offence. *See* **Magistrates** (Right of accused to claim trial by jury for summary offence).

Special jury—

Right to—Discretion of court—Extent—Administration of Justice (Miscellaneous Provisions) Act 1933, s 6. **Hope v Great Western Rly Co** [1937] **1** 625, CA.

Speeches of counsel—

Civil action—No witnesses called for defence—Right of defendants' counsel to invite jury to stop case. **Alexander v Burgoine (H) & Sons Ltd** [1939] **4** 568, CA.

Submission of no case to answer—

Duty of judge to put defendants to election whether to call evidence—Defendants not put to election whether to call evidence—Discretion of judge. **Young v Rank** [1950] **2** 166, KBD.

Transfer of proceedings to Queen's Bench Division to obtain jury trial—

Fraud in issue. *See* **Practice** (Transfer of proceedings between Divisions of High Court—Jury trial available as of right in action begun in Queen's Bench Division where fraud in issue—Action begun in Chancery Division including allegation of fraud).

Trials on indictment without a jury—

Application by prosecution for trial to be conducted without a jury where danger of jury tampering—Discharge of jury because of jury tampering—Guidance—Criminal Justice Act 2003, ss 44-46. **R v T** [2009] **3** 1002, CA.

Application by prosecution for trial to be conducted without a jury where danger of jury tampering—Discharge of jury because of jury tampering—Jury retiring—Judge discharging jury—Judge having presided over ten connected trials—Judge ordering trial to continue without jury—Relevant principles—Whether actual or apparent bias—Criminal Justice Act 2003, s 46. **R v S** [2010] **1** 1084, CA.

Unanimity of jury—

Direction. *See* Direction to jury—Requirement of unanimity in decision, *above*.

Verdict—

Appeal against—

Case stated. *See* **Case stated** (Appeal from Crown Court—Jury verdict).

Conviction or acquittal—

Plea of autrefois acquit or convict. *See* **Criminal law** (Autrefois acquit—Verdict of jury).

Criminal proceedings—

Generally. *See* **Criminal law** (Verdict).

Direction to jury. *See* **Criminal law** (Trial—Direction to jury—Verdict).

General verdict—

Questions as to reasons for verdict—Libel action—Justification and privilege pleaded—General verdict for defendant—Question as to which defence jury found to be established put to jury—Whether jury should be asked grounds on which verdict given. **Barnes v Hill** [1967] **1** 347, CA.

Inconsistent verdicts—

Burden on appellant to satisfy the court that the verdicts cannot stand together. **R v Durante** [1972] **3** 962, CA.

JURY (cont)—
  Verdict (cont)—
    Inconsistent verdicts (cont)—
      Burden on appellant to satisfy the court that the verdicts cannot stand together—Charges of grievous bodily harm to B and of assault occasioning actual bodily harm to H—Charges arising out of acts on same occasion—Issue of identity of single assailant—Appellant acquitted of causing grievous bodily harm to B but convicted of assault occasioning actual bodily harm to H—Whether verdicts could stand together. **R v Hunt** [1968] **2** 1056, CA.
      Separate trials—Charges arising out of same offence—Accused tried separately on charges arising out of same offence—Juries returning different verdicts in separate trials—Whether verdict of guilty necessarily unsafe—Corruption—Officer of public body—Charges of giving and receiving bribes—One accused acquitted of giving bribe—Other accused convicted at separate trial of receiving bribe. **R v Andrews Weatherfoil Ltd** [1972] **1** 65, CA.
      Separate trials—No absolute rule that first verdict of guilty will be set aside. **R v Andrews** [1967] **1** 170, CA.
    Inquest. See **Coroner** (Inquest—Verdict).
    Majority verdict. See Majority verdict, above.
    Time for verdict—
      Necessity for jury to hear summing-up on defence of accused before returning verdict of guilty. **R v Young** [1964] **2** 480, CCA.
    Trinidad and Tobago. See **Trinidad and Tobago** (Jury—Verdict).
    Unanimity—
      Direction as to requirement of unanimity. See Direction to jury—Requirement of unanimity in decision, above.
    Unreasonable verdict—
      Setting aside on appeal. See **Criminal law** (Appeal—Unreasonable verdict).
    Verdict announced as unanimous—
      Juror subsequently stating that she had disagreed with verdict—Verdict returned in sight and hearing of all jurors without protest—Whether evidence of juror that she disagreed with verdict admissible. **R v Roads** [1967] **2** 84, CA.
    Verdict announced by foreman—
      Impression that verdict unanimous—Foreman subsequently announcing verdict was a majority verdict—Whether jury functus officio immediately verdict given. **R v Bateson** [1969] **3** 1372, CA.
    Verdict given in judge's absence—
      Validity. **Hawksley v Fewtrell** [1953] **2** 1486, CA.
  View by jury—
    Criminal proceedings—
      Accused declining to attend. **Karamat v R** [1956] **1** 415, PC.
      Presence of judge. **Tameshwar v R** [1957] **2** 683, PC.
      Presence of judge—Material irregularity if judge not present at view by jury. **R v Hunter** [1985] **2** 173, CA.
    Statutory procedure—
      Procedure to be strictly followed—Jury divided up into groups at locus delicti, each group being asked impressions—Procedure altogether irregular—Criminal Procedure Code 1898 (Ceylon), s 238. **Seneviratne v R** [1936] **3** 36, PC.
  Warning—
    Disputed signature. See **Criminal evidence** (Handwriting—Signature disputed—Warning to jury).
    Evidence of accomplice—
      Corroboration. See **Criminal evidence** (Corroboration—Accomplice—Warning to jury).
  Withdrawal of issue from jury—
    Negligence. See **Negligence** (Withdrawal of issue from jury).

JUS TERTII
  Money recovered by agent on behalf of principal—
    Duty to account. See **Agent** (Account—Duty to account—Money recovered on behalf of principal).

JUSTICE
  Interference with due administration of justice—
    Contempt of court. See **Contempt of court** (Interference with due administration of justice).
  Natural. See **Natural justice**.
  Obstructing the course of justice. See **Criminal law** (Obstructing course of justice).

JUSTICES
  Bail. See **Criminal law** (Bail).
  Case stated. See **Case stated**.
  Certiorari. See **Certiorari** (Justices).
  Committal proceedings—
    Generally. See **Criminal law** (Committal—Preliminary hearing before justices).
  Contempt of court. See **Contempt of court**.
  Costs in criminal cases. See **Criminal law** (Costs—Magistrates' court).
  Family proceedings. See **Family proceedings**.
  Generally. See **Magistrates**.
  Licensing—
    Betting office. See **Gaming** (Betting—Licensed betting office—Application for licence).
    Discretion to grant occasional licence. See **Licensing** (Occasional licence—Grant—Discretion of justices).
    Gaming. See **Gaming**.
    Generally. See **Licensing**.
    Intoxicating liquor. See **Licensing**.
    Power to state a case. See **Licensing** (Justices—Case stated—Power of licensing justices to state a case).
    Public music and dancing. See **Entertainment** (Music and dancing licence).

JUSTICES (cont)—
    Natural justice—
        Generally. *See* **Natural justice** (Magistrates).
        Practice. *See* **Practice** (Magistrates' courts).

JUSTIFICATION
    Interlocutory injunction—
        Defamation cases. *See* **Libel and slander** (Injunction—Interlocutory—Justification).

JUVENILE
    Criminal proceedings—
        Detention in custody. *See* **Criminal law** (Detention in custody—Juvenile).
        Sentence—
            Murder—Tariff period. *See* **Sentence** (Young person—Serious criminal offence—Murder).
        Police interview. *See* **Criminal evidence** (Police interview—Interview of juvenile).
        Prosecution of juvenile—
            Decision of Crown Prosecution Service—
                Judicial review of decision—Availability of remedy. *See* **Judicial review** (Availability of remedy—Decision to prosecute—Juvenile).

JUVENILE COURT
    Adoption proceedings—
        Guardian ad litem. *See* **Adoption** (Practice—Guardian ad litem—Juvenile court).
    Appeal—
        Adoption proceedings. *See* **Adoption** (Practice—Appeal—Appeal from juvenile court).
    Care proceedings—
        Generally. *See* **Children and young persons** (Care proceedings in juvenile court).
        Legal aid. *See* **Legal aid—Care proceedings in juvenile court**.
    Generally. *See* **Magistrates** (Juvenile court).
    Irish warrant—
        Application for indorsement—
            Hearing in open court. *See* **Magistrates** (Indorsement of Irish warrant—Application for indorsement—Hearing in open court—Juvenile).

K

KEEPING A BROTHEL
    See **Criminal law** (Brothel—Keeping a brothel).

KEEPING A DISORDERLY HOUSE
    See **Criminal law** (Disorderly house).

KENYA
    Appeal—
        Judgment to be drawn up in formal decree before appeal—
            Time limit—Duty of appellant to move for formal decree within time limit—Order for an
            account—No formal decree—Account taken—Report confirmed—Decree drawn up and
            ante-dated according to date of judgment—Whether appellant entitled to appeal. **Ribeiro
            (Rozendo Avres) v Siqueira (Olivia da Ritta) e Facho** [1936] **1** 537, PC.
    Hypothecation—
        Letter of hypothecation—
            Validity—Unattested letter—Bank overdraft secured by letter of hypothecation over stock-in-trade
            and other articles—Letter of hypothecation unattested and unregistered—Cheques drawn in
            excess of extended overdraft—Seizure of stock-in-trade—Letter authorising seizure as overdraft
            could not be reduced—Whether unattested letter of hypothecation valid as between parties
            thereto—Chattels Transfer Ordinance (No 24) 1930, s 15. **National and Grindlays Bank Ltd v
            Dharamshi Vallabhji** [1966] **2** 626, PC.
    Mortgage—
        Moneylending transaction—
            Exemption—Loan by moneylenders by instalments, some of which were made before the date of
            the charge—Security given by charge on land—Charge attested by one witness only—Individuals
            joining as guarantors for repayment—Whether charge enforceable as being within exemption
            conferred by statute—Money-Lenders Ordinance (Cap 307 of the Revised Laws of Kenya 1948 as
            amended by the Money-Lenders Ordinance, Cap 56, 1959), s 3(1)(b)—Registration of Titles
            Ordinance, s 58—Indian Transfer of Property Act 1882, s 59. **Coast Brick & Tile Works Ltd v
            Premchand Raichand Ltd** [1966] **1** 819, PC.
    Sale of mortgaged property—
        Proviso for redemption—Whether proviso for redemption in mortgage a contract to the
        contrary—Indian Transfer of Property Act 1882 (No 4 of 1882), s 67. **Karachiwalla (Mohamedali
        Jaffer) v Nanji (Noorally Rattanshi Rajan)** [1959] **1** 137, PC.

KIDNAPPING
    Child—
        Child abduction. *See* **Minor** (Abduction).
        Removal by parent from foreign jurisdiction—
            Wardship proceedings. *See* **Ward of court** (Jurisdiction—Kidnapping).
    Crime. *See* **Criminal law** (Kidnapping).

KING'S PROCTOR
    Intervention—
        Divorce. *See* **Divorce** (Intervention—King's Proctor showing cause why a decree nisi should not be
        made absolute).
        Nullity proceedings. *See* **Nullity** (King's Proctor).

KITTYSCOOP
    Lawfulness. *See* **Gaming** (Lawful and unlawful gaming—Variant of roulette—Kittyscoop).

KNIFE
    Butterfly knife—
        Whether dangerous article per se. *See* **Criminal law** (Dangerous article—Article 'made or adapted for
        use for causing injury'—Butterfly knife).
    Flick knife—
        Whether an offensive weapon per se. *See* **Criminal law** (Offensive weapons—Article made or adapted
        for use for causing injury—Flick knife).

KNOCK-FOR-KNOCK AGREEMENT
    Motor insurance. *See* **Motor insurance** (Knock-for-knock agreement).

KNOW-HOW
    Consideration for imparting know-how—
        Income tax—
            Capital or income. *See* **Income tax** (Capital or income receipts—Know-how).

L

LABEL
Food and drugs. *See* **Food and drugs** (Label).
Goods—
European Community. *See* **European Union** (Freedom of movement—Goods—Description and labelling).

LABORATORY TEST
Specimen to determine driver's blood-alcohol proportion. *See* **Road traffic** (Specimen for laboratory test to determine driver's blood-alcohol proportion).

LABOUR PARTY
Gift to—
Rule against perpetuities. *See* **Rule against perpetuities** (Unincorporated association—Gift to association—Absolute gift to members on trust for association—Bequest in will—Gift to committee of local political party).
Rules. *See* **Unincorporated association** (Rules—National Executive Committee of Labour Party).

LABOUR RELATIONS
See **Industrial relations**.

LACHES
See **Equity** (Laches).

LADDERS
Building operations. *See* **Building** (Building operations—Ladders).

LANCASTER CHANCERY COURT
Trust—
Variation—
Jurisdiction. *See* **Variation of trusts** (Jurisdiction—Lancaster Chancery Court).

LAND
Activities on land—
Occupier's liability. *See* **Occupier's liability** (Activities on land).
Adverse possession—
Limitation of action. *See* **Limitation of action** (Land—Adverse possession).
Registration. *See* **Land registration** (Acquisition of title by possession).
River bed or foreshore—
Limitation of action. *See* **Limitation of action** (Land—Adverse possession—Acts amounting to possession—Unregistered land—Vessel moored and anchored in tidal river).
Agricultural holding. *See* **Agricultural holding**.
Agricultural land—
Capital allowances. *See* **Capital allowances** (Agricultural land and buildings).
Exemption from rates. *See* **Rates** (Exemption—Agricultural land).
Inheritance tax—
Relief. *See* **Inheritance tax** (Exemptions and relief—Agricultural property relief).
Mortgagor's power of leasing. *See* **Mortgage** (Power of leasing—Agricultural land).
Planning control. *See* **Town and country planning** (Agricultural land).
Agricultural Land Tribunal. *See* **Agricultural Land Tribunal**.
Appropriation by local authority—
Accommodation of working classes, for. *See* **Housing** (Accommodation of working classes).
Generally. *See* **Local authority** (Land—Power to appropriate land).
Armed forces—
Use by—
Crown—Immunity from suit. *See* **Crown** (Proceedings against—Liability of Crown—Immunity from suit in respect of land used for purpose of armed forces).
Artificial transactions—
Tax avoidance. *See* **Income tax** (Avoidance—Artificial transactions in land).
Boundary. *See* **Boundary**.
Building land—
Value added tax—
Exemption—European Community. *See* **European Union** (Value added tax—Exemptions—Building land).
Burial ground. *See* **Burial** (Burial ground).
Capital gains tax—
Exemption—
Private residence—Land occupied with residence as garden. *See* **Capital gains tax** (Exemptions and reliefs—Private residence—Land occupied and enjoyed with residence as its garden or grounds).
Land held on 6th April 1965—
Computation of chargeable gain. *See* **Capital gains tax** (Computation of chargeable gains—Asset held on 6th April 1965—Land).
Caravan site—
Generally. *See* **Caravan site**.
Certificate—
Charge created by deposit of land certificate. *See* **Land registration** (Charge—Deposit of land certificate).
Charge. *See* **Land charge**.
Charging order. *See* **Execution** (Charging order—Land).
Charitable trust—
Planning control. *See* **Town and country planning** (Land held on charitable trusts).

LAND (cont)—
Common land. *See* **Commons.**
Compensation—
Compulsory purchase. *See* **Compulsory purchase** (Compensation).
Displacement from land. *See* **Compensation** (Displacement from land).
Injurious affection. *See* **Compensation** (Injurious affection).
Rehousing—
Persons displaced from residential accommodation. *See* **Housing** (Rehousing—Duty of local authority—Persons displaced from residential accommodation).
Compulsory purchase—
Generally. *See* **Compulsory purchase.**
Housing. *See* **Housing** (Compulsory purchase).
Compulsory resumption of—
New South Wales. *See* **New South Wales** (Compulsory resumption of land).
Consecrated ground—
Secular use—
Faculty. *See* **Ecclesiastical law** (Faculty—Secular use of consecrated ground).
Conservation area. *See* **Town and country planning** (Conservation area).
Contamination—
Remediation. *See* **Environment** (Protection—Contaminated land—Remediation).
Contract concerning land—
Part performance. *See* **Contract** (Part performance).
Sale of land. *See* **Sale of land** (Contract).
Conveyance—
Conveyance under School Sites Acts. *See* **Education** (School—Conveyance under School Sites Acts).
Exception and reservation—
Minerals—Land acquired through private and statutory conveyance—Reservations as to metals, stones and minerals under land—Owners extracting mudstone from bedrock—Owners of retained rights objecting—Whether reservations extending to mudstone—Meaning of 'minerals'—Arwystli Enclosure Act 1816. **Wynne-Finch v Natural Resources Body for Wales** [2022] 3 162, CA.
Fraudulent conveyance. *See* **Fraudulent conveyance.**
Generally. *See* **Sale of land** (Conveyance).
Land erroneously included in conveyance—
Rectification of land register. *See* **Land registration** (Rectification of register—Rectification affecting title of proprietor in possession—Proprietor contributing to mistake in registration).
Covenant running with land—
Landlord and tenant. *See* **Landlord and tenant** (Covenant—Covenant running with land).
Positive covenant, burden of—
Registration. *See* **Land registration** (Effect of registration of dispositions of freeholds—Positive covenant—Burden).
Restrictive covenant. *See* **Restrictive covenant affecting land.**
Damages—
Breach of contract—
Injury to land. *See* **Contract** (Damages for breach—Injury to land).
Sale of land. *See* **Sale of land** (Damages for breach of contract).
Measure of damages for injury to land. *See* **Damages** (Land—Measure of damages for injury to land).
Dealing with land—
Fiji. *See* **Fiji** (Land—Dealing with land).
Development—
Development land tax. *See* **Development land tax.**
Town and country planning. *See* **Town and country planning.**
Displacement from land—
Compensation. *See* **Compensation** (Displacement from land).
Disposal of interest in land—
Development land tax. *See* **Development land tax** (Disposal of interest in land).
Evidence—
Company minute book. *See* **Company** (Minute book—Evidence—Evidence of disposal of interest in land).
Offer to settle—
Statutory requirements for contract for sale or other disposition of interest in land. *See* **Practice** (Offer to settle—Offer including disposition of interest in land).
Disposal of land—
Power to demise land—
Duty to obtain best consideration—Lessor of local authority land covenanting to use best endeavours to employ specified number of employees—Whether job creation relevant to local authority's obligation to obtain best consideration—Local Government Act 1972, s 123. **R v Pembrokeshire CC, ex p Coker** [1999] 4 1007, QBD.
Drainage. *See* **Land drainage.**
Easement. *See* **Easement.**
Educational purposes, for—
Conveyance under School Sites Acts. *See* **Education** (School—Conveyance under School Sites Acts).
Treasury grant. *See* **Education** (Land—Acquisition for educational purposes—Treasury grant).
Electricity lines over—
Power of undertakers to place lines over land. *See* **Electricity** (Overhead lines—Power of undertakers to place lines over land).
Environmental protection—
Site of scientific interest. *See* **Environment** (Protection—Site of special scientific interest).
Equitable burden on land—
Estoppel—
Acquiescence in expenditure being made in reliance on right over land of another. *See* **Acquiescence** (Estoppel).
Estate agent. *See* **Estate agent.**

LAND (cont)—
Estates or interests capable of subsisting at law—
Rights of entry exercisable over or in respect of a legal term of years absolute—
Right of entry on breach of covenant—Assignment of leasehold interest in part of premises—Assignment reserving to assignor right of entry on breach of covenant—Right of entry limited to perpetuity period—Whether right of entry a legal interest—Law of Property Act 1925, s 1(2). **Shiloh Spinners Ltd v Harding** [1973] **1** 90, HL.
European Community—
Value added tax—
Exemption. See **European Union** (Value added tax—Exemptions—Land).
Fiji. See **Fiji** (Land).
Fixtures—
Annexation to land. See **Landlord and tenant** (Fixtures—Annexation to land).
Lease. See **Landlord and tenant** (Lease—Fixtures).
Mortgage. See **Mortgage** (Fixtures).
Flooding—
Protection. See **Water and watercourses** (Flooding—Protection of land from flooding).
Forcible entry and detainer. See **Criminal law** (Forcible entry and detainer).
Foreign land—
Conflict of laws. See **Conflict of laws** (Foreign land).
Fraudulent transfer—
Generally. See **Fraudulent conveyance**.
Malaysia. See **Malaysia** (Land—Transfer).
General equitable charge. See **Land charge** (General equitable charge—Charge on land).
Gift—
Donatio mortis causa. See **Gift** (Donatio mortis causa—Land).
Glebe land—
Disposition. See **Ecclesiastical law** (Glebe land—Disposition of land).
Harassment of occupier—
Residential occupier. See **Criminal law** (Harassment—Residential occupier of land).
Hong Kong—
New Territories—
Land tenure. See **Hong Kong** (New Territories—Land tenure).
Improvement of land—
Loan for improvement of land—
Interest—Income tax relief. See **Income tax** (Interest—Relief—Loan for purchase or improvement of land).
Income tax—
Generally. See **Income tax** (Land).
Loan for improvement of land. See **Income tax** (Interest—Relief—Loan for purchase or improvement of land).
Injurious affection—
Compensation. See **Compensation** (Injurious affection—Land).
Interest in land—
Charging order. See **Execution** (Charging order—Land—Interest in land).
Creation—
Agreement for lease—Building agreement providing for grant of lease by owner to developer on completion of buildings—Developer granting to plaintiff equitable mortgage of his interest under agreement—Mortgage including covenant to execute legal mortgage of lease granted under building agreement—Equitable charge registered under Companies Act 1948 but not under land charges legislation—Owner granting lease to developer—Legal mortgage not executed in favour of plaintiff—Developer assigning lease to defendant—Money remaining due under mortgage—Whether mortgage creating equitable charge enforceable against defendant—Whether mortgage creating single charge on developer's interest under building agreement—Whether mortgage creating separate charges on developer's chose in action against owner requiring owner to grant lease and on covenant to execute legal mortgage of lease which though registrable under land charges legislation was not registered. **Property Discount Corp Ltd v Lyon Group Ltd** [1981] **1** 379, CA.
Disposal—
Development land tax. See **Development land tax** (Disposal of interest in land).
Joint tenancy—
Charging order. See **Execution** (Charging order—Land—Interest in land—Joint tenancy).
Generally. See **Joint tenancy**.
Power of sale. See **Settlement** (Powers of tenant for life—Joint tenants—Power of sale).
Whether tenants' interest an 'interest' within Administration of Justice Act 1956, s 351. See **Execution** (Charging order—Land—Interest in land—Property held legally and beneficially by joint tenants).
Land registration. See **Land registration**.
Landlocked land—
Access to—
Right of way. See **Easement** (Right of way—Creation—Right of way to one plot of land used as means of access to another plot lying beyond it).
Lease. See **Landlord and tenant** (Lease).
Licence to occupy—
Generally. See **Licence** (Licence to occupy land).
Grant exempt from value added tax. See **Value added tax** (Exemptions—Grant of right over or licence to occupy land).
Tenancy distinguished. See **Landlord and tenant** (Tenancy—Tenancy distinguished from licence).
Limitation of action. See **Limitation of action** (Land).
Local authority. See **Local authority** (Land).
London—
Building. See **Building** (London).
Lost modern grant, doctrine of. See **Easement** (Right of way—Prescription—Lost modern grant).

LAND (cont)—

Metropolitan open land—
 Development. *See* **Town and country planning** (Permission for development—Metropolitan open land).

Mortgage. *See* **Mortgage**.

Native lands—
 Alienation—
  Nigeria. *See* **Nigeria** (Native lands in Lagos—Alienation of land).
 Statutory charge on lands—
  Validity of statutory charge on lands. *See* **New Zealand** (Native lands—Charge on lands—Statutory charge).
 Unlawful dealing—
  Fiji. *See* **Fiji** (Land—Dealing with land—Native land).

Non-natural use of land—
 Escape in consequence of—
  Nuisance. *See* **Nuisance** (Escape in consequence of non-natural use of land).

Nuisance. *See* **Nuisance**.

Occupancy—
 Rights of person in actual occupation. *See* **Land registration** (Overriding interest—Rights of person in actual occupation of land).
 Tanganyika. *See* **Tanganyika** (Land—Occupancy).

Occupier—
 Liability of. *See* **Occupier's liability**.
 Right to sue—
  Nuisance. *See* **Nuisance** (Right to sue—Occupier of land).

Open space—
 Appropriation for accommodation of working classes. *See* **Housing** (Accommodation of working classes—Appropriation of land—Open space).

Operation on land—
 Town and country planning—
  Discontinuance order. *See* **Town and country planning** (Discontinuance order—Use of land—Jurisdiction to make order—Operations carried out on land).

Option to purchase—
 Conditional bequest in will. *See* **Will** (Condition—Conditional bequest—Option to purchase land).
 Generally. *See* **Option** (Option to purchase).

Owner—
 Negligence—
  Hidden defects in premises—Duty to subsequent purchaser. *See* **Negligence** (Duty to take care—Owner of realty—Duty to subsequent purchaser in respect of hidden defects).
 Partnership. *See* **Partnership** (Partnership property).
 Purchase notice. *See* **Town and country planning** (Purchase notice—Owner of land).

Pending land action. *See* **Land charge** (Pending action).

Planning. *See* **Town and country planning**.

Planning permission. *See* **Town and country planning** (Permission for development).

Possession—
 Adverse possession. *See* **Limitation of action** (Land—Adverse possession).
 Summary proceedings for possession. *See* Summary proceedings for possession, *below*.

Possession proceedings. *See* Summary proceedings for possession—Extent of court's jurisdiction—Persons unlawfully occupying woodland, *below*.

Profit à pendre. *See* **Profit à prendre**.

Protected tenancy—
 Let together with house. *See* **Rent restriction** (Land let together with house).

Purchase of land—
 Loan for purchase of land—
  Interest—Income tax relief. *See* **Income tax** (Interest—Relief—Loan for purchase or improvement of land).

Rates. *See* **Rates**.

Recovery of possession—
 Limitation. *See* **Limitation of action** (Land).
 Minister of Crown. *See* **Crown** (Recovery of possession of land—Power of Minister to recover possession).
 Mortgaged property—
  Jurisdiction of county court. *See* **County court** (Jurisdiction—Mortgage).
 Order for possession. *See* **Landlord and tenant** (Recovery of possession—Order for possession).
 Palestine. *See* **Palestine** (Recovery of land).
 Protected tenancy. *See* **Rent restriction** (Possession).
 Sale for purpose of administration of deceased's estate. *See* **Administration of estates** (Sale for purposes of administration—Recovery of possession for purposes of sale).
 Summary proceedings. *See* Summary proceedings for possession, *below*.

Redevelopment—
 War damage—
  Compulsory purchase. *See* **War damage** (Redevelopment of land—Compulsory purchase).

Registration—
 Common land. *See* **Commons** (Registration).
 Generally. *See* **Land registration**.
 New Zealand. *See* **New Zealand** (Land registration).

Rentcharge. *See* **Rentcharge**.

Requisition—
 Development value of requisitioned land. *See* **Town and country planning** (Development value—Determination—Land requisitioned at relevant date).
 Generally. *See* **Requisition** (Land).

Restrictive covenant affecting. *See* **Restrictive covenant affecting land**.

LAND (cont)—
Reverter—
Possibility of reverter on determination of determinable fee—
Whether such a possibility capable of being devised—Wills Act 1837, ss 1, 3. **Bath and Wells Diocesan Board of Finance v Jenkinson** [2002] **4** 245, Ch D.
Right in, to or on property conveyed—
Statutory provision providing that every conveyance effectual to pass such right—
Whether applying only to right touching and concerning land—Law of Property Act 1925, s 63. **Harbour Estates Ltd v HSBC Bank plc** [2004] **3** 1057, Ch D.
Right of entry on land—
Drainage board. *See* **Land drainage** (Drainage board—Right of entry on land).
Right of way to. *See* **Easement** (Right of way—Creation).
River bed or foreshore—
Acquisition of title by adverse possession—
Limitation of action. *See* **Limitation of action** (Land—Adverse possession—Acts amounting to possession—Unregistered land—Vessel moored and anchored in tidal river).
Sale—
Charity estate. *See* **Charity** (Sale of charity estate).
Church—
Unconsecrated curtilage—Faculty jurisdiction. *See* **Ecclesiastical law** (Faculty—Unconsecrated curtilage of church—Sale—Power to authorise sale).
Generally. *See* **Sale of land**.
Specific performance. *See* **Specific performance** (Sale of land).
Settled land. *See* **Settled land**.
Settlement—
Capital gains tax. *See* **Capital gains tax** (Settlement).
Generally. *See* **Settlement**.
Sporting and recreational facilities—
Easement. *See* **Easement** (Sporting and recreational facilities).
Summary proceedings for possession—
Abridgement of time for making order—
Urgency—Procedure for applying for abridgement of time—Application to be made to judge hearing summons—Plaintiff serving properly constituted summons and establishing clear right to possession of premises against defendant—Summons heard by Queen's Bench judge within five clear days of date of service of summons—Judge taking view case not one of urgency—Judge dismissing summons—Whether judge should have adjourned summons until five day period elapsed before making final order—RSC Ord 113, r 6(1). **Westminster City Council v Monahan** [1981] **1** 1050, CA.
Challenge to summary proceedings—
Action by local authority against trespassers—Challenge to local authority's right to bring proceedings—Trespassers wishing to assert public law right—Whether challenge to right to bring proceedings can be made in eviction proceedings—Whether defendant required to bring separate application for judicial review—RSC Ord 113. **Avon CC v Buscott** [1988] **1** 841, CA.
Execution of possession order—
Execution against persons in occupation but not parties to proceedings—County court—Warrant of possession—Right of bailiff to evict anyone in possession of land—CCR Ord 26, r 6. **R v Wandsworth County Court, ex p Wandsworth London Borough** [1975] **3** 390, QBD.
Writ of restitution—Leave to issue writ of restitution—Plaintiffs' land occupied by group of squatters—Order for possession obtained by plaintiffs in 1983—In 1985 group of squatters found to be living on same land—Plaintiffs seeking to issue writ of restitution—Whether necessary to show that all those occupying land were in unlawful occupation when original order for possession obtained. **Wiltshire CC v Frazer** [1986] **1** 65, QBD.
Extent of court's jurisdiction—
Part of university premises occupied by students—Premises vacated—Threat by students to occupy other parts of premises—Application by university for possession order in respect of whole of its premises—Whether court having jurisdiction to grant order for possession of whole premises or only that part of premises actually occupied—RSC Ord 113. **University of Essex v Djemal** [1980] **2** 742, CA.
Persons unlawfully occupying woodland—Owner obtaining possession order against unlawful occupiers in respect of woodland unlawfully occupied by them and in respect of other separate areas of woodland within 20-mile radius—Whether court having jurisdiction to grant order for possession in relation to other separate areas—CPR Pt 55. **Drury v Secretary of State for the Environment, Food and Rural Affairs** [2004] **2** 1056, CA.
Persons unlawfully occupying woodland—Owner obtaining possession order against unlawful occupiers in respect of woodland unlawfully occupied by them—Court finding real danger of decampment to other sites—Judge refusing wider possession order in respect of other sites—Judge refusing injunction in respect of other sites—Whether court having discretion to make wider possession order where real danger of decampment established—Whether remedy of injunction available. **Secretary of State for the Environment, Food and Rural Affairs v Meier** [2009] **1** 614, CA; [2010] **1** 855, SC.
Form of originating summons—
Plaintiff unable to identify every person in occupation—Affidavit stating plaintiff has taken all reasonable steps to identify persons in occupation—All reasonable steps—Meaning—Large number of students occupying university building—Only ringleaders identified and named in summons as defendants—University officials and staff who witnessed occupation unable to identify other students—Whether university having taken all reasonable steps to identify them—RSC Ord 113, rr 2(2), 3. **Warwick University v De Graaf** [1975] **3** 284, CA.
Summons against unnamed defendants—Reasonable steps to identify occupiers before issue of summons—Failure to take reasonable steps invalidating proceedings from start—RSC Ord 113, r 2(2), form 11A. **Orpen Road (9), Stoke Newington, Re** [1971] **1** 944, Ch D.

LAND (cont)—
    Summary proceedings for possession (cont)—
        Land occupied solely by persons who entered into or remained in occupation without licence or
            consent—
            Licence or consent of plaintiff or predecessor in title—Meaning of 'entered into or remained in
                occupation without licence or consent'—Whether including case when person enters property
                with licence or consent but remains in possession after licence terminated—RSC Ord 113 r 1.
                Bristol Corp v Persons unknown [1974] **1** 593, Ch D.
            Licensee's right to bring proceedings—Respondent needing to carry out certain work on land
                owned by third party—Appellants unlawfully occupying land—Owner granting respondent
                licence to occupy land for purpose of carrying out works—Respondent not having occupation of
                land—Respondent seeking summary possession order against appellants—Whether respondent
                had sufficient interest in land to rely on summary possession proceedings. **Dutton v Manchester**
                Airport plc [1999] **2** 675, CA.
            Persons entering into possession with licence or consent but remaining in possession after licence
                terminated—Availability of summary procedure—Discretion of court—Licence granted for
                substantial period—Whether court has a discretion to prevent use of summary procedure where
                licensee holds over after termination of licence—CCR Ord 26, r 1(1). **Greater London Council v**
                Jenkins [1975] **1** 354, CA.
        Procedure—
            Abridgement of time for making order. *See* Summary proceedings for possession—Abridgement of
                time for making order, *above.*
            Adjournment to judge—Appointment before master not required. **Practice Direction** [1983] **1** 131,
                Ch D.
        Service of originating summons or application—
            Failure to comply with rules of court—Effect—Irregularity not necessarily nullifying proceedings—
                Respondents not all identified—Summons or application to be served by affixing copy to main
                door or other conspicuous part of premises—Copy of originating application and notice of date of
                hearing put in envelope addressed to 'persons unknown' and pushed through letterbox—
                Envelope subsequently opened and application read by all respondents—Respondents appearing
                in court at hearing—Whether irregularity in service nullifying proceedings—RSC Ord 2, r 1—CCR
                Ord 26, r 3(2). **Westminster City Council v Chapman** [1975] **2** 1103, CA.
            Method of service—Alternative methods prescribed—Personal service or service by leaving copy of
                summons and affidavit at premises—Whether service by leaving documents at premises
                permissible where personal service practicable—RSC Ord 113, r 4(1). **Crosfield Electronics Ltd v**
                Baginsky [1975] **3** 97, CA.
        Suspension of possession order—
            County court—Whether county court has discretion to suspend order in absence of consent—CCR
                Ord 26. **Swordheath Properties Ltd v Floydd** [1978] **1** 721, CA.
            Plaintiff having established right to possession and that defendant a trespasser—Whether court
                having power to suspend operation of order—RSC Ord 113. **Dept of the Environment v James**
                [1972] **3** 629, Ch D.
            Squatters—Whether court having discretion to suspend order—Whether equitable jurisdiction to
                suspend Order—RSC Ord 113. **McPhail v persons, names unknown** [1973] **3** 393, CA.
        Tenant holding over not liable to summary proceedings—
            Unlawful sub-tenant—Flat let to tenant with absolute prohibition against assigning, underletting or
                parting with possession—Tenant unlawfully sub-letting flat to other persons without knowledge
                or consent of landlord—Tenant subsequently leaving flat and determining tenancy—Landlord
                discovering unlawful sub-tenant still in possession—Landlord issuing summary proceedings for
                possession—Whether unlawful sub-tenant a 'tenant holding over after the termination of the
                tenancy'—RSC Ord 113, r 1. **Moore Properties (Ilford) Ltd v McKeon** [1977] **1** 262, Ch D.
    Support—
        Easement—
            Generally. *See* **Easement** (Support).
        Natural right of support—
            Whether servient owner under positive duty to provide support for neighbour's land. **Holbeck Hall**
                Hotel Ltd v Scarborough BC [2000] **2** 705, CA.
            Withdrawal of support of underlying solid salt strata—Dissolution of salt by natural water and
                extraction by brine pumping—Whether loss of support occasioned by removal of liquefied strata
                actionable. **Lotus Ltd v British Soda Co Ltd** [1971] **1** 265, Ch D.
        Support from underground water—
            Water percolating beneath land—Works on neighbouring land causing loss of water and
                subsidence in land—Whether actionable in negligence or nuisance. **Langbrook Properties Ltd v**
                Surrey CC [1969] **3** 1424, Ch D.
    Telegraph line across private land. *See* **Telegraphs etc** (Telegraphic lines—Placing of telegraph line across
        private land).
    Tenure—
        Hong Kong—
            New Territories. *See* **Hong Kong** (New Territories—Land tenure).
    Tidal lands—
        Drainage rates—
            Exemption. *See* **Land drainage** (Drainage rates—Exemption—Tidal lands).
    Tithe and tithe rentcharge. *See* **Tithe and tithe rentcharge**.
    Title—
        Acknowledgment—
            Limitation of action. *See* **Limitation of action** (Acknowledgment—Title to land).
        Landlord. *See* **Landlord and tenant** (Title).
        Registration. *See* **Land registration**.
        Sale of land—
            Generally. *See* **Sale of land** (Title).
    Town and country planning. *See* **Town and country planning**.
    Town or village green—
        Registration. *See* **Commons** (Registration—Town or village green).

LAND (cont)—
    Transactions in land—
        Tax avoidance. *See* **Income tax** (Avoidance—Artificial transactions in land).
    Transfer for fraudulent purpose—
        Generally. *See* **Fraudulent conveyance**.
        Malaysia. *See* **Malaysia** (Land—Transfer).
    Trespass—
        Animal, by. *See* **Animal** (Trespass).
        Damages. *See* **Damages** (Trespass to land).
        Generally. *See* **Trespass to land**.
        Interlocutory injunction. *See* **Injunction** (Interlocutory—Trespass).
        Occupier's liability. *See* **Occupier's liability** (Trespasser).
    Tribunal—
        Agricultural Land Tribunal. *See* **Agricultural Land Tribunal**.
    Trust of land. *See* **Trust and trustee** (Trust of land).
    Trust property—
        Trust for sale. *See* **Trust and trustee** (Trust for sale—Trust property including land).
    Underground—
        Drainage rates—
            Exemption. *See* **Land drainage** (Drainage rates—Exemption—Underground land).
    Unlawful occupation—
        Injunction. *See* Summary proceedings for possession—Extent of court's jurisdiction—Persons unlawfully occupying woodland, *above*.
    Unoccupied—
        Planning permission. *See* **Town and country planning** (Permission for development—Land unoccupied on appointed day).
    Use and occupation—
        Action by owner of land against occupier. *See* **Landlord and tenant** (Use and occupation—Action for use and occupation in absence of lease).
    Use of land—
        Town and country planning—
            Discontinuance order. *See* **Town and country planning** (Discontinuance order—Use of land).
    Valuation—
        Appeal—
            Income tax. *See* **Income tax** (Appeal—Valuation of land).
        'Valuation agreed for probate'. *See* **Will** (Valuation of effects—Probate valuation—Direction to executors to transfer land at 'valuation agreed for probate').
    Value added tax—
        Exemption—
            Grant of right over or licence to occupy land. *See* **Value added tax** (Exemptions—Grant of right over or licence to occupy land).
        Supply of goods or services—
            Lease of land. *See* **Value added tax** (Supply of goods or services—Supply—Lease of land).
    Village green—
        Registration. *See* **Commons** (Registration—Town or village green).
    War damage—
        Payment in respect of damage to land. *See* **War damage** (Payments in respect of damage to land).
        Redevelopment—
            Compulsory purchase. *See* **War damage** (Redevelopment of land—Compulsory purchase).
    Waste land of a manor—
        Common land—
            Registration. *See* **Commons** (Registration—Common land and rights of common—Waste land of a manor).
    Water supply—
        Acquisition of land for purposes of water supply. *See* **Water supply** (Acquisition of land for purposes of water supply).
    Wayleave—
        Electricity—
            Compensation. *See* **Electricity** (Wayleave—Compensation).
    Will—
        Specific bequests. *See* **Will** (Gift—Specific bequests—Land).
    Work on land under statutory authority—
        Drainage board. *See* **Land drainage** (Drainage board).

LAND CHARGE
    Certificate—
        Negligence—
            False certificate. *See* **Negligence** (Information or advice—Assumption of liability—Statutory duty to give information—Register of local land charges).
    Creation—
        Joint tenancy—
            Land held on trust for sale—Severance of joint tenancy. *See* **Joint tenancy** (Severance—Land held on trust for sale—Severance of joint tenancy—Creation of charge by joint tenant on property held jointly).
    Equitable easement—
        Right or privilege over or affecting land being an equitable interest—
            Employee's position worsened—Need for registration of interest of requisitioning authority—Whether 'right or privilege over or affecting land'—Defence (General) Regulations 1939, reg 51(1)—Land Charges Act 1925, s 10(1), Class D(iii). **Lewisham BC v Maloney** [1947] **2** 36, CA.

LAND CHARGE (cont)—
Equitable easement (cont)—
Right or privilege over or affecting land being an equitable interest (cont)—
Right of re-entry—Re-entry on breach of covenant—Assignment of leasehold interest in part of premises—Covenant to perform and observe stipulations for benefit of retained premises—Covenant by purchaser that successors in title would observe stipulations—Whether right of re-entry void against successor in title to purchaser for want of registration—Land Charges Act 1925, s 10(1), Class C (iv), Class D (iii). **Shiloh Spinners Ltd v Harding** [1971] **2** 307, CA; [1973] **1** 90, HL.
Right to remove fixtures at end of tenancy—
Business premises. *See* **Landlord and tenant** (Business premises—Fixtures).
Equitable estoppel—
Mutual benefit and burden—
Right of passage with vehicles over land of another in return for allowing trespass by the foundations of his building—Acquiescence or estoppel giving rise subsequently to such a right—Whether registrable as estate contract or equitable easement—Whether invalidated as against purchaser with notice for want of registration—Land Charges Act 1925, ss 10(1), 13(2)—Law of Property Act 1925, s 199(1)(i). **Ives (E R) Investments Ltd v High** [1967] **1** 504, CA.
Estate contract—
Agreement for sale of land—
Failure to register prior to subsequent equitable mortgage—Priority. *See* **Mortgage** (Equitable interest—Priority—Agreement for sale of land).
Contract to convey or create a legal estate—
Contract appointing and authorising agent to make contract for sale of land—Whether a contract 'to convey or create a legal estate'—Land Charges Act 1925, s 10(1), Class C (iv). **Thomas v Rose** [1968] **3** 765, Ch D.
Contract—Meaning—Obligation binding on one party only—Absence of money consideration—Lease—Surrender—Obligation on lessee to offer to surrender lease to lessor before asking lessor's consent to assignment—Lessor having right to accept surrender without any consideration—Release of lessee from obligations of lease valuable consideration for surrender—Whether obligation on lessee a 'contract to convey' a legal estate—Land Charges Act 1972, s 2(4), Class C (iv). **Greene v Church Comrs for England** [1974] **3** 609, CA.
Exceptional rate—Whether registrable as an 'estate contract'—Land Charges Act 1925, s 10(1), Class C (iv). **Rayleigh Weir Stadium, Re** [1954] **2** 283, Ch D.
Notice to treat for a compulsory purchase—Whether registrable as estate contract—Land Charge Act 1925, s 10(1), Class C (iv). **Capital Investments Ltd v Wednesfield UDC** [1964] **1** 655, Ch D.
Failure to register. *See* Failure to register—Estate contract, *below*.
Name of estate owner—
Registration of estate contract in name of 'Frank David Blackburn' when true name of estate owner was 'Francis David Blackburn'—Registration not a nullity, but effective against purchaser who did not search or searched in wrong name—Search by subsequent intending mortgagee in name that was not estate owner's correct name—Whether mortgagee deemed to have notice of estate contract—Law of Property Act 1925, s 198(1)—Land Charges Act 1925, s 10(2). **Oak Co-op Building Society v Blackburn** [1968] **2** 117, CA.
Option to purchase—
Registration as estate contract—Generally. *See* **Option** (Option to purchase—Land charge—Registration as estate contract).
Option to purchase, right of pre-emption or other like right—
Absence of money consideration—Lease—Surrender—Obligation on lessee to offer to surrender lease to lessor before asking lessor's consent to assignment—Lessor having right to accept surrender without any consideration—Lessor thereby having first call on residue of lease should lessee wish to dispose of it—Release of lessee from obligations of lease valuable consideration for surrender—Whether lessor's right to call for surrender a right 'like' a right of pre-emption—Land Charges Act 1972, s 2(4), Class C (iv). **Greene v Church Comrs for England** [1974] **3** 609, CA.
Option to renew lease—
Registrability as land charge—Land Charges Act 1925, s 10(1), Class C(iv), s 13(2). **Beesly v Hallwood Estates Ltd** [1960] **2** 314, Ch D.
Registrability as land charge—Whether covenant in lease giving tenant option to renew lease registrable as land charge—Land Charges Act 1972, ss 2(4), Class C(iv), 4(6). **Phillips v Mobil Oil Co Ltd** [1989] **3** 97, CA.
Tenancy agreement—
Effect of registration on subsequent mortgages—Law of Property Act 1925, s 199(1). **Coventry Permanent Economic Building Society v Jones** [1951] **1** 901, Ch D.
Vacation of entry in register. *See* Vacation of entry in register, *below*.
Yearly tenancy under written agreement—
Undertaking to grant ten years' lease—Landlord himself holding under yearly tenancy at time of agreement—Fee simple later vested in landlord—Validity of undertaking against purchaser of land—Land Charges Act 1925, ss 10(1), Class C (iv), 13(2). **Sharp v Coates** [1948] **2** 871, CA.
Failure to register—
Estate contract—
Contract to grant underlease—Contract not registered—Breach—Enforcement by lessees against purchaser with notice—Liability of vendors—Damages—Land Charges Act 1925, ss 10(1), Class C (iv), 13(2). **Hollington Bros Ltd v Rhodes** [1951] **2** 578, Ch D.
Contract void against purchaser of legal estate for money or money's worth—Mortgagee—Defendant agreeing to purchase property—Agreement not registered—Defendant paying purchase price but title not conveyed to defendant—Legal owner charging property to bank—Bank claiming possession on legal owner's default—Whether defendant entitled to assert bare trust, constructive trust or proprietary estoppel against bank—Land Charges Act 1972, s 4(6). **Lloyds Bank plc v Carrick** [1996] **4** 630, CA.

LAND CHARGE (cont)—
  Failure to register (cont)—
    Estate contract (cont)—
      Contract void against purchaser of legal estate for money or money's worth—Purchaser—Sale of land by husband to wife for consideration substantially less than real value of land—Substantial element of gift in transaction—Transaction executed for ulterior motive of defeating option to purchase land—Option not registered—Whether wife a 'purchaser' of the legal estate for money or money's worth—Whether option binding on her estate—Land Charges Act 1925, s 13(2). **Midland Bank Trust Co Ltd v Green** [1981] **1** 153, HL.
      Solicitor's liability. *See* **Solicitor** (Negligence—Cause of action—Parallel claims in tort and contract—Solicitor drawing up option to purchase land—Solicitor acting for both grantor and grantee of option—Solicitor omitting to register option as estate contract—Grantor selling land to third party and defeating option—Grantee suing solicitor for negligence).
  General equitable charge—
    Charge on land—
      Contract to divide proceeds of sale of land—Whether charge on land—Whether registrable only general equitable charge—Land Charges Act 1925, s 10(1), Class C(iii). **Thomas v Rose** [1968] **3** 765, Ch D.
      Loss of deficiency payment—Whether charge on 'land'—Whether registrable as general equitable charge—Land Charges Act 1925, s 10(1), Class C(iii). **Georgiades v Edward Wolfe & Co Ltd** [1964] **3** 433, CA.
    Contract for sale of one-eighth share of partnership property—
      Freehold vested in one partner—Land Charges Act 1925, s 10(1), Class C(iii),(iv). **Rayleigh Weir Stadium, Re** [1954] **2** 283, Ch D.
    Vacation of entry in register. *See* Vacation of entry in register—General equitable charge, *below*.
  Interlocutory motion—
    Vacation of entry in register. *See* Vacation of entry in register—Interlocutory motion—Jurisdiction to order vacation on motion, *below*.
  Land certificate—
    Charge created by deposit of land certificate—
      Protection on register. *See* **Land registration** (Charge—Deposit of land certificate—Protection on register).
  Lis pendens. *See* Pending action, *below*.
  Local land charge—
    Registration—
      Certificate—Conclusiveness—Town and country planning—Compensation notice—Whether certificate conclusive. *See* **Town and country planning** (Compensation—Notice—Registration—Rules—Ultra vires—Whether power to make certificates issued by local land registrar conclusive as to existence of compensation notice).
      Town planning—Prohibition or restriction—Permission for development subject to time limit and for particular purpose only—Whether the permission was a restriction required to be registered under the repealed para (ii) of Land Charges Act 1925, s 15(7)(b), as substituted by Law of Property (Amendment) Act 1926, s 7, Sch. **Rose v Leeds Corp** [1964] **3** 618, CA.
  Matrimonial home—
    Costs—
      Legal aid. *See* **Legal aid** (Costs—Matrimonial home).
    Registration. *See* **Husband and wife** (Matrimonial home—Land charge—Registration).
  Option—
    Estate contract. *See* Estate contract, *above*.
    Lease—
      Renewal of lease—Registration as land charge. *See* General equitable charge—Contract for sale of one-eighth share of partnership property, *above*.
      Tenant's option conferred by lease. *See* **Option** (Option to purchase—Tenant's option conferred by lease—Registration as land charge).
  Partnership—
    Contract for sale of share of partnership property. *See* General equitable charge—Contract for sale of one-eighth share of partnership property, *above*.
  Pending action—
    Registration—
      Action 'relating to land'—Action must be one in which claim to land or interest in land is asserted—Registration of action by non-counterclaiming defendants—Whether registration wrongful—Land Charges Act 1925, s 2(1). **Heywood v BDC Properties Ltd (No 2)** [1964] **2** 702, CA.
      Pending land action—Action relating to interest in land—Action in which existence of easement over land is directly in issue—Whether action relating to interest in land—Land Charges Act 1972, s 17. **Allen v Greenhi Builders Ltd** [1978] **3** 1163, Ch D.
      Pending land action—Application by spouse for transfer of property other than matrimonial home—Whether application registrable—Whether claim required to be to an existing proprietary interest in the land—Land Charges Act 1972, ss 5(1) (a), 17(1)—Matrimonial Causes Act 1973, s 24. **Whittingham v Whittingham (National Westminster Bank Ltd intervening)** [1978] **3** 805, Ch D and CA.
      Pending land action—Application by wife for transfer of matrimonial home—Wife registering claim for ancillary relief as pending action—Husband obtaining loan from bank secured by first charge on matrimonial home—Bank not searching land charges register—Whether wife's application for property adjustment order having priority over bank's charge—Land Charges Act 1972, s 5—Matrimonial Causes Act 1973, ss 24(1), 37. **Perez-Adamson v Perez-Rivas (Barclays Bank plc, third party)** [1987] **3** 20, CA.
      Pending land action—Application for leave to commence action for breach of repairing covenant in lease—Whether application registrable—Whether application a proceeding 'relating to' land—Whether a proceeding which if successful would destroy an interest in land can 'relate to' land—Leasehold Property (Repairs) Act 1938, s 1(3). Land Charges Act 1972, ss 5(1), 17(1). **Selim Ltd v Bickenhall Engineering Ltd** [1981] **3** 210, Ch D.

LAND CHARGE (cont)—
Pending action (cont)—
Registration (cont)—
Pending land action—Meaning—Action relating to land or any interest in or charge on land—Action in respect of expenditure incurred by plaintiff in hope of obtaining contract relating to land and in furtherance of that contract when made—Plaintiff claiming payment of fair sum in respect of such expenditure and an order that until payment such sum should be a charge on the land—Whether 'an action relating to an interest in the land'—Land Charges Act 1972, s 17(1). **Haslemere Estates Ltd v Baker** [1982] **3** 525, Ch D.

Pending land action—Meaning—Action relating to land or any interest in or charge on land—Action to restrain owner of land from exercising power of disposition—Whether 'action relating to land' limited to action claiming some proprietary right in land—Land Charges Act 1972, ss 1(1), 5(1), 17(1). **Calgary & Edmonton Land Co Ltd v Dobinson** [1974] **1** 484, Ch D.

Pending land action—Tenants' action against landlord for damages for breach of landlord's repairing covenant in lease—Claim for damages coupled with claim for mandatory order requiring landlord to carry out repairs—Whether action registrable—Whether action relating to tenants' 'interest in land'—Land Charges Act 1972, ss 5(1), 17(1). **Regan & Blackburn Ltd v Rogers** [1985] **2** 180, Ch D.

Vacation of entry in register. See Vacation of entry in register—Pending action, *below.*
Vacation of entry in register. See Vacation of entry in register—Pending action, *below.*
Register—
Production—
Practice. See **Land registration** (Production of register of title).
Vacation of entry in. See Vacation of entry in register, *below.*
Registration—
Charge created by company—
Equitable charge affecting land. See **Company** (Charge—Registration—Equitable charge affecting land).
Compensation notice. See **Town and country planning** (Compensation—Notice—Registration).
Dispute regarding registration—
Service of originating summons to determine dispute impossible—Diplomatic privilege—Local authority registering local land charges in respect of building formerly used as Iranian embassy—Authority issuing summons to determine whether charges could be registered in land registry—Summons unable to be served on Iranian government—Whether court could hear and determine summons in absence of service on Iranian government—State Immunity Act 1978, s 12(1)—RSC Ord 32, r 5(1). **Westminster City Council v Government of the Islamic Republic of Iran** [1986] **3** 284, Ch D.

Equitable easement. See Equitable easement, *above.*
Estate contract. See Estate contract, *above.*
General equitable charge. See General equitable charge, *above.*
Matrimonial home. See **Husband and wife** (Matrimonial home—Land charge—Registration).
Obligation affecting land—
Obligation binding on successors in title—Right of pre-emption—Local authority—Sale of house by authority—Local authority exercising statutory power to impose condition precluding purchaser or successor in title from selling house without first offering to resell to authority—Whether condition an 'obligation affecting land'—Whether registrable as an estate contract—Housing Act 1957, s 104(3)(c)—Land Charges Act 1972, s 2(1)(4). **First National Securities Ltd v Chiltern DC** [1975] **2** 766, Ch D.

Order appointing receiver—
Re-registration—Receiving order in bankruptcy made in 1927—Discharge of bankrupt in 1930—Re-registration by Official Receiver in 1946—Vacation of entry in register—Land Charges Act 1925, s 6(1)(c), (3), (5). **A Receiving Order (In Bankruptcy), Re** [1947] **1** 843, Ch D.

Receiver appointed by court to manage property—Tenanted property in disrepair—Tenant obtaining order appointing receiver to manage property—Tenant lodging caution against landlords' title in respect of receivership order—Whether receivership order registrable against landlords' title—Whether tenant a 'person interested' in land—Land Registration Act 1925, ss 54(1), 59(5)—Land Charges Act 1925, s 6(1)(b). **Clayhope Properties Ltd v Evans** [1986] **2** 795, CA.

Pending action. See Pending action—Registration, *above.*
Registered land—
Exemption from requirement to register land charge where charge capable of being protected by caution under Land Registration Act—Option to renew underlease—Headlease not registered at time of creation of underlease—Assignment of headlease—Headlease registered subsequently to assignment—Whether option exempt from requirement to be registered as land charge—Whether underlessee entitled to lodge caution as person having or claiming interest in land not already registered—Land Charges Act 1925, s 23(1)—Land Registration Act 1925, s 53(1). **Kitney v MEPC Ltd** [1978] **1** 595, CA.

Registration in appropriate register—
Middlesex Deeds Registry—Land charge created after 1st January 1926—Land charge created in area not at time a compulsory registration area—Option in lease—Option to renew lease—Memorial of lease recorded in Middlesex Deeds Registry—Whether Middlesex Deeds Register an 'appropriate register'—Whether registration of lease in Middlesex Deeds Registry sufficient to ensure validity of option—Land Charges Act 1925, ss 13(2), 18. **Kitney v MEPC Ltd** [1978] **1** 595, CA.

Registration in name of estate owner—
Relayer inspecting line to determine lengths of metal later required for relaying—Meaning—Owner of legal estate unless context otherwise requires—Contract for sale of land—Purchaser registering land charge in name of vendor—Vendor at date of registration having only equitable interest under contract of sale with owner of legal estate—Vendor subsequently acquiring legal estate—Whether registration valid—Law of Property Act 1925, s 205(1)(v)—Land Charges Act 1972, ss 3(1), 17(1). **Barrett v Hilton Developments Ltd** [1974] **3** 944, CA.

LAND CHARGE (cont)—
 Registration (cont)—
  Restrictive covenant—
   Covenant for benefit of demised land—Whether covenant between lessor and lessee within
   meaning of exception in Land Charges Act 1925, s 10(1), Class D(ii). **Dartstone Ltd v Cleveland
   Petroleum Co Ltd** [1969] **3** 668, Ch D.
 Restrictive covenant. *See* Registration—Restrictive covenant, *above.*
 Search—
  Official certificate of search—
   Conclusiveness—Search in name that was a version of estate owner's name but not his full correct
   name—Search in name 'Francis Davis Blackburn', when true name was 'Francis David
   Blackburn'—Estate contract registered in name 'Frank David Blackburn' not revealed by
   search—Effect of certificate of search—Land Charges Act 1925, s 17(3). **Oak Co-op Building
   Society v Blackburn** [1968] **2** 117, CA.
 Tenancy agreement—
  Effect of registration on subsequent mortgages. *See* Estate contract—Tenancy agreement—Effect of
  registration on subsequent mortgages, *above.*
 Unpaid rates or taxes—
  Surcharge on unused commercial building. *See* **Rates** (Surcharge on unused commercial
  building—Unpaid surcharge constituting charge on land comprised in hereditament).
 Vacation of entry in register—
  Contract registered as estate contract—
   Conditional contract relating to land—Condition to be satisfied not by parties but by some
   extraneous person—Motion to vacate entry. **Haslemere Estates Ltd v Baker** [1982] **3** 525, Ch D.
   Contract authorising agent to make contract for sale of land—Motion to vacate entry—Land
   Charges Act 1925, s 10(1), Class C(iv). **Thomas v Rose** [1968] **3** 765, Ch D.
   Failure by purchaser to complete—Summons to vacate entry—Competency. **Engall's Agreement,
   Re** [1953] **2** 503, Ch D.
   Whether an estate contract—Land Charges Act 1925, ss 8(3), 10(1), Class C(iv). **Turley v Mackay**
   [1943] **2** 1, Ch D.
  County court—
   Jurisdiction—Registered land. *See* **County court** (Jurisdiction—Land registration—Rectification of
   register—Notice of charge).
  General equitable charge—
   Entry of general equitable charge for estate agents' commission charged on purchase
   money—Bona fide dispute whether estate agents entitled to commission—Vendor's application
   to vacate entry—Whether application should be disposed of prior to determination of dispute as
   to commission—Judicial discretion—Determination of application by Court of Appeal—Land
   Charges Act 1925, s 10(8). **Georgiades v Edward Wolfe & Co Ltd** [1964] **3** 433, CA.
  Interlocutory motion—
   Jurisdiction to order vacation on motion—Estate contract—Contract for sale of land—Registration
   of land charge by purchaser—Purchaser failing to complete contract—Action by vendor for
   damages and vacation of entry—Motion by vendor for vacation of entry—Whether power of court
   to order vacation on motion limited to cases where defendant never having had a charge which
   could be registered—Land Charges Act 1925, s 10(8). **Hooker v Wyle** [1973] **3** 707, Ch D.
   Jurisdiction to order vacation on motion—Land Charges Act 1972, s 1(b). **Calgary & Edmonton
   Land Co Ltd v Dobinson** [1974] **1** 484, Ch D.
   Jurisdiction to order vacation on motion—Land charge registered by defendants in respect of an
   estate contract evidenced by specified correspondence—Action by plaintiffs for declaration that
   no contract existed and for vacation of entry in land charges register—Motion in action for order
   for vacation of entry granted—Land Charges Act 1925, s 10(8)—RSC Ord 55, r 14A. **Heywood v
   BDC Properties Ltd** [1963] **2** 1063, CA.
   Triable issue—Appropriate order to preserve parties interests—Pending action—Action prosecuted
   in good faith—Court having no power to vacate registration of pending action—Power to secure
   vacation by indirect means—Order to stay action unless entry vacated—Intimation to plaintiff that
   on vacating entry he would be granted interlocutory injunction on giving cross-undertaking as to
   damages—Whether proper for court to make order. **Norman v Hardy** [1974] **1** 1170, Ch D.
  Order—
   Form of order—Personal or impersonal form—Order that entry 'be vacated'—Whether order should
   require defendant to remove caution. **Calgary & Edmonton Land Co Ltd v Dobinson** [1974] **1** 484,
   Ch D.
  Pending action—
   Action struck out by court as scandalous, frivolous and vexatious and an abuse of the process of
   the court—Decision upheld by Court of Appeal—Petition to appeal pending before House of
   Lords—Whether entry be vacated as proceedings not prosecuted in good faith—Land Charges
   Act 1925, s 2(6). **Calgary & Edmonton Land Co Ltd v Discount Bank (Overseas) Ltd** [1971] **1** 551,
   Ch D.
   Matrimonial proceedings—Summons under Married Women's Property Act 1882—Wife,
   respondent in divorce suit, claiming declaration of entitlement to half share in proceeds of sale of
   the matrimonial home, and asking for sale, etc—Property in name of husband who had
   contracted to sell it—Registration vacated—Land Charges Act 1925, ss 2(1)(6), 20(6). **Taylor v
   Taylor** [1968] **1** 843, CA.
   Power of court to order vacation of registration—Mareva injunction registered in land
   register—Whether injunction registered for 'purpose of enforcing a judgment'—Land Charges Act
   1972, s 6(1)(a). **Stockler v Fourways Estates Ltd** [1983] **3** 501, QBD.
   Power of court to order vacation of registration—Order during pendency of proceedings—Court
   satisfied proceedings not being prosecuted in good faith—Power to order vacation limited to
   cases where proceedings not being prosecuted in good faith—Land Charges Act 1972, ss 1(6),
   5(10). **Norman v Hardy** [1974] **1** 1170, Ch D.
   Power of court to order vacation of registration—Order during pendency of proceedings—No claim
   or counterclaim for interest in land—Whether power to order vacation during pendency of
   proceedings—Land Charges Act 1925, s 2(6). **Heywood v BDC Properties Ltd (No 2)** [1964] **2** 702,
   CA.

LAND CHARGE (cont)—
Vacation of entry in register (cont)—
Pending action (cont)—
Power of court to order vacation of registration—Summons—Action registered as lis pendens by non-counterclaiming defendants—Defendants not prosecuting proceedings—No power in court to vacate registration under statute—Order, as if on motion, for vacation under court's inherent jurisdiction—Land Charges Act 1925, s 2(6). **Heywood v BDC Properties Ltd (No 2)** [1964] **2** 702, CA.
Power of court to order vacation of registration—Whether power restricted to cases where absence of good faith in prosecuting proceedings—Whether general power to vacate registration of pending action—Land Charges Act 1972, ss 1(6), 5(10). **Northern Development (Holdings) Ltd v UDT Securities** [1977] **1** 747, Ch D.

LAND DRAINAGE
Banks—
Deposit of soil on banks of watercourse. *See* Drainage board—Right to deposit spoil on banks of watercourse—Banks, *below*.
Catchment board—
Commutation of obligation to repair—
Contractual obligation to keep ditch clean—Land Drainage Act 1930, s 9(1). **Eton RDC v River Thames Conservators** [1950] **1** 996, Ch D.
Contract to widen, deepen and make good banks of river—
Bursting of banks—Flooding of adjoining land owned by successor in title to party to contract—Liability of board. **Smith v River Douglas Catchment Board** [1949] **2** 179, CA.
Precept—
Amount of demand—Aggregate not to exceed estimated amount which would be produced by rate of 2d in £—'Estimated amount'—Whether allowance to be made for cost of calculation and bad debts—Land Drainage Act 1930, ss 20, 22(2). **R v Cambridgeshire CC** [1936] **3** 352, KBD.
Drainage board—
Exercise of statutory powers—
Injury sustained by person by reason of exercise of board's statutory powers—Statutory remedy—Compensation—Catchment board cleansing watercourse—Damage to plaintiff's bridge—Dredgings deposited on bank—Diversion of flood waters—Action for nuisance, alternatively, negligence, by plaintiff—Competence—Land Drainage Act 1930, ss 34(1) (3), 38(1). **Marriage v East Norfolk Rivers Catchment Board** [1949] **2** 1021, CA.
Maintenance and repair of drainage works—
Failure to keep drainage works in repair—Flooding—Breach of statutory duty. **Smith v Cawdle Fen, Ely (Cambridge), Comrs** [1938] **4** 64, KBD.
Maintenance and repair of drains—
Failure to keep drains in fit and proper condition—Nonfeasance—Clearing weeds—Action for negligence and breach of statutory duty—Liability of board—Land Drainage Act 1930, ss 12, 34. **Gillett v Kent Rivers Catchment Board** [1938] **4** 810, KBD.
Maintenance and repair of dyke—
Positive duty to repair dyke imposed by local Act—Whether duty superseded by provisions of Land Drainage Act 1930, ss 4(1)(a)(b), 34. **Rippingale Farms Ltd v Black Sluice Internal Drainage Board** [1963] **3** 726, CA.
Maintenance and repair of river bank—
Bank some distance from main river—protection against flood—Whether 'bank' within Land Drainage Act 1930—Land Drainage Act 1930, ss 1, 7, 9, 11, 81. **North Level Comrs v River Welland Catchment Board** [1937] **4** 684, Ch D.
Maintenance and repair of river wall—
Negligent repair—Liability for misfeasance—Land Drainage Act 1930, s 34. **East Suffolk Rivers Catchment Board v Kent** [1940] **4** 527, HL.
Right of entry on land—
Circumstances in which right exercisable—Whether for maintenance of existing works only—Land Drainage Act 1930, s 34(4)—Land Drainage Act 1961, s 40(1). **Pattinson v Finningley Internal Drainage Board** [1970] **1** 790, QBD.
Right to deposit spoil on banks of watercourse—
Banks—Meaning—River board cleansing watercourse—Dredgings deposited on adjoining land—Exclusion of compensation where matter so removed deposited on the banks of the watercourse—Whether adjoining land 'banks'—Construction of enactment—Land Drainage Act 1930, s 38(1). **Jones v Mersey River Board** [1957] **3** 375, CA.
Drainage rates—
Annual value of hereditament—
Determination of annual value—Whether 'determined' when annual value in dispute for income tax purposes—Land Drainage Act 1930, s 29(1). **BP Refinery (Kent) Ltd v Kent River Board** [1956] **2** 834, QBD.
New premises not assessed to income tax under Sch A—Rate assessed on basis of current annual value of premises—Other properties in board's area assessed on Sch A value at figure based on their value in 1936—Whether for reason of equality new premises should be assessed on that basis—Land Drainage Act 1930, ss 24(4), 29(2). **R v Hastings Justices, ex p Pevensey Levels Internal Drainage Board** [1962] **1** 278, QBD.
Valuation—Duty to board—Whether board required to make fresh valuation in each year—Land Drainage Act 1930, ss 24, 26, 29. **Port of London Authority v Essex Rivers Catchment Board** [1944] **2** 507, CA.
Exemption—
Tidal lands—Extent of exemption—Whether tidal lands other than those vested in Crown exempt—Land Drainage Act 1930, s 77. **Collard v River Stour (Kent) Catchment Board** [1937] **1** 436, KBD.
Underground land—Application for determination that no rate should be levied in respect of underground workings more than 500 ft below surface—Whether horizontal section of underground workings can be portion of the district within Land Drainage Act 1930, s 24(7). **Trent River Authority v National Coal Board** [1970] **1** 558, HL.

255

LAND DRAINAGE (cont)—
  Drainage rates (cont)—
    Owners's rate—
      Covenant in lease—Covenant by tenant to pay 'all rates, taxes and outgoings'—Owner's rate paid by tenant—Whether entitled to be recouped by landlord. **Smith v Smith** [1939] **4** 312, KBD.
  Dyke—
    Maintenance and repair. *See* Drainage board—Maintenance and repair of dyke, *above*.
  Embankment—
    Statutory duty to maintain under local Act—
      Transfer of obligation to river board—Breach of duty—Whether right of action for damages conferred—Whether right of action excluded by enactment conferring default powers on minister of Crown—Scarisbrick Estate Drainage Act 1924, s 16(2)—Land Drainage Act 1930, s 12—River Boards Act 1948, s 22. **Sephton v Lancashire River Board** [1962] **1** 183, Assizes.
  Implied Crown grant—
    Right to drain from seaward to landward side of sea wall. *See* Sea wall—Right to drain from seaward to landward side of wall—Implied Crown grant, *below*.
  Mutual licences—
    Drainage to and from adjoining properties—
      Unilateral revocation. *See* **Licence** (Mutual licences—Unilateral revocation—Drainage to and from adjoining properties).
  Restriction on erection of structures on bank of river—
    Byelaw prohibiting structure on bank of river—
      Row of tanks filled with earth kept in position by own weight—Whether a 'structure'. **Hobday v Nicol** [1944] **1** 302, KBD.
  River bank—
    Erection of structures on. *See* Restriction on erection of structures on bank of river, *above*.
    Maintenance and repair. *See* Drainage board—Maintenance and repair of river bank, *above*.
  River wall—
    Maintenance and repair. *See* Drainage board—Maintenance and repair of river wall, *above*.
  Sea wall—
    Negligence—
      Duty of catchment board to repair—Footpath on wall—Collapse of wall—Injury to person on path—Liability of board. **Hunwick v Essex Rivers Catchment Board** [1952] **1** 765, Assizes.
    Right to drain from seaward to landward side of wall—
      Implied Crown grant—Rights of drainage of upper landowner. **Symes and Jaywick Associated Properties Ltd v Essex Rivers Catchment Board** [1936] **3** 908, CA.
  Tidal lands—
    Drainage rates exemption. *See* Drainage rates—Exemption—Tidal lands, *above*.

LAND IMPLEMENT
  Trailer. *See* **Road traffic** (Trailer—Land implement).

LAND REGISTRATION
  Acquisition of title by possession—
    Dispute—
      Oral agreement to compromise dispute—Statutory requirements for contract for sale or other disposition of interest in land—Whether compromise agreement being 'for the sale or other disposition of an interest in land'—Law of Property (Miscellaneous Provisions) Act 1989, s 2(1). **Yeates v Line** [2013] **2** 84, Ch D.
    Leaseholds—
      Effect of surrender of lease on rights of squatter acquired by adverse possession against lessee—Land Registration Act 1925, s 75. **Central London Commercial Estates Ltd v Kato Kagaku Co Ltd (Axa Equity and Law Life Assurance Society plc, third party)** [1998] **4** 948, Ch D.
    Registration of adverse possession—
      Offence of squatting in a residential building—Whether required period of adverse possession could include period during which offence of squatting in residential building committed—Land Registration Act 2002, Sch 6—Legal Aid, Sentencing and Punishment of Offenders Act 2012, s 144. **R (on the application of Best) v Chief Land Registrar (Secretary of State for Justice, interested party)** [2014] **3** 637, QBD; [2015] **4** 495, CA.
      Treatment of application—Adjacent land—Reasonable belief for at least ten years ending on date of application that land belonged to applicant—Nature of reasonable belief—Land Registration Act 2002, Sch 6, para 5(4). **Zarb v Parry** [2012] **2** 320, CA.
  Adverse possession—
    Priority of pending application. *See* Priority—Pending application—Day list showing date and time at which applications made—Application for registration of title by adverse possession entered on day list, *below*.
  Appeal—
    Notice of appeal—
      Caution against dealings. *See* Caution against dealings—Notice of appeal, *below*.
    Procedure—
      Appeal to nominated judge of Chancery Division from decision of registrar—Whether re-hearing or trial de novo—RSC Ord 54D, r 6. **Gilbert's Application, Re** [1961] **2** 313, Ch D.
  Boundary—
    Description of registered land. *See* Description of registered land—Boundary, *below*.
  Caution—
    Caution against dealings. *See* Caution against dealings, *below*.
    Charging order—
      Protection on register. *See* Charging order—Protection on register—Caution, *below*.
    Rectification of register. *See* Rectification of register—Caution, *below*.

LAND REGISTRATION (cont)—
 Caution against dealings—
  Lodging of caution by person interested in land—
   Effect—Registrar not to register any dealing until notice served on cautioner—Purchaser applying
    for official search—Cautioner subsequently lodging caution against dealings—Purchaser then
    lodging application to register instrument effecting purchase within priority period—Registrar
    cancelling cautioner's application without giving notice to cautioner—Whether cautioner entitled
    to statutory protection—Land Registration Act 1925, s 55. **Smith v Morrison** [1974] **1** 957, Ch D.
   Sale of land held on trust for sale by registered proprietor—Cautioner having an interest in
    proceeds of sale—Whether an interest in land—Whether cautioner having locus standi to lodge
    caution in respect of land—Land Registration Act 1925, ss 3(xv), 54(1). **Elias v Mitchell**
    [1972] **2** 153, Ch D.
  Notice of appeal—
   Appeal from 'decision or order...of the Court'—Entry of notice of appeal from decision or order of
    court in register—Whether only notice of appeal from decision of court on appeal from registrar
    need be entered in register—Whether any notice of appeal affecting property required to be
    registered—Land Registration Rules 1925, r 301. **Belcourt v Belcourt** [1989] **2** 34, Ch D.
 Charge—
  Deposit of land certificate—
   Protection on register—Notice—Caution—Land Registration Act 1925, s 49—Land Registration
    Rules 1925 (SR & O 1925 No 1093), r 239. **White Rose Cottage, Re** [1965] **1** 11, CA.
  Legal mortgage—
   Date when charge takes effect—Land Registration Act 1925, ss 20(1), 27(3). **Rymer (Grace)**
    Investments Ltd v Waite [1958] **2** 777, CA.
   Legal mortgage by estoppel—Legal mortgage executed in favour of bank—Grantor not being
    registered proprietor of property or entitled to be so registered at date of charge—Grantor
    subsequently obtaining legal estate and becoming registered proprietor—Mortgagee applying to
    register charge—Whether legal mortgage created by estoppel—Whether doctrine of feeding the
    estoppel applicable in absence of clear and unambiguous recital in grant that grantor seised of
    legal estate—Whether doctrine of feeding the estoppel applicable to creation of legal charge of
    registered land—Land Registration Act 1925, ss 25, 37. **First National Bank plc v Thompson**
    [1996] **1** 140, CA.
  Transfer—
   Powers of proprietor of charge—Powers of proprietor remaining in transferor until
    registration—Appointment of receiver between transfer and registration—Land Registration Act
    1925, ss 33, 34. **Lever Finance Ltd v Trustee of Property of Needleman** [1956] **2** 378, Ch D.
 Charging order—
  Protection on register—
   Caution—Caution registered at Land Registry to protect charge over or interest in property—Land
    Registry registering subsequent charge over same property, in one case without notice to
    cautioners—Whether cautioners in first case entitled to indemnity from registrar—Whether
    cautioners' interest in land having priority over subsequently registered charge—Whether
    charging order giving cautioners charge over legal estate—Land Registration Act 1925, ss 55,
    56(2), 83(2)—Charging Orders Act 1979, s 2(1)(b)(iii). **Clark v Chief Land Registrar** [1993] **2** 936,
    Ch D; [1994] **4** 96, CA.
   Caution—Official search on sale of property—Failure to disclose caution—Mistake of Land
    Registry—Transfer to purchaser—Charge on property by purchaser in favour of third
    party—Transfer and charge lodged for registration—Cautioner's objection to registration—
    Whether caution effective—Priority as between cautioners, transferee and chargee—Land
    Registration Act 1925, ss 55(1)(2), 59(1)—Land Registration Rules 1925 (SR & O 1925 No 1093),
    r 295. **Parkash v Irani Finance Ltd** [1969] **1** 930, Ch D.
 Common land. *See* **Commons** (Registration).
 Concurrent applications for registration—
  Priority. *See* Priority—Concurrent applications for registration, *below.*
 Contract to divide proceeds of sale of land—
  Whether registrable as general equitable charge. *See* **Land charge** (General equitable charge—Charge
   on land—Contract to divide proceeds of sale of land—Whether charge on land—Whether registrable
   only general equitable charge).
 Costs—
  Transfer of registered land on sale—
   Scale fee—Not all work done to which scale fee applied—Whether scale fee chargeable—Solicitors'
    Remuneration (Registered Land) Order 1925 (SR & O 1926 No 2), art 1(d)(i), Sch (as substituted by
    Solicitors' Remuneration (Registered Land) Order 1953 (SI 1953 No 118)). **Solicitor, Re a**
    [1957] **1** 427, CA.
   Scale fee—Sale by order of court—Not all work completed to which scale fee applied—Whether
    scale fee chargeable—Solicitors' Remuneration (Registered Land) Order 1925 (S R & O 1926
    No 2), art 1(d)(i), Sch (as substituted by Solicitors' Remuneration (Registered Land) Order 1953
    (SI 1953 No (SI 1953 No 118)). **Terrace (10), The, Hampton Wick, Middlesex, Re** [1957] **1** 87, Ch D.
 Deposit of land certificate—
  Charge. *See* Charge—Deposit of land certificate, *above.*
 Description of registered land—
  Boundary—
   Filed plan—Plan on land certificate at variance with plan attached to transfer—Which plan
    prevails—Land Registration Act 1925, ss 19, 69, 76—Land Registration Rules 1925 (SR & O 1925
    No 1093), r 278. **Lee v Barrey** [1957] **1** 191, CA.
  Roof space—
   Freeholder granting new development lease to claimant—New lease comprising roof space already
    included in demise of existing leases—Registrar registering new lease concurrently with existing
    leases—Property register referring to existing leases as first floor 'only'—Whether necessary to
    examine both register and registered leases when determining extent demised—Land
    Registration Act 2002, ss 60, 66—Land Registration Rules 2003, SI 2003/1417, rr 4, 5, 6, 26. **R (on**
    the application of HCP (Hendon) Ltd) v Chief Land Registrar (Henley Court Properties Ltd,
    interested party) [2021] **1** 667, QBD.

LAND REGISTRATION (cont)—
  Easement—
    Equitable easement—
      Overriding interest. *See* Overriding interest—Equitable easement, *below.*
    Sale of land. *See* **Sale of land** (Easements—Registration).
  Effect of registration of dispositions of freeholds—
    Positive covenant—
      Burden—Whether burden of positive covenant required to be registered—Land Registration Act 1925, s 20(1). **Elwood v Goodman** [2013] **4** 1077n, CA.
  Effect of registration of dispositions of leaseholds—
    Effect on forfeiture—
      Possessory leasehold title assigned to foreign corporation—No licence in mortmain or statutory authority to hold land—Effect of registration—Land Registration Act 1925, ss 23, 80. **Morelle Ltd v Wakeling** [1955] **1** 708, CA.
  Effect of registration on legal estate—
    Possessory title—
      Leaseholds—Registration of title acquired by squatter under Limitation Acts by adverse possession—Whether squatter's registered title defeasible by surrender of lease by documentary lessee to freeholder—Whether surrender by documentary lessee after removal of title from register effecting surrender of lease—Whether 'transfer' of registered land including surrender—Land Registration Act 1925, ss 21(1), 75(3). **Spectrum Investment Co v Holmes** [1981] **1** 6, Ch D.
      Leaseholds—Vesting of one-day reversion after sale of leasehold term created by mortgage of leaseholds by sub-demise—Land Transfer Act 1875, s 13—Land Transfer Rules 1903 (SR & O 1903 No 1081), r 57—Land Registration Act (Apportionment) s 69(1). **King (decd), Re** [1963] **1** 781, CA.
  Effect of registration on title of registered proprietor—
    Notice of lease—
      Option in lease—Option having been invalidated for want of registration as land charge—Merger of freehold interest with headlease—Headlease subject to underlease—Option contained in underlease—Option to renew underlease—Merger resulting in registration of new title to freehold interest with title absolute—Charges register of new title containing entry referring to underlease—Whether registration of new freehold title validating option. **Kitney v MEPC Ltd** [1978] **1** 595, CA.
  Estate contract—
    Failure to register. *See* **Land charge** (Failure to register—Estate contract).
  First registration—
    Leasehold—
      Application to register sub-lease—Whether entry of land certificate of head-lease necessary—Refusal to accept application without land certificate of head-lease—Whether production effective as from date of application—Land Registration Act 1925, s 64(1)(a)—Land Registration Rules 1925 (SR & O 1925 No 1093), r 83. **Strand Securities Ltd v Caswell** [1965] **1** 820, CA.
  Fraud—
    Rectification of register on ground of fraud. *See* Rectification of register—Circumstances justifying rectification—Entry obtained by fraud, *below.*
  Implied covenants on transfer of leaseholds. *See* Transfer—Leaseholds—Implied covenants on transfer of leaseholds, *below.*
  Land charge—
    Generally. *See* **Land charge**.
  Legal mortgage—
    Charge. *See* Charge—Legal mortgage, *above.*
  Local land charge. *See* **Land charge** (Local land charge).
  Minor interests—
    Protection—
      Class of rights and interests constituting minor interests—Class limited to interests capable of subsisting as interests in unregistered land—Right of first refusal to purchase freehold premises—Right of first refusal not an interest in land—Right of first refusal not capable of protection by registration of a caution—Land Registration Act 1925, s 3(xv). **Murray v Two Strokes Ltd** [1973] **3** 357, Ch D.
      Transfer for valuable consideration—Transferee not acting in good faith—Notice of minor interest—House held on trust by defendant for himself and plaintiff in equal shares—Defendant registered owner—Trust not entered in land registry—Defendant transferring whole beneficial interest in house to wife as part of divorce settlement—Defendant and wife aware of trust affecting house—Whether wife taking house free of trust—Whether transferee who is a purchaser for valuable consideration entitled to protection against unregistered minor interest if acting in bad faith—Land Registration Act 1925, ss 20(1)(4), 59(6). **Peffer v Rigg** [1978] **3** 745, Ch D.
  Mortgage—
    Equitable mortgage—
      Deposit of land certificate. *See* **Mortgage** (Equitable mortgage—Priority—Memorandum of deposit and deposit of land certificate).
  Name of estate owner—
    Registration of estate contract in incorrect name. *See* **Land charge** (Estate contract—Name of estate owner).
  New Zealand. *See* **New Zealand** (Land registration).
  Notice—
    Notice of charge—
      Rectification of register—County court—Jurisdiction. *See* **County court** (Jurisdiction—Land registration—Rectification of register—Notice of charge).
    Notice of restrictive covenant—
      Binding effect of covenant—Restrictive covenant entered on register against freehold title—Lease—Assignment of lease—No actual notice of covenant to assignee—Constructive notice—Land Registration Act 1925, ss 20, 50, 52. **White v Bijou Mansions Ltd** [1938] **1** 546, CA.

LAND REGISTRATION (cont)—
Notice (cont)—
Positive covenant noted on register—
Whether binding on subsequent purchaser—Land Registration Act 1925, s 20. **Cator v Newton and Bates** [1939] **4** 457, CA.
Notices and restrictions—
Notices—
Entry on application—Unilateral notices—Cancellation—Jurisdiction of High Court to cancel unilateral notice—Land Registration Act 2002, Pt 4. **Nugent v Nugent** [2014] **2** 313, Ch D.
Overriding interest—
Deserted wife's equity to remain in matrimonial home—
Whether an overriding interest. See **Husband and wife** (Deserted wife's right to remain in matrimonial home—Registered land—Overriding interest).
Equitable easement—
Easement 'not ... required to be protected by notice on the register'—Landlord granting lease of garage to tenant—Lease including right of way over driveway leading to garage—Tenant using garage—Right of way not protected by notice on register—Landlord leasing part of driveway to petrol company—Whether tenant of garage in 'actual occupation'—Whether petrol company's lease subject to right of way—Whether right of way an 'overriding interest'—Land Registration Act 1925, s 70(1)(a)(g)—Land Registration Rules 1925, r 258. **Celsteel Ltd v Alton House Holdings Ltd** [1985] **2** 562, Ch D.
Right of way—Interests of persons in actual occupation—Access to dominant tenement obtained by metal staircase and landing constructed on servient tenement by unregistered agreement between claimant and defendant's predecessor in title—Defendant acquiring servient tenement—Defendant subsequently taking down metal staircase—Whether claimant having prior interest—Whether claimant in actual occupation of part of servient land—Land Registration Act 2002, s 29(2)(a)(ii), Sch 3, paras 2, 3. **Chaudhary v Yavuz** [2012] **2** 418, CA.
Extent of interest—
Land affected—Tenant occupying shop premises on part of development site—Tenant entitled to lease of new shop on its premises if site redeveloped—Agreement for lease of new shop giving rise to overriding interest—Whether overriding interest extending to whole redevelopment site—Whether tenant entitled to lease of new shop anywhere on whole site—Whether tenant entitled to insist that new shop be built on existing premises. **Ashburn Anstalt v Arnold** [1988] **2** 147, CA.
Lease for term not exceeding 21 years granted at a rent without taking a fine—
Granted—Oral agreement, evidenced by memorandum in writing, to grant a tenancy for term exceeding three years—Whether 'overriding interest'—Land Registration Act 1925, s 70(1)(k). **City Permanent Building Society v Miller** [1952] **2** 621, CA.
Rectification of land register to give effect to overriding interest. See Rectification of register—Overriding interest—Rectification to give effect to overriding interest, *below*.
Right to remove fixtures at end of lease—
Whether an overriding interest. See **Landlord and tenant** (Business premises—Fixtures).
Rights of person in actual occupation of land—
Actual occupation—Date for ascertaining whether interest in registered land is protected by actual occupation—Son buying leasehold house on mortgage for occupation by mother—Mother having beneficial interest in property—Mother entering into occupation after completion but before registration of mortgagee's charge—Son defaulting on mortgage—Mortgagee seeking to enforce security—Whether mother having overriding interest—Whether beneficial interest created after charge but before it was registered having priority over charge—Whether entry into property to plan decorations as measure for furnishing prior to completion constituting 'actual occupation'—Land Registration Act 1925, ss 23(1), 70(1)(g). **Abbey National Building Society v Cann** [1990] **1** 1085, HL.
Actual occupation—Lessee allowing relative to occupy flat, rent free—Whether lessee in actual occupation of flat—Land Registration Act 1925, s 70(1)(g). **Strand Securities Ltd v Caswell** [1965] **1** 820, CA.
Actual occupation—Relevant date for determining actual occupation—Occupation through agent—Husband exchanging contracts for purchase of house requiring repairs and renovation—Common intention of husband and wife that wife should have beneficial interest in property—Vendors permitting builders engaged by husband and wife to enter onto property prior to completion—Husband executing charge over property on completion without wife's knowledge to secure overdraft—Bank seeking possession and sale of property to obtain repayment of overdraft—Whether wife having rights in property—Whether relevant date for ascertaining wife's rights date of execution or date of registration of charge—Whether wife in actual occupation of property—Whether wife having beneficial interest in property—Whether wife having overriding interest which took priority over bank's charge—Land Registration Act 1925, ss 20(1), 70(1)(g). **Lloyds Bank plc v Rosset** [1988] **3** 915, CA.
Actual occupation—Vendor in occupation—Whether person other than vendor may be in actual occupation—Land Registration Act 1925, s 70(1). **Hodgson v Marks** [1971] **2** 684, CA.
Agreement for sale and purchase—Agreement before exchange of contracts for vendor to remain in occupation as tenant—Contract not reflecting agreement for tenancy—Exchange of contracts, completion and execution of mortgage taking place on same day—Tenancy subsequently granted by purchaser to vendor—Purchaser defaulting on mortgage loan—Whether vendor having priority over mortgagee—Whether vendor having overriding interest—Land Registration Act 2002, s 29(2)(a)(ii), Sch 3, para 2. **Scott v Southern Pacific Mortgages Ltd** [2015] **1** 277, SC.
Building society granting mortgage conditional on occupying tenants signing consent forms postponing their interests to interest of society—Effect of consent forms on tenants' mandatory rights—Land Registration Act 1925, s 70(1)(g). **Woolwich Building Society v Dickman** [1996] **3** 204, CA.

LAND REGISTRATION (cont)—
Overriding interest (cont)—
Rights of person in actual occupation of land (cont)—
Doctrine of overreaching—Vendors selling land including yard to defendant—Right of way over yard not reserved in favour of vendors—Vendors subsequently selling adjoining land to claimants with right of way over yard—Claimants' title registered prior to defendant's title—Whether grant of easement to claimants being 'conveyance to a purchaser of a legal estate in land' so that grant of easement capable of overreaching defendant's equitable interest—Law of Property Act 1925, ss 1, 2(1). **Baker v Craggs** [2018] **4** 627, CA.
Husband and wife's joint purchase of matrimonial home—Conveyance in husband's sole name—Husband leaving home—Wife continuing to live there—Whether wife in actual occupation—Whether overriding interest—Land Registration Act 1925, s 70(1)(g). **Bird v Syme Thomson** [1978] **3** 1027, Ch D.
Husband and wife's joint purchase of matrimonial home—Conveyance in husband's sole name—Husband mortgaging home without wife's knowledge—Possession sought by mortgagee—Whether mortgagee having priority over wife's equitable interest—Whether wife in 'actual occupation'—Whether wife having an 'overriding interest'—Land Registration Act 1925, s 70(1)(g). **Williams & Glyn's Bank Ltd v Boland** [1980] **2** 408, HL.
Option in lease for lessee to purchase freehold reversion—Lessee in actual occupation—Whether option an overriding interest—Option not protected by entry of notice, etc on register—Whether enforceable against purchaser of reversion—Land Registration Act 1925, s 70(1)(g). **Webb v Pollmount Ltd** [1966] **1** 481, Ch D.
Option in lease of part of premises giving tenant option to purchase reversion in whole of premises—Tenant in actual occupation—Whether option overriding interest—Whether option enforceable against purchaser of reversion—Land Registration Act 1925, s 70(1)(g). **Wallcite Ltd v Ferrishurst Ltd** [1999] **1** 977, CA.
Parents and daughter and son-in-law jointly purchasing house—Conveyance in names of daughter and son-in-law only—Parents occupying house as their home—Daughter and son-in-law mortgaging property without parents' knowledge or consent—Daughter and son-in-law defaulting on mortgage repayments—Possession sought by mortgagee—Whether parents having an 'overriding interest'—Whether disposition by two trustees for sale overreaching parents' equitable interest—Law of Property Act 1925, ss 2(1)(ii), 14—Land Registration Act 1925, s 70(1)(g). **City of London Building Society v Flegg** [1987] **3** 435, HL.
Right to rectification of title—Sale of land under mutual mistake as to position of boundary—Vendor having right to rectification of title—Whether right to rectification capable of enduring through different ownerships of land—Whether vendor having overriding interest as against purchaser's successors in title—Land Registration Act 1925, s 70(1)(g). **Blacklocks v JB Developments (Godalming) Ltd** [1981] **3** 392, Ch D.
Tenant in occupation of dwelling-house—Purchase and mortgage of house by landlord—Registration subject to overriding interest of tenant in occupation—Land Registration Act 1925, s 70(1). **Mornington Permanent Building Society v Kenway** [1953] **1** 951, Ch D; **Woolwich Equitable Building Society v Marshall** [1951] **2** 769, Ch D.
Transferee agreeing to act as agent for transferors in finding purchaser for property—Transferee representing that transfer being made to named third party—Third party non-existent and transferee using that name as alias—Transferors transferring property into third party's name and transferee registering himself as proprietor under that name—Transferee granting legal charge over property to building society but transferors remaining in actual occupation—Whether transferors having overriding interest in property—Land Registration Act 1925, s 70(1)(g). **Collings v Lee** [2001] **2** 332, CA.
Trustees for sale mortgaging land to bank as security for discharge on demand of present and future liabilities—No capital money being advanced by mortgagee contemporaneously with the mortgage—Trustees failing to satisfy demand for payment—Possession sought by mortgagee—Whether beneficiaries under trust for sale in actual occupation having overriding interests—Whether equitable interests of beneficiaries overreached by mortgage—Whether capital money required to be advanced contemporaneously with conveyance for overreaching to occur—Law of Property Act 1925, s 2(1)(ii)—Land Registration Act 1925, s 70(1)(g). **State Bank of India v Sood** [1997] **1** 169, CA.
Unpaid vendor's lien—Vendor remaining in occupation as lessee after sale of registered land—Subsequent charge on property by purchaser in favour of third party—Vendor later going out of occupation—Whether overriding interest extinguished—Land Registration Act 1925, s 70(1)(g). **London and Cheshire Insurance Co Ltd v Laplagrene Property Co Ltd** [1971] **1** 766, Ch D.
Pending action—
Caution—
Rectification of register. *See* Rectification of register—Caution, *below.*
Plan—
Description of registered land. *See* Description of registered land—Boundary—Filed plan, *above.*
Positive covenant—
Notice. *See* Notice—Positive covenant noted on register, *above.*
Possessory title—
Effect of registration on legal estate. *See* Effect of registration on legal estate—Possessory title, *above.*
Priority—
Concurrent applications for registration—
Applications for first registration of sub-lease and for transfer of head lease taking effect on same day—Whether sub-lease had precedence—Land Registration Act 1925, s 23(1)(b). **Strand Securities Ltd v Caswell** [1965] **1** 820, CA.
Effect of notices on dispositions—
Priority of legal charges—Plaintiffs' charge first in time—Defendants' charge protected by notice—Plaintiffs' charge not protected by notice—Whether plaintiffs' charge having priority over defendants' charge notwithstanding defendants' charge protected by notice—Land Registration Act 1925, s 52. **Mortgage Corp Ltd v Nationwide Credit Corp Ltd** [1993] **4** 623, CA.

LAND REGISTRATION (cont)—
Priority (cont)—
Entries protecting dealings off the register—
Deposit of land certificate with bank by registered proprietors to secure debt—Notice of deposit registered—Agreement by registered proprietors to execute legal mortgage in favour of bank on demand—Subsequent execution of mortgage under seal—Registered proprietors thereafter contracting to sell land—Purchasers entering caution against dealings on register in their favour—Subsequent application by bank to register mortgage as a charge—Whether bank entitled to rely on notice of deposit to protect mortgage—Whether mortgage subject to purchasers' interest under contract—Land Registration Act 1925, s 106. **Barclays Bank Ltd v Taylor** [1973] **1** 752, CA.
Official search by purchaser—
Priority period—Definition of purchaser—Person who in good faith and for valuable consideration acquires legal estate in land—Meaning of 'in good faith'—Land Registration (Official Searches) Rules 1969 (SI 1969 No 1179), r 2. **Smith v Morrison** [1974] **1** 957, Ch D.
Overriding interest. *See* Overriding interest, *above.*
Pending application—
Day list showing date and time at which applications made—Application for registration of title by adverse possession entered on day list—Adjudicator cancelling application—Application removed from day list—Applicants appealing cancellation—Judge ordering reinstatement of application—Subsequent registration of third party charges—Judge making further order requiring restoration of application with original priority date—Whether judge having jurisdiction to make order—Land Registration Act 2002—Land Registration Rules 2003, SI 2003/1417, rr 12, 20—Adjudicator to Her Majesty's Land Registry (Practice and Procedure) Rules 2003, SI 2003/2171. **Franks v Chief Land Registrar** [2012] **1** 326, CA.
Production of register of title—
Application for inspection of register etc—
Procedure—Ex parte application in High Court—Affidavit that judgment debtor is proprietor of land or charge thereon—Procedure where sum not exceeding county court limit—Land Registration Act 1925, s 112(2), (3)—Charging Orders Act 1979, s 1(2). **Practice Direction** [1983] **1** 352, QBD.
Protection of minor interests. *See* Minor interests—Protection, *above.*
Rectification of register—
Caution—
Cautions entered against mortgagee's interest in land—Mortgage the subject of High Court action—Action struck out by High Court and Court of Appeal—Petition to appeal pending before House of Lords—Whether a court had decided that mortgagee entitled to any estate right or interest to any registered land—Land Registration Act 1925, s 82(1). **Calgary & Edmonton Land Co Ltd v Discount Bank (Overseas) Ltd** [1971] **1** 551, Ch D.
Circumstances justifying rectification—
Circumstances in which rectification deemed just—Overriding interest noted on first registration—Exception and reservation of right of way for all persons entitled to the same contained in conveyance of 1939—Whether easement created by the exception or whether exception referred to existing rights—Whether decision to cancel entry would determine existence of easement so as to give rise to res judicata—Discretion of chief land registrar—Land Registration Act 1925, ss 70(2), 82(1)(h)—Land Registration Rules 1925 (S R & O 1925 No 1093), r 298. **Dances Way, West Town Hayling Island, Hants, Re Freehold Land in** [1962] **2** 42, CA.
Entry obtained by fraud—Circumstances in which court satisfied—Entry obtained by fraud—Costs—Land Registration Act 1925, s 82(1)(d). **Leighton's Conveyance, Re** [1936] **3** 1033, CA.
Registered owner executing power of attorney—Donee of power of attorney tricked into signing transfer of property—Building society granting mortgage on property—Whether court having power to order rectification of register by removal of building society's charge—Land Registration Act 1925, s 82(1). **Norwich and Peterborough Building Society v Steed (No 2)** [1993] **1** 330, CA.
Correction of mistake—
Meaning of 'mistake'—Land Registration Act 2002, Sch 4, paras 1, 5, 6, Sch 6, paras 1, 2. **Baxter v Mannion** [2011] **2** 574, CA.
County court—
Jurisdiction. *See* **County court** (Jurisdiction—Land registration—Rectification of register).
Date from which rectification effective—
Effect on dispositions before date of rectification—Restrictive covenant—Title of servient tenement unregistered—Covenant registered against servient tenement—Title of servient tenement subsequently registered—Notice of restrictive covenant omitted from register—Lease of servient tenement subsequently granted—Lease assigned to defendants—Defendants having no knowledge of covenant—Plaintiff owner of dominant tenement—Plaintiff obtaining rectification of register—Notice of restrictive covenant entered—Whether covenant binding on defendants—Land Registration Act 1925, s 82. **Freer v Unwins Ltd** [1976] **1** 634, Ch D.
Decision of land registrar—
Construction of conveyance—Res judicata. *See* **Estoppel** (Res judicata—Land registration—Rectification of register—Decision of land registrar—Construction of conveyance).
Disposition of freehold estate—
Subrogated liens and charges affecting land—subrogated rights not appearing as entries on register—Entries on register relating to unenforceable charges in favour of lenders—Right of lender to apply for register to be rectified—Land Registration Act 1925, ss 20(1), 82(1)(a), (h). **Orakpo v Manson Investments Ltd** [1977] **1** 666, CA.
Entry obtained by mistake—
Landowner granting lease of strip of road—Registrar erroneously recording against lessor's title general right of way over landowner's land for duration of lease—Plaintiff purchasing land after expiry of lease but claiming right of way in reliance on register—Whether right of way enforceable—Whether plaintiff having knowledge of error—Whether defendant entitled to rectification—Registered Land Ordinance 1970 (British Virgin Islands), ss 38, 140. **Racoon Ltd v Turnbull** [1996] **4** 503, PC.

LAND REGISTRATION (cont)—
  Rectification of register (cont)—
    Entry obtained by mistake (cont)—
      Mortgage obtained fraudulently by claimant's husband without claimant's knowledge—Claimant applying for rectification of register by removal of bank's charge—Whether 'exceptional circumstances' justifying not rectifying register—Land Registration Act 2002, Sch 4, para 3(3). **Dhillon v Barclays Bank plc** [2021] **1** 421, CA.
      Two registered titles mistakenly including same land—Proprietor of first title applying for rectification—Proprietor of second title in exclusive possession of land—Whether proprietor of second title obtaining possessory title—Land Registration Act 1925, s 82—Limitation Act 1980, s 15. **Parshall v Hackney** [2013] **3** 224, CA.
    Interlocutory motion—
      Motion to vacate caution—Jurisdiction—Applications to by 'summons at chambers'—Inherent jurisdiction to order vacation of caution on motion—Land Registration Act 1925, ss 82(1), 138(2). **Calgary & Edmonton Land Co Ltd v Dobinson** [1974] **1** 484, Ch D.
      Motion to vacate caution—Jurisdiction—Cautioner alleging existence of contract for sale of land—Cautioner failing to make out prima facie case—Failure to adduce memorandum of contract—Jurisdiction to vacate caution on motion. **Tiverton Estates Ltd v Wearwell Ltd** [1974] **1** 209, CA.
      Triable issue—Appropriate order to preserve parties' interests—Contract for sale of land—Cautions lodged by purchasers to protect interest in land—Notice to complete served by vendor—Vendor purporting to rescind contract on expiry of notice—Action by purchasers for specific performance—Motion by vendor to vacate cautions—Evidence that period of notice extended by oral agreement justifying trial—Appropriate order to preserve purchasers' rights to specific performance and vendor's right to damages if purchasers should fail in action. **Clearbrook Property Holdings Ltd v Verrier** [1973] **3** 614, Ch D.
    Loss suffered by reason of rectification—
      Indemnity—Overriding interest alleged—Time at which to determine whether person was in actual occupation of land—Land Registration Act 1925, ss 70(1)(g), 83(1). **Boyle's Claim, Re** [1961] **1** 620, Ch D.
    Overriding interest—
      Rectification to give effect to overriding interest—Actual occupation—Use of land to park car—Strip of disputed land between adjoining properties—Strip conveyed to plaintiffs' predecessor with one property—Strip used for purpose of parking car—Strip mistakenly included in conveyance of adjoining property to defendants' predecessor—Defendants' predecessor registering title—Filed plan including strip—Whether plaintiffs' predecessor having overriding interest—Whether use of strip for parking car amounting to actual occupation—Land Registration Act 1925, ss 70(1)(g), 82(3). **Epps v Esso Petroleum Co Ltd** [1973] **2** 465, Ch D.
    Rectification affecting title of proprietor in possession—
      Proprietor contributing to mistake in registration—Discretion of court—Owner conveyed plot to plaintiff and later, owing to mistake, conveyed land, including plaintiff's plot, to defendant—Defendant applied for registration, lodged transfer, and was registered as proprietor—Defendant did not know of plaintiff's title to plot—After long absence plaintiff visited plot and saw defendant's building work on it—Plaintiff applied for rectification of register—Defendant's lodgment of transfer containing misdescription of land held to have contributed to registrar's mistake—Exercise of court's discretion where defendant contributed to mistake or stood by—Land Registration Act 1925, s 82(1),(3)(a). **Sea View Gardens, Re** [1966] **3** 935, Ch D.
      Proprietor contributing to mistake in registration—Land erroneously included in registered title of adjoining land—Contribution to mistake by registered proprietor—'Void' disposition—Land Registration Act 1925, s 82(3)(a), (b). **High Street, Deptford, Re 139** [1951] **1** 950, Ch D.
      Unjust not to rectify register against proprietor in occupation—Circumstances making it unjust not to order rectification—Indemnity—Entitlement of proprietor to indemnity on rectification—Applicants not entitled to indemnity on refusal of rectification—Land Registration Act 1925, s 82(3)(c). **Epps v Esso Petroleum Co Ltd** [1973] **2** 465, Ch D.
  Register of title—
    Charges and other interests appearing or protected on register—
      Rights and interests appearing on adjoining site—Covenant for title—Adjoining owner's land mistakingly included in conveyance of registered land—Whether 'register' referring to register of individual title of which vendor was registered proprietor—Whether 'register' extending to global register of all registered titles—Whether covenant for title only subject to charges and other interests appearing on vendor's title—Law of Property Act 1925, s 76, Sch 2—Land Registration Rules 1925, r 77(1)(a). **Dunning (A J) & Sons (Shopfitters) Ltd v Sykes & Son (Poole) Ltd** [1987] **1** 700, CA.
    Inspection—
      Documents in registrar's custody not referred to in register—Index of proprietors' names—Refusal of inspection—Appeal—Whether right of appeal against registrar's refusal to allow inspection of documents in registrar's custody but not referred to in register—Whether right of appeal against registrar's refusal to search proprietors' index—Land Registration Act 1925, s 112(2)(b)—Land Registration Rules 1925, rr 9(2), 298, 299. **Quigly v Chief Land Registrar** [1993] **4** 82, CA.
    Order for production. *See* Production of register of title, *above*.
  Registration—
    Matrimonial home—
      Rights of non-occupying spouse—Registration as a land charge. *See* **Husband and wife** (Matrimonial home—Land charge—Registration).
  Rentcharge. *See* **Rentcharge**.
  Restrictive covenant—
    Notice. *See* Notice—Notice of restrictive covenant, *above*.
  Search—
    Mistake by Land Registry—
      Failure to disclose caution. *See* Charging order—Protection on register—Caution—Official search on sale of property—Failure to disclose caution—Mistake of Land Registry, *above*.

LAND REGISTRATION (cont)—
  Search (cont)—
    Mistake by Land Registry (cont)—
      Part of property acquired by claimant already registered—Filed plan and search certificate issued by Land Registry failing to disclose registration—Whether claimant entitled to indemnity in respect of losses suffered as a result of errors of Land Registry—Land Registration Act 1925, s 83. **Prestige Properties Ltd v Scottish Provident Institution** [2003] **2** 1145, Ch D.
  Sub-lease—
    Application to register sub-lease. *See* First registration—Leasehold—Application to register sub-lease, *above*.
  Transfer—
    Charge. *See* Charge—Transfer, *above*.
    Leaseholds—
      Implied covenants on transfer of leaseholds—Covenants for title—Assignment of leasehold premises compulsorily acquired in dilapidated condition—Breaches of repairing covenants during currency of lease—Whether acquiring authority should covenant to indemnify assignor—Assignor a personal representative of deceased lessee—Land Registration Act 1925, s 24(1)—Land Registration Rules 1925 (SR & O 1925 No 1093), r 115. **King (decd), Re** [1963] **1** 781, CA.
    Merger—
      Agreement for sale of registered land and transfer—Whether contract merged in transfer. **Knight Sugar Co Ltd v Alberta Rly and Irrigation Co** [1938] **1** 266, PC.
    Purchase price remaining unpaid—
      Deed of transfer containing acknowledgment of receipt of purchase price—Purchase price entered on proprietorship register—Subsequent charge on property in favour of third party—Chargee unaware of acknowledgment of receipt of purchase money in deed of transfer—Whether entry on register sufficient evidence of payment of purchase money to preclude vendor enforcing lien against chargee—Law of Property Act 1925, s 68—Land Registration Rules 1925 (SR & O 1925 No 1093), r 247(1). **London and Cheshire Insurance Co Ltd v Laplagrene Property Co Ltd** [1971] **1** 766, Ch D.
    Validity—
      Transfer not in prescribed form—Land Registration Rules 1925 (S R & O 1925 No 1093), rr 74, 121(1), 123(1), 322(1). **Morelle Ltd v Wakeling** [1955] **1** 708, CA.
  Vendor's lien—
    Overriding interest—
      Rights of person in actual occupation of land. *See* Overriding interest—Rights of person in actual occupation of land—Unpaid vendor's lien, *above*.

LAND SETTLEMENT
  Palestine. *See* **Palestine** (Land settlement).

LANDFILL TAX
  Disposal—
    Taxable disposal—
      Statutory provision rendering disposal subject to landfill tax if four conditions satisfied—Whether disposal taxable only if all conditions satisfied at same time—Finance Act 1996, s 40(2). **Customs and Excise Comrs v Parkwood Landfill Ltd** [2003] **1** 579, CA.

LANDLORD AND TENANT
  Action for possession—
    Claim for mesne profits—
      Interim payments order—Application by landlord for interim payments order pending determination of action—Counterclaim by defendant for damages for harassment—Counterclaim exceeding amount of claim for mesne profits—Defendant liable for rent or mesne profits whether he won or lost counterclaim—Whether court having power to make order for interim payments—RSC Ord 29, r 18. **Old Grovebury Manor Farm Ltd v W Seymour Plant Sales & Hire Ltd** [1979] **1** 573, Ch D.
  Agreement for lease—
    Conditional acceptance—
      Conditional agreement becoming unconditional on obtaining of planning permission free from unacceptable conditions before specified 'end date'—Agreement providing for developer forwarding planning decision to tenant—Tenant thereafter having ten days to give written notice if conditions unacceptable—Whether on true construction of agreement planning condition not fulfilled if developer failing to forward planning decision ten days before end date—Whether tenant entitled to rescind agreement. **Gregory Projects (Halifax) Ltd v Tenpin (Halifax) Ltd** [2010] **2** Comm 646, Ch D.
    Subject to a lease to be drawn up by our clients' solicitors. **Berry (HC) Ltd v Brighton and Sussex Building Society** [1939] **3** 217, Ch D.
    Subject to the terms of a formal lease. **Spottiswoode Ballantyne & Co Ltd v Doreen Appliances Ltd** [1942] **2** 65, CA.
  County court jurisdiction. *See* **County court** (Jurisdiction—Equity jurisdiction—Landlord and tenant—Agreement for lease).
  Creation of interest in land. *See* **Land** (Interest in land—Creation—Agreement for lease).
  Effect in equity. *See* **Equity** (Agreement for lease).
  Illegality—
    Use of premises—Town and country planning—User requiring planning permission—Permission refused—Landlord's right to recover rent—Town and Country Planning Act 1947, s 12(1). **Best v Glanville** [1960] **3** 478, CA.
  Interest in land. *See* **Land** (Interest in land—Creation—Agreement for lease).

LANDLORD AND TENANT (cont)—
  Agreement for lease (cont)—
    Occupation pending completion—
      Tenant or licensee—National Conditions of Sale applied so far as applicable to sale by private treaty
        and not inconsistent—Condition that purchaser let into occupation should be licensee—Rent paid
        in advance—Whether occupation pending completion and during period covered by rent paid
        was that of tenant or licensee—National Conditions of Sale (17th Edn) conditions, 7. **Joel v
        Montgomery & Taylor Ltd** [1966] **3** 763, Ch D.
    Premium—
      Balance of premium not paid—Rent paid in advance—Action by proposing lessor for
        rescission—Application for payment of balance of premium into court and, in default, delivery of
        possession—Greenwood v Turner order—Order inappropriate where rent paid to future date.
        Joel v Montgomery & Taylor Ltd [1966] **3** 763, Ch D.
    Repudiation—
      Test. See **Contract** (Repudiation—Test—Agreement for lease).
      What amounts to repudiation—Whether objecting to form of draft lease amounting to repudiation.
        Sweet & Maxwell Ltd v Universal News Service Ltd [1964] **3** 30, CA.
    Specific performance. See **Specific performance** (Lease—Agreement for lease).
  Agreement for rent increase. See Rent—Agreement for increase, *below.*
  Agricultural holding—
    Compulsory purchase—
      Compensation—Assessment. *See* **Compulsory purchase** (Compensation—Assessment—
        Agricultural holding).
    Generally. See **Agricultural holding**.
  Agricultural worker—
    Rent restriction. See **Rent restriction** (Agricultural worker).
    Tied cottage. See **Agriculture** (Agricultural worker—Tied cottage).
  Allotment. See **Allotment**.
  Alterations—
    Breach of covenant. See Covenant—Alterations—Breach of covenant against alterations, *below.*
  Apportionment of rent—
    Lease—
      Implied term. See Lease—Implied term—Apportionment of rent, *below.*
  Arrears of rent—
    Forfeiture of lease. See Forfeiture of lease—Arrears of rent, *below.*
    Re-entry. See Re-entry—Arrears of rent, *below.*
  Assignment of lease—
    Assignment —
      Covenants against alienation—Tenant transferring economic benefits and burdens to third party
        without assigning leasehold interest—Whether tenant breaching covenants against alienation—
        Law of Property Act 1925, s 205(1)(xix). **Clarence House Ltd v National Westminster Bank plc**
        [2009] **2 Comm** 273, Ch D; [2009] **3** 175, Ch D; [2010] **2** 201, CA; [2010] **2 Comm** 1065, CA.
    Assignment by company—
      Voluntary winding up of lessee company—Assignment of lease for value—Permitted
        assignment—Future performance of covenants—Landlord's right to have sufficient assets of
        company set aside to meet future rent and provide for performance of other covenants. **House
        Property and Investment Co Ltd, Re** [1953] **2** 1525, Ch D.
    Consent of landlord not to be unreasonably withheld—
      Consent withheld in interests of good estate management—Whether withholding of consent
        reasonable—Landlord and Tenant Act 1927, s 19(1). **Bromley Park Garden Estates Ltd v Moss**
        [1982] **2** 890, CA.
      Consent withheld on grounds of apprehended depreciation of value of reversion—Whether
        landlord need only take into account his own interests when considering whether to withhold
        consent. **International Drilling Fluids Ltd v Louisville Investments (Uxbridge) Ltd** [1986] **1** 321, CA.
      Covenant by lessee to use premises only for purposes of printers' business—Proposed assignment
        by lessee—Intention of proposed assignee to use premises as offices—Refusal of
        consent—Whether breach of covenant a necessary consequence of assignment—Whether
        consent unreasonably withheld. **Killick v Second Covent Garden Property Co Ltd** [1973] **2** 337,
        CA.
      Express provision in lease for consent not to be unreasonably withheld—Covenant that tenant, if
        wishing to assign, should first offer to surrender lease—Validity of covenant—Landlord and
        Tenant Act 1927, s 19(1). **Bocardo SA v S & M Hotels Ltd** [1979] **3** 737, CA.
      Express provision in lease for consent not to be unreasonably withheld—Provision that tenant, if
        wishing to assign, should first offer to surrender lease—Validity of proviso—Landlord and Tenant
        Act 1927, s 19(1)(a). **Adler v Upper Grosvenor Street Investment Ltd** [1957] **1** 229, QBD.
      Express provision in lease for consent not to be withheld in favour of a respectable and responsible
        person—Proposed assignee such a person—Consent withheld—Assignment without consent—
        Action for declaration that assignment valid—Assignees not essential parties. **Theodorou v
        Bloom** [1964] **3** 399, Ch D.
      Express provision that consent would not be withheld in the case of a respectable and responsible
        person—Need to imply proviso that lease not to be unreasonably withheld—Landlord and Tenant
        Act 1927, s 19(1). **Moat v Martin** [1949] **2** 646, CA.
      Landlord failing to request information about financial standing of proposed assignee—Landlord
        seeking to rely on absence of such information in proceedings brought by tenant following
        landlord's failure to give consent—Whether landlord entitled to do so—Landlord and Tenant Act
        1988, s 1(3). **Norwich Union Life Insurance Society v Shopmoor Ltd** [1998] **3** 32, Ch D.
      Landlord giving unjustified reasons for withholding consent—Whether landlord can later justify
        withholding consent on other grounds. **Lovelock v Margo** [1963] **2** 13, CA.
      Landlord refusing consent to assignment on ground that prospective assignee's proposed use of
        premises would breach covenant restricting use of premises—Whether covenant restricting use
        of premises—Whether landlord's refusal to consent to assignment necessarily unreasonable if
        based solely on belief that proposed assignee intended to breach user covenant. **Ashworth
        Frazer Ltd v Gloucester City Council** [2002] **1** 377, HL.

LANDLORD AND TENANT (cont)—
　Assignment of lease (cont)—
　　Consent of landlord not to be unreasonably withheld (cont)—
　　　No grounds for objection to proposed assignee—Landlord wishing to obtain vacant possession—Whether withholding of consent reasonable. **Swanson's Agreement, Re** [1946] **2** 628, Ch D.
　　　Prevention of creation of statutory tenancy. **Lee v Carter (K) Ltd** [1948] **2** 690, CA; **Swanson v Forton** [1949] **1** 135, CA.
　　　Prevention of creation of statutory tenancy—Seven and a half months of term unexpired—Intention of tenant and assignee. **Bookman (Thomas) Ltd v Nathan** [1955] **2** 821, CA.
　　　Prevention of creation of statutory tenancy—Tenant in possession at date of assignment. **Dollar v Winston** [1949] **2** 1088, Ch D.
　　　Property intended to be used by proposed assignee in accordance with specific purpose permitted under lease—Consent withheld on grounds of proposed use—Whether consent unreasonably withheld. **International Drilling Fluids Ltd v Louisville Investments (Uxbridge) Ltd** [1986] **1** 321, CA.
　　　Provision in lease that consent not to be unreasonably withheld in case of assignment to respectable and 'responsible' assignee—Proposed assignee a subsidiary company of large well-known company—Guarantee by holding company required by landlord as a condition of consent—Whether consent unreasonably withheld. **Greater London Properties Ltd's Lease, Re** [1959] **1** 728, Ch D.
　　　Redevelopment scheme planned by landlords and others—Assignees' intention to participate in landlords' redevelopment scheme by means of nuisance value of lease—Landlord and Tenant Act 1927, s 19(1). **Pimms Ltd v Tallow Chandlers in the City of London** [1964] **2** 145, CA.
　　　Right of proposed assignee to acquire freehold—Reasonable ground for refusing consent—Limited company tenant of property including mews houses—Company proposing to assign leasehold interest in one of houses to private individual—Assignee as individual qualifying for statutory right to acquire freehold of house after five years' residence—Not purpose of assignment to enable assignee to acquire freehold—Assignment adversely affecting value of landlords' reversion in consequence of proposed assignee's prospective right to acquire freehold—Whether reasonable ground for landlords' refusing consent to assignment. **Norfolk Capital Group Ltd v Kitway Ltd** [1976] **3** 787, CA.
　　　Right of proposed assignee to acquire freehold—Reasonable ground for refusing consent—Relevant circumstances—Refusal relating to attribute of personality of proposed assignee and user of premises—Premises part of large estate owned by landlords—Management and development of estate likely to be impeded if tenant enabled to acquire freehold—Landlords liable to suffer financial loss—Whether refusal of consent to assignment reasonable. **Bickel v Duke of Westminster** [1976] **3** 801, CA.
　　　Sale of land. *See* **Sale of land** (Leasehold interest—Consent to assignment).
　　　Statutory provision requiring landlord within reasonable time to serve notice on tenant of decision whether or not to give consent to assignment—Whether service of such notice terminating reasonable time allowed to landlord—Landlord and Tenant Act 1988, s 1(3). **Go West Ltd v Spigarolo** [2003] **2** 141, CA.
　　　Statutory provision—Provision in lease for circumstances in which refusal not to be deemed unreasonable—Validity—Landlord and Tenant Act 1927, s 19(1). **Smith's Lease, Re** [1951] **1** 346, Ch D.
　　Covenant against assignment—
　　　Absolute covenant against assignment—Whether term to be implied that consent to assignment not to be unreasonably withheld—Landlord and Tenant Act 1927, s 19(1). **Property and Bloodstock Ltd v Emerton** [1967] **3** 321, CA.
　　　Consent of landlord not to be unreasonably withheld. *See* Assignment of lease—Consent of landlord not to be unreasonably withheld, *above.*
　　　Forfeiture of lease for breach of covenant. *See* Forfeiture of lease—Breach of covenant prohibiting assignment, *below.*
　　　Generally. *See* Covenant against assignment without consent, *below.*
　　　Mortgaged property. *See* **Mortgage** (Sale—Leasehold property—Covenant by lessee in lease not to assign).
　　Effect of assignment—
　　　Whether landlord's liability for breach of repairing covenant surviving assignment. *See* Repair—Landlord's covenant—Breach of covenant—Assignment of lease—Effect of assignment, *below.*
　　Estoppel—
　　　Underlessee in possession and paying rent—Whether defendants estopped from denying that they were assignees of head lease. **Official Trustee of Charity Lands v Ferriman Trust Ltd** [1937] **3** 85, KBD.
　　Implied covenant—
　　　Indemnity for unpaid rent—Exclusion of covenant—Assignor paying unpaid rent to landlord when called on to do so—Assignor seeking to wind up assignee company for failure to reimburse its expenditure—Whether exclusion of covenant ousting general law obligation of reimbursement—Whether assignee indebted to assignor—Law of Property Act 1925, s 77(1)(C), Sch 2, Pt IX. **Healing Research Trustee Co Ltd, Re** [1992] **2** 481, Ch D.
　　　Indemnity for unpaid rent—Reversioner claiming rent from original tenant after current tenant defaulting—Original tenant claiming under implied covenant—Whether original tenant liable for rent—Whether notice of liability valid—Whether notice served within specified period of date when rent became due—Landlord and Tenant (Covenants) Act 1995, s 17(2). **Scottish & Newcastle plc v Raguz** [2006] **4** 524, Ch D; [2007] **2** 871, CA; [2009] **1** 763, HL; [2009] **2 Comm** 447, HL.
　　Notice of assignment—
　　　Covenant in head lease to give notice of assignment or underlease—Term derived out of underlease—Application of covenant. **Portman v J Lyons & Co Ltd** [1936] **3** 819, Ch D.

LANDLORD AND TENANT (cont)—
  Assignment of lease (cont)—
    Notice to quit—
      Assignment of contractual tenancy after notice to quit given but before its expiration—Assignee becoming statutory tenant on expiration of notice. **Regional Properties Ltd v Frankenschwerth** [1951] **1** 178, CA.
    Obligation to pay rent—
      Assignee liable to landlord for rent arrears—Assignee entering into voluntary arrangement with creditors including landlord—Creditors accepting terms of voluntary arrangement in full and final settlement of all claims—Landlord claiming arrears from original lessees—Whether voluntary arrangement extinguishing liability of original lessees. **Mytre Investments Ltd v Reynolds** [1995] **3** 588, QBD.
      Assignee liable to landlord for rent arrears—Assignee entering into voluntary arrangement with creditors—Landlord but not original lessee bound by arrangement—Landlord claiming arrears from original lessee—Effect of voluntary arrangement on claim—Whether original lessee entitled to rely on arrangement to avoid liability—Whether arrangement amounting to accord and satisfaction—Insolvency Act 1986, s 5(2). **RA Securities Ltd v Mercantile Credit Co Ltd** [1995] **3** 581, Ch D.
      Assignee with licence of landlord re-assigning lease—Express covenant by assignee with landlord included in licence to assign—Liability of assignee after re-assignment. **Lyons (J) & Co Ltd v Knowles** [1943] **1** 477, CA.
      Assignee—Assignee executing deed of variation with lessor to increase rent—Subsequent assignee falling into arrears—Whether lessee liable under personal covenant for payment of original or increased rent—Whether deed of variation releasing assignee and lessee from liability for original rent. **Friends' Provident Life Office v British Railways Board** [1996] **1** 336, CA.
      Assignee—Express covenant with assignor to pay rent—Assignment of benefit of covenant to landlord. **Butler Estates Ltd v Bean** [1941] **2** 793, CA.
      Assignment by original lessees to company assignee—Express covenant by assignee with lessor to pay rent in licence to assign—Assignee further assigning lease with lessor's consent—Assignee going into liquidation—Liquidator disclaiming lease as onerous property—Lessor claiming from original lessee rent falling due after disclaimer—Whether obligation to pay rent remaining with original lessee or surety for original lessee notwithstanding liquidator's disclaimer—Insolvency Act 1986, s 178(4). **Hindcastle Ltd v Barbara Attenborough Associates Ltd** [1996] **1** 737, HL.
      Assignments with indemnity against rents and covenants—One assignment to limited company—Assignment to original lessee of benefit of subsequent covenant of indemnity on the liquidation of company. **Josselson v Borst (Gliksten, third party)** [1937] **3** 722, CA.
      Assignor's obligation—Accord and satisfaction—Assignee directly covenanting with landlord to perform covenants and conditions of headlease—Assignee falling into arrears with rent—Landlord agreeing to release assignee from obligations in return for immediate surrender of lease—Whether accord and satisfaction—Whether assignor also released from obligations under lease. **Deanplan Ltd v Mahmoud** [1992] **3** 945, Ch D.
      Covenant by assignor to pay rent in event of non-payment by assignee—Mortgage of lease by assignee—Non-payment of rent by assignee—Payment by assignor under guarantee—Order for possession against assignee granted to mortgagee—New lease granted to assignor by head landlord subject to and with benefit of assignee's lease—Whether receipt of payments from assignor under guarantee waived landlord's rights to forfeit assignee's lease—Whether right to forfeit waived by making new lease subject to assignee's lease—Whether assignor as reversioner to assignee's lease entitled to forfeit that lease for rent in arrear when assignor became reversioner. **London and County (A & D) Ltd v Wilfred Sportsman Ltd (Greenwoods (Hosiers and Outfitters) Ltd, third party)** [1970] **2** 600, CA.
      Covenant by assignor with landlord—Covenant by lessee to pay rent and service charges—Default in payment—Assignment of lease by lessee—Receipt for unpaid instalments of rent, etc given by lessor to facilitate assignment—Subsequent assignment by lessor of reversion—Whether obligation to pay rent etc remaining with original lessee after assignment of lease—Whether assignees of reversion entitled to enforce obligation against original lessee. **Arlesford Trading Co Ltd v Servansingh** [1971] **3** 113, CA.
      Liability of assignee—Assignee covenanting to pay rent reserved by lease 'at the time and in the manner therein provided for'—Assignee assigning lease—Landlord claiming arrears of rent from assignee and surety after further assignment—Whether assignee and surety liable for unpaid rent. **Estates Gazette Ltd v Benjamin Restaurants Ltd** [1995] **1** 129, CA.
    Release of covenant. *See* Covenant—Release—Assignment of lease, *below.*
    Rights and liabilities of assignee—
      Assignee of part of premises—Division of premises included in lease—Assignee of part forced to pay whole rent—Contribution from assignee of other part—Recoupment. **Whitham v Bullock** [1939] **2** 310, CA.
    Sale of land. *See* **Sale of land** (Leasehold interest—Assignment).
    Validity—
      Transfer of tenancy—Whether assignment effective only if made by deed—Law of Property Act 1925, ss 52-54. **Crago v Julian** [1992] **1** 744, CA.
  Assured tenancy—
    Creation. *See* Tenancy—Creation—Assured tenancy, *below.*
    Recovery of possession. *See* Recovery of possession—Order for possession—Assured tenancy, *below.*
    Tenancy deposit schemes—
      Requirements—Money intended to be held as security—Whether final payment under contract for sale and lease back tenancy deposit—Housing Act 2004, Pt 6, Ch 4. **UK Housing Alliance (North West) Ltd v Francis** [2010] **3** 519, CA.
  Tenancy under which a dwelling-house is let as a separate dwelling—
    Whether cooking facilities prerequisite of dwelling-house—Housing Act 1988, s 1(1). **Uratemp Ventures Ltd v Collins** [2002] **1** 46, HL.
  Avoidance of lease. *See* Lease—Avoidance, *below.*
  Beneficiary granting tenancy. *See* Tenancy—Grant—Beneficiary granting tenancy, *below.*
  Breach of covenant—
    Agricultural holding. *See* **Agricultural holding** (Breach of covenant).

LANDLORD AND TENANT (cont)—
Breach of covenant (cont)—
Persons entitled to sue tenant in respect of breach—
Assignment of reversion on lease—Breach occurring before assignment—Whether assignor of reversion entitled to sue after assignment for breach of covenant before assignment—Law of Property Act 1925, s 141. **King (decd), Re** [1963] **1** 781, CA.
Quiet enjoyment, as to. *See* Covenant—Quiet enjoyment—Breach, *below.*
Remedy—
Capable of remedy—Notice of breach—Requirement to remedy breach—Breach capable of remedy—Covenant to reconstruct interior of demised premises by specified date or within reasonable time thereafter—Tenant failing to reconstruct—Whether breach capable of remedy—Whether notice required to call on tenant to remedy breach—Law of Property Act 1925, s 146. **Expert Clothing Service and Sales Ltd v Hillgate House Ltd** [1985] **2** 998, CA.
Repairing covenant. *See* Breach of covenant to repair, *below.*
Underletting without consent. *See* Covenant against underletting without consent—Breach, *below.*
Breach of covenant to repair—
Damages—
Landlord's covenant. *See* Repair—Landlord's covenant—Damages for breach, *below.*
Defence—
Regulations prohibiting repair above certain cost without licence—Whether breach excused by regulations—Defence (General) Regulations 1939, reg 56A. **Eyre v Johnson** [1946] **1** 719, KBD.
Regulations prohibiting repair above certain cost without licence—Whether breach excused by regulations—Defence (General) Regulations 1939, reg 56A, para 2, Sch 6, Pt 3—Control of Building Operations Order 1941 (SR & O 1941 No 1986), para 2. **Maud v Sandars** [1943] **2** 783, KBD.
Expenses of landlord in relation to breach—
Declaration on grant of leave to institute proceedings—Law of Property Act 1925, s 146(3)—Leasehold Property (Repairs) Act 1938, s 2. **Phillips and Price (Intended Action), Re** [1958] **3** 386, Ch D.
Declaration on grant of leave to institute proceedings—Surveyors' and solicitors' costs—Law of Property Act 1925, s 146(3)—Leasehold Property (Repairs) Act 1938, s 2. **Metropolitan Film Studios Ltd v Twickenham Film Studios Ltd, Re (Intended Action)** [1962] **3** 508, Ch D.
Surveyors' and solicitors' charges. **Lloyds Bank Ltd v Lake** [1961] **2** 30, QBD.
Landlord's covenant to 'maintain repair amend renew' and 'otherwise keep in good and tenantable condition'—
Inherent defect in building—Water leaking through anodised aluminium and glass cladding—Whether landlord in breach of covenant—Whether landlord liable for cost of putting building into tenantable condition—Whether landlord's liability extending to replacement of cladding. **Crédit Suisse v Beegas Nominees Ltd** [1994] **4** 803, Ch D.
Leave to institute proceedings—
Conditions to be satisfied before leave may be given—Clearance order and compulsory purchase order made by local authority—Leasehold Property (Repairs) Act 1938, s 1(5), as amended by Landlord and Tenant Act 1954, s 51(2)(c), (d). **Phillips and Price (Intended Action), Re** [1958] **3** 386, Ch D.
Conditions to be satisfied before leave may be given—Service by lessor of notice under s 146 of the Law of Property Act 1925—Notice served by lessor after he had caused repairs to be executed—Whether notice valid—Whether leave could be given to institute proceedings—Law of Property Act 1925, s 146(1)—Leasehold Property (Repairs) Act 1938, s 1. **SEDAC Investments Ltd v Tanner** [1982] **3** 646, Ch D.
Conditions to be satisfied before leave may be given—Time at which satisfaction of statutory conditions to be ascertained—Discretion of court to grant leave—Exercise of discretion—Interlocutory nature of relief—Leasehold Property (Repairs) Act 1938, s 1(5), as amended by Landlord and Tenant Act 1954, s 51(2)(c), (d). **Metropolitan Film Studios Ltd v Twickenham Film Studios Ltd, Re (Intended Action)** [1962] **3** 508, Ch D.
Discretion of court—Standard of proof of alleged breach of covenant—Prima facie case sufficient—Court having discretion to refuse leave even though prima facie case made out—Circumstances in which discretion will be exercised—Leasehold Property (Repairs) Act 1938, s 1(5). **Land Securities plc v Receiver for the Metropolitan Police District** [1983] **2** 254, Ch D.
Necessity where counter-notice served by lessee—Action against former assignee who had assigned his leasehold interest before action—Defence of want of notice specifying breaches and of leave to proceed—Whether defendant 'lessee'—Law of Property Act 1925, s 146—Leasehold Property (Repairs) Act 1938, s 1(3). **Cusack-Smith v Gold** [1958] **2** 361, QBD.
Premises mortgaged by lessee by way of legal charge—Lessee in possession of premises—Notice of breach given to lessee and also to mortgagee—No counter-notice by lessee—Counter-notice by mortgagee—Whether leave of court required by lessors before commencing action against lessee for damages and possession—Leasehold Property (Repairs) Act 1938, s 1(2), (3). **Church Comrs for England v Ve-Ri-Best Manufacturing Co Ltd** [1956] **3** 777, QBD.
Proceedings to recover cost of repairs already carried out by landlord—Landlord carrying out repairs and bringing action against tenant to recover cost of repairs—Whether claim for debt due under lease or claim for damages for breach of repairing covenant—Whether leave required to bring action—Leasehold Property (Repairs) Act 1938, s 1. **Hamilton v Martell Securities Ltd** [1984] **1** 665, Ch D.
Standard of proof of alleged breach of covenant—Prima facie case sufficient—Leasehold Property (Repairs) Act 1938, s 1(4),(5), as amended by Landlord and Tenant Act 1954, s 51(2). **Sidnell v Wilson** [1966] **1** 681, CA.
Whether mortgagee in possession entitled to serve counter-notice to landlord's notice to remedy breach of covenant to repair— Law of Property Act 1925, s 146—Leasehold Property (Repairs) Act 1938, s 1(3). **Smith v Spaul** [2003] **1** 509, CA.
Notice of forfeiture—
Retrospective operation of statute—Leasehold Property (Repairs) Act 1938, ss 1, 5. **National Real Estate and Finance Co Ltd v Hassan** [1939] **2** 154, CA.

267

LANDLORD AND TENANT (cont)—
  Breach of covenant to repair (cont)—
    Notice to remedy breach served on tenant—
      Counter-notice served by tenant—Assignment of lease—Leave obtained to commence proceedings
        against tenant only—Judgment in default of appearance against assignee—Whether judgment
        irregular—Law of Property Act 1925, s 146(1)—Leasehold Property (Repairs) Act 1938, s 1(3).
        Church Comrs for England v Kanda [1957] **2** 815, CA.
      Counter-notice served by tenant—Assignment of lease—Surrender by assignee—Action for
        damages for breach of covenant commenced by landlord without obtaining leave of
        court—Whether action maintainable—Leasehold Property (Repairs) Act 1938, s 1(3). **Baker v Sims
        (Alsen Properties Ltd, third party)** [1958] **3** 326, CA.
      Counter-notice served by tenant—Landlord requiring leave to institute proceedings—Conditions to
        be satisfied before leave given—Lease of dry dock which had ceased to be used—Lease having
        60 years to run—Landlord proving that tenant in breach of repairing covenant—Landlord having
        to prove that immediate remedying of breach necessary to prevent substantial diminution in
        value of reversion—Standard of proof required—Whether prima facie or arguable case
        sufficient—Leasehold Property (Repairs) Act 1938, s 1(5). **Associated British Ports v C H Bailey plc**
        [1990] **1** 929, HL.
      Notice also alleging breach of non-existent covenant not to sub-let—Validity of notice—Law of
        Property Act 1925, s 146(1)—Leasehold Property (Repairs) Act 1938, s 1(2), as amended by
        Landlord and Tenant Act 1954, s 51(2)(b). **Silvester v Ostrowska** [1959] **3** 642, QBD.
      Tenant refusing landlord entry—Underlease of property containing clause giving landlord right to
        enter and effect repairs in default—Landlord seeking injunction to restrain tenant from preventing
        him from entering premises and carrying out repairs—Whether landlord's right to enter and
        effect repairs himself and recover cost from tenant being a claim for damages for breach of
        repairing covenant or claim for debt—Whether leave required to bring action—Leasehold
        Property (Repairs) Act 1938, s 1. **Jervis v Harris** [1996] **1** 303, CA.
    Specific performance—
      Jurisdiction to make order requiring landlord to repair—Circumstances in which order will be
        made. **Jeune v Queens Cross Properties Ltd** [1973] **3** 97, Ch D; **Rainbow Estates Ltd v Tokenhold
        Ltd** [1998] **2** 860, Ch D.
  Brothel—
    Immoral user of premises—
      Forfeiture of lease—Relief against forfeiture. See Relief against forfeiture—Immoral user of
        premises—Suffering premises to be used as a brothel, below.
    Letting premises for use as brothel. See **Criminal law** (Brothel—Landlord letting premises for use as
      brothel).
  Building lease—
    Consent of lessor to plans—
      Plans approved by lessor—Later application by lessee for approval of new plans—Refusal of
        approval by lessor—Whether discretion to withhold approval absolute—Whether lessee bound to
        build in accordance with approved plans. **Comr for Railways v Avrom Investments Pty Ltd**
        [1959] **2** 63, PC.
      Power to amend deleted assessment—Whether lessor had absolute discretion to withhold consent.
        Comr for Railways v Avrom Investments Pty Ltd [1959] **2** 63, PC.
    Frustration of contract—
      Applicability—Whether doctrine of frustration applicable to building lease. **Cricklewood Property
        and Investment Trust Ltd v Leighton's Investment Trust Ltd** [1945] **1** 252, HL.
    Leasehold enfranchisement—
      House. See Leasehold enfranchisement—House—Building lease, below.
  Business premises—
    Application for new tenancy—
      Amendment—Landlord a company—Wrong company made respondent to tenant's originating
        summons—Summons amended by making landlord company respondent—Amendment not
        made within time prescribed for making application—Whether amendment to be allowed—
        Landlord and Tenant Act 1954, s 29(3)—RSC Ord 53D, r 6(3), Ord 70, r 1. **Holmes Road, Kentish
        Town, Re Nos 55 & 57** [1958] **2** 311, Ch D.
      Amendment—Whether court having power to allow tenant to amend claim for new tenancy by
        adding or substituting party after expiry of limitation period—Landlord and Tenant Act 1954,
        s 29(3)—CPR 19.5. **Parsons v George** [2004] **3** 633, CA.
      Answer—Statement of landlord's objections to proposed terms—Failure of landlord to state, in his
        answer to tenants' originating application, his objection to terms proposed by tenants—Whether
        court required to hear evidence as to reasonableness of terms—Landlord and Tenant Act 1954,
        ss 29(1), 33, 34, 69(2)—County Court Rules 1936 (as amended), Ord 40, r 8(2), Form 336. **Morgan
        v Jones** [1960] **3** 583, CA.
      Application by tenant not served—Whether landlord may apply for dismissal for want of
        prosecution. **Pike v Michael Nairn & Co Ltd** [1960] **2** 184, Ch D.
      Application out of time—Tenancy having terminated—Locus standi of tenant—Request by tenant
        for new tenancy—Date specified for beginning of new tenancy—Existing tenancy terminating
        immediately before that date—Tenant failing to make application for new tenancy until after that
        date—Whether application should be struck out—Landlord and Tenant Act 1954, ss 24(1), 26(5).
        Meah v Sector Properties Ltd [1974] **1** 1074, CA.
      Cost of proceedings for. See Business premises—Costs of proceedings for new tenancy, below.
      County court procedure—Failure to serve documents relating to application within prescribed time
        limit—Jurisdiction to enlarge time for service—Exercise of discretion to enlarge time where
        jurisdiction—CCR 1981 Ord 7, r 20, Ord 13, r 4, Ord 43, r 6(3). **Baxendale (Robert) Ltd v Davstone
        (Holdings) Ltd** [1982] **3** 496, CA; **Ward-Lee v Linehan** [1993] **2** 1006, CA.
      Filing of answer by landlords—Fixing of date for hearing—No objection made by landlords to
        validity of application until after time limits for application expired—Jurisdiction of court to hear
        application—Whether time limits procedural and capable of being waived—Landlord and Tenant
        Act 1954, s 29(3). **Kammins Ballrooms Co Ltd v Zenith Investments (Torquay) Ltd** [1970] **2** 871,
        HL.

LANDLORD AND TENANT (cont)—
Business premises (cont)—
Application for new tenancy (cont)—

Form—Tenant requesting new tenancy 'upon terms of current tenancy'—Current lease for seven years—Tenant intending to ask for lease for 14 years—Validity of request—Need to state duration of new term—Landlord and Tenant Act 1954, ss 24(1), 26(1), (3), (5), (6)—Landlord and Tenant (Notices) Regulations 1954 (SI 1954 No 1107), Appendix, Form 8. **Bolsom (Sidney) Investment Trust Ltd v E Karmios & Co (London) Ltd** [1956] 1 536, CA.

Joint tenants—One joint tenant only applying—Applicant in sole occupation, carrying on former partnership business—Whether applicant 'the tenant' and so entitled to apply for grant of new tenancy—Landlord and Tenant Act 1954, ss 24(1), 41. **Jacobs v Chaudhuri** [1968] 2 124, CA.

Judgment for forfeiture before issue of application for new tenancy—Subsisting claim by tenant for relief from forfeiture—Landlord seeking to dismiss application for new tenancy on ground that tenancy had already come to an end by forfeiture—Whether tenant entitled to apply for new tenancy—Whether judgment for forfeiture resulting in 'coming to an end of ... tenancy by ... forfeiture'—Whether tenancy not coming to an end by forfeiture until claim for relief determined—Whether undue delay in applying for relief indicating application not genuine and forfeiture fully effective—Landlord and Tenant Act 1954, s 24(2). **Meadows v Clerical Medical and General Life Assurance Society** [1980] 1 454, Ch D.

Landlord intending demolition or reconstruction of premises or substantial work of reconstruction—Whether proposed works necessarily involving structure of building—Landlord and Tenant Act 1954, s 30(1)(f). **Ivorygrove Ltd v Global Grange Ltd** [2004] 4 144, Ch D.

Landlord issuing counter summons for interim rent—Withdrawal of tenant's application—Action discontinued—Whether counter-summons surviving as a counterclaim. **Artoc Bank and Trust Ltd v Prudential Assurance Co plc** [1984] 3 538, Ch D.

Landlord local authority—Reversion acquired by local authority after date of tenant's request for new tenancy—Opposition to grant of new tenancy—Application to government department for certificate—Notice served on tenant within two months of request—Effect of notice on tenant's application—Landlord and Tenant Act 1954, s 57(4)(b). **XL Fisheries Ltd v Leeds Corp** [1955] 2 875, CA.

Parties to application—Landlord—Mortgagee—Receiver in receipt of rents and profits appointed by mortgagee of landlord between making and hearing of tenant's application—Mortgagee in possession—Landlord and Tenant Act 1954, ss 44(1), 67—CCR Ord 40, r 21(2). **Meah v Mouskos** [1963] 3 908, CA.

Parties to application—Landlord—Whether landlord ceased to be such on becoming a statutory tenant—Whether proceedings thereafter properly constituted without joining superior landlords—Landlord and Tenant Act 1954, s 44(1). **Piper v Muggleton** [1956] 2 249, CA.

Premature application—Landlords objecting to validity of application—Desirability of setting out objection in landlords' answer. **Kammins Ballrooms Co Ltd v Zenith Investments (Torquay) Ltd** [1970] 2 871, HL.

Premature application—Landlords objecting to validity of application—Effect of landlords deliberately withholding notice of objection until time limits for application expired. **Kammins Ballrooms Co Ltd v Zenith Investments (Torquay) Ltd** [1970] 2 871, HL.

Request by tenant for new tenancy—Lease of office premises for term of years with option to determine—Lessee serving notice to determine on landlord together with request for new tenancy—New tenancy commencing before expiry of existing tenancy but after date of option to determine—Whether notice to determine effective—Whether request for new tenancy effective to determine existing tenancy—Landlord and Tenant Act 1954, s 26. **Garston v Scottish Widows' Fund and Life Assurance Society** [1998] 3 596, CA.

Request by tenant for new tenancy—Request specifying date for commencement of new tenancy—Tenant not applying to court for new tenancy within prescribed period—Tenant serving second request for new tenancy two days before current tenancy due to terminate by virtue of first request—Second request specifying later date for commencement of new tenancy than that in first request—Tenant purporting to withdraw first request—Whether tenancy automatically determined immediately before date specified in first request—Whether tenant entitled to withdraw valid request for a new tenancy and serve fresh request specifying later commencement date—Landlord and Tenant Act 1954, ss 26(5), 29(3). **Stile Hall Properties Ltd v Gooch (1968)** [1979] 3 848, CA.

Request by tenant for new tenancy—Request specifying date for commencement of new tenancy—Tenant not applying to court for new tenancy within prescribed period—Tenant serving second request for new tenancy—Second request specifying same date for commencement as in first request—Tenant applying to court for new tenancy on basis of second request—Whether second request valid—Whether tenant entitled to serve second request where valid request already served—Whether application based on second request valid—Landlord and Tenant Act 1954, ss 26(5), 29(3). **Polyviou v Seeley** [1979] 3 853, CA.

Request by tenant for new tenancy—Whether tenant of business premises required to have genuine intention to take up new tenancy when making request for such a tenancy—Landlord and Tenant Act 1954, ss 26(3), 37. **Sun Life Assurance plc v Thales Tracs Ltd** [2002] 1 64, CA.

Service of application out of time—Extension of time—Jurisdiction. *See* **County court** (Practice—Service of summons—Time for service of default summons—Extension of time—Jurisdiction—Landlord and tenant—Business premises—Application for new tenancy—Service of application out of time).

Time—Computation of time—Four months from giving of landlord's notice terminating tenancy—Landlord's notice given on last day of short month, namely on 30th September—Whether four months' period expiring on 30th or 31st of following January—Landlord and Tenant Act 1954, s 29(3). **Dodds v Walker** [1981] 2 609, HL.

Time—Computation of time—Four months from giving of landlord's notice terminating tenancy—Landlord's notice sent by recorded delivery—Whether notice served on date of posting or date of delivery—Landlord and Tenant Act 1927, s 23—Landlord and Tenant Act 1954, s 25—Interpretation Act 1978, s 7—Human Rights Act 1998, Sch 1, Pt I, art 6, Pt II, art 1. **Beanby Estates Ltd v Egg Stores (Stamford Hill) Ltd** [2004] 3 184, Ch D.

LANDLORD AND TENANT (cont)—

Business premises (cont)—

Application for new tenancy (cont)—

Time—Computation of time—Not less than two months after the giving of landlord's notice terminating tenancy—Landlord's notice given on 23 March and tenant's notice given on 23 May—Whether two-month period expiring on midnight of 23-24 May—Whether tenant's notice premature and out of time—Landlord and Tenant Act 1954, s 29(3). **Riley (E J) Investments Ltd v Eurostile Holdings Ltd** [1985] **3** 181, CA.

Time—Period expiring on Sunday or holiday. *See* **County court** (Time—Period prescribed by statute expiring on a Sunday or holiday—Period within which application to be made to court for new business tenancy expired on Easter Monday).

Tribunal—Application refused by tribunal and notice of appeal served by tenant before commencement of Landlord and Tenant Act 1954—Prohibition imposed by 1954 Act on continuation of proceedings pending an application to tribunal—Whether appeal from tribunal 'Proceedings ... pending on an application ... to the tribunal'—Landlord and Tenant Act 1954, Sch IX, para 8. **Etam Ltd v Forte** [1954] **3** 311, CA.

Withdrawal of application—Date of withdrawal—High Court application for new tenancy—Leave to withdraw application necessary in High Court but not in county court—Whether 'the date of withdrawal' was the date of the judgment giving leave to withdraw the application or the date of issue of summons for leave to withdraw—Whether court having jurisdiction to backdate order giving leave to withdraw application—Landlord and Tenant Act 1954, s 64(2)—RSC Ord 21, r 3. **Covell Matthews & Partners v French Wools Ltd** [1978] **2** 800, CA.

Withdrawal of application—Leave to discontinue proceedings—Notice of withdrawal of application given before any evidence filed—Whether leave to discontinue necessary—RSC Order 21, r 2(3A)—RSC Ord 28, r 1A—RSC Ord 97. **Artoc Bank and Trust Ltd v Prudential Assurance Co plc** [1984] **3** 538, Ch D.

Withdrawal of application—Leave to discontinue proceedings—Terms on which leave given—Tenants entitled to compensation on withdrawal of application—Landlords withdrawing opposition to grant of new tenancy before tenants deciding to seek leave to withdraw application—Whether court in giving leave to discontinue should impose condition that tenants should not pursue claim for compensation—Landlord and Tenant Act 1954, s 37(1)—RSC Ord 21, r 3(1). **Lloyds Bank Ltd v City of London Corp** [1983] **1** 92, CA.

Withdrawal of application—Leave to discontinue proceedings—Terms on which leave given—Tenants entitled to compensation on withdrawal of application—Tenants withdrawing application because they had moved elsewhere and no longer wished to apply for renewal of tenancies—If application had proceeded tenants not entitled to compensation—Whether court in giving leave to discontinue entitled to impose term that tenant should not pursue claim for compensation—Landlord and Tenants Act 1954, s 37(1) (as amended by the Law of Property Act 1969, s 11)—RSC Ord 21, r 3(1). **Young Austen & Young Ltd v British Medical Association** [1977] **2** 884, Ch D.

Business—

Sunday school carried on by tenant for one hour a week in loft or part of premises which had been a shop—No payment demanded by tenant—Whether a 'business'—Landlord and Tenant Act 1954, s 23(1), (2). **Abernethie v AM & J Kleiman Ltd** [1969] **2** 790, CA.

Compensation for disturbance—

Agreement by landlord and tenant excluding tenant's statutory right to compensation for disturbance—Restriction on such agreements—Agreement void if tenant occupying premises 'for the whole of the five years immediately preceding' expiry of lease—Tenant leaving premises 12 days before expiry of lease—Whether tenant occupying premises for five years immediately preceding expiry of lease—Whether agreement void—Whether compensation payable—Landlord and Tenant Act 1954, ss 37, 38(2). **Bacchiocchi v Academic Agency Ltd** [1998] **2** 241, CA.

Amount of compensation—Amount altered by amendment of statutory provision—Landlord serving notice to terminate tenancy before amendment coming into force—Landlord entitled to possession after amendment coming into force—Amount of compensation payable by landlord to tenant on quitting premises—Whether compensation payable according to statutory scale in force at date of landlord's notice or at date tenant quitting holding—Landlord and Tenant Act 1954, s 37(2)—Local Government, Planning and Land Act 1980, Sch 33, para 4(1)—Landlord and Tenant Act 1954 (Appropriate Multiplier) Regulations 1981. **Cardshops Ltd v John Lewis Properties Ltd** [1982] **3** 746, CA; **International Military Services Ltd v Capital and Counties plc** [1982] **2** 20, Ch D.

Capital gains tax—Capital sum received for loss of asset. *See* **Capital gains tax** (Disposal of assets—Capital sum derived from asset notwithstanding no asset acquired by person paying sum—Capital sum received from loss of asset—Termination of tenancy—Statutory compensation for termination of business tenancy).

Premises 'being or comprised in the holding' and continously occupied by tenant for 14 years for business premises—Premises—Amount of compensation—Entitlement to double compensation—Tenant not entitled to double compensation if change in occupier of 'the premises' and new tenant not the successor of previous occupier's business—Whether 'premises' referring to any premises in holding or particular premises in holding used by tenant for his business—Whether tenant entitled to double compensation if at least part of relevant holding continously occupied by him for business purposes—Landlord and Tenant Act 1954, s 37(3)(a), (b). **Edicron Ltd v William Whiteley Ltd** [1984] **1** 219, CA.

Compensation for goodwill in respect of business premises. *See* Compensation for goodwill in respect of business premises, *below.*

Compensation for refusal of new tenancy—

Premises continuously occupied for five years for the purposes of carrying on the tenants' business—Successive businesses of same type conducted by successive tenants—Landlord and Tenant Act 1954, Sch 9, para 5(1). **Cramas Properties Ltd v Connaught Fur Trimmings Ltd** [1965] **2** 382, HL.

Construction of licence agreement. *See* **Contract** (Construction—Licence agreement—Licence for occupation of premises).

LANDLORD AND TENANT (cont)—
Business premises (cont)—
Continuation of tenancy—
Severance of reversion—Notice to determine—Part of premises ceasing to be protected—Tenants of business premises subletting part of premises—Sub-tenants occupying part for business purposes—Sub-tenants acquiring lease from landlord of their part of premises to commence on expiry of tenants' term—Right of sub-tenants after expiry of tenants' lease to give tenants notice to quit part of premises occupied by sub-tenants—Law of Property Act 1925, s 140(1)—Landlord and Tenant Act 1954, ss 23(1), 24(3)(a). **Skelton (William) & Son v Harrison & Pinder Ltd** [1975] **1** 182, QBD.

Surrender—Provision for continuation of no effect if tenancy coming to end by surrender—Continuation despite surrender in case of an instrument of surrender executed within specified period—Instrument of surrender—Meaning—Lease conferring option on tenant to acquire freehold—Option exercisable by three months' notice in writing—Exercise of option by tenant—Whether on expiry of three months' notice tenancy coming to end by surrender—Whether notice exercising option an 'instrument of surrender'—Landlord and Tenant Act 1954, s 24(2)(as amended by the Law of Property Act 1969, s 4(1). **Watney v Boardley** [1975] **2** 644, Ch D.

Tenant ceasing to occupy premises for purposes of its business before expiration of contractual term—Tenant serving statutory notice terminating tenancy on date after expiration of contractual term—Whether tenancy continuing after expiration of contractual term until expiration of statutory notice—Landlord and Tenant Act 1954, ss 23, 24(1), 27(2). **Esselte AB v Pearl Assurance plc** [1997] **2** 41, CA.

Whether tenant having continuing liability for rent after disposal of application for new tenancy if not in occupation of premises on contractual term date—Landlord and Tenant Act 1954, ss 24(1), 25(1), 64(1)(c). **Surrey CC v Single Horse Properties Ltd** [2002] **4** 143, CA.

Contracting out—
Agreement by landlord and tenant excluding statutory provisions governing security of tenure—Court authorising agreement—Whether agreement invalid if terms of lease differing from draft placed before court—Landlord and Tenant Act 1954, s 38(4). **Metropolitan Police District Receiver v Palacegate Properties Ltd** [2000] **3** 663, CA.

Agreement by landlord and tenant excluding statutory provisions governing security of tenure—Order of court authorising agreement—Acceptance of rent pending application for court order—Application for order never made—Whether payment and receipt of rent creating periodic tenancy—Whether parties intending to create periodic tenancy—Landlord and Tenant Act 1954, s 38(4). **Cardiothoracic Institute v Shrewdcrest Ltd** [1986] **3** 633, Ch D.

Agreement by landlord and tenant excluding statutory provisions governing security of tenure—Order of court authorising agreement—Agreement to be contained in or endorsed on instrument creating tenancy—Tenant in possession—Agreement for new tenancy for one year certain—Agreement that statutory provisions to be excluded—Order of court embodying terms of agreement—No formal lease executed—Agreement to exclude statutory provisions not therefore contained in or endorsed on lease contemplated by court order—Whether agreement to exclude statutory provisions effective—Whether landlord entitled to possession on expiry of term—Landlord and Tenant Act 1954, s 38(4) (added by the Law of Property Act 1969, s 5). **Tottenham Hotspur Football & Athletic Co Ltd v Princegrove Publishers Ltd** [1974] **1** 17, QBD.

Applications to court—Court's power to authorise contracting out of statutory provisions where tenancy for term of years certain—Joint applications for authorisation—Appointments for hearing—Urgent cases—Landlord and Tenant Act 1954, s 38(4) (added by the Law of Property Act 1969, s 5). **Practice Direction** [1973] **1** 769, QBD.

Term of years certain—Court's power to authorise contracting out of statutory provisions where tenancy for term of years certain—Proposed tenancy for fixed period of six months—Whether six months 'term of years'—Landlord and Tenant Act 1954, s 38(4), (added by the Law of Property Act 1969, s 5). **Land and Premises at Liss, Hants, Re** [1971] **3** 380, Ch D.

Costs of proceedings for new tenancy—
County court. *See* **County court** (Costs—Landlord and tenant—Business premises—Application for new tenancy).

Terms of tenancy in dispute—No dispute that new tenancy should be granted—Rent determined at figure intermediate between rents proposed by the two parties—Proper order no costs on either side—Landlord and Tenant Act 1954, ss 24(1), 29(1). **Le Witt v Cannon Brookes** [1956] **3** 676, CA.

Terms of tenancy in dispute—Tenants asking for 14 year lease, seven year lease granted—Rent nearer to figure of tenants' proposal—Landlord to pay half tenants' costs. **Harewood Hotels Ltd v Harris** [1958] **1** 104, CA.

Duration of new tenancy—
Matters to be considered—Landlord and Tenant Act 1954, s 33. **Upsons Ltd v Robins (E) Ltd** [1955] **3** 348, CA.

Power to insert option for landlord to determine during term—Factors to be considered—Discretion of court—Landlord and Tenant Act 1954, s 33. **London and Provincial Millinery Stores Ltd v Barclays Bank Ltd** [1962] **2** 163, CA.

Power to insert option for landlord to determine during term—Landlord and Tenant Act 1954, ss 30(1)(f), 33. **McCombie v Grand Junction Co Ltd** [1962] **2** 65, CA.

Regard had to terms of previous leases granted to tenant in respect of the premises—Landlord and Tenant Act 1954, s 33. **Betty's Cafés Ltd v Phillips Furnishing Stores Ltd** [1958] **1** 607, HL.

Fixtures—
Continuation by statute of contractual sub-tenancy—Right of mesne landlord, conferred by the lease, to remove fixtures lost by continuation of sub-tenancy beyond the duration of the mesne landlord's lease—Whether sub-tenant had constructive notice of right of removal—Right of removal not an equitable easement and not registrable as a land charge—Land Charges Act 1925, s 10(1), Class D(iii)—Landlord and Tenant Act 1954, ss 23(1), (3), 24(1)—Land Registration Act 1925, s 70(1). **Poster v Slough Estates Ltd** [1968] **3** 257, Ch D.

Forfeiture of lease—
Underlessee—Relief against forfeiture. *See* Relief against forfeiture—Underlessee—Business premises, *below.*

Goodwill—
Compensation for. *See* Compensation for goodwill in respect of business premises, *below.*

271

LANDLORD AND TENANT (cont)—
  Business premises (cont)—
    Improvements—
      Compensation. *See* Improvements—Business premises—Compensation, *below.*
    Improvements. *See* Improvements—Business premises, *below.*
    Interim continuation of tenancy pending determination by court—
      Premature application for new tenancy—No waiver or acquiescence by landlords—Whether premature application an 'application to the court' having effect of prolonging tenancy—Landlord and Tenant Act 1954, s 64. **Zenith Investments (Torquay) Ltd v Kammins Ballrooms Co Ltd (No 2)** [1971] **3** 1281, CA.
      Tenancy terminating at expiration of three months from date when application finally disposed of—Notice by landlord to terminate tenancy—Application for new tenancy refused—Appeal dismissed—Leave to appeal to the House of Lords refused by Court of Appeal—Date of termination of tenancy—When proceedings on appeal are 'finally disposed of'—'Time for appealing'—Landlord and Tenant Act 1954, ss 64(1)(c), 64(2). **Exchange Street (20), Manchester, Re (No 2)** [1956] **3** 490, Ch D.
    Interim rent. *See* Rent—Business premises—Interim rent, *below.*
    Landlord's notice of willingness to grant new tenancy—
      Landlord—Notice served only by superior landlord more than two months after tenant's claim—Whether valid—Landlord and Tenant Act 1927, ss 4(1), proviso(b), 5(1), 8(1). **Rackett v Aston & Co Ltd** [1948] **2** 19, CA.
      What term and rent appropriate for new lease—Landlord and Tenant Act 1927, ss 4(1)(b), (3), 5(5). **Rialto Cinemas Ltd v Wolfe** [1955] **2** 530, QBD.
    Licensed premises—
      Exclusion of statutory protection. *See* Business premises—Tenancy—Exclusion of statutory protection—Licensed premises, *below.*
    Modification of use or occupation—
      Public interest. *See* Business premises—Public interest—Modification of use or occupation, *below.*
    New tenancy—
      Application for new tenancy. *See* Business premises—Application for new tenancy, *above.*
      Compensation for refusal of new tenancy. *See* Business premises—Compensation for refusal of new tenancy, *above.*
      Costs of proceedings for new tenancy. *See* Business premises—Costs of proceedings for new tenancy, *above.*
      Duration of new tenancy. *See* Business premises—Duration of new tenancy, *above.*
      Opposition. *See* Opposition to grant of new tenancy of business premises, *below.*
      Opposition to grant of new tenancy. *See* Opposition to grant of new tenancy of business premises, *below.*
      Refusal—Compensation. *See* Business premises—Compensation, *above.*
      Terms of new tenancy. *See* Business premises—Terms of new tenancy, *below.*
    Notice by landlord to terminate tenancy—
      Application by tenant for new tenancy—Landlord creating trust in favour of children within five-year period preceding termination of tenancy—Whether landlord's interest created within five-year period—Whether landlord barred from opposing grant of new tenancy—Landlord and Tenant Act 1954, ss 30(1)(g), (2), 41(2). **Morar v Chauhan** [1985] **3** 493, CA.
      Application by tenant for new tenancy—Requirements for making application—Notice by tenant to landlord of unwillingness to give up possession—Landlord to be 'duly notified' of tenant's unwillingness—Tenant's notice not received by landlord within two months of landlord's notice—Tenant applying for new tenancy—Whether landlord 'duly notified'—Whether court having power to entertain tenant's application—Landlord and Tenant Act 1954, ss 25(5), 29(2). **Chiswell v Griffon Land and Estates Ltd** [1975] **2** 665, CA.
      Compensation—Tenant giving counter-notice of intention to vacate premises—Whether counter-notice revocable—Whether landlord obtaining indefeasible right to obtain possession without payment of compensation—Landlord and Tenant Act 1954, ss 25(5), 29(2). **Grafton Street (14), London W1, Re** [1971] **2** 1, Ch D.
      Generally. *See* Notice to quit—Business premises, *below.*
      Notice specifying date earlier than date on which apart from statute tenancy would have come to an end by effluxion of time—Date tenancy would have come to an end—Notice purporting to terminate tenancy on last date of term—Whether notice specifying date earlier than date tenancy would have come to an end—Landlord and Tenant Act 1954, s 25(4). **Crowhurst Park, Re** [1974] **1** 991, Ch D.
      Statement of grounds on which landlord would oppose application for new tenancy—Inaccurate statement—Landlord trustee for company—Intention that company should occupy premises for purpose of company's business—Statement that landlord intended to occupy for purposes of landlord's business—Validity of notice—Landlord and Tenant Act 1954, s 25. **Sevenarts Ltd v Busvine** [1969] **1** 392, CA.
      Tenant giving counter-notice erroneously indicating willingness to give up possession—Tenant giving second counter-notice within prescribed period correctly indicating unwillingness to give up possession—Whether first counter-notice binding—Landlord and Tenant Act 1954, ss 25(5), 29(2)—Human Rights Act 1998, s 3, Sch 1, Pt I, art 6(1), Pt II, art 1. **Pennycook v Shaws (EAL) Ltd** [2003] **3** 1316, Ch D; [2004] **2** 665, CA.
      Time—Computation of time—Not less than six months before date of termination specified in notice—Landlord's notice sent by recorded delivery—Whether notice served on date of posting or date of delivery—Landlord and Tenant Act 1927, s 23—Landlord and Tenant Act 1954, s 25—Interpretation Act 1978, s 7, Human Rights Act 1998, Sch 1, Pt I, art 6, Pt II, art 1. **CA Webber (Transport) Ltd v Railtrack plc** [2004] **3** 202, CA.
      Time—Computation of time—Tenant entitled to 'not less than 3 months' previous notice'—Landlord requiring tenant to vacate premises 'within' three months—Whether notice having effect of giving tenant less than three months' notice—Whether notice valid. **Manorlike Ltd v Le Vitas Travel Agency and Consultancy Services Ltd** [1986] **1** 573, CA.

LANDLORD AND TENANT (cont)—
　Business premises (cont)—
　　Notice by landlord to terminate tenancy (cont)—
　　　Validity—Form of notice—Prescribed form—Notice substantially to like effect—Notice informing
　　　tenant of right to apply for new tenancy within specified time limit—Notice stating that time
　　　running from receipt of notice by tenant—Prescribed form stating that time running from giving
　　　of notice by landlord—Whether notice given by landlord 'substantially to the like effect' as
　　　prescribed form—Landlord and Tenant (Notices) Regulations 1957 (SI 1957 No 1157),
　　　reg 4—Landlord and Tenant (Notices) Regulations 1969 (SI 1969 No 1771), reg 3, Appendix I,
　　　Form 7. **Sun Alliance and London Assurance Co Ltd v Hayman** [1975] **1** 248, CA.
　　　Validity—Notice failing to identify landlord correctly—Whether notice valid—Landlord and Tenant
　　　Act 1954, s 25(1). **Morrow v Nadeem** [1987] **1** 237, CA.
　　　Waiver by tenant of invalidity of notice—Notice failing to identify landlord correctly—Notice given
　　　by 'solicitors and agents of' person who controlled landlord company—Tenant serving
　　　counter-notice on solicitors—Whether tenant waiving invalidity of notice—Landlord and Tenant
　　　Act 1954, s 25(1). **Morrow v Nadeem** [1987] **1** 237, CA.
　　Notice to quit—
　　　Generally. *See* Notice to quit—Business premises, *below*.
　　　Validity. *See* Validity of notice to quit—Business premises, *below*.
　　Occupied for business purposes—
　　　Business purposes—Activity carried on by single person—Tenant of house taking in
　　　lodgers—Lodgers charged very small amounts and tenant making no profit—Whether tenant
　　　occupying house partly for purposes of a 'business'—Whether if tenant a single person the
　　　activity carried on was required to be a 'trade, profession or employment' to constitute a
　　　'business'—Whether tenant carried on a 'trade'—Landlord and Tenant Act 1954, s 23(1), (2). **Lewis
　　　v Weldcrest Ltd** [1978] **3** 1226, CA.
　　　Business purposes—Cottage let to hotel proprietor to house hotel staff—Occupation by staff
　　　convenient for hotel proprietor's business—No evidence that occupation by staff necessary for
　　　proprietor's business—Whether hotel proprietor occupying cottage 'for the purposes of a
　　　business carried on by him'—Landlord and Tenant Act 1954, s 23(1). **Chapman v Freeman**
　　　[1978] **3** 878, CA.
　　　Business purposes—Government department—Occupation for purposes of government
　　　department—Lease of premises to Secretary of State for Social Services—Premises converted
　　　into flats occupied by persons employed in national health service hospitals—Flats managed by
　　　local area health authority under delegated powers and let to employees of health
　　　authority—Whether Secretary of State entitled to new tenancy—Whether Secretary of State in
　　　occupation of premises—Whether premises 'occupied for any purposes of a Government
　　　department'—Whether area health authority acting as agent for Secretary of State—Whether
　　　authority's occupation to be treated as occupation by Secretary of State—Landlord and Tenant
　　　Act 1954, ss 23(1), (3), 56(3). **Linden v Dept of Health and Social Security** [1986] **1** 691, Ch D.
　　　Flat and garage let to company—Covenant to use garage for standing 'private cars' only—Garage
　　　used by company to store cartons of samples and cars in garage used to transport customers and
　　　to carry cartons—Whether garage occupied for business purposes—Whether business user in
　　　breach of covenant to use garage for private cars only. **Bell v Alfred Franks & Bartlett Co Ltd**
　　　[1980] **1** 356, CA.
　　　Occupation of residential tenancy for business purposes—Test of occupation for business
　　　purposes—Business activity on premises required to be a significant purpose of the
　　　occupation—Business activity which is merely incidental to the residential occupation not
　　　constituting occupation for business purposes—Landlord and Tenant Act 1954, s 23(1). **Cheryl
　　　Investments Ltd v Saldanha** [1979] **1** 5, CA.
　　　Occupation—Premises—Incorporeal right—Lease granting right of way over private road for term
　　　of years for purposes connected with lessee's business—Permitted user intermittent and
　　　non-exclusive—Lessor opposing grant of new tenancy—Whether tenancy of right of way a
　　　protected business tenancy—Whether incorporeal right such as an easement of way capable of
　　　being 'premises ... occupied' for business purposes—Landlord and Tenant Act 1954, s 23(1). **Land
　　　Reclamation Co Ltd v Basildon DC** [1978] **2** 1162, Ch D; [1979] **2** 993, CA.
　　　Occupation—Tenant carrying on business as market operator—Market hall fitted out with stalls let
　　　to individual traders—Tenant supplying certain facilities and services—Notice by landlord to
　　　terminate tenancy—Whether tenant entitled to apply for grant of new tenancy—Whether tenancy
　　　a protected tenancy—Whether tenant occupying hall for purposes of its business—Landlord and
　　　Tenant Act 1954, s 23(1). **Graysim Holdings Ltd v P & O Property Holdings Ltd** [1995] **4** 831, HL.
　　　Occupation—Vacation of premises by tenant—Circumstances forcing tenant to leave premises—
　　　Premises damaged by fire and incapable of occupation for business purposes—Tenant vacating
　　　premises with intention of returning to carry on business when premises repaired—Whether
　　　during absence of tenant premises continuing to be 'occupied' by him—Landlord and Tenant Act
　　　1954, s 23(1). **Morrison Holdings Ltd v Manders Property (Wolverhampton) Ltd** [1976] **2** 205, CA.
　　　Residential flat used by tenant for his business—Business having no trade premises—Tenant
　　　placing office equipment in hall of flat—Business notepaper giving same telephone number as
　　　for flat—Considerable volume of trade carried on from flat—Landlords serving notice to
　　　quit flat—Tenant claiming protection of Rent Acts—Whether tenancy a business tenancy—
　　　Whether flat occupied by tenant 'for the purposes of a business carried on by him'—Whether
　　　business activity a significant purpose of occupation of flat—Landlord and Tenant Act 1954,
　　　s 23(1). **Cheryl Investments Ltd v Saldanha** [1979] **1** 5, CA.
　　　Residential premises let to tenant who was a medical practitioner—Tenant having his consulting
　　　rooms nearby—Tenant minded to see patients occasionally at residence and obtaining landlords'
　　　consent to do so—Both addresses entered in Medical Directory—Telephone numbers for both
　　　addresses printed on the separate notepaper used for each address—Tenant seeing patients at
　　　residence only once or twice a year in an emergency—Landlords serving notice to quit—Tenant
　　　claiming protection of Rent Acts—Whether tenancy a business tenancy—Whether flat occupied
　　　by tenant 'for the purposes of a business carried on by him'—Whether use of residence for
　　　professional purposes a significant use—Landlord and Tenant Act 1954, s 23(1). **Cheryl
　　　Investments Ltd v Saldanha** [1979] **1** 5, CA.

LANDLORD AND TENANT (cont)—
 Business premises (cont)—
  Occupied for business purposes (cont)—
   Seasonal business—Active only in holiday seasons, inactive in winter—Agreement by tenant to employ a manager for a year—Manager to have full control of business and all profits in return for agreed sum—Keys of premises returned to tenant at end of summer season—Agreement a sham as regards employment of manager—Whether premises occupied by tenant for the purposes of a business during next winter—Landlord and Tenant Act 1954, ss 23(1), 25(1). **Teasdale v Walker** [1958] **3** 307, CA.
   Tenant carrying on business of letting furnished service apartments in premises—Tenant living in basement flat of premises—Tenant and servants having access to all apartments for purpose of running business and providing services—Occupants of each apartment having exclusive occupation of apartment 'as a residence' for purposes of Rent Act 1968—Whether tenant occupying whole of premises including apartments for purposes of business—Landlord and Tenant Act 1954, s 23(1). **Lee-Verhulst (Investments) Ltd v Harwood Trust** [1972] **3** 619, CA.
   Tenant carrying on business of sub-letting parts of premises as flats—Occupation by landlord of ancillary parts of premises—Application of Landlord and Tenant Act 1954, Part II—Landlord and Tenant Act 1954, ss 23(1), (2), (3), 32(1). **Bagettes Ltd v GP Estates Co Ltd** [1956] **1** 729, CA.
  Opposition to grant of new tenancy. *See* Opposition to grant of new tenancy of business premises, *below.*
  Part only of holding—
   Jurisdiction—Whether jurisdiction to order tenancy of part of premises used by tenant for business purposes—Landlord and Tenant Act 1954, ss 23(3), 29(1), 32(1). **Fernandez v Walding** [1968] **1** 994, CA.
  Premises—
   Tenancy of gallops for training racehorses—Whether gallops were 'premises' within Landlord and Tenant Act 1954, s 23(1). **Bracey v Read** [1962] **3** 472, Ch D.
  Public interest—
   Modification of use or occupation—Land requisite for public purposes—Meaning—Minister deciding that appellant's land reasonably necessary for local authority's purposes—Whether land 'requisite' for local authority's purposes—Landlord and Tenant Act 1954, s 57(1). **R v Secretary of State for the Environment, ex p Powis** [1981] **1** 788, CA.
  Recovery of possession. *See* Recovery of possession—Business premises, *below.*
  Rent. *See* Rent—Business premises, *below.*
  Right to new tenancy conditional on tenant's continuing throughout proceedings to be tenant under business tenancy—
   Continuity of business user—Tenant ceasing to trade from premises and premises left empty for period during pendency of application for new tenancy—Tenant's intention to discontinue lines of existing business and, if granted new tenancy, to start another but similar line of business—Whether tenant ceased to occupy premises for the purposes of a business—Landlord and Tenant Act 1954, s 23(1). **Caplan (I & H) Ltd v Caplan (No 2)** [1963] **2** 930, Ch D.
  Surrender of tenancy—
   Restriction on agreements purporting to preclude tenant applying for new tenancy—Purporting to preclude—Lease requiring tenant to offer to surrender lease before he is entitled to consent to assign—Tenant offering to surrender lease and offer accepted by landlord but tenant subsequently withdrawing offer—Landlord suing tenant to enforce agreement—Whether agreement void as 'purporting to preclude' tenant from applying for new tenancy at end of term—Landlord and Tenant Act 1954, s 38(1). **Allnatt London Properties Ltd v Newton** [1984] **1** 423, CA.
  Tenancy—
   Exclusion of statutory protection—Business user in breach of covenant in lease—Consent—Acquiescence—Consent to breach by immediate landlord or predecessor in title—Predecessor in title noticing business user of premises in breach of covenant and not objecting—Whether 'consent' to business user—Whether standing by and not objecting to breach consent or merely acquiescence—Whether consent requiring positive action accepting breach—Whether tenancy within statute—Landlord and Tenant Act 1954, s 23(4). **Bell v Alfred Franks & Bartlett Co Ltd** [1980] **1** 356, CA.
   Exclusion of statutory protection—Effect of provision purporting to exclude statutory protection of tenancy. **Manfield & Son Ltd v Botchin** [1970] **3** 143, QBD.
   Exclusion of statutory protection—Licensed premises—Restaurant business—Whether business comprising restaurant has to be carried on wholly on demised premises for tenancy to be protected—Landlord and Tenant Act 1954, s 43(1)(d). **Ye Olde Cheshire Cheese Ltd v Daily Telegraph** [1988] **3** 217, Ch D.
   Renewal by agreement between landlord and tenant—Landlord—Reversionary lease granted by head lessor to person then tenant of intermediate landlord—Whether intermediate landlord the 'landlord'—Whether interest of intermediate landlord a tenancy which would not expire within fourteen months of the grant of the 'reversionary tenancy'—Landlord and Tenant Act 1954, ss 28, 44(1)(b). **Bowes-Lyon v Green** [1961] **3** 843, HL.
   Surrender of. *See* Business premises—Surrender of tenancy, *above.*
   Tenancy at will—Tenancy created by express agreement—Whether protected tenancy. **Hagee (London) Ltd v AB Erikson and Larson (a firm)** [1975] **3** 234, CA.
   Tenancy at will—Whether protected tenancy—Landlord and Tenant Act 1954, ss 25(3), (4), 43(3), 69(1). **Wheeler v Mercer** [1956] **3** 631, HL.
   Tenant at will—Plaintiff occupying premises under two successive agreements of less than six months—Plaintiff holding over after expiry of second agreement while negotiating for grant of lease—Defendant terminating plaintiff 's right of occupation more than 12 months after it first occupied premises—Whether plaintiff had been in occupation of premises as tenant for period exceeding 12 months—Landlord and Tenant Act 1954, s 43(3). **Cricket Ltd v Shaftesbury plc** [1999] **3** 283, Ch D.
  Terms of new tenancy. *See* Business premises—Terms of new tenancy, *below.*

LANDLORD AND TENANT (cont)—
Business premises (cont)—
Tenant's claim for new lease in lieu of compensation—

Claim by tenant seeking new lease that old lease still subsisting—Right of tenant to claim old lease still subsisting—Landlord and Tenant Act 1927, ss 4(1)(i), 5(1). **Davis (W) (Spitalfields) Ltd v Huntley** [1947] **1** 246, KBD.

Claim for compensation bad—Effect on claim for new lease—Landlord and Tenant Act 1927, s 5(1). **British and Colonial Furniture Co Ltd v William McIlroy Ltd** [1952] **1** 12, KBD.

Factors to be considered—Covenant by tenant not to apply for new lease—Landlord and Tenant Act 1927, ss 5(2), 9. **Etam Ltd v Forte** [1954] **3** 311, CA.

Grant of new lease subject to condition—Provision for determination by landlord and payment of compensation to tenant—Tribunal's power to fix compensation on determination—Landlord and Tenant Act 1927, s 5(2). **Lambert v Ve-Ri-Best Manufacturing Co Ltd** [1954] **1** 961, CA.

Interim continuation of tenancy pending determination by court—Undertaking by landlord not to dispossess tenant during proceedings for new lease—Right of tenant to interim order—Landlord and Tenant Act 1927, s 5(1),(13). **British and Colonial Furniture Co Ltd v William McIlroy Ltd (No 1)** [1951] **1** 404, CA.

Opposition by landlord—Premises required for occupation by landlord—Joint landlords—Premises required for occupation by two of three landlords—Two landlords sons of third landlord—Reasonableness—Landlord and Tenant Act 1927, s 5(2), (3)(b)(i). **Wetherall & Co Ltd v Stone** [1950] **2** 1209, CA.

Opposition by landlord—Premises required for occupation by landlord—'Landlord'—Relevant date for determining reasonableness—Landlord and Tenant Act 1927, s 5(3). **Nuthall (GC & E) (1917) Ltd v Entertainments & General Investment Corp Ltd** [1947] **2** 384, KBD.

Reference to referee—Report by referee—Private conversation between county court judge and referee—Validity of judge's subsequent decision—Landlord and Tenant Act 1927, ss 4(1), 5(1), 20(2)—CCR Ord 19, r 2(f),(g),(h), Ord 40, r 5. **Schooley v Nye** [1949] **2** 950, CA.

Time for making claim—Within two months after service of notice—Landlord and Tenant Act 1927, s 5(2). **Kerridge v Lamdin** [1950] **2** 1110, CA.

Term of lease—

Assignment of unexpired term—Assignee's tenancy extended by operation of statute—Liability of original tenant for breaches of covenant by assignee occurring after expiry of original tenant's contractual term—Assignee compulsorily wound up—Lessors claiming outstanding rent from original tenants for period following expiry of contractual term—Whether term of lease covering statutorily extended period of tenancy—Whether obligations of original tenants ceasing on expiry of contractual term of lease—Whether original tenants liable for outstanding rent—Landlord and Tenant Act 1954, s 24(1). **City of London Corp v Fell** [1992] **3** 224, QBD; [1993] **4** 968, HL.

Terms of new tenancy—

Agreed terms—Agreement between landlord and tenant subject to contract and without prejudice to tenants statutory rights—Application to court for new tenancy—Negotiations between parties in endeavour to dispose of matter out of court—Negotiations without prejudice to tenant's rights under Landlord and Tenant Act 1954—Negotiations subject to contract—Agreed terms embodied in draft lease—Lease engrossed but not executed—Tenant wishing to reconsider agreed terms because of changes in property market—Parties failing to agree on tenant's proposed amendments—Tenant withdrawing from negotiations—Whether parties had 'agreed' terms of new tenancy—Whether court in granting new tenancy bound by terms embodied in engrossed lease—Landlord and Tenant Act 1954, ss 33, 34(1), 35. **Derby & Co Ltd v ITC Pension Trust Ltd** [1977] **2** 890, Ch D.

Covenant in former lease not to assign without consent—New covenant requiring offer first to surrender lease—Need for court to have regard to terms of former tenancy—Whether new covenant such that court might approve—Rent fixed before terms settled—Whether rent should stand—Landlord and Tenant Act 1954, s 35. **Cardshops Ltd v Davies** [1971] **2** 721, CA.

Date of commencement of new tenancy—Landlord and Tenant Act 1954, ss 25(1), 33, 64(1). **High Road, Kilburn, Re 88** [1959] **1** 527, Ch D.

Duration of tenancy. *See* Business premises—Duration of new tenancy, *above.*

Inclusion of new restrictions on use—Proposed term preventing use for substantial part of existing business—County court judge's discretion—Landlord and Tenant Act 1954, s 35. **Gold v Brighton Corp** [1956] **3** 442, CA.

Inclusion of personal right—Licence to exhibit advertising signs—Jurisdiction to include licence in new lease—Landlord and Tenant Act 1954, ss 32(3), 35. **Albemarle Street (No 1), W1, Re** [1959] **1** 250, Ch D.

Inclusion of service charge over and above reserved rent—Landlord offering tenant new three-year lease containing new provisions as to service charge—Landlord claiming proportion of amount expended by him on services and repairs to building as service charge from tenant—Reserved rent to be consequentially reduced—Landlord thus obtaining clear lease free of burden of services and repairs—Whether service charge merely part of rent payable or variation of terms of tenancy—Whether transfer of risk and burden of services and repairs from landlord to tenant fair and reasonable—Landlord and Tenant Act 1954, ss 34, 35. **O'May v City of London Real Property Co Ltd** [1982] **1** 660, HL.

Inclusion of term that tenant pay landlord's costs in respect of preparation of lease—Whether court should exercise discretion to approve such term—Landlord and Tenant Act 1954, s 35—Costs of Leases Act 1958, s 1. **Cairnplace Ltd v CBL (Property Investment) Co Ltd** [1984] **1** 315, CA.

Inclusion of term that tenant provide guarantor of his obligations under new lease—Whether court having jurisdiction to order inclusion of such term—Landlord and Tenant Act 1954, ss 35, 41A(6). **Cairnplace Ltd v CBL (Property Investment) Co Ltd** [1984] **1** 315, CA.

Property to be comprised in new tenancy—Holding—Occupation of part of premises resumed by tenant after date of application for new tenancy—Occupation for purpose of extending right to new lease—Whether colourable—Landlord and Tenant Act 1954, ss 23(3), 32(1). **Narcissi v Wolfe** [1959] **3** 71, Ch D.

Property to be comprised in new tenancy—Proper date for designating holding—Landlord and Tenant Act 1954, s 32(1). **Caplan (I & H) Ltd v Caplan** [1961] **3** 1174, HL.

LANDLORD AND TENANT (cont)—
Business premises (cont)—
  Terms of new tenancy (cont)—
    Rent—Controlled sub-tenancy—All circumstances relevant to what rent might be expected to be
      obtained in open market to be taken into consideration—Landlord and Tenant Act 1954, s 34.
      Oscroft v Benabo [1967] **2** 548, CA.
    Rent—Evidence—Evidence of earnings of occupant—Admissibility—Landlord and Tenant Act 1954,
      s 34(a),(b). **Harewood Hotels Ltd v Harris** [1958] **1** 104, CA.
  Underlessee—
    Relief against forfeiture. *See* Relief against forfeiture—Underlessee—Business premises, *below*.
  User of premises—
    Covenant against use except as business premises. *See* Covenant—User of premises—Covenant
      against use except as business premises, *below*.
Certificate of managing agents as to landlord's costs of maintaining building. *See* Contribution by tenant to
  landlord's costs of maintaining building—Certificate of managing agents as to amount of contribution,
  below.
Collective compulsory acquisition by tenants of landlord's interest. *See* Flats—Compulsory acquisition by
  tenants of their landlord's interest, *below*.
Collective enfranchisement. *See* Leasehold enfranchisement, *below*.
Compensation—
  Compensation for disturbance—
    Business premises. *See* Business premises—Compensation for disturbance, *above*.
  Compensation for goodwill in respect of business premises. *See* Compensation for goodwill in respect
    of business premises, *below*.
  Improvements—
    Business premises. *See* Improvements—Business premises—Compensation, *below*.
  Notice by landlord to terminate tenancy—
    Business premises. *See* Business premises—Notice by landlord to terminate tenancy—
      Compensation, *above*.
  Refusal of new tenancy—
    Business premises. *See* Business premises—Compensation for refusal of new tenancy, *above*.
Compensation for goodwill in respect of business premises—
  Apportionment—
    Business carried on in two separate premises—Apportionment of goodwill—Landlord and Tenant
      Act 1927, ss 4, 5. **Morell (H) & Sons Ltd v Canter** [1947] **2** 533, CA.
  Business carried on by tenant or predecessors in title for period of not less than five years—
    Computation of period—Continuous period covering two contracts of tenancy—Whether
      compliance with condition—Landlord and Tenant Act 1927, s 4(1). **Lawrence v Sinclair**
      [1949] **1** 418, CA.
    Need for business to be carried on by predecessors as tenants—Business carried on for part of
      period under friendly arrangement with previous tenant—Landlord and Tenant Act 1927, s 4(1).
      Corsini v Montague Burton Ltd [1953] **2** 8, CA.
    Predecessor in title—Similar business carried on for part of period by sub-tenant under
      sub-lease—Landlord and Tenant Act 1927, ss 4(1), 25(1). **Williams v Portman** [1951] **2** 539, CA.
    Predecessor in title—Title to premises, not to business—Landlord and Tenant Act 1927, ss 4(1),
      25(1). **Pasmore v Whitbread & Co Ltd** [1953] **1** 361, CA.
  Carrying on of trade or business—
    Trade or business—Solicitor—Agent for insurance companies and building societies—Relevant
      goodwill—Landlord and Tenant Act 1927, ss 4(1), 17(1). **Stuchbery & Son v General Accident, Fire
      and Life Assurance Corp Ltd** [1949] **1** 1026, CA.
  Claim—
    Form—Failure by tenant to state amount of compensation claimed—Validity of claim—Jurisdiction
      to allow amendment of claim—Landlord and Tenant Act 1927, s 4(1)—RSC Ord 53D, r 1. **British
      and Colonial Furniture Co Ltd v William McIlroy Ltd** [1952] **1** 12, KBD.
  Claim for new lease—
    Reasonableness—Premises required by landlord for occupation by his firm—Absence of adherent
      goodwill—Landlord and Tenant Act 1927, ss 4(1), 5(1), (3)(b)(i), (iv). **Clift v Taylor** [1948] **2** 113, CA.
  Goodwill arising from activities of sub-lessees or licensees—
    Alternative claims for new lease or compensation—Landlord and Tenant Act 1927, ss 4(1), 5(3).
      Butlins Ltd v Fytche [1948] **1** 737, CA.
  Letting of premises at higher rent—
    New lease—Premises used for purpose prohibited by head lease—Premises 'required' for
      occupation by landlord—Landlord and Tenant Act 1927, ss 4(1), 5(1), (2), (3)(b)(i). **Ireland v Taylor**
      [1948] **2** 450, CA.
  Licensed premises—
    Right to new lease—Attracting particular classes of customers to the premises—Landlord and
      Tenant Act 1927, ss 4(1), 5(1). **Dartford Brewery Co Ltd v Freeman** [1938] **4** 78, KBD.
  Practice—
    Admission of evidence on consideration of report by county court judge—Whether or not
      proceedings before county court judge an appeal. **British and Argentine Meat Co Ltd v Randall**
      [1939] **4** 293, .
  Value of premises enhanced for similar business—
    Landlord requiring premises for own purposes—Landlord and Tenant Act 1927, ss 4, 5. **Mullins v
      Wessex Motors Ltd** [1947] **2** 727, CA.
Conditions and covenants in lease distinguished. *See* Lease—Condition—Conditions and covenants
  distinguished, *below*.
Consent—
  Assignment. *See* Covenant against assignment without consent, *below*.
  Underletting. *See* Covenant against underletting without consent, *below*.
Construction—
  Lease. *See* Lease—Construction, *below*.
Continuation of tenancy—
  Business premises. *See* Business premises—Continuation of tenancy, *above*.

LANDLORD AND TENANT (cont)—
Contract to grant underlease—
Failure to register. *See* **Land charge** (Failure to register—Estate contract—Contract to grant underlease).
Contracting out of statutory provisions regarding security of tenure—
Business premises. *See* Business premises—Contracting out, *above*.
Contribution by tenant to landlord's costs of maintaining building—
Certificate of managing agents as to amount of contribution—
Validity of certificate—Independence of agents from landlords—Agents required to assess and certify amounts of contribution acting as experts and not arbitrators—Landlords and agents in effect same person—Whether certificate issued by agents to tenant valid. **Finchbourne Ltd v Rodrigues** [1976] **3** 581, CA.
Implied term—
Amount of contribution—Fair and reasonable amount—Amount to be assessed and certified by landlord's managing agents acting as experts and not as arbitrators—Whether an implied term that amount certified should be limited to an amount which is fair and reasonable. **Finchbourne Ltd v Rodrigues** [1976] **3** 581, CA.
Cost of repairs. *See* Repair—Cost of repairs, *below*.
Costs—
County court—
Generally. *See* **County court** (Costs—Landlord and tenant).
Proceedings for new tenancy—
Business premises. *See* Business premises—Costs of proceedings for new tenancy, *above*.
Recovery of possession by landlord—
High Court action. *See* Recovery of possession—Costs—Action in High Court, *below*.
Council houses. *See* **Housing** (Local authority houses).
County court—
Costs. *See* **County court** (Costs—Landlord and tenant).
Equity jurisdiction—
Agreement for lease. *See* **County court** (Jurisdiction—Equity jurisdiction—Landlord and tenant).
Procedure—
Application for new tenancy of business premises. *See* Business premises—Application for new tenancy, *above*.
Rent restriction. *See* **Rent restriction** (County court).
Covenant—
Agreement excluding, modifying or frustrating operation of statutory provisions—
Landlord's covenant in sublease for quiet enjoyment and payment of rent reserved by head lease—Landlord's covenant in sublease excluding liability after landlord disposing of its interest—Landlord assigning reversion—Assignee defaulting on rent reserved by head lease—Whether landlord's covenant void—Whether agreement excluding, modifying or frustrating operation of statutory provisions—Landlord and Tenant (Covenants) Act 1995, ss 3, 6, 7, 8, 25. **London Diocesan Fund v Phithwa (Avonridge Property Co Ltd, Pt 20 defendant)** [2006] **1** 127, HL.
Alienation, covenant against. *See* Assignment of lease—Assignment —Covenants against alienation, *above*.
Alterations—
Breach of covenant against alterations—Measure of damages—Injury to reversion. **Espir v Basil Street Hotel Ltd** [1936] **3** 91, CA.
Breach of covenant against alterations—Measure of damages—Landlord and Tenant Act 1927, s 18. **Eyre v Rea** [1947] **1** 415, KBD.
Covenant to complete alterations in a proper and workmanlike manner etc—Whether imposing obligation to carry out alterations as distinct from obligation to do them in particular manner, if done at all. **Ridley v Taylor** [1965] **2** 51, CA.
Assignment of lease—
Assignment of benefit of covenant to pay rent. *See* Assignment of lease—Obligation to pay rent—Assignee—Express covenant with assignor to pay rent, *above*.
Consent. *See* Covenant against assignment without consent, *below*.
Breach of covenant—
Agricultural holding. *See* **Agricultural holding** (Breach of covenant).
Generally. *See* Breach of covenant, *above*.
Quiet enjoyment, as to. *See* Covenant—Quiet enjoyment—Breach, *below*.
Repairing covenant. *See* Breach of covenant to repair, *above*.
Underletting without consent. *See* Covenant against underletting without consent—Breach, *below*.
Contribution to landlord's costs of maintaining building. *See* Contribution by tenant to landlord's costs of maintaining building, *above*.
Covenant against change of use without consent—
Consent not to be unreasonably withheld—Landlord refusing consent to apply for planning permission for change of use from business to residential on basis of increased risk of enfranchisement—Whether consent unreasonably withheld. **Sequent Nominees Ltd (formerly Rotrust Nominees Ltd) v Hautford Ltd** [2020] **1** 1003, SC.
Covenant benefiting demised land—
Registration. *See* **Land charge** (Registration—Restrictive covenant—Covenant for benefit of demised land).
Covenant running with land—
Covenant by surety to accept new lease if tenant becoming insolvent and disclaiming lease—Whether surety's covenant running with land—Whether covenant enforceable by landlord against surety if tenant becoming insolvent and disclaiming lease. **Coronation Street Industrial Properties Ltd v Ingall Industries plc** [1989] **1** 979, HL.
Covenant to guarantee lessee's payment of rent—Assignment of lease—Sureties guaranteeing payment of rent by new lessee—Sureties executing assignment—Whether sureties' covenant touching and concerning the land—Whether assignee of reversion entitled to benefit of sureties' covenant. **Kumar v Dunning** [1987] **2** 801, CA.

277

LANDLORD AND TENANT (cont)—
  Covenant (cont)—
    Covenant running with land (cont)—
      Covenant to guarantee underlessee's payment of rent—Assignment of reversion—No express assignment of benefit of surety's covenant—Whether reversion of a lease 'land'—Whether surety's covenant touching and concerning land—Whether assignee of reversion entitled to benefit of surety's covenant. **Swift (P & A) Investments (a firm) v Combined English Stores Group plc** [1988] **2** 885, HL.
      Lease of petrol filling service station—Landlord covenanting to supply motor fuel to tenant—Tenant covenanting to sell only motor fuel marketed by landlord—Landlord assigning reversion of lease—Whether covenants enforceable by assignee against tenant—Whether assignee subject to landlord's sale obligations—Whether covenants touching and concerning land—Law of Property Act 1925, ss 78, 141. **Caerns Motor Services Ltd v Texaco Ltd** [1995] **1** 247, Ch D.
      Lease of restaurant premises—Premises intended for use as a licensed victualling house—Company third party in lease and described as 'the surety'—Covenant by lessee not to let person named be concerned directly or indirectly in business of company or in business carried on upon demised premises—Lease assigned to company with consent of lessor—Reversion of lease assigned to plaintiff—Breach of the covenant relating to named person—Action by assignee of reversion of lease against assignee of lessee—Whether covenant running with land. **Lewin v American and Colonial Distributors Ltd** [1945] **2** 271, CA.
      Lease—Deposit paid by tenant to landlord returnable at end of term if tenant's covenants observed—Whether assignee of reversion liable to return deposit—Whether covenant to repay touching and concerning land. **Hua Chiao Commercial Bank Ltd v Chiaphua Industries Ltd** [1987] **1** 1110, PC.
      Proviso for payment of £500 if lease not renewed—Liability of assignee of reversion. **Hunter's Lease, Re** [1942] **1** 27, Ch D.
      Restriction on right to determine tenancy for three years—Repugnancy—Quarterly tenancy—Law of Property Act 1925, s 142(1). **Breams Property Investment Co Ltd v Stroulger** [1948] **1** 758, CA.
    Derogation from grant—
      Use as private dwelling only—Implied covenant—Common scheme—Top floor of house let as residential flat by oral tenancy agreement—Other floors originally let as flats by written agreements containing similar covenants as to user—User as private dwelling only—Whole house, excepting top floor, converted into hotel—Rights of tenant of top floor. **Kelly v Battershell** [1949] **2** 830, CA.
    Enforcement covenant—
      Landlord's covenant to enforce covenants in leases of other lessees—Leases containing absolute covenant against waste, spoil or destruction—Lessee seeking landlord's approval to carry out works breaching absolute covenant—Claimant lessee objecting—Whether landlord having power to license works—Whether licensing works breaching landlord's covenant to other lessees. **Duval v 11-13 Randolph Crescent Ltd** [2020] **4** 537, SC.
      Restraint of trade. *See* **Restraint of trade by agreement** (Lessor and lessee—Enforceability of covenant).
    Implied covenant—
      Fitness of property for human habitation—Scope of covenant. *See* **Housing** (Fitness of property for human habitation—Scope of implied condition of lease).
      Maintenance of access to demised premises—Stairway leading to tenant's flat—Lighting—Whether implied covenant to maintain reasonable standard of lighting on stairway. **Devine v London Housing Society Ltd** [1950] **2** 1173, KBD.
      Repair. *See* Implied covenant to repair, *below*.
      Use of landlord's fixtures and fittings granted by tenancy agreement—Fixtures and fittings including refrigerator—Covenant for quiet enjoyment—Whether covenant to supply motive power to refrigerator in premises demised implied in agreement. **Penn v Gatenex Co Ltd** [1958] **1** 712, CA.
    Insurance—
      Covenant by lessee to insure in joint names—Covenant to reinstate—Premises destroyed by fire—Reinstatement impossible—Insurance moneys invested in names of lessor and lessee—Agreement that policy moneys not to form part of lessee's estate on his decease—Premises subsequently compulsorily acquired by local authority—Whether lessee entitled to insurance money—Fires Prevention (Metropolis) Act 1774, s 83. **King (decd), Re** [1963] **1** 781, CA.
      Fire—Estoppel. *See* **Estoppel** (Landlord and tenant—Fire insurance—Covenant by tenant to insure premises against fire).
      Fire—Landlord covenanting to insure premises to full value—Tenant covenanting to pay additional rent to cover premiums—Landlord covenanting in case of destruction or damage to premises to apply insurance moneys received in respect of insurance in reinstating premises—Policy naming insured as landlord and tenant 'for their respective rights and interests'—Premises destroyed by fire—Premises underinsured—Tenant not wishing to occupy premises if rebuilt—Landlord deciding not to rebuild—Tenant surrendering lease to landlord—Right of tenant to damages for landlord's breach of covenant to insure to full value—Rights of landlord and tenant in insurance moneys. **Beacon Carpets Ltd v Kirby** [1984] **2** 726, CA.
      Fire—Landlord letting part of premises to tenant—Landlord covenanting to insure premises and tenant covenanting to pay portion of premiums—Landlord agreeing to apply insurance moneys received in reinstating premises—Premises destroyed by fire caused by tenant's negligence—Landlord receiving insurance moneys for cost of rebuilding premises—Whether landlord precluded from recovering damages for negligence from tenant—Whether landlord's insurers entitled by subrogation to recover damages from tenant. **Rowlands (Mark) Ltd v Berni Inns Ltd** [1985] **3** 473, CA.
      Fire—Landlord's covenant to insure adequately—Tenant to pay insurance premiums—Landlord following advice of insurance company as to amount for which insurance effected—Premises severely damaged by fire—Insurance cover inadequate—Whether breach of covenant—Reinstatement—No covenant that policy moneys be applied in reinstatement—Whether landlord under implied obligation to apply moneys in reinstating property. **Mumford Hotels Ltd v Wheler** [1963] **3** 250, Ch D.

Covenant (cont)—
Insurance (cont)—
Repayment by lessee of amount of fire insurance premiums paid by lessor—Lessor to insure with reputable insurers—Whether implied term against lessor imposing unnecessarily heavy burden on lessees in respect of premium. **Bandar Property Holdings Ltd v JS Darwen (Successors) Ltd** [1968] **2** 305, QBD.
Notice of covenant—
Tenant precluded from inquiring into lessor's title—Notice of restrictive covenants—Onus of proving tenant had notice of covenant—Law of Property Act 1925, s 44(2),(5). **Shears v Wells** [1936] **1** 832, Ch D.
Parting with possession—
Breach—Covenant against parting with possession and sharing possession—Tenant sharing possession—Landlord serving notice specifying breach of covenant against parting with possession and forfeiting lease—Whether forfeiture valid—Law of Property Act 1925, s 146. **Akici v LR Butlin Ltd** [2006] **2** 872, CA.
Covenant against parting with possession without consent—Breach—Tenant assigning tenancy without landlord's consent—No restriction on assignment in terms—Whether tenant in breach of covenant not to part with possession without consent. **Marks v Warren** [1979] **1** 29, Ch D.
Covenant against parting with possession—Breach—Evidence—Lessee carrying on business in partnership on demised premises—Partners forming company to carry on business—Lessee having majority shareholding in company—Other former partners holding remaining shares—Company carrying on business thereafter—Cheque drawn by company tendered for instalment of rent—Forfeiture proceedings by lessor for breach of covenant not to part with possession—Lessee denying breach of covenant on ground company belonged to him. **Lam Kee Ying Sdn Bhd v Lam Shes Tong** [1974] **3** 137, PC.
Payment of all assessments, impositions and outgoings whatsoever—
Road charges—Charges not paid by landlord at date of issue of writ—Right of landlord to recover charges. **Francis v Squire** [1940] **1** 45, KBD.
Payment of rates—
Rates imposed on the demised premises—Water rate—Water facilities used by tenant not in demised premises—Whether tenant liable for water rate. **King v Cave-Browne-Cave** [1960] **2** 751, QBD.
Payment of rent and service charge without deduction or set-off—
Action by landlord for non-payment of service charge and late payment of rent—Tenant seeking set-off for breaches of landlord's repairing covenant—Whether anti-set-off covenant an unfair contract term—Unfair Contract Terms Act 1977, Sch 1. **Electricity Supply Nominees Ltd v IAF Group plc** [1993] **3** 372, QBD.
Personal occupation—
Breach—Lease vesting in trustee—Trustee's failure to occupy—Waiver—Occupation by one of two trustees and later by a beneficiary. **Lower Onibury Farm, Onibury, Shropshire, Re** [1955] **2** 409, CA.
Proper working order—
Installation for supply of gas, water and electricity—Covenant to keep in proper working order installation for supply of gas, water and electricity—Test of proper working order—Landlord and Tenant Act 1985, s 11(1)(b). **O'Connor v Old Etonian Housing Association Ltd** [2002] **2** 1015, CA.
Quiet enjoyment—
Breach—Building operations on adjoining part of premises—Conditional consent by lessor—Condition not fulfilled—Nuisance—Building operations—Dust and noise—Independent contractor—Danger of works amounting to nuisance. **Matania v National Provincial Bank Ltd and Elevenist Syndicate Ltd** [1936] **2** 633, CA.
Breach—Damages—Measure—'Eviction'—Gas and electricity supply cut off by landlord with intention of forcing statutory tenant to quit premises. **Perera v Vandiyar** [1953] **1** 1109, CA.
Breach—Lock-up shop—Erection of scaffolding outside shop window. **Owen v Gadd** [1956] **2** 28, CA.
Breach—Pleading—Departure from pleading—Facts pleaded sufficient to warrant claim for trespass. See **Pleading** (Departure—Legal consequences of pleaded facts—Pleading setting out material facts and alleging interference with right to quiet enjoyment of premises—Facts pleaded sufficient to warrant claim for trespass).
Breach—Threats of eviction—Whether direct physical interference with possession necessary to constitute breach—Measure of damages when no special damage proved. **Kenny v Preen** [1962] **3** 814, CA.
Damages—Injured feelings and mental distress—Whether damages recoverable for injured feelings and mental distress resulting from breach of covenant for quiet enjoyment—Whether covenant for quiet enjoyment a contract to provide peace of mind or freedom from distress. **Branchett v Beaney** [1992] **3** 910, CA.
Implied covenant—Crown lease—Extent of covenant implied—Exception of acts done in performance of executive duty. **Comrs of Crown Lands v Page** [1960] **2** 726, CA.
Implied covenant—Express covenant's effect as excluding implied covenants. **Miller v Emcer Products Ltd** [1956] **1** 237, CA.
Limited covenant—Protection provided by covenant—Persons against whose acts covenant protects lessee—Persons claiming under landlord—Covenant that tenant entitled to hold demised premises without interruption by landlord or any person lawfully claiming through or under landlord—Predecessor in title of landlord granting right of way to other tenants—Landlord granting lease to tenant to build car wash over right of way granted to other tenants—Other tenants obtaining injunction restraining construction of car wash—Tenant claiming contribution from landlord—Whether injunction an interruption of tenant's quiet enjoyment by persons 'claiming under' landlord—Whether other tenants 'claiming under' landlord—Whether landlord liable to tenant under covenant for quiet enjoyment. **Celsteel Ltd v Alton House Holdings Ltd (No 2)** [1987] **2** 240, CA.
Noise—Local authority landlords letting flats with inadequate soundproofing—Tenants hearing everyday activities of their neighbours—Whether landlords breaching covenant for quiet enjoyment. **Baxter v Camden London BC** [1999] **4** 449, HL.

LANDLORD AND TENANT (cont)—
 Covenant (cont)—
  Reinstatement of premises at end of term—
   Breach—Damages—Measure—Covenant to reinstate premises at end of term—No actual damage suffered by landlord—Landlord and Tenant Act 1927, s 19(2). **James v Hutton** [1949] **2** 243, CA.
  Release—
   Assignment of lease—Statutory provisions providing mechanism for release of 'landlord covenants' on assignment—Whether personal covenants capable of being released under statutory provisions—Landlord and Tenant (Covenants) Act 1995, ss 3(6), 8, 28(1). **BHP Petroleum Great Britain Ltd v Chesterfield Properties Ltd** [2001] **2** 914, Ch D; [2002] **1** 821, CA.
  Renewal of lease—
   Renewal for once only—Lease renewed—New lease supplemental to original lease and providing for benefit of covenants in original lease—Whether covenant for renewal incorporated in supplementary lease—Letters of parties disclosing intentions. **Plumrose Ltd v Real and Leasehold Estates Investment Society Ltd** [1969] **3** 1441, Ch D.
  Rent, covenant or provision annexed and incident to reversion—
   Rent, covenant or provision capable of being recovered, received, enforced and taken advantage of by person entitled to the income of the land leased—Landlord assigning reversion by transfer of registered title—Transferee giving notice to tenant of transfer—Transfer remaining unregistered—Transferee forfeiting lease for arrears of rent—Whether transferee person entitled to the income of the land—Law of Property Act 1925, s 141(2). **Scribes West Ltd v Relsa Anstalt** [2005] **2** 690, CA.
  Repair—
   Breach. *See* Breach of covenant to repair, *above.*
   Generally. *See* Repair, *below.*
   Implied. *See* Implied covenant to repair, *below.*
  Restraint of trade. *See* **Restraint of trade by agreement** (Lessor and lessee).
  Restrictive covenant. *See* Restrictive covenant, *below.*
  Service agreement—
   Covenant in lease to execute service agreement—Specific performance. *See* **Specific performance** (Personal services—Service agreement in lease—Covenant in lease to execute service agreement).
  Tenancy by estoppel—
   Enforcement of covenant against lessee out of possession. *See* Tenancy—Tenancy by estoppel—Enforcement of covenant against lessee out of possession, *below.*
  Underletting—
   Consent. *See* Covenant against underletting without consent, *below.*
   Unusual covenants in underlease—Duty of solicitor to advise and/or warn client of effect. *See* **Solicitor** (Client—Negotiation of grant of underlease to architects—Unusual convenants in underlease restricting user—Omission of solicitor to advise and/or warn client on effect).
  User of premises—
   Covenant against change of use without consent—Consent not to be unreasonably withheld—Whether conditions restricting user protecting landlord's trading interests reasonable. **Sargeant v Macepark (Whittlebury) Ltd** [2004] **4** 662, Ch D.
   Covenant against change of use without consent—No fine or sum of money to be payable in respect of consent—Undertaking by tenants to assign debt in consideration of consent—Whether a fine or sum in nature of a fine—Whether undertaking enforceable—Landlord and Tenant Act 1927, s 19(3). **Comber v Fleet Electrics Ltd** [1955] **2** 161, Ch D.
   Covenant against fixing nameplate without consent—Consent not to be unreasonably withheld—Construction—Reasonableness of refusal. **Berry (Frederick) Ltd v Royal Bank of Scotland** [1949] **1** 706, KBD.
   Covenant against use except as business premises—Construction of lease—Reference to drafts—Consideration of history and of conduct of parties after the grant—Consideration of nature of demised premises. **City & Westminster Properties (1934) Ltd v Mudd** [1958] **2** 733, Ch D.
   Covenant against use for business—User in breach of covenant. *See* Business premises—Tenancy—Exclusion of statutory protection—Business user in breach of covenant in lease, *above.*
   Use as dwellings for 'the working classes'—Covenant requiring demised premises to be used as dwellings for the working classes—'Working classes' to be construed in terms of housing legislation for time being in force—Housing legislation no longer referring to 'working classes'—Whether covenant still effective or obsolete. **Westminster City Council v Duke of Westminster** [1991] **4** 136, Ch D.
   Use as private dwelling only—Covenant not to use premises for any purpose other than as a private dwelling-house—'Private dwelling-house'—Sub-lease of part of premises as private residence—Whether breach of covenant. **Dobbs v Linford** [1952] **2** 827, CA.
   Use as private dwelling only—Covenant to use as private residence only—Paying guest—Sharing accommodation—Whether breach of covenant. **Segal Securities Ltd v Thoseby** [1963] **1** 500, QBD.
   Use as private dwelling only—Implied covenant common scheme—Block of flats—Property subject to restriction—Letting for purposes inconsistent with restriction. **Newman v Real Estate Debenture Corp Ltd and Flower Decorations Ltd** [1940] **1** 131, KBD.
   Use as supermarket—Covenants to use premises as supermarket and to keep open during business hours—Tenant breaching covenants by closing supermarket—Whether decree of specific performance or award of damages appropriate remedy. **Co-op Insurance Society Ltd v Argyll Stores (Holdings) Ltd** [1997] **3** 297, HL.
  Usual covenants—
   Determination by court—Meaning in open contract as distinct from agreement to assign existing lease—Evidence on which court determines usual covenants—Open contract made in 1971 for grant by landlord to tenant of lease of garage and workshop in residential area of London—Draft lease settled by a conveyancing counsel of the court because parties failing to agree terms of lease—Landlord objecting to draft lease and wishing to insert further tenant's covenants and to enlarge proviso for re-entry—Matter referred to court—Whether landlord wishing to insert 'usual covenants' in lease—Whether 'usual covenants' in open contract more limited than in agreement to assign lease. **Chester v Buckingham Travel Ltd** [1981] **1** 386, Ch D.

LANDLORD AND TENANT (cont)—
  Covenant against alienation—
    Assignment of lease. See Assignment of lease—Assignment —Covenants against alienation, *above*.
  Covenant against assignment without consent—
    Binding on tenant and successors in title—
      Tenant becoming bankrupt—Trustee in bankruptcy wishing to assign lease—Whether trustee
      'successor in title' to tenant. **Wright (a bankrupt), Re, ex p Landau (a creditor) v The Trustee**
      [1949] 2 605, Ch D.
    Consent not to be unreasonably withheld. See Assignment of lease—Consent of landlord not to be
      unreasonably withheld, *above*.
    Covenant against assigning or underletting 'any part' of premises without consent—
      Whether tenant entitled to assign or underlet whole of premises without consent—Whether 'any
      part' of the premises including the whole. **Field v Barkworth** [1986] 1 362, Ch D.
    Covenant as to use of premises for residential purposes—
      Duty of tenant in relation to sub-tenant where also covenant not to use premises for other than
      residential purposes. **Glass v Kencakes Ltd** [1964] 3 807, QBD.
    Enforcement by head lessor—
      Assignment of sub-lease—Head lessor not party to sub-lease—Law of Property Act 1925, s 56(1).
      Drive Yourself Hire Co (London) Ltd v Strutt [1953] 2 1475, CA.
    Forfeiture of lease for breach of covenant—
      Notice of forfeiture—Persons to be served with notice. See Forfeiture of lease—Notice of
      breach—Persons to be served with notice, *below*.
    Licence to assign granted by landlord—
      No legal assignment—Entry on premises—Action for rent—Estoppel. **Rodenhurst Estates Ltd v W
      H Barnes Ltd** [1936] 2 3, CA.
    Sub-lease—
      Covenant requiring consent of lessor or superior lessors—Consent unreasonably withheld by
      superior lessors—Sub-lessors willing to grant consent subject to consent of superior lessors
      being obtained—Declaration that consent unreasonably withheld by sub-lessors made in the
      absence of superior lessors. **Vienit Ltd v W Williams & Son (Bread Street) Ltd** [1958] 3 621, Ch D.
    Waiver of breach—
      Effect—Whether waiver renders unlawful sub-letting lawful ab initio. **Muspratt v Johnston**
      [1963] 2 339, CA.
      Implied waiver—Requirements of personal occupation—Application of covenant to trustees—
      Occupation by one only of two trustees and later by a beneficiary. **Lower Onibury Farm, Onibury,
      Shropshire, Re** [1955] 2 409, CA.
  Covenant against parting with possession. See Covenant—Parting with possession, *above*.
  Covenant against underletting without consent—
    Breach—
      Sub-letting part—Whether covenant broken by sub-letting part of demised premises. **Esdaile v
      Lewis** [1956] 2 357, CA.
      Tenant subletting land in breach of covenant—Possibility of tenant giving notice of intention to quit
      to landlord—Whether landlord entitled to possession against subtenant. **Pennell v Payne**
      [1995] 2 592, CA.
    Consent not to be unreasonably withheld—
      Landlord absent at time of application for consent—Necessity for landlord to have time for
      consideration—Lessees not to permit premises 'to be used otherwise than as offices for the
      purposes of their business'—Sub-lessees' business different from that of lessees. **Wilson v Fynn**
      [1948] 2 40, KBD.
      Landlord refusing consent on ground that proposed rent was lower than market rent and so might
      be detrimental to future rent levels of other properties owned by landlord in vicinity—Whether
      landlord's refusal of consent unreasonable—Landlord and Tenant Act 1988, s 1(3). **Norwich Union
      Life Insurance Society v Shopmoor Ltd** [1998] 3 32, Ch D.
      Landlord refusing consent on grounds that proposed use inappropriate for location and would
      diminish value of reversion and that accounts of proposed subtenant not strong
      enough—Landlord communicating reasons for refusing consent by telephone—Whether landlord
      entitled to rely on oral reasons to justify refusal of consent—Whether landlord's refusal of
      consent unreasonable—Landlord and Tenant Act 1988, s 1(3)(b). **Footwear Corp Ltd v Amplight
      Properties Ltd** [1998] 3 52, Ch D.
      Low rent in consideration of substantial premium—Lack of security—Depreciation in future value of
      property. **Town Investments Ltd Underlease, Re** [1954] 1 585, Ch D.
      Proposed underlessee entitled to diplomatic privilege. **Parker v Boggan** [1947] 1 46, KBD.
      Subletting adversely affecting value of premises—Butcher's shop with residential accommodation
      for shop staff above shop—Lessee proposing to sublet residential accommodation to someone
      unconnected with shop—Sublessee entitled to security of tenure through statutory
      protection—Statutory protection not available to sublessee at time lease granted—Whether
      landlord's refusal of consent to subletting unreasonable. **West Layton Ltd v Ford** [1979] 2 657,
      CA.
  Covenant against assigning or underletting 'any part' of premises without consent. See Covenant
    against assignment without consent—Covenant against assigning or underletting 'any part' of
    premises without consent, *above*.
  Damages for failure to repair—
    Application of statutory provisions—
      Covenant by lessee to spend £500 per annum on repairs or pay the difference between £500 and
      the amount actually spent—Whether sums payable under covenant payable as 'damages for
      breach of covenant to repair'—Landlord and Tenant Act 1927, s 18(1). **Moss' Empires Ltd v
      Olympia (Liverpool) Ltd** [1939] 3 460, HL.
    Damages not recoverable when it is proposed to demolish building—
      Intention to demolish—Material date for proof of intention to demolish—Landlord and Tenant Act
      1927, s 18(1). **Keats v Graham** [1959] 3 919, CA.
      Intention to demolish—Material date for proof of intention to demolish—Landlord and Tenant Act
      1927, ss 4, 5, 18(1). **Salisbury v Gilmore & Marcel** [1942] 1 457, CA.

LANDLORD AND TENANT (cont)—
  Damages for failure to repair (cont)—
    Damages not recoverable when it is proposed to demolish building (cont)—
      Local authority as lessee—Local authority declaring premises unfit for human habitation—Premises unfit by reason of local authority's breach of covenant to repair—Premises included in slum clearance order—Premises to be demolished under slum clearance order—Whether landlords entitled to damages for breach of covenant to repair—Landlord and Tenant Act 1927, s 18(1). **Hibernian Property Co Ltd v Liverpool Corp** [1973] **2** 1117, QBD.
      Proof—Onus on tenant to prove definite decision or intention—Landlord and Tenant Act 1927, s 18(1). **Cunliffe v Goodman** [1950] **1** 720, CA.
    Diminution in value of reversion—
      Breach of covenant to leave or put premises in state of repair at termination of lease—Whether value of reversion increased by value of hypothetical lease to new tenant—Landlord and Tenant Act 1927, s 18(1). **Van Dal Footwear Ltd v Ryman Ltd** [2010] **1** 883, CA.
      Cost of re-decoration—Repairs necessary to make premises fit for re-letting—Landlord and Tenant Act 1927, s 18(1). **Jones v Herxheimer** [1950] **1** 323, CA.
      Landlord letting premises to new tenant on expiry of old lease—New tenant covenanting with landlord to put premises into repair—Claim by landlord against former tenant for damages for breach of repairing covenant—Whether agreement going in diminution of damage to reversion—Landlord and Tenant Act 1927, s 18(1). **Haviland v Long (Dunn Trust Ltd, third party)** [1952] **1** 463, CA.
      Premises containing shop and dwelling accommodation—Requisitioned premises—Landlord and Tenant Act 1927, s 18(1). **Smiley v Townshend** [1950] **1** 530, CA.
      Underlease—Reversion momentary or notional—Underlessee without notice that demise was underlease—Landlord liable to head lessor under repairing covenant in head lease—Whether landlord's surveyor's and solicitor's charges for schedule of dilapidation on both head lease and underlease recoverable from underlease—Landlord and Tenant Act 1927, s 18(1). **Lloyds Bank Ltd v Lake** [1961] **2** 30, QBD.
  Dangerous installation—
    Landlord's liability. *See* **Negligence** (Dangerous things—Landlord's liability for dangerous installation).
  Death of tenant—
    Agricultural holding—
      Succession. *See* **Agricultural holding** (Tenancy—Death of tenant).
    Statutory tenancy. *See* **Rent restriction** (Death of tenant).
    Validity of notice to quit. *See* Validity of notice to quit—Death of tenant, *below*.
  Defective title of landlord—
    Tenancy by estoppel. *See* Tenancy—Tenancy by estoppel, *below*.
  Demand for payment—
    Service charge. *See* Service charge—Flat—Limitation on service charges—Time limit on making demands—Demand for payment of service charge, *below*.
  Demise—
    Extent. *See* Lease—Extent of demise, *below*.
  Demolition of business premises—
    Intention—
      Opposition to grant of new tenancy. *See* Opposition to grant of new tenancy of business premises—Intention of landlord to demolish or reconstruct premises comprised in holding, *below*.
  Denial of landlord's title—
    Forfeiture of lease. *See* Forfeiture of lease—Denial of landlord's title, *below*.
  Deposit—
    Tenancy deposit schemes. *See* Tenancy—Tenancy deposit schemes, *below*.
  Determination of lease—
    Impossibility of performance—
      Frustration—Whether doctrine of frustration applicable to demise of real property. **Denman v Brise** [1948] **2** 141, CA.
    Premises required by landlord—
      Part only required—Power for landlords to determine 21 years' lease at end of 14 years if landlords 'shall require the premises for the purpose of the business carried on by them'—Premises not required immediately at end of 14 years—Only part of premises required. **Parkinson v Barclays Bank Ltd** [1950] **2** 936, CA.
    Requisition of premises—
      Frustration of tenancy agreement. **Swift v Macbean** [1942] **1** 126, KBD.
  Distress—
    Company—
      Winding up—Stay or restraint of proceedings—Distress levied by landlord against company before commencement of winding up. *See* **Company** (Winding up—Stay or restraint of proceedings against company—Distress levied against company before commencement of winding up).
    Generally. *See* **Distress**.
  Duration of lease. *See* Lease—Duration, *below*.
  Duty of care to visitors—
    Landlord's duty. *See* **Occupier's liability** (Landlord—Duty of care to visitors).
  Dwelling-house let together with land other than site of dwelling-house—
    Camping site and bungalow—
      Intention to demolish buildings and let land as smallholding—Intention to demolish subsidiary to purpose of letting—Whether necessary for intention to demolish to be landlord's primary purpose—Landlord and Tenant Act 1954, s 30(1)(f). **Craddock v Hampshire CC** [1958] **1** 449, CA.
  Encroachment by tenant—
    Encroachment on other land owned by landlord and not included in tenancy—
      Purchase by tenant of house subject to tenancy—Sale by landlord of adjoining land—Right of purchaser of land to possession. **King v Smith** [1950] **1** 553, CA.
      Tenant claiming possession under lease—Acquiescence by landlords in de facto possession—Claim for cost of repairs. **Perrott (JF) & Co Ltd v Cohen** [1950] **2** 939, CA.

LANDLORD AND TENANT (cont)—
Encroachment by tenant (cont)—
Encroachment on other land owned by landlord and not included in tenancy (cont)—
Title of tenant to land taken—Failure to communicate to landlord any disclaimer of landlord's title—Presumption that land taken as part of holding comprised in tenancy. **Smirk v Lyndale Developments Ltd** [1974] **2** 8, Ch D.
Enemy alien—
Lease—
Forfeiture. *See* Forfeiture of lease—Lessee enemy alien abroad, *below*.
Enforcement of judgment for possession. *See* Recovery of possession—Judgment for possession, *below*.
Enfranchisement. *See* Leasehold enfranchisement, *below*.
Estoppel—
Assignment of lease. *See* Assignment of lease—Estoppel, *above*.
Generally. *See* **Estoppel** (Landlord and tenant).
Right of tenant to question landlord's title. *See* Title—Right of tenant to question landlord's title—Estoppel, *below*.
Tenancy by estoppel. *See* Tenancy—Tenancy by estoppel, *below*.
Eviction—
Characteristics of act of eviction—
Crown lease—Covenant for quiet enjoyment implied—Extent of covenant in relation to acts done in performance of Crown's executive duty—Requisition by Crown under Defence (General) Regulations 1939, reg 51. **Comrs of Crown Lands v Page** [1960] **2** 726, CA.
Judgment for possession—
Recovery of possession. *See* Recovery of possession—Judgment for possession—Eviction, *below*.
Protection from eviction—
Premises occupied under licence other than excluded licence—Licence by which housing authority providing accommodation to homeless person providing for enforced sharing of accommodation—Whether excluded licence—Whether conferring right of occupation in hostel—Whether separate and self-contained accommodation—Protection from Eviction Act 1977, ss 3(2B), 3A(8)—Housing Act 1985, s 622. **Rogerson v Wigan Metropolitan BC** [2005] **2** 1000, QBD.
Validity of notice to quit—Date for termination—Agreement between landlord and one joint tenant to accept less than statutory minimum notice—Whether notice binding on other joint tenant—Protection from Eviction Act 1977, s 5(1). **Hounslow London BC v Pilling** [1994] **1** 432, CA.
Trespass by landlord—
Exemplary damages—Landlord unlawfully evicting tenant from demised premises. *See* **Damages** (Exemplary damages—Trespass to land—Landlord unlawfully evicting tenant from demised premises).
Unlawful eviction of tenant—
Damages—Joint secure tenancy—Wife obtaining ouster injunction requiring husband to leave property—Short notice to quit served by wife ineffective to determine joint tenancy—Local authority believing notice to be effective and excluding husband from property—Whether unlawful eviction—Whether husband entitled to damages—Measure of damages—Housing Act 1988, ss 27, 28. **Osei-Bonsu v Wandsworth London BC** [1999] **1** 265, CA.
Damages—Measure of damages—Difference in value between value of landlord's interest on assumption residential occupier continuing to have same right to occupy and value of landlord's interest on assumption residential occupier ceasing to have that right—Effect on value of landlord's interest on change in tenancy from secure tenancy to assured tenancy on hypothetical sale—Housing Act 1988, ss 27, 28. **Loveridge v Lambeth London BC** [2013] **3** 261, CA; [2015] **1** 513, SC.
Damages—Measure of damages—Whether damages for unlawful eviction will be reduced if offer of reinstatement is made before proceedings for damages are commenced—Whether damages for unlawful eviction will be reduced if proceedings to obtain injunction to force reinstatement have been commenced—Housing Act 1988, s 27(7)(b). **Tagro v Cafane** [1991] **2** 235, CA.
Offer of reinstatement—What amounts to proper offer of reinstatement—Whether tenant having option to accept offer of reinstatement or to press for damages for unlawful eviction—Housing Act 1988, ss 27, 28. **Tagro v Cafane** [1991] **2** 235, CA.
Exclusion clause in lease. *See* Lease—Exclusion clause, *below*.
Exclusion of statutory protection—
Business premises. *See* Business premises—Tenancy—Exclusion of statutory protection, *above*.
Execution—
Lease. *See* Lease—Execution, *below*.
Possession order—
Jurisdiction of county court to postpone execution. *See* Recovery of possession—County court action—Order for possession—Jurisdiction to postpone execution of order, *below*.
Fair rent. *See* **Rent restriction** (Fair rent).
Fire—
Insurance—
Covenant. *See* Covenant—Insurance—Fire, *above*.
Insurable interest. *See* **Insurance** (Fire insurance—Insurable interest—Landlord and tenant).
Fishing rights—
Lease. *See* Lease—Fishing rights, *below*.
Fitness of premises—
Escape of gas—
Removal of gas fire—Fitting not required by tenant removed by landlord and previous occupier—Whether contract to remove. **Davis v Foots** [1939] **4** 4, CA.
Innocent misrepresentation inducing contract—
Recovery of rent paid—Implied warranty—Unilateral mistake—Money had and received. **Edler v Auerbach** [1949] **2** 692, KBD.

LANDLORD AND TENANT (cont)—
   Fitness of premises (cont)—
      Legal or physical fitness—
         Warranty—No implied warranty—Sub-lessee requiring premises, to sub-lessor's knowledge, for use for particular business—Grant of sub-lease with restriction of certain uses, but an exception for the particular use—Particular use prohibited by covenant in head lease, and stopped by freeholder. **Hill v Harris** [1965] **2** 358, CA.
   Fixtures—
      Annexation to land—
         House—House resting on concrete foundation blocks—No physical attachment to land—Whether house a fixture or chattel. **Elitestone Ltd v Morris** [1997] **2** 513, HL.
      Business premises. See Business premises—Fixtures, above.
      Generally. See Lease—Fixtures, below.
   Flats—
      Compulsory acquisition by tenants of their landlord's interest—
         Preliminary notice by tenants—Applications for acquisition orders—Conditions for making acquisition orders—Contents of preliminary notice—Landlord and Tenant Act 1987, ss 27(2)(b), (c), (d), 28(2)(a), 29(3). **Arrowgame Ltd v Wildsmith** [2013] **2** 128, Ch D.
      Residential flat—
         Service charge. See Service charge—Flat, below.
      Tenants' right to acquire landlord's reversion—
         Disposal by landlord—Any estate or interest—Landlord disposing of estate or interest in property to freeholder by agreement for surrender of headlease and regrant—Tenants serving notice on freeholder applicable where disposal consisting of entering into contract—Whether notice applicable where disposal consisting of surrender by landlord of tenancy—Landlord and Tenant Act 1987, ss 4A(1), 12B, 12C, 16. **Kensington Heights Commercial Co Ltd v Campden Hill Developments Ltd** [2007] **2** 751, CA.
         Disposal by landlord—Tenants' rights of first refusal—Block of flats—Landlord disposing of reversion without giving tenants prior notice of disposal—New landlord granting new reversionary leases to associated company before tenants giving notice of wish to exercise their right to purchase reversion—Whether grant of new reversionary leases a sham for purpose of depriving tenants of their right to purchase reversion—Whether new reversionary leases amounting to 'incumbrances'—Whether original landlord having given good notice of disposal to tenants—Extent of tenants' right of first refusal—Landlord and Tenant Act 1987, ss 12(4), 16. **Belvedere Court Management Ltd v Frogmore Developments Ltd** [1996] **1** 312, CA.
         Disposal by landlord—Tenants' rights of first refusal—Building—Disposal of more than one building—Whether several structures and appurtenant premises more than one building—Meaning of 'building'—Landlord and Tenant Act 1987, ss 1(2)(a), 5(3). **Long Acre Securities Ltd v Karet** [2005] **4** 413, Ch D.
         Disposal by landlord—Tenants' rights of first refusal—Building—Whether 'building' including appurtenances expressly or impliedly included in demise of flat to tenant—Landlord and Tenant Act 1987, s 1(2). **Denetower Ltd v Toop** [1991] **3** 661, CA.
         Disposal by landlord—Tenants' rights of first refusal—Disposal of reversion to landlord's subsidiary company—Subsidiary's shares sold to company wishing to purchase flats—Landlord failing to give notice to tenants prior to disposal—Whether disposal a 'relevant disposal'—Whether defendant a subsidiary of landlord at time of disposal—Landlord and Tenant Act 1987, Pt I, ss 4(2), 20(1). **Michaels v Harley House (Marylebone) Ltd** [1999] **1** 356, CA.
         Disposal by landlord—Tenants' rights of first refusal—Landlord disposing of reversion without giving tenants prior notice of disposal—Service of purchase notice by tenants on new landlord—Whether new landlord under a duty to comply with purchase notice—Whether purchase notice served by requisite majority of tenants—Whether purchase notice valid—Landlord and Tenant Act 1987, ss 1, 12. **Kay Green v Twinsectra Ltd** [1996] **4** 546, CA.
         Disposal by landlord—Tenants' rights of first refusal—Landlord disposing of reversion without giving tenants prior notice of disposal—Tenants serving notice requiring particulars of disposal—Notice omitting tenants' addresses—Whether notice valid—Landlord and Tenant Act 1987, ss 11A, 54. **M25 Group Ltd v Tudor** [2004] **2** 80, CA.
         Disposal by landlord—Tenants' rights of first refusal—Purchase notice—Validity—Reference to buildings in which flats situated—Notice requiring assignment be on same terms as sale by original landlord with necessary modifications—Whether valid notice requiring transfer of block of flats and appurtenances—Landlord and Tenant Act 1987, s 12(3). **Denetower Ltd v Toop** [1991] **3** 661, CA.
         Disposal by landlord—Tenants' rights of first refusal—Qualifying tenants—Tenancy consisting of or including flat and any common parts of building—Common parts—Whether tenant qualifying tenant if flat itself containing common parts—Landlord and Tenant Act 1987, ss 3(2)(a)(ii), 60. **Denetower Ltd v Toop** [1991] **3** 661, CA.
      Tenants' right to apply to court for appointment of manager—
         Appointment of manager by the court—Appointment of manager to act in relation to premises to which statutory provision applying—Extent of property over which management functions exercisable—Landlord and Tenant Act 1987, ss 21(1), 24(1). **Cawsand Fort Management Co Ltd v Stafford** [2008] **3** 353, CA.
   Forfeiture of lease—
      Action for possession by lessor—
         Injunctions to restrain breaches of covenant also claimed, without prejudice to claim for possession—Motion for injunctions—Whether writ on unequivocal demand for possession constituting election to determine term—Whether plaintiff entitled to ask for relief by way of injunction on footing that covenant in lease still subsisted. **Calabar Properties Ltd v Seagull Autos Ltd** [1968] **1** 1, Ch D.
         Landlord electing to forfeit for breach of covenant prohibiting parting with possession without consent—Tenant accepting breach and entitlement to forfeiture—Lease determined by service of writ—Landlord subsequently realising that tenant had not parted with possession—Landlord challenging validity of its own action in effecting forfeiture—Whether landlord entitled to challenge forfeiture—Whether landlord entitled to challenge forfeiture on basis that writ served under mistake as to breach of covenant. **GS Fashions Ltd v B & Q plc** [1995] **4** 899, Ch D.

LANDLORD AND TENANT (cont)—
  Forfeiture of lease (cont)—
    Application for relief—
      Lessee making informal application during course of hearing—No claim for relief included in pleadings—No application for leave to amend pleadings—Jurisdiction to grant relief—National Land Code (Malaysia), s 237. **Lam Kee Ying Sdn Bhd v Lam Shes Tong** [1974] 3 137, PC.
    Arrears of rent—
      County court action—Form of order—Relief from forfeiture—Order in wrong form—No indication forfeiture avoidable if rent paid—Non-compliance with statute—Tenant absent from court when order for possession made—Warrant for possession—Arrears paid before date for execution—Application to set aside—Not a case for amending order—Order discharged—Possession restored to tenant as lessee—County Courts Act 1959, s 191(1)—County Court Rules 1936 (SR & O 1936 No 626), App A, Forms 134, 136. **Spurgeons Homes v Gentles** [1971] 3 902, CA.
      County court action—Relief against forfeiture—Cesser of action following payment into court by lessee of arrears and costs—Arrears and costs paid in over five days before return day—Payment not made by or on behalf of lessee—No cesser of action—County Courts Act 1959, s 191(1)(a). **Matthews v Dobbins** [1963] 1 417, CA.
      County court action—Relief against forfeiture—Jurisdiction of High Court—'Lessee shall be barred from all relief' if lessee failing to pay arrears of rent specified in possession order made by county court—Whether lessee merely barred from seeking further relief in county court—Whether jurisdiction of High Court to grant relief against forfeiture ousted—County Courts Act 1959, s 191(1)(c). **Di Palma v Victoria Square Property Co Ltd** [1985] 2 676, CA; **Jones v Barnett** [1984] 3 129, Ch D.
      County court action—Relief against forfeiture—Relief to be granted if lessee paying into court 'all the rent in arrear'—Meaning of 'all the rent in arrear'—Whether including sums falling due after service of summons—County Courts Act 1984, s 138(3). **Maryland Estates Ltd v Bar-Joseph** [1998] 3 193, CA.
    Relief. See Relief against forfeiture—Arrears of rent, *below*.
    Breach of covenant prohibiting assignment—
      Secure tenancy—Tenant assigning secure tenancy in breach of lease—Statute preserving secure tenancy on assignment if assignee meeting statutory requirements—Assignee satisfying statutory requirements—Landlord treating assignee as a trespasser and seeking possession order—Landlord not complying with statutory notice requirements for possession proceedings against tenant—Whether assignment in breach of tenancy of no effect—Whether statutory provisions preserving secure tenancy on assignment only applicable to assignments not in breach of the tenancy—Whether landlord required to comply with notice provisions—Housing Act 1980, ss 28, 30, 33, 37(1). **Peabody Donation Fund (Governors) v Higgins** [1983] 3 122, CA.
    Breach of repairing covenant—
      Landlord unable to ascertain name of lessee—Notice requiring premises to be repaired served on 'the lessee' of premises—Leave given to proceed for forfeiture and damages—Whether lessee entitled to withold name—Leasehold Property (Repairs) Act 1938, s 1(3). **Pascall v Galinski** [1969] 3 1090, CA.
      Leave to institute proceedings. See Breach of covenant to repair—Leave to institute proceedings, *above*.
      Notice—Statement of lessee's right to serve counter-notice—Statement in characters not less conspicuous than those used in any other part of notice—Statement to specify manner in which counter-notice may be served—Name and address for service of lessor to be specified—Notice served on tenant—Standard form used—Blank spaces for insertion of details—Details filled in in bigger blacker type—Statement of tenant's rights in ordinary type—Statement only specifying some of the ways in which counter-notice could be served—Statement only giving name and address for service of landlords' solicitor—Whether statutory requirements complied with—Law of Property Act 1925, s 146—Leasehold Property (Repairs) Act 1938, s 1(4). **Middlegate Properties Ltd v Messimeris** [1973] 1 645, CA.
    Denial of landlord's title—
      Application for relief against forfeiture—Law of Property Act 1925, s 146(2). **Warner v Sampson (No 2)** [1958] 1 314, QBD.
      Denial by tenant—Whether sufficient to cause forfeiture. **Wisbech St Mary Parish Council v Lilley** [1956] 1 301, CA.
      Denial in pleadings—Action for possession for breach of covenants—Defence containing general traverse—Claim for forfeiture in reply—Whether sufficient denial of landlord's title—Administration of Estates Act 1925, ss 2(2), 55(1)(iii). **Warner v Sampson** [1959] 1 120, CA.
      Denial in pleadings—Amendment of pleading to remove disclaimer—Whether amendment effective to counter landlord's claim to possession based on disclaimer of landlord's title. **Clark (WG) (Properties) Ltd v Dupre Properties Ltd** [1992] 1 596, Ch D.
      Denial in pleadings—Partial denial of landlord's title—Property owned by landlord's neighbour included in lease granted to tenant—Landlord claiming ownership of disputed property from neighbour by adverse possession—Neighbour bringing action against tenant for removal of building erected on disputed property—Tenant bringing separate action against landlord claiming damages for misrepresentation of title—Whether tenant disclaiming landlord's title—Whether tenant's partial disclaimer of landlord's title sufficient to constitute disclaimer of whole. **Clark (WG) (Properties) Ltd v Dupre Properties Ltd** [1992] 1 596, Ch D.
      Relief against forfeiture—Whether relief against forefeiture available to tenant where forfeiture arises out of disclaimer of landlord's title—Law of Property Act 1925, s 146. **Clark (WG) (Properties) Ltd v Dupre Properties Ltd** [1992] 1 596, Ch D.
    Effect—
      Rent—Entitlement to rent—Lessee subletting and mortgaging property—Receiver appointed by mortgagee to collect rents from sublessees—Action by landlord for forfeiture of headlease and mesne profits—Forfeiture of lease and payment of mesne profits by lessee ordered by court—Receiver satisfying judgment for mesne profits out of rents received from sublessees—Whether landlords entitled to balance of rents paid to receiver by sublessees between commencement of forfeiture action and date of judgment. **Official Custodian for Charities v Mackey (No 2)** [1985] 2 1016, Ch D.

LANDLORD AND TENANT (cont)—
  Forfeiture of lease (cont)—
    Forfeiture—
      Action for possession by lessor—Issue of writ not sufficient to bring about forfeiture—Service of writ necessary to effect forfeiture and terminate lease. **Canas Property Co Ltd v KL Television Services Ltd** [1970] **2** 795, CA.
    Forfeiture clause—
      Provision enabling landlord to determine lease for breach of covenant to pay rent on giving notice in writing—Tenancy agreement containing clause entitling either party to determine lease on giving twelve months' notice—Landlord entitled to give three months' notice for breach of covenant to pay rent—Whether provision enabling landlord to give three months' notice to determine tenancy operating as a forfeiture clause—Whether tenant entitled to relief against forfeiture. **Richard Clarke & Co Ltd v Widnall** [1976] **3** 301, CA.
    Interim payments order—
      Action for forfeiture and mesne profits—Application by landlord for interim payments order pending determination of action—Jurisdiction of court to make order—Claim by landlord for sum by way of interim payment corresponding to minimum amount he would receive by way of compensation for use of land—No rule of court expressly authorising making of such an order—Whether court having inherent jurisdiction to make order—Administration of Justice Act 1969, s 20. **Moore v Assignment Courier Ltd** [1977] **2** 842, CA.
    Lessee enemy alien abroad—
      No person authorised to pay rent or perform covenants—Re-entry by grant of weekly tenancy to another tenant. **Lewis (EH) & Son Ltd v Morelli** [1948] **1** 433, KBD.
    Notice of breach—
      Failure to give notice—Breach of condition complained of—Bankruptcy of surety—Lease providing for re-entry on bankruptcy of surety for lessee—Action for repossession on ground of bankruptcy of surety—No statutory notice served specifying surety's bankruptcy as breach of condition complained of—Whether surety's bankruptcy a 'breach of condition'—Whether service of statutory notice necessary—Law of Property Act 1925, s 146(1). **Halliard Property Co Ltd v Jack Segal Ltd** [1978] **1** 1219, Ch D.
      Failure to give notice—Deed of surrender—Surrender executed and delivered in escrow to third party conditional on compliance with positive covenant—Surrender delivered to landlord by third party on failure to comply with covenant—Whether surrender void as device to circumvent statutory provisions requiring notice of breach—Law of Property Act 1925, s 146. **Plymouth Corp v Harvey** [1971] **1** 623, Ch D.
      Persons to be served with notice—Assignment of lease—Assignment in breach of covenant not to assign without lessor's consent—Whether notice should be served on original lessee or on assignee—Law of Property Act 1925, s 146. **Old Grovebury Manor Farm Ltd v W Seymour Plant Sales & Hire Ltd (No 2)** [1979] **3** 504, CA.
      Persons to be served with notice—Lease vested in co-owners—Covenant to repair—Notice to repair served on one lessee only—Notice requiring work not within covenant—Vesting of lease in Public Trustee—Law of Property Act 1925, s 146, Sch I, Part IV, para 1(4). **Blewett v Blewett** [1936] **2** 188, CA.
      Requirement to remedy breach—Breach incapable of remedy—Covenant not to sublet without lessor's consent—Lessee subletting without necessary consent—Whether breach capable of remedy—Whether notice required to call on lessee to remedy breach—Law of Property Act 1925, s 146(1). **Scala House and District Property Co Ltd v Forbes** [1973] **3** 308, CA.
      Requirement to remedy breach—Requirement where breach capable of remedy—Covenant against user of premises for other than residential purposes—User for purposes of prostitution—User by sub-tenant without knowledge of tenants—Notice not requiring breach to be remedied—Whether notice invalid—Validity of notice requiring remedy of breach if capable of being remedied—Law of Property Act 1925, s 146(1). **Glass v Kencakes Ltd** [1964] **3** 807, QBD.
      Requirement to remedy breach—Requirement where breach capable of remedy—Covenant not to contravene any of the laws of the land—User of premises as brothel—Notice not containing requirement that breach should be remedied—Validity—Whether breach capable of remedy—Whether notice required to call on lessee to remedy breach—Law of Property Act 1925, s 146(1), (2). **Egerton v Esplanade Hotels, London Ltd** [1947] **2** 88, KBD.
      Requirement to remedy breach—Requirement where breach capable of remedy—Covenant to conduct club in proper and orderly manner—Permitting premises to be used for purpose of gaming—Notice not containing requirement that breach should be remedied—Validity—Law of Property Act 1925, s 146(1)(2). **Hoffman v Fineberg** [1948] **1** 592, Ch D.
    Premises let as a dwelling—
      Enforcement of right of re-entry or forfeiture unlawful otherwise than by proceedings in court—Lease of shop premises and residential flat—Landlord peaceably re-entering shop premises—Whether lease forfeit—Whether premises let as a dwelling—Meaning of 'let as a dwelling'—Protection from Eviction Act 1977, s 2. **Patel v Pirabakaran** [2006] **4** 506, CA.
    Re-entry. See Re-entry, *below.*
    Receiving order made against tenant—
      Subsequent action for possession by landlord. *See* **Bankruptcy** (Legal proceedings against debtor following receiving order—Remedy of creditor against property or person of debtor in respect of debt—Forfeiture of lease).
    Relief against forfeiture. *See* Relief against forfeiture, *below.*
    Right of re-entry—
      Appellants in breach of covenant to pay rent—Landlords requesting payment—Landlords peaceably re-entering—Appellants obtaining interim orders preventing proceedings being commenced against them without leave of court—Whether landlords having waived forfeiture—Whether effect of interim orders being that leave of court required for peaceable re-entry—Whether 'other proceedings' and 'other legal process' referring to peaceable re-entry—Insolvency Act 1986, ss 11(3), 252(2)(b). **Debtor (No 13A/IO/95), Re a** [1996] **1** 691, Ch D.

LANDLORD AND TENANT (cont)—
  Forfeiture of lease (cont)—
    Right of re-entry (cont)—
      Restrictions on forfeiture—Forfeiture under lease for tenant's breach of covenant—Statutory right of re-entry not enforceable until landlord serving notice on tenant specifying particular breach complained of, requiring tenant to remedy breach and tenant failing to remedy breach in reasonable time—Whether notice valid if given before right of re-entry accruing under lease—Law of Property Act 1925, s 146(1). **Toms v Ruberry** [2019] 3 170, CA.
    Waiver of forfeiture—
      Acceptance of rent—Covenants against underletting without consent and against user otherwise than as private dwelling-house—Unlawful underletting—Acceptance by landlord of rent—Waiver of forfeiture for breach of covenant as to user. **Downie v Turner** [1951] 1 416, CA.
      Acceptance of rent—Whether question of fact or of law. **Windmill Investments (London) Ltd v Milano Restaurant Ltd** [1962] 2 680, QBD.
      Act of landlord relied on not involving demand for or acceptance of rent—Whether landlord's act so unequivocal as to be only consistent with continued existence of tenancy—Law of Property Act 1925, s 146. **Expert Clothing Service and Sales Ltd v Hillgate House Ltd** [1985] 2 998, CA.
      Demand for rent—Demand by landlord for future rent in advance—Landlord having sufficient knowledge of facts constituting breach to put him to election—Whether demand for future rent capable of amounting to waiver. **Blackstone (David) Ltd v Burnetts (West End) Ltd** [1973] 3 782, QBD.
      Demand for rent—Rent payable in advance—Demand expressed to be without prejudice—Whether an unqualified demand effecting a waiver—Whether a waiver in respect of the future period to which the rent related. **Segal Securities Ltd v Thoseby** [1963] 1 500, QBD.
      Knowledge of breach of covenant—Knowledge sufficient to put landlord to election—Knowledge of landlord's solicitor of facts constituting breach of covenant—Solicitor uncertain whether facts constituting a breach of covenant in law. **Blackstone (David) Ltd v Burnetts (West End) Ltd** [1973] 3 782, QBD.
      Knowledge of breach of covenant—Landlords' managing agents having knowledge of tenant's breach—Agents instructing their staff not to demand or accept rent from tenant—Clerk, ignorant of instruction, demanding rent from tenant—Rent paid by tenant well knowing landlords still intended to forfeit lease—Whether landlords' right to forfeiture waived—Law of Property Act 1925, s 146. **Central Estates (Belgravia) Ltd v Woolgar (No 2)** [1972] 3 610, CA.
      Promise by landlord before execution of lease that tenant could continue to live on premises—Enforceability of landlord's promise. **City & Westminster Properties (1934) Ltd v Mudd** [1958] 2 733, Ch D.
  Form of application for new tenancy—
    Business premises. *See* Business premises—Application for new tenancy—Form, *above*.
  Freehold—
    Acquisition by long leaseholder. *See* Leasehold enfranchisement, *below*.
  Frustration—
    Building lease. *See* Building lease—Frustration of contract, *above*.
  Furnished tenancy—
    Reference of contract to rent tribunal. *See* **Rent tribunal** (Reference of contract).
    Rent restriction. *See* **Rent restriction** (Furnished letting).
  Goodwill—
    Business premises—
      Compensation for goodwill. *See* Compensation for goodwill in respect of business premises, *above*.
  Harassment—
    Civil liability. *See* **Statutory duty** (Breach—Civil liability—Landlord and tenant—Harassment).
  Holding over—
    Wilful. *See* Tenancy—Wilfully holding over after determination of term—Wilfully, *below*.
  House—
    Leasehold enfranchisement. *See* Leasehold enfranchisement—House, *below*.
  Illegality—
    Agreement for lease—
      Use of premises. *See* Agreement for lease—Illegality—Use of premises, *above*.
    Illegal user of premises. *See* Lease—Illegal purpose—Illegal user of premises, *below*.
  Immoral user of premises—
    Forfeiture of lease—
      Discretion to grant relief. *See* Relief against forfeiture—Immoral user of premises—Court's discretion to grant relief, *below*.
  Implied covenant—
    Generally. *See* Covenant—Implied covenant, *above*.
    Repair. *See* Implied covenant to repair, *below*.
  Implied covenant to repair—
    Covenant by landlord—
      Common parts of block of flats—Block in multiple occupation—Landlord retaining possession of common parts—No express covenant to repair in tenancy agreement—Tenancy agreement containing implied easements for the purpose of access to dwellings—Circumstances requiring implication of covenant on part of landlord with regard to easements—Nature of obligation—Obligation to take reasonable care to keep stairs, lifts etc in state of reasonable repair and efficiency. **Liverpool City Council v Irwin** [1976] 2 39, HL.
      Flat let on weekly tenancy by local authority—No obligation on landlords to repair expressed in tenancy—Landlord having right of entry to repair—Restriction on tenant's doing repairs—Duty on tenant to deliver up in tenantable repair—Whether obligation on landlord to repair implied. **Sleafer v Lambeth Metropolitan BC** [1959] 3 378, CA.
      Implication of repairing covenant—Implication necessary to give business efficacy to tenancy agreement—Express covenant by tenant to repair inside of premises—Agreement silent on obligation to repair outside—Whether covenant by landlord to repair outside correlative to tenant's obligation to repair inside should be implied. **Barrett v Lounova (1982) Ltd** [1989] 1 351, CA.

LANDLORD AND TENANT (cont)—
  Implied covenant to repair (cont)—
    Covenant by landlord (cont)—
      Landlord's duty at common law to repair—Lease of commercial premises—Drain partly under demised premises and partly under landlord's property—No express landlord's covenant to repair—Lease containing detailed scheme regarding repairs to demised premises including drains—Lease including implied easement of drainage over part of drain under landlord's property—Whether landlord's covenant to repair could be implied—Whether landlord under common law duty to repair drain. **Westminster (Duke) v Guild** [1984] **3** 144, CA.
    Short lease of dwelling house—
      Defect requiring repair—Knowledge of defect—Relevance—Latent defect in ceiling—Ceiling falling in and injuring tenant—Tenant having no knowledge of defect before fall—Tenant not in a position to inform landlord of defect—Landlord having no knowledge of defect—Whether landlord liable for breach of implied covenant to keep structure of dwelling-house in repair—Housing Act 1961, s 32(1). **O'Brien v Robinson** [1973] **1** 583, HL.
      Duty of landlord to keep in repair and working order installations—Installations in the dwelling-house—Meaning—Duty limited to installations within physical confines of the relevant dwelling-house—Flat in block of flats—Flat the relevant dwelling-house—Duty to repair limited to installations within the flat—Installations outside the flat, though affecting proper functioning of installations within the flat, not within duty to repair—Housing Act 1961, s 32(1)(b). **Campden Hill Towers Ltd v Gardner** [1977] **1** 739, CA.
      Duty of landlord to keep in repair structure and exterior of the dwelling-house—Demised premises consisting of top floor flat in building—Whether roof immediately above flat capable of being part of the structure and exterior of flat—Housing Act 1961, s 32(1)(a). **Douglas-Scott v Scorgie** [1984] **1** 1086, CA.
      Duty of landlord to keep in repair structure and exterior of the dwelling-house—Exterior—Meaning—Yard behind house—Paving slabs in yard—Yard not a means of access to the house—Whether slabs part of 'exterior' of house—Housing Act 1961, s 32(1)(a). **Hopwood v Cannock Chase DC** [1975] **1** 796, CA.
      Duty of landlord to keep in repair structure and exterior of the dwelling-house—Landlord holding leasehold interest in flat from freeholder—Landlord granting tenancy of flat to tenant—Tenant tripping on paved area outside building whilst taking rubbish to bin—Tenant suffering personal injury—Tenant bringing proceedings for damages relying on breach of repairing covenant by landlord—Whether paved area part of exterior of front hall of building—Whether landlord having estate or interest in front hall—Whether landlord liable for disrepair notwithstanding he had no notice of it before tenant's accident—Landlord and Tenant Act 1985, s 11. **Edwards v Kumarasamy** [2017] **2** 624, SC.
      Duty of landlord to keep in repair structure and exterior of the dwelling-house—Particular part of building demised—Flat in block of flats—'Exterior' of flat—'Exterior' of flat including anything which in ordinary language was part of the exterior—Exterior not limited to parts included in demise—Outside walls of flat expressly excluded from demise—Outside walls part of exterior of flat—Other parts of structure included in 'exterior' of the flat—Housing Act 1961, s 32(1)(a). **Campden Hill Towers Ltd v Gardner** [1977] **1** 739, CA.
      Duty of landlord to keep in repair structure and exterior of the dwelling-house—Repair—Premises let by local authority—Demised premises having inherent defect causing severe condensation and damp—Whether premises in disrepair—Whether local authority under duty to eradicate inherent defect—Whether local authority in breach of implied covenant to 'repair'—Housing Act 1961, s 32(1). **Quick v Taff-Ely BC** [1985] **3** 321, CA.
      Short lease—Lease for term of less than seven years—Determination of length of term—Agreement for lease for term of seven years beginning on date of agreement—Lease executed shortly after but not delivered to tenant until two weeks later—Fair rent assessed and correspondence passing between landlord and tenant on basis that landlord liable for repair under implied covenant—Whether lease for term of 'less than seven years' because grant took effect from date of delivery—Whether agreement for lease for term of seven years beginning on or after date of agreement constituting a lease for term of seven years and therefore having no implied covenant to repair—Whether landlord estopped from denying implied covenant to repair—Housing Act 1961, ss 32(1), 33(1)(3)(5). **Brikom Investments Ltd v Seaford** [1981] **2** 783, CA.
      Short lease—Lease for term of less than seven years—Lease determinable at option of lessor before expiration of seven years from commencement of term—Lease for term of 90 years—Lease conferring option on either party to determine lease on death of landlord—Whether lease 'determinable at the option of the lessor before the expiration of seven years from the commencement of the term'—Housing Act 1961, s 33(2). **Parker v O'Connor** [1974] **3** 257, CA.
      Steps and flagstones forming access to house—Whether implied covenant included steps and flagstones—Housing Act 1961, s 32(1)(a). **Brown v Liverpool Corp** [1969] **3** 1345, CA.
  Weekly tenancy—
    Extent of obligation of weekly tenant to repair. **Warren v Keen** [1953] **2** 1118, CA.
Implied grant of lease—
  Death of statutory tenant—
    Death of second statutory tenant—Permission to member of family to remain in occupation—Payment of rent—Occupation continuing for six months. **Marcroft Wagons Ltd v Smith** [1951] **2** 271, CA.
    Son and daughter residing with statutory tenant at his death and continuing in occupation thereafter—Acceptance of rent from son, etc—Correct inference—Son succeeding as statutory tenant under Increase of Rent and Mortgage Interest (Restrictions) Act 1920, s 12(1)(g). **Dealex Properties Ltd v Brooks** [1965] **1** 1080, CA.
  General words—
    Inclusion of rights appertaining to premises—Flats supplied with hot water and central heating by landlords—Whether right conferred on tenant by general words—Law of Property Act 1925, s 62. **Regis Property Co Ltd v Redman** [1956] **2** 335, CA.
    Tenancy agreement—Right enjoyed with land at time of agreement—Coal shed—Shed being used by tenant, with landlord's permission, at date of agreement—Law of Property Act 1925, s 62(1). **Wright v Macadam** [1949] **2** 565, CA.
Implied grant of tenancy agreement. *See* Tenancy agreement—Implied grant, *below.*

LANDLORD AND TENANT (cont)—
Improvements—
Business premises—
Compensation—Limitation on tenant's right to compensation—Contractual obligation to make improvement—Proposed installation of new lavatories—Subsequent contract by tenants with underlessee to make the improvement—Whether tenant entitled to claim compensation—Landlord and Tenant Act 1927, s 2(1)(b). **Owen Owen Estate Ltd v Livett** [1955] **2** 513, Ch D.
Meaning of improvement—Lessee proposing to demolish all buildings demised and rebuild them—Objection by landlord—Application in Chancery Division for declaration proposed works improvements—Jurisdiction of Chancery Division—Landlord and Tenant Act 1927, ss 1, 2, 3, 16, 17, 21. **National Electric Theatres Ltd v Hudgell** [1939] **1** 567, Ch D.
Tenant serving notice on landlord of intention to carry out works of improvement—Landlord offering to carry out works in consideration of reasonable increase in rent in accordance with statutory provision—Tenant not accepting offer and withdrawing notice—Whether landlord entitled to carry out works notwithstanding tenant's withdrawal of notice—Landlord and Tenant Act 1927, s 3. **Norfolk Capital Group Ltd v Cadogan Estates Ltd** [2004] **3** 889, Ch D.
Housing legislation, under—
Notice. *See* **Housing** (Improvement notice).
Licence or consent of landlord—
Alteration to premises—Installation of individual hot water system—Whether an 'improvement'—Whether installation trespass to landlord's property—Landlord and Tenant Act 1927, s 19(2). **Tideway Investment and Property Holdings Ltd v Wellwood** [1952] **1** 1142, Ch D.
Licence or consent not to be unreasonably withheld—Unreasonable withholding—Compensation substantial but uncertain in amount—Right of landlord to consider self-interest—Covenant against making alterations—Landlord and Tenant Act 1927, s 19(2). **Lambert v F W Woolworth & Co Ltd (No 2)** [1938] **2** 664, CA.
Licence or consent not to be unreasonably withheld—Unreasonable withholding—Demand of sum of money considered excessive by lessee—Counter-offer of lesser sum as compensation—Power of court to order reference to official or special referee—Meaning of 'improvements'—Improvements from tenants' point of view—Demised premises as part of composite premises—Landlord and Tenant Act 1927, s 19(2), (3). **Woolworth (F W) & Co Ltd v Lambert** [1936] **2** 1523, Ch D.
Income tax—
Excess rent. *See* **Income tax** (Profits—Excess rent).
Land—
Person chargeable—Landlord. *See* **Income tax** (Land—Person chargeable—Landlord).
Indemnity clause—
Lease. *See* Lease—Indemnity clause, *below.*
Injunction—
Injunction restraining breach of tenancy agreement—
Whether court having jurisdiction to grant landlord injunction based on tenancy agreement restraining tenant from acting in anti-social manner to other tenants after termination of tenancy. **Medina Housing Association Ltd v Case** [2003] **1** 1084, CA.
Landlord—
Locus standi. *See* **Injunction** (Locus standi—Landlord).
Innocent misrepresentation—
Fitness of premises. *See* Fitness of premises—Innocent misrepresentation inducing contract, *above.*
Insurance—
Covenant. *See* Covenant—Insurance, *above.*
Interim rent—
Business premises. *See* Rent—Business premises—Interim rent, *below.*
Intestacy—
Service of notice to quit. *See* Notice to quit—Service—Intestacy, *below.*
Introductory tenancy—
Possession. *See* **Housing** (Local authority houses—Possession—Introductory tenancy).
Joint tenants—
Business premises—
Application for new tenancy. *See* Business premises—Application for new tenancy—Joint tenants, *above.*
Death of one of two joint tenants—
Liability of executors for rent. *See* Rent—Joint tenancy—Death of one of two joint tenants—Tenancy of committee rooms—Liability of executors, *below.*
Determination of periodic tenancy by one joint tenant without consent of other. *See* Tenancy—Joint tenancy—Determination, *below.*
Judgment for possession—
Enforcement. *See* Recovery of possession—Judgment for possession, *below.*
Judicial review—
Public authority—
Registered social landlord. *See* **Human rights** (Public authority—Private person performing functions of public nature—Registered social landlord bringing action against tenant for possession on mandatory grounds).
Landlord—
Registered social landlord. *See* **Human rights** (Public authority—Private person performing functions of public nature—Registered social landlord bringing action against tenant for possession on mandatory grounds).
Landlord's duty of care to visitors. *See* **Occupier's liability** (Landlord—Duty of care to visitors).
Lease—
Agreement for lease. *See* Agreement for lease, *above.*
Agreement to purchase lease—
Breach of agreement—Assignor to use best endeavours to obtain landlord's consent—Alternatively option to take a declaration of trust or direct method of dealing with property—Landlord's consent refused—Refusal to exercise option—Breach of contract—Return of deposit. **Pincott v Moorstons Ltd** [1937] **1** 513, CA.

LANDLORD AND TENANT (cont)—
　Lease (cont)—
　　Agreement to purchase lease (cont)—
　　　Delay—Damages for delay. **Phillips v Lamdin** [1949] **1** 770, KBD.
　　Agricultural holding. *See* **Agricultural holding**.
　　Assignment. *See* Assignment of lease, *above*.
　　Avoidance—
　　　Mistake as to identity of lessee—Fraudulent misrepresentation by lessee—Lessor's right to avoid
　　　lease. **Sowler v Potter** [1939] **4** 478, KBD.
　　Building lease. *See* Building lease, *above*.
　　Business lease. *See* Business premises, *above*.
　　Coal mining—
　　　New South Wales. *See* **New South Wales** (Coal mining—Lease).
　　Condition—
　　　Conditions and covenants distinguished—Stipulations possibly having the characters of both.
　　　Bashir v Comr of Lands [1960] **1** 117, PC.
　　Construction—
　　　Clause in lease providing that no 'goods' were to be 'placed outside the said premises' if forbidden
　　　by landlord—Demised premises originally having open basement but that area later being
　　　completely covered by skylights at pavement level—Whether clause preventing lessee from
　　　parking cars on skylights outside building but within demised premises. **Spring House (Freehold)**
　　　Ltd v Mount Cook Land Ltd [2002] **2** 822, CA.
　　　Service charge clause—Lease for leisure park chalets containing service charge clause providing
　　　for annual compound interest increase—Tenants disputing interpretation of compound interest
　　　clause—County court finding for tenants—Landlord appealing to High Court—High Court and
　　　Court of Appeal ruling in landlord's favour—Correct interpretation of service charge
　　　clause—Whether clause providing for compound interest. **Arnold v Britton** [2016] **1** 1, SC.
　　　What surrounding circumstances should be taken into consideration. **City & Westminster**
　　　Properties (1934) Ltd v Mudd [1958] **2** 733, Ch D.
　　Covenant. *See* Covenant, *above*.
　　Creation of tenant's interest—
　　　Date of creation—Whether date of execution of lease or of subsequent commencement of term.
　　　Northcote Laundry Ltd v Donnelly (Frederick) Ltd [1968] **2** 50, CA.
　　Determination. *See* Determination of lease, *above*.
　　Diplomatic agent's residence—
　　　Diplomatic privilege. *See* **Constitutional law** (Diplomatic privilege—Immunity from legal
　　　process—Residence of diplomatic agent—Lease of residence).
　　Disclaimer—
　　　Bankruptcy. *See* **Bankruptcy** (Disclaimer of onerous property—Lease).
　　　Compulsory winding up of company. *See* **Company** (Compulsory winding up—Disclaimer of
　　　onerous property—Lease).
　　　Voluntary winding up of company. *See* **Company** (Voluntary winding up—Disclaimer of onerous
　　　property—Lease).
　　Duration—
　　　Certainty—Lease not created when grant for uncertain term—Clause in occupancy agreement
　　　purporting to limit circumstances in which fully mutual housing association landlord could serve
　　　notice to quit—Agreement expressed to take effect from month to month and to be terminable by
　　　association only in event of breach of agreement by occupant—Agreement not expressly giving
　　　landlord right to terminate by the giving of notice to quit—Tenant temporarily falling into
　　　arrears—Landlord giving notice to quit—Whether agreement capable of taking effect as a
　　　tenancy—Law of Property Act 1925, s 149(6). **Mexfield Housing Co-operative Ltd v Berrisford**
　　　[2012] **1** 1393, SC.
　　　Certainty—Lease not created when grant for uncertain term—Clause in occupancy agreement
　　　purporting to limit circumstances in which fully mutual housing association landlord could serve
　　　notice to quit—Whether contract contained in occupancy agreement could be enforced by tenant
　　　as if creating interest in land—Whether occupancy agreement contractual licence. **Mexfield**
　　　Housing Co-operative Ltd v Berrisford [2011] **2** 273, CA.
　　　Certainty—Lease not created when grant for uncertain term—Strip of land let to tenant in 1930 on
　　　terms that tenancy would continue until land required by landlord for road widening—Land never
　　　required for road widening—Notice to quit served on tenant purporting to terminate
　　　tenancy—Whether notice to quit valid. **Prudential Assurance Co Ltd v London Residuary Body**
　　　[1992] **3** 504, HL.
　　　Certainty—Possession to be given up 'by' specified date. **Joseph v Joseph** [1966] **3** 486, CA.
　　Exclusion clause—
　　　Express language required—Clauses exempting lessor from liability for damage to property leased
　　　or goods therein, and providing indemnity against claims by third parties—Need of express
　　　language to exempt from liability for negligence—Existence of other ground of damage. **Canada**
　　　Steamship Lines Ltd v R [1952] **1** 305, PC.
　　Execution—
　　　Counterpart lease and lease both executed but not exchanged—Lessor a limited company—
　　　Whether company bound by sealed lease. **Beesly v Hallwood Estates Ltd** [1961] **1** 90, CA.
　　　Counterpart lease and lease both executed but not exchanged—Lessor a limited company—
　　　Whether tenant—Whether executed lease in escrow—Absence of evidence of intention of those
　　　executing lease on behalf of company—Law of Property Act 1925, s 74(1). **D'Silva v Lister House**
　　　Development Ltd [1970] **1** 858, Ch D.
　　Extent of demise—
　　　Lease of one-storey shop—Shop flanked on two sides by higher buildings—Whether air space
　　　above shop demised to tenant. **Kelsen v Imperial Tobacco Co (of GB and Ireland) Ltd** [1957] **2** 343,
　　　QBD.
　　　Lease of part of building—External walls—External fixtures—Extent to which included in demise.
　　　Sturge v Hackett [1962] **3** 166, CA.

LANDLORD AND TENANT (cont)—

Lease (cont)—

Extent of demise (cont)—

Owner of houses and gardens converting houses into shops—Gardens asphalted—Owner leasing to tenant 'all that messuage and shop with appurtenances thereto'—'Appurtenances'—Whether including forecourt—Law of Property Act 1925, s 62. **Owens v Scott & Sons (Bakers) Ltd, and Wastall** [1939] **3** 663, Assizes.

Fishing rights—

Grant for term of years—Retention by owner of 'one rod for her own use'—Effect of retention. **Vicker's Lease, Re** [1947] **1** 707, CA.

Fixtures—

Fixtures annexed by tenant—Tenant's right to remove fixtures on surrender of lease—Surrender by operation of law—Lease expiring by effluxion of time and being replaced by new lease—Rent under new lease to be open market rental value—Whether tenant losing right to remove fixtures on surrender of lease—Whether rent to be assessed without regard to tenant's fixtures. **New Zealand Government Property Corp v H M & S Ltd** [1982] **1** 624, CA.

Removal after contract for assignment of lease—Order to replace. **Phillips v Lamdin** [1949] **1** 770, KBD.

Trade fixtures—Mode of annexation—Corrugated iron shed erected upon concrete floor—Superstructure removable without material injury—Whether concrete foundation and superstructure single unit. **Webb v Frank Bevis Ltd** [1940] **1** 247, CA.

Trade fixtures—Mode of annexation—Petrol pumps and tanks—Whether pumps and tanks single unit—Removal within reasonable time—On failure to remove, property in fixtures to vest in landlord. **Smith v City Petroleum Co Ltd** [1940] **1** 260, Assizes.

Trade fixtures—Removal of trade fixtures—Waste—Pipes and extractor fans installed by 'drilling holes in walls of building—Subsequent tenant or licensee lawfully removing fixtures but without filling in holes—Building ceasing to be weatherproof—Whether subsequent tenant or licensee under obligation to fill in holes—Whether waste occurring when holes made or when fixtures removed. **Mancetter Developments Ltd v Garmanson Ltd** [1986] **1** 449, CA.

Use of landlord's fixtures and fittings granted by tenancy agreement—Refrigerator operated by central plant in landlord's control—Plant in disrepair—Whether landlord liable to repair plant and supply refrigeration. **Penn v Gatenex Co Ltd** [1958] **1** 712, CA.

What constitutes fixtures—Electric plant—Storage battery. **Jordan v May** [1947] **1** 231, CA.

Forfeiture. *See* Forfeiture of lease, *above.*

Frustration—

Building lease. *See* Building lease—Frustration of contract, *above.*

Change of circumstances. *See* **Contract** (Frustration—Change of circumstances—Lease).

Grant—

Generally. *See* **Lease** (Grant).

Illegal premium. *See* **Rent restriction** (Premium).

Illegal purpose—

Illegal user of premises—Permission to use premises for professional purposes—Regulation forbidding such use without consent of local housing authority—Enforceability of lease—Illegal object of lessor not pleaded, but disclosed, and dealt with, in evidence—Defence (General) Regulations 1939, reg 68CA(1). **Edler v Auerbach** [1949] **2** 692, KBD.

Implied covenant. *See* Covenant—Implied covenant, *above.*

Implied grant. *See* Implied grant of lease, *above.*

Implied term—

Apportionment of rent—Rent payable in advance—Commercial leases requiring payment of rent quarterly in advance—Termination of lease by tenant exercising break clause—Tenant seeking repayment of portion of rent paid for period following termination—Whether term to be implied allowing recovery of apportioned sum—Apportionment Act 1870, s 2. **Marks and Spencer plc v BNP Paribas Securities Services Trust Co (Jersey) Ltd** [2016] **4** 441, SC.

Contribution by tenant to landlord's costs of maintaining building. *See* Contribution by tenant to landlord's costs of maintaining building—Implied term, *above.*

Indemnity clause—

Scope—Lease of premises by railway company to wagon repairing company—Indemnity clause against damages, etc, for injury to repairing company's employees—Employee injured away from demised premises—Whether indemnity restricted to injury connected with demised premises—Construction. **Henson v London and North Eastern Rly Co** [1946] **1** 653, CA.

Land registration—

Effect of registration on title of registered proprietor—Notice of lease. *See* **Land registration** (Effect of registration on title of registered proprietor—Notice of lease).

Licence distinguished. *See* **Licence** (Licence to occupy premises).

Long lease—

Acquisition of freehold or extended lease. *See* Leasehold enfranchisement, *below.*

Mining lease—

Coal. *See* **Coal mining** (Mining lease).

Mortgage of lease—

Forfeiture—Relief of mortgagees. *See* Relief against forfeiture—Underlessee—Lease mortgaged—Relief of mortgagees, *below.*

Mortgagor's power of leasing. *See* **Mortgage** (Power of leasing).

Option to determine—

Break clause on premises becoming unfit—Service flat—No damage to flat—Damage to building rendering service impossible—Whether tenant entitled to exercise option—Landlord and Tenant (War Damage) Act 1939, s 1. **Johnstone v Swan Estates Ltd** [1941] **3** 446, Ch D.

Break clause—Lease containing break clause expressed to be personal to original tenant but allowing assignment of benefit in specified circumstances—Original tenant assigning lease to company which fell within category of persons to whom benefit of break clause could be assigned—Assignment of lease containing no express assignment of benefit of break clause—Whether benefit of break clause passing on assignment of lease as right touching and concerning land or having reference to subject-matter of lease—Law of Property Act 1925, ss 63, 142. **Harbour Estates Ltd v HSBC Bank plc** [2004] **3** 1057, Ch D.

LANDLORD AND TENANT (cont)—
  Lease (cont)—
    Option to determine (cont)—
      Break clause—Notice under break clause effective where tenant had materially complied with all obligations under lease—Meaning of material compliance. **Fitzroy House Epworth Street (No 1) Ltd v The Financial Times Ltd** [2006] **2** 776, CA.
      Break clause—Notice under break clause must be expressed to be given pursuant to s 24(2) of the Landlord and Tenant Act 1954—Notice did not contain those words—Whether notice valid notwithstanding its failure to include prescribed words—Landlord and Tenant Act 1954, s 24(2). **Friends Life Ltd v Siemes Hearing Instruments Ltd** [2015] **1 Comm** 1068, CA.
      Break clause—Vacant possession—Notice under break clause effective where tenant had delivered up vacant possession—Meaning of vacant possession. **Ibrend Estates BV v NYK Logistics (UK) Ltd** [2011] **4** 539, CA.
      Lease for fixed term commencing on 13 January containing break clause—Break clause providing for determination on expiry of six months' notice on third anniversary of commencement of lease—Notice given expiring on 12 January—Whether notice valid. **Mannai Investment Co Ltd v Eagle Star Life Assurance Co Ltd** [1997] **3** 352, HL.
      Notice must follow terms of clause—Notice given for 21st December instead of 25th December—Invalid. **Hankey v Clavering** [1942] **2** 311, CA.
    Option to purchase. See **Option** (Option to purchase—Tenant's option conferred by lease).
    Option to renew—
      Covenant to provide services previously supplied voluntarily—Impossibility of performance—Option to renew at rack rent—Meaning of 'rack rent'—Regulated tenancy—Registered rent—Option to renew at rent to be agreed—Failing agreement rent for renewed term to be 'commercial yearly rack rent' at which premises might be expected to be let in open market—Purported exercise of option—Subsequent registration of fair rent—Fair rent less than commercial yearly rack rent which could be expected in open market—Whether option capable of being exercised. **Newman v Dorrington Developments Ltd** [1975] **3** 928, Ch D.
      Estoppel—Representation. See **Estoppel** (Representation—Knowledge of falsity—Representor's knowledge of falsity—Relevance—Lease containing option to renew).
      Fixing of rent—Option for renewal at a rent to be fixed having regard to the market value of the premises at the time of exercising option—No machinery for fixing rent—Whether void. **Brown v Gould** [1971] **2** 1505, Ch D.
      Lease for duration of hostilities—Lessee's option for further term—Time for exercise of option—Validation of War-Time Leases Act 1944, ss 1, 3(3), 7. **Dungey v Tunbridge Wells Properties Ltd** [1947] **1** 785, Ch D.
      Notice of renewal—Note in rent book—Whether sufficient in memorandum in writing—Law of Property Act 1925, s 40. **Hill v Hill** [1947] **1** 54, CA.
      Observance of covenants—Condition of exercise of option performance of covenants—Delay in performance—Obligation satisfied before date for renewal of lease although not at date specified in agreement—Right to renewal. **Robinson v Thames Mead Park Estates Ltd** [1947] **1** 366, Ch D.
      Observance of covenants—Condition of exercise of option that 'all covenants ... have been observed'—Trivial breaches of covenant—Covenants by tenant to keep interior in repair and paint every three years and in last year of term—Tenant kept interior in fair decorative repair, but failed to paint ceiling at all, or to paint at all in last year of term—Notice given before last year of term to exercise option—Landlord frequently visited premises but said nothing—Whether breaches waived or landlord estopped from relying on them—Whether option exercisable. **West Country Cleaners (Falmouth) Ltd v Saly** [1966] **3** 210, CA.
      Observance of covenants—Condition of exercise of option that all covenants 'have been performed and observed' up to date of exercise of option—Breaches of positive and negative covenants occurring prior to exercise of option—All breaches spent by date option exercised—Whether condition precedent requiring observance and performance of all covenants up to date of option—Whether distinction between breach of positive and negative covenants—Whether tenant precluded from exercising option by past breach of negative covenant. **Bass Holdings Ltd v Morton Music Ltd** [1987] **2** 1001, CA.
      Option of 'continuing for an extension of seven or fourteen years'—Option exercisable providing tenant had 'reasonably' fulfilled his covenants—Whether option exercised by tenant's conduct in remaining in occupation after expiry of original term and paying rent reserved by lease—Whether, if tenant in breach of covenant to repair, option exercisable. **Gardner v Blaxill** [1960] **2** 457, QBD.
      Option of taking a further lease granted by agreement in writing (but not under seal), executed on same date as lease—Whether option for renewal of lease or void as infringing rule against perpetuities—Whether obligation to grant new lease run with reversion—Whether agreement was 'covenant' within Law of Property Act 1925, s 142(1). **Weg Motors Ltd v Hales** [1961] **3** 181, CA.
      Registration as estate contract. See **Land charge** (Estate contract—Option to renew lease).
      Time for exercise of option—Lease for 35 years—Covenant to renew on request of lessees 'made 6 months before the expiration of the term'—Request to renew made within 10 days of date of lease. **Biondi v Kirklington and Piccadilly Estates Ltd** [1947] **2** 59, Ch D.
      Uncertainty—Option for renewal at such rental as may be agreed—Whether void. **King's Motors (Oxford) Ltd v Lax** [1969] **3** 665, Ch Ct County Palatine of Lanca.
    Options relating to land—
      Rule against perpetuities—Option to acquire interest reversionary on term of a lease—Option exercisable only by lessee or his successors in title—Option for extension of lease—Whether void for perpetuity—Whether only existing superior interest capable of being 'interest reversionary' on term of lease—Whether chargee of charge by way of legal mortgage capable of being successor in title of lessee—Perpetuities and Accumulations Act 1964, s 9(1). **Souglides v Tweedie** [2012] **3** 189, Ch D.
    Parol lease—
      Statutory requirements. See Lease—Statutory requirements—Parol lease, below.
    Perpetual right of renewal. See Renewal of lease—Perpetual right of renewal, below.
    Premium—
      Agreement for lease. See Agreement for lease—Premium, above.

LANDLORD AND TENANT (cont)—
Lease (cont)—
Premium (cont)—
Protected tenancy. *See* **Rent restriction** (Premium).
Rectification—
Absence of common intention to include words in lease. **City & Westminster Properties (1934) Ltd v Mudd** [1958] **2** 733, Ch D.
Common intention of parties—Unilateral mistake—Lease not giving effect to parties' common intention due to landlord's mistake—Tenant aware of mistake at date of execution of lease—Mistake contrary to landlord's interest and beneficial to tenant's interest—Tenant not drawing landlord's attention to mistake—Failure by landlord to provide machinery in rent review clause for fixing rent in default of agreement between parties—Whether landlord entitled to rectification of clause—Whether standard of proof of common intention higher than balance of probability. **Bates (Thomas) & Son Ltd v Wyndham's (Lingerie) Ltd** [1981] **1** 1077, CA.
Renewal. *See* Renewal of lease, *below*.
Rent. *See* Rent, *below*.
Repudiation—
Acceptance of repudiation—Effect—Continuance of lease—Solus agreement—Petrol filling station—Lease of petrol station by oil company—Tenant agreeing to take all supplies of fuel from landlord—Payment cash on delivery—Landlord repudiating agreement by requiring payment by banker's draft prior to despatch of order—Tenant accepting repudiation and obtaining supplies elsewhere—Landlord subsequently offering to revert to original terms of cash on delivery—Tenant continuing to obtain supplies elsewhere—Claim by landlord for injunction—Whether lease continuing to subsist after acceptance of repudiation—Whether landlord entitled to enforce agreement after offering to revert to original terms for payment. **Total Oil GB Ltd v Thompson Garages (Biggin Hill) Ltd** [1971] **3** 1226, CA.
Reservation—
Right of entry—Derogation from grant—Tenancy agreement reserving landlord's right of entry for 'all reasonable purposes'—Landlord proposing entry to carry out ecological survey and other activities to comply with development requirements—Whether reservation to be construed strictly—Extent of permitted activities. **Earl of Plymouth v Rees** [2021] **2** 1013, CA.
Sporting rights—Right to take rabbits reserved to landlord—Right to tenant farmer to kill rabbits in interests of good farming—Right to agree to destruction of rabbits by agricultural executive committee—Right of landlord to set snares in tenant's fields—Profit à prendre—Oral grant—Part performance—Ground Game Act 1880, s 1(1)(b)—Law of Property Act 1925, s 40. **Mason v Clarke** [1955] **1** 914, HL.
Resulting trust. *See* **Trust and trustee** (Constructive trust—Tenancy agreement).
Reversion—
Acquisition by trustee—Matrimonial home. *See* **Trust and trustee** (Profit from trust—Matrimonial home).
Flats—Disposal by landlord—Tenants' right to acquire reversion. *See* Flats—Tenants' right to acquire landlord's reversion, *above*.
Option granted to tenant to purchase freehold reversion—Purchase price—Valuation—Value of reversion or of freehold with vacant possession—Presumption that price to be determined at value of reversion—Rebuttal of presumption by inconsistent directions—Price to represent 'fair market price of the demised premises'—Fair market price having regard to values of comparable properties—Impossibility of valuing reversion by reference to comparable properties—Inference that price to be determined by reference to value of freehold with vacant possession. **Nagel's Lease, Re** [1974] **3** 34, Ch D.
Option to purchase—Generally. *See* **Option** (Option to purchase—Tenant's option conferred by lease).
Right to acquire new lease—
Landlord intending to redevelop—Redevelopment of any premises in which tenant's flat contained—Whether 'any premises in which the tenant's flat is contained' referring to existing recognisable unit—Leasehold Reform, Housing and Urban Development Act 1993, s 47. **Majorstake Ltd v Curtis** [2006] **4** 1326, CA; [2008] **2** 303, HL.
Qualifying tenant—Whether head lessee having right to individual lease extension—Leasehold Reform, Housing and Urban Development Act 1993, ss 39(1), (4), 56(1)(a). **Aggio v Howard de Walden Estates Ltd** [2007] **3** 910, CA.
Qualifying tenant—Whether head lessee having right to individual lease extension—Leasehold Reform, Housing and Urban Development Act 1993, ss 39(1), (4), 57(1)(a), 101(3). **Aggio v Howard de Walden Estates Ltd** [2008] **4** 382, HL.
Sporting rights—
Reservation. *See* Lease—Reservation—Sporting rights, *above*.
Statutory requirements—
Lease exceeding three years to be in writing—Agreement not under seal—Term of 14 years determinable by tenant at end of any year—Whether lease for term exceeding three years—Whether valid—Law of Property Act 1925, ss 52(1), (2)(d), 54(2). **Kushner v Law Society** [1952] **1** 404, KBD.
Parol lease—Lease taking effect in possession for a term not exceeding three years—Whether letter confirming tenancy to commence three weeks later operating as a lease 'taking effect in possession'—Law of Property Act 1925, s 54(2). **Long v Tower Hamlets London BC** [1996] **2** 683, Ch D.
Surrender—
Generally. *See* Surrender of tenancy, *below*.
Surrender by operation of law—Right of tenant to remove fixtures. *See* Lease—Fixtures—Fixtures annexed by tenant, *above*.
Winding up of lessee company—Informal surrender of lease by liquidator—Breach of covenant at time of surrender—Whether provable in liquidation. *See* **Company** (Winding up—Proof and ranking of claims—Claim for breach of covenant—Covenant to yield up demised premises with full vacant possession—Informal surrender of lease by liquidator).
Underlease. *See* Underlease, *below*.

LANDLORD AND TENANT (cont)—
  Lease (cont)—
    Validity—
      Grant of lease by nominee to principal. *See* **Lease** (Grant—Grant of lease by nominee to principal—Validity).
    Variation—
      Effect of variation—Lessor executing deed of variation with assignee—Deed increasing yearly rent and changing covenants as to user and alienation—Nature of changes to demised estate—Whether deed effecting surrender and regrant by operation of law. **Friends' Provident Life Office v British Railways Board** [1996] **1** 336, CA.
      Implied variation—Tenancy agreement under which tenant undertook responsibility for repairs—Repairs carried out by landlords for many years—Whether variation of agreement implied. **London Hospital (Board of Governors) v Jacobs** [1956] **2** 603, CA.
    War time lease. *See* War time lease, *below*.
  Lease extension. *See* Leasehold enfranchisement—Lease extension—Valuation, *below*.
  Leasehold enfranchisement—
    Acquisition of new lease—
      Valuation —Marriage value—Hope value—Whether hope value to be taken into account in valuation—Leasehold Reform Act 1967, ss 9(1), (1A)—Leasehold Reform, Housing and Urban Development Act 1993, Sch 6, paras 3, 4, Sch 13, paras 3, 4. **Cadogan v Sportelli (sub nom Cadogan v Pitts)** [2009] **3** 365, HL.
    Agreement relating to tenancy—
      Agreement purporting to exclude or modify right to acquire freehold—Purports to exclude or modify—Freeholder granting concurrent lease of house to third party before service of tenant's notice to acquire freehold—Concurrent lease having effect of increasing price payable by tenant for freehold—Whether concurrent lease modifying tenant's right to acquire freehold—Whether concurrent lease providing for imposition of penalty or disability on tenant seeking to acquire freehold—Leasehold Reform Act 1967, s 23(1). **Jones v Wrotham Park Settled Estates** [1979] **1** 286, HL.
    Claim by tenant—
      Proceedings to enforce right of re-entry or forfeiture during currency of claim—Leave—Leave only where claim not made in good faith—Good faith—Tenant claiming extended lease—Serious breaches by tenant of repairing covenants—Proceedings by landlord to forfeit lease for breach of covenant—Notice by tenant of claim to extended lease—No prospect of tenant being able to fulfil repairing obligations under extended lease—Whether tenant's claim made in good faith—Leasehold Reform Act 1967, Sch 3, para 4(1). **Liverpool Corp v Husan** [1971] **3** 651, CA.
      Proceedings to enforce right of re-entry or forfeiture during currency of claim—Leave—Leave only where claim not made in good faith—Good faith—Tenant claiming freehold—Claim following conviction of keeping a brothel on the premises—Tenant in breach of covenant for keeping brothel on premises—Lease liable to forfeiture for breach—Landlord wishing to bring proceedings to enforce right of forfeiture—Whether tenant's claim made in 'good faith'—Leasehold Reform Act 1967, Sch 3, para 4(1). **Central Estates (Belgravia) Ltd v Woolgar** [1971] **3** 647, CA.
    Enfranchisement where landlord cannot be found—
      Determination of amount to be paid into court—Determination of 'amount remaining unpaid of any pecuniary rent payable'—Whether including arrears of rent which have become statute-barred—Limitation Act 1939, s 17—Leasehold Reform Act 1967, ss 9(5), 27(5). **Howell's Application, Re** [1972] **3** 662, Ch D.
      Identity of freeholder unknown—Tenant under long lease wishing to acquire freehold—Procedure—Leasehold Reform Act 1967, s 27. **Robertson's Application, Re** [1969] **1** 257, Ch D.
      Identity of freeholder unknown—Tenant under long lease wishing to acquire freehold—Rent reserved under lease of 1869 at 1d per annum in respect of greater area than that held by tenant—Determination of amount to be paid into court in respect of rent unpaid—Form of order—Leasehold Reform Act 1967, s 27(5). **Frost's Application, Re** [1970] **2** 538, Ch D.
    Entitlement—
      Flat forming part of house let to qualifying tenant—Tenant of house having right to enfranchise only when occupying house or part as only or main residence—Company being tenant of house and qualifying tenant of each flat—Whether company required to occupy house or part as only or main residence—Leasehold Reform Act 1967, s 1(1ZB). **Cadogan v Search Guarantees plc** [2005] **1** 280, CA.
    House—
      Building designed or adapted for living in and reasonably so called—Meaning of 'designed or adapted for living in'—House reasonably so called—Relevance of use—Leasehold Reform Act 1967, s 2(1). **Day v Hosebay Ltd** [2010] **4** 36, CA; [2012] **4** 1347, SC.
      Building designed or adapted for living in and reasonably so called—Whether 'designed or adapted for living in' meaning fit for immediate residential occupation—Leasehold Reform Act 1967, s 2(1). **Boss Holdings Ltd v Grosvenor West End Properties** [2008] **2** 759, HL.
      Building lease—Whether construction of house under terms of building lease an 'improvement' to 'house and premises' for purposes of determining price payable by tenant for transfer of freehold—Leasehold Reform Act 1967, ss 2(3), 9(1A). **Rosen v Trustees of Camden Charities** [2001] **2** 399, CA.
      Ground floor sublet—Whether building ground floor of which sublet as betting shop a house reasonably so called—Leasehold Reform Act 1967, s 2(1). **Lake v Bennett** [1970] **1** 457, CA.
      House reasonably so called—Purpose-built shop with flat above in parade of similar premises—Shop occupying equal or greater area of premises than flat depending on whether covered yard and stable included as part of premises—Whether building 'reasonably ... called' a house—Leasehold Reform Act 1967, s 2(1). **Tandon v Trustees of Spurgeon's Homes** [1982] **1** 1086, HL.
      Lease of building comprising shop on ground floor with tenant's residential accommodation above—Shop joined up with the shop on the ground floor of next-door building by an opening in the wall—Tenant also lessee of next-door building—Whether building designed or adapted for living in and reasonably called a house—Leasehold Reform Act 1967, s 2(1). **Peck v Anicar Properties Ltd** [1971] **1** 517, CA.

LANDLORD AND TENANT (cont)—
Leasehold enfranchisement (cont)—
House (cont)—
Lease of house comprised in agricultural holding—Partition and severance of leasehold interest of agricultural holding between several assignees—Partition of house from agricultural land—Landlord's consent to partition and severance not obtained—Assignee of house applying to purchase freehold—Whether partition creating two separate tenancies of two separate holdings in absence of landlord's consent—Whether house still comprised in agricultural holding—Whether assignee having right of leasehold enfranchisement—Leasehold Reform Act 1967, s 1(3)(b). **Lester v Ridd** [1989] **1** 1111, CA.

Material part of house lying above or below structure not comprised in house—Meaning of 'material part'—Leasehold Reform Act 1967, s 2. **Malekshad v Howard De Walden** [2003] **1** 193, HL.

Material part of house lying above or below structure not comprised in house—Occupation of 'house' by tenant as residence for period of five years—Semi-detached house—Opening made in wall between ground floor front room and front room of adjoining house—Door between front room and hall of adjoining house bricked up—Rooms restored to original condition year before tenant's application—Whether house occupied by tenant excluding front room of adjoining house—Whether tenant having occupied 'house' for requisite period—Leasehold Reform Act 1967, ss 1(1), 2(2). **Gaidowski v Gonville and Caius College, Cambridge** [1975] **2** 952, CA.

Material part of house lying above part of structure not comprised in house—House not structurally detached—Meaning of 'structurally detached'—Material part of house lying above part of structure not comprised in house—House having own entrance and separated from rest of structure by walls, ceiling and floor—Whether house 'structurally detached' from rest of structure—Leasehold Reform Act 1967, s 2(2). **Parsons v Viscount Gage and ors (trustees of Henry Smith's Charity)** [1974] **1** 1162, HL.

Material part of house lying below part of structure not comprised in house—Tenant seeking enfranchisement of house including basement lying under other premises—House not structurally detached—Meaning of 'house'—Whether premises a 'house' if material part lying above or below part of structure not comprised in it—Whether tenant's premises a 'house'—Whether tenant entitled to enfranchise property—Leasehold Reform Act 1967, ss 1(1), 2(1), (2). **Westminster (Duke) v Birrane** [1995] **3** 416, CA.

Rateable value—House and premises—Leasehold including two houses—Only one occupied by tenant—Material part of house occupied by tenant overhanging part of structure not comprised in house—Appropriate rateable value—Rateable value of whole of premises in leasehold not appropriate rateable value—Appropriate rateable value that of whole building including part of structure not comprised in house occupied by tenant—Leasehold Reform Act 1967, s 1(1)(a). **Parsons v Viscount Gage and ors (trustees of Henry Smith's Charity)** [1973] **3** 23, CA.

Rateable value—Reduction—Improvement by execution of works amounting to structural alteration, extension or addition—Central heating system—Whether installation of central heating system a 'structural alteration...or addition'—Housing Act 1974, Sch 8, para 1(2). **Pearlman v Keepers and Governors of Harrow School** [1979] **1** 365, CA.

Intermediate leasehold interests—
Valuation—Marriage value—Hope value—Development value - Whether development value to be taken into account in valuation—Leasehold Reform, Housing and Urban Development Act 1993, Sch 6, para 3(1). **Cravecrest Ltd v Trustees of the Will of the second Duke of Westminster** [2013] **4** 456, CA.

Landlord's counter-notice—
Additional leaseback proposals—Landlord's counter-notice specifying no additional leaseback proposals—Landlord subsequently serving leaseback notice—Whether notice valid—Leasehold Reform, Housing and Urban Development Act 1993, ss 21(3), 36, Sch 9, Pt III, para 5. **Cawthorne v Hamdan** [2007] **2** 116, CA.

Tenant serving notice on landlord claiming new lease of flat—Landlord purporting to serve counter-notice—Counter-notice not stating whether tenant's claim admitted or not admitted and which if any of tenant's proposals accepted—Whether counter-notice valid—Leasehold Reform, Housing and Urban Development Act 1993, s 45. **Burman v Mount Cook Land Ltd** [2002] **1** 144, CA.

Tenants serving notice of wish to exercise right to collective enfranchisement and specifying proposed purchase price—Landlord serving counter-notice proposing higher purchase price—Whether counter-notice valid—Whether purchase price proposed in counter-notice required to be realistic—Leasehold Reform, Housing and Urban Development Act 1993, ss 13, 21, 25. **Cornwall Crescent (9) London Ltd v Kensington and Chelsea Royal London BC** [2005] **4** 1207, CA.

Lease extension—
Valuation—Marriage value—Hope value—Whether hope value to be taken into account in valuation—Leasehold Reform, Housing and Urban Development Act 1993, Schs 6, 13. **Cadogan v Sportelli (sub nom Cadogan v Pitts)** [2008] **2** 220, CA.

Leaseback. *See* Leasehold enfranchisement—Landlord's counter-notice—Additional leaseback proposals, *above*.

Limitation of action—
Tenant giving notice of desire to acquire freehold—Landlord opposing claim and citing current legal authority under which tenant's lease not qualifying as at low rent—Five years later legal decision defining letting value and thereby tenant becoming entitled to claim enfranchisement—Over six years after original notice tenant seeking to proceed on original notice—Whether cause of action statute-barred by limitation—Whether cause of action a statutory cause of action—Whether statutory cause of action a 'specialty' and accordingly limitation period of 12 years—Leasehold Reform Act 1967, s 8—Limitation Act 1980, s 8. **Collin v Duke of Westminster** [1985] **1** 463, CA.

LANDLORD AND TENANT (cont)—
  Leasehold enfranchisement (cont)—
    Long tenancy—
      Commencement—Tenancy granted for term exceeding 21 years—Grant of lease for 21 1/4 years expressed to take effect on date prior to date of execution and delivery of lease—Contract to grant lease of 10 1/4 years—Agreement two years later to extend term to 21 1/4 years from date of original contract—Date of subsequent execution of lease less than 21 years from date of expiry of term—Whether tenancy a long tenancy—Leasehold Reform Act 1967, s 3. **Roberts v Church Comrs for England** [1971] **3** 703, CA.
      Tenancy deemed to be long tenancy—Tenant under long tenancy becoming tenant of same property under short tenancy—Tenant deemed to be holding property under long tenancy—Assignment of short tenancy to third party—Third party occupying property as his residence for five years—Whether third party deemed to be tenant under long tenancy—Whether third party entitled to acquire freehold—Leasehold Reform Act 1967, s 3(2). **Austin v Dick Richards Properties Ltd** [1975] **2** 75, CA.
      Tenancy for term of years certain—Tenancy granted by housing association—Tenancy granted for term of years exceeding 21 years 'or until this Lease shall cease ... to be vested in a Member of the Association'—Tenant becoming and remaining a member of the association—Tenant claiming right to acquire freehold—Whether tenancy for a 'term of years certain'—Whether tenancy a 'long tenancy'—Leasehold Reform Act 1967, s 3(1). **Eton College v Bard** [1983] **2** 961, CA.
    Notice by qualifying tenants of claim to exercise right to collective enfranchisement—
      Discontinuance and subsequent proceedings—Tenants serving notice on freeholder—Freeholder serving counter-notice—Nominee company applying to court for declarations—Nominee company discontinuing proceedings—Tenants serving fresh notice—Freeholder serving fresh counter-notice—Nominee company applying again to court for declarations—Permission of court required for claimant to make another claim against same defendant arising out of same facts after discontinuing—Whether nominee company requiring permission of court—Leasehold Reform, Housing and Urban Development Act 1993, s 13—CPR 38.7. **Westbrook Dolphin Square Ltd v Friends Life Ltd** [2012] **4** 148, CA.
      Notice to be signed by each of the tenants—Execution of documents by companies—Company executing document by affixing common seal or by signature of two directors or director and secretary expressed to be executed by company—One director of corporate qualifying tenant signing notice—Whether notice signed by tenant—Whether notice a document requiring execution—Companies Act 1985, s 36A—Leasehold Reform, Housing and Urban Development Act 1993, ss 13, 99(5). **Hilmi & Associates Ltd v 20 Pembridge Villas Freehold Ltd** [2010] **3** 391, CA.
      Premises—Self-contained building or part of building—Whether self-contained part of building capable of comprising two or more self-contained parts—Leasehold Reform, Housing and Urban Development Act 1993, ss 3(2), 4. **Craftrule Ltd v 41-60 Albert Palace Mansions (Freehold) Ltd** [2010] **3** 952, Ch D; [2011] **2** 925, CA.
      Tenants serving notice on freeholder—Freeholder serving counter-notice claiming notice invalid—Tenants serving corrected notice—Freeholder claiming service of invalid notice precluding tenants from serving second notice—Whether second notice valid—Leasehold Reform, Housing and Urban Development Act 1993, s 13. **Sinclair Gardens Investments (Kensington) Ltd v Poets Chase Freehold Co Ltd** [2008] **2** 187, Ch D.
    Premises—
      Common parts—Common facilities—Acquisition on behalf of qualifying tenants of interest in any common parts where acquisition reasonably necessary for proper management and maintenance of common parts—Lessor covenanting to provide services of full-time caretaker in caretaker's flat for performance of specified duties—Whether caretaker's flat within common parts—Leasehold Reform, Housing and Urban Development Act 1993, ss 2(1)(b), (3), 19(1)(a)(ii), 101(1). **Cadogan v Panagopoulos** [2011] **2** 21, CA.
      Flat—Appurtenance let with flat—Outhouse let with flat—Tenant having fixed term lease of second floor flat in block together with separate fixed term lease of storeroom on sixth floor—Tenant claiming new lease of flat on same terms as existing lease but including storeroom within demise—Whether tenant entitled to have storeroom included in new lease—Whether storeroom 'appurtenance'—Whether storeroom 'outhouse'—Whether storeroom part of flat—Leasehold Reform, Housing and Urban Development Act 1993, ss 62(2), 101(1). **Cadogan v McGirk** [1996] **4** 643, CA.
      House and other premises—Appurtenance let with house—Paddock demised and occupied with house on land to be enfranchised—Whether paddock an 'appurtenance' to house—Whether 'appurtenance' restricted to incorporeal right where principal subject-matter land—Whether 'appurtenance' limited to land within curtilage of house—Whether paddock within curtilage of house—Leasehold Reform Act 1967, s 2(3). **Methuen-Campbell v Walters** [1979] **1** 606, CA.
      House and other premises—House and other premises occupied therewith—House connected with adjoining house by doorway—Whether adjoining house other premises—Leasehold Reform Act 1967, s 3(6). **Wolf v Crutchley** [1971] **1** 520, CA.
      House and other premises—Premises let to the tenant with the house—Meaning of 'let with'—Necessity for reasonably close connection between transactions of letting house and other premises—House and other premises let by landlords to separate tenants—Tenant of house subsequently acquiring tenancy of other premises—Whether house let to tenant with other premises—Leasehold Reform Act 1967, s 2(3). **Gaidowski v Gonville and Caius College, Cambridge** [1975] **2** 952, CA.
    Resident landlord exception—
      Whether continuity of interest required to satisfy resident landlord exception—Leasehold Reform, Housing and Urban Development Act 1993, s 10. **Slamon v Planchon** [2004] **4** 407, CA.
    Retention of management powers—
      Approval of scheme by court—Clause in lease imposing obligation on tenants to join association which would be responsible for upkeep of gardens—Scheme incorporating substance of clause—Scheme also providing that after enfranchisement powers and duties of landlords to be exercised by tenants' association—Provisions ancillary to power of management and control—Leasehold Reform Act 1967, s 19(1). **Abbots Park Estate, Re** [1972] **2** 177, Ch D.

LANDLORD AND TENANT (cont)—
  Leasehold enfranchisement (cont)—
    Retention of management powers (cont)—
      Approval of scheme by court—Obligations imposed on enfranchised tenants—Insurance—
        Obligation to insure property up to current cost of rebuilding—Whether power to enforce
        insurance included in powers of management—Leasehold Reform Act 1967, s 19(1). **Sherwood**
        Close (Barnes) Management Co Ltd, Re [1971] **3** 1293, Ch D.
      Approval of scheme by court—Tenants members and directors of landlord management
        company—Scheme including obligation designed to ensure that person acquiring enfranchised
        property became member of company—Provision not constituting 'powers of management'—
        Leasehold Reform Act 1967, s 19(1). **Sherwood Close (Barnes) Management Co Ltd, Re**
        [1971] **3** 1293, Ch D.
      Scheme—Charge in favour of landlord—Building society—Society prohibited from advancing
        money on property subject to charge in favour of landlord—Clause postponing charge arising
        under scheme to legal charge or mortgage being a first charge on property—Leasehold Reform
        Act 1967, s 19(8)—Building Societies Act 1962, s 32. **Abbots Park Estate, Re (No 2)** [1972] **3** 148,
        Ch D.
  Tenancy at a low rent—
    Letting value—Premium paid for grant of lease—Determination of 'letting value'—Whether letting
      value to be construed as including or excluding decapitalised annual value of premium—Whether
      annual value of premium should be determined on purely actuarial basis—Leasehold Reform Act
      1967, s 4(1) proviso. **Johnston v Duke of Westminster** [1986] **2** 613, HL.
    Rateable value—Appropriate day—House—House and premises—Leasehold including two
      houses—Tenant renovating two derelict adjoining cottages and erecting garages on
      forecourt—Cottages and garages appearing in valuation list for first time on different
      days—Tenant later converting cottages into single dwelling house—Appropriate day for
      determining rateable value of house—Leasehold Reform Act 1967, ss 1(1), 4(1)(a)—Rent Act 1977,
      s 25(3), (4). **Dixon v Allgood** [1987] **3** 1082, HL.
    Tenancy granted between end of August 1939 and beginning of April 1963—Rent payable at
      commencement of tenancy exceeding two-thirds of letting value of property—Determination of
      'letting value'—Rent obtainable in market—Tenancy subject to Rent Acts—Whether letting value
      restricted to rent permitted under Rent Acts—Leasehold Reform Act 1967, s 4(1) proviso.
      Gidlow-Jackson v Middlegate Properties Ltd [1974] **1** 830, CA.
    Tenancy granted between end of August 1939 and beginning of April 1963—Tenancy by way of
      building lease—Meaning of 'building lease'—Lease in consideration of agreement for substantial
      reconstruction of whole or part of house in question—Meaning of 'substantial reconstruction'—
      Distinction between 'reconstruction' and improvement—Leasehold Reform Act 1967, s 4(1)(d).
      Gidlow-Jackson v Middlegate Properties Ltd [1974] **1** 830, CA.
    Tenancy granted during period of rent restriction—Rent payable at commencement of tenancy
      exceeding two-thirds of letting value of property—Premium paid for grant of lease—
      Determination of letting value—Landlords obtaining maximum rent permitted under Rent Acts
      but not obtaining maximum premium on open market—When premium decapitalised total rent
      then not exceeding two-thirds of letting value—Whether letting value restricted to rent or
      including maximum premium obtainable in open market—Leasehold Reform Act 1967, s 4(1)
      proviso. **Manson v Duke of Westminster** [1981] **2** 40, CA.
  Tenant entitled to enfranchisement or extension—
    Leaseholder occupying basement and subletting other three floors—Whether entitled to acquire
      freehold—Leasehold Reform Act 1967, s 1(2)(a). **Harris v Swick Securities Ltd** [1969] **3** 1131, CA.
  Tenant occupying house as his residence—
    Occupation in right of the tenancy—Mortgage term to be disregarded in determining in what right
      tenant occupies—Meaning of 'mortgage term'—Purchaser having acquired term from mortgagee
      exercising power of sale—Whether term created under mortgage which no longer applies to the
      term a 'mortgage term'—Leasehold Reform Act 1967, s 1(2)(b). **Fairview, Church Street,**
      Bromyard, Re [1974] **1** 1233, Ch D.
    Occupation in right of the tenancy—Tenant not physically in occupation for three of past five
      years—Tenant making arrangements to sublet property—Mortgagees taking possession of
      property for part of five year period—Whether tenant 'occupying the house as his
      residence'—Whether tenant qualified to acquire freehold—Leasehold Reform Act 1967, s 1(1)(b).
      Poland v Earl Cadogan [1980] **3** 544, CA.
  Tenant's notice—
    Prescribed notice—Notice of desire to have 'the freehold or an extended lease'—Failure to delete
      alternative—Validity of notice—Transitional provisions—Leasehold Reform Act 1967, ss 5(1), 34.
      Byrne Road (33), Balham, Re [1969] **2** 311, CA.
    Tenant giving notice to landlords of desire to acquire freehold—Landlords opposing claim and
      citing current legal authority under which tenant's lease not qualifying as at low rent—Five years
      later legal decision defining letting value and thereby tenant becoming entitled to claim
      enfranchisement—Whether notice by tenant abandoned—Whether abandonment by conduct—
      Leasehold Reform Act 1967, s 20. **Collin v Duke of Westminster** [1985] **1** 463, CA.
    Tenant giving notice to landlords of desire to acquire freehold—Notice extending to property not
      properly included—Tenant subsequently giving notice to landlord relating to property not
      properly included in first notice—Tenant seeking to amend first notice—Whether amendment
      required—Whether conditions to be imposed—Whether tenant entitled to serve second
      notice—Leasehold Reform Act 1967, Sch 3, paras 3(1), 6(3). **Malekshad v Howard De Walden**
      Estates Ltd (No 2) [2004] **4** 162, Ch D.
  Tenants' rights of first refusal—
    Relevant disposal—Landlord contracting to sell premises subject to tenants' rights to purchase
      freehold, but without serving notices conferring rights of first refusal—Contract providing that
      service of statutory notices subject to satisfaction of condition precedent—Prospective purchaser
      serving notices inquiring whether tenants wished to exercise rights of first refusal—Tenant
      seeking service of notices by landlord—Whether 'relevant disposal' made—Whether landlord
      'proposing' to make relevant disposal—Point at which notices conferring rights of first refusal
      required to be served—Landlord and Tenant Act 1987, ss 4, 5, 18. **Mainwaring v Trustees of Henry**
      Smith's Charity [1996] **2** 220, CA.

LANDLORD AND TENANT (cont)—
    Leasehold enfranchisement (cont)—
        Valuation—
            Improvement—Former lessee converting property from single house into flats—Current lessee converting property back into single house and thereby increasing value of property—Whether lessee's works an 'improvement' for purposes of leasehold valuation if merely reversing work done by previous lessee that had depressed value of property—Leasehold Reform Act 1967, s 9(1A)(d). **Shalson v Keepers and Governors of the Free Grammar School of John Lyon** [2002] **3** 1119, CA; [2003] **3** 975, HL.
            Improvement—Statutory assumption requiring comparison between value of property in improved state and value if never improved—Whether assumption requiring value of potential for improvement to be excluded from valuation of unimproved house—Leasehold Reform Act 1967, s 9(1A)(d). **Fattal v Keepers and Governors of the Free Grammar School of John Lyon** [2005] **1** 466, CA.
    Leave to institute proceedings for breach of covenant to repair. *See* Breach of covenant to repair—Leave to institute proceedings, *above*.
    Licence to occupy land. *See* **Licence** (Licence to occupy land).
    Licence to occupy premises—
        Generally. *See* **Licence** (Licence to occupy premises).
        Tenancy distinguished. *See* Tenancy—Tenancy distinguished from licence, *below*.
        Whether notice to quit needed. *See* Notice to quit—Tenancy at will—Licence to occupy premises—Whether any notice needed, *below*.
    Licensed premises—
        Compensation for goodwill. *See* Compensation for goodwill in respect of business premises—Licensed premises, *above*.
        Tenancy—
            Exclusion of statutory protection for business tenancies. *See* Business premises—Tenancy—Exclusion of statutory protection—Licensed premises, *above*.
        Unauthorised licensable activities. *See* **Licensing** (Premises —Licensable activity—Unauthorised licensable activities).
    Limitation of action. *See* **Limitation of action** (Land—Adverse possession).
    Local authority—
        Generally. *See* **Housing** (Local authority).
        Local authority houses. *See* **Housing** (Local authority houses).
        Tenant's right to buy. *See* **Housing** (Local authority houses—Tenant's right to buy).
    Local authority. *See* **Housing**.
    Long leasehold—
        Acquisition of freehold or extended lease. *See* Leasehold enfranchisement, *above*.
    Long tenancy at low rent—
        Acquisition of freehold or extended lease. *See* Leasehold enfranchisement, *above*.
        Continuation as statutory tenancy—
            Contractual tenancy held by joint tenants but only one tenant resident in premises on expiration of tenancy by effluxion of time—Tenant declared bankrupt and trustee in bankruptcy disclaiming lease—Whether bankrupt tenant having right to remain in premises after determination date—Whether continuation tenancy part of bankrupt tenant's estate—Landlord and Tenant Act 1954, Pt I—Insolvency Act 1986, s 283. **De Rothschild v Bell (a bankrupt)** [1999] **2** 722, CA.
            Liabilities under former tenancy—Effect of statutory tenancy—Service charge—Lease of flat—Covenant in lease requiring tenant to pay service charge—Whether liability to pay service charge extinguished under provisions relating to statutory tenancy—Whether arrears of service charge amounting to 'failure to pay rent'—Whether liability to pay service charge amounting to 'liability ... related to property other than the dwelling-house'—Landlord and Tenant Act 1954, s 10(1). **Blatherwick (Services) Ltd v King** [1991] **2** 874, CA.
            Terms of statutory tenancy—Determination of terms by court—Principles applicable in determining terms—Fairness and justice as between parties—Relevance of terms of contractual tenancy—Lease of maisonette—Tenancy limited to residential use for one household only—Whether prohibition on sharing maisonette justified as term of statutory tenancy—Landlord and Tenant Act 1954, s 7(1). **Etablissement Commercial Kamira v Schiazzano** [1984] **2** 465, CA.
        Protection. *See* **Rent restriction** (Long tenancy at low rent).
    Magistrates—
        Procedure before magistrates—
            Recovery of possession. *See* Recovery of possession—Procedure before magistrates, *below*.
    Management of premises—
        Right to manage. *See* Right to manage, *below*.
    Mesne profits—
        Action for forfeiture of lease—
            Order pending determination of action. *See* Forfeiture of lease—Interim payments order—Action for forfeiture and mesne profits—Application by landlord for interim payments order pending determination of action, *above*.
    Mining lease—
        Coal. *See* **Coal mining** (Mining lease).
    Mortgage of lease—
        Forfeiture—
            Relief of mortgagees—Generally. *See* Relief against forfeiture—Mortgagee, *below*.
            Relief of mortgagees—Underlease. *See* Relief against forfeiture—Underlessee—Lease mortgaged—Relief of mortgagees, *below*.
            Relief of underlessees. *See* Relief against forfeiture—Underletting without consent—Mortgage, *below*.
    Mortgaged property—
        Covenant against assignment. *See* **Mortgage** (Sale—Leasehold property—Covenant by lessee in lease not to assign).
        Receiver. *See* **Mortgage** (Receiver—Tenancy).

LANDLORD AND TENANT (cont)—
  Mortgaged property (cont)—
    Unauthorised tenancy—
      Action by mortgagee for possession. *See* **Mortgage** (Action by mortgagee for possession—House subject to statutory tenancy under Rent Acts—Unauthorised tenancy of mortgaged property).
  Negligence—
    Duty to take care—
      Person to whom duty owed. *See* **Negligence** (Duty to take care—Person to whom duty owed—Social landlord).
    Information or advice—
      Assumption of duty of care—Duty to give information about change of circumstances affecting statement previously made. *See* **Negligence** (Information or advice—Assumption of duty of care—Duty to give information about change of circumstances affecting statement previously made—Landlord and tenant).
    Landlord's liability—
      Defective premises—Landlord's duty of care by virtue of obligation to repair. *See* **Negligence** (Defective premises—Landlord's duty of care by virtue of obligation to repair).
      Generally. *See* **Negligence** (Landlord's liability).
  New tenancy—
    Business premises—
      Generally. *See* Business premises, *above*.
      Opposition to grant of new tenancy. *See* Opposition to grant of new tenancy of business premises, *below*.
      Rent. *See* Rent—Business premises—New tenancy, *below*.
    Shop—
      Application to be made by occupier of shop—Occupier—Company carrying on business—Tenancy held by managing director—Application for renewal by managing director—Whether 'occupier'—Leasehold Property (Temporary Provisions) Act 1951, s 10(1). **Pegler v Craven** [1952] 1 685, CA.
      Form of application—Omission of particulars in application—Validity of application—Leasehold Property (Temporary Provisions) Act 1951, s 10(1)—County Court Rules 1936, Ord 40A, r 7, Form 342A, para 2(h), (k) (added by County Court (Amendment) Rules 1951). **Osborne v Snook** [1953] 1 332, CA.
      Opposition by landlord—Premises reasonably required for demolition or re-construction—Reasonableness—Leasehold Property (Temporary Provisions) Act 1951, s 12(3)(c). **Smart (JW) (Modern Shoe Repairs) Ltd v Hinckley & Leicestershire Building Society** [1952] 2 846, CA.
      Premises occupied wholly or mainly for purposes of a retail trade or business—Builders and decorators—Whether their premises shop within statutory definition—Leasehold Property (Temporary Provisions) Act 1951, ss 10(1), 20(1). **Frawley (M & F) Ltd v Ve-Ri-Best Manufacturing Co Ltd** [1953] 1 50, CA.
      Premises occupied wholly or mainly for purposes of a retail trade or business—Dairy business—Premises used for storage of milk bottles and refrigerator—No sales on premises—Whether premises a shop within statutory definition—Leasehold Property (Temporary Provisions) Act 1951, ss 10(2)(c), 20(1). **Deeble v Robinson** [1953] 2 1348, CA.
      Premises occupied wholly or mainly for purposes of a retail trade or business—Nine-tenths of products sold wholesale—Whole premises used from time to time for production for retail sale—Whether premises a shop within statutory definition—Leasehold Property (Temporary Provisions) Act 1951, ss 10(1)(a), 20(1). **Berthelemy v Neale** [1952] 1 437, CA.
      Reasonableness of grant—Matters for consideration of court—Rent—Quantum—Hardship—Financial disadvantage to landlord—Leasehold Property (Temporary Provisions) Act 1951, s 12(1), 3(e). **Kay (John) Ltd v Kay** [1952] 1 813, CA.
      Tenancy at will—Tenancy coming 'to an end...by the expiration of a notice to quit'—Determination by service of writ in action for possession—Leasehold Property (Temporary Provisions) Act 1951, s 10(1). **Martinali v Ramuz** [1953] 2 892, CA.
  Notice—
    Failure to give notice of breach of covenant—
      Forfeiture. *See* Forfeiture of lease—Notice of breach—Failure to give notice, *above*.
    Forfeiture—
      Breach of repairing covenant. *See* Forfeiture of lease—Breach of repairing covenant—Notice, *above*.
      Persons to be served with notice. *See* Forfeiture of lease—Notice of breach—Persons to be served with notice, *above*.
    Notice to quit. *See* Notice to quit, *below*.
    Opposition to grant of new tenancy—
      Business premises. *See* Opposition to grant of new tenancy of business premises—Notice of opposition, *below*.
    Termination of tenancy—
      Business premises. *See* Business premises—Notice by landlord to terminate tenancy, *above*.
  Notice to quit—
    Agricultural holding. *See* **Agricultural holding** (Notice to quit).
    Allotment. *See* **Allotment** (Allotment garden—Termination of tenancy).
    Assignment of lease. *See* Assignment of lease—Notice to quit, *above*.
    Business premises—
      Date for which statutory notice may be given—Monthly tenancy—Rent payable monthly in advance on first day of each calendar month—Landlord's notice to terminate on eleventh day of month—Effect—Landlord and Tenant Act 1954, s 25(1)(2). **Commercial Properties Ltd v Wood** [1967] 2 916, CA.
      Generally. *See* Business premises—Notice by landlord to terminate tenancy, *above*.
      Lease for 14 years determinable by either party by notice of desire to determine at end of seventh year—Notice given by landlord in statutory form under the Landlord and Tenant Act 1954—Effect of notice—Landlord and Tenant Act 1954, ss 25(1), 69(1). **Scholl Mfg Co Ltd v Clifton (Slim-Line) Ltd** [1966] 3 16, CA.

LANDLORD AND TENANT (cont)—
  Notice to quit (cont)—
    Business premises (cont)—
      Power of landlord to give notice—Landlord—Sub-tenancy of part of premises—Expiration of sub-tenancy and sub-tenant holding over as tenant from year to year—Notice by owner of freehold purporting to terminate sub-tenancy—Notice given before termination of tenant's lease—Date specified in notice as date of termination of sub-tenancy later than date on which tenancy would terminate—Whether notice effective—Landlord and Tenant Act 1954, ss 25(3)(4), 44(1). **Westbury Property & Investment Co Ltd v Carpenter** [1961] **1** 481, Ch D.
      Power of landlord to give notice—Notice specifying date for termination of tenancy—Notice by head landlord—Notice to sub-tenant—Notice specifying date for termination before date on which mesne landlord's tenancy due to expire—Whether notice valid—Landlord and Tenant Act 1954, ss 25(3) (4), 44(1) (as amended by the Law of Property Act 1969, s 14(1)). **Lewis v MTC (Cars) Ltd** [1975] **1** 874, CA.
      Power of landlord to give notice—Tenancy comprising two properties—Severance of reversion between properties—Apportionment of landlord's rights on severance—Power to give notice to terminate tenancy—Whether landlord of one property having power to give notice—Law of Property Act 1925, s 140—Landlord and Tenant Act 1954, s 25. **Dodson Bull Carpet Co Ltd v City of London Corp** [1975] **2** 497, Ch D.
      Service of notice—Registered letter addressed to tenants' former address forwarded to new address—Validity of service—Waiver of invalidity—Landlord and Tenant Act 1927, s 23(1)—Landlord and Tenant Act 1954, s 66(4). **Stylo Shoes Ltd v Prices Tailors Ltd** [1959] **3** 901, Ch D.
      Service of notice—Service at 'place of abode'—Delivery at business premises to which notice related—Validity—Counter-notice refusal—Landlord within period specified in notice, if measured from date of actual receipt by tenant—Whether any effect of reference to receipt of notice, as distinct from the giving of notice, in prescribed form, would be ultra vires—Landlord and Tenant Act 1927, s 23(1)—Landlord and Tenant Act 1954, ss 25(1), (5), 29(3), 66(1), s (2)—Landlord and Tenant (Notices) Regulations 1957 (SI 1957 No 1157), Form 7. **Price v West London Investment Building Society** [1964] **2** 318, CA.
      Validity of notice. See Validity of notice to quit—Business premises, *below*.
    Double rent—
      Tenant exercising option to determine lease—Landlord contending that notice of determination invalid—Tenant remaining in occupation of premises after expiry of notice—Landlord claiming arrears of rent on basis of continuing tenancy but alternatively claiming double rent against tenant for holding over—Whether landlord precluded from claiming double rent if not treating tenant as trespasser. **Ashworth (Oliver) (Holdings) Ltd v Ballard (Kent) Ltd** [1999] **2** 791, CA.
    Local authority housing. See **Housing** (Local authority houses—Notice to quit).
    Option to determine. See Lease—Option to determine, *above*.
    Service—
      Agricultural holding. See **Agricultural holding** (Notice to quit—Service).
      Business premises. See Notice to quit—Business premises—Service of notice, *above*.
      Intestacy—Service on President of Family Division—Address for service. **Practice Direction** [1985] **1** 832, Fam D.
      Intestacy—Service on President of Probate, Divorce and Admiralty Division. **Practice Direction** [1965] **3** 230, Prob.
      Intestacy—Service on Public Trustee—Address for service. **Practice Direction** [1995] **3** 192, Fam D.
      Mode of service—Mode of service different from that prescribed by statute—Notice received by tenant—Whether service effective—Landlord and Tenant Act 1927, s 23(1)—Landlord and Tenant Act 1954, s 66(4). **Stylo Shoes Ltd v Prices Tailors Ltd** [1959] **3** 901, Ch D.
    Tenancy at will—
      Licence to occupy premises—Whether any notice needed—Rent Act 1957, s 16. **Crane v Morris** [1965] **3** 77, CA.
      Sufficiency of notice—Letter from landlord's solicitors to tenant—Letter informing tenant that in absence of settlement solicitors have instructions to take proceedings against tenant for possession and damages. **Fox v Hunter-Paterson** [1948] **2** 813, KBD.
    Validity. See Validity of notice to quit, *below*.
    Waiver—
      Acceptance of rent in respect of period after termination of tenancy. **Clarke v Grant** [1949] **1** 768, CA.
      Service of second notice to quit—Effect. **Loewenthal v Vanhoute** [1947] **1** 116, KBD.
    Yearly tenancy—
      Tenant holding over on expiration of lease—Term in lease enabling landlord to determine lease by giving six month's notice expiring on any day—Consistency with yearly tenancy. **Thornfield (Godfrey) Ltd v Bingham** [1946] **2** 485, KBD.
      When yearly tenancy is determined—Whether fixed term is substituted by notice to quit—Tenancy for purposes of Landlord and Tenant Act 1954, s 25. **Rhyl UDC v Rhyl Amusements Ltd** [1959] **1** 257, Ch D.
  Nuisance—
    Liability of landlord for nuisance. See **Nuisance** (Landlord's liability).
    Possession—
      Recovery—Generally. See Recovery of possession, *below*.
  Objection to rent determined as fair rent. See **Rent restriction** (Rent—Determination of fair rent—Objection).
  Opposition to grant of new tenancy of business premises—
    Breach of covenant—
      Breaches of covenant to repair—Negotiations for rebuilding premises—Discretion of court over refusal of grant of tenancy—Landlord and Tenant Act 1954, ss 30(1)(a), 31. **Lyons v Central Commercial Properties Ltd** [1958] **2** 767, CA.
      Disclosure—Discovery relating to tenants' ability to perform covenants—Landlord and Tenant Act 1954, s 30(1)(a), (c), (g). **St Martin's Theatre, Re** [1959] **3** 298, Ch D.
      Judge taking into account matters not specified in notice of opposition—Whether judge could take into account tenant's general conduct towards obligations under tenancy—Landlord and Tenant Act 1954, s 30(1)(a), (b), (c). **Eichner v Midland Bank Exor and Trustee Co Ltd** [1970] **2** 597, CA.

LANDLORD AND TENANT (cont)—
  Opposition to grant of new tenancy of business premises (cont)—
    Intention of landlord to carry out substantial work of construction on part of holding—
      Proposed work involving substantial construction of part of premises—Tenant willing to allow access for work to be carried out—Whether work could reasonably be done without obtaining possession—Landlord and Tenant Act 1954, s 30(1)(f). **Whittingham v Davies** [1962] **1** 195, CA.
      Whether work could reasonably be done without obtaining possession of holding—Landlord and Tenant Act 1954, s 30(1)(f). **Fernandez v Walding** [1968] **1** 994, CA.
    Intention of landlord to carry out substantial work of reconstruction on the holding—
      Landlord showing that he could not reasonably carry out proposed work without obtaining possession—Meaning of 'possession'—Lease reserving to landlord right of entry to carry out necessary repairs—Proposed work of reconstruction requiring exclusive occupation of premises by landlord for period of months—Landlord entitled to carry out work as necessary repairs under reservation in lease—Similar reservation to be included in proposed new tenancy—Whether possession meaning legal right to possession—Whether landlord able to carry out work without obtaining possession—Landlord and Tenant Act 1954, s 30(1)(f). **Heath v Drown** [1972] **2** 561, HL.
      New tenancy on economically separable part of holding—Remainder of holding reasonably sufficient to enable landlord to carry out intended work—Landlord having bona fide intention to construct building for particular purpose occupying whole area of holding—Tenant wishing to have new lease of small part of holding—Whether open to tenant to argue that landlord's purpose could be achieved by building confined to remainder of holding—Landlord and Tenant Act 1954, ss 30(1)(f), 31A(1)(inserted by the Law of Property Act 1969, s 7(1)). **Decca Navigator Co Ltd v Greater London Council** [1974] **1** 1178, CA.
      Premises comprised in holding—Wooden garage and a wall covering part only of site—Whole of site to be concreted, but no building to be erected—Notice stating ground of opposition not following working of s 30(1)(f) of Landlord and Tenant Act 1954—Sufficiency of notice—Landlord and Tenant Act 1954, s 30(1)(f). **Housleys Ltd v Bloomer-Holt Ltd** [1966] **2** 966, CA.
    Intention of landlord to demolish or reconstruct premises comprised in holding—
      Conditional intention—Landlord opposing grant of new lease to tenant on ground of intended works—Works designed with material intention of leading to tenant's eviction—Whether open to landlord to oppose grant of new tenancy if works having no purpose other than to remove tenant—Landlord and Tenant Act 1954, ss 30(1)(f), 31A. **S Franses Ltd v Cavendish Hotel (London) Ltd** [2019] **2** 463, SC.
      Counter-notice by immediate landlords of sub-tenant—Freeholders' intention to develop site including premises sub-leased—Surrender by immediate landlords of their tenancy to freeholders before hearing—Validity of counter-notice—Whether freeholders intending 'to demolish or reconstruct' premises—Landlord and Tenant Act 1954, ss 26(6), 30(1)(f). **Marks v British Waterways Board** [1963] **3** 28, CA.
      Date at which fixed and genuine intention to reconstruct must exist—Landlord and Tenant Act 1954, s 30(1)(f). **Betty's Cafés Ltd v Phillips Furnishing Stores Ltd** [1958] **1** 607, HL.
      'Eggshell tenancy'—Tenant having 'eggshell' tenancy excluding load-bearing parts of building—Landlord intending to demolish 'eggshell' and opposing grant of new tenancy—Whether 'eggshell tenancy' constituting 'premises' capable of being demolished—Whether court entitled to look beyond programme of intended works when considering whether landlord could reasonably carry them out without obtaining possession—Landlord and Tenant Act 1954, ss 30(1)(f), 31A(1)(a). **Pumperninks of Piccadilly Ltd v Land Securities plc** [2002] **3** 609, CA.
      Intention to grant building lease providing for demolition and reconstruction—Whether 'intention to demolish or reconstruct' premises—Landlord and Tenant Act 1954, s 30 (1)(f). **Gilmour Caterers Ltd v St Bartholomew's Hospital (Governors)** [1956] **1** 314, CA.
      Local authority landlord—No resolution passed expressing intention—Intention inferred from relevant evidence—Landlord and Tenant Act 1954, s 30 (1)(f). **Poppett's (Caterers) Ltd v Maidenhead BC** [1970] **3** 289, CA.
      Proof of intention—Intention of limited company—Proposed expansion of company associated with landlord—No consideration by associated company—Whether firm intention to carry out reconstruction—When intention must be held—Landlord and Tenant Act 1954, s 30(1)(f). **Fleet Electrics Ltd v Jacey Investments Ltd** [1956] **3** 99, CA.
      Proof of intention—Intention stated to reconstruct whole of premises—Evidence of intention to reconstruct substantial part of premises only—Landlords joint owners—Death of one co-owner—Evidence by surviving co-owner and executor of deceased co-owner before probate—Whether intention proved—Landlord and Tenant Act 1954, ss 25(1), 30(1)(f). **Biles v Caesar** [1957] **1** 151, CA.
      Proposed demolition and reconstruction of premises—Intention to use for landlord's own business—Whether genuine intention to demolish and reconstruct—Landlord and Tenant Act 1954, s 30(1)(f)(g). **Fisher v Taylors Furnishing Stores Ltd** [1956] **2** 78, CA.
      Proposed demolition and reconstruction of substantial part of premises—Primary object use for landlord's own business—Whether necessary that primary object should be reconstruction—Landlord and Tenant Act 1954, s 30(1)(f). **Atkinson v Bettison** [1955] **3** 340, CA.
      Proposed inclusion of site in development scheme—Whether firm intention to carry out scheme—Date at which fixed and genuine intention to reconstruct must exist—Landlord and Tenant Act 1954, s 30 (1)(f). **Reohorn v Barry Corp** [1956] **2** 742, CA.
      Proposed work involving demolition of all buildings and replacement by others—Tenant willing to allow access for work to be carried out—Term of existing tenancy that landlord could do such work during tenancy and that tenant should allow access for it—Whether work could reasonably be done without obtaining possession—Landlord and Tenant Act 1954, s 30(1)(f). **Little Park Service Station Ltd v Regent Oil Co Ltd** [1967] **2** 257, CA.
      Reconstruct—Meaning—Landlord and Tenant Act 1954, s 30(1)(f). **Cadle (Percy E) & Co Ltd v Jacmarch Properties Ltd** [1957] **1** 148, CA.
      Reconstruct—Proposed work including alteration to shop-front involving considerable changes in physical character of premises—Totality of proposed work to be considered—Landlord and Tenant Act 1954, s 30(1)(f). **Bewlay (Tobacconists) Ltd v British Bata Shoe Co Ltd** [1958] **3** 652, CA.
      Reconstruct—Substantial interference with structure—Landlord and Tenant Act 1954, s 30(1)(f). **Joel v Swaddle** [1957] **3** 325, CA.

Opposition to grant of new tenancy of business premises (cont)—
Intention of landlord to occupy holding for purposes of business to be carried on by him—
Change of landlord between date of notice terminating tenancy and hearing of application for new tenancy—Effect—Whether landlord opposing application entitled to rely on notice served by previous landlord—Landlord and Tenant Act 1954, s 30(1)(g). **Wimbush (A D) & Son Ltd v Franmills Properties Ltd** [1961] 2 197, Ch D.

Disclosure relating to intention to occupy—Intention to occupy for business purposes—Discovery relating to landlord's financial position—Whether order for discovery appropriate—Landlord and Tenant Act 1954, s 30(1)(g). **St Martin's Theatre, Re** [1959] 3 298, Ch D.

Disclosure relating to intention to occupy—Undertaking to occupy premises—Landlord and Tenant Act 1954, s 30(1)(g). **Miller (John) (Shipping) Ltd v Port of London Authority** [1959] 2 713, Ch D.

Holding—Demised premises consisting of vacant site used as car park—Landlord's intention to use site in connection with his existing garage business by building workshop on part of site for car testing—Whether landlord intending to occupy 'the holding' comparised in the tenancy—Whether proposed development of site creating new holding—Landlord and Tenant Act 1954, s 30(1)(g). **Cam Gears Ltd v Cunningham** [1981] 2 560, CA.

Holding—Demised property buildings—Landlord's intention at time of hearing to demolish buildings and to convert and occupy site—Whether intention to occupy the holding—Landlord and Tenant Act 1954, ss 23(3), 30 (1)(g). **Nursey v P Currie (Dartford) Ltd** [1959] 1 497, CA.

Hospital governors—Board of governors of hospital as landlord—Premises to be conveyed by board to Minister of Health—Whether premises would be 'occupied' by the board for purposes of business carried on by it—Landlord and Tenant Act 1954, ss 23(2), 30(1)(g). **Hills (Patents) Ltd v University College Hospital Board of Governors** [1955] 3 365, CA.

Landlord providing accommodation, equipment and staff for Universities Central Council on Admissions—Council separate entity—Landlord a limited company—Voluntary winding-up of landlord to transfer property to chartered company taking over landlord's activities—Transfer not complete at date of hearing of tenant's application for new tenancy—Whether provision of accommodation, etc, was an 'activity' and thus a business—Whether landlord could carry on business after resolution for winding-up—Whether sufficient intention on part of landlord for purposes of s 30(1)(g) of Act of 1954—Companies Act 1948, s 281—Landlord and Tenant Act 1954, ss 23(2), 30(1)(g). **Willis v Association of Universities of the British Commonwealth** [1964] 2 39, CA.

Landlord's interest, a leasehold interest, created within five years—Date of creation—Whether date of execution of lease or of commencement of term—Sub-tenant's interest arising only on commencement of term, sub-tenant being also freeholder—Whether leasehold landlord debarred from opposition under s 30(1)(g)—Landlord and Tenant Act 1954, s 30(2). **Northcote Laundry Ltd v Donnelly (Frederick) Ltd** [1968] 2 50, CA.

Only part of holding to be used immediately for purposes of business—Whether necessary to show intention to make actual physical use of whole of holding—Landlord and Tenant Act 1954, s 30(1)(g). **Method Developments Ltd v Jones** [1971] 1 1027, CA.

Partnership business—Landlord intending to carry on business in partnership with wife—Whether intention that business should be carried on by him—Landlord and Tenant Act 1954, s 30(1)(g). **Crowhurst Park, Re** [1974] 1 991, Ch D.

Proof of intention—Proof that reasonable prospect of being able to occupy premises by voluntary act—Objective test—Intention—Planning permission—Doubt whether planning permission necessary and, if so, whether obtainable—Landlord and Tenant Act 1954, s 30(1)(g). **Gregson v Cyril Lord Ltd** [1962] 3 907, CA.

Reasonable prospect of carrying out intention to use premises for business purposes—Landlord requiring planning permission for change of use—Whether landlord having reasonable prospect of obtaining planning permission—Landlord and Tenant Act 1954, s 30(1)(g). **Westminster City Council v British Waterways Board** [1984] 3 737, HL.

Resolution of board passed—Landlord negotiating for lease of other premises—Undertaking given to court to occupy—Intention—Landlord and Tenant Act 1954, s 30(1)(g). **Espresso Coffee Machine Co Ltd v Guardian Assurance Co Ltd** [1959] 1 458, CA.

Restriction on landlord's right to oppose application—Landlord's interest purchased less than five years before end of tenancy—Acquisition of interest by landlords under contract made in June, 1954—No pecuniary consideration from landlords—Tenancy expiring in March, 1959—Landlord's notice not having effect for certain purposes until three months after application disposed of—Whether landlords' interest purchased after beginning of the period of five years ending with the termination of the current tenancy—Landlord and Tenant Act 1954, ss 25(1), proviso, 30(2), 64. **Lawrence (Frederick) Ltd v Freeman, Hardy & Willis Ltd** [1959] 3 77, CA.

Restriction on landlord's right to oppose application—Landlord's interest purchased or created less than five years before end of tenancy—Competent landlord—Person whose interest in tenancy will not come to an end within 14 months by effluxion of time—Immediate landlord having interest purchased or created more than five years before end of tenancy—Immediate landlord having successive interests—Immediate landlord not being competent landlord throughout five year period—Whether landlord entitled to oppose application for grant of new tenancy of business premises—Landlord and Tenant Act 1954, ss 30(1)(g), (2), 44(1), Sch 6, para 1. **Frozen Value Ltd v Heron Foods Ltd** [2012] 3 1328, CA.

Restriction on landlord's right to oppose application—Landlord's interest purchased or created less than five years before end of tenancy—Landlord's intention to occupy premises on termination of current sub-tenancy—Acquisition of lease in March, 1960—Fresh lease in April, 1960—Sub-tenancy granted in November, 1963—Termination of sub-tenancy in October, 1965—Landlord's interest within s 30(2) created more than five years before termination of sub-tenancy—Landlord and Tenant Act 1954, s 30(1)(g), (2). **Artemiou v Procopiou** [1965] 3 539, CA.

Restriction on landlord's right to oppose application—Landlord's interest purchased or created less than five years before end of tenancy—Lease of landlord expired—Landlord holding over as business tenant—Acceptance of conditional offer to grant lease—Conditions not fulfilled—Whether interest of landlord created within five years ending with termination of current tenancy—Landlord—Competent landlord—Landlord and Tenant Act 1954, ss 30(1)(g), (2), 44(1), 69(1), Sch 6, para 1. **Cornish v Brook Green Laundry Ltd** [1959] 1 373, CA.

LANDLORD AND TENANT (cont)—
  Opposition to grant of new tenancy of business premises (cont)—
    Intention of landlord to occupy holding for purposes of business to be carried on by him (cont)—
      Restriction on landlord's right to oppose application—Landlord's interest purchased or created less than five years before end of tenancy—Surrender of intermediate tenants' tenancy for no consideration within five years—Whether 'interest' 'purchased' by superior landlords—Evidence of intention of landlord—Landlord a limited company—No board meeting—Whether director's intention imputed to company—Landlord and Tenant Act 1954, s 30(1)(g), (2). **Bolton (HL) Engineering Co Ltd v TJ Graham & Sons Ltd** [1956] **3** 624, CA.
      Restriction on landlord's right to oppose application—Merger of interest, which but for merger would be interest of landlord purchased or created less than five years before end of tenancy—Surrender of intermediate lease less than five years before end of tenancy—Less than fourteen months of surrendered term remaining (but for merger) at time of request for new tenancy—Whether right to oppose application excluded—Landlord and Tenant Act 1954, ss 30(2), 44(1). **Diploma Laundry Ltd v Surrey Timber Co Ltd** [1955] **2** 922, CA.
      Restriction on landlord's right to oppose application—Railway board letting station car park to tenant and having successive freehold and leasehold interests in premises—Board transferring lease to company in same group—New landlord opposing grant of new tenancy—Ground for opposition available only if landlord acquiring interest in premises over five years before termination of tenancy—Landlord relying on board's successive interests to satisfy qualifying period—Whether successive interests qualifying where landlord first a freeholder and then lessee—Landlord and Tenant Act 1954, s 30(2). **VCS Car Park Management Ltd v Regional Rlys North East Ltd** [2000] **1** 403, CA.
      Transfer of business—Landlord's business transferred to company—Company virtually wholly owned by landlord—Whether to be treated as business carried on by landlord—Landlord and Tenant Act 1954, s 30(1)(g). **Tunstall v Steigmann** [1962] **2** 417, CA.
      Trustee—Landlord a trustee—Intention that cestui que trust should occupy for purposes of cestui que trust's business—Landlord and Tenant Act 1954, ss 30(1)(g), 41(2). **Sevenarts Ltd v Busvine** [1969] **1** 392, CA.
      Trustee—Term landlord to include 'beneficiaries under the trust or any of them'—Intended letting to beneficiary on commercial basis—Only beneficiaries having right as against trustee to occupy trust property by virtue of beneficial interests—'beneficiaries'—Landlord and Tenant Act 1954, ss 30(1)(g), 41(2). **Frish Ltd v Barclays Bank Ltd** [1955] **3** 185, CA.
    Interim rent. *See* Rent—Business premises—Interim rent, *below*.
    Notice of opposition—
      Form and sufficiency—Landlord and Tenant Act 1954, s 26(6). **Marks v British Waterways Board** [1963] **3** 28, CA.
      Intention to demolish premises on termination of current tenancy and carry out substantial work of construction—Work reasonably be done without obtaining possession—Notice stating ground of opposition—Notice did not state that landlord could not reasonably do the work without obtaining possession of the holding—Whether notice valid—Landlord and Tenant Act 1954, ss 25(1), 30(1)(f). **Bolton's (House Furnishers) Ltd v Oppenheim** [1959] **3** 90, CA.
      Sufficiency. **Housleys Ltd v Bloomer-Holt Ltd** [1966] **2** 966, CA.
    Procedure—
      Opposition on basis of intention to demolish or reconstruct premises—Determination in two stages—Issue whether opposition succeeds determined first—Terms of new tenancy, if any, to be settled at subsequent hearing—Landlord and Tenant Act 1954, s 30(1)(f). **Dutch Oven Ltd v Egham Estate and Investment Co Ltd** [1968] **3** 100, Ch D.
  Option—
    Determination of lease. *See* Lease—Option to determine, *above*.
    Purchase—
      Freehold reversion—Option separately assigned to mortgagee—Option exercised by mortgagee—Whether mortgagor entitled to conveyance of reversion on redemption. *See* **Mortgage** (Redemption—Lease with option to purchase freehold reversion).
      Tenant's option conferred by lease. *See* **Option** (Option to purchase—Tenant's option conferred by lease).
    Renewal of lease—
      Building lease. *See* Building lease, *above*.
      Generally. *See* Lease—Option to renew, *above*.
      Registration as estate contract. *See* **Land charge** (Estate contract—Option to renew lease).
  Order for possession. *See* Recovery of possession—Order for possession, *below*.
  Periodic tenancy—
    Creation. *See* Tenancy—Periodic tenancy—Creation, *below*.
  Possession—
    Action for. *See* Action for possession, *above*.
    Forfeiture. *See* Forfeiture of lease—Action for possession by lessor, *above*.
    Local authority. *See* **Housing** (Local authority—Possession).
    Local authority houses. *See* **Housing** (Local authority houses—Possession).
    Protected tenancy—
      Recovery of poseession. *See* **Rent restriction** (Possession).
      Sale of land. *See* **Sale of land** (Protected tenancy—Possession).
    Recovery—
      Generally. *See* Recovery of possession, *below*.
      Protected tenancy. *See* **Rent restriction** (Possession).
      Small tenement. *See* Small tenement—Recovery of possession, *below*.
      Statutory tenancy. *See* **Rent restriction** (Possession).
    Tenancy deposit schemes. *See* Tenancy—Tenancy deposit schemes—Notice for possession, *below*.
  Premises—
    Business premises—
      Generally. *See* Business premises, *above*.
    Fitness. *See* Fitness of premises, *above*.

LANDLORD AND TENANT (cont)—
Premises (cont)—
Occupied wholly or mainly for purposes of retail trade or business—
Shop—New tenancy. *See* New tenancy—Shop—Premises occupied wholly or mainly for purposes of a retail trade or business, *above.*
Premium—
Agreement for lease. *See* Agreement for lease—Premium, *above.*
Protected tenancy. *See* **Rent restriction** (Premium).
Proof of intention of landlord to demolish or reconstruct—
Business premises. *See* Opposition to grant of new tenancy of business premises—Intention of landlord to demolish or reconstruct premises comprised in holding—Proof of intention, *above.*
Proof of intention of landlord to occupy holding—
Business premises. *See* Opposition to grant of new tenancy of business premises—Intention of landlord to occupy holding for purposes of business to be carried on by him—Proof of intention, *above.*
Protected tenancy—
Generally. *See* **Rent restriction** (Protected tenancy).
Possession. *See* **Rent restriction** (Possession).
Premium. *See* **Rent restriction** (Premium).
Sale of land. *See* **Sale of land** (Protected tenancy).
Termination—
Joint tenancy. *See* **Rent restriction** (Statutory tenancy—Protected tenant in occupation on termination of protected tenancy—Joint tenancy).
Statutory tenancy. *See* **Rent restriction** (Termination of protected tenancy).
Transfer on termination of marriage. *See* **Divorce** (Property—Protected or statutory tenancy—Transfer of protected or statutory tenancy on termination of marriage).
Qualifying tenant—
Right to acquire new lease. *See* Lease—Right to acquire new lease, *above.*
Quarterly rent—
Time at which rent becomes due. *See* Rent—Time at which rent becomes due—Quarterly rent, *below.*
Quiet enjoyment—
Covenant. *See* Covenant—Quiet enjoyment, *above.*
Re-entry—
Arrears of rent—
Peaceable re-entry by landlord—Landlord changing locks but permitting underlease to continue—Whether lease forfeited by re-entry—Whether continuation of underlease consistent with re-entry—Whether tenant entitled to relief from forfeiture. **Ashton v Sobelman** [1987] **1** 755, Ch D.
Forfeiture of lease. *See* Forfeiture of lease—Right of re-entry, *above.*
Right of. *See* Relief against forfeiture—Right of re-entry, *below.*
Reconstruction—
Intention to reconstruct business premises—
Opposition to grant of new tenancy—Meaning of reconstruct. *See* Opposition to grant of new tenancy of business premises—Intention of landlord to demolish or reconstruct premises comprised in holding—Reconstruct—Meaning, *above.*
Recovery of possession—
Action for possession. *See* Action for possession, *above.*
Assured tenancy—
Mandatory grounds for possession—Unpaid rent—Tenant receiving housing benefit—Maladministration in payment of housing benefit causing rent arrears—Whether court could adjourn possession proceedings to allow tenant to pay rent arrears so defeating possession claim—Housing Act 1988, ss 7(3), 9(6), Sch 2, Pt 1, ground 8. **North British Housing Association Ltd v Matthews** [2005] **2** 667, CA.
Assured tenancy. *See* Recovery of possession—Order for possession—Assured tenancy, *below.*
Business premises—
Defence of absence of notice under Landlord and Tenant Act 1954—Tennis courts and premises let to tennis club—Club registered society under Industrial and Provident Societies Act 1893—Whether club carried on business—Landlord and Tenant Act 1954, s 23(1), (2). **Addiscombe Garden Estates Ltd v Crabbe** [1957] **3** 563, CA.
Closing order—
Local authority serving closing order on landlord—Landlord not serving notice to quit on tenant—Whether landlord entitled to possession order without serving notice to quit—Housing Act 1985, ss 276, 277. **Aslan v Murphy (Nos 1 and 2)** [1989] **3** 130, CA.
Costs—
Action in High Court—Claim arising out of Rent Restrictions Acts raised in defence—Right of landlord to costs in High Court—Increase of Rent and Mortgage Interest (Restrictions) Act 1920, s 17(2). **Lee v Carter (K) Ltd** [1948] **2** 690, CA.
Action in High Court—House within Rent Restrictions Acts—Acts not pleaded in defence—Right of landlord to costs in High Court. **Jaslowitz v Burstein** [1948] **1** 40, KBD.
County court action—
Order for possession—Jurisdiction to postpone execution of order. **Jones v Savery** [1951] **1** 820, CA.
Order for possession—No warrant to issue without leave of court—Limit to period of refusal of leave. **Air Ministry v Harris** [1951] **2** 862, CA.
Debt relief order. *See* **Insolvency** (Debt relief order—Moratorium from qualifying debts—Assured tenancy).
Insolvency. *See* **Insolvency** (Bankruptcy—Restriction on proceedings and remedies—Assured tenancy).
Judgment for possession—
Eviction—Tenant ejected by landlord without intervention of sheriff—Right of landlord personally to evict tenant. **Aglionby v Cohen** [1955] **1** 785, QBD.
Leave to proceed. *See* **Emergency legislation** (Landlord and tenant—Action for possession and rent—Leave to proceed).

LANDLORD AND TENANT (cont)—
    Recovery of possession (cont)—
      Local authority dwelling—
        Defence to claim for possession—Abuse of power. *See* **Housing** (Local authority houses—Management—Abuse of powers—Defence to claim for possession).
        Generally. *See* **Housing** (Local authority houses—Management—Eviction).
      Notice of proceedings for possession—
        Assured shorthold tenancy—Company landlord—Requirements relating to tenancy deposits—Prescribed form notice requiring signature by landlord or agent—Notice signed by authorised landlord company's property agent—Requirement that landlord confirm with signed certificate having provided information about deposit scheme—Certificate signed by director of landlord company—Whether company authentication required—Whether notice/certificate valid—Housing Act 1988, s 8—Housing Act 2004, s 213—Housing (Tenancy Deposits) (Prescribed Information) Order 2007, SI 2007/797, art 2—Assured Tenancies and Agricultural Occupancies (Forms) (England) Regulations 2015, SI 2015/620, reg 2. **Northwood (Solihull) Ltd v Fearn** [2022] **4** 399, CA.
        Assured shorthold tenancy—Domestic tenancy—Welsh legislation requiring landlords be licensed before serving notice to terminate tenancy—Whether notice of proceedings for possession 'notice to terminate a tenancy'—Whether notice served in breach of licensing requirement valid—Housing Act 1988, s 8—Housing (Wales) Act 2014, s 7(1), (2)(f). **Jarvis v Evans (Shelter Cymru intervening)** [2021] **2** 359, CA.
        Assured shorthold tenancy—Statutory provision requiring notice of proceedings for possession to specify earliest date for commencement of proceedings—Notices served with error specifying date as previous year—Whether reasonable recipient test applying—Whether notices valid—Housing Act 1988, s 8(3)(b), (4B). **Pease v Carter** [2020] **4** 519, CA.
      Order for possession—
        Application for permission to appeal—Order for possession stayed—Application to set aside stay—Statute providing for limitation on period of stay—Whether statutory provision applying to proceedings in court exercising appellate jurisdiction—Housing Act 1980, s 89(1). **Admiral Taverns (Cygnet) Ltd v Daniel** [2009] **4** 71, CA.
        Assured shorthold tenancy—Break clause—Landlord terminating tenancy during starter period—Whether at least six months' notice required—Meaning of 'term certain'—Housing Act 1988, ss 5, 21. **Livewest Homes Ltd v Bamber** [2020] **2** 181, CA.
        Assured shorthold tenancy—Recovery of possession on expiry or termination of assured shorthold tenancy—Mandatory grounds for possession—Right to respect for private and family life—Respect for home—Private landlord—Whether making of possession order on mandatory ground on application of private landlord breach of right to respect for private and family life—Whether proportionality test applicable—Housing Act 1988, s 21(4)—Human Rights Act 1998, Sch 1, Pt I, art 8. **McDonald v McDonald** [2015] **1** 1041, CA.
        Assured shorthold tenancy—Recovery of possession on expiry or termination of assured shorthold tenancy—Mandatory grounds for possession—Right to respect for private and family life—Respect for home—Private landlord—Whether making of possession order on mandatory ground on application of private landlord breach of right to respect for private and family life—Whether proportionality test applicable—Human Rights Act 1998, Sch 1, Pt I, art 8, Pt II, art 1. **McDonald v McDonald** [2017] **1** 961, SC.
        Assured tenancy—Periodic tenancy—Statutory provision requiring court to make order for possession of assured shorthold periodic tenancy if landlord serving notice specifying last date of period of tenancy and requiring possession thereafter—Whether notice valid if not specifying last date of period of tenancy but requiring possession on day known to be day immediately following last day of period—Housing Act 1988, s 21(4)(a). **Fernandez v McDonald** [2003] **4** 1033, CA.
        Assured tenancy—Suspended order for possession on condition as to payment of arrears of rent—Tenant seeking to exercise right to buy—Whether tenant eligible—Whether tenancy ending only when possession given up—Housing Act 1988, s 9(2), (3), (4). **Knowsley Housing Trust v White** [2007] **4** 800, CA; [2009] **2** 829, HL.
        Assured tenancy—Tenant holding property on assured fixed term tenancy—Tenant falling into arrears and landlord obtaining order for possession—Tenant applying for suspension of order and paying off arrears—Whether county court's power to grant relief from forfeiture applicable to proceedings for possession of property held under assured tenancy—County Courts Act 1984, s 138—Housing Act 1988, ss 5(1), 7(6), 45(4). **Artesian Residential Investments Ltd v Beck** [1999] **3** 113, CA.
        Enforcement order—Writ of possession stayed—Application to set aside stay—Statute providing for limitation on period of stay—Whether statutory provision applying to proceedings in High Court—Whether statutory provision applying to consent orders—Housing Act 1980, s 89(1). **Hackney London BC v Side by Side (Kids) Ltd** [2004] **2** 373, QBD.
        Secure tenancy—Suspended order for possession on condition as to payment of arrears of rent—Tenant breaching conditions of suspended possession order—Housing association obtaining warrant for possession—Tenant paying off arrears—Whether open to tenant to seek discharge or rescission of possession order—Housing Act 1985, s 85. **Knowsley Housing Trust v White** [2009] **2** 829, HL.
        Secure tenancy—Suspended order for possession on condition as to payment of arrears of rent—Tenant breaching conditions of suspended possession order—Whether tenancy ending on breach of conditions—Tenant dying—Whether right to apply for postponement of date for possession terminating on tenant's death—Housing Act 1985, ss 82(2), 85(2). **Austin v Southwark London BC** [2010] **4** 16, SC.
        Secure tenancy—Suspended order for possession on conditions as to payment of arrears of rent—Tenant becoming 'tolerated trespasser'—Tolerated trespasser liable for mesne profits—Whether liability for mesne profits continuing after giving up of possession until former landlord notified of giving up of possession—Housing Act 1985, s 85(3). **Jones v Merton London BC** [2008] **4** 287, CA.
        Secure tenancy—Suspended order for possession on conditions as to payment of arrears of rent—Whether date for possession having to appear on face of order—Appropriate form of order—Housing Act 1985, s 85(2). **Bristol City Council v Hassan** [2006] **4** 420, CA.

LANDLORD AND TENANT (cont)—
Recovery of possession (cont)—
Order for possession (cont)—
Suspension of order—Discretion—Protection from Eviction Act 1964, s 2(4). **Crane v Morris** [1965] **3** 77, CA.
Procedure before magistrates—
Application to magistrates for warrant—Notice of application—Service of notice—Service on tenant personally—Substituted service where tenant cannot be found—Need to prove due diligence to find missing tenant before substituted service permissible—Small Tenements Recovery Act 1838, s 2. **Stoker v Stansfield** [1972] **1** 938, QBD.
Evidence—Evidence required to be taken on commission—No power in justices to order evidence to be taken on commission—Right of party to obtain declaration in High Court—Small Tenements Recovery Act 1838. **Sivyer v Amies** [1940] **3** 285, Ch D.
Warrant for possession—Action by tenant for trespass—Application for stay of execution of warrant—Magistrates' refusal to suspend execution pending hearing of action for trespass—Whether magistrates bound to bind over tenant if proper sureties provided—Small Tenements Recovery Act 1838, ss 1-4. **R v Droxford Justices, ex p Knight** [1943] **1** 209, KBD.
Protected tenancy. See **Rent restriction** (Possession).
Rent restricted tenancy—
Offer of suitable alternative accommodation. See **Rent restriction** (Alternative accommodation).
Small tenement. See Small tenement—Recovery of possession, *below*.
Statutory tenancy. See **Rent restriction** (Possession).
Summary proceedings—
Tenant holding over not liable to summary proceedings. See **Land** (Summary proceedings for possession—Tenant holding over not liable to summary proceedings).
Suspended order for possession—
Leave to issue execution. See **Execution** (Leave to issue execution—Application—Suspended order for possession).
Unauthorised tenancy of mortgaged property—
Action by mortgagee for possession. See **Mortgage** (Action by mortgagee for possession—House subject to statutory tenancy under Rent Acts—Unauthorised tenancy of mortgaged property).
Winding up of company—
Possession order against liquidator. See **Company** (Winding up—Possession of property—Landlord of property leased to company applying to Companies Court for possession order against liquidator).
Rectification—
Lease. See Lease—Rectification, *above*.
Tenancy agreement. See Tenancy agreement—Rectification, *below*.
Reduction of rent. See Rent—Reduction, *below*.
Reinstatement of premises—
Covenant. See Covenant—Reinstatement of premises at end of term, *above*.
Relief against forfeiture—
Arrears of rent—
County court action. See Forfeiture of lease—Arrears of rent—County court action, *above*.
Discretion—Judgment for possession and arrears of rent obtained against one of two joint tenants—Court's discretion to grant relief—Supreme Court of Judicature (Consolidation) Act 1925, s 46—Common Law Procedure Act 1852, s 212. **Gill v Lewis** [1956] **1** 844, CA.
Long residential leases granted for premium at low rent mortgaged by subdemise—Lessor forfeiting leases for non-payment of rent and service charge—Mortgagee seeking relief from forfeiture—Whether service charge reserved in lease as additional rent constituting rent for purposes of relief against forfeiture—Whether mortgagee entitled to claim retrospective relief by way of reinstatement of lease—Law of Property Act 1925, s 146(2), (5)(b)—Supreme Court Act 1981, s 38—County Courts Act 1984, s 138. **Escalus Properties Ltd v Robinson** [1995] **4** 852, CA.
Mortgage expressly excluding power to let premises—Arrears for three months—Payment into court—Whether proceedings should be stayed under Common Law Procedure Act 1852, s 212—Whether statutory provisions applicable only where one half year's rent in arrear. **Standard Pattern Co Ltd v Ivey** [1962] **1** 452, Ch D.
Terms of relief—Mortgagee's application for relief—Whether previous history of mortgagee as tenant taken into consideration—Common Law Procedure Act 1852, s 210—Supreme Court of Judicature (Consolidation) Act 1925, s 46—Law of Property Act 1925, s 146(4). **Belgravia Insurance Co Ltd v Meah** [1963] **3** 828, CA.
Terms of relief—Power to extend time. **Chandless-Chandless v Nicholson** [1942] **2** 315, CA.
Terms of relief—Sub-lessees of part of premises—Whether sub-lessees required to pay total arrears in respect of whole of premises or only that part protection the arrears attributable to the premises sub-let to them—Law of Property Act 1925, s 146(4). **Chatham Empire Theatre (1955) Ltd v Ultrans Ltd** [1961] **2** 381, QBD.
Terms of relief—Whether lessor having to give credit for benefits accruing from exercise of right of re-entry when determining price to be paid by lessee for obtaining relief. **Bland v Ingram's Estates Ltd (No 2)** [2002] **1** 244, CA.
Underlessee—Exceptional case—Sub-sub-lessee's application for relief—Bombed site—No rent paid for twenty-two years—Covenant to rebuild unlikely to be performed—Intervention of rights of innocent third party—Whether relief should be granted—Law of Property Act 1925, s 146(4). **Public Trustee v Westbrook** [1965] **3** 398, CA.
Company—
Insolvency of company—Forfeiture of company's lease because of winding up—Company not entitled to apply for statutory relief—Whether court having equitable jurisdiction to grant company relief against forfeiture—Law of Property Act 1925, s 146(10). **Official Custodian for Charities v Parway Estates Developments Ltd** [1984] **3** 679, CA.
Insolvency of company—Forfeiture of company's lease because of winding up—Procedure to be followed to obtain relief against forfeiture. **Brompton Securities Ltd, Re (No 2)** [1988] **3** 677, Ch D.

LANDLORD AND TENANT (cont)—
Relief against forfeiture (cont)—
  Conditional relief—
    Breach of covenant—House converted into flats—Impracticability of reinstatement—Measure of damages. **Westminster (Duke) v Swinton, Adams (third party) and Williams (fourth party)** [1948] **1** 248, KBD.
  County court action—
    Arrears of rent. See Forfeiture of lease—Arrears of rent—County court action, *above*.
  Denial of landlord's title—
    Whether relief against forfeiture available to tenant where forfeiture arises out of disclaimer of landlord's title. See Forfeiture of lease—Denial of landlord's title—Relief against forfeiture, *above*.
  Immoral user of premises—
    Court's discretion to grant relief—Extent—Lease of ground floor and basement—Sublease of basement—Lessee and sublessee both guilty of permitting basement to be used for immoral purposes—Whether court able to restrict order for possession to basement part of demised premises only—Law of Property Act 1925, s 146(2). **GMS Syndicate Ltd v Gary Elliott Ltd** [1981] **1** 619, Ch D.
    Court's discretion to grant relief—Law of Property Act 1925, s 146(2). **Central Estates (Belgravia) Ltd v Woolgar (No 2)** [1972] **3** 610, CA.
    Suffering premises to be used as a brothel—User by sub-tenant—Knowledge of tenant—Imputation of knowledge—Court's discretion to grant relief—Law of Property Act 1925, s 146(2). **Borthwick-Norton v Romney Warwick Estates Ltd** [1950] **1** 798, CA.
  Jurisdiction—
    Breach of covenant—Non-payment of rent—Peaceable re-entry by landlord. **Lovelock v Margo** [1963] **2** 13, CA.
  Lease of chattels. See **Equity** (Forfeiture—Relief—Hiring of chattels—Machines leased to plaintiff).
  Mortgagee—
    Mortgagee not taking part in forfeiture proceedings—Whether mortgagee bound by forfeiture order. **Official Custodian for Charities v Mackey** [1984] **3** 689, Ch D.
  Refusal of relief—
    Grounds for refusal—Personal qualifications of tenant—Circumstances in which personal qualifications of tenant a relevant consideration—Personal qualifications of importance for preservation of value and character of property—Lease of country house to American citizen—Tenant banned from re-entering United Kingdom. **Bathurst (Earl) v Fine** [1974] **2** 1160, CA.
  Right of re-entry—
    Rent—Entitlement to rent—Lessee subleasing and mortgaging property—Receivers appointed by mortgage to collect rents from underlessees—Landlord obtaining forfeiture against lessee—Landlord obtaining order excluding mortgagees and receivers from demanding and receiving rent from underlessees—Whether landlord's receipt of rents from underlessees constituting full enforcement of right of re-entry—Whether underlessee's right to apply for relief against forfeiture ending when landlord obtaining exclusive entitlement to demand and receive rent—Law of Property Act 1925, s 146(4). **Hammersmith and Fulham London BC v Top Shop Centres Ltd** [1989] **2** 655, Ch D.
  Right to apply for relief—
    Charging order—Creditors obtaining charging order over flat to secure payment of debt owed to them by tenant—Creditors registering caution to protect charging order—Landlords bringing proceedings against tenant for non-payment of rent and obtaining possession order—Creditors not being informed of possession order but later applying to intervene in possession action—Whether holder of charging order entitled to apply for relief against forfeiture—Whether creditors should have been notified of possession proceedings—County Courts Act 1984, s 138—CCR Ord 6, r 3. **Croydon (Unique) Ltd v Wright (Crombie and anor intervening)** [1999] **4** 257, CA.
    Equitable chargee—Chargee not entitled to possession of property—Judgment creditor of lessee obtaining charging order absolute secured on lessee's lease—Lease forfeited for non-payment of rent—Judgment creditor seeking relief against forfeiture of lease—Whether court having jurisdiction to grant equitable chargee relief against forfeiture—Whether necessary for chargee to have interest in lease entitling him to possession. **Ladup Ltd v Williams & Glyn's Bank plc** [1985] **2** 577, Ch D.
    Equitable chargee—Claimant having equitable charge over lease—Landlord forfeiting lease for non-payment of rent—Tenants failing to claim relief from forfeiture—Whether equitable chargee of lease having right to claim indirect relief from forefeiture for non-payment of rent under High Court's inherent jurisdiction. **Bland v Ingram's Estates Ltd** [2002] **1** 221, CA.
    Loss of right—Re-entry by landlord—Effect of re-entry—Breach of covenant—Landlord effecting peaceable re-entry of premises for breach of covenant—Tenant regaining possession after re-entry—Landlord seeking possession order from court—Whether landlord 'proceeding' to enforce his rights of re-entry or forfeiture—Whether court having statutory jurisdiction to grant tenant relief against forfeiture—Law of Property Act 1925, s 146(2). **Billson v Residential Apartments Ltd** [1992] **1** 141, HL.
    Occupant of property acquiring title by adverse possession against landlord—Rent under lease paid by occupant and accepted by landlord—Landlord unaware that occupant not lessee nor acting on his behalf—Forfeiture of lease and re-entry by landlord—Whether occupant held under a yearly tenancy—Whether landlord estopped from denying occupant held under lease—Whether squatter having acquired title by adverse possession against leaseholder although not against freeholder, entitled to claim relief against forfeiture. **Tickner v Buzzacott** [1965] **1** 131, Ch D.
  Underlessee—
    Breach of covenant other than for payment of rent—Mortgage—Assignment of lease intended as security—Breach of covenant against assignment, etc—Winding-up of the company that was lessee and assignor—Whether mortgagee entitled to relief against forfeiture—Costs—Law of Property Act 1925, s 146(4). **Grangeside Properties Ltd v Collingwoods Securities Ltd** [1964] **1** 143, CA.

LANDLORD AND TENANT (cont)—
Relief against forfeiture (cont)—
Underlessee (cont)—
Business premises—Forfeiture of underlease in consequence of forfeiture of superior lease—Underlessee applying for vesting order granting him new lease of premises—Contractual term of underlease expiring before application heard—Landlord not terminating underlease in accordance with Landlord and Tenant Act 1954—Whether jurisdiction to make vesting order—Whether 'term' of underlease including period during which sublease continues prior to termination under 1954 Act—Whether 'term' of underlease limited to term specified in sublease—Law of Property Act 1925, s 146(4)—Landlord and Tenant Act 1954, s 24(1). **Cadogan v Dimovic** [1984] **2** 168, CA.

Lease mortgaged—Relief of mortgagees—Conditions of relief—Full indemnity to landlord in respect of all costs in proceedings for breach of covenant and relief from forfeiture—Law of Property Act 1925, s 146(4). **Egerton v Jones** [1939] **3** 889, CA.

Lease mortgaged—Relief of mortgagees—Loan to lessee by mortgagees secured by charge by way of legal mortgage—Action for possession by lessor for non-payment of maintenance contribution—Proceedings unknown to mortgagees until after forfeiture of lease—Relief barred by statute—Whether court having equitable jurisdiction to grant relief—Law of Property Act 1925, s 146(4). **Abbey National Building Society v Maybeech Ltd** [1984] **3** 262, Ch D.

Meaning of underlessee—Charge by way of legal mortgage—Relief to chargee against forfeiture—Law of Property Act 1925, ss 87(1), 146(4). **Grand Junction Co Ltd v Bates** [1954] **2** 385, QBD.

Meaning of underlessee—Written undertaking by lessee to execute legal charge or mortgage in favour of third party as security under guarantee—Payment by third party under guarantee—Application by third party for relief against forfeiture—Law of Property Act 1925, s 146(4), (5)(d). **Good's Lease, Re** [1954] **1** 275, Ch D.

Mortgaged lease—Tenant failing to pay costs of action for service charges—Lessor repossessing flat for failure to pay costs—Plaintiff mortgagee failing to apply for relief against forfeiture within six months of repossession—Whether restrictions on lessee applying for relief against forfeiture apply to mortgagee—Whether plaintiff as mortgagee entitled to apply for relief against forfeiture—County Courts Act 1984, ss 138, 140. **United Dominions Trust Ltd v Shellpoint Trustees Ltd** [1993] **4** 310, CA.

Relief to mortgagee—Whether new lease subject to mortgagor's right to redeem. **Chelsea Estates Investment Trust Co Ltd v Marche** [1955] **1** 195, Ch D.

Vesting order—Effect of vesting order—Lessee subleasing and mortgaging property—Landlord obtaining forfeiture against lessee—Mortgagee of lease obtaining vesting order granting new lease—Whether vesting of new lease in mortgagee automatically reinstating underlessee's leases—Law of Property Act 1925, s 146(4). **Hammersmith and Fulham London BC v Top Shop Centres Ltd** [1989] **2** 655, Ch D.

Vesting order—Effect of vesting order—Lessee subleasing and mortgaging property—Landlord obtaining forfeiture against lessee—Mortgagee of lessee intending to obtain vesting order for new mortgage—Whether vesting order would have retrospective effect—Whether landlord or mortgagee entitled to receive rents from sublessees prior to vesting order being made—Law of Property Act 1925, s 146(4). **Official Custodian for Charities v Mackey** [1984] **3** 689, Ch D.

Underletting without consent—
Grounds for relief—Law of Property Act 1925, s 146(2). **House Property and Investment Co Ltd v James Walker, Goldsmith and Silversmith Ltd** [1947] **2** 789, KBD.

Mortgage—Sub-demise by way of security—Underlessees of sound financial standing—Winding-up of company that was lessee—Whether underlessees entitled to relief. **Grangeside Properties Ltd v Collingwoods Securities Ltd** [1964] **1** 143, CA.

Relief of underlessee—Period of lease granted to underlessee—Property controlled under Rent Restrictions Acts—Increase of Rent and Mortgage Interest (Restrictions) Act 1920, s 15(3)—Law of Property Act 1925, s 146(4)—Underlessee an assisted person—Contribution assessed at nil—Order to pay sum equal to party and party costs as condition of relief under Law of Property Act 1925, s 146(4)—Legal Aid and Advice Act 1949, s 2(2)(e). **Factors (Sundries) Ltd v Miller** [1952] **2** 630, CA.

Renewal of lease—
Covenant. See Covenant—Renewal of lease, *above.*
Option. See Lease—Option to renew, *above.*
Perpetual right of renewal—
Construction—Lease for three years with option to renew for further period of three years on same terms 'including the present covenant for renewal'—Law of Property Act 1922, s 145, Sch XV, para 5. **Greenwood's Agreement, Re** [1950] **1** 436, CA.

Construction—Notice to quit by head landlords—Landlord for five years with option to renew for further period of five years on the same terms 'as are herein contained (including an option to renew such lease for the further term of five years at the expiration thereof)'—Whether lease perpetually renewable—Law of Property Act 1922, Sch 15, para 5. **Hopkins's Lease, Re** [1972] **1** 248, CA.

Construction—Option to renew tenancy for a 'period of months on the same terms and conditions including this clause'—Whether tenant has perpetual right of renewal. **Green v Palmer** [1944] **1** 670, Ch D.

Rent—
Review. See Rent—Review—Renewal of lease, *below.*

Rent—
Administrator of deceased tenant—
Liability for rent. See **Executor and administrator** (Contract—Liability of administrator—Tenancy agreement—Implied obligation—Obligation to pay rent so long as tenancy subsisting).

Agreement for increase—
Rent book required by law not supplied by landlord—Whether rent recoverable by action—Landlord and Tenant Act 1962, s 4. **Shaw v Groom** [1970] **1** 702, CA.

Agricultural holding—
Arbitration. See **Agricultural holding** (Arbitration—Rent).

LANDLORD AND TENANT (cont)—
  Rent (cont)—
    Arrears—
      Action to recover—Limitation of action. *See* **Limitation of action** (Land—Action for recovery of arrears of rent).
      Forfeiture of lease. *See* Forfeiture of lease—Arrears of rent, *above.*
      Insolvency. *See* **Insolvency** (Bankruptcy—Restriction on proceedings and remedies—Assured tenancy—Arrears of rent).
      Re-entry. *See* Re-entry—Arrears of rent, *above.*
      Relief against forfeiture of lease. *See* Relief against forfeiture—Arrears of rent, *above.*
    Assignment of lease—
      Obligation to pay rent. *See* Assignment of lease—Obligation to pay rent, *above.*
    Business premises—
      Interim rent—Application by landlord for determination of rent during continuance of tenancy—Date from which rent payable—Landlord and Tenant Act 1954, s 24A. **Stream Properties Ltd v Davis** [1972] 2 746, Ch D.
      Interim rent—Application by landlord for determination of rent during continuance of tenancy—Determination of interim rent—Application by landlord—Discretion of court—Rent which it would be reasonable for tenant to pay—Market rent of hypothetical yearly tenancy—Regard to be had to rent payable under terms of existing tenancy—Landlord and Tenant Act 1954, ss 24A (added by the Law of Property Act 1969, ss 3(1)), 34. **English Exporters (London) Ltd v Eldonwall Ltd** [1973] 1 726, Ch D.
      Interim rent—Application by landlord for determination of rent during continuance of tenancy—Determination of interim rent—Determination of rent for new tenancy—Factors to be taken into consideration—State of disrepair of premises—Power of court to award differential rent—Landlord and Tenant Act 1954, ss 24A (as inserted by the Law of Property Act 1969, s 3(1)), 34. **Fawke v Viscount Chelsea** [1979] 3 568, CA.
      Interim rent—Application by landlord for determination of rent during continuance of tenancy—Determination of rent—Landlord and Tenant Act 1954, s 24A(3) (added by Law of Property Act 1969, s 3(1)). **Regis Property Co Ltd v Lewis & Peat Ltd** [1970] 3 227, Ch D.
      Interim rent—Date from which interim rent payable—Tenant applying for new tenancy—Landlord applying for determination of interim rent in answer to the tenant's application—Landlord subsequently giving notice of application for determination of interim rent—Whether rent to be fixed at date of landlord's answer or date of notice of application—Landlord and Tenant Act 1954, s 24A(2)—CCR Ord 13, r 1. **Thomas v Hammond-Lawrence** [1986] 2 214, CA.
      Limitation—Prohibition on increase in rate of rent—Counter-inflation legislation—Rent not payable at rate exceeding standard rate—Standard rate—Rate at which rent was payable in respect of premises on specified date—Different tenancies of separate parts of premises subsisting on specified date—Subsequent lease of premises—Single tenancy of whole premises—Whether 'standard rate' for premises as a whole—Counter-inflation (Business Rents) Order 1972 (SI 1972 No 1850), paras 2(2), 4—Counter-Inflation (Business Rents) Order 1973 (SI 1973 No 741), arts 3-5. **Number 20 Cannon Street Ltd v Singer & Friedlander Ltd** [1974] 2 577, Ch D.
      New tenancy—Determination of rent—Disregard of improvements carried out by tenant—Whether improvements made before current tenancy to be disregarded in determining rent payable on grant of new tenancy—Landlord and Tenant Act 1954, s 34(c). **Wonderland, Cleethorpes, Re** [1963] 2 775, HL.
      New tenancy—Determination of rent—Evidence of trading records—Admissibility—Landlord and Tenant Act 1954, s 34(1). **Barton (W J) Ltd v Long Acre Securities Ltd** [1982] 1 465, CA.
      New tenancy—Power of tribunal to fix rent above standard rent—Increase of Rent and Mortgage Interest (Restrictions) Act 1920, s 1—Landlord and Tenant Act 1927, s 5(2). **Rose v Hurst** [1949] 2 24, CA.
      Terms of new tenancy. *See* Business premises—Terms of new tenancy—Rent, *above.*
    Certainty—
      Rent review—Retrospective operation. *See* Rent—Review—Retrospective operation—Certainty of rent, *below.*
    Claim for rent—
      Distress for rent—Set-off—Cross-claim for damages—Whether tenant entitled to invoke set-off against claim by landlord to levy distress. **Eller v Grovecrest Investments Ltd** [1994] 4 845, CA.
      Set-off—Whether tenant entitled to set off against rent due to transferee of reversion a claim for unliquidated damages against original landlord for breach of lease or agreement under which lease was granted—Law of Property Act 1925, ss 136, 141—Landlord and Tenant (Covenants) Act 1995, s 3. **Edlington Properties Ltd v JH Fenner and Co Ltd** [2006] 1 98, QBD; [2006] 3 1200, CA.
    Coal mining lease, under. *See* **Coal mining** (Mining lease—Rent).
    Collection—
      Appointment of receiver to collect rent. *See* **Receiver** (Appointment—Protection or preservation of property—Landlord failing to collect rents or to repair).
    Covenant to pay on gold basis—
      Payment to be either in gold or in Bank of England notes to the equivalent value in gold sterling of specified sum—Whether fixing amount to be paid or determining manner in which fixed amount to be discharged. **Treseder-Griffin v Co-op Insurance Society Ltd** [1956] 2 33, CA.
    Covenant to pay rent and service charge without deduction or set-off—
      Whether unfair contract term. *See* Covenant—Payment of rent and service charge without deduction or set-off, *above.*
    Distress—
      Distress on goods comprised in hire-purchase agreement. *See* **Hire-purchase** (Distress—Landlord and tenant).
      Generally. *See* **Distress** (Distress for rent).
    Eviction for non-payment—
      Local authority dwelling. *See* **Housing** (Local authority houses—Management—Eviction—Non-payment of rent).

LANDLORD AND TENANT (cont)—
Rent (cont)—
    Exclusive use of part of house given in return for services—
        Whether performance of services constituting rent. *See* **Rent restriction** (Rent—Exclusive use of
        part of house given in return for services).
    Fair rent—
        Generally. *See* **Rent restriction** (Fair rent).
        Local authority houses. *See* **Housing** (Local authority houses—Rent—Fair rent).
    Forfeiture of lease—
        Effect. *See* Forfeiture of lease—Effect—Rent, *above*.
    Grant of new lease to existing tenant—
        New lease increasing rent payable—Time from which new rent operative—Covenant by tenant to
        pay new rent from date before execution of new lease—Whether tenant liable to pay rent at new
        rate from prior date or only from date of execution of lease. **Bradshaw v Pawley** [1979] **3** 273,
        Ch D.
    House constructed under building licence—
        Permitted rent. *See* **Housing** (House constructed under building licence—Permitted rent).
    Income tax—
        Annual value of land. *See* **Income tax** (Land—Annual value—Rent).
        Damages in lieu of rent. *See* **Income tax** (Capital or income receipts—Damages—Loss of profit in
        respect of property—Damages awarded to landlord against tenant unlawfully remaining in
        occupation of property).
        Mining rents. *See* **Income tax** (Mining rents).
    Increase—
        Notice—Local authority housing. *See* **Housing** (Local authority houses—Rent—Notice of increase).
        Rent of rural worker. *See* **Agriculture** (Housing—Rural worker—Rent—Right to increase).
    Interim payment order—
        Jurisdiction of county court to make order. *See* **County court** (Jurisdiction—Interim payment).
    Joint tenancy—
        Death of one of two joint tenants—Tenancy of committee rooms—Liability of executors for
        contribution towards payment of rent—Law of Property Act 1925, ss 34(2), 36. **Cunningham-Reid
        v Public Trustee and Underwood** [1944] **2** 6, CA.
    Limitation—
        Prohibition on increase in rate of rent—Business premises—Premises occupied by the tenant for
        the purposes of a business carried on by him—Business—Government business—Premises
        leased to Secretary of State on behalf of Crown—Crown tenant of premises—Premises occupied
        as government offices—Whether premises occupied by tenant 'for the purposes of a business
        carried on by him'—Counter-Inflation (Business Rents) Order 1972 (SI 1972 No 1850), art 2(2).
        Town Investments Ltd v Dept of the Environment [1977] **1** 813, HL.
        Prohibition on increase in rate of rent—Business premises—Premises occupied by the tenant for
        the purposes of a business carried on by him—Premises leased to Secretary of State on behalf of
        Crown—Crown tenant of premises—Premises occupied by Crown servants in other government
        departments—Whether premises 'occupied' by Crown—Counter-Inflation (Business Rents) Order
        1972 (SI 1972 No 1850), art 2(2). **Town Investments Ltd v Dept of the Environment** [1977] **1** 813,
        HL.
        Prohibition on increase in rate of rent—Business premises—Premises occupied by the tenant for
        the purposes of a business carried on by him—Tenant of premises—Premises leased to Secretary
        of State on behalf of Crown—Whether Secretary of State or Crown the tenant—Counter-Inflation
        (Business Rents) Order 1972 (SI 1972 No 1850), art 2(2). **Town Investments Ltd v Dept of the
        Environment** [1977] **1** 813, HL.
    Local authority houses. *See* **Housing** (Local authority houses—Rent).
    Low rent—
        Tenancy at low rent—Continuation as statutory tenancy. *See* Long tenancy at low rent, *above*.
    Payment—
        Covenant to guarantee payment of rent—Whether covenant touching and concerning the land. *See*
        Covenant—Covenant running with land—Covenant to guarantee lessee's payment of rent, *above*.
        Payment of rent 'without any deduction'—Meaning of 'deduction'—Landlord's breach of covenant
        causing tenant damage—Tenant withholding payment of rent—Landlord claiming possession of
        premises and arrears of rent—Tenant counterclaiming for damages in respect of disruption to
        business—Whether tenant entitled to claim equitable right of set-off—Whether right of set-off
        excluded by words 'without any deduction'. **Connaught Restaurants Ltd v Indoor Leisure Ltd**
        [1994] **4** 834, CA.
        Recognition of landlord's title—Estoppel. *See* Title—Right of tenant to question landlord's
        title—Estoppel, *below*.
        Recognition of landlord's title—Payment in ignorance of true state of title—Onus of proof. **Hindle v
        Hick Bros Manufacturing Co Ltd** [1947] **2** 825, CA.
    Permitted rent—
        House constructed under building licence. *See* **Housing** (House constructed under building
        licence—Permitted rent).
    Rebate—
        Local authority houses. *See* **Housing** (Local authority houses—Rent—Rebate).
    Recovery—
        Limitation of action—Evacuation area. *See* **Emergency legislation** (Evacuation area—Recovery of
        rent—Limitation of action).
    Reduction of rent—
        Sub-letting room without consent—No consideration—Reduced rent paid—Binding effect of
        promise—Effect of ending of war-time conditions. **Central London Property Trust Ltd v High Trees
        House Ltd (1946)** [1956] **1** 256, KBD.
    Registered rent. *See* **Rent restriction** (Rent).
    Renewal of lease—
        Option to renew at rent stated. *See* Lease—Option to renew, *above*.

LANDLORD AND TENANT (cont)—
  Rent (cont)—
    Rent reserved—
      Sub-letting without consent—Lease—Estate agent's commission—Commission calculated as percentage of year's rent—Rent defined as 'rent reserved by the letting'—Amount of rent payable under lease restricted by statute—Counter-inflation legislation—Restrictions on rent of business premises—Agreed rent under lease £20,000—Rent payable restricted by statute to £600—Whether 'rent reserved' rent provided for by lease or rent payable by virtue of statute. **Brecker Grossmith & Co v Canworth Group Ltd** [1974] **3** 561, QBD.
      Suspension of payment of rent—Lease providing for rack rent and 'additional rents' in respect of service charge and insurance—Clause providing for suspension of 'rent hereby reserved' during period in which premises rendered unfit for occupation by insured event—Whether rent suspension extending to additional rents. **P & O Property Holdings Ltd v International Computers Ltd** [2000] **2** 1015, Ch D.
    Rent restriction. *See* **Rent restriction**.
    Review—
      Arbitration—Commencement—Extension of time fixed by agreement. *See* **Arbitration** (Commencement—Extension of time fixed by agreement—Rent review).
      Arbitration—Evidence—Rents at which comparable properties recently let—Whether award of another arbitrator in review of rent of comparable property admissible evidence in arbitration. **Land Securities plc v Westminster City Council** [1993] **4** 124, Ch D.
      Arbitration—Leave to appeal against award. *See* **Arbitration** (Award—Leave to appeal against award—Factors to be considered by court when deciding whether to grant leave—Rent review).
      Basis of rent review—Review of ground rent—Rent to be reviewed on basis of 'reasonable current ground rental value of the demised premises'—Whether notional letting to be on same terms and conditions as original lease—Whether notional letting to be on terms and conditions of hypothetical lease of a bare site for development. **Basingstoke and Deane BC v Host Group Ltd** [1988] **1** 824, CA.
      Basis of rent review—Terms 'other than as to the yearly rent'—Rent review to be undertaken on basis of terms of lease 'other than as to the yearly rent'—Whether terms 'as to the yearly rent' referring only to amount of rent payable immediately before rent review—Whether terms 'as to the yearly rent' including terms relating to rent reviews—Whether provisions for future rent reviews to be taken into account on rent review. **British Gas Corp v Universities Superannuation Scheme Ltd** [1986] **1** 978, Ch D.
      Basis of rent review—Terms 'other than the amount of rent hereby reserved'—Rent review to be undertaken on basis of terms of lease 'other than the amount of rent hereby reserved'—Whether 'amount of rent' referring only to fixed amount of rent payable immediately before rent review—Whether 'amount of rent' including rent ascertained by a formula under a rent review—Whether provisions for future rent reviews to be taken into account on rent review. **Datastream International Ltd v Oakeep Ltd** [1986] **1** 966, Ch D.
      Basis of rent review—Terms 'other than those relating to rent'—Rent review to be undertaken on basis of terms of lease 'other than those relating to rent'—Whether terms 'relating to rent' referring only to amount of rent payable immediately before rent review—Whether terms 'relating to rent' including terms relating to rent reviews—Whether provisions for future rent reviews to be taken into account on rent review. **MFI Properties Ltd v BICC Group Pension Trust Ltd** [1986] **1** 974, Ch D.
      Failure to comply with time limits—Construction of clause—Presumption that time not of the essence—Rebuttal of presumption—Contra-indications in express words of lease or in interrelation of rent review clause itself and other clauses or in surrounding circumstances—Failure to comply vith time limit not precluding landlord from invoking clause unless presumption that time not of the essence rebutted. **United Scientific Holdings Ltd v Burnley BC** [1976] **2** 220, CA; [1977] **2** 62, HL.
      Failure to comply with time limits—Effect—Clause providing machinery for determination of rent for specified period of term—No other provision in lease for rent during that period—Notice to operate clause to be given by landlord within specified time limits before termination of preceding period of term—Failure of landlord to give notice within time limits—Validity of notice given subsequently. **Kenilworth Industrial Sites Ltd v EC Little & Co Ltd** [1975] **1** 53, CA.
      Failure to comply with time limits—Effect—Clause providing machinery for determination of rent for specified period of term—No other provision in lease for rent during that period—Notice to operate clause to be given by landlord within specified time limits before termination of preceding period of term—Lease expressly providing that time of the essence—Failure of landlord to give notice within time limits—Whether failure precluding recourse to machinery for determination of rent—Whether proper inference that parties would have intended old rent to continue. **Weller v Akehurst** [1981] **3** 411, Ch D.
      Failure to comply with time limits—Effect—Delay in serving assessment notice to initiate rent review—Time not of the essence in serving notice—Whether delay, however unreasonable, precluding landlord from relying on notice. **Amherst v James Walker Goldsmith & Silversmith Ltd** [1983] **2** 1067, CA.
      Failure to comply with time limits—Effect—Lease providing that rent might be reviewed at option of lessor at end of seventh year of term—Condition precedent that lessor serve notice of intention to exercise option 'not later than two quarters before the expiry' of the seventh year—Seventh year expiring on 7th July 1971—Notice served by lessor on 22nd February—Notice served 'later than two quarters' before expiry of seventh year—Whether strict adherence to time limit necessary—Whether lessor entitled to equitable relief. **Samuel Properties (Developments) Ltd v Hayek** [1972] **3** 473, CA.
      Failure to comply with time limits—Option to require review—Right conferred on landlord in nature of option—Right conferred on landlord to require arbitration in event of failure to agree on revised rent—Right to be exercised within specified time limit—Whether time limit mandatory—Whether landlord capable of making valid application for arbitration after expiry of time limit. **Mount Charlotte Investments Ltd v Leek and Westbourne Building Society** [1976] **1** 890, Ch D.

311

LANDLORD AND TENANT (cont)—
  Rent (cont)—
    Review (cont)—

Failure to comply with time limits—Presumption that time not of essence—Correlation between rent review clause and time limit in tenant's break clause—Both parties having option to initiate rent review—Rent review clause providing for arbitration to determine new rent on parties' failure to agree—Arbitrator's decision to be obtained within specified time limit—Landlord serving notice of rent review after expiry of time limit—Whether correlation between rent review clause and break clause making time of essence—Whether presumption that time not of the essence displaced. **Metrolands Investments Ltd v JH Dewhurst Ltd** [1986] **3** 659, CA.

Failure to comply with time limits—Presumption that time not of the essence—Whether express deeming provision sufficient to displace presumption that time not of the essence in rent review clause. **Starmark Enterprises Ltd v CPL Distribution Ltd** [2002] **4** 264, CA.

Issue estoppel. *See* **Estoppel** (Issue estoppel—Rent review clause).

Reasonable rent—Improvements made to demised premises—Rent to be stated rent or a reasonable rent for the demised premises—Improvements made pursuant to landlord's licence and at tenant's expense—Improvements becoming part of demised premises—Whether improvements to be taken into account in assessing reasonable rent. **Cuff v J & F Stone Property Co Ltd** [1978] **2** 833, Ch D.

Reasonable rent—Improvements made to demised premises—Rent to be the higher of existing rent or a reasonable rent for the demised premises—Improvements made pursuant to landlord's licence and at tenant's expense—Improvements becoming part of demised premises—Whether improvements to be taken into account in assessing reasonable rent. **Ponsford v HMS Aerosols Ltd** [1978] **2** 837, HL.

Renewal of lease—New rent payable to be rent agreed between parties or fixed by arbitrator in default of agreement—Whether rent to be fair rent as between parties or market rent—Whether improvements made by tenant's predecessor in title to be taken into account—Whether premium to be added to take account of anticipated inflation. **Lear v Blizzard** [1983] **3** 662, QBD.

Rent payable on review to be fixed by agreement between the parties—Rent not to be less than original rent payable under lease—No arbitration clause or other machinery for fixing rent in default of agreement—Parties failing to agree rent on rent review—Whether court could imply term that market rent was payable in order to give business efficacy to lease—Whether in absence of agreement original rent payable under lease continuing to be payable. **Beer v Bowden** [1981] **1** 1070, CA.

Rent payable on review to be rent agreed between the parties or fixed by arbitration in default of agreement—Rent fixed by arbitration after tenant surrendering lease—Whether surrender before arbitrator's determination discharging tenant's liability to pay new rent—Whether tenant liable to pay new rent even though new rent not determined until after surrender of lease. **Torminster Properties Ltd v Green** [1982] **1** 420, Ch D; [1983] **2** 457, CA.

Rent payable on review to be rent agreed between the parties or fixed by arbitration in default of agreement—Whether rent on review to be reasonable rent as between the parties or market rent. **Bates (Thomas) & Son Ltd v Wyndham's (Lingerie) Ltd** [1981] **1** 1077, CA.

Retrospective operation—Certainty of rent—Increased rent determined under review clause payable from specified date—Increased rent not determined until after specified date—Whether increased rent payable retrospectively from specified date. **United Scientific Holdings Ltd v Burnley BC** [1977] **2** 62, HL.

Retrospective operation—Rent to be paid on usual quarter days—Lease providing for forfeiture of lease if rent 21 days in arrears—Increased rent determined under review clause payable from specified date—Increased rent not determined until after specified date—Whether rent due and payable until quarter day following award of increased rent—Whether rent due and payable on date of award. **South Tottenham Land Securities Ltd v R & A Millett (Shops) Ltd** [1984] **1** 614, CA.

Retrospective operation—Time for review—Date for ascertainment of new rent—Increased rent payable from specified date—Landlords failing to take steps to secure a review on or before specified date—Effect—Provision for increase in rent if market rental value 'found' to exceed existing rent on specified date—Increased rent to be 'substituted from such date'—Market value on specified date eventually determined over three years later—Whether landlords entitled to invoke rent review clause—Whether increased rent payable from specified date or from date of ascertainment. **Bailey (C H) Ltd v Memorial Enterprises Ltd** [1974] **1** 1003, CA.

Review clause—Time limits—Review clause providing notice of increase to be given by four weeks' notice in writing and providing for increase in rent payable annually with effect from first Monday in June of each year—Landlord not increasing rent in June—Landlord giving notice of increase in following February with effect from first Monday in April—Whether notice valid. **Riverside Housing Association Ltd v White (Housing Corporation intervening)** [2007] **4** 97, HL.

Review clause—Time limits—Review clause providing notice to be given 'at any time not more than twelve months before the expiration of ... every fifth year thereof but not at any other time'—Whether notice to be given before end of relevant five-year period. **First Property Growth Partnership LP v Royal & Sun Alliance Property Services Ltd** [2003] **1** 533, CA.

Surveyor appointed under rent review clause to determine rent increase—Negligence—Immunity from suit. *See* **Negligence** (Immunity from suit—Surveyor—Rent review).

Time limits. *See* Rent—Review—Review clause—Time limits, *above*.

Waiver by landlord of breach of covenant against sub-letting—Effect—Clause providing machinery for determination of rent for specified period of term—No other provision in lease for rent during that period—Notice to operate clause to be given by landlord within specified time limits before termination of preceding period of term—Unreasonable delay—Failure of landlord to give notice before termination of preceding period—Notice given six months after commencement of review period—Whether time of the essence—Whether notice effective. **Accuba Ltd v Allied Shoe Repairs Ltd** [1975] **3** 782, Ch D.

  Stamp duty—

Lease—Consideration consisting of rent. *See* **Stamp duty** (Lease or tack—Consideration consisting of rent).

LANDLORD AND TENANT (cont)—
Rent (cont)—
Suspension of rent—
Eviction by title paramount—Demolition under dangerous structure notice—Frustration of lease—Breach of covenant of quiet enjoyment. **Popular Catering Association Ltd v Romagnoli** [1937] **1** 167, KBD.
Time at which rent becomes due—
Quarterly rent—Right of action arising at last moment of quarter day—Apportionment. **Aspinall (decd), Re** [1961] **2** 751, Ch D.
Underlease—
Rent due from undertenant—Tenant a company in receivership—Future rent assigned in equity under debenture to bank—Landlord serving notice requiring undertenant to pay direct to landlord rent due to tenant—Whether landlord entitled to rent under statutory assignment effected by notice—Whether bank entitled to rent under equitable assignment effected by appointment of receiver—Law of Distress Amendment Act 1908, ss 3, 6. **Rhodes v Allied Dunbar Pension Services Ltd** [1988] **1** 524, Ch D.
Rent control. *See* **Rent control**.
Rent restriction—
Bona fide let at rent which includes payments in respect of attendance or use of furniture—
Attendance—Furniture—Amount fairly attributable to attendance or use of furniture—'Substantial portion' of 'whole rent'—Rent and Mortgage Interest Restrictions Act 1923, s 10(1)—Rent and Mortgage Interest Restrictions Act 1939, s 3(2)(b). **Property Holding Co Ltd v Mischeff** [1948] **1** 1, HL.
Generally. *See* **Rent restriction**.
Repair—
Breach of covenant—
Forfeiture of lease. *See* Forfeiture of lease—Breach of repairing covenant, *above*.
Generally. *See* Breach of covenant to repair, *above*.
Construction of covenant—
Covenant to keep external walls in tenantable repair—Old house—Dampness—'External wall'. **Pembery v Lambdin** [1940] **2** 434, CA.
Covenant to keep premises in repair—Covenant by tenant to keep demised premises in good and substantial repair—Demised premises having defect in original construction caused by bad workmanship—Defect resulting in flooding of basement—No damage caused to premises by defect—Whether building in disrepair—Whether tenant liable under covenant to eradicate defect. **Post Office v Aquarius Properties Ltd** [1987] **1** 1055, CA.
Covenant to 'repair and renew'—'Renew'—'Repair' covers renewal of part of premises, but not an improvement to eliminate inherent defects. **Collins v Flynn** [1963] **2** 1068, QBD.
Covenant to repair 'main walls' of dwelling-house—Whether windows form part of main walls. **Holiday Fellowship Ltd v Viscount Hereford** [1959] **1** 433, CA.
Covenant 'to repair'—Covenant to repay landlord cost of repairs—Inherent defect—Building constructed of concrete frame and stone claddings—Expansion joints omitted from structure—Not standard practice to include expansion joints at date of erection—Cladding becoming loose and in danger of falling due mainly to lack of expansion joints but also because of defective workmanship in tying in stones—Landlord executing remedial works by removing cladding and reinstating it with expansion joints and proper ties—Whether tenant liable to repay cost of inserting expansion joints—Whether repair caused by inherent defect in premises falling within covenants to repair or pay for repairs. **Ravenseft Properties Ltd v Davstone (Holdings) Ltd** [1979] **1** 929, QBD.
Covenant to undertake 'structural repairs of a substantial nature'. **Granada Theatres Ltd v Freehold Investment (Leytonstone) Ltd** [1959] **2** 176, CA.
Necessary work—Whether necessary work to be considered as whole, or piecemeal, to determine whether it is 'repair', or so great that outside covenant—Overlapping covenants. **Brew Bros Ltd v Snax (Ross) Ltd** [1970] **1** 587, CA.
Obligation to keep premises in good and tenantable condition—Agreement authorising alterations—Whether necessary for landlord to give written notification requiring repairs before expiry of lease—Whether necessary for landlord to give written notification requiring removal of alterations and reinstatement of premises. **Batley (L) Pet Products Ltd v North Lanarkshire Council (Note)** [2014] **3** 64n, SC.
Power to determine lease for seven years at end of five years—Covenant to paint in 'the last quarter of the said term'—Whether covenant applies when lease determined at end of five years. **Dickinson v St Aubyn** [1944] **1** 370, CA.
Cost of repairs—
Repair done by landlord at request of prospective tenant—Breakdown of negotiations—Fault of tenant—Work done for tenant's benefit—Liability for cost of work. **Brewer Street Investments Ltd v Barclays Woollen Co Ltd** [1953] **2** 1330, CA.
Waiver—Agreement by landlord not to seek contribution towards cost from tenants—Lease not incorporating agreement but providing that landlord entitled to contribution—Tenants entering into leases on faith of agreement—Whether landlord entitled to demand contribution from tenants—Whether landlord entitled to demand contribution from assignees of original tenants. **Brikom Investments Ltd v Carr** [1979] **2** 753, CA.
Damages for breach of covenant to repair. *See* Damages for failure to repair, *above*.
Damages for failure to repair at end of tenancy—
Allegation that tenancy of dwelling-house notionally continued by statute—Whether daughter residing in house 'in right of the tenancy'—Leasehold Property (Temporary Provisions) Act, 1951 (c 38), s 2(1)(a), s 5(1)(a). **Richmond v McGann** [1954] **3** 97, QBD.
Defective premises—
Landlord under obligation to tenant for maintenance or repair of premises—Tenant suffering injury due to defective inspection cover in garden—Whether landlord could be liable by reason of a defect which would have been discovered if landlord implemented system of regular inspection—Whether duty satisfied by purely visual inspection—Defective Premises Act 1972, s 4. **Rogerson v Bolsover DC** [2019] **4** 962, CA.

Repair (cont)—
Delay—
Effect—Undertaking by landlord to repair—Delay in effecting repairs—Tenant injured by fall of ceiling—Reasonableness of tenant in using room. **Porter v Jones** [1942] **2** 570, CA.
Enforcement of covenant—
Covenant to keep premises in repair—Covenant contained in underlease and made between tenant and subtenant—Subtenant assigning underlease and reversion in headlease transferred to plaintiff—Whether plaintiff able to enforce covenants directly against subtenants—Whether previous head landlord entitled to enforce covenants against subtenants—Law of Property Act 1925, s 56(1). **Amsprop Trading Ltd v Harris Distribution Ltd** [1997] **2** 990, Ch D.
Failure to repair—
Reversion. *See* Damages for failure to repair—Diminution in value of reversion, *above*.
Implied covenant. *See* Implied covenant to repair, *above*.
Landlord's covenant—
Breach of covenant—Appointment of receiver. *See* **Receiver** (Appointment—Protection or preservation of property—Landlord failing to collect rents or to repair).
Breach of covenant—Arbitration—Reference to small claims procedure—Grant of injunction or specific performance—Landlord and Tenant Act 1985, s 11. **Joyce v Liverpool City Council** [1995] **3** 110, CA.
Breach of covenant—Assignment of lease—Effect of assignment—Whether landlord's liability for breach of repairing covenant surviving assignment—Whether tenant entitled to sue for damages for breach after assignment. **City and Metropolitan Properties Ltd v Greycroft Ltd** [1987] **3** 839, Ch D.
Breach of covenant—Time when obligation to repair arises—Obligation to repair whole building within which demised premises situated—Defect arising in part of building not comprised in demised premises—Whether obligation arising immediately building ceased to be in state of good repair or on expiry of reasonable period thereafter. **British Telecommunications plc v Sun Life Assurance Society plc** [1995] **4** 44, CA.
Covenant to keep structure in repair— Damage to plasterwork of wall and ceiling—Whether plasterwork part of 'structure'—Landlord and Tenant Act 1985, s 11(1)(a). **Grand v Gill** [2011] **3** 1043, CA.
Damages for breach—Measure of damages—Premises acquired as a home becoming uninhabitable due to landlord's breach of repairing covenant—Tenant having to move into alternative accommodation—Whether measure of damages the diminution in market value of the premises—Whether cost of alternative accommodation recoverable by tenant. **Calabar Properties Ltd v Stitcher** [1983] **3** 759, CA.
Implication of repairing covenant. *See* Implied covenant to repair—Covenant by landlord, *above*.
Notice of intention to do repairs—Sufficiency. **Granada Theatres Ltd v Freehold Investment (Leytonstone) Ltd** [1959] **2** 176, CA.
Repairing prevented by tenant—Whether tenant entitled to damages for breach of covenant to repair. **Granada Theatres Ltd v Freehold Investment (Leytonstone) Ltd** [1959] **2** 176, CA.
Time when obligation to repair arises—Obligation to repair not arising in the absence of notice of want of repair or actual knowledge—Collapse of floor owing to dry rot—Injury to manager of lessee company—Action by lessee to recover compensation paid to manager. **Uniproducts (Manchester) Ltd v Rose Furnishers Ltd** [1956] **1** 146, Assizes.
Lien. *See* **Lien** (Mortgaged property).
Machinery or plant—
Wear and tear allowance. *See* **Income tax** (Deduction in computing profits—Wear and tear of machinery or plant—Lessor and lessee).
Tenancy by estoppel—
Enforcement of covenant against lessee out of possession. *See* Tenancy—Tenancy by estoppel—Enforcement of covenant against lessee out of possession—Repairing covenant by lessee, *below*.
Want of—
Liability to adjoining owners—Collapse of house on adjoining premises—Landlord liable to do repairs—Knowledge of landlord. **Wringe v Cohen** [1939] **4** 241, CA.
Repudiation—
Agreement for lease. *See* Agreement for lease—Repudiation, *above*.
Lease. *See* Lease—Repudiation, *above*.
Residential property—
Occupation for business purposes. *See* Business premises—Occupied for business purposes— Occupation of residential tenancy for business purposes, *above*.
Security of tenure—
Statutory protection—Agreement purporting to exclude statutory provisions void—Statute not preventing surrender of tenancy—Surrender—Agreement to surrender in futuro—Agreement giving landlord option to purchase residue of term in certain events—Agreement by tenant to surrender tenancy in those events—Whether agreement to surrender tenancy in futuro void by virtue of statute—Landlord and Tenant Act 1954, s 17. **Hennessey's Agreement, Re** [1975] **1** 60, Ch D.
Restraint of trade by agreement. *See* **Restraint of trade by agreement** (Lessor and lessee).
Restrictive covenant—
Covenant benefiting demised land—Registration. *See* **Land charge** (Registration—Restrictive covenant—Covenant for benefit of demised land).
Landlord's covenant—
Enforceability against third party—Landlord letting part of building to claimant as gift shop and covenanting not to permit other gift shop to be operated in building—Landlord letting other part of building to defendant but not placing restriction on use as gift shop—Whether covenant binding on defendant—Land Registration Act 1925, s 50(1)—Landlord and Tenant (Covenants) Act 1995, s 3(5). **Oceanic Village Ltd v United Attractions Ltd** [2000] **1** 975, Ch D.

LANDLORD AND TENANT (cont)—
  Restrictive covenant (cont)—
    Restriction on landlord's user of adjoining premises—
      Premises let to tobacconist—Landlord's covenant not to permit adjoining premises to be used for
      'business of sale of tobacco, cigars and cigarettes'—Adjoining premises let to caterers—Caterers
      selling cigarettes on premises—Whether business of 'sale of tobacco, cigars and cigarettes'.
      Lewis (A) & Co (Westminster) Ltd v Bell Property Trust Ltd [1940] **1** 570, Ch D.
  Reversion—
    Damages for failure to repair. *See* Damages for failure to repair—Diminution in value of reversion,
    above.
    Lease—
      Flats—Tenant's right to acquire reversion. *See* Flats—Tenants' right to acquire landlord's reversion,
      above.
      Option to purchase. *See* Lease—Reversion—Option granted to tenant to purchase freehold
      reversion, *above*.
  Reversionary tenancy. *See* Tenancy—Reversionary tenancy, *below*.
  Right to manage—
    Acquisition and exercise of rights in relation to management of premises—
      RTM company—Claim notice—Costs in consequence of claim notice—RTM company giving notice
      of claim to acquire right to manage premises—Freehold owner giving counter-notice—RTM
      company applying to tribunal for determination as to its acquisition of right to manage
      premises—Tribunal issuing directions and fixing hearing date—RTM company giving notice of
      withdrawal—Whether freehold owner entitled to costs in consequence of claim notice—Whether
      tribunal retaining jurisdiction—Whether consent of tribunal required for withdrawal—
      Commonhold and Leasehold Reform Act 2002, ss 84, 88. **R (on the application of O Twelve
      Baytree Ltd) v Leasehold Valuation Tribunal** [2014] **3** 732, QBD.
      Scope of right to manage—Premises forming part of larger estate—Whether acquisition of right to
      manage premises extending to right to manage shared estate facilities—Commonhold and
      Leasehold Reform Act 2002, ss 72, 73, 96, 97, 112. **Settlers Court RTM Co Ltd v FirstPort Property
      Services Ltd** [2022] **2** 1085, SC.
  Road charges—
    Covenant—
      Payment of all assessments, impositions and outgoings whatsoever. *See* Covenant—Payment of all
      assessments, impositions and outgoings whatsoever—Road charges, *above*.
  Sale of land—
    Local authority house—
      Offer by local authority to sell house to sitting tenant. *See* **Sale of land** (Exchange of
      contracts—Necessity for exchange—Concluded contract before exchange—Intention of
      parties—Offer by council in printed form to sell council house to sitting tenant).
    Tenant in occupation. *See* **Sale of land** (Notice—Tenant in occupation).
  Secure tenancy—
    Forfeiture of lease—
      Breach of covenant prohibiting assignment. *See* Forfeiture of lease—Breach of covenant
      prohibiting assignment—Secure tenancy, *above*.
    Possession. *See* **Rent restriction** (Possession).
    Succession on death of secure tenant. *See* **Housing** (Local authority houses—Security of
    tenure—Secure tenancy—Succession on death of secure tenant).
  Security of tenure—
    Agricultural worker. *See* **Rent restriction** (Agricultural worker).
    Contracting out of statutory provisions governing security of tenure—
      Business premises. *See* Business premises—Contracting out, *above*.
    Council house tenants. *See* **Housing** (Local authority houses—Security of tenure).
    Gipsies occupying caravans on local authority site. *See* **Local authority** (Caravan sites—Provision of
    caravan sites—Duty of local authority—Duty to provide accommodation for gipsies).
    Homeless person—
      Temporary housing accommodation. *See* **Housing** (Homeless person—Security of tenure).
    Public sector housing—
      Action for possession. *See* **Housing** (Local authority houses—Possession—Security of tenure).
      Generally. *See* **Housing** (Local authority houses—Security of tenure).
    Residential property. *See* Residential property—Security of tenure, *above*.
  Service charge—
    Business premises—
      Terms of new tenancy. *See* Business premises—Terms of new tenancy—Inclusion of service charge
      over and above reserved rent, *above*.
    Construction of lease. *See* Lease—Construction—Service charge clause, *above*.
    Consultation requirements. *See* Service charge—Dwelling—Limitation on service charges—
    Consultation requirements, *below*.
    Covenant to pay rent and service charge without deduction or set-off—
      Whether unfair contract term. *See* Covenant—Payment of rent and service charge without
      deduction or set-off, *above*.
    Dwelling—
      Building or part of building occupied or intended to be occupied as separate dwelling—Headlessee
      owning flats and common parts—Headlessee letting individual flats on subleases—Whether
      maintenance charge paid by headlessee to freeholder service charge—Whether maintenance
      charge amount payable by tenant of dwelling—Landlord and Tenant Act 1985, ss 18(1), 38. **Ruddy
      v Oakfern Properties Ltd** [2007] **1** 337, CA.
      Headlessee owning flats and common parts—Headlessee letting individual flats on subleases—
      Headlessee paying maintenance charge to freeholder under headlease—Subtenants paying
      amount equal to proportionate part of maintenance charge to headlessee under
      subleases—Subtenant applying for determination as to amount of maintenance charge
      payable—Whether subtenant having standing to make application—Landlord and Tenant
      Act 1985, s 27A. **Ruddy v Oakfern Properties Ltd** [2007] **1** 337, CA.

LANDLORD AND TENANT (cont)—
  Service charge (cont)—
    Dwelling (cont)—
      Limitation on service charges—Consultation requirements—Dispensation from consultation requirements—Landlord failing to comply with statutory consultation requirements in carrying out works—No evidence as to specific prejudice caused to tenants by failure—Landlord applying for dispensation—Correct approach to applications for dispensation—Whether dispensation could be granted on terms—Landlord and Tenant Act 1985, ss 20, 20ZA—Service Charges (Consultation Requirements) (England) Regulations 2003, SI 2003/1987, Sch 4, Pt 2. **Daejan Investments Ltd v Benson** [2013] **2** 375, SC.
    Flat—
      Limitation on service charges—Time limit on making demands—Demand for payment of service charge—Notification that costs incurred—Requirements of valid demand—Requirements of valid notification—Landlord and Tenant Act 1985, s 20B. **Brent London BC v Shulem B Association Ltd** [2011] **4** 778, Ch D.
      Limitation on service charges—Time limit on making demands—Whether landlord entitled to recover payments on account—Landlord and Tenant Act 1985, s 20B. **Gilje v Charlegrove Securities Ltd** [2004] **1** 91, Ch D.
      Restriction on recovery of service charge—Recovery in advance—Lease providing for payment in advance of interim sums on account of service charge—Interim sums paid into separate bank account maintained by landlord's managing agents to meet service costs during year—Whether landlord entitled to require interim sums to be paid in advance—Whether interim sums held by managing agents as stakeholders—Whether interim sums received by managing agents trust moneys—Housing Finance Act 1972, s 91A(1)(b). **Frobisher (Second Investments) Ltd v Kiloran Trust Co Ltd** [1980] **1** 488, Ch D.
      Restriction on recovery of service charge—Supervening legislation rendering recovery of service charge in advance unlawful—Landlord obliged to borrow in order to carry out obligations under lease if unable to recover service charge in advance—Whether landlord entitled to include interest charges in fees payable to him for carrying out obligations under lease—Whether term implied in lease that tenant should pay interest charges—Housing Finance Act 1972, s 91A. **Frobisher (Second Investments) Ltd v Kiloran Trust Co Ltd** [1980] **1** 488, Ch D.
    Request for summary of relevant costs—
      Request to inspect supporting accounts, etc—Failure to comply with requests a criminal offence—Landlord failing to comply with request for summary of relevant costs and request to inspect supporting accounts—Whether tenant entitled to civil remedy to compel landlord to comply with requests—Landlord and Tenant Act 1985, ss 21, 22. **Morshead Mansions Ltd v Di Marco** [2014] **2** 773, CA.
  Service occupancy—
    Agricultural worker—
      Suspended order for possession—Costs. *See* **Agriculture** (Agricultural worker—Tied cottage—Possession—Suspended order for possession).
    Small tenement—
      Recovery of possession. *See* Small tenement—Recovery of possession—Service occupancy, *below*.
  Service of notice to quit. *See* Notice to quit—Service, *above*.
  Shared accommodation—
    Accommodation shared by tenant and sub-tenant—
      Weekly tenancy—Implication of liability of landlord—Right to enter and effect repairs. **Mint v Good** [1950] **2** 1159, CA.
  Shop—
    New tenancy. *See* New tenancy—Shop, *above*.
  Short lease—
    Dwelling house—
      Implied covenant to repair. *See* Implied covenant to repair—Short lease of dwelling house, *above*.
  Small tenement—
    Recovery of possession—
      Notice of intention to proceed—Form of notice—Statutory tenancy—Small Tenements Recovery Act 1838, s 1, Sch. **Bowden v Rallison** [1948] **1** 841, KBD.
      Notice of intention to proceed—Signature—Notice of intended application signed by housing manager as agent of local authority—Whether notice validly signed—Small Tenements Recovery Act 1838, ss 1, 7—Housing Act 1957, 158(2), 166(2). **R v Berkshire (Forest) Justices, ex p Dallaire** [1961] **3** 1138, QBD.
      Oral permission to occupy for life—Licence or tenancy—Law of Property Act 1925, s 54—Small Tenements Recovery Act 1838, s 1. **Buck v Howarth** [1947] **1** 342, KBD.
      Service occupancy—Occupation as licensee—House occupied free of rent by farm stockman—Small Tenements Recovery Act 1838, s 1. **Ramsbottom v Snelson** [1948] **1** 201, KBD.
  Specific performance—
    Covenant to repair. *See* Breach of covenant to repair—Specific performance, *above*.
  Sporting rights—
    Reservation in lease. *See* Lease—Reservation—Sporting rights, *above*.
  Statutory tenancy—
    Continuation. *See* Long tenancy at low rent—Continuation as statutory tenancy, *above*.
    Creation—
      Death of resident landlord. *See* **Rent restriction** (Resident landlord—Death of resident landlord or transfer of landlord's interest inter vivos).
    Implied grant of lease—
      Death. *See* Implied grant of lease—Death of statutory tenant, *above*.
    Possession. *See* **Rent restriction** (Possession).
    Rent restriction. *See* **Rent restriction** (Statutory tenancy).
    Succession to tenancy on death of original tenant. *See* **Rent restriction** (Death of tenant).
    Terms of tenancy on termination of contractual long tenancy at low rent. *See* Long tenancy at low rent—Continuation as statutory tenancy—Terms of statutory tenancy, *above*.
    Transfer on termination of marriage. *See* **Divorce** (Property—Protected or statutory tenancy—Transfer of protected or statutory tenancy on termination of marriage).

LANDLORD AND TENANT (cont)—

Statutory tenancy (cont)—

Transmission on death. *See* Tenancy—Tenancy by estoppel—Transmission of statutory tenancy on death of tenant, *below*.

Statutory tenant. *See* **Rent restriction** (Statutory tenant).

Sub-lease—

Assignment—

Consent. *See* Covenant against assignment without consent—Enforcement by head lessor—Assignment of sub-lease, *above*.

Sub-tenancy—

Business premises—

Notice to quit. *See* Notice to quit—Business premises—Power of landlord to give notice—Landlord—Sub-tenancy of part of premises, *above*.

Sub-tenancy of flat forming part of property let as business premises—Whether on determination of superior tenancy of business premises residential sub-tenancy of part of property continuing to qualify for statutory protection. *See* **Rent restriction** (Sub-tenancy—Determination of superior tenancy—Business premises).

Statutory tenancy. *See* **Rent restriction** (Sub-tenancy).

Summary proceedings to recover possession—

Tenant holding over not liable to summary proceedings. *See* **Land** (Summary proceedings for possession—Tenant holding over not liable to summary proceedings).

Surrender of tenancy—

Business premises. *See* Business premises—Surrender of tenancy, *above*.

Continuation by statute—

Business premises. *See* Business premises—Continuation of tenancy—Surrender, *above*.

Restriction on agreements purporting to preclude tenant applying for new tenancy—

Agreement by tenants to give up possession at future date—Business premises—Whether agreement void in so far as it 'purports' to preclude tenants from applying for new tenancy—Whether agreement takes effect as surrender of existing tenancy for longer term—Landlord and Tenant Act 1954, s 38(1). **Joseph v Joseph** [1966] 3 486, CA.

Surrender by deed in consideration of new lease—

New lease invalid—Effectiveness of surrender. **Rhyl UDC v Rhyl Amusements Ltd** [1959] 1 257, Ch D.

Surrender by operation of law—

Agreement between landlord and tenant for increase of rent—Whether agreement amounted to surrender of existing tenancy and grant of new tenancy. **Lewis (Jenkin R) & Son Ltd v Kerman** [1970] 3 414, CA.

Creation of new tenancy—No express grant of new lease—Parties not intending tenant to have new tenancy on different terms from former tenancy—Whether doctrine of surrender of tenancy and creation of new tenancy by operation of law applying. **Take Harvest Ltd v Liu** [1993] 2 459, PC.

Grant of option to extend term—Operation as surrender and grant of new lease—Effective from grant rather than exercise of option—Liability of lessee assigning after grant but before exercise of option—Rent and dilapidations after end of original term. **Baker v Merckel** [1960] 1 668, CA.

Sub-letting of room subject to Rent Acts—Subsequent taking over of three other rooms—Three other rooms not let and not subject to Rent Acts—Whether implied surrender of one room. **Fredco Estates Ltd v Bryant** [1961] 1 34, CA.

Surrender on grant of new tenancy—Agreement—Inference of agreement to surrender tenancy and substitute new tenancy—Weekly tenancy—Transfer of reversion to new landlord—New landlord giving tenant new rent book—Terms stated in rent book differing in some respects from terms stipulated by previous landlord—New rent book stating that house let on terms stated where such terms not inconsistent with existing tenancy—Rent unchanged—Whether terms in new rent book supporting inference of agreement—Whether agreement to substitute new tenancy. **Smirk v Lyndale Developments Ltd** [1975] 1 690, CA.

Surrender on grant of new tenancy—New tenancy not effective—Whether existing tenancy surrendered if new tenancy not effective. **Barclays Bank Ltd v Stasek** [1956] 3 439, Ch D.

Surrender on sale of land subject to lease in favour of vendor—Sale of part of land—Whether lease still subsisting in relation to unsold land—Whether surrender operating in respect of unsold land. **Allen v Rochdale BC** [1999] 3 443, CA.

Tenancy from year to year—Termination—Grant of licence to former tenant to occupy premises rent free. **Foster v Robinson** [1950] 2 342, CA.

Suspended order for possession—

Termination of tenancy on breach. *See* Recovery of possession—Order for possession—Secure tenancy—Suspended order for possession on condition as to payment of arrears of rent, *above*.

Suspension of possession order—

Discretion to suspend. *See* Recovery of possession—Order for possession—Suspension of order—Discretion, *above*.

Suspension of rent. *See* Rent—Suspension of rent, *above*.

Tenancy—

Agreement—

Death of tenant—Liability of administrator of tenant's estate for rent. *See* **Executor and administrator** (Contract—Liability of administrator—Tenancy agreement—Implied obligation—Obligation to pay rent so long as tenancy subsisting).

Estoppel. *See* **Estoppel** (Contract—Agreement granting tenancy of land).

Generally. *See* Tenancy agreement, *below*.

Agricultural holding. *See* **Agricultural holding**.

Assured tenancy—

Creation. *See* Tenancy—Creation—Assured tenancy, *below*.

Creation—Order for possession. *See* Recovery of possession—Order for possession—Assured tenancy, *above*.

Business premises. *See* Business premises, *above*.

Contribution to rent—

Informal arrangement—Constructive trust. *See* **Trust and trustee** (Constructive trust—Tenancy agreement—Contribution to rent).

LANDLORD AND TENANT (cont)—

Tenancy (cont)—

Creation—

Assured tenancy—Tenant of premises held on assured tenancy falling into arrears of rent—Landlord obtaining order for possession together with payment of arrears and mesne profits—Tenant offering to pay off arrears in monthly instalments—Landlord accepting proposal and not enforcing order—Whether landlord's acceptance of tenant's proposal creating new assured tenancy—Housing Act 1988. **Stirling v Leadenhall Residential 2 Ltd** [2001] **3** 645, CA.

Estate agent—Authority to create tenancy. *See* **Estate agent** (Authority—Authority to create tenancy).

Tenancy at will. *See* Tenancy—Tenancy at will—Creation, *below*.

Wartime—Cottage let rent free for period for war—Subsequent lease of land including cottage—Claim by lessee for possession of cottage for occupation by labourer—Whether existing occupier entitled to retain possession. **Booker v Palmer** [1942] **2** 674, CA.

Devolution—

Statutory tenancy. *See* **Rent restriction** (Death of tenant).

Duration—

Presumption of yearly tenancy—Tenancy for one year at weekly rent—Holding over at weekly rent—Rebuttal of presumption of yearly tenancy—Notice to quit on basis of weekly tenancy—Claim for compensation or new lease under Landlord and Tenant Act 1927, ss 4(1), 5(1), (2). **Adler v Blackman** [1952] **2** 945, CA.

Presumption of yearly tenancy—Tenant for years remaining in possession—Rent payable weekly. **Covered Markets Ltd v Green** [1947] **2** 140, KBD.

Terms of years or from year to year—Letting for successive periods of 364 days. **Land Settlement Association Ltd v Carr** [1944] **2** 126, CA.

Grant—

Beneficiary granting tenancy—Premises held by trustees on trust for sale—Life tenant let into possession—Life tenant granted weekly tenancy—Whether valid contractual tenancy. **Stratford v Syrett** [1957] **3** 363, CA.

Inference of agricultural tenancy from occupation for an annual payment. **Holder v Holder** [1968] **1** 665, CA.

Overlap in identity of landlords and tenants—Whether A and B permitted to grant tenancy to A, B and C—Whether such tenancy entitled to protection as agricultural holding—Meaning of 'agricultural holding'—Law of Property Act 1925, ss 53, 54, 72—Agricultural Holdings Act 1986, s 2. **Procter v Procter** [2022] **1** 358, CA.

Joint tenancy—

Determination—Assured weekly tenancy of matrimonial home held jointly by husband and wife—Wife determining tenancy by serving notice to quit—Landlord bringing possession proceedings against husband following expiry of notice—Husband wishing to apply for property adjustment order—Whether notice to quit a 'disposition' of property intended to prevent or reduce financial relief in matrimonial proceedings—Whether court having power to set aside notice to quit in order to make property adjustment order—Whether tenancy 'property' for purposes of property adjustment order—Whether husband having defence to possession claim—Matrimonial Causes Act 1973, ss 24, 37(2). **Newlon Housing Trust v Alsulaimen** [1998] **4** 1, HL.

Determination—Determination of periodic tenancy held by two or more joint tenants—Joint tenant giving notice terminating tenancy without consulting other joint tenant—Whether breach of trust—Law of Property Act 1925, s 26(3). **Crawley BC v Ure** [1996] **1** 724, CA.

Determination—Determination of periodic tenancy held by two or more joint tenants—Weekly tenancy—Notice to quit accepted by landlord as terminating tenancy three days after notice given by one joint tenant—Whether notice binding on other joint tenant. **Hounslow London BC v Pilling** [1994] **1** 432, CA.

Determination—Determination of periodic tenancy held by two or more joint tenants—Whether one joint tenant may determine tenancy by notice to quit without consent of other. **Hammersmith and Fulham London BC v Monk** [1992] **1** 1, HL.

Determination—Determination of secure tenancy held by two or more joint tenants—Determination of tenancy by one joint tenant by notice to quit without consent of the other—Tenant giving notice to quit to landlord while subject to non-molestation order—Landlord taking possession proceedings against other tenant—Whether notice to quit constituting breach of non-molestation order—Whether landlord in contempt by taking possession proceedings. **Harrow London BC v Johnstone** [1997] **1** 929, HL.

Determination—Local authority granting joint secure periodic tenancy to husband and wife—Wife serving notice to quit following separation from husband—Local authority accepting notice to quit and seeking order for possession—Whether tenancy brought to an end by service of notice to quit—Whether infringement of right to respect for home—Whether infringement of right to protection of property—Human Rights Act 1998, Sch 1, Pt I, art 8, Pt II, art 1. **Sims v Dacorum BC (Secretary of State for Communities and Local Government, interested party)** [2015] **All ER** 834, SC.

Licence distinguished. *See* **Licence** (Licence to occupy land—Licence distinguished from tenancy).

Manager, appointment of. *See* Flats—Tenants' right to apply to court for appointment of manager, *above*.

New tenancy of business premises—

Failure of Solicitor to give notice of tenant's unwillingness to give up possession. *See* **Solicitor** (Negligence—Damages—New tenancy of business premises).

Generally. *See* Business premises, *above*.

Occupation in return for services—

Whether tenancy or licence to occupy. *See* **Rent restriction** (Rent—Exclusive use of part of house given in return for services).

LANDLORD AND TENANT (cont)—
Tenancy (cont)—
Periodic tenancy—
Creation—Inference—Entry into possession while negotiations proceed—Prospective tenant entering into possession while negotiations proceeded on terms of proposed lease—Periodic payments of rent—Proposed lease not in fact granted—Landlord giving notice to quit—Whether prospective tenant having secure tenancy or tenancy at will—Whether notice to quit effective. **Javad v Aqil** [1991] **1** 243, CA.
Creation—Sub-tenant going into possession—Payment of rent—Whether sub-tenant entitled to protection of interest valid between himself and immediate landlord—Sub-tenant not party to headlease—Landlord and Tenant Act 1954, s 23(4). **D'Silva v Lister House Development Ltd** [1970] **1** 858, Ch D.
Reversionary tenancy—
Agreement to grant future tenancy—Landlord and Tenant Act 1954, ss 28, 65(3). **Bowes-Lyon v Green** [1961] **3** 843, HL.
Surrender. See Surrender of tenancy, above.
Tenancy at will—
Accrual of right of action of person entitled to land. See **Limitation of action** (Land—Adverse possession—Tenancy at will).
Business premises. See Business premises—Tenancy—Tenancy at will, above.
Creation—Inference—Factors to be considered—Intention of parties—Evidence. **Cobb v Lane** [1952] **1** 1199, CA.
Creation—Inference—Permission to occupy premises conditional on payments being made to third party—Whether tenancy at will or licence. **Errington v Errington** [1952] **1** 149, CA.
Express agreement for tenancy at will of business premises—Whether protected tenancy. **Manfield & Son Ltd v Botchin** [1970] **3** 143, QBD.
Tenancy by estoppel—
Enforcement of covenant against lessee out of possession—Repairing covenant by lessee—Lessor having no title to demise legal estate—Lessee paying rent and enjoying undisturbed exclusive possession during currency of lease—Covenant to yield up premises in good and tenantable repair on termination of lease—Premises in bad state of repair on termination of lease—No prospect of any adverse claim against lessee by title paramount—Owner of freehold estate alter ego of lessor—Action by lessor for breach of repairing covenant—Whether lessee out of possession estopped from denying lessor's title. **Industrial Properties (Barton Hill) Ltd v Associated Electrical Industries Ltd** [1977] **2** 293, CA.
Feeding the estoppel—Underlease purported to be granted by equitable mortgagor whose statutory power of leasing was excluded—Legal term subsequently acquired by mortgagor—Whether doctrine of feeding the estoppel of any avail against mortgagee. **Rust v Goodale** [1956] **3** 373, Ch D.
Passing of tenant's right to enforce estoppel to tenant's personal representative—Conversion of right into tenancy. **Mackley v Nutting** [1949] **1** 413, CA.
Repairing covenant by lessee—Lease granted by one of several proving executors—Lessor not having power to demise legal estate—Whether lessee estopped from denying lessor's title after surrendering tenancy—Whether repairing covenant enforceable by lessor's successor in title. **Harrison (Exor of B M Tulk-Hart, decd) v Wells** [1966] **3** 524, CA.
Transmission of statutory tenancy on death of tenant—Vesting of legal estate in President of Probate, Divorce and Admiralty Division—Member of family residing with tenant—Increase of Rent and Mortgage Interest (Restrictions) Act 1920, s 12(1)(g). **Whitmore v Lambert** [1955] **2** 147, CA.
Tenancy deposit schemes—
Assured tenancy. See Assured tenancy—Tenancy deposit schemes, above.
Letting agent lodging tenancy deposit with an authorised scheme two months after receipt of deposit—Whether initial requirement of scheme that deposit be paid into scheme within 14 days—Whether breach of requirements relating to tenancy deposits—Whether county court could make order against landlord to pay tenant sum of money equal to three times amount of deposit in circumstances where deposit lodged, after 14 days of receipt of deposit, but before tenant commencing proceedings in county court—Whether for purposes of that order 'landlord' could include a letting agent—Housing Act 2004, ss 212(9), 213(3), 214(4). **Draycott v Hannells Letting Ltd (t/a Hannells Letting Agents)** [2010] **3** 411, QBD.
Notice for possession—Whether landlord's notice of possession being valid absent payment of deposit into tenancy deposit scheme—Housing Act 1988, s 21—Housing Act 2004, ss 213-215—Localism Act 2011 (Commencement No 4 and Transitional, Transitory and Saving Provisions) Order 2012, SI 2012/628, art 16. **Charalambous v Ng** [2015] **3** 814, CA.
Requirements relating to tenancy deposits—Proceedings relating to tenancy deposits—Landlord not complying with requirements relating to tenancy deposits—Tenants bringing proceedings after end of tenancy—Whether statutory provisions applying after end of tenancy—Housing Act 2004, ss 213, 214. **Gladehurst Properties Ltd v Hashemi** [2011] **4** 556, CA.
Requirements relating to tenancy deposits—Proceedings relating to tenancy deposits—Relevant date for performance of requirements—Housing Act 2004, ss 213(3), (6), 214. **Tiensia v Vision Enterprises Ltd (t/a Universal Estates)** [2011] **1** 1059, CA.
Tenancy distinguished from licence—
Agreement granting exclusive occupation without payment of rent until landlords giving notice in writing terminating occupation—Whether reservation of rent necessary for creation of tenancy—Whether tenancy or licence—Whether occupation giving rise to overriding interest enforceable against purchaser—Land Registration Act 1925, s 70(1)(g). **Ashburn Anstalt v Arnold** [1988] **2** 147, CA.
Agreement to occupy furnished flat—Flat-sharing arrangement—Landlord granting occupancy of furnished flat granted to four occupants under separate short-term agreements—Agreements made at different times on different terms—Occupants paying different monthly amounts—Agreements expressed to be 'licences'—Agreements providing that occupants having no right to exclusive possession of any part of flat—Whether occupants jointly having exclusive possession of accommodation at rent for a term—Whether tenancy or licence created. **AG Securities v Vaughan** [1988] **3** 1058, HL.

LANDLORD AND TENANT (cont)—
  Tenancy (cont)—
    Tenancy distinguished from licence (cont)—
      Agreement to occupy furnished flat—Landlord granting occupancy of small flat to unmarried couple by two contemporaneous agreements expressly not granting exclusive possession and stating intention of parties to create licence—Whether tenancy or licence created. **Antoniades v Villiers** [1988] **2** 309, CA.

      Agreement to occupy furnished house—Occupancy granted to family—Agreement expressed to be bare licence—Agreement providing that occupiers having no right of exclusive possession of house—Landlord retaining key but not providing services—Whether tenancy or licence created. **Aslan v Murphy (Nos 1 and 2)** [1989] **3** 130, CA.

      Agreement to occupy furnished room—Agreement granting exclusive occupation for a fixed or periodic term at stated rent—Agreement expressed to be a licence—Parties believing they had created a licence—Whether intention of parties relevant—Whether tenancy or licence created. **Street v Mountford** [1985] **2** 289, HL.

      Agreement to occupy small furnished room—Agreement expressed to be licence—Occupier not entitled to occupy room for 90 minutes out of every 24 hours—Agreement providing that occupier having no right of exclusive possession of room—Whether provisions for sharing room and licensing occupier for only part of day a pretence—Whether tenancy or licence created. **Aslan v Murphy (Nos 1 and 2)** [1989] **3** 130, CA.

      Agreement to occupy two-room flat—Flat only suitable for occupation by persons acceptable to each other—Defendant and another person signing separate but identical agreements to occupy flat—Agreements expressed to be licences—Defendant and other occupant having separate obligation to pay share of rent—Whether provisions for payment of rent creating separate obligations to pay share of rent or joint obligation to pay whole rent—Whether identical agreements conferring on two occupants a right of exclusive joint occupation creating a tenancy—Whether unity of interest between occupants. **Mikeover Ltd v Brady** [1989] **3** 618, CA.

      Almsperson enjoying exclusive occupation of flat in almshouse administered by charitable trust and paying weekly charge—Whether tenancy or licence created. **Gray v Taylor** [1998] **4** 17, CA.

      Homeless person having priority need—Agreement to occupy temporary accommodation provided by housing association for homeless families referred to it by council—Agreement expressed to be licence—Agreement providing that occupier having no right of exclusive possession of premises—Payment of weekly accommodation charge—Retention of key by landlord—Whether tenancy or licence created. **Family Housing Association v Jones** [1990] **1** 385, CA.

      Homeless person having priority need—Agreement to occupy temporary accommodation provided by local authority at hostel for homeless single men—Agreement expressed to be licence—Agreement providing that occupier having no right to exclusive possession of accommodation allotted to him at hostel—Payment of weekly accommodation charge—Occupier having to comply with directions of staff at hostel—Whether tenancy or licence created. **Westminster City Council v Clarke** [1992] **1** 695, HL.

      Intentionally homeless person having priority need—Local authority required to provide accommodation for sufficient period to enable homeless person to find other accommodation—Local authority providing temporary accommodation in discharge of statutory function—Homeless person being granted exclusive possession of accommodation—Whether tenancy or licence created—Housing Act 1985, s 65(3). **Ogwr BC v Dykes** [1989] **2** 880, .

      Occupation of residential accommodation where public or local authority is landlord—Secure tenancy—Agreement granting occupation of flat to homeless person having priority need—Whether agreement creating tenancy or licence—Whether agreement giving security of tenure against possession order sought by authority—Purpose for which authority permitting occupier to occupy premises—Housing Act 1985, ss 63(1), 65(2), 79(3). **Family Housing Association v Jones** [1990] **1** 385, CA.

      Occupation of residential accommodation where public or local authority is landlord—Secure tenancy—Agreement granting occupation of room in hostel for single homeless men having priority need—Whether agreement creating tenancy or licence—Whether agreement giving security of tenure against possession order sought by authority—Housing Act 1985, ss 59(1), 65(2). **Westminster City Council v Clarke** [1992] **1** 695, HL.

      Provision of temporary accommodation for homeless and other persons in need of accommodation—Housing trust granted licence by local authority of short-life properties for use for occupation under short-term occupancy agreements by people on trust's waiting list—Plaintiff signing agreement with trust to occupy short-life accommodation on temporary basis on weekly licence—Plaintiff aware that trust had no title to premises—Whether tenancy or licence created—Whether tenancy by estoppel. **Bruton v London and Quadrant Housing Trust** [1997] **4** 970, CA.

      Provision of temporary accommodation for homeless—Housing trust granted licence by local authority of block of flats for use for occupation by persons in need of accommodation—Plaintiff signing agreement with trust to occupy flat on temporary basis on weekly licence—Plaintiff aware trust having no title to premises—Whether tenancy or licence created. **Bruton v London and Quadrant Housing Trust** [1999] **3** 481, HL.

      Two persons signing separate 'licences' to occupy flat—Landlord entitled to nominate new occupant if one of existing occupants left—Both occupants responsible for payment of total rent rather than merely their share—Whether tenancy or licence created. **Hadjiloucas v Crean** [1987] **3** 1008, CA.

  Termination of tenancy. See Termination of tenancy, *below.*
  Terms of tenancy—
    Evidence—Rent book. **Moses v Lovegrove** [1952] **1** 1279, CA.
  Transfer of tenancy—
    Assignment of lease. See Assignment of lease, *above.*
  Wilfully holding over after determination of term—
    Wilfully—Action for double value—Landlord and Tenant Act 1730, s 1. **French v Elliott** [1959] **3** 866, QBD.

LANDLORD AND TENANT (cont)—
   Tenancy agreement—
      Implied grant—
         Right enjoyed with land at time of agreement—Use of coal shed. **Wright v Macadam** [1949] **2** 565, CA.
      Indemnity. *See* **Indemnity** (Tenancy agreement).
      Re-grant of—
         Construction. *See* **Contract** (Construction—Contractual term—Landlord and tenants engaging in rent arbitration).
      Rectification—
         Repairs provision misconstrued by tenant and original landlord—Farm occupied country tenant sold by landlord to purchaser for value—Constructive notice—Inquiries—Tenant's equity to rectify not effective against purchaser—Law of Property Act 1925, s 199(1)(ii)(a). **Smith v Jones** [1954] **2** 823, Ch D.
      Registration as estate contract—
         Effect on subsequent mortgages. *See* **Land charge** (Estate contract—Tenancy agreement—Effect of registration on subsequent mortgages).
   Tenancy at will—
      Business premises. *See* Business premises—Tenancy—Tenancy at will, *above*.
      Generally. *See* Tenancy—Tenancy at will, *above*.
      New tenancy—
         Shop. *See* New tenancy—Shop—Tenancy at will, *above*.
      Notice to quit. *See* Notice to quit—Tenancy at will, *above*.
   Termination of tenancy—
      Allotment. *See* **Allotment** (Allotment garden—Termination of tenancy).
      Compensation to landlord for deterioration of agricultural holding. *See* **Agricultural holding** (Termination of tenancy—Compensation—Landlord).
      Compensation to tenant of agricultural holding for disturbance. *See* **Agricultural holding** (Termination of tenancy—Compensation—Tenant).
      Notice to quit. *See* Notice to quit, *above*.
      Statutory tenancy. *See* **Rent restriction** (Statutory tenant—Termination of tenancy).
      Tenancy deposit schemes. *See* Tenancy—Tenancy deposit schemes—Notice for possession, *above*.
      Tenancy from year to year—
         Denial of landlord's title—Whether sufficient to cause termination of tenancy. **Wisbech St Mary Parish Council v Lilley** [1956] **1** 301, CA.
   Title—
      Right of tenant to question landlord's title—
         Estoppel. **Lewis (EH) & Son Ltd v Morelli** [1948] **2** 1021, CA.
         Estoppel—Tenant paying rent to landlord in ignorance of fact that landlord's title had been determined—Tenant refusing to pay rent on discovering true facts about landlord's title—Tenant unable to show that there was a third party who had a better title than landlord—Whether tenant estopped from denying landlord's title. **National Westminster Bank Ltd v Hart** [1983] **2** 177, CA.
   Trade fixtures. *See* Lease—Fixtures—Trade fixtures, *above*.
   Trespass by landlord—
      Unlawful eviction of tenant from demised premises—
         Exemplary damages. *See* **Damages** (Exemplary damages—Trespass to land—Landlord unlawfully evicting tenant from demised premises).
   Underlease—
      Arrears of rent—
         County court action—Forfeiture of lease—Relief against forfeiture. *See* Forfeiture of lease—Arrears of rent—County court action—Relief against forfeiture, *above*.
      Contract to grant underlease—
         Failure to register as estate contract. *See* **Land charge** (Failure to register—Estate contract—Contract to grant underlease).
      Forfeiture of lease—
         Arrears of rent—Relief. *See* Relief against forfeiture—Arrears of rent—Underlessee, *above*.
         Relief against forfeiture—Generally. *See* Relief against forfeiture—Underlessee, *above*.
      Rent—
         Arrears of rent—Relief against forfeiture. *See* Relief against forfeiture—Arrears of rent—Underlessee, *above*.
         Generally. *See* Rent—Underlease, *above*.
      Term of underlease—
         Underlease for whole term of lease operating as assignment—Reversion sufficient to support underlease—Indefinite but defeasible term—Business premises—Term continuing after date of expiry by virtue of statute—Term liable to be determined by notice—Underlease for term expiring after date of expiry of lease—Whether sufficient reversion to support underlease. **Skelton (William) & Son v Harrison & Pinder Ltd** [1975] **1** 182, QBD.
      Unusual covenants restricting user—
         Omission of solicitor to advise and/or warn client of effect. *See* **Solicitor** (Client—Negotiation of grant of underlease to architects—Unusual convenants in underlease restricting user—Omission of solicitor to advise and/or warn client on effect).
   Underletting without consent—
      Covenant. *See* Covenant against underletting without consent, *above*.
      Forfeiture of lease—
         Relief. *See* Relief against forfeiture—Underletting without consent, *above*.
   Undertaking to grant lease—
      Validity against purchaser of land. *See* **Land charge** (Estate contract—Yearly tenancy under written agreement—Undertaking to grant ten years' lease).
   Unincorporated association—
      Status—
         Separate entity—Landlord's opposition to grant of new tenancy. *See* **Unincorporated association** (Status—Separate entity—Landlord's opposition to grant of new tenancy).

LANDLORD AND TENANT (cont)—

Use and occupation—

Action for use and occupation in absence of lease—

Necessity for agreement express or implied—Husband and wife—Matrimonial home owned by wife—Husband remaining in home after divorce against wife's will—Husband a trespasser—Absence of intention to create relationship of landlord and tenant—Wife not entitled to action for use and occupation. **Morris v Tarrant** [1971] **2** 920, QBD.

User of premises—

Covenant. *See* Covenant—User of premises, *above*.

Vacant possession—

Break clause. *See* Lease—Option to determine—Break clause—Vacant possession, *above*.

Validity of notice to quit—

Agreement for tenancy for three months 'and afterwards from year to year'—

Tenancy determinable on three months' notice at any time. **Simonds (H & G) Ltd v Heywood** [1948] **1** 260, KBD.

Ambiguity—

Notice to terminate tenancy 'at the end of the last quarter of this year'—Whether ambiguous. **Winchester Court Ltd v Holmes** [1941] **2** 542, KBD.

Notice to terminate tenancy 'by the date'—Whether ambiguous. **Eastaugh v Macpherson** [1954] **3** 214, CA.

Notice to terminate tenancy on or before specified date—Whether ambiguous—Rent and Mortgage Interest Restrictions (Amendment) Act 1933, s 3, Sch I(h). **Dagger v Shepherd** [1946] **1** 133, CA.

Business premises—

Lease for 20 years determinable by either party by notice at end of seventh year—Notice, in accordance with lease, given by landlord after Landlord and Tenant Act 1954 in operation—Notice not in form required by Act—Landlord and Tenant Act 1954, ss 24(1), 25(1). **Bleachers' Association Ltd's Leases, Re** [1957] **3** 663, Ch D.

New tenancy for three years 'from' 1st May 1963—First rent payable on 1st May 1963—Rent payable in advance—Notice terminating tenancy on 30th April 1966—Landlord and Tenant Act 1954, s 25(4). **Ladyman v Wirral Estates Ltd** [1968] **2** 197, Assizes.

Notice to quit given before but expiring after decontrol by Rent Act 1957—Notice not in form required by Landlord and Tenant Act 1954—Whether notice effective—Landlord and Tenant Act 1954, s 24(3)(b). **Brown v Jamieson** [1959] **1** 144, CA.

Notice to quit given, in accordance with lease, after Landlord and Tenant Act 1954 came into operation—Notice not in form required by 1954 Act—Whether notice effective—Landlord and Tenant Act 1954, ss 24(1), 25(1). **Bleachers' Association Ltd's Leases, Re** [1957] **3** 663, Ch D.

Prescribed form—Date incomplete—Year of termination of tenancy left blank—Landlord and Tenant Act 1954, s 25, s 66(2)—Landlord and Tenant (Notices) Regulations 1957 (SI 1957 No 1157), reg 4(vii). **Sunrose Ltd v Gould** [1961] **3** 1142, CA.

Prescribed form—Landlord accidentally failing to strike out one of alternative sentences—Notice stating that landlord would not oppose application by tenant for new tenancy and that landlord would oppose application—Landlord intending to oppose—Notice stating grounds of opposition—Whether notice to be construed as stating landlord would oppose application—Landlord and Tenant Act 1954, s 25(6). **Lewis v MTC (Cars) Ltd** [1974] **3** 423, Ch D.

Prescribed form—Notice stating landlord would not oppose application to court for new tenancy provided rent and performance of covenants guaranteed by person approved by landlord—Notice on prescribed form containing notes which set out grounds on which landlord entitled to oppose application to court under Landlord and Tenant Act 1954—Notice did not state of of opposition—Landlord and Tenant Act 1954, s 25(6). **Barclays Bank Ltd v Ascott** [1961] **1** 782, QBD.

Second notice—First notice to quit given before operation of Landlord and Tenant Act 1954—Notice expiring after Act in operation—Notice under Landlord and Tenant Act 1954 served after expiry of first notice—Validity of second notice—Landlord and Tenant Act 1954, s 25. **Castle Laundry (London) Ltd v Read** [1955] **2** 154, QBD.

Statute coming into force during period of notice—Notice to quit given after the Landlord and Tenant (Notices) Regulations 1954 (SI 1954 No 1107), but before Landlord and Tenant Act 1954 in operation—Notice expiring after Act in operation—Notice not in prescribed form—Landlord and Tenant Act 1954, s 24(1), (3), Sch 9, para 1. **Orman Bros Ltd v Greenbaum** [1955] **1** 610, CA.

Conveyance of legal estate in land to minor—

Imposition of trusts—Local housing authority granting tenancy to minor—Notice to quit served on minor—Whether property held in trust for minor by authority—Whether notice to quit validly served—Law of Property Act 1925, s 1(6)—Trusts of Land and Appointment of Trustees Act 1996, Sch 1, para 1(1). **Hammersmith and Fulham London BC v Alexander-David** [2009] **3** 1098, CA.

Date for termination—

Lease determinable by three months' notice at any time—No date for possession specified in notice. **Davis (W) (Spitalfields) Ltd v Huntley** [1947] **2** 371, CA.

Lease for fixed term then quarterly—Notice served before expiration of fixed term. **British Iron and Steel Corp Ltd v Halpern** [1946] **1** 408, KBD.

Lease for two years and thereafter for consecutive periods of two quarters—Lease determinable on or after given date by two quarters' previous notice in writing—Lease determined by landlords by notice expiring on given date. **Associated London Properties Ltd v Sheridan** [1946] **1** 20, KBD.

Tenancy for fixed term followed by tenancy from year to year—Notice to quit at 'expiration of your tenancy which will expire next after the end of one half year from the service of this notice'. **Addis v Burrows** [1948] **1** 177, CA.

Death of tenant—

Notice given before grant of letters of administration—No service on President of Probate Division—Service on persons in occupation—Notice addressed to 'tenants' executors...and to all others whom it may concern'—Grant of letters of administration before date of operation of notice to quit. **Harrowby (Earl) v Snelson** [1951] **1** 140, Staffordshire Autumn Assizes.

LANDLORD AND TENANT (cont)—
  Validity of notice to quit (cont)—
    Error or mistake—
      Meaning of notice clear to tenant—Erroneous date given for termination of tenancy—Landlord
        having right to determine lease on 27th September 1975 by giving 12 months' notice—Notice
        given in 1974 referring to termination of lease on 27th September 1973—Clerical error—Whether
        a valid notice to terminate lease on 27th September 1975. **Carradine Properties Ltd v Aslam**
        [1976] **1** 573, Ch D.
    Landlord a company—
      Director who acted on behalf of company named as landlord in notice to quit—Notice expressed to
        be given on behalf of director as landlord—Director had acted as if landlord and tenant
        understood him to be landlord. **Harmond Properties Ltd v Gajdzis** [1968] **3** 263, CA.
    Notice by mortgagor—
      Notice given by mortgagor after service on him of mortgagee's summons for possession. **Bolton
        Building Society v Cobb** [1965] **3** 814, Ch D.
    Notice by purchaser—
      Notice given by purchaser after execution of conveyance, but before payment of purchase money
        in full. **Thompson v McCullough** [1947] **1** 265, CA.
    Notice to quit dwelling—
      Notice to be given not less than four weeks before date on which it is to take effect—Four
        weeks—Four clear weeks necessary—Rent Act 1957, s 16. **Thompson v Stimpson** [1960] **3** 500,
        QBD.
    Periodic tenancy—
      Certainty of duration—Weekly tenancy—Written memorandum of agreement—Memorandum
        expressing tenancy 'to continue until determined by the lessee'—Whether lessor having right to
        determine—Whether tenancy void for uncertainty—Whether fetter on lessor's right to determine
        void as being repugnant to nature of periodic tenancy. **Centaploy Ltd v Matlodge Ltd**
        [1973] **2** 720, Ch D.
      Certainty of duration—Written agreement—Notice to be three months by either party—Proviso that
        landlord might give notice only if premises required for specified purposes—Whether proviso
        void as creating a term of uncertain duration—Whether proviso void as repugnant to nature of
        periodic tenancy. **Clay (Charles) & Sons Ltd v British Railways Board** [1971] **1** 1007, CA.
      Date of expiration—Expiration at end of current period—Date of last day of period. **Crate v Miller**
        [1947] **2** 45, CA.
    Reference to demised property—
      Reference to part only of demised property. **Woodward v Earl of Dudley** [1954] **1** 559, Ch D.
    Reversion severed—
      Notice as to severed part by owner of that part. **Smith v Kinsey** [1936] **3** 73, CA.
    Signature—
      Agreement providing for signature by landlord's valuer—Signature by valuer's assistant in valuer's
        name—No indication that signature not valuer's. **London CC v Vitamins Ltd** [1955] **2** 229, CA.
      Agreement providing for signature on behalf of local authority's director of housing and
        valuer—Department split into two—Notice signed by valuer—No evidence that valuer authorised
        to sign it. **London CC v Farren** [1956] **3** 401, CA.
    Time for service—
      Notice served before commencement of tenancy. **Lower v Sorrell** [1962] **3** 1074, CA.
    Weekly tenancy—
      Month's notice given to quit on 4th May—Subsequent week's notice to quit on 20th April.
        Thompson v McCullough [1947] **1** 265, CA.
      Notice to be given not less than four weeks before the date on which it is to take effect—Notice
        given on Friday, 4th March, for Friday, 1st April—Rent Act 1957, s 16. **Schnabel v Allard**
        [1966] **3** 816, CA.
    Written agreement purporting to be a sub-lease—
      Sub-term expressed to extend beyond date of expiry of head lease—No reversion left in head
        tenant—Head tenant not entitled to serve notice to quit—No contractual obligation on so-called
        sub-lessee to deliver up possession to head tenant. **Milmo v Carreras** [1946] **1** 288, CA.
  Valuation—
    Lease extension. See Leasehold enfranchisement—Lease extension—Valuation, above.
    Leasehold enfranchisement, for. See Leasehold enfranchisement—Valuation, above.
  Variation of lease. See Lease—Variation, above.
  Waiver—
    Forfeiture. See Forfeiture of lease—Waiver of forfeiture, above.
    Notice to quit. See Notice to quit—Waiver, above.
  Want of repair. See Repair—Want of, above.
  War damage—
    Disclaimer of lease. See **War damage** (Disclaimer of lease).
    Multiple lease. See **War damage** (Landlord and tenant—Multiple lease).
  War time lease—
    Commencement and termination defined with reference to commencement and termination of war—
      Certainty of duration. **Swift v Macbean** [1942] **1** 126, KBD.
      Date of termination of European war—Declaration by government that national emergency
        ended—Notice to quit—Validity—Validation of War-time Leases Act 1944, ss 1, 2—Tenancy
        Agreements (End of the War in Europe) Order 1945 (SR & O 1945 No 703). **Hawtrey v Beaufront
        Ltd** [1946] **1** 296, KBD.
    Option for further term—
      Lease for term of years or duration of hostilities, whichever the longer—Lessee's option for further
        term—Validation of War-Time Leases Act 1944, ss 1, 3(3), 7(3). **M W Investments Ltd v Kilburn
        Envoy Ltd** [1947] **1** 710, CA.
    Termination 12 months after date of end of emergency—
      Termination also on happening of specified events—Validation of War-Time Leases Act 1944,
        s 1(1)-(3). **Manchester Royal Exchange Ltd v The Manchester Ltd** [1949] **2** 1037, CA.

LANDLORD AND TENANT (cont)—
War time lease (cont)—
Uncertainty—
Term—Lease to continue until cessation of hostilities—Cessation of hostilities meaning actual day of cease fire order—Whether tenancy void for uncertainty—Whether tenancy within Validation of War-Time Leases Act 1944, s 1. **Eker v Becker** [1946] **1** 721, KBD.
Term—Termination defined with reference to termination of war—Whether void for uncertainty. **Lace v Chandler** [1944] **1** 305, CA.
War-time tenancy—
Creation. See Tenancy—Creation—Wartime, *above*.
Warrant for possession—
Procedure before magistrates. See Recovery of possession—Procedure before magistrates—Warrant for possession, *above*.
Warranty—
Fitness of premises—
Legal or physical fitness. See Fitness of premises—Legal or physical fitness—Warranty, *above*.
Weekly tenancy—
Repair—
Implied covenant. See Implied covenant to repair—Weekly tenancy, *above*.

LANDS TRIBUNAL
Appeal to tribunal—
Development value. See **Town and country planning** (Development value—Determination—Appeal to Lands Tribunal).
Permission to appeal—
Judicial review—Application to Lands Tribunal for permission to appeal from determination of leasehold valuation tribunal relating to residential service charges—Whether judicial review available in respect of refusal of Lands Tribunal to grant such permission—Approach to be adopted by High Court on such application for judicial review—Lands Tribunal Act 1949, s 3(4)—Landlord and Tenant Act 1985. **R (on the application of Sinclair Gardens Investments (Kensington) Ltd) v Lands Tribunal** [2006] **3** 650, CA.
Rating appeal. See **Rates** (Lands Tribunal—Appeal).
Case stated—
Contention not pressed before tribunal—
Change of law—Consideration on appeal—Discretion of court. See **Court of Appeal** (Ground of appeal—Contention not pressed in court of first instance—Discretion of court—Lands Tribunal decision—Change in law after decision and before appeal).
Decision—
Final decision on point of law—Application for discovery at commencement of hearing of appeal—Dismissal of application—Application renewable later in proceedings if circumstances requiring it—Tribunal refusing to state case on determination of application for discovery— Whether determination a final 'decision' on a point of law—Lands Tribunal Act 1949, ss 1(3)(e), 3(4). **R v Lands Tribunal, ex p City of London Corp** [1982] **1** 892, CA.
Form. See Practice—Case stated—Form, *below*.
Compensation—
Coal mining subsidence damage. See **Coal mining** (Subsidence—Compensation for subsidence damage).
Exclusivity of jurisdiction over disputes as to compensation. See **Declaration** (Jurisdiction— Hypothetical question—Basis of assessing compensation for compulsory acquisition of land).
Costs—
Compulsory purchase—
Claim for compensation. See **Compulsory purchase** (Compensation—Claim—Costs).
Costs awarded on county court scale—
Application for increased charges—Time for application—Costs awarded on county court scale 3—Appeal to Court of Appeal—No application for increased charges for a year—Subsequent application for certificate for increased charges—Delay—Effect—County Court Rules 1936, Ord 13, r 5, Ord 47, r 21(4)—Lands Tribunal Rules 1949 (SI 1949 No 2263), r 42(2). **Sandown Park Ltd v Castle (Valuation Officer)** [1955] **2** 634, CA.
Discretion—
Judicial exercise—Determination of development value by Central Land Board—Appeal to Lands Tribunal—Successful party overstating case—Deprived of costs—Hearing fees—Lands Tribunal Act 1949, s 3(5), (6)—Lands Tribunal Rules 1949 (SI 1949 No 2263), r 52. **Wootton v Central Land Board** [1957] **1** 441, CA.
Order that costs of one party be borne by other party—Claim for compensation—Acquisition of land—Unconditional offer by acquiring authority—Offer rejected—Tribunal rejecting claim for compensation—Order by tribunal that authority pay claimant's costs before date of offer—Jurisdiction to make order—Discretion to be exercised judicially—Special reasons for order to be stated—Lands Tribunal Act 1949, s 3(5)—Land Compensation Act 1961, s 4(1). **Pepys v London Transport Executive** [1975] **1** 748, CA.
Decisions—
Precedent value—
Ability of tribunal to give guidance. **Cadogan v Sportelli (sub nom Cadogan v Pitts)** [2008] **2** 220, CA.
Previous decisions on points of law—
Whether binding on tribunal. **Birmingham City Corp v West Midland Baptist (Trust) Association (Inc)** [1968] **1** 205, CA.
Jurisdiction—
Application for discharge or modification of restrictive covenants—
Covenant requiring demised premises to be used as dwellings for the working classes—Whether tribunal having jurisdiction to discharge or modify covenant—Whether covenant constituting negative restriction on user or positive obligation as to user—Law of Property Act 1925, s 84(1). **Westminster City Council v Duke of Westminster** [1991] **4** 136, Ch D.

LANDS TRIBUNAL (cont)—
 Jurisdiction (cont)—
  Application for discharge or modification of restrictive covenants (cont)—
   Investigation of title of objectors—Assumption of their title—Determination of facts on which
    jurisdiction depends—Existence of building scheme—Whether determination effective. **Purkiss'**
    Application, Re [1962] **2** 690, CA.
  Compensation—
   Disputes—Compensation for coal mining subsidence damage. *See* **Coal mining** (Subsidence—
    Compensation for subsidence damage—Determination of disputes).
   Disputes—Exclusivity of jurisdiction over disputes as to compensation. *See* **Declaration**
    (Jurisdiction—Hypothetical question—Basis of assessing compensation for compulsory
    acquisition of land—Whether planning permission might reasonably have been expected to be
    granted).
  Consent—
   Statutory tribunal—Jurisdiction not conferred by consent without statutory authority—Purchase
    notice under Town and Country Planning Act 1959, s 39—Counter-notice stating only grounds
    within s 40(1)(f)—Preliminary point of law raised later by consent—Point of law a ground of
    objection under s 40(1)(e), but had not been specified in the counter-notice—Tribunal had no
    jurisdiction to determine point of law, nor had appellate court on appeal from it—Town and
    Country Planning Act 1959, s 41(2). **Essex CC v Essex Incorporated Congregational Church Union**
    [1963] **1** 326, HL.
  Water rates—
   Transfer of jurisdiction from county court—Extent of tribunal's jurisdiction—Lands Tribunal Act
    1949, s 1(3)(e). **Sowerby Bridge UDC v Stott** [1956] **2** 264, CA.
 Practice—
  Case stated—
   Decision. *See* Case stated—Decision, *above*.
   Form. **Practice Direction** [1956] **3** 117, CA.
  Rating appeal. *See* **Rates** (Lands Tribunal—Appeal).
  Restrictive covenants—
   Discharge or modification. *See* **Restrictive covenant affecting land** (Discharge or modification—
    Application for leave to apply to Lands Tribunal).
  Water rates—
   Jurisdiction. *See* Jurisdiction—Water rates, *above*.

LANGUAGE
 Court proceedings. *See* **Practice** (Conduct of proceedings—Language).
 Maori—
  Protection of. *See* **New Zealand** (Treaty of Waitangi—Protection of Maori taonga—Maori language).
 Trial—
  Ceylon. *See* **Ceylon** (Criminal law—Trial—Language).
 Welsh language—
  Use in Crown Court. *See* **Crown Court** (Practice—Wales—Use of Welsh language).

LARCENY
 See **Criminal law** (Larceny).

LAST OPPORTUNITY
 Contributory negligence—
  Causation. *See* **Negligence** (Contributory negligence—Causation—Last opportunity doctrine inappro-
   priate).
  Generally. *See* **Negligence** (Contributory negligence—Last opportunity of avoiding accident).

LATE NIGHT REFRESHMENT HOUSE
 Licence. *See* **Licensing** (Late night refreshment house).

LATENT DAMAGE
 Limitation of action. *See* **Limitation of action** (Latent damage).

LATENT DEFECT
 Implied warranty of fitness—
  Effect on. *See* **Contract** (Implied term—Warranty of fitness—Latent defect).
 Negligence—
  Defence. *See* **Negligence** (Defence—Latent defect).

LAUNDERETTE
 Coin operated—
  Sunday closing. *See* **Shop** (Sunday closing—Premises to be closed for the serving of
   customers—Serving of customers—Coin-operated launderette).

LAUTRO
 Investment business—
  Duty to hear representations before intervening in member's business. *See* **Investment business**
   (Self-regulating organisation—LAUTRO—Intervention in member's business).

LAVATORY ACCOMMODATION
 Right to use—
  Creation of easement. *See* **Easement** (Lavatory accommodation—Right to use lavatory accommoda-
   tion).

LAW
 Mistake of law. *See* **Mistake** (Mistake of law).
 Preliminary point of law. *See* **Practice** (Preliminary point of law).

LAW REPORT
Alteration by judge. *See* **Precedent** (Alteration to judgment by judge).
Citation—
    Court of Appeal, Civil Division. *See* **Court of Appeal** (Practice—Civil Division—Citation of cases—Reports).
    Generally. *See* **Practice** (Citation of cases—Reports).
Decision not reported in any major series—
    Duty of solicitor. *See* **Solicitor** (Duty—Knowledge—Case not reported in any major series of law reports).
Duty of advocate. *See* **Practice** (Law reports—Duty of advocates to keep up to date with recent reported authority).
Expenditure on acquisition of law reports—
    Barrister—
        Capital allowances—Law reports and textbooks purchased by barrister in first year of practice. *See* **Capital allowances** (Plant—Books—Books purchased by barrister for purpose of carrying on his profession—Law reports and textbooks purchased by barrister in first year of practice).
List of authorities—
    Court of Appeal. *See* **Court of Appeal** (Practice—List of authorities).
    House of Lords—
        Division of list into two parts. *See* **House of Lords** (Procedure—List of authorities—Division of list into two parts).
    Queen's Bench Division. *See* **Practice** (List of authorities—Procedure—Queen's Bench Division).
Publication—
    Company publishing law reports—
        Whether a charity. *See* **Charity** (Benefit to community—Law—Development and administration of judge-made law—Law reports).

LAW SOCIETY
Compensation fund. *See* **Solicitor** (Compensation fund).
Disciplinary Committee—
    Solicitor—
        Professional misconduct. *See* **Solicitor** (Disciplinary proceedings).
Injunction against solicitor. *See* **Solicitor** (Law Society—Injunction).
Insurance—
    Professional indemnity insurance—
        Group scheme—Commission. *See* **Trust and trustee** (Profit from trust—Account of profits—Commission—Professional indemnity insurance).
Intervention in solicitor's practice—
    Dishonesty. *See* **Solicitor** (Dishonesty—Intervention by Law Society in solicitor's practice).
    Generally. *See* **Solicitor** (Law Society—Intervention).
Legal aid. *See* **Legal aid**.
Locus standi. *See* **Practice** (Parties—Law Society).
Power to require solicitor to produce books for inspection. *See* **Solicitor** (Clients' account—Inspection of books of account, bank pass books, vouchers etc—Law Society's power to require solicitor to produce books for inspection).
Solicitor. *See* **Solicitor** (Law Society).

LAWYER
Access to—
    Prisoner. *See* **Prison** (Access to legal adviser).
Attorney at law—
    Trinidad and Tobago. *See* **Trinidad and Tobago** (Legal profession—Attorney at Law).
Barrister. *See* **Counsel**.
European Union—
    Court of First Instance—
        Guidance for counsel. *See* **European Union** (Court of First Instance—Guidance for counsel).
    Freedom of establishment—
        Mutual recognition of qualifications. *See* **European Union** (Freedom of establishment—Mutual recognition of qualifications—Practising as lawyer on permanent basis in member state other than that in which qualification obtained).
    Restriction on freedom to provide services. *See* **European Union** (Freedom of establishment—Restriction on freedom to provide services—Lawyers).
Fees—
    European Union Treaty obligations. *See* **European Union** (Treaty provisions—Obligations under treaty—Failure to fulfil obligations—Freedom of establishment—Freedom to provide services—Lawyers—Fees).
Foreign lawyer—
    Costs. *See* **Costs** (Taxation—Litigant appearing in person—Assistance of foreign lawyer).
    Legal professional privilege. *See* **Privilege** (Legal professional privilege—Legal advice privilege—Scope—Foreign lawyer).
Legal professional privilege. *See* **Privilege** (Legal professional privilege).
Professional indemnity insurance. *See* **Insurance** (Liability insurance—Professional indemnity insurance).
Solicitor. *See* **Solicitor**.

LAY DAYS
Commencement. *See* **Shipping** (Commencement of lay days).

LAYETTE
Expenditure on layette—
    Affiliation order—
        Expenses incidental to the birth of the child. *See* **Affiliation** (Affiliation order—Payment of expenses incidental to the birth of the child—Incidental to—Layette for new-born child).

LAYTIME
Commencement of lay days. *See* **Shipping** (Commencement of lay days).
Computation—
    Time lost waiting for berth—
        Demurrage. *See* **Shipping** (Demurrage—Time lost waiting for berth—Computation of time).
Expiry—
    Demurrage. *See* **Shipping** (Demurrage—Expiry of laytime).

LEARNER DRIVER
Examiner—
    Duty of care. *See* **Negligence** (Duty to take care—Driving examiner).
Instructor—
    Contributory negligence—
        Accident. *See* **Negligence** (Contributory negligence—Road accident—Learner-driver and instructor).
Motor insurance—
    Extent of cover. *See* **Motor insurance** (Compulsory insurance against third party risks—Extent of cover—Learner being taught to drive).

LEARNING
Article in interests of learning—
    Defence to charge of publishing obscene publication. *See* **Criminal law** (Obscene publications—Defence of public good—Publication justified on ground that article in interests of science, literature, art or learning or other objects of general concern).

LEASE
Agreement for lease. *See* **Landlord and tenant** (Agreement for lease).
Agreement relating to services—
    Restrictive trading agreement—
        Registration. *See* **Restrictive trade practices** (Registration of agreement—Agreement relating to services—Agreement—Trading nexus between parties—Leases).
Agreement to purchase. *See* **Landlord and tenant** (Lease—Agreement to purchase lease).
Agricultural holding. *See* **Agricultural holding**.
Animal—
    Property in progeny. *See* **Hire-purchase** (Livestock—Progeny—Property in progeny).
Assignment—
    Landlord and tenant. *See* **Landlord and tenant** (Assignment of lease).
    Sale of land. *See* **Sale of land** (Leasehold interest—Assignment).
    Supply of goods and services—
        Value added tax. *See* **Value added tax** (Supply of goods or services—Supply in the course of a business—Assignment of lease).
Building lease—
    Generally. *See* **Landlord and tenant** (Building lease).
Business premises. *See* **Landlord and tenant** (Business premises).
Chattels—
    Forfeiture—
        Relief. *See* **Equity** (Forfeiture—Relief—Hiring of chattels—Machines leased to plaintiff).
Coal mining—
    New South Wales. *See* **New South Wales** (Coal mining—Lease).
Company—
    Disclaimer of lease—
        Compulsory winding up of company. *See* **Company** (Voluntary winding up—Disclaimer of onerous property—Lease).
        Voluntary winding up. *See* **Company** (Voluntary winding up—Disclaimer of onerous property—Lease).
    Winding up—
        Liability for rent. *See* **Company** (Winding up—Proof and ranking of claims—Rent).
Consecrated ground. *See* **Ecclesiastical law** (Consecrated ground—Lease).
Construction. *See* **Landlord and tenant** (Lease—Construction).
Contribution by tenant to landlord's costs of managing building. *See* **Landlord and tenant** (Contribution by tenant to landlord's costs of maintaining building).
Covenants. *See* **Landlord and tenant** (Covenant).
Determination of tenancy—
    Generally. *See* **Landlord and tenant** (Determination of lease).
    Notice to quit. *See* **Landlord and tenant** (Notice to quit).
Diplomatic agent's residence—
    Action to enforce obligations under lease—
        Whether diplomatic agent protected from suit by diplomatic immunity. *See* **Constitutional law** (Diplomatic privilege—Immunity from legal process—Residence of diplomatic agent—Lease of residence).
Disclaimer—
    Bankruptcy. *See* **Bankruptcy** (Disclaimer of onerous property—Lease).
    Compulsory winding up of company. *See* **Company** (Compulsory winding up—Disclaimer of onerous property—Lease).
    Voluntary winding up of company. *See* **Company** (Voluntary winding up—Disclaimer of onerous property—Lease).
Duration. *See* **Landlord and tenant** (Lease—Duration).
Encroachment by tenant. *See* **Landlord and tenant** (Encroachment by tenant).
Enfranchisement. *See* **Landlord and tenant** (Leasehold enfranchisement).
Excess rent—
    Income tax. *See* **Income tax** (Profits—Excess rent—Rent payable under).
Execution of lease by limited company. *See* **Landlord and tenant** (Lease—Execution).
Extent of demise. *See* **Landlord and tenant** (Lease—Extent of demise).

LEASE (cont)—
Finance lease—
Contract. *See* **Contract** (Finance lease).
Fishing rights. *See* **Landlord and tenant** (Lease—Fishing rights).
Fixtures—
Business premises. *See* **Landlord and tenant** (Business premises).
Generally. *See* **Landlord and tenant** (Fixtures).
Forfeiture—
Dwelling. *See* **Landlord and tenant** (Forfeiture of lease—Premises let as a dwelling).
Generally. *See* **Landlord and tenant** (Forfeiture of lease).
Relief—
Generally. *See* **Equity** (Forfeiture—Relief—Jurisdiction of court).
Frustration—
Building lease. *See* **Landlord and tenant** (Building lease—Frustration of contract).
Change of circumstances. *See* **Contract** (Frustration—Change of circumstances—Lease).
Grant—
Grant of lease by nominee to principal—
Validity—Whether breach of principle that person cannot contract with himself. **Ingram and anor (exors of the estate of Lady Ingram (decd)) v IRC** [1997] **4** 395, CA; [1999] **1** 297, HL.
Intent to defraud creditors. *See* **Fraudulent conveyance** (Conveyance of property with intent to defraud creditors).
Holiday letting—
Exclusion from protection of Rent Acts. *See* **Rent restriction** (Protected tenancy—Excluded tenancies—Holiday letting).
Illegal premium. *See* **Rent restriction** (Premium).
Implied covenant—
Generally. *See* **Landlord and tenant** (Covenant—Implied covenant).
Repair. *See* **Landlord and tenant** (Implied covenant to repair).
Implied grant of lease. *See* **Landlord and tenant** (Implied grant of lease).
Implied reservation—
Right to display advertisements. *See* **Easement** (Implied reservation—Lease—Right to display advertisements).
Implied term—
Contribution to landlord's costs of maintaining building. *See* **Landlord and tenant** (Contribution by tenant to landlord's costs of maintaining building—Implied term).
Income tax—
Expenditure to secure modification of rent obligation—
Deduction in computing profits—Capital or revenue expenditure. *See* **Income tax** (Deduction in computing profits—Capital or revenue expenditure—Payment to secure improvement in asset—Payment to secure modification of rent obligation in lease).
Insurance—
Covenant. *See* **Landlord and tenant** (Covenant—Insurance).
Land registration—
Effect of registration on title of registered proprietor—
Notice of lease. *See* **Land registration** (Effect of registration on title of registered proprietor—Notice of lease).
Landlord and tenant. *See* **Landlord and tenant** (Lease).
Long lease—
Enfranchisement. *See* **Landlord and tenant** (Leasehold enfranchisement).
Mining lease—
Coal. *See* **Coal mining** (Mining lease).
Mortgage of lease—
Forfeiture—
Relief of mortgagees. *See* **Landlord and tenant** (Relief against forfeiture—Underlessee—Lease mortgaged—Relief of mortgagees).
Mortgagor's power of leasing. *See* **Mortgage** (Power of leasing).
Option—
Purchase—
Freehold reversion—Option separately assigned to mortgagee—Option exercised by mortgagee—Whether mortgagor entitled to conveyance of reversion on redemption. *See* **Mortgage** (Redemption—Lease with option to purchase freehold reversion).
Freehold reversion—Overriding interest. *See* **Land registration** (Overriding interest—Rights of person in actual occupation of land—Option in lease for lessee to purchase freehold reversion).
Generally. *See* **Landlord and tenant** (Lease—Reversion).
Leasehold reversion—Enforcement. *See* **Option** (Option to purchase—Enforcement—Option to purchase leasehold reversion).
Tenant's option conferred by lease. *See* **Option** (Option to purchase—Tenant's option conferred by lease).
Renewal—
Generally. *See* **Landlord and tenant** (Lease—Option to renew).
Settled land. *See* **Settlement** (Purchaser dealing in good faith with tenant for life—Protection of purchaser—Agreement for lease with option to renew).
Parol lease—
Statutory requirements. *See* **Landlord and tenant** (Lease—Statutory requirements—Parol lease).
Perpetual right of renewal—
Construction. *See* **Landlord and tenant** (Renewal of lease—Perpetual right of renewal—Construction).
Possession—
Forfeiture. *See* **Landlord and tenant** (Forfeiture of lease—Forfeiture—Action for possession by lessor).
Premium—
Protected tenancy. *See* **Rent restriction** (Premium).
Railway rolling stock, of—
Proper law. *See* **Conflict of laws** (Contract—Proper law of contract—Lease of railway rolling stock).

LEASE (cont)—
    Renewal—
        Option to renew. *See* **Landlord and tenant** (Lease—Option to renew).
    Rent—
        Generally. *See* **Landlord and tenant** (Rent).
        Income tax—
            Excess rent. *See* **Income tax** (Profits—Excess rent—Rent payable under lease).
        Rent restriction—
            Generally. *See* **Rent restriction**.
        Review clause—
            Issue estoppel. *See* **Estoppel** (Issue estoppel—Rent review clause).
    Repair. *See* **Landlord and tenant** (Repair).
    Representation—
        Negligent misrepresentation. *See* **Misrepresentation** (Negligent misrepresentation—Lease of office premises).
    Repudiation. *See* **Landlord and tenant** (Lease—Repudiation).
    Restraint of trade—
        Covenant—
            Election between observing unenforceable covenant and surrendering lease. *See* **Restraint of trade by agreement** (Lessor and lessee—Election).
    Resulting trust. *See* **Trust and trustee** (Constructive trust—Tenancy agreement).
    Reversion—
        Flats—
            Disposal by landlord—Tenants' right to acquire reversion. *See* **Landlord and tenant** (Flats—Tenants' right to acquire landlord's reversion).
        Generally. *See* **Landlord and tenant** (Lease—Reversion).
    Right to acquire new lease. *See* **Landlord and tenant** (Lease—Right to acquire new lease).
    Sale of land—
        Disclosure. *See* **Sale of land** (Title—Leasehold—Disclosure).
    Service agreement in lease—
        Specific performance. *See* **Specific performance** (Personal services—Service agreement in lease).
    Short lease of dwelling house—
        Implied covenant to repair. *See* **Landlord and tenant** (Implied covenant to repair—Short lease of dwelling house).
    Small house—
        Implied condition—
            Fitness of property for human habitation. *See* **Housing** (Fitness of property for human habitation—Scope of implied condition of lease).
    Specific performance—
        Agreement for lease. *See* **Specific performance** (Lease).
    Stamp duty. *See* **Stamp duty** (Lease or tack).
    Students—
        Premises let to educational institution—
            Protected tenancy. *See* **Rent restriction** (Protected tenancy—Tenancy under which a dwelling-house is let as a separate dwelling—Premises let to educational institution).
    Surrender—
        Consideration—
            Income tax—Capital or income. *See* **Income tax** (Capital or income receipts—Surrender of lease).
        Contract to convey or create a legal estate—
            Registration as estate contract. *See* **Land charge** (Estate contract—Contract to convey or create a legal estate—Contract—Meaning—Obligation binding on one party only—Absence of money consideration—Lease).
        Generally. *See* **Landlord and tenant** (Surrender of tenancy).
        Lessee's obligation to offer to surrender lease to lessor before asking lessor's consent to assignment—
            Registration as land charge. *See* **Land charge** (Estate contract—Option to purchase, right of pre-emption or other like right—Absence of money consideration—Lease—Surrender).
        Statutory compensation—
            Capital gains tax—Surrender of agricultural tenancy following notice to quit—Disposal of asset. *See* **Capital gains tax** (Disposal of assets—Capital sum derived from asset notwithstanding no asset acquired by person paying sum—Capital sum received for surrender of rights—Surrender of lease—Statutory compensation paid to agricultural tenant for disturbance).
        Value added tax—
            Whether surrender exempt under Community law. *See* **European Union** (Value added tax—Exemptions—Land—Surrender of lease).
        Winding up of lessee company—
            Informal surrender of lease by liquidator—Breach of covenant at time of surrender—Whether provable in liquidation. *See* **Company** (Winding up—Proof and ranking of claims—Claim for breach of covenant—Covenant to yield up demised premises with full vacant possession—Informal surrender of lease by liquidator).
    Underlease—
        Forfeiture—
            Relief. *See* **Landlord and tenant** (Relief against forfeiture—Underlessee).
        Generally. *See* **Landlord and tenant** (Underlease).
    Undertaking to grant ten-years' lease—
        Registration as land charge—
            Validity against purchaser of land. *See* **Land charge** (Estate contract—Yearly tenancy under written agreement—Undertaking to grant ten years' lease).
    Usual covenants. *See* **Landlord and tenant** (Covenant—Usual covenants).
    Value added tax—
        Supply of goods or services. *See* **Value added tax** (Supply of goods or services—Supply—Lease of land).
    War damage—
        Disclaimer of lease. *See* **War damage** (Disclaimer of lease).

LEASE (cont)—
War time lease. *See* **Landlord and tenant** (War time lease).

LEASEHOLD ENFRANCHISEMENT
See **Landlord and tenant** (Leasehold enfranchisement).

LEASEHOLD INTEREST
Assignment. *See* **Sale of land** (Leasehold interest—Assignment).
Contract for sale of—
Rescission of contract. *See* **Sale of land** (Rescission of contract—Contract for sale of leasehold interest).
Disposition—
Effect of registration of disposition on forfeiture. *See* **Land registration** (Effect of registration of dispositions of leaseholds—Effect on forfeiture).
Easement—
Right of way—
Whether right of way can be acquired by leaseholder under doctrine of lost modern grant. *See* **Easement** (Right of way—Prescription—Lost modern grant—Leasehold interest).
Possessory title—
Effect of registration on legal estate. *See* **Land registration** (Effect of registration on legal estate—Possessory title—Leaseholds).
Registration—
Sub-lease. *See* **Land registration** (First registration—Leasehold—Application to register sub-lease).

LEAVE
Amendment—
Notice of appeal. *See* **Court of Appeal** (Notice of appeal—Amendment—Leave).
Pleadings. *See* **Pleading** (Amendment).
Annual leave—
Organisation of. *See* **Health and safety at work** (Organisation of working time—Paid annual leave).
Appeal—
Arbitration award. *See* **Arbitration** (Award—Leave to appeal against award).
County court. *See* **County court** (Appeal—Leave).
Court of Appeal—
Appeal as to costs only. *See* **Costs** (Appeal to Court of Appeal—Leave—Requirement of leave—Appeal as to costs only).
Criminal proceedings—Jurisdiction. *See* **Criminal law** (Court of Appeal—Jurisdiction—Application for leave to appeal).
Generally. *See* **Court of Appeal** (Leave to appeal).
Court-Martial Appeal Court. *See* **Court-martial** (Appeal—Application for leave to appeal).
Criminal proceedings. *See* **Criminal law** (Appeal—Leave to appeal).
House of Lords—
Generally. *See* **House of Lords** (Leave to appeal).
Petition for leave to appeal—Costs. *See* **House of Lords** (Costs—Petition for leave to appeal).
Immigration appeal. *See* **Immigration** (Appeal—Leave to appeal).
Official reference, from. *See* **Appeal** (Official referee—Leave).
Out of time—
War pension. *See* **War pension** (Appeal—Leave to appeal—Leave to appeal out of time).
Privy Council—
Ceylon. *See* **Ceylon** (Appeal to Privy Council—Leave).
Generally. *See* **Privy Council** (Leave to appeal).
Registrar's order, from. *See* **Judgment** (Order—Consent order—Appeal).
Third party. *See* **Court of Appeal** (Third party—Appeal against judgment in favour of plaintiff in main action—Leave).
Change of surname—
Divorce of parents. *See* **Minor** (Change of surname—Divorce of parents—Leave of court to change surname in absence of parent's consent).
Continuation of proceedings. *See* **Vexatious proceedings** (Leave to institute or continue vexatious proceedings).
Criminal appeal—
Generally. *See* **Criminal law** (Appeal—Leave to appeal).
Privy Council—
Special leave to appeal. *See* **Privy Council** (Criminal appeal—Special leave to appeal).
Criminal libel—
Leave to commence proceedings. *See* **Criminal law** (Libel—Leave to commence proceedings).
Divorce—
Answer—
Leave to file answer out of time. *See* **Divorce** (Practice—Answer—Time—Leave to file answer out of time).
Application for financial provision—
Application subsequent to petition or answer. *See* **Divorce** (Financial provision—Application—Application subsequent to petition or answer—Leave of court).
Application for leave to apply for decree nisi to be made absolute. *See* **Divorce** (Decree absolute—Application for leave to apply for decree to be made absolute).
Application for maintenance. *See* **Divorce** (Maintenance—Application—Leave of judge).
Fresh petition. *See* **Divorce** (Petition—Fresh petition—Leave).
Presentation of petition within three years of marriage. *See* **Divorce** (Petition—Petition within three years of marriage—Leave to present).
Enforcement of judgment or order. *See* **Emergency legislation** (Leave to enforce judgment or order).
Ex parte application, on. *See* **Practice** (Leave on ex parte application).
Execution. *See* **Execution** (Leave to issue execution).
Immigration—
Leave to enter. *See* **Immigration** (Leave to enter).
Leave to remain. *See* **Immigration** (Leave to remain).

LEAVE (cont)—
  Immigration (cont)—
    Mistake in giving leave to enter and stay indefinitely—
      Entry in breach of immigration laws—Detention of entrant. *See* **Immigration** (Detention—Illegal entrant—Entry in breach of immigration laws—Immigration officer mistakenly giving entrant leave to enter and stay indefinitely).
  Interlocutory appeal—
    Appeal from county court—
      Point of law. *See* **County court** (Appeal—Right of appeal—Point of law—Interlocutory appeal—Leave).
  Judicial review—
    Leave to apply for judicial review—
      Generally. *See* **Judicial review** (Leave to apply for judicial review).
  Leave to defend—
    Summary judgment—
      Practice. *See* **Practice** (Summary judgment—Leave to defend).
  Mental Health Acts—
    Proceedings in respect of acts done in pursuance of statute. *See* **Mental health** (Protection in respect of acts done in pursuance of statute—Leave to bring proceedings).
  Non-patrial—
    Entry into United Kingdom. *See* **Immigration** (Leave to enter).
  Patent specification—
    Leave to amend. *See* **Patent** (Specification—Amendment of specification with leave of the court).
  Privy Council—
    Leave to appeal. *See* **Privy Council** (Leave to appeal).
    Special leave to appeal. *See* **Privy Council** (Criminal appeal—Special leave to appeal).
  Quarter sessions. *See* **Quarter sessions** (Appeal to—Leave).
  Service of respondent's notice on third party—
    Court of Appeal. *See* **Court of Appeal** (Respondent's notice—Service—Service on third party—Leave).
  Service of writ out of jurisdiction. *See* **Practice** (Service out of the jurisdiction).
  Summary judgment—
    Leave to defend. *See* **Practice** (Summary judgment—Leave to defend).
  Vexatious proceedings—
    Leave to institute or continue vexatious proceedings. *See* **Vexatious proceedings** (Leave to institute or continue vexatious proceedings).
  Wardship proceedings—
    Removal of ward from jurisdiction. *See* **Ward of court** (Removal of ward from jurisdiction—Leave).

LEGACY
  Estate duty. *See* **Estate duty** (Incidence).
  Fund for payment of legacies. *See* **Administration of estates** (Fund for payment of legacies).
  Generally. *See* **Will** (Gift).
  Hospital. *See* **National Health Service** (Legacy to hospital).
  Interest. *See* **Interest** (Legacy).
  Legacy duty. *See* **Legacy duty.**
  Payment—
    Generally. *See* **Administration of estates** (Legacy).
    Payment pending application for reasonable provision for maintenance. *See* **Family provision** (Interim payment—Appropriate procedure for executors where applicant is entitled to benefit under deceased's will).
  Satisfaction of debt. *See* **Debt** (Satisfaction by legacy).

LEGACY DUTY
  Exemption—
    Event occurring after commencement of Finance Act 1949—
      Determination of interest—Completion of administration and distribution of estate after 30th July 1949—Finance Act 1949, s 27(2)(b), (e). **Cunliffe-Owen (decd), Re** [1953] **2** 196, CA.
      Instalments of legacy duty falling due—Ascertainment of residuary estate—Finance Act 1949, s 27(2)(e). **Gibbs, Re** [1951] **2** 63, Ch D.
  Incidence—
    Duties on sums paid for duty on gifts free of duty—
      Legacy duty on sums paid in respect of estate duty and succession duty—Whether payable by beneficiary or out of residue—Legacy Duty Act 1796, s 21. **King, Re** [1942] **2** 182, CA.
    Foreign duty—
      Legacy to foreign national 'free of duty'—Whether foreign duty as well as English duty to be paid out of testator's estate. **Norbury, Re** [1939] **2** 625, Ch D.
    Freedom from duty—
      Foreign duties. **Cunliffe-Owen, Re** [1951] **2** 220, Ch D.
    Further legacy duty—
      Settled legacy of £20,000—Duty payable on death of tenant for life—Payment out of capital of legacy or residue—Finance Act 1947, s 49. **Shepherd, Re** [1948] **2** 932, Ch D.
    Legacies expressly given free of duty—
      Direction to pay 'death duties (payable in consequence of my death)'—Incidence of legacy duty in respect of legacies not expressed to be free of duty. **Borough, Re** [1938] **1** 375, Ch D.
    Settled legacy at discretion of trustees—
      Contingent legacy. **Fenwick, Re** [1936] **2** 1096, Ch D.
  New South Wales. *See* **New South Wales** (Legacy duty).
  Rate of duty—
    Assessment—
      Legal costs incurred by executor in connection with will. **Comr of Stamp Duties of New South Wales v Pearse** [1954] **1** 19, PC.

LEGAL ADVISER

Access to—
Right of person in custody. *See* **Solicitor** (Access to—Right of person in custody).
Right of prisoner. *See* **Prison** (Access to legal adviser).
Barrister. *See* **Counsel**.
Correspondence with legal adviser—
Prisoner. *See* **Prison** (Letters—Prisoner's letters—Correspondence with legal adviser).
Legal professional privilege. *See* **Privilege** (Legal professional privilege).
Solicitor. *See* **Solicitor**.

LEGAL AID

Advice and assistance—
Advice and assistance provided by specialist in particular field of law—
Specialist not a barrister or solicitor—Whether specialist's fees can be recovered from Legal Aid Board as disbursement under green form scheme—Legal Aid Act 1988, ss 2(2)(6), (4)(4), 10(3), 32(1). **Bruce v Legal Aid Board** [1992] **3** 321, HL.
Financial limit on prospective cost of advice and assistance—
Provision of advice and assistance to value exceeding prescribed limit—Whether charges for advice and assistance provided to value exceeding prescribed limit without Legal Aid Board's prior approval may be recovered out of legal aid fund—Whether board's approval of charges in excess of limit may be given retrospectively—Legal Aid Act 1988, s 10(1). **Drummond & Co WS v Lamb** [1992] **1** 449, HL.
Proceedings before magistrates' court—
Advice by solicitor to party to proceedings—Care proceedings in juvenile court—Parent of child—Care proceedings in respect of child—Whether parent of child a 'party to proceedings'—Whether parent entitled to legal advice and assistance—Children and Young Persons Act 1969, s 1—Legal Aid Act 1974, s 2(4). **R v Worthing Justices, ex p Stevenson** [1976] **2** 194, QBD.
Agent—
Foreign agent—
Costs—Taxation. *See* Taxation of costs, *below*.
Amendment of certificate. *See* Certificate—Amendment, *below*.
Appeal—
Costs. *See* Costs—Appeal, *below*.
Criminal cases. *See* Criminal cases—Appeal, *below*.
Security for costs. *See* Security for costs—Costs of appeal, *below*.
Assisted person's liability to pay costs—
Assessment—
Costs of appeal—Dismissal of assisted plaintiff's appeal against amount of damages for personal injuries awarded—Damages awarded to plaintiff to be taken into account in assessing defendants' costs of the appeal—Assessment of costs by Court of Appeal—Legal Aid and Advice Act 1949, s 2(2)(e)—Legal Aid (General) Regulations 1950 (SI 1950 No 1359), reg 17, as substituted by Legal Aid (General) (Amendment No 1) Regulations 1954 (SI 1954 No 166). **Bloomfield v British Transport Commission** [1960] **2** 54, CA.
Postponement of assessment—Legal Aid (General) Regulations 1960 (SI 1960 No 408), reg 18(1), proviso. **W v W (No 3)** [1962] **1** 736, Div.
Assisted person unsuccessful litigant—
Application by opponent for costs—Costs in House of Lords. *See* **House of Lords** (Costs—Application for costs or expenses against legally-aided party—Application for costs by successful respondent).
Certificate limited to part of issues in action or petition—
Certificate limited to defending claims for ancillary relief in divorce petition—Whether assisted person liable to pay costs of petition—Legal Aid and Advice Act 1949, s 2(2)(e). **Mills v Mills** [1963] **2** 237, CA.
Certificate limited to steps or procedures to be taken by legal advisers—
Certificate limited to obtaining counsel's opinion on plaintiff's claim—Before counsel's opinion obtained defendant succeeding on interlocutory application for further and better particulars of claim—Whether plaintiff liable to pay costs of interlocutory application—Legal Aid Act 1974, s 8(1)(e). **Boorman v Godfrey** [1981] **2** 1012, CA.
Certificate limited to settling proceedings—Plaintiff issuing proceedings without obtaining extension of certificate—Proceedings later discontinued—Plaintiff's liability for costs for steps taken beyond scope of certificate—Legal Aid Act 1988, s 17. **Turner v Plasplugs Ltd** [1996] **2** 939, CA.
Date on which person ceases to be assisted party for purposes of costs liability—
Legal Aid Act 1988, ss 2, 17, 18—Civil Legal Aid (General) Regulations 1989, reg 3. **Burridge v Stafford** [1999] **4** 660, CA.
Legal aid certificates discharged and reinstated in course of proceedings—Litigant acting in person without legal representation for certain period of litigation—Whether litigant legally assisted person while acting in person—Legal Aid Act 1988, ss 2(11), 17(1). **Mohammadi v Shellpoint Trustees Ltd** [2010] **1** 433, Ch D.
Determination of amount of liability—
Time for determination—Trial or hearing of action—Dismissal of action for want of prosecution—Legal aid certificate discharged before dismissal of action—Whether there had been a trial or hearing of action—Whether defendants entitled to costs incurred prior to discharge of assisted person's certificate—Legal Aid and Advice Act 1949, s 2(2)(e)—Legal Aid (General) Regulations 1962 (SI 1962 No 148), reg 18(1). **Cope v United Dairies (London) Ltd** [1963] **2** 194, QBD.
Wife assisted person with nil contribution—
Matrimonial home—Property in issue being matrimonial home vested at law in wife alone—Husband claiming beneficial interest on account of work of improvement done by him—Husband awarded some beneficial interest—Costs awarded against wife—Whether award of costs should stand—Legal Aid and Advice Act 1949, s 2(2)(e)—Legal Aid (General) Regulations 1962 (SI 1962 No 148), reg 18(2). **Pettitt v Pettitt** [1968] **1** 1053, CA.

LEGAL AID (cont)—
  Bail applications—
    Crown Court. *See* **Crown Court** (Bail—Applications).
  Bill of costs—
    Form—
      Claimant bringing action against defendant NHS Trust—Community Legal Services funding
        certificate issued—Funding inadequate to pursue claim to completion—Claimant and solicitor
        entering into Conditional Fee Arrangement (CFA) to enable completion of action—Claim being
        settled—Defendant claiming public funding certificate not discharged at time CFA made and
        therefore CFA unenforceable—Master dismissing challenge—Defendant appealing—Whether
        master erring—Access to Justice Act 1999, ss 10(1), 22(2). **Milton Keynes NHS Foundation Trust v
        Hyde** [2016] **4** 874, QBD.
      Transitional provisions—Work done partly before and partly after 1st January 1961—Composite
        fee—Divorce—Legal Aid and Advice Act 1949—Rules of Supreme Court (No 3) 1959 (SI 1959
        No 1958), Sch 2—Legal Aid (General) (Amendment No 4) Regulations 1960 (SI 1960 No 2369).
        Practice Note [1961] **1** 329, PDA.
      Transitional provisions—Work done partly before and partly after 1st January 1961—Composite
        fee—Rules of Supreme Court (No 3) 1959 (SI 1959 No 1958), Sch 2—Legal Aid (General)
        (Amendment No 4) Regulations 1960 (SI 1960 No 2369). **Practice Direction** [1961] **1** 64,
        SC Taxing Office.
    Lodgment—
      Attendance—Appointment to tax—Divorce Division. **Practice Direction** [1962] **3** 465,
        Div; [1963] **1** 230, Div.
  Care proceedings in juvenile courts—
    Person who may be granted legal aid—
      Person brought before juvenile court—Parent of child—Care proceedings brought in respect of
        child—Child in custody and care of parent—Issue between local authority and parent over
        competence of parent to look after child—Whether parent a 'person...brought before'
        court—Whether court having power to grant parent legal aid—Children and Young Persons Act
        1969, s 1—Legal Aid Act 1974, s 28(3). **R v Worthing Justices, ex p Stevenson** [1976] **2** 194, QBD.
  Certificate—
    Amendment—
      Appeal by husband against maintenance order—Adultery by wife after making of order—Need to
        inform legal aid committee—Legal Aid (General) Regulations 1950 (SI 1950 No 1359), regs 8(1),
        18(3). **Minkley v Minkley** [1953] **1** 1176, Div.
      Mistake—Circumstances in which legal aid certificate amendable on grounds of mistake—Civil
        Legal Aid (General) Regulations 1989, reg 51(a). **R v Legal Aid Board, ex p Edwin Coe (a firm)**
        [2000] **3** 193, CA.
      Retrospective amendment—Criminal cases—Powers of court. **R v Gibson** [1983] **3** 263, CA.
      Retrospective amendment—Jurisdiction—Civil aid certificate issued for appeal in regard to amount
        of damages—Transcript of shorthand note of evidence and judgment bespoken by plaintiff's
        solicitors—Not authorised by certificate—Whether certificate could be amended retrospectively—
        Legal Aid (General) Regulations 1950 (SI 1950 No 1359), regs 8(1)(a), 14(3)(b). **Wallace v Freeman
        Heating Co Ltd** [1955] **1** 418, QBD.
    Ante-dating certificate—
      Power of local committee to ante-date—Legal Aid (General) Regulations 1950 (SI 1950 No 1359),
        regs 2(2), 5(14). **Lacey v W Silk & Son Ltd** [1951] **2** 128, KBD.
    Certificate limited to obtaining opinion of counsel in regard to contemplated proceedings—
      No proceedings taken—Validity of certificate—Legal Aid and Advice Act 1949, s 1(5), (6). **Law
        Society v Elder** [1956] **2** 65, CA.
      Responsibilities of counsel. **Hanning v Maitland (No 2)** [1970] **1** 812, CA.
    Certiorari to quash certificate—
      Assisted person unsuccessful litigant—Executors of small estate—Means of executors above limit
        for legal aid—Area committee looked only to means of widow beneficially interested in
        estate—Certificate granted in respect of proceedings—Whether certiorari lay to quash
        certificate—Legal Aid and Advice Act 1949, s 2(1)—Legal Aid (General) Regulations 1962 (SI 1962
        No 148), reg 5(5), (11). **R v Area Committee No 9 (North Eastern) Legal Aid Area, ex p Foxhill Flats
        (Leeds) Ltd** [1970] **1** 1176, QBD.
    Criminal cases—
      Grant. *See* Criminal cases—Grant, *below.*
    Discharge—
      Assisted person's requiring unreasonable conduct of proceedings causing unjustifiable
        expense—Solicitor and counsel still acting for assisted person—Discharge under reg 12(3)(b)—
        Whether that or reg 12(2)(d) applicable—Legal Aid (General) Regulations 1962 (SI 1962 No 148),
        reg 12(2)(d), 3(b). **R v Area Committee No 14 (London West) Legal Aid Area, ex p Dhargalkar**
        [1968] **1** 225, CA.
    Extension of time for issue of full certificate—
      Power of court to extend time—Assessment of contribution after expiration of emergency
        certificate—Legal Aid (General) Regulations 1950 (SI 1950 No 1359), regs 10(9), 12(1)—RSC
        Ord 64, r 7. **Ward v Mills** [1953] **2** 398, CA.
      Power of court to extend time—Issue of certificate more than three months after grant of
        emergency certificate—Validity—Legal Aid (General) Regulations 1950 (SI 1950 No 1359),
        regs 10(9), 12(1), 15(9)—RSC Ord 64, r 7. **Greenwood v Sketcher** [1951] **1** 750, CA.
    Filing—
      Time for—Extension of time—Application for—Procedure for obtaining extension—Postal facilities.
        Practice Direction [1969] **2** 1140, QBD.
    Grant—
      Criminal cases. *See* Criminal cases—Grant, *below.*
      Matters to be taken into consideration by legal aid committee in determining whether to grant or
        refuse certificate. **R v Area Committee No 1 (London) Legal Aid Area, ex p Rondel** [1967] **2** 419,
        QBD.

LEGAL AID (cont)—
  Certificate (cont)—
    Grant (cont)—
      Matters to be taken into consideration by legal aid committee in determining whether to grant or refuse certificate—Bankruptcy proceedings—Application by trustee in bankruptcy—Legal Aid and Advice Act 1949, s 2(1)—Legal Aid (General) Regulations 1950 (SI 1950 No 1359), reg 4(1), (3). **R v Manchester Legal Aid Committee, ex p R A Brand & Co Ltd** [1952] **1** 480, QBD.
      Matters to be taken into consideration by legal aid committee in determining whether to grant or refuse certificate—Responsibilities of committee. **Hanning v Maitland (No 2)** [1970] **1** 812, CA.
    Grounds for discharge—
      Alteration of circumstances—Failure to inform area committee—Whether such breach of regulations as justified court in discharging certificate—Legal Aid (Assessment of Resources) Regulations 1950 (SI 1950 No 1358), reg 1(2), Sch I, Part I, para 2(1)—Legal Aid (General) Regulations 1950 (SI 1950 No 1359), as amended by Legal Aid (General) (Amendment No 1) Regulations 1954 (SI 1954 No 166), regs 8(5), 11(2A), (4). **Moss v Moss** [1956] **1** 291, Div.
      False statement made by wife in application for legal aid—Wife's failure to disclose adultery—Whether wife's certificate should be discharged by court—Legal Aid (General) Regulations 1950 (SI 1950 No 1359), reg 11(4). **Nevill v Nevill (Lewis cited)** [1959] **1** 619, Div.
    Inspection—
      Procedure. **Practice Note** [1956] **2** 416, Div.
    Issue of certificate—
      Notice to unassisted party of issue of certificate—Failure to serve notice on unassisted party—Effect—Legal Aid (General) Regulations 1950 (SI 1950 No 1359), reg 15(2). **King v T and W Farmiloe Ltd** [1953] **1** 614, QBD.
    Refusal—
      Conclusiveness of legal aid committee's decision—View taken by committee on merits conclusive in absence of fresh evidence—Proceedings—Appeal to House of Lords—Certiorari and mandamus against refusal of certificate not granted—Legal Aid (General) Regulations 1962 (SI 1962 No 148), reg 7(f). **R v Area Committee No 1 (London) Legal Aid Area, ex p Rondel** [1967] **2** 419, QBD.
    Revocation—
      Applicant obtaining legal aid to sue former employer—Legal Aid Board revoking certificate on grounds of untrue statement as to resources or failure to disclose material fact concerning them—Whether revocation a punitive measure—Whether decision unreasonable and disproportionate—Civil Legal Aid (General) Regulations 1989, reg 78(1)(a). **R v Legal Aid Board, ex p Parsons** [1999] **3** 347, CA.
      Costs, recovery of. *See* **Limitation of action** (Accrual of cause of action—Action to recover sums recoverable by virtue of statute— Recovery of costs paid or payable under revoked legal aid certificate).
    Revocation by court—
      Charge against assisted person of furnishing false information—Disclosure of information supplied to Law Society and National Assistance Board—Jurisdiction of court—Legal Aid and Advice Act 1949, ss 4(6), 14(1)(a)—Legal Aid (General) Regulations 1950 (SI 1950 No 1359), reg 11(4). **Whipman v Whipman** [1951] **2** 228, Div.
      Charge against assisted person of furnishing false information—Investigation of allegation that assisted person furnished false information to Law Society—Disclosure of information to court—Whether court should itself investigate the question of discharge or revocation or should adjourn to enable the area committee to consider the matter—Legal Aid and Advice Act 1949, s 14(1)(a)—Legal Aid (General) Regulations 1962 (SI 1962 No 148, reg 12(5),(6). **Neill v Glacier Metal Co Ltd** [1963] **3** 477, QBD.
    Scope of certificate—
      Certificate covering proceedings exempt from charge on property recovered and proceedings in which property recovered—Whether charge extending to all costs incurred under certificate—Legal Aid Act 1974, s 9(7)—Legal Aid (General) Regulations 1980, reg 96(c). **Watkinson v Legal Aid Board** [1991] **2** 953, CA.
      Counsel's fees—Certificate to 'brief counsel'—Whether certificate covering counsel's fees for work done before delivery of brief—Whether discretion to allow unauthorised costs incurred in instructing counsel where no party and party taxation—Legal Aid (General) Regulations 1980, regs 60(1), 64(4). **Din v Wandsworth London BC (No 3)** [1983] **2** 841, QBD.
      Counsel's fees—Queen's Counsel—Certificate authorising taking of proceedings—Solicitors instructing Queen's Counsel without authority in certificate to do so—Judgment entered for defendant after trial—Taxing master disallowing costs incurred in instructing Queen's Counsel—Whether taxing master having discretion to allow costs incurred in instructing Queen's Counsel—Legal Aid (General) Regulations 1980, reg 60(1), 64(4), (5). **Hunt v East Dorset Health Authority** [1992] **2** 539, QBD.
      Enforcement proceedings—Civil aid certificate granted to prosecute action to include enforcement proceedings in High Court in respect of judgment obtained—Assisted person obtained judgment for damages against company, which remained unpaid—Petitioned for, and obtained, winding-up order against company—Civil aid certificate covered winding-up proceedings—Legal Aid (General) Regulations 1962 (SI 1962 No 148), reg 6(2). **Peretz Co Ltd, Re** [1964] **3** 633, Ch D.
      Matrimonial cause—Certificate to prosecute or defend a suit for divorce—Certificate to enforce order for ancillary relief, costs or damages—Scope of usual form of certificate. **Practice Direction** [1965] **3** 732, Div.
      Matrimonial cause—Certificate to prosecute suit for divorce, to continue property proceedings and to apply for an injunction—Single contribution assessed 'in respect of proceedings'—Proceedings—Whether certificate covering ancillary proceedings—Legal Aid Act 1974, s 9(6). **Hanlon v Law Society** [1980] **2** 199, HL.
      Winding up petition—Certificate for action and 'to enforce any order made therein'—Winding up petition after judgment obtained. **Parker, Davis and Hughes Ltd, Re** [1953] **2** 1158, Ch D.
  Certiorari to quash legal aid certificate. *See* Certificate—Certiorari to quash certificate, *above*.

LEGAL AID (cont)—
Charge on property recovered for deficiency of costs—
  Duty of assisted person's solicitor—
    Enforcement of charge—Exemptions from charge—Discretion of Law Society—Money recovered in proceedings—Assisted person's solicitor under absolute duty to pay money recovered to Law Society forthwith—No question of charge or exemption therefrom arising once payment made—Legal Aid Act 1974, s 9(6)—Legal Aid (General) Regulations 1980, regs 88, 91, 96(d), 97(2). **Simmons v Simmons** [1984] **1** 83, CA.

Enforcement of charge—
  Charge for costs on damages recovered—Infant plaintiff—Money paid into court—Balance remitted to county court for plaintiff's benefit—Whether charge enforceable by payment out to Law Society—Legal Aid and Advice Act 1949, s 3(4)—Legal Aid (General) Regulations 1950 (SI 1950 No 1359), reg 19(1), (2)—CCR Ord 16, r 13(4). **Law Society v Rushman** [1955] **2** 544, CA.

  Discretion of Law Society—Charge on matrimonial home—Wife recovering lump sum in ancillary proceedings—Whether Law Society having discretion to transfer charge from home to lump sum instead of requiring payment over of lump sum—Legal Aid Act 1974, ss 9(6), 17(9)—Legal Aid (General) Regulations 1980, regs 91(1)(b), 97(2). **R v Law Society, ex p Sexton** [1984] **1** 92, CA.

  Discretion of Law Society—Matrimonial home occupied by wife and children of family—Court likely to postpone order for possession if charge sought to be enforced—Wife wishing to sell matrimonial home and buy smaller house—Whether Law Society bound to enforce charge—Whether Law Society having discretion to postpone enforcement—Whether charge able to be transferred to substitute home—Legal Aid Act 1974, s 9(6)—Legal Aid (General) Regulations 1971 (SI 1971 No 62, as amended by SI 1976 No 628), regs 18(10)(c), 19(1). **Hanlon v Law Society** [1980] **2** 199, HL.

  Discretion of Law Society—Money recovered in proceedings—Court ordering sale of matrimonial home and division of proceeds between husband and wife—Whether Law Society having discretion to postpone statutory charge to permit wife to use proceeds to purchase new home—Legal Aid Act 1974, s 9(6). **Simpson v Law Society** [1987] **2** 481, HL.

  Discretion of Law Society—Money recovered in proceedings—Court ordering sale of matrimonial home and division of proceeds between husband and wife—Whether wife's share of proceeds 'property recovered or preserved in proceedings'—Whether property recovered or preserved in proceedings including money recovered in proceedings—Legal Aid Act 1974, s 9(6)—Legal Aid (General) Regulations 1980, reg 97(2). **Simmons v Simmons** [1984] **1** 83, CA.

  Duty of Law Society—Law Society bound to enforce charge—Manner of enforcement discretionary—Legal Aid and Advice Act 1949, s 3(4)—Legal Aid (General) Regulations 1971 (SI 1971 No 62), reg 19(2). **Till v Till** [1974] **1** 1096, CA.

  Duty of assisted person's solicitor. *See* Charge on property recovered for deficiency of costs—Duty of assisted person's solicitor—Enforcement of charge, *above*.

  Enforcement deferred if property recovered to be used by order of court for home for assisted person—Court order that property recovered to be used for home for assisted person—Form of order—Civil Legal Aid (General) Regulations 1989, reg 90(3). **Practice Direction** [1991] **3** 896, Fam D.

  Nil contribution of assisted person—Whether any enforceable charge—Legal Aid and Advice Act 1949, s 3(4)—Legal Aid (General) Regulations 1950 (SI 1950 No 1359), reg 19(1), (2). **R v Judge Fraser Harrison, ex p Law Society** [1955] **1** 270, QBD.

Exemptions from charge—
  Assisted person's dwelling-house—Contract for exchange of dwelling-houses—Assisted person awarded decree of specific performance—No order as to costs except taxation—Maximum contribution paid—Whether Law Society entitled to a charge for remainder on assisted person's dwelling-house—Legal Aid and Advice Act 1949, s 3(4). **Wagg v Law Society** [1957] **2** 274, Ch D.

  Assisted person's dwelling-house—Whether dwelling-house exempt from charge—Legal Aid and Advice Act 1949, s 3(4)—Legal Aid (General) Regulations 1971 (SI 1971 No 62), reg 18(10). **Till v Till** [1974] **1** 1096, CA.

Property recovered or preserved in proceedings—
  Compromise of proceedings—Legally-aided party obtaining property under compromise—Property not in issue in proceedings—Whether charge for benefit of legal aid fund extending to property received under compromise notwithstanding that such property never in issue in proceedings—Legal Aid Act 1974, s 9(7). **Van Hoorn v Law Society** [1984] **3** 136, QBD.

  Compromise of proceedings—Terms of compromise designed to avoid charge attaching to sum accepted by plaintiff in settlement of action—Action by legally aided plaintiff for breach of contract arising out of defendant's refusal to exploit his invention—Plaintiff incurring debts in developing invention—Under terms of compromise defendants paying sum to parties' solicitors in settlement of action—Solicitors buying plaintiff's debts for defendants and paying balance to plaintiff—Terms of compromise disclosed to court and Law Society and embodied in consent order—Whether charge attaching to whole sum paid by defendants to solicitors or only to balance paid over to plaintiff—Whether amount provided by defendant's property recovered for plaintiff's benefit—Legal Aid Act 1974, s 9(6), (7). **Manley v Law Society** [1981] **1** 401, QBD and CA.

  Compromise of proceedings—Test for determining whether legal aid charge attaching to property not in issue in proceedings but dealt with in compromise agreement—Legal Aid Act 1988, s 16. **Morgan v Legal Aid Board** [2000] **3** 974, Ch D.

  Preserved—Assisted person successfully resisting adverse claim to property—Assisted person not making any claim to declaration or other relief—Whether property 'preserved' for assisted person in proceedings—Legal Aid and Advice Act 1949, s 3(4). **Till v Till** [1974] **1** 1096, CA.

  Priority of charge—Order for payment of costs—Declaration that plaintiff entitled to share in proceeds of sale of property—Defendant ordered to pay plaintiff's costs of proceedings—Both parties legally aided—Charge on sum preserved by defendant—Whether charge attaching to whole sum or to balance remaining after effect given to court's order to pay plaintiff's costs—Legal Aid and Advice Act 1949, s 3(4). **Cooke v Head (No 2)** [1974] **2** 1124, CA.

LEGAL AID (cont)—
   Charge on property recovered for deficiency of costs (cont)—
      Property recovered or preserved in proceedings (cont)—
         Property adjustment order in matrimonial proceedings—Husband conceding wife's share to half-interest in property but wishing to postpone sale—Title to property not in issue in proceedings—Consent order that wife transfer her interest to husband in return for sum representing her half-share—Whether charge for benefit of legal aid fund extending to sum so received notwithstanding that title to property never in issue in proceedings—Legal Aid Act 1974, s 9(6). **Curling v Law Society** [1985] **1** 705, CA.
         Property recovered or preserved—Home of unmarried couple held in joint names on trust for sale—Respondent issuing proceedings for immediate sale with vacant possession—Appellant obtaining legal aid and defending proceedings—Consent order permitting appellant to remain in occupation—Whether charge for benefit of legal aid fund extending to appellant's continued enjoyment of right of possession—Whether shares of beneficial interests in issue—Law of Property Act 1925, s 30—Legal Aid Act 1988, s 16. **Parkes v Legal Aid Board** [1996] **4** 271, CA.
         Recovered or preserved—Property adjustment order in matrimonial proceedings—No concession that husband's share limited to a half share nor any agreement that wife had any share at all—Matrimonial home ordered to be transferred to wife absolutely—Whether matrimonial home 'recovered or preserved' by wife—Legal Aid Act 1974, s 9(6)—Legal Aid (General) Regulations 1971 (SI 1971 No 62, as amended by SI 1976 No 628), reg 18(10)(c). **Hanlon v Law Society** [1980] **2** 199, HL.
      Set-off—
         First charge for benefit of legal aid fund—Discretion to allow damages or costs to be set off against other damages or costs—Order that solicitors of other party personally pay assisted party's costs—Assisted party ordered to pay sum to other party—Execution stayed on payment by assisted party—Other party assigning rights to payment of sum to solicitors—Whether solicitors entitled to set off sum against costs—Whether charge in favour of legal aid fund having priority—Legal Aid and Advice Act 1949, s 3(4), (6). **Currie & Co v Law Society** [1976] **3** 832, QBD.
   Civil legal aid—
      Exceptional cases funding—
         Exceptional cases funding scheme—Regulations and guidance concerning operation of scheme—Whether scheme unlawful—Whether regulations and guidance unlawful—Legal Aid, Sentencing and Punishment of Offenders Act 2012, s 10—Civil Legal Aid (Merits Criteria) Regulations 2013, SI 2013/104. **R (on the application of S) v Director of Legal Aid Casework** [2017] **2** 642, CA.
         Lord Chancellor's guidance that exceptional cases funding only available in very limited cases where failure to do so being breach of human right to fair hearing and access to court—Guidance stating that failure to provide legal aid in immigration cases not breach of human right to family life—Whether guidance misstating effect of domestic legislation, Convention jurisprudence and EU law—Legal Aid, Sentencing and Punishment of Offenders Act 2012, s 10—Human Rights Act 1998, Sch 1, Pt I, arts 6, 8—Charter of Fundamental Rights of the European Union, art 47. **R (on the application of Gudanaviciene) v Director of Legal Aid Casework (British Red Cross Society intervening)** [2015] **3** 827, QBD and CA.
   Civil legal services—
      General cases—
         Orders, regulations and directions—Variation or omission of services—Provision of services by reference to services provided for particular class of individual—Test of residence—Whether test lawful—Whether amending instrument intra vires—Whether test discriminatory—Legal Aid, Sentencing and Punishment of Offenders Act 2012, ss 9, 41, Sch 1, Pt 1. **R (on the application of the Public Law Project) v Lord Chancellor and Secretary of State for Justice** [2017] **2** 423, CA, SC; **R (on the application of the Public Law Project) v Secretary of State for Justice** [2015] **2** 689, DC.
      Judicial review—
         Procedure in which court required by an enactment to make a decision applying the principles applied on an application for judicial review—Review of decision of local housing authority—Right of appeal to county court on point of law—Whether county court required by enactment to make decision applying judicial review principles—Housing Act 1996, s 204—Legal Aid, Sentencing and Punishment of Offenders Act 2012, Sch 1, Pt 1, para 19(10). **Bhatia Best Ltd v Lord Chancellor** [2014] **3** 573, QBD.
   Community legal service funding. *See* **Community legal service funding**.
   Company—
      Minority shareholder—
         Action for benefit of company. *See* **Company** (Minority shareholder—Representative action—Legal aid).
      Winding up petition—
         Legal aid certificate—Scope of certificate. *See* Certificate—Scope of certificate—Winding up petition, *above*.
   Compromise—
      Costs of giving effect to compromise. *See* Costs—Compromise—Costs of giving effect to compromise, *below*.
   Contribution order—
      Order made prior to trial on indictment—
         Jurisdiction of High Court to review order. *See* **Crown Court** (Supervisory jurisdiction of High Court—Trial on indictment—High Court having no supervisory jurisdiction in matters relating to trial on indictment—Relating to trial on indictment—Legal aid contribution order).
   Costs—
      Appeal—
         Certificate—Discharge—Certificate limited to obtaining transcript of judgment and counsel's opinion as to appeal—Costs incurred by opponent while certificate current—Certificate discharged before appeal heard—Appeal dismissed—Whether costs incurred during currency of certificate should be awarded against assisted person—Legal Aid and Advice Act 1949, ss 1(5), (6), 2(2)(e)—Legal Aid (General) Regulations 1962 (SI 1962 No 148), reg 13(6)(b). **Dugon v Williamson** [1963] **3** 25, CA.

LEGAL AID (cont)—
  Costs (cont)—
    Appeal (cont)—
      Costs payable by unsuccessful assisted person—Adjournment to master in chambers for determination—Legal Aid (General) Regulations 1960 (SI 1960 No 408), reg 18(1), proviso (a). **Blatcher v Heaysman** [1960] **2** 721, CA.

      Costs payable by unsuccessful assisted person—Sum reasonable for person to pay—Jurisdiction of Court of Appeal—Substitution of own view for trial judge's—Legal Aid and Advice Act 1949, s 2(2)(e)—Legal Aid (General) Regulations 1962 (SI 1962 No 148) reg 18(1)-(3). **Gooday v Gooday** [1968] **3** 611, CA.

      Security for costs. *See* Security for costs—Costs of appeal, *below*.

    Assisted person resident abroad—
      Costs of attendance at court—Prior approval of Law Society—Legal Aid (General) Regulations 1950 (SI 1950 No 1359), reg 3(4)—Legal Aid (General) (Amendment No 1) Regulations 1954 (SI 1954 No 166), reg 23(1). **Ammar v Ammar** [1954] **2** 365, Div.

      Right to order against defendant for full costs—Legal Aid and Advice Act 1949, s 1(7)(b). **Starkey v Railway Executive** [1951] **2** 902, CA.

    Assisted person successful plaintiff—
      Right to costs—Legal Aid and Advice Act 1949, s 1(7)(b). **Daley v Diggers Ltd** [1951] **1** 116, KBD.

    Assisted person's liability to pay costs. *See* Assisted person's liability to pay costs, *above*.

    Bill of costs. *See* Bill of costs, *above*.

    Charge on property recovered for deficiency of costs. *See* Charge on property recovered for deficiency of costs, *above*.

    Compromise—
      Costs of giving effect to compromise—Conveyancing matters—Legal Aid and Advice Act 1949, s 1(5). **Trusts Affecting 26 Clarendon Villas, Hove, Re** [1955] **3** 178, Ch D.

    Criminal cases—
      Crown Court and Court of Appeal, Criminal Division—Generally. *See* **Criminal law** (Costs—Power to award costs).

    Deficiency of costs—
      Charge on property recovered for deficiency of costs. *See* Charge on property recovered for deficiency of costs, *above*.

    Divorce—
      Damages—Costs of prayer for damages not included on legal aid taxation. **Practice Direction** [1967] **3** 177, Div.

      Divorce by consent. **Hymns v Hymns** [1971] **3** 596, Div.

      Divorce by consent—Legally aided petitioner—Omission of prayer for costs. *See* **Divorce** (Separation—Two year separation—Consent to decree by respondent—Petitioner legally aided—Consent on terms that there be no order as to costs).

      Queen's Proctor's intervention—Certificate granted for divorce suit—Whether covering costs of intervention—Legal Aid (General) Regulations 1950 (SI 1950 No 1359), reg 5(2). **Wallis v Wallis (Queen's Proctor Showing Cause)** [1952] **1** 915, Div.

      Security for costs. *See* Security for costs—Matrimonial causes, *below*.

      Wife's costs—Wife's petition for divorce on ground of husband's cruelty—Husband's petition for divorce on ground of wife's adultery with co-respondent—Suits consolidated—Wife in receipt of legal aid covering both suits—Order for security for costs against husband—Husband and wife reconciled and petitions dismissed by consent—Wife's instructions to legal representatives not to ask for order for costs against husband—Wife's solicitor would have applied for costs on her behalf but for her veto—Whether Law Society as guardian of legal aid fund entitled to apply for order for costs against husband—Legal Aid and Advice Act 1949, s 1(7)(b). **Carter v Carter** [1964] **2** 968, Div.

    House of Lords. *See* **House of Lords** (Costs—Application for costs or expenses against legally-aided party).

    Indemnity costs—
      Whether court entitled to make award of indemnity costs in favour of assisted person notwithstanding that he would not himself recover difference between standard costs and indemnity costs. **Brawley v Marczynski (No 2)** [2002] **4** 1067, CA.

    Liability of assisted person. *See* Assisted person's liability to pay costs, *above*.

    Magistrates' jurisdiction—
      Award of costs against local authority—Award of costs prior to Legal Aid Board assessment. *See* **Costs** (Order for costs—Jurisdiction—Magistrates—Order against local authority—Legally aided applicant).

    Matrimonial home—
      Sub-tenancy of dwelling-house forming part of premises let as a whole on superior letting—Registration of wife's charge. **Practice Direction** [1968] **1** 456, Div.

    No order made as to costs—
      Taxation. *See* Taxation of costs—No order made as to costs, *below*.

    Order for costs. *See* Order for costs, *below*.

    Payment into court—
      Recovery by legally assisted person of amount less than that paid in—Discretion of court—Contest as to incidence of costs, after payment in, lying substantially between legal aid fund and defendant—Action against solicitor for negligence—Costs of defendant after payment in exceeding damages recovered by plaintiff—Costs after payment in given to defendant and set-off against damages and plaintiff's costs before payment in—Legal Aid and Advice Act 1949, s 2(2)(e). **Cook v S** [1967] **1** 299, CA.

      Recovery by legally assisted person of amount less than that paid in—Liability for defendants' costs after date of payment into court—Legal Aid and Advice Act 1949, s 2(2)(e). **Nolan v C & C Marshall Ltd** [1954] **1** 328, CA.

LEGAL AID (cont)—
Costs (cont)—
Remuneration of persons giving legal aid—
Restriction on payment otherwise than from legal aid fund—Legal aid certificate issued in connection with proceedings—Proceedings—Proceedings incidental to main action—Whether solicitor giving legal aid in connection with incidental proceedings precluded from charging for work done in connection with main action—Whether solicitor precluded from claiming lien on papers pertaining to main action—Legal Aid (General) Regulations 1980, reg 65. **Littaur v Steggles Palmer (a firm)** [1986] **1** 780, CA.
Security for costs. *See* Security for costs, *below*.
Set-off—
Assisted person successful defendant—Retention of fund in court pending satisfaction of costs of defendant—'Means'—Legal Aid and Advice Act 1949, ss 2(2)(e), 3(4)—Legal Aid (General) Regulations 1950 (SI 1950 No 1359), regs 16, 17. **Carr v Boxall** [1960] **1** 495, Ch D.
County court. *See* **County court** (Costs—Set-off—Legal aid).
Unassisted party's costs—Set-off of unassisted party's costs against damages or costs to which legally aided party becomes entitled in action—Costs of interlocutory application—Whether permissible to make order directing set-off of unassisted defendant's costs of interlocutory application against damages or costs to which legally aided plaintiff becomes entitled in action—Whether precondition of order that there be assessment of amount reasonable for legally aided person to pay by way of costs—Legal Aid Act 1988, ss 16(6), (8), 17(1)—Civil Legal Aid (General) Regulations 1989, reg 124(1). **Lockley v National Blood Transfusion Service** [1992] **2** 589, CA.
Whether statutory provisions protecting assisted person from liability for amount exceeding reasonable sum preventing party awarded costs from setting off those costs against costs and other sums awarded in favour of an assisted person—Access to Justice Act 1999, s 11. **Hill v Bailey** [2004] **1** 1210, Ch D.
Solicitor's failure to give notice of legal aid certificate—
Personal liability of solicitor for costs. *See* **Solicitor** (Payment of costs by solicitor personally—Failure to give notice of legal aid certificate).
Successful third party—
Plaintiff legally aided—Discretion. *See* **Costs** (Order for costs—Discretion—Successful third party—Plaintiff legally aided).
Taxation of costs. *See* Taxation of costs, *below*.
Transcript—
Shorthand notes—Transcript of shorthand notes of Divisional Court of Probate, Divorce and Admiralty Division—Legal Aid (General) Regulations 1950 (SI 1950 No 1359), reg 14(3). **Harvey v Harvey** [1955] **3** 82, Div.
Trustee's costs—
Solicitor-trustee approaching retirement and completely exculpated in action for breach of trust—Plaintiffs of of co-trustee claiming that their school fees had been paid out of trust fund in breach of trust—Plaintiffs absolutely entitled to trust fund—Father and mother divorced—Whether order for solicitor-trustee's costs out of trust fund an order made against plaintiffs—Legal Aid and Advice Act 1949, s 2(2)(e)—Legal Aid (General) Regulations 1962 (SI 1962 No 148), regs 12(3)(b), 18(3)(a). **Spurling's Will Trusts, Re** [1966] **1** 745, Ch D.
Counsel—
Criminal cases. *See* Criminal cases—Representation by counsel, *below*.
Duty to legally-aided client. *See* **Counsel** (Duty—Legally-aided client).
Fees. *See* Counsel's fees, *below*.
Counsel's fees—
Criminal cases. *See* Criminal cases—Counsel's fees, *below*.
Payment out of legal aid fund—
Need for counsel to check whether certificate authorising instruction of counsel if looking to fund for remuneration—Civil Legal Aid (General) Regulations 1989, reg 59. **Hunt v East Dorset Health Authority** [1992] **2** 539, QBD.
Scope of legal aid certificate. *See* Certificate—Scope of certificate—Counsel's fees, *above*.
Taxation of costs—
Generally. *See* Taxation of costs—Counsel's fee, *below*.
Counsel's fees—
Civil legal aid certificate—
Legal Services Commission paying money to counsel on account of fees in respect of work done under civil legal aid certificate—Commission claiming for recovery of alleged overpayment of money paid to counsel six years after work carried out—Whether Commission's cause of action for recoupment accruing from date demand made or from date work under certificate completed—Limitation Act 1980, s 9—Civil Legal Aid (General) Regulations 1989, SI 1989/339, reg 100(8). **Legal Services Commission v Henthorn** [2012] **2** 439, CA.
Criminal cases—
Appeal—
Application for leave to appeal—Application to full court when single judge refused leave to appeal—Scope of legal aid certificate—Assistance in preparation of application for leave to appeal—Certificate also covering assistance regarding application to full court where single judge refuses leave—No need for court to amend certificate—Criminal Appeal Act 1968, s 31(3)—Legal Aid Act 1974, ss 28(7), 30(1), (7), (9), 31—Criminal Appeal Rules 1968, r 12. **R v Gibson** [1983] **3** 263, CA.
Application for leave to appeal—Application to full court when single judge refuses leave to appeal—Whether grant of legal aid for purposes of appeal covers legal representation at hearing of application before full court—Whether full court can grant legal aid to cover legal representation at hearing—Legal Aid Act 1974, ss 28(8), 30(7)(a), (9)—Legal Aid in Criminal Proceedings (General) Regulations 1968, reg 12. **R v Kearney** [1983] **3** 270, CA.
Court of Appeal—Powers of Court of Appeal—Power to amend legal aid order made by single judge when giving leave to appeal—Legal Aid Act 1974, s 31. **R v Gibson** [1983] **3** 263, CA.
Bail applications—
Crown Court. *See* **Crown Court** (Bail—Applications).

Criminal cases (cont)—
Costs payable to assisted person—
Sums on account of fees payable to counsel or solicitor and disbursements incurred by solicitor—Fees and disbursements incurred before date of order and remaining payable at date of order—Legal aid order made at conclusion of trial—Whether sums allowable in respect of fees and disbursements incurred before date of order—Legal Aid Act 1974, s 37(2). **R v Tullett** [1976] **2** 1032, Crown Ct.
Counsel's fees—
Determination—Matters to be considered—Fee paid to opposing counsel—Whether 'other relevant information'—Legal Aid in Criminal and Care Proceedings (Costs) Regulations 1989, reg 9(1). **Lord High Chancellor v Wright** [1993] **4** 74, QBD.
Evidence—
Accused cross-examined on contents of his legal aid application for purpose of discrediting him—Whether witness properly examined on his legal aid application entitled to warning against self-incrimination—Whether privilege from disclosure afforded to information furnished for civil legal aid extending to information furnished for criminal legal aid—Legal Aid Act 1974, ss 22(1), 23(1). **R v Stubbs** [1982] **1** 424, CA.
Grant—
Committal proceedings—Complete discretion—Criminal Justice Act 1967, ss 73(2), 74(1), (2). **R v Derby Justices, ex p Kooner** [1970] **3** 399, QBD.
Committal proceedings—Contempt committed other than in face of court—Breach of court order—Whether committal proceedings for contempt committed other than in face of court amounting to criminal proceedings for purposes of legal aid—Whether High Court having power to determine application for legal aid—Legal Aid, Sentencing and Punishment of Offenders Act 2012, ss 14(h), 16(1), 19(1)—Criminal Legal Aid (General) Regulations 2013, SI 2013/9, regs 9(v), 21—Criminal Legal Aid (Determinations by a Court and Choice of Representative) Regulations 2013, SI 2013/614, regs 4(2), 5(1), 7(2). **King's Lynn and West Norfolk Council v Bunning (Legal Aid Agency, interested party)** [2014] **2** 1095, QBD.
Committal proceedings—Contempt committed other than in face of court—County Court—Appellant committed to prison for contempt of court for breach of injunctions in County Court proceedings—Appellant appearing unrepresented—Whether publicly-funded legal representation available—Whether fair trial—Legal Aid, Sentencing and Punishment of Offenders Act 2012, ss 14, 16, 18, 19—Criminal Legal Aid (General) Regulations 2013, SI 2013/9, regs 9(v), 10. **Brown v Haringey London BC** [2016] **4** 754, CA.
Committal proceedings—Murder—Legal aid should include representation by counsel—Criminal Justice Act 1967, s 74(2). **R v Derby Justices, ex p Kooner** [1970] **3** 399, QBD.
Defence certificate—Nature of right given—Poor Prisoners' Defence Act 1930, s 1(1). **R v Sowden** [1964] **3** 770, CCA.
Jurisdiction—Jurisdiction to grant legal aid in criminal proceedings—Meaning of criminal proceedings—Legal Aid Act 1988, s 19. **R v Bow Street Magistrates' Court, ex p Shayler** [1999] **1** 98, QBD.
Solicitor and counsel—Serious case—Prisoner charged with serious offence carrying heavy penalty should be given legal aid for representation by solicitor and counsel. **R v Howes** [1964] **2** 172, CCA.
Withdrawal of solicitors—Whether fresh certificate for solicitors should be granted—Grant of services of counsel only an emergency measure—Discretion of court—Poor Prisoner's Defence Act 1930 ss 1(1), 3(3). **R v Sowden** [1964] **3** 770, CCA.
Legal aid costs and contributions—
Generally. *See* **Criminal law** (Costs—Power to award costs).
Offer of legal aid—
Guilty plea—Offer of legal aid to be made by court where heavy sentence likely even though accused pleads guilty—Sentence of 30 months marginal—Duty of court to ensure representation where circumstances clearly require careful inquiry. **R v Green** [1968] **2** 77, CA.
Guilty plea—Offer to be made by court where heavy sentence likely even though accused pleads guilty. **R v Serghiou** [1966] **3** 637, CA.
Guilty plea—Offer to be made by court where heavy sentence likely even though accused pleads guilty—Offer of legal aid, or explanation why legal aid not offered, should be on record of trial court even though accused declines legal aid. **R v Hooper** [1967] **1** 766, CA.
Order for purpose of proceedings before magistrates' court—
Reference of question to European Court—Proceedings before magistrates' court including proceedings before European Court—Applicability of legal aid order to proceedings before European Court—Defendant a national of member state of European Economic Community—Defendant migrant worker in United Kingdom—Defendant charged with drugs offence in magistrates' court—Defendant granted legal aid for purpose of proceedings before magistrates' court—Reference to European Court of question whether magistrates' court having power to make deportation order—Whether legal aid order covering proceedings before European Court—Legal Aid Act 1974, s 28(2)—EEC Treaty, arts 48, 177. **R v Marlborough Street Stipendiary Magistrate, ex p Bouchereau** [1977] **3** 365, QBD.
Power to award costs. *See* **Criminal law** (Costs—Power to award costs).
Practice—
Appeal—Legal aid order—Legal Aid Act 1974, s 30(7). **Practice Note** [1974] **2** 805, CA.
Refusal of legal aid—
Failure to provide complete statement of means before conclusion of proceedings—Applicant solicitors applying for legal aid for client on day of client's summary trial and conviction—Documentary evidence required to support statement of means sent two weeks later—Justices' clerk refusing legal aid on ground that supporting documentary evidence received after conclusion of proceedings—Whether legal aid order could be granted after conclusion of proceedings to cover work earlier undertaken—Legal Aid in Criminal and Care Proceedings (General) Regulations 1989, regs 11, 23, 44(7). **R v Highbury Corner Magistrates' Court, ex p D J Sonn & Co (a firm)** [1995] **4** 57, QBD.

LEGAL AID (cont)—
  Criminal cases (cont)—
    Refusal of legal aid (cont)—
      Review of decision to refuse legal aid—When application for review to be made—Application required to be made no later than 21 days before 'date fixed for ... trial ... or ... inquiry'—Offence triable either way—Magistrates refusing legal aid—Magistrates refusing to allow review of refusal because application made within 21 days of defendant's first appearance in court—Whether first appearance in court is 'date fixed for ... trial ... or ... inquiry'—Legal Aid in Criminal Proceedings (General) Regulations 1968, reg 6E(2)(c). **R v Bury Magistrates, ex p N (a minor)** [1986] **3** 789, QBD.
    Representation by counsel—
      Assignment of two counsel—Application for order for two counsel—Procedure—Legal Aid in Criminal and Care Proceedings (General) Regulations 1989, reg 48(3). **Practice Note** [1989] **2** 479, QBD.
      Assignment of two counsel—Entitlement to two counsel—Requirement that one counsel be Queen's Counsel or senior counsel—Whether defendant entitled to avail himself of two junior counsel—Whether defendant entitled to choose own counsel—Whether refusal to allow defendant ability to choose counsel breach of convention rights—Human Rights Act 1998, Sch 1, Pt I, art 6—Criminal Aid Certificate Rules (Northern Ireland) 2012, SR 2012/135, r 4—Code of Conduct for the Bar of Northern Ireland, r 20.11. **Maguire's application for judicial review (Northern Ireland), Re** [2018] **3** 30, SC.
      Assignment of two or three counsel—Application for order for two counsel—Procedure—Legal Aid in Criminal and Care Proceedings (General) Regulations 1989, reg 48(14)(a), (b). **Practice Note** [1995] **1** 307, CA.
      Indictable offence—Legal aid not including representation by counsel except in the case of an indictable offence—Meaning of 'indictable offence'—Whether including offence triable either summarily or on indictment—Legal Aid Act 1974, s 30(2)(a). **R v Guildhall Justices, ex p Marshall** [1976] **1** 767, QBD.
      Joint defendants—Defendants' right to separate representation—Defendants assigned same solicitor—Whether solicitor having right to select separate counsel to represent defendants—Whether each counsel entitled to be paid out of legal aid fund—Legal Aid in Criminal Proceedings (General) Regulations 1968, regs 9, 14. **R v O'Brien** [1985] **1** 971, QBD.
    Revocation of legal aid for non-payment of contributions—
      Fresh application for legal aid made to trial court after revocation of legal aid order—Whether application may be made at pre-trial proceedings—Legal Aid in Criminal and Care Proceedings (General) Regulations 1989, reg 10. **R v Liverpool City Magistrates' Court, ex p Pender (No 2)** [1994] **2** 897, QBD.
      Refusal by clerk to justices of fresh application for legal aid—Whether clerk to justices having power to grant fresh application following revocation of legal aid—Whether person wishing to reapply for legal aid must do so to court at trial—Legal Aid in Criminal and Care Proceedings (General) Regulations 1989, regs 10, 11, Pts II, IV. **R v Liverpool City Magistrates' Court, ex p Shacklady** [1993] **2** 929, QBD.
    Solicitors' fees—
      Uplift in fees for cases which 'relate to' serious or complex fraud—Meaning of 'relate to'—Legal Aid in Criminal and Care Proceedings (Costs) Regulations 1989, Sch 1, Pt 1, para 3(5). **Murria (a firm) v Lord Chancellor** [2000] **2** 941, QBD.
    Solicitors' fees—
      Duty provider work (DPW)—Judicial review of Lord Chancellor's decision to introduce tendering process for limited number of DPW contracts—Whether failure to take account of investment costs required—Whether failure to investigate extent and financial implications of investment costs—Whether proposed measures of support legally sufficient—Whether decision irrational. **R (on the application of the London Criminal Courts Solicitors' Association) v Lord Chancellor** [2016] **3** 296, CA.
    Taxation of costs—
      Generally. *See* Taxation of costs—Criminal proceedings, *below.*
      Solicitor's fees and expenses. *See* Taxation of costs—Solicitor's fees and expenses—Criminal proceedings, *below.*
    Trial—
      Time when application must be made—Committal for trial to Crown Court—Application to Crown Court for legal aid—Application made at conclusion of trial—Whether court having jurisdiction to entertain application—Legal Aid Act 1974, s 28(7). **R v Tullett** [1976] **2** 1032, Crown Ct.
  Defence certificate—
    Criminal appeal. *See* **Criminal law** (Appeal—Defence certificate).
  Discharge of certificate. *See* Certificate—Discharge, *above.*
  Divorce—
    Costs. *See* Costs—Divorce, *above.*
    Generally. *See* **Divorce** (Legal aid).
  Domestic violence. *See* Entitlement—Domestic violence, *below.*
  Entitlement—
    Assessment of resources—
      Exclusion of subject-matter of dispute—Divorce—Application by wife for legal aid to defend petition, to cross-petition and to claim maintenance—Alimony pending suit ordered subsequently—Whether alimony taken into account in computing wife's disposable income—Whether maintenance so taken into account where application is to reduce the amount payable—Legal Aid and Advice Act 1949, s 4(3)—Legal Aid (Assessment of Resources) Regulations 1950 (SI 1950 No 1358), reg 2. **Taylor v National Assistance Board** [1957] **3** 703, HL.
      Trustee in bankruptcy—Proposed proceedings by petitioning creditor in name of trustee—Impropriety of joining petitioning creditor as co-applicant. **Crossley (a debtor), Re** [1954] **3** 296, Ch D.

LEGAL AID (cont)—
  Entitlement (cont)—
    Domestic violence—
      Supporting documents—Claimant seeking judicial review of regulation requiring supporting evidence of domestic violence within 24 months of application for legal aid—Whether regulation ultra vires—Whether regulations frustrating statutory purpose of primary legislation—Legal Aid, Sentencing and Punishment of Offenders Act 2012, s 12—Civil Legal Aid (Procedure) Regulations 2012, SI 2012/3098, reg 33. **R (on the application of Rights of Women) v Lord Chancellor and Secretary of State for Justice** [2016] 3 473, CA.
    Judicial review—
      'No permission, no fee' arrangement—Whether 'no permission, no fee' arrangement for making legally-aided application for judicial review ultra vires or inconsistent with statutory purpose—Legal Aid, Sentencing and Punishment of Offenders Act 2012, s 2(3)—Civil Legal Aid (Merits Criteria) Regulations 2013, SI 2013/104—Civil Legal Aid (Remuneration) Regulations 2013, SI 2013/422, reg 5A. **R (on the application of Ben Hoare Bell Solicitors) v Lord Chancellor** [2016] 2 46, DC.
  Exceptional cases funding. See Civil legal aid—Exceptional cases funding, above.
  Expert evidence—
    Remuneration of expert witness—
      Expert witness claiming under alleged contract for payment of fees by solicitor—Solicitor acting for legally aided defendant in criminal proceedings—Whether such contract precluded by law and therefore unenforceable—Legal Aid in Criminal and Care Proceedings (General) Regulations 1989, reg 55. **Goulden v Wilson Barca (a firm)** [2000] 1 169, CA.
    Taxation of costs. See Taxation of costs—Expert evidence, below.
  Expert's fee. See Taxation of costs, below.
  Extension of time for issue of full certificate. See Certificate—Extension of time for issue of full certificate, above.
  False information—
    Revocation of certificate. See Certificate—Revocation by court—Charge against assisted person of furnishing false information, above.
  Family proceedings—
    Funding from HM Courts Service—
      Private law cases involving children—Correct approach where 'exceptional' funding via legal aid unavailable—Whether court could properly direct that cost of certain activities should be borne by HM Courts and Tribunals Service—Matrimonial and Family Proceedings Act 1984, s 31G(6)—Human Rights Act 1998, Sch 1, Pt I, arts 8, 10—Legal Aid, Sentencing and Punishment of Offenders Act 2012, s 10—Family Procedure Rules 2010, SI 2010/2955, r 1.1(1). **Q v Q** [2015] 3 759, Fam Ct.
  Financial conditions of legal aid—
    Calculation of capital—
      Interest in land—Civil legal aid to fund private family law proceedings—Legal aid refused on basis applicant's interest in property co-owned with former partner exceeding threshold—Applicant unable to sell or borrow against property—Whether Director of Legal Aid Casework having discretion to value property at nil—Whether refusal of legal aid breach of applicant's convention rights—Human Rights Act 1998, Sch 1, Pt I, arts 6, 8—Civil Legal Aid (Financial Resources and Payment for Services) Regulations 2013, SI 2013/480, regs 31, 37. **R (on the application of GR) v Director of Legal Aid Casework (Lord Chancellor, interested party)** [2021] 3 1166, QBD.
  Liability of assisted person not to exceed amount which is reasonable having regard to circumstances—
    Means of assisted person—Divorce—Ancillary proceedings—Lump sum payable to wife under court order wife's 'means'—Court entitled to take lump sum into account in assessing wife's liability to pay husband's costs of successful appeal against transfer of property order—Legal Aid Act 1974, s 8(1)(e). **McDonnell v McDonnell** [1977] 1 766, CA.
  House of Lords—
    Costs—
      Application for costs or expenses against legally-aided party. See **House of Lords** (Costs—Application for costs or expenses against legally-aided party).
  Inquest—
    State's obligation to investigate death. See **Human rights** (Right to life—State's obligation to investigate death in circumstances where state arguably in breach of substantive obligation under convention right to life).
  Land charge—
    Matrimonial home—
      Costs. See Costs—Matrimonial home, above.
  Legal Aid Board—
    Judicial review of decision—
      Availability of remedy. See **Judicial review** (Availability of remedy—Justiciable issue—Legal Aid Board).
  Legal aid committee—
    Certiorari to quash decision of. See **Certiorari** (Jurisdiction—Legal aid committee).
    Matters to be taken into consideration in determining whether to grant or refuse certificate. See Certificate—Grant—Matters to be taken into consideration by legal aid committee in determining whether to grant or refuse certificate, above.
  Legal aid fund—
    Charge for benefit of fund on property recovered or preserved. See Charge on property recovered for deficiency of costs, above.
    Garnishee proceedings—
      Sum representing damages paid to legal aid fund—Existing debt to assisted person—Garnishee order obtained against Law Society—Legal Aid (General) Regulations 1950 (SI 1950 No 1359), reg 16(6). **Dawson v Preston (Law Society, garnishee)** [1955] 3 314, QBD Divl Ct.
    Unassisted person's costs out of legal aid fund. See Unassisted person's costs out of legal aid fund, below.

LEGAL AID (cont)—
Legal services—
    Civil legal services. *See* Civil legal services, *above.*
Legal Services Commission. *See* **Community legal service funding** (Legal Services Commission).
Magistrates' court—
    Criminal cases. *See* Criminal cases, *above.*
Matrimonial cause—
    Legal aid certificate. *See* Certificate—Scope of certificate—Matrimonial cause, *above.*
Matrimonial home—
    Registration of land charge—
        Costs. *See* Costs—Matrimonial home, *above.*
Minority shareholder—
    Representative action. *See* **Company** (Minority shareholder—Representative action—Legal aid).
Mortgaged property—
    Mortgagor plaintiff challenging mortgagee's sale—
        Whether mortgagee could recover costs under mortgage if action failed. *See* **Mortgage** (Costs—Protecting security).
Multi-party action arrangements—
    Procedure—
        Contract to represent generic plaintiffs—Decision-making process of committee considering solicitors' tender applications. **R v Legal Aid Board, ex p Donn & Co (a firm)** [1996] **3** 1, QBD.
Order for costs—
    Award of costs against assisted person—
        Costs to be taxed on indemnity basis—Whether court's jurisdiction to award costs limited by legal aid rules—Whether court having discretion to award inter partes costs on indemnity basis—Supreme Court Act 1981, s 51—Civil Legal Aid (General) Regulations 1989, reg 107—RSC Ord 62, r 12. **Willis v Redbridge Health Authority** [1996] **3** 114, CA.
        Enforcement of order—Assessment of legally assisted person's resources—Whether interest of spouse of legally assisted person in matrimonial home to be aggregated—Whether costs order should be enforced—Legal Aid Act 1988, s 17—Civil Legal Aid (General) Regulations 1989, reg 126. **Waterford Wedgwood plc v David Nagli Ltd (Haughton and anor, third parties)** [1999] **3** 185, Ch D.
        Enforcement of order—Assisted party's action against unassisted defendants struck out for want of prosecution and costs awarded to defendants, not to be enforced without leave of court—Plaintiff bringing action against solicitors and settlement of action including indemnity against liability for defendants' costs—Defendants seeking to enforce costs order on grounds that plaintiff's circumstances had changed—Whether defendants entitled to enforce order—Civil Legal Aid (General) Regulations 1989, reg 130. **Wraith v Wraith** [1997] **2** 526, CA.
        Enforcement of order—Assisted persons ordered to pay successful litigants' costs—Charging order made against assisted persons' house in respect of costs—Enforcement of charge ordered against proceeds of sale of house—Whether charging order 'execution'—Whether court entitled to make charging order against assisted litigants' house—Whether court entitled to order enforcement of charge against proceeds of sale of house—Legal Aid Act 1988, s 17(3)(b). **Parr v Smith** [1995] **2** 1031, CA.
        Enforcement of order—Costs to be paid out of proceeds of sale of dwelling house—Whether proceeds of sale forming disposable capital of assisted person—Legal Aid Act 1988, s 17. **Chaggar v Chaggar** [1997] **1** 104, CA.
        Enforcement of order—Court of Appeal, following appeal from county court, making order for costs against assisted person, not to be enforced without leave of the court—Whether leave of Court of Appeal or of county court required to enforce order—Supreme Court Act 1981, ss 15(4), 17(1)—County Courts Act 1984, s 76. **Ager v Ager** [1998] **1** 703, CA.
        Form of order. **Practice Direction** [1954] **1** 255, HL.
        Order not complied with—Assisted person serving statutory demand for payment of costs with consent of Legal Aid Board—Whether order for costs debt—Whether assisted person having locus standi to serve statutory demand—Whether Legal Aid Board having power to authorise service of statutory demand—Legal Aid Act 1988, s 16(5)—Civil Legal Aid (General) Regulations 1989, regs 87(1)(a), 91(2). **Debtor (No 68/5D/97), Re a** [1998] **4** 779, Ch D.
    Exercise of discretion—
        Nil contribution of assisted person—Legal Aid and Advice Act 1949, s 2(2)(e). **Crystall v Crystall** [1963] **2** 330, CA.
        Nil contribution of assisted person—Order to pay full taxed costs of hire-purchase action—Legal Aid and Advice Act 1949, s 2(2)(e). **Mercantile Credit Co Ltd v Cross** [1965] **1** 577, CA.
        Substantial justice between parties—Matrimonial proceedings—Legal Aid and Advice Act 1949, s 1(7)(b). **Corbett v Corbett (orse Ashley) (No 2)** [1970] **2** 654, Div.
        Successful plaintiff in action for fraud—All parties legally aided—Judgment against defendant husband and wife but wife not dishonest—Contributions of defendants different—Costs awarded in proportion to and subject to limit of contributions—Legal Aid and Advice Act 1949, ss 1(7)(b), 2(2)(e). **Blatcher v Heaysman** [1960] **2** 721, CA.
    Order against successful party—
        Relief of legal aid fund—Relevance—Order in favour of unsuccessful petitioner against successful party cited. **Howell v Howell** [1953] **2** 628, CA.
    Variation—
        Application—Chancery Division—Practice—Legal Aid (General) Regulations 1950 (SI 1950 No 1359), reg 17(4), as substituted by Legal Aid (General)(Amendment No 1) Regulations 1954 (SI 1954 No 166). **Wing v Spring** [1958] **3** 43, Ch D.
        Factors to be considered—Change in circumstances—Variation of order against legally assisted person—Legal Aid (General) Regulations 1950 (SI 1950 No 1359), reg 17(4), as substituted by Legal Aid (General) (Amendment No 1) Regulations 1954 (SI 1954 No 166). **Corrick v Northam** [1956] **2** 174, QBD.
        Whether court having jurisdiction to vary costs order against assisted person whose legal aid certificate was subsequently revoked—Civil Legal Aid (General) Regulations 1989, regs 74(2), 130(b). **DEG-Deutsche Investitions und Entwicklungsgesellschaft mbH v Koshy** [2001] **3** 878, CA.

LEGAL AID (cont)—
  Overpayment—
    Recoupment—
      Counsel's fees. *See* Counsel's fees—Civil legal aid certificate, *above.*
  Payment into court—
    Costs. *See* Costs—Payment into court, *above.*
    Taxation of costs. *See* Taxation of costs—Payment into court, *below.*
  Privilege—
    Absolute privilege—
      Document sent by defendants to financial regulator in course of investigation—Whether defence of absolute privilege applying to document. **Mahon v Rahn (No 2)** [1999] **2 Comm** 789, QBD; [2000] **2 Comm** 1, CA; [2000] **4** 41, CA.
  Queen's Proctor's intervention—
    Costs—
      Divorce. *See* Costs—Divorce—Queen's Proctor's intervention, *above.*
  Remuneration of persons giving legal aid. *See* Costs—Remuneration of persons giving legal aid, *above.*
  Remuneration of providers—
    Criminal cases—
      Lord Chancellor reducing maximum number of pages of prosecution evidence counted in fixing graduated fees—Whether decision procedurally unfair—Whether decision irrational—Whether implementing regulations unlawful—Criminal Legal Aid (Remuneration) (Amendment) Regulations 2017, SI 2017/1019. **R (on the application of the Law Society) v Lord Chancellor** [2019] **1** 638, DC.
  Representation by counsel—
    Criminal cases. *See* Criminal cases—Representation by counsel, *above.*
  Revocation of certificate by court. *See* Certificate—Revocation by court, *above.*
  Scale of costs—
    Taxation. *See* Taxation of costs—Scale of costs, *below.*
  Security for costs—
    Action founded on tort commenced in High Court—
      Remittance of action to county court unless security given by plaintiff for defendant's costs—Legal aid certificate issued to plaintiff—Jurisdiction to remit action—County Courts Act 1934, s 46(1), (2). **Burton v Holdsworth** [1951] **2** 381, CA.
    Appeal in bankruptcy proceedings—
      Application for dispensation from payment—Certificate authorising bringing of appeal—Whether bankrupt automatically entitled to a dispensation—Bankruptcy Rules 1952 (SI 1952 No 2113), r 129. **Traviss (a bankrupt), Re, ex p the Bankrupt v Official Receiver** [1971] **2** 1257, Ch D.
      Costs of appeal—Bankrupt's appeal. **Cohen (a bankrupt), Re, ex p the Bankrupt v Trustee of the Property of the Bankrupt** [1961] **1** 646, CA.
    Costs of appeal—
      Bankrupt's appeal. *See* Security for costs—Appeal in bankruptcy proceedings—Costs of appeal, *above.*
      Circumstances in which assisted person ordered to give security for costs. **Wyld v Silver (No 2)** [1962] **2** 809, CA.
      Plaintiff not assisted person when order first made—Subsequent grant of emergency certificate—Effect on order—Legal Aid and Advice Act 1949, s 12(2)(b)(ii). **Conway v Wimpey (George) & Co Ltd** [1951] **1** 56, CA.
      'Special circumstance'—Plaintiff 'assisted person' in court of first instance—Substantial contribution then ordered—RSC, Ord 58, r 15(2). **Bampton v Cook** [1954] **1** 457, CA.
    Discretion—
      County court claim by company—Assignment of company including claim to director—Director but not company eligible for legal aid—Director added as co-plaintiff—Whether joinder a device to avoid rule that company not eligible for legal aid—Whether joinder should be set aside. **Eurocross Sales Ltd v Cornhill Insurance plc** [1995] **4** 950, CA.
      Exercise—Substantial justice between parties—Matrimonial proceedings—Legal Aid and Advice Act 1949, s 1(7)(b). **Corbett v Corbett (orse Ashley) (No 2)** [1970] **2** 654, Div.
    Matrimonial causes—
      Right of wife to apply for security for costs—Application by wife in divorce proceedings—Husband an 'assisted person'—Legal Aid and Advice Act 1949, s 12(2)(b)(ii). **Evans v Evans** [1953] **1** 70, CA; **Vincent v Vincent** [1952] **2** 978, Div.
      Wife respondent to divorce petition an assisted person—Respondent's answer and cross-prayer abandoned at hearing in view of respondent's evidence—Whether respondent entitled to order for costs, the husband having given security. **Mines v Mines** [1957] **1** 667, Div.
    Plaintiff an assisted person resident out of the jurisdiction—
      Relevance of fact plaintiff assisted person—Relevance as to quantum. **Friedmann v Austay (London) Ltd** [1954] **1** 594, Ch D.
      Right of defendant to security—Whether fact that plaintiff assisted person disentitling defendant to order for security—Legal Aid and Advice Act 1949, s 1(7)(b). **Jackson v John Dickinson & Co (Bolton) Ltd** [1952] **1** 104, CA.
    Right of assisted person to order—
      Matrimonial cause—Amount of order—Wife's case conducted by salaried solicitor—Wife poor person when application first made—Legal Aid (General) Regulations 1950 (SI 1950 No 1359), reg 5(10). **Wigley v Wigley** [1950] **2** 1218, CA.
      Need of evidence of means. **Williams v Williams** [1953] **2** 474, CA.
  Set-off—
    Costs. *See* Costs—Set-off, *above.*
  Solicitor—
    Duty to legally assisted client. *See* Solicitor (Client—Legally assisted client—Duty to).

LEGAL AID (cont)—
Taxation of costs—
Advice and assistance—
Client receiving advice and assistance under green form scheme—Client signing general retainer instructing solicitors to act on indemnity basis—Client successful in claim against defendants—Solicitors submitting bill including amount for pre-legal aid certificate costs—Whether client could at same time be subject to both statutory and private retainers—Whether general retainer a sham to enable solicitors to recover costs incurred outwith the green form scheme from unsuccessful defendant on indemnity basis—Whether solicitors entitled to recover pre-legal aid certificate costs from defendants—Legal Advice and Assistance Regulations (No 2) 1980, reg 15. **Joyce v Kammac (1988) Ltd** [1996] **1** 923, QBD.
Agreement as to costs—
Proceedings to which assisted person a party—Assessment of costs by area director of Legal Aid Board—Procedure—Civil Legal Aid (General) Regulations 1989, reg 106(1), (2). **Practice Direction** [1989] **3** 960, SC Taxing Office.
Proceedings to which assisted person a party—Assessment of costs by Law Society—Matrimonial causes—Procedure—Legal Aid Act 1974, Sch 2—Legal Aid (General) Regulations 1980, reg 100A. **Practice Direction** [1984] **1** 944, Fam D.
Proceedings to which assisted person a party—Assessment of costs by Law Society—Procedure—Legal Aid (General) Regulations 1980, reg 100A. **Practice Direction** [1984] **1** 919, SC Taxing Office.
Assessment of resources—
Income exceeding prescribed figure—Income—Income including benefits and privileges—Sums received as benefits and privileges rather than by way of legal right—Element of recurrence—Gifts and loans—Whether gifts and loans from friends and relations constituting 'income'—Legal Aid (Assessment of Resources) Regulations 1960 (SI 1960 No 1471), reg 1(2), Sch 1, para 1. **R v Supplementary Benefits Commission, ex p Singer** [1973] **2** 931, QBD.
Certificate—
Transitional provisions—Work done partly before 1961 and partly after 1960—Legal Aid (General) (Amendment No 4) Regulations 1960 (SI 1960 No 2369). **Practice Direction** [1961] **1** 64, SC Taxing Office.
Counsel's and solicitors' fees—
Attendance of country solicitor on examination of witness on commission—Fees for instructions to counsel on examination and for supplemental instructions—Attendance of country solicitor at conference, consultations, and trial in London—Legal Aid and Advice Act 1949, Sch III, para 4(1). **Theocharides v Joannou** [1955] **1** 615, Ch D.
Country solicitor attending trial in London—Leading counsel advising attendance. **McCullie v Butler** [1961] **2** 554, QBD.
Disallowance—Advice on evidence before delivery of defence—Attendance of country solicitor at consultation in London—Conference to advise plaintiff to agree to settlement—Legal Aid and Advice Act 1949, Sch III, para 4(1). **Warman v Barclays Bank Ltd** [1953] **2** 1575, Ch D.
Counsel's fee—
Additional fee—Case outside London or large assize centres—Right of assisted litigant to select counsel from appropriate panel—Fair and reasonable remuneration—Legal Aid and Advice Act 1949, s 6(4), Sch III, para 4(1). **Self v Self** [1954] **2** 550, Div.
Appeal to taxing master against fees allowed in criminal proceedings—Counsel appearing at appeal on behalf of another barrister—Whether counsel's fee for attending appeal should be allowed if appeal successful—Legal Aid in Criminal Proceedings (Costs) Regulations 1982, reg 11. **R v Boswell** [1987] **2** 513, QBD.
Counsel's and solicitors' fees. See Taxation of costs—Counsel's and solicitors' fees, above.
Divorce petition heard outside London—Undefended suit—Counsel appearing in two cases on same day—Legal Aid and Advice Act 1949, Sch III, para 4(1)—Legal Aid (General) Regulations 1950 (SI 1950 No 1359), reg 18(3). **Isaacs v Isaacs** [1955] **2** 811, Div.
Divorce petition heard outside London—Undefended suit—Hearing at assize town—Legal Aid and Advice Act 1949, Sch III, para 1(1)—Legal Aid (General) Regulations 1950 (SI 1950 No 1359), reg 18(3). **Young v Young and Kohler** [1955] **1** 796, Div.
Divorce petition heard outside London—Undefended suit—Normal fee for counsel reduced on taxation—No special facts or circumstances stated by taxing officer—Legal Aid and Advice Act 1949, Sch III, para 4(1). **Eaves v Eaves and Powell** [1955] **3** 849, Div.
Leading counsel—Duty of solicitor acting for legally aided client—Duty not to brief leading counsel without client's authority—Duty to explain to client effect of cost of briefing leading counsel—When leading counsel should not be briefed for legally aided client—Whether court entitled under inherent jurisdiction to inquire into propriety of briefing leading counsel—Solicitors Act 1974, s 50(2)—Legal Aid (General) Regulations 1980, regs 60(1), 64(2). **Solicitors, Re, Re Taxation of Costs** [1982] **2** 683, Ch D.
Matrimonial causes. **Practice Note** [1957] **2** 604, Div.
Scope of certificate. See Certificate—Scope of certificate—Counsel's fees, above.
Criminal proceedings—
Appeal from decision of costs judge—Certification of principle of general importance—Whether High Court judge having power on appeal from costs judge to permit solicitor to make new claims—Whether appeal from decision of costs judge restricted to principle of general importance certified—Legal Aid in Criminal and Care Proceedings (Costs) Regulations 1989, regs 15, 16. **Patten (t/a Anthony Patten & Co) v Lord Chancellor** [2001] **3** 886, QBD.
Appeal from decision of taxing master—Procedure—Legal Aid in Criminal Proceedings (Fees and Expenses) Regulations 1968 (SI 1968 No 1230), reg 10. **Practice Direction** [1968] **3** 869, .
Appeal to High Court against review of taxation—Amendment of provision for awarding costs taking place between review and appeal—Solicitors' fees and expenses in criminal proceedings—Whether court entitled to take amendment into consideration—Whether amendment a procedural amendment—Whether nevertheless court required to deal with matter on same basis as that applicable when taxation was initiated—Legal Aid in Criminal Proceedings (Fees and Expenses) Regulations 1968 (SI 1968 No 1230), regs 7(6) (as substituted by the Legal Aid in Criminal Proceedings (Fees and Expenses) (Amendment) Regulations 1977 (SI 1977 No 875)), 10(4). **R v Dunwoodie** [1978] **1** 923, QBD.

LEGAL AID (cont)—
    Taxation of costs (cont)—
        Criminal proceedings (cont)—
            Crown Court—Attendance of solicitor at trial. *See* Taxation of costs—Solicitor's fees and expenses—Criminal proceedings—Attendance of solicitor at trial, *below*.

            Crown Court—Disallowance by taxing authority of fees and expenses—Work unreasonably done—Duty of judge to make observations for attention of taxing authority—Opportunity for counsel or solicitors whose fees or expenses might be affected to make representations—Matters to which taxing authority should have regard. **Practice Direction** [1977] **1** 542, Crown Ct.

            Crown Court—Preparation by solicitor of case for trial. *See* Taxation of costs—Solicitor's fees and expenses—Criminal proceedings—Method of charging for work of preparing case for trial, *below*.

            Crown Court—Review of decision of taxing authority—Procedure—Legal Aid in Criminal Proceedings (Fees and Expenses) Regulations 1968 (SI 1968 No 1230), reg 9. **Practice Direction** [1972] **2** 984, SC Taxing Office.

            Crown Court—Work undertaken and disbursements incurred by solicitor prior to assignment to client under legal aid order—Claim by solicitor for payment in respect of that work and those disbursements—Whether payment could be authorised for work undertaken and disbursements incurred before grant of legal aid order—Legal Aid Act 1974, s 28(7). **R v Rogers** [1979] **1** 693, Sup Ct Tax Office.

            Review of decision of taxing authority—Judicature fee—Payment—Legal Aid in Criminal Proceedings (Fees and Expenses) Regulations 1968 (SI 1968 No 1230), reg 9. **Practice Direction** [1971] **1** 576, SC Taxing Office.

            Review of decision of taxing authority—Procedure—Legal Aid in Criminal Proceedings (Fees and Expenses) Regulations 1968 (SI 1968 No 1230), reg 9. **Practice Direction** [1968] **3** 870, QBD.

        Direction for taxation—
            Effect—Interlocutory proceedings—Costs of interlocutory application reserved to trial judge—Direction by trial judge for legal aid taxation—No specific order as to costs of interlocutory applications—Costs reserved inter partes—Effect of direction for taxation—Legal Aid and Advice Act 1949, Sch III, para 4(1)—Legal Aid (General) Regulations 1950 (SI 1950 No 1359), reg 18(3) (as amended by SI 1954 No 166). **Paice v Paice** [1957] **2** 721, Div.

        Disallowance—
            View before trial. **Rolph v Marston Valley Brick Co Ltd** [1956] **2** 50, QBD.

        Dispensing with taxation—
            Procedure. *See* Taxation of costs—Procedure—Dispensing with taxation, *below*.

        Expert evidence—
            Solicitor and client costs—Disallowance, or partial disallowance, of items allowed in full on party and party taxation—Disbursements not previously authorised—Amounts received in full by legal aid fund from defendants—Legal Aid and Advice Act 1949, s 12(1)—Legal Aid (General) Regulations 1950 (SI 1950 No 1359), reg 14(4),(5),(6), as amended by Legal Aid (General) (Amendment No 1) Regulations 1954 (SI 1954 No 166), and Legal Aid (General) (Amendment No 2) Regulations 1955 (SI 1955 No 1829). **Ullah v Hall Line Ltd** [1960] **3** 488, QBD.

        Further allowance—
            Full value of work done—Costs representing full value of work done allowed on taxation as between party and party—No further allowance on solicitor-and-client basis—Legal Aid and Advice Act 1949, Sch III, para 4(1). **Lyon v Lyon** [1952] **2** 831, CA.

        Master's duty—
            Duty to consider each item—Solicitors agreeing quantum of profit costs in bill—Master allowing profit costs as agreed—Master taxing counsel's fees—Master disallowing item representing counsel's fee for conference on basis that no evidence conference had taken place—Solicitors' profit costs as allowed containing item for same conference—Master on disallowing one item bound to consider effect on other items in bill of costs. **Seabrook v Gascoignes (Reading) Ltd** [1973] **1** 1023, Ch D.

        Matrimonial causes—
            Direction for taxation of assisted person's costs. *See* **Divorce** (Costs—Taxation—Judgment or final order must include direction for taxation of costs of assisted person unless otherwise directed).

            Registration of ancillary order—Registration in magistrates' court of order for ancillary relief obtained in matrimonial cause. **Practice Note** [1959] **1** 576, PDA.

        Negotiations between solicitors and insurers—
            Personal injuries case—Costs of negotiations between plaintiff's solicitors and defendant's insurers recoverable against fund—Scottish solicitors acting as agents not solicitors within Legal Aid and Advice Act 1949—Proper method of taxing charges incurred by Scottish solicitors—Country solicitors' fee for attending trial in London—Costs of review of taxation—Legal Aid and Advice Act 1949, Sch 111, para 2(3). **McCullie v Butler** [1961] **2** 554, QBD.

        No order made as to costs—
            Duty of court to make order for taxation—Legal Aid and Advice Act 1949, ss 6(5), 6(6), Sch III—Legal Aid (General) Regulations 1950 (SI 1950 No 1359), reg 18(3). **Metcalf v Wells** [1953] **1** 626, CA.

            Need of order for taxation—Legal Aid and Advice Act 1949, Sch III, para 4(1)—Legal Aid (General)Regulations 1950 (SI 1950 No 1359), reg 18(3). **Brown v Brown** [1952] **1** 1018, CA.

            Power to make order for taxation—Legal Aid and Advice Act 1949, Sch III, para 4(1)—Legal Aid (General) Regulations 1950 (SI 1950 No 1359), reg 18(3). **Frost v Frost** [1952] **2** 1125, Div.

            Settlement by parties during trial—No term in settlement as to costs—Legal Aid (General) Regulations 1950 (SI 1950 No 1359), reg 18(3). **Metcalf v Wells** [1953] **1** 626, CA.

        Payment into court—
            Acceptance of money paid into court—Notice of acceptance—Taxation on notice of acceptance—Legal Aid and Advice Act 1949, Sch III—RSC Ord 62, r 10(2). **Practice Direction** [1971] **1** 576, SC Taxing Office.

        Principles to be applied—
            More generous allowance than in party and party taxation—Legal Aid and Advice Act 1949, Sch III, para 4(1)—RSC Ord 65, r 27(29). **Gibbs v Gibbs** [1952] **1** 942, Div.

LEGAL AID (cont)—
Taxation of costs (cont)—
Principles to be applied (cont)—
Solicitor's duty to assisted client—Advice of counsel—What costs properly incurred—Divorce—Inquiry by respondent wife for evidence of husband's adultery where not alleged by her in answer—Legal Aid and Advice Act 1949, s 1(7)(a), Sch III, para 4(1)—Legal Aid (General) Regulations 1950 (SI 1950 No 1359), reg 18(3), as amended by Legal Aid (General) (Amendment No 1) Regulations 1954 (SI 1954 No 166), reg 27. **Francis v Francis and Dickerson** [1955] **3** 836, Div.
Procedure—
Assisted person having financial interest in taxation—Notice to assisted person—Certificate—Legal aid summary—Certification of castings of bill of costs—Civil Legal Aid (General) Regulations 1989, regs 106(1)(2), 118, 119. **Practice Direction** [1993] **1** 263, SC Taxing Office.
Assisted person having financial interest in taxation—Notice to assisted person—Certificate—Legal aid summary—Certification of castings of bill of costs—Civil Legal Aid (General) Regulations 1989, regs 118, 119. **Practice Direction** [1991] **1** 703, SC Taxing Office.
Chancery Division—Consent orders made without personal attendance—Orders for taxation in legally aided cases. **Practice Direction** [1977] **2** 173, Ch D.
Chancery Division—Ex parte application—Written request for order for taxation—Papers to be lodged. **Practice Direction** [1969] **2** 1127, Ch D.
Chancery Division—Use of postal facilities. *See* **Practice** (Chancery Division—Applications by post or telephone).
Dispensing with taxation—Agreement regarding costs to be paid to assisted person—Acceptance by solicitor and counsel in full satisfaction of work done—Duty of taxing master or registrar to fix amount to be paid—Legal Aid (General) Regulations 1971 (SI 1971 No 62). **Practice Direction** [1972] **2** 624, SC Taxing Office.
Taxation of bills having both legal aid and inter partes element. **Practice Direction** [1994] **3** 125, SC Taxing Office.
Review of taxation—
Application for authority for review of taxation of legally-aided party's solicitor's costs—Principles to be applied by Legal Aid Board when considering application. **R v Legal Aid Board, ex p Bateman** [1992] **3** 490, QBD.
Costs of review. **McCullie v Butler** [1961] **2** 554, QBD.
Jurisdiction of court to order review—Application stated to be by plaintiff's solicitor—Legal Aid and Advice Act 1949, Sch III, para 4(1)—Legal Aid (General) Regulations 1950 (SI 1950 No 1359), reg 18(3)(b), as substituted by S I 1954 No 166, reg 27. **Sutton v Sears** [1959] **3** 545, QBD.
Jurisdiction of court to order review—Assisted person not financially interested and not having obtained authority of area committee to apply for review—Legal Aid and Advice Act 1949, Sch III, para 4(1)—Legal Aid (General) Regulations 1950 (SI 1950 No 1359), reg 18(3)(b), as substituted by SI 1954 No 166. **Hammond v Hammond** [1957] **3** 16, Div.
Jurisdiction of court to order review—Law Society refusing to give authority for review of taxation by judge—Solicitors applying to judge to have taxation reviewed in same way as an ordinary non-legal aid taxation—Whether legal aid costs able to be taxed and reviewed under ordinary procedure—Whether judge able to review legal aid taxation without Law Society's authority to do so—Legal Aid (General) Regulations 1971 (SI 1971 No 62), reg 23(7)—RSC Ord 62, r 35. **Storer v Wright** [1981] **1** 1015, CA.
Scale of costs—
Issue as to domicile—Both parties assisted—Law Society Divorce Department entitled to profit costs—Recommendation for increased fee for counsel—Legal Aid (General) Regulations 1950 (SI 1950 No 1359), reg 18(5) and schedule, as amended by Legal Aid (General) (Amendment No 1) Regulations 1954 (SI 1954 No 166), regs 12, 13. **Bezzi v Bezzi** [1955] **3** 785, Div.
Solicitor's fees and expenses—
Attendance fee for petitioner in divorce suit—Petitioner's evidence disbelieved by trial judge—Expenses of attendance at court—Whether vexatious and improper charge—Legal Aid and Advice Act 1949, Sch III, para 4(1). **Bock v Bock** [1955] **2** 793, Div.
Attendance of country solicitor at trial in London—Costs incurred on behalf of unsuccessful defendants in arranging payment of judgment debt—Legal Aid and Advice Act 1949, s 1(5), Sch III, para 4(1)—RSC Ord 65, r 27(29). **Marshall (W F) Ltd v Barnes and Fitzpatrick (a firm)** [1953] **1** 970, QBD.
Counsel's and solicitors' fees. *See* Taxation of costs—Counsel's and solicitors' fees, *above*.
Criminal proceedings—Attendance of solicitor at trial—Whether fee should be daily attendance fee or be calculated on same basis as that for preparation of case for trial—Legal Aid in Criminal Proceedings (Fees and Expenses) Regulations 1968 (SI 1968 No 1230) regs 2 and 17(6) (as substituted by the Legal Aid in Criminal Proceedings (Fees and Expenses) Amendment Regulations 1977 (SI 1977 No 875), reg 10(4)). **R v Wilkinson** [1980] **1** 597, QBD.
Criminal proceedings—Fair remuneration—Power of taxing authority to certify that owing to exceptional circumstances sums payable under regulations would not provide fair remuneration—Exceptional circumstances—Inflation—Whether effect of inflation an 'exceptional circumstance'—Legal Aid in Criminal Proceedings (Fees and Expenses) Regulations 1968 (SI 1968 No 1230), reg 7(6). **R v Dunwoodie** [1978] **1** 923, QBD.
Criminal proceedings—Method of charging for work of preparing case for trial—Solicitors adopting method based on hourly expense rate recorded on time record sheet by partner etc occupied directly on work for client—Whether that method providing reliable basis for taxation of costs. **R v Wilkinson** [1980] **1** 597, QBD.
Criminal proceedings—Principles to be applied—Effect of notes for guidance on taxation contained in non-statutory document issued to taxing officers—Effect of inflation on figures given in document—Assessment of hourly rate for work done—Degree of difficulty of case and status of person doing work relevant factors—Allowance for travelling time—Basis of assessment—Fee for attending court—Assessment—Application of broad average figures in taxations—Whether charges for criminal work should be higher or lower than those applicable in other types of work. **R v Dunwoodie** [1978] **1** 923, QBD.
Time limit. *See* **Costs** (Taxation—Time limit).
Transitional provisions—
Costs. *See* Bill of costs—Form—Transitional provisions, *above*.

Unassisted person's costs out of legal aid fund—

Appeal against refusal of order for payment—

Judge finding that unassisted party would not suffer severe financial hardship if order not made—Whether appeal lying from judge's decision—Legal Aid Act 1974, s 13(5). **Kelly v London Transport Executive** [1982] **2** 842, CA.

Circumstances in which order may be made—

Liability of assisted party to pay costs apart from Act—Divorce—Ancillary proceedings—Appeal—Husband unassisted person—Husband appealing against order transferring home to wife subject to fixed charge in his favour—Compromise offer by husband—Offer made without prejudice—Wife rejecting offer—Husband's appeal successful—Rejection of offer factor in exercise of court's discretion to award costs against wife on the merits—Rejection of offer unreasonable—Circumstances justifying order for payment by wife of husband's costs of appeal—Circumstances enabling court to make order for payment to husband of costs out of legal aid fund—Legal Aid Act 1974, s 13(1), (4). **McDonnell v McDonnell** [1977] **1** 766, CA.

Costs incurred by unassisted party—

Costs incurred in proceedings between him and party receiving legal aid—Costs incurred on appeal—District registrar entering judgment for plaintiff—Legally aided defendant appealing unsuccessfully to judge in chambers—Whether judge in chambers acting as appellate court—Legal Aid Act 1974, s 13(3). **Megarity v Law Society** [1981] **1** 641, HL.

Costs incurred in proceedings between him and party receiving legal aid—Costs of counterclaim where defendant legally aided—Counterclaim raising issues common to both claim and counterclaim—Judge ordering payment of plaintiff's costs of counterclaim out of legal aid fund and directing that the costs attributable to the common issues should be apportioned equally to the claim and counterclaim—Whether jurisdiction to make direction—Whether costs incurred in claim can be appropriated to counterclaim—Legal Aid Act 1974, s 13(1). **Millican v Tucker** [1980] **1** 1083, CA.

Costs incurred in proceedings between him and party receiving legal aid—Costs of counterclaim where defendant legally aided—Defendant admitting claim but pleading set off of counterclaim against claim—Application for legal aid for defendant limited to defence of claim—No application for legal aid to prosecute counterclaim—Legal aid certificate giving authority only to defend claim—Shortly before hearing certificate amended to cover counterclaim—Action settled in plaintiff's favour—Plaintiff applying for order for costs of counterclaim out of legal aid fund—Whether judge entitled to hold original certificate issued by mistake and that certificate covered counterclaim—Whether certificate conclusive of proceedings covered by it—Legal Aid Act 1974, s 13(1)—Legal Aid (General) Regulations 1971 (SI 1971 No 62), regs 2(2), 9(1). **Thew (R & T) Ltd v Reeves** [1981] **2** 964, CA.

Costs incurred in proceedings between him and party receiving legal aid—Proceedings finally decided in favour of unassisted party—Proceedings for judicial review—Appeal—Only one of decisions originally challenged forming subject of appeal—Order by appellate court—Whether 'proceedings finally decided' by appellate court—Whether 'proceedings' including all proceedings in court below—Whether appellate court entitled to order payment of costs incurred in connection with proceedings in court below—Legal Aid Act 1988, s 18(1), (2), (7). **R v Greenwich London BC, ex p Lovelace (No 2)** [1992] **1** 679, CA.

Costs incurred in proceedings between him and party receiving legal aid—Proceedings—Appeal—Order by appellate court—Whether 'proceedings' including proceedings in court below—Whether appellate court entitled to order payment of costs incurred in connection with proceedings in court below—Legal Aid Act 1964, s 1(1). **Shiloh Spinners Ltd v Harding (No 2)** [1973] **1** 966, HL.

Costs incurred in proceedings between him and party receiving legal aid—Proceedings—Interlocutory appeal—Interlocutory appeal in action in Queen's Bench Division for damages for personal injuries—Interlocutory appeal by legally aided plaintiff dismissed—Whether power to order payment of unassisted defendant's costs of appeal out of legal aid fund—Whether interlocutory appeal 'proceedings' in connection with which plaintiff receiving legal aid—Legal Aid Act 1974, s 13(1). **Megarity v Law Society** [1981] **1** 641, HL.

Incurred by—Agreement by insurance company to pay unassisted person's costs—No agreement by unassisted party's solicitors not to look to him for payment of costs—Whether costs 'incurred by' unassisted party—Legal Aid Act 1964, s 1(1). **Davies v Taylor (No 2)** [1973] **1** 959, HL.

Incurred by—Unassisted party member of Automobile Association—Association undertaking proceedings on behalf of unassisted party and paying solicitors—Whether costs 'incurred by' unassisted party—Legal Aid Act 1964, s 1(1). **Lewis v Averay (No 2)** [1973] **2** 229, CA.

Provisional order for payment of unassisted party's costs out of legal aid fund—Such orders not to be made as of course whenever unassisted party is successful—Legal Aid Act 1974, s 13. **Din v Wandsworth London BC (No 2)** [1982] **1** 1022, HL.

Costs incurred in court of first instance—

Divisional Court—Judicial review proceedings—Judicial review of county court order—Respondent to judicial review application granted legal aid—Divisional Court granting unassisted applicant relief sought—Court ordering that applicant's costs be paid out of legal aid fund—Whether Divisional Court a 'court of first instance'—Whether costs of application for judicial review 'costs incurred in a court of first instance'—Whether Divisional Court having power to order unassisted party's costs to be paid out of legal aid fund—Legal Aid Act 1974, s 13(3). **R v Leeds County Court, ex p Morris** [1990] **1** 550, QBD.

Divisional Court—Judicial review proceedings—Judicial review of decision of local authority—Whether Divisional Court hearing application for judicial review of decision of local authority a 'court of first instance'—Whether local authority's costs in defending judicial review proceedings 'costs incurred in a court of first instance'—Legal Aid Act 1988, s 18(4)(b). **R v Greenwich London BC, ex p Lovelace (No 2)** [1992] **1** 679, CA.

LEGAL AID (cont)—
    Unassisted person's costs out of legal aid fund (cont)—
        Costs incurred in proceedings in which apart from Act no order for costs would have been made—
            No order to be made in favour of unassisted party—Divorce proceedings—Petition by impecunious wife—Unsuccessful petition—Practice of divorce courts not to make order for costs against impecunious wife—Statutory discretion as to costs—Wife legally aided with nil contribution—Whether proceedings in which apart from Act order would have been made against wife—Whether court precluded from making order for payment to husband of costs out of legal aid fund—Supreme Court of Judicature (Consolidation) Act 1925, s 50—Legal Aid Act 1964, s 1(4). **Stewart v Stewart** [1974] **2** 795, CA.
        Costs recoverable where assisted person granted legal aid for part only of proceedings—
            Costs attributable to that part of proceedings—Attributable—Assisted party granted legal aid certificate for hearing only on day before hearing commenced—Successful unassisted party incurring substantial costs prior to grant of legal aid certificate in respect of preparation and reading of counsel's briefs for the hearing—Whether costs 'attributable to' part of proceedings for which legal aid granted limited to costs incurred while legal aid certificate in force—Whether costs of preparing and reading briefs 'attributable to' the hearing—Legal Aid Act 1974, s 14(5). **S v S (unassisted party's costs)** [1978] **1** 376, Fam D.
        Just and equitable—
            Action for personal injuries—Assisted plaintiff's claim without foundation—Plaintiff refusing £750 paid into court and offer of £4,000 before trial—Plaintiff awarded damages of £75—Defendant put to trouble and expense to expose plaintiff's groundless claim—Whether 'just and equitable' to order payment of defendant's costs out of legal aid fund—Legal Aid Act 1974, s 13(2). **Kelly v London Transport Executive** [1982] **2** 842, CA.
            Circumstances surrounding grant of certificate irrelevant—Legal Aid Act 1964, s 1(2). **Hanning v Maitland (No 2)** [1970] **1** 812, CA.
            Divorce proceedings—Unsuccessful petition by wife—Husband's costs—Wife's petition for divorce dismissed—Wife legally aided with a nil contribution—Husband an unassisted person—Application by husband at hearing for his costs out of legal aid fund—No order for costs made against wife—Whether making of order for husband's costs out of legal aid fund just and equitable—Legal Aid Act 1964, ss 1(2), (3)(b), (4), 6(3)—Matrimonial Causes Rules 1957 (SI 1957 No 619), rr 4(4), 17(8). **Nowotnik v Nowotnik (Hyatt intervening)** [1965] **3** 167, CA.
            Divorce proceedings—Unsuccessful petition by wife—Petition containing false and scandalous allegations—Wife legally aided—Decree awarded to husband on answer—Parties found equally to blame for breakdown of marriage in subsequent ancillary proceedings—Husband ordered to pay costs of ancillary proceedings—Whether just and equitable that husband should be awarded costs of divorce proceedings out of legal aid fund—Legal Aid Act 1964, s 1(2). **Stewart v Stewart** [1974] **2** 795, CA.
            Financial position of unassisted party—Relevance—Appeal to Court of Appeal—Fact that he has vast financial resources not of itself bar to application for costs—Unassisted party an insurance company—Legal Aid Act 1964, s 1(2). **General Accident, Fire and Life Assurance Corp Ltd v Foster** [1972] **3** 877, CA.
            Infant's custody—Appeal by mother from order of magistrates' court giving custody to father—Prospects of success of appeal small—Father's hypothetical contribution to legal aid fund would have exceeded his costs of appeal if he had been an assisted party—Whether just and equitable that an order for payment of his costs out of the legal aid fund should be made—Legal Aid Act 1964, s 1(2). **SL (infants), Re** [1967] **3** 538, Ch D.
            Judicial review proceedings—Judicial review of decision of local authority—Applicants for judicial review granted legal aid—Divisional Court refusing applicants relief sought—Unsuccessful appeal by applicants to Court of Appeal—Substantial proportion of local authority's expenditure met by local residents and businesses—Whether just and equitable that local authority's costs in Court of Appeal be paid out of legal aid fund—Legal Aid Act 1988, s 18(4)(c). **R v Greenwich London BC, ex p Lovelace (No 2)** [1992] **1** 679, CA.
            Leapfrog appeal—Appeal direct to House of Lords from High Court on point of law of general public importance—Legal aid granted to appellant in connection with appeal—Appeal dismissed—Costs incurred by respondent—Whether just and equitable that order for payment of costs out of legal aid fund be made—Legal Aid Act 1964, s 1(1), (2). **O'Brien v Robinson (No 2)** [1973] **1** 969, HL.
            Merits of proceedings—Court entitled to consider merits of proceedings by assisted party—Court entitled to consider course of events after legal aid certificate granted—Appeal by assisted party—Appeal a device for winning more time to avoid payment—Spurious defence put forward by assisted party—Legal aid enabling assisted party to pursue appeal—Unassisted party incurring costs as a result of grant of legal aid—Legal Aid Act 1964, s 1(2). **General Accident, Fire and Life Assurance Corp Ltd v Foster** [1972] **3** 877, CA.
            Order for payment if (and only if) court satisfied that it is just and equitable in all the circumstances—Discretion—Scope of discretion—Circumstances justifying order—Whether fact that unassisted party successful alone sufficient to justify an order—Legal Aid Act 1964, s 1(2). **Davies v Taylor (No 2)** [1973] **1** 959, HL.
            Refusal of legal aid—Unassisted party alleging legal aid unreasonably refused—Whether relevant in considering whether in force—Duration and equitable to make order—Legal Aid Act 1964, s 1(2). **Lewis v Averay (No 2)** [1973] **2** 229, CA.
            Successful appeal to Court of Appeal against decision in favour of assisted party—Onus of proving that it is just and equitable that order should be made—Onus on unassisted party—Evidence that successful unassisted party of limited means—Whether evidence sufficient to discharge onus—Legal Aid Act 1964, s 1(2). **Clifford v Walker** [1972] **2** 806, CA.
            Successful appeal to Court of Appeal against decision in favour of assisted party—Whether just and equitable that order for payment of costs out of legal aid fund should be made—Legal Aid Act 1964, s 1(2). **Saunders (exrx of the estate of Rose Maud Gallie (decd)) v Anglia Building Society (formerly Northampton Town and County Building Society) (No 2)** [1971] **1** 243, HL.
            Unassisted party bringing action on himself—Legal Aid Act 1964, s 1(2). **Hanning v Maitland (No 2)** [1970] **1** 812, CA.

LEGAL AID (cont)—
Unassisted person's costs out of legal aid fund (cont)—
  Just and equitable (cont)—
    Unsuccessful appeal to Court of Appeal by assisted party—Appeal on a point of constitutional importance—Unassisted party a police authority funded out of central funds—Whether just and equitable that police authority's costs be paid out of legal aid fund—Legal Aid Act 1974, s 13(2). **Maynard v Osmond (No 2)** [1979] **1** 483, CA.
  Matrimonial proceedings—
    Appeal against refusal of leave to implement collusive agreement with a view to divorce—Appeal by wife—Husband an assisted person—Appeal allowed—Husband not a person against whom an order for costs could be made apart from Act—Wife not entitled to costs out of legal aid fund—Legal Aid Act 1964, s 1(4). **Gosling v Gosling** [1967] **2** 510, CA.
  Order—
    Order by judge in chambers—Final or interlocutory order. **Hanning v Maitland** [1969] **3** 1558, CA.
    Suspended order—Whether suspended order to take effect after lapse of time in absence of objection by the Legal Aid Board contravening prohibition on making order 'forthwith'—Civil Legal Aid (General) Regulations 1989, reg 143. **H and anor (minors) (abduction: custody rights) (No 2), Re** [1992] **3** 380, HL.
  Proceedings finally decided in favour of unassisted party—
    Court by which proceedings finally decided in favour of unassisted party—Proceedings for judicial review—Appeal—Notice of appeal served but appeal later abandoned—Whether 'appeal' brought—Legal Aid Act 1988, s 18(7). **R v Greenwich London BC, ex p Lovelace (No 2)** [1992] **1** 679, CA.
    Sufficient if unassisted party substantially successful—Legally-aided plaintiff given judgment for considerably less than amount paid into court by unassisted defendant—Whether proceedings determined in favour of plaintiff because judgment given for him—Whether proceedings determined in favour of defendant because award less than amount paid into court—Legal Aid Act 1974, s 13(1). **Kelly v London Transport Executive** [1982] **2** 842, CA.
    Sufficient if unassisted party substantially successful—Order for summary judgment against assisted party—Variation of order below on appeal by assisted party—Assisted party failing to obtain unconditional leave to defend as to whole sum claimed by unassisted party—Whether unassisted party having substantially succeeded on appeal—Legal Aid Act 1964, s 1(1). **General Accident, Fire and Life Assurance Corp Ltd v Foster** [1972] **3** 877, CA.
  Severe financial hardship—
    Broad interpretation—Divorce proceedings—Financial hardship to husband—Husband enjoying substantial salary—Husband living in house too large for needs—Husband subject to heavy financial commitments—Legal Aid Act 1964, s 1(3)(b). **Hanning v Maitland (No 2)** [1970] **1** 812, CA; **Stewart v Stewart** [1974] **2** 795, CA.
    Company—Whether company able to suffer severe financial hardship—Legal Aid Act 1974, s 13(3)(b). **Thew (R & T) Ltd v Reeves** [1981] **2** 964, CA.
    Corporation—Large public transport undertaking—Corporation having £100,000 overdraft on its operations after receiving local government grant of £179m—Whether corporation would suffer severe financial hardship if its costs of £8,000 in successfully defending action not paid out of legal aid fund—Legal Aid Act 1974, s 13(3)(b). **Kelly v London Transport Executive** [1982] **2** 842, CA.
    Effect of hardship—Extent to which costs payable out of legal aid fund—Unassisted person establishing that he would suffer severe financial hardship if costs not paid out of legal aid fund—Whether unassisted person entitled to have whole of his costs paid out of legal aid fund—Whether unassisted person only entitled to have that part of his costs paid which would cause him severe financial hardship—Legal Aid Act 1974, s 13(3). **Adams v Riley** [1988] **1** 89, QBD.
    Local authority—Whether local authority would suffer severe financial hardship if its costs of between £70,000 and £80,000 in successfully defending judicial review proceedings not paid out of legal aid fund—Legal Aid Act 1988, s 18(4)(b). **R v Greenwich London BC, ex p Lovelace (No 2)** [1992] **1** 679, CA.
    Resources to be taken into account—Affidavit of resources—Failure to file affidavit within prescribed time limit—Whether court having power to grant extension of time—Legal Aid Act 1988, s 18—Civil Legal Aid (General) Regulations 1989, regs 7(2), 142(a). **Middleton v Middleton** [1994] **3** 236, CA.
    Resources to be taken into account—Affidavit of resources—Unassisted applicant for costs required to file affidavit of costs and resources to prove severe financial hardship—Unassisted person filing affidavit which did not contain specified matters or cover three years prior to application being made for costs—Whether court can make costs order where unassisted person's affidavit of costs and resources defective—Legal Aid Act 1988, s 18(4)(b)—Civil Legal Aid (General) Regulations 1989, Sch 2. **Jones v Zahedi** [1993] **4** 909, CA.
    Resources to be taken into account—Spouse's resources—Whether spouse's means to be taken into account in determining hardship—Extent to which spouse's means can be taken into account—Legal Aid Act 1974, s 13(3). **Adams v Riley** [1988] **1** 89, QBD.
  Successful appeal—
    Variation of maintenance order—Unassisted husband's appeal against order of magistrates varying maintenance order and making attachment of earnings order—Whether order for costs would be made against assisted wife—Legal Aid Act 1964, s 1(2), (4). **Povey v Povey** [1970] **3** 612, Div.
  Successful in defence and on appeal—
    No severe financial hardship—Costs of appeal, but not of defence, granted out of legal aid fund—No need to show severe financial hardship as regards costs of appeal—Whether application to court should be necessary in a plain case—Legal Aid Act 1964, s 1(1), (3)(b). **Parker v Thompson** [1966] **3** 766, CA.
  Trustee—
    Breach of trust—Plaintiffs legally aided—Defendants successful in severed defences and separately represented—Trust fund insufficient to meet costs—Plaintiffs the daughters of one trustee-defendant—Defendants completely exculpated—Defendants entitled to two sets of costs—Father not given costs out of legal aid fund—No application to legal aid committee to discharge certificate—Legal Aid Act 1964, ss 1, 2. **Spurling's Will Trusts, Re** [1966] **1** 745, Ch D.

LEGAL AID (cont)—
Unassisted person's costs out of legal aid fund (cont)—
Unassisted person—
Person who is unassisted for only part of proceedings—Costs incurred while unassisted—Proceedings finally decided in favour of that person—Whether court having jurisdiction to order payment by Legal Aid Board of that person's costs incurred before issue of legal aid certificate—Legal Aid Act 1988, s 18. **H and anor (minors) (abduction: custody rights) (No 2), Re** [1992] **3** 380, HL.
Unavailability of legal aid—
Funding. *See* **Legal representation** (Funding—Procedure—Unavailability of legal aid).
Winding up petition—
Scope of certificate. *See* Certificate—Scope of certificate—Winding up petition, *above*.
Writ—
Extension of validity—
Legal aid needs not a factor. *See* **Writ** (Extension of validity—Action statute-barred—Writ issued before action statute-barred but not served).

LEGAL CAPACITY
Child—
Criminal capacity. *See* **Criminal law** (Criminal capacity—Child).
Criminal capacity. *See* **Criminal law** (Criminal capacity).
Mental capacity. *See* **Mental health** (Persons who lack capacity).

LEGAL COSTS
Community legal service funding. *See* **Community legal service funding**.
Generally. *See* **Costs**.
Income tax—
Deduction of costs in computing profits. *See* **Income tax** (Deduction in computing profits—Legal costs).
Legal aid. *See* **Legal aid**.
Recovery as head of damages—
Legal expenses involved in investigating plaintiff's claim. *See* **Damages** (Costs—Recovery of legal costs as damages—Legal expenses involved in investigating plaintiff's claim).

LEGAL EXPENSES INSURANCE
See **Insurance** (Legal expenses insurance).

LEGAL MORTGAGE
Charge—
Registered land. *See* **Land registration** (Charge—Legal mortgage).
Generally. *See* **Mortgage**.

LEGAL PROFESSIONAL PRIVILEGE
Care proceedings—
Medical report concerning welfare of child—
Whether court entitled to disclose report to police. *See* **Family proceedings** (Confidential information in care proceedings—Disclosure to police—Medical report concerning welfare of child—Privilege—Legal professional privilege).
Disclosure of documents. *See* **Disclosure and inspection of documents** (Legal professional privilege).
Expert evidence—
Criminal proceedings. *See* **Criminal evidence** (Expert evidence—Legal professional privilege).
Generally. *See* **Privilege** (Legal professional privilege).
New Zealand. *See* **New Zealand** (Legal professional privilege).

LEGAL REPRESENTATION
Criminal proceedings—
Defendant—
Generally. *See* **Criminal law** (Trial—Defendant—Representation).
Jamaica. *See* **Jamaica** (Constitutional law—Fundamental rights and freedoms—Right of defendant in criminal proceedings to be permitted to defend himself by legal representative of his choice).
Generally. *See* **Criminal law** (Trial—Counsel).
Legal aid. *See* **Legal aid** (Remuneration of providers—Criminal cases).
Exclusion of legal representative from hearing—
Tribunal. *See* **Tribunal** (First-tier Tribunal—Hearing).
Fees—
European Union Treaty obligations. *See* **European Union** (Treaty provisions—Obligations under treaty—Failure to fulfil obligations—Freedom of establishment—Freedom to provide services—Lawyers—Fees).
Foreign lawyer—
Costs. *See* **Costs** (Taxation—Litigant appearing in person—Assistance of foreign lawyer).
Legal professional privilege. *See* **Privilege** (Legal professional privilege—Legal advice privilege—Scope—Foreign lawyer).
Funding—
Litigation funding agreements ('LFAs')—
Whether LFAs enforceable—Whether LFAs 'damages-based agreements'—Meaning of 'claims management services'—Courts and Legal Services Act 1990, s 58AA—Financial Services and Markets Act 2000, s 419A—Compensation Act 2006, s 4(2). **PACCAR Inc v Road Haulage Association Ltd (Association of Litigation Funders of England and Wales intervening)** [2021] **4** 737, CA, DC; [2022] **1** Comm 51, CA, DC.

LEGAL REPRESENTATION (cont)—
Funding (cont)—
Procedure—
Unavailability of legal aid—Whether court having power to order Lord Chancellor to provide public funding for legal representation outside legal aid scheme provided by statute—Matrimonial and Family Proceedings Act 1984, s 31G(6)—Prosecution of Offences Act 1985, s 19(3)—Human Rights Act 1998, s 3, Sch 1, Pt I, arts 6, 8—Courts Act 2003, s 1—Legal Aid, Sentencing and Punishment of Offenders Act 2012, s 19(1). **K (children) (unrepresented father: cross-examination of a child), Re** [2016] **1** 102, CA.
Immigration and asylum—
Duty to court. *See* **Solicitor** (Duty—Duty to court—Solicitors Regulation Authority—Referral—Immigration and asylum).
Insurance—
Legal expenses insurance. *See* **Insurance** (Legal expenses insurance).
Litigant in person—
Assistance of foreign lawyer—
Costs. *See* **Costs** (Taxation—Litigant appearing in person—Assistance of foreign lawyer).
Costs—
Legal aid. *See* **Legal aid** (Assisted person's liability to pay costs—Date on which person ceases to be assisted party for purposes of costs liability).
Police—
Disciplinary proceedings. *See* **Police** (Discipline—Procedure at disciplinary hearing—Legal representation).
Prisoner—
Charge of offending against prison discipline. *See* **Prison** (Discipline—Offence against discipline—Charge—Rights of prisoner charged—Legal representation).
Solicitor. *See* **Solicitor**.
Trade union—
Legal proceedings. *See* **Trade union** (Legal proceedings).

LEGATEE
Residuary legatee—
Residue. *See* **Will** (Residue—Residuary legatee).
Will—
Gift—
Misdescription of legatee. *See* **Will** (Gift—Misdescription—Legatee).

LEGISLATION
Legislative power—
Devolution. *See* **Constitutional law** (Devolution—National Assembly for Wales—Legislative power).
Statute. *See* **Statute**.

LEGISLATIVE COUNCIL
Uganda. *See* **Uganda** (Constitutional law—Legislative Council).

LEGISLATURE
Northern Ireland. *See* **Northern Ireland** (Parliament).
Parliament. *See* **Parliament**.

LEGITIMACY
Child of void marriage—
Belief of parents that marriage valid—
Child born after ceremony of marriage between parents—One parent reasonably believing marriage valid—Declaration of legitimacy—Legitimacy Act 1959, s 2—Matrimonial Causes Act 1950, s 17. **Sheward v A-G** [1964] **2** 324, Div.
Objective test whether either parent reasonably believed that marriage was valid—Legitimacy Act 1959, s 2(1). **Hawkins v A-G** [1966] **1** 392, Div.
Bigamous marriage—
Child born before ceremony of marriage between parents—Whether person born before void marriage can be treated as legitimate—Legitimacy Act 1976, s 1(1). **Spence (decd), Re** [1990] **2** 827, CA.
Conflict of laws. *See* **Conflict of laws** (Legitimacy).
Declaration of legitimacy—
Binding effect. *See* **Legitimation** (Declaration of legitimacy—Binding effect).
Costs—
Failure of petition—Costs of Attorney General and interveners out of estate. **Cleave v A-G, Headley, Channon and Barclays Bank Ltd, Intervening** [1952] **2** 283, Prob.
Fraud. *See* **Legitimation** (Declaration of legitimacy—Declaration obtained by fraud).
Jurisdiction—
Declaration of legitimacy of uncle—Whether 'ancestor'—Whether jurisdiction to make declaration—Legitimacy Act 1926, s 2(1)—RSC Ord 25, r 5, Ord 34, r 1. **Knowles v A-G** [1950] **2** 6, Div.
Legitimacy of person other than petitioner—Whether court has jurisdiction to make a declaration of the legitimacy of some person other than the petitioner—Whether a declaration on a bare claim for it should be made, assuming that there were jurisdiction—Supreme Court of Judicature (Consolidation) Act 1925, s 21(b)—Matrimonial Causes Act 1965, s 39(1)—RSC Ord 15, r 16. **Aldrich v A-G (Rogers intervening)** [1968] **1** 345, Prob.
Rebutting evidence—
Legitimacy not contested in divorce proceedings—Custody order treating child as legitimate—Settlement treating child as legitimate—Whether husband in divorce suit entitled in subsequent legitimacy proceedings to deny paternity—Admissibility of admissions by wife (still living) and another man (deceased) as to paternity of child. **B v A-G (NEB intervening)** [1965] **1** 62, Div.

LEGITIMACY (cont)—
Divorce—
   Decree absolute—
      Setting aside—Remarriage of petitioner—Birth of child of second marriage—Effect on child's
      legitimacy of decree absolute being set aside. **Wiseman v Wiseman** [1953] **1** 601, CA.
Jurisdiction—
   Declaration—
      Declaration of illegitimacy on cross-prayer—Blood test evidence—Matrimonial Causes Act 1950,
      s 17. **B v A-G (B intervening)** [1966] **2** 145, Div.
Legitimation by subsequent marriage. *See* **Legitimation** (Legitimation by subsequent marriage of parents).
Polygamous marriage—
   Children of second polygamous marriage in England—
      Second marriage recognised as valid by law of husband's domicile—Husband domiciled in
      Pakistan—First marriage in Pakistan—Second marriage to Englishwoman after coming to
      England—Second marriage whilst first marriage subsisting—Second marriage valid by Pakistani
      law—Children recognised as legitimate by Pakistani law—Whether children legitimate by English
      law. **Hashmi v Hashmi** [1971] **3** 1253, Leeds Assizes.
Presumption of legitimacy—
   Nature of presumption—
      Duration of presumption—Conception after decree nisi—Husband and wife living apart—
      Presumption in favour of conception before decree absolute. **Knowles v Knowles** [1962] **1** 659,
      Div.
   Onus of proof—
      Blood test. *See* **Paternity** (Blood test—Onus of proof).
   Rebuttal—
      Adultery by wife—Marital intercourse also at time of conception—Use of contraceptives—Parties
      regarding child as illegitimate—Whether presumption of legitimacy rebutted. **Francis v Francis**
      [1959] **3** 206, Div.
      Evidence of non-access—Admissibility—Separation deed. **Ettenfield v Ettenfield** [1940] **1** 293, CA;
      Stafford v Kidd [1936] **3** 1023, KBD.
      Evidence of non-access—Necessity for evidence of non-access—Maintenance order with no
      provision for non-cohabitation—Whether sufficient to rebut presumption. **Bowen v Norman**
      [1938] **2** 776, KBD.
      Evidence of non-access—Sufficiency—Whether evidence tendered sufficient. **Cotton v Cotton**
      [1954] **2** 105, CA.
      Evidence of use of contraceptives—Whether sufficient to rebut presumption. **W v W** [1953] **2** 1013,
      Div.
      Statement in will suggesting child illegitimate. **Hamer's Estate, Re** [1937] **1** 130, Ch D.
      Statements by mother during lifetime—Statements by natural father—Admissibility—Matrimonial
      Causes Act 1950, s 32(1), (2). **Jenion (decd), Re** [1952] **1** 1228, CA.
   Relevant presumption—
      Mother twice married—Child born within nine months of termination of first marriage by death of
      husband—Second marriage of mother before birth of child—Paternity of child. **Overbury (decd),**
      Re [1954] **3** 308, Ch D.
Succession to intestate's estate. *See* **Intestacy** (Succession—Legitimacy).
Will. *See* **Will** (Legitimacy).

LEGITIMATED PERSON
Child—
   Custody. *See* **Minor** (Custody—Legitimated child).
   Gift in will. *See* **Will** (Lapse—Statutory exception from lapse—Residuary bequest to illegitimate
      child—Legitimation and death of child leaving issue before death of testatrix).
Right of legitimated persons to take interests in property. *See* **Legitimation** (Right of legitimated persons to
   take interests in property).
Will—
   Disposition to legitimated person. *See* **Will** (Children—Legitimated person—Disposition).

LEGITIMATION
Belief of parents in validity of marriage—
   Test of reasonable belief. *See* **Legitimacy** (Child of void marriage—Belief of parents that marriage
      valid—Objective test whether either parent reasonably believed that marriage was valid).
Conflict of laws. *See* **Conflict of laws** (Legitimation).
Declaration of legitimacy—
   Binding effect—
      Crown—Peerage claim—Advice to Crown of House of Lords on peerage claim—Father disputing
      paternity of claimant in legitimacy proceedings—Father's evidence of non-access to mother
      inadmissible at hearing—Succession to hereditary title of honour—Claimant petitioning Crown
      on death of father to allow succession to title—Whether declaration binding—Whether Crown
      bound by declaration—Legitimacy Declaration Act 1858, ss 1, 8—Law Reform (Miscellaneous
      Provisions) Act 1949, s 7. **Ampthill Peerage Case, The** [1976] **2** 411, HL.
   Declaration obtained by fraud—
      Meaning of fraud—Conscious and deliberate dishonesty by means of which the declaration was
      obtained—Requirement that party alleging fraud particularise charge—Whether fraud having to
      be proved before case reopened—Legitimacy Declaration Act 1858, s 8. **Ampthill Peerage Case,**
      The [1976] **2** 411, HL.
   Generally. *See* **Legitimacy** (Declaration of legitimacy).
Foreign legitimation—
   Recognition. *See* **Conflict of laws** (Legitimation—Recognition).
Legitimation by subsequent marriage of parents—
   Child born before annulment of mother's first marriage for incapacity—
      Whether deemed to be legitimate child of first marriage—Legitimacy Act 1926, s 1(2)—Law Reform
      (Miscellaneous Provisions) Act 1949 s 4(1). **Adams (decd), Re** [1951] **1** 1037, Ch D.

LEGITIMATION (cont)—
    Legitimation by subsequent marriage of parents (cont)—
        Child born before, but on same day as, decree of divorce of mother made absolute—
            Father then free to marry—Subsequent marriage of father and mother—Whether child
            legitimated—Legitimacy Act 1926, s 1(1). **Kruhlak v Kruhlak (No 2)** [1958] **2** 294, QBD.
        Child conceived pending its mother's divorce proceedings—
            Presumptive issue of dissolved marriage—Rebutting evidence—Marriage of mother and putative
            father—Custody prayed in divorce petition by second husband—Declaration of legitimacy—
            Supreme Court of Judicature (Consolidation) Act 1925, s 188—Legitimacy Act 1926, ss 1, 2.
            Maturin v A-G [1938] **2** 214, Div.
        Domicile of father at date of marriage—
            Evidence—Statements made by deceased father to petitioner—Admissibility—Legitimacy Act 1926,
            s 1(1). **Scappaticci v A-G** [1955] **1** 193, Div.
            Father domiciled at child's birth in foreign country in which legitimation by subsequent marriage
            was permitted by law—Whether child legitimated—Legitimacy Act 1926, s 8(1). **Hurll, Re**
            [1952] **2** 322, Ch D.
        Exception where one parent married to third person at date of birth of illegitimate person—
            Onus of proof—Presumption as to continuance of life—Legitimacy Act 1926, s 1(2). **MacDarmaid v**
            A-G [1950] **1** 497, Div.
    Practice—
        Hearing of petition in camera—
            Infants' petitions—Application for hearing in camera—Fact that petitioners were infants did not
            given them greater rights than those of an adult litigant—Deterrence of litigant by prospect of
            publicity of trial not a ground for ordering hearing in private. **B (orse P) v A-G** [1965] **3** 253, Div.
            Power of court to order hearing in camera—Discretion—Exercise of discretion—Factors to be
            considered—Domestic and Appellate Proceedings (Restriction of Publicity) Act 1968, s 2. **Barritt v**
            A-G [1971] **3** 1183, Div.
    Right of legitimated persons to take interests in property—
        Disposition coming into operation after date of legitimation—
            Settlement made in 1934 including trust for 'any child' of settlor's son—Plaintiff illegitimate child of
            settlor's son born in 1936—Plaintiff subsequently legitimated by parents' marriage in
            1937—Whether plaintiff entitled to take under 1934 settlement—Whether plaintiff claiming under
            'disposition coming into operation after date of legitimation'—Whether plaintiff's interest arising
            on date of his legitimation—Whether relevant disposition the instrument creating the trust or the
            trust itself—Legitimacy Act 1926, s 3(1)(b). **Billson's Settlement Trusts, Re** [1984] **2** 401, CA.
            Special power of appointment given by will—Will before and appointment after legitimation—
            'Disposition'—Legitimacy Act 1926, ss 3(1), 10(2), 11. **Hoff, Re** [1942] **1** 547, Ch D.

LESOTHO
    Refugee—
        Expulsion—
            Refugee claiming immunity by virtue of international convention—Whether outside own country as
            result of events before 1st January 1951—Convention Relating to the Status of Refugees 1951,
            art 1—Aliens Control Act (Basutoland)(No 16 of 1966), s 38(1). **Molefi v Legal Adviser** [1970] **3** 724,
            PC.
    Treaty—
        Accession to treaty—
            Positive manifestation of intention to accede—Letter to United Nations after independence
            adhering to treaties, pending review of commitments, subject to reciprocity. **Molefi v Legal**
            Adviser [1970] **3** 724, PC.

LETTER
    Demanding money with menaces—
        Criminal jurisdiction. *See* **Criminal law** (Jurisdiction—Demanding with menaces—Demand by letter).
    Prisoner—
        Letters to and from a prisoner. *See* **Prison** (Letters—Prisoner's letters).
    Threat to kill. *See* **Criminal law** (Threatening letters—Sending letter threatening to kill).

LETTER BOX
    Service of writ through letter box. *See* **Practice** (Service—Service through letter box).

LETTER OF ATTORNEY
    Stamp duty. *See* **Stamp duty** (Letter or power of attorney).

LETTER OF CREDIT
    Generally. *See* **Bank** (Documentary credit).
    Proper law. *See* **Conflict of laws** (Contract—Proper law of contract—Commercial credit).
    Sale of goods—
        Payment—
            Whether confirmed irrevocable letter of credit constituting payment. *See* **Sale of goods**
            (Payment—Confirmed letter of credit—Confirmed irrevocable letter of credit established).

LETTERS OF ADMINISTRATION
    Intestacy. *See* **Intestacy** (Grant of administration).

LIABILITIES ADJUSTMENT
    Liabilities adjustment order—
        Application—
            Protection order made—Applicant's affairs referred to liabilities adjustment officer for investigation
            and report—Officer applying for directions—Power to revoke protection order on such
            application—Liabilities (War-Time Adjustment) Act 1941. **Marten (F W), Re** [1943] **2** 196, CA.

LIABILITIES ADJUSTMENT (cont)—

Liabilities adjustment order (cont)—

Interim order—

Jurisdiction—Proceedings for recovery of possession of land—Monthly tenancy determined before date of protection order—Action for recovery of possession of premises—All proceedings for recovery of possession of land stayed pending investigation when protection order made—Interim adjustment order extending debtor's occupation of premises—No extension permissible, as debtor already trespasser before date of protection order—'Tenant'—Liabilities (War-Time Adjustment) Act 1941, s 3(2), (5)—Liabilities (War-Time Adjustment) Act 1944, ss 6, 21, 22. **Alsop's Affairs, Re** [1945] 2 43, CA.

Propriety—Order in respect of insolvent company—Postponement of liabilities—Whether practical and proper—Liabilities (War-Time Adjustment) Property 1941, ss 3(6), 15. **Royal Albion Hotel Ltd, Re** [1943] 2 192, CA.

Jurisdiction—

Interim order. See Liabilities adjustment order—Interim order—Jurisdiction, above.

Mortgages—Mortgage deed—Variation—Power of court to reopen past payments—Liabilities (War-Time Adjustment) Act 1941, s 7(3)(a), as amended by Liabilities (War-Time Adjustment) Act 1944, s 7(1). **Ginger, Re** [1948] 1 18, CA.

Reduction of debt—Landlord a judgment creditor for rent—Inland Revenue a creditor for Sched A tax—Application by debtor for reduction of judgment debt by amount of Sch A income tax—Jurisdiction of court—Liabilities (War-Time Adjustment) Act 1941, s 4(1). **Farquhar's Affairs, Re** [1943] 2 781, CA.

Variation of order—Order by consent—Application to vary on ground of mistake—Jurisdiction of court—Liabilities (War-Time Adjustment) Act 1941. **Elstein's Affairs, Re** [1945] 1 272, CA.

Order in favour of assignee of lease—

Effect on liability for rent of original lessee—Liabilities (War-Time Adjustment) Act 1947, s 12(1). **House Property and Investment Co Ltd v Benardout** [1947] 2 753, KBD.

Possession of property—

Extension of tenant's term—No extension beyond contractual term—Continuance of term after forfeiture for non-payment of rent—Liabilities (War-Time Adjustment) Act 1941, s 8. **Kirby's Affairs, Re** [1944] 1 166, CA.

Relief from payment of rent—

Proceedings to enforce covenant—Discretion of court—'Lettable value'—Development of shopping centre arrested—Liabilities (War-Time Adjustment) Act 1941, s 6—Liabilities (War-Time Adjustment) Act 1944, s 6. **Davey, Re** [1947] 1 90, CA.

Validity—

Dispute—Procedure—Proper course to appeal against order and not to ask for variation—Liabilities (War-Time Adjustment) Act 1941, s 10(2). **Smith, Re** [1943] 2 740, CA.

Protection order—

Effect on other proceedings—

Petition for compulsory winding-up of company—Protection order made two days before petition due to be heard—Jurisdiction to entertain petition—Liabilities (War-Time Adjustment) Act 1941, s 3(2). **Johnson (R W) Ltd, Re** [1942] 1 175, Ch D.

Practice—

Preliminary hearing to be ex parte—Notice given to creditor by registrar of county court—Appearance of creditor's solicitor at hearing—Whether irregularity such as to vitiate proceedings—Liabilities (War-Time Adjustment) Act 1941—Liabilities (War-Time Adjustment) Rules 1942 (SR & O 1942 No 1302), rr 12(1), 14, 16, 20-22—Liabilities (War-Time Adjustment) Rules 1943 (S R& O 1943 No 1336). **Evans and Evans Affairs, Re** [1944] 1 348, CA.

Restriction on remedies—

Action to recover possession and arrears of rent—

Conditions of application of the Courts (Emergency Powers) Acts—Liabilities (War-Time Adjustment) Act 1941, s 26. **Lawrence v Johnson** [1943] 2 301, CA.

LIABILITY INSURANCE

See **Insurance** (Liability insurance).

LIBEL AND SLANDER

Anonymous publication—

Power of court to proceed in absence of party. See **Judgment** (Default of acknowledgment of service—Power of court to proceed in absence of party—Anonymous defendants).

Apology—

Qualified privilege. See Qualified privilege—Apology, below.

Vindication of plaintiff's character—

Necessity for—Newspaper—Article not containing recantation of criticisms of plaintiff's conduct nor an apology—Article not a sufficient vindication of his character. **Associated Newspapers Ltd v Dingle** [1962] 2 737, HL.

Appeal—

Damages. See Damages—Appeal, below.

Further evidence—

Use of reasonable diligence to obtain evidence before trial—Defendants accusing well-known rugby player of infringing amateur status by writing book for money—Damages awarded against defendants—Defendants seeking leave to adduce fresh evidence relating to receipt of 'boot money' by plaintiff—Defendants making no attempt to obtain fresh evidence before trial—New trial granted—Whether defendants entitled to produce boot money evidence at new trial. **Williams v Reason (1983)** [1988] 1 262, CA.

Blasphemous libel. See **Criminal law** (Blasphemy—Blasphemous libel).

Comment or fact. See Fair comment—Meaning of words complained of—Comment or fact, below.

Conflict of laws. See **Conflict of laws** (Jurisdiction—Libel).

Consolidation of actions. See **Practice** (Consolidation of actions—Libel actions).

LIBEL AND SLANDER (cont)—
  Contempt of court—
    Action pending—
      Republication of alleged libel. *See* **Contempt of court** (Republication of alleged libel—Pending proceedings).
  Costs—
    Conditional fee agreement. *See* **Costs** (Order for costs—Conditional fee agreement—Defamation).
    Joint tortfeasors. *See* Joint tortfeasors—Costs, *below*.
    Slander of woman—
      Costs exceeding damages—Certificate—Application—Plaintiff not entitled to damages unless certificate of reasonable grounds for bringing action—Costs of sucessful plaintiff exceeding damages—Plaintiff awarded costs at trial—Judge not asked at trial for certificate that there was reasonable ground for bringing action—Jurisdiction to grant certificate on subsequent application—Slander of Women Act 1891, s 1. **Russo v Cole** [1965] 3 822, QBD.
  County court—
    Jurisdiction—
      Counterclaim for slander. *See* **County court** (Jurisdiction—Counterclaim—Counterclaim for slander).
  Criminal libel. *See* **Criminal law** (Libel).
  Damages—
    Appeal—
      Excessive award—Power of Court of Appeal to order new trial or substitute own award on ground that jury's award excessive—When power should be exercised—Whether reasonable jury could have thought award necessary to compensate plaintiff and re-establish reputation—Courts and Legal Services Act 1990, s 8(1)—RSC Ord 59, r 11(4)—Convention for the Protection of Human Rights and Fundamental Freedoms, art 10. **Rantzen v Mirror Group Newspapers (1986) Ltd** [1993] 4 975, CA.
      Excessive award—Power of Court of Appeal to substitute own award on ground that jury's award excessive—Circumstances in which power to be exercised—Courts and Legal Services Act 1990, s 8. **Kiam v MGN Ltd** [2002] 2 219, CA.
      Unreasonable award—Injury to reputation and grief at publication—Equating incommensurables—Scale of values applicable for physical injuries not to be disregarded. **McCarey v Associated Newspapers Ltd** [1964] 3 947, CA.
      Unreasonable award—Jury—Award by jury—Right to appeal against award. **Lewis v Daily Telegraph Ltd** [1963] 2 151, HL.
      Unreasonable award—When Court of Appeal can order new trial or substitute its own award—Guidance for jury regarding financial implications and real value of sum to be awarded—Amount awarded so large as to contain exemplary element even though case not appropriate for exemplary award—Whether new trial should be ordered—Whether any new trial should be limited to issue of damages—Whether defendant entitled to put forward evidence in support of unsuccessful plea of justification at any new trial. **Sutcliffe v Pressdram Ltd** [1990] 1 269, CA.
      Unreasonable award—When Court of Appeal can order new trial or substitute its own award—Test whether no reasonable jury properly directed and properly considering evidence could have made award—No power to order new trial or substitute different award merely because Court of Appeal considers award to be excessive—£45,000 aggravated damages awarded to former civil servant for libel that he was dismissed from Civil Service for incompetence—Whether award so high that no reasonable jury properly directed and properly considering the evidence could have made such an award. **Blackshaw v Lord** [1983] 2 311, CA.
    Apportionment of damages between defendants—
      Judge—Statute empowering jury to apportion damages in consolidated libel action—Trial before judge sitting alone—Whether judge having power to apportion damages—Law of Libel (Amendment) Act 1888, s 5. **Mitchell v Hirst, Kidd and Rennie Ltd** [1936] 3 872, Assizes.
    Assessment—
      Aggravated damages—Libel in newspaper—Whether in awarding damages distinction should be drawn between publisher, editor and journalist. **Hayward v Thompson** [1981] 3 450, CA.
      Factors to be taken into account—Failure to offer apology—Knowledge of special facts indicating that libel referred to plaintiff limited to a few readers—Absence of belief on part of readers in truth of libel. **Morgan v Odhams Press Ltd** [1971] 2 1156, HL.
      Offer of amends—Principles to be applied—Defamation Act 1996, s 3. **Abu v MGN Ltd** [2003] 2 864, QBD.
      Vindication of plaintiff's character—Judge sitting without jury—Right to award heavy damages—Judge not disentitled to award heavy damages because in judgment he expresses opinion of libel. **Bull v Vazquez** [1947] 1 334, CA.
      Vindication of plaintiff's character—Judgment in suit—Judge sitting without jury—Plaintiff's character vindicated by judgment—Whether judge should take vindication into account in assessing damages. **Rook v Fairrie** [1941] 1 297, CA.
      Vindication of plaintiff's character—Reduction of damages—Vindication by judgment in suit—Judge sitting without jury—Whether vindication of plaintiff's reputation by judgment in suit a ground for reducing damages. **Associated Newspapers Ltd v Dingle** [1962] 2 737, HL.
      Whether House of Lords having jurisdiction to substitute award of damages for jury's award—Appellate Jurisdiction Act 1876, s 4. **Grobbelaar v News Group Newspapers Ltd** [2002] 4 732, HL.
    Conduct of defendant—
      Plaintiff's feelings—No withdrawal of libel or apology—Conduct of defendant taken into account, although exemplary or punitive damages not to be awarded—Damages not confined to pecuniary damage—Whether permissible to take into account defendant's conduct in assessing damages. **Fielding v Variety Inc** [1967] 2 497, CA.

355

LIBEL AND SLANDER (cont)—
  Damages (cont)—
    Direction to jury—
      Matters to which trial judge may refer in summing up—Whether permissible to refer to previous awards of Court of Appeal on appeal from excessive jury awards—Whether permissible to refer to previous jury awards in defamation actions or to awards made in personal injury actions—Courts and Legal Services Act 1990, s 8(1). **Rantzen v Mirror Group Newspapers (1986) Ltd** [1993] 4 975, CA.
      Matters to which trial judge may refer in summing up—Whether permissible to refer to previous awards of Court of Appeal on appeal from excessive jury awards—Whether permissible to refer to previous jury awards in defamation actions or to awards made in personal injury actions—Whether judge and counsel entitled to indicate to jury appropriate level of award—Whether award excessive. **John v MGN Ltd** [1996] 2 35, CA.
    Exemplary damages. See Exemplary or punitive damages, below.
    Heads of damage—
      Injury to health—Whether admissible head of damage. **Wheeler v Somerfield** [1966] 2 305, CA.
    Loss of income—
      Income tax—Whether tax to be taken into account where loss of income results. **Lewis v Daily Telegraph Ltd** [1963] 2 151, HL.
    Mitigation—
      Contemporaneous publication of same libel—Previous publication in privileged Parliamentary papers—Subsequent publication with additional actionable defamatory material by defendant newspaper—Whether ground for mitigating damages. **Associated Newspapers Ltd v Dingle** [1962] 2 737, HL.
      Pleading. See Pleading—Mitigation of damages, below.
      Reputation—Established bad reputation only taken into account in mitigation—Prior publication of same libel not evidence of such reputation. **Associated Newspapers Ltd v Dingle** [1962] 2 737, HL.
      Reputation—Evidence of general bad reputation—Previous convictions—Relevant previous convictions of criminal offences admissible. **Goody v Odhams Press Ltd** [1966] 3 369, CA.
      Reputation—Evidence of reputation plaintiff ought to have—Evidence of general bad reputation only admissible in mitigation of damages—Evidence of specific instances of misconduct designed to show character plaintiff ought to have in public estimation inadmissible. **Plato Films Ltd v Speidel** [1961] 1 876, HL.
      Reputation—Specific acts of misconduct—Unsuccessful plea of justification—Whether specific acts of misconduct adduced in support of unsuccessful plea of justification can be relied on by defendant in mitigation of damages. **Pamplin v Express Newspapers Ltd (No 2) (1985)** [1988] 1 282, CA.
    Offer to make amends—
      Compensation determined on same principles as damages in defamation proceedings—Effect of offer to make amends on damages—Defamation Act 1996, s 3(5). **Nail v News Group Newspapers Ltd** [2005] 1 1040, CA.
      Compensation determined on same principles as damages in defamation proceedings—Mitigation of damages—Evidence relevant to the damage caused—Defamation Act 1996, s 3. **Turner v News Group Newspapers Ltd** [2006] 4 613, CA.
    Repetition of libel—
      Letter to editor of journal—Letter republished in journal—Letter intended for publication in journal—Whether damage from repetition of publication to be taken into account in assessing damages for original publication. **Cutler v McPhail** [1962] 2 474, QBD.
      Press reviews of television film—Defendants broadcasting on television a film defamatory of plaintiff—Reviews repeating sting of libel—Whether defendants liable for unauthorised publications—Whether foreseeable and natural and probable consequence that reviews would contain sting of libel—Whether damages recoverable for repetition of libel. **Slipper v BBC** [1991] 1 165, .
    Separate actions for similar libels—
      Libels in different newspapers—Direction to jury to consider whether and how far damage attributable solely to the libel in one action—Defamation Act 1952, s 12. **Lewis v Daily Telegraph Ltd** [1963] 2 151, HL.
    Special damage—
      Dismissal from employment—Dismissal lawful—Dismissal in consequence of publication of libel—Determination of service not in breach of contract—Whether plaintiff entitled to special damages in respect of loss of employment. **Longdon-Griffiths v Smith** [1950] 2 662, KBD.
      Particularity in pleading—Plea that words calculated to cause pecuniary damage—Special damage not pleaded—Evidence of actual loss inadmissible—Defamation Act 1952, s 3(1)(b). **Calvet v Tomkies** [1963] 3 610, CA.
  Defamatory statement—
    Requirement of serious financial loss—
      Solicitors firm alleging defamatory statements published on website by anonymous defendants—Whether firm suffering 'serious financial loss'—Whether court having jurisdiction to determine claim—Whether defendants 'editors' of statements—Defamation Act 1996, s 1(2)—Defamation Act 2013, ss 1(1), (2), 10(1), (2). **Brett Wilson LLP v Person(s) Unknown, responsible for the operation and publication of the website www.solicitorsfromhelluk.com** [2016] 1 1006, QBD.
    Requirement of serious harm—
      Claimant bringing libel claims in respect of articles published in print and online—Whether publications causing or likely to cause serious harm to reputation of claimant—Whether tendency to cause serious harm sufficient—Whether other publications of same libel admissible—Defamation Act 1952, ss 2, 12—Defamation Act 2013, s 1(1). **Lachaux v Independent Print Ltd** [2016] 4 140, QBD.
      Requirement of serious harm introduced by statute—Whether common law presumption of general damages surviving—Whether serious harm in fact having to be shown—Whether special categories of slander actionable per se surviving—Defamation Act 2013, s 1. **Lachaux v Independent Print Ltd** [2019] 4 485, SC.

356

LIBEL AND SLANDER (cont)—
  Defamatory statement (cont)—
    Requirement of serious harm (cont)—
      Statement whose publication has caused or is likely to cause serious harm to reputation of claimant—Date of considering causing of harm—Meaning of 'serious harm'—Proof of serious harm—Defamation Act 2013, s 1(1). **Cooke v MGN Ltd** [2015] **2** 622, QBD.
  Defamatory words—
    Accusation of being informer—
      Report of crime to police—Club—Gambling machines on club premises—Complaint to police—Plaintiff member of club—Allegation that plaintiff had informed on club to police—Whether allegation capable of being defamatory. **Byrne v Deane** [1937] **2** 204, CA.
    Breach of undertaking given to the court—
      Special circumstances—Words defamatory to persons having knowledge of special circumstances—Whether necessary to prove person did understand them in that sense. **Hough v London Express Newspaper Ltd** [1940] **3** 31, CA.
    Business ethics—
      Statement that plaintiff was not conversant with normal business ethics—Words connoting dishonourable behaviour. **Angel v HH Bushell & Co Ltd** [1967] **1** 1018, QBD.
    Debt to servant—
      Imputation of pecuniary difficulties—Implication that plaintiff had borrowed from maid-servant—Telegram referring to 'the money you borrowed'—Whether words complained of reasonably capable of defamatory meaning. **Sim v Stretch** [1936] **2** 1237, HL.
    Dishonourable conduct—
      Refusal to accept award of conciliation—Allegation that plaintiff firm had refused to accept interim wages award of a joint conciliation board—Whether words in natural and ordinary meaning defamatory. **Holdsworth Ltd v Associated Newspapers Ltd** [1937] **3** 872, CA.
  Meaning of words complained of—
    Social media post—Parties formerly married—Defendant stating on Facebook that claimant 'tried to strangle her'—Judge holding words meaning claimant had tried to kill her—Whether judge erred in approach—Whether words meaning claimant tried to kill defendant. **Stocker v Stocker** [2019] **3** 647, SC.
  Words capable of defamatory meaning—
    Accusation of being involved in murder plot—Newspaper reports that name of person 'connected with' plot given to police—Plaintiff identified as person whose name was given to police—Whether words capable of bearing defamatory meaning. **Hayward v Thompson** [1981] **3** 450, CA.
    Determination of meaning by jury—Ambiguous words—Words true in ordinary meaning—Headline in large type—'False profit return charge against society'—Question whether meaning returns incorrect or fraudulent for jury to determine. **English and Scottish Co-op Properties Mortgage and Investment Society Ltd v Odhams Press Ltd** [1940] **1** 1, CA.
    Dismissal from employment—Statement by employer that servant dismissed—Plea that words meaning servant had been guilty of some discreditable conduct—Whether words capable of defamatory meaning—Statement by employer that servant dismissed. **Morris v Sandess Universal Products** [1954] **1** 47, CA.
    Publication of words regarding financial viability of plaintiffs' family company—Defendants seeking to amend plea of justification following settlement between corporate plaintiffs and defendants so as to reflect on plaintiff directors instead of companies—Whether words capable of bearing defamatory meaning—RSC Ord 82, r 3A. **Aspro Travel Ltd v Owners Abroad Group plc** [1995] **4** 728, CA.
    Publication of words regarding physical appearance of plaintiff—Plaintiff claiming that words meant that he was 'hideously ugly' and were therefore defamatory—Whether meaning pleaded capable of being defamatory. **Berkoff v Burchill** [1996] **4** 1008, CA.
  Exemplary or punitive damages—
    Calculation that profit would exceed compensation payable to the injured person—
      Deliberate act—Newspaper article—Direction to jury—Punitive damages only if publication of defamatory matter was a deliberate act calculated to make profit out of publishing something known to be false or without caring whether it was true or false—Course of criminal conduct falsely alleged—Justification not pleaded and no direct evidence of motive for publication. **Manson v Associated Newspapers Ltd** [1965] **2** 954, QBD.
      Publication in profitable newspaper—Fact of publication of defamatory matter in profitable newspaper not sufficient of itself to justify punitive damages—Unreasonable award—Appeal—New trial. **Broadway Approvals Ltd v Odhams Press Ltd** [1965] **2** 523, CA.
      What must be proved—Necessity to show knowledge that what was done was against law and decision to persist with it because prospects of material advantage outweighed prospects of material loss—Unnecessary to show defendant had made arithmetical calculation that profit would exceed loss. **Cassell & Co Ltd v Broome** [1972] **1** 801, HL.
    Distinction between compensatory and punitive damages—
      Punishment for wrongdoing—Distinction applicable to damages for libel and also in tort generally—Damages not recoverable by way of punishment for wrongdoing. **McCarey v Associated Newspapers Ltd** [1964] **3** 947, CA.
    Insufficiency of compensatory damages—
      Direction to jury—Direction that exemplary damages to be awarded 'if, but only if' proposed compensatory damages insufficient to punish defendant—Direction to jury that exemplary damages to be additional to compensatory damages—Whether sufficient. **Cassell & Co Ltd v Broome** [1972] **1** 801, HL.
    Joint defendants—
      Award of single sum—Degrees of blameworthiness—One defendant more blameworthy than other—No necessity to split damages between defendants according to blameworthiness—Sum to be that appropriate for least blameworthy. **Cassell & Co Ltd v Broome** [1972] **1** 801, HL.
    Principles on which exemplary damages awarded—
      Categories—Whether appropriate cases for award restricted to categories laid down in Rookes v Barnard. **Cassell & Co Ltd v Broome** [1972] **1** 801, HL.

LIBEL AND SLANDER (cont)—
Exemplary or punitive damages (cont)—
Principles on which exemplary damages awarded (cont)—
Insufficiency of compensatory damages—Test of recklessness—Newspaper libelling well-known singer—Whether publisher having no genuine belief in truth of words published, suspecting words were untrue and deliberately refraining from checking—Whether award of compensatory damages adequately reflecting gravity of defendant's conduct—Whether exemplary damages award excessive. **John v MGN Ltd** [1996] 2 35, CA.

New South Wales. *See* **New South Wales** (Libel—Exemplary or punitive damages—Principles on which exemplary damages awarded).

Several plaintiffs—
Appropriate direction to jury—Jury awarding each of ten plaintiffs £25,000 exemplary damages—Whether jury should only award exemplary damages if total compensatory damages insufficient to punish defendant—Whether jury should make single award divided among plaintiffs—Whether jury entitled to make separate awards for each plaintiff. **Riches v News Group Newspapers Ltd** [1985] 2 845, CA.

Fair comment—
Comment or fact—
Communication to press—Letter in response to newspaper article complaining of author's racialist and anti-semitic views—Whether words complained of in letter capable of being understood as comment or fact—Whether words complained of to be read in isolation or in context of letter and/or article—Whether defence of fair comment capable of being based on extrinsic evidence. **Telnikoff v Matusevitch** [1991] 4 817, HL.

Facts relied on—
Elements of defence of fair comment—Extent to which defence of fair comment requiring comment to identify the matter or matters to which it relates—Claimants alleging internet posting defamatory—Defendants raising defence of fair comment—Defendants relying on fact to which no reference made in posting. **Joseph v Spiller** [2011] 1 947, SC.

Existence at date of publication—Facts relied on to support plea must be facts existing at date of publication—Particulars pleaded in support of defence of fair comment included events occurring after publication of alleged libel—Particulars struck out. **Cohen v Daily Telegraph Ltd** [1968] 2 407, CA.

Existence at date of publication—Whether facts having to be referred to or indicated in words complained of—Whether commentator having to have been aware of facts at date of publication. **Lowe v Associated Newspapers Ltd** [2006] 3 357, QBD.

Facts distinguished from comment—Communication to press—Letter deploring simultaneous termination of engagements privately by four artistes in a play running at London theatre—Simultaneous giving of notices a matter of public interest—Whether statements in letter comment or fact—One fact not proved—Defence of fair comment—Necessity to distinguish between fact and comment—Whether question whether comment or fact could have been left to jury. **London Artists Ltd v Littler** [1969] 2 193, CA.

Facts including unproven statements made on privileged occasion—Publishers seeking to republish and rely on privileged statements—Whether publishers entitled to rely on privileged statements—Whether publishers required to give fair and accurate report of occasion on which they were made. **Brent Walker Group plc v Time Out Ltd** [1991] 2 753, CA.

Statement of facts in libel—Need for facts on which comment made to be stated in alleged libel—Article criticising conduct of newspaper—Proof of truth of facts stated in particulars. **Kemsley v Foot** [1952] 1 501, HL.

Honest expression of opinion—
Honesty of comment—Criticism of dramatic work—Misstatements in criticism—Criticism contained in letter to newspaper—False name and address. **Lyon v Daily Telegraph Ltd** [1943] 2 316, CA.

Personal imputation—Defence available against personal imputation—Test is whether an honest expression of genuine opinion. **Slim v Daily Telegraph Ltd** [1968] 1 497, CA.

Test of fair comment—Burden of proof—Criticism of newspaper article—Criticism contained in letter written by defendant to newspaper—Whether test of fair comment subjective as well as objective—Whether defendant required to prove not only that comment was reasonable but also that it was honest expression of his own opinion. **Telnikoff v Matusevitch** [1991] 4 817, HL.

Test to be applied—Defence available even though comment exaggerated, obstinate or prejudiced. **Silkin v Beaverbrook Newspapers Ltd** [1958] 2 516, QBD.

Truth—Relevance—Plea of justification of defamatory statements of fact on which comment based—Plea of justification failing—Whether honest expression of opinion actionable if untrue. **Broadway Approvals Ltd v Odhams Press Ltd** [1965] 2 523, CA.

Malice—
Evidence—Admissibility—Evidence of plaintiff's qualities and reputation at date of trial—Direction on damages to jury. **Cornwell v Myskow** [1987] 2 504, CA.

Evidence—Newspaper publishing company—Factors that can or cannot be evidence of malice—One department of defendant company ignorant of activities of another—Advertisement in similar form to that criticised by editorial department of large newspaper accepted by advertising department—Editing of reporter's report—Amendments and omissions—Failure to retract or apologise and persistence in plea of justification. **Broadway Approvals Ltd v Odhams Press Ltd** [1965] 2 523, CA.

Interrogatory. *See* Interrogatory—Fair comment—Malice, *below*.

Meaning of words complained of—
Comment or fact—Honest expression of opinion—Role of appellate court—Review of opera in newspaper—Claimant composer and co-librettist alleging defamatory meaning—Defendant seeking summary judgment—Judge refusing application—Judge ruling words complained of not incapable of bearing meaning pleaded by claimant—Whether appellate court to interfere with judge's ruling—Whether words capable of meeting requirements for defence of fair comment. **Burstein v Associated Newspapers Ltd** [2007] 4 319, CA.

Particulars. *See* Particulars—Fair comment, *below*.

LIBEL AND SLANDER (cont)—
 Fair comment (cont)—
  Pleading fair comment—
   Comments inseparable from assertions of fact not sought to be justified—Whether defendant required to identify comment claimed to be fair comment. **Control Risks Ltd v New English Library Ltd** [1989] **3** 577, CA.
  Public benefit—
   Burden of proof—Publication for public benefit—Whether it was necessary to show that to publish the words was for the public benefit—Defamation Act 1912-1948 (No 32 of 1912), s 7. **Jones v Skelton** [1963] **3** 952, PC.
  Truth of facts commented on—
   Findings that words complained of untrue but fair comment—Comment founded on inaccurate statement of witness in judicial proceedings—Whether findings inconsistent or comment unfair. **Grech v Odhams Press Ltd** [1958] **2** 462, CA.
 Friendly society—
  Action against trustees—
   Competence. *See* **Friendly society** (Action against trustees—Tort—Libel—Competence).
 Identification of plaintiff as person defamed—
  Ascertainable class—
   Words referring to a group—No reference to individual member of group—Proof required that words would reasonably lead people acquainted with plaintiff to conclusion he was person referred to—Words reasonably understood to refer to each member of group—Whether individual member can claim damages for defamation. **Knupffer v London Express Newspaper Ltd** [1944] **1** 495, HL.
  Evidence—
   Extrinsic evidence—Article in newspaper—Nothing in article itself pointing to plaintiff—Inference that article referred to plaintiff based on extrinsic evidence—Whether article could constitute libel on plaintiff. **Morgan v Odhams Press Ltd** [1970] **2** 544, CA.
  Name—
   Person of same name as plaintiff—True statement about existing person of same name—Whether referable also to plaintiff. **Newstead v London Express Newspaper Ltd** [1939] **4** 319, CA.
  Practice—
   Statements made after publication of libel—Statements made at meetings—Anonymous telephone communications—Whether admissible as evidence that published libel referred to plaintiff. **Jozwiak v Sadek** [1954] **1** 3, QBD.
  Separate publications—
   First publication bearing defamatory meaning but not identifying plaintiff—Second publication identifying plaintiff as being person referred to in first publication—Whether jury entitled to look at second publication in order to identify person referred to in first publication. **Hayward v Thompson** [1981] **3** 450, CA.
 Identity—
  Persons to whom publication made—
   Innuendo—Persons having knowledge of facts rendering published words defamatory—Duty to plead particulars identifying those persons. *See* Innuendo—Particulars—Duty of plaintiff to plead facts on which he relies for his claim—Identity of persons to whom publication made and who have knowledge of facts which render published words defamatory, *below*.
  Reference to plaintiff—
   Innuendo. *See* Innuendo—Reference to plaintiff—Identity, *below*.
 Injunction—
  Exercise of discretion—
   Justification—No plea of justification—No admission of falsity of statements—Plea of qualified privilege—Plea rejected—No finding that words complained of false—Whether perpetual injunction restraining publication should be granted. **Bryanston Finance Ltd v De Vries** [1975] **2** 609, CA.
  Interlocutory—
   Jurisdiction—Defendant threatening to publish libel unless financial claim satisfied—Plaintiffs seeking injunction restraining defendant from publication—Defendant pleading justification—Whether injunction should be granted—Whether defendant's motive relevant. **Holley v Smyth** [1998] **1** 853, CA.
   Jurisdiction—Generally. *See* **Injunction** (Interlocutory—Jurisdiction).
   Jurisdiction—Plaintiff seeking injunction restraining publication—Publication referring to spent convictions—Grant of injunction restraining publication if publication is malicious—Rehabilitation of Offenders Act 1974, s 1(1). **Herbage v Pressdram Ltd** [1984] **2** 769, CA.
   Justification—Defendant pleading justification and fair comment—Whether injunction should be granted. **Fraser v Evans** [1969] **1** 8, CA.
   Justification—Defendant pleading justification—Plaintiff seeking injunction restraining publication—Truth of words published not in question—Words published in pursuance of conspiracy having sole or dominant purpose of injuring plaintiff—Whether injunction restraining further publication should be granted. **Gulf Oil (GB) Ltd v Page** [1987] **3** 14, CA.
   Justification—Defendant pleading justification—Whether injunction restraining further publication should be granted. **Harakas v Baltic Mercantile and Shipping Exchange Ltd** [1982] **2** 701, CA.
   Justification—Inseparable allegations—Common sting—Article containing a number of inseparable allegations—Defendants unable to prove particular allegation complained of—Defendants intending to justify common sting of allegations—Whether plaintiff entitled to interlocutory injunction restraining publication of article. **Khashoggi v IPC Magazines Ltd** [1986] **3** 577, CA.
   Justification—Whether human rights legislation abrogating rule precluding court from imposing prior restraint in defamation action unless clear that no defence could succeed at trial—Human Rights Act 1998, ss 6, 12(3), Sch 1, Pt I, arts 8, 10. **Greene v Associated Newspapers Ltd** [2005] **1** 30, CA.
 Innocent dissemination of libel. *See* Publication—Innocent dissemination of libel, *below*.

LIBEL AND SLANDER (cont)—
Innuendo—
Extrinsic facts—
Facts coming to light after publication complained of—Whether such facts capable of supporting innuendo. **Grappelli v Derek Block (Holdings) Ltd** [1981] **2** 272, CA.
No extrinsic evidence to support innuendo—Innuendo meaning allegedly implicit in ordinary meaning—Whether defendants entitled to ruling whether words capable of bearing innuendo meaning—Newspaper report that police fraud squad inquiring into company's affairs, and naming chairman—Admission that words defamatory in ordinary meaning—Innuendo that chairman guilty of fraud—Whether words capable of imputing guilt of fraud as distinct from suspicion—Pleading innuendoes—RSC Ord 19, r 6(2). **Lewis v Daily Telegraph Ltd** [1963] **2** 151, HL.
Inference—
Words capable of bearing imputed meaning—Inquiry by police fraud squad alleged—Innuendo that X guilty of fraud—Inference of guilt or any suspicion—Whether words capable of bearing imputed meaning of guilt by fraud. **Lewis v Daily Telegraph Ltd** [1963] **2** 151, HL.
Interlocutory decision—
Effect on discretion of trial judge—Particulars of plaintiff's claim relied on to show that words complained of referred to him—Interlocutory application to strike out particulars of claim—Decision of Court of Appeal that particulars should not be struck out as claim arguable—Whether trial judge bound by reason of decision to leave case to jury—Duty of trial judge after hearing argument and evidence to rule whether words reasonably capable of being understood to refer to plaintiff. **Morgan v Odhams Press Ltd** [1971] **2** 1156, HL.
Natural and ordinary meaning complained of—
Defamatory inferences from words in their natural and ordinary meaning pleaded—Effect of pleading particular inferences—Whether plaintiffs entitled to select particular imputations—Whether plaintiffs confined to particular inferences pleaded. **Slim v Daily Telegraph Ltd** [1968] **1** 497, CA.
Particulars—
Duty of plaintiff to plead facts on which he relies for his claim—Identity of persons to whom publication made and who have knowledge of facts which render published words defamatory—Publication by newspaper—Usual practice not to plead particular acts of publication where words complained of published in newspaper—Ordinary reader of newspaper not deriving from published words imputation alleged by way of innuendo—Allegation that words having a defamatory meaning to persons having knowledge of special circumstances—Ordinary readers of newspaper unlikely to have knowledge of special circumstances pleaded by plaintiff in support of innuendo—Whether plaintiff required to give particulars identifying the readers of the newspaper with knowledge of the special circumstances—RSC Ord 18, r 7, Ord 82, r 3(1). **Fullam v Newcastle Chronicle and Journal Ltd** [1977] **3** 32, CA.
Particulars of facts to support secondary meaning—Application to strike out innuendo—RSC Ord 19, rr 6(2), 27, Ord 25, r 4. **Greenslade v Swaffer** [1955] **3** 200, CA.
Practice—
Actual words of statement—Plaintiff relying solely on actual words of statement alleged to be defamatory—No facts or matters relied on in support—Whether plaintiff entitled to plead innuendo—RSC Ord 19, r 6(2). **Loughans v Odhams Press Ltd** [1962] **1** 404, CA.
Innuendo must be supported by extrinsic facts—Meaning of innuendo—True and false innuendoes—Extrinsic fact needed to support extended meaning alleged by true innuendo—Interpretation of words not properly a subject of innuendo—Particulars to be pleaded of facts supporting true innuendo—Striking out innuendo where unsupported by extrinsic facts—RSC Ord 19, r 6(2). **Grubb v Bristol United Press Ltd** [1962] **2** 380, CA.
Similar articles about others in same newspaper—Other articles exposing malpractices and dishonesty of other people—Innuendo attributing consequential like character to article in question—Whether prior articles about others relevant. **Wheeler v Somerfield** [1966] **2** 305, CA.
Publication—
Limited publication. *See* Publication—Limited publication—Innuendo, *below*.
Reference to plaintiff—
Identity—Previous statements by persons other than defendant about 'Mr X'—Statement in alleged libel that plaintiff was 'Mr X'—Previous statements by others not expressly or implicitly adopted or repeated in statement sued on—Innuendo—Plaintiff not entitled by pleading innuendoes to make defendant responsible for statements made by others. **Astaire v Campling** [1965] **3** 666, CA.
Knowledge of special facts—Newspaper article—Nothing in article itself pointing to plaintiff—Extrinsic evidence of special facts indicating that article referred to plaintiff—Whether extrinsic evidence admissible to import meaning that article referred to plaintiff—Knowledge of special facts limited to a few readers—Discrepancies between story in article and facts relating to plaintiff—Whether readers with special knowledge could reasonably understand article referred to plaintiff. **Morgan v Odhams Press Ltd** [1971] **2** 1156, HL.
Words and illustrations—
Juxtaposition of photograph and text—Picture of plaintiff as outdoor photographer—Facing picture of naked woman—Text explaining that for payment customer could have photograph like that of naked woman—Allegation that juxtaposition of illustrations and text implied plaintiff dealt in indecent pictures—Whether pictures and text capable of defamatory meaning. **Garbett v Hazell, Watson and Viney Ltd** [1943] **2** 359, CA.
Interlocutory injunction. *See* Injunction—Interlocutory, *above*.
Interrogatory—
Author not a party—
Printer's information as to state of author's mind at date of publication. **Crozier v Wishart & Co Ltd and Western Printing Services Ltd** [1936] **1** 1, CA.
Fair comment—
Malice—Interrogatories as to defendants' sources of information or grounds of belief—RSC Ord 31, r 1A. **Adams v Sunday Pictorial Newspapers (1920) Ltd** [1951] **1** 865, CA.
Newspaper—
Action against contributor—Interrogatory as to identity of informant. **South Suburban Co-op Society Ltd v Orum** [1937] **3** 133, CA.

LIBEL AND SLANDER (cont)—
  Interrogatory (cont)—
    Newspaper (cont)—
      Action against person not involved in publication—Plaintiff seeking to compel defendant to answer interrogatories concerning identity of publishers and printers of newspaper—Defendant having knowledge of identities but not involved in publication—Newspaper not established to have been published in United Kingdom—Whether defendant compellable to disclose information—Newspapers, Printers and Reading Rooms Repeal Act 1869, Sch 2. **Ricci v Chow** [1987] **3** 534, CA.
      Defence of fair comment—Interrogatory to writer of article as to identity of informant—Writer paid servant of newspaper. **Lawson v Odhams Press Ltd** [1948] **2** 717, CA.
  Source of information—
    Annual reference book. **Georgius v Oxford University Press (Delegates)** [1949] **1** 342, CA.
  Joint tortfeasors—
    Costs—
      Judgment—Damages of scheme—Minimum halfpenny—Action against author, publishers, and printers of book—Settlement with printers on payment of £500 damages some months prior to hearing—Action continued against author and publishers—Payment into court of forty shillings by publishers—No payment in by author—Verdict for plaintiff for halfpenny damages—Whether plaintiff entitled to judgment—Order as to costs—RSC, Ord 82, r 4(2). **Dering v Uris** [1964] **2** 660, QBD.
  Release or covenant not to sue—
    Implied term—Defamation action settled against second and third defendants (publishers and printers)—No express reservation of rights against first defendant (author)—Whether agreement not to sue or release of all three defendants. **Gardiner v Moore** [1966] **1** 365, QBD.
    Release of one joint tortfeasor by accord and satisfaction—No express reservation of rights against another joint tortfeasor—Whether release or covenant not to sue. **Cutler v McPhail** [1962] **2** 474, QBD.
  Jurisdiction—
    Conflict of laws. See **Conflict of laws** (Jurisdiction—Libel).
    County court—
      Counterclaim for slander. See **County court** (Jurisdiction—Counterclaim—Counterclaim for slander).
  Jury—
    Answers—
      Finality. See **Jury** (Answers—Finality—Defamation).
    Trial by jury—
      Libel. See **Jury** (Trial by jury—Libel).
  Justification—
    Alternative meaning of words complained of—
      Words capable of a meaning alternative to that alleged by plaintiff—Whether defendant entitled to plead justification to alternative meaning. **Prager v Times Newspapers Ltd** [1988] **1** 300, CA.
    Duty of defendant—
      Evidence to support plea—Duty of defendant not to place plea on record until clear and sufficient evidence to support it. **Associated Leisure Ltd v Associated Newspapers Ltd** [1970] **2** 754, CA.
      Particulars of justification—Defendant required to make clear meaning he seeks to justify. **Lucas-Box v News Group Newspapers Ltd** [1986] **1** 177, CA.
    Facts sufficient to support plea—
      Newspaper report of issue of writ alleging conspiracy—Particulars of justification repeating fact of issue of writ—Whether sufficient to support justification. **Cadam v Beaverbrook Newspapers Ltd** [1959] **1** 453, CA.
    Interlocutory injunction. See **Injunction** (Interlocutory).
    Jury—
      Intervention—Jury returning verdict before conclusion of defence—Plaintiff intending to give evidence in rebuttal of justification—Need for ruling by judge whether such evidence should be permitted—Whether jury entitled to intervene. **Beevis v Dawson** [1956] **3** 837, CA.
      Newspaper accusing claimant of serious wrongdoing and relying on taped admissions—Claimant alleging that he had fabricated admissions to expose wrongdoing of person to whom they were made—Jury finding for claimant—Court of Appeal setting aside jury's verdict as perverse—Whether Court of Appeal's decision correct. **Grobbelaar v News Group Newspapers Ltd** [2001] **2** 437, CA; [2002] **4** 732, HL.
    Newspaper report repeating allegations in pending High Court proceedings—
      Particulars of justification on ground allegations were in fact made—Whether repetition of allegations in anticipation of open court proceedings libellous—Whether justification maintainable. **Stern v Piper** [1996] **3** 385, CA.
    Offer to make amends. See Pleading—Amendment—Offer to make amends, *below.*
    Partial justification—
      Severable allegation—Plea of partial justification substituted by amendment in place of justification of whole of alleged libel—Alleged defamation by statement of commission of robbery—Conviction not admissible as evidence of truth of facts found—Costs thrown away by amendments reserved to trial judge. **Goody v Odhams Press Ltd** [1966] **3** 369, CA.
    Particulars. See Particulars—Justification, *below.*
    Pleading justification—
      Particulars—Justification required to be pleaded clearly and without obfuscation. **Morrell v International Thomson Publishing Ltd** [1989] **3** 733, CA.
    Substantial justification—
      Pleading—Reliance by defendant on substantial justification—Necessary to plead substantial justification if sought to rely on it—Defamation Act 1952, s 5. **Moore v News of the World Ltd** [1972] **1** 915, CA.
    Wider meaning—
      Justification of wider meaning than that pleaded by plaintiff—Evidence of other facts capable of justifying wider meaning—When evidence of other facts capable of justifying wider meaning admissible. **Williams v Reason (1983)** [1988] **1** 262, CA.

LIBEL AND SLANDER (cont)—
  Justification (cont)—
    Wider meaning (cont)—
      Justification of wider meaning than that pleaded by plaintiff—Plaintiff pleading particular and general charges of squandering public funds—Defendant pleading justification of specific issue and wider meaning—Plaintiff withdrawing general charge—Whether defendant entitled to continue to rely on general charge to support plea of justification. **Bookbinder v Tebbit** [1989] **1** 1169, CA.
  Knowledge of libel—
    Innocent dissemination—
      Absence of prior knowledge. *See* Publication—Innocent dissemination of libel—Absence of prior knowledge of libel, *below*.
  Limitation of action—
    Extension of time limit—
      Discretion to extend time limit. *See* **Limitation of action** (Extension of time limit—Discretion—Exercise of discretion—Defamation action).
    'Facts relevant'—
      Knowledge of fact relevant to cause of action—Newspapers publishing allegations made by a party to proceedings—Plaintiff receiving information outside limitation period that allegations not privileged—Whether information constituting fact relevant to cause of action—Whether grounds for extension of time limit—Limitation Act 1980, s 32A. **C v Mirror Group Newspapers** [1996] **4** 511, CA.
    Multiple publication rule—
      Whether multiple publication rule infringing right to freedom of expression by inhibiting maintenance of Internet archives of press reports—Limitation Act 1980, s 4A—Human Rights Act 1998, Sch 1, Pt I, art 10. **Loutchansky v Times Newspapers Ltd (No 2)** [2002] **1** 652, CA.
  Malice—
    Fair comment—
      Malice pleaded to displace defence of fair comment. *See* Fair comment—Malice, *above*.
    Qualified privilege—
      Malice avoiding privilege. *See* Qualified privilege—Malice avoiding privilege, *below*.
  Malicious falsehood. *See* **Malicious falsehood**.
  Meaning of words complained of. *See* Fair comment—Meaning of words complained of, *above*.
  New trial—
    Jury taking into account impermissible factors—
      Burden of costs—Jury having regard to burden of costs when awarding damages—Whether new trial should be ordered. **Pamplin v Express Newspapers Ltd (No 2) (1985)** [1988] **1** 282, CA.
  Offer of amends—
    Damages—
      Assessment. *See* Damages—Assessment—Offer of amends, *above*.
      Generally. *See* Damages—Offer to make amends, *above*.
    Refusal of offer of amends giving rise to defence unless defendant having 'reason to believe' that statement complained of was false—
      Meaning of 'reason to believe'—Defamation Act 1996, s 4(3). **Milne v Express Newspapers Ltd** [2003] **1** 482, QBD; [2005] **1** 1021, CA.
      Whether defence of refusal of amends based on absence of negligence—Defamation Act 1996, s 4. **Milne v Express Newspapers Ltd** [2003] **1** 482, QBD.
    Resilement—
      Pleading. *See* Pleading—Amendment—Offer to make amends, *below*.
  Ordinary and natural meaning—
    Headline and photograph in tabloid newspaper—
      Accompanying article not defamatory—Severance of headline and photograph—Headline and photograph defamatory—Accompanying article negating libel—Whether plaintiffs entitled to sever and rely on headline and photograph in claim for libel. **Charleston v News Group Newspapers Ltd** [1995] **2** 313, HL.
  Parliamentary proceedings. *See* Qualified privilege, *below*.
  Particulars—
    Defamatory meaning of words complained of—
      Claim based on natural and ordinary meaning of words—No allegation that words used in defamatory sense other than ordinary meaning—Desirability of pleading innuendo setting out alleged defamatory meaning. **S & K Holdings Ltd v Throgmorton Publications Ltd** [1972] **3** 497, CA.
      Claim based on natural and ordinary meaning of words—No allegation that words used in defamatory sense other than ordinary meaning—Desirability of setting out particulars of alleged defamatory meaning—Uncertainty as to meaning attributable to words complained of—Whether necessary that particulars of defamatory meaning should be pleaded—Whether order for particulars should be made. **Allsop v Church of England Newspaper Ltd** [1972] **2** 26, CA.
      Claim based on natural and ordinary meaning of words—Words complained of bearing different possible meanings—Necessity of pleading particulars of defamatory meaning alleged. **DDSA Pharmaceuticals Ltd v Times Newspapers Ltd** [1972] **3** 417, CA.
    Fair comment—
      General plea—Particulars of facts on which plea based—Plaintiff entitled to particulars. **Cunningham-Howie v FW Dimbleby & Sons Ltd** [1950] **2** 882, CA.
      Particulars of defence—Fact and comment—Particulars of facts relied on—Defendant raising general plea of fair comment—Defendant not required to particularise which words complained of are fact and which are comment—Defendant required to give particulars of the facts supporting the plea—RSC Ord 82, r 3(2), applicable only to rolled-up plea and not to a general plea of fair comment. **Lord v Sunday Telegraph Ltd** [1970] **3** 504, CA.
      Rolled-up plea—Particulars of facts relied on. **Tudor-Hart v British Union for the Abolition of Vivisection** [1937] **4** 475, CA.
    Innuendo. *See* Innuendo—Particulars, *above*.
    Justification—
      Duty of defendant. *See* Justification—Duty of defendant—Particulars of justification, *above*.

LIBEL AND SLANDER (cont)—
  Particulars (cont)—
    Justification (cont)—
      Fair comment—Particulars of words not complained of in statement of claim—Publication not severable into parts—Natural and ordinary meaning—Plaintiff applying to strike out particulars in defence not concerned with words complained of—Whether defendant entitled to plead justification or fair comment as to whole publication—Whether defamatory statement complained of separate and distinct from other defamatory statements contained in publication. **Polly Peck (Holdings) plc v Trelford** [1986] **2** 84, CA.
      Fair comment—Particulars of words not complained of in statement of claim—Single publication not severable into parts—Natural and ordinary meaning of words relied on—Jury entitled to see whole publication—Defendant entitled to plead justification or fair comment as to whole publication—Long article in journal alleging that directors of company guilty of improper accountancy practices—Seventh paragraph of article referring to one director's previous involvement in accounting controversies when chairman of another company—Statement of claim complaining of whole article except seventh paragraph—Particulars of defence justifying seventh paragraph admissible. **S & K Holdings Ltd v Throgmorton Publications Ltd** [1972] **3** 497, CA.
      Fair comment—Two or more distinct charges against plaintiff—Newspaper article—Plaintiff complaining of certain words in article—Words complained of containing only one charge—Whether defendant entitled to rely on whole article to justify separate charges in article against plaintiff—Defamation Act 1952, s 5. **Polly Peck (Holdings) plc v Trelford** [1986] **2** 84, CA.
      Giving of particulars—Whether before or after discovery—RSC Ord 19, rr 4, 27. **Goldschmidt v Constable & Co** [1937] **4** 293, CA.
      Hearsay and rumour—Publication of words regarding financial viability of plaintiffs' family company—Whether particulars of hearsay and rumour capable of supporting plea of justification. **Aspro Travel Ltd v Owners Abroad Group plc** [1995] **4** 728, CA.
      Order for full particulars—No rule that particulars of facts and matters relied on should always be ordered—Charges sufficiently specific—No general order for particulars—RSC Ord 19, r 6. **Marks v Wilson-Boyd** [1939] **2** 605, CA.
      Reasonable suspicion of guilt—Hearsay statements—Republication of reports or repetition of assertions alleging involvement in money laundering scheme—Whether defence of justification of reasonable suspicion of guilt having to focus on some conduct of plaintiff giving rise to suspicion—Whether such conduct having to be pleaded and proved—Whether reliance on hearsay statements to support plea of reasonable suspicion of guilt infringing repetition rule. **Shah v Standard Chartered Bank** [1998] **4** 155, CA.
      Relevance of particulars to pleading—Plaintiff producing television documentary alleging conspiracy to murder republicans in Northern Ireland—Defendants publishing article claiming that programme was a hoax—Plaintiff bringing proceedings for libel and defendants pleading justification—Defendants applying to reamend particulars of justification to add new particulars challenging existence of conspiracy—Whether cost and expense of litigating issues raised by amendment disproportionate. **McPhilemy v Times Newspapers Ltd** [1999] **3** 775, CA.
      Relevance of particulars to pleading—Plaintiffs a computer school and directors of school—Allegations by defendants that school a financial racket and guilty of publishing misleading advertisements—Allegation that founder and manager of school unfit to run a school—Whether defendants entitled to give particulars of founder's criminal record. **London Computer Operators Training Ltd v BBC** [1973] **2** 170, CA.
    Letters alleged to be defamatory—
      Plaintiff ignorant of contents—Plaintiff ignorant of contents—Whether particulars to be delivered. **Collins v Jones** [1955] **2** 145, CA.
    Material facts—
      Reference to plaintiff—Plaintiff not referred to by name on description other than nationality. **Bruce v Odhams Press Ltd** [1936] **1** 287, CA.
    Passages alleged to be defamatory—
      Need to specify passages—Newspaper article—Parts only of article capable of being defamatory of plaintiffs—Statement of claim alleging that defendants had published 'an article' which seriously injured plaintiffs in their reputation—Copy of complete article delivered with statement of claim—Statement of claim defective. **DDSA Pharmaceuticals Ltd v Times Newspapers Ltd** [1972] **3** 417, CA.
    Publication of alleged libel—
      Date, time and place of publication—Necessary for plaintiff to set out in pleading with reasonable certainty words complained of—Duty to give sufficient particulars to ensure he has proper case—Letters alleged to be defamatory—Plaintiff ignorant of contents—Defendant entitled to particulars including date, time and place of publication of letters. **Collins v Jones** [1955] **2** 145, CA.
    Quia timet injunction—
      Action for injunction to restrain publication of threatened libel—Particularity of pleadings—Whether prior restraint requiring exact words of libel to be set out verbatim in statement of claim—Requirement of reasonable certainty. **British Data Management plc v Boxer Commercial Removals plc** [1996] **3** 707, CA.
  Parties—
    Right to sue—
      Corporation—Foreign corporation—Right to freedom of expression—Common law presumption of damage under English law once publication of libel established—Whether right to freedom of expression modifying common law presumption in relation to foreign corporation—Human Rights Act 1998, Sch 1, Pt I, art 10(2). **Jameel v Wall Street Journal Europe SPRL** [2004] **2** 92, QBD; [2005] **4** 356, CA; [2006] **4** 1279, HL.
      Corporation—Local government corporation—Right of local authority to sue—Publication relating to administration by local authority of its superannuation fund—Local authority alleging defamatory of it—Whether entitled to sue for libel. **Derbyshire CC v Times Newspapers Ltd** [1993] **1** 1011, HL.

363

LIBEL AND SLANDER (cont)—
  Parties (cont)—
    Right to sue (cont)—
      Corporation—Local government corporation—Right of local authority to sue—Publication relating to administration by local authority of its superannuation fund—Publication insinuating maladministration of pension funds—Whether non-trading corporation entitled to sue for libel if damage not pleaded. **Derbyshire CC v Times Newspapers Ltd** [1993] **1** 1011, HL.
      Corporation—Local government corporation—Statements reflecting on personal reputation of corporation—Statements not affecting property of corporation—Statements reflecting on 'governing' reputation of corporation. **Bognor Regis UDC v Campion** [1972] **2** 61, QBD.
      Political party—Right of political party to sue—Publication relating to political party withdrawing from General Election—Political party alleging publication defamatory of it—Whether political party entitled to sue in defamation. **Goldsmith v Bhoyrul** [1997] **4** 268, QBD.
      Trade union—Libel against union—Right of union to sue—Allegation of 'rigging' a ballot. **Willis v Brooks** [1947] **1** 191, KBD.
  Pleading—
    Amendment—
      Defence—Amendment to plead justification at a late stage—Amendment allowed because in interests of justice—Any hardship to plaintiffs compensatable by increased damages if plea failed—Due diligence exercised by defendants in placing plea on the record. **Associated Leisure Ltd v Associated Newspapers Ltd** [1970] **2** 754, CA.
      Defence—Amendment to plead justification at a late stage—Amendment raising allegation of fraud—Whether late amendment alleging fraud should be allowed. **Atkinson v Fitzwalter** [1987] **1** 483, CA.
      Leave—Appeal against order giving leave—Test to be applied in determining appeal—Striking out of amended plea only in plain and obvious cases. **Cadam v Beaverbrook Newspapers Ltd** [1959] **1** 453, CA.
      Offer to make amends—Right to fair trial—Right to freedom of expression—Defendant making offer to make amends in respect of a defamatory imputation—Claimant accepting offer and apology read in open court—Whether defendant able to resile from offer to make amends after acceptance and plead justification in respect of that imputation—Whether defendant's right to a fair trial and freedom of expression infringed if unable to plead justification—Whether particulars directly relevant to contextual background of publication for purposes of assessment of damages—Defamation Act 1996 s (4)—Human Rights Act 1998, Sch 1, Pt I, arts 6, 10. **Warren v Random House Group Ltd** [2009] **2** 245, CA.
    Mitigation of damages—
      Character of plaintiff—Evidence in mitigation of damages—Plea of justification—Intention of defendant to adduce evidence as to character of plaintiff—Issues of fact not arising out of preceding pleadings—RSC Ord 19, r 15. **Plato Films Ltd v Speidel** [1961] **1** 876, HL.
    Particulars. See Particulars, *above.*
  Preliminary point of law—
    Application for trial of preliminary issue on point of law—
      Suitability of question for determination as preliminary issue. *See* **Practice** (Preliminary point of law—Application for trial of preliminary issue on point of law—Libel action).
  Privilege—
    Absolute privilege—
      Action —Immunity from suit—Defendant instigating police investigation by making oral and written complaints regarding claimant—No criminal proceedings ensuing—Claimant commencing proceedings seeking damages for defamation—Whether defendant's statements to police protected by absolute privilege and immunity from suit. **Westcott v Westcott** [2009] **1** 727, CA.
      Communications between officials of foreign government—Internal embassy document—Acting ambassador of foreign embassy causing memorandum concerning plaintiff to be published within embassy to another embassy official—Whether action for libel by plaintiff justiciable in English court—Whether publication of embassy document protected by absolute privilege—Diplomatic Privileges Act 1964, Sch 1, art 24. **Fayed v Al-Tajir** [1987] **2** 396, CA.
      Document sent by defendants to financial regulator in course of investigation—Whether defence of absolute privilege applying to document. **Mahon v Rahn (No 2)** [2000] **2 Comm** 1, CA; [2000] **4** 41, CA.
      Judicial proceedings—Defendant council serving contribution notice on plaintiff 's husband in respect of costs of fostering their adoptive son—Plaintiff 's solicitor requesting information from defendants' solicitor as to who had initiated removal of son into foster accommodation—Whether answer given absolutely privileged. **Waple v Surrey CC** [1998] **1** 624, CA.
      Tribunal recognised by law—Benchers of Inn of Court—Initiation of proceedings—Communication to Bar Council—Alleged libel contained in letters of complaint against Queen's Counsel addressed to secretary of Bar Council—No complaint made to Benchers of Inn of Court—Whether Benchers a tribunal recognised by law—Whether letters initiation of proceedings before Benchers—Whether protected by absolute privilege. **Lincoln v Daniels** [1961] **3** 740, CA.
      Tribunal recognised by law—EC Commission—Complaint made to Commission—Complaint containing defamatory remarks—Commission investigating and adjudicating on complaint—Company complained about suing complainant for libel—Whether voluntary complaint to EC Commission protected by absolute privilege—Whether public interest for complaint not to be produced in libel proceedings—EEC Regulation No 17 of 6 February 1962, arts 11, 20. **Hasselblad (GB) Ltd v Orbinson** [1985] **1** 173, CA.
    Communications between officials of foreign government—
      Communications made in England—Official communications on state matters—Government in exile in London—Letter from state prosecutor to office of head of state—Letter containing defamatory allegations against plaintiff—Plaintiff a citizen of foreign state—Whether letter protected by absolute privilege. **Szalatnay-Stacho v Fink** [1946] **2** 231, CA.
    Judicial proceedings—
      Coroner's court—Newspaper report of proceedings in coroner's court—Whether proceedings in coroner's court judicial proceedings—Law of Libel Amendment Act 1888, s 3. **McCarey v Associated Newspapers Ltd** [1964] **3** 947, CA.

LIBEL AND SLANDER (cont)—
  Privilege (cont)—
    Judicial proceedings (cont)—
      Disciplinary committee of Law Society—Proceedings before committee—Judicial character of proceedings—Whether proceedings absolutely privileged—Solicitors Act 1957, s 46. **Addis v Crocker** [1959] **2** 773, QBD.
      Interruption—Application to court by interrupter—Newspaper report of interruption—Whether application made in course of judicial proceedings—Whether reports of interruption privileged—Law of Libel Amendment Act 1888, s 3. **Farmer v Hyde** [1937] **1** 773, CA.
    Official communications on State matters—
      Extent of privilege—Whether applying to official communications sent in England by Czechoslovak military prosecutor. *See* **Conflict of laws** (Tort—Libel—Defence—Privilege—Official communications on State matters—Official communication sent in England by Czechoslovak military prosecutor).
    Police report—
      Assistant Commissioner's report on chief officer of Metropolitan Sub-Division—Whether report absolutely privileged. **Merricks v Nott-Bower** [1964] **1** 717, CA.
    Proceedings in Parliament—
      Communication to member of Parliament within precincts of Parliament—Publication not connected with proceedings of Parliament—Contempt of court—Breach of injunction against repetition of libel. **Rivlin v Bilainkin** [1953] **1** 534, QBD.
      Evidence of words spoken in Parliament in support of claim—Evidence of malice—Words complained of spoken by member of Parliament in television interview—Defence of fair comment in good faith and without malice—Evidence of words spoken by defendant in Parliament adduced in order to prove malice—Evidence inadmissible. **Church of Scientology of California v Johnson-Smith** [1972] **1** 378, QBD.
      Questioning proceedings in Parliament—Committee of House of Commons—Former member of Parliament claiming damages for defamatory allegations during television interview—Allegations subject of inquiry by Parliamentary Commissioner for Standards and dealt with in report by Committee on Standards and Privileges—House of Commons approving report—Whether action should be stayed on ground that issues could not be determined fairly because of parliamentary privilege—Defamation Act 1996, s 13. **Hamilton v Al Fayed** [1999] **3** 317, CA; [2000] **2** 224, HL.
      Questioning proceedings in Parliament—Committee of House of Commons—Member of Parliament claiming damages against defendants for defamatory article—Plaintiff claiming that article causing him to be deselected from standing committee and not appointed as chairman of select committee and causing opposition member of Parliament to complain to Speaker—Plaintiff seeking to adduce evidence to support claims—Whether appointment and deselection of members of committee of House forming part of proceedings of House—Whether proceedings of committee protected by parliamentary privilege—Bill of Rights (1688), art 9. **Rost v Edwards** [1990] **2** 641, QBD.
      Questioning proceedings in Parliament—Committee of House of Commons—Repetition outside Parliament of statements made to Parliament—Bill of Rights (1688), art 9. **Makudi v Baron Triesman of Tottenham** [2014] **3** 36, CA.
    Qualified privilege—
      Common law privilege—Responsible journalism—Politician making statement defaming public official—Whether politician protected by qualified privilege—Whether defence of responsible journalism limited to press and broadcasting media. **Seaga v Harper** [2008] **1** 965, PC.
      Common law privilege—Responsible journalism—Public interest—Newspaper publishing article stating allegations against named police officer had led to police investigation into corruption—Whether publication in public interest—Whether responsible journalism. **Flood v Times Newspapers Ltd** [2012] **4** 913, SC.
    Qualified privilege. *See* Qualified privilege, *below*.
    Solicitor. *See* **Solicitor** (Disciplinary proceedings—Disciplinary committee—Privilege against liability for defamation).
    Unemployment insurance claim—
      Communication to labour exchange—Letter from employer—Letter sent in response to request from labour exchange for information concerning former employee—Letter defamatory and malicious—Whether absolutely privileged—Unemployment Insurance Act 1920, s 11—Unemployment Insurance Act 1935, s 44. **Mason v Brewis Bros Ltd** [1938] **2** 420, KBD.
    Visiting forces—
      Communications between members of visiting forces—Consequent dismissal of civilian employee—Whether communication absolutely privileged. **Richards v Naum** [1966] **3** 812, CA.
  Professional description—
    Boxing title. *See* **Slander of title** (Professional description—Boxing title—Defendant represented as holding title held by plaintiff).
  Public interest defence—
    Whether Reynolds criteria applying to statutory defence—
      Defamation Act 2013, s 4. **Serafin v Malkiewicz** [2020] **4** 711, SC.
  Publication—
    Innocent dissemination of libel—
      Absence of prior knowledge of libel—Distributor of periodicals—Whether necessary to prove that distributor knew or ought to have known that particular issue of periodical contained a libel on the plaintiff which could not be justified or excused. **Goldsmith v Sperrings Ltd** [1977] **2** 566, CA.
    Internet posting—
      Internet service provider—Internet service provider performing passive role in facilitating postings on internet—Whether internet service provider a publisher. **Bunt v Tilley** [2006] **3** 336, QBD.
      Posting defamatory of plaintiff being placed on Internet—Internet service provider failing to act on plaintiff's request to remove posting—Whether service provider having published defamatory posting—Defamation Act 1996, s 1. **Godfrey v Demon Internet Ltd** [1999] **4** 342, QBD.
      Search engine—Search engine provider—Claimant bringing action for defamation based on comments left on website—Search engine results including links to allegedly defamatory material—Whether search engine provider a publisher. **Metropolitan International Schools Ltd (t/a SkillsTrain and/or Train2Game) v Designtechnica Corp (t/a Digital Trends)** [2010] **3** 548, QBD.

LIBEL AND SLANDER (cont)—
  Publication (cont)—
    Internet posting (cont)—
      Whether in action for libel on internet publication there was presumption of law that substantial publication had taken place within jurisdiction of English court. **Al Amoudi v Brisard** [2006] **3** 294, QBD.
    Limited publication—
      Innuendo—Extrinsic facts supporting innuendo—Identification of persons knowing extrinsic facts—Whether plaintiff must identify persons knowing extrinsic facts when publication complained of is limited. **Grappelli v Derek Block (Holdings) Ltd** [1981] **2** 272, CA.
    Multiple publication rule—
      Limitation of action. *See* Limitation of action—Multiple publication rule, *above*.
    Notice on wall of premises—
      Allowing notice to remain on wall—Club premises—Proprietary club—Notice containing defamatory statement posted on club wall—Proprietors of club permitting notice to remain on wall—Whether notice published by proprietors. **Byrne v Deane** [1937] **2** 204, CA.
    Republication pending action—
      Contempt of court. *See* **Contempt of court** (Republication of alleged libel—Pending proceedings).
    Third party—
      Circumstances in which defendant can be liable for damage caused to claimant by press reporting of defendant's slanderous words. **McManus v Beckham** [2002] **4** 497, CA.
      Employer and employee—Publication by one employee of company to another—Action against company—Acts of employees treated as acts of company—Inter-departmental memorandum—Memorandum about one of company's employees dictated by another employee to his secretary—Memorandum containing defamatory words—Memorandum received and read by another employee—Whether memorandum published by company. **Riddick v Thames Board Mills Ltd** [1977] **3** 677, CA.
  Qualified privilege—
    Apology—
      Apology defamatory of third party—Whether position of person publishing apology and person at whose instance it was published to be considered separately—Whether apology protected by qualified privilege. **Watts v Times Newspapers Ltd (Schilling & Lom (a firm), third party)** [1996] **1** 152, CA.
    Common and corresponding interest—
      Whether communications between Bar Council and Bar on matters of compliance with professional rules attracting qualified privilege without need to evaluate quality of information. **Kearns v General Council of the Bar** [2002] **4** 1075, QBD.
    Common law privilege—
      Duty to publish—Public interest—Whether exercise of responsible journalism equating to test for qualified privilege. **Jameel v Wall Street Journal Europe SPRL** [2005] **4** 356, CA; [2006] **4** 1279, HL.
      Duty to publish—Standard to be applied by court when considering whether newspaper had been under duty to publish defamatory words—Guidance. **Loutchansky v Times Newspapers Ltd (No 2)** [2002] **1** 652, CA.
      Plaintiff resigning as Prime Minister of Ireland following political crisis—Newspaper publishing article on resignation and plaintiff suing for libel—Newspaper claiming qualified privilege—Whether publication of political information automatically attracting qualified privilege—Whether test for qualified privilege including 'circumstantial test' distinct from duty-interest test. **Reynolds v Times Newspapers Ltd** [1999] **4** 609, HL.
      Public interest—Newspaper publishing series of sensational articles accusing footballer of taking bribes to fix football matches—Whether newspaper entitled to rely on defence of qualified privilege. **Grobbelaar v News Group Newspapers Ltd** [2001] **2** 437, CA.
      Report in newspaper—When newspaper report entitled to protection of common law privilege—Journalist inferring from statement made to him by government official that plaintiff dismissed from Civil Service for incompetence—Allegations against plaintiff not substantiated at time of publication—Whether public at large having legitimate interest in publication of inference—Whether newspaper having duty to publish inference—Whether fair information on matter of public interest a defence open to newspaper at common law. **Blackshaw v Lord** [1983] **2** 311, CA.
      Responsible journalism—Principles to be applied—Defendants publishers and author of book concerning police corruption—Whether publication of book an occasion of qualified privilege. **Charman v Orion Publishing Group Ltd** [2007] **1** 622, QBD; [2008] **1** 750, CA.
      Whether qualified privilege protecting publication to public at large where plaintiff an elected politician and defamatory words complained of relating to his conduct in his public role rather than his private or personal life. **Reynolds v Times Newspapers Ltd** [1998] **3** 961, CA.
    Duty and interest—
      Agreement not to offer to supply goods in response to an invitation to tender until after discussions with other persons invited to tender—Privilege ordinarily attributable to communications between persons in a particular relationship not lost merely by absence of duty or common interest to make the particular communication that was made—Statement that plaintiff not conversant with normal business ethics—Communicated by letter to mutual friend who had introduced plaintiff to the writer with a view to business. **Angel v HH Bushell & Co Ltd** [1967] **1** 1018, QBD.
      Bank—Cheque marked 'not sufficient'—Sufficient funds in account—Duty of bank to make communication. **Davidson v Barclays Bank Ltd** [1940] **1** 316, KBD.
      Belief of defendant—Defamatory communication about conduct of third party—Genuine but mistaken belief by defendant that recipient of communication has interest in receiving it—Whether belief sufficient to attract qualified privilege. **Beach v Freeson** [1971] **2** 854, QBD.
      Clerical staff—Publication to clerical staff for purpose of preparing document—Interest of employer and employee in publication—Publication to intended recipient never made—Whether publication to clerical staff protected by original privilege—Whether publication must be made to intended recipient to attach ancillary privilege. **Bryanston Finance Ltd v De Vries** [1975] **2** 609, CA.

LIBEL AND SLANDER (cont)—
 Qualified privilege (cont)—
  Duty and interest (cont)—
   Member of Parliament—Allegation of improper conduct by public official—Communication to member of Parliament seeking interview with Minister—Whether member of Parliament having sufficient interest in communication. **R v Rule** [1937] 2 772, CCA.
   Member of Parliament—Complaint by constituent concerning conduct of solicitor—Letters sent by member to Law Society and Lord Chancellor setting out details of complaint—Duty or interest of member in passing on complaint—Interest of Lord Chancellor in complaint—Whether publication of letters protected by qualified privilege. **Beach v Freeson** [1971] 2 854, QBD.
   Official organ of body or association—Notice published in organ—Racehorse trainer—Licence withdrawn—Publication in 'Racing Calendar'. **Russell v Duke of Norfolk** [1949] 1 109, CA.
   Presence of bystanders—Statement to person having interest in hearing it—Words spoken in presence of bystanders—Words overheard by bystanders—Bystanders having no interest or duty in respect of statement—Whether occasion privileged. **White v J & F Stone Ltd** [1939] 3 507, CA.
   Privileged occasion—Report to commanding officer—Allegation that serviceman had failed to pay debt—Communication by creditor to commanding officer—Interest of commanding officer in payment of debt. **Winstanley v Bampton** [1943] 1 661, KBD.
   Protection of common interest—Alleged breach of copyright—Letter by owner of copyright to firms selling publication in which copyright infringed—Whether letter written on privileged occasion. **Cramp (G A) & Sons Ltd v Smythson (Frank) Ltd** [1943] 1 322, CA.
   Ship's log—Entry in log—Statutory duty to make entry when seaman left behind—Entry stating seaman had deserted the ship—Master not informed that seaman in hospital—Absence of malice. **Moore v Canadian Pacific Steamship Co** [1945] 1 128, Assizes.
   Statutory duty—Common interest—No common interest to make and receive communication—Report of committee to borough council—Publication of report in public libraries for perusal of ratepayers and others—Metropolis Management Amendment Act 1856, s 9. **De Buse v McCarty and Stepney BC** [1942] 1 19, CA.
  Established relationship—
   Whether lack of verification relevant for purposes of determining whether qualified privilege attaching to defamatory communications between parties in established relationship. **Kearns v General Council of the Bar** [2003] 2 534, CA.
  Malice avoiding privilege—
   Anger—Libel published unnecessarily and in anger—Statement that plaintiff not conversant with normal business ethics—Statement communicated by letter to mutual friend who had introduced plaintiff to defendant with a view to business—Anger at sales not being forthcoming. **Angel v HH Bushell & Co Ltd** [1967] 1 1018, QBD.
   Employer and workman—Workman suffering from dermatitis caused by conditions of employment—Certificate of disablement—Application for compensation—Letter to company's insurers disclaiming liability—Letter containing defamatory statements of workman's uncleanliness and exposure of fellow workers to risk of infection—Appeal to medical referee—Appeal out of time—Purported appointment of medical referee by registrar—Repetition of certain defamatory statements in insurers' letter to medical referee—Privilege—Proceedings before medical referee not judicial in character—Workmen's Compensation (Medical Referees in England and Wales) Regulations 1932 (SR & O 1932 No 960),, regs 25, 26, 27, 30. **Smith v National Meter Co Ltd** [1945] 2 35, KBD.
   Evidence of malice—Motive—Financial considerations—Expression of opinion—Opinion actuated by financial considerations—Right of defence against written attack—Procedure at trial. **Turner v Metro-Goldwyn-Mayer Pictures Ltd** [1950] 1 449, HL.
   Gross and unreasoning prejudice—Honest belief of defendant in truth of defamatory allegation—Honest belief induced by gross and unreasoning prejudice—Gross and unreasoning prejudice not itself amounting to malice—Honest belief in truth of defamatory allegation inconsistent with malice. **Horrocks v Lowe** [1974] 1 662, HL.
   Joint publication—Malice of one defendant—Partners—Malice found against only one of the partners—Act performed by another partner without malice—Liability of partner against whom malice found—Partnership Act 1890, s 10. **Meekins v Henson** [1962] 1 899, QBD.
   Joint publication—Principal and agent—Malice of principal—Liability of agent—Letter written by assistant secretary on instructions of committee—Malice found against some committee members only—No malice found against assistant secretary—Effect of malice of some members on privilege of innocent members of committee—Effect of malice of principal on privilege of agent. **Egger v Viscount of Chelmsford** [1964] 3 406, CA.
   Joint publication—Trustees of friendly society—Malice of one trustee—Effect on qualified privilege of other trustees—Whether privilege of trustees avoided by malice of one. **Longdon-Griffiths v Smith** [1950] 2 662, KBD.
   Judge withdrawing issue of malice from jury—Whether judge in error. **Alexander v Arts Council of Wales** [2001] 4 205, CA.
   Master and servant—Corporation—Publication by one employee of corporation to another—Liability of corporation where employee actuated by malice—Inter-departmental memorandum—Company's assistant personnel manager instructed to investigate manner of employee's dismissal—Assistant personnel manager telephoning F and S, two employees who had dealt with dismissal—Assistant personnel manager preparing memorandum—Memorandum dictated to secretary and sent to personnel manager—Action brought by dismissed employee against company for defamation in memorandum—Malice proved against F and S—Whether memorandum infected by malice of F and S—Whether company should be liable for libel contained in confidential memorandum made by one employee about another even if memorandum infected by malice. **Riddick v Thames Board Mills Ltd** [1977] 3 677, CA.
   Solicitor—Admission of negligence by client—Evidence of malice—Plaintiff involved in motor accident—Plaintiff not to blame for accident—Conduct of litigation in hands of insurance company—Company's solicitor admitting plaintiff's negligence cause of accident—Action for libel against solicitor—Evidence that solicitor actuated by malice. **Groom v Crocker** [1938] 2 394, CA.

LIBEL AND SLANDER (cont)—
Qualified privilege (cont)—
Notice or other matter issued by government department—
Fair and accurate report of notice or other matter issued by government department—Report in newspaper—What constitutes matter issued by government department—Whether statement given by government official to journalist over telephone can constitute 'matter issued' by government department—Whether statement made without authority by government official in answer to journalist's questions can constitute 'matter issued' by government department—Defamation Act 1952, s 7(1), Schedule, para 12. **Blackshaw v Lord** [1983] **2** 311, CA.

Parliamentary proceedings—
Fair and accurate report—Additional non-privileged material—Whether privilege lost—Test for fairness and accuracy—Defamation Act 1996, s 15, Sch 1, para 1. **Curistan v Times Newspapers Ltd** [2007] **4** 486, QBD; [2008] **3** 923, CA.

Fair and honest report—Selective report in newspaper—'Parliamentary sketch'—Sketch consisting of selective report of part of proceedings considered by reporter to be of public interest—Sketch giving reporter's impression of that part of proceedings—Sketch privileged if fair and honest presentation of what took place—Debate in House of Lords—Sketch giving prominence to one speech strongly critical of the plaintiff—Sketch also referring to rebuttal of criticism in another speech. **Cook v Alexander** [1973] **3** 1037, CA.

Newspaper comment—Parliamentary papers—Report of select committee—Comment on proceedings and report of committee—Parliamentary Papers Act 1840, s 3. **Associated Newspapers Ltd v Dingle** [1960] **1** 294, QBD.

Privilege subject to explanation or contradiction—
Refusal to publish explanation or contradiction—Letter requesting full apology—Request not setting out words of statement to be published by way of explanation—Whether a request to publish 'letter or statement by way of explanation or contradiction'—Defamation Act 1952, s 7(2). **Khan v Ahmed** [1957] **2** 385, QBD.

Protection of common interest—
Examination—Allegation of cheating—Common interest of examinees—Words alleging cheating in examination—Statement made by invigilator to remainder of examinees. **Bridgman v Stockdale** [1953] **1** 1166, QBD.

Public interest—
Common law privilege. See Qualified privilege—Common law privilege—Public interest, above.

Duty to communicate information to public—Communication to press—Simultaneous termination of their engagements at London theatre by four artistes privately giving contractual month's notice—Unusual happening likely to curtail run of successful play—Coincidence of notice with alleged wish to transfer another play to that theatre—Letter to artistes by employing impressario deploring their simultaneous notice—Communication of letter to national press—Alleged defamation of artistes' theatrical agents and other plaintiffs who were not the artistes—Whether letter subject of qualified privilege. **London Artists Ltd v Littler** [1968] **1** 1075, QBD.

Duty to communicate information to public—Whether defendant entitled to rely on matters not known at time of publication in support of plea of qualified privilege—Human Rights Act 1998, Sch 1, Pt I, art 10(2). **Loutchansky v Times Newspapers Ltd** [2001] **4** 115, CA.

Election—Address by candidate—Statement by candidate in election address—Whether subject of qualified privilege. **Braddock v Bevins** [1948] **1** 450, CA.

Election—Limitation of privilege at elections—Statement in election address—Whether plea of qualified privilege barred by statute—Defamation Act 1952, s 10. **Plummer v Charman** [1962] **3** 823, CA.

Election—Limitation of privilege at elections—Whether election candidate precluded from relying on defence of qualified privilege in respect of statement in election that was material to question in issue in election—Defamation Act 1952, s 10—Human Rights Act 1998, s 3, Sch 1, Pt I, arts 6, 10. **Culnane v Morris** [2006] **2** 149, QBD.

Public meeting—
Meeting for furtherance or discussion of matter of public concern—Report of meeting in newspaper—Meeting organised by Pakistani students to honour distinguished statesman—Meeting open to anyone—Whether public meeting—Defamation Act 1952, s 7(1), Sch, para 9. **Khan v Ahmed** [1957] **2** 385, QBD.

Press conference—Newspaper reporting defamatory comments made at press conference—Report referring to contents of press release distributed at press conference but not read aloud—Newspaper relying on defence of qualified privilege attaching to fair and accurate report of proceedings at 'public meeting'—Whether press conference a 'public meeting' for purposes of qualified privilege—Whether contents of press release capable of forming subject matter of report of proceedings at public meeting if not read aloud at meeting—Defamation Act (Northern Ireland) 1955, s 7, Schedule, para 9. **McCartan Turkington Breen (a firm) v Times Newspapers Ltd** [2000] **4** 913, HL.

Report of judicial proceedings—
Accuracy—Newspaper report—Criminal proceedings—Charges of theft and of taking car without owner's consent—Charge of theft withdrawn—Reporter through inattention failing to realise charge of theft withdrawn—Plaintiffs convicted of taking without consent—Report referring to conviction for 'theft'. **Mitchell v Hirst, Kidd and Rennie Ltd** [1936] **3** 872, Assizes.

Advocate's speech—Verification—Newspaper report—Whether duty to verify advocate's statement. **Burnett & Hallamshire Fuel Ltd v Sheffield Telegraph & Star Ltd** [1960] **2** 157, Assizes.

Foreign proceedings—Confession—Report of criminal trial abroad of British subject in which he confessed to crimes in England, including murder of which he had previously been acquitted by English court—Whether report protected by qualified privilege—Scope of such privilege—Whether extending to report of statement concerning murdered man having been father of child of the murderer's wife. **Webb v Times Publishing Co Ltd** [1960] **2** 789, QBD.

Report of notice issued by public authority for information of public—
Police notice—Broadcast—Circular letter by auctioneers to other auctioneers—Theft of pigs at auction—Television flash arranged through chief officer of police containing offer of reward by auctioneers—Whether matter of public concern and for public benefit—Defamation Act 1952, ss 7, 9, Sch, para 12. **Boston v WS Bagshaw & Sons** [1966] **2** 906, CA.

LIBEL AND SLANDER (cont)—
    Qualified privilege (cont)—
        Report of planning inquiry—
            Newspaper report of evidence given at planning inquiry—Witness at inquiry alleging plaintiffs guilty of corruption—Whether newspaper's report of inquiry fair and accurate—Whether report a matter publication of which was of public concern and for public benefit—Whether issues of fairness and accuracy and public concern and public benefit matters for judge or jury—Defamation Act 1952, s 7(3), Sch, para 10(c). **Kingshott v Associated Kent Newspapers Ltd** [1991] **2** 99, CA.
        Report of proceedings of public inquiry—
            Newspaper article referring to proceedings of special inquiry set up in Ghana to inquire into murder of three High Court judges—Special inquiry naming plaintiff as conspirator—Whether paragraph in article a 'report' and 'fair and accurate'—Whether report of special inquiry 'proceedings in public'—Whether publication 'not of public concern and ... not for the public benefit'—Defamation Act 1952, s 7(1)(3), Sch, para 5. **Tsikata v Newspaper Publishing plc** [1997] **1** 655, CA.
        Right to respect for private and family life—
            Claimant being placed on defendant local authority's 'Potentially Violent Persons Register'—Authority publishing register to employees and external 'partner organisations' by e-mail—Claimant issuing libel proceedings—Whether defence of qualified privilege available—Human Rights Act 1998, Sch 1, Pt I, art 8. **Clift v Slough BC** [2009] **4** 756, QBD; [2011] **3** 118, CA.
            Whether fact occasion of publication attracting qualified privilege precluding claim on basis of violation of claimant's right to respect for private and family life—Human Rights Act 1998, s 7, Sch 1, Pt 1, art 8. **W v Westminster City Council** [2005] **4** 96n, QBD.
    Responsible journalism, defence of. *See* Privilege—Qualified privilege—Common law privilege—Responsible journalism, *above.*
    Seditious libel. *See* **Criminal law** (Sedition—Seditious libel).
    Serious harm to reputation. *See* Defamatory statement—Requirement of serious harm, *above.*
    Settlement of action—
        Statement in open court. *See* Statement in open court, *below.*
    Severance of causes of action—
        Actions for libel and slander—
            Statements that plaintiff was referred to in alleged libel—Statements pleaded as slander—Application for severance of the two causes of action on ground statements irrelevant and inadmissible on issue of libel—Application refused—Statements relevant on question of damages for libel. **Bridgmont v Associated Newspapers Ltd** [1951] **2** 285, CA.
    Slander actionable per se—
        Imputation of criminal offence—
            Conviction—Allegation that plaintiff has been convicted—Words not putting defamed person in jeopardy of prosecution. **Gray v Jones** [1939] **1** 798, KBD.
        Imputation of unchastity against woman—
            Lesbianism—Words spoken imputing lesbianism—Whether imputation of unchastity—Slander of Women Act 1891. **Kerr v Kennedy** [1942] **1** 412, KBD.
        Official, professional or business reputation of plaintiff—
            Employee—Plaintiff employed by Jew—Statement by defendant to employer that plaintiff a 'Jew hater'—Whether words spoken of plaintiff in relation to his business—Special damage. **De Stempel v Dunkels** [1938] **1** 238, CA.
            Office or duty—Firewatcher—Firewatcher entrusted with keys of house—Allegation that keys improperly used—No proof of special damage—Whether firewatching an office or a duty. **Cleghorn v Sadler** [1945] **1** 544, KBD.
            Party enjoined—Limited liability company—Defamatory statements relating to company's business—Limited liability company—Whether slander of company actionable at suit of company without proof of actual damage. **D & L Caterers Ltd v D'Anjou** [1945] **1** 563, CA.
            Professional examination—Allegation that examinee had cheated—Examination for professional qualification—Inference that examinee unable to qualify without cheating—Whether words spoken of examinee in way of profession. **Bridgman v Stockdale** [1953] **1** 1166, QBD.
            Publication at a time when plaintiff pursuing that profession—Slander published while plaintiff on indefinite leave—Whether pursuing profession of army officer at time of slander. **Bull v Vazquez** [1947] **1** 334, CA.
            Solicitor—Acting in non-professional capacity—Testimonial by solicitor for friend—Statement that testimonial worthless—Whether statement spoken of solicitor in way of his professional reputation. **Hopwood v Muirson** [1945] **1** 453, CA.
    Slander of goods. *See* **Slander of goods**.
    Slander of title. *See* **Slander of title**.
    Solicitor advocate—
        Conflict of interest—
            Duty. *See* **Solicitor** (Duty—Conflict of interest—Solicitor advocate—Libel action).
    Statement in open court—
        Money paid into court—
            Whether defendant who had made payment into court normally liable for incidental costs incurred by claimant in making unilateral statement in open court—CPR Pt 36. **Phillipps v Associated Newspapers Ltd** [2004] **2** 455, QBD.
        No money paid into court—
            Statement to be approved by judge in chambers—RSC Ord 22, r 2(4). **Liebrich v Cassell & Co Ltd** [1956] **1** 577, QBD.
        Settlement of plaintiff's action against one of two defendants—
            Plaintiff continuing action against other defendant—Factors to be considered by court in deciding whether to allow statement to be made—Whether making of statement should be postponed until after conclusion of trial of outstanding claim—RSC Ord 82, r 5. **Barnet v Crozier** [1987] **1** 1041, CA.
    Stay of proceedings. *See* **Practice** (Stay of proceedings—Appropriate forum—Libel).

LIBEL AND SLANDER (cont)—
  Summary disposal of claim—
    Quantum—
      Whether procedure for summary disposal available in respect of quantum after separate trial on liability—Defamation Act 1996, s 8. **Loutchansky v Times Newspapers Ltd (No 2)** [2002] **1** 652, CA.
    Relief—
      Damages—Injunction—Claimant obtaining default judgment in absence of anonymous defendants—Whether claimant entitled to summary relief in damages and injunctions—Defamation Act 1996, ss 8, 9. **Brett Wilson LLP v Person(s) Unknown, responsible for the operation and publication of the website www.solicitorsfromhelluk.com** [2016] **1** 1006, QBD.
  Trade union—
    Right to sue. *See* **Trade union** (Legal proceedings—Right of union to sue—Defamatory statements relating to reputation of trade union).
  Trial by jury—
    Generally. *See* **Jury** (Trial by jury—Defamation).
    Libel. *See* **Practice** (Trial—Trial by jury—Libel).
    Slander. *See* **Practice** (Trial—Trial by jury—Slander).
  Verdict—
    Separate libels—
      Defamatory words published on separate occasions—Single verdict—Validity—Defendants' counsel at trial asking for separate verdicts—Judge directing jury to make single award of damages if they found in favour of plaintiff—Whether judge having discretion to direct jury to give single verdict—Whether judge exercised discretion correctly. **Hayward v Thompson** [1981] **3** 450, CA.
    Separate slanders—
      Words spoken on different occasions—Single verdict—Validity—Defendants' counsel at trial not asking for separate verdicts. **Barber v Pigden** [1937] **1** 115, CA.

LIBERTY TO APPLY
  Family Division. *See* **Family Division** (Applications to the court—Liberty to apply).

LIBRARY
  Public library—
    Duty of library authority—
      Duty to provide efficient library service—Making books etc available to public—Extent of duty—Book subject to injunction restraining publication of confidential information—Whether duty to make books available qualified by requirement not to interfere with due administration of justice—Whether library authority interfering with due administration of justice if it made injuncted book available to public—Public Libraries and Museums Act 1964, s 7. **A-G v Observer Ltd** [1988] **1** 385, Ch D.

LICENCE
  Accounts—
    Inspection by licensor—
      Principle of settled accounts—Relevance—Licence to manufacture and sell road-making specialities—Payment of royalties—Provision for licensor to inspect accounts—Request to inspect after agreement terminated and receipt given for payment of final royalty—Licensors entitled to ask for inspection—Principle of settled account not applicable. **Anglo-American Asphalt Co Ltd v Crowley Russell & Co Ltd** [1945] **2** 324, Ch D.
      Scope of licensee's obligation. *See* **Accounts** (Inspection—Scope of obligation—Licence agreement).
  Advertisement. *See* **Town and country planning** (Advertisement—Licence).
  Aerodrome. *See* **Aerodrome** (Licence).
  Agricultural worker—
    Licence to occupy farm cottage. *See* Licence to occupy premises—Agricultural worker, *below*.
  Betting office. *See* **Gaming** (Betting—Licensed betting office—Application for licence).
  Broadcasting without licence—
    Wireless. *See* **Wireless** (Broadcasting—Broadcasting without licence).
  Building licence. *See* **Building control** (Building licence).
  Cab licence—
    Revocation—
      Certiorari to quash revocation. *See* **Certiorari** (Jurisdiction—Licensing committee—Cab licence—Decision of Commissioner of Metropolitan Police to revoke).
  Caravan site—
    Generally. *See* **Caravan site** (Licence).
  Carrier's licence—
    Goods vehicle. *See* **Road traffic** (Goods vehicle—Carrier's licence).
  Charity—
    Licence to occupy premises. *See* Licence to occupy premises—Charity, *below*.
  Cinema. *See* **Cinema** (Licence).
  Cinematograph exhibition—
    Licensing of premises used for exhibition. *See* **Cinema** (Cinematograph exhibition—Licensing of premises).
  Condition—
    Severability—
      Licence granted under statutory power. *See* **Public authority** (Statutory powers—Licence granted under statutory power—Condition—Severability).
  Consideration for grant of licence—
    Income tax—
      Capital or income. *See* **Income tax** (Capital or income receipts—Licence).
  Construction—
    Generally. *See* **Contract** (Construction—Licence agreement).

LICENCE (cont)—
  Construction (cont)—
    Interpretation—
      Construction of bridge over highway. *See* **Highway** (Restriction on construction of bridges over highway—Need for licence from highway authority).
  Contractual—
    Licence to occupy land. *See* Licence to occupy land—Contractual licence, *below*.
    Rights of licensee against purchaser with notice—
      Constructive trust—Agreement in writing by landlord to allow tenant to occupy premises rent-free pending redevelopment—Landlord selling freehold to purchaser—Sale subject to agreement between landlord and tenant—Whether purchaser bound by agreement. **Ashburn Anstalt v Arnold** [1988] **2** 147, CA.
  Copyright. *See* **Copyright** (Licence).
  Custodial sentence. *See* **Sentence** (Custodial sentence—Licence).
  Dealing in securities—
    Dealing without licence. *See* **Criminal law** (Dealing in securities without a licence).
  Deserted wife's right to occupy matrimonial home. *See* Licence to occupy premises—Deserted wife's right to occupy matrimonial home, *below*.
  Dock workers—
    Licence to employ registered dock workers—
      Refusal of licence—Compensation for refusal—Application for licence—Withdrawal of application before decision—Application for licence to employ five workers—Licensing authority notifying applicants that they proposed to issue licence subject to condition that 13 workers employed—Appeal to Minister—Applicants deciding to close down business—Applicants notifying Minister before decision on appeal that they were withdrawing application—Minister subsequently notifying applicants that application refused—Whether Minister having jurisdiction to refuse application after withdrawal—Whether applicants entitled to compensation for refusal—Docks and Harbours Act 1966, ss 4(1), 13(1). **Boal Quay Wharfingers Ltd v King's Lynn Conservancy Board** [1971] **3** 597, CA.
      Refusal of licence—Compensation for refusal—Licence granted with conditions—Whether grant of licence with conditions a refusal of licence—Docks and Harbours Act 1966, s 13. **Limb & Co (Stevedores) (a firm) v British Transport Docks Board** [1971] **1** 828, QBD.
  Drainage—
    Mutual licences—
      Unilateral revocation. *See* Mutual licences—Unilateral revocation—Drainage to and from adjoining properties, *below*.
  Driving licence—
    Disqualification. *See* **Road traffic** (Disqualification for holding licence).
    Endorsement—
      Penalty points. *See* **Road traffic** (Penalty points—Disqualification—Endorsement of licence).
    Generally. *See* **Road traffic** (Driving licence).
  Entertainments licence. *See* **Entertainment** (Public entertainment—Entertainments licence).
  Entry—
    Revocation of licence—
      Licence to enter premises—Police officers approaching front door of house through unlocked garden gate—Revocation of oral licence to enter house—Reasonable time to leave. **Robson v Hallett** [1967] **2** 407, QBD Divl Ct.
  Fishing—
    European Community—
      Licence to fish against British quotas. *See* **European Union** (Fishing rights—Common fishing policy—Licence to fish against British quotas).
    Salmon and trout. *See* **Fish** (Salmon and trout—Licence to fish).
  Free travel pass—
    Whether contract or licence. *See* **Carriers** (Negligence—Exclusion of liability—Passengers—Free pass—Contractual animus, not merely a licence).
  Funfair. *See* **Entertainment** (Fun-fair—Obligation to obtain licence).
  Game. *See* **Game** (Licence).
  Gaming—
    Application for licence. *See* **Gaming** (Licensing of premises—Application for licence).
    Generally. *See* **Gaming** (Gaming licence).
  Hackney carriage. *See* **Road traffic** (Hackney carriage—Licence).
  Heavy goods vehicle driver's licence. *See* **Road traffic** (Heavy goods vehicle driver's licence).
  Horse-racing—
    Trainer's licence—
      Refusal of licence to woman on ground of sex—Monopoly control—Whether contrary to public policy arbitrarily to exclude from work—Whether horse-racing a vocation within Sex Disqualification (Removal) Act 1919, s 1. **Nagle v Feilden** [1966] **1** 689, CA.
  Human fertilisation. *See* **Medical treatment** (Human fertilisation—Licence).
  Import licence—
    Duty to obtain—
      Person on whom duty rests—Prohibition against import without licence—Buyer's duty to obtain licence—Customs (Consolidation) Act 1876, s 284—Import, Export and Customs Powers (Defence) Act 1939, ss 1(1), 3(1), 9(2)—Anthrax Order 1935 (SR & O 1935 No 164)—Import of Goods (Control) Order, 1940 (SR & O 1940 No 873). **Mitchell Cotts & Co (Middle East) Ltd v Hairco Ltd** [1943] **2** 552, CA.
  Inspection of accounts by licensor. *See* Accounts—Inspection by licensor, *above*.
  Intoxicating liquor. *See* **Licensing**.
  Irrevocable licence. *See* Licence to occupy land—Contractual licence—Irrevocable licence, *below*.
  Land—
    Licence to enter—
      Trespass—Defence. *See* **Trespass to land** (Defence—Leave and licence).
    Licence to occupy—
      Generally. *See* Licence to occupy land, *below*.

LICENCE (cont)—
  Land (cont)—
    Licence to occupy (cont)—
      Revocation—Interlocutory injunction. *See* **Injunction** (Interlocutory—Trespass—Revocation of licence).
      Trespass. *See* **Trespass to land** (Right to maintain action).
  Licence to assign lease granted—
    Covenant against assignment without consent—
      No legal assignment. *See* **Landlord and tenant** (Covenant against assignment without consent—Licence to assign granted by landlord—No legal assignment).
  Licence to occupy land—
    Agreement whereby person granted licence to occupy land for use as agricultural land—
      Agreement to take effect with necessary modifications as agreement for tenancy from year to year. *See* **Agricultural holding** (Tenancy—Agreement whereby person granted licence to occupy land for use as agricultural land).
    Agricultural worker—
      Suspended order for possession—Costs. *See* **Agriculture** (Agricultural worker—Tied cottage—Possession—Suspended order for possession—Costs).
    Contractual licence—
      Enforcement of rights by licensor—Equitable remedies. **Hounslow London Borough v Twickenham Garden Developments Ltd** [1970] **3** 326, Ch D.
      Irrevocable licence—Implied term that licensor would not revoke licence during term of contract. **Hounslow London Borough v Twickenham Garden Developments Ltd** [1970] **3** 326, Ch D.
      Nature of licence. **Hounslow London Borough v Twickenham Garden Developments Ltd** [1970] **3** 326, Ch D.
      Rights of licensee against third parties—Constructive trust—Agreement in writing by licensor to allow licensee to occupy premises rent free for life or so long as she may desire—Undertaking by licensee to maintain premises—Sale of licensor's interest to third party—Agreement for sale stated to be subject to agreement with licensee—Agreement for sale constituting constructive trust in favour of licensee—Third party bound by licensee's interest under trust. **Binions v Evans** [1972] **2** 70, CA.
    Deserted wife in occupation of matrimonial home—
      Notice of licence. *See* **Husband and wife** (Deserted wife's right to remain in matrimonial home—Notice of licence to occupy).
    Estoppel as between licensor and licensee—
      Ceylon. *See* **Ceylon** (Estoppel—Licensor and licensee—Licence granted by deputy Viharadhipathi—Implied renewal of licence after death of Viharadhipathi—Implied resumption of possession).
    Grant—
      Value added tax—Exemption. *See* **Value added tax** (Exemptions—Grant of right over or licence to occupy land).
    Licence distinguished from tenancy—
      Agreement granting licence to occupy and use, as agricultural land, land forming part of airfield—Grantor a government department—Part of land under requisition, and rest owned, by grantor—Agreement containing covenants usual in tenancy agreements, but expressly excluding creation of tenancy—Same protection conferred on grantee as tenant of agricultural holding, other than conditional security of tenure—Whether tenancy created. **Finbow v Air Ministry** [1963] **2** 647, QBD.
      Tenancy distinguished from licence. *See* **Landlord and tenant** (Tenancy—Tenancy distinguished from licence).
    Occupation in return for services—
      Whether licence or tenancy. *See* **Rent restriction** (Rent—Exclusive use of part of house given in return for services).
    Summary proceedings for possession—
      Availability of proceedings. *See* **Land** (Summary proceedings for possession—Land occupied solely by persons who entered into or remained in occupation without licence or consent—Persons entering into possession with licence or consent but remaining in possession after licence terminated—Availability of summary procedure).
    Tenancy distinguished—
      Generally. *See* **Landlord and tenant** (Tenancy—Tenancy distinguished from licence).
      Protected tenancy. *See* **Rent restriction** (Protected tenancy—Tenancy or licence).
  Licence to occupy premises—
    Agricultural worker—
      Exclusive possession of farm cottage—Recovery of possession—Suspension of order—Protection from Eviction Act 1964, ss 1(6), 2(4). **Crane v Morris** [1965] **3** 77, CA.
      Protection of widow's occupancy—Question of protection to be decided on assumption Rent (Agriculture) Act 1976 in force at all material times—At all material times—Husband an agricultural worker in 1968—Employment terminated through illness but employer permitting him to remain in house—Employer selling house in 1972 to purchasers not engaged in agricultural work—Purchasers permitting husband to remain in house because of his illness—Widow remaining in house after husband's death—Purchaser bringing action for possession against widow—Whether widow a statutory tenant—Whether 'at all material times' meaning Act retrospectively effective at all times material to licence to occupy at date Act came into force or whether retrospective effect limited to period commencing with licence to occupy at date Act came into force—Rent (Agricultural) Act 1976, ss 2, 4, Sch 9, para 3. **Skinner v Cooper** [1979] **2** 836, CA.
    Charity—
      Old people's home run by a society—Unfurnished room—Agreement for occupation of room on weekly payment—Society reserved right to take possession of room at discretion on one month's notice—Possession to be taken only if society considered it essential in the interests of residents—Bona fide decision by society to take possession—Occupier a licensee, not a tenant—Society entitled to possession. **Abbeyfield (Harpenden) Society Ltd v Woods** [1968] **1** 352, CA.

372

LICENCE (cont)—
Licence to occupy premises (cont)—
Contractual licence—
Enforcement by assignees—Restrictive covenants affecting property other than land—Agreement for front of the house rights. **Clore v Theatrical Properties Ltd, and Westby & Co Ltd** [1936] 3 483, CA.

Implied term—Fitness for purpose—Licence to occupy factory—Factory becoming unsuitable and dangerous forcing licensee to relocate and suffer loss—Whether term to be implied in licence that factory fit for purpose required by licensee. **Wettern Electric Ltd v Welsh Development Agency** [1983] 2 629, QBD.

Specific performance. *See* **Specific performance** (Defence to action—Licence—Contract to let hall to political party).

Terms of licence providing that fixtures not to be removed at end of licence—Licensee expending money on fixtures—Licensor ejecting licensee in breach of contract—Licensee moving to rent free premises until after licence would have expired—Licensee claiming cost of fixtures as damages—Whether licensee entitled to be put in same position as before contract—Whether licensee only entitled to be put in position he would have been in if contract performed. **C & P Haulage (a firm) v Middleton** [1983] 3 94, CA.

Terms to be inferred—Man and mistress—Man buying house from mistress and her husband at substantially below market price—Mistress and husband living apart—House occupied by mistress and her children—Man intending to move into house to live with mistress and children in due course—Relationship between man and mistress ending six weeks after purchase of house—Whether possible to infer licence for mistress to occupy house for life—Whether license terminable on reasonable notice. **Chandler v Kerley** [1978] 2 942, CA.

Unmarried couple—Circumstances in which contract will be inferred—Circumstances indicating meeting of minds with intention to affect legal relationship—Contractual terms reasonably clearly made out—House acquired by man to provide accommodation for mistress and children—House owned by man—Relationship of man and mistress continuing over period of 17 years until death of man—Mistress generously supported by man—Whether contractual licence for mistress to remain in house to be inferred. **Horrocks v Forray** [1976] 1 737, CA.

Unmarried couple—Consideration to support contractual licence—House acquired by man to provide accommodation for mistress and children—Couple not intending to marry—Mistress giving up own rent-controlled flat to live in house with children—Implied licence to occupy house so long as children of school age and accommodation reasonably required by mistress and children—Whether consideration to support contractual licence—Whether mistress's licence revocable at will—Whether mistress entitled to compensation for revocation of licence. **Tanner v Tanner** [1975] 3 776, CA.

Unmarried couple—Terms to be inferred. *See* Licence to occupy premises—Contractual licence—Terms to be inferred—Man and mistress, *above.*

Description in document—
Terms of agreement indicating licence—Occupiers not having exclusive possession—Agreement personal in nature—Petrol filling station—Licensees undertaking not to impede licensors in exercise of their rights of possession—Licensees undertaking to promote sales of licensors' products. **Shell-Mex and BP Ltd v Manchester Garages Ltd** [1971] 1 841, CA.

Terms of agreement indicating licence—Terms appearing to make occupation non-exclusive—Two agreements to share residential accommodation—Unmarried couple signing separate agreements to share room—Agreements identical except for name of grantee—Condition of each agreement that grantee would be willing to share room with grantor or such other grantee as licensor might from time to time permit to use it—Whether condition void as contrary to public policy or illegal—Whether tenancy or licence created. **Somma v Hazlehurst** [1978] 2 1011, CA.

Terms of agreement indicating tenancy—Description of document not conclusive—Terms showing an intention to give exclusive possession and create a tenancy—Whether tenancy created. **Addiscombe Garden Estates Ltd v Crabbe** [1957] 3 563, CA.

Deserted wife's right to occupy matrimonial home—
Revocation of licence—Family enterprise—Family arrangement whereby husband's mother purchasing house for husband and wife on payment of monthly sums by them—Nature of legal relationship between mother and husband and wife—Licence—Marriage breaking down early on—Husband leaving wife for another woman—Wife and baby remaining in house—Wife offering to make monthly payments to mother—Mother claiming possession of house—Whether licence to occupy house joint licence in favour of husband and wife—Whether licence revocable as against wife on breakdown of marriage. **Hardwick v Johnson** [1978] 2 935, CA.

Revocation of licence—Length of notice to deliver up possession. **Vaughan v Vaughan** [1953] 1 209, CA.

Undertakings by husband—Licence not a contractual licence by virtue of husband's undertakings in maintenance order. **Debtor, Re a, ex p the Trustee v Solomon** [1966] 3 255, Ch D.

Employee—
Occupation in return for services—Defendant employee permitted to reside in employer's house adjacent to employer's business on condition that he obtained PSV licence—Employee disqualified from driving—Employer dismissing employee and seeking possession of house—Whether employee occupying house under service tenancy or licence—Whether statutory requirements as to giving of notice applying—Protection from Eviction Act 1977, s 5(1A). **Norris v Checksfield** [1991] 4 327, CA.

Equitable licence—
Revocation—Revocation claimed by legal owner because of licensee's subsequent conduct—Effect of conduct on licensee's right to claim equitable relief—Excessive user of property or bad behaviour towards legal owner not conduct justifying revocation of licence—Defendant occupying one of two adjoining cottages under equitable licence for life pronounced by court in action for possession brought by previous legal owner of property—Present legal owner living in other cottage claiming possession on ground of defendant's subsequent conduct—Conduct as pleaded and found by judge consisting of trifling acts—Disturbance of legal owner's quiet enjoyment not pleaded—Judge determining licence—Whether conduct sufficient to justify revocation of licence—Whether court entitled to grant defendant equitable relief. **Williams v Staite** [1978] 2 928, CA.

LICENCE (cont)—
Licence to occupy premises (cont)—
  Gift of house to common law wife—
    Representation to common law wife that house given to her. *See* **Estoppel** (Conduct—Conduct leading representee to act to his detriment—Representation—Licence—Representee led to believe house in which she was living had been given to her).
  House—
    Furnished room—Separate rooms provided in house, formerly an hotel, for daily or weekly charges—Terms including daily cleaning of room, but no meals—Use of bathroom, etc, in common with others—Whether occupant of room a tenant or a licensee—Door of room having mortice lock and insecure Yale lock—Failure of proprietor to provide occupant with key to mortice lock—Occupant's room broken into and her goods stolen—Whether proprietor negligent. **Appah v Parncliffe Investments Ltd** [1964] **1** 838, CA.
  Licence distinguished from tenancy—
    Agreement to share residential accommodation—Right of access reserved by licensor—Licensor explaining that right of access a 'legal formality' to ensure agreement was a licence—Licensees understanding that they would in fact have exclusive possession of premises—Whether reservation of right of access destroyed licensees' right to exclusive possession—Whether agreement a licence to occupy premises or a tenancy. **Walsh v Griffiths-Jones** [1978] **2** 1002, Cty Ct.
    Exclusive possession—Payment and acceptance of amount of rent due to landlord of licensor—Intention of parties—Whether licence or lease. **Isaac v Hotel de Paris Ltd** [1960] **1** 348, PC.
    Factors determining whether agreement creating licence or lease. **Cobb v Lane** [1952] **1** 1199, CA.
    Occupation conditional on payments being made to third party—Whether occupiers licensees or tenants. **Errington v Errington** [1952] **1** 149, CA.
    Permission to occupy furnished flat—Weekly payment—No agreement as to notice—Whether occupiers licensees or tenants. **Moss (E) Ltd v Brown** [1946] **2** 557, CA.
    Protected tenancy. *See* **Rent restriction** (Protected tenancy—Tenancy or licence).
  Licence distinguished from tenancy at will—
    Exclusive occupation—Right to exclude owner from premises—Evidence of tenancy—Evidence not conclusive—Inference of licence when grant of exclusive occupation—Inference where personal advantage to occupier intended or grant a result of family arrangement or act of friendship or generosity. **Heslop v Burns** [1974] **3** 406, CA.
  Notice to terminate occupation—
    Length of notice—Evacuees—Reasonable time for removal—Evacuees from abroad granted licence to occupy premises—Terms of notice of revocation—No necessity to state date of removal—Notice good though time stated for removal too short. **Minister of Health v Bellotti** [1944] **1** 238, CA.
  Occupation in return for services—
    Licence or tenancy—Employer and employee—Retention by employee of possession of flat by consent after termination of service—Work of confidential nature—Direct access of flat to offices. **Murray, Bull & Co Ltd v Murray** [1952] **2** 1079, QBD.
  Revocation—
    Deserted wife's right to occupy matrimonial home. *See* Licence to occupy premises—Deserted wife's right to occupy matrimonial home—Revocation of licence, *above*.
    Equitable licence. *See* Licence to occupy premises—Equitable licence—Revocation, *above*.
    Notice—Length of notice—Reasonable notice—Licence for use of theatre—Express term entitling licensee to determine licence—No provision for determination by licensor. **Winter Garden Theatre (London) Ltd v Millenium Productions Ltd** [1947] **2** 331, HL.
    Specific performance. *See* **Specific performance** (Defence to action—Licence).
  Tenancy distinguished—
    Generally. *See* **Landlord and tenant** (Tenancy—Tenancy distinguished from licence).
    Whether notice to quit needed. *See* **Landlord and tenant** (Notice to quit—Tenancy at will—Licence to occupy premises—Whether any notice needed).
Licence to use quay for business of repairing boats—
  Notice to terminate licence—
    Length of notice—Whether seven days' notice to terminate use unreasonably short. **Iveagh (Earl) v Martin** [1960] **2** 668, QBD.
Licensing. *See* **Licensing**.
Local taxation licences. *See* **Local government—Local taxation licence**.
Malicious refusal—
  Action—
    Statutory licensing power—Duty owed by licensing authority in regard to execution of statutory power—Refusal by authority to grant licence for cinema—Whether action lies for wrongful and malicious refusal to grant licence. **David (Asoka Kumar) v MAMM Abdul Cader** [1963] **3** 579, PC.
Market—
  Stallholder—
    Grant of licence by owner to erect stall. *See* **Markets and fairs** (Right of public to attend market—Stallholder—Grant of licence by owner of market to erect stall in specified place).
Marriage licence—
  Grant—
    Wales—Effect of dis-establishment of Church in Wales on. *See* **Ecclesiastical law** (Church in Wales—Dis-establishment—Effect on grant of marriage licences).
Matrimonial home—
  Deserted wife's right to occupy—
    Revocation of licence. *See* Licence to occupy premises—Deserted wife's right to occupy matrimonial home, *above*.
Milk. *See* **Food and drugs** (Milk—Licence to sell).
Mineral licence—
  New Zealand. *See* **New Zealand** (Mine—Mineral licence).
Mining—
  New South Wales. *See* **New South Wales** (Licence—Mining licence).

LICENCE (cont)—
  Mining (cont)—
    Termination—
      Right to mine for magnesite—Non-exclusive licence—Whether licence terminable at will—Whether dated notice necessary—Whether distinction between period of grace after termination of revocable licence and period of reasonable notice to terminate licence. **Australian Blue Metal Ltd v Hughes** [1962] **3** 335, PC.
  Moneylender. *See* **Moneylender** (Licence).
  Movable dwellings. *See* **Housing** (Movable dwellings—Licence).
  Music and dancing. *See* **Entertainment** (Music and dancing licence).
  Mutual licences—
    Unilateral revocation—
      Drainage to and from adjoining properties—Whether licence revocable by one owner while retaining benefit of the licence of the other owner. **Hopgood v Brown** [1955] **1** 550, CA.
  Notice to terminate occupation—
    Date—
      Earliest date that agreement can lawfully be terminated—Advertising hoardings—Agreements between contractors and site owners giving licences to maintain display hoardings—Site owners authorising another advertising contractor, a company, to determine existing licence agreements—Notice to terminate occupation given by letter signed by solicitors—Letter addressed to parent company and associated companies, but not separately sent or addressed to associated companies by name—Sufficiency of notice. **Allam & Co Ltd v Europa Poster Services Ltd** [1968] **1** 826, Ch D.
  Occupation of premises. *See* Licence to occupy premises—Notice to terminate occupation, *above.*
  Nuisance—
    Liability of occupier for nuisance committed by licensees. *See* **Nuisance** (Occupier—Licensees).
  Nurses—
    Agency for supply of nurses—
      Licence by local authority. *See* **Nurse** (Agency for supply of nurses—Licence by local authority).
  Operator's licence—
    Goods vehicle. *See* **Road traffic** (Goods vehicle—Operator's licence).
  Oral—
    Possession of land by oral licence for more than 12 years. *See* **Limitation of action** (Land—Adverse possession—Possession by oral licence for more than 12 years).
  Parole licence. *See* **Prison** (Release on licence).
  Patent—
    European Community. *See* **European Union** (Patent—Licence).
    Generally. *See* **Patent** (Licence).
  Pilot—
    Carriage by air—
      Private pilot's licence. *See* **Carriage by air** (Private pilot's licence).
  Possession—
    Burden of proof in criminal proceedings. *See* **Criminal evidence** (Burden of proof—Facts peculiarly within knowledge of accused—Licence).
  Prison—
    Release on licence. *See* **Prison** (Release on licence).
  Prisoner—
    Release on licence—
      Custodial sentence. *See* **Sentence** (Custodial sentence—Licence—Statutory scheme providing for release of offender on licence rather than unconditionally).
      Generally. *See* **Prison** (Prisoner—Release on licence).
  Private hire vehicle. *See* **Road traffic** (Private hire vehicle—Licence).
  Product licence—
    Medicine. *See* **Medicine** (Product licence).
  Provisional driving licence. *See* **Road traffic** (Driving licence—Provisional licence).
  Public service vehicle—
    Suspension of licence. *See* **Road traffic** (Public service vehicle—Suspension of licence).
  Revocation—
    Excessive punishment—
      Certiorari. *See* **Certiorari** (Jurisdiction—Excessive punishment—Revocation of licence).
    Licence to occupy premises. *See* Licence to occupy premises—Revocation, *above.*
  Road service licence—
    Express carriage. *See* **Road traffic** (Express carriage—Road service licence).
    Public service vehicle. *See* **Road traffic** (Public service vehicle—Road service licence).
  Salmon and trout fishing. *See* **Fish** (Salmon and trout—Licence to fish).
  Sex establishment. *See* **Sex establishment** (Control—Licensing).
  Ship repairs and alterations, for. *See* **Dock** (Shiprepairs and alterations—Licence).
  Street trading. *See* **Street trading** (Licence).
  Suspension—
    Public service vehicle. *See* **Road traffic** (Public service vehicle—Suspension of licence).
  Tenancy at will distinguished. *See* Licence to occupy premises—Licence distinguished from tenancy at will, *above.*
  Tenancy distinguished. *See* Licence to occupy land—Licence distinguished from tenancy, *above.*
  Theatre. *See* **Theatre** (Licence for the performance of stage plays).
  Trade licence—
    Vehicle. *See* **Road traffic** (Trade licence).
  Trainer's licence. *See* Horse-racing—Trainer's licence, *above.*
  Unmarried couple—
    House—
      Licence to occupy. *See* Licence to occupy premises—Contractual licence—Unmarried couple, *above.*
  Vehicle excise licence. *See* **Road traffic** (Excise licence).
  Wireless. *See* **Telegraphs etc** (Wireless—Licence).

LICENSED COAL MERCHANT

Distribution of coal, by. *See* **Coal** (Distribution—Licensed merchant).

LICENSED HOUSE

Excess rent—
  Income tax. *See* **Income tax** (Profits—Excess rent—Licensed houses).

LICENSED PREMISES

Business tenancy—
  Compensation for goodwill. *See* **Landlord and tenant** (Compensation for goodwill in respect of business premises—Licensed premises).
Compulsory purchase—
  Compensation—
    Assessment. *See* **Compulsory purchase** (Compensation—Assessment—Licensed premises).
Conveyance—
  Stamp duty. *See* **Stamp duty** (Conveyance on sale—Instrument whereby property or estate or interest in property on sale thereof transferred to or vested in purchaser—Conveyance of licensed premises).
Drunk on licensed premises. *See* **Licensing** (Found drunk on licensed premises).
Gaming on. *See* **Licensing** (Gaming on licensed premises).
Generally. *See* **Licensing**.
Police constable's right of entry. *See* **Intoxicating liquor** (Licensed premises—Constable—Right of entry).
Tenancy—
  Exclusion of statutory protection for business tenancies. *See* **Landlord and tenant** (Business premises—Tenancy—Exclusion of statutory protection—Licensed premises).

LICENSEE

Nuclear installation—
  Liability to pay compensation—
    Ionising radiation emitted from waste matter discharged from nuclear site. *See* **Nuclear installation** (Licensee—Liability to pay compensation).
Occupier's liability—
  Duty to licensee. *See* **Occupier's liability** (Duty to licensee).
  Invitee or licensee—
    Distinction. *See* **Occupier's liability** (Invitee or licensee).
Prison—
  Release on licence. *See* **Prison** (Release on licence).

LICENSING

Age—
  Knowingly selling liquor to person under age. *See* Knowingly selling liquor to person under age, *below*.
Air travel organisers—
  Accommodation in aircraft. *See* **Air traffic** (Civil Aviation Authority—Licensing of provision of accommodation in aircraft).
Alteration of premises—
  Consent. *See* Justices—Consent to alteration of premises, *below*.
Appeal—
  Appeal to quarter sessions—
    Costs. *See* Costs—Appeal to quarter sessions, *below*.
  Notice of appeal—
    Service—Time for service—Extension of time—Notice of appeal served, within 14 days allowed by s 22, on clerk to licensing justices—Notice of appeal served on grantee of licence after expiry of 14 days—Whether notice had to be served on grantee of licence—Whether quarter sessions could extend time for service—Licensing Act 1964, s 22. **R v Pembrokeshire Quarter Sessions, ex p Bennell** [1968] **1** 940, QBD.
Application for licence—
  Hearing. *See* Justices—Hearing of application for licence, *below*.
Betting office—
  Application for licence. *See* **Gaming** (Betting—Licensed betting office—Application for licence).
Bingo—
  Played on licensed premises. *See* Gaming on licensed premises—Bingo, *below*.
Brewers—
  Expense of obtaining new licence—Capital or revenue expenditure. *See* **Income tax** (Deduction in computing profits—Capital or revenue expenditure—Brewers—New licences).
Broadcasting—
  Radio—
    Independent radio services. *See* **Broadcasting** (Government control over broadcasting—Radio—Licensing of independent radio services).
Caravan site—
  Town and country planning. *See* **Town and country planning** (Caravan site licence).
Case stated—
  Power of licensing justices to state a case. *See* Justices—Case stated—Power of licensing justices to state a case, *below*.

LICENSING (cont)—
    Certificate of non-objection—
        Duty of licensing planning committee to try to secure that number, nature and distribution of licensed premises accord with local requirements—
            Adoption by committee of policy of equation of barrelage—Policy to refuse applications for certificates unless applicant had acquired licence in suspense covering barrelage equal to estimated barrelage of new premises—Licences only obtainable from existing holders by purchase—Object of policy to relieve local authority of need to compensate existing holders in respect of licences which would not be re-sited—Whether proper ground for refusing certificate that applicant had not purchased licence covering required barrelage—Licensing Act 1964, s 119(2). **Kennedy v Birmingham Licensing Planning Committee (sub nom R v Birmingham Licensing Planning Committee, ex p Kennedy)** [1972] **2** 305, CA.
            Factors to be considered—Conduct of premises an extraneous consideration—Licensing Act 1964, s 119(2). **R v London (Metropolis) Licensing Planning Committee, ex p Baker** [1970] **3** 269, QBD.
            Nature of licensed premises—Meaning—Club premises—Admission to membership of club—Delay between application for and admission to membership—Application for licence containing condition that delay should be 24 hours—Committee refusing to grant certificate unless period increased to 48 hours—Whether period of delay affecting nature of licensed premises—Whether committee having jurisdiction to refuse certificate on that ground—Licensing Act 1964, s 119(2). **Fletcher v London (Metropolis) Licensing Planning Committee** [1975] **2** 916, HL.
    Cinema—
        Censorship of films for exhibition. *See* **Cinema** (Censorship).
        Generally. *See* **Cinema** (Licence).
    Cinematograph exhibition—
        Licensing of premises used for exhibition. *See* **Cinema** (Cinematograph exhibition—Licensing of premises).
    Club—
        Application for registration certificate—
            Compliance with statutory requirements—Specification of address of club—Address of club—Meaning—Licensing Act 1964, Sch 5, para 1. **R v City and County of Exeter Justices, ex p Fowler** [1966] **3** 49, QBD.
        Public dancing, music or other entertainment. *See* **Entertainment** (Music and dancing licence).
        Search warrant—
            Search of licensed premises—Execution on Sunday—Sunday Observance Act 1677, s 6—Magistrates' Courts Act 1952, s 102(3)—Licensing Act 1953, s 152(1). **Magee v Morris** [1954] **2** 276, QBD.
        Striking off register—
            Licensing offences—Summons against secretary to show cause—Order for costs for sum in excess of costs of prosecution—Power of justices to make order. **R v Highgate Justices, ex p Petrou** [1954] **1** 406, QBD.
    Consumption of intoxicating liquor after permitted hours—
        Aiding and abetting by licensee—
            Consumption by customers—Licensee unaware of offence—Whether aiding and abetting—Licensing Act 1921, s 4(b). **Thomas v Lindop** [1950] **1** 966, KBD.
            Knowledge of offence by licensee's servants—No knowledge in licensee—Liability of licensee—Licensing Act 1921, s 4(b). **Ferguson v Weaving** [1951] **1** 412, KBD.
            Passive assistance with knowledge of facts. **Tuck v Robson** [1970] **1** 1171, QBD.
    Costs—
        Appeal to quarter sessions—
            Appellant technically successful—Whether appellant can be ordered to pay licensing justices' costs—Licensing Act 1953, ss 36(1), 37(1)(a). **R v Hampshire Justices, ex p Maggs** [1963] **1** 818, QBD.
    Disorderly conduct on premises. *See* Knowingly permitting disorderly conduct on premises, *below*.
    Drunk on licensed premises—
        Found drunk. *See* Found drunk on licensed premises, *below*.
    Duty to cause person smoking in smokefree premises to stop smoking—
        Revocation of licence. *See* Licensing objectives—Prevention of crime and disorder—Revocation of licence, *below*.
    Failure to comply with condition of licence—
        Late night refreshment house. *See* Late night refreshment house—Failure to comply with condition of licence, *below*.
    Forfeiture of intoxicating liquor and vessels. *See* Unauthorised sale of intoxicating liquor—Forfeiture of intoxicating liquor and vessels, *below*.
    Found drunk on licensed premises—
        Licensed premises—
            Upper room let to private party—Defendants found drunk there—Whether 'licensed' premises—Licensing Act 1872, s 12. **Stevens v Dickson** [1952] **2** 246, QBD.
    Gaming—
        Gaming on licensed premises. *See* Gaming on licensed premises, *below*.
        Licensing of premises. *See* **Gaming** (Licensing of premises).
    Gaming on licensed premises—
        Bingo—
            Free bingo played on licensed premises—Prizes other than intoxicating liquor provided—No chance of losing—Whether gaming—Betting, Gaming and Lotteries Act 1963, ss 34(1), 55(1)—Licensing Act 1964, s 177. **McCollom v Wrightson** [1968] **1** 514, HL.
        Small lottery—
            Exemption—Whether a small lottery that was exempted from illegality under Betting and Lotteries Act 1934, s 21, could lawfully be conducted on licensed premises—Licensing Act 1953, s 141(1)—Small Lotteries Gaming Act 1956, ss 1, 5(1). **Smith v Wyles (or Wiles)** [1958] **3** 279, QBD.
    Intoxicating liquor—
        Consumption after permitted hours. *See* Consumption of intoxicating liquor after permitted hours, *above*.
    Jurisdiction to confirm licence. *See* Licence—Confirmation—Jurisdiction, *below*.

LICENSING (cont)—
Justices—
Appeal—
Music and dancing—Whether appeal lies from licensing justices to quarter sessions. *See* **Quarter sessions** (Appeal to—Licensing appeal—Licensing justices refusing to renew dancing and music licence).
Bias—
Natural justice. *See* **Natural justice** (Magistrates—Bias).
Case stated—
Power of licensing justices to state a case—Magistrates' Courts Act 1952, ss 87(1), 124(1). **Jeffrey v Evans** [1964] **1** 536, QBD.
Consent to alteration of premises—
Alterations involving extension of licensed premises—Whether alterations 'in' premises—Licensing Act 1902, s 11—Licensing (Consolidation) Act 1910, s 71. **R v Weston-super-Mare Licensing Justices, ex p Powell** [1939] **1** 212, CA.
Factors to be considered—Proposed structural alterations—Destruction of identity of premises—Relevant consideration—Change from hotel to public house—Licensing (Consolidation) Act 1910, s 71. **R v Pontypridd Licensing Justices, ex p Ely Brewery Co Ltd** [1948] **2** 581, KBD.
Disqualification—
Bias—Publican's licence—Order of removal by confirming authority—Justices also members of city council—Subject previously considered by council under planning scheme—Public statements showing hostile attitude. **R v Sheffield Confirming Authority, ex p Truswell's Brewery Co Ltd** [1937] **4** 114, KBD.
Interest in profits of premises—Exception—Application by co-operative society for off-licence—All justices either members, or spouses of members, of the society—Interest in profits of business carried on at premises—Whether justices disqualified—Whether licence invalidated—Licensing Act 1953, s 48(4), (5). **R v Barnsley County Borough Licensing Justices, ex p Barnsley and District Licensed Victuallers' Association** [1960] **2** 703, CA.
General annual licensing meeting—
Adjournment—Statutory time limit of one month—Decision re-opened at adjourned meeting—Further adjournment to meeting not within the month—Whether permissible—Licensing (Consolidation) Act 1910, s 10—Licensing Act 1921, ss 1, 2—Licensing Rules 1921 (SR & O 1921 No 1313), r 9. **R v Wandsworth Licensing Justices** [1936] **2** 394, KBD.
Hearing of application for licence—
General rule not to issue full licence to holder of restricted licence—Duty to consider facts of each case. **R v Torquay Licensing Justices, ex p Brockman** [1951] **2** 656, KBD.
Provisional licence—Full off-licence sought for supermarket—Supermarket in course of construction—Provisional licence only capable of being granted—Failure to specify in application that provisional licence sought—Whether necessary to apply specifically for provisional licence—Justices' finding that application a nullity—Whether mandamus to justices lay—Licensing Act 1964, ss 1(3), 6(1), Sch 2, para 4(d)—Finance Act 1967, s 5, Sch 7, para 1. **R v Merthyr Tydfil Licensing Justices, ex p Duggan** [1970] **2** 540, QBD.
Time—Second session inadvertently fixed more than one month after first session—Refusal of justices to hear applications—Whether mandamus to justices lay—Licensing Act 1953, Sch 2, Part 1, para 5. **R v Woodbury Licensing Justices, ex p Rouse** [1960] **2** 205, QBD.
Knowingly allowing person under age to consume intoxicating liquor in bar of licensed premises—
Intoxicating liquor including beer—
Consumption of shandy—Whether sale of beer that was mixed to form the shandy and thus a consumption of the beer sold—Licensing Act 1964, s 169(1). **Hall v Hyder** [1966] **1** 661, QBD.
Knowingly permitting disorderly conduct on premises—
Co-licensees—
'Keepers'—Management and sole control in one of two co-licensees—Liability—Metropolitan Police Act 1839, s 44. **Linnett v Metropolitan Police Comr** [1946] **1** 380, KBD.
Knowingly selling liquor in breach of condition of licence—
Knowingly—
Imputation of knowledge to licensee—Condition of restaurant licence that liquor not to be sold except to persons taking meals—Waitress authorised to serve drinks only if meal ordered—Sale by waitress of drink without meal—Licensee not having actual knowledge of such sale—Imputation of knowledge only if management delegated—Licensing Act 1961, s 22(1)(a). **Vane v Yiannopoullos** [1964] **3** 820, HL.
Licensee systematically conducting club in breach of condition—
Licensee delegated management during his absence, intending system to continue—Condition of on-licence for club that liquor should be supplied only to members and their guests—Whether licensee had knowledge of acts in breach of condition committed during his absence—Licensing Act 1961, s 22(1)(a). **Ross v Moss** [1965] **3** 145, QBD.
Knowingly selling liquor to person under age—
Evidence of age—
Person under age of 18. **Wallworth v Balmer** [1965] **3** 721, QBD.
Knowingly—
Imputation of knowledge to licensee—Barman selling liquor—Barman in sole charge of bar—Licensee present on another part of premises—Justices' finding that licensee had delegated responsibility for bar to barman—Barman guilty of offence of knowingly selling liquor—Licensee having no actual knowledge of sale—Whether licensee having effectively delegated responsibility although on premises—Whether licensee also liable for knowingly selling liquor—Licensing Act 1964, s 169(1). **Howker v Robinson** [1972] **2** 786, QBD.
Servant of holder of licence—
Wife of holder of licence left in charge of licensed premises during his temporary absence—Sale of cider to boy of 14—No evidence that wife was contractually servant of or was being paid by, or under control of licence-holder—Whether wife a 'servant of holder of licence' for the purposes of the Licensing Act 1964, s 169(1). **Brandish v Poole** [1968] **2** 31, QBD.

LICENSING (cont)—
  Late night refreshment house—
    Failure to comply with condition of licence—
      Exemption from liability—On-licence—Licensee owning restaurant—Licensee also holding justices'
      on-licence for same premises—Licensee acting in breach of condition of late night refreshment
      house licence—Whether possession of justices' on-licence exempting him from liability—Late
      Night Refreshment Houses Act 1969, ss 1, 7(2). **Portsmouth Corp v Nishar Ali** [1973] **1** 236, QBD.
    House, room, shop or building kept open for public refreshment, resort and entertainment—
      Building inside which public may congregate for refreshment—Stall from which refreshment could
      only be served to members of public standing outside—Stall a permanent structure—Whether a
      refreshment house—Late Night Refreshment Houses Act 1969, s 1. **Bucknell (Frank) & Son Ltd v
      Croydon London Borough** [1973] **2** 165, QBD.
  Licence—
    Confirmation—
      Jurisdiction—General annual licensing meeting—Application for new licence—Bench equally
      divided—Adjournment of meeting—Application granted at adjourned meeting—Confirming
      authority—Jurisdiction to confirm licence. **Fussell v Somerset Quarter Sessions Licensing
      Committee** [1947] **1** 44, KBD.
    Grant—
      Off-licence—Grant subject to undertaking—Undertaking contrasted with condition—Whether
      justices entitled to grant off-licence subject to undertaking from applicant how he will operate
      licence—Whether applicant bound to observe undertaking if granted licence—Whether departure
      from undertaking relevant on objection to renewal of licence—Licensing Act 1964, s 3. **R v
      Edmonton Licensing Justices, ex p Baker** [1983] **2** 545, QBD.
    New licence—
      Grant where increase of 25 per cent of population—Whether increase relates to city or ward or
      district electoral division—Government of Ireland Act 1920, s 49(a)(b)—Intoxicating Liquor Act
      (Northern Ireland), 1923, s 9(c)—Intoxicating Liquor and Licensing Act (Northern Ireland), 1927,
      s 3(6)(iv). **Jennings v Kelly** [1939] **4** 464, HL.
      Jurisdiction—Jurisdiction to grant new licence in substitution for current licence. **R v Godalming
      Licensing Committee, ex p Knight** [1955] **2** 328, QBD.
    Occasional licence. *See* Occasional licence, *below.*
    Off-licence—
      Grant. *See* Licence—Grant—Off-licence, *above.*
      Renewal. *See* Licence—Renewal—Off-licence, *below.*
    On-licence subject to condition—
      Condition restricting use of licence to off-sales and for obtaining occasional licences—Power of
      justices to impose condition—Validity of licence—Licensing Act 1964, ss 1(2), 4(1) (as amended by
      the Finance Act 1967, ss 5(1), 45(8), Sch 16, Part I). **R v Dudley Justices, ex p Curlett** [1974] **2** 38,
      QBD.
      Payment required in pursuance of condition prohibited—Condition prohibiting supply of
      intoxicating liquor to persons other than holders of admission tickets purchased for not less than
      specified amount—Whether condition requiring payments to be made to licensee valid—
      Licensing Act 1964, s 4(1) (as amended by the Finance Act 1967, ss 5(1), 45(8), Sch 16, Pt I). **R v
      Crown Court at Leeds, ex p City of Bradford Chief Constable** [1975] **1** 133, QBD.
      Restriction of sale to a limited class—Power of justices to impose condition—Validity of
      licence—Licensing (Consolidation) Act 1910, s 14(1). **R v Sussex Confirming Authority, ex p
      Tamplin & Sons' Brewery (Brighton) Ltd** [1937] **4** 106, KBD.
    Premises disqualified for renewing licence—
      Premises containing less than two rooms for the accommodation of the public—Whether necessary
      for the two rooms to be licensed for service of intoxicating liquor—Licensing Act 1953, ss 32(1),
      34(2). **R v Middlesex County Confirming and Compensation Committee, ex p Frost** [1956] **2** 921,
      QBD.
    Provisional licence—
      Hearing. *See* Justices—Hearing of application for licence—Provisional licence, *above.*
    Removal—
      Ordinary removal—Confirmation—Jurisdiction—Death of licensee, after grant of removal subject to
      confirmation, but before confirmation—Whether personal representative of deceased licensee
      can be granted confirmation of removal—Licensing Act 1953, ss 22, 25. **R v Derby Borough
      Justices Confirming Authority, ex p Blackshaw** [1957] **2** 823, QBD.
      Ordinary removal—Jurisdiction—Removal from county licensing division to borough within same
      county—Jurisdiction of borough justices to hear the application—Licensing (Consolidation) Act
      1910, s 24(3). **R v Leamington Spa Licensing Justices, ex p Pinnington** [1947] **1** 114, KBD.
      Planning removal—Conditional confirmation of proposal by planning authority—Condition
      complied with—Duty to grant removal—Licensing Act 1953, s 58(2). **R v City of London Licensing
      Justices, ex p Stewart** [1954] **3** 270, QBD.
      Special removal—Old on-licence—Removal on the ground that premises for which licence granted
      are or are about to be pulled down or occupied for any public purpose—Date on which question
      whether premises are or are about to be pulled down or occupied to be asked—Date on which
      specified conditions must subsist—Licensing Act 1964, s 15(1)(a). **R (on the application of
      Bushell) v Newcastle upon Tyne Licensing Justices** [2004] **3** 493, CA.
      Special removal—Old on-licence—Removal on the ground that premises for which licence granted
      are or are about to be pulled down or occupied for any public purpose—Whether public authority
      obtaining possession—Licensing Act 1964, s 15(1)(a). **R (on the application of Bushell) v
      Newcastle upon Tyne Licensing Justices** [2006] **2** 161, HL.
    Renewal—
      Off-licence—Application for renewal—Guidelines on the approach which the justices should adopt.
      R v Windsor Licensing Justices, ex p Hodes [1983] **2** 551, CA.

LICENSING (cont)—
  Licence (cont)—
    Renewal (cont)—
      Off-licence—Original licence for sale of beer only—Amendment of law to reduce forms of off-licence to two only—One form was for intoxicating liquor of all descriptions, the other was for sale of beer, cider and wine only—Renewal to be for licence of type nearest to the previously existing licence, viz, for sale of beer, cider and wine—Such licence similar to previously existing licence within s 3(3)(a) of Licensing Act 1964—Licensing Act 1964, s 1(3) as amended by Finance Act 1967, ss 5(1)(c), Sch 7, para 1(b)(ii), 3(3)(a). **R v Leicester Licensing Justices, ex p Bisson** [1968] **2** 351, QBD.

      Off-licence—Original licence for sale of intoxicating liquor on self-service basis in multiple store—Subsequent change of policy by licensing justices—Justices deciding as matter of policy to renew licences for multiple stores only if store agreed to sell liquor in supervised area with separate check-out—Notification sent to licensee—Store not complying with policy—Justices objecting to renewal of licence—No other objections to renewal—No reason for justices' objection given on oath—Application for renewal refused without licensee having opportunity of dealing with justices' objection—Whether justices entitled to refuse to renew licence—Licensing Act 1964, s 7(4). **R v Windsor Licensing Justices, ex p Hodes** [1983] **2** 551, CA.

    Surrender—
      What constitutes surrender—Application for new licence—Existing licence handed to justices' clerk before hearing—New licence refused—Original licence returned to licensee—Whether original licence 'surrendered'—Licensing (Consolidation) Act 1910, s 65(1). **Carter v Pickering** [1949] **1** 340, KBD.

    Transfer—
      Employee of unlimited company applying for transfer of licence—Shareholders not disclosing their identities—Whether licence could be refused because of failure to disclose identities of shareholders—Licensing Act 1964, s 3(1). **R v Warrington Crown Court, ex p RBNB (a company)** [2002] **4** 131, HL.

      Production of documents—Agreement or assurance under which licence to be transferred and held—Mortgage of licensed premises by proposed transferee to owners—Jurisdiction of justices to make production order—Licensing (Consolidation) Act 1910, s 25(2). **R v Newington Licensing Justices, ex p Conrad** [1948] **1** 346, KBD.

      Unlimited company owning public house—Shareholders not disclosing their identities—Company employee applying for transfer of licence—Application being refused because of failure to disclose shareholders' identities—Whether license could be refused merely because of refusal to disclose identities of shareholders—Licensing Act 1964, s 3(1). **R v Warrington Crown Court, ex p RBNB (a company)** [2001] **2** 851, CA.

  Licensed premises—
    Assault on police officer. *See* **Police** (Assault on constable in execution of duty—Execution of duty—Failure to leave licensed premises).

  Licensing agreement—
    Trade mark. *See* **Trade mark** (Licensing agreement).

  Licensing authorities—
    Decisions—
      Appeals against decisions of licensing authorities—Approach to appeals—Guidance—Licensing Act 2003, s 181, Sch 5—Magistrates' Courts Rules 1981, SI 1981/552. **R (on the application of Hope and Glory Public House Ltd) v City of Westminster Magistrates' Court (Lord Mayor and Citizens of the City of Westminster, interested party)** [2011] **3** 579, CA.

    General duties of licensing authorities—
      Licensing objectives—Licensing guidance—Application for licence—Licensing authority granting licence—Local objectors appealing to magistrates' court—Magistrates' court imposing restrictions—Whether restrictions necessary to promote licensing objectives—Whether magistrates' court having proper regard to guidance—Licensing Act 2003, s 4. **R (on the application of Daniel Thwaites plc) v Wirral Borough Magistrates' Court** [2009] **1** 239, QBD.

  Licensing objectives—
    Premises licence—
      Conditions—Appeals—Responsible authority—Licensing authority granting premises licence subject to conditions sought by responsible authority—Applicant appealing against conditions—Responsible authority applying to be joined as party to appeal proceedings—Whether magistrates having power to allow responsible authority to appear at appeal—Licensing Act 2003, Sch 5. **R (on the application of Chief Constable of Nottinghamshire Police) v Nottingham Magistrates' Court** [2010] **2** 342, DC.

    Prevention of crime and disorder—
      Revocation of licence—Licensee convicted of offence of failing to comply with statutory duty to cause person smoking in smokefree premises to stop smoking—Whether revoking of licence promoting licensing objectives—Licensing Act 2003, s 4. **Blackpool BC v Howitt** [2009] **4** 154, QBD.

  Licensing policy—
    Application for variation to extend permitted hours—
      Authority refusing variation—Authority relying on statement of policy adopting cumulative impact policy to refuse variation—Whether reliance on cumulative impact policy precluded by statute, Secretary of State's guidance, or authority's statement of policy—Licensing Act 2003. **R (on the application of JD Wetherspoon plc) v Guildford BC** [2007] **1** 400, QBD.

  Music and dancing. *See* **Entertainment** (Music and dancing licence).

  New licence. *See* Licence—New licence, *above*.

  Notice of appeal—
    Service. *See* Appeal—Notice of appeal—Service, *above*.

LICENSING (cont)—
Occasional licence—
  Grant—
    Circumstances in which occasional licence may be granted—Applicant forgetting to renew on-licence for premises—Applicant holder of on-licence for other premises—Whether magistrate entitled to grant occasional licences for purpose of allowing liquor to be sold lawfully until application for late renewal of on-licence heard—Whether 'occasional licence' can only be granted for a particular event or function—Licensing Act 1964, s 180(1)(2). **R v Bow Street Stipendiary Magistrate, ex p Comr of Police of the Metropolis** [1983] 2 915, QBD.

    Discretion of justices—Exercise of discretion—General rule of justices restricting number of such licences to same applicant in any one year to two—Whether rule illegal—Licensing (Consolidation) Act 1910, s 64. **R v Rotherham Licensing Justices, ex p Chapman** [1939] 2 710, KBD.

    Jurisdiction to grant applications for consecutive periods of three days each—Applications in respect of events at festival lasting two months—Revenue Act 1862, s 13—Licensing (Consolidation) Act 1910, s 64(1), (2), (4). **R v Bath Licensing Justices, ex p Chittenden** [1952] 2 700, QBD.

    Jurisdiction to grant applications made regularly—Application in respect of premises regularly used for dance functions—Licensing (Consolidation) Act 1910, s 64. **Chandler v Emerton** [1940] 3 146, KBD.

    Jurisdiction to grant in respect of premises which already fully licensed—Licensing (Consolidation) Act 1910, s 64(1), (3). **Brown v Drew** [1953] 2 689, QBD.

    Jurisdiction to grant to holder of off-licence—Undertaking by licensee not to sell for consumption on premises—Licensing Act 1953, s 148(1). **R v Brighton Justices, ex p Jarvis** [1954] 1 197, QBD.

  Right to apply for licence—
    Applicant nominee of a club licence—Justices' on-licence granted to applicant as nominee of proprietory club—Whether same applicant entitled to apply for occasional licence in respect of premises separate from club—Licensing Act 1961, s 35(2)(a). **Birt v Swansea Justices** [1963] 2 769, QBD.

Occasional permission—
  Grant—
    Period of permission—Number of permissions required—Occasional permission sought for series of periods on successive days—Performances by operatic society on successive nights—Total time for which permission sought not exceeding 24 hours—Whether separate permissions required for each period—Licensing (Occasional Permissions) Act 1983, s 1(1). **R v Bromley Licensing Justices, ex p Bromley Licensed Victuallers' Association** [1984] 1 794, QBD.

  Persons entitled to object to grant of occasional permission—
    Whether only police may object—Whether trade association such as a licensed victuallers' association entitled to object—Licensing (Occasional Permissions) Act 1983, s 1(1). **R v Bromley Licensing Justices, ex p Bromley Licensed Victuallers' Association** [1984] 1 794, QBD.

Off-licence—
  Grant. *See* Licence—Grant—Off-licence, *above*.
  Renewal. *See* Licence—Renewal—Off-licence, *above*.

Offence—
  Bookmaking—
    Business other than bookmaking—Carried on in licensed office. *See* **Gaming** (Betting—Bookmaker—Business of bookmaker receiving or negotiating bets—Bet—Offence for bookmaker to carry on business other than bookmaking in licensed office).

  Club—
    Striking off register. *See* Club—Striking off register—Licensing offences, *above*.

  Refusal to admit constable to licensed premises—
    Constable's right of entry—Circumstances in which right exercisable. *See* **Intoxicating liquor** (Licensed premises—Constable—Right of entry).

On-licence—
  Disqualification—
    Conviction of offence—Appeal—Order prohibiting licence for premises in respect of which offence committed—Licence holder convicted in Crown Court of offence—Owner of premises convicted in same court of aiding and abetting offence—Owner liable to be punished as principal offender—Court making disqualification order in respect of premises—Owner applying for leave to appeal against order—Whether order a 'sentence' passed on owner—Whether Court of Appeal, Criminal Division, having jurisdiction to entertain an appeal by owner—Accessories and Abettors Act 1861, s 8—Licensing Act 1964, s 100 (as amended by the Refreshment Houses Act 1964, s 3(3), Sch)—Criminal Appeal Act 1968, ss 9, 50(1). **R v Ioannou** [1975] 3 400, CA.

  Grant subject to condition. *See* Licence—On-licence subject to condition, *above*.

Passenger vessel—
  Sale of intoxicating liquor on board—
    Permitted hours—Whether sale restricted to permitted hours—Finance (1909-10) Act 1910, Sch I, Pt D—Licensing Act 1921, ss 1(1), 18. **Green v Thames Launches Ltd** [1952] 2 332, QBD.

Permitted hours—
  Extension—
    Registered club—Entertainment—Gaming rooms—Whether proprietors were using the club for providing other 'entertainment as distinct from facilities for entertainment'—Licensing Act 1961, s 9(1). **Rous de Horsey v Rignell** [1963] 1 38, QBD.

    Special requirements of the district—Licensing Act 1921, s 1(1). **R v Bradford Licensing Justices, ex p Illingworth** [1939] 3 106, CA; **R v Wisbech (Isle of Ely) Licensing Justices, ex p Payne** [1937] 3 767, KBD.

    Supper-hour—Requirement that there should be a supply of substantial refreshment to which sale and supply of intoxicating liquor was ancillary—Liquor ancillary to refreshment—Whether necessary for total sale of liquor to be ancillary to total sale of food—Licensing Act 1953, s 104(1)(a). **R v Liverpool Licensing Justices, ex p Tynan** [1961] 2 363, QBD.

LICENSING (cont)—
Permitted hours (cont)—
General order of exemption—
Application—Jurisdiction—Unregistered club—Membership composed of workers in same factory—Workers working normal hours—Whether justices have jurisdiction to hear application—Licensing Act 1953, s 106(1)—Licensing Act 1961, s 38(3) and Sch 9, Pt 2. **Young v North Riding Justices** [1965] **1** 141, QBD.
Passenger vessel. *See* Passenger vessel—Sale of intoxicating liquor on board—Permitted hours, *above*.
Prohibition of sale or consumption of intoxicating liquor outside permitted hours—
Drinking-up time—Consumption by person taking meal—Consumption permitted for half hour after end of any period of permitted hours—Whether exception limited to restaurants—Whether applicable to all licensed premises—Licensing Act 1964, s 63(1)(b). **Jackson v Sinclair** [1973] **3** 42, QBD.
Supply to private friends of licensee bona fide entertained by him at own expense—Private friends of licensee supplied by assistant manager in the absence of licensee—Implied authority of assistant manager—Bona fide entertainment—Licensing Act 1921, ss 4, 5(c). **Jones v Cockcroft** [1945] **2** 333, KBD.
Supply to private friends of licensee bona fide entertained by him at own expense—Supply of drinks to staff—No payment by staff—Whether supply to private friends of licensee—Licensing Act 1953, s 100(2)(c). **Schofield v Jones** [1955] **3** 337, QBD.
Special hours certificate—
Application—Who may apply—Holder of justices' licence in respect of premises—Licensed premises—Premises in respect of which in theatre licence in force—Premises exempt from need for Justices' licence—No holder of Justices' licence—Whether justices having jurisdiction to entertain application for certificate in respect of theatre premises—Licensing Act 1964, ss 77, 199 (as amended by the Theatres Act 1968, s 19(1) Sch 2) 200(1). **R v Licensing Justices for South Westminster, ex p Raymond** [1973] **3** 106, QBD.
Permitted hours for premises for which certificate in force—Bar in premises—Permitted hours not applicable to bar—Meaning of 'bar'—Place mainly or exclusively used for sale and consumption of intoxicating liquor—Premises consisting of dancing area with tables and chairs and counter from which intoxicating liquor served—Special hours certificate in force for whole premises—Nothing separating counter from rest of premises—Whether counter a 'bar'—Licensing Act 1964, ss 76(5), 201(1). **Carter v Bradbeer** [1975] **3** 158, HL.
Premises for which music and dancing licence in force for part of premises—Whether possible to have special hours certificate in force for whole premises—Licensing Act 1964, s 77A. **Westminster City Council v O'Reilly** [2003] **3** 237, QBD.
Whether music and dancing and substantial refreshment having to be provided simultaneously throughout permitted hours of special hours certificate—Licensing Act 1964, ss 76, 77. **Northern Leisure plc v Schofield** [2001] **1** 660, QBD.
Whether possible in law for two or more special hours certificates to co-exist in respect of same premises—Licensing Act 1964, ss 76(7), 77, 81(3). **R v Crown Court at Stafford, ex p Chief Constable of Staffordshire Police** [1998] **2** 812, QBD.
Whether special hours certificate 'bolt-on' addition to ordinary permitted hours or in substitution therefor—Whether licensing justices having power to limit commencement time of special hours certificate—Licensing Act 1964, s 78A. **R v Crown Court at Stafford, ex p Shipley** [1998] **2** 465, CA.
Special order of exemption for special occasion—
Dances at hotel—Organised by licensee—Held regularly twice a week—No connection with local or national event—Whether 'special occasion'—Licensing Act 1964, s 74(4). **Lemon v Sargent** [1971] **3** 936, QBD.
Football match—Match nearly every week—Whether 'special occasion'—Licensing Act 1964, s 74(4). **R v Llanidloes (Lower) Justices, ex p Thorogood** [1971] **3** 932, QBD.
Special occasion—Principles to be applied by justices in deciding whether occasion a 'special occasion'—Licensing Act 1964, s 74(4). **Martin v Spalding** [1979] **2** 1193, QBD; **R v Corwen Justices, ex p Edwards** [1980] **1** 1035, QBD.
Special occasion—Registered club—Sporting club—Annual sporting occasions held by club—Whether 'special occasions'—Whether event held by club itself on club premises could be a 'special occasion'—Licensing Act 1964, s 74(4). **Knole Park Golf Club v Chief Superintendent Kent County Constabulary** [1979] **3** 829, QBD.
Planning committee—
Certificate of non-objection. *See* Certificate of non-objection—Duty of licensing planning committee to try to secure that number, nature and distribution of licensed premises accord with local requirements, *above*.
Premises —
Licensable activity—
Unauthorised licensable activities—Landlord holding premises licence—Tenant and designated premises supervisor carrying on unauthorised licensable activities—Whether acts of tenant and premises supervisor to be imputed to freeholder—Licensing Act 2003, s 136(1)(a). **Hall & Woodhouse Ltd v Poole BC** [2010] **1** 425, DC.
Premises licence—
Variation of licences—Application to vary premises licences—Determination of application—Promotion of licensing objectives—Holder of premises licence applying for variation of licence—Relevant licensing authority receiving relevant representations within prescribed period—Licence holder revising application—Licensing authority determining application and granting variation of licence without inviting further representations—Whether determination lawful—Licensing Act 2003, s 35. **Taylor v Manchester City Council** [2013] **2** 490, QBD.
Private hire vehicles—
Passenger contract—
Obligations of London operators—Passengers booking transport via operator's smartphone app—Whether licensed operator to contract with passenger as principal or as driver's agent—Whether drivers plying for hire—Meaning of 'plies for hire'—Metropolitan Public Carriage Act 1869, s 4—Private Hire Vehicles (London) Act 1998, ss 4, 5. **Uber London Ltd v Transport for London (Transopco (UK) Ltd (t/a Free Now) intervening)** [2022] **2** 797, DC.

LICENSING (cont)—
Private Security—
Licensing criteria—
Licences to engage in licensable conduct—Appeals—Applicants for licences having previous criminal convictions—Whether licensing rules permitting licensing authority and appellate courts to take into account circumstances of applicants' previous convictions in determining whether to grant licence—Private Security Industry Act 2001, ss 7, 8(3), 11(5). **Security Industry Authority v Stewart** [2008] 2 1003, DC.
Security Industry Authority—
Functions of authority—Power of authority to do anything it considered calculated to facilitate or incidental or conducive to carrying out of any of its functions—Conduct prohibited without a licence—Offences—Whether authority having power to prosecute—Private Security Industry Act 2001, s 1(2), (3). **R (on the application of Securiplan) v Security Industry Authority** [2009] 2 211, DC.
Provisional licence—
Hearing of application. *See* Justices—Hearing of application for licence—Provisional licence, *above*.
Public entertainments. *See* **Entertainment** (Public entertainment—Entertainments licence).
Public motor vehicles—
Australia. *See* **Australia** (Transport—Freedom of inter-state trade—Licensing of public motor vehicles).
Registration certificate—
Application—
Club. *See* Club—Application for registration certificate, *above*.
Removal of licence. *See* Licence—Removal, *above*.
Renewal of licence. *See* Licence—Renewal, *above*.
Sale of intoxicating liquor to person under 18—
Statutory provision rendering it an offence for a 'person' in licensed premises to sell intoxicating liquor to person under 18—
Whether 'person' including owner of business or employer who was not licensee and/or individual involved in sale—Licensing Act 1964, ss 3, 160, 169A. **Haringey London BC v Marks & Spencer plc** [2004] 3 868, DC.
Sale of liquor by retail without licence—
Absolute offence—
Sale to non-member of working men's club in erroneous belief that customer was a member of the club—Licensing Act 1964, s 160(1)(a), (2). **French v Hoggett** [1967] 3 1042, QBD Divl Ct.
Dismissal of informations—
Appeal by excise officer to quarter sessions—Appeal suspended pending application for order of prohibition—Excise officer person 'aggrieved'—Statutory right of appeal—Excise Management Act 1827, ss 82-85—Finance (1909-10) Act 1910, s 50(3). **R v London County Quarter Sessions (Appeal Committee)** [1945] 2 298, KBD.
Incorporated members' club—
Sale to members—Liquor served to members and honorary members in exchange for money payment—Liquor purchased in club's name as authorised by club committee—Agency—Whether club separate legal entity apart from its members—Whether service of liquor to members a sale—Licensing (Consolidation) Act 1910, s 65. **Trebanog Working Men's Club and Institute Ltd v Macdonald** [1940] 1 454, KBD.
Place of sale—
Order at licensed premises—Delivery postponed pending instructions—Liquor collected and delivered to and paid for at unlicensed club after permitted hours—Appropriation—Finance (1909-10) Act 1910, s 50(3). **Furby v Hoey** [1947] 1 236, KBD.
Sale—
Social party—No justices' licence—Payment made in advance for entertainment and drink—Drinks, including intoxicants, available to guests to help themselves—No payment at party and no restriction on amount consumed—Whether a sale of intoxicating liquor at the party—Whether what took place was in the nature of a sale of intoxicating liquor within the meaning of the Licensing Act 1953, ss 120(1), 154(1). **Doak v Bedford** [1964] 1 311, QBD.
Sale of bottled beer by servants of hotel to guests—
Liability of manager and proprietors—Finance (1909-10) Act 1910, s 50(3). **Hotel R (Torquay) Ltd v Moon** [1940] 2 495, KBD.
Search warrant—
Search of licensed premises—
Club. *See* Club—Search warrant—Search of licensed premises, *above*.
Sex establishment. *See* **Sex establishment** (Control—Licensing).
Slaughterhouses. *See* **Food and drugs** (Slaughterhouse—Licensing).
Small lottery—
Conducted on licensed premises. *See* Gaming on licensed premises—Small lottery, *above*.
Special hours certificate. *See* Permitted hours—Special hours certificate, *above*.
Special occasion—
Special order of exemption. *See* Permitted hours—Special order of exemption for special occasion, *above*.
Supper-hour extension. *See* Permitted hours—Extension—Supper-hour, *above*.
Surrender of licence. *See* Licence—Surrender, *above*.
Taking from licensed premises intoxicating liquor outside permitted hours—
Offence—
Take from—Whether offence incomplete until liquor is outside the licensed premises—Licensing Act 1953, s 100(1)(b). **Pender v Smith** [1959] 2 360, QBD.
Tobacco—
Sale by unlicensed person. *See* **Tobacco** (Sale by unlicensed person).
Transfer of licence. *See* Licence—Transfer, *above*.
Unauthorised sale of intoxicating liquor—
Forfeiture of intoxicating liquor and vessels—
Circumstances in which liquor and vessels forfeited—Members' club—Only one member convicted—Whether forfeiture incurred—Licensing Act 1953, s 152(2). **R v Lewes Justices, ex p Trustees of the Plumpton and District Club** [1960] 2 476, QBD.

LICENSING (cont)—
    Variation of licence—
        Application to extend permitted hours. *See* Licensing policy—Application for variation to extend permitted hours, *above*.

LIEN
    Accountant. *See* **Accountant** (Lien).
    Administration of estates—
        Gift cum onere—
            Paramount lien for debts due to company. *See* **Administration of estates** (Gift—Gift cum onere—Paramount lien for debts due to company).
    Animals—
        Distrainor's lien. *See* **Animal** (Distress damage feasant—Lien of distrainor).
        Maintenance of animals. *See* Maintenance of animals, *below*.
    Auctioneer. *See* **Auctioneer** (Lien).
    Banker's lien. *See* **Bank** (Lien).
    Broker's lien—
        Marine insurance policy. *See* **Marine insurance** (Composite policy—General lien).
    Carriers. *See* **Carriers** (Contract—Carriage of goods—International carriage of goods by road—Lien).
    Common law lien—
        Possession—
            Electronic database—Database manager offering customers service of holding electronic databases and amending them as necessary—Database manager refusing to release database or give customer access to it until all outstanding fees paid—Whether electronic database property capable of possession—Whether database manager entitled to exercise lien over database. **Your Response Ltd v Datateam Business Media Ltd** [2014] **2 Comm** 899, CA; [2014] **4** 928, CA.
    Company—
        Shares—
            Equitable lien—Purchase of shares. *See* Equitable lien—Purchase of shares, *below*.
            Generally. *See* **Company** (Shares—Lien).
    Contract for work and materials. *See* **Contract** (Contract for work and materials—Lien).
    Crew—
        Wages. *See* **Shipping** (Crew—Wages—Claim for wages—Lien for wages).
    Deposit of documents of title—
        Equitable charge by way of sub-mortgage—
            Common law lien on documents deposited—Ancillary rights destroyed when equitable charge avoided as against liquidator under Companies Act 1948, s 95(1),(2)—RSC Ord 50, r 2. **Molton Finance Ltd, Re** [1967] **3** 843, CA.
    Distrainor's lien—
        Cattle straying. *See* **Animal** (Distress damage feasant—Lien of distrainor).
    Enforcement—
        Sale. **Larner v Fawcett** [1950] **2** 727, CA.
    Equitable lien—
        Purchase of shares—
            Money advanced by father to son—Arrangement for repayment out of dividends—Whether father entitled to retain shares until all sums paid. **Crossman, Re** [1939] **2** 530, Ch D.
        Solicitor. *See* **Solicitor** (Lien—Equitable lien).
    Innkeeper. *See* **Inn** (Lien).
    Life insurance—
        Policy moneys. *See* **Insurance** (Life insurance—Policy moneys—Lien on policy moneys).
    Maintenance of animals—
        Pigs—
            Farmer agreeing with company to care for sows and their litters—Boars supplied by company for servicing sows—No element of improvement but merely maintenance and natural increase—Whether farmer had particular lien on pigs in his possession for sums owing to him for such care. **Southern Livestock Producers Ltd, Re** [1963] **3** 801, Ch D.
    Marine insurance policy—
        Broker's lien. *See* **Marine insurance** (Composite policy—General lien).
    Maritime lien—
        Admiralty action. *See* **Admiralty** (Jurisdiction—Action in rem—Maritime lien or other charge on ship).
        Generally. *See* **Shipping** (Maritime lien).
        Proceeds of insurance policy. *See* **Marine insurance** (Proceeds of policy—Lien).
    Mechanics' lien—
        Oil well—
            Canada. *See* **Canada** (Lien—Mechanics' lien—Oil well).
    Mortgaged property—
        Tenant's contract to purchase property on landlord's undertaking to repair—
            Mortgage of property by landlord to third party—Repairs carried out by tenant on landlord's failure to do so—Claim for possession by mortgagee—Whether tenant entitled to lien in respect of repairs. **Lee-Parker v Izzet** [1971] **3** 1099, Ch D.
    Motor vehicle—
        Repairers' lien. *See* Repairer's lien—Motor repairer, *below*.
    Purchaser's lien—
        Sale of land. *See* **Sale of land** (Purchaser's lien).
    Repairer's lien—
        Motor repairer—
            Motor car let on hire-purchase agreement—Repairs at request of hirer after determination of agreement—Whether repairer having lien on car against owner. **Bowmaker Ltd v Wycombe Motors Ltd** [1946] **2** 113, KBD.
    Sale—
        Enforcement of lien. *See* Enforcement—Sale, *above*.
    Shares—
        Company. *See* **Company** (Shares—Lien).

LIEN (cont)—
    Shares (cont)—
        Equitable lien. *See* Equitable lien—Purchase of shares, *above*.
    Shipowner's lien—
        Contribution to general average. *See* **Shipping** (General average—Contribution by cargo owners—Enforcement—Lien).
        Freight. *See* **Shipping** (Freight—Lien).
        Non-payment of hire—
            Time charterparty. *See* **Shipping** (Time charterparty—Hire—Lien for non-payment of hire).
    Solicitor. *See* **Solicitor** (Lien).
    Specific performance. *See* Vendor's lien—Specific performance, *below*.
    Subrogation. *See* **Subrogation**.
    Vendor's lien—
        Registered land—
            Overriding interest. *See* **Land registration** (Overriding interest—Rights of person in actual occupation of land—Unpaid vendor's lien).
        Registration—
            Charge—Sale of property to company. *See* **Company** (Charge—Registration—Unpaid vendor's lien—Property sold to company).
        Sale of land. *See* **Sale of land** (Vendor's lien).
        Specific performance—
            Preservation of lien—Purchase of shares—Transfer of shares conditional on payment of purchase price—Calculation of purchase price in accordance with prescribed formula—Calculation not possible until future date—Vendor agreeing to execute transfer of shares in company to plaintiffs forthwith on termination of his employment with company—Price payable to be determined by valuation from company's accounts for two years following date of transfer—Whether plaintiffs entitled to order to execute transfer in advance of payment of purchase price. **Langen & Wind Ltd v Bell** [1972] **1** 296, Ch D.

LIES
    Defendant's lies—
        Direction to jury—
            Criminal proceedings. *See* **Criminal law** (Trial—Direction to jury—Lies).

LIFE
    Loss of expectation of life—
        Damages. *See* **Damages** (Personal injury—Loss of expectation of life).
    Right to—
        Human rights legislation and. *See* **Human rights** (Right to life).
    Shortened expectation of life—
        Loss of future earnings—
            Damages. *See* **Damages** (Personal injury—Loss of future earnings—Shortened expectation of life).

LIFE ASSURANCE
    Capital investment bond—
        Whether policy of life assurance. *See* **Insurance** (Contract of insurance—Nature of contract—Capital investment bond).
    European Community. *See* **European Union** (Insurance—Life assurance).
    Generally. *See* **Insurance** (Life insurance).
    Loans by insurance company—
        Annual payments for income tax purposes. *See* **Income tax** (Annual payment—Annuity—Monthly loans by insurance company—Life assurance).
    Policy—
        Variation of settlement—
            Post-nuptial settlement. *See* **Variation of Settlement (Matrimonial Causes)** (Post-nuptial settlement—Life assurance policy).

LIFE ASSURANCE COMPANY
    Management expenses—
        Income tax. *See* **Income tax** (Management expenses—Life assurance company).

LIFE DIRECTOR
    See **Company** (Director—Life director).

LIFE IMPRISONMENT
    Appeal—
        Discretionary life sentence. *See* **Sentence** (Appeal—Right of appeal—Discretionary life sentence).
    Category A prisoner—
        Annual review of categorisation by Category A section. *See* **Prison** (Life sentence—Mandatory life sentence—Category A prisoner).
    Generally. *See* **Sentence** (Life imprisonment).
    Mandatory life sentence. *See* **Sentence** (Mandatory life sentence).
    Murder—
        Generally. *See* **Sentence** (Murder—Life imprisonment).
        Mandatory life sentence. *See* **Sentence** (Mandatory life sentence—Murder).
    Post-tariff mandatory life prisoner—
        Release on licence. *See* **Prison** (Release on licence—Refusal to release on licence—Post-tariff mandatory life prisoner).
    Prison. *See* **Prison** (Life sentence).
    Release of prisoner on licence. *See* **Prison** (Release on licence—Life sentence).

LIFE INTEREST
Determination of—
Estate duty. *See* **Estate duty** (Determination of life interest).
Surrender—
Consideration for compromise of dispute arising over trust—
Power of trustee—Exercise of power. *See* **Trust and trustee** (Powers of trustee—Compromise—Exercise of power—Consideration for compromise—Consideration including surrender by adverse claimant of life interest under trust).

LIFE TENANT
Continuance of life—
Burden of proof. *See* **Trust and trustee** (Life interest—Continuance of life of life tenant—Burden of proof).
Income tax—
Liability. *See* **Income tax** (Persons chargeable—Life tenant).

LIFT
Factory, in. *See* **Factory** (Hoists or lifts).

LIFTING EXCESSIVE WEIGHTS
Factory. *See* **Factory** (Lifting excessive weights).

LIFTING OPERATIONS
Construction of a building—
Secureness of loads. *See* **Building** (Lifting operations—Secureness of loads).
Undertaking building operation. *See* **Building** (Building operations—Lifting operation—Undertaking building operation).

LIFTING TACKLE
Factory—
Safety. *See* **Factory** (Lifting tackle).

LIGHT
Easement. *See* **Easement** (Light).

LIGHT LOCOMOTIVE
See **Road traffic** (Light locomotive).

LIGHT RAILWAY
Amending order—
Sale of railway—
Application for order authorising sale of railway to company formed to operate it—Matters to be taken into account by Minister in determining application—Whether Minister entitled to take public interest into account—Light Railways Act 1896, ss 7 and 24. **Rother Valley Rly Co Ltd v Ministry of Transport** [1970] 3 805, CA.

LIGHT SIGNALS
Road traffic. *See* **Road traffic** (Traffic sign—Light signals).

LIGHTERAGE
See **Shipping** (Lighterage).

LIGHTING
Dock—
Loading and unloading operations, for. *See* **Dock** (Loading and unloading—Lighting).
Repair of ship in dry dock. *See* **Dock** (Repair of ship in dry dock—Lighting).
Electricity. *See* **Electricity**.
Factory. *See* **Factory** (Lighting).
Film. *See* **Cinema** (Film—Production—Lighting).
Inn—
Lighting of passages. *See* **Inn** (Safety of premises—Lighting of passages).
Motor vehicles. *See* **Road traffic** (Lighting of vehicles).
Obstruction on highway. *See* **Highway** (Obstruction—Lighting of obstruction).
Restriction. *See* **Lighting restriction**.
Safe system of working. *See* **Safe system of working** (Reasonable care not to expose employee to unnecessary risk—Lighting).
Working places—
Building. *See* **Building** (Working places—Lighting).

LIGHTING RESTRICTION
Bicycles—
Statutory provision that only one lamp need be carried—
Cycle with two headlamps—Whether offence to carry two headlamps—Road Transport Lighting Act 1927, s 5(1)(a)—Lighting (Restrictions) Order 1940 (SR & O 1940 No 74), para 31. **Blackshaw v Chambers** [1942] 2 678, KBD.
Obstructions on highway—
Lighting obstructions—
Air-raid shelter in highway—Cyclist injured by collision with shelter—Power of local authority to erect shelter—Lighting—Civil Defence Act 1939, ss 9, 13—Lighting (Restrictions) Order, 1939 (SR & O 1939 No 1098). **Fox v Newcastle-upon-Tyne City Council** [1941] 2 563, CA.
Sand-bin on pavement—How far affecting obligation to light obstructions in street—Metropolis Management Act 1855, s 130—London County Council (General Powers) Act 1928, s 33—Lighting (Restrictions) Order 1939 (SR & O 1939 No 1098), para 1. **Lyus v Stepney BC** [1940] 4 463, CA.

LIGHTING RESTRICTION (cont)—

Obstructions on highway (cont)—

Lighting obstructions (cont)—

Sandbag-barrier on pavement—Pedestrian injured by colliding with barrier—Power of local authority to erect barrier—Lighting—Contributory negligence—Civil Defence Act 1939, s 9—Emergency Powers (Defence) Act 1939, s 1—Defence (General) Regulations 1939, reg 51—Lighting (Restrictions) Order 1939, (SR & O 1939 No 1098). **Jelley v Ilford BC** [1941] **2** 468, CA.

Street refuge—How far affecting obligation to light obstructions in street—Metropolis Management Act 1855, ss 108, 130—Lighting (Restrictions) Order 1939 (SR & O 1939 No 1098), paras 1, 4(d). **Greenwood v Central Service Co Ltd** [1940] **3** 389, CA; **Wodehouse v Levy (St Marylebone BC, third party)** [1940] **4** 14, CA.

Prohibition against illuminating advertising sign—

Licence to erect sign—

Licensee having right to determine agreement if sign required to be altered or amended—Whether prohibition requiring alteration or amendment to sign—Right of licensee to determine licence to erect sign—Lighting (Restrictions) Order 1939 (SR & O 1939 No 1098). **Williams v Mercer** [1940] **3** 292, CA.

LIKE WORK

Equality of treatment between men and women. *See* **Employment** (Equality of treatment of men and women).

LIMITATION

Estoppel—

Recovery of social security arrears. *See* **Social security** (Arrears of contributions—Recovery—Limitation).

Social security—

Recovery of arrears. *See* **Social security** (Arrears of contributions—Recovery—Limitation).

Value added tax—

Input tax, claim for deduction of. *See* **Value added tax** (Input tax—Claim for deduction of input tax—Late claim for repayment of under-claimed input tax).

LIMITATION FUND

Admiralty proceedings—

Interest on fund. *See* **Admiralty** (Practice—Interest—Rate of interest on limitation fund).

LIMITATION OF ACTION

Account—

Action for account—

Husband and wife. *See* Action—Action for an account—Meaning—Husband and wife, *below*.

Accrual of cause of action—

Action to recover principal sum of money secured by charge on property—

Action not to be brought after expiration of twelve years from date on which right to receive money accrued—Trustee in bankruptcy obtaining charging order over property belonging to bankrupt—Trustee over twelve years later applying for enforcement of charge and sale of property—Whether action for principal sum—Whether action time-barred—Limitation Act 1980, s 20(1)—Insolvency Act 1986, s 313(2). **Gotham v Doodes** [2007] **1** 527, CA.

Action to recover sums recoverable by virtue of statute—

Recovery of costs paid or payable under revoked legal aid certificate—Whether cause of action accruing at date of revocation of certificate or date of assessment or taxation of costs—Limitation Act 1980, s 9—Legal Aid Act 1988—Civil Legal Aid (General) Regulations 1989, SI 1989/339, reg 86(1). **Legal Services Commission v Rasool** [2008] **3** 381, CA.

Compulsory purchase—Entry on land by acquiring authority—Claim for compensation referred to Lands Tribunal after the expiration of six years from date of entry—Whether claim for compensation time-barred—Compulsory Purchase Act 1965, s 11—Limitation Act 1980, s 9. **Hillingdon London BC v ARC Ltd** [1997] **3** 506, Ch D.

Compulsory purchase—Entry on land by acquiring authority—Interest payable on compensation for cost of reasonable reinstatement—Whether claim for interest statute-barred—Compulsory Purchase Act 1965, s 11—Limitation Act 1980, s 9. **Halstead v Manchester City Council** [1998] **1** 33, CA.

Legal Services Commission claiming for recovery of alleged overpayment of money paid to counsel on account of fees—When Commission's cause of action accruing—Limitation Act 1980, s 9—Civil Legal Aid (General) Regulations 1989, SI 1989/339, reg 100(8). **Legal Services Commission v Henthorn** [2012] **2** 439, CA.

Recovery of expenses incurred by local authority in carrying out works under housing legislation—Council carrying out repairs to house in defendant's control—Council seeking recovery of expenses incurred by it in carrying out repairs—Summons for recovery of expenses issued more than six years after completion of works but less than six years from service of demand for payment—Whether cause of action accruing when works completed or when demand for payment served on defendant—Whether action time-barred—Housing Act 1957, s 10—Limitation Act 1980, s 9. **Swansea City Council v Glass** [1992] **2** 680, CA.

Cause of action—

Facts essential for bringing actions as distinct from evidence of facts—Local authority formerly electricity undertakers—Funds of electricity undertaking transferred to electricity board on nationalisation—Minister's decision that funds were held as electricity undertakers—Decision not a condition precedent to cause of action accruing, but evidence of an essential fact—Time ran from vesting date, not date of Minister's decision—Electricity Act 1947, s 15(3). **Central Electricity Generating Board v Halifax Corp** [1962] **3** 915, HL.

Claim to personal estate of deceased person or to any share or interest in any such estate—

Date on which the right to receive the share or interest accruing—Limitation Act 1980, s 22(a). **Loftus (decd), Re** [2005] **2** 700, Ch D; [2006] **4** 1110, CA.

Indemnity. *See* Indemnity—Accrual of cause of action, *below*.

LIMITATION OF ACTION (cont)—
  Accrual of cause of action (cont)—
    Negligence—
      Accountant—Accountant providing negligent report on solicitor's accounts—Clients suffering loss claiming compensation from fund administered by Law Society—Law Society seeking to recover costs of compensation from accountant—When cause of action accruing. **Law Society v Sephton & Co** [2006] **3** 401, HL.
      Accountant—Client seeking to reduce potential capital gains tax liability by investing in qualifying company for purposes of roll-over relief—Accountants failing to advise on need for qualifying company to establish subsidiaries and client subsequently incurring corporation tax liability—When cause of action accruing. **Pegasus Management Holdings SCA v Ernst & Young** [2010] **2 Comm** 191, CA; [2010] **3** 297, CA.
      Brokers—Insurance—Plaintiffs engaging brokers to procure goods in transit insurance—Brokers failing to exercise due care and skill in effecting policy of insurance—Insurers electing to avoid insurance contract on discovery of material facts—Whether plaintiff's cause of action against brokers accruing when contract executed or when insurers electing to avoid contract—Whether plaintiff's cause of action time-barred. **Islander Trucking Ltd (in liq) v Hogg Robinson & Gardner Mountain (Marine) Ltd** [1990] **1** 826, QBD.
      Brokers—Reinsurance—Plaintiffs engaging brokers to place marine quota share reinsurance in respect of underwriting accounts—Brokers negligently placing reinsurance—Reinsurers electing to avoid reinsurance contracts on discovery of material facts—Whether plaintiffs' cause of action against brokers accruing when contracts executed or when reinsurers electing to avoid contracts—Whether plaintiffs' cause of action time-barred. **Iron Trade Mutual Insurance Co Ltd v J K Buckenham Ltd** [1990] **1** 808, QBD.
      Solicitor—Economic loss suffered in consequence of solicitor's negligent advice—Plaintiff executing mortgage as guarantor following solicitor's negligent advice—Date from which limitation period running—Whether cause of action against solicitor complete when plaintiff incurred contingent liability on executing mortgage—Whether cause of action not complete until mortgagee demanding payment under mortgage. **Forster v Outred & Co (a firm)** [1982] **2** 753, CA.
      Solicitor—Negligent drafting of contract—Solicitor negligently drafting restrictive covenant—Plaintiffs unable to enforce covenant—Whether plaintiffs' cause of action against solicitor accruing when executed or when defect in covenant discovered—Whether plaintiffs' cause contract executed or when defect in covenant discovered—Whether plaintiffs' cause of action time-barred. **Moore (DW) & Co Ltd v Ferrier** [1988] **1** 400, CA.
      Solicitor—Parallel claims in tort and contract. See **Solicitor** (Negligence—Cause of action—Parallel claims in tort and contract).
      Valuer—Bank making loan on security of lease—Bank relying on valuer's valuation of lease as at future date—Borrower defaulting on loan—Security insufficient to cover debt owed by insolvent borrower—Bank claiming damages for negligent valuation—Whether bank's cause of action time-barred—Point when cause of action accrued. **First National Commercial Bank plc v Humberts (a firm)** [1995] **2** 673, CA.
      Valuer—Plaintiffs purchasing flat in reliance on valuation report prepared by defendants—Defects in property subsequently coming to light—Plaintiffs bringing actions for negligence more than six years after exchange of contracts but less than six years after completion—Whether action time-barred—Whether cause of action accruing when contracts were exchanged or when purchase was completed—Limitation Act 1980, s 2. **Byrne v Hall Pain & Foster (a firm)** [1999] **2** 400, CA.
    Patent—
      Infringement. See **Patent** (Infringement—Accrual of cause of action).
    Shipping—
      General average contribution by cargo owners. See **Shipping** (General average—Contribution by cargo owners—Accrual of cause of action for contribution).
    Standstill agreement—
      Construction—Parties entering into standstill agreement to avoid claims becoming statute barred—Standstill period extended in subsequent agreements—Claimants issuing proceedings on day following expiry of final standstill agreement—Defendants seeking to strike out claims on basis they had become statute barred with expiry of final standstill agreement—Whether standstill agreements suspending time for purposes of limitation or extending time. **Russell v Stone (t/a PSP Consultants)** [2018] **1 Comm** 839, TCC.
  Accrued defence—
    Effect of subsequent legislation—
      Claimant commencing action against defendants alleging abuse by defendants during education—Defendants relying on time bar accruing to them under previous legislation—Whether subsequent legislation depriving defendants of accrued right to rely on time bar—Limitation Act 1939, s 2(1), Limitation Act 1963, s 1, Limitation Act 1980, Sch 2, para 9(1)(a). **McDonnell v Congregation of Christian Brothers Trustees (formerly Irish Christian Brothers)** [2004] **1** 641, HL.
      Deceased employed by defendant from 1938 to 1943—Deceased diagnosed in 1981 as suffering from asbestos-related disease—Action commenced in 1984 alleging deceased contracted disease during employment with defendant—Defendant relying on time-bar accruing to it in 1944—Whether subsequent legislation depriving defendant of accrued right to rely on time-bar. **Arnold v Central Electricity Generating Board** [1987] **3** 694, HL.
  Acknowledgment—
    Acknowledgment by agent—
      Agent—Loan to company by director—Balance sheet signed by creditor director—Signature of accountants to their certificate of the balance sheet and accounts—Whether accountants agents to give acknowledgment—Limitation Act 1939, ss 23(4), 24(2)—Companies Act 1948, s 155(1). **Transplanters (Holding Co) Ltd, Re** [1958] **2** 711, Ch D.
      Agent—Mortgage of interest under will comprising realty and personalty—Estate accounts and distribution statement sent by trustees of will to mortgagee—Whether trustees agents of beneficiary—Real Property Limitation Act 1874, s 8. **Edwards' Will Trusts, Re** [1937] **3** 58, Ch D.

Acknowledgment in writing—
Balance sheets of company showing loans—Loans including loans on which the plaintiffs claimed—Balance sheets signed by director months after date at which they showed financial position of company—Whether an acknowledgment of an existing liability—Whether fresh limitation period began from signing of balance sheets—Indian Limitation Act 1908 (No 9 of 1908), s 19. **Consolidated Agencies Ltd v Bertram Ltd** [1964] **3** 282, PC.
Signature—Balance sheet of company—Company director—Fiduciary duty—Debt owed by company to director—Signature of balance sheet by director not capable of constituting effective acknowledgment in writing—Balance sheet approved by members of company in general meeting—Whether balance sheet thereby becoming an effective acknowledgment—Limitation Act 1939, ss 23(4), 24. **Gee & Co (Woolwich) Ltd, Re** [1974] **1** 1149, Ch D.
Date of acknowledgment—
Fresh cause of action accruing on date of acknowledgment of claim—Balance sheet of company—Signature of directors—Balance sheet signed 11 months after end of relevant financial year—Balance sheet acknowledging debt to claimant—Whether capable of operating as acknowledgment of debt as at date of balance sheet—Limitation Act 1939, s 23(4). **Gee & Co (Woolwich) Ltd, Re** [1974] **1** 1149, Ch D.
Debt—
Acknowledgment of a claim—Fresh accrual of action on acknowledgment or part payment—Debt or other liquidated pecuniary claim—Solicitors' claim for costs billed but not fixed by assessment or agreement—Whether debt or other liquidated pecuniary claim—Limitation Act 1980, s 29(5). **Phillips & Co (a firm) v Bath Housing Co-operative Ltd** [2013] **2** 475, CA.
Acknowledgment of a claim—Need for admission that debt or other liquidated amount outstanding and unpaid—Limitation Act 1939, s 23(4). **Good v Parry** [1963] **2** 59, CA.
Acknowledgment of a claim—Need to establish admission by debtor of legal liability to pay amount creditor seeking to recover—Denial of liability on ground of set-off or cross-claim—Alleged right of set-off or cross-claim reducing amount of creditor's claim in part—Acknowledgment of debt subject to cross-claim constituting acknowledgment of indebtedness for balance of claim only—Limitation Act 1939, s 23(4). **Surrendra Overseas Ltd v Government of Sri Lanka** [1977] **2** 481, QBD.
Arrangement in lieu of payment of interest—Creditor living rent-free on debtor's farm and receiving free farm produce—Continuous acknowledgment. **Wilson, Re** [1937] **3** 297, Ch D.
Balance sheet of debtor company despatched to shareholders—Receipt by shareholder not proved—Whether 'acknowledgment'—Whether acknowledgment 'made to' shareholder—Whether acknowledgment effective—Limitation Act 1939, s 24(2). **Cia de Electricidad de la Provincia de Buenos Aires Ltd, Re** [1978] **3** 668, Ch D.
Cause of action—Whether new cause of action—Whether to be pleaded in statement of claim or in reply—Limitation Act 1939, s 23(4). **Busch v Stevens** [1962] **1** 412, QBD.
Company—Acknowledgment contained in company's statement of affairs and summaries thereof made in company's receivership and subsequent liquidation—Whether statement of affairs and summaries thereof capable of constituting acknowledgment—Whether acknowledgment in documents only an acknowledgment of indebtedness as at date to which statement of affairs relates and not as at later date when documents signed—Whether creditors' claims statute-barred in liquidation—Limitation Act 1939, ss 23(4), 24. **Overmark Smith Warden Ltd, Re** [1982] **3** 513, Ch D.
Company—Contract depending on contingency—Acknowledgment in balance sheet—Acknowledgment by board of debt owed to themselves as trustees. **Ledingham v Bermejo Estancia Co Ltd** [1947] **1** 749, KBD.
Debt due to executor mentioned in Inland Revenue affidavit—Debt mentioned in statement to trustee in bankruptcy of creditor—Same hand to pay and receive—Debt due to executor—Suspension of operation of statute. **Bowring-Hanbury's Trustee in Bankruptcy v Bowring-Hanbury** [1943] **1** 48, CA.
Defence in foreign action denying liability—Whether acknowledgment for purposes of Limitation Act—Limitation Act 1939, s 23(4). **Flynn (decd), Re (No 2)** [1969] **2** 557, Ch D.
Interrogatory answer to which might constitute acknowledgment—Whether interrogatory necessary to dispose fairly of cause or matter—Limitation Act 1939, s 23(4)—RSC Ord 26, r 1(3). **Lovell v Lovell** [1970] **3** 721, CA.
Part payment—Debt secured against property—Debtor becoming insolvent—Mortgagee taking possession of property—Debtor's solicitor making payment to mortgagee in possession on account of rental income from property—Mortgagee in possession making payment to debtor's account in respect of proceeds of sale of property—Whether those payments amounting to re-accrual of claim—Limitation Act 1980, ss 29, 30, 31. **UCB Corporate Services Ltd v Kohli** [2004] **2 Comm** 422, Ch D.
What amounts to an acknowledgment—Action to recover money lent—Denial of indebtedness—Plaintiff relying on letter sent to defendant—Letter not in terms referring to debt sued on—Letter suggesting no debt but possibly obligation of another nature—Letter not an 'acknowledgment of for debt'. **Ward v Tibbatts** [1936] **2** 656, KBD.
What amounts to an acknowledgment—Balance sheets of debtor company handed to shareholder creditor—Parol evidence to explain entries—Debt due to creditor included in sum set out as total of company's debts—Whether capable of operating as acknowledgment of debt as at date of balance sheet—Limitation Act 1939, ss 23(4), 24(1)(2). **Jones v Bellegrove Properties Ltd** [1949] **2** 198, CA.
What amounts to an acknowledgment—Letter acknowledging indebtedness but not specifying amount of debt—Parole evidence of amount—Tax deduction certificates—Whether acknowledgments—Limitation Act 1939, s 23(4). **Dungate v Dungate** [1965] **3** 818, CA.
Whether acknowledgments confined to admissions of debts which were indisputable as to quantum as well as liability—Limitation Act 1980, s 29(5). **Bradford & Bingley plc v Rashid** [2006] **2 Comm** 951, HL; [2006] **4** 705, HL.
Whether sufficient acknowledgment of claim to prevent limitation period expiring—Limitation Act 1980, s 29. **Habib Bank Ltd v Central Bank of Sudan** [2007] **1 Comm** 53, QBD.

LIMITATION OF ACTION (cont)—
  Acknowledgment (cont)—
    Interrogatory—
      Interrogatory to obtain evidence that document written before issue of writ amounted to acknowledgment—Whether interrogatory necessary to dispose fairly of cause or matter—Limitation Act 1939, s 23(4)—RSC Ord 26, r 1(3). **Lovell v Lovell** [1970] **3** 721, CA.
    Mortgage—
      Payments made to mortgagee by receiver appointed under a different mortgage—Receiver's appointment contrary to Companies Act 1929, s 306. **Portman Building Society v Gallwey** [1955] **1** 227, Ch D.
    Title to land—
      Acknowledgment of plaintiff's title—Acknowledgment by agent of defendant—Mortgage—Acknowledgment by mortgagor's solicitor—Limitation Act 1939, ss 4(3), 23(1)(a). **Wright v Pepin** [1954] **2** 52, Ch D.
      Offer, subject to contract, to owner's agent by person in possession to purchase the land—Limitation Act 1939, ss 23(1)(a), 24 (1), (2). **Edginton v Clark (Macassey and ors (Trustees of Whitely House Trust) third parties)** [1963] **3** 468, CA.
  Action—
    Action for an account—
      Meaning—Husband and wife—Property—Claim under, s 17 of Married Women's Property Act 1882. **Spoor v Spoor** [1966] **3** 120, Div.
    Action on contract—
      Settlement agreement scheduled to Tomlin Order staying proceedings but providing for enforcement of foreign judgment in event of defendant defaulting on payment obligations—Defendant failing to make all payments and claimants applying to lift stay and enter judgment after six years—Whether claim time barred—Whether 'action founded on simple contract' and subject to six-year time limit—Whether new claim—Limitation Act 1980, ss 5 and 35(3)—CPR 17.4. **Bostani (in their capacity as trustees of the Alfred E Mann Living Trust) v Pieper** [2019] **2 Comm** 276, QBD.
    Action on judgment—
      Plaintiffs seeking to enforce judgment after 111/2 years—Whether execution of judgment or bringing of fresh action barred after six years—Whether, when judgment executed after six years, interest on judgment limited to period of six years before date of execution—Limitation Act 1980, s 24(1)(2). **Lowsley v Forbes (t/a L E Design Services)** [1998] **3** 897, HL.
      Warrant for possession—Application to extend time—Warrant obtained 14 years before claim for order to extend time for execution—Whether court will give leave to issue execution when right of action barred—Limitation Act 1939, s 2(4)—Increase of Rent and Mortgage Interest (Restrictions) Act 1920, s 5(4). **Lougher v Donovan** [1948] **2** 11, CA.
      Warrant for possession—Suspension of warrant—Non-enforcement for more than 12 years since date of issue—Small Tenements Recovery Act 1838, s 1—Rent and Mortgage Interest Restrictions Act 1923, s 4(2)—Limitation Act 1939, s 2(4). **Mills v Allen** [1953] **2** 534, CA.
      Warrant for possession—Warrant not executed—Judgment creditor renewing warrant more than six years after action for possession commenced—Creditor seeking to have warrant set aside—Whether application for leave to issue warrant an 'action'—Whether renewal of warrant or issue of new warrant time-barred—Whether court having discretion to order renewal of warrant or issue of new warrant—How court should exercise discretion—Limitation Act 1980, ss 24, 29(2), 38(1)—CCR Ord 26, rr 5, 6, 17. **National Westminster Bank plc v Powney** [1990] **2** 416, CA.
      Winding up petition brought by judgment creditor—Whether action on judgment—Limitation Act 1980, ss 24(1), 38(1). **Ridgeway Motors (Isleworth) Ltd v ALTS Ltd** [2005] **2** 304, CA.
    Action on statute—
      Action based on Consumer Credit Act 1974—Action on specialty—Appropriate period of limitation—Whether claim to reopen an extortionate credit bargain an action upon a specialty—Whether claim an entitlement to invoke jurisdiction of court—Consumer Credit Act 1974, s 139(1)—Limitation Act 1980, ss 8, 38(1). **Nolan v Wright** [2009] **2 Comm** 503, Ch D; [2009] **3** 823, Ch D.
      Action based on Consumer Credit legislation—Action on specialty—Claim for relief from unfair relationship between creditors and debtors—Whether cause of action accruing at date of credit agreement—Whether 12-year limitation period running from date of credit agreement—Consumer Credit Act 1974, ss 140A, 140B. **Patel v Patel** [2010] **1 Comm** 864, QBD.
      Action based on Gaming Act—Action on specialty—Appropriate period of limitation—Gaming Act 1835, s 2—Limitation Act 1939, s 2(3). **Brueton v Woodward** [1941] **1** 470, KBD.
    Proceeding in a court of law—
      Application to issue distress warrant in respect of arrears of general rates—Application for warrant more than six years after demand—Whether application 'proceeding in a court of law'—'Date on which cause of action accrued'—Limitation Act 1939, ss 2(1)(d), 31(1). **China v Harrow UDC** [1953] **2** 1296, QBD.
    Tort, in, against estates of deceased persons—
      Period of limitation—Action brought after lapse of more than six years after accident but within six months of administration—Whether action against tortfeasor's administrator barred—Law Reform (Miscellaneous Provisions) Act 1934, s 1(3)—Limitation Act 1939, ss 2, 32. **Airey v Airey** [1958] **2** 571, CA.
  Action on contract. See Action—Action on contract, above.
  Adjudication award—
    Building contract. See **Building contract** (Adjudication—Award—Payment of damages made by unsuccessful party pursuant to adjudication award).
  Adverse possession. See Land—Adverse possession, below.
  Agent—
    Concealment of right of action by fraud. See Concealment of right of action by fraud—Concealment by agent, below.
  Amendment of pleading—
    New claim. See **Pleading** (Amendment—Leave to amend after expiry of limitation period—New claim).
  Arbitration—
    Action to enforce award. See **Arbitration** (Award—Enforcement—Action to enforce award).

LIMITATION OF ACTION (cont)—
  Arbitration (cont)—
    Commencement. *See* **Arbitration** (Commencement).
    Jurisdiction, challenge to. *See* **Arbitration** (Award—Challenge to award on grounds of lack of jurisdiction—Claimant making challenge to jurisdiction after expiry of time limit).
  Bank. *See* **Bank** (Limitation of action).
  Bankruptcy proceedings—
    Statutory demand—
      Petitioning creditor obtaining judgment in default against debtor in 1987—Creditor serving statutory demand for payment in 1995—Whether proceedings statute-barred—Whether making of statutory demand and subsequent bankruptcy proceedings an 'action'—Limitation Act 1980, s 24(1). **Debtor (No 50A/SD/95), Re a** [1997] **2** 789, Ch D.
  Breach of statutory duty—
    Action for damages. *See* When time begins to run—Action for damages for breach of statutory duty, *below*.
  Broker—
    Negligence—
      Accrual of cause of action. *See* Accrual of cause of action—Negligence—Brokers, *above*.
  Carriage of goods by sea—
    Damages for breach of contract. *See* **Shipping** (Carriage by sea—Damages for breach of contract—Time limit for bringing action).
  Carriage of passengers by sea—
    Personal injury. *See* **Shipping** (Passengers—Carriage by sea—Limitation of action).
  Cause of action—
    Accrual. *See* Accrual of cause of action, *above*.
  Charge on land—
    Enforcement. *See* When time begins to run, *below*.
  Charitable trust—
    Trust property. *See* Trust property—Charitable trust, *below*.
  Child—
    Disability. *See* Persons under disability—Extension of limitation period in case of disability—Person who is an infant or lacks capacity, *below*.
  Child in care of local authority. *See* Persons under disability—Custody of parent—Child in care of local authority, *below*.
  Claim for declaratory relief—
    HMRC bringing claim for declaration that settlement agreement lawfully rescinded on basis of fraudulent misrepresentation—
      Whether six-year limitation period for deceit applying by analogy—Limitation Act 1980, ss 32(1), 36(1). **Revenue and Customs Comrs v IGE USA Investments Ltd (formerly IGE USA Investments)** [2022] **2** 139, CA.
  Claim to personal estate of deceased person—
    Action by next-of-kin against beneficiary—
      Action to recover sums paid under invalid residuary bequest—Whether 'action in respect of claim to personal estate of deceased'—Limitation Act 1939, s 20. **Ministry of Health v Simpson** [1950] **2** 1137, HL.
  Company—
    Debt—
      Acknowledgment. *See* Acknowledgment—Debt—Company, *above*.
    Restoration to register—
      Period of limitation. *See* **Company** (Restoration to register—Period of limitation).
  Competition—
    Follow-on claims. *See* **Competition** (Competition Appeal Tribunal—Follow-on claims—Limitation of action).
  Compulsory purchase—
    Compensation—
      Accrual of cause of action. *See* Accrual of cause of action—Action to recover sums recoverable by virtue of statute—Compulsory purchase, *above*.
    Compulsory purchase order—
      Application to quash order—Time limit. *See* **Compulsory purchase** (Compulsory purchase order—Application to quash order—Time limit).
  Computation of limitation period. *See* When time begins to run, *below*.
  Concealment of right of action—
    Breach of duty—
      Action based on Consumer Credit Act 1974—Loan agreement and related payment protection insurance policy—Lender receiving undisclosed commission—Whether creation of unfair relationship amounting to breach of duty for limitation purposes—Whether failure to disclose existence and size of commission 'concealment'—Whether deliberate commission of breach of duty—Whether recklessness sufficient—Consumer Credit Act 1974, s 140A—Limitation Act 1980, s 32(1)(b), (2). **Potter v Canada Square Operations Ltd** [2020] **2** Comm 984, QBD; [2020] **4** 1114, QBD; [2021] **2** Comm 1319, CA; [2021] **4** 1036, CA.
      Claimant bringing action for professional negligence more than six years after alleged breach of duty—Defendant raising limitation defence—Claimant contending that concealment of breach of duty prevented time from running but not alleging that defendant dishonest or aware of breach of duty—Whether limitation provisions on concealment applying only to wrongful concealment of facts—Limitation Act 1980, s 32. **Liverpool Roman Catholic Archdiocese Trustees Incorporated v Goldberg** [2001] **1** 182, Ch D.
      Defendant solicitors raising limitation defence in action for negligence—Claimant relying on statutory provision postponing limitation period where defendant had concealed from claimant any fact relevant to his right of action—Statute providing that deliberate breach of duty amounting to concealment if claimant unlikely to discover it for some time—Whether person committing deliberate act of concealment required to be aware of its legal consequences—Limitation Act 1980, s 32(1)(b), (2). **Brocklesby v Armitage & Guest (a firm)** [2001] **1** 172, CA.

LIMITATION OF ACTION (cont)—
  Concealment of right of action (cont)—
    Breach of duty (cont)—
      Defendant solicitors raising limitation defence in action for negligence—Claimant relying on statutory provision postponing limitation period where defendant had concealed from claimant any fact relevant to his right of action—Statute providing that deliberate commission of breach of duty amounting to concealment if claimant unlikely to discover it for some time—Whether defendant committing deliberate breach of duty for limitation purposes if unaware of breach—Limitation Act 1980, s 32(2). **Cave v Robinson Jarvis & Rolf (a firm)** [2002] **2** 641, HL.
      Deliberate commission of breach of duty in circumstances in which breach is unlikely to be discovered for some time—Lender registering default in respect of arrears under unenforceable consumer credit agreement with credit reference agencies—Discovery of registration by claimant outside six-year limitation period—Whether lender in deliberate breach of duty—Whether claimant entitled to postponement of running of time—Limitation Act 1980, s 32(2). **Grace v Black Horse Ltd** [2015] **2 Comm** 465, CA; [2015] **3** 223, CA.
      Deliberate concealment—Certificate of quality for cargo of gasoline—Certifier using wrong test—Certifier subsequently retesting samples—Whether certifier under duty to disclose existence and content of retests to certificate holder—Whether deliberate concealment of retests—Limitation Act 1980, s 32. **AIC Ltd v ITS Testing Services (UK) Ltd** [2007] **1 Comm** 667, CA.
      Transactions defrauding creditors—Transactions entered into at an undervalue—Deliberate commission of breach of duty in circumstances in which breach is unlikely to be discovered for some time—Whether action under provisions relating to transactions at an undervalue an allegation of breach of duty—Limitation Act 1980, s 32(2)—Insolvency Act 1986, s 423. **Giles v Rhind** [2008] **3** 697, CA.
    Continued concealment—
      Defendant under fiduciary duty to inform plaintiff if security for loan becoming insufficient—Whether defendant's continuing failure to inform plaintiff a continuing breach of defendant's fiduciary duty—Whether continuing breach of duty preventing time from running—Limitation Act 1980, s 32(1)(b). **UBAF Ltd v European American Banking Corp** [1984] **2** 226, CA.
    Defendant solicitors raising limitation defence in action for negligence—
      Claimant relying on statutory provision postponing limitation period where defendant had concealed from claimant any fact relevant to his right of action—Whether mistaken belief of defendant that consequences of its negligent act could be cured together with its wish to avoid embarrassment by revealing negligent act constituting deliberate concealment—Limitation Act 1980, s 32(1)(b). **Williams v Fanshaw Porter & Hazelhurst (a firm)** [2004] **2** 616, CA.
    Discovery with reasonable diligence—
      Claimant company in administration when facts relevant to discovery emerging—Reasonably diligent insolvency practitioner not put on notice of need for further enquiry—Whether claimant could have discovered concealment with reasonable diligence—Limitation Act 1980, s 32(1). **OT Computers Ltd (in liq) v Infineon Technologies AG** [2021] **4** 1095, CA.
    Fraud, by. *See* Concealment of right of action by fraud, *below.*
  Concealment of right of action by fraud—
    Concealment by agent—
      Building contract—Developer party to contract—Developer employing builder to construct house in accordance with contract—Builder an independent contractor—Builder concealing defects in foundations—Whether builder 'agent' of developer—Limitation Act 1939, s 26(b). **Archer v Moss** [1971] **1** 747, CA.
      Defendant acting as broker for insurance pool which included claimant—Agreement containing fronting provision—Defendant using claimant to front large number of risks—Claimant bringing contractual and tortious claims against defendant in respect of fronting outside primary limitation period—Claimant relying on same facts to ground claim for breach of fiduciary duty—Whether limitation period applied to breach of fiduciary duty claim—Limitation Act 1980, s 36. **Cia de Seguros Imperio (a body corporate) v Heath (REBX) Ltd (formerly C E Heath & Co (North America) Ltd)** [1999] **1 Comm** 750, QBD; [2000] **2 Comm** 787, CA.
      Defendant acting as broker for insurance pool which included plaintiff—Agreement containing fronting provision—Defendant using plaintiff to front large number of risks—Plaintiff querying its liability under fronting provision but defendant failing to explain why plaintiff had been used to front—Plaintiff bringing contractual and tortious claims against defendant in respect of fronting outside primary limitation period—Plaintiff relying on same facts to ground claim for breach of fiduciary duty—Plaintiff alleging concealment of relevant facts by defendant—Whether plaintiff had been aware of facts relevant to claim more than six years before commencing proceedings—Whether limitation period applied to breach of fiduciary duty claim—Limitation Act 1980, s 32. **Cia de Seguros Imperio (a body corporate) v Heath (REBX) Ltd (formerly C E Heath & Co (North America) Ltd)** [1999] **1 Comm** 750, QBD.
    Conduct such as to hide from plaintiff existence of right of action—
      Equitable fraud—Building contract—House—Foundations not of sufficient standard and not in accordance with contract—Concrete mixture not of standard specified—Foundations covered up when plaintiff bought house—House unfit to live in—Defects discovered eight years later—Limitation Act 1939, s 26(b). **Archer v Moss** [1971] **1** 747, CA.
      Knowledge on part of defendants of facts giving plaintiff right of action—Building contract—Contract for sale of land and erection of house thereon—Implied term that foundations reasonably fit for house—House built on site of old chalk pit—Pit having been filled in in haphazard fashion and in part with organic matter—Failure of defendants as vendors to warn plaintiff of nature of site and risk of building thereon—Knowledge of defendants that house not having properly reinforced foundations—Subsidence after lapse of years—Whether failure to warn plaintiff of nature of site and risk amounting to concealment of right of action by fraud—Limitation Act 1939, s 26(b). **King v Victor Parsons & Co (a firm)** [1973] **1** 206, CA.
    Conversion—
      Action based on fraud—Right of action concealed by fraud—Bailment of goods—Owner abroad during war—Bailee's business closing down—Goods given away as worthless—Owner not notified—Limitation Act 1939, s 26(a)(b). **Beaman v ARTS Ltd** [1949] **1** 465, CA.

LIMITATION OF ACTION (cont)—
  Concealment of right of action by fraud (cont)—
    Conversion (cont)—
      Action based on fraud—Right of action concealed by fraud—Sale of heirloom by tenant for life to defendants—Resale by defendants to third party—Trustees' action for damages for conversion—Whether defendants claiming through tenant for life—Whether action statute-barred—Limitation Act 1939, ss 26(b), 31(4). **Eddis v Chichester Constable** [1969] 2 912, CA.
    Due diligence to discover defects—
      Reliance on expert knowledge and honesty—Building contract for house—Facing bricks used were of a type different from that specified and some were defective—Plaintiff relied on builder's expert knowledge and honesty—Defects not discovered by plaintiffs, using reasonable diligence, for some eight years—Whether action for breach of contract state statute-barred—Measure of damages—Limitation Act 1939, s 26(b). **Clark v Woor** [1965] 2 353, QBD.
    Fraud—
      Action against trustee for breach of trust—Bank trustee of a fund consisting of controlling interest in a company—Bank failing to secure adequate information from board on company's activities—Company sustaining loss through speculative investment—Loss to trust fund—Action by beneficiaries against trustee—Whether bank's omission to secure information unconscionable conduct amounting to fraud—Limitation Act 1939, s 26(b). **Bartlett v Barclays Bank Trust Co Ltd** [1980] 1 139, Ch D.
    Marriage contract—
      Invalid marriage—Breach of promise—Breach of implied warranty that party was legally in a position to marry—Plaintiff unaware of illegality—Postponement of limitation period—Limitation Act 1939, ss 2(1)(a), 26(b). **Shaw v Shaw** [1954] 2 638, CA.
    Negligence—
      Failure by solicitor to commence an action on behalf of client within statutory period—Ex gratia payment subsequently made by intended defendant for client's benefit—Concealment of source of gift—Limitation Act 1939, s 26(b). **Kitchen v Royal Air Forces Association** [1958] 2 241, CA.
    Trover. *See* Trover (Limitation of action—Postponement of limitation period—Action based on fraud).
  Consumer credit agreement—
    Concealment of right of action. *See* Concealment of right of action—Breach of duty—Deliberate commission of breach of duty in circumstances in which breach is unlikely to be discovered for some time, *above*.
    Unfair relationship between creditors and debtors. *See* **Consumer credit** (Unfair relationships between creditors and debtors—Credit agreement—Limitation period).
  Consumer protection—
    Product liability—
      European Union. *See* **European Union** (Consumer protection—Product liability—Limitation period).
  Contract—
    Limitation clause. *See* **Contract** (Construction—Limitation clause).
  Conversion—
    Action based on fraud—
      Concealment of right of action. *See* Concealment of right of action by fraud—Conversion—Action based on fraud, *above*.
  Counterclaim—
    Immunity from accrued limitation defence—
      Plaintiff commencing proceedings against defendant for unpaid professional fees—Defendant not entering defence but pursuing unsuccessful action against plaintiff in United States for damages for fraud, negligence and breach of contract at considerable cost to plaintiff—Defendant subsequently purporting to pursue negligence action in High Court by way of counterclaim to fees action in order to avoid limitation consequences—Whether counterclaim appropriate vehicle for negligence action—Whether subject matter of counterclaim ought to be disposed of in separate action—Limitation Act 1980, s 35(1)(a)—RSC Ord 15, r 5(2). **Ernst & Young (a firm) v Butte Mining plc (No 2)** [1997] 2 471, Ch D.
  Court's power to override time limit in personal injury or fatal accident claim—
    Exercise of discretion—
      Service of claim form—Extension of time for serving claim form—Failure to serve claim form within time—Second claim form issued—Whether discretion exerciseable—Principles—Limitation Act 1980, s 33. **Davidson v Aegis Defences Services (BVI) Ltd** [2014] 2 216, CA.
  Court's power to override time limit in personal injury or fatal accident claim—
    Court required to have regard to any unreasonable delay by plaintiff and nature of legal advice received—
      Legal professional privilege—Interrogatory. *See* **Disclosure and inspection of documents** (Interrogatory—Privilege—Legal professional privilege—Application for leave to bring action outside limitation period—Court required to have regard to any unreasonable delay by plaintiff and nature of legal advice received).
    Exercise of discretion—
      Absence of fault on part of defendant—Prejudice to plaintiff if action not allowed to proceed—Plaintiff having cast-iron case against solicitor for negligence if action not allowed to proceed—Whether appropriate to lay down guideline that if defendant not at fault limitation period ought to be enforced against plaintiff unless delay has been minimal especially if plaintiff has good claim against his solicitor—Limitation Act 1980, s 33(1). **Ramsden v Lee** [1992] 2 204, CA.
      Appeal against exercise of discretion—When Court of Appeal will interfere with judge's exercise of his discretion—Limitation Act 1980, ss 11, 33. **Conry v Simpson** [1983] 3 369, CA.
      Burden of proof—Discharge of burden of proof—Limitation Act 1980, s 33. **Sayers v Lord Chelwood** [2013] 2 232, CA.
      Carriage of passengers by sea—Passenger injured while travelling on ferry—Convention setting limitation period of two years—Whether court having discretion to extend or exclude time limit—Merchant Shipping Act 1979, Sch 3, art 16(1)(3)—Limitation Act 1980, ss 33, 39. **Higham v Stena Sealink Ltd** [1996] 3 660, CA.
      General guidance as to exercise of judicial discretion—Whether fair and just in circumstances—Limitation Act 1980, s 33. **Cain v Francis** [2009] 2 579, CA.

LIMITATION OF ACTION (cont)—
Court's power to override time limit in personal injury or fatal accident claim (cont)—
Exercise of discretion (cont)—
Limitation Act 1980, ss 11, 33. **Horton v Sadler** [2006] **3** 1177, HL.

Service of claim form—Extension of time for serving claim form—Failure to serve claim form within time—Second claim form issued—Whether abuse of process—Whether discretion exerciseable—Limitation Act 1980, s 33—CPR 7.5, 7.6. **Aktas v Adepta (a registered charity)** [2011] **2** 536, CA.

Unfettered discretion to allow action to proceed where equitable to do so—Discretion not limited to difficult or exceptional cases—Formal delay on part of plaintiff's solicitor—Failure to apply for extension of validity of writ within limitation period—No prejudice to defendant in allowing action to proceed—Whether proper case in which to override time limit—Limitation Act 1939, s 2D (as inserted by the Limitation Act 1975, s 1). **Firman v Ellis** [1978] **2** 851, CA.

Unfettered discretion to allow action to proceed where equitable to do so—Discretion not limited to exceptional cases—Failure of plaintiff's solicitor to issue writ in time—Delay in issuing writ due to solicitor's difficulty in identifying defendant, one of a group of companies, because defendant not identified in statement of terms of plaintiff's employment or his payslips and group's insurers not identifying defendant—Whether prejudice to plaintiff in allowing action to proceed caused by provisions of s 2A of Limitation Act 1939 or by solicitor's delay—Whether proper case to exercise discretion to override time limit—Limitation Act 1939, s 2D(1)(as inserted by Limitation Act 1975, s 1). **Simpson v Norwest Holst Southern Ltd** [1980] **2** 471, CA.

Whether unfettered discretion—Plaintiff sustaining injury at work when aged 16—Plaintiff notifying employer five years later of claim in respect of injury to knee arising out of accident—Plaintiff not issuing writ until 51/2 months after expiry of limitation period—Whether defendant prejudiced by expiry of limitation period—Whether court entitled to have regard to matters occurring before expiry of limitation period—Whether delay in notifying claim relevant—Limitation Act 1980, ss 11, 28, 33(1)(3)(4). **Donovan v Gwentoys Ltd** [1990] **1** 1018, HL.

Whether unfettered discretion—Whether plaintiff barred from commencing second action and seeking court's discretion to override time limit where failure to serve writ in first action commenced within primary limitation period or where first action struck out for want of prosecution or discontinued—Limitation Act 1939, s 2D(1)(as inserted by the Limitation Act 1975, s 1(1)). **Chappell v Cooper** [1980] **2** 463, CA.

Whether unfettered discretion—Whether plaintiff having cast-iron case in negligence against own solicitor equal to claim against defendant prejudiced by expiry of limitation period—Limitation Act 1939, s 2D (as inserted by the Limitation Act 1975, s 1(1)). **Thompson v Brown Construction (Ebbw Vale) Ltd** [1981] **2** 296, HL.

Matters to which court may have regard—

Action claiming damages for personal injury sustained in road accident—Defendant's insurers disclaiming liability—Motor Insurers' Bureau liable to meet judgment against defendant—Plea of limitation actions raised—Whether discretion to override time limit should be exercised—Whether fact that Motor Insurers' Bureau would meet judgment a matter to be taken into consideration—Limitation Act 1939, s 2D(1)(a)(as inserted by Limitation Act 1975, s 1(1)). **Liff v Peasley** [1980] **1** 623, CA.

Evidence to be adduced by defendant likely to be less cogent than if action brought within prescribed time—Presumption that defendant would be prejudiced where delay exceeding five years—12 years' delay in bringing action—Action for damages for pneumoconiosis—Similar claims brought against defendants and settled by them during the 12 years—Inference that because of those claims cogent evidence to defend plaintiff's claim available to defendants—Whether presumption of prejudice rebutted—Limitation Act 1939, s 2D(3)(b)(as inserted by the Limitation Act 1975, s 1). **Buck v English Electric Co Ltd** [1978] **1** 271, QBD.

Length of delay—Delay of one day in issuing writ—Plaintiff personally not at fault—Defendant's ability to defend action on merits not affected—Defendant presented with windfall of cast-iron defence—Plaintiff having cast-iron case against own solicitor for negligence—Whether defendant's loss of unexpected windfall limitation defence constituting prejudice—Whether action should not be allowed to proceed because plaintiff having cast-iron case against solicitor—Whether discretion should be exercised where very short period of delay in commencing action not affecting defendant's ability to defend on merits—General guidelines on exercise of discretion—Limitation Act 1980, ss 11, 33(1)(3). **Hartley v Birmingham City DC** [1992] **2** 213, CA.

Length of delay—Extreme length of delay alone not a reason for refusing to allow case to proceed—All facts of case required to be considered—12 years' delay in bringing action from date of knowledge that injury was significant—Whether length of delay ground for refusing to allow action to proceed—Limitation Act 1939, s 2D(3) (a) (as inserted by the Limitation Act 1975, s 1). **Buck v English Electric Co Ltd** [1978] **1** 271, QBD.

Plaintiff's ignorance of legal rights—Inability of defendant to meet judgment—Second defendant tried for but acquitted of murder of plaintiff's daughter—Plaintiff having strong suspicions as to involvement of defendants in killing of daughter at time of second defendant's acquittal—First defendant not tried for murder of plaintiff's daughter—Plaintiff obtaining legal advice as to availability of civil claim against defendants more than six years later—Delay not jeopardising fairness of trial by rendering evidence against defendants less cogent—Whether inability of defendants to meet judgment legitimate reason for preventing plaintiff from pursuing civil claim—Whether court should exercise discretion to disapply limitation period—Limitation Act 1980, s 33. **Halford v Brookes** [1991] **3** 559, CA.

Prejudice to plaintiff—Remedy against solicitor—Plaintiff having remedy against solicitor for negligence if application to override time limit refused—Whether a relevant consideration in determining whether action should be allowed to proceed—Limitation Act 1939, s 2D(1) (as inserted by the Limitation Act 1975, s 1). **Firman v Ellis** [1978] **2** 851, CA.

LIMITATION OF ACTION (cont)—
  Court's power to override time limit in personal injury or fatal accident claim (cont)—
    Matters to which court may have regard (cont)—
      Reasons for not bringing action—Express and subconscious reasons—Claim by employee against
        employer—Reason given by employee for not bringing action that he regarded injury to his
        hearing merely as an irritating nuisance—Inference that reason for not bringing action was that
        employee did not wish to jeopardise employment and wished to preserve harmonious relations
        with employer—Whether subconscious reason a matter to which court could have regard in
        determining whether it would be equitable to allow action to proceed—Limitation Act 1939,
        s 2D(1)(3)(as added by the Limitation Act 1975, s 1). **McCafferty v Metropolitan Police District**
        Receiver [1977] **2** 756, CA.
    Practice—
      Application to extend validity of writ—Application made after expiry of limitation period—Proper
        course for master or registrar to decline to consider whether action should be allowed to proceed
        under statutory power to override time limit—Onus on plaintiff to issue fresh writ and apply to
        judge for order overriding time limit—Limitation Act 1939, s 2D (as inserted by the Limitation Act
        1975, s 1)—RSC Ord 6, r 8. **Firman v Ellis** [1978] **2** 851, CA.
      Claim by one defendant against another—Appropriate time for applying for court to override time
        limit—Plaintiff claiming damages for personal injury against first defendant—First defendant
        seeking contribution from and claiming damages against second defendant for personal
        injury—First defendant's claim against second defendant outside limitation period—Whether first
        defendant entitled to bring claim before seeking to disapply limitation period—Limitation Act
        1980, ss 33(1), 35(1)(b), (3). **Kennett v Brown** [1988] **2** 600, CA.
      Plaintiff injured by defendant driving company car—Summons issued against company within
        limitation period—Plaintiff failing to serve summons in time so action struck out—Plaintiff
        commencing proceedings against defendant outside limitation period—Whether plaintiff barred
        from commencing second action—Whether court entitled to exercise discretion to disapply
        limitation period—Whether court should do so—Limitation Act 1980, s 33. **Shapland v Palmer**
        [1999] **3** 50, CA.
      Plaintiff issuing writ within time but failing to serve defendant—Whether plaintiff barred from
        commencing second action and seeking court's discretion to override time limit where plaintiff's
        first action failed—Whether conduct of defendant leading to estoppel—Limitation Act 1980,
        s 33(1). **Forward v Hendricks** [1997] **2** 395, CA.
    Transitional provisions on commencement of statute introducing power—
      Action commenced and pending at date of commencement of statute—Order made before
        commencement of statute dismissing application made outside limitation period to extend
        validity of writ—Effect of order—Whether order rendering proceedings a nullity—Whether action
        having been commenced and determined before commencement of statute—Limitation Act 1975,
        s 3. **Firman v Ellis** [1978] **2** 851, CA.
    Whether plaintiff barred from commencing second action and seeking court's discretion to override
      time limit where plaintiff's first action liable to be dismissed for want of prosecution—
      Whether criteria for exercise of discretion to override time limit different from criteria for exercise
        of discretion to dismiss action for want of prosecution—Limitation Act 1939, s 2D(1)(as inserted
        by the Limitation Act 1975, s 1). **Walkley v Precision Forgings Ltd** [1979] **2** 548, HL.
  Crown—
    Proceedings against. *See* Proceeding against Crown, *below.*
    Requisites for establishing title against. *See* Land—Adverse possession—Foreshore—Requisites for
      establishing title against the Crown, *below.*
  Current account—
    Part payment. *See* Part payment—Current account, *below.*
  Damages—
    Negligence of solicitor—
      Action not brought within limitation period. *See* **Solicitor** (Negligence—Damages—Action not
        brought within limitation period).
  Debt—
    Acknowledgment. *See* Acknowledgment—Debt, *above.*
    Mortgage debt. *See* Mortgage—Debt, *below.*
  Detinue. *See* When time begins to run—Actions in tort—Detinue, *below.*
  Disability. *See* Persons under disability, *below.*
  Dispossession—
    Land. *See* Land—Adverse possession—Dispossession of true owner, *below.*
  Dwelling house—
    Adverse possession—
      Period of adverse possession. *See* Land—Adverse possession—Period of adverse possession,
        below.
  Ecclesiastical law. *See* **Ecclesiastical law** (Limitation of action).
  Employment—
    Deduction from wages. *See* **Employment** (Remuneration—Deduction from wages—Period of limitation
      applying to claim for unlawful deductions).
    Disability discrimination—
      Omission to act. *See* **Employment** (Disability—Discrimination—Complaint of discrimination—
        Period within which proceedings must be brought—Unlawful act—Deliberate omission).
  European Union—
    Action for annulment. *See* **European Union** (Procedure—Action for annulment—Time limit).
    Consumer protection. *See* **European Union** (Consumer protection).
  Evidence of adverse possession—
    Land. *See* Land—Adverse possession—Evidence, *below.*
  Expert knowledge—
    Reliance on. *See* Concealment of right of action by fraud—Due diligence to discover defects—Reliance
      on expert knowledge and honesty, *above.*
  Expiry of limitation period—
    Dismissal of claim—
      Estoppel. *See* **Estoppel** (Issue estoppel—Dismissal of claim—Expiry of limitation period).

Extension of time limit—
  Amendment of statute—
    Whether amendment retrospective. *See* Statute—Amendment—Construction—Extension of limitation period, *below.*
  Discretion—
    Exercise of discretion—Defamation action—Facts relevant to plaintiff's cause of action not becoming known until after expiry of three-year limitation period—Plaintiff applying for leave to issue writ after expiry of statutory period—Master granting leave ex parte—Whether grant of leave ex parte an irregularity—Whether judge having discretion to refuse leave—Limitation Act 1980, ss 4A, 32A—RSC Ord 2, r 1(2), Ord 32, r 9. **Oyston v Blaker** [1996] 2 106, CA.
    Principle governing determination whether leave should be granted—Reasonable prospect of winning action and obtaining adequate damages on known position, if completely advised—Preliminary issue without evidence directed—Severe injury to plaintiff in 1961—Deterioration in 1965—Plaintiff alleged want of knowledge of future deterioration before 1965—Limitation Act 1963, ss 1(3), 7(4). **Goodchild v Greatness Timber Co Ltd** [1968] 2 255, CA.
  Ignorance of claim against employer—
    Plaintiff leaving cotton mill because of ill health caused by conditions at work—Plaintiff not knowing that he was suffering from byssinosis as result of inhaling cotton dust—Plaintiff bringing action for damages after expiry of limitation period—Whether plaintiff knowing that condition due in whole or in part to breach of employers' statutory duty at time of leaving employment—Whether plaintiff statute-barred from bringing action—Whether court should exercise discretion to allow action to continue—Whether prejudice to plaintiff if denied right to litigate greater than that suffered by employer if action allowed to continue—Limitation Act 1980, ss 11, 33. **Brooks v J & P Coates (UK) Ltd** [1984] 1 702, QBD.
  Material fact of decisive character outside knowledge of plaintiff—
    Action for damages for personal injuries due to unsafe premises—Identity of occupier unknown to plaintiff until after expiration of limitation period—Whether identity of occupier a 'material fact'—Limitation Act 1963, ss 1(3), 7(3)(c)(5). **Clark v Forbes Stuart (Thames Street) Ltd (intended action), Re** [1964] 2 282, CA.
    Ignorance of claim against employer—Application by member of trade union to union for advice—All reasonable steps taken by member—Attributability of injury first known by member when union's advice communicated to him in July, 1967—Nature of applicant's illness known to him in September, 1966—Disease contracted in employment before 1960—Leave granted ex parte—Limitation Act 1963, s 7(5). **Pickles v National Coal Board** [1968] 2 598, CA.
    Ignorance of claim against employer—Application by member of trade union to union for advice—All reasonable steps taken by member—Nature of member's illness known to him in 1966—Trade union's advice that action statute-barred based on mistaken belief that nature of member's illness known to him in 1962—Member not informed by trade union that illness caused by breach of statutory duty or negligence of employers—Whether lack of knowledge of material facts relating to the cause of action—Limitation Act 1963, ss 1(3), 7(3). **Drinkwater v Joseph Lucas (Electrical) Ltd** [1970] 3 769, CA.
    Lack of knowledge of extent of injury—Plaintiff injured on employers' premises in 1948—Full extent of injury not realised until after six year limitation period expired—Plaintiff receiving offer of workmen's compensation in settlement in 1968 when became redundant—Plaintiff's union advising him throughout no common law claim—Plaintiff only seeking legal advice after became redundant—Plaintiff bringing negligence action within 12 months of receiving legal advice—Whether claim statute-barred—Limitation Act 1939, s 2(1)—Limitation Act 1963, ss 1, 7. **Knipe v British Railways Board** [1972] 1 673, CA.
    Lack of knowledge that facts founding worthwhile cause of action—Reasonable steps taken by plaintiff to ascertain whether a cause of action—Whether time beginning to run when plaintiff acquiring knowledge of relevant facts or when discovering that he has worthwhile cause of action—Limitation Act 1963, s 1(3) (as amended by the Law Reform (Miscellaneous Provisions) Act 1971, s 1(1)). **Harper v National Coal Board** [1974] 2 441, CA.
    Lack of knowledge that injuries attributable to negligence, nuisance or breach of duty—Plaintiff knowing that injury resulting from acts and knowing extent of injury—Plaintiff reasonably believing that acts did not afford him grounds for an action at law—Plaintiff not knowing that injuries caused by defendants' wrongful conduct—Plaintiff contracting asbestosis in defendants' employment—Disease caused by defendants' breaches of statutory regulations—Plaintiff receiving disablement benefit in respect of the disease—Works manager informing plaintiff that he could not receive benefit and claim damages against defendants—Limitation Act 1963, ss 1(3), 7(3). **Central Asbestos Co Ltd v Dodd** [1971] 3 204, CA; [1972] 2 1135, HL.
    Lack of knowledge that injury due to negligence or breach of duty giving rise to cause of action—Claim not statute-barred—Limitation Act 1963, s 7(4). **Newton v Cammel Laird & Co (Shipbuilders and Engineers) Ltd** [1969] 1 708, CA, Assizes.
    Mistaken belief that claim statute-barred—Whether mistaken belief by plaintiff amounts to mistake as to material fact—Limitation Act 1963, s 7(3). **Drinkwater v Joseph Lucas (Electrical) Ltd** [1970] 3 769, CA.
  Order for extension—
    Application by defendants to set aside order—Refusal of application—Appeal to Court of Appeal—Whether appeal lies to House of Lords from refusal to set aside order giving leave. **Cozens v North Devon Hospital Management Committee** [1966] 2 799, CA.
    Application by defendants to set aside order—Whether defendants had right to make such application—Limitation Act 1963, ss 1(1)(a), 2(1)(2)(4). **Cozens v North Devon Hospital Management Committee** [1966] 2 799, CA.
  Persons under disability. *See* Persons under disability, *below.*
  Trespass to the person. *See* Trespass to the person—Period of limitation—Extension, *below.*
Extension of validity of writ. *See* Writ (Extension of validity).
Fatal accident—
  Amendment of writ. *See* Writ (Amendment—Amendment after expiry of limitation period—Claim under Fatal Accidents Acts).

LIMITATION OF ACTION (cont)—
  Fatal accident (cont)—
    Application of statutory limitation period—
      Third-party insurance—Liability admitted by insurance company—Writ issued more than 12 months after death—Fatal Accidents Act 1846, s 3. **Cohen v Snelling** [1943] 2 577, CA.
    Court's power to override time limit. *See* Court's power to override time limit in personal injury or fatal accident claim, *above.*
    Material facts of decisive character unknown to deceased—
      Application for leave to join new defendant to action—Application more than 12 months after death—Limitation Act 1963, s 3(4). **Lucy v Henleys (WT) Telegraph Works Co Ltd (ICI Ltd, third party)** [1969] 3 456, QBD and CA.
  Foreign limitation periods—
    Relevant law relating to limitation—
      Interruption of limitation period—Claims brought by Iraqi civilians in tort regarding actions of British troops in Iraq—Coalition Provisional Authority (CPA) Order rendering troops immune from action in Iraq—Whether claims time-barred under Iraqi law—Whether time bar suspended by operation of CPA Order under Iraqi law—Foreign Limitation Periods Act 1984, ss 1, 2, 4—Iraqi Civil Code, arts 232, 435—Coalition Provisional Authority Order No 17. **Iraqi Civilians v Ministry of Defence (No 2)** [2016] 2 300, CA.
      Interruption of limitation period—Claims brought by Iraqi civilians in tort regarding actions of British troops in Iraq—Coalition Provisional Authority (CPA) Order rendering troops immune from action in Iraq—Whether claims time-barred under Iraqi law—Whether time bar suspended by operation of CPA Order under Iraqi law—Foreign Limitation Periods Act 1984, ss 1, 4—Iraqi Civil Code, art 435—Coalition Provisional Authority Order No 17. **Iraqi Civilians v Ministry of Defence (No 2)** [2017] 2 79, SC.
  Foreshore—
    Adverse possession of. *See* Land—Adverse possession—Foreshore, *below.*
  Fraud—
    Claim for declaratory relief based on fraudulent misrepresentation. *See* Claim for declaratory relief, *above.*
    Concealment of right of action. *See* Concealment of right of action by fraud, *above.*
    Fraudulent breach of trust. *See* Period of limitation—Fraudulent breach of trust, *below.*
    Trust property. *See* Trust property—Fraud or fraudulent breach of trust to which trustee a party, *below.*
  Future interests—
    Accrual of right of action in case of future interests. *See* Land—Accrual of right of action in case of future interests, *below.*
  Husband and wife—
    Property—
      Claim under, s 17 of Married Women's Property Act 1882. *See* **Husband and wife** (Property—Summary proceedings—Limitation of time).
  Immigration appeal. *See* **Immigration** (Appeal—Time limit for appealing).
  Indemnity—
    Accrual of cause of action—
      Charterparty—Charterparty requiring master to sign bills of lading as presented—Bills of lading containing more onerous terms than charterparty and exposing owners to greater liability to consignees of cargo—Charterers owing implied indemnity to owners—Whether implied indemnity against incurring of liability or against consequences of master signing more onerous bills—Whether owners' right to indemnity arising when damage ascertained or when owners' liability to consignees ascertained—Whether owners' claim against charterers for indemnity time-barred. **Telfair Shipping Corp v Inersea Carriers SA** [1985] 1 243, QBD.
      Policy of fidelity insurance—Whether cause of action accruing when loss occurred or when fraud discovered—Limitation Act 1980, s 5. **Universities Superannuation Scheme Ltd v Royal Insurance (UK) Ltd** [2000] 1 Comm 266, QBD.
      Third party granted right to tip material on to land owned by defendants—Third party agreeing to indemnify defendants against all consequent liabilities—Plaintiffs alleging damage to neighbouring land from third party's activities—Whether defendants' claim against third party for indemnity statute-barred—Whether general indemnity an indemnity against liabilities arising under principal claim or against payment and discharge of those liabilities—Whether time not beginning and discharge of those liabilities—Whether time not beginning to run against person claiming indemnity until he is called on to pay principal claim. **Green (R & H) & Silley Weir Ltd v British Railways Board (Kavanagh, third party)** [1985] 1 237, Ch D.
    Contribution proceedings—
      Employers' liability insurance—Employee contracting malignant mesothelioma—Claimant insurer reaching settlement with employee—Defendant being earlier provider of employers' liability insurance—Claimant seeking contribution from defendant—Whether claimant's action being statute barred—Civil Liability (Contribution) Act 1978, s 1(1)—Limitation Act 1980, s 10. **RSA Insurance plc v Assicurazoni Generali SpA** [2019] 1 Comm 115, QBD.
  Interest on mortgage money—
    Entitlement of mortgagee in redemption action to arrears of interest. *See* **Mortgage** (Redemption—Mortgagee's entitlement to arrears of interest).
  Interrogatory—
    Acknowledgment. *See* Acknowledgment—Interrogatory, *above.*
  Invalid marriage—
    Concealment of right of action by fraud. *See* Concealment of right of action by fraud—Marriage contract—Invalid marriage, *above.*
  Joint tortfeasors. *See* When time begins to run—Joint tortfeasors, *below.*
  Judgment—
    Action on judgment. *See* Action—Action on judgment, *above.*
  Judicial review—
    Time for application. *See* **Judicial review** (Leave to apply for judicial review—Promptness).

LIMITATION OF ACTION (cont)—
Land—
Accrual of right of action in case of future interests—
Estate or interest in reversion or remainder—Freeholder holding subject to a term of years—Squatter on demised land—Date at which freeholder's right of action against squatter deemed to accrue—Registered land—Limitation Act 1939, ss 6(1), 16—Land Registration Act 1925, s 75(1). **Fairweather v St Marylebone Property Co Ltd** [1962] **2** 288, HL.
Acquisition of title by squatter—
Dispossession of true owner—Requirements of 'dispossession' and 'possession'—Limitation Act 1980, s 15, Sch 1, para 1. **Pye (JA) (Oxford) Ltd v Graham** [2002] **3** 865, HL.
Action for recovery of arrears of rent—
Action against guarantor of tenant's undertaking to pay rent—Lease and guarantee under seal—Whether action against guarantor being action to recover 'damages in respect of arrears of rent'—Whether six-year limitation period applying to action—Limitation Act 1980, s 19. **Romain v Scuba TV Ltd** [1996] **2** 377, CA.
Adverse possession—
Accrual of cause of action—Whether intervention of Crown's ownership defeating claim—Limitation Act 1980, Sch 1, para 12. **Hill v Transport for London** [2005] **3** 677, Ch D.
Acknowledgment of title—Owner bringing possession proceedings—Defendant admitting owner's title in defence but counter-claiming for tenancy—Defendant making without prejudice offer to purchase freehold—Possession proceedings eventually stayed and struck out—Owner bringing fresh proceedings—Defendant claiming title by adverse possession—Whether acknowledgment of title made in defence or without prejudice letter—Limitation Act 1980, ss 15(1), 29. **Ofulue v Bossert** [2009] **3** 93, HL.
Acts amounting to possession—Acts tending to prove possession of part of land—Acts tending to prove possession of part tending to prove possession of whole—Land not enclosed by wall or other physical barrier—Boundaries of land known and not in dispute—Whether acts tending to prove possession of part capable of proving possession of whole. **Higgs v Nassauvian Ltd** [1975] **1** 95, PC.
Acts amounting to possession—Unregistered land—Vessel moored and anchored in tidal river—Vessel resting on river bed or foreshore at low tide—Whether owner of vessel could acquire title by adverse possession to river bed or foreshore—Limitation Act 1980, s 15(1). **Port of London Authority v Ashmore** [2009] **4** 665, Ch D; [2010] **1** 1139n, CA.
Claim by true owner to recover possession—True owner sending letter requiring squatter to vacate—Whether letter conferring possession on true owner—Whether squatter prevented by letter from acquiring title by adverse possession—Limitation Act 1980, s 15(1). **Mount Carmel Investments Ltd v Peter Thurlow Ltd** [1988] **3** 129, CA.
Co-tenants—Devise of land in undivided shares—Co-tenants entitled to some only of the undivided shares were in exclusive possession of the whole land for over 20 years for their own benefit—Whether right of entry and right of action accrued on death of testator—Whether time ran notwithstanding possession of co-tenants was not wrongful—Real Property Limitation (No 1) Act 1833, s 3—Real Property Limitation (1874) Act, s 1. **Paradise Beach and Transportation Co Ltd v Price-Robinson** [1968] **1** 530, PC.
Dispossession of true owner—Acts amounting to dispossession—Land held by owner for purpose of future property development—Owner having no immediate use for land—Land forming part of field belonging to farm—Land not fenced off from rest of field—Owner of farm using land as part of field for statutory period of limitation—Farm owner cutting grass, grazing cattle and on one occasion ploughing land—Whether acts amounting to dispossession of owner—Whether farm owner having enjoyed adverse possession for requisite period—Limitation Act 1939, ss 4(3), 5(1), 10(1). **Wallis's Cayton Bay Holiday Camp Ltd v Shell-Mex and BP Ltd** [1974] **3** 575, CA.
Dispossession of true owner—Acts amounting to possession—Land held by owner for purpose of future road development—Owner having no immediate use for land—Occupier of neighbouring house maintaining land as part of his garden—Land not fenced off from garden—Whether occupier's acts amounting to dispossession of owner—Whether occupier having adverse possession for requisite period—Whether occupier prevented from claiming adverse possession by owner's plans for its future use—Limitation Act 1980, s 15(1). **Buckinghamshire CC v Moran** [1989] **2** 225, CA.
Dispossession of true owner—Original registered proprietor of land deprived of title by forged documents—New registered proprietor transferring land to appellant complicit in fraud—Appellant entering into occupation—Whether claim for rectification of register defeated by appellant's adverse possession—Land Registration Act 1925, ss 69, 75, 114—Limitation Act 1980, ss 18(1), 21, Sch 1, paras 1, 8—Land Registration Act 2002, Sch 4, para 3(3), Sch 12, para 18. **Nasrullah v Rashid** [2019] **4** 424, CA.
Dispossession of true owner—Possession with permission of true owner—Landlord permitting occupation of land for agricultural use—Landlord allowing occupier to remain on land with exclusive occupation at his own risk and on condition that he give up possession at short notice—Landlord seeking to regain possession of land after more than 12 years—Whether landlord's title to land extinguished—Whether occupier acquiring title to land by adverse possession—Whether permission to remain on land amounting to grant of estate or interest in land—Whether permission creating licence to occupy land—Whether licence creating agricultural tenancy from year to year—Limitation Act 1939, s 4(3)—Agricultural Holdings Act 1948, s 2(1). **Colchester BC v Smith** [1991] **2** 29, Ch D.
Evidence—Equivocal acts—Blocking of public access to land used as hotel garden—Owners of hotel had rights to use garden as such—Whether acts of exclusion showed intention to exclude owner of garden land—Limitation Act 1939, s 4(3), s 10. **Wimpey (George) & Co Ltd v Sohn** [1966] **1** 232, CA.
Foreshore—Requisites for establishing title against the Crown. **Fowley Marine (Emsworth) Ltd v Gafford** [1968] **1** 979, CA.
Highways—Highways maintainable at public expense—Statutory vesting in highway authority—Squatter occupying caravan on byway open to all traffic applying for registration of title—Whether title could be acquired by adverse possession—Highways Act 1980, s 263(1)—Limitation Act 1980, s 17. **R (on the application of Smith) v Land Registry (Cambridgeshire County Council, interested party)** [2010] **3** 113, CA.

LIMITATION OF ACTION (cont)—
  Land (cont)—
    Adverse possession (cont)—
      Period of adverse possession—Decontrolled dwelling-house—No rent paid by tenant—Accrual of
      right of action—House again controlled—Limitation Act 1939, ss 9(2), 10(1), 16. **Moses v
      Lovegrove** [1952] **1** 1279, CA.

      Period of adverse possession—Landlord confirming grant of quarterly tenancy by letter—Tenant in
      possession for many years without paying rent—Tenant claiming beneficial entitlement to
      premises—Whether letter a 'lease in writing'—Whether letter sufficient to create leasehold estate
      in land—Limitation Act 1980, Sch 1, para 5(1). **Long v Tower Hamlets London BC** [1996] **2** 683,
      Ch D.

      Period of adverse possession—Owner bringing action for recovery of land—Action being struck out
      nine years later for want of prosecution—Owner bringing fresh action for recovery of
      land—Whether issue of writ in first action stopping time running in trespasser's favour for
      purposes of second action—Limitation Act 1980, s 15. **Markfield Investments Ltd v Evans**
      [2001] **2** 238, CA.

      Possession by defendant not inconveniencing owner—Derelict land—Owner not intending to use
      land for any special purpose—Acts of defendant not causing inconvenience to owner—Defendant
      grazing cattle and dumping spoil on land—Acts amounting to taking possession of land by
      defendant—Whether necessary to show that owner had been inconvenienced in order to
      establish that possession adverse—Limitation Act 1939, ss 4(3), 5(1), 10(1). **Treloar v Nute**
      [1977] **1** 230, CA.

      Possession by oral licence for more than 12 years—Limitation Act 1939, ss 4(3), 5(3), 10(1). **Hughes
      v Griffin** [1969] **1** 460, CA.

      Possession by successive squatters—First squatter abandoning claim to possession—Whether
      second squatter can obtain title by combined period of adverse possession by successive
      squatters. **Mount Carmel Investments Ltd v Peter Thurlow Ltd** [1988] **3** 129, CA.

      Purchaser paying purchase price and taking possession—No conveyance—Acquisition by
      purchaser of title by adverse possession—Person in whose favour the period of limitation can
      run—Limitation Act 1939, ss 9(1), 10(1). **Bridges v Mees** [1957] **2** 577, Ch D.

      Purchaser taking possession before completion of contract of sale—Conveyance never
      completed—Purchaser in possession for 14 years—Vendor subsequently conveying property to
      third party—Third party dispossessing purchaser—Purchaser claiming title to property by
      adverse possession for period exceeding limitation period—Whether purchaser merely a licensor
      of vendor—Whether purchaser having 'adverse possession' for period of his occupancy—
      Whether third party entitled to possession—Limitation Act 1939, ss 4(3), 10. **Hyde v Pearce**
      [1982] **1** 1029, CA.

      Right to property—Trespasser successfully establishing possession of registered land and expiry of
      limitation period—Trespasser becoming beneficial owner of registered land—Whether breach of
      right to property—Land Registration Act 1925, s 75—Human Rights Act 1998, s 3, Sch 1, Pt II,
      art 1. **Beaulane Properties Ltd v Palmer** [2005] **4** 461, Ch D.

      Seasonal tenancy—Tenancy granted by adverse possessor of field to tenant who, unknown to
      either party, had the documentary title to the freehold—User of field for cattle during winter
      months, when seasonal tenancy not current, not bringing adverse possession to an end—Mutual
      mistake—Seasonal tenancy extending also to other lands—Whether tenancy of field
      void—Whether adverse possessor established title by virtue of Limitation Act 1939, s 10(3). **Bligh
      v Martin** [1968] **1** 1157, Ch D.

      Squatter acquiring rights by adverse possession against lessee of registered land—Lessee
      surrendering lease to freeholder—Whether freeholder thereby obtaining right to immediate
      possession against squatter—Land Registration Act 1925, s 75. **Central London Commercial
      Estates Ltd v Kato Kagaku Co Ltd (Axa Equity and Law Life Assurance Society plc, third party)**
      [1998] **4** 948, Ch D.

      Statutory tenant—Non-payment of rent—Accrual of right of action to recover land—Weekly tenancy
      granted to defendant—Defendant becoming statutory tenant of premises—Defendant
      subsequently ceasing to pay rent—No demand made for rent for period of 12 years—Whether
      statutory tenant in adverse possession—Whether statutory tenant capable of acquiring a
      possessory title against landlord—Limitation Act 1939, ss 9(2), 10(1). **Jessamine Investment Co v
      Schwartz** [1976] **3** 521, CA.

      Tenancy at will—Oral repetition of permission to stay some years after tenancy at will
      granted—Whether adverse possession thereby ended. **Hughes v Griffin** [1969] **1** 460, CA.

      Tenancy not in writing—No rent paid by tenant—Tenant incumbent of benefice—Land used as
      garden of glebe cottage—Succession to rights of corporation sole—Limitation Act 1939, ss 4(3),
      9(2), 10. **Hayward v Challoner** [1967] **3** 122, CA.

    Co-owners—
      Receipt of rent and profits by one co-owner—Co-owner trustee of legal estate—Real Property
      Limitation Act 1833, s 12—Law of Property Act 1925, s 12. **Landi, Re** [1939] **3** 569, CA.

    Discontinuance of possession—
      Dispossession—Vacant land—Owners' intention to develop land in future—Owners' minor acts of
      use—Defendants' war-time cultivation and subsequent use for greyhound breeding—Limitation
      Act 1939, s 5(1). **Williams Bros Direct Supply Stores Ltd v Raftery** [1957] **3** 593, CA.

    Land held in undivided shares before 1926—
      Mortgage—Statutory trusts—Proceeds of sale—Whether claim of mortgagees barred—Real
      Property Limitation Act 1874, s 8—Law of Property Act 1925, s 35, Sch I, Part IV, para 1(4). **Milking
      Pail Farm Trusts, Re** [1940] **4** 54, Ch D.

    Recovery—
      Action within 12 years from date on which right of action accrued—Date on which right of action
      accrued—Tenancy agreement to let cottage and shed—Tenant quitting cottage but retaining
      possession of shed—No rent paid for 17 years—Landlord's right to recover possession of shed
      barred—Limitation Act 1939, ss 4(3), 9(2). **Mason v Warlow** [1941] **1** 475, CA.

LIMITATION OF ACTION (cont)—
    Land (cont)—
        Recovery (cont)—
            Action within 12 years next after right to make entry or right of action accrued—Date when right of entry accrued—Contract for sale of land—Purchase price payable in quarterly instalments—Purchaser in possession—Default in payment of instalments—On default for specified period vendor having alternative remedies under contract—Right to enforce contract or to rescind contract and re-enter land—Whether right of entry accruing after lapse of specified period following default in payment or when vendor exercises option to rescind contract—Real Property Limitation Act 1874 (Fiji), s 1. **Lakshmijt v Sherani** [1973] **3** 737, PC.
            Sea-bed—Whether possession sufficiently exclusive—Limitation Act 1939, s 4(1), proviso. **Fowley Marine (Emsworth) Ltd v Gafford** [1967] **2** 472, QBD.
    Latent damage—
        Three-year limitation period—
            Three-year limitation period for negligence actions where facts relevant to cause of action not known at date of accrual—Claimant seeking to rely on three-year limitation period in negligence action in respect of latent damage—Loss adjuster aware of potential claim—Whether knowledge of loss adjuster appointed by claimant's insurers in subrogated claim attributable to claimant—Whether claimant's cause of action prima facie time-barred—Limitation Act 1980, s 14(5). **Graham v Entec Europe Ltd (t/a Exploration Associates)** [2003] **2 Comm** 811, CA; [2003] **4** 1345, CA.
            Three-year limitation period for negligence actions where facts relevant to cause of action not known at date of accrual—Plaintiff seeking to rely on three-year limitation period in negligence action in respect of latent damage—Defendant applying to strike out action—Whether plaintiff's cause of action prima facie time-barred—Whether appropriate to decide question of when plaintiff possessed sufficient relevant knowledge to commence proceedings on application to strike out—Limitation Act 1980, s 14A. **Iron Trade Mutual Insurance Co Ltd v J K Buckenham Ltd** [1990] **1** 808, QBD.
            Three-year limitation period for negligence actions where facts relevant to cause of action not known at date of accrual—Time limit applying to 'any action for damages for negligence'—Whether 'any action for damages for negligence' including action for damages for breach of contractual duty founded on allegation of negligent conduct—Limitation Act 1980, s 14A. **Société Commerciale de Réassurance v ERAS (International) Ltd (note)** [1992] **2** 82, CA.
            Three-year limitation period for negligence actions where facts relevant to cause of action not known at date of accrual—Time limit applying to 'any action for damages for negligence'—Whether 'any action for damages for negligence' including action for damages for breach of contractual duty founded on allegation of negligent conduct—Whether three-year limitation period for latent damage applying to cause of action in contract as well as in tort—Limitation Act 1980, s 14A. **Iron Trade Mutual Insurance Co Ltd v J K Buckenham Ltd** [1990] **1** 808, QBD.
    Leasehold enfranchisement. See **Landlord and tenant** (Leasehold enfranchisement—Limitation of action).
    Leave to add party to proceedings—
        Writ issued before expiration of limitation period—
            Leave sought after expiration. See Fatal accident—Material facts of decisive character unknown to deceased—Application for leave to join new defendant to action, *above*.
            Whether limitation period ceases to run to defendant's advantage when defendant added as party—Whether limitation period ceases to run on date of issue of writ or on date when defendant added as party. **Gawthrop v Boulton** [1978] **3** 615, Ch D.
    Legal aid, recoupment of. See **Legal aid** (Counsel's fees—Civil legal aid certificate).
    Libel and slander—
        Substitution of parties after expiry of limitation period. See **Practice** (Parties—Substitution—Substitution after expiry of limitation period).
    Libel and slander. See **Libel and slander** (Limitation of action).
    Limitation period—
        Generally. See Period of limitation, *below*.
        Postponement of. See Postponement of limitation period, *below*.
        Trespass to the person. See Trespass to the person—Period of limitation, *below*.
    Loss of life—
        Collision at sea. See **Shipping** (Collision—Limitation of action—Loss of life).
    Magistrates. See **Magistrates** (Limitation of time).
    Mistake—
        Action for relief from consequences of mistake. See Postponement of limitation period—Action for relief from consequences of mistake, *below*.
        Belief claim statute barred. See Extension of time limit—Material fact of decisive character outside knowledge of plaintiff—Mistaken belief that claim statute-barred, *above*.
        Money paid under mistake of law—
            Restitution. See **Mistake** (Mistake of law—Money paid under mistake of law).
    Moneylender—
        Proceedings for recovery of money lent by moneylender. See **Moneylender** (Limitation of action—Proceedings for recovery of money lent by moneylender).
    Mortgage—
        Acknowledgment. See Acknowledgment—Mortgage, *above*.
        Mortgage debt—
            Mortgagees selling mortgaged properties and subsequently bringing proceedings against mortgagors for recovery of shortfall on mortgage debt—Whether action to recover sum of money secured by mortgage—Limitation Act 1980, s 20(1). **West Bromwich Building Society v Wilkinson** [2005] **4** 97, HL.
            Mortgagees selling mortgaged properties and subsequently bringing proceedings against mortgagors for recovery of shortfall on mortgage debt—Whether proceedings subject to six-year or twelve-year limitation period—Limitation Act 1980, ss 5, 8, 20. **Bristol & West plc v Bartlett** [2002] **2 Comm** 1105, CA; [2002] **4** 544, CA.

LIMITATION OF ACTION (cont)—
  Mortgage (cont)—
    Mortgage money—
      Interest—Entitlement of mortgagee in redemption action to arrears of interest. *See* **Mortgage** (Redemption—Mortgagee's entitlement to arrears of interest).
    Mortgages vested in trustees—
      One common trustee—Receipt of rents for more than statutory period—Application by common trustee for benefit of first mortgagees in possession—Same hand to pay and receive. **Hodgson v Salt** [1936] **1** 95, Ch D.
  Motor insurers' bureau. *See* **Motor insurance** (Rights of third parties against insurers—Motor Insurers' Bureau—Untraced driver—Limitation).
  Negligence—
    Accountant—
      Accrual of cause of action. *See* Accrual of cause of action—Negligence—Accountant, *above*.
    Accrual of cause of action—
      Negligence. *See* Accrual of cause of action—Negligence, *above*.
    Action for damages—
      Unwanted pregnancy—Plaintiff giving birth following unsuccessful sterilisation operation—Action brought more than three years after cause of action accrued—Plaintiff claiming not for personal injury but for economic loss stemming from cost of rearing child—Whether claim for economic loss a separate cause of action from potential claim for personal injury—Whether plaintiff's claim an action for damages 'in respect of personal injuries'—Whether plaintiff's claim time-barred—Limitation Act 1980, s 11(1). **Walkin v South Manchester Health Authority** [1995] **4** 132, CA.
    Concealment of right of action by fraud. *See* Concealment of right of action by fraud—Negligence, *above*.
    Latent damage. *See* Latent damage, *above*.
    New Zealand. *See* **New Zealand** (Negligence—Duty of care—Limitation of action).
    Solicitor—
      Parallel claims in tort and contract—Accrual of cause of action. *See* **Solicitor** (Negligence—Cause of action—Parallel claims in tort and contract).
    When time begins to run. *See* When time begins to run—Actions in tort—Accrual of cause of action—Negligence, *below*.
  New claim—
    Amendment of pleading. *See* **Pleading** (Amendment—Leave to amend after expiry of limitation period—New claim).
    New claims in pending actions—
      Effect of non-payment of court fee—Running of time—Application to strike out amended particulars of claim as time-barred—Whether non-payment of court fee preventing new claim being 'made'—Limitation Act 1980, s 35(1)(b). **Hayes v Butters (No 2)** [2021] **4** 1185, CA.
  New Zealand—
    Action against electric-power board. *See* **New Zealand** (Limitation of action—Action against electric-power board).
    Negligence. *See* **New Zealand** (Negligence—Duty of care—Limitation of action).
  Oral licence—
    Possession by oral licence for more than 12 years. *See* Land—Adverse possession—Possession by oral licence for more than 12 years, *above*.
  Overriding time limit—
    Personal injury and fatal accident claims. *See* Court's power to override time limit in personal injury or fatal accident claim, *above*.
  Part payment—
    Current account—
      Payment made on account generally—Whether made in respect of balance on account—Limitation Act 1939, s 23(4). **Footman Bower & Co Ltd, Re** [1961] **2** 161, Ch D.
    Payment in respect of claim—
      Need to establish that part payment constituting admission of liability to pay balance of sum claimed—Denial of liability to pay balance on ground of cross-claim—Whether payment made a payment in respect of the claim—Whether payment reviving cause of action—Limitation Act 1939, s 23(4). **Surrendra Overseas Ltd v Government of Sri Lanka** [1977] **2** 481, QBD.
  Period of limitation—
    Action for general damages for breach of contract under seal—
      Whether action upon a specialty—Whether specialty relating simply to action for specific performance of debt or other obligation created by specialty or including also action for damages for breach of obligation in contract—Limitation Act 1980, s 8(1). **Aiken v Stewart Wrightson Members' Agency Ltd** [1995] **3** 449, QBD.
    Bond issued by company—
      Bondholder not claiming payment of interest or capital—Right to payment of interest statute-barred after six years—Right to payment of capital statute-barred after 12 years—From what moment period begins to run—Limitation Act 1939, s 18(1), (5). **Cia de Electricidad de la Provincia de Buenos Aires Ltd, Re** [1978] **3** 668, Ch D.
    Breach of statutory duty—
      Public law decisions—Claims for damages for breach of statutory duty alleged to have occurred during public procurement exercise for rail franchises—Whether claims subject to three-month limitation period for judicial review—CPR Pts 7, 54. **Stagecoach East Midlands Trains Ltd v Secretary of State for Transport** [2020] **3** 948, CA.
    Carriage by sea—
      Claim for damages arising out of death of passenger—Claim brought on behalf of passenger's child more than two years after event but within three years—Whether claim time-barred—Whether domestic legislation suspending limitation period—Meaning of 'suspension'—Prescription and Limitation (Scotland) Act 1973, s 18—Merchant Shipping Act 1995, s 183, Sch 6, Pt I, art 16. **Warner v Scapa Flow Charters** [2019] **2 Comm** 1, SC; [2019] **2** 1042, SC.

LIMITATION OF ACTION (cont)—
    Period of limitation (cont)—
        Claim for freight—
            Defence not subject to limitation period. *See* **Shipping** (Freight—Claim for freight—Defence—Cross-claim—Limitation period for cross-claim).
        Fraudulent breach of trust—
            Claimant Nigerian national commencing proceedings alleging defendant bank party to fraudulent breach of trust—Proceedings being commenced 24 years after alleged breach—Claimant being granted permission to serve claim form on defendant—Defendant appealing—Defendant alleging claim time-barred—Claimant relying on provision disapplying time bar where action in respect of fraud or fraudulent breach of trust—Defendant contending disapplication only occurring in respect of trustee, not dishonest assister of trustee—Whether claim time-barred—Limitation Act 1980, s 21. **Williams v Central Bank of Nigeria** [2012] 3 579, CA; [2014] 2 489, SC.
        Personal injury claim—
            Claims made by adults relating to sexual, physical or emotional abuse during childhood by staff at children's homes—Date of knowledge of claimants that injury 'significant'—Whether employer of staff vicariously liable—Whether claims statute-barred—Whether judge should exercise discretion to disapply limitation period—Limitation Act 1980, ss 11, 14, 33. **KR v Bryn Alyn Community (Holdings) Ltd (in liq)** [2004] 2 716, CA.
            Damages for negligence, nuisance or breach of duty—Damages consisting of or including damages in respect of personal injuries—In respect of—Meaning—Contract between plaintiff and defendants whereby defendants to effect insurance cover on vehicle on behalf of plaintiff—Defendants failing to effect adequate cover—Plaintiff injured when vehicle involved in accident—Plaintiff unable to obtain compensation for injuries from insurers—Action against defendants for damages for breach of contract more than three and less than six years after cause of action accrued—Whether an action for damages consisting of or including damages in respect of personal injuries—Whether action statute-barred—Limitation Act 1939, s 2(1) (as amended by the Law Reform (Limitation of Actions, etc) Act 1954, s 2(1)). **Ackbar v CF Green & Co Ltd** [1975] 2 65, QBD.
            Date of knowledge of claimant that injury significant—Injury significant if person whose date of knowledge is in question would reasonably have considered it significantly serious to justify instituting proceedings—Claim relating to sexual abuse while a minor—Date of knowledge of claimant—Whether test objective—Whether special features justifying court in exercising power to disapply limitation period—Limitation Act 1980, ss 14(2), 33. **A v Hoare and other appeals** [2008] 2 1, HL; **Young v South Tyneside Metropolitan BC** [2007] 1 895, CA.
            When proceedings 'brought' for purposes of limitation period—Whether claim 'brought' on date on which claim form issued by court—Whether claim 'brought' when court requested to issue claim form—Limitation Act 1980, s 11—CPR Pt 7 PD 5.1. **Barnes v St Helens Metropolitan BC** [2007] 3 525, CA.
            Writ claiming damages for negligence and/or breach of statutory duty—Statement of claim alleging breach of implied term or warranty that agricultural machinery supplied by defendant would be fit for purpose and of merchantable quality—Plaintiff's claim outside three-year limitation period—Order made disapplying three-year limitation period—Plaintiff thereafter seeking to amend writ by adding second plaintiff and claim by himself and father in partnership—Partnership claiming in contract and tort under proposed amendment—Whether limitation period three years or six years in respect of firm's claim—Whether damages claimed by firm for negligence and breach of contractual duty consisting of and including damages in respect of personal injuries—Limitation Act 1980, s 11(1)—RSC Ord 15, r 6(5). **Howe v David Brown Tractors (Retail) Ltd (Rustons Engineering Co Ltd, third party)** [1991] 4 30, CA.
        Return of capital by company to shareholders under scheme of arrangement—
            Dividends declared by company—Share warrants issued by company to bearer—Members not claiming payment—Right to payment statute-barred after six years—Limitation Act 1939, s 2(1). **Cia de Electricidad de la Provincia de Buenos Aires Ltd, Re** [1978] 3 668, Ch D.
        When time begins to run—
            Claim alleging respondent discriminating against appellant in pursuing disciplinary proceedings against her—Whether claim time-barred—Whether disciplinary proceedings a series of discrete acts or single continuing act—Whether act ending with first instance decision or acquittal on appeal—Human Rights Act 1998, ss 6, 7(5). **O'Connor v Bar Standards Board** [2018] 2 779, SC.
            Claim made by claimant relating to failure of defendant to assess and treat him for dyslexia—Whether claim for personal injury—Date of knowledge of claimant that injury significant—Constructive knowledge—Test for constructive knowledge—Whether claim statute-barred—Whether special features justifying court in exercising power to disapply limitation period—Limitation Act 1980, ss 11, 14(3), 33. **Adams v Bracknell Forest BC** [2004] 3 897, HL.
    Personal injury claim—
        Action for damages—
            Extension of time. *See* Extension of time limit—Material fact of decisive character outside knowledge of plaintiff, *above*.
            Court's power to override time limit. *See* Court's power to override time limit in personal injury or fatal accident claim, *above*.
            Generally. *See* Period of limitation—Personal injury claim, *above*.
        Plaintiff's knowledge—
            Date of plaintiff's knowledge of identity of defendant—Defendant plaintiff's employer and one of several companies forming part of group—Statement of plaintiff's terms of employment and his payslips not identifying which company was his employer because group name used in statement and payslips—Plaintiff injured on 4th August 1976 but defendant's identity not discovered until 4th July 1979 when group's insurers informing plaintiff's solicitor which company was the employer—Solicitor commencing action on 17th August 1979 more than three years from date cause of action accrued—Whether action time-barred—Whether plaintiff knew or could reasonably have been expected to acquire knowledge of defendant's identity before 17th August 1976—Limitation Act 1939, s 2A(4)(b), (6), (8) (as inserted by the Limitation Act 1975, s 1). **Simpson v Norwest Holst Southern Ltd** [1980] 2 471, CA.

LIMITATION OF ACTION (cont)—
Personal injury claim (cont)—
Plaintiff's knowledge (cont)—
Date of plaintiff's knowledge that injury was significant—Date on which plaintiff first had knowledge that injury attributable to defendant's act or omission—Group action—Product liability—Plaintiffs suffering side effects after taking drug manufactured by defendants—Whether actions statute-barred—Exercise of discretion—Whether court should have regard to group action structure when exercising discretion—Limitation Act 1980, ss 11, 14, 33. **Nash v Eli Lilly & Co** [1993] **4** 383, CA.
Date of plaintiff's knowledge that injury was significant—Date on which plaintiff first had knowledge that injury attributable to defendant's act or omission—Point when knowledge fixing cause of action—Limitation Act 1980, ss 11, 14. **Broadley v Guy Clapham & Co** [1994] **4** 439, CA.
Date of plaintiff's knowledge that injury was significant—Date on which plaintiff first had knowledge that injury attributable to defendant's act or omission—Whether action statute-barred—Exercise of discretion by court—Limitation Act 1980, ss 11, 14, 33. **Forbes v Wandsworth Health Authority** [1996] **4** 881, CA.
Date of plaintiff's knowledge that injury was significant—Discretion to disapply limitation period—Plaintiff failing to issue writ within three-year limitation period—Time running from when plaintiff had knowledge that injury was attributable to act or omission of defendant—Whether plaintiff should know that act or omission tortious—Whether court should exercise discretion to allow action to proceed—Limitation Act 1980, ss 11(4)(b), 14(1), 33. **Dobbie v Medway Health Authority** [1994] **4** 450, CA.
Date of plaintiff's knowledge that injury was significant—When reasonable for plaintiff to have considered injury sufficiently serious to justify instituting proceedings—Plaintiff contracting pneumoconiosis first certified in 1959—In 1963 disability from disease assessed at 20 per cent and plaintiff becoming aware that disease was progressively worsening—Between 1963 and 1970 plaintiff aware that other employees had claimed damages for pneumoconiosis against the defendants—Plaintiff not bringing action for damages until February 1975 when disability assessed at 100 per cent and he was no longer able to work—Plaintiff not bringing action earlier because he was in employment and receiving disability pension and therefore not in need of damages—Whether deceased must reasonably have considered more than three years prior to issue of writ that injury was sufficiently serious to justify instituting proceedings—Limitation Act 1939, s 2A(4)(b)(7). **Buck v English Electric Co Ltd** [1978] **1** 271, QBD.
Date on which plaintiff first had knowledge that injury attributable to defendant's act or omission—Plaintiff under disability—Plaintiff alleging sexual abuse by adoptive father and brother during childhood—Plaintiff claiming damages for mental illness and psychological disturbance—Whether injury on which action founded 'significant'—Whether plaintiff aware that injury attributable to acts of defendants—Court's power to override time limit in personal injury or fatal accident claim—Exercise of discretion—Limitation Act 1980, ss 11, 14, 33. **Stubbings v Webb** [1991] **3** 949, CA.
Untraced driver—
Motor insurance. *See* **Motor insurance** (Rights of third parties against insurers—Motor Insurers' Bureau—Untraced driver—Limitation).
When time begins to run. *See* When time begins to run—Personal injury claim, *below*.
Persons under disability—
Custody of parent—
15 year old boy living and working on farm away from parents and financially independent on agricultural wages—Whether in custody of parent—Limitation Act 1939, s 22(2)(b), (as amended by the Law Reform (Limitation of Actions, &c) Act 1954, s 2(2)). **Hewer v Bryant** [1969] **3** 578, CA.
Capacity to manage own affairs—Plaintiff rendered unconscious and unable to manage his own affairs from date of accident until issue of writ—Plaintiff living with his mother—Writ issued more than three years after date of accident—Whether plaintiff of 'unsound mind'—Whether 'in custody of a parent'—Limitation Act 1939, ss 2(1) proviso, 22(2)(b), 31(2) (as amended by the Law Reform (Limitation of Actions, &c) Act 1954, ss 2(1)(2)(b), 8(3)). **Leather v Kirby** [1965] **3** 927, HL.
Child in care of local authority—Whether in custody of parent—Limitation Act 1939, s 22(2)(b)—Law Reform (Limitation of Actions, &c) Act 1954, s 2(2). **Duncan v Lambeth London Borough** [1968] **1** 84, QBD.
Effective care and control—Capacity of parent to exercise effective care and control—Infant living with parents at time when cause of action accrued—Parents incapable of exercising adequate care or control over infant—Whether quality of care and control exercised by parents relevant in determining issue of custody—Limitation Act 1939, s 22(2)(b), (as amended by the Law Reform (Limitations of Actions, &c) Act 1954, s 2(2)). **Todd v Davison** [1971] **1** 994, HL.
Legitimated son—Right of action for personal injuries accruing to infant 18 years old, economically independent and free to live where he chose but residing with parents—Father declining to apply for legal aid to act as next friend—Writ issued more than three years after right of action accrued, plaintiff having attained 21—Whether plaintiff was in the custody of a parent at the time of the accident—Limitation Act 1939, s 22(2)(b)—Law Reform (Limitation of Actions, &c) Act 1954, s 2(2). **Brook v Hoar** [1967] **3** 395, QBD.
Extension of limitation period in case of disability—
Person who is an infant or lacks capacity—Infant claimant with subsequent mental illness—Whether time beginning to run when infant claimant attaining his majority regardless of whether he was under other disability at that date—Whether lack of capacity to be determined under statutory test applicable at date proceedings commenced or test at date cause of action accrued—Limitation Act 1980, ss 28(1), 38. **Seaton v Seddon** [2013] **1** 29, Ch D.
Trespass to the person—
Extension of limitation period. *See* Trespass to the person—Period of limitation—Extension—Person under disability, *below*.
Pleading—
Amendment—
Leave to amend after expiry of limitation period. *See* **Pleading** (Amendment—Leave to amend after expiry of limitation period).
Statute. *See* Statute—Pleading, *below*.

LIMITATION OF ACTION (cont)—
    Possession—
        Land. *See* Land—Adverse possession, *above*.
    Postponement of limitation period—
        Action for breach of contract and duty—
            Deliberate concealment of relevant facts—Plaintiffs issuing proceedings outside statutory six-year limitation period—Plaintiffs alleging that defendants had deliberately concealed facts relevant to their right of action—Concealment occurring after plaintiffs' cause of action arose—Whether running of limitation period postponed—Whether later concealment capable of defeating time bar—Limitation Act 1980, s 32(1)(b). **Sheldon v R H M Outhwaite (Underwriting Agencies) Ltd** [1994] **4** 481, QBD and CA; [1995] **2** 558, HL.
        Action for relief from consequences of mistake—
            Bank seeking recovery of payments made to local authorities under swap agreements—Whether bank's claim time-barred—Whether 'mistakes' including mistake of law—Limitation Act 1980, s 32(1)(c). **Kleinwort Benson Ltd v Lincoln City Council** [1998] **4** 513, HL.
            Claim for account—Underpayment of money due under contract—Whether 'action for relief from consequences of a mistake'—Limitation Act 1939, s 26(c). **Phillips-Higgins v Harper** [1954] **2** 51, CA.
            Mistake of law—Claims for repayment of tax—Whether 'mistake' including mistake of law—When time begins to run—When mistake of law discoverable—Limitation Act 1980, s 32(1)(c). **Test Claimants in the Franked Investment Income Group Litigation v Revenue and Customs Comrs** [2021] **1** 1001, SC.
            Plaintiff buying drawing believed to be original—Drawing discovered to be reproduction ten years after purchase—Whether plaintiff's claim for rescission time-barred—Whether plaintiff could 'with reasonable diligence' have discovered the mistake six years prior to institution of proceedings—Whether plaintiff obliged to have independent valuation of drawing soon after purchase—Whether plaintiff entitled to rely on reputation of defendants—Limitation Act 1980, s 32(1)(e). **Peco Arts Inc v Hazlitt Gallery Ltd** [1983] **3** 193, QBD.
        Fraud. *See* Concealment of right of action by fraud, *above*.
    Proceeding against Crown—
        Revival of cause of action—
            Cause of action statute barred before commencement of Crown Proceedings Act 1947—Whether cause of action revived by Crown Proceedings Act 1947, s 1. **Benson v Home Office** [1949] **1** 48, KBD.
    Public authority—
        Generally. *See* **Public authority** (Limitation of action).
        Harbour board—
            Singapore. *See* **Singapore** (Public authority—Limitation of action—Harbour board).
        Public utility undertaking. *See* **Public utility undertaking** (Limitation of action).
    Recovery of land. *See* Land—Recovery, *above*.
    Recovery of rent—
        Evacuation area. *See* **Emergency legislation** (Evacuation area—Recovery of rent—Limitation of action).
    Registered land—
        Overriding interest. *See* **Land registration** (Overriding interest).
    Restitution—
        Money paid under mistake of law. *See* **Mistake** (Mistake of law—Money paid under mistake of law).
    Revival of cause of action—
        Part payment. *See* Part payment, *above*.
        Proceeding against Crown. *See* Proceeding against Crown—Revival of cause of action, *above*.
    Salvage—
        Shipping. *See* **Shipping** (Salvage—Right to claim salvage—Limitation).
    Sea-bed—
        Recovery. *See* Land—Recovery—Sea-bed, *above*.
        Salvage. *See* **Shipping** (Salvage—Right to claim salvage—Limitation).
    Set-off or counterclaim—
        Acknowledgment of debt—
            Need to establish admission by debtor of legal liability to pay what creditor seeking to recover—Denial of liability on ground of set-off or cross-claim. *See* Acknowledgment—Debt—Acknowledgment of a claim—Need to establish admission by debtor of legal liability to pay amount creditor seeking to recover—Denial of liability on ground of set-off or cross-claim, *above*.
        Set-off or counterclaim deemed to be subject of separate action—
            Cross-claim arising out of same transaction as claim—Cross-claim in respect of damage other than that resulting in reduction of value of goods sold or work done—Whether cross-claim a defence to action for price or other remuneration—Whether cross-claim a set-off or counterclaim deemed to be the subject of a separate action—Limitation Act 1939, s 28. **Henriksens Rederi A/S v PHZ Rolimpex** [1973] **3** 589, CA.
    Setting aside—
        Order for extension of time. *See* Extension of time limit, *above*.
    Shipping—
        Bill of lading. *See* **Shipping** (Bill of lading—Time for bringing claims).
        Carriage of passengers by sea. *See* **Shipping** (Passengers—Carriage by sea—Limitation of action).
        Claim for freight—
            Cross-claim—Limitation period for cross-claim. *See* **Shipping** (Freight—Claim for freight—Defence—Cross-claim—Limitation period for cross-claim).
        Collision. *See* **Shipping** (Collision—Limitation of action).
        Limitation of liability. *See* **Shipping** (Limitation of liability).
        Loss of or damage to cargo. *See* **Shipping** (Cargo—Loss or damage—Limitation of action).
    Signature—
        Acknowledgment in writing. *See* Acknowledgment—Acknowledgment in writing—Signature, *above*.
    Specialty—
        Right of action conferred by statute—
            Period of limitation. *See* Action—Action on statute—Action based on Consumer Credit Act 1974—Action on specialty—Appropriate period of limitation, *above*.

LIMITATION OF ACTION (cont)—
  Specialty (cont)—
    Right of action conferred by statute (cont)—
      Period of limitation—Civil Procedure Act 1833, s 3. **Pratt v Cook & Co (St Paul's) Ltd** [1940] **1** 410, HL.
  Statement of claim—
    Amendment. *See* **Statement of case** (Amendment—Limitation of action).
    Cause of action accruing before statutory period—
      Possibility plaintiff pleading exceptions to statute. *See* **Statement of case** (Striking out—Limitation period—Statement of claim showing cause of action accruing before statutory period).
  Statute—
    Amendment—
      Construction—Extension of limitation period—Cause of action time-barred before amendment—Cause of action within limitation period if amendment retrospective—Whether amendment retrospective—Whether classification of amending statute as procedural or substantive relevant to retrospectivity—Whether cause of action revived by amending statute—Public Authorities Protection Ordinance 1948 (Malaysia), s 2(a)—Public Authorities Protection (Amendment) Act 1974 (Malaysia). **Yew Bon Tew v Kenderaan Bas Mara** [1982] **3** 833, PC.
    Pleading—
      Limitation period under Limitation Act 1623, expiring in 1938—Whether Limitation Act 1939, should be pleaded in action after 1939. **Rhyl UDC v Rhyl Amusements Ltd** [1959] **1** 257, Ch D.
  Substitution of parties after expiry of limitation period. *See* **Practice** (Parties—Substitution—Substitution after expiry of limitation period).
  Sum recoverable by virtue of an enactment—
    Specialty—
      Action on statute—Whether period of limitation six years or 12 years—Limitation Act 1939, s 2(1)(d)(3). **Central Electricity Generating Board v Halifax Corp** [1962] **3** 915, HL.
  Time—
    When time begins to run. *See* When time begins to run, *below*.
  Time limit—
    Extension of. *See* Extension of time limit, *above*.
  Title to land—
    Acknowledgment. *See* Acknowledgment—Title to land, *above*.
  Tort—
    Actions founded on—
      Estate of deceased person against. *See* Action—Tort, in, against estates of deceased persons, *above*.
      Generally. *See* When time begins to run—Actions in tort, *below*.
    Shipping—
      Loss or damage to cargo. *See* **Shipping** (Cargo—Loss or damage—Limitation of action).
  Trade description. *See* **Trade description** (False trade description—Time limit for prosecutions).
  Transaction at undervalue—
    Concealment of right of action. *See* Concealment of right of action, *above*.
  Trespass to the person—
    Period of limitation—
      Causes of action pleaded in negligence and alternatively in trespass—Whether claim in trespass was an action for 'breach of duty' for which limitation period reduced to three years by Law Reform (Limitation of Actions, &c) Act 1954, s 2(1). **Letang v Cooper** [1964] **2** 929, CA.
      Extension—Actions alleging sexual offences—Claimants bringing actions long after the events—Whether claims actions for negligence, nuisance or breach of duty—Whether court should exercise discretion to disapply limitation period—Limitation Act 1980, ss 11, 33. **A v Hoare and other appeals** [2008] **2** 1, HL.
      Extension—Person under disability—Action alleging indecent assault and rape during childhood—Plaintiff claiming damages for mental illness and psychological disturbance—Plaintiff bringing action more than six years after reaching majority but within three years of knowledge of psychological injury—Whether personal injury claim—Whether claim an action for breach of duty—Whether breach of duty including deliberate assault—Whether claim subject to six-year limitation period—Whether claim statute-barred—Limitation Act 1980, ss 2, 11, 14, 28. **Stubbings v Webb** [1993] **1** 322, HL.
      Intentional trespass causing personal injuries—Whether claim for trespass was an action for 'breach of duty' statute barred by lapse of three years—Limitation Act 1939, s 2(1)(a), (as amended by proviso added by Law Reform (Limitation of Actions, &c) Act 1954, s 2(1)). **Long v Hepworth** [1968] **3** 248, QBD.
  Tribunal—
    Competition Appeal Tribunal. *See* **Competition** (Competition Appeal Tribunal—Monetary claims before tribunal).
  Trover. *See* **Trover** (Limitation of action).
  Trust property—
    Breach of fiduciary duty to account—
      Plaintiff alleging under-accounting by defendants—Allegation forming basis of claims for breach of duty to account and fraud which were vulnerable to limitation defence—Plaintiff relying on same allegation to ground breach of fiduciary duty and constructive trust claims—Whether a simple duty to account could be a fiduciary duty—Whether equitable claims time-barred—Limitation Act 1980, s 5. **Coulthard v Disco Mix Club Ltd** [1999] **2** 457, Ch D.
      Plaintiff musician bringing action against business manager to account for income—Whether cause of action in contract or breach of fiduciary duty to recover property under constructive trust—Applicable limitation period—Limitation Act 1980, s 21(1)(b). **Nelson v Rye** [1996] **2** 186, Ch D.
    Charitable trust—
      Action by Attorney General for accounts to be taken of trust property—Action brought nearly 35 years after trust created—Whether there can be beneficiaries of public charitable trust with right to enforce trust—Whether Attorney General's claim statute-barred—Limitation Act 1980, s 21(3). **A-G v Cocke** [1988] **2** 391, Ch D.

LIMITATION OF ACTION (cont)—
  Trust property (cont)—
    Company—
      Proceedings for unlawful distribution in specie of shareholding in subsidiary company by directors in breach of fiduciary duty—Shareholding placed in legal and beneficial ownership of succession of corporate entities—Whether proceedings time-barred—Whether shareholding in possession of directors, or previously received by directors and converted to their use—Limitation Act 1980, s 21(1)(b). **Burnden Holdings (UK) Ltd (in liq) v Fielding** [2018] **2** 1083, SC.
    Fraud or fraudulent breach of trust to which trustee a party—
      Dishonest assistance—Whether normal primary period of limitation applying—Whether claims by beneficiaries time-barred—Limitation Act 1980, ss 21(1)(a), (3), 32. **Cattley v Pollard** [2007] **2** 1086, Ch D.
      Father vesting shares in children—Subsequent dealing with shares and proceeds of sale of shares for his own benefit. **Shephard v Cartwright** [1954] **3** 649, HL.
      Innocent trustees—Partnership—Whether innocent partners to be regarded as party or privy to dishonest partner's breaches of trust—Partnership Act 1890, ss 9-13—Limitation Act 1980, s 21. **Bishop of Leeds v Dixon Coles & Gill** [2022] **1 Comm** 1155, CA; [2022] **2** 1019, CA.
      Payment by trustee to innocent third party—Whether third party can rely on any period of limitation—When time begins to run in favour of third party—Limitation Act 1939, ss 19(1)(a)(2), 26(a)(b). **Baker (GL) Ltd v Medway Building & Supplies Ltd** [1958] **3** 540, CA.
    Occupation of trust property by trustee—
      Liability to account for rents and profits—Application of period of limitation—Limitation Act 1939, s 19(1)(b). **Howlett (decd), Re** [1949] **2** 490, Ch D.
    Trustee in bankruptcy—
      Knowledge of bankrupt's interest. *See* **Insolvency** (Bankruptcy—Bankrupt's estate—Matrimonial home—Transaction at undervalue).
  Unfair industrial practice—
    Complaint. *See* **Industrial relations** (Unfair industrial practice—Complaint—Time limit).
  Warrant—
    Distress—
      Arrears of rates—Application to issue warrant more than six years after demand. *See* **Action**—Proceeding in a court of law—Application to issue distress warrant in respect of arrears of general rates, *above*.
  When time begins to run—
    Accrual of cause of action—
      Fraud—Deceit—Whether time begins to run when claimant knew it had been defrauded without knowing the elements of the deceit it was alleging—Limitation Act 1980, s 32(1)(a). **Barnstaple Boat Co Ltd v Jones** [2008] **1** 1124, CA.
      Midnight deadline—Whether day following midnight deadline should be included or excluded in computation of limitation period—Limitation Act 1980, ss 2, 5, 21(3). **Matthew v Sedman** [2021] **4** 477, SC.
      Negligence—Damage—Accountants advising that company to be acquired by purchaser requiring injection of cash before profitability possible—Purchaser purchasing company and injecting substantially greater amounts of cash but company remaining insolvent—Purchaser alleging negligence by accountants—Whether claim statute-barred—Date of knowledge of purchaser that advice negligent—Limitation Act 1980, s 14A(8)(a). **Haward v Fawcetts (a firm)** [2006] **3** 497, HL.
      Negligence—Damage—Solicitor—Solicitors failing to advise leaseholder to obtain fire insurance and to name subtenant's parents as guarantors in underlease—Property destroyed by fire and subtenant defaulting on obligations—Leaseholder claiming damages for negligence against solicitors—Whether damage necessary for accrual of action occurring at time lease entered into or when fire and defaults taking place. **Elliott v Hattens (a firm)** [2022] **1** 635, CA.
      Plaintiffs obtaining order for addition of defendants—Plaintiffs serving defendants with writs not resealed and reissued—Plaintiffs obtaining ex parte order extending time for service and re-serving properly sealed and issued writs—Order made outside limitation period—Whether court allowing new claim outside limitation period—Whether action time-barred—Limitation Act 1980, s 35. **Bank of America National Trust and Savings Association v Chrismas** [1994] **1** 401, QBD.
      Whether cause of action against dissolved company accruing only on order restoring company to register—Companies Act 1985, s 651(1). **Smith v White Knight Laundry Ltd** [2001] **3** 862, CA.
    Action arising from contract for carriage of goods. *See* **Carriers** (Contract—Carriage of goods—Action arising out of carriage—Limitation period).
    Action for damages for breach of statutory duty—
      Accrual of cause of action—Crown breaching obligation under Community law in relation to domestic copyright law—Whether single cause of action commencing on date of breach of obligation—Limitation Act 1980, s 2—Council Directive (EEC) 92/100, art 8(2). **Phonographic Performance Ltd v Dept of Trade and Industry** [2005] **1** 369, Ch D.
      Accrual of cause of action—Crown breaching obligations under Community law in relation to domestic law—Personal injury—Claimants bringing proceedings against Crown for breach of statutory duty—Whether time running from date of personal injury—Limitation Act 1980, s 2—Council Directive (EEC) 84/5—Council Directive (EEC) 89/391. **Spencer v Secretary of State for Work and Pensions** [2009] **1** 314, CA.
      Accrual of cause of action—When serious harm suffered—Pneumoconiosis—Injury caused by acts outside statutory period—Injury first discovered within statutory period—Disablement within statutory period—Limitation Act 1939, s 2(1)(a). **Cartledge v E Jopling & Sons Ltd** [1963] **1** 341, HL.
      Injury caused by acts outside statutory period—Injury first discovered within statutory period—Limitation Act 1939, s 2(1)(a). **Archer v Catton & Co Ltd** [1954] **1** 896, Leeds Assizes.
      Plaintiff unaware of presence of serious disease—Writ issued six years after breach of statutory duty—Presence of disease not discovered until shortly before writ issued—Whether writ issued out of time—Limitation Act 1939, s 2(1)(a). **Cartledge v E Jopling & Sons Ltd** [1963] **1** 341, HL.
      Pneumoconiosis contracted by workman—Disease probably initially contracted through breaches of statutory duty outside period of limitation—Materially aggravated by breaches within period of limitation—Limitation Act 1939, s 2(1)(a). **Clarkson v Modern Foundries Ltd** [1958] **1** 33, Assizes.

LIMITATION OF ACTION (cont)—
  When time begins to run (cont)—
    Action for relief from consequences of mistake. *See* Postponement of limitation period—Action for relief from consequences of mistake, *above*.
    Action on marine insurance—
      Accrual of cause of action—Plaintiffs giving notice to insurers of abandonment of vessel as total constructive loss—Plaintiffs commencing action more than six years after date of casualty but less than six years after notice to insurers of abandonment as total constructive loss—Policies providing that vessel free from particular average—Whether policies precluding claim for partial loss—Whether policies precluding election of alternative remedies—Whether notice of abandonment essential part of cause of action—Whether cause of action accruing at date of casualty or notice of abandonment—Marine Insurance Act 1906, s 61. **Bank of America National Trust and Savings Association v Chrismas** [1994] **1** 401, QBD.
    Actions in tort—
      Accrual of cause of action—Negligence—Damage—Lapse of time between alleged negligent act and occurrence of damage—Action against surveyors in respect of survey report on building—Plaintiffs entering into lease of building in reliance on report—Defects in building developing after plaintiffs entered into lease—Whether limitation period running from date when plaintiffs acted on report or from date damage appearing. **Secretary of State for the Environment v Essex Goodman & Suggitt (a firm)** [1986] **2** 69, QBD.
      Accrual of cause of action—Negligence—Damage—Lapse of time between discovery of defect and damage to other property—Time when cause of action arises—Economic loss—Defendants supplying alloy tubing for use in plaintiffs' chemical production plant—Plaintiffs discovering cracks in pipe—Plaintiffs unable to discover cause of cracking despite reasonable investigation—Plaintiffs repairing and continuing to use pipe—Pipe exploding a year later causing physical damage to other property and economic loss to plaintiffs—Writ issued within six years of explosion but more than six years after discovery of cracks—Whether limitation period running from discovery of cracks or date of explosion—Whether damage caused by explosion irrecoverable economic loss. **Nitrigin Eireann Teoranta v Inco Alloys Ltd** [1992] **1** 854, QBD.
      Accrual of cause of action—Negligence—Damage—Lapse of time between negligent act and occurrence of damage—Action against architects in respect of negligent design and supervision of construction of buildings—Buildings completed outside limitation period—Damage occurring within limitation period—Whether buildings doomed from the start—Whether limitation period running from date when damage occurring or date when buildings completed. **Ketteman v Hansel Properties Ltd** [1988] **1** 38, HL; **London Congregational Union Inc v Harriss & Harriss (a firm)** [1988] **1** 15, CA.
      Accrual of cause of action—Negligence—Damage—Lapse of time between negligent act and occurrence of damage—Action against architects in respect of negligent supervision of the fixing of stone mullions to facade of building—Cracks occurring within six years before action brought—Inevitability of damage at date of erection of mullions—Whether mullions doomed from the start—Whether limitation period running from date when damage occurred or date works completed. **Kensington and Chelsea and Westminster Area Health Authority v Wettern Composites Ltd** [1985] **1** 346, QBD.
      Accrual of cause of action—Negligence—Damage—Lapse of time between negligent act and occurrence of damage—Action against burglary prevention specialist for negligent installation of security door—Burglar forcing security door to gain entry—Writ issued more than six years after negligence work completed but less than six years after burglary—Whether limitation period running from date of completion or from date of burglary. **Dove v Banhams Patent Locks Ltd** [1983] **2** 833, QBD.
      Accrual of cause of action—Negligence—Damage—Lapse of time between negligent act and occurrence of damage—Action against consultant engineers in respect of negligent design of chimney—Cracks occurring in chimney more than six years before action brought—Writ issued within six years of date when cracks could reasonably have been discovered—Whether limitation period running from date when damage occurred or when damage could reasonably have been discovered—Limitation Act 1939, s 2(1)(a). **Pirelli General Cable Works Ltd v Oscar Faber & Partners (a firm)** [1983] **1** 65, HL.
      Accrual of cause of action—Negligence—Damage—Lapse of time between negligent act and occurrence of damage—Action against local authority for breach of duty to secure compliance with building byelaws—Construction of block of maisonettes—Block built on inadequate foundations—Consequent damage to structure occurring more than six years after first conveyance of maisonettes—Writ issued within six years of discovery of damage—Whether cause of action accrued on date of first conveyance or on date when damage occurred—Whether action 'brought after expiration of six years from the date on which the cause of action accrued'—Limitation Act 1939, s 2(1)(a). **Anns v Merton London Borough** [1977] **2** 492, HL.
      Accrual of cause of action—Negligence—Damage—Lapse of time between negligent act and occurrence of damage—Action against local authority for breach of duty to secure compliance with building byelaws—Construction of house—Authority approving house with defective foundations—Action brought by purchaser of house—Purchaser not discovering defective condition of house until three years after purchase—Damage occurring when purchaser discovered or ought reasonably to have discovered defect—Accrual of cause of action at that date—Writ issued by purchaser within six years of discovering cracks in brickwork due to defective foundations but more than six years after inspection and approval of house by local authority—Action not statute-barred—Limitation Act 1939, s 2(1)(a). **Sparham-Souter v Town and Country Developments (Essex) Ltd** [1976] **2** 65, CA.
      Accrual of cause of action—Negligence—Damage—Lapse of time between negligent act and occurrence of damage—Action against local authority for breach of duty to take reasonable care in considering and approving plans of house—Plans showing house to be constructed on raft foundations—Raft and foundations inadequate—Cracks appearing in brick work of house more than six years before action brought—Writ issued within six years of discovery of cause of cracks—Whether limitation period accruing from date when damage first appeared or when cause of cracks discovered—Limitation Act 1939, s 2(1)(a). **Dennis v Charnwood BC** [1982] **3** 486, CA.

LIMITATION OF ACTION (cont)—
When time begins to run (cont)—
Actions in tort (cont)—
Accrual of cause of action—Negligence—Damage—Lapse of time between negligent act and occurrence of damage—Action against local authority in respect of negligent approval of plans and failure to supervise construction of dwelling house—Subsidence and dampness occurring more than six years after construction of dwelling house—Whether limitation period running from date when dwelling house constructed or when damage occurring—Whether dwelling house 'doomed from the start'—Whether cause of action not accruing until condition of property giving rise to danger to health or safety of occupants. **Jones v Stroud DC** [1988] **1** 5, CA.

Accrual of cause of action—Negligence—Damage—Lapse of time between negligent act and occurrence of damage—Construction of house—Defective foundations—Wet rot subsequently developing—Action brought within six years of discovery of wet rot but more than six years after original sale with defective foundations—Whether period of limitation running from time of original sale or discovery of wet rot—Limitation Act 1939, s 2(1). **Higgins v Arfon BC** [1975] **2** 589, QBD.

Accrual of cause of action—Negligence—Solicitor. *See* Accrual of cause of action—Negligence—Solicitor, *above*.

Computation of limitation period—Exclusion of day of accident. **Seabridge v H Cox & Sons (Plant Hire) Ltd** [1968] **1** 570, CA.

Computation of limitation period—Whether day of event causing injuries excluded—Limitation Act 1939, s 2(1)—Law Reform (Limitation of Actions, etc) Act 1954, s 2(1). **Marren v Dawson Bentley & Co Ltd** [1961] **2** 270, Assizes; **Pritam Kaur (administratrix of Bikar Singh (decd)) v Russell (S) & Sons Ltd** [1973] **1** 617, CA.

Detinue—Date of accrual of action—Car stolen by unknown person—Discovery in hands of innocent purchaser for value—Action for recovery brought seven years after theft—Limitation Act 1939, ss 2(1), 3(1). **R B Policies at Lloyd's v Butler** [1949] **2** 226, KBD.

Contribution proceedings—
Claim for contribution following settlement—Building contract—Whether time running only from binding settlement agreement—Whether incomplete agreement or agreement in principle sufficient—Meaning of 'agreed'—Civil Liability (Contribution) Act 1978, s 1—Limitation Act 1980, s 10. **RG Carter Building Ltd v Kier Business Services Ltd (formerly Mouchel Business Services Ltd)** [2018] **4** 456, TCC; [2019] **1** Comm 150, TCC.

Claim for contribution not made within two years of judgment on liability but made within two years of judgment on quantum—Whether claim statute-barred—Civil Liability (Contribution) Act 1978—Limitation Act 1980, s 10. **Aer Lingus plc v Gildacroft Ltd** [2006] **2** 290, CA.

Indemnity. *See* Indemnity—Contribution proceedings, *above*.

Patient bringing action against surgeon—Parties settling proceedings and subsequently embodying settlement agreement in consent order—Surgeon bringing contribution proceedings in respect of liability to patient—Whether time running for limitation purposes from date of agreement or date of consent order—Civil Liability (Contribution) Act 1978—Limitation Act 1980, s 10. **Knight v Rochdale Healthcare NHS Trust** [2003] **4** 416, QBD.

Joint tortfeasors—
Contribution—Third party claim against driver—Claim not made within 12 months of negligent act but made within 12 months of judgment against defendant—Third party not liable for contribution—Law Reform (Married Women and Tortfeasors) Act 1935, s 6(1)(c)—Limitation Act 1939, s 21(1). **Merlihan v Pope (A C) Ltd & Hibbert** [1945] **2** 449, KDD.

Judgment—
Execution postponed—Ascertainment of debt in German court. *See* **Conflict of laws** (Foreign judgment—Enforcement—Limitation period—When time begins to run—Judgment subject to stay of execution—Final and conclusive judgment—German bankruptcy proceedings).

Patent—
Infringement. *See* **Patent** (Infringement—Accrual of cause of action).

Personal injury claim—
Claimant's knowledge—Date on which claimant first had knowledge that injury attributable to defendant's act or omission—Claims for personal injury following exposure to radiation during experimental explosions of thermonuclear devices—Whether claims time-barred—Nature of knowledge required—Limitation Act 1980, ss 11, 14. **AB v Ministry of Defence** [2012] **3** 673, SC.

Claimant's knowledge—Date on which claimant first had knowledge that injury attributable to defendant's act or omission—Knowledge claimant might reasonably have been expected to acquire—Relevant circumstances—Limitation Act 1980, s 11, 14(3). **London Strategic Health Authority v Whiston** [2010] **3** 452, CA.

Plaintiff's knowledge—Date of plaintiff's knowledge that injury was significant—When reasonable for plaintiff to have considered injury sufficiently serious to justify instituting proceedings—Plaintiff contracting pneumoconiosis first certified in 1959—In 1963 disability from disease assessed at 20 and plaintiff becoming aware that disease progressively worsening—Between 1963 and 1970 plaintiff aware that others claiming damages for pneumoconiosis against defendants—Plaintiff not bringing action until 1975 when disability assessed at 100 and no longer able to work—Plaintiff not bringing action earlier because he was employed and receiving pension and not in need of damages—Whether plaintiff must reasonably have considered more than three years prior to issue of writ that injury sufficiently serious to justify instituting proceedings—Limitation Act 1939, s 2A(4)(b)(7). **Buck v English Electric Co Ltd** [1978] **1** 271, QBD.

Plaintiff's knowledge—Date on which plaintiff first had knowledge that injury attributable to defendant's act or omission—Attributable—Plaintiff aware of broad failure by employer to provide safe working conditions—Plaintiff not knowing particular breaches of duty by employer—Whether time running from date when plaintiff became aware of employer's broad failure—Whether time not running until defendant's acts or omissions could be particularised—Limitation Act 1980, ss 11(4)(b), 14(1)(b)(3)(b). **Wilkinson v Ancliff (BLT) Ltd** [1986] **3** 427, CA.

LIMITATION OF ACTION (cont)—
When time begins to run (cont)—
Personal injury claim (cont)—
Plaintiff's knowledge—Plaintiff's knowledge of identity of defendant—Plaintiff employed by defendant company—Defendant one of several companies forming part of group—Statement of plaintiff's terms of employment and payslips referring only to group name and not identifying defendant—Plaintiff injured on 4 August 1976 but defendant's identity not discovered until 4 July 1979—Solicitor commencing action on 17 August 1979—Action commenced more than three years from date cause of action accrued—Whether action time-barred—Whether plaintiff knew or could reasonably have been expected to acquire knowledge of defendant's identity before 17 August 1976—Limitation Act 1939, s 2A(4)(b), (6)(c), (8). **Simpson v Norwest Holst Southern Ltd** [1980] **2** 471, CA.
Plaintiff's knowledge—Plaintiff's knowledge of identity of defendant—Solicitors failing to establish identity of defendant within limitation period—Whether action statute-barred—Whether plaintiff fixed with constructive knowledge which her solicitors ought to have acquired—Limitation Act 1980, s 14(3). **Henderson v Temple Pier Co Ltd** [1998] **3** 324, CA.
Plaintiff's knowledge—Second defendant tried for but acquitted of murder of plaintiff's daughter—Plaintiff having strong suspicions as to involvement of defendants in killing of daughter at time of second defendant's acquittal—First defendant not tried for murder of plaintiff's daughter—Plaintiff obtaining legal advice as to availability of civil claim against defendants more than six years later—Whether legal advice that civil proceedings could be brought against defendants, 'expert advice' without which plaintiff did not have knowledge of facts relevant to claim against defendants—Whether time running from when plaintiff realised that daughter's death attributable to defendants' acts—Whether time running from when plaintiff advised of availability of civil claim—Whether primary limitation period had expired—Limitation Act 1980, s 14(1). **Halford v Brookes** [1991] **3** 559, CA.
Transaction at undervalue—
Claim in relation to transaction at undervalue by trustee in bankruptcy—Whether time running from date of bankruptcy order—Insolvency Act 1986, s 423. **Hill v Spread Trustee Co Ltd** [2007] **1** 1106, CA.
Writ—
Amendment after expiry of limitation period. *See* **Writ** (Amendment—Amendment after expiry of limitation period).
Issued but not served. *See* **Writ** (Extension of validity).
Issued more than 12 months after death. *See* Fatal accident, *above*.

LIMITATION OF AUTHORITY
Agent. *See* **Agent** (Authority—Limitation of authority).

LIMITATION OF LIABILITY
Bailment for reward. *See* **Bailment** (Bailment for reward—Liability of bailee—Limitation of liability).
Bill of lading. *See* **Shipping** (Bill of lading—Limitation of liability).
Building contract—
Contractor—
Liability for loss or damage. *See* **Building contract** (Contractor—Liability for loss or damage—Limitation of liability).
Insurance in joint names, provision for. *See* **Building contract** (Contractor—Liability for loss or damage—Limitation of liability—Contract requiring employer to take out joint names insurance in respect of specified perils).
Liability for loss or damage—
Generally. *See* **Building contract** (Liability for loss or damage—Limitation of liability).
Sub-contractors—
Liability for loss or damage. *See* **Building contract** (Sub-contractors—Liability for loss or damage—Limitation of liability).
Taking-over certificate. *See* **Building contract** (Sub-contractors—Taking-over certificate—Limitation of liability).
Carrier—
Carriage by road. *See* **Carriers** (Limitation of liability).
Carriage by sea—
Damages for breach of contract. *See* **Shipping** (Carriage by sea—Damages for breach of contract—Loss of or damage to goods—Limitation of liability).
Carriage of goods by air—
Damage to baggage or cargo. *See* **Carriage by air** (Damage to baggage or cargo—Limitation of liability).
International carriage. *See* **Carriage by air** (Carriage of goods—International carriage—Limitation of carrier's liability).
Carriage of passengers by air—
Domestic carriage. *See* **Carriage by air** (Carriage of passengers—Domestic carriage—Limitation of carrier's liability).
International carriage. *See* **Carriage by air** (Carriage of passengers—International carriage—Limitation of carrier's liability).
Generally. *See* **Contract** (Limitation of liability).
Insurance—
Professional indemnity policy—
Solicitor. *See* **Insurance** (Liability insurance—Professional indemnity insurance—Solicitor—Limitation of liability).
Limitation clause—
Construction. *See* **Contract** (Construction—Limitation clause).
Magistrates—
Damages. *See* **Magistrates** (Civil liability—Limitation of damages).
Shipping. *See* **Shipping** (Limitation of liability).

LION
Damage caused by lion—
Liability of owner or keeper. *See* **Animal** (Dangerous animal—Damage—Liability—Lion).

LIQUIDATION
Company. *See* **Company** (Winding up).
Insurer—
Protection of policyholder. *See* **Insurance** (Protection of policyholders—Liquidation of insurer).

LIQUIDATOR
Company—
Compulsory winding up—
Generally. *See* **Company** (Compulsory winding up—Liquidator).
Priority of liquidator's fees before corporation tax. *See* **Company** (Compulsory winding up—Corporation tax on chargeable gains—Priority of liquidator's fees over tax).
Provisional liquidator. *See* **Company** (Compulsory winding up—Provisional liquidator).
Examination of officer of company. *See* **Company** (Compulsory winding up—Examination of officer of company etc).
Voluntary winding up. *See* **Company** (Voluntary winding up—Liquidator).
Winding up. *See* **Company** (Winding up—Liquidator).
Constructive trustee. *See* **Trust and trustee** (Constructive trust—Shares in company—Transfer by company in liquidation of shares in another company).
Generally. *See* **Insolvency** (Liquidator).
Insurance company—
Indemnity—
Protection of policyholders. *See* **Insurance** (Protection of policyholders—Liquidation of insurance company—Interim payments to policyholders—Indemnity to liquidator).
Trade—
Income tax. *See* **Income tax** (Trade—Liquidator).

LIQUOR LICENSING
See **Licensing**.

LIS ALIBI PENDENS
Admiralty proceedings. *See* **Admiralty** (Practice—Lis alibi pendens).

LIS PENDENS
Jurisdiction—
Conflict of laws. *See* **Conflict of laws** (Jurisdiction—Challenge to jurisdiction—Lis pendens).
Registration as land charge. *See* **Land charge** (Pending action—Registration).
Stay of proceedings—
Conflict of laws. *See* **Conflict of laws** (Stay of proceedings—Lis pendens).

LISTED BUILDING
Church—
Alterations—
Faculty. *See* **Ecclesiastical law** (Faculty—Alterations to church—Church listed as being of special architectural or historic interest).
Planning control. *See* **Town and country planning** (Building of special architectural or historic interest).
Rates—
Exemption. *See* **Rates** (Exemption—Listed building).
School chapel—
Jurisdiction of consistory court in respect of listed school chapel. *See* **Ecclesiastical law** (Faculty—Consecrated school chapel—Planning and listed building controls).

LISTS
Chancery Division—
Bankruptcy appeals—
Appeals to Divisional Court. *See* **Bankruptcy** (Appeal—Appeal from county court—Appeal to Divisional Court of Chancery Division—Practice—List of appeals to be heard during term).
Non-witness list. *See* **Practice** (Chancery Division—Non-witness list).
Revenue list. *See* **Practice** (Chancery Division—Revenue list).
Short causes list. *See* **Practice** (Chancery Division—Short Causes List).
Warned list. *See* **Practice** (Chancery Division—Warned List).
Witness list. *See* **Practice** (Chancery Division—Witness list).
Court of Appeal—
Generally. *See* **Court of Appeal** (Practice—Lists).
Queen's Bench Division—
Chambers proceedings. *See* **Practice** (Chambers proceedings—Queen's Bench Division—Lists).
Short cause list. *See* **Practice** (Trial—Lists—Short cause list).
Short summons list. *See* **Practice** (Summons—Hearing—Short summonses and applications—List).

LITERARY AND SCIENTIFIC INSTITUTION
Dissolution—
Application of funds on dissolution. *See* **Unincorporated association** (Dissolution—Application of funds on dissolution—Literary and scientific institution).

LITERARY EXECUTOR
See **Executor and administrator** (Executor—Literary executor).

LITERARY WORK
Copyright. *See* **Copyright** (Literary work).

LITIGANT

Privilege from arrest while attending court. *See* **Arrest** (Privilege from arrest—Persons attending court).

LITIGANT IN PERSON

Assistance—
Chambers proceedings. *See* **Practice** (Chambers proceedings—Party acting in person—Right to assistance).
Right to. *See* **Practice** (Trial—Party acting in person—Right to assistance).
Contempt of court—
Application for committal by litigant in person. *See* **Contempt of court** (Committal—Application—Litigant in person).
Costs—
County court. *See* **County court** (Costs—Jurisdiction—Litigant in person).
Taxation—
Generally. *See* **Costs** (Taxation—Litigant appearing in person).
Review of taxation—Jurisdiction. *See* **Costs** (Taxation—Review of taxation—Jurisdiction—Litigant in person).
Court of Appeal—
Right of audience. *See* **Court of Appeal** (Right of audience—Litigant in person).
Foreigner unable to speak or understand English—
Conduct of proceedings. *See* **Practice** (Conduct of proceedings—Language—Foreign litigant in person—Foreign litigant unable to speak or understand English).
McKenzie friend. *See* **Practice** (Trial—Party acting in person—Right to assistance—McKenzie friend).
Right of audience—
Application for certiorari. *See* **Certiorari** (Application—Right of audience—Litigant in person).
Vexatious proceedings. *See* **Vexatious proceedings** (Litigant in person).

LITIGATION SERVICES

Generally. *See* **Solicitor** (Costs—Conditional fee agreement—Litigation services).

LITTER

Depositing and leaving litter—
Offence. *See* **Criminal law** (Litter).

LIVERPOOL

Commercial List—
Practice. *See* **Practice** (Commercial cases—Northern Circuit).

LIVERPOOL COURT OF PASSAGE

Appeal from—
Provision of judge's note. *See* **Court of Appeal** (Judge's note—Practice—Appeal from Liverpool Court of Passage).
Trial of action by registrar by consent—
Whether appeal lies to Divisional Court or Court of Appeal. *See* **Court of Appeal** (Jurisdiction—Appeal from Liverpool Court of Passage).
Certiorari—
Removal of action—
Removal to High Court for trial—Discretion—Liverpool Corporation Act 1921, s 256. **R v Liverpool Court of Passage Registrar, ex p Braund (William) Ltd** [1965] **3** 693, QBD.

LIVESTOCK

Agriculture—
Pheasants—
Keeping and rearing of pheasants for sport. *See* **Rent restriction** (Agricultural worker—Agriculture—Livestock keeping—Animals kept for production of food—Keeping and rearing of pheasants for sport).
Buildings used for keeping or breeding livestock—
Rates—
Exemption. *See* **Rates** (Exemption—Agricultural buildings—Buildings used for keeping or breeding of livestock).

LIVING APART

Husband and wife—
Divorce. *See* **Divorce** (Separation).

LIVING ON EARNINGS OF PROSTITUTION

See **Criminal law** (Prostitution—Living on earnings of prostitution).

LLOYD'S

Insurance. *See* **Insurance** (Society of Lloyd's).
Jewellers' block policy. *See* **Insurance** (Contract of insurance—Construction of terms—Lloyd's jewellers' block policy).
Responsibilities of Society of Lloyd's—
Negotiation—
Implied contractual obligation. *See* **Contract** (Implied term—Duty to negotiate—Responsibilities of Society of Lloyd's).

LLOYD'S UNDERWRITING AGENT

Insurance—
Liability of agent. *See* **Insurance** (Underwriter—Liability—Lloyd's underwriting agent).
Negligence—
Duty to take care. *See* **Negligence** (Duty to take care—Insurance—Lloyd's underwriting agent).

LOAD LINE
See **Shipping** (Load line).

LOADING
Dock, in—
    Statutory regulation of. See **Dock** (Loading and unloading).
Load line. See **Shipping** (Load line).
Shipping. See **Shipping** (Loading).
Vehicle—
    Waiting and loading restrictions. See **Road traffic** (Waiting and loading restrictions).

LOAN
Agreement—
    Construction. See **Contract** (Construction—Loan agreement).
Bank. See **Bank** (Bank loan).
Banker / client relationship. See **Bank** (Banker/client relationship).
Company director, to. See **Company** (Director—Loan to director).
Constructive trust—
    Expenditure on property of another. See **Trust and trustee** (Constructive trust—Expenditure on property of another).
Delivery of gift by donor with intention that donee should receive as a gift—
    Donee receiving and keeping thing given—
        Donee intending to treat it merely as a loan—Relevance of intention of donee. See **Gift** (Acceptance—Intention of donor).
Employee—
    Income tax—
        Car loan scheme. See **Income tax** (Emoluments from office or employment—Benefits in kind—Car loan scheme).
Gaming—
    Loan for lawful gaming. See **Gaming** (Loan for lawful gaming).
Guarantee. See **Guarantee**.
Hire-purchase, by. See **Hire-purchase** (Refinancing arrangements).
Illegal loan—
    Enforceability of contract. See **Contract** (Illegality—Enforceability of contract—Loan).
Income tax—
    Car loan scheme. See **Income tax** (Emoluments from office or employment).
    Interest—
        Loan for purchase or improvement of land—Relief. See **Income tax** (Interest—Relief—Loan for purchase or improvement of land).
    Loan for purchase or improvement of land—
        Interest. See **Income tax** (Interest—Relief—Loan for purchase or improvement of land).
    Loan scheme for training of employee. See **Income tax** (Emoluments from office or employment—Reward for services—Loan scheme for course of training).
Interest—
    Income tax—
        Relief—Loan for purchase or improvement of land. See **Income tax** (Interest—Relief—Loan for purchase or improvement of land).
Loan agreement—
    Conflict of laws. See **Conflict of laws** (Contract—Proper law of contract—Loan agreement).
    Construction. See **Contract** (Construction—Loan agreement).
Loan capital—
    Stamp duty. See **Stamp duty** (Issue of loan capital).
Loan facility—
    Joint venture agreement. See **Contract** (Construction—Joint venture agreement—Loan facility).
Loan Market Association (LMA) standard terms—
    Construction. See **Contract** (Construction—Loan Market Association (LMA) standard terms).
Moneylender. See **Moneylender**.
Mortgage. See **Mortgage**.
Nature of transaction. See **Money** (Loan—Nature of transaction).
Priority—
    Equitable interest. See **Equity** (Equitable interest—Loan).
Recovery—
    Loan secured by mortgage—
        High Court—Action triable as commercial action or mortgage action. See **Court** (Jurisdiction—High Court of Justice—Divisions of High Court—Action triable as commercial action or mortgage action).
Repayment of loan index-linked to foreign currency. See **Money** (Loan—Repayment of loan index-linked to foreign currency).
Servant—
    Vicarious liability. See **Vicarious liability** (Loan of servant).
Student—
    Higher education. See **Education** (Higher education—Student loans).

LOCAL AUTHORITY
Accommodation—
    Caravan site, on. See Caravan sites, *below*.
    Community care services. See **Community care services** (Assessment of needs—Duty of local authorities to provide accommodation).
    Duty to provide accommodation—
        Enforcement. See Statutory duty—Enforcement—Accommodation, *below*.
    Generally. See **Housing**.
    Provision of accommodation for children. See Statutory powers—Children—Provision of accommodation for children, *below*.

412

LOCAL AUTHORITY (cont)—
   Accounts—
      Audit. *See* **Local government** (Audit).
      Inspection. *See* **Local government** (Documents—Inspection—Accounts of local authority).
   Action—
      Action against local authority—
         Action by ratepayer against local authority—Ratepayer's locus standi-Ratepayer bringing action in own name against local authority—Whether Attorney General's consent to relator proceedings necessary. **Barrs v Bethell** [1982] **1** 106, Ch D.
      Action by local authority—
         Reasonableness—Local authority resolving to institute proceedings to obtain removal of unauthorised caravans—Local authority not issuing writ until public inquiry completed—Whether reasonableness of local authority's decision to institute proceedings to be determined as at date of resolution or date of issue of writ. **Waverley BC v Hilden** [1988] **1** 807, Ch D.
      Charity—
         Locus standi to sue for declaration of charitable trust. *See* **Practice** (Parties—Proceedings relating to charities—Local authority).
      Competence to bring in own name. *See* **Practice** (Parties—Local authority).
      Practice. *See* **Practice** (Local authority).
      Right of action. *See* Right of action, *below*.
   Adoption proceedings—
      Production of records and giving of evidence. *See* **Adoption** (Practice—Production of records and giving of evidence by adoption society or local authority).
   Advances—
      Purchase of small dwellings, for. *See* **Housing** (Small dwellings—Purchase of house by means of advance by local authority).
   After-care services—
      Mental health patient. *See* **Mental health** (Patient—After-care services).
   Age assessment—
      Judicial review. *See* Statutory powers—Children—Provision of accommodation for children in need—Person seeking asylum stating himself to be under age of 18 years, *below*.
   Alteration of area. *See* **Local government** (Alteration of area).
   Amusements with prizes—
      Permit. *See* **Gaming** (Amusements with prizes—Permit for provision of amusements with prizes).
   Animal—
      Importation of animal by air—
         Charges for use of local authority's quarantine station at airport. *See* **Animal** (Importation of animal—Quarantine—Provision by local authority of quarantine station).
   Appeal to quarter sessions—
      Right of person aggrieved by order of court of summary jurisdiction—
         Appeal against local authority restrictions allowed by justices—Local authority ordered to pay costs—Right of council to appeal to quarter sessions against costs order—Whether 'Person aggrieved'—Public Health Act 1936, s 301—Nurseries and Child-Minders Regulation Act 1948, s 6(4). **R v Surrey Quarter Sessions Appeal Committee, ex p Lilley** [1951] **2** 659, KBD.
   Appointment of committee—
      Delegation of functions to committee—
         Committee—Committee of one—Local authority delegating enforcement proceedings to chairman of planning committee—Whether local authority able to delegate functions to single councillor—Whether committee of one constituting a 'committee'—Local Government Act 1972, s 101(1). **R v Secretary of State for the Environment, ex p Hillingdon London BC** [1986] **2** 273, CA.
         Extent of delegation—Member appointed for one year—Membership revoked by local authority before expiration of year—Whether local authority having power to revoke membership—Local Government Act 1933, s 85. **Manton v Brighton Corp** [1951] **2** 101, KBD.
   Assumption of parental rights—
      Child in care—
         Resumption of care by parent. *See* **Child** (Care—Resumption of care by parent—Resolution assuming parental rights).
   Audit. *See* **Local government** (Audit).
   Boundary. *See* **Local government** (Alteration of area).
   Building control—
      Prosecution by local authority for failure to obtain building licence. *See* **Building control** (Building licence—Failure to obtain—Prosecution by local authority).
   Caravan sites—
      Provision of caravan sites—
         Duty of local authority—Duty to provide accommodation for gipsies—Definition of 'gipsies'—Question of whether particular persons 'gipsies' being a matter for the relevant local authority—Whether local authority's decision open to challenge—Caravan Sites Act 1968, s 16. **R v South Hams DC, ex p Gibb** [1994] **4** 1012, CA.
         Duty of local authority—Duty to provide accommodation for gipsies—Gipsies occupying caravans on site seasonally as main or only residence—Whether sites 'protected sites'—Whether occupants entitled to security of tenure—Caravan Sites Act 1968, s 6—Mobile Homes Act 1983, s 5(1). **Greenwich London BC v Powell** [1989] **1** 65, HL.
         Duty of local authority—Duty to provide adequate accommodation for gipsies 'resorting to' its area—Caravan Sites Act 1968, s 6(1). **West Glamorgan CC v Rafferty** [1987] **1** 1005, CA.
         Duty of local authority—Judicial review of authority's decision—Authority in breach of duty to provide caravan sites—Authority deciding to evict gipsies from site required for redevelopment—Whether authority giving sufficient weight to its own breach of duty and consequences thereof—Whether decision to evict void for unreasonableness—Caravan Sites Act 1968, s 6. **West Glamorgan CC v Rafferty** [1987] **1** 1005, CA.

LOCAL AUTHORITY (cont)—
  Caravan sites (cont)—
    Provision of caravan sites (cont)—
      Duty of local authority—Judicial review of authority's decision—Authority providing site in accordance with duty—Site provided proving unsuitable for human habitation—Authority deciding to cease to provide site and not providing alternative site—Secretary of State refusing to direct authority to comply with duty to provide site—Whether gipsy living on existing site having sufficient interest to apply for judicial review of local authority's and Secretary of State's decisions—Whether relevant that authority's area designated as area in which unauthorised camping prohibited—Whether court should grant relief—Caravan Sites Act 1968, ss 6(1), 9, 12(1)—Supreme Court Act 1981, s 31(3)—RSC Ord 53, r 3(7). **R v Secretary of State for the Environment, ex p Ward** [1984] 2 556, QBD.
  Caravans—
    Permission to place on land. *See* **Public health** (Movable dwellings).
    Sites for. *See* Caravan sites, *above*.
  Censorship—
    Films. *See* **Cinema** (Censorship—Local authority).
  Certiorari—
    Jurisdiction. *See* **Certiorari** (Jurisdiction—Local authority).
  Child—
    Accommodation. *See* Statutory powers—Children—Provision of accommodation for children, *below*.
    Care. *See* **Child** (Care—Local authority).
    Care order. *See* **Family proceedings** (Orders in family proceedings—Care order).
    Child abuse register. *See* **Child** (Child abuse—Child abuse register—Register maintained by local authority).
    Child in need—
      Provision of services for. *See* Statutory powers—Children—Provision of services for children in need, *below*.
    Child-minder—
      Registration. *See* **Child** (Registration of child-minders).
    Detention of child in place of safety. *See* **Children and young persons** (Detention—Place of safety order).
    Looked after child. *See* **Child** (Care—Local authority—Looked after child).
    Negligence—
      Existence of duty of care. *See* **Negligence** (Duty to take care—Existence of duty—Children).
    Statutory powers. *See* Statutory powers—Children, *below*.
    Welfare. *See* **Child** (Welfare—Local authority).
  Committee—
    Appointment. *See* Appointment of committee, *above*.
    Meeting—
      Voting. *See* **Local government** (Meeting—Voting—Committee meetings).
    Membership of. *See* **Local government** (Councillor—Membership of council committee).
  Common lodging-house—
    Registration. *See* **Public health** (Common lodging-house—Registration).
  Communications between departments—
    Privilege—
      Disclosure of documents. *See* **Disclosure and inspection of documents** (Privilege—Local authority).
  Community care services. *See* **Community care services**.
  Community charge. *See* **Local government** (Community charge).
  Compensation—
    Acquisition of land by local authority—
      Displacement from land. *See* **Compensation** (Displacement from land—Home loss payment—Displacement from dwelling—Land acquired by local authority and held by authority for purpose for which it was acquired).
    Compensation order—
      Offence committed by child in care. *See* **Sentence** (Compensation—Parent or guardian's liability—Local authority as guardian).
  Compulsory acquisition of land—
    Generally. *See* **Compulsory purchase**.
    Housing. *See* **Housing** (Compulsory purchase).
  Consultation. *See* **Natural justice** (Duty to act fairly—Consultation).
  Contract—
    Accordance with standing orders—
      Duty to make contract in accordance with standing orders—Local Government Act 1933, s 266(2). **R v Hereford Corp, ex p Harrower** [1970] 3 460, QBD.
      Non-compliance with standing orders—Local authority—Contract—Accordance with standing orders—Non-compliance with standing orders—Validation of non-compliance with standing orders if contract otherwise valid—Council clerk agreeing to amend terms of contract—Clerk having no authority to agree amendment—Contract sealed but not in accordance with council's standing orders—Whether contract 'otherwise valid'—Whether clerk's lack of authority resulting in void contract which was unable to be subsequently validated—Local Government Act 1933, s 266(2). **North West Leicestershire DC v East Midlands Housing Association Ltd** [1981] 3 364, CA.
    Seal—
      Necessity for seal—Agent signing contract in writing—Law of Property Act 1925, s 74(2)—Local Government Act 1933, s 266(2). **Wright (A R) & Son Ltd v Romford Corp** [1956] 3 785, QBD.
  Corruption of officer or employee. *See* **Criminal law** (Corruption).
  Costs—
    Proceedings against local authority—
      Jurisdiction—Magistrates. *See* **Costs** (Order for costs—Jurisdiction—Magistrates—Order against local authority).
      Statutory nuisance. *See* **Nuisance** (Statutory nuisance—Complaint to justices—Proceedings against local authority—Costs).
  Council tax. *See* **Local government** (Council tax).

LOCAL AUTHORITY (cont)—
  Crowd control—
    Premises open to public—
      Danger from rush of people—Duty to institute crowd control. *See* **Negligence** (Duty to take care—Premises open to public—Danger from rush of people—Duty to institute crowd control—Local authority).
  Damages—
    Exemplary damages—
      Oppressive, arbitrary or unconstitutional act in exercise of public powers. *See* **Damages** (Exemplary damages—Oppressive, arbitrary or unconstitutional act in exercise of public powers).
  Decision of local authority—
    Validity—
      Challenge to validity by way of application for judicial review. *See* **Judicial review** (Challenge to validity of public authority's decision).
  Delegation of functions to committee. *See* Appointment of committee—Delegation of functions to committee, *above*.
  Disabled persons—
    Provision of care—
      Local authority developing support plan for profoundly disabled person—Local authority providing payment for disabled person to obtain services—Local authority failing to provide explanation for basis of calculation of payment—Whether assessment of payment unlawful for want of explanatory reasons—Whether assessment irrational—Chronically Sick and Disabled Persons Act 1970, s 2—National Assistance Act 1948, s 29—Community Care, Services for Carers and Children's Services (Direct Payments) (England) Regulations 2009, SI 2009/1887. **R (on the application of KM) (by his mother and litigation friend JM) v Cambridgeshire CC** [2012] 3 1218, SC.
  Discovery—
    Powers—
      Canada. *See* **Canada** (Local government—Local authority—Powers of discovery).
  Discretion—
    Exercise—
      Fetter—Whether local authority entitled to have fixed policy on how it will exercise discretion conferred on it. **R v Rochdale Metropolitan BC, ex p Cromer Ring Mill Ltd** [1982] 3 761, QBD.
  Disqualification for office as member of local authority—
    Office in gift or disposal of local authority—
      Assistant schoolmaster—Local Government Act 1933, s 59(1)(a). **Lamb v Jeffries** [1956] **1** 317, QBD.
      Head teacher—Appointments to office of head teacher to be made by joint committee of which half the members were appointed by the local authority—Local Government Act 1933, s 59(1)(a). **Boyd v Easington RDC** [1963] 3 747, Ch D.
  Documents—
    Generally. *See* **Local government** (Documents).
    Local education authority. *See* **Education** (Local education authority—Documents).
  Education—
    Duty of local education authority to secure provision in area of sufficient schools. *See* **Education** (School—Duty of local education authority to secure provision in area of sufficient schools).
    Generally. *See* **Education** (Local education authority).
  Entertainment licence—
    Condition—
      Severability. *See* **Public authority** (Statutory powers—Licence granted under statutory power—Condition—Severability).
  Expenses. *See* **Local government** (Expenses).
  Facilities for disabled persons—
    Structures—
      Rating relief—Structures of a similar kind to those provided by authority. *See* **Rates** (Structures supplied for use of invalids, disabled or handicapped persons—Structure supplied for use of person in pursuance of arrangements for after-care of any person suffering from illness—Structure of a kind similar to structures which could be provided by local authority or voluntary organisation).
  Financial transactions—
    Power to enter financial transactions—
      Interest rate swap transactions. *See* Statutory powers—Implied power—Implied power used for improper purpose—Interest rate swap transactions, *below*.
  Gift of property—
    Power to accept—
      Charitable trust—Eleemosynary charity. *See* **Charity** (Charitable trust—Eleemosynary charity—Local authority).
  Gipsies—
    Caravan site—
      Duty of local authority to provide site. *See* Caravan sites—Provision of caravan sites—Duty of local authority, *above*.
  Greater London Council—
    Statutory powers—
      Excessive exercise of statutory powers. *See* **Public authority** (Statutory powers—Excessive exercise of statutory powers—Greater London Council).
  Guardianship of minors—
    Compensation order—
      Liability of local authority to pay compensation. *See* **Sentence** (Compensation—Parent or guardian's liability—Local authority as guardian).
    Evidence. *See* **Minor** (Guardianship—Evidence—Production of records and giving of evidence by adoption society or local authority).

LOCAL AUTHORITY (cont)—
Hackney carriage—
  Grant of licence—
    Duty to act fairly. *See* **Road traffic** (Hackney carriage—Licence—Grant of licence—Natural justice—Duty of licensing authority to act fairly).
Health authority—
  National Health Service. *See* **National Health Service** (Health authority).
Highway and bridge authority—
  Notification of abnormal indivisible load. *See* **Road traffic** (Heavy motor car—Abnormal indivisible load—Notification to highway and bridge authority).
Highway authority—
  Duty to assert and protect rights of public to use and enjoy highway. *See* **Highway** (Protection of public rights—Highway authority's duty to assert and protect rights of public to use and enjoy highway).
  Generally. *See* **Highway** (Highway authority).
  Negligence—
    Generally. *See* **Negligence** (Highway).
Homeless persons—
  Housing. *See* **Housing** (Homeless person).
Hospitals vested in local authority—
  Transfer to Minister of Health. *See* **National Health Service** (Transfer of hospital to Minister—All hospitals vested in local authority).
Housing—
  Generally. *See* **Housing**.
  Housing assistance. *See* **Housing** (Local authority—Housing assistance).
  Housing benefit. *See* **Social security** (Housing benefit).
  Tenant's right to buy. *See* **Housing** (Local authority houses—Tenant's right to buy).
Improvement grants. *See* **Housing** (Improvement grant).
Income tax—
  Annual payment—
    Deduction of tax. *See* **Income tax** (Annual payment—Deduction of tax—Local authority).
  Interest on loan—
    Deduction in computing profits. *See* **Income tax** (Deduction in computing profits—Local authority—Interest on loans on security of general rate fund).
Injunction—
  Inability of authority to comply with injunction. *See* **Injunction** (Compliance outside defendant's control—Local authority).
Interest on loan—
  Income tax—
    Deduction in computing profits. *See* **Income tax** (Deduction in computing profits—Local authority—Interest on loans on security of general rate fund).
Judicial review—
  Lease of premises. *See* **Judicial review** (Application for judicial review—Amenability to judicial review—Local authority refusing to renew solicitor's lease for office premises).
Land—
  Common land—
    Land acquired for purposes of 'benefit, improvement or development' of area—Authority banning hunting on land on ethical grounds—Whether ban valid—Whether ban a lawful exercise of authority's powers to manage land—Whether authority having regard to relevant considerations—Whether authority entitled to rely solely on ethical grounds—Local Government Act 1972, s 120(1)(b). **R v Somerset CC, ex p Fewings** [1995] **3** 20, CA.
  Development—
    Permission for development. *See* **Town and country planning** (Permission for development).
  Disposal of land—
    Power to demise land—Duty to obtain best consideration—Lessor of local authority land covenanting to use best endeavours to employ specified number of employees—Whether job creation relevant to local authority's obligation to obtain best consideration—Local Government Act 1972, s 123. **R v Pembrokeshire CC, ex p Coker** [1999] **4** 1007, QBD.
  Housing—
    Right to respect for private and family life—Local authority granting licence to gipsies to occupy caravan site—Local authority seeking possession—Special statutory regime—Whether breach of right to respect for private and family life—Whether statutory regime incompatible with convention right—Whether authority's decision challengeable on reasonableness grounds—Caravan Sites and Control of Development Act 1960—Caravan Sites Act 1968, s 4(6)—Mobile Homes Act 1983, s 5(1)—Human Rights Act 1998, s 3(1), Sch 1, Pt I, art 8. **Doherty v Birmingham City Council** [2009] **1** 653, HL.
    Right to respect for private and family life—Right to fair trial—Possession order—Prohibition of eviction without due process of law—Local authority seeking possession from occupier of premises let as dwelling after termination of secure tenancy—Occupier seeking to rely on personal circumstances and proportionality—Whether statutory regime compatible with convention rights—Protection from Eviction Act 1977, s 3—Human Rights Act 1998, Sch 1, Pt I, arts 6, 8. **R (on the application of Coombes) v Secretary of State for Communities and Local Government** [2010] **2** 940, QBD.
    Right to respect for private and family life—Tenants of housing trust occupying properties owned by local authority and leased to housing trust—Gipsies occupying local authority land without licence or consent—Local authorities seeking possession orders—Whether breach of right to respect for private and family life—Human Rights Act 1998, s 2, Sch 1, Pt I, art 8. **Lambeth London BC v Kay** [2006] **4** 128, HL.
    Right to respect for private and family life—Tenants of housing trust occupying properties owned by local authority and leased to housing trust—Lease to housing trust ending—Local authority seeking possession orders—Whether breach of right to respect for private and family life—Whether authority required to have regard to personal circumstances of occupiers—Human Rights Act 1998, Sch 1, Pt I, art 8. **Central Bedfordshire Council (formerly Bedfordshire CC) v Taylor (Secretary of State for Communities and Local Government, intervening)** [2010] **1** 516, CA.

LOCAL AUTHORITY (cont)—
  Land (cont)—
    Open space—
      Disposal—Trust to administer open space for enjoyment of public—Power to sell open space—Open Spaces Act 1906, s 10—Local Government Act 1933, ss 165, 179. **Laverstock Property Co Ltd v Peterborough Corp** [1972] 3 678, Ch D.
      Power to appropriate. See Land—Power to appropriate land—Land forming part of common, open space or fuel or field garden allotment, *below*.
    Power to appropriate land—
      Authorisation—Procedure—Common. See **Compulsory purchase** (Authorisation—Procedure—Common).
      Exercise of power—Consent of Minister—Land acquired by authority in exercise (directly or indirectly) of compulsory powers—Acquisition of land for purposes of airfield—Authority prepared to acquire land compulsorily if necessary—Compulsory purchase order made but not confirmed—Agreement with owner for purchase of land instead—Authority subsequently resolving to appropriate land for other purposes—Whether land having been acquired in the exercise (directly or indirectly) of compulsory powers—Whether consent of Minister to subsequent appropriation necessary—Town and Country Planning Act 1959, ss 23(2)(b), 30(5). **Dowty Boulton Paul Ltd v Wolverhampton Corp (No 2)** [1973] 2 491, CA.
      Exercise of power—Local authority appropriating by resolutions under power to acquire land immediately for planning purposes—Whether planning purpose required to be implemented immediately—Whether resolutions invalid if planning purpose not implemented immediately—Town and Country Planning Act 1971, s 112(1). **Thames Water Authority v Elmbridge BC** [1983] 1 836, CA.
      Land forming part of common, open space or fuel or field garden allotment—Claimant seeking judicial review of inspector's decision refusing registration of land as town or village green—Whether appropriation of land to open space could be inferred—Whether relevant considerations as to implied licence being considered—Local Government Act 1972, s 122. **R (on the application of Goodman) v Secretary of State for Environment, Food and Rural Affairs** [2016] 2 701, QBD.
      Land forming part of common, open space or fuel or field garden allotment—Open space—Appropriation for planning purposes—Land held by authority on trust as open space—Land having been built on—Land de facto having ceased to be open space—Whether power exercisable if land held for purposes of an open space—Town and Country Planning Act 1971, s 121(1). **Third Greytown Properties Ltd v Peterborough Corp** [1973] 3 731, Ch D.
      Land no longer required for purpose for which acquired—Decision of local authority that land no longer required for those purposes—Jurisdiction of courts to review decision—Local authority acquiring land for purposes of aerodrome—Local authority conveying site adjoining land to plaintiffs to build factory—Plaintiffs aircraft manufacturers—Conveyance containing covenant by local authority to allow plaintiffs to use airfield for defined period for purposes of test, delivery and other flights in connection with their business—Local authority deciding that land no longer required for purposes of aerodrome—Resolution to appropriate land for purposes of housing scheme—Validity of resolution—Whether test flights, etc of plaintiffs' aircraft a purpose for which land acquired—Whether court having jurisdiction to review local authority's decision that land no longer required for original purposes—Local Government Act 1933, s 163(1). **Dowty Boulton Paul Ltd v Wolverhampton Corp (No 2)** [1973] 2 491, CA.
    Power to demise land—
      Failure to obtain consent of Ministry of Health—Validity of lease—Ultra vires—Estoppel—Effect of invalidity of lease on surrender made in consideration of the grant of the lease—Public Health Act 1875, s 177—Rhyl Improvement Act 1892, s 43. **Rhyl UDC v Rhyl Amusements Ltd** [1959] 1 257, Ch D.
    Power to sell land—
      Land subject to charitable trust—Statutory power—Whether power to dispose of land subject to charitable trust—Local Government Act 1933, s 165. **Hauxwell v Barton-upon-Humber UDC** [1973] 2 1022, Ch D.
      Statutory provision prohibiting local authorities from disposing of land for less than best possible consideration without Secretary of State's consent—Respondent authority entering into contract for sale of land in breach of that provision—Applicant obtaining injunction restraining completion of sale—Authority contending that transaction valid by virtue of statutory provision protecting third parties on 'disposal' of property—Whether disposal taking place on entry into contract or on conveyance—Local Government Act 1972, ss 123, 128(2). **R (on the application of Structadene Ltd) v Hackney London BC** [2001] 2 225, QBD.
    Redevelopment of land—
      Home loss payment. See **Compensation** (Displacement from land—Home loss payment).
    Restrictive covenant affecting land—
      Discharge or modification—Acquisition of land by local authority for statutory purposes. See **Restrictive covenant affecting land** (Discharge or modification—Acquisition of land by defendant for statutory purposes).
  Legal proceedings—
    By and against local authority. See Action, *above*.
    Practice—
      Generally. See **Practice** (Local authority).
  Libel—
    Qualified privilege. See **Libel and slander** (Qualified privilege—Right to respect for private and family life—Claimant being placed on defendant local authority's 'Potentially Violent Persons Register').
    Right to sue for libel. See **Libel and slander** (Parties—Right to sue—Corporation—Local government corporation).
  Library—
    Duty of library authority. See **Library** (Public library—Duty of library authority).
  Licence—
    Agency for supply of nurses. See **Nurse** (Agency for supply of nurses—Licence by local authority).
    Sex establishment. See **Sex establishment** (Control—Licensing).
  Local education authority. See **Education** (Local education authority).

LOCAL AUTHORITY (cont)—
  Local Government Commission—
    Restructuring of local government—
      Policy guidance—Guidance urging substantial increase in unitary authorities at expense of existing two-tier structure of local government—Secretary of State issuing policy guidance on restructuring of local government—Secretary of State rejecting commission's recommendations and directing further review—Commission directed to conduct review having regard to policy guidance—Whether Secretary of State bound to implement commission's recommendations—Whether Secretary of State having power to direct further review of wide-ranging scope—Local Government Act 1992, s 15(6). **R v Secretary of State for the Environment, ex p Lancashire CC** [1994] **4** 165, QBD.
      Policy guidance—Guidance urging substantial increase in unitary authorities at expense of existing two-tier structure of local government—Secretary of State issuing policy guidance on restructuring of local government and directing commission to review local authorities having regard to policy guidance—Local authorities seeking judicial review of Secretary of State's guidance and directions—Whether policy guidance being outside Secretary of State's powers and unlawful—Local Government Act 1992, s 13. **R v Secretary of State for the Environment, ex p Lancashire CC** [1994] **4** 165, QBD.
  Maladministration. *See* **Local government** (Maladministration).
  Meetings—
    Admission of public. *See* **Public authority** (Meeting—Admission of public).
    Disability of members of authorities for voting on account of pecuniary interest in contracts etc—
      Exception—Interest relating to terms on which right to participate in service offered to public—Tenants of council—Question relating to rent of council houses—Whether housing a 'service'—Local Government Act 1933, s 76(1). **Brown v DPP** [1956] **2** 189, QBD.
      Pecuniary interest in any contract or other matter—Direct and indirect interest—Discussion on council's policy regarding tenders for building contracts—Councillor managing director and shareholder of building company which did not intend to tender but had tendered in the past—Local Government Act 1933, s 76(1),(2). **Rands v Oldroyd** [1958] **3** 344, QBD.
    Generally. *See* **Local government** (Meeting).
  Member—
    Disability for voting at meetings. *See* Meetings—Disability of members of authorities for voting on account of pecuniary interest in contracts etc, *above.*
    Disqualification for office. *See* Disqualification for office as member of local authority, *above.*
    Expenses. *See* **Local government** (Expenses—Member of local authority).
    Inspection of documents. *See* **Local government** (Documents—Inspection—Inspection by councillor).
  Mental defective—
    Responsibility for providing accommodation. *See* **Mental health** (Mental defective—Local authority responsible for providing accommodation).
  Minutes—
    Inspection. *See* **Local government** (Documents—Inspection—Minutes of local authority).
  Misbehaviour in public office—
    Common law offence. *See* **Criminal law** (Misbehaviour in public office).
  Misuse of statutory powers—
    Application to prevent misuse of powers—Locus standi of applicant. *See* **Prohibition** (Locus standi of applicant—Application to prevent local authority misusing powers).
    Generally. *See* **Public authority** (Statutory powers—Misuse of powers).
  Mortgage—
    Power of sale. *See* **Mortgage** (Sale—Exercise of power of sale by mortgagee—Local authority).
  Natural justice. *See* **Natural justice** (Local authority).
  Negligence—
    Duty to take care—
      Act performed in exercise of statutory powers. *See* **Negligence** (Duty to take care—Statutory powers—Act performed in exercise of powers—Local authority).
      Children—Existence of duty. *See* **Negligence** (Duty to take care—Existence of duty—Children).
      Existence of duty. *See* **Negligence** (Duty to take care—Existence of duty—Local authority).
      New Zealand. *See* **New Zealand** (Negligence—Duty of care—Statutory powers—Local authority).
    Highway—
      Generally. *See* **Negligence** (Highway).
  New tenancy—
    Business premises—
      Landlord local authority. *See* **Landlord and tenant** (Business premises—Application for new tenancy—Landlord local authority).
      Opposition to grant of new tenancy of business premises—Intention to demolish or reconstruct. *See* **Landlord and tenant** (Opposition to grant of new tenancy of business premises—Intention of landlord to demolish or reconstruct premises comprised in holding—Local authority landlord).
  Nuisance—
    Exercise of statutory powers—
      Remedy. *See* **Nuisance** (Local authority—Exercise of statutory powers—Remedy).
    Injunction—
      Form of order. *See* **Injunction** (Form of order—Nuisance—Local authority).
    Sewage—
      Pollution of river by sewage. *See* **Nuisance** (Sewage—Local authority's liability—Pollution of river by sewage).
    Statutory nuisance. *See* **Nuisance** (Statutory nuisance).
    Summary proceedings to abate, prohibit or restrict nuisance—
      Noise. *See* **Nuisance** (Noise—Summary proceedings by local authority to abate, prohibit or restrict nuisance).
  Occupier's liability—
    Occupation of house compulsorily acquired. *See* **Occupier's liability** (Occupation—Local authority).
  Offensive trades. *See* **Public health** (Offensive trades).
  Officer—
    Generally. *See* **Local government** (Officer).

LOCAL AUTHORITY (cont)—
  Officer (cont)—
    Officer or employee—
      Corruption. *See* **Criminal law** (Corruption).
    Registration officer—
      Superannuation. *See* **Local government** (Superannuation—Interim registrar of births and deaths).
  Open space—
    Facilities for public recreation. *See* **Commons** (Right of common—Facilities for public recreation).
    Power to erect building on open space—
      Caretaker's lodge—Extent of power—Calculation of area withdrawn from public purposes—Public Health Act 1875, s 164—Poole Corporation Act 1919, ss 39, 40, 88. **A-G v Poole Corp** [1937] **3** 608, CA.
    Trust to administer open space for enjoyment of public—
      Disued burial ground—Churchyard converted into open space for benefit of parish—Monument—Proposal to erect monument in open space—Monument unconnected with parish and politically controversial—Monument taking up large part of open space—Whether erection of monument by local authority a breach of trust—Open Spaces Act 1906, s 10. **St Luke's, Chelsea, Re** [1976] **1** 609, Con Ct.
  Opposition to grant of new tenancy of business premises—
    Intention to demolish or reconstruct. *See* **Landlord and tenant** (Opposition to grant of new tenancy of business premises—Intention of landlord to demolish or reconstruct premises comprised in holding—Local authority landlord).
  Parental rights—
    Child in care—
      Resumption of care by parent—Local authority's power to assume parental rights. *See* **Child** (Care—Resumption of care by parent—Resolution assuming parental rights—Power to make resolution assuming parental rights).
  Party to civil proceedings—
    Practice. *See* **Practice** (Parties—Local authority).
  Persons in need of care and attention—
    Housing. *See* **Housing** (Persons in need of care and attention).
  Persons who lack capacity—
    Right to liberty and security. *See* **Mental health** (Persons who lack capacity—Right to liberty and security—Local authority removing person lacking capacity from placement).
  Planning authority. *See* **Town and country planning**.
  Possession proceedings—
    Children. *See* Statutory duty—Children—Possession proceedings, *below*.
  Powers—
    Designation of paying parking places on highways—
      Financial provision relating to designation orders—Exercise of functions by local authorities—Local authority increasing charges for residents' parking permits and visitor vouchers in designated paying parking places—Charges increased for purpose of raising surplus to use for other transport expenditure—Whether decision lawful—Road Traffic Regulation Act 1984, ss 45, 55, 122. **R (on the application of Attfield) v Barnet London BC** [2014] **1** 304, QBD.
    Discovery—
      Canada. *See* **Canada** (Local government—Local authority—Powers of discovery).
    Local authority having management regulation and control of local housing authority's houses—
      Local authority having power to do any thing calculated to facilitate, or conducive or incidental to, the discharge of any of their functions—Whether local housing authority having power to operate parking scheme in local authority housing estate—Local Government Act 1972, s 111(1)—Housing Act 1985, s 21(1). **Akumah v Hackney London BC** [2005] **2** 148, HL.
    Misuse of powers—
      Application to prevent misuse of local authority's powers—Locus standi of applicant. *See* **Prohibition** (Locus standi of applicant—Application to prevent local authority misusing powers).
    Power of local authority to do anything it considers likely to achieve promotion or improvement of economic and social well-being of its area—
      Whether power including provision of student assistance—Local Government Act 2000, s 2. **R (on the application of Theophilus) v Lewisham London BC** [2002] **3** 851, QBD.
    Powers to prosecute—
      Whether local authority having power to prosecute for using motor vehicle without insurance—Local Government Act 1972, s 222—Road Traffic Act 1988, s 143—Road Traffic Offenders Act 1988, s 4. **Middlesbrough BC v Safeer** [2001] **4** 630, QBD DC.
    Statutory powers. *See* Statutory powers, *below*.
    Subsidiary powers—
      Power to do any thing calculated to facilitate or conducive or incidental to discharge of functions—Whether local council having power to say prayers as part of formal business of council meeting—Local Government Act 1972, s 111(1). **R (on the application of National Secular Society) v Bideford Town Council** [2012] **2** 1175, QBD.
      Power to do any thing calculated to facilitate which is conducive or incidental to discharge of functions—Power to make charges—Local authority making charges for pre-application planning consultations—Whether charges calculated to facilitate or conducive or incidental to discharge of planning functions—Whether local authority having statutory authority to levy charges—Local Government Act 1972, s 111. **McCarthy & Stone (Developments) Ltd v Richmond upon Thames London BC** [1991] **4** 897, HL.

LOCAL AUTHORITY (cont)—
  Property—
    Reorganisation of local government—
      Vesting of property in newly consituted authorities—More than one authority succeeding to
        different functions of former authority—Land held by former authority for two or more
        purposes—Determination by former authority that land used mainly for one purpose—Building
        used for purposes of fire service and library—Building one of number on fire station
        site—Remaining buildings on site used solely for purposes of fire service—Determination that
        building used mainly for library purposes—Validity of determination—Whether building or fire
        station site as a whole 'any land used for two or more purposes 'London Authorities (Property
        etc) Order 1964 (SI 1964 No 1464), art 4(1). **Greater London Council v Croydon London Borough**
        [1971] **2** 906, Ch D.
      Vesting of property in newly constituted authorities—Water and sewerage functions transferred
        from local authorities to regional water authorities—Whether assets and property in water
        undertakings transferred to and vested in regional water authorities absolutely—Whether local
        authorities retaining beneficial interest in assets—Whether local authorities entitled to proceeds
        of sale on privatisation of water undertakings. **Sheffield City Council v Yorkshire Water Services**
        Ltd [1991] **2** 280, Ch D.
    Reorganisation of National Health Service—
      Transfer of property to Minister. *See* **National Health Service** (Reorganisation—Transfer from local
        authorities to Minister of property held by local authorities for their former health functions).
  Public entertainments—
    Licensing. *See* **Entertainment** (Public entertainment—Entertainments licence).
  Public health—
    Generally. *See* **Public health**.
  Public spaces protection order. *See* Statutory powers—Public spaces protection order, *below*.
  Public transport. *See* **Road traffic** (Public transport—Local authority).
  Quarantine stations for animals—
    Imported animals. *See* **Animal** (Importation of animal—Quarantine—Provision by local authority of
      quarantine station).
  Race relations. *See* **Race relations** (Local authority).
  Rates. *See* **Rates**.
  Redevelopment of land—
    Home loss payment. *See* **Compensation** (Displacement from land—Home loss payment).
  Registration officer—
    Superannuation. *See* **Local government** (Superannuation—Interim registrar of births and deaths).
  Rehousing—
    Duty to rehouse persons displaced from residential accommodation. *See* **Housing** (Rehousing—Duty of
      local authority—Persons displaced from residential accommodation).
  Relator action. *See* **Practice** (Parties—Local authority).
  Rent control—
    Reference of contract to rent tribunal. *See* **Rent tribunal** (Reference of contract—Jurisdiction—
      Reference by local authority).
  Representation by Treasury Solicitor—
    Appeal concerning validity of traffic order—
      Interest of Crown in subject-matter of litigation—Whether representation proper. **Brownsea Haven**
        Properties Ltd v Poole Corp [1958] **1** 205, CA.
  Residential care home—
    Elderly persons—
      Closure of local authority home—Consultation—Duty to act fairly—Whether local authority under
        duty to consult permanent residents prior to making decision on closure—Whether duty to
        consult part of duty to act fairly. **R v Devon CC, ex p Baker** [1995] **1** 73, CA.
      Closure of local authority home—Statutory duty to make arrangements for providing residential
        accommodation for old people in need of care and attention—Nature of such arrangements—
        Whether local authority can discharge statutory duty entirely by means of arrangements made
        with third parties—Whether local authority required to maintain some accommodation for old
        people in premises under its own management—National Assistance Act 1948, ss 21(1)(4), 26. **R**
        v Wandsworth London BC, ex p Beckwith [1996] **1** 129, HL.
    Services provided to resident under arrangement between service provider and local authority
      exercising statutory duty to provide accommodation—
      Local authority subsequently indicating to care home that resident to be charged for his care—Care
        home seeking recovery of fees from resident's estate—Whether estate or local authority liable for
        payment of fees—National Assistance Act 1948, ss 21, 26(2)—National Health Service and
        Community Care Act 1990, s 47(5). **Aster Healthcare Ltd v Estate of Shafi** [2016] **2** 316, CA.
  Restructuring. *See* Local Government Commission—Restructuring of local government, *above*.
  Restructuring of local government —
    Powers —
      Reorganisation —Secretary of State inviting proposals for new governance arrangements—
        Secretary of State not acting under existing legislative machinery—Secretary of State rejecting
        objections to proposals—Local authorities challenging Secretary of State's decisions by way of
        judicial review—Judge dismissing applications—Parliament passing new Act subsequently—
        Secretary of State making decisions under new Act to proceed with proposals—Whether subject
        of appeal including pre-Act decisions—Whether Secretary of State acting inconsistently with
        existing legislation—Local Government Act 1992—Local Government and Public Involvement in
        Health Act 2007. **R (on the application of Shrewsbury and Atcham BC) v Secretary of State for**
        Communities and Local Government (Shropshire CC, interested party) [2008] **3** 548, CA.
  Right of action—
    Assertion and protection of rights of public. *See* **Practice** (Parties—Local authority).
    Protection of interest of inhabitants of area. *See* **Practice** (Parties—Local authority—Promotion or
      protection of interests of inhabitants of their area).
    Unlawful closure of railway line—
      Interim injunction—Local Government Act 1933, s 276. **Warwickshire CC v British Railways Board**
      [1969] **3** 631, Ch D.

LOCAL AUTHORITY (cont)—
  Right of pre-emption—
    Right imposed by local authority on sale of house—
      Obligation affecting land—Registration. *See* **Land charge** (Registration—Obligation affecting land—Obligation binding on successors in title—Right of pre-emption—Local authority).
  Seal—
    Contract—
      Necessity for seal. *See* Contract—Seal—Necessity for seal, *above*.
  Sewers—
    Agreement to vest sewer in local authority. *See* **Public health** (Sewerage—Public sewer—Agreement to vest sewer in local authority).
    Provision of public sewers. *See* **Public health** (Sewerage—Public sewer—Provision of).
  Sex establishments—
    Licensing. *See* **Sex establishment** (Control—Licensing).
  Shops—
    Sunday closing—
      Enforcement. *See* **Shop** (Sunday closing—Enforcement by local authority).
  Signature—
    Document. *See* **Local government** (Documents—Signature).
  Social care—
    Exclusion of nursing care from community care services—
      Whether NHS or local authority responsible for funding work of registered nurses in social care settings—Meaning of 'nursing care by a registered nurse'—Health and Social Care Act 2001, s 49. **R (on the application of Forge Care Homes Ltd) v Cardiff and Vale University Health Board** [2018] **1** 449, SC.
  Social services—
    Generally. *See* **Social security**.
    Powers—
      Local authority setting up inquiry into children's home—Terms of reference of inquiry including vulnerable adults living at children's home—Whether inquiry into circumstances of adults within local authority's powers—Local Authority Social Services Act 1970, s 7. **Local Authority v Health Authority (disclosure: restriction on publication)** [2004] **1** 480, Fam D.
    Residential care home. *See* Residential care home, *above*.
  Standing orders—
    Contract in accordance with standing orders. *See* Contract—Accordance with standing orders, *above*.
    Power to suspend—
      Exercise of power only by special resolution. **R v Hereford Corp, ex p Harrower** [1970] **3** 460, QBD.
  Statutory duty—
    Breach of statutory duty—
      Careless performance of statutory duty—Exercise of statutory discretion—Justiciability of decisions involving policy matters—Application of principles of negligence—Whether fair, just and reasonable to impose duty of care. **X and ors (minors) v Bedfordshire CC** [1995] **3** 353, HL.
      Duty owed in relation to welfare of children. *See* Statutory duty—Statutory duty owed in relation to welfare of children, *below*.
    Children—
      Possession proceedings—Duty to have regard to need to safeguard and promote welfare of children—Whether breach of statutory duty providing defence to possession proceedings—Children Act 2004, s 11. **Hertfordshire CC v Davies** [2018] **4** 831, CA.
    Discretion. *See* **Mandamus** (Discretion—Local authority—Statutory duty—Enforcement—Housing).
    Enforcement—
      Accommodation—Duty to provide accommodation for persons in urgent need—Scope of duty—Remedy for breach of duty—Specific remedy provided for by statute—Exclusion of other remedies—Homeless family—Occupation by homeless family of empty property owned by local authority—Whether local authority in breach of duty to provide accommodation for homeless—Whether breach of duty justifying occupation of property—National Assistance Act 1948, s 21(1)(b). **Southwark London Borough v Williams** [1971] **2** 175, CA.
    Public sector equality duty—
      Council resolution—Council passing resolution to boycott produce originating from illegal Israeli settlements in West Bank—Whether resolution contrary to council's public sector equality duty—Equality Act 2010, s 149. **R (on the application of Jewish Rights Watch t/a Jewish Human Rights Watch) v Leicester City Council** [2018] **4** 1040, CA.
      Council resolution—Councils passing resolutions critical of Israel and its policies—Whether resolutions contrary to councils' public sector equality duty—Whether resolutions having improper regard to non-commercial matters in relation to public supply or works contracts—Local Government Act 1988, s 17—Equality Act 2010, s 149. **R (on the application of Jewish Rights Watch t/a Jewish Human Rights Watch) v Leicester City Council** [2017] **3** 505, DC.
    Statutory duty owed in relation to welfare of children—
      Breach—Whether children and parents affected by breach of statutory duty having right of action—Children and Young Persons Act 1969—Child Care Act 1980—Children Act 1989. **X and ors (minors) v Bedfordshire CC** [1994] **4** 602, CA.
    Vulnerable adult—
      Vulnerable adult seeking assisted suicide abroad—Husband proposing to make necessary arrangements and to accompany her—Husband thereby potentially committing criminal offence—Duties of local authority—Whether duty lying on local authority to seek injunctive relief against husband—Whether court would act of its own motion—Local Government Act 1972, s 222. **Z (local authority: duty), Re** [2005] **3** 280, Fam D.
    Whether statutory duty to promote road safety creating parallel common law duty—
      Road Traffic Act 1988, s 39(2),(3). **Gorringe v Calderdale Metropolitan BC** [2004] **2** 326, HL.

LOCAL AUTHORITY (cont)—
Statutory powers—
Children—
Provision of accommodation for children in need—Person seeking asylum stating himself to be under age of 18 years—First-tier Tribunal (Immigration and Asylum Chamber) finding person seeking asylum to be a child—High Court in distinct judicial review proceedings finding person seeking asylum to be an adult—Upper Tribunal (Immigration and Asylum Chamber) finding error in First-tier Tribunal decision and attaching weight to High Court decision—Whether Upper Tribunal entitled to place reliance on High Court decision. **MWA (Afghanistan) v Secretary for State for the Home Dept** [2015] **3** 111, CA.

Provision of accommodation for children in need—Person seeking asylum stating himself to be under age of 18 years—Local authority determining age of person as 18 years—Claim for judicial review of age assessment—Whether burden of proof lying on claimant or on local authority. **R (on the application of CJ) v Cardiff City Council** [2012] **2** 836, CA.

Provision of accommodation for children in need—Person seeking asylum stating himself to be under age of 18 years—Person seeking asylum determined by immigration judge to be a child—Local authority assessing person seeking asylum as adult—Whether local authority acting unlawfully by failing to comply with joint protocol on age assessments—Whether EU law requiring local authority to be bound by age assessment of Secretary of State—Children Act 1989, s 20. **R (on the application of K) v Birmingham City Council (Secretary of State for the Home Dept, interested party)** [2013] **1** 945, CA.

Provision of accommodation for children in need—Person seeking asylum stating himself to be under age of 18 years—Person seeking asylum referred to local children's services authority for assessment of age—Local authority determining age of person as 18 years—Whether decision as to whether person a child a decision of objective fact—Children Act 1989, ss 17(10), 20(1), 105(1). **R (on the application of A) v Croydon London BC** [2010] **1** 469, SC.

Provision of accommodation for children in need—Provision of services for children in need—Child aged 17 years excluded from family home—Local authority determining child not 'requiring accommodation' although needing help with accommodation—Local authority providing child with accommodation under homelessness provisions—Whether decision lawful—Children Act 1989, ss 7(1), (10), 20(1). **R (on the application of G) v Southwark London BC** [2009] **3** 189, HL.

Provision of accommodation for children—Secure accommodation—Arrested juvenile—Police requesting secure accommodation for arrested juvenile—Whether duty of local authority to provide accommodation falling only on authority within whose area police station located—Whether duty of local authority to provide secure accommodation—Police and Criminal Evidence Act 1984, s 38(6)—Children Act 1989, s 21(2)(b). **R (on the application of M) v Gateshead Council** [2007] **1** 1262, CA.

Provision of accommodation—Use of accommodation for restricting liberty—Relevant criteria for secure accommodation order—Meaning of 'secure accommodation'—Children Act 1989, s 25—Human Rights Act 1998, Sch 1, Pt I, arts 5, 8—Children (Secure Accommodation) Regulations 1991, SI 1991/1505, reg 3. **B (a child) (Association of Lawyers for Children intervening), Re** [2020] **3** 375, CA.

Provision of services for children in need—Arrangements for the provision of assistance—Duty of local authority— Whether means of parents relevant to local authority in determining whether to provide assistance—Chronically Sick and Disabled Persons Act 1970, s 2—Children Act 1989, ss 17, 29. **R (on the application of Spink) v Wandsworth London BC** [2005] **2** 954, CA.

Provision of services for children in need—Child aged 17 presenting herself to local authority housing department as homeless—Local authority providing temporary accommodation—Child not referred to children's services department—Whether local authority should have identified child as child in need—Whether local authority to be treated as if it had provided child with accommodation in the exercise of its social services functions—Children Act 1989, ss 20, 22—Housing Act 1996, s 188. **R (on the application of M) v Hammersmith and Fulham London BC** [2008] **4** 271, HL.

Provision of services for children in need—Children of failed asylum seeker—Whether availability of support for failed asylum seekers from Secretary of State entitling local authority to refuse to provde support to children 'in need'—Children Act 1989, s 17—Immigration and Asylum Act 1999, ss 4, 95. **R (on the application of VC) v Newcastle City Council (Secretary of State for the Home Dept, interested party)** [2012] **2** 227, DC.

Provision of services for children in need—Extent of local authority powers—Claimant part of travelling fairground family—Defendant local authority assessing claimant as child 'in need'—Support services not being afforded to claimant when outside area of authority—Whether power to provide services to children in need extending to those outside area of authority—Children Act 1989, s 17(1). **R (on the application of J) (by his litigation friend, W) v Worcestershire CC (Equality and Human Rights Commission intervening)** [2015] **2** 792, CA.

Provision of services for children in need—Home Office having policy of not normally proceeding with enforced removal or deportation in case involving child with seven or more years' residence in United Kingdom—Whether local authority having to take account of reasons underlying that policy when carrying out duty to such a child who was in need—Children Act 1989, s 17—Human Rights Act 1998, Sch 1, Pt I, art 8—Nationality, Immigration and Asylum Act 2002, Sch 3, paras 1, 3, 7. **R (on the application of C) v Birmingham City Council** [2009] **1** 1039, QBD.

Provision of services for children in need—Whether local social services authority having duty to provide accommodation for entire family of child in need requiring residential accommodation—Whether local social services authority looking after child having duty to provide accommodation for child's parent—Children Act 1989, ss 17(1), 23(6). **R (on the application of G) v Barnet London BC** [2004] **1** 97, HL.

Provision of services for children in need—Whether local social services authority having power to provide accommodation for families with dependent children—Children Act 1989, s 17. **R (on the application of W) v Lambeth London BC** [2002] **2** 901, CA.

Whether lawful basis for children's accommodation once 72 hours of police protection expiring—Children Act 1989, ss 20, 46—Human Rights Act 1998, Sch 1, Pt I, art 8. **Williams v Hackney London BC** [2018] **4** 396, SC.

LOCAL AUTHORITY (cont)—
  Statutory powers (cont)—
    Continuing functions—
      Former relevant child—Person seeking asylum assessed as under 18 years—Local authority providing asylum seeker with accommodation—Claim for asylum dismissed—Local authority subsequently terminating support for failed asylum seeker—Whether local authority empowered to provide accommodation to former relevant child—Whether local authority entitled to take into account support that might be given to former relevant child by National Asylum Support Service—Children Act 1989, s 23C(4)(c)—Immigration and Asylum Act 1999, s 95(1). **R (on the application of O) v Barking and Dagenham London BC Council (Secretary of State for the Home Dept, interested party; The Children's Society, intervening)** [2011] **2** 337, CA.
    Generally. *See* **Public authority** (Statutory powers).
    Implied power—
      Implied power used for improper purpose—Interest rate swap transactions—Local authority incorporated by charter entering into financial transactions involving speculation on interest rate movements—Auditor claiming that local authority having no power to enter into transactions—Auditor seeking declaration that local authority's capital market activity ultra vires—Whether local authority having capacity to enter into swap transactions—Whether capacity conferred to statute—Whether local authority having capacity to enter into swap transactions for limited purpose of interest rate risk management—Whether swap transactions tainted with improper purpose of speculative trading—London Government Act 1963, s 1(2)—Local Government Act 1972, s 111(1)—Local Government Finance Act 1982, s 19. **Hazell v Hammersmith and Fulham London BC** [1991] **1** 545, HL.
      Local authority forming and partly owning company to fund property acquisitions—Local authority guaranteeing company's obligations to bank and indemnifying company against losses—Company entering into speculative property transactions—Company incurring losses following collapse of property market—Whether local authority liable under indemnity and guarantee—Whether local authority having implied power to form company and give indemnity and guarantee—Local Government Act 1972, s 111—Housing Act 1985, ss 65, 69. **Crédit Suisse v Waltham Forest London BC** [1996] **4** 176, CA.
      Local authority forming company to finance capital project and avoid statutory controls on borrowing—Company borrowing finance to fund leisure pool and time-share development—Local authority guaranteeing loan to company—Company defaulting on loan repayments—Whether local authority liable under guarantee—Whether local authority acting ultra vires in forming company and giving guarantee—Whether guarantee enforceable—Local Government Act 1972, s111—Local Government (Miscellaneous Provisions) Act 1976, s 19. **Crédit Suisse v Allerdale BC** [1996] **4** 129, CA.
    Injunction—
      Local authority granted injunction against 'persons unknown' prohibiting car cruising in area—Whether injunction should have been refused on basis local authority should have made public spaces protection order instead—Local Government Act 1972, s 222—Anti-social Behaviour, Crime and Policing Act 2014, s 59. **Birmingham City Council v Sharif** [2021] **3** 176, CA.
    Interference with flow of water to mill. *See* **Water and watercourses** (Flow of water—Mill deriving water power from river—Interference with flow of water by local authority executing works under statutory powers).
    Power to provide accommodation for persons in need—
      Claimant making application for local authority assistance when application for indefinite leave to remain not yet determined—Defendant authority refusing to exercise power but offering claimant and her children assistance—Whether authority erring in approach to determining application for assistance—Children Act 1989, s 17—Human Rights Act 1998, Sch 1, Pt I, art 8—Nationality, Immigration and Asylum Act 2002, Sch 3. **R (on the application of C) v Birmingham City Council (sub nom R (on the application of Clue) v Birmingham City Council)** [2010] **4** 423, CA.
    Public spaces protection order—
      Claimants challenging public spaces protection order providing for 'safe zone' around abortion clinic—Whether statutory requirements established—Whether right to privacy engaged—Whether any interference with rights proportionate—Meaning of 'those in the locality'—Human Rights Act 1998, Sch 1, Pt I, arts 8-11—Anti-social Behaviour, Crime and Policing Act 2014, ss 59, 66. **Dulgheriu v Ealing London BC** [2018] **4** 881, QBD; **Dulgheriu v Ealing London BC (National Council for Civil Liberties (t/a Liberty) intervening)** [2020] **3** 545, CA.
  Street trading—
    Licence—
      Revocation—Application of the rules of natural justice. *See* **Natural justice** (Local authority—Street trading—Revocation of licence).
  Summary proceedings to abate, prohibit or restrict nuisance—
    Noise. *See* **Nuisance** (Noise—Summary proceedings by local authority to abate, prohibit or restrict nuisance).
  Sunday closing of shops—
    Enforcement. *See* **Shop** (Sunday closing—Enforcement by local authority).
  Superintendent registrar of births, deaths and marriages—
    Remuneration. *See* **Registrar** (Superintendent registrar of births, deaths and marriages—Remuneration).
  Tenancy of local authority dwelling—
    Transfer of tenancy—
      Order in divorce proceedings. *See* **Divorce** (Property—Adjustment order—Transfer of property—Local authority tenancy).
  Town and country planning—
    Exercise of discretion—
      Estoppel. *See* **Estoppel** (Statutory body—Local planning authority—Exercise of discretion).
    Generally. *See* **Town and country planning**.
  Tramway. *See* **Tramway**.

LOCAL AUTHORITY (cont)—
　Transport—
　　Free pass—
　　　Exclusion of liability for negligence. *See* **Carriers** (Negligence—Exclusion of liability—Passengers—
　　　Free pass).
　　Schoolchildren, for. *See* **Education** (Local education authority—Provision of transport for pupils).
　　Travel concessions—
　　　Free travel facilities for aged persons—Discrimination in favour of class—Whether ultra vires.
　　　Prescott v Birmingham Corp [1954] **3** 698, CA.
　　　Local authority running public services in area of another local authority—Contribution to
　　　cost—Basis of calculation—Public Service Vehicles (Travel Concessions) Act 1955, s 1(4).
　　　Litherland UDC v Liverpool Corp [1958] **2** 489, Ch D.
　Tree preservation—
　　Duty to protect areas of natural beauty. *See* **Practice** (Parties—Local authority—Promotion or protection
　　of interests of inhabitants of their area—Local authority obtaining injunction to restrain breaches by
　　defendant of tree preservation order).
　Vicarious liability for employee—
　　Remedies. *See* **Employment** (Discrimination—Remedies—Vicarious liability).
　Wardship proceedings—
　　Jurisdiction of court to commit ward of court to care of local authority. *See* **Ward of court** (Care and
　　control—Power to commit ward of court to care of local authority).
　　Minor in care of local authority—
　　　Generally. *See* **Child** (Care—Local authority—Wardship proceedings).
　　　Parties. *See* **Ward of court** (Application to make minor ward of court—Parties—Respondent where
　　　minor in care of local authority).
　Water charges—
　　Recovery of charges on behalf of water authority—
　　　Sewerage services. *See* **Water supply** (Charges—Power of water authority to make
　　　charges—Charges for services performed—Liability of person who has not received
　　　services—Power of water authority to make such charges for services performed, facilities
　　　provided or rights made available by them as they think fit—Sewerage services).
　Water supply—
　　Generally. *See* **Water supply**.
　Weekly tenancy—
　　Implied covenant by landlord to repair. *See* **Landlord and tenant** (Implied covenant to repair—Covenant
　　by landlord—Flat let on weekly tenancy by local authority).

LOCAL CHARITY
　Action to establish existence of charitable trust—
　　Parties—
　　　Local inhabitants—Attorney General. *See* **Charity** (Proceedings—Parties—Attorney General—Local
　　　charity).
　Powers—
　　Subsidiary powers—
　　　Power to do any thing calculated to facilitate or conducive or incidental to discharge of
　　　functions—Power to make charges—Local authority making charges for pre-application planning
　　　consultations—Whether charges calculated to facilitate or conducive or incidental to discharge of
　　　planning functions—Whether local authority having statutory authority to levy charges—Local
　　　Government Act 1972, s 111. **McCarthy & Stone (Developments) Ltd v Richmond upon Thames
　　　London BC** [1991] **4** 897, HL.

LOCAL COMMISSIONER
　Complaint of maladministration—
　　Local government. *See* **Local government** (Maladministration—Complaint to local commissioner).

LOCAL EDUCATION AUTHORITY
　Estoppel. *See* **Estoppel** (Local education authority).
　Generally. *See* **Education** (Local education authority).

LOCAL GOVERNMENT
　Alteration of area—
　　Extension of city boundaries to include part of county area—
　　　Loss to county ratepayers—Whether city council liable to compensate county council—Local
　　　government Act 1888, s 62—Local Government Act 1894, s 68 Sch 1 Part 11—Local Government
　　　(Adjustments) Act 1913, s 1(1)(b)—Local Government (County Borough and Adjustments) Act
　　　1926, s 5—Oxford Extension Act 1928, ss 33 61—Local Government Act 1929, ss 30. **Oxford City
　　　Council v Oxfordshire CC** [1938] **4** 721, HL.
　　Extension of county borough boundaries to include part of administrative county area—
　　　Financial adjustments—Claims presented by county council against corporation of borough more
　　　than six years after alteration of areas—Limitation of time—Date from which time runs—Local
　　　Government Act, s 151(1)(3)—Limitation Act 1939, ss 2(1)(d), 27(1)(6). **West Riding of
　　　Yorkshire CC v Huddersfield Corp** [1957] **1** 669, QBD.
　　Extension of county borough boundaries to include parts of rural districts—
　　　Loss to rural district ratepayers—Abolition of rural district councils affected and districts
　　　amalgamated—Right of new rural district council to financial adjustment with county
　　　borough—Local Government Act 1933, s 152(1)(b), Sch 1, r 1(a). **Magor and St Mellons RDC v
　　　Newport Corp** [1951] **2** 839, HL.
　　Extension of county borough to include part of county area—
　　　Financial adjustments—Increased burden on county ratepayers—Method of assessing
　　　compensation—Arbitrator's duty—Interest on amount awarded—Local Government Act 1933,
　　　ss 151, 152(1)(b), Sch V, r 1—Newport Extension Act 1934, s 58. **Newport BC v Monmouthshire
　　　CC** [1947] **1** 900, HL.

LOCAL GOVERNMENT (cont)—
Alteration of area (cont)—
Financial adjustments—
Settlement—Capital sum plus interest, less tax—Transaction treated by income tax authorities as capital payment—Tax deducted not accounted for—Claim to recover tax deducted—Whether settlement could be re-opened. **Bullingdon RDC v Oxford Corp** [1936] **3** 875, KBD.
Order adjusting boundaries—
Letter adjourning decision on amalgamation—Subsequent order for amalgamation of authorities—Whether second order barred—Local Government Act 1929, s 47(1). **R v Minister of Health, ex p Hampton UDC** [1936] **3** 169, KBD.
Proposal—
Objection by local authority—Action by local authorities on ground that inquiry invalid—Whether production of departmental briefs for guidance of inspectors and correspondence between inspectors and ministry necessary in interest of justice. **Wednesbury Corp v Ministry of Housing and Local Government** [1965] **1** 186, CA.
Objection by local authority—Action by local authority on ground that boundary commission's proposals invalid—Commission required to observe rules laid down for considering electoral arrangements—Commission required to achieve electoral equality between wards—Commission appointing assistant commissioner to hold local inquiry and to report—Assistant commissioner recommending scheme based on size of council and not on electoral equality—Commission accepting recommendations but modifying scheme to improve balance of representation between wards—Commission submitting modified scheme to Secretary of State—Whether commission complied with rules—Whether modified scheme achieved required electoral equality—Local Government Act 1972, Sch 11, para 3(2)(3). **Enfield London Borough v Local Government Boundary Commission for England** [1978] **2** 1073, QBD.
Objection by local authority—Local inquiry into objection—Action by local authorities on ground that inquiry invalid—Whether production of departmental briefs for guidance of inspectors and correspondence between inspectors and ministry necessary in interest of justice. **Wednesbury Corp v Ministry of Housing and Local Government** [1965] **1** 186, CA.
Objection by local authority—Local inquiry into objection—Minister giving instructions to holders of inquiry—No statutory obligation on persons holding the inquiry to express judgment on merits of the proposals—Holders of inquiry instructed by Minister not to make recommendations on matter on which by statute he was to decide—Right of Minister to give such instructions—Validity of inquiry—Local Government Act 1958, s 23(2). **Wednesbury Corp v Ministry of Housing and Local Government (No 2)** [1965] **3** 571, CA.
Audit—
Auditor's duty—
Duty owed to local authority—Duty owed to local authority's officers—Local authority bringing action against its officers for making payments without authority—Officers claiming to have acted on advice of district auditor—Whether district auditor owing statutory duty to local authority—Whether duty enforceable by action for damages by local authority—Whether district auditor owing statutory duty of care to officer of local authority—Whether district auditor owing common law duty of care to officer of local authority—Local Government Finance Act 1982, s 15. **West Wiltshire DC v Garland (Cond and ors, third parties)** [1995] **2** 17, CA.
Duty of auditor to disallow item of account which contrary to law and to surcharge amount disallowed on person responsible—
Contrary to law—Contract to dispose of refuse—Decision to increase remuneration of contractor—Whether payment in excess of those council contractually bound to pay 'contrary to law'—Local Government Act 1933, s 228(1). **Hurle-Hobbs, Re Decision of** [1944] **2** 261, CA.
Rent on de-requisition—Council undertaking full cost of any increases under Rent Act 1957—Discretion of councillors not properly exercised—Surcharge properly made—Local Government Act 1933, s 228—Requisitioned Houses and Housing (Amendment) Act 1955, s 4(4). **Taylor v Munrow** [1960] **1** 455, QBD.
Duty of auditor to surcharge amount of any loss or deficiency on any person by whose negligence or misconduct loss or deficiency incurred—
Negligence or misconduct—Loss or deficiencey—Failure to increase revenue of authority—Local authority refusing to implement statutory duty to increase rents of council houses tenants—Refusal in consequence of pledge to electorate—Whether local authority guilty of 'negligence or misconduct'—Whether failure to increase rents resulting in a 'loss or deficiency'—Local Government Act 1933, s 228(1)(d). **Asher v Lacey** [1973] **3** 1008, QBD.
Negligence or misconduct—Loss or deficiency—Resolution authorising payment passed after warning by clerk that purpose of resolution unlawful—Whether councillors guilty of misconduct in passing resolution—Whether loss or deficiency caused by councillors' misconduct—Liability to be surcharged—Local Government Act 1933, s 228(1)(d). **Davies v Cowperthwaite** [1938] **2** 685, KBD Divl Ct.
Negligence—Local Government Act 1933, s 228(1)(d). **Pentecost v London District Auditor** [1951] **2** 330, KBD.
Production of and declarations as to documents—
Statutory power of district auditor to compel witness to attend audit—Failure of witness to comply with notice to attend—Witness fined—Issue of subpoena ad testificandum and duces tecum—Jurisdiction—Whether auditor precluded from applying to court for issue of subpoena—Local Government Act 1933, s 225(1)(2). **R v Hurle-Hobbs, ex p Simmons** [1945] **1** 273, KBD.
Surcharge—
Appeal—Relief—Refusal by district auditor to surcharge—Appeal to Minister by aggrieved elector allowed—Consequent surcharge by district auditor pursuant to instructions of Minister—Appeal against such surcharge—Application for relief against such surcharge—Jurisdiction of High Court—Local Government Act 1933, ss 229, 230. **Dean v District Auditor for Ashton-in-Makerfield** [1959] **2** 577, QBD Divl Ct.
Appeal—Right of appeal of person aggrieved by disallowance or surcharge—Auditor disallowing payments by council to contractor in excess of contractual sum—Appeal by contractor—Whether 'person aggrieved'—Local Government Act 1933, s 229(1). **Hurle-Hobbs, Re Decision of** [1944] **2** 261, CA.

LOCAL GOVERNMENT (cont)—
 Audit (cont)—
  Surcharge (cont)—
   Application for relief—Circumstances to be considered by the court—Discretion of court to grant—Local Government Act 1933, s 230. **Annison v St Pancras Metropolitan Borough (District Auditor)** [1961] **3** 914, QBD.
   Auditor's inquiry—Procedure—Whether auditor required to invite oral representations before issuing certificate of surcharge—Whether auditor acting unfairly in inviting written representations only—Whether unfairness by auditor curable on appeal—Local Government Finance Act 1982, s 20(1)(3). **Lloyd v McMahon** [1987] **1** 1118, CA and HL.
   Powers of district auditor—Fraud by company—Surcharge on managing director—Local Government Act 1933, s 228. **Dickson, Re** [1948] **1** 713, CA.
   Ruling party on local authority formulating and implementing new policy on sale of authority's properties designed to increase party's voting base in key wards— Auditor finding authority's leader and deputy leader guilty of wilful misconduct which had caused authority loss—Whether auditor correct—Whether auditor's calculation of loss correct—Local Government Finance Act 1982, s 20. **Porter v Magill** [2002] **1** 465, HL.
 Authority. *See* **Local authority**.
 Committee—
  Membership of council committee. *See* Councillor—Membership of council committee, *below*.
 Community charge—
  Charge capping—
   Power of Secretary of State to charge cap local authorities—Whether Secretary of State's decision to charge cap local authorities susceptible to judicial review—Local Government Finance Act 1988, s 100. **Hammersmith and Fulham London BC v Secretary of State for the Environment** [1990] **3** 589, HL, QBD and CA.
  Enforcement—
   Distress. *See* **Distress**.
 Council tax—
  Sole or main residence—
   Council taxpayer owning cottage—Council taxpayer and his wife moving to house provided by employer—Whether cottage sole or main residence—Local Government Finance Act 1992, s 6(2), (5). **Williams v Horsham DC** [2004] **3** 30, CA.
 Councillor—
  Access to meetings. *See* Meeting—Access—Access by councillor, *below*.
  Conduct—
   Freedom of expression—Adjudication Panel for Wales—Case tribunal disqualifying councillor for breach of codes of conduct—Councillor challenging tribunal's decision with Public Services Ombudsman for Wales named as respondent—Whether appropriate respondent—Whether tribunal applying wrong standard of proof—Whether tribunal erring in finding breaches of codes in the light of councillor's right to freedom of expression—Whether period of disqualification manifestly excessive—Human Rights Act 1998, Sch 1, Pt I, art 10. **Heesom v Public Services Ombudsman for Wales** [2014] **4** 269, QBD.
  Inspection of documents in council's possession. *See* Documents—Inspection—Inspection by councillor, *below*.
  Membership of council committee—
   Removal from committee—Applicant councillor member of housing committee—Applicant refusing to vote along party lines on committee—Council passing resolution to change constitution of housing committee—Resolution effectively removing applicant from housing committee—Whether removal of applicant constituting sanction or punishment—Whether council acting ultra vires. **R v Greenwich London BC, ex p Lovelace** [1991] **3** 511, CA.
 Documents—
  Audit—
   Production of and declarations as to documents. *See* Audit—Production of and declarations as to documents, *above*.
  Inspection—
   Accounts of local authority—Omnibus board constituted by local statute—Whether board a local authority—Provisions relating to accounts of local authority incorporated in local statute—Repeal of provisions of 1894 Act—Effect on local Act—Whether elector entitled to inspection of auditor's report on accounts of board—Interpretation of statutes—Local Government Act 1894, s 58—Local Government Act 1933, s 283(4). **R v West Monmouthshire Omnibus Board, ex p Price** [1938] **1** 220, KBD.
   Inspection by councillor—Application for adoption order—Social services committee report on suitability of prospective adoptive parents—Councillor of housing sub-committee requesting disclosure of social services report—Councillor claiming disclosure necessary to enable her to perform duties as councillor—Social services committee withholding report—Whether councillor entitled to see report. **Birmingham City DC v O** [1983] **1** 497, HL.
   Inspection by councillor—Councillor a member of public services committee—Council setting up public services sub-committee to look after direct labour organisations employed by council—Councillor seeking access to documents of sub-committee—Councillor claiming access to documents necessary to enable him to perform his duties as councillor—Council holding that documents confidential and refusing access to documents—Whether councillor entitled to access to documents. **R v Hackney London BC, ex p Gamper** [1985] **3** 275, QBD.
   Inspection by councillor—Documents relating to pending litigation—Sufficient production for proper discharge of duties—Prejudice of council's interest by production. **R v Barnes BC, ex p Conlan** [1938] **3** 226, KBD.
   Inspection by councillor—Inspection for performance of duties as member of council—Application for adoption order—Social services committee report on suitability of prospective parents to adopt foster child—Councillor of housing sub-committee requesting disclosure of social services report—Councillor claiming disclosure necessary to enable her to perform duties as councillor—Social services committee withholding report—Whether social services committee required to produce report. **Birmingham City DC v O** [1982] **2** 356, CA.

LOCAL GOVERNMENT (cont)—
  Documents (cont)—
    Inspection (cont)—
      Inspection by councillor—Inspection necessary for performance of duties as member of local government committee—Disclosure matter for committee's discretion—Test of proper exercise of discretion—Report to police committee on conduct of chief constable—Report containing defamatory allegations against third parties based on rumour and gossip—Consideration of full report by committee resulting in tribunal of inquiry into chief constable's conduct—Copies of full report then withdrawn from committee because of disclosure to press—Applicant becoming member of committee after full report considered and acted on by committee—Applicant requesting to see full report—Applicant claiming disclosure necessary to enable him to perform his duties as member of committee—Counsel advising against disclosure of full report to applicant and other new members of committee because republication of report to committee might not be subject to qualified privilege—Committee deciding to act on counsel's advice and withold full disclosure—Whether committee properly exercising its discretion. **R v Clerk to Lancashire Police Committee, ex p Hook** [1980] 2 353, CA.

      London. *See* **London** (Local government—Inspection of documents).

      Minutes of local authority—Matters involving accounts and finance—Inspection by agent of elector. **R v Glamorganshire CC, ex p Collier** [1936] 2 168, KBD.

  Signature—
    Facsimile signature—No evidence how signature affixed or with what authority document issued—Notice required to be signed by clerk or his lawful deputy—Document bearing purported signature deemed authoritatively given until contrary proved—Housing Act 1957, s 166(2)—Local Government Act 1933, s 287B added by London Government Act 1963, s 8(2) Sch 4. **Plymouth City Corp v Hurrell** [1967] 3 354, CA.

  Elections. *See* **Elections** (Local government).

  Electoral arrangements—
    Proposal for change of arrangements—
      Objection by local authority—Commission required to observe rules laid down for considering electoral arrangements—Failure to observe rule to achieve electoral equality between wards—Commission rejecting scheme based on electoral equality and adopting scheme not based on electoral equality—Scheme adopted by commission in interests of effective and convenient local government—Whether proposals valid—Whether commission required to comply with rules—Whether interests of effective and convenient local government an overriding consideration—Local Government Act 1972, s 47(1), Sch 11, para 3(2)(a). **Enfield London Borough v Local Government Boundary Commission for England** [1979] 3 747, HL.

  Expenditure—
    Payment out of general rate fund—
      Forward funding—Rates limited to amount 'sufficient ... to defray ... expenditure which may fall to be defrayed'—Greater London Council making forward funding arrangements for voluntary organisations in anticipation of GLC's abolition—Whether local authority's expenditure has to be referable to year in which rate levied—Whether GLC's forward funding proposals ultra vires—General Rate Act 1967, s 11. **Westminster City Council v Greater London Council** [1986] 2 278, HL.

      Payment in respect of employment of valuer by rating authority—Whether ultra vires the rating authority—Local Government Act 1933, s 187(2). **Grainger v Liverpool Corp** [1954] 1 333, QBD.

      Purchase of undertaking of omnibus company—Payment for goodwill—Ultra vires—Payment out of reverse fund of local authority's undertaking—Local Government Act 1933, ss 185, 187—Leicester Corporation Act 1930, s 45(2)(b). **A-G (ex rel Birmingham and Midland Motors Omnibus Co Ltd) v Leicester Corp** [1943] 1 146, Ch D.

  Expenses—
    Member of local authority—
      Attendance allowance payable to member of local authority who is a councillor—Whether allowance payable to deemed member of local authority who is a councillor of another local authority—Local Government Act 1972, s 173(1). **Hopson v Devon CC** [1978] 1 1205, Ch D.

    Members of council—
      Expenses necessarily incurred in travelling—Whether including expenses incurred for purpose of bodily subsistence while travelling—Local Government Act 1933, s 294(1). **Glamorgan CC v Ayton** [1936] 3 210, KBD.

  General rate fund—
    Payment out of fund. *See* Expenditure—Payment out of general rate fund, *above*.

  Housing. *See* **Housing**.

  Local taxation licences—
    Distribution of proceeds between county and county borough—
      Statutory provision for distribution of proceeds of licences and grants—Grants discontinued—Whether necessary for new agreement to be made as to distribution of proceeds of licences—Local Government Act 1929, s 85(5). **Liverpool Corp v Lancashire CC** [1936] 3 945, CA.

  London. *See* **London** (Local government).

  Maladministration—
    Complaint to local commissioner—
      Children taken into care by local authority, separated and placed with different foster parents—Care proceedings in respect of children—Foster parents bringing adoption proceedings—Mother of children complaining direct to commissioner about local authority's acts in respect of children—Complaint out of time—Whether complaint required to specify expressly or by inference acts of maladministration—Whether commissioner properly exercising discretion to dispense with requirement that complaint be referred by member of local authority—Whether extension of time for entertaining complaint justified—Whether investigation of complaint precluded because remedy by way of court proceedings—Whether investigation into 'decision' by local authority permissible—Children and Young Persons Act 1963, s 1—Local Government Act 1974, ss 26(2)(a)(3)(4)(6)(c)(10), 34(3). **R v Local Comr for Administration for the North and East Area of England, ex p Bradford Metropolitan City Council** [1979] 2 881, QBD and CA.

LOCAL GOVERNMENT (cont)—
   Maladministration (cont)—
      Complaint to local commissioner (cont)—
         Commissioner's report—Commissioner finding council guilty of maladministration in respect of
         planning application—Commissioner applying tests set out in National Code of Local
         Government Conduct—Whether commissioner applying correct tests. **R v Local Comr for
         Administration in North and North East England, ex p Liverpool City Council** [1999] 3 85, QBD.
         Commissioner's report—Commissioner finding maladministration in respect of planning
         decision—Whether commissioner applying correct tests—Whether commissioner erring in
         undertaking investigation—Local Government Act 1974, s 26. **R v Local Comr for Administration
         in North and North East England, ex p Liverpool City Council** [2001] 1 462, CA.
         Commissioner's report—Defect in sewer connected to complainant's house—Complaint regarding
         council's inspection of sewer during its construction—Report on complaint concluding that there
         had been maladministration by council and that complainant had suffered injustice as result of
         maladministration—Whether commissioner's report susceptible to judicial review—Whether
         local commissioner exceeding his powers—Local Government Act 1974, ss 26(1), 34(3). **R v Comr
         for Local Administration, ex p Eastleigh BC** [1988] 3 151, CA.
         Jurisdiction of commissioner—Exclusion of jurisdiction—Action taken in exercise of administrative
         functions—Action in respect of which aggrieved person has remedy by way of proceedings in
         any court of law—Decision of education appeal committee—Complaint to local commissioner
         regarding committee's decision—Finding of injustice by reason of maladministration—Whether
         committee's decision administrative or judicial function—Whether persons aggrieved having
         legal remedy by way of judicial review of committee's decision—Whether commissioner having
         jurisdiction to investigate complaint—Whether findings of maladministration justified—Local
         Government Act 1974, s 26(1)(6). **R v Comr for Local Administration, ex p Croydon London BC**
         [1989] 1 1033, QBD.
         Production of documents or information to commissioner for purpose of investigating
         complaint—Notice served by local authority on commissioner that disclosure of documents
         would be contrary to public interest—Effect of service of notice—Documents or information not
         authorised or required to be communicated by any persons to any other person—Records
         relating to child in care of local authority—Commissioner issuing subpoena requiring production
         of records—Whether commissioner 'any other person' to whom communication of document or
         information not authorised or required to be made—Whether local authority required to produce
         records—Local Government Act 1974, s 32(3). **Liverpool CC, Re a complaint against** [1977] 2 650,
         QBD.
   Meeting—
      Access—
         Access by councillor—Councillor a member of public services committee—Council setting up
         public services sub-committee to look after direct labour organisations employed by
         council—Councillor seeking access to meetings of sub-committee—Councillor claiming access to
         meetings necessary to enable him to perform his duties as councillor—Council holding that
         meetings confidential and refusing access to meetings—Whether councillor entitled to access to
         meetings. **R v Hackney London BC, ex p Gamper** [1985] 3 275, QBD.
         Remote meetings—Temporary provision made in response to COVID-19 pandemic for local
         authority meetings to be held remotely—Whether permanent provision possible—Whether
         possible to construe existing provisions as permitting remote meetings or whether primary
         legislation required—Local Government Act 1972, Sch 12. **R (on the application of Hertfordshire
         CC) v Secretary of State for Housing, Communities and Local Government (Local Government
         Association and ors, interested parties)** [2022] 1 1058, DC.
      Committee meeting—
         Council member having personal interest in matter under consideration excluded from
         meeting—Whether provisions for exclusion of council member having personal interest applying
         only to members of council committee—Whether council member having personal interest able
         to remain in meeting in personal but not representative capacity—Local Authorities (Model Code
         of Conduct) (England) Order 2001, Sch 1. **R (on the application of Richardson) v North Yorkshire
         CC** [2004] 2 31, CA.
      Parish meeting—
         Poll—Question not put to vote—Whether poll demandable—Local Government Act 1933, Sch 3,
         Part 6, para 5(4). **Bennett v Chappell** [1965] 3 130, CA.
      Voting—
         Chairman's casting vote—Manner of exercise of casting vote—Council resolution to increase
         council house rents—Resolution passed on mayor's casting vote—Duty of mayor when using
         casting vote—Whether mayor entitled to exercise casting vote in favour of his party's
         policy—Whether mayor required to exercise casting vote in favour of status quo—Whether
         council resolution valid—Local Government Act 1972, Sch 12, para 39(2). **R v Bradford
         Metropolitan City Council, ex p Corris** [1989] 3 156, CA.
         Chairman's casting vote—Manner of exercise of casting vote—Council resolution to sell old
         people's home—Resolution passed on mayor's casting vote—Duty of mayor when using casting
         vote—Whether mayor entitled to exercise casting vote in favour of his party's policy—Whether
         mayor required to exercise casting vote in favour of status quo—Whether council resolution
         valid—Local Government Act 1972, Sch 12, para 39(2). **R v Bradford Metropolitan City Council,
         ex p Wilson** [1989] 3 140, QBD.
         Committee meetings—Prohibition on county councillor voting on matter involving expenditure on
         account of which district not liable to be charged—County councillor representing separate
         district for purposes of Maternity and Child Welfare Act 1918—Member of public health and
         housing committee of county council and of maternity and child welfare sub-committee—Right
         to vote at committee and sub-committee meetings—Local Government Act 1933, s 75. **Alderton v
         Essex CC** [1937] 3 219, Ch D.
         Duty of councillor when voting—Resolution to fix general rate—Councillor voting in accordance
         with party 'whip'—Whether councillor entitled to take party policy into account when
         voting—Whether voting in accordance with party whip amounting to fetter on councillor's
         discretion—Whether council resolution valid. **R v Waltham Forest London BC, ex p Baxter**
         [1987] 3 671, CA.

LOCAL GOVERNMENT (cont)—

Meeting (cont)—
 Voting (cont)—
  Resolution passed by nod of head without ballot or show of hands—Whether resolution validly passed—Local Government Act 1972, Sch 12, para 39. **R v Highbury Corner Magistrates' Court, ex p Ewing** [1991] 3 192, CA.

Office—
 Appointment—
  Restriction—Members of local authority not to be appointed to paid office—Appointment of councillor as clerk to council in honorary capacity on his undertaking to resign from council—Whether 'paid office'—Local Government Act 1933, s 122. **A-G v Ulverston UDC** [1944] 1 475, Ch D.

Officer—
 Compensation for loss of employment—
  London Passenger Transport Board—Transfer of officer to Board. See **London Passenger Transport Board** (Transfer of officer or servant to Board—Compensation of officer of company ceasing to exist on formation of board).
  Long-term compensation—Assessment—Deduction—Factors to be considered—Prospects of other employment—Size of salary officer likely to command in other employment—Local Government (Compensation) Regulations 1963 (SI 1963 No 999), reg 14(1)(c), (f). **Myrddin-Baker v Teesside County BC (No 2)** [1971] 1 567, QBD.
  Loss of employment attributable to reorganisation of local government—Attributable to—Causal connection between reorganisation and loss of employment—Applicant town clerk of a borough council due to disappear under reorganisation—Applicant appointed to office of chief executive of a district council created under reorganisation—District council reviewing its management structure after one year of being in operation—District council deciding to abolish post of chief executive because of economic conditions—Applicant's employment as chief executive terminated—Whether loss of employment 'attributable to' reorganisation of local government—Whether sufficient causal connection between reorganisation and loss of employment—Local Government Act 1972, s 259(1)—Local Government (Compensation) Regulations 1974 (SI 1974 No 463), reg 4(1). **Walsh v Rother DC** [1978] 3 881, CA.
  Loss of employment attributable to reorganisation of local government—Attributable to—Material contributory cause of loss of employment—Applicant employed by council as airport manager—Under reorganisation council ceasing to exist and replaced by new council—New council continuing to employ applicant as airport manager—New council deciding for financial reasons to hand over management of airport to a company—Termination of applicant's employment with new council—Whether sufficient to show that reorganisation of local government a material contributory cause of loss of employment—Whether sufficient to prove that new council's change of policy about managing the airport would not have been adopted by the former council—Local Government (Compensation) Regulations 1974 (SI 1974 No 463), regs 7(1)(a), 11(1)(a). **Mallet v Restormel BC** [1978] 1 503, QBD.
  Resettlement and long-term compensation—Appeal to industrial tribunal of tribunal to hear further evidence on appeal from compensating authority—Local Government (Compensation) Regulations 1963 (SI 1963 No 999), regs 14(1), 38(1), 43(3). **Myrddin-Baker v Teesside County BC** [1970] 1 1108, QBD.
  Resettlement compensation—Assessment—Deduction—Net emoluments received from work or employment in place of employment lost—Part only of salary to which entitled in new employment paid—Local Government (Compensation) Regulations 1963 (SI 1963 No 999), reg 8(1). **Myrddin-Baker v Teesside County BC (No 2)** [1971] 1 567, QBD.
  Resettlement compensation—Local government—Officer—Compensation for loss of employment—Resettlement compensation—Time for making claim for compensation—Claim to be made not later than 13 weeks after loss of employment which was the cause of the claim—Applicant employed as airport manager—Council ceasing to operate airport—Applicant refusing alternative employment but negotiating for early retirement with pension—Applicant retained as employee for two months after date in which he ceased to manage airport—During those two months applicant employed on duties connected with winding up airport and on other unspecified duties—Claim for compensation made more than 13 weeks after date on which applicant ceased to manage airport but within 13 weeks of date employment terminated as result of negotiations—Whether claim in time—Local Government (Compensation) Regulations 1974 (SI 1974 No 463), reg 7(1)(d). **Mallet v Restormel BC** [1978] 1 503, QBD.
  Transferred officer. See Officer—Transferred officer—Compensation, below.
 Corruption. See **Criminal law** (Corruption).
 Loss of employment—
  Ill-health—Payment of gratuity to employee—Resolution to grant—Enforceability by employee—Resolution to pay gratuity in weekly instalments—Whether decision vires—Poplar Borough Council Superannuation and Pensions Act 1911, s 8(2). **Holloway v Poplar BC** [1939] 4 165, KBD.
 Remuneration—
  Children's allowances—Fair and reasonable—Discretion of local authority—Local Government Act 1933, ss 106, 228, 229, 230. **Walker, Re** [1944] 1 614, CA.
  Reduction—Sickness—Poor law relieving officer—Contract of service—Clause relating to sick pay—Public Assistance Order 1930 (SR & O 1930 No 185), art 162. **Littlejohn v London CC** [1937] 3 43, CA.
  Reduction—Sickness—Poor law relieving officer—Contract of service—Recovery of pay—Regulations of council relating to sick pay—Public Authorities Protection Act 1893, s 1—Public Assistance Order 1930 (SR & O 1930 No 185), arts 142(1), 162. **Compton v West Ham County BC** [1939] 3 193, Ch D.
  Transferred officer—Rate collector—Amalgamation of districts. **Cowan v Ennerdale RDC** [1936] 3 684, Assizes.
  War time. See **Emergency legislation** (Local government—Remuneration of officer).
 Transferred officer—
  Compensation—Emoluments for which compensation granted—Increases of salary in new employment—Power to review compensation—Local Government Act 1929, s 123, Sch VIII, para 14. **Dodds v Durham CC** [1950] 2 1090, Durham Assizes.

LOCAL GOVERNMENT (cont)—
Officer (cont)—
Transferred officer (cont)—
Remuneration. *See* Officer—Remuneration—Transferred officer, *above*.
Superannuation. *See* Superannuation—Transferred officer, *below*.
Pension scheme. *See* **Pension** (Pension scheme—Local government pensions).
Public sector equality duty. *See* **Local authority** (Statutory duty—Public sector equality duty).
Public utility undertaking—
Reserve fund—
Application of fund—Relief of unemployed. **A-G v Oldham Corp** [1936] **2** 1022, Ch D.
Rates. *See* **Rates**.
Reorganisation—
Local Government Commission. *See* **Local authority** (Local Government Commission—Restructuring of local government).
Loss of employment attributable to reorganisation—
Compensation. *See* Officer—Compensation for loss of employment—Loss of employment attributable to reorganisation of local government, *above*.
Powers of local authority. *See* **Local authority** (Restructuring of local government —Powers —Reorganisation).
Vesting of property in newly constituted authorities. *See* **Local authority** (Property—Reorganisation of local government).
Superannuation—
Assessment of allowance—
Area public assistance officer acting also as interim superintendent registrar of births and deaths—Inclusion of fees as registrar in calculation of average remuneration—Calculation to be based on gross fees—Local Government Superannuation Act 1937, ss 8(2)(5)(c), 40(1)(3). **Jobbins v Middlesex CC** [1948] **2** 610, CA.
Remuneration of borough treasurer acting as local fuel overseer—Superannuation rights regulated by local Act—Local Government Superannuation Act 1937, s 40(3), not applicable to employees of local Act authorities—Employment not to be treated as two separate employments—'Officer'— 'Emoluments'—Paddington Borough Council (Superannuation and Pensions) Act 1911, ss 3, 4, 5, 13—London County Council (General Powers) Act 1928, Part VII—Local Government Superannuation Act 1937, ss 1, 3, 8, 26, 40(3)—Local Government Superannuation (Administration) Regulations, 1938 (SR & O 1938 No 574), art 4—Fuel and Lighting Order 1939 (SR & O 1939 No 1028), art 16(1)—Paddington Borough Council Superannuation Scheme 1938, arts 4, 13(2), 15. **Wickham and the Mayor, Aldermen and Burgesses of the Metropolitan Borough of Paddington, Re an arbitration between** [1946] **2** 68, KBD.
Decision on claim by authority concerned—
Authority concerned—Scheme administered by county council—Employees of rural district council entitled to participate—Claim to annual superannuation allowance by former employee of rural district council—Claim admitted by rural district council but rejected by county council—Local Government Superannuation Act 1937, ss 8, 35. **Walter v Eton RDC** [1950] **2** 588, CA.
Interim registrar of births and deaths—
Originally contributory employee as Poor Law Officer—Request for assurance that superannuation rights protected on change of appointment—No reply to request—Estoppel—Contributory employee since commencement of appointment as 'interim registrar'—Births and Deaths Registration Act 1874, ss 24, 25—Local Government Act 1929, ss 21, 22, 119—Local Government Superannuation Act 1937, ss 3(2)(d), 27(1), 35. **Algar v Middlesex CC** [1945] **2** 243, KBD.
London. *See* **London** (Local government—Employee—Superannuation).
Right to annual superannuation allowance on ceasing to be employed—
Question to be decided by Minister—Claim after cessation of employment—Whether claimant 'employee' at material time—Local Government Superannuation Act 1937, s 35. **Wilkinson v Barking Corp** [1948] **1** 564, CA.
Scheme apart from Superannuation Acts—
Powers of local authority—Contract—Registration—Superannuation and other Trusts Funds (Validation) Act 1927. **Armour v Liverpool Corp** [1939] **1** 363, Ch D.
Transferred officer—
Officer transferred in 1930—Whether 'in the service on 28th July 1925'—Poor Law Officers' Superannuation Act 1896—Local Government Act 1929, ss 119, 124. **Clay v London CC** [1939] **2** 67, Ch D.
Town and country planning. *See* **Town and country planning**.
Transfer of functions—
More than one authority succeeding to different functions of former authority—
Vesting of property. *See* **Local authority** (Property—Reorganisation of local government).
Travel concessions. *See* **Local authority** (Transport—Travel concessions).

LOCAL GOVERNMENT COMMISSION
See **Local authority** (Local Government Commission).

LOCAL INQUIRY
Appeal against refusal of permission for development. *See* **Town and country planning** (Appeal to Minister against refusal of permission for development—Local inquiry).

LOCAL LAND CHARGE
See **Land charge** (Local land charge).

LOCAL VALUATION COURT
Appeal. *See* **Rates** (Local valuation court—Appeal).
Contempt of court—
Publications concerning legal proceedings. *See* **Contempt of court** (Publications concerning legal proceedings—Court—Inferior court—Local valuation court).

LOCK-OUT AGREEMENT
Enforceability. *See* **Contract** (Enforceability—Lock-out agreement).
Sale of land. *See* **Sale of land** (Lock-out agreement).

LOCOMOTIVE
Factory, in—
Safety regulations. *See* **Factory** (Locomotive—Safety regulations).
Light locomotive. *See* **Road traffic** (Light locomotive).

LODGING
Innkeeper—
Duty to provide. *See* **Inn** (Duty to supply refreshment and lodging to traveller).
Overcrowding. *See* **Housing** (Overcrowding—Lodgings).

LODGING-HOUSE
Registration of common lodging-house. *See* **Public health** (Common lodging-house—Registration).

LOITERING
Prostitution—
Loitering for purposes of prostitution—
Generally. *See* **Criminal law** (Prostitution—Loitering or soliciting for purposes of prostitution).
Male prostitute—Whether offence capable of being committed only by female prostitute. *See* **Criminal law** (Prostitution—Common prostitute—Male prostitute—Male prostitute charged with loitering in street for purposes of prostitution).
Suspected person. *See* **Criminal law** (Vagrancy—Suspected person).

LONDON
Building. *See* **Building** (London).
Chancery business—
Transfer from High Court to county court. *See* **County court** (Transfer of action—Transfer from High Court—Chancery business—London).
Club—
Music and dancing licence. *See* **Entertainment** (Music and dancing licence—London—Club).
Damage to property vested in local authority—
Recovery of expenses incurred in repairing damage—
Accidental damage—Recovery of cost of repairs—London Government Act 1939, s 181(3). **Kensington BC v Walters** [1959] 3 652, QBD.
Diocese of London—
Confirmatory faculty—
Costs. *See* **Ecclesiastical law** (Faculty—Confirmatory faculty—Costs—Diocese of London).
Employment agencies—
Licensing—
Carrying on business at licensed address—London County Council (General Powers) Act 1921, ss 11, 16. **Arram v Walters** [1936] 2 959, KBD.
Housing—
Accommodation of working classes. *See* **Housing** (Accommodation of working classes—Administrative County of London).
Local government—
City of London ward election—
Election petition. *See* **Elections** (Local government—Election petition—City of London ward elections).
Consultation between authorities—
Greater London Council required to consult London boroughs about proposals involving expenditure—GLC deciding to make grants to voluntary organisations without consulting London boroughs—Whether grants ultra vires—Local Government (Interim Provisions) Act 1984, s 11. **Westminster City Council v Greater London Council** [1986] 2 278, HL.
Election—
Borough council—Ballot papers—Inspection. *See* **Elections** (Local government—Ballot papers—Inspection—London borough council election).
Employee—
Retirement compensation—Employee made redundant at 60—Retiring age 65—Whether compensation based on actual average salary of last five years preceding date of retirement or on national average of five years between 60 and 65—Local Government Superannuation Act 1937, s 8(5)—London Government (Compensation) Regulations 1964 (SI 1964 No 1953), reg 2(1). **Minister of Housing and Local Government v Lambert** [1969] 1 447, QBD.
Superannuation—Established officer or servant—Option of contributing to superannuation fund in respect of previous continous temporary service—Continuous temporary service—Period of rendering services broken by employee's participation in strike—City of London (Various Powers) Act 1944, s 9(2). **Cardy v City of London Corp** [1950] 2 475, KBD.
Inspection of documents—
Minutes—Inspection by local government elector—Planning committee of local planning authority—Whether minutes of committee acting under delegated powers were minutes of London County Council—London Government Act 1939, s 173(1)(7). **Wilson v Evans** [1962] 1 247, QBD.
Orders for payment of money by council—Request by local government elector to see all orders for payment of money without specifying which particular order or orders—Alleged obstruction by council official in charge of documents—Considerations to be observed in assessing whether elector's request abuse of his rights—London Government Act 1939, s 173(3)(7). **Evans v Lloyd** [1962] 1 239, QBD.

LONDON (cont)—

Local government (cont)—

Transfer of liabilities—

Children's home transferred from London County Council to London borough—Whether liability for personal injury to child transferred—London Government Act 1963, s 84—London Authorities (Property etc) Order 1964 (SI 1964 No 1464), art 11. **Duncan v Lambeth London Borough** [1968] **1** 84, QBD.

London County Council—

Consent to erection of building over 100 feet in height. *See* **Building** (London—Height—Consent to building over one hundred feet in height by London County Council).

London Passenger Transport Board. *See* **London Passenger Transport Board**.

London Transport Executive. *See* **London Transport Executive**.

Mayor and City of London Court—

Appeal from—

Jurisdiction of Court of Appeal. *See* **Court of Appeal** (Jurisdiction—Appeal from Mayor's and City of London Court).

Nuisance—

Statutory nuisance—

Summons—Service. *See* **Nuisance** (Statutory nuisance—Metropolis—Summons—Service).

Obstruction—

Road traffic. *See* **Road traffic** (Obstruction—London).

Petrol-filling station—

Consent of county council to establishment of station adjacent to street—

Refusal permissible only if proposed station would cause 'obstruction to traffic'—Evidence of obstruction—Site of proposed station at intersection of several roads—Part of an adjacent road designated as site for street trading—Refusal of consent by local authority—Whether on appeal evidence of danger to traffic resulting from obstruction of traffic admissible—Whether evidence in regard to street traders admissible—London County Council (General Powers) Act 1933, s 69(1). **London CC v Cutts** [1961] **1** 600, QBD.

Road traffic—

Obstruction. *See* **Road traffic** (Obstruction—London).

Parking—

Traffic sign. *See* **Road traffic** (Traffic sign—Parking—London).

Statutory nuisance—

Summons—

Service. *See* **Nuisance** (Statutory nuisance—Metropolis—Summons—Service).

Street—

Prohibition on erection of posts etc by way of inclosure without licence—

Erection of dead shores without licence—Whether licence necessary—Metropolitan Paving Act 1817, s 75—Metropolis Management Act 1855, ss 122, 123. **Smith v Benabo** [1937] **1** 523, KBD.

Street trading. *See* **Street trading**.

Transport—

London Passenger Transport Board. *See* **London Passenger Transport Board**.

London Transport Executive. *See* **London Transport Executive**.

Waiting and loading restrictions. *See* **Road traffic** (Waiting and loading restrictions—London).

LONDON COUNTY COUNCIL

Building—

Consent of council to erection of building over 100 feet in height. *See* **Building** (London—Height—Consent to building over one hundred feet in height by London County Council).

LONDON GAZETTE

Company—

Winding up order—

Publication in Gazette—Effect. *See* **Company** (Compulsory winding up—Order—Notice—Notice of order—Publication of winding up order in London Gazette).

LONDON PASSENGER TRANSPORT BOARD

Tramway—

Liability for repair. *See* **Tramway** (Repair of road—Liability for repair).

Transfer of officer or servant to Board—

Compensation of officer for worsening of conditions of employment—

Opportunity of promotion—Limitation of time—London Passenger Transport Act 1933, ss 73, 85(2)—Limitation Act 1939, s 27. **Layen v London Passenger Transport Board** [1944] **1** 432, KBD.

Compensation of officer of company ceasing to exist on formation of board—

Compensation for loss of employment—Assessment of compensation—London Passenger Transport Act 1933, s 73(4)(6). **Allen v London Passenger Transport Board** [1936] **2** 122, KBD.

Transfer of rights to London Transport Executive. *See* **London Transport Executive** (Transfer to executive of rights of London Passenger Transport Board).

LONDON TRANSPORT

Public-private partnership agreements—

Administration order. *See* **Company** (Administration order—Public-private partnership administration order).

Underground train network—

Public-private partnership administration order. *See* **Company** (Administration order—Public-private partnership administration order).

LONDON TRANSPORT EXECUTIVE

Duty to consult with local authorities before altering bus services—
Traffic considerations—
Convenience of passengers—Whether duty to consult only in relation to traffic considerations—Whether duty extending also to convenience of public transport passengers—Transport (London) Act 1969, s 23(3). **Sinfield v London Transport Executive** [1970] 2 264, CA.
Fares—
Reduction—
Greater London Council requiring LTE to reduce fares by 25 per cent—Whether GLC acting in excess of statutory power—Transport (London) Act 1969, ss 5(1), 7(3)(b), 7(6). **Bromley London BC v Greater London Council** [1982] 1 129, CA and HL.
Greater London Council requiring LTE to reduce fares—Whether GLC acting in excess of statutory power—Transport (London) Act 1969, ss 1, 5(1), 7(3)(b)(6). **R v London Transport Executive, ex p Greater London Council** [1983] 2 262, QBD.
Transfer to executive of rights of London Passenger Transport Board—
Existing right of board to make alterations to certain bus services—
Right of board not subject to any fetter—Whether right after transfer to executive subject to general statutory provisions requiring executive to consult with local authorities—Transport (London) Act 1969, ss 16(1), 23(3). **Sinfield v London Transport Executive** [1970] 2 264, CA.

LONG LEASE

Acquisition of freehold or extended lease. See **Landlord and tenant** (Leasehold enfranchisement).
Long tenancy at low rent—
Generally. See **Landlord and tenant** (Long tenancy at low rent).
Protection. See **Rent restriction** (Long tenancy at low rent).

LONG VACATION

Commercial Court—
Sittings in Long Vacation. See **Practice** (Commercial Court—Sittings in Long Vacation).
Companies Court—
Applications in Long Vacation. See **Practice** (Companies Court—Applications in Long Vacation).
Court of Appeal—
Practice. See **Court of Appeal** (Practice—Long Vacation).
Family Division—
Practice. See **Practice** (Long Vacation—Family Division).
Hearing during. See **Practice** (Long Vacation—Hearing during vacation).
Queen's Bench Division—
Practice. See **Practice** (Long Vacation—Queen's Bench Division).

LONG-TERM INSURANCE BUSINESS

Transfer of. See **Insurance** (Transfer of long-term insurance business).

LOOK-OUT

Duty of railway authority to provide. See **Railway** (Look-out).

LORD CHANCELLOR

Bail—
Jurisdiction. See **Criminal law** (Bail—Successive applications—Jurisdiction of Lord Chancellor).
Judicial review of Lord Chancellor's decision. See **Judicial review** (Lord Chancellor).
Magistrates' courts—
Abolition of magistrates' courts committees—
Transfer of property, rights or liabilities—Lord Chancellor empowered to make scheme for transfer to Minister of the Crown—Whether Lord Chancellor having power to effect grant by local authority of leases of magistrates' courts—Whether Lord Chancellor having power to effect transfer by local authority of freehold or leasehold interest in entirety of building part of which occupied by magistrates' court—Courts Act 2003, Sch 2, para 1(1)(b). **R (on the application of the Lord Chancellor) v Chief Land Registrar (Barking and Dagenham LBC, interested party)** [2005] 4 643, QBD.
Rules made by Lord Chancellor—
Aid to construction of statute. See **Statute** (Construction—Statutory instrument—Use of rules made by Lord Chancellor for interpretation of section of statute).
University—
Visitor—
No appointment of visitor. See **University** (Visitor—Modern university—Charter establishing university providing for appointment of visitor by crown—No appointment made—Whether university having a visitor—Whether visitatorial powers exercisable by Lord Chancellor on behalf of Crown in absence of appointment).

LORD CHANCELLOR'S VISITOR

Report. See **Mental health** (Lord Chancellor's visitor—Report).

LORRY

Heavy motor vehicle. See **Road traffic** (Heavy motor car).

LOSS
    Constructive total loss—
        Fire causing significant damage to vessel at sea—
            Notice of abandonment (NOA) given more than five months after casualty—Owners seeking to be indemnified by insurers on constructive total loss basis—Whether expenditure incurred before service of NOA to be included in computing cost of repair—Whether relevant costs include charges payable to salvors under special compensation, protection and indemnity clause contained in Lloyd's Open Form—Marine Insurance Act 1906, s 60(2)(ii). **Connect Shipping Inc v Sveriges Anfgartygs Assurans Forening (The Swedish Club)** [2019] **2 Comm** 627, SC; [2019] **4** 885, SC.

LOSS OF BARGAIN
    Damages for breach of contract. *See* **Sale of land** (Damages for breach of contract—Loss of bargain).

LOSS OF OFFICE
    Compensation—
        Company director. *See* **Company** (Director—Compensation for loss of office).
        Income tax. *See* **Income tax** (Emoluments from office or employment—Compensation—Loss of office).

LOSS OF SERVICE
    Injury to servant through negligence of third person. *See* **Employment** (Loss of service).

LOST GRANT
    Commons—
        Creation of right of common. *See* **Commons** (Right of common—Creation—Prescription—Lost modern grant).
    Drainage. *See* **Easement** (Drainage—Prescription—Lost modern grant).
    Pleading—
        Particulars. *See* **Pleading** (Particulars—Lost grant).
    Right of way. *See* **Easement** (Right of way—Prescription—Lost modern grant).

LOST PROPERTY
    Larceny by finding. *See* **Criminal law** (Larceny—Finding—Lost property).

LOTTERY
    European Community, within—
        Freedom of movement—
            Advertisements, applications and tickets for lottery. *See* **European Union** (Freedom of movement—Services—Lottery).
    Generally. *See* **Gaming** (Lottery).
    Illegality not constituting offence. *See* **Statute** (Offence—Illegality not constituting an offence—Enactment declaring lotteries unlawful).
    Licensed premises—
        Small lottery. *See* **Licensing** (Gaming on licensed premises—Small lottery).

LUGGAGE
    Innkeeper's lien. *See* **Inn** (Lien—Luggage).

LUMP SUM CONTRACT
    See **Contract** (Lump sum contract).

LUMP SUM PAYMENT
    Divorce. *See* **Divorce** (Financial provision—Lump sum order).

M

MACHINERY
Capital allowances—
  Income tax—
    Machinery or plant. *See* **Capital allowances** (Machinery or plant).
Circular saw—
  Safe system of working. *See* **Safe system of working** (Dangerous machinery—Circular saw).
Cleaning—
  Factory. *See* **Factory** (Cleaning machinery).
Coal mine, in—
  Statutory duty. *See* **Coal mining** (Statutory duty—Machinery).
Dangerous—
  Building operations—
    Fencing of machinery. *See* **Building** (Building operations—Fencing of machinery—Dangerous machinery).
  Coal mine. *See* **Coal mining** (Statutory duty—Machinery—Dangerous machinery).
  Factory—
    Negligence. *See* **Negligence** (Dangerous things—Factory occupier—Duty to avoid leaving machinery in potentially dangerous condition).
    Statutory duty. *See* **Factory** (Dangerous parts of machinery).
  Generally. *See* **Safe system of working** (Dangerous machinery).
Fencing—
  Building operations. *See* **Building** (Building operations—Fencing of machinery).
Income tax—
  Allowance. *See* **Capital allowances**.
  Deduction in computing profits—
    Wear and tear. *See* **Income tax** (Deduction in computing profits—Wear and tear of machinery or plant).
Investment grant. *See* **Investment grant** (Machinery and plant).
Manufacturer's duties. *See* **Health and safety at work** (Manufacturer's duties—Manufacture and supply of machines).
Negligence—
  Dangerous machinery—
    Factory—Duty to avoid leaving machinery in potentially dangerous condition. *See* **Negligence** (Dangerous things—Factory occupier—Duty to avoid leaving machinery in potentially dangerous condition).
    Foreseeable harm. *See* **Negligence** (Duty to take care—Foreseeable harm—Dangerous machinery).
Sale of, for use in factory—
  Failure to comply with statutory requirements—
    Liability of seller for injury to workman. *See* **Factory** (Sale of machinery—Machinery not complying with statutory requirements).
Threshing machine. *See* **Agriculture** (Threshing machine).
Wear and tear—
  Deduction in computing profits for income tax. *See* **Income tax** (Deduction in computing profits—Wear and tear of machinery or plant).

MAGAZINE
Obscenity. *See* **Criminal law** (Obscene publications).
Title—
  Passing off. *See* **Passing off** (Magazine).

MAGISTRATES
Acts of justices for which action may be maintained—
  Act done by justice of peace without jurisdiction—
    Maintenance order—Wife's allegation of cruelty not proved but consent order for maintenance made—Husband committed to prison for failure to comply with order—Order discharged by Divisional Court—Action against justices for damages for false imprisonment and for sums paid to wife under order—Justices Protection Act 1848, ss 2, 3, 13. **O'Connor v Isaacs** [1956] **2** 417, CA.
Adjournment—
  Adjournment for hearing by different bench—
    Party prejudiced by evidence. **Elkington v Kesley** [1948] **1** 786, KBD.
  Adjournment for medical examination and report—
    Power of magistrates' court to make hospital order or guardianship order without convicting accused—Defence of insanity—Defendant admitting facts of offence and indicating defence of insanity would be advanced—District judge adjourning for psychiatric report with a view to proceeding to make hospital or guardianship order without conviction—Whether defence of insanity available in magistrates' court—Whether district judge obliged to proceed to verdict—Mental Health Act 1983, s 37(3)—Powers of Criminal Courts (Sentencing) Act 2000, s 11(1). **R (on the application of Singh) v Stratford Magistrates' Court** [2007] **4** 407, DC.
  Adjournment pending change in law—
    Magistrates adjourning trial to await coming into force of change in law on following day—Whether magistrates entitled to adjourn trial pending change in law. Children and Young Persons Act 1933, s 38(1) proviso—Magistrates' Courts Act 1980, s 10(1)—Criminal Justice Act 1988, s 34(1). **R v Walsall Justices, ex p W (a minor)** [1989] **3** 460, QBD.
  Application by prosecution for adjournment during submission of no case—
    Discretion—Adjournment to permit evidence on formal requirement—Special road—Failure by prosecution to prove notices and regulations—Whether magistrates justified in refusing application—Road Traffic Act 1960, ss 20(5), 37(5)—Special Roads (Notice of Opening) Regulations 1962 (SI 1962 No 1320), reg 1. **Royal v Prescott-Clarke** [1966] **2** 366, QBD.

MAGISTRATES (cont)—
  Adjournment (cont)—
    Bench of two justices unable to agree—
      Duty to adjourn case to bench of three justices—Magistrates' Courts Act 1980, s 9(2). **R v Redbridge Justices, ex p Ram** [1992] **1** 652, QBD.
    Discretion of justices—
      Review by appellate court of exercise of discretion by justices—Refusal by magistrates to grant adjournment of hearing in absence of party—Fine imposed in absentia—Power of appellate court to review exercise of discretion. **M (J) v M (K)** [1968] **3** 878, Ch D.
      Review by appellate court of exercise of discretion by justices—Summons by wife alleging cruelty and desertion—Application by husband to adjourn hearing—Husband unable to attend on date fixed, being sent abroad for twelve months on business—Adjournment refused—Finding of desertion on wife's uncontradicted evidence—Injustice to husband in that his side of case not heard—Re-hearing ordered. **Walker v Walker** [1967] **1** 412, Div.
    Jurisdiction—
      Closure order—Power to adjourn hearing of application for closure order for not more than 14 days—Whether magistrates having jurisdiction to adjourn application for closure order more than once for not more than 14 days—Magistrates' Courts Act 1980, s 54—Anti-social Behaviour Act 2003, s 2(3), (6), (7). **Metropolitan Police Comr v Hooper** [2005] **4** 1095, QBD.
    Late arrival of prosecuting counsel—
      Court informed that counsel would arrive late—Justices refusing to prolong adjournment to await arrival of counsel—Justices dismissing charges before arrival of prosecuting counsel—Whether justices exercising discretion wrongly. **R v Sutton Justices, ex p DPP** [1992] **2** 129, QBD.
    Summary trial—
      Adjournment after conviction and before sentence—Disqualification—Conviction of accused in his absence—Restriction on disqualifying accused in his absence—Disqualification for holding driving licence—Justices imposing fine on accused and adjourning consideration of disqualification—Justices purporting to disqualify accused at subsequent hearing in his presence—Whether justices having power to adjourn question after imposing fine—Whether purported disqualification valid—Magistrates' Courts Act 1952, s 14(3)—Criminal Justice Act 1967, s 26(2). **R v Talgarth Justices, ex p Bithell** [1973] **2** 717, QBD.
      Power to remand accused in custody for medical examination—Offence not punishable with imprisonment—Magistrates' Courts Act 1952, s 14(3). **Boaks v Reece** [1956] **3** 986, CA.
  Adoption—
    Appeal from magistrates' court to Divisional Court of Family Division. *See* **Adoption** (Practice—Appeal—Appeal from magistrates' court to Divisional Court of Family Division).
    Overlapping jurisdictions. *See* Juvenile court—Jurisdiction—Adoption, *below*.
  Affiliation proceedings. *See* **Affiliation**.
  Amendment of information. *See* Information—Amendment, *below*.
  Anonymity—
    Policy of withholding names of justices—
      Bench adopting policy of withholding names of justices—Justices withholding names from newspaper reporter—Whether policy contrary to principle of open justice—Whether reporter entitled to declaration that policy contrary to law. **R v Felixstowe Justices, ex p Leigh** [1987] **1** 551, QBD.
  Anti-social behaviour order—
    Practice. *See* **Practice** (Magistrates' courts—Anti-social Behaviour Orders).
    Whether proceedings criminal or civil. *See* Proceedings—Anti-social behaviour order, *below*.
  Appeal—
    Adoption proceedings—
      Generally. *See* **Adoption** (Practice—Appeal—Appeal from magistrates' court to Divisional Court of Family Division).
    Contempt of court. *See* **Contempt of court** (Appeal—Jurisdiction).
    Review of justices' decision. *See* Review of justices' decision, *below*.
  Assault—
    Dismissal of charge—
      Assault so trifling as not to merit any punishment. *See* **Criminal law** (Assault—Dismissal of charge—Trifling assault).
  Bail. *See* **Criminal law** (Bail).
  Bias—
    Circumstances in which likelihood of bias—
      Active connection between magistrate and victim of alleged offence—Trader charged with supplying underweight goods to schools in county—Magistrate hearing case member of county council education committee—Whether magistrate's interest sufficient to disqualify her from acting. **R v Altrincham Justices, ex p Pennington** [1975] **2** 78, QBD.
      Application for possession of cottage—Clerk to justices having acted for vendor of cottage on sale to applicant several years previously—Advice to justices on evidence—Comment after decision of justices—Conclusion of justices that no case to answer—Decision announced during respondent's examination, and before cross-examination. **R v Lower Munslow Justices, ex p Pudge** [1950] **2** 756, KBD.
      Chairman of justices member of fishery board instituting proceedings. **R v Pwllheli Justices, ex p Soane** [1948] **2** 815, KBD.
      Magistrate acquainted with mother of one party—Party stating before proceedings that this magistrate would 'put the defendant through it'. **Cottle v Cottle** [1939] **2** 535, Div.
      Prosecution by officer of county council of which justices' clerk was a member. **R v Camborne Justices, ex p Pearce** [1954] **2** 850, QBD.
    Knowledge of other charges against defendant—
      Discretion not to continue hearing charge where possible bias arising from knowledge of other charges—Test of bias—Proper test whether appearance of bias and not whether actual bias—Appearance of bias where fair-minded person sitting in court with knowledge of relevant facts would think fair trial impossible. **R v Liverpool City Justices, ex p Topping** [1983] **1** 490, QBD.
    Natural justice—
      Generally. *See* **Natural justice** (Magistrates—Bias).

MAGISTRATES (cont)—
Binding over—
Accused bound over to keep the peace on adjournment of case—
Necessity for reasonable grounds that future breach of the peace might occur—Justices of the Peace Act 1361—Magistrates' Courts Act 1952, s 91. **R v Aubrey-Fletcher, ex p Thompson** [1969] **2** 846, QBD.
Appeal to Crown Court—
Procedure. *See* **Crown Court** (Appeal to Crown Court—Procedure at appeal—Appeal against binding over order made by magistrates).
Conditions to be satisfied before binding over order may be made—
Magistrate's duties. **R v South Molton Justices, ex p Ankerson** [1988] **3** 989, QBD.
Forfeiture of recognisance—
Appeal—Conviction—Whether order of forfeiture a 'conviction' in respect of an offence—Whether right of appeal to quarter sessions—Summary Jurisdiction Act 1879, ss 9(1), (2), 19—Criminal Justice Administration Act 1914, s 37—Criminal Justice Act 1925, s 26(1). **R v Keeper of the Peace and Durham Justices, ex p Laurent** [1944] **2** 530, KBD.
Standard of proof—Recognisance to keep peace or be of good behaviour—No conviction when recognisance entered into—Forfeiture of recognisance only liability on breach of recognisance—Application to forfeit recognisance for breach—Whether breach of recognisance to be determined according to civil or criminal standard of proof. **R v Marlow Justices, ex p O'Sullivan** [1983] **3** 578, QBD.
Freedom of movement—
European Community—Workers. *See* **European Union** (Workers—Freedom of movement—Extent of freedom guaranteed by Treaty—Restrictions applying in territory of member state on movement of persons subject to its domestic criminal jurisdiction—Binding over).
Natural justice—
Acquitted defendant—Opportunity to make representations—Defendant bound over to keep the peace—Defendant neither warned of proposed binding-over order nor given opportunity to make representations—Whether order should be set aside as being made in breach of rules of natural justice. **R v Woking Justices, ex p Gossage** [1973] **2** 621, QBD.
Complainant—Opportunity to make representations—Complainant bound over to keep peace—Complainant neither warned of proposed binding-over order nor given opportunity to make representations—Whether order should be set aside as being made in breach of rules of natural justice. **R v Hendon Justices, ex p Gorchein** [1974] **1** 168, QBD.
Disturbance in face of court—Likelihood of breach of peace—Complainant—Applications by two complainants for summonses against each other—Argument breaking out between complainants—Magistrate refusing summonses and ordering complainants to be bound over—Magistrate giving no warning of intention to make order—Whether breach of rules of natural justice. **R v North London Metropolitan Magistrate, ex p Haywood** [1973] **3** 50, QBD.
Opportunity to make representations—Applicant bound over to keep peace—Binding over requiring applicant to pay sum in his own recognisance and requiring a surety—Applicant not given an opportunity to make representations before order made—Whether order to be set aside as being in breach of natural justice—Justices of the Peace Act 1361. **R v Clerkenwell Metropolitan Stipendiary Magistrate, ex p Hooper** [1998] **4** 193, QBD.
Witnesses—Witnesses bound over to keep the peace without knowing that justices had that in mind and without being given opportunity of making answer to it—Whether justices acted contrary to natural justice. **Sheldon v Bromfield Justices** [1964] **2** 131, QBD.
Refusal to enter into recognisance—
Young person under 17—Whether power to imprison for refusing to enter into recognisance—Whether prohibition on imprisonment of persons under 17 applying to power to bind over—Whether binding-over order can be made unilaterally by the court without defendant's consent to be bound over in sum fixed by court—Justices of the Peace Act 1361—Powers of Criminal Courts Act 1973, s 19(1). **Veater v G** [1981] **2** 304, QBD.
Right of appeal—
Magistrate's order binding over accused under Stat (1360-1)—1), 34 Edw III, c 1—Whether order involving a 'conviction'—Whether accused entitled to appeal to quarter sessions. **R v London County Quarter Sessions, ex p Metropolitan Police Comrs** [1948] **1** 72, KBD.
Borstal sentence—
Committal for sentence. *See* Committal for sentence—Committal with a view to a borstal sentence, *below*.
Caravan sites—
Jurisdiction. *See* Jurisdiction—Caravan sites, *below*.
Case stated—
Costs—
Payment by justices. *See* Costs—Payment by justices—Appeal by way of case stated, *below*.
Generally. *See* **Case stated**.
Certiorari—
Excess of jurisdiction. *See* **Certiorari** (Justices—Excess of jurisdiction).
Ground of complaint—
Failure to grant adjournment. *See* **Certiorari** (Ground of complaint—Failure to grant adjournment—Magistrates' court).
Natural justice. *See* **Certiorari** (Justices—Natural justice).
Child—
Care proceedings. *See* **Children and young persons** (Care proceedings in juvenile court).
Custody. *See* **Minor** (Custody).
Removal from jurisdiction. *See* Jurisdiction—Removal of child from jurisdiction, *below*.
Civil debt—
Summary recovery—
Order by court of summary jurisdiction for payment—Direction to levy distress in default of payment—Whether precluding issue of bankruptcy notice under Bankruptcy Act 1914, s 1(1)(2). **Debtor (No 48 of 1952), Re a, ex p Ampthill RDC v The Debtor** [1953] **1** 545, CA.

MAGISTRATES (cont)—

Civil liability—

Appointment by debenture holder—

Action against justices for false imprisonment—Plaintiff committed to prison for failure to comply with maintenance order—Order made without jurisdiction—Last period of imprisonment ending in 1945—Order discharged in October 1954—Action commenced in December 1954—Justices Protection Act 1848, s 2—Limitation Act 1939, s 21(1). **O'Connor v Isaacs** [1956] **2** 417, CA.

Excess or absence of jurisdiction—

Sentence—Imposing sentence which magistrates had no power to impose—Extent of magistrates' civil liability for acting without jurisdiction—Magistrates' Court Act (Northern Ireland) 1984, s 15. **McC v Mullan** [1984] **3** 908, HL.

Limitation of damages—

Magistrates acting without jurisdiction—Magistrates committing applicant to prison for default in maintenance order payments—Maintenance order subsequently found not to have been registered—Magistrates having no jurisdiction to commit applicant—Applicant granted certiorari quashing committal order—Applicant claiming damages against magistrates—Whether damages limited to 1p—Justices of the Peace Act 1979, s 52(1). **R v Waltham Forest Justices, ex p Solanke** [1986] **2** 981, CA.

Magistrates acting without jurisdiction—Wrongful imprisonment—Magistrates committing applicant to prison for non-payment of rates—Non-payment not caused by applicant's wilful refusal or culpable neglect—Applicant granted certiorari quashing committal order—Applicant seeking damages against magistrates for unlawful imprisonment—Whether magistrates liable in damages—Whether damages limited to one penny—General Rate Act 1967, ss 96(1), 102, 103(1)—Justices of the Peace Act 1979, ss 45, 52. **R v Manchester City Magistrates' Court, ex p Davies** [1989] **1** 90, CA.

Malicious action within jurisdiction—

Whether magistrates under civil liability for acting within jurisdiction but maliciously and without reasonable and probable cause—Justices of the Peace Act 1979, s 44. **McC v Mullan** [1984] **3** 908, HL.

Order for maintenance of wife—

Marriage polygamous or potentially so—Magistrate acting within jurisdiction in issuing summons—No duty then to inquire on his own into alleged facts on which summons based—Evidence of complainant that she was married—Respondent not present at hearing—Subsequent enforcement of maintenance order by attachment of earnings—Whether magistrates protected—Justices Protection Act 1848, s 1—Maintenance Orders Act 1958, s.6(1). **Sammy-Joe v GPO Mount Pleasant Office** [1966] **3** 924, Ch D.

Clerk—

Examination of witnesses by clerk—

General principles to be applied. **Simms v Moore** [1970] **3** 1, QBD.

Inherent power of justices to permit—Prosecution not legally represented at trial—Prosecution witness examined by clerk—Whether defendant prejudiced—Magistrates' Courts Rules 1968 (SI 1968 No 1920), r 13. **Simms v Moore** [1970] **3** 1, QBD.

Functions—

Advice on questions of law, mixed law and fact, practice and procedure—Evidence and issues—Penalties—Manner of performance of functions. **Practice Direction** [1981] **2** 831, LCJ.

Authorised legal adviser and. *See* Clerk and authorised legal adviser—Functions and responsibilities, *below*.

Intervention in examination of witnesses—

Notes of evidence based on proof of a witness—Desirability of taking notes in bound notebook. **Hobby v Hobby** [1954] **2** 395, Div.

Presence in retiring room while justices consider decision—

Circumstances in which permissible—Function of clerk. **R v Barry (Glamorgan) Justices, ex p Kashim** [1953] **2** 1005, QBD; **R v East Kerrier Justices, ex p Mundy** [1952] **2** 144, QBD; **R v Welshpool Justices, ex p Holley** [1953] **2** 807, QBD.

Clerk cross-examining witnesses and ordering witnesses out of court—Whether conviction should be quashed. **R v Consett Justices, ex p Postal Bingo Ltd** [1967] **1** 605, QBD.

Justices' deliberations revealed—Consequences of order based on cruelty in regard to divorce taken into account—Miscarriage of justice—Cumulative effect of various factors—Matrimonial Causes Rules 1957 (SI 1957 No 619), r 73(7). **Hudson v Hudson** [1965] **2** 82, Div.

Matrimonial proceedings. **Practice Direction** [1954] **1** 230, PDA.

Merits of case not affected—Complaint to Lord Chancellor. **How, ex p** [1953] **2** 1562, QBD.

Note from police officer obtained by justices' clerk and taken into retiring room—No statement in court as regards contents—Certiorari to quash conviction. **R v East Kerrier Justices, ex p Mundy** [1952] **2** 144, QBD.

Shorthand note—Clerk with approval of justices inviting assistant clerk who had taken shorthand note to retire with justices—Both present throughout Justices' deliberations—Whether presence of clerk and assistant clerk in retiring room grounds for invalidating decision. **R v Consett Justices, ex p Postal Bingo Ltd** [1967] **1** 605, QBD.

Shorthand writer also present—Shorthand writer sent for by justices—Part of shorthand note read to justices—No statement in court as regards purpose for which her presence required—Whether presence of clerk and shorthand writer in retiring room grounds for invalidating justices' decision. **R v Welshpool Justices, ex p Holley** [1953] **2** 807, QBD.

Witness—

Magistrates' clerk to be called as witness—Whether he should act as clerk retiring with magistrates at hearing of case. **Jolliffe v Jolliffe** [1963] **3** 295, Div.

Clerk and authorised legal adviser—

Functions and responsibilities. **Practice Note** [2000] **4** 895, QBD.

Committal for sentence—

Committal with a view to a borstal sentence—

Offender previously convicted or previously discharged on probation—Offender placed on probation—Failure to observe recognisance—Conviction for offence for which offender placed on probation—Whether liable to be sent to borstal—Criminal Justice Administration Act 1914, s 10—Criminal Justice Act 1925, s 46(1). **Martin v Nolan** [1944] **2** 342, KBD.

MAGISTRATES (cont)—
  Committal for sentence (cont)—
    Committal with a view to a borstal sentence (cont)—
      Power of committing justices to order disqualification and to commit for sentence—Magistrates'
        Courts Act 1952, ss 28, 83(3)(d)—Road Traffic Act 1960, ss 104(1), 105(1). **R v Surrey Quarter**
        Sessions, ex p Comr of Police of the Metropolis [1962] 1 825, QBD.
      Power to commit—Magistrates purporting to commit under new enactment—Proceedings
        commenced before new enactment in operation—Committal required to be made under previous
        enactment—New and old enactments in similar terms—Minute of adjudication and copy sent to
        Crown Court stating committal made under new enactment—Magistrates' courts rules not
        requiring minute or copy sent to Crown Court to state statute under which committal
        made—Whether committal void—Whether defendant entitled to certiorari to quash committal—
        Magistrates' Courts Act 1980, s 37(1), Sch 8, para 2. **R v Folkestone and Hythe Juvenile Court, ex**
        p R (a juvenile) [1981] 3 840, QBD.
      Procedure—Criminal Justice Administration Act 1914, s 10. **R v Riordan** [1937] 2 62, CCA.
    Crown Court. *See* **Crown Court** (Committal of offender to Crown Court for sentence).
    Offence triable summarily or on indictment—
      Defendant indicating guilty plea to offence triable either way—Whether defendant should be
        committed to Crown Court for sentence—Guidelines—Magistrates' Courts Act 1980, s 38. **R v**
        Warley Magistrates' Court, ex p DPP [1999] 1 251, QBD.
      Discontinuance of summary trial and committal to Crown Court—Circumstances of offence—
        Character and antecedents of accused—Accused charged with offences triable either
        way—Justices agreeing to try case summarily—Whether stipendiary magistrate having power to
        commit accused to Crown Court for sentence—Whether circumstances of offence part of
        accused's character and antecedents—Whether decision of one bench to try case summarily
        precluding subsequent committal to Crown Court for sentence by another bench—Principles to
        be applied when committing for sentence—Magistrates' Courts Act 1980, ss 19(1), 38. **R v**
        Doncaster Magistrates' Court, ex p Goulding [1993] 1 435, QBD.
    Practice—
      Options to commit under s 28 or s 29—Normally commit under s 29—Magistrates' Courts Act 1952,
        ss 28(1), 29. **R v Moore** [1968] 1 790, CA.
    Quarter sessions. *See* **Quarter sessions** (Committal of offender for sentence—Factors to be considered
      by quarter sessions before sentencing offender).
    Restitution order—
      Jurisdiction. *See* **Sentence** (Restitution order—Magistrates—Committal of accused to Crown Court
        for sentence).
    Sentence for indictable offence tried summarily—
      Committal following plea of guilty—Power of quarter sessions to remit case to justices to consider
        whether to allow accused to alter plea—At what stage a conviction comes into existence. **R v**
        Riley [1963] 3 949, Liverpool Crown Ct.
      Court of opinion that greater punishment should be inflicted for offence than court has power to
        inflict—Conviction of three offences—Court of opinion suspended sentence exceeding six
        months appropriate if coupled with supervision order—Court having no power to impose that
        sentence—Supervision order only possible if suspended sentence for any one offence exceeding
        six months—Court having power to impose consecutive sentences of up to 12 months—Whether
        court of opinion that greater punishment should be inflicted than court having power to
        inflict—Whether committal ultra vires—Magistrates' Courts Act 1952, s 29. **R v Rugby Justices, ex**
        p Prince [1974] 2 116, QBD.
      Offender 17 years old—Advisability of committal under s 29, rather than under s 28, of Magistrates'
        Courts Act 1952, ss 28, 29. **R v Dangerfield** [1959] 3 88, CCA.
  Committal proceedings—
    Committal for trial—
      Bail—Committal to Central Criminal Court. *See* **Criminal law** (Bail—Central Criminal
        Court—Committal for trial).
      Indictment quashed following committal. *See* **Indictment** (Committal supporting indictment—
        Indictment quashed following committal).
      Jurisdiction. *See* **Crown Court** (Committal to Crown Court for trial—Jurisdiction).
      Procedure. *See* **Crown Court** (Committal to Crown Court for trial).
      Young person. *See* **Children and young persons** (Trial of persons under 17—Committal for trial).
    Costs. *See* **Criminal law** (Costs—Magistrates' court—Indictable offences—Summary trial or inquiry as
      examining justices).
    Generally. *See* **Criminal law** (Committal—Preliminary hearing before justices).
    Guilty plea—
      Admissibility in evidence. *See* **Criminal evidence** (Admissions and confessions—Plea of guilty at
        magistrates' court).
    Judges' Rules. *See* **Criminal evidence** (Admissions and confessions—Committal proceedings—Judges'
      Rules).
    Judicial review—
      Availability of remedy. *See* **Judicial review** (Availability of remedy—Quashing of committal
        proceedings).
    Material evidence—
      Witness summons. *See* Witness summons—Material evidence—Committal proceedings, *below*.
    Offence triable summarily or on indictment. *See* Summary trial—Offence triable summarily or on
      indictment—Committal proceedings, *below*.
  Committees—
    Abolition. *See* **Lord Chancellor** (Magistrates' courts—Abolition of magistrates' courts committees).
  Complaint—
    Adjournment—
      Different justices at different hearings of same complaint—Propiety. *See* **Husband and wife**
        (Summary proceedings—Adjournment of complaint—Different justices at different hearings of
        same complaint).

Complaint (cont)—
Dismissal—
Complaint in respect of refusal of fire certificate—Whether an order. *See* **Fire** (Certificate—Refusal to issue—Appeal from refusal to justices—Dismissal of complaint by justices—Appeal to quarter sessions—Jurisdiction to hear appeal—Order).
Minute of adjudication. *See* **Husband and wife** (Summary proceedings—Complaint—Dismissal—Minute of adjudication).
Failure to comply with abatement notice. *See* **Nuisance** (Statutory nuisance—Abatement notice—Failure to comply—Complaint to justices).
Hearing—
Practice where related criminal proceedings—Inadvisability of civil and criminal proceedings being heard together—Complaint should be heard separately after criminal proceedings have been determined. **R v Dunmow Justices, ex p Anderson** [1964] **2** 943, QBD.
Unsworn statement by defendant—Admissibility—Matrimonial proceedings—Magistrates' Courts Rules 1968 (SI 1968 No 1920), rr 13(2), 14(2). **Aggas v Aggas** [1971] **2** 1497, Div.
Jurisdiction. *See* Jurisdiction—Complaint, *below*.
Limitation of time—
Matrimonial proceedings—Complaint of adultery. *See* **Husband and wife** (Summary proceedings—Adultery—Limitation of time).
Matrimonial proceedings—Generally. *See* **Husband and wife** (Summary proceedings—Complaint—Limitation of time).
Matrimonial proceedings—
Adultery. *See* **Husband and wife** (Summary proceedings—Adultery).
Desertion. *See* **Husband and wife** (Summary proceedings—Desertion).
Generally. *See* **Husband and wife** (Summary proceedings—Complaint).
Persistent cruelty. *See* **Husband and wife** (Summary proceedings—Persistent cruelty).
Right to stop case at conclusion of complainant's evidence—
Matrimonial proceedings. *See* **Husband and wife** (Summary proceedings—Right to stop case at conclusion of complainant's evidence).
Statutory nuisance. *See* **Nuisance** (Statutory nuisance—Complaint to justices).
Condemnation proceedings. *See* Proceedings—Condemnation proceedings, *below*.
Contempt of court. *See* **Contempt of court** (Magistrates' court).
Conviction—
Not recorded—
Autrefois convict. *See* **Criminal law** (Autrefois convict—Conviction—Conviction by justices in absence of accused—Conviction not recorded in court register).
Costs—
Criminal cases. *See* **Criminal law** (Costs—Magistrates' court).
Jurisdiction—
Generally. *See* **Costs** (Order for costs—Jurisdiction—Magistrates).
Payment by justices—
Appeal by way of case stated—Judicial review proceedings—Jurisdiction to award costs against justices—Guidelines for making costs orders against justices—Supreme Court Act 1981, ss 28A(3), 51(1)(b). **R v Newcastle-under-Lyme Justices, ex p Massey** [1995] **1** 120, QBD.
Mandamus. *See* **Mandamus** (Costs—Payment by justices).
Payment by police—
Property in possession of police—Delivery to owner. *See* **Police** (Property in possession of police—Delivery to owner—Costs of application for delivery to owner).
Court—
Constitution of bench—
Desirability of uneven number of justices. **Barnsley v Marsh** [1947] **1** 874, KBD.
Open court—
Petty sessional or occasional court-house—Requirement that sitting be in open court—Accused arriving at court-house with over 20 supporters—Only seats for five members of the public in courtroom—Five supporters occupying the five seats—Five supporters interrupting proceedings shortly after start of hearing—Five having to leave courtroom as a result—Five seats remaining empty for rest of hearing—Member of press present during hearing—Whether hearing in 'open court'—Magistrates' Courts Act 1952, s 98(4). **R v Denbigh Justices, ex p Williams** [1974] **2** 1052, QBD.
Court list—
Procedure. *See* Procedure—Court list, *below*.
Court register—
Procedure. *See* Procedure—Court register, *below*.
Criminal jurisdiction and procedure—
Offences triable on indictment or summarily—
Initial procedure: accused to indicate intention as to plea—Matters to be explained by court in ordinary language before court asking accused to indicate intention as to plea—Magistrates' court not explaining to accused that if he indicated he would plead guilty he could be committed for sentence to Crown Court—Accused pleading guilty—Accused committed for sentence to Crown Court—Whether magistrates' court having jurisdiction to commit accused for sentence—Magistrates' Courts Act 1980, s 17A. **R (on the application of Rahmdezfouli) v Wood Green Crown Court** [2014] **1** 567, DC.
Crown Court—
Justices as judges. *See* **Crown Court** (Justices as judges).
Custody—
Access. *See* **Ward of court** (Custody—Prior custody order made by magistrates).
Appeal from magistrates court. *See* **Minor** (Custody—Appeal from magistrates' court).
Jurisdiction to divide custody. *See* **Minor** (Division of custodial rights—Jurisdiction of justices to divide custody).
Jurisdiction to make custody order while divorce pending. *See* **Minor** (Custody—Jurisdiction—Magistrates' court—Divorce pending).

MAGISTRATES (cont)—
   Custody (cont)—
      Refusal to stay execution of order. *See* **Minor** (Custody—Order—Breach—Breach by father of order made in favour of mother).
      Removal of proceedings instituted in court of summary jurisdiction to High Court. *See* **Minor** (Custody—Jurisdiction—Removal of proceedings to High Court).
   Damages—
      Limitation of liability. *See* Civil liability—Limitation of damages, *above*.
   Debt—
      Summary recovery of. *See* Civil debt—Summary recovery, *above*.
   Default of payment of fine—
      Committal to prison. *See* Fine—Committal to prison in default of payment, *below*.
   Deferment of sentence. *See* **Sentence** (Deferment of sentence).
   Depositions—
      Committal for trial. *See* **Criminal evidence** (Committal for trial—Depositions).
      Evidence at trial. *See* **Criminal evidence** (Trial—Depositions as evidence).
   Discretion—
      Discretion as to offence to be charged. *See* **Criminal law** (Prosecutor—Discretion—Offence to be charged).
      Review of exercise of discretion—
         Duty of appellate court. *See* **Appeal** (Review of exercise of discretion).
      Whether to accept change of plea after plea of guilty—
         Generally. *See* **Criminal law** (Trial—Plea—Withdrawal of plea of guilty—Application—Application before sentence passed).
   Dismissal of charge—
      Judicial review—
         Whether on application for judicial review court has power to interfere with magistrates' dismissal of charge. *See* Proceedings—Control by judicial review—Magistrates dismissing charge without giving prosecution opportunity to present case, *below*.
   Disqualification—
      Driver—
         Adjournment. *See* **Road traffic** (Disqualification for holding licence—Adjournment in order to enable disqualification to be imposed).
   Dogs—
      Dangerous dogs—
         Proceedings in respect of. *See* **Animal** (Dog—Dangerous dog).
   Domestic proceedings. *See* **Husband and wife**.
   Double jeopardy, rule against. *See* Rule against double jeopardy, *below*.
   Driving test—
      Jurisdiction of magistrate. *See* **Road traffic** (Driving licence—Test conducted in accordance with regulations—Jurisdiction of magistrate).
   Drugs offences. *See* **Drugs**.
   Duty to act openly, impartially and fairly. *See* **Natural justice** (Magistrates—Duty to act openly, impartially and fairly).
   Election to be tried by jury—
      Indictable offence triable summarily—
         Graver offences added on indictment—Sentence. *See* **Sentence** (Indictable offence tried summarily—Election by accused at summary trial for trial by jury).
   Evidence—
      Admission—
         Admission by probation officer of desertion on behalf of respondent husband unable to attend hearing—Appeal by husband on ground that admission was unauthorised—Probation officer authorised to ask for adjournment on husband's behalf but not to make admission of desertion—Re-trial ordered. **Smith v Smith** [1957] **2** 397, Div.
      Character of defendant—
         Defendant conducting own defence attacking character of prosecution witness—Warning of consequent admissibility of questions as to defendant's character—How given. **R v Weston-super-Mare Justices, ex p Townsend** [1968] **3** 225, QBD.
      Closure order—
         Evidence in support of application for closure order—Hearsay evidence—Disclosure of documents in possession of police—Guidance—Anti-social Behaviour Act 2003, s 2—Magistrates' Courts (Hearsay Evidence in Civil Proceedings) Rules 1999, SI 1999/681, rr 3, 4. **R (on the application of Cleary) v Highbury Corner Magistrates' Court** [2007] **1** 270, DC.
      Consideration of evidence—
         Matrimonial proceedings. *See* **Husband and wife** (Summary proceedings—Consideration of evidence).
      Specialised knowledge of magistrate—
         Specialised knowledge of circumstances forming background of particular case—Advice to other justices after retirement to consider verdict—Propriety—Medical evidence given at hearing—Member of bench a medical practitioner—Extent to which medical practitioner may draw on specialised knowledge to advise himself and other justices in considering evidence. **Wetherall v Harrison** [1976] **1** 241, QBD.
      Witness summons. *See* Witness summons, *below*.
      Written statement—
         Admissibility—Employers' letter showing arrangements for employee litigant to go abroad on business—Receivable on application for adjournment—Evidence Act 1938, s 1. **Walker v Walker** [1967] **1** 412, Div.
         Committal proceedings—Copy to be given to each of the other parties to the proceedings—Whether sufficient to give copy to solicitor representing accused—Criminal Justice Act 1967, s 2(2)(c). **R v Bott** [1968] **1** 1119, Assizes.

MAGISTRATES (cont)—
    Examination of witnesses by court—
        Domestic proceedings—
            Procedure—Party appearing in person and giving evidence—Unable effectively to cross-examine—Party's case not put to witnesses on other side—Duty of court—Magistrates' Courts Act 1952, s 61. **Fox v Fox** [1954] **3** 526, Div.
    Examining justices—
        Generally. *See* **Criminal law** (Committal).
        Remand—
            Adjournment granted at request of Crown before any evidence called—Whether magistrate has discretion to remand accused in custody or must remand on bail—Magistrates' Courts Act 1952, ss 6(1), 105(1). **R v Guest, ex p Metropolitan Police Comr** [1961] **3** 1118, Vacation Ct.
    Excess or absence of jurisdiction—
        Civil liability. *See* Civil liability—Excess or absence of jurisdiction, *above*.
    Extradition. *See* **Extradition**.
    Family proceedings. *See* **Family proceedings**.
    Fine—
        Committal to prison in default of payment—
            Adult offenders—Statutory requirements in relation to warrants of commitment—Whether magistrates having to state reasons for not making money payment supervision order—Whether magistrates having to state reasons for not making alternative order in open court—Magistrates' Courts Act 1980, s 82(4), (6). **R v Stockport Justices, ex p Conlon** [1997] **2** 204, QBD.
            Inquiry as to means—Criminal Justice Administration Act 1914, ss 1(1), 5—Money Payments (Justices Procedure) Act 1935, s 1(3). **R v Dunne, ex p Sinnatt** [1943] **2** 222, KBD.
            Inquiry as to means—Money Payments (Justices Procedure) Act 1935, ss 1, 11. **R v Woking Justices, ex p Johnstone** [1942] **2** 179, KBD.
            Issue of committal warrant without a hearing—Issue of committal warrant without notice—Offender serving term of imprisonment—Failure to notify offender that committal warrant to be issued—Whether breach of natural justice—Whether power to issue warrant without hearing including power to issue warrant without notice to offender—Criminal Justice Act 1967, s 44(6). **R v Dudley Magistrates' Court, ex p Payne** [1979] **2** 1089, QBD.
            Issue of committal warrant without a hearing—Issue of committal warrant without notice—Whether breach of natural justice—Whether power to dispense with presence of defendant at hearing including power to dispense with notice—Criminal Justice Act 1967, s 44(6). **Forrest v Brighton Justices** [1981] **2** 711, HL.
            Issue of committal warrant without a hearing—Issue of warrant postponed subject to conditions—Defendant failing to comply with conditions—Warrant issued without notice to defendant—Whether issue or warrant breach of natural justice—Magistrates' Courts Act 1980, s 77(2). **R v Chichester Justices, ex p Collins** [1982] **1** 1000, QBD.
            Maximum period of imprisonment—Committal for non-payment of several fines—Whether maximum period that applicable to aggregate of fines not paid or to total of maxima applicable to individual fines—Magistrates' Courts Act 1952, s 64, Sch 3. **R v Southampton Justices, ex p Davies** [1981] **1** 722, QBD.
            National insurance contributions and fine—Whether sum enforceable as a civil debt for the purpose of fixing the maximum period of committal in default of payment—Magistrates' Courts Act 1952, s 64(3), Sch 3, para 4. **R v Marlow (Bucks) Justices, ex p Schiller** [1957] **2** 783, QBD.
        Supervision order—
            Effect—Committal to prison in default of payment—Limitation on power where supervision order in force—Meaning of 'commit ... to prison'—Term of imprisonment fixed for defaulter but issue of warrant of committal postponed subject to conditions—Defaulter not subject to supervision order—Effect of making supervision order subsequently—Defaulter failing to comply with conditions of postponement—Whether court bound to issue warrant of commitment despite supervision order—Magistrates' Courts Act 1952, ss 65(2), 71(6). **R v Clerkenwell Stipendiary Magistrate, ex p Mays** [1975] **1** 65, QBD.
    Fingerprints—
        Evidence in criminal proceedings—
            Order to take fingerprints—Place where fingerprints to be taken. *See* **Criminal evidence** (Fingerprints—Place where fingerprints to be taken—Justices' order to take fingerprints).
    Food and drugs—
        Condemnation of food by magistrate as unfit for human consumption—
            Magistrate acting in administrative or executive capacity—No appeal lies against his order. **R v Cornwall Quarter Sessions Appeal Committee, ex p Kerley** [1956] **2** 872, KBD.
    Guardianship of minors. *See* **Minor** (Guardianship).
    Hearing—
        Adjournment. *See* Adjournment, *above*.
        Duty to hear parties etc. *See* **Natural justice** (Magistrates).
        Procedure—
            Generally. *See* Procedure—Court hearing, *below*.
    Hospital order. *See* **Sentence** (Hospital order).
    Husband and wife—
        Generally. *See* **Husband and wife**.
        Hearing—
            Witnesses—Counsel's right to choose sequence in which to call witnesses. *See* **Counsel** (Authority—Authority in respect of witnesses—Right to call witnesses in sequence chosen by him).
        Matrimonial order—
            Income tax—Small maintenance order. *See* **Divorce** (Maintenance—Income tax—Small maintenance payments).
        Protection of young persons—
            Potentially polygamous marriage—Wife under sixteen. *See* **Children and young persons** (Protection—Recognition of foreign marriage—Potentially polygamous marriage—Fit person order).
    Imprisonment. *See* **Sentence** (Imprisonment—Magistrates' court).

MAGISTRATES (cont)—

Indictable offence triable summarily. *See* Summary trial for indictable offence, *below*.

Indorsement of Irish warrant—

  Application for indorsement—

    Hearing in open court—Juvenile—Hearing before juvenile court behind locked doors—Whether hearing of application for indorsement of Irish warrant in respect of juvenile required to be in open court—Whether restrictions on public access to juvenile court proceedings applying—Whether juvenile court having inherent power to take security precautions to prevent subject of warrant absconding—Children and Young Persons Act 1933, s 47—Backing of Warrants (Republic of Ireland) Act 1965, s 4(1), Sch, para 2. **R v Westminster City Council, ex p L** [1992] **1** 917, QBD.

  Irish warrant indorsed for execution in England—

    Indorsement required by prescribed officer of Royal Irish Constabulary—Royal Irish Constabulary disbanded—No United Kingdom legislation substituting another officer—Warrant indorsed by Deputy Commissioner of Garda Siochana—Indorsement insufficient—Sufficiency of statement of cause of complaint—Whether English magistrate has discretion to refuse execution of a warrant—Indictable Offences Act 1848, s 12, as amended by Magistrates' Courts Act 1952, s 131 and Sch 5—Petty Sessions (Ireland) Act 1951, s 27(3). **Metropolitan Police Comr v Hammond** [1964] **2** 772, HL.

  Obligation of English magistrate to indorse warrant—

    Offence in Republic of Ireland triable only on indictment—In England triable summarily or on indictment—Whether offence alleged corresponded with English offence—Whether magistrate must be satisfied prima facie case made out—Backing of Warrants (Republic of Ireland) Act 1965, s 1(1), s 2(2), Sch, para 3. **Arkins, Re** [1966] **3** 651, QBD.

  Order for return—

    Irish warrants indorsed for execution in England charging applicant with various offences—Whether offences specified corresponding with English offences—Whether magistrate having sufficient material to conclude that they did—Whether magistrate having jurisdiction to entertain an abuse of process application—Backing of Warrants (Republic of Ireland) Act 1965, s 2(2). **Gilligan, Re** [1998] **2** 1, QBD; [2000] **1** 113, HL.

    Likelihood of prosecution for another offence of political character—Evidence to show political character of offence or likelihood of prosecution for another offence of political character not tendered before magistrates—Whether fresh or additional evidence admissible on application for habeas corpus—Backing of Warrants (Republic of Ireland) Act 1965, s 2(2). **Nobbs, Re** [1978] **3** 390, QBD.

    Likelihood of prosecution or detention for another offence—Offence of political character—'Another offence'—Backing of Warrants (Republic of Ireland) Act 1965, s 2(2)(b). **Keane v Governor of Brixton Prison** [1971] **1** 1163, HL.

    Refusal to make order—Likelihood of prosecution or detention for another offence—Offence of a political character—Evidence that offence of a political character—Trial for offence in Irish special court—Court established because Irish government of view that ordinary courts inadequate to secure effective administration of justice—Applicant convicted of armed robbery by special court—Applicant sentenced to imprisonment—Applicant escaping from prison and arrested in United Kingdom—Applicant arrested under Irish warrant—Whether applicant likely to be detained for an 'offence of a political character'—Whether trial in special court showing that robbery was an 'offence of a political character'—Backing of Warrants (Republic of Ireland) Act 1965, s 2(2)(b). **R v Governor of Winson Green Prison, Birmingham, ex p Littlejohn** [1975] **3** 208, QBD.

  Prima facie case—

    Inquiry—Whether inquiry into existence of prima facie case necessary. **Keane v Governor of Brixton Prison** [1971] **1** 1163, HL.

Information—

  Abuse of process—

    Two informations arising out of same incident—Second information laid in general terms—Second information capable of being consistent or inconsistent with first information—Prosecution failing to give further particulars of second information—Whether second information should be dismissed as abuse of process of court. **R v Newcastle-upon-Tyne Justices, ex p Hindle** [1984] **1** 770, QBD.

  Amendment—

    New offence—Time limit for laying information—Amendment outside limitation period—Amendment substituting new offence—Discretion of justices to allow amendment—No injustice to defendant—Notice of facts served on defendant with original summons—Facts constituting new offence fully disclosed in notice—Whether permissible for justices to allow amendment substituting new offence outside limitation period—Magistrates' Courts Act 1952, s 104. **R v Newcastle-upon-Tyne Justices, ex p John Bryce (Contractors) Ltd** [1976] **2** 611, QBD.

    Three offences charged in one information—Accused charged with one offence only at hearing—Amendment of information allowed after commencement of trial—Whether jurisdiction to try accused or to amend information—Magistrates' Courts Rules 1952 (SI 1952 No 2190), r 14. **Hargreaves v Alderson** [1962] **3** 1019, QBD.

  Civil matter—

    Nullity of proceedings by information. **R v Dunmow Justices, ex p Anderson** [1964] **2** 943, QBD.

  Computer used for issuing process—

    Summons produced from information fed into computer—No need for production of separate information—Unsigned summons to be treated as information—Information 'laid' on date contents of summons brought to attention of magistrate or justices' clerk—Magistrates' Courts Act 1952, s 104. **Hill v Anderton** [1981] **3** 72, QBD.

  Dangerous driving. *See* **Road traffic** (Dangerous driving—Information).

  Defect—

    No offence disclosed—Information void ab initio—Poaching Prevention Act 1862, s 2—Magistrates' Courts Act 1952, s 100(1). **Garman v Plaice** [1969] **1** 62, QBD.

    Statement of offence—Particulars—Lack of 'such particulars as may be necessary for giving reasonable information of the nature of the charge'—Magistrates' Courts Rules 1952 (SI 1952 No 2190), r 77(1), (2)—Milk Distributive Wages Council (England and Wales) Wages Regulation Order 1952 (SI 1952 No 986), Sch, para 6(2)(b)(i). **Stephenson v Johnson** [1954] **1** 369, QBD.

Information (cont)—
Defect (cont)—
Statement of offence—Statement of offence not specifying correct enactment constituting offence—Particulars deficient—Road traffic offence—Objection taken at outset of hearing—No amendment—Whether conviction should be quashed—Magistrates' Courts Act 1952, s 100—Magistrates' Courts Rules 1952 (SI 1952 No 2190), r 77. **Hunter v Coombs** [1962] **1** 904, QBD.

Two or more offences charged in one information—Whether 'defect in substance or form'—Whether justices entitled to hear information—Summary Jurisdiction Act 1848, ss 1, 10. **Edwards v Jones** [1947] **1** 830, KBD.

Variance between information and evidence of prosecution—Risk of grave injustice to accused—Whether information should be amended—Magistrates' Courts Act 1952, s 100(1), (2). **Wright v Nicholson** [1970] **1** 12, QBD.

Duplicity—
Contravention of enforcement notice—Information alleging initial failure to comply with notice 'on and since' certain date—Whether continuing offence—Whether information bad for duplicity—Town and Country Planning Act 1971, s 89(5). **Chiltern DC v Hodgetts** [1983] **1** 1057, HL.

Drug offence. See **Drugs** (Dangerous drugs—Cannabis—Being concerned in the management of premises used for smoking or dealing in cannabis—Information charging managing premises for purposes of smoking and dealing in cannabis—Whether bad for duplicity).

Handling stolen goods. See **Criminal law** (Handling stolen goods—Information—Magistrates' court).

Having charge of motor vehicle when under influence of drink or a drug—Uncertainty of conviction—Words of statute creating one offence—In charge of vehicle while in state of self-induced incapacity—Road Traffic Act 1930, s 15(1). **Thomson v Knights** [1947] **1** 112, KBD.

Information alleging more than one breach of regulations—Sale of motor vehicle in unroadworthy condition in breach of regulations—Information alleging car sold with dangerous parts and defective steering—Whether information bad for duplicity—Road Traffic Act 1972, s 60(3)—Motor Vehicles (Construction and Use) Regulations 1978. **Streames v Copping** [1985] **2** 122, QBD.

Obtaining pecuniary advantage by deception—Evasion or deferment of debt—Information alleging dishonest obtaining of pecuniary advantage by evasion or deferment of debt—Whether more than one offence charged—Whether information bad for duplicity—Theft Act 1968, s 16(1). **Bale v Rosier** [1977] **2** 160, QBD.

Separate charges of two offences—Charge of selling rationed food naming two different kinds of rationed food. **Kite v Brown** [1940] **4** 293, KBD.

Taking or killing game without a licence—Information alleging killing of two deer in one charge—Shots fired within seconds from same geographical location—Shots separate acts—Whether shots constituting single activity—Whether information bad for duplicity—Game Licences Act 1860, s 4. **Jemmison v Priddle** [1972] **1** 539, QBD.

Hearing two or more together—
Consent of defendant—Separate informations against one or more defendants—Connected facts—Whether court having power to hear informations together without consent of defendants. **Clayton v Chief Constable of Norfolk** [1983] **1** 984, HL.

Consent of defendant—Separate informations against two or more defendants—Whether court having power to hear informations together without consent of defendants. **Aldus v Watson** [1973] **2** 1018, QBD.

Summons and cross-summons arising out of informations—Informations founded on same incident and same facts—Whether magistrates having jurisdiction to hear summons and cross-summons together—Whether consent of either party material. **R v Epsom Justices, ex p Gibbons** [1983] **3** 523, QBD.

Jurisdiction. See Jurisdiction—Trial of information, *below.*

Laying of information—
Fax. See Information—Time limit for laying information, *below.*
Meaning of 'laying'. See Jurisdiction—Trial of information—Validity of information—Laying of information, *below.*
Time limit for laying information. See Information—Time limit for laying information, *below.*

Obtaining pecuniary advantage. See **Criminal law** (Obtaining pecuniary advantage by deception—Information).

Particularity of charge—
Right to reasonable particulars at any time after charge preferred—Charge of perjury—Evidence alleged to be perjured not identified in particulars of charge supplied to accused—Accused arrested on charge—Whether accused entitled to see sworn written information leading to his arrest before committal proceedings completed—Magistrates' Courts Rules 1952 (SI 1952 No 2190), rr 13, 77. **R v Aylesbury Justices, ex p Wisbey** [1965] **1** 602, QBD.

Statement of offence—
Document commencing prosecution charging more than one offence—Preamble containing particulars common to all offences and ensuing paragraphs charging individual offences alleged to have been committed—Whether document containing five informations or one information charging five offences—Whether document valid—Magistrates' Courts Rules 1981, rr 12, 100. **Shah v Swallow** [1984] **2** 528, HL.

Summons or information—
Road traffic offence. See **Road traffic** (Offence—Summons or information).

Theft—
Information charging accused with stealing specified articles—Proof only that accused stole some of the articles specified—Whether necessary that prosecution should prove all articles specified in information to have been stolen—Theft Act 1968, s 9. **Machent v Quinn** [1970] **2** 255, QBD.

Time limit for laying information—
Amendment alleging new offence. See Information—Amendment—New offence, *above.*
Information laid just within time limit but decision to prosecute not taken until later—Delay in service of summons—Whether abuse of process of court—Whether justices having discretion to dismiss summons—Magistrates' Courts Act 1952, s 104. **R v Brentford Justices, ex p Wong** [1981] **1** 884, QBD.

MAGISTRATES (cont)—
Information (cont)—
Time limit for laying information (cont)—
Institution of proceedings—Information laid by fax within time limit—Later date indorsed on summons by court staff—Whether information laid by fax within time limit constituting institution of proceedings—Forestry Act 1967, s 17(2). **Dept for Environment, Food and Rural Affairs v Rockall** [2007] **3** 258, DC.
Jurisdiction of magistrates after expiry of time limit. *See* Jurisdiction—Trial of information, *below.*
Trial of information—
Jurisdiction. *See* Jurisdiction—Trial of information, *below.*
Two informations for one offence—
Pleas of guilty entered—Whether certiorari lies to quash conviction. **R v Campbell, ex p Nomikos** [1956] **2** 280, QBD.
Two informations relating to same facts—
Conviction on one information—Whether precluding conviction on second information. **R v Burnham Justices, ex p Ansorge** [1959] **3** 505, QBD.
Insanity, defence of—
Availability of defence of insanity in magistrates' court. *See* Adjournment—Adjournment for medical examination and report, *above.*
Irish warrant—
Indorsement. *See* Indorsement of Irish warrant, *above.*
Judicial review—
Control of proceedings by. *See* Proceedings—Control by judicial review, *below.*
Costs—
Payment by justices. *See* Costs—Payment by justices—Appeal by way of case stated—Judicial review proceedings, *above.*
Jurisdiction—
Access order—
Enforcement of order. *See* **Minor** (Custody—Access—Enforcement of order).
Accessory after the fact—
Summary trial—Whether jurisdiction to try summarily—Accessories and Abettors Act 1861, s 7. **R v West** [1962] **2** 624, CCA.
Affiliation order—
Variation. *See* **Affiliation** (Affiliation order—Variation—Jurisdiction of magistrates).
Byelaw—
Challenge to validity of byelaw in summary proceedings—Jurisdiction of magistrates to determine issue of validity. *See* **Byelaw** (Validity—Summary proceedings).
Caravan sites—
Appeal against condition imposed by local authority in site licence—Condition same as that imposed by local planning authority—Whether magistrates had power to vary condition—Caravan Sites and Control of Development Act 1960, s 7(1). **R v Kent Justices, ex p Crittenden** [1963] **2** 245, QBD.
Control of unauthorised encampments—Gypsies—Power of justices to order removal of unlawful encampments on complaint of local authority—Local authority laying complaint—Justices fixing date for hearing without issuing summonses on caravan owners and occupiers—Jurisdiction of justices to entertain ex parte complaint—Caravan Sites Act 1968, ss 10, 11. **R v Havering Justices, ex p Smith** [1974] **3** 484, QBD.
Children and young persons—
Fine—Child in care of local authority—Power to order local authority to pay fine instead of child. *See* **Children and young persons** (Fine—Imposition—Court's power to order parent or guardian to pay fine instead of child or young person).
Claim of right—
Letting house in excess of permitted rent—Building Materials and Housing Act 1945, s 7(1). **Duplex Settled Investment Trust Ltd v Worthing BC** [1952] **1** 545, KBD.
Common assault—
Ouster of jurisdiction—Execution under the process of any court of justice—Service of summons by county court bailiff—Jurisdiction of justices—Procedure to be followed—Offences against the Person Act 1861, s 46—County Courts Act 1934, s 31. **R v Holsworthy Justices, ex p Edwards** [1952] **1** 411, KBD.
Complaint—
Maintenance order in favour of wife—Complaint by wife to increase amount of order—Application by husband for discharge of order after wife's desertion—No complaint by husband—Complaint necessary for application for discharge of order—Discharge of order—Magistrates' Courts Act 1952, ss 43, 45(2). **Trathan v Trathan** [1955] **2** 701, PDA.
Costs. *See* **Costs** (Order for costs—Jurisdiction—Magistrates).
Court hearing. *See* Procedure—Court hearing—Powers, *below.*
Criminal jurisdiction and procedure. *See* Criminal jurisdiction and procedure, *above.*
Disclosure of prosecution evidence to defence—
Whether magistrates having jurisdiction to rule on disclosure issues. **R v Bromley Magistrates, ex p Smith** [1995] **4** 146, QBD.
Excess of jurisdiction—
Certiorari. *See* **Certiorari** (Justices—Excess of jurisdiction).
Gaming—
Gaming machines—Order for destruction of. *See* **Gaming** (Gaming machine—Forfeiture and destruction—Jurisdiction of justices to order destruction of gaming machines).
Highway—
Obstruction of free passage—Bona fide claim that there was no public right of way—Whether magistrates' jurisdiction ousted—Highways Act 1959, ss 121(1), 269. **R v Ogden, ex p Long Ashton RDC** [1963] **1** 574, QBD.
Implied jurisdiction from enactment creating offence—
Territorial waters—Wireless broadcast from disused fort more than three nautical miles from low-water mark off Kent coast—Wireless Telegraphy Act 1949, ss 1(1), 6(1)(a). **R v Kent Justices, ex p Lye** [1967] **1** 560, QBD.

MAGISTRATES (cont)—
  Jurisdiction (cont)—
    Indictable offence—

      Compensation order. *See* **Sentence** (Compensation—Order—Indictable offence).

    Jurisdiction—

      Costs. *See* **Costs** (Order for costs—Jurisdiction—Magistrates).

    Juvenile court. *See* Juvenile court—Jurisdiction, *below.*

    Magistrate—

      Proceedings partly heard by one metropolitan magistrate—Continuation by another magistrate—Conflict of evidence between the parties. **Bolton v Bolton** [1949] **2** 908, Div.

    Mode of trial—

      Young person appearing with adult before magistrates on committal proceedings—No case to answer in relation to adult—Case to answer in relation to young person—Magistrates referring young person to youth court for that court to determine mode of trial—Whether magistrates having power to do so—Children and Young Persons Act 1933, s 53—Magistrates' Courts Act 1980, s 24. **R v Tottenham Youth Court, ex p Fawzy** [1998] **1** 365, QBD.

    Nuisance order—

      Terms of order. *See* **Nuisance** (Statutory nuisance—Nuisance order—Terms of order—Jurisdiction of justices to add terms to order).

    Offence in respect of property in or on vehicle—

      Carriage of goods—Breach of condition of A licence—Whether offence consisting of unlawful use of vehicle is 'in or on a vehicle'—Summary Jurisdiction Act 1879, s 46(3). **Wardhaugh (A F) Ltd v Mace** [1952] **2** 28, QBD.

    Probation—

      Breach of probation order—Power to make fresh probation order for period of three years from date of fresh order—Effect of supervising court's decision on existing probation order—Criminal Justice Act 1948, ss 3(1), 6(3), Sch 1, para 3, proviso (a). **R v Havant Justices, ex p Jacobs** [1957] **1** 475, QBD.

    Removal of child from jurisdiction—

      Order forbidding removal—Whether magistrates' court having jurisdiction to make order. **T v T** [1968] **3** 321, Div.

    Reopening case to rectify mistake etc—

      Justices ruling no case to answer due to mistaken belief as to admissibility of evidence—Justices rescinding decision and convicting defendant—Whether justices functi officio. **Steward v DPP** [2003] **4** 1105, DC.

      Plea of guilty—Sentence passed—Invalid sentence—Whether magistrates had jurisdiction to substitute valid sentence—Sentence substituted by Divisional Court on application for certiorari—Administration of Justice Act 1960, s 16—Criminal Justice Act 1967, s 39. **R v Uxbridge Justices, ex p Clark** [1968] **2** 992, QBD.

      Trial of information adjourned—Accused receiving no notice of date of adjourned hearing—Magistrates under statutory duty not to proceed unless satisfied that notice had been served on accused—Magistrates convicting accused in his absence without considering whether there was proof of service of notice on him—Whether magistrates having jurisdiction to order rehearing of case—Whether magistrates functus officio as soon as conviction announced—Magistrates' Courts Act 1980, ss 10, 142—Magistrates' Courts Rules 1981, 1981/552), rr 15, 99. **R v Seisdon Justices, ex p Dougan** [1983] **1** 6, QBD.

    Statement of case. *See* Statement of case by magistrates' court—Jurisdiction to state case, *below.*

    Statutory nuisance. *See* **Nuisance** (Statutory nuisance—Jurisdiction of justices).

    Summary offence—

      Offence committed by tinner in stannaries area of Cornwall—Ancient right of tinners to be tried only by Stannaries Court—Abolition of Stannaries Court in 1896—Transfer of jurisdiction to county court—County court dealing only with civil claims—Whether summary offences committed within stannaries area now triable by magistrates' court—Stannaries Court (Abolition) Act 1896, s 1(1)—Magistrates' Courts Act 1952, s 2(1). **R v East Powder Magistrates' Court, ex p Lampshire** [1979] **2** 329, QBD.

    Trial of information—

      Duty of considering information delegated by justices' clerk to his assistant—Assistant considering information against accused within time limit for instituting proceedings—Accused appearing before justices after expiry of time limit—Whether information validly laid before assistant—Whether justices having jurisdiction to try information—Magistrates' Courts Act 1952, s 1(1)—Justices' Clerks Rules 1970 (SI 1970 No 231), r 3. **R v Gateshead Justices, ex p Tesco Stores Ltd** [1981] **1** 1027, QBD.

      Invalid summons—Trial following issue of invalid summons—Accused appearing before justices within six months of date of alleged offence—Copy of summons containing details of information before justices—Whether justices having jurisdiction to try accused despite invalidity of summons. **R v Brentford Justices, ex p Catlin** [1975] **2** 201, QBD.

      Validity of information—Laying of information—Identity of informant—Information stated to have been preferred by named police force—Identity of informant not stated in information—Whether information invalid. **Rubin v DPP** [1989] **2** 241, QBD.

      Validity of information—Laying of information—Information laid on behalf of company—Decision to instruct solicitors to lay information following alleged assault during company's annual general meeting—Whether company able to institute proceedings—Whether prosecution matter of public policy and utility and concerning public morals. **R (on the application of Gladstone plc) v Manchester City Magistrates' Court (Guiver, interested party)** [2005] **2** 56, DC.

MAGISTRATES (cont)—
Jurisdiction (cont)—
Trial of information (cont)—
Validity of information—Laying of information—Invalid process issued on invalidly laid information—Defendant not required to attend court on first hearing of information and not present—Court having before it register setting out particulars of offence on which prosecution intended to proceed—Court at first hearing not considering information for purpose of issuing process in belief that valid process already issued—Case adjourned—Adjourned hearing taking place after time limit for commencing proceedings—Whether court having jurisdiction at adjourned hearing to try case—Whether information 'laid' at first hearing—Whether consideration of information for purpose of issuing process an essential ingredient of laying information—Magistrates' Courts Act 1980, s 127. **Hill v Anderton** [1981] **3** 72, QBD; [1982] **2** 963, HL.
Validity of information—Laying of information—Laying of information by means of data entries in computer system—Time of laying of information where data entries capable of being added to or amended—Magistrates' Courts Act 1980, s 127. **Atkinson v DPP** [2004] **3** 971, DC.
Validity of information—Laying of information—Time limit—Information in relation to Companies Act offence not laid within time limit contained in statutory provision—Offence charged triable either way—Whether statutory provision applying to offences triable either way or solely to offences triable only summarily—Whether magistrate having jurisdiction to try case—Magistrates' Courts Act 1980, s 127(1), (2)—Companies Act 1985, s 731(2). **R v Thames Magistrates' Court, ex p Horgan** [1998] **1** 559, QBD.
Validity of information—Laying of information—Time limit—Informations when laid not accompanied by proper certificate of compliance with time limit—Informations in fact laid within time limit—Proper certificate not produced until after expiry of time limit—Magistrate declining jurisdiction to hear informations—Whether magistrate entitled to decline jurisdiction—Gas Act 1972, s 43(2). **R v Clerkenwell Metropolitan Stipendiary Magistrate, ex p DPP** [1984] **2** 193, QBD.
Ward of court—
Overlapping jurisdictions. *See* **Ward of court** (Previous custody order of magistrates made under jurisdiction conferred by guardianship legislation—Circumstances in which High Court will make different order under wardship jurisdiction).
Warrant for distress for non-payment of rates—
Unincorporated association and various different entities using premises—Claim for rates made against member of association—Defence of non-occupation of premises—Whether magistrate having jurisdiction to entertain defence of non-occupation when defence not raised by way of appeal to Crown Court—General Rate Act 1967, s 7. **Verrall v Hackney London BC** [1983] **1** 277, CA.
Warrant of commitment—
Postponement—Further postponement or variation of conditions of previous postponement—Whether magistrates' court having jurisdiction to order further postponement or vary conditions—Interpretation Act 1978, s 12(1)—Magistrates' Courts Act 1980, s 77(2). **Wilson v Colchester Justices** [1985] **2** 97, HL.
Youth court—
Power of youth court to appoint intermediary for defendant—Funding for intermediary appointed for defendant—Effective participation in trial—Youth Justice and Criminal Evidence Act 1999, s 29—Costs in Criminal Cases (General) Regulations 1986, SI 1986/1335, reg 20—Crim PR, rr 1.11, 3.10(b)(v). **R (on the application of C) v Sevenoaks Youth Court** [2010] **1** 735, DC.
Power of youth court to commit young persons to Crown Court—Challenging decision of Youth Court on jurisdiction—Procedure—Magistrates' Court Act 1980, s 24(1)—Powers of Criminal Courts (Sentencing) Act 2000, s 91. **R (on the application of the DPP) v Camberwell Youth Court** [2004] **4** 699, DC.
Power of youth court to commit young persons to Crown Court—Guidance—Magistrates' Courts Act 1980, s 24(1)—Crime and Disorder Act 1998, s 51A. **R (on the application of the DPP) v South East Surrey Youth Court (Ghanbari, interested party)** [2006] **2** 444, DC.
Remittal for sentence to adult magistrates' court—Seventeen-year-old charged with offence triable in relation to an adult only on indictment—Youth court finding offender guilty and remitting him for sentence to adult magistrates court as he had attained the age of 18—Whether remittal lawful—Magistrates' Courts Act 1980, s 142(1)—Powers of Criminal Courts (Sentencing) Act 2000, s 9(1). **R (on the application of Denny) v Acton Youth Court JJ (DPP, interested party)** [2004] **2** 961, DC.
Jury trial for summary offence—
Right of accused. *See* Right of accused to claim trial by jury for summary offence, *below*.
Juvenile court—
Care proceedings—
Generally. *See* **Children and young persons** (Care proceedings in juvenile court).
Legal aid. *See* **Legal aid—Care proceedings in juvenile court**.
Witness summons—Child. *See* Witness summons—Child—Care proceedings, *below*.
Child—
Application for interim order. *See* **Children and young persons** (Detention—Interim order—Application).
Irish warrant—
Application for indorsement—Hearing in open court. *See* Indorsement of Irish warrant—Application for indorsement—Hearing in open court—Juvenile, *above*.
Jurisdiction—
Adoption—Overlapping jurisdictions—Order conflicting with previous order of superior court—Divorce—Custody order—Parents of child divorced—County court consent order giving custody of child to mother and access to father—Remarriage of mother—Application by mother and stepfather for adoption order—Whether magistrates having power to make adoption order. **B (a minor) (adoption: jurisdiction), Re** [1975] **2** 449, Fam D.
Conviction—Maximum penalty fine of 40s—Remand in custody—Excess of jurisdiction—Children and Young Persons Act 1933, ss 47(3), 107(1)—Summary Jurisdiction (Children and Young Persons) Rules 1933 (S R & O 1933 No 819), r 11. **R v Toynbee Hall Juvenile Court Justices, ex p Joseph** [1939] **3** 16, KBD.

MAGISTRATES (cont)—
  Juvenile court (cont)—
    Jurisdiction (cont)—
      Summary trial of non-summary offence—Defendant remanded with a view to summary trial for wounding with intent—Defendant attained 17 while on remand—Subsequently charged with attempted murder based on same facts—Whether latter charge triable summarily—Magistrates' Courts Act 1952, s 20(1)—Children and Young Persons Act 1933, s 48(1). **R v Chelsea Justices, ex p DPP** [1963] **3** 657, QBD.
    Procedure—
      Application by parent for access order—Appeal from decision of juvenile court—Child in care—Adoption proceedings simultaneously on foot in High Court—Juvenile court refusing to adjourn application for access order pending determination of adoption proceedings—Whether refusal to adjourn a 'decision of juvenile court' appealable to High Court—Whether juvenile court right not to adjourn access proceedings—Whether desirable that question of access be determined before adoption proceedings heard—Child Care Act 1980, ss 12B(1), 12C(1), (5). **Southwark London BC v H** [1985] **2** 657, Fam D.
      Hearing—Persons who may be present—Persons directly concerned in the case—Exclusion from hearing—Effect—Child in care of local authority—Social worker having supervision of child—Social worker wishing to attend hearing of case against child—Social worker excluded from hearing—Whether social worker a person 'directly concerned in that case'—Whether exclusion of social worker depriving court of jurisdiction—Whether certiorari should be granted to quash proceedings—Children and Young Persons Act 1933, s 47(2). **R v Southwark Juvenile Court, ex p NJ** [1973] **3** 383, QBD.
      Summons—Service—Child in care of local authority—Whether summons should be served on local authority. **R v Southwark Juvenile Court, ex p NJ** [1973] **3** 383, QBD.
  Landlord and tenant—
    Proceedings by landlord for recovery of possession. *See* **Landlord and tenant** (Recovery of possession—Procedure before magistrates).
  Legal aid—
    Order for purpose of proceedings before magistrates' court. *See* **Legal aid** (Criminal cases—Order for purpose of proceedings before magistrates' court).
  Licensing—
    Betting office. *See* **Gaming** (Betting—Licensed betting office—Application for licence).
    Cinema. *See* **Cinema** (Licence).
    Cinematograph exhibition—
      Licensing of premises used for exhibition. *See* **Cinema** (Cinematograph exhibition—Licensing of premises).
    Generally. *See* **Licensing**.
    Public dancing, music or other entertainment. *See* **Entertainment** (Music and dancing licence).
  Limitation of time—
    Date from which time runs—
      Charge of failing to fence machinery—Whether time running from date when machinery installed and operated or whether from date machinery proved to be in unfenced condition—Metalliferous Mines Regulation Act 1872, s 34(1)—Quarries General Regulations 1938, (S R & O 1938 No 632), reg 14. **Rowley v Everton (T A) & Sons Ltd** [1940] **4** 435, KBD.
    Laying information. *See* Information—Time limit for laying information, *above*.
    Misdemeanour—
      Aiding and abetting—Accessory before fact a principal offender—Whether information out of time—Summary Jurisdiction Act 1848, s 5—Road Traffic Act 1930, s 7(5). **Homolka v Osmond** [1939] **1** 154, KBD.
    Prosecution under Defence (Price Control) Regulations 1945, reg 6—
      Period of limitation—Supplies and Services (Transitional Powers) Act 1945, s 2(1), (3)—Defence (Price Control) Regulations 1945 (SR & O 1945 No 1613), reg 10(1). **Wallace v Clench** [1947] **1** 175, KBD.
  Maintenance—
    Children—
      Statutory jurisdiction under Summary Jurisdiction Acts. *See* **Minor** (Maintenance—Statutory jurisdiction).
    Husband and wife—
      Generally. *See* **Husband and wife** (Maintenance).
      Summary proceedings. *See* **Husband and wife** (Summary proceedings—Financial provision).
  Majority decision. *See* Procedure—Majority decision, *below*.
  Malicious action within jurisdiction—
    Civil liability. *See* Civil liability—Malicious action within jurisdiction, *above*.
  Matrimonial proceedings. *See* **Husband and wife**.
  Mitigation of penalties—
    Fine—
      Power to sentence accused to fine of less than amount specified—Extent of power—National insurance contribution arrears recoverable as a penalty—Whether court can reduce amount of arrears adjudged recoverable—Magistrates' Courts Act 1952, ss 27(1), 126(1), (3)—National Insurance Act 1946, s 8—National Insurance (Contributions) Regulations 1948 (SI 1948 No 1417), reg 19(5). **Leach v Litchfield** [1960] **3** 739, QBD.
    Fine in lieu of imprisonment—
      Act under which offender prosecuted only providing penalty of imprisonment—Amount of fine—Summary Jurisdiction Act 1879, ss 4, 5—Merchant Shipping Act 1894, s 376(1)(d). **Lowther v Smith** [1949] **1** 943, KBD.
  Music and dancing licences. *See* **Entertainment** (Music and dancing licence).
  Names of justices—
    Policy of withholding names of justices. *See* Anonymity—Policy of withholding names of justices, *above*.
  Natural justice—
    Affiliation order—
      Enforcement. *See* **Affiliation** (Affiliation order—Enforcement—Natural justice).

MAGISTRATES (cont)—
    Natural justice (cont)—
        Binding over order. *See* Binding over—Natural justice, *above.*
        Breach of rules of—
            Certiorari. *See* **Certiorari** (Justices—Natural justice).
            Generally. *See* **Natural justice** (Magistrates).
    Newspaper report of committal proceedings. *See* **Criminal law** (Committal—Newspaper report).
    No case to answer. *See* Procedure—No case to answer, *below.*
    Nuisance—
        Statutory nuisance—
            Complaint to justices. *See* **Nuisance** (Statutory nuisance—Complaint to justices).
    Obscene publications—
        Destruction. *See* **Criminal law** (Obscene publications—Destruction).
        Forfeiture—
            Appeal—Right of appeal by case stated. *See* **Case stated** (Right of appeal by—Party to proceedings—Informant—Obscene publications—Forfeiture order by justices in respect of certain obscene publications, no order in respect of others).
            Articles seized under warrant of justices—Justices examining articles to decide whether summons should be issued—Hearing of summons by same justices—Whether same justices precluded from hearing summons—Obscene Publications Act 1959, s 3(3). **Morgan v Bowker** [1963] **1** 691, QBD.
            Defence of public good—Defence a separate issue from issue of obscenity—Magistrates determining issue of obscenity before hearing evidence on issue of public good—Obscene Publications Act 1959, s 4. **Olympia Press Ltd v Hollis** [1974] **1** 108, QBD.
            Reading of books by justices—Necessity for justices to be acquainted with books as a whole—Not necessary for justices to read every word of books—Collection of 34 different titles—Bench of six justices all reading some of books—Each book read by at least two justices—No book read by all the justices—Justices deliberating on books as a whole and forming collective opinion that books obscene—Obscene Publications Act 1959, s 3(3). **Olympia Press Ltd v Hollis** [1974] **1** 108, QBD.
    Offence triable summarily or on indictment—
        Committal for sentence. *See* Committal for sentence—Offence triable summarily or on indictment, *above.*
        Summary trial. *See* Summary trial—Offence triable summarily or on indictment, *below.*
    Order—
        Fingerprints. *See* **Criminal evidence** (Fingerprints—Place where fingerprints to be taken—Justices' order to take fingerprints).
        Matrimonial proceedings—
            What constitutes an order—Order is that which magistrates pronounce at the conclusion of the proceedings. **Jolliffe v Jolliffe** [1963] **3** 295, Div.
        Sex offender order—
            Whether conditions for imposition of sex offender order having to be established on criminal standard of proof—Crime and Disorder Act 1998, s 2. **B v Chief Constable of Avon and Somerset Constabulary** [2001] **1** 562, QBD.
        Sexual offences prevention order—
            Applications and grounds—Whether conditions for imposition of sexual offences prevention order having to be established on criminal standard of proof—Sexual Offences Act 2003, s 104. **R (on the application of the Chief Constable of Cleveland Police) v Haggas** [2010] **3** 506, QBD.
    Penalties—
        Mitigation of. *See* Mitigation of penalties, *above.*
    Perverse decision—
        Jurisdiction of High Court to interfere—
            Decision to which no reasonable bench could have come—Remittance by High Court of case stated with direction to convict. **Bracegirdle v Oxley** [1947] **1** 126, KBD.
    Place of safety order—
        Ward of court. *See* **Ward of court** (Protection of ward—Place of safety order).
    Plea of guilty—
        Absence of accused—
            Adjournment of proceedings before ordering disqualification—Disqualification—Road traffic offence—No adjournment to enable accused to be present and to be heard in mitigation—Circumstances of disqualification within s 5(3) of Road Traffic Act 1962—Whether order for disqualification should be quashed—Magistrates' Courts Act 1957, s 1(2), proviso (iii). **R v Llandrindod Wells Justices, ex p Gibson** [1968] **2** 20, QBD.
            Notice sent to accused of procedure for pleading guilty without appearing—Adjournments—Notification in writing on behalf of accused of desire to plead guilty—Prosecution's witnesses present on date of adjourned trial—Police and other evidence heard in accused's absence—Whether court could proceed under Magistrates' Courts Act 1952, s 15, or was bound to proceed under Magistrates' Courts Act 1957, s 1. **R v Norham and Islandshire Justices, ex p Sunter Bros Ltd** [1961] **1** 455, QBD.
            Plea of guilty notified in writing—Adjournment of case for purpose of enabling sentence of imprisonment, detention or disqualification to be imposed—Notice of adjournment must include reason therefor—Magistrates' Courts Act 1952, s 14(2)—Magistrates' Courts Act 1957, s 1(2), proviso (iii), (3). **R v Mason** [1965] **2** 308, Crown Ct Liverpool.
            Written submission by accused with view to mitigation of sentence—Necessity for submission to be read out in court before accused convicted in his absence—Magistrates' Courts Act 1957, s 1(2), proviso (ii). **R v Davis, ex p Brough** [1958] **3** 559, QBD.
        Conviction—
            Application to withdraw plea of guilty—Refusal by magistrate—Whether magistrates' court functus officio. **R v Guest, ex p Anthony** [1964] **3** 385, QBD.
            Plea entered by accused's solicitor—Accused not asked how he pleaded—Whether certiorari lay to quash conviction—Magistrates' Courts Act 1952, s 13(1). **R v Wakefield Justices, ex p Butterworth** [1970] **1** 1181, QBD.
            Subsequent application that plea be amended to not guilty—Whether plea of guilty can be withdrawn after judgment. **R v Campbell, ex p Hoy** [1953] **1** 684, QBD.

MAGISTRATES (cont)—
Plea of guilty (cont)—
    Conviction (cont)—
        When plea finally accepted—Accused, youth subnormal mentally, not represented—Statement made by accused produced and accused and father given opportunity to explain position—Whether justices right in disallowing subsequent application to change plea. **R v Gore Justices, ex p N (an infant)** [1966] **3** 991, QBD.
        When plea finally accepted—Summary Jurisdiction (Children and Young Persons) Rules 1933 (SR & O 1933 No 819), r 6. **R v Blandford Justices, ex p G (an infant)** [1966] **1** 1021, QBD.
    Evidence—
        Need to hear evidence on 'oath. **R v Grimsby Recorder, ex p Purser** [1951] **2** 889, KBD.
    Practice—
        Hearing—
            Civil and criminal proceedings. *See* Complaint—Hearing—Practice where related criminal proceedings, *above*.
        Procedure. *See* Procedure, *below*.
    Preliminary hearing—
        Committal. *See* **Criminal law** (Committal—Preliminary hearing before justices).
        Statement by accused. *See* **Criminal law** (Preliminary hearing before justices—Statement made by accused).
    Presence of clerk in retiring room while justices consider decision. *See* Clerk—Presence in retiring room while justices consider decision, *above*.
    Prison—
        Disciplinary proceedings before visiting justices—
            Escape from prison—Autrefois convict. *See* **Criminal law** (Autrefois convict—Escape from prison—Disciplinary proceedings before visiting justices).
    Private prosecution—
        Summons—
            Refusal to issue summons. *See* Summons—Refusal to issue summons—Private prosecution, *below*.
    Probation—
        Jurisdiction. *See* Jurisdiction—Probation, *above*.
        Order—
            Generally. *See* **Sentence** (Probation order).
    Procedure—
        Advice by justices' clerk. *See* Clerk—Functions, *above*.
        Committal for trial at Crown Court. *See* **Crown Court** (Committal to Crown Court for trial—Procedure).
        Complaint—
            Dismissal—Minute of adjudication—Matrimonial proceedings. *See* **Husband and wife** (Summary proceedings—Complaint—Dismissal—Minute of adjudication).
            Hearing—Generally. *See* Complaint—Hearing, *above*.
            Matrimonial proceedings. *See* **Husband and wife** (Summary proceedings—Complaint).
            Statutory nuisance—Failure to comply with abatement notice. *See* **Nuisance** (Statutory nuisance—Abatement notice—Failure to comply—Complaint to justices—Procedure).
        Conviction—
            Justices in error pronouncing conviction immediately after defence submission of no case to answer—Defendants applying for order of certiorari to quash conviction—Effect of pronouncement of conviction by justices—Whether justices thereupon becoming functi officio—Whether order of certiorari necessary. **R v Midhurst Justices, ex p Thompson** [1973] **3** 1164, QBD.
            Previous convictions—Justices' decision not announced before inquiry into accused's previous history—Advisability of justices announcing decision to convict before inquiring into previous convictions. **Davies v Griffiths** [1937] **2** 671, KBD.
            Release on licence—Conviction of further offence—Duty of magistrates. *See* **Prison** (Release on licence—Conviction of further offence—Duty of magistrates' court).
            Subsequent alteration of determination to acquittal—Whether functus officio at moment conviction announced. **R v Essex Justices, ex p Final** [1962] **3** 924, QBD.
        Court hearing—
            Powers—Whether magistrates having power to sit in camera—Whether magistrates having power to impose restriction on publication of defendant's address—Magistrates' Courts Act 1980, s 121(4). **R v Evesham Justices, ex p McDonagh** [1988] **1** 371, QBD.
        Court list—
            Court list listing all charges against defendant for hearing on same day—Whether practice of putting court list containing list of all charges before magistrates wrong in law. **R v Weston-super-Mare Justices, ex p Shaw** [1987] **1** 255, QBD.
        Court register—
            Computer used to produce sheets forming register—Sheets containing all outstanding charges against defendant and convictions on which he awaited sentence—Whether practice of putting such court sheets before magistrates wrong in law—Magistrates' Courts Rules 1981, r 66(1)(2). **R v Liverpool City Justices, ex p Topping** [1983] **1** 490, QBD.
        Criminal jurisdiction and procedure. *See* Criminal jurisdiction and procedure, *above*.
        Evidence—
            Witness called after magistrates had retired to consider their decision—In absence of special circumstances magistrates not to allow evidence to be called after retirement. **Webb v Leadbetter** [1966] **2** 114, QBD.
            Witness called after magistrates had retired to consider their decision—Magistrates allowing witness to be recalled by prosecution to give evidence dealing with point made by defence for first time in final speech—Whether special circumstances allowing recall of witness—Crim PR 1.1(1), 3.2, 3.3(a). **Malcolm v DPP** [2007] **3** 578, DC.
        Generally. *See* **Practice** (Magistrates' courts).
        Justices' reasons—
            Content—Decision founded on matter not in clerk's note. **Bond v Bond** [1964] **3** 346, Div.

MAGISTRATES (cont)—
  Procedure (cont)—
    Justices' reasons (cont)—
      Content—Evidence—Which party's evidence accepted—Precise findings of fact. **Hudson v Hudson** [1965] **2** 82, Div.
      Content—Evidence—Which party's evidence accepted—Precise findings of fact—Signing of reasons by justices—Matrimonial Causes Rules 1957 (SI 1957 No 619), r 73(3). **Theobald v Theobald** [1962] **2** 863, Div.
      Justices' clerk requesting assistance of successful party's counsel to draft reasons—Reasons so drafted approved by justices with minor amendments—Irregularity. **Johnson v Johnson** [1961] **1** 153, Div.
      Time for stating—Practice that reasons stated initially by justices' clerk and later superseded by statement signed by magistrates disapproved. **Griffiths v Griffiths** [1964] **3** 929, Div.
    Juvenile court. *See* Juvenile court—Procedure, *above.*
    Majority decision—
      Reasons of dissentient—Whether any need for dissentient to give reasons. **Kemp v Kemp** [1953] **2** 553, Div.
    No case to answer—
      Criminal charge—Clear statement whether evidence is to be called should be required. **R v Birkenhead Justices, ex p Fisher** [1962] **3** 837, QBD.
      Criminal charge—Considerations for guidance of justices. **Practice Note** [1962] **1** 448, QBD.
      Criminal charge—Election—Accused not to be put to his election. **Jones v Metcalfe** [1967] **3** 205, QBD.
      No evidence called for defendants—What amounts to election to call no evidence. **Laurie v Raglan Building Co Ltd** [1941] **3** 332, CA.
      Proper time to make submission. **Vye v Vye** [1969] **2** 29, Div.
      Rejection of submission—Counsel's right to address court—No case to answer submitted as submission of law—No evidence adduced on husband's behalf—Whether husband's counsel entitled to address bench on the facts, after submission of no case was rejected—Magistrates' Courts Rules 1952 (SI 1952 No 2190), r 18(2). **Disher v Disher** [1963] **3** 933, Div.
      Submission—Reservation of right to call evidence—Question to be put whether defendant making submission of no case reserving right to call evidence if submission unsuccessful. **R v Gravesend Justices, ex p Sheldon** [1968] **3** 466, QBD.
      Successful submission of no case on one count—Charge no longer subsisting—Verdict should not subsequently be taken on that count. **R v Plain** [1967] **1** 614, CA.
      Undertaking not to call further evidence—Whether undertaking obligatory. **Muller (William H) & Co (NV), etc v Ebbw Vale Steel, Iron and Coal Co Ltd** [1936] **2** 1363, KBD.
    Re-opening case for prosecution—
      Material fact not proved by prosecution—Discretion of justices. **Middleton v Rowlett** [1954] **2** 277, QBD.
    Rehearing—
      Matrimonial proceedings. *See* **Husband and wife** (Summary proceedings—Rehearing—Procedure).
    Service of documents—
      Document required to be served on defendant. *See* **Practice** (Service—Document required to be served on defendant—Magistrates' court proceedings).
  Proceedings—
    Anti-social behaviour order—
      Breach—Respondent raising validity of order as defence—District judge determining order unenforceable and invalid—Whether district judge having jurisdiction to rule original order invalid. **DPP v T** [2006] **3** 471, DC.
      Interim anti-social behaviour order—Without notice applications—Justices' clerk granting applications for permission to apply for interim orders without notice—District judge granting applications—Whether procedure lawful—Whether proceedings a determination of the claimants' rights for the purposes of their right to a fair trial—Test to be applied when making interim orders—Crime and Disorder Act 1998, s 1D—Human Rights Act 1998, Sch 1, Pt I, art 6(1)—Magistrates' Courts (Anti-Social Behaviour Orders) Rules 2002, r 5. **R (on the application of Kenny) v Leeds Magistrates' Court** [2004] **1** 1333, QBD; **R (on the application of M) v Secretary of State for Constitutional Affairs and Lord Chancellor** [2004] **2** 531, CA.
      Order prohibiting defendant from doing anything described by the order—Prohibition in the nature of a curfew—Whether lawful—Whether curfew prohibitory in nature—Whether curfew penal—Crime and Disorder Act 1998, s 1(4), (6). **R (on the application of Lonergan) v Lewes Crown Court (Secretary of State for the Home Dept, interested party)** [2005] **2** 362, QBD Divl Ct.
      Variation of order—Application to vary order by extending its duration—Whether magistrates' court having power to extend duration of order—Crime and Disorder Act 1998, ss 1(1), (8), 1D(4). **Leeds City Council v G** [2007] **4** 652, DC.
      Whether proceedings for imposition of anti-social behaviour orders criminal or civil—Whether criminal or civil standard of proof to be applied in such proceedings—Crime and Disorder Act 1998, s 1—Human Rights Act 1998, Sch 1, Pt I, art 6. **R (on the application of McCann) v Crown Court at Manchester** [2001] **4** 264, CA; [2002] **4** 593, HL.
    Condemnation proceedings—
      Representation order not generally available in magistrates' court for civil proceedings—Whether condemnation proceedings civil or criminal—Access to Justice Act 1999, s 12—Customs and Excise Management Act 1979, Sch 3, para 6. **R (on the application of Mudie) v Kent Magistrates' Court** [2003] **2** 631, CA.
    Control by judicial review—
      Magistrates dismissing charge without giving prosecution opportunity to present case—Magistrates dismissing information because date of adjournment sought by prosecution not convenient for defence—Prosecutor applying for certiorari to quash dismissal and mandamus directing justices to hear prosecution evidence against defendant—Whether on application for judicial review court has power to interfere with magistrates' dismissal of charge—Whether rehearing of information would place defendant in double jeopardy—Whether relevant that magistrates acted in breach of rules of natural justice in acquitting defendant—Magistrates' Courts Act 1980, s 9(2). **Harrington v Roots** [1984] **2** 474, HL.

MAGISTRATES (cont)—
  Proceedings (cont)—
    Control by judicial review (cont)—
      Magistrates dismissing charge without giving prosecution opportunity to present case—Whether magistrates having power to dismiss charge without hearing any evidence on ground that unjust or prejudicial to defendant for hearing to continue. **R v Birmingham Justices, ex p Lamb** [1983] **3** 23, QBD.
      Non-appearance of prosecution—Justices dismissing charge without giving prosecution opportunity to present case—Prosecutor applying for certiorari to quash dismissal—Whether justices acting unreasonably—Whether certiorari can issue to quash acquittal arising from dismissal of information which was a nullity—Magistrates' Courts Act 1980, s 15. **R v Hendon Justices, ex p DPP** [1993] **1** 411, QBD.
    Criminal behaviour order—
      Burden and standard of proof—Conditions for order—Discretion of court—Judge refusing order prohibiting offender from entering geographical area—Whether burden of proof on prosecution—Whether order to contain positive requirement helping to prevent criminal behaviour—Relevant considerations—Crime and Disorder Act 1998, s 1C—Violent Crime Reduction Act 2006, s 27—Anti-social Behaviour, Crime and Policing Act 2014, s 22. **DPP v Bulmer** [2016] **3** 860, DC.
  Prohibition. *See* **Prohibition** (Justices—Right to issue).
  Property in possession of Customs and Excise—
    Power of magistrates court—
      Property taken from arrested person's premises—Power to order Customs and Excise to return seized property—Whether magistrates have power to order Customs and Excise to return property or documents taken from arrested person's premises—Whether magistrates restricted to ordering return of property found on arrested person and 'taken from him' on his arrest—Magistrates Court's Act 1980, s 48. **R v Southampton Magistrates' Court, ex p Newman** [1988] **3** 669, QBD.
  Property in possession of police—
    Power of magistrates' court. *See* **Police** (Property in possession of police—Delivery to owner—Power of magistrates' court to order property to be delivered to person appearing to court to be owner).
  Prosecutor—
    Discretion as to offence to be charged. *See* **Criminal law** (Prosecutor—Discretion—Offence to be charged).
  Publicity—
    Committal proceedings. *See* **Criminal law** (Committal—Preliminary hearing before justices—Publicity).
  Reasons—
    Content—
      Generally. *See* Procedure—Justices' reasons—Content, *above*.
      Matrimonial proceedings. *See* **Husband and wife** (Summary proceedings—Justices' reasons).
    Drafting—
      Irregularity. *See* Procedure—Justices' reasons—Justices' clerk requesting assistance of successful party's counsel to draft reasons, *above*.
    Failure of justices to supply to High Court statement of reasons—
      Matrimonial proceedings. *See* **Husband and wife** (Summary proceedings—Appeal to Divisional Court—Failure of justices to supply to High Court statement of reasons for their decision).
    Majority decision—
      Need of dissenting justice to give reasons. *See* **Husband and wife** (Summary proceedings—Justices' reasons—Majority decision—Need of dissenting justice to give reasons).
    Time for stating. *See* Procedure—Justices' reasons—Time for stating, *above*.
  Recognisance—
    Case stated. *See* **Case stated** (Magistrates' courts—Recognisance).
  Reference to European Court—
    Jurisdiction of magistrates to refer question regarding validity of EEC enactment. *See* **European Union** (Reference to European Court—Referral by court of member state of question regarding validity of EEC enactment—Referral by magistrates' court).
  Remand in custody. *See* **Criminal law** (Committal—Remand in custody).
  Reopening case to rectify mistake—
    Jurisdiction. *See* Jurisdiction—Reopening case to rectify mistake etc, *above*.
  Restitution order. *See* **Sentence** (Restitution order—Magistrates).
  Return of property taken from accused—
    Person charged—
      Money taken from person without any charge preferred—Subsequent charge of theft of articles in postal packets not including money—Direction by magistrates at trial for return of money—Jurisdiction—Summary Jurisdiction Act 1879, s 44. **Arnell v Harris** [1944] **2** 522, KBD.
  Review of exercise of discretion on appeal—
    Duty of appellate court. *See* **Appeal** (Review of exercise of discretion).
  Review of justices' decision—
    Adoption proceedings. *See* **Adoption** (Appeal—Review of decision of justices).
    Appeal to Divisional Court—
      Mode of appeal—Case stated or application for judicial review—Case stated inappropriate in cases where defendant seeking quashing of conviction and not answer to question whether magistrates had power to quash conviction. **Hill v Anderton** [1981] **3** 72, QBD.
    Case stated. *See* **Case stated** (Magistrates' courts).
    Conduct of proceedings by justices impugned—
      Affidavit tendered on appeal to establish relevant fact—Copy should be served on clerk to justices. **Walker v Walker** [1967] **1** 412, Div.
    Duty of appellate court. *See* **Appeal** (Review of exercise of discretion).
    Family proceedings. *See* **Practice** (Family proceedings—Appeals—Appeals from magistrates' courts).
    Guardianship of Infants Acts—
      Leave to appeal out of time. **Practice Direction** [1955] **3** 591, Ch D.

MAGISTRATES (cont)—
    Review of justices' decision (cont)—
        Matrimonial proceedings—
            Appeal to High Court against matrimonial order. *See* **Husband and wife** (Matrimonial order—Appeal to High Court against order of magistrates).
        Sentence—
            Appeal to Divisional Court—Whether appeal against sentence imposed by magistrates by way of case stated appropriate—Whether appeal should be to Crown Court. **Tucker v DPP** [1992] **4** 901, QBD.
    Right of accused to claim trial by jury for summary offence—
        Election by accused to go for trial to quarter sessions—
            Substitution of new charge—Whether permissible—Summary Jurisdiction Act 1879, s 17(1). **R v Phillips** [1953] **1** 968, CCA.
        Exception—
            Assault—Assault on police constable in execution of his duty—Whether accused entitled to claim trial by jury—Magistrates' Courts Act 1952, s 25(1)—Police Act 1964, s 51(1). **Toohey v Woolwich Justices** [1966] **2** 429, HL.
        Need for accused to be personally informed of right and asked for his election—
            Answer may be given by his legal representative—Magistrates' Courts Act 1952, s 25(3). **R v Kettering Justices, ex p Patmore** [1968] **3** 167, QBD.
        Offence triable summarily and also indictable at common law—
            Charge brought under Criminal Law Amendment Act 1885, s 13(1)—Whether accused entitled to claim trial by jury. **Waroquiers v Marsden** [1950] **1** 93, KBD.
        Omission to inform accused of right—
            Election by accused, after hearing of charge begun to be tried summarily—Effect of omission to inform accused of right to trial by jury—Summary Jurisdiction Act 1879, s 17(1). **Stefani v John** [1947] **2** 615, KBD.
    Road traffic offences. *See* **Road traffic**.
    Rule against double jeopardy—
        Defective summons—
            Summons dismissed before defendant pleading to it—Issue of fresh summons—Whether defendant placed in peril of conviction on first summons—Whether defect in first summons such that defendant never in danger of conviction—Whether rule against double jeopardy applying. **Williams v DPP** [1991] **3** 651, QBD.
    Sentence—
        Committal for sentence. *See* Committal for sentence, *above*.
        Generally. *See* **Sentence**.
    Sex offender order. *See* Order—Sex offender order, *above*.
    Statement of case by magistrates' court—
        Generally. *See* **Case stated** (Magistrates' courts).
        Jurisdiction to state case—
            Preliminary objection to jurisdiction upheld—Whether justices having power to state a case where preliminary objection to jurisdiction upheld by justices—Summary Jurisdiction Act 1857, ss 2-5—Summary Jurisdiction Act 1879, s 33(1). **Pratt v A A Sites Ltd** [1938] **2** 371, KBD.
    Summary trial—
        Arson. *See* **Criminal law** (Damage to property—Arson—Trial—Summary trial).
        Attempt to commit crime—
            Merger with completed offence. *See* **Criminal law** (Attempt—Full offence committed—Merger—Summary proceedings).
        Indictable offence triable summarily—
            Election by accused to be tried by jury—Graver offences added on indictment—Sentence. *See* **Sentence** (Indictable offence tried summarily—Election by accused at summary trial for trial by jury).
            Generally. *See* Summary trial for indictable offence, *below*.
        Information—
            Three informations heard at same time without defendant's consent—Convictions on each information—Validity. **Brangwynne v Evans** [1962] **1** 446, QBD.
        Offence triable summarily or on indictment—
            Application to re-elect as to mode of trial—Factors to be taken into account—Accused electing summary trial intending to plead guilty in mistaken belief that he had no defence to charge—Application to re-elect for jury trial after receiving legal advice that he had a defence—Whether accused who intends to plead guilty should be put to election as to mode of trial—Whether accused entitled to re-elect for jury trial—Whether accused properly understanding nature and significance of his election for summary trial—Magistrates' Courts Act 1980, ss 19, 20. **R v Birmingham Justices, ex p Hodgson** [1985] **2** 193, QBD.
            Application—Whether application for summary trial by prosecutor may be implied—Magistrates' Courts Act 1952, s 18(1)(2). **Rigby, ex p** [1958] **3** 30, QBD.
            Committal for sentence. *See* Committal for sentence—Offence triable summarily or on indictment, *above*.
            Committal proceedings—Defendant charged with indictable offence—Magistrates deciding evidence only supported lesser offence triable either way—Whether magistrates entitled to try lesser offence summarily—Whether magistrates obliged to commit defendant for trial—Magistrates' Courts Act 1980, ss 2(4), 6(1), 25(3). **R v Cambridge Justices, ex p Fraser** [1985] **1** 667, QBD.
            Decision to proceed with summary trial of juvenile—Differently constituted bench refusing to proceed with summary trial and committing defendant for trial at Crown Court—Whether magistrates having power to review a properly considered decision as to mode of trial before summary or committal proceedings commence—Magistrates' Courts Act 1980, s 24(1)(a). **R v Newham Juvenile Court, ex p F (a minor)** [1986] **3** 17, QBD.

MAGISTRATES (cont)—
Summary trial (cont)—
Offence triable summarily or on indictment (cont)—
Determination of mode of trial of person attaining age of 17 after pleading to charge—Mode of trial determined before defendant attaining age of 17—Whether fact that defendant turns 17 before trial affecting mode of trial—Whether defendant must be tried summarily as if he was still 16 years of age—Magistrates' Courts Act 1980, s 24. **R v Nottingham Justices, ex p Taylor** [1991] **4** 860, QBD.

Determination of mode of trial of person attaining age of 17 after pleading to charge—Trial by juvenile court or in magistrates' court with right to elect trial by jury—Date when defendant's age relevant for determining mode of trial—Defendant attaining 17 before commencement of trial but after pleading to charge—Whether defendant entitled to elect trial by jury on attaining 17—Magistrates' Courts Act 1980, ss 18, 22. **Daley, Re** [1982] **2** 974, HL.

Determination of mode of trial of person attaining age of 17 after pleading to charge—Trial by juvenile court or in magistrates' court with right to elect trial by jury—Date when defendant's age relevant for determining mode of trial—Defendant attaining 17 before commencement of trial but after pleading to charge—Whether defendant entitled to elect trial by jury on attaining 17—Whether magistrates' decision to try case summarily when plea taken a final decision as to mode of trial—Whether juvenile court having discretion as to mode of trial after defendant attaining 17—Children and Young Persons Act 1963, s 29(1) as amended—Children and Young Persons Act 1969, s 6(1)—Criminal Law Act 1977, s 19(1). **R v Amersham Juvenile Court, ex p Wilson** [1981] **2** 315, QBD.

Determination of mode of trial of person attaining age of 17 after pleading to charge—Trial by juvenile court or in magistrates' court with right to elect trial by jury—Defendant attaining 17 before commencement of trial but after pleading to charge—Whether defendant entitled to elect trial by jury on attaining 17—Whether magistrates' decision to try case summarily when plea taken a final decision as to mode of trial—Whether juvenile court having discretion as to mode of trial after defendant attaining 17—Children and Young Persons Act 1963, s 29(1) as amended—Criminal Law Act 1977, ss 19(1), 21. **R v St Albans Juvenile Court, ex p Godman** [1981] **2** 311, QBD.

Discontinuance of summary trial and committal to Crown Court—Discontinuance at any time before conclusion of prosecution evidence—Magistrates accepting jurisdiction over offence and accused electing summary trial—Accused entering unequivocal plea of guilty—Magistrates accepting plea—Prosecution not calling further evidence—Magistrates then deciding to discontinue summary proceedings and act as examining justices in committal proceedings—Whether magistrates having power to discontinue summary proceedings—Magistrates' Courts Act 1980, s 25(2). **Chief Constable of West Midlands Police v Gillard** [1985] **3** 634, HL.

Factors justices entitled to take into account in determining mode of trial—Previous conviction—Corporation—No power of committal for sentence if offence tried summarily—Offence punishable by larger fine if tried on indictment—Whether justices entitled to be informed of company's previous conviction for a similar offence when deciding whether offence should be tried summarily—Magistrates' Courts Act 1952, s 29, Sch 2, para 7 (as amended by the Courts Act 1971, Sch 8, para 34(1). **R v Colchester Justices, ex p North Essex Building Co Ltd** [1977] **3** 567, QBD.

Magistrate accepting jurisdiction and accused entering not guilty plea—Possible defence of insanity arising after plea but before commencement of evidence—Magistrate committing accused to Crown Court for trial—Whether magistrate having jurisdiction to reopen mode of trial—Whether trial having 'begun'—Magistrates' Courts Act 1980, ss 19, 25(2). **R v Horseferry Road Magistrates' Court, ex p K** [1996] **3** 719, QBD.

Matters to be taken into account in determining mode of trial—Guidelines—Duty of magistrates to consider each case individually and on its own merits—General considerations—Defendants to whom guidelines apply—Either way offences generally to be tried summarily unless certain features present or court's sentencing powers insufficient—Burglary—Theft and fraud—Handling—Social security frauds—Violence against the person—Public order offences—Violent disorder—Affray—Violence to and neglect of children—Indecent assault—Unlawful sexual intercourse—Drugs—Reckless driving—Criminal damage—Offences against the Person Act 1861, ss 20, 47—Criminal Damage Act 1971, s 1—Magistrates' Courts Act 1980, s 19, Sch 1, para 28(c), Sch 2—Public Order Act 1986. **Practice Note** [1990] **3** 979, QBD.

Minor offence of criminal damage—Offence triable summarily only unless offence forming part of series of offences of same or similar character—Factors constituting offences of similar character—Accused charged with damaging police uniform valued at £23 and using threatening words and behaviour likely to occasion breach of peace, assaulting a constable and wilfully obstructing constable—Last three offences triable summarily only—Whether offence of criminal damage to uniform triable summarily only—Whether one of several offences of 'similar character'—Criminal Law Act 1977, s 23(7)(a). **R v Hatfield Justices, ex p Castle** [1980] **3** 509, QBD.

Need of formal application by prosecutor for summary trial—Criminal Justice Act 1948, s 28(1). **James v Bowkett** [1952] **2** 320, QBD.

Several defendants jointly charged with single offence triable either way—Magistrates determining that offence suitable for summary trial—One defendant electing trial on indictment—Whether magistrates required to commit all defendants for trial by jury—Magistrates' Courts Act 1980, ss 19(1), 20(3). **Nicholls v Brentwood Justices** [1991] **3** 359, HL.

Time limit for trying information—Whether time limit for trying summary offences applicable to summary trial of offences triable either way—Interpretation Act 1978, Sch 1, definition of 'indictable offence'—Magistrates' Courts Act 1980, s 127(1), (2). **Kemp v Liebherr-GB Ltd** [1987] **1** 885, QBD.

Summary trial for indictable offence—
Consent of accused to summary trial—
Withdrawal of consent—Case adjourned for a week after evidence of first prosecution witness—Whether accused entitled to withdraw consent at adjourned hearing—Whether summary trial begun—Magistrates' Courts Act 1952, ss 19(5), 24. **R v Bennett, ex p R** [1960] **1** 335, QBD.

454

MAGISTRATES (cont)—
Summary trial for indictable offence (cont)—
Consent of accused to summary trial (cont)—
Withdrawal of consent—Plea of guilty—Committal to quarter sessions for sentence—Change of plea after committal—Case remitted to magistrates for disposal—Claim by accused to withdraw consent to summary trial and to elect trial by jury—Discretion of justices to grant request. **R v Southampton City Justices, ex p Briggs** [1972] **1** 573, QBD.
Withdrawal of consent—Withdrawal after plea and before evidence given—Whether trial begun—Whether accused entitled to withdraw consent and elect for trial by jury. **R v Craske, ex p Comr of Police of the Metropolis** [1957] **2** 772, QBD.
Costs. *See* **Criminal law** (Costs—Magistrates' court—Indictable offences—Summary trial or inquiry as examining justices).
Duty of court to explain to accused liability to be committed to quarter sessions for sentence—
Failure to explain liability to accused—Effect—Summary Jurisdiction Act 1879, s 17(2), and Criminal Justice Act 1925, s 24(2), (as amended by Criminal Justice Act 1948, Sch IX). **R v Kent Justices, ex p Machin** [1952] **1** 1123, QBD.
Serious offence—
Necessity for judicial exercise of jurisdiction—Criminal Justice Act 1925, s 24(1). **R v Bodmin Justices, ex p McEwen** [1947] **1** 109, KBD.
Prosecution not to invite summary trial—Justices' duty—Committal on bail—Propriety—Magistrates' Courts Act 1952, ss 19(2), 29. **R v Coe** [1969] **1** 65, CA.
Summons—
Consent to institution of proceedings—
Omnia praesumuntur rite esse acta. **Price v Humphries** [1958] **2** 725, QBD.
Form of summons—
Signature—Summons to be signed by issuing justice or to state his name and be authenticated by clerk's signature—Facsimile signature—Validity—Summons issued bearing facsimile signature of justice—Justice's facsimile signature applied by clerk—Clerk having general authority to apply justice's signature—Justice not giving specific instructions for his facsimile signature to be applied to defendant's summons—Whether summons valid—Magistrates' Courts Rules 1968 (SI 1968 No 1920), r 81. **R v Brentford Justices, ex p Catlin** [1975] **2** 201, QBD.
Issue of summons—
Discretion of prosecutor over offence charged. **R v Nuneaton Justices, ex p Parker** [1954] **3** 251, QBD.
Enquiry into facts when issuing summons—Whether magistrate under duty to enquire. **Sammy-Joe v GPO Mount Pleasant Office** [1966] **3** 924, Ch D.
Issue of second summons for same offence—Abuse of process—Respondent bound over to Keep the peace at hearing of first summons—Complainant laying fresh information and magistrates issuing fresh summons in respect of same offence—Whether issue of second summons an abuse of process. **R v Grays Magistrates, ex p Low** [1988] **3** 834, QBD.
Issue outside justices' county—Exercise of discretion. **R v Blandford** [1955] **1** 681, CCA.
Issue upon information being laid—Delay—Effect—No time limit for issuing summons—Prejudice to defendant—Summons issued several months after information laid—Whether a requirement that summons should be issued promptly on information being laid—Whether delay invalidating summons—Magistrates' Courts Act 1952, s 1(1). **R v Fairford Justices, ex p Brewster** [1975] **2** 757, QBD.
Objection to issue of summons—Whether proposed defendant having locus standi to be heard on complainant's application for summons—Whether magistrate having discretion to hear proposed defendant—Magistrates' Courts Act 1952, s 1(1). **R v West London Justices, ex p Klahn** [1979] **2** 221, QBD.
Refusal to issue summons—
Private prosecution—Driver prosecuted by Crown for driving without due care and attention in respect of collision in which claimant's child killed—Crown discontinuing prosecution—Claimant seeking issue of summons against driver—Magistrate refusing to issue summons in absence of special circumstances—Whether magistrate properly refusing to issue summons. **R (on the application of Charlson) v Guildford Magistrates' Court** [2007] **3** 163, QBD.
Private prosecution—Private prosecution against defendant already charged in respect of same matter—Driver charged with minor traffic offences in respect of collision in which applicant's son killed—Applicant seeking issue of summons against driver for causing death by reckless driving—Magistrate refusing to issue summons—Whether magistrate required to take into account existence of prosecution by Crown Prosecution Service—Whether magistrate properly refusing to issue summons—Magistrates' Courts Act 1980, s 1—Prosecution of Offences Act 1985, s 6. **R v Tower Bridge Metropolitan Stipendiary Magistrate, ex p Chaudhry** [1994] **1** 44, QBD.
Road traffic offence—
Summons or information. *See* **Road traffic** (Offence—Summons or information).
Summons and cross-summons—
Whether magistrates having jurisdiction to hear summons and cross-summons together. *See* Information—Hearing two or more together—Summons and cross-summons arising out of informations, *above*.
Withdrawal of summons—
Withdrawal on ground of informality—Whether bar to second summons. **Owens v Minoprio** [1942] **1** 30, KBD.
Summons or information—
Road traffic offence. *See* **Road traffic** (Offence—Summons or information).
Supervision order—
Effect. *See* Fine—Supervision order—Effect, *above*.
Territorial waters—
Jurisdiction—
Implied jurisdiction from enactment creating offence. *See* Jurisdiction—Implied jurisdiction from enactment creating offence—Territorial waters, *above*.
Theft—
Information. *See* Information—Theft, *above*.

MAGISTRATES (cont)—
  Trial of criminal charge—
    Generally. *See* **Criminal law** (Trial).
  Unsworn statement by defendant. *See* Complaint—Hearing—Unsworn statement by defendant, *above.*
  Variation of decision by quarter sessions. *See* **Quarter sessions** (Appeal to—Variation of decision of court of summary jurisdiction).
  Variation or discharge of maintenance order—
    Order registered in magistrates' court—
      Variation. *See* **Husband and wife** (Variation or discharge of maintenance order—Variation of order registered in magistrates' court).
  Wardship proceedings—
    Order forbidding removal of child—
      Jurisdiction. *See* **Ward of court** (Jurisdiction—Magistrates—Order forbidding removal—Order a nullity).
  Warrant—
    Execution—
      Warrant of commitment—Non-payment of fine—Unknown to justices defaulter already remanded in custody on other charges at time warrant issued—Warrant not executed during period of custody—Defaulter eventually acquitted on other charges—Warrant thereafter executed and defaulter arrested—Whether delayed execution of warrant an abuse of power. **R v Leeds Prison Governor, ex p Huntley** [1972] **2** 783, QBD.
      Warrant of commitment—Person committed already detained in prison—Whether essential to validity of execution that warrant be delivered to governor of prison—Magistrates' Courts Rules 1968 (SI 1968 No 1920), r 80(5). **R v Leeds Prison Governor, ex p Huntley** [1972] **2** 783, QBD.
    Indorsement—
      Indorsement pinned to warrant—Validity—Indictable Offences Act 1848, s 12. **R v Metropolitan Police Comr, ex p Melia** [1957] **3** 440, QBD.
      Irish warrant. *See* Indorsement of Irish warrant, *above.*
    Possession—
      Landlord and tenant—Procedure. *See* **Landlord and tenant** (Recovery of possession—Procedure before magistrates—Warrant for possession).
    Powers of seizure—
      Notice of seizure—Traders suspected of breaching food safety laws—Magistrates' court issuing warrant to enter premises and search and seize property—Crown Court finding warrant should not have been granted and ordering return of property—Whether warrant defective—Whether seizure unlawful—Whether Crown Court acting without jurisdiction or otherwise making irrational decision—Food Safety Act 1990, s 32(2)—Criminal Justice and Police Act 2001, ss 52, 59. **R (on the application of Dulai) v Chelmsford Magistrates' Court** [2012] **3** 764, DC.
    Warrant for arrest of witness—
      Witness refusing to attend court—Witness's evidence critical to defence case—Magistrates refusing to issue warrant for arrest of witness—Whether magistrates acting in breach of natural justice—Magistrates' Courts Act 1980, s 97(3). **R v Bradford Justices, ex p Wilkinson** [1990] **2** 833, QBD.
  Witness—
    Presence in court during examination of earlier witnesses—
      Maintenance proceedings. *See* **Husband and wife** (Maintenance—Procedure—Magistrates' court—Presence of witness during hearing).
    Procedure. *See* Procedure—Evidence, *above.*
    Summons—
      Generally. *See* Witness summons, *below.*
    Warrant for arrest of. *See* Warrant—Warrant for arrest of witness, *above.*
  Witness summons—
    Child—
      Care proceedings—Child making allegations against father of sexual abuse—Father applying for witness summons to compel attendance of child as witness in care proceedings—Whether witness summons should be issued to compel attendance of child as witness—Magistrates' Courts Act 1980, s 97. **R v B - CC, ex p P** [1991] **2** 65, CA.
    Material evidence—
      Committal proceedings—Documents likely to be material evidence—Legal professional privilege—Witness having previously made inconsistent statement to his solicitor—Witness's instructions to solicitor when he himself was charged with same crime with which accused charged—Witness refusing to waive legal professional privilege—Whether privilege overriding public interest in securing that all relevant and admissible evidence made available to accused for his defence—Whether magistrate having jurisdiction to issue witness summons for production of witness's instructions to solicitor—Criminal Procedure Act 1865, ss 4, 5—Magistrates' Courts Act 1980, s 97. **R v Derby Magistrates' Court, ex p B** [1995] **4** 526, HL.
      Transcripts of evidence given by witnesses at investigation into company's affairs—Summons to inspector requiring him to produce transcripts in criminal proceedings resulting from investigation—Whether documents material evidence in criminal proceedings—Sole purpose of documents for use in cross-examination of witnesses at trial—Companies Act 1948, s 165. **R v Cheltenham Justices, ex p Secretary of State for Trade** [1977] **1** 460, QBD.
      Witness not voluntarily making statement or producing document or other exhibit—Taking evidence as deposition—Whether deposition taking place in open court—Whether justices required to investigate claim for privilege against self-incrimination—Crime and Disorder Act 1998, Sch 3, para 4. **R (on the application of CPS) v Bolton Magistrates' Court** [2005] **2** 848, DC.
  Youth court—
    Jurisidiction. *See* Jurisdiction—Youth court, *above.*

MAGISTRATES' COURT

Anti-social behaviour—
Dispersal of groups and removal of persons under 16 to their place of residence—
Authorisation—Where authorisation in force—Guidance—Anti-social behaviour Act 2003, ss 30, 31.
Carter v CPS [2010] **4** 990, DC.
Police authorisation of powers. *See* Anti-social behaviour—Dispersal of groups and removal of persons under 16 to their place of residence—Authorisation, *above*.
Premises where drugs used unlawfully—
Closure notice—Closure order—Extension and discharge of closure order—Guidance—Anti-social Behaviour Act 2003, ss 2, 5(4). **R (on the application of Smith) v Snaresbrook Crown Court** [2009] **1** 547, DC.

MAIL

Generally. *See* **Post Office**.
Prisoner—
Letters to and from prisoner. *See* **Prison** (Letters—Prisoner's letters).

MAIL ORDER BUSINESS

Master and servant—
Restraint of trade by agreement. *See* **Restraint of trade by agreement** (Employer and employee).

MAINTENANCE

Action, of. *See* **Maintenance of action**.
Affiliation proceedings. *See* **Affiliation**.
Animals—
Lien for cost of maintenance. *See* **Lien** (Maintenance of animals).
Arrears. *See* **Husband and wife** (Maintenance—Arrears).
Bridge. *See* **Bridge** (Maintenance).
Building—
Value added tax—
Zero-rating. *See* **Value added tax** (Zero-rating—Building works—Alteration of building—Work of repair or maintenance).
Child—
Divorce. *See* **Divorce** (Financial provision—Child—Maintenance).
Generally. *See* **Child** (Maintenance).
Church. *See* **Ecclesiastical law** (Church—Repairs and maintenance).
Dependant—
Family provision. *See* **Family provision** (Dependant).
Divorce—
Generally. *See* **Divorce** (Maintenance).
Estoppel—
Child of the family. *See* **Divorce** (Estoppel—Maintenance—Child of the family).
Divorce. *See* **Divorce** (Financial provision—Estoppel in maintenance proceedings).
Factory floor. *See* **Factory** (Floor—Maintenance).
Family provision. *See* **Family provision**.
Former spouse—
Maintenance from estate of deceased former spouse. *See* **Divorce** (Financial provision—Deceased former spouse—Maintenance for surviving spouse out of deceased's estate).
Highway. *See* **Highway** (Maintenance).
Husband and wife—
Generally. *See* **Husband and wife** (Maintenance).
Variation or discharge of maintenance order. *See* **Husband and wife** (Variation or discharge of maintenance order).
Maintenance assessment by Child Support Agency—
Arrears accumulating under assessment—
Jurisdiction to grant freezing order. *See* **Practice** (Pre-trial or post-judgment relief—Freezing order—Jurisdiction—Maintenance assessment by Child Support Agency).
Matrimonial proceedings—
Generally. *See* **Husband and wife** (Maintenance).
Order made in husband's absence—
Personal liability of solicitor for costs. *See* **Solicitor** (Payment of costs by solicitor personally—Matrimonial proceedings—Maintenance order made in husband's absence).
Nullity suit. *See* **Nullity** (Financial provision and property adjustment—Maintenance).
Order—
Income tax. *See* **Income tax** (Annual payment—Order of court—Maintenance order).
Variation—
Divorce proceedings. *See* **Divorce** (Maintenance—Variation of order).
Generally. *See* **Husband and wife** (Variation or discharge of maintenance order).
Road—
Coal mine, in—
Statutory duty. *See* **Coal mining** (Statutory duty—Road—Construction and maintenance).
Safe means of access to place of work—
Factory. *See* **Factory** (Safe means of access to place of work).
Trust—
Statutory power. *See* **Trust and trustee** (Maintenance—Statutory power).
Variation of maintenance agreement. *See* **Husband and wife** (Variation of maintenance agreement).
Variation of settlement—
Application by wife for maintenance. *See* **Variation of Settlement (Matrimonial Causes)** (Application by wife for maintenance).
Wife—
Arrears—
Judgment summons—Substituted service. *See* **Divorce** (Practice—Service—Substituted service—Judgment summons).

MAINTENANCE (cont)—
Wife (cont)—
Divorce. *See* **Divorce** (Maintenance).
Wilful neglect to maintain—
Maintenance order after divorce—
Discretion to make order. *See* **Husband and wife** (Wilful neglect to maintain—Divorce—Discretion to make maintenance order after parties divorced).

MAINTENANCE OF ACTION
Assignment of right of action—
Bare right to litigate—
When assignment of bare right to litigate is void for maintenance and champerty—Whether assignment of action champertous if assignee's intention is to sell cause of action to stranger for a profit rather than to pursue action himself. **Brownton Ltd v Edward Moore Inbucon Ltd** [1985] **3** 499, CA.
Champerty—
Abuse of process—
Shipbuilders agreeing to build vessels for buyer—Brokers being entitled to 4 or 5% commission on instalments paid by buyer—Buyer not paying instalments and shipbuilders bringing action against buyer and other defendants—Brokers' agent agreeing with shipbuilders to fund litigation—Agreement providing for funder to receive larger share of recovery from proceedings—Whether nature of agreement rendered proceedings abuse of process. **Stocznia Gdanska SA v Latvian Shipping Co (No 2)** [1999] **3** 822, QBD.
Bona fide dispute test—
Assignment of debt—Debtor acknowledging debt due but refusing to pay voluntarily—Whether assignment of debt valid where necessity for litigation to recover contemplated—Whether assignment champertous—Law of Property Act 1925, s 136. **Camdex International Ltd v Bank of Zambia** [1996] **3** 431, CA.
Contingency fee agreement—
Claimants instructing accountants to prepare and submit claims for damages after obtaining judgment on liability—Claimants agreeing that accountants' fees to be percentage of final settlement—Accountants providing services ancillary to conduct of litigation by claimants' solicitors—Whether agreement champertous—Courts and Legal Services Act 1990, s 58. **Factortame Ltd v Secretary of State for the Environment, Transport and the Regions (No 2)** [2002] **4** 97, CA.
Conditional fee agreement—Agreement between solicitors and client including provision for indemnity against payment by client of opponent's costs on failure of claim—Whether agreement enforceable—Whether indemnity champertous—Courts and Legal Services Act 1990, s 58. **Morris v Southwark London BC (Law Society intervening)** [2011] **2** 240, CA.
Insurer instructing maritime claims and recovery agent—Agreement that agent's fees to be percentage of recovered amount—Agent providing services relating or incidental to conduct of litigation by claimants' solicitors—Whether agreement champertous. **Papera Traders Co Ltd v Hyundai Merchant Marine Co Ltd** [2002] **2 Comm** 1083, QBD.
Provision of hire car to victim of non-fault accident—
Car hire reimbursed out of damages recovered by plaintiff—Plaintiff motorist involved in motor vehicle accident caused by negligence of defendant motorist—Plaintiff entering into agreement for hire of car while own car repaired—Plaintiff under no obligation to pay hire charges until damages awarded for cost of car hire—Whether agreement champertous—Whether plaintiff suffering loss—Whether plaintiff entitled to interest on award of damages for cost of car hire. **Giles v Thompson** [1993] **3** 321, CA and HL.
Statutory exemption—
Action by liquidator against directors for wrongful trading—Assignment of fruits of litigation to third party in return for funding of action—Damages recovered to be split between liquidator and third party—Whether assignment of fruits of litigation within liquidator's statutory powers—Whether assignment within liquidator's power to sell any of company's property—Whether assignment within liquidator's power to do all such other things as may be necessary for winding up company's affairs and distributing its assets—Whether assignment unlawful as being champertous—Insolvency Act 1986, s 214, Sch 4, paras 6, 13. **Oasis Merchandising Services Ltd (in liq), Re** [1997] **1** 1009, CA.
Assignment of fruits of litigation to third party by liquidator of insolvent company—Liquidator assigning fruits of cause of action and control over action—Whether assignment objectionable as being champertous—Insolvency Act 1986, Sch 4, para 6. **Ruttle Plant Ltd v Secretary of State for the Environment Food and Rural Affairs (No 3)** [2009] **1** 448, QBD.
Liquidator of insolvent company selling beneficial interest in proceeds of litigation in consideration for contributions towards costs—Whether arrangement within liquidators' statutory exemption from prohibition of maintenance—Whether stay of action should be granted on ground of champertous arrangement—Insolvency Act 1986, ss 165, 166, Sch 4, para 6. **Grovewood Holdings plc v James Capel & Co Ltd** [1994] **4** 417, Ch D.
Common interest—
Cause of action—
Assignment—Assignment of cause of action in tort for damages for personal injury—Whether assignment valid—Whether assignee having sufficient interest in subject matter of action. **Simpson v Norfolk and Norwich University Hospital NHS Trust** [2012] **1** 1423, CA.
Commercial and financial interest—
Cause of action—Assignment—Bank financing corporation in commercial transaction—Corporation bringing action against third party in respect of that transaction—Bank guaranteeing corporation's legal costs—Corporation assigning to bank its rights of action against third party—Whether assignment valid—Whether bank having sufficient interest in subject matter of action. **Trendtex Trading Corp v Crédit Suisse** [1981] **3** 520, HL.

458

MAINTENANCE OF ACTION (cont)—
Common interest (cont)—
Commercial and financial interest (cont)—
Cause of action—Assignment—Plaintiff suing defendant in negligence—Defendant in its defence alleging breach of contract by third party—Plaintiff then suing third party—Defendant settling claim against it—Plaintiff assigning to defendant its right of action against third party—Whether assignment valid—Whether defendant having sufficient interest in subject matter of action. **Brownton Ltd v Edward Moore Inbucon Ltd** [1985] **3** 499, CA.
Pollution action—
Action brought by riparian owner and owners of fishing rights—Deeds of indemnity executed by trustees of anglers' association to provide for plaintiff's costs—Application by defendants to stay proceedings. **Martell v Consett Iron Co Ltd** [1955] **1** 481, CA.
Trade union employing salaried officials—
Action by officials against union member for defamation in respect of their conduct in course of their duties—Union executive supporting legal action in good faith—Whether this constituted maintenance—Express authority to defray costs of officials not given by union's rules—Whether power to do so implied. **Hill v Archbold** [1967] **3** 110, CA.
Unincorporated body—
Funds used to pay personal legal costs of members—Legal interest in result of action. **Baker v Jones** [1954] **2** 553, QBD.
Identity of maintainer—
Disclosure of identity of maintainer—
Plaintiff commencing action against defendants for damages for assisting or procuring breaches of contract—Plaintiff refusing to accede to defendants' requests to disclose identity of any third parties providing funds for his legal costs—Whether court having jurisdiction to order disclosure of identity of person maintaining action—Whether court having power to stay proceedings on grounds concerning financing of action. **Abraham v Thompson** [1997] **4** 362, CA.

MAINTENANCE OF THE PEACE
Royal prerogative. *See* **Crown** (Prerogative—Maintenance of the peace).

MAJORITY DECISION
Magistrates. *See* **Magistrates** (Procedure—Majority decision).

MAJORITY VERDICT
Jury. *See* **Jury** (Majority verdict).

MAKING OFF WITHOUT PAYMENT
Crime. *See* **Criminal law** (Theft—Making off without payment).

MALADMINISTRATION
Building society. *See* **Building society** (Maladministration).
Local government. *See* **Local government** (Maladministration).
Pension scheme. *See* **Pension** (Pension scheme—Maladministration of pension scheme).

MALAYA
Wrongful dismissal. *See* **Employment** (Wrongful dismissal).

MALAYSIA
Administration of estates—
Costs—
Order—Nullity—Order approving sale of partnership property of which intestate trustee and part owner—Order made in absence of persons entitled to be heard—Order a nullity—Costs against administrator personally set aside—Malayan Rules of the Supreme Court 1957, Ord 55, r 5(a), Ord 70. **Chettiar v Chettiar (No 2)** [1962] **2** 238, PC.
Appeal—
Court of Appeal. *See* Court of Appeal, *below.*
Criminal cases. *See* Criminal law—Appeal, *below.*
Right to appeal to Judicial Committee—
Where appeal lies as of right and where it is discretionary—Courts of Judicature Act 1964, s 74. **Lopes v Valliappa Chettiar** [1968] **2** 136, PC.
Compensation—
Act done for another person—
Expenditure on making road to mineral lands—Appellant granted prospector's licence—Agreement by appellant with company for sub-lease of mineral lands to company—Assignments of benefit of agreement vesting benefit in first respondents—Road to mineral lands built by respondents when they were prospectively entitled to mining rights and sub-lease by virtue of assigned agreement—Whether respondents entitled to compensation from appellant for building road, they having ceased to be entitled to the benefit of the agreement—Contract Ordinance, s 71. **Siow Wong Fatt v Susur Rotan Mining Ltd** [1967] **2** 492, PC.
Court of Appeal—
Extension of time—
Filing of record of appeal—Refusal by Court of Appeal—Review by Judicial Committee of discretion exercised by Court of Appeal—Rules of the Supreme Court of the Federation of Malaya, Ord 58, r 22(6), Ord 64, r 7. **Ratnam v Cumarasamy (sub nom Thambro Ratnam v Thambro Cumarasamy)** [1964] **3** 933, PC.
Criminal law—
Appeal—
New ground for upholding conviction—Presentation of a different case involved—Leave to advance new ground refused—Criminal Procedure Code, s 155. **Liew Sai Wah v Public Prosecutor** [1968] **2** 738, PC.

MALAYSIA (cont)—
  Criminal law (cont)—
    Emergency legislation—
      Charge of unlawfully carrying a firearm—Intention to surrender to authorities—'Lawful excuse'—'Lawful authority'—Malaya Emergency Regulations 1951, reg 4(1), as amended by Emergency (Amendment No 11) Regulations 1952, reg 2. **Wong Pooh Yin, alias Kwang Sin, alias Kar Sin v Public Prosecutor** [1954] **3** 31, PC.
  Elections—
    Petition—
      Appeal—Interlocutory order to strike out petition for want of service—Competency of appeal court—No address for service left with registrar by candidate—Advertisement of petition outside time prescribed for service—Whether appeal lay from interlocutory order—Whether rule prescribing time limit for service was mandatory—Election Offences Ordinance (No 906 of 1954), ss 33(4), 36—Courts of Judicature Act 1964, ss 67, 74. **Nair v Teik** [1967] **2** 34, PC.
  Estoppel—
    Licensor and licensee—
      Licence granted by government to plaintiff—Licence to occupy alluvium formed by recession of sea adjoining plaintiff's land—Government subsequently granting lease of alluvium to third party—Plaintiff giving up possession—Subsequent claim by plaintiff that alluvium forming part of his own land by reason of gradual and imperceptible recession of sea—Whether plaintiff estopped from denying government's title—Evidence Ordinance (Malaysia) 1950, s 116. **Government of the State of Penang v Beng Hong Oon** [1971] **3** 1163, PC.
  False imprisonment—
    Arrest without warrant—
      Reasonable suspicion that offence committed—Whether prima facie proof necessary—Criminal Procedure Code, s 23(1)(a). **Shaabin Bin Hussien v Chong Fook Kam** [1969] **3** 1626, PC.
  Income tax—
    Compensation for loss of employment—
      Exemption from income tax—Ex gratia payment—Payment of lump sum to employee on termination of employment—Prospect of future employment—Lump sum based on scale under scheme for compensation operated by employers—Scale providing for reduced payments on termination after age of 45—Evidence that sum paid as compensation for loss of prospect of future employment—Whether payment 'compensation for loss of employment' or a 'gratuity...in respect of having or exercising employment'—Income Tax Act 1967 (Malaysia), s 13(1)(a), Sch 6, Part I, para 15. **Heywood v Comptroller-General of Inland Revenue** [1974] **3** 872, PC.
  Industrial Court—
    Jurisdiction of High Court to quash decision of Industrial Court—
      Exclusion by statute. *See* **Certiorari** (Jurisdiction—Exclusion by statute—Industrial Court of Malaysia).
  Internal security—
    Consorting in a security area with persons who carried arms—
      Accused consorted with Indonesian soldiers only—Whether offence under Internal Security Act 1960 (No 18 of 1960), ss 57, 58. **Public Prosecutor v Koi** [1968] **1** 419, PC.
    Possession of ammunition—
      Hand grenade bodies—Whether parts of hand granades 'ammunition'—Internal Security Act 1960 (No 18 of 1960), ss 2, 57(1). **Liew Sai Wah v Public Prosecutor** [1968] **2** 738, PC.
  Land—
    Transfer—
      Deceit of public administration—Transfer of land by father to son for purpose of avoiding regulations controlling rubber production—Transaction ostensibly a sale—No consideration paid and father remaining in possession after transfer—Fraudulent purpose effected—Whether father could obtain re-transfer of land. **Chettiar v Chettiar** [1962] **1** 494, PC.
  Prisoner of war—
    Privileges—
      Burden of proof—Proof whether prisoner entitled to privileges of protected prisoner of war within Geneva Convention—Effect of raising doubt at trial—Proceedings at trial not sustainable in the absence of notice—Geneva Conventions Act 1962 (No 5 of 1962), s 4(1), Sch 3, arts 4, 5. **Public Prosecutor v Koi** [1968] **1** 419, PC.
    Uniform not worn—
      Sabotage of non-military building—Entitlement to protection of Geneva Convention—Emergency (Criminal Trials) Regulations 1964—Geneva Convention Act 1962 (No 5 of 1962). **Mohamed Ali v Public Prosecutor** [1968] **3** 488, PC.
  Statutory duty—
    Breach—
      Failure to maintain motor vehicle in proper condition—Whether right of action in favour of person claiming to have been injured by reason of breach—Motor Vehicles (Construction and Use) Rules 1959 (Malaysia) (Legislative notification 170 of 1959). **Tan Chye Choo v Chong Kew Moi** [1970] **1** 266, PC.

MALE PROSTITUTION
  Living on earnings of male prostitution. *See* **Criminal law** (Prostitution—Living on earnings of prostitution—Male prostitution).

MALICE
  Damage to property. *See* **Criminal law** (Damage to property).
  Grievous bodily harm. *See* **Criminal law** (Grievous bodily harm—Maliciously causing grievous bodily harm).
  Libel action—
    Malice avoiding privilege. *See* **Libel and slander** (Qualified privilege—Malice avoiding privilege).
    Malice pleaded to displace defence of fair comment. *See* **Libel and slander** (Fair comment—Malice).
  Malicious falsehood. *See* **Malicious falsehood**.
  Malicious prosecution. *See* **Malicious prosecution**.
  Malicious wounding. *See* **Criminal law** (Wounding—Unlawful and malicious wounding).

MALICE (cont)—
    Slander of title. *See* **Slander of title** (No proof of malice or damage—Power of court to declare right to title).

MALICIOUS DAMAGE
    See **Criminal law** (Damage to property).

MALICIOUS FALSEHOOD
    Damages—
        Nature of damages recoverable—
            Damages for anxiety and distress—Aggravated damages—Whether aggravated damages recoverable for malicious falsehood—Defamation Act 1952, s 3. **Khodaparast v Shad** [2000] **1** 545, CA.
            Damages for anxiety and distress—Aggravated damages—Whether plaintiff who is unable to prove any compensatable pecuniary loss restricted to nominal damages—Whether damages for anxiety and distress or aggravated damages recoverable for malicious falsehood—Defamation Act 1952, s 3. **Joyce v Sengupta** [1993] **1** 897, CA.
        Pecuniary loss—
            Damages for injured feelings not recoverable—Damages reduced from £10,000 to £100—Defamation Act 1952, s 3(1). **Fielding v Variety Inc** [1967] **2** 497, CA.
            Special damage not pleaded—Whether evidence of actual loss admissible—Defamation Act 1952, s 3(1)(b). **Calvet v Tomkies** [1963] **3** 610, CA.
    Libel and slander—
        Choice of action—
            Defendant making false statement about plaintiff—Plaintiff choosing to sue for malicious falsehood rather than defamation—Legal aid available for action for malicious falsehood but not for action for defamation—Defendant not entitled to jury trial as of right in action for malicious falsehood—Whether plaintiff having choice of action—Whether malicious falsehood and defamation incompatible causes of action—Defamation Act 1952, s 3. **Joyce v Sengupta** [1993] **1** 897, CA.
            Single meaning rule—Whether single meaning rule applying to tort of malicious falsehood. **Ajinomoto Sweeteners Europe SAS v Asda Stores Ltd** [2010] **2** 311, QBD.
    Malice—
        Test of malice—
            Whether same test for malicious falsehood as for libel and slander—Whether honest belief or positive belief in truth of what was published good defence to action for malicious falsehood. **Spring v Guardian Assurance plc** [1993] **2** 273, CA.
    Meaning of words complained of—
        Single meaning rule—
            Whether single meaning rule in defamation also applying to malicious falsehood. **Ajinomoto Sweeteners Europe SAS v Asda Stores Ltd** [2010] **4** 1029, CA.
    Slander of goods. *See* **Slander of goods**.
    Slander of title. *See* **Slander of title**.

MALICIOUS PROSECUTION
    Abuse of process of court—
        Tort of abuse of process distinguished from malicious prosecution. *See* **Tort** (Abuse of process—Actionable abuse of process—Elements of tort).
    Action—
        Essentials to action for malicious prosecution—
            Setting law in motion—Defendant providing false information to financial regulator—Serious Fraud Office bringing criminal proceedings against claimants—Prosecution collapsing—Claimants bringing action for malicious prosecution against defendants—Test to determine whether Serious Fraud Office or defendants prosecutor. **Mahon v Rahn (No 2)** [2000] **2 Comm** 1, CA; [2000] **4** 41, CA.
            Setting law in motion—Defendant providing false information to police—Police charging plaintiff with indecent exposure—Prosecution offering no evidence at hearing of charge—Plaintiff bringing action for malicious prosecution against defendant—Whether defendant setting law in motion—Whether defendant liable for malicious prosecution of plaintiff. **Martin v Watson** [1995] **3** 559, HL.
            Setting law in motion—Defendants allegedly providing false information to financial regulator—Serious Fraud Office bringing criminal proceedings against claimants—Prosecution collapsing—Claimants bringing action for malicious prosecution against defendants—Test for determining whether informant prosecutor for purposes of tort of malicious prosecution. **Mahon v Rahn (No 2)** [2000] **2 Comm** 1, CA; [2000] **4** 41, CA.
            Setting law in motion—Pathologist preparing post-mortem report for police—Plaintiff charged with murder after report considered by Director of Public Prosecutions—Whether pathologist setting law in motion—Whether plaintiff entitled to bring action for malicious prosecution against pathologist. **Evans v London Hospital Medical College** [1981] **1** 715, QBD.
            Unsuccessful prosecution—Plaintiff bound over by court of summary jurisdiction—Whether action for malicious prosecution appropriate—Summary Jurisdiction Act 1879, s 25. **Everett v Ribbands** [1952] **1** 823, CA.
            Whether tort extending to civil proceedings. **Crawford Adjusters v Sagicor General Insurance (Cayman) Ltd** [2013] **4** 8, PC; **Willers v Joyce (No 1)** [2017] **2** 327, SC.
            Whether tort extending to domestic disciplinary proceedings. **Gregory v Portsmouth City Council** [2000] **1** 560, HL.
    Damage necessary to support action—
        Costs of defence and appeal—
            Actual costs less lump sum costs awarded by quarter sessions—Whether sufficient to support an action. **Berry v British Transport Commission** [1961] **3** 65, CA.

MALICIOUS PROSECUTION (cont)—

Damage necessary to support action (cont)—
Injury to plaintiff's reputation—
Charge of statutory offence punishable by fine only—Insufficient damage entailed to support action unless charge injures fair fame of plaintiff—What amounts to injury to fair fame—Whether difference between solicitor and client costs and costs awarded to a successful appellant in criminal proceedings is sufficient damage to support an action for malicious prosecution—Prosecution for pulling communication cord contrary to the Regulation of Railways Act 1868, s 22. **Berry v British Transport Commission** [1961] 3 65, CA.
Damages. See **Damages** (Measure of damages—Malicious prosecution).
Honest belief of defendant in plaintiff's guilt—
Question for jury—
Circumstances in which question to be put to jury—Evidence of witnesses known to prosecution rendering accused's guilt improbable—Positive identification of accused by another witness—Statements of witnesses supporting accused's innocence not disclosed to committing magistrate, but made available to defence—Whether question of defendant's honest belief in guilt should be left to jury. **Dallison v Caffery** [1964] 2 610, CA.
Circumstances in which question to be put to jury—Questions not to be put to jury in absence of evidence on which to base a finding of want of such belief—Legal advice as defence. **Glinski v McIver** [1962] 1 696, HL.
Form of question for jury. **Tempest v Snowden** [1952] 1 1, CA.
Malice—
Motive—
Recovery of sum of which prosecutor had been defrauded the ultimate aim—Prosecution for felony before civil action a duty imposed by law—Whether malice established. **Abbott v Refuge Assurance Co Ltd** [1961] 3 1074, CA.
Malicious arrest or detention—
Immunity from suit. See **Action** (Immunity from suit—Witness).
Pleading—
Defence—
Denial of absence of reasonable or probable cause—Whether particulars of denial could be ordered. See **Pleading** (Particulars—Malicious prosecution).
Prosecutor—
Police officer—
Police officer alleging claimant had struck him and asking another police officer to arrest claimant—Second police officer acting in good faith based on information provided by first police officer—Whether first or second police officer 'prosecutor' -Whether jury's verdict perverse. **Copeland v Metropolitan Police Comr** [2015] 3 391, CA.
Private citizen—
Prosecution at invitation of police—Private citizen who had reported matter to police, signed charge, being invited to do so by police officer—Prosecution conducted by solicitor and counsel retained by police—Whether private citizen was 'prosecutor'. **Malz v Rosen** [1966] 2 10, QBD.
Reasonable and probable cause for prosecution—
Director of Public Prosecutions—
Prosecution instigated by Director of Public Prosecutions—Whether conclusive that reasonable and probable cause for prosecution. **Riches v DPP** [1973] 2 935, CA.
Factors to be considered—
Need to take steps to obtain information—Admissible evidence only to be considered—Need for legal advice—Weight to be attributed to counsel's opinion—Subsequent stages of trial—Resisting submission of no case to answer—Contesting successful appeal against conviction. **Abbott v Refuge Assurance Co Ltd** [1961] 3 1074, CA.
Police advice—Advice of apparently responsible police officer to whom prosecutor has given honest and reasonably accurate account of incident. **Malz v Rosen** [1966] 2 10, QBD.
Question for judge—
Prosecution successful at first instance—Conviction quashed in the Court of Criminal Appeal—Whether reasonable and probable cause for prosecution. **Herniman v Smith** [1938] 1 1, HL.
Single question whether one witness had positively identified accused put to jury—Judge need put only salient issues of fact on which jury's help needed. **Dallison v Caffery** [1964] 2 610, CA.
When question for jury—
Reasonable cause in respect of part of money alleged to have been stolen—Belief of defendant in truth of charge against plaintiff—When question for jury. **Leibo v Buckman (D) Ltd** [1952] 2 1057, CA.
Trial by jury—
Practice. See **Practice** (Trial—Trial by jury—Malicious prosecution, misfeasance in public office and conspiracy).
Queen's Bench Division. See **Jury** (Trial by jury—Cases where party entitled to trial by jury—Queen's Bench Division).

MALICIOUS WOUNDING

See **Criminal law** (Wounding—Unlawful and malicious wounding).

MALTA

Constitutional law—
Fundamental democratic freedoms—
Freedom of expression—Church condemnation of certain newspapers—Government circular prohibiting entry of condemned newspapers to hospitals and health department branches—Whether issue of circular an interference with constitutional rights—Malta (Constitution) Order in Council 1961, Constitution, ss 13, 14. **Olivier v Buttigieg** [1966] 2 459, PC.

MALTA (cont)—
Criminal law—
Appeal—
First review of summing-up—Homicide—Untruthfulness in relation to accused's evidence—Loss of memory—Judge's views indicated too freely—Whether appellant deprived of substance of a fair trial—Criminal Code of Malta, ss 35(4), 225, 234. **Broadhurst v R** [1964] **1** 111, PC.
Right to legislate in colonies—
Settlements—
Ceded territories—Cession by general consent of inhabitants—Royal prerogative—British Settlements Act 1887, s 6—Foreign Jurisdiction Act 1890, s 1. **Sammut v Strickland** [1938] **3** 693, PC.
Tort—
Personal injuries—
Action in England—Damages—Assessment. *See* **Conflict of laws** (Tort—Damages—Assessment—Accident in Malta between servicemen normally resident in England but stationed in Malta).

MAN
Employment—
Discrimination against a man—
Equality of treatment—Generally. *See* **Employment** (Equality of treatment of men and women).
European Community. *See* **European Union** (Equality of treatment of men and women).

MANAGEMENT
Brothel. *See* **Criminal law** (Brothel—Keeping a brothel—Management).
Local authority houses. *See* **Housing** (Local authority houses—Management).
Powers—
Retention—
Leasehold enfranchisement. *See* **Landlord and tenant** (Leasehold enfranchisement—Retention of management powers).

MANAGER
Charity—
Receiver and manager. *See* **Charity** (Receiver and manager).
School. *See* **Education** (School—Managers).

MANAGING CLERK
Solicitor—
Conduct of case left to managing clerk—
Payment of costs by solicitor personally. *See* **Solicitor** (Payment of costs by solicitor personally—Conduct of case left to managing clerk).

MANAGING DIRECTOR
See **Company** (Director—Managing director).

MANCHESTER
Commercial List—
Practice. *See* **Practice** (Commercial cases—Northern Circuit).

MANDAMUS
Applicant—
Sufficiency of interest—
Bookmakers—Off-course betting premises licence—Collection of duty by Commissioners of Customs and Excise—Statutory provision for method of payment—Purported authority given by Ministry to commissioners to accept payment otherwise than as provided by statute—Application by bookmakers for mandamus requiring commissioners to comply with statute—Whether applicants had sufficient interest to support application for mandamus—Finance Act 1969, s 2, Sch 8. **R v Customs and Excise Comrs, ex p Cooke and Stevenson** [1970] **1** 1068, QBD.
Ratepayer—Failure of local authority to comply with own standing orders. **R v Hereford Corp, ex p Harrower** [1970] **3** 460, QBD.
Application for—
Expedited hearing. *See* **Divisional Court** (Expedited hearings).
Attorney General—
Certificate authorising appeal to House of Lords—
Attorney General—Refusal of application for certificate—Whether duty to re-consider application—Whether mandamus would lie—Criminal Appeal Act 1907, s 1(6)—Criminal Justice Act 1925, s 16(1). **Blackburn, Ex p** [1956] **3** 334, CA.
Availability of remedy. *See* **Judicial review** (Availability of remedy—Mandamus).
Chairman of university convocation—
Performance of duty imposed by university statutes—
Alleged refusal to perform duty imposed by university statutes—Refusal to re-employ teacher in school—Whether mandamus would lie. **R v Dunsheath, ex p Meredith** [1950] **2** 741, KBD.
Chief officer of police—
Enforcement of law—
Gaming—Unlawful gaming in clubs—Policy decision reversed—Whether mandamus would lie to Commissioner of Police of the Metropolis—Whether applicant had sufficient interest to maintain proceedings for mandamus—Whether criminal cause or matter so as to exclude appeal to Court of Appeal—Supreme Court of Judicature (Consolidation) Act 1925, s 31(1)(a). **R v Metropolitan Police Comr, ex p Blackburn** [1968] **1** 763, CA.

463

MANDAMUS (cont)—
Chief officer of police (cont)—
  Enforcement of law (cont)—
    Obscene publications—Sale in shops of pornographic material—Police procedure to enforce law
    against sale of pornography ineffective—Policy of referring all prima facie cases for prosecution
    to the Director of Public Prosecutions for advice—Procedure of police in cautioning and taking
    'disclaimers' of material seized not conforming with the law—Cause of ineffectiveness of police
    efforts largely due to difficulty of enforcing Obscene Publications Act 1959—Whether mandamus
    would lie to Commissioner of Police of the Metropolis requiring him to enforce the
    law—Prosecution of Offences Regulations 1946 (SR & O 1946 No 1467), reg 6(2)(d). **R v
    Metropolitan Police Comr, ex p Blackburn (No 3)** [1973] **1** 324, CA.
Costs—
  Payment by justices—
    Motion for mandamus opposed by justices—Justices appearing by counsel—Motion granted—
    Justices liable for costs as parties to motion—Justices entitled to file affidavits in lieu of taking
    an appearance—No costs then payable—Review of Justices Decisions Act 1872, s 2. **R v
    Llanidloes Licensing Justices, ex p Davies** [1957] **2** 610, QBD.
Crown Court. *See* **Crown Court** (Supervisory jurisdiction of High Court—Orders of mandamus, prohibition
  or certiorari).
Delay—
  Discretion—
    Exercise of discretion. **R v Senate of the University of Aston, ex p Roffey** [1969] **2** 964, QBD.
Discretion—
  Delay. *See* Delay—Discretion, *above*.
  Local authority—
    Statutory duty—Enforcement—Housing—Duty to rehouse persons displaced from residential
    accommodation by housing order—Circumstances in which order of mandamus inappropriate—
    Authority unable to comply with duty—Authority able to comply with duty only at expense of
    other housing applicants. **R v Bristol Corp, ex p Hendy** [1974] **1** 1047, CA.
Immigration officer, to—
  Refusal of admission to United Kingdom to Commonwealth citizen. *See* **Commonwealth immigrant**
  (Admission—Refusal of admission—Discretion of immigration officer—Duty to act fairly).
Industrial Court—
  Failure to hear and determine reference by Minister. *See* **Industrial Court** (Reference by
  Minister—Failure to hear and determine reference—Industrial Court acting as arbitral tribunal—
  Whether mandamus lay).
Justices, to—
  Committal proceedings—
    Refusal to allow cross-examination. *See* **Criminal law** (Committal—Preliminary hearing before
    justices—Prerogative order—Magistrate refusing to allow cross-examination during committal
    proceedings—Whether mandamus would issue directing magistrate to allow cross-examination).
  Licensing justices, to. *See* **Licensing** (Justices—Hearing of application for licence—Provisional licence).
Parliamentary Commissioner for Administration—
  Whether mandamus lies. *See* **Parliamentary Commissioner for Administration** (Mandamus).
Quarter sessions—
  Refusal to state case—
    Power of High Court to issue mandamus. **R v Somerset Justices, ex p Cole (Ernest J) & Partners
    Ltd** [1950] **1** 264, KBD.
Registrar-General—
  Correction or erasure of entry in register—
    Bigamous marriage. *See* **Registration** (Births, deaths and marriages—Correction or erasure of entry
    in register—Bigamous marriage—Correction of register—Whether mandamus to correct register
    lies).
Secretary of State—
  Implementation of European Community obligations—
    Equal treatment of men and women in employment field—Equal Opportunities Commission
    alleging that United Kingdom legislation in breach of Community obligations—Whether court
    having jurisdiction to grant mandamus to compel Secretary of State to introduce
    legislation—European Communities Act 1972, s 2(2). **Equal Opportunities Commission v
    Secretary of State for Employment** [1992] **1** 545, QBD.
Valuation officer—
  Statutory duty—
    Rating—Valuation list—Whether mandamus can lie to compel valuation officer to carry out his
    statutory duty, to prepare list in accordance with law—Whether certiorari to quash list was a
    necessary prerequisite of such an application for mandamus—Rating and Valuation
    (Miscellaneous Provisions) Act 1955, s 1(2). **R v Paddington Valuation Officer, ex p Peachey
    Property Corp Ltd** [1965] **2** 836, CA.

MANDATORY INJUNCTION
Generally. *See* **Injunction** (Mandatory injunction).
Interlocutory—
  Generally. *See* **Injunction** (Interlocutory—Mandatory injunction).
  Housing authority's duty to provide accommodation for homeless person pending enquiries—
    Enforcement of duty by interlocutory injunction. *See* **Housing** (Homeless person—Preliminary duty
    to house pending inquiries—Enforcement of duty by interim mandatory injunction).

MANDATORY SENTENCE
Life sentence—
  Release of prisoner on licence. *See* **Prison** (Release on licence—Life sentence).

MANITOBA
Business tax. *See* **Canada** (Business tax—Manitoba).

MANOR

Privileges of tenants. *See* **Tolls** (Ancient demesne—Privileges of tenants in manor of ancient demesne).
Waste land of manor—
    Common land—
        Registration. *See* **Commons** (Registration—Common land and rights of common—Waste land of a manor).

MANSION HOUSE

Settlement. *See* **Settlement** (Mansion house).

MANSLAUGHTER

Causing death by reckless driving. *See* **Road traffic** (Reckless driving—Causing death by reckless driving).
Generally. *See* **Criminal law** (Manslaughter).
Murder—
    Reduction to manslaughter. *See* **Criminal law** (Murder—Manslaughter—Reduction to manslaughter).
Sentence. *See* **Sentence** (Manslaughter).
Will of victim—
    Exclusion from benefit under will. *See* **Will** (Benefit—Exclusion from benefit—Public policy—Manslaughter).

MANUFACTURER'S LIABILITY

False trade description. *See* **Trade description** (Offences due to fault of another person—Manufacturer and retailer).
Health and safety at work. *See* **Health and safety at work** (Manufacturer's duties).
Negligence—
    Dangerous things. *See* **Negligence** (Dangerous things—Manufacturer's liability).
    Defective work or product. *See* **Negligence** (Duty to take care—Defective work or product).
    Generally. *See* **Negligence** (Manufacturer's liability).
Supply of defective trailer coupling—
    User of trailer injured in accident. *See* **Sale of goods** (Implied condition as to fitness—Defective trailer coupling supplied by garage to vehicle owner for use with trailer—Coupling unsafe for purpose for which it was designed by manufacturer).

MANUSCRIPT

Copyright. *See* **Copyright**.

MAORI TAONGA

Protection of—
    New Zealand. *See* **New Zealand** (Treaty of Waitangi—Protection of Maori taonga).

MAP

Highway—
    Dedication—
        Evidence. *See* **Highway** (Dedication—Evidence—Definitive map).
    Definitive map—
        Classification. *See* **Highway** (Classification—Definitive map).
        Generally. *See* **Highway** (Definitive map).

MAREVA INJUNCTION

Affidavit in support of application—
    Affidavit containing references to prior criminal proceedings against defendant—
        Admissibility. *See* **Affidavit** (Admissibility in evidence—Affidavit in support of Mareva application).
Bank—
    Duty of care. *See* **Bank** (Duty of care—Freezing order).
Generally. *See* **Practice** (Pre-trial or post-judgment relief—Freezing order).
Service out of the jurisdiction. *See* **Practice** (Service out of the jurisdiction—Pre-trial or post-judgment relief—Freezing order).
Specific performance order combined with freezing order—
    Sale of land. *See* **Specific performance** (Sale of land—Freezing order).
Writ of ne exeat regno in support of. *See* **Equity** (Ne exeat regno—Writ—Application for writ and freezing order).

MARGINAL NOTE

Statute—
    Aid to construction. *See* **Statute** (Construction—Headings and marginal notes).

MARINE INSURANCE

Claim—
    Fraud—
        Presentation of claim supported by fraudulent device—Water ingress causing damage to vessel—Owners seeking indemnity under policy of hull and machinery insurance—Owners making recklessly untrue statement to fortify and accelerate payment under policy—Lie irrelevant to owners right to recover but insurer not liable to pay claim by reason of 'collateral lie'—Whether fraudulent claims rule at common law applying to justified claims supported by collateral lies. **Versloot Dredging BV v HDI Gerling Industrie Versicherung AG** [2016] **2 Comm** 955, SC; [2016] **4** 907, SC.
        Presentation of claim supported by fraudulent device—Water ingress causing damage to vessel—Owners seeking indemnity under policy of hull and machinery insurance—Owners writing letter to underwriters' solicitor containing allegations underwriters alleging to be false—Whether allegations false—Whether fraud such as to vitiate owners' claim. **Versloot Dredging BV v HDI Gerling Industrie Versicherung AG, The DC Merwestone** [2013] **2 Comm** 465, QBD.

MARINE INSURANCE (cont)—
  Composite policy—
    General lien—
      Proceeds of policy—Whether general rule that broker who has lien over policy of marine insurance is normally entitled, when he collects under policy, to apply proceeds collected in discharge of debt that was protected by lien, extends to cases of composite insurance—Marine Insurance Act 1906, s 53(2). **Eide UK Ltd v Lowndes Lambert Group Ltd** [1998] **1** 946, CA.
  Constructive loss. *See* Loss—Constructive total loss, *below*.
  Contract of marine insurance—
    Condition survey—
      Plaintiff purchasing Swedish dry dock with intention of towing it to England—Defendants providing 12 months' insurance cover on dry dock—Policy requiring towage survey and condition survey before dry dock set sail—Surveyor carrying out survey for purposes of towage only—Defendants noting and agreeing surveyor's report—Plaintiff claiming under policy—Whether policy required survey only for purposes of tow—Whether surveyor had been acting for defendants—Whether defendants estopped from relying on discharge of policy. **Kirkaldy & Sons Ltd v Walker** [1999] **1 Comm** 334, QBD.
    Disclosure—
      Duty to disclose—Duty of utmost good faith—Scope of pre-contract duty to disclose—Whether shipowners under a continuing duty of utmost good faith to disclose information material to the claim after commencement of litigation—Marine Insurance Act 1906, s 17. **Manifest Shipping Co Ltd v Uni-Polaris Shipping Co Ltd** [2001] **1 Comm** 193, HL; [2001] **1** 743, HL.
      Duty to disclose—Duty of utmost good faith—Whether application of fraudulent claim rule and statutory duty of utmost good faith restricted to pre-litigation period—Marine Insurance Act 1906, s 17. **Agapitos v Agnew** [2002] **1 Comm** 714, CA.
      Duty to disclose—Duty of utmost good faith—Whether duty of utmost good faith arising under implied term of contract—Whether damages available for breach of duty of utmost good faith. **Bank of Nova Scotia v Hellenic Mutual War Risks Association (Bermuda) Ltd** [1989] **3** 628, CA.
      Duty to disclose—Implied term of undertaking—Shipowners assigning war risk insurance on vessels to bank as mortgagee—Insurer undertaking to inform bank promptly if it ceased to cover any vessel—Shipowners dishonestly jeopardising war risk cover—Insurer aware of shipowners' deception—Whether insurer owing duty to disclose shipowners' deception to bank under implied term of undertaking. **Bank of Nova Scotia v Hellenic Mutual War Risks Association (Bermuda) Ltd** [1989] **3** 628, CA.
      Duty to disclose—Insurer providing insurance for towing of floating dock from Vladivostok to Vietnam—Dock sinking in rough seas—Insurer alleging material non-disclosure of wave height restrictions in towage plan—Whether non-disclosure. **Garnat Trading and Shipping (Singapore) Pte Ltd v Baominh Insurance Corp** [2012] **1 Comm** 790, CA.
      Duty to disclose—Waiver -Insurer providing insurance for towing of floating dock from Vladivostok to Vietnam—Insurance provided on basis that classification society approved towage plan which specified maximum wave height for safe tow—Express towage plan warranty removed from final version of insurance policy on basis of classification society's approval—Insurer not seeing towage plan itself—Dock sinking in rough seas—Insurer alleging material non-disclosure of wave height restrictions in towage plan—Whether non-disclosure—Whether duty to disclose—Whether disclosure of wave height restrictions waived by insurer—Marine Insurance Act 1906, s 18. **Garnat Trading and Shipping (Singapore) Pte Ltd v Baominh Insurance Corp** [2011] **1 Comm** 573, QBD.
      Misrepresentation—Right to avoid contract—Election—Insurer declining claim under policy on grounds of non-disclosure and misrepresentation—Insurer not returning premium or invoking right to avoid policy—Seven years later insurer alleging entitlement to avoid policy—Whether insurer having elected to affirm contract—Whether insurer able to avoid contract. **Argo Systems Fze v Liberty Insurance (Pte)** [2011] **1 Comm** 1111, QBD.
    Reinsurance —
      Formation —Parties negotiating marine reinsurance contract via e-mail—Terms agreed in e-mail correspondence including class warranty—Final slip as sent to reinsurer omitting class warranty—Reinsurer accepting cover 'as we had quoted'—Whether contract concluded—Whether contract incorporating class warranty. **Allianz Insurance Co v Aigaion Insurance Co SA** [2009] **2 Comm** 745, CA.
    Valuation of vessel—
      Misrepresentation of value of vessel—Whether misrepresentation material—Whether presentation of supporting documents fraudulent—Whether insurer entitled to avoid contract of insurance—Whether insurer discharged from liability in respect of claim. **Eagle Star Insurance Co Ltd v Games Video Co (GVC) SA** [2004] **1 Comm** 560, QBD.
  Deviation—
    Trade custom—
      Evidence—Ship proceeding from Poti to Istanbul—Voyage via Constantza—Deviation—Whether evidence of trade custom admissible—Absence of ambiguity in terms of charter-party. **Reardon Smith Line Ltd v Black Sea and Baltic General Insurance Co Ltd, The Indian City** [1939] **3** 444, HL.
  Disclosure—
    Duty to disclose. *See* Contract of marine insurance—Disclosure—Duty to disclose, *above*.
    Non-disclosure—
      Material non-disclosure. *See* **Insurance** (Disclosure—Non-disclosure—Material non-disclosure—Marine insurance—War risks policy—Marine and non-marine insurance).
  Discovery. *See* **Disclosure and inspection of documents** (Marine insurance actions).
  Excepted perils—
    Civil war—
      Liability of underwriters. **Pesquerias Y Secaderos de Bacalao de Espana SA v Beer** [1949] **1** 845, HL.

MARINE INSURANCE (cont)—
Excepted perils (cont)—
Infringement of customs regulations—
War risks policy—Institute war and strike clauses—Exclusion of liability for loss by reason of infringement of customs regulations—Confiscation of ship by order of foreign court on smuggling charge—Validity of order of foreign court—Burden of proof—Special court set up by decree of government of South Vietnam—Evidence that court acting under political direction and in excess of jurisdiction—Whether loss of ship attributable to political act of government of South Vietnam. **Panamanian Oriental Steamship Corp v Wright** [1971] 2 1028, CA.
Infringement of trading regulations—
Operation of ordinary judicial process—Failure to provide security—War risks policy—Institute war and strike clauses—Seizure of vessel following breach of Australian national law—Owners failing to pay security required by Australian authorities—Whether Australian fisheries management law 'trading regulation'—Whether vessel detained by operation of ordinary judicial process and failure to provide security. **Handelsbanken ASA v Dandridge** [2002] 2 Comm 39, CA.
Freight—
Exemption clause—
Claim consequent on loss of time—Off-hire clause in charterparty—Machinery breakdown on chartered vessel and consequent stranding—Vessel off-hire during period of repair—Claim by shipowners under policy for loss of freight—Whether claim 'consequent on loss of time'—Whether exemption clause applicable—Institute Time Clauses, Freight, cl 8. **Naviera de Canarias SA v Nacional Hispanica Aseguradora SA** [1977] 1 625, HL.
Claim consequent on loss of time—Time charter—Off-hire clause in charterparty—Machinery breakdown on chartered vessel and consequent stranding—Two months taken to effect repairs—Claim by shipowners under policy for loss of freight—Whether claim 'consequent on loss of time' or consequent on peril insured against—Whether exemption clause applicable—Institute Time Clauses, Freight, cl 8. **Naviera de Canarias SA v Nacional Hispanica Aseguradora SA** [1976] 3 167, CA.
Indemnity—
Loss. *See* Loss—Indemnity, *below*.
Measure of indemnity. *See* Measure of indemnity, *below*.
Indemnity insurance. *See* **Insurance** (Indemnity insurance—Marine insurance).
Limitation of action—
When time begins to run. *See* **Limitation of action** (When time begins to run—Action on marine insurance).
Loss—
Actual total loss—
Condition—Subject to survey condition—Survey incorporating previous government survey—Whether insured entitled to rely upon the findings of more than one surveyor in satisfying condition. **Zeus Tradition Marine Ltd v Bell** [2000] 2 Comm 769, CA.
Constructive total loss—Barratry—True facts at time of abandonment—Marine Insurance Act 1906, ss 57, 60(1), (2)(i). **Marstrand Fishing Co Ltd v Beer** [1937] 1 158, KBD.
Seizure of vessel by pirates—Shipowner entering into negotiations with pirates—Vessel subsequently released following payment of ransom—Whether seizure of vessel by pirates actual total loss—Marine Insurance Act 1906, ss 57(1), 78(4). **Masefield AG v Amlin Corporate Member Ltd** [2011] 2 Comm 764, CA; [2011] 3 554, CA.
Seizure of vessel by pirates—Shipowner entering into negotiations with pirates—Vessel subsequently released following payment of ransom—Whether seizure of vessel by pirates an actual total loss—Marine Insurance Act 1906, s 57(1). **Masefield AG v Amlin Corporate Member Ltd** [2010] 1 Comm 1067, QBD; [2010] 2 593, QBD.
Constructive total loss—
Actual total loss caused by uninsured peril following constructive total loss—Actual total loss occurring before insured acquiring knowledge of constructive total loss—No notice of abandonment served—Whether insured permitted to recover for constructive total loss. **Kastor Navigation Co Ltd v AGF MAT** [2003] 1 Comm 277, QBD; [2005] 2 Comm 720, CA.
Fire causing significant damage to vessel at sea—Notice of abandonment (NOA) given more than five months after casualty—Owners seeking to be indemnified by insurers on constructive total loss basis—Whether NOA given too late—Whether any basis to limit cost of recovery and repair to post-NOA costs—Marine Insurance Act 1906, ss 60, 62(3). **Connect Shipping Inc v Sveriges Anfgartygs Assurans Forening (The Swedish Club)** [2017] 2 Comm 1122, QBD; [2018] 2 Comm 575, CA.
Fire causing significant damage to vessel at sea—Notice of abandonment (NOA) given more than five months after casualty—Owners seeking to be indemnified by insurers on constructive total loss basis—Whether expenditure incurred before service of NOA to be included in computing cost of repair—Whether relevant costs include charges payable to salvors under special compensation, protection and indemnity clause contained in Lloyd's Open Form—Marine Insurance Act 1906, s 60(2)(ii). **Connect Shipping Inc v Sveriges Anfgartygs Assurans Forening (The Swedish Club)** [2019] 2 Comm 627, SC; [2019] 4 885, SC.
First claimant's vessel insured under policy of marine insurance issued by defendant insurers—Fire rendering vessel constructive total loss—Claimants claiming under policy—Defendant disputing liability on grounds of misrepresentation/non-disclosure, breach of warranty and illegality—Whether defences made out—Marine Insurance Act 1906, s 41. **Sea Glory Maritime Co v Al Sagr National Insurance Co, The Nancy** [2013] 2 Comm 913, QBD.
Freight—Agreement to pay if vessel a total loss—Cost of repairs greater than insured value of hull—Vessel worth more, when repaired, than insured value—No notice of abandonment—Whether constructive total loss—Marine Insurance Act 1906, s 60—Institute Time Clauses (Freight), cl 5. **Robertson v Nomikos (Petros M) Ltd** [1939] 2 723, HL.
Freight—Institute voyage clauses—Perils of the sea—Ship and cargo abandoned to salvors—Cost of repair for completion of contracted voyage. **Kulukundis v Norwich Union Fire Insurance Society** [1936] 2 242, CA.

467

Loss (cont)—
Constructive total loss (cont)—
Freight—Loss of freight not recoverable if arising from constructive total loss of vessel—Vessel abandoned either because loss appeared unavoidable or because cost of repairs would exceed value of vessel when repaired—Institute Time Clauses (Freight), cll 5, 6. **Vrondissis v Stevens** [1940] **3** 74, KBD.

Insurance against total loss of estimated earnings due to constructive total loss of vessel—Constructive total loss of vessel—Losses after repair occasioned by fluctuation in charter market—No total loss of earnings—Losses not due to constructive total loss of vessel. **Continental Grain Co Inc v Twitchell** [1945] **1** 575, CA.

Seizure of vessel by pirates—Shipowner entering into negotiations with pirates—Cargo owners serving notice of abandonment—Vessel subsequently released following payment of ransom—Whether constructive total loss of cargo—Marine Insurance Act 1906, s 60(1). **Masefield AG v Amlin Corporate Member Ltd** [2010] **1 Comm** 1067, QBD; [2010] **2** 593, QBD.

Ship sheltering in Italian port—Perishable cargo not transhipped or released—Constructive total loss—Marine Insurance Act 1906, s 60(2)(i). **Czarnikow (C) Ltd v Java Sea and Fire Insurance Co Ltd** [1941] **3** 256, KBD.

Statutory definition—Exclusion of common law—Partial loss—Termination of risk—Abandonment of voyage—Amount of indemnity—Marine Insurance Act 1906, ss 60(1), (2), 69(3), 78(4). **Irvin v Hine** [1949] **2** 1089, KBD.

Vessel owned by first defendant becoming constructive total loss following collision—Claimant excess layer underwriters paying first defendant amount due in respect of loss of vessel—Claimants also settling salvage claim—Majority of claimants and primary underwriters expressly electing to take over interest of first defendant in remainder of vessel—First defendant subsequently attempting to sell vessel to related fourth defendant company without claimants' consent—Minority claimants and primary underwriters subsequently expressly electing to take over interest of first defendant—Whether claimants acquiring proprietary interest in vessel in form of equitable lien—Whether majority claimants' election to take over vessel effective for statutory purposes—Whether claimants having beneficial interest in ship—Marine Insurance Act 1906, ss 63, 79. **Dornoch Ltd v Westminster International BV** [2009] **2 Comm** 399, QBD.

Indemnity—
Constructive total loss attributable to unseaworthiness—Insurer's liability excluded when ship sent to sea in unseaworthy state with privity of the assured—Meaning of privity—Degree of knowledge necessary—'Blind-eye' knowledge—Whether gross negligence sufficient to establish 'blind-eye' knowledge—Marine Insurance Act 1906, s 39(5). **Manifest Shipping Co Ltd v Uni-Polaris Shipping Co Ltd** [2001] **1 Comm** 193, HL; [2001] **1** 743, HL.

Indemnity for loss of hire—Vessel on hire to third party—Policy of insurance for loss of hire—Vessel suffering mechanical failure—Owners performing unrelated maintenance while awaiting completion of repairs—Vessel suffering subsequent mechanical failure during maintenance—Whether second mechanical failure broke chain of causation—Whether owners mitigated loss—Whether insurance policy provided for separate periods of excess for each failure—Whether owners entitled to recover full indemnity under policy. **Sealion Shipping Ltd v Valiant Insurance Co, The Toisa Pisces** [2013] **1 Comm** 1179, CA.

Loss of goods attributable to unseaworthiness—Exclusion clause—Insurer's liability excluded where ship sent to sea in unseaworthy state with privity of the assured—Meaning of 'privity'—Degree of knowledge necessary—Knowledge of facts constituting unseaworthiness—Knowledge that ship rendered unseaworthy—Whether negligence or fault on part of assured sufficient to establish privity—Marine Insurance Act 1906, s 39(5). **Cia Maritima San Basilio SA v The Oceanus Mutual Underwriting Association (Bermuda) Ltd** [1976] **3** 243, CA.

Measure of indemnity. See Measure of indemnity, below.

Settlement—Insured commencing action against insurers claiming indemnities under policies—Insured agreeing to accept sum in full and final settlement of claims under policy against 'Underwriters'—Insured subsequently bringing proceedings in Greece against insurers and employees of insurers—Judge finding Greek proceedings against insurers in breach of settlement agreements—Whether findings extending to employees and agents of insurers—Whether declaratory relief, specific performance and damages to be granted—Contracts (Rights of Third Parties) Act 1999, ss 1(1)(b), (2), (3)—GAFTA form 78, cl 17. **Starlight Shipping Co v Allianz Marine and Aviation Versicherungs AG** [2015] **2 Comm** 747, QBD.

Suing and labouring clause—Claim for constructive total loss—Additional claim for sue and labour expenses—Whether sue and labour claim adequately pleaded—Whether sue and labour claim separate cause of action to claim for loss of vessel. **North Star Shipping Ltd v Sphere Drake Insurance plc** [2005] **1 Comm** 112, QBD.

Whether policy covering storage of cargoes beyond 30 days—
Whether intention to make transfer by substitution inferable from existence of sufficient stock with which to do so. **Glencore International AG v Alpina Insurance Co Ltd (No 2)** [2004] **1 Comm** 858, QBD.

Measure of indemnity—
Bailee clause—
Expenses incurred by assured in bringing action against carriers to preserve time-bar—Clause providing that assured under duty to ensure that all rights against carriers were properly preserved and exercised—No express provision in contract entitling assured to recover expenses of preserving rights against carriers—Whether term could be implied—Whether expenses recoverable from insurers—Institute Cargo Clauses (All Risks) 1 January 1963 edn, cl 9. **Netherlands Insurance Co Est 1845 Ltd v Karl Ljungberg & Co AB** [1986] **3** 767, PC.

Suing and labouring clause—
Expenses due to condition of goods at time of shipment—Clause providing that insurance was not to cover loss, damage, or expense proximately caused by 'inherent vice' of goods insured—Whether expenses recoverable from insurers—Marine Insurance Act 1906, s 55(2)(c)—Institute Cargo Clauses (Wartime Extension), cl 6. **Berk (F W) & Co Ltd v Style** [1955] **3** 625, QBD.

MARINE INSURANCE (cont)—
  Measure of indemnity (cont)—
    Suing and labouring clause (cont)—
      Plaintiff companies operating dredging fleet in Iraq under contract with Iraqi government—
      Plaintiffs insured against war risks by defendants under agreement providing cover for 'suing and
      labouring' charges—Iraqi government seizing plaintiffs' assets following Iraqi invasion of
      Kuwait—Plaintiffs waiving claims under dredging contract in return for demobilisation of
      assets—Whether plaintiff entitled to recover value of waived claims from defendants under 'sue
      and labour' clause—Whether plaintiffs' claim against defendants affected by enforceability of
      waiver—Whether defendants discharged from liability through duress and illegality—Marine
      Insurance Act 1906, s 41. **Royal Boskalis Westminster NV v Mountain** [1997] **2** 929, CA.
  Misrepresentation—
    Damages—
      Insurer seeking damages for misrepresentation as alternative to avoiding contract—Whether
      damages available to insurer in absence of right to avoid. **Argo Systems Fze v Liberty Insurance
      (Pte)** [2011] **1 Comm** 1111, QBD.
  Non-disclosure—
    Material non-disclosure. See **Insurance** (Disclosure—Non-disclosure—Material non-disclosure—Marine
      insurance—War risks policy—Marine and non-marine insurance).
    War risks policy. See **Insurance** (Disclosure—Non-disclosure—Material non-disclosure—Marine
      insurance—War risks policy).
  Open policy—
    Jurisdiction—
      Certificate of insurance issued in respect of particular goods—Condition in policy that claim be
      referred to local tribunal of commerce—Jurisdiction of English court. **Macleod Ross & Co Ltd v
      Cie d'Assurance Generales l'Helvetia of St Gall** [1952] **1** 331, CA.
    Oil storage facility—
      Insurers seeking to avoid policy—Consideration of duty of utmost good faith in relation to open
      cover policy—Whether claimant exposed to uninsured credit risk by allowing dealings with oil
      before property transferred—Whether losses relating to oil storage facility single or multiple.
      Glencore International AG v Alpina Insurance Co Ltd [2004] **1 Comm** 766, QBD.
  Order for ship's papers. See **Disclosure and inspection of documents** (Marine insurance actions—Order for
    ship's papers).
  Perils insured against—
    All risks—
      Inherent vice—Incorporation of cl 6 of Institute Cargo Clauses (Wartime Extension)—Whether
      expenses due to inherent vice of subject-matter of insurance covered—Marine Insurance Act
      1906, s 55(2)(c). **Berk (F W) & Co Ltd v Style** [1955] **3** 625, QBD.
      Inherent vice—Policy incorporating provisions in Institute Cargo Clauses (A) excluding loss caused
      by inherent vice—Policy insuring oil rig during towage on barge—Legs of oil rig lost at sea during
      towage—Whether loss due to inherent vice. **Global Process Systems Inc v Syarikat Takaful
      Malaysia Bhd** [2009] **2 Comm** 795, QBD; [2010] **2 Comm** 224, CA; [2010] **3** 248, CA; [2011] **1** 869,
      SC; [2012] **1 Comm** 111, SC.
      Inherent vice—Whether contract providing insured with additional cover in respect of pure
      economic loss—Marine Insurance Act 1906, s 55. **Shell UK Ltd v CLM Engineering Ltd** [2000] **1
      Comm** 940, QBD.
      'Warehouse to warehouse' clause—Vessel not arriving at destination specified in policy—Statutory
      provision providing that policy not applying upon vessel sailing for destination other than that
      specified—Whether 'warehouse to warehouse' clause affecting operation of statutory
      provision—Marine Insurance Act 1906, s 44. **Nima SARL v Deves Insurance Public Co Ltd** [2002] **2
      Comm** 449, CA.
    Collision clause—
      Liability of insurer—Collision with Admiralty tug—Liability of insured under contract. **Furness,
      Withy & Co Ltd v Duder** [1936] **2** 119, KBD.
      Policy covering collision with other ship or vessel—Collision with flying boat—Whether flying boat
      a 'ship or vessel'. **Polpen Shipping Co Ltd v Commercial Union Assurance Co Ltd** [1943] **1** 162, .
      Sum payable by way of damages—Indemnity to French pilot boat. **Hall Bros Steamship Co Ltd v
      Young** [1939] **1** 809, CA.
    Fire—
      Loss of vessel by fire—Burden of proof. **Slattery v Mance** [1962] **1** 525, QBD.
    General average—
      Obedience to orders—Convoy instructed by Admiralty to return to port—Whether obedience to
      orders a general average act—Marine Insurance Act 1906, ss 66, 87—York-Antwerp Rules 1924,
      rr A, C, E. **Athel Line Ltd v Liverpool and London War Risks Insurance Association Ltd** [1944] **1** 46,
      KBD.
    Latent defect—
      Inchmaree clause—Damage to hull or machinery caused through breakage of shafts or through any
      latent defect—Latent defect in shaft—Breakage—Liability of insurer—Marine Insurance Act 1906,
      s 55(2)(c). **Scindia Steamships (London) Ltd v London Assurance** [1937] **3** 895, KBD.
    Negligence of crew—
      Want of due diligence by owners or managers—Watering ingress as result of failure of crew to
      close valve—Water traveling from bowthruster room to engine room through unsealed apertures
      in bulkheads—Substantial damage caused to vessel—Whether loss caused by negligence of crew
      and/or contractors—Whether want of due diligence by owners or managers. **Versloot Dredging
      BV v HDI Gerling Industrie Versicherung AG, The DC Merwestone** [2013] **2 Comm** 465, QBD.
    Perils of the sea—
      Burden of proving ship lost by perils of the sea—Incorporation of cl 9 of Institute Yacht
      Clauses—Identification of peril relied upon in claim—Proximate cause of loss—Warranty for
      'professional skipper and crew'—Burden of proving ship deliberately cast away with connivance
      of owner. **Brownsville Holdings Ltd v Adamjee Insurance Co Ltd** [2000] **2 Comm** 803, QBD.

MARINE INSURANCE (cont)—
   Perils insured against (cont)—
      Perils of the sea (cont)—
         Burden of proving ship lost by perils of the sea—Judge choosing between two possible explanations as to proximate cause of loss—One explanation virtually impossible and the other extremely improbable—Where burden of proof remaining on shipowners—Whether shipowners discharging burden of proof. **Rhesa Shipping Co SA v Edmunds** [1985] **2** 712, HL.
         Damage to cargo in rough weather usual at the time of year—Whether a fortuitous happening. **Neter (N E) & Co Ltd v Licenses and General Insurance Co Ltd** [1944] **1** 341, KBD.
         Negligence of crew—Burden of proving salvage liabilities incurred owing to perils of sea or negligence of crew—Proximate cause—Whether salvage liabilities incurred to avoid or in connection with the avoidance of a loss caused by an insured peril. **Seashore Marine SA v Phoenix Assurance plc** [2002] **1 Comm** 152, QBD.
         Negligence of crew—Crew leaving pump valve full of water and open—Valve icing up and cracking—Water entering vessel through valve—Water ingress causing engine room to flood—Substantial damage caused to vessel—Whether damage caused by perils of sea. **Versloot Dredging BV v HDI Gerling Industrie Versicherung AG, The DC Merwestone** [2013] **2 Comm** 465, QBD.
         Rice damaged through lack of ventilation—Ventilators closed on account of rough weather—Damage caused by perils of the sea. **Canada Rice Mills Ltd v Union Marine and General Insurance Co Ltd** [1940] **4** 169, HL.
      Piracy—
         Actual total loss. *See* Loss—Actual total loss—Seizure of vessel by pirates, *above*.
         Constructive total loss. *See* Loss—Constructive total loss—Seizure of vessel by pirates, *above*.
         Riot—Ship's equipment stolen when ship anchored within port limits—Thieves using or threatening to use force to make good escape after theft—Whether theft arising from act of piracy or a riot. **Athens Maritime Enterprises Corp v Hellenic Mutual War Risks Association (Bermuda) Ltd** [1983] **1** 590, QBD.
      Riot—
         Piracy. *See* Perils insured against—Piracy—Riot, *above*.
      Seizure—
         Total loss—Customs officials wrongfully taking vehicles—Whether customs compound 'final place of storage' of cargo—Whether vehicles confiscated during period of cover—Whether vehicles having been 'seized' by customs officials. **Bayview Motors Ltd v Mitsui Marine and Fire Insurance Co Ltd** [2002] **1 Comm** 967, QBD; [2002] **2 Comm** 1095, CA.
         Total loss—Seizure by peoples—Confiscation by workmen—Acts of workmen subsequently recognised by de facto government. **Société Belge des Betons Société Anonyme v London and Lancashire Insurance Co Ltd** [1938] **2** 305, KBD.
      Taking at sea—
         Loss of cargo—Shipowner and captain diverting ship to unauthorised port and off-loading most of cargo—Off-loaded cargo fraudulently sold to third party—Ship taken out to sea and scuttled with remainder of cargo—Whether diversion of ship to unauthorised port a 'taking at sea'—Wheter off-loading in port a 'taking at sea'—Whether diversion of ship and off-loading of cargo a deemed barratry—Whether loss of remainder of cargo when ship scuttled caused by 'perils' of the sea—Lloyd's SG policy. **Shell International Petroleum Co Ltd v Gibbs** [1983] **1** 745, HL.
         Loss of goods—Recovery—Expenses properly incurred in recovery of goods—Cargo diverted by shipowners and mortgaged—Goods recovered by owners—Expenditure reasonably and properly incurred in recovery—Goods lost by reason of taking at sea—Indemnity for expenses and theft. **Nishina Trading Co Ltd v Chiyoda Fire and Marine Insurance Co Ltd** [1969] **2** 776, CA.
      War—
         Collision with requisitioned ship—Requisitioned ship proceeding to be used as transport. **Wharton (J) (Shipping) Ltd v Mortleman** [1941] **2** 261, CA.
         Government decree controlling shipping—Ship attempting to return to enemy country in obedience to decree—Scuttling of ship—Frustration of voyage—Liability of insurers of cargo. **Rickards v Forestal Land Timber and Rlys Co Ltd** [1941] **3** 62, HL.
         Insurable interest—Vessel sequestrated by Spanish insurgents while on lawful contract voyage—Documentation of vessel—Loss of anticipated freight—Marine Insurance Act 1906, s 67—Institute Time Clauses (Freight), cl 5. **Papadimitriou v Henderson** [1939] **3** 908, KBD.
         Loss caused through restraint, warlike operations, and civil war etc—Frustration clause if voyage or adventure lost through restraint of prices—Proximate cause of loss—Delay—Institute Time Clauses (Freight), cl 8. **Atlantic Maritime Co Inc v Gibbon** [1953] **2** 1086, CA.
         Prolongation of voyage—Insurance against expenses incurred by 'prolongation' of voyage in compliance with orders or directions or with approval of a government department or insurers—Admiralty warning issued advising merchant shipping to avoid Suez Canal area as a result of hostilities—Vessels diverted round Cape because of warning—Diversions notifed to insurers—Whether assured entitled to recover expenses incurred in diversions—Whether voyages prolonged. **Union Castle Mail Steamship Co Ltd v Mutual War Risks Association Ltd** [1958] **1** 431, QBD.
      Warlike operation—
         Consequences of warlike operations—Ship carrying war material including heavy deck cargo—Necessity to maintain speed and take zigzag course for fear of enemy submarines—Damage caused by effect of heavy seas on deck cargo and aggravated by reason of speed of ship. **Liverpool and London War Risks Insurance Association Ltd v Ocean Steamship Co Ltd** [1947] **2** 586, HL.
         Ship in convoy carrying petrol to war base for use of armed forces—Alteration of course to avoid enemy action—Unexpected and unexplained tidal set—Stranding. **Yorkshire Dale Steamship Co Ltd v Minister of War Transport** [1942] **2** 6, HL.
         Ship returning home in ballast after discharging cargo at war base—Ship stranded. **Larrinaga Steamship Co Ltd v R** [1945] **1** 329, HL.
         Ship stranded while anchored according to instructions from naval authorities before discharging cargo—'Proceeding through the water'—Damage consequence of warlike operations. **Athel Line Ltd v Liverpool and London War Risks Insurance Association Ltd** [1945] **2** 694, CA.

MARINE INSURANCE (cont)—
  Perils insured against (cont)—
    Warlike operation (cont)—
      Vessel carrying raw material for armaments—Carriage from England to France—Material not ready for use by army in the field. **Clan Line Steamers Ltd v Liverpool and London War Risks Insurance Association Ltd** [1942] **2** 367, KBD.
  Piracy—
    Actual total loss. *See* Loss—Actual total loss—Seizure of vessel by pirates, *above*.
    Constructive total loss. *See* Loss—Constructive total loss—Seizure of vessel by pirates, *above*.
  Pleading—
    Particulars. *See* **Pleading** (Particulars—Marine insurance).
  Policy—
    Construction—
      All risks marine cargo policy—Shipment of copper ingots not received and no such cargo ever existing—Whether policy covering losses for non-existent cargo. **Engelhart CTP (US) LLC v Lloyd's Syndicate 1221 for the 2014 Year of Account** [2019] **1 Comm** 583, QBD.
      Follow the settlements clause—Policy underwritten by three underwriters—Policy containing clause under which following underwriters agreed to follow lead underwriter in respect of all decisions, surveys and settlements—Assured making claim under policy in respect of constructive total loss of tug—Lead underwriter settling its share of the claim—Defendant underwriter refusing to pay its share on basis of breach of warranty by claimant and fraudulent misrepresentation subsequent to settlement of claim by lead underwriter—Whether defendant obliged to follow settlement of leader notwithstanding breach of warranty—Whether alleged fraudulent misrepresentations discharging defendant. **PT Buana Samudra Pratama v Maritime Mutual Insurance Association (NZ) Ltd** [2012] **1 Comm** 581, QBD.
      Non-avoidance clause—Policy containing non-standard transaction premium clause and non-avoidance clause—Bank suffering loss and seeking indemnity—Certain underwriters claiming to be unaware of existence of transaction premium clause and non-avoidance clause—Whether insured estopped by convention from claiming against those underwriters—Whether non-avoidance clause preventing underwriters claiming estoppel by convention—Whether broker liable for negligence/breach of contract. **ABN Amro Bank NV v Royal & Sun Alliance Insurance plc** [2022] **2 Comm** 665, CA.
      Sanctions clause—Defendant underwriters resisting payment of claim under policy on basis payment would result in exposure to sanctions against Iran—Whether payment of claim would expose defendants to any sanctions within meaning of sanctions clause. **Mamancochet Mining Ltd v Aegis Managing Agency Ltd** [2019] **1 Comm** 335, QBD.
      Schedule specifying 'sum insured'—Whether policy valued or unvalued policy—Marine Insurance Act 1906, s 27(2). **Kyzuna Investments Ltd v Ocean Marine Mutual Insurance Association (Europe)** [2000] **1 Comm** 557, QBD.
    Open policy. *See* Open policy, *above*.
    Time policy. *See* Time policy, *below*.
  Practice—
    Disclosure of documents—
      Order for ship's papers on summons for directions. *See* **Disclosure and inspection of documents** (Marine insurance actions—Order for ship's papers).
  Proceeds of policy—
    Lien—
      Premiums for reinsurance paid by placing broker—Reinsured failing to reimburse broker for premiums—Broker bringing claim for payment of premiums against reinsured and reinsured's intermediary—Reinsured counterclaiming for loss proceeds arising from subsequent marine average claim—Broker asserting lien in respect of loss proceeds—Whether lien attaching—Marine Insurance Act 1906, s 53(2). **Heath Lambert Ltd v Sociedad de Corretaje de Seguros** [2006] **2 Comm** 543, QBD.
  Reinsurance—
    Named ships—
      Named ships 'and/or steamers held covered at premiums to be arranged'—Cargo in fact carried by another ship which was lost at date of reinsurance—Whether policy effective to cover loss. **Marine Insurance Co Ltd v Grimmer** [1944] **2** 197, CA.
  Right of action—
    Assignment—
      Chose in action. *See* **Chose in action** (Assignment—Right of action—Legal assignment—Marine insurance).
  Risk—
    Description of risk—
      Dinghy insurance—Policy covering loss or damage 'whilst within the United Kingdom ashore or afloat'—Accident to craft in middle of English Channel. **Navigators and General Insurance Co Ltd v Ringrose** [1962] **1** 97, CA.
    Termination—
      Custom of port—Cargo sorted by port authority after discharge from ship. **Renton (GH) & Co Ltd v Black Sea and Baltic General Insurance Co Ltd** [1941] **1** 149, KBD.
  Safe port—
    Charterparty. *See* **Shipping** (Charterparty—Safe port—Insurance).
  Subrogation—
    Interest—
      Payment by own insurers—Loss due to defendants' breach of contract with insured paid to insured by own insurers—Whether insured can recover interest on damages awarded against defendant in respect of period after insurers' payment of loss—Marine Insurance Act 1906, s 79. **Cousins (H) & Co Ltd v D & C Carriers Ltd** [1971] **1** 55, CA.
    Payment as for total loss—
      Salvage—Contribution to underwriters of increased value policies. **Boag v Standard Marine Insurance Co Ltd** [1937] **1** 714, CA.

MARINE INSURANCE (cont)—
  Subrogation (cont)—
    Total loss—
      Assured recovering damages from third party at fault of amount exceeding sum paid by insurer—Insurer not entitled to recover excess amount from assured—Valued policy—Policy value of vessel less than actual value—Marine Insurance Act 1906, s 79(1). **Yorkshire Insurance Co Ltd v Nisbet Shipping Co Ltd** [1961] **2** 487, QBD.
  Taking at sea—
    Taking by shipowner—
      Time and place at which taking occurs. **Shell International Petroleum Co Ltd v Gibbs** [1982] **1** 225, QBD.
  Third parties' rights against insurers—
    Protection and indemnity association—
      'Pay to be paid' rule—Association member incurring liability to third party—Member wound up prior to discharging liability to third party—Third party claiming member's right to indemnity against club transferred under statute—Whether third party entitled to indemnity against club—Whether member having existing right to be indemnified by club in respect of third party liability prior to winding up—Whether 'pay to be paid' provision altering member's contractual rights against club on insolvency and thereby rendered ineffective by statute—Third Parties (Rights against Insurers) Act 1930, s 1(1), (3). **Firma C-Trade SA v Newcastle Protection and Indemnity Association** [1990] **2** 705, HL.
  Time policy—
    Contract for a definite period of time—
      Contract determinable on notice by either side and, if not determined, continued automatically from year to year—Whether contract for 'a definite period of time'—Whether a time policy—Marine Insurance Act 1906, s 25(1). **Cia Maritima San Basilio SA v The Oceanus Mutual Underwriting Association (Bermuda) Ltd** [1976] **3** 243, CA.
  Trade custom. *See* Deviation—Trade custom, *above*.
  War. *See* Perils insured against—War, *above*.
  War risks policy—
    Arbitration clause—
      Incorporation of arbitration clause contained in rules of association—Jurisdiction clause—Whether arbitration clause incorporated—Whether jurisdiction clause a non-exclusive jurisdiction clause. **Sea Trade Maritime Corp v Hellenic Mutual War Risks Association (Bermuda) Ltd (No 2)** [2007] **1 Comm** 183, QBD.
    Exception clause—
      Exclusion of liability by reason of infringement of customs regulations—Detainment of vessel by foreign court following discovery of attachment of drugs to hull—Owner's abandonment of vessel to foreign court—Owner's claim under policy of insurance for constructive total loss of vessel—Whether war risks insurers entitled to rely on exclusions in policy relating to losses arising from detainment by reason of infringement of customs regulations—Whether loss attributable to infringement of customs regulations—Institute War and Strikes Clauses (Hulls-Time) 1/10/83, cl 4.1.5. **Atlasnavios - Navegação, Lda v Navigators Insurance Company Ltd** [2015] **1 Comm** 439, QBD; [2017] **1 Comm** 401, CA.
      Exclusion of liability by reason of infringement of customs regulations—Detainment of vessel by foreign court following discovery of attachment of drugs to hull—Owner's abandonment of vessel to foreign court—Owner's claim under policy of insurance for constructive total loss of vessel—Whether war risks insurers entitled to rely on exclusions in policy relating to losses arising from detainment by reason of infringement of customs regulations—Whether loss attributable to infringement of customs regulations—Institute War and Strikes Clauses (Hulls-Time) 1/10/83, cll 1.5, 4.1.5.
      Exclusion of liability for loss by reason of infringement of customs regulations—Confiscation of ship by order of foreign court on smuggling charge—Whether 'customs regulations' including narcotics offences—Whether loss attributable to infringement of customs regulations—Institute War and Strikes Clauses (Hulls-Time), cl 4.1.5. **Sunport Shipping Ltd v Tryg-Baltica International (UK) Ltd** [2002] **2 Comm** 350, QBD; [2003] **1 Comm** 586, CA.
      Exclusion of liability for loss by reason of infringement of customs regulations—Detainment of vessel by foreign court following discovery of attachment of drugs to hull—Owner's abandonment of vessel to foreign court—Owner's claim under policy of insurance for constructive total loss of vessel—Whether war risks insurers entitled to rely on exclusions in policy relating to losses arising from detainment by reason of infringement of customs regulations—Whether loss attributable to infringement of customs regulations—Institute War and Strikes Clauses (Hulls-Time) 1/10/83, cll 1.5, 4.1.5. **Atlasnavios - Navegação, Lda v Navigators Insurance Company Ltd** [2018] **2 Comm** 671, SC; [2018] **4** 589, SC.
  Material non disclosure. *See* **Insurance** (Disclosure—Non-disclosure—Material non-disclosure—Marine insurance—War risks policy).
  Warranty—
    Breach—
      Claimant obtaining insurance for towage of vessel—Policy containing warranty that 'no release, waiver or "hold harmless" given to tug and towers'—Towage contract releasing tower and tug from liability to claimant—Insurer declining claim under policy but not on ground of breach of warranty—Claimant consequently not relying on warranty point in separate proceedings against broker—Insurer relying on breach of warranty seven years later—Whether insurer having made unequivocal representation that it no longer intended to rely on breach—Whether insurer having waived breach. **Argo Systems Fze v Liberty Insurance (Pte)** [2012] **2 Comm** 126, CA.
      Claimant obtaining insurance for towage of vessel—Policy containing warranty that 'no release, waiver or "hold harmless" given to tug and towers'—Towage contract releasing tower and tug from liability to claimant—Insurer declining claim under policy but not on ground of breach of warranty—Claimant consequently not relying on warranty point in separate proceedings against broker—Insurer relying on breach of warranty seven years later—Whether claimant in breach of warranty—Whether insurer estopped from relying on breach. **Argo Systems Fze v Liberty Insurance (Pte)** [2011] **1 Comm** 1111, QBD.

MARINE INSURANCE (cont)—
  Warranty (cont)—
    Breach (cont)—
      Fishing trawler damaged in port whilst crew ashore—Warranty that 'owner and/or owner's experienced skipper on board and in charge at all times and one experienced crew member'—Construction of warranty—Whether requirement only applicable when trawler at sea—Meaning of 'at all times'. **Pratt v Aigaion Insurance Co SA** [2008] **2 Comm** 574, QBD; [2009] **2 Comm** 387, CA.
      Inception of this insurance—Warranty that all arrangements for conversion of ship made at 'inception of this insurance'. **Simons (t/a Acme Credit Services) v Gale** [1958] **2** 504, PC.
      Reinsurance. *See* **Insurance** (Reinsurance—Breach of warranty).
      Seaworthiness—Sea towage of floating dock permissible only in certain sea force and wave height conditions—Dock meeting conditions exceeding those permissible and sinking—Insurer alleging breach of implied warranty of seaworthiness—Whether implied warranty of seaworthiness satisfied if dock fit to encounter ordinary perils of the sea as specified for insured voyage. **Garnat Trading and Shipping (Singapore) Pte Ltd v Baominh Insurance Corp** [2012] **1 Comm** 790, CA.
      Vessel damaged by fire whilst laid up alongside berth—Warranty that vessel be 'fully crewed at all times'—Construction of warranty—Whether crew member to be physically present whilst vessel laid up—Meaning of 'at all times'. **GE Frankona Reinsurance Ltd v CMM Trust No 1400** [2006] **1 Comm** 665, QBD.
    Promissory warranty—
      Breach—Effect of breach—Shipowners assigning war risk insurance on vessels to bank as mortgagee—Insurer undertaking to inform bank promptly if it ceased to cover any vessel—Vessel lost while trading in prohibited war zone in breach of promissory warranty—Whether breach of promissory warranty automatically discharging insurer from liability or entitling him to avoid insurance—Whether insurer obliged to inform bank of breach—Whether insurer in breach of express contractual term of undertaking—Marine Insurance Act 1906, s 33(3). **Bank of Nova Scotia v Hellenic Mutual War Risks Association (Bermuda) Ltd** [1991] **3** 1, HL.
  Worldwide freezing order—
    Pre-trial or post-judgment relief. *See* **Practice** (Pre-trial or post-judgment relief—Freezing order—Worldwide freezing order).

MARINER
  Will. *See* **Will** (Soldier's or mariner's privileged will).

MARITAL COMMUNICATIONS
  Breach of confidence. *See* **Equity** (Breach of confidence—Marital communications).

MARITAL STATUS
  Declaration as to—
    Jurisdiction. *See* **Declaration** (Jurisdiction—Declaration as to marital status).

MARITIME LAW
  Generally. *See* **Shipping**.
  Prize law. *See* **Prize law**.

MARITIME LIEN
  Admiralty proceedings. *See* **Admiralty** (Jurisdiction—Action in rem—Maritime lien or other charge on ship).
  Generally. *See* **Shipping** (Maritime lien).

MARITIME TRANSPORT
  Freedom of establishment—
    European Community. *See* **European Union** (Freedom of establishment—Maritime transport).
  Freedom of movement—
    European Union. *See* **European Union** (Freedom of movement—Services—Maritime transport).
  International maritime transport—
    EC rules on competition—
      Abuse of dominant position. *See* **European Union** (Rules on competition—Abuse of dominant position—Collective dominant position—International maritime transport).

MARK
  Origin, of—
    Imported food. *See* **Food and drugs** (Marks of origin—Imported food).
  Trade mark—
    European Community. *See* **European Union** (Trade marks).
    Generally. *See* **Trade mark**.

MARKET
  Extinction of use. *See* **Town and country planning** (Development—Extinction of use—Open site used for market trading).
  Generally. *See* **Markets and fairs**.
  Sunday trading—
    Jewish shop—
      Place where any retail trade is carried on—Market held in field. *See* **Shop** (Sunday closing—Exemption—Jewish shop—Place where any retail trade is carried on—Market held in field).
    Market stall—
      Place where any retail trade or business carried on. *See* **Shop** (Sunday closing—Retail trading elsewhere than in shop).

MARKETING SCHEME

Apple and Pear Publicity Scheme. *See* **Agriculture** (Marketing scheme—Validity—Apple and Pear Publicity Scheme).

MARKETS AND FAIRS

Disturbance—
Annual fair or wake—
Right of inhabitants of parish by ancient usage to hold annual fair or wake—Enclosure award made pursuant to private Act of Parliament appointing certain parcels of land in parish on which inhabitants might hold fair—Declaration in award of future right of inhabitants to hold fair annually and bar against disturbing surface—Annual fair or wake had not then been held within living memory—Planning permission obtained by defendant and building begun—Inhabitants of parish claimed to be entitled to preserve right to hold fair—Whether right established—Whether action maintainable by plaintiffs as representatives of inhabitants of parish—Whether Attorney General a necessary party—Whether right vested in parish council—Local Government Act 1894, s 6(1)(a). **Wyld v Silver** [1962] 3 309, CA.

Levying of rival market—
Common law remedy—Disturbance of statutory market by levying of rival market—Whether common law remedy available to protect a statutory market—Markets and Fairs Clauses Act 1847, s 13. **Wakefield City Council v Box** [1982] 3 506, Ch D.

Damages—Defendants holding unlawful rival market within common law distance of local authority's statutory market—Rival market causing no loss to local authority's market—Assessment of damages—Whether local authority entitled to substantial damages or restricted to nominal damages. **Stoke-on-Trent City Council v W & J Wass Ltd** [1988] 3 394, CA.

Market rights conveyed subject to purported reservation of right to hold same-day market, within common law distance, dealing in same commodities—Whether market rights capable of severance by purported reservation—Whether market held in reliance of reservation properly established. **Sevenoaks DC v Pattullo & Vinson Ltd** [1984] 1 544, CA.

Market rights extending to live pigs for slaughter of bacon weight and pig carcases—Establishment of abattoir and live pig collecting centre outside market—Withdrawal of bacon pig market from market. **Scottish Co-op Wholesale Society Ltd v Ulster Farmers' Mart Co Ltd** [1959] 2 486, HL.

Rival market within common law distance—Measurement of common law distance—Whether distance to be measured from place where lawful market held or from boundary of area over which monopoly granted. **Birmingham City Council v Anvil Fairs (a firm)** [1989] 1 147, Ch D.

Rival market within common law distance—Statutory market—Defendant holding rival market within common law distance of plaintiff local authority's market but outside plaintiff's district—Whether local authority's market entitled to protection from rival market. **Halton BC v Cawley** [1985] 1 278, Ch D.

Rival market within common law distance—Whether such nuisance actionable without proof of damage. **Sevenoaks DC v Pattullo & Vinson Ltd** [1984] 1 544, CA.

Highway, on—
Obstruction. *See* **Highway** (Obstruction—Market).

Local authority—
Proceedings for injunction to prevent use of premises for Sunday market—
Action by local authority in own name. *See* **Practice** (Parties—Local authority—Assertion and protection of rights of public—Local authority instituting proceedings for injunction to prevent use of premises for Sunday market).

Market authority—
Certiorari. *See* **Certiorari** (Jurisdiction—Bodies amenable to jurisdiction—Market authority).

Market owner—
Duty—
Liability of market owner for injuries by animals brought to market—Injury to member of public on highway—Whether market owner liable. **Brackenborough v Spalding UDC** [1942] 1 34, HL.

Planning permission—
Market franchise granted by letters patent from Crown in 1638—
Weekly market held on original site until 1923 when removed to another site—Market discontinued in 1957 for 9 years and then revived on original site—Resumption constituting material change in use of site—Whether planning permission required for market—Whether market owner acting on behalf of Crown and therefore exempt from having to obtain planning permission. **Spook Erection Ltd v Secretary of State for the Environment** [1988] 2 667, CA.

Rates—
Valuation. *See* **Rates** (Valuation—Market).

Right of public to attend market—
Stallholder—
Grant of licence by owner of market to erect stall in specified place—Nature of stallholder's right—Whether a common law right—Whether decision to determine licence affecting stallholder's common law rights. **R v Barnsley Metropolitan BC, ex p Hook** [1976] 3 452, CA.

Stall—
Whether a shop. *See* **Medicine** (Sale by retail—Shop).

Stallage—
Amount properly chargeable—
No amount fixed by charter or custom—No compulsion to take stalls—Whether amount charged excessive and unreasonable. **A-G v Colchester Corp** [1952] 2 297, Ch D.

Statutory market—
Market for the sale of horticultural produce—
Power for market authority with consent of minister to carry out other activities with a view to making the best use of any of their assets—Market authority obtaining consent of minister to authorisation of trade in meat and fish—Whether minister empowered to consent to activities unconnected with sale of horticultural produce—Covent Garden Market Act 1961, s 18(1)(f). **R (on the application of Corporation of London) v Secretary of State for Environment, Food and Rural Affairs** [2006] 3 1130, HL.

Street trading. *See* **Street trading**.

MARRIAGE

Banns—

Due publication—

Delivery of particulars of true Christian name and surname—Married woman giving her maiden name—Publication in maiden name—Knowledge of both parties—Whether 'due publication'—Marriage Act 1823, s 22. **Chipchase v Chipchase** [1941] **2** 560, Div.

Delivery of particulars of true Christian name and surname—Surname acquired by repute—Banns published in name acquired by repute—Whether 'due publication'—Absence of fraud—Marriage Act 1823, ss 7, 22. **Dancer v Dancer** [1948] **2** 731, Div.

Bigamy. *See* **Criminal law** (Bigamy).

Breach of promise of marriage—

Action for damages—

Ceylon—No right of action unless promise made in writing—'Writing'—Ceylon Marriage Registration Ordinance (Vol III, Legislative Enactments of Ceylon), s 19, proviso. **Udalagama v Boange** [1959] **3** 403, PC.

Fraudulent concealment of previous marriage—Action long after pretended marriage. **Beyers v Green** [1936] **1** 613, KBD.

Prerequisite for action—Statutory requirement that promise made in writing—Evidence necessary to satisfy statutory requirements—Ceylon. **Udalagama v Boange** [1959] **3** 403, PC.

Promise by married man after decree nisi of divorce but before decree absolute—Public policy. **Fender v Mildmay** [1937] **3** 402, HL.

Promise made by person already married—Enforceability—Public policy—Whether promise unenforceable as performance would involve bigamy—Promisee unaware of illegality—Promisor deceased—Special damages—Law Reform (Miscellaneous Provisions) Act 1934, s 1(1). **Shaw v Shaw** [1954] **2** 638, CA.

Costs—

Security for costs—Plaintiff ordinarily resident out of jurisdiction. *See* **Costs** (Security for costs—Plaintiff ordinarily resident out of the jurisdiction—Action for breach of promise of marriage).

Breakdown—

Divorce. *See* **Divorce** (Irretrievable breakdown of marriage).

Building registered for solemnisation of marriages—

Place of meeting for religious worship—

Church of Scientology—Whether chapel of Church of Scientology place of meeting for religious worship—Places of Worship Registration Act 1855, s 2. **R (on the application of Hodkin) v Registrar General of Births, Deaths and Marriages** [2014] **1** 737, SC.

Capacity to marry—

Validity. *See* Validity—Declaration—Person lacking capacity marrying abroad, *below.*

Ceremony—

Failure to comply with form—

Validity—Failure to comply literally with form of marriage service—Effect—Marriage Act 1904, (Laws of Barbados, No 9 of 1904), s 2. **Hill v Hill** [1959] **1** 281, PC.

Certificate—

Affidavit supporting. *See* **Practice** (Chancery Division—Affidavit—Affidavit supporting—Certificate of birth, marriage or death).

Evidence, as. *See* Evidence—Marriage certificate, *below.*

Certificate and licence for solemnisation of marriage—

Impediment—

Foreign domicile—Foreign domicile of both parties and legal incapacity of intending husband to remarry validly by foreign law—Husband an Italian national divorced in Switzerland and by Italian law, recognised in Switzerland, not free to remarry—Legal incapacity for remarriage inapplicable by foreign law to husband's ex-wife—Whether such discriminatory incapacity recognised by English court—Whether lawful impediment to the granting of a certificate and licence to marry in England—Marriage Act 1949, s 32(2)(a). **R v Brentwood Superintendent Registrar of Marriages, ex p Arias** [1968] **3** 279, QBD.

Child of void marriage—

Legitimacy—

Generally. *See* **Legitimacy** (Child of void marriage).

Civil partnership—

Opposite-sex couple—

Legislation precluding opposite-sex couples registering as civil partners—Whether incompatible with prohibition on discrimination and right to respect for private and family life—Human Rights Act 1998, Sch 1, Pt I, arts 8, 14—Civil Partnership Act 2004, ss 1, 3(1)—Marriage (Same Sex Couples) Act 2013. **Steinfeld v Secretary of State for Education** [2016] **4** 421, QBD.

Legislation precluding opposite-sex couples registering as civil partners—Whether incompatible with prohibition on discrimination and right to respect for private and family life—Whether potential breach justified—Human Rights Act 1998, Sch 1, Pt I, arts 8, 14—Civil Partnership Act 2004, ss 1, 3(1)(a)—Marriage (Same Sex Couples) Act 2013. **Steinfeld v Secretary of State for Education** [2017] **4** 47, CA.

Legislation precluding opposite-sex couples registering as civil partners—Whether incompatible with prohibition on discrimination and right to respect for private and family life—Whether potential breach justified—Whether justification including time to investigate how best to eliminate inequality—Human Rights Act 1998, Sch 1, Pt I, arts 8, 14—Civil Partnership Act 2004, ss 1, 3—Marriage (Same Sex Couples) Act 2013. **R (on the application of Steinfeld) v Secretary of State for International Development** [2018] **4** 1, SC.

Consanguinity. *See* Prohibited degrees of consanguinity, *below.*

Consent—

Degree of soundness of mind required—

Test to be applied—Capacity to understand nature of contract. **Park, In the Estate of** [1953] **2** 1411, CA.

Marriage of minor—

Refusal of consent by justices. *See* **Minor** (Marriage—Refusal of consent by justices).

MARRIAGE (cont)—
  Contract—
    Proper law. *See* **Conflict of laws** (Contract—Proper law of contract—Contract of marriage).
  Death—
    Presumption of death before remarriage. *See* **Husband and wife** (Presumption of death).
  Declaration as to marital status. *See* **Declaration** (Jurisdiction—Declaration as to marital status).
  Declaration as to validity of. *See* Validity—Declaration, *below*.
  Declaration of subsistence of marriage—
    Jurisdiction—
      Foreign divorce—Husband domiciled abroad—Wife resident in England—At time of marriage husband and wife domiciled in England—Wife's petition for declaration that marriage still subsisting—Whether court had jurisdiction to entertain petition—Supreme Court of Judicature (Consolidation) Act 1925, s 225—RSC, Ord 15, r 17. **Garthwaite v Garthwaite** [1964] **2** 233, CA.
  Dissolution. *See* **Divorce**.
  Evidence—
    Foreign marriage—
      Divorce. *See* **Divorce** (Evidence—Foreign marriage).
    Marriage certificate—
      Certificate of marriage according to law of Southern Rhodesia—Whether displaced by husband's evidence of mistaken belief that marriage was polygamous. **Kassim (orse Widmann) v Kassim (orse Hassim)** [1962] **3** 426, Div.
      Conclusiveness—Wife described as widow—No proof of death of first husband. **Peete, Re** [1952] **2** 599, Ch D.
  Forced marriage—
    Forced marriage protection orders—
      Applications—Relevant third party—Standing—Sixteen-year-old child applying for forced marriage protection order—Child made subject of forced marriage protection order—Child subsequently undergoing form of marriage—Police arresting child's mother and aunt—Police applying for committal of mother and aunt to prison for contempt of court—Whether police having standing to make application—Family Law Act 1996, s 63C—Family Law Act 1996 (Forced Marriage) (Relevant Third Party) Order 2009, SI 2009/2023. **Bedfordshire Police Constabulary v RU** [2014] **1** 1068, Fam D.
  Foreign domicile—
    Certificate and licence for solemnisation of marriage—
      Impediment. *See* Certificate and licence for solemnisation of marriage—Impediment—Foreign domicile, *above*.
  Foreign marriage—
    Evidence—
      Divorce. *See* **Divorce** (Evidence—Foreign marriage).
    Recognition—
      Marriage by proxy—Validity. **Apt (orse Magnus) v Apt** [1947] **2** 677, CA; **Ponticelli v Ponticelli (orse Giglio) (by her guardian)** [1958] **1** 357, Div.
    Validity—
      Common law—Marriage in Italy—Husband domiciled in Poland and serving with Polish forces in Italy—Wife domiciled in Italy—Ceremony performed by Roman Catholic priest—Civil ceremony—Not valid by Italian or Polish law—Whether valid at common law. **Lazarewicz (orse Fadanelli) v Lazarewicz** [1962] **2** 5, Div.
      Essential requirements of valid marriage distinguished from procedural requirements—Foreign Marriage Act 1892, s 8. **Collett (orse Sakazova) v Collett** [1967] **2** 426, Div.
      Essential validity. *See* **Conflict of laws** (Marriage—Validity—Essential validity).
      Forms and ceremonies—Burden of proof. **Preston v Preston** [1963] **2** 405, CA.
      Lex loci celebrationis—Invalid marriage—Retrospective validation—Requirement of registration not complied with. **Pilinski v Pilinska** [1955] **1** 631, Div.
      Marriage in Germany of Polish nationals domiciled in Poland—Husband and wife members of Allied Army of Occupation in Germany—Ceremony performed by Polish army chaplain according to rites of Roman Catholic church—Not valid by lex loci celebrationis—Valid by English law. **Merker v Merker** [1962] **3** 928, Div.
      Marriage in Germany of Polish nationals domiciled in Poland—Not valid by German law—No subjection to German law—Separate community—Displaced persons—Common law marriage. **Kochanski v Kochanska** [1957] **3** 142, Div.
      Marriage in Germany of domiciled Poles—Husband a member of Polish forces in Polish camp in Germany—Camp under control of allies—Allies in belligerent occupation of Germany—Ceremony of marriage performed by chaplain in accordance with Roman Catholic rites—Whether marriage valid as English common law marriage abroad. **Preston v Preston** [1962] **3** 1057, PDA.
      Marriage in Italy of Polish nationals domiciled in Poland—Husband a member of the Allied forces in belligerent occupation of Italy—Ceremony performed by Polish army chaplain according to rites of Roman Catholic church—Not valid by lex loci celebrationis or under Polish law then in force, although valid under earlier Polish law—Whether valid at common law—Whether validated as an act of 'internal administration' of Polish forces—Whether ceremony performed by chaplain 'officiating under the orders of the commanding officer of a British army serving abroad'—Foreign Marriage Act 1892, s 22—Allied Forces Act 1940, s 1(1)—Polish Resettlement Act 1947, s 9. **Taczonowska (orse Roth) v Taczanowski (Lystek cited)** [1957] **2** 563, CA.
      Marriage in Russia—Parties domiciled in England—Requirements of Soviet law not observed—'Mistake'—Wife forbidden to leave Russia—Avoidance for failure of condition. **Way v Way** [1950] **2** 297, CA.
      Petitioner Canadian by birth but domiciled in England—Petitioner in China on consular service—Marriage of petitioner to Canadian lady in China—Ceremony not performed by an episcopally ordained priest—Extent of English law applicable to British subjects abroad—Marriage valid—Foreign Marriages Act 1892, s 23—China Order in Council 1925 (SR & O 1925 No 602), art 104. **Wolfenden v Wolfenden** [1945] **2** 539, Div.
  Immigration—
    Right to respect for private and family life. *See* **Immigration** (Leave to enter—Leave to remain—Right to respect for private and family life—Right to marry).

MARRIAGE (cont)—
  Invalid—
    Concealment of right of action by fraud—
      Limitation of action. *See* **Limitation of action** (Concealment of right of action by fraud—Marriage contract—Invalid marriage).
  Invalidity—
    Declaration—
      Marriage terminated by foreign decree of divorce—Divorce obtained under duress. *See* **Divorce** (Foreign decree—Invalidity—Basis of invalidity—Lack of consent to divorce proceedings—Duress).
  Irretrievable breakdown—
    Divorce. *See* **Divorce** (Irretrievable breakdown of marriage).
  Licence—
    Grant—
      Wales—Effect of dis-establishment of Church in Wales on. *See* **Ecclesiastical law** (Church in Wales—Dis-establishment—Effect on grant of marriage licences).
    Misdescription of party—
      Validity of marriage. *See* Validity—Declaration—Discretion to grant declaration—Marriage by licence—Misdescription of party, *below*.
  Minor—
    Refusal of consent by justices. *See* **Minor** (Marriage—Refusal of consent by justices).
  Nullity—
    Generally. *See* **Nullity**.
    Marriage in articulo mortis—
      Mauritius. *See* **Mauritius** (Nullity—Marriage in articulo mortis).
  Polygamous—
    Family provision—
      Widow of polygamous marriage. *See* **Family provision** (Jurisdiction—Polygamous marriage).
    Intestacy. *See* **Intestacy** (Succession—Surviving spouse—Polygamous spouses).
    Legitimacy of children. *See* **Legitimacy** (Polygamous marriage).
    Maintenance of wife and children. *See* **National assistance** (Recovery of cost of assistance from husband—Polygamous marriage).
    Potentially polygamous—
      Acquisition of domicile of choice in England—Jurisdiction of English courts over alleged matrimonial offences—Whether marriage converted into monogamous union. **Ali v Ali** [1966] **1** 664, Div.
      Chinese customary marriage—Regarded as monogamous by Hong Kong law—Question whether monogamous marriage to be determined according to English law. **Lee v Lau** [1964] **2** 248, Div.
      Christian spouses—Whether religious belief of parties justified court in treating marriage as monogamous. **Ohochuku v Ohochuku** [1960] **1** 253, Div.
      Dower payable under marriage contract—Whether right to dower enforceable in English court. **Shahnaz v Rizwan** [1964] **2** 993, QBD.
      Monogamous at date of proceedings—Civil monogamous marriage—Mistaken belief of husband that marriage into which he was entering was a polygamous marriage—Consent to marriage not vitiated—Subsequent re-marriage of husband bigamous. **Kassim (orse Widmann) v Kassim (orse Hassim)** [1962] **3** 426, Div.
      Monogamous at date of proceedings—Whether English court had nullity jurisdiction. **Cheni (orse Rodriguez) v Cheni** [1962] **3** 873, Div.
      Protection of young person. *See* **Children and young persons** (Protection—Recognition of foreign marriage—Potentially polygamous marriage—Fit person order).
      Right to matrimonial relief—Marriage celebrated abroad under law permitting polygamy—Wife domiciled abroad and husband domiciled in England—Neither party permitted by law of their domiciles to marry second spouse during subsistence of marriage—Whether marriage void—Matrimonial Causes Act 1973, ss 11(b), (d), 47. **Hussain v Hussain** [1982] **3** 369, CA.
      Right to matrimonial relief—Summary proceedings. *See* **Husband and wife** (Summary proceedings—Potentially polygamous marriage—Right to matrimonial relief).
    Property—
      Summary proceedings. *See* **Husband and wife** (Property—Summary proceedings—Jurisdiction—Polygamous marriage).
    Right to contract polygamous marriage—
      Ceylon. *See* **Ceylon** (Polygamous marriage—Right to contract polygamous marriage).
    Widows' benefits. *See* **Social security** (Benefit—Widows' benefits).
  Presumption of marriage from cohabitation—
    Rebuttal of presumption—
      Absence of entry in marriage resgister in area where registration compulsory—Date and place of marriage referred to in children's birth certificates—Contrary suggestion in deed of covenant by husband's father—Whether presumption rebutted. **Taplin, Re** [1937] **3** 105, Ch D.
      Clear evidence necessary to rebut presumption. **Taylor (decd), Re** [1961] **1** 55, CA.
      Subsequent marriage ceremony—Parties described as bachelor and spinster in certificate of ceremony. **Bradshaw, Re** [1938] **4** 143, Ch D.
  Prohibited degrees of consanguinity—
    Uncle and niece—
      Jewish marriage in Egypt between uncle and niece—Whether valid. **Cheni (orse Rodriguez) v Cheni** [1962] **3** 873, Div.
  Prospects—
    Damages for personal injuries—
      Loss of future earnings. *See* **Damages** (Personal injury—Loss of future earnings—Marriage prospects).
  Public policy—
    Gift subject to condition encouraging separation of spouses. *See* **Will** (Condition—Family matters—Condition inducing future separation of spouses—Public policy).
  Recognition of foreign marriage. *See* Foreign marriage—Recognition, *above*.
  Registration. *See* **Registration** (Births, deaths and marriages).

MARRIAGE (cont)—
  Remarriage—
    Divorced person—
      Application for financial provision. *See* **Divorce** (Financial provision—Application—Remarriage of party).
      Capacity to remarry immediately after grant of decree absolute. *See* **Divorce** (Decree absolute—Remarriage—Capacity of divorced person to remarry immediately after grant of decree absolute).
  Restraint of marriage—
    Condition—
      Will. *See* **Will** (Condition—Restraint of marriage).
  Right to marry—
    Immigration—
      Discrimination—Requirement for persons subject to immigration control wishing to marry other than according to rites of Church of England to obtain written permission of Secretary of State—Secretary of State refusing permission to person present in United Kingdom unlawfully—Whether breach of right to marry—Whether discriminatory—Human Rights Act 1998, Sch 1, Pt I, arts 12, 14—Asylum and Immigration (Treatment of Claimants, etc) Act 2004, s 19. **R (on the application of Baiai) v Secretary of State for the Home Dept** [2006] **3** 608, QBD; [2007] **4** 199, CA; **R (on the application of Baiai) v Secretary of State for the Home Dept (No 2)** [2006] **4** 555, QBD; [2007] **4** 199, CA.
      Discrimination—Requirement for persons subject to immigration control wishing to marry other than according to rites of Church of England to obtain written permission of Secretary of State—Whether breach of right to marry—Whether discriminatory—Human Rights Act 1998, Sch 1, Pt I, arts 12, 14—Asylum and Immigration (Treatment of Claimants, etc) Act 2004, s 19. **R (on the application of Baiai) v Secretary of State for the Home Dept** [2007] **4** 199, CA.
      Discrimination—Requirement for persons subject to immigration control wishing to marry other than according to rites of Church of England to obtain written permission of Secretary of State—Whether breach of right to marry—Whether discriminatory—Human Rights Act 1998, Sch 1, Pt I, arts 12, 14—Asylum and Immigration (Treatment of Claimants, etc) Act 2004, s 19. **R (on the application of Baiai) v Secretary of State for the Home Dept** [2008] **3** 1094, HL.
    Person in detention—
      Illegal entrant awaiting deportation—Temporary release. *See* **Immigration** (Detention—Illegal entrant—Detention pending deportation—Rights of entrant—Temporary release—Right to marry).
      Remand prisoner—Whether non-compellability of witness if marrying remand prisoner constituting public policy ground entitling authorities to refuse consent to marriage before trial—Marriage Act 1949, ss 27A(3)(b), 31(2)—Police and Criminal Evidence Act 1984, s 80. **R (on the application of CPS) v Registrar General of Births, Deaths and Marriages** [2003] **1** 540, CA.
  Rule against perpetuities. *See* **Rule against perpetuities** (Impossibility of infringing rule—Age of lawful marriage).
  Settlement—
    Generally. *See* **Settlement** (Marriage settlement).
    Proper law of settlement. *See* **Conflict of laws** (Settlement—Proper law of settlement—Marriage settlement).
  Solemnisation—
    Licence for. *See* Certificate and licence for solemnisation of marriage, *above*.
    Offences relating to solemnisation of marriages—
      False pretence of being in Holy Orders—Knowingly and wilfully solemnizing a marriage according to the rites of the Church of England falsely pretending to be in Holy Orders—Mens rea—Intent to deceive—Whether honest belief that all persons knew ceremony to be charade by way of repetition of prior wedding was a defence—Marriage Act 1949, s 75(1)(d). **R v Ali Mohammed (1943)** [1964] **1** 653, Assizes; **R v Kemp** [1964] **1** 649, CCA.
      Knowingly and wilfully solemnising a 'marriage' in place other than church or registered building—Indictment—Form of indictment—Islamic ceremony—Ceremony in private house—Marriage Act 1836, s 39. **R v Rahman** [1949] **2** 165, Assizes.
      Knowingly and wilfully solemnising a 'marriage' in place other than church or registered building—Potentially polygamous Mohammedan marriage solemnised in private house—Whether ceremony a marriage—Marriage Act 1949, s 75(2)(a). **R v Bham** [1965] **3** 124, CCA.
  Validity—
    Declaration—
      British subject domiciled in England—Procedure to obtain declaration—Matrimonial Causes Act 1965, s 39—Matrimonial Causes Rules 1957 (SI 1957 No 619), r 74. **Collett (orse Sakazova) v Collett** [1967] **2** 426, Div.
      Discretion to grant declaration—Marriage by licence—Misdescription of party—Husband and wife marrying by licence in England—Wife fraudulently impersonating another woman—Wife having German domicile of origin—Wife presenting petition to have marriage declared valid—Wife seeking declaration so as to claim status of British subject and immunity from extradition—Whether marriage invalid by reason of misdescription—Whether wife domiciled in England when petition presented—Whether court having discretion to refuse decree—Marriage Act 1949, s 49—Matrimonial Causes Act 1973, s 45(1)(5)—Domicile and Matrimonial Proceedings Act 1973, s 1. **Puttick v A-G and Puttick** [1979] **3** 463, Fam D.
      Foreign nullity decree—Jurisdiction to grant declaration that decree effective in England for purpose of establishing validity of subsequent marriage—Discretion in exercise of jurisdiction—Discretion where foreign decree entitled to recognition under binding international convention—Petitioner entitled to claim real estate in England if subsequent marriage valid—Petitioner seeking declaration that foreign decree declaring earlier marriage to respondent invalid entitled to recognition—Respondent but not petitioner resident in England at date of petition—Whether petitioner entitled to declaration under RSC Ord 15, r 16, that foreign decree entitled to recognition—Whether jurisdiction to grant declaration—Whether if jurisdiction court having discretion in matter and should exercise discretion by refusing declaration on ground petitioner could claim declaration of validity of subsequent marriage under Matrimonial Causes Act 1973, s 45(1). **Vervaeke v Smith (Messina and A-G intervening)** [1981] **1** 55, Fam D, CA.
    Jurisdiction. **Aldrich v A-G (Rogers intervening)** [1968] **1** 345, Prob.

MARRIAGE (cont)—
  Validity (cont)—
    Declaration (cont)—
      Jurisdiction—RSC, Ord 25, r 5. **Woyno v Woyno** [1960] **2** 879, Div.
      Jurisdiction—Suit for declaration—Venue. **Practice Direction** [1965] **3** 916, Div.
      Parties to proceedings—Validity of marriage dependent on recognition of foreign decree of divorce—Whether first wife should be served—Natural justice—RSC, Ord 15, rr 6, 16. **Kunstler v Kunstler** [1969] **3** 673, Div.
      Person lacking capacity marrying abroad—Whether court having jurisdiction to make declaration of non-recognition of valid marriage in England and Wales. **XCC v AA** [2013] **2** 988, Ct of Protection.
      Whether person whose sex had been correctly classified at birth could later become person of opposite sex for purposes of marriage—Whether non-recognition of gender reassignment for purposes of marriage incompatible with convention rights—Matrimonial Causes Act 1973, s 11(c)—Human Rights Act 1998, Sch 1, Pt I, arts 8, 12. **Bellinger v Bellinger** [2002] **1** 311, CA; [2003] **2** 593, HL.
    Foreign marriage—
      Essential validity. *See* **Conflict of laws** (Marriage—Validity—Essential validity).
      Generally. *See* Foreign marriage—Validity, *above.*
    Party to marriage under 16—
      Marriage celebrated abroad—Wife domiciled abroad—Husband domiciled in England—Marriage legal under lex celebrationis and law of wife's domicil—Marriage illegal under Age of Marriage Act 1929, s 1(1). **Pugh v Pugh** [1951] **2** 680, Div.
    Presumption of validity—
      Cohabitation before as well as after marriage ceremony—Whether presumption applicable. **Hill v Hill** [1959] **1** 281, PC.
      Omnia praesumuntur rite esse acta—Omnia praeseumuntur pro matrimonio—Ceremony followed by cohabitation—Conclusiveness of marriage certificate—Standard of proof to rebut presumption. **Mahadervan v Mahadervan** [1962] **3** 1108, Div.
  Void—
    Child of marriage—
      Legitimacy. *See* **Legitimacy** (Child of void marriage).
  Voidable marriage—
    Revocation of will. *See* **Will** (Revocation—Marriage—Voidable marriage).
  Widow—
    Social security. *See* **Social security** (Benefit—Widows' benefits).
  Will—
    Revocation by marriage. *See* **Will** (Revocation—Marriage).
    Revocation by remarriage. *See* **Will** (Revocation—Covenant not to revoke—Revocation by remarriage).
    Will expressed to be in contemplation of marriage—
      Revocation. *See* **Will** (Revocation—Will expressed to be made in contemplation of a marriage).

MARRIAGE GUIDANCE
  Conciliation—
    Divorce—
      Certificate with regard to reconciliation. *See* **Divorce** (Reconciliation—Certificate with regard to—Names etc of persons qualified to help).
    Privilege attaching to communications. *See* **Evidence** (Privilege—Confidential relationships—Marriage guidance).

MARRIED WOMAN
  Affiliation proceedings by. *See* **Affiliation** (Application for order—Single woman—Married mother—Living apart from husband).
  Bankruptcy. *See* **Bankruptcy** (Married woman).
  Domicile—
    Abandonment of domicile of choice—
      Deemed domicile of choice. *See* **Domicile** (Abandonment of domicile of choice—Deemed domicile of choice—Married woman).
    Generally. *See* **Domicile** (Husband and wife—Wife's domicile).
  Financial provision for, on dissolution of marriage. *See* **Divorce** (Financial provision).
  Property—
    Disputes as to. *See* **Husband and wife** (Property).
  Tax advantage. *See* **Income tax** (Tax advantage—Married woman).
  United Kingdom citizenship—
    Entitlement of woman married to United Kingdom citizen. *See* **Citizenship** (United Kingdom citizenship—Entitlement—Entitlement of woman married to United Kingdom citizen).
  Witness fee. *See* **Witness** (Fee—Amount—Married woman not gainfully employed).

MASONIC LODGE
  Will—
    Gift. *See* **Will** (Gift—Specific donees—Masonic lodge).

MASSAGE PARLOUR
  Offering sexual services—
    Whether a 'brothel'. *See* **Criminal law** (Brothel—Keeping a brothel—Meaning of brothel—Massage parlour offering sexual services not including full sexual intercourse).

MASTER
  Chancery Division—
    Chambers proceedings—
      Masters' powers. *See* **Practice** (Chambers proceedings—Master's powers).
  Queen's Bench Division—
    Appeal. *See* **Appeal** (Master of Queen's Bench Division).
    Lists. *See* **Practice** (Queen's Bench Division—Lists—Masters' lists).

MASTER (cont)—
Summons—
Practice—
Masters' summonses. *See* **Practice** (Summons—Masters' summonses).

MASTER AND SERVANT
Breach of undertaking in contract of service—
Injunction. *See* **Injunction** (Breach of covenant—Breach of undertaking—Contract of service).
Generally. *See* **Employment**.
Race relations. *See* **Race relations**.
Seduction. *See* **Seduction**.
Unfair dismissal—
Generally. *See* **Unfair dismissal**.
Vicarious liability. *See* **Vicarious liability** (Employer and employee).

MATCH
Football match—
Public order offences. *See* **Public order** (Football).

MATERNITY GRANT
See **Social security** (Maternity grant).

MATRIMONIAL CAUSE
Cause list. *See* **Divorce** (Matrimonial causes list).
Costs—
Taxation. *See* **Costs** (Taxation—Matrimonial causes).
Legal aid—
Certificate. *See* **Legal aid** (Certificate—Scope of certificate—Matrimonial cause).
Practice—
Generally. *See* **Practice** (Matrimonial causes).
Psychiatric examination of minor—
Practice. *See* **Minor** (Psychiatric examination—Wardship and matrimonial causes).
Security for costs—
Legal aid. *See* **Legal aid** (Security for costs—Matrimonial causes).
Taxation of costs—
Generally. *See* **Costs** (Taxation—Matrimonial causes).
Legal aid. *See* **Legal aid** (Taxation of costs—Matrimonial causes).
Transfer of proceedings between High Court and county courts—
Practice. *See* **Practice** (Transfer of proceedings between High Court and county court—Family business and family proceedings).
Trial—
Practice. *See* **Practice** (Matrimonial causes—Trial).

MATRIMONIAL HOME
Ante-nuptial settlement. *See* **Variation of Settlement (Matrimonial Causes)** (Ante-nuptial settlement—House purchased before marriage to provide matrimonial home).
Bankruptcy—
Bankrupt's estate. *See* **Insolvency** (Bankruptcy—Bankrupt's estate—Matrimonial home).
Property available for distribution. *See* **Bankruptcy** (Property available for distribution—Matrimonial home).
Costs—
Registration of land charge—
Legal aid. *See* **Legal aid** (Costs—Matrimonial home).
Deserted wife's right to remain in. *See* **Husband and wife** (Deserted wife's right to remain in matrimonial home).
Divorce—
Property adjustment order. *See* **Divorce** (Property—Adjustment order).
Exclusion from matrimonial home—
Injunction. *See* **Injunction** (Exclusion of party from matrimonial home).
Protection order. *See* **Husband and wife** (Summary proceedings—Order for protection of party to marriage or child of the family—Exclusion from matrimonial home).
Specific issue order—
Family proceedings. *See* **Family proceedings** (Orders in family proceedings—Specific issue order—Exclusion of party from matrimonial home).
Generally. *See* **Husband and wife** (Matrimonial home).
Injunction—
Exclusion of party from matrimonial home. *See* **Injunction** (Exclusion of party from matrimonial home).
Generally. *See* **Injunction** (Husband and wife—Matrimonial home).
Insolvency—
Property available for distribution. *See* **Insolvency** (Property available for distribution—Matrimonial home).
Intestacy—
Rights of surviving spouse—
Generally. *See* **Intestacy** (Rights of surviving spouse—Rights as respects matrimonial home).
Right of surviving spouse to acquire home. *See* **Intestacy** (Appropriation by personal representatives—Surviving spouse—Matrimonial home).
Leasehold property—
Husband trustee for himself and wife—
Bought freehold after divorce suit begun by wife—Whether freehold held on same trusts. *See* **Trust and trustee** (Profit from trust—Matrimonial home—Leasehold premises).
Licence to occupy—
Deserted wife's right to occupy matrimonial home. *See* **Licence** (Licence to occupy premises—Deserted wife's right to occupy matrimonial home).

MATRIMONIAL HOME (cont)—

Mortgage—
    Deserted wife's right to be joined in proceedings by mortgagee against husband for possession. *See* **Mortgage** (Action by mortgagee for possession—Parties).
    Priority of wife's equitable interest. *See* **Mortgage** (Equitable interest—Priority—Husband and wife's joint purchase of matrimonial home).

Occupation by wife—
    Overriding interest—
        Priority of wife's equitable interest. *See* **Land registration** (Overriding interest—Rights of person in actual occupation of land—Husband and wife's joint purchase of matrimonial home).

Rateable occupation—
    Former matrimonial home. *See* **Rates** (Rateable occupation—Occupation by relatives—Husband and wife—Former matrimonial home).

Registered land—
    Overriding interest—
        Person in actual occupation. *See* **Land registration** (Overriding interest—Rights of person in actual occupation of land—Husband and wife's joint purchase of matrimonial home).

Sale—
    Divorce—
        Sale under trust for sale. *See* **Husband and wife** (Matrimonial home—Sale under trust for sale—Divorce).
    Pending action—
        Wife's summons—Land charge. *See* **Land charge** (Vacation of entry in register—Pending action—Matrimonial proceedings).
    Vacant possession—
        Duty of vendor to bring proceedings to obtain possession. *See* **Specific performance** (Sale of land—Sale with vacant possession—Duty of vendor to bring proceedings to obtain possession).

Transfer to deserted wife—
    Agreement as to—
        Enforceability. *See* **Contract** (Intention to create legal relationship—Presumption against intention—Presumption inapplicable—Husband and wife not living in amity—Evidence disclosing intention to create legal relationship—Agreement after separation—Husband providing for wife—Wife paying off mortgage on matrimonial home).

MATRIMONIAL OFFENCE

Burden of proof. *See* **Divorce** (Evidence—Proof—Burden of proof of matrimonial offence).

MATRIMONIAL ORDER

See **Husband and wife** (Matrimonial order).

MATRIMONIAL PROCEEDINGS

County court—
    Appeal to Court of Appeal—
        Jurisdiction of Court of Appeal. *See* **Court of Appeal** (Jurisdiction—Appeal from county court—Matrimonial proceedings).

Decree granted in absence of party—
    Personal liability of solicitor for costs. *See* **Solicitor** (Payment of costs by solicitor personally—Matrimonial proceedings—Decree granted in absence of party).

Generally. *See* **Husband and wife**.

Injunction—
    Application—
        High Court. *See* **Injunction** (High Court—Applications in matrimonial proceedings).
    Breach of injunction—
        Committal for contempt of court. *See* **Contempt of court** (Committal—Breach of injunction—Divorce).
    Ex parte injunction. *See* **Injunction** (Ex parte injunction—Matrimonial proceedings).

Freezing order—
    Worldwide injunction. *See* **Practice** (Pre-trial or post-judgment relief—Freezing order—Worldwide freezing order—Matrimonial proceedings).

Jurisdiction—
    European Union. *See* **European Union** (Jurisdiction—Matrimonial matters and matters of parental responsibility).

Probation officer—
    Extent of authority. *See* **Probation** (Officer—Extent of authority—Matrimonial proceedings).

Solicitor acting for petitioner—
    Practice. *See* **Practice** (Family Division—Solicitor acting in matrimonial proceedings for petitioner).

Welfare report—
    Child—
        Practice. *See* **Child** (Welfare—Welfare report).

MAURITIUS

Constitutional law—
    Human rights and freedoms—
        Protection of law—Criminal trial—Accused's right to interpreter—Accused's right to be present at trial—Right of accused to hear evidence against him so that he can decide what course to take at his trial—Whether constitutional right to interpreter replacing common law principles—Constitution of Mauritius, s 10(2)(f). **Kunnath v The State** [1993] **4** 30, PC.

MAURITIUS (cont)—
  Constitutional law (cont)—
    Human rights and freedoms (cont)—
      Right not to be deprived of property without compensation—Pay dispute between marine authority and workers referred to arbitration—Arbitrator recommending increases of salary and allowances—Minister directing authority not to implement award—Minister authorised to give directions in the public interest to authority 'in relation to the exercise of the powers of the Authority'—Attorney General authorised to object to enforcement of arbitration award—Whether minister exceeding powers—Attorney General's objection to enforcement of award depriving workers of property without compensation—Constitution of Mauritius 1968, ss 3(c), 8(1)—Ports Act 1979 (Mauritius), s 9(1)—Code of Civil Procedure (Amendment) Act 1981 (Mauritius). **Société United Docks v Government of Mauritius** [1985] **1** 864, PC.
      Right not to be deprived of property without compensation—Statute creating corporation having monopoly to store and load sugar—Consequent loss of business by dock and stevedore companies—No provision in statute for payment of compensation—Whether companies deprived of property without compensation—Constitution of Mauritius 1968, ss 3(c), 8(1)—Mauritius Sugar Terminal Corporation Act 1979, s 5. **Société United Docks v Government of Mauritius** [1985] **1** 864, PC.
    Separation of judicial and executive power—
      Director of Public Prosecutions having statutory power to prosecute importers of prohibited drugs either before judge without jury in Supreme Court or in intermediate or district court—Mandatory death penalty for conviction in Supreme Court of importation and trafficking—Penalty of fine and imprisonment in intermediate and district courts—Director deciding to prosecute appellants in Supreme Court—Whether Director having discretion as to court before which person accused of being drug trafficker to be tried—Whether Director of Public Prosecutions' discretion to select court of trial unconstitutional as enabling him to select penalty—Dangerous Drugs Act 1986 (Mauritius), ss 28(1)(c), (8), 38(4). **Ali v R** [1992] **2** 1, PC.
  Drug trafficking—
    Offences—
      Penalties—Drug offences carrying heavier sentences if amounting to drug trafficking—Mandatory death penalty for conviction in Supreme Court of importation and trafficking—Whether separate offence of 'importing-cum-drug trafficking'—Whether drug trafficking merely aggravating circumstance going to penalty—Whether separate offence of 'importing-cum-drug trafficking' must be charged in Supreme Court—Dangerous Drugs Act 1986 (Mauritius), ss 28(1)(c), 38. **Ali v R** [1992] **2** 1, PC.
  Nullity—
    Marriage in articulo mortis—
      Lack of consent through mental infirmity—Whether collaterals entitled to sue for nullity—Matrimonial Causes Ordinance 1949 (cap 91), s 14. **Choppy v Bibi (orse Choppy)** [1966] **1** 203, PC.
  Passport—
    Passport issued by Governor of Mauritius—
      Whether holder of passport holder of United Kingdom passport within Commonwealth Immigrants Act 1962, s 1. See **Commonwealth immigrant** (Commonwealth citizen other than person holding United Kingdom passport—United Kingdom passport—Passport issued to holder by government of United Kingdom—Passport issued by Governor of Mauritius).
  Public authorities—
    Colonial government—
      Liability on debenture—Contract or tort—Petition of right. **Guerard v Mauritius Government** [1939] **2** 178, PC.
    Commission of inquiry—
      Contempt of court—Whether law of contempt applying to commission of inquiry—Commissions of Inquiry Ordinance (Mauritius). **Badry v DPP of Mauritius** [1982] **3** 973, PC.

MAYOR'S AND CITY OF LONDON COURT
  Appeal from—
    Jurisdiction of Court of Appeal. See **Court of Appeal** (Jurisdiction—Appeal from Mayor's and City of London Court).

MCKENZIE FRIEND
  Litigant in person—
    Chambers proceedings—
      Right to assistance of McKenzie friend. See **Practice** (Chambers proceedings—Party acting in person—Right to assistance).
    Right to assistance of 'McKenzie Friend'. See **Practice** (Trial—Party acting in person—Right to assistance).
    Scope of right to assistance. See **Practice** (Trial—Party acting in person—Right to assistance—McKenzie friend).

MEALS
  School. See **Education** (School meals).

MEASURE
  Weights and. See **Weights and measures**.

MEASURE OF DAMAGES
  Conversion. See **Conversion** (Damages—Measure of damages).
  Generally. See **Damages** (Measure of damages).

MEAT
  Prepacked. See **Weights and measures** (Prepacked goods).

MECHANICALLY PROPELLED VEHICLE
  See **Road traffic** (Motor vehicle—Mechanically propelled vehicle).

MEDIA
- Broadcasting. *See* **Broadcasting**.
- Confidential information—
  - Breach of confidence. *See* **Equity** (Breach of confidence—Confidential information—Disclosure by media).
- Freedom of information. *See* **Freedom of information**.
- Legal proceedings—
  - Anonymity—
    - Human rights. *See* **Human rights** (Freedom of expression—Right to a fair trial—Right to respect for private and family life—Principle of open justice—Anonymity).
  - Reporting restrictions—
    - Human rights. *See* **Human rights** (Right to respect for private and family life—Freedom of expression—Legal proceedings—Principle of open justice—Reporting restrictions).
- Privacy rights—
  - Police investigation. *See* **Human rights** (Right to respect for private and family life—Freedom of expression—Police investigation—Media coverage).
- Reporting restrictions—
  - Court proceedings—
    - Children and young persons. *See* **Children and young persons** (Court proceedings—Protection of child concerned in proceedings).
- Restrictions on publication—
  - Intentional infliction of harm. *See* **Tort** (Intentional infliction of harm—Restrictions on publication).

MEDIATION
- Pre-action mediation—
  - Security for costs. *See* **Costs** (Security for costs—Company—Limited company as plaintiff—Company likely to be unable to pay costs of defendant if successful in his defence—Costs of and incidental to proceedings).

MEDICAL APPEAL TRIBUNAL
- Duty to make due enquiry—
  - Extent of duty. *See* **Natural justice** (Medical appeal tribunal—Duty to make due enquiry—Extent of duty).

MEDICAL BOARD
- Industrial injury. *See* **Industrial injury** (Medical board).

MEDICAL CARE
- European Union—
  - Freedom of movement. *See* **European Union** (Freedom of movement—Services—Medical care).
- Value added tax—
  - Exemption—
    - European Community. *See* **European Union** (Value added tax—Exemptions—Medical care).
    - Generally. *See* **Value added tax** (Exemptions—Medical care).

MEDICAL DEFENCE UNION
- Aid for medical practitioners—
  - Contract for a benefit other than money—
    - Insurance contract. *See* **Insurance** (Contract of insurance—Nature of contract—Contract for a benefit other than money or money's worth—Medical Defence Union).

MEDICAL EVIDENCE
- Appeal. *See* **Appeal** (Evidence—Medical evidence).
- Criminal proceedings—
  - Generally. *See* **Criminal evidence** (Medical evidence).
  - Summing-up. *See* **Criminal law** (Trial—Summing up—Medical evidence).
- Diminished responsibility—
  - Murder. *See* **Criminal law** (Murder—Diminished responsibility).
- Generally. *See* **Evidence** (Medical evidence).
- Road traffic offence—
  - Driving while unfit to drive through drink or drugs. *See* **Road traffic** (Driving while unfit to drive through drink or drugs).

MEDICAL EXAMINATION
- National service. *See* **National service** (Medical examination).
- Personal injuries claim—
  - Stay of proceedings. *See* **Practice** (Stay of proceedings—Medical examination of plaintiff at defendant's request).

MEDICAL EXPENSES
- Income tax—
  - Deduction in computing profits. *See* **Income tax** (Deduction in computing profits—Expenses wholly and exclusively laid out for purposes of trade—Medical expenses).

MEDICAL INSPECTION
- Divorce—
  - Fees of inspectors on London rates. *See* **Divorce** (Fees—Medical inspection—Fees of inspectors on London rates).
- Nullity suit—
  - Evidence of inspector. *See* **Nullity** (Evidence—Medical inspector's evidence).
  - Generally. *See* **Nullity** (Medical inspection).

MEDICAL PRACTICE
Will—
    Advancement clause—
        Advancement in business. *See* **Will** (Advancement clause—Advancement in 'business'—Medical practice).

MEDICAL PRACTICES COMMITTEE
Race relations. *See* **Race relations** (Medical Practices Committee).

MEDICAL PRACTITIONER
Abortion—
    Defence. *See* **Criminal law** (Abortion—Defence).
    Negligence. *See* Negligence—Abortion, *below*.
Advertising—
    Restriction on press advertising—
        Doctor wishing to establish independent practice in holistic medicine—Doctor experiencing difficulty in establishing practice while abiding by General Medical Council's guidance as to dissemination of practice information by doctors—Whether guidance ultra vires and void—Whether guidance unreasonable, irrational and disproportionate to purpose of protecting legitimate interests of medical practitioners—Whether prevention of competition between doctors an irrelevant consideration—Whether guidance in breach of international obligations—Whether guidance an unreasonable restraint on professional activities of doctor—Medical Act 1983, s 35—Convention for the Protection of Human Rights and Fundamental Freedoms, art 10. **R v General Medical Council, ex p Colman** [1990] **1** 489, CA.
Appeal against determination of disciplinary committee—
    Defects in conduct of inquiry alleged—
        Charge of professional misconduct by adultery with patient—Corroboration—Letter sent by appellant to committee before hearing—Statutory declaration of complainant for purposes of initiating proceedings produced at hearing—Complainant sole witness at hearing—Whether defects of sufficient significance to invalidate finding. **Sivarajah v General Medical Council** [1964] **1** 504, PC.
    Powers of Privy Council—
        Finding by disciplinary committee that appellant guilty of infamous conduct in a professional respect—Sentence—Erasure of name from register—Whether appellate tribunal would interfere with disciplinary committee's discretion as to sentence—Medical Act 1956, s 33(1). **McCoan v General Medical Council** [1964] **3** 143, PC.
        Nature of appeal to Privy Council—Medical Act 1956, s 33(1)(b). **Fox v General Medical Council** [1960] **3** 225, PC.
    Right of appeal—
        Nature of appeal—Circumstances in which Privy Council may reverse a decision of disciplinary committee. **Libman v General Medical Council** [1972] **1** 798, PC.
Data protection—
    Personal data. *See* **Data protection** (Processing of information—Personal data—Mixed data case).
Disciplinary committee—
    Appeal against determination of. *See* Appeal against determination of disciplinary committee, *above*.
    Committee—
        Suspension from register—Successive periods of suspension—Powers of committee—Whether committee having power to direct successive periods of suspension for punitive reasons—Whether further period of suspension can only be directed if practitioner commits further offence or is guilty of other misconduct or fails to respond to treatment during period of suspension—Medical Act 1983, s 36(3). **Taylor v General Medical Council** [1990] **2** 263, PC.
    Erasure of name from register—
        Discretion of committee to consider evidence of previous offences—Powers of legal assessor. **Daly v General Medical Council** [1952] **2** 666, PC.
        Duty of committee to hold due inquiry prior to erasure—'Infamous conduct in a professional respect'—Practitioner found guilty by divorce court of adultery—Refusal by council to hear evidence not given before divorce court—'Due inquiry'—Evidence Act 1851, s 16—Medical Act 1858, s 29. **R v General Medical Council, ex p Spackman** [1943] **2** 337, HL.
        Practitioner convicted in Malaya of criminal offence—Portions of record of convicting court excised before disciplinary committee—Admissibility—Medical Disciplinary Committee (Procedure) Rules 1951 (SI 1951 No 665), r 63. **Ong Bak Hin v General Medical Council** [1956] **2** 257, PC.
    Fitness to practise—
        Sanction—Doctor convicted of manslaughter by gross negligence—Medical Practitioners Tribunal finding impairment of fitness to practise and suspending from register for one year—Whether tribunal in error—Whether erasure from register appropriate sanction—Medical Act 1983, s 1—General Medical Council (Fitness to Practise) Rules Order in Council 2004, SI 2004/2608, Sch 1, r 34. **General Medical Council v Bawa-Garba (British Medical Association intervening)** [2019] **1** 500, CA.
        Sanction—Review following suspension—Committee directing removal of pharmacist from register as sanction for impairment of fitness to practise by reason of criminal convictions—Whether review committee having power to direct suspension beyond 12 months to reflect gravity of misconduct—Whether removal from register disproportionate—Pharmacy Order 2010, SI 2010/231, art 54. **Khan v General Pharmaceutical Council (Scotland)** [2017] **3** 873, SC.
    Natural justice—
        Disclosure of information received by committee—Withholding information from practitioner—Committee entitled to withhold information as to practitioner's behaviour since the original hearing—Committee obtaining medical reports on practitioner's fitness to practice—Whether committee entitled to withhold reports from practitioner—General Medical Council Disciplinary Committee (Procedure) Rules Order in Council 1970, Appendix, r 47. **Crompton v General Medical Council** [1982] **1** 35, PC.
        Natural justice before committee—Ambiguous charges preferred before committee—Charges leading to conviction whether true or false. **Sloan v General Medical Council** [1970] **2** 686, PC.

MEDICAL PRACTITIONER (cont)—
    Disciplinary committee (cont)—
        Whether a 'court'. *See* **Contempt of court** (Publications concerning disciplinary proceedings—
        Professional Conduct Committee of the General Medical Council).
    Disciplinary panel—
        Erasure of name from register—
            Medical practitioner forming relationship with vulnerable patient—Panel of opinion erasure
            appropriate penalty save in exceptional circumstances—Whether panel applying correct test.
            Giele v General Medical Council [2005] **4** 1242, QBD.
        Immunity from suit—
            Expert giving medical evidence in criminal trial—Complaint that evidence flawed—Disciplinary
            proceedings brought—Panel finding serious professional misconduct proved and ordering
            erasure of name of expert—Whether panel having jurisdiction—Whether immunity from suit
            providing immunity from disciplinary proceedings. **Meadow v General Medical Council**
            [2006] **2** 329, QBD; [2007] **1** 1, CA.
        Reference to High Court—
            Reference of final decision—Fitness to practise panel excluding evidence and staying proceedings
            as abuse of process on basis of entrapment—Whether final decision not to take any disciplinary
            measure—Whether panel in error—National Health Service Reform and Health Care Professions
            Act 2002, s 29. **Saluja (Reference of decision by General Medical Council in disciplinary**
            proceedings), Re [2007] **2** 905, QBD.
    Disciplinary proceedings—
        Disciplinary committee. *See* Disciplinary committee, *above*.
        Disciplinary panel. *See* Disciplinary panel, *above*.
        General Medical Council—
            Fitness to practise—Functions of the investigation committee—First claimant qualified as both
            solicitor and medical practitioner—General Medical Council investigating first claimant in relation
            to allegations arising in capacity as solicitor—Whether General Medical Council having
            jurisdiction—Medical Act 1983, s 35C—General Medical Council (Fitness to Practise) Rules Order
            of Council 2004, SI 2004/2608, r 4. **Ogunsanya v General Medical Council** [2021] **1** 887, QBD.
            Interim Orders Panel—Interim suspension order—Application to court for extension of
            order—Guidance—Medical Act 1983, s 41A. **General Medical Council v Hiew** [2007] **4** 473, CA.
        National Health Service. *See* **National Health Service** (Medical practitioner—Disciplinary procedures).
        Procedure—
            Categorisation of proceedings—Professional conduct—Requirement to have independent doctor
            on panel in cases concerning professional conduct—Dismissal for gross misconduct—Whether
            charges concerning 'professional conduct'. **Idu v East Suffolk and North Essex NHS Foundation**
            Trust [2020] **2** 793, CA.
            Categorisation of proceedings—Whether professional or personal conduct—Department of Health
            Circular HC(90)9. **Skidmore v Dartford & Gravesham NHS Trust** [2003] **3** 292, HL.
        Professional Conduct Committee of the General Medical Council—
            Procedure—Charge of serious professional misconduct—Whether committee to take into account
            personal mitigation advanced by medical practitioner in deciding on guilt—General Medical
            Council Preliminary Proceedings Committee and Professional Conduct Committee (Procedure)
            Rules 1988, SI 1988/2255, r 28. **R (on the application of Campbell) v General Medical Council**
            [2005] **2** 970, CA.
        Right to a fair hearing. *See* **Human rights** (Right to a fair hearing—Disciplinary proceedings—Medical
        practitioner).
    Doctor and patient—
        Disclosure of confidential information—
            Company seeking to persuade doctors and pharmacists to disclose prescription information which
            did not reveal identity of patients—Department of Health advising that such disclosure would
            constitute breach of duty of confidence owed to patients—Whether disclosure of anonymous
            information by doctors and pharmacists could be breach of confidence. **Muman v Nagasena**
            [1999] **4** 178, CA; **R v Dept of Health, ex p Source Informatics Ltd** [2000] **1** 786, CA.
            Disclosure at request of patient—Patient suffering from venereal disease—Proceedings for decree
            of nullity contemplated—Request by patient for disclosure of confidential information to named
            person—Duty of doctor. **C v C** [1946] **1** 562, Assizes.
            Health authority seeking disclosure of medical records and case papers relating to Children Act
            proceedings in Family Division—Disclosure sought in connection with disciplinary proceedings—
            Judge ordering disclosure of documents subject to conditions—Whether judge in error—National
            Health Service (General Medical Services) Regulations 1992, Sch 2, para 36(6). **A Health Authority**
            v X [2002] **2** 780, CA.
            Public interest—Doctor's duty to patient and to public—Disclosure of report on patient in public
            interest—Psychiatrist instructed by patient detained in secure hospital to prepare independent
            report on patient's mental condition—Psychiatrist disclosing report to hospital charged with
            patient's care and encouraging hospital to disclose report to public authorities responsible for
            making decisions about patient's future—Whether psychiatrist barred by duty of confidence
            owed to patient from disclosing contents of report—Whether duty of confidence subordinate to
            duty owed to public—Whether doctor's public duty requiring him to disclose report to public
            authorities responsible for patient's treatment and future. **W v Egdell** [1990] **1** 835, CA.
    Duty of care. *See* Negligence—Duty of care, *below*.
    Evidence—
        Appeal. *See* **Appeal** (Evidence—Medical evidence).
        Criminal trial. *See* **Criminal evidence** (Medical evidence—Weight—Position of doctor giving medical
        evidence at criminal trial).
        Expert evidence—
            Negligence cases—Disclosure to other parties. *See* **Practice** (Evidence—Expert evidence—
            Disclosure to other parties—Action for medical negligence).
        Generally. *See* **Evidence** (Medical evidence).
        Nullity suit. *See* **Nullity** (Medical inspection).
    Family planning clinic—
        Advice on contraception. *See* **National Health Service** (Family planning clinics—Contraception).

MEDICAL PRACTITIONER (cont)—
    Gift—
        Undue influence. *See* **Equity** (Undue influence—Presumption of undue influence—Doctor and patient).
    Hospital—
        House physician—
            Contract—Implied term. *See* **Contract** (Implied term—Hospital—House physician).
        Staff—
            Negligence. *See* Negligence, *below.*
    Hospital patient—
        Specimen for laboratory test to determine blood-alcohol proportion—
            Drinking and driving offence—Practitioner's objection to test. *See* **Road traffic** (Specimen for laboratory test to determine driver's blood-alcohol proportion—Hospital patient—Right of medical practitioner to object).
    Hours of work—
        Contract of service. *See* **Employment** (Contract of service—Hours of work—Employer's duty not to injure employee—Doctor).
    Immigration rules—
        Statement of changes in immigration rules. *See* **Immigration** (Rules—Statement of changes in immigration rules—Presumption against retrospectivity).
    Income tax—
        Annual payments—
            Payments by Minister of Health. *See* **Income tax** (Annual payment—Personal debt or obligation by virtue of contract—Receipts payable as a personal debt or obligation—Medical practitioner).
        Avoidance—
            Australia. *See* **Australia** (Income tax—Avoidance—Agreement or arrangement having purpose or effect of avoiding liability—Partnership of medical practitioners dissolved).
        Travelling expenses. *See* **Income tax** (Deduction in computing profits—Travelling expenses—Medical practitioner).
    Insurance—
        Medical Defence Union—
            Contract for a benefit other than money. *See* **Insurance** (Contract of insurance—Nature of contract—Contract for a benefit other than money or money's worth—Medical Defence Union).
    Medical Defence Union—
        Insurance—
            Contract for a benefit other than money. *See* **Insurance** (Contract of insurance—Nature of contract—Contract for a benefit other than money or money's worth—Medical Defence Union).
    Medical performers list—
        Protection of property. *See* Professional misconduct—Suspension—Protection of property—Medical practitioner suspended from medical performers list, *below.*
    Medical treatment—
        Generally. *See* **Medical treatment**.
    National Health Service—
        Generally. *See* **National Health Service** (Medical practitioner).
        Medical services. *See* **National Health Service** (General medical services).
    Negligence—
        Abortion—
            Failure to detect foetal deformity in ultrasound scans when mother more than 27 weeks pregnant—Foetus capable of being born alive—Termination of pregnancy unlawful—Whether failure to discover abnormality and advise on possibility of abortion amounting to negligence if termination would have been unlawful—Infant Life (Preservation) Act 1929, s 1—Abortion Act 1967. **Rance v Mid-Downs Health Authority** [1991] **1** 801, QBD.
        Burden of proof—
            Causation, as to. *See* Negligence—Causation—Burden of proof, *below.*
        Causation—
            Burden of proof—Breach of duty causing or materially contributing to damage—Enhancement of existing risk—Doctor's negligence merely one of several factors which could have caused injury—Existence and extent to which doctor's negligence contributed to plaintiff's injury not able to be ascertained—Whether plaintiff discharging burden of proof as to causation—Whether doctor liable for breach of duty. **Wilsher v Essex Area Health Authority** [1986] **3** 801, CA; [1988] **1** 871, HL.
            Doctor negligently failing to make correct diagnosis—Disease carrying statistical probability of patient not surviving for ten years if treated promptly—Probability of patient surviving for ten years lessening during delay in diagnosis—Whether damages to be awarded for reduction in chance of survival. **Gregg v Scott** [2005] **4** 812, HL.
            Failure to warn of risks of operation—Surgeon negligently failing to advise patient of risk inherent in operation—Patient suffering injury when risk materialising during operation—Patient establishing that she would not have had immediate operation if properly advised—Whether causation established only if patient also proving that she would never have had operation at any time if properly advised. **Chester v Afshar** [2002] **3** 552, CA; [2004] **4** 587, HL.
        Conformity with practices accepted as proper by responsible members of profession—
            Unsuccessful operation—Operation departing from orthodox course of treatment—Plaintiff left disabled—Onus of proof shifting to defendants to prove departure from established practice not a breach of duty—Onus of proof on defendants to prove that plaintiff's injuries not caused by breach of duty—Whether defendants negligent. **Clark v MacLennan** [1983] **1** 416, QBD.
        Costs—
            Order for costs—Discretion. *See* Costs (Order for costs—Discretion—Claim for professional medical negligence).
        Damages—
            Aggravated damages. *See* **Damages** (Personal injury—Aggravated damages—Medical negligence).
            Grief. *See* **Damages** (Personal injury—Grief—Medical negligence).
            Unwanted pregnancy. *See* **Damages** (Unwanted pregnancy—Negligence).

Negligence (cont)—
Diagnosis and treatment—
Decision to operate—Operation involving risk to patient—Conflicting medical opinion as to necessity of operation—Whether negligence if operation supported by body of competent professional opinion. **Maynard v West Midlands Regional Health Authority** [1985] **1** 635, HL.
Duty of care—
Duty to exercise reasonable skill and care. *See* **Negligence** (Professional person—Duty to exercise reasonable skill and care).
Standard of care—Advice—Contraceptive advice—Failure to warn of risk that sterilisation operation might not succeed—Substantial body of responsible doctors would not have given warning of risk of failure of operation—Whether failure to give warning amounting to negligence—Whether context in which advice given relevant—Whether relevant that advice given in contraceptive context and not therapeutic context. **Gold v Haringey Health Authority** [1987] **2** 888, CA.
Standard of care—Alternative medical practitioner—Patient suffering liver failure and dying after taking remedy prescribed by Chinese herbal medicine practitioner—Patient's widow bringing action for negligence and relying on orthodox medical literature suggesting such remedies giving rise to risk of liver failure—Whether alternative medical practitioner to be judged by standards of reasonably careful practitioner of alternative medicine or by standards applicable to orthodox medical practitioners. **Shakoor (administratrix of the estate of Shakoor (decd)) v Situ (t/a Eternal Health Co)** [2000] **4** 181, QBD.
Standard of care—Specialist hospital unit—Duty and standard of care required of specialist unit—Junior doctor in unit inserting catheter into baby's vein instead of artery—Junior doctor consulting senior registrar who failed to notice error—Senior registrar subsequently making same error—Baby given excess oxygen as result of error—Whether health authority could be directly liable for failure to provide proper staff for unit—Whether any concept of team negligence—Whether inexperience of doctor a defence. **Wilsher v Essex Area Health Authority** [1986] **3** 801, CA.
Duty owed to foetus—
Extent of duty—Mother contracting infection during pregnancy—Infection involving risk of damage to foetus—Whether doctor having legal obligation to foetus to terminate its life to prevent existence in disabled state. **McKay v Essex Area Health Authority** [1982] **2** 771, CA.
Expert evidence—
Disclosure to other parties. *See* **Practice** (Evidence—Expert evidence—Disclosure to other parties—Action for medical negligence).
Liability of hospital. *See* **Hospital** (Liability for negligence of members of staff—Medical practitioner).
Limitation of action—
Act done in execution of public duty—Specialist at hospital administered by hospital board—Action for negligence commenced more than one year after cause of action accrued—Whether act done in execution of public duty. **Higgins v North West Metropolitan Hospital Board** [1954] **1** 414, QBD.
Surgery—
Failure to warn of result of surgery—Failure to warn that result of surgery might be naturally reversed—Vasectomy—Failure to warn that patient might regain fertility—Patient's wife becoming pregnant—Wife not aware of pregnancy until too late for abortion—Whether failure to give warning a breach of surgeon's duty of care—Whether damage consisting of pregnancy or of not knowing of pregnancy until too late for abortion. **Thake v Maurice** [1986] **1** 497, CA.
Sterilisation of female patient—Statement by doctor that operation 'irreversible'—Patient becoming pregnant—Whether statement amounting to negligent misrepresentation that operation would be successful. **Gold v Haringey Health Authority** [1987] **2** 888, CA.
Test of liability—
Conforming with practice accepted as proper by responsible members of the profession—Expert evidence of practice accepted as proper—Circumstances in which expert evidence not to be relied on as establishing proper level of skill and competence—Omission to intubate infant prior to respiratory failure resulting in cardiac arrest—Expert evidence both for and against intubation—Whether evidence for defendants reasonable and responsible—Whether evidence capable of withstanding logical analysis. **Bolitho (administratrix of the estate of Bolitho (decd)) v City and Hackney Health Authority** [1997] **4** 771, HL.
Conformity with practices accepted as proper by responsible members of the profession—Whether doctor under duty, when advising electroconvulsive therapy, to warn of risks. **Bolam v Friern Hospital Management Committee** [1957] **2** 118, QBD.
Error of judgment—Hospital registrar testing forceps delivery—Registrar pulling foetus several times with obstetric forceps—Baby born with brain damage—Whether error of clinical judgment negligence—Whether negligence to be inferred from fact baby born with brain damage— Whether registrar negligent. **Whitehouse v Jordan** [1981] **1** 267, HL.
Risk of misfortune inherent in treatment proposed by doctor—Doctor's duty to warn of inherent risk of misfortune. **Chatterton v Gerson** [1981] **1** 257, QBD.
Risk of misfortune inherent in treatment proposed by doctor—Doctor's duty to warn of inherent risk of misfortune—High risk pregnancy and delivery due to small stature of mother with diabetes—Failure of doctor to advise on risks of vaginal delivery and possible need for caesarean section—Baby sustaining serious birth injuries during vaginal delivery -Whether negligence where failure to warn of risks accepted as proper by responsible body of medical opinion. **Montgomery v Lanarkshire Health Board (General Medical Council intervening)** [2015] **2** 1031, SC.
Risk of misfortune inherent in treatment proposed by doctor—Doctor's duty to warn of inherent risk of misfortune—Operation to cure neck deformity resulting in patient's complete paralysis— Patient electing to have operation—Inherent risk of paralysis following operation—Whether standard of care required of doctor in giving advice before operation the same as that normally required of medical practitioners in course of diagnosis and treatment—Whether higher standard requiring full disclosure to patient before operation of all details and risks. **Hills v Potter** [1983] **3** 716, QBD.

MEDICAL PRACTITIONER (cont)—
  Negligence (cont)—
    Test of liability (cont)—
      Risk of misfortune inherent in treatment proposed by doctor—Doctor's duty to warn of inherent risk
        of misfortune—Operation to relieve persistent pain in neck resulting in serious disablement of
        patient—Doctor warning patient of material risks but not of all risks inherent in
        operation—Whether standard of care required of doctor in giving advice before operation the
        same as that normally required of medical practitioner in course of diagnosis and
        treatment—Whether higher standard requiring full disclosure to patient of all details and risks
        before operation. **Sidaway v Bethlem Royal Hospital Governors** [1985] **1** 643, HL.
    Unwanted pregnancy—
      Damages. *See* **Damages** (Unwanted pregnancy—Negligence).
    Vicarious liability—
      Locum GP—Psychiatric injury—Claimant alleging she suffered psychiatric harm as result of
        religious practices and doctrines imposed on her through locum GP—Whether locum GP
        tortiously liable for harm caused—Whether GP practice vicariously liable for torts of locum GP.
        Brayshaw v Partners of Apsley Surgery [2019] **2** 997, QBD.
  Nullity suit—
    Medical inspection. *See* **Nullity** (Medical inspection).
  Partnership—
    Goodwill. *See* **National Health Service** (Medical practitioner—Partnership—Goodwill).
    Restraint of trade. *See* **Restraint of trade by agreement** (Partnership—Medical partnership).
  Personal injury—
    Loss of future earnings—
      Damages. *See* **Damages** (Personal injury—Loss of future earnings—Doctor).
  Professional Conduct Committee—
    Interim suspension powers. *See* **Osteopath** (Professional conduct and fitness to practise—Professional
      Conduct Committee—Interim suspension powers).
  Professional misconduct—
    Charge of professional misconduct—
      Duplicity—Single charge of improperly supplying drugs to 'individual patients' on different
        occasions—Whether charge bad for duplicity—Whether charge alleging single course of
        professional misconduct. **Gee v General Medical Council** [1987] **1** 1204, QBD and CA; [1987] **2** 193,
        HL.
      Duplicity—Single charge of improperly supplying drugs to 'individual patients' over four-year
        period—Whether charge bad for duplicity—Whether charge alleging single course of professional
        misconduct. **Peatfield v General Medical Council** [1987] **1** 1197, PC.
    Charge of serious professional misconduct—
      Evidence—Corroboration—Acts of dishonesty—Committee sitting in Scotland—Whether English or
        Scots law applicable—Whether acts of dishonesty required to be proved by corroborated
        evidence—Civil Evidence (Scotland) Act 1988, ss 1(1), 9. **McAllister v General Medical Council**
        [1993] **1** 982, PC.
      Expert giving medical evidence in criminal trial—Whether flawed expert evidence amounting to
        serious professional misconduct. **Meadow v General Medical Council** [2007] **1** 1, CA.
      Misconduct in course of medical examination of two female patients—Charge founded on
        complaints of both patients—Whether complaints on which charge founded ought to have been
        heard separately. **Lanford v General Medical Council** [1989] **2** 921, PC.
      Particulars of charge—Making improper and indecent remarks and/or behaving improperly to four
        employees and two patients—Whether complaints should be heard separately—Whether
        complaints relating to employees should be heard by same committee as complaints relating to
        patients—General Medical Council Preliminary Proceedings Committee and Professional Conduct
        Committee (Procedure) Rules Order of Council 1988, App. rr 27-31. **Reza v General Medical
        Council** [1991] **2** 796, PC.
    Disciplinary proceedings—
      Disciplinary committee. *See* Disciplinary committee, *above*.
      Procedure—Whether charge of professional misconduct required to be considered by General
        Medical Council's preliminary proceedings committee before being referred to professional
        conduct committee—Whether charge can be amended by professional conduct committee by
        adding further particulars without being referred back to preliminary proceedings committee—
        General Medical Council Preliminary Proceedings Committee and Professional Conduct
        Committee (Procedure) Rules Order of Council 1980. **Gee v General Medical Council**
        [1987] **1** 1204, QBD and CA; [1987] **2** 193, HL.
    Infamous conduct in professional respect—
      Shareholder in company advertising medical services—Power to control company—Failure to
        exercise power to prevent advertising—Whether capable of amounting to infamous conduct.
        Faridian v General Medical Council [1971] **1** 144, PC.
    Suspension—
      Protection of property—Medical practitioner suspended from medical performers list—Whether
        breach of right to protection of property—Whether inclusion in list a 'possession'—Human Rights
        Act 1998, Sch 1, Pt II, art 1—National Health Service (Performers Lists) Regulations 2004,
        SI 2004/585—Primary Medical Services (Sales of Goodwill and Restrictions on Sub-contracting)
        Regulations 2004, SI 2004/906. **R (on the application of Malik) v Waltham Forest Primary Care
        Trust (Secretary of State for Health, interested party)** [2007] **4** 832, CA.
      Right to a fair trial—Protection of property—Medical practitioner suspended from medical
        performers list—Whether suspension unlawful—Whether breach of right to a fair trial—Whether
        breach of right to protection of property—Human Rights Act 1998, Sch 1, Pt I, art 6, Pt II, art 1. **R
        (on the application of Malik) v Waltham Forest Primary Care Trust (Secretary of State for Health,
        interested party)** [2006] **3** 71, QBD.
    Using obscene and indecent language and behaving improperly to two female patients—
      Corroboration—Admissibility of similar fact evidence—Similar obscene language used to both
        patients—No striking similarity in what was done to patients—Whether evidence of what was
        said to one patient capable of corroborating evidence of indecency by other patient. **Lanford v
        General Medical Council** [1989] **2** 921, PC.

MEDICAL PRACTITIONER (cont)—
    Sterilisation of child—
        Consent of court—
            Liability of doctor carrying out sterilisation operation on child without consent of court. *See* **Sterilisation** (Child—Consent).
    Surgery—
        Contract with patient—
            Collateral warranty—Breach. *See* **Contract** (Warranty—Collateral warranty—Breach—Surgery).
            Nature of contract. *See* **Contract** (Surgery—Nature of contract).
        Negligence. *See* Negligence—Surgery, *above*.
    Suspension from register. *See* Disciplinary committee—Committee—Suspension from register, *above*.
    Trespass to the person—
        Consent to medical treatment—
            Prison—Prison medical officer administering drug to prisoner—Prisioner contending that drug administered by force without his consent—Whether prisoner's consent required to be informed consent—Whether sufficient that prisoner consenting in broad terms. **F v Home Office** [1984] **1** 1036, CA.
        Consent to operation—
            Operation on or other treatment of person unable to give consent—Lawfulness of operation or other treatment—Operation or other treatment in person's best interests—Whether operation or other treatment lawful—Whether lawful only if carried out to save life or to ensure improvement or prevent deterioration in physical or mental health. **F v West Berkshire Health Authority (Mental Health Act Commission intervening)** [1989] **2** 545, HL.
            Operation on person without consent—Vitiation of patient's consent—Doctor explaining nature of operation in broad terms to patient—Whether lack of consent by patient to operation. **Chatterton v Gerson** [1981] **1** 257, QBD.
            Operation to cure neck deformity resulting in patient's complete paralysis—Patient electing to have operation—Inherent risk of paralysis following operation—Doctor not explaining all aspects of operation to patient before operating—Whether patient's consent to operation vitiated—Whether doctor committing assault and battery by performing operation—Whether claim for assault and battery appropriate. **Hills v Potter** [1983] **3** 716, QBD.
    Venereal disease—
        Disclosure of confidential information—
            Nullity suit. *See* **Nullity** (Venereal disease—Disclosure of confidential information by doctor).
    Water supply—
        Domestic purposes. *See* **Water supply** (Supply of water for domestic purposes—Domestic purposes—Water supplied to medical practitioner).
    Wilfully and falsely pretending to be a registered person—
        Honest belief in use of title—
            Accused using title 'physician'—Accused holding diploma of drugless therapy—Honest belief in use of title 'physician'—Reasonable ground for belief—Matters for consideration by court—Medical Act 1858, s 40. **Wilson v Inyang** [1951] **2** 237, KBD.
        Need to prove wilful falsity—
            Accused using title 'doctor of medicine'—Doctor of medicine of Berlin University—Medical Act 1858, s 40. **Younghusband v Luftig** [1949] **2** 72, KBD.
    Withdrawal of treatment. *See* **Medical treatment** (Withdrawal of treatment).

MEDICAL RECORDS
    Access to medical records by patient—
        National Health Service. *See* **National Health Service** (Medical records—Access to medical records by patient).

MEDICAL REFEREE
    Reference to. *See* **Workmen's compensation** (Reference to medical referee).

MEDICAL REPORT
    Agreed report—
        Order for. *See* **Practice** (Medical reports—Agreed report—Order for agreed medical reports).
        Trial of case on. *See* **Practice** (Medical reports—Agreed report—Trial of case on agreed medical report).
    Care proceedings in juvenile court. *See* **Children and young persons** (Care proceedings in juvenile court—Evidence—Medical reports).
    Disclosure—
        Action for medical negligence. *See* **Practice** (Evidence—Expert evidence—Disclosure to other parties—Action for medical negligence).
        Privilege—
            Waiver of privilege. *See* **Disclosure and inspection of documents** (Privilege—Waiver of privilege—Medical reports).
    Order for exchange of. *See* **Practice** (Medical reports—Order for exchange).
    Refusal—
        Costs. *See* **Costs** (Order for costs—Discretion—Disallowing costs of successful plaintiff—Misconduct or neglect—Medical report).

MEDICAL SCHOOL
    Contingent gift—
        Hospital—
            Effect of National Health Service Act, 1946. *See* **National Health Service** (Legacy to hospital—Gift to medical school of hospital—Gift over if hospital nationalised or passes into public ownership).

MEDICAL TREATMENT
Adult patient—
  Consent to treatment—
    Adult lacking capacity refusing treatment—Approach to grant of interim declaration—CPR 25.1(1)(b). **NHS Trust v T (adult patient: refusal of medical treatment)** [2005] **1** 387, Fam D.
    Force feeding—Mentally ill patient refusing to eat—Patient applying for injunction to restrain health authority from feeding her without consent—Whether feeding by nasogastric tube constituting 'medical treatment ... for the mental disorder'—Whether treatment without consent lawful—Mental Health Act 1983, ss 3, 58, 62, 63, 145. **B v Croydon Health Authority** [1995] **1** 683, CA.
    Force feeding—Prisoner on hunger strike—Whether lawful to permit hunger strike and allow prisoner to die—Whether prison officials and medical staff having duty to force feed prisoner. **Secretary of State for the Home Dept v Robb** [1995] **1** 677, Fam D.
    Pregnancy—Substantial risk of becoming incapacitous during labour—Whether anticipatory and contingent declarations should be made allowing medical treatment and authorising the deprivation of liberty of patient—Mental Capacity Act 2005, ss 15, 16, 24-26. **Guys and St Thomas' NHS Foundation Trust v R** [2020] **4** 312, COP.
    Pregnancy—Substantial risk of becoming incapacitous during labour—Whether anticipatory and contingent declarations should be made allowing medical treatment and authorising the deprivation of liberty of patient—Mental Capacity Act 2005, ss 4B, 15, 16. **An NHS Trust v CD** [2020] **2** 630, COP.
    Right to refuse consent—Mentally ill patient contracting gangrene in leg—Hospital proposing amputation of leg—Patient refusing to consent to amputation—Patient applying for injunction to restrain hospital from amputating leg without his written consent—Whether patient's refusal impaired by mental illness—Whether court should grant injunction—Whether court having jurisdiction to grant injunction restraining future treatment. **C (adult: refusal of medical treatment), Re** [1994] **1** 819, Fam D.
    Right to refuse consent—Refusal of consent to treatment affected by undue influence—Refusal on religious grounds—Religious sect believing blood transfusion to be a sin—Medical treatment involving administration of blood transfusion—Patient not a Jehovah's Witness but under influence of mother who was a member of sect—Patient refusing consent to blood transfusions—Whether refusal effective—Whether patient's refusal affected by undue influence of mother—Guidance for doctors and hospitals. **T (adult: refusal of medical treatment), Re** [1992] **4** 649, CA.
    Right to refuse consent—Refusal on religious grounds—Discretion of court to authorise emergency operation—Health authority seeking authority to carry out emergency Caesarian section operation on pregnant woman—Operation in vital interests of patient and unborn child—Patient objecting to operation on religious grounds—Whether court should exercise inherent jurisdiction to authorise operation. **S (adult: refusal of medical treatment), Re** [1992] **4** 671, Fam D.
    Right to refuse treatment—Patient 36 weeks pregnant diagnosed with pre-eclampsia and advised she needed to be admitted to hospital for an induced delivery—Patient rejecting advice as wishing her baby to be born naturally—Patient admitted against her will to mental hospital and later transferred to general hospital—Judge on ex parte application disposing with patient's consent to medical treatment and patient delivered of baby by Caesarean section—Patient transferred back to mental hospital and later discharged herself—Whether judge right in dispensing with patient's consent—Whether patient's detention, treatment and transfer lawful—Mental Health Act 1983, s 2. **St George's Healthcare NHS Trust v S** [1998] **3** 673, CA.
    Right to refuse treatment—Tetraplegic patient being kept alive by ventilator—Patient wishing to have ventilator turned off—Whether patient competent to refuse treatment—Whether treatment of patient unlawful. **B (adult: refusal of medical treatment), Re** [2002] **2** 449, Fam D.
    Right to respect for private and family life—Do not attempt cardio-pulmonary resuscitation notice—Decision—Requirement for consultation—Obligation of clinicians to involve patient in decision—Availability of sufficiently clear and precise policy—Secretary of State's duty to promote comprehensive health service—Duty as to the NHS Constitution—Human Rights Act 1998, Sch 1, Pt I, art 8—National Health Service Act 2006, ss 1, 1B. **R (on the application of Tracey) v Cambridge University Hospitals NHS Foundation Trust** [2015] **1** 450, CA.
Child. *See* **Minor** (Medical treatment).
Consent to medical treatment—
  Absence of—
    Trespass to the person. *See* **Medical practitioner** (Trespass to the person).
  Adult patient. *See* Adult patient—Consent to treatment, *above*.
Consent to treatment—
  Child. *See* **Minor** (Medical treatment—Consent).
Declaration as to lawfulness of proposed treatment—
  Experimental treatment—
    Patients suffering from incurable neurodegenerative disease and lacking capacity—Patients' parents wishing them to receive treatment which had not been tested on humans—Approach to be adopted by court in such circumstances. **Simms v Simms** [2003] **1** 669, Fam D.
  Generally. *See* **Declaration** (Procedure—Declaration as to lawfulness of proposed conduct—Proposed medical treatment).
Human fertilisation—
  Consent to use—
    Posthumous use—Regulatory authority refusing to permit export of deceased donor's eggs for fertilisation and implantation in donor's mother on basis of lack of effective consent by donor—Whether authority in error—Meaning of 'effective consent'—Human Fertilisation and Embryology Act 1990, Sch 3. **R (on the application of M) v Human Fertilisation and Embryology Authority** [2017] **3** 77, CA.
  Embryo—
    Cell nuclear replacement—Whether organism created by cell nuclear replacement falling within statutory definition of embryo—Human Fertilisation and Embryology Act 1990, s 1(1). **R (on the application of Quintavalle) v Secretary of State for Health** [2001] **4** 1013, QBD.

MEDICAL TREATMENT (cont)—
　Human fertilisation (cont)—
　　Embryo (cont)—
　　　Frozen stored embryos—Consent to treatment together of each of male and female gamete
　　　　providers in treatment involving in vitro fertilisation, freezing and storage of embryos—Whether
　　　　consent effective after couple separating—Whether implantation of embryo in female gamete
　　　　provider 'treatment together'—Whether requirement for consent by both partners contrary to
　　　　right to respect for private and family life and discriminatory—Human Fertilisation and
　　　　Embryology Act 1990, Sch 3, para 6(3)—Human Rights Act 1998, Sch 1, Pt I, arts 8, 14. **Evans v
　　　　Amicus Healthcare Ltd** [2003] **4** 903, Fam D; [2004] **3** 1025, CA.
　　　Licence—
　　　　Keeping embryos—'Person responsible' securing proper arrangements made for keeping
　　　　　embryos—Whether 'person responsible' person keeping embryos—Human Fertilisation and
　　　　　Embryology Act 1990, ss 3(1)(b), 17(1), 41(2). **A-G's Reference (No 2 of 2003)** [2005] **3** 149, CA.
　　　Sperm taken without written consent from comatose husband who subsequently died—
　　　　Sperm placed in storage—Wife seeking to be inseminated with husband's sperm—Statutory body
　　　　　refusing to release sperm in absence of written consent or to consent to export of sperm for
　　　　　treatment abroad—Wife seeking judicial review of authority's decision—Whether authority acting
　　　　　within its powers—Whether exception to requirement of written consent applicable—Whether
　　　　　refusal to permit export of sperm infringement of freedom to obtain medical services elsewhere
　　　　　in European Community—Human Embryology and Fertilisation Act 1990, s 4, Sch 3—EC Treaty,
　　　　　arts 59, 60. **R v Human Fertilisation and Embryology Authority, ex p Blood** [1997] **2** 687, CA.
　　Human reproduction—
　　　Embryo—
　　　　Cell nuclear replacement—Cell nuclear replacement not involving fertilisation—Statute defining
　　　　　embryo as 'live human embryo where fertilisation is complete'—Whether embryo created by cell
　　　　　nuclear replacement falling within statutory definition—Human Fertilisation and Embryology Act
　　　　　1990, s 1(1). **R (on the application of Quintavalle) v Secretary of State for Health** [2002] **2** 625,
　　　　　CA; [2003] **2** 113, HL.
　　　　Tissue typing—Whether statutory authority having power to permit tissue typing in conjunction
　　　　　with pre-implantation genetic diagnosis—Human Fertilisation and Embryology Act 1990, ss 2(1),
　　　　　3(1)(b), Sch 2, para 1(1). **R (on the application of Quintavalle) v Human Fertilisation and
　　　　　Embryology Authority** [2003] **2** 105, QBD; [2003] **3** 257, CA.
　Immunisation—
　　Child in care. *See* **Child** (Care—Local authority—Immunisation).
　Medicinal product—
　　European Union. *See* **European Union** (Medicinal products).
　Mental patient—
　　Generally. *See* **Mental health** (Patient—Medical treatment).
　Minor—
　　Generally. *See* **Minor** (Medical treatment).
　Minor aged 16 years—
　　Right to refuse treatment—
　　　Minor suffering from anorexia nervosa refusing medical treatment—Medical condition of minor
　　　　such that she would suffer permanent physical damage without treatment—Whether court
　　　　exercising inherent jurisdiction can order medical treatment against minor's wishes—Whether
　　　　minor's wishes can be disregarded by court—Whether minor having exclusive right to consent
　　　　and absolute right to refuse medical treatment—Family Law Reform Act 1969, s 8—Children Act
　　　　1989, s 100. **W (a minor) (medical treatment), Re** [1992] **4** 627, CA.
　Persons who lack mental capacity. *See* **Mental health** (Persons who lack capacity—Inability to make
　　decisions—Medical treatment).
　Ward of court—
　　Jurisdiction of court. *See* **Ward of court** (Jurisdiction—Medical treatment).
　Withdrawal of treatment—
　　Insensate patient—
　　　Patient in persistent vegetative state with no hope of recovery—Patient requiring operation if he
　　　　was to continue to be fed—Medical opinion that in patient's best interests for no action to be
　　　　taken and that he be allowed to die naturally—Hospital applying as matter of urgency for
　　　　declaration authorising no action to be taken—Official Solicitor not having time to explore
　　　　facts—Judge granting declaration—Whether judge right to grant declaration—Whether court
　　　　should necessarily accept medical opinion as to patient's best interests—Whether in patient's
　　　　best interests to take no action and allow patient to die. **Frenchay Healthcare NHS Trust v S**
　　　　[1994] **2** 403, CA.
　　　Patient in persistent vegetative state with no hope of recovery—Whether in patient's best interests
　　　　not to prolong his life—Whether continuance of medical care would confer any benefit on
　　　　patient—Whether lawful to withdraw life support and allow patient to die. **Airedale NHS Trust v
　　　　Bland** [1993] **1** 821, Fam D, CA & HL.
　　　Patient in persistent vegetative state without hope of recovery—Whether withdrawal of artificial
　　　　nutrition and hydration from patients in permanent vegetative state infringing right of
　　　　life—Whether withdrawal or continuance of such nutrition constituting inhuman or degrading
　　　　treatment—Human Rights Act 1998, Sch 1, arts 2, 3. **NHS Trust A v M** [2001] **1** 801, Fam D.
　　　Patient in persistent vegetative state—Practice—Sanction of High Court judge required before
　　　　treatment terminated—Confirmation of diagnosis—Form of application—Parties to application—
　　　　Evidence—Views of patient—Consultation with Official Solicitor. **Practice Note** [1996] **4** 766, .
　　Judicial visits—
　　　Contested application to Court of Protection for declaration that not in best interests of patient to
　　　　continue artificial ventilation—Judge visiting patient before judgment—Proper approach to
　　　　judicial visits—Guidance. **AH (Court of Protection: judicial visits), Re** [2022] **2** 909n, CA.
　　Minor. *See* **Minor** (Medical treatment—Withdrawal of treatment).

MEDICAL TREATMENT (cont)—
    Withdrawal of treatment (cont)—
        Patient in minimally conscious state—
            Withdrawal of artificial nutrition and hydration—Application to determine whether withdrawal of treatment in best interests of patient—Application brought under statutory provisions applicable to deprivation of liberty—Non-means tested legal aid available for applications on deprivation of liberty but not for applications on medical treatment—Whether application brought under appropriate statutory provision—Mental Capacity Act 2005, ss 16, 21A. **Briggs (incapacitated person), Re** [2018] **2** 990, CA.
        Patient in minimally conscious state with no hope of recovery—
            Whether clinically assisted nutrition and hydration should be withdrawn from patient—Whether legal proceedings necessary where parties agreeing on withdrawal of clinically assisted nutrition and hydration—Whether patient's mother to be appointed litigation friend—Human Rights Act 1998, Sch 1, Pt I, art 2—Mental Capacity Act 2005, ss 5, 21A—Court of Protection Rules 2007, SI 2007/1744, Practice Direction 9E. **M (incapacitated person: withdrawal of treatment), Re** [2018] **2** 551, COP.
        Patient in state of prolonged disorder of consciousness—
            Withdrawal of clinically assisted nutrition and hydration—Whether legal proceedings necessary where parties agreeing on withdrawal—Human Rights Act 1998, Sch 1, Pt I—Mental Capacity Act 2005. **NHS Trust v Y (Intensive Care Society intervening)** [2019] **1** 95, SC.
    Persons who lack mental capacity. *See* **Mental health** (Persons who lack capacity—Inability to make decisions—Medical treatment—Withholding of treatment).
    Refusal to allocate funds—
        Judicial review—Minor aged 10 years—Minor suffering from acute myeloid leukaemia—Doctors in charge of minor's treatment advising that no further treatment could usefully be administered—Medical experts retained by minor's father advising that further treatment worthwhile—Health authority refusing to fund further treatment—Whether decision lawful—Role of courts in determining whether health authority's decision lawful. **R v Cambridge Health Authority, ex p B** [1995] **2** 129, CA.

MEDICINAL PRODUCTS
    Freedom of movement—
        European Community. *See* **European Union** (Freedom of movement—Goods—Medicinal products).
    Supply of medicinal product not of nature or quality specified in prescription—
        Level of fine. *See* **Sentence** (Fine—Not-for-profit organisation carrying out work for public benefit).

MEDICINE
    Drugs. *See* **Drugs**.
    Importation—
        Product licence. *See* Product licence, *below*.
    National Health Service—
        Generally. *See* **National Health Service**.
        Prescription—
            Supply not sale of medicine. *See* **National Health Service** (Pharmaceutical services).
    Patent—
        Licence—
            Compulsory licence. *See* **Patent** (Licence—Compulsory licence—Medicine).
    Prescription only medicine—
        Sale by retail. *See* Sale by retail—Prescription only medicine, *below*.
    Product licence—
        Generic product—
            Essential similarity—Demonstrating essential similarity—Use of originator's confidential information—Originator supplying details of research and testing in development of drug when applying to licensing authority for product licence—Generic companies subsequently applying for product licence for similar generic product—Whether licensing authority entitled to use information supplied by originator when considering subsequent applications for product licences—EEC Council Directive 65/65, art 4(8)(a)(iii)—EC Council Directive 87/21. **Smith Kline & French Laboratories Ltd v Licensing Authority (Generics (UK) Ltd intervening)** [1989] **1** 578, HL.
            Essential similarity—Demonstrating essential similarity—Use of originator's confidential information—Originator supplying details of research and testing in development of drug when applying to licensing authority for product licence—Originator granted product licence for similar generic product by reference to original product—Generic company subsequently applying for product licence for similar generic product by reference to originator's first product—Whether confidential information provided originator in course of product licencing procedure for second generic product to be accorded further period of protection—Council Directive (EEC) 65/65, art 4(8)(a). **R (on the application of Novartis Pharmaceuticals UK Ltd) v Licensing Authority (Case C-106/01)** [2005] **EC** 192, ECJ.
    Importation—
        Parallel imports—Licence for parallel import of medicine from other EEC states—Infringement of trade mark rights—Secretary of State granting licences for parallel imports—Imported medicines infringing applicants' trade marks—Whether infringement of trade marks a relevant consideration in decision to issue parallel import licence—Medicines Act 1968, ss 19(1), 20. **Wellcome Foundation Ltd v Secretary of State for Social Services** [1988] **2** 684, HL.
    Sale by retail—
        Disclosure of composition—
            Article consisting of or comprising a substance recommended as a medicine—Appropriate designation on label or container—Tonic (beverage)—'Hall's Wine'—Whether 'substance recommended as medicine'—Pharmacy and Medicines Act 1941, ss 11(1), 17(1). **Nairne and Nairne v Smith (Stephen) & Co Ltd and Pharmaceutical Society of GB** [1942] **2** 510, KBD.

MEDICINE (cont)—
    Sale by retail (cont)—
        Disclosure of composition (cont)—
            Article consisting of or comprising a substance recommended as a medicine—Sale by retail chemist—Article so sold prepacked and labelled when supplies purchased wholesale—Label purporting to state the active constituents of the article—Omission of one of the active constituents on label—Charge of selling a medicine without disclosing its composition—Pharmacy and Medicines Act 1941, ss 11(1)(a), 13(1)(a). **Pharmaceutical Society of GB v Heppells (1932) Ltd** [1945] **2** 33, KBD.
            Article consisting of or comprising substance recommended as a medicine—Sale by unauthorised persons—Substance known to public as supposed remedy for particular ailment—Name of substance and dosage given on label, but no reference to any ailment—Pharmacy and Medicines Act 1941, ss 11(1), 12(1), (5), 17. **Potter & Clarke Ltd v Pharmaceutical Society of GB** [1947] **1** 802, CA.
        Prescription only medicine—
            Offence—Sale or supply otherwise than in accordance with prescription—Whether offence of strict liability—Whether prosecution must prove mens rea where prescription only medicine supplied in accordance with forged prescription—Medicines Act 1968, s 58(2)(a). **Pharmaceutical Society of GB v Storkwain Ltd** [1985] **3** 4, QBD; [1986] **2** 635, HL.
        Shop—
            Stall in market place—Movable structure but retail business carried on at same place in market five days a week—Whether stall was a shop for the purposes of Shops Act 1912, s 19(1) and Pharmacy and Medicines Act 1941, ss 12(1), 17(1). **Greenwood v Whelan** [1967] **1** 294, QBD.
            Stall in market place—Movable structure but retail business carried on at same place in market twice a week—Whether stall a 'shop'—Shops Act 1912, s 19—Pharmacy Act 1941, s 12(2). **Summers v Roberts** [1943] **2** 757, KBD.
    Sale of drugs. *See* **Drugs** (Sale of drugs).

MEETING
    Building society. *See* **Building society** (Meeting).
    Committee meeting—
        Presence of non-member—
            Participation—Validity of decision reached by meeting. **Leary v National Union of Vehicle Builders** [1970] **2** 713, Ch D.
    Company. *See* **Company** (Meeting).
    Creditors'—
        Bankruptcy. *See* **Bankruptcy** (Meeting of creditors).
    Disorder—
        Unincorporated association. *See* **Unincorporated association** (Meeting—Disorder).
    Local authority—
        Admission of public. *See* **Public authority** (Meeting—Admission of public).
        Generally. *See* **Local government** (Meeting).
    Local government. *See* **Local government** (Meeting).
    Student meeting on university premises—
        Freedom of speech. *See* **University** (Freedom of speech—Duty to ensure freedom of speech—Student meeting on university premises).

MEMBER OF PARLIAMENT
    Privilege—
        Libel—
            Qualified privilege. *See* **Libel and slander** (Qualified privilege—Duty and interest—Member of Parliament).

MEMBER STATES
    European Community—
        Application of treaty provisions in. *See* **European Union** (Treaty provisions—Direct application in member states).
        Enforceability of directives by individuals. *See* **European Union** (Directives—Direct application in member states—Circumstances in which rights conferred by directives enforceable by individuals in courts of member states).

MEMBERS' CLUB
    False trade description—
        No application to transactions with members. *See* **Trade description** (False or misleading indication as to price—Scope of offence).
    Generally. *See* **Club** (Members' club).

MEMORANDUM
    Contract—
        Generally. *See* **Contract** (Memorandum or note).
    Guarantee—
        Note or memorandum in writing. *See* **Guarantee** (Note or memorandum of agreement in writing).
    Moneylender's contract. *See* **Moneylender** (Memorandum).
    Sale of goods. *See* **Sale of goods** (Note or memorandum in writing).
    Sale of land—
        Auction—
            Signing of memorandum by auctioneer on behalf of vendor—Whether auctioneer owes duty to purchaser to sign on behalf of vendor. *See* **Auctioneer** (Memorandum—Signature—Duty to purchaser—Auctioneer signing on behalf of vendor).
        Evidence of contract. *See* **Sale of land** (Memorandum of contract).

MEMORANDUM OF ASSOCIATION
    See **Company** (Memorandum of association).

MEMORIAL

Churchyard. *See* **Ecclesiastical law** (Memorial).
Plaque—
  Faculty for memorial plaque within churchyard to person not buried there. *See* **Ecclesiastical law**
  (Memorial—Memorial plaque within churchyard to person not buried there).
Tablet within church—
  Ecclesiastical law. *See* **Ecclesiastical law** (Monument—Memorial tablet within church).
Trust for memorial to testator—
  Validity. *See* **Trust and trustee** (Purpose—Memorial to testator—Public non-charitable trust).

MEMORY

Expert evidence of childhood memory—
  Admissibility—
    Criminal proceedings involving sexual offences. *See* **Criminal evidence** (Expert evidence—
    Admissibility—Sexual offences—Expert evidence on childhood memory).

MEN AND WOMEN

Discrimination—
  Employment—
    Discrimination against a man. *See* **Employment** (Discrimination against a man).
    Discrimination against a woman. *See* **Employment** (Discrimination against a woman).
    Generally. *See* **Employment** (Discrimination).
  Generally. *See* **Sex discrimination**.
Equality of treatment—
  Employment. *See* **Employment** (Equality of treatment of men and women).
  European Community. *See* **European Union** (Equality of treatment of men and women).
  Pension. *See* **Pension** (Equality of treatment of men and women).

MENACES

Demanding money with menaces. *See* **Criminal law** (Demanding money with menaces).

MENS REA

Absolute liability. *See* **Criminal law** (Absolute liability).
Accessory before the fact. *See* **Criminal law** (Accessory before the fact—Knowledge).
Aiding and abetting. *See* **Criminal law** (Aiding and abetting—Mens rea).
Conspiracy. *See* **Criminal law** (Conspiracy—Mens rea).
Dangerous driving. *See* **Road traffic** (Dangerous driving—Mens rea).
Statute—
  Construction of statute. *See* **Statute** (Offence—Mens rea).

MENTAL CAPACITY

Generally. *See* **Mental health** (Persons who lack capacity).
Gift inter vivos—
  Capacity to make gift. *See* **Gift** (Inter vivos gift—Mental capacity to make gift).
Persons who lack capacity. *See* **Mental health** (Persons who lack capacity).

MENTAL DEFECTIVE

See **Mental health** (Mental defective).

MENTAL DISTRESS

Damages—
  Breach of contract. *See* **Contract** (Damages for breach—Mental distress).

MENTAL HEALTH

Abortion—
  Mentally handicapped person—
    Consent. *See* **Abortion** (Legal abortion—Consent—Mentally handicapped person).
Action—
  Action on behalf of patient—
    Generally. *See* Legal proceedings brought on behalf of patient, *below*.
  Leave to bring—
    Refusal of leave to bring action for acts done in pursuance of Mental Health Act
    1959—Appeal—Whether leave required. *See* **Court of Appeal** (Interlocutory appeal—Leave to
    appeal—Necessity—Appeal against order refusing leave to bring proceedings in respect of acts
    done in pursuance of Mental Health Act 1959).
Administration of estate—
  Intestacy—
    Person incapable of managing his own affairs. *See* **Intestacy** (Grant of administration—Person
    incapable of managing his own affairs).
Admission of patient to hospital—
  Admission for assessment—
    Remand to hospital for report on accused's mental condition for purpose of obtaining evidence for
    use at trial by prosecution—Whether judge entitled to do so—Mental Health Act 1983, s 35. **R (on
    the application of M) v Kingston Crown Court (Crown Prosecution Service, interested party)**
    [2015] 4 1026, DC.
    Right to liberty and security—Patient admitted for assessment—Patient not competent to avail
    herself of statutory provision allowing for application for discharge—Whether breach of right to
    liberty and security—Mental Health Act 1983, ss 2, 66—Human Rights Act 1998, Sch 1, Pt I,
    art 5(4). **R (on the application of H) v Secretary of State for Health** [2005] **3** 468, CA; [2005] **4** 1311,
    HL.

MENTAL HEALTH (cont)—
  Admission of patient to hospital (cont)—
    Admission for assessment (cont)—
      Right to liberty and security—Patient admitted for assessment—Statutory period for detention for
        assessment—Hospital applying for court order relating to nearest relative before end of statutory
        period—Effect of application extending statutory period until application finally disposed
        of—Whether breach of right to liberty and security—Mental Health Act 1983, s 29(4)—Human
        Rights Act 1998, Sch 1, Pt I, art 5(4). **R (on the application of H) v Secretary of State for Health**
        [2005] **3** 468, CA; [2005] **4** 1311, HL.
    Admission for treatment—
      Application—Approved mental health professional making application for admission of patient to
        hospital acting in mistaken belief that patient's nearest relative having no objection to
        admission—Hospital trust acting on application—Admission subsequently found to be
        unlawful—Whether detention unlawful from outset—Mental Health Act 1983, ss 3, 6(3), 11(4)(a),
        12(2), 139(1)—Human Rights Act 1998, Sch 1, Pt I, art 5. **M (by his litigation friend TM) v Hackney**
        London BC [2011] **3** 529, CA.
      Application—Nearest relative—Consent to application—Consent of nearest relative not obtained in
        proper form—Effect on patient's admission—Whether patient's admission unlawful—Mental
        Health Act 1983, ss 6(3), 11(4), 26. **R v South Western Hospital Managers, ex p M** [1994] **1** 161,
        QBD.
      Application—Nearest relative—Consent to application—Unreasonable objection to application—
        Application for substitution of acting nearest relative—Evidence in support of application—
        Respondent to application required to be told substance of medical report—Whether
        communication of report to respondent's solicitor sufficient compliance with requirement—
        Whether non-compliance with statutory form of report vitiating proceedings—Mental Health Act
        1959, s 52(3)(c)—CCR Ord 46, r 18(5). **B v B (mental health patient)** [1979] **3** 494, CA.
      Application—Nearest relative—Consent to application—Unreasonable objection to application—
        Application for substitution of acting nearest relative—Unreasonable objection—Test of
        unreasonableness—What reasonable person would do in all the circumstances—Mental Health
        Act 1959, ss 27(1), (2), 52(3)(c). **W v L (mental health patient)** [1973] **3** 884, CA.
      Application—Nearest relative—Father objecting to application—Social worker consulting mother as
        to compulsory admission of adult son—Father being nearest relative—Application not made in
        proper form—Effect on patient's admission—Whether patient's admission unlawful—Whether
        writ of habeas corpus appropriate remedy—Mental Health Act 1983, ss 3, 6(3), 11(4). **S-C (mental**
        patient: habeas corpus), Re [1996] **1** 532, CA.
      Compulsory admission—Application—Grounds for admission—Discharge—Entitlement to
        discharge—Application stating that patient suffering from mental illness—Patient 40 years of
        age—Mental health review tribunal reclassifying patient as suffering from psycholpathic
        disorder—Psychopathic disorder in person over 21 not a ground for admission—Tribunal
        concluding that necessary in patient's interests and for protection of others that she should
        continue to be detained—Whether patient entitled to be discharged—Mental Health Act 1959,
        ss 26, 123. **V E (mental health patient), Re** [1972] **3** 373, QBD.
      Compulsory admission—Compulsory admission after conditional discharge of patient by mental
        health review tribunal—Whether hospital entitled to compulsorily detain conditionally discharged
        restricted patient—Whether conditionally discharged patient only capable of compulsory
        detention in hospital if recalled to hospital by Secretary of State—Mental Health Act 1983, ss 3,
        37, 41, 42, 73. **R v North West London Mental Health NHS Trust, ex p Stewart** [1997] **4** 871, CA.
      Compulsory admission—Compulsory admission after discharge of patient by mental health review
        tribunal—Whether patient can be compulsorily admitted to hospital for treatment after mental
        health review tribunal ordering patient's discharge—Whether change of circumstances necessary
        since tribunal's decision—Mental Health Act 1983, ss 2, 3. **R (on the application of Von**
        Brandenburg (aka Hanley)) v East London and the City Mental Health NHS Trust [2004] **1** 400, HL.
      Compulsory admission—Compulsory admission after discharge of patient by mental health review
        tribunal—Whether patient can be compulsorily admitted to hospital for treatment immediately
        following discharge by mental health review tribunal—Whether doctors, social workers and
        hospital managers required to exercise independent judgment irrespective of tribunal's
        decision—Whether change of circumstances necessary since tribunal's decision—Mental Health
        Act 1983, ss 3, 6(3), 13, 72(1). **R v South Western Hospital Managers, ex p M** [1994] **1** 161, QBD.
      Detention of patient in hospital—Absence without leave from hospital—Whether patient unlawfully
        at large—Whether patient deemed to have escaped from legal custody—Mental Health Act 1983,
        ss 6(2), 17, 18(1)—Police and Criminal Evidence Act 1984, s 17(1)(d). **D'Souza v DPP** [1992] **4** 545,
        HL.
      Detention of patient in hospital—Out-patient refusing medication—Out-patient detained in hospital
        for one night and next day granted leave of absence subject to conditions—Whether 'admission
        for treatment' restricted to treatment in hospital as an in-patient—Whether doctor entitled to
        detain patient with a view to attaching conditions to him being an out-patient—Whether patient's
        liberty infringed—Mental Health Act 1983, ss 3, 20(3), (4)(c). **R v Hallstrom, ex p W (No 2)**
        [1986] **2** 306, QBD.
      Detention of patient in hospital—Whether hospital entitled to detain patient admitted on informal
        basis under common law doctrine of necessity—Mental Health Act 1983, s 131. **R v Bournewood**
        Community and Mental Health NHS Trust, ex p L (Secretary of State for Health intervening)
        [1998] **3** 289, HL.
      Leave of absence—Revocation of leave of absence—Patient ceasing to be liable to be recalled to
        hospital if on leave of absence continuously for six months—Whether leave of absence can be
        revoked to prevent patient being continuously on leave of absence for six months—Mental Health
        Act 1983, s 17(4), (5). **R v Hallstrom, ex p W (No 2)** [1986] **2** 306, QBD.
      Mental illness—Meaning—Patient suffering from psychopathic disorder—Patient over
        21—Expression 'mental illness' not having special medical significance—Ordinary words of
        English language to be construed as ordinary sensible people would construe them—Whether
        finding of psychopathic disorder precluding finding that patient suffering from mental
        illness—Mental Health Act 1959, ss 4(4), 26(2). **W v L (mental health patient)** [1973] **3** 884, CA.

MENTAL HEALTH (cont)—
  Admission of patient to hospital (cont)—
    Application—
      Nearest relative—Unreasonable objection to application—Application for substitution of acting
        nearest relative—Whether county court having jurisdiction to make ex parte or interim order for
        substitution—County Courts Act 1984, s 38—Mental Health Act 1983, s 29. **R v Central London
        County Court, ex p London** [1999] **3** 991, CA.
    Jurisdiction of mental health review tribunal. *See* Mental health review tribunal—Jurisdiction—
      Admission to hospital, *below.*
  After-care—
    Hospital order. *See* Hospital order—Person admitted to hospital in pursuance of hospital
      order—After-care services, *below.*
  Asylum officer—
    Dismissal—
      Notice—Supperannuation—Return of payments—Lunacy Act 1890, s 276—Asylums Officers'
        Superannuation Act 1909. **McManus v Bowes** [1937] **3** 227, CA.
    Superannuation—
      Disputes to be settled by Minister of Health—Jurisdiction of Minister to determine whether
        employee 'established'—Asylums Officers' Superannuation Act 1909, ss 1, 15, 17. **R v Minister of
        Health, ex p Staffordshire Mental Hospitals Board** [1942] **1** 551, CA.
  Bankruptcy—
    Jurisdiction to make receiving order in respect of person of unsound mind. *See* **Bankruptcy** (Person of
      unsound mind—Jurisdiction to make receiving order).
  Capacity. *See* Persons who lack capacity, *below.*
  Civil proceedings in respect of acts purporting to be done in pursuance of statute. *See* Protection in respect
    of acts done in pursuance of statute, *below.*
  Community treatment order—
    Release of compulsorily detained patient into community by responsible clinician—
      Conditions attached to order—Whether responsible clinician could impose conditions in
        community treatment order amounting to deprivation of liberty—Mental Health Act 1983, ss 17A,
        17B—Human Rights Act 1998, Sch 1, Pt I, art 5. **Welsh Ministers v PJ** [2019] **2** 766, SC.
  Compulsory admission of patient to hospital. *See* Admission of patient to hospital—Admission for
    treatment—Compulsory admission, *above.*
  Consent—
    Admission to hospital—
      Consent of nearest relative to admission of patient to hospital. *See* Admission of patient to
        hospital—Admission for treatment—Application—Nearest relative—Consent to application,
        above.
    Consent to medical treatment—
      Adult patient. *See* **Medical treatment** (Adult patient—Consent to treatment).
  Court of Protection—
    Appeal to Court of Appeal. *See* **Court of Appeal** (Jurisdiction—Appeal from Court of Protection).
    Contempt of court. *See* Persons who lack capacity—Declaration—Contempt of court, *below.*
    Fee for management of patient's property. *See* Patient's property—Fee for management of property,
      below.
    Jurisdiction—
      Decision. *See* **Court of Appeal** (Jurisdiction—Appeal from Court of Protection).
      Incapacity—Paternity—Best interests—Individual believ-ing herself to be daughter of person
        suffering from dementia—Solicitor appointed as deputy for property and affairs—Person having
        refused to provide sample for DNA purposes before onset of dementia—Whether in best interests
        of person to provide DNA sample—Whether court having jurisdiction notwithstanding absence of
        specific application within proceedings putting parentage in issue - Family Law Reform Act 1969,
        ss 20(1), 21(4)—Family Law Act 1986, s 55A. **LG v DK** [2012] **2** 115, COP.
      Property and affairs of patient—Patient—Person incapable of managing property or affairs—
        Jurisdiction only extending to person of whose incapacity a judge is satisfied—Mental Health Act
        1959, ss 4, 101, 103(1). **S (FG) (mental health patient), Re** [1973] **1** 273, Ch D.
    Jurisdiction. *See* Court of Protection—Jurisdiction, *below.*
    Practice—
      Application to the court—Matters requiring formal application—Trustee Act 1925, ss 36(9),
        54—Variation of Trusts Act 1958, s 1(3)—Mental Health Act 1983, ss 96(1)(d)(e)(k), 99—Court of
        Protection Rules 1984, r 6, Form B. **Practice Direction** [1985] **1** 642, Ct of Protection.
      Application to the court—Notification of hearing of application—Application by receiver for
        exercise of patient's power of appointment—Persons to be notified of receiver's
        application—Receiver seeking to refrain from notifying persons affected by exercise of power
        because it would exacerbate family dissension—Whether persons adversely affected by
        application required to be notified of it—Mental Health Act 1983, s 96(1)(k)—Court of Protection
        Rules 1984, rr 18, 37. **B (Court of Protection: notice of proceedings), Re** [1987] **2** 475, Ch D.
      Appointment of new trustee in place of trustee of unsound mind—Form of originating summons.
        Practice Direction [1957] **1** 581, Ct of Protection.
      Costs—Solicitors' costs—Agreeing costs without taxation—Discretion to direct taxation of costs.
        Practice Direction [1991] **1** 438, Ct of Protection.
      Costs—Solicitors' costs—Fixed costs. **Practice Direction** [1983] **3** 192, Ct of Protection.
      Costs—Solicitors' costs—Fixed costs—Extension of categories of work—Certifying accounts.
        Practice Direction [1985] **1** 884, Ct of Protection.
      Enduring powers of attorney. *See* **Power of attorney** (Enduring power of attorney—Court of
        Protection).
      Evidence—Evidence by affidavit. **Practice Direction** [1984] **3** 128, Ct of Protection.
      Execution of will. *See* Patient's property—Execution of will, *below.*
      Personal welfare deputies—Appointment—Guidance—Mental Capacity Act 2005, s 16. **Lawson, Re**
        [2020] **2** 120, COP.

MENTAL HEALTH (cont)—
   Court of Protection (cont)—
      Practice (cont)—
         Power to make declarations and decisions—Case management—Dispute as to provision or funding of care between care provider and person lacking capacity or his/her family—Whether court to perform 'best-interest' analysis—Mental Capacity Act 2005, ss 15, 16. **N v A Clinical Commissioning Group** [2017] 3 719, SC.
         Power to make declarations and decisions—Anticipatory and contingent declarations. *See* **Medical treatment** (Adult patient—Consent to treatment—Pregnancy).
         Right to liberty and security—Deprivation of liberty—Streamlined process to deal with increase in cases—Guidance—Human Rights Act 1998, Sch 1, Pt I, art 5. **X (deprivation of liberty), Re** [2015] 2 1154, Ct of Protection.
         Right to liberty and security—Deprivation of liberty—Streamlined process to deal with increase in cases—Guidance—Human Rights Act 1998, Sch 1, Pt I, arts 5, 6—Court of Protection Rules 2007, SI 2007/1744, r 141(1). **X (deprivation of liberty) (No 2), Re** [2015] 2 1165, Ct of Protection.
         Right to respect for private and family life—Freedom of expression—Person lacking capacity having public profile due to musical talents—Family members applying for order to act as his deputies—Media applying for order enabling designated representatives to attend hearing—Whether 'good reason' existing for making order sought by media—Whether media's right to receive and impart information only engaged once 'good reason' established—Human Rights Act 1998, Sch 1, Pt I, arts 8, 10—Mental Capacity Act 2005—Court of Protection Rules 2007, SI 2007/1744, rr 90-93. **Independent News and Media Ltd v A (by his litigation friend, the Official Solicitor)** [2010] 3 32, CA.
         Right to respect for private and family life—Freedom of expression—Publication of information in relation to proceedings—Mother of person lacking capacity (M) seeking reporting restriction order restraining publication of information likely to lead to identification of M, family members and care staff—Approach to be followed by Court of Protection considering such an application—Human Rights Act 1998, Sch 1, Pt I, arts 6, 8, 10—Mental Capacity Act 2005—Court of Protection Rules 2007, SI 2007/1744, rr 90, 92. **W (by her litigation friend B) v M (by her litigation friend, the Official Solicitor)** [2011] 4 1295, COP.
         Title of proceedings under Trustee Act 1925. **Practice Note** [1959] 3 320, Ct of Protection.
         Variation of trusts. *See* Patient's property—Variation of trusts—Court of Protection, *below*.
   Criminal law—
      Defence of automatism. *See* **Criminal law** (Automatism).
      Defence of insanity. *See* **Criminal law** (Insanity).
   Detained patient—
      Conditional discharge—
         Deprivation of liberty—Applications for authorisations relating to care plans involving deprivation of liberty—Whether deprivation of liberty of conditionally discharged patients lawful—Mental Health Act 1983, ss 17, 42, 73(2)—Human Rights Act 1998, Sch 1, Pt I, art 5—Mental Capacity Act 2005, Sch 1A. **Birmingham City Council v SR** [2020] 3 438, COP.
         Hospital order coupled with restriction order—Patient applying for conditional discharge—Whether conditional discharge possible on conditions amounting to detention or deprivation of liberty—Mental Health Act 1983, ss 42, 73—Human Rights Act 1998, Sch 1, Pt I, art 5. **Secretary of State for Justice v MM** [2019] 2 749, SC.
   Detention by police—
      Leave to bring proceedings. *See* Protection in respect of acts done in pursuance of statute, *below*.
   Detention order. *See* Mental defective—Detention order, *below*.
   Diminished responsibility—
      Defence to murder charge. *See* **Criminal law** (Murder—Diminished responsibility).
   Discharge of restricted patient—
      Mental health review tribunal. *See* Mental health review tribunal—Discharge of restricted patient, *below*.
   Divorce—
      Insanity as ground for. *See* **Divorce** (Insanity).
      Mental disorder—
         Cruelty. *See* **Divorce** (Cruelty—Mental disorder).
   Education—
      Statutory duty of local education authority to ascertain what children mentally defective. *See* **Education** (Local education authority—Statutory duty to ascertain what children mentally defective).
   Enduring power of attorney. *See* **Power of attorney** (Enduring power of attorney).
   Epilepsy—
      Criminal law—
         Defence—Insanity or automatism. *See* **Criminal law** (Automatism—Insanity distinguished—Epileptic seizure).
   Forfeiture clause—
      Settlement. *See* Patient's property—Settlement—Forfeiture clause, *below*.
   Homes for mentally disordered persons. *See* Registration of residential homes for mentally disordered persons, *below*.
   Hospital order—
      Criminal proceedings. *See* **Sentence** (Hospital order).
      Person admitted to hospital in pursuance of hospital order—
         After-care services—After-care by local social services authority for the area in which person resident or sent on discharge—Person resident in area A made subject to hospital order—Person conditionally discharged into area B—Person recalled to hospital and conditionally discharged again to area B—Whether person resident in area A or area B—Mental Health Act 1983, s 117(3). **R (on the application of Wiltshire Council) v Hertfordshire CC** [2015] 2 518, CA.
   Legal proceedings brought on behalf of patient—
      Function of next friend in legal proceedings—
         Waiver of right of appeal—Whether patient bound by next friend's waiver of right of appeal. **E (mental health patient), Re** [1985] 1 609, CA.

MENTAL HEALTH (cont)—

Legal proceedings brought on behalf of patient (cont)—

Ownership of papers in legal proceedings—

Action brought on behalf of patient by Official Solicitor as next friend—Patient's father wishing to appeal against judgment—Whether papers 'property' of patient—Whether father as new next friend entitled to possession of papers in existence as result of proceedings—Whether Official Solicitor entitled to withhold papers—Mental Health Act 1983, ss 95, 96, 112. **E (mental health patient), Re** [1985] **1** 609, CA.

Lord Chancellor's visitor—

Report—

Cross-examination of visitor on report—Application by patient for restoration to management of own affairs—Medical visitor's report disclosed to parties—Views expressed by visitor conflicting with affidavits filed by patient's medical witnesses—Application by patient for leave to issue witness summons requiring attendance of visitor to give oral evidence—Power of court to procure attendance of visitor—Power of court to allow cross-examination of visitor on report—Circumstances in which visitor's report should be disclosed—Mental Health Act 1959, s 109(5). **WLW, Re** [1972] **2** 433, Ch D.

Medical treatment—

Patient. *See* Patient—Medical treatment, *below*.

Mental capacity—

Lack of capacity. *See* Persons who lack capacity, *below*.

Mental defective—

Detention order—

Continuation of order—Report to Board of Control by visitors recommending continuation of order—Certiorari to quash report. **R v Statutory Visitors to St Lawrence's Hospital, Caterham, ex p Pritchard** [1953] **2** 766, QBD.

Continuation of order—Whether imperative that continuance order should be made on date of expiry of previous order—Mental Deficiency Act 1913, ss 10, 11. **R v Board of Control, ex p Winterflood** [1938] **2** 463, CA.

Detention order in case of indictable offence—Jurisdiction to make order if satisfied on medical evidence that the offender was a defective—Evidence by prison doctor that offender was a feeble-minded person within the Act—Whether justices had jurisdiction to make order for detention in institution for defectives—Mental Deficiency Act 1913, s 8(1). **Sage, Re** [1958] **1** 477, QBD.

Grant of leave of absence—

Factors to be considered—Past history of patient—Inquiry by officers and committee—Negligence. **Holgate v Lancashire Mental Hospitals Board, Gill and Robertson** [1937] **4** 19, Assizes.

Local authority responsible for providing accommodation—

Council of county or county borough in which defective resided—Person certified while in a general hospital—Place of residence immediately before admission to certified institution—Whether general hospital 'place of residence immediately before'—Liability for maintenace—Mental Deficiency Act 1913, ss 43(1), 71—Mental Deficiency Act 1927, s 9. **London CC v Ipswich County BC** [1939] **2** 660, KBD.

Person committed to certified institution following conviction of criminal offence—Determination of his place of residence prior to conviction—Mental Deficiency Act 1913, s 44. **London CC v Cambridgeshire CC** [1936] **2** 15, KBD.

Order for transfer to institution for defectives—

Date of expiration of order—Power of Board of Control to make a general order for extension—Mental Deficiency Act 1913, s 11. **R v Board of Control (Secretary), ex p Abdul Kayum** [1948] **2** 853, KBD.

Reception order on ground of being found neglected—

Found neglected—Mental Deficiency Act 1913, s 2(1)(b)(i), as amended by Mental Deficiency Act 1927, s 2. **R v Board of Control, ex p Rutty** [1956] **1** 769, QBD.

Removal to place of safety of person found neglected by person reasonably believing him to be defective—

Found neglected—Order for removal of defective to place of safety—Whether defective 'found neglected'—Subsequent order for detention made by judicial authority in 1925 on petition of one parent—Other parent abroad—Whether other parent's consent in writing necessary—Mental Deficiency Act 1913, ss 6 (3), proviso (a), 15(1). **Richardson v London CC** [1957] **2** 330, CA.

Mental disorder—

Mentally disordered person—

Liability in tort. *See* **Tort** (Mentally disordered person).

Person believed to be suffering from mental disorder being ill-treated, neglected, kept otherwise than under proper control, or living alone being unable to care for himself—

Warrant to remove person to place of safety—Warrant specifying named professionals to accompany constable—Named professionals not accompanying constable on execution of warrant—Whether execution lawful—Mental Health Act 1983, s 135. **Ward v Metropolitan Police Comr** [2005] **3** 1013, HL.

Person not suffering from mental disorder by reason only of sexual deviancy—

Sexual deviancy—Whether 'sexual deviancy' including mere tendency to deviation—Mental Health Act 1983, s 1(3). **R v Mental Health Review Tribunal, ex p Clatworthy** [1985] **3** 699, QBD.

Mental health review tribunal—

Contempt of court—

Whether mental health review tribunal a 'court'. *See* **Contempt of court** (Publications concerning legal proceedings—Court—Inferior court—Mental health review tribunal).

MENTAL HEALTH (cont)—
Mental health review tribunal (cont)—
Decision—
Reasons for decision—Adequacy of reasons—Decision not to direct discharge of patient—Tribunal
stating that they were not satisfied as to specified matters—Tribunal not indicating whether they
considered patient was suffering from mental disorder or whether patient's detention was
necessary for protection of others—Tribunal merely stating they were not satisfied patient's
improved behaviour within hospital would be maintained in community—Whether tribunal's
reasons adequate—Whether patient and doctor in charge of treatment entitled to know why
application for discharge not succeeding—Mental Health Act 1983, s 72(1)(b)(i), (ii). **R v Mental
Health Review Tribunal, ex p Pickering** [1986] **1** 99, QBD.

Reasons for decision—Adequacy of reasons—Decision not to direct discharge of patient—
Tribunal's reasons merely a traverse of circumstance in which discharge could be
contemplated—Tribunal not giving reasons for not accepting evidence of medical witnesses—
Tribunal relying on patient's sexual deviancy and diagnoses while in hospital—Whether tribunal's
reasons adequate—Mental Health Act 1983, s 1(3). **R v Mental Health Review Tribunal, ex p
Clatworthy** [1985] **3** 699, QBD.

Reasons for decision—Adequacy of reasons—Decision not to direct discharge of patient—Whether
tribunal required to give reasons if it refuses to direct discharge of patient because it is not
satisfied as to specified matters—Mental Health Act 1983, ss 72(1), (4), 73(1), (2)—Mental Health
Review Tribunal Rules 1983, r 23(2). **Bone v Mental Health Review Tribunal** [1985] **3** 330, QBD.

Discharge of restricted patient—
Applicant applying for discharge of restriction order—Medical evidence—Statute requiring tribunal
to discharge patient if not satisfied as to statutory criteria—Applicable standard of proof—Mental
Health Act 1983, ss 72, 73. **R (on the application of N) v Mental Health Review Tribunal (Northern
Region)** [2006] **4** 194, CA.

Applicant applying for discharge of restriction order—Mental health review tribunal refusing
application, but recommending transfer to a regional secure unit—Applicant's responsible
medical officer making proposal for trial leave—Secretary of State referring matter to Advisory
Board on Restricted Patients—Board finding that applicant still dangerous and refusing to
support proposal—Secretary of State refusing consent to proposal—Applicant not invited to
make representations—Further information not disclosed to applicant—Whether Secretary of
State's decisions to refer proposal to board and to act on its recommendation
irrational—Whether Secretary of State bound to follow recommendations of tribunal—Mental
Health Act 1983, s 73(1). **R v Secretary of State for the Home Dept, ex p Harry** [1998] **3** 360, QBD.

Conditional discharge—Patient—Applicant subject to restriction order applying for absolute
discharge from restriction order—Mental Health review tribunal making finding that applicant not
suffering from any mental disorder but refusing to grant absolute discharge—Whether applicant
a 'patient' if tribunal making finding that he was not suffering from any mental
disorder—Whether applicant entitled to absolute discharge—Mental Health Act 1983, ss 41(1), 73,
145(1). **R v Merseyside Mental Health Review Tribunal, ex p K** [1990] **1** 694, CA.

Discharge—Conditional discharge. See Mental health review tribunal—Discharge of restricted
patient—Conditional discharge, *above*.

Discharge—Decision directing conditional discharge of restricted patient—Direction imposing
condition on conditional discharge requiring patient to continue to reside in a hospital—
Condition deferring conditional discharge until arrangements could be made for admission of
patient to another hospital—Whether condition valid—Mental Health Act 1983, ss 72(1), 73(1), (2),
(4), (7). **Secretary of State for the Home Dept v Mental Health Review Tribunal for the Mersey
Regional Health Authority** [1986] **3** 233, QBD.

Discharge—Decision directing conditional discharge of restricted patient—Direction subject to
arrangements being made for support of patient—District health authority declining to supply
psychiatric supervision for patient—Whether health authority under duty to supply psychiatric
supervision for patient if released into community—Mental Health Act 1983, s 117. **R v Ealing
District Health Authority, ex p Fox** [1993] **3** 170, QBD.

Discharge—Decision directing conditional discharge of restricted patient—Direction subject to
arrangements being made for support of patient—District health authority failing to find
psychiatrist to supervise patient—Patient continuing to be detained—Power of tribunal to
reconsider decision ordering conditional discharge—Mental Health Act 1983, s 73. **R (on the
application of H) v Secretary of State for the Home Dept** [2004] **1** 412, HL.

Discharge—Decision directing conditional discharge of restricted patient—Direction subject to
arrangements being made for support of patient—District health authority failing to find
psychiatrist to supervise patient—Patient continuing to be detained—Whether continued
detention unlawful—Human Rights Act 1998, Sch 1, Pt I, art 5(1)(e), (4). **R (on the application of H)
v Secretary of State for the Home Dept** [2004] **1** 412, HL.

Discharge—Decision directing conditional discharge of restricted patient—Direction subject to
arrangements being made for support of patient—Whether decision directing conditional
discharge a provisional or final decision—Whether tribunal having power to reconsider
decision—Whether decision vitiated by failure to inform Secretary of State of date of
hearing—Mental Health Act 1983, s 73(2), (7). **Secretary of State for the Home Dept v Oxford
Regional Mental Health Review Tribunal** [1987] **3** 8, HL.

Discharge—Tribunal imposing conditions on release of restricted patient and deferring direction for
discharge until necessary arrangements put in place—Local social services and health authorities
denying responsibility and failing to make necessary arrangements—Patient continuing to be
detained because of non-implementation of conditions—Whether tribunal having duty to ensure
conditions could be implemented within reasonable time—Mental Health Act 1983, s 73(7). **R v
Mental Health Review Tribunal, ex p Hall** [1999] **3** 132, QBD; [1999] **4** 883, CA.

Jurisdiction—
Admission to hospital—Whether tribunal having jurisdiction to consider validity of admission
giving rise to liability to be detained in hospital—Mental Health Act 1983, s 72. **R v Hallstrom, ex
p W** [1985] **3** 775, CA.

MENTAL HEALTH (cont)—
 Mental health review tribunal (cont)—
  Proceedings—
   Irregularity—Failure to send documents and notice of hearing to Secretary of State in case of application by restricted patient—Effect of failure—Whether failure an irregularity—Whether failure an irregularity which be cured—Whether failure amounting to breach of rules of natural justice—Whether Secretary of State entitled to apply for judicial review—Mental Health Tribunal Rules 1983, rr 12(1), 20, 28. **Secretary of State for the Home Dept v Oxford Regional Mental Health Review Tribunal** [1986] **3** 239, CA.
   Publication of information in relation to proceedings—Restricted patient applying for release from detention—Whether publication of fact that patient had applied for release, date of hearing and result of proceedings prohibited—Whether publication of information would be contempt—Whether patient having sufficient interest to bring proceedings to restrain publication—Administration of Justice Act 1960, s 12(1)(b)—Mental Health Review Tribunal Rules 1983, r 21(5). **Pickering v Liverpool Daily Post and Echo Newspapers plc** [1991] **1** 622, HL.
   Publication of information in relation to proceedings—Tribunal sitting in private unless patient requesting hearing in public and tribunal satisfied public hearing not contrary to patient's interests—Tribunal granting patient's application for public hearing—Whether tribunal empowered to limit publication of information from public hearing—Whether tribunal having discretion to refuse public hearing if conditions satisfied—Mental Health Review Tribunal Rules 1983, SI 1983/942, r 21(1), (5). **R (on the application of Mersey Care NHS Trust) v Mental Health Review Tribunal (Brady and anor, interested parties)** [2005] **2** 820, QBD.
  Right to liberty and security—
   Admission for assessment—Admission for treatment—Applications to tribunals—References to tribunals by Secretary of State—Patient admitted for assessment—Patient applying for review of detention for assessment—Application treated as being out of time—Patient admitted for treatment—Patient having right to apply for review of detention for treatment—Secretary of State declining patient's request for discretionary reference to tribunal—Whether decision lawful—Whether breach of right to liberty and security—Mental Health Act 1983, ss 2, 3, 66(1)(a), (b), 67(1)—Human Rights Act 1998, Sch 1, Pt I, art 5(4). **R (on the application of Modaresi) v Secretary of State for Health** [2013] **4** 318, SC.
 Mental hospital—
  Recall of patient to hospital. *See* Patient—Recall to hospital, *below.*
  Staff—
   Pay—Emergency during war—Nurse required to stand by for duty if necessary—Overtime—'Subject to standing orders, regulations and rules'—Whether nurse entitled to overtime pay in respect of periods when standing by. **Farmer v London CC** [1943] **2** 32, CA.
 Nearest relative to patient. *See* Patient—Nearest relative, *below.*
 Nullity of marriage—
  Grounds for nullity. *See* **Nullity** (Insanity).
 Patient—
  Admission to hospital. *See* Admission of patient to hospital, *above.*
  After-care services—
   After-care by local social services authority for the area in which person resident or sent on discharge—Patient voluntarily admitted to hospital and then discharged into the community—Patient placed at residential college in area A—Patient subsequently voluntarily admitted to hospital in area B—Residential college withdrawing placement and licence to occupy accommodation—Whether patient resident in area A or area B—Mental Health Act 1983, s 117. **R (on the application of Sunderland City Council) v South Tyneside Council** [2013] 1 394, CA.
   Duty to provide after-care services—Leave of absence from hospital—Patient granted leave of absence to go on day trips in custody of hospital staff—Whether mother's travel expenses recoverable—Whether duty to provide after-care services applying—Whether patient ceasing to be detained or leaving hospital—Mental Health Act 1983, ss 17, 117. **R (on the application of CXF (by his mother, his litigation friend)) v Central Bedfordshire Council** [2019] **3** 20, CA.
   Negligence—Health authority—Duty of care. *See* **Negligence** (Duty to take care—Existence of duty—Health authority—Health authority owing statutory duty to provide after-care services for discharged mental patients).
   Whether local authorities having duty or right to charge discharged patients for accommodation provided as after-care services—Mental Health Act 1983, s 117. **R v Manchester City Council, ex p Stennett** [2001] **1** 436, CA; [2002] **4** 124, HL.
  Discharge from hospital—
   Discharge of restricted patient—Mental health review tribunal. *See* Mental health review tribunal—Discharge of restricted patient, *above.*
   Psychopathic disorder—Treatability—Patient suffering from psychopathic disorder detained in hospital—Patient not mentally handicapped or suffering from mental deficiency—Whether patient suffering from psychopathic disorder entitled to be discharged if condition not able to be alleviated by treatment—Mental Health (Scotland) Act 1984, ss 17, 64. **Reid v Secretary of State for Scotland** [1999] **1** 481, HL.
   Psychopathic disorder—Treatability—Patient suffering from psychopathic disorder detained in hospital—Patient refusing to co-operate in appropriate treatment—Alternative treatment unlikely to alleviate or prevent deterioration of patient's condition—Mental health review tribunal refusing discharge—Whether patient suffering from psychopathic disorder entitled to be discharged if condition not able to be alleviated by treatment—Whether patient untreatable if unwilling to co-operate with suitable treatment—Mental Health Act 1983, ss 3, 16(2), 72. **R v Canons Park Mental Health Review Tribunal, ex p A** [1994] **2** 659, CA.
  Evidence—
   Corroboration—Criminal proceedings. *See* **Criminal evidence** (Corroboration—Direction to jury—Mental patient with criminal conviction detained in special hospital).
  Force feeding—
   Consent. *See* **Medical treatment** (Adult patient—Consent to treatment—Force feeding—Mentally ill patient refusing to eat).

MENTAL HEALTH (cont)—
  Patient (cont)—
    Jurisdiction—
      Inherent jurisdiction—Vulnerable adults within definition of 'patients' potentially identifiable by publication of anonymised report commissioned by local authority—Whether inherent jurisdiction of court exercisable to consider whether publication of report could be restrained in relation to welfare of vulnerable adults—Whether publication harmful to vulnerable adults—Whether breach of right to private and family life balanced by public interest and right to freedom of expression—Human Rights Act 1998, Sch 1, Pt I, arts 8, 10. **Local Authority v Health Authority (disclosure: restriction on publication)** [2004] **1** 480, Fam D.
    Legal proceedings involving patient—
      Anonymity order—Patient seeking judicial review of decision of Secretary of State refusing consent for unescorted community leave—Whether anonymity order should be maintained in respect of patient—CPR, r 39.2(4). **R (on the application of C) v Secretary of State for Justice** [2017] **1** 513, SC.
      Appeal—Official Solicitor—Power to appeal to Court of Appeal in cases involving patients—Supreme Court Act 1981, s 90(3)(b)—Mental Health Act 1983—RSC Ord 80, r 1. **Practice Direction** [1989] **1** 764, LC.
      Parties. *See* **Practice** (Parties—Actions and proceedings by and against patients).
    Management of property and affairs of patient—
      Jurisdiction. *See* Patient's property—Jurisdiction—Management of property of patient, *below*.
      Management by judicial authorities—Whether 'affairs of patient' extending to medical treatment or limited to business affairs etc—Mental Health Act 1983, s 93(1). **F v West Berkshire Health Authority (Mental Health Act Commission intervening)** [1989] **2** 545, HL.
      Statutory powers. *See* Patient's property—Statutory powers—Management of property of patient, *below*.
    Medical treatment—
      Mental disorder of patient subject to restriction order specified as mental illness—Consent of patient not required for medical treatment given him for mental disorder from which he was suffering—Patient treated for psychopathic disorder—Whether treatment for psychopathic disorder requiring patient's consent—Mental Health Act 1983, s 63. **R (on the application of B) v Ashworth Hospital Authority** [2003] **4** 319, CA; [2005] **2** 289, HL.
      Patient compulsorily detained in hospital under mental health provisions—Whether detained patient prevented by public policy or legislation from paying for own care and treatment—Mental Health Act 1983—National Health Service Act 2006, s 1. **Coombs v North Dorset NHS Primary Care Trust** [2013] **4** 429, CA.
      Right to refuse consent. *See* **Medical treatment** (Adult patient—Consent to treatment—Right to refuse consent—Mentally ill patient contracting gangrene in leg).
    Nearest relative—
      Removal or change of nearest relative—Compatibility with right to respect for private life—Mental Health Act 1983, ss 26, 29—Human Rights Act 1998, Sch 1, Pt I, art 8. **R (on the application of M) v Secretary of State for Health** [2003] **3** 672n, QBD.
    Property of. *See* Patient's property, *below*.
    Recall to hospital—
      Recall of conditionally discharged patient by Secretary of State—Duty to give reasons for recall—Oral reasons given at time of recall—Failure to give written reasons within three days of recall—Further oral reasons given after 15 days—Whether initial explanation legally sufficient—Whether detention unlawful—Whether damages and/or declaratory relief appropriate—Mental Health Act 1983, s 42(3)—Human Rights Act 1998, s 8, Sch 1, Pt I, art 5(2). **R (on the application of Lee-Hirons) v Secretary of State for Justice** [2017] **3** 97, SC.
      Recall of conditionally discharged patient by Secretary of State—Patient having history of sexual offences and ordered to be detained in secure hospital—Patient conditionally discharged from hospital by mental health review tribunal—Uncontroverted medical evidence that patient not suffering psychopathic disorder—Secretary of State issuing warrant for recall of patient—Whether Secretary of State required to act on medical opinion when exercising power—Whether Secretary of State acting reasonably in issuing warrant for recall of patient—Mental Health Act 1983, ss 42(3), 73(2). **R v Secretary of State for the Home Dept, ex p K** [1990] **3** 562, CA.
    Right to life—
      Patient absconding from hospital and committing suicide—Whether breach of right to life—Obligations of state—General duty—Operational duty—Mental Health Act 1983—Human Rights Act 1998, Sch 1, Pt I, art 2. **Savage v South Essex Partnership NHS Foundation Trust** [2009] **1** 1053, HL.
      Patient admitted to hospital as informal patient for treatment for depressive disorder following suicide attempt—Hospital assessing patient as being at high risk of further suicide attempt—Patient being released on home leave from hospital—Patient committing suicide—Claimants alleging negligence and breach of right to life by health care trust—Negligence claim being settled—Whether operational obligation owing to mentally ill hospital patient not detained under Mental Health Act 1983—Whether 'real and immediate' risk to life of claimant on date of release to home leave of which trust knew or ought to have known and failed to take reasonable steps to avoid—Whether claimants 'victims' within meaning of art 34 of convention—Whether claimants lost victim status because trust made adequate redress and sufficiently acknowledged breach of duty—Human Rights Act 1998 Sch 1, art 2. **Rabone v Pennine Care NHS Foundation Trust** [2012] **2** 381, SC.
    Seclusion—
      Prohibition of inhuman or degrading treatment—Right to respect for private and family life—Code of practice issued by Secretary of State in relation to admission and medical treatment of patients suffering from mental disorder—Code of practice requiring hospitals to have written guidelines on use of seclusion—High security hospital's policy set out in guidelines differing from code of practice—Whether policy unlawful—Whether policy breaching prohibition of inhuman or degrading treatment—Whether policy breaching right to respect for private and family life—Mental Health Act 1983, s 118(1)—Human Rights Act 1998, Sch 1, Pt I, arts 3, 8. **R (on the application of Munjaz) v Mersey Care NHS Trust** [2006] **4** 736, HL.

Suicide—
Right to life. *See* Patient—Right to life, *above*.
Patient's property—
Damages—
Damages awarded in Queen's Bench Division action—Transfer of damages to Court of Protection—Procedure—Provision for transfer in judgment—Form of provision—Similar provision in order approving compromise—Access to award to meet patient's needs—Appointment of receiver—Statutory charge in legally aided cases—Mental Health Act 1983—Legal Aid Act 1988—Court Funds Rules 1987, Pt II—Court Funds Office Form 200. **Practice Direction** [1991] **1** 436, Ct of Protection and QBD.
Enduring power of attorney. *See* **Power of attorney** (Enduring power of attorney).
Execution of will—
Application to judge—Power to order or direct execution of will for patient—Exercise of jurisdiction—Factors to be considered in making will for patient—Procedure on application to master or deputy master of Court of Protection for making of will—Jurisdiction of master or deputy master—Whether execution of will ought to be stayed pending appeal—Whether judge having unfettered discretion on appeal—Mental Health Act 1959, ss 100(4), 102(1)(c), 103(1)(dd) (as amended by the Administration of Justice Act 1969, s 17). **D (J), Re** [1982] **2** 37, Ch D.
Application to judge—Power to order or direct execution of will for patient—Patient suffering from severe mental disability since birth—Patient inheriting substantial fortune—Patient assumed to have been normal decent person acting in accordance with contemporary standards of morality—Nature of bequests and gifts directed by court—Mental Health Act 1983, s 95. **C (a patient), Re** [1991] **3** 866, Ch D.
Application to judge—Practice—Respondents to summons—Persons interested in relief sought by summons—Prospective legatees under existing will—Attorney General—Whether prospective legatees or Attorney General persons 'interested'—Whether prospective legatees or Attorney General should be joined as respondents to summons—Mental Health Act 1959, s 103(1)(dd) (as amended by the Administration of Justice Act 1969, s 17)—Court of Protection Rules 1960 (SI 1960 No 1146), r 12(1). **HMF (mental patient: will), Re** [1975] **2** 795, Ch D.
Application—Parties—Evidence—Evidence of lack of testamentary capacity—Execution and attestation—Evidence of patient's domicile and situation of immovable property affected by proposed will—Mental Health Act 1983, ss 96(4), 97—Court of Protection Rules 1982, r 21. **Practice Direction** [1983] **3** 255, Ct of Protection.
Attestation—Mental Health Act 1959, s 103A, as added by Administration of Justice Act 1969, s 18. **Practice Direction** [1970] **1** 15, Ct of Protection.
By whom statutory powers exercisable—Mental Health Act 1959, s 103(1)(dd)—Administration of Justice Act 1969, s 17(1). **Practice Direction** [1970] **1** 208, Ct of Protection.
Execution pursuant to order of master of Court of Protection—Execution in accordance with statutory requirements—Whether High Court having jurisdiction to discharge order and set aside will—Mental Health Act 1959, ss 103 (1)(dd) 103 (1), (3). **Davey (decd), Re** [1980] **3** 342, Ch D.
Order for execution of will—Respondents to order—Discretion not to make interested person a respondent—Matters to be considered—Urgency of case—Elderly patient in poor health—Patient married in suspicious circumstances to man many years younger—Patient executing will shortly before marriage—Will automatically revoked by marriage—Statutory will executed in same terms as earlier will without notice to husband—Husband not made respondent to application for statutory will—Whether Court of Protection having discretion not to make husband a respondent—Whether urgency of case sufficient reason for not making husband a respondent—Whether Court of Protection may take into account opportunity for husband to make subsequent application under family provision legislation—Mental Health Act 1959, s 103A(1)(dd)—Court of Protection Rules 1960 (SI 1960 No 1146), rr 12, 21(2). **Davey (decd), Re** [1980] **3** 342, Ch D.
Powers to make decisions and appoint deputies. *See* Persons who lack capacity—Principles —Best interests—Powers to make decisions and appoint deputies, *below*.
Fee for management of property—
Percentage fee calculated by reference to clear income at patient's disposal—Clear income—Calculation—Elderly patient—Court of Protection exercising its authority on three occasions only—Constant attendance allowance, age, allowance and sums received gross before deduction by tax included in clear income—No deduction made for court fees and solicitors' fees—Whether those items should be included in 'clear income'—Whether fee ought to be remitted—Court of Protection Rules 1960 (SI 1960 No 1146), rr 87, 94. **N (decd), Re** [1977] **2** 687, CA.
Functions of judge—
Doing or securing the doing of all such things as appear necessary and expedient for the benefit of the patient—Benefit of patient—Meaning—Mental Health Act 1959, s 102(1)(a)(b). **W, Re** [1970] **2** 502, Ct of Protection.
Doing or securing the doing of all such things as appear necessary and expedient for the maintenance or other benefit of patient's family—Meaning of 'family'—Whether nephews and nieces included—Mental Health Act 1959, s 102(1)(b). **DML, Re** [1965] **2** 129, Ch D.
Exercise of functions—Requirements of patient—Meaning—Mental Health Act 1959, s 102(2). **W, Re** [1970] **2** 502, Ct of Protection.
Gift—
Application to court for order etc—Application normally to be heard and determined by master—Parties—Evidence—Mental Health Act 1983, s 96(1)(d)—Court of Protection Rules 1982, rr 21, 45. **Practice Direction** [1983] **3** 255, Ct of Protection.
Sanctioning of gift to private independent mental hospital. *See* **Equity** (Undue influence—Presumption of undue influence—Mental hospital and patient—Gift by patient to private independent mental hospital—Sanctioning of gift by Court of Protection).
Jurisdiction—
Management of property of patient—Beneficiary of unsound mind absolutely entitled—Trustees seeking to retain capital—Summonses heard in Chancery Division—Whether within Chancery jurisdiction—Discretion. **K's Settlement Trusts, Re** [1969] **1** 194, Ch D.

MENTAL HEALTH (cont)—
   Patient's property (cont)—
      Receiver—

         Appointment of Public Trustee as receiver—Certain applications to be referred to Court of Protection—Form of order of appointment—Dealings with land—Execution of documents—Inquiries, applications and correspondence—Trustee Act 1925, ss 36(9), 54—Variation of Trusts Act 1958, s 1(3)—Mental Health Act 1983, ss 96(1)(d), (e)(i), (k), 98, 99, 100, 104—Enduring Powers of Attorney Act 1985,Public Trustee and Administration of Funds Act 1986. **Practice Direction** [1987] **1** 403, Ct of Protection.

         Discharge of receiver—Discharge where judge considers it expedient—Expedient—Whether meaning expedient for patient or expedient in interests of all persons connected with receivership—Mental Health Act 1959, s 105(2). **N (decd), Re** [1977] **2** 687, CA.

         Settlement. *See* Patient's property—Settlement—Receiver, *below.*

      Settlement—

         Costs—Taxation—Costs of successful applicants, interested parties and receiver, when respondent qua receiver, should be taxed on common fund basis—Costs of Official Solicitor, appearing for patient, should be taxed on solicitor and own client basis—Supreme Court Costs Rules 1959, r 28—Court of Protection Rules 1960 (SI 1960 No 1146), r 98. **CEFD, Re** [1963] **1** 685, Ct of Protection.

         Distribution of capital of trust fund during patient's lifetime—Power to vary settlement during patient's lifetime—Settlement on trusts to pay income to patient's sister for her life and thereafter to hold capital and income on trusts for her children and remoter issue—Settlement incorporating statutory power of advancement—Court varying settlement by partitioning trust fund between sister and remaindermen—Variation extending statutory power of advancement to whole of beneficiary's expectant or presumptive share—Whether court having power during patient's lifetime to authorise distribution of capital to beneficiaries—Whether court's power to vary trusts merely power to vary trusts of property comprised in settlement at date of the variation—Mental Health Act 1959, s 103(1), (4). **CWHT, Re** [1978] **1** 210, Ch D.

         Forfeiture clause—Forfeiture in event of income to which patient entitled becoming charged in favour of another—Receiver of life tenant's property appointed—Percentage charged on lunatic's estate—Whether patient forfeiting interest under settlement. **Westby's Settlement, Re** [1950] **1** 479, CA.

         Illegitimate son—Recognition of moral obligation for care of son, and inclusion of son in father's family home—Patient not of testamentary capacity and without chance of mental improvement—Patient had made no will—His next of kin were cousins who had not visited him—Proposed revocable settlement of patient's property on illegitimate son and son's family approved in principle—Mental Health Act 1959, ss 102(1)(c), 103(1)(d). **TB, Re** [1966] **3** 509, Ct of Protection.

         Persons for whom patient might be expected to provide—Assumptions regarding circumstances—Circumstances assumed to be those of patient while incapacitated, save that he was assumed sane and reasonably advised—Patient maintained in state hospital at small annual expense—No prospect of recovery—No will made and intestacy certain—Voluntary settlement on nephews and niece and their families, and a sum for family chauffeur who had looked after patient—Mental Health Act 1959, ss 102(1)(c), 103(1)(d). **WJGL, Re** [1965] **3** 865, Ch D.

         Persons for whom patient might be expected to provide—Funds settled by patient's father on her for life and after her death for remaindermen—Remaindermen were patient's nephews and nieces—Patient obtained £35,000 capital from partition of settled funds under sanction of court—Proposed provision by spending £35,000 in purchase of an annuity and out of surplus income of patient augmented by annuity paying premiums on 22 policies, one for benefit of each remainderman—No evidence any of remaindermen in special need—No evidence patient felt any special affection for them—Whether court would sanction proposed provision—Mental Health Act 1959, ss 102(1)(c), 103(1)(d). **DML, Re** [1965] **2** 129, Ch D.

         Receiver—Receiver settling patient's property in form of settlement bringing about liability to inheritance tax—Rule of equity requiring trustee to take into account all relevant considerations and not take into account any irrelevant considerations when exercising power—Whether settlement to be set aside—Whether rule of equity applying to receiver. **Pitt v Holt** [2010] **2** 774, Ch D; [2011] **2** 450, CA; [2013] **3** 429, SC.

         Reservation of power of revocation to patient—Law of Property Act 1925, s 171(5). **CWM, Re** [1951] **2** 707, CA.

         Resettlement of settled property—Object to provide for poorer members of wealthy patient's family—Patient a bachelor aged 48 incapable of managing affairs but not insane—Fiscal aspect—Primogeniture where no mansion house or estate, but valuable town property—Patient capable of marrying—Discretionary settlement to confer power of revocation on patient's behalf during first 15 years—Mental Health Act 1959, s 103(1)(d), (j), (2). **RHC, Re** [1963] **1** 524, Ct of Protection.

         Restraint from squandering property—Form of settlement—Law of Property Act 1925, s 171(1)(5)(7). **C, Re** [1960] **1** 393, Ct of Protection.

   Statutory powers—

         Management of property of patient—Settlement or gift of any property of patient for maintenance or benefit of patient's family, or for making provision for other persons—By whom statutory powers exercisable—Mental Health Act 1959, ss 102(1)(b)(c), 103 (1)(d). **Practice Direction** [1960] **3** 447, .

   Surrender of property under order of the court—

         War savings certificates—Nomination—Succession to fund in court on death of lunatic—Lunacy Act 1890, s 123(1). **Stillwell, Re** [1936] **1** 757, Ch D.

   Trustee—

         Powers of trustee. *See* Patient's property—Settlement—Receiver, *above.*

MENTAL HEALTH (cont)—
  Patient's property (cont)—
    Variation of trusts—
      Benefit of patient—Form of application to court—Patient's income substantially in excess of her requirements—Arrangement proposed whereby patient should give up, for the benefit of adopted children, a protected life interest and a contingent interest in remainder—Proposed arrangement one that patient would make if she were capable of managing her affairs—Approval of Chancery judge necessary on behalf of adult patient—Whether proposed arrangement for benefit of patient, although financially to her detriment—Variation of Trusts Act 1958, s 1(3). **CL, Re** [1968] **1** 1104, Ct of Protection.
      Court of Protection—Application to determine question whether proposed arrangement beneficial to person of unsound mind—Practice under Variation of Trusts Act 1958, s 1(3). **Practice Note** [1959] **3** 897, Ct of Protection.
    Will—
      Drafting—Reasons for disposing of patient's property in manner intended—Mental Health Act 1959, s 103A(5) (as added by Administration of Justice Act 1969, s 18). **Practice Direction** [1970] **1** 15, Ct of Protection.
      Execution. *See* Patient's property—Execution of will, *above*.
      Sealing—Mental Health Act 1959, s 103A(1) (as added by the Administration of Justice Act 1969, s 18). **Practice Direction** [1970] **1** 15, Ct of Protection.
  Person of unsound mind—
    Contract—
      Capacity of person of unsound mind to make contract. *See* **Contract** (Parties—Capacity—Insanity).
    Trustee—
      Appointment of new trustee in place of trustee of unsound mind. *See* **Trust and trustee** (Appointment of new trustee—Trustee of unsound mind—Appointment in place of person of unsound mind).
  Persons who lack capacity—
    Compromise of action. *See* **Practice** (Compromise of action—Approval of court—Compromise by or on behalf of child or protected party).
    Declaration—
      Contempt of court—Court of Protection making best interests declaration in relation to individual—Individual's relatives acting contrary to declaration by removing her from jurisdiction—Whether contempt of court to act contrary to declaration—Correct approach to declarations of the Court of Protection—Mental Capacity Act 2005, ss 15, 16, 48. **M (incapacitated adult) (best interests declaration: potential contempt), Re** [2016] **1** 71, Ct of Protection.
    Deprivation of liberty—
      Community treatment order. *See* Community treatment order, *above*.
      Conditional discharge of patient. *See* Detained patient—Conditional discharge, *above*.
      Placements in small group or domestic setting authorised by court as being in best interests of person concerned—No objection or lack of compliance by persons subject to placements—Whether deprivation of liberty—Test for deprivation of liberty—Human Rights Act 1998, Sch 1, Pt I, art 5—Mental Capacity Act 2005. **P v Cheshire West and Chester Council** [2014] **2** 585, SC.
      Restriction on deprivation of liberty—Powers to make decisions and appoint deputies—Persons ineligible to be deprived of liberty—Mental Capacity Act 2005, ss 4A, 16, 16A, Sch 1A. **W Primary Care Trust v TB** [2010] **2** 331, Ct of Protection.
      Right to liberty and security—Right to private and family life—Son in respite care at father's request—Son subsequently being admitted to residential support unit—Son kept in support unit against his and his father's wishes—Local authority authorising deprivation of liberty requests—Whether authority acting unlawfully—Human Rights Act 1998, Sch 1, Pt I, arts 5, 8—Mental Capacity Act 2005, Pt 8, Sch A1. **Hillingdon London BC v Neary (by his litigation friend the Official Solicitor)** [2011] **4** 584, COP.
      Streamlined process to deal with increase in cases—Guidance—Human Rights Act 1998, Sch 1, Pt I, art 5. **X (deprivation of liberty), Re** [2015] **2** 1154, Ct of Protection.
      Streamlined process to deal with increase in cases—Guidance—Human Rights Act 1998, Sch 1, Pt I, arts 5, 6—Court of Protection Rules 2007, SI 2007/1744, r 141(1). **X (deprivation of liberty) (No 2), Re** [2015] **2** 1165, Ct of Protection.
      Withdrawal of medical treatment. *See* **Medical treatment** (Withdrawal of treatment).
    Ill-treatment or neglect—
      Criminal law. *See* **Criminal law** (Ill-treatment or neglect of person lacking capacity).
    Inability to make decisions—
      Medical treatment—Withdrawal of artificial nutrition and hydration—Best interests of patient—Patient in minimally conscious state—Patient having some awareness of self and environment but being totally dependent on others for care—Application for declaration allowing doctors to lawfully discontinue and withhold all life-sustaining treatment—Whether in patient's best interests for artificial nutrition and hydration to be withdrawn—Guidelines for future applications—Mental Capacity Act 2005, ss 4, 24-26. **W (by her litigation friend B) v M (by her litigation friend the Official Solicitor)** [2012] **1** 1313, Fam D.
      Medical treatment—Withholding of treatment—Best interests of patient—Futile treatment, overly burdensome to patient or where no prospect of recovery—How 'futility' of treatment to be judged—Mental Capacity Act 2005, s 1(5). **Aintree University Hospitals NHS Foundation Trust v James** [2013] **4** 67, CA; [2014] **1** 573, SC.
      Payment for necessary goods or services—Statutory provision requiring person lacking contractual capacity to pay reasonable price for necessary goods or services supplied to him—Whether provision applying where services provided under arrangement between service provider and local authority exercising statutory duty to provide accommodation—National Assistance Act 1948, s 26—Mental Capacity Act 2005, s 7. **Aster Healthcare Ltd v Estate of Shafi** [2014] **3** 283, QBD; [2016] **2** 316, CA.
    Loss of mental capacity—
      Solicitor's retainer. *See* **Solicitor** (Retainer—Termination of retainer—Mental incapacity of client).
    Marriage, validity of. *See* **Marriage** (Validity—Declaration—Person lacking capacity marrying abroad).

MENTAL HEALTH (cont)—
    Persons who lack capacity (cont)—
        Mental capacity—
            Inability to make decisions—Capacity to consent to sexual relations—Test for determining
                capacity—Mental Capacity Act 2005, ss 2, 3. **D Borough Council v AB** [2011] **3** 435, COP.
            Inability to make decisions—Capacity to consent to sexual relations -Test for determining
                capacity—Whether test person-specific—Extent of judicial investigation required—Mental
                Capacity Act 2005, ss 3(1)(c), 27. **IM v LM** [2014] **3** 491, CA.
            Inability to make decisions—Capacity to engage in sexual relations—Test for determining
                capacity—Whether 'information relevant to the decision' including understanding that consent of
                other person required—Mental Capacity Act 2005, s 3. **A Local Authority v JB (by his litigation
                friend, the Official Solicitor)** [2021] **1** 1103, CA.
            Inability to make decisions—Capacity to engage in sexual relations—Test for determining
                capacity—Whether 'information relevant to the decision' including understanding that consent of
                other person required—Mental Capacity Act 2005, ss 1, 2, 3, 27. **A Local Authority v JB (by his
                litigation friend, the Official Solicitor)** [2022] **3** 697, SC.
            Inability to make decisions—Vulnerable adults—Capacity to make decisions as to contraception—
                Test of capacity—Mental Capacity Act 2005, ss 2, 3. **Local Authority (A) v A (capacity:
                contraception)** [2011] **3** 706, COP.
        Principles —
            Best interests—Police—Severely autistic boy becoming fixated by water at swimming pool—Police
                taking action without consulting carers causing boy to jump into pool—Police removing him from
                pool, forcibly restraining and detaining him in police van—Whether practicable and appropriate
                for police to consult carers before taking action—Whether police acting in best interests of
                boy—Mental Health Act 2005, ss 4, 5. **ZH v Metropolitan Police Comr** [2013] **3** 113, CA.
            Best interests—Powers to make decisions and appoint deputies—Property and affairs—Execution
                of will for person lacking capacity—Mental Capacity Act 2005, ss 1, 4, 16. **P, Re** [2009] **2** 1198, COP.
            Best interests—Powers to make decisions and appoint deputies—Property and affairs—Statutory
                will—Directing execution of statutory will—Mental Capacity Act 2005, s 4. **D (statutory will), Re**
                [2011] **1** 859, COP.
            Best interests—Powers to make decisions and appoint deputies—Property and affairs—Statutory
                will—Mental Capacity Act 2005, ss 1, 4. **M, Re** [2010] **3** 682, Ct of Protection.
        Right not to be subject to torture or to inhuman or degrading treatment or punishment—
            Police removing autistic boy from swimming pool, forcibly restraining and detaining him in police
                van—Whether treatment crossing threshold of severity to amount to breach of Convention
                right—Human Rights Act 1998, Sch 1, Pt 1, art 3. **ZH v Metropolitan Police Comr** [2013] **3** 113, CA.
        Right to liberty and security—
            Local authority removing person lacking capacity from placement—Sister seeking declarations that
                person lacking capacity detained unlawfully by local authority—Interim declaration being made
                that it was in his best interests to remain at local authority placement—Judge subsequently
                finding that interim declaration had rendered previously unlawful detention lawful—Whether
                judge erring as to effect of interim declaration—Application of deprivation of liberty
                safeguards—Whether necessary for threshold conditions to be satisfied before best interests
                assessment undertaken—Human Rights Act 1998, Sch 1, Pt I, art 5—Mental Capacity Act 2005. **G
                v E (by his litigation friend, the Official Solicitor)** [2010] **4** 579, CA.
            Police forcibly restraining and detaining autistic boy in police van—Whether breach of Convention
                right—Human Rights Act 1998, Sch 1, Pt 1, art 5. **ZH v Metropolitan Police Comr** [2013] **3** 113, CA.
    Power of attorney. *See* **Power of attorney**.
    Prisoner—
        Life sentence—
            Release on licence. *See* **Prison** (Release on licence—Life sentence—Mandatory or discretionary life
                sentence—Detention in mental hospital).
        Prison hospital—
            Negligence—Duty to take care. *See* **Negligence** (Duty to take care—Prison hospital—Mentally ill
                prisoner).
        Transfer to hospital—
            Secretary of State directing transfer of prisoner to secure hospital—Responsible medical officer
                notifying Secretary of State that patient not treatable—Secretary of State directing patient's
                return to prison—Role and duties of responsible medical officer and Secretary of State under
                procedure—Mental Health Act 1983, s 50(1). **R (on the application of Morley) v Nottinghamshire
                Health Care NHS Trust** [2003] **1** 784, CA.
    Protection in respect of acts done in pursuance of statute—
        Extent of protection—
            Judicial review—Person not liable to 'civil … proceedings' in respect of act done in pursuance of
                statute—Whether protection extending to exclude application for judicial review—Mental Health
                Act 1983, s 139(1). **R v Hallstrom, ex p W** [1985] **3** 775, CA.
        Leave to bring proceedings—
            Applicant to satisfy judge of substantial ground for contention that proposed defendant has acted
                in bad faith or without reasonable care—Application for leave to bring action against duly
                authorised officer-Removal to mental hospital—Whether reasonable ground for believing that
                person was of unsound mind—Lunacy Act 1890, ss 14(1), 20 (as amended by National Health
                Service Act 1946, s 50, Sch 9, Part 1), 330(2) (as amended by Mental Treatment Act 1930, s 16(1).
                Buxton v Jayne (Intended action), Re [1960] **2** 688, CA.
            Applicant to satisfy judge of substantial ground for contention that proposed defendant has acted
                in bad faith or without reasonable cause—Substantial ground—Lunacy Act 1890, s 330(2) (as
                substituted by Mental Treatment Act 1930, s 16(1)). **Richardson v London CC** [1957] **2** 330, CA.
            Civil proceedings brought without leave of High Court—Whether proceedings a nullity—Mental
                Health Act 1983, s 139(2). **Seal v Chief Constable of South Wales Police** [2007] **4** 177, HL.
            Onus on applicant—Applicant to satisfy judge of substantial ground for contention that proposed
                defendant has acted in bad faith or without reasonable care—Duty of judge to consider all
                evidence including that adduced on behalf of proposed defendant—Not enough for applicant to
                show conflict of evidence—Duty of judge to consider inherent probabilities of matter—Mental
                Health Act 1959, s 141(2). **Carter v Comr of Police for the Metropolis** [1975] **2** 33, CA.

MENTAL HEALTH (cont)—
  Protection in respect of acts done in pursuance of statute (cont)—
    Leave to bring proceedings (cont)—
      Patient in hospital—Act of nurse exercising duty of controlling patients—Act of nurse in exercise of duty not expressly provided for in statute—Patient alleging assault by nurse—Whether alleged assault done or purportedly done 'in pursuance of' statute—Whether leave required to bring criminal proceedings—Mental Health Act 1959, s 141(1), (2). **Pountney v Griffiths** [1975] **2** 881, HL.
      Test appropriate to grant of leave—Test appropriate to grant of leave—Whether applicant required to establish prima facie case against respondent—Mental Health Act 1983, s 139. **Winch v Jones** [1985] **3** 97, CA.
      Wrongful detention—Application for leave to bring action for wrongful detention—Mental Treatment Act 1930, s 16(2). **Frost, Re an intended action by** [1936] **2** 182, CA.
  Rate-aided patient—
    Maintenance—
      Old age pension—Public assistance officer appointed receiver—Form of order—Widows', Orphans' and Old Age Contributory Pensions Act 1936, s 21(1), Sch III. **TRM, Re** [1938] **4** 194, CA.
  Registration of residential homes for mentally disordered persons—
    Conditions of registration—
      Appeal—Whether refusal to re-register—Whether right of appeal to magistrates—National Assistance Act 1948, s 37(3)—Mental Health Act 1959, s 20. **Retarded Children's Aid Society Ltd v Barnet London Borough** [1969] **1** 300, QBD.
  Right to liberty and security—
    Mental health review tribunal. See Mental health review tribunal—Right to liberty and security, *above*.
    Persons who lack capacity—
      Deprivation of liberty. See Persons who lack capacity—Deprivation of liberty—Right to liberty and security, *above*.
  Right to respect for private and family life. See **Human rights** (Right to respect for private and family life—Mental health).
  Settlement—
    Patient's property. See Patient's property—Settlement, *above*.
  Sexual intercourse with patient. See **Criminal law** (Sexual intercourse—Mental defective).
  Statutory powers—
    Management of patient's property. See Patient's property—Statutory powers, *above*.
  Sterilisation—
    Mentally handicapped person—
      Consent to abortion and sterilisation. See **Abortion** (Legal abortion—Consent—Mentally handicapped person—Consent to abortion and sterilisation).
      Consent to sterilisation—Generally. See **Sterilisation** (Mentally handicapped person—Consent).
      Declaration as to lawfulness of proposed treatment—Procedure. See **Declaration** (Procedure—Declaration as to lawfulness of proposed conduct—Proposed medical treatment—Medical treatment of person unable to consent thereto—Mentally handicapped person—Sterilisation).
  Succession on intestacy. See **Intestacy** (Succession—Person of unsound mind).
  Tort—
    Mentally disordered person—
      Liability. See **Tort** (Mentally disordered person).
  Trustee of unsound mind. See Court of Protection—Practice—Appointment of new trustee in place of trustee of unsound mind, *above*.
  Vulnerable adults—
    Inherent jurisdiction of High Court—
      Human rights infringement. See **Human rights** (Infringement of human rights—Inherent jurisdiction of High Court in respect of vulnerable adults).
    Mental capacity. See Persons who lack capacity—Mental capacity—Inability to make decisions—Vulnerable adults, *above*.
  Will. See Patient's property—Will, *above*.
  Witness—
    Mentally handicapped witness—
      Competence as witness. See **Criminal evidence** (Competence as witness—Mentally handicapped witness).

MENTAL HEALTH OFFICER
  National Health Service—
    Superannuation. See **National Health Service** (Superannuation of officers—Determination of questions by Minister of Health—Mental health officer).

MENTAL HEALTH REVIEW TRIBUNAL
  See **Mental health** (Mental health review tribunal).

MENTAL HOSPITAL
  See **Mental health** (Mental hospital).

MENTAL INJURY
  Assault occasioning bodily harm. See **Criminal law** (Assault—Occasioning bodily harm—Mental injury).

MENTAL SHOCK
  Damages for. See **Damages** (Remoteness of damage—Mental shock).
  Negligence—
    Damages. See **Damages** (Personal injury—Nervous shock).
    Rescue work—
      Duty to rescuer. See **Negligence** (Duty to take care—Rescuer—Mental shock).

MERCANTILE AGENT
  See **Agent** (Mercantile agent).

MERCANTILE COURT
Bristol—
> Practice. *See* **Practice** (Commercial cases—Bristol—Bristol Mercantile Court).
>
> Costs management scheme. *See* **Costs** (Assessment—Detailed assessment—Mercantile Courts and Technology and Construction Courts costs management scheme).

MERCANTILE LIST
Cardiff and Chester—
> Practice. *See* **Practice** (Queen's Bench Division—Mercantile lists—Cardiff and Chester).

Leeds and Newcastle upon Tyne—
> Practice. *See* **Practice** (Queen's Bench Division—Mercantile lists—Leeds and Newcastle upon Tyne).

MERCANTILE MARINE
War pension. *See* **War pension** (Mercantile marine).

MERCHANT SHIP
Crew member—
> Right of master at common law to arrest and confine. *See* **False imprisonment** (Merchant ship—Member of crew—Right of master, at common law, to arrest and confine).

MERCHANT SHIPPING
See **Shipping**.

MERCHANTABLE QUALITY
Sale of goods—
> Implied term as to merchantable quality. *See* **Sale of goods** (Implied condition as to merchantable quality).

MERCY
Prerogative of mercy—
> Bahamas. *See* **Bahamas** (Prerogative of mercy).
>
> Judicial review—
> > Availability of remedy. *See* **Judicial review** (Availability of remedy—Royal prerogative—Prerogative of mercy).

MERGER
Assets—
> Capital gains tax—
> > Disposal of assets—Value of assets derived from other asset. *See* **Capital gains tax** (Disposal of assets—Value of asset derived from another asset—Merger of assets).

Assignment of life interest to beneficiary contingently entitled to absolute reversionary interest in trust property. *See* **Trust and trustee** (Merger of beneficial interests—Absolute entitlement—Assignment of life interest to beneficiary contingently entitled to absolute reversionary interest in trust property).

Attempt to commit crime—
> Full offence committed. *See* **Criminal law** (Attempt—Full offence committed—Merger).

Cause of action—
> Proceedings in High Court and Employment tribunal for wrongful dismissal—
> > Judgment of Employment tribunal. *See* **Employment tribunal** (Decision of tribunal—Merger—Wrongful dismissal).

City Code on Take-overs and Mergers—
> Construction. *See* **Document** (Construction—City Code on Take-overs and Mergers).

Competition. *See* **Competition** (Merger).

Contract. *See* **Contract** (Merger).

European Community regulations. *See* **European Union** (Rules on competition—Mergers).

Interest—
> Merger of right to interest in judgment for principal sum and interest. *See* **Interest** (Debt—Merger of right to interest in judgment for principal sum and interest).

Life interest, of—
> Estate duty. *See* **Estate duty** (Passing of property—Enlargement of life interest).

Monopolies and Mergers Commission—
> Reference. *See* **Monopolies and mergers**.

Panel on Take-overs and Mergers—
> Judicial review of decision of panel—
> > Whether panel's decisions subject to judicial review. *See* **Judicial review** (Availability of remedy—Take-over Panel).

Registered land—
> Transfer. *See* **Land registration** (Transfer—Merger).

Sale of land—
> Merger of contract in conveyance. *See* **Sale of land** (Merger of contract in conveyance).

Succession to trade for tax purposes. *See* **Income tax** (Succession to trade—Merger).

MESNE PROFITS
Action for forfeiture of lease—
> Interim payments order—
> > Order pending determination of action. *See* **Landlord and tenant** (Forfeiture of lease—Interim payments order—Action for forfeiture and mesne profits—Application by landlord for interim payments order pending determination of action).

Action for possession by landlord—
> Claim for mesne profits. *See* **Landlord and tenant** (Action for possession—Claim for mesne profits).

Administration of deceased's estate—
> Recovery of possession and mesne profits. *See* **Administration of estates** (Sale for purposes of administration—Recovery of possession for purposes of sale—Recovery of mesne profits).

METAL
  Precious metal—
    Hallmarking. *See* **Hallmarking**.

METAL EXCHANGE BROKER
  Fiduciary duty. *See* **Equity** (Fiduciary duty—Metal exchange broker).

METHODIST MINISTER
  Dismissal—
    Complaint of unfair dismissal—
      Whether contract between minister and Church. *See* **Employment** (Contract of service—Incidents of contract—Minister of religion—Methodist minister dismissed by the Church after disciplinary hearing—Minister alleging unfair dismissal).

METRICATION
  Paper sizes—
    Taxation of costs. *See* **Costs** (Taxation—Documents—System of charging—Page basis method).

METROPOLITAN POLICE
  Assault on constable in execution of duty. *See* **Police** (Assault on constable in execution of duty).

MIDDLESEX DEEDS REGISTRY
  Appropriate register—
    Land charge—
      Registration in appropriate register. *See* **Land charge** (Registration—Registration in appropriate register—Middlesex Deeds Registry).

MIDLAND AND OXFORD CIRCUIT
  Commercial cases—
    Practice. *See* **Practice** (Commercial cases—Midland and Oxford Circuit).

MIDWIVES
  Equality of treatment of men and women—
    European Economic Community—
      United Kingdom restriction for men of access to employment as midwives—Validity—Sex Discrimination Act 1975, s 20—EEC Council Directive 76/207, arts 2(2), 9(2). **EC Commission v United Kingdom** [1984] **1** 353, ECJ.

MILEOMETER
  False trade description. *See* **Trade description** (False trade description—Meaning of trade description).

MILITARY
  Detention in non-convention state—
    Human rights. *See* **Human rights** (Right to liberty and security—Military detention in non-convention state).
  Equipment and technology—
    Export control. *See* **Export control** (Control powers—Control orders—Exercise of functions under control orders—Guidance about exercise of functions under control orders—Military equipment and technology).

MILITARY LAND
  Byelaw regulating use of military land—
    Byelaw prejudicially affecting rights of common—
      Validity. *See* **Byelaw** (Validity—Byelaw wider than authorised by statute—Prohibited action within scope of byelaws if byelaws properly made—Military land byelaws prejudicially affecting rights of common).

MILITARY SERVICE
  Compulsory military service—
    European Community—
      Equality of treatment of men and women. *See* **European Union** (Equality of treatment of men and women—Derogation from principle of equal treatment—Compulsory military service).
  Soldier's or mariner's privileged will—
    Actual military service. *See* **Will** (Soldier's or mariner's privileged will—Actual military service).

MILK
  Dairy produce quotas. *See* **Agriculture** (Dairy farming—Dairy produce quotas).
  Generally. *See* **Food and drugs** (Milk).
  Marketing. *See* **Milk marketing**.
  Misrepresentation as to quantity. *See* **Weights and measures** (Misrepresentation as to quantity of goods).

MILK MARKETING
  Complaint—
    Reference to committe of investigation—
      Duty of Minister in relation to complaint—Mandamus—Agricultural Marketing Act 1958, s 19(3). **Padfield v Minister of Agriculture Fisheries and Food** [1968] **1** 694, HL.
  Contract—
    Provision for stop notices on seven days' default by purchaser—
      Subsidiary agreement for non-issue of stop notices on certain conditions—Implied term that stop notices issuable immediately on breach of subsidiary agreement. **Milk Marketing Board v Lawrence** [1939] **3** 483, KBD.

MILK MARKETING (cont)—
    Explanatory leaflet—
        Representation—
            Warranty—Reference to prevention of undercutting. **Milk Marketing Board v C Warman & Sons** [1937] **3** 541, KBD.
    Scheme—
        Costs of operating scheme—
            Method of computing contributions payable by milk producers—Whether costs include loss from sale of surplus milk—Agricultural Marketing Act 1931, s 1(8)—Scottish Milk Marketing Scheme (Approval) Order 1933, s 24(2). **Ferrier v Scottish Milk Marketing Board** [1936] **2** 1131, HL.
        Determination of prices—
            Exceptional quotations—Average of mean prices—Milk Act 1934, s 4. **United Dairies (Wholesale) Ltd v Lemon** [1937] **2** 618, CA.

MILL
    Interference of flow of river to mill by local authority. *See* **Water and watercourses** (Flow of water—Mill deriving water power from river—Interference with flow of water by local authority).

MILL GEARING
    Fencing—
        Factory. *See* **Factory** (Dangerous parts of machinery—Duty to fence—Mill gearing).

MINE
    Application for ancillary rights—
        Jurisdiction of Railway and Canal Commission Court—
            Declaration—Repair of highway—Mines (Working Facilities and Support) Acts 1923 and 1925. **Somerville (T Ryan) & Co Ltd, Re an Application by** [1937] **1** 507, Ry and Can Com.
    Coal mine—
        Generally. *See* **Coal mining**.
        New South Wales. *See* **New South Wales** (Coal mining—Lease).
    Drainage rates—
        Exemption. *See* **Land drainage** (Drainage rates—Exemption—Underground land).
    Flooding—
        Coal mine. *See* **Coal mining** (Flooding).
    Gold mine—
        Tributer's agreement—
            Australia. *See* **Australia** (Mine—Gold mine—Tributer's agreement).
    Grant of working facilities—
        Application—
            Interim order pending determination of status quo—Jurisdiction—Implied or inherent jurisdiction to make interim order—Company working hardstone under lease of quarry—Company applying for right to continue working on expiry of lease—Lessor opposing application—Lease expiring before application heard—Company applying for interim order to continue working pending hearing—Whether court having jurisdiction to make interim order—Mines (Working Facilities and Support) Act 1966, s 1 (as amended by the Mines (Working Facilities and Support) Act 1974, s 1). **King (W J) & Sons Ltd's Application, Re** [1976] **1** 770, CA.
    Isle of Man. *See* **Isle of Man** (Mines and minerals).
    Lease—
        Coal mine—
            New South Wales. *See* **New South Wales** (Coal mining—Lease).
        Settlement. *See* **Settlement** (Mining leases).
    Licence to mine—
        Generally. *See* **Licence** (Mining).
        New South Wales. *See* **New South Wales** (Licence—Mining licence).
    Machinery—
        Maintenace—
            Statutory duty—Coal mine. *See* **Coal mining** (Statutory duty—Machinery—Maintenance of machinery).
    Manager—
        Duty—
            Security of road and working place—Coal mine. *See* **Coal mining** (Statutory duty—Security of road and working place—Duty of manager).
    Mineral licence—
        New Zealand. *See* **New Zealand** (Mine—Mineral licence).
    Minerals—
        Access rights—
            Compensation —Defendants laying pipelines to extract oil beneath claimant's land without obtaining rights of access—Whether actionable trespass—Remedy available to claimant—Mines (Working Facilities and Support) Act 1966, s 8(2). **Bocardo SA v Star Energy UK Onshore Ltd** [2009] **1** 517, Ch D; [2010] **1** 26, CA; [2010] **3** 975, SC.
        Exception and reservation—
            Underground workings—Right to win, work, get and carry away minerals—Whether licensees were, by virtue of the exception, entitled to go on surface of the land in search of gypsum. **General Accident Fire and Life Assurance Corp Ltd v British Gypsum Ltd** [1967] **3** 40, Ch D.
        Reservation—
            Implied term—Right to work implied in reservation—Reservation in respect of petroleum—Meaning of 'petroleum'—Vernacular, not scientific, meaning to be sought—Right of occupier of land to natural gas within the land. **Borys v Canadian Pacific Rly Co** [1953] **1** 451, PC.
            Implied term—Right to work implied in reservation—Reservation in respect of petroleum and natural gas—Grant by Crown in 1880 of right to coal, culm, ironstone and fireclay and 'all other mines and minerals (if any)' in or under certain land—Whether grant including oil and natural gas. **Lonsdale (Earl) v A-G** [1982] **3** 579, Ch D.

MINE (cont)—

Minerals (cont)—

Right to work—

Application for grant of right to work—Power to confer right on any person having an interest in the minerals—Interest—Meaning—Proprietary interest—Gravel and sand quarries—Mining lease—Application by tenant a week before expiry of lease—Tenant having no proprietary interest in minerals when application heard—Mines (Working Facilities and Support) Act 1923, s 1(1). **East Yorkshire Gravel Co Ltd's Application, Re** [1954] **3** 631, Ch D.

Compensation to be paid in respect of right—Brickearth—Applicants obtained planning permission to win and work brick earth in site on respondents' farm—Site allocated to be used for winning and working brick earth by development plan—Application to court for right to work—Agreed grant by way of lease for 21 years—Nature of compensation—Scope of compensation—Compensation should be in form of lump sum with no deduction in respect of tax—Mines (Working Facilities and Support) Act 1923, ss 6(1), 9(1), (2). **Associated Portland Cement Manufacturers Ltd's Application, Re** [1965] **2** 547, Ch D.

Compensation to be paid in respect of right—'Fair and reasonable between a willing grantor and a willing grantee'—Right of electricity board to have condition imposed on mineral undertaker not to withdraw support from pylons on the land—Mines (Working Facilities and Support) Act 1923, ss 8(1), 9(2), 11. **Naylor Benzon Mining Co Ltd, Re** [1950] **1** 518, Ch D.

Compensation to be paid in respect of right—Grant of right subject to compensation of owners—Whether owners could be awarded compensation for apprehended damage. **Beckermet Mining Co Ltd's Application, Re** [1938] **1** 389, Ry and Can Com.

Mining operations—

Town and country planning—

Enforcement notice—Validity. *See* **Town and country planning** (Enforcement notice—Validity—Mining operations).

Mining rent—

Income tax. *See* **Income tax** (Mining rents).

Railway lines above ground at mines—

Safety precautions—

Duty to ensure that if material placed at distance less than three feet from track and employee required to pass it material so placed that employee could pass without risk of exposure to injury—Railway above ground—Bank of spoil placed less than three feet from track—Loose material on route for shunter going in course of duty from one point to another—Route, formerly safe, obstructed and side of bank sloping steeply towards track—Shunter not warned—Shunter preceding train, slipped on bank, fell between railway wagons and was killed—Whether negligence on part of employers of shunter—Whether shunter 'required' in the course of his duty to pass on foot over that material or between it and the line—Whether breach of statutory duty—Whether contributory negligence by shunter—Coal and Other Mines (Sidings) Order 1956, (SI 1956 No 1773), Sch, reg 20. **Smith (formerly Westwood) v National Coal Board** [1967] **2** 593, HL.

Road—

Construction and maintenace—

Statutory duty—Coal mine. *See* **Coal mining** (Statutory duty—Road—Construction and maintenance).

Safety of. *See* Safety of roads and working places, *below*.

Roof support—

Construction and maintenance—

Coal mine. *See* **Coal mining** (Statutory duty—Support of roof).

Generally. *See* Support—Support of roof, *below*.

Safety of roads and working places—

Statutory duty to secure safety of roads and working places—

Duty of keeping road secure—Methods of security prescribed by statute must be adopted, though other proper methods available—Obligation involving duty to prevent foreseeable insecurity emerging—Clay mine—Manager having knowledge that shot-firing likely to affect sides of road—Failure to prevent movement of strata or to provide support before shot-firing—Evidence that putting up supports to prop up clay walls was contrary to good mining practice—Fall of clay on workman—Workman in course of inspecting and trimming site which fell on him—Mines and Quarries Act 1954, s 48(1). **Stein (John G) & Co Ltd v O'Hanlon** [1965] **1** 547, HL.

Scope of duty—Latent defect—Road cut through good, strong limestone—Junction of roadways creating wider span—Widening roadway—Roof tested after firing charges—Employee killed by subsequent fall of roof—Fall due to latent defect, cause undetectable—Whether breach of statutory duty—Mines and Quarries Act 1954, s 48(1). **Tomlinson v Beckermet Mining Co Ltd** [1964] **3** 1, CA.

Security of roof—Gypsum mine—Duty of mine owner—So far as may be reasonably practicable—Metalliferous Mines Regulation Act 1872, s 23—Metalliferous Mines General Regulations 1938, (S R & O 1938 No 630), reg 7(3). **Marshall v Gotham & Co Ltd** [1954] **1** 937, HL.

Shaft—

Safety precautions—

Entrance barrier—Coal mine. *See* **Coal mining** (Statutory duty—Safety precautions at entrance to shafts—Barriers to be maintained).

Shot-firing—

Coal mine, in—

Statutory duty. *See* **Coal mining** (Statutory duty—Shot-firing).

Support—

Support of roof—

Coal mine. *See* **Coal mining** (Statutory duty—Support of roof).

Duty of master to servant to provide safe system of work—Contractor undertaking tunnelling and following expert advice of mine owner—Accident to contractor's employee due to insufficient support to roof—Whether contractor liable. **Szumczyk v Associated Tunnelling Co Ltd** [1956] **1** 126, Assizes.

MINE (cont)—
　Ventilation—
　　Statutory duty—
　　　Coal mine. *See* **Coal mining** (Statutory duty—Provision of ventilation).
　Working facilities—
　　Application—
　　　Costs. *See* **Costs** (Mining application—Application in respect of working facilities).
　　Coal mine. *See* **Coal mining** (Working facilities).
　　Grant—
　　　Ancillary rights—Coal. *See* **Coal mining** (Ancillary rights—Grant).

MINEFIELD
　Foreshore—
　　Injuries to children—
　　　Exclusion of right of action for damages. *See* **War injury** (Exclusion of right of action for damages—Exclusion of right where injury war injury—Minefield on foreshore—Injuries to children by exploded mines).

MINERALS
　Compensation to be paid in respect of right to work minerals.　　*See* **Mine** (Minerals—Right to work—Compensation to be paid in respect of right).
　Crown—
　　Right to minerals etc—
　　　Isle of Man. *See* **Isle of Man** (Mines and minerals—Crown rights to minerals, flagg, slate and stone).
　Exception and reservation, of—
　　Land. *See* **Land** (Conveyance—Exception and reservation).
　　Mine. *See* **Mine** (Minerals—Exception and reservation).
　Mineral licence—
　　New Zealand. *See* **New Zealand** (Mine—Mineral licence).
　Reservation. *See* **Mine** (Minerals).
　Right to work minerals—
　　Mine. *See* **Mine** (Minerals—Right to work).
　　Quarry. *See* **Quarry** (Minerals—Right to work).

MINES AND QUARRIES
　Mine. *See* **Mine**.
　Quarry. *See* **Quarry**.

MINI-CAB
　Plying for hire. *See* **Road traffic** (Hackney carriage—Plying for hire—Mini-cab).

MINIMUM WAGE
　Coal mine—
　　Workman. *See* **Coal mining** (Workman—Minimum wage).

MINING
　Coal mining. *See* **Coal mining**.
　Enforcement notice—
　　Validity. *See* **Town and country planning** (Enforcement notice—Validity—Mining operations).
　Generally. *See* **Mine**.
　Lease—
　　Coal mine. *See* **Coal mining** (Mining lease).
　　Settlement. *See* **Settlement** (Mining leases).
　Permitted development. *See* **Town and country planning** (Development—Permitted development—Development by mineral undertakers).

MINING LEASE
　Coal. *See* **Coal mining** (Mining lease).
　Settlement. *See* **Settlement** (Mining leases).

MINING RENTS
　Income tax. *See* **Income tax** (Mining rents).

MINISTER OF CROWN
　Action against—
　　Competency. *See* **Crown** (Action against Minister of Crown—Competency).
　　Generally. *See* **Crown** (Proceedings against).
　Appeal against refusal of planning permission. *See* **Town and country planning** (Appeal to Minister against refusal of permission for development).
　Contempt of court. *See* **Contempt of court** (Crown).
　Delegation of powers—
　　Secretary of State for Trade—
　　　Petition to wind up company presented on behalf of Secretary of State. *See* **Company** (Compulsory winding up—Petition by Secretary of State—Secretary of State taking view that it is expedient in the public interest that the company be wound up—Secretary of State—Petition presented mis-spelt—Errors by Inspector of Companies on behalf of Secretary of State).
　Discretion—
　　Judicial control. *See* **Public authority** (Statutory powers—Duty of Minister).
　Ministerial Code—
　　Justiciability. *See* **Judicial review** (Availability of remedy—Ministerial Code).
　Powers—
　　Control of local education authority. *See* **Education** (Local education authority—Power of Secretary of State to prevent unreasonable exercise of functions).

MINISTER OF CROWN (cont)—
Powers (cont)—
Quasi-judicial. *See* **Natural justice** (Quasi-judicial function—Minister).

MINISTER OF HEALTH
Duty to provide treatment by means of service of specialists. *See* **National Health Service** (Specialist services—Duty of Minister to provide treatment by means of service of specialists).
Hospital—
Vesting in Minister of Health—
Effect. *See* **National Health Service** (Hospital—Vesting in Minister of Health—Effect).

MINISTER OF RELIGION
Dismissal—
Complaint of unfair dismissal—
Whether agreement between Minister and Church a contract of service. *See* **Employment** (Contract of service—Incidents of contract—Minister of religion).
Income tax—
Perquisites or profits from office or employment—
Occupation of house. *See* **Income tax** (Emoluments from office or employment—Perquisites or profits—Occupation of house—Rates and property tax paid by employers—Minister of religion).
Official residence—
Rates—
Occupation—Premises left empty. *See* **Rates** (Rateable occupation—Premises left empty—Intention to occupy—Charity—Ecclesiastical corporation).

MINOR
Abduction—
Criminal proceedings. *See* **Criminal law** (Child abduction).
Ethnic minority—
Parents taking child abroad against her will—Sister bringing wardship proceedings—Court's approach where traditional values of parents and individual integrity of child conflict. **KR (a child) (abduction: forcible removal by parents), Re** [1999] **4** 954, Fam D.
Habitual residence—
Father a US serviceman stationed in Iceland—US court restraining mother from removing children from Iceland—Mother removing children to Wales without consent of US court—Father applying for order that children be returned to United States—Iceland not signatory to Hague Convention—Meaning of 'habitual residence'—Whether children habitually resident in Iceland or United States for purpose of convention—Whether court should order children's return—Child Abduction and Custody Act 1985, Sch 1, art 4. **A and ors (minors) (abduction: habitual residence), Re** [1996] **1** 24, Fam D.
Habitual residence of children in state where request for return made—Whether summary return under Convention available—Hague Convention on the Civil Aspects of International Child Abduction 1980. **C (children: anticipatory retention), Re** [2018] **3** 1, SC.
Inherent jurisdiction—US court granting mother return order under Hague Convention—Mother removing child to England—US appeal court subsequently overturning return order -Father seeking return of child to US—Whether child habitually resident in England and Wales by date in issue—Whether child should be returned to US under court's inherent jurisdiction for dispute to be decided there—Hague Convention on the Civil Aspects of International Child Abduction 1980. **KL (a child) (abduction: habitual residence: inherent jurisdiction), Re** [2014] **1** 999, SC.
Parental intentions—Mother giving birth to two children in France and family residing there—Mother and children going to live in Scotland with father's agreement soon after birth of second child for the duration of mother's maternity leave—Mother seeking residence order in Scotland and interdict against father removing children from Scotland—Father seeking order for return of children to France under Hague Convention—Whether shared parental intention to move permanently an essential element in alteration of children's habitual residence—Whether children habitually resident in Scotland at material time—Child Abduction and Custody Act 1985, Sch 1. **AR v RN** [2015] **3** 749, SC.
Jurisdiction—
Cases of urgency—Child born in United Kingdom to Moroccan parents—Family moving to Morocco—Moroccan court granting residential custody to mother and visiting rights to father following divorce—Mother removing child from Morocco to UK without father's consent—English court ordering child's return—Whether court having jurisdiction—Whether order for return of child to country of habitual residence constituting 'measure of protection' for purposes of 1996 Hague Convention—Whether pre-condition to jurisdiction that impossible or impracticable for courts of country of habitual residence to exercise jurisdiction—Hague Convention on Jurisdiction, Applicable Law, Recognition, Enforcement and Co-operation in Respect of Parental Responsibility and Measures for the Protection of Children 1996, art 11—Council Regulation 2201/2003/EC, art 20. **J (a child) (1996 Hague Convention: cases of urgency), Re** [2016] **4** 1048, SC.
Removal outside jurisdiction. *See* Removal outside jurisdiction—Abduction, *below*.
Rights of custody. *See* Custody—Rights of custody—Foreign custody rights—Wrongful removal or retention, *below*.
Ward of court—
Custody rights. *See* Custody—Rights of custody—Ward of court—Abduction of ward of court, *below*.
Acceptance of child as one of family—
Assumption of parental responsibility—
Liability for maintenance—Children of wife by previous marriage—Whether children accepted as members of the new family—Whether and to what extent husband had assumed responsibility for children's maintenance—Liability of former husband for maintenance—Matrimonial Proceedings (Magistrates' Courts) Act 1960, ss 2(1)(h), (5), 16(1). **Bowlas v Bowlas** [1965] **3** 40, CA.

MINOR (cont)—
  Acceptance of child as one of family (cont)—
    Child en ventre de sa mère at time of marriage—
      Child not husband's child—Acceptance of child by husband before marriage as child of the family—Liability of putative father—No proceedings taken by wife against putative father—Effect as regards maintenance order against husband—Matrimonial Proceedings (Magistrates' Courts) Act 1960, ss 2(1)(h), (5), 16(1). **Caller v Caller (by her guardian)** [1966] 2 754, PDA.
    Discretion as to maintenance—
      Children not children of husband—Children illegitimate children of wife—Children accepted by husband as children of the family—Wife in desertion—Exercise of discretion to award maintenance in respect of children. **Kirkwood v Kirkwood** [1970] 2 161, Div.
    Divorce proceedings. See **Divorce** (Infant—Child of the family—Acceptance of child as one of the family).
    Effect of acceptance—
      Maintenance—Child not a child of husband—Child accepted by husband as one of the family—Liability of child's father to maintain child—Matrimonial Proceedings (Magistrates' Courts) Act 1960, s 2(5). **Roberts v Roberts** [1962] 2 967, Div.
    Knowledge of material facts necessary for acceptance—
      Material fact—Failure to disclose child's illegitimacy—Whether wife's failure to disclose illegitimacy of children material fact—Matrimonial Proceedings (Magistrates' Courts) Act 1960, s 16(1). **Kirkwood v Kirkwood** [1970] 2 161, Div.
    Mutuality—
      Child of previous marriage—Whether mutuality necessary for acceptance of child as child of the family—Matrimonial Proceedings (Magistrates' Courts) Act 1960, ss 2(5), 16(1). **Dixon v Dixon** [1967] 3 659, Div.
    Time for acceptance—
      Marriage—Acceptance by husband of wife's child—Unconditional acceptance at time of marriage—Mutuality of parties—Exercise by husband of parental control prior to and at time of marriage with wife's consent—Subsequent withdrawal by wife of children from husband's control within short time of marriage—Acceptance of child at time of marriage constituting it child of the family—Subsequent events irrelevant—Matrimonial Proceedings (Magistrates' Courts) Act 1960, ss 2(1)(h), 16(1). **Snow v Snow** [1971] 3 833, CA, Div.
  Access—
    Adoption. See **Adoption** (Access).
    Child in care of local authority—
      Access by putative father. See **Child** (Welfare—Child in care of local authority—Access by putative father).
    Generally. See Custody—Access, below.
    Ward of court—
      Welfare of ward. See **Child** (Welfare—Access—Wardship proceedings).
  Action—
    Adoption of action on attaining full age. See **Practice** (Persons under disability—Minor—Proceeding by next friend—Adoption of action on attaining majority).
    Settlement of—
      Approval of court for. See **Practice** (Compromise of action—Approval of court—Approval on behalf of infant).
  Adoption—
    Generally. See **Adoption**.
    Illegitimate child—
      Putative father's application. See Custody—Illegitimate child—Putative father's application, below.
    Leave to enter United Kingdom for purposes of adoption. See **Immigration** (Leave to enter—Adoption—Entry of child for purposes of adoption).
  Adoption society—
    Evidence. See Guardianship—Evidence—Production of records and giving of evidence by adoption society or local authority, below.
  Affiliation. See **Affiliation**.
  Agent—
    Disposition of minor's property—
      Disposition by agent—Voidability. **G (A) v G (T)** [1970] 3 546, CA.
  Applications in respect of—
    Chancery Division—
      Chambers—Contested applications in which witnesses to be cross-examined. See **Practice** (Chancery Division—Chambers proceedings—Adjournment to judge—Infants—Contested applications relating to infants in which witnesses are to be cross-examined).
    Family Division—
      Practice. See **Child** (Practice—Matrimonial causes—Applications relating to children).
  Arrangement affecting interest of minor—
    Variation of trusts—
      Evidence. See **Variation of trusts** (Practice—Arrangement—Evidence—Arrangement affecting interests of infants or unborn beneficiaries).
  Arrears of maintenance. See Maintenance—Arrears, below.
  Assignment of property—
    Copyright—
      Written contract—Effect of subsequent repudiation—Copyright passing by assignment by virtue of words of written contract—Contract by infant and adult with publishers for the writing of a book for infant and that publishers should have exclusive right to print, publish and sell—Infant and adult joint owners of copyright—Contract voidable if not for infant's benefit—Election by infant to repudiate contract—Validity of assignment on infant's subsequent election not to be bound by contract—Whether contract for infant's benefit—Copyright Act 1956, ss 19(1), 37(1). **Chaplin v Leslie Frewin (Publishers) Ltd** [1965] 3 764, CA.
  Blood test to determine paternity. See **Paternity** (Blood test).
  Care—
    Local authority. See **Child** (Care—Local authority).

MINOR (cont)—
Care and control—
 Divorce. *See* **Divorce** (Custody—Care and control).
 Generally. *See* Custody—Care and control, *below*.
 Ward of court. *See* **Ward of court** (Care and control).
Care and upbringing—
 Arrangements required before decree absolute of divorce between parents. *See* **Divorce** (Decree absolute—Arrangements for care and upbringing of children).
Caution in lieu of criminal proceedings—
 Ward of court. *See* **Ward of court** (Criminal proceedings—Caution in lieu of criminal proceedings).
Change of surname—
 Correction of entry in register of births. *See* **Registration** (Births, deaths and marriages—Correction or erasure of entry in register—Surname of child).
 Deed poll—
  Consent of parent—Application by parent having custody or care and control of child—Consent in writing of other parent required—Procedure where application not supported by consent of other parent—RSC Ord 63, r 10. **Practice Direction** [1977] **3** 451, QBD; [1995] **1** 832, QBD.
  Consent of parent—Application by parent not having custody or care and control of child—Consent of other parent—Leave to enrol deed to be granted if consent in writing of other parent produced or other parent dead, beyond the seas or cannot be found despite exercise of reasonable diligence—RSC Ord 63, r 10. **Practice Direction** [1977] **3** 451, QBD; [1995] **1** 832, QBD.
 Divorce of parents—
  Custody. *See* **Divorce** (Custody—Change of surname).
  Leave of court to change surname in absence of parent's consent—Best interests of child—Mother leaving father before birth of child and going to live with co-respondent—Mother proposing to marry co-respondent and bring up child as child of co-respondent's family—Father wishing child to have his name—Whether in best interests of child to have father's name. **D v B (orse D) (child: surname)** [1979] **1** 92, CA.
  Mother having custody—Remarriage of mother—Deed-poll executed without father's consent purporting to change infant's surname to that of her second husband—Whether deed-poll effective. **T (orse H) (an infant), Re** [1962] **3** 970, Ch D.
  Mother having custody—Remarriage of mother—Rights of mother as custodian—Rights of father as natural guardian—Interests of child—Whether mother or father having unilateral right to change surname of child. **Y v Y (child: surname)** [1973] **2** 574, PDA.
 Importance—
  Proper approach by court to decision to change surname—Parents divorced and each remarried—Parents having joint custody of children and mother having care and control—Father agreeing to mother and children going out of the jurisdiction with mother's second husband provided mother gave undertaking that children would continue to use father's surname—Mother and children wishing second husband's surname to be used by children—Change of surname matter of importance to be decided by reference to child's best interests in the circumstances—Whether judge right not to pay regard to children's wishes—Guardianship of Minors Act 1971, s 1. **W v A (child: surname)** [1981] **1** 100, CA.
 Procedure—
  Statutory declaration—Execution of deed poll—Consent of minor over 16—Consent of both parents—Affidavit in support. **Practice Direction** [1969] **3** 288, .
 Unborn child—
  Consent of both parents—Husband and wife separating before birth—Wife adopting new surname by deed poll—Deed poll not enrolled—Birth of child registered in wife's adopted name—Whether judge entitled to direct mother to execute fresh deed poll and alter entry in register to ensure child known by father's name—Whether judge entitled to direct that child be known by father's name until aged 18—Births and Deaths Registration Act 1953, s 29(3)—Registration of Births, Deaths and Marriages Regulations 1968 (SI 1968 No 2049), reg 18(3). **D v B (orse D) (child: surname)** [1979] **1** 92, CA.
 Unmarried parents—
  Mother known by former husband's name—Parents separating shortly after birth of child—Birth of child registered in mother's name—Father applying to change child's name—Judge granting application, but Court of Appeal allowing appeal—Whether Court of Appeal had exercised its discretion correctly—Children Act 1989, ss 1, 8. **Dawson v Wearmouth** [1999] **2** 353, HL.
  Mother known by former husband's name—Parents separating shortly after birth of child—Birth of child registered in mother's name—Father applying to change register—Whether court can make order for change of name where no residence order in force—Whether court can make specific issue order for change of name—Children Act 1989, ss 8, 13. **Dawson v Wearmouth** [1998] **1** 271, CA.
Child—
 Generally. *See* **Child**.
Child of the family—
 Acceptance as. *See* Acceptance of child as one of family, *above*.
 Maintenance—
  Divorce proceedings. *See* **Divorce** (Financial provision—Child—Maintenance).
Child of unmarried parents—
 Financial relief—
  Application for order—Second application—Res judicata—First application dismissed on ground of want of corroboration—Mother making fresh application for financial relief for child—Mother intending to adduce further evidence to establish paternity—Whether mother estopped from making second application—Whether paternity issue res judicata—Whether doctrine of res judicata applicable in proceedings for financial relief—Whether mother precluded from making fresh application. **Hager v Osborne** [1992] **2** 494, Fam D.
  Child born before statutory provisions providing for financial relief for children coming into effect—Whether statutory provisions having retrospective effect—Guardianship of Minors Act 1971, s 11B. **Hager v Osborne** [1992] **2** 494, Fam D.

MINOR (cont)—
Compromise of action—
Approval of court for. *See* **Practice** (Compromise of action—Approval of court—Approval on behalf of infant).
Contempt of court—
Magistrates' court—
Wilfully interrupting proceedings—Restriction on imprisoning or committing person under 21 for contempt. *See* **Contempt of court** (Magistrates' court—Wilfully interrupting proceedings of court—Minor).
Contract—
Apprenticeship—
Benefit of minor. *See* **Employment** (Apprenticeship—Benefit of infant).
Capacity to contract—
Nature of contract with minor—Contracts for necessaries, services and apprenticeships—Footballer entering representation contract—Footballer being minor at time of contract—Whether contract enforceable against minor—Whether contract constituting contract for necessaries, services or apprenticeship—Whether contract for benefit of minor. **Proform Sports Management Ltd v Proactive Sports Management Ltd** [2007] **1 Comm** 356, Ch D; [2007] **1** 542, Ch D.
Inducing or procuring a breach of contract. *See* **Tort** (Interference with contractual relations—Inducing or procuring a breach of contract—Contract with a minor).
Liability—
Liability in tort for act founded on contract. *See* Torts—Tort founded on contract, *below*.
Whether contract for minor's benefit. *See* Assignment of property—Copyright, *above*.
Necessaries—
Agreement to purchase motor lorry—Whether a contract for necessaries. **Mercantile Union Guarantee Corp Ltd v Ball** [1937] **3** 1, CA.
Gifts to person to whom minor engaged to be married—Rings—Whether necessaries. **Elkington & Co Ltd v Amery** [1936] **2** 86, CA.
Conveyance of legal estate in land to minor—
Tenancy. *See* **Landlord and tenant** (Validity of notice to quit—Conveyance of legal estate in land to minor).
Copyright—
Assignment. *See* Assignment of property—Copyright, *above*.
Court proceedings in relation to children—
Practice. *See* **Child** (Practice—Court proceedings in relation to children).
Criminal capacity. *See* **Criminal law** (Criminal capacity—Child).
Criminal offence—
Compensation—
Parent or guardian's liability. *See* **Sentence** (Compensation—Parent or guardian's liability).
Custody—
Access—
Adopted child—Welfare of child—Right of access—Access to be regarded as a right of child rather than parent—Fact that child adopted irrelevant—Custody awarded to father—Circumstances in which mother may be deprived of access. **M v M (child: access)** [1973] **2** 81, Fam D.
Allegation of sexual abuse—Evidence—Hearsay—Matrimonial proceedings—Father implicated in sexual abuse of his brother's children—Judge relying on hearsay evidence of social worker who interviewed brother's children—Whether hearsay evidence admissible in access proceedings. **H v H and C (Kent CC intervening) (child abuse: evidence)** [1989] **3** 740, CA.
Allegation of sexual abuse—Standard of proof—Matrimonial proceedings—Father alleged to have sexually abused daughter during access visits—Conflicting medical evidence—Judge relying on evidence of social worker—Whether civil standard of balance of probabilities to be applied—Whether allegation of sexual abuse to be proved on balance of probabilities—Whether in deciding whether to permit future access by father judge can take into account evidence which points to real possibility or real risk of future abuse. **H v H and C (Kent CC intervening) (child abuse: evidence)** [1989] **3** 740, CA.
Application for order regarding right of access—Extent of court's jurisdiction—High Court—County court—Mother having custody of infant—Father having right of access—Mother living in England with infant—Father living in Switzerland—Father applying for order permitting infant to visit him in Switzerland—Whether court having jurisdiction to make order permitting removal of infant out of jurisdiction—Guardianship of Minors Act 1971, s 9. **F (a minor) (access out of jurisdiction), Re** [1973] **3** 493, Fam D.
Character of parties seeking access to ward of court. *See* **Ward of court** (Custody—Character of parties seeking access to child).
Child in care of local authority—Access by putative father. *See* **Child** (Welfare—Child in care of local authority—Access by putative father).
Divorce proceedings—Generally. *See* **Divorce** (Custody).
Enforcement of order—Order of magistrates' court—Jurisdiction of justices to enforce access order by imposing monetary penalty or by committal to prison—Guardianship of Minors Act 1971, s 9—Domestic Proceedings and Magistrates' Courts Act 1978, s 8—Magistrates' Courts Act 1980, s 63(3). **P v W** [1984] **1** 866, Fam D.
Enforcement of order—Order of magistrates' court—Whether power to enforce order by imposing monetary penalty or by committal to prison—Magistrates' Courts Act 1952, s 54(3)—Guardianship of Minors Act 1971, s 9(1). **K (a minor) (access order: breach), Re** [1977] **2** 737, Fam D.
Enforcement of order—Proceedings for contempt—When such proceedings should be instituted—What must be proved in such proceedings—Form of summons—Magistrates' Courts Act 1980, s 63(3). **P v W** [1984] **1** 866, Fam D.

MINOR (cont)—
    Custody (cont)—
        Access (cont)—
            Foreign right of access—Enforcement of foreign custody order—Belgian court granting access to father—Mother removing children to England—Foreign order registered in English court—Father applying to enforce rights under Belgian order—Enforcement of order no longer in accordance with child's welfare—Whether order should be enforced in English court—Whether enforcement of foreign order automatically following recognition and registration—Child Abduction and Custody Act 1985, Sch 2, art 10. **H (a minor) (foreign custody order: enforcement), Re** [1994] **1** 812, CA.

            Foreign right of access—Enforcement of foreign right of access—Application to make arrangements for organising or securing effective exercise of rights—Application for residence, contact or other order with respect to child—Duty of central authority—Provision of English solicitors to act on behalf of applicant—Consideration to be given to commencing proceedings in High Court—Invitation to Official Solicitor to act on behalf of children—Child Abduction and Custody Act 1985, Sch 1, art 21—Children Act 1989, s 8. **T and ors (minors) (international child abduction: access) (note), Re** [1993] **3** 127, Fam D.

            Foreign right of access—Enforcement of foreign right of access—Contracting state—Ontario court giving mother custody of child and father specific access—Mother and child returning to England with consent of Ontario court—Father applying to enforce access rights in Ontario under Ontario order—Mother refusing access—Judge granting father limited access in England pending future access in Ontario—Whether Convention on the Civil Aspects of International Child Abduction applying where child habitually resident in contracting state other than state where access rights arose—Whether provisions of convention relating to access creating rights in private law—Child Abduction and Custody Act 1985, Sch 1, arts 4, 21—Children Act 1989, ss 1(1), 8. **G (a minor) (enforcement of access abroad), Re** [1993] **3** 657, CA.

            Foreign right of access—Enforcement of foreign right of access—Ontario court giving mother custody of children and father reasonable access—Mother removing children to England—Father applying to enforce his rights under Ontario order—Whether court having jurisdiction to entertain father's application—Child Abduction and Custody Act 1985, s 2(2), Sch 1, arts 4, 21. **B v B (minors: enforcement of access abroad)** [1988] **1** 652, Fam D.

            Practice—Divorce proceedings. *See* **Divorce** (Practice—Children—Custody).

            Practice—Wardship and guardianship proceedings. *See* Practice—Wardship and guardianship proceedings—Custody and access, *below.*

            Stay of order—Appeal—Whether power to stay access order pending appeal. **K (a minor) (access order: breach), Re** [1977] **2** 737, Fam D.

            Supervised access—Application to court for supervised access—Consent of person to supervise access—Welfare officers to be asked to supervise access only in exceptional circumstances. **Practice Direction** [1980] **1** 1040, Fam D.

            Variation of order—Jurisdiction of court of summary jurisdiction where applicant resides—Guardianship and Maintenance of Infants Act 1951, s 1(1)—Children Act 1948, s 53. **D (an infant), Re** [1953] **2** 1318, CA.

        Appeal from magistrates' court—
            Change of custody—Stay pending appeal—Magistrates' order transferring custody from mother to father—Principles regulating grant of stay pending appeal. **S (an infant), Re** [1958] **1** 783, Ch D.

            Costs—Award against mother whose appeal fails. **SL (infants), Re** [1967] **3** 538, Ch D.

            Review of exercise of discretion—Duty of appellate court. *See* **Appeal** (Review of exercise of discretion—Duty of appellate court—Extent of duty—Custody cases).

        Application—
            Application of mother or father—Jurisdiction of court to award custody to person other than parent or guardian—Guardianship of Minors Act 1971, s 9(1). **R (an infant) (custody to non-parent), Re** [1974] **1** 1033, Fam D.

            Applications which may be made to registrar—Wardship and guardianship proceedings—Application for access where other party consents to access and only issue extent of the access—Such applications to be made in first instance to registrar unless exceptional circumstances make it desirable to apply to a judge. **Practice Direction** [1980] **1** 813, Fam D.

        Boy—
            Custody of father—Boy of eight—Whether a principle that he should be with father. **C (A) (an infant), Re** [1970] **1** 309, CA.

        Care and control—
            Divorce. *See* **Divorce** (Custody—Care and control).

            Religious education—Whether custody, in addition to care and control, should be granted. **M (infants), Re** [1967] **3** 1071, CA.

            Ward of court. *See* **Ward of court** (Care and control).

        Child of tender years—
            Custody of mother—No rule of law that mother is entitled to custody. **B (an infant), Re** [1962] **1** 872, CA.

        Conflict of laws. *See* **Ward of court** (Jurisdiction).

        Custody as between parents—
            Factors to be considered—Interest of minor paramount consideration—Continuity of care an important factor—Father applying for custody—Mother having had adulterous relations with several men—Whether unimpeachable character of father a relevant consideration—Whether mother entitled to retain care and control of children. **S (BD) v S (DJ) (infants: care and consent)** [1977] **1** 656, CA.

        Division of custodial rights. *See* Division of custodial rights, *below.*

        Divorce proceedings. *See* **Divorce** (Custody).

        Divorce proceedings—Practice. *See* **Divorce** (Practice—Children—Custody).

        Enforcement of custody order—
            Overseas order. *See* Custody—Order—Enforcement of overseas order, *below.*

MINOR (cont)—
  Custody (cont)—
    Enforcement of custody order (cont)—
      Unlawful removal—Illegitimate child removed from England to Ireland by relatives on mother's death without father's knowledge or consent—Father not having right to determine child's place of residence at date of removal—Two days later father granted interim care and control of child by English court and return of child ordered—Whether removal of child thereafter unlawful—Child Abduction and Custody Act 1985, s 23(2), Sch 2, art 12. **S (a minor) (custody: habitual residence), Re** [1997] 4 251, HL.
  Illegitimate child—
    Conflict between mother and natural father—Welfare of child paramount consideration. **A (an infant), Re** [1955] 2 202, CA.
    Putative father's application—Adoption application made by mother, in whose custody child was, and her husband—Advantage to child of ceasing to be a bastard outweighing loss of connection with real father. **E (P) (an infant), Re** [1969] 1 323, CA.
    Putative father's application—Adoption application made by proposing adopters—Both applications to be heard before judgment given on either—Legitimacy Act 1959, s 3. **O (an infant), Re** [1964] 1 786, CA.
    Putative father's application—Adoption application made by proposing adopters—Boy placed by mother with adopters—Adopters in every way suitable, and Roman Catholics, in which religion mother wanted boy brought up—Father wanting custody of boy and offering home with his wife—Wife wishing to accept boy—Father and wife Protestants, but not practising members of their religious denomination—Father and wife 47 years of age, boy 18 months—Adopters younger than the father—Blood tie between father and son. **C (MA) (an infant), Re** [1966] 1 838, CA.
    Putative father's application—Jurisdiction of justices—Jurisdiction of judge of Chancery Division of High Court on appeal by putative father from decision of justices—Guardianship of Infants Act 1886, s 5 (as amended by Administration of Justice Act 1928, s 16). **T (infants), Re** [1956] 3 500, Ch D.
    Weight to be given to father's wishes. **C (A) (an infant), Re** [1970] 1 309, CA.
  Income tax relief. *See* **Income tax** (Child relief—Entitlement—Custody of child).
  Joinder of child as party to proceedings. *See* Practice—Wardship and custody proceedings—Joinder of child as party, *below.*
  Jurisdiction—
    Habitual residence—Illegitimate child habitually resident in England removed to Ireland by relatives on mother's death without father's knowledge or consent—Two days later father granted interim care and control of child by English court and child made ward of court—Whether court having jurisdiction to make order—Whether child habitually resident in England at date of order—Whether relatives changing child's habitual residence by taking him out of jurisdiction—Family Law Act 1986, ss 2(3), 3(1)(a)—Children Act 1989, s 3(5). **S (a minor) (custody: habitual residence), Re** [1997] 4 251, HL.
    Magistrates' court—Divorce pending—Adjournment of proceedings—Propriety—Party proposing to bring divorce suit—Justices adjourning custody proceedings pending divorce—Effect to suspend decision on child's future for considerable period—Jurisdiction of justices to make custody order while divorce proceedings pending. **Jones (E G) v Jones (E F)** [1974] 3 702, CA.
    Removal of proceedings to High Court—Proceedings instituted in court of summary jurisdiction—Whether proceedings can be removed into High Court—Guardianship of Infants Act 1886, ss 5, 9, 10—Guardianship of Infants Act 1925, s 7—R S C Ord 55A, r 5. **Beaumont v Beaumont** [1938] 2 226, Ch D and CA.
  Legitimated child—
    Child of the marriage—No formal declaration of legitimacy—Summary Jurisdiction (Married Women) Act 1895, s 5(b)—Married Women (Maintenance) Act 1920, s 1(1)—Supreme Court of Judicature (Consolidation) Act 1925, ss 188(1), 193(1)—Legitimacy Act 1926, s 1(1). **C v C** [1947] 2 50, Div.
  Order—
    Breach—Breach by father of order made in favour of mother—Committal of father to prison for fixed term—Sentence suspended—Refusal to grant stay of execution—Power of Divisional Court to review committal order—Powers of magistrates—Magistrates' Courts Act 1952, s 54(3)—Administration of Justice Act 1960, s 13—Criminal Justice Act 1967, s 39—R S C Ord 109, r 2(2). **B (B) v B (M)** [1969] 1 891, Div.
    Enforcement of overseas order—Order made by Australian court—Enforcement in England. **Harris v Harris** [1949] 2 318, Div.
    Previous order of foreign court—Variation of order—Welfare of infant paramount consideration. **B's Settlement, Re** [1951] 1 949, Ch D; **McKee v McKee** [1951] 1 942, PC.
    Reasons for decision—County court. *See* **County court** (Judgment or order—Reasons for decision—Custody cases).
    Revocation of order in wife's favour—No misconduct by wife—Welfare of child paramount consideration—Guardianship of Infants Act 1925, s 1. **Chipperfield v Chipperfield** [1952] 1 1360, Div.
  Orphan—
    Religious upbringing—Conflict between grandparents—Father's direction as to religion of child—Welfare of child paramount consideration—Guardianship of Infants Act 1925, s 1. **Collins (an infant), Re** [1950] 1 1057, CA.
  Proceedings in private—
    Transcripts. *See* **Child** (Practice—Court proceedings in relation to children—Proceedings in private—Publication of information—Transcripts).

MINOR (cont)—
   Custody (cont)—
      Rights of custody—

Foreign custody rights—Jurisdiction—Wrongful removal or retention—Removal from non-convention country—Father removing child from Israel to England in breach of mother's rights of custody—Mother obtaining interim custody order from Israeli court—Father subsequently obtaining similar order from English court—Principles applicable in deciding appropriate forum to determine child's welfare—Whether English court should order child to be returned to Israel—Child Abduction and Custody Act 1985, Sch 1, art 13. **F (minor: abduction: jurisdiction), Re** [1990] **3** 97, CA.

Foreign custody rights—Wrongful removal or retention—Acquiescence—Mother removing children from Israel to England without father's knowledge or consent—Father as Orthodox Jew initially pursuing remedies in religious court in Israel—Father asking mother to allow children to visit him and promising to return them—Whether father acquiescing in removal of children from Israel—What amounts to acquiescence—Child Abduction and Custody Act 1985, Sch 1, art 13(a). **H and ors (minors) (abduction: acquiescence), Re** [1997] **2** 225, HL.

Foreign custody rights—Wrongful removal or retention—Acquiescence—Mother secretly removing children from Australia to England and then notifying father—Father writing letter to mother stating that he knew mother's action was illegal but that he was not going to fight it—Father subsequently seeking return of children to Australia alleging unlawful abduction—Whether father acquiescing in removal of children from Australia—What amounts to acquiescence—Child Abduction and Custody Act 1985, s 2(2), Sch 1, art 13(a). **A and anor (minors) (abduction: acquiescence), Re** [1992] **1** 929, CA.

Foreign custody rights—Wrongful removal or retention—Australian court giving custody of child to mother but providing that neither parent should be entitled to remove child from Australia without consent of the other—Mother removing child to England without father's consent—Father applying for order that child be returned to Australia—Whether father's right to prevent child being removed from Australia without his consent constituting a custody right—Whether return of child to Australia exposing child to grave risk of psychological harm—Child Abduction and Custody Act 1985, Sch 1, arts 3, 5, 13. **C v C (minor: abduction: rights of custody abroad)** [1989] **2** 465, CA.

Foreign custody rights—Wrongful removal or retention—Child living with mother in Republic of Ireland—Father applying to Irish court for guardianship of child—Mother removing child to England while application pending—Father bringing proceedings in England for return of child to Ireland—Whether Irish court having rights of custody in respect of child—Whether father entitled to rely on custody rights of Irish court—Child Abduction and Custody Act 1985, Sch 1, art 3. **H (child abduction: rights of custody), Re** [2000] **2** 1, CA and HL.

Foreign custody rights—Wrongful removal or retention—Child not physically present within jurisdiction—Father removing child from California without consent of parties or leave of court—Application made by mother in anticipation of child's arrival in England from California—Whether court having jurisdiction to make order before child physically present within jurisdiction—Child Abduction and Custody Act 1985, s 5. **N (child abduction: jurisdiction), Re** [1995] **2** 417, Fam D.

Foreign custody rights—Wrongful removal or retention—Discretion of court to refuse to order immediate return of child—Exercise of discretion—Parents entering into separation agreement under which mother and child would live in France and father would have unrestricted access to child—Mother removing child to England—Father applying for return of child to France—Child objecting to return—No evidence that return of child to France would expose her to grave risk of psychological harm—Whether child had attained age and maturity at which it was appropriate to take account of her views—Whether court could refuse to order return of child to France even though return would not expose her to grave risk of psychological harm—Child Abduction and Custody Act 1985, Sch 1, art 13. **S (a minor) (abduction), Re** [1993] **2** 683, CA.

Foreign custody rights—Wrongful removal or retention—Grave risk that return would place child in intolerable situation—Canadian court giving custody to mother and interim access to father—Mother removing child to England without consent of Canadian court—Father applying for order that child be returned to Canada—Whether father having rights of custody—Whether removal of child wrongful—Whether grave risk of intolerable situation for child if return to Canada ordered—Child Abduction and Custody Act 1985, Sch 1, arts 3, 13. **B v B (abduction: custody rights)** [1993] **2** 144, CA.

Foreign custody rights—Wrongful removal or retention—Habitual residence—Israeli parents agreeing to reside in England for specified period of time—Mother deciding to remain in England with children and claiming that children's habitual residence in England—Father applying for return of children to Israel before expiry of agreed period—Parents having equal custody rights under Israeli law—Whether mother wrongfully retaining children—Whether father having agreed or acquiesced to retention—Whether mother's decision changing children's habitual residence—Child Abduction and Custody Act 1985, s 1, Sch 1, arts 3, 13. **S and anor (minors) (abduction: wrongful retention), Re** [1994] **1** 237, Fam D.

Foreign custody rights—Wrongful removal or retention—Illegitimate child—Mother having sole right to custody under Australian law unless order made vesting that right in father—Mother removing child to England without father's consent and with intention of leaving Australia permanently—Father subsequently obtaining order from Australian court granting him sole guardianship and custody of child—Whether removal of child from Australia constituting 'wrongful removal or retention' of child in breach of father's custody rights—Child Abduction and Custody Act 1985, Sch 1, art 3. **C v S (minor: abduction: illegitimate child)** [1990] **2** 961, HL.

Foreign custody rights—Wrongful removal or retention—Inchoate rights of custody—Child living with maternal grandparents in Lithuania—Mother taking child to Northern Ireland—Whether 'rights of custody' under Hague Convention including inchoate rights—Whether grandmother having rights of custody—Child Abduction and Custody Act 1985, Sch 1, art 3—Council Regulation (EC) 2201/2003. **K (a child) (abduction: rights of custody), Re** [2014] **3** 149, SC.

MINOR (cont)—
  Custody (cont)—
    Rights of custody (cont)—

      Foreign custody rights—Wrongful removal or retention—Inherent jurisdiction—Child present in UK—Father seeking child's return to Israel—Whether court having jurisdiction to order child's return under inherent jurisdiction—Factors to be taken into account—Child Abduction and Custody Act 1985, Sch 1—Children Act 1989, s 1(3)—FPR PD 12D, para 1.1. **NY (a child), Re** [2020] **1** 923, SC.

      Foreign custody rights—Wrongful removal or retention—Mother granted care and custody of child by Colorado court—Mother secretly removing child from Colorado—No order prohibiting removal of child from jurisdiction—Father applying for order that child be returned to Colorado—Whether removal of child constituting 'wrongful removal' of child in breach of father's 'rights of custody'—Whether return of child to Colorado exposing him to grave risk or otherwise placing him in intolerable situation—Whether court should exercise its discretion to refrain from ordering child's return—Child Abduction and Custody Act 1985, Sch 1, arts 3, 12, 13(b). **F (minor: abduction: rights of custody abroad), Re** [1995] **3** 641, CA.

      Foreign custody rights—Wrongful removal or retention—Mother having right of custody under order of foreign court—Father removing children outside jurisdiction in breach of court's order—Mother applying to English court for return of children to jurisdiction of foreign court—Whether removal of children from their habitual place of residence abroad constituting wrongful removal in breach of mother's custody rights—Whether mother entitled to order for return of children if removal from jurisdiction occurring before Convention on the Civil Aspects of International Child Abduction having effect—Child Abduction and Custody Act 1985, s 2(2), Sch 1. **H and anor (minors) (abduction: custody rights), Re** [1991] **1** 836, CA; [1991] **3** 230, HL.

      Foreign custody rights—Wrongful removal or retention—Mother removing child from Romania without knowledge or consent of divorced father—Father requesting return of child—Whether removal wrongful—Whether removal in breach of rights of custody—Judge directing determination of Romanian court as to effect of orders made on parents' divorce as to rights of custody—Romanian court determining that father not having rights of custody—English judge ordering expert evidence as to Romanian law—Expert disagreeing with Romanian court—Judge ordering return of child—Whether child should be returned—Child Abduction and Custody Act 1985, Sch 1, arts 3, 15. **D (a child) (abduction: rights of custody), Re** [2007] **1** 783, HL.

      Foreign custody rights—Wrongful removal or retention—Mother removing children from Tenerife without father's consent and in breach of Spanish court order—Mother applying for residence order in respect of children—Father protesting to court by letter but making no application under Hague Convention for return of children—Whether court having received 'notice of a wrongful removal or retention' of children—Whether court bound to refrain from deciding on merits of rights of custody—Whether court required to secure that father informed of his rights under convention—Child Abduction and Custody Act 1985, Sch 1, arts 3, 16—Family Proceedings Rules 1991, r 6.11. **R v R (residence order: child abduction)** [1995] **4** 115, Fam D.

      Foreign custody rights—Wrongful removal or retention—Return of child—Welfare of child—Mother wrongfully removing children from Australia—Father acquiescing in removal of children to or their retention in England—Father applying for return of children to Australia—Whether appropriate for court to consider welfare interests of children—Whether court restricted to considering degree of acquiescence by father—Whether if acquiescence by father established court free to consider welfare interests of children—Child Abduction and Custody Act 1985, Sch 1, art 13(a)(b). **A and anor (minors) (abduction: acquiescence), Re (No 2)** [1993] **1** 272, CA.

      Removal outside jursidiction—Parental responsibility—Mother and father marrying in Islamic ceremony not recognised as valid under English law—Mother giving birth to child—Father registering child's birth—Father named on birth certificate as father—Mother removing child to the Netherlands without father's consent—Father applying for child's return pursuant to Hague Convention—Hague District Court requesting determination from central authority in UK regarding whether removal wrongful—Whether father having parental responsibility by virtue of being named on birth certificate—Whether father having inchoate rights of custody—Whether statutory scheme incompatible with father and child's human rights—Births and Deaths Registration Act 1953, s 10(1)—Hague Convention on the Civil Aspects of International Child Abduction 1980, art 3—Human Rights Act 1998, Sch 1, Pt 1, art 8. **A v H (Registrar General for England and Wales intervening)** [2009] **4** 641, Fam D.

      Ward of court—Abduction of ward of court—Mother taking ward to United States without consent of court—Father applying for declaration that custody rights vested in court had been breached—Whether court having rights of custody in respect of ward—Whether court 'person, an institution or ... other body' to which rights of custody to be attributed—Child Abduction and Custody Act 1985, Sch 1, arts 3, 5. **J (minor: abduction: ward of court), Re** [1989] **3** 590, Fam D.

      Wrongful removal or retention—Anticipatory retention—Mother failing to return children to father in Australia following agreed period of living in UK—Father seeking summary return of children—Judge refusing father's application—Whether principle of anticipatory retention recognised in law—Proper approach—Hague Convention on the Civil Aspects of International Child Abduction 1980, art 3. **C (children: anticipatory retention), Re** [2018] **1** 476, CA.

      Wrongful removal or retention—Discretion of court to refuse to order immediate return of child—Exercise of discretion—Mother wrongfully removing children from Zimbabwe—Father applying for return of children—Father delaying in making application—Children being settled in United Kingdom and objecting to return—Whether necessary for case to be exceptional before court could exercise discretion to refuse to return—Principles on which discretion should be exercised—Child Abduction and Custody Act 1985, Sch 1, art 12. **M (children) (abduction), Re** [2008] **1** 1157, HL.

      Wrongful removal or retention—Habitual residence—Family moving from Australia to France—Mother refusing to return child to France following holiday in England and Wales—Where child habitually resident—Whether possible to order return to third state—Hague Convention on the Civil Aspects of International Child Abduction 1980, art 12. **B (a child) (abduction: habitual residence), Re** [2021] **2** 1246, CA.

MINOR (cont)—
  Custody (cont)—
    Rights of custody (cont)—
      Wrongful removal or retention—Habitual residence—Family residing in Germany—Parents separating and father agreeing to mother and children living in England for 12 months—Children attending school and registering with doctor in England—Mother informing father of intention to remain in England—Father seeking order for return of children to Germany—Correct approach to habitual residence—Relevance of question whether previous habitual residence 'lost'—Hague Convention on the Civil Aspects of International Child Abduction 1980. **M (children) (habitual residence: 1980 Hague Child Abduction Convention), Re** [2021] **2** 1227, CA.
      Wrongful removal or retention—Illegitimate child removed from England to Ireland by relatives on mother's death without father's knowledge or consent—Father having no rights of custody at date of removal—Two days later father granted interim care and control of child by English court and return of child ordered—Whether retention of child in Ireland thereafter wrongful—Child Abduction and Custody Act 1985, Sch 1, art 3. **S (a minor) (custody: habitual residence), Re** [1997] **4** 251, HL.
      Wrongful removal or retention—Repudiatory retention—Mother failing to return children to father in Australia following agreed period of living in UK—Father seeking summary return of children—Judge refusing father's application—Whether principle of repudiatory retention recognised in law—Proper approach—Hague Convention on the Civil Aspects of International Child Abduction 1980, art 3. **C (children: anticipatory retention), Re** [2018] **3** 1, SC.
    Summons incidental to divorce proceedings—
      Costs. *See* **Divorce** (Costs—Co-respondent—Costs of incidental proceedings after decree).
    Welfare of minor as first and paramount consideration—
      Parents—Right of parents to custody subordinate to welfare of minor—Order for custody and adoption order contrasted—No consideration of comity arising out of nationality of parents—Guardianship of Infants Act 1925, s 1. **J v C** [1969] **1** 788, HL.
      Relevance of other considerations—Mother's conduct—Weight to be attached to other considerations dependent on how they affect children's welfare—Guardianship of Minors Act 1971, ss 1, 9(1). **D (minors) (wardship: jurisdiction), Re** [1973] **2** 993, Fam D.
      Welfare not the exclusive consideration—Consideration of all relevant circumstances—Guardianship of Infants Act 1925, s 1. **F (an infant), Re** [1969] **2** 766, Ch D.
  Damages—
    Control of money recovered for personal injury. *See* Money recovered—Control, *below*.
    Generally. *See* **Damages** (Infant).
    Jurisdiction of court to postpone entitlement until after attainment of majority. *See* **Variation of trusts** (Jurisdiction—Damages recovered by infant).
  Death of divorced father—
    Maintenance. *See* Maintenance—Child of divorced parents—Death of divorced father, *below*.
  Death of mother—
    Fatal accident—
      Damages for loss of services as mother. *See* **Fatal accident** (Damages—Death of mother—Loss of services as mother).
  Deprivation of liberty. *See* **Child** (Deprivation of liberty).
  Division of custodial rights—
    Jurisdiction of justices to divide custody—
      Circumstances in which division of custody rights appropriate—Guardianship of Minors Act 1971, s 9. **Jussa v Jussa** [1972] **2** 600, Fam D.
      Custody granted to one parent, care and control to other—Magistrates not empowered to make such order—Matrimonial Proceedings (Magistrates' Courts) Act 1960, ss 2(1)(d), 4. **W (C) v W (R)** [1968] **3** 608, Div.
      Order of magistrates' court giving legal right to custody of infant to father and possession to mother—Whether court had jurisdiction to divide custody—Guardianship of Infants Act 1886, s 5. **W (JC) (an infant), Re** [1963] **3** 459, CA.
  Divorce—
    Inclusion of name in petition. *See* **Divorce** (Petition—Form of petition).
    Protection of minors. *See* **Divorce** (Infant).
  Divorced parents—
    Choice of school. *See* **Divorce** (Infant—Education—Choice of school).
    Maintenance of children. *See* Maintenance—Child of divorced parents, *below*.
  Education—
    Child over 16. *See* Maintenance—Education or training, *below*.
    Divorced parents—
      Choice of school—Information. *See* **Divorce** (Infant—Education—Choice of school—Means available to court to obtain information thereon).
    Maintenance. *See* Maintenance—Education or training, *below*.
  Enforcement—
    High Court order. *See* Maintenance—Enforcement of High Court order, *below*.
    Justices' order. *See* Maintenance—Enforcement of justices' order, *below*.
    Overseas order. *See* Custody—Order—Enforcement of overseas order, *above*.
  Estate of—
    Appointment of guardian—
      Application. *See* **Practice** (Chancery Division—Infant's estate—Application for appointment of guardian).
  Evidence—
    Care proceedings in juvenile court. *See* **Children and young persons** (Care proceedings in juvenile court—Evidence).
    Criminal proceedings. *See* **Criminal evidence** (Child).
    Hearsay evidence—
      Civil proceedings. *See* **Evidence** (Hearsay—Child).
  Family proceedings. *See* **Family proceedings.**

MINOR (cont)—
  Financial provision—
    Divorce proceedings—
      Generally. *See* **Divorce** (Financial provision—Child).
      Lump sum order—Generally. *See* **Divorce** (Financial provision—Lump sum order—Lump sum for
      children).
  Foreign custody order. *See* Custody—Order—Enforcement of overseas order, *above.*
  Foreign right of access. *See* Custody—Access—Foreign right of access, *above.*
  Funds in court—
    County court—
      Transfer of funds to High Court. *See* **Practice** (Funds in court—Transfer to High Court from county
      court—Minors' funds).
  Grandparents—
    Religious upbringing of orphan. *See* Custody—Orphan—Religious upbringing, *above.*
  Gross indecency with minor. *See* **Criminal law** (Gross indecency—Child).
  Guardian—
    Appointment by the court—
      Jurisdiction—Infant aliens resident in England—Parents abroad—No property belonging to infants
      within the jurisdiction which the court is asked to administer. **D (Infants), Re** [1943] **2** 411, Ch D.
    Appointment of guardian—
      Palestine. *See* **Palestine** (Infant—Appointment of guardian).
    Guardian's allowance. *See* **Social security** (Guardian's allowance).
    Maintenance—
      Expenditure of private income by guardian—Statutory power of maintenance—Reimbursement of
      guardian—Conveyancing Act 1881, s 43. **Senior, Re** [1936] **3** 196, Ch D.
  Guardian ad litem—
    Disclosure of information to guardian—
      Care order in family proceedings. *See* **Family proceedings** (Orders in family proceedings—Care
      order—Guardian ad litem).
    Variation of trusts. *See* **Variation of trusts** (Infant).
  Guardianship—
    Appeals from county courts or courts of summary jurisdiction—
      Practice—Guardianship of Infants Act 1886 and 1925. **Practice Direction** [1955] **2** 115, Ch D.
    Appeals from courts of summary jurisdiction—
      Applications in regard to two or more children of same parents—Guardianship of Infants Acts 1886
      and 1925—R S C Ord 55A, r 6. **Practice Direction** [1957] **1** 32, Ch D.
      Exercise of discretion—Circumstances changed after magistrates' decision. **B (TA) (an infant), Re**
      [1970] **3** 705, Ch D.
      Legal aid in connection with appeal—Extension of time—Procedure. **Practice Direction**
      [1969] **2** 1220, Ch D.
      Review of exercise of discretion—Duty of appellate court. *See* **Appeal** (Review of exercise of
      discretion).
      Title of proceedings—Application for leave to adduce further evidence—Date of hearing of
      appeal—Guardianship of Infants Acts 1886 and 1925—RSC Ord 55A, Ord 59, r 34(2), (3), (4).
      Practice Direction [1960] **2** 862, Ch D.
      Title of proceedings—Application for leave to adduce further evidence—Guardianship of Infants
      Acts 1886 and 1925—RSC Ord 55, r 3(1), (2), Ord 91, r 7(1), (2). **Practice Direction** [1967] **2** 1232,
      Ch D.
    Application—
      Contested application—Second application to justices—First application dismissed on merits—No
      further evidence—Not res judicata—Whether justices should hear. **F (W) (an infant), Re**
      [1969] **3** 595, Ch D.
      Contested application—Witnesses to be cross-examined. *See* **Practice** (Chancery Division—
      Chambers proceedings—Adjournment to judge—Infants—Contested applications relating to
      infants in which witnesses are to be cross-examined).
      Minor having no parent, guardian or other person having parental rights—Parental
      rights—Stepfather—Minor living in household with stepfather—Father and mother deceased—
      Whether stepfather a 'person having parental rights'—Guardianship of Minors Act 1971, s 5(1). **N**
      (minors) (parental rights), Re [1974] **1** 126, Fam D.
    Evidence—
      Production of records and giving of evidence by adoption society or local authority—Contested
      applications—Application to court for directions. **Practice Direction** [1968] **1** 762, Ch D.
      Statements exhibited to affidavits. **Practice Direction** [1967] **2** 299, Ch D.
    Joint guardianship—
      Relevant factors—Benefit to minor the sole determining factor in deciding whether joint guardian
      should be appointed—Order not to be made for collateral purpose—Appeal from magistrates'
      order—Guardianship of Infants Act 1925, s 4(2). **H (an infant), Re** [1959] **3** 746, Ch D.
    Originating summons—
      Form. *See* **Originating summons** (Guardianship of infant—Form).
    Parents' position—
      Illegitimate child—Whether any pre-eminence of rights of parents—Legitimacy Act 1959, s 3(1).
      Adoption Application No 41/61, Re [1962] **3** 553, CA.
    Proceedings in private—
      Transcripts. *See* **Child** (Practice—Court proceedings in relation to children—Proceedings in
      private—Publication of information—Transcripts).
    Removal of minor from jurisdiction. *See* Removal outside jurisdiction, *below.*
  High Court order—
    Enforcement. *See* Maintenance—Enforcement of High Court order, *below.*
  Housing—
    Child in need—
      Duty of housing authority to provide accommodation for homeless person. *See* **Housing** (Homeless
      person—Duty of housing authority to provide accommodation—Children in need).

MINOR (cont)—

Illegitimate child—
 Access. *See* Custody—Illegitimate child, *above.*
 Affiliation proceedings. *See* **Affiliation.**
 Generally. *See* **Child** (Illegitimate child).
 Maintenance. *See* Maintenance—Illegitimate child, *below.*

Immigration—
 Child subject to immigration legislation—
  Wardship jurisdiction of court. *See* **Ward of court** (Jurisdiction—Child subject to immigration legislation).
 Detention. *See* **Immigration** (Detention—Minor).
 Leave to enter—
  Entry for purposes of adoption. *See* **Immigration** (Leave to enter—Adoption—Entry of child for purposes of adoption).

Income tax relief. *See* **Income tax** (Child relief).

Indecent photograph of—
 Obscene publication. *See* **Criminal law** (Obscene publications—Indecent photographs of children).

Intoxicating liquor—
 Sale to. *See* **Licensing** (Sale of intoxicating liquor to person under 18).

Joint guardianship. *See* Guardianship—Joint guardianship, *above.*

Legacy—
 Payment to minor. *See* **Administration of estates** (Legacy—Payment to infant).

Legitimacy—
 Declaration. *See* **Legitimation** (Declaration of legitimacy).
 Generally. *See* **Legitimacy.**
 Succession to intestate's estate. *See* **Intestacy** (Succession—Legitimacy).

Legitimated child. *See* Custody—Legitimated child, *above.*

Limitation—
 Rights of third parties against insurers—
  Motor Insurers' Bureau. *See* **Motor insurance** (Rights of third parties against insurers—Motor Insurers' Bureau—Untraced driver—Limitation).

Local authority—
 Care. *See* **Child** (Care—Local authority).
 Evidence. *See* Guardianship—Evidence—Production of records and giving of evidence by adoption society or local authority, *above.*

Magistrates—
 Enforcement of order. *See* Maintenance—Enforcement of justices' order, *below.*
 Jurisdiction to make custody order while divorce pending. *See* Custody—Jurisdiction—Magistrates' court—Divorce pending, *above.*

Maintenance—
 Application—
  Application to justices by mother for order against father—Venue—Child living out of England—Power of justices to make order. **R v Sandbach Justices, ex p Smith** [1950] **2** 781, KBD.
  Form of summons—Parties—Condition of making order that mother should have applied for custody. **Dulles' Settlement Trusts, Re** [1950] **2** 1013, CA.
 Arrears—
  Judgment summons—No application by husband for variation of maintenance order—Order for payment of arrears by instalments and for suspension of maintenance order—Whether county court judge had jurisdiction to suspend maintenance order—Debtors Act 1869, s 5, proviso (2)—Matrimonial Causes (Judgment Summons) Rules 1952 (SI 1952 No 2209), r 6(1), (2). **Cockburn v Cockburn** [1957] **3** 260, CA.
 Child of divorced parents—
  Age of child—Order for unsecured maintenance for child extending beyond age of 21—Matrimonial Causes Act 1950, s 26(1). **Le Mare v Le Mare** [1960] **2** 280, Div.
  Child of wife by previous marriage—Child accepted as one of the family after wife's re-marriage—Adultery by wife four months after marriage—Husband granted decree—Exercise of discretion to award maintenance in respect of children—Matrimonial Causes Act 1950, s 26(1)—Matrimonial Proceedings (Children) Act 1958, s 1(1). **Smith v Smith and Brown** [1962] **3** 369, CA.
  Death of divorced father—Order made against him in his lifetime to pay maintenance for children—Whether maintenance payable out of his estate after his death—proper method of securing that maintenance should continue after husband's death—Meaning of 'cause of action'—Law Reform (Miscellaneous Provisions) Act 1934, s 1(1). **Sugden v Sugden** [1957] **1** 300, CA.
  Guilty wife—Order made against wife—Supreme Court of Judicature (Consolidation) Act 1925, s 193(1). **Hering v Hering and Wilson** [1943] **2** 424, Div.
  Investment of divorce damages for benefit of child—Death of child while an infant—Further order regarding application of fund—Form of original order. **Collins v Collins** [1952] **2** 1133, CA.
  Lump sum—Jurisdiction to order lump sum payment for liabilities incurred in the past by the mother—Matrimonial Causes Act 1950, s 26(1). **Freeman-Thomas v Freeman-Thomas** [1963] **1** 17, Div.
 Child support—
  Absent parent—Maintenance assessment—Exempt income—Housing costs—Housing costs necessarily incurred for purpose of purchasing, renting or otherwise securing possession of home—Absent parent remortgaging home and incurring higher housing costs—Meaning of 'necessarily incurred'—Child Support (Maintenance Assessments and Special Cases) Regulations 1992, SI 1992/1815, Sch 3, para 4(1)(a). **Pabari v Secretary of State for Work and Pensions** [2005] **1** 287, CA.
 Child support. *See* **Child** (Maintenance—Child support).
 Custody—
  Summonses by wife under both Summary Jurisdiction and Guardianship of Infants Acts—Proper course for justices to follow. **Heworth v Heworth** [1948] **2** 715, Div.

MINOR (cont)—
  Maintenance (cont)—
    Discharge of order—
      Need of fresh evidence—Evidence not available when order made—Question for court—Confirmation of wife's adultery—Guardianship of Infants Act 1925, s 3(4). **Wakeman, Re** [1947] **2** 74, Ch D.
    Divorce Division of the High Court—
      Application to High Court while magistrates' court's order existing—Copy of maintenance order of magistrates' court to be lodged. **Practice Direction** [1961] **3** 1200, Div.
      Application—Leave of judge—Claim not included in wife's petition—Whether leave needed—Rule 43(3) ultra vires Matrimonial Causes Act 1950, s 29—Matrimonial Causes Rules 1957 (SI 1957 No 619), r 43(3). **Bancroft v Bancroft** [1963] **1** 367, CA.
    Education or training—
      Continuance of order after age of 16—Matters to be considered—Interests of child—Means of parties—Married Women (Maintenance) Act 1949, s 2(2). **Nowell v Nowell** [1951] **1** 474, Div.
      Infant aged more than 16—Continuation of payments under previous order—Application after cessation of order—Married Women (Maintenance) Act 1949, s 2(2). **Norman v Norman** [1950] **1** 1082, Div.
      Maintenance order including element in respect of school fees—Orders intended to run until earlier or later of child's seventeenth birthday or ceasing full-time education—Form of order—Correction of existing orders—Certificate of tax deduction—RSC Ord 20, r 11—CCR Ord 15, r 5. **Practice Direction** [1987] **2** 1084, Fam D.
      Maintenance order including element in respect of school fees—Payment to minor—Custodial parent applying for periodical payments order to be made against himself—Purpose of application to reduce tax liability—No issue before court—Whether court having jurisdiction to make order—Whether court should have regard to tax considerations when making financial provision n order—Matrimonial Causes Act 1973, s 23(1)(d). **Sherdley v Sherdley** [1987] **2** 54, HL.
      Maintenance order including element in respect of school fees—Provision for automatic adjustment to allow for increase in fees—Amount paid direct to school—Tax relief—Form of order—Contract for child's education to be between child and school—Form of contract. **Practice Direction** [1983] **2** 679, Fam D.
    Enforcement of High Court order—
      Attachment—Default in payment of amount of school fees—Whether writ of attachment will issue—Debtors Act 1869, s 4. **Farrant v Farrant** [1957] **1** 204, Div.
      Judgment summons—Order for maintenance of two children of marriage—No payment under order—Separate summons in respect of debt due to each child. **Easterbrook v Easterbrook** [1957] **2** 117, Div.
      Order of commitment against husband—Suspended order—Order directed to issue—Whether husband entitled to release on payment of amount not including arrears accrued since committal order made—Matrimonial Causes (Judgment Summons) Rules 1952 (SI 1952 No 2209), r 6(3). **Riding v Riding** [1958] **1** 65, CA.
      Summons by wife as infant's next friend—Debtors Act 1869, s 5—Matrimonial Causes Rules 1950 (SI 1950 No 1940), r 64(1). **Shelley v Shelley** [1952] **1** 70, PDA.
    Enforcement of justices' order—
      Appeal—Justices' order enforcing previous maintenance order—Right of appeal to High Court—Guardianship of Infants Act 1925, s 7(3). **Stern, Re** [1950] **2** 160, Ch D.
    Illegitimate child—
      Infant born before marriage—Not legitimated per subsequens matrimonium—Matrimonial Causes Act 1950, s 26(1). **Galloway v Galloway** [1955] **3** 429, HL; **Packer v Packer** [1953] **2** 127, CA.
    Income tax—
      Small maintenance payments. See **Divorce** (Maintenance—Income tax—Small maintenance payments—Payments to be made direct to children included).
    Jurisdiction—
      Divorce proceedings. See **Divorce** (Financial provision—Child—Maintenance—Jurisdiction).
      Father foreign citizen resident abroad—Submission of father to jurisdiction of High Court. **Dulles' Settlement Trusts, Re** [1950] **2** 1013, CA.
      Statutory jurisdiction. See Maintenance—Statutory jurisdiction, below.
    Means of parent—
      Mother granted custody—Means of mother taken into consideration in assessing sum payable by father—Guardianship of Infants Act 1925, s 3(2). **T (an infant), Re** [1953] **2** 830, Ch D; **W (infants), Re** [1956] **1** 368, CA.
    Order varying maintenance—
      Appeal against order—Whether leave to appeal necessary. See **Court of Appeal** (Interlocutory appeal—Leave to appeal—Necessity—Appeal against order varying maintenance of infants).
    Payment to minor—
      Payment directly to child or to person with whom child has his home—Registration of order in magistrates' court—Right of person with whom child has his home to proceed in his own name for variation, revival or revocation or for enforcement of order—Orders for payment direct to minor not to be made where of no benefit to parties or no tax advantage—Magistrates' Courts Act 1952, s 53A. **Practice Direction** [1980] **1** 1007, Fam D.
      Receipt of custodial parent—Avoidance of allegation by minor when of age that maintenance never received—Registration of order in magistrates' court—Order to provide that receipt of custodial parent valid receipt for payment to minor—Right of custodial parent to apply for enforcement of order—Orders for payment direct to minor not to be made where of no benefit to parties or no tax advantage—Nominal orders, orders pending suit and interim orders not to be registered except in special circumstances. **Practice Direction** [1977] **3** 942, Fam D.
    Statutory jurisdiction—
      Discharge of order—Order made under Summary Jurisdiction Acts—Order discharged—Order for custody under Guardianship of Infants Acts—Summary Jurisdiction (Married Women) Act 1895, s 5(b). **Flood v Flood** [1948] **2** 712, Div.

MINOR (cont)—
Maintenance (cont)—
Statutory jurisdiction (cont)—
Order made under Summary Jurisdiction Acts—Wife's subsequent application to justices for custody of children and weekly sum for their maintenance under Guardianship of Infants Acts—Competence—Summary Jurisdiction (Married Women) Act 1895, s 5(b)—Guardianship of Infants Act 1925, s 3(2). **Kinseth, Re** [1947] **1** 201, Ch D.
Trust in favour of children—
Order for payment of annual sum to be held in trust for children—Power of court to create trust—Supreme Court of Judicature (Consolidation) Act 1925, s 193(1), (3) (added by Matrimonial Causes Act 1937, s 10(4)). **Yates (Inspector of Taxes) v Starkey** [1951] **1** 732, CA.
Undertaking not to take proceedings for maintenance—
Undertaking in deed by wife petitioner—Covenant by husband to pay annuity for child—Illegality of wife's undertaking. **Bennett v Bennett** [1951] **1** 1088, KBD.
Variation of order—
Application—Reference to High Court—Competency—Guardianship of Infants Act 1925, s 7(3). **L (infants), Re** [1951] **1** 912, Ch D.
Wilful neglect. *See* Wilful neglect to maintain, *below*.
Marriage—
Refusal of consent by justices—
Appeal—No jurisdiction in High Court to hear appeal—Marriage Act 1823—Guardianship of Infants Act 1886—Guardianship of Infants Act 1925, ss 7(3), 9(1)(a), (4), 11(2). **Queskey, Re** [1946] **1** 717, Ch D.
Means of parent. *See* Maintenance—Means of parent, *above*.
Medical treatment—
Consent—
Nature of consent which minor can give to medical treatment without obtaining parental consent. **Gillick v West Norfolk and Wisbech Area Health Authority** [1985] **3** 402, HL.
Puberty-supressing drugs—Administration to persons under 18 experiencing gender dysphoria—Whether lawful—Whether child capable of consenting—Whether sanction of court required—Whether declaration and judicial guidance appropriate—Family Law Reform Act 1969, s 8. **R (on the application of Bell) v Tavistock and Portman NHS Foundation Trust (University College London Hospitals NHS Foundation Trust intervening)** [2022] **1** 416, DC and CA.
Invasive surgery—
Conjoined twins—Twins born conjoined at abdomen but only one capable of independent existence—Non-viable twin surviving only because viable twin circulating blood for both of them—Both twins facing certain death unless separated but operation inevitably causing death of non-viable twin—Parents refusing consent to operation—Whether court should permit operation—Whether operation would be lawful—Human Rights Act 1998, Sch 1, art 2. **A (children) (conjoined twins: surgical separation), Re** [2000] **4** 961, CA.
Mother refusing consent—Child born with life-threatening liver defect—Medical opinion that liver transplant which would prolong child's life had good chance of success—Mother refusing consent to operation because of pain and distress it would cause to child—Whether mother's views relevant—Whether in child's best interests to require him to undergo liver transplant. **T (a minor) (wardship: medical treatment), Re** [1997] **1** 906, CA.
Parental wishes—
Parents requesting treatment of minor—Treating clinician concluding treatment not in minor's best interests and affront to conscience—Whether clinician compelled to give treatment. **Wyatt, Re** [2005] **4** 1325, Fam D.
Right to refuse treatment—
Minor aged 16 years. *See* **Medical treatment** (Minor aged 16 years—Right to refuse treatment).
Ward of court—
Jurisdiction of court. *See* **Ward of court** (Jurisdiction—Medical treatment).
Withdrawal of treatment—
Alternative treatment—Hospital applying for declarations that lawful and in child's best interests for artificial ventilation to be withdrawn, for child to receive palliative care only and for child not to undergo alternative treatment overseas—Parents seeking alternative treatment—Judge granting declarations—New evidence on likelihood of success of alternative treatment—Whether declarations to be affirmed. **Great Ormond Street Hospital for Children NHS Foundation Trust v Yates (No 2)** [2018] **1** 623n, Fam D.
Alternative treatment—Hospital applying for declarations that lawful and in child's best interests for artificial ventilation to be withdrawn, for child to receive palliative care only and for child not to undergo alternative treatment overseas—Parents seeking alternative treatment—Judge granting declarations—Whether judge in error. **Great Ormond Street Hospital for Children NHS Foundation Trust v Yates** [2018] **1** 569, Fam D, CA.
Transfer for medical treatment in other European Union member state—Disagreement between parents and treating doctors as to medical treatment of child—Determination of best interests of child—Proper approach where child's EU rights engaged—Children Act 1989, s 8—Article 56 TFEU—Charter of Fundamental Rights of the European Union, art 24. **Raqeeb (by her litigation friend, XX) v Barts NHS Foundation Trust** [2020] **3** 663, QBD.
Money recovered—
Control—
Appointment of receiver—Damages recovered for personal injuries including brain damage whereby infant would require supervision for life—Application to be made for the appointment of a receiver—Money to be transferred to Court of Protection for administration. **M v Lester** [1966] **1** 207, QBD.
Name—
Change of surname. *See* Change of surname, *above*.
Negligence—
Duty to take care. *See* **Negligence** (Duty to take care—Existence of duty—Children).
Generally. *See* **Child** (Negligence).
Parental contact—
Generally. *See* **Child** (Care—Parental contact).

MINOR (cont)—
    Negligence (cont)—
        Proceedings in juvenile court. *See* **Children and young persons** (Care proceedings in juvenile court).
        Voluntary assumption of risk. *See* **Negligence** (Volenti non fit injuria—Infant).
    Next friend—
        Adoption, by minor, of action on attaining majority. *See* **Practice** (Persons under disability—Minor—
        Proceeding by next friend—Adoption of action on attaining majority).
        Parent—
            Removal as next friend—Removal where parent acting improperly and against interests of
            infant—application for removal of five parents as next friends—Five parents of thalidomide
            children refusing to accept settlement proposed by company marketing thalidomide drug—Drug
            taken during pregnancy causing deformity in children—Some 400 thalidomide children in
            England—Claims in respect of 62 children brought within limitation period previously
            settled—Company under that settlement paying average of £15,000 in respect of each child—260
            parents subsequently given leave to apply to extend limitation period—Negotiations for
            settlement—Company offering to set up trust fund for benefit of children who had not benefited
            from earlier settlement—Trustees in applying fund for benefit of children to have 'due and proper
            regard for the differing needs and resources of and for the differing degrees of handicap or
            disability of individual beneficiaries'—Condition of proposed settlement that should be accepted
            by all parents—Five parents refusing—Whether refusal reasonable in circumstances. **Taylor's**
            Application, Re [1972] **2** 873, CA.
    Occupier's liability. *See* **Occupier's liability** (Children).
    Orphan—
        Religious upbringing. *See* Custody—Orphan—Religious upbringing, *above*.
    Parens patriae jurisdiction. *See* **Statute** (Crown—Parens patriae jurisdiction).
    Parental responsibility—
        Specific issue order—
            Father dying intestate in France—Mother applying for specific issue order authorising her to accept
            French inheritance and enter into contract of sale of French property on minor's behalf—Whether
            court having power to authorise sale—Meaning of 'parental responsibility'—Children Act 1989,
            ss 3, 8—Hague Convention on Jurisdiction, Applicable Law, Recognition, Enforcement and
            Co-operation in Respect of Parental Responsibility and Measures for the Protection of Children
            1996, art 3(g). **B (a child), Re** [2022] **3** 1036, Fam Ct.
    Parental rights—
        Assumption by local authority. *See* **Child** (Care—Local authority—Assumption by authority of parental
        rights).
        European Community—
            Jurisdiction. *See* **European Union** (Jurisdiction—Matrimonial matters and matters of parental
            responsibility).
        Illegitimate child. *See* **Child** (Illegitimate child—Parental rights and duties).
        Marriage—
            Unrecognised marriage ceremony. *See* Custody—Rights of custody—Removal outside
            jursidiction—Parental responsibility—Mother and father marrying in Islamic ceremony not
            recognised as valid under English law, *above*.
        Stepfather. *See* Guardianship—Application—Minor having no parent, guardian or other person having
        parental rights, *above*.
    Party to proceedings—
        Family proceedings. *See* **Family proceedings** (Parties—Minor).
        Wardship proceedings. *See* **Ward of court** (Practice—Parties to proceedings—Minor).
    Paternity. *See* **Paternity**.
    Payment out of court—
        Money recovered by minors in High Court and transferred to county court. *See* **County court** (Payment
        out of court—Money recovered by infants etc in High Court and transferred to county court).
    Place of safety order—
        Generally. *See* **Children and young persons** (Detention—Place of safety order).
        Ward of court. *See* **Ward of court** (Protection of ward—Place of safety order).
    Practice—
        Appeal to Divisional Court—
            Family Division. *See* **Practice** (Family Division—Divisional Court—Appeal to Divisional
            Court—Child).
        Chancery Division—
            Chambers applications relating to minors—Adjournment to judge within stated time. **Practice**
            Direction [1966] **3** 84, Ch D.
        Divorce proceedings. *See* **Divorce** (Practice—Children).
        Generally. *See* **Child** (Practice).
        Wardship and custody proceedings—
            Joinder of child as party—Official Solicitor as guardian ad litem—Joinder not to be ordered, even
            by consent, unless special reasons shown—Note of special reasons etc to be taken for guidance
            of Official Solicitor. **Practice Direction** [1982] **1** 319, Fam D.
        Wardship and guardianship proceedings—
            Custody and access—Care and control and access—Contested applications—Conciliation—
            Conciliation before registrar. **Practice Direction** [1984] **3** 800, Fam D.
            Custody and access—Care and control and access—Residence, contact and other orders—
            Contested applications—Conciliation—Conciliation before district judge and court welfare
            officer—Attendance of parties—Applications for adjournment—Directions where conciliation
            unsuccessful—Urgent applications—Children Act 1989, s 8. **Practice Direction** [1992] **1** 421,
            Fam D.
            Custody and access—Residence, contact and other orders—Contested applications—Conciliation—
            Conciliation before district judge and Children and Family Court Advisory and Support Service
            officer—Attendance of parties—Applications for adjournment—Directions where conciliation
            unsuccessful—Urgent applications—Children Act 1989, ss 8, 13. **Practice Direction** [2004] **2** 463,
            Fam D.

MINOR (cont)—
Practice (cont)—
    Welfare report—
        Family Division. *See* **Child** (Welfare—Welfare report).
Proceeding by next friend—
    Adoption of action on attaining majority. *See* **Practice** (Persons under disability—Minor—Proceeding by next friend—Adoption of action on attaining majority).
    Generally. *See* Next friend, *above*.
Psychiatric examination—
    Wardship and matrimonial causes—
        Circumstances in which leave to subject child to psychiatric examination appropriate—Leave not necessary where examination is purely physical. **Practice Direction** [1985] **3** 576, Fam D.
        Costs of examination. **Practice Direction** [1985] **1** 832, Fam D.
Publication—
    Protection of child. *See* **Child** (Protection—Freedom of publication).
Religious education. *See* Custody—Care and control—Religious education, *above*.
Removal of proceedings instituted in court of summary jurisdiction to High Court. *See* Custody—Jurisdiction—Removal of proceedings to High Court, *above*.
Removal outside jurisdiction—
    Abduction—
        Exceptions to the requirements to order return—Asylum proceedings—Mother wrongfully removing child from South Africa to England and applying for asylum—Child named as dependant on mother's asylum application—Father applying for return of child—Whether naming child as dependant on parent's asylum application providing protection from refoulement—Child Abduction and Custody Act 1985, Sch 1, art 13—Nationality, Immigration and Asylum Act 2002, s 104—Council Directive 2005/85/EC, art 7—Geneva Convention Relating to the Status of Refugees 1951. **G v G (Secretary of State for the Home Dept intervening)** [2021] **4** 113, SC.
        Exceptions to the requirements to order return—Grave risk of harm—Hague Convention on the Civil Aspects of International Child Abduction 1980, art 13(b). **E (children) (wrongful removal: exceptions to return), Re** [2011] **4** 517, SC; **S (a child), Re** [2012] **2** 603, SC.
        Habitual residence—Degree of integration of child in social and family environment—Consideration of child's own state of mind —Hague Convention on the Civil Aspects of International Child Abduction 1980. **LC (children) (abduction: habitual residence: state of mind of child), Re** [2014] **1** 1181, SC.
        Removal out of United Kingdom—Abduction of child under 16 or removal of ward without leave of court—Danger of removal real and imminent—Application to police to institute 'port-alert'—Information to accompany application—Notification to Passport Department—Guardianship of Minors Act 1971—Guardianship Act 1973—Child Abduction Act 1984, ss 1, 2. **Practice Direction** [1986] **1** 983, Fam D.
        Ward of court—Rights of custody. *See* Custody—Rights of custody—Ward of court—Abduction of ward of court, *above*.
    Application for order prohibiting or allowing removal of child out of England and Wales—
        Practice. *See* **Child** (Practice—Matrimonial causes—Applications relating to children—Application for order prohibiting removal of child out of England and Wales).
    Application to set aside return order under 1980 Hague Convention—
        Proper approach—FPR 12.52A—Child Abduction and Custody Act 1985, Sch 1, art 13(b). **B (a child) (abduction: art 13(b)), Re** [2021] **1** 1138n, CA.
    Application under Guardianship of Infants Acts—
        Custody and access the subject of an order of Canadian court—Guardianship of Infants Act 1886, s 5 (as amended by Administration of Justice Act 1928, s 16). **E (an infant), Re** [1955] **3** 174, Ch D.
    Custody granted to father by Divorce Court—
        Minors made wards of court in Chancery Division—Application by father to Chancery Division that minors should cease to be wards of court—Law Reform (Miscellaneous Provisions) Act 1949, s 9(3). **Andrews (Infants), Re** [1958] **2** 308, Ch D.
        Minors made wards of court in Chancery Division—Application by father to Divorce Division for leave to take minors out of jurisdiction—Law Reform (Miscellaneous Provisions) Act 1949, s 9(2)—Matrimonial Causes Act 1950, s 26(1)—RSC Ord 54P, r 3. **Andrews v Andrews and Sullivan** [1958] **2** 305, Div.
    Habitual residence. *See* **Family proceedings** (Orders in family proceedings—Jurisdiction—Habitual residence).
    Injunction—
        Notification to Passport Office. **Practice Direction** [1983] **2** 253, Fam D.
    Jurisdiction of magistrates. *See* **Magistrates** (Jurisdiction—Removal of child from jurisdiction).
    Magistrates' order—
        Order forbidding removal—Order a nullity. **T v T** [1968] **3** 321, Div.
    Order of court prohibiting removal—
        Risk of unauthorised removal—Home Office assistance to prevent such removal—Circumstances in which application for assistance to be made—Form of application—Matrimonial Causes Rules 1971 (SI 1971 No 1953), r 94(1) (as amended by the Matrimonial Causes (Amendment) Rules 1973 (SI 1973 No 777), s 4). **Practice Direction** [1973] **3** 194, Fam D.
    Passport—
        Notice to Passport Office—Home Office assistance to prevent unauthorised removal of infant. **Practice Note** [1963] **3** 66, Ch D.
    Permission to relocate—
        Unmarried parents sharing residence of children—Mother applying for permission to remove children to relocate to Abu Dhabi with new husband—Judge granting relocation order but requiring husband to provide financial security to ensure compliance by mother with contact arrangements and making children wards of court—Whether provision of financial security enforceable—Whether use of wardship appropriate—Children Act 1989, s 8. **B (children) (relocation outside jurisdiction: enforcement of contact: wardship), Re** [2017] **1 Comm** 1099, CA.

MINOR (cont)—
Removal outside jurisdiction (cont)—
Powers of court—
Removal of family's passport as coercive measure. *See* **Ward of court** (Contempt of court in wardship proceedings—Removal of ward from jurisdiction without leave—Proceedings to locate parent and ward).
Removal in defiance of court order—
Advice on recovery of custody. **Practice Direction** [1984] **3** 640, Fam D.
Removal of child normally to be dealt with as contempt of court rather than as subject of criminal prosecution—Criminal prosecution only appropriate for exceptional cases—Private prosecution of parent for kidnapping own child extremely undesirable. **R v D** [1984] **2** 449, HL.
Removal in defiance of undertaking given to court—
Specific issue and prohibited steps orders—Parent who removed child not within jurisdiction and having no assets within jurisdiction—Whether court could issue specific issue and prohibited steps orders to assist return of child—Whether orders could be made ex parte—Children Act 1989, s 8(1). **D (a minor), Re** [1992] **1** 892, CA.
Removal to or retention in European member state—
Return procedure—Whether court having power to make order for summary return—Whether court should do so or wait until determination of proceedings under international convention—Child Abduction and Custody Act 1985, Sch 1—Council Regulation 2201/2003/EC, arts 1, 11. **S (abduction: Hague Convention or BIIa), Re** [2018] **4** 806, CA.
Ward of court—
Leave. *See* **Ward of court** (Removal of ward from jurisdiction).
Wardship and guardianship cases—
Application for leave to remove child normally to be made to judge—Cases where application may be made to registrar. **Practice Direction** [1984] **2** 407, Fam D.
Residence order—
Family proceedings. *See* **Family proceedings** (Orders in family proceedings—Residence order).
Sentence. *See* **Sentence** (Young person).
Settlement—
Accumulation of income during minority—
Surplus income. *See* **Accumulation** (Surplus income—Accumulation during minority).
Financial provision—
Divorce of parents. *See* **Divorce** (Financial provision—Child—Settlement).
Generally. *See* **Settlement** (Children).
Income tax. *See* **Income tax** (Settlement—Children).
Sexual offences against—
Sentence. *See* **Sentence** (Sexual offences against children).
Statutory jurisdiction under Summary Jurisdiction Acts. *See* Maintenance—Statutory jurisdiction, *above*.
Stepfather—
Parental rights. *See* Guardianship—Application—Minor having no parent, guardian or other person having parental rights, *above*.
Sterilisation—
Generally. *See* **Sterilisation** (Child).
Ward of court—
Jurisdiction of court to authorise sterilisation. *See* **Ward of court** (Jurisdiction—Sterilisation).
Surname—
Change of surname. *See* Change of surname, *above*.
Torts—
Tort founded on contract—
Independent act outside contract—Liability for act in tort. **Ballett v Mingay** [1943] **1** 143, CA.
Training—
Child over 16. *See* Maintenance—Education or training, *above*.
Maintenance. *See* Maintenance—Education or training, *above*.
Trust—
Relative advantages between infant and adult beneficiaries—
Variation of trusts by the court. *See* **Variation of trusts** (Benefit—Infant beneficially interested).
Variation of maintenance order. *See* Maintenance—Variation of order, *above*.
Ward of court—
Child in care of local authority—
Generally. *See* **Child** (Care—Local authority—Wardship proceedings).
Generally. *See* **Ward of court**.
Welfare of minor—
Adoption proceedings. *See* **Adoption** (Welfare of infant).
Generally. *See* **Child** (Welfare).
Welfare of minor as first and paramount consideration. *See* Custody—Welfare of minor as first and paramount consideration, *above*.
Whereabouts. *See* **Child** (Whereabouts).
Wilful neglect to maintain—
Amount of maintenance to be ordered—
National assistance—Whether national assistance taken into account. **Ashley v Ashley** [1965] **3** 554, Div.
Order against husband—Liability of person other than party to marriage to maintain child—Husband not father of child—Liability of natural father—Liability of father not exceeding amount which would be awarded against him under maintenance order—Matrimonial Proceedings (Magistrates' Courts) Act 1960, s 2(1)(h), (5). **Snow v Snow** [1971] **3** 833, CA, Div.
Child's maintenance and wife's maintenance separate subjects of complaint—
Whether husband's reasonable belief in wife's adultery a defence to her application for maintenance for child—Summary Jurisdiction (Married Women) Act 1895, s 4. **Cooke v Cooke** [1960] **3** 39, Div.

MINOR (cont)—
  Wilful neglect to maintain (cont)—
    Consensual separation—
      Court's power to found on that neglect an order for provision for the wife, in addition to maintenance for the child—Provision such as to enable wife to discharge obligations to child impairing her earning power—Matrimonial Proceedings (Magistrates' Courts) Act 1960, s 2(1)(b), (h). **Northrop v Northrop** [1967] **2** 961, CA.
      No agreement as to maintenance—Liability of husband. **Starkie v Starkie (No 2)** [1953] **2** 1519, Div.
    Desertion—
      Wife in state of desertion—Jurisdiction to make orders for custody and maintenance of child—Matrimonial Proceedings (Magistrates' Courts) Act 1960, ss 1(1)(h), 2(1)(d), (h), 4(1). **Vaughan v Vaughan** [1963] **2** 742, Div.
      Wife in state of desertion—Right to claim maintenance suspended—Summary Jurisdiction (Married Women) Act 1895, s 4. **Naylor v Naylor** [1961] **2** 129, Div.
    Order in favour of wife—
      Validity. **Kinnane v Kinnane** [1953] **2** 1144, Div.
    Wife's maintenance—
      Failure to maintain child—Whether wife disentitled to maintenance for herself by reason of husband's failure to maintain child—Matrimonial Proceedings (Magistrates' Courts) Act 1960, ss 1(1)(h), 2(1)(b), (h). **Young v Young** [1962] **3** 120, Div.
  Wrongful removal or retention. See Custody—Rights of custody—Wrongful removal or retention, *above*.
  Youthful offender—
    Sentence. See **Sentence** (Youthful offender).

MINOR INTEREST
  Land—
    Registration. See **Land registration** (Minor interests).

MINORITY SHAREHOLDER
  Foreign company—
    Conflict of laws. See **Conflict of laws** (Company—Foreign company—Minority shareholder).
  Generally. See **Company** (Minority shareholder).

MIRROR
  Goods vehicle. See **Road traffic** (Goods vehicle—Mirrors).

MISAPPROPRIATION
  Trust money—
    Breach of trust. See **Trust and trustee** (Breach of trust—Misappropriation of trust money).

MISBEHAVIOUR IN PUBLIC OFFICE
  See **Criminal law** (Misbehaviour in public office).

MISCARRIAGE
  Procuring—
    Offence. See **Criminal law** (Abortion).

MISCARRIAGE OF JUSTICE
  Compensation—
    Crime. See **Compensation** (Crime—Scheme).

MISCONDUCT
  Arbitration—
    Setting aside award. See **Arbitration** (Award—Setting aside award—Misconduct).
  Costs—
    Taxation. See **Costs** (Taxation—Misconduct, neglect etc).
  Professional misconduct—
    Counsel. See **Counsel** (Professional misconduct).
    Dentist. See **Dentist** (Professional misconduct).
    Medical practitioner. See **Medical practitioner** (Professional misconduct).
    Solicitor. See **Solicitor** (Disciplinary proceedings—Professional misconduct).
  Public office, in. See **Criminal law** (Misconduct in public office).

MISDESCRIPTION
  Sale of land—
    Generally. See **Sale of land** (Misdescription).
    Rescission of contract. See **Sale of land** (Rescission of contract—Misdescription).
  Will—
    Gift—
      False description of beneficiary. See **Will** (Gift—Misdescription—False description of beneficiary).

MISFEASANCE
  Company officer, by. See **Company** (Winding up—Misfeasance).
  Public officer, by—
    Damages—
      Exemplary damages. See **Damages** (Exemplary damages—Misfeasance in public office).
      Generally. See **Public office** (Abuse of—Misfeasance by a public officer).
      Jury trial. See **Jury** (Trial by jury—Cases where party entitled to trial by jury).
  Public officer, by. See **Public office** (Abuse of—Misfeasance by a public officer).

MISLEADING ADVERTISEMENT
  Control. See **Advertisement** (Control—Misleading advertisements).

MISLEADING LABEL
Food and drugs. *See* **Food and drugs** (Label—Misleading label).

MISNOMER
Parties. *See* **Practice** (Parties—Misnomer).

MISPRISION OF FELONY
See **Criminal law** (Misprision of felony).

MISREPRESENTATION
Agent—
    Fraudulent misrepresentation—
        Liability of principal for misrepresentation of agent. *See* Fraudulent misrepresentation—Agent, *below*.
    Innocent misrepresentation—
        Liability of principal for misrepresentation of agent. *See* Innocent misrepresentation—Agent, *below*.
    Liability—
        Agent's liability for misrepresentation inducing another to enter into contract—Whether liability for agent's misrepresentation attaching to principal only—Whether agent personally liable to innocent party for misrepresentation—Misrepresentation Act 1967, s 2(1). **Resolute Maritime Inc v Nippon Kaiji Kyokai** [1983] **2** 1, QBD.
Charterparty. *See* **Shipping** (Charterparty—Conditions and warranties—Misrepresentation).
Condition distinguished. *See* Distinction from condition and warranty, *below*.
Conflict of laws—
    Proper law of tort. *See* **Conflict of laws** (Tort—Proper law of tort—Misrepresentation).
Continuing representation—
    True representation when made but subsequently becoming untrue—
        Rescission. **With v O'Flanagan** [1936] **1** 727, CA.
Credit. *See* Misrepresentation as to person's credit, *below*.
Damages—
    Deceit—
        Fraudulent misrepresentation contrasted with deceit—Defendant conceding that plaintiff entitled to rescission for misrepresentation—Whether defendant's concession precluding plaintiff from recovering damages for deceit. **Archer v Brown** [1984] **2** 267, QBD.
        Measure of damages—Loss of profits—Claim for loss of profits on trading stocks and contracts for differences—Claimant deceitfully induced to enter into trades—Whether claimant entitled to damages for lost profits that it would otherwise have made after the discovery of the fraud with the funds of which it had been defrauded. **Parabola Investments Ltd v Browallia Cal Ltd** [2011] **1 Comm** 210, CA.
        Measure of damages—Loss of profits—Claim for loss of profits on trading stocks and contracts for differences—Whether claimant required to show specific and profitable alternative transaction for loss to be recoverable—Whether loss in relation to contracts for differences too speculative to be recoverable—Whether loss of profits recoverable to date of trial. **Parabola Investments Ltd v Browallia Cal Ltd** [2009] **2 Comm** 589, QBD.
        Measure of damages—Loss of profits—Plaintiffs purchasing hairdressing business in reliance on defendant's representation that he would not trade in opposition to plaintiffs—Plaintiffs suffering loss of profits by reason of defendant's competing business—Whether loss of profits damage directly flowing from fraudulent inducement—Whether loss of profits recoverable in action for deceit—Whether loss of profits to be assessed on basis of compensating plaintiffs for all loss suffered—Whether loss of profits to be assessed on basis of putting plaintiffs in as good a position as if representation had been true. **East v Maurer** [1991] **2** 733, CA.
    Fraudulent misrepresentation—
        Deceit contrasted. *See* Damages—Deceit—Fraudulent misrepresentation contrasted with deceit, *above*.
        Measure of damages. *See* **Damages** (Measure of damages—Fraudulent misrepresentation).
    Innocent misrepresentation—
        Measure of damages—Reasonable ground for belief—Insurers entering into contracts on basis of presentation by insurance brokers—Presentation indicating particular underwriter's involvement and specifying underwriting criteria—Whether underwriter's lesser involvement and alleged non-compliance with criteria constituting misrepresentation—Whether alleged misrepresentation induced contract—Whether correct measure of loss for innocent misrepresentation measure for fraud—Misrepresentation Act 1967, s 2(1). **Avon Insurance plc v Swire Fraser Ltd** [2000] **1 Comm** 573, QBD.
        Measure of damages—Unforeseeable loss—Finance company entering into hire-purchase agreement with purchaser of motor vehicle—Motor dealer misrepresenting amount of deposit paid by purchaser to induce finance company to enter into hire-purchase agreement—Purchaser defaulting on payment of hire-purchase instalments and dishonestly disposing of vehicle—Finance company claiming damages from dealer for innocent misrepresentation—Whether measure of damages for innocent misrepresentation measure of damages in tort or contract—Whether measure of damages for innocent misrepresentation same as measure of damages for fraudulent misrepresentation—Whether innocent party entitled to recover unforeseeable loss flowing from misrepresentation—Misrepresentation Act 1967, s 2(1). **Royscot Trust Ltd v Rogerson** [1991] **3** 294, CA.
    Measure of damages—
        Distributor seeking to recover expenses defrayed from promotional activities carried out under contract—Supplier providing no calculation of hypothetical losses had distributor entered contract later—Whether distributor able to recover expenses on reliance basis when likely to have entered into similar arrangement with supplier. **Yam Seng Pte Ltd v International Trade Corp Ltd** [2013] **1 Comm** 1321, QBD.
    Innocent misrepresentation. *See* Damages—Innocent misrepresentation—Measure of damages, *above*.

MISREPRESENTATION (cont)—
Damages (cont)—
  Measure of damages (cont)—
    Misrepresentation not discovered until value of article had fallen by reason of defect. *See* **Contract** (Damages for breach—Misrepresentation—Misrepresentation not discovered until value of article had fallen by reason of defect).
  Negligent misrepresentation. *See* Negligent misrepresentation—Damages for breach of duty of care, *below*.
  Non-fraudulent misrepresentation—
    Loss—Defendants providing guarantee—Claimant demanding debt under guarantee—Defendants making misleading disclosure of means—Claimant providing waiver on basis of disclosure—Whether claimant suffering loss—Misrepresentation Act 1967, s 2(2). **UCB Corporate Services Ltd v Thomason** [2005] **1 Comm** 601, CA.
  Reasonable ground for belief that facts represented true—
    Contract for hire of barges—Representation as to capacity of barges—Barge owners overstating capacity of barges—Owners relying on deadweight capacity stated in Lloyd's Register—Register giving wrong figure—Owners having in their possession ship's documents stating correct figure—Misrepresentation inducing charterers to enter into a contract of hire—Whether owners having reasonable ground to believe that statement as to capacity of barges true—Misrepresentation Act 1967, s 2(1). **Howard Marine and Dredging Co Ltd v A Ogden & Sons (Excavations) Ltd** [1978] **2** 1134, CA.
  Sale of land. *See* Innocent misrepresentation—Sale of land—Innocent misrepresentation as to size of site, *below*.
Disclosure—
  Duty to disclose—
    Claimant providing services to defendant in respect of its annual trade show under fixed term contract—Defendant insisting on inclusion of new clause in contract with claimant that the contract would not be enforced if for some 'unforeseen circumstance' the show was cancelled or did not take place—Defendant confidentially contemplating sale of its business and trade show to third party—Whether defendant had to provide reasons for insistence on inclusion of new clause—Whether reasons had to be truthful. **Burntcopper Ltd (t/a Contemporary Design Unit) v International Travel Catering Association Ltd** [2014] **2 Comm** 1055, QBD.
    Duty of good faith between partners—Whether duty of good faith existing between persons negotiating entry into partnership. **Conlon v Simms** [2006] **2** 1024, Ch D; [2007] **3** 802, CA.
    Duty of utmost faith—Failure to disclose material facts—Whether silence amounting to misrepresentation—Whether misrepresentation 'made' to other party if there is a failure to disclose material facts—Misrepresentation Act 1967, s 2(1). **Banque Financière de la Cité SA v Westgate Insurance Co Ltd** [1989] **2** 952, CA.
Distinction from condition and warranty—
  Construction—
    Effect. **Chess (Oscar) Ltd v Williams** [1957] **1** 325, CA.
Estoppel. *See* **Estoppel** (Representation).
Exclusion of liability for misrepresentation—
  Avoidance of provision excluding liability—
    Liability for misrepresentation by agent—Condition excluding authority of agent to make representation on behalf of principal—Misrepresentation by agent—Whether condition limiting authority of agent liable to be avoided—Whether principal liable for misrepresentation by agent—Misrepresentation Act 1967, s 3. **Overbrooke Estates Ltd v Glencombe Properties Ltd** [1974] **3** 511, Ch D.
  Non-contractual notice—
    Claimant alleging induced to buy subordinated loan notes by representation contained in bank's investor presentation document—Whether representation made to claimant—Whether bank entitled to rely on disclaimer in document—Misrepresentation Act 1967, s 2(1)—Unfair Contract Terms Act 1977, s 2. **Taberna Europe CDO II plc v Selskabet af 1 September 2008 A/S (formerly Roskilde Bank A/S)** [2017] **2 Comm** 605, CA; [2017] **3** 1046, CA.
  Unfair terms. *See* **Contract** (Unfair terms—Exclusion of liability for misrepresentation).
Fraudulent misrepresentation—
  Action founded on tort committed within jurisdiction—
    Service out of the jurisdiction. *See* **Practice** (Service out of the jurisdiction—Action founded on tort committed within jurisdiction—Fraudulent or negligent misrepresentation).
  Agent—
    Liability of principal for misrepresentation of agent—Misrepresentation by agent made before appointment and continuing thereafter—Ratification. **Briess v Woolley** [1954] **1** 909, HL.
  Belief in truth of representation as understood by representor—
    Circular letter inducing purchase of shares. **Akerhielm v De Mare** [1959] **3** 485, PC.
    Letters read together amounting to representation which writer knew to be untrue—Such representation unintentional—Liability of writer. **Gross v Lewis Hillman Ltd** [1969] **3** 1476, CA.
  Builders' brochure—
    Builders having pool agreement with building society—Whether co-adventurers—Liability of society. **Bradford Third Equitable Benefit Building Society v Borders** [1941] **2** 205, HL.
  Company—
    Prospectus. *See* **Company** (Prospectus—Misrepresentation—Fraud).
    Signature of company—Fraudulent misrepresentation made in letter signed by assistant secretary of company—Whether misrepresentation 'signed' by company—Statute of Frauds Amendment Act 1828, s 6. **UBAF Ltd v European American Banking Corp** [1984] **2** 226, CA.
  Damages—
    Generally. *See* **Damages** (Measure of damages—Fraud).
    Measure of damages. *See* **Damages** (Measure of damages—Fraudulent misrepresentation).
    Mitigation of loss. *See* **Damages** (Mitigation of loss—Plaintiff not required to expend money—Plaintiff induced by fraudulent misrepresentation to advance money on debenture).
  Deceit—
    Fraudulent misrepresentation contrasted with deceit. *See* Damages—Deceit—Fraudulent misrepresentation contrasted with deceit, *above*.

MISREPRESENTATION (cont)—
Fraudulent misrepresentation (cont)—
Dimensions of garden—
Rescission—National Conditions of Sale, cl 10—Costs. **Bellotti v Chequers Developments Ltd** [1936] **1** 89, KBD.
Grant of protected tenancy. *See* **Rent restriction** (Protected tenancy—Misrepresentation—Fraudulent misrepresentation).
Loss of protected tenancy—
Action—Whether loss sufficient to support action. **Mafo v Adams** [1969] **3** 1404, CA.
Reliance—
Contract for long term loans—Local authorities seeking rescission of loans made to them by bank on ground of fraudulent misrepresentation—Bank contending local authorities having no awareness of any representations—Correct test for reliance. **Leeds City Council v Barclays Bank plc** [2022] **1 Comm** 569, Comm Ct.
Contract for supply of dried egg products by Netherlands supplier to US company—Representation made that additional costs to be incurred to comply with inspection procedures of US regulatory authorities—Price increased under revised contract—US company rejecting egg products—Netherlands supplier claiming damages for breach of contract—Whether fraudulent misrepresentation inducing US company to enter into revised contract—Whether breach of warranties by Netherlands supplier. **BV Nederlandse Industrie van Eiprodukten v Rembrandt Enterprises Inc** [2019] **1 Comm** 543, QBD.
Contract for supply of dried egg products by Netherlands supplier to US company—Representation made that additional costs to be incurred to comply with inspection procedures of US regulatory authorities—Price increased under second contract—Sister company of Netherlands supplier supplying some products—US company suspending its contractual obligations—Netherlands supplier claiming damages for breach of contract—Whether fraudulent misrepresentation inducing US company to enter into second contract—Whether Netherlands supplier entitled to claim for transferred loss of sister company. **BV Nederlandse Industrie van Eiprodukten v Rembrandt Enterprises Inc** [2019] **2 Comm** 501, CA; [2019] **4** 612, CA.
Whether presumption of reliance arising on fraudulent misrepresentation having no force once representee gives evidence—Whether representor inducing acts flowing from erroneous belief if falsely answering question touching that belief after it had been reached. **County NatWest Ltd v Barton (note)** [2002] **4** 494, CA.
Rescission—
Agreement to settle claim for damages—Employee seeking damages for personal injury sustained at work—Employer's insurer suspecting employee dishonestly exaggerating effect of injury but unable to obtain satisfactory evidence to prove fraud—Insurer settling claim by way of Tomlin order—Insurer subsequently obtaining evidence as to fraudulent claim and seeking rescission of agreement on basis of inducement due to employee's misrepresentation as to extent of injury—Whether requirement to prove representee believed misrepresentation true—Whether mere suspicion of fraudulent claim precluding rescission. **Hayward v Zurich Insurance Co plc** [2016] **2 Comm** 755, SC; [2016] **4** 628, SC.
Duty of good faith—Bribery—Parties entering contract—Parties subsequently negotiating second contract for sale of asset whose value depending on first contract—Payment made to managing director of negotiating company—Managing director disclosing payment to one other director—Whether first contract creating duty of good faith—Whether agent making fraudulent misrepresentations—Whether payment to director bribery—Whether company having knowledge of payment—Whether rescission available in relation to first contract. **Ross River Ltd v Cambridge City Football Club Ltd** [2008] **1** 1004, Ch D; [2008] **1 Comm** 1028, Ch D.
Share distribution agreements—Scope of equitable discretion in rescission claims—Whether misrepresentee entitled to rescind part of contract. **De Molestina v Ponton** [2002] **1 Comm** 587, QBD.
Sale of company—
Misrepresentation inducing contract—No dishonesty in making misrepresentation—Whether damages can be claimed for fraudulent misrepresentation if no dishonesty in making misrepresentation. **Witter (Thomas) Ltd v TBP Industries Ltd** [1996] **2** 573, Ch D.
Sale of goods—
Financing agreement—Misrepresentation of price by seller—Sale of used car represented as new car—Fraud. **United Motor Finance Co v Addison & Co Ltd** [1937] **1** 425, PC.
Sale of shares—
Shares pledged to bank—Bank charge redeemed since sale—Rescission—Restitutio in integrum—One party released from obligations which cannot be restored. **Spence v Crawford** [1939] **3** 271, HL.
Standard of proof—
Balance of probabilities. **Hornal v Neuberger Products Ltd** [1956] **3** 970, CA.
Undisclosed principal. *See* **Agent** (Contract—Undisclosed principal—Fraud of principal).
Guarantee—
Non-disclosure. *See* **Guarantee** (Enforcement—Misrepresentation by non-disclosure).
Husband and wife—
Undue influence—
Misrepresentation by spouse exercising influence—Effect. *See* **Equity** (Undue influence—Misrepresentation by person exercising influence—Effect of misrepresentation—Husband and wife).
Indemnity. *See* **Indemnity** (Misrepresentation).
Innocent misrepresentation—
Agent—
Defendant alleging misrepresentation and applying to amend defence and counterclaim to include further allegations of misrepresentation—Judge refusing permission to amend—Judge granting summary judgment—Whether judge correct to refuse permission to amend—Whether judge correct to give summary judgment. **MCI WorldCom International Inc v Primus Telecommunications Inc** [2004] **1 Comm** 138, QBD; [2004] **2 Comm** 833, CA.
Liability of principal for misrepresentation of agent—Knowledge of true facts by principal—No fraud on part of principal. **Armstrong v Strain** [1952] **1** 139, CA.

MISREPRESENTATION (cont)—
Innocent misrepresentation (cont)—
Contract to buy shares in partnership from one partner—
Rescission—Restitutio in integrum—Whether acting as partner made contract an executed contract—Claim for rescission timely and fair. **Senanayake v Cheng** [1965] 3 296, PC.
Damages. *See* Damages—Innocent misrepresentation, *above.*
Fitness of premises. *See* **Landlord and tenant** (Fitness of premises—Innocent misrepresentation inducing contract).
Misrepresentation as to condition of motor lorry—
Acceptance of delivery—Buyer's claim to rescind contract within week of delivery. **Long v Lloyd** [1958] 2 402, CA.
Misrepresentation as to extent of exception clause. *See* **Contract** (Exception clause—Innocent misrepresentation as to extent of clause).
Reasonable ground for belief—
Sale of reversion in trust fund set aside to pay an annuity—Statement, in particulars of sale, that annuitant was believed to have no aggregable estate—No reasonable ground for belief—Rescission of contract. **Brown v Raphael** [1958] 2 79, CA.
Rescission—
Contract for sale of goods—Representation as to place of storage of goods—Whether claimant relying on representation—Whether agreement subsisting—Misrepresentation Act 1967, s 2(2). **Huyton SA v Distribuidora Internacional de Productos Agricolas SA de CV** [2004] 1 Comm 402, CA.
Sale of goods—
Misrepresentation as to quality of article sold—Rescission of contract—Acceptance by buyer of delivery—Claim to rescind contract after five years. **Leaf v International Galleries** [1950] 1 693, CA.
Motor cycle—Wrong entry in registration book—Effect. **Routledge v McKay** [1954] 1 855, CA.
Warranty as to car—When misrepresentation gives rise to warranty. **Bentley (Dick) Productions Ltd v Harold Smith (Motors) Ltd** [1965] 2 65, CA.
Sale of land—
Damages—Limitation of damages—Innocent misrepresentation by vendor of land—Claim by purchaser for damages under statute—Damages recoverable in tort—Whether statutory cause of action having effect of removing limitation on damages recoverable in contract—Misrepresentation Act 1967, s 2(1). **Sharneyford Supplies Ltd v Edge (Barrington Black Austin & Co (a firm), third party)** [1985] 1 976, Ch D.
Innocent misrepresentation as to size of site—Contract incorporating Law Society's Conditions of Sale, 1953, condition 35—Area of property substantially smaller than that stated in particulars of sale—Purchaser prejudiced by reason of difference—Contract rescinded. **Watson v Burton** [1956] 3 929, Ch D.
Preliminary inquiries before contract—Exclusion of liability for errors, mis-statements or omissions in answers to preliminary inquiry—Vendor stating in answer to preliminary inquiry that no boundary disputes affecting property—Property affected by boundary dispute—Vendor acting innocently but ought to have known of dispute—Contract containing condition that error, mis-statement or omission in answer to preliminary inquiry not to annul sale—Purchaser claiming to rescind sale because boundary dispute not disclosed—Whether exception clause precluding rescission—National Conditions of Sale (19th edn), condition 17(1). **Walker v Boyle** [1982] 1 634, Ch D.
Statement of rents—Representation or warranty—Remedy—Reduction in purchase price. **Gilchester Properties Ltd v Gomm** [1948] 1 493, Ch D.
Insurance—
Generally. *See* **Insurance** (Misrepresentation).
Motor insurance—
Policy obtained by misrepresentation of material fact. *See* **Motor insurance** (Rights of third parties against insurers—Duty of insurers to satisfy judgments against insured persons—Insurers not liable where policy obtained by non-disclosure or misrepresentation of material fact).
Reinsurance. *See* **Insurance** (Reinsurance—Misrepresentation).
Misrepresentation as to person's credit—
Defence of absence of writing—
Defence restricted to representations as to creditworthiness—Statute of Frauds Amendment Act 1828, s 6. **Diamond v Bank of London & Montreal Ltd** [1979] 1 561, CA.
Representation as to credit or ability of third party to pay—Statutory requirements—Purpose or intent of representation—Defendant company owing money to claimant—Directors of company making oral representations as to ability to repay outstanding sums—Company ceasing trading and transferring assets to third party—Claimant bringing claim in tort of deceit against directors—Directors seeking to rely on statutory defence—Whether statutory defence applicable only if purpose of representation to obtain money or goods upon credit—Whether directors could rely on statutory defence—Statute of Frauds Amendment Act 1828, s 6. **Roder UK Ltd v Titan Marquees Ltd** [2012] 1 Comm 659, CA; [2012] 1 1305, CA.
Negligence—
Oral representation—Whether defence of absence of writing maintainable under Statute of Frauds Amendment Act 1828, s 6. **Anderson (WB) & Sons Ltd v Rhodes (Liverpool) Ltd** [1967] 2 850, Assizes.
Negligent misrepresentation—
Agent—
Liability to principal for misrepresentation to agent—Continuing representations—Misrepresentation made to individual as to subject-matter of lease—Individual incorporating limited liability partnership—Limited liability partnership entering into lease—Whether representors liable for misrepresentation to limited liability partnership—Whether representors owing duty of care to limited liability partnership. **Cramaso LLP v Ogilvie-Grant** [2014] 1 Comm 830, SC; [2014] 2 270, SC.
Credit reference—
Whether reference amounting to negligent misstatement. **Turner v Royal Bank of Scotland plc (No 2)** [2001] 1 Comm 1057, CA.

MISREPRESENTATION (cont)—
   Negligent misrepresentation (cont)—
      Damages for breach of duty of care—
         Contributory negligence—Plaintiff claiming damages for negligence at common law and under statute—Whether defence of contributory negligence available to claim under statute—Law Reform (Contributory Negligence) Act 1945, s 1—Misrepresentation Act 1967, s 2(1). **Gran Gelato Ltd v Richcliff (Group) Ltd** [1992] **1** 865, Ch D.
         Medical brochures detailing cosmetic skin rejuvenation therapy—Brochures and relevant information provided by manufacturer of treatment—Statements in brochures that relevant injectate contained only patient's own cells and no extraneous matter—Possibility that injectate contained traces of extraneous matter—Whether statements in brochures misleading—Whether clinicians responsible for content of brochures—Whether statements materially accurate. **Webster v Liddington** [2015] **1 Comm** 427, CA.
      Lease of office premises—
         Lessor describing premises as offices and offering them for 15 year letting as offices—Planning permission available for use as offices for two years only—Use of premises thereafter subject to review—Lessor failing to check facts at date of grant of lease—Alleged acquiesence on part of lessee—Whether lessee entitled to rescission of lease on ground of negligent misrepresentation. **Laurence v Lexcourt Holdings Ltd** [1978] **2** 810, Ch D.
      Pre-contractual negotiations—
         Silence in course of pre-contractual negotiations—Effect of silence—Banks making loans to companies guaranteed by credit insurance policies arranged by broker—Broker's employee dishonestly issuing cover notes when part of cover missing—Banks lending large sums in reliance on cover notes—Insurers aware of broker's employee's deception—Whether insurers owing duty of care to disclose broker's employee's deception to banks—Whether party's right to withhold material fact during pre-contractual negotiations preventing duty of care arising. **Banque Financière de la Cité SA v Westgate Insurance Co Ltd** [1989] **2** 952, CA.
      Sale of company—
         Misrepresentation inducing contract—Damages—Award of damages where plaintiff entitled to rescind contract by reason of innocent misrepresentation inducing contract—Whether damages can be awarded if rescission no longer a viable remedy—Misrepresentation Act 1967, s 2(1), (2). **Witter (Thomas) Ltd v TBP Industries Ltd** [1996] **2** 573, Ch D.
      Solicitor. *See* **Solicitor** (Negligence—Negligent misrepresentation).
   Protected tenancy—
      Grant of tenancy induced by fraudulent misrepresentation. *See* **Rent restriction** (Protected tenancy—Misrepresentation—Fraudulent misrepresentation).
      Loss through fraudulent misrepresentation. *See* Fraudulent misrepresentation—Loss of protected tenancy, *above*.
   Quantity, as to. *See* **Weights and measures—Misrepresentation as to quantity**.
   Sale of goods—
      Fraudulent misrepresentation. *See* Fraudulent misrepresentation—Sale of goods, *above*.
      Innocent misrepresentation. *See* Innocent misrepresentation—Sale of goods, *above*.
      Warranty distinguished. *See* Distinction from condition and warranty, *above*.
   Sale of land—
      Damages. *See* **Sale of land** (Damages for breach of contract—Misrepresentation).
      Fraudulent misrepresentation. *See* Fraudulent misrepresentation—Dimensions of garden, *above*.
      Generally. *See* **Sale of land** (Misrepresentation).
      Innocent misrepresentation. *See* Innocent misrepresentation—Sale of land, *above*.
      Rescission of contract. *See* **Sale of land** (Rescission of contract—Misrepresentation).
   Standard of proof—
      Fraudulent misrepresentation. *See* Fraudulent misrepresentation—Standard of proof, *above*.
   Supplementary benefit. *See* **Social security** (Supplementary benefit—Overpayment—Recovery—Misrepresentation or non-disclosure).
   Undue influence—
      Misrepresentation by person exercising influence. *See* **Equity** (Undue influence—Misrepresentation by person exercising influence).
      Undue influence or misrepresentation—
         Equitable relief. *See* **Equity** (Undue influence—Undue influence or misrepresentation).
   Warranty distinguished from. *See* Distinction from condition and warranty, *above*.

MISSING PERSON
   Child—
      Disclosure of whereabouts. *See* **Child** (Whereabouts—Disclosure of whereabouts).
   Ward of court. *See* **Ward of court** (Missing ward).

MISTAKE
   Action for relief from consequences of mistake—
      Postponement of limitation period. *See* **Limitation of action** (Postponement of limitation period—Action for relief from consequences of mistake).
   Agreement to compromise—
      Mistake as to validity of claim—
         Agreement to compromise insurance claim—Mistake that insurance policy on which claim based valid—Whether agreement to compromise void for mistake—Whether voidable in equity. **Magee v Pennine Insurance Co Ltd** [1969] **2** 891, CA.
   Appearance entered by mistake—
      Withdrawal of appearance—
         Jurisdiction to allow withdrawal. *See* **Practice** (Appearance—Withdrawal of appearance—Jurisdiction—Appearance entered by mistake).
   Articles of association—
      Rectification of mistake—
         Jurisdiction of court. *See* **Company** (Articles of association—Mistake—Rectification of mistake—Jurisdiction of court).

MISTAKE (cont)—

Bank—
    Dishonour of cheque. *See* **Bank** (Cheque—Dishonour—Mistake).
Common mistake—
    Contract. *See* **Contract** (Mistake—Common mistake).
    Mistake of fact. *See* Mistake of fact—Common mistake, *below*.
Contract. *See* **Contract** (Mistake).
Criminal charge—
    Mistake as a defence. *See* **Criminal law** (Mistake—Mistake as a defence).
Defence—
    Criminal charge. *See* **Criminal law** (Mistake—Mistake as a defence).
    Trade description. *See* **Trade description** (Defence to proceedings—Mistake).
Disclosure of documents—
    Production of privileged documents. *See* **Disclosure and inspection of documents** (Production of documents—Inspection—Disclosure carried out under pressure of time and without due care—Privileged documents mistakenly disclosed).
Driving while disqualified. *See* **Road traffic** (Driving while disqualified for holding licence—Mens rea—Mistake).
Estoppel by representation. *See* **Estoppel** (Representation—Mistake).
Fire insurance—
    Payment of loss. *See* **Insurance** (Fire insurance—Payment of loss—Mistake).
Firearm—
    Possession without certificate—
        Mistaken belief as to nature of firearm. *See* **Firearms** (Possession—Possession of firearm without a certificate—Mistaken belief as to nature of firearm).
Habeas corpus—
    Return to writ—
        Enquiry into truth of facts set out in return—Mistake in return. *See* **Habeas corpus** (Return to writ—Enquiry into truth of facts set out in return—Mistake in return).
Identity of party—
    Contract. *See* **Contract** (Mistake—Identity of party).
    Lease. *See* **Landlord and tenant** (Lease—Avoidance—Mistake as to identity of lessee).
Income tax—
    Additional assessment. *See* **Income tax** (Additional assessment).
    Mistake, defect or omission not invalidating assessment. *See* **Income tax** (Assessment—Mistake, defect or omission not invalidating assessment).
Land Registration—
    Rectification of register, for. *See* **Land registration** (Rectification of register—Correction of mistake).
Lease—
    Identity of lessee—
        Avoidance. *See* **Landlord and tenant** (Lease—Avoidance—Mistake as to identity of lessee).
    Rectification. *See* **Landlord and tenant** (Lease—Rectification).
Legal aid certificate—
    Amendment. *See* **Legal aid** (Certificate—Amendment—Mistake).
Limitation of action. *See* **Limitation of action** (Postponement of limitation period—Action for relief from consequences of mistake).
Magistrates—
    Reopening case to rectify mistake etc—
        Jurisdiction. *See* **Magistrates** (Jurisdiction—Reopening case to rectify mistake etc).
Maintenance order—
    Order registered in magistrates' court—
        Variation of order—Power to fix maintenance de novo—Mistake by original court. *See* **Husband and wife** (Variation or discharge of maintenance order—Variation of order registered in magistrates' court—Power to fix maintenance de novo—Mistake by original court).
Marriage ceremony—
    Nature of ceremony. *See* **Nullity** (Mistake as to nature of ceremony).
Mistake of fact—
    Alteration of dwelling-house—
        New dwelling—Mistake whether a dwelling-house had been so substantially altered as to become a new and separate dwelling under the Rent Restrictions Acts—Estoppel. **Solle v Butcher** [1949] **2** 1107, CA.
    Common mistake—
        Existence of mistake at date of contract—Belief of parties at date of contract that planning permission available without restriction for use of premises as offices—Planning permission available for limited period only—Planning permission subject to review thereafter—Lessee taking possession without making any enquiries or searches—Whether lessee entitled to rescission of contract on ground of common mistake. **Laurence v Lexcourt Holdings Ltd** [1978] **2** 810, Ch D.
        Plaintiff buying drawing believed to be original—Drawing discovered to be reproduction ten years after purchase—Whether plaintiff's claim for rescission time-barred—Whether plaintiff could 'with reasonable diligence' have discovered the mistake six years prior to institution of proceedings—Limitation Act 1980, s 32(1)(c). **Peco Arts Inc v Hazlitt Gallery Ltd** [1983] **3** 193, QBD.
        Sale of freehold property for £850 subject to existing tenancy—Mistake as to existence of statutory tenancy—Vendor believed property to be in occupation of statutory tenant—Market value of property with vacant possession would have been approximately £2,250—Original tenant might be wife or husband, but both of them had died—Their son was in occupation but did not claim protection under Rents Acts—Whether vendor entitled to rescission of agreement. **Grist v Bailey** [1966] **2** 875, Ch D.

MISTAKE (cont)—
   Mistake of fact (cont)—
      Common mistake (cont)—
         Subject-matter of contract essentially and radically different from that which both parties believed
            to exist at time contract executed—Sale and leaseback transaction with lessee's obligations
            secured by guarantee—Parties to guarantee mistaken about existence of subject-matter of
            transaction—Subject-matter of lease and guarantee non-existent—Whether guarantee void ab
            initio for common mistake. **Associated Japanese Bank (International) Ltd v Crédit du Nord SA**
            [1988] 3 902, QBD.
      Equity—
         Mistake as to commercial effect of agreement—Claimants bringing proceedings for breach of
            alleged agreement—Defendant alleging that it had failed to appreciate commercial effect of
            agreement—Whether defendant entitled to have agreement set aside in equity for mistake as to
            subject matter. **Clarion Ltd v National Provident Institution** [2000] 2 265, Ch D.
         Transferor making transfers potentially exempt from charge to inheritance tax if transferor
            surviving seven years—Transferor subsequently diagnosed with cancer—Transferor dying less
            than three years following transfers—Transfers becoming chargeable to inheritance
            tax—Transferor's executors applying to set aside transfers as voluntary dispositions made on
            basis of mistake of fact as to transferor's state of health—Whether circumstances amounting to
            mistake of fact—Whether necessary for executors to show what transferor would have done if he
            had not made mistake—Whether disposition capable of relief in equity void or voidable. **Griffiths
            (deceased), Re** [2008] 2 654, Ch D.
   Money paid under mistake of fact—
      Contract—Modification of payment—Contract providing for sampling of goods—Contract providing
         for complaints regarding sampling to be raised within time period—Independent tester
         discovering clerical error after expiration of time period—Whether error could be corrected
         subsequent to contractual time period. **Soules CAF v Louis Dreyfus Negoce SA** [2000] 2
         Comm 154, QBD.
      Contract—Modification of terms of payment—Payment upon old terms—Account passed by agent
         ignorant of new terms—Mistake of principal—Effect of knowledge of another agent.
         Anglo-Scottish Beet Sugar Corp Ltd v Spalding UDC [1937] 3 335, KBD.
      Defence to claim to recover money paid under mistake of fact—Change of position of payee in
         reliance on payment—Whether change of position a defence—Circumstances in which payee's
         change of position a defence to claim to recover money paid under mistake of fact. **Rover
         International Ltd v Cannon Film Sales Ltd (No 3)** [1989] 3 423, CA.
      Employment—Employee acting fraudulently in conjunction with other employees to detriment of
         employer—Employee obtaining discretionary pension benefits on retiring before fraud
         discovered—Payment would not have been made if employer had known of fraud—Whether
         payment recoverable as money paid under mistake of fact induced by employee's breach of duty
         to disclose his or others' fraud. **Sybron Corp v Rochem Ltd** [1983] 2 707, CA.
      Equitable right to trace money paid under mistake of fact—Basis of right—American company
         paying sum into New York bank for the account of an English company—Payment made as a
         result of a factual mistake by employee of American company—English company insolvent and
         compulsory winding-up order made in respect of it—Action brought against English company by
         American company to trace and recover sum paid—Whether American company entitled to trace
         and recover sum paid—Whether winding-up of English company affecting right of American
         company to trace and recover sum paid. **Chase Manhattan Bank NA v Israel-British Bank
         (London) Ltd** [1979] 3 1025, Ch D.
      Equitable right to trace money paid under mistake of fact—Production of bankers' books—Plaintiff
         seeking to trace money paid under mistake of fact induced by fraud—Power to make
         interlocutory order for disclosure of bankers' books and correspondence between bank and
         customer to show amount standing in defendant's account—Defendants outside jurisdiction—
         Plaintiff unable to effect service on defendants but effecting service on bank—Bank not implicated
         in fraud—Whether interlocutory order for disclosure may be made against bank. **Bankers Trust
         Co v Shapira** [1980] 3 353, CA.
      Estoppel by representation—Prejudice suffered by person misled making it inequitable to require
         him to make restitution—Money paid to party misled under mistake of fact. *See* **Estoppel**
         (Representation—Prejudice suffered by party misled by representation—Prejudice making it
         inequitable to require party misled to make restitution—Money paid to party misled under
         mistake of fact).
      First mortgagee selling mortgaged property and remitting incorrect balance to second
         mortgagee—Mistake in calculation of interest—Mistake inter partes—Estoppel. **Weld Blundell v
         Synott** [1940] 2 580, KBD.
      Long lease—Rent paid without deduction of tax at standard rate—Recovery of overpayments—
         Income Tax Act 1918, General Rules Applicable to All Schedules, r 19(2)—Finance Act 1940,
         s 17(1)(a), (2). **Turvey v Dentons (1923) Ltd** [1952] 2 1025, QBD.
      Recovery—Bank—Cheque stopped by drawer—Cheque paid by bank due to oversight—Whether
         bank intended payee to have money at all events—Whether payment made for valuable
         consideration—Whether payee changing his position—Whether money recoverable from
         payee—Whether payee can invoke defence that he had been deprived of opportunity of giving
         notice of dishonour—Bills of Exchange Act 1882, s 50(2)(c). **Barclays Bank Ltd v W J Simms Son
         & Cooke (Southern) Ltd** [1979] 3 522, QBD.
      Recovery—Bank—Payer owing debt to payee—Payee instructing payer to make payment
         discharging debt to solicitors—Payer making payment to payee's bank—Bank applying payment
         to payee's overdraft—Payee complaining that payer had failed to comply with instructions for
         payment—Payer making second payment to solicitors and seeking recovery of payment to
         bank—Whether bank authorised to receive payment—Whether payer entitled to recovery of
         payment from bank. **Customs and Excise Comrs v National Westminster Bank plc** [2003] 1
         Comm 327, Ch D.
      Recovery—Overpayment of betting winnings. **Morgan v Ashcroft** [1937] 3 92, CA.
      Resolution of local authority to make up to employees difference between war service pay and
         civilian pay—Right of authority to recover overpayments. **Larner v London CC** [1949] 1 964, CA.
      Restitution. *See* **Restitution** (Money paid under mistake of fact).

MISTAKE (cont)—
  Mistake of fact (cont)—
    Money paid under mistake of fact (cont)—
      Totalisator bet—Winnings paid partly in five-pound notes in mistake for one-pound notes—Whether excess recoverable—Racecourse Betting Act 1928, ss 2(8), 3(3), 4. **Racecourse Betting Control Board v Mount** [1938] **3** 547, CA.
  Mistake of law—
    Correction—
      Availability of judicial review as means of correcting mistake. *See* **Judicial review** (Availability of remedy—Correction of mistakes of law).
    Law subsequently changed by decision of House of Lords—
      Money paid into court taken out in satisfaction—Right to removal of stay of action. **Derrick v Williams** [1939] **2** 559, CA.
    Limitation of action. *See* **Limitation of action** (Postponement of limitation period—Action for relief from consequences of mistake—Mistake of law).
    Money paid under mistake of law—
      Money paid to charitable institutions by executors under a mistake as to the construction of a will. *See* **Trust and trustee** (Following trust property—Payment under mistake—Money paid to charitable institutions by executors under a mistake as to the construction of a will).
      Money paid under threat of legal proceedings—Law subsequently changed—Whether recoverable—Landlord and Tenant (War Damage) (Amendment) Act 1941, s 13. **Sawyer v Windsor Brace Ltd** [1942] **2** 669, KBD.
      Payment to Commissioners of Customs and Excise for purchase tax while liability to tax sub judice. **Sebel Products Ltd v Customs and Excise Comrs** [1949] **1** 729, Ch D.
      Recovery—Claim in equity—Residue of testator's estate paid to charitable institutions by executors—Directions in will void for uncertainty—Rights of those entitled under intestacy to recover from institutions sums paid. **Ministry of Health v Simpson** [1950] **2** 1137, HL.
      Recovery—Parties not in pari delicto. **Kiriri Cotton Co Ltd v Dewani** [1960] **1** 177, PC.
      Restitution—Generally. *See* **Contract** (Restitution—Mistake—Payment made under mistake of law).
      Restitution. *See* **Restitution** (Unjust enrichment—Compensation—Money paid under mistake of law).
      Restitution—Limitation of action—Claimant company United Kingdom subsidiary of German parent—Claimant unable to utilise group income election to avoid paying advance corporation tax on dividends paid to parent as election only available if both subsidiary and parent resident in United Kingdom—European Court of Justice finding that such treatment contrary to Community law—Claimant commencing action for restitution—Whether action time-barred—Whether payments of advance corporation tax made under mistake of law—Whether English law recognising claim in restitution to recover taxes paid under mistake of law—Limitation Act 1980, s 32(1)(c). **Deutsche Morgan Grenfell Group plc v IRC** [2003] **4** 645, Ch D; [2005] **3** 1025, CA; [2007] **1** 449, HL.
      Restitution. *See* **Restitution** (Payment under mistake of law).
      Restitution—Limitation of action—Claimant company United Kingdom subsidiary of German parent—Claimant unable to utilise group income election to avoid paying advance corporation tax on dividends paid to parent as election only available if both subsidiary and parent resident in United Kingdom—European Court of Justice finding that such treatment contrary to Community law—Claimant commencing action for restitution—Whether action time-barred—Whether payments of advance corporation tax made under mistake of law—Whether English law recognising claim in restitution to recover taxes paid under mistake of law—Limitation Act 1980, s 32(1)(c). **Deutsche Morgan Grenfell Group plc v IRC** [2003] **4** 645, Ch D; [2005] **3** 1025, CA; [2007] **1** 449, HL.
      Taxation—European Union. *See* **European Union** (Taxation—Claims for repayment of sums unduly levied or benefits unduly claimed—Advance corporation tax—Payment under mistake of law).
  Mistaken belief—
    Belief action statute-barred—
      Whether mistake as to material fact. *See* **Limitation of action** (Extension of time limit—Material fact of decisive character outside knowledge of plaintiff—Mistaken belief that claim statute-barred).
  Mutual mistake—
    Mutual mistake as to freehold title—
      Tenancy including also other lands—Whether tenancy void as regards land affected by mutual mistake. **Bligh v Martin** [1968] **1** 1157, Ch D.
  Nature of document—
    Non est factum—
      Burden of proof—Proof that reasonable care exercised—Failure to exercise reasonable care not giving rise to estoppel. **Saunders (exrx of the estate of Rose Maud Gallie (decd)) v Anglia Building Society (formerly Northampton Town and County Building Society)** [1970] **3** 961, HL.
      Fundamental difference—Mistake as to personality. **Saunders (exrx of the estate of Rose Maud Gallie (decd)) v Anglia Building Society (formerly Northampton Town and County Building Society)** [1970] **3** 961, HL.
      Generally. *See* **Document** (Non est factum).
      Hire-purchase transaction—Documents signed by car-owner in blank in belief that they were to procure her a loan on the security of her car—Non est factum—Defence not established—No sufficient misrepresentation as result sought by car-owner would have been attained. **Mercantile Credit Co Ltd v Hamblin** [1964] **3** 592, CA.
      Hire-purchase transaction—Indemnity form signed by hirer in respect of hire-purchase agreement of car in belief that it was release of his rights as hire-purchaser of same car under another hire-purchase agreement—Non est factum. **Muskham Finance Ltd v Howard** [1963] **1** 81, CA.
      To whom plea available. **Saunders (exrx of the estate of Rose Maud Gallie (decd)) v Anglia Building Society (formerly Northampton Town and County Building Society)** [1970] **3** 961, HL.
  Notice to quit—
    Validity of notice. *See* **Landlord and tenant** (Validity of notice to quit—Error or mistake).
  Payment out of court—
    Jurisdiction of county court to order money to be repaid into court. *See* **County court** (Jurisdiction—Order for repayment of money paid out of court in error).

MISTAKE (cont)—
Payment subject to deduction of tax—
Receipt in full settlement—
Inland Revenue decision that no tax payable—Re-opening accounts. **Bullingdon RDC v Oxford Corp** [1936] **3** 875, KBD.
Pension scheme. *See* **Pension** (Pension scheme—Company pension scheme—Mistake).
Price of subject-matter of transaction—
Goods offered at certain prices per pound instead of per piece—
Offeree's knowledge of mistake—Whether acceptance of such offer binding contract. **Hartog v Colin and Shields** [1939] **3** 566, KBD.
Recovery of money paid—
Estoppel. *See* **Estoppel** (Representation—Mistake—Payment of money).
Income tax—
Insufficient deduction of tax. *See* **Income tax** (Annual payment—Deduction of tax—Insufficient deduction—Recovery of money overpaid).
Money paid—
Mistake of fact, under. *See* Mistake of fact—Money paid under mistake of fact—Recovery, *above.*
Mistake of law, under. *See* Mistake of law—Money paid under mistake of law—Recovery, *above.*
Nature of mistake—
Mistake of law or of fact—Burden of proof—Overpayment of salary by mistake—Action by employer to recover money overpaid—Overpayment recoverable only if paid under mistake of fact—Burden of proof that money paid under mistake of fact lying on employer. **Avon CC v Howlett** [1983] **1** 1073, CA.
Rectification—
Agreement containing arbitration clause—
Parties proceeding to arbitration and award made—Claim for rectification of agreement in action to enforce award—Estoppel. **Crane v Hegeman-Harris Co Inc** [1939] **4** 68, CA.
Antecedent expressed accord on particular point before written contract. *See* **Contract** (Rectification—Written contract—Antecedent expressed accord on particular point).
Covenant to pay sum free of tax—
Words used ineffectual to secure result. **Jervis v Howle & Talke Colliery** [1936] **3** 193, Ch D.
Deed—
Estoppel. *See* **Estoppel** (Deed—Rectifiable deed).
Generally. *See* **Deed** (Rectification).
Estoppel—
Deed. *See* **Estoppel** (Deed—Rectifiable deed).
Evidence of mistake—
Annuity granted without sufficient reference to deduction of tax—Grantor paying annuity in full for 30 years. **Fredensen v Rothschild** [1941] **1** 430, Ch D.
Jurisdiction of magistrates. *See* **Magistrates** (Jurisdiction—Reopening case to rectify mistake etc).
Land register—
Rectification affecting title of proprietor in possession. *See* **Land registration** (Rectification of register—Rectification affecting title of proprietor in possession—Proprietor contributing to mistake in registration).
Lease. *See* **Landlord and tenant** (Lease—Rectification).
Sale of goods—
Written contract correctly stating terms agreed orally—Mutual error as to meaning of expression used. **Rose (Frederick E) (London) Ltd v Pim (Wm H) Junr & Co Ltd** [1953] **2** 739, CA.
Unilateral mistake—
Estoppel—Building contract—Time for completion of building specified in plaintiff's tender as eighteen months—Contract drawn up by defendants specifying thirty-month period for completion—Plaintiff executed contract believing that eighteen-month period for completion specified therein—Defendants knowing of plaintiff's mistake did nothing to correct it—Whether plaintiff entitled to rectification. **Roberts (A) & Co Ltd v Leicestershire CC** [1961] **2** 545, Ch D.
Estoppel—Deed. *See* **Estoppel** (Deed—Rectifiable deed).
Lease—Common intention of parties. *See* **Landlord and tenant** (Lease—Rectification—Common intention of parties).
Lease—Mistake of lessor in drafting lease—Lessee unaware of mistake—Mistake not attributable to anything said or done by lessee—Claim by lessor for rescission subject to rectification at lessee's option—Whether mere unilateral mistake ground for rescission. **Riverlate Properties Ltd v Paul** [1974] **2** 656, CA.
Unconscionable conduct by one party—Availability of rectification—Tenant negotiating with landlord to acquire without landlord's knowledge put option enjoyed by predecessor—Tenant's representatives deliberately misleading landlord's representatives in ambiguous discussions and correspondence—Whether contract to be construed as including grant of put option—Whether landlord's representatives having authority to grant put option—Whether rectification available on ground of landlord's unilateral mistake—Whether tenant's conduct sufficiently unconscionable—Whether tenant's representatives having actual knowledge of landlord's mistake. **Commission for the New Towns v Cooper (GB) Ltd** [1995] **2** 929, CA.
Return to writ of habeas corpus—
Enquiry into truth of facts set out in return. *See* **Habeas corpus** (Return to writ—Enquiry into truth of facts set out in return—Mistake in return).
Royalties—
Deduction of tax—
Accord and satisfaction. *See* **Accord and satisfaction** (Royalties—Deduction of tax—Acceptance of deduction under mistake of law).
Social security—
Recovery of overpayment. *See* **Social security** (Benefit—Overpayment—Recovery).
Trust and trustee—
Trustees of company pension scheme. *See* **Trust and trustee** (Trustees of company pension scheme—Mistake in rules of scheme).

MISTAKE (cont)—
  Unilateral mistake—
    Claimant entering into settlement agreement on basis of unilateral mistake—
      Defendant knowing of claimant's mistake but keeping silent—Whether settlement agreement void at common law—Whether court having equitable jurisdiction to grant rescission of contract on ground of unilateral mistake where mistake not rendering contract void at common law. **Statoil ASA v Louis Dreyfus Energy Services LP** [2009] **1 Comm** 1035, QBD.
    Rectification. *See* Rectification—Unilateral mistake, *above*.
  Valuation. *See* **Valuer** (Valuation—Mistake).
  Weights and measures—
    Defence to proceedings. *See* **Weights and measures** (Defence to proceedings—Mistake, accident or some other cause beyond defendant's control).

MISTRESS
  Joint acquisition of property with man—
    Resulting trust. *See* **Trust and trustee** (Constructive trust—Unmarried couple).
  Licence to occupy premises—
    Contractual licence—
      Terms to be inferred. *See* **Licence** (Licence to occupy premises—Contractual licence—Terms to be inferred—Man and mistress).
      Unmarried couple. *See* **Licence** (Licence to occupy premises—Contractual licence—Unmarried couple).
  Man and woman living with each other in same household—
    Domestic violence—
      Injunction—Exclusion of party from home—County court. *See* **Injunction** (Exclusion of party from matrimonial home—County court—Man and woman who are living with each other in the same household as husband and wife).
  Property acquired by joint contributions. *See* **Trust and trustee** (Constructive trust—Unmarried couple).

MISUSE OF COMPUTER
  Criminal proceedings. *See* **Criminal law** (Computer—Misuse of computer).

MISUSE OF DRUGS
  Generally. *See* **Drugs**.
  Sentence—
    Forfeiture order. *See* **Sentence** (Forfeiture order—Forfeiture of profits made by offender out of offence—Forfeiture order made under Misuse of Drugs Act 1971).

MISUSE OF POWER
  Public authority. *See* **Public authority** (Statutory powers—Misuse of power).

MITIGATION
  Contempt of court. *See* **Contempt of court** (Mitigation).
  Damages—
    Breach of contract. *See* **Contract** (Damages for breach—Mitigation of loss).
    Generally. *See* **Damages** (Mitigation of loss).
    Wrongful dismissal. *See* **Contract** (Damages for breach—Wrongful dismissal—Mitigation of loss).
  Sentence—
    Criminal trial. *See* **Sentence** (Factors in assessing sentence—Mitigation).

MOBILE HOME
  Agreement offered by site owner to occupier of mobile home—
    Dispute—
      Occupier dissatisfied with terms of agreement—Application to court for determination of matter in dispute—Criteria to be applied in determining matter in dispute—Mobile Homes Act 1975, s 4(5), (7). **Grant v Allen** [1980] **1** 720, CA.
    Term of agreement offered by owner—
      Date of commencement of agreement omitted—Term that owner could move mobile home for purpose of better management of park—Term imposing on occupier obligation to pay commission to owner where mobile home not sold to assignee of agreement—Term giving owner right of access to pitch for purpose of inspecting and maintaining property other than his own—County court's power to make date of commencement of agreement retrospective—Whether terms offered valid—Mobile Homes Act 1975, s 3(f), (h), (i), (j). **Grant v Allen** [1980] **1** 720, CA.
      Term of agreement to be not less than five years—Owner offering agreement for term of five years—Occupier applying to county court for longer term—County court judge exercising discretion under power to settle matters in dispute by extending term to eight years—Whether county court judge had discretion to extend term—Whether length of term could be 'a matter in dispute'—Mobile Homes Act 1975, ss 2(1), 4(5). **Taylor v Calvert** [1978] **2** 630, CA.
  Agreement to occupy mobile home—
    Termination of agreement—
      Termination for non-occupation of mobile home—Occupation of mobile home—Whether occupation to be determined on date application made to court by site owner or on date application heard—Mobile Homes Act 1983, Sch 1, Pt I, para 5. **Omar Parks Ltd v Elkington** [1993] **1** 282, CA.
      Termination where occupier has breached term of agreement and after service by site owner of notice to remedy breach has not complied with notice within reasonable time—Agreement containing covenant against anti-social behaviour—Occupier breaching covenant—Owner serving notice—Requirements of compliance with notice—Effect of obligation to comply within reasonable time—Mobile Homes Act 1983, Sch 1, Pt I, Ch 2, para 4(a). **Telchadder v Wickland Holdings Ltd** [2015] **1** 855, SC.

MOBILE HOME (cont)—
Application to county court—
Statutory provision conferring jurisdiction on a particular court—
Proceedings commenced in wrong court—Transfer of proceedings to correct court. *See* **County court** (Transfer of action—Transfer to another county court—Proceedings commenced in wrong court—Statutory provision conferring jurisdiction on a particular court).

MOBILE VAN
Equipped as shop—
Sunday trading. *See* **Shop** (Sunday closing—Retail trading elsewhere than in shop—Mobile van equipped as shop).

MOBILITY ALLOWANCE
See **Social security** (Mobility allowance).

MOCK AUCTION
See **Criminal law** (Mock auction).

MODEL
Damages—
Personal injury—
Loss of future earnings. *See* **Damages** (Personal injury—Loss of future earnings).
Production in evidence. *See* **Practice** (Document—Production in evidence—Leave to produce plan, photograph or model as evidence without giving other party opportunity to inspect it).

MODERN SLAVERY
Trafficking people for exploitation. *See* **Criminal law** (Trafficking people for exploitation).

MODERN UNIVERSITY
Visitor—
Generally. *See* **University** (Visitor—Modern university).

MOLESTATION
Injunction—
Generally. *See* **Injunction** (Molestation).
Husband or wife. *See* **Injunction** (Husband and wife—Molestation).

MONEY
Award—
Arbitration. *See* **Arbitration** (Award).
Bank. *See* **Bank**.
Borrowing—
Treasury control—
Issue of shares and debenture stock in consideration of sale of land—Whether transaction 'borrowing of money' within Borrowing (Control and Guarantees) Act 1946, s 4(2)(a)—Control of Borrowing Order 1947 (SR & O 1947 No 945), art 2(1). **London and Country Commercial Property Investments Ltd v A-G** [1953] **1** 436, Ch D.
Building society. *See* **Building society**.
Currency—
Alteration of currency—
Annuity payable under will and family arrangement—Sum expressed in marks—Assessment of amount to be paid after alteration of German currency—Whether exercise of discretion of court. **Kornatski v Oppenheimer** [1937] **4** 133, Ch D.
Appraisement and sale of ship by Admiralty marshal. *See* **Admiralty** (Appraisement and sale—Currency of sale).
Currency in which debt payable—
Bond issued by British Government in America—Law applicable—Gold clause—American legislation—Effect of option to pay in England. **R v International Trustee for the Protection of Bondholders Akt** [1937] **2** 164, HL.
Contract governed by Turkish law—Pension based on salary—Whether payable on a gold basis—Unconditional receipts for 'net amount payable'—Release. **Ottoman Bank, Haifa v Menni (Clement)** [1939] **4** 9, PC.
Contract of service made in England to be performed in New Zealand—Payment in sterling—Whether English or New Zealand currency. **De Bueger v J Ballantyne & Co Ltd** [1938] **1** 701, PC.
Contract with Turkish corporation—Pension based on salary—Whether payable on a gold basis. **Ottoman Bank of Nicosia v Chakarian** [1937] **4** 570, PC.
Covenant to pay on gold basis—Redemption of debenture—Payment of interest—Construction of bond—Construction of provisions for payment of interest. **New Brunswick Rly Co v British and French Trust Corp Ltd** [1938] **4** 747, HL.
Debenture bond and coupons payable at the option of the holder in London or Auckland—Local Bodies Loans Act 1913, (NZ). **Auckland City Council v Alliance Assurance Co Ltd** [1937] **1** 645, PC.
Lease—Governed by Chilean law—Proof of law of country where decisions not binding precedents—Rent reserved in pesos of a certain weight in gold—'Remit'. **St Pierre v South American Stores (Gath & Chaves) Ltd & Chilean Stores (Gath & Chaves) Ltd** [1937] **3** 349, .
Loan in French liras—Payment of interest on gold basis—Palestinian law. **Apostolic Throne of St Jacob v Saba Eff Said** [1940] **1** 54, PC.
Rent—Payment to be either in gold sterling or Bank of England notes to the equivalent value in gold sterling of a specified sum—'Gold sterling'—'Value'. **Treseder-Griffin v Co-op Insurance Society Ltd** [1956] **2** 33, CA.
Repayment of loan—Loan in Gibraltar in pesetas—Subsequent restriction by Spanish government on export of currency. **Pyrmont Ltd v Schott** [1938] **4** 713, PC.

MONEY (cont)—
    Currency (cont)—
        Currency in which government stock repayable—
            New Zealand inscribed stock—Principal and interest repayable at Melbourne free of exchange—Whether payable in Australian currency or New Zealand currency. **National Mutual Life Association of Australasia Ltd v A-G for New Zealand** [1956] **1** 721, PC.
        Currency to which amount referable—
            Appeal as of right to Privy Council dependant on amount of the matter in dispute—Whether '£500 sterling' referred to Australian pounds. **Skelton v Jones** [1962] **3** 85, PC.
        Date at which rate of exchange calculated—
            Charterparty providing for demurrage to be calculated in dollars—No provision for payment in sterling—Freight payable in sterling in London at rate of exchange on bill of lading date—Charterers paying demurrage in sterling at rate of exchange on bill of lading date—Fall in value of sterling between bill of lading date and date of payment—Whether demurrage required to be paid at rate of exchange on bill of lading date or date of payment. **Veflings (George) Rederi A/S v President of India** [1979] **1** 380, CA.
            Damages for breach of contract—Foreign judgment sued on in the United Kingdom—Rate at date of judgment. **East India Trading Co Inc v Carmel Exporters and Importers Ltd** [1952] **1** 1053, QBD.
            Liquidated demand—Debt in marks payable in Germany—Whether action in debt or for breach of contract—Rate of exchange prevailing when payment should have been made. **Graumann v Treitel** [1940] **2** 188, KBD.
            Liquidated sum—Balance of current account with English branch of foreign bank—Bank dissolved abroad. **Russian Commercial & Industrial Bank, Re** [1955] **1** 75, Ch D.
            Trust—Rentals due to trustee under American lease of railway rolling stock in Cuba—Sums due from trustee to cestuis que trust for service of equipment trust certificate—Trustee's expenses—Default in payment of rentals—Liquidation of railway company in England—At what dates rents payable to trustee and sum due to beneficiaries should be converted into English currency for purposes of proof in liquidation. **United Rlys of the Havana and Regla Warehouses Ltd, Re** [1960] **2** 332, HL.
        Debenture bonds and coupons—
            Payable at option of the holder in London or New Zealand—Currency in which payable. *See* **New Zealand** (Currency—Debenture bonds and coupons—Payable at option of the holder in London or New Zealand).
    Decimal currency—
        Change to. *See* **Decimalisation**.
    Foreign currency—
        Award of arbitrator—Generally. *See* **Arbitration** (Award—Foreign currency).
        Award of arbitrator—Validity of award for payment expressed in foreign currency. *See* **Arbitration** (Award—Payment of sum of money—Foreign currency).
        Judgment. *See* **Judgment** (Foreign currency).
    Palestine. *See* **Palestine** (Money—Currency).
    Rate of exchange—
        Damages—Contract or tort. **United Rlys of the Havana and Regla Warehouses Ltd, Re** [1960] **2** 332, HL.
        Date at which calculated. *See* Currency—Date at which rate of exchange calculated, *above*.
        Debt due in foreign country—Payment into court in England—Distinction between payment in foreign country and payment into court in this country. **Vionnet (Madeleine) et Cie v Wills** [1939] **4** 136, CA.
        Promissory notes payable in Turkish gold pounds—Paid in Palestinian currency—Date for calculating exchange—Binding effect of decisions of Supreme Court of Palestine—Palestine Order in Council 1922, art 46. **Khoury, Syndic in Bankruptcy of Nasrallah v Khayat** [1943] **2** 406, PC.
        Rate applicable—Loan in Gibraltar in pesetas—Repayment. **Marrache v Ashton** [1943] **1** 276, PC.
        Redemption of bonds—Floating currencies—Bonds redeemable at rate of exchange 'determined by the par values of the currencies concerned in force on the appropriate date as agreed with the International Monetary Fund'—Payment in United States dollars of nominal amount of bonds to be reconverted into sterling at appropriate rate of exchange—Dollar and sterling floating currencies on appropriate date and not confined within parity margins—International Monetary Fund not notified of new rates of exchange—Whether previous rates of exchange notified to fund 'in force on the appropriate date'. **Lively Ltd v City of Munich** [1976] **3** 851, QBD.
    Currency control. *See* **Currency control**.
    Decimalisation. *See* **Decimalisation**.
    Divorce—
        Financial provision. *See* **Divorce** (Financial provision).
    Exchange control. *See* **Currency control**.
    Following money—
        Following trust money—
            Generally. *See* **Trust and trustee** (Following trust property).
            Mixing trust money with trustee's own money. *See* **Trust and trustee** (Breach of trust—Mixing trust moneys with trustee's own money).
        Plaintiff seeking to trace money paid under mistake of fact induced by fraud—
            Power to make interlocutory order for disclosure of banker's books to show amount standing in defendant's account. **A v C** [1980] **2** 347, QBD.
    Foreign currency—
        Award of arbitrator. *See* **Arbitration** (Award—Foreign currency).
        Judgment. *See* **Judgment** (Foreign currency).
    Foreign exchange control. *See* **Currency control** (Exchange control—Foreign exchange control).
    Forged bank note—
        Possession—
            Sentence. *See* **Sentence** (Imprisonment—Length of sentence—Forgery).
    Inducement to invest money—
        Criminal liability. *See* **Criminal law** (Inducement to invest money).

MONEY (cont)—
  Interest—
    Generally. *See* **Interest**.
    Income tax—
      Persons chargeable—Receipt of interest. *See* **Income tax** (Persons chargeable—Receipt of income—Person receiving income chargeable—Interest on money).
  Investment—
    Charity—
      Chartered corporation—Power to invest. *See* **Charity** (Chartered corporation—Investments).
  Judgment—
    Foreign currency. *See* **Judgment** (Payment of sum of money—Foreign currency).
  Loan—
    Burden of proof—
      Receipt of money admitted by defendant—Allegation by defendant that money a gift, alternatively that it was not repayable when the action was brought—No presumption of advancement arising—Whether burden of proof lay on defendant. **Seldon v Davidson** [1968] **2** 755, CA.
    Moneylender. *See* **Moneylender**.
    Nature of transaction—
      Bills purchased at discount—Post-dated cheques given as collateral security—Purchaser not a bank or discount house—Whether contract for repayment of money lent—Whether moneylending transaction. **Chow Yoong Hong v Choong Fah Rubber Manufactory** [1961] **3** 1163, PC.
    Power to borrow—
      Parochial church council. *See* **Ecclesiastical law** (Parochial church council—Conduct of financial affairs of church—Borrowing powers).
    Priority—
      Equitable interest. *See* **Equity** (Equitable interest—Loan).
    Repayment of loan index-linked to foreign currency—
      Enforceability—Public policy—Mortgage—Parties within United Kingdom—Principal and interest due under mortgage to be repaid in sterling—Clause in mortgage index-linking sums concerned to Swiss franc—Whether index-linking of money obligation contrary to public policy—Whether clause void or unenforceable. **Multiservice Bookbinding Ltd v Marden** [1978] **2** 489, Ch D.
  Mistake—
    Money paid under mistake of fact. *See* **Mistake** (Mistake of fact—Money paid under mistake of fact).
    Money paid under mistake of law. *See* **Mistake** (Mistake of law—Money paid under mistake of law).
    Payment of money—
      Estoppel by representation. *See* **Estoppel** (Representation—Mistake—Payment of money).
  Money had and received—
    Cause of action—
      Tort—Whether cause of action in tort—Law Reform (Miscellaneous Provisions) Act 1934, s 1(3) as amended by Law Reform (Limitation of Actions &c) Act 1954, s 4. **Chesworth v Farrar** [1966] **2** 107, QBD.
    Creditor instructing debtor to pay third person out of fund—
      Acceptance of instructions by debtor—Action by third person against debtor—What constitutes a sufficient fund to enable the action to lie—Whether consideration moving from the third person to the creditor is necessary. **Shamia v Joory** [1958] **1** 111, QBD.
    Defence—
      Change of position. *See* **Restitution** (Money had and received—Defence—Change of position).
    Failure of consideration—
      Company—Invalid issue of shares—Transfer by shareholder to transferees—Subsequent claim against company for repayment of price of shares. **Linz v Electric Wire Co of Palestine Ltd** [1948] **1** 604, PC.
    Origin of cause of action—
      Money paid under mistake of law recoverable when parties not in pari delicto—Money paid for illegal premium. **Kiriri Cotton Co Ltd v Dewani** [1960] **1** 177, PC.
    Recovery—
      Cheques obtained by fraud and paid into wife's account—No privity of contract between wife and plaintiff—Wife agent of husband—Money paid out by wife without notice of fraud and under instructions of husband—Whether contract to repay money to be implied. **Transvaal and Delagoa Bay Investment Co Ltd v Atkinson** [1944] **1** 579, KBD.
    Restitution—
      Quasi-contract. *See* **Restitution** (Quasi-contract—Money had and received).
    Right to trace funds at common law—
      Funds transmitted to bank by telegraphic transfer—Plaintiff's employee forging payment order in favour of nominee company set up and controlled by defendant accountants—Plaintiff's bank transmitting funds by telegraphic transfer to nominee company's London bank account—London bank reimbursed by correspondent bank in New York via New York clearing system—Whether plaintiff having title to bring action—Whether funds recoverable as money had and received—Whether origin of funds identifiable. **Agip (Africa) Ltd v Jackson** [1992] **4** 451, CA.
  Money paid—
    Nature of claim—
      Distinction between claim for money paid and claim for money lent. **HPC Productions Ltd, Re** [1962] **1** 37, Ch D.
    Recovery of money paid—
      Failure of consideration. *See* **Contract** (Failure of consideration—Recovery of money paid).
  Moneylender. *See* **Moneylender**.
  Payment into court. *See* **Practice** (Payment into court).
  Payment out of court. *See* **Practice** (Payment out of court).
  Promissory note—
    Implied request to third party to discharge promisor's liability—
      Payment made by third party—Note not enforceable. **Chetwynd's Estate, Re** [1937] **3** 530, CA.
  Rate of exchange. *See* Currency—Rate of exchange—Promissory notes payable in Turkish gold pounds, *above*.

MONEY (cont)—
Rate of exchange—
Currency. *See* Currency—Rate of exchange, *above.*
Date at which rate calculated. *See* Currency—Date at which rate of exchange calculated, *above.*
Receipt—
Evidence of receipt—
Purchase money from sale of registered land—Entry on proprietorship register. *See* **Land registration** (Transfer—Purchase price remaining unpaid—Deed of transfer containing acknowledgment of receipt of purchase price).
Receiving stolen money. *See* **Criminal law** (Receiving stolen property—Stolen property—Money).
Recovery of money paid by mistake—
Generally. *See* **Mistake** (Recovery of money paid).
Repayment—
Guarantee. *See* **Guarantee.**
Smuggling of—
Prohibition on export of money. *See* **Currency control** (Exchange control—Prohibition of export of money—Smuggling money, Bank of England notes, out of the country).
Will—
Gift—
Construction. *See* **Will** (Gift—Specific bequests—Any money I may leave).

MONEY JUDGMENT
Execution and enforcement—
Garnishee order. *See* **Execution** (Garnishee order).

MONEY LAUNDERING
Authorised disclosure to Serious Organised Crime Agency. *See* **Proceeds of crime** (Criminal property—Knowledge or suspicion of arrangement facilitating acquisition, retention, use or control of criminal property).
Conspiracy—
Mens rea. *See* **Criminal law** (Conspiracy—Mens rea—Money laundering).
Criminal conduct. *See* **Criminal law** (Proceeds of crime—Criminal conduct).
European Community. *See* **European Union** (Directives—Direct application in member states—Directive on prevention of use of financial system for money laundering).
Financial Services Authority—
Powers of. *See* **Financial services** (Financial Services Authority (FSA)—Powers—Prosecution of criminal offences).
Prevention of use of financial system for purposes of—
European Union. *See* **European Union** (Freedom of movement—Services—Restriction on freedom—Prevention of use of financial system for purposes of money laundering and terrorist financing).
Proceeds of crime. *See* **Proceeds of crime.**

MONEYLENDER
Ceylon, in. *See* **Ceylon** (Moneylending).
Discovery—
Securities alleged void on ground that lenders were moneylenders and that acts were not complied with—
Transactions after loan—Whether disclosure should be ordered of transactions after as well as before the loan in question. **Marshall v Goulston Discount (Northern) Ltd** [1966] 3 994, CA.
Document issued by moneylender for purpose of his business—
Document which implies that moneylender carries on banking business—
Moneylender described as 'Merchant Bankers' on cheque issued by him—Cheque drawn by moneylender in part payment of loan—Whether loan unenforceable by moneylender—Whether civil remedy available to borrower in addition to criminal penalties—Moneylenders Act 1927, s 4(3). **London and Harrogate Securities Ltd v Pitts** [1976] 3 809, CA.
Exception from definition of moneylender—
Person bona fide carrying on business not having for its primary object lending of money—
Belief that refraining from making loans to customers would lose custom—Materiality of belief—Immateriality of correctness of belief in fact. **Koh Hor Khoon (Official Assignee of the Property), Bankrupts v Ek Liong Hin Ltd** [1960] 1 440, PC.
Hire-purchase finance company—Discounting notes issued against hire-purchase agreement—Whether moneylending transaction—Companies Act 1929, s 266. **Transport and General Credit Corp Ltd v Morgan** [1939] 2 17, Ch D.
Hire-purchase finance company—Loans to motor dealers—No direct connexion with hire-purchase transactions—Whether finance company within exception—Whether loans recoverable—Moneylenders Act 1900, s 6(d). **Premor Ltd v Shaw Bros** [1964] 2 583, CA.
Hire-purchase finance company—Sale of book debts—Whether moneylending transaction—Whether unenforceable as made by unlicensed moneylender—Moneylenders Act 1927, s 1. **Olds Discount Co Ltd v John Playfair Ltd** [1938] 3 275, KBD.
Issuing house—Joint loans by issuing house and others—Whether unenforceable as made by unlicensed moneylender—Moneylenders Act 1900, s 6(1)(d). **Wright (Frank H) (Constructions) Ltd v Frodoor Ltd** [1967] 1 433, QBD.
Person carrying on the business of banking—
Effect of longstanding reputation as banker—Burden of proof—Moneylenders Act 1900, s 6(d). **United Dominions Trust Ltd v Kirkwood** [1966] 1 968, CA.
Interest—
Rate—
Forty-five per cent—Personal loan and legal charge on ten-year lease at a rack rent—Whether rate harsh and unconscionable—Moneylenders Act 1900, s 1—Moneylenders Act 1927, s 10(1). **Albion Street (22), Westminster, Re** [1967] 3 943, Ch D.
Memorandum. *See* Memorandum—Rate of interest charged on loan, *below.*
Issuing house—
Whether exempt from Moneylenders Acts. *See* Exception from definition of moneylender, *above.*

MONEYLENDER (cont)—
  Licence—
    Address—
      Licensed moneylender a company having registered office at one place and authorised address at another—Memorandum of contract, and a guarantee, bearing authorised address—Negotiation by telephone—Moneylenders Act 1927, s 1(3)(b). **Albion Street (22), Westminster, Re** [1967] **3** 943, Ch D.
  Limitation of action—
    Proceedings for recovery of money lent by moneylender—
      Proceedings for enforcement of security taken in respect of loan made by moneylender—Unenforceable loan contract—Loan and charge securing loan unenforceable—Subrogation of moneylender to rights of paid-off creditor—Action by moneylender in exercise of subrogated rights to recover amount of loan—Whether 'proceedings ... for the recovery ... of ... money lent' by moneylender—Whether 'proceedings ... for the enforcement of any ... security taken ... in respect of any loan made' by moneylender—Whether proceedings subject to 12 month limitation period—Moneylenders Act 1927, s 13(1). **Orakpo v Manson Investments Ltd** [1977] **1** 666, CA; [1977] **3** 1, HL.
  Loan—
    Nature of loans and contracts for loans—
      Bills purchased at discount—Post-dated cheques maturing on same day as bills given as collateral security—Purchaser not a bank or discount house—Whether contract for the repayment of money lent—Malayan Moneylenders Ordinance 1951, (No 42 of 1951), ss 15, 16. **Chow Yoong Hong v Choong Fah Rubber Manufactory** [1961] **3** 1163, PC.
    Unenforceable transaction—
      Relief—Terms—Repayment of moneys borrowed—Whether borrower obtaining relief put on terms to repay moneys borrowed. **Kasumu v Baba-Egbe** [1956] **3** 266, PC.
  Memorandum—
    Contents—
      Element of machinery for effecting transaction, not essential term of contract—Loan to be secured on lease—Borrower to pay premium for lease—Part of loan intended to be used, and used, to meet premium—Premium in fact paid, and lease obtained, by lender's solicitor as agent for borrower's solicitor before loan completed—Memorandum not stating that premium to be met out of loan—Whether memorandum complied with Moneylenders Act 1927, s 6(2). **Albion Street (22), Westminster, Re** [1968] **2** 960, CA.
    Delivery to borrower—
      Loan to joint and several borrowers—Copy of memorandum sent to only one borrower—Whether sufficient compliance with statutory requirements—Moneylenders Act 1927, s 6(1). **Grahame (John W) (English Financiers) Ltd v Ingram** [1955] **2** 320, CA.
    Interest—
      Provision for payment of compound interest—Partial illegality—Legality of loan to discharge partially illegal loan by moneylender. *See* **Contract** (Illegality—Enforceability of contract—Subsequent transaction—Loan to discharge obligation under illegal contract—Partial illegality—Loan by registered moneylender—Provision in agreement for payment of compound interest).
    Rate of interest charged on loan—
      Actual rate stated—Instalments—Allocation to principal and interest—Interest upon interest—Moneylenders Act 1927, ss 6(2), 7, 15(2). **Mutual Loan Fund Association Ltd v Sanderson** [1937] **1** 380, KBD.
      Alternative statutory requirements—Actual or notional rate—Total interest, as defined in statute, spread over period of repayment loan in order to compute actual rate stated—Whether compliance with the alternative statutory requirement for statement of an actual rate—Moneylenders Act 1927, ss 6(2), 15(1), Sch 1. **Askinex Ltd v Green** [1967] **1** 65, CA.
      Memorandum required to show interest expressed in terms of a rate per cent per annum—Memorandum providing that interest 'be calculated at the true rate of 23% on the balance'—Omission of words 'per annum'—True meaning of memorandum clear—Whether statutory requirement complied with—Whether memorandum unenforceable—Moneylenders Act 1927, s 6(2). **London and Harrogate Securities Ltd v Pitts** [1976] **3** 809, CA.
      Necessity to state interest—Moneylenders Act 1927, s 6. **Mason and Wood Ltd v Greene** [1936] **2** 509, CA.
    Signature by borrower—
      Statutory requirement that memorandum to be signed personally by borrower—Personally—Loan to company—Signature to memorandum by company official—Sufficiency of memorandum—Sufficiency of affidavit of proof—Moneylenders Act 1927, ss 6, 9—Companies Act 1929, s 29. **British Games Ltd, Re** [1938] **1** 230, Ch D.
    Sufficiency—
      Collateral transactions not stated—Moneylenders Act 1927, s 6(2). **Askinex Ltd v Green** [1967] **1** 65, CA.
      Composite documents—Discrepancies between terms of conjoined documents—Loan secured by legal charge on property—Memorandum incorporating legal charge—Discrepancies between terms of memorandum and terms of legal charge—Whether composite memorandum contained all the terms of the contract—Whether necessity for reference to court to resolve discrepancies rendering memorandum insufficient—Moneylenders Act 1927, s 6(1)(2). **Holiday Credit Ltd v Erol** [1977] **2** 696, HL.
      Guarantee and bill of sale—Clause that if bill of sale became invalid, guarantors would repay loan and interest—Clause not referred to in memorandum—Moneylenders Act 1927, s 6. **Central Advance and Discount Corp Ltd v Marshall** [1939] **3** 695, CA.
      Loan made up of previous loans and new loans—Principal and interest payable in lump sum on stated date—No power to charge interest after stated date—Whether sum paid for stamp duties to be included in memorandum—Inclusion of schedule in copy of bill of sale attached to memorandum—Moneylenders Act 1927, s 6. **Allighan v London and Westminster Loan and Discount Co Ltd** [1940] **3** 530, KBD.
      Loan of purchase price of property mortgaged to secure loan—Mortgage debt—Date of loan not in mortgage deed when signed—Requirements of statute—Moneylenders Act 1927, s 6(1), (2). **Congresbury Motors Ltd v Anglo-Belge Finance Co Ltd** [1969] **3** 545, Ch D.

MONEYLENDER (cont)—
  Memorandum (cont)—
    Sufficiency (cont)—
      Loan secured by bill of sale—Borrower receiving copy of bill of sale—No reference in memorandum to power of seizure and sale contained in bill of sale—Moneylenders Act 1927, s 6. **Hoare v Smith (Adam) (London) Ltd** [1938] **4** 283, KBD.
      Loan secured by bill of sale—Copy of bill of sale attached to memorandum—Whether two documents can be read together—Moneylenders Act 1927, s 6. **Tooke v TW Bennett & Co Ltd** [1939] **4** 200, KBD.
      Loan secured by bill of sale—No reference in memorandum to power of seizure and sale contained in bill of sale—Moneylenders Act 1927, s 6. **Mitchener v Equitable Investment Co Ltd** [1938] **1** 303, KBD.
      Loan secured by promissory note—Ambiguity in stating effect of promissory note—Promissory note only consistent with one view of memorandum—Whether sufficient compliance with statutory provisions—Moneylenders Act 1927, s 6. **Mills Conduit Investments Ltd v Tattersall** [1940] **1** 281, KBD.
      Omission of reference to part of security—Borrower fully aware of terms of contract—Moneylenders Act 1927, s 6. **Kent Trust Ltd v Cohen** [1946] **2** 273, CA.
      Omitted terms—Reference therein to promissory note which contained the omitted words—Not permissible to look at promissory note unless copy thereof delivered or sent to borrower—Moneylenders Act 1927, s 6(2). **Edgware Trust Ltd v Lawrence** [1961] **3** 141, QBD.
      Promissory note payable by instalments—Post-dated cheques in respect of instalments—No reference in memorandum to payment by cheque—Moneylenders Act 1927, s 6. **Collings v Charles Bradbury Ltd** [1936] **3** 369, Ch D.
      Statement of one promissory note for £100—Two notes for £50 each actually given—Moneylenders Act 1927, s 6(2). **Debtor (No 18 of 1937), Re a** [1938] **2** 759, Ch D.
  Re-opening of transactions of moneylender—
    Jurisdiction—
      Loan at high rate of interest—Principal and interest consolidated in new loan at moderate rate of interest—Moneylenders Act 1900, s 1. **Lyle (B S) Ltd v Pearson and Medlycott** [1941] **3** 128, CA.
  Security—
    Enforcement—
      Limitation of time for proceedings—Loan secured by second mortgage—Sale of mortgaged property by first mortgagee—Claim by moneylender of surplus proceeds—Whether claim to enforce 'security taken in respect of a loan'—Law of Property Act 1925, s 105—Moneylenders Act 1927, s 13(1). **Martin's Mortgage Trusts, Re** [1951] **1** 1053, CA.
      Security given by the borrower or by his agent—Security given by third party—Memorandum insufficient—Security given by borrower not enforceable—Security given by third party—Whether 'security given by the borrower'—Whether enforceable—Moneylenders Act 1927, s 6(1). **Barclay v Prospect Mortgages Ltd** [1974] **2** 672, Ch D.
      Security given by the borrower or by his agent—Subrogated rights—Unenforceable loan contract—Sum advanced used to pay off existing charge on property—Term of contract that loan to be secured by charge on property in respect of which loan made—Charge executed but unenforceable—Lender entitled by subrogation to security represented by existing charge on property—Whether subrogated right a 'security given by the borrower'—Whether subrogated right enforceable—Moneylenders Act 1927, s 6(1). **Orakpo v Manson Investments Ltd** [1977] **3** 1, HL.
      Security not enforceable—Meaning of 'enforceable'—Mode of enforcement—Deposit of assets by surety with lender as security for loan—Memorandum of loan insufficient—Whether security enforceable by means other than legal proceedings—Whether surety entitled to order for delivery up of assets—Moneylenders Act 1927, s 6(1). **Barclay v Prospect Mortgages Ltd** [1974] **2** 672, Ch D.
    Return of security—
      Unenforceable contract—Right of borrower to return of security for loan—Whether plaintiff put upon terms—Moneylenders Act 1927, ss 5(6), 6. **Cohen v J Lester Ltd** [1938] **4** 188, KBD.
  West Africa—
    No memorandum of loan. *See* **West Africa** (Moneylender—No memorandum of loan).

MONEYLENDING
  Ceylon. *See* **Ceylon** (Moneylending).

MONITORING OF TELEPHONE CONVERSATION
  Powers of police. *See* **Police** (Powers—Telephone tapping).

MONOPOLIES AND MERGERS
  Monopolies and Mergers Commission—
    Chairman's powers—
      Reference of take-over bid to commission—Chairman of commission deciding bid abandoned—Chairman deciding commission should lay aside reference—Whether chairman having power to act alone. **R v Monopolies and Mergers Commission, ex p Argyll Group plc** [1986] **2** 257, CA.
    Commission's powers—
      Disclosure of confidential information—Disclosure to affected party in course of contested take-over—Commission acting 'for the purpose of facilitating the performance of [its] functions'—Commission receiving confidential information from bidder and disclosing it to company bid for—Whether commission acting fairly to bidder—Whether commission acting for purpose of facilitating performance of its functions—Whether commission entitled to disclose confidential information—Fair Trading Act 1973, s 133. **R v Monopolies and Mergers Commission, ex p Elders IXL Ltd** [1987] **1** 451, QBD.
      Disclosure of confidential information—Refusal to disclose confidential information to affected party—Commission receiving submission from bidder in course of contested take-over bid—Commission not divulging information from bidder to company bid for—Whether commission acting fairly—Whether commission entitled to withhold information from company bid for. **R v Monopolies and Mergers Commission, ex p Matthew Brown plc** [1987] **1** 463, QBD.

MONOPOLIES AND MERGERS (cont)—
Reference to Monopolies and Mergers Commission—
Discretion of Secretary of State whether to make reference to commission—
Whether Secretary of State entitled to act on advice of Director General of Fair Trading in deciding whether to refer bid to commission. **Lonrho v Secretary of State for Trade and Industry** [1989] **2** 609, HL.
Laying aside of reference to commission—
Commission entitled to lay reference aside if 'arrangements such as are mentioned in the reference' are abandoned by take-over bidder—Bidder making offer to take over company—Take-over bid referred to commission—Bidder substituting new bid—Whether 'arrangements ... mentioned in the reference' referring only to original bid or including new bid—Whether commission entitled to lay reference aside—Fair Trading Act 1973, s 75. **R v Monopolies and Mergers Commission, ex p Argyll Group plc** [1986] **2** 257, CA.
Merger affecting substantial part of United Kingdom—
Substantial part of United Kingdom—Merger of local bus undertakings—Reference area being 1·65% of United Kingdom and containing 3·2% population—Whether reference area 'a substantial part of the United Kingdom'—Whether commission having jurisdiction to hear reference—Fair Trading Act 1973, s 64(1)(a), (3). **South Yorkshire Transport Ltd v Monopolies and Mergers Commission** [1993] **1** 289, HL.
Report of Monopolies and Mergers Commission—
Order of Secretary of State on merger reference—
Discretion of Secretary of State—Reference of takeover bid to Monopolies and Mergers Commission—Majority report by commission that takeover against public interest—Commission's recommendation overruled by Secretary of State—Whether Secretary of State entitled to permit takeover—Fair Trading Act 1973, s 73(2), (3). **R v Secretary of State for Trade, ex p Anderson Strathclyde plc** [1983] **2** 233, QBD.

MONUMENT
Ancient monument—
Generally. See **Ancient monuments**.
Secretary of State's refusal to schedule ancient monument—
Judicial review. See **Judicial review** (Availability of remedy—Scheduling of ancient monument).
Headstone in churchyard. See **Ecclesiastical law** (Monument—Headstone in churchyard).
Memorial tablet within church. See **Ecclesiastical law** (Monument—Memorial tablet within church).
Sale—
Faculty jurisdiction. See **Ecclesiastical law** (Faculty—Sale of chattel—Monument).

MOORINGS
Laying and maintenance of permanent moorings—
Ordinary incidents of navigation. See **Water and watercourses** (Navigation—Ordinary incidents of navigation—Laying and maintenance of permanent moorings).

MORAL CHARACTER
Disclosure—
Insurance—
Duty to disclose such facts as a reasonable or prudent insurer might treat as material. See **Insurance** (Disclosure—Duty to disclose such facts as a reasonable or prudent insurer might treat as material—Moral character of insured).

MORTGAGE
Accounts—
Date from which account to commence—
Appointment of receiver by first mortgagee after appointment of receiver by subsequent mortgagee—Date from which account to commence where leave under Courts (Emergency Powers) Act 1939 necessary. **Belbridge Property Trust Ltd, Re** [1941] **2** 48, Ch D.
Mortgagee in possession—
Sum received for principal and interest—Whether mortgagee entitled to deduct amount of tax on interest. **Hollis v Wingfield** [1940] **1** 531, CA.
Receiver's duty to account. See Receiver—Duty to account, below.
Acknowledgment—
Limitation of action. See **Limitation of action** (Acknowledgment—Mortgage).
Action by mortgagee for possession—
Acknowledgment of title—
Acknowledgment by mortgagor's solicitor—Limitation Act 1939, ss 4(3), 23(1)(a). **Wright v Pepin** [1954] **2** 52, Ch D.
Action commenced by writ—
Judgment entered in default of appearance—Irregular procedure—Judgment set aside. **Redditch Benefit Building Society v Roberts** [1940] **1** 342, CA.
Flat subject to Rent Restrictions Acts—
Building society granting mortgage under mistaken belief no formal tenancy existing—Occupying tenants signing consent forms postponing their interests to interest of society as first mortgagee—Whether building society bound by protected tenancy—Whether consent forms effective—Rent Act 1977, s 98. **Woolwich Building Society v Dickman** [1996] **3** 204, CA.
House subject to Rent Restrictions Acts—
Unauthorised lease of mortgaged property—Default in payment of instalments due under mortgage—Position of tenant—Increase of Rent and Mortgage Interest (Restrictions) Act 1920, s 12(1)(g)—Law of Property Act 1925, s 99(1)—Rent and Mortgage Interest Restrictions (Amendment) Act 1933, s 3(1), Sch 1. **Dudley and District Benefit Building Society v Emerson** [1949] **2** 252, CA.

MORTGAGE (cont)—
  Action by mortgagee for possession (cont)—
    House subject to statutory tenancy under Rent Acts—
      Unauthorised lease of mortgaged property by mortgagors—Tenant becoming statutory tenant on expiry of lease—Mortgagee subsequently registering legal charge at Land Registry—Mortgagee seeking possession of property—Whether statutory tenancy binding on mortgagee—Whether mortgagee entitled to recover possession from tenant. **Barclays Bank plc v Zaroovabli** [1997] **2** 19, Ch D.
      Unauthorised lease of mortgaged property by mortgagor—Tenants becoming statutory tenants on expiry of lease—Mortgagor defaulting in payment of sums due under mortgage—Mortgagee seeking possession of property—Position of tenants—Whether tenants statutory tenants as against mortgagee as well as against mortgagor—Whether mortgagee entitled to recover possession from tenants—Rent Act 1977, s 98. **Britannia Building Society v Earl** [1990] **2** 469, CA.
      Unauthorised tenancy of mortgaged property—Tenancy not binding on mortgagee—Mortgagor wishing to obtain vacant possession in order to sell property—Mortgagee bringing action for possession against tenant on mortgagor's behalf—Whether mortgagee acting bona fide to protect security—Whether mortgagee entitled to possession against tenant. **Quennell v Maltby** [1979] **1** 568, CA.
    Jurisdiction of High Court—
      Action by mortgagee for foreclosure or sale—County court having exclusive jurisdiction to hear and determine action in which claim for possession made unless action is an action for foreclosure or sale—Mortgagee in reality seeking payment or possession—Claim for foreclosure or sale added as colourable device—Whether 'an action for foreclosure or sale'—Whether High Court having jurisdiction to hear and determine it—Administration of Justice Act 1970, ss 37, 38. **Trustees of Manchester Unity Life Insurance Collecting Society v Sadler** [1974] **2** 410, Ch D.
      Net annual value of property for rating—Property not liable to be rated—County court having exclusive jurisdiction if net annual value for rating less than county court limit—Mortgaged property comprising two hereditaments one of which not liable to be rated and the other having net annual value for rating below county court limit—Net annual value for rating of property not consisting of one or more hereditaments having separate net annual value—Property to be taken to have net annual value for rating equal to its value by the year—Whether annual value by the year of hereditament not liable to be rated to be taken as its net annual value for rating—Whether combined net annual value for rating of both hereditaments exceeding county court limit—Administration of Justice Act 1970, s 37(1)—County Courts Act 1959, ss 48, 200(2)(b). **Frost (P B) Ltd v Green** [1978] **2** 206, Ch D.
  Order for possession. *See* Order for possession of mortgaged property, *below*.
  Originating summons—
    Affidavit in support—Particulars of every person to best of plaintiff's knowledge in possession—Affidavit to contain only such facts as to his own knowledge deponent able to prove—Plaintiff a building society—Affidavit to state deponent's office in society—Affidavit to contain only an unqualified assertion giving particulars of persons in possession to best of society's knowledge—RSC Ord 41, r 5(1), Ord 88, r 6(4). **Nationwide Building Society v Bateman** [1978] **1** 999, Ch D.
    Affidavit in support—Particulars of the amount of the repayments—Affidavit to state total amount of the repayments of principal down to its date—RSC Ord 88, r 6(3)(b). **Nationwide Building Society v Bateman** [1978] **1** 999, Ch D.
    Service of certain notices—Default of appearance—Notice to proceed after a year's delay—RSC Ord 55, r 5A, Ord 64, r 13, Ord 67, r 4. **Practice Direction** [1958] **2** 384, Ch D.
    Service—Joint mortgagors—Service effected on one mortgagor who was in possession—No service on other mortgagor whose whereabouts was unknown—Order for possession made—RSC Ord 55, r 5A. **Alliance Building Society v Yap** [1962] **3** 6, Ch D.
    Substituted service—Courts (Emergency Powers) Act 1939, s 1(2)(a)(ii), (v). **Temperance Permanent Benefit Building Society v Isles** [1940] **1** 75, CA.
  Parties—
    Action against wife of mortgagor—Mortgagor serving soldier—Judgment in default of appearance—Certificate—RSC Ord 13, rr 8, 17, Ord 55, r 5A, B. **Temperance Permanent Benefit Building Society v Nevitt** [1940] **3** 237, CA.
    Deserted wife in occupation of former matrimonial home—Default by husband in mortgage payments—No notice to wife of proceedings against husband until after judgment—Whether wife entitled to be joined as defendant in action against husband—Whether husband after order for possession entitled to occupy dwelling-house—Matrimonial Homes Act 1967, s 1(5), (8). **Hastings and Thanet Building Society v Goddard** [1970] **3** 954, CA.
    Deserted wife in occupation of former matrimonial home—Default by husband in mortgage payments—Originating summons for possession by mortgagee against husband alone—Order for delivery of possession—Wife added as defendant—Wife having no independent right against mortgagee—Summons and order not void—Person having independent right against mortgagee entitled to be heard and thus to be added as defendant, but summons against mortgagor alone not void—RSC Ord 55, r 5B. **Pfizer Corp v Ministry of Health** [1965] **1** 450, HL.
    Mortgagor entitled to possession as registered proprietor—Mortgagor not in actual possession—Action for possession not a proceeding for enforcement of mortgage—Mortgagor not a proper party to action for possession. **Esso Petroleum Co Ltd v Alstonbridge Properties Ltd** [1975] **3** 358, Ch D.
    Mortgagor not in occupation. *See* Possession of mortgaged property—Mortgagor not in occupation, *below*.
    Mortgagor—Personal representatives of deceased mortgagor not necessary parties if possession would not prejudice mortgagor's estate. **Barclays Bank Ltd v Kiley** [1961] **2** 849, Ch D.
    Person in possession of the property—Stranger to mortgage—RSC Ord 55, r 5A. **Alliance Building Society v Varma** [1949] **2** 261, CA.
    Trustee in bankruptcy—RSC Ord 55, rr 5A, 5B. **Martins Bank Ltd v Kavanagh** [1948] **2** 448, Ch D.
  Remedy, as. *See* Remedies of mortgagee—Possession proceedings, *below*.
  Transfer of proceedings to High Court. *See* **Practice** (Transfer of proceedings between High Court and county court—Proceedings which must be in county court—Mortgagee possession actions).

MORGAGE (cont)—

Action on covenant—
  Building society—
    Mortgagor transferring property and shares in society—No release from covenant. **West Bromwich Building Society v Bullock** [1936] **1** 887, KBD.
Action to recover loan secured by mortgage—
  Action triable as commercial action or mortgage action—
    High Court. *See* **Court** (Jurisdiction—High Court of Justice—Divisions of High Court—Action triable as commercial action or mortgage action).
Advance—
  Further advances—
    Mortgage varied by extending term and increasing rate of interest—Whether extension of term at increased rate of interest amounting to 'further advances'. **Burnes v Trade Credits Ltd** [1981] **2** 122, PC.
Agreement for a loan—
  Repayment as to the first ten years only agreed—
    Damages for breach of agreement. **Astor Properties Ltd v Tunbridge Wells Equitable Friendly Society** [1936] **1** 531, KBD.
Application—
  False accounting. *See* **Criminal law** (False accounting—Document made or required for an accounting purpose—Falsifying account or document—Falsifying mortgage application forms).
Application of proceeds of sale. *See* Sale—Application, *below*.
Apportionment of principal—
  Effect of Rent Restriction Acts. *See* Payment—Apportionment of principal, *below*.
Attornment clause—
  Charge by way of legal mortgage—
    Leasehold interest—Chargee having same protection as if mortgage by sub-demise—Effect of attornment clause—Assignment of lease—Whether assignee liable on covenants, contained in charge, to take motor fuel supplies from chargee by way of legal mortgage—Tied petrol filling station—Law of Property Act 1925, s 87(1)(b). **Regent Oil Co Ltd v Gregory (JA) (Hatch End) Ltd** [1965] **3** 673, CA.
    Tenancy by estoppel—Whether tenancy by estoppel created. **Regent Oil Co Ltd v Gregory (JA) (Hatch End) Ltd** [1965] **3** 673, CA.
  Creation of relationship of landlord and tenant—
    Application of Rent Restrictions Acts. **Portman Building Society v Young** [1951] **1** 191, CA.
    Notice to quit—Length of notice required—Whether property let as a dwelling—Rent Act 1957, s 16. **Alliance Building Society v Pinwill** [1958] **2** 408, Ch D.
    Notice to quit—Need of notice—Breach of covenant to repay principal by instalments—Claim by mortgagee to possession. **Hinckley and Country Building Society v Henny** [1953] **1** 515, Ch D.
    Notice to quit—Validity—Application of Agricultural Holdings Acts—Agricultural Holdings Act 1948, ss 2(1), 23(1). **Steyning and Littlehampton Building Society v Wilson** [1951] **2** 452, Ch D.
Bankruptcy—
  Mortgaged property subject to joint tenancy—
    Bankruptcy of one of joint tenants—Right of mortgagee to prove for debt. *See* **Bankruptcy** (Proof—Secured creditor—Joint tenancy of property charged to secure loan).
Breach of statutory duty—
  Measure of damages. *See* **Damages** (Measure of damages—Breach of statutory duty—Mortgage).
Building society. *See* **Building society** (Mortgage).
Charge—
  Registered land. *See* **Land registration** (Charge).
Charge by way of legal mortgage—
  Estate of mortgagee—
    Term of years—Whether legal term of years vested in chargee—Law of Property Act 1925, s 87(2). **Weg Motors Ltd v Hales** [1961] **3** 181, CA.
  Statutory protection, powers and remedies of mortgagee—
    Effect as if mortgage by sub-demise—Tied petrol filling station—Covenants in mortgage to take motor fuel from chargee were covenants protecting security—Enforceable against assignee by virtue of Law of Property Act 1925, s 87(1)(b). **Regent Oil Co Ltd v Gregory (JA) (Hatch End) Ltd** [1965] **3** 673, CA.
Charging order of judgment creditor—
  Remedy—
    Foreclosure—Sale—Judgments Act 1938, s 14. **Daponte v Schubert** [1939] **3** 495, Ch D.
Clog on equity of redemption—
  Applicability of rule—
    Defendant advancing money for purchase of long lease of flat by relatives—Oral agreement that defendant to acquire leasehold interest after relatives' death—Charge granted to defendant over flat in respect of purchase money—Second charge granted to defendant in respect of increase in base value of flat—Whether defendant's second charge void as clog on equity of redemption—Whether arrangement between defendant and relatives constituting mortgage. **Brighton & Hove City Council v Audus** [2010] **1 Comm** 343, Ch D.
  Option to purchase—
    Transfer of mortgage—Option to purchase mortgaged property granted by mortgagor to transferees as part of arrangement for transferees lending a sum slightly larger than the amount secured by the mortgage—Whether option was void as a clog on the equity of redemption. **Lewis v Love (Frank) Ltd** [1961] **1** 446, Ch D.
  Postponement of redemption—
    Principal repayable by instalments over period of 40 years—Company—Loan deemed by mortgage of property—Reasonableness of postponement of redemption—Clog on equity—Rule against perpetuities—Whether mortgage a debenture—Companies Act 1929, ss 74, 380. **Knightsbridge Estates Trust Ltd v Byrne** [1940] **2** 401, HL.

MORTGAGE (cont)—
Clog on equity of redemption (cont)—
Restraint of trade—
Petrol filling station—Solus terms incorporated into mortgage—Mortgage repayable by instalments over twenty-one years—Not redeemable otherwise—Whether doctrine of restraint of trade applied to covenants in mortgage—Whether mortgage oppressive and therefore redeemable on notice. **Esso Petroleum Co Ltd v Harper's Garage (Stourport) Ltd** [1967] **1** 699, HL.
Collateral advantage—
Premium—
Security for premium and moneys lent—Charge on mortgagor's house on occasion of expiration of lease and his purchase of freehold from landlords—Loan of £2,900 by landlords—Purchase price £3,500—£600 provided by mortgagor—Sum charged by mortgage £4,553, payable by seventy-two equal monthly instalments—Premium (£1,653) included in the sum charged—On default whole of money lent and premium would become due—Mortgagor in default—Mortgagees sought to enforce mortgage—Whether charge should stand as security for premium as well as for moneys lent—Whether interest should be allowed. **Cityland and Property (Holdings) Ltd v Dabrah** [1967] **2** 639, Ch D.
Consumer credit—
Multiple agreements. *See* **Consumer credit** (Agreement—Multiple agreements—Mortgage).
Costs—
Challenge—
Mortgagee having contractual right to recover or retain costs out of mortgaged property—Mortgagor challenging items included in mortgagee's account of costs as being of unreasonable amount—Whether mortgagor entitled to object to items in account. **Gomba Holdings UK Ltd v Minories Finance Ltd (No 2)** [1992] **4** 588, CA.
Contractual entitlement to costs—
Statutory discretion to order payment of costs—Mortgagee having contractual right to recover or retain costs out of mortgaged property on full indemnity basis—Whether statutory discretion to be exercised in accordance with mortgagee's contractual entitlement to costs—Whether court having power to curtail mortgagee's contractual entitlement to costs—Supreme Court Act 1981, s 51(1). **Gomba Holdings UK Ltd v Minories Finance Ltd (No 2)** [1992] **4** 588, CA.
Enforcing security—
Mortgagee's costs—Scale—Costs, charges and expenses properly incurred. **Adelphi Hotel (Brighton) Ltd, Re** [1953] **2** 498, Ch D.
Litigation costs and non-litigation costs—
Quantification—Taxation—Mortgagee having contractual right to recover or retain costs from mortgaged property—Whether mortgagee's entitlement to litigation costs and non-litigation costs to be quantified by means of taxation—Whether non-litigation costs amenable to taxation—RSC Ord 62, rr 19, 24. **Gomba Holdings UK Ltd v Minories Finance Ltd (No 2)** [1992] **4** 588, CA.
Protecting security—
Mortgagee defending his title—Action by legally-aided person—Costs added to security—Legal Aid and Advice Act 1949, s 2(2). **Saunders (exrx of the estate of Rose Maud Gallie (decd)) v Anglia Building Society (formerly Northampton Town and County Building Society) (No 2)** [1971] **1** 243, HL.
Mortgagee defending his title—Action by poor person—Costs added to security—RSC Ord 16, r 28(1), Ord 65, r 1. **Leighton's Conveyance, Re** [1936] **3** 1033, CA.
Mortgagee defending his title—Action by stranger—Costs of defending action by stranger impugning mortgagee's exercise of statutory power of sale—Whether costs recoverable out of mortgage security—Whether general obligation on court to order payment of costs out of mortgaged security—RSC Ord 62, r 6(2). **Parker-Tweedale v Dunbar Bank plc (No 2)** [1990] **2** 588, CA.
Not recoverable from mortgagor personally as distinct from being allowed as condition of redeeming mortgage—Legally aided mortgagor challenging sale by mortgagee—Whether mortgagor would be declared personally liable for mortgagee's costs if action failed—Legal Aid and Advice Act 1949, s 2(2)(e). **Sinfield v Sweet** [1967] **3** 479, Ch D.
Covenant—
Action on. *See* Action on covenant, *above*.
Restraint of trade. *See* **Restraint of trade by agreement** (Petrol filling station—Solus agreement—Mortgage).
Debt—
Limitation of action. *See* **Limitation of action** (Mortgage—Mortgage debt).
Repayment—
Joint and several liability—Bank making advances to defendants jointly and to one of them solely—Defendants covenanting as 'mortgagor' in standard form mortgage to pay all sums advanced to 'mortgagor'—Mortgage defining 'mortgagor' as referring to all or any of the mortgagors when there was more than one—Mortgage declaring obligations of all such persons to be joint and several—Whether payment covenant rendering joint mortgagor liable for advances made solely to other joint mortgagor. **AIB Group (UK) plc (formerly Allied Irish Banks plc and AIB Finance Ltd) v Martin** [2002] **1** Comm 209, HL; [2002] **1** 353, HL; **AIB Group (UK) plc v Martin** [2000] **2** Comm 686, CA.
Mortgagee retaining debt out of proceeds of mortgaged policy. *See* Repayment—Mortgagee retaining debt out of proceeds of mortgaged policy, *below*.
Security—
Individual voluntary arrangement (IVA)—Mortgagee making claim in IVA in respect of anticipated shortfall on mortgage debt—Mortgagee accepting payment of dividend in respect of claim—Whether mortgagee to be treated as having abandoned its security in respect of that part of mortgage debt which formed subject matter of its claim in IVA. **Whitehead v Household Mortgage Corp plc** [2003] **1** Comm 263, CA; [2003] **1** 319, CA.
Deeds—
Deposit of—
India, in. *See* **India** (Mortgage by deposit of deeds).

MORTGAGE (cont)—
Deeds (cont)—
Preparation—
Unqualified person. *See* **Solicitor** (Unqualified person—Preparation of documents etc—Clerk to local authority—Mortgage deeds).
Demand for repayment—
Death of mortgagor. *See* Repayment—Demand—Service—Death of mortgagor, *below*.
Deposit of deeds—
India. *See* **India** (Mortgage by deposit of deeds).
Devise of mortgaged property. *See* **Administration of estates** (Gift—Gift cum onere—Real property mortgaged).
Discharge—
Counterclaim by mortgagor—
Failure of mortgagor to repay loan secured by charge on his property—Writ issued by mortgagee—Counterclaim by mortgagor for unliquidated damages—Counterclaim possibly exceeding amount of debt due—Whether mortgage debt discharged by existence of counterclaim. **Keller (Samuel) (Holdings) Ltd v Martins Bank Ltd** [1970] **3** 950, CA.
Sale of land. *See* **Sale of land** (Title—Discharge of mortgage).
Statutes of Limitation, by—
Return of documents of title to mortgagor. **Lewis v Plunket** [1937] **1** 530, Ch D.
Equitable interest—
Priority—
Agreement for sale of land—Subsequent equitable mortgage of land by vendor company—Mortgagee's notice of agreement—Failure to register agreement as estate contract until after equitable mortgage—Mortgagee acquiring legal mortgage after registration of agreement—Agreement between vendor company and builder for sale and purchase of property for development—Builder to develop site by building houses building houses thereon—Builder to obtain planning permission—Vender company to provide finance for building of houses—Finance obtained from mortgagee by means of mortgage on property—Mortgagee's knowledge of agreement for sale—Provision in agreement for builder to give option to complete on giving 14 days' notice—Whether builder obtaining equitable interest under agreement—Whether mortgage obtaining priority through failure to register agreement prior to equitable mortgage—Whether mortgagee taking precedence over builder's equitable interest by obtaining legal mortgage. **McCarthy & Stone Ltd v Julian S Hodge & Co Ltd** [1971] **2** 973, Ch D.
Equitable interests ranking in order of time—Law of Property Act 1925, s 113. **Beddoes v Shaw** [1936] **2** 1108, Ch D.
Husband and wife's joint purchase of matrimonial home—Conveyance in husband's sole name—Creation of mortgage by husband—Possession sought by mortgagee—Whether mortgagee having priority over wife's equitable interest. **Bird v Syme Thomson** [1978] **3** 1027, Ch D.
Husband and wife's joint purchase of matrimonial home—Conveyance in husband's sole name—Creation of three legal charges by husband without wife's knowledge—Whether mortgagee had priority over wife's equitable interest—Constructive notice—Reasonable enquiry—Law of Property Act 1925, s 199(1)(ii). **Caunce v Caunce** [1969] **1** 722, Ch D.
Husband and wife's joint purchase of matrimonial home—Conveyance in husband's sole name—Husband mortgaging home without wife's knowledge—Possession sought by mortgagee—Whether mortgagee having priority over wife's equitable interest—Whether wife's interest 'subsisting in reference' to land—Land Registration Act 1925, s 70(1). **Williams & Glyn's Bank Ltd v Boland** [1980] **2** 408, HL.
Notice of equitable interest—Inspection—Such inspections as ought reasonably to have been made—Unregistered land—Occupation—Evidence of occupation—Residential property—Inspection by pre-arranged appointment—Occupation of matrimonial home by wife concealed by husband—Whether inspection by pre-arranged appointment amounting to 'such ... inspections ... as ought reasonably to have been made'—Law of Property Act 1925, s 199(1)(ii). **Kingsnorth Trust Ltd v Tizard** [1986] **2** 54, Ch D.
Notice of equitable interest—Notice—Constructive notice—Notice to agent—Matrimonial home in sole name of husband—Husband subsequently obtaining loan on security of mortgage of matrimonial home—Husband describing himself to mortgagee as single—Mortgagee's surveyor inspecting matrimonial home during temporary absence of wife—Husband concealing wife's occupation—Whether surveyor's knowledge that husband had a wife to be taken to be mortgagee's knowledge—Whether mortgagee put on further inquiry—Whether wife's equitable interest having priority over mortgagee's interest—Law of Property Act 1925, s 199(1)(ii)(a). **Kingsnorth Trust Ltd v Tizard** [1986] **2** 54, Ch D.
Notice of equitable interest—Person in occupation—Occupation—Actual occupation—Physical presence—Whether physical presence must be exclusive or continuous and uninterrupted to amount to actual occupation—Whether presence on land with occupation excluding possibility of occupation of others. **Kingsnorth Trust Ltd v Tizard** [1986] **2** 54, Ch D.
Possession of mortgaged property—Generally. *See* Possession of mortgaged property—Adverse interest—Equitable interest, *below*.
Equitable mortgage—
Equitable mortgagee paid off by subsequent lender—
Presumption of intention to keep equitable mortgage alive—Whether presumption negatived by taking of an invalid legal mortgage. **Ghana Commercial Bank v Chandiram** [1960] **2** 865, PC.
Financial collateral arrangements—
Enforcement—Appropriation—Equitable mortgage of shares—Collateral-taker giving notice of exercise of right of appropriation of shares—Whether power of appropriation validly exercised—Whether necessary for collateral-taker to become registered holder of shares—Financial Collateral Arrangements (No 2) Regulations 2003, SI 2003/3226, reg 17—Council Directive (EC) 2002/47, art 4. **Cukurova Finance International Ltd v Alfa Telecom Turkey Ltd** [2009] **3** 849, PC; [2010] **1** Comm 1173, PC.

549

MORTGAGE (cont)—
Equitable mortgage (cont)—
  Financial collateral arrangements (cont)—
    Enforcement—Appropriation—Equitable mortgage of shares—Relief from forfeiture—Terms of relief—Basis of relief. **Cukurova Finance International Ltd v Alfa Telecom Turkey Ltd (No 2)** [2013] **4** 936, PC; **Cukurova Finance International Ltd v Alfa Telecom Turkey Ltd (No 3)** [2013] **4** 989n, PC.
  Priority—
    Memorandum of deposit and deposit of land certificate—Registered title to land—Notice of deposit (not of the memorandum) entered on register—Charging orders subsequently obtained by judgment creditors and two cautions lodged—Whether charge created by the deposit of the land certificate had priority to judgment creditors' charge—Mortgagees by deposit had power of attorney to convey legal estate—Whether equitable mortgagees by deposit could sell so as to override judgment creditors' charges—Law of Property Act 1925, ss 101, 104(1)—Land Registration Act 1925, s 49—Land Registration Rules 1925 (S R & O 1925 No 1093), r 239. **White Rose Cottage, Re** [1965] **1** 11, CA.
    Unregistered equitable mortgage—Registered lien of contractor—Mortgage not registered while contractor's work done—Subsequent application for registration of mortgage—Delay as result of requisition of district registrar—Registration in respect of first lien action—Caveat registered by mortgagee—Registration in respect of second lien action—Alteration unilaterally by mortgagee of mortgage, expressing it to be subject to liens—Alteration made only for purpose of meeting requisition of district registrar and procuring registration—Whether mortgage as unaltered could be invoked for purposes of obtaining priority over liens—Wages Protection and Contractors' Liens Act 1939 (No 27 of 1939), s 41. **Farrier-Waimak Ltd v Bank of New Zealand** [1964] **3** 657, PC.
Equity of redemption—
  Clog on equity of redemption. *See* Clog on equity of redemption, *above*.
  Limitation of action—
    Second mortgagee's estate and right to recover possession statute-barred—Equity of redemption incapable of surviving in gross. **Cotterell v Price** [1960] **3** 315, Ch D.
Execution—
  Sequence of execution of conveyance and mortgage—
    Vendor of land leaving part of purchase price on mortgage—Whether vendor's lien excluded or abandoned. **Cityfield Properties Ltd, Re** [1968] **3** 625, CA.
Extortionate credit bargain. *See* Consumer credit (Extortionate credit bargain—Mortgage).
Financial collateral arrangements. *See* Equitable mortgage—Financial collateral arrangements, *above*.
Fire insurance. *See* **Insurance** (Fire insurance—Mortgage).
Fixtures—
  Degree of annexation necessary—
    Machines attached to driving apparatus attached to realty. **Hulme v Brigham** [1943] **1** 204, KBD.
Foreclosure—
  Application for foreclosure nisi—
    Affidavit of due execution—No longer required. **Practice Direction** [1969] **2** 639, Ch D.
  Leave to commence proceedings—
    War time. *See* **Emergency legislation** (Mortgage—Foreclosure proceedings—Leave to commence).
  Order for delivery of possession contained in order absolute—
    Mortgagee's right to possession without leave of court—Courts (Emergency Powers) Act 1939, s 1(2)(b)—Possession of Mortgaged Land (Emergency Powers) Act 1939. **Wood v Smallpiece** [1942] **1** 252, CA.
  Power to authorise sale of mortgaged property in action for foreclosure. *See* Sale—Power to authorise sale—Action for foreclosure, *below*.
  Redemption—
    Orders nisi—Notice of intention to redeem—Place of redemption. **Practice Direction** [1954] **3** 364, Ch D; [1955] **1** 30, Ch D.
Forfeiture of lease—
  Rights of mortgagee. *See* Lease—Forfeiture, *below*.
Illegal consideration—
  Betting debt secured by deed of charge—
    Covenant to repay. **Hill (William) (Park Lane) Ltd v Hofman** [1950] **1** 1013, Ch D.
Implied term. *See* **Contract** (Implied term—Mortgage).
Insurance—
  Fire insurance. *See* **Insurance** (Fire insurance—Mortgage).
  Insurance against war risks—
    Breach of covenant—Impossibility of performance—Waiver. **Moorgate Estates Ltd v Trower and Barstow** [1940] **1** 195, Ch D.
Interest—
  Compound interest—
    Bank's right to charge compound interest. *See* **Interest** (Compound interest—Bank).
  Higher than usual rate of interest—
    Extortionate credit bargain. *See* **Consumer credit** (Extortionate credit bargain—Mortgage).
  Income tax. *See* **Income tax** (Interest—Mortgage interest).
  Matrimonial home—
    Interest payments. *See* **Husband and wife** (Matrimonial home—Mortgage repayments—Interest payments).
  Mortgagee's entitlement to arrears of interest. *See* Redemption—Mortgagee's entitlement to arrears of interest, *below*.
  Notice by mortgagor to pay off—
    Failure to pay on date named—Sum due not set aside and available on date of expiry of notice—Right to interest subsequent to date of expiry. **Barratt v Gough-Thomas** [1951] **2** 48, Ch D.
  Option to pay interest at variable rate—
    Mortgagees falling into arrears—Calculation of arrears—Construction of contract—Whether mortgagees paying at fixed rate or variable rate. **Bank of Scotland v Ladjadj** [2000] **2 Comm** 583, CA.
  Restrictions. *See* Statutory restrictions, *below*.

MORTGAGE (cont)—
   Interest (cont)—
      Variation of interest rate payable—
         Mortgage offer providing for variable rate of interest by reference to Bank of England base rate plus additional margin over base rate—Mortgage conditions providing for lender to vary interest rate in specified circumstances—Lender increasing margin over base rate pursuant to conditions for reasons other than change in base rate—Whether terms of conditions contradicting terms of offer—Whether irreconcilable discrepancy between terms of offer and conditions. **Alexander (as representative of the 'Property 118 Action Group') v West Bromwich Mortgage Co Ltd** [2015] **2 Comm** 224, QBD.
   Jurisdiction of High Court. *See* Action by mortgagee for possession—Jurisdiction of High Court, *above.*
   Lease—
      Forfeiture—
         Breach of repairing covenant—Whether mortgagee entitled to notice of breach—Leasehold Property (Repairs) Act 1938, s 1(2), (3). **Church Comrs for England v Ve-Ri-Best Manufacturing Co Ltd** [1956] **3** 777, QBD.
         Protection of mortgagee—'Underlessee'—Law of Property Act 1925, ss 87(1), 146(1). **Grand Junction Co Ltd v Bates** [1954] **2** 385, QBD.
         Relief against forfeiture—Underlessee. *See* **Landlord and tenant** (Relief against forfeiture—Underlessee—Mortgaged lease).
         Relief of mortgagees—Generally. *See* **Landlord and tenant** (Relief against forfeiture—Mortgagee).
         Relief of mortgagees—Underlessee. *See* **Landlord and tenant** (Relief against forfeiture—Underlessee—Lease mortgaged—Relief of mortgagees).
      Option to purchase freehold reversion—
         Option separately assigned to mortgagee—Option excercised by mortgagee—Whether mortgagor entitled to conveyance on redemption. *See* Redemption—Lease with option to purchase freehold reversion, *below.*
      Underlease—
         Forfeiture of lease—Relief of underlessees. *See* **Landlord and tenant** (Relief against forfeiture—Underletting without consent—Mortgage).
   Leasehold—
      Assignment by way of mortgage after 1925—
         Intended to be security only but not so expressed—Whether assignment operated as sub-demise—Law of Property Act 1925, s 86(2). **Grangeside Properties Ltd v Collingwoods Securities Ltd** [1964] **1** 143, CA.
      Leaseholds mortgaged by subdemise—
         No trust of nominal reversion—Equity of redemption statute-barred before 1926—Transitional provisions—Privity of estate between lessor and mortgagee—Law of Property Act 1925, s 89(3), Sch I, Part II, para 3. **St Germans (Earl) v Barker** [1936] **1** 849, Ch D.
   Lien—
      Mortgaged property subject to contract of sale. *See* **Lien** (Mortgaged property).
   Limitation of action—
      Generally. *See* **Limitation of action** (Mortgage).
      Interest—
         Arrears. *See* Redemption—Mortgagee's entitlement to arrears of interest, *below.*
   Loan index-linked to foreign currency—
      Repayment—
         Enforceability—Public policy. *See* **Money** (Loan—Repayment of loan index-linked to foreign currency—Enforceability—Public policy—Mortgage).
   Loan secured by mortgage—
      Recovery—
         High Court—Action triable as commercial action or mortgage action. *See* **Court** (Jurisdiction—High Court of Justice—Divisions of High Court—Action triable as commercial action or mortgage action).
   Matrimonial home—
      Deserted wife's right to be joined in proceedings against husband by mortgagee. *See* Action by mortgagee for possession—Parties, *above.*
      Mortgage repayments. *See* **Husband and wife** (Matrimonial home—Mortgage repayments).
   Mortgage action—
      Mortgage conditions—
         Disclosure—Affidavit in support of originating summons—Standard mortgage conditions, offer letter or other side letter incorporated into mortgage to be exhibited to affidavit—Administration of Justice Act 1970, s 36—Administration of Justice Act 1973, s 8—RSC Ord 88, r 5(2). **Practice Direction** [1991] **3** 768, Ch D.
   Mortgagee in possession—
      Accounts. *See* Accounts—Mortgagee in possession, *above.*
      Action for possession. *See* Action by mortgagee for possession, *above.*
   Mortgagee's right to recover possession. *See* Possession of mortgaged property—Mortgagee's right to recover possession, *below.*
   Mortgagor not in occupation—
      Possession of mortgaged property. *See* Possession of mortgaged property—Mortgagor not in occupation, *below.*
   Mortgagor's right of possession. *See* Possession of mortgaged property—Mortgagor's right to possession, *below.*
   Notice to mortgagee—
      Application for order for transfer of mortgaged property—
         Matrimonial proceedings. *See* **Husband and wife** (Matrimonial home—Transfer—Order of court—Application for order on decree of divorce, nullity or judicial separation—Mortgaged property).
   Notice to redeem—
      Interest payable after expiry of notice. *See* Interest—Notice by mortgagor to pay off, *above.*

MORTGAGE (cont)—

Option—
Grant of option by mortgagee. *See* Sale—Option—Grant of option by building society mortgagee, *below.*

Purchase—
Clog on equity of redemption. *See* Clog on equity of redemption—Option to purchase, *above.*

Order for possession of mortgaged property—

Counterclaim—
Mortgagee bringing action for possession against mortgagor—Counterclaim by mortgagor for unliquidated damages—Counterclaim alleged to exceed amount of debt due—Mortgagor claiming equitable set-off—Whether mortgagee entitled to possession notwithstanding counterclaim—Whether counterclaim a defence to mortgagee's claim to possession. **National Westminster Bank plc v Skelton** [1993] **1** 242, CA.

Mortgagee bringing action for possession against mortgagor—Mortgagor guaranteeing debts of principal debtor—Guarantor counterclaiming that principal debtor having cross-claims against mortgagee giving rise to equitable set-off for unliquidated sum—Whether existence of cross-claims for unliquidated sum defeating order for possession—Whether position of guarantor different from position of principal debtor—Whether mortgagee entitled to possession. **Ashley Guarantee plc v Zacaria** [1993] **1** 254, CA.

Joint mortgagors—
Mortgagee applying for order for possession against husband and wife in respect of matrimonial property—Wife having arguable defence to application—Court granting possession order as against husband pending outcome of proceedings against wife—Whether court having power to make order for possession as against one of two joint mortgagors. **Albany Home Loans Ltd v Massey** [1997] **2** 609, CA.

Stay of execution of order—
Legal mortgagees obtained order for possession—Mortgagor sought stay of execution—Nothing had occurred since making of order which if it had occurred before order was made would have prevented its being made—Whether court had power to grant stay of execution on an order for possession—RSC Ord 45, r 11. **London Permanent Benefit Building Society v De Baer** [1968] **1** 372, Ch D.

Suspension of execution of order—
Likelihood that mortgagor will be able to pay sums due within a reasonable period—Counterclaim—Whether court entitled to consider mortgagor's counterclaim in exercising discretion to postpone order for possession—Administration of Justice Act 1970, s 36. **Citibank Trust Ltd v Ayivor** [1987] **3** 241, Ch D.

Likelihood that mortgagor will be able to pay sums due within a reasonable period—Execution of order suspended for 13 months to give mortgagor opportunity to sell mortgaged property—Whether court only having power to defer order for possession where sale to take place within short period of time—Administration of Justice Act 1970, s 36—Administration of Justice Act 1973, s 8. **National and Provincial Building Society v Lloyd** [1996] **1** 630, CA.

Likelihood that mortgagor will be able to pay sums due within a reasonable period—Likelihood a question of fact—Proposal by mortgagor to sell property in order to pay sums due—Whether court entitled to take prospective sale into account for purpose of determining whether sums likely to be paid within reasonable period—Administration of Justice Act 1970, s 36(1). **Royal Trust Co of Canada v Markham** [1975] **3** 433, CA.

Likelihood that mortgagor will be able to pay sums due within a reasonable period—Proposal by mortgagor to sell property in order to pay sums due—Whether sale better effected by mortgagors in occupation or by mortgagee—Whether sale by mortgagors in occupation serving best interests of both mortgagors and mortgagee—Whether court should suspend execution of order for possession to enable sale of property by mortgagors—Administration of Justice Act 1970, s 36—Administration of Justice Act 1973, s 8. **Target Home Loans Ltd v Clothier** [1994] **1** 439, CA.

Likelihood that mortgagor will be able to pay sums due within a reasonable period—Repayment by instalments—Whether execution of order should be suspended if amount of instalments to clear arrears within reasonable time is beyond debtor's means—Whether execution of order should be suspended if order which is within debtor's means will not clear arrears within reasonable time and cover current instalments—Administration of Justice Act 1970, s 36. **First National Bank plc v Syed** [1991] **2** 250, CA.

Likelihood that mortgagor will be able to pay sums due within a reasonable period—Sums due—Arrears or whole of redemption moneys—Power to suspend execution conditional on likelihood of mortgagor paying sums due—Mortgagor failing to pay instalments—Mortgagee entitled to redemption—Mortgagee seeking possession—Mortgagor likely to be able to pay arrears within reasonable period and to pay future instalments—No prospect of mortgagor paying redemption moneys within reasonable period—Mortgagor not entitled to suspension of possession order—Administration of Justice Act 1970, s 36(1), (2). **Halifax Building Society v Clark** [1973] **2** 33, Ch D.

Mortgagee falling into arrears and bank obtaining possession order—Possession order suspended on terms mortgagee pay unpaid instalments in addition to current instalments due—Bank agreeing to consolidate arrears with outstanding balance of the loan—Mortgagee falling into arrears again and bank seeking warrant of possession—Mortgagee contending discharge of arrears by consolidation extinguishing possession order—Whether consolidation extinguishing possession order—Whether terms of possession order disproportionate or otherwise unlawful—Administration of Justice Act 1970, s 36(3). **Bank of Scotland plc v Zinda** [2011] **2** Comm 839, CA.

Mortgagor negotiating sale of property—Mortgagee refusing consent since proceeds of sale not sufficient to discharge mortgage debt—Mortgagor applying to county court for suspension of possession order pending determination of High Court application for sale of property under s 91(2) of the Law of Property Act 1925—Whether county court having jurisdiction to suspend possession order—Administration of Justice Act 1970, s 36—Administration of Justice Act 1973, s 8. **Cheltenham and Gloucester plc v Krausz** [1997] **1** 21, CA.

MORTGAGE (cont)—
    Order for possession of mortgaged property (cont)—
        Suspension of execution of order (cont)—
            Mortgagor permitted to defer payment of principal sum but provision also made for earlier payment in event of default by mortgagor—Dwelling-house mortgaged to secure repayment of loan—Loan to be repaid six months from date of mortgage—Interest to be payable quarterly on so much of the loan as unpaid—In default of payment of interest, loan deemed to be due forthwith and mortgagee entitled to possession—Mortgagor defaulting in payment of interest—Mortgagee obtaining order for possession—Mortgagor applying for order to suspend execution of possession order—Whether a mortgage whereby 'mortgagor permitted to defer payment of principal sum but whereby provision also made for earlier payment in event of default by mortgagor'—Whether execution of order for possession should be suspended—Administration of Justice Act 1970, s 36—Administration of Justice Act 1973, s 8. **Centrax Trustees Ltd v Ross** [1979] 2 952, Ch D.

            Mortgagor permitted to defer payment of principal sum but provision also made for earlier payment in event of default by mortgagor—Mortgagor charging dwelling house to secure repayment of bank overdraft on current account—Mortgage containing covenant by mortgagor to repay principal sum secured by charge on bank's written demand for payment—Mortgagor exceeding overdraft and bank making written demand for repayment of principal sum and interest—Whether court entitled to exercise discretion to postpone order for possession to give mortgagor reasonable time to repay sums due—Whether mortgage permitting mortgagor 'to defer payment' of principal sum—Whether mortgage providing for 'earlier payment' in event of default—Administration of Justice Act 1970, s 36(1)—Administration of Justice Act 1973, s 8(1). **Habib Bank Ltd v Tailor** [1982] 3 561, CA.

            Mortgagor permitted to defer payment of principal sum but provision also made for payment in event of default by mortgagor—Endowment mortgage—Whether mortgagor under an endowment mortgage from bank entitled to same relief as mortgagor under instalment mortgage from building society—Administration of Justice Act 1970, s 36—Administration of Justice Act 1973, s 8(1). **Bank of Scotland v Grimes** [1985] 2 254, CA.

            Period of suspension—Definite or indefinite period—Whether court's jurisdiction limited to suspending execution for definite or ascertainable period—Administration of Justice Act 1970, s 36(1), (2)—Administration of Justice Act 1973, s 8(2). **Royal Trust Co of Canada v Markham** [1975] 3 433, CA.

            Persons 'deriving title under the ... mortgagor'—Unauthorised lease of mortgaged property by mortgagor in breach of mortgage terms—Mortgagor defaulting in payment of sums due under mortgage—Action by mortgagee for possession—Tenants seeking adjournment of proceedings to enable them to pay off sums due under mortgage—Whether tenants 'deriving title under ... mortgagor'—Whether breach of mortgage terms capable of being remedied—Whether court having power to adjourn proceedings—Administration of Justice Act 1970, ss 36, 39(1). **Britannia Building Society v Earl** [1990] 2 469, CA.

            Statutory power to defer possession for a 'reasonable period'—Assessment of a 'reasonable period'—Mortgagor defaulting under terms of suspension order requiring payment of interest instalments and arrears within four years—Whether remaining term of mortgage a 'reasonable period' for repayment—Whether in position of shorter fixed period of two or more years 'reasonable' for statutory purposes—Administration of Justice Act 1970, s 36—Administration of Justice Act 1973, s 8. **Cheltenham and Gloucester Building Society v Norgan** [1996] 1 449, CA.

        Time for possession—
            Twenty-eight days order. **Barclays Bank Ltd v Kiley** [1961] 2 849, Ch D.

    Originating summons—
        Service—
            Mortgagee's action for possession. See Action by mortgagee for possession—Originating summons, *above*.

    Payment—
        Apportionment of principal—
            Effect of Rent Restrictions Acts—Mortgage of dwelling-house divided into six flats—Four flats outside Rent Restrictions Acts and two flats within them on basis of rateable values—Apportionment of principal secured by mortgage between the two flats and the four flats—Whether protection of Rent Restrictions Acts removed from principal apportioned to four flats—Increase of Rent and Mortgage Interest (Restrictions) Act 1920, s 12(5) (as applied by Rent and Mortgage Interest Restrictions Act 1939, s 3(1)). **Coutts & Co v Duntroon Investment Corp Ltd** [1958] 1 51, Ch D.

        Summary judgment—
            Leave—Action to recover principal moneys and interest due under second mortgage—Default of appearance by mortgagor—Mortgaged property sold by first mortgagee before issue of writ—Whether judgment could be entered summarily by plaintiff or whether leave required—Meaning of 'mortgage'—RSC Ord 13, r 1, Ord 55, rr 5A, 5C, 5E(a). **Newnham v Brown** [1966] 2 229, CA.

    Possession of mortgaged property—
        Action by mortgagee for possession. See Action by mortgagee for possession, *above*.

        Adverse interest—
            Equitable interest—Priority between mortgagee's interest and equitable interest—Matrimonial home—Man sole owner at law—Mortgage first legal charge on property—Mortgage granted with woman's knowledge and approval—Man ceasing to pay mortgage instalments—Whether woman having beneficial interest in property—Whether woman having irrevocable licence to remain in house—Whether woman's interest having priority over mortgagee's interest. **Bristol and West Building Society v Henning** [1985] 2 606, CA.

MORTGAGE (cont)—
  Possession of mortgaged property (cont)—
    Adverse interest (cont)—
      Equitable interest—Priority between mortgagee's interest and equitable interest—Remortgage of property—Matrimonial home—Man sole owner at law—Home purchased with cash contributed by woman and mortgaged in sole name of man—Woman aware that mortgage and conveyance in man's sole name—Man remortgaging home for greater amount without woman's knowledge—Man redeeming original mortgage and keeping balance—New mortgagee seeking possession for non-payment of mortgage instalments—Whether consent of woman to remortgage to be imputed—Whether woman's beneficial interest having priority over new mortgagee's interest—Whether substituted incumbrance ranking ahead of woman's beneficial interest to extent of her imputed consent. **Equity and Law Home Loans Ltd v Prestidge** [1992] **1** 909, CA.
      Equitable interest—Wife's equitable interest—Matrimonial home purchased and owned by company—Wife a director of company—Husband arranging for company to mortgage property without wife's knowledge—Company incurring overdraft—Wife making contribution to reduce company overdraft—Mortgagee seeking possession of property from company—Whether any connection between contribution and acquisition of matrimonial home—Whether wife's contribution giving her equitable interest in home—Whether wife acting in breach of duty as director. **Winkworth v Edward Baron Development Co Ltd** [1987] **1** 114, HL.
    Matrimonial home—
      Deserted wife in occupation. *See* **Husband and wife** (Deserted wife's right to remain in matrimonial home—Mortgage).
    Mortgagee's right to recover possession—
      Discretion to allow mortgagor time to assign mortgage. **Braithwaite v Winwood** [1960] **3** 642, Ch D.
      Instalment mortgage—Mortgage providing that on default by mortgagor loan immediately repayable and mortgagee entitled to possession—Whether jurisdiction to refuse order for possession and to make order for payment on terms—Jurisdiction to adjourn application. **Birmingham Citizens Permanent Building Society v Caunt** [1962] **1** 163, Ch D.
      Mortgage containing no restriction on mortgagee's right—Judges' Practice Directions—RSC Ord 55, r 5A. **Fourmaids Ltd v Dudley Marshall (Properties) Ltd** [1957] **2** 35, Ch D.
      Mortgagee taking possession of mortgaged property unoccupied by mortgagor and exercising power of sale—Mortgagee not first obtaining possession order—Whether mortgagee entitled to take possession without first obtaining order of court—Administration of Justice Act 1970, s 36. **Ropaigealach v Barclays Bank plc** [1999] **4** 235, CA.
      Nature of mortgagee's action—Whether mortgagee's action for possession an action for recovery of land or for enforcement of the mortgage—County Courts Act 1934, ss 48, 52—County Courts Act 1955, s 2, Sch I, para 4. **R v Judge Dutton Briant, ex p Abbey National Building Society** [1957] **2** 625, QBD.
      No default under mortgage—Failure of collateral security—Obligation to pay principal and interest deferred for ten years—Mortgagor not in default under mortgage—Life assurance policy as collateral security—Mortgagor allowing policy to lapse—Whether implied term in mortgage that mortgagee not entitled to recover possession except in case of default by mortgagor. **Western Bank Ltd v Schindler** [1976] **2** 393, CA.
      Order for possession—Furniture left on premises—Application for order for removal of furniture—Whether order for possession was for vacant possession—RSC App H, Form No 8. **Norwich Union Life Insurance Society v Preston** [1957] **2** 428, Ch D.
    Mortgagor not in occupation—
      Agreement between occupier and mortgagor made before mortgagor had any title to mortgaged premises—Payment of lump sums to mortgagor by tenant said to be rent for a specified period—Whether payments constituted rent or a fine—Whether tenancy binding on mortgagee—Law of Property Act 1925, s 99(6), s 205(1)(xxiii). **Hughes v Waite** [1957] **1** 603, Ch D.
      Mortgage subject to existing tenancy—New tenancy granted—New tenancy effecting surrender of old tenancy by operation of law as between tenant and mortgagor—New tenancy not binding on mortgagee—Whether old tenancy surrendered as between tenant and mortgagee. **Barclays Bank Ltd v Stasek** [1956] **3** 439, Ch D.
      Mortgagor's power of leasing excluded except with consent of mortgagees—Mortgagees having knowledge of tenancy for eight months prior to notice to quit—Implied confirmation of tenancy. **Parker v Braithwaite** [1952] **2** 837, Ch D.
      Need to join occupier as defendant to claim for possession by mortgagee—RSC Ord 55, r 5A. **Leicester Permanent Building Society v Shearley** [1950] **2** 738, Ch D.
      Order for possession against occupier although mortgagor not joined in proceedings—RSC Ord 55, rr 5A, 8A. **Alliance Building Society v Shave** [1952] **1** 1033, Ch D.
      Power of leasing only with consent in writing of mortgagee—Tenancy granted by mortgagor—No evidence of consent in writing—Mortgagee having knowledge of tenancy—Mortgagee going without interest for many years—Whether mortgagee entitled to recover possession against tenant as trespasser—Law of Property Act 1925, s 99. **Taylor v Ellis** [1960] **1** 549, Ch D.
      Registered land—Oral tenancy agreed and completed by tenant's entry before mortgagor has completed purchase of property—Purchase completed and mortgage granted on same day—Whether mortgagee entitled to possession as against tenant—Land Registration Act 1925, ss 20(1), 27(3), 70(1)(g)—Law of Property Act 1925, s 55(c). **Rymer (Grace) Investments Ltd v Waite** [1958] **2** 777, CA.
    Mortgagor's right to possession—
      Circumstances in which term will be implied that mortgagor entitled to possession against mortgagee—Instalment mortgage—Mortgagor only in technical possession—Whether an implied term that mortgagor entitled to possession as against mortgagee. **Esso Petroleum Co Ltd v Alstonbridge Properties Ltd** [1975] **3** 358, Ch D.
      Instalment mortgage—Implied term that mortgagor entitled to possession so long as instalments paid—Default in payment of instalments—Subsequent tender of arrears—Whether tender capable of reviving implication that mortgagor entitled to possession. **Esso Petroleum Co Ltd v Alstonbridge Properties Ltd** [1975] **3** 358, Ch D.
    Order for possession. *See* Order for possession of mortgaged property, *above*.

MORTGAGE (cont)—

Possession of mortgaged property (cont)—

Persons not parties to mortgage claiming to be entitled to possession—

Adjournment of originating summons into open court. **Practice Note** [1958] **1** 128, Ch D.

Occupiers claiming protection from eviction—Practice—Whether summons necessary—Whether mortgagee was 'owner' for the purposes of the Protection from Eviction Act 1964, s 1(2). **Bolton Building Society v Cobb** [1965] **3** 814, Ch D.

Premises subject to Rent Restrictions Acts—

Default in payment of mortgaged interest for more than 21 days—Subsequent payment—Loss of protection—Increase of Rent and Mortgage Interest (Restrictions) Act 1920, s 7. **Nichols v Walters** [1953] **2** 1516, CA.

Second mortgagee—

Subsequent encumbrances—Enquiry of prior mortgagees before applying for possession. **Practice Direction** [1968] **1** 752, Ch D; [1970] **1** 671, Ch D.

Suspension of execution of order for possession—

Discretion of court—Mortgagee obtaining order for possession of dwelling-house—Mortgagor not in default under mortgage—Failure of collateral security—Obligation to pay principal and interest deferred for ten years—Whether court having power to suspend order for possession where mortgagor not in default—Whether court bound to exercise discretion in favour of mortgagor—Administration of Justice Act 1970, s 36(1). **Western Bank Ltd v Schindler** [1976] **2** 393, CA.

Postponement of redemption. *See* Clog on equity of redemption—Postponement of redemption, *above*.

Power of leasing—

Agricultural land—

Statutory power of leasing although contrary intention expressed in deed—Covenant by mortgagor against letting without consent of mortgagee—Effect of covenant—Avoiding lease or tenancy granted outside statutory powers—Law of Property Act 1925, s 99—Agricultural Holdings Act 1948, Sch 7, para 2. **Rhodes v Dalby** [1971] **2** 1144, Ch D.

Consent of mortgagee—

Lease created without consent—Whether mortgages entitled to regard themselves as no longer bound by their own covenants—Common law power of leasing—Law of Property Act 1925, ss 99, 152. **Iron Trades Employers Insurance Association Ltd v Union Land and House Investors Ltd** [1937] **1** 481, Ch D.

No power to lease without consent but lessee not concerned to see that consent given—Lease granted by mortgagor in possession without consent of mortgagee—Tenancy by estoppel. **Lever Finance Ltd v Trustee of Property of Needleman** [1956] **2** 378, Ch D.

Underlease without consent—Sale by mortgagee of mortgaged premises to second mortgagee—Sale expressed in contract to be subject to underlease but underlease not mentioned in conveyance—Rights of purchaser against underlessee—Law of Property Act 1925, s 89(1)(a). **Rust v Goodale** [1956] **3** 373, Ch D.

Rent—

Reservation of best rent that can reasonably be obtained—Lease providing for rent to be fixed by a valuer after execution—Whether compliance with statutory requirements—Law of Property Act 1925, s 99. **Lloyds Bank Ltd v Marcan** [1973] **3** 754, CA.

Statutory power—

Oral tenancy—Mortgagee granting oral tenancy for two years of bungalow on mortgaged premises—Whether necessary to include condition of re-entry for non-payment of rent—Whether necessary to deliver particulars of tenancy to mortgagor—Law of Property Act 1925, s 99(7)(11). **Rhodes v Dalby** [1971] **2** 1144, Ch D.

Oral tenancy—Oral agreement by mortgagors for tenancy from year to year—Tenancy agreement containing no provision for re-entry—Whether tenancy validated—Law of Property Act 1925, ss 99(7), 152(1), (6). **Pawson v Revell** [1958] **3** 233, CA.

Tenancy by estoppel—

Tenancy agreement entered into by mortgagor before completion of purchase of mortgaged property. **Woolwich Equitable Building Society v Marshall** [1951] **2** 769, Ch D.

Tenancy agreement entered into by mortgagor before completion of purchase of mortgaged property—Mortgage granted to facilitate purchase—Exclusion of mortgagor's power of leasing. **Coventry Permanent Economic Building Society v Jones** [1951] **1** 901, Ch D.

Tenancy agreement entered into by mortgagor before completion of purchase of mortgaged property—Mortgage of premises by purchaser by deed dated day after completion—Exclusion of mortgagor's power of leasing—Position of tenant. **Universal Permanent Building Society v Cooke** [1951] **2** 893, CA.

Tenancy granted by mortgagor before completion of purchase of mortgaged property—Legal charge granted to facilitate purchase—Recital that property vested in mortgagor. **Church of England Building Society v Piskor** [1954] **2** 85, CA.

Priority—

Apparent owner charging fund—

Appointment of settled fund so that investments could be deposited at Lloyd's by underwriter—Trusts declared by deed in relation to investments deposited—Investments subject by the deed of appointment to trusts of settlement in priority to interests of underwriter under deed declaring trusts—Charge of interest of underwriter under deed declaring trusts—Charge of interest of underwriter under deed declaring trust to secure repayment of money lent to him—Priority as between chargee and trustees of settlement—Rule in Dearle v Hall. **Lyle (B S) Ltd v Rosher** [1958] **3** 597, HL.

Equitable interest. *See* Equitable interest—Priority, *above*.

Equitable mortgage. *See* Equitable mortgage—Priority, *above*.

Registered land. *See* **Land registration** (Priority—Concurrent applications for registration).

Successive mortgages of same property—

Whether mortgagees can alter priority of mortgages—Whether consent of mortgagor required to alteration of priority. **Cheah v Equiticorp Finance Group Ltd** [1991] **4** 989, PC.

Proviso for redemption. *See* Redemption—Proviso for redemption, *below*.

MORTGAGE (cont)—
Receiver—
  Appointment—
    Appointment under debenture—Remuneration—Debenture not specifying rate of commission—Debenture extending statutory powers of receiver by giving power of sale and providing that receiver's remuneration 'and the costs of realisation' to be paid out of proceeds of sale—Whether receiver entitled to retain commission at rate of 5 out of gross proceeds of sale without application to court—Whether agents' fees and expenses, costs of conveyance and caretaker's wages pending sale deductible from commission as part of 'costs charges and expenses' incurred by receiver—Law of Property Act 1925, s 109(6). **Marshall v Cottingham** [1981] **3** 8, Ch D.
    By mortgagee in possession—Collateral mortgage of policy of insurance—Non-payment of premiums—Whether breach of provision in mortgage—Law of Property Act 1925, s 101(1)(iii), 103(iii). **Refuge Assurance Co Ltd v Pearlberg** [1938] **3** 231, CA.
    Interest in arrear—Whether receiver under any statutory duty to rating authority to pay rates—Law of Property Act 1925, s 109(8). **Liverpool Corp v Hope** [1938] **1** 492, CA.
    War-time. See **Emergency legislation** (Mortgage—Appointment of receiver).
  Duty to account—
    Account to mortgagee—Receiver agent of mortgagor—Statutory duty to account—Law of Property Act 1925, s 109. **Leicester Permanent Building Society v Butt** [1943] **2** 523, Ch D.
  Liability for breach of statutory duty on mortgaged premises—
    Failure to maintain fire escape in good order—Employee on premises injured by fire—'Owner'—London Building Acts (Amendment) Act 1939, ss 33, 133(2). **Solomons v Gertzenstein Ltd** [1954] **1** 1008, QBD.
  Mortgaged property—
    Receiver's right to possession—Additional powers of court in action by mortgagee for possession of dwelling-house—Receivers appointed under mortgage of property owned by individuals—Receivers making claim for possession of mortgaged property against mortgagors in occupation—Whether receivers entitled to possession—Whether receivers 'deriving title under the original mortgagee'—Whether court having usual discretion to postpone possession—Law of Property Act 1925, s 109—Administration of Justice 1970, ss 36, 39. **Pask v Menon** [2020] **1 Comm** 990, Ch D.
  Receiver's duties to mortgagor—
    Mortgagee appointing receivers over mortgaged property—Receivers managing business carried on at mortgaged property—Whether receivers owed mortgagor a duty of care in managing mortgaged business. **Medforth v Blake** [1999] **3** 97, CA.
    Whether receiver owing duty to mortgagor to take steps to increase value of mortgaged property before exercising power of sale. **Silven Properties Ltd v Royal Bank of Scotland plc** [2004] **4** 484, CA.
  Tenancy—
    Acceptance of tenant of mortgagor as mortgagees' tenant—Mortgagor's covenant not to create any underlease or tenancy—Order for possession obtained against mortgagor—Subsequent letting by mortgagors to weekly tenant—Morgagees' appointment of receiver of rents—Letter to tenant referring to mortgagors as 'your former Landlord'—Mortgages' claim for possession—Whether new tenancy created. **Chatsworth Properties Ltd v Effiom** [1971] **1** 604, CA.
    Acceptance of tenant of mortgagor as mortgagee's tenant—Mortgagor's power of leasing restricted to leasing with consent in writing of mortgagee—Tenancy granted without consent—Receipt of rent by receiver appointed by mortgagee—Notice to quit given by mortgagee and containing statement that tenant held as tenant of mortgagee. **Stroud Building Society v Delamont** [1960] **1** 749, Ch D.
    Repairs done by occupier on advice of receiver—Whether sufficient to show that relationship of landlord and tenant constituted. **Barclays Bank Ltd v Kiley** [1961] **2** 849, Ch D.
Redemption—
  Clog on equity of redemption. See Clog on equity of redemption, above.
  Lease mortgaged by legal charge—
    Mortgagee obtained relief against forfeiture of lease on default of mortgagor—Order giving relief granted new lease for full residue of term—Whether new lease subject to mortgagor's right of redemption—Law of Property Act 1925, s 146(4). **Chelsea Estates Investment Trust Co Ltd v Marche** [1955] **1** 195, Ch D.
  Lease with option to purchase freehold reversion—
    Option separately assigned to mortgagee—Option exercised by mortgagee—Whether mortgagor entitled to conveyance of reversion on redemption. **Nelson v Hannam and Smith** [1942] **2** 680, CA.
  Mortgagee's entitlement to arrears of interest—
    Action for redemption by mortgagor—Sale of mortgaged property by agreement—Whether mortgagee entitled to more than six years' arrears of interest out of proceeds of sale—Whether six year limitation period for recovery of interest by mortgagee applicable to redemption action—Limitation Act 1939, s 18(5). **Holmes v Cowcher** [1970] **1** 1224, Ch D.
  Order for sale—
    Application for sale of mortgaged property by mortgagor—Price negotiated for sale of property not sufficient to discharge mortgage debt—Mortgagee refusing to consent to sale—Mortgagee wishing to rent house and wait for improvement in house prices—Rental income likely to be well below amount of interest saved by mortgagor if property sold—Whether court can direct sale of mortgaged property against mortgagee's wishes when large part of debt remaining unsecured and outstanding—How court should exercise discretion to direct sale of mortgaged property against mortgagee's wishes—Law of Property Act 1925, s 91(2). **Palk v Mortgage Services Funding plc** [1993] **2** 481, CA.
  Proviso for redemption—
    Construction of mortgage providing for repayment by instalments and redemption on date when last instalment repayable. **Karachiwalla (Mohamedali Jaffer) v Nanji (Noorally Rattanshi Rajan)** [1959] **1** 137, PC.

MORTGAGE (cont)—
  Redemption (cont)—
    Relief against contractual terms in mortgage transaction—
      Circumstances in which court will grant relief—Terms unfair and unconscionable—Mortgage to secure borrowed money—Mortgagor required to repay mortgagee principal and interest in sterling—Clause in mortgage index-linking to Swiss franc actual amount to be repaid—Depreciation of sterling against Swiss franc—Principal and interest to be repaid far exceeding in value nominal amount of sum lent—Whether clause unfair and unconscionable and therefore unenforceable. **Multiservice Bookbinding Ltd v Marden** [1978] **2** 489, Ch D.
  Relief against contractual terms—
    Redemption of mortgage. *See* Redemption—Relief against contractual terms in mortgage transaction, *above.*
  Remedies of mortgagee—
    Action for the recovery of land—
      Jurisdiction of county court. *See* **County court** (Jurisdiction).
    Enforcement of remedy—
      Courts' emergency powers—Bankruptcy of mortgagor—Trustee respondent to application. **Legal Charge Dated 26 November 1937, Re** [1949] **1** 477, Ch D.
    Foreclosure or sale—
      House subject to Rent Restrictions Acts—Transfer of mortgage to statutory tenant—Whether statutory tenancy abandoned. **Silsby v Holliman** [1955] **2** 373, Ch D.
    Moneylender's security—
      Originating summons for repayment—Whether particulars required by RSC Ord 20, r 10, and RSC Ord 3, r 10, must be included in summons or affidavit in support—RSC Ord 55, r 5A. **Lewis v Packer** [1960] **1** 720, Ch D.
    Possession proceedings—
      Mortgagor's spouse successfully defending possession proceedings on ground of undue influence—Mortgagee subsequently commencing action in debt against mortgagor—Whether abuse of process. **Alliance and Leicester plc v Slayford** [2001] **1 Comm** 1, CA.
    Puisne mortgagee—
      Title to mortgaged property extinguished—Sale by first mortgagee—Right of puisne mortgagee to surplus profits—Law of Property Act 1925, ss 104, 105, 107, 116—Limitation Act 1939, ss 12, 16. **Young v Clarey** [1948] **1** 197, Ch D.
    Rectification of register to remove caution. *See* **Land registration** (Rectification of register—Caution—Cautions entered against mortgagee's interest in land).
    Rent Restrictions Acts—
      Interest in arrear for 21 days—Subsequent payment—Whether protection restored—Increase of Rent and Mortgage Interest (Restrictions) Act 1920, s 7 (as applied by Rent and Mortgage Interest Restrictions Act 1939, s 3(1)). **Coutts & Co v Duntroon Investment Corp Ltd** [1958] **1** 51, Ch D.
    Sale. *See* Sale, *below.*
  Rent—
    Best rent—
      Lease granted by mortgagor. *See* Power of leasing—Rent, *above.*
    Rent restriction—
      Loss of protection. *See* Possession of mortgaged property—Premises subject to Rent Restrictions Acts, *above.*
  Repayment—
    Demand—
      Service—Death of mortgagor—Letter demanding repayment in accordance with instrument of charge addressed by mortgagee to mortgagor six months after his death—Whether demand validly made—Whether receiver's acts established relationship of landlord and tenant between mortgagee and occupiers—Possession—Parties—Personal representatives of deceased mortgagor not necessary parties if not prejudiced by order. **Barclays Bank Ltd v Kiley** [1961] **2** 849, Ch D.
    Mortgagee retaining debt out of proceeds of mortgaged policy—
      Acting as agent for mortgagor. **Hodge's Policy, Re** [1957] **3** 584, CA.
    Sale of mortgaged property—
      Unliquidated claim by mortgagor against mortgagee related to mortgage debt—Whether mortgagee entitled to repayment out of proceeds. **Keller (Samuel) (Holdings) Ltd v Martins Bank Ltd** [1970] **3** 950, CA.
  Requisition of land subject to mortgage—
    Application of compensation—
      Land leased to company—Covenant by lessee to insure against fire—Insurance to be laid out in re-building—Mortgage by lessee—Property destroyed by fire while requisitioned—Insurance policy not kept up—Whether compensation to be applied in same manner as money receivable under policy. **Radnor (Earl) v Folkestone Pier and Lift Co** [1950] **2** 690, Ch D.
  Restraint of trade. *See* Clog on equity of redemption—Restraint of trade, *above.*
  Restrictions on interest. *See* Statutory restrictions—Interest, *below.*
  Restrictions on mortgagee's powers. *See* Sale—Statutory restrictions on mortgagee's powers, *below.*
  Sale—
    Application of proceeds—
      Claim by moneylender as second mortgagee—Claim against mortgagor statute-barred—'Person entitled to the mortgaged property'—Law of Property Act 1925, s 105—Moneylenders Act 1927, s 13(1). **Martin's Mortgage Trusts, Re** [1951] **1** 1053, CA.
      Claim by mortgagee for surplus proceeds of sale in addition to recovery of sums due under mortgage—Mortgage advance obtained by fraudulent deception—Confiscation order and charging order made in criminal proceedings in respect of mortgagor's interest in surplus—Whether mortgagee entitled to surplus proceeds—Law of Property Act 1925, s 105. **Halifax Building Society v Thomas** [1995] **4** 673, CA.
      Duty of first mortgagee to subsequent encumbrancers. **Weld Blundell v Synott** [1940] **2** 580, KBD.

MORTGAGE (cont)—
 Sale (cont)—
  Application of proceeds (cont)—
   Mortgagee having purchased properties through mortgage obtained fraudulently—Mortgagee applying proceeds of sale of properties to purchase of house—Fraudulent mortgage applications made with assistance of co-owners—Mortgagee remortgaging house without knowledge of co-owners—Bank seeking possession of house—Co-owners asserting equitable interest in house by virtue of contribution to purchase price and improvements—Whether claim to equitable interest defeated by previous illegality. **Mortgage Express v Robson** [2001] **2 Comm** 886, CA.
  Appropriation of proceeds of sale—
   Validity as against liquidator of company—Secured creditor of company in creditors' voluntary winding-up realised security and appropriated proceeds to satisfying non-preferential part of company's indebtedness—Secured creditor, a bank, also creditor for preferential indebtedness in respect of moneys advanced—Whether appropriation valid against liquidators—Companies Act 1948, s 319(4). **Hall (William) (Contractors) Ltd, Re** [1967] **2** 1150, Ch D.
  Duties of mortgagee—
   Aircraft mortgage—Mortgagee's power of sale triggered—Mortgagee holding auction—Mortgagee purchasing aircraft at auction—Mortgagee transferring aircraft to second defendant—Whether mortgagee in breach of duty—Whether mortgagee's conduct amounting to wilful misconduct—Whether unlawful conspiracy between mortgagee and second defendant. **Alpstream AG v PK Airfinance Sarl** [2014] **1 Comm** 441, QBD.
  Duty of mortgagee—
   Duty when exercising power of sale—Duty to take care to obtain proper price—Whether duty owed to beneficiary under trust of mortgaged property. **Parker-Tweedale v Dunbar Bank plc (No 1)** [1990] **2** 577, CA.
   Ship—Mortgagee arresting ship laden with perishable cargo—Mortgagee disposing of cargo overboard in order to sell ship—Expense of disposal deducted from proceeds of sale—Whether mortgagee in breach of duty—Whether ship mortgage inherently different from mortgage on land. **Den Norske Bank ASA v Acemex Management Co Ltd** [2003] **2 Comm** 318, QBD; [2004] **1 Comm** 904, CA.
   Standard of duty in exercising power of sale—Duty to take reasonable care to obtain price equal to market value—Mortgagee not obtaining market value of security—Whether failure to obtain market value extinguishing mortgagor's liability or reducing liability pro tanto—Whether loss to be calculated on difference from market value or loss of a chance—Building Societies Act 1986, Sch 4, para 1(1)(a). **Skipton Building Society v Stott** [2000] **1 Comm** 257, CA; [2000] **2** 779, CA.
   Standard of duty in exercising power of sale—Duty to take reasonable care to obtain price equal to market value—Principles to be applied. **Meftah v Lloyds TSB Bank plc** [2001] **2 Comm** 741, Ch D.
   Standard of duty in exercising power of sale—Duty to take reasonable care to obtain price equal to market value—Sale by auction—Sale to company in which mortgagee has an interest—Reserve price fixed by mortgagee—Advertisements announcing bare fact of auction with minimum description of property—Conditions of sale containing bare legal requirements—Mortgagee not obtaining expert or independent advice about sale—Property purchased by family company of mortgagee for reserve price—No competitive bidding at auction—Mortgagee providing interest-free loan to company to enable it to purchase property—Whether sale valid. **Tse Kwong Lam v Wong Chit Sen** [1983] **3** 54, PC.
   Standard of duty in exercising power of sale—Duty to take reasonable care to obtain price equal to market value—Site with planning permission for development with flats—Planning permission also for development with houses—Advertisement of sale referring only to permission for houses—Mortgagees aware of both permissions—Estate agents handling sale unaware of permission for flats at time advertisements distributed—Estate agents subsequently apprised of permission for flats—Allowing sale to go ahead without further advertisement—Evidence that site would have realised substantially higher price if permission for flats advertised—Whether mortgagees liable to mortgagors for their own and agents' negligence in failing to realise full market price. **Cuckmere Brick Co Ltd v Mutual Finance Ltd** [1971] **2** 633, CA.
   Standard of duty in exercising power of sale—Duty to take reasonable care to obtain price equal to market value—Whether mortgagee sufficiently marketed property—Whether mortgagee breached duty by failing to obtain 'Red Book' valuations of property—Whether property value tainted by repossession and forced sale—Whether 'facility fee' in loan to mortgagor a penalty. **Aodhcon LLP v Bridgeco Ltd** [2014] **2 Comm** 928, Ch D.
   Standard of duty in exercising power of sale—Security including business—Whether duty to preserve business pending realisation of security. **AIB Finance Ltd v Debtors** [1997] **4** 677, Ch D; [1998] **2** 929, CA.
  Exercise of power of sale—
   Breach of right to peaceful enjoyment of possession—Mortgagors falling into arrears on mortgage payments and losing equity of redemption—Mortgagee appointing receiver—Receiver selling property—Purchaser transferring property to new owner—New owner seeking possession of property—Whether loss of equity of redemption amounting to deprivation of right to 'possession'—Whether loss attributable to state intervention—Whether current statutory framework compatible with human rights law—Law of Property Act 1925, s 101—Administration of Justice Act 1970, s 36—Human Rights Act 1998, Sch 1, Pt II, art 1. **Horsham Properties Group Ltd v Clark (GMAC RFC Ltd, third party)** [2009] **1 Comm** 745, Ch D.
  Exercise of power of sale by mortgagee—
   Equitable estoppel—Conduct estopping mortgagee from exercising power. **Braithwaite v Winwood** [1960] **3** 642, Ch D.
   Local authority—House sold by local authority to tenant subject to mortgage in favour of authority—Local authority reserving right of pre-emption under statutory powers—Statutory power of sale becoming exercisable on default by mortgagor—House transferred by local authority to itself—Whether transfer valid—Law of Property Act 1925, s 101(1)—Housing Act 1957, s 104. **Williams v Wellingborough BC** [1975] **3** 462, CA.
   Purity of purpose—Whether mortgagee required to have purity of purpose in order for exercise of power of sale to be valid. **Meretz Investments NV v ACP Ltd** [2006] **3** 1029, Ch D.

MORTGAGE (cont)—
  Sale (cont)—
    Exercise of power of sale by mortgagee (cont)—
      Sale overreaching prior dealing by mortgagor—Mortgagor contracting to sell mortgaged property to plaintiffs—Registration of contract by plaintiffs as land charge—Subsequent contract entered into by mortgagee in exercise of power of sale and with notice of the previous contract—Whether mortgagee can be restrained from exercising power of sale. **Duke v Robson** [1973] **1** 481, Ch D and CA.
      Setting aside—Deception by purchaser—Purchaser deceiving vendor mortgagee—Relevance of deception to mortgagor—Whether sale liable to set aside—Law of Property Act 1925, s 104(2). **Corbett v Halifax plc** [2003] **2 Comm** 384, CA; [2003] **4** 180, CA.
    Leasehold property—
      Covenant by lessee in lease not to assign—Contract for sale by lessee's mortgagee—Condition that sale subject to mortgagee's obtaining consent to assignment of lease to purchaser—Date fixed by contract for completion passed—Mortgagee obtained order for possession—Lessee tendered redemption moneys before time for delivering possession under the order arrived—Lessee applied for a stay of proceedings for possession, and brought an action to redeem the mortgage—Whether contract for sale put an end to the right of redemption—Law of Property Act 1925, ss 101(1), 104(1). **Property and Bloodstock Ltd v Emerton** [1967] **3** 321, CA.
    Option—
      Grant of option by building society mortgagee—Validity. **Cottrill v Steyning and Littlehampton Building Society** [1966] **2** 295, QBD.
    Power to authorise sale—
      Action for foreclosure—Right to foreclosure—Breach of covenant to pay interest—Mortgage debt not due—No express proviso for redemption—Mortgagee bound to accept payment of principal in instalments if covenant to pay interest punctually observed—Whether mortgagor having forfeited right to redemption on breach of covenant to pay interest on loan—Whether mortgagee having right to foreclosure—Whether court having power to authorise sale—Law of Property Act 1925, s 91(2). **Twentieth Century Banking Corp Ltd v Wilkinson** [1976] **3** 361, Ch D.
      Jurisdiction—Whether court should sanction sale where mortgagee having full power to affect sale without order and purchaser having statutory protection—Law of Property Act 1925, ss 91(2), 104. **Arab Bank plc v Merchantile Holdings Ltd** [1994] **2** 74, Ch D.
    Statutory restrictions on mortgagee's powers—
      Sale with consent of mortgagor—Validity—Courts (Emergency Powers) Act 1914. **Colebrook v Watson Investment Co** [1944] **2** 115, Ch D.
    Uncompleted contract of sale rescinded—
      Resale by mortgagee at lower price to another purchaser—Mortgagee not accountable to mortgagor for purchase price under first sale which he had never received. **Wright v New Zealand Farmers' Co-operative Association of Canterbury Ltd** [1939] **2** 701, PC.
  Scale fee—
    Solicitor—
      Acting for both mortgagor and mortgagee—Charging below scale fee. *See* **Solicitor** (Remuneration—Charging below scale fee—Solicitor acting for both mortgagor purchaser and mortgagee).
  Search—
    Land charge—
      Name of estate owner. *See* **Land charge** (Search—Official certificate of search—Conclusiveness).
  Service of demand for repayment—
    Death of mortgagor. *See* Repayment—Demand—Service—Death of mortgagor, *above*.
  Small dwellings legislation. *See* **Housing** (Small dwellings).
  Solicitor—
    Duty, breach of. *See* **Solicitor** (Breach of duty—Solicitor acting for both purchaser and mortgagee in conveyancing transaction).
    Lien. *See* **Solicitor** (Lien—Mortgage).
    Trust, breach of. *See* **Solicitor** (Duty—Breach of trust—Mortgage transaction).
  Solus agreement. *See* Clog on equity of redemption—Restraint of trade, *above*.
  Stamp duty. *See* **Stamp duty** (Mortgage, bond, debenture or covenant).
  Statutory power of leasing. *See* Power of leasing—Statutory power, *above*.
  Statutory restrictions—
    Interest—
      Interest reserved as amount payable after deduction of tax—Restriction on gross rate payable—Rent and Mortgage Interest Restrictions Act 1939, s 3, Sch I. **Warrilow v Ward** [1942] **1** 366, Ch D.
  Subrogation—
    Generally. *See* **Subrogation**.
  Summary judgment—
    Mortgagee's action to recover principal moneys and interest under second mortgage. *See* Payment—Summary judgment—Leave—Action to recover principal moneys and interest due under second mortgage, *above*.
  Tenancy agreement—
    Registration as estate contract—
      Effect on subsequent mortgages. *See* **Land charge** (Estate contract—Tenancy agreement—Effect of registration on subsequent mortgages).
  Transfer—
    No notice to mortgagor—
      Debt due from original mortgage to mortgagor—Set-off. **Parker v Jackson** [1936] **2** 281, Ch D.
    Transfer of mortgage by way of gift—Stamp duty. *See* **Stamp duty** (Voluntary disposition inter vivos—Mortgage—Transfer of mortgage by way of gift).
  Two properties mortgaged together—
    Sale of one subject to the mortgage—
      Debt discharged by property retained—Exoneration or contribution. **Mainwaring's Settlement Trusts, Re** [1936] **3** 540, CA.

MORTGAGE (cont)—
    Unconsionable bargain—
        Equitable relief. *See* **Equity** (Unconscionable bargain—Mortgage).
    Unfair terms. *See* **Contract** (Unfair terms—Mortgage).
    Variation. *See* **Contract** (Variation—Mortgage).

MORTMAIN
    See **Charity** (Mortmain).

MOSLEM LAW
    Divorce—
        Talaq—
            Recognition. *See* **Divorce** (Foreign decree—Recognition by English court—Foreign divorce not judicial act—Marriage celebrated and divorce occurring in England—Divorce by talaq).

MOTHER
    Death—
        Fatal accident—
            Damages for loss of services as mother. *See* **Fatal accident** (Damages—Death of mother—Loss of services as mother).

MOTION
    Adjournment. *See* **Practice** (Motion—Adjournment).
    Bankruptcy proceedings—
        Service out of jurisdiction. *See* **Bankruptcy** (Service—Service out of jurisdiction).
    Committal order—
        Contempt of court. *See* **Contempt of court** (Committal—Application).
    Disclosure of documents—
        Application for. *See* **Disclosure and inspection of documents** (Interlocutory motion).
    Listing—
        Chancery Division. *See* **Practice** (Chancery Division—Listing—Motions).
    Order on—
        Drawing up. *See* **Practice** (Chancery Division—Order—Order on motion—Drawing up of order).
    Practice—
        Generally. *See* **Practice** (Motion).

MOTOR CYCLE
    Crash helmet—
        Failure to wear—
            Contributory negligence. *See* **Negligence** (Contributory negligence—Road accident—Crash helmet).
    Hire-purchase—
        Fundamental breach of contract—
            Effect on exception clause. *See* **Contract** (Fundamental breach—Effect on exception clause—Affirmation of contract—Hire-purchase of motor cycle).
    Modified motor cycle—
        Whether a 'motor vehicle'. *See* **Road traffic** (Motor vehicle—Motor cycle).
    Provisional licence—
        Bicycle not having sidecar attached—
            Conditions attached to licence. *See* **Road traffic** (Driving licence—Conditions attached to provisional licences—Motor bicycle not having sidecar attached).

MOTOR INSURANCE
    Breach of statutory duty. *See* Using vehicle or causing or permitting vehicle to be used on road without policy being in force—Cause or permit—Breach of statutory duty, *below*.
    Certificate—
        Delivery to insured—
            Certificate received by third party—Policy prepared for and signed by insured—Premium paid by third party—Third party to be repaid by insured in instalments—Certificate retained by third party pending repayment—Whether certificate delivered to third party as agent for insured—Road Traffic Act 1930, ss 36, 40. **Starkey v Hall** [1936] **2** 18, KBD.
        False statement to obtain insurance certificate—
            Gain or advantage to proposer—Whether necessary to prove gain or advantage resulting from deception—Road Traffic Act 1930, s 112(2). **Jones v Meatyard** [1939] **1** 140, KBD.
            Offence under Road Traffic Act 1960. *See* Compulsory insurance against third party risks—Certificate of insurance—False statement for purpose of obtaining insurance certificate, *below*.
    Ceylon. *See* **Ceylon** (Motor insurance).
    Compulsory insurance against third party risks—
        Breach of statutory duty—
            Owner uninsured—Claim against owner on ground of breach of statutory duty not to permit an uninsured person to drive—Road Traffic Act 1934, s 35(1). **Daniels v Vaux** [1938] **2** 271, KBD.
            Rights of third party—Driver without means—Liability of owner of vehicle to satisfy judgment against driver—Effect on owner's liability of independent contract of insurance—Road Traffic Act 1930, s 35(1). **Corfield v Groves** [1950] **1** 488, KBD.
        Certificate of insurance—
            False statement for purpose of obtaining insurance certificate—Withholding material information for the like purpose—Whether guilty mind an element of the offence—Road Traffic Act 1960, s 235(2). **R v Cummerson** [1968] **2** 863, CA.
        Disqualification for using etc vehicle on road without policy being in force. *See* Disqualification for using etc vehicle on road without policy being in force, *below*.
        Extension clause—
            Person driving with consent of insured. *See* Compulsory insurance against third party risks—Persons driving with consent of insured, *below*.

Compulsory insurance against third party risks (cont)—
Extent of cover—

Driver under age of 16—Licence obtained by false pretences—Motor car driven with owner's permission—Insurers willing to admit liability, under misapprehension of legal effect of policy—Road Traffic Act 1930, ss 7(4), 9(1)(2)(5), 35(1). **Mumford v Hardy** [1956] 1 337, QBD.

Insured being covered to drive another's car with permission—Insured having sold car in respect of which policy issued—Whether insured covered to drive another's car with permission having sold own car without replacement. **Dodson v Peter H Dodson Insurance Services (a firm)** [2001] 1 **Comm** 300, CA; [2001] 3 75, CA.

Learner being taught to drive—Instructor's policy covering user of vehicle while he was driving it or any other person with his permission provided that person had a driving licence—Instructor holding steering wheel and handbrake—Learner not insured—Instructor and learner both 'drivers'—Use of vehicle by learner covered by instructor's policy—Road Traffic Act 1930, s 35(1). **Langman v Valentine** [1952] 2 803, QBD.

Negligence of permitted driver for which owners of vehicle not liable—Road Traffic Act 1930, ss 35, 36. **Sutch v Burns** [1944] 1 520, CA.

Son under 17 driving father's car—Father, licensed to drive, sitting in passenger's front seat but not touching any controls—Policy in force but excepting liability where car driven by unlicensed driver—Road Traffic Act 1930, s 35(1). **Evans v Walkden** [1956] 3 64, QBD.

Liabilities required to be covered—

Driver deliberately crashing car, causing damage to property—Driver's motor insurance policy not covering damage arising out of his deliberate acts—Insurer of damaged property bringing subrogated claim in name of property owner—Whether property insurer entitled to recover from motor insurer—Road Traffic Act 1988, ss 145, 151. **Bristol Alliance Limited Partnership v EUI Ltd** [2013] 1 **Comm** 257, CA.

Employer—Whether employer required to take out policy covering personal liability of servant while driving vehicle in the course of his employment—Road Traffic Act 1930, ss 35(1), 36(1), 121. **Lister v Romford Ice and Cold Storage Co Ltd** [1957] 1 125, HL.

Insured motorist driving car into building—Property insurer bringing subrogated claim against motorist and his insurer—Motorist's insurer arguing that policy not covering deliberate acts—Whether liability for third party's loss caused by deliberate acts of insured required to be covered—Road Traffic Act 1988, ss 145, 151. **Bristol Alliance Limited Partnership v Williams** [2011] 2 **Comm** 1113, QBD.

Owner insured against third party risks incurred by use of vehicle on road—Passenger sustaining injury in public car park—Whether injury arising out of use of vehicle on road—Whether car park a 'road'—Road Traffic Act 1988, ss 145, 151, 192. **Cutter v Eagle Star Insurance Co Ltd** [1997] 2 311, CA; [1998] 4 417, HL.

Permitted driver—Owner of vehicle permitting another person to drive it—Permitted driver injured because of defective brakes—Whether owner's liability to permitted driver required to be covered by third party insurance—Whether injury to permitted driver an injury to 'any person ... arising out of' use of vehicle—Road Traffic Act 1972, ss 143(1), 145(3)(a). **Cooper v Motor Insurers' Bureau** [1985] 1 449, CA.

Passengers carried for hire or reward in private vehicle—

Owner of car regularly over period of years driving fellow workers to place of work—Regular and understood arrangement that passengers would pay for journey—Payment sometimes in kind—Owner of car not advertising service or soliciting custom—Whether passengers being carried for 'hire or reward'—Road Traffic Act 1960, s 203(4). **Albert v Motor Insurers' Bureau** [1971] 2 1345, HL.

Owner of minibus regularly over period of 11 months driving fellow workers to place of work—Minibus fitted with seats for 11 passengers—Informal arrangement among regular passengers to pay cost of petrol—Owner not buying petrol for any of the journey—Whether passengers being carried for 'hire or reward'—Road Traffic Act 1960, s 203(4). **Motor Insurers' Bureau v Meanen** [1971] 2 1372, HL.

Passenger on private solo motor cycle—Regular voluntary contribution towards expenses—Vehicle in which passengers are carried for hire or reward—Whether carriage for 'reward' includes a case where no legal obligation to pay—Whether passenger so carried compulsorily insurable—Road Traffic Act 1930, ss 35(1), 36(1)(b)(ii). **Coward v Motor Insurers' Bureau** [1962] 1 531, CA.

Passenger on three occasions paying owner 10s for a lift—Passenger injured—Vehicle not habitually used for hire or reward—Whether owner bound to insure against liability to passenger—Whether Motor Insurers' Bureau liable—Road Traffic Act 1960, s 203. **Connell v Motor Insurers' Bureau** [1969] 3 572, CA.

Payment for journey—Private car policy—Whether compulsory third-party insurance necessary—Road Traffic Act 1930, s 36(1). **Wyatt v Guildhall Insurance Co Ltd** [1937] 1 792, KBD.

Regular voluntary contribution towards expenses—Policy not covering carriage of passengers for hire or reward—'Hire'—'Reward'—Whether carriage for 'reward' included a case where there was no legal obligation to pay'—Road Traffic Act 1930, ss 35, 36, 38. **Bonham v Zurich General Accident & Liability Insurance Co Ltd** [1945] 1 427, CA.

Payment for hospital expenses—

Passenger injured—Voluntary passenger—Policy extending to voluntary passengers—Hospital expenses of passenger's treatment sought to be recovered by hospital from insurers—Insurers ignorant of hospital treatment at time when they paid passenger—Whether hospital subsequently entitled to recover their expenses from insurers—Whether payment by insurers made in consequence of policy issued under Act of 1930—Whether voluntary passenger was a person within s 36(2) of Act of 1930—Road Traffic Act 1930, s 36(2) (as substituted by Road and Rail Traffic Act 1933, s 33). **Barnet Group Hospital Management Committee v Eagle Star Insurance Co Ltd** [1959] 3 210, QBD.

MOTOR INSURANCE (cont)—
Compulsory insurance against third party risks (cont)—
Person carried by reason of or in pursuance of a contract of employment—
Employee carrying fellow employee back to work—Employee under no obligation to carry fellow employees—Employee entitled to passenger allowance from employer—Fact of allowance reason for employee carrying fellow employee—Fellow employee a person being carried by reason of his contract of employment—Indemnity under policy for liability to passenger arising from employee's negligent driving. **Nottingham v Aldridge (The Prudential Assurance Co Ltd, third party)** [1971] **2** 751, QBD.
Employee provided with transport within certain limits—Employee injured when travelling beyond those limits—Whether insurance compulsory—Road Traffic Act 1930, s 36(1)(b)(ii). **Baker v Provident Accident and White Cross Insurance Co Ltd** [1939] **2** 690, KBD; **Izzard v Universal Insurance Co Ltd** [1937] **3** 79, HL.
Loan of car to employee on condition that fellow employee given lifts to work—Whether fellow employee passenger in car 'by reason of or in pursuance of contract of employment'—Whether insurance compulsory—Acceptance of liability by Motor Insurers' Bureau—Road Traffic Act 1960, s 203(4). **Vandyke v Fender (Sun Insurance Office Ltd, third party)** [1970] **2** 335, CA.
Persons driving with consent of insured—
Indemnity in like manner of authorised driver while driving against liability in respect of any claim by any person including passengers—Claim against authorised driver by policy-holder—Road Traffic Act 1930, ss 35(1), 36(1)(b),(4). **Digby v General Accident, Fire and Life Assurance Corp Ltd** [1942] **2** 319, HL.
Indemnity of authorised driver—Injury to employees excluded—Employee injured—Whether authorised driver can claim under policy. **Richards v Cox** [1942] **2** 624, CA.
Insurers of permitted driver indemnified driver—Whether entitled to contribution from insurers of owner—Road Traffic Act 1930, s 36(4). **Austin v Zurich General Accident & Liability Insurance Co Ltd** [1945] **1** 316, CA.
Owner's son named driver in policy—Unlimited permission given by owner to son to drive car and never withdrawn—Owner died—Accident while car still part of deceased's estate—Executrix of owner had not revoked son's permission to drive—Whether son protected by policy against third party claims. **Kelly v Cornhill Insurance Co Ltd** [1964] **1** 321, HL.
Using vehicle or causing or permitting vehicle to be used on road without policy being in force. *See* Using vehicle or causing or permitting vehicle to be used on road without policy being in force, *below*.
Conditions—
Absolute conduct and control of proceedings—
Claim for damages—Settlement without consulting insured—Liability of insured for first £5 of sum paid in settlement. **Beacon Insurance Co Ltd v Langdale** [1939] **4** 204, CA.
Duty of insurance company and its legal advisers. **Groom v Crocker** [1938] **2** 394, CA.
Breach of condition—
Policy indemnifying insured against loss, theft and damage—Liability excluded if car stolen when keys left in or on car—Insured leaving key in ignition—Car being stolen—Meaning of 'left in or on the car'—Whether insurer liable to indemnify insured. **Hayward v Norwich Union Insurance Ltd** [2001] **1 Comm** 545, CA.
Waiver of breach—Insured failing to comply with condition to inform insurers within five days of claim—Insurers' delay in electing whether to refuse to indemnify. **Allen v Robles (Compagnie Parisienne De Garantie, third party)** [1969] **3** 154, CA.
Notice of claim—
Notification to insurers—Failure of insured to inform insurers of accident and to forward notice of prosecution and summons—Insurers informed by other persons before hearing of summons—No prejudice to insurers—Whether condition a bar to recovery under policy—Waiver of condition. **Lickiss v Milestone Motor Policies at Lloyds** [1966] **2** 972, CA.
Roadworthiness—
Condition that (a) imposed duty to take precautions to keep vehicle in good repair and (b) excluded liability if vehicle driven in unsafe condition—Whether sentence (a) imposed personal obligation on insured but not vicarious liability for casual negligence of employee—Whether exclusion, by virtue of (b), applied where no breach of (a)—Failure of insured, owners of a fleet of motor coaches, to operate an adequate system of maintenance and repair—Unsafe condition of vehicle due to that failure—Whether insurers liable—Whether insurers entitled to indemnity claimed under Road Traffic Act 1960, s 206. **Liverpool Corp v T & HR Roberts (a firm) (Garthwaite, third party)** [1964] **3** 56, Assizes.
Policy originally giving comprehensive cover—Modification to cover third party risks only by deletion of loss and damage section—Condition requiring insured to safeguard vehicle from loss or damage and maintain it in efficient condition—Claim against insured by third party—Satisfaction by insurers of sum awarded—Insurers claiming reimbursement by insured—Breach of condition—Whether condition applicable after deletion of loss and damage section. **New India Assurance Co Ltd, The v Yeo Beng Chow alias Yeo Beng Chong** [1972] **3** 293, PC.
Cost of hire of replacement vehicle. *See* **Damages** (Measure of damages—Motor insurance—Cost of hire of replacement vehicle).
Cost of repair—
Damages. *See* **Damages** (Measure of damages—Motor insurance—Cost of repair).
Cover note—
Duration of cover—
Commencement 11.45 am on 2nd December 1959—Cover note expressed to be valid for 15 days from commencement date of risk—Insurance continued for 15 days from midnight on day of commencement—Insurers liable in respect of accident occurring at 5.45 pm on 17th December. **Cartwright v MacCormack** [1963] **1** 11, CA.
Damages. *See* **Damages** (Measure of damages—Motor insurance).
Deliberate acts—
Liability of insurer to third parties. *See* Compulsory insurance against third party risks—Liabilities required to be covered—Driver deliberately crashing car, causing damage to property, *above*.

562

MOTOR INSURANCE (cont)—
Disclosure—
Material non-disclosure. *See* **Insurance** (Disclosure—Non-disclosure—Material non-disclosure—Marine insurance—War risks policy—Motor insurance).
Disqualification for using etc vehicle on road without policy being in force—
Power to limit disqualification to driving of vehicle of the same class or description as vehicle in relation to which offence committed—
Disqualification limited to 'five hundredweight vehicles'—No such vehicle mentioned in Act—Road Traffic Act 1930, ss 2(1), 6(1), proviso. **Petherick v Buckland** [1955] **1** 151, QBD.
Lorry driver using private car—Whether recorder having power to limit disqualification to private motor vehicle—Road Traffic Act 1930, s 6(1), s 35(2). **Burrows v Hall** [1950] **2** 156, KBD.
Special reasons for not disqualifying—
Assured misled as to effect of policy—Proposal form signed for general cover—Temporary general cover certificate issued, but policy limited to named driver—Road Traffic Act 1930, s 35(2). **Labrum v Williamson** [1947] **1** 824, KBD.
Desirability of stating special reasons. **R v Recorder of Leicester, ex p Gabbitas** [1946] **1** 615, KBD.
Farm labourer driving uninsured tractor—Road Traffic Act 1930, s 35(2). **Blows v Chapman** [1947] **2** 576, KBD.
Insurers willing to admit liability—Taxi-cab under repair—Insurance cover suspended during overhaul—Renewed user through oversight—Road Traffic Act 1930, s 35(2). **Pilbury v Brazier** [1950] **2** 835, KBD.
Misapprehension of legal effect of policy—Date from which disqualification runs where quarter sessions allow appeal against disqualification—Road Traffic Act 1930, s 35(1)(2). **Rennison v Knowler** [1947] **1** 302, KBD.
No special reasons found—Conditional discharge not applicable—Road Traffic Act 1930, s 35(1),(2)—Criminal Justice Act 1948, s 7(1). **Surtees v Benewith** [1954] **3** 261, QBD.
No special reasons found—Conditional discharge—Exercise of discretion—Road Traffic Act 1930, s 35(2)—Criminal Justice Act 1948, ss 7(1), 12(2). **Taylor v Saycell** [1950] **2** 887, KBD.
Owner's policy covering only owner and persons in his employ—Lorry driven back to owner's premises by garage proprietor—Garage proprietor not in owner's employ—Garage proprietor not insured—Road Traffic Act 1930, s 35(1)(2). **Lyons v May** [1948] **2** 1062, KBD.
Penalty considered too severe—Whether a 'special reason'—Road Traffic Act 1930, s 35(1)(2). **Williamson v Wilson** [1947] **1** 306, KBD.
Reasons special to the offence—Lonely road, absence of traffic, short distance—Road Traffic Act 1930, s 35(1)(2). **Reay v Young** [1949] **1** 1102, KBD.
Use of motor vehicle not covered by insurance policy—Dismissal of charge under Probation of Offenders Act 1907, s 1(1)—Good character—Road Traffic Act 1930, s 35(1)(2). **Gardner v James** [1948] **2** 1069, KBD.
Driving school—
Implied duty to insure against third party risks—
Car provided by school for driving lessons and driving test—Pupil not covered by insurance—Implied term in contract with school that cover is provided. **British School of Motoring Ltd v Simms (A R Stafford (t/a Mini Countryman School of Motoring) and Cooper, third parties)** [1971] **1** 317, Assizes.
Duty of insurers to satisfy judgments against insured persons. *See* Rights of third parties against insurers—Duty of insurers to satisfy judgments against insured persons, *below*.
Employer—
Liabilities required to be covered. *See* Compulsory insurance against third party risks—Liabilities required to be covered—Employer, *above*.
European Union. *See* **European Union** (Insurance—Compulsory insurance of motor vehicles).
Exception—
Member of the assured's household—
Meaning. **English v Western** [1940] **2** 515, CA.
Overloading—
Liability of insurers excluded if 'car conveying load in excess of that for which it was constructed'—Car carrying one person in excess of normal seating accommodation. **Houghton v Trafalgar Insurance Co Ltd** [1953] **2** 1409, CA.
Passenger other than one carried by reason of or in pursuance of a contract of employment—
By reason of contract of employment—Passenger's contract of employment containing no provision for him to obtain lift—Forester whose duty it was to inspect lorry loads of logs requesting lift from driver of timber lorry for personal reasons—Forester's contract making no provision for him to obtain lifts from timber lorries—Driver giving lift to forester because he thought it might help his employer—Lorry overturning and killing forester—Driver and employer ordered to pay damages to forester's estate—Whether forester being carried 'by reason of...[his] contract of employment'—Whether insurer liable under policy to indemnify driver and employer. **Tan Keng Hong v New India Assurance Co Ltd** [1978] **2** 380, PC.
Policy excluding loss or damage occurring while vehicle driven by person other than policyholder—
Policy stating limitation of use of vehicle not breached by delivery of vehicle into custody or control of member of motor trade for repair—Vehicle stolen while in charge of repairer—Whether policy holder entitled to be indemnified—Whether vehicle in custody or control of member of motor trade for purpose of repair when stolen—Whether vehicle on risk while being driven by or in charge of person other than policyholder. **Samuelson v National Insurance and Guarantee Corp Ltd** [1986] **3** 417, CA.
Policy excluding 'use for hire or reward other than private hire'—
Supply of car 'direct from garage'—Car used to take owner's fellow workmen home from work—Car taken to place of work hours before. **Lyons v Denscombe** [1949] **1** 977, KBD.
Unroadworthiness—
Liability of insurers excluded if car being driven in unsafe or unroadworthy condition—Steering, braking and control of car seriously impaired when being driven at speed by reason of overloading. **Clarke v National Insurance and Guarantee Corp Ltd** [1963] **3** 375, CA.
Extent of cover—
Compulsory insurance against third party risks. *See* Compulsory insurance against third party risks—Extent of cover, *above*.

Extent of cover (cont)—

Driving vehicle not owned by insured—

Driving vehicle with consent of owner—Insured permitted under personal insurance policy to drive vehicles not belonging to him provided he had 'consent' of owner—Insured borrowing vehicle not owned by him—Vehicle owner giving consent to use vehicle—Consent subject to implied limitation—Insured using vehicle for purpose outside owner's consent—Insured involved in accident while negligently driving vehicle for purpose outside owner's consent—Whether use covered by insured's insurance policy. **Singh v Rathour (Northern Star Insurance Co Ltd, third party)** [1988] **2** 16, CA.

Indemnity—

'Owner driver only' insurance policy—Accident whilst car driven by employee—Insurer settling third party claim then seeking to recover sum paid from owner—Whether breach of contract—Whether contractual or statutory indemnity—Whether judicial interpretation of legislation operating retrospectively—Whether unjust enrichment—Whether payment under legal compulsion—Motor Vehicles Insurance (Third Party Risks) Act (Trinidad and Tobago), s 4(7). **Capital Insurance Co Ltd v Samsoondar** [2021] **2 Comm** 353, PC; [2021] **2** 1105, PC.

Use of vehicle—

Damage caused by fire breaking out while insured repairing vehicle on garage premises—Insured employee of garage and carrying out repairs to his own vehicle with consent of employer—Whether policy providing cover for accidents occurring whilst vehicle off road—Whether carrying out of repairs amounting to 'use' of vehicle. **UK Insurance Ltd v Holden** [2016] **3** 727, QBD.

Damage caused by fire breaking out while insured repairing vehicle on garage premises—Insured employee of garage and carrying out repairs to his own vehicle with consent of employer—Whether policy providing cover for accidents occurring whilst vehicle off road—Whether carrying out of repairs amounting to 'use' of vehicle—Road Traffic Act 1988, s 145(3)—European Parliament and Council Directive 2009/103/EC, art 3. **UK Insurance Ltd v Holden** [2019] **2 Comm** 793, SC; [2019] **3** 917, SC.

European Union. *See* **European Union** (Insurance—Compulsory insurance of motor vehicles—Insurance against civil liability in respect of use of motor vehicles).

False statement to obtain insurance certificate. *See* Certificate—False statement to obtain insurance certificate, *above*.

Indemnity of authorised driver. *See* Compulsory insurance against third party risks—Persons driving with consent of insured—Indemnity of authorised driver, *above*.

Insurer liable to pay amount in respect of liability of a person not insured by a policy—

Causing or permitting use of vehicle giving rise to liability—

Road Traffic Act 1988, s 151(8)(b). **Lloyd-Wolper v Moore (National Insurance Guarantee Corp plc, Pt 20 claimant, Moore and anor, Pt 20 defendants)** [2004] **3** 741, CA.

Excluded liability—

Liability excluded where person allowing himself to be carried knew or had reason to believe vehicle stolen or unlawfully taken—Meaning of 'reason to believe'—Meaning of 'unlawfully taken'—Road Traffic Act 1988, s 151(4). **McMinn v McMinn** [2006] **3** 87, QBD.

Insurer's entitlement to recover amount paid out from person insured by policy who caused or permitted the use of the vehicle which gave rise to the liability—

Person insured injured in road traffic accident caused by person not insured by policy—Whether insurer's right to recover amount paid out to injured insured person prohibited by EC law—Whether English law capable of being interpreted so as to comply with EC law—Road Traffic Act 1988, s 151(8)—Council Directive (EEC) 84/5, art 2(1). **Wilkinson v Churchill Insurance Co Ltd (Secretary of State for Transport intervening)** [2010] **1** 198, QBD; [2010] **1 Comm** 278, QBD; [2013] **1 Comm** 881, CA; [2013] **1** 1146, CA.

Knock-for-knock agreement—

Claim by insured against another car owner—

Effect of knock-for-knock agreement—Assignment of right of action—Insured recovering part of damage from insurers—Claim against other car owner for full amount of damage—Whether knock-for-knock agreement between insured's insurers and other party's insurers effecting equitable assignment of insured's right of action for amount recovered from own insurers—Whether insured precluded from bringing action for full amount of damages. **Hobbs v Marlowe** [1977] **2** 241, CA and HL.

Whether claim barred by knock-for-knock agreement. **Morley v Moore** [1936] **2** 79, CA.

Learner driver. *See* Compulsory insurance against third party risks—Extent of cover—Learner being taught to drive, *above*.

Licence obtained by false pretence—

Compulsory insurance against third party risks—

Extent of cover. *See* Compulsory insurance against third party risks—Extent of cover—Driver under age of 16—Licence obtained by false pretence, *above*.

Misrepresentation of material fact. *See* Rights of third parties against insurers—Duty of insurers to satisfy judgments against insured persons—Insurers not liable where policy obtained by non-disclosure or misrepresentation of material fact, *below*.

Motor Insurers' Bureau—

Liability of bureau to compensate following insurer's insolvency—

Claimant sustaining personal injuries in road traffic accident occurring in member state other than member state of residence—Foreign insurer failing to provide reply to claim for compensation within prescribed time limit—Injured person becoming entitled to present claim to Motor Insurers' Bureau (MIB)—Injured party presenting claim to MIB after insolvency of foreign insurer and revocation of its licence—Whether MIB liable—Motor Vehicles (Compulsory Insurance) (Information Centre and Compensation Body) Regulations 2003, SI 2003/37, regs 11, 12—European Parliament and Council Directive 2000/26/EC, art 6. **Wigley-Foster v Wilson** [2017] **1 Comm** 715, CA.

Motor Insurers' Bureau (cont)—
  Liability of bureau to satisfy judgment against uninsured driver—
    Claimant seeking compensation for injuries suffered in motor vehicle accident in Greece—Whether claim to be determined in accordance with English or Greek law—Motor Vehicles (Compulsory Insurance) (Information Centre and Compensation Body) Regulations 2003, SI 2003/37, regs 12(4)(b), 13(2)(b)—European Parliament and Council Directive 2009/103/EC. **Moreno v Motor Insurers' Bureau** [2017] **4** 28, SC.
    Uninsured driver driving from road and then footpath onto private land and colliding with claimant—UK law requiring compulsory insurance in respect of use of vehicles on road or other public place—Requirement of compulsory insurance under EU law extending to use of vehicle on private land—Whether EU obligation to hold insurance for using vehicle on private land having direct effect—Whether Motor Insurers' Bureau emanation of state—Road Traffic Act 1988, s 145—European Parliament and Council Directive 2009/103/EC, arts 3, 10. **Lewis (by his litigation friend, Lewis) v Tindale** [2019] **2 Comm** 936, CA; [2019] **3** 1064, CA.
    Uninsured driver driving from road and then footpath onto private land and colliding with claimant—Whether requirement of compulsory insurance applicable—Whether domestic law to be 'read down' to include requirement of compulsory insurance in respect of use of vehicle on private land—Whether EU obligation to hold insurance for using vehicle on private land having direct effect—Whether Motor Insurers' Bureau emanation of state—Road Traffic Act 1988, ss 143, 145—European Parliament and Council Directive 2009/103/EC, arts 3, 10. **Lewis (by his litigation friend, Lewis) v Tindale** [2019] **1 Comm** 747, QBD; [2019] **1** 870, QBD.
Motor Insurers' Bureau—
  Dependants. *See* Motor Insurers' Bureau—Liability of bureau to satisfy judgment against uninsured driver—Passenger allowing himself/herself to be carried in vehicle s/he knew to be uninsured—Passenger dying in road traffic accident—Dependant of passenger bringing claim, *below*.
  Exclusion of bureau's obligation to pay compensation. *See* Motor Insurers' Bureau—Liability of bureau to satisfy judgment against uninsured driver—Passenger allowing himself/herself to be carried in vehicle s/he knew to be uninsured, *below*.
  Liability of bureau to satisfy judgment against uninsured driver—
    Bureau agreeing with Secretary of State to satisfy awards of damages made against uninsured drivers—Agreement intended to give effect to European Community directive—Agreement absolving bureau from liability in respect of claims by passengers who 'knew or ought to have known' that vehicle uninsured—Directive providing for exception from liability where passenger 'knew' driver was uninsured—Whether exclusion covering negligence or carelessness on part of passenger as to driver's insurance status—Second Council Directive (EEC) 84/5, art 1(4)—Motor Insurers' Bureau (Compensation of Victims of Uninsured Drivers) Agreement (1988), cl 6(1)(e)(ii). **White v White** [2001] **1 Comm** 1105, HL; [2001] **2** 43, HL.
    Bureau agreeing with Secretary of State to satisfy awards of damages made against uninsured drivers—Agreement intended to give effect to European Community directive—Agreement absolving bureau from liability in respect of claims by passengers who knew or ought to have known that vehicle was being used in the course or furtherance of a crime—Whether exclusion from liability compatible with Directive—Second Council Directive (EEC) 84/5, art 1(4)—Motor Insurers' Bureau (Compensation of Victims of Uninsured Drivers) Agreement (1999), cl 6(1)(e)(iii). **Delaney v Secretary of State for Transport** [2015] **3** 329, CA.
    Bureau agreeing with Secretary of State to satisfy awards of damages made against uninsured drivers—Agreement intended to give effect to European Community directive—Compatibility of agreement with directive—Whether nature of bureau sufficient to comply with directive—Whether procedural arrangements of bureau sufficient to ensure protection to which victims entitled under directive—Whether bureau required to pay interest on awards of compensation to victims—Whether bureau required to reimburse costs incurred by victims in processing applications for compensation—Whether directive properly transposed—Council Directive (EEC) 84/5, art 1(4). **Evans v Secretary of State for the Environment, Transport and the Regions (Case C-63/01)** [2005] **EC** 763, ECJ.
    Passenger allowing himself/herself to be carried in vehicle s/he knew to be uninsured—Passenger dying in road traffic accident—Dependant of passenger bringing claim—Exclusion of bureau's obligation to pay compensation where claimant allowing himself to be carried in vehicle knowing vehicle uninsured—Whether dependant's claim within exclusion—Motor Insurers' Bureau (Compensation of Victims of Uninsured Drivers) Agreement 1999, cll 1, 6(1)(e). **Phillips v Rafiq** [2007] **2 Comm** 484, CA; [2007] **3** 382, CA.
    Passenger allowing himself/herself to be carried in vehicle s/he knew to be uninsured—Passenger telling driver to stop vehicle when driver driving dangerously—Whether passenger withdrawing consent to be carried—Motor Insurers' Bureau (Compensation of Victims of Uninsured Drivers) Agreement 1988, cl 6(1)(e). **Pickett v Roberts** [2004] **2** 685, CA.
  Rights of third parties against insurers. *See* Rights of third parties against insurers—Motor Insurers' Bureau, *below*.
Motor vehicle—
  Meaning. *See* Using vehicle or causing or permitting vehicle to be used on road without policy being in force—Motor vehicle—Cycle fitted with auxiliary engine, *below*.
Notice of claim. *See* Conditions—Notice of claim, *above*.
Overloading—
  Exception. *See* Exception—Overloading, *above*.
Passengers carried for hire or reward in private vehicle. *See* Compulsory insurance against third party risks—Passengers carried for hire or reward in private vehicle, *above*.
Passenger's negligence injuring third party. *See* Using vehicle or causing or permitting vehicle to be used on road without policy being in force—Use—Passenger's negligence injuring third party, *below*.
Payment of hospital expenses. *See* Compulsory insurance against third party risks—Payment for hospital expenses, *above*.
Permit—
  Meaning. *See* Using vehicle or causing or permitting vehicle to be used on road without policy being in force—Permit, *below*.

Person carried by reason of or in pursuance of a contract of employment. *See* Compulsory insurance against third party risks—Person carried by reason of or in pursuance of a contract of employment, *above*.

Person driving with consent of insured. *See* Compulsory insurance against third party risks—Persons driving with consent of insured, *above*.

Repairs to car at request of car owner—

Repairs authorised by insurers—

Agreement by insurers with repairers to pay for repairs—Liability of repairers to owner for failure to carry out repairs within a reasonable time. **Charnock v Liverpool Corp** [1968] **3** 473, CA.

Replacement vehicle, hire of—

Damages recoverable. *See* **Damages** (Measure of damages—Motor insurance—Cost of hire of replacement vehicle).

Rights of third parties against insurers—

Duty of insurers to satisfy judgments against insured persons—

Claimant's vehicle damaged in road traffic accident with vehicle hired by insured from car hire company—Insured permitting unidentified driver to use vehicle without insurance in breach of statutory duty—Claimant obtaining judgment against insured—Whether statutory requirement that liability of insured be covered by insurance—Whether car hire company's insurance policy requiring liability of car hirer to be covered by insurance—Road Traffic Act 1988, ss 143, 145, 151—Second Council Directive 84/5/EEC. **Sahin v Havard** [2017] **2 Comm** 851, CA; [2017] **4** 157, CA.

Exception—Declaration obtained by insurer entitling it to avoid liability—Claimant seeking compensation after being injured in road traffic accident—Relevant policy not covering driver—Whether insurer falling within exception and thereby claim against it to be dismissed—Whether order extending time for service of claim form on first defendant to be set aside—Whether permission to be granted for joining Secretary of State for Transport as additional defendant—Whether permission to be granted to amend Particulars of Claim—Road Traffic Act 1988, s 152(2)—Consumer Insurance (Disclosure Representations) Act 2012—European Parliament and Council Directive 2009/103/EC. **Colley v Shuker** [2019] **2 Comm** 1060, QBD.

Exception—Insured deliberately driving into claimant's car off road—Insured convicted of criminal damage—Claimant obtaining judgment against insured—Whether contrary to public policy to permit an assured to recover indemnity in respect of a deliberate criminal act—Third Parties (Rights against Insurers) Act 1930. **Charlton v Fisher** [2001] **1 Comm** 769, CA.

Exception—Policy covering only 'social, domestic and pleasure purposes'—Payment made to insured by passenger in respect of expenses—Policy not covering use for hiring—Insurers not liable—Road Traffic Act 1934, s 10(1). **McCarthy v British Oak Insurance Co** [1938] **3** 1, KBD.

Insurers not liable where no notice of proceedings by third party against insured—Sufficiency of casual conversation with agent as notice of proceedings—Road Traffic Act 1934, s 10. **Herbert v Rly Passengers Assurance Co** [1938] **1** 650, KBD.

Insurers not liable where no notice of proceedings by third party against insured—Sufficiency of letter to insurers as notice of proceedings—Motor Car Ordinance of Ceylon (No 45 of 1938), s 134(a). **Ceylon Motor Insurance Association Ltd v Thambugala** [1953] **2** 870, PC.

Insurers not liable where no notice of proceedings by third party against insured—Time at which proceedings 'commenced'—Road Traffic Act 1934, s 10(2)(a). **Cross v British Oak Insurance Co Ltd** [1938] **1** 383, KBD.

Insurers not liable where policy obtained by non-disclosure or misrepresentation of material fact—Action by insurance company for declaration—Clause negativing right to declaration—Declaration based on admissions by insured binding on all parties to action—Road Traffic Act 1934, s 10(3). **Merchants' and Manufacturers' Insurance Co Ltd v Hunt** [1941] **1** 123, CA.

Insurers not liable where policy obtained by non-disclosure or misrepresentation of material fact—Action by insurance company for declaration—Notice to third party of matters relied upon—Insurance company subsequently discovering further non-disclosure—Insurance company restricted to matters stated in notice as against third party—Road Traffic Act 1934, s 10(3). **Zurich General Accident and Liability Insurance Co Ltd v Morrison** [1942] **1** 529, CA.

Insurers not liable where policy obtained by non-disclosure or misrepresentation of material fact—Declaration under Road Traffic Act 1934, s 10(3)—Meaning of 'policy of insurance' within Road Traffic Act 1930, s 36(4)—Nature of indemnity under Road Traffic Act 1930, s 36(4)—Right to declaration in absence of defendant. **Guardian Assurance Co Ltd v Sutherland** [1939] **2** 246, KBD.

Insurers not liable where policy obtained by non-disclosure or misrepresentation of material fact—Misrepresentation in proposal form—Action by insurance company for declaration—Right of third parties to strict proof of falsity of representations—Road Traffic Act 1934, s 10. **Merchants' and Manufacturers' Insurance Co Ltd v Hunt** [1941] **1** 123, CA.

Exception—

Weight or physical characteristics of goods vehicle carries—Use of vehicle in connection with business or profession—Profession stated in policy—Insured also carrying on other business—Physical characteristics of goods carried—Road Traffic Act 1934, s 12(d). **Jones v Welsh Insurance Corp Ltd** [1937] **4** 149, KBD.

Motor Insurers' Bureau—

Adding as defendant—Action by insurers to avoid policy—Notice to third party of matters relied on—Motor Insurers' Bureau—Liability of bureau to satisfy judgment obtained by third party if that judgment not satisfied by insured or insurers—Whether bureau entitled to be joined in insurers' action—Road Traffic Act 1960, s 207(3)—RSC Ord 15, r 6(2)(b). **Fire, Auto and Marine Insurance Co Ltd v Greene** [1964] **2** 761, QBD.

Adding as defendant—Whether insurers can be added as parties to running down action where policy does not contain clause giving them conduct of the defence. **Gurtner v Circuit** [1968] **1** 328, CA.

Bodily injury suffered by person just within boundary of private land—Motor lorry partly on road—Whether injury caused by, or arising out of, use of vehicle on a road—Road Traffic Act 1960, s 203(3)(a). **Randall v Motor Insurers' Bureau** [1969] **1** 21, QBD.

MOTOR INSURANCE (cont)—

Rights of third parties against insurers (cont)—

Motor Insurers' Bureau (cont)—

Dependants. *See* Motor Insurers' Bureau—Liability of bureau to satisfy judgment against uninsured driver—Passenger allowing himself/herself to be carried in vehicle s/he knew to be uninsured—Passenger dying in road traffic accident—Dependant of passenger bringing claim, *above*.

Liability in respect of intentional criminal act—Road Traffic Act 1960, ss 203(3)(a), 207. **Hardy v Motor Insurers' Bureau** [1964] **2** 742, CA.

Liability in respect of intentional criminal act—Road Traffic Act 1972, s 145(3). **Gardner v Moore** [1984] **1** 1100, HL.

Liability of bureau to satisfy judgment against uninsured driver—Liability required to be covered by insurance—Owner of vehicle permitting another person to drive it—Permitted driver injured because of defective brakes—Owner not insured—Whether bureau obliged to satisfy judgment against owner—Whether owner's liability to permitted driver required to be covered by insurance—Whether injury to permitted driver an injury to 'any person ... arising out of' use of vehicle—Road Traffic Act 1972, ss 143(1), 145(3)(a). **Cooper v Motor Insurers' Bureau** [1985] **1** 449, CA.

Policy of insurance taken out by employer covering liability for death of any person caused by use of lorry owned by employer—Exclusion of liability in respect of death arising out of and in course of employment of person in employment of insured—Employee killed in accident with lorry—Judgment in favour of widow unsatisfied—Liability of Motor Insurers' Bureau—Road Traffic Act 1930, ss 35(1), 36(b), proviso (i). **Lees v Motor Insurers' Bureau** [1952] **2** 511, QBD.

Untraced driver—Agreement between Motor Insurers' Bureau and Minister of Transport—Death or injury caused by untraced person—Duty of bureau to award compensation—Discretion of bureau to refuse compensation—Right of appeal to arbitrator against refusal—Applicant suing bureau instead of appealing to arbitrator—Whether claim should be struck out as showing no cause of action—Agreement between Minister of Transport and Motor Insurers' Bureau (21st April 1969), cll 3, 7. **Persson v London Country Buses** [1974] **1** 1251, CA.

Untraced driver—Limitation—Agreement between Motor Insurers' Bureau and Secretary of State—Death or injury caused by untraced person—Obligation of member states to set up or authorise body with task of providing compensation for damage to property or personal injuries caused by unidentified vehicle—Application to bureau required to be made within three years of accident—Minor making unsuccessful application more than three years after accident but within limitation period applicable in proceedings in tort—Whether United Kingdom in breach of Community obligations—Whether minor having remedy against bureau—Whether breach sufficiently serious to give rise to claim for damages—Second Council Directive (EEC) 84/5, art 1(4). **Byrne v Motor Insurers' Bureau** [2007] **3** 499, QBD; [2008] **4** 476, CA.

Rights under statute—

Retrospective operation of statute—Road Traffic Act 1934, s 10. **Croxford v Universal Insurance Co Ltd** [1936] **1** 151, CA; **Dolan v Dominion of Canada General Insurance Co** [1936] **2** 1354, Liverpool Summer Assizes.

Risk—

Description of risk—

Loss of car—Car bought from owner on false pretence and for worthless cheque. **Eisinger v General Accident, Fire and Life Assurance Corp Ltd** [1955] **2** 897, QBD.

Loss of car—Car sold contrary to owner's authority and proceeds of sale retained. **Webster v General Accident Fire and Life Assurance Corp Ltd** [1953] **1** 663, QBD.

Double insurance—

Right in equity to a contribution—Term in policy limiting insurer's liability to half of loss in event of double insurance—Insurer paying loss in full—Insurer expressly reserving right to claim from other insurer—Whether insurer a volunteer in paying in full—Whether insurer entitled to equitable contribution. **Drake Insurance plc v Provident Insurance plc** [2004] **2 Comm** 65, CA.

Duration of risk—

Sale of vehicle—Insured person covered (i) when driving named vehicle and (ii) when driving other vehicles—Condition that insured take all reasonable steps to maintain named vehicle in efficient condition and to allow insurers free access at all times to examine it—Whether second indemnity continued after named vehicle sold—Road Traffic Act 1960, s 201(1). **Boss v Kingston** [1963] **1** 177, QBD.

Sale of vehicle—Purported assignment of policy by seller of car—Policy handed to purchaser—Whether person injured by purchaser can recover from insurers. **Peters v General Accident Fire and Life Assurance Corp Ltd** [1938] **2** 267, CA.

Roadworthiness. *See* Conditions—Roadworthiness, *above*.

Sale of vehicle—

Duration of risk. *See* Risk—Duration of risk—Sale of vehicle, *above*.

Settlement without consulting insured. *See* Conditions—Absolute conduct and control of proceedings—Claim for damages—Settlement without consulting insured, *above*.

Statutory rights of third parties against insurers. *See* Rights of third parties against insurers—Rights under statute, *above*.

Temporary cover note—

Using vehicle or causing or permitting vehicle to be used on road without policy being in force. *See* Using vehicle or causing or permitting vehicle to be used on road without policy being in force—Policy of insurance—Temporary cover note, *below*.

Third parties—

Rights of third parties against insurers. *See* Rights of third parties against insurers, *above*.

Third party risks. *See* Compulsory insurance against third party risks, *above*.

Uninsured driver—

Causing or permitting use of vehicle by uninsured driver. *See* Using vehicle or causing or permitting vehicle to be used on road without policy being in force, *below*.

Unlicensed driver. *See* Using vehicle or causing or permitting vehicle to be used on road without policy being in force—Vehicle driven by unlicensed driver, *below*.

Unroadworthiness. *See* Exception—Unroadworthiness, *above*.

MOTOR INSURANCE (cont)—

Untraced driver—
> Injury caused by untraced driver. *See* Rights of third parties against insurers—Motor Insurers' Bureau—Untraced driver, *above.*

Using vehicle or causing or permitting vehicle to be used on road without policy being in force—

Accused not the driver—
> Evidence that occupants of motor vehicle were acting in concert—Sufficiency of evidence—Road Traffic Act 1930, s 35. **Ross v Rivenall** [1959] **2** 376, QBD.

Cause or permit—
> Breach of statutory duty—Road Traffic Act 1930, s 35(1). **Watkins v O'Shaughnessy** [1939] **1** 385, CA.
> Person other than owner of vehicle—Person assisting driver to obtain insurance policy—Policy avoided by reason of misrepresentation in proposal form—Whether person other than owner capable of causing or permitting use of vehicle—Road Traffic Act 1930, s 35(1). **Goodbarne v Buck** [1940] **1** 613, CA.
> Use of commercial van for private purposes when insured for commercial use only—No evidence of owner's knowledge of such user or of his express permission to driver—Road Traffic Act 1930, s 35(1). **McLeod (or Houston) v Buchanan** [1940] **2** 179, HL.

Charge of using motor vehicle and trailer while uninsured—
> Wrong description of offence—Charge not amended—Road Traffic Act 1930, s 35(1). **Rogerson v Stephens** [1950] **2** 144, KBD.

Extenuating circumstances—
> Owner honestly believing himself covered—Dismissal of charge under Probation of Offenders Act 1907, s 1(1)—Road Traffic Act 1930, s 35. **Quelch v Collett** [1948] **1** 252, KBD.

In force—
> Company's servant driving company's car on authorised journey—Instructing unlicensed person to drive—Whether policy 'in force'—Road Traffic Act 1930, s 35(1). **Marsh v Moores** [1949] **2** 27, KBD.
> Insurance covering the 'proposer or his paid driver'—Car driven by paid driver not in general employment of proposer—Whether insurance 'in force'—Road Traffic Act 1930, s 35(1). **Bryan v Forrow** [1950] **1** 294, KBD.
> Policy covering facts constituting offence against Road Traffic Acts—Use of tractor with two trailers covered—Whether policy 'in force'—Road Traffic Act 1930, s 18(1), s 35(1). **Leggate v Brown** [1950] **2** 564, KBD.
> Statement by insurance company that it regards policy as 'on risk'—Whether policy 'in force'—Road Traffic Act 1930, s 35(1). **Carnill v Rowland** [1953] **1** 486, QBD.

Liability of insurance company for injury to insured. *See* Insurer liable to pay amount in respect of liability of a person not insured by a policy, *above.*

Motor vehicle—
> Cycle fitted with auxiliary engine—Use as pedal cycle—No removal of essential parts of engine—Whether 'motor vehicle'. **Floyd v Bush** [1953] **1** 265, QBD.
> Cycle fitted with auxiliary engine—Use as pedal cycle after removal of essential parts of engine—Whether 'motor vehicle'. **Lawrence v Howlett** [1952] **2** 74, QBD.

Permit—
> Permission given by person in charge of vehicle, not the owner—Whether owner alone can give permission—Road Traffic Act 1930, s 35(1). **Lloyd v Singleton** [1953] **1** 291, QBD.

Person not to use vehicle or cause or permit vehicle to be used—
> Any person—Whether persons other than owner of vehicle can be guilty of the offence—Road Traffic Act 1930, s 35(1). **Williamson v O'Keeffe** [1947] **1** 307, KBD.

Policy of insurance—
> Temporary cover note—Effect—Former policy of insurance expired—Car owner intending to change insurers—Cover note issued by former insurers—No renewal premium paid—Cover note having effect as offer by former insurers—Owner not relying on cover note and not having accepted former insurers' offer—Former insurers ready to assume liability on cover note—Whether car owner insured by virtue of the cover note for the purposes of Road Traffic Act 1960, s 201. **Taylor v Allon** [1965] **1** 557, QBD.

Policy stating vehicle could be driven by any person with policy holder's permission provided not disqualified for holding licence—
> Defendant driving with policy holder's permission—Defendant mental defective—Whether 'insured'—Road Traffic Act 1930, s 35(1). **Edwards v Griffiths** [1953] **2** 874, QBD.

Use—
> Broken down car parked on road outside owner's house—Car not completely immovable, but in such condition that it could not be mechanically propelled—Owner having no intention of driving or moving car at material time—Whether car in use on road—Road Traffic Act 1930, s 35(1). **Elliott v Grey** [1959] **3** 733, QBD.
> Passenger's negligence injuring third party—Owner not insured against third party liability of passenger—Whether breach of statutory duty to insure against third party risks—Whether there was a 'user' of the vehicle by the passenger within Road Traffic Act 1930, s 35(1). **Brown v Roberts** [1963] **2** 263, QBD.

Using vehicle taken and driven away without owner's consent—
> Appellant boy 15 years old not party to original wrongful taking of motor cycle by another boy of same age—Riding on cycle subsequently as pillion passenger—Road Traffic Act 1930, s 35(1). **D (an infant) v Parsons** [1960] **2** 493, QBD Divl Ct.

Vehicle driven by unlicensed driver—
> Exception if vehicle driven by unlicensed driver—Need for policy to cover driver's liability—Knowledge of owner—Constructive knowledge—Road Traffic Act 1930, s 35(1). **Ellis (John T) Ltd v Hinds** [1947] **1** 337, KBD.

Waiver of breach of condition. *See* Conditions—Breach of condition—Waiver of breach, *above.*

MOTOR INSURERS' BUREAU

Generally. *See* **Motor insurance** (Motor Insurers' Bureau).

Rights of third parties against insurers. *See* **Motor insurance** (Rights of third parties against insurers—Motor Insurers' Bureau).

MOTOR TRACTOR

See **Road traffic** (Motor tractor).

MOTOR VEHICLE

Abandoned or broken down vehicle on road. See **Road traffic** (Motor vehicle—Abandoned or broken down vehicle on road).

Articulated vehicle. See **Road traffic** (Articulated vehicle).

Car—

    Displaying for sale notice in vehicle. See **Street trading** (Offence—Displaying for sale notice in private vehicle).

    False trade description—

        Indication of previous history including ownership or use—Previous use—Mileage. See **Trade description** (False trade description—Meaning of trade description—Indication of history including previous ownership or use—Previous use—Motor car—Mileage).

    Insurance. See **Motor insurance**.

    Sale of. See **Sale of goods** (Motor car).

Collision on road—

    Negligence—

        Contributory negligence. See **Negligence** (Contributory negligence—Collision between vehicles on road).

Cycle fitted with auxiliary engine. See **Motor insurance** (Using vehicle or causing or permitting vehicle to be used on road without policy being in force—Motor vehicle—Cycle fitted with auxiliary engine).

Driving offences. See **Road traffic**.

Excise licence. See **Road traffic** (Excise licence).

False trade description—

    Defence to proceedings. See **Trade description** (Defence to proceedings—Reasonable precautions and due diligence to avoid commission of offence—Sale of car by motor dealer).

Generally. See **Road traffic** (Motor vehicle).

Goods vehicle. See **Road traffic** (Goods vehicle).

Hackney carriage. See **Road traffic** (Hackney carriage).

Heavy goods vehicle. See **Road traffic** (Goods vehicle—Heavy goods vehicle).

Heavy motor car. See **Road traffic** (Heavy motor car).

Hire-purchase. See **Hire-purchase** (Motor vehicle).

Insurance. See **Motor insurance**.

Latent defect—

    Defence to action for negligence. See **Negligence** (Defence—Latent defect—Motor vehicle).

Lien—

    Repairers' lien. See **Lien** (Repairer's lien—Motor repairer).

Loan, on. See **Hire-purchase** (Refinancing arrangements—Loan by borrower on security of own car).

Mercantile agent—

    Possession of car—

        Document of title. See **Agent** (Mercantile agent—Possession of goods—Consent of owner—Document of title—Motor car registration book).

Negligence. See **Negligence** (Vehicles).

New car—

    Sale. See **Sale of goods** (Motor car—New car).

Plant—

    Investment grant. See **Investment grant** (Machinery and plant—Vehicle).

Presence on road—

    Accident—

        Breath test. See **Road traffic** (Breath test—Accident owing to presence of motor vehicle on road).

Private hire vehicle. See **Road traffic** (Private hire vehicle).

Registration mark—

    Assignment. See **Chose in action** (Assignment—Vehicle registration mark).

Road traffic. See **Road traffic** (Motor vehicle).

Sale—

    Fitness for purpose—

        Implied condition. See **Sale of goods** (Implied condition as to fitness—Particular purpose made known to seller—Vehicle).

Secondhand car—

    Sale—

        Fitness for purpose. See **Sale of goods** (Implied condition as to fitness—Reasonably fit—Secondhand motor car).

Taking vehicle without authority. See **Road traffic** (Taking vehicle without authority).

Title—

    Hire-purchase. See **Hire-purchase** (Title—Motor vehicle).

    Private purchaser without notice of hire-purchase agreement. See **Hire-purchase** (Title—Motor vehicle—Private purchaser without notice of hire-purchase agreement under which owner reclaiming vehicle).

Value added tax—

    Input tax—

        Disallowance. See **Value added tax** (Input tax—Disallowance of input tax—Motor vehicles).

Vicarious liability—

    Owner's liability for driver's negligence. See **Vicarious liability** (Vehicle owner's liability for driver's negligence).

MOTORING OFFENCES

See **Road traffic**.

MOTORWAY

Improvements and stopping-up of slip roads—

    Compulsory purchase—

        Compensation. See **Compulsory purchase** (Compensation—Injurious affection).

MOTORWAY (cont)—
　　Road traffic. *See* **Road traffic** (Motorway).

MOVABLE DWELLINGS
　　Licence. *See* **Housing** (Movable dwellings—Licence).

MOVABLE STRUCTURE
　　Occupier's duty—
　　　　Duty to independent contractor. *See* **Occupier's liability** (Duty to independent contractor—Movable structure).

MOVEMENT, FREEDOM OF
　　Bermuda—
　　　　Construction of Constitution. *See* **Bermuda** (Constitutional law—Construction of Constitution—Protection of freedom of movement).
　　European Community—
　　　　Goods. *See* **European Union** (Freedom of movement—Goods).
　　　　Workers. *See* **European Union** (Workers—Freedom of movement).

MULTIPLE OCCUPATION HOUSES
　　See **Housing** (House in multiple occupation).

MULTIPLIER
　　Damages—
　　　　Fatal accident. *See* **Fatal accident** (Damages—Multiplier).
　　　　Personal injury—
　　　　　　Loss of future earnings. *See* **Damages** (Personal injury—Loss of future earnings—Multiplier).

MULTIRACIAL JURY
　　See **Jury** (Composition—Multiracial jury).

MUNICIPAL CEMETERY
　　Faculty jurisdiction. *See* **Ecclesiastical law** (Faculty—Confirmatory faculty—Availability of remedy—Municipal cemetery).
　　Restoration order. *See* **Ecclesiastical law** (Restoration order—Municipal cemetery).
　　Scheme of management. *See* **Ecclesiastical law** (Cemetery—Municipal cemetery—Scheme of management).

MUNICIPAL LAW
　　European Community—
　　　　Treaty provisions superseding municipal law of member states. *See* **European Union** (Treaty provisions—Direct application in member states—Municipal law no longer applicable).
　　International law—
　　　　Relationship. *See* **International law** (Municipal law—Relationship).

MURAL TABLET
　　Memorial tablet within church—
　　　　Ecclesiastical law. *See* **Ecclesiastical law** (Monument—Memorial tablet within church).

MURDER
　　Attempted murder—
　　　　When attempt begins. *See* **Criminal law** (Attempt—Acts preparatory to offence—When attempt begins).
　　Autrefois convict. *See* **Criminal law** (Autrefois convict—Murder).
　　Belize. *See* **Belize** (Criminal law—Murder).
　　Concerted action. *See* **Criminal law** (Murder—Concerted action).
　　Court-martial. *See* **Court-martial** (Civil offence—Jurisdiction—Murder).
　　Duress as a defence. *See* **Criminal law** (Duress as a defence—Murder).
　　Generally. *See* **Criminal law** (Murder).
　　Incitement. *See* **Criminal law** (Incitement—Commission of crime—Murder).
　　Joint unlawful enterprise. *See* **Criminal law** (Murder—Concerted action—Joint unlawful enterprise).
　　Reduction to manslaughter. *See* **Criminal law** (Murder—Manslaughter—Reduction to manslaughter).
　　Sentence—
　　　　Generally. *See* **Sentence** (Murder).
　　　　Mandatory life sentence. *See* **Sentence** (Mandatory life sentence—Murder).
　　　　Young person. *See* **Sentence** (Young person—Serious criminal offence—Murder).
　　Succession—
　　　　Intestacy—
　　　　　　Exclusion from benefit. *See* **Intestacy** (Succession—Exclusion from benefit—Public policy—Murder of deceased).

MUSIC
　　Advancement of composer's works—
　　　　Trust for—
　　　　　　Whether charitable. *See* **Charity** (Benefit to community—Music—Advancement of composer's works).
　　Copyright. *See* **Copyright** (Musical work).
　　Licence. *See* **Entertainment** (Music and dancing licence).
　　Live performance—
　　　　Bootlegging recordings—
　　　　　　Person entitled to bring action to prevent bootlegging. *See* **Copyright** (Conflict of laws—Right of action—Bootlegging).

MUSIC (cont)—
    Training of singer—
        Gift to promote training of singers—
            Whether charitable purpose. *See* **Charity** (Benefit to community—Music—Training of singers).

MUSLIM
    Oath—
        Legal proceedings. *See* **Evidence** (Oath—Person who is neither Christian nor Jewish).

MUTINY
    Royal forces. *See* **Court-martial** (Mutiny).

MUTUAL DEALINGS
    Bankruptcy—
        Proof—
            Set-off. *See* **Bankruptcy** (Proof—Set-off—Mutual credits, mutual debts or other mutual dealings).
    Set-off—
        Insolvency. *See* **Insolvency** (Set-off—Mutual dealings).

MUTUAL MISTAKE
    See **Mistake** (Mutual mistake).

MUTUAL WILLS
    Generally. *See* **Will** (Mutual wills).

NAME
    Change—
        Minor's surname. *See* **Minor** (Change of surname).
        Parties to proceedings—
            Practice. *See* **Practice** (Parties—Change of name).
    Company—
        Generally. *See* **Company** (Name).
        Prohibited name. *See* **Company** (Prohibited name).
    Divorce—
        Custody—
            Change of surname. *See* **Divorce** (Custody—Change of surname).
    Election—
        Local government election—
            Nomination paper—Names of candidates. *See* **Elections** (Local government—Nomination papers—Names of candidates).
    Fictitious—
        Bank account opened in fictitious name. *See* **Criminal law** (Forgery—Cheque—Bank account opened in fictitious name).
    Magistrates—
        Policy of withholding names of justices. *See* **Magistrates** (Anonymity—Policy of withholding names of justices).
    Name of estate owner—
        Registration in incorrect name. *See* **Land charge** (Estate contract—Name of estate owner).
    Passing off—
        Descriptive name. *See* **Passing off** (Descriptive name).
        Geographical name. *See* **Passing off** (Geographical name).
        Name of maker—
            Use of own name. *See* **Passing off** (Name of maker).
        Trade name. *See* **Passing off** (Trade name).
    Trade mark—
        Infringement. *See* **Trade mark** (Infringement—Name).
    Will—
        Name and arms clause. *See* **Will** (Condition—Name and arms clause).

NAME AND ARMS CLAUSES
    Generally. *See* **Will** (Condition—Name and arms clause).
    Will—
        Revocation. *See* **Will** (Revocation—Conditional revocation—Name and arms clauses).

NARCOTIC DRUGS
    Drug trafficking. *See* **Drugs** (Drug trafficking).

NATIONAL ARBITRATION COUNCIL
    Trade dispute. *See* **Employment** (National Arbitration Tribunal).

NATIONAL ARBITRATION TRIBUNAL
    See **Employment** (National Arbitration Tribunal).

NATIONAL ASSISTANCE
    Bastardy order—
        Recovery of expenses. *See* Recovery of expenses—Application for bastardy order, *below*.
    Board—
        Affiliation proceedings by. *See* **Affiliation** (Application for order—National Assistance Board).
    Damages for personal injuries—
        Whether material assistance taken into account. *See* **Damages** (Personal injury—Loss of future earnings—National assistance).
    Recovery of cost of assistance from husband—
        Polygamous marriage—
            Separation of husband and wife—Polygamous marriage validly entered into according to the law of the spouses' domicil—Wife and children in receipt of national assistance—Whether sums recoverable from husband towards their maintenance—National Assistance Act 1948, ss 42(1)(a), 43(1). **Din v National Assistance Board** [1967] **1** 750, QBD.
        Separation of husband and wife—
            Deed of separation—Grant of national assistance to wife—Liability of husband to National Assistance Board—National Assistance Act 1948, ss 42(1)(a), 43(2). **National Assistance Board v Prisk** [1954] **1** 400, QBD.
            Deed of separation—Grant of national assistance to wife—Wife's covenant under deed not to claim any financial provision from husband—Liability of husband to National Assistance Board—National Assistance Act 1948, ss 42(1)(a), 43(1)(2). **National Assistance Board v Parkes** [1955] **1** 700, QBD; [1955] **3** 1, CA.
            No agreement and no misconduct—Difference between remedy of National Assistance Board for recovering cost of assistance and liability of husband for wilful neglect to maintain—National Assistance Act 1948, ss 42, 43—Summary Jurisdiction (Married Women) Act 1895, s 4. **Lilley v Lilley** [1959] **3** 283, CA.
            Polygamous marriage. *See* Recovery of cost of assistance from husband—Polygamous marriage, *above*.
        Wife deserting husband—
            National assistance given to wife—Liability of husband to National Assistance Board—National Assistance Act 1948, s 42(1)(a). **National Assistance Board (by J R Beattie) v Wilkinson** [1952] **2** 255, QBD.

NATIONAL ASSISTANCE (cont)—
  Recovery of expenses—
    Application for bastardy order—
      Right of National Assistance Board to apply—National Assistance Act 1948, s 44(2)(3). **National Assistance Board v Mitchell** [1955] **3** 291, QBD.
      Right of National Assistance Board to apply—Whether proof necessary that mother a single woman—National Assistance Act 1948, s 44(2). **National Assistance Board v Tugby** [1957] **1** 509, QBD.
  Supplementary benefit. *See* **Social security** (Supplementary benefit).

NATIONAL DEFENCE CONTRIBUTION
  Computation of profits—
    Chargeable accounting period—
      Underwriting agents—Commission not ascertainable and not payable until two years after underwriting of risk—When earned—Finance Act 1937, ss 19, 20 Sch IV, para 1. **Gardner, Mountain and D'Ambrumenil Ltd v IRC** [1947] **1** 650, HL.
    Deductions in computing profits—
      Payments made by company to retiring directors—Payments made in consideration of covenants in restraint of trade—Whether payments capital or revenue expenditure—Finance Act 1937, Sch IV. **Associated Portland Cement Manufacturers Ltd v IRC** [1946] **1** 68, CA.
      Repairs to premises—Premises kept open for business during rehabilitation work—Increased cost of work. **Mann, Crossman & Paulin Ltd v Compton (Inspector of Taxes), Same v IRC** [1947] **1** 742, KBD.
    Income received from investments or other property—
      Bank interest on current account—Whether excluded from computation—Finance Act 1937, Sch IV, para 7. **IRC v Imperial Tobacco Co (of GB and Ireland) Ltd** [1940] **3** 248, KBD.
      Income received by way of dividend from another company in which company having controlling interest—Controlling interest in company—Whether including indirect control—Finance Act 1937, Sch IV, paras 4, 7(b), 11. **British American Tobacco Co Ltd v IRC** [1941] **2** 651, CA; [1943] **1** 13, HL.
      Income received indirectly by way of dividend—Dividends received by British company from American company which held shares in British companies—Whether income received 'indirectly' from a company liable to be assessed to national defence contribution—Finance Act 1937, Sch IV para 7(a)(1). **Selection Trust Ltd v Devitt (Inspector of Taxes)** [1943] **2** 727, KBD.
      Royalties in respect of licence to manufacture patented aluminium alloy—Deduction of cost of alloy purchased—Finance Act 1937, Sch IV, para 7. **IRC v Rolls Royce Ltd** [1942] **1** 196, KBD.

NATIONAL ENTERPRISE BOARD
  Declaration—
    Breach of statutory duty. *See* **Originating summons** (Striking out—Declaration—Breach of statutory duty—Public corporation).

NATIONAL HEALTH INSURANCE
  Approved society—
    Power to institute proceedings on behalf of member—
      Accident to member of approved society—Proceedings not instituted by society—Whether duty of committee to institute proceedings on behalf of member—Whether society liable for failure to institute proceedings. **Butler v Alcock** [1941] **3** 411, CA.
  Dental benefit. *See* Medical and dental benefit, *below*.
  Employment—
    Persons in employment within statutory meaning—
      Canvasser—Payment of fixed sum weekly for expenses—Remuneration by payment of value of first order from new customers—Whether employment within meaning of National Health Insurance Act 1936—National Health Insurance Act 1936, Sch I. **Belcher, appeal of, Re Essex Flour and Grain Co Ltd** [1938] **3** 244, KBD.
      Employment by reference to contract of bailment—Bailee of motor car used for plying for hire—Whether in 'employment' of bailor—National Health Insurance Act 1936, s 161, Sch I, Part I, cl (e). **Thompson, Appeal of, Re Johnson (A) (Hove) Ltd** [1939] **4** 277, KBD.
      Lavatory attendant working two shifts a week—Whether employed as relief employee—National Health Insurance Act 1936, Sch I, Part II—National Health Insurance (Subsidiary Employments) Order 1932, (SR & O 1932 No 501). **Mackley, Appeal of** [1943] **2** 19, KBD.
      Sub-postmaster—Remuneration by scale payment—Whether compulsorily insurable—National Health Insurance Act 1936, Sch I. **Roberts, Re appeal of, Re Postmaster-General** [1939] **4** 269, KBD.
  Exemption—
    Person employed in military service of Crown—
      Territorial officer—Whether exempt. **Cousens, Re** [1938] **1** 17, KBD.
    Remuneration in excess of prescribed amount—
      Calculation of remuneration—Unpaid assistance of employee's wife—Whether value of such assistance may be deducted from remuneration—National Health Insurance Act 1936, s 161, Sch I, Part II, cl (k). **Sherwood, Appeal of, Re Brown (G F & A) & Sons Ltd** [1939] **4** 291, KBD.
  Failure to insure—
    Breach of statutory duty—
      Civil proceedings—Whether breach actionable at common law—National Health Insurance Act 1936, ss 1, 174(1). **Chadwick v Pioneer Private Telephone Co Ltd** [1941] **1** 522, Assizes.
  Insured person—
    Proof that insured person available for but unable to obtain employment—
      Franking of contribution card at labour exchange—Conclusive evidence of genuine unemployment—National Health Insurance Act 1924, s 3(3)(a)(b)—National Health Insurance Act 1928, s 1(3)—National Health Insurance (Arrears) Regulations 1930, (SR & O 1930 No 187)—Circular AS 267. **Donovan v National Amalgamated Approved Society** [1939] **2** 718, KBD Divl Ct.

NATIONAL HEALTH INSURANCE (cont)—

Medical and dental benefit—
  Dental benefit—
    Right of dentist to recover payment under statutory scheme—Dental treatment given to member of approved society by medical practitioner not on dentists' register—Whether dentist entitled to payment by approved society—Dentists Act 1921, s 1(3)(a)—Dental Benefit Regulations 1930, (S R & O 1930 No 1060), regs 2, 21(1). **Bynoe v General Federation of Trades Unions Approved Society (110)** [1937] **4** 184, CA.

NATIONAL HEALTH SERVICE

Act done in pursuance of public duty or authority—
  Limitation of action. *See* **Public authority** (Limitation of action).
Board of governors—
  Hospital. *See* Hospital—Board of governors, *below*.
Charges—
  England. *See* England—Charges, *below*.
Compensation to medical practitioner for loss of right to sell practice. *See* Medical practitioner—Compensation for loss of right to sell practice, *below*.
Consultant—
  Remuneration—
    Reports on candidates for Royal Ulster Constabulary—Examination of X-ray photographs of chests with a view to the prevention of tuberculosis in the constabulary—Duty assigned to whole-time consultant in tuberculosis and chest diseases employed under health service—Whether consultant entitled to remuneration in addition to fixed salary—National Health Service Terms and Conditions of Service of Hospital Medical and Dental Staff (England and Wales), dated 7th June 1949, para 14—Public Health (Tuberculosis) Act (Northern Ireland) 1946, s 2. **Northern Ireland Hospitals Authority v Whyte** [1963] **3** 343, HL.
Consultants and specialists—
  Position. *See* Specialist services—Duty of Minister to provide treatment by means of service of specialists—Position of consultants and specialists, *below*.
Contraception—
  Family planning clinics. *See* Family planning clinics—Contraception, *below*.
Drug—
  Supply of medicine or drug. *See* Pharmaceutical services—Supply of medicine or drug, *below*.
Duty to provide healthcare services—
  Abortion—
    Secretary of State failing to exercise power to enable United Kingdom citizens resident in Northern Ireland to undergo abortions in England free of charge—Whether unlawful—Whether breaching human rights—Whether justified—Human Rights Act 1998, Sch 1, Pt I, arts 8, 14—National Health Service Act 2006, ss 1, 3. **R (on the application of A) v Secretary of State for Health** [2017] **4** 353, SC.
  Right to respect for private and family life—
    Primary care trust—Policy—Primary care trust establishing general policy for authorisation of treatment—Primary care trust establishing policy requiring exceptionality for considering request for treatment falling outside general policy—Exceptionality determined exclusively by reference to clinical factors—Whether exclusion of social or non-clinical factors breach of right to respect for private and family life—Human Rights Act 1998, Sch 1, Pt I, art 8—National Health Service Act 2006. **R (on the application of Condliff) v North Staffordshire Primary Care Trust** [2012] **1** 689, CA.
England—
  Charges—
    Charges in respect of non-residents—Overseas visitor—Person not ordinarily resident in United Kingdom—Exemption from charges for overseas visitor lawfully resident in United Kingdom for period of not less than one year—Guidance issued by Secretary of State—Whether failed asylum seeker ordinarily resident—Whether person temporarily admitted to United Kingdom and lawfully present also lawfully resident—Whether guidance lawful—Immigration Act 1971, Sch 2, para 21—National Health Service Act 2006, ss 1, 175—National Health Service (Charges to Overseas Visitors) Regulations 1989, SI 1989/306, reg 4(1)(b). **R (on the application of YA) v Secretary of State for Health** [2010] **1** 87, CA.
    Charges in respect of non-residents—Overseas visitor—Regulations amended to provide advance payment and recording of information requirements—Public consultation on extension of charging of overseas visitors but no consultation on advance payment or recording of information requirements—Whether amendments unlawful—Whether legitimate expectation of consultation arising—National Health Service Act 2006, s 175—National Health Service (Charges to Overseas Visitors) Regulations 2015, SI 2015/238, regs 3(1A), 3A. **R (on the application of MP) v Secretary of State for Health and Social Care** [2021] **4** 326, CA.
Family planning clinics—
  Contraception—
    Circular containing guidance to area health authorities—Legality of advice contained in circular—Advice given regarding contraception for girls under 16—Whether doctor may give advice and treatment on contraception to girl under 16 without parental consent—Whether doctor committing criminal offence or acting unlawfully by giving advice on contraception to girl under 16—Whether doctor interfering with parental rights—Sexual Offences Act 1956, ss 6(1), 28(1). **Gillick v West Norfolk and Wisbech Area Health Authority** [1985] **3** 402, HL.
General medical services—
  Provision of general medical services to family health services authority—
    Whether medical practitioner providing services to authority pursuant to contract. **Roy v Kensington and Chelsea and Westminster Family Practitioner Committee** [1992] **1** 705, HL.
Gift—
  Legacy to hospital—
    Diversion of gift. *See* Legacy to hospital—Diversion of gift, *below*.

NATIONAL HEALTH SERVICE (cont)—
Health authority—
  Facilities appropriate as part of health service—
    Facilities for prevention of illness, care of persons suffering from illness and after-care of persons
    who have suffered from illness—Meaning of 'facilities'—National Health Service Act 1977,
    s 3(1)(e). **R (on the application of Keating) v Cardiff Local Health Board (Secretary of State for
    Health, intervening)** [2005] **3** 1000, CA.
  Nursing care—
    Respondent local authority providing appellant with carer to enable her to access commode at
    night—Authority seeking to reduce cost of appellant's care package by replacing night-time carer
    with incontinence pads—Whether authority in breach of statutory duty—Whether proposal
    violating appellant's right to private life—Whether authority's decision a 'practice, policy, or
    procedure' within meaning of disability discrimination legislation—Whether authority failing to
    have regard to the need to promote equality of opportunity for disabled persons—National
    Assistance Act 1948, s 29—National Health Service and Community Care Act 1990,
    s 47—Disability Discrimination Act 1995, ss 21, 49A—Human Rights Act 1998, Sch 1, Pt I, art 8.
    McDonald v Kensington and Chelsea Royal London BC [2011] **4** 881, SC.
    Whether provision of nursing care sole responsibility of health authorities—National Assistance Act
    1948, s 21—National Health Service Act 1977, ss 1, 3. **R v North and East Devon Health Authority,
    ex p Coughlan (Secretary of State for Health intervening)** [2000] **3** 850, CA.
Health Service Commissioner—
  Complaint—
    Investigation—Clinical judgment—Test to be applied in considering matters of clinical
    judgment—Whether test same as one applied for determining issues of clinical negligence—
    Whether commissioner had intimated that test to be applied should be same as one applied to
    issues of clinical negligence—Health Service Commissioners Act 1993, s 3(1). **R (on the
    application of Attwood) v Health Service Comr** [2009] **1** 415, QBD.
    Investigation—Powers of commissioner investigating complaint—Complaint made to commis-
    sioner in consequence of failure of health service body to provide a service—Commissioner
    bespeaking expert reports as to clinical judgment and practice—Expert reports criticising treating
    doctors—Report of commissioner based on expert reports—Whether investigation and report
    within commissioner's powers—Health Service Commissioners Act 1993, ss 3, 11. **R (on the
    application of Cavanagh) v Health Service Comr** [2006] **3** 543, CA.
Hospital—
  Board of governors—
    Occupation of property—Whether board of governors occupy premises of teaching hospital—
    National Health Service Act 1946, s 12(3). **Hills (Patents) Ltd v University College Hospital Board
    of Governors** [1955] **3** 365, CA.
  Endowment of bed—
    Absence of recognised amount and scheme—Acceptance by governors of sum subject to
    conditions of will. **Mills (decd), Re** [1953] **1** 835, Ch D.
  Institution for the reception and treatment of persons—
    Clinic maintained in connection with any such institution—Clinic maintained for treatment of
    out-patients—Not confined to ex-patients of any particular hospital—Whether a 'hospital'—
    National Health Service Act 1946, s 79(1). **Couchman's Will Trusts, Re** [1952] **1** 439, Ch D.
    Treatment—Home for incurables—Whether a 'hospital'—National Health Service Act 1946, ss 6(1),
    s 79(1). **Minister of Health v Royal Midland Counties Home for Incurables, Leamington Spa,
    General Committee** [1954] **1** 1013, CA.
  Legacy. *See* Legacy to hospital, *below.*
  Protection of members and officers against liability in respect of acts done in pursuance of statute—
    Scope of protection—Whether hospital group management committee liable for negligence of one
    of its servants—National Health Service Act 1946, s 72. **Bullard v Croydon Hospital Group
    Management Committee** [1953] **1** 596, QBD.
  Staff—
    Continuance of employment of consultant after nationalisation—Contract subject to terms and
    conditions of service issued by Minister—Termination of employment by regional hospital
    board—Non-compliance with clause of terms of service for reference to Minister before
    termination of employment—Remedies—Measure of damages—Declaration—Discretionary
    remedy—Breach of contract of employment—Breach of statutory duty under National Health
    Service Act 1946, ss 12, 14, 68. **Barber v Manchester Regional Hospital Board** [1958] **1** 322, QBD.
    Post-graduate training positions—International medical graduates—International medical gradu-
    ates allowed entry into United Kingdom for post-graduate training positions without work permit
    under permit-free training and highly skilled migrant programme schemes—Highly skilled
    migrants having leave for entry periodically renewed—Highly skilled migrants eligible for
    indefinite leave to remain after five years—Immigration Rules amended so that only United
    Kingdom medical school graduates could benefit from permit-free training—Secretary of State
    for Health issuing guidance that NHS Trusts should only offer post-graduate training posts to
    international medical graduates whose leave to remain in United Kingdom did not extend beyond
    duration of post if resident labour market test satisfied—Whether guidance lawful. **R (on the
    application of BAPIO Action Ltd) v Secretary of State for the Home Dept** [2009] **1** 93, HL.
    Terms and conditions of service—Dismissal—Hospital medical and dental staff—Representations
    against dismissal—Member of staff considering that employment being unfairly terminated—
    Terminated—Medical assistant—Appointment for two year period renewable, subject to
    confirmation, indefinitely—Medical assistant's appointment not confirmed—Whether appoint-
    ment being 'terminated'—Terms and Conditions of Service of Hospital Medical and Dental Staff
    (England and Wales) and Administrative Medical Staff of Regional Hospital Boards (England and
    Wales) (January 1971), para 190. **R v Secretary of State for Social Services, ex p Khan**
    [1973] **2** 104, CA.
  Vesting in Minister of Health—
    Effect—Charity—Whether hospital remaining a charity—National Health Service Act 1946,
    s 59(1)(2). **Frere (decd), Re** [1950] **2** 513, Ch D.

Legacy to hospital—
Continuance of work of hospital after National Health Service Act 1946—
Payment of legacy to body administering hospital under Act. **Meyers (decd), Re** [1951] **1** 538, Ch D.
Destruction of object—
Vesting of hospital in Minister of Health after date of will but before death of testator—National Health Service Act 1946, s 6. **Glass' Will Trusts, Re** [1950] **2** 953, Ch D; **Morgan's Will Trusts, Re** [1950] **1** 1097, Ch D.
Vesting of hospital in Minister of Health after death of testator but before legacy paid over. **Hunter (decd), Re** [1951] **1** 58, Ch D.
Diversion of gift—
Discretion to trustees to divert gift if hospital becomes amalgamated or absorbed—National Health Service Act 1946, ss 11(8), 60(1). **Bawdens Settlement, Re** [1953] **2** 1235, Ch D.
Discretion to trustees to divert gift if impracticable or inequitable in consequence of amalgamation—Effect of National Health Service Act 1946. **Hayes' Will Trusts, Re** [1953] **2** 1242, Ch D.
Gift of half share of residue of testator's estate to twelve named charities—
Proviso that if any of the charities ceased to exist as an independent charity fund to be divided among charities then in existance—Three of charities became subject to National Health Service Act 1946—Whether they ceased thereby to exist as independent charities. **Lowry's Will Trusts, Re** [1966] **3** 955, Ch D.
Gift of residue—
Gift 'to the trustees for the time being' of the hospital 'and by them to be appropriated for or towards the building funds' of the hospital—Vesting of hospital and endowment funds in Minister of Health after date of will, but before death of testatrix—National Health Service Act 1946, ss 6, 7(4). **Little (decd), Re** [1953] **2** 852, Ch D.
Gift of share of residue—
Estate fully administered—Right to require transfer of funds—National Health Service Act 1946, ss 60(1), 79(1). **Gartside, Re** [1949] **2** 546, Ch Ct, County Palatine of Lanc.
Gift 'to any three hospitals in Devon which are most in need of it'—'Need' of hospitals vested in Minister of Health—National Health Service Act 1946, s 54(1) (2). **Perreyman (decd), Re** [1953] **1** 223, Ch D.
Gift of share of residue to teaching hospital—
Gift to lapse if the funds should have come under 'government control'—National Health Service Act 1946, s 7(1)(2). **Buzzacott (decd), Re** [1952] **2** 1011, Ch D.
Institution taken over by State between death of testatrix and grant of probate—Disposition of gifts—Provisions for arbitration—'Rights to which any governing body were entitled immediately before the appointed day'—'Endownment' of hospital—Application of trust property in making payments to board of governors—National Health Service Act 1946, ss 6(1), 7(1) (10), 60(1)(a), 78(1)(c)—National Health Service (Apportionment and Transfer) Regulations 1948 (SI 1948 No 888), reg 30. **Kellner's Will Trusts, Re** [1949] **2** 774, CA.
Gift to hospital 'if not taken over by the State'—
Residuary gift to same hospital—Effect of condition on residuary gift. **Frere (decd), Re** [1950] **2** 513, Ch D.
Gift to medical school of hospital—
Gift over if hospital nationalised or passes into public ownership—Medical school not nationalised. **Royal College of Surgeons of England v National Provincial Bank Ltd** [1951] **1** 494, CA; [1952] **1** 984, HL.
'Specific purpose of hospital'—
Payment to board of governors—Gift to infirmary 'for the purposes of a home of rest for the nurses'—National Health Service Act 1946, s 60(1) (2). **White's Will Trusts, Re** [1951] **1** 528, Ch D.
Medical practitioner—
Compensation for loss of right to sell practice—
Assessment—Calculated by reference to the last two accounting years immediately preceding the appointed day—National Health Service Act 1946, s 36(1)—National Health Service (Medical Practices Compensation) Regulations 1948 (SI 1948 No 1506), reg 2(1), reg 7(2). **R v Minister of Health, ex p Dingle** [1950] **1** 875, KBD.
Assessment—Calculated by reference to the last two accounting years immediately preceding the appointed day—Powers of arbitrator—National Health Service Act 1946, s 36(1)—National Health Service (Medical Practices Compensation) Regulations 1948 (SI 1948 No 1506), reg 7(2)(a). **Carter v Minister of Health** [1950] **1** 904, KBD.
Disciplinary procedures—
Medical practitioners employed by NHS trusts—Professional capability—Professional conduct—Disciplinary policies—Guidance—Employer NHS trust carrying out disciplinary conduct process in relation to charges of gross misconduct by employee medical practitioner in breach of patient confidentiality—Whether disciplinary process fair. **West London Mental Health NHS Trust v Chhabra** [2014] **1** 943, SC.
Failure to comply with terms of service—
Recommendation by executive council to Minister of Health to withhold sum from practitioner's remuneration—Purported appeal by complainant to Minister on quantum of penalty—Application by practitioner for order of prohibition against proceeding with appeal—Implicit that appeal lay only against adverse decisions—National Health Service Act 1946, s 33—National Health Service (Service Committees and Tribunal) Regulations 1956 (SI 1956 No 1077), reg 7 (as amended by National Health Service (Service Committees and Tribunal) Amendment Regulations 1965 (SI 1965 No 1366)). **R v Minister of Health, ex p Ellis** [1967] **3** 65, QBD.
National disqualification—
Review of disqualification—Family Health Services Appeal Authority Tribunal—Scope of powers—National Health Service Act 1977, s 49N(7), (8). **Kataria v Essex Strategic Health Authority** [2004] **3** 572, QBD.
Partnership—
Goodwill—Clause in partnership agreement prohibiting retiring partner from carrying on practice within ten-mile radius—Validity—National Health Service Act 1946, s 35(1)—National Health Service (Amendment) Act 1949, s 1(1). **Whitehill v Bradford** [1952] **1** 115, CA.

NATIONAL HEALTH SERVICE (cont)—
  Medical practitioner (cont)—
    Partnership (cont)—
      Restraint of trade by agreement—Generally. *See* **Restraint of trade by agreement** (Partnership—
        Medical partnership—National Health Service practice).
  Medical records—
    Access to medical records by patient—
      Former psychiatric patient requesting access to his medical records—Health authorities refusing to
        allow direct access—Whether patient having unconditional right of access to his records at
        common law—Whether health authority entitled to deny patient access to his records if
        disclosure would be detrimental to his health. **R v Mid Glamorgan Family Health Services
        Authority, ex p Martin** [1995] **1** 356, CA.
  Medical school of hospital—
    Gift—
      Gift over if hospital nationalised or passes into public ownership. *See* Legacy to hospital—Gift to
        medical school of hospital—Gift over if hospital nationalised or passes into public ownership,
        above.
  Medicine—
    Supply of medicine or drug. *See* Pharmaceutical services—Supply of medicine or drug, *below.*
  Minister of Health—
    Hospital vesting in—
      Effect. *See* Hospital—Vesting in Minister of Health—Effect, *above.*
  National Health Service Commissioning Board—
    Commissioning of preventative medication—
      Anti-retroviral drug (PrEP) to be used on preventative basis for those at high risk of contracting
        AIDS—Whether defendant National Health Service Commissioning Board having power to
        commission preventative treatment for HIV—Whether provision of PrEP within 'public health
        functions' exception—National Health Service Act 2006, ss 1H, 2—National Health Service
        Commissioning Board and Clinical Commissioning Groups (Responsibilities and Standing Rules)
        Regulations 2012, SI 2012/2996, reg 11, Sch 4, para 17. **R (on the application of National Aids
        Trust) v National Health Service Commissioning Board (NHS England)** [2017] **3** 993, QBD and CA.
  Officer—
    Compensation for loss of employment—
      Factors to be considered—Application by clerk to hospital board—Also clerk to local
        authority—Consideration of service with local authority—National Health Service (Transfer of
        Officers and Compensation) Regulations 1948 (SI 1948 No 1475), reg 2. **R v Northumberland
        Compensation Appeal Tribunal, ex p Shaw** [1952] **1** 122, CA.
    Superannuation. *See* Superannuation of officers, *below.*
  Ophthalmic services—
    Ophthalmic optician—
      Qualification—Advisory committee—Duties and powers—Scope and method of investigation—
        National Health Service (Executive Council) Regulations 1947 (SR & O 1947 No 889), reg 19(2). **R
        v Central Professional Committee for Opticians, ex p Brown** [1949] **2** 519, KBD.
  Patented drug. *See* Pharmaceutical services—Supply of medicine or drug—Patented drug, *below.*
  Pension scheme—
    Maladministration. *See* **Pension** (Pension scheme—Maladministration of pension scheme—National
      Health Service).
  Pharmaceutical services—
    Supply of medicine or drug—
      Contractual relationship between chemist and National Health Service Executive Council that of
        contract for services—Supply of drug by chemist against a prescription—Whether a sale to
        executive council—Sliver of glass in bottle of medicine—Whether offence of selling drug out of
        the nature, etc demanded—National Health Service Act 1946, s 38—National Health Service
        (General Medical and Pharmaceutical Services) Regulations 1966 (SI 1966 No 1210), reg 23, Sch 4,
        Part 1—Food and Drugs Act 1955, s 2(1). **Appleby v Sleep** [1968] **2** 265, QBD.
      Patented drug—Drug supplied to hospital out-patients and prescribed charges made—Whether sale
        of drug to patient—National Health Service Act 1946, s 5. **Pfizer Corp v Ministry of Health**
        [1965] **1** 450, HL.
  Remuneration—
    Consultant. *See* Consultant—Remuneration, *above.*
  Reorganisation—
    Dissolution and establishment of NHS Trusts—
      Transfer order transferring all property rights and liabilities of dissolved NHS Trust to new NHS
        Trust—Whether transfer order transferring criminal liability—National Health Service and
        Community Care Act 1990, Sch 2, para 30. **R v Pennine Acute Hospitals NHS Trust** [2004] **1** 1324,
        CA.
    Transfer from local authorities to Minister of property held by local authorities for their former health
      functions—
      Determination of question whether immediately before 1 April 1974 property was held for health
        functions of a local authority—Question to be determined by 'the local authority' in which
        property was vested immediately before 1 April 1974—Whether determination can be made after
        appointed day—Whether determination can be made by local authority which only came into
        existence after appointed day under reorganisation of local government—National Health Service
        Reorganisation Act 1973, s 16(1)(2)—National Health Service (Transferred Local Authority
        Property) Order 1974, art 3(1). **Sheffield Area Health Authority v Sheffield City Council**
        [1983] **2** 384, QBD.
  Scotland—
    Proceedings against Scottish health board—
      Whether action against health board a proceeding against Crown. *See* **Crown** (Proceedings
        against—Health authority—Scottish Health Board).

NATIONAL HEALTH SERVICE (cont)—
Specialist services—
Duty of Minister to provide treatment by means of service of specialists—
Position of consultants and specialists—National Health Service Act 1946, s 3(1)(c). **Razzel v Snowball** [1954] **3** 429, CA.
Staff—
Hospital. *See* Hospital—Staff, *above.*
Superannuation of officers—
Determination of questions by Minister of Health—
Mental health officer—Shoemaker employed in mental hospital—Periodically in charge of working patients—Finality of determination of status by Minister—National Health Service Act 1946, s 67(1)(i)—National Health Service (Superannuation) Regulations 1950 (SI 1950 No 497), regs 1(3), 60. **Healey v Ministry of Health** [1954] **3** 449, CA.
Terms and conditions of service—
Hospital staff. *See* Hospital—Staff—Terms and conditions of service, *above.*
Transfer of hospital to Minister—
All hospitals vested in local authority—
All hospitals—National Health Service Act 1946, s 6(2). **Ministry of Health v Stafford Corp** [1952] **2** 386, CA.
Vested—Two local authorities respectively owning freehold and leasehold interests in hospital premises—Whether freehold interest vesting in Minister—National Health Service Act 1946, s 6(2). **Ministry of Health v Stafford Corp** [1952] **2** 386, CA.
Interests in voluntary hospitals—
'Interest held by trustees solely for the purposes of that hospital'—Trustees having liberty to pay or apply income of fund to or for a hospital until further order of court—National Health Service Act 1946, s 7(4) (10). **Galloway (decd), Re** [1952] **1** 1379, Ch Ct, County Palatine of Lanc.
Interest held by trustees solely for the purposes of that hospital—Power of trustees to sell property and apply proceeds of sale to other charitable purposes—National Health Service Act 1946, s 6(1). **Marjoribank's Indenture, Re** [1952] **1** 191, CA.
Interest held by trustees solely for the purposes of that hospital—Transfer of property and endowment—Power of trustees to divert property and endowment to other charitable purposes—National Health Service Act 1946, ss 6(1), 7(4). **Ministry of Health v Fox** [1950] **1** 1050, Ch D.

NATIONAL HOUSE-BUILDING COUNCIL
Guarantee required by council—
Construction. *See* **Guarantee** (Construction—Guarantee by housebuilding company's directors to National House-Building Council).

NATIONAL INDUSTRIAL RELATIONS COURT
Contempt of court—
Breach of injunction—
Evidence of contempt. *See* **Contempt of court** (Committal—Breach of injunction—Evidence of contempt—National Industrial Relations Court).
Generally. *See* **Industrial relations** (National Industrial Relations Court).
Precedent—
Decisions binding on court. *See* **Precedent** (National Industrial Relations Court).

NATIONAL INSURANCE
See **Social security.**

NATIONAL INSURANCE COMMISSIONER
Certiorari—
Jurisdiction. *See* **Certiorari** (Jurisdiction—National insurance commissioners).
Finality of decision. *See* **Social security** (Determination of claims and questions—Finality of decision of National Insurance Commissioner).

NATIONAL MINIMUM WAGE
See **Employment** (Remuneration—National minimum wage).

NATIONAL REGISTRATION
See **Emergency legislation** (National registration).

NATIONAL RULES
European Community. *See* **European Union** (National rules).

NATIONAL SAVINGS
Certificate—
Additions to sum invested—
Capital or income. *See* **Administration of estates** (Capital or income—National savings certificates).
Death of holder—
Transfer of certificate. **Note** [1954] **1** 519, .
National development bonds—
Dispute as to holding on register—
Reference to Chief Registrar of Friendly Societies—Bank having equitable charge over customer's holding of bonds, and an application for encashment signed by customer, as security for her overdraft—On failure to discharge overdraft bank applying to Director of Savings to encash bonds—Customer countermanding encashment order—Whether 'dispute' between Director of Savings and bank—Whether bank person 'claiming to be entitled' to the bonds—National Debt Act 1958, s 4(1). **R v Chief Registrar of Friendly Societies, ex p Mills** [1970] **3** 1076, QBD.
National Savings Bank investment deposit account—
Attachment of money in judgment debtor's account. *See* **Execution** (Attachment of money payable by Crown to judgment debtor—Jurisdiction—National Savings Bank investment deposit account).

NATIONAL SECURITY

Civil proceedings—
 Closed material procedure. *See* **Practice** (Civil litigation—Closed material procedure).
Deportation of alien—
 Natural justice—
  Validity of order. *See* **Alien** (Deportation—Order—Validity—Natural justice—Deportation in the interest of national security).
Deportation of immigrant on grounds of—
 Appeal. *See* **Immigration** (Appeal—Deportation—Appeal against deportation on grounds of national security).
Deprivation of citizenship. *See* **Citizenship** (British citizen—Deprivation of citizenship—Dual national—Deprivation of British citizenship on grounds of national security).
Disclosure and inspection of documents—
 Closed material procedure. *See* **Disclosure and inspection of documents** (Privilege—Production contrary to public interest—Disclosure of sensitive material—Closed material procedure).
 Public interest immunity. *See* **Disclosure and inspection of documents** (Privilege—Production contrary to public interest).
 Sensitive material. *See* **Disclosure and inspection of documents** (Privilege—Production contrary to public interest—Disclosure of sensitive material).
Employment tribunal—
 Right to a fair trial. *See* **Employment tribunal** (Procedure—Right to a fair trial—Interests of national security).
Exercise of prerogative on grounds of national security—
 Judicial review. *See* **Judicial review** (Availability of remedy—National security).
Interception of communications. *See* **Telecommunications** (Interception of communications—Directions in the interests of national security).
Judicial review—
 Availability of remedy. *See* **Judicial review** (Availability of remedy—National security).
Port and border controls—
 Terrorism, prevention of. *See* **Terrorism** (Prevention of—Port and border controls).
Risk to national security—
 Suspicion that a person is a terrorist—
  Secretary of State issuing certificate and detaining person suspected of being a terrorist—Special Immigration Appeals Commission cancelling certificate—Whether reasonable grounds existing for belief that the person's presence a risk to national security and suspicion that he was a terrorist—Whether suspicious circumstances necessarily establishing reasonable suspicion—Anti-terrorism, Crime and Security Act 2001, ss 21(1), 25. **M v Secretary of State for the Home Dept** [2004] **2** 863, CA.

NATIONAL SERVICE

Call up—
 British subjects—
  Ordinarily resident in Great Britain—Exception—Residence for temporary purpose—Residence in Great Britain for more than two years—Citizen of Republic of Ireland—Domicil in Ireland and intention to return thereto—Whether liable to be called up—National Service Act 1948, s 34(4)(b)(c)—British Nationality Act 1948 s 3(2)—Ireland Act 1949, ss 3(1)(a)(i), 3(2)(a). **Bicknell v Brosnan** [1953] **1** 1126, QBD.
  Person domiciled in Eire—Whether subject to be called up for service—British Nationality and Status of Aliens Act 1914, s 1(1)(a)—Irish Free State (Agreement) Act 1922—Irish Free State Constitution Act 1922—Eire (Confirmation of (Agreements) Act 1938—National Service (Armed Forces) Act 1939, s 1. **Murray v Parkes** [1942] **1** 558, KBD.
 Deferment—
  False statement—Liability of secretary of company—National Service (Armed Forces) Act 1939, s 16(a). **Dellow v Busby** [1942] **2** 439, KBD Divl Ct.
Conscientious objector—
 Registration—
  Failure to comply with condition of registration—Reasonable excuse—Exemption from requirement to register—Minister of religious denomination—Claim to exemption not proceeded with at time of registration—As registered conscientious objector minister bound to comply with condition—National Service (Armed Forces) Act 1939, ss 5(6)(b), 11(1)(e)—National Service Act 1941. **Emery v Sage** [1943] **1** 509, KBD.
Exemption from National Service—
 Regular minister of religious denomination—
  Jehovah's Witnesses—Whether regular minister of a religious denomination—National Service Act 1948, Sch In para 2. **Walsh v Lord Advocate** [1956] **3** 129, HL.
Medical examination—
 Notice requiring person to submit to medical examination—
  Failure to comply with notice—Conscientious objector—Refusal to undergo medical examination—Punishment—Probation—Jurisdiction to deal with offence under Probation of Offenders Act 1907—National Service (Armed Forces) Act 1939, ss 4, 5. **Eversfield v Story** [1942] **1** 268, KBD.
Reinstatement in civil employment—
 Decision of umpire—
  Dissatisfaction of employer—Certiorari—Reinstatement in Civil Employment Act 1944, ss 1(1), 9(1)(2), 10(1)(2). **R v Ludlow, ex p Barnsley Corp** [1947] **1** 880, KBD.
Reserved occupation—
 Enlistment notice—
  Claim to be in reserved occupation—Whether Schedule of Reserved Occupations binding upon the Minister—National Service (Armed Forces) Act 1939. **Roeder v Bevin** [1942] **2** 90, CA.

NATIONAL SERVICE (cont)—
　　Termination of civilian employment—
　　　Restriction on employers terminating employment by reason of duties employees may be liable to
　　　　perform or discharge—
　　　　　Regulations making it offence—Dismissal of conscientious objector—Validity of regulation—
　　　　　　Whether employers in breach of regulation—National Service (Armed Forces) Act 1939, ss 5
　　　　　　14(4)—National Service (Armed Forces) Prevention of Evasion Regulations 1939, (S R & O 1939
　　　　　　No 1099) reg 2(1)(a)(b) (2). **Downsborough v Huddersfield Industrial Society Ltd** [1941] **3** 434,
　　　　　　KBD.

NATIONAL SOCIETY FOR THE PREVENTION OF CRUELTY TO CHILDREN
　　Disclosure of documents—
　　　Privilege—
　　　　Confidential information—Public interest. See **Disclosure and inspection of documents**
　　　　　(Privilege—Production contrary to public interest—Persons entitled to resist disclosure on ground
　　　　　of public interest—Bodies other than central departments of government—Society incorporated
　　　　　by royal charter for protection of children).

NATIONAL TRUST
　　Enclosure of common land—
　　　Nuisance. See **Nuisance** (Land—Enclosure of common land—National Trust).
　　Restrictive covenant—
　　　Discharge or modification. See **Restrictive covenant affecting land** (Discharge or modification—Status
　　　　of covenantee—National Trust).

NATIONALISATION
　　Anti-nationalisation campaign—
　　　Deduction of expenses for tax purposes. See **Income tax** (Deduction in computing profits—Expenses
　　　　wholly and exclusively laid out for purposes of trade—Prevention of seizure of business by
　　　　state—Anti-nationalisation campaign).
　　Coal mining industry. See **Coal mining** (Nationalisation of industry).
　　Compensation—
　　　Income tax—
　　　　Annual payment. See **Income tax** (Annual payment—Compensation for nationalisation).
　　Compulsory acquisition of property—
　　　Act of State. See **Constitutional law** (Act of State—Acts of foreign government—Justiciability in English
　　　　courts—Foreign government nationalising claimant company).
　　Contract—
　　　Frustration. See **Contract** (Frustration—Nationalisation).
　　Denationalisation—
　　　Compensation—
　　　　Iron and steel industry. See **Iron and steel industry** (Compensation—Denationalisation).
　　Electricity. See **Electricity** (Nationalisation).
　　Foreign—
　　　No compensation—
　　　　Application to register trade mark. See **Trade mark** (Opposition to registration—Confusion—
　　　　　Contrary to morality—Mark formerly used by opponent in connection with his business in
　　　　　Czechoslovakia and Central Europe—Business nationalised in 1948 by Czechoslovakian law).
　　Foreign government, by—
　　　Act of State. See **Constitutional law** (Act of State—Acts of foreign government—Justiciability in English
　　　　courts—Foreign government nationalising claimant company).
　　Gas. See **Gas** (Nationalisation).
　　Property abroad—
　　　Compensation—
　　　　Claim. See **Foreign compensation** (Claim—Nationalisation or expropriation).

NATIONALITY
　　Adoption—
　　　Relevant consideration. See **Adoption** (Order—Discretion—Nationality).
　　British nationality—
　　　Acquisition. See **Alien** (British nationality—Acquisition).
　　　Citizenship. See **Citizenship** (British citizen).
　　Citizenship. See **Citizenship**.
　　Discrimination on grounds of—
　　　European Community—
　　　　Corporation tax. See **European Union** (Freedom of establishment—Discrimination on grounds of
　　　　　nationality—Corporation tax).
　　　　Freedom of establishment—Principle of non-discrimination. See **European Union** (Freedom of
　　　　　establishment—Principle of non-discrimination).
　　　　Generally. See **European Union** (Discrimination—Discrimination on grounds of nationality).
　　　　Principle of non-discrimination. See **European Union** (Freedom of establishment—Principle of
　　　　　non-discrimination).
　　　　Security for costs. See **European Union** (Costs—Security for costs—Discrimination on grounds of
　　　　　nationality).
　　　　Workers. See **European Union** (Workers—Freedom of movement—Discrimination on grounds of
　　　　　nationality).
　　Divorce—
　　　Jurisdiction based on nationality—
　　　　Recognition of foreign decree. See **Divorce** (Foreign decree—Recognition by English court—Basis
　　　　　of recognition—Nationality and habitual residence).

NATIONALITY (cont)—
  Dual nationality—
    Citizenship—
      European Union. *See* **European Union** (Citizenship—Freedom to reside and move freely within territory of member states—Dual nationality).
  Enemy alien—
    Deprivation of nationality—
      Recognition by English courts—Deprivation by decree of enemy state in wartime—Public policy precluding recognition of change of status—Recognition once war terminated—War terminating as soon as fighting ceases. **Oppenheimer v Cattermole (Inspector of Taxes)** [1975] **1** 538, HL.
    Naturalisation during war—
      Alien becoming naturalised British subject—Compatability of allegiance to Crown with allegiance to enemy state—Whether alien ceasing in English law to be national of enemy state on naturalisation. **Oppenheimer v Cattermole (Inspector of Taxes)** [1975] **1** 538, HL.
  Fugitive offender—
    Extradition—
      Possibility, if returned, of punishment by reason of nationality. *See* **Extradition** (Fugitive offender—Restrictions on return—Punishment by reason of race, religion, nationality or political opinions).
  National origins—
    Discrimination on grounds of national origins—
      European Community—Workers. *See* **European Union** (Workers—Freedom of movement—Discrimination on grounds of nationality).
      Generally. *See* **Race relations** (Discrimination).

NATIVE COURTS
  West Africa—
    Jurisdiction. *See* **West Africa** (Courts—Native courts—Jurisdiction).

NATIVE LANDS
  Alienation—
    Nigeria. *See* **Nigeria** (Native lands in Lagos—Alienation of land).
  Dealing with native land—
    Meaning of dealing—
      Fiji. *See* **Fiji** (Land—Dealing with land—Native land).
  Statutory charge on—
    Validity—
      New Zealand. *See* **New Zealand** (Native lands—Charge on lands—Statutory charge).

NATURAL GAS
  Crown rights. *See* **Petroleum rights** (Crown—Rights vested in Crown—Petroleum and natural gas situated inside and outside territorial waters).

NATURAL HAZARD
  Nuisance. *See* **Nuisance** (Natural processes).

NATURAL JUSTICE
  Adjudicator—
    Bias—
      Adjudicator adjudicating on issue without jurisdiction—Adjudicator acquiring jurisdiction and adjudicating on same issue—Whether apparent bias. **AMEC Capital Projects Ltd v Whitefriars City Estates Ltd** [2005] **1** 723, CA.
  Affiliation order—
    Enforcement. *See* **Affiliation** (Affiliation order—Enforcement—Natural justice).
  Appeal—
    Appeal from domestic tribunal—
      Composition of appellate body. *See* Domestic tribunal—Appeal, *below*.
  Architect's notice. *See* **Building contract** (Architect—Architect's notice—Requirements of natural justice).
  Bahamas Public Disclosure Commission—
    Duty to hear parties etc. *See* Hearing—Duty to hear parties etc—Bahamas Public Disclosure Commission, *below*.
  Bias—
    Professional regulatory body. *See* Professional regulatory body, *below*.
  Board of Trade investigation of company's affairs—
    Proceedings before inspectors. *See* **Company** (Investigation by Board of Trade—Proceedings before inspectors—Natural justice).
  British Boxing Board of Control. *See* Domestic tribunal—British Boxing Board of Control, *below*.
  Chief constable—
    Dismissal by watch committee—
      Whether rules of natural justice applicable to proceedings. *See* **Police** (Chief constable—Dismissal—Natural justice).
  College—
    Dismissal of student. *See* **Education** (College—Governing body—Natural justice).
  Commission for Racial Equality—
    Investigation of complaint—
      Duty to act fairly. *See* **Race relations** (Investigation of complaint—Commission for Racial Equality—Duty to act fairly).
  Company—
    Board of Trade investigation—
      Appointment of inspectors. *See* **Company** (Investigation by Board of Trade—Appointment of inspectors—Natural justice).
      Proceedings before inspectors. *See* **Company** (Investigation by Board of Trade—Proceedings before inspectors—Natural justice).

NATURAL JUSTICE (cont)—

Company (cont)—
    Director—
        Disqualification—Notice of allegations required to be given to director sought to be disqualified. **Lo-Line Electric Motors Ltd, Re** [1988] 2 692, Ch D.
    Expulsion from company—
        Absolute and unfettered power to expel conferred by articles—Property rights livelihood or reputation not infringed by expulsion—Whether natural justice ousted by express terms of articles. **Gaiman v National Association for Mental Health** [1970] 2 362, Ch D.
Compulsory purchase order—
    Inquiry following objection to order—
        Inquiry conducted in breach of rules of natural justice—Ground for quashing order. *See* **Housing** (Quashing of clearance order or compulsory purchase order—Requirement of Act not complied with—Natural justice).
Crown Court—
    Binding over order—
        Whether court required to give defendant opportunity to make representations against order. *See* **Crown Court** (Binding over—Powers of court—Terms of order—Opportunity to make representations against order).
Deportation of alien—
    Validity of order. *See* **Alien** (Deportation—Order—Validity—Natural justice).
Disciplinary board—
    Legal advice to board—
        Presence of parties—Hong Kong—Architect—Disciplinary board consisting of three authorised architects, the building authority and a legal adviser—Legal adviser having conduct of inquiry—Deliberation of board in private on submissions made on behalf of architect—Rulings given by legal adviser in presence of parties after deliberations concluded—Whether any legal advice given to board by legal adviser must be given in presence of parties and so to appear on the record—Whether breach of rules of natural justice—Hong Kong Buildings Ordinance 1955, (No 68 of 1955), s 5B(2). **Chien Sing-Shou, Re** [1967] 2 1228, PC.
Disclosure to parties of information before court—
    Court empowered to seek information—
        Power to withhold information from parties—Whether fair hearing in accordance with principles of fundamental Justice—Industrial Stabilisation Act 1965, (Trinidad and Tobago) (No 8 of 1965), s 11(2) (as substituted by Act No 6 of 1967)—Trinidad and Tobago (Constitution) Order in Council 1962, (SI 1962 No 1875) Sch 2, s 2(e). **Collymore v A-G of Trinidad and Tobago** [1969] 2 1207, PC.
    Wardship proceedings—
        Discretion of court to withhold confidential reports—Letter written by social worker to court registrar not disclosed to applicant—Disclosure not harmful to children—Court relying on letter to reach its conclusions—Whether court in breach of rules of natural justice. **B v W (wardship: appeal)** [1979] 3 83, HL.
Dismissal—
    Employee, of—
        Public authority. *See* Public authority—Dismissal of employee, *below.*
    Schoolmaster, of. *See* **Tribunal** (Membership—Bias—Inquiry into dismissal).
    Student, of—
        Duty to hear parties etc. *See* Educational establishment—Dismissal of student, *below.*
Divorce—
    Foreign decree obtained under duress. *See* **Divorce** (Foreign decree—Invalidity—Basis of invalidity—Lack of consent to divorce proceedings—Duress).
Domestic tribunal—
    Appeal—
        Composition of appellate body—Appellate body hearing appeal from domestic tribunal—Whether member of domestic tribunal disabled from sitting on appeal from tribunal's decision. **Hamlet v General Municipal Boilermakers and Allied Trades Union** [1987] 1 631, Ch D.
    British Boxing Board of Control—
        Application for manager's licence—Reasons for refusal of licence not given—Request for oral hearing not granted—Whether board required to give applicant an oral hearing—Whether board required to give reasons for refusing licence. **McInnes v Onslow Fane** [1978] 3 211, Ch D.
    Dismissal of schoolmaster. *See* **Tribunal** (Membership—Bias).
    Expulsion from union. *See* **Trade union** (Expulsion of member).
    Jockey club—
        Appeal—Effect of appeal—Stewards' inquiry—Owner disqualified from running horses and from membership of Jockey Club—Conduct of stewards' inquiry not in accordance with rules of natural justice—Appeal by owner to committee of club—Hearing de novo—Whether committee had jurisdiction to hear appeal from stewards' decision if decision void—Whether defects in stewards' inquiry could be cured by fair hearing of appeal. **Calvin v Carr** [1979] 2 440, PC.
        Withdrawal of trainer's licence—Discretion of Jockey Club to withdraw licence—Need to hold inquiry before withdrawal—Conduct of inquiry according to rules of natural justice. **Russell v Duke of Norfolk** [1949] 1 109, CA.
    Legal representation—
        Appeal to tribunal on point of law—Refusal by tribunal to allow represenation—Declaration more appropriate remedy than appeal. **Enderby Town Football Club Ltd v Football Association Ltd** [1971] 1 215, CA.
        Inquiry into matter affecting licence-holder's reputation and livelihood—National club rules silent as to procedure—Stewards of dog racing track inquiring into doping of dog and requiring trainer's presence at inquiry—Whether trainer entitled to oral hearing—Whether entitled to be represented by counsel and solicitor. **Pett v Greyhound Racing Association Ltd** [1968] 2 545, CA.

NATURAL JUSTICE (cont)—
  Domestic tribunal (cont)—
    Legal representation (cont)—
      Inquiry into matter affecting licence-holder's reputation and livelihood—National club rules silent as to procedure—Stewards of dog-racing track inquiring into drugging of dog and requiring trainer's presence at inquiry—Whether trainer entitled to be represented by counsel and solicitor—Duties of domestic tribunal exercising quasi-judicial powers—Whether requirements of natural justice included legal representation. **Pett v Greyhound Racing Association Ltd (No 2)** [1969] 2 221, QBD.
    Political party—
      National Executive Committee of Labour Party—Resolution to 'suspend activities' of constituency party—No charges made and no opportunity of being heard—Whether contrary to principles of natural justice. **John v Rees** [1969] 2 274, Ch D.
      National Executive Committee of Labour Party—Resolution to suspend constituency officers and committees pending enquiry—Persons concerned given no opportunity to be heard before suspensions became effective—Whether breach of rules of natural justice. **Lewis v Heffer** [1978] 3 354, CA.
    Procedure—
      No rules prescribed. *See* **Tribunal** (Procedure—No rules prescribed).
    Trade union. *See* Trade union, *below*.
  Duty to act fairly—
    Commission for Racial Equality—
      Investigation of complaint. *See* **Race relations** (Investigation of complaint—Commission for Racial Equality—Duty to act fairly).
    Consultation—
      Local authority conducting consultation on new council tax reduction scheme—Local authority adopting new scheme following consultation—Whether authority complying with statutory duty to consult—Local Government Finance Act 1992, Sch 1A, para 3(1)(c). **R (on the application of Moseley) v Haringey London BC** [2015] 1 495, SC.
    Equal treatment—
      Judicial review—Office of Fair Trading making mistaken assurance to one respondent in investigation of tobacco market—OFT subsequently repaying penalties paid by that party but not penalties paid by other respondents—Whether principle of equal treatment requiring OFT to replicate mistake—Relevance of 'conspicuous unfairness'. **R (on the application of Gallaher Group Ltd) v Competition and Markets Authority** [2018] 4 183, SC.
    Immigration officer—
      Admission of Commonwealth immigrant. *See* **Commonwealth immigrant** (Admission—Refusal of admission—Discretion of immigration officer—Duty to act fairly).
    Local authority—
      Closure of residential care home—Consultation with permanent residents. *See* **Local authority** (Residential care home—Elderly persons—Closure of local authority home—Consultation—Duty to act fairly).
      Permission for development of land by local authority. *See* **Town and country planning** (Permission for development—Development by local authority—Duty to act fairly).
  Duty to act openly, impartially and fairly—
    Hackney carriage—
      Grant of licence. *See* **Road traffic** (Hackney carriage—Licence—Grant of licence—Natural justice).
  Duty to hear parties. *See* Hearing—Duty to hear parties, *below*.
  Educational establishment—
    Complaint against teacher—
      Duty to hear parties etc—Preliminary investigation—Complaint to school board—Board under statutory duty to appoint sub-committee to make preliminary investigation of complaint—Sub-committee reporting to board in accordance with statutory duty—Teacher knowing nothing of complaint and having no opportunity of making representations to sub-committee—Board suspending teacher following report—Charges referred to disciplinary committee for final determination—Teacher having right to a hearing before disciplinary committee—Whether teacher having right to be heard before decision to suspend taken—Education Act 1964 (New Zealand), s 158—Secondary and Technical Institute Teachers Disciplinary Regulations 1969 (New Zealand), regs 4, 5. **Furnell v Whangarei High Schools Board** [1973] 1 400, PC.
    Dismissal of student—
      Duty to hear parties etc—College—Academic board—Board composed of heads of department and other academic staff—Board having power to recommend dismissal of student on academic grounds—Board recommending dismissal of student—Board taking into account adverse comments by tutors on student's performance and capabilities—Student not accorded hearing before recommendation made—Whether breach of rules of natural justice. **Herring v Templeman** [1973] 3 569, CA.
      Duty to hear parties etc—University—Student sent down for failing examination—Whether student to be heard in defence before decision to send down. **R v Senate of the University of Aston, ex p Roffey** [1969] 2 964, QBD.
    Inquiry into examination offence—
      Principal witness not tendered by commission of inquiry for cross-examination by alleged offender—Whether failure to comply with principles of natural justice. **University of Ceylon v Fernando** [1960] 1 631, PC.
    Suspension of student—
      Duty to hear parties etc—University—Quasi-judicial function—Vice-Chancellor—Power to suspend students—Exercise of power quasi-judicial function—Decision to exclude student from residence—No opportunity given to student to be heard—Whether decision breach of rules of natural justice—Whether decision a matter of internal discipline. **Glynn v Keele University** [1971] 2 89, Ch D.
  Employment—
    Suspension of employee. *See* **Employment** (Suspension).

NATURAL JUSTICE (cont)—
  Evidence—
    Duty to hear and consider evidence—
      Board set up by statute for (among other functions) determining zoning orders—Committee appointed by board to investigate and report—Committee held public hearing—Report did not state evidence—Evidence not taken, and written evidence not considered, by board—Recommendation of committee adopted by board—Zoning order quashed. **Jeffs v New Zealand Dairy Production and Marketing Board** [1966] **3** 863, PC.
      Industrial injuries tribunal. *See* Industrial injuries tribunal—Evidence, *below*.
  Expulsion from company. *See* Company—Expulsion from company, *above*.
  Expulsion from trade union—
    Curability of deficiency of natural justice before trial tribunal. *See* Trade union—Deficiency of natural justice before trial tribunal—Curability, *below*.
    Generally. *See* **Trade union** (Expulsion of member).
  Extradition—
    Committal. *See* **Extradition** (Committal—Power of magistrate to refuse to commit fugitive—Natural justice).
  Gaming Board for Great Britain—
    Application to board for gaming licence—
      Duty of board to observe rules of natural justice. *See* **Gaming** (Licensing of premises—Application for licence—Certificate of consent for purposes of application for licence—Whether Gaming Board for Great Britain bound to observe rules of natural justice).
  General Medical Council—
    Disciplinary committee. *See* **Medical practitioner** (Disciplinary committee—Natural justice).
  Hearing—
    Duty to hear parties etc—
      Airports authority—Mini-cab driver prohibited from entering airport—No opportunity to protest given to driver—Whether driver having legitimate expectation of being heard—Whether rules of natural justice observed. **Cinnamond v British Airports Authority** [1980] **2** 368, CA.
      Bahamas Public Disclosure Commission—Complaint as to incomplete declarations of financial affairs—Whether complainant entitled to be given opportunity to rebut finding of commission—Public Disclosure Act 1976 (Bahamas). **Public Disclosure Commission v Isaacs** [1989] **1** 137, PC.
      Company—Investigation by Board of Trade—Appointment of inspectors. *See* **Company** (Investigation by Board of Trade—Appointment of inspectors—Natural justice—Duty to hear parties).
      Company—Investigation by Board of Trade—Proceedings before inspectors. *See* **Company** (Investigation by Board of Trade—Proceedings before inspectors—Natural justice—Duty to hear parties).
      Crown Court—Binding over order. *See* **Crown Court** (Binding over—Powers of court—Terms of order—Opportunity to make representations against order).
      Determination whether prima facie case—No hearing. *See* **Income tax** (Tax advantage—Counteracting—Tribunal—Determination whether there is a prima facie case—Procedure—Determination on documents).
      Educational establishment. *See* Educational establishment, *above*.
      Hong Kong Immigration Authority—Illegal immigrant—Government announcement that each illegal immigrant's case would be dealt with on its own merits—Order made for removal of applicant as an illegal immigrant without giving him a hearing—Whether announcement creating legitimate or reasonable expectation of a hearing—Whether applicant entitled to hearing before removal. **A-G of Hong Kong v Ng Yuen Shiu** [1983] **2** 346, PC.
      Immigration adjudicator—Applicant deprived of hearing through negligence of his own solicitors—Adjudicator not at fault—Whether breach of rules of natural justice—Whether adjudicator's decision subject to judicial review. **Al-Mehdawi v Secretary of State for the Home Dept** [1989] **3** 843, HL.
      Immigration adjudicator—Applicant not given hearing through fault of her own advisers—Adjudicator not at fault—Whether breach of rules of natural justice—Whether adjudicator's decision reviewable. **Rahmani v Diggines** [1985] **1** 1073, CA.
      Income tax appeal. *See* **Income tax** (Appeal—Hearing—Natural justice—Duty to hear parties).
      Income tax tribunal. *See* Income tax tribunal, *below*.
      Legitimate expectation—Immigration—Secretary of State issuing circular setting out criteria and procedure for certain entrants—Secretary of State applying different criteria and procedure to applicant—Whether circular creating legitimate expectation that Secretary of State would apply criteria and procedure set out in it—Whether Secretary of State entitled to apply different criteria. **R v Secretary of State for the Home Dept, ex p Khan** [1985] **1** 40, CA.
      Magistrates. *See* Magistrates—Duty to hear parties etc, *below*.
      Opportunity to be heard—Secretary of State granting permit enabling Romanian pilots to operate charter aircraft to and from United Kingdom—Secretary of State provisionally suspending permit pending inquiry into Romanian licence requirements and pilots' ability to comply with them—Interested parties given no opportunity to be heard prior to suspension—Whether emergency involving safety of aircraft and passengers outweighing duty to hear parties—Whether Secretary of State's action reasonable. **R v Secretary of State for Transport, ex p Pegasus Holidays (London) Ltd** [1989] **2** 481, QBD.
      Opportunity to be heard—Tribunal wishing to proceed on point not put before it—Necessity for person affected to be alerted to tribunal's intention. **R v Mental Health Review Tribunal, ex p Clatworthy** [1985] **3** 699, QBD.
      Public inquiry. *See* Public inquiry—Duty to hear parties, *below*.
      Rent assessment committee. *See* Rent assessment committee—Duty to hear parties, *below*.
      Royal Commission. *See* Royal Commission—Duty to hear parties, *below*.
    Presence of parties—
      Deliberations of committee exercising quasi-judicial functions—Prosecuting party present during deliberations of committee—Accused party absent when evidence against him given to committee—Whether breach of rules of natural justice. **R v Barnsley Metropolitan BC, ex p Hook** [1976] **3** 452, CA.

NATURAL JUSTICE (cont)—
    Immigration—
        Leave to remain. *See* **Immigration** (Leave to remain—Natural justice).
    Immigration officer—
        Admission of Commonwealth immigrant. *See* **Commonwealth immigrant** (Admission—Refusal of admission—Discretion of immigration officer—Duty to act fairly).
        Examination of entrant. *See* **Immigration** (Immigration officer—Examination of entrant—Natural justice).
    Income tax tribunal—
        Duty to hear parties etc—
            Determination of prima facie case—Determination an administrative decision—No requirement that in determining whether prima facie case tribunal must hear both parties—Duty of tribunal to act fairly. **Pearlberg v Varty (Inspector of Taxes)** [1972] **2** 6, HL.
    Industrial injuries tribunal—
        Evidence—
            Oral hearing—Further medical evidence obtained by tribunal after hearing and before decision—Parties not informed—Whether failure to comply with principles of natural justice. **R v Deputy Industrial Injuries Comr, ex p Jones** [1962] **2** 430, QBD.
            Oral hearing—Medical opinions in previous cases put to expert witnesses—Incorporation of previous medical opinions in decision of industrial injuries commissioner—Whether failure to comply with principles of natural justice. **R v Deputy Industrial Injuries Comr, ex p Moore** [1965] **1** 81, CA.
    Inquiry into examination offence. *See* Educational establishment—Inquiry into examination offence, *above*.
    Jockey Club. *See* Domestic tribunal—Jockey club, *above*.
    Judge—
        Bias—
            Apparent bias—Circumstances capable of giving rise to possibility of bias on part of judge—Guidance. **Taylor v Lawrence** [2002] **2** 353, CA.
            Apparent bias—Judge a member of international association of Jewish lawyers and jurists—Judge dismissing petition for review of refusal of leave to appeal against refusal of asylum claim by supporter of Palestinian Liberation Organisation—Whether apparent bias. **Helow v Secretary of State for the Home Dept** [2009] **2** 1031, HL.
            Apparent bias—Judge sitting on aborted criminal trial and making number of rulings—Defendants convicted following subsequent retrial—Judge from aborted trial sitting on appeal from retrial—Whether apparent bias—Whether judge ought to have recused himself. **R v Stubbs** [2019] **1** 581, PC.
            Apparent bias—Waiver—Circumstances capable of giving rise to possibility of bias on part of judge—Requirements for valid waiver. **Smith v Kvaerner Cementation Foundations Ltd (Bar Council intervening)** [2006] **3** 593, CA.
            Apparent bias—Witness proposed to be called during trial personally known to judge—Whether judge should recuse himself from trying case—Whether judge having discretion. **AWG Group Ltd v Morrison** [2006] **1** 967, CA.
            Disqualification of judge on grounds of bias—Principles and guidelines. **Locabail (UK) Ltd v Bayfield Properties Ltd** [2000] **1** 65, CA.
            Fair trial—Judge making numerous interventions during presentation of case by litigant in person—Whether trial unfair—Whether full retrial necessary. **Serafin v Malkiewicz** [2020] **4** 711, SC.
            Non-pecuniary interest in outcome of proceedings—Law Lord serving as director of charity closely associated with party to an extradition appeal—Law Lord hearing appeal, but failing to disclose connection—Whether Law Lord automatically disqualified from hearing appeal. **R v Bow Street Metropolitan Stipendiary Magistrate, ex p Pinochet Ugarte (No 2)** [1999] **1** 577, HL.
            Subconscious bias—Leading counsel appearing on appeal before Employment Appeal Tribunal having previously sat as part-time judge with lay member hearing appeal—Whether real possibility of subconscious bias on part of lay member. **Lawal v Northern Spirit Ltd** [2004] **1** 187, HL.
            Test for determining apparent bias. **Porter v Magill** [2002] **1** 465, HL.
        Removal from office—
            Trinidad and Tobago. *See* **Trinidad and Tobago** (Judge—Removal from office—Suspension from judicial duties—Natural justice).
        'Without prejudice' correspondence—
            Disqualification of judge on grounds of having seen such correspondence—Test and guidance—Human Rights Act 1998, Sch 1, Pt I, art 6. **Berg v IML London Ltd** [2002] **4** 87, QBD.
    Juror —
        Bias—
            Prosecution witness known to juror—Test for determining apparent bias. **A-G of the Cayman Islands v Tibbetts** [2010] **3** 95, PC.
    Legal representation—
        Domestic tribunal. *See* Domestic tribunal—Legal representation, *above*.
        Police—
            Disciplinary proceedings. *See* **Police** (Discipline—Procedure at disciplinary hearing—Legal representation).
        Prison board of visitors, before. *See* Prison board of visitors—Exercise of disciplinary powers—Request by prisoner for legal representation or assistance of friend or adviser, *below*.
    Local authority—
        Planning permission—
            Development of land by local authority—Duty of authority to act fairly. *See* **Town and country planning** (Permission for development—Development by local authority—Duty to act fairly).
            Permission for development of land by local authority—Duty to act fairly. *See* **Town and country planning** (Permission for development—Development by local authority—Duty to act fairly).

NATURAL JUSTICE (cont)—
Local authority (cont)—
  Street trading—
    Revocation of licence—Street trader having informal licence to trade from town market place—Local authority giving street trader notice to quit—Local authority giving no prior notification or reasons—Whether local authority required to act in accordance with rules of natural justice—Whether local authority required to observe rules of natural justice only when regulating trading in statutory market. **R v Wear Valley DC, ex p Binks** [1985] **2** 699, QBD.
Magistrates—
  Bias—
    Fair hearing not possible—Member of local licensing committee sitting on appeal from committee's decision—Applicants applying for full liquor licence—Application refused by local licensing committee—Applicants making unsuccessful second application and then appealing to Crown Court—Appeal heard by bench which included justice who had been member of licensing committee which dismissed applicants' first application—Whether reasonable suspicion that applicants would not have fair hearing of appeal—Whether statutory prohibition on licensing justice acting in hearing or determination of appeal from any decision in which he took part exhaustive of circumstances in which justice disqualified for acting on grounds of bias—Licensing Act 1964, s 22(7)—Crown Court Rules 1982, r 5. **R v Crown Court at Bristol, ex p Cooper** [1990] **2** 193, CA.
  Binding over. *See* **Magistrates** (Binding over—Natural justice).
  Breach of rules of natural justice—
    Certiorari. *See* **Certiorari** (Justices—Natural justice).
  Duty to act openly, impartially and fairly—
    Information received prior to hearing—Meeting with local government officials—Inspection of subject-matter—Objectors at hearing aware of point in issue—No unfairness—Food and Drugs Act 1955, s 9(1)(3). **R v Birmingham City Justice, ex p Chris Foreign Foods (Wholesalers) Ltd** [1970] **3** 945, QBD.
    Retirement to take advice—Advice received not made known to objectors—Breach of rules of natural justice—Food and Drugs Act 1955, s 9(1)(3). **R v Birmingham City Justice, ex p Chris Foreign Foods (Wholesalers) Ltd** [1970] **3** 945, QBD.
  Duty to hear parties etc—
    Commitment—Warrant of commitment—Magistrates not to issue warrant of commitment without giving offender opportunity to be heard. **Wilson v Colchester Justices** [1985] **2** 97, HL.
    Opportunity to prepare case—Party allocated time for case to be heard—Party not given reasonable opportunity to prepare case—Whether breach of rules of natural justice. **R v Thames Magistrates' Court, ex p Polemis** [1974] **2** 1219, QBD.
    Venue of proceedings—Transfer of proceedings to another court—Maintenance order—Complaint for revocation of maintenance order—Transfer of complaint to another petty sessional division—Whether respondent to complaint entitled to make representations objecting to transfer—Magistrates' Courts Rules 1981, r 41(4). **R v Wareham Magistrates' Court, ex p Seldon** [1988] **1** 746, QBD.
Master and servant—
  Dismissal of servant—
    Trade union official—Applicability of rules of natural justice—Grounds for dismissal prescribed by union rules—Status as a senior officer of union rendering dismissal a serious matter to official—Meeting of executive committee to consider dismissal of official for misconduct—Whether committee bound to comply with rules of natural justice. **Stevenson v United Road Transport Union** [1976] **3** 29, Ch D.
Medical appeal tribunal—
  Duty to make due enquiry—
    Extent of duty. **R v National Insurance Comr, ex p Viscusi** [1974] **2** 724, CA.
Minister—
  Quasi-judicial function. *See* Quasi-judicial function—Minister, *below*.
Negligence—
  Whether breach of rules of natural justice amounting to breach of duty of care owed to person affected. *See* **Negligence** (Duty to take care—Breach of duty—Breach of rules of natural justice).
Non-judicial body—
  Investigation of complaint—
    Duty to act fairly—Race Relations Board. *See* **Race relations** (Investigation of complaint—Race Relations Board—Duty to act fairly).
Parole Board—
  Refusal to release prisoner on licence—
    Refusal to inform prisoner of reason—Whether contrary to rules of natural justice. *See* **Prison** (Release on licence—Refusal to release on licence—Reasons for refusal—Whether Parole Board or local review committee required to inform prisoner of reasons for refusal to recommend release).
    Review by Parole Board—Whether natural justice requiring disclosure to prisoner of reports to be presented to Parole Board. *See* **Prison** (Release on licence—Refusal to release on licence—Review by Parole Board).
Police—
  Dismissal of probationer constable. *See* **Police** (Dismissal—Constable—Probationer constable—Natural justice).
Prison—
  Discipline—
    Bias—Deputy prison governor present when governor approving squat search order—Prisoners refusing to comply with order—Deputy prison governor later adjudicating at prisoners' disciplinary hearings—Whether apparent bias. **R (on the application of Al-Hasan) v Secretary of State for the Home Dept** [2005] **1** 927, HL.
Prison board of visitors—
  Exercise of disciplinary powers—
    Certiorari. *See* **Certiorari** (Jurisdiction—Prison board of visitors—Exercise of disciplinary powers).

NATURAL JUSTICE (cont)—
Prison board of visitors (cont)—
Exercise of disciplinary powers (cont)—
Disciplinary hearing—Chairman of board also a member of local review committee—Chairman having background knowledge of prisoner as a result of sitting on review committee—Whether chairman disqualified from hearing case—Whether breach of the rules of natural justice. **R v Frankland Prison Board of Visitors, ex p Lewis** [1986] **1** 272, QBD.

Procedure—Duty of board to give fair hearing to prisoner charged with disciplinary offence—Extent of board's duty—Prisoner's right to be heard himself and to call witnesses—Chairman's power to limit right to call witnesses—Whether board bound by technical rules of evidence—Prison Act 1952, s 47(2)—Prison Rules 1964 (SI 1964 No 388), r 49(2). **R v Hull Prison Board of Visitors, ex p St Germain (No 2)** [1979] **3** 545, QBD.

Request by prisoner for legal representation or assistance of friend or adviser—Whether prisoner entitled as of right to legal representation or assistance of friend or adviser at disciplinary hearing before board—Whether board having discretion to allow legal representation or assistance of friend or adviser—What matter should be taken into consideration in exercising discretion—Prison Act 1952, s 47(2)—Prison Rules 1964, r 49(2). **R v Secretary of State for the Home Dept, ex p Tarrant** [1984] **1** 799, QBD.

Prison control unit—
Transfer of prisoner from ordinary prison to control unit—
Control unit involving separation from other prisoners and strict regime—Whether Secretary of State under duty to inform prisoner of reason for transfer and to give him opportunity of making representations. **Williams v Home Office (No 2)** [1981] **1** 1211, QBD.

Professional regulatory body—
Bias—
Apparent bias—Institute of Legal Executives (ILEX) appeal tribunal—Disciplinary proceedings against student member of ILEX—Vice-president of ILEX council member of appeal tribunal—Whether apparent bias—Whether appeal tribunal member automatically disqualified. **R (on the application of Kaur) v Institute of Legal Executives Appeal Tribunal** [2012] **1** 1435, CA.

Public authority—
Dismissal of employee—
Appointment during authority's pleasure—Statutory protection—Dismissal invalid unless employee receiving not less than three weeks' notice of motion for dismissal—Scottish education authority dismissing teacher for failure to register—Regulations providing every teacher employed by authority to be registered teacher—Refusal to afford teacher opportunity to be heard before dismissal—Right of teacher to be heard before passing of resolution for dismissal—Validity of dismissal—Education (Scotland) Act 1962, ss 82(1), 85(1)—Schools (Scotland) Code 1956 (SI 1956 No 894), reg 4(2), as amended by the Teachers (Education, Training and Registration) (Scotland) Regulations 1967, (SI 1967 No 1162). **Malloch v Aberdeen Corp** [1971] **2** 1278, HL.

Public inquiry—
Duty to hear parties—
Departmental advice received by Minister after inquiry closed—Department changing method of forecasting traffic growth after inquiry closed—Whether Minister required to communicate change of method to objectors and reopen inquiry—Whether Minister required to disclose departmental advice received after inquiry. **Bushell v Secretary of State for the Environment** [1980] **2** 608, HL.

Effect of government policy—Secretary of State wishing to increase tolls levied on users of bridge—Public inquiry held to consider objections to proposed increase—Inspector deciding certain objections falling within matters of government policy—Inspector not considering or evaluating objections—Whether inspector entitled to ignore objections because of policy—Whether public inquiry and order increasing tolls invalid—Severn Bridge Tolls Act 1965, ss 1(1), 3(3), 4, Sch 2—Severn Bridge Tolls Order 1985. **R v Secretary of State for Transport, ex p Gwent CC** [1987] **1** 161, CA.

Opportunity to be heard—Adjournment of inquiry—Local inquiry into refusal of planning permission—Application for adjournment to allow applicant to prepare case and instruct counsel—Secretary of State refusing adjournment—Inspector having power to adjourn inquiry in interests of justice—Town and Country Planning (Inquiries Procedure) Rules 1974 (SI 1974 No 419), r 10(8). **Co-op Retail Services Ltd v Secretary of State for the Environment** [1980] **1** 449, CA.

Opportunity to be heard—Religion prohibiting party from attending on date set for hearing—Housing—Compulsory purchase order—Inquiry by inspector—Objector to order unable to attend on date of inquiry on religious grounds—Objector requesting either deferment of inquiry or special hearing at later date—Request made two months after date for inquiry fixed and three weeks before inquiry held—Secretary of State refusing request—Secretary of State suggesting that objector arrange to be represented at inquiry—Objector not replying to Secretary of State's suggestion—Whether objector acquiescing in Secretary of State's suggestion—Whether inquiry conducted in breach of rules of natural justice—Whether ground for quashing order. **Ostreicher v Secretary of State for the Environment** [1978] **3** 82, CA.

Opportunity to consider reasons for decision—Reasons not put forward at hearing—Housing—Compulsory purchase order—Inquiry by inspector—Houses unfit for habitation—Local authority's case that houses unfit because of settlement and rehabilitation not feasible—Inspection of houses by inspector at end of inquiry—Inspector concluding that houses unfit because of foundations and in consequence rehabilitation not feasible—Inadequacy of foundations not part of local authority's case—Owner of houses having no opportunity to refute finding as to inadequacy of foundations—Whether owner prejudiced by breach of rules of natural justice—Whether compulsory purchase order should be quashed. **Fairmount Investments Ltd v Secretary of State for the Environment** [1976] **2** 865, HL.

NATURAL JUSTICE (cont)—
Public inquiry (cont)—
Duty to hear parties (cont)—
Opportunity to deal with evidence relating to matter on which decision based—Party not alerted to fact that issue one which would be taken into account—Planning inquiry—Appeal against refusal of planning permission to extract sand and gravel from agricultural land—Refusal on ground extraction and refilling would reduce quality and productivity of land—Applicant's evidence at inquiry directed to dealing with that issue—Bare reference in objector's evidence to function of sand and gravel in attracting moisture to topsoil—Applicant's appeal dismissed on ground replacement of gravel would put at risk supply of moisture to topsoil—Whether decision in breach of rules of natural justice. **Sabey (H) & Co Ltd v Secretary of State for the Environment** [1978] **1** 586, BD.

Right to cross-examine witnesses—Ministerial policy—Methods used in formulating policy—Local inquiry to hear objections to motorway scheme—Objectors wishing to cross-examine departmental witnesses on methods used to predict future traffic volumes—Cross-examination disallowed—Whether breach of rules of natural justice. **Bushell v Secretary of State for the Environment** [1980] **2** 608, HL.

Quasi-judicial function—
Exercise of statutory power—
Minister's order superseding municipal council for incompetence—Duty to act judicially—Inquiry—No opportunity given to council to be heard in defence—Order voidable only in proceedings by or on behalf of council—Municipal Ordinance (cap 252) of Ceylon, s 277(1). **Durayappah v Fernando** [1967] **2** 152, PC.

Minister—
Determination whether contravention of statute—Duty to act judicially—Unaided school—No notification of one of two alleged statutory breaches—Reliance on breach not notified shown by subsequent broadcast statement—Failure to consider present as distinct from past conduct of school in deciding statutory breach—Assisted Schools and Training Colleges (Special Provisions) Act, No 5 of 1960—Assisted Schools and Training Colleges (Supplementary Provisions) Act, No 8 of 1961. **Maranda Mosque (Board of Trustees) v Badi-Ud-Din Mahmud** [1966] **1** 545, PC.

Remedies for breach of rules of natural justice—
Injunctions—
Discretion. *See* **Injunction** (Discretion—Natural justice).
Remedies for conduct of proceedings being contrary to natural justice—
Necessity for contractural relationship—Whether proceedings of joint investigating committee of film renters protection society and trade union of exhibitors conducted in accordance with natural justice. **Byrne v Kinematograph Renters Society Ltd** [1958] **2** 579, Ch D.

Rent assessment committee—
Duty to hear parties—
Objection by tenant to rent officer's determination of fair rent—Reference to committee—Tenant purporting to withdraw objection before hearing—Tenant believing objection withdrawn and not attending hearing—Committee at hearing considering increase in rent—After hearing and before decision committee realising reason for tenant's absence—Whether committee bound to give tenant opportunity of being heard before deciding whether to increase rent. **Hanson v Church Comrs for England** [1977] **3** 404, CA.

Royal Commission—
Duty to hear parties—
Opportunity to rebut proposed findings—Royal commissioner making finding that witnesses had engaged in conspiracy to commit perjury before commission—Witnesses not given opportunity to rebut finding—Whether Royal commission finding made in breach of rules of natural justice. **Mahon v Air New Zealand Ltd** [1984] **3** 201, PC.

Solicitors Disciplinary Tribunal—
Bias —
Clerk to tribunal—Clerk employed by Law Society—Clerk retiring with tribunal members—Whether apparent bias. **Virdi v Law Society (Solicitors Disciplinary Tribunal intervening)** [2010] **3** 653, CA.

Suspension of student—
Duty to hear parties etc. *See* Educational establishment—Suspension of student—Duty to hear parties etc, *above.*

Taxation of costs—
Whether rules of natural justice apply to taxation proceedings. *See* **Costs** (Taxation—Review of taxation—Right to see documents lodged with taxing master).

Teacher—
Complaint against teacher—
Duty to hear parties etc. *See* Educational establishment—Complaint against teacher—Duty to hear parties etc, *above.*
Dismissal. *See* **Tribunal** (Membership—Bias).

Trade union—
Deficiency of natural justice before trial tribunal—
Adjudication on union member's conduct—Appeal by member to annual conference of delegates—Whether member could thereafter seek redress in the courts. **Annamunthodo v Oilfields Workers' Trade Union** [1961] **3** 621, PC.
Curability—Sufficiency of natural justice in subsequent proceedings—Expulsion from trade union. **Leary v National Union of Vehicle Builders** [1970] **2** 713, Ch D.

Dismissal of union official from office—
Applicability of rules of natural justice—Executive committee of union—Union rule that official to hold office so long as he gave satisfaction to committee—Dismissal on ground that performance of official unsatisfactory—Official not informed before hearing of charges being made against him—Request at hearing for charges and evidence to be put into writing refused—Refusal to adjourn hearing to allow official to prepare defence—Whether executive committee bound to comply with rules of natural justice—Whether decision of committee made in breach of natural justice void ab initio. **Stevenson v United Road Transport Union** [1977] **2** 941, CA.

NATURAL JUSTICE (cont)—
 Trade union (cont)—
  District committee of union—
   Discretion to refuse member's election as shop steward—Reasons for decision—Reason given for
    refusal at time of decision erroneous and prejudicial to member—Evidence given at trial five
    years later of real reason for decision—Evidence to show what happened at committee
    meeting—Committee not precluded from asserting that reason given to member was not real
    reason for decision. **Breen v Amalgamated Engineering Union** [1971] **1** 1148, CA.
  Duty to act judicially—
   Chairman acting as accuser—Official of union employed on terms of union rules—Dismissed by
    general secretary for insubordination—Dismissal might involve disabilities as a member of
    union—Appeal by official in exercise of right conferred by rules to executive council—Duty of
    council under rules to act judicially—Consequences in issue on appeal not merely termination of
    employment but also ineligibility under rules to certain positions in union—Chairman of council
    acting as accuser and prejudicial matter introduced in plaintiff's absence—Whether declaration of
    continuance of employment etc should be made. **Taylor v National Union of Seamen**
    [1967] **1** 767, Ch D.
  Right to be heard—
   Refusal of district committee to endorse member's election as shop steward—Functions of
    committee under union rules discretionary—Requirement to exercise discretion fairly—Member
    not invited to attend meeting at which endorsement of election refused—Reasons for
    decision—Committee entitled to come to decision in absence of member on basis of valid
    reasons—Right of member to be present to refute prejudicial reason based on erroneous facts.
    Breen v Amalgamated Engineering Union [1971] **1** 1148, CA.
  Termination of membership. *See* **Trade union** (Membership—Termination of membership).
 Witness—
  Presence in court. *See* **Witness** (Presence in court during examination of earlier witnesses).

NATURAL PARENT
 Access to child—
  Adoption of child. *See* **Adoption** (Access—Access by natural parent).
 Care and control of child—
  Ward of court—
   Contest between natural parent and foster parents. *See* **Ward of court** (Care and control—Contest
    between natural parent and foster parents).
 Wardship proceedings by natural parent—
  Child in care of local authority—
   Jurisdiction of court to review decisions of local authority. *See* **Child** (Care—Local
    authority—Wardship proceedings—Jurisdiction of court to review decisions of local
    authority—Wardship proceedings by natural parent).

NATURALISATION
 Alien—
  British nationality. *See* **Alien** (British nationality—Acquisition—Naturalisation).
 Citizenship, acquisition of—
  British citizen. *See* **Citizenship** (British citizen—Acquisition—Acquisition by naturalisation).

NATURE CONSERVANCY COUNCIL
 Environment, protection of. *See* **Environment** (Protection).

NATURE RESERVE
 Harbour. *See* **Harbour** (Nature reserve).

NAVIGATION
 Air navigation. *See* **Air traffic**.
 Ordinary incidents of navigation—
  Laying and maintenance of permanent moorings. *See* **Water and watercourses** (Navigation—Ordinary
   incidents of navigation—Laying and maintenance of permanent moorings).
 Public right of navigation—
  Generally. *See* **Water and watercourses** (Navigation—Public right of navigation (PRN)).
  Interference—
   Public nuisance. *See* **Water and watercourses** (Navigation—Public right of navigation
    (PRN)—Public nuisance).
 Reservoir. *See* **Water and watercourses** (Navigation—Reservoir).
 Shipping—
  Generally. *See* **Shipping** (Navigation).
 Tidal waters—
  Public right to navigate. *See* **Water and watercourses** (Navigation—Public right of navigation (PRN)).

NAVY
 Court-martial. *See* **Court-martial**.
 Discipline—
  Regulations—
   Drunkenness—Serviceman at naval base becoming drunk and dying of asphyxiation following
    inhalation of own vomit—Naval regulations imposing duty on officers to discourage drunkenness
    and to take appropriate action to prevent injury or fatality—Serviceman's widow suing Navy for
    damages—Whether Navy owing duty of care to serviceman—Whether Navy liable for
    serviceman's death—Whether regulations and standing orders indicating standards to be applied
    in assessing liability—Queen's Regulations for the Royal Navy 1967, art 1810. **Barrett v Ministry
    of Defence** [1995] **3** 87, CA.

NAVY (cont)—
  Discipline (cont)—
    Summary jurisdiction of captain—
      Naval officer disobeying orders—'Wilful disobedience'—'Highly insubordinate conduct'—Meaning
      of terms—Naval Discipline Act 1866, s 17, s 56(2)—King's Regulations and Admiralty Instructions,
      arts 540, 552. **Jenkins v Shelley** [1939] **1** 786, KBD.
  Pay, pensions etc—
    Avoidance of assignment of, or charge on, pay, pensions etc—Financial provision order—Divorce
    proceedings. *See* **Divorce** (Financial provision—Military pay, pensions etc—Avoidance of assignment
    of, or charge on, military pay, pensions etc).

NE EXEAT REGNO
  Writ of. *See* **Equity** (Ne exeat regno).

NEAREST RELATIVE
  Mental health patient. *See* **Mental health** (Patient—Nearest relative).

NECESSITY
  Agency of necessity. *See* **Agent** (Agency of necessity).
  Defence of—
    Criminal charge. *See* **Criminal law** (Necessity as a defence).
    Trespass to land. *See* **Trespass to land** (Defence—Necessity).
  Easement—
    Implied grant. *See* **Easement** (Implied grant—Necessity).
  Way of—
    Private right of way. *See* **Easement** (Way of necessity).

NEGATIVE AVERMENT
  Burden of proof—
    Criminal proceedings. *See* **Criminal evidence** (Burden of proof—Negative averment).

NEGLECT
  Child—
    Criminal offence. *See* **Criminal law** (Child—Wilful neglect of child).
    Proceedings in juvenile court. *See* **Children and young persons** (Care proceedings in juvenile
    court—Conditions to be satisfied before making order—Neglect or ill-treatment of child).
  Clergyman—
    Neglect of duty—
      Ecclesiastical law. *See* **Ecclesiastical law** (Clergyman—Offence—Neglect of duty).
  Costs—
    Taxation. *See* **Costs** (Taxation—Misconduct, neglect etc).
  Income tax—
    Additional assessment. *See* **Income tax** (Additional assessment—Neglect).
    Adjournment of appeal—
      Crown alleging fraud, wilful default or neglect by taxpayer. *See* **Income tax** (Appeal—
      Commissioners—Adjournment of appeal—Taxpayer appealing to commissioners against
      assessments—Crown alleging fraud, wilful default or neglect by taxpayer).
  Infirm person, of—
    Manslaughter—
      Breach of duty amounting to recklessness. *See* **Criminal law** (Manslaughter—Recklessness or gross
      negligence—Assumption of duty of care for infirm person—Breach of duty amounting to
      recklessness).
  Nuisance. *See* **Nuisance** (Neglect).
  Verdict—
    Inquest. *See* **Coroner** (Inquest—Verdict—Neglect).
  Wife—
    Wilful neglect to maintain. *See* **Husband and wife** (Wilful neglect to maintain).

NEGLIGENCE
  Abortion—
    Medical practitioner. *See* **Medical practitioner** (Negligence—Abortion).
  Accountant—
    Duty to take care. *See* Duty to take care—Accountant, *below.*
    Information or advice—
      Generally. *See* Information or advice—Accountant, *below.*
    Limitation of action. *See* **Limitation of action** (Accrual of cause of action—Negligence—Accountant).
  Accrual of cause of action. *See* **Limitation of action** (When time begins to run—Actions in tort—Accrual of
  cause of action—Negligence).
  Adjudication officer—
    Duty to take care. *See* Duty to take care—Existence of duty—Adjudication officer, *below.*
  Admission—
    Judgment. *See* **Judgment** (Judgment on admission of facts—Negligence).
  Advice. *See* Information or advice, *below.*
  Aiding and abetting offence. *See* **Criminal law** (Aiding and abetting—Mens rea—Negligence).
  Ambulance service—
    Duty to take care. *See* Duty to take care—Ambulance service, *below.*
  Animal. *See* **Animal** (Negligence).
  Apportionment of liability—
    Contributory negligence. *See* Contributory negligence—Apportionment of liability, *below.*
    Shipping collision. *See* **Shipping** (Negligence in collision cases—Apportionment of liability).
  Architect—
    Building contract. *See* **Building contract** (Architect—Negligence).
    Duty to take care. *See* Duty to take care—Architect, *below.*

NEGLIGENCE (cont)—

Armed forces, negligent performance of duty in. *See* **Court-martial** (Negligent performance of duty).
Auctioneer—
    Duty to take care. *See* Duty to take care—Auctioneer, *below*.
Auditor—
    Audit of company's accounts. *See* **Company** (Auditor—Negligence).
    Damages. *See* **Damages** (Measure of damages—Negligence—Auditor).
    Duty to take care—
        Existence of duty. *See* Duty to take care—Existence of duty—Auditor, *below*.
        Generally. *See* Duty to take care—Auditor, *below*.
    Information or advice—
        Knowledge third party might rely on information. *See* Information or advice—Knowledge third party might rely on information—Auditor, *below*.
Bailee—
    Contract of bailment—
        Exception clause. *See* **Contract** (Exception clause—Bailment).
    Generally. *See* **Bailment**.
Bank—
    Bank of England—
        Duty to take care. *See* Duty to take care—Existence of duty—Bank of England, *below*.
    Duty of care. *See* **Bank** (Duty of care).
Barrister. *See* **Counsel** (Negligence).
Bill of lading—
    Issue. *See* **Shipping** (Bill of lading—Negligent issue of bill of lading).
Blind persons on highway—
    Duty of care to blind. *See* Duty to take care—Person to whom duty owed—Blind persons on highway, *below*.
Broker. *See* Professional person—Duty to exercise reasonable skill and care—Broker on commodities market, *below*.
Builder—
    Defective premises—
        Liability. *See* Defective premises—Builder's liability, *below*.
    Duty to take care. *See* Duty to take care—Builder, *below*.
Building—
    Building in course of construction. *See* **Building** (Building in course of construction—Negligence).
    Building operations—
        Persons to whom duty of care owed. *See* Duty to take care—Person to whom duty owed—Building operations, *below*.
    Damages—
        Measure of damages. *See* **Damages** (Measure of damages—Negligence—Building).
Burden of proof—
    Evidence of conviction in action for negligence. *See* **Burden of proof** (Civil action—Conviction as evidence—Negligence).
Cargo—
    Bill of lading—
        Cargo damaged by negligence. *See* **Shipping** (Bill of lading—Transfer of rights and liabilities—Cargo damaged by negligence).
Carriage by air—
    Carriage of passengers. *See* **Carriage by air** (Carriage of passengers—Negligence).
Carriers. *See* **Carriers** (Negligence).
Casino—
    Duty to take care. *See* Duty to take care—Existence of duty—Casino, *below*.
Casualty officer—
    Hospital—
        Liability of hospital. *See* **Hospital** (Liability for negligence of members of staff—Casualty officer).
Catchment board—
    Duty to repair sea wall. *See* **Land drainage** (Sea wall—Negligence—Duty of catchment board to repair).
Causation—
    Breach of duty causing or contributing to damage—
        Advice to workman—Likelihood of advice being taken—Duty of employer to give information or advice—Effect of unlikelihood of plaintiff's taking advice if given. **Qualcast (Wolverhampton) Ltd v Haynes** [1959] **2** 38, HL.
        Balance of probabilities—Plaintiff injured and having 75 per cent chance of permanent disability developing—Hospital wrongly diagnosing injury for five days—Wrong diagnosis making permanent disability inevitable—Whether plaintiff entitled to damages for loss of 25 per cent chance of full recovery—Whether plaintiff having to prove that disability caused by hospital's negligence—Whether loss of chance of better medical result an issue of causation or of quantum. **Hotson v East Berkshire Area Health Authority** [1987] **2** 909, HL.
        Highway—Relevant cause of accident—Initial act of negligence by one driver followed by reckless driving on part of another driver—Car breaking down at night in fog on dual carriageway—Driver negligently leaving car on carriageway instead of moving car onto verge—Lorry driven recklessly colliding with stationary car and then going out of control—Lorry ending up overturned on opposite carriageway—Two other cars colliding with overturned lorry—Whether negligent driver of car liable to contribute to damages payable by lorry driver to persons injured in collision with overturned lorry—Whether lorry driver's reckless driving sole cause of accident on opposite carriageway. **Wright v Lodge** [1993] **4** 299, CA.
        Investor seeking investment for proceeds of sale of real estate—Investor telling bank's financial advisor he could not afford to take risk with capital sum—Financial advisor recommending insurance fund product—Financial advisor telling investor that fund equivalent to a deposit in bank account—Financial market crash occurring—Investor withdrawing his investment for sum below original capital investment—Whether negligent advice causing investor's loss—Whether market crash breaking chain of causation. **Rubenstein v HSBC Bank plc** [2013] **1 Comm** 915, CA.

NEGLIGENCE (cont)—
  Causation (cont)—
    Breach of duty causing or contributing to damage (cont)—
      Onus of proof—Onus on plaintiff—Employer and employee—Proof of breach of statutory duty—Whether onus of proving breach did not contribute to plaintiff's injury on employer. **Bonnington Castings Ltd v Wardlaw** [1956] **1** 615, HL.
      Safety equipment—Provision of safety appliance—Instruction or exhortation to use appliance—Safety belt not available to experienced steel erector on day of accident—Fatal fall from tower crane under construction—Deceased would not have worn belt if available—Practice among steel erectors not to wear safety belts for job that deceased was doing—Employer not under duty to order or to exhort employees to wear belts—Factories Act 1937, s 26(2)—Building (Safety, Health and Welfare) Regulations 1948, (SI 1948 No 1145), reg 97. **McWilliams v Sir William Arrol & Co Ltd** [1962] **1** 623, HL.
    Breach of duty causing or materially contributing to damage—
      Causal connection between breach of duty and damage—Causal connection between breach of duty and damage not established—Employer using working methods which exposed employee to asbestos dust—Employee contracting asbestos-related disease—Existence and extent to which employer's breach of duty contributed to employee contracting disease not established—Whether employer liable. **Bryce v Swan Hunter Group plc** [1988] **1** 659, QBD.
      Causal connection between breach of duty and damage—Causal connection between breach of duty and damage not established—Overdose of penicillin negligently administered in hospital during treatment for pneumococcal meningitis—Patient subsequently suffering from deafness—Deafness a common sequela of pneumococcal meningitis—No positive evidence that patient would not have suffered deafness if he had not been given penicillin overdose—Whether hospital authority liable for deafness suffered by patient. **Kay v Ayrshire and Arran Health Board** [1987] **2** 417, HL.
      Causal connection between breach of duty and damage—Employee developing mesothelioma after being exposed to asbestos dust by successive employers in breach of duty and by self-employment—Whether exposure during self-employment precluding employee from recovering damages from employers. **Barker v Corus (UK) Ltd** [2006] **3** 785, HL; **Barker v Saint-Gobain Pipelines plc** [2005] **3** 661, CA.
      Causal connection between breach of duty and damage—Employee developing mesothelioma after being exposed to asbestos dust by successive employers in breach of duty—Employee unable to establish that either employer or both of them responsible for mesothelioma on 'but for' test of causation—Whether employee precluded from recovering damages for mesothelioma against any employer when employed by successive employers during period of exposure to asbestos. **Fairchild v Glenhaven Funeral Services Ltd** [2002] **3** 305, HL.
      Causal connection between breach of duty and damage—Victim developing mesothelioma after being exposed to asbestos dust by person owing a duty of care—Special rule governing attribution of causation—Statutory rule making provision about damages for mesothelioma—Whether special rule applying to exposure to asbestos dust by single defendant—Compensation Act 2006, s 3. **Sienkiewicz v Greif (UK) Ltd** [2011] **2** 857, SC.
      Contributory negligence. *See* Contributory negligence—Causation, *below.*
      Damage caused or contributed to by two or more persons—Claimant being exposed to asbestos over several years while working for various employers—Claimant contracting asbestosis but suing only one former employer—Judge holding defendant liable only for part of disability and reducing damages accordingly—Whether claimant entitled to recover damages in full from defendant who had materially contributed only to part of disability—Whether defendant having to plead and prove that others partly responsible for disability. **Holtby v Brigham & Cowan (Hull) Ltd** [2000] **3** 421, CA.
      Enhancement of existing risk—Medical practitioner. *See* **Medical practitioner** (Negligence—Causation—Burden of proof—Breach of duty causing or materially contributing to damage).
      Enhancement of existing risk—Plaintiff hit by two cars while crossing road—Both drivers negligent—Whether second defendant liable to plaintiff when plaintiff cannot establish whether and to what extent second driver's negligence caused or contributed to plaintiff's injuries. **Fitzgerald v Lane** [1987] **2** 455, CA.
      Increase in risk of damage—Damage caused or contributed to by factors for which defendant not responsible—Defendant's breach of duty materially increasing risk of damage to plaintiff—No positive evidence that plaintiff would not have suffered damage in absence of defendant's breach of duty—Whether defendant liable to plaintiff in respect of breach of duty. **McGhee v National Coal Board** [1972] **3** 1008, HL.
      Medical practitioner. *See* **Medical practitioner** (Negligence—Causation).
  Child—
    Allurement. *See* Child—Allurement—Causal connection between allurement and injury, *below.*
    Contributory negligence. *See* Contributory negligence—Causation, *below.*
  Intervening act—
    Conduct of claimant—Contamination of parcel of ethylene—Coolant parcel indicating vessel unsuitable for carriage of ethylene—Loading continuing notwithstanding indication—Master playing little part in loading process—Owners admitting vessel unfit to carry ethylene—Whether decision to continue loading constituting intervening act. **Vinmar International Ltd v Theresa Navigation SA** [2001] **2** Comm 243, QBD.
    Conduct of plaintiff—Collision at sea—Refusal by plaintiffs of defendants' offer to tow—Plaintiffs' ship subsequently sinking and becoming a total loss—Reasonableness of refusal—Whether refusal breaking chain of causation. **Guildford, The** [1956] **2** 915, Admin Ct.
  Intervention of third party—
    Children—Foreseeability of interference by children—Vehicle park—Open parking ground—Motor coach adjacent to boundary—Explosion caused by child throwing lighted match into petrol tank—Injury to another child outside vehicle park—Whether occupiers of vehicle park liable. **Perry v Kendricks Transport Ltd** [1956] **1** 154, CA.
    Damage direct result of breach of duty of care—Security of premises—Decorator leaving house with front door unlocked during known absence of tenants—Entry and theft by third party—Liability of decorator for loss occasioned by theft. **Stansbie v Troman** [1948] **1** 599, CA.

NEGLIGENCE (cont)—
  Causation (cont)—
    Intervention of third party (cont)—
      Damage natural consequence of negligence—Immediate cause of damage unexplained—Onus of proving intervention of third party on defendant—Escape of water from pipe with open end and without drain—No explanation for cause of escape. **Prosser (A) & Son Ltd v Levy** [1955] **3** 577, CA.

      Dangerous things—Deliberate act of third party necessary to constitute novus actus interveniens—Onus of proof—Inflammable material—Delivery by defendants to plaintiffs by mistake—Explosion caused by cigarette of plaintiffs' employee—Onus on defendants to prove that employee deliberately set material alight. **Philco Radio and Television Corp of GB Ltd v J Spurling Ltd** [1949] **2** 882, CA.

      Reasonable act in circumstances not breaking chain of causation—Plaintiff's act the natural consequence of position in which he was placed—Direct consequence of defendants' negligence—Collision at sea—Men ordered to boats—Death of seaman through boat capsizing—Whether death direct consequence of collision. **Lord v Pacific Steam Navigation Co Ltd** [1943] **1** 211, CA.

    Loss of chance—
      Loss dependent on hypothetical action of third party—Plaintiffs negligently advised by defendant solicitors in take-over—Plaintiffs unknowingly assuming vendors first tenant liability after take-over—Plaintiffs suing solicitors for negligent advice—Whether plaintiffs if properly advised would have sought to obtain protection from vendor—Whether substantial chance that plaintiffs would have been successful in negotiating protection—Whether loss of chance to be assessed as a matter of causation or quantum of damages. **Allied Maples Group Ltd v Simmons & Simmons (a firm)** [1995] **4** 907, CA.

    Predominant cause—
      Railway track—Bomb crater caused by enemy action—Engine-driver ordered to proceed 'at caution'—Train driven down line and into crater—Whether negligence of railway company in ordering driver to proceed predominant cause of accident—Personal Injuries (Emergency Provisions) Act 1939, ss 3(1), 8. **Greenfield v London and North Eastern Rly Co** [1944] **2** 438, CA.

  Cause of action—
    Damage—
      Negligent exposure of employees by employers to asbestos—Employees developing pleural plaques—Employees at risk of asbestos related diseases—Employees suffering anxiety or psychiatric illness—Whether development of pleural plaques capable of founding cause of action—Whether cause of action could be founded by aggregating heads of claim—Whether employers owing duty of care in respect of psychiatric illness caused by anxiety about future health. **Rothwell v Chemical & Insulating Co Ltd** [2006] **4** 1161, CA; [2007] **4** 1047, HL.

      Personal injury—Employer's breach of statutory duty—Exposure of employees to platinum salts causing platinum salt sensitivity—Sensitivity not itself having physical symptoms but further exposure to platinum salts would result in allergic reactions—Employees dismissed or redeployed to prevent further exposure—Whether claimants suffering actionable personal injury. **Dryden v Johnson Matthey plc** [2018] **3** 755, SC.

      Plaintiff requesting agent or bailee to enter car in auction and account to him for proceeds—Agent or bailee delegating performance to third party—Third party negligently paying proceeds to wrong person—Whether plaintiff entitled to sue agent or bailee in contract and third party in tort in respect of same damage—Whether plaintiff having direct cause of action against third party. **Balsamo v Medici** [1984] **2** 304, Ch D.

    Foreseeability—
      Criterion for culpability and for compensation the same—Whether damage could reasonably have been foreseen. **Wagon Mound, The (No 1)** [1961] **1** 404, PC.

  Charity Commissioners—
    Duty to take care. *See* Duty to take care—Existence of duty—Charity Commissioners, *below*.

  Child—
    Allurement—
      Causal connection between allurement and injury—Child injuring itself on obvious danger not part of allurement—Road works—Pile of metal left on part of road fenced off—Children allowed to play on nearby sand heap—Child leaving sand and injuring itself on metal—Metal not itself an allurement—Whether any causal connection between injury and allurement constituted by sand. **Morley v Staffordshire CC** [1939] **4** 92, CA.

      Child trespasser—Liability of persons other than occupier—Contractors—Electricity undertakers—High-voltage electric overhead wires—Easily climbed tree immediately below wires—Child electrocuted while climbing tree—Liability of undertakers. **Buckland v Guildford Gas Light & Coke Co** [1948] **2** 1086, KBD.

      Child trespasser—Liability of persons other than occupier—Standard of care—Trailer left by contractors on land adjoining road in course of construction—Contractors not in occupation of land—Child injured while playing with trailer—Duty of contractors to child. **Creed v John McGeoch & Sons Ltd** [1955] **3** 123, Assizes.

      Duty to protect thing from interference by children—Flagpole—Flagpole erected in public place—Children attracted to pole and swinging on rope—Inadequate steps taken to prevent them from doing so—Pole falling and injuring plaintiff. **Shiffman v St John of Jerusalem (Grand Priory in the British Realm of the Venerable Order of the Hospital)** [1936] **1** 557, KBD.

      Lorry on highway constituting an allurement—Lorry laden with sacks of sugar—Sugar escaping on to highway—Provision of look-out man at rear—Child running on to highway to catch sugar—Look-out man unable to see child—Child injured by lorry's trailer—Whether owners of lorry liable to child. **Culkin v McFie & Sons Ltd** [1939] **3** 613, Assizes.

      Nature of an allurement—Something attractive but dangerous to children—Hole in the ground not of itself an allurement—Child trespasser injured by falling into pit. **Perry v Thomas Wrigley Ltd** [1955] **3** 243, Assizes.

      Reasonable steps taken to avoid danger—Scaffold—Erection for repair of house—Children injured by scaffold being pulled over by boys—Foreseeable danger of young persons interfering with scaffolding—Whether defendants could reasonably have foreseen events which caused scaffolding to fall. **Cuttress v Scaffolding (GB) Ltd** [1953] **2** 1075, CA.

NEGLIGENCE (cont)—
  Child (cont)—
    Apprehension of danger to children—
      Objects left on highway—Pile of lime mortar left by defendant in gutter outside his house—Piece thrown by boy injuring child plaintiff—Whether evidence of negligence by occupier—Whether defendant could reasonably be expected to apprehend danger to children. **Prince v Gregory** [1959] **1** 133, CA.
    Contributory negligence. *See* Contributory negligence—Child, *below*.
    Foreseeable harm. *See* Duty to take care—Foreseeable harm—Child, *below*.
    Intervention by children breaking chain of causation. *See* Causation—Intervention of third party—Children, *above*.
    Local authority's duty to child in its care. *See* Duty to take care—Existence of duty—Children—Local authority, *below*.
    Parent's liability. *See* **Child** (Negligence—Parent's liability).
  Club. *See* **Club** (Negligence).
  Coastguard—
    Duty to take care. *See* Duty to take care—Coastguard, *below*.
  Collision at sea—
    Contributory negligence. *See* Contributory negligence—Collision at sea, *below*.
    Generally. *See* **Shipping** (Negligence in collision cases).
    Towage—
      Negligent navigation. *See* **Shipping** (Collision—Towage—Negligent navigation).
  Collision between vehicles on road—
    Contributory negligence. *See* Contributory negligence—Collision between vehicles on road, *below*.
    Proof of negligence. *See* Proof of negligence—Collision between vehicles on road, *below*.
  Company—
    Director—
      Information or advice—Knowledge third party might rely on information. *See* Information or advice—Knowledge third party might rely on information—Company—Directors, *below*.
    Minority shareholder—
      Representative action—Negligence alleged against majority shareholders. *See* **Company** (Minority shareholder—Representative action—Negligence alleged against majority shareholders).
    Take-over bid—
      Information or advice—Knowledge third party might rely on information. *See* Information or advice—Knowledge third party might rely on information—Company—Take-over bid, *below*.
  Concealment of right of action by fraud. *See* **Limitation of action** (Concealment of right of action by fraud—Negligence).
  Concurrent remedies—
    Negligence and contract. *See* Contract—Concurrent remedies, *below*.
  Consequential loss—
    Damage to property—
      Damage to property of another. *See* Duty to take care—Damage to property of another—Consequential loss to plaintiffs, *below*.
      Economic loss—Duty to take care. *See* Duty to take care—Economic loss—Damage to property, *below*.
  Construction work—
    Building. *See* **Building** (Construction—Negligence).
  Consultant engineer—
    Duty to take care. *See* Duty to take care—Consultant engineer, *below*.
  Contract—
    Concurrent remedies—
      Duty of care—Insurance—Lloyd's underwriting agent—Duty owed to names—Implied term of contract between underwriting agents and names that agents would exercise due care and skill—Whether agents owing duty of care in tort—Whether duty of care in tort excluded by contract—Whether names free to choose most advantageous remedy. **Henderson v Merrett Syndicates Ltd** [1994] **3** 506, HL.
      Duty of care—Insurance—Lloyd's underwriting agent—Duty owed to names—Name selecting syndicates and portfolio allocations independently—Name requesting advice on allocations to excess of loss syndicates—Agent failing to warn name of dangers of excess of loss reinsurance or advise on proper spread of risk—Agent in breach of contract—Extent of agent's duty to warn—Measure of name's damages—Availability of set-off of underwriting profits against losses incurred in other years—Remoteness of damage. **Brown v KMR Services Ltd** [1995] **4** 598, CA.
      Duty of care—Insurance—Lloyd's underwriting agent—Duty owed to names—Names informing members' agents of wish to follow cautious underwriting strategy—Agents recommending high risk excess of loss syndicates—Agents failing to warn names of dangers of excess of loss reinsurance—Whether agents in breach of contract—Whether agents in breach of duty of care, irrespective of whether name a sophisticated investor or whether agent recommended stop-loss insurance—Whether agents liable for names' losses. **Brown v KMR Services Ltd** [1994] **4** 385, QBD.
  Contributory negligence—
    Appeal—
      Inference of contributory negligence—Rejection of plea of contributory negligence by judge—Shunter injured by fall from railway engine caused by ground lever working points—Whether inference of contributory negligence from circumstances permissible on appeal. **Hicks v British Transport Commission** [1958] **2** 39, CA.
      Principle on which appellate court will interfere with apportionment of liability. *See* Contributory negligence—Principle on which appellate court will interfere with apportionment of liability, *below*.

NEGLIGENCE (cont)—
 Contributory negligence (cont)—
  Apportionment of liability—
   Deceit—Bank paying seller under letter of credit—Payment made against presentation of false bill of lading—Bank presenting documents to issuing bank knowing them to be false—Issuing bank refusing payment by reference to other discrepancies—Whether contributory negligence defence to action for deceit—Law Reform (Contributory Negligence) Act 1945, ss 1(1), 4. **Standard Chartered Bank v Pakistan National Shipping Corp (No 2)** [2002] **2 Comm** 931, HL; [2003] **1** 173, HL; **Standard Chartered Bank v Pakistan National Trading Corp (No 3)** [2000] **2 Comm** 929, CA.
   Jurisdiction—Defence of contributory negligence not pleaded—Whether court can apportion liability in absence of plea of contributory negligence. **Fookes v Slaytor** [1979] **1** 137, CA.
   Method of apportionment—Assessment of damages—Proportion of sums claimed—Claim and counterclaim arising out of collision—Liability apportioned two-thirds to plaintiffs and one-third to defendant—Plaintiffs entitled to one-third and defendants to two-thirds of respective sums claimed by them—Law Reform (Contributory Negligence) Act 1945, s 1. **Jay (William A) & Sons v Veevers (J S) Ltd** [1946] **1** 646, Assizes.
   Road traffic accident—Pedestrian struck by vehicle while crossing the road—Principles to be applied in apportionment of liability for contributory negligence—Circumstances in which appellate court can interfere with trial judge's apportionment of liability—Whether apportionment of liability to pedestrian should be reduced—Law Reform (Contributory Negligence) Act 1945, s 1(1). **Jackson v Murray** [2015] **2** 805, SC.
  Assault and battery. *See* **Tort** (Assault and battery—Contributory negligence).
  Breach of contract—
   Damages. *See* **Contract** (Damages for breach—Contributory negligence).
  Breach of Highway Code—
   Plaintiff in breach of code—Breach creating no presumption of negligence making a real contribution to cause of accident—Plaintiff a pedestrian—Walking at night along pavement in straight, lighted street in built-up area—Walking in or near gutter where pavement slushy—Dark clothing—Not facing oncoming traffic—Plaintiff struck from behind by fast moving car—Driver solely responsible for accident—Road Traffic Act 1960, s 74(5). **Powell v Phillips** [1972] **3** 864, CA.
  Breach of statutory directions—
   Employer and employee—Employee acting in breach of statutory directions—Employee injured in coal mining accident—Breach of statutory duty by employers and of statutory directions by employee—Employee acting in accordance with orders of immediate superior—Law Reform (Contributory Negligence) Act 1945, s 1(1). **Laszczyk v National Coal Board** [1954] **3** 205, Assizes.
  Burden of proof—
   Allegation that plaintiff's negligence contributed to damage suffered—Road accident—Failure to wear seat belt—No evidence that failure contributed to extent of plaintiff's injuries—Whether burden on defendant to prove that injuries in whole or in part attributable to failure to wear a seat belt. **Owens v Brimmell** [1976] **3** 765, QBD.
  Causation—
   Collision between vehicles on road. *See* Contributory negligence—Collision between vehicles on road—Causation, *below.*
   Last opportunity doctrine inappropriate—Negligence of plaintiff must be a factor contributing to accident—No need to prove breach of duty to defendant—Lack of reasonable care by deceased for his own safety—Law Reform (Contributory Negligence) Act 1945, ss 1(1), 4. **Davies v Swan Motor Co (Swansea) Ltd (Swansea Corp and James, third parties)** [1949] **1** 620, CA.
   Proximate cause of injury—Plaintiff's failure to take care—Fall down lift shaft—Plaintiff stepping backwards through lift door—Lift defective in that door opened when lift at another level—Whether entitled to assume presence of lift if door opened. **Kerry v Keighley Electrical Engineering Co Ltd** [1940] **3** 399, CA.
   Proximate cause of injury—Prisoner addicted to drugs and alcohol allocated top bunk bed—Prisoner suffering withdrawal seizure falling from bed and suffering head injury—Prisoner suffering recurrent seizures without recovery of consciousness—Prisoner suffering permanent brain damage—Whether prisoner contributorily negligent—Whether prisoner suffering damage as result partly of own fault—Whether drug addiction being prisoner's own fault—Whether drug addiction cause of damage—Law Reform (Contributory Negligence) Act 1945, s 1(1). **St George v Home Office** [2008] **4** 1039, CA.
  Child—
   Explosive substance given to child—Sale of petrol to child—Sale procured by untruth told by child—Injury by explosion of ignited petrol—Liability of seller—Whether contributory negligence could be inputed to child. **Yachuk v Blais (Oliver) Co Ltd** [1949] **2** 150, PC.
  Collision at sea—
   Last opportunity of avoiding accident—Vessel improperly anchored athwart fairway. *See* Contributory negligence—Last opportunity of avoiding accident—Continuing negligence—Vessel improperly anchored athwart fairway, *below.*
   Vessel overtaking in swept channel—Narrow berth given—Overtaken vessel changing course. **Admiralty Comrs v North of Scotland and Orkney and Shetland Steam Navigation Co Ltd** [1947] **2** 350, HL.
  Collision between vehicles on road—
   Ambulance with left-hand drive—Warning notice on back—Back of ambulance shut in—Ambulance driver unable to see cars close behind—Ambulance driver turning to right when motor omnibus close behind—Correct hand signals given by ambulance driver—Negligence of omnibus driver—Whether ambulance driver guilty of contributory negligence. **Daborn v Bath Tramways Motor Co Ltd and Trevor Smithey** [1946] **2** 333, CA.
   Car emerging from minor to major road—Driver's vision blocked by stationary vehicle—Driver inching out slowly in front of stationary vehicle even though vision blocked—Motor cyclist overtaking stationary vehicle and crashing into emerging car—Whether motor cyclist solely responsible for accident—Whether driver of emerging car also responsible for accident. **Worsfold v Howe** [1980] **1** 1028, CA.

NEGLIGENCE (cont)—
  Contributory negligence (cont)—
    Collision between vehicles on road (cont)—
      Causation—Obstruction of highway—Danger to road users—Danger to road users failing to keep proper look-out—Collision caused by negligent driving of following vehicle—Obstruction contributing to collision—Driver negligently causing lorry to jack-knife and obstruct two lanes of motorway at night—Lorry behind stopping and illuminating scene with headlights—Third party driving lorry too fast and failing to observe obstruction until too late—Collision following belated attempt of third party to avoid obstruction—Collision caused by negligent driving of third party—Whether negligence of driver of jack-knifed lorry contributing to collision. **Rouse v Squires** [1973] **2** 903, CA.
      Duty to have regard to danger created by other driver—Collision at cross-roads—Major and minor road—'Slow, Major road ahead' sign in minor road—Motor cyclist emerging from minor road without observing sign and without slowing down, at speed of twenty miles an hour—Omnibus travelling on major road at speed of not more than twenty miles an hour—Possibility of danger emerging—Duty of omnibus driver to take precautions—Whether omnibus driver guilty of contributory negligence. **Lang v London Transport Executive** [1959] **3** 609, QBD.
      Failure to observe signals—Parked car aiminq to cut across near traffic stream—Bus in stream stopping to allow it—Bus driver's flashing of lights—Car pulling out—Collision with moped overtaking bus—Moped solely responsible. **Clark v Winchurch** [1969] **1** 275, CA.
      Traffic lights—Relevance of green light signal—Collision at road junction—Fiveway road junction controlled by traffic lights—Collision between pedal cyclist and motor car—Plaintiff cyclist legitimately on junction when lights in his favour—Defendant motorist entering junction from cyclist's left when lights changing in his favour—Cyclist failing to see car—No absolute right to enter road junction merely because lights are green—Duty of care to road users already legitimately on the junction—Cyclist failing to take action to avoid collision—Burden of proof on defendant to show that cyclist could have avoided accident. **Radburn v Kemp** [1971] **3** 249, CA.
  Cross-claims—
    Costs—Both parties to blame—Proper order as to costs. **Smith v W H Smith & Sons Ltd** [1952] **1** 528, CA.
  Damages—
    Jurisdiction of court—Damages before apportionment assessed at sum in excess of that which court had jurisdiction to award—Reduced to amount within limits of jurisdiction—County Courts Act 1934, s 40(1)—Law Reform (Contributory Negligence) Act 1945, s 1(1)(2). **Kelly v Stockport Corp** [1949] **1** 893, CA.
  Defence to action for breach of contract. *See* **Contract** (Damages for breach—Contributory negligence).
  Emergency act—
    Rescue of child—Highway—Plaintiff escorting child—Child stepping on to road—plaintiff running into road to rescue child from danger—Plaintiff injured by motor cycle—Whether plaintiff guilty of contributory negligence. **Morgan v Aylen** [1942] **1** 489, KBD.
    Rescue—Rescuer injured while attempting rescue—Rescuer failing to reduce danger to himself and contributing to own injuries—Whether rescuer contributorily negligent. **Harrison v British Railways Board** [1981] **3** 679, QBD.
  Employer and employee—
    Employee acting outside scope of employment—Deceit—Whether contributory negligence a defence to action for deceit—Law Reform (Contributory Negligence) Act 1945. **Alliance and Leicester Building Society v Edgestop Ltd** [1994] **2** 38, Ch D.
    Employee prepared mould for casting with handle obstructing pouring aisle—Stumbled over handle and suffered injury—Employers in breach of Iron and Steel Foundries Regulations 1953—Whether just or equitable to reduce employee's damages—Law Reform (Contributory Negligence) Act 1945, s 1. **Hawkins v Ian Ross (Castings) Ltd** [1970] **1** 180, QBD.
  Failure to disclose disability—
    Employer and employee—Breach of building regulations—Fatal accident—Employee's fall from platform—Employee failing to disclose liability to epileptic fits—Law Reform (Contributory Negligence) Act 1945, s 1(1). **Cork v Kirby Maclean Ltd** [1952] **2** 402, CA.
  Fatal accident. *See* **Fatal accident** (Damages—Deduction from damages—Contributory negligence).
  Inadventure—
    Accidental contribution to injury—Mechanical fitter accidently touching with screwdriver uncovered electric junction box while adjusting mechanism of machine—No contributory negligence. **Kansara v Osram (GEC) Ltd** [1967] **3** 230, CA.
  Judge's reasons—
    Appeal—Need for copy of judge's notes of evidence and of his reasons. **Johnson v Rea Ltd** [1961] **3** 816, CA.
  Knowledge of danger—
    Blackout during wartime—Duty of pedestrian on highway—Duty of pedestrian to look behind or get off road—Bus using sidelights placed too high and no headlights—Pedestrian knocked down by bus. **Franklin v Bristol Tramways and Carriage Co Ltd** [1941] **1** 188, CA.
  Lack of reasonable care by claimant for own safety—
    Contractor undertaking building work for farmer—Farmer providing farm ladder for use in building work—Contractor not rejecting ladder as unsuitable—Contractor injured when ladder collapsed—Whether contractor contributorily negligent. **Wheeler v Copas** [1981] **3** 405, QBD.
    Existence of contributory negligence not depending on duty of care—Collision between vehicles on highway—Duty of plaintiff towards other road users. **Nance v British Columbia Electric Rly Co Ltd** [1951] **2** 448, PC.
    Motor accident—Duty to other road users—Collision between motor car and unlighted motor cycle combination in which plaintiff a passenger—Plaintiff's knowledge that motor cycle combination had no lights—Lack of reasonable care by plaintiff for her own safety—Whether plaintiff guilty of contributory negligence. **Dawrant v Nutt** [1960] **3** 681, Stafford Assizes.
    Smoking—Deceased exposed to asbestos in workplace—Deceased smoking for most of adult life—Deceased dying from lung cancer—Both asbestos exposure and smoking causative of lung cancer—Whether deceased's continued smoking amounting to contributory negligence. **Badger v Ministry of Defence** [2006] **3** 173, QBD.

NEGLIGENCE (cont)—
  Contributory negligence (cont)—
    Last opportunity of avoiding accident—
      Continuing negligence—Vessel improperly anchored athwart fairway—Colliding vessel failing to keep proper look-out—Continuing negligence by anchored vessel—Neither vessel having last opportunity of avoiding accident—Both vessels equally to blame. **Corstar (owners) v Eurymedon (owners)** [1938] **1** 122, CA.
    Negligent misrepresentation—
      Claim under Misrepresentation Act 1967 for damages for negligence—Whether defence of contributory negligence available to claim under the Act. *See* **Misrepresentation** (Negligent misrepresentation—Damages for breach of duty of care—Contributory negligence).
    Principle on which appellate court will interfere with apportionment of liability—
      Change in ground of liability—Finding of common law negligence substituted on appeal for finding of breach of statutory duty—Duty of appellate court to reconsider apportionment of liability in light of changed ground of liability. **Quintas v National Smelting Co Ltd** [1961] **1** 630, CA.
      Error in principle—Apportionment by trial judge not interfered with save for error in principle or where clearly erroneous—Law Reform (Contributory Negligence) Act 1945, s 1(1). **Brown v Thompson** [1968] **2** 708, CA.
      Error in principle—Apportionment by trial judge not interfered with save for error in principle or where clearly erroneous—Pedestrian struck by motor car when crossing road—Pedestrian and driver with clear view of each other—No evasive action taken—Whether trial judge's apportionment to be amended. **Baker v Willoughby** [1969] **3** 1528, HL.
      Factual basis of assessment—Substantial misjudgment by trial judge of factual basis on which he made his assessment. **Jennings v Norman Collison (Contractors) Ltd** [1970] **1** 1121, CA.
      Misdirection by trial judge—Substantial misdirection. **Kerry v Carter** [1969] **3** 723, CA.
    Road accident—
      Collision between vehicles. *See* Contributory negligence—Collision between vehicles on road, *above*.
      Crash helmet—Failure to fasten securely—Defendant wholly to blame for accident—Plaintiff in part responsible for injuries—Plaintiff riding a moped—Plaintiff failing to secure strap of crash helmet—Helmet coming off before plaintiff's head striking road—Whether plaintiff contributorily negligent—Whether plaintiff's damages should be reduced—Law Reform (Contributory Negligence) Act 1945, s 1—Motor Cycles (Protective Helmets) Regulations 1980, reg 4. **Capps v Miller** [1989] **2** 333, CA.
      Crash helmet—Failure to wear—Motor cyclist not wearing crash helmet—Whether contributory negligence. **Hilder v Associated Portland Cement Manufacturers Ltd** [1961] **3** 709, QBD.
      Crash helmet—Failure to wear—Plaintiff's share of responsibility for injury—Defendant wholly to blame for accident—Plaintiff's lack of care contributing to extent of injury—Liability of plaintiff for contributory negligence—Plaintiff a motor cyclist—Failure to wear crash helmet. **O'Connell v Jackson** [1971] **3** 129, CA.
      Lack of care by plaintiff. *See* Contributory negligence—Lack of reasonable care by claimant for own safety—Motor accident, *above*.
      Learner-driver and instructor—Instructor injured by reason of driver's negligence—Instructor in part control of car—Failure of instructor to avoid accident—Whether instructor guilty of contributory negligence. **Nettleship v Weston** [1971] **3** 581, CA.
      Passenger in car—Driver and passenger intoxicated—Passenger seriously injured—Passenger's knowledge of driver's intoxication—Whether passenger contributorily negligent—Whether passenger able to rely on their own intoxication to avoid finding of contributory negligence or reduce apportionment of responsibility. **Campbell v Advantage Insurance Co Ltd** [2022] **4** 1007, CA.
      Passenger in car—Passenger knowing that driver under influence of drink—Passenger having accompanied driver on drinking session—Effect of alcohol to diminish driver's capacity to drive safely and passenger's capacity to appreciate the danger—Passenger injured in consequence of accident caused by driver's negligence—Whether passenger guilty of contributory negligence in riding with driver under influence of drink. **Owens v Brimmell** [1976] **3** 765, QBD.
      Seat belt—Failure to wear—Plaintiff's share of responsibility for injury—Plaintiff front seat passenger—Car belonging to and driven by defendant—Car fitted with seat belts—Plaintiff failing to wear seat belt—Defendant failing to draw attention to seat belt—Accident caused by driver's negligence—Plaintiff suffering injury—Evidence that injury caused or contributed to by failure to wear seat belt—Plaintiff's share of responsibility for injury. **Pasternack v Poulton** [1973] **2** 74, QBD.
      Seat belt—Failure to wear—Plaintiff's share of responsibility for injury—Vehicle fitted with seat belts—Plaintiff not wearing seat belt—Accident caused wholly by negligence of defendant—Plaintiff suffering injuries which would have been avoided if he had been wearing a seat belt—Plaintiff in part responsible for injuries—Plaintiff guilty of contributory negligence—Amount by which damages should be reduced. **Froom v Butcher** [1975] **3** 520, CA.
  Standard of care imposed on plaintiff—
    Duty to take precautions—Scalding water from shower—Whether person entering shower should have tested water first. **Foulder v Canadian Pacific Steamships Ltd** [1969] **1** 283, Liverpool Summer Assizes.
  Two defendants—
    Contribution—Road accident—Plaintiff hit by two cars while crossing road—All three parties equally to blame—Whether defendants to be considered separately or collectively when apportioning liability—Whether plaintiff entitled to half or two-thirds of amount awarded. **Fitzgerald v Lane** [1988] **2** 961, HL.
  Two plaintiffs—
    Contributory negligence of one—Recovery of damages by defendant from plaintiff partly to blame—Judgment for first plaintiff against defendant—Second plaintiff one third to blame—Right of defendant to recover from second plaintiff one third of damages payable to first plaintiff—Law Reform (Contributory Negligence) Act 1945, s 1(1). **Drinkwater v Kimber** [1952] **1** 701, CA.

NEGLIGENCE (cont)—
  Contributory negligence (cont)—
    Unsafe system of work—
      Workman's knowledge of danger—Failure of employer to provide proper appliance—Method adopted less safe than recognised method—Failure by employers to provide proper tackle for rigging operation—Skilled rigger wishing to use proper tackle resorting to make-shift tackle in order to get on with job—Whether rigger guilty of contributory negligence. **Machray v Stewarts and Lloyds Ltd** [1964] 3 716, Assizes.
    Workman and fellow employee—
      Breach of statutory duty—Vicarious liability of employer—Deceased and fellow workmen in breach of statutory regulations—Vicarious liability of employer in respect of death of deceased—Deceased's share in responsibility assessed at 80 per cent—Employers liable for 20 per cent of liability—Law Reform (Contributory Negligence) Act 1945, s 1(1). **Stapley v Gypsum Mines Ltd** [1953] 2 478, HL.
      Dangerous method of work adopted by plaintiff and fellow employees—Method contrary to employers' instructions—Duty owed by each of employees to other—Plaintiff injured—Employers incautiously liable for breach of duty by fellow employees—Plaintiff's share of blame 50 per cent—Law Reform (Contributory Negligence) Act 1945, s 1(1). **Williams v Port of Liverpool Stevedoring Co Ltd** [1956] 2 69, Assizes.
  Copyright—
    Infringement of copyright. *See* **Copyright** (Conflict of laws—Negligence).
  Costs—
    Counsel—
      Payment of costs by counsel personally. *See* **Counsel** (Payment of costs by counsel personally—Costs incurred negligently).
    Medical negligence action—
      Discretion. *See* **Costs** (Order for costs—Discretion—Claim for professional medical negligence).
  Counsel. *See* **Counsel** (Negligence).
  Crown Prosecution Service—
    Duty to take care. *See* Duty to take care—Existence of duty—Crown Prosecution Service, *below.*
  Damage—
    Admission of negligence but denial of damage—
      Judgment. *See* **Judgment** (Judgment on admission of facts—Negligence).
    Cause of action. *See* Cause of action—Damage, *above.*
    Damage to property—
      Dust caused by construction work—Plaintiffs' properties adversely affected by dust from construction of road—Whether excessive deposits of dust capable of giving rise to action in negligence. **Hunter v Canary Wharf Ltd** [1996] 1 482, CA.
      Economic loss—Duty to take care. *See* Duty to take care—Economic loss—Damage to property, *below.*
    Men undergoing chemotherapy treatment at NHS trust hospital for cancer—
      Men advised treatment might damage fertility—NHS trust freezing and storing men's semen for future use—Semen thawing—Whether trust negligent—Whether men suffering damage—Whether damage to sperm personal injury—Whether sperm property of men—Whether statutory provisions precluding ownership of sperm—Human Fertilisation and Embryology Act 1990. **Yearworth v North Bristol NHS Trust** [2009] 2 986, CA.
    Nature of damage giving rise to cause of action—
      Negligence in construction of house—Present or imminent danger to health or safety of occupier—House built on top of hill—Garden on slope of hill—Foundations of house and bricks and mortar properly constructed by builder—House liable to collapse at any time owing to instability of hillside—Part of garden damaged in landslip—Danger to house having mental and physical effect on occupier—Whether occupier having cause of action against builder for negligent construction of house. **Batty v Metropolitan Property Realizations Ltd** [1978] 2 445, CA.
  Damages—
    Assessment—
      Appeal—Principle on which appellate court will intervene. *See* **Damages** (Assessment—Principle on which appellate court will intervene).
    Date at which damages assessed. *See* **Damages** (Assessment—Date at which damages assessed).
    Economic loss—
      Duty to take care. *See* Duty to take care—Economic loss, *below.*
      Loss not consequent on physical damage. *See* **Damages** (Remoteness of damage—Economic loss not consequent on physical damage).
    Fatal accident. *See* **Fatal accident** (Damages).
    Interest—
      Generally. *See* **Interest** (Damages—Negligence).
      Jurisdiction of Privy Council to award interest. *See* **Privy Council** (Jurisdiction—Interest—Interest on award of damages).
      Personal injury cases. *See* **Interest** (Damages—Personal injury).
    Jurisdiction of county court. *See* **County court** (Jurisdiction—Negligence—Damages).
    Limitation of action—
      Generally. *See* **Limitation of action** (Negligence—Action for damages).
    Measure of damages. *See* **Damages** (Measure of damages—Negligence).
    Nervous shock. *See* **Damages** (Personal injury—Nervous shock).
    Personal injury. *See* **Damages** (Personal injury).
    Recoverability independent of claim against third party. *See* **Damages** (Contract and tort—Recoverability independent of claim against third party).
    Remoteness of damage—
      Foreseeable harm. *See* Remoteness of damage, *below.*
      Generally. *See* **Damages** (Remoteness of damage).
    Solicitor. *See* **Solicitor** (Negligence—Damages).
    Unwanted pregnancy. *See* **Damages** (Unwanted pregnancy—Negligence).

Damages (cont)—
Wrongful entry into life—
Foetus. *See* Duty to take care—Person to whom duty owed—Foetus—Wrongful entry into life, *below*.
Dangerous machinery. *See* **Safe system of working** (Dangerous machinery).
Dangerous things—
Causation—
Intervention of third party. *See* Causation—Intervention of third party—Dangerous things, *above*.
Danger in purchaser's hands—
Duty to warn purchaser or refrain from sale—Sale of pistol and blank cartridges to child aged 12—Liability of vendor to stranger injured. **Burfitt v A & E Kille** [1939] **2** 372, KBD.
Sale of bow and arrow to boy of ten years—Injury to schoolchild—Liability of vendor—Whether bow and arrow dangerous thing to put into hands of particular purchaser. **Ricketts v Erith BC** [1943] **2** 629, KBD.
Defect discoverable by reasonable diligence—
Car in dangerous condition—Car purchased by plaintiff from dealer—Condition discoverable by dealer using reasonable diligence—Liability of dealer for failure to examine car or warn purchaser. **Andrews v Hopkinson** [1956] **3** 422, Leeds Assizes.
Distributor's liability—
Exclusion of intermediate examination by advertising safety of goods—Hair dye—Distributors advertising product as absolutely safe and harmless and needing no preliminary test—Hairdresser applying dye to customer's head—Liability of distributors to customer. **Watson v Buckley, Osborne, Garrett & Co Ltd and Wyrovoys Products Ltd** [1940] **1** 174, Assizes.
Duty to take special precautions—
Gas cylinder—Danger from leakage—Cylinder introduced into ship by contractor—Special care needed to move cylinder—No instructions to others working on ship as to how it should be moved when necessary to do so—Explosion caused by leakage of gas—Contractors responsible for explosion. **Beckett v Newalls Insulation Co Ltd** [1953] **1** 250, CA.
Employer's liability to workmen—
No opportunity for intermediate examination—Tool supplied for use in trade—Tool obtained from reputable suppliers—Workman injured in consequence of defect—Whether employers having used reasonable care and skill in providing tool. **Davie v New Merton Board Mills Ltd** [1959] **1** 346, HL.
Factory occupier—
Duty to avoid leaving machinery in potentially dangerous condition—Electrically driven machine (circular saw) being connected up by electrical contractor—Machine left by factory occupier in condition which would be dangerous if machine switched on—Contractor's workman wiring up machine with duty to test, and to ask occupiers' permission first—Failure to ask permission—Contributory negligence. **Field v Jeavons (E E) & Co Ltd** [1965] **2** 162, CA.
Knowledge of danger—
Appearance not indicating danger to defendants—Disposal of refuse in barge—Refuse including metal shavings—Shavings mainly magnesium and liable to ignite when brought into contact with other refuse—Shavings generating fire in barge—Whether defendants liable to barge owners for negligence in loading shavings. **Burley (C) Ltd v Stepney Corp** [1947] **1** 507, KBD.
Conversion of article into dangerous thing—Assembling of article in manner as to make it dangerous—Steam valve—Defendants assembling valve into one part upside down then by winding it dangerous—Escape of steam injuring plaintiff—Defendants liable for danger which to their knowledge they had evcated. **Howard v Furness-Houlder Argentine Lines Ltd and A & R Brown Ltd** [1936] **2** 781, KBD.
Plaintiff's knowledge of defect avoiding duty on part of defendant—Factory owner and servant of contractor working factory—Chains supplied by factory owner for use by contractor's servants in factory—Chains unsuitable for purpose for which required—Injury to servant of contractor—Nature and quality of chains well known both to servant and to contractor—Whether factory owner liable to servant of contractor. **Gledhill v Liverpool Abattoir Utility Co Ltd** [1957] **3** 117, CA.
Landlord's liability for dangerous installation—
Gas geyser—Defective installation by landlord—Landlord's attention drawn to defect by gas company—Lodger or tenant gassed in bathroom because of defective installation—Whether landlord liable to lodger. **Travers v Gloucester Corp** [1946] **2** 506, KBD.
Gratuitous installation—Domestic boiler installed in dwelling-house by landlord—Boiler in dangerous condition—Tenant's daughter injured by explosion. **Ball v London CC** [1949] **1** 1056, CA.
Manufacturer's liability—
Onus of proof—Lapse of time since purchase—Windscreen manufactured by defendants and bought by plaintiff—Windscreen shattering year after being fitted to plaintiff's car—No explanation for accident—Whether breach of duty proved against defendant. **Evans v Triplex Safety Glass Co Ltd** [1936] **1** 283, KBD.
Reasonable steps to be taken before putting dangerous article on market—Warning to ultimate recipient—Necessity for—Hair dye—Warning given by manufacturers to hairdresser—Character of preparation not brought to knowledge of customer—Failure of hairdresser to take precautions—Injury to customer—Whether manufacturers liable to customer. **Holmes v Ashford** [1950] **2** 76, CA.
Warning to customer—Sale for purposes of resale—Opportunity for intermediate examination—Chemicals supplied for experiments in school—Warning in invoice not transmitted—Explosion injuring schoolgirl—Liability of manufacturer to schoolgirl—Law Reform (Married Women and Tortfeasors) Act 1935, s 6. **Kubach v Hollands (Frederick Allen & Son (Poplar) Ltd, third party)** [1937] **3** 907, KBD.
Occupier of premises—
Standard of care owed to invitee—Work of kind requiring special care—Manufacture of high explosives in ordnance factory—Injury to invitee from explosion—Liability of occupier to invitee. **Read v J Lyons & Co Ltd** [1946] **2** 471, HL.

Dangerous things (cont)—

Opportunity for examination—

Manufacturer's liability to retailer—Sale for purposes of resale—Opportunity for intermediate examination after sale for purposes of resale—Sweets—Retailer's finger injured by wire in one of sweets. **Barnett v H & J Packer & Co Ltd** [1940] **3** 575, KBD.

Proximate relationship—Manufacturer's liability to third party—Kiosk housing electrical transformer—Kiosk supplied by manufacturers to electrical suppliers—Faulty construction rendering kiosk dangerous—Ample opportunity for examination by suppliers—Manufacturers not liable for death of workman killed in consequence of faulty construction. **Paine v Colne Valley Electricity Supply Co Ltd** [1938] **4** 803, KBD.

Reasonable expectation of examination—Sale of article for immediate use—Reconditioned car—Accident due to defective condition of car—Opportunity for examination of car—No expectation that opportunity would be used—Liability of supplier. **Herschtal v Stewart & Ardern Ltd** [1939] **4** 123, KBD.

Repairer's liability—

Duty to execute repairs carefully—Lift—Contract of maintenance—Repair improperly carried out by repairer causing defect in lift—User of lift injured when lift fell to bottom of well—Liability to repairer to user of lift. **Haseldine v Daw & Son Ltd** [1941] **3** 156, CA.

Inefficient repair—Defect not discoverable by owner of article repaired—Repair of motor lorry—Accident on highway—Latent defect due to inefficient repair—Defect not discoverable on inspection—Liability of repairer to person injured in accident. **Stennett v Hancock and Peters** [1939] **2** 578, KBD.

Wholesaler's liability to ultimate customer—

Warning to customer—Failure to give warning—Description stating substance dangerous in certain cases—Hair dye applied by hairdresser to customer—Dye causing dermatitis—Liability of manufacturer to customer. **Parker v Oloxo Ltd and Senior** [1937] **3** 524, Assizes.

Data protection—

Loss of data. *See* **Data protection** (Processing of information—Personal data—Consumer seeking damages for distress caused by compromise or loss of personal data following cyber-attack on retailer's systems).

Defective premises—

Builder's liability—

Cost of repair—Economic loss. *See* Duty to take care—Economic loss—Building—Defect in building—Cost of repair, *below*.

Extent of duty to take care—Duty to potential occupier of house which he builds. *See* Duty to take care—Builder—Extent of duty—Duty to potential occupier of house which he builds, *below*.

Owner of premises—Duty to subsequent purchaser. *See* Duty to take care—Owner of realty—Duty to subsequent purchaser in respect of hidden defects, *below*.

Personal injury—Proximity of relation—Builders of house for occupation by local authority tenant—Fault in construction—Plaintiff injured by canopy falling in consequence of fault—Fall occurring eight years after construction—Whether duty of care owed to plaintiff by builder. **Sharpe v ET Sweeting & Son Ltd** [1963] **2** 455, York Assizes.

Contractor's liability—

Safety of visitors—Duty to take precautions for the safety of others—Building contractors removing ramp giving access to house—Effect of removal to prevent safe access to house—Liability of contractors for injury caused to visitor. **Billings (A C) & Sons Ltd v Riden** [1957] **3** 1, HL.

Creation of dangerous conditions—

Duty to take precautions for safety of others—Extent of duty—Whether to warn or to take steps to protect others from injury—Stevedores loading cargo on to ship—Shed floor rendered slippery by soda ash in cargo—No steps taken to remedy this—Lorry man bringing cargo injured through slipping on floor. **Johnson v Rea Ltd** [1961] **3** 816, CA.

Danger not apparent—

Reasonable care by plaintiff avoiding danger—Stairs—No electric light—Handrail ending before bottom of stairs—Visitor on premises falling down stairs—Whether occupiers in breach of common duty of care. **Wheat v E Lacon & Co Ltd** [1966] **1** 582, HL.

Duty to build dwelling properly—

Scope of duty—Claim for damages arising out of alleged defective construction of flats—Whether statutory duty extending to approved inspectors in performance of their statutory function—Meaning of 'for or in connection with the provision of a dwelling'—Defective Premises Act 1972, s 1(1). **Lessees and Management Company of Herons Court v Heronslea Ltd** [2020] **2** 145, CA.

Scope of duty—Date for determining whether duty applies—Work taken on before commencement of defective premises legislation—Taking on work—Work completed shortly after commencement of legislation—Whether statutory duty applied—Whether duty to ensure that on completion of work dwelling fit for human habitation provided—Whether duty merely to ensure during carrying out of work that work done in proper manner with proper materials—Defective Premises Act 1972, s 1(1). **Alexander v Mercouris** [1979] **3** 305, CA.

Scope of duty—Liability for non-feasance—Failure to carry out necessary work—Duty on person taking on work to see work is done in workmanlike or professional manner with proper materials so that dwelling fit for habitation when completed—Whether duty imposing liability for non-feasance as well as misfeasance—Whether dwelling lacking some essential attribute when completed fit for habitation if problems only manifested later—Defective Premises Act 1972, s 1. **Andrews v Schooling** [1991] **3** 723, CA.

Landlord's duty of care by virtue of obligation to repair—

Enforcement of duty—An injunction requiring landlord to repair premises—Defective Premises Act 1972, s 4(1). **Barrett v Lounova (1982) Ltd** [1989] **1** 351, CA.

NEGLIGENCE (cont)—
  Defective premises (cont)—
    Landlord's duty of care by virtue of right to repair—
      Implied right to repair—Local authority landlord—Tenancy requiring tenant to give council access to premises 'for any purpose which might from time to time be required by council'—Tenant sustaining personal injuries due to defective garden step—Whether tenancy expressly or impliedly giving council right to carry out repairs to garden step—Whether council owing duty of care to tenant by virtue of right to carry out repairs to garden step—Defective Premises Act 1972, s 4(1)(4). **McAuley v Bristol City Council** [1992] **1** 749, CA.
  Defence—
    Acceptance of statutory compensation—
      Onus of proof—Knowledge of common law rights—Employer and employee—Acceptance by employee of compensation under Workmen's Compensation Acts—Onus on employer of proving that workman accepted compensation with knowledge of his common law right to recover damages for negligence—Workmen's Compensation Act 1925, s 29(1). **Olsen v Magnesium Castings and Products Ltd** [1947] **1** 333, CA.
    Contributory negligence. *See* Contributory negligence, *above*.
    Ex turpi causa non oritur actio—
      Auditor. *See* Duty to take care—Auditor—Defence of ex turpi causa non oritur actio, *below*.
      Joint illegal enterprise—Duty of care. *See* Duty to take care—Joint illegal enterprise—Defence of ex turpi causa non oritur actio, *below*.
    Exclusion of liability—
      Breach of trust—Guernsey. *See* **Trust and trustee** (Breach of trust—Guernsey—Exclusion of liability).
      Extent of exclusion—Manufacturer of products incorporated in supplier's goods excluding liability for damage consequent on defects in products—Supplier selling goods to purchaser—Whether manufacturer entitled to rely on exclusion in action brought directly against him by purchaser for negligence arising out of such defects. **Muirhead v Industrial Tank Specialities Ltd** [1985] **3** 705, CA.
      Notice—Implied agreement—Freedom to choose whether to submit to terms of notice—Employee acting in course of employment—Plaintiff employed as lighterman on barge—Train of barges being brought into dock by means of capstan rope provided and operated by defendants—Notice excluding liability of defendants to lightermen availing themselves of assistance provided by defendants—Plaintiff injured by reason of defect in rope caused by defendants' negligence—Notice apt to cover accident—Plaintiff not free to refuse to avail himself of assistance provided by defendants—Whether notice protecting defendants from liability. **Burnett v British Waterways Board** [1973] **2** 631, CA.
      Statutory board—Duty to have regard to safety of operations in provision of services and facilities—Power to make use of services and facilities subject to such terms and conditions as board think fit—Power to exclude liability for negligence in providing services and facilities—Power to exclude liability in absence of contract—British Waterways Board—Plaintiff employed as lighterman on barge—Barge being brought into dock by means of capstan rope provided by board—Notice excluding liability for board's negligence—Plaintiff injured by reason of board's negligence—Whether board protected by notices—Transport Act 1962, ss 10(1), 43(3). **Burnett v British Waterways Board** [1973] **2** 631, CA.
    Latent defect—
      Evidential burden of proof—Failure of defence to show all proper steps taken to avoid accident—Vehicle—Failure of brakes—Accident caused by failure of brakes—Liability of defendants as owners of vehicle—Defendants relying on plea of latent defect—Burden on defendants to prove all proper steps taken. **Henderson v Henry E Jenkins & Sons** [1969] **3** 756, HL.
      Motor vehicle—Collision caused by latent defect in vehicle—Whether owner guilty of negligence in maintenance. **Tan Chye Choo v Chong Kew Moi** [1970] **1** 266, PC.
    Manufacturer's liability. *See* Manufacturer's liability—Defence, *below*.
    Pleading. *See* Pleading—Defence, *below*.
    Practice of trade—
      Roof ladder—Plaintiff slipping on roof ladder—Set-up in accord with established practice—Whether conclusive answer to negligence that good practice followed. **Cavanagh v Ulster Weaving Co Ltd** [1959] **2** 745, HL.
    Sudden event or affliction—
      Malfunction of mind—Road accident—Driver suffering stroke shortly before accident—Stroke causing impairment of driver's consciousness—Driver's control of vehicle impaired—Driver not aware of stroke—Driver aware of feeling queer at time of accident—Whether impairment of consciousness a defence—Whether driver liable for damage caused by accident. **Roberts v Ramsbottom** [1980] **1** 7, QBD.
    Volenti non fit injuria. *See* Volenti non fit injuria, *below*.
  Demolition contractor. *See* **Building contract** (Contractor—Demolition contractor—Negligence).
  Dog—
    Liability of owner or keeper. *See* **Animal** (Negligence—Domestic animal—Liability of owner or keeper).
  Driver of motor vehicle—
    Duty to take care. *See* Duty to take care—Driver of motor vehicle, *below*.
  Duty to take care—
    Accountant—
      Accountants giving advice in relation to disposal of shares in UK company—Client born in Iran and potentially non-domiciled for UK tax purposes—Whether accountants owing duty of care to advise client of potential tax advantages arising from non-domicile status—Whether accountants owing duty of care to advise client to seek specialist tax advice in relation to non-domicile status—Whether accountants in breach of duty of care. **Mehjoo v Harben Barker (a firm)** [2014] **4** 806, CA.
      Valuation—Valuation of company shares. **Caribbean Steel Co Ltd v Price Waterhouse (a firm)** [2013] **4** 338n, PC.
    Act of third party—
      Duty of management of nightclub to its guests in respect of actions of third parties. **Everett v Comojo (UK) Ltd (t/a The Metropolitan)** [2011] **4** 315, CA.

NEGLIGENCE (cont)—
  Duty to take care (cont)—
    Act of third party (cont)—
      Duty of owner of building to occupier of adjoining building in respect of act of third party—Respondents purchasing cinema and closing it prior to redeveloping site—Children gaining access to empty and unattended cinema—Respondents unaware of children's incursions—Children starting fire in cinema—Fire demolishing and damaging adjoining properties—Whether respondents owing duty of care to owners of adjoining properties—Whether respondents liable for adjoining owners' loss. **Smith v Littlewoods Organisation Ltd (Chief Constable, Fife Constabulary, third party)** [1987] **1** 710, HL.

      Duty of owner of building to occupier of adjoining building in respect of act of third party—Thieves gaining access to defendants' unoccupied and unsecured premises—Thieves then making hole in common wall between defendants' and plaintiffs' premises in order to steal from plaintiffs—Whether defendants owing duty to plaintiffs to act positively to prevent third party entering defendants' premises—Whether defendants liable for plaintiffs' loss. **Perl (P) (Exporters) Ltd v Camden London BC** [1983] **3** 161, CA.

      Duty of owner of building to occupier of adjoining building in respect of act of third party—Vandals gaining access to defendant's unoccupied and unsecured premises and damaging water system—Plaintiff's adjacent property flooded—Whether defendant owing duty to plaintiff for acts of third party—Whether defendant liable for plaintiff's loss. **King v Liverpool City Council** [1986] **3** 544, CA.

      Duty to highway user in respect of third party's criminal act—Defendant's carelessness providing opportunity for third party's criminal act—Plaintiff's wife killed when run over by defendants' minibus stolen by unknown third party—Minibus stolen by criminal driver after being left unlocked with ignition keys in it for nine hours—Whether foreseeable that minibus would be stolen and driven negligently—Whether minibus constituting an allurement—Whether defendants owing duty of care to plaintiff's wife. **Topp v London Country Bus (South West) Ltd** [1993] **3** 448, QBD and CA.

      Existence of duty—Limitation of action—Duty of shipowner to non-employee—Widow bringing negligence claim against shipowner company arising from husband's death in Bangladeshi shipyard whilst working on vessel—Company having sold vessel to third party for demolition prior to accident—Company applying for strike out and/or reverse summary judgment—Whether widow having 'reasonable grounds' for claim or 'no real prospect of succeeding'—Whether claim time-barred if Bangladeshi law applied—CPR 3.4, 24.2—European Parliament and Council Regulation 864/2007/EC, arts 7, 26. **Begum (on behalf of Mollah) v Maran (UK) Ltd** [2022] **1 Comm** 940, CA.

  Ambulance service—
    Doctor calling ambulance for patient suffering asthma attack—Ambulance failing to arrive within reasonable time and patient suffering respiratory arrest—Whether ambulance service owing duty of care to patient. **Kent v Griffiths** [2000] **2** 474, CA.

  Animal—
    Owner or keeper of domestic animal. *See* **Animal** (Negligence—Domestic animal—Liability of owner or keeper).

  Architect—
    Inadequate design for building—Liability for defects in building—Plaintiffs engaging defendant architects to design and act as contractor for church—Architects submitting plans to plaintiffs for approval—Whether inadequate plans amounting to negligent misstatements made without care—Whether cost of putting right defects purely economic loss—Whether defendants owing duty of care to prevent loss sustained by plaintiffs as building owners. **Lancashire and Cheshire Association of Baptist Churches Inc v Howard & Seddon Partnership (a firm)** [1993] **3** 467, QBD.

  Arising out of foreseeable risk of injury—
    Liability for escape of animal onto highway. *See* **Animal** (Negligence—Highway—Animal straying on to highway).

  Armed forces—
    Jurisdiction of court. *See* **Armed forces** (Terms of service—Jurisdiction of court).

  Assumption of duty—
    Information or advice. *See* Information or advice—Assumption of duty of care, *below*.
    Third party, by. *See* Duty to take care—Assumption of duty by third party, *below*.

  Assumption of duty by third party—
    Bailment of goods—Bailment to company—Assumption of duty of care by director of company with respect to goods—Personal liability of director for damage to goods. **Fairline Shipping Corp v Adamson** [1974] **2** 967, QBD.

  Auctioneer—
    Valuation of painting—Artist unknown—Standard of skill and care required of provincial auctioneer undertaking to research value of painting prior to auction. **Luxmoore-May v Messenger May Baverstock (a firm)** [1990] **1** 1067, CA.

    Valuation of painting—Claimant issuing proceedings against defendant leading international auction house for negligence and breach of contract—Scope of defendant's duty of care—Whether defendant breaching duty of care. **Thwaytes v Sotheby's** [2016] **1** 423, Ch D.

  Auditor—
    Defence of ex turpi causa non oritur actio—Claimant company used as vehicle for fraud—Claimant becoming insolvent due to proceedings by victims of fraud—Liquidator of company contending defendant auditors negligent in failing to discover fraud—Claimant bringing proceedings against auditors in negligence and fraud—Auditors applying to strike out claim—Whether claim precluded by ex turpi causa non oritur actio rule. **Stone & Rolls Ltd (in liq) v Moore Stephens (a firm)** [2009] **4** 431, HL; [2010] **1 Comm** 125, HL.

    Existence of duty of care. *See* Duty to take care—Existence of duty—Auditor, *below*.
    Foreseeable harm—Causation—Audited accounts of companies containing substantial inaccuracies—Continued trading by companies resulting in losses—Whether auditors' negligence causing companies' losses. **Galoo Ltd (in liq) v Bright Grahame Murray (a firm)** [1995] **1** 16, CA.

NEGLIGENCE (cont)—
  Duty to take care (cont)—
    Bailee for reward—
      Duty to owner of goods—No contractual relation with owner—Carriage of goods by road to order of independent contractors with owners—Goods stolen in transit—Whether duty of care owed by carrier to owner of goods with whom carrier was not in contractual relation. **Lee Cooper Ltd v Jeakins (CH) & Sons Ltd** [1965] **1** 280, QBD.
    Bank—
      Contractual duty to customer. *See* **Bank** (Duty of care—Contractual duty to exercise care and skill).
      Existence of duty. *See* Duty to take care—Existence of duty, *below*.
      Generally. *See* **Bank** (Duty of care).
    Breach of duty—
      Action taken as result of legal advice—Local authority passing invalid resolution affecting plaintiff—Resolution passed on legal advice—Whether local authority in breach of duty of care to plaintiff not to pass ultra vires resolution. **Dunlop v Woollahra Municipal Council** [1981] **1** 1202, PC.
      Breach of rules of natural justice—Local authority breaching rules of natural justice—Whether breach of rules of natural justice amounting to breach of duty of care owed to person affected. **Dunlop v Woollahra Municipal Council** [1981] **1** 1202, PC.
      Burden of proof—Evidential burden—Accident not one that would ordinarily have occurred if defendants had complied with duty—Absence of explanation by defendants showing that they had complied with duty—Defendants owners and managers of supermarket—Duty to keep floors clean and clear of spillage—Customer slipping on yoghurt spilt on floor—No evidence how long yoghurt had been on floor or whether defendants had had reasonable opportunity to clear it up—Whether judge entitled to infer that defendants in breach of duty in absence of explanation by them. **Ward v Tesco Stores Ltd** [1976] **1** 219, CA.
      Horseplay—Test for determining whether participant in horseplay breaching duty of care by causing injury to another participant. **Blake v Galloway** [2004] **3** 315, CA.
    Builder—
      Extent of duty—Defect in building—Cost of repair—Economic loss. *See* Duty to take care—Economic loss—Building—Defect in building—Cost of repair, *below*.
      Extent of duty—Defect in building—Cost of repair—No contractual relationship—Whether builder liable to lessee for cost of repair or defect. **D & F Estates Ltd v Church Comrs for England** [1988] **2** 992, HL.
      Extent of duty—Duty to potential occupier of house which he builds—Defective support from adjoining land—Builder constructing house financed by development company on land owned by company—Builder and company inspecting site before decision to build taken—Foundations of house and bricks and mortar properly constructed—House sold by company to purchaser—House liable to collapse at any time owing to defective support from adjoining land—Defect discoverable before house built—Purchaser suing builder for negligence—Liability of builder. **Batty v Metropolitan Property Realizations Ltd** [1978] **2** 445, CA.
      Extent of duty—Liability for acts of independent contractor—Defendant agreeing to be contractor for erection of factory building—Defendant sub-contracting erection to independent contractor—Building erected according to faulty design—Whether defendant liable in negligence for failing to see that building properly designed and built. **Cynat Products Ltd v Landbuild (Investment and Property) Ltd (Sanders & Forster Ltd, third parties)** [1984] **3** 513, QBD.
      Extent of duty—Liability for acts of sub-contractor—Builder employing sub-contractor to carry out plastering on building—Sub-contractor negligent—Whether builder liable for sub-contractor's negligence. **D & F Estates Ltd v Church Comrs for England** [1988] **2** 992, HL.
    Carriage of passengers by rail. *See* Railway—Duty to passengers and invitees, *below*.
    Club—
      Members' club—Member injured by reason of condition of club premises—Whether club owing duty of care to members to maintain club premises in reasonable state of safety and repair. **Robertson v Ridley** [1989] **2** 474, CA.
    Coastguard—
      Negligence in rescue operation—Duty of coastguard in relation to persons known to be in an emergency—Persons to whom duty owed—Members of canoeing party rescued after unnecessary delay and frustration of rescue attempts by coastguard—Whether duty limited to circumstances where coastguard's positive acts increased or created direct physical injury. **OLL Ltd v Secretary of State for Transport** [1997] **3** 897, QBD.
    Conductor of tramcar—
      Starting signal given by unauthorised person—Conductor absent from platform—Injury caused to person attempting to board tramcar. **Davies v Liverpool Corp** [1949] **2** 175, CA.
    Consultant engineer—
      Consultant engineer retained by employer to supervise contract works—Contractor making claims for additional payments—Engineer rejecting claims—Contractor claiming engineer negligent in rejecting claims—Whether engineer owing duty of care to contractor. **Pacific Associates Inc v Baxter** [1989] **2** 159, CA.
    Contributory negligence—
      Lack of reasonable care for own safety. *See* Contributory negligence—Lack of reasonable care by claimant for own safety, *above*.
      Standard of care imposed on plaintiff. *See* Contributory negligence—Standard of care imposed on plaintiff, *above*.
    Criminal activities—
      Duty owed by criminal to fellow participant in crime—Plaintiff injured while a passenger in get-away car fleeing from crime—Whether driver of get-away car owing a duty of care to plaintiff—Whether public policy preventing duty of care being owed to plaintiff. **Ashton v Turner** [1980] **3** 870, QBD.

NEGLIGENCE (cont)—
Duty to take care (cont)—
Custody of prisoners—
Liability for acts of prisoners—Borstal trainees—Escape of trainees from custody and control of officers—Trainees working on island—Trainees escaping at night and taking yacht—Collison with, and damage to, second yacht—Whether officers owed duty of care to owners of second yacht—Whether officers responsible for damage caused by act of third persons—Whether officers immune from liability on grounds of public policy. **Home Office v Dorset Yacht Co Ltd** [1970] **2** 294, HL.
Damage to property of another—
Consequential loss to plaintiffs—Electric cable severed causing power failure in plaintiffs' factory—Cable not property of plaintiffs—Physical damage leading to loss of profit. **SCM (UK) Ltd v WJ Whittall & Son Ltd** [1970] **3** 245, CA.
Title to property—Right of cif buyer to sue—Goods sold during shipment to cif buyer—Goods damaged by shipowner's negligence before buyer becoming holder of bill of lading—Whether buyer entitled to sue shipowner in tort even though not the owner of goods when damage occurring. **Schiffahrt und Kohlen GmbH v Chelsea Maritime Ltd** [1982] **1** 218, QBD.
Title to sue—Loss caused to person having no title to property—Indirect interest in property—Collision causing damage to chartered vessel—Whether charterers entitled to sue for economic loss. **Candlewood Navigation Corp Ltd v Mitsui OSK Lines Ltd** [1985] **2** 935, PC.
Title to sue—Loss caused to person having no title to property—Indirect interest in property—Whether duty owed to person not having title to property damaged. **Margarine Union GmbH v Cambay Prince Steamship Co Ltd** [1967] **3** 775, QBD.
Title to sue—Right of c & f buyer to sue—Goods sold during shipment to c & f buyer—Goods damaged by shipowner's negligence before buyer becoming holder of bill of lading—Whether buyer entitled to sue shipowner in tort even though not owner of goods when damage occurring. **Leigh & Sillavan Ltd v Aliakmon Shipping Co Ltd** [1986] **2** 145, HL.
Dangerous things. *See* Dangerous things, *above.*
Defective work or product—
Duty to avoid producing defective work or product—Proximity—Defendants laying defective floor in plaintiffs' factory—Defective floor not causing damage to the person or to plaintiffs' other property—No contractual relationship between plaintiffs and defendants—Whether defendants liable to plaintiffs in negligence for cost of replacing defective floor—Whether parties in sufficient proximity for duty of care to arise. **Junior Books Ltd v Veitchi Co Ltd** [1982] **3** 201, HL.
Duty to avoid producing defective work or product—Proximity—Reliance on manufacturer—Defendants manufacturing defective motors for pumps supplied through intermediaries to plaintiff—Defective pumps causing damage to plaintiff's property—Defendants claiming damages from manufacturer for economic loss—Whether close proximity or relationship between parties—Whether plaintiff placing real reliance on defendants—Whether plaintiff restricted to claiming against vendor. **Muirhead v Industrial Tank Specialities Ltd** [1985] **3** 705, CA.
Driver of motor vehicle—
Duty to passenger in vehicle—Duty to drive with standard of skill and care to be expected of competent and experienced driver—Relevance of driver's experience—Learner-driver—Driving instructor as passenger—Driving instructor's knowledge of driver's lack of experience—Whether learner-driver under a duty to drive with degree of care of a competent driver. **Nettleship v Weston** [1971] **3** 581, CA.
Duty to passenger in vehicle—Emergency stop—Sudden stopping of omnibus to avoid running over dog—Injury to passenger—Whether driver in breach of duty to take reasonable care of passengers. **Parkinson v Liverpool Corp** [1950] **1** 367, CA.
Foreseeable harm. *See* Duty to take care—Foreseeable harm—Duty to take care to avoid injury to persons who might foreseeably suffer injury from want of care—Driver of motor vehicle, *below.*
Obstruction above level of road—Omnibus—Overhanging branch—Omnibus brushing branch—Injury through breaking of window—Presumption of negligence—Duty to avoid obstruction above the level of the road. **Radley v London Passenger Transport Board** [1942] **1** 433, KBD.
Police officer—Police officer pursuing person attempting to avoid arrest for arrestable offence—Extent of policeman's duty of care to that person. **Marshall v Osmond** [1983] **2** 225, CA.
Standard of care—Driving in blackout—Duty to take all necessary steps to minimise danger—Excessive speed—Collision at cross-roads—Duty to minimise inherent risk of operation. **Miller v Liverpool Co-op Society Ltd** [1941] **1** 379, CA.
Traffic lights—Road junction controlled by traffic lights—Lights not functioning properly—Requisite duty of care—Liability of driver for collision. **Ramoo son of Erulapan v Gan Soo Swee** [1971] **3** 320, PC.
Driving examiner—
Supervision of learner-driver—Driver undertaking driving test—Only duty to interfere with driving when necessary to avoid danger to public. **British School of Motoring Ltd v Simms (A R Stafford (t/a Mini Countryman School of Motoring) and Cooper, third parties)** [1971] **1** 317, Assizes.
Economic loss—
Building—Defect in building—Cost of repair—Building unfit for intended use—No imminent threat of physical injury to occupants—Remedial works required to render building fit for intended use—Whether builder liable for cost of repair. **Dept of the Environment v Thomas Bates & Son Ltd (New Towns Commission, third party)** [1990] **2** 943, HL.
Building—Defect in building—Cost of repair—Whether cost of repair economic loss—Whether builder liable for cost of repair. **D & F Estates Ltd v Church Comrs for England** [1988] **2** 992, HL.
Contract between parties—Sub-contractor's negligence—Sub-contractor engaged for piling operations—Sub-contractor and building owner entering into collateral contract—Collateral contract making no provision for manner in which piling works to be executed—Sub-contractor's negligence in carrying out piling works causing economic loss to building owner—Whether collateral contract exhaustively defining liability—Whether sub-contractor liable to building owner for economic loss. **Greater Nottingham Co-op Society Ltd v Cementation Piling and Foundations Ltd** [1988] **2** 971, CA.

NEGLIGENCE (cont)—
  Duty to take care (cont)—
    Economic loss (cont)—
      Damage to property—Consequential loss to beneficial owner of property—Whether defendant liable for consequences of physical loss—Whether duty of care owed to beneficial owner. **Shell UK Ltd v Total UK Ltd** [2010] 3 793, CA.
      Damage to property—Consequential loss to plaintiffs who did not own the property damaged—Collision causing damage to chartered vessel—Whether charterers entitled to sue for economic loss. **Candlewood Navigation Corp Ltd v Mitsui OSK Lines Ltd** [1985] 2 935, PC.
      Damage to property—Consequential loss to plaintiffs who did not own the property damaged—Defendants damaged hydrant on industrial estate—Water supply cut off for repairs—Loss of a day's work at plaintiff's factory on same estate owing to water being cut off—Plaintiffs having no cause of action against defendants for negligence. **Electrochrome Ltd v Welsh Plastics Ltd** [1968] 2 205, Glamorgan Assizes.
      Damage to property—Loss of revenue caused by damage to revenue-generating property—Railway lines temporarily closing due to damage caused by negligence of defendants' employees—Claimant owner of railway network liable to pay train operating companies under its contracts with them—Whether loss recoverable from defendants. **Network Rail Infrastructure Ltd v Conarken Group Ltd** [2012] 1 Comm 692, CA.
      Digital currency—Digital asset network developers—Company unable to access bitcoin following hack of its computers—Whether developers under tortious duty to assist company in regaining control and use of its bitcoin. **Tulip Trading Ltd (a Seychelles co) v Bitcoin Association for BSV** [2022] 2 Comm 624, Ch D.
      Employer—Plaintiff employed by defendants and posted to Ethiopia—Plaintiff injured by uninsured driver in course of employment in Ethiopia—Whether defendants owing duty of care to plaintiff to insure him against third party negligence—Whether defendants owing duty of care to plaintiff to advise him to obtain insurance cover against third party's negligence—Whether implied term in contract of employment that defendants would insure plaintiff—Whether employer owing duty of care to protect employee from economic loss. **Reid v Rush & Tompkins Group plc** [1989] 3 228, CA.
      Loss of profit on contract—Defective product—Defendants supplying wrong coloured glass to sub-contractor to install in factory being constructed by main contractor—Building owner withholding payment to main contractor—Main contractor suffering economic loss because payment withheld—No contract between main contractor and glass supplier—Whether glass supplier owing duty of care to main contractor—Whether main contractor entitled to sue glass supplier for economic loss. **Simaan General Contracting Co v Pilkington Glass Ltd (No 2)** [1988] 1 791, CA.
    Employer—
      Character reference given by employer on former employee—Reference required by new employer—Whether employer owing duty to former employee when giving character reference to new employer of that employee. **Lawton v BOC Transhield Ltd** [1987] 2 608, QBD.
      Duty to prevent employee becoming drunk—Liability for employee's death or injury due to drunkenness—Employee becoming drunk and dying of asphyxiation following inhalation of own vomit while in employer's control—Employee's widow suing employer for damages—Whether employer owing duty of care to employee to prevent drunkenness and injury or death caused thereby—Whether employer in breach of such duty—Whether and to what extent employer liable for employee's death—Whether and to what extent employee himself liable. **Barrett v Ministry of Defence** [1995] 3 87, CA.
      Duty to protect employee from economic loss. *See* Duty to take care—Economic loss—Employer, *above.*
      Duty to protect employee from foreseeable risk of danger to health. *See* **Employment** (Duty of master—Safety of employees—Common law duty to protect employee from foreseeable risk of danger to health).
      Duty to protect employee from foreseeable risk of danger to health—Liability for employee's psychiatric illness caused by stress at work—Guidance. **Barber v Somerset CC** [2004] 2 385, HL; **Hatton v Sutherland** [2002] 2 1, CA.
      Duty to protect employee from foreseeable risk of danger to health—Liability for employee's psychiatric illness caused by stress at work—Whether provision of counselling services discharging duty of care. **Daw v Intel Corporation UK Ltd** [2007] 2 126, CA.
      Duty to provide safe system of work—Plaintiff suffering nervous breakdown owing to overwork—Plaintiff suffering further nervous breakdown owing to pressure of work—Whether employer in breach of duty to provide safe system of work—Whether risk of nervous breakdown reasonably foreseeable. **Walker v Northumberland CC** [1995] 1 737, QBD.
      Employee developing symptoms of repetitive strain injury—Employee claiming damages for negligence in respect of injury allegedly caused by amount of typing work—Employee failing to satisfy judge that her condition was organic in origin—Judge also holding that her employer was not under a duty to instruct her to take rest breaks and dismissing claim—Whether Court of Appeal entitled to reverse judge on burden of proof and findings of fact. **Pickford v Imperial Chemical Industries plc** [1998] 3 462, HL.
      Employer's parent company. *See* Duty to take care—Existence of duty—Employer's parent company, *below.*
      Reference given by employer on former employee—Reference required by new employer—Whether employer owing duty to former employee when giving character reference to new employer—Whether employer under duty to take reasonable care in preparing reference in respect of employee. **Spring v Guardian Assurance plc** [1994] 3 129, HL.
    Existence of duty—
      Adjudication officer—Claim for unemployment benefit disallowed by adjudication officer—Payment allowed on appeal—Plaintiff alleging that adjudication officer negligent when disallowing claim for benefit—Whether adjudication officer acting judicially when determining claim for benefit—Whether adjudication officer owing duty of care to plaintiff—Whether adjudication officer's negligence actionable—Crown Proceedings Act 1947, s 2(5)—Social Security Act 1975, s 117. **Jones v Dept of Employment** [1988] 1 725, CA.

NEGLIGENCE (cont)—
Duty to take care (cont)—
Existence of duty (cont)—

Auditor—Company claiming to have suffered losses because of fraud and theft committed by dominant figure within group—Company claiming that auditors under duty to warn of fraud discovered in course of audit—Whether auditors having such a duty. **Sasea Finance Ltd (in liq) v KPMG (formerly KPMG Peat Marwick McLintock (a firm))** [2000] **1** 676, CA.

Auditor—Purchase of company's shares—Company's auditors providing accounts to enable purchaser to determine purchase price—Purchaser subsequently purchasing further shares and making loans to company and wholly-owned subsidiary—Whether auditors owing duty of care to purchaser—Whether degree of proximity sufficient to establish duty of care. **Galoo Ltd (in liq) v Bright Grahame Murray (a firm)** [1995] **1** 16, CA.

Bank of England—Bank's supervisory role over commercial banks in United Kingdom—Commercial bank incurring substantial losses on loan portfolio—Bank of England joined as third party by auditors in actions brought against them by bank and its parent company for damages in negligence—Whether Bank of England under legal obligation to individual bank to exercise reasonable care and skill in carrying out supervisory functions—Whether Bank of England owing duty of care to bank to protect it from financial losses resulting from imprudent dealings. **Minories Finance Ltd v Arthur Young (a firm) (Bank of England, third party)** [1989] **2** 105, QBD.

Bank—Bank providing advice to claimants in relation to operation of Sharia-compliant investment fund—Contractual chain excluding liability between defendant and third claimant company embodying investment fund—Whether permissible to impose duty of care on the defendant towards the fund where contractual chain of liability existing. **Riyad Bank v Ahli United Bank (UK) plc** [2006] **2 Comm** 777, CA.

Bank—Claimant company refinancing its borrowing with defendant banks—Claimant entering into interest rate hedging product as condition of loan—Banks providing advice and/or recommendations on suitability of product—Claimant issuing proceedings for economic loss suffered as result of advice or statements—Whether banks owing claimant duty to use reasonable skill and care—Whether banks breaching duty to give information. **Crestsign Ltd v National Westminster Bank plc** [2015] **2 Comm** 133, Ch D.

Bank—Claimant underwriters authorising agent to underwrite insurance on their behalf—Authority requiring operation of separate client account—Bank issuing letter describing account as 'client account'—Bank and agent entering into 'sweeper' arrangement whereby funds transferred from 'client account' to general account—Whether bank owing duty of care to claimant underwriters—Whether bank acting negligently—Whether claimants acting in reliance on letter when renewing contractual relationship with agent. **Mann v Coutts & Co** [2004] **1 Comm** 1, QBD.

Bank—Islamic financing—Bank arranging Sukuk transaction—Promissory note providing Sukuk certificate holders with means of enforcement not properly executed in accordance with Saudi law—Whether bank owing duty of care to take reasonable care to ensure proper execution—Breach of duty—Whether certificate holders suffering loss—Measure of damages. **Golden Belt 1 Sukuk Co BSC(c) v BNP Paribas** [2018] **1 Comm** 1126, QBD; [2018] **3** 113, QBD.

Bank—Negligent misstatement—Casino seeking customer reference from bank via intermediary to preserve confidentiality—Reference addressed by appellant bank to intermediary in strict confidence—Casino seeking to recover from bank when customer's cheques returned unpaid—Whether bank owing duty of care to casino. **Playboy Club London Ltd v Banca Nazionale del Lavoro SpA** [2017] **1 Comm** 309, CA.

Bank—Negligent misstatement—Casino seeking customer reference from bank via intermediary to preserve confidentiality—Reference addressed by bank to intermediary in strict confidence—Casino seeking to recover from bank when customer's cheques returned unpaid—Whether bank owing duty of care to casino. **Playboy Club London Ltd v Banca Nazionale del Lavoro SpA** [2019] **1 Comm** 693, SC; [2019] **2** 478, SC.

Bank—Negligent misstatement—Interest rate swaps—Defendant bank selling four interest rate swaps to claimant—Proceedings issued wherein claimant seeking rescission of swaps and/or damages—Claims made in negligent misstatement founded on bank's failure to disclose cost of breaking swaps in future and misrepresentation that swaps were a 'hedge'—Whether bank under duty to disclose size of future break costs—Whether bank misrepresenting nature of swaps. **Property Alliance Group Ltd v Royal Bank of Scotland plc** [2018] **2 Comm** 695, CA.

Casino—Whether casino having a duty of care to restrain player from gambling. **Ritz Hotel Casino Ltd v Al Daher** [2015] **4** 222, QBD.

Charity Commissioners—Action in negligence against commissioners—Commissioners giving opinion or advice that local charity comprising educational trust had failed—Local inhabitants claiming that commissioners' opinion and advice erroneous and that commissioners had failed to exercise due care and skill in giving opinion and advice—Whether commissioners owing duty of care to potential objects of charity—Whether action lying against commissioners in negligence. **Mills v Winchester Diocesan Board of Finance** [1989] **2** 317, Ch D.

Children—Accusations of child abuse made against parents—Local authority—Accusations later proving unfounded—Whether duty of care owed to parents and children. **D v East Berkshire Community Health NHS Trust** [2003] **4** 796, CA; [2005] **2** 443, HL.

Children—Department of Social Welfare, New Zealand—Complaint of sexual abuse of child made against parent—Parent and children bringing proceedings in respect of alleged failure to investigate complaint of sexual abuse properly—Whether duty of care owed to parents and children. **B v A-G of New Zealand** [2003] **4** 833, PC.

Children—Local authority—Care—Negligent misstatement—Statutory duty of local authority to maintain register—Power to refuse to register child-minder and to cancel registration—Local authority deciding not to suspend or deregister child-minder under investigation—Local authority's officer advising infant plaintiff's mother that he could be safely left with child-minder—Infant seriously injured while in child-minder's care—Whether local authority having duty to take reasonable care in exercising its statutory obligations to register and deregister child-minders—Whether local authority liable for negligent misstatement. **T (a minor) v Surrey CC** [1994] **4** 577, QBD.

NEGLIGENCE (cont)—
Duty to take care (cont)—
Existence of duty (cont)—

Children—Local authority—Duty to act as a parent of child after child taken into care—Decisions taken as to future of child—Child suffering deep-seated psychological and psychiatric problems—Whether local authority owing direct duty of care. **Barrett v Enfield London BC** [1997] **3** 171, CA; [1999] **3** 193, HL.

Children—Local authority—Education authority—Duty owed in relation to welfare of children or children with special education needs—Whether local authority owing direct duty of care—Whether local authority vicariously liable for negligent professional advice given by or on behalf of authority. **X and ors (minors) v Bedfordshire CC** [1995] **3** 353, HL.

Children—Local authority—Local authorities placing children in their care with foster parents—Children claiming to have suffered damage due to sexual abuse by foster fathers—Children bringing negligence actions against local authorities—Whether claims should be struck out or summary judgment given against claimants—CPR 3.4(2), 24.2. **S v Gloucestershire CC** [2000] **3** 346, CA.

Children—Local authority—Social services—Statutory duty to safeguard and promote welfare of children in need—Statutory duty to enquire whether action should be taken if reasonable cause to suspect child suffering or likely to suffer significant harm—Whether local authority owing common law duty of care to children—Whether local authority vicariously liable for employees—Children Act 1989, ss 17, 47. **N (by his litigation friend, the Official Solicitor) v Poole BC** [2019] **4** 581, SC.

Crown Prosecution Service—Actions in negligence against Crown Prosecution Service—Plaintiffs charged with offences by Crown Prosecution Service and detained in custody—Crown Prosecution Service later abandoning prosecutions—Whether Crown Prosecution Service owing duty of care to those it prosecutes—Whether Crown Prosecution Service in breach of duty of care—Whether Crown Prosecution Service negligent in not discontinuing prosecutions sooner. **Elguzouli-Daf v Comr of Police of the Metropolis** [1995] **1** 833, CA.

Crown Prosecution Service—Duty owed to accused in criminal case—Administrative responsibility as prosecutor to keep court informed as to state of adjourned criminal case—Crown Prosecution Service undertaking to inform magistrates' court that plaintiff's offences had been taken into consideration by Crown Court—Crown Prosecution Service failing to inform magistrates' court—Plaintiff not appearing before magistrates to answer charges—Plaintiff arrested and kept in custody under warrant of arrest issued by magistrates—Whether Crown Prosecution Service under duty to inform magistrates' court that plaintiff's offences had been taken into consideration by Crown Court—Whether Crown Prosecution Service owing duty of care to plaintiff—Whether Crown Prosecution Service immune from proceedings—Crown Proceedings Act 1947, s 2(5). **Welsh v Chief Constable of Merseyside Police** [1993] **1** 692, QBD.

Defendant publishing hydrogeological report on water samples from Bangladesh—Implied statement in report as to absence of arsenic—Claimant seeking to recover damages for personal injury caused by drinking water contaminated by arsenic—Whether defendant owing duty of care to claimant. **Sutradhar v Natural Environment Research Council** [2006] **4** 490, HL.

Duty of sub-contractor to employer—Construction contract distinguishing between nominated and domestic sub-contractors—Contract requiring employer to insure against fire risk and providing that nominated sub-contractors to be treated as insured parties or to have benefit of waiver of insurer's subrogation rights—Employer suing domestic sub-contractor for damage caused by fire—Whether insurance provisions of contract rendering it unfair, unjust and unreasonable to impose duty of care on domestic sub-contractor. **British Telecommunications plc v James Thomson & Sons (Engineers) Ltd** [1999] **2** 241, HL.

Economic loss. See Duty to take care—Economic loss, above.

Education officer—Child with special educational needs—Whether duty of care owed by education officer to child with special educational needs. **Carty v Croydon London BC** [2005] **2** 517, CA.

Educational psychologist—Plaintiff, as a child, having history of lack of educational progress—Educational psychologist employed by local education authority examining plaintiff but failing to diagnose dyslexia—Plaintiff seeking to recover damages from local education authority as employer—Whether educational psychologist owing duty of care to plaintiff. **Phelps v Hillingdon London BC** [1999] **1** 421, CA.

Employer's parent company—Claimant exposed to asbestos dust during course of employment—Claimant contracting asbestosis as a result of exposure—Employer ceasing to exist and claimant bringing proceedings against defendant parent company—Whether parent company assuming responsibility for duty of care to claimant. **Chandler v Cape plc** [2012] **3** 640, CA.

Exposure to asbestos dust—Whether, given relatively low level of deceased's exposure to asbestos and state of knowledge in late 1960s, defendant under duty to take protective measures. **Bussey v 00654701 Ltd (formerly Anglia Heating Ltd)** [2018] **3** 354, CA.

Health and safety inspector—Plaintiff operating bungee jumping business from mobile crane—Plaintiff prevented from continuing with business by local authorities on incorrect advice from health and safety inspector—Whether inspector owing duty of care to plaintiff as to content of advice—Health and Safety at Work etc Act 1974. **Harris v Evans** [1998] **3** 522, CA.

Health authority—Health authority owing statutory duty to provide after-care services for discharged mental patients—Responsible medical officer appointed for plaintiff but plaintiff failing to attend appointments arranged—Plaintiff killing man in unprovoked attack, pleading guilty to manslaughter by reason of diminished responsibility and ordered to be detained in secure hospital—Plaintiff bringing action against health authority for negligence—Whether health authority's statutory obligations giving rise to common law duty of care—Whether fair, just and reasonable to impose duty of care—Whether plaintiff 's action barred on grounds of public policy—Mental Health Act 1983, s 117. **Clunis v Camden and Islington Health Authority** [1998] **3** 180, CA.

NEGLIGENCE (cont)—
  Duty to take care (cont)—
    Existence of duty (cont)—
      Inspection company—Inspection certificate to be presented under letter of credit—Inspection company issuing inspection certificate by reference to bill of lading—Bill of lading false—Seller's bank paying away money remitted in settlement of letter of credit liability on instructions of seller—No goods delivered to buyer—Buyer's bank remitting payment and debiting buyer's account—Whether inspection company negligent—Whether inspection company owing duty of care to buyer of goods—Whether scope of duty owed to buyer extending to duty to verify independently truth of contents of bill of lading. **Niru Battery Manufacturing Co v Milestone Trading Ltd** [2002] **2 Comm** 705, QBD; [2004] **1 Comm** 193, CA.

      Insurance broker—Construction all risks open cover placed and operated through first defendant broker—Projects having to be declared under terms of policy in order to be covered—Declarations handled by brokers—Declarations having to be made to each insurer within period of cover—Claimant issuing proceedings for damages arising from failure of broker to make declarations to certain following insurers within period of cover—Whether broker owing claimant duty of care. **BP plc v Aon Ltd** [2006] **1 Comm** 789, QBD.

      Local authority—Fostering agreement—Plaintiff foster parents stipulating that they did not want to foster a known or suspected sexual abuser—Defendants placing known sexual abuser with plaintiff family—Defendants assuring plaintiffs that fostered child not a known or suspected abuser—Fostered child abusing foster parents' children—Whether local authority liable in negligence to foster parents or children where performing duties imposed by statute. **W v Essex CC** [1998] **3** 111, CA.

      Local education authority—Educational psychologist—Teacher—Failure to provide competent advice—Failure to provide appropriate educational services—Whether educational psychologist or teacher owing duty of care to claimant—Whether authority liable for negligence of employee—Whether authority directly liable. **Phelps v Hillingdon London BC** [2000] **4** 504, HL.

      Matters to be considered in determining whether duty existing—Statutory powers—Regulatory powers—Isle of Man—Treasurer and Finance Board having regulatory powers in regard to banks—Treasurer having power to issue, with or without conditions, to refuse or to revoke bank's licence or to suspend or discontinue bank's business—Plaintiffs depositing funds with Isle of Man bank licensed by Treasurer—Bank collapsing with loss of depositors' funds—Whether Treasurer and Finance Board owing duty of care to depositors in respect of licensing of banks. **Davis v Radcliffe** [1990] **2** 536, PC.

      Parties in contractual relationship—Plaintiffs engaging defendant architects to design and act as contractor for church—Building unsatisfactory—Plaintiffs issuing writ outside limitation period for contract—Plaintiffs suing in negligence—Whether duty of care actionable in negligence existing when parties in contractual professional relationship—Whether limitation period for contract applying to action in tort. **Lancashire and Cheshire Association of Baptist Churches Inc v Howard & Seddon Partnership (a firm)** [1993] **3** 467, QBD.

      Parties in non-contractual relationship akin to employment—Whether such relationship precluding existence of duty of care arising from voluntary assumption of responsibility. **Lennon v Metropolitan Police Comr** [2004] **2** 266, CA.

      Public authority—Police—Officers attending scene of road traffic accident caused by black ice—Officers leaving without taking measures to notify road users of presence of black ice—Fatal road traffic accident occurring some 20 minutes later—Whether police in breach of duty of care. **Tindall v Chief Constable of Thames Valley Police** [2022] **4** 372, CA.

      Solicitor drafting loan agreement on basis loan to finance property development—Developer using loan for different purpose—Transaction failing—Whether solicitor liable for lender's loss—Whether loss falling within scope of duty owed. **Hughes-Holland v BPE Solicitors** [2017] **3** 969, SC.

      Test to establish whether duty existing—Statutory powers—Regulatory powers—Hong Kong—Commissioner of Deposit-taking Companies having regulatory powers in regard to deposit-taking companies—Commissioner having power to refuse or revoke registration if company not fit and proper to be registered—Plaintiffs relying on registration when depositing money with company—Company operated fraudulently, speculatively and to detriment of depositors—Company going into liquidation and plaintiffs losing deposits—Whether commissioner owing duty of care to plaintiffs—Deposit-taking Companies Ordinance 1976 (Hong Kong). **Yuen Kun-yeu v A-G of Hong Kong** [1987] **2** 705, PC.

    Extent of duty to contractor—
      Equipment provided for contractor—Duty to exercise care and control over equipment—Owner providing scaffolding for contractor—Scaffolding made a danger by unknown person—Planks on scaffolding collapsing under contractor's weight—Contractor injured in subsequent fall—Res ipsa loquitur—Whether owner discharging duty of care—Whether contractor contributorily negligent. **Kealey v Heard** [1983] **1** 973, QBD.

      Equipment provided for contractor—Duty to provide suitable equipment for work undertaken—Contractor undertaking building work for farmer—Farmer providing farm ladder for use in building work—Ladder unsuitable for building work—Contractor injured when ladder collapsed—Whether farmer liable for contractor's injuries. **Wheeler v Copas** [1981] **3** 405, QBD.

    Fire. *See* Fire, *below.*
    Fire brigade—
      Negligence in attendance at fire—Duty of fire brigade in relation to fire—Persons to whom duty owed—Plaintiffs' property damaged by fire—Whether fire brigade owing duty of care to plaintiffs—Whether fire brigade liable for breach of statutory duty—Whether fire brigade having statutory immunity—Fire Services Act 1947, ss 13, 30(1). **Capital and Counties plc v Hampshire CC** [1997] **2** 865, CA.

    Foreseeable harm—
      Child—Test of foreseeability—15-year-old plaintiff injured during game with defendant of same age at school—Game not considered dangerous or prohibited by school authorities—Whether accident foreseeable to 15-year-old child—Whether defendant negligent. **Mullin v Richards** [1998] **1** 920, CA.

NEGLIGENCE (cont)—
  Duty to take care (cont)—
    Foreseeable harm (cont)—

Dangerous machinery—Duty of owner—Permission for use—Portable pneumatic grinding machine hired by sub-contractors from plant hire company—Plaintiff employee of head contractors—Plaintiff given permission by sub-contractors to use machine—Plaintiff injured by grinding wheel of machine shattering—Speed of machine too fast for diameter of grinding wheel—Liability of subcontractors and plant hire company. **Griffiths v Arch Engineering Co (Newport) Ltd** [1968] **3** 217, Assizes.

Duty to take care to avoid injury to persons who might foreseeably suffer injury from want of care—Driver of motor vehicle—Duty to other road users and owners of property—Plaintiff suffering nervous shock on hearing that family involved in road accident—Plaintiff at home at time of accident—Whether duty of care owed to plaintiff by driver causing accident. **McLoughlin v O'Brian** [1982] **2** 298, HL.

Duty to take care to avoid injury to persons who might foreseeably suffer injury from want of care—Driver of motor vehicle—Duty to other road users—Collision—Shock from noise of collision—Pregnant woman near to scene of collision suffering shock and consequent injury—Whether duty of care owed to woman. **Bourhill v Young** [1942] **2** 396, HL.

General practice not to take precautionary measures—Ship—Open unfenced hatch—Seaman injured by falling down an open hatch in grain ship while at sea—General practice of grain ships not to fence hatches while at sea—Whether shipowners in breach of duty of care. **Morris v West Hartlepool Steam Navigation Co Ltd** [1956] **1** 385, HL.

Knowledge of previous occurrence causing harm—Escape of substance from premises—Metal foil—Factories on trading estate receiving electric power from same power station—Escape from factory of metal foil blown on to power station causing power failure and consequential damage to other years earlier—Knowledge of defendants that escape of foil could cause power failure—Whether duty to prevent escape. **British Celanese Ltd v AH Hunt (Capacitors) Ltd** [1969] **2** 1252, QBD.

Need to prove harm foreseeable—Water—Damage from burst pipe—Defendant having good reason to believe that water turned off. **Tilley v Stevenson** [1939] **4** 207, CA.

Reasonable grounds for suspecting danger—Submarine—Torpedoe tube—Test cock made dangerous by contractors' painting—Submarine sinking in consequence—Painting negligent—No reason to suspect danger caused thereby—Liability of contractors. **Duncan v Cammell Laird & Co Ltd** [1946] **1** 420, HL.

Unforeseen danger—Spilling of boiling water from tea urn—Water scalding children in shop—Hold of bearer of urn slipping and water thereby spilt—Whether danger foreseeable—Whether a duty to clear children out of way. **Glasgow Corp v Muir** [1943] **2** 44, HL.

  Hospital. *See* **Hospital** (Duty to take care).

  Information or advice. *See* Information or advice, *below.*

  Insurance—

Duty owed by insurer to insured—Application for life assurance—Insurer repeatedly sending completed direct debit form to wrong bank branch—Claim made and policy treated by insurer as void—Claim for damages by estate—Whether duty of care in negligence arising from relation of insurer and insured. **Weldon v GRE Linked Life Assurance Ltd** [2000] **2 Comm** 914, QBD.

Lloyd's underwriting agent—Duty owed to names—Direct and indirect names—Duty owed by members' agents and managing agents—Whether members' agents and managing agents owing duty of care to direct and indirect names because of assumption of responsibility for conduct of underwriting business. **Henderson v Merrett Syndicates Ltd** [1994] **3** 506, HL.

Lloyd's underwriting agent—Duty owed to names—Duty owed by members' agents and managing agents—Managing agent failing to disclose material facts when entering into run-off reinsurance contract with reinsurer on behalf of Lloyd's syndicates—Reinsurer subsequently lawfully avoiding contract on grounds of material non-disclosure—Whether members' agents and/or managing agents owing duty in contract and/or tort to act with reasonable skill and care in relation to placing of run-off reinsurance. **Aiken v Stewart Wrightson Members' Agency Ltd** [1995] **3** 449, QBD.

Names—Future names—Members of syndicates for whom managing agents did not act at time of negligence complained of—Whether managing agents owing any duty of care to future names in respect of reinsurance. **Aiken v Stewart Wrightson Members' Agency Ltd** [1995] **3** 449, QBD.

Pensions and life cover—Insurance company negligently advising customer to join personal pension scheme rather than occupational scheme—Customer's dependants suffering loss in consequence—Whether insurance company owing customer's dependants duty of care when advising on pension and life cover—Financial Services Act 1986. **Gorham v British Telecommunications plc** [2000] **4** 867, CA.

  Insurance broker. *See* **Insurance** (Broker—Duty).

  Insurer—

Duty owed by insurer to insured's assignee—Shipowners dishonestly jeopardising war risk insurance cover on mortgaged vessels—Insurer aware of shipowners' deception—Whether insurer owing duty of care to disclose shipowners' deception to mortgagee bank as assignee of insurance. **Bank of Nova Scotia v Hellenic Mutual War Risks Association (Bermuda) Ltd** [1989] **3** 628, CA.

Duty owed by insurer to insured—Banks making loans to companies guaranteed by credit insurance policies arranged by broker—Broker's employee dishonestly issuing cover notes when part of cover missing—Banks lending large sums in reliance on cover notes—Insurers aware of broker's employee's deception—Whether insurers owing duty of care to disclose broker's employee's deception to banks. **Banque Financière de la Cité SA v Westgate Insurance Co Ltd** [1987] **2** 923, QBD; [1989] **2** 952, CA.

NEGLIGENCE (cont)—
   Duty to take care (cont)—
      Joint illegal enterprise—
         Defence of ex turpi causa non oritur actio—Pillion passenger encouraging rider of motor cycle to
         drive recklessly and dangerously after both had been drinking together—Pillion passenger
         injured in collision between motor cycle and oncoming car—Car driver not to blame for
         accident—Whether motor cyclist owing pillion passenger duty of care—Whether plaintiff barred
         from recovering damages by public policy, maxim ex turpi causa non oritur actio or 100%
         contributory negligence—Whether volenti non fit injuria a defence to negligent driving—Law
         Reform (Contributory Negligence) Act 1945, s 1—Road Traffic Act 1972, s 148(3). **Pitts v Hunt**
         [1990] **3** 344, CA.
      Knowledge of risk—
         Risk so small as to be disregarded—Defendant occupying land adjoining highway—Children
         permitted to use land for play with a football—Land abutting on highway and separated only by
         low wall—Motor cyclist on highway injured as result of football kicked over wall on to highway
         by child—Whether risk to injury to persons using highway so small that it could be safely
         disregarded. **Hilder v Associated Portland Cement Manufacturers Ltd** [1961] **3** 709, QBD.
      Landlord—
         Landlord also designer and builder of premises. *See* Landlord's liability—Landlord also designer
         and builder of premises, *below*.
      Liquidator. *See* **Company** (Voluntary winding up—Liquidator—Duty of liquidator).
      Litigation—
         Conduct of litigation—Defendant serving winding-up petition on company—Petition served at
         wrong address—Company wound up without knowing of winding-up proceedings—Company
         subsequently incurring costs in setting aside order and suffering damage to reputation—
         Company claiming damages for defendant's negligence in serving petition at wrong
         address—Whether defendant owing duty of care to company in relation to service of
         petition—Whether litigant owing duty of care to another litigant in conduct of litigation. **Business
         Computers International Ltd v Registrar of Companies** [1987] **3** 465, Ch D.
      Local education authority—
         Existence of duty. *See* Duty to take care—Existence of duty—Children—Local authority—Education
         authority, *above*.
         Generally. *See* **Education** (Local education authority—Negligence).
      Manufacturer's liability—
         User of manufacturer's product—Proximity—Plaintiff's goods shipped to Kuwait in pails—Pails
         collapsing under heat when left in sun on quayside—Whether manufacturer of pails owing duty
         of care to plaintiff. **Aswan Engineering Establishment Co v Lupdine Ltd (Thurgar Bolle Ltd, third
         party)** [1987] **1** 135, CA.
      Medical practitioner. *See* **Medical practitioner** (Negligence—Duty of care).
      Nervous shock—
         Defendant suffering injuries in road traffic accident caused by his own negligence—Defendant's
         father attending scene as fire officer—Father suffering post-traumatic stress disorder as a result
         of accident and bringing proceedings against son—Whether victim of self-inflicted injuries owing
         third party duty of care not to cause him psychiatric injury. **Greatorex v Greatorex (Pope, Pt 20
         defendant)** [2000] **4** 769, QBD.
         Employer—Rescuer—Employee suffering psychiatric injury in course of rescue—Police officers
         suffering psychiatric injury in aftermath of football stadium disaster caused by police
         negligence—Whether plaintiffs rescuers—Whether plaintiffs entitled to recover for psychiatric
         injury—Whether plaintiffs owed duty of care by employer as employees or rescuers. **White v
         Chief Constable of South Yorkshire Police** [1997] **1** 540, CA; [1999] **1** 1, HL.
         Foreseeability of harm—Duty to take care to avoid injury to persons who might foreseeably suffer
         nervous shock from want of care—Driver of school bus carrying plaintiff's son colliding with
         lorry—Plaintiff's son killed in accident—Plaintiff at home at time of accident and receiving news
         of accident at home—Plaintiff suffering emotional trauma and consequently developing reactive
         depression—Whether consequential illness suffered by plaintiff foreseeable—Whether defendant
         liable for consequential illness following mental shock suffered when receiving news of
         accident—Whether proximity of time and place of learning of accident relevant factors in
         determining liability of defendant. **Hevican v Ruane** [1991] **3** 65, QBD.
         Foreseeability of harm—Duty to take care to avoid injury to persons who might foreseeably suffer
         nervous shock from want of care—Plaintiff's son killed in accident at work—Accident caused by
         defendants' negligence—Plaintiff informed of son's death at hospital—Plaintiff suffering
         emotional trauma and consequently developing reactive depression—Whether consequential
         illness suffered by plaintiff foreseeable—Whether defendants liable for consequential illness
         following mental shock suffered when receiving news of son's death—Whether proximity of time
         and place of learning of accident relevant factors for liability of defendants. **Ravenscroft v
         Rederiaktiebølaget Transatlantic** [1991] **3** 73, QBD; [1992] **2** 470, CA.
         Plaintiff suffering from post-traumatic stress disorder and pathological grief disorder—Plaintiff
         witnessing aftermath of car crash in which children killed—Plaintiff vulnerable to
         stress—Whether plaintiff entitled to recover damages for mental injury. **Vernon v Bosley (No 1)**
         [1997] **1** 577, CA.
      Non-delegable duty of care—
         Liability of local authority for acts of foster carers. *See* **Child** (Care—Local authority—Liability for
         acts of foster carers).
         Local education authority—School—Local education authority school contracting with independent
         contractor to provide swimming lessons for school pupils—Independent contractor providing
         swimming teacher and lifeguard—Pupil having swimming lesson suffering injury through
         negligence of swimming teacher and lifeguard—Whether local education authority liable in
         negligence—Whether local education authority owing non-delegable duty of care. **Woodland v
         Essex CC** [2014] **1** 482, SC.
      Occupier of premises. *See* **Occupier's liability**.

Duty to take care (cont)—
Owner of realty—
Builder—Duty to subsequent purchaser in respect of hidden defects—Negligence in construction of house—Inadequate foundations—Defect causing damage to house after purchase by subsequent purchaser—Builder in breach of duty of care to subsequent purchaser—Immaterial that builder owner of house when defect created. **Anns v Merton London Borough** [1977] **2** 492, HL.

Duty to neighbour—Beekeeper. *See* Duty to take care—Person to whom duty owed—Beekeeper—Duty owed by neighbouring farmer, *below*.

Duty to subsequent purchaser in respect of hidden defects—Builder—Negligence in construction of house—Foundations badly laid so as to create hidden defect—Defective foundations causing damage to house after purchase by subsequent purchaser—Builder owing duty of care to a purchaser of the house—Builder liable for negligence to subsequent purchaser—Immaterial that builder owner of realty. **Dutton v Bognor Regis United Building Co Ltd** [1972] **1** 462, CA.

Duty to subsequent purchaser in respect of hidden defects—Builder—Negligent in construction of house—Liability in tort to person injured. **Otto (M) & E Otto v Bolton & Norris** [1936] **1** 960, KBD.

Participants in sporting event—
Duty owed by one participant to another—Plaintiff injured by defendant's tackle during football match—Whether defendant owing plaintiff duty of care. **Condon v Basi** [1985] **2** 453, CA.

Person to whom duty owed—
Beekeeper—Duty owed by neighbouring farmer—Farmer spraying crops in vicinity of beehives—Farmer using pesticide known to be harmful to bees at a time when crops attractive to bees—Whether farmer owing duty of care to beekeeper—Whether farmer liable in negligence for loss of bees. **Tutton v A D Walter Ltd** [1985] **3** 757, QBD.

Blind persons on highway—Duty of care extends to the blind when it is reasonably foreseeable that they may use highway—Trench dug along pavement in London—Guard at end of trench inadequate and an obstruction to a blind person, but a sufficient guard to protect normal road users—Reasonably foreseeable that blind person might use city pavement—Assumption that blind person exercises proper care to protect himself—Breach of duty to blind person injured by fall caused by the obstruction. **Haley v London Electricity Board** [1964] **3** 185, HL.

Building operations—Liability of contractor to servant of sub-contractor—Retention by contractor of control over manner of performance of work—Building (Safety, Health and Welfare) Regulations 1948 (SI 1948 No 1145), reg 4, reg 31(1). **Mulready v JH & W Bell Ltd** [1953] **2** 215, CA.

Building operations—Liability of sub-contractor to servant of contractor—Dangerous scaffolding erected or altered by sub-contractor—Contractor responsible for scaffolding. **Simmons v Bovis Ltd** [1956] **1** 736, Assizes.

Duty owed only to those whose persons or property may be foreseeably injured—Escape of virus from research premises leading to infection of cattle in the vicinity—Closing of cattle markets—Consequent economic loss to auctioneers who did not own cattle—Whether auctioneers within scope of duty owed by research institute. **Weller & Co v Foot and Mouth Disease Research Institute** [1965] **3** 560, QBD.

Fireman—Duty of care owed to fireman—Nature of duty—Fireman attending premises to put out fire—Fire caused by occupier's negligence—Fireman injured by steam created by fighting fire with water—Fireman wearing protective clothing—Whether person starting fire owing duty of care to fireman—Whether fireman's injuries reasonably foreseeable—Whether duty of care to fireman limited to special or exceptional risks. **Ogwo v Taylor** [1987] **3** 961, HL.

Foetus—Child injured in utero—Hospital negligent in carrying out gynaecological operation on plaintiffs' mothers while they were pregnant—Hospital negligent in carrying out medical care of plaintiffs' mothers while they were pregnant and during plaintiffs' birth—Plaintiffs born with physical deformities—Whether plaintiffs having cause of action against hospital even though plaintiffs having no legal status at time of wrongful act. **De Martell v Merton and Sutton Health Authority** [1992] **3** 833, CA.

Foetus—Wrongful entry into life—Mother contracting infection during pregnancy—Doctor failing to diagnose and treat infection—Child born severely disabled—Child claiming damages against doctor for wrongful entry into life—Whether doctor owing duty to foetus to terminate pregnancy in order to prevent existence in disabled state—Whether child's claim disclosing reasonable cause of action—Whether claim should be struck out—RSC Ord 18, r 19(1). **McKay v Essex Area Health Authority** [1982] **2** 771, CA.

Owner of building—Duty to occupier of adjoining building in respect of acts of third party. *See* Duty to take care—Act of third party—Duty of owner of building to occupier of adjoining building in respect of act of third party, *above*.

Police. *See* **Police** (Negligence—Duty to take care—Persons to whom duty owed).

Social landlord—Right to life—Tenant of social landlord—Tenant threatening neighbouring tenant of same landlord—Landlord serving notice of proceedings for recovery of possession on tenant—Landlord meeting with tenant to inform him of continuing monitoring of complaints about his behaviour—Tenant returning home and attacking neighbouring tenant—Neighbouring tenant dying from injuries—Whether landlord owing duty of care to neighbouring tenant to give warning of meeting—Whether breach of right to life—Whether landlord knew or ought to have known of real and immediate risk—Human Rights Act 1998, Sch 1, Pt I, art 2. **Mitchell v Glasgow City Council** [2009] **3** 205, HL.

Trespasser—Plaintiff injured by defendant while attempting to break into defendant's premises—Whether defendant owing duty of care to plaintiff—Occupiers' Liability Act 1984, s 1. **Revill v Newbery** [1996] **1** 291, CA.

Police—
Generally. *See* **Police** (Negligence—Duty to take care).

Police driver. *See* Duty to take care—Driver of motor vehicle—Police officer, *above*.

Premises open to public—
Danger from rush of people—Duty to institute crowd control—Local authority—Air-raid shelter—Steps down to shelter—Steps uneven, inadequately illuminated and without centre hand-rail—Duty of local authority as occupier of premises to guard against danger from rush of people. **Baker v Bethnal Green Corp** [1945] **1** 135, CA.

NEGLIGENCE (cont)—
  Duty to take care (cont)—
    Prevention of theft—
      Theatrical producer—Failure of producer to take reasonable care to prevent theft—Actor's clothing stolen from dressing room—Liability of producer. **Deyong v Shenburn** [1946] **1** 226, CA.
    Prison authorities. *See* **Prison** (Negligence—Prison authorities—Duty to prisoner).
    Prison hospital—
      Mentally ill prisoner—Suicide risk—Prisoner ordered to be detained in remand prison pending admission to hospital—Prisoner known to have suicidal tendancies—Prison medical staff deciding that prisoner should be observed in cell at 15-minute intervals—Prisoner committing suicide in between inspections—Whether standard of care provided for mentally ill prisoner in prison hospital required to be as high as standard of care provided in psychiatric hospital—Whether medical staff negligent in failing to keep prisoner under continuous observation. **Knight v Home Office** [1990] **3** 237, QBD.
    Professional person—
      Exercise of reasonable skill and care. *See* Professional person—Duty to exercise reasonable skill and care, *below*.
    Proximity of relation—
      Building contract—Safety consultants—Consultants engaged by contractors—Failure to give advice which would have prevented accident to labourer employed by contractors—Liability of consultants in damages to labourer—Apportionment of liability between contractors and consultants—Liability of consultants to contractors for damages for breach of contract. **Driver v William Willett (Contractors) Ltd** [1969] **1** 665, Sussex Assizes.
      Constructional company having conduct of work—Sub-contractors. *See* **Building** (Construction—Negligence—Sub-contractors liable to servant of other sub-contractors—Liability of constructional company having conduct of work for building owner, to servant of sub-contractors).
    Railway—
      Duty to fence railway line—Entrant taking short cut through gap in fence—Entrant familiar with line and aware of dangers—Whether occupier owing entrant duty to repair fence—Occupiers' Liability (Scotland) Act 1960, s 2(1). **Titchener v British Railways Board** [1983] **3** 770, HL.
      Duty to passengers and invitees. *See* Railway—Duty to passengers and invitees, *below*.
      Footpath crossing railway line—Stile erected at edge of crossing to line—Stile in disrepair—Child walking through stile on to line—Child hit by train—Whether railway under duty to take car in relation to maintenance of stile—Whether liable for child's injuries. **Thomas v British Railways Board** [1976] **3** 15, CA.
    Registrar of Companies—
      Winding-up order erroneously registered against wrong company name—Company going into administration—Whether registrar owing duty of care under common law—Whether error on register causing company's administration. **Sebry v Companies House** [2015] **4** 681, QBD.
    Reliance on defendant—
      Motor vehicles—Motor cyclist leading second motor cycle—Agreement by leading one to act as pilot to second motor cyclist carrying pillion-rider—Accident due to pilot accidentally leaving road—Whether injured pillion-rider entitled to recover damages from driver of first motor cycle—Undertaking by first driver imposing duty not to put second motor cycle in danger. **Sharp v Avery and Kerwood** [1938] **4** 85, CA.
    Rescuer—
      Danger to property—Intervention to avert danger to property natural consequence of negligence—Fire breaking out owing to defendant's negligence—Fire constituting danger to property—Plaintiff injured trying to extinguish fire—Whether entitled to damages. **Hyett v Great Western Rly Co** [1947] **2** 264, CA.
      Duty owed by master to servant—Rescue of servant—Duty to rescuer—Negligence placing workmen in imminent peril from gas on their descending a well—Doctor descending well to rescue them—Whether duty of care owed by master to servant extended to doctor. **Baker v T E Hopkins & Son Ltd** [1959] **3** 225, CA.
      Mental shock—Voluntary assistance in rescue work—Foreseeability—Railway collision causing many casualties among passengers—Rescuer voluntarily assisting in rescue work—Rescuer subsequently suffering prolonged mental shock—Defendants admitting liability for collision—Whether under duty of care to rescuer—Whether mental shock to rescuer reasonably foreseeable. **Chadwick v British Transport Commission** [1967] **2** 945, QBD.
      Nervous shock—Generally. *See* Duty to take care—Nervous shock, *above*.
      Person being rescued creating danger—Passenger attempting to board train while it was moving—Rescuer attempting to assist passenger aboard—Both passenger and rescuer falling off train—Rescuer injured—Whether person being rescued owing duty of care to rescuer. **Harrison v British Railways Board** [1981] **3** 679, QBD.
      Railway—Negligent driving of trolley by railway employee—Child trespassing on line—Stationmaster killed in rescuing child—Liability of railway. **Videan v British Transport Commission** [1963] **2** 860, CA.
      Rescuer injured while attempting to reach scene of danger—Whether reasonably foreseeable that rescuer would be injured while attempting to reach scene of danger. **Crossley v Rawlinson** [1981] **3** 674, QBD.
    Safe system of working. *See* **Safe system of working** (Reasonable care not to expose employee to unnecessary risk).
    Safety rules—
      Coal mine—Rules prohibiting employees riding on conveyors—Practice of employees to ride conveyors in breach of rules—Whether employers negligent in failing to prevent employees from doing what employees knew to be prohibited and unsafe. **Storey v National Coal Board** [1983] **1** 375, QBD.
    School—
      Generally. *See* School—Duty of care, *below*.
      Non-delegable duty of care. *See* Duty to take care—Non-delegable duty of care, *above*.

NEGLIGENCE (cont)—

Duty to take care (cont)—

Serviceman—

Duty to provide safe systems of work and safe equipment—Soldiers serving in Iraq killed by improvised explosive devices—Soldiers serving in Iraq killed or injured by friendly fire—Whether state owing duty of care—Whether issues relating to procurement of equipment and to training justiciable—Whether claims within scope of 'combat immunity'. **Smith v Ministry of Defence** [2013] **1** 778, CA; [2013] **4** 794, SC.

Soldier engaging enemy in battle conditions—Soldier sustaining personal injury—Injury caused by negligence of fellow soldier—Whether soldier owing duty of care to fellow servicemen when engaging enemy during hostilities. **Mulcahy v Ministry of Defence** [1996] **2** 758, CA.

Solicitor. *See* **Solicitor** (Negligence—Duty of care).

Special relationship giving rise to duty of care—

Information or advice. *See* Information or advice—Special relationship giving rise to duty of care, *below*.

Spectator at game or competition—

Child—No duty to protect child spectator against danger incidental to game—Ice-hockey—Child spectator injured by puck—Implied contract—Reasonable care for safety—Foreseeable danger incident to entertainment. **Murray v Harringay Arena Ltd** [1951] **2** 320, CA.

Duty not to show reckless disregard for spectator's safety—Duty not to make error of judgment which cannot be regarded as reasonable—Competitor in race—Motor cycle scramble—Competitor going all out to win. **Wilks (formerly an infant) v Cheltenham Home Guard Motor Cycle and Light Car Club** [1971] **2** 369, CA.

Standard of care—

Social utility—Security services in Iraq—Contractors and civilian interpreters being required to participate in fitness for role exercises—Interpreter causing injury to contractor during FFR exercise—Whether breach of duty of care—Whether social utility factor only applying if measures required to reduce level of risk entirely preventing continuation of activity. **Humphrey v Aegis Defence Services Ltd** [2017] **2** 235, CA.

Statutory regulations—Safety—Circumstances not quite within regulations—Whether regulation relevant in determining standard of care. **Chipchase v British Titan Products Co Ltd** [1956] **1** 613, CA.

Statement—

Careless statement causing damage to person or property—Statements actionable in negligence—Instructions negligently issued by architect to bricklayer resulting in bricklayer's personal injuries. **Clayton v Woodman & Sons (Builders) Ltd** [1962] **2** 33, CA.

Information or advice. *See* Information or advice, *below*.

Traffic signal. *See* Duty to take care—Traffic signal, *below*.

Statutory duty—

Relation of statutory duty to common law duty—Factory—Protection of eyes—Melting and founding non-ferrous metals—Employers under statutory duty to provide goggles to employee—Employers complying with statutory duty—Employers failing to instruct and persuade employee to wear goggles—Whether employers in breach of duty to provide reasonably safe system of work—Whether compliance with statutory duty absolving employers from breach of common law duty—Non-Ferrous Metals (Melting and Founding) Regulations 1962 (SI 1962 No 1667), reg 13(1). **Bux v Slough Metals Ltd** [1974] **1** 262, CA.

Statutory powers—

Act performed in exercise of powers—Local authority—Building operations—Duty of care owed to building owner—Duty of care to supervise building works—Developer employing builder to erect building—Local authority inspector inspecting foundations—Inspector's instructions regarding depth of foundations carried out—Instructions not complying with building regulations—Foundations inadequate for site—Subsequent damage occurring to building after occupation—Whether local authority owing duty of care to building owner—Whether negligence of building owner the source of his own loss—Whether building owner's opportunities for inspection and control removing him from scope of local authority's duty of care. **Acrecrest Ltd v W S Hattrell & Partners (a firm)** [1983] **1** 17, CA.

Act performed in exercise of powers—Local authority—Building operations—Duty of care owed to building owner—Duty of care when granting building regulation approval—Extent of liability—Whether liability extending to liability for economic loss. **Cynat Products Ltd v Landbuild (Investment and Property) Ltd (Sanders & Forster Ltd, third parties)** [1984] **3** 513, QBD.

Act performed in exercise of powers—Local authority—Building operations—Legislation giving authority control over building operations—Byelaws requiring approval of foundations of building by authority's inspector before being covered up—Inspector carrying out inspection but failing to take reasonable care to ensure that foundations adequate—Building constructed on inadequate foundations—Subsequent damage to structure of building resulting from inadequate foundations—Whether local authority in breach of duty of care to owner or occupier of building at time damage occurs. **Anns v Merton London Borough** [1977] **2** 492, HL.

Act performed in exercise of powers—Local authority—Building operations—Legislation giving authority control over building operations—Byelaws requiring approval of foundations of building by authority—Authority referring plans of foundations to independent consulting engineers for checking—Engineers negligently recommending approval of plans—Authority approving plans—House constructed on inadequate foundations—Subsequent damage to building resulting from inadequate foundations—Whether local authority in breach of duty of care to owner or occupier of house—Whether local authority discharging duty by engaging independent consulting engineers to check plans—Public Health Act 1936, s 64. **Murphy v Brentwood DC** [1990] **2** 269, CA.

NEGLIGENCE (cont)—
   Duty to take care (cont)—
      Statutory powers (cont)—
         Act performed in exercise of powers—Local authority—Building operations—Legislation giving authority control over building operations—Plans—Building byelaws requiring approval of plans—Plans disclosing that house to be supported by concrete raft—Local authority passing plans on assumption that concrete raft would be adequate for its purpose—Raft constructed partly on natural soil and partly on fills of mixed composition—Raft inadequate and badly constructed—Raft and foundations constructed in breach of building byelaws—Subsequent damage to structure of building resulting from inadequate foundations—Extent of local authority's duty in considering and approving plans—Whether local authority liable for breach of duty to owner of building at time damage occurs. **Dennis v Charnwood BC** [1982] **3** 486, CA.

         Act performed in exercise of powers—Local authority—Building operations—Local authority's building byelaws requiring approval of foundations of building—Local authority negligently approving inadequate foundations—House constructed on inadequate foundations—Subsequent damage to building resulting from inadequate foundations—Whether local authority owing duty of care to owner or occupier of house when approving plans. **Murphy v Brentwood DC** [1990] **2** 908, HL.

         Act performed in exercise of powers—Local authority—Coast protection authority—Authority lowering groyne in purported exercise of statutory power—Landowner's property adjoining groyne subsequently washed away—Landowner claiming loss of land due to authority's negligence—Whether authority owing duty of care to landowner at common law—Whether authority could be liable for loss of land. **Fellowes v Rother DC** [1983] **1** 513, QBD.

         Compliance with statutory requirements—Building operations—Duty of care owed to building owner—Building owner not adhering to approved plans for drainage system—Local authority aware of building owner's non-compliance with its requirements but taking no action to enforce compliance—Drainage system proving defective—Building owner suffering loss by having to replace drains—Whether local authority owing duty of care to building owner to force him to comply with its requirements—London Building Act 1963, Sch 9, Part III, paras 13, 15. **Peabody Donation Fund (Governors) v Sir Lindsay Parkinson & Co Ltd** [1984] **3** 529, HL.

         Compliance with statutory requirements—Building operations—Duty of care owed to building owner—Original building owner—Owner's architects and structural engineers submitting plans for warehouses to be erected on infilled site—Foundations proposed by structural engineers inadequate—Plans approved by local authority—Warehouses suffering damage from subsidence and having to be demolished—Whether owner responsible for breach of building regulations—Whether local authority owing duty of care to original building owner to ensure building erected in compliance with building regulations—Public Health Act 1936, s 64. **Investors in Industry Commercial Properties Ltd v South Bedfordshire DC (Ellison & Partners (a firm), third parties)** [1986] **1** 787, CA.

         Compliance with statutory requirements—Building operations—Duty of care owed to building owner—Original building owner—Plaintiff submitting plan for proposed extension to roof space—Plan never specifically approved by local authority—Plan defective in detail—Local authority not inspecting roof space during construction—Extension defective—Whether local authority owing duty of care to original building owner to ensure building erected in compliance with building regulations. **Richardson v West Lindsey DC** [1990] **1** 296, CA.

         Compliance with statutory requirements—Non-compliance with statutory requirements—Whether duty to prevent person acting unlawfully to his own detriment. **Peabody Donation Fund (Governors) v Sir Lindsay Parkinson & Co Ltd** [1984] **3** 529, HL.

         Construction of statute conferring power on Minister of State—Application for consent of minister—Minister taking into account irrelevant consideration and refusing consent—Whether erroneous construction of statute and consequential consideration of irrelevant matters amounting to negligence—Whether minister in breach of duty of care—Reserve Bank of New Zealand Act 1964 (NZ), s 28—Capital Issues (Overseas) Regulations 1965 (NZ), reg 3. **Rowling v Takaro Properties Ltd** [1988] **1** 163, PC.

         Exercise of statutory power conferred by statute—Secretary of State obtaining undertaking from plaintiff not to acquire more than 30% of company's share capital—Monopolies and Mergers Commission subsequently reporting that plaintiff's take-over of company not against public interest—Rival making take-over bid for company—Secretary of State releasing plaintiff from undertaking after rival had acquired control of company—Whether Secretary of State and Department of Trade and Industry negligent in failing to release undertaking in due time—Whether Secretary of State and department in breach of duty of care owed to plaintiff—Whether public law nature of claim requiring plaintiff to seek judicial review rather than proceed by action. **Lonrho plc v Tebbit** [1992] **4** 280, CA.

         Housing—Improvement grant—Extension to house built with aid of improvement grant—Payment of grant conditional on works being executed 'to the satisfaction of' authority making grant—Plaintiffs purchasing house with knowledge of grant—Extension defective—Whether payment of grant giving rise to duty of care on authority—Whether authority owing duty of care to plaintiffs to ensure extension properly constructed—Housing (Northern Ireland) Order 1976, art 60(5). **Curran v Northern Ireland Co-ownership Housing Association Ltd (Stewart, third party)** [1987] **2** 13, HL.

         Local authority—Building operations—Duty to secure or enforce compliance with building regulations—To whom duty owed—Duty owed to occupier—Whether duty owed to non-resident occupier. **Investors in Industry Commercial Properties Ltd v South Bedfordshire DC (Ellison & Partners (a firm), third parties)** [1986] **1** 787, CA.

         Local authority—Building operations—Legislation giving authority control over building operations—Byelaws requiring approval of foundations of building by authority's building inspector before being covered up—Inspector failing to make proper inspection before giving approval—Foundations laid by builder of house inadequate to carry load of building—Consequent damage to structure of house occurring after house coming into hands of subsequent purchaser—Liability of authority for inspector's negligence. **Dutton v Bognor Regis United Building Co Ltd** [1972] **1** 462, CA.

         Local authority—New Zealand. See **New Zealand** (Negligence—Duty of care—Statutory powers—Local authority).

NEGLIGENCE (cont)—
  Duty to take care (cont)—
    Statutory powers (cont)—
      Local education authority—Education authority employing head teacher—Head teacher suffering stress due to acrimonious disputes within governing body of school—Head teacher bringing claim in negligence against education authority—Whether claim justiciable—Whether actions of education authority wholly within its public law functions. **Connor v Surrey CC** [2010] **3** 905, CA.
      Non-exercise of power—Circumstances in which non-exercise of power capable of amounting to a breach of duty of care—Local authority—Building operations—Legislation giving authority control over building operations—Byelaws requiring approval of foundations of building by authority's inspector before being covered up—Authority not carrying out inspection of foundations—Building constructed on inadequate foundations—Subsequent damage to structure of buildings resulting from inadequate foundations—Local authority not under statutory duty to inspect foundations—Whether failure to carry out inspection capable of amounting to breach of duty of care. **Anns v Merton London Borough** [1977] **2** 492, HL.
      Registration authority—Nursing home—Registration authority applying ex parte and without notice for cancellation of nursing home registration—Magistrate granting order—Nursing home owners bringing proceedings in negligence against authority for economic loss suffered—Whether authority owing duty of care to claimants in making application—Registered Homes Act 1984, s 30. **Jain v Trent Strategic Health Authority** [2009] **1** 957, HL.
      Test to establish whether duty existing. *See* Duty to take care—Existence of duty—Test to establish whether duty existing—Statutory powers, *above*.
    Survey of ship—
      Duty of classification society arranging for survey of ship—Vessel carrying cargo developing crack in hull—Vessel inspected by surveyor acting on behalf of classification society—Temporary repairs effected—Surveyor recommending vessel continue and that repairs be further examined after cargo discharged—Vessel sinking with total loss of cargo—Whether classification society owing duty of care to cargo owners for carelessness of surveyor—Whether fair, just and reasonable to impose duty of care on classification society. **Rich (Marc) & Co AG v Bishop Rock Marine Co Ltd** [1995] **3** 307, HL.
    Surveyor. *See* Surveyor—Duty to take care, *below*.
    Traffic signal—
      Duty owed to driver—Signal to car driver to proceed—Driver acting on signal—Collision inevitable after driver proceeds—Duty of care of third party—Duty of care of driver. **Grange Motors (Cymbran) Ltd v Spencer (Post Office, Third Party)** [1969] **1** 340, CA.
    Tree adjacent to highway—
      Duty of occupier to property—Standard of care—Elm tree adjoining road—Fall on passing car—Fall due to disease—Duty of reasonable and prudent landowner—Knowledge to be expected of landowner as to likelihood of trees suffering from disease. **Caminer v Northern & London Investment Trust Ltd** [1950] **2** 486, HL.
      Knowledge of dangerous condition—Duty of occupying landowners—Beech trees growing on property alongside highway—Portion of tree, old and top-heavy and showing some indications of unhealthiness falling across highway—Collision caused between vehicles on the road at the time—Whether breach of duty of care by occupying landowner. **Quinn v Scott** [1965] **2** 588, QBD.
    Trespasser—
      Duty of occupier to. *See* **Occupier's liability** (Trespasser).
      Highway—Duty owed by user of highway to trespasser on highway—Lorry laden with container driven under too low a bridge—Boy running behind lorry injured by fall of container—Extent of duty of care required of user of highway—Boy technically a trespasser on highway—Duty not confined to people defendants could reasonably expect to be on highway. **Farrugia v Great Western Rly Co** [1947] **2** 565, CA.
  Economic loss—
    Defective work or product. *See* Duty to take care—Defective work or product, *above*.
    Duty to take care. *See* Duty to take care—Economic loss, *above*.
  Educational officer—
    Duty of care. *See* Duty to take care—Existence of duty—Education officer, *above*.
  Educational psychologist—
    Duty of care. *See* Duty to take care—Existence of duty—Educational psychologist, *above*.
  Employer—
    Duty to protect employee from foreseeable risk of danger to health. *See* **Employment** (Duty of master—Safety of employees—Common law duty to protect employee from foreseeable risk of danger to health).
    Duty to take care—
      Generally. *See* Duty to take care—Employer, *above*.
      Nervous shock. *See* Duty to take care—Nervous shock—Employer, *above*.
    Liability—
      Generally. *See* **Employment** (Liability of master—Negligence).
  Estoppel—
    Cause of action estoppel. *See* **Estoppel** (Res judicata—Cause of action estoppel—Negligence).
    Generally. *See* **Estoppel** (Negligence).
    Res judicata. *See* **Estoppel** (Res judicata—Negligence).
  Ex turpi causa non oritur actio, defence of—
    Auditor. *See* Duty to take care—Auditor—Defence of ex turpi causa non oritur actio, *above*.
  Exceptions—
    Bill of lading—
      Neglect of agents or servants. *See* **Shipping** (Bill of lading—Exceptions—Cause arising without actual fault or neglect of agents or servants of carrier).
  Exclusion of liability—
    Carriage by sea—
      Passengers. *See* **Shipping** (Passengers—Carriage by sea—Negligence—Exclusion of liability).
    Exception clause. *See* **Contract** (Exception clause—Negligence).
    Generally. *See* Defence—Exclusion of liability, *above*.

NEGLIGENCE (cont)—
  Exclusion of liability (cont)—
    Passenger in vehicle—
      Agreement to exclusion of liability. *See* Volenti non fit injuria—Consent to risk of injury—Agreement to exclude liability—Passenger in vehicle, *below*.
    Unfair term of contract. *See* **Contract** (Unfair terms—Exclusion of liability for negligence).
  Fatal Accidents Acts. *See* **Fatal accident**.
  Fire—
    Damage to neighbouring premises—
      Heat, smoke and water used to put out fire—Fire started negligently—Water used to put out fire escaping on to neighbouring premises—Damage to neighbouring premises caused to neighbouring premises by heat and smoke—Fires Prevention (Metropolis) Act 1774, s 86. **Mulholland & Tedd Ltd v Baker** [1939] **3** 253, KBD.
    Duty to occupier of neighbouring land—
      Failure to put out fire—Fire caused by lightning—Steps initially taken to deal with source of danger—Subsequently fire left to burn itself out—Negligence in leaving fire to burn itself out—Escape of fire to adjacent premises—Fires so escaping did not accidentally begin—Fires Prevention (Metropolis) Act 1774, s 86. **Goldman v Hargrave** [1966] **2** 989, PC.
      Reasonable steps to extinguish fire—Tree struck by lightning—Burning tree felled—Fire left to burn out—Revival—Escape to adjacent premises—Liability of occupier—Action necessary to put out fire within capacity and resources. **Goldman v Hargrave** [1966] **2** 989, PC.
    Escape to adjoining premises—
      Burden of disproving negligence—Liability of occupier as such—Non-natural user of land by occupier—Yard used as store for machinery greased and stacked in wooden cases pending sale—Serious fire risk to adjoining occupiers—Destruction by fire of neighbour's hedge and garden plants—Whether burden of disproving negligence on occupier—Fires Prevention (Metropolis) Act 1774, s 86. **Mason v Levy Auto Parts of England Ltd** [1967] **2** 62, Assizes.
      Independent contractor—Liability of occupier for acts of independent contractor—Fires Prevention (Metropolis) Act 1774, s 86. **Balfour v Barty-King (Hyder & Sons (Builders) Ltd, third parties)** [1957] **1** 156, CA.
      Liability of occupier as such—Rag ignited by occupier used by him to ignite bird's nest—Fire spreading from nest to adjoining premises. **Sturge v Hackett** [1962] **3** 166, CA.
      Liability of occupier for negligence of third party—Liability for acts of third parties other than strangers—Demolition of bungalows on site by contractors—Site owned by local authority—Local authority requesting Ministry of Works to remove bungalows—Contractors engaged by Ministry—Contractors forbidden to burn rubbish on site by terms of agreement with Ministry—Contractors starting fire in accordance with usual practice—Sparks causing fire on adjoining premises—Whether local authority occupiers of site—Whether contractors strangers. **Emanuel (H & N) Ltd v Greater London Council** [1971] **2** 835, CA.
    Fire brigade—
      Duty of care. *See* Duty to take care—Fire brigade, *above*.
    Police action—
      Police firing CS gas container into building to flush out armed intruder under seige—Building catching fire—No fire-fighting equipment available when police firing canister—Whether police negligent. **Rigby v Chief Constable of Northamptonshire** [1985] **2** 985, QBD.
  Flood—
    Occupier's liability—
      Factory flooded in exceptional storm. *See* **Occupier's liability** (Negligence—Factory flooded in exceptional storm).
  Foreseeable harm—
    Duty of care. *See* Duty to take care—Foreseeable harm, *above*.
    Remoteness of damage. *See* Remoteness of damage—Foreseeable harm, *below*.
  Foster parents—
    Child in care of local authority boarded out with foster parents—
      Whether local authority vicariously liable for foster parents' negligence in respect of child. *See* **Child** (Care—Local authority—Child boarded out with foster parents—Whether foster parents agents of local authority).
  Gas undertakers. *See* **Gas** (Undertakers—Negligence).
  Gross negligence—
    Manslaughter. *See* **Criminal law** (Manslaughter—Recklessness or gross negligence).
  Hairdresser—
    Failure to exercise care and skill—
      Permanent waving—Bleached hair—Failure of hairdresser to have regard to danger of permanent waving bleached hair. **Dobbin v Waldorf Toilet Saloons Ltd** [1937] **1** 331, Manchester Michaelmas Assizes.
  Harbour authority. *See* **Harbour** (Harbour authority—Negligence).
  Health and safety inspector—
    Duty to take care. *See* Duty to take care—Existence of duty—Health and safety inspector, *above*.
  Health authority—
    Duty to take care—
      Existence of duty. *See* Duty to take care—Existence of duty—Health authority, *above*.
  Highway—
    Breach of duty causing or contributing to damage—
      Relevant cause of accident. *See* Causation—Breach of duty causing or contributing to damage—Highway, *above*.
    Breach of Highway Code—
      Contributory negligence. *See* Contributory negligence—Breach of Highway Code, *above*.
    Child—
      Allurement—Lorry on highway constituting an allurement. *See* Child—Allurement—Lorry on highway constituting an allurement, *above*.
    Collision between vehicles—
      Contributory negligence. *See* Contributory negligence—Collision between vehicles on road, *above*.

NEGLIGENCE (cont)—
  Highway (cont)—
    Duty of highway authority—
      Icy patch on road—Warning of danger—Whether highway authority under duty to give warning. **Burton v West Suffolk CC** [1960] **2** 26, CA.

      Obstruction of visibility—Duty to remove obstruction—Bank on land adjoining highway restricting visibility—Defendant alleging highway authority negligent in not reducing risk to road users caused by restricted visibility at road junction—Highway authority having power to compel removal of embankment—Whether authority owing duty of care in respect of omission to take action—Whether compensation payable in respect of loss arising from omission to take action—Highways Act 1980, ss 41, 79. **Stovin v Wise (Norfolk CC, third party)** [1996] **3** 801, HL.

      Restriction of visibility—Collision at junction—Defendant contending visibility severely restricted by vegetation on land owned by highway authority bordering junction, not on or over highway itself—Whether highway authority owing duty of care. **Sumner v Colborne (Denbighshire County Council and anor, Part 20 defendants)** [2018] **3** 1049, CA.

      Tree overhanging highway—Injury to passenger in passing omnibus—Liability of highway authority. **Hale v Hants and Dorset Motor Services Ltd** [1947] **2** 628, CA.

    Duty of local planning authority—
      Obstruction of visibility—Planning authority requiring developer to construct footpath before commencing development works—Authority allowing footpath to be opened to public despite knowing that it lacked adequate sightlines—Car striking claimant when emerging from footpath—Claimant bringing proceedings against planning authority—Whether local planning authority having blanket immunity for anything done in exercise of planning functions—Whether authority liable for danger on highway which it had created. **Kane v New Forest District Council** [2001] **3** 914, CA.

    Duty to highway user in respect of third party's criminal act. *See* Duty to take care—Act of third party—Duty to highway user in respect of third party's criminal act, *above*.

    Maintenance. *See* **Highway** (Maintenance—Negligence).

    Opening of vehicle door—
      Injury to passer-by—Injury to cyclist by driver opening door of stationary motor vehicle—Highway Act 1835, s 78. **Shears v Matthews** [1948] **2** 1064, KBD; **Watson v Lowe** [1950] **1** 100, KBD.

    Parking of vehicle—
      Collision—Vehicle parked near blind corner at night—Vehicle having lights on—Room for other vehicles to pass—Second vehicle rounding corner and colliding with rear of stationary vehicle—Passenger in second vehicle injured—Liability of driver of stationary vehicle to passenger—Whether bad parking capable of giving rise to liability in negligence. **Chop Seng Heng v Thevannasan s/o Sinnapan** [1975] **3** 572, PC.

    Pavement—
      Hole dug in pavement. *See* **Highway** (Maintenance—Negligence—Street works—Hole dug in pavement by local authority workmen for junction box).

      Proximity of vehicle to edge of pavement—Injury to pedestrian on pavement by van passing so close to kerb that door-handle passed over pavement. **Watson v Whitney (Thomas S) & Co Ltd** [1966] **1** 122, CA.

      Unguarded opening. *See* Highway—Unguarded opening on pavement, *below*.

    Police—
      Knowledge of dangerous condition of highway—Whether police under duty of care to protect or warn road users. *See* **Police** (Negligence—Duty to take care—Dangerous condition of highway).

    Traffic—
      Giving way—Priority due to traffic coming on driver's right. **MacIntyre v Coles** [1966] **1** 723, CA.

    Tree adjacent to highway—
      Duty to take care. *See* Duty to take care—Tree adjacent to highway, *above*.

    Trespasser—
      Duty of care to trespasser. *See* Duty to take care—Trespasser—Highway, *above*.

    Unguarded opening on pavement—
      Opening to coal-cellar left unguarded during delivery of coal to premises—Pedestrian stepping into hole—Liability of coal merchant and occupier of premises—Law Reform (Married Women and Tortfeasors) Act 1935, s 6(2). **Daniel v Rickett Cockerell & Co Ltd and Raymond** [1938] **2** 631, KBD.

      Street works. *See* **Highway** (Maintenance—Negligence—Street works).

    Unlighted vehicle—
      Danger to other traffic—Unlighted motor cycle stationary at night—Negligence in failing to take all reasonable precautions to prevent danger to other traffic. **Hill-Venning v Beszant** [1950] **2** 1151, CA.

      Presumption of negligence—Rebuttal of presumption—Adequate lighting from street lamp—Unlighted motor vehicle stationary on dark night—Prima facie evidence of negligence rebutted since street lamp nearby afforded ample warning to drivers keeping proper look out. **Parish v Judd** [1960] **3** 33, QBD.

      Presumption of negligence—Unlighted motor vehicle stationary on dark night—Prima facie evidence of negligence, there being no street lighting—Rebuttal of presumption of negligence. **Moore v Maxwells of Emsworth Ltd** [1968] **2** 779, CA.

      Proper look-out—Collision despite plaintiff keeping proper look-out—Plaintiff motor cyclist colliding with unlighted stationary car. **Stewart v Hancock** [1940] **2** 427, PC.

  House—
    Construction of house—
      Nature of damage giving rise to cause of action. *See* Damage—Nature of damage giving rise to cause of action—Negligence in construction of house, *above*.

NEGLIGENCE (cont)—
  Immunity from suit—
    Arbitrator—
      Person acting in arbitral capacity—Immunity from liability for failure to exercise care and professional skill—Circumstances in which professional man acting in arbitral capacity—Determination of dispute—Agreement by parties to accept determination as final—Architect—Interim certificate—Building contract—Architect appointed to supervise works under building contract between employer and contractor—Contract in RIBA form—Duty of architect to act fairly between employer and contractor—Interim certificate issued by architect over-certifying amount due to contractor—Whether architect acting in arbitral capacity in issuing certificates—Whether immune from liability to employer for negligent over-certification. **Sutcliffe v Thackrah** [1974] **1** 859, HL.
    Counsel. *See* **Counsel** (Negligence—Immunity).
    Expert witness. *See* **Action** (Immunity from suit—Witness—Expert witness).
    Sequestrator—
      Whether sequestrator immune from all liability for negligence—Whether sequestrator liable only for gross misconduct etc. **IRC v Hoogstraten** [1984] **3** 25, CA.
    Shipowner—
      Bill of lading. *See* **Shipping** (Bill of lading—Immunities of shipowner—Neglect in management of ship).
    Solicitor. *See* **Solicitor** (Negligence—Immunity).
    Surveyor—
      Rent review—Surveyor appointed under rent review clause to determine rent increase—Surveyor appointed by terms of lease as expert and not as arbitrator—Surveyor to consider but not be limited or fettered by reasons or valuations submitted to him—Surveyor entitled to rely on own judgment and opinion—Whether surveyor acting as arbitrator or quasi-arbitrator—Whether surveyor immune from action for damages for negligence. **Palacath Ltd v Flanagan** [1985] **2** 161, QBD.
    Valuer—
      Valuation of property—Valuation determining price to be paid for property under contract of sale—Liability of valuer to parties to sale for negligent valuation—Auditor appointed to value shares as expert and not as arbitrator—Shareholder selling shares to controlling shareholder in company on basis of valuation—Company prospectus subsequently issued by same auditor—Value placed on shares six times greater than value previously given by auditor to shareholder—Whether shareholder having cause of action in negligence against auditor. **Arenson v Casson Beckman Rutley & Co** [1975] **3** 901, HL.
  Indemnity—
    Construction of indemnity clause—
      Indemnity against consequence of own negligence. *See* **Indemnity** (Construction of indemnity clause—Indemnity against consequence of own negligence).
    Generally. *See* **Indemnity** (Negligence).
  Information or advice—
    Accountant—
      Statutory provision requiring solicitors' practices to deliver annual accountant's report to Law Society—Defendant accountants preparing annual reports on firm of solicitors—Firm's clients being defrauded—Law Society making payments from compensation fund—Whether accountant owing Law Society duty of care in preparing annual report on solicitors' practice—Solicitors Act 1974, s 34. **Law Society v KPMG Peat Marwick (sued as KPMG Peat Marwick McLintock)** [2000] **1** 515, Ch D; [2000] **4** 540, CA.
    Assumption of duty of care—
      Duty to give information about change of circumstances affecting statement previously made—Landlord and tenant—Covenant by tenant to insure premises against fire—Landlord informing tenant premises insured under block policy—Landlord arranging to insure premises under policy for two years thereafter and charging tenant with appropriate proportion of premium—Block policy cancelled without notice to tenant—Premises uninsured when damaged by fire—Liability of landlord to tenant—Whether landlord under duty to inform tenant block policy not being renewed. **Argy Trading Development Co Ltd v Lapid Developments Ltd** [1977] **3** 785, QBD.
    Assumption of liability—
      Statutory duty to give information—Register of local land charges—False certificate issued by employee of local authority—Conclusiveness of certificate resulting in loss of incumbrancer's rights—Whether employee owed duty of care to incumbrancer. **Ministry of Housing and Local Government v Sharp** [1970] **1** 1009, CA.
    Causing or contributing to damage—
      Advice to workman. *See* Causation—Breach of duty causing or contributing to damage—Advice to workman, *above*.
    Counsel—
      Immunity. *See* **Counsel** (Negligence—Immunity—Preliminary advice on matters connected with pending or contemplated litigation).
    Damage giving rise to liability—
      Danger to life, limb or health—Valuation of property—Valuer instructed by promoters of company to be formed—Valuation of property to be acquired by company—Duty to company—Liability for negligent overvaluation—Whether liability confined to negligence resulting in danger to life, limb or health. **Old Gate Estates Ltd v Toplis and Harding and Russell** [1939] **3** 209, KBD.
    Fact peculiarly within knowledge of defendant—
      Specific fact which plaintiff has no ready means of ascertaining—Owners and prospective charterers of barges to be employed for specific purpose known to owners—Owners innocently misrepresenting capacity of barges—Misrepresentation inducing charterers to enter into contract of hire—Whether owners under a duty of care to give accurate information as to capacity of barges. **Howard Marine and Dredging Co Ltd v A Ogden & Sons (Excavations) Ltd** [1978] **2** 1134, CA.

NEGLIGENCE (cont)—
  Information or advice (cont)—
    Hire-purchase agreement—
      Failure to register—Estoppel. *See* **Estoppel** (Negligence—Need to establish duty of care in order to found estoppel by negligence—Hire-purchase agreement—Registration).
    Knowledge third party might rely on advice—
      Accountant—Preparation of company's accounts—Duty to prospective investor—Knowledge that accounts to be shown to prospective investor in company—Accounts failing to give true statement of financial position of company—Liability of accountant to investor. **Candler v Crane Christmas & Co** [1951] **1** 426, CA.
    Knowledge third party might rely on information—
      Auditor—Auditor of deposit-taking company—Report to trustee of unsecured depositors—Auditor under statutory duty to report to trustee if he became aware of any matter that 'in his opinion' was relevant to exercise or performance of trustee's powers or duties—Auditor notifying trustee of company's probable insolvency some time after prudent auditor would have formed opinion that company insolvent—Trustee required to indemnify unsecured depositors—Whether auditor under common law duty of care to notify trustee of company's probable insolvency when prudent auditor would have done so—Whether auditor merely under statutory duty to report when he subjectively formed opinion that company insolvent—Whether any breach of duty by auditor had caused trustee loss—Securities Act 1978 (NZ), s 50(2). **Deloitte Haskins & Sells v National Mutual Life Nominees Ltd** [1993] **2** 1015, PC.
      Auditor—Preparation of company's accounts—Duty to company's creditors—Plaintiff banks lending money to company to enable it to finance business operations—Banks relying on audited accounts when making loans—Audited accounts failing to show company insolvent—Advances made by banks to company irrecoverable—Banks bringing action against auditors claiming damages for auditors' negligence—Whether sufficient proximity between auditors and company's creditors or potential creditors—Whether auditors owing duty of care to company's creditors or potential creditors to carry out audit with reasonable care and skill. **Al Saudi Banque v Clark Pixley (a firm)** [1989] **3** 361, Ch D.
      Auditor—Preparation of company's accounts—Duty to prospective investor—Auditor negligent in preparing accounts—Auditor aware when preparing accounts that company requiring outside financial support—Accounts made available to plaintiffs—Plaintiffs taking over company—Whether plaintiffs incurring loss because of reliance on accounts. **JEB Fasteners Ltd v Marks Bloom & Co (a firm)** [1983] **1** 583, CA.
      Auditor—Preparation of company's accounts—Duty to shareholder—Duty to potential investor—Plaintiffs owning shares in public company—Plaintiffs making successful take-over bid for company in reliance on audited accounts of company—Accounts showing profit instead of loss—Whether reasonably foreseeable that shareholders and potential investors might rely on auditor's report when dealing in company's shares—Whether sufficient proximity between auditor and shareholders or potential investors—Whether auditor owing duty of care to shareholders or potential investors to carry out audit with reasonable care and skill. **Caparo Industries plc v Dickman** [1990] **1** 568, HL.
      Auditor—Preparation of company's accounts—Duty to shareholder—Duty to prospective investor—Plaintiffs owning shares in public company—Plaintiffs making successful take-over bid for company in reliance on audited accounts of company—Accounts showing profit instead of loss—Whether reasonably foreseeable that shareholders and potential investors might rely on auditor's report when dealing in company's shares—Whether sufficient proximity between auditor and shareholders or potential investors—Whether just and reasonable to impose duty of care on auditor—Whether auditor owing duty of care to shareholders or potential investors to carry out audit with reasonable care and skill. **Caparo Industries plc v Dickman** [1989] **1** 798, CA.
      Clinician—Clinician providing prospective patients with brochures and information prepared by third party—Whether clinicians responsible for possible misrepresentations in brochure—Whether statements materially accurate. **Webster v Liddington** [2015] **1 Comm** 427, CA.
      Company—Directors—Prospects and company report—Liability of directors for inaccuracies in prospectus and report—Shareholder relying on prospectus and report when buying company's shares on stock market—Shareholder suffering loss on shares—Whether directors owing duty of care to shareholder or anyone else who relied on prospectus to purchase shares in company on stock market. **Al-Nakib Investments (Jersey) Ltd v Longcroft** [1990] **3** 321, Ch D.
      Company—Prospectus for initial allotment of shares and after-market purchase on unlisted securities market—Prospectus allegedly misrepresenting company's financial position—Plaintiffs making after-market share purchases in reliance on prospectus—Plaintiffs suffering loss—Whether persons issuing prospectus owing duty of care to purchasers of after-market shares. **Possfund Custodian Trustee Ltd v Diamond (McGrigor Donald (a firm), third party)** [1996] **2** 774, Ch D.
      Company—Take-over bid—Duty of care to bidder—Preparation of target company's financial statements and profit forecast—Duty to potential or actual bidder—Financial statements of company issued before announcement of bid for company—After announcement of bid target company issuing circulars and profit forecast—Circulars issued to and for guidance of shareholders—Whether board and advisers of target company owing duty of care to bidder—Whether sufficient proximity between bidder and board and advisers of target company to found action in negligence. **Morgan Crucible Co plc v Hill Samuel Bank Ltd** [1991] **1** 148, CA.
      Company—Take-over bid—Target company's accountants—Preparation of company's accounts—Accountants preparing draft accounts at request of target company for use in take-over negotiations—Whether accountants owing duty of care to bidder. **McNaughton (James) Papers Group Ltd v Hicks Anderson & Co (a firm)** [1991] **1** 134, CA.
      Special relationship giving rise to duty of care—Claimants seeking to employ contractor for swimming pool installation—Defendant being swimming pool installer trade association—Claimants obtaining contact details for contractor from website of defendant—Claimants relying on statements made on website in relation to members of association without further inquiry—Contractor becoming insolvent—Claimants suffering financial loss—Claimants claiming statements made on website being negligent statements—Whether sufficient proximity between parties to establish duty of care. **Patchett v Swimming Pool and Allied Trades Association Ltd** [2010] **2 Comm** 138, CA.

NEGLIGENCE (cont)—
    Information or advice (cont)—
        Knowledge third party might rely on information (cont)—
            Surveyor and valuer—Valuation report to building society—Surveyor's report stating that property adequate security for amount of loan sought by purchaser of property—Building society offering to lend that amount to purchaser in reliance on report—Surveyor negligent in failing to discover defects in foundations of property—Property inadequate security for loan—Purchaser accepting building society's offer and purchasing property—Whether surveyor liable to purchaser for negligent statement in report to building society—Whether relationship between surveyor and purchaser sufficiently proximate for duty of care to arise. **Yianni v Edwin Evans & Sons (a firm)** [1981] **3** 592, QBD.

            Vasectomy operation—Vasectomy not permanent—Liability to woman made pregnant—Man advised after vasectomy that he would not need to use contraception in future—Plaintiff having sexual relationship with man three years later and becoming pregnant—Whether person performing vasectomy operation could have known advice to man would be communicated to and acted on by plaintiff—Whether person performing vasectomy operation owing duty of care to plaintiff. **Goodwill v British Pregnancy Advisory Service** [1996] **2** 161, CA.

        Pre-contract negotiations—
            Statement made by one party to other in course of negotiations—Statement inducing other party to enter agreement—Whether fact that statement made in course of pre-contract negotiations excluding duty to take care in making statement. **Esso Petroleum Co Ltd v Mardon** [1976] **2** 5, CA.

        Professional person—
            Duty to exercise reasonable skill and care—Valuation of property. *See* Professional person—Duty to exercise reasonable skill and care—Estate agent—Valuation of property, *below*.

        Reliance on skill and judgment—
            Knowledge of informant or adviser—Knowledge that he was being trusted or that reliance was placed on his skill or judgment—Bankers—Advice as to financial stability of company—Whether duty to exercise care imposed on person giving information or advice. **Hedley Byrne & Co Ltd v Heller & Partners Ltd** [1963] **2** 575, HL.

            Likelihood of physical injury—Statement by professional adviser—No need to prove reliance on advice by plaintiff where negligence in giving advice on safety of buildings etc likely to result in bodily injury—Surveyor—Building inspector—Failure to make proper inspection of foundations of house before giving byelaw approval—Foundations inadequate—Subsequent damage to structure of building caused by settlement—Liability for cost of repairs. **Dutton v Bognor Regis United Building Co Ltd** [1972] **1** 462, CA.

            Professional advice—Advisor not engaged in business or profession of giving advice on subject-matter of enquiry—Whether duty to exercise care imposed on advisor. **Mutual Life and Citizens' Assurance Co Ltd v Evatt** [1971] **1** 150, PC.

            Valuer—Valuation and survey of landed property—House purchased in reliance on surveyor's report—Measure of damages. **Philips v Ward** [1956] **1** 874, CA.

        Reply to enquiry—
            Credit-worthiness of third party—Representation of credit-worthiness of purchaser—Wholesaler and commission agent's buyer purchasing in vegetable market for third party—Negligence by manager of wholesaler in not informing buyer about state of account of third party with wholesaler—Whether wholesaler owed duty of care to prospective vendor to the third party. **Anderson (WB) & Sons Ltd v Rhodes (Liverpool) Ltd** [1967] **2** 850, Assizes.

        Solicitor—
            Cause of action. *See* **Solicitor** (Negligence—Cause of action—Negligent advice).

        Special relationship giving rise to duty of care—
            Reliance on adviser's knowledge and expertise—Company engaged in distribution of petrol—Negotiations by company to let new petrol station—Forecast by company of prospective petrol sales from station—Forecast inducing tenant to enter into tenancy agreement—Forecast inaccurate—Whether company under duty of care to tenant. **Esso Petroleum Co Ltd v Mardon** [1976] **2** 5, CA.

        Tax advice—
            Accountants advising claimant that proposed transaction would incur no tax liability—Revenue asserting that transaction giving rise to tax charge—Claimant paying tax and bringing proceedings for negligence on basis that accountants' advice had been wrong in law—Judge finding for claimant without deciding whether or not advice had been correct—Whether necessary for judge to determine whether tax advice had been correct. **Grimm v Newman** [2003] **1** 67, CA.

    Insurer—
        Duty of care. *See* Duty to take care—Insurer, *above*.

    Intoxicated driver of vehicle—
        Passenger—
            Consent to risk of injury. *See* Volenti non fit injuria—Knowledge of risk—Passenger in car—Intoxicated driver, *below*.

    Invitee—
        Ship—
            Injury to employee of independent contractor during ship's trial—Ship under command of employee of shipbuilders—Negligence of purchasers' servants on board—Common interest of shipbuilders and purchasers in success of trial—Control of purchasers' servants by shipbuilders' employee—Liability of shipbuilders. **Hobson v Bartram and Sons Ltd** [1950] **1** 412, CA.

    Joint illegal enterprise—
        Duty of care. *See* Duty to take care—Joint illegal enterprise, *above*.

    Joint tortfeasors—
        Contribution—
            Settlement between plaintiff and some defendants—Remaining defendant issuing contribution notice against co-defendants—Plaintiff issuing notice of discontinuance against co-defendants—Whether new contribution notice required—Whether contribution notice rendered invalid by discontinuance of action against co-defendants—Whether co-defendants capable of being 'joint tortfeasors'—Law Reform (Married Women and Tortfeasors) Act 1935, s 6(1)(c). **Harper v Gray & Walker (a firm)** [1985] **2** 507, QBD.

NEGLIGENCE (cont)—
Judgment—
Admission of negligence. *See* **Judgment** (Judgment on admission of facts—Negligence).
Knowledge of danger—
No reason to suspect danger—
Water board—Pipe laid under highway—Leakage in pipe—Paving-stones on footpath affected—Water board not aware of danger—Pedestrian injured by movement of paving stone affected by leakage—Whether board liable in negligence. **Longhurst v Metropolitan Water Board** [1948] **2** 834, HL.
Landlord's liability—
Exemption from liability—
Defective state of demised premises—Yard attached to demised premises over which tenants had right to pass—Fall of chimneystack due to want of repair—Tenant's daughter injured in yard by fall—Whether yard part of demised premises—Whether landlord exempted from liability. **Taylor v Liverpool Corp** [1939] **3** 329, Assizes.
Operations carried out by landlord on demised premises—Duty of care to persons on Premises—Gratuitous operation at request of tenant—Installation of domestic boiler—Boiler in dangerous condition—Explosion injuring tenant's daughter—Whether landlord absolved from liability by virtue of his status as landlord. **Ball v London CC** [1949] **1** 1056, CA.
Landlord also designer and builder of premises—
Liability of defendant as landlord and/or designer and builder of premises—Access to council house down two flights of steps—Steps not provided with handrail—No lighting in immediate vicinity of steps—Tenant falling down steps and injuring leg—Whether council owing duty of care to tenant as landlord and/or as builder and designer of premises. **Targett v Torfaen BC** [1992] **3** 27, CA.
Liability of defendant as landlord and/or designer and builder—Council designing and building flats containing panel of thin and easily breakable glass—Tenant of flat breaking glass and injuring hand—Whether council owing duty of care to tenant as landlord and/or as builder and designer. **Rimmer v Liverpool City Council** [1984] **1** 930, CA.
Last opportunity—
Contributory negligence. *See* Contributory negligence—Last opportunity of avoiding accident, *above*.
Latent defect—
Defence. *See* Defence—Latent defect, *above*.
Res ipsa loquitur. *See* Res ipsa loquitur—Latent defect, *below*.
Liability of master. *See* **Employment** (Liability of master—Negligence).
Lighting of film. *See* **Cinema** (Film—Production—Lighting—Negligence).
Limitation of action—
Accrual of cause of action. *See* **Limitation of action** (Accrual of cause of action—Negligence).
Brokers—
Accrual of cause of action. *See* **Limitation of action** (Accrual of cause of action—Negligence—Brokers).
Generally. *See* **Limitation of action** (Negligence).
New Zealand. *See* **New Zealand** (Negligence—Duty of care—Limitation of action).
Personal injury claim. *See* **Limitation of action** (Period of limitation—Personal injury claim).
Valuer—
Accrual of cause of action. *See* **Limitation of action** (Accrual of cause of action—Negligence—Valuer).
Limitation of liability—
Carriage of passengers by air—
Domestic carriage. *See* **Carriage by air** (Carriage of passengers—Domestic carriage—Limitation of carrier's liability—Negligence).
Lloyd's underwriting agent—
Duty to take care. *See* Duty to take care—Insurance—Lloyd's underwriting agent, *above*.
Local authority—
Children in care—
Duty of local authority to take care. *See* Duty to take care—Existence of duty—Children—Local authority, *above*.
Duty of care in exercising statutory powers—
Existence of duty. *See* Duty to take care—Existence of duty—Children, *above*.
Education authority—
Duty to take care. *See* Duty to take care—Existence of duty—Children—Local authority—Education authority, *above*.
Existence of duty to take care. *See* Duty to take care—Existence of duty—Local authority, *above*.
Local government—
Loss or deficiency—
Surcharge—Audit. *See* **Local government** (Audit—Duty of auditor to surcharge amount of any loss or deficiency on any person by whose negligence or misconduct loss or deficiency incurred—Negligence).
Machinery—
Dangerous machinery—
Foreseeable harm. *See* Duty to take care—Foreseeable harm—Dangerous machinery, *above*.
Manslaughter. *See* **Criminal law** (Manslaughter—Negligence).
Manufacturer's liability—
Defective trailer coupling for trailer—
User of trailer injured in accident. *See* **Sale of goods** (Implied condition as to fitness—Defective trailer coupling supplied by garage to vehicle owner for use with trailer).
Defective work or product. *See* Duty to take care—Defective work or product, *above*.
Defence—
Proof of good system of work and adequate supervision—Wooden packing case—Lorry driver standing on case while loading lorry injured when case broke—Case badly nailed—Whether proof of good system of work and adequate supervision defence to action against manufacturer of case. **Hill v James Crowe (Cases) Ltd** [1978] **1** 812, QBD.

NEGLIGENCE (cont)—
  Manufacturer's liability (cont)—
    Extent of manufacturer's duty to take care—
      Generally. *See* Duty to take care—Manufacturer's liability, *above*.
    Opportunity for intermediate examination—
      Latent defect—Breakage of ring causing death of workman—Examination by workman's employers
      would have revealed defect—Whether manufacturers liable for death. **Dransfield v British
      Insulated Cables Ltd** [1937] **4** 382, KBD.
  Measure of damages. *See* **Damages** (Measure of damages—Negligence).
  Medical practitioner—
    Costs—
      Order for costs—Discretion. *See* **Costs** (Order for costs—Discretion—Claim for professional medical
      negligence).
    Expert evidence—
      Disclosure to other parties. *See* **Practice** (Evidence—Expert evidence—Disclosure to other
      parties—Action for medical negligence).
    Generally. *See* **Medical practitioner** (Negligence).
    Hospital—
      Liability of hospital. *See* **Hospital** (Liability for negligence of members of staff—Medical
      practitioner).
  Members' club—
    Duty to take care. *See* Duty to take care—Club—Members' club, *above*.
  Mental shock—
    Damages. *See* **Damages** (Personal injury—Nervous shock).
    Rescuer—
      Duty to rescuer. *See* Duty to take care—Rescuer—Mental shock, *above*.
  Misrepresentation—
    Misrepresentation as to person's credit. *See* **Misrepresentation** (Misrepresentation as to person's
    credit—Negligence).
    Negligent misrepresentation. *See* **Misrepresentation** (Negligent misrepresentation).
    Solicitor. *See* **Solicitor** (Negligence—Negligent misrepresentation).
  Misstatement—
    Conflict of laws. *See* **Conflict of laws** (Jurisdiction—Challenge to jurisdiction—Negligent
    mis-statement).
    Information or advice. *See* Information or advice, *above*.
  Mortgagee—
    Exercise of power of sale. *See* **Mortgage** (Sale—Duty of mortgagee).
  Negligent mistatement—
    Information or advice. *See* Information or advice, *above*.
  Nervous shock—
    Damages. *See* **Damages** (Personal injury—Nervous shock).
    Duty to take care. *See* Duty to take care—Nervous shock, *above*.
  New Zealand. *See* **New Zealand** (Negligence).
  Nuisance—
    Need to prove negligence. *See* **Nuisance** (Negligence—Need to prove).
  Nurse—
    Hospital—
      Liability of hospital. *See* **Hospital** (Liability for negligence of members of staff—Nurses).
  Occupier. *See* **Occupier's liability**.
  Owner of realty—
    Duty to take care. *See* Duty to take care—Owner of realty, *above*.
  Passenger—
    Car—
      Knowledge of risk. *See* Volenti non fit injuria—Knowledge of risk—Passenger in car, *below*.
    Railway—
      Duty to passengers. *See* Railway—Duty to passengers and invitees, *below*.
  Pavement—
    Hole dug in pavement. *See* **Highway** (Maintenance—Negligence—Street works—Hole dug in pavement
    by local authority workmen for junction box).
  Personal injury—
    Damages—
      Generally. *See* **Damages** (Personal injury).
      Interest. *See* **Interest** (Damages—Personal injury).
      Special damage—Particulars of claim. *See* **Practice** (Personal injuries action—Special damage).
    Expert evidence—
      Disclosure to other parties—Action for medical negligence. *See* **Practice** (Evidence—Expert
      evidence—Disclosure to other parties—Action for medical negligence).
      Reports—Practice. *See* **Practice** (Personal injuries action—Experts' reports).
    Limitation of action—
      Court's power to override time limit in personal injury or fatal accident claim. *See* **Limitation of
      action** (Court's power to override time limit in personal injury or fatal accident claim).
      Fatal accident. *See* **Limitation of action** (Fatal accident).
      Generally. *See* **Limitation of action** (Personal injury claim).
      When time begins to run. *See* **Limitation of action** (When time begins to run—Personal injury
      claim).
    Transfer of action from High Court to county court—
      Generally. *See* **County court** (Transfer of action—Transfer from High Court—Personal injuries
      action).
    Trial by jury—
      Practice. *See* **Practice** (Trial—Trial by jury—Personal injuries claim).
    Writ—
      Practice. *See* **Practice** (Personal injuries action—Writ).

NEGLIGENCE (cont)—
Pleading—
Breach of statutory duty only pleaded—
Finding of liability based on negligence—Whether finding maintainable. **Morris v National Coal Board** [1963] **3** 644, CA.
Contributory negligence not pleaded—
Apportionment of liability—Jurisdiction. *See* Contributory negligence—Apportionment of liability—Jurisdiction—Defence of contributory negligence not pleaded, *above.*
Defence—
Act of third party—Defendants relying on act of third party—Necessary to plead specific act relied on—Ground of defence that tool was supplied by reputable suppliers—RSC, Ord 19, r 4, r 15. **Davie v New Merton Board Mills Ltd** [1956] **1** 379, QBD.
Insufficiency. *See* **Practice** (Trial—Departure from case originally pleaded—Particulars of negligence).
Particulars. *See* **Pleading** (Particulars—Negligence).
Res ipsa loquitur. *See* Res ipsa loquitur—Pleading, *below.*
Stranding of vessel—
Unseaworthiness—Need to plead—Damage arising from stranding of vessel—Pleading of negligence in navigation—No allegation of unseaworthiness in statement of claim—Whether plaintiffs entitled to rely on negligence in sending ship to sea. **Esso Petroleum Co Ltd v Southport Corp** [1955] **3** 864, HL.
Police—
Fire. *See* Fire—Police action, *above.*
Generally. *See* **Police** (Negligence).
Practice of trade—
Defence. *See* Defence—Practice of trade, *above.*
Predominant cause. *See* Causation—Predominant cause, *above.*
Pregnancy—
Unwanted pregnancy—
Damages. *See* **Damages** (Unwanted pregnancy—Negligence).
Prison authorities. *See* **Prison** (Negligence—Prison authorities).
Prison hospital—
Duty to take care. *See* Duty to take care—Prison hospital, *above.*
Professional person—
Causation—
Approach to issue of causation of loss—Honesty of claim—Claim against solicitors for failing to make claim—Solicitors admitting breach of duty of care—Whether breach of duty of care causing loss. **Perry v Raleys Solicitors** [2019] **2** 937, SC.
Damages—
Solicitor. *See* **Damages** (Measure of damages—Negligence—Solicitor).
Duty to exercise reasonable skill and care—
Accountant. *See* Duty to take care—Accountant, *above.*
Broker on commodities market—Broker carrying out 46 transactions for investor—Broker giving advice to investor but investor usually making own decision in regard to transactions—Transactions resulting in substantial losses—Whether broker negligent having regard to unpredictable nature of commodities market—Whether error of judgment amounting to negligence—Whether fact of losses establishing negligence by virtue of res ipsa loquitur. **Stafford v Conti Commodity Services Ltd** [1981] **1** 691, QBD.
Duty where work done for standard fee—Whether duty of care modified by fact that work done may involve more time than expected or fee structure contemplated. **Roberts v J Hampson & Co (a firm)** [1989] **2** 504, QBD.
Estate agent—Valuation of property—Advance by way of mortgage on footing of valuation—Valuation excessive—Reliance on valuation by mortagee—Measure of damages. **Baxter v F W Gapp & Co Ltd** [1939] **2** 752, CA.
Minor surgical operation—Jeweller undertaking minor surgical operation often done by jewellers—Ear-piercing—Jeweller only required to show skill of jewellers doing that work and not skill of doctor. **Philips v Whiteley (William) Ltd** [1938] **1** 566, KBD.
Proof of negligence—Question for consideration by court—Failure on balance of probabilities to exercise care required of professional person—Whether additional burden of proof on person alleging negligence. **Ashcroft v Mersey Regional Health Authority** [1985] **2** 96, CA.
Reliance on specialist consultant—Circumstances in which professional person may rely on specialist consultant—Architect—Architect relying on consulting engineer. **Investors in Industry Commercial Properties Ltd v South Bedfordshire DC (Ellison & Partners (a firm), third parties)** [1986] **1** 787, CA.
Solicitor. *See* **Solicitor** (Negligence—Duty to exercise reasonable skill and care).
Steps to be taken to fulfil duty depending on circumstances—Consultant engineers—Design of building—Building required for purpose of storing oil drums and moving them about by fork-lift trucks—Knowledge of purpose for which building required—New mode of construction—Warning of danger of vibrations in code of practice interpreted too narrowly—Design rendering floor of warehouse inadequate for its purpose—Engineers liable for breach of duty. **Greaves & Co (Contractors) Ltd v Baynham Meikle and Partners** [1975] **3** 99, CA.
Hairdresser. *See* Hairdresser, *above.*
Medical practitioner. *See* **Medical practitioner** (Negligence).
Real property—
Valuation—Commercial mortgage-backed security—Defendant valuing commercial property as security for loan—Tenant becoming insolvent and property sold at undervalue—Claimant bringing claim for professional negligence—Judge finding defendant negligent and claimant entitled to sue for damages—Whether judge erring. **Titan Europe 2006-3 plc v Colliers International UK plc (in liq)** [2016] **1 Comm** 999, CA.
Valuation—Commercial mortgage-backed security—Defendant valuing commercial property as security for loan—Tenant becoming insolvent and property sold at undervalue—Claimant bringing claim for professional negligence—Whether claimant entitled to pursue claim—Whether defendant negligently overvaluing property. **Titan Europe 2006-3 plc v Colliers International UK plc (in liq)** [2015] **2 Comm** 479, QBD.

NEGLIGENCE (cont)—
 Professional person (cont)—
  Solicitor. *See* **Solicitor** (Negligence).
  Surgeon—
   Operation—Conformity with practices accepted as proper by responsible members of profession. *See* **Medical practitioner** (Negligence—Conformity with practices accepted as proper by responsible members of profession).
   Operation—Duty to search for swabs—Duty to count swabs—Swab left in patient—Whether surgeon under a duty to count or search for swabs. **Mahon v Osborne** [1939] **1** 535, CA.
   Operation—Res ipsa loquitur—Evidence sufficient to raise presumption. *See* Res ipsa loquitur—Evidence sufficient to raise presumption—Surgical operation, *below*.
 Proof of negligence—
  Collision between vehicles on road—
   Drivers equally to blame—Right of owner of one car to recover in full against driver of other car—Collision at cross-roads—Roads of equal status—Inference that both drivers equally to blame—Car hired from plaintiff by driver—Defendant driver of other car—Plaintiff's right to recover full damages from defendant. **France v Parkinson** [1954] **1** 739, CA.
  Conviction in criminal court—
   Burden of proof. *See* **Burden of proof** (Civil action—Conviction as evidence—Negligence).
  Duty of judge—
   Contradictory allegations in claim and counterclaim—No decision which was proved—Claim and counterclaim dismissed—Whether judge entitled to dismiss claim and counterclaim on ground he was unable to decide which was right—Whether new trial should be ordered. **Bray v Palmer** [1953] **2** 1449, CA.
  Expert evidence—
   Plaintiff not bound to show how accident happened—Reliance on expert evidence—No direct evidence of how accident happened—Plaintiff by competent evidence showing that his explanation of what happened the more probable one. **Dawson v Murex Ltd** [1942] **1** 483, CA.
 Psychologist—
  Educational psychologist—
   Duty of care. *See* Duty to take care—Existence of duty—Educational psychologist, *above*.
 Radiographer—
  Hospital—
   Liability of hospital. *See* **Hospital** (Liability for negligence of members of staff—Radiographer).
 Railway—
  Crossing—
   Duty to persons using crossing—Closing of gates. *See* **Railway** (Accommodation works—Accommodation crossing—Extent of obligations of railway authority—Closing of gates).
  Duty to passengers and invitees—
   Infant passenger's fall through door of guard's van—Passengers having to pass through van to reach restaurant car—Door capable of being opened by small child. **O'Connor v British Transport Commission** [1958] **1** 558, CA.
   Liability of passenger to other persons—Opening of carriage door—Door striking person on platform—Passenger boarding moving train—Open door striking porter on platform. **Booker v Wenborn** [1962] **1** 431, CA.
   Open door of guard's van—Plaintiff on platform injured by open door when train was starting—Whether any duty to shut door before departure of train. **Hare v British Transport Commission** [1956] **1** 578, QBD.
   Safety of station platform—Duty of railway to provide safe means of egress from train—Snow on platform following sudden snowstorm—Delay in sanding and salting—Porter responsible otherwise urgently engaged—Passenger injured by slipping on snow when alighting from train—Whether railway executive having exercised reasonable care. **Tomlinson v Railway Executive** [1953] **1** 1, CA.
   Safety of station platform—Passenger slipping on patch of oil—No delay in taking precautionary measures. **Blackman v Railway Executive** [1953] **2** 323, CA.
   Shutting of doors before departure—Underground train—Train departing with open doors—Passenger thrown out of open door in consequence of motion of train—Whether company's servants under a duty to shut doors before departure of train. **Brookes v London Passenger Transport Board** [1947] **1** 506, KBD.
  Engine-driver—
   Duty to persons on line—Extent of duty of care to railway employees on the line. **Trznadel v British Transport Commission** [1957] **3** 196, CA.
  Licensees on railway track—
   Duty to licensees—Involuntary encroachment on track. *See* **Occupier's liability** (Duty to licensee—Involuntary encroachment—Railway track).
  Railway line—
   Duty to fence. *See* Duty to take care—Railway—Duty to fence railway line, *above*.
 Registrar of Companies. *See* Duty to take care—Registrar of Companies, *above*.
 Reliance on skill and judgment—
  Information or advice. *See* Information or advice—Reliance on skill and judgment, *above*.
 Remoteness of damage—
  Direct result of breach of duty—
   Foreseeability—Need to prove that risk of damage foreseeable—Not sufficient to prove damage direct result of breach if damage not foreseeable. **Wagon Mound, The (No 2)** [1966] **2** 709, PC.
  Foreseeable harm—
   Damage foreseeable but not extent—Dangerous chattels—Chemical liable to explode on contact with water—No adequate research by seller—No adequate warning given by seller to purchaser—Purchaser entitled to expect adequate warning—Explosion causing death and extensive destruction of property—Whether damage too remote—Whether seller liable. **Vacwell Engineering Co Ltd v BDH Chemicals Ltd** [1970] **3** 553, CA.

NEGLIGENCE (cont)—
  Remoteness of damage (cont)—
    Foreseeable harm (cont)—
      Damage suffered entirely different in kind to that foreseeable—Rare disease—Agricultural worker contracting Weil's disease—Little-known disease carried by rats rarely contracted by humans—Disease different in kind from other infections transmitted by rats—Other infections from rats foreseeable—Whether employer liable. **Tremain v Pike** [1969] 3 1303, Assizes.
      Novus actus interveniens—Third party's negligence intervening between defendant's negligence and plaintiffs injuries—Test for determining whether chain of causation between tort and damage broken by novus actus interveniens. **Knightley v Johns** [1982] 1 851, CA.
      Physical condition of victim—Personal injury—Tortfeasor bound to take victim as he finds him—Cancer developing from pre-malignant condition—Liability of defendant for damage resulting from death. **Smith v Leech Brain & Co Ltd** [1961] 3 1159, QBD.
      Precise damage suffered by plaintiff not foreseeable—Type of damage suffered foreseeable—Lobsters in tank on fish farm dying when pump used to recirculate water breaking down—Whether pump manufacturers liable in respect of loss of lobsters and consequent financial loss. **Muirhead v Industrial Tank Specialities Ltd** [1985] 3 705, CA.
      Precise nature of injury not reasonably foreseeable—Type of accident reasonably foreseeable but actual development of events not reasonably foreseeable—Allurement—Children exploring shelter covering manhole uncovered for repairs in street—Shelter unattended but marked by lighted paraffin lamps—Lamp accidentally kicked into manhole by child—Explosion—Child injured by burns—Accident by burns reasonably foreseeable, but explosion not reasonably foreseeable—Liability. **Hughes v Lord Advocate** [1963] 1 705, HL.
      Precise nature of injury not reasonably foreseeable—Type of injury reasonably foreseeable—Frostbite—Plaintiff required by employers to make long journey in unheated motor van in severe weather conditions—Some injury to health reasonably foreseeable—Plaintiff permanently injured by frostbite—Liability of employers. **Bradford v Robinson Rentals Ltd** [1967] 1 267, .
      Type of accident not foreseeable—Different accident foreseeable—Dropping of object into molten liquid causing unforeseeable eruption injuring plaintiff—Dangerous splashing foreseeable—Plaintiff not injured by splashing, but injured by eruption after danger of splashing had passed. **Doughty v Turner Manufacturing Co Ltd** [1964] 1 98, CA.
    Generally. *See* **Damages** (Remoteness of damage).
  Res ipsa loquitur—
    Accident raising presumption of negligence—
      Cause of accident unexplained—Inference of negligence from occurrence of accident—Motor cycle scramble—Motor cycle and competitor veering off course across safety fence into spectators—Absence of evidence as to how accident occurred—Liability of competitor—Fence not under control of competitor—Accident consistent with misjudgment not amounting to negligence. **Wilks (formerly an infant) v Cheltenham Home Guard Motor Cycle and Light Car Club** [1971] 2 369, CA.
    Application of doctrine—
      Complicated surgical operation—Swab left in patient—Ordinary reasonable man knowing facts unable to say what had happened was due to negligence—Whether doctrine of res ipsa loquitur applicable. **Mahon v Osborne** [1939] 1 535, CA.
    Control of defendant over events—
      Acts of independant contractor—Contractors engaged on conversion of building—Building adjacents to highway—Conversion heing carried out on behalf of occupier—Adjacent building being re-constructed by contractors for occupiers—Unexplained fall of brick on passer-by—Res ipsa loquitur raising presumption against occupier and contractors—Negligence disproved. **Walsh v Holst & Co Ltd** [1958] 3 33, CA.
      Railway train—Security of doors—Infant passenger falling through door of corridor train in motion—Opening of door unexplained—Whether doctrine of res ipsa loquitur applicable—Whether doors to be regarded as under control of railway company. **Easson v London and North Eastern Rly Co** [1944] 2 425, CA.
    Evidence required to discharge onus on defendant—
      Defendant's evidence that he was not negligent—Sufficiency—Evidence required to discharge onus—Defendant driving hired motor car—Unexplained swerve by motor car being driven at 60 mph on motorway—Defendant's evidence that he was not negligent in any way—Whether sufficient to discharge onus. **Ludgate v Lovett** [1969] 2 1275, CA.
      Evidence that accident could have happened without negligence—Workman employed by defendant fatally injured by explosion of gas apparatus on defendant's premises—Expert evidence that accident could have happened without negligence of defendant—Whether onus discharged. **Moore v Fox (R) & Sons** [1956] 1 182, CA.
      Evidence that defendant not negligent—No need for defendant to prove how and why accident happened—Sufficient for plaintiff to satisfy court he personally was not negligent. **Duncan v Cammell Laird & Co Ltd** [1946] 1 420, HL.
      Expert evidence—No reasonable steps available to avoid danger—Explosion caused by escape of gas from underground metal gas main—Expert evidence that fracture of pipe due to frost, but pipe in good condition and no reasonable steps available to safeguard public from consequences of such fractures—Negligence not established. **Pearson v North Western Gas Board** [1968] 2 669, Assizes.
      Explanation of accident—Finding of trial judge—Explanation excluding negligence—Pile-driving operations—Collapse of crane—Injury to servant—Finding by judge that collapse caused by ground giving way—Burden on defendant discharged. **Swan v Salisbury Construction Co Ltd** [1966] 2 138, PC.
      Explanation of res not requiring positive proof—Plaintiff injured jumping off platform after explosion—No evidence that defendant's explanation consistent with absence of negligence. **Colvilles Ltd v Devine** [1969] 2 53, HL.
      Malicious act of third party—Identity of third party—Possibility that third party servant of defendants—Plaintiff injured through breaking of hoist rope—Proof that rope had been cut maliciously. **Birchall v Bibby (J) & Sons Ltd** [1953] 1 163, Assizes.

NEGLIGENCE (cont)—

Res ipsa loquitur (cont)—

  Evidence sufficient to raise presumption—

    Dentist—Extraction of tooth—Fracture of jaw—Whether sufficient evidence to raise presumption of negligence. **Fish v Kapur** [1948] **2** 176, KBD.

    Surgical operation—Tube left in body—Surgeon not having direct control, charge or power over patient during relevant period—Action for negligence against surgeon—Whether finding of tube sufficient to raise presumption of negligence. **Morris v Winsbury-White** [1937] **4** 494, KBD.

  Highway—

    Omnibus—Accident due to tyre burst—Impact fracture of tyre—Supervision of condition of tyre—Duty of owners of vehicle—Breach of regulation—Right of action—Motor Vehicles (Construction and Use) Regulations 1941 (SR & O 1941, No 398), reg 71. **Barkway v South Wales Transport Co Ltd** [1950] **1** 392, HL.

  Latent defect—

    Presumption of negligence not discharged by proof of latent defect—Defect not discoverable by exercise of reasonable care by defendant—Purchase of secondhand machine—Injury caused by broken bolt—Metal fatigue in bolt not discoverable by routine inspection—Onus on defendant to proof that they had exercised reasonable care when machine purchased. **Pearce v Round Oak Steel Works Ltd** [1969] **3** 680, CA.

  Nature of doctrine—

    Onus on plaintiff—Plaintiff's evidence to explain cause of accident—Evidence giving rise to inference that cause of accident involved failure by defendant to take due care—Onus on plaintiff to adduce evidence—Rebuttal of inference. **Lloyde v West Midlands Gas Board** [1971] **2** 1240, CA.

  Pleading—

    Adequacy—Particulars of negligence—Accident which prima facie could not have happened without defendants' negligence—Accident to plaintiff steel erector at site works—Electrical control panels stacked against wall—Removal to instal in prescribed places—Plaintiff supervising—Move to prevent pile toppling—Two panels falling and injuring plaintiff—No explanation of cause of fall—Terms of pleading—'Workmen caused or permitted one or both panels to fall'—Whether pleading adequately covered claim in negligence. **Bennett v Chemical Construction (GB) Ltd** [1971] **3** 822, CA.

  Road accident—

    Collision between stationary and moving vehicle—Stationary vehicle on highway hit in daylight by agricultural tractor and baler—Narrow margin of space for passing—Onus on driver of moving vehicle to disprove negligence. **Randall v Tarrant** [1955] **1** 600, CA.

Res judicata. *See* **Estoppel** (Res judicata—Negligence).

Rescue—

  Contributory negligence—

    Rescue of child—Emergency act. *See* Contributory negligence—Emergency act—Rescue of child, *above*.

  Duty to rescuer. *See* Duty to take care—Rescuer, *above*.

Risk—

  Consent to risk of injury. *See* Volenti non fit injuria—Consent to risk of injury, *below*.

  Knowledge of risk—

    Duty to take care. *See* Duty to take care—Knowledge of risk, *above*.

Road accident—

  Contributory negligence. *See* Contributory negligence—Road accident, *above*.

  Res ipsa loquitur. *See* Res ipsa loquitur—Road accident, *above*.

  Vehicles. *See* Vehicles, *below*.

School—

  Duty of care—

    Non-delegable duty of care. *See* Duty to take care—Non-delegable duty of care, *above*.

    Sport—Injury to pupil—Pupil injured during rugby match at school—Whether school under duty to insure pupils against injuries received while playing sport—Whether school under duty to advise parents to take out personal accident insurance. **Van Oppen v Clerk to the Bedford Charity Trustees** [1989] **3** 389, CA.

  Local education authority. *See* **Education** (Local education authority—Negligence).

Sea wall—

  Duty of catchment board to repair. *See* **Land drainage** (Sea wall—Negligence).

Seaworthiness—

  Bill of lading—

    Due diligence to make ship seaworthy. *See* **Shipping** (Bill of lading—Implied undertaking to use due diligence to make ship seaworthy).

  Charterparty—

    Due diligence to make ship seaworthy. *See* **Shipping** (Charterparty—Seaworthiness of vessel—Due diligence).

Sequestrator—

  Immunity from suit. *See* Immunity from suit—Sequestrator, *above*.

Serviceman—

  Duty to take care. *See* Duty to take care—Serviceman, *above*.

Ship—

  Invitee—

    Injury to employee of independent contractor during ship's trial. *See* Invitee—Ship—Injury to employee of independent contractor during ship's trial, *above*.

  Survey—

    Duty to take care. *See* Duty to take care—Survey of ship, *above*.

Shipowners—

  Immunities of shipowners—

    Bill of lading—Management of ship. *See* **Shipping** (Bill of lading—Immunities of shipowner—Neglect in management of ship).

Shipping—

  Collision. *See* **Shipping** (Negligence in collision cases).

NEGLIGENCE (cont)—
  Skill and care—
    Professional person. *See* Professional person—Duty to exercise reasonable skill and care, *above*.
  Solicitor—
    Accrual of cause of action. *See* **Limitation of action** (Accrual of cause of action—Negligence—Solicitor).
    Damages—
      Generally. *See* **Solicitor** (Negligence—Damages).
      Measure of damages. *See* **Damages** (Measure of damages—Negligence—Solicitor).
    Generally. *See* **Solicitor** (Negligence).
  Specialist anaesthetist—
    Liability of hospital. *See* **Hospital** (Liability for negligence of members of staff—Specialist anaesthetist).
  Spectator—
    Duty to spectator at game or competition. *See* Duty to take care—Spectator at game or competition, *above*.
    Voluntary assumption of risk. *See* Volenti non fit injuria—Spectator at game or competition, *below*.
  Sporting event—
    Participants—
      Duty of care owed by one participant to another. *See* Duty to take care—Participants in sporting event, *above*.
  Statement—
    Careless statement causing damage to person or property. *See* Duty to take care—Statement—Careless statement causing damage to person or property, *above*.
    Information or advice. *See* Information or advice, *above*.
  Statutory powers—
    Damage caused by exercise of powers—
      Statutory remedy excluding liability in negligence—Catchment board—Power to deposit on banks of river matter removed by dredging—Diversion of flood water as result of dredging operations—Statutory liability for damage—Whether owner of bridge entitled to maintain action for negligence. **Marriage v East Norfolk Rivers Catchment Board** [1949] **2** 1021, CA.
    Duty to take care. *See* Duty to take care—Statutory powers, *above*.
  Sterilisation operation—
    Unwanted pregnancy—
      Damages. *See* **Damages** (Unwanted pregnancy—Negligence).
  Street works—
    Pavement—
      Hole dug in pavement. *See* **Highway** (Maintenance—Negligence—Street works—Hole dug in pavement by local authority workmen for junction box).
  Sub-contractor—
    Builder's liability for acts of sub-contractor. *See* Duty to take care—Builder—Extent of duty—Liability for acts of sub-contractor, *above*.
    Defective work—
      Liability. *See* Duty to take care—Defective work or product, *above*.
  Subsidence in land. *See* **Land** (Support).
  Surgeon. *See* Professional person—Surgeon, *above*.
  Survey of ship—
    Duty to take care. *See* Duty to take care—Survey of ship, *above*.
  Surveyor—
    Duty to take care—
      Surveyor making report to building society for mortgage application—Survey and valuation carried out negligently—Surveyor not following trial of suspicion when suspicions aroused as to defect—Purchaser relying on report—Surveyor knowing that purchaser likely to rely on report—Whether surveyor owing purchaser duty to exercise reasonable skill and care in carrying out valuation—Whether surveyor under duty to follow trail of suspicion—Whether surveyor liable for negligence. **Roberts v J Hampson & Co (a firm)** [1989] **2** 504, QBD.
      Surveyor making report to building society or local authority for mortgage application—Survey and valuation carried out negligently—Application form and report containing disclaimer of responsibility for condition of property—Purchaser relying on report—Surveyor knowing that purchaser likely to rely on report—Whether surveyor owing purchaser duty to exercise reasonable skill and care in carrying out valuation—Whether disclaimer reasonable—Whether disclaimer effective to exclude liability—Whether surveyor liable for negligence—Unfair Contract Terms Act 1977, s 2(2). **Harris v Wyre Forest DC** [1989] **2** 514, HL.
      Surveyor relying on vendors' statement that property connected to main drainage—Failure to qualify statement in survey report—Property not connected to main drainage—Whether failure to qualify report amounting to breach of duty of care. **Strover v Harrington** [1988] **1** 769, Ch D.
    Exclusion of liability—
      Unfair term of contract. *See* **Contract** (Unfair terms—Exclusion of liability for negligence—Surveyor).
    Immunity from suit. *See* Immunity from suit—Surveyor, *above*.
  Take-over bid—
    Information or advice—
      Knowledge third party might rely on information. *See* Information or advice—Knowledge third party might rely on information—Company—Take-over bid, *above*.
  Theft—
    Prevention—
      Duty to take care. *See* Duty to take care—Prevention of theft, *above*.
  Third party—
    Duty of care for acts of. *See* Duty to take care—Act of third party, *above*.
  Third party's intervention. *See* Causation—Intervention of third party, *above*.
  Title to sue—
    Damage to property of another. *See* Duty to take care—Damage to property of another—Title to sue, *above*.
  Traffic signal—
    Duty to take care. *See* Duty to take care—Traffic signal, *above*.

NEGLIGENCE (cont)—

Tramcar—

Duty of conductor to take care. *See* Duty to take care—Conductor of tramcar, *above*.

Trespasser—

Duty of occupier to. *See* **Occupier's liability** (Trespasser).

Unwanted pregnancy—

Damages. *See* **Damages** (Unwanted pregnancy—Negligence).

Valuer—

Accrual of cause of action. *See* **Limitation of action** (Accrual of cause of action—Negligence—Valuer).

Damages—

Interest. *See* **Interest** (Damages—Negligence—Valuer).

Measure of damages. *See* **Damages** (Measure of damages—Negligence—Valuer).

Real property valuation. *See* Professional person—Real property—Valuation, *above*.

Vehicles—

Contributory negligence—

Collision. *See* Contributory negligence—Collision between vehicles on road, *above*.

Duty of driver to take care. *See* Duty to take care—Driver of motor vehicle, *above*.

Employer's liability—

Driver suffering from heart condition—Disease undiscoverable by prior medical examination—Accident due to death of driver while driving—Whether employer liable in negligence. **Ryan v Youngs** [1938] **1** 522, CA.

Failure to keep proper look-out—

Inability to pull up within limits of vision. *See* Volenti non fit injuria—Knowledge of risk—Passenger in car, *below*.

Person riding in dark negligent if unable to pull up within limits of vision—Cyclist colliding with air-raid shelter during black-out—Principle that person must be able to pull up within limits of vision not generally applicable—Special circumstances of each case proper test. **Morris v Luton Corp** [1946] **1** 1, CA.

Opening of vehicle door. *See* Highway—Opening of vehicle door, *above*.

Parking on highway. *See* Highway—Parking of vehicle, *above*.

Passenger injured while alighting from omnibus—

Omnibus moving at time—Signal for omnibus to proceed already given by another passenger—Conductress not on platform. **Mottram v South Lancashire Transport Co** [1942] **2** 452, CA.

Omnibus stopping short of request stop—No warning by conductor. **Prescott v Lancashire United Transport Co Ltd** [1953] **1** 288, CA.

Public service vehicle—

Duty of conductor to passengers—Starting signal—Conductor absent from platform while vehicle stationary at request stop—Starting signal given by unauthorised person—Vehicle starting while plaintiff having one foot on step of car—Plaintiff injured—Whether conductor in breach of duty of care. **Davies v Liverpool Corp** [1949] **2** 175, CA.

Duty of driver to keep to time schedule—Conflict with duty of care—Injury to elderly pedestrian—Driver able to avoid accident—Plaintiff unable to tell whether pedestrian sufficiently young to avoid accident—Driver not blameworthy—Avoidance of accident conflicting with duty to observe time schedule—Whether driver liable in negligence. **Daly v Liverpool Corp** [1939] **2** 142, Liverpool Hilary Assizes.

Reliance on defendant. *See* Duty to take care—Reliance on defendant—Motor vehicles, *above*.

Skid—

Evidence of negligence—Unexplained and violent skid itself evidence of negligence. **Richley v Faull (Richley, third party)** [1965] **3** 109, QBD.

Vehicle mounting pavement—Skid not due to negligence on part of driver—Time and space available to remedy skid not sufficient. **Hunter v Wright** [1938] **2** 621, CA.

Vehicle projecting over pavement—Presumption of negligence—Dangerous road covered with frozen snow—Heavy laden lorry driven at 10 to 12 mph. **Laurie v Raglan Building Co Ltd** [1941] **3** 332, CA.

Speed—

Police vehicle—Relevance of speed limit to liability for negligence—Police motor cyclist travelling at 60 mph in pursuance of police duties—Speed limit 40 mph—Whether police motor cyclist exonerated from civil liability for negligence by statute—Road Traffic Act 1934, s 3. **Gaynor v Allen** [1959] **2** 644, QBD.

Sudden and unexpected danger—Fall of tree—Motor vehicle passing two others on main country road at 70 mph—Sudden fall of tree across road ahead—Collision with motor vehicle on far side of fallen tree—Whether driver of motor vehicle negligent in overtaking at that speed on that road. **Quinn v Scott** [1965] **2** 588, QBD.

Sudden stoppage of vehicle—

Failure of following vehicle to avoid collision—Liability of driver of following vehicle—Motor cyclists—String of motor cyclists engaged on treasure-hunt—Sudden braking by leading cyclist—Injury to pillion-rider on fourth motor cycle—Liability of first and fourth cyclists to pillion rider. **Smith v Harris** [1939] **3** 960, CA.

Traffic lights—

Road crossing controlled by traffic lights—Collision on crossing—Presumption that lights in proper working order. **Tingle Jacobs & Co v Kennedy** [1964] **1** 888, CA.

Vicarious liability. *See* **Vicarious liability**.

Visiting forces. *See* **Visiting forces** (Negligence).

NEGLIGENCE (cont)—

Volenti non fit injuria—

Consent to risk of injury—

Agreement to exclude liability—Passenger in vehicle—Notice on windscreen that passengers riding at own risk and on condition no claim made against driver—Driver informing passenger that he is 'not insured for passenger liability'—Driver pointing to notice and telling passenger it is to do with the insurance—Passenger injured in collision caused by driver's negligence in overtaking car when dangerous—Driver exempt from liability—Driver doing all that is reasonably necessary to draw limitation of liability to passenger's attention—No misrepresentation as to disclaimer of responsibility for driver's negligence—Driver's conduct within protection of notice. **Birch v Thomas** [1972] **1** 905, CA.

Voluntary consent—Duty of employee—Night watchman—Fire in building—Watchman returning to building and injured—Watchman acting in accordance with duties of employment and not voluntarily. **D'Urso v Sanson** [1939] **4** 26, KBD.

Voluntary consent—Notice by defendants excluding liability for injury—Plaintiff undergoing risk of injury in course of employment—Plaintiff a lighterman employed on barge—Train of barges being brought into dock by means of capstan rope provided and operated by defendants—Notice excluding liability of defendants to lightermen availing themselves of assistance provided by defendants—Plaintiff having no freedom to choose not to submit to terms of notice—Plaintiff injured by reason of defect in rope caused by defendants' negligence—Whether plaintiff having freely and voluntarily consented to risk of injury. **Burnett v British Waterways Board** [1973] **2** 631, CA.

Voluntary consent—Workman injured on premises not owned by employer—Workman working in house damaged by blast—Voluntarily incurring risk of latent defect—House not owned by or in occupation of employer. **Taylor v Sims & Sims** [1942] **2** 375, KBD.

Employee—

Risk to employee's health—Employee susceptible to dermatitis—Work entailing slight risk of disease—Employee and employer knowing of susceptibility—Whether employer under duty to refuse employment on ground of risk to employee's health—Whether employee having voluntarily assumed risk. **Withers v Perry Chain Co Ltd** [1961] **3** 676, CA.

Infant—

Capacity to waive right to sue for negligence—Infant passenger injured in collision—Driver of car also an infant—Infant passenger knowing that driver not insured. **Buckpitt v Oates** [1968] **1** 1145, Assizes.

Knowledge of risk—

Knowledge essential to establish consent to risk of injury—Spectator at race meeting—Motor racing—Injury caused to spectator by organisers' failure to take adequate safety precautions—Spectator having no knowledge of risk he was running owing to organisers' default—Defence of volenti not available to organisers. **White v Blackmore** [1972] **3** 158, CA.

Passenger in car—Disability of driver—Lack of driving experience—Passenger's knowledge—Learner-driver and instructor—Instructor's knowledge of risk of accident—Instructor obtaining assurance that he was covered by insurance policy before commencing lessons—Whether instructor voluntarily accepting risk of accident. **Nettleship v Weston** [1971] **3** 581, CA.

Passenger in car—Intoxicated driver—Car being used to escape from scene of crime—Car crashing causing injuries to passenger—Whether defence of volenti available to driver. **Ashton v Turner** [1980] **3** 870, QBD.

Passenger in car—Intoxicated driver—No compulsion to travel in car with knowledge of intoxication of driver—Passenger injured in consequence of accident caused by drunkenness of driver. **Dann v Hamilton** [1939] **1** 59, KBD.

Passenger in light aircraft piloted by drunken pilot—Plaintiff aware that pilot very drunk—Plaintiff seriously injured when aircraft crashed—Whether plaintiff's claim against pilot's estate barred by defence of volenti non fit injuria. **Morris v Murray** [1990] **3** 801, CA.

Person crossing railway line through gap in fence injured by train—Train not being driven negligently—Entrant fully aware of, and accepting, risks—Whether occupier liable—Occupiers' Liability (Scotland) Act 1960, s 2(3). **Titchener v British Railways Board** [1983] **3** 770, HL.

Risk of negligence—Licensee walking on defendants' railway track—Knowledge of danger from running of railway in usual way—No consent to risk of injury resulting from train driver's negligence. **Slater v Clay Cross Co Ltd** [1956] **2** 625, CA.

Spectator at game or competition—

Knowledge of risk. *See* Volenti non fit injuria—Knowledge of risk—Knowledge essential to establish consent to risk of injury—Spectator at race meeting, *above*.

Risk of damage from act of participant—Error of judgment—Consent presumed to damage from act of participant even though resulting from error of judgment—No consent to risk from reckless disregard for spectators' safety—Horse show—Spectator injured by competing horse not entitled to damages. **Wooldridge v Sumner** [1962] **2** 978, CA.

State of mind of plaintiff—

Evidence—Subjective or objective test—Passenger injured in car accident—Warning notice that passengers travelled at own risk—Passenger's knowledge that driver insured—Passenger's mistaken belief that he could claim against insurance company even though driver exempt from liability. **Bennett v Tugwell (an infant)** [1971] **2** 248, QBD.

Water—

Supply of water for domestic purposes—

Infected water. *See* **Water supply** (Supply of water for domestic purposes—Duty of undertakers as respects sufficiency and purity—Infected water).

Underground water—

Abstraction. *See* **Water and watercourses** (Underground water—Abstraction—Negligence).

Will—

Solicitor—

Duty of care. *See* **Solicitor** (Negligence—Will—Duty of care).

NEGLIGENCE (cont)—
Withdrawal of issue from jury—
Suspected terrorists shot dead in Northern Ireland by army patrol of four soldiers protecting bank—
Action by widow against Ministry of Defence claiming damages—Allegation in statement of claim
that soldiers negligent—No allegation of negligence made against anyone else in planning
operation to protect bank—Trial judge withdrawing issue of negligence from jury—Whether issue
of negligence should have been withdrawn from jury. **Farrell v Secretary of State for Defence**
[1980] **1** 166, HL.

NEGOTIATIONS
Contract to negotiate—
Enforceability. *See* **Contract** (Enforceability—Contract to negotiate).
Correspondence forming part of negotiations—
Without prejudice correspondence—
Admissibility in evidence. *See* **Evidence** (Without prejudice correspondence—Correspondence
forming part of negotiations).
Dispute resolution—
Contractual provisions. *See* **Contract** (Dispute resolution—Provision for negotiations).
Negotiations with a view to reconciliation—
Privilege—
Family proceedings. *See* **Family proceedings** (Evidence—Privilege—Negotiations with view to
reconciliation).
Without prejudice negotiations—
Evidence. *See* **Evidence** (Without prejudice negotiations).

NERVOUS SHOCK
Damages for. *See* **Damages** (Personal injury—Nervous shock).
Negligence—
Driver of motor vehicle—
Foreseeable harm. *See* **Negligence** (Duty to take care—Foreseeable harm—Duty to take care to
avoid injury to persons who might foreseeably suffer injury from want of care—Driver of motor
vehicle).
Duty to take care—
Generally. *See* **Negligence** (Duty to take care—Nervous shock).

NET
Seine net—
Prohibition—
Seafishing. *See* **Fish** (Seafishing—Prohibition by byelaw of fishing with seine net within three-mile
limit).

NET BOOK AGREEMENT
European Community rules on competition. *See* **European Union** (Rules on competition—Agreements
preventing, restricting or distorting competition—Sale of books—Net Book Agreements).

NEUROSIS
Damages for. *See* **Damages** (Remoteness of damage—Neurosis).

NEVIS
See **St Christopher, Nevis and Anguilla**.

NEW SOUTH WALES
Appeal—
Appeal as of right where value of matter in dispute £500 sterling—
Whether Australian or English pound measure of value—Australian pound worth less than English
pound—Verdict of £500 damages given in Australia set aside—Whether plaintiff had appeal as of
right—SR & O 1909 No 1521, r 2(a). **Skelton v Jones** [1962] **3** 85, PC.
Findings of fact—
Trial judge sitting without jury—Whether appeal lay only on questions of law or to direct trial de
novo—Supreme Court Procedure Act (N S W) 1900—57, s 5—Order in Council Regulating
Appeals (NSW) SR & O 1909 No 1521. **Woolworths Ltd v Stirling Henry Ltd** [1968] **1** 81, PC.
Coal mining—
Lease—
Rent and fluctuating royalties for coal mined—Statutory deductions—Whether statutory deductions
to be taken into account in computing amount due—Landlord and Tenant (Amendment) Act
1932-1947 (NSW)—Commonwealth National Security Act 1939-1949—Commonwealth National
Security (Prices) Regulations, reg 3(b), reg 23(2)—Commonwealth Prices Regulation Order
No 985, para 2(c)—Prices Regulation Act 1948 (No 26) (NSW), s 2(1). **Perpetual Trustee Co (Ltd) v
Pacific Coal Co Pty Ltd** [1956] **1** 92, PC.
Company—
Shares—
Acquisition of shares of dissenting shareholder—Acquisition by transferee company—Whether
transferee company necessarily a single company—Companies Act 1961 (NSW) (No 71 of 1961),
s 185—Interpretation Act 1897 (NSW) (No 4 of 1897), s 21(b). **Blue Metal Industries Ltd v RW
Dilley** [1969] **3** 437, PC.
Compulsory resumption of land—
Assessment of compensation—
Land resumed when subject to land sales control—Admissibility of evidence relating to sales of
land after removal of land sales control—Commonwealth Lands Acquisition Act 1906-1936 (No 13
of 1906-No 60 of 1936), s 28(1)(a). **Minister, The v Thistlethwayte** [1954] **2** 843, PC.
Resumption for settlement of ex-servicemen—Date for valuation of land—Closer Settlement
(Amendment) Act 1907 (No 12 of 1907), s 4(4)(b), proviso (as amended). **Pye v Minister for Lands
for New South Wales** [1954] **3** 514, PC.

NEW SOUTH WALES (cont)—
  Death duty—
    Dutiable estate—
      Classes of property—Property disposed of by deceased by a settlement—Settlement containing trust to take effect after deceased's death—Property deemed to be included in estate being property subject to trust at time of death—Whether limited to actual property disposed of by deceased remaining subject to trust at time of death—Stamp Duties Act 1920-1964 (NSW), s 102(2)(a). **Comr of Stamp Duties v Atwill** [1973] **1** 576, PC.
      Classes of property—Property disposed of by deceased by a settlement—Settlement containing trust to take effect after deceased's death—Settlement containing trust to take effect on failure of preceding trusts—Trust for next-of-kin of settlor—'Next-of-kin' meaning next-of-kin at time of settlor's death—Trust to take effect after deceased's death—Stamp Duties Act 1920-1959 (NSW), s 102(2)(a). **Falkiner v Comr of Stamp Duties** [1973] **1** 598, PC.
      Classes of property—Property to which any person becomes entitled—Gift to trustees for charitable purposes—Trustees selecting university as beneficiary—Whether university 'any person...entitled' to property—Whether property exempt from duty—Stamp Duties Act 1920 (NSW), s 102(1)(a). **Perpetual Trustee Co Ltd v Comr of Stamp Duties** [1976] **2** 792, PC.
      Classes of property—Trust to take effect after death—Reservation of benefit—New South Wales Stamp Duties Act 1920-1949, s 102(2)(a)(c)(d). **Comr of Stamp Duties of New South Wales v Way** [1952] **1** 198, .
      Exemption—Gift of residuary estate to educational institution—Testator expressing wish in will that trustees should apply residuary estate towards building of arts centre—Direction to trustees to transfer residuary estate for that purpose to any one of several institutions—Executor selecting university—Whether gift for educational purposes or gift to educational institution—Whether residuary estate exempt from duty as gift to educational institution—Educational Institutions (Stamp Duties Exemption) Act 1961 (NSW), s 2(1), (3)(a). **Perpetual Trustee Co Ltd v Comr of Stamp Duties** [1976] **2** 792, PC.
    Interest limited to cease on death—
      Interest in property within and outside New South Wales—Validity of relevant statutory provisions—New South Wales Stamp Duties Act 1920-1952, s 102(2)(g)(2A)—New South Wales Constitution Act 1902 (No 32), s 5. **Johnson v Comr of Stamp Duties** [1956] **1** 502, PC.
    Power of appointment—
      Exercise of general power by will of person domiciled in New South Wales—Trust fund comprising shares situate outside New South Wales—Validity of legislation of New South Wales imposing death duty—Construction of New South Wales Stamp Duties Act 1920-1965, s 102(2)(a)(2A). **Thompson v Comr of Stamp Duties** [1968] **2** 896, PC.
  Jurisdiction—
    Cause of action arising within the jurisdiction—
      Negligence—Ingredients of cause of action occurring outside the jurisdiction—English company manufacturing drugs and supplying them to Australian company for sale in Australia—English company not resident within jurisdiction—Failure by English company to give warning or notice of danger of taking drug in early months of pregnancy—Plaintiff born malformed as result of mother taking drug—Action in negligence by plaintiff against English company—Whether cause of action arising within jurisdiction—Common Law Procedure Act (No 21 of 1899), s 18(4)(a). **Distillers Co (Biochemicals) Ltd v Thompson** [1971] **1** 694, PC.
  Legacy duty—
    Legal costs incurred by executor in connection with will—
      Rate of duty—New South Wales Stamp Duties Act 1920-1940, s 101D, Sch VII. **Comr of Stamp Duties of New South Wales v Pearse** [1954] **1** 19, PC.
  Libel—
    Exemplary or punitive damages—
      Principles on which exemplary damages awarded—Categories—Competency of Australian courts to award exemplary damages—Limitation of categories laid down in Rookes v Barnard not applicable in Australia. **Australian Consolidated Press Ltd v Uren** [1967] **3** 523, PC.
  Licence—
    Mining licence—
      Right to mine for magnesite—Non-exclusive licence—Whether licence terminable at will—Whether dated notice required. **Australian Blue Metal Ltd v Hughes** [1962] **3** 335, PC.
  Magistrates—
    Audience—
      Conduct of prosecution—Discretionary power to allow person not being the informant, or his counsel or attorney, to conduct prosecution—No statutory limitation on exercise of discretionary power—Justices Act 1902 (No 27 of 1902), s 70(2). **O'Toole v Scott** [1965] **2** 240, PC.
  Mining licence. *See* Licence—Mining licence, *above.*
  Rates—
    Exemption—
      Land owned by public hospital—No physical use of land—'Used'—'Occupied'—New South Wales Local Government Act 1919 (No 41 of 1919), s 132(1)(d). **Newcastle City Council v Royal Newcastle Hospital** [1959] **1** 734, PC.
    Valuation—
      Land—Meaning of 'land'—Stratum—Assessment of unimproved capital value—Improvements to land—Parcels defined by reference to improvements and having no recognisable connection with surface—Strata—Horizontal layers above and below ground level—Property demised with spaces above and below ground level excepted from lease—Hotel and office block—Whether 'land' meaning land defined by vertical boundaries usque as coelum et ad inferos—Whether demised property as a whole to be valued as 'land'—Whether to be valued as 'strata'—Valuation of Land Act 1916 (NSW), ss 4(1), 6(1), 7B(1) (as amended by Act 66 of 1961). **Comr for Railways v Valuer-General** [1973] **3** 268, PC.
      Racecourse—Land subject to restrictive trusts, conditions and provisos materially affecting its value—Whether, in ascertaining 'unimproved value' of land, valuation should take into account existence of restrictions—New South Wales Valuation of Land Act 1916-1951, s 6. **Golland v Randwick Municipal Council** [1960] **3** 449, PC.

NEW SOUTH WALES (cont)—
    Sale of reversion—
        Undervalue—
            Independent professional advice—Sales of Reversions Act 1867, s 1—New South Wales
            Conveyancing Act 1919 (No 6), s 30. **Permanent Trustee Co of New South Wales Ltd v
            Bridgewater** [1936] **3** 501, PC.
    Statutory instrument—
        Ultra vires—
            Breach of regulation alleged—Whether regulation ultra vires—Scaffolding and Lifts Act 1912-1960,
            s 22(1)(2)(g)(iv)(v)—Regulations 98, 73(2)(5). **Utah Construction & Engineering Pty Ltd v Pataky**
            [1965] **3** 650, PC.

NEW TENANCY
    Business premises. *See* **Landlord and tenant** (Business premises).
    Generally. *See* **Landlord and tenant** (New tenancy).

NEW TOWN
    Compulsory acquisition of land—
        Compensation. *See* **Compulsory purchase** (Compensation—Town development).
    Order designating area as site for proposed new town—
        Statutory requirements to be fulfilled prior to order—
            Consultation—Duty of Minister to consult—New Towns Act 1946, s 1(1). **Fletcher v Minister of Town
            and Country Planning** [1947] **2** 496, KBD.
            Consultation—Information as to proposed new town—New Towns Act 1946, s 1(1), Sch I, para 1.
            Rollo v Minister of Town and Country Planning [1948] **1** 13, CA.
            Draft order—Objections—Public inquiry—Scope of inquiry—Nature of Minister's duties—Need to
            support proposed order by public inquiry—Bias—New Towns Act 1946, s 1(1), Sch I, para 3.
            Franklin v Minister of Town and Country Planning [1947] **2** 289, HL.

NEW TRIAL
    County court action. *See* **County court** (New trial).
    Court of Appeal—
        Generally. *See* **Court of Appeal** (New trial).
    Criminal appeal—
        Order for new trial—
            Jamaica. *See* **Jamaica** (Criminal law—Appeal—Allowing appeal—New trial).
    Defamation case. *See* **Libel and slander** (New trial).
    Evidence—
        Admiralty proceedings. *See* **Admiralty** (Practice—Evidence—New trial).
    Jurisdiction. *See* **Court of Appeal** (Jurisdiction—Order for new trial).
    Order for new trial. *See* **Court of Appeal** (Order for new trial).

NEW ZEALAND
    Company—
        Director—
            Breach of duty—Director nominated by major shareholder. *See* **Company** (Director—Breach of
            duty—Director nominated by major shareholder).
    Conflict of laws—
        Interest on debentures—
            Debentures issued in New Zealand by borough council and secured on a rate thereof—Whether
            interest thereon reduced by effect of Financial Emergency Act 1931 (No 3961 of Victoria),
            s 19(1)—Distinction between obligation and performance of the obligation. **Mount Albert BC v
            Australasian Temperance and General Mutual Life Assurance Society Ltd** [1937] **4** 206, PC.
    Costs—
        Jurisdiction—
            Order for costs—Payment of costs by non-party—Whether jurisdiction existing to make order for
            payment of costs by non-party after final order—Circumstances in which non-party may be
            ordered to pay costs of proceedings. **Dymocks Franchise Systems (NSW) Pty Ltd v Todd**
            [2005] **4** 195, PC.
    Court of Appeal—
        Precedent. *See* **Precedent** (New Zealand Court of Appeal).
    Currency—
        Debenture bonds and coupons—
            Payable at option of the holder in London or New Zealand—Currency in which such payments may
            be made—Local Bodies Loans Act 1913. **Auckland City Council v Alliance Assurance Co Ltd**
            [1937] **1** 645, PC.
    Damages—
        Interest—
            Jurisdiction to include interest in award of damages. *See* **Interest** (Damages—Jurisdiction to
            include interest in award of damages—New Zealand).
    Estate duty—
        Allowance—
            Obligation of deceased to pay life annuity—Contingent debt—What amount allowable as a
            debt—New Zealand Death Duties Act 1921 (1921, No 21), s 9(2)(d). **Comr of Stamp Duties v New
            Zealand Insurance Co Ltd** [1956] **1** 598, PC.
        Annuity—
            Transfer of property by deceased to his sons in 1932—Covenant by sons to pay deceased annuity
            for his life—Deceased dying in 1949—Whether property liable to duty—New Zealand Death
            Duties Act 1921 (1921, No 21), s 5(1)(j). **Ward v Comr of Inland Revenue** [1956] **1** 571, PC.

NEW ZEALAND (cont)—
Executor and administrator—
Notice to creditors and others to send in claims—
Executor with notice of persons disputing the validity of will—Liability for payment of legacies—Trustee Act (New Zealand) 1908, s 74. **Guardian Trust and Exors Co of New Zealand Ltd v Public Trustee of New Zealand** [1942] **1** 598, PC.
Husband and wife—
Division of matrimonial property—
Distinction between matrimonial and separate property—Business started after marriage with property belonging to husband before marriage—Whether proceeds of sale of business available for division in matrimonial proceedings—Exercise of discretion of local courts—Whether Privy Council entitled to interfere—New Zealand Matrimonial Property Act 1976 (No 166 of 1976), ss 8(e), 9(2). **Reid v Reid** [1982] **3** 328, PC.
Income tax—
Assessable income—
Deductions in computing income—Expenditure or loss incurred in production of assessable income—Rights obtained in return for expenditure—Expenditure on acquisition of stock-in-trade—Rights under purchase contracts the only legally enforceable rights obtained by taxpayer company—Indirect benefit resulting from expenditure—Taxpayer company not a party to agreements whereby benefit secured on its behalf—Benefit equivalent to a calculated discount on purchase price of stock-in-trade—Benefit obtained by means of dividends paid by third company to subsidiary of taxpayer company—Dividends arising in consequence of agreement between ultimate supplier of stock-in-trade and third company—Whether whole of taxpayer company's expenditure incurred in production of assessable income—Land and Income Tax Act 1954 (New Zealand), s 111 (as amended by the Land and Income Tax Act 1968, s 12). **Europa Oil (NZ) Ltd v IRC** [1976] **1** 503, PC.
Assessment out of time. *See* **Income tax** (Assessment—Assessment out of time—New Zealand).
Avoidance—
Arrangement having purpose or effect of altering incidence of tax—Paddock trust—Yearly lease by taxpayer to trustees of different parts of land when sown to wheat—Income from land held on trust for taxpayer's family—Whether arrangement altering the incidence of tax—Whether income derived by the taxpayer—Land and Income Tax Act 1954, s 108. **Mangin v IRC** [1971] **1** 179, PC.
Arrangement having purpose or effect of altering incidence of tax—Purpose or effect—Meaning—No real distinction in meaning—Arrangement having particular effect treated as having that purpose—Motive irrelevant—Arrangement void if one of its effects is to alter incidence of tax—Purpose or effect of arrangement to be determined by reference to the arrangement only—Land and Income Tax Act 1954, s 108. **Ashton v IRC** [1975] **3** 225, PC.
Exemption—
Income derived by trustees in trust for charitable purposes—Crown settling tax-exempt income on trust for use for charitable purposes with ultimate trust of undistributed income in favour of the Crown—Whether income liable to tax—Income Tax Act 1976 (New Zealand), s 61(25). **Crown Forestry Rental Trust, Re** [2004] **4** 558, PC.
Information—
Information relevant to enforcement of Inland Revenue Acts—Notice to sharebrokers and bankers requiring information disclosing names of possible taxpayers—Whether commissioner having power to require information relating to unidentified taxpayers—Whether commissioner's request unreasonable or an abuse of power—Inland Revenue Department Act 1974 (NZ), s 17(1)—Bill of Rights Act 1990 (NZ), s 21. **New Zealand Stock Exchange v IRC** [1991] **4** 443, PC.
Mutual life insurance company—
Assessment—Reversionary bonuses—Allotment of surplus funds for reversionary bonuses—Declared face value of maturing reversionary bonuses irrelevant—Deduction of income exempt from taxation—Income not 'exempt' unless it would be subject to New Zealand taxation but for the exemption—Income from investments in Australian and English companies not therefore 'exempt' from taxation and not deductible—Whether income from Australian investments held by branch in New Zealand of Australian life insurance company income 'derived from' a business carried on in New Zealand'New Zealand Land and Income Tax Act 1954 (No 67), ss 149(2), 86(1)(i), 167(a). **Australian Mutual Provident Society v IRC** [1961] **3** 1051, PC.
Profits or gains derived from sale of property—
Profits or gains—Meaning—Conversion of sterling funds into New Zealand currency—Purchase of United Kingdom securities with sterling funds and simultaneous sale of securities for New Zealand currency—Transactions yielding premium over amount of New Zealand currency receivable by converting sterling at official rate of exchange—Transactions of that kind in common use for purpose of converting sterling into New Zealand currency—Whether premium a profit derived from sale of United Kingdom securities—Land and Income Tax Act 1954, s 88(1)(c). **Holden v IRC** [1974] **2** 819, PC.
Land registration—
Indefeasibility of title of registered proprietors—
Mortgage—Forgery—Mortgage of fee simple by one joint owner forging other joint owner's signature—Memorandum of mortgage registered—Power of sale exercised by mortgagees—Memorandum of transfer registered—Mortgagees and purchaser acting in good faith—Whether purchaser and mortgagees acquired title as against the joint owner who had not known of the mortgage—Land Transfer Act 1952 (No 52 of 1952), ss 63, 85. **Frazer v Walker** [1967] **1** 649, PC.
Legal professional privilege—
Documents—
Law society investigating complaint against law firm—Whether statutory power to requisition documents overriding legal professional privilege—Law Practitioners Act 1982 (New Zealand), s 101(3)(d). **B v Auckland District Law Society** [2004] **4** 269, PC.
Limitation of action—
Action against electric-power board—
Breach of implied term in employee's contract—Breach of duty—Electric-power Boards Act 1925, s 127. **Vincent v Tauranga Electric-Power Board** [1936] **3** 884, PC.

NEW ZEALAND (cont)—

Mine—

Mineral licence—

Grant not registered under Land Transfer Act—Grant not confined to mining gold—Whether grantee's successor in title bound by licence—New Zealand Mining Act 1926 (No 15), s 58—New Zealand Land Transfer Act 1952 (No 52), ss 62, 143, 145. **Miller v Minister of Mines** [1963] **1** 109, PC.

Native lands—

Charge on lands—

Statutory charge—Validity—Claim for indemnity of legislature of New Zealand to impose charge—Power to legislate in derogation of treaty right—Treaty of Waitangi 1840—New Zealand Constitution Act 1852, ss 53, 72, 73—New Zealand Constitution (Amendment) Act 1857—Colonial Laws Validity Act 1865—Native Land Act (New Zealand) 1873—Native Purposes Act (New Zealand) 1935, s 14. **Hoani Te Heuheu Tukino v Aotea District Maori Land Board** [1941] **2** 93, PC.

Negligence—

Duty of care—

Limitation of action—Latent defect—Latent defect caused by local authority's building inspector negligently approving defective foundations—Whether cause of action accruing when house built or when reasonably prudent homeowner would have discovered latent defect. **Invercargill City Council v Hamlin** [1996] **1** 756, PC.

Statutory powers—Local authority—Building byelaws—Byelaws requiring approval of foundations by local authority's building inspector—Inspector negligently approving defective foundations—Defective foundations causing damage to house—Whether local authority owing duty of care to owner of house. **Invercargill City Council v Hamlin** [1996] **1** 756, PC.

Parliament—

Parliamentary privilege—

Bill of Rights—Libel action by member of Parliament—Plea of justification—Allegation that plaintiff made misleading statements to Parliament and caused legislation to be passed as part of fraudulent conspiracy—Whether particulars infringing Parliamentary privilege should be struck out—Whether plaintiff's action should be stayed if privilege not waived by Parliament—Bill of Rights (1688), art 9. **Prebble v Television New Zealand Ltd** [1994] **3** 407, PC.

Bill of Rights—Member of Parliament making defamatory statement in Parliament—Member of Parliament affirming content of statement but not repeating it outside Parliament—Person referred to in statement bringing proceedings for defamation—Whether member of Parliament protected by parliamentary privilege—Bill of Rights (1688), art 9. **Buchanan v Jennings** [2005] **2** 273, PC.

Pharmacy—

Wholesale dealer in drugs—

Prohibition on dealer having an interest in the business carried on in pharmacy—Application for permission to open a new pharmacy in New Zealand—Applicant a subsidiary of a United Kingdom wholesale dealer in drugs but which exercised no control over the business of the applicant—Wholesale dealer doing no business of its own in New Zealand—Whether applicant disentitled to open new pharmacy—Pharmacy Act 1939, as amended by Pharmacy Amendment Act 1954, s 13(1). **Boots The Chemists (New Zealand) Ltd v Chemists' Service Guild of New Zealand, Inc** [1967] **3** 234, PC.

Precedent—

Court of Appeal. *See* **Precedent** (New Zealand Court of Appeal).

Price control—

Sale of imported motor cars—

Licence for importation conditional on purchaser entering into covenant restricting resale—Purchase of imported car at maximum control price and resale at profit in breach of covenant—Validity of covenant—Measure of damages for breach of covenant—New Zealand Control of Prices Act 1947 (No 51 of 1947), s 2(1). **Mouat v Betts Motors Ltd** [1958] **3** 402, PC.

Service out of the jurisdiction. *See* **Practice** (Service out of the jurisdiction—New Zealand).

Statute—

Enforcement of New Zealand statute in England—

New Zealand statute providing for forfeiture of historic articles unlawfully removed from New Zealand—Whether statute enforceable in England. **A-G of New Zealand v Ortiz** [1982] **3** 432, QBD.

Interpretation—

New Zealand statutes deemed to be 'remedial'—Whether all statutes to receive purposive construction—New Zealand Acts Interpretation Act 1924, s 5(j). **A-G of New Zealand v Ortiz** [1982] **3** 432, QBD.

Statute providing that historic articles unlawfully removed 'shall be forfeited' to Her Majesty—Whether goods so removed automatically forfeited on removal from New Zealand—Whether forfeiture dependent on seizure of goods—Whether Crown's title accruing only on seizure—Historic Articles Act 1962 (NZ), s 12(2). **A-G of New Zealand v Ortiz** [1982] **3** 432, QBD; [1983] **2** 93, HL.

Treaty of Waitangi—

Protection of Maori taonga—

Maori language—Restructuring of New Zealand broadcasting—Possible detrimental effect on survival of Maori language—New Zealand government proposing to transfer state-controlled television operations and assets to state enterprise—Principal objective of state enterprise to operate as successful business by being as profitable and efficient as comparable private business—Whether transfer of television assets to state enterprise incompatible with Crown's obligation under Treaty of Waitangi to protect and preserve Maori taonga including Maori language—Nature of Crown's obligation under Treaty of Waitangi—Treaty of Waitangi 1840—State-Owned Enterprises Act 1986, ss 4(1), 7, 9. **New Zealand Maori Council v A-G of New Zealand** [1994] **1** 623, PC.

NEW ZEALAND (cont)—
  Water supply—
    Domestic purposes—
      Pure water—Addition of fluoride—Local authority which was also health authority empowered to supply 'pure water'—Water supply 'pure' in its natural state but deficient in fluoride—Fluoride added solely to improve dental health—Whether local authority entitled to make addition—Municipal Corporations Act 1954 (No 76), s 240. **A-G for New Zealand (ex rel Lewis and Elliott) v Lower Hutt Corp** [1964] **3** 179, PC.

NEWLY ERECTED BUILDING
  Rates. *See* **Rates** (Unoccupied property—Newly erected building).

NEWSPAPER
  Article—
    Copyright—
      Ownership. *See* **Copyright** (Ownership—Proof of ownership—Newspaper articles).
      False attribution of authorship. *See* **Copyright** (False attribution of authorship—Attribution—Newspaper article).
    Contempt of court—
      Publications concerning legal proceedings. *See* **Contempt of court** (Publications concerning legal proceedings).
    Copyright—
      Infringement. *See* **Copyright** (Conflict of laws—Newspaper).
    Freedom of expression—
      Antigua. *See* **Antigua** (Fundamental rights and freedoms—Freedom of expression).
      Child—
        Protection of child—Generally. *See* **Child** (Protection—Freedom of publication).
      Ward of court—
        Protection—Publication of matter likely to be harmful to ward. *See* **Ward of court** (Jurisdiction—Protection of ward—Freedom of publication).
    Journalist—
      Evidence—
        Privilege. *See* **Evidence** (Privilege—Press—Newspaper reporter).
      Income tax—
        Newspaper allowance. *See* **Income tax** (Emoluments from office or employment—Expenses wholly, exclusively and necessarily incurred—Newspaper allowance).
      Refusal to disclose source of information—
        Contempt of court. *See* **Contempt of court** (Refusal to disclose source of information—Journalist).
    Libel proceedings—
      Generally. *See* **Libel and slander**.
      Innuendo—
        Particulars—Identity of readers who have knowledge of special facts which render published words defamatory. *See* **Libel and slander** (Innuendo—Particulars—Duty of plaintiff to plead facts on which he relies for his claim—Identity of persons to whom publication made and who have knowledge of facts which render published words defamatory—Publication by newspaper).
      Qualified privilege—
        Common law privilege. *See* **Libel and slander** (Qualified privilege—Common law privilege—Report in newspaper).
    News story—
      Whether copyright in news story. *See* **Copyright** (Infringement).
    Passing off—
      Alteration of copies without authority. *See* **Passing off** (Journal).
    Previous convictions of accused—
      Report disclosing previous convictions. *See* **Criminal evidence** (Character of accused—Previous conviction—Newspaper report).
    Prize competition. *See* **Gaming** (Prize competition—Forecast of result of future event—Newspaper competition).
    Publishing—
      Selective employment tax—
        Premium. *See* **Selective employment tax** (Premium—Activity in which establishment engaged—Publishing).
    Report—
      Committal proceedings. *See* **Criminal law** (Committal—Newspaper report).
      Restrictions on reporting proceedings concerning children or young persons. *See* **Children and young persons** (Court proceedings—Protection of child concerned in proceedings—Order that no report shall reveal particulars calculated to lead to identification of child concerned in proceedings).
    Reporter—
      Privilege—
        Evidence. *See* **Evidence** (Privilege—Press—Newspaper reporter).
      Refusal to disclose source of information. *See* **Tribunal** (Tribunal of inquiry—Evidence—Newspaper reporter).

NEXT FRIEND
  Mental patient, for—
    Function in legal proceedings. *See* **Mental health** (Legal proceedings brought on behalf of patient—Function of next friend in legal proceedings).
  Minor. *See* **Minor** (Next friend).
  Nullity suit—
    Petition by next friend. *See* **Nullity** (Petition—Parties—Petition by next friend).

NEXT-OF-KIN
Claims to personal estate of deceased person—
Limitation of action. *See* **Limitation of action** (Claim to personal estate of deceased person—Action by next-of-kin against beneficiary).
Enquiries for—
Chancery Division. *See* **Practice** (Chancery Division—Inquiries for next-of-kin).
Gift. *See* **Will** (Gift—Specific donees—Next-of-kin).
Right of possession—
Human tissue. *See* **Human tissue** (Property—Right of possession—Next-of-kin).

NIGERIA
Constitutional law—
Dismissal of Premier by Governor—
No adverse vote in House of Assembly—Whether Governor may remove Premier on material other than decision or resolution in the House—Nigeria (Constitution) Order in Council 1960 (SI 1960 No 1652), Sch 4, s 33(10). **Adegbenro v Akintola** [1963] **3** 544, PC.
Contempt of court—
Right of appeal to West African Court of Appeal—
Convicted—Person in contempt ordered to pay fine, with imprisonment in default—West African Court of Appeal Ordinance, s 10. **Izuora v R** [1953] **1** 827, PC.
Native lands in Lagos—
Alienation of land—
Laches—Alienation of part of compound, by headman without the consent of the chief and family—Acquiescence of family by laches. **Oshodi v Balogun and Scottish Nigerian Mortgage and Trust Co Ltd** [1936] **2** 1632, PC.
Reference—
Interpretation of Constitution—
Interpretation referred to Federal Supreme Court—Whether decision of reference a final decision—Nigeria (Constitution) Order in Council 1960 (SI 1960 No 1652), Sch 2, ss 108, 114(1). **Adegbenro v Akintola** [1963] **3** 544, PC.
Title to property—
Royal palace at Lagos—
Rights of previous ruler—Crown grant of palace to previous ruler—Right of successor of occupying palace—Treaty of Cession 1861—Crown Grants (Township of Lagos) Ordinance (Laws of Nigeria 1948), s 3. **Oyekan v Adele** [1957] **2** 785, PC.

NIGHT OFFENCES
See **Criminal law** (Night offences).

NO CASE TO ANSWER
Criminal trial. *See* **Criminal law** (Trial—No case to answer).
Practice. *See* **Practice** (No case to answer).

NO REASONABLE CAUSE OF ACTION
Pleading—
Striking out. *See* **Pleading** (Striking out—No reasonable cause of action).

NOISE
Easement—
Nuisance. *See* **Nuisance** (Noise—Motor racing—Easement).
Landlord and tenant—
Covenant for quiet enjoyment. *See* **Landlord and tenant** (Covenant—Quiet enjoyment).
Nuisance—
Air traffic. *See* **Air traffic** (Noise nuisance).
Generally. *See* **Nuisance** (Noise).
Highway. *See* **Nuisance** (Highway—Noise).
Motor racing. *See* **Nuisance** (Noise—Motor racing).
Safety of employee—
Duty of employer to protect employee from foreseeable risk of danger to health—
Generally. *See* **Employment** (Duty of master—Safety of employees—Common law duty to protect employee from foreseeable risk of danger to health—Noise).
Need to take competent advice about precautions—Danger to hearing from noise. *See* **Employment** (Duty of master—Safety of employees—Common law duty to protect employee from foreseeable risk of danger to health—Need to take competent advice about precautions—Noise).

NOMINAL PLAINTIFF
Security for costs. *See* **Costs** (Security for costs—Nominal plaintiff).

NOMINATION
Elections—
Local government. *See* **Elections** (Local government—Nomination papers).
Parliamentary. *See* **Elections** (Parliamentary—Nomination).
Pension scheme—
Power of nomination. *See* **Pension** (Pension scheme—Power of nomination).
Will—
Testamentary disposition—
Exercise of power. *See* **Will** (Testamentary disposition—Exercise of power—Nomination).

NON EST FACTUM
Plea—
Document. *See* **Document** (Non est factum).
Mistake. *See* **Mistake** (Nature of document—Non est factum).

NON-CONTENTIOUS BUSINESS
Solicitor—
    Costs—
        Generally. *See* **Solicitor** (Costs—Non-contentious business).
        Taxation of costs. *See* **Costs** (Taxation—Solicitor—Non-contentious business).

NON-CONTENTIOUS PROBATE
Practice. *See* **Probate** (Practice—Non-contentious probate).

NON-CONTRIBUTORY INVALIDITY PENSION
See **Social security** (Non-contributory invalidity pension).

NON-DOMESTIC RATES
Distress—
    Company—
        Generally. *See* **Company** (Distress—Rates).
    Generally. *See* **Rates**.

NON-MOLESTATION ORDER
Power of arrest attached to non-molestation order. *See* **Family proceedings** (Orders in family proceedings—Power of arrest attached to non-molestation order).

NON-PARTY
Costs—
    Payment. *See* **Costs** (Order for costs—Payment of costs by non-party).

NON-PATRIAL
Deportation. *See* **Immigration** (Deportation).
Illegal entry into United Kingdom. *See* **Immigration** (Illegal entry and other offences).
Immigration. *See* **Immigration**.
Right to enter United Kingdom. *See* **Immigration** (Leave to appeal—Non-patrial—Right of entry).

NON-PECUNIARY LOSS
Damages—
    Personal injury claim. *See* **Damages** (Personal injury—Pain, suffering and loss of amenities).

NON-REPAIR OF HIGHWAY
Civil liability. *See* **Highway** (Maintenance—Civil liability for non-repair).

NON-RESIDENT
Habeas corpus—
    Jurisdiction of English courts. *See* **Habeas corpus** (Jurisdiction—Places to which writ may run—Northern Ireland).
Income tax. *See* **Income tax** (Non-resident).

NON-RESIDENT PARENT
Child support. *See* **Child** (Maintenance—Child support—Non-resident parent).

NONSUIT
County court practice. *See* **County court** (Practice—Nonsuit).

NORTH EASTERN CIRCUIT
Practice—
    Appeals. *See* **Practice** (Chancery Division—Northern Area—Appeals).

NORTHERN CIRCUIT
Practice—
    Appeals. *See* **Practice** (Chancery Division—Northern Area—Appeals).
    Commercial cases. *See* **Practice** (Commercial cases—Northern Circuit).

NORTHERN IRELAND
Arrest without warrant—
    False imprisonment. *See* **False imprisonment** (Arrest without warrant—Northern Ireland).
Commissioner for Complaints—
    Powers and duties—
        Investigation of complaint—Power to recommend monetary redress—Power to make special report—Commissioner investigating general medical practitioner following complaint—Whether commissioner having power to recommend payment by general medical practitioner to complainant—Whether commissioner having power to make special report to legislature—Commissioner for Complaints (Northern Ireland) Order 1996, SI 1996/1297, arts 7, 8, 9, 11, 16, 17. **application by JR55 for Judicial Review (Northern Ireland), Re an** [2016] 4 779, SC.
Company—
    Compulsory winding up. *See* **Company** (Compulsory winding up—Northern Ireland company).
Coroner's inquest—
    Practice and procedure. *See* **Coroner** (Inquest—Practice and procedure—Northern Ireland).
Criminal evidence. *See* **Criminal evidence** (Northern Ireland).
Criminal law—
    Sexual intercourse—
        Girl under 14—Reasonable belief as to age—Defence -Availability of defence—Criminal Law Amendment Acts (Northern Ireland) 1885-1923, s 4. **R v Brown** [2013] 4 860, SC.

NORTHERN IRELAND (cont)—
Employment—
Discrimination against a woman—
Less favourable treatment—Staff appraisal duties removed from employee—Identification of appropriate comparator—Whether employee discriminated against on ground of her sex—Sex Discrimination (Northern Ireland) Order 1976, arts 3(1)(a), 7. **Shamoon v Chief Constable of Royal Ulster Constabulary** [2003] **2** 26, HL.
Provision in relation to retirement—Female employees required to retire at 60 whereas men retiring at 65—Northern Ireland and English legislation identical—English legislation passed before adoption of EEC equal treatment directive whereas Northern Ireland legislation passed subsequent to directive—Whether Northern Ireland provision passed to implement directive—Whether Northern Ireland provision to be construed differently from English provision—Whether unlawful discrimination for women to be required to retire earlier than men—Whether necessary to refer question to European Court—Sex Discrimination (Northern Ireland) Order 1976, art 8(2)(4)—Council Directive (EEC) 76/207, art 5(1). **Finnegan v Clowney Youth Training Programme Ltd** [1990] **2** 546, HL.
Parliament—
Legislative power—
Restrictions on power—Non-interference with trade—Legislation imposing restrictions on sale of milk—Whether interference with trade—Whether ultra vires—Government of Ireland Act 1920, s 4(1),(7)—Milk and Milk Products Act (Northern Ireland) 1934, ss 1(1)(c), 2(2). **Gallagher v Lynn** [1937] **3** 598, HL.
Prisoner—
Legal representation—
Charge of offence against prison discipline. *See* **Prison** (Discipline—Offence against discipline—Charge—Rights of prisoner charged—Legal representation).
Rates—
Exemption—
Charity—School not of eleemosynary character—Whether exempt from rates—Contemporanea expositio—Stare decisis—Effect of long-standing practice—Valuation (Ireland) Amendment Act 1854, s 2—Poor Relief (Ireland) Act 1838, s 63, proviso. **Campbell College Belfast (Governors) v Comr of Valuation for Northern Ireland** [1964] **2** 705, HL.
Reference—
Taxation—
Powers of Government of Northern Ireland—Tax substantially the same as income tax—Government of Ireland Act 1920, s 21—Finance Act (Northern Ireland) 1934, s 3. **Government of Ireland Act 1920, s 51, Re a reference under** [1936] **2** 111, PC.
Terrorist—
Arrest without warrant. *See* **Arrest** (Arrest without warrant—Terrorist).
Town and country planning—
Compensation—
Refusal of permission to develop—Statutory exclusion of right to compensation—Constitutional invalidity of law made to take any property without compensation—Validity of exclusion of right to compensation—Government of Ireland Act 1920, s 5(1)—Planning and Housing Act (Northern Ireland) 1931, s 10(2)—Planning (Interim Development) Act (Northern Ireland) 1944, s 2, s 6(4). **Belfast Corp v O D Cars Ltd** [1960] **1** 65, HL.
Refusal of permission to develop—Statutory exclusion of right to compensation—Evidence—Evidence of Ministry's view as to reasonableness of restrictive provisions in a planning scheme—Adequacy of oral evidence. **Belfast Corp v O D Cars Ltd** [1960] **1** 65, HL.
Trust—
Marriage settlement. *See* **Variation of trusts** (Jurisdiction—Northern Ireland marriage settlement).

NORWICH PHARMACAL ORDER
See **Disclosure and inspection of documents** (Defendant for purposes of disclosure only—Norwich Pharmacal order).

NOT GUILTY
Plea. *See* **Criminal law** (Trial—Plea—Not guilty).

NOTE OF JUDGMENT
Appeal from Chancery Division or Queen's Bench Division—
Practice. *See* **Practice** (Note of judgment—Appeal from Chancery Division or Queen's Bench Division).
Appeal from county court. *See* **County court** (Appeal—Note of county court judgment).

NOTE OR MEMORANDUM
Guarantee. *See* **Guarantee** (Note or memorandum of agreement in writing).

NOTES OF TRIAL
Judge's notes—
Criminal proceedings. *See* **Criminal law** (Trial—Judge—Notes of trial).

NOTICE OF APPEAL
Appeal against committal for contempt of court. *See* **Contempt of court** (Committal—Appeal against committal—Notice of appeal).
Bankruptcy appeal from county court. *See* **Bankruptcy** (Appeal—Appeal from county court—Notice of appeal).
Court of Appeal. *See* **Court of Appeal** (Notice of appeal).
Criminal cases. *See* **Criminal law** (Appeal—Notice of appeal).
Matrimonial proceedings—
Appeal to Divisional Court. *See* **Husband and wife** (Summary proceedings—Appeal to Divisional Court—Notice of appeal).

NOTICE OF APPEAL (cont)—
Matrimonial proceedings (cont)—
Appeal to High Court against order of magistrates—
Form of notice of appeal. *See* **Husband and wife** (Matrimonial order—Appeal to High Court against order of magistrates—Procedure—Form of notice of appeal).

NOTICE TO COMPLETE
Sale of land. *See* **Sale of land** (Notice to complete).

NOTICE TO QUIT
Agricultural holding. *See* **Agricultural holding** (Notice to quit).
Allotment. *See* **Allotment** (Allotment garden—Termination of tenancy).
Landlord and tenant. *See* **Landlord and tenant** (Notice to quit).
Local authority house. *See* **Housing** (Local authority houses—Notice to quit).

NOTICE TO TREAT
Compulsory acquisition of land. *See* **Compulsory purchase** (Notice to treat).

NOTORIOUS FACTS
Judicial notice. *See* **Judicial notice** (Notorious facts).

NOVATION
See **Contract** (Novation).

NOXIOUS MATTER
Entry into river. *See* **Water and watercourses** (Pollution of river—Causing poisonous, noxious or polluting matter to enter river).

NOXIOUS THING
Administration of. *See* **Criminal law** (Administering poison or other destructive or noxious thing).

NUCLEAR INSTALLATION
Application of Building Regulations. *See* **Building** (Building regulations—Application—Construction of a building—Nuclear reactor).
Licensee—
Liability to pay compensation—
Ionising radiation emitted from waste matter discharged from nuclear site—Plaintiffs selling family home because of high level of radioactive contamination and perceived increase in health risks to children—Plaintiffs selling home for substantially less than expected—Plaintiffs claiming compensation for damage to property and increased risk of injury to health due to radioactive contamination from licensee's site—Whether Plaintiffs entitled to compensation—Whether licensee in breach of statutory duty to secure that no ionising radiations emitted from discharge of nuclear waste caused personal injury or damage to property—Whether licensee's liability extending to risk or increased risk of personal injury or damage to property—Nuclear Installations Act 1965, ss 7(1)(b)(ii), 12(1)—Convention on Civil Liability for Nuclear Damage 1963, art I(k)(i). **Merlin v British Nuclear Fuels plc** [1990] 3 711, QBD.
Plaintiff's land becoming contaminated with radioactive material—Plaintiff unable to sell land—Whether contamination causing 'damage' to property—Whether amount of compensation limited to damage to land or extending to diminution in value or saleability of land—Nuclear Installations Act 1965, ss 7, 12. **Blue Circle Industries plc v Ministry of Defence** [1998] 3 385, CA.

NUISANCE
Abatement notice. *See* Statutory nuisance—Abatement notice, *below.*
Byelaw—
Validity. *See* **Byelaw** (Validity—Repugnant to statute—Bye-law prohibiting nuisance by noisy animals).
Continuing nuisance—
Right to sue—
Generally. *See* Right to sue—Continuing nuisance, *below.*
Occupier of land. *See* Right to sue—Occupier of land—Continuing nuisance, *below.*
Creation of nuisance—
Flooding—
Interference with course of stream—Culvert constructed in 1926 by highway authority to carry stream under highway—Entrance to culvert not protected by grid—Property on lower side of highway flooded owing to entrance to culvert being blocked by debris—Liability of highway authority—Liability of occupiers of fields—Apportionment of liability. **Pemberton v Bright** [1960] 1 792, CA.
Sewer—
Overflow—Flooding of neighbouring premises—Overloading of sewer resulting in repeated flooding of claimant's property—Statutory sewerage undertaker failing to take steps to prevent flooding—Whether sewerage undertaker liable at common law for failure to prevent flooding—Whether failure infringing claimant's right to respect for home and right to peaceful enjoyment of possessions under human rights convention—Water Industry Act 1991—Human Rights Act 1998, Sch 1, Pt I, art 8, Pt II, art 1. **Marcic v Thames Water Utilities Ltd** [2004] 1 135, HL.
Overflow—Flooding of neighbouring premises—Overloading of sewers—Sanitary authority under statutory duty to allow occupiers of houses to discharge sewage into sewers—Liability of sanitary authority—Whether authority having created or continued nuisance—Public Health Act 1936, ss 31, 34(1). **Smeaton v Ilford Corp** [1954] 1 923, Ch D.
Damage—
Continuing threat of damage—
Injunction. *See* **Injunction** (Nuisance—Continuing threat of damage).
Escape in consequence of non-natural use of land. *See* Escape in consequence of non-natural use of land—Damage, *below.*

NUISANCE (cont)—
   Damage (cont)—
      Foreseeability—
         Need to establish damage foreseeable—Necessary element in measure of damages for nuisance—Distinction between measure of damage in all actions in nuisance and special damage required to render public nuisance actionable at suit of member of public—On measure of damages the criterion of foreseeability arises as in negligence actions. **Wagon Mound, The (No 2)** [1966] **2** 709, PC.
      Property held under grant from defendant—
         Implied agreement—Lease by quarry owner of land next to quarry—Injury to land from working of quarry—Working not improper—Whether open to lessee to complain of injury to property land subject to grant. **Thomas v Lewis** [1937] **1** 137, Ch D.
      Smuts emanating from defendant's land—
         Acid smuts—Damage to clothes hung out to dry in plaintiff's garden—Smuts created by defendant's carrying on trade on neighbouring property—Oil depot—Whether defendant's liable for damage to clothes as resulting from private nuisance. **Halsey v Esso Petroleum Co Ltd** [1961] **2** 145, QBD.
      Wall on adjoining property—
         Mound of earth piled against wall—Date when cause of action arose—Appropriate remedy—Damage to adjoining wall and land by percolation of injurious chemicals deposited on mound—No substantial damage sustained up to date of proceedings—Whether cause of action arose when undue burden placed on wall or when damage first occurred—Whether damages or injunction appropriate remedy. **Maberley v Peabody & Co of London Ltd, Rowland Smith Motors Ltd and Rowland Smith** [1946] **2** 192, KBD.
   Damages—
      Defence—
         Statutory authority. See Defence—Statutory authority, below.
      Exemplary damages. See **Damages** (Exemplary damages—Nuisance).
      Interference with trade—
         Trade having increased during period of nuisance—Hoarding erected outside shop following fire—Hoarding interfering with access to shop—Trade in fact having increased while hoarding there—Whether owner of shop entitled to damages. **Collingwood v Home and Colonial Stores Ltd** [1936] **1** 74, KBD.
      Nuisance by smell. See Smell—Damages, below.
      Public nuisance. See Public nuisance—Damages , below.
      Repairs to building—
         Cost of repairs—Flying freehold—Claimant owning freehold of ground floor of property—Defendant owning freehold of upper floors and roof—Defendant allowing roof to fall into disrepair—Claimant repairing roof pursuant to court order—Principles governing apportionment of cost of repairs in such cases. **Abbahall Ltd v Smee** [2003] **1** 465, CA.
         Cost of repairs—Pile driving operations causing damage to next door building—Owners deferring carrying out repairs until after trial of action 10 years later—Owners deferring repairs partly for financial reasons and partly for commercial reasons—Whether damages to be assessed at date physically reasonable to commence repairs—Whether owners entitled to damages assessed at date of hearing. **Dodd Properties (Kent) Ltd v Canterbury City Council** [1980] **1** 928, CA.
   Damages in lieu of injunction. See Noise—Motor racing—Remedies—Damages in lieu of injunction, below.
   Defence—
      Statutory authority—
         Action for damages arising out of construction of ferry terminals in river—Design of terminals causing 75 more siltation than necessary—Local authority constructing terminals under statute authorising it to 'execute ... works'—Whether local authority able to rely on defence of statutory authority in action for nuisance—London County Council (Improvements) Act 1962, ss 17, 50(3)(a). **Tate & Lyle Industries Ltd v Greater London Council** [1983] **1** 1159, HL.
         Action for damages for nuisance arising from escape of water from burst water main under street—Water main laid by water authority under statutory duty to supply water—Street authority claiming cost of repairs to street from water authority—Whether water authority liable for nuisance caused without negligence—Public Utilities Street Works Act 1950, s 18(2). **Dept of Transport v North West Water Authority** [1983] **3** 273, HL.
         Action for damages for nuisance arising out of construction and operation of oil refinery—Statute authorising oil company to acquire land compulsorily for construction of oil refinery—Oil company authorised to construct certain works and to construct and use certain subsidiary works in connection with refinery—Whether oil company able to rely on defence of statutory authority in action for nuisance—Gulf Oil Refining Act 1965 (c xxiv), ss 5, 15, 16. **Allen v Gulf Oil Refining Ltd** [1981] **1** 353, HL.
   Disturbance of easement—
      Light. See **Easement** (Light—Interference with light—Test whether interference complained of amounting to nuisance).
      Right of way. See **Easement** (Right of way—Disturbance—Remedy).
   Escape in consequence of non-natural use of land—
      Act of stranger—
         Dangerous substance on land—Explosion—Motor vehicle in parking ground—Explosion caused by act of strangers—Whether occupiers of parking ground liable. **Perry v Kendricks Transport Ltd** [1956] **1** 154, CA.
      Consent of plaintiff to condition causing escape—
         Implied consent—Knowledge of condition—Storage for benefit of plaintiff—Plaintiff taking tenancy of shop forming part of building belonging to defendant—Escape of water from choked gutter damaging plaintiff's stock—Not open to plaintiff to complain of structure of building—Arrangements for collection and carrying away of water for joint benefit of plaintiff and defendant. **Kiddle v City Business Properties Ltd** [1942] **2** 216, KBD.
         Knowledge and implied consent—Water—Flooding from sprinkler system—Damage to lower part of same building—Sprinkler system installed before possession taken. **Peters v Prince of Wales Theatre (Birmingham) Ltd** [1942] **2** 533, CA.

NUISANCE (cont)—
    Escape in consequence of non-natural use of land (cont)—
        Damage—
            Personal injury—Fairground roundabout—Part of revolving apparatus becoming detached and causing injury—Accident caused by recklessness of third party—Liability of owner of fairground. **Hale v Jennings Bros** [1938] **1** 579, CA.

            Proximity of loss—Escape of virus—Cattle infected by disease—Plaintiffs cattle auctioneers—Cattle markets closed because of disease—Loss of business—Whether loss sufficiently proximate. **Weller & Co v Foot and Mouth Disease Research Institute** [1965] **3** 560, QBD.

        Escape from premises—
            Deliberate release of dangerous thing an escape—Whether defence of necessity available. **Rigby v Chief Constable of Northamptonshire** [1985] **2** 985, QBD.

            Fire—Fire on premises of motor vehicle tyre supplier and fitter spreading to adjacent property—Whether escape from premises—Whether non-natural use of land. **Gore v Stannard (t/a Wyvern Tyres)** [2013] **1** 694, CA.

            Need to establish—Shell burst in ordnance factory. **Read v J Lyons & Co Ltd** [1946] **2** 471, HL.

            Steam—Defective valve—Steamship—Plaintiff working on ship injured by escape of steam from defectively assembled valve—Steamship owners not liable—No escape of steam off the premises. **Howard v Furness-Houlder Argentine Lines Ltd and A & R Brown Ltd** [1936] **2** 781, KBD.

        Escape to premises of third party—
            Damage to plaintiff—Escape of metal foil to premises of electricity board—Damage to plaintiff through loss of electric power—Whether actionable. **British Celanese Ltd v AH Hunt (Capacitors) Ltd** [1969] **2** 1252, QBD.

        Foreseeability of damage—
            Ultra-hazardous operations on land—Water containing solvent percolating 1·3 miles from tannery to borehole used for extraction of domestic water supply—Water supply contaminated by solvent—Contamination resulting from regular spillages of relatively small amounts of solvent onto tannery floor and seepage into sub-strata—Whether tannery owners liable for contamination—Whether foreseeability of damage if there was an escape of dangerous things from land a prerequisite of liability. **Cambridge Water Co Ltd v Eastern Counties Leather plc** [1994] **1** 53, CA and HL.

        Harmful substance—
            Acid smuts—Smuts emanating from neighbouring land—Smuts damaging clothes in plaintiff's garden and plaintiff's car on highway—Smuts created by defendant's carrying on trade on neighbouring property—Oil depot—Whether defendants liable for damage caused to plaintiff's car and clothes. **Halsey v Esso Petroleum Co Ltd** [1961] **2** 145, QBD.

        Natural processes. *See* Natural processes, *below.*
        Non-natural use—
            Accumulation of waters for business purposes—Accumulation for defendant's benefit—User for extraordinary purpose—Escape of water on to adjoining premises—Liability without proof of specific acts of negligence. **Western Engraving Co v Film Laboratories Ltd** [1936] **1** 106, CA.

            Electrical wiring for domestic use—Fire caused by fault in electric lighting circuit—Damage to adjoining premises by water—No negligence whether use of electricity for domestic purposes non-natural use of land. **Collingwood v Home and Colonial Stores Ltd** [1936] **3** 200, CA.

            Metal foil—Foil stored on land in connection with manufacture of electrical and electronic components—Escape of metal foil causing damage—Whether special use of land. **British Celanese Ltd v AH Hunt (Capacitors) Ltd** [1969] **2** 1252, QBD.

            Pipe carrying water from mains to storage tanks in block of flats belonging to local authority for domestic purposes of residents—Escape of water by prolonged leakage causing collapse of embankment supporting gas main—Whether non-natural use of land—Whether local authority bringing onto land something likely to cause danger or mischief on escaping. **Transco plc (formerly BG plc and BG Transco plc) v Stockport Metropolitan BC** [2004] **1** 589, HL.

        Statutory power—
            Mandatory power—Absence of negligence—Gas board—Obligation to supply gas—Escape of water from water main—Consequential breakage of, and escape of gas from, gas main—Explosion of gas—Whether gas board liable for resulting personal injuries—Gas Act 1948, s 1(1)(a), Sch 3, paras 33, 42—Waterworks Clauses Act 1847, s 27. **Dunne v North Western Gas Board** [1963] **3** 916, CA.

            Permissive power—Absence of negligence—Statutory undertakers having done merely what statute authorised—Water undertakers—Escape of water from water main—Consequential breakage of and escape of gas from gas main—Explosion of gas—Whether water undertakers liable for resulting personal injuries—Gas Act 1948, s 1(1)(a), Sch 3, paras 33, 42—Waterworks Clauses Act 1847, s 27. **Dunne v North Western Gas Board** [1963] **3** 916, CA.

    Failure to remedy—
        Creation of nuisance by lapse of time—
            Pipe in river bed—Sewer—Obstruction to flow of river caused by pipe of sewer constructed by local authority beneath river bed not becoming exposed as river bed washed away—Damage to plaintiff's property from eddies caused—Sewer not out of repair—Whether any breach of duty to plaintiff's by statute or common law established—Covenant, in lease demising sewerage rights, that local authority would not interfere with flow of water in river—Benefit of covenant not assigned to plaintiff's subsequently becoming riparian owners—Statutory powers of sewage disposal overriding lease. **Radstock Co-op and Industrial Society Ltd v Norton-Radstock UDC** [1968] **2** 59, CA.

        Creation unknown to occupier—
            Creation by trespasser—Adoption and continuation by occupier—Culvert or pipe laid on occupier's land by trespasser—Used by occupiers to drain field—Culvert liable to blockage thereby causing flooding—Whether occupier having adopted and continued nuisance—Whether occupier liable for failure to abate nuisance. **Sedleigh-Denfield v O'Callagan** [1940] **3** 349, HL.

NUISANCE (cont)—
> Failure to remedy (cont)—
>> Knowledge of owner or occupier—
>>> Awareness that situation constitutes a nuisance—Tree—Branch of tree intruding over trunk road at height of sixteen feet—Tree belonging to adjoining landowner but growing in verge forming part of highway—Intrusion of branch patent but no reasonable cause to realise branch constituted a nuisance—Nuisance not created by landowner—Whether landowner liable as having failed to remedy nuisance. **British Road Services Ltd v Slater** [1964] **1** 816, Assizes.
>>> Building in want of repair—Lack of knowledge—Owner liable to do repairs—House in disrepair—House collapsing on adjoining premises—Whether owner liable dispite lack of knowledge of danger from want of repair. **Wringe v Cohen** [1939] **4** 241, CA.
>>> Creation of nuisance by stranger—Creation unknown to occupier—Not discoverable on reasonable examination—Tile on roof loosened in consequence of enemy action—Blown down by high wind—Whether occupier liable. **Cushing v Peter Walker & Son (Warrington & Burton) Ltd** [1941] **2** 693, Assizes.
>>> Natural conditions—Snow—Accumulation of snow on roof of defendant's house—Fall of snow from roof injuring person on highway—Whether accumulation of snow a nuisance of which defendant deemed to have knowledge. **Slater v Worthington's Cash Stores (1930) Ltd** [1941] **3** 28, CA.
>>> Presumed knowledge—Building unoccupied—Building damaged in air raid—Glass falling from premises five days later in consequence of damage—Owner having no actual knowledge of state of building—Whether knowledge to be presumed—Whether liable for continuing nuisance. **Leanse v Egerton** [1943] **1** 489, KBD.
> Fire—
>> Escape to adjoining premises—
>>> Negligence. *See* **Negligence** (Fire—Escape to adjoining premises).
>> Non-natural user of land. *See* Escape in consequence of non-natural use of land—Escape from premises—Fire, *above*.
> Flats—
>> Noise. *See* Noise—Flats, *below*.
> Flooding—
>> Creation of nuisance. *See* Creation of nuisance—Flooding, *above*.
>> Generally. *See* Natural processes—Flooding, *below*.
> Highway—
>> Danger arising from ordinary use—
>>> Butcher's shop—Piece of fat escaping on to pavement. **Dollman v Hillman Ltd** [1941] **1** 355, CA.
>> Debris left by kerb—
>>> No obstruction—Small heap of debris left by repairers of property for collection—Pedestrian tripping over pile—No negligence on part of pedestrian—Whether repairers liable in nuisance. **Almeroth v W E Chivers & Sons Ltd** [1948] **1** 53, CA.
>> Highway authority's liability—
>>> Flooding—Interference with course of stream. *See* Creation of nuisance—Flooding—Interference with course of stream—Culvert constructed in 1926 by highway authority to carry stream under highway, *above*.
>>> Warning of danger—Bridge over road—Headroom reduced below statutory limit by highway authority in repairing road—Negligent exercise of statutory powers—Head of passengers in lorry struck when passing under bridge—Warning signs indicating reduced height placed on bridge—Whether authority liable for creating and failing to abate nuisance. **Lewys v Burnett and Dunbar** [1945] **2** 555, KBD.
>> Interference with business—
>>> Queues—Access to shop—Formation of queues at adjacent shop—Defendant carrying on business as greengrocer—Queues forming outside shop when goods available—Queues interfering with access to neighbouring shops—Defendant doing nothing unnecessary or unreasonable—Whether defendant liable in nuisance. **Dwyer v Mansfield** [1946] **2** 247, KBD.
>> Liability of owner or occupier of adjoining premises—
>>> Grating in pavement—Want of repair—Grating admitting light to cellar of adjoining premises—Dedicated as part of highway—Liability of owner or occupier of adjoining premises for accident resulting from want of repair—Public Health Acts Amendment Act 1890, s 35(1). **MacFarlane v Gwalter** [1958] **1** 181, CA.
>>> Nuisance created by highway authority—Cover of cellar of adjoining premises not lying flush with pavement after reconstruction by highway authority—Whether owner of adjoining premises liable for resulting accident—Public Health Acts Amendment Act 1890, s 35(1). **Penney v Berry** [1955] **3** 182, CA.
>> Negligence—
>>> Statutory power to break up highway—Water board—Acts carried out under statutory power—Need to prove negligence—Leakage in water pipe—Paving stones on footpath affected—Water board not aware of danger—Pedestrian injured by movement of paving stone affected by leakage—Whether water board liable in absence of negligence. **Longhurst v Metropolitan Water Board** [1948] **2** 834, HL.
>> Noise—
>>> Nuisance caused by passage of heavy goods vehicles to and from defendants' port—Port operated 24 hours a day in accordance with planning permission granted by plaintiff council—Whether claim in nuisance to be judged by reference to character of neighbourhood as affected by planning permission—Whether use in accordance with planning permission can amount to actionable nuisance. **Gillingham BC v Medway (Chatham) Dock Co Ltd** [1992] **3** 923, QBD.
>> Nuisance adjoining highway—
>>> Defective paving of forecourt adjoining highway—Need to cross forecourt to reach shop—Forecourt not fenced off from highway—Injury to customer leaving highway to visit shop—Act of customer in leaving highway deliberate—Whether occupier liable on ground defective pavement constituted a public nuisance adjoining highway. **Jacobs v London CC** [1950] **1** 737, HL.

NUISANCE (cont)—
  Highway (cont)—
    Nuisance adjoining highway (cont)—
      Trailer left on land adjoining road—Child leaving road to play on trailer and injured—Whether
        contractors who left lorry by road liable in nuisance. **Creed v John McGeoch & Sons Ltd**
        [1955] **3** 123, Assizes.
    Obscuring visibility of users of highway—
      Smoke and steam—Coke ovens—Smoke and steam escaping across highway—Collision on
        highway because view obscured—Liability in nuisance of factory owners for allowing smoke and
        steam to escape. **Holling v Yorkshire Traction Co Ltd** [1948] **2** 662, Assizes.
    Obstruction of highway—
      Basis of liability—Causation—Negligence—Danger—Accident causing injury to plaintiff—Nuisance
        as cause of accident—Relevance of negligence in creating obstruction—Obstruction as a source
        of danger—Vehicle parked on highway—Vehicle constituting a public nuisance—Parking of
        vehicle not negligent—Collision of motor cycle with parked vehicle injuring pillion
        passenger—Accident wholly caused by negligence of driver of motor cycle—Nuisance not a
        cause of accident—Nuisance not a source of danger. **Dymond v Pearce** [1972] **1** 1142, CA.
      Unlighted vehicle left on highway—Need to prove vehicle a dangerous obstruction—Unlighted
        motor vehicle on road in darkness—Vehicle being towed by lorry—Lorry and vehicle stopped at
        place where vehicle within light of street lamp—Vehicle not a nuisance because not a dangerous
        obstruction. **Parish v Judd** [1960] **3** 33, QBD.
    Reasonableness of user—
      Hosepipe laid across highway—House adjoining highway—Hosepipe laid across highway to supply
        water in time of drought—Plaintiff tripping over hosepipe—Whether defendant absolved from
        liability on ground user reasonable. **Trevett v Lee** [1955] **1** 406, CA.
      Obstruction of highway—Demonstration—Lawful user—Test whether user reasonable or
        not—Demonstration in public street. **R v Clark** [1963] **3** 884, CCA.
    Tree on land adjoining highway—
      Dangerous condition—Knowledge of occupier of land—Reasonable care taken in management of
        land—No sign of danger in tree—Tree falling on passing car—Fall due to disease—Liability of
        occupier of land. **Caminer v Northern & London Investment Trust Ltd** [1950] **2** 486, HL.
    Unlighted vehicle on highway—
      Negligence—Absence of negligence—Whether unlighted vehicle left on highway ipso facto a
        nuisance. **Maitland v R T & J Raisbeck & Hewitt Ltd** [1944] **2** 272, CA.
      Negligence—Liability for negligence. *See* **Negligence** (Highway—Unlighted vehicle).
      Negligence—Need to prove—Motor lorry broken down on highway—Rear lamp of trailer left alight
        but subsequently going out—Plaintiff on motor cycle colliding with lorry—Whether lorry a
        nuisance despite absence of negligence on part of those who left it there. **Ware v Garston
        Haulage Co Ltd** [1943] **2** 558, CA.
      Obstruction of highway. *See* Highway—Obstruction of highway—Unlighted vehicle left on highway,
        above.
    Unreasonable use. *See* **Highway** (Public nuisance—Unreasonable use of highway).
    Vehicle subject to defect—
      Driver suffering from heart condition—Disease undiscoverable by prior medical examination—
        Driver employed by defendant to drive lorry—Accident due to sudden death of driver while
        driving—Whether employer liable in nuisance. **Ryan v Youngs** [1938] **1** 522, CA.
    Watching and besetting premises. *See* Watching and besetting premises, *below.*
  Injunction. *See* **Injunction** (Nuisance).
  Isolated occurrence—
    Escape of substance causing power failure—
      Damage caused to other electricity users—Metal foil blown onto electricity board's equipment so
        as to cause power failure—Whether isolated occurrence actionable. **British Celanese Ltd v AH
        Hunt (Capacitors) Ltd** [1969] **2** 1252, QBD.
    Single negligent act causing damage—
      Defendant's act causing physical damage to electric cable supplying plaintiffs' factory—Whether
        actionable nuisance. **SCM (UK) Ltd v WJ Whittall & Son Ltd** [1970] **2** 417, QBD.
  Land—
    Enclosure of common land—
      National Trust—Whether Trust having power to erect fences or walling on Trust property—National
        Trust Act 1907, s 29—National Trust Act 1971, s 23. **National Trust for Places of Historic Interest or
        Natural Beauty v Ashbrook** [1997] **4** 76, Ch D.
    Natural right to support. *See* **Land** (Support—Natural right of support).
    Subsidence in land. *See* **Land** (Support).
  Landlord's liability—
    Defective electric wiring—
      House let with defect—Landlord liable for repairs—Fire caused by defect—Live wire inadequately
        protected owing to negligence of contractor—Adjoining premises destroyed—Whether defective
        wiring a nuisance—Whether landlord liable for damage caused by fire—Fires Prevention
        Metropolis) Act 1774, s 86. **Spicer v Smee** [1946] **1** 489, KBD.
    Nuisance created by tenants—
      Landlord's consent to nuisance—Ordinary and necessary consequence of use of land by
        occupier—Council letting land to go-kart club for use as go-kart track—Plaintiffs claiming
        injunction against council to restrain continuation of use as go-kart track—Whether council liable
        for nuisance—Whether nuisance an ordinary and necessary consequence of operation of
        track—Whether plaintiffs entitled to injunction. **Tetley v Chitty** [1986] **1** 663, QBD.
      Local authority landlord letting flat to appellant—Appellant hearing everyday activities of
        neighbouring tenants because of inadequate soundproofing—Whether ordinary use of flat
        capable of constituting actionable nuisance—Whether landlord liable to appellant in tort of
        nuisance. **Baxter v Camden London BC** [1999] **4** 449, HL.
      Nuisance impliedly authorised by landlords—Landlord's knowledge when tenants let into
        possession that likely to create nuisance—Conditions of tenancy expressly prohibiting tenants
        from creating nuisance—Whether landlord's knowledge that tenants likely to create nuisance
        sufficient to render him liable therefor. **Smith v Scott** [1972] **3** 645, Ch D.

NUISANCE (cont)—
Landlord's liability (cont)—
Nuisance created by tenants (cont)—
Nuisance impliedly authorised by landlords—Occupiers of stadium and track used for speedway racing and motorcycle racing liable in nuisance for noise to owners of nearby residential property—Whether landlords also liable—Whether landlords had authorised nuisance by letting property to tenants—Whether landlords had participated in tenants' nuisance. **Lawrence v Fen Tigers Ltd (No 2)** [2014] **4** 517, SC.
Plaintiffs owning property on housing estate owned by defendant council and alleging that council's tenants had racially harassed them—Plaintiffs alleging that council had failed to take appropriate steps to halt harassment—Whether plaintiffs having cause of action in nuisance or negligence against council. **Hussain v Lancaster City Council** [1999] **4** 125, CA.
Right to enter and repair—
Defective paving—Shop—Defective paving of forecourt—Injury to customer—No covenant by landlord to repair—Right of entry to inspect and repair—Repairs previously carried out by landlord—Whether landlord liable for want of repair. **Howard v Walker** [1947] **2** 197, KBD.
Periodic tenancy of small dwelling-house—Implied right to enter and repair—No right of entry reserved to landlord—Liability of landlord in nuisance for want of repair—Collapse of wall—Increase of Rent and Mortgage Interest (Restrictions) Act 1920, s 16(2). **Mint v Good** [1950] **2** 1159, CA.
Tenant's covenant to repair—
Danger of collapse of wall of building into adjoining premises—Danger known to landlords of building when building let to tenants—Full repairing covenant taken from tenants—Whether taking of covenant sufficient to exculpate landlords from liability to lessees of adjoining premises—Landlords and tenants jointly liable. **Brew Bros Ltd v Snax (Ross) Ltd** [1970] **1** 587, CA.
Light—
Interference with light—
Test whether interference complained of amounting to nuisance. *See* **Easement** (Light—Interference with light—Test whether interference complained of amounting to nuisance).
Local authority—
Exercise of statutory powers—
Remedy—Injunction against authority—Pollution of river—Sewage works—Sewage entering river in condition and quantity to cause nuisance—Injunction granted—Suspension of injunction. **Pride of Derby and Derbyshire Angling Association Ltd v British Celanese Ltd** [1953] **1** 179, CA.
Motive—
Acts done on own land—
Acts done maliciously to injure neighbour's business—Plaintiffs breeding silver foxes on their land—Defendant maliciously causing son to fire gun on edge of his land with intention of disturbing breeding of foxes. **Hollywood Silver Fox Farm Ltd v Emmett** [1936] **1** 825, KBD.
Natural processes—
Change in nature of land itself—
Change giving rise to state of affairs constituting hazard to neighbouring properties—Claimants owning hotel on top of cliff owned by defendant—Cliff prone to land slips because of erosion—Defendant aware of problem but not investigating hazard to claimants' land—Land beneath hotel collapsing in land slip caused by defect on both sides of boundary—Whether defendant owing claimants duty of care to prevent hazard—Scope of duty. **Holbeck Hall Hotel Ltd v Scarborough BC** [2000] **2** 705, CA.
Change giving rise to state of affairs constituting hazard to neighbouring properties—Occupier aware of hazard—Duty of occupier to abate hazard—Plaintiffs' houses adjacent to steep mound owned and occupied by defendant—Earth movements taking place in mound as a result of natural causes—Movements giving rise to danger of bank collapsing onto houses—Whether defendant under a duty to take reasonable steps to abate danger. **Leakey v National Trust for Places of Historic Interest or Natural Beauty** [1980] **1** 17, CA.
Flooding—
Percolation of water from higher land to lower land—Occupier of lower land filling in land and preventing free flow of water from higher land—Filling operations also squeezing water onto higher land—Filling operations causing flooding—Whether occupier of higher land entitled to passage of natural unconcentrated water from his land onto lower land—Whether occupier of lower land entitled to prevent water flowing onto his land from higher land. **Home Brewery plc v William Davis & Co (Loughborough) Ltd** [1987] **1** 637, QBD.
Watercourse—Bridge over river—Claimant regarding bridge responsible for flooding to his property—Claimant seeking to persuade defendant to serve abatement notice on highway authority responsible for bridge—Defendant refusing to serve abatement notice on authority—Claimant applying for judicial review—Claimant seeking declaration that word 'choked' in statute capable of including obstruction of proper flow of river by bridge—Defendant subsequently serving abatement notice—Meaning of 'choked'—Whether application academic—Public Health Act 1936, s 259(1)(b). **R (on the application of Robinson) v Torridge DC (Devon CC, interested party)** [2006] **3** 1148, QBD.
Things naturally on defendant's land—
Thistles—Thistledown blown on to neighbouring land—Whether action will lie for damage from thistledown. **Davey v Harrow Corp** [1957] **2** 305, CA.
Tree—
Roots causing damage. *See* Tree—Roots causing damage, *below*.
Neglect—
Need to prove—
State of defendant's property—Tree—Diseased tree falling on to highway—Defendant having taken all reasonable steps to ascertain condition of tree—Could not have realised tree likely to fall—Whether liable in nuisance. **Cunliffe v Bankes** [1945] **1** 459, Assizes.

NUISANCE (cont)—
  Neglect (cont)—
    Neglect of house—
      Neglect interfering with easement of support—Neglect resulting in loss of support for neighbouring house—Owner of neighbouring house having right to enter neglected house and abate nuisance—Whether owner of neglected house owing duty to neighbour to prevent damage occurring to neighbour's house—Whether right to enter and abate nuisance freeing owner of neglected house from liability to neighbour for nuisance. **Bradburn v Lindsay** [1983] 2 408, Ch D.
  Negligence—
    Need to prove—
      Pollution of shore—Ship—Discharge of oil to lighten vessel stranded in estuary—Damage to adjoining foreshore—Whether necessary to prove negligence. **Esso Petroleum Co Ltd v Southport Corp** [1955] 3 864, HL.
  Noise—
    Abatement notice. *See* Statutory nuisance—Abatement notice—Noise, *below*.
    Air traffic. *See* **Air traffic** (Noise nuisance).
    Building operations—
      Reasonable steps to ensure no undue inconvenience to neighbours—Demolition and rebuilding operations—Damage limited to matters going over permissible line. **Andrae v Selfridge & Co Ltd** [1937] 3 255, CA.
    Emanation from defendant's land—
      Necessity for—Noise associated with operations on defendant's land—Lorries on highway—Road tankers entering and leaving defendant's oil depot at night—Noise partly from tankers partly from highways outside depot and partly from depot itself—Liability in nuisance for noise of tankers on highway—Whether private nuisance. **Halsey v Esso Petroleum Co Ltd** [1961] 2 145, QBD.
    Flats—
      Building converted into flats—Local authority landlord letting flats—Noise from ordinary use of flats constituting undue interference with plaintiff's enjoyment of her flat—Whether local authority liable in nuisance. **Baxter v Camden London BC** [1999] 1 237, CA.
      Building converted into flats—Roof terrace constructed above plaintiff's flat—Roof terrace so constructed as to allow noise to penetrate to flat below—Tenant in occupation of terrace using it in normal way and for purpose contemplated by lease—Tenant's use of terrace interfering with use and enjoyment by plaintiff of his flat—Roof terrace constructed by landlord's predecessor in title—Landlord taking assignment of reversion with knowledge of disturbance created by use of roof terrace—Plaintiff's lease containing covenant for quiet enjoyment—Whether landlord liable for nuisance. **Sampson v Hodson-Pressinger** [1981] 3 710, CA.
    Highway. *See* Highway—Noise, *above*.
    Inconvenience materially affecting ordinary physical comfort—
      Night time operations—Boilers on neighbouring oil depot operating at night—At peak noise making doors and windows and doors in plaintiff's house to vibrate and preventing plaintiff sleeping—Whether sufficient noise to constitute nuisance. **Halsey v Esso Petroleum Co Ltd** [1961] 2 145, QBD.
    Motor racing—
      Easement—Acquisition by prescription—Whether easement of noise recognised in law. **Lawrence v Fen Tigers Ltd** [2011] 4 1314n, QBD.
      Motor racing stadium and motocross circuit operated in accordance with planning permission—Character of locality—Whether noise constituting nuisance—Whether character of locality having changed consequent on grant and implementation of planning permission. **Lawrence v Fen Tigers Ltd** [2012] 3 168, CA; [2014] 2 622, SC.
      Remedies—Damages in lieu of injunction—Principles governing exercise of judicial discretion in respect of remedies. **Watson v Croft Promosport Ltd** [2008] 3 1171, QBD; [2009] 3 249, CA.
    Poultry farm—
      Crowing of cocks—Defendant making no effort to move cockerels further from plaintiff's property after complaints—Injunction granted. **Leeman v Montagu** [1936] 2 1677, KBD.
    Statutory power—
      Local authority serving notice requiring abatement of nuisance—Relevant statute repealed and re-enacted—Whether obligation under notice continuing—Control of Pollution Act 1974, s 58—Environmental Protection Act 1990, s 80. **Aitken v South Hams DC** [1994] 3 400, HL.
    Summary proceedings by local authority to abate, prohibit or restrict nuisance—
      Alternative remedies—Proceedings in High Court to secure remedy—Appeal to magistrates' court against notice pending—Power of High Court to grant relief—Centre for taxis in quiet residential street—Disturbance to residents at night—Local authority serving notice requiring operators of centre to cease use of centre throughout the night—Operators lodging appeal against notice to magistrates' court—Notice remaining in force pending appeal—Failure to comply with notice—Summary remedy by way of prosecution for failing to comply with notice available to local authority—Before appeal to magistrates' court heard local authority applying to High Court for injunction to restrain use of centre at night—Whether injunction should be granted—Control of Pollution Act 1974, s 58(3)(4)(8). **Hammersmith London Borough v Magnum Automated Forecourts Ltd** [1978] 1 401, CA.
  Nuisance order. *See* Statutory nuisance—Nuisance order, *below*.
  Occupier—
    Duty to abate hazard—
      Occupier aware of hazard—Change in nature of land giving rise to hazard. *See* Natural processes—Change in nature of land itself—Change giving rise to state of affairs constituting hazard to neighbouring properties—Occupier aware of hazard—Duty of occupier to abate hazard, *above*.
    Licensees—
      Council owning land adjacent to plaintiffs' land—Plaintiffs alleging that travellers based on council's land had committed various activities on their land—Plaintiffs bringing action for nuisance against council in respect of travellers' activities—Whether occupier of land could be liable in nuisance for acts committed by its licensees on plaintiff's land. **Lippiatt v South Gloucestershire Council** [1999] 4 149, CA.

NUISANCE (cont)—
  Occupier (cont)—
    Nuisance on land of which plaintiff in occupation—
      Plaintiff and defendant in joint occupation—Plaintiff in sole occupation of land affected by nuisance—Whether action will lie at suit of plaintiff. **Hooper v Rogers** [1974] **3** 417, CA.
    Occupation—
      Statutory power—Recreation ground dedicated to public—Local authority having statutory powers of management and control of recreation ground—Noise from model aircraft flown in recreation ground—No contravention of bye-laws—Whether local authority liable as occupier—Public Health Act 1875, s 164. **Hall v Beckenham Corp** [1949] **1** 423, KBD.
      Statutory power—Stream—Power of local authority to remove obstructions—Authority exercising statutory power to place sewer in stream—Flooding due to weir erected and maintained by riparian owner—Whether exercise of statutory powers constituting local authority occupier of stream—Nelson Local Board Act 1879, ss 20, 21, 22. **Bank View Mill Ltd v Nelson Corp and Fryer & Co (Nelson) Ltd** [1943] **1** 299, CA.
      Right to sue. See Right to sue—Occupier of land, below.
  Overlooking—
    Privacy—
      Private properties overlooked by public viewing gallery—Whether overlooking capable of giving rise to cause of action in private nuisance at common law—Significance of convention right to respect for private and family life—Human Rights Act 1998, Sch 1, Pt I, art 8. **Fearn v Board of Trustees of the Tate Gallery** [2021] **1** 60, CA.
  Picketing. See **Trade dispute** (Picketing—Nuisance).
  Principle of Rylands v Fletcher. See Escape in consequence of non-natural use of land, above.
  Prostitution—
    Use of premises for prostitution—
      Interference with comfortable and convenient enjoyment of neighbouring properties—Good class residential street—Defendants soliciting men in nearby streets and bringing them to house in street for purposes of prostitution—Whether prima facie case of nuisance. **Thompson-Schwab v Costaki** [1956] **1** 652, CA.
  Protected tenancy—
    Order for possession. See **Rent restriction** (Possession—Nuisance or annoyance to adjoining occupiers).
  Protective costs order. See **Costs** (Protective costs order—Nuisance).
  Public nuisance—
    Action by local authority—
      Institution of proceedings. See **Practice** (Parties—Local authority).
    Criminal proceedings. See **Criminal law** (Public nuisance).
    Damages —
      Whether damages for personal injury recoverable in public nuisance. **Corby Group Litigation, Re** [2009] **4** 44, CA.
    Generally—
      Watercourse. See **Water and watercourses** (Navigation—Public right of navigation (PRN)—Public nuisance).
    Highway. See **Highway** (Public nuisance).
    Injunction. See **Injunction** (Nuisance—Public nuisance).
    Pollution of shore—
      Discharge of oil to lighten vessel stranded in estuary—Damage to adjoining foreshore—Failure by defendants to prove inevitable accident. **Esso Petroleum Co Ltd v Southport Corp** [1955] **3** 864, HL.
    Private nuisance distinguished—
      Who must be affected to constitute public nuisance—Isolated act capable of constituting public nuisance—Dust and vibration from quarry affecting adjoining householders—Evidence—Injunction—Remedial measures taken since action begun—Whether injunction should be granted. **A-G (ex rel Glamorgan CC and Pontardawe RDC) v PYA Quarries Ltd** [1957] **1** 894, CA.
    Right of corporation to sue—
      Franchise ferry—Curtailment of hours of operation—Proposal to discontinue late evening sailings—Late evening sailings used by some of corporation's employees—Likelihood of disruption of corporation's business and financial loss if sailings discontinued—Corporation bringing action for public nuisance against ferry owner—Whether disruption of business and expense involved capable of being regarded as particular damage giving corporation cause of action. **Gravesham BC v British Railways Board** [1978] **3** 853, Ch D.
    Special damage—
      Damage to unadopted road—Frontagers. **Medcalf v R Strawbridge Ltd** [1937] **2** 393, KBD.
  Right to sue—
    Continuing nuisance—
      Roots of defendant's tree desiccating ground beneath property and causing structural cracking—Claimant acquiring freehold of property after cracks occurring and carrying out reasonable remedial work—Whether reasonable remedial expenditure recoverable by current owner in respect of pre-transfer damage arising from continuing nuisance. **Delaware Mansions Ltd v Westminster City Council** [2001] **4** 737, HL.
    Corporation—
      Public nuisance. See Public nuisance—Right of corporation to sue, above.
    Occupier of land—
      Continuing nuisance—Damage occurring while land occupied by plaintiff's predecessor in title—Roots of tree planted by neighbour causing subsidence of wall of house—Plaintiff purchasing house and carrying out necessary repairs—Whether nuisance a continuing nuisance—Whether right to sue accruing only to predecessor in title. **Masters v Brent London Borough** [1978] **2** 664, QBD.
      Tolerated trespasser—Whether tolerated trespasser having sufficient interest in premises to bring action for nuisance against local authority landlord—Housing Act 1985, Pt IV. **Pemberton v Southwark London BC** [2000] **3** 924, CA.

NUISANCE (cont)—

Right to sue (cont)—

Persons without right to affected land—

Dust caused by construction work—Whether persons having no right to land affected by nuisance can bring action in private nuisance. **Hunter v Canary Wharf Ltd** [1997] 2 426, HL.

Tenant—

Original tenant who has assigned lease—Nuisance by noise created by landlords after assignment—Assignee tenant having absconded—Whether original tenant having right to sue. **Metropolitan Properties Ltd v Jones** [1939] 2 202, KBD.

Rylands v Fletcher principle. *See* Escape in consequence of non-natural use of land, *above.*

Sewage—

Local authority's liability—

Pollution of river by sewage—Local authority in control of sewer—Sewer originally constructed by rural sanitary authority—Subsequent legislation vesting rights and duties of sanitary authority in local authority—Injunction against local authority at suit of private individual. **Haigh v Deudraeth RDC** [1945] 2 661, Ch D.

Sewer—

Creation of nuisance. *See* Creation of nuisance—Sewer, *above.*

Effectually dealing with contents of sewer—

Sewage treatment works causing odour and mosquitoes—Statutory sewerage undertaker failing to take steps preventing odour and mosquitoes—Whether sewerage undertaker effectually dealing with contents of sewer—Whether sewerage undertaker potentially liable at common law—Whether sewerage undertaker potentially liable for breach of rights for respect for home and peaceful enjoyment of possessions—Approach to extension of limitation period for breach of human rights—Water Industry Act 1991, s 94(1)(b)—Human Rights Act 1998, s 7(5)(b). **Dobson v Thames Water Utilities Ltd (Water Services Regulation Authority (Ofwat) intervening)** [2008] 2 362, QBD.

Overflow—

Flooding of neighbouring premises—Overloading of sewer resulting in repeated flooding of claimant's property—Statutory sewerage undertaker failing to take steps to prevent flooding—Whether sewerage undertaker liable at common law for failure to prevent flooding—Whether failure infringing claimant's right to respect for home and right to peaceful enjoyment of possessions under human rights convention—Human Rights Act 1998, Sch 1, Pt I, art 8, Pt II, art 1. **Marcic v Thames Water Utilities Ltd** [2001] 3 698, QBD; [2002] 2 55, CA.

Smell—

Claim in respect of landfill site—

Odour from pre-treated waste emanating from site—Site immediately neighbouring residential estate—Residents making complaints—Relevance of statutory scheme. **Barr v Biffa Waste Services Ltd** [2012] 3 380, CA.

Odour from pre-treated waste emanating from site—Site immediately neighbouring residential estate—Residents making complaints—Whether site operator having defence of statutory authority—Whether landfill reasonable user of land—Environmental Protection Act 1990, s 33. **Barr v Biffa Waste Services Ltd** [2011] 4 1065, QBD.

Damages—

Loss of amenity—Non-pecuniary damage—Smell from neighbouring pig farm interfering with plaintiff's enjoyment of property—Nuisance continuing intermittently for period of over 12 years—Analogy with damages for loss of amenity in personal injury cases—Award of damages at £500 a year—Whether award excessive. **Bone v Seale** [1975] 1 787, CA.

Loss of amenity—Smell from neighbouring pig farm interfering with plaintiffs' enjoyment of property—Pig housing units erected in close proximity to neighbouring dwellings pursuant to planning permission—Whether grant of planning permission constituting defence to action in nuisance—Whether plaintiffs entitled to damages and injunction. **Wheeler v J J Saunders Ltd** [1995] 2 697, CA.

Injury to health—

Need to prove—Smell emanating from defendant's oil depot—No injury to plaintiff's health—Whether injury to health a necessary ingredient in cause of action for nuisance by smell. **Halsey v Esso Petroleum Co Ltd** [1961] 2 145, QBD.

Statutory nuisance—

Abatement notice—

Failure to comply—Complaint to justices—Expenses of complainant—Proceedings against local authority. *See* Statutory nuisance—Complaint to justices—Proceedings against local authority—Expenses of complainant, *below.*

Failure to comply—Complaint to justices—Procedure—Initiation of proceedings—Complaint by individual—Information laid by person aggrieved by nuisance—Jurisdiction of justices—Whether person entitled to lay information against local authority—Public Health Act 1936, ss 94, 99. **R v Newham Justices, ex p Hunt** [1976] 1 839, QBD.

Failure to comply—Complaint to justices—Procedure—Initiation of proceedings—Information laid by local authority—Jurisdiction of justices—Whether failure to comply with abatement notice an 'offence'—Whether laying of information proper method of initiating proceedings—Public Health Act 1936, s 94(1) (2)—Magistrates' Courts Act 1952, s 42. **Northern Ireland Trailers Ltd v County Borough of Preston** [1972] 1 260, QBD.

Form—Method of abating nuisance specified—Abatement notice specifying manner in which nuisance to be abated—Validity—Words specifying method of abating nuisance mere surplasage—Power of justices to make nuisance order in terms other than those of abatement notice—Public Health Act 1936, ss 93, 94(1) (2), 95(1). **McGillivray v Stephenson** [1950] 1 942, KBD.

NUISANCE (cont)—
   Statutory nuisance (cont)—
      Abatement notice (cont)—
         Noise—Noise emitted by lift and its motor in block of flats—Complaint by tenants of flats adjoining lift shaft—Abatement notice served by local authority on managers of flats—Right of appeal given by statute where notice alleged to be invalid—No notice of appeal given by managers—No steps taken by managers to abate nuisance—Managers charged with failure to comply with abatement notice—Managers pleading by way of defence that by signing leases the tenants had assented to noise from lift—Whether that defence available in criminal proceedings—Whether managers had a 'reasonable excuse' for not complying with abatement notice—Control of Pollution Act 1974, s 58. **Lambert (A) Flat Management Ltd v Lomas** [1981] **2** 280, QBD.

         Owner of premises—Person receiving the rackrent as agent—Bank—Rackrent paid into owner's account at bank—Bank paying rates on behalf of owner to local authority—Whether special circumstances constituting bank agent for owner—Whether local authority entitled to serve notice on bank as 'owner'—Public Health Act 1936, s 343(1). **Midland Bank Ltd v Conway BC** [1965] **2** 972, QBD.

         Owner of premises—Person receiving the rackrent as agent—Local authority serving abatement notice on managing agent—Whether managing agent could be owner of premises for such purpose—Environmental Protection Act 1990, s 80(2)(b). **Camden London BC v Gunby** [1999] **4** 602, QBD.

         Owner of premises—Person receiving the rackrent as agent—Secretary of owner receiving cheques for rent and paying them into owner's account—Whether secretary receiving the rent as 'as agent or trustee' for owner—Public Health Act 1936, ss 93, 343(1). **Bottomley v Harrison** [1952] **1** 368, KBD.

         Proceedings against local authority—Whether abatement notice should be served before laying information. *See* Statutory nuisance—Complaint to justices—Proceedings against local authority—Abatement notice, *below.*

         Watercourse—Health authority serving abatement notice requiring cessation of discharge of sewage into estuary—Notice describing estuary as 'watercourse' and relying on statutory nuisance involving watercourses—Notice failing to specify works required to abate nuisance—Whether enforcing authority having duty to consult alleged perpetrator before serving abatement notice—Whether abatement notice having to specify works or steps required where nuisance only abatable by execution of works—Whether estuary capable of being 'watercourse'—Public Health Act 1936, s 259(1)(a). **R v Falmouth and Truro Port Health Authority, ex p South West Water Ltd** [2000] **3** 306, CA.

      Accumulation or deposit prejudicial to health or a nuisance—
         Nuisance—Visual impact—Accumulation of rubbish visible to neighbouring houses—Whether accumulation capable of being a statutory nuisance by reason of its visual impact—Public Health Act 1936, s 92(1)(c). **Coventry City Council v Cartwright** [1975] **2** 99, QBD.

         Prejudicial to health—Likelihood of physical injury—Injury to persons coming on to site—Local authority allowing accumulation on site of inert material including tins and broken glass—Public permitted to come on to land—Likelihood of injury to persons coming on to land—Whether accumulation prejudicial to health—Public Health Act 1936, s 92(1)(c). **Coventry City Council v Cartwright** [1975] **2** 99, QBD.

      Appeal against justices' order—
         Nuisance order made by justices on failure to comply with abatement notice—Appeal a rehearing—Circumstances relating to the offence at date of 'hearing of the complaint'—Whether circumstances at date of hearing before justices or at date of appeal to be considered—Public Health Act 1936, s 94(2). **Northern Ireland Trailers Ltd v County Borough of Preston** [1972] **1** 260, QBD.

      Complaint to justices—
         Proceedings against company—Service of statutory notice prior to commencement of proceedings—Complainant sending notice to company but not to its registered office—Whether notice properly served—Environmental Protection Act 1990, ss 82, 160. **Hewlings v McLean Homes East Anglia Ltd** [2001] **2** 281, QBD.

         Proceedings against local authority—Abatement notice—Whether person entitled to lay information against local authority without first serving abatement notice—Public Health Act 1936, s 99. **Sandwell Metropolitan BC v Bujok** [1990] **3** 385, HL.

         Proceedings against local authority—Compensation for statutory nuisance—Extent of period of offence for which compensation payable—Whether magistrates entitled to consider whole of period for which statutory nuisance existing—Powers of Criminal Courts Act 1973, s 35—Environmental Protection Act 1990, s 82. **R v Crown Court at Liverpool, ex p Cooke** [1996] **4** 589, QBD.

         Proceedings against local authority—Competence—Public Health Act 1936, ss 92(1)(c), 99. **R v Epping (Waltham Abbey) Justices, ex p Burlinson** [1947] **2** 537, KBD.

         Proceedings against local authority—Costs—Mandatory award of costs against defendant—Whether magistrates required to award costs against local authority if nuisance order made against local authority in proceedings brought against it without abatement notice first being served—Whether costs in discretion of magistrates—Public Health Act 1936, s 94(3). **Sandwell Metropolitan BC v Bujok** [1990] **3** 385, HL.

         Proceedings against local authority—Costs—Mandatory award of costs against defendant—Whether magistrates required to award costs against local authority—Whether magistrates having discretion not to allow costs if in opinion of court it was unnecessary for proceedings to be instituted—Environmental Protection Act 1990, s 82(12). **R v Dudley Magistrates' Court, ex p Hollis** [1998] **1** 759, QBD.

         Proceedings against local authority—Expenses of complainant—Nuisance abated at date of hearing of complaint—Whether complainant entitled to reasonable expenses—Public Health Act 1936, ss 94(3), 99. **Coventry City Council v Doyle** [1981] **2** 184, QBD.

         Proceedings against local authority—Service of statutory notice prior to commencement of proceedings—Statutory notice sent to address specified by local authority—Whether notice properly served—Whether justices having jurisdiction to entertain complaint—Environmental Protection Act 1990, ss 82(6), 160. **Hall v Kingston upon Hull City Council** [1999] **2** 609, QBD.

NUISANCE (cont)—
    Statutory nuisance (cont)—
        Complaint to justices (cont)—
            Proceedings against local authority—Statutory nuisance still existing at date of hearing—Whether magistrates having right to adjourn proceedings to enable local authority to abate nuisance—Magistrates' Courts Act 1980, ss 10, 54—Environmental Protection Act 1990, s 82(2). **R v Dudley Magistrates' Court, ex p Hollis** [1998] **1** 759, QBD.
        Costs properly incurred in proceedings—
            Whether complainant seeking order for such costs required to adduce evidence of personal liability to pay solicitor's costs—Environmental Protection Act 1990, s 82(12). **Hazlett v Sefton Metropolitan BC** [2000] **4** 887, QBD.
        Defence—
            War damage—Liability of landlord for want of repair—Roofs of houses in state of disrepair—Damage to roofs caused by enemy action—Statutory nuisance—Abatement notice served on landlord—Failure to carry out repairs—Whether landlord entitled to relief from obligation in case of war damage—Public Health Act 1936, ss 91 to 94—Landlord and Tenant (War Damage) Act 1939, s 1. **Turley v King** [1944] **2** 489, KBD.
        Jurisdiction of justices—
            Premises occupied for the public service of the Crown—Hospital transferred to minister under National Health Service Act 1946—Whether justices had jurisdiction to hear complaint—Public Health Act 1936, s 106. **Nottingham Area No 1 Hospital Management Committee v Owen** [1957] **3** 358, QBD.
        Metropolis—
            Summons—Service—Summons on complaint of local authority—Public Health (London) Act 1936, s 301(1)(a)(i)—London Government Act 1939, s 183(1). **R v Wilson, ex p Battersea BC** [1947] **2** 569, KBD.
        Notice of intended proceedings—
            Summary proceedings by persons aggrieved by statutory nuisances—Service on body corporate—Whether service on secretary, clerk or identifiable person required—Meaning of 'may'—Environmental Protection Act 1990, ss 82, 160. **Allen v Ealing London BC** [2022] **1** 554, DC.
        Nuisance order—
            Date to be considered by justices in deciding whether nuisance exists—Whether relevant date is date of complaint or date of hearing by justices—Public Health Act 1936, s 94(2). **Coventry City Council v Doyle** [1981] **2** 184, QBD.
            Defence—House subject to clearance order—House acquired by local authority for purpose of demolition—Demolition postponed on ground house could be rendered capable of providing accommodation adequate for time being—Finding by justices that house in such a state as to be prejudicial to health—Whether justices bound to make nuisance order—Whether a defence that house occupied as one capable of providing adequate accommodation pending demolition—Public Health Act 1936, ss 92(1)(a), 94(2), 99—Housing Act 1957, s 48(1). **Salford City Council v McNally** [1975] **1** 597, QBD; [1975] **2** 860, HL.
            Duty of justices to make order on finding that nuisance exists—Discretion as to implementation of order—Power to delay operation of order—Duty of justices to take into account surrounding circumstances—House constituting nuisance subject to unconfirmed compulsory purchase order under slum clearance programme—Power of justices to delay operation of order in view of prospective demolition of house—Public Health Act 1936, s 94(2). **Nottingham Corp v Newton** [1974] **2** 760, QBD.
            House subject to clearance order—Defence. *See* Statutory nuisance—Nuisance order—Defence—House subject to clearance order, *above.*
            Terms of order—Jurisdiction of justices to add terms to order—Form of additional terms—Complaint of noise emanating from public house—Justices making nuisance order and requiring that noise level should not exceed 70 decibels—Whether justices having jurisdiction to make requirement—Whether requirement void for uncertainty—Public Health Act 1936, ss 94(2)(a), 99 (as amended by the Noise Abatement Act 1960, s 1(2)(a)). **R v Fenny Stratford Justices, ex p Watney Mann (Midlands) Ltd** [1976] **2** 888, QBD.
        Premises in such a state as to be prejudicial to health—
            Lavatory in tenant's house lacking washbasin—Lavatory users having to wash hands in kitchen sink or go through kitchen to bathroom—Tenant bringing proceedings for statutory nuisance against landlord—Whether layout or lack of facility capable in themselves of rendering premises in such a state as to be prejudicial to health—Environmental Protection Act 1990, s 79(1)(a). **Birmingham City Council v Oakley** [2001] **1** 385, HL.
        Premises in such a state as to be prejudicial to health or a nuisance—
            Local authority premises—Plaintiffs living in premises with parents—Local authority convicted of criminal offence in relation to state of premises—Plaintiffs bringing civil action for damages for ill-health resulting from state of premises—Whether commission of criminal offence rendering local authority liable in civil action for damages for loss or damage thereby suffered by plaintiffs—Public Health Act 1936, ss 92(1)(a), 94(2), 99. **Issa v Hackney London BC** [1997] **1** 999, CA.
            Or a nuisance—Discomfort to tenant—Walls and ceilings of rooms and landing stained, dirty, and flaking, and in need of decorative repair—Whether a 'nuisance'—Public Health (London) Act 1936, s 82(1)(a)—Public Health Act 1936, s 92(1)(a). **Springett v Harold** [1954] **1** 568, QBD.
            Or a nuisance—Injury or danger of injury to health—Interference with personal comfort of occupier—Landlord removing doors and windows of dwelling-house—Whether necessary to establish injury or danger of injury to health—Whether sufficient if occupier only affected—Public Health Act 1936, s 92(1)(a). **Betts v Penge UDC** [1942] **2** 61, KBD.
            Or a nuisance—Need to prove existence of common law public or private nuisance—Premises in disrepair—State of premises such as to interfere with comfort of occupiers—No evidence of interference with comfort of public or with use and enjoyment of neighbouring property—Whether a 'nuisance'—Public Health Act 1936, s 92(1)(a). **National Coal Board v Neath BC** [1976] **2** 478, QBD.
        Premises likely to cause personal injury as a result of steep internal staircase—Whether premises capable in law of constituting a statutory nuisance—Environmental Protection Act 1990, s 79(1)(a). **R v Bristol City Council, ex p Everett** [1998] **3** 603, QBD.

NUISANCE (cont)—
  Statutory nuisance (cont)—
    Premises in such a state as to be prejudicial to health or a nuisance (cont)—
      Risk of physical injury arising from state of premises—Council serving abatement notice on landlord requiring replacement of steep staircase—Council withdrawing notice following legal advice that steep staircase could not be statutory nuisance—Tenant seeking judicial review of decision—Whether risk of physical injury arising from state of premises could be statutory nuisance—Environmental Protection Act 1990, s 79(1)(a)(7). **R v Bristol City Council, ex p Everett** [1999] **2** 193, CA.
      Unoccupied premises—Relevance of fact that premises unoccupied—Public Health Act 1936, s 92(1)(a). **Coventry City Council v Doyle** [1981] **2** 184, QBD.
    Prohibition notice—
      Local authority resolution to issue complaint passed before service of prohibition notice and recurrence of nuisance—Propriety—Public Health (Recurring Nuisances) Act 1969, s 2. **Peaty v Field** [1971] **2** 895, QBD.
      Requirements to be fulfilled before service—Local authority to be satisfied statutory nuisance has 'occurred'—Public Health (Recurring Nuisances) Act 1969, 2 1(1). **Peaty v Field** [1971] **2** 895, QBD.
    Watercourse—
      Natural watercourse—Obstruction impeding flow of water and causing flooding—Liability of owner for failing to abate—Nuisance not due to owner's act or default—Land Drainage Act 1930, ss 35(1), 57(1) (2)—Public Health Act 1936, ss 93, 259(1)(b), proviso. **Neath RDC v Williams** [1950] **2** 625, KBD.
  Statutory tenancy—
    Order for possession. *See* **Rent restriction** (Possession—Nuisance or annoyance to adjoining occupiers).
  Television—
    Interference with reception—
      Defendant erecting tall building which caused interference with plaintiffs' television reception—Whether interference with television reception capable of constituting actionable nuisance. **Hunter v Canary Wharf Ltd** [1997] **2** 426, HL.
      Recreational facility—Plaintiffs relayed television broadcasts—Defendant electricity board erected 66 kv overhead power line that might cause interference with television reception—Quia timet action—Injunction refused because evidence showed interference due to remediable defects in line—Exceptional sensitivity of plaintiffs' business to electrical interference did not entitle them under law of nuisance to greater protection than ordinary householder—Whether actionable nuisance. **Bridlington Relay Ltd v Yorkshire Electricity Board** [1965] **1** 264, Ch D.
  Tenant creating nuisance—
    Landlord's liability. *See* Landlord's liability—Nuisance created by tenants, *above*.
  Tree—
    Diseased tree falling on to highway—
      Neglect. *See* Neglect—Need to prove—State of defendant's property—Tree—Diseased tree falling on to highway, *above*.
    Roots causing damage—
      Creation of nuisance—Liability of person who planted trees—Roots of trees causing damage to adjoining owners' houses. **Butler v Standard Telephones and Cables Ltd** [1940] **1** 121, KBD.
      Owner's liability—Roots of tree causing damage to adjoining property. **Davey v Harrow Corp** [1957] **2** 305, CA.
      Remedy—Injunction—Encroachment of roots—Roots causing damage to neighbour's house—Continuing damage—Injunction granted—Form of injunction. **McCombe v Read** [1955] **2** 458, QBD.
    Tree on land adjoining highway—
      Dangerous condition—Knowledge of occupier of land. *See* Highway—Tree on land adjoining highway—Dangerous condition—Knowledge of occupier of land, *above*.
  Watching and besetting premises—
    Watching and besetting plaintiff's premises with a view to compelling him to do or not to do something—
      Existence of tort—Picketing on highway—Plaintiffs' offices picketed by defendants—Picketing not for purpose of trade dispute—Evidence that picketing interfering with conduct of plaintiffs' business—Purpose of picketing to compel plaintiffs to comply with demands made by defendants—No evidence of unlawful acts—Whether defendants' acts capable of constituting an actionable nuisance. **Hubbard v Pitt** [1975] **3** 1, CA.
      Existence of tort—Picketing on highway—Whether offence of watching and besetting also constituting nuisance—Conspiracy and Protection of Property Act 1875, s 7. **Thomas v National Union of Mineworkers (South Wales Area)** [1985] **2** 1, Ch D.
  Water—
    Flooding—
      Generally. *See* Natural processes—Flooding, *above*.

NULLITY
  Alimony pendente lite—
    Application to discharge order—
      Order remaining effective after decree pending appeal—Discretion—Fair and reasonable. **Corbett v Corbett (orse Ashley) (No 2)** [1970] **2** 654, Div.
      Retrospective operation—Ground of nullity not a reason for discharging order ab initio. **Corbett v Corbett (orse Ashley) (No 2)** [1970] **2** 654, Div.
    Duration of order—
      Wilful refusal by wife—Whether alimony pendente lite continues until decree absolute. *See* **Divorce** (Alimony—Pendente lite—Nullity—Wilful refusal by wife).
  Appeal—
    Time limit—
      Appeal against decree absolute—No time and opportunity to appeal against decree nisi—Appeal subject to normal time limit—Supreme Court of Judicature (Consolidation) Act 1925, ss 27(1)(2), 31(1)(e). **Whitehead v Whitehead (orse Vasbor)** [1962] **3** 800, CA.

NULLITY (cont)—
  Bar to relief—
    Approbation of unconsummated marriage—
      Adoption of child by spouses—Recognition of existence of marriage by petitioner. **W v W** [1952] **1** 858, CA.
      Adoption of children by spouses—Recognition of existence of marriage by petitioner—Common law doctrine of approbation replaced by statutory bar—Whether public policy still a factor to be considered—Nullity of Marriage Act 1971, s 3. **D v D (nullity)** [1979] **3** 337, Fam D.
      Artificial insemination of wife with husband's seed—Birth of child—Estoppel—Public policy— Bastardisation of child by nullity decree. **L v L** [1949] **1** 141, Div.
      Birth of child—Fecundation ab extra—Approbation—Sincerity. **Clarke (orse Talbott) v Clarke** [1943] **2** 540, Div.
      Knowledge of facts and law—Husband permanently sterilised before marriage by medical operation—Avoidance of procreation of children—Wife's knowledge of operation at time of marriage—Whether bar to decree—Lack of sincerity—Matrimonial Causes Act 1937, s 7(1)(a). **J (orse S) v J** [1947] **2** 43, CA.
      Knowledge of facts and law—Reliance on validity of marriage for purpose of other proceedings—Decree inequitable and against public policy. **Tindall v Tindall** [1953] **1** 139, CA.
      Knowledge of facts and law—Treatment by way of artificial insemination—Adoption of child by spouses. **Slater v Slater** [1953] **1** 246, CA.
      Nature of bar—Whether or not a discretionary bar. **G v G (orse H)** [1960] **3** 56, Div.
      Pre-marital understanding between spouses regarding sexual intercourse—Acquiescence by petitioner for over four years—Wilful refusal to consummate marriage—Matrimonial Causes Act 1950, s 8(1)(a). **Scott v Scott (orse Fone)** [1959] **1** 531, Div.
    Insincerity—
      Approbation of marriage—Desire of petitioner husband to be relieved from financial liability to wife. **Clifford v Clifford** [1948] **1** 394, CA.
      Factors to be considered—Time of knowledge of husband's impotence—Motives inducing marriage—Relevance. **Nash v Nash** [1940] **1** 206, Div.
  Bigamous marriage—
    Children of marriage—
      Custody—Power of court to make order—Matrimonial Causes Act 1950, s 26(1). **Bryant v Bryant** [1955] **2** 116, CA.
    Estoppel—
      Parties to bigamous marriage aware that earlier marriage still in existence—Duty of court to inquire into facts alleged—Matrimonial Causes Act 1950, s 4(1). **Hayward v Hayward** [1961] **1** 236, Div.
      Wife deserted by first husband in 1926—First husband last heard of in 1930—Wife married second husband in 1944—Second husband had then full knowledge of facts—Allegation by second husband in 1959 that 1944 marriage bigamous—Whether second husband estopped from disputing validity of 1944 marriage. **Bullock v Bullock** [1960] **2** 307, Div.
    Financial provision—
      Conduct of parties. *See* Financial provision—Conduct of parties—Bigamous marriage, *below*.
    Onus of proof as to death—
      Husband going through second ceremony of marriage 16 years after wife last known to be alive—Presumption of continuance of life. **Chard v Chard (orse Northcott)** [1955] **3** 721, Div.
  Birth of child—
    Approbation of unconsummated marriage. *See* Bar to relief—Approbation of unconsummated marriage—Birth of child, *above*.
    Evidence. *See* Pregnancy at date of marriage by person other than petitioner—Evidence—Birth of child, *below*.
  Blood test—
    Power of court to order blood tests. *See* Pregnancy at date of marriage by person other than petitioner—Application for order for blood tests, *below*.
  Child of void marriage—
    Legitimacy and legitimation. *See* **Legitimacy** (Child of void marriage).
  Children—
    Arrangements for care and upbringing—
      Generally. *See* **Divorce** (Infant—Child of the family—Arrangements for care and upbringing).
      Petition—Petition filed before 1st January 1971. *See* **Divorce** (Infant—Child of the family— Arrangements for care and upbringing—Practice—Petitions filed before 1st January 1971—Divorce or nullity proceedings or proceedings for judicial separation).
  Confidential information—
    Venereal disease. *See* Venereal disease, *below*.
  Consent to marriage—
    Duress—
      Absence of duress—Purpose of marriage to enable wife, a German, to live in England with another man with whom she had been living as his wife—No cohabitation between the parties to the marriage. **Silver (orse Kraft) v Silver** [1955] **2** 614, Div.
      Capacity of petitioner to resist—Respondent threatening to kill petitioner if she refused to marry him—Respondent Egyptian subject—Ceremony performed in England—Jurisdiction. **Hussein (orse Blitz) v Hussein** [1938] **2** 344, Div.
      Degree of fear necessary to vitiate consent—Fear must be of sufficient degree to vitiate consent, reasonably entertained and arise from some external circumstance for which petitioner not responsible. **Buckland v Buckland** [1967] **2** 300, PDA.
      Degree of fear necessary to vitiate consent—Obedience to parents' wishes and religious customs—Arranged marriage—Sikh marriage—Marriage arranged by parents—Wife never having seen husband prior to marriage ceremony—Wife taking dislike to husband at first meeting on occasion of marriage ceremony—Wife proceeding with ceremony in obedience to parents' wishes and out of respect for Sikh customs. **Singh v Singh** [1971] **2** 828, CA.
      Father of petitioner inducing her by fear to go through marriage ceremony with respondent. **Parojcic (orse Ivetic) v Parojcic** [1959] **1** 1, Div.
      Marriage in country under Communist government—Marriage to foreigner to obtain passport—No consummation of marriage. **H (orse D) v H** [1953] **2** 1229, Div.

NULLITY (cont)—
  Consent to marriage (cont)—
    Duress (cont)—
      Will of one party overborne by fear—Fear genuine and reasonably held relating to danger to life, limb or liberty—Ceremony of marriage in Polish prison—Attempt to save detainee from ill-effects of long prison term. **Szechter (orse Karsov) v Szechter** [1970] **3** 905, DPA.
  Consummation of marriage—
    Allegation of wilful refusal—
      Practice. *See* Practice—Allegation of wilful refusal, *below*.
    Incapacity. *See* Incapacity to consummate marriage, *below*.
    Wilful refusal. *See* Wilful refusal to consummate marriage, *below*.
  Costs—
    Security for costs—
      Order—Form—Petitioner resident out of jurisdiction—Uncertainty whether order made under Matrimonial Causes Rules 1968 (SI 1968 No 219) r 37, or RSC Ord 23—Order to state rules under which made. **Corbett v Corbett (orse Ashley)** [1970] **2** 33, Div.
  Death of spouse—
    Bigamous marriage. *See* Bigamous marriage—Onus of proof as to death, *above*.
  Declaration—
    Jurisdiction—
      Jewish bill of divorcement—Declaratory judgment sought that marriage be dissolved—Jurisdiction of court to make declaratory order—Husband domiciled in Israel—Wife resident in England—RSC Ord 25, r 5. **Har-Shefi v Har-Shefi** [1953] **1** 783, CA.
    Marital status, as to. *See* **Declaration** (Jurisdiction—Declaration as to marital status).
    Marriage void—
      Banns not published—Marriage abroad between two British subjects according to rites of Church of England—Marriage Act 1949, s 25. **Hooper (orse Harrison) v Hooper** [1959] **2** 575, Div.
      Discretion as to declaration—Discretionary jurisdiction under RSC Ord 25, r 5, to make declaration not applicable—Decree of nullity in fact a declaration and not discretionary. **Kassim (orse Widmann) v Kassim (orse Hassim)** [1962] **3** 426, Div.
      Wife a man—Power of court to make bare declaratory order—RSC Ord 15. **Corbett v Corbett (orse Ashley)** [1970] **2** 33, Div.
  Decree—
    Decree absolute—
      Time limit for appeal. *See* Appeal—Time limit, *above*.
    Effect—
      Application under Inheritance (Family Provision) Act 1938—Locus standi of daughter whose marriage had been annulled before will made. *See* **Family provision** (Daughter—Daughter who has not been married—Application for reasonable provision to be made for her maintenance—Locus standi of daughter whose marriage annulled before will made).
      Decree nisi. *See* Decree nisi, *below*.
      Separation agreement entered into between the parties prior to the decree of annulment—Whether provision made for the wife under the agreement enforceable. **Adams v Adams** [1941] **1** 334, CA; **Fowke v Fowke** [1938] **2** 638, Ch D.
    Order for transfer of property on grant of decree. *See* **Husband and wife** (Matrimonial home—Transfer—Order of court—Application for order on decree of divorce, nullity or judicial separation).
    Status—
      Decree operates on status of parties to the marriage. **Merker v Merker** [1962] **3** 928, Div.
  Decree nisi—
    Effect—
      Remarriage—Wife granted decree nisi of nullity on the ground of husband's incapacity—Remarriage of wife before decree made absolute—Whether second marriage bigamous. **Wiggins v Wiggins (orse Brooks) and Ingram** [1958] **2** 555, Registry.
  Domicile—
    Jurisdiction. *See* Jurisdiction—Domicile, *below*.
    Marriage by proxy of Italians in Italy—
      Wilful refusal by wife to consummate marriage—Husband domiciled in England at time of marriage and at time of suit—Law applicable for determining issue of nullity. **Ponticelli v Ponticelli (orse Giglio) (by her guardian)** [1958] **1** 357, Div.
  Duress vitiating consent to marriage. *See* Consent to marriage—Duress, *above*.
  Estoppel—
    Bigamous marriage. *See* Bigamous marriage—Estoppel, *above*.
  Evidence—
    Incapacity to consummate marriage. *See* Incapacity to consummate marriage, *below*.
    Medical inspector's evidence—
      Written statement—Affidavit—Evidence Act 1938, s 1(2)—Matrimonial Causes Rules 1957 (SI 1957 No 619), r 25(1). **Practice Direction** [1967] **3** 828, Div.
  Financial provision—
    Conduct of parties—
      Bigamous marriage—Whether person who knowingly enters into bigamous marriage entitled to claim ancillary relief—Matrimonial Causes Act 1973, s 25. **Whiston v Whiston** [1998] **1** 423, CA.
      Duty of court to have regard to conduct—Void marriage—Transsexual making false declarations that no impediment to marriage—Other party being deceived as to gender—Transsexual claiming ancillary relief following decree of nullity—Whether claim barred in limine on grounds of public policy—Whether court having discretion to grant relief—Matrimonial Causes Act 1973, ss 11(c), 25(1). **S-T (formerly J) v J** [1998] **1** 431, CA.
  Financial provision and property adjustment—
    Decree against male respondent—
      Maintenance and variation of settlements—Short cohabitation—Petitioner having means. **Clifton (orse Packe) v Clifton** [1936] **2** 886, Div.

NULLITY (cont)—

Financial provision and property adjustment (cont)—
Maintenance—
Conduct of parties—Matters to be taken into consideration—Refusal of intercourse by wife without contraceptives—Assent of husband—Ignorance of parties of legal position—Age of wife at time of decree—Supreme Court of Judicature (Consolidation) Act 1925, s 190(1). **Dailey v Dailey (orse Smith)** [1947] 2 269, CA.

Foreign decree—
Recognition. *See* Recognition of foreign decree, *below.*

Foreign marriage—
Second marriage—
Lex loci celebrationis not providing for divorce—Husband's first marriage in Eire dissolved by English court, parties being then domiciled in England—Second marriage of husband in Republic of Ireland—Whether second marriage void—Constitution of Ireland, art 41, s 3(3). **Breen (orse Smith) v Breen** [1961] 3 225, Div.

Impotent spouse. *See* Incapacity to consummate marriage—Petition by impotent spouse, *below.*

Incapacity to consummate marriage—
Consummate—
Erectio and intromissio without ejaculatio—Whether 'consummation'. **R v R (orse F)** [1952] 1 1194, Div.

Evidence—
Corroboration—Sole evidence of petitioner—Need of corroboration. **Hodgkins v Hodgkins** [1950] 1 619, CA.

Husband's incapacity—
Children born in wedlock—Wife's evidence as to paternity—Admissibility. **Burgess (orse Leadbetter) v Burgess** [1937] 1 374, Div.
Failure to consummate after reasonable time—Seven days' cohabitation—Husband giving false reasons for failure to attempt intercourse. **B (orse S) v B** [1958] 2 76, Div.
Penetration—Whether any penetration, however transient, amounts to consummation of the marriage. **W (orse K) v W** [1967] 3 178, Div.

Impotency quoad hunc—
Birth of child to respondent—Evidence by petitioner of non-access—Admissibility. **Farnham v Farnham** [1936] 3 776, Div.

Petition by impotent spouse—
Competency—Need of repudiation of marriage by potent spouse. **Harthan v Harthan** [1948] 2 639, CA.
Factors to be considered—All the circumstances, including respondent spouses' attitude and reaction to the position, to be regarded—Whether a decree just and equitable in all the circumstances. **Pettit v Pettit** [1962] 3 37, CA.
Pre-marital agreement that marriage should be for companionship only—Mental reservation by petitioner regarding consummation later—Parties both of advanced years at time of marriage. **Morgan v Morgan (orse Ransom)** [1959] 1 539, Div.

Practical impossibility of consummation—
Date for ascertaining—Remediable by minor operation without danger. **S v S (orse C)** [1954] 3 736, Div.
Failure to undergo operation or treatment—Offer at trial to undergo operation—Genuineness of offer. **M v M (orse B)** [1956] 3 769, Div.
Onus of proof—Admissibility of evidence up to time of hearing—Adjournment—Further evidence on appeal as regards medical examination after the trial—Matrimonial Causes Rules 1957, (SI 1957 No 619), r 24(2)—RSC Ord 58, r 9(2). **S v S (orse W)** [1962] 2 816, CA.

Wife's incapacity—
Invincible repugnance—Psychiatric or physical aversion rendering wife incapable of intercourse—Arranged marriage—Wife taking dislike to husband at first meeting on occasion of marriage ceremony—Wife proceeding with marriage in obedience to parents' wishes—Wife unwilling to marry husband or to have sexual intercourse with him. **Singh v Singh** [1971] 2 828, CA.
Physical defect of wife—Operation for enlargement of vagina having good chance of success—Consummation with partly artificial vagina. **S v S (orse W) (No 2)** [1962] 3 55, CA.
Physical defect of wife—Provision of artificial vagina—Incurability of defect. **D v D** [1954] 2 598, PDA.
Wife registered as male at birth—Wife later undergoing sex-change operation—Provision of artificial vagina—Whether wife a woman for purposes of marriage—Whether wife capable of consummating marriage. **Corbett v Corbett (orse Ashley)** [1970] 2 33, Div.

Income tax—
Married person's allowance—
Effect of nullity decree. *See* **Income tax** (Husband and wife—Married person's allowance—Nullity decree).

Indian divorce. *See* Remarriage—Former marriage dissolved by decree under Indian and Colonial Divorce Jurisdiction Act 1926 and 1940, *below.*

Insanity—
Party at time of marriage of unsound mind or subject to recurrent fits of insanity—
Fits—Unsound mind—Insanity—Matrimonial Causes Act 1937, s 7(1)(b). **Smith v Smith (orse Hand) (by her guardian)** [1940] 2 595, Div.
Party suffering from mental disorder of such a kind as to be unfitted for marriage and the procreation of children—
Subject to recurrent attacks of insanity—Insanity—Mental disorder—Mental Health Act 1959, s 4—Matrimonial Causes Act 1965, s 9(1)(b) (ii) (iii). **Bennett v Bennett** [1969] 1 539, Div.

Jurisdiction—
Celebration of marriage in England—
Husband domiciled in Italy marrying woman in Italy—Husband obtaining decree of divorce in Mexico and thereafter marrying Danish wife in England—Husband petitioner neither resident nor domiciled in England. **Padolecchia v Padolecchia** [1967] 3 863, Div.
Parties domiciled in Scotland—Petitioner resident in England—Petition on ground of respondent's impotence. **Hill (orse Petchey) v Hill** [1959] 3 754, Div.

NULLITY (cont)—
  Jurisdiction (cont)—
    Celebration of marriage in England (cont)—
      Wife petitioner domiciled and resident in England—Husband neither domiciled nor resident in England when petition presented—Nullity jurisdiction over void marriages by reason of celebration of marriage in England but not over voidable marriages. **Ross Smith v Ross Smith (orse Radford)** [1962] **1** 344, HL.
    Domicile—
      French person's marriage in England—French domicile—Marriage invalid according to French law—Nullity decree pronounced by French court—Competency of English petition. **Galene v Galene (orse Galice)** [1939] **2** 148, Div.
      Marriage in England—Petitioner domiciled and resident in England at time of marriage and resident in England when petition presented—Husband domiciled and resident in Canada. **Casey v Casey** [1949] **2** 110, CA.
      Marriage in France—Petitioner wife born in England of English parents, and resident in England when petition presented—Respondent domiciled and resident in France. **De Reneville v De Reneville** [1948] **1** 56, CA.
      Petitioner domiciled in America—Both parties resident in England—Ceremony in England—Petition for decree of nullity on ground of wilful refusal to consummate. **Hutter v Hutter** [1944] **2** 368, Div.
      Petitioner domiciled in Canada—Both parties resident in England—Ceremony in England—Petition for decree of nullity on ground of wilful refusal to consummate—No appearance by respondent. **Easterbrook v Easterbrook (orse Jervis)** [1944] **1** 90, Div.
      Petitioner domiciled in England—Ceremony in Australia—Respondent neither resident nor domiciled in England—No appearance by respondent. **White (orse Bennett) v White** [1937] **1** 708, Div.
      Petitioner wife domiciled in England—Hindu husband—Marriage in India according to rites of Arya Samaj sect—Marriage monogamous in its inception—Hindu husband if becoming orthodox Hindu free to marry second wife—Possibility of husband's subsequent polygamous marriage no bar to relief sought under matrimonial law of England. **Mehta (orse Kohn) v Mehta** [1945] **2** 690, Div.
    Polygamous marriage—
      Marriage potentially polygamous at date of ceremony—Monogamous at date of proceedings. **Cheni (orse Rodriguez) v Cheni** [1962] **3** 873, Div.
    Residence—
      Petition alleging husband's wilful refusal and incapacity—Husband domiciled in Scotland—Husband and wife resident in England—Matrimonial Causes Act 1950, s 8(1)(a). **Ramsay-Fairfax (orse Scott-Gibson) v Ramsay-Fairfax** [1955] **3** 695, CA.
      Petitioner resident in England at time of petition—Respondent resident in Guernsey—Marriage in Guernsey—Wilful refusal to consummate—Law to be applied. **Robert (orse De La Mare) v Robert** [1947] **2** 22, Div.
      Real and substantial connection with England—Celebration of marriage in England—Husband domiciled in Ohio—Wife resident and domiciled in England at date of marriage—Parties living in England for six months after marriage and then moving to Ohio—Non-consummation of marriage—Wife leaving husband and returning to England—Wife presenting petition for nullity after five months' residence in England—Whether court having jurisdiction on basis of original matrimonial residence or wife's real and substantial connection with England—Matrimonial Causes Act 1965, s 40(1). **Kern v Kern** [1972] **3** 207, Fam D.
  King's Proctor—
    Intervention to show cause against decree nisi being made absolute—
      Onus of proof—Undefended petition for nullity—Wilful refusal to consummate marriage—Decree nisi granted—King's Proctor alleging marriage consummated—Whether affirmative proof necessary. **Bluff v Bluff (orse Kelly)** [1946] **2** 63, Div.
  Maintenance. *See* Financial provision and property adjustment—Maintenance, *above*.
  Marriage by proxy. *See* Domicile—Marriage by proxy, *above*.
  Medical evidence. *See* Evidence—Medical inspector's evidence, *above*.
  Medical inspection—
    Appointment of medical inspectors—
      Principles to be applied in determining whether inspectors should be appointed—Practice. **Practice Direction** [1963] **1** 611, Div.
    Defended cases—
      Appointment of inspector. **Practice Direction** [1971] **2** 1310, Div.
    Examination and report by inspector appointed by court—
      Procedure—Attendance not required to give evidence—Payment of fees. **Practice Direction** [1968] **3** 828, Div.
    Fees—
      Fees of inspectors on London rates. **Practice Direction** [1971] **2** 736, Div.
    Venereal disease. *See* Venereal disease, *below*.
  Mistake as to nature of ceremony—
    Petitioner agreeing to be converted to Hindu faith—
      Ceremony of conversion conducted in Hindustani and in presence of respondent—Conversion ceremony also marriage ceremony—Marriage ceremony a nullity. **Mehta (orse Kohn) v Mehta** [1945] **2** 690, Div.
  Next friend. *See* Petition—Parties—Petition by next friend, *below*.
  Non-access. *See* Pregnancy at date of marriage by person other than petitioner—Evidence—Birth of child, *below*.
  Petition—
    Cross-petition—
      Petition by husband on ground of wife's impotence—Cross-charge of desertion—Need to file cross-petition—Inclusion in same document as answer. **Pickett v Pickett (orse Moss)** [1951] **1** 614, Div.
      Petition for decree of nullity—Cross-petition by husband alleging adultery—Whether issues should be tried together or issue of nullity tried first. **S (orse P) v S (J and P cited)** [1970] **2** 251, Div.

NULLITY (cont)—
  Petition (cont)—
    Form of petition—
      Children or issue—Reference to there being no other children of the family. **Practice Note** [1959] **2** 163, Div.
      Use of printed forms sold by law stationers—Matrimonial Causes Rules 1971 (SI 1971 No 953), r 9, App 2, Form 2. **Practice Direction** [1971] **3** 288, Fam D.
    Parties—
      Petition by next friend—Petitioner said to be 'of unsound mind, not so found by inquisition'—Reasonable ground for thinking petitioner capable of managing affairs—Dismissal of petition. **J (orse B) (by her next friend) v J** [1952] **2** 1129, Div.
    Title of suit—
      Inclusion of surname of wife prior to marriage ceremony no longer necessary. **Practice Direction** [1973] **2** 880, Fam D.
  Polygamous marriage—
    Jurisdiction. *See* Jurisdiction—Polygamous marriage, *above*.
    Relief—
      Marriage in England—Marriage with Indian already lawfully married in India according to Hindu law—Hindu law permitting polygamy—Hindu marriage recognised as valid in English law—Whether English ceremony of marriage a nullity. **Baindail v Baindail** [1946] **1** 342, CA.
      Petitioner domiciled in England—Marriage in Egypt with Moslem domiciled in Egypt—Law Reform (Miscellaneous Provisions) Act 1949, s 1(1) (2). **Risk (orse Yerburgh) v Risk** [1950] **2** 973, Div.
      Petitioner going through a form of marriage with Hindu temporarily resident in England—Respondent already married to Hindu woman in India—Hindu law permitting polygamy—Hindu law recognised in England—Hindu marriage valid—English ceremony of marriage a nullity. **Srini Vasan v Srini Vasan** [1945] **2** 21, Div.
  Practice—
    Allegation of wilful refusal—
      Investigation—Petition alleging fits of epilepsy and wilful refusal to consummate marriage—Cross-charge of wilful refusal to consummate marriage—Finding that respondent subject to recurrent fits of epilepsy at time of marriage—Question of wilful refusal to consummate not investigated—Whether necessary to investigate question of wilful refusal—Matrimonial Causes Act 1950, s 8(1)(b). **Iddenden (orse Brians) (by her next friend) v Iddenden** [1958] **3** 241, Div.
    Cross-petitions. *See* Petition—Cross-petition, *above*.
    Particulars—
      Incapacity—Whether particulars will be ordered of plea contained in the petition of a female petitioner alleging incapacity. **W (orse B) v W** [1944] **1** 446, Div.
    Petition. *See* Petition, *above*.
    Recognition of foreign decree. *See* Recognition of foreign decree—Practice, *below*.
    Trial—
      Circuit—Trial of matrimonial causes on circuit. **Practice Note** [1958] **3** 352, Div.
  Pregnancy at date of marriage by person other than petitioner—
    Application for order for blood tests—
      Power of court to order blood tests—Supreme Court of Judicature (Consolidation) Act 1925, ss 32, 103(1)—Matrimonial Causes Act 1950, s 8(1)(d)—Matrimonial Causes Rules 1957, (SI 1957 No 619), r 24, RSC Ord 37A, r 1, Ord 50, r 3. **W v W (No 4)** [1963] **2** 841, CA.
    Blood tests. *See* **Paternity** (Blood test—Nullity).
    Discovery of existence of grounds for decree—
      Belief of husband—Matrimonial Causes Act 1937, s 7(1)(d), proviso (iii). **Smith v Smith** [1947] **2** 741, CA.
    Evidence—
      Birth of child—Admissibility of evidence of non-access before marriage ceremony—Rule in Russell v Russell—Matrimonial Causes Act 1937, s 7(1)(d). **Jackson v Jackson (orse Prudom)** [1939] **1** 471, Div.
    Time limit for institution of proceedings—
      Petition filed more than a year after marriage—Concealment by wife—Whether time limit could be extended—Matrimonial Causes Act 1937, s 7(1)(d), proviso (ii). **Chaplin v Chaplin** [1948] **2** 408, CA.
  Proof of death—
    Bigamous marriage. *See* Bigamous marriage—Onus of proof as to death, *above*.
  Property adjustment. *See* Financial provision and property adjustment, *above*.
  Recognition of foreign decree—
    Basis of recognition—
      Decree granted to wife on basis of six month's residence in foreign court's jurisdiction—Evidence before court that wife residing in jurisdiction for three years prior to application for decree—Decree not recognised by law of husband's domicile—Husband remarrying in England—Whether re-marriage valid—Whether foreign decree based on wife's residence within foreign court's jurisdiction capable of being recognised—Whether English court ought to recognise decree. **Perrini v Perrini** [1979] **2** 323, Fam D.
      Real and substantial connection between petitioner and foreign country—Wife leaving husband to go and live in foreign country with intention of marrying national of that country—Wife obtaining decree of nullity in competent court of foreign country after 12 months' residence there—Whether decree should be recognised by English court. **Law v Gustin (formerly Law)** [1976] **1** 113, Fam D.
    Contrary to justice—
      Maltese husband marrying English wife at register office in England—Husband a Roman Catholic—Marriage valid by English law but voidable by Maltese law—Decree of nullity granted to husband in Malta—Whether decree recognised in English court. **Lepre v Lepre** [1963] **2** 49, Div.
      Maltese husband with domicile of choice in England marrying English wife at register office—Husband a Roman Catholic—Husband resuming domicile of origin in Malta—Refusal of wife to go to Malta—Decree of nullity granted to husband in Malta based on Maltese domicile of parties by virtue of husband's resumed domicile—Whether decree recognised by English court—Whether husband in desertion. **Formosa v Formosa** [1962] **3** 419, CA.

NULLITY (cont)—
Recognition of foreign decree (cont)—
Decree granted to wife on ground of religious incapacity—
Wife domiciled in foreign country at date of marriage—Decreee by court of country where marriage celebrated—Recognition of decree by English court. **Corbett v Corbett** [1957] **1** 621, PDA.
Domicile of parties in Italy—
Residence in Switzerland—Swiss decree of nullity on ground of husband's impotence recognised by Italian courts—Recognition by English court. **Abate v Cauvin (formerly Abate orse Cauvin)** [1961] **1** 569, Div.
Practice—
Oath as to domicile or full statement of facts to be submitted as case requires. **Practice Direction** [1968] **1** 400, Prob.
Residence of parties within jurisdiction of German court—
Decree of German court annulling marriage but not treating it as non-existent—Decree a nullity by German law owing to its not having treated the marriage as non-existent—Recognition of decree by English court. **Merker v Merker** [1962] **3** 928, Div.
Right to recognition—
Marriage celebrated in England—Previous decision of English court that marriage valid under English law—Previous decision based on petitioner's consent to marriage—Foreign decree based on ground that marriage a sham although consented to—That ground not raised in English proceedings—Whether foreign decree entitled to recognition by English court. **Vervaeke v Smith (Messina and A-G intervening)** [1982] **2** 144, HL.
Remarriage—
Former marriage dissolved by decree under Indian and Colonial Divorce Jurisdiction Act 1926 and 1940—
Remarriage of wife less than six months after decree—Earlier Indian statute prohibiting re-marriage for six months after decree—Whether second marriage valid—Indian Divorce Act 1869, (Act No 4 of 1869), s 57—Indian and Colonial Divorce Jurisdiction Act 1926, s 1(1), proviso (b). **Buckle v Buckle (orse Williams)** [1955] **3** 641, Div.
Residence. See Jurisdiction—Residence, above.
Security for costs. See Costs—Security for costs, above.
Status—
Parties to marriage. See Decree—Status, above.
Time limit for appeal against decree absolute. See Appeal—Time limit, above.
Unconsummated marriage—
Approbation as bar to relief. See Bar to relief—Approbation of unconsummated marriage, above.
Variation of settlement. See **Variation of Settlement (Matrimonial Causes)** (Post-nuptial settlement—House purchased by spouses on trust for sale—Decree nisi of nullity to wife).
Venereal disease—
Disclosure of confidential information by doctor—
Duty of doctor—Doctor requested by patient to disclose confidential information to named person before presentation of petition—Matrimonial Causes Act 1937, s 7(1)(c). **C v C** [1946] **1** 562, Assizes.
Wilful refusal to consummate marriage—
Consummate—
Agreement by parties to use contraceptives for limited period—Wife wishing to have child—Husband persisting in use of contraceptive—Coitus interruptus—Whether marriage consummated—Whether acquiesence by wife agreement not to have sexual intercourse for a limited period bar to relief—Matrimonial Causes Act 1937, s 7(1)(a). **Cowen v Cowen** [1945] **2** 197, CA.
Coitus interruptus—Whether amounting to consummation. **Cackett (orse Trice) v Cackett** [1950] **1** 677, Div.
Coitus interruptus—Whether amounting to consummation—Matrimonial Causes Act 1937, s 7(1)(a). **Grimes (orse Edwards) v Grimes** [1948] **2** 147, Div; **White (orse Berry) v White** [1948] **2** 151, Div.
Insistence by wife on use of contraceptives by husband—
Acquiescence by husband—Whether preventing consummation of marriage—Matrimonial Causes Act 1937, s 7(1)(a). **Baxter v Baxter** [1947] **2** 886, HL.
Refusal—
Indecision not refusal—Refusal distinguished from neglect. **S v S (orse C)** [1954] **3** 736, Div.
Refusal to arrange religious ceremony—
Marriage at register office—Mutual intention to have subsequent church ceremony—Parties being Roman Catholics knew that consummation could only follow after church ceremony—Failure by husband to arrange religious ceremony despite repeated requests by wife—Refusal constituting wilful refusal to consummate. **Jodla v Jodla (orse Czarnomska)** [1960] **1** 625, Div.
Marriage at register office—Mutual intention to hold subsequent religious ceremony—Parties being Sikhs knowing that consummation could only follow religious ceremony—Refusal by husband to arrange ceremony—Refusal constituting refusal to consummate. **Kaur v Singh** [1972] **1** 292, CA.
Relevant considerations—
Result of decree to bastardise child—Wife pregnant by husband at date of marriage—Child born subsequently—Delay—Whether grounds for withholding decree—Matrimonial Causes Act 1937, s 7(1)(a). **Dredge v Dredge** [1947] **1** 29, Div.
Wilful refusal—
Definite decision arrived at without just excuse—Duty of judge—Matrimonial Causes Act 1937, s 7(1)(a). **Horton v Horton** [1947] **2** 871, HL.

NURSE
Agency for supply of nurses—
Licence by local authority—
Condition—Limitation on fees receivable by agency—Nurses Act 1943, s 8(2). **Middlesex CC v Miller** [1948] **1** 192, KBD.
Negligence—
Hospital—
Liability of hospital. See **Hospital** (Liability for negligence of members of staff—Nurses).

NURSING
Damages—
Personal injury—
Cost of nursing. *See* **Damages** (Personal injury—Nursing).
Gift—
Charitable purpose. *See* **Charity** (Benefit to community—Nursing).
Home of rest for nurses—
Gift of funds for—
Whether charitable purpose. *See* **Charity** (Benefit to community—Hospital—Home of rest for nurses of institution).
Nursing care—
Health authority's responsibilities. *See* **National Health Service** (Health authority—Nursing care).

NURSING HOME
Charges—
Whether deductible in assessing professional man's income. *See* **Income tax** (Deduction in computing profits—Expenses wholly and exclusively laid out for purposes of trade—Medical expenses).
Registration—
Cancellation of—
Exercise of statutory powers. *See* **Negligence** (Duty to take care—Statutory powers—Registration authority—Nursing home).

657

O

OATH
    Administrator—
        Grant of administration on intestacy. *See* **Intestacy** (Grant of administration—Practice—Oath of administrator).
    Child—
        Ability to understand nature of oath—
            Criminal proceedings. *See* **Criminal evidence** (Child—Oath—Ability to understand nature of oath).
        Witness in criminal proceedings. *See* **Criminal evidence** (Child—Oath).
    Generally. *See* **Evidence** (Oath).
    Juror. *See* **Jury** (Juror—Oath).
    Probate—
        Grant of representation. *See* **Probate** (Practice—Non-contentious probate—Grant of representation—Oath in support of application).
    Trust corporation—
        Application for grant of probate. *See* **Probate** (Grant—Trust corporation—Application for grant—Oath in support of application).
    Witness—
        Affirmation—
            Perjury. *See* **Criminal law** (Perjury—Lawfully sworn as a witness—Affirmation).

OBITER DICTUM
    Binding effect. *See* **Precedent** (Ratio decidendi—Obiter dictum).

OBJECTS CLAUSE
    Company. *See* **Company** (Objects clause).

OBSCENE PUBLICATIONS
    Criminal proceedings. *See* **Criminal law** (Obscene publications).
    Enforcement of law—
        Mandamus directed to chief officer of police. *See* **Mandamus** (Chief officer of police—Enforcement of law).
    Forfeiture—
        Magistrates. *See* **Magistrates** (Obscene publications—Forfeiture).

OBSCENITY
    Test—
        Tendency to deprave or corrupt—
            Publications. *See* **Criminal law** (Obscene publications—Tendency to deprave or corrupt).

OBSTRUCTION
    Constable. *See* **Criminal law** (Obstructing constable in execution of duty).
    Course of justice—
        Conspiracy. *See* **Criminal law** (Conspiracy—Obstruction of course of justice).
        Generally. *See* **Criminal law** (Obstructing course of justice).
    Factory floor. *See* **Factory** (Floor—Obstruction).
    Factory passage. *See* **Factory** (Passage—Duty to keep free from obstruction).
    Highway—
        Generally. *See* **Highway** (Obstruction).
        Lighting obstructions. *See* **Lighting restriction** (Obstructions on highway—Lighting obstructions).
        Obstruction of streets in neighbourhood of Parliament. *See* **Parliament** (Prevention of obstruction of streets in neighbourhood of Parliament).
    Legal proceedings, of—
        Contempt of court. *See* **Contempt of court** (Obstruction of legal proceedings).
    Police. *See* **Criminal law** (Obstructing constable in execution of duty).
    Road traffic. *See* **Road traffic** (Obstruction).

OBTAINING CREDIT
    Undischarged bankrupt. *See* **Bankruptcy** (Offences—Undischarged bankrupt obtaining credit).

OBTAINING PECUNIARY ADVANTAGE BY DECEPTION
    See **Criminal law** (Obtaining pecuniary advantage by deception).

OBTAINING PROPERTY BY DECEPTION
    Conspiracy to obtain money by deception. *See* **Criminal law** (Conspiracy—Conspiracy to obtain money by deception).
    Generally. *See* **Criminal law** (Obtaining property by deception).

OCCASIONAL LICENCE
    Grant. *See* **Licensing** (Occasional licence—Grant).

OCCUPATION
    Land—
        Income tax. *See* **Income tax** (Land—Occupation of land).
    Occupier's liability—
        Meaning of occupation. *See* **Occupier's liability** (Occupation).
    Premises—
        Business purposes. *See* **Landlord and tenant** (Business premises—Occupied for business purposes).
        Licence to occupy premises. *See* **Licence** (Licence to occupy premises).
    Rateable occupation. *See* **Rates** (Rateable occupation).

OCCUPATION (cont)—
  Single room—
    Tenancy or licence—
      Protected tenancy. *See* **Rent restriction** (Protected tenancy—Tenancy or licence—Occupant of single room).

OCCUPATIONAL PENSION INSURANCE
  European Community—
    Freedom of movement. *See* **European Union** (Freedom of movement—Services—Occupational pension insurance).

OCCUPATIONAL PENSION SCHEME
  Company. *See* **Pension** (Pension scheme—Company pension scheme).
  European Community—
    Freedom of movement. *See* **European Union** (Freedom of movement—Services—Occupational pension insurance).
  Generally. *See* **Pension** (Pension scheme).
  Income tax—
    Approved scheme. *See* **Income tax** (Pension—Approved occupational pension scheme).

OCCUPIER
  Cellar under street—
    Statutory duty. *See* **Highway** (Cellars under streets—Statutory duty of owner or occupier to keep cellar openings and cellar in good condition and repair).
  Dangerous premises etc—
    Liability for. *See* **Occupier's liability**.
  Dock—
    Statutory duty—
      Repair of ship in dry dock—Protection of openings in decks and tank tops. *See* **Dock** (Repair of ship in dry dock—Protection of openings in decks and tank tops—Statutory duty of occupier).
  Enforcement notice. *See* **Town and country planning** (Enforcement notice—Validity—Owner and occupier).
  Factory—
    Contravention of statutory provisions by—
      Offence. *See* **Factory** (Offence—Contravention of statutory provisions by occupier).
  Harrassment—
    Residential occupier of land. *See* **Criminal law** (Harassment—Residential occupier of land).
  Independent contractor, liability for—
    Acts outside control of occupier—
      Erection of scaffold—Erection by electrical contractors working on premises—Erection by servant of occupier on instructions of contractor—Servant of contractor injured on scaffold—Whether occupier liable. **Clelland v Edward Lloyd Ltd** [1937] **2** 605, KBD.
  Liability—
    Generally. *See* **Occupier's liability**.
  Mobile home—
    Agreement offered by site owner to occupier of mobile home. *See* **Mobile home** (Agreement offered by site owner to occupier of mobile home).
  Negligence—
    Accommodation works. *See* **Railway** (Accommodation works—Duty of railway authority to maintain works—Persons to whom duty owed).
  Nuisance—
    Generally. *See* **Nuisance** (Occupier).
    Right to sue. *See* **Nuisance** (Right to sue—Occupier of land).
  Overriding interest—
    Registered land—
      Person in actual occupation. *See* **Land registration** (Overriding interest—Rights of person in actual occupation).
  Permitting premises to be used for activities in connection with dangerous drugs. *See* **Drugs** (Dangerous drugs—Occupier of premises permitting activities in connection with drugs to take place there).
  Premises used for smoking of cannabis or dealing in cannabis—
    Penalisation of. *See* **Drugs** (Dangerous drugs—Cannabis).
  Rateable occupation. *See* **Rates** (Rateable occupation).
  Residential occupier of premises—
    Unlawful eviction and harassment. *See* **Criminal law** (Unlawful eviction and harassment of residential occupier of premises).

OCCUPIER'S LIABILITY
  Acceptance of risk—
    Foreseeable but improbable risk—
      Rugby football club in occupation of football ground—Concrete wall seven feet three inches from touchline—Compliance in that respect with byelaws of Rugby Football League—Injury to visiting player in collision with wall—Such an injury foreseeable but improbable—Whether occupier liable—Whether player had willingly accepted risk of playing on football ground which complied with league's byelaws—Occupiers' Liability Act 1957, s 2(1), (2), (5). **Simms v Leigh Rugby Football Club Ltd** [1969] **2** 923, Assizes.
  Act of unauthorised persons—
    Reasonable precautions—
      Lift in business premises—Accident to tenant—Liability of landlord for unauthorised tampering with lift. **Rochman v J & E Hall Ltd** [1947] **1** 895, KBD.

OCCUPIER'S LIABILITY (cont)—

Activities on land—

Static conditions of land connected with activities—

Railway—Level crossing—Licensee—Level crossing only access to village—Plaintiff inhabitant of village—Lawfully using crossing—Fell on uneven sleepers and was injured by train—Whether general duty of care on part of corporate body charged with running the railway extended to static conditions of railway track—Whether that duty limited by common law duty owned by the occupier of the railway lines to the plaintiff as licensee. **Railways Comr v McDermott** [1966] **2** 162, CA.

Carriage of passengers—

Safety of premises—

Implied warranty—Defective paving near edge of station platform—Injury to passenger—Breach of implied warranty that premises reasonably safe. **Protheroe v Railway Executive** [1950] **2** 1093, KBD.

Station platform—Fall from platform—Edge marked by white lines—Fog. **Schlarb v London and North Eastern Rly Co** [1936] **1** 71, KBD.

Station platform—Snow on platform—Delay in sanding and salting—Porter responsible otherwise urgently engaged—Liability of Railway Executive for injury to passenger. **Tomlinson v Railway Executive** [1953] **1** 1, CA.

Child trespasser—

Air raid shelter on public green—

Shelter maintained by local authority—Electric cable placed on ground and connected to ventilating fans in shelter—Child electrocuted while playing in air-raid shelter—Liability of local authority—Child a trespasser and therefore liability excluded. **Walder v Hammersmith BC** [1944] **1** 490, KBD.

Concealed danger—

Duty to child trespasser likely to come on to property—Danger created by occupier—Child not capable of appreciating danger—Contractors engaged in demolition of warehouse—Contractors lighting fires on premises—Contractors leaving premises unguarded—Plaintiff five year old child—Plaintiff entering premises and falling into fire—Contractors having warned off children, including plaintiff, on previous occasions. **Pannett v P McGuinness & Co Ltd** [1972] **3** 137, CA.

Duty to child trespasser likely to come on to property—Danger created by occupier—Child not capable of appreciating danger—Electrified railway line—Failure by occupier to maintain adequate fence—Railway line passing alongside field open to public—Chain link fence marking boundary of railway line with field—Fence broken down and giving easy access to short cut across railway—Occupier notified that children had been seen on line—Failure to inspect or repair fence—Child walking on to line seriously injured by electrified rail—Whether occupier liable for breach of duty to child. **British Railways Board v Herrington** [1972] **1** 749, HL.

Duty to child trespasser likely to come on to property—Danger created by occupier—Dangerous thing or something near it constituting allurement to child—Duty of occupier to consider the possibility of protecting potential trespassers—Circumstances in which occupier under a duty to take steps to protect potential trespassers—Relevant factors—Chance of trespassers coming on to land—Expense to occupier of taking appropriate steps—Occupiers piling rubble beneath high tension electric cable—Child trespasser playing on mound of rubble injured by touching cable. **Southern Portland Cement Ltd v Cooper** [1974] **1** 87, PC.

Duty to trespassing child—

Presence of child on land reasonably foreseeable—Child injured on railway line adjacent to home at railway station—Negligent driving of trolley by railway employee—Whether presence of child reasonably foreseeable—Whether duty of care owed to child. **Videan v British Transport Commission** [1963] **2** 860, CA.

Presence of children on land a likely occurrence—Demolition of house—Liability of demolition contractors—Site easily approached from open space—Wall in unsafe condition—Interference with wall by child—Collapse on child—Whether contractor's under a duty of care to child. **Davis v St Mary's Demolition and Excavation Co Ltd** [1954] **1** 578, QBD.

Children—

Adequate measures to avoid danger to children—

Public park—Paddling-pool maintained by local authority—Sand at side of pool—Local authority aware of danger of broken glass—Sand raked by park-keeper—Raking not sufficient to remove glass embedded in sand—Whether steps taken by authority to remove glass adequate. **Ellis v Fulham BC** [1937] **3** 454, CA.

Breach of duty to warn child of danger—

Factors to be taken into account when determining whether breach—Duty of parents to protect child—Child of tender years—Licensee on land—Injured by falling into trench on housing estate in occupation of local authority—Danger obvious, but child too young to appreciate it—Whether authority in breach of duty. **Phipps v Rochester Corp** [1955] **1** 129, QBD.

Danger or trap to child—

Accident on land owned by local authority—Foreseeability—Council negligently failing to remove abandoned boat from amenity land—Fourteen-year-old boy attempting to repair boat—Boat falling on boy and causing injury—Whether accident reasonably foreseeable. **Jolley v Sutton London BC** [1998] **3** 559, CA; [2000] **3** 409, HL.

Tramway track used by public and children—Slow-moving trucks—Child riding on trucks—Whether child a licensee on truck—Whether defendants as owners of track under a duty of care. **Gough v National Coal Board** [1953] **2** 1283, CA.

Waste land used for tipping—Child rolling down sloping bank and injured by broken glass—Whether presence of bank coupled with tins and broken glass constituting a trap. **Williams v Cardiff Corp** [1950] **1** 250, CA.

Duty to guard against existence of danger—

Recreation ground—Chain fixed to chute by child—Chain injuring plaintiff child on slide—Chain left unsecured by attendant—Danger known to local authority occupiers. **Coates v Rawtenstall BC** [1937] **3** 602, CA.

Ignorance of danger—

Avoidance of duty to warn of danger—Recreation ground—Injuries caused by defective swing—Local authority ignorant of defect. **Sutton v Bootle Corp** [1947] **1** 92, CA.

OCCUPIER'S LIABILITY (cont)—
    Children (cont)—
        Licensee or trespasser—
            Inference of licence—Rebuttal of inference—Knowledge of intrusion by children on to land—Steps taken to prevent intrusions—Injury on railway line adjacent to recreation ground—Access to line through hole made by children in fence—No evidence that occupier had acquiesced in intrusion by children—Whether child plaintiff a trespasser. **Edwards v Railway Executive** [1952] **2** 430, HL.
        Playground controlled by local authority—
            Playground open to children of all ages—Chute with platform—Child of four and a half years falling through gap between rails on platform—Whether local authority liable. **Dyer v Ilfracombe UDC** [1956] **1** 581, CA.
            Playground open to children of all ages—Chute with platform—Child of three years falling through gap between rails and floor of platform—Liability of local authority—Forseeable danger—Similar accident in 1934—Damages—Injuries resulting in blindness. **Bates v Stone Parish Council** [1954] **3** 38, CA.
        Trespassing. *See* Child trespasser, *above.*
    Common duty of care—
        Liability in contract—
            Option to claim in contract or tort for breach of duty—Building occupied by building contractors—Building in course of erection—Plaintiff engaged as independent sub-contractor to work on building—Building contractors in breach of common duty of care—Plaintiff injured—Breach a cause of injury—Plaintiff guilty of contributory negligence—Contributory negligence precluding claim in contract—Whether plaintiff entitled to claim in tort for breach of duty to him as visitor—Occupiers' Liability Act 1957, ss 2(1), 5(1). **Sole v WH Hallt Ltd** [1973] **1** 1032, QBD.
        Nature of duty—
            Reasonable care—Building site—Duty of building contractor—Duty of care towards servant of specialist sub-contractor coming on the building site—Bank on site muddy and slippery—Servant injured on slope—Whether contractors as occupiers having used reasonable care—Occupiers' Liability Act 1957, s 2(1). **Savory v Holland, Hannen and Cubitts (Southern) Ltd** [1964] **3** 18, CA.
            Reasonable care—Lake open to the public—Occupier posting notices prohibiting swimming—Occupier aware of further steps which could minimise likelihood of swimming—Claimant running into lake, diving, and suffering injury—Whether occupier having taken such care as in all the circumstances was reasonable to see that claimant would be reasonably safe—Occupiers' Liability Act 1957, s 2. **Tomlinson v Congleton BC** [2003] **3** 1122, CA and HL.
    Concealed danger—
        Child trespasser. *See* Child trespasser—Concealed danger, *above.*
        Licensee. *See* Duty to licensee—Concealed danger or trap, *below.*
    Damages—
        Financial loss—
            Loss following from damage to property—Whether damages recoverable for financial loss as well as for physical damage—Occupiers' Liability Act 1957, s 1(3)(b). **AMF International Ltd v Magnet Bowling Ltd** [1968] **2** 789, QBD.
    Dangerous things—
        Liability in negligence. *See* **Negligence** (Dangerous things—Occupier of premises).
    Duty to independent contractor—
        Duty to contractor's employees—
            Safe system of work—Occupier entering into contract for demolition of building—Contractor sub-contracting demolition without occupier's authority—Sub-contractor using unsafe system of work—Sub-contractor's employee injured—Whether occupier owing duty to employee to see that safe system of work used—Occupiers' Liability Act 1957, s 2(2). **Ferguson v Welsh** [1987] **3** 777, HL.
        Movable structure—
            Ladder—Contractor undertaking building work for farmer—Farmer providing farm ladder for use in building work—Whether farmer 'occupying' ladder—Occupiers' Liability Act 1957, s 1(3)(a). **Wheeler v Copas** [1981] **3** 405, QBD.
        Safe means of access—
            Window cleaner—Engaged as independent contractor to clean factory windows—No safe means of access—Liability of occupier. **Lavender v Diamints Ltd** [1949] **1** 532, CA.
    Duty to invitee—
        Customers in shops etc—
            Reasonable care—Unusual danger—Onus of proof that reasonable steps taken to avoid accident—Customer injured because of slippery substance on floor of shop—Burden on shopkeeper to explain how accident occurred or adduce evidence that reasonable steps taken to avoid accident. **Turner v Arding & Hobbs Ltd** [1949] **2** 911, KBD.
        Duty of shipowners to stevedores—
            Duty to ensure that beams left in position secure—Beam left insecure by shipowners—Beam falling and injuring stevedores unloading ship—Cause of accident—Effect of failure to examine beam by stevedores or their employers—Factories Act 1937, s 60—Docks Regulations 1934 (S R & O 1934 No 279), Duties, para (d), reg 42. **Jerred v T Roddam Dent & Son Ltd (Glen Line Ltd, third party)** [1948] **2** 104, Leeds Assizes.
        Duty to ensure premises reasonably safe—
            Theatre—Ceiling damaged by enemy bomb blast—Failure to maintain premises—Member of audience injured by fall of ceiling—Whether defendants in breach of duty to ensure that theatre reasonably safe for purpose for which it was used. **Pope v St Helen's Theatre Ltd** [1946] **2** 440, KBD.
        Goods of invitee on premises—
            Theft—Publican—Customer's motor cycle stolen from yard of public house—Whether breach of occupier's duty of care. **Tinsley v Dudley** [1951] **1** 252, CA.

OCCUPIER'S LIABILITY (cont)—

Duty to invitee (cont)—

Independent contractor—

Employment of independent contractor to do work requiring special skill—Electrical wiring of offices defective—Premises re-wired by reputable electrical engineering company five years before date of accident—Defect not apparent—Whether occupier liable as a consequence of contractor's negligence. **Green v Fibreglass Ltd** [1958] 2 521, Assizes.

Innkeeper—

Extent of invitation—Private door—Plaintiff passing along unlighted passage and through door marked 'Private'. **Lee v Luper** [1936] 3 817, KBD.

Railway passengers—

Safety of station platform—Negligence. *See* **Negligence** (Railway—Duty to passengers and invitees—Safety of station platform).

Scope of invitation—

Stevedore—Stevedore working on defendant's ship—Stevedore going to after part of ship to find suitable skid for unloading work—Falling down hatch in badly lighted part of ship and injured—Whether an invitee. **Henaghan v Rederiet Forangirene** [1936] 2 1426, Assizes.

Standard of care—

Reasonable steps to guard against danger—Yard forming part of licensed premises—Customer slipping on vomit in yard late at night—Yard unlighted—Landlord having inspected yard earlier and cleaned it out—Whether danger one which landlord could reasonably be expected to guard against. **Simons v Winslade** [1938] 3 774, CA.

Unusual danger—

Fireman—Explosion—Exceptional and unnecessary dangers of fire and explosion created by occupiers—Fireman fighting fire on premises—Injured by explosion. **Merrington v Ironbridge Metal Works Ltd** [1952] 2 1101, Assizes.

Fireman—Mains supply of electricity to lighting circuit not cut off—Obsolete type of mechanism—Fireman electrocuted. **Hartley v Mayoh & Co** [1954] 1 375, CA.

Invitee's knowledge of danger—Appreciation of nature of risk—Defective doors of machine house on roof to which access had by ladder—Invitee's knowledge of defect—No warning or safeguards by occupier—Liability of occupier. **Smith v Austin Lifts Ltd** [1959] 1 81, HL.

Invitee's knowledge of danger—Workman—Complaints made by workman—Workman engaged on ship repairs—Faulty staging—Despite complaints defects not remedied by ship repairers—Workman falling from staging—Whether workman's knowledge of danger exonerating ship repairers from liability. **London Graving Dock Co Ltd v Horton** [1951] 2 1, HL.

Railway station—Person visiting railway station to meet passenger—Oily patch on platform. **Stowell v Railway Executive** [1949] 2 193, KBD.

Window cleaner—Defective window sash—Window safe for ordinary purposes. **General Cleaning Contractors Ltd v Christmas** [1952] 2 1110, HL.

Window cleaner—Plywood panel in window—Occupier's removal of bolts—Failure to inform cleaner. **Bates v Parker** [1953] 1 768, CA.

Use of chattels—

Defective chattel—Knowledge of occupier—Building operations—Defective ladder removed from building operation—Ladder put back by unknown person—Invitee injured using ladder—Onus on invitee to prove invitor's responsibility for or knowledge of replacement of ladder. **Woodman v Richardson and Concrete Ltd** [1937] 3 866, CA.

Works on premises—

Occupier carrying out work himself—Work not requiring special skill and knowledge—Standard of care and skill required—Outside door handle fixed by householder—Handle coming off door when pulled by tradesman—Tradesman injured—Whether occupier liable. **Wells v Cooper** [1958] 2 527, CA.

Duty to licensee—

Concealed danger or trap—

Bridge over ditch—Canvasser visiting premises after dark—Only means of access to house over road across concrete bridge over ditch—Canvasser tripping and falling into ditch—Whether bridge over ditch a concealed danger. **Dunster v Abbott** [1953] 2 1572, CA.

Diving board over tidal area of bay—Board erected by defendants some years previously—Water outside area of defendants' occupation—Licensee injured in consequence of diving off board at low tide—No defect in board—Whether board a concealed danger—Whether fact that board had been erected by defendants some years previously altered the duty—Whether fact that danger arose from use of shallow sea outside area of defendants' occupation displaced duty. **Perkowski v Wellington Corp (City of)** [1958] 3 368, PC.

Duty to give warning—Passenger in lorry—Railway bridge over road—Headroom of bridge reduced—Passenger killed by contact with low bridge—No warning given to deceased—Duty of lorry driver to warn passenger. **Lewys v Burnett and Dunbar** [1945] 2 555, KBD.

Polished linoleum—Guest in house—Guest having observed that linoleum was polished but not suspecting it was slippery—Guest injured by slipping—Whether linoleum constituting a trap. **Pitt v Jackson** [1939] 1 129, KBD.

Requisitioned property—Duty to repair—Liability of requisitioning authority—Unsafe ceiling—Occupation by family of five—Authority's agreement with husband—Injury to wife—Whether agreement for occupation by family a licence rather than tenancy—Whether requisitioning authority under duty of care to members of family as licensees. **Greene v Chelsea BC** [1954] 2 318, CA.

Duty of care—

Distinction between duty to licensee and duty to invitee—Whether any distinction. **Slater v Clay Cross Co Ltd** [1956] 2 625, CA.

Involuntary encroachment—

Railway track—Licensees on walkway adjoining track—Duty to keep look-out for licensees on walkway adjoining track—Licensee involuntarily putting foot on sleepers of track following warning shout—Licensee struck by van on track. **Braithwaite v South Durham Steel Co Ltd** [1958] 3 161, Assizes.

OCCUPIER'S LIABILITY (cont)—
 Duty to licensee (cont)—
  Licensor's knowledge of danger—
   Actual knowledge—Knowledge of potential danger—Public convenience—Injury caused by children tampering with grille—Liability of local authority. **Pearson v Lambeth BC** [1950] **1** 682, CA.
   Reasonable appreciation of risk—Knowledge by licensor of facts constituting danger—Accident in dark—Risk not obvious to licensee—Defective steps of requisitioned house—Liability of requisitioning authority. **Hawkins v Coulsdon and Purley UDC** [1954] **1** 97, CA.
 Exclusion of liability—
  Notice—
   Knowledge of terms of notice—Notice on land purporting to exclude liability—Knowledge of licensee of existence of notice but allegation of ignorance of most of its terms—Whether liability of licensor for negligence excluded—Whether conditions sufficiently brought to licensee's notice—Construction of licence—Whether exclusion of liability limited to static condition of the land. **Ashdown v Samuel Williams & Sons Ltd** [1957] **1** 35, CA.
   Race meeting—Safety precautions for spectators—Duty of organisers to spectators—Motor racing—Jalopy racing in field—Failure to take reasonable safety precautions—Notice at entrance to field excluding liability for accidents to spectators 'howsoever caused'—Notice addressed to 'the public'—Deceased a competitor in race—Deceased not a member of club organising meeting—Deceased signing on in morning at field as competitor in races to be held in afternoon—Notice not in position at entrance to field in morning—Exclusion of liability not drawn to deceased's attention when signing on—Deceased entering field in afternoon when notice in position—Deceased fatally injured while watching race in which not taking part—Injuries caused by inadequacy of safety ropes—Whether deceased's licence to enter field variable summarily on terms stated in notice at entrance to field—Whether notice effective to exclude organisers' liability for negligence—Occupiers' Liability Act 1957, s 2(1). **White v Blackmore** [1972] **3** 158, CA.
  Warning to visitor—
   Sufficiency—Chimney sweep killed by carbon monoxide fumes while sealing up sweep-hole—Warnings by occupier disregarded—Special risks ordinarily incident to calling—Whether occupier liable—Occupiers' Liability Act 1957, s 2(2),(3)(b),(4)(a). **Roles v Nathan** [1963] **2** 908, CA.
 Financial loss. *See* Duty to invitee—Goods of invitee on premises, *above*.
 Fire—
  Escape to adjoining premises—
   Negligence. *See* **Negligence** (Fire—Escape to adjoining premises).
  Fireman—
   Duty of care owed to fireman—Nature of duty—Fireman attending premises to put out fire—Fire caused by occupier's negligence—Fire causing explosion injuring fireman—Likelihood of explosion not unusual in type of fire involved—Whether occupier owing common duty of care to fireman—Whether duty of care to fireman limited to protection from special or exceptional risks—Occupiers' Liability Act 1957, s 2. **Salmon v Seafarer Restaurants Ltd (British Gas Corp, third party)** [1983] **3** 729, QBD.
 Goods—
  Liability for goods of invitee. *See* Duty to invitee—Goods of invitee on premises, *above*.
 Independent contractor—
  Duty to. *See* Duty to independent contractor, *above*.
  Liability for. *See* Liability for independent contractor, *below*.
 Invitee or licensee—
  Common interest in visit—
   Hospital—Relative visiting sick patient in state hospital—Visit a matter of material common interest to plaintiff and hospital authority. **Slade v Battersea and Putney Group Hospital Management Committee** [1955] **1** 429, QBD.
  Entry on to premises on own business—
   Canvasser—Visit to defendant's premises in order to do business with him—Defendant unwilling to do business—Canvasser injured on premises—Whether an invitee or licensee. **Dunster v Abbott** [1953] **2** 1572, CA.
  Forecourt of shop adjoining highway—
   Forecourt not fenced off—Foot passenger stepping from highway on to forecourt—Injured because of defective paving of forecourt to shop—Forecourt in occupation of landlord of shop—Whether foot passenger an invitee or licensee on forecourt. **Jacobs v London CC** [1950] **1** 737, HL.
  Material interest of occupier in visit—
   Neighbour entering premises to attend invalid—Neighbour entering occupier's house at request of occupier to tend occupier's bedridden wife—Fall and injury to leg—Whether neighbour an invitee. **Jennings v Cole** [1949] **2** 191, KBD.
  Permission to use tools of occupier—
   Plaintiff an invitee on premises—Plaintiff servant of contractors working on premises—Permission by occupier to plaintiff to use ladder—Choice by servant of defective ladder—Whether occupier liable to plaintiff as invitee for defect on ladder. **Johnson v Croggon & Co Ltd** [1954] **1** 121, QBD.
  Railway station—
   Passenger—Part of station used for unloading mail bags—Passenger going on to that part—Nothing to show passengers should not go on that part—Passenger slipping on patch of oil—Whether passenger an invitee. **Blackman v Railway Executive** [1953] **2** 323, CA.
  Wife of tenant—
   Business interest in common with landlord—Tenant of flat in block of flats—Wife keeping house for tenant—Defect in surface of courtyard to flats—Wife of tenant injured—Whether wife having sufficient business interest in common with landlord to make her an invitee—Whether landlord liable. **Anderson v Guinness Trust** [1949] **1** 530, KBD.
 Joint occupation. *See* Occupation—Occupation through licensee—Joint occupation, *below*.

OCCUPIER'S LIABILITY (cont)—
  Landlord—
    Duty of care to visitors—
      Lift in block of flats—Lift in occupation of landlord—Duty to take care that lift safe—Duty to invitees and licensees—Employment competent engineers to maintain lift—Defective repair carried out by engineers—Visitor in lift injured—Whether landlord liable. **Haseldine v Daw & Son Ltd** [1941] **3** 156, CA.
  Liability for independent contractor—
    Danger or trap—
      Lift—Door left open—Occupier having contracted with independent contractor to keep lift in good working order—Plaintiff stepping through open lift door and falling down shaft—Liability of occupier. **Morgan v Girls' Friendly Society (Inc Central Council of)** [1936] **1** 404, KBD.
      Nut and bolt weighing machine protruding above path level in railway station—Machine maintained by competent contractors—Whether occupiers liable. **Bloomstein v Railway Executive** [1952] **2** 418, QBD.
    Duty to invitee—
      Performance entrusted to independent contractor—Liability for negligence of independent contractor—Stevedore's labourer injured by shore while unloading cargo from ship—Shore fixed by independent contractor—Whether an excuse that performance of duty of care entrusted to independent contractor. **Thomson v Cremin** [1953] **2** 1185, HL.
    Supervision of contractor—
      Construction works—Valuable property of third party brought on to site—Duty to employ supervising architect—Building owner—Installation of equipment by separate specialist contractor—Firm of architects engaged by architect-employee of company associated with building owner—Specialist contractor's equipment damaged by flood water during erection of building—Building owner relying on building contractors—Liability of building owner—Occupiers' Liability Act 1957, ss 1, 2(4)(b). **AMF International Ltd v Magnet Bowling Ltd** [1968] **2** 789, QBD.
    Works of construction, maintenance or repair—
      Incidental works—Protection against flooding—Construction works—Valuable property of third party brought on to site—Liability of site to flooding—Work necessary to protect third party's property from flooding—Whether works of 'construction, maintenance or repair'—Occupiers' Liability Act 1957, s 2(4)(b). **AMF International Ltd v Magnet Bowling Ltd** [1968] **2** 789, QBD.
  Licensee—
    Duty to. *See* Duty to licensee, *above.*
    Invitee or licensee. *See* Invitee or licensee, *above.*
    Occupation through. *See* Occupation—Occupation through licensee, *below.*
  Negligence—
    Delegation of occupier's duties—
      Railway and transport executives—Railway station—Passenger on premises of different executive—Delegation of liabilities by British Transport Commission—Transport Act 1947, s 5(9)(a). **Bloomstein v Railway Executive** [1952] **2** 418, QBD.
    Factory flooded in exceptional storm—
      Water mixed with oil—Floor rendered dangerously slippery—No want of care by occupiers—Accident through workman slipping—Liability of occupiers. **Latimer v AEC Ltd** [1953] **2** 449, HL.
  Occupation—
    Local authority—
      House unoccupied in consequence of compulsory purchase order—Notice of entry served on owner and tenant of house following compulsory purchase order—Notice stating local authority would enter and take possession of house on expiry of 14 days—House subsequently vacated by tenant and left unoccupied—House not secured or bricked up by local authority—House made ruinous in consequence of activities of vandals—Child trespasser entering house—Child injured in consequence of ruinous condition—Whether local authority occupiers—Whether liable to child for breach of duty. **Harris v Birkenhead Corp** [1976] **1** 341, CA.
    Occupation through licensee—
      Joint occupation—Proprietors of club managed by licensees—Redecoration of club premises—Common duty of care towards servant of decorators—Plaster work on ceiling of restaurant—Bare electric wiring—Electricity switched on—Accident to plasterer—Whether proprietors in occupation of premises—Occupiers' Liability Act 1957, s 1. **Fisher v CHT Ltd** [1966] **1** 88, CA.
    Occupation through servant—
      Inn managed by licensee employed by brewers—Manager having control of part of inn where business of sale of intoxicants not carried on—Manager's wife allowed to run own boarding-house business upstairs in private part of the inn—Second staircase (back stairs) to first floor not used by public or usually by lodgers—Handrail of back staircase from first floor ended above bottom of stairs—Back staircase unlit, but absence of light not due to negligence of manager—Lodger in private part of inn fell down stairs of back staircase—Whether brewers liable as 'occupiers'—Occupiers' Liability Act 1957, s 1(2). **Wheat v E Lacon & Co Ltd** [1966] **1** 582, HL.
    Scaffolding—
      Contractor on building site—Scaffolding and staging for making working platforms provided by contractors—Staging positioned by sub-contractors—Accident to servant of sub-contractors caused by unstable working platform—Whether contractors in occupation or having control of working platform so as to be under common duty of care—Occupiers' Liability Act 1957, s 1(3). **Kearney v Eric Waller Ltd** [1965] **3** 352, QBD.
  Practice—
    Option to claim in contract or tort for breach of duty. *See* Common duty of care—Liability in contract—Option to claim in contract or tort for breach of duty, *above.*
  Property adjoining highway—
    Forecourt indistinguishable from pavement—
      Duty to repair forecourt—Liability to passer-by. **Owens v Scott & Sons (Bakers) Ltd, and Wastall** [1939] **3** 663, Assizes.
  Railway—
    Duty to fence railway line. *See* **Negligence** (Duty to take care—Railway—Duty to fence railway line).

OCCUPIER'S LIABILITY (cont)—
    Railway (cont)—
        Duty to passengers and invitees—
            Safety of station platform—Negligence. *See* **Negligence** (Railway—Duty to passengers and invitees—Safety of station platform).
    Right of way—
        Liability of owner of land over which right of way runs—
            Liability to persons using right of way—Plaintiff injured when tripping in hole in right of way—Whether owner of land over which right of way liable for negligent nonfeasance towards members of public—Whether person exercising public right of way a licensee or invitee of occupier of soil over which right of way—Whether occupier's liability duty owed to person exercising public right of way—Occupiers' Liability Act 1957, s 2. **McGeown v Northern Ireland Housing Executive** [1994] **3** 53, HL.
    Standard of care—
        Duty to invitee. *See* Duty to invitee—Standard of care, *above*.
    Trespasser—
        Child trespasser. *See* Child trespasser, *above*.
        Duty of care—
            Whether test of existence of duty of care to be determined having regard to circumstances prevailing at time of accident—Occupiers' Liability Act 1984, s 1(3)(b). **Donoghue v Folkestone Properties Ltd** [2003] **3** 1101, CA.
        Duty of occupier limited to avoidance of wilful or reckless acts—
            Foreseeability test not relevant criterion—Degree of knowledge sufficient to impose duty—Trespasser injured by train on private level crossing—Fact that occupier knew there was a likelihood of trespassers on crossing at some time or another not sufficient to impose duty. **Railways Comr v Quinlan** [1964] **1** 897, PC.
        Trespasser injured while engaged in criminal activities—
            Plaintiff attempting to break into defendant's premises—Defendant firing shotgun and wounding plaintiff—Action for damages for personal injury—Whether defendant negligent—Whether plaintiff barred from recovering damages by maxim ex turpi causa non oritur actio—Occupiers' Liability Act 1984, s 1. **Revill v Newbery** [1996] **1** 291, CA.
    Visitor—
        Permission to be on premises—
            Involuntary act causing scope of permission to be exceeded—Railway—Employee of company owning rail track—Licence from proprietors of adjoining track to use walkway between tracks—Warning of danger from train on adjoining track causing employee to encroach on to adjoining track—Involuntary act—Licence not extending to adjoining track—Whether proprietors of adjoining track still under duty to employee as licensee. **Braithwaite v South Durham Steel Co Ltd** [1958] **3** 161, Assizes.
            Right of way—Defendant owning and occupying land over which right of way granted—Milkman using right of way to deliver milk to third party having right of access over right of way—Milkman injured when falling through defective manhole in right of way—Whether milkman an invitee or licensee or would be treated as such at common law—Whether milkman a visitor of owner of land over which right of way granted—Whether defendant owing duty of care to milkman—Occupiers' Liability Act 1957, s 1(2). **Holden v White** [1982] **2** 328, CA.
            Time limit—Effect of expiry of time limit—Visitor remaining on premises after expiry of time limit—Duty of occupier to make clear to visitor that permission subject to time limit—Public house—Owners permitting customer to be on premises for party—Party continuing after closing time—Whether customer a visitor or trespasser on premises after closing time. **Stone v Taffe** [1974] **3** 1016, CA.
        Warning to visitor. *See* Exclusion of liability—Warning to visitor, *above*.
        Works on premises. *See* Duty to invitee—Works on premises, *above*.

OFF-HIRE CLAUSE
    See **Shipping** (Charterparty—Off-hire clause).

OFF-LICENCE
    Grant. *See* **Licensing** (Licence—Grant—Off-licence).
    Renewal. *See* **Licensing** (Licence—Renewal—Off-licence).

OFFENCES TAKEN INTO CONSIDERATION
    Criminal proceedings. *See* **Criminal law** (Trial—Other offences taken into consideration).

OFFENDERS
    Dangerous—
        Custodial sentence. *See* **Sentence** (Custodial sentence—Dangerous offenders).

OFFENSIVE TRADES
    See **Public health** (Offensive trades).

OFFENSIVE WEAPON
    Generally. *See* **Criminal law** (Offensive weapons).
    Possession in public place—
        Sentence. *See* **Sentence** (Possession of an offensive weapon in a public place).
    Smuggling—
        Armed with offensive weapon. *See* **Customs and excise** (Armed with offensive weapon).

OFFER
    Contract. *See* **Contract** (Offer and acceptance).
    Invitation to treat distinguished. *See* **Animal** (Protection—Bird—Restriction on sale or offer for sale of live wild bird—'Offer for sale').
    Offer to settle. *See* **Practice** (Offer to settle).

OFFER (cont)—
    Sale of dangerous weapon. *See* **Criminal law** (Dangerous weapons—Manufacture, sale or hire—Offer to
    sell or hire).

OFFER OF AMENDS
    Defamation cases—
        Assessment of damages. *See* **Libel and slander** (Damages—Assessment—Offer of amends).
        Damages. *See* **Libel and slander** (Damages—Offer to make amends).
        Generally. *See* **Libel and slander** (Offer of amends).

OFFER TO SETTLE
    CPR Pt 36—
        Costs. *See* **Costs** (Offers to settle—CPR Pt 36 offer).
        Effect of apparent time limit for acceptance—
            Principles of construction for Pt 36 offers. **C v D** [2012] **1** 302, CA.

OFFICEHOLDER
    Costs—
        Assessment. *See* **Costs** (Assessment—Detailed assessment—Costs of officeholder).

OFFICES, SHOPS AND RAILWAY PREMISES
    Fire certificate. *See* **Fire** (Certificate).
    Safety of employees—
        Breach of statutory duty. *See* **Employment** (Duty of master—Offices, shops and railway premises).

OFFICIAL CUSTODIAN FOR CHARITIES
    Party—
        Charity proceedings. *See* **Charity** (Proceedings—Parties—Official Custodian for Charities).

OFFICIAL RECEIVER
    Company—
        Winding up—
            Petition. *See* **Company** (Compulsory winding up—Petition by Official Receiver).

OFFICIAL REFEREE
    Appeal—
        Generally. *See* **Appeal** (Official referee).
        Leave to appeal. *See* **Court of Appeal** (Leave to appeal—Requirement of leave—Official referee).
    Discretion—
        Exercise of—
            Review. *See* **Court of Appeal** (Discretion of Official Referee—Review of exercise of discretion).
    Note—
        Court of Appeal—
            Official Referee's note used in absence of agreed note taken on behalf of parties. *See* **Court of
                Appeal** (Judge's note—Substitution of note taken by solicitors—Appeal from official referee).
    Reference to—
        Procedure. *See* **Practice** (Reference to referee).
        Summary proceedings in relation to matrimonial property. *See* **Husband and wife** (Property—
        Summary proceedings—Reference to official referee).
    Trial before. *See* **Practice** (Reference to referee).

OFFICIAL SECRETS
    Diplomatic privilege. *See* **Constitutional law** (Diplomatic privilege—Inviolable archives and documents of
    diplomatic missions).
    Offences. *See* **Criminal law** (Official secrets).
    Sentence—
        Consecutive sentences—
            Spying—Separate offences. *See* **Sentence** (Consecutive sentences—Series of offences—Separate
            and distinct offences—Spying).

OFFICIAL SOLICITOR
    Costs—
        Generally. *See* **Costs** (Official Solicitor).
        Taxation. *See* **Costs** (Taxation—Solicitor—Official Solicitor).
        Wardship proceedings—
            Taxation. *See* **Costs** (Taxation—Solicitor—Official Solicitor—Guardian ad litem—Wardship
            application).
    Guardian ad litem—
        Adoption proceedings—
            Practice. *See* **Adoption** (Practice—Guardian ad litem—Official Solicitor as guardian ad litem or
            reporting officer).
        Costs. *See* **Costs** (Taxation—Solicitor—Official Solicitor—Guardian ad litem).
        Divorce—
            Infant—Blood test. *See* **Paternity** (Blood test—Divorce—Guardian ad litem—Official Solicitor).
            Insanity. *See* **Divorce** (Insanity—Guardian ad litem—Official Solicitor).
        Wardship proceedings—
            Application by ward to continue proceedings without guardian ad litem. *See* **Ward of court**
            (Practice—Official Solicitor—Official Solicitor appointed as guardian ad litem—Application by
            ward of court to continue proceedings without guardian ad litem).
            Appointment. *See* **Ward of court** (Practice—Appointment of Official Solicitor as guardian ad litem).
            Costs—Taxation. *See* **Costs** (Taxation—Solicitor—Official Solicitor—Guardian ad litem—Wardship
            application).

OFFICIAL SOLICITOR (cont)—
  Guardian ad litem (cont)—
    Wardship proceedings (cont)—
      Criminal injuries compensation claim—Application by Official Solicitor for leave to make claim as guardian ad litem of ward. *See* **Ward of court** (Practice—Criminal injuries compensation claim—Application for leave to claim compensation).
      Institution of proceedings—No duty on Official Solicitor to institute proceedings. **D (a minor) (wardship: sterilisation), Re** [1976] **1** 326, Fam D.
      Seeking to control question of access. *See* **Ward of court** (Care and control—Interim care and control—Access—Official Solicitor as guardian ad litem, seeking control of question of access by parents).
  Mental patient—
    Legal proceedings involving patient—
      Power to appeal to Court of Appeal. *See* **Mental health** (Patient—Legal proceedings involving patient—Appeal—Official Solicitor).
  Powers and duties—
    Contempt of court—
      Authority to apply to Court of Appeal by way of appeal against committal order—Person committed not moving court himself—Industrial Court making committal orders against dockers—Appeal to Court of Appeal by Official Solicitor on ground that insufficient evidence to support committals. **Churchman v Joint Shop Stewards' Committee of the Workers of the Port of London** [1972] **3** 603, CA.
  Report—
    Disclosure—
      Wardship proceedings. *See* **Ward of court** (Practice—Official Solicitor—Official Solicitor' report—Disclosure).
  Representation of deceased defendant—
    Notice of change of solicitors by Official Solicitor—
      Substitution of Official Solicitor for solicitor on record. **Watts v Official Solicitor** [1936] **1** 249, CA.

OIL
  Bachaquero Crude—
    Contamination by paraffin. *See* **Shipping** (Freight—Claim for freight—Freight payable on delivery—Cargo contaminated on delivery—Shipment of Bachaquero Crude Oil).
  Discharge of oil—
    Damage to adjoining land. *See* **Trespass to land** (Oil—Discharge of oil into public navigable waters—Damage to adjoining land).
  Extraction by pipeline—
    Access rights. *See* **Mine** (Minerals—Access rights).
  Hydrocarbon oil—
    Duty on. *See* **Customs and excise** (Hydrocarbon oils).
  Navigable waters, in—
    Damage to adjoining land. *See* **Trespass to land** (Oil—Discharge of oil into public navigable waters—Damage to adjoining land).
    Generally. *See* **Shipping** (Oil in navigable waters).
  Nuisance—
    Discharge of oil to lighten vessel stranded in river—
      Damage to adjoining foreshore—Need to prove negligence. *See* **Nuisance** (Negligence—Need to prove—Pollution of shore—Ship—Discharge of oil to lighten vessel stranded in estuary).
    Public nuisance—
      Discharge of oil to lighten vessel stranded in estuary—Damage to adjoining foreshore. *See* **Nuisance** (Public nuisance—Pollution of shore—Discharge of oil to lighten vessel stranded in estuary).

OIL REFINERY
  Operation—
    Nuisance—
      Defence—Statutory authority. *See* **Nuisance** (Defence—Statutory authority—Action for damages for nuisance arising out of construction and operation of oil refinery).

OLD PEOPLE
  Residential care home—
    Local authority. *See* **Local authority** (Residential care home—Elderly persons).

OMBUDSMAN
  Financial services—
    Regulation of financial services. *See* **Financial services** (Financial Services Authority (FSA)—Regulation of financial services—Ombudsman scheme).
  Local government—
    Maladministration—
      Complaint to local ombudsman. *See* **Local government** (Maladministration—Complaint to local commissioner).
  Pensions—
    Costs of appeal—
      Liability of ombudsman for costs of successful appeal against his determination. *See* **Costs** (Order for costs—Costs of appeal—Pensions Ombudsman).
    Jurisdiction—
      Maladministration of pension scheme. *See* **Pension** (Pension scheme—Maladministration of pension scheme—Jurisdiction of Pensions Ombudsman).

OMNIBUS
    Driver—
        Duty of care—
            Obstruction above level of road. *See* **Negligence** (Duty to take care—Driver of motor vehicle—Obstruction above level of road—Omnibus).
    Free pass—
        Exclusion of liability of carriers for negligence. *See* **Carriers** (Negligence—Exclusion of liability—Passengers—Free pass).
    Passenger—
        Injury alighting from omnibus. *See* **Negligence** (Vehicles—Passenger injured while alighting from omnibus).
    Service—
        London—
            Alteration of service. *See* **London Transport Executive** (Duty to consult with local authorities before altering bus services).
    Stage carriage. *See* **Road traffic** (Stage carriage).

ON-LICENCE
    Disqualification from holding—
        Conviction of offence. *See* **Licensing** (On-licence—Disqualification—Conviction of offence).
    Intoxicating liquor—
        Grant subject to condition. *See* **Licensing** (Licence—On-licence subject to condition).

ONE-THIRD RULE
    Maintenance—
        Husband and wife. *See* **Husband and wife** (Maintenance—Amount—One-third rule).

ONEROUS PROPERTY
    Disclaimer—
        Bankruptcy. *See* **Bankruptcy** (Disclaimer of onerous property).
        Company—
            Voluntary winding up. *See* **Company** (Voluntary winding up—Disclaimer of onerous property).

ONUS OF PROOF
    Adultery—
        Divorce. *See* **Divorce** (Adultery—Proof—Onus and standard of proof).
    Bailment—
        Liability of bailee—
            Gratuitous bailment. *See* **Bailment** (Gratuitous bailment—Liability of bailee—Onus of proof).
    Generally. *See* **Burden of proof**.
    Proceedings related to customs or excise—
        Improper importation of goods—
            Forfeiture of goods. *See* **Customs and excise** (Forfeiture—Imported goods—Goods on which duty chargeable and unpaid—Onus of proof).

OPEN COURT
    Bankruptcy petition—
        Hearing—
            Exclusion of public. *See* **Bankruptcy** (Petition—Hearing—Exclusion of public).
    Criminal proceedings. *See* **Criminal law** (Trial—Open court).
    Divorce proceedings—
        Hearing—
            Chambers or open court. *See* **Divorce** (Practice—Hearing—Chambers or open court).

OPEN SPACE
    Commons. *See* **Commons**.
    Facilities for public recreation. *See* **Commons** (Right of common—Facilities for public recreation).
    Incumbent—
        Power to convey land for use as open space. *See* **Ecclesiastical law** (Incumbent—Freehold—Power to convey land for statutory purpose—Open space).
    Land scheduled as open space—
        Compensation—
            Town and country planning. *See* **Town and country planning** (Compensation—Land scheduled as open space).
    Local authority's powers. *See* **Local authority** (Open space).

OPERATION
    Surgical operation—
        Negligence of surgeon. *See* **Negligence** (Professional person—Surgeon—Operation).
        Trespass to the person. *See* **Medical practitioner** (Trespass to the person—Consent to operation).

OPERATOR'S LICENCE
    Goods vehicle. *See* **Road traffic** (Goods vehicle—Operator's licence).

OPHTHALMIC OPTICIAN
Erasure of name from register—
Infamous conduct in a professional respect—
'Profession'—'Infamous'—Canvassing by means of a letter—Letters sent to official of students' union at two colleges—Letters in breach of a previous undertaking to disciplinary committee not to advertise for clients—Letters criticising other members of profession and making careless statement as to price of contact lenses—Prominent advertisements placed in students' magazine and in professional magazine—Whether advertisements 'dignified and restrained'—Opticians Act 1958, s 11(1)(b)(3)—General Optical Council (Rules on Publicity) Order of Council 1981, rr 4, 5. **Le Scroog v General Optical Council** [1982] **3** 257, PC.
Ophthalmic services. See **National Health Service** (Ophthalmic services—Ophthalmic optician).

OPPRESSION
Company matters—
Oppression of minority. See **Company** (Oppression).
Statements obtained by oppression—
Admissibility in criminal proceedings—
Brunei. See **Brunei** (Criminal evidence—Admissions and confessions—Oppression).
Generally. See **Criminal evidence** (Admissions and confessions—Answers and statements to police—Oppression).
Subpoena ad testificandum—
Discretion to refuse issue. See **Practice** (Subpoena ad testificandum—Issue—Discretion to refuse issue—Oppression).

OPTICIAN
Ophthalmic optician. See **Ophthalmic optician**.

OPTION
Assignment—
Equitable assignment—
Assignee's right to exercise option—Absence of notice to grantor of assignment of option—Contract conferring option to extend period of contract—Rights of grantee under contract assignable—Grantee assigning rights under contract—No notice of assignment given to grantor of option—Whether assignee entitled to exercise option in own name so as to bind grantor. **Warner Bros Records Inc v Rollgreen Ltd** [1975] **2** 105, CA.
Lease—
Tenant's option conferred by lease. See Option to purchase—Tenant's option conferred by lease—Assignment of lease, below.
Bequest—
Option to purchase shares. See **Administration of estates** (Order of application of assets—Shares—Option to purchase).
Capital gains tax—
Contingent liability of grantor to refund consideration for grant. See **Capital gains tax** (Computation of chargeable gains—Contingent liabilities—Option).
Creditor's option to take land in place of money—
Option to take one acre of land to be selected by creditor—Measure of damages in default. **Thomas v Kensington** [1942] **2** 263, KBD.
Equitable assignment. See Assignment—Equitable assignment, above.
Exercise—
Notice—
Service of notice in writing—Service by post. See **Contract** (Offer and acceptance—Acceptance—Acceptance by post—Mode of acceptance prescribed—Notice in writing to offeror—Option).
Hire-purchase agreement—
Option to terminate—
Exercise of option. See **Hire-purchase** (Termination of agreement—Exercise of option).
Income tax—
Exercise of option to purchase shares—
Appropriate year of assessment. See **Income tax** (Assessment—Appropriate year—Option to purchase shares).
Year of assessment—
Option granted to employee to purchase shares. See **Income tax** (Emoluments from office or employment—Year of assessment—Option to purchase shares).
Lease—
Determination. See **Landlord and tenant** (Lease—Option to determine).
Option to purchase reversion—
Option separately assigned to mortgagee—Whether mortgagor entitled to conveyance of reversion on redemption. See **Mortgage** (Redemption—Lease with option to purchase freehold reversion).
Registered land—Overriding interest. See **Land registration** (Overriding interest—Rights of person in actual occupation of land—Option in lease for lessee to purchase freehold reversion).
Sale of leasehold interest. See **Sale of land** (Leasehold interest—Option to purchase reversion).
Tenant's option conferred by lease. See Option to purchase—Tenant's option conferred by lease, below.
Renewal—
Generally. See **Landlord and tenant** (Lease—Option to renew).
Perpetual right of renewal. See **Landlord and tenant** (Renewal of lease—Perpetual right of renewal).
Registration as estate contract. See **Land charge** (Estate contract—Option to renew lease).
Settled land. See **Settlement** (Purchaser dealing in good faith with tenant for life—Protection of purchaser—Agreement for lease with option to renew).
Mortgaged property—
Grant of option by mortgagee. See **Mortgage** (Sale—Option).

OPTION (cont)—
  Option to purchase—
    Breach of option contract—
      Damages—Measure—Repudiation of option by vendor—Intention of purchaser to develop property—Vendor having knowledge of purchaser's intention—Damages for loss of profits. **Cottrill v Steyning and Littlehampton Building Society** [1966] **2** 295, QBD.
    Condition in will—
      Option to purchase freehold property—Conditional bequest. *See* **Will** (Condition—Conditional bequest—Option to purchase freehold property).
    Covenant to grant purchaser first option to purchase additional land—
      Option at a figure to be agreed upon—No machinery to settle figure—Whether option void for uncertainty—Method by which figure to be determined. **Smith v Morgan** [1971] **2** 1500, Ch D.
    Duration—
      Clause conferring option and also right of pre-emption—Whether option continued after failure to exercise right of pre-emption. **Du Sautoy v Symes** [1967] **1** 25, Ch D.
      Three years certain—Provision for notice—Whether determinable at the expiration of three years. **Downes and Lobbs' Contract, Re** [1937] **4** 324, Ch D.
    Enforcement—
      Option to purchase leasehold reversion expectant on term of years granted by tenancy agreement—Option contained in deed of licence to assign term and exercisable only by assignee—Assignee not party to deed—Whether 'agreement respecting land'—'Interest in land'—Law of Property Act 1925, s 56(1). **Stromdale & Ball Ltd v Burden** [1952] **1** 59, Ch D.
    Exercise of option—
      Deposit—Provision for payment of deposit to purchaser on exercising option—Purchaser exercising option but inadvertently failing to pay deposit—Whether vendor entitled to cancel option agreement—Whether vendor required to give purchaser opportunity to pay deposit before cancelling agreement. **Millichamp v Jones** [1983] **1** 267, Ch D.
      Shipbuilding contract—Commitment fee—Commitment fee to be paid simultaneously with declaration of option—Claimant declaring option but not paying commitment fee—Whether valid exercise of option. **Haugland Tankers AS v RMK Marine Gemi Yapim Sanayii ve Deniz Tasimaciligi Isletmesi AS** [2005] **1 Comm** 679, QBD.
    Farm—
      Option granted to colliery concern—Acquisition of assets of colliery concern by National Coal Board—Purported exercise of option by National Coal Board—Coal Industry Nationalisation Act 1946, s 5(1), (2), (7), Sch I, Part I, Part II, paras 9, 14, Sch II. **National Coal Board v Hornby** [1949] **2** 615, Ch D.
    Implied term—
      Implied term that grantor would retain subject-matter of option during option period—Option not exercisable until after grantor's death—Grantee accepting lease from grantor of part of option land at high rent because lease granted him option to purchase whole of land at favourable price after grantor's death—Right of pre-emption of option land granted prior to grant of option—Right of pre-emption exercised before grantor's death—Whether term to be implied in option that grantor would not sell land during option period. **Pritchard v Briggs** [1980] **1** 294, CA.
    Land—
      Formation of contract—Electronic communication. *See* **Contract** (Signature—Real property—Option to purchase).
      Formation of contract—Part performance. *See* **Contract** (Part performance—Contract concerning land—Option to purchase).
    Land charge—
      Registration as estate contract—Exercise of option—No registration of further estate contract after exercise of option—Sale of land by grantor to third party—Whether further registration of contract of sale necessary to protect option—Land Charges Act 1972, s 2(4). **Armstrong & Holmes Ltd v Holmes** [1994] **1** 826, Ch D.
      Registration as estate contract—Failure to register. *See* **Land charge** (Failure to register—Estate contract—Contract void against purchaser of legal estate for money or money's worth).
      Registration as estate contract—Official certificate of search obtained by subsequent purchaser of land showing no entry in respect of option—Application for search containing insufficiently clear description of land—Whether certificate conclusive in favour of purchaser—Whether option-holder entitled to specific performance against purchaser—Land Charges Act 1925, s 17(3). **Du Sautoy v Symes** [1967] **1** 25, Ch D.
      Registration as estate contract—Option to purchase, right of pre-emption or other like right. *See* **Land charge** (Estate contract—Option to purchase, right of pre-emption or other like right).
    Notice to exercise option to purchase—
      Whether notice a contract for sale of interest in land. *See* **Sale of land** (Memorandum of contract—Option to purchase—Contract for sale or other disposition of interest in land).
    Realty—
      Will. *See* **Will** (Option—Option to purchase realty).
    Shares—
      Construction of scheme rules—Remedy for unlawful decision under scheme rules. **McCarthy v McCarthy & Stone plc** [2006] **4** 1127, Ch D; [2008] **1** 221, CA.
      Option available to employees of company and its subsidiaries—Whether option lapsing on sale of subsidiary. *See* **Contract** (Condition subsequent—Company—Share option).
      Re-purchase of shares—Conditions—Time limits—Observance—Separate times for election and for payment—Time for payment of essence of contract. **Hare v Nicoll** [1966] **1** 285, CA.
      Stamp duty. *See* **Stamp duty** (Conveyance on sale—Instrument whereby property or estate or interest in property on sale thereof transferred to or vested in purchaser—Transfer of shares).
    Specific performance—
      Option to purchase land. *See* **Specific performance** (Option to purchase land).
    Tenant's option conferred by lease—
      Assignment of lease—Subsequent assignment of option to assignee of lease—Whether option enforceable by assignee. **Griffith v Pelton** [1957] **3** 75, CA.

OPTION (cont)—
Option to purchase (cont)—
    Tenant's option conferred by lease (cont)—
        Implication that vacant possession be given on exercise of option—Proviso that tenant should 'accept without objection the title of the landlord'—Whether reference to title at date of lease or on exercise of option. **Crosby's Contract, Re** [1949] **1** 830, Ch D.
        Nature of option—Assignability—Whether benefit of option prima facie assignable where assigns not mentioned in lease. **Button's Lease, Re** [1963] **3** 708, Ch D.
        New lease—Inclusion in new lease of option to purchase. **Hill v Hill** [1947] **1** 54, CA.
        Notice of exercise of option—Notice to grantor's personal representatives—Whether valid. **Kennewell v Dye** [1949] **1** 881, Ch D.
        Notice of exercise of option—Option conferred by tenancy agreement to purchase 'at any time' at fixed price—Term of tenancy agreement a five year's term—Property becoming subject to Rent Restrictions Acts after date of agreement—Tenant holding over as statutory tenant—Exercise of option while statutory tenant—Validity. **Longmuir v Kew** [1960] **3** 26, Ch D.
        Option price—Option price stated to be full market value of agricultural land or open space suitable for development as golf course—Change in planning guidelines creating possibility of development for housing—Whether option price including hope value. **Multi-Link Leisure Developments Ltd v North Lanarkshire Council** [2011] **1** 175, SC.
        Provision for payment of interest on purchase money on expiration of notice—Lease then determined—Liability of original lessees for rent. **Cockwell v Romford Sanitary Steam Laundry Ltd** [1939] **4** 370, CA.
        Registration as land charge—Option not registered as land charge—Sale of reversion—Rejection by purchaser of purported exercise of option—Liability of lessor—Measure of damages. **Wright v Dean** [1948] **2** 415, Ch D.
        Uncertainty of option—Agreement to agree—Option to purchase at price to be fixed by valuers nominated by parties—Tenant seeking to exercise option—Landlord refusing to appoint valuer—Tenant asking court to order specific performance or to appoint valuer—Whether option uncertain—Whether court should order specific performance—Whether court having power to appoint valuer. **Sudbrook Trading Estate Ltd v Eggleton** [1981] **3** 105, CA; [1982] **3** 1, HL.
    Will—
        Conditional bequest. *See* **Will** (Condition—Conditional bequest—Option to purchase land).
    Personal to donee. *See* **Will** (Option—Option to purchase realty—Business premises).
Pre-emption—
    Creation of interest in land—
        Option to purchase land granted subsequently to grant of right of pre-emption—Right of pre-emption registered as land charge prior to grant and registration of option—Right of pre-emption exercised before option exercised—Grantor of right of pre-emption and option patient under Mental Health Act—Sale of land purportedly pursuant to exercise of right of pre-emption—Authorisation of sale by Court of Protection—Payment of two cheques together amounting to purchase at market value—Right of pre-emption providing for purchase at low price—Whether right of pre-emption taking priority over option—Whether right of pre-emption creating interest in land—Whether sale pursuant to exercise of right of pre-emption genuine sale pursuant to right—Whether order of Court of Protection constituting lawful justification for sale—Law of Property Act 1925, s 204—Mental Health Act 1959, s 116. **Pritchard v Briggs** [1980] **1** 294, CA.
    Implication of prohibition of making gift to defeat right. *See* **Contract** (Implied term—First refusal—Right of pre-emption—Gift of land, the subject of the right of pre-emption, made subsequently by grantor of right).
Purchase—
    Generally. *See* Option to purchase, *above.*
    Option to purchase, right of pre-emption or other like right—
        Registration as estate contract. *See* **Land charge** (Estate contract—Option to purchase, right of pre-emption or other like right).
    Reversion—
        Landlord and tenant. *See* **Landlord and tenant** (Lease—Reversion).
Registration as land charge—
    Option to renew underlease—
        Registered land—Exemption from requirement to register charge when charge capable of being protected by caution under Land Registration Act. *See* **Land charge** (Registration—Registered land—Exemption from requirement to register land charge where charge capable of being protected by caution under Land Registration Act—Option to renew underlease).
Renewal of lease. *See* **Landlord and tenant** (Lease—Option to renew).
Rent review—
    Option to require review—
        Time limits for exercise of option—Failure to comply with time limit. *See* **Landlord and tenant** (Rent—Review—Failure to comply with time limits—Option to require review).
Resulting trust. *See* **Trust and trustee** (Resulting trust—Option).
Reversion—
    Purchase. *See* **Landlord and tenant** (Lease—Reversion).
Sale of land—
    Option to take income of property in lieu of interest on unpaid purchase money. *See* **Sale of land** (Interest on unpaid purchase money—Option to take income of property in lieu).
    Specific performance. *See* **Specific performance** (Option to purchase land).
Shares—
    Option to purchase. *See* Option to purchase—Shares, *above.*
    Stock exchange dealings. *See* **Stock Exchange** (Options).
Specific performance—
    Sale of land. *See* **Specific performance** (Sale of land).
Stamp duty—
    Option to purchase land. *See* **Stamp duty** (Conveyance on sale—Instrument whereby property or estate or interest in property on sale thereof transferred to or vested in purchaser—Option to purchase land).

OPTION (cont)—
  Stamp duty (cont)—
    Option to purchase shares. *See* **Stamp duty** (Conveyance on sale—Instrument whereby property or estate or interest in property on sale thereof transferred to or vested in purchaser—Transfer of shares).
  Tenant's option to purchase freehold reversion—
    Registered land—
      Overriding interest. *See* **Land registration** (Overriding interest—Rights of person in actual occupation of land—Option in lease for lessee to purchase freehold reversion).
  Trust. *See* **Trust and trustee** (Resulting trust—Option).
  Will—
    Creation of option by testamentary gift—
      Option to purchase realty at reasonable valuation. *See* **Will** (Option—Option to purchase realty—Option to purchase at reasonable valuation).
    Generally. *See* **Will** (Option).
    Option or right of pre-emption conferred by will. *See* **Will** (Option).
    Purchase of freehold property—
      Conditional bequest. *See* **Will** (Condition—Conditional bequest—Option to purchase freehold property).

ORAL CONTRACT
  Sale of land—
    Memorandum—
      Oral contract to enter into formal written contract for sale of land. *See* **Sale of land** (Memorandum of contract—Contract for disposition of land—Oral contract for disposition of land).

ORAL DECISION
  Industrial tribunal—
    Res judicata. *See* **Employment tribunal** (Jurisdiction—Res judicata—Oral decision).
  Written reasons for decision—
    Duty of court regarding written reasons. *See* **Criminal law** (Appeal—Oral decision—Written reasons for decision stated to be given later).

ORAL DECLARATION
  Will—
    Soldier's or mariner's privileged will—
      Testamentary intention. *See* **Will** (Soldier's or mariner's privileged will—Oral declaration—Testamentary intention).

ORAL PROMISE
  Incorporation in contract. *See* **Contract** (Incorporation of terms—Express oral term).

ORAL SNUFF
  Safety regulations banning supply of—
    Duty to consult affected parties before making regulations. *See* **Consumer protection** (Safety regulations—Duty to consult affected parties before making regulations—Prohibition on supply of product—Oral snuff).

ORDER
  Amendment—
    Accidental slip or omission. *See* **Judgment** (Order—Correction—Accidental slip or omission).
    Court of Appeal—
      Criminal appeal. *See* **Criminal law** (Court of Appeal—Order of court—Alteration).
    Crown Court. *See* **Crown Court** (Order—Amendment).
  Bankruptcy—
    Bankruptcy restrictions order. *See* **Bankruptcy** (Bankruptcy restrictions order).
  Consent order—
    Generally. *See* **Practice** (Consent order).
  Copy—
    Postal despatch—
      Crown Office and Associate's Department. *See* **Practice** (Order—Postal despatch of copy order—Crown Office and Associates' Department).
      Queen's Bench Divisional Court. *See* **Divisional Court** (Queen's Bench Division—Queen's Bench Divisional Court orders—Postal despatch of copy orders).
  Correction—
    Accidental slip or omission. *See* **Judgment** (Order—Correction—Accidental slip or omission).
  Costs—
    Criminal proceedings. *See* **Criminal law** (Costs—Order to pay).
    Generally. *See* **Costs** (Order for costs).
  County court—
    Committal order—
      Contempt of court. *See* **Contempt of court** (Committal—Order—County court).
    Generally. *See* **County court** (Judgment or order).
    Reference of proceedings to arbitration—
      Terms of order. *See* **County court** (Arbitration—Reference of proceedings to arbitration—Terms of order).
  Court of unlimited jurisdiction. *See* **Court** (Order—Court of unlimited jurisdiction).
  Cross-examination of deponent—
    Chancery Division. *See* **Practice** (Chancery Division—Affidavit—Cross-examination of deponent—Order for cross-examination).
  Crown Court. *See* **Crown Court** (Order).
  Disclosure—
    Generally. *See* **Disclosure and inspection of documents** (Order for disclosure).

ORDER (cont)—
   Disclosure (cont)—
      Order for production of documents for inspection. *See* **Disclosure and inspection of documents** (Production of documents—Order for production for inspection).
   Drawing-up. *See* **Practice** (Order—Drawing-up).
   Early trial. *See* **Practice** (Trial—Order for early trial).
   Family proceedings—
      Generally. *See* **Family proceedings** (Orders in family proceedings).
   Foreign order. *See* **Conflict of laws** (Foreign order).
   Judgment. *See* **Judgment**.
   Practice. *See* **Practice** (Order).
   Restoration of company to register, for. *See* **Company** (Restoration to register).
   Suspension of court order—
      Orders in Council, relating to validity of. *See* **Terrorism** (Sanctions—Freezing of funds and economic resources—United Nations Resolutions requiring freezing of funds and economic resources of terrorists).
   'Unless' orders and other peremptory orders. *See* **Practice** (Order—'Unless' orders and other peremptory orders).

ORDER IN COUNCIL
   See **Statutory instrument**.

ORGAN
   Reconstruction of church organ—
      Faculty. *See* **Ecclesiastical law** (Faculty—Reconstruction of church organ).

ORGANIC DISEASE
   Aggravation thereof—
      War injury—
         Compensation. *See* **War injury** (Compensation—Physical injury—Organic disease and aggravation thereof).

ORGANISATION OF WORKERS
   See **Industrial relations** (Organisation of workers).

ORIGINATING APPLICATION
   Industrial tribunal. *See* **Employment tribunal** (Procedure—Originating application).

ORIGINATING MOTION
   Third party proceedings—
      Whether proceedings begun by originating motion can be treated as third party proceedings. *See* **Practice** (Third party proceedings—Originating motion).

ORIGINATING SUMMONS
   Adjournment—
      Adjournment into court or chambers for hearing with witnesses—
         Certificate of length of hearing. **Practice Direction** [1963] **1** 766, Ch D.
      Adjournment to judge—
         Chancery Division—Chambers proceedings. *See* **Practice** (Chambers proceedings—Adjournment to judge—Originating summons).
   Adoption proceedings—
      Removal of proceedings from county court to High Court. *See* **Adoption** (Practice—Removal of proceedings from county court to High Court—Application to be made by originating summons).
   Amendment—
      New questions—
         Order made on questions originally made—Exhaustion of summons—Whether new summons required. **Pattman's Will Trusts, Re** [1965] **2** 191, Ch D.
      Parties—
         Substituting different party as respondent to originating summons—Time for making application expired before amendment—Whether misnomer—Whether amendment allowed—Landlord and Tenant Act 1954, s 29(3)—RSC, Ord 53D, r 6(3), Ord 70, r 1. **Holmes Road, Kentish Town, Re Nos 55 & 57** [1958] **2** 311, Ch D.
   Application to make minor ward of court—
      Contents of summons. *See* **Ward of court** (Application to make minor ward of court—Originating summons—Contents).
   Chancery Division—
      Chambers proceedings—
         Adjournment to judge. *See* **Practice** (Chambers proceedings—Adjournment to judge—Originating summons).
   Continuation of proceedings as if begun by writ—
      Opposition by plaintiff—
         Plaintiff seeking inquiry what common rights, and who commoners, were, and declarations regarding compensation fund—Plaintiff uncertain of his own legal position—Action to proceed as if begun by writ so that issues might be clarified—RSC Ord 28, r 8. **Old Wood Common Compensation Fund, Re** [1967] **2** 1146, Ch D.
      Proceedings involving allegation of fraud—
         Amendment of claim to include alternative allegation of fraud—Whether proceedings must be commenced by writ or whether may continue as though commenced by writ—RSC, Ord 5 r 2, Ord 28, r 8. **Deadman (decd), Re** [1971] **2** 101, Ch D.
         Power to order continuance as if begun by writ—RSC Ord 5, r 2, Ord 28, r 8. **Green Lane (462), Ilford, Re** [1971] **1** 315, Ch D.
   Costs. *See* **Costs** (Originating summons).

ORIGINATING SUMMONS (cont)—

Counsel—
Parties. *See* Parties—Construction summons—Parties with same interest represented by separate counsel, *below.*

Date of hearing—
Requirement of fixed date for hearing—
Adjournment—Hearing 'on a day to be fixed'—New business tenancy—Application to determine interm rent—Procedure to bring summons on for hearing—Landlord and Tenant Act 1954, s 24A—RSC Appendix A, Forms 10, 12. **Practice Direction** [1976] **1** 672, Ch D.

Declaration on originating summons—
Application—
Another procedure afforded by statute—Competence—RSC Ord 54A, r 14A. **Bagettes Ltd v GP Estates Co Ltd** [1956] **1** 729, CA.

Declaration as to powers—
Powers under Settled Land Act 1925, and under private Act—Whether powers extended by public Act—Discretion of court—RSC Ord 54A, r 1A. **Thomas v A-G** [1936] **2** 1325, Ch D.

Duties and procedure of inferior tribunal—
Inappropriate procedure—Tribunal under Finance Act 1960, s 28(5), (7). **Wiseman v Borneman** [1967] **3** 1045, CA.

Jurisdiction—
Discretion—Construction of statute—RSC Ord 54A, rr 1A, 4. **Punton v Ministry of Pensions and National Insurance (No 2)** [1964] **1** 448, CA.

Statutory tribunal's decision final by statute—Decision involving question of interpretation of enactment—Whether High Court has jurisdiction on originating summons to determine whether tribunal's decision on interpretation bad in law—RSC Ord 54A, r 1A—National Insurance Act 1946, s 13(1), s 43(1). **Punton v Ministry of Pensions and National Insurance** [1963] **1** 275, CA.

Town and country planning—
Validity of enforcement notice. *See* **Town and country planning** (Enforcement notice—Validity—Application by originating summons for declaration that notice invalid).

Disclosure in proceedings begun by. *See* **Disclosure and inspection of documents** (Proceedings begun by originating summons).

Dismissal of action commenced by—
Dismissal for want of prosecution. *See* **Practice** (Dismissal of action for want of prosecution—Originating summons).

Family provision—
Affidavit in support. *See* **Family provision** (Application—Form—Affidavit in support).

Fraud—
Proceedings involving allegation of fraud—
Continuance of action begun by originating summons—Whether allegation of fraud fatal to continuance of action—RSC Ord 2, r 1(3), Ord 5, r 2. **Deadman (decd), Re** [1971] **2** 101, Ch D; **Green Lane (462), Ilford, Re** [1971] **1** 315, Ch D.

Guardianship of infant—
Form—
Parties—Condition of making order for maintenance that mother should have applied for custody—Guardianship of Infants Act 1886, s 5—Guardianship of Infants Act 1925, s 3(2)—RSC Ord 55A, rr 2, 3. **Dulles' Settlement Trusts, Re** [1950] **2** 1013, CA.

Guardianship proceedings—
Removal of proceedings from county court to High Court. *See* **Guardianship of minor** (Practice—Removal of proceedings from county court to High Court—Application to be made by originating summons).

Indorsement—
Wardship proceedings—
Removal of ward from jurisdiction without leave—Indorsement on originating summons applying to make child a ward. *See* **Ward of court** (Removal of ward from jurisdiction—Removal without leave of court—Indorsement on originating summons applying to make child a ward).

Issue—
Issue out of Central Office—
Application—Application by post—Practice. *See* **Practice** (Chancery Division—Applications by post or telephone).
Application—Application by post—RSC Ord 7. **Practice Direction** [1971] **1** 510, Central Office.

New practice and procedure. *See* **Practice** (Queen's Bench Division and Chancery Division—New practice and procedure).

Seal—
District registry—Issue of originating summons in district registry other than Manchester or Liverpool—Application by plaintiff to remove cause to Central Office—Summons under Inheritance (Family Provision) Act 1938—Whether proceedings a nullity or irregular only—Supreme Court of Judicature (Consolidation) Act 1925, s 225(1)—RSC Ord 54, r 4B, Ord 70, r 1. **Pritchard (decd), Re** [1963] **1** 873, CA.

Mortgaged property—
Action by mortgagee for possession. *See* **Mortgage** (Action by mortgagee for possession—Originating summons).
Adjournment into open court. *See* **Mortgage** (Possession of mortgaged property—Persons not parties to mortgage claiming to be entitled to possession).

Parties—
Amendment. *See* Amendment—Parties, *above.*
Construction summons—
Parties with same interest represented by separate counsel—Costs—RSC, Ord 65, r 1. **Amory (decd), Re** [1951] **2** 947, Ch D.
Joinder of Crown as party—
Future liability to estate duty—Crown Proceedings Act 1947, ss 13, 23(2)(b)—RSC Ord 1A, r 1, Ord 54A, r 1A, Ord 55, rr 3, 5. **Barnato (decd), Re** [1949] **1** 515, CA.

ORIGINATING SUMMONS (cont)—

Parties (cont)—

Summons by mortgagees for possession—

Mortgagor adjudicated bankrupt—Need to join trustee in bankruptcy. **Martins Bank Ltd v Kavanagh** [1948] **2** 448, Ch D.

Mortgagor not in occupation—Person in occupation under agreement with mortgagor—Need to join occupier as defendant to claim for possession by mortgagees—RSC Ord 55, r 5A. **Leicester Permanent Building Society v Shearley** [1950] **2** 738, Ch D.

Service—

Mortgagee's action for possession. *See* **Mortgage** (Action by mortgagee for possession—Originating summons).

Service impossible—

Diplomatic privilege—Local authority issuing originating summons against Iranian government—Summons unable to be served on Iranian government—Whether court could hear and determine summons in absence of service on Iranian government—State Immunity Act 1978, s 12(1)—RSC Ord 32, r 5(1). **Westminster City Council v Government of the Islamic Republic of Iran** [1986] **3** 284, Ch D.

Substituted service—

Copy of notice placed on door of premises—Newspaper advertisement—RSC Ord 67, r 6. **Temperance Permanent Benefit Building Society v Isles** [1940] **1** 75, CA.

Summary proceedings for possession of land. *See* **Land** (Summary proceedings for possession—Service of originating summons or application).

Waiver—

Originating summons to which appearance not required—Whether service can be waived and application made for dismissal for want of prosecution—RSC Ord 53D, r 5, Ord 54, r 4E—Landlord and Tenant Act 1954, s 64(1)(b). **Pike v Michael Nairn & Co Ltd** [1960] **2** 184, Ch D.

Statutory tribunal—

Jurisdiction of the court. *See* Declaration on originating summons—Jurisdiction—Statutory tribunal's decision final by statute, *above.*

Striking out—

Declaration—

Breach of statutory duty—Public corporation—Corporation entering into agreement with private company—Corporation purporting to act in compliance with its statutory duty—Persons affected by agreement claiming declaration that corporation acting in breach of its statutory duty—No provision in statute establishing corporation for remedy for breach of statutory duty—Application by corporation for summons to be struck out on ground plaintiffs had no locus standi to sue—Whether summons should be struck out. **Booth & Co (International) Ltd v National Enterprise Board** [1978] **3** 624, QBD.

Hypothetical question. **Argosam Finance Co Ltd v Oxby (Inspector of Taxes)** [1964] **3** 561, CA.

Hypothetical question—

Preliminary issue—Whether summons should be treated as preliminary issue—Whether summons should be struck out as abuse of process. **Hampshire CC v Shonleigh Nominees Ltd** [1970] **2** 144, Ch D.

No reasonable cause of action. *See* **Pleading** (Striking out—No reasonable cause of action—Originating summons).

Summary proceedings—

Husband and wife—

Absence of respondent—Powers of registrar. *See* **Husband and wife** (Property—Summary proceedings—Application—Procedure by originating summons—Absence of respondent—Powers of registrar).

Possession of land—

Form of originating summons. *See* **Land** (Summary proceedings for possession—Form of originating summons).

Service of originating summons. *See* **Land** (Summary proceedings for possession—Service of originating summons or application).

Summons to which appearance not required—

Procedure—

Insertion of particulars of hearing by master—RSC Appendix A, Form 10. **Practice Direction** [1974] **2** 566, Ch D.

Title—

Application under Inheritance (Family Provision) Act 1938—

Amendment of 1938 Act by Intestate Estates Act 1952—Correct form of title. **Riglar (decd), Re** [1956] **3** 703, Ch D.

New practice. *See* **Practice** (Queen's Bench Division and Chancery Division—New practice and procedure).

Wardship proceedings—

Application to make minor ward of court. *See* **Ward of court** (Application to make minor ward of court—Originating summons).

Writ—

Continuation of proceedings as if begun by writ. *See* Continuation of proceedings as if begun by writ, *above.*

ORNAMENTS

Church. *See* **Ecclesiastical law** (Ornaments).

ORPHAN

Custody. *See* **Minor** (Custody—Orphan).

OSTENSIBLE AUTHORITY

Agent. *See* **Agent** (Authority—Ostensible authority).

OSTEOPATH
Professional conduct and fitness to practise—
Professional Conduct Committee—
Interim suspension powers—Committee empowered to make interim suspension order if satisfied order necessary to protect members of public—Appeal—Committee finding osteopath guilty of professional incompetence—Committee ordering removal of name from register—Committee making interim suspension order—Osteopath appealing to High Court against interim suspension order—Power of court on appeal—Osteopaths Act 1993, s 24(2), (6)—CPR 52.11(3). **Moody v General Osteopathic Council** [2008] **2** 532, QBD.

OUT-OF-COURT STATEMENT
Admissibility in evidence. *See* **Document** (Admissibility in evidence—Out-of-court statement).

OUTGOINGS
Sale of land—
Apportionment of outgoings. *See* **Sale of land** (Condition—Apportionment of outgoings).
Rights of parties pending completion. *See* **Sale of land** (Outgoings—Rights of parties pending completion).

OUTLINE PLANNING PERMISSION
See **Town and country planning** (Permission for development—Outline permission).

OUTRAGING PUBLIC DECENCY
Common law offence. *See* **Criminal law** (Public decency—Act outraging public decency).
Conspiracy. *See* **Criminal law** (Conspiracy—Outrage to public decency).

OVERALL LENGTH
Heavy motor car. *See* **Road traffic** (Heavy motor car—Overall length).

OVERALL WIDTH
Motor tractor. *See* **Road traffic** (Motor tractor—Overall width).

OVERCHARGING
Hackney carriage—
Fare. *See* **Road traffic** (Hackney carriage—Fare—Overcharging).

OVERCROWDING
Housing. *See* **Housing** (Overcrowding).

OVERDUE TAX
Interest. *See* **Income tax** (Interest—Overdue tax).

OVERFLOW
Sewer—
Nuisance. *See* **Nuisance** (Creation of nuisance—Sewer).

OVERHANG
Heavy motor car. *See* **Road traffic** (Heavy motor car—Overhang).

OVERLAPPING OFFENCES
Public order—
Threatening, abusive or insulting words or behaviour. *See* **Public order** (Offensive conduct conducive to breaches of peace—Threatening, abusive or insulting words or behaviour—Overlapping offences).

OVERLOADING
Exception—
Motor insurance policy. *See* **Motor insurance** (Exception—Overloading).

OVERPAYMENT OF TAX
Value added tax. *See* **Value added tax** (Overpayment of tax).

OVERRIDING INTEREST
Rectification of land register to give effect to overriding interest. *See* **Land registration** (Rectification of register—Overriding interest).
Registered land. *See* **Land registration** (Overriding interest).

OVERSEA COMPANY
Charge created by oversea company—
Registration. *See* **Company** (Charge—Registration—Charge created by oversea company with place of business in England).
Generally. *See* **Company** (Oversea company).

OVERSEAS AID
Judicial review of Ministerial decision to grant overseas aid. *See* **Judicial review** (Availability of remedy—Overseas aid).

OVERSEAS DIVORCE
Financial relief after divorce—
Jurisdiction of English court to grant relief. *See* **Divorce** (Financial provision—Order—Order following decree—Jurisdiction—Foreign decree).
Recognition. *See* **Divorce** (Foreign decree—Recognition by English court—Overseas divorce).

OVERSEAS ORDER
    Maintenance—
        Enforcement. *See* **Husband and wife** (Maintenance—Overseas order—Enforcement).

OVERSEAS TRADER
    Value added tax—
        Zero rating—
            Services to overseas traders or for overseas purposes. *See* **Value added tax** (Zero-rating—Services
            to overseas traders or for overseas purposes).

OVERTAKING
    Vehicle—
        Zebra crossing. *See* **Road traffic** (Pedestrian crossing—Zebra crossing—Overtaking).
    Vessel—
        Collision regulations. *See* **Shipping** (Collision regulations—Overtaking vessel).

677

PACKAGE TRAVEL
Consumer protection—
European Community. *See* **European Union** (Consumer protection—Package travel).
Contract. *See* **Contract** (Holiday—Package holiday).

PADDOCK
Leasehold enfranchisement. *See* **Landlord and tenant** (Leasehold enfranchisement—Premises—House and other premises).

PAGER
Interception of communications—
Use of pager messages as evidence—
Criminal proceedings. *See* **Criminal evidence** (Interception of communications—Telephone intercepts—Pager).

PAIN
Damages. *See* **Damages** (Personal injury—Pain, suffering and loss of amenities).

PAINTING
Removal from exhibition in public place. *See* **Criminal law** (Removal of articles from public building).
Sale—
Implied condition—
Correspondence with description. *See* **Sale of goods** (Implied condition goods correspond with description—Sale by description—Painting).
Merchantable quality. *See* **Sale of goods** (Implied condition as to merchantable quality—Merchantable quality—Painting).
Valuation—
Negligence—
Auctioneer. *See* **Negligence** (Duty to take care—Auctioneer—Valuation of painting).

PALESTINE
Criminal law—
Prosecution witnesses—
Discretion of prosecuting counsel to call witnesses named on indictment or information—Constitution of Court of Criminal Assize—Order made by the High Commissioner—Ultra vires—Palestine Interpretation Ordinance 1933 (1933 No 69), s 7—Palestine Criminal Code Ordinance 1936, ss 214, 216—Emergency Powers (Defence) Act 1939, s 1—Palestine Defence (Judicial) Regulations 1942, reg 3. **Adel Muhammed El Dabbah v A-G for Palestine** [1944] **2** 139, PC.
Damages—
Breach of contract—
Penalty or liquidated damages—Ottoman Code of Civil Procedure, arts 111, 112—Palestine Order in Council 1922, s 46. **Michel Habib Raji Ayoub v Sheikh Suleiman el Taji el Farouqi** [1941] **1** 507, PC.
Grazing rights—
Person—
Fluctuating body of persons—Members of tribe and village—Interpretation Ordinance (Palestine) 1929 (No 34), s 3—Cultivators (Protection) Ordinance (Palestine) 1933 (No 37), ss 18(1), 19(1). **Keren Kayemeth Leisrael Ltd v Mazareeb (Tribe) and Ma'loul (Villagers)** [1943] **2** 570, PC.
Infant—
Appointment of guardian—
Ecclesiastical Court of the Greek Orthodox Patriarchate, Jerusalem—Jurisdiction—Palestine Order in Council 1922 (SR & O 1922 No 1282), art 54(ii). **Kawas v Kawas** [1943] **2** 530, PC.
Intestacy—
Succession—
Lebanese subject owning mulk land situate in Palestine—National law of deceased—Application of the law of the situation of the property—Palestine Order in Council 1922 (SR & O 1922 No 1282), arts 46, 51, 58, 59, 64—Palestine Succession Ordinance 1923, ss 2, 3, 4, 11—Palestine (Amendment) Order in Council 1935. **Jaber Elias Kotia v Katr Bint Jiryes Nahas** [1941] **3** 20, PC.
Land settlement—
Jurisdiction of settlement officer—
Appeal—Right of appeal from decision of settlement officer—Palestine Land Settlement Ordinance 1928. **Aaronson v Ghadieh** [1936] **2** 1670, PC.
Money—
Currency—
Contract governed by Turkish law—Pension based on salary—Whether payable on a gold basis—Unconditional receipts for 'net amount payable'—Release. **Ottoman Bank, Haifa v Menni (Clement)** [1939] **4** 9, PC.
Rating—
Exemption from payment of rates—
Taxation—Whether 'taxation' includes municipal rates—Edicts and firmans overridden by statutory liability—Municipal Corporations Ordinance (Palestine) 1934, s 102—Rates and Taxes (Exemption) Ordinance (Palestine) 1938, s 15(b). **Orthodox Patriarchate of Jerusalem v Municipal Corp of Jerusalem** [1944] **1** 130, PC.
Recovery of land—
Rectification of land registry—
Onus of proof—Disagreement of two judges—Procedure—Land Court Rules 1921, r 2—Establishment of Courts Orders 1924-1931—Court Amendment Ordinance 1939—Land (Settlement of Title) Ordinance 1928-1939. **Mohamed Selim (Prince) v A-G of Palestine** [1941] **2** 321, PC.

PALESTINE (cont)—
  Supreme Court of Palestine—
    Decision—
      Binding effect of decision—Palestine Order in Council 1922 (SR & O 1922 No 1282), art 46. **Khoury, Syndic in Bankruptcy of Nasrallah v Khayat** [1943] 2 406, PC.

PANEL ON TAKE-OVERS AND MERGERS
  Judicial review of decision of panel—
    Whether panel's decisions subject to judicial review. *See* **Judicial review** (Availability of remedy—Take-over Panel).

PARDON
  Habeas corpus—
    Application for habeas corpus on basis of pardon—
      Nature and effect of pardon. *See* **Habeas corpus** (Application for habeas corpus in criminal matter—Pardon).
  Royal prerogative—
    Generally. *See* **Crown** (Prerogative—Pardon).
    Judicial review—
      Availability of remedy. *See* **Judicial review** (Availability of remedy—Royal prerogative—Prerogative of mercy).
  Trinidad and Tobago, in. *See* **Trinidad and Tobago** (Pardon).

PARENS PATRIAE JURISDICTION
  Infants. *See* **Statute** (Crown—Parens patriae jurisdiction).

PARENT
  Access to child—
    Child in care of local authority. *See* **Child** (Welfare—Child in care of local authority—Access of natural parent to child).
    Generally. *See* **Minor** (Custody—Access).
    Ward of court—
      Welfare of ward. *See* **Child** (Welfare—Access—Wardship proceedings).
  Adoption of child—
    Application by parent and step-parent. *See* **Adoption** (Application—Married couple—Parent and step-parent of child).
    Consent—
      Dispensing with consent of parent. *See* **Adoption** (Dispensing with consent of parent or guardian).
      Generally. *See* **Adoption** (Consent—Parent or guardian).
    Progress report to former parents. *See* **Adoption** (Progress report to former parents).
  Affiliation proceedings. *See* **Affiliation**.
  Care proceedings in juvenile court—
    Legal aid. *See* **Legal aid** (Care proceedings in juvenile courts—Person who may be granted legal aid—Person brought before juvenile court—Parent of child).
  Child—
    Detention—
      Application for interim order. *See* **Children and young persons** (Detention—Interim order—Application—Persons who may make application—Parent).
  Child-stealing—
    Defence—
      Right to possession of child. *See* **Criminal law** (Child-stealing—Defence—Person claiming right to possession of child not liable to prosecution).
  Compensation order—
    Offence committed by child or young person. *See* **Sentence** (Compensation—Parent or guardian's liability).
  Contact with child in care—
    Generally. *See* **Child** (Care—Parental contact).
  Custody of child—
    Custody as between parents. *See* **Minor** (Custody—Custody as between parents).
  Dependent parent—
    Admission to United Kingdom. *See* **Immigration** (Leave to enter—Dependent parents).
  Education—
    Duty to secure regular attendance of child. *See* **Education** (School attendance—Duty of parent to secure regular attendance of pupil).
    Wishes of parent—
      Duty of local authority to have regard to wishes. *See* **Education** (Local education authority—Regard to wishes of parents).
  Financial provision—
    Family proceedings. *See* **Family proceedings** (Orders in family proceedings—Financial provision—Parent).
  Income tax—
    Child relief. *See* **Income tax** (Child relief).
  Kidnapping. *See* **Criminal law** (Kidnapping—Parent).
  Maintenance order in favour of child—
    Payment to child—
      Receipt of custodial parent. *See* **Minor** (Maintenance—Payment to minor—Receipt of custodial parent).
  Medical treatment of minor—
    Wishes of parent. *See* **Minor** (Medical treatment—Parental wishes).

PARENT (cont)—
  Natural parent—
    Wardship proceedings by natural parent—
      Child in care of local authority—Jurisdiction of court to review decisions of local authority. *See* **Child** (Care—Local authority—Wardship proceedings—Jurisdiction of court to review decisions of local authority—Wardship proceedings by natural parent).
  Negligence—
    Liability for child. *See* **Child** (Negligence—Parent's liability).
  Next friend—
    Minor. *See* **Minor** (Next friend—Parent).
  Parental responsibility—
    Deprivation of liberty of child. *See* **Child** (Deprivation of liberty—Consent—Parental responsibility).
    Generally. *See* **Minor** (Parental responsibility).
  Parental responsibility agreement—
    Child in local authority care. *See* **Child** (Care—Local authority—Parental responsibility agreement).
  Parental responsibility order and contact order. *See* **Family proceedings** (Orders in family proceedings—Parental responsibility order and contact order).
  Registration on birth certificate—
    Gender. *See* **Registration** (Births, deaths and marriages—Parental status—Gender).
  Rights in respect of child—
    Assumption by local authority. *See* **Child** (Care—Local authority—Assumption by authority of parental rights).
    Illegitimate child. *See* **Child** (Illegitimate child—Parental rights and duties).
    Unlawful interference with parental rights—
      Tort—Children taken into local authority care and placed with long-term foster parents—Mother claiming damages for loss of parental rights—Whether right of action in tort for interference with parental rights. **F v Wirral Metropolitan BC** [1991] 2 648, CA.
  Surname of child—
    Consent to change of surname—
      Consent of both parents—Unborn child. *See* **Minor** (Change of surname—Unborn child—Consent of both parents).
      Deed poll. *See* **Minor** (Change of surname—Deed poll—Consent of parent).
      Leave of court to change of surname in absence of consent—Divorce of parents. *See* **Minor** (Change of surname—Divorce of parents—Leave of court to change surname in absence of parent's consent).
  Undue influence. *See* **Equity** (Undue influence—Presumption of undue influence—Parent and child).
  Ward of court—
    Care and control—
      Factors to be considered—Welfare of child—Wishes of unimpeachable parent. *See* **Ward of court** (Care and control—Factors to be considered—Welfare of minor first and paramount consideration—Wishes of unimpeachable parent).

PARISH
  Church—
    Generally. *See* **Ecclesiastical law**.
  Meeting. *See* **Local government** (Meeting—Parish meeting).
  Parishioner—
    Right of burial in churchyard. *See* **Ecclesiastical law** (Churchyard—Right of burial in churchyard—Parishioner).

PARK
  Exhibition of agricultural and horticultural produce—
    Charitable object. *See* **Charity** (Benefit to community—Showground, park and recreation—Exhibition of agricultural and horticultural produce).

PARKING
  Negligence—
    Parking of vehicle on highway. *See* **Negligence** (Highway—Parking of vehicle).
  Obstruction—
    Parking place. *See* **Road traffic** (Obstruction—Parking place).
  Parking place—
    Generally. *See* **Road traffic** (Parking place).
    Local authority powers. *See* **Local authority** (Powers—Designation of paying parking places on highways).
    Obstruction. *See* **Road traffic** (Obstruction—Parking place).
  Private car park—
    Distress damage feasant. *See* **Distress** (Distress damage feasant—Private car park).
  Right to park cars—
    Easement. *See* **Easement** (Right to park cars).
  Traffic sign. *See* **Road traffic** (Traffic sign—Parking).
  Unlighted vehicle—
    Nuisance. *See* **Nuisance** (Highway—Unlighted vehicle on highway).
  Waiting and loading restrictions. *See* **Road traffic** (Waiting and loading restrictions).
  Wheelclamping—
    Wrongful interference with goods. *See* **Tort** (Wrongful interference with goods—Cause of action—Plaintiff parking vehicle on private property without authority).

PARLIAMENT
  Act of Parliament. *See* **Statute**.
  Ceylon. *See* **Ceylon** (Parliament).
  Defamation—
    Proceedings in Parliament—
      Privilege of members. *See* **Libel and slander** (Privilege—Proceedings in Parliament).

PARLIAMENT (cont)—
  Election—
    Corrupt practice. *See* **Elections** (Corrupt practice—Parliamentary election).
    Generally. *See* **Elections** (Parliamentary).
  European Parliament. *See* **European Union** (European Parliament).
  Hansard—
    Reference to Hansard—
      Construction of statute. *See* **Statute** (Construction—Hansard).
  House of Lords—
    Generally. *See* **House of Lords**.
  Injunction—
    Opposition to private bill. *See* **Injunction** (Parliamentary affairs—Opposition to private Bill).
  Legislative power. *See* **Constitutional law** (Parliament—Legislative power).
  Member—
    Libel—
      Qualified privilege. *See* **Libel and slander** (Qualified privilege—Duty and interest—Member of Parliament).
    Personal data—
      Freedom of information. *See* **Freedom of information** (Exempt information—Personal data—Members of Parliament).
  Ministerial Code—
    Justiciability. *See* **Judicial review** (Availability of remedy—Ministerial Code).
  New Zealand. *See* **New Zealand** (Parliament).
  Northern Ireland. *See* **Northern Ireland** (Parliament).
  Practice—
    Practice in relation to proceedings sub judice. *See* **Contempt of court** (Publications concerning legal proceedings—Pending proceedings—Discussion in Parliament—Practice of Parliament in relation to proceedings sub judice).
  Prevention of obstruction of streets in neighbourhood of Parliament—
    Assemblies—
      Sessional order of Parliament—Directions issued by the Commissioner of Police of the Metropolis—Validity of directions—Metropolitan Police Act 1839, s 52. **Papworth v Coventry** [1967] **2** 41, QBD.
  Privilege—
    Action against member of Parliament—
      Issue of writ as breach of privilege—Writ beginning action against member of Parliament in respect of a speech or proceeding by him in Parliament—Whether to treat the issue of such a writ as a breach of Parliamentary privilege was contrary to statute—Parliamentary Privilege Act 1770, s 1. **Parliamentary Privilege Act, 1770, In the matter of** [1958] **2** 329, PC.
    Consultation—
      Consultation process to inform decision-making as to design of primary legislation—Judicial review challenge to decisions made regarding design of consultation process on grounds of indirect discrimination and failure to comply with common law requirements of lawful consultation—Whether justiciable—Equality Act 2010, ss 19, 29(6), 149, Sch 3, para 2, Sch 18, para 4. **R (on the application of A) v Secretary of State for the Home Dept** [2022] **4** 615, Admin Ct.
    Libel and slander. *See* **Libel and slander** (Privilege—Proceedings in Parliament).
    New Zealand. *See* **New Zealand** (Parliament—Parliamentary privilege).
    Proceedings in Parliament—
      Members of Parliament charged with offences of false accounting—Charges relating to claims for parliamentary expenses—Whether Crown Court having jurisdiction—Whether making expenses claims 'proceedings in Parliament'—Whether making expenses claims within exclusive cognisance of Parliament—Bill of Rights (1688), art 9. **R v Chaytor** [2011] **1** 805, SC.
      Motion for an unopposed return—Report of inquiry ordered to be published by House of Commons following motion for an unopposed return—Whether report constituting 'proceedings in Parliament'—Whether privileged—Whether panel of inquiry 'public authority'—Bill of Rights (1688), art 9—Human Rights Act 1998, s 6(3), Sch 1, Pt I, art 8. **Warsama v Foreign and Commonwealth Office (Speaker of the House of Commons, interested party)** [2020] **4** 486, CA.
      Secretary of State seeking to rely on parliamentary debates to show compliance with statutory duty—Whether reliance on parliamentary debates contrary to parliamentary privilege—Bill of Rights 1688, art 9. **R (on the application of the Project for the Registration of Children as British Citizens) v Secretary of State for the Home Dept** [2021] **4** 445, CA.
    Proceedings in Parliament. *See* Proceedings in Parliament, *below*.
    Report of parliamentary proceedings. *See* **Libel and slander** (Qualified privilege—Parliamentary proceedings).
    Report of select committee—
      Impugning validity of report contrary to Bill of Rights—Whether comment on report permitted—Bill of Rights, s 1, art 9. **Associated Newspapers Ltd v Dingle** [1960] **1** 294, QBD.
    Saint Vincent and the Grenadines. *See* **Saint Vincent and the Grenadines** (Parliament—Parliamentary privilege).
  Proceedings in Parliament—
    Construction of statute—
      Reference to Hansard. *See* **Statute** (Construction—Hansard—Reference to proceedings in Parliament as an aid to construction).
    Construction of statutory instrument—
      Reference to Hansard. *See* **Statutory instrument** (Construction—Hansard).
    Defamation—
      Admissibility of evidence—Words complained of spoken by member of Parliament in television interview. *See* **Libel and slander** (Privilege—Proceedings in Parliament—Evidence of words spoken in Parliament in support of claim).
      Privilege—Generally. *See* **Libel and slander** (Privilege—Proceedings in Parliament).
      Qualified privilege. *See* **Libel and slander** (Qualified privilege—Parliamentary proceedings).
    Libel and slander—
      Privilege. *See* **Libel and slander** (Privilege—Proceedings in Parliament).

PARLIAMENT (cont)—
Proceedings in Parliament (cont)—
Register of members' interests—
Whether practice and procedure relating to register part of 'proceedings in Parliament'—Whether practice and procedure relating to register protected by Parliamentary privilege—Bill of Rights (1688), art 9. **Rost v Edwards** [1990] **2** 641, QBD.

PARLIAMENTARY COMMISSIONER FOR ADMINISTRATION
Judicial review of decision of. *See* **Judicial review** (Parliamentary Commissioner for Administration).
Mandamus—
Failure of commissioner to investigate complaint—
Jurisdiction to order commissioner to investigate—Discretion of commissioner—Whether leave would be given for mandamus against commissioner—Parliamentary Commissioner Act 1967, s 5. **Fletcher's Application, Re** [1970] **2** 527, CA.
Report by Commissioner—
Commissioner finding maladministration and making recommendations—
Secretary of State deciding not to accept findings of maladministration and rejecting Commissioner's recommendations—Whether findings of Commissioner binding on Secretary of State—Parliamentary Commissioner Act 1967. **R (on the application of Bradley) v Secretary of State for Work and Pensions** [2008] **3** 1116, CA.

PARLIAMENTARY COMMISSIONER FOR STANDARDS
Judicial review of decision of. *See* **Judicial review** (Availability of remedy—Parliamentary Commissioner for Standards).

PARLIAMENTARY ELECTION
Ceylon—
Validity. *See* **Ceylon** (Election—No appeal to Crown—Validity of Parliamentary election).
Generally. *See* **Elections** (Parliamentary).

PAROCHIAL CHURCH COUNCIL
See **Ecclesiastical law** (Parochial church council).

PAROL LEASE
Statutory requirements. *See* **Landlord and tenant** (Lease—Statutory requirements—Parol lease).

PAROLE
Generally. *See* **Prison** (Release on licence).
Parole Board. *See* **Prison** (Release on licence—Parole Board).
Release from prison. *See* **Prison** (Release on licence).

PART EXCHANGE
Sale of goods. *See* **Sale of goods** (Price—Sale for cash and part exchange).

PART PAYMENT
Limitation of action—
Revival of cause of action. *See* **Limitation of action** (Part payment).

PART PERFORMANCE
Acts constituting part performance—
Contract for sale of land. *See* **Sale of land** (Part performance of contract).
Contract. *See* **Contract** (Part performance).

PART TIME EMPLOYMENT
Generally. *See* **Employment** (Employee—Part-time employee).

PARTIAL INTESTACY
Hotchpot. *See* **Administration of estates** (Partial intestacy—Hotchpot).

PARTICULARS
Census return—
Private household. *See* **Census** (Form of return—Private household—Particulars).
Claim, of—
Generally. *See* **Particulars of claim**.
Criminal offence—
Further particulars. *See* **Criminal evidence** (Character of accused—Evidence against co-accused).
Unspecified particulars. *See* **Indictment** (Conviction of lesser offence—Causing grievous bodily harm with intent—Particulars of way grievous bodily harm caused not specified—Whether open to court to accept plea to and verdict of unlawful wounding).
Libel proceedings—
Generally. *See* **Libel and slander** (Particulars).
Innuendo. *See* **Libel and slander** (Innuendo—Particulars).
Pleading. *See* **Pleading** (Particulars).
Service of particulars of claim. *See* **Particulars of claim**.

PARTICULARS OF CLAIM
Amendment—
Abandonment—
Claim made in claim form not repeated or adopted in points of claim—Whether claim abandoned—Discretion of court. **British Credit Trust Holdings v UK Insurance Ltd** [2004] **1** Comm 444, QBD.

PARTICULARS OF CLAIM (cont)—
  Service—
    Extension of time for service—
      Application for extension of time prior to expiry of time limit—Procedure on application prior to expiry of time limit—CPR 3.1(2)(a). **Robert v Momentum Services Ltd** [2003] **2** 74, CA.
      Factors to be considered in deciding whether to grant extension of time—Grant of extension of time subject to conditions—CPR 3.1, 3.9. **Price v Price (t/a Poppyland Headware)** [2003] **3** 911, CA.
      Whether court having discretion to grant extension of time for service of particulars of claim—CPR 7.4, 7.6. **Totty v Snowden** [2001] **4** 577, CA.

PARTIES
  Absence of. *See* **Practice** (Absence of party).
  Action in name of company incorporated in foreign state. *See* **Writ** (Parties—Action in name of company incorporated in foreign state).
  Adding persons as parties. *See* **Practice** (Parties).
  Arbitration—
    Arbitration clause. *See* **Arbitration** (Agreement—Arbitration clause—Parties).
  Capacity. *See* **Practice** (Parties—Capacity).
  Change of parties. *See* **Practice** (Parties—Change of parties).
  Charity proceedings. *See* **Charity** (Proceedings—Parties).
  Civil proceedings. *See* **Practice** (Parties).
  Contract. *See* **Contract** (Parties).
  Death of party—
    Criminal appeal—
      Death before appeal heard. *See* **Criminal law** (Appeal—Death of appellant).
    Privy Council—
      Death before appeal heard. *See* **Privy Council** (Abatement of appeal—Death of party).
  Declaration—
    Validity of marriage. *See* **Marriage** (Validity—Declaration—Parties to proceedings).
  Defamation action—
    Corporation—
      Right to sue. *See* **Libel and slander** (Parties—Right to sue—Corporation).
  Defamation action. *See* **Libel and slander** (Parties).
  Defendant—
    Unnamed defendant. *See* **Practice** (Parties—Unnamed defendant).
  Description of parties. *See* **Practice** (Parties—Description of parties).
  Divorce proceedings. *See* **Divorce** (Parties).
  Existence of party—
    Plaintiff. *See* **Practice** (Parties—Existence of plaintiff).
  Generally. *See* **Practice** (Parties).
  Hearing—
    Natural justice—
      Duty to hear parties—Generally. *See* **Natural justice** (Hearing—Duty to hear parties etc).
      Duty to hear parties—Rent assessment committee. *See* **Natural justice** (Rent assessment committee—Duty to hear parties).
  Joinder—
    Civil action. *See* **Practice** (Parties—Joinder of parties).
  Local authority. *See* **Practice** (Parties—Local authority).
  Misnomer—
    Amendment. *See* **Practice** (Parties—Misnomer—Amendment).
    Generally. *See* **Practice** (Parties—Misnomer).
    Warranty by solicitor. *See* **Practice** (Parties—Misnomer—Solicitor).
  Mortgage—
    Proceedings by mortgagee. *See* **Mortgage** (Action by mortgagee for possession—Parties).
  Mortgaged property—
    Possession of mortgaged property. *See* **Mortgage** (Possession of mortgaged property—Persons not parties to mortgage claiming to be entitled to possession).
  New tenancy—
    Application—
      Business premises. *See* **Landlord and tenant** (Business premises—Application for new tenancy—Parties to application).
  Nullity suit. *See* **Nullity** (Petition—Parties).
  Originating summons—
    Separate representation of parties with same interest. *See* **Originating summons** (Parties—Construction summons—Parties with same interest represented by separate counsel).
  Practice. *See* **Practice** (Parties).
  Representation—
    Consistory court. *See* **Ecclesiastical law** (Consistory court—Representation of parties).
  Representative proceedings. *See* **Practice** (Parties—Representative proceedings).
  Res judicata—
    Privy of party to proceedings. *See* **Estoppel** (Res judicata—Privity of party to proceedings).
  Specific performance. *See* **Specific performance** (Parties).
  Standing to bring proceedings—
    Human rights proceedings. *See* **Human rights** (Proceedings—Standing to bring proceedings for breach of convention rights).
  Striking out party. *See* **Practice** (Parties—Striking out party).
  Substitution. *See* **Practice** (Parties—Substitution).
  Unnamed defendant. *See* **Practice** (Parties—Unnamed defendant).
  Wardship proceedings. *See* **Ward of court** (Application to make minor ward of court—Parties).

PARTNERSHIP

Accounts—
Audit—
Auditor's certificate—Circumstances in which court having jurisdiction to set aside auditor's certificate. *See* **Auditor** (Certificate—Circumstances in which court having jurisdiction to interfere—Partnership agreement providing for retirement of partner—Agreement providing for account to be taken by auditor of income and expenditure of partnership practice).

Agreement—
Characteristics—
Whether agreement for payment of commission on orders obtained partnership agreement. *See* **Canada** (Quebec—Partnership—Agreement for payment of commission on orders obtained—Whether partnership agreement).

Arbitration—
Clause in partnership agreement. *See* **Arbitration** (Arbitration clause—Partnership agreement).
Dissolution of partnership. *See* Dissolution—Arbitration, *below*.

Authority of one partner to bind firm—
Partnership with third party for single venture—
Transaction involved was one that would be in usual way of partnership business—Firm of produce merchants—Joint venture with plaintiff in purchase and re-sale of potatoes arranged by one partner—Whether partnership bound—Partnership Act 1890, s 5. **Mann v D'Arcy** [1968] **2** 172, Ch D.

Breach of trust—
Liability of firm—
Beneficiaries bringing action for breach of trust against trustee who was partner in firm of solicitors—Beneficiaries contending that breaches of trust 'in ordinary course' of firm's business and that firm vicariously liable—Whether breaches of trust by partner-trustee capable of being in ordinary course of firm's business—Partnership Act 1890, ss 10, 13. **Walker v Stones** [2000] **4** 412, CA.

Company in substance a partnership—
Compulsory winding up of company—
Just and equitable. *See* **Company** (Compulsory winding up—Just and equitable—Company in substance a partnership).

Demonstrative legacy. *See* **Administration of estates** (Legacy—Demonstrative legacy—Partnership).

Dissolution—
Appointment of receiver—
Fund in court—Partnership insolvent—Charging orders on fund in court—Priority—Solicitors Act 1932, s 69. **Newport v Pougher** [1937] **1** 276, CA.
Retirement of partner. *See* Receiver—Appointment—Retirement of partner, *below*.

Arbitration—
Stay of proceedings—Partnership deed providing for reference of disputes to arbitration—Action for dissolution started by partner—Application for receiver and manager—Claim that dissolution 'just and equitable'—Whether action would be stayed pending arbitration—Partnership Act 1890, s 35(d), (f). **Olver v Hillier** [1959] **2** 220, Ch D.

Continuing authority for purposes of winding up firm—
Claimant entering into merger with another firm—Claimant commencing proceedings post-merger against its professional indemnity insurers—Claimant seeking to bind former partners to litigation—Whether general dissolution of firm—Whether claimant entitled to bring action on behalf of former partners as a result of powers arising on dissolution of a firm—Whether claimant entitled to bring action on behalf of former partners under terms of partnership deed—Partnership Act 1890, s 38. **HLB Kidsons (formerly Kidsons Impey) v Lloyd's Underwriters subscribing to Policy No 621/PKID00101** [2009] **1 Comm** 760, QBD.

Death—
Partnership at will—Death of partner—Profits—Estate entitled pending final settlement to receive share of profits or interest on deceased's share of assets—Executor electing to take interest—Value of assets of partnership business increasing after date of death—Whether executor's election to take interest depriving estate of right to receive share of increased value of assets—Whether 'profits' of partnership business after date of death including increase in value of assets—Partnership Act 1890, s 42(1). **Barclays Bank Trust Co Ltd v Bluff** [1981] **3** 232, Ch D.
Partnership for joint lives—Whether interest in partnership business passed on death. **Burdett-Coutts v IRC** [1960] **3** 153, Ch D.
Right to profits—Partnership at will—Death of partner—Share of deceased settled—Apportionment—Partnership Act 1890, s 33(1). **Robbins, Re** [1941] **2** 601, Ch D.

Discretion of court—
Appropriate remedy—Farming partnership—Termination of partnership—Injunction sought to restrain one partner from entering on land—Winding-up the proper remedy. **Harrison-Broadley v Smith** [1964] **1** 867, CA.

Dissolution by the court—
Applicability of contractual principles of repudiation and affirmation—Partnership Act 1890, s 35(d). **Golstein v Bishop** [2014] **3** 397, CA.

Effect—
Agreement signed by partners prematurely dissolving partnership without consent of one partner—Partner treating agreement as repudiatory breach of partnership deed and accepting repudiation—Whether repudiatory breach of partnership deed discharging innocent partner from obligation to contribute towards partnership liabilities. **Hurst v Bryk** [1997] **2** 283, CA; [2000] **2** 193, HL.
Partnership carrying on business as hotel developers—Two developments in progress at time of dissolution—Whether partnership obliged to complete developments in order to wind up business—Partnership Act 1890, s 38. **Boghani v Nathoo** [2011] **2 Comm** 743, Ch D.
Partnership property—Boxing promoters entering into partnership agreement relating to promotion and management of boxing—Promoter purporting to assign to partnership benefit and burden of existing agreements with boxers—Whether non-assignable property could be partnership property—Partnership Act 1890, s 20. **Don King Productions Inc v Warren** [1999] **2** 218, CA.

684

PARTNERSHIP (cont)—
  Dissolution (cont)—
    Effect (cont)—
      Partnership property—Duties of partners—Good faith—Leasehold interest—Interest remaining undistributed asset after dissolution—Acquisition of freehold reversion by one of former partners—Whether partner accountable to other former partners in respect of freehold interest. **Thompson's trustee in bankruptcy v Heaton** [1974] **1** 1239, Ch D.
      Profits—Profits earned by partnership business after dissolution—Outgoing partner entitled to share of profits attributable to use of his share of partnership assets—Meaning of 'share of partnership assets'—Partnership Act 1890, s 42(1). **Sandhu v Gill** [2005] **1** 990, Ch D; [2006] **2** 22, CA.
      Whether accepted repudiatory breach of partnership deed dissolving partnership. **Mullins v Laughton** [2003] **4** 94n, Ch D.
    Incapacity of partner—
      Incapacity to perform fair share of the work of the practice—Medical partnership—Provision that if either partner incapacitated from performing fair share of work for nine consecutive months other partner might by notice determine partnership—Partner suffering cerebral haemorrhage—Partner returning to practice nine months later—Evidence that partner fit to resume work only on part-time basis under supervision—No prospect of resuming work on full-time basis for further two months—Validity of notice to determine partnership. **Peyton v Mindham** [1971] **3** 1215, Ch D.
    Indemnity of outgoing partner—
      Partnership debts and liabilities—Income tax. **Stevens v Britten** [1954] **3** 385, CA.
    Notice—
      Partnership to continue notwithstanding retirement of one partner—Notice of dissolution by one partner—Partnership at will—Partnership Act 1890, ss 26(1), 32(c). **Abbott v Abbott** [1936] **3** 823, Ch D.
    Persons who may apply—
      Salaried partner—Partnership having ceased in fact—Circumstances in which winding-up order may be refused. **Stekel v Ellice** [1973] **1** 465, Ch D.
    Profits—
      Profits earned by partnership business after dissolution—Partnership determinable at will—Plaintiff terminating partnership but leaving capital in business—Remaining partner carrying on business and then selling at profit—Whether plaintiff entitled to equal share of capital profit made on sale of business—Partnership Act 1890, ss 24(1), 42(1). **Popat v Shonchhatra** [1997] **3** 800, CA.
    Ranking of claims—
      Partnership carried on by two companies—Ranking of creditors of partnership and creditors of individual companies—Whether partnership creditors entitled to preference similar to that available in winding up of individual companies—Bankruptcy Act 1914, s 33(6)—Companies Act 1948, s 319. **Rudd & Son Ltd, Re** [1984] **3** 225, Ch D.
    Solicitors. *See* **Solicitor** (Partnership—Dissolution).
  Employment—
    Period of continuous employment—
      Change of partners. *See* **Employment** (Continuity—Change of employer—Partnership—Employment by partnership—Change in partners).
  Executor—
    Appointment of firm as. *See* **Executor and administrator** (Executor—Appointment—Appointment of firm).
    Trading for tax purposes—
      Partnership business—Dealing in land. *See* **Income tax** (Trade—Executors—Partnership business—Dealing in land).
  Existence of partnership disputed—
    Appointment of receiver sought—
      Interlocutory application. **Floydd v Cheney** [1970] **1** 446, Ch D.
    Injunctions—
      Delivering up of documents wrongfully taken by purported partner—Restraint on use of documents or confidential information. **Floydd v Cheney** [1970] **1** 446, Ch D.
    Persons working together to commence business—
      Parties incurring liabilities and acquiring assets in connection with prospective restaurant business—Relationship between parties breaking down before opening of restaurant—Whether parties to joint venture not becoming partners until actual trading commenced. **Khan v Miah** [2001] **1** 20, HL; [2001] **1 Comm** 282, HL.
    Persons working together to form a company—
      Question of mixed fact and law—Partnership Act 1890, s 1(1). **Spicer (Keith) Ltd v Mansell** [1970] **1** 462, CA.
  Expulsion—
    Misconduct—
      Power of partners—Exercise by single partner—Provision in partnership deed that if any partner guilty of default the other partners might by notice expel him from the partnership—Notice given by one partner to expel the other two for misconduct—Whether he had power to do so under partnership deed—Effect of Law of Property Act 1925, s 61. **Solicitors' Arbitration, Re a** [1962] **1** 772, Ch D.
  Farming—
    Income tax. *See* **Income tax** (Farming—Mixed farm—Partnership).
  Fiduciary relationship. *See* Relations between partners—Good faith—Fiduciary relationship, *below*.
  Foreign judgment against—
    Enforcement—
      Action in England. *See* **Conflict of laws** (Foreign judgment—Enforcement—Action in England—Foreign judgment against partnership).
  Foreign partnership—
    Action against Swiss general partnership—
      Whether partnership should be named as defendant. *See* **Practice** (Parties—Description of parties—Defendants sued as individual partners in Swiss general partnership).

PARTNERSHIP (cont)—

Guarantee—
    Validity. *See* **Guarantee** (Validity—Partnership guarantee).
Husband and wife—
    Beneficial interest—
        Assessment. *See* **Husband and wife** (Property—Partnership business—Beneficial interests).
Illegality—
    Betting office. *See* **Gaming** (Betting—Licensed betting office—Partnership).
Incapacity of partner. *See* Dissolution—Incapacity of partner, *above*.
Income tax—
    Additional assessment—
        Time limit. *See* **Income tax** (Additional assessment—Time limit—Partnership).
    Generally. *See* **Income tax** (Partnership).
    Income arising from possessions out of United Kingdom—
        Partnership between taxpayer and Bahamian company. *See* **Income tax** (Foreign possessions—
        Income arising from possessions out of United Kingdom—Partnership between taxpayer and
        Bahamian company).
    Retired partner—
        Earned income relief. *See* **Income tax** (Earned income relief—Earned income—Income immediately
        derived from carrying on or exercise of trade, profession or vocation—Immediately
        derived—Partnership).
    Total income for tax purposes—
        Share of partnership profits. *See* **Income tax** (Total income—Share of profits—Partnership).
Indemnity of outgoing partner. *See* Dissolution—Indemnity of outgoing partner, *above*.
Insolvency. *See* **Insolvency** (Partnership).
Joint lives. *See* Dissolution—Death—Partnership for joint lives, *above*.
Liability of firm—
    Vicarious liability of firm to third parties in respect of 'wrongful act or omission' of partner 'acting in the
    ordinary course' of firm's business—
        Whether 'wrongful act or omission' confined to common law torts—Whether firm not vicariously
        liable unless all wrongful acts for which partner responsible had been committed in course of
        firm's business—Partnership Act 1890, s 10. **Dubai Aluminium Co Ltd v Salaam (Livingstone and
        ors, third parties)** [2003] **1** 97, HL; [2003] **2** Comm 451, HL.
Limited liability partnership—
    Employment. *See* **Employment** (Limited liability partnership).
    Liability of general partner to limited partners—
        Liability of manager to limited partners—Limited partners seeking to sue general partner and
        manager for breaches of terms of partnership agreement and management deed—Whether
        claimant limited partners entitled to bring derivative claim against general partner or against
        manager—Whether claimant limited partners entitled to pre-emptive costs order—Limited
        Partnerships Act 1907, s 6(1). **Certain Limited Partners in Henderson PFI Secondary Fund II LLP (a
        firm) v Henderson PFI Secondary Fund II LP (a firm)** [2013] **2** Comm 189, QBD; [2013] **3** 887, QBD.
    Member—
        Disqualification—Conduct as a director—Disqualification proceedings against members of
        LLP—Members not involved in management of LLP—Whether all members of LLP potentially
        liable to be disqualified—Whether members' non-participation in management excluded them
        from liability—Company Directors Disqualification Act 1986, s 6—Limited Liability Partnerships
        Regulations 2001, SI 2001/1090, reg 4(2). **Bell Pottinger LLP, Re** [2022] **1** Comm 815, Ch D.
    Winding up. *See* **Winding up** (Limited partnership).
Medical practitioner—
    Clause in partnership agreement prohibiting retiring partner carrying on practice within ten mile
    radius—
        Validity. *See* **National Health Service** (Medical practitioner—Partnership—Goodwill—Clause in
        partnership agreement prohibiting retiring partner from carrying on practice within ten-mile
        radius—Validity).
    Restraint of trade—
        Generally. *See* **Restraint of trade by agreement** (Partnership—Medical partnership).
Misconduct of partner—
    Expulsion. *See* Expulsion—Misconduct, *above*.
Nature—
    Relationship of partners—
        Salaried partnership—Two partners—One partner providing all capital and taking profits—Other
        partner paid a fixed salary—Other partner held out as partner—Circumstances in which
        relationship one of partnership rather than employment—Partnership Act 1890, ss 1(1), 27(1).
        Stekel v Ellice [1973] **1** 465, Ch D.
Notice of dissolution by one partner. *See* Dissolution—Notice, *above*.
Partner—
    Liability to limited partners. *See* Limited liability partnership—Liability of general partner to limited
    partners, *above*.
Partnership business—
    Winding up—
        Dissolution. *See* Dissolution—Effect—Partnership carrying on business as hotel developers, *above*.
Partnership property—
    Contract for sale of share of partnership property—
        Registration as general equitable charge. *See* **Land charge** (General equitable charge—Contract for
        sale of one-eighth share of partnership property).
    Conversion—
        Joinder of parties—Conversion of partnership property by one of two partners—Cheques payable
        to partnership indorsed by one partner and paid into third person's banking account—Right of
        aggrieved partner to sue alone without joining guilty partner—RSC Ord 16, r 11. **Baker v Barclays
        Bank Ltd** [1955] **2** 571, Assizes.
    Dissolution—
        Effect. *See* Dissolution—Effect—Partnership property, *above*.

PARTNERSHIP (cont)—
  Partnership property (cont)—
    Ownership of assets—
      No partnership agreement except as to division of profits. **Miles v Clarke** [1953] **1** 779, Ch D.
    Share of partnership property—
      Contract for sale of share—Registration as estate contract. *See* **Land charge** (Estate contract—Contract to convey or create a legal estate).
    Theft of, by one partner in partnership. *See* **Criminal law** (Theft—Property belonging to another—Partnership property).
    Valuation—
      Partnership operating family business from freehold premises—Partnership deed providing for annual general account on basis of 'just valuation'—Accounts showing premises at historic cost value—Whether deceased partner's share in partnership capital to be calculated by reference to book or market value of premises. **White (decd), Re** [1999] **2** 663, Ch D; [2000] **3** 618, CA.
      Partnership operating family farm—Partnership deed providing for fixed capital not increased to take account of increase in value of farm land—Partnership deed providing that on retirement or death outgoing partner or his estate to receive payment equal to share in capital and profits as determined by last annual general account—Annual general accounts not revaluing farm land—One partner dying and two partners retiring from partnership due to loss of capacity—Last general account not signed by all partners—Whether payment to outgoing partners to be determined by reference to historic or market value of land. **Drake v Harvey** [2011] **1 Comm** 344, Ch D.
      Partnership operating family farm—Partnership deed providing that on retirement or death of partner outgoing partner or his personal representatives entitled to amount representing his share in the capital and his 'undrawn profits' as at the date of the last general accounts—Value of farming land recorded at cost in annual general accounts and never revalued—Partner dying—Dispute as to correct value to be attributed to capital assets—Whether capital assets to be valued at book value or fair value. **Drake v Harvey** [2012] **1 Comm** 617, CA.
  Powers and liabilities of partners—
    Limited liability partnership. *See* Limited liability partnership—Liability of general partner to limited partners, *above*.
  Property. *See* Partnership property, *above*.
  Receiver—
    Appointment—
      Dissolution of partnership. *See* Dissolution—Appointment of receiver, *above*.
      Retirement of partner—Remaining partners continuing in partnership—Agreement for retirement making no provision for valuation of retiring partner's share in partnership assets—Agreement not effecting dissolution—Professional firm—Circumstances in which court will appoint receiver—Whether retiring partner entitled to sale—Whether receiver should be appointed. **Sobell v Boston** [1975] **2** 282, Ch D.
  Relations between partners—
    Good faith—
      Fiduciary relationship—When partner a trustee. **Gordon v Gonda** [1955] **2** 762, CA.
      Partnership property—Leasehold interest—Underlease of premises where partnership business carried on—Acquisition of leasehold reversion by one of the partners—Dissolution of partnership—Appointment of receiver—Rent in arrears—Landlord's right to claim possession with leave of court—Whether fact that landlord a partner raising any equity which would preclude court from giving leave. **Brenner v Rose** [1973] **2** 535, Ch D.
  Restraint of trade. *See* **Restraint of trade by agreement** (Partnership).
  Retiring partner—
    Liability—
      Person holding out—Debts incurred after dissolution—Liability of retiring partner—Unauthorised use of retiring partner's name—Partnership Act 1890, ss 14(1), 36(1), (3). **Tower Cabinet Co Ltd v Ingram** [1949] **1** 1033, KBD.
  Single venture—
    Authority of one partner to bind firm. *See* Authority of one partner to bind firm—Partnership with third party for single venture, *above*.
  Solicitor—
    Advice to partnership—
      Duty. *See* **Solicitor** (Duty—Advice to partnership).
    Generally. *See* **Solicitor** (Partnership).
    Liability for acts of his partners—
      Negligence. *See* **Solicitor** (Negligence—Partnership).
    Solicitor employed by partnership—
      Restraint of trade by agreement. *See* **Restraint of trade by agreement** (Employer and employee—Employee of partnership—Solicitor).
  Theft by one partner of partnership property. *See* **Criminal law** (Theft—Property belonging to another—Partnership property).
  Tort—
    Liability of firm—
      Ordinary course of business of firm—Libel—Qualified privilege—Communication on behalf of firm sent by one partner without malice—Another partner actuated by malice—Latter liable although partner sending the communication was not liable—Partnership Act 1890, s 10. **Meekins v Henson** [1962] **1** 899, QBD.
  Value added tax—
    Registration. *See* **Value added tax** (Registration—Partnership).
  Writ—
    Service on partnership. *See* **Writ** (Service on partnership).

PARTY WALL
  Boundary. *See* **Boundary** (Party wall).

PASS
Free travel—
Exclusion of liability of carriers for negligence. *See* **Carriers** (Negligence—Exclusion of liability—Passengers—Free pass).

PASSENGER
Aircraft—
Carriage. *See* **Carriage by air** (Carriage of passengers).
Contract of carriage. *See* **Carriers** (Contract—Carriage of passengers).
Contributory negligence—
Road accident. *See* **Negligence** (Contributory negligence—Road accident—Passenger in car).
Express carriage. *See* **Road traffic** (Express carriage).
Motor vehicle—
Duty of driver to take care. *See* **Negligence** (Duty to take care—Driver of motor vehicle—Duty to passenger in vehicle).
Insurance—
Exception—Passenger other than one carried by reason of or in pursuance of a contract of employment. *See* **Motor insurance** (Exception—Passenger other than one carried by reason of or in pursuance of a contract of employment).
Private motor vehicle—
Carried for hire or reward. *See* **Motor insurance** (Compulsory insurance against third party risks—Passengers carried for hire or reward in private vehicle).
Negligence—
Exclusion of liability to passenger in vehicle. *See* **Negligence** (Volenti non fit injuria—Consent to risk of injury—Agreement to exclude liability—Passenger in vehicle).
Injuring third party. *See* **Motor insurance** (Using vehicle or causing or permitting vehicle to be used on road without policy being in force—Use—Passenger's negligence injuring third party).
Occupier's liability—
Safety of premises. *See* **Occupier's liability** (Carriage of passengers—Safety of premises).
Omnibus—
Injury to passenger alighting from bus. *See* **Negligence** (Vehicles—Passenger injured while alighting from omnibus).
Railway—
Duty of care to passengers. *See* **Negligence** (Railway—Duty to passengers and invitees).
Safety—
Endangering. *See* **Railway** (Offence—Unlawful act endangering safety of person conveyed on a railway).
Sea, carriage by. *See* **Shipping** (Passengers).
Transport—
Value added tax—
Zero-rating. *See* **Value added tax** (Zero-rating—Transport of passengers).
Volenti non fit injuria—
Knowledge of risk. *See* **Negligence** (Volenti non fit injuria—Knowledge of risk—Passenger in car).

PASSENGER VEHICLE
See **Road traffic** (Passenger vehicle).

PASSENGER VESSEL
Intoxicating liquor—
Sale on board—
Permitted hours. *See* **Licensing** (Passenger vessel—Sale of intoxicating liquor on board—Permitted hours).

PASSING OFF
Business—
Representation that employers had gone out of business—
Employee commencing similar business on own account—Malice—Special damage. **Worsley (E) & Co Ltd v Cooper** [1939] **1** 290, Ch D.
Conflict of laws—
Challenge to jurisdiction. *See* **Conflict of laws** (Jurisdiction—Challenge to jurisdiction—Passing off).
Confusion—
Get-up of goods. *See* Get-up of goods—Confusion, *below*.
Damages—
Right to substantial damages—
Sales to middleman. **Draper v Trist** [1939] **3** 513, CA.
Descriptive material—
Imitation of advertising campaign—
Slogans and themes made familiar to market in radio and television advertising campaign—Whether plaintiff acquiring an intangible property right in advertised descriptions. **Cadbury Schweppes Pty Ltd v Pub Squash Co Pty Ltd** [1981] **1** 213, PC.
Descriptive name—
Imitation of advertising campaign—
Slogans and themes made familiar to market in radio and television advertising campaign—Whether plaintiff acquiring of an intangible property right in advertised descriptions. **Cadbury Schweppes Pty Ltd v Pub Squash Co Pty Ltd** [1981] **1** 213, PC.
Reputation of product gained under particular name—
Plaintiff's members of class producing product—Plaintiffs manufacturing and selling alcoholic drink known as 'advocaat'—Advocaat made out of eggs and spirits—Defendants manufacturing alcoholic drink out of eggs and wine and marketing it as 'Old English Advocaat'—Whether name 'advocaat' distinctive or merely descriptive—Whether plaintiff's entitled to injunction against defendants. **Erven Warnink BV v J Townend & Sons (Hull) Ltd** [1979] **2** 927, HL.

688

PASSING OFF (cont)—
   Endorsement—
      False endorsement—
         Liability—Assessment of damages. **Irvine v Talksport Ltd** [2002] **2** 414, Ch D; [2003] **2 Comm** 141, CA; [2003] **2** 881, CA.
   False attribution of authorship—
      Attribution—
         Newspaper article—Article by journalist in form of diary, parodying published diaries of plaintiff—Plaintiff seeking injunction restraining defendant from publishing work falsely attributed to him—Whether article attributing authorship to plaintiff—Whether plaintiff entitled to injunction. **Clark v Associated Newspapers Ltd** [1998] **1** 959, Ch D.
   Foreign corporation—
      Authority to sue—
         Want of authority. *See* **Solicitor** (Payment of costs by solicitor personally—Want of authority to institute action).
   Geographical name—
      False trade description—
         Admixture of single malt whisky and cane spirit sold as Scotch whisky—Whether plaintiffs producers of Scotch whisky—Supply by defendant in England of means to produce and retail admixture as Scotch whisky in Ecuador—Whether defendant committed tort of passing-off. **Walker (John) & Sons Ltd v Henry Ost & Co Ltd** [1970] **2** 106, Ch D.
      Geographical name descriptive of particular district of France—
         Plaintiffs a class of producers within that district—Champagne—Non-alcoholic beverage made from elderflowers produced and offered for sale in England under description 'Elderflower Champagne'—Whether likelihood of substantial damage to plaintiffs' goodwill. **Taittinger v Allbev Ltd** [1994] **4** 75, CA.
         Plaintiffs a class of producers within that district—Champagne—Wine produced in Spain offered for sale in England under the description 'Spanish Champagne'—Whether calculated to deceive. **Bollinger (J) v Costa Brava Wine Co Ltd (No 2)** [1961] **1** 561, Ch D.
      Geographical name descriptive of particular region of France—
         Unfair competition—'Spanish Champagne' used to describe wine produced in Spain—Whether action lay to restrain such unfair competition. **Bollinger (J) v Costa Brava Wine Co Ltd** [1959] **3** 800, Ch D.
   Get-up of goods—
      Common field of activity—
         Similarity to well known name in broadcasting—'Uncle Mac' of 'Children's Hour' broadcasting programme—'Uncle Mac's Puffed Wheat'—No common field of activity. **McCulloch v Lewis A May (Produce Distributors) Ltd** [1947] **2** 845, Ch D.
      Confusion—
         Descriptive name—Misuse of descriptive terms—Defendant selling alcoholic drink made of vodka and fermented alcohol of 22% alcohol by volume in similar get-up to vodka of 37·5% alcohol by volume under brand name similar to word 'vodka'—Claimant bringing passing-off action—Whether 'cachet' of superior class of product required—Whether 'vodka' denoting defined class of goods—Whether 'vodka' defining class of goods having reputation giving rise to goodwill amongst significant section of public. **Diageo North America Inc v InterContinental Brands (ICB) Ltd** [2010] **3** 147, Ch D; [2011] **1** 242, CA.
         Foreign market—Emphasis in respondent's labels on essential part of appellant's trade mark borne on labels of his goods—Labels not causing actual confusion, but calculated to enable respondent's goods to be passed off to customers as appellant's goods—Customer illiterate persons, who ordered goods by reference to a prominent feature on the label—No infringement of appellant's registered trade mark, but relief granted on the ground of passing off. **Lee Kar Choo (t/a Yeen Thye Co) v Lee Lian Choon (t/a Chuan Lee Co)** [1966] **3** 1000, PC.
         Foreign market—Importance of get-up where goods retailed to non-English speaking customers by description—Sweets wrapped in red wrappers sold in Singapore loose from unlabelled glass jars—Different names of appellants' and respondents' sweets printed on wrappers, but many customers unable to read English names. **White Hudson & Co Ltd v Asian Organisation Ltd** [1965] **1** 1040, PC.
         Known public susceptibility to confusion—De facto monopoly in particular goods or services—Competitor competing with monopolist—Whether competitor subject to duty to distinguish his product from connection with monopolist. **British Sky Broadcasting Group plc v Sky Home Services Ltd (Note)** [2007] **3** 1066, Ch D.
      Container allusive of contents—
         Lemon juice sold in squeeze pack coloured and shaped like natural lemon—Whether get-up entitled to protection—Whether fact that get-up is allusive of contents depriving get-up of entitlement to protection. **Reckitt & Colman Products Ltd v Borden Inc** [1990] **1** 873, HL.
      Get-up common to the trade—
         Common to the trade—Containers for lemon juice—Container consisting of plastic squeeze pack coloured and shaped like natural lemon—One trader dominating United Kingdom market in lemon juice sold in containers—Trader not first to use such containers and technique of marketing juice in such containers common outside United Kingdom—Whether device of selling juice in such containers 'common to the trade'—Whether such container acquiring secondary significance of indicating particular trader's lemon juice. **Reckitt & Colman Products Ltd v Borden Inc** [1990] **1** 873, HL.
      Similarity of get-up—
         Similarity of part of get-up—Separation of similar and dissimilar parts of get-up—Protection for similar part of get-up—Containers for lemon juice—Container consisting of plastic squeeze pack coloured and shaped like natural lemon—One trader dominating market in lemon juice sold in such containers—Rival introducing similar containers—Rival's containers distinguished by different label—Evidence establishing that rival's action effectively deceiving public regarding source of rival's juice—Whether dissimilar part of get-up may be separated from similar part so as to confer protection against passing off on similar part—Whether defence to action for passing off that more careful, literate or perspicacious shopper would not be deceived. **Reckitt & Colman Products Ltd v Borden Inc** [1990] **1** 873, HL.

PASSING OFF (cont)—
Injunction—
Form of order. *See* **Injunction** (Form of order—Passing off).
Journal—
Alteration of copies without authority—
Insertion of advertising matter in illustrated newspapers by means of supplement—Representation that supplement part of advertisements of newspaper—Misrepresentation for trading purposes. **Illustrated Newspapers Ltd v Publicity Services (London) Ltd** [1938] **1** 321, Ch D.
Newspaper—Insertion of advertising material in newspapers without consent of newspaper proprietor—Whether advertising inserts amounting to misrepresentation—Whether advertising inserts causing damage to goodwill and reputation attaching to newspapers. **Associated Newspapers plc v Insert Media Ltd** [1991] **3** 535, CA.
Known public susceptibility to confusion. *See* Get-up of goods—Confusion, *above.*
Magazine—
Title to magazine—
Amalgamation with and incorporation in another magazine—Magazine 'Today' published by plaintiffs from 1945 to 1953—Incorporation then with another magazine of plaintiffs—'Today' not included in title of other magazine but statement of incorporation on inside page—No intention to abandon right to title—Whether proprietary right protected by law had been lost through discontinuance of user. **Norman Kark Publications Ltd v Odhams Press Ltd** [1962] **1** 636, Ch D.
Name of company—
Injunction to restrain continued use of word in company's name. *See* **Company** (Name—Use of name—Restraining use of name by company).
Name of maker—
Bona fide use by defendant of own name—
Confusion of defendants' goods with plaintiffs'—Whether defendant's use of own name constituting passing off. **Baume & Co Ltd v A H Moore Ltd** [1958] **2** 113, CA.
Newspaper. *See* Journal, *above.*
Professional description—
Boxing title—
Confusion with defendant—Plaintiff newcomer to England—Whether reputation to protect—Whether likelihood of confusion with defendant. **Serville v Constance** [1954] **1** 662, Ch D.
Fanciful name—
Musician arranging music and conducting band under fanciful name—Name invented by producer, plaintiff's employer, but associated exclusively with plaintiff. **Hines v Winnick** [1947] **2** 517, Ch D.
Trade name—
Business carried on abroad and in England—
Business enjoying international reputation and goodwill—International business setting up branch in England—International business losing control of management of English branch and setting up another branch—Whether goodwill and reputation continuing to attach to international business or becoming exclusive property of English branch. **Habib Bank Ltd v Habib Bank AG Zurich** [1981] **2** 650, CA.
Business carried on abroad but not in England—
Business enjoying reputation and goodwill in England—Restaurant in Paris—Defendant opening restaurant in England under name of plaintiff's restaurant and furnishing it in same style—Whether plaintiff entitled to injunctions restraining defendant from using plaintiff's name and passing off her business as that of plaintiff—Whether existence of goodwill and reputation in England without carrying on business there sufficient to entitle plaintiff to relief. **Maxim's Ltd v Dye** [1978] **2** 55, Ch D.
Goodwill—Whether goodwill requiring business within jurisdiction—Whether reputation sufficient. **Starbucks (HK) Ltd v British Sky Broadcasting Group plc** [2015] **3** 469, SC.
Charity enjoying reputation and goodwill in England—
Plaintiff charity known as British Diabetic Association—Defendants setting up new charity named Diabetic Society—Whether plaintiff entitled to injunction restraining defendant from using name Diabetic Society—Whether existing charity enjoying exclusive reputation and goodwill in society as well as in association—Whether Society sufficiently differentiated from Association. **British Diabetic Association v Diabetic Society Ltd** [1995] **4** 812, Ch D.
Discontinuance of user—
Name of business—Closure of business—Goodwill—Retention of goodwill after closure—Goodwill attached to name of business—Action to protect name maintainable after closure so long as goodwill retained—Whether goodwill retained question of fact. **Ad-Lib Club Ltd v Granville** [1971] **2** 300, Ch D.
Game—
Plaintiffs manufacturing chess sets of particular design with which name Staunton associated—Defendant selling chess-sets described as 'Genuine Staunton chessmen'—Made to Staunton design but not manufactured by plaintiffs—'Genuine'—Whether calculated to deceive. **Jaques (John) & Son Ltd v Chess (A Firm)** [1940] **2** 285, CA.
Internet domain names—
Registration of company names as Internet domain names—Registration of names carried out by dealer in domain names—Judge granting injunction against dealer—Whether judge right to do so—Whether passing off or threatened passing off established—Whether registered domain names instruments of fraud. **British Telecommunications plc v One In A Million Ltd** [1998] **4** 476, CA.
Service or process—
Knowingly purporting to give named process using other than branded articles—Misrepresentation analogous to passing off. **Sales Affiliates Ltd v Le Jean Ltd** [1947] **1** 287, Ch D.
Name descriptive of business—Fraud expressly negatived—Right to injunction—Office Cleaning Services—Office Cleaning Association. **Office Cleaning Services Ltd v Westminster Window and General Cleaners Ltd** [1946] **1** 320, HL.

PASSING OFF (cont)—
　Trade name (cont)—
　　Unincorporated association—
　　　Unincorporated trade association holding exhibition known as the Long Point exhibition—
　　　Association expelling defendant as member—Defendant registering 'Long Point' as trade mark
　　　and announcing that it controlled Long Point exhibition—Claimant bringing passing off
　　　proceedings against defendant as representative of association members—Whether unincorpo-
　　　rated association able to maintain action for passing off. **Artistic Upholstery Ltd v Art Forma
　　　(Furniture) Ltd** [1999] **4** 277, Ch D.
　Voice—
　　Simulation of voice—
　　　Remedy—Alleged simulation of actor's voice in broadcast of advertising commentaries—Action for
　　　libel and for passing off—Interlocutory injunction not appropriate on the ground of
　　　libel—Whether interlocutory injunction would be granted on the ground of passing off. **Sim v H J
　　　Heinz Co Ltd** [1959] **1** 547, CA.

PASSPORT
　Alien—
　　Allegiance to Crown—
　　　Treason. *See* **Criminal law** (Treason—Allegiance to Crown—Alien—Holder of British passport).
　Refusal to issue—
　　Crown prerogative. *See* **Crown** (Prerogative—Passport).
　Reliance on stamp in passport—
　　Mistake in giving leave to enter and stay indefinitely—
　　　Passport so stamped—Entry in breach of immigration laws—Leave not obtained by fraud or
　　　misrepresentation—Detention of entrant. *See* **Immigration** (Detention—Illegal entrant—Entry in
　　　breach of immigration laws—Immigration officer mistakenly giving entrant leave to enter and
　　　stay indefinitely—Passport so stamped—Entrant not obtaining leave by fraud or
　　　misrepresentation—Entrant subsequently detained as illegal entrant—Whether entrant entitled to
　　　rely on stamp in passport).
　United Kingdom passport—
　　Gender—
　　　Whether application requirement to declare gender as either male or female unlawful—Whether
　　　issue of passport only bearing 'M' or 'F' indicator in sex field, rather than 'X' indicating
　　　unspecified sex, unlawful—Human Rights Act 1998, Sch 1, Pt I, arts 8, 14. **R (on the application of
　　　Elan-Cane) v Secretary of State for the Home Dept (Human Rights Watch intervening)**
　　　[2018] **4** 519, QBD; [2021] **1** 25, CA; [2022] **2** 1, SC.
　　Meaning in Commonwealth Immigrants Act 1962. *See* **Commonwealth immigrant** (Commonwealth
　　citizen other than person holding United Kingdom passport—United Kingdom passport).

PASTORAL SCHEME
　Appeal. *See* **Ecclesiastical law** (Appeal—Pastoral scheme).

PASTURE
　Common of pasture by reason of vicinage—
　　Whether a right of common. *See* **Commons** (Right of common—Common of pasture by reason of
　　vicinage).
　Rights of pasture—
　　Sale of land. *See* **Sale of land** (Conveyance—Construction—Rights of pasture).

PATENT
　Action—
　　Costs—
　　　Taxation. *See* **Costs** (Taxation—Patent action).
　　Amendment of specification. *See* Specification—Amendment of specification with leave of the court,
　　below.
　Appeal—
　　Comptroller's opinion as to validity or infringement—
　　　Review of Comptroller's opinion—Appeal from review to High Court—Appellant applying to
　　　Comptroller for opinion as to infringement of patent relating to shower tray by third party's
　　　product—Examiner issuing opinion of no infringement—Hearing officer agreeing with conclusion
　　　of examiner upon review—Appellant seeking to appeal to High Court—Whether appellant having
　　　right of appeal against decision of Comptroller—Patents Act 1977, ss 74A, 74B,
　　　97—Patent Rules 1995, SI 1995/2093, r 77K. **DLP Ltd's Patent, Re** [2008] **1** 839, Ch D.
　　Appeal to Court of Appeal—
　　　Application for leave to appeal—
　　　　Determination of applications—CPR 52.5. **Teva UK Ltd v Boehringer Ingelheim Pharma GmbH & Co
　　　　KG** [2017] **4** 976, CA.
　　　　Time for application—Extension of time for service of notice of appeal—RSC Ord 59, r 18—Patents
　　　　Act 1949, s 87(1)(c). **Practice Direction** [1969] **2** 544, PAT.
　　　　Time for application—Time for service of notice of appeal if leave granted by tribunal—Ex parte
　　　　application to Court of Appeal if leave refused—Patents Act 1949, s 87(1)(aa), (c)—RSC Ord 59,
　　　　rr 14, 18. **Practice Direction** [1973] **1** 976, PAT.
　　Appeal to House of Lords—
　　　Appeal from High Court. *See* **House of Lords** (Appeal from High Court—Patent appeal).
　　Appeal tribunal—
　　　Certiorari to quash decision of tribunal—
　　　　Circumstances in which certiorari will lie. **Baldwin & Francis Ltd v Patents Appeal Tribunal**
　　　　[1959] **2** 433, HL;　**R v Patents Appeal Tribunal, ex p Champion Paper and Fibre Co** [1957] **1** 227,
　　　　QBD;　**R v Patents Appeal Tribunal, ex p Geigy (J R), Société Anonyme** [1963] **1** 850, QBD.
　　　Practice—
　　　　Appointment of scientific adviser—Notice that appointment of scientific adviser appropriate—
　　　　Patents Appeal Tribunal Rules 1972 (SI 1972 No 1940) r 15. **Practice Direction** [1977] **2** 431, PAT.

PATENT (cont)—
  Appeal tribunal (cont)—
    Practice (cont)—
      Dates of sitting. **Practice Direction** [1961] **2** 512, PAT.
    Public hearing—
      Jurisdiction to direct hearing or judgment to be in public. **Practice Direction** [1958] **3** 720, PAT.
  Application—
    Examination of application—
      Function of Comptroller-General and of Patents Appeal Tribunal—Patents Act 1949, s 6. **R v Patents Appeal Tribunal, ex p Swift & Co** [1962] **1** 610, QBD.
    Extension of term. *See* Extension of term—Application, *below.*
    Refusal—
      Process for treatment of human beings—Method of contraception—Process for treatment of human beings to cure or prevent disease only excluded from patent protection—Whether claim to method of contraception allowable. **Schering Aktiengesellschaft's Application, Re** [1971] **3** 177, PAT.
  Biotechnological inventions, legal protection of—
    European Union. *See* **European Union** (Patent—Industrial and commercial property—Legal protection of biotechnological inventions).
  Canada. *See* **Canada** (Patent).
  Cause of action estoppel. *See* **Estoppel** (Res judicata—Cause of action estoppel—Patent).
  Certificate of contested validity—
    Action for infringement—
      Counterclaim for revocation—Order for affidavit of documents—Failure to comply with order—Defence and counterclaim struck out—Trial of action—Certificate of validity—Certificate that particulars of breaches were reasonable—Whether action 'proceeded to trial'—Patents and Designs Acts 1907-1938, s 35—RSC Ord 31, r 21, Ord 53A, r 20. **Superma Ltd v Tenconi** [1939] **2** 427, Ch D.
  Certiorari—
    Patent appeal tribunal. *See* Appeal tribunal—Certiorari to quash decision of tribunal, *above.*
  Comptroller-General of Patents, Designs and Trade Marks—
    Opinion as to validity or infringement—
      Appeal. *See* Appeal—Comptroller's opinion as to validity or infringement, *above.*
    Reference to Comptroller of Patents. *See* Practice—Reference to Comptroller of Patents, *below.*
  Compulsory licence. *See* Licence—Compulsory licence, *below.*
  Condition—
    Licence. *See* Licence—Condition, *below.*
  Conflict of laws—
    Jurisdiction—
      Challenge to jurisdiction. *See* **Conflict of laws** (Jurisdiction—Challenge to jurisdiction—Patent).
      Exclusive jurisdiction. *See* **Conflict of laws** (Jurisdiction—Exclusive jurisdiction—Patent).
    Jurisdiction. *See* **Conflict of laws** (Jurisdiction—Challenge to jurisdiction—Patent).
  Convention for Protection of Industrial Property. *See* Licence—Compulsory licence—Medicine, *below.*
  Covenant by licensee. *See* Licence—Covenant by licensee to communicate improvements, *below.*
  Crown use—
    Importation—
      Drug made abroad and imported by British firm—Drug supplied to Ministry of Health—Use in National Health Service hospitals—Use for the services of the Crown—Minister's power to authorise transaction—Patents Act 1949, s 46(1). **Pfizer Corp v Ministry of Health** [1965] **1** 450, HL.
    Patent for whole article, not for component part—
      Application to unpatented article of statute—Patents and Designs Act 1907, s 29(1)(1A) (as amended to 1946) and Defence (Patents, Trade Marks etc) Regulations 1941 (SR & O 1941 No 1780), reg 3(5). **American Flange and Manufacturing Co Inc v Van Leer** [1948] **2** 698, KBD.
    Rights of third parties in respect of Crown use—
      Contract—Covenant by patentees not to sell fuel economisers except exclusively through agents—Patentees becoming contractors to Government department—Written authority to use patents for service of Crown—Whether authority rendered ineffective contractual obligation with third parties—'Agents, contractors, or others'—Patents and Designs Acts 1907-1942, s 29—RSC Ord 53A, r 22. **Foster Wheeler Ltd v Green & Son Ltd** [1946] **1** 63, CA.
  Damages. *See* Infringement—Damages, *below.*
  Declaration of non-infringement. *See* Infringement—Declaration of non-infringement, *below.*
  Delivery up. *See* Infringement—Order for delivery up, *below.*
  Determination of questions about entitlement to foreign and convention patents—
    Service out of jurisdiction. *See* **Practice** (Service out of the jurisdiction—Appropriate forum—English and American technology companies entering non-disclosure agreement).
  Employee's invention—
    Payment to employee—
      Patents registered in name of employer and employee—Understanding as to payment to employee but no agreement—Apportionment of benefits of inventions—Patents Act 1949, s 56(2). **Sterling Engineering Co Ltd v Patchett** [1955] **1** 369, HL.
    Right of employer to benefit of invention—
      Invention by technical adviser in charge of design and development—Not specifically called on for advice as to design—Invention relating to employer's business—Duty of employee. **British Syphon Co Ltd v Homewood** [1956] **2** 897, Ch D.
      Invention of employee belonging to employer if made in course of 'normal' or 'specifically assigned' duties and circumstances such that an invention might reasonably be expected to result from carrying out of employee's duties—Approach to be adopted in determining whether invention made in course of 'normal' duties—Approach to be adopted in determining whether an invention might reasonably be expected to result from carrying out of employee's duties—Patents Act 1977, s 39(1)(a). **LIFFE Administration and Management v Pinkava** [2007] **4** 981, CA.

PATENT (cont)—

Employee's invention—

Payment to employee—

Award and assessment of just compensation—Size and nature of employer's undertaking—Employee inventing system for measuring glucose—Employer part of group of companies—Whether invention of outstanding benefit to employer—Determination of just compensation—Meaning of 'outstanding benefit'—Patents Act 1977, ss 40, 41. **Shanks v Unilever plc** [2020] **2** 733, SC.

European Patent Office—

Authority of European Patent Office Boards of Appeal decisions. *See* **Precedent** (Court of Appeal—Binding effect of previous decisions of court—Power of court to depart from previous decision—Authority of European Patent Office Boards of Appeal decisions).

European Union. *See* **European Union** (Patent).

Extension of term—

Application—

Advertisement—Amendment of application—Natural justice—Period of extension—Application specifying period of extension sought—Application amended after expiry of original term—Amendment specifying greatly increased period of extension—No advertisement of amended application—Comptroller granting application for period slightly in excess of period originally sought—No opportunity for persons wishing to oppose extended period to do so—Whether amended application a fresh application made out of time—Whether comptroller acting ultra vires or contrary to the principles of natural justice—Patents Act 1949, s 24(1), (3)—Patent Rules 1968 (SI 1968 No 1389) rr 70(2), 71, 152. **R v Comptroller-General of Patents, ex p Farmacy Supplies Ltd** [1971] **2** 419, QBD.

Advertisement—Form—RSC Ord 53A, r 4(d). **Practice Direction** [1963] **2** 1048, Ch D.

Discontinuance—Procedure. **Practice Direction** [1975] **1** 992, Ch D.

Procedure—Fixing appointed day—Patents Act 1949, ss 24, 25—RSC Ord 53A, r 4(c), (d). **Practice Direction** [1961] **2** 625, Ch D.

Extension on ground of loss due to hostilities between His Majesty and any foreign state—

Matters to be considered—Applicant prohibited by foreign law from giving necessary information—Patented article manufactured abroad—Corresponding foreign patent already expired—Patents and Designs Acts 1907-1942, s 18(6). **Von Kantzow's Patent, Re** [1944] **1** 630, Ch D.

Matters to be considered—Whether sales to Government to be taken into consideration. **Van Berkel's Patents, Re** [1944] **1** 545, Ch D.

No order to be made on application of person who subject of such foreign state—Deprivation of nationality by decree of enemy state—Patents and Designs Acts 1907-1946, s 18(6). **Lowenthal v A-G** [1948] **1** 295, Ch D.

Patents acquired from German company—English company paying under agreement one-quarter of moneys received under patents to German company—German company majority shareholders in English company—Loss or damage suffered due to hostilities—Whether English company carried on wholly or mainly for benefit of German company—Custodian of enemy property—Vesting order—Shares sold by Custodian to directors of English company—Patents and Designs Act 1907-1942, s 18(6). **Ring Springs Ltd's Patents, Re** [1944] **2** 421, Ch D.

Recognition—North Korea not recognised—Whether a 'state'—Patents Act 1949, s 24(1). **Al-Fin Corp's Patent, Re** [1969] **3** 396, Ch D.

Foreign judgment—

Recognition—

Foreign judgment affecting rights of English company in regard to English patents—English company neither subject to jurisdiction of foreign court nor party to foreign proceedings. **British Nylon Spinners Ltd v Imperial Chemical Industries Ltd** [1952] **2** 780, CA.

Grant—

Entitlement—

Reference to Comptroller of Patents—Entitlement to patent registered in another's name—Requirements of proof—Whether sufficient to prove referrer being 'inventor'—Whether necessary to prove registered proprietor procuring registration by breach of other rule of law—Patents Act 1977, s 7, 37(1). **Yeda Research and Development Co Ltd v Rhône-Poulenc Rorer International Holdings Inc (Comptroller General for Patents, Designs and Trade Marks intervening)** [2008] **1** 425, HL.

Opposition—

Anticipation—Novelty—State of the art—Disclosure—Enablement—Validity of patent—Patents Act 1977, s 2(3). **Synthon BV v SmithKline Beecham plc** [2006] **1** 685, HL.

Prior use—Invention used in United Kingdom before priority date of claim—Used—Use without appreciating qualities of product or principles on which based—Product blended with other substances to make it commercially saleable—Identity of product lost in blended article—Manufacture and sale of blended product in commercial quantities—Ampicillin trihydrate—Ampicillin trihydrate blended with other substances to make it commercially saleable in form of capsules—Special qualities of ampicillin trihydrate unknown to manufacturers—Whether manufacturers 'used' ampicillin trihydrate—Patents Act 1949, s 14(1)(d). **Bristol-Myers Co v Beecham Group Ltd** [1974] **1** 333, HL.

Prior use—Secret use—No account to be taken of any secret use—Meaning of 'secret'—Intention to conceal use—Nature of product not discoverable by public—Product blended with other substances to make it commercially saleable—Manufacturers unaware of qualities of product—Sale of blended product in commercial quantities—Nature of product not discoverable in existing state of scientific knowledge after blending—Manufacturers having no intention to conceal product—Whether manufacture and sale of product a 'secret use'—Patents Act 1949, s 14(3). **Bristol-Myers Co v Beecham Group Ltd** [1974] **1** 333, HL.

Industrial application. *See* Validity—Industrial application, *below*.

PATENT (cont)—
  Infringement—
    Accrual of cause of action—
      Infringement committed after publication of complete specification but before sealing of
      patent—Action brought more than six years after infringement committed—Whether cause of
      action accruing when infringement committed or when patent granted—Whether action
      time-barred—Patents Act 1949, s 13(4)—Limitation Act 1980, s 2. **Sevcon Ltd v Lucas CAV Ltd**
      [1986] **2** 104, HL.
    Damages—
      Effect of amendment of specification on recovery of damages—Effect upon existing domestic
      proceedings—European Patent Office—Concurrent proceedings—Res judicata—Estoppel—Court
      of Appeal finding patent valid and infringed and ordering inquiry as to damages—Concurrent
      proceedings before European Patent Office (EPO) in respect of patent—EPO subsequently finding
      patent invalid and amending patent to remove infringing claims—Whether defendant able to
      contend at inquiry as to damages that patent retrospectively amended so as to remove infringing
      claims and therefore no damage resulting—Whether defendant estopped from relying on
      revocation or amendment of patent in answer to claim for damages. **Virgin Atlantic Airways Ltd
      v Zodiac Seats UK Ltd** [2013] **4** 715, SC.
      Effect of amendment of specification on recovery of damages—Original claim framed in good faith
      and with reasonable skill and knowledge—Patent invalid at time infringed—Patent as amended
      valid—Jurisdiction to award damages in respect of infringements—Patents and Designs Acts
      1907-1932, s 23. **Molins and Molins Machine Co Ltd v Industrial Machinery Co Ltd** [1937] **4** 295,
      CA.
      Interest—Discretion to include interest on whole or part of the debt—Damages in respect of
      infringing use over period of years—Infringing use starting before grant of patent but after
      publication of complete specification—Exercise of discretion—Evidence of commercial
      practice—Evidence that royalties in respect of use not expected to be paid until grant—No
      evidence that interest expected or paid for period prior to grant—Discretion to limit interest so as
      to run from date of grant—Law Reform (Miscellaneous Provisions) Act 1934, s 3(1)—Patents Act
      1949, s 13(4). **General Tire and Rubber Co v Firestone Tyre and Rubber Co Ltd** [1975] **2** 173, HL.
      Measure of damages—Basis of assessment—Amount payable by way of royalties under licence for
      use—Evidence of amount of royalties defendant would have had to pay—Licensing agreements
      entered into by plaintiff with other users—Damages to be assessed on basis of what defendant
      would in fact have had to pay rather than on sum defendant ought to have paid. **General Tire and
      Rubber Co v Firestone Tyre and Rubber Co Ltd** [1975] **2** 173, HL.
    Declaration of non-infringement—
      Construction of patent—Defendant company proprietor of European Patent in respect of use of
      pemetrexed disodium in combination with vitamin B12 or pharmaceutical derivative
      thereof—Claimant intending to launch generic pemetrexed product—Claimant seeking
      declaration of non-infringement in respect of French, German, Italian, Spanish and United
      Kingdom designations of patent—Whether direct and/or indirect infringement—Applicable
      law—Whether abuse of process—Meaning of 'evidence and procedure'—European Patent
      Convention 2000, art 69—Protocol on the Interpretation of Article 69 of the European Patent
      Convention, arts 1, 2—EP and Council Regulation 864/2007/EC, arts 1(3), 15, 22. **Actavis UK Ltd v
      Eli Lilly & Co** [2014] **2 Comm** 669, Ch D; [2014] **4** 331, Ch D.
      Construction of patent—Defendant company proprietor of European Patent in respect of use of
      pemetrexed disodium in combination with vitamin B12 or pharmaceutical derivative
      thereof—Claimant intending to launch generic pemetrexed product—Claimant seeking
      declaration of non-infringement in respect of French, Italian, Spanish and United Kingdom
      designations of patent—Whether direct and/or indirect infringement—Proper approach to history
      of claim—Patents Act 1977, s 60(2)—European Parliament and Council Regulation 864/2007/EC,
      art 15. **Actavis UK Ltd v Eli Lilly & Co** [2016] **4** 666, CA; [2017] **1 Comm** 24, CA.
      Construction of patent—Defendant company proprietor of European Patent in respect of use of
      pemetrexed disodium in combination with vitamin B12 or pharmaceutical derivative
      thereof—Claimant intending to launch generic pemetrexed product—Claimant seeking
      declaration of non-infringement in respect of French, Italian, Spanish and United Kingdom
      designations of patent—Whether direct and/or indirect infringement—Proper approach to history
      of claim—European Patent Convention 2000, art 69—Protocol on the Interpretation of Article 69 of
      the European Patent Convention, arts 1, 2. **Actavis UK Ltd v Eli Lilly & Co** [2018] **1** 171,
      SC; [2018] **2 Comm** 1, SC.
    Indirect infringement—
      Supplying in United Kingdom a person with any of the means relating to essential element of
      invention for putting invention 'into effect' in United Kingdom—Bookmakers supplying punter
      with computer program making punter's computer a terminal for bookmakers' gaming
      system—Bookmakers' host computer held abroad—Whether host computer having to be within
      United Kingdom to constitute supply for purpose of putting invention 'into effect' in United
      Kingdom—Patents Act 1977, s 60(2). **Menashe Business Mercantile Ltd v William Hill
      Organisation Ltd** [2002] **3** 597, Ch D; [2003] **1** 279, CA.
    Infringement by making—
      Claimant being exclusive licensee of patent relating to intermediate bulk containers (IBCs)—IBCs
      consisting of cages into which bottles fitted—Bottles having limited lifespan—Defendant
      replacing claimant's original bottles with own bottles and offering for sale—Whether defendant
      'making' patented product—Whether infringement of patent—Patents Act 1977, s 60(1)(a). **Schütz
      (UK) Ltd v Werit (UK) Ltd** [2013] **2** 177, SC.
      Plaintiffs having patents for improvements to sifting screens—Screens consisting of frame to which
      meshes were secured—Defendants stripping down plaintiffs' frames and replacing mesh—
      Whether defendants making patented product—Patents Act 1977, s 60(1)(a). **United Wire Ltd v
      Screen Repair Services (Scotland) Ltd** [2000] **4** 353, HL.
    Injunction—
      Form of order—Judge upholding claim for patent infringement but granting injunction only
      restraining defendants from infringing in manner proved at trial—Whether judge should have
      granted injunction restraining defendants from infringing patent in suit. **Coflexip SA v Stolt
      Comex Seaway MS Ltd** [1999] **2** 593, Ch D; [2001] **1** 952n, CA.

PATENT (cont)—
  Infringement (cont)—
    Jurisdiction—
      Standard essential patent ('SEP')—Fair, reasonable and non-discriminatory ('FRAND') licence—
      Whether court having jurisdiction to determine terms of FRAND licence—Whether injunction to
      be granted—Whether breach of EU competition law—Appropriate remedies—Article 102 TFEU.
      Unwired Planet International Ltd v Huawei Technologies (UK) Co Ltd [2021] **1 Comm** 885,
      SC; [2021] **1** 1141, SC.
    Order for delivery up—
      Infringement by particular user only. **Electric and Musical Industries Ltd v Lissen Ltd** [1936] **3** 234,
      Ch D.
    Proceedings for infringement—
      Practice. *See* Practice—Proceedings for infringement or revocation of patent, *below*.
    Validity of patent—
      Ambiguity—Construction of claim—'Substantially as hereinbefore described'—Claim of principal—
      Widening words. **Crabtree (R W) & Sons Ltd v Hoe (R) & Co Ltd** [1936] **2** 1639, CA.
      Insufficiency—Product by process claim—Patents relating to production of erythropoietin—
      Recombinant DNA technology—Whether patents valid—Patents Act 1977, s 72(1)(c)—Convention
      on the Grant of European Patents 1973, arts 64(2), 69. **Kirin-Amgen Inc v Hoechst Marion Roussel
      Ltd** [2005] **1** 667, HL.
      Novelty—Novelty dependent on anterior discovery—Ambiguity and obscurity in specification—
      Indication of inventive step—Width of claim—Limitation of claim by reference to plan. **Raleigh
      Cycle Co Ltd v H Miller & Co Ltd** [1948] **1** 308, HL.
      Novelty—Patentable subject-matter—Prior publication—Prior grant—Patents and Designs Act 1907,
      s 25(2). **Mullard Radio Valve Co Ltd v Philco Radio & Television Corp of GB Ltd** [1936] **2** 920, HL.
      Sufficiency—Patent claim for range of transgenic mice—Whether sufficiency requiring disclosure of
      whole range of products claimed or only some—Whether invention disclosing beneficial principle
      of general application—Whether patent valid—Patents Act 1977, s 14—European Patent
      Convention, art 83. **Regeneron Pharmaceuticals Inc v Kymab Ltd** [2021] **1** 475, SC.
      Sufficiency—Pharmaceutical patent—Second medical use—Pregabalin—Claimant proprietor of
      second medical use patent for pregabalin for treating pain, inflammatory pain and neuropathic
      pain—Defendants applying for authorisation to market pregabalin under 'skinny label' restricted
      to treating epilepsy and anxiety—Whether patent valid—Whether patent infringed—Test for
      sufficiency—Patents Act 1977, ss 14, 72(1)—European Patent Convention 2000, arts 83, 84,
      138—Protocol on the Interpretation of Article 69. **Warner-Lambert Co LLC v Generics (UK) Ltd (t/a
      Mylan) (Secretary of State for Health intervening)** [2019] **3** 95, SC.
  Infringement. *See* Infringement—Validity of patent, *below*.
  Injunction—
    Interim injunction—
      Cross-undertaking in damages—Ex turpi causa non oritur actio—Claimant patent holder obtaining
      interim injunction against defendant selling products infringing its European patent enforceable
      in UK—Claimant giving cross-undertaking in damages—Patent subsequently held invalid and
      injunction discharged—Inquiry as to damages on cross-undertaking—Goods defendant would
      have sold in UK but for interim injunction would have been manufactured in Canada in breach of
      valid patent enforceable in Canada—Whether ex turpi causa rule providing defence to claim on
      cross-undertaking in damages. **Les Laboratoires Servier v Apotex Inc** [2015] **1** 671, SC.
  Insufficiency—
    Revocation. *See* Petition for revocation—Insufficiency, *below*.
  Invention—
    Breach of confidence—
      Invention unpatented. *See* **Equity** (Breach of confidence—Damages—Use of information obtained
      in confidence—Springboard for activities detrimental to informant—Unpatented device disclosed
      by inventor as alternative in course of negotiation for marketing his patented device).
    Emoloyee's. *See* Employee's invention, *above*.
    Exclusions from patentability—
      Business methods—Computer programs—Test to be applied—Convention on the Grant of
      European Patents 1973, art 52(2), (3). **Aerotel Ltd v Telco Holdings Ltd** [2007] **1** 225, CA.
      Computer programs—Test to be applied—Convention on the Grant of European Patents 1973,
      art 52. **Astron Clinica Ltd v Comptroller General of Patents, Designs and Trade Marks**
      [2008] **2** 742, Ch D.
    Manner of manufacture—
      Agricultural process—Method of tenderising meat by injection of enzyme before slaughter—Statute
      of Monopolies (1623), s 6—Patents Act 1949, s 101(1). **R v Patents Appeal Tribunal, ex p Swift &
      Co** [1962] **1** 610, QBD.
    Publication—
      Meaning of publication—Patents Act 1949, s 101(1). **R v Patents Appeal Tribunal, ex p Løvens
      Kemiske Fabriks Handelsaktieselskab** [1968] **3** 536, QBD.
  Invention by importation—
    Jamaica. *See* **Jamaica** (Patent—Validity—Invention by importation).
  Inventive step. *See* Petition for revocation—Obviousness —Inventive step, *below*.
  Jurisdiction—
    Conflict of laws. *See* **Conflict of laws** (Jurisdiction—Challenge to jurisdiction—Patent).
  Law—
    Development—
      Homogeneous development in all countries with like system. **R v Patents Appeal Tribunal, ex p
      Swift & Co** [1962] **1** 610, QBD.
  Leave to amend specification. *See* Specification—Amendment of specification with leave of the court,
  below.

PATENT (cont)—
   Licence—
      Compulsory licence—
         Medicine—Application for compulsory licence within three years from grant—Effect of International Convention for Protection of Industrial Property 1934 (1938, Cmd 5833) art 5(A)(4)—Patents Act 1949, ss 41(1)(b), 45(3). **Parke Davis & Co v Comptroller-General of Patents, Designs and Trade Marks** [1954] **1** 671, HL.
         Medicine—Date from which licence effective—Licence not able to be granted with retroactive effect and thus not to be back-dated—Interlocutory injection granted to restrain infringement pending grant of compulsory licence—Patents Act 1949, s 41(1). **Hoffmann-La Roche (F) & Co AG v Inter-Continental Pharmaceuticals Ltd** [1965] **2** 15, CA.
      Condition—
         Condition restricting sale price of patented article—Retailer obtaining supplies of patented article from licensee—Sale by retailer at less than fixed price—Knowledge of condition as to price—Infringement of patent by retailer. **Dunlop Rubber Co Ltd v Longlife Battery Depot (a firm)** [1958] **3** 197, Ch D.
         Sale in violation of condition—Time when knowledge of condition essential—Certificate of validity—Practice as to grant of certificate of validity. **Gillette Industries Ltd v Bernstein** [1941] **3** 248, CA.
         Validity—Condition in licence that compensation payable to licensors if quantity of contract material sold or used by licensees exceeds certain quota in any month—Whether condition void—Patents and Designs Act 1907, s 38(1). **Tool Metal Manufacturing Co Ltd v Tungsten Electric Co Ltd** [1955] **2** 657, HL.
      Covenant by licensee to communicate improvements—
         Assignment of patent—Enforcement of covenant. **National Carbonising Co Ltd v British Coal Distillation Ltd** [1936] **2** 1012, CA.
      European Community. *See* **European Union** (Patent—Licence).
      Royalties—
         Information for ascertaining royalties—Licensors' auditors to be given 'all such other information as may be necessary or appropriate to enable the amount of the royalties payable' to be ascertained—Whether auditors entitled to information related to articles which were similar to patented articles but which licensees stated were not patented. **Fomento (Sterling Area) Ltd v Selsdon Fountain Pen Co Ltd** [1958] **1** 11, HL.
         Payment—Licensees, sub-contractors to Government department—Written authority to use patents for service of Crown—Whether royalties payable under licence—Minimum royalty clause—patents and Designs Acts 1907-1939, s 29. **No-Nail Cases Pty Ltd v No-Nail Boxes Ltd** [1944] **1** 528, CA; [1946] **1** 523, HL.
         Payment—Most favoured licensee clause—Condition in licence that if sub-licence granted at lower royalties such royalties should be substituted for those in the licence—Royalty structure in sub-licence different from that in licence—Whether royalties payable under sub-licence substituted for those payable under licence. **Fomento (Sterling Area) Ltd v Selsdon Fountain Pen Co Ltd** [1958] **1** 11, HL.
      Specific performance of agreement to grant—
         Judgment of American court affecting rights of English company in regard to English patents—Conflict of law. **British Nylon Spinners Ltd v Imperial Chemical Industries** [1954] **3** 88, Ch D.
   Licensing agreement—
      Inspection of account. *See* **Accounts** (Inspection—Scope of obligation—Licence agreement—Agreement in relation to patents and trade marks).
   Making patented product—
      Infringement. *See* Infringement—Infringement by making, *above.*
   Medicine—
      Compulsory licence. *See* Licence—Compulsory licence—Medicine, *above.*
   Obviousness. *See* Petition for revocation—Obviousness , *below.*
   Opposition to grant of patent. *See* Grant—Opposition, *above.*
   Patents Court—
      Appeal from Comptroller-General of Patents, Designs and Trade Marks—
         Constitution of court—Patents Act 1977, s 97(2). **Practice Direction** [1978] **2** 464, Pat Ct.
         Practice—Appeal to be brought by originating motion—Fees—Registrar of Patent Appeals—Proper officer—RSC Ord 104 (as inserted by RSC (No 3) 1978, r 12), r 14(1) (9) (17). **Practice Direction** [1978] **2** 464, Pat Ct.
      Numbering of judgment. *See* **Judgment** (Numbering of judgments).
      Procedure—
         Draft orders—Experiments for litigation purposes—Assessment of costs—Notices to admit facts—Applications for interlocutory injunctions—RSC Ord 104, rr 10, 11(1)(a), 12. **Practice Note** [1997] **1** 383, Ch D.
      Procedure to be followed—
         Specimen minute of order for directions—Guidance—RSC Ord 104. **Practice Direction** [1998] **1** 279, Pat Ct; [1998] **3** 372, Pat Ct.
   Petition for revocation—
      Appeal from order for revocation—
         Appeal from High Court to House of Lords—Procedure. *See* **House of Lords** (Appeal from High Court—Patent appeal—Appeal from order for revocation of patent—Procedure).
      Application to comptroller—
         Matters which may not be considered by the comptroller—Want of utility, prior user, want of subject-matter—Application to amend specification—Restrictions on amendments under s 11—Patents and Designs Acts 1907-1932, ss 11, 21, 25, 26. **Johnson and Johnson (GB) Ltd's Patent, Re** [1937] **4** 561, CA.
      Insufficiency—
         Fair basis—Patent for antibiotic and process of manufacture—Micro-organism described in specification—Micro-organism deposited in collection—Whether patentee must make essential starting material available to public—Patents Act 1949, s 32(1). **American Cyanamid Co v Upjohn Co** [1970] **3** 785, HL.

PATENT (cont)—
Petition for revocation (cont)—
Insufficiency (cont)—
Product claims in patents—Claim to a single chemical compound—Whether product claim to a single chemical compound restricted to invention's technical contribution to the art—Whether contribution to the art meaning inventive concept. **Generics (UK) Ltd v H Lundbeck A/S** [2009] **2** 955, HL.
Obviousness —
Inventive step—How to identify inventive step—Whether specification having to demonstrate by experiment that invention would work or explain why it would work—Patents Act 1977, s 1(1)(b)—Convention on the Grant of European Patents, art 56. **Conor Medsystems Inc v Angiotech Pharmaceuticals Inc** [2008] **4** 621, HL.
Inventive step—Swiss form claim—Dosage patent—Treatment for sexual dysfunction—Low dosage patent—Whether patent obvious—Patents Act 1977, s 3—European Patent Convention, art 56. **Actavis Group PTC EHF v ICOS Corp** [2020] **1** 213, SC.
Particulars of prior use—
Earliest and latest dates—RSC Ord 53A, r 16. **Martin's Patents, Re** [1936] **1** 711, Ch D.
Practice—
Appeal from High Court to House of Lords. See **House of Lords** (Appeal from High Court—Patent appeal).
Appeal tribunal. See Appeal tribunal, *above*.
Application—
Generally. See Application, *above*.
Consent order made without personal attendance—
Minutes of order signed by counsel for all parties—Specimen form of order for directions. **Practice Direction** [1977] **2** 173, Ch D.
Motions—
Motions to be made to patents judge—Patents Act 1949—RSC Ord 53A. **Practice Direction** [1960] **3** 593, Ch D.
Patents Appeal Tribunal. See Appeal tribunal—Practice, *above*.
Patents Court—
Generally. See Patents Court, *above*.
Petition for revocation. See Petition for revocation, *above*.
Preparation for trial—
Reading guide for judge—Estimated length of trial—Estimate of time needed to read documents—Time for lodging documents—Content of reading guide. **Practice Note** [1990] **1** 192, Ch D.
Proceedings for infringement or revocation of patent—
Discontinuance—Costs—Guidance. **Fresenius Kabi Deutschland GMBH v CareFusion 303 inc** [2012] **1** 794, CA.
European Patent (UK)—Proceedings in both domestic court and European Patent Office—Domestic court finding patent valid and infringed—No further appeal lying—Claimant seeking directions for inquiry for damages or account of profits—Defendants seeking stay pending European Patent Office opposition proceedings—Whether claimant's entitlement to inquiry for damages or account of profits res judicata—Whether defendants estopped from challenging claimant's entitlement if patent revoked in European Patent Office opposition proceedings—Convention on the Grant of European Patents 1973, arts 64, 68—Patents Act 1977, s 77. **Unilin Beheer BV v Berry Floor NV** [2008] **1** 156, CA.
Order for inspection of machinery—Application for leave to inspect allegedly infringing machines—No prima facie case for inspection—Power of court to order inspection in special circumstances—Application for particulars of defendants' contentions—Agreement between the parties that no written statements of contentions should be made—Whether court should order particulars—RSC Ord 53A, r 21A(2). **American Chain and Cable Co Inc v Hall's Barton Ropery Co Ltd** [1938] **4** 129, Ch D.
Petition for revocation. See Petition for revocation, *above*.
Statements of contentions of parties—Interlocutory application—Tests and experiments— Experiments to be limited to issues of infringement and validity—Statements of contentions of parties—Form of such statements—RSC Ord 53A, r 21A(2)(b), (d). **British Thomson-Houston Co Ltd v Tungstalite Ltd** [1938] **4** 177, Ch D.
Summons for directions—Action for infringement—Counterclaim for revocation—Statements signed by counsel—What particulars may be ordered—RSC Ord 53A, r 21A(2). **Whatmough v Morris Motors Ltd** [1938] **4** 584, Ch D.
Summons for directions—Application by post or telephone. See **Practice** (Chancery Division— Applications by post or telephone).
Summons for directions—Procedure where parties agreed as to form of order—Procedure where parties not agreed on terms of order—Procedure for obtaining other interlocutory relief—RSC Ord 103, r 26. **Practice Direction** [1974] **1** 40, Ch D.
Rectification of register—
Application for rectification. See Rectification of register—Application for rectification of register of patents or designs, *below*.
Reference to Comptroller of Patents—
Amendment to statement of case—Referrer seeking to amend claim from joint entitlement to patent to sole entitlement to patent—Whether amendment allowed after expiry of limitation period for making reference—Patents Act 1977, s 37(1), (5). **Yeda Research and Development Co Ltd v Rhône-Poulenc Rorer International Holdings Inc (Comptroller General for Patents, Designs and Trade Marks intervening)** [2008] **1** 425, HL.
Reference to High Court—
Comptroller a party—Costs. **Al-Fin Corp's Patent, Re** [1969] **3** 396, Ch D.
Summons suitable for hearing by judge—
Issue of summons—Stamp—Adjournment into court—Setting down for hearing. **Practice Direction** [1970] **1** 17, Ch D.

PATENT (cont)—
  Practice (cont)—
    Telephone summonses—
      Agreed interlocutory orders—Information sheets—Pre-trial reviews—Solicitors' rights of audience on hearing of summons—Sittings out of London. **Practice Direction** [1996] **1** 63, Ch D.
  Price of patented article—
    Condition restricting price. *See* Licence—Condition—Condition restricting sale price of patented article, *above*.
  Product claim—
    Insufficiency. *See* Petition for revocation—Insufficiency—Product claims in patents, *above*.
  Public hearing of appeal tribunal. *See* Appeal tribunal—Public hearing, *above*.
  Rectification of register—
    Application for rectification of register of patents or designs—
      Agreed directions—Procedure—RSC Ord 104, r 17. **Practice Direction** [1985] **1** 192, Ch D.
    Vesting order—
      Enemy alien bare trustee for British company—Interference with comptroller's emergency powers—Trading with the Enemy Act 1939, s 4—Patents, Designs, Copyright and Trade Marks (Emergency) Act 1939, s 2. **IG Farbenindustrie Aktiengesellschaft and Bayer Products Ltd, Re** [1940] **4** 486, Ch D.
  Refusal of application. *See* Application—Refusal, *above*.
  Restriction of sale price of patented article. *See* Licence—Condition—Condition restricting sale price of patented article, *above*.
  Revocation. *See* Petition for revocation, *above*.
  Royalties. *See* Licence—Royalties, *above*.
  Royalty or other sum paid in respect of the user of a patent—
    Capital gains tax—
      Exemption—Disposal of right to annual payments due under personal covenant not secured on property. *See* **Capital gains tax** (Exemptions and reliefs—Disposal of right to annual payments due under personal covenant not secured on property—Annual payment—Royalty or other sum paid in respect of the user of a patent).
  Scientific adviser—
    Appointment in proceedings before appeal tribunal—
      Practice. *See* Appeal tribunal—Practice—Appointment of scientific adviser, *above*.
  Second medical use—
    Different dosage regime—
      Validity. *See* Validity—Novelty—Obviousness—Second medical use—Swiss form claim—Different dosage regime, *below*.
  Specific performance of agreement to grant licence. *See* Licence—Specific performance of agreement to grant, *above*.
  Specification—
    Amendment of specification by way of disclaimer—
      By way of disclaimer—Whether amendment claims or describes matter not in substance disclosed in unamended specification—Amendment adding further integer to combination constituting invention—Additional integer disclosed in unamended specification but not shown therein as a distinctive part of the invention or as an inventive step—Patents Act 1949, s 31(1). **Amp Inc v Hellerman Ltd** [1962] **1** 673, HL.
    Amendment of specification with leave of the court—
      Application for leave—Advertisement of intention to apply for leave—Identification of pending proceedings—Patents Act 1949, s 30—RSC Ord 53A, r 19(a). **Practice Direction** [1957] **3** 697, Ch D.
      Application for leave—Advertisement of intention to apply for leave—Title of invention to be included—RSC Ord 95, r 19(a). **Practice Direction** [1965] **2** 799, Ch D.
    Construction—
      Disconformity—Legitimate development—Patents and Designs Acts 1907-1932, ss 25(2), 91. **Electric and Musical Industries Ltd v Lissen Ltd** [1938] **4** 221, HL.
    Content. *See* Petition for revocation—Obviousness—Inventive step—How to identify inventive step, *above*.
  Swiss form claim—
    Different dosage regime—
      Validity. *See* Validity—Novelty—Obviousness—Second medical use—Swiss form claim—Different dosage regime, *below*.
  Threats of infringement proceedings—
    Remedy for groundless threats of infringement proceedings—
      Action by person aggrieved—Whether threats action lies where genuine intention to enforce patent—Whether interlocutory injunction against threats granted—Patents Act 1949, s 65. **HVE (Electric) Ltd v Cufflin Holdings Ltd** [1964] **1** 674, CA.
    Threats—
      What constitutes a threat—Patents and Designs Acts 1907-1932, s 36. **Surridge's Patents Ltd v Trico-Folberth Ltd** [1936] **3** 26, Ch D.
  Validity—
    Industrial application—
      Biotechnological invention—Revocation proceedings—Principles to be applied in determining whether invention having industrial application—Patents Act 1977, ss 1(1)(c), 72(1)(a)—European Patent Convention 2000, art 57. **Eli Lilly and Co v Human Genome Sciences Inc** [2012] **1** 1154, SC.
    Novelty—
      Obviousness—Second medical use—Swiss form claim—Different dosage regime—Claimant seeking revocation of defendant's European patent for second medical use in Swiss form—Finasteride drug for treatment of androgenic alopecia—Claimant alleging defendant's previous European patent disclosing same therapeutic application—Whether claim lacking novelty—Whether new dosage regime enough to confer novelty on Swiss form claim—Whether Swiss form claim limited to claim for treatment of a different disease or extending to different method of using a compound for treatment of a particular disease when its use in treating that disease by a different method already known—Convention on the Grant of European Patents 1973, art 54. **Actavis UK Ltd v Merck & Co Inc** [2009] **1** 196, CA.

PATENT (cont)—
Validity. *See* Infringement—Validity of patent, *above*.

PATENTS APPEAL TRIBUNAL
Appeal from. *See* **Patent** (Appeal to Court of Appeal).
Generally. *See* **Patent** (Appeal tribunal).

PATENTS COURT
See **Patent** (Patents Court).

PATERNITY
Affiliation proceedings. *See* **Affiliation**.
Appeal—
Leave to appeal out of time—
Divorce—Decree granted in favour of husband—Child held to be child of family—Appeal by husband on issue of paternity—Six years delay—Reasons for refusal—Failure to show due diligence—Changes in law relating to burden of proof of illegitimacy working to disadvantage of child. **McC (R D) v McC (J A)** [1971] **2** 1097, CA.
Blood test—
Application—
Jurisdiction of registrar to entertain application—Circumstances in which summons should be adjourned to judge—Summons opposed or matter of principle likely to arise—Family Law Reform Act 1969, s 20(1). **R v R (blood test: jurisdiction)** [1973] **3** 933, Fam D.
Child under 16 in care of mother—
Applicants obtaining orders for the testing of children's blood to determine paternity—Children's mothers refusing to consent to tests—Whether court having jurisdiction to compel mothers to consent to tests—Family Law Reform Act 1969, ss 20(1), 21(3)—Children Act 1989, s 37. **O (a child) (blood tests: constraint), Re** [2000] **2** 29, Fam D.
Divorce—
Adultery—Evidence—Blood groups. **H v H (H, by his guardian, intervening)** [1966] **1** 356, Div.
Adultery—Evidence—Legitimacy of child in issue—Standard of proof. **F v F** [1968] **1** 242, Div.
Criterion whether test should be ordered—Interest of child—Application for purpose of claiming custody. **B v B and E (B intervening)** [1969] **3** 1106, CA.
Criterion whether test should be ordered—Interest of child—Inconclusiveness of result. **B v B and E (B intervening)** [1969] **3** 1106, CA; **S v S, W v Official Solicitor** [1970] **1** 1157, CA.
Criterion whether test should be ordered—Interest of child—Inconclusiveness of result—Allegation of adultery—Child ten years old—Purpose of test provision of evidence of adultery. **M (D) v M (S) and G (M (D A) intervening)** [1969] **2** 243, CA.
Criterion whether test should be ordered—Interest of child—Interest of justice. **S v S, W v Official Solicitor** [1970] **1** 1162, CA.
Criterion whether test should be ordered—Interest of child—Whether interest of child paramount. **S v S, W v Official Solicitor** [1970] **3** 107, HL.
Guardian ad litem—Consent—Whether consent of guardian ad litem necessary—Matrimonial Causes Act 1965, ss 33, 34. **L, Re** [1968] **1** 20, CA.
Guardian ad litem—Official Solicitor—Appointment of Official Solicitor as guardian ad litem where blood test likely to be directed—Appointment usually unnecessary in first instance—Circumstances in which appointment should be made. **Practice Direction** [1975] **1** 223, Fam D.
Guardian ad litem—Official Solicitor—Appointment of Official Solicitor—Notice to Official Solicitor of intention to cause child to undergo medical examination—Matrimonial Causes Rules 1968 (SI 1968 No 219), r 108. **Practice Direction** [1968] **3** 607, Div.
Jurisdiction to order test—County court. **B R B v J B** [1968] **2** 1023, CA.
Jurisdiction to order test—High Court—Advantage to child essential. **H v H** [1966] **3** 560, Div.
Jurisdiction to order test—High Court—Divorce Division. **L, Re** [1967] **2** 1110, PDA.
Refusal of test—Presumption of legitimacy—Whether refusal reasonable. **B v B and E (B intervening)** [1969] **3** 1106, CA.
Nullity—
Pregnancy at date of marriage—Pregnancy by person other than petitioner—Haptoglobin tests. **Stocker (by his next friend) v Stocker (orse Woodruff, by her guardian)** [1966] **2** 147, Div.
Onus of proof—
Presumption of legitimacy—Blood test not conclusive—Inference to be drawn—Test showing that husband could be father of child—Evidence that child had blood group compatible with paternity of one man in nine or ten of western Europeans—Family Law Reform Act 1969, s 26. **T (H) v T (E)** [1971] **1** 590, Div.
Procedure—
Direction for use of blood tests—Arrangements for taking and testing of samples. **Practice Direction** [1972] **1** 640, Fam D.
Wardship proceedings—
Circumstances in which court will order blood test in wardship proceedings. **J S (a minor), Re** [1980] **1** 1061, CA.
Declaration of legitimacy. *See* **Legitimation** (Declaration of legitimacy).
Declaration of paternity—
Appeal against declaration—
Child born after IVF treatment with donor sperm—Unmarried mother having started treatment together with partner—Parties having separated before implantation of embryo which resulted in birth of child—Whether former partner legal father of child—Human Fertilisation and Embryology Act 1990, s 28(3). **R (a child), Re** [2003] **2** 131, CA; [2005] **4** 433, HL.
Family proceedings court making declaration that appellant was father of child—Subsequent medical evidence confirming that appellant could not be father of child—Whether appellant able to appeal to High Court against declaration—Child Support Act 1991, s 27. **T v Child Support Agency** [1997] **4** 27, Fam D.

PATERNITY (cont)—
    Declaration of paternity (cont)—
        DNA testing—
            Jurisdiction to order—DNA sample of deceased person—Whether court having power to direct scientific testing of deceased person to establish paternity—Whether testing to be ordered—Family Law Reform Act 1969—Family Law Act 1986, s 55A—FPR 20.2. **Spencer v Anderson** [2017] **2** 846, Fam D.
        DNA testing—
           Jurisdiction to order—
            Court of protection. *See* **Mental health** (Court of Protection—Jurisdiction—Incapacity—Paternity).
    Estoppel—
        Divorce—
            Order for custody of child—Child subsequently petitioning for declaration of legitimacy—Husband in divorce suit denying paternity—Order for custody not a judgment in rem. **B v A-G (NEB intervening)** [1965] **1** 62, Div.
            Order for maintenance of child—Application to vary order on ground that child not child of marriage—Registrar not competent to determine issue of paternity—Matrimonial Causes Act 1950, s 26(1)—Matrimonial Causes Rules 1950 (SI 1950 No 1940), rr 27, 29(1). **Nokes v Nokes** [1957] **2** 535, CA.
            Undefended proceedings—Custody order—Custody awarded to mother—Application for maintenance—Application opposed by father—Whether father estopped from denying paternity by reason of custody order. **G (S D) v G (H H)** [1970] **3** 844, Div.
    Evidence—
        Admissibility—
            Photographic evidence—Evidence of facial resemblance between child and near relations—Whether photographic evidence admissible. **C v C and C (legitimacy: photographic evidence)** [1972] **3** 577, Fam D.
        Title. *See* **Title** (Honour—Succession—Paternity).
    Leave to appeal out of time. *See* Appeal—Leave to appeal out of time, *above*.
    Legitimation of child. *See* **Legitimation**.
    Presumption of legitimacy—
        Onus of proof—
            Blood test. *See* Blood test—Onus of proof—Presumption of legitimacy, *above*.
    Succession—
        Title. *See* **Title** (Honour—Succession—Paternity).
    Ward of court—
        Declaration of paternity—
            Jurisdiction to make grant bare declaration in wardship proceedings. *See* **Ward of court** (Jurisdiction—Declaration of paternity).

PATIENT
    After-care services—
        Mental health patient. *See* **Mental health** (Patient—After-care services).
    Doctor and patient—
        Confidential information—
            Disclosure—Generally. *See* **Medical practitioner** (Doctor and patient—Disclosure of confidential information).
    Hospital—
        Driver—
            Breath test. *See* **Road traffic** (Breath test—Hospital patient).
    Medical treatment—
        Generally. *See* **Medical treatment**.
    Mental health—
        Seclusion. *See* **Mental health** (Patient—Seclusion).
    Mental health. *See* **Mental health** (Patient).
    National Health Service—
        Medical records—
            Access to medical records by patient. *See* **National Health Service** (Medical records—Access to medical records by patient).

PATRIAL
    Immigration. *See* **Immigration** (Patrial).

PAVEMENT
    Negligence—
        Hole dug in pavement. *See* **Highway** (Maintenance—Negligence—Street works—Hole dug in pavement by local authority workmen for junction box).
        Proximity of vehicle to edge of pavement. *See* **Negligence** (Highway—Pavement—Proximity of vehicle to edge of pavement).
    Unguarded opening—
        Negligence. *See* **Negligence** (Highway—Unguarded opening on pavement).

PAWN
    Sale of pawned articles—
        Interest. *See* **Interest** (Sale of pawned articles).

PAY
    Equal pay—
        Men and women—
            Equality of treatment—European Community. *See* **European Union** (Equality of treatment of men and women—Equal pay for equal work).
            Equality of treatment—Generally. *See* **Employment** (Equality of treatment of men and women).
    Generally. *See* **Employment** (Remuneration).

PAY AS YOU EARN
    See **Income tax** (Pay as you earn system).

PAYMENT INTO COURT
    Acceptance—
        Interest—
            Person under a disability. *See* **Practice** (Payment into court—Interest—Claimant under a disability).
        Statement in open court—
            Action for assault. *See* **Practice** (Statement in open court—Action for assault).
    Application for specific performance. *See* **Sale of land** (Purchaser—Purchaser in possession).
    Costs—
        Generally. *See* **Costs** (Payment into court).
        Interest on costs. *See* **Costs** (Interest on costs—Payment into court by defendant).
        Legal aid cases. *See* **Legal aid** (Costs—Payment into court).
        Order for costs—
            Discretion. *See* **Costs** (Order for costs—Discretion—Payment into court).
        Practice. *See* **Practice** (Payment into court—Costs).
    County court—
        Effect on costs. *See* **County court** (Costs—Payment into court).
        Generally. *See* **County court** (Practice—Payment into court).
    Damages—
        Personal injury—
            Interest. *See* **Interest** (Damages—Personal injury—Payment into court).
    Delay by solicitor—
        Payment of costs by solicitor personally. *See* **Solicitor** (Payment of costs by solicitor personally—Delay by solicitor—Payment into court).
    Generally. *See* **Practice** (Payment into court).
    Interim remedy, as—
        Payment of specific fund. *See* **Practice** (Interim remedy—Payment into court of specified fund where there was dispute over party's right to fund).
    Investment of funds—
        Practice. *See* **Practice** (Funds in court—Investment of funds in court).
    Legal aid—
        Costs. *See* **Legal aid** (Costs—Payment into court).
    Non-disclosure—
        Appeal as to quantum of damages. *See* **Court of Appeal** (Practice—Payment into court—Non-disclosure—Appeal as to quantum of damages).
        Practice. *See* **Practice** (Payment into court—Non-disclosure of payment into court).
    Person under a disability—
        Interest. *See* **Practice** (Payment into court—Interest—Claimant under a disability).
    Stay of proceedings. *See* **Practice** (Payment into court—Stay of proceedings).

PAYMENT OUT OF COURT
    Admiralty. *See* **Admiralty** (Practice—Payment out of court).
    Compensation for compulsory acquisition of land. *See* **Compulsory purchase** (Compensation—Payment out of compensation paid into court).
    County court. *See* **County court** (Payment out of court).
    Generally. *See* **Practice** (Payment out of court).
    Mistake—
        Payment into court—
            Jurisdiction of county court to order. *See* **County court** (Jurisdiction—Order for repayment of money paid out of court in error).

PEACEFUL PICKETING
    Generally. *See* **Trade dispute** (Picketing).
    Unfair industrial practice. *See* **Industrial relations** (Unfair industrial practice—Peaceful picketing).

PECUNIARY ADVANTAGE
    Obtaining by deception. *See* **Criminal law** (Obtaining pecuniary advantage by deception).

PECUNIARY INTEREST
    Member of local authority—
        Disability for voting at meeting. *See* **Local authority** (Meetings—Disability of members of authorities for voting on account of pecuniary interest in contracts etc).

PECUNIARY LEGACY
    Amount. *See* **Will** (Gift—Amount of pecuniary legacy).
    Estate duty. *See* **Estate duty** (Incidence—Pecuniary legacies).
    Payment before testamentary expenses. *See* **Administration of estates** (Order of application of assets—Statutory order—Variation—Pecuniary legacies to be paid before testamentary expenses).

PECUNIARY LOSS
    Fatal accident—
        Damages. *See* **Fatal accident** (Damages—Pecuniary loss).

PEDESTRIAN CROSSING
    See **Road traffic** (Pedestrian crossing).

PEDIATRICIAN
    Expert witness—
        Divorce proceedings. *See* **Evidence** (Expert witness—Pediatrician—Divorce proceedings).

PEDLAR
Definition. *See* **Street trading** (Pedlar—Definition).
Street trading. *See* **Street trading** (Pedlar).

PEER
Parliamentary election—
    Disqualification as candidate. *See* **Elections** (Parliamentary—Validity—Disqualification of candidate—
    Peer).
Privilege from arrest. *See* **Arrest** (Privilege from arrest—Peer of the realm).

PEERAGE
Claim to peerage—
    House of Lords Committee for Privileges—
        Precedent. *See* **Precedent** (House of Lords—Committee for Privileges—Claim to peerage).
Creation—
    Title—
        Grant in same name as earlier title—Concurrent grant or grant on more than one
        occasion—Whether Sovereign can grant same title of nobility to more than one person
        concurrently—Whether Sovereign can grant title to individual on more than one occasion without
        resignation of prior grant. **Annandale and Hartfell Peerage Claim** [1985] 3 577, HL.
Hereditary peerage—
    Peerage confirmed by letters patent—
        Whether inalienable. **Bristol South East Parliamentary Election, Re** [1961] 3 354, QBD.
Succession—
    Legitimacy—
        Declaration—Binding effect on Crown. *See* **Legitimation** (Declaration of legitimacy—Binding
        effect—Crown—Peerage claim).

PENAL STATUTE
Generally. *See* **Statute** (Penal statute).
Retrospective operation. *See* **Statute** (Retrospective operation—Penal statute).

PENALTY
Bankruptcy—
    Whether penalty a 'debt provable in bankruptcy'. *See* **Bankruptcy** (Debts provable in
    bankruptcy—Penalty).
Continuing penalty—
    Value added tax. *See* **Value added tax** (Penalty—Continuing penalty).
Contract. *See* **Contract** (Penalty).
Hire-purchase agreement. *See* **Hire-purchase** (Penalty).
Hiring agreement. *See* **Hire** (Damages for breach of contract of hiring—Repudiation of contract by
    hirer—Agreed damages percentage of outstanding rentals—Whether penalty).
Importation of prohibited goods. *See* **Customs and excise** (Importation of prohibited goods—Penalty).
Income tax. *See* **Income tax** (Penalty).
National insurance—
    Arrears of contributions—
        Recoverable as a penalty. *See* **Social security** (Arrears of contributions—Recovery—Recoverable as
        a penalty).
Relief against. *See* **Equity** (Penalty—Relief against penalty).
Value added tax. *See* **Value added tax** (Penalty).
Witness exposed to risk of penalty—
    Privilege against self-incrimination—
        Answer to question tending to expose witness or spouse to penalties provided for by law of United
        Kingdom. *See* **Evidence** (Privilege—Incrimination of witness or spouse—Answer to question
        tending to expose witness or spouse to penalties provided for by law of United Kingdom).
        Belief that evidence would expose witness to proceedings for offence or recovery of penalty. *See*
        Evidence (Privilege—Incrimination of witness or spouse—Belief that evidence would expose
        witness to proceedings for offence or recovery of penalty).

PENALTY POINTS
Road traffic offences. *See* **Road traffic** (Penalty points).

PENDING ACTION
Comment prejudicial to fair trial—
    Contempt of court. *See* **Contempt of court** (Publications concerning legal proceedings—Pending
    proceedings).
Effect of retrospective legislation. *See* **Statute** (Retrospective operation—Pending proceedings).
Interlocutory injunction. *See* **Injunction** (Interlocutory—Pending proceedings).
Land action—
    Registration as land charge. *See* **Land charge** (Pending action).
    Vacation of entry in land register. *See* **Land charge** (Vacation of entry in register—Pending action).

PENDING APPEAL
Practice. *See* **Practice** (Appeal—Pending appeal).

PENSION

Annuities—

Transfers—

Scheme proposed providing for transfer of annuity policies from one provider to another—Independent expert concluding scheme will not materially affect interests or reasonable expectations of policyholders—Regulators not objecting to scheme—Policyholders raising objections to scheme—Whether appropriate in all the circumstances for discretion to be exercised to sanction scheme—Financial Services and Markets Act 2000, s 111(3). **Prudential Assurance Company Ltd, Re** [2020] **1 Comm** 955, Ch D; [2021] **2 Comm** 1051, CA.

Appeal. *See* **Pensions Appeal Tribunal.**

Appeal tribunal. *See* **Pensions Appeal Tribunal.**

Attachment of earnings. *See* **Husband and wife** (Maintenance—Attachment of earnings—Husband in receipt of pension).

Civil service pension scheme—

Amendment. *See* Pension scheme—Amendment—Civil service pension scheme, *below*.

Company pension scheme—

Surplus fund—

Pensions scheme requiring employers to make arrangements to deal with actuarial surplus but precluding amendment 'making any of the moneys of the Scheme payable to any of the Employers'—Employers making arrangements to treat their accrued liabilities to fund as discharged out of surplus funds—Whether release of debt owed to fund by employers amounting to payment to them out of fund—Whether amendment required before arrangements could be made to treat employers' accrued liabilities as discharged out of surplus funds—Pensions Act 1995, s 37. **National Grid Co plc v Mayes** [2001] **2** 417, HL.

Contributions—

Employer and employee—

Failure of employer to pay contributions. *See* **Employment** (Contract of service—Breach of contract—Damages—Pension fund contributions).

Equality of treatment of men and women—

European Community. *See* **European Union** (Equality of treatment of men and women—Pension contributions).

Damages for personal injuries—

Whether pension to be taken into account. *See* **Damages** (Personal injury—Loss of future earnings—Pension).

Damages under Fatal Accidents Acts—

Payments made to widow from husband's pension fund consequent on his death—

Whether payments to widow to be disregarded in assessing damages for husband's death. *See* **Fatal accident** (Damages—Benefits excluded in assessing damages—Pension).

Whether pension deductible. *See* **Fatal accident** (Damages—Deduction from damages—Pension).

Widow—

Lost opportunity of post-retirement pension. *See* **Fatal accident** (Damages—Lost opportunity of widow's post-retirement pension).

Discrimination—

Discrimination on grounds of age. *See* **Employment** (Discrimination—Discrimination on grounds of age—Occupational pension scheme).

Divorce—

Pension sharing order. *See* **Divorce** (Financial provision—Pension sharing order).

Equal treatment in employment and occupation—

European Community. *See* **European Union** (Employment—Equal treatment in employment and occupation—Pension).

Part-time worker—

Calculation of pension entitlement—Fee-paid part-time judges claiming statutory entitlement to pension—Whether three-month limitation period running from end of appointment or date of retirement—Whether claims time-barred—Judicial Pensions and Retirement Act 1993, s 1(1), (6), Sch 1—Part-time Workers (Prevention of Less Favourable Treatment) Regulations 2000, SI 2000/1551, regs 5, 8. **Miller v Ministry of Justice** [2020] **3** 621, SC.

Calculation of pension entitlement—Whether calculation to account for part-time employment prior to transposition of prohibition of discrimination against part-time workers in national law—Whether Directive having retroactive effect—Council Directive 97/81/EC. **O'Brien v Ministry of Justice** [2017] **1** 1078, CA; [2017] **4** 997n, SC.

Sexual orientation—

Surviving spouse's pension—Whether surviving spouse's pension payable where employee retiring prior to transposition of prohibition of discrimination on grounds of sexual orientation—Equality Act 2010, Sch 9, para 18—Council Directive 2000/78/EC. **O'Brien v Ministry of Justice** [2017] **1** 1078, CA.

Surviving spouse's pension—Whether surviving spouse's pension payable where employee retiring prior to transposition of prohibition of discrimination on grounds of sexual orientation—Whether domestic law compatible with EU law—Equality Act 2010, Sch 9, para 18—Council Directive 2000/78/EC. **Walker v Innospec Ltd** [2017] **4** 1004, SC.

Equality of treatment of men and women—

Equal pay for equal work—

European Community. *See* **European Union** (Equality of treatment of men and women—Equal pay for equal work—Pension).

European Community—

Equal pay for equal work. *See* **European Union** (Equality of treatment of men and women—Equal pay for equal work—Pension).

Pension contributions. *See* **European Union** (Equality of treatment of men and women—Pension contributions).

PENSION (cont)—
Equality of treatment of men and women (cont)—
Legislation equalising state pension age for women and men—
Pension age for women raised incrementally—Whether direct age discrimination—Whether indirect sex or sex/age discrimination—Whether legislation justified—Whether notification required—Whether relief to be granted—Pensions Act 1995—Human Rights Act 1998, Sch 1, Pt I, art 14, Pt II, art 1—Pensions Act 2007—Pensions Act 2011—Pensions Act 2014—Council Directive 79/7/EEC, arts 4, 7. **R (on the application of Delve) v Secretary of State for Work and Pensions** [2021] **3** 115, CA.
Part-time employees' retrospective claims time-barred and restricted by national legislation—
Meaning of 'the employment'—Equal Pay Act 1970, s 2(4). **Preston v Wolverhampton Healthcare NHS Trust** [1998] **1** 528, HL.
Whether legislation compatible with Community law—Equal Pay Act 1970, s 2(4)—EC Treaty, art 119 (now art 141 EC). **Preston v Wolverhampton Healthcare NHS Trust** [2001] **3** 947, HL.
European Community—
Non-discrimination, principle of—
Income tax. *See* **European Union** (Freedom of movement—Principle of non-discrimination—Income tax—Retirement pension).
Final salary pension—
Parliamentary Commissioner for Administration, report by. *See* **Parliamentary Commissioner for Administration** (Report by Commissioner).
Fireman. *See* **Fire brigade** (Fireman—Pension).
Freedom of movement—
Income tax. *See* **European Union** (Freedom of movement—Principle of non-discrimination—Income tax—Retirement pension).
Income tax. *See* **Income tax** (Pension).
Increase—
Right to increase—
Pensions 'payable by local authority solely in respect of local government service'—Transfer of servant to transport board—Continuance as member of pension fund of local authority—'Enactment by which fund regulated'—London Passenger Transport Act 1933, 2 80(9), (10)—Pensions (Increase) Act 1944, Sch I, Pt II, para 1. **Abbott v London CC** [1951] **2** 697, CA.
Invalidity—
Non-contributory invalidity pension. *See* **Social security** (Non-contributory invalidity pension).
Local government pension. *See* Pension scheme—Local government pensions, *below.*
Loss of pension rights—
Damages for breach of contract. *See* **Contract** (Damages for breach—Loss of pension rights).
Damages for loss of pension rights—
Company's pension scheme—Wrongful dismissal—Discretionary pension scheme referred to in service agreement—Whether discharge or early retirement with consent. **Bold v Brough, Nicholson & Hall Ltd** [1963] **3** 849, QBD.
Damages for personal injuries. *See* **Damages** (Personal injury—Loss of future earnings—Pension).
Military pension—
Avoidance of assignment of, or charge on, pay, pensions etc—
Financial provision order—Divorce proceedings. *See* **Divorce** (Financial provision—Military pay, pensions etc—Avoidance of assignment of, or charge on, military pay, pensions etc).
Negligence—
Duty to take care—
Insurance. *See* **Negligence** (Duty to take care—Insurance—Pensions and life cover).
Occupational pension scheme—
Discrimination—
Discrimination on grounds of age. *See* **Employment** (Discrimination—Discrimination on grounds of age—Occupational pension scheme).
Winding up. *See* Pension scheme—Company pension scheme—Winding up, *below.*
Order for costs—
Costs of reference—
Pensions Ombudsman—Ombudsman refusing to make direction for costs—Whether ombudsman having power to make direction as to costs—Whether ombudsman entitled to refuse to make direction for costs in instant case. **Sheffield v Kier Group plc** [2019] **3** 1086, Ch D.
Payment through bank. *See* **Bank** (Pension—Payment of pension through bank).
Pension scheme—
Amendment—
Civil service pension scheme—Civil service compensation scheme—Protection of property—Freedom of assembly and association—Whether entitlements under scheme constituting possessions—Whether amendment to scheme constituting unlawful interference with possessions or with right to freedom of assembly and association—Human Rights Act 1998, Sch 1, Pt I, art 11, Pt II, art 1—Superannuation Act 2010. **R (on the application of the Public and Commercial Services Union) v Minister for the Civil Service** [2012] **1** 985, Admin Ct.
Civil service pension scheme—Civil service compensation scheme—Requirement for consultation over amendment reducing any amount referable to rights accrued—Whether requirement for consultation extending to compensation scheme—Superannuation Act 1972, s 2(3). **R (on the application of the Public and Commercial Services Union) v Minister for the Civil Service** [2011] **3** 54, QBD; **R (on the application of the Public and Commercial Services Union) v Minister for the Civil Service (No 2)** [2011] **3** 73n, QBD.
Employees' pension and life assurance scheme—Provision for change of scheme reserving the right to employers to discontinue the scheme in the event of 'unforeseen circumstance'—Whether amendments changing beneficial interests validly made. **Herbert (Alfred) Ltd Pension and Life Assurance Scheme Trusts, Re** [1960] **1** 618, Ch D.
Approved scheme—
Income tax. *See* **Income tax** (Pension—Approved scheme).

Pension scheme (cont)—
Company pension scheme—
Action by members of pension scheme—Costs—Pre-emptive order as to costs—Indemnity—Action brought concerning administration of pension scheme—Plaintiffs applying for pre-emptive costs order requiring their costs and any costs they might be ordered to pay to be paid on indemnity basis out of pension fund—Judge granting order—Whether judge having jurisdiction to do so—Whether judge's discretion properly exercised. **McDonald v Horn** [1995] **1** 961, CA.
Appointment and removal of trustees—Insolvent company—Whether administrators having power to amend definitive trust deed of employee pension scheme—Whether administrators having power to remove independent trustee after pension scheme fully paid up—Validity of removal and appointment of trustee—Social Security Pensions Act 1975, s 57C—Occupational Pension Schemes (Independent Trustee) Regulations 1990, reg 4. **Denny v Yeldon** [1995] **3** 624, Ch D.
Damages for loss of pension rights. *See* Loss of pension rights—Damages for loss of pension rights—Company's pension scheme, *above.*
Deficit—Buy-out deficit—Power of trustee to determine appropriate contributions from employer company—Whether trustee having power to demand contribution to make good buy-out deficit. **K & J Holdings Ltd, Re** [2005] **4** 449, CA.
Dissolution of scheme—Calculation of deferred annuities—Whether trustees should have regard to member's projected salary and/or future period of service in determining amount of mandatory benefits. **Mettoy Pension Trustees Ltd v Evans** [1991] **2** 513, Ch D.
Employer contributions—Overriding statutory provisions where occupational pension scheme provisions conflicting with legislation—Pension trustee demanding contributions from employer—Whether demand valid—Whether scheme contribution rule conflicting with legislation—Pensions Act 2004, s 306—Occupational Pension Schemes (Scheme Funding) Regulations 2005, SI 2005/3377. **British Vita Unlimited v British Pension Fund Trustees Ltd** [2008] **1** 37, Ch D.
Improper application of pension funds—Funds improperly paid into overdrawn bank account—Whether equitable tracing remedy available—Whether fact of overdrawn account defeating equitable remedy. **Bishopsgate Investment Management Ltd (in liq) v Homan** [1995] **1** 347, CA.
Members terminating pensionable service and applying to exercise their right to a transfer value of cash equivalent of accrued pension benefits—Company going into receivership and thereafter pension scheme commencing winding up—Statutory time period for payment of transfer value expiring—Occupational Pensions Board granting scheme trustee's application for extension—Whether extension of statutory period validly granted—Whether right to cash equivalent lost on termination of scheme—Whether members' right to cash equivalent an overriding right which remained unaffected by winding up—Social Security Pensions Act 1975, Sch 1A, paras 15(3)(c), 16(3)(a), (5), 18(2). **Law Debenture Trust Corp plc v Pensions Ombudsman** [1997] **3** 233, Ch D.
Minimum funding requirement—Minimum funding requirement applicable to schemes other than money purchase schemes—Whether scheme money purchase scheme—Pension Schemes Act 1993, s 181—Pensions Act 1995, s 67. **Aon Trust Corp Ltd v KPMG (a firm)** [2005] **3** 587, Ch D; [2006] **1** 238, CA.
Mistake—Mistake in rules of scheme—Whether relief for mistake available in equity. **Smithson v Hamilton** [2008] **1** 1216, Ch D.
New rules for administration of scheme—Execution of deed bringing new rules into operation—Trustees not fully aware of consequences of new winding-up provisions—Whether trustees would have executed deed as drafted if they had been fully aware of such consequences—Whether deed should be set aside. **Mettoy Pension Trustees Ltd v Evans** [1991] **2** 513, Ch D.
Occupational pension scheme—Winding up—Deficiencies in assets—Valuation of pension liabilities—Date of assessment—Pensions Act 1995, s 75—Occupational Pension Schemes (Employer Debt) Regulations 2005, SI 2005/678, reg 5. **BESTrustees plc (trustee of the Singer & Friedlander Ltd Pension & Assurance Scheme) v Kaupthing Singer & Friedlander Ltd (in admin)** [2012] **3** 874, Ch D.
Pension benefits payable to members—Increase in pension benefits payable to members—Consent of company to increases—Company pension scheme managed by committee of management—Scheme having substantial surplus—Increases in pension benefits made by amendment of rules with consent of company—Right to increase pension benefits payable to members of scheme—Whether committee of management having power to increase pension benefits without company's consent—Whether company entitled to withhold consent—Whether company's right to give or withhold consent subject to obligation to act in good faith. **Imperial Group Pension Trust Ltd v Imperial Tobacco Ltd** [1991] **2** 597, Ch D.
Pensions Regulator—Determinations Panel—Financial support direction—Standard procedure—References—Determination notice—Reference by person directly affected by determination—Relevant time—Determination issuing direction for financial support to group companies securing support for company pension scheme—Trustees of pension scheme applying for reference to add further group companies—Whether trustees of pension scheme persons directly affected by determination—Whether relevant time limit excluding addition of further group companies—Pensions Act 2004, ss 43, 96, 103. **Trustees of the Lehman Brothers Pension Scheme v Pensions Regulator** [2013] **4** 744, CA.
Pensions Regulator—Standard procedure—Warning notices—Decision of the Determination Panel to issue financial support directions referred to Upper Tribunal—Whether regulator could rely on additional grounds and arguments not stated in warning notices—Applicable test for permitting regulator to raise new case—Pensions Act 2004, s 96. **ITV plc v Pensions Regulator** [2015] **4** 919, CA.
Privatisation of statutory corporation leading to winding up of employee pension funds—Surpluses in funds being distributed to government—Trustee commencing proceedings for recovery of surpluses—Trustee asking for directions on application of statutory provisions—Whether funds remained occupational pension schemes—Whether schemes had any members—Pension Schemes Act 1993, s 1—Pensions Act 1995, s 124(1)—Register of Occupational and Personal Pension Schemes Regulations 1997, reg 1(4). **Bus Employees Pension Trustees Ltd v Harrod** [1999] **2** 993, Ch D.

PENSION (cont)—

Pension scheme (cont)—

Company pension scheme (cont)—

Surplus fund—Company in liquidation—Dissolution of scheme—Distribution of surplus fund—Trustee's discretion surrendered to court—Manner in which discretion to be exercised—Whether employer precluded from taking surplus out of scheme unless provision made for all pensions under scheme to be increased by statutory limited price index—Social Security Act 1990, s 11(3). **Thrells Ltd (in liq) v Lomas** [1993] **2** 546, Ch D.

Surplus fund—Discretion to augment benefits—Fiduciary power—Group of companies establishing contributory pension scheme for employees—Rules of scheme conferring discretion on employer, exercisable on termination of scheme, to use surplus fund to augment benefits payable—Fund in surplus on termination of scheme—Whether discretion to augment benefits amounting to full fiduciary power—Whether discretion exercisable by receivers of liquidators. **Mettoy Pension Trustees Ltd v Evans** [1991] **2** 513, Ch D.

Surplus fund—Distribution of surplus funds of two occupational pension schemes—Whether trustees able to make taxable payments—Whether trustees able to purchase run-off insurance to cover claims by known beneficiaries—Whether trustees able to purchase insurance to cover claims by unknown beneficiaries and untraced known beneficiaries—Trustee Act 1925, s 57. **NBPF Pension Trustees Ltd v Warnock-Smith** [2008] **2 Comm** 740, Ch D.

Surplus fund—Employees belonging to company pension scheme—Company's scheme in substantial actuarial surplus—Part of company sold and employees transferred to purchaser's employment—Employees joining purchaser's pension scheme—Company's pension scheme giving trustee discretion to transfer to purchaser's scheme such assets as it deemed appropriate—Trustee transferring amount equal only to past service reserve of transferring employees, leaving surplus in company's scheme—Plaintiff employees seeking disclosure of documents indicating reasons for trustee's decision—Whether trustee of pension fund required to give reasons for exercise of discretion. **Wilson v Law Debenture Trust Corp plc** [1995] **2** 337, Ch D.

Surplus fund—Enhanced benefits payable to members who accepted voluntary redundancy—Employer having contractual obligation to pay into fund a sum equal to additional cost of providing enhanced benefits—Scheme precluding any amendment which would make fund moneys payable to employer—Employer paying additional cost in instalments—Whether employer entitled to set off outstanding instalments against surplus—Whether set-off would amount to payment out to employer. **British Coal Corp v British Coal Staff Superannuation Scheme Trustees Ltd** [1995] **1** 912, Ch D.

Surplus fund—Group of companies establishing contributory pension scheme for employees by interim trust deed—Interim deed containing provision for execution of definitive trust deed—Definitive deed incorporating rules for administration of surplus fund—Execution of definitive deed occurring after termination of scheme—Whether definitive deed and rules governing surplus fund valid—Whether interim deed creating enforceable executory trust—Whether surplus fund devolving by way of resulting trust for scheme contributors or as bona vacantia. **Davis v Richards & Wallington Industries Ltd** [1991] **2** 563, Ch D.

Valuation of fund—Transfer of part of fund—Company selling subsidiary and transferring portion of its pension fund to purchaser's fund—Fund in surplus—Appropriate method of valuation of separate portion—Whether past service reserve or share of fund appropriate method of valuation. **Imperial Foods Ltd's Pension Scheme, Re** [1986] **2** 802, Ch D.

Variation of scheme—Alteration of rules—Removal of surplus in scheme by company—Company pension scheme managed by committee of management—Scheme having substantial surplus—Company taken over—New holding company wishing to substitute itself as 'the company' in the scheme and to remove surplus for own use—New company requesting committee of management to execute deeds amending trust deeds and rules of scheme—Whether amendments altering purposes of scheme and ultra vires—Whether committee of management at liberty or bound to execute amending deeds. **Courage Group's Pension Schemes, Re** [1987] **1** 528, Ch D.

Winding up—Priority—Priority where person's entitlement to payment of pension or other benefit has arisen—Whether entitlement arising only where pension actually in payment—Pensions Act 1995, s 73(3)(b). **Trustee Solutions Ltd v Dubery** [2007] **1** 308, Ch D; [2008] **1** 826, CA.

Winding up—Priority—Salary related occupational pension scheme benefits—Money purchase benefits—Underpin benefits—Protected rights—Whether application of actuarial factors necessarily precluding benefits from being money purchase benefits—Meaning of payments 'derived from' voluntary contributions—Analysis of scheme—Pensions Act 1995, s 73—Occupational Pension Schemes (Winding up) Regulations 1996, SI 1996/3126, reg 13. **Bridge Trustees Ltd v Houldsworth (Secretary of State for Work and Pensions, intervener)** [2012] **1** 659, SC.

Winding up—Priority—Salary related occupational pension scheme benefits—Money purchase benefits—Underpin benefits—Protected rights—Whether application of actuarial factors necessarily precluding benefits from being money purchase benefits—Meaning of payments 'derived from' voluntary contributions—Analysis of scheme—Pensions Act 1995, s 73—Occupational Pension Schemes (Winding up) Regulations 1996, SI 1996/3126, reg 13. **Bridge Trustees Ltd v Houldsworth (Secretary of State for Work and Pensions, intervener)** [2010] **4** 1069, CA.

Construction—

Index of price inflation—Whether pension scheme rules allowing trustees to adopt index of price inflation, such as consumer price index, when official body responsible for compiling retail price index not discontinuing it, thereby requiring its replacement. **Barnardo's v Buckinghamshire** [2019] **2** 175, SC.

Pensions increase provision—Whether 'any other rate' in pension scheme provision should be read as 'any higher rate'—Whether obvious mistake in drafting of pension scheme. **Britvic plc v Britvic Pensions Ltd** [2022] **2** 457, CA.

Endowment assurance—

Power for company to select beneficiaries after death of employee. *See* **Trust and trustee** (Discretionary trust—Uncertainty—Power of selection).

PENSION (cont)—
  Pension scheme (cont)—
    Equality of treatment of men and women—
      European Community. *See* **European Union** (Equality of treatment of men and women—Equal pay for equal work—Pension).
      Generally. *See* **Employment** (Equality of treatment of men and women—Pensions).
    Forfeiture provision—
      Member of scheme becoming bankrupt—Whether benefits to which member entitled vesting in trustee in bankruptcy—Whether forfeiture provision effective to prevent such vesting. **Trusts of the Scientific Investment Pension Plan, Re** [1998] **3** 154, Ch D.
    Jurisdiction of Pensions Ombudsman—
      Appellant referring dispute to ombudsman—Ombudsman making determination as to date from which pension payable—Whether reference extending to such issues—Whether ombudsman having jurisdiction to determine issues outside reference—Pension Schemes Act 1993, s 146. **Sheffield v Kier Group plc** [2019] **3** 1086, Ch D.
      Jurisdiction of Ombudsman to investigate complaint against person 'concerned with the administration of the scheme'—Whether person carrying out administrative acts in connection with pension scheme a person 'concerned with the administration of the scheme'—Pension Schemes Act 1993, s 146(4)—Personal and Occupational Pension Schemes (Pensions Ombudsman) Regulations 1996, regs 1(2), 2(1). **R (on the application of Britannic Asset Management Ltd) v Pensions Ombudsman** [2002] **4** 860, CA.
    Local government pensions—
      Non-contractual overtime—Regulations providing that 'non-contractual overtime' not constituting remuneration for purposes of calculating retirement pension—Meaning of 'non-contractual overtime'—Local Government Pension Scheme Regulations 1995, reg C2(2)(a). **Newham London BC v Skingle** [2002] **3** 287, Ch D; [2003] **2** 761, CA.
      Secretary of State's guidance on investment strategy for local government pension scheme—Guidance prohibiting scheme administrators from pursuing policies contrary to UK foreign policy or UK defence policy—Whether relevant parts of guidance unlawful—Public Service Pensions Act 2013, s 3, Sch 3, para 12—Local Government Pension Scheme (Management and Investment of Funds) Regulations 2016, SI 2016/946, reg 7. **R (on the application of Palestine Solidarity Campaign Ltd) v Secretary of State for Housing, Communities and Local Government** [2020] **4** 347, SC.
    Maladministration of pension scheme—
      Jurisdiction of Pensions Ombudsman—Complaint to Pensions Ombudsman—Local authority operating severance and compensation scheme in addition to statutory pension scheme—Local authority reducing monthly payments to pensioner under own scheme after receiving legal advice as to legality of payments—Pensioner alleging misinformation as to pension entitlement—Pensions Ombudsman finding maladministration and directing local authority to reinstate payments and pay compensation for distress and inconvenience—Whether ombudsman having jurisdiction to entertain complaint—Limit to ombudsman's payment order. **Westminster City Council v Haywood** [1996] **2** 467, QBD.
      Jurisdiction of Pensions Ombudsman—Exercise of jurisdiction of Pensions Ombudsman—Maladministration by Pensions Ombudsman—Necessity for statutory procedure to be followed—Necessity for the rules of natural justice to be applied—Pension Schemes Act 1993, ss 149(1), 151. **Seifert v Pensions Ombudsman** [1997] **1** 214, QBD.
      Jurisdiction of Pensions Ombudsman—Exercise of jurisdiction of Pensions Ombudsman—Trustees of pension scheme amending rules by deed of amendment—Amendment giving extra benefits to one class of members—Pensions Ombudsman holding that trustees had acted in breach of trust and directing scheme to be administered under pre-amendment rules—Direction depriving persons who were not parties to proceedings of proprietary rights—Whether trustees under duty to act impartially when exercising discretionary powers between various beneficiaries—Whether ombudsman entitled to make direction affecting rights of third parties to proceedings—Pension Schemes Act 1993, s 146. **Edge v Pensions Ombudsman** [1998] **2** 547, Ch D; [1999] **4** 546, CA.
      Jurisdiction of Pensions Ombudsman—Injury allowance scheme—Local authority at first refusing to entertain application for allowance and then making small award—Pensions Ombudsman finding maladministration and directing local authority to back date allowance and pay damages for distress—Whether ombudsman having jurisdiction to entertain complaint—Pension Schemes Act 1993, s 1. **Swansea City and County v Johnson** [1999] **1** 863, Ch D.
      Jurisdiction of Pensions Ombudsman—Local authority operating severance scheme in addition to pension scheme—Local authority reducing monthly payments to former employee under severance scheme following legal advice—Employee not in pensionable service under severance scheme—Pensions Ombudsman finding maladministration and directing local authority to reinstate payments and pay compensation for distress and inconvenience—Whether ombudsman having jurisdiction to investigate complaint—Whether ombudsman's directions should be set aside—Pension Schemes Act 1993, ss 146(1), 151(2). **Westminster City Council v Haywood** [1997] **2** 84, CA.
      Jurisdiction of Pensions Ombudsman—Trust deed authorising transfer of assets and liabilities to another approved scheme but prohibiting transfer of assets to employer and amendment of scheme for that purpose—Trustees transferring assets and liabilities of scheme to another pension scheme—Trustees of other scheme amending scheme to enable payment of surplus funds to employer—Whether exercise of power to transfer used for collateral purpose—Jurisdiction of ombudsman with regard to remedies—Liability of employer to make repayment—Pension Schemes Act 1993, s 151(2). **Hillsdown Holdings plc v Pensions Ombudsman** [1997] **1** 862, QBD.
      Jurisdiction of Pensions Ombudsman—Trustees offering pension or transfer value guaranteed for three months—Beneficiary applying for transfer value to be paid to new scheme within guarantee period—Transfer value reduced—Effect of guarantee—Whether application for transfer value valid—Whether Pensions Ombudsman having jurisdiction to award compensation for distress and inconvenience—Pension Schemes Act 1993, ss 95, 151. **Miller v Stapleton** [1996] **2** 449, QBD.

PENSION (cont)—
    Pension scheme (cont)—
        Maladministration of pension scheme (cont)—
            Jurisdiction of Pensions Ombudsman—Whether party having right of appeal to High Court from determination by Pensions Ombudsman on preliminary issues—Whether ombudsman having jurisdiction to consider fairness of insurance contract used as scheme's investment vehicle—Pension Schemes Act 1993, s 151(4). **Legal & General Assurance Society Ltd v Pensions Ombudsman** [2000] **2** 577, Ch D and QBD.

            Jurisdiction of Pensions Ombudsman—Winding up of pension scheme—Retirement of member agreed prior to winding up but payment of pension not commenced—Member informed funding sufficient to pay 63% of his entitlement but later told funds sufficient to pay 83%—Member making complaint to Pensions Ombudsman—Whether member claiming 100% of pension entitlement—Whether complaint having any substance. **Seifert v Pensions Ombudsman** [1997] **4** 947, CA.

            National Health Service—Initial occupational pension increasing annually by compound percentage increase—Initial pension subject to reduction on entitlement to state pension—Department of Health determining reduction to be from initial pension, not from increased pension—Whether correct—Pensions (Increase) Act 1971, s 17—Social Security Pensions Act 1975, s 59—National Health Service (Superannuation) Regulations 1980, reg 56(3)(c). **Dept of Health v Pensions Ombudsman** [1998] **4** 508, CA.

        Post-nuptial settlement—
            Variation. *See* **Variation of Settlement (Matrimonial Causes)** (Post-nuptial settlement—Pension scheme).

        Power of nomination—
            Power to appoint nominee to receive benefits payable if employee died while still in employment—Nominations subject to prior approval of management committee of scheme—Deceased nominating brother as beneficiary—Deceased subsequently marrying without varying or revoking nomination—Deceased dying while still employed—Death-in-employment benefit claimed by both brother and widow—Whether power to appoint non-assignable death-in-employment benefit a testamentary disposition—Whether power to appoint only valid if executed as if it was a will—Whether brother or widow entitled to death-in-employment benefit. **Baird v Baird** [1990] **2** 300, PC.

            Power to appoint nominee to receive contributions in event of employee's death before entitlement to pension—Form of appointment provided for by rules of scheme—Power to cancel nomination and appoint new nominee—Exercise of power—Employee cancelling nomination and requesting new nomination by letter to secretary of pension fund—Original nomination form amended by secretary in accordance with letter—Validity of new nomination. **Danish Bacon Co Ltd Staff Pension Fund, Re** [1971] **1** 486, Ch D.

            Prohibition of discrimination—Protection of property—Scheme requiring nomination of cohabiting partner as condition of eligibility for survivor's pension—Whether interference with convention rights justified or proportionate—Human Rights Act 1998, Sch 1, Pt I, art 14, Pt II, art 1—Local Government Pension Scheme (Benefits, Membership and Contributions) Regulations (Northern Ireland) 2009, SI 2009/32, regs 24, 25. **Brewster's application for judicial review (Northern Ireland), Re** [2017] **2** 1001, SC.

        Power to determine scheme—
            Rule against perpetuities. *See* **Rule against perpetuities** (Pension scheme—Register of pensionable employees).

        Provision excluding employer's liability for injuries caused by persons in common employment with injured person—
            Agreement collateral to contract of service—Validity. **Smith v British European Airways Corp** [1951] **2** 737, KBD.

        Registered pension scheme—
            Payments by registered pension schemes—Authorised member payment—Benefits—Pension reciprocation plan—Reciprocal loans being made from scheme Y to scheme Z and from scheme Z to scheme Y—Whether loans valid—Whether loans constituting unauthorised member payments—Finance Act 2004, ss 160(2), 164(1), 173. **Dalriada Trustees Ltd v Faulds** [2012] **2** 734, Ch D.

            Unauthorised payment charge—Meaning of 'payment'—HMRC issuing discovery assessment against taxpayer on basis unauthorised payments made from registered pension scheme—FTT upholding assessment but on different basis—Whether 'payment' requiring transfer of beneficial title—Whether discovery assessment encompassing FTT's conclusion—Taxes Management Act 1970, s 29—Finance Act 2004, s 160. **Clark v Revenue and Customs Comrs** [2020] **4** 652, CA.

        Restraint of trade. *See* **Restraint of trade by agreement** (Pension scheme).
        Surplus fund—
            Industry-wide pension scheme for non-associated employers—Scheme divided into sections with each section representing different employer or group of employers—Whether each section of scheme constituting separate 'qualifying scheme' for purposes of satisfying preconditions on distribution of surplus to employer—Whether new requirement on giving of notice applying to scheme governed by previous statutory regime—Pension Schemes Act 1993, ss 1, 102(2), 108—Pensions Act 1995, s 76(3)(d)—Pensions Act 1995 (Commencement No 10) Order 1997, art 6. **BEC Pension Trustee Ltd v Sheppeck** [2002] **3** 154, Ch D.

        Trustees—
            Liability to members—Winding up. *See* Pension scheme—Winding up—Pension trustee posting statutory advertisement for former members of scheme to notify it of claims before final distribution of assets, *below*.

            Powers of investment—Duty towards beneficiary. *See* **Trust and trustee** (Duty of trustee—Duty towards beneficiary—Investments—Power of investment—Pension fund).

PENSION (cont)—
    Pension scheme (cont)—
        Unfunded scheme—
            Private sector hospital operating unfunded occupational pension scheme—Scheme providing no benefits for early leavers—Employee leaving early and claiming right to deferred pension under statutory provisions requiring defined category of occupational pension scheme to preserve short service benefit for early leavers—Whether preservation requirements applying to unfunded private sector occupational pension schemes—Pension Schemes Act 1993, ss 69(3), 181. **Royal Masonic Hospital v Pensions Ombudsman** [2001] **3** 408, Ch D.
        Winding up—
            Pension trustee posting statutory advertisement for former members of scheme to notify it of claims before final distribution of assets—Existing members not receiving share of final distribution as not recorded as members at time of joining scheme—Trustee having actual knowledge of members at time of contribution but forgetting existence at time of final distribution—Whether trustee having notice of claims at time of distribution for purposes of statute—Whether 'notice' meaning 'knowledge' for purposes of statute—Trustee Act 1925, s 27. **MCP Pension Trustees Ltd v AON Pension Trustees Ltd** [2011] **1 Comm** 228, CA.
            Pension trustee posting statutory advertisement for former members of scheme to notify it of claims before final distribution of assets—Members not notifying it of claims—Trustee having previously been aware of members' claims but not aware of claims at time of final distribution—Whether trustee having 'notice' of claims at time of distribution for purposes of statute—Whether 'notice' meaning knowledge for purposes of statute—Whether trustee liable to members—Trustee Act 1925, s 27. **MCP Pension Trustees Ltd v AON Pension Trustees Ltd** [2010] **1 Comm** 323, Ch D.
    Pensions Ombudsman—
        Costs of appeal. See **Costs** (Order for costs—Costs of appeal—Pensions Ombudsman).
        Jurisdiction—
            Generally. See Pension scheme—Jurisdiction of Pensions Ombudsman, *above*.
            Maladministration of pension scheme. See Pension scheme—Maladministration of pension scheme—Jurisdiction of Pensions Ombudsman, *above*.
    Pensions Regulator—
        Company pension scheme. See Pension scheme—Company pension scheme—Pensions Regulator, *above*.
    Police. See **Police** (Pension).
    Registered pension scheme. See Pension scheme—Registered pension scheme, *above*.
    Retirement annuity contracts—
        Final bonus—
            Policy providing policyholders with various options including annuity at guaranteed rate—Policy-provider deciding to pay policyholders opting for guaranteed rate lower final bonus than other policyholders—Whether policy-provider entitled to declare differential final bonuses. **Equitable Life Assurance Society v Hyman** [2000] **2** 331, CA; [2000] **3** 961, HL.
    Scheme. See Pension scheme, *above*.
    Social security. See **Social security** (Retirement pension).
    Surplus fund—
        Company pension scheme. See Pension scheme—Company pension scheme—Surplus fund, *above*.
    Teacher. See **Education** (Teacher—Pension).
    Transfer—
        Inheritance tax. See **Inheritance tax** (Exemptions and relief—Purchase exemption—Associated operations—Transfer of pension plan).
    War service. See **War pension**.
    Widow—
        Damages under Fatal Accidents Acts—
            Lost opportunity of widow's post-retirement pension. See **Fatal accident** (Damages—Lost opportunity of widow's post-retirement pension).

PENSION SHARING ORDER
    Divorce. See **Divorce** (Financial provision—Pension sharing order).

PENSIONS APPEAL TRIBUNAL
    Holder of service pension applying for leave to appeal to High Court from tribunal's decision—
        President of Pensions Appeal Tribunals (England and Wales) setting aside tribunal's decision and ordering rehearing—
            Whether direction within President's power—Pensions Appeal Tribunals Act 1943, s 6(2), (2A)—Pensions Appeal Tribunal (England and Wales) Rules 1980, rr 20, 21, 37. **R (on the application of the Secretary of State for Defence) v President of the Pensions Appeal Tribunals (England and Wales) (Jones, interested party)** [2004] **2** 159, QBD.
    War pension—
        Procedure. See **War pension** (Pensions appeal tribunal—Procedure).

PENSIONS OMBUDSMAN
    Costs of appeal—
        Liability of ombudsman for costs of successful appeal against his determination. See **Costs** (Order for costs—Costs of appeal—Pensions Ombudsman).
    Jursidiction—
        Costs. See **Pension** (Order for costs—Costs of reference—Pensions Ombudsman).
        Generally. See **Pension** (Pension scheme—Jurisdiction of Pensions Ombudsman).
        Maladministration of pension scheme. See **Pension** (Pension scheme—Maladministration of pension scheme—Jurisdiction of Pensions Ombudsman).

PER INCURIAM
    Circumstances in which decision regarded as given per incuriam. See **Precedent** (Decision per incuriam).
    Judicial decision—
        Court of Appeal. See **Precedent** (Court of Appeal—Decision per incuriam).

PEREMPTORY ORDER
Arbitration—
Powers of court. *See* **Arbitration** (Practice—Powers of court in relation to arbitral proceedings—Peremptory order).
Child—
Order for return of child to foreign jurisdiction—
Wardship proceedings—Child removed by parent from foreign jurisdiction. *See* **Ward of court** (Jurisdiction—Kidnapping—Peremptory order for return of wards to foreign jurisdiction).
Form of order. *See* **Practice** (Order—'Unless' orders and other peremptory orders—Form of order).

PERFECTING INCOMPLETE GIFT
See **Gift** (Incomplete gift—Perfecting gift).

PERFORMANCE BOND
Building contract. *See* **Building contract** (Bond—Performance bond).
Documentary credit—
Generally. *See* **Bank** (Documentary credit—Performance bond).
Generally. *See* **Contract** (Bond—Performance bond).
Interim injunction to restrain call on. *See* **Injunction** (Interim—Injunction to restrain call on performance bond).

PERFORMER
Right of action—
Infringement of copyright. *See* **Copyright** (Conflict of laws—Right of action—Performer).

PERILS OF THE SEA
Insurance against. *See* **Marine insurance** (Perils insured against—Perils of the sea).

PERIOD OF TIME
Duration. *See* **Time**.

PERIODIC TENANCY
Creation. *See* **Landlord and tenant** (Tenancy—Periodic tenancy—Creation).

PERIODICAL PAYMENTS
Divorce. *See* **Divorce** (Financial provision—Periodical payments).
Inheritance (Family Provision) Act 1938, under. *See* **Family provision** (Order—Periodical payments).
Maintenance—
Husband and wife. *See* **Husband and wife** (Maintenance—Periodical payments order by High Court).
Personal injury—
Damages. *See* **Damages** (Personal injury—Amount of damages—Periodical payments).
Stamp duty. *See* **Stamp duty** (Conveyance on sale—Periodical payments).

PERJURY
Certiorari to quash order obtained as a result of perjured evidence. *See* **Certiorari** (Fraud—Perjury).
Civil action—
Right of injured party—
Civil action at suit of injured party—Whether action lies. **Hargreaves v Bretherton [1958] 3 122, QBD.**
Civil liability. *See* **Criminal law** (Perjury—Civil action).
Criminal liability. *See* **Criminal law** (Perjury).
Witness—
Whether civil cause of action. *See* **Evidence** (Witness—Perjury—No civil cause of action).

PERMITTED DEVELOPMENT
Generally. *See* **Town and country planning** (Development—Permitted development).

PERMITTED HOURS
Licensing. *See* **Licensing** (Permitted hours).

PERPETUITIES
Rule against perpetuities. *See* **Rule against perpetuities**.

PERQUISITE
Income tax—
Emoluments from office or employment. *See* **Income tax** (Emoluments from office or employment—Perquisites or profits).

PERSISTENT CRUELTY
Summary matrimonial jurisdiction. *See* **Husband and wife** (Summary proceedings—Persistent cruelty).

PERSON OF UNSOUND MIND
Bankruptcy jurisdiction. *See* **Bankruptcy** (Person of unsound mind—Jurisdiction to make receiving order).
Generally. *See* **Mental health**.
Succession—
Intestacy. *See* **Intestacy** (Succession—Person of unsound mind).
Trustee—
Appointment of new trustee in place of trustee of unsound mind. *See* **Trust and trustee** (Appointment of new trustee—Trustee of unsound mind—Appointment in place of person of unsound mind).

PERSON UNDER DISABILITY
Injunction—
Whether fact of disability bar to grant of injunction. *See* **Injunction** (Person under disability).

PERSON UNDER DISABILITY (cont)—
Limitation period—
Extension—
Trespass to the person. *See* **Limitation of action** (Trespass to the person—Period of limitation—Extension—Person under disability).
Generally. *See* **Limitation of action** (Persons under disability).
Minor—
Generally. *See* **Minor**.
Person of unsound mind—
Generally. *See* **Mental health**.
Practice—
Generally. *See* **Practice** (Persons under disability).

PERSONAL ACCIDENT INSURANCE
Damages—
Deduction of proceeds of insurance policy. *See* **Damages** (Personal injury—Insurance).
Generally. *See* **Insurance** (Accident insurance).
School—
Sport—
Injury to pupil—Whether school under duty to insure pupils against injuries received while playing sport. *See* **Negligence** (School—Duty of care—Sport—Injury to pupil).

PERSONAL ATTENDANCE
Chambers proceedings—
Classes of business which may be transacted without personal attendance—
Communications by post or telephone. *See* **Practice** (Chambers proceedings—Communications by post or telephone—Chancery Division—Classes of business which may be transacted without personal attendance).

PERSONAL CHATTELS
Intestacy—
Rights of surviving spouse. *See* **Intestacy** (Rights of surviving spouse—Personal chattels).

PERSONAL CONTRACT
See **Contract** (Personal contract).

PERSONAL DATA
Processing of. *See* **Data protection** (Processing of information—Personal data).

PERSONAL INJURIES
Action—
Action for benefit of deceased's estate—
Damages. *See* **Damages** (Personal injury—Action for benefit of deceased's estate).
Costs—
After-the-event (ATE) insurance premium. *See* **Costs** (Order for costs—Jurisdiction—After-the-event (ATE) insurance premium—Personal injury claims).
Cross-examination—
Video evidence. *See* **Practice** (Cross-examination—Personal injury action—Video evidence).
Disclosure—
Order for disclosure against person not a party to proceedings. *See* **Disclosure and inspection of documents** (Disclosure against persons not parties to proceedings—Claim in respect of personal injuries or death).
Production of documents before commencement of proceedings. *See* **Disclosure and inspection of documents** (Production of documents—Production before commencement of proceedings—Claim in respect of personal injuries).
Experts' reports—
Disclosure to other parties—Action for medical negligence. *See* **Practice** (Evidence—Expert evidence—Disclosure to other parties—Action for medical negligence).
Generally. *See* **Practice** (Personal injuries action—Experts' reports).
Fundamental dishonesty. *See* **Practice** (Personal injuries action—Fundamental dishonesty).
Interlocutory injunction—
Danger that defendant may transfer assets out of jurisdiction—Injunction restraining removal of assets out of jurisdiction—Power of court to grant such an injunction in a personal injuries action. *See* **Practice** (Pre-trial or post-judgment relief—Freezing order—Injunction restraining removal of assets out of the jurisdiction—Personal injuries claim).
Limitation of time—
Court's power to override time limit. *See* **Limitation of action** (Court's power to override time limit in personal injury or fatal accident claim).
Extension of time. *See* **Limitation of action** (Extension of time limit—Material fact of decisive character outside knowledge of plaintiff).
Generally. *See* **Limitation of action** (Period of limitation—Personal injury claim).
Plaintiff's knowledge. *See* **Limitation of action** (Personal injury claim—Plaintiff's knowledge).
When time begins to run. *See* **Limitation of action** (When time begins to run—Personal injury claim).
Medical evidence—
Number of expert witnesses. *See* **Evidence** (Medical evidence—Expert witnesses—Number of witnesses).
Practice. *See* **Practice** (Personal injuries action).
Statement of claim—
Particulars. *See* **Pleading** (Particulars—Personal injuries actions).
Transfer of action from High Court to county court—
Generally. *See* **County court** (Transfer of action—Transfer from High Court—Personal injuries action).

PERSONAL INJURIES (cont)—
  Action (cont)—
    Transfer of action from High Court to county court (cont)—
      Practice. *See* **County court** (Transfer of action—Transfer from High Court—Actions suitable for transfer—Personal injury actions).
    Trial by jury. *See* **Practice** (Trial—Trial by jury—Personal injuries claim).
    Writ—
      Practice. *See* **Practice** (Personal injuries action—Writ).
  Carriage by air—
    Injury to passenger. *See* **Carriage by air** (Carriage of passengers—International carriage—International convention imposing liability on carrier for 'bodily injury' to passenger arising from 'accident').
  Cause of action—
    Damage. *See* **Negligence** (Cause of action—Damage—Personal injury).
  Compensation—
    Criminal injuries—
      Compensation order. *See* **Sentence** (Compensation—Order—Compensation for personal injury, loss or damage resulting from the offence).
      Generally. *See* **Compensation** (Criminal injuries).
  Costs—
    Fixed costs. *See* **Costs** (Fixed costs—Low value personal injury claims in road traffic accidents).
    Qualified one-way costs shifting. *See* **Costs** (Order for costs—Qualified one-way costs shifting).
  Damages—
    Action for benefit of deceased's estate. *See* **Damages** (Personal injury—Action for benefit of deceased's estate).
    Fatal accident. *See* **Fatal accident** (Damages).
    Generally. *See* **Damages** (Personal injury).
    Interest. *See* **Interest** (Damages—Personal injury).
    Periodical payments. *See* **Damages** (Personal injury—Amount of damages—Periodical payments).
    Provisional damages—
      Practice. *See* **Practice** (Personal injuries action—Damages—Provisional damages).
    Special damage—
      Particulars of claim. *See* **Practice** (Personal injuries action—Special damage).
  Defective premises—
    Builder's liability. *See* **Negligence** (Defective premises—Builder's liability—Personal injury).
  Disclosure—
    Order for disclosure against person not party to proceedings. *See* **Disclosure and inspection of documents** (Disclosure against persons not parties to proceedings—Claim in respect of personal injuries or death).
    Production of documents before commencement of proceedings. *See* **Disclosure and inspection of documents** (Disclosure against persons not parties to proceedings—Claim in respect of personal injuries or death).
  Experts' reports—
    Road traffic accidents. *See* **Practice** (Personal injuries action—Experts' reports—Road traffic accidents).
  Extent of injury—
    Lack of knowledge on part of plaintiff—
      Extension of limitation period. *See* **Limitation of action** (Extension of time limit—Material fact of decisive character outside knowledge of plaintiff—Lack of knowledge of extent of injury).
  Freezing order—
    Jurisdiction to grant. *See* **Practice** (Pre-trial or post-judgment relief—Freezing order—Injunction restraining removal of assets out of jurisdiction).
  Indemnity—
    Building contract—
      Contract between builders and scaffolding contractors. *See* **Indemnity** (Contract between builders and scaffolding contractors—Personal injuries).
  Interest on damages. *See* **Interest** (Damages—Personal injury).
  Limitation of action—
    Court's power to override time limit. *See* **Limitation of action** (Court's power to override time limit in personal injury or fatal accident claim).
    Generally. *See* **Limitation of action** (Personal injury claim).
    Period of limitation. *See* **Limitation of action** (Period of limitation—Personal injury claim).
    When time begins to run. *See* **Limitation of action** (When time begins to run—Personal injury claim).
  Loss of expectation of life—
    Damages. *See* **Damages** (Personal injury—Loss of expectation of life).
  Low value personal injury claims in road traffic accidents—
    Costs. *See* **Costs** (Fixed costs—Low value personal injury claims in road traffic accidents).
  Mareva injunction—
    Jurisdiction to grant. *See* **Practice** (Pre-trial or post-judgment relief—Freezing order—Injunction restraining removal of assets out of the jurisdiction—Personal injuries claim).
  Medical evidence. *See* **Evidence** (Medical evidence).
  Medical examination of plaintiff—
    Stay of proceedings. *See* **Practice** (Stay of proceedings—Medical examination of plaintiff at defendant's request).
  Occupier's liability. *See* **Occupier's liability**.
  Special damage—
    Future losses—
      Pleading. *See* **Pleading** (Damage—Special damage—Personal injuries).
  Statement of claim—
    Allegation of failure to provide safe system of working. *See* **Statement of case** (Personal injuries action).
  Visiting forces—
    Personal injuries claim by member of visiting force—
      Liability of United Kingdom. *See* **Visiting forces** (Negligence—Personal injuries claim by member of visiting force).

PERSONAL PROPERTY

Conflict of laws. *See* **Conflict of laws** (Movables).
Succession—
    Legitimacy. *See* **Will** (Legitimacy—Succession to personal property in England).

PERSONAL REPRESENTATIVES

Appropriation of intestate's estate. *See* **Intestacy** (Appropriation by personal representatives).
Capital transfer tax—
    Liability for tax. *See* **Capital transfer tax** (Liability for tax—Persons liable as executor or trustee).
Contract—
    Power of personal representative to contract with himself as individual—
        Employment—Employee appointed personal representative of employer—Employee continuing in employment on death of employer—Employee taken into employment of himself as personal representative. *See* **Employment** (Continuity—Death of employer—Employee taken into employment of deceased's personal representative—Employee and personal representative same person—Power as personal representative to contract with himself as individual).
Distribution of estate—
    Generally. *See* **Administration of estates** (Distribution).
Generally. *See* **Executor and administrator**.
Legacy to personal representatives of deceased legatee—
    Lapse—
        Substituted gifts. *See* **Will** (Lapse—Substituted gifts—Legacy to personal representatives of deceased legatee).

PERSONAL SERVICE

Documents. *See* **Practice** (Service—Personal service).

PERSONAL SERVICES

Injunction—
    Breach of contract for personal services. *See* **Injunction** (Breach of contract—Contract for personal services).

PERSONALTY

Settlement. *See* **Settlement** (Personalty).
Will—
    Proceeds of sale of settled land—
        Will made abroad. *See* **Will** (Will made abroad—Proceeds of sale of settled land—Whether personalty).

PERVERTING COURSE OF JUSTICE

See **Criminal law** (Obstructing course of justice).

PESTS

Rats and mice—
    Destruction—
        Notice to owner of land—Validity—Instruction to carry out 'poison treatment or other work of no less effectual character'—Prevention of Damage by Pests Act 1949, s 4(1). **Perry v Garner** [1953] **1** 285, QBD.

PETITION

Advertisement—
    Petition to wind up company. *See* **Company** (Compulsory winding up—Advertisement of petition).
Appeal—
    House of Lords—
        Leave to appeal—Costs. *See* **House of Lords** (Costs—Petition for leave to appeal).
        Leave to appeal—Generally. *See* **House of Lords** (Leave to appeal).
Bankruptcy—
    Creditor's petition—
        Death of creditor—Effect on proceedings. *See* **Bankruptcy** (Appeal—Divisional Court—Jurisdiction—Appeal against receiving order—Death of petitioning creditor prior to hearing of appeal).
        Proceedings under Insolvency Act 1986. *See* **Insolvency** (Proceedings on creditor's petition).
    Generally. *See* **Bankruptcy** (Petition).
    Proceedings under Insolvency Act 1986. *See* **Insolvency** (Petition).
    Service—
        Evidence. *See* **Bankruptcy** (Appeal—Appeal against adjudication—Allegation that petition not served on debtor).
Company—
    Administration order. *See* **Company** (Administration order—Petition).
    Compulsory winding up—
        Advertisement of petition. *See* **Company** (Compulsory winding up—Advertisement of petition).
        Board of Trade's petition. *See* **Company** (Compulsory winding up—Petition by Board of Trade).
        Contributory's petition. *See* **Company** (Compulsory winding up—Petition by contributory).
        Costs—Dismissal petition. *See* **Company** (Compulsory winding up—Costs—Dismissed petition).
        Creditor's petition. *See* **Company** (Compulsory winding up—Petition by creditor).
        Official Receiver's petition. *See* **Company** (Compulsory winding up—Petition by Official Receiver).
        Procedure—Generally. *See* **Company** (Compulsory winding up—Procedure).
        Secretary of State's petition. *See* **Company** (Compulsory winding up—Petition by Secretary of State).
    Oppression of minority—
        Petition for order under Companies Act 1948, s 210. *See* **Company** (Oppression—Petition).
    Petition for order confirming reduction of share capital. *See* **Company** (Reduction of capital—Petition).
    Restoration of name to register. *See* **Company** (Restoration to register—Application).

PETITION (cont)—
Divorce. *See* **Divorce** (Petition).
Election petition—
Local government election. *See* **Elections** (Local government—Election petition).
Faculty. *See* **Ecclesiastical law** (Faculty—Petition).
House of Lords—
Leave to appeal. *See* **House of Lords** (Leave to appeal—Petition for leave to appeal).
Insolvency—
Generally. *See* **Insolvency** (Petition).
Judicial separation—
Form of petition. *See* **Husband and wife** (Judicial separation—Form of petition).
Leave to appeal to House of Lords. *See* **House of Lords** (Leave to appeal—Petition for leave to appeal).
Legitimation—
Power of court to order hearing in camera. *See* **Legitimation** (Practice—Hearing of petition in camera).
Nullity. *See* **Nullity** (Petition).
Patent—
Revocation of patent. *See* **Patent** (Petition for revocation).
Right, of. *See* **Petition of right**.
Service—
Bankruptcy proceedings. *See* **Bankruptcy** (Petition—Service).
Divorce—
Generally. *See* **Divorce** (Practice—Service—Petition).
Infant. *See* **Divorce** (Infant—Service).
Service out of jurisdiction—
Bankruptcy petition. *See* **Bankruptcy** (Petition—Service—Service out of jurisdiction).

PETITION OF RIGHT
Colonial government—
Mauritius. *See* **Mauritius** (Public authorities—Colonial government).
Colonial stock—
Claim by stockholder for interest on stock—
Judgment or order—Compliance with order—Duty of registrar of colonial government to comply with order—Failure to comply—Examination of registrar as judgment debtor—Jurisdiction of court to order examination of registrar—Whether order made on petition order against Crown or against registrar—Whether registrar a judgment debtor—Whether order an order for the payment of money—Colonial Stock Act 1877, s 20—RSC Ord 48, r 1(1), Ord 77, rr 1, 15(1). **Franklin v R** [1973] **3** 861, QBD and CA.
Remedy—Procedure—Plaintiff claiming to be interested in Government of Southern Rhodesia stock—Bank of England paying agents and registrars of stock—Government of Southern Rhodesia failing to provide bank with funds to pay interest—Whether plaintiff limited to civil proceedings against bank in respect of funds held by them as registrars—Whether plaintiff entitled to present petition of right—Form of petition—Colonial Stock Act 1877, s 20—Crown Proceedings Act 1947, ss 39, 40, Sch 2—Cyprus Act 1960, s 3, Sch para 9. **Franklin v A-G** [1973] **1** 879, QBD.
Suppliant holding stock jointly with others—Other stockholders not joined in petition—Whether suppliant entitled to petition on his own. **Barclays Bank Ltd v R** [1974] **1** 305, QBD.
Right of any person claiming to be interested in stock to present petition of right—
Beneficial interest—Claim by stockholder to interest on stock—Suppliant not at date of petition registered holder of stock—Suppliant having beneficial interest in stock—Suppliant registered holder by date of judgment—Whether essential for success of petition that suppliant be registered holder at date of petition—Colonial Stock Act 1877, s 20. **Barclays Bank Ltd v R** [1974] **1** 305, QBD.
Salvage—
Crown acting as salvor—
Claim against Crown as salvor—Whether petition of right lies against Crown when acting as salvor—Merchant Shipping (Salvage) Act 1940, s 1(1). **Anglo-Saxon Petroleum Co Ltd v Damant** [1947] **2** 465, CA.
Stockholder—
Colonial stock. *See* Colonial stock, *above*.
Stock transferred by statutory authority to Crown—
Action for rectification of register—Need to apply for relief by way of petition of right. **Lovibond v Grand Trunk Rly Co of Canada** [1936] **2** 495, PC.

PETROL
Filling station—
Agreement in restraint of trade. *See* **Restraint of trade by agreement** (Petrol filling station).
Change of use for planning purposes. *See* **Town and country planning** (Development—Material change of use—Petrol filling station).
London—
Consent to establishment of station adjacent to street. *See* **London** (Petrol-filling station—Consent of county council to establishment of station adjacent to street).
Solus agreement—
Implied term—Retail price maintenance. *See* **Contract** (Implied term—Retail price maintenance—Petrol filling station—Solus agreement).
Restraint of trade. *See* **Restraint of trade by agreement** (Petrol filling station—Solus agreement).
Garage—
Sunday closing. *See* **Shop** (Sunday closing—Garage—Lawful opening for sale of petrol, oil and motor accessories).
Offence—
Having commercial petrol in tank of private car—
Prima facie evidence—Analysis—Result possibly produced by derivatives of diphenylamine—Motor Spirit (Regulation) Act 1948, s 2(1). **Taylor v Ciecierski** [1950] **1** 319, KBD.

PETROL (cont)—
Offence (cont)—
Keeping petroleum spirit on premises without a licence—
Petrol sold direct from tanker into car tanks in café forecourt—Whether owner of forecourt occupier of premises on which petrol 'kept' without licence—Whether owners of tanker occupiers of 'premises', viz petrol tanker, for keeping petrol without licence—Whether owners of tanker conveying petrol—Petroleum (Consolidation) Act 1938, ss 1(1), (2), 6(2)—Petroleum-Spirit (Conveyance by Road) Regulations 1957 (SI 1957 No 191), reg 9. **Grandi v Milburn** [1966] **2** 816, QBD.
Petroleum rights. *See* **Petroleum rights**.
Rationing. *See* **Rationing** (Petrol).
Sale to child—
Negligence—
Contributory negligence. *See* **Negligence** (Contributory negligence—Child—Explosive substance given to child—Sale of petrol to child).

PETROL BOMB
Whether an 'explosive substance'. *See* **Explosives** (Offence—Making explosive substance with intent to endanger life or cause serious injury to property—Explosive substance).

PETROLEUM RIGHTS
Crown—
Rights vested in Crown—
Petroleum and natural gas situated inside and outside territorial waters—Rights included in mineral grant made by Crown—Whether rights to oil and natural gas statutorily revesting in Crown—Petroleum (Production) Act 1934—Continental Shelf Act 1964. **Lonsdale (Earl) v A-G** [1982] **3** 579, Ch D.
Western Australia. *See* **Western Australia**.

PEWS
Church—
Removal of pews—
Faculty. *See* **Ecclesiastical law** (Faculty—Pews—Removal of pews).

PHARMACEUTICAL INDUSTRY
Pharmaceutical Price Regulation Scheme—
Arbitration. *See* **Arbitration** (Award—Appeal—Jurisdiction—Appeal from reasoned opinion of Pharmaceutical Price Regulation Scheme Arbitration Panel).

PHARMACEUTICAL SERVICES
National Health Service—
Supply of medicine or drug. *See* **National Health Service** (Pharmaceutical services—Supply of medicine or drug).

PHARMACIST
Poison—
Sale by retail. *See* **Poison** (Sale by retail—Sale to be effected by or under supervision of registered pharmacist).

PHARMACY
Freedom of establishment—
European Community. *See* **European Union** (Freedom of establishment—Restriction on freedom to provide services—Public health—Pharmacies).
Wholesale dealer in drugs—
Prohibition on dealer having interest in business carried on in pharmacy—
New Zealand. *See* **New Zealand** (Pharmacy—Wholesale dealer in drugs—Prohibition on dealer having an interest in the business carried on in pharmacy).

PHEASANTS
Livestock—
Agriculture—
Pheasants kept for sport. *See* **Rent restriction** (Agricultural worker—Agriculture—Livestock keeping—Animals kept for production of food—Keeping and rearing of pheasants for sport).

PHOTOCOPY OF DOCUMENT
Legal professional privilege. *See* **Privilege** (Legal professional privilege—Documents—Copies).

PHOTOFIT PICTURE
Criminal proceedings—
Admissibility in evidence. *See* **Criminal evidence** (Identity—Photofit picture—Admissibility).

PHOTOGRAPH
Breach of confidence. *See* **Equity** (Breach of confidence—Photographs).
Evidence—
Criminal proceedings—
Prejudice to accused. *See* **Criminal evidence** (Improper conduct of accused on other occasions—Prejudice to accused—Photograph of accused).
Leave to produce photograph without giving other party opportunity to inspect it. *See* **Practice** (Document—Production in evidence—Leave to produce plan, photograph or model as evidence without giving other party opportunity to inspect it).
Indecent photographs of children—
Fraudulent evasion of prohibition or restriction. *See* **Criminal law** (Indecent photographs of persons under 16—Fraudulent evasion of prohibition or restriction).

PHOTOGRAPH (cont)—
    Indecent photographs of children (cont)—
        Making indecent photographs of children. *See* **Criminal law** (Indecent photographs or pseudo-photographs of children).
        Obscene publications. *See* **Criminal law** (Obscene publications—Indecent photographs of children).

PHYSICIAN
    See **Medical practitioner.**

PICKETING
    Breach of peace. *See* **Trade dispute** (Picketing—Breach of peace).
    Highway—
        Obstruction of highway. *See* **Trade dispute** (Picketing—Obstruction of highway).
        Unreasonable use. *See* **Highway** (Public nuisance—Unreasonable use of highway—Circumstances constituting unreasonable use—Picketing).
    Nuisance. *See* **Trade dispute** (Picketing—Nuisance).
    Peaceful picketing—
        Generally. *See* **Trade dispute** (Picketing).
        Unfair industrial practice. *See* **Industrial relations** (Unfair industrial practice—Peaceful picketing).
    Watching and besetting premises—
        Whether actionable nuisance. *See* **Nuisance** (Watching and besetting premises).

PICTURES
    Estate duty—
        Exception. *See* **Estate duty** (Exemption—Pictures and objects of artistic interest).
    Purchase tax. *See* **Purchase tax** (Chargeable goods—Pictures, prints, engravings etc).

PIGEON
    Spoiling crops—
        Right of landowner to kill. *See* **Animal** (Pigeon—Spoiling crops—Right to kill).

PIGS
    Lien. *See* **Lien** (Maintenance of animals—Pigs).

PILOT
    Charter aircraft—
        Permit to operate—
            International flights. *See* **Air traffic** (International civil aviation—Permit to operate charter flights).
    Licence—
        Carriage by air—
            Private pilot's licence. *See* **Carriage by air** (Private pilot's licence).

PILOTAGE DISTRICT
    See **Harbour** (Pilotage district).

PIPES
    Title to—
        Pipes laid in servient land pursuant to easement. *See* **Easement** (Pipes—Right to lay and maintain pipes on servient land).

PIT BULL TERRIER
    Dangerous dog. *See* **Animal** (Dog—Dangerous dog—Pit bull terrier).

PLACE OF ABODE
    Possession of articles for stealing—
        Possession when not at place of abode. *See* **Criminal law** (Going equipped for stealing—Possession of articles when not at place of abode).

PLACE OF SAFETY ORDER
    Children and young persons. *See* **Children and young persons** (Detention—Place of safety order).
    Ward of court. *See* **Ward of court** (Protection of ward—Place of safety order).

PLACE OF TRIAL
    Criminal trial. *See* **Criminal law** (Trial—Place of trial).

PLACE OF WORK
    Safety—
        Building. *See* **Building** (Working places).

PLAN
    Building lease—
        Consent of lessor to plans. *See* **Landlord and tenant** (Building lease—Consent of lessor to plans).
    Conveyance—
        Reference to plan. *See* **Sale of land** (Conveyance—Parcels—Reference to plan).
    Description of registered land. *See* **Land registration** (Description of registered land—Boundary—Filed plan).
    Evidence—
        Leave to produce plan as evidence without giving other party opportunity to inspect it. *See* **Practice** (Document—Production in evidence—Leave to produce plan, photograph or model as evidence without giving other party opportunity to inspect it).

PLANNING
    Appeal—
        Non-party, application to appeal by. *See* **Court of Appeal** (Permission to appeal—Application for permission to appeal—Jurisdiction—Planning authority adopting local plan).
    Generally. *See* **Town and country planning**.
    Planning inquiry—
        Report—
            Libel—Qualified privilege. *See* **Libel and slander** (Qualified privilege—Report of planning inquiry).
    Planning permission—
        Development—
            Generally. *See* **Town and country planning**.
        Sale of land—
            Condition. *See* **Sale of land** (Condition—Planning permission to be obtained).
    Town and country planning. *See* **Town and country planning**.

PLANNING SCHEME
    Enforcement of planning control. *See* **Town and country planning** (Enforcement of planning control—Land subject to resolution to prepare planning scheme).

PLANT
    Capital allowances—
        Income tax—
            Generally. *See* **Capital allowances** (Plant).
            Machinery or plant. *See* **Capital allowances** (Machinery or plant).
    Factory—
        Explosive or inflammable substance—
            Plant, etc containing substance. *See* **Factory** (Explosive or inflammable substance).
    Hire—
        Contract—
            Unfair terms—Exclusion of liability for negligence. *See* **Contract** (Unfair terms—Exclusion of liability for negligence—Contract for hire of plant).
    Income tax—
        Allowance. *See* **Capital allowances**.
        Wear and tear—
            Deduction in computing profits for income tax. *See* **Income tax** (Deduction in computing profits—Wear and tear of machinery or plant).
    Investment grant. *See* **Investment grant** (Machinery and plant).
    Rates—
        Plant deemed to be part of hereditament. *See* **Rates** (Plant and machinery deemed to be part of hereditament).
        Valuation. *See* **Rates** (Valuation—Plant and machinery).
    Safe system of working. *See* **Safe system of working** (Plant).

PLAQUE
    Memorial plaque—
        Faculty for memorial plaque within churchyard to person not buried there. *See* **Ecclesiastical law** (Memorial—Memorial plaque within churchyard to person not buried there).

PLATE
    Church plate—
        Sale of—
            Faculty. *See* **Ecclesiastical law** (Faculty—Sale of chattel—Church plate).
    Gold plate—
        Wedding ring—
            Need to bear hall-mark—Plate (Offences) Act 1738, ss 1, 5—Gold Plate (Standard) Act 1798, ss 1, 2, 6—Wedding Rings Act 1855, s 1—Gold Wares (Standard of Fineness) Order 1932 (S R & O 1932 No 654), art 2. **Westwood v Cann** [1952] 2 349, CA.
    Silver plate—
        Exposure to sale of silver plate below statutory standard—
            Cigarette case—Absence of hall-mark—Obligation to mark sub-standard goods—Liability of seller to penalty—Forfeiture of article—Stat 8 & 9 Will 3 c 8, s 8 (as amended by Plate Duty Act 1719, s 3)—Plate (Offences) Act 1738, ss 1, 5. **Westwood v Cann** [1950] 2 805, KBD.

PLATFORM
    Railway station—
        Whether 'public place' within meaning of Public Order Act 1936. *See* **Public order** (Public place—Offensive conduct conducive to breaches of peace—Disturbance on railway station platform).

PLATING
    Certificate—
        Goods vehicle. *See* **Road traffic** (Plating and test certificates for goods vehicles).

PLATINUM
    Hallmarking. *See* **Hallmarking**.

PLAY
    Copyright—
        Rights of owner of copyright in title of work. *See* **Copyright** (Rights of owner of copyright—Rights in title of work—Play).

PLEA
    Criminal cases—
        Legal aid. *See* **Legal aid** (Criminal cases—Offer of legal aid—Guilty plea).

PLEA (cont)—
    Trial. *See* **Criminal law** (Trial—Plea).

PLEA-BARGAINING
    Criminal trial. *See* **Criminal law** (Trial—Plea—Plea-bargaining).

PLEADING
    Admission—
        Divorce—
            Irretrievable breakdown of marriage—Duty of court to enquire into facts. *See* **Divorce** (Irretrievable
               breakdown of marriage—Duty of court to enquire into facts).
        Illegality—
            Admission of consent—Consent given under illegal hire-purchase agreement—Whether admission
               effective. **Belvoir Finance Co Ltd v Harold G Cole & Co Ltd** [1969] 2 904, QBD.
        Particulars. *See* Particulars—Admission, *below*.
    Amendment—
        Amendment at trial or hearing—
            Defence—Defence struck out for failure to comply with order for discovery—Judgment in default of
               defence entered against defendant as personal representative—Enquiry into damages
               ordered—Application by personal representative before enquiry held to serve a defence pleading
               plene administravit—Whether jurisdiction to give leave—RSC Ord 24, r 17, Ord 35, r 2. **Midland
               Bank Trust Co Ltd v Green (No 2)** [1979] 1 726, Ch D.
            Defence—Procedural defence—Application to amend at end of trial—Defendant applying during
               closing speech for leave to plead limitation defence—Whether leave should be granted.
               Ketteman v Hansel Properties Ltd [1988] 1 38, HL.
            Late amendment substantially altering case against defendant—Whether amendment necessary to
               enable all issues between parties to be determined—Whether amendment would result in
               prejudice or injustice to defendant which could not properly be compensated in costs—Whether
               amendment should be allowed. **Beoco Ltd v Alfa Laval Co Ltd** [1994] 4 464, CA.
            Necessity for amendment where new case set up at hearing. **Leavey (J) & Co Ltd v Hirst (George H)
               & Co Ltd** [1943] 2 581, CA.
            Statement of claim—Damages for breach of contract—Application at trial to alter whole basis of
               claim. **Perestrello E Companhia Ltda v United Paint Co Ltd** [1969] 3 479, CA.
        Appeal—
            Appeal against refusal to amend. *See* Amendment—Appeal against refusal of leave to amend,
               below.
            Review of exercise of judge's discretion. *See* **Appeal** (Review of exercise of discretion—
               Circumstances in which appellate court will interfere—Pleading—Amendment).
        Appeal against refusal of leave to amend—
            Application to amend defence before trial—Defendants applying for leave to amend defence five
               years after filing of defence—Action not ready for trial—Whether leave to amend should be
               granted. **Easton v Ford Motor Co Ltd** [1993] 4 257, CA.
            Refusal of leave to amend defence at trial—Principle on which discretion to give leave to amend
               should be exercised—Whether Court of Appeal would interfere with exercise of discretion by trial
               judge—Whether amendment should be formulated in writing at trial or on appeal—RSC Ord 28,
               r 1, Ord 58, r 3(2). **Derrick v Williams** [1939] 2 559, CA.
            Test—Libel action. **Cadam v Beaverbrook Newspapers Ltd** [1959] 1 453, CA.
        Application for leave to amend—
            Application for summary judgment—Related proceedings concerning claim on bank loan and in
               relation to interest rate swap—Judge refusing defendants' application to amend defence—
               Whether judge correct. **Deutsche Bank AG v Unitech Global Ltd** [2016] 2 Comm 689,
               CA; [2017] 1 570, CA.
            Application for summary judgment—Related proceedings concerning claim on bank loan and in
               relation to interest rate swap—Whether defendants to be granted permission to amend
               defence—Whether claimants entitled to summary judgment in respect of certain issues. **Deutsche
               Bank AG v Unitech Global Ltd** [2014] 2 Comm 268, QBD.
            Judge striking out particulars of claim but not claim form in order to enable claimants to
               reformulate claim—Claimants applying to amend re-amended particulars of claim by pleading
               re-re-amended particulars of claim—New claims pleaded arguably time-barred—Judge allowing
               amendments by comparing re-re-amended particulars with re-amended particulars—Whether
               court having power to amend—Whether new claims arising out of same or substantially same
               facts as 'are already in issue'—Whether strike out order to be corrected under slip rule or
               varied—Limitation Act 1980, s 35(5)(a)—CPR 3.1(7), 17.4(2), 40.12(1). **Libyan Investment Authority
               v King** [2022] 1 Comm 279, CA.
            Necessity for amendment to be reduced into writing. **Derrick v Williams** [1939] 2 559, CA.
            Perjured evidence—Defendants seeking leave to reamend points of defence on ground that
               plaintiffs' witnesses had given perjured evidence—Whether evidence of perjury admissible.
               Westacre Investments Inc v Jugoimport-SDPR Holding Co Ltd [1998] 4 570, QBD.
        Application for permission to amend after judgment but before formal completion of order—
            Judge giving summary judgment for defendants—Claimant applying for permission to amend
               pleading before issue of order—Whether judge having jurisdiction to review decision before
               formal completion of order—CPR 3.1. **Stewart v Engel** [2000] 3 518, CA.
        Application to amend pleadings and adduce further evidence after judgment but before drawing up of
            order—
            Principles applicable on such an application. **Charlesworth v Relay Road Ltd (in liq)** [1999] 4 397,
              Ch D.
        Effect—
            Landlord's action for possession—Defence and counterclaim containing general traverse—
               Subsequent amendment admitting landlord's title—Claim of forfeiture based on denial of
               landlord's title by the original defence—Whether amendment removed effect of original denial.
               Warner v Sampson [1959] 1 120, CA.

Amendment (cont)—
Leave to amend after close of case—
Application for leave to amend after close of case but before judgment. **Loutfi v C Czarnikow Ltd** [1952] **2** 823, QBD.
Leave to amend after close of pleadings—
Amendment at trial—Allegation of breach of statutory duty—RSC Ord 28, r 1. **Hunt v Rice & Son Ltd** [1937] **3** 715, CA.
Claim for injunction—Effect of new legislation—Legislation enacted after close of Pleadings— Question whether injunction should be granted to be determined by reference to law at date of trial—New legislation giving effect to law of European Economic Community—Action for infringement of copyright—Leave to amend defence—Allegation that injunction would assist plaintiff to abuse dominant position and to restrict competition in breach of community laws—Whether leave to amend should be given. **Application des Gaz SA v Falks Veritas Ltd** [1974] **3** 51, CA.
Defence—Leave given to amend statement of claim—Implied leave to amend defence—Scope of power to amend defence without special leave—Whether defendant entitled to amend defence without limit—Whether right to amend defence limited to matters consequential on amendments to statement of claim. **Squire v Squire** [1972] **1** 891, CA.
Leave to amend defence at trial—Necessity of pleading peculiar sense of document under foreign law—Document agreed translation of foreign agreement—Special meaning of terms— Adjournment on security for costs being given—Necessity. **Ascherberg, Hopwood and Crew Ltd v Casa Musicale Sonzogno Di Piero Ostali, Societa in Nome Collettivo** [1971] **3** 38, CA.
Time for amendments to be made—Leave to amend pleadings given at trial but amendments not made until after judgment delivered—Judgment to be post-dated to date when all amendments of pleadings have been made. **Luby v Newcastle-under-Lyme Corp** [1964] **3** 169, CA.
Leave to amend after expiry of limitation period—
Claimants applying to re-amend claim—Limitation defence raised by defendant—Judge allowing amendment application—Whether judge correct—Whether new claim arising out of 'the same facts or substantially the same facts' as previous claim—CPR 17.4(2). **Akers v Samba Financial Group** [2020] **1 Comm** 111, CA.
Defence—Action for damages for personal injury—Negligence of plaintiff sought to be raised by amendment after three years after accident—Alleged failure to wear safety helmet provided by employers—Employers not parties to action—No allegation of fault on part of employers— Amendment sought after time for joining employers as defendants—Plaintiff not prejudiced by amendment. **Turner v Ford Motor Co Ltd** [1965] **2** 583, CA.
Defence—Damage—Novus actus interveniens in chain of causation of damages—Discovered by defendant after delivery of defence and after expiry of period of limitation for action by plaintiff against third person—Defendant not at fault—Whether defendant entitled to leave to amend. **Weait v Jayanbee Joinery Ltd** [1962] **2** 568, CA.
New cause of action—Prejudice—Proposed amendments raising new causes of action—Factors to be considered—Whether prejudice to defendants outweighing plaintiff's need to make amendments—Whether prejudice limited to matters relating to delay after expiry of time limit—Whether leave should be granted—RSC Ord 20, r 5(2). **Hancock Shipping Co Ltd v Kawasaki Heavy Industries Ltd** [1992] **3** 132, CA.
New claim—Claimant unable to rely on facts pleaded in defence but not in statement of case on application for post-limitation amendment to add new claim—Unsatisfactory nature of rule prohibiting such reliance—Limitation Act 1980, s 35(5)—CPR 17.4(2). **Goode v Martin** [2001] **3** 562, QBD.
New claim—New cause of action arising out of same facts or substantially same facts as already in issue in original action—Limitation Act 1980, s 35(5)(a). **Finlan v Eyton Morris Winfield (a firm)** [2007] **4** 143, Ch D.
New claim—New claim in pending action—Addition or substitution of new cause of action or new party—Addition of new party permitted if addition necessary—Beneficiary under will bringing proceedings in negligence in personal capacity—Beneficiary seeking to amend proceedings after expiry of limitation period to continue personal action and add derivative action—Whether addition of personal representative necessary for derivative action—Whether addition of personal representative necessary for personal action—Limitation Act 1980, s 35(2)—CPR 19.5. **Roberts v Gill & Co** [2010] **4** 367, SC.
New claim—New claim in pending action—Original set-off or counterclaim—Meaning of original counterclaim—Limitation Act 1980, s 35(3). **Law Society v Wemyss** [2009] **1** 752, Ch D.
Plaintiffs claiming damages for negligence—Limitation period expiring—Plaintiffs seeking leave to amend statement of claim—Amendment constituting new claim—Whether plaintiffs entitled to leave to amend statement of claim—Limitation Act 1980, s 35(1), (3)—RSC Ord 20, r 5(5). **Welsh Development Agency v Redpath Dorman Long Ltd** [1994] **4** 10, CA.
Plaintiffs claiming damages for negligence—Plaintiffs seeking leave to amend statement of claim to allege fraud—Whether amendment constituting new claim—Whether amendment involving same facts as original claim—Whether leave to amend should be granted—RSC Ord 20, r 5. **Paragon Finance plc v D B Thakerar & Co (a firm)** [1999] **1** 400, CA.
Statement of claim—Amendment to be allowed if just—RSC Ord 20, r 5. **Chatsworth Investments Ltd v Cussins (Contractors) Ltd** [1969] **1** 143, CA.
Statement of claim—Negligence or breach of statutory duty alleged by employee against employers—Extension of original claim for negligence or breach of duty by alleging vicarious responsibility—Not new cause of action—Whether amendment should be allowed. **Dornan v JW Ellis & Co Ltd** [1962] **1** 303, CA.
Statement of claim—Partners—Claim by three partners for damages for breach of contract— Statement of claim alleging contract made by one partner on behalf of all three—Amendment sought after expiration of limitation period to allege contract made by one partner on behalf of himself or on behalf of himself and his other partner—Rights assigned in equity to present partners—Whether new cause of action raised. **Robinson v Unicos Property Corp Ltd** [1962] **2** 24, CA.

PLEADING (cont)—
 Amendment (cont)—
  Leave to amend after expiry of limitation period (cont)—
   Statement of claim—Statute-barred cause of action introduced by amendment—Alleged negligence of solicitor—Allegation of breach of duty under joint retainer by two clients—Amendment by alleging separate retainers by each client. **Hall v Meyrick** [1957] **2** 722, CA.
   Statutory bar—Sunday Observance Act 1780, s 5. **Green v Kursaal (Southend-on-Sea) Estates Ltd** [1937] **1** 732, KBD.
  Leave to amend after trial of action—
   Statement of claim—Issue which trial judge bound to find against plaintiff or on which no evidence given at trial—Whether Court of Appeal should refuse leave to amend statement of claim—Whether Court of Appeal should give leave to appeal to House of Lords against refusal of leave to amend. **Williams v Home Office (No 2)** [1982] **2** 564, CA.
  Leave to amend statement of claim—
   Generally. *See* **Statement of case** (Leave to amend).
  New cause of action—
   Adding new cause of action—Cause of action accruing since original pleading—Plaintiffs seeking declaration entitling them to reject delivery of goods—Defendants counterclaiming for price of goods—Defendants subsequently seeking to amend counterclaim to plead repudiation—Whether repudiation a new cause of action accruing since counterclaim—Whether defendants entitled to amend counterclaim. **Tilcon Ltd v Land and Real Estate Investments Ltd** [1987] **1** 615, CA.
  New claim. *See* Amendment—Leave to amend after expiry of limitation period—New claim, *above*.
  Permission to amend after expiry of limitation period—
   New claim—Claimant seeking permission for post-limitation amendment to statement of claim to add alternative claim based on facts put forward in the defence—Rule of procedure allowing post-limitation amendment to add new claim only if new claim arising out of same facts as a claim in respect of which claimant had already claimed a remedy—Whether possible to interpret rule in manner giving effect to claimant's right of access to court under human rights convention—Human Rights Act 1998, s 3(1), Sch 1, Pt I, art 6—CPR 17.4(2). **Goode v Martin** [2002] **1** 620, CA.
  Statement of claim—
   Generally. *See* **Statement of case** (Amendment).
 Answer—
  Divorce petition. *See* **Divorce** (Practice—Answer).
 Appeal against refusal of leave to amend. *See* Amendment—Appeal against refusal of leave to amend, *above*.
 Condition of mind. *See* Particulars—Condition of mind, *below*.
 Conversion—
  Unidentified goods. *See* Particulars—Conversion, *below*.
 Copyright—
  Infringement—
   Reproduction. *See* **Copyright** (Conflict of laws—Reproduction—Pleading).
 Counterclaim—
  Charterparty—
   Breach of obligation to provide cargo delay ship's becoming an arrived ship—Whether defence to action or matter of counterclaim. **Sociedad Financiera de Bienes Raices SA v Agrimpex Hungarian Trading Co for Agricultural Products** [1960] **2** 578, HL.
  When counterclaim can be made—
   Plaintiff obtaining RSC Ord 14 judgment against defendant and defendant satisfying judgment—Counterclaim raised but not pleaded prior to Ord 14 judgment—Whether defendant entitled to serve counterclaim after judgment obtained and satisfied—Whether power to 'make' counterclaim entitling defendant to plead counterclaim after final judgment obtained—Supreme Court of Judicature (Consolidation) Act 1925, s 39(1)—RSC Ord 15, r 2. **CSI International Co Ltd v Archway Personnel (Middle East) Ltd** [1980] **3** 215, CA.
 County court—
  Claim for exemplary damages. *See* **County court** (Practice—Exemplary damages).
  Generally. *See* **County court** (Pleadings).
 Damage—
  Exemplary damages—
   Grounds justifying award of exemplary damages—No need to plead. **Cassell & Co Ltd v Broome** [1972] **1** 801, HL.
   Need to plead claim—County court proceedings. *See* **County court** (Practice—Exemplary damages—Need to plead claim for exemplary damages).
  Special damage—
   Need to plead—Breach of contract—Damage of a kind which is not the necessary and immediate consequence of the breach—Damage which can be precisely calculated—Claim particularising expenditure by plaintiff rendered abortive by breach—Plaintiff at trial seeking to lead evidence of, and recover, loss of profits had expenditure not been rendered abortive by breach. **Perestrello E Companhia Ltda v United Paint Co Ltd** [1969] **3** 479, CA.
   Need to plead—Breach of contract—Sale of goods—Goods supplied alleged to be valueless—Full purchase price claimed—Alternative claim where goods not valueless, but depreciated. **Anglo-Cyprian Trade Agencies Ltd v Paphos Wine Industries Ltd** [1951] **1** 873, KBD.
   Need to plead—Personal injuries—Loss of wages between accident and trial not pleaded as special damage—No power to include in general damages. **Ilkiw v Samuels** [1963] **2** 879, CA.
   Personal injuries—Special circumstances likely to lead plaintiff to sustain future losses other than those reasonably to be expected to flow from accident—Intention of plaintiff employee to set up in business on own account frustrated by accident—Claim for compensation for loss of profits plaintiff would have earned in own business. **Domsalla v Barr (t/a AB Construction)** [1969] **3** 487, CA.
  Wrongful dismissal—
   Loss of remuneration—Whether claimant must give particulars of his taxable income and tax assessments and allowances. **Phipps v Orthodox Unit Trusts Ltd** [1957] **3** 305, CA.

PLEADING (cont)—

    Damage (cont)—

        Wrongful dismissal (cont)—

            Remuneration during period of alleged contractual notice. **Hayward v Pullinger & Partners Ltd** [1950] **1** 581, KBD.

    Defamation—

        Fair comment. *See* **Libel and slander** (Fair comment—Pleading fair comment).

        Generally. *See* **Libel and slander** (Pleading).

        Justification—

            Generally. *See* **Libel and slander** (Justification—Pleading justification).

            Particulars. *See* **Libel and slander** (Particulars).

    Default of pleading—

        Counterclaim—

            Default in delivering reply—Motion for judgment—Action still pending—Subject-matter of action and counterclaim indivisible—RSC Ord 27, r 11. **Rogers v Wood** [1948] **1** 38, Ch D.

    Defence—

        Contents—

            Whether defendant required to make reasonable enquiries of third parties before pleading that he is unable to admit or deny an allegation—Meaning of 'unable to admit or deny'—CPR 16.5(1). **SPI North Ltd v Swiss Post International (UK) Ltd** [2019] **2** 512, CA.

        Counterclaim. *See* Counterclaim, *above*.

        Filing a defence—

            Whether CPR requiring defence to be served by defendants making summary judgment application against claim—CPR Pt 15. **King v Stiefel** [2022] **1 Comm** 990n, Comm Ct.

        Particulars before defence. *See* Particulars—Particulars before defence, *below*.

    Delivery—

        Long Vacation—

            Irregularity—Statement of claim delivered in long vacation—No defence filed within time allowed—Judgment signed in default of defence—Whether statement of claim void or voidable—Whether judgment should be set aside—RSC Ord 64, r 4, Ord 70, r 1. **MacFoy v United Africa Co Ltd** [1961] **3** 1169, PC.

        Time—

            Order dismissing action unless statement of claim be served on or before specified date—Delivery after 4 pm on specified date—RSC Ord 64, r 11. **Kaye v Levinson** [1950] **1** 594, CA.

    Departure—

        Legal consequences of pleaded facts—

            Pleading setting out material facts and alleging interference with right to quiet enjoyment of premises—Facts pleaded sufficient to warrant claim for trespass—Judge in course of trial raising issue of trespass—Whether judge entitled to his own motion to raise issue—Whether defendant taken by surprise. **Drane v Evangelou** [1978] **2** 437, CA.

            Pleading setting out material facts and legal consequences sought to be drawn from facts—Party not precluded at hearing from seeking to draw different consequences from pleaded facts. **Vandervell's Trusts, Re (No 2)** [1974] **3** 205, CA.

        New ground inconsistent with previous pleading—

            Inconsistency—Mutually exclusive or merely different—Claim by personal representatives to set aside gift by deceased to defendant—Allegation in statement of claim of undue influence over deceased by defendant—Defendant alleging that gift made on advice of deceased's husband—Plaintiffs alleging in reply that gift procured by undue influence of deceased's husband—Whether reply inconsistent with statement of claim—RSC Ord 18, r 10(1). **Herbert v Vaughan** [1972] **3** 122, Ch D.

    Disclosure—

        Particulars before disclosure. *See* Particulars—Particulars before disclosure, *below*.

        Production of documents. *See* **Disclosure and inspection of documents** (Production of documents—Documents referred to in pleadings or affidavits).

    Divorce. *See* **Divorce** (Practice—Pleading).

    Document referred to in pleading—

        Production. *See* **Disclosure and inspection of documents** (Production of documents—Documents referred to in pleadings or affidavits).

    Easement—

        Lost grant. *See* Particulars—Lost grant—Easement, *below*.

    Estoppel—

        Generally. *See* **Estoppel** (Pleading).

        Matters pleaded in previous proceedings—

            Effect—Whether confessions of truth of facts stated. **Park, In the Estate of** [1953] **2** 408, PDA.

        Striking out pleading. *See* Striking out—Estoppel per rem judicatam, *below*.

    Exemplary damages. *See* Damage—Exemplary damages, *above*.

    Facts on which party relies for claim or defence—

        Duty to plead—

            Libel proceedings—Innuendo—Particulars. *See* **Libel and slander** (Innuendo—Particulars—Duty of plaintiff to plead facts on which he relies for his claim).

    Fair comment—

        Libel—

            Generally. *See* **Libel and slander** (Fair comment—Pleading fair comment).

            Particulars. *See* **Libel and slander** (Particulars—Fair comment).

    Foreign currency—

        Pleading claims in foreign currency. *See* **Judgment** (Payment of sum of money—Foreign currency—Claims in foreign currency).

    Forfeiture of lease—

        Defence. *See* Particulars—Defence—Forfeiture of lease, *below*.

    Indictment. *See* **Indictment**.

    Intention. *See* Particulars—Condition of mind—Plaintiff's state of mind, *below*.

    Interest—

        Practice. *See* **Practice** (Interest—Pleading).

PLEADING (cont)—
Interrogatories—
    Defamation actions. *See* **Libel and slander** (Interrogatory).
Justification—
    Libel—
        Particulars. *See* **Libel and slander** (Particulars—Justification).
Land—
    Acknowledgment of title in defence. *See* **Limitation of action** (Land—Adverse possession—Acknowledgment of title).
Leave to amend. *See* Amendment, *above*.
Limitation—
    New claim. *See* Amendment—Leave to amend after expiry of limitation period—New claim, *above*.
Limitation period—
    Leave to amend pleadings after expiry of limitation period. *See* Amendment—Leave to amend after expiry of limitation period, *above*.
Lodging—
    Chancery Division. *See* **Practice** (Summons for directions—Chancery Division—Pleadings).
Long Vacation—
    Delivery. *See* Delivery—Long Vacation, *above*.
Loss of wages between accident and trial—
    Special damage—
        Need to plead. *See* Damage—Special damage—Need to plead—Personal injuries—Loss of wages between accident and trial not pleaded as special damage, *above*.
Lost grant—
    Particulars. *See* Particulars—Lost grant, *below*.
Negligence—
    Generally. *See* **Negligence** (Pleading).
    Particulars. *See* Particulars—Negligence, *below*.
Notice—
    Allegation that person had notice. *See* Particulars—Notice, *below*.
Ownership of property—
    Particulars. *See* Particulars—Ownership of property, *below*.
Particulars—
    Account—
        Particulars sought by defendant of sums paid to him by plaintiff—RSC Ord 19, r 7(b). **Sharer v Wallace** [1950] **2** 463, Ch D.
    Admission—
        Occurrence of accident in course of employment admitted—No admission made as to the circumstances—Whether particulars of the accident admitted should be ordered. **Fox v H Wood (Harrow) Ltd** [1962] **3** 1100, CA.
    Application for particulars—
        Power of Master to order particulars to be given by reference to plan. **Tarbox v St Pancras BC** [1952] **1** 1306, CA.
    Bad faith—
        Local authority dwelling—Management. *See* **Housing** (Local authority houses—Management—Bad faith—Pleading).
    Condition of mind—
        Condition of mind alleged as a fact—Whether particulars can be ordered—RSC Ord 19, rr 4, 7, 22, 23. **Burgess v Beethoven Electric Equipment Ltd** [1942] **2** 658, CA.
        Plaintiff's state of mind—Absence of intention to make a gift to woman with whom plaintiff lived as his wife—Particulars of facts relied on—House conveyed into name of defendant, the unmarried wife—Plaintiff claimed half share in proceeds of sale of house—Alleged that contributions made by him towards purchase of house were never intended as gift to the defendant—Whether particulars of allegation of absence of intention would be ordered—RSC, Ord 18, r 12(1)(b). **Feeney v Rix** [1968] **3** 22, CA.
    Constructive trust—
        Knowledge of fraudulent or dishonest breach of trust—Foreign organisation claiming damages against former employee for fraudulent breach of trust—Statement of claim alleging that defendant's wife accountable as constructive trustee on ground that with actual or constructive knowledge of defendant's breach of trust she had actively assisted in breach—Wife alleging that particulars of claim inadequate to support allegation of knowledge sufficient to impose liability—Whether plaintiff entitled to frame pleading in general terms and defer particularisation until after discovery. **Arab Monetary Fund v Hashim (No 2)** [1990] **1** 673, Ch D.
        Knowledge of fraudulent or dishonest breach of trust—Pleading of fraud or dishonesty—Directors of company enabling third party to purchase shares with financial assistance from company—Company pleading conspiracy between directors and third party and claiming damages—Statement of claim alleging defendants 'aware or ought to have been aware' of facts which showed dishonest breach of trust—Whether allegation a clear and unequivocal pleading of knowledge of fraudulent breach of trust—Whether knowledge of dishonesty of breach of trust required to be pleaded—RSC Ord 18, r 15(1). **Belmont Finance Corp Ltd v Williams Furniture Ltd** [1979] **1** 118, CA.
    Conversion—
        Unidentified goods—Whether goods must be specified and conversion of particularised goods proved—Value and general nature of goods pleaded. **Brightside and Carbrock (Sheffield) Co-op Society Ltd v Phillips** [1964] **1** 49, CA.
    Defence—
        Forfeiture of lease—Onus on plaintiff to prove case—Defendant's denial involving double negative. **Duke's Court Estates Ltd v Associated British Engineering Ltd** [1948] **2** 137, Ch D.
        No obligation to plead to particulars. **Chapple v Electrical Trades Union** [1961] **3** 612, Ch D.
    Knowledge—
        Allegation that man knew or ought to have known. **Fox v H Wood (Harrow) Ltd** [1962] **3** 1100, CA.

PLEADING (cont)—
    Particulars (cont)—
        Libel—
            Fair comment—Rolled-up plea—Particulars of facts relied on. **Tudor-Hart v British Union for the Abolition of Vivisection** [1937] 4 475, CA.
            Generally. *See* **Libel and slander** (Particulars).
            Innuendo. *See* **Libel and slander** (Innuendo—Particulars).
            Justification—Particulars of justification—Whether before or after discovery—RSC Ord 19, rr 4, 27. **Goldschmidt v Constable & Co** [1937] 4 293, CA.
            Letters alleged to be defamatory—Plaintiff ignorant of contents—Whether particulars to be delivered. **Collins v Jones** [1955] 2 145, CA.
            Material facts—Plaintiff not referred to by name or description other than nationality. **Bruce v Odhams Press Ltd** [1936] 1 287, CA.
        Lost grant—
            Easement—Whether particulars should be ordered. **Wade (Gabriel) & English Ltd v Dixon & Cardus** [1937] 3 900, Ch D.
            Particulars of lost grant which may be ordered—Particulars of whether lost grant alleged to have been made before or after certain dates. **Tremayne v English Clays Lovering Pochin & Co Ltd** [1972] 2 234, Ch D.
        Malicious prosecution—
            Denial by defendant of absence of reasonable or probable cause—Whether particulars of defence would be ordered. **Stapeley v Annetts** [1969] 3 1541, CA.
        Marine insurance—
            Particulars of defence—Shipowner's claim against insurer for loss of ship—Insurer alleging loss due to wilful casting away of ship—Shipowner applying for further and better particulars of insurer's defence—Practice of Commercial Court not to order such particulars—Validity of practice—RSC Ord 18, r 12(1)(a), Ord 72, r 7(2). **Astrovlanis Compania Naviera SA v Linard** [1972] 2 647, CA; **Dias, The** [1972] 2 1112, CA.
        Negligence—
            Action for damages for negligence—Plaintiff relying on 'all the provisions of the Highway Code applicable'—Whether further and better particulars invited. **Wells v Weeks** [1965] 1 77, QBD.
            Departure from case originally pleaded. *See* **Practice** (Trial—Departure from case originally pleaded—Particulars of negligence).
        Notice—
            Allegation that person had notice—Notice contrasted with knowledge—Notice that cheque being dealt with without owner's authority alleged against bankers—Materiality of form and precise terms of notice, or of circumstances from which notice was to be inferred—RSC Ord 19, rr 22, 23. **Cresta Holdings Ltd v Karlin** [1959] 3 656, CA.
        Ownership of property—
            Personalty—Ownership claimed by both parties—Neither party in position to allege possession—Whether particulars of title should be ordered. **Kemlo v Heath** [1964] 2 591, Ch D.
        Particulars before defence—
            Allegation that defendant was in breach of the duty that as banker it owed to plaintiff as customer—Allegation ambiguous as to nature of duty—Plaintiff should specify with precision the relation under which duty arose. **Selangor United Rubber Estates Ltd v Cradock** [1964] 3 709, Ch D.
            Matters within knowledge of defendant—Action for breach of contract—Breach of term as to time for delivery of car—RSC Ord 19, r 7. **Ross v Blakes Motors Ltd** [1951] 2 689, CA.
            Racial discrimination—Identity of persons alleged to have been discriminated against—Proceedings against local authority based on allegation that authority had discriminated against Asian children by dispersing them to schools outside areas where they lived—Large number of children affected by dispersal policy—Difficulty of local authority in giving discovery in absence of particularisation—Whether local authority entitled to particulars of identity of children against whom it was alleged they had discriminated before delivering their defence and before discovery. **Race Relations Board v Ealing London Borough (No 2)** [1978] 1 497, CA.
        Particulars before disclosure—
            Special circumstances—Action by managing agents for wrongful dismissal—Defence alleging breaches of duty as managing agents—Allegations couched in general terms—Order that defendants give particulars of breaches known to them on which intending to rely at trial—Particulars not limited to breaches known to defendants at date of dismissal. **Leonard (Cyril) & Co v Simo Securities Trust Ltd** [1971] 3 1313, Ch D and CA.
        Personal injuries actions—
            Particulars to give plaintiff's age or date of birth. **Practice Note** [1974] 3 976, QBD.
        Secret process—
            Expert's inspection—Order for inspection by expert in lieu of order for particulars—Claimant for order should take initiative in explaining process in detail to expert. **Printer and Finishers Ltd v Holloway** [1964] 3 54, Ch D.
        Traverse of negative allegation—
            Negative pregnant with affirmative allegation—Defendant denying negative allegations in statement of claim—Burden of proof on plaintiff—Defence importing nothing beyond that which was in any event to be implied from a mere denial of plaintiff's allegations—Whether particulars of defence should be ordered. **Howard v Borneman** [1972] 2 867, Ch D.
            Negative pregnant with affirmative allegation—Denial that defendant 'failed to furnish any such particulars without reasonable excuse'—RSC Ord 19, rr 7, 19. **IRC v Jackson** [1960] 3 31, CA.
            Negative pregnant with affirmative allegation—Evasive denial—Amendment—RSC Ord 19, rr 7, 19. **Pinson v Lloyds & National Provincial Foreign Bank Ltd** [1941] 2 636, CA.
            Not pregnant with affirmative—Whether particulars of traverse should be ordered. **Chapple v Electrical Trades Union** [1961] 3 612, Ch D.
        Wrongful dismissal—
            Particulars of employment and earnings since dismissal—Period claimed by plaintiff as reasonable notice—Claim for particulars before defence—RSC Ord 19, r 7B. **Monk v Redwing Aircraft Co Ltd** [1942] 1 133, CA.

PLEADING (cont)—
 Particulars (cont)—
  Wrongful dismissal (cont)—
   Special damage—Loss of remuneration—Whether particulars of taxable income must be given. **Phipps v Orthodox Unit Trusts Ltd** [1957] **3** 305, CA.
 Parties—
  Substitution of parties after expiry of limitation period. *See* **Practice** (Parties—Substitution— Substitution after expiry of limitation period).
 Personal injuries actions—
  Particulars of plaintiff's age or date of birth. *See* Particulars—Personal injuries actions—Particulars to give plaintiff's age or date of birth, *above*.
 Point of law—
  Admission of facts alleged and objection in point of law—
   Evidence on behalf of plaintiff—Whether evidence admissible on behalf of plaintiff. **Pioneer Plastic Containers Ltd v Customs and Excise Comrs** [1967] **1** 1053, Ch D.
  Preliminary point—
   Expediency of pleading point of law that may dispose of whole matter—Whether preliminary point of law may be raised at trial although not pleaded—RSC Ord 25, r 2. **Independent Automatic Sales Ltd v Knowles & Foster** [1962] **3** 27, Ch D.
 Prescription—
  Right of way. *See* **Easement** (Right of way—Prescription—Pleadings).
 Probate. *See* **Probate** (Pleading).
 Reply—
  Estoppel—
   Estoppel arising after issue of writ—Amendment by plaintiff to pleading. **Morrison Rose & Partners (a firm) v Hillman** [1961] **2** 891, CA.
  Service. *See* **Practice** (Service—Reply to defence).
 Restraint of trade. *See* **Restraint of trade by agreement** (Pleading).
 Sale of goods—
  Special damage. *See* Damage—Special damage—Need to plead—Breach of contract, *above*.
 Secret process—
  Particulars. *See* Particulars—Secret process, *above*.
 Service. *See* **Practice** (Service).
 Special damage. *See* Damage—Special damage, *above*.
 Statement of case—
  Delivery—
   Delay—Dismissal of action for want of prosecution. *See* **Practice** (Dismissal of action for want of prosecution—Delay—Delay in delivering statement of claim).
  Generally. *See* **Statement of case**.
 Statute—
  Limitation period. *See* **Limitation of action** (Statute—Pleading).
 Striking out—
  Abuse of process of the court—
   Claim form—Claimant issuing claim form and seeking extension of time for service of claim—Claimant unable to particularise claim—Claimant issuing claim form in order to protect its limitation position—Defendants applying to strike out claim form—Whether issuing of claim form an abuse of process. **Nomura International plc v Granada Group Ltd** [2007] **2 Comm** 878, QBD.
   Claim form—Solicitor issuing claim form without authorisation of all named claimants—Whether issue of proceedings without authority abuse of process of the court—CPR 3.4(2). **Adams v Ford** [2012] **3** 247, CA.
   Libel—Defendants pleading justification and fair comment—Parts of defence and particulars struck out on grounds of insufficient supporting evidence—Criteria for pleading justification and fair comment—Principles to be applied by court in considering interlocutory application to strike out for abuse of process—RSC Ord 18, r 19. **McDonald's Corp v Steel** [1995] **3** 615, CA.
  Application—
   Need for precise indication of what should be struck out. **Carl-Zeiss-Stiftung v Rayner & Keeler Ltd (No 3)** [1969] **3** 897, Ch D.
  County court—
   Generally. *See* **County court** (Pleadings—Striking out).
   Jurisdiction. *See* **County court** (Jurisdiction—Striking out pleading).
  Defence—
   County court practice. *See* **County court** (Practice—Striking out—Defence).
   Defence tending to prejudice, embarrass or delay fair trial—General denial of every allegation of fact in statement of claim—Each allegation not set out separately and denied specifically— Effective denial of every allegation—RSC Ord 19, r 27. **Lancaster (John) Radiators Ltd v General Motor Radiator Co Ltd** [1946] **2** 685, CA.
   Defendant making pre-action admission—Defendant withdrawing pre-action admission and filing defence—Claimant applying to strike out defence as abuse of process or likely to obstruct just disposal of proceedings—Applicable test—CPR 3.4(2). **Walley v Stoke-on-Trent City Council** [2006] **4** 1230, CA.
   Order that paragraphs be struck out in default of further and better particulars within 21 days—Imperfect particulars delivered in time—No default warranting striking out of paragraphs—Automatic striking out on default. **Reiss v Woolf** [1952] **2** 112, CA.
   Vexatious and oppressive—Inherent jurisdiction of Court of Appeal to strike out. **Oxford (Charles) Ltd v Gonshaw Ltd** [1948] **2** 229, CA.
  Divorce. *See* **Divorce** (Practice—Pleading—Striking out).
  Embarassing material—
   Pleaded facts not within defendant's knowledge—Whether pleading should be struck out as embarassing—RSC Ord 18, r 19(1)(c). **Paterson Zochonis & Co Ltd v Merfarken Packaging Ltd** [1986] **3** 522, CA.

PLEADING (cont)—
    Striking out (cont)—
        Estoppel per rem judicatam—
            Claim for damage to and loss of cargo—Judgment obtained in India in respect of part of goods—Action brought in England in respect of whole of loss—Whether cause of action in England identical to that in India—Whether English action barred—Whether action should be struck out—Civil Jurisdiction and Judgments Act 1982, s 34. **Indian Endurance, The** [1993] **1** 998, HL.
            Issue determined in earlier action against different defendant—Failure of plaintiff to add defendant in second action as defendant in first action—No privity of interest between defendants in first and second action—Issue raised in second action determined against plaintiff in first action—Whether defendant in second action should have been added as defendant in first action by plaintiff—Whether pleadings in second action should be struck out—RSC Ord 15, r 6(2)(b)(ii). **Gleeson v J Wippell & Co Ltd** [1977] **3** 54, Ch D.
            Refusal to strike out—Complexity of issue not a ground for refusal. **Carl-Zeiss-Stiftung v Rayner & Keeler Ltd (No 3)** [1969] **3** 897, Ch D.
        Exercise of court's powers—
            Jurisdiction discretionary—RSC Ord 18, r 19. **Carl-Zeiss-Stiftung v Rayner & Keeler Ltd (No 3)** [1969] **3** 897, Ch D.
        Jurisdiction of county court. *See* **County court** (Jurisdiction—Striking out pleading).
        Mid-trial. *See* **Practice** (Striking out—Mid-trial—Application made to strike out part of counterclaim during trial).
        No reasonable cause of action—
            Claim based on implied collateral contract—Sale of shares in breach of covenant—Transferee acquiring shares with knowledge of covenants—Claim that transferee bound by covenants under implied collateral contract—Whether claim should be struck out. **Law Debenture Trust Corp plc v Ural Caspian Oil Corp Ltd** [1993] **2** 355, Ch D.
            Defendant having defence under Limitation Acts—Whether pleading may be struck out as disclosing no reasonable cause of action merely because defendant may have defence under Limitation Acts—RSC Ord 18, r 19. **Ronex Properties Ltd v John Laing Construction Ltd (Clarke, Nicholls & Marcel (a firm), third parties)** [1982] **3** 961, CA.
            Originating summons—Evidence inadmissible on an application to strike out—Affidavit in support of originating summons—Affidavit consituting evidence and not pleading—Originating summons containing nothing to show no reasonable cause of action—Defendants relying for purpose of application on contents of plaintiff's affidavit in support of originating summons—Whether affidavit constituting 'evidence on an application' to strike out—Whether court entitled to have regard to affidavit in determining application—RSC Ord 18, r 19(1)(a), (2), (3). **Caines (decd), Re** [1978] **2** 1, Ch D.
        Order of Court of Appeal—
            Reliance on decision at nisi prius—Gaming debt—Action brought as on an account stated—Gaming Act 1892, s 1—RSC Ord 25, r 4. **Law v Dearnley** [1950] **1** 124, CA.
        Order striking out pleading—
            Appeal against order—Whether order interlocutory for purposes of leave to appeal—Supreme Court of Judicature (Consolidation) Act 1925, s 31(1)(i)—RSC Ord 25, r 4. **Hunt v Allied Bakeries Ltd** [1956] **3** 513, CA.
        Statement of claim. *See* **Statement of case** (Striking out).
    Striking-out—
        No reasonable cause of action—
            Claimants alleging unlawful means conspiracy by defendant banks and chairman of company in which they held shares—Whether claim to be struck out in absence of reasonable grounds to bring it—Whether claimants entitled to amend particulars of claim—CPR 3.4(2)(a). **Standish v Royal Bank of Scotland plc** [2019] **1 Comm** 97, Ch D.
    Sufficiency. *See* **Practice** (Trial—Departure from case originally pleaded).
    Traverse—
        Effect—
            Action for possession—Whether general traverse denial of landlord's title entailing forfeiture. **Warner v Sampson** [1959] **1** 120, CA.
        Negative allegation. *See* Particulars—Traverse of negative allegation, *above*.
    Wrongful dismissal—
        Particulars. *See* Particulars—Wrongful dismissal, *above*.

PLEASURE GROUND
    Right to enjoy. *See* **Easement** (Pleasure ground—Right to enjoy pleasure ground).

PLEDGE
    Consumer credit agreement—
        Form and content of agreement. *See* **Consumer credit** (Agreement—Form and content of agreement—Pledges).
    Mercantile agent—
        Possession of goods—
            Pledge of documents. *See* **Agent** (Mercantile agent—Possession of goods—Consent of owner—Pledge of documents).
    Pledge of chattel—
        Registration—
            Need of registration. **Waight v Waight and Walker** [1952] **2** 290, Div.
    Sale of goods—
        Documents of title to goods sent by unpaid vendors to merchant bankers. *See* **Bank** (Documentary credit—Irrevocable credit—Undertaking to provide funds to meet drafts—Selling agents opening for their foreign principals, timber exporters, an irrevocable credit with merchant bankers on sale of a shipment to foreign buyers).

PLYING FOR HIRE
    Hackney carriage. *See* **Road traffic** (Hackney carriage—Plying for hire).

POINT OF LAW

Appeal—
County court to Court of Appeal—
Point of law not argued in county court. *See* **Court of Appeal** (Ground of appeal—Point of law not argued in court below—Appeal from county court).
Criminal cause or matter—
Refusal of court below to certify point of law of general public importance involved. *See* **House of Lords** (Leave to appeal—Criminal cause or matter—Refusal of court below to certify point of law of general public importance involved).
Income tax. *See* **Income tax** (Appeal—Point of law).
Income tax—
Appeal. *See* **Income tax** (Appeal—Point of law).
Error or mistake—
Relief—Case stated. *See* **Income tax** (Case stated—Relief in respect of error or mistake—Point of law).
Preliminary point of law—
Pleading. *See* **Pleading** (Point of law—Preliminary point).
Practice. *See* **Practice** (Preliminary point of law).
Reference following acquittal of accused. *See* **Criminal law** (Appeal—Reference of point of law following acquittal of accused).
Tribunal—
Appeal to Divisional Court. *See* **Tribunal** (Appeal to Divisional Court on point of law).
Interpretation of word in statute. *See* **Tribunal** (Appeal on point of law—Interpretation of word in statute).

POISON

Administering unlawfully. *See* **Criminal law** (Administering poison or other destructive or noxious thing).
Pollution of river. *See* **Water and watercourses** (Pollution of river—Causing poisonous, noxious or polluting matter or solid waste to enter controlled waters).
Sale by retail—
Corporate body—
Sale under supervision of superintendent—Sufficiency of supervision—Pharmacy and Poisons Act 1933, s 9(1), (2). **Hygienic Stores Ltd v Coombes** [1938] **1** 63, KBD.
Prohibition on sale by person other than authorised seller—
Exemption with respect to sale by way of wholesale dealing—Wholesaler selling drugs containing poison to retail shop for sale by retail—Neither proprietor of retail shop nor her employees authorised sellers—Whether wholesalers committed offence—Pharmacy and Poisons Act 1933, ss 18(1)(a)(i), 20(1), 29. **Oxford v Sangers Ltd** [1965] **1** 96, QBD.
Sale to be effected by or under supervision of registered pharmacist—
Exemption with respect to medicines—Failure to comply with conditions of exemption—Whether in itself an offence—Meaning of 'medicine'—Pharmacy and Poisons Act 1933, ss 18, 19, 24. **R v Staincross Justices, ex p Teasdale** [1960] **3** 572, QBD.
Registered pharmacist in another room on premises—Pharmacist out of sight and hearing—Sufficiency of supervision—Pharmacy and Poisons Act 1933, s 18(1)(a)(iii). **Roberts v Littlewoods Mail Order Stores Ltd** [1943] **1** 271, KBD.
Time at which sale effected—Chemist's self-service shop—Pharmacist supervising transaction at time of payment—Pharmacy and Poisons Act 1933, s 18(1)(a)(iii). **Pharmaceutical Society of GB v Boots Cash Chemists (Southern) Ltd** [1953] **1** 482, CA.

POLICE

Accident—
Report to police—
Traffic accident. *See* **Road traffic** (Accident—Duty to stop and furnish particulars—Report to police).
Admissions and confessions to police—
Admissibility in criminal proceedings. *See* **Criminal evidence** (Admissions and confessions—Answers and statements to police).
Allocation of police resources—
Discretion—
Police operation mounted in response to animal rights protests against export of livestock—Operation mounted at considerable cost but unlikely to meet Home Office criteria for special financial assistance—Chief constable deciding not to apply for special financial assistance but to reduce levels of policing and restrict operation to specific days—Whether decision in breach of chief constable's duties to enforce law and keep peace—Whether decision constituting unreasonable exercise of discretion. **R v Chief Constable of Sussex, ex p International Trader's Ferry Ltd** [1997] **2** 65, CA; [1999] **1** 129, HL.
Armament of police—
Powers of Secretary of State—
Prerogative power to maintain peace. *See* **Crown** (Prerogative—Maintenance of the peace—Powers of Secretary of State—Disposition and armament of police).
Arrest—
Terrorist, suspicion of being a. *See* **Arrest** (Terrorist —Suspicion of being a terrorist).
Arrest without warrant. *See* **Arrest** (Arrest without warrant).
Assault on constable in execution of duty—
Arrest without warrant. *See* **Arrest** (Arrest without warrant—Constable).
Assault—
Meaning—Accused driving car on to constable's foot when parking car on constable's direction—Car remaining on constable's foot after request to move car—Whether assault—Police Act 1964, s 51(1). **Fagan v Metropolitan Police Comr** [1968] **3** 442, QBD.
Defence—
Assault to free son from custody—Son's arrest lawful—Whether genuine belief that son's restraint unlawful a defence—Police Act 1964, s 51(1). **R v Fennell** [1970] **3** 215, CA.

POLICE (cont)—
Assault on constable in execution of duty (cont)—
Defence (cont)—
Self-defence—Police officers in plain clothes detaining boys in order to put questions to them—Technical assault by police officers as they were not effecting arrest of the boys—Assault by boys on police officers—Genuine misunderstanding on both sides—Self-defence—Police Act 1964, s 51(1). **Kenlin v Gardiner** [1966] 3 931, QBD.
Self-defence—Mistaken belief that self-defence justified. *See* **Criminal law** (Assault—Self-defence).
Duty—
Attempt to stop suspect to make enquiries—No charge or arrest at that time—Constable touched suspect on shoulder—Suspect struck constable—Alleged assault on constable in execution of duty. **Donnelly v Jackman** [1970] 1 987, QBD.
Detention of person in street for questioning—Police officer taking hold of woman's arm to question her whether she was a prostitute—Woman assaulting officer—Officer not exercising power of arrest—Whether officer acting in execution of duty when detaining woman—Whether taking hold of woman's arm lawful contact or battery—Street Offences Act 1959, s 1—Police Act 1964, s 51(1). **Collins v Wilcock** [1984] 3 374, QBD.
Police officers entering garden of house and knocking on front door to inquire about alleged offence—Police sergeant invited inside and leaving when requested to do so by tenant of house—Other officers remaining in garden of house—Assault on police sergeant as he was leaving house—Other officers coming to sergeant's assistance—Assault on sergeant and officer in general mêlée—Whether officers were trespassers—Implied licence to enter garden and approach front door—Whether officers were acting in execution of duty—Police Act 1964, s 51(1). **Robson v Hallett** [1967] 2 407, QBD Divl Ct.
Preventing removal of privately owned car, the subject-matter of evidence of crime—No charge nor arrest at that time—Alleged assault of constable in execution of duty—Whether constable acting within the execution of his duty in trying to prevent removal of car—Whether statutory power so to do under Road Traffic Act 1960, s 223. **R v Waterfield** [1963] 3 659, CCA.
Execution of duty—
Entry on premises without search warrant—Refusal to leave when asked—Constable trespasser no longer acting in execution of duty. **Davis v Lisle** [1936] 2 213, KBD.
Execution of search warrant relating to property and persons therein—Police officers restricting movement of persons on premises while premises being searched—Whether police officers acting in execution of duty—Police and Criminal Evidence Act 1984, s 117. **DPP v Meaden** [2004] 4 75, DC.
Failure to leave licensed premises—Landlord requesting constable to help expel from licensed premises person who was drunk or disorderly—Constable using physical force to expel person from licensed premises—Ejected person assaulting constable—Whether assault on constable in execution of duty—Whether constable empowered to use reasonable force—Licensing Act 2003, s 143(4). **Semple v Luton and South Bedfordshire Magistrates' Court** [2010] 2 353, DC.
Forcible attempt to take fingerprints—Attempt to take fingerprints pursuant to justices' order—Justices' order only authorising fingerprints to be taken at courthouse—Forcible attempt to take fingerprints at police station—Appellant forcibly resisting attempt to take fingerprints—Whether appellant assaulting police officers in execution of their duty—Police Act 1964, s 1(1). **R v Jones (Yvonne)** [1978] 3 1098, CA.
Metropolitan police constable stopping and searching suspect—Constable detaining suspect against his will but not arresting him—Suspect assaulting constable—Whether at time of assault constable acting unlawfully or in execution of his duty—Metropolitan Police Act 1839, s 66—Police Act 1964, s 51(1). **Pedro v Diss** [1981] 2 59, QBD.
Borough police force—
Consolidation of borough and county police force. *See* Consolidation of borough and county police force, *below.*
Constable—
Dismissal-Chief constable. *See* Chief constable—Dismissal—Natural justice—County borough police force, *below.*
Dismissal—Confirmation by watch committee—Right of member dismissed—Policeman acting as fireman—Public authority—Public Authorities Protection Act 1893, s 1—Police Act 1919, s 4(1)—Police Regulations 1920 (SR & O 1920 No 1484), regs 15, 16, 18, 94. **Kilduff v Wilson** [1939] 1 429, CA.
Resignation—Acceptance—Cancellation—Dismissed after expiration of notice—Validity—Power to dismiss—Right to declaration—Municipal Corporations Act 1882, s 191(4)—Police Act 1919—Police Pensions Act 1921—Police (Appeals) Act 1927. **Cooper v Wilson** [1937] 2 726, CA.
Breach of the peace—
Entry to premises to prevent apprehended breach of the peace—
Powers. *See* Powers—Entry to private premises without warrant—Entry to prevent apprehended breach of the peace, *below.*
Caution—
Answers and statements to the police. *See* **Criminal evidence** (Admissions and confessions—Answers and statements to police—Caution).
Ward of court—
Caution in lieu of criminal proceedings. *See* **Ward of court** (Criminal proceedings—Caution in lieu of criminal proceedings).
Chief constable—
Dismissal—
Natural justice—County borough police force—Summary dismissal of chief constable by watch committee—Whether rules of natural justice applicable to proceedings for dismissal—Chief constable previously indicted for alleged criminal offences—Acquitted, but conduct severely criticised by trial judge—Appeal against decision of watch committee dismissed by Home Secretary—Whether action by chief constable thereby barred—Municipal Corporations Act 1882, s 191(4)—Police Act 1919, s 4(1)—Police (Appeals) Act 1927, s 2(3)—Police (Discipline) (Deputy Chief Constables, Assistant Chief Constables and Chief Constables) Regulations 1952 (SI 1952 No 1706), regs 1, 18. **Ridge v Baldwin** [1963] 2 66, HL.

POLICE (cont)—

Children—

Duty to safeguard and promote welfare of. *See* **Children and young persons** (Children's services in England—Arrangements to safeguard and promote welfare).

Co-operation with judiciary—

Criminal matters—

European community. *See* **European Union** (Police and judicial co-operation in criminal matters).

Compensation—

Criminal injuries. *See* **Compensation** (Criminal injuries).

Complaint against police—

Investigation—

Independent Police Complaints Commission—Direction and control matters—Handling of complaints and conduct matters—Complaint against chief officer of police—Meaning of 'conduct'—Meaning of 'direction and control'- Police Reform Act 2002, ss 10(8), 12, 14(1), Sch 3. **R (on the application of North Yorkshire Police Authority) v Independent Police Complaints Commission (Chief Constable of North Yorkshire Police and anor, interested parties)** [2011] **3** 106, QBD.

Independent Police Complaints Commission—General functions of Commission—Duties of Commission on references of death and serious injury matters—Person suffering serious injury in police custody—Whether Commission having power or duty to investigate events before involvement of police possibly causative of injury—Whether independent inquiry required— Police Reform Act 2002, s 10, Sch 3, para 14D. **R (on the application of Reynolds) v Independent Police Complaints Commission** [2009] **3** 237, CA.

Independent Police Complaints Commission—Removal centres and detained persons—Custody and movement of detained persons—Arrangements for the provisions of escorts and custody—Escorts for persons removed from the United Kingdom under direction—Exclusion of Commission's functions in relation to enforcement of specified immigration and asylum functions—Secretary of State directing removal of detained person—Detained person escorted on enforced removal from United Kingdom to Iraq—Detained person complaining to Commission alleging assault on him by Iraqi police officers while he was restrained by escorts—Whether Commission having jurisdiction to investigate—Whether Commission's functions excluded—Whether escorts enforcing specified immigration and asylum functions— Immigration and Asylum Act 1999, ss 14, 156(1)(b)—UK Border Agency (Complaints and Misconduct) Regulations 2010, SI 2010/782, reg 3(2). **R (on the application of Salimi) v Secretary of State for the Home Dept** [2012] **1** 244, QBD.

Independent Police Complaints Commission—Right to life—State's obligation to investigate death—General functions of Commission—General duties of police authorities, chief officers and inspectors—Duty to provide information for other persons—Duty to preserve evidence relating to death or serious injury matters—Commission investigating circumstances of fatal shootings by police officers—Police officers conferring before giving first accounts of shootings—Whether breach of state's obligation to investigate death—Whether Commission having general power to direct chief officers to put in place procedures to prevent conferring—Whether Commission having duty in specific circumstances to direct such procedures—Extent of duty to provide information—Human Rights Act 1998, s 6, Sch 1, Pt I, art 2—Police Reform Act 2002, ss 10, 15, 21, Sch 3, para 14B. **R (on the application of Saunders) v Independent Police Complaints Commission** [2009] **1** 379, QBD.

Police Complaints Authority—Discharge of functions of authority—Statements taken by police in statutory investigation into complaint by member of public—Member of public seeking disclosure of statements—Whether disclosure necessary for proper discharge of functions of authority—Whether prohibition of inhuman or degrading treatment necessitating disclosure— European Convention for the Protection of Human Rights and Fundamental Freedoms 1950, art 3—Police Act 1996, s 80(1)(a). **R (on the application of Green) v Police Complaints Authority** [2004] **2** 209, HL.

Statements taken by police during investigation—Privilege—Disclosure—Production contrary to public interest. *See* **Disclosure and inspection of documents** (Privilege—Production contrary to public interest—Class of documents—Statements taken by police in statutory investigation into complaints by member of the public).

Police Complaints Board—

Discharge of board's functions—Board required to 'have regard' to guidance given by Secretary of State—Secretary of State's guidance stating that disciplinary proceedings should not be taken if Director of Public Prosecutions decided that evidence against police officer was insufficient for criminal prosecution—Whether board bound to comply with Secretary of State's guidance— Whether board abdicating statutory function by not considering complaint if DPP decided not to prosecute—Whether board unlawfully fettering its discretion—Police Act 1976, s 3(2). **R v Police Complaints Board, ex p Madden** [1983] **2** 353, QBD.

Compulsory purchase of land for. *See* Land—Acquisition of land for police purposes, *below*.

Compulsory retirement—

Permanent disablement—

Reference to medical practitioner—Medical practitioner's decision of judicial character— Application of natural justice to determination—Independent medical practitioner—Material medical practitioner entitled to consider—Police officer's medical advisers entitled to see same material—Police force's medical officer of health disqualified from deciding question of officer's disablement where he has already expressed an opinion on officer's health—Police Pensions Regulations 1971 (SI 1971 No 232), reg 70(2). **Godden, Re** [1971] **3** 20, CA.

Conduct—

Commission of offence to secure evidence against offender—

Accomplice—Car used by police officer in such a way as to enable prostitute to solicit—Whether officer using car accomplice for purpose of doctrine of corroboration. **Sneddon v Stevenson** [1967] **2** 1277, QBD.

Undesirability. **Brannan v Peek** [1947] **2** 572, KBD.

Use of informer—

Mitigating consequences of proposed offence—Participation in commission of offence. **R v Birtles** [1969] **2** 1131, CA.

POLICE (cont)—
    Confession to police—
        Admissibility in criminal proceedings. *See* **Criminal evidence** (Admissions and confessions—Answers and statements to police).
    Consolidation of borough and county police force—
        Powers to be exercised by police authority—
            Police authority—Police Pensions Act 1921, s 30, Sch III—House to House Collections Act 1939. **Swindon BC v Herbert** [1941] 3 481, KBD.
    Constable—
        Arrest without warrant by. *See* **Arrest** (Arrest without warrant—Constable).
        Chief constable. *See* Chief constable, *above*.
        Dismissal. *See* Dismissal—Constable, *below*.
        Duty—
            Position of constable while off duty. **Davis v Minister of Pensions** [1951] 2 318, KBD.
        Impartial discharge of duties—
            Activity likely to interfere with impartial discharge of duties—Service on school appointments committee—Whether service on appointments committee compatible with impartial discharge of duties—Police Regulations 1979, Sch 2, para 1. **Champion v Chief Constable of Gwent Constabulary** [1990] 1 116, HL.
        Misbehaviour in public office. *See* **Criminal law** (Misbehaviour in public office).
        Nature of office—
            Servant of Crown—Loss of services of police officer due to negligence of third person—Whether action per quod servitium amisit lay at suit of Crown. **A-G for New South Wales v Perpetual Trustee Co (Ltd)** [1955] 1 846, PC.
        Obstructing constable in execution of his duty. *See* **Criminal law** (Obstructing constable in execution of duty).
        Power to stop, search and detain person suspected of having or conveying stolen property—
            Metropolis—Suspicion of possession of stolen property—'Having or conveying' property in street—Search during voluntary visit to police station—Metropolitan Police Act 1839, s 66. **Willey v Peace** [1950] 2 724, KBD.
        Service of billeting notice by. *See* **Billeting** (Billeting notice—Service—Service by police constable in presence of billeting officer).
    County police force—
        Consolidation of borough and county police force. *See* Consolidation of borough and county police force, *above*.
        Police expenses paid out of county fund—
            Accident to police officer through negligence of third party—Officer's wages and allowances during illness paid by county council—Right of county council to recover recover expenses from third party—Local Government Act 1888, s 30(3). **Metropolitan Police District Receiver v Croydon Corp** [1957] 1 78, CA.
    Custody—
        Generally. *See* **Criminal law** (Detention in custody).
        Injury in police custody—
            Investigation. *See* Complaint against police—Investigation—Independent Police Complaints Commission, *above*.
    Custody officer—
        Appointment of custody officer—
            Appointment of custody officers for each designated police station—Chief constable required to appoint 'one or more custody officers ... for each designated police station'—Whether chief constable only required to appoint one custody officer at each designated station—Whether chief constable required to appoint sufficient custody officers to ensure at least one custody officer normally available at each designated station—Police and Criminal Evidence Act 1984, s 36(1). **Vince v Chief Constable of Dorset Police** [1993] 2 321, CA.
        Duties of custody officer before charge. *See* **Arrest** (Arrest without warrant—Duties of custody officer before charge).
    Dangerous drugs—
        Evidence. *See* Search warrant—Dangerous drugs, *below*.
    Database—
        Right to respect for private and family life. *See* **Human rights** (Right to respect for private and family life—Police—Evidence gathering—Database).
    Detention and questioning of suspects—
        Admissings and confessions—
            Evidence in criminal proceedings. *See* **Criminal evidence** (Admissions and confessions).
    Discipline—
        Disciplinary offence of being 'found guilty of criminal offence'—
            Conviction—Conditional—Conditional discharge—Police officer convicted of criminal offence and given conditional discharge—Discharge having effect that conviction deemed not to be conviction for purpose of other proceedings—Whether finding of guilt equivalent to conviction—Whether police disciplinary authority entitled to have regard to finding of guilty—Powers of Criminal Courts Act 1973, s 13(1)—Police (Discipline) Regulations 1977, Sch 2, para 15. **R v Secretary of State for the Home Dept, ex p Thornton** [1986] 2 641, CA.
        Disciplinary proceedings—
            Discrimination. *See* **Employment** (Disability—Discrimination—Police).
            Investigation—Conduct of proceedings—Duty of care—Police officer under investigation alleging that investigation carried out in breach of statutory duty and negligently—Whether chief constable and investigating officer owing common law duty of care to police officer under investigation—Whether police officer having right of action for damages for breach of duty of care—Whether breach of statutory duty under Police Acts and regulations giving rise to right of action—Whether investigating officer guilty of misfeasance in public office—Police Act 1964—Police (Discipline) Regulations 1977, reg 7. **Calveley v Chief Constable of Merseyside Police** [1989] 1 1025, HL.

POLICE (cont)—
  Discipline (cont)—
    Disciplinary proceedings (cont)—
      Judicial review of decision in disciplinary proceedings—Availability of remedy. *See* **Judicial review** (Availability of remedy—Alternative remedy available—Discretion of court to grant relief—Disciplinary proceedings—Complaint against police officer).
      Judicial review of decision in disciplinary proceedings—Two officers charged with disciplinary offences—Chief constable permitting retirement of one officer prior to hearing—Charges against officer withdrawn—Charges against second officer dismissed as an abuse of process—Whether officer facing disciplinary process able to avoid adjudication by retiring—Whether decision to dismiss proceedings against second officer justified. **R v Chief Constable of Devon and Cornwall Constabulary, ex p Hay** [1996] **2** 711, QBD.
    Metropolitan Police Force. *See* Metropolitan Police Force—Discipline, *below*.
    Procedure at disciplinary hearing—
      Legal representation—Case against accused to be presented by member of police force—Accused given right to conduct defence in person or by member of police force—Whether accused entitled to be legally represented—Whether chief constable having discretion to allow accused legal representation—Police (Discipline) Regulations 1965 (SI 1965 No 543), reg 8(3), (6). **Maynard v Osmond** [1977] **1** 64, QBD.
    Punishment—
      Infliction of disqualification or disability—Whether punishment for breach of police discipline imposing disqualification or disability on officer—Powers of Criminal Courts Act 1973, s 13(3)—Police (Discipline) Regulations 1977, reg 22. **R v Secretary of State for the Home Dept, ex p Thornton** [1986] **2** 641, CA.
    Regulations—
      Ultra vires—Unreasonableness—Power of Secretary of State to make regulations for maintenance of discipline—Regulations denying legal representation at disciplinary hearing to junior officers—Legal representation allowed in proceedings against senior officers—Whether regulations denying legal representation ultra vires the Secretary of State—Police Act 1964, s 33(2)—Police (Discipline) Regulations 1965 (SI 1965 No 543), reg 8(6). **Maynard v Osmond** [1977] **1** 64, QBD.
    Suspension from membership of police force—
      Effect of suspension—Whether suspended police officer ceasing to be member of police force for all purposes during period of suspension—Whether suspended police officer retaining membership of Police Federation—Whether suspended officer entitled to attend federation meetings—Whether chief officer having power to instruct suspended officer not to attend federation meetings—Police Federation Regulations 1969, reg 4—Police (Discipline) Regulations 1985, reg 27(1). **R v Deputy Chief Constable of North Wales Police, ex p Hughes** [1991] **3** 414, CA.
      Suspension lifted pending completion of investigations—Chief constable failing to have regard to Home Office guidance—Whether guidance statutory—Whether Chief constable having obligation to consider guidance—Whether decision taken to lift suspension flawed—Police Act 1996, ss 50, 87—Police (Conduct) Regulations 1999, SI 1999/730, reg 5. **R (on the application of Coghlan) v Chief Constable of Greater Manchester Police (Independent Police Complaints Commission, interested party)** [2005] **2** 890, QBD.
    Transfer of officers. *See* Metropolitan Police Force—Discipline, *below*.
  Disclosure of information—
    Criminal convictions and cautions—
      Reprimand—Persons applying to become police constable or cadet—Requirement to disclose any previous convictions or cautions, including those received as child—Right to respect for private and family life—Whether requirement to disclose reprimand received as child contrary to convention right—Human Rights Act 1998, Sch 1, Pt I, art 8—Rehabilitation of Offenders Act 1974 (Exceptions) Order 1975, SI 1975/1023. **R (on the application of RD) v Secretary of State for Justice** [2021] **3** 477, CA.
    Criminal record certificates—
      Right to respect for private and family life—Statutory scheme for rehabilitation of offenders—Scheme requiring disclosure of spent convictions, cautions or reprimands by persons with multiple convictions or convictions for serious offences when applying to work with children or vulnerable adults—Whether infringing convention right—Rehabilitation of Offenders Act 1974, s 4—Police Act 1997, ss 113A, 113B—Human Rights Act 1998, Sch 1, Pt I, art 8—Rehabilitation of Offenders Act 1974 (Exceptions) Order 1975, SI 1975/1023, art 2A—Rehabilitation of Offenders (Northern Ireland) Order 1978, SI 1978/1908—Rehabilitation of Offenders (Exceptions) Order (Northern Ireland) 1979, SR 1979/195, art 1A. **Gallagher's application for judicial review (Northern Ireland), Re** [2019] **3** 823, SC.
    Enhanced criminal record certificate—
      Provision of non-conviction information—Information which 'might be relevant'—Information which 'ought to be included'—Right to respect for private and family life—Whether scheme for provision of non-conviction information within scope of right to respect for private and family life—Whether scheme compatible with right to respect for private and family life—Police Act 1997, s 115(7)—Human Rights Act 1998, Sch 1, Pt I, art 8. **R (on the application of L) v Metropolitan Police Comr** [2010] **1** 113, SC.
      Provision of non-conviction information—Information which 'might be relevant'—Whether information limited to information of criminal or potentially criminal activity—Police Act 1997, s 115(7). **R (on the application of L) v Metropolitan Police Comr** [2007] **4** 128, CA.
      Provision of non-conviction information—Whether decision to disclose governed by common law and convention principles—Whether duty to act with procedural fairness requiring person affected to make representations—Whether decision to disclose information lawful—Police Act 1997, s 115—Human Rights Act 1998, Sch 1, Pt I, art 8. **R (on the application of X) v Chief Constable of West Midlands Police** [2004] **2** 1, QBD; [2005] **1** 610, CA.
      Right to respect for private and family life—Enhanced criminal record certificate disclosing details of criminal charge against appellant and of acquittal—Whether admitted interference with appellant's private life justified—Police Act 1997, s 113B—Human Rights Act 1998, Sch 1, arts 6(2), 8. **R (on the application of R) v Chief Constable of Greater Manchester Police** [2019] **1** 391, SC.

POLICE (cont)—
Disclosure of information (cont)—
Enhanced criminal record certificate (cont)—
Right to respect for private and family life—Statutory scheme for rehabilitation of offenders—Convictions, cautions, warnings and reprimands in respect of certain offences deemed spent after specified periods of time—Statutory scheme for disclosing records of convictions and cautions held for use of police forces generally—Whether provisions for disclosure breaching right to respect for private and family life—Rehabilitation of Offenders Act 1974—Police Act 1997, Pt V—Human Rights Act 1998, Sch 1, Pt I, art 8—Rehabilitation of Offenders Act 1974 (Exceptions) Order 1975, SI 1975/1023. **R (on the application of T) v Chief Constable of Greater Manchester** [2013] **2** 813, CA; [2014] **4** 159, SC.
Right to respect for private and family life—Statutory scheme for rehabilitation of offenders—Convictions, cautions, warnings and reprimands in respect of certain offences deemed spent after specified periods of time—Statutory scheme for disclosing records of convictions and cautions held for use of police forces—Disclosure of spent convictions and cautions for specified offences—Disclosure of spent conviction where person had more than one conviction—Whether provisions for disclosure requiring mechanism for independent review—Whether provisions for disclosure breaching right to respect for private and family life—Whether retention of spent caution in records breaching right to respect for private and family life—Rehabilitation of Offenders Act 1974—Police Act 1997, Pt V—Human Rights Act 1998, Sch 1, Pt I, art 8—Rehabilitation of Offenders Act 1974 (Exceptions) Order 1975, SI 1975/1023. **R (on the application of P) v Secretary of State for the Home Dept** [2018] **2** 794, CA.
Extent of powers—
Police formulating a policy of disclosing information about paedophiles resident in area to persons potentially at risk—Police acquiring information on two convicted paedophiles staying at a caravan site in area—Police concluding that public interest requiring them to disclose identity of paedophiles to site owner—Whether police treating paedophiles in procedurally unfair manner—Whether disclosure lawful. **R v Chief Constable of North Wales Police, ex p AB** [1997] **4** 691, QBD; [1998] **3** 310, CA.
Interview—
Caution—Police officer interviewing suspect without a solicitor present—Suspect making admission—Officer concluding that admission rendering suspect suitable for caution—Police refusing request by suspect's solicitor to disclose contents of interview—Non-disclosure preventing solicitor from giving informed advice on whether to accept caution—Police charging suspect—Whether police having duty to disclose contents of interview to suspect's solicitor for purpose of enabling him to advise on acceptance of caution—Whether failure to give such disclosure rendering subsequent prosecution an abuse of process. **DPP v Ara** [2001] **4** 559, QBD DC.
Dismissal—
Chief constable—
Natural justice. *See* Chief constable—Dismissal—Natural justice, *above*.
Constable—
Confirmation by watch committee. *See* Borough police force—Constable—Dismissal—Confirmation by watch committee, *above*.
Probationer constable—Natural justice—Chief constable deciding to dispense with services of constable on basis of certain allegations and rumours—Constable informed that if he did not resign he would be dismissed—Constable not given opportunity to refute allegations and rumours—Whether chief constable having absolute discretion to discharge constable—Whether chief constable required to observe rules of natural justice before exercising discretion—Police Regulations 1971, reg 16(1). **Chief Constable of North Wales Police v Evans** [1982] **3** 141, HL.
Special constable—Discrimination on grounds of race—Whether special constable holding office of constable—Whether special constable deemed to be in employment as constable—Whether special constable entitled to protection against unlawful discrimination in employment on racial grounds—Race Relations Act 1976, ss 4, 16. **Sheikh v Chief Constable of Greater Manchester Police** [1989] **2** 684, CA.
Power of Commissioner. *See* Metropolitan Police Force—Dismissal, *below*.
DNA samples—
Powers as to. *See* Powers—Fingerprints and DNA samples, *below*.
Documents—
Seizure—
Disclosure of documents to third party—Breach of confidence—Injunction. *See* **Equity** (Breach of confidence—Injunction—Information and documents obtained by police or public authority from citizen under compulsory powers of seizure).
Powers. *See* Powers—Seizure of documents, *below*.
Driver—
Dangerous driving. *See* **Road traffic** (Dangerous driving—Driving dangerously—Driving below standard of competent and careful driver).
Enforcement of law—
Mandamus. *See* **Mandamus** (Chief officer of police—Enforcement of law).
Enhanced criminal record certificate—
Disclosure. *See* Disclosure of information—Enhanced criminal record certificate, *above*.
Entry and search of premises—
Powers—
Generally. *See* Powers—Entry and search of premises, *below*.
Search warrant. *See* Search warrant, *below*.
Equipment—
Riot equipment—
Central services—Establishment of central store by Secretary of State—Power of Secretary of State to supply riot equipment from central store to chief constable without consent of local police authority—Whether right to supply equipment restricted to emergency—Police Act 1964, ss 4(4), 41. **R v Secretary of State for the Home Dept, ex p Northumbria Police Authority** [1988] **1** 556, CA.

POLICE (cont)—

European Union—
    Police and judicial co-operation in criminal matters. *See* **European Union** (Police and judicial co-operation in criminal matters).

Evidence by police—
    Disclosure of DNA profiles. *See* Powers—Fingerprints and DNA samples—Disclosure of DNA profiles, *below*.
    Disclosure of sources of information. *See* **Criminal evidence** (Prosecution evidence—Disclosure of sources of information).

    Exclusion of evidence—
        Evidence obtained by undercover police operation. *See* **Criminal evidence** (Exclusion of evidence—Evidence obtained by undercover police operation).
        Generally. *See* **Criminal evidence** (Exclusion of evidence).

    Human rights—
        Right to respect for private and family life. *See* **Human rights** (Right to respect for private and family life—Police—Evidence gathering).

    Production of notebooks—
        Denial of collaboration in preparing notes—Refusal by court to allow jury to inspect notebooks. **R v Bass** [1953] **1** 1064, CCA.

Evidence gathering—
    Right to respect for private and family life. *See* **Human rights** (Right to respect for private and family life—Police—Evidence gathering).

False allegation to police—
    Obstructing course of justice. *See* **Criminal law** (Obstructing course of justice—False allegation to police).

Fingerprints—
    Powers as to. *See* Powers—Fingerprints and DNA samples, *below*.

Fire—
    Negligence. *See* **Negligence** (Fire—Police).

Firearms—
    Exemption from general prohibition. *See* **Firearms** (Possession—Prohibited weapons—Crown servants).

Forced marriage protection order—
    Enforcement. *See* **Marriage** (Forced marriage—Forced marriage protection orders—Applications).

Human rights—
    Duty to protect life. *See* **Human rights** (Right to life—Prohibition of inhuman or degrading treatment—Positive duty to take measures to avert real and immediate risk to life—Operational duty of police).

    Right to respect for private and family life—
        Surveillance. *See* **Human rights** (Right to respect for private and family life—Surveillance—Police).
    State's obligation to prevent inhuman or degrading treatment. *See* **Human rights** (Inhuman or degrading treatment—State's obligation to prevent inhuman or degrading treatment).

Identification parade—
    Evidence of identification. *See* **Criminal evidence** (Identity—Identification parade).

Impartial discharge of duties. *See* Constable—Impartial discharge of duties, *above*.

Impersonation—
    Wearing articles of police uniform—
        Appearance so nearly resembling that of police officer as to be calculated to deceive—Calculated to deceive—Meaning—Whether requiring an intention to deceive—Police Act 1964, s 52(2). **Turner v Shearer** [1973] **1** 397, QBD.

Independent Police Complaints Commission. *See* Complaint against police—Investigation—Independent Police Complaints Commission, *above*.

Inducement—
    Statement obtained by inducement—
        Admissibility in criminal proceedings. *See* **Criminal evidence** (Admissions and confessions—Inducement—Police).

Industrial injury—
    Accident arising out of and in course of employment—
        Recreational activities—Police officer expected to take part in activities but under no duty to do so—Constable injured in football match. *See* **Social security** (Disablement benefit—Accident arising out of and in course of employment—Recreational activities—Employee expected to take part in activities but under no duty to do so—Police constable injured in football match).

Informer—
    Disclosure to court by prosecution. *See* **Criminal law** (Trial—Prosecution—Informer).
    Duty owed by police. *See* Negligence—Duty to take care—Persons to whom duty owed—Informer, *below*.

    Identity—
        Disclosure to court. *See* **Criminal evidence** (Prosecution evidence—Informer—Disclosure of police informer's identity).

    Use of informer. *See* Conduct—Use of informer, *above*.

Interception of telephone conversations. *See* Powers—Telephone tapping, *below*.

Interference with police—
    Vicinity of a prohibited place. *See* **Criminal law** (Official secrets—Interference with police officers or members of HM forces—Vicinity of a prohibited place).

Interview with suspect—
    Juvenile. *See* **Criminal evidence** (Police interview—Interview of juvenile).

    Tape recording—
        Evidence in criminal proceedings. *See* **Criminal evidence** (Tape recording—Tape recording of police interviews).

POLICE (cont)—
  Investigation of crime—
    Automated facial recognition technology ('AFR')—
      Judicial review of police deployment of AFR—Whether AFR contrary to human rights—Whether AFR contrary to data protection legislation—Whether AFR failing to comply with public sector equality duty—Data Protection Act 1998, s 4(4)—Human Rights Act 1998, Sch 1, Pt I, art 8—Equality Act 2010, s 149—Data Protection Act 2018, ss 34, 64. **R (on application of Bridges) v Chief Constable of South Wales Police (Secretary of State for the Home Dept, interested party) (Information Comr and Surveillance Camera Comr intervening)** [2020] **1** 864, QBD; [2021] **2** 1121, CA.
    Negligence—
      Duty to take care. *See* Negligence—Duty to take care—Negligence in investigation of crime, *below*.
    Privacy rights. *See* **Human rights** (Right to respect for private and family life—Freedom of expression—Police investigation).
  Investigatory powers. *See* **Investigatory Powers**.
  Juror. *See* **Jury** (Juror—Bias—Persons concerned with administration of justice).
  Land—
    Acquisition of land for police purposes—
      Duty of county council. **Wiltshire Standing Joint Committee v Wiltshire CC** [1951] **1** 1041, KBD.
  Licensed premises—
    Right of entry for purposes of preventing or detecting commission of offence. *See* **Intoxicating liquor** (Licensed premises—Constable—Right of entry).
  Metropolitan Police Force—
    Accident to police officer through negligence of third party—
      Officer's wages and allowances during illness paid by Receiver—Right of Receiver to recover amount of wages from third party. **Monmouthshire CC v Smith** [1957] **1** 78, CA.
    Discipline—
      Transfer of officers after receipt of report—Whether transfer procedure can be used as a punishment—Disciplinary procedure not followed—Whether claim for declaration that transfer was without regard to Police (Discipline) Regulations 1952 (SI 1952 No 1705), should be struck out. **Merricks v Nott-Bower** [1964] **1** 717, CA.
    Dismissal—
      Summary dismissal—Power of Commissioner—Officer convicted of theft—Metropolitan Police Act 1829, s 5—General Orders of Metropolitan Police Force, s 5(9). **Hogg v Scott** [1947] **1** 788, KBD.
    Power to arrest—
      Suspicion of possession of stolen property—'Having or conveying' property in street—Search during voluntary visit to police station. **Willey v Peace** [1950] **2** 724, KBD.
    Receiver for Metropolitan Police District—
      Treasurer of fund for the purposes of the police—Power to sue—Accident to police officer through negligence of third party—Hospital charges and officer's wages during illness paid by Receiver—Right of Receiver to recover expenses from third party—Metropolitan Police Act 1829, s 12—Metropolitan Police (Receiver) Act 1861, s 1. **Metropolitan Police District Receiver v Tatum** [1948] **1** 612, KBD.
  Misconduct in public office—
    Sentence. *See* **Sentence** (Misconduct in public office—Police).
  Motor vehicle—
    Removal and disposal—
      Abandoned or broken down vehicle on road. *See* **Road traffic** (Motor vehicle—Abandoned or broken down vehicle on road—Removal—Police powers of removal).
  Negligence—
    Duty to take care—
      Appropriate adult—Plaintiff acting as appropriate adult during interviews of murder suspect considered to be mentally disordered—Plaintiff claiming damages against police for psychological injury—Whether police owing duty of care to plaintiff—Code of Practice for the Detention, Treatment and Questioning of Persons by Police Officers. **Leach v Chief Constable of Gloucestershire Constabulary** [1999] **1** 215, CA.
      Breach of duty of confidentiality—Persons to whom duty owed—Informant—Informant giving information to police in confidence about suspect—Police knowing suspect to be violent—Information left in unattended police vehicle—Vehicle broken into and suspect obtaining information—Informant and family threatened with violence and arson and suffering psychiatric damage—Whether special relationship of proximity between informant and police giving rise to duty of care—Whether public policy precluding prosecution of claim. **Swinney v Chief Constable of Northumbria Police** [1996] **3** 449, CA.
      Conduct of police operations—Persons to whom duty owed—Police officer involved in operations—Police officer injured during violent public disorder—Officer part of police force attempting to keep order—Officer suing chief constable for negligently exposing plaintiff to excessive and avoidable risk of injury—Whether chief constable liable to individual officers injured by attacks from rioters—Whether contrary to public policy for senior police officer charged with controlling serious public disorder to be liable to officer injured by attacks from rioters—Police Act 1964, s 48(1). **Hughes v National Union of Mineworkers** [1991] **4** 278, QBD.
      Dangerous condition of highway—Police having knowledge of hazard on road—No warning given to users of highway—Whether police under duty of care to protect or warn road users. **Ancell v McDermott** [1993] **4** 355, CA.
      Female police officer claiming to have been raped by fellow officer—Other officers allegedly subjecting female officer to campaign of harassment for reporting attack—Female officer bringing action against police commissioner for negligently failing to deal with her complaint and allowing campaign of harassment by other officers—Whether claim should be struck out. **Waters v Comr of Police of the Metropolis** [2000] **4** 934, HL.
      Investigation of complaint against police officer—Whether chief constable and investigating officer owing duty of care to police officer under investigation. *See* Discipline—Disciplinary proceedings—Investigation—Conduct of proceedings—Duty of care, *above*.

POLICE (cont)—
  Negligence (cont)—
    Duty to take care (cont)—
      Malfunctioning of traffic lights—Police aware of malfunction—Plaintiff and defendant colliding at intersection where traffic lights malfunctioning—Plaintiff bringing action against defendant for damages for personal injuries—Defendant claiming injury to plaintiff occurring because of malfunctioning of traffic lights—Defendant bringing third party proceedings against police—Whether police owing duty of care to defendant—Whether third party proceedings should be struck out. **Clough v Bussan (West Yorkshire Police Authority, third party)** [1990] **1** 431, QBD.

      Negligence in investigation of crime—Persons to whom duty owed—Victim of crime—Entry by burglars to premises activating alarm call to police station—Police officer failing properly to inspect premises—Whether police owing duty of care to occupier of premises—Whether special relationship existing between police and occupier of premises giving rise to duty of care—Whether occupier having cause of action in negligence against police. **Alexandrou v Oxford** [1993] **4** 328, CA.

      Negligence in investigation of crime—Persons to whom duty owed—Victim of crime—Husband of first plaintiff murdered—Second plaintiff severely wounded—Police failing to apprehend criminal prior to crimes—Whether police owing duty of care to victims—Whether special relationship existing between police and victims—Whether plaintiffs having cause of action for negligence against police. **Osman v Ferguson** [1993] **4** 344, CA.

      Negligence in investigation of crime—Persons to whom duty owed—Victim of crime—Plaintiff's daughter murdered by notorious criminal—Police failing to apprehend criminal prior to murder of plaintiff's daughter—Whether police owing duty of care to plaintiff's daughter—Whether special relationship existing between police and victim—Whether plaintiff having cause of action for negligence against police—Police Act 1964, s 48(1). **Hill v Chief Constable of West Yorkshire** [1988] **2** 238, HL.

      Negligence in investigation of crime—Persons to whom duty owed—Victim of crime—Witness of crime—Whether police owing duty of care to primary victim of crime and eye witness to crime. **Brooks v Metropolitan Police Comr** [2005] **2** 489, HL.

      Person in custody—Escape—Whether police having duty of care to prevent person suffering injury in foreseeable attempt to escape from police custody. **Vellino v Chief Constable of Greater Manchester** [2002] **3** 78, CA.

      Person in custody—Suicide risk—Police taking person with suicidal tendencies into custody—Police having knowledge of prisoner's suicidal tendencies—Prisoner committing suicide by hanging himself using shirt tied through spyhole on outside of cell door—Administratrix on behalf of prisoner's estate bringing action for negligence against police—Whether police failing to take reasonable steps to prevent prisoner committing suicide—Whether defences of volenti non fit injuria and novus actus interveniens available—Whether prisoner contributorily negligent. **Reeves v Comr of Police of the Metropolis** [1998] **2** 381, CA; [1999] **3** 897, HL.

      Person in custody—Suicide risk—Police taking person with suicidal tendencies into custody—Police having knowledge of prisoner's suicidal tendencies—Prisoner remanded in custody and taken to remand centre—Police not informing prison authorities of prisoner's suicidal tendencies—Prisoner committing suicide at remand centre—Whether police under duty to pass on to remand centre all available information relevant to risk of suicide by prisoner—Whether police owing duty of care to prevent prisoner committing suicide—Whether police in breach of duty of care—Whether cause of action barred by maxim ex turpi causa non oritur actio or public policy because claim arising out of suicide. **Kirkham v Chief Constable of Greater Manchester Police** [1990] **3** 246, CA.

      Persons to whom duty owed—Informer—Authorised covert human intelligence source—Informer becoming suspect in investigation arising out of information provided to police—Restraint order obtained against informer—Court making restraint order unaware of informer's status—No criminal proceedings brought and restraint order discharged—Informer bringing claim against police for breach of duty of care—Whether police having duty to take reasonable care to safeguard informer against economic loss as result of investigation—Extent of duty—Regulation of Investigatory Powers Act 2000, s 29. **Informer v Chief Constable** [2012] **3** 601, CA.

      Persons to whom duty owed—Personal injury caused to passer-by by police officers during attempt to arrest suspect—Whether duty of care owed—Whether police immune from claims in negligence when investigating and preventing crime—Whether police liable—Test for duty of care. **Robinson v Chief Constable of West Yorkshire Police** [2018] **2** 1041, SC.

      Persons to whom duty owed—Victim of crime—Claimant informing police of threats of violence toward him made by third party—Claimant suffering violence from third party—Whether police owing duty of care to claimant. **Van Colle v Chief Constable of Hertfordshire Police** [2008] **3** 977, HL.

      Persons to whom duty owed—Victim of crime—Woman making emergency call to police reporting threat to kill her—Police not responding in time—Woman murdered before arrival of police—Whether police owing duty of care. **Michael and others v Chief Constable of South Wales Police (Refuge and Liberty intervening)** [2015] **2** 635, SC.

      Persons to whom duty owed—Whether police commissioner owing duty of care to protect officers from economic or reputational harm in conduct of third party proceedings—Whether duty of care deriving from employer's duty of trust and confidence—Whether imposition of duty of care fair, just or reasonable. **James-Bowen v Metropolitan Police Comr** [2018] **4** 1007, SC.

      Plaintiff police officer injured by prisoner—Fellow police officer failing to come to plaintiff's assistance—Whether fellow police officer owing plaintiff a duty of care—Whether chief constable vicariously liable—Police Act 1964, s 48. **Costello v Chief Constable of the Northumbria Police** [1999] **1** 550, CA.

      Police driver pursuing person attempting to avoid arrest for arrestable offence. See **Negligence** (Duty to take care—Driver of motor vehicle—Police officer).

    Fire. See **Negligence** (Fire—Police action).
  Notebooks—
    Use in evidence. See Evidence by police—Production of notebooks, above.

POLICE (cont)—
Notice—
Libel—
Qualified privilege. *See* **Libel and slander** (Qualified privilege—Report of notice issued by public authority for information of public—Police notice).
Observation posts in private premises—
Protection of occupiers of premises used as police observation posts—
Exclusion of evidence which would reveal identity etc of occupiers of premises used as observation posts. *See* **Criminal evidence** (Prosecution evidence—Disclosure of sources of information—Confidentiality of sources—Police observation posts in private premises).
Obstruction—
Obstructing constable in execution of his duty. *See* **Criminal law** (Obstructing constable in execution of duty).
Obstructing course of justice—
False allegation to police. *See* **Criminal law** (Obstructing course of justice—False allegation to police).
Picketing. *See* **Trade dispute** (Picketing—Breach of peace anticipated—Obstruction of police).
Pension—
Appeal to quarter sessions—
Appeal against decision of medical referee—Jurisdiction of quarter sessions—Police Pensions Act 1948, s 5(1)—Police Pensions Regulations 1949 (SI 1949 No 1241), reg 45(1). **Ead v Home Secretary** [1954] **1** 386, QBD Divl Ct.
Damages—
Whether pension taken into account when accessing police officer's damages for personal injuries. *See* **Damages** (Personal injury—Loss of future earnings—Pension—Compulsory contributory police pension).
Payment of pension—
Payment to persons ceasing to be members of force by reason of injury received in execution of duty—Duodenal ulcer contracted in consequence of conditions of service—Whether 'injury received in execution of duty'—Police Pensions Act 1921, s 2(1)(c). **Huddersfield Police Authority v Watson** [1947] **2** 193, KBD.
Payment to persons ceasing to be members of force by reason of injury received in execution of duty—Tuberculosis contracted during period of service—Whether an 'injury'—Police Pensions Act 1921, s 2(1)(c). **Garvin v City of London Police Authority** [1944] **1** 378, KBD.
Widow's special pension—Non-accidental injury—Special risks—Heart disease aggravated by duty—Police Pensions Act 1921, ss 3(b), 33(3). **Gordon v Barnsley Police Authority** [1948] **2** 79, KBD.
Personal data—
Data protection. *See* **Data protection** (Processing of information—Personal data—Police).
Police authority—
Powers of police authority—
Private prosecutions being brought against retired police officers for actions in course of duty—DPP refusing to intervene in proceedings—Officers seeking judicial review of DPP's decision—Police authority refusing to fund judicial review proceedings and officers' defences to private prosecutions—Whether police authority having power to fund legal representation of police officers—Local Government Act 1972, s 111(1)—Police Act 1996, s 6(1). **R v DPP, ex p Duckenfield** [1999] **2** 873, QBD.
Powers to be exercised by police authority. *See* Consolidation of borough and county police force—Powers to be exercised by police authority, *above*.
Police Complaints Board. *See* Complaint against police—Police Complaints Board, *above*.
Power—
Removal of peaceful protesters—
Actual or threatened breach of peace—Whether police and local authorities having power to exclude and eject from council meetings—Whether use of force against claimants being reasonable - Human Rights Act 1998, Sch 1, Pt I, arts 10, 11. **Laporte v Metropolitan Police Comr** [2015] **3** 438, QBD.
Powers—
Anti-social behaviour—
Authorised dispersal—Authorisation given in relation to certain anti-social behaviours not including protests—Protest taking place in area covered by authorisations—Police giving dispersal direction—Whether direction lawful—Whether dispersal power applying to protests—Whether authorisation empowering police to issue dispersal direction in relation to anti-social behaviour not contemplated when authorisation given—Anti-social Behaviour Act 2003, s 30. **R (on the application of Singh) v Chief Constable of West Midlands Police** [2007] **2** 297, CA.
Authorised dispersal—Power to remove person under 16 from dispersal area to his place of residence—Whether power to remove coercive—Anti-social Behaviour Act 2003, s 30(6). **R (on the application of W) v Metropolitan Police Comr (Secretary of State for the Home Dept, interested party)** [2005] **3** 749, DC; [2006] **3** 458, CA.
Arrest—
Arrest without warrant. *See* **Arrest** (Arrest without warrant).
Suspicion of possession of stolen property. *See* Metropolitan Police Force—Power to arrest—Suspicion of possession of stolen property, *above*.
Control and restraint—
Disability discrimination—Duty to make reasonable adjustments—Police forcibly restraining and detaining severely autistic boy without consulting carers—Whether failure to make reasonable adjustments to policy on control and restraint—Disability Discrimination Act 1995, s 21E. **ZH v Metropolitan Police Comr** [2013] **3** 113, CA.

POLICE (cont)—
Powers (cont)—
Entry and search of premises—
Entry and search of premises by force without warrant—Right of constable to enter private premises by force without warrant to recapture person 'unlawfully at large and whom he is pursuing'—Pursuing—Constables resorting to premises and entering by force to recapture absconding mental patient whom they reasonably believed to be within premises—Other occupants of house assaulting police and charged with assaulting police in execution of their duty—Whether police 'pursuing' patient—Whether police acting in execution of duty—Police and Criminal Evidence Act 1984, s 17(1)(d). **D'Souza v DPP** [1992] **4** 545, HL.

Entry to private premises—
Entry to effect arrest without warrant. See **Arrest** (Arrest without warrant—Constable—Power to enter (if need be by force) place to effect arrest).

Entry to private premises without warrant—
Entry to prevent apprehended breach of the peace—Whether power of entry restricted to premises where public meeting being held—Police and Criminal Evidence Act 1984, s 17(6). **McLeod v Comr of Police of the Metropolis** [1994] **4** 553, CA.

Fingerprints and DNA samples—
Disclosure of DNA profiles—Right to respect for private and family life—Care proceedings—Paternity—Judge ordering Metropolitan Police Commissioner during course of care proceedings to disclose DNA profiles from crime scene—Whether use of DNA profiles prohibited other than for criminal law enforcement purposes—Police and Criminal Evidence Act 1984, Pt II, ss 19, 22, Pt V, s 63T—Human Rights Act 1998, Sch 1, Pt I, art 8. **Z (children) (disclosure of DNA profile), Re** [2015] **4** 205, CA.

Retention of fingerprints and DNA samples lawfully taken from persons convicted of recordable offence—Retention for indefinite period—Conviction for driving with excess alcohol—Whether policy for retention lawful—Whether policy breaching convention rights—Police and Criminal Evidence (Northern Ireland) Order 1995—Human Rights Act 1998, Sch 1, Pt I, art 8. **Gaughran v Chief Constable of the Police Service of Northern Ireland** [2015] **3** 655, SC.

Retention of fingerprints and DNA samples lawfully taken from persons who are not convicted—Right to respect for private and family life—Policy of destruction of samples only in exceptional circumstances—Whether scheme of statute and policy compatible with right to respect for private life—Whether scheme unlawful—Police and Criminal Evidence Act 1984, s 64(1A)—Human Rights Act 1998, ss 6(1), (2)(b), 8(1), Sch 1, Pt I, art 8. **R (on the application of GC) v Metropolitan Police Comr** [2011] **3** 859, SC.

Retention of fingerprints and DNA samples lawfully taken from persons who are not convicted—Whether power of retention compatible with convention right to privacy and prohibition on discrimination—Police and Criminal Evidence Act 1984, s 64(1A)—Human Rights Act 1998, Sch 1, Pt I, arts 8, 14. **R (on the application of S) v Chief Constable of South Yorkshire** [2003] **1** 148, CA; [2004] **4** 193, HL.

Interception of telephone conversation. See Powers—Telephone tapping, below.

Photographs—
Retention of photographs lawfully taken of persons who are not convicted—Right to respect for private and family life—Whether retention of photographs of arrested persons who are not subsequently convicted compatible with right to respect for private and family life—Whether retention of information concerning non-conviction constituting disproportionate interference with right to respect for private and family life—Police and Criminal Evidence Act 1984, s 64A—Human Rights Act 1998, Sch 1, Pt I, art 8. **R (on the application of RMC) v Metropolitan Police Comr** [2012] **4** 510, DC.

Police authority, of. See Police authority—Powers of police authority, above.

Power to detain stopped vehicle—
Vehicle stopped for purpose of investigating possible road traffic offences—Police officers suspecting vehicle stolen and attempting to detain it—Driver assaulting police officer—Whether police officer having power to detain vehicle—Whether police officer acting in execution of duty—Road Traffic Act 1972, s 159. **Lodwick v Sanders** [1985] **1** 577, QBD.

Power to remove trespassers on land—
Direction requiring trespassers to leave land—Local authority requiring travellers to leave its land in two days—Police immediately giving statutory direction requiring travellers to leave site in two days—Whether direction requiring trespassers to leave land valid if not giving trespassers opportunity to comply with occupier's request to leave—Whether direction for trespassers to leave land valid if requiring them to leave at future time—Criminal Justice and Public Order Act 1994, s 61. **R (on the application of Fuller) v Chief Constable of Dorset Police** [2002] **3** 57, QBD.

Power to retain property relevant to criminal proceedings—
Accused obtaining money by deception on forged instruments—Accused putting stolen money into his own bank account—Police seeking to freeze money in bank account—Whether police having sufficient interest to apply for injunction freezing moneys in bank account obtained from another by criminal means—Extent of court's power to grant injunction in favour of police—Supreme Court Act 1981, s 37(1). **Chief Constable of Kent v V** [1982] **3** 36, CA.

Police arresting claimants on suspicion of drug dealing and seizing cash from them—Police claiming that cash derived from drug dealing and retaining it despite failure to secure convictions—Whether unconvicted claimants entitled to recover cash when police establishing on balance of probabilities that it derived from drug dealing—Whether public policy precluding recovery in such circumstances. **Webb v Chief Constable of Merseyside Police** [2000] **1** 209, CA.

Police lawfully seizing property from claimants for purpose of a criminal prosecution—Crown Prosecution Service deciding not to prosecute claimants—Police retaining claimants' property for purpose of assisting private prosecution by private commercial organisation—Whether police entitled to retain property—Police and Criminal Evidence Act 1984, s 22. **Scopelight Ltd v Chief of Police for Northumbria** [2010] **2** 431, CA.

POLICE (cont)—
  Powers (cont)—
    Power to retain property relevant to criminal proceedings (cont)—
      Retention as material evidence in respect of charges against accused—Police finding and seizing stolen property and English and foreign currency in accused's house—Police believing currency to be used to purchase stolen property—Accused charged in respect of stolen property—No charge made in respect of currency—Currency not made an exhibit—Whether currency material evidence in respect of charges against plaintiff—Whether police entitled to retain currency as material evidence. **Malone v Comr of Police of the Metropolis** [1979] **1** 256, CA.
      Retention in respect of anticipated restitution, compensation or forfeiture order—Police finding and seizing stolen property and English and foreign currency in accused's house—Accused charged in respect of stolen property—No charge made in respect of currency—Whether police entitled to retain currency in anticipation of restitution, compensation or forfeiture order being made against accused if convicted in respect of stolen property—Theft Act 1968, s 28(1)(c)—Powers of Criminal Courts Act 1973, ss 35, 43. **Malone v Comr of Police of the Metropolis** [1979] **1** 256, CA.
    Power to seize and retain property relevant to criminal proceedings—
      Electronic data—Electronic copies of data—Return of copies—Whether data 'seized property'—Whether 'return' of data possible—Whether return reasonably practicable—Police and Criminal Evidence Act 1984, s 21—Criminal Justice and Police Act 2001, ss 53, 59. **R (on the application of Business Energy Solutions Ltd) v Crown Court at Preston (Cheshire West and Chester Trading Standards, interested party)** [2018] **4** 1053, DC.
      Whether police having power to seize whole premises where premises movable—Police and Criminal Evidence Act 1984, ss 18(2), 19(3). **Cowan v Comr of Police of the Metropolis** [2000] **1** 504, CA.
    Power to stop, search and detain—
      Powers to stop and search in anticipation of, or after, violence—Senior police officer authorising officers to stop and search members of public for offensive weapons whether or not grounds for suspicion existing—Whether stop and search power in accordance with law—Whether breach of right to respect for private life—Whether sufficient safeguards against power being used in arbitrary or discriminatory manner—Criminal Justice and Public Order Act 1994, s 60—Human Rights Act 1998, ss 4, 6, Sch 1, Pt I, art 8. **R (on the application of Roberts) v Metropolitan Police Comr** [2016] **2** 1005, SC.
      Protestors—Right to freedom of expression—Right to freedom of assembly and association—Protest demonstration at RAF base—Police stopping coaches en route to protest—Police forming opinion occupants of coaches likely to cause breach of the peace at protest—Police escorting coaches back to departure point—Whether police entitled to take measures to prevent breach of the peace—Whether enforced return lawful—Human Rights Act 1998, Sch 1, Pt I, arts 10, 11. **R (on the application of Laporte) v Chief Constable of Gloucestershire Constabulary (Chief Constable of Thames Valley Police and Comr of Police of the Metropolis, interested parties)** [2007] **2** 529, HL.
      Searching for articles of a kind which could be used in connection with terrorism—Senior police officer issuing authorisation—Secretary of State confirming authorisation—Whether authorisation and confirmation lawful—Whether exercise of search powers lawful—Human Rights Act 1998, Sch 1, Pt I, arts 5, 8, 10, 11—Terrorism Act 2000, ss 44, 45, 46. **R (on the application of Gillan) v Metropolitan Police Comr** [2005] **1** 970, CA; [2006] **4** 1041, HL.
      Stolen property. See Constable—Power to stop, search and detain person suspected of having or conveying stolen property, *above*.
    Powers derived from emergency legislation—
      Use of powers—Right to require production of identity cards. **Willcock v Muckle** [1951] **2** 367, KBD.
    Processions and assemblies—
      Imposing conditions on public assemblies—Police imposing condition that any assembly linked to Extinction Rebellion Autumn Uprising ('XRAU') to cease protests within London—Whether power to impose condition on basis XRAU one public assembly—Meaning of 'public assembly'—Public Order Act 1986, s 14. **R (on the application of Baroness Jones) v Comr of Police of the Metropolis** [2020] **3** 509, DC.
    Removal of peaceful protesters—
      Actual or apprehended breach of peace—Protesters obstructing survey of site for nuclear power plant—Protest peaceful and non-violent—Whether police having power to remove or assist in removal of protesters. **R v Chief Constable of Devon and Cornwall Constabulary, ex p Central Electricity Generating Board** [1981] **3** 826, CA.
    Search. See Right of search, *below*.
    Search warrant—
      Extent of powers under warrant. See Search warrant—Extent of police powers under warrant, *below*.
    Seizure of documents—
      Retention—Disclosure to third party—Whether police entitled to disclose seized documents to third party for use in civil litigation—Whether police liable to produce to court on subpoena duces tecum documents which true owner would be so liable to produce if documents still in his possession—Police and Criminal Evidence Act 1984, s 22. **Marcel v Comr of Police of the Metropolis** [1992] **1** 72, CA.
    Telephone tapping—
      Citizen's rights of property, privacy and confidentiality—Violation of human rights and freedoms—Police obtaining warrant from Home Secretary to tap plaintiff's telephone—Plaintiff's telephone tapped by Post Office on behalf of police—Whether telephone tapping by Post Office on behalf of police lawful—Whether plaintiff's rights of property, privacy or confidentiality breached—Whether plaintiff's human rights and freedoms violated—Post Office Act 1969, s 80—European Convention for the Protection of Human Rights and Fundamental Freedoms 1950, art 8. **Malone v Comr of Police of the Metropolis (No 2)** [1979] **2** 620, Ch D.
  Previous convictions at trial. See **Criminal law** (Trial—Previous convictions—Police).
  Private premises—
    Power to enter and remove instrument of crime. See Right of search—Right of search and seizure—Entry to private premises, *below*.

POLICE (cont)—
  Proceeds of crime—
    Interlocutory injunction to restrain dealings with proceeds of crime. *See* **Injunction** (Interlocutory—
    Preservation of proceeds of crime).
  Property in possession of police—
    Delivery to owner—
      Costs of application for delivery to owner—Jurisdiction of justices to make order for
      costs—Justices having power to award costs where proceedings initiated by way of
      complaint—Whether 'application' by claimant for order for delivery of property to him properly
      made by way of complaint—Whether justices having power to order police to pay costs—Police
      (Property) Act 1897, s 1(1)—Magistrates' Courts Act 1952, s 55(1). **R v Uxbridge Justices, ex p
      Comr of Police of the Metropolis** [1981] **3** 129, CA.
      Power of magistrates' court to order property to be delivered to person appearing to court to be
      owner—Owner—Meaning—Application by person having good title save against true owner by
      virtue of possession—True owner untraceable—Whether applicant 'owner'—Police (Property) Act
      1897, s 1(1) (as amended by the Criminal Justice Act 1972, s 58). **Raymond Lyons & Co Ltd v
      Metropolitan Police Comr** [1975] **1** 335, QBD.
    Recovery of property—
      Plaintiff's property seized by police in connection with theft—Delivered under magistrates' order in
      respect of stolen property—Conviction of plaintiff quashed—Action to recover property—
      Whether burden of proof on plaintiff to establish title to the property—Police (Property) Act 1897,
      s 1. **Irving v National Provincial Bank Ltd** [1962] **1** 157, CA.
  Prosecutor—
    Costs—
      Police constable laying information and giving evidence—Police not legally represented—
      Prosecutor acting on behalf of Metropolitan Police—Costs—Costs in Criminal Cases Act 1952,
      s 17. **R v Burt, ex p Presburg** [1960] **1** 424, QBD.
  Records—
    Production for inspection—
      Privilege. *See* **Disclosure and inspection of documents** (Privilege—Production contrary to public
      interest—Police records).
  Recreational facilities—
    Provision of—
      Whether charitable purpose. *See* **Charity** (Benefit to community—Recreational facilities—
      Encouragement of athletic sports of police force).
  Remand prisoner—
    Right of person in custody to have access to solicitor. *See* **Solicitor** (Access to—Right of person in
    custody—Remand prisoner).
  Resignation of constable—
    Cancellation of resignation and subsequent dismissal. *See* Borough police force—Constable—
    Resignation, *above*.
  Retirement—
    Compulsory retirement. *See* Compulsory retirement, *above*.
  Right of search—
    Arrested person—
      Extent of right of search—Whether general right of search—Whether reason for search required to
      be given—Police Act 1964, s 51(1). **Brazil v Chief Constable of Surrey** [1983] **3** 537, QBD.
      Good reason for search—Trespass to person—Police officer acting in accordance with standard
      procedure—Police officer required to have good reason to search detained person. **Middleweek v
      Chief Constable of Merseyside Police (1985)** [1990] **3** 662, CA.
      Search unrelated to offence for which suspect arrested—Search of suspect's house—Suspect
      arrested at place other than house—Contents of house having no apparent relation to offence
      charged or evidence required to support it—Whether search unlawful. **Jeffrey v Black**
      [1978] **1** 555, QBD.
    Right of search and seizure—
      Entry to private premises—Power to enter and remove instrument of crime—Police entering private
      premises without warrant and removing instrument of crime after defendant charged—Occupier
      of premises objecting to entry and resisting removal—Extent of police powers to enter premises
      without warrant in order to seize instrument of crime. **McLorie v Oxford** [1982] **3** 480, QBD.
      Extradition—Whether police having common law power of search and seizure in respect of
      premises where person arrested pursuant to provisional warrant of arrest for extradition
      crime—Police and Criminal Evidence Act 1984, ss 18, 19—Extradition Act 1989, s 8—Criminal
      Justice (International Co-operation) Act 1990, s 7. **R (on the application of Rottman) v Comr of
      Police of the Metropolis** [2002] **2** 865, HL.
  Riot damage—
    Liability for compensation—
      Immigration detention centre. *See* **Riot** (Damage—Compensation—Police authority).
  Riot equipment. *See* Equipment—Riot equipment, *above*.
  Road traffic—
    Direction by constable engaged in regulation of traffic—
      Failure to comply with direction. *See* **Road traffic** (Directions—Failure to comply with
      direction—Direction by constable engaged in regulation of traffic).
    Power to stop vehicles—
      Whether including power to detain stopped vehicle. *See* Powers—Power to detain stopped vehicle,
      above.
    Speeding—
      Exemption from restriction on driving at excessive speed. *See* **Road traffic** (Excessive
      speed—Exemption—Police).
      Negligence. *See* **Negligence** (Vehicles—Speed—Police vehicle).
  Search—
    Right of search. *See* Right of search, *above*.
    Search warrant. *See* Search warrant, *below*.

POLICE (cont)—
Search warrant—
Conspiracy to defraud—
Extent of police powers under search warrant—Seizure of documents not authorised by warrant—Magistrate issuing search warrants for documents relating to advance fee fraud by group of companies—Police removing from premises whole files believed to contain relevant documents and some material unconnected with group—Companies and managers applying for judicial review—Whether scope of warrants too wide—Whether seizure of documents not authorised by warrant rendering whole search unlawful—Police and Criminal Evidence Act 1984, ss 8, 15, 16. **R v Chief Constable of Warwickshire Constabulary, ex p Fitzpatrick** [1998] **1** 65, QBD.
Dangerous drugs—
Evidence—Admissibility—Search of premises authorised by warrant—Warrant did not authorise search—Accused found on premises and searched—Warrant for search of person should expressly authorise such search—Dangerous drug found on accused—Discretion of court to admit evidence obtained as result of search. **King v R** [1968] **2** 610, PC.
Extent of police powers under warrant—
Police entering premises to search plaintiff's premises for forged documents—Police removing large quantity of documents etc—Whether necessary in relation to each item for police officer to have reasonable cause to believe that it might contain forged material or evidence showing that plaintiff guilty of some other crime—Whether police committing trespass to goods—Forgery Act 1913, s 16(1). **Reynolds v Comr of Police of the Metropolis** [1984] **3** 649, CA.
Power to retain documents other than those specified which are relevant to criminal proceedings—Police obtaining warrant to search solicitor's premises for forged documents belonging to client—Solicitor giving police permission to take all client's files for searching and sorting—Client already charged with conspiracy—Police on sorting documents finding evidence that they believed was material to conspiracy charge—Whether police entitled to retain documents relating to conspiracy charge. **Truman (Frank) Export Ltd v Metropolitan Police Comr** [1977] **3** 431, QBD.
Forged documents or instruments—
Any forged document—Documents custody or possession of which a criminal offence—Jurisdiction to issue search warrant in respect of forged documents possession of which not a criminal offence—Forgery Act 1913, ss 8, 16(1). **R v Justice of the Peace for Peterborough, ex p Hicks** [1978] **1** 225, QBD.
Extent of police powers under warrant—Seizure of genuine document—Warrant authorising police to seize any forged documents—Documents seized including one genuine document—Police believing genuine document to be material evidence that other seized documents forgeries—Whether police entitled to seize and retain genuine document—Forgery Act 1913, s 16(1). **Truman (Frank) Export Ltd v Metropolitan Police Comr** [1977] **3** 431, QBD.
Lawful authority or excuse for possession of forged documents—Solicitor—Legal professional privilege—Document in possession of solicitor in connection with preparation of client's defence to criminal charges—Whether document privileged—Whether solicitor having lawful authority or excuse for possession of forged documents—Forgery Act 1913, s 16(1). **R v Justice of the Peace for Peterborough, ex p Hicks** [1978] **1** 225, QBD.
Reasonable and probable cause for belief that person having forged documents in his possession—Seizure of person's documents pursuant to warrant—Person alleging police having no reasonable and probable grounds for belief that person having forged documents in his possession—Whether burden of proving that no reasonable and probable cause for belief lay on person alleging tort—Whether for judge to decide on objective test whether there was reasonable and probable cause for belief that forged documents on premises—Forgery Act 1913, s 16(1). **Reynolds v Comr of Police of the Metropolis** [1984] **3** 649, CA.
Issue of warrant—
Information in support—Disclosure—Whether magistrates' court on ex parte application for search and seizure warrant could rely on information which in public interest could not be disclosed—Whether Crown Court on inter partes application to retain unlawfully seized material could operate closed procedure—Whether High Court in judicial review proceedings could have regard to evidence not disclosed—Whether principles concerning minimum disclosure applying to proceedings concerning search warrants—Police and Criminal Evidence Act 1984, ss 8, 15(3)—Criminal Justice and Police Act 2001, s 59. **R (on the application of Haralambous) v St Albans Crown Court (Secretary of State for the Home Dept intervening)** [2018] **2** 303, SC.
Power of justice of the peace to authorise entry and search of premises—Pro forma application for warrant listing certain statutory conditions for issue of warrant and requiring deletion of inapplicable alternatives—No deletions made in application for warrant—Whether issue of warrant lawful—Whether statutory conditions fulfilled—Police and Criminal Evidence Act 1984, s 8(3). **Redknapp v Comr of Police for City of London** [2009] **1** 229, DC.
Power of justice of the peace to authorise entry and search of premises—Safeguards—Entry and search after arrest—Reasonable grounds for believing material not consisting of or including items subject to legal privilege—Premises occupied by person under arrest for indictable offence—Whether necessary to disclose that occupant of premises to be searched a solicitor—Nature of 'occupation' of premises by person under arrest for indictable offence—Police and Criminal Evidence Act 1984, ss 8, 15(6), 18(1). **R (on the application of AB) v Huddersfield Magistrates' Court** [2014] **4** 500, QBD.
Requirements for issue of search and seizure warrant—Failure to make full disclosure in application for search and seizure warrant—Consequence of non-disclosure—Whether warrant to be set aside—Test—Proceeds of Crime Act 2002, ss 352, 353. **R (on the application of Mills) v Sussex Police** [2015] **2** 956, DC.
Warrant issued in Scotland for execution in England—Warrant in respect of special procedure material—Warrant indorsed by English magistrate—Whether issue of warrant in Scotland for search of special procedure material in England precluded by statute—Summary Jurisdiction (Process) Act 1881, s 4—Police and Criminal Evidence Act 1984, s 9(2). **R v Manchester Stipendiary Magistrate, ex p Granada Television Ltd** [2000] **1** 135, HL.
Obscene publications—
Validity of warrant. *See* **Criminal law** (Obscene publications—Power of search and seizure—Validity of warrant).

POLICE (cont)—
    Search warrant (cont)—
        Retention of documents unlawfully seized—
            Application to judge for warrant—Warrant consisting of authorisation and schedule—Judge signing authorisation—When searching premises police using original authorisation and photocopy of schedule—Whether warrant issued lawfully—Whether search and seizure lawful—Whether police entitled to retain documents unlawfully seized—Police and Criminal Evidence Act 1984, s 16. **R v Chief Constable of Lancashire Constabulary, ex p Parker** [1993] **2** 56, QBD.
            Documents being seized by Revenue and Customs as part of investigation into possible fraud—Warrants being quashed - Revenue and Customs applying to retain documents - Whether Crown Court having jurisdiction to entertain Revenue's application - Criminal Justice and Police Act 2001, s 59. **R (on the application of Panesar) v Central Criminal Court (Revenue and Customs Comr, interested party)** [2015] **4** 754, DC.
        Safeguards —
            Execution of warrants—Copy warrants—Supply of copy warrant to occupier of premises—Copy warrants not replicating original warrant—Whether entry, search and seizure lawful—Police and Criminal Evidence Act 1984, ss 15, 16. **R (on the application of Bhatti) v Croydon Magistrates' Court** [2010] **3** 671, DC.
        Seizure of documents—
            Privileged material and items falling outside scope of warrant—Principles applicable—Police and Criminal Evidence Act 1984, ss 8, 19. **R v Chesterfield Justices, ex p Bramley** [2000] **1** 411, QBD.
        Seizure of goods believed on reasonable grounds to be stolen goods—
            Goods seized not of manufacture specified in warrant—Constable entered company's premises and seized goods of other manufacture believing on reasonable grounds them to be stolen goods received by an officer or officers of the company—Explanation subsequently made on behalf of company and accepted by police and goods returned—Whether police liable in action for trespass to goods. **Chic Fashions (West Wales) Ltd v Jones** [1968] **1** 229, CA.
    Seized materials—
        Retention of documents unlawfully seized. *See* Search warrant—Retention of documents unlawfully seized, *above.*
    Special constable—
        Dismissal. *See* Dismissal—Constable—Special constable, *above.*
    Special police services—
        Police attendance at football matches—
            Attendance inside football club's ground necessary to maintain law and order and protect life and property—Chief constable needing to use off-duty officers to police club's matches—Large overtime payment necessary—Whether attendance of police at club's matches constituting 'special police services'—Whether police attendance at matches merely part of police's public duty to maintain law and order—Whether club required to pay for attendance of police—Whether club impliedly requesting special police services—Police Act 1964, s 15(1). **Harris v Sheffield United Football Club Ltd** [1987] **2** 838, CA.
            Attendance outside football club's ground at request of football club on public land—Whether attendance on public land 'special police services'—Whether part of police's public duty to maintain law and order—Police Act 1996, s 25(1). **Leeds United Football Club Ltd v Chief Constable of West Yorkshire Police** [2013] **2** 760, CA.
    Special procedure material—
        Appeal against order for production of material—
            Whether order for production of material an order in a 'criminal cause or matter'. *See* **Criminal law** (Appeal—Criminal cause or matter—Order of Crown Court—Order for production of special procedure material).
        Generally. *See* **Criminal evidence** (Special procedure material).
    Speeding—
        Exemption from restriction on driving at excessive speed. *See* **Road traffic** (Excessive speed—Exemption—Police).
        Negligence. *See* **Negligence** (Vehicles—Speed—Police vehicle).
    Statements to police—
        Admissibility in criminal proceedings. *See* **Criminal evidence** (Admissions and confessions—Answers and statements to police).
    Stop, search and detain—
        Powers as to. *See* Powers—Power to stop, search and detain, *above.*
    Surveillance—
        Human rights. *See* **Human rights** (Right to respect for private and family life—Surveillance—Police).
    Tape recording of police interview—
        Evidence in criminal proceedings. *See* **Criminal evidence** (Tape recording—Tape recording of police interviews).
    Telephone tapping. *See* Powers—Telephone tapping, *above.*
    Terrorism—
        Notification order. *See* **Terrorism** (Prevention of—Notification order).
    Trap—
        Admission obtained by trap. *See* **Criminal evidence** (Admissions and confessions—Trap—Police).
    Unlawful conduct—
        Action for damages—
            Compensatory damages—Exemplary damages—Directions to be given to jury as to appropriate level of damages recoverable. **Thompson v Comr of Police of the Metropolis** [1997] **2** 762, CA.
    Ward of court—
        Caution in lieu of criminal proceedings. *See* **Ward of court** (Criminal proceedings—Caution in lieu of criminal proceedings).
        Witness in criminal proceedings—
            Leave of court for police to interview child. *See* **Criminal evidence** (Child—Ward of court—Witness in criminal proceedings).

POLICE (cont)—
    Witness—
        Imputation on character of police witness. *See* **Criminal evidence** (Character of accused—Imputation on character of prosecutor or witness—Police).

POLICE COMPLAINTS BOARD
    Investigation of complaint against officer. *See* **Police** (Complaint against police—Police Complaints Board).

POLICY
    Insurance—
        Generally. *See* **Insurance** (Policy).
        Husband and wife. *See* **Husband and wife** (Insurance policy).
        Jurisdiction. *See* **Conflict of laws** (Jurisdiction—Challenge to jurisdiction—Insurance policy).
        Life insurance. *See* **Insurance** (Life insurance—Policy).
        Motor vehicle. *See* **Motor insurance**.
        Proper law. *See* **Conflict of laws** (Contract—Proper law of contract—Insurance policy).
        Protection of policyholders. *See* **Insurance** (Protection of policyholders).
        Stamp duty. *See* **Stamp duty** (Insurance policy).
        Variation of settlement. *See* **Variation of Settlement (Matrimonial Causes)** (Insurance policy).

POLITICAL ADVERTISEMENT
    Commercial radio—
        Ban on political advertising—
            Judicial review of Radio Authority's decision. *See* **Judicial review** (Radio Authority—Ban on political advertising).

POLITICAL FUND
    Trade union—
        Member contracting out. *See* **Trade union** (Political fund—Member contracting out).

POLITICAL LAW
    Foreign law—
        Recognition. *See* **Conflict of laws** (Foreign law—Recognition—Political law).

POLITICAL OFFENCE
    Extradition—
        Fugitive offender—
            Restrictions on return. *See* **Extradition** (Fugitive offender—Restrictions on return—Political offence).
            Restriction on surrender of fugitive criminal. *See* **Extradition** (Restrictions on surrender—Political offence).
        Return of offender to Ireland—
            Irish warrant—
                Indorsement for execution in England. *See* **Magistrates** (Indorsement of Irish warrant—Irish warrant indorsed for execution in England).

POLITICAL PARTIES
    Donations. *See* **Elections** (Political parties—Registered parties—Control of donations to registered parties and their members).
    Elections. *See* **Elections** (Political parties).

POLITICAL PARTY
    Gift to—
        Rule against perpetuities. *See* **Rule against perpetuities** (Unincorporated association—Gift to association—Absolute gift to members on trust for association—Bequest in will—Gift to committee of local political party).
    Labour Party—
        Rules. *See* **Unincorporated association** (Rules—National Executive Committee of Labour Party).
    Libel and slander—
        Right of political party to sue. *See* **Libel and slander** (Parties—Right to sue—Political party).
    Natural justice—
        Domestic tribunal. *See* **Natural justice** (Domestic tribunal—Political party).
    Unincorporated association. *See* **Unincorporated association** (Requirements of unincorporated association—Political party constituted by members of local constituency associations and both Houses of Parliament).

POLITICAL PURPOSE
    Charity—
        Change in law. *See* **Charity** (Political object—Change in law).
        Public benefit. *See* **Charity** (Public benefit—Political purposes).

POLITICS
    Political indoctrination—
        Education. *See* **Education** (School—Duty of local education authority, governing body and head teachers to forbid political indoctrination).

POLLUTION
    Brook. *See* **Water and watercourses** (Pollution of brook).
    Controlled water. *See* **Water and watercourses** (Pollution of controlled water).
    Environmental protection. *See* **Environment** (Protection—Pollution).
    Foreshore—
        Public nuisance. *See* **Nuisance** (Public nuisance—Pollution of shore).

POLLUTION (cont)—
  Noise—
    Nuisance. *See* **Nuisance** (Noise).
  Oil—
    Discharge into navigable waters—
      Damage to adjoining land. *See* **Trespass to land** (Oil—Discharge of oil into public navigable
        waters—Damage to adjoining land).
      Generally. *See* **Shipping** (Oil in navigable waters).
  Pollution offences—
    Sentence—
      Polluting of controlled water. *See* **Sentence** (Pollution offences—Polluting controlled waters).
  River. *See* **Water and watercourses** (Pollution of river).
  Ship-source pollution—
    European Community. *See* **European Union** (Environment—Ship-source pollution).
  Waste disposal—
    Control. *See* **Public health** (Waste disposal).
  Water and watercourses—
    Controlled water. *See* **Water and watercourses** (Pollution of controlled water).

POLYGAMOUS MARRIAGE
  Conspiracy—
    Husband and wife. *See* **Criminal law** (Conspiracy—Husband and wife—Polygamous marriage).
  Family provision—
    Wife. *See* **Family provision** (Jurisdiction—Polygamous marriage).
  Generally. *See* **Marriage** (Polygamous).
  Maintenance—
    Wife and children. *See* **National assistance** (Recovery of cost of assistance from husband—
      Polygamous marriage).
  Nullity suit—
    Jurisdiction. *See* **Nullity** (Jurisdiction—Polygamous marriage).
    Relief. *See* **Nullity** (Polygamous marriage—Relief).
  Potentially polygamous—
    Right to summary matrimonial relief. *See* **Husband and wife** (Summary proceedings—Potentially
      polygamous marriage—Right to matrimonial relief).
  Property—
    Summary proceedings. *See* **Husband and wife** (Property—Summary proceedings—Jurisdiction—
      Polygamous marriage).
  Right to contract polygamous marriage—
    Ceylon. *See* **Ceylon** (Polygamous marriage—Right to contract polygamous marriage).

POOL BETTING
  See **Gaming** (Pool betting).

POOR LAW
  Idle and disorderly person—
    Running away and leaving wife and child whereby they became chargeable to public assistance
    committee—
      Maintenance order against accused made by another court already in existence—Whether charge
        sustainable—Vagrancy Act 1824, s 4. **Batty v Lee** [1938] **4** 207, KBD.
  Order for maintenance—
    Enforcement—
      Jurisdiction. **London CC v Betts** [1936] **1** 144, KBD.
  Relief—
    Disability pension—
      Factors to be considered—Whether first one pound of pension should be disregarded in
        considering application for relief—Poor Law (Scotland) Act 1934, s 11(1)(d). **Duncan v Aberdeen
        CC** [1936] **2** 911, HL.
    Duty to grant relief—
      Enforcement—Public assistance committee—Recommendation of medical officer—How far binding
        on committee—Discretion of committee—Poor Law Act 1930, s 15(1)—Public Assistance Order
        1930 (SR & O 1930 No 185), reg 167—Relief Regulation Order 1930 (SR & O 1930 No 186), reg 10.
        Cresswell and Cresswell v Liverpool Corp [1939] **2** 824, Assizes.
  Settlement—
    Change of residence—
      Former residence—Immediately before—Newport Extension Act 1934, s 26. **Newport BC v
        Leicester CC** [1937] **1** 439, KBD.
    Husband and wife living apart—
      Wife and children deserted by husband—Wife and children in receipt of poor relief—Wife and
        children on change of residence becoming chargeable to another local authority—Order for
        removal to former locality—Validity—Maintenance order against husband—Poor Law Act 1930,
        ss 13, 18, 19(1), 84(1), (2), 85 (1), 86(1), (2), 93(1)(f), (4). **Middlesex CC v Essex CC** [1940] **1** 460,
        KBD.
    State of irremovability—
      Mental patient—Married woman—Settlement of husband—Mental Treatment Act 1930, s 18(1)(b).
        Rochdale Corp v Lancashire CC [1937] **1** 559, KBD.

POOR PERSON
  Costs. *See* **Costs** (Poor person).

PORT

Charterparty—
  Arrived ship—
    Commencement of lay days. *See* **Shipping** (Commencement of lay days—Arrived ship under port charterparty).
    Generally. *See* **Shipping** (Port charterparty).
Dock labour—
  Dock labour scheme—
    Application. *See* **Employment** (Dock labour scheme—Application—Port).
  Licence to employ registered dock workers—
    Refusal of licence. *See* **Licence** (Dock workers).
Meaning—
  Dock Labour Scheme for South Wales Ports. *See* **Employment** (Dock labour scheme—Application—Port—Port of Port Talbot—Meaning).
Safe port—
  Charterparty. *See* **Shipping** (Charterparty—Safe port).

PORTABLE GRINDING MACHINES

Exemption from Grinding of Metals (Miscellaneous Industries) Regulations 1925. *See* **Factory** (Grinding machines—Regulations—Exemption of portable grinding machines).

PORTIONS

Accumulation of income—
  Provision for raising portion. *See* **Accumulation** (Excessive period—Exception—Provision for raising portion).
Ademption. *See* **Administration of estates** (Ademption—Double portions).
Settlement. *See* **Settlement** (Portions).

POSSESSION

Adulterated milk. *See* **Food and drugs** (Milk—Adulteration of milk—Possession of adulterated milk for purpose of sale).
Adverse—
  Land—
    Limitation of action. *See* **Limitation of action** (Land—Adverse possession).
Apparent possession—
  Bill of sale. *See* **Bill of sale** (Absolute bill of sale—Apparent possession).
Bankruptcy—
  Property held by bankrupt on trust for sale—
    Order for possession. *See* **Bankruptcy** (Property available for distribution—Trust for sale—Powers of court—Order for possession).
Cannabinol derivative—
  Unlawful possession. *See* **Drugs** (Dangerous drugs—Cannabinol derivative—Unlawful possession).
Chattel found on another's property—
  Building operation—
    Workmen in cellar of demolished building finding bank notes in safe built in wall—True owners unknown—Whether freeholders, building leaseholders or finders entitled to notes—Whether, if finders entitled, they would be bound in law to account to their employers, who were independent contractors—Equitable title of freeholders by virtue of a provision of the building lease. **London Corp v Appleyard** [1963] 2 834, QBD.
  Rights of finder—
    Right of finder to possession. **Hannah v Peel** [1945] 2 288, KBD.
  Title to chattel—
    Owner not shown to have surrendered title—Owner's title indefeasible. **Moffatt v Kazana** [1968] 3 271, Assizes.
Controlled drugs—
  Unlawful possession. *See* **Drugs** (Controlled drugs—Unlawful possession).
Conversion. *See* **Conversion** (Possession).
Dangerous drugs—
  Generally. *See* **Drugs** (Dangerous drugs—Possession).
  Unauthorised possession. *See* **Drugs** (Dangerous drugs—Unauthorised possession).
Finder—
  Right of possession—
    Trover. *See* **Trover** (Right of possession—Finder).
Firearm—
  Five years after sentence—
    Suspended sentence. *See* **Sentence** (Firearms offence—Prohibition on possession of firearms within five years of sentence—Suspended sentence).
  Generally. *See* **Firearms**.
Forged document. *See* **Criminal law** (Forgery—Possession of forged document).
Goods—
  Mercantile agent. *See* **Agent** (Mercantile agent—Possession of goods).
Hereditament—
  Owner having legal possession—
    Rateable occupation. *See* **Rates** (Rateable occupation—Owner having legal possession).
Housebreaking implements. *See* **Criminal law** (Housebreaking—Implements—Possession of housebreaking implements by night).
Implements of forgery. *See* **Criminal law** (Forgery—Implements of forgery).
Injunction—
  Possession action. *See* **Injunction** (Possession action).
Interest in possession under settlement—
  Capital transfer tax. *See* **Capital transfer tax** (Settlement—Interest in possession).
Land—
  Defence to action for trespass. *See* **Trespass to land** (Defence—Lawful possession).

POSSESSION (cont)—
  Land (cont)—
    Limitation of action. *See* **Limitation of action** (Land).
    Possession before completion of sale. *See* **Sale of land** (Possession before completion).
    Summary proceedings to recover possession. *See* **Land** (Summary proceedings for possession).
  Landlord—
    Action for possession. *See* **Landlord and tenant** (Action for possession).
    Parting with possession. *See* **Landlord and tenant** (Covenant—Parting with possession).
    Recovery of possession—
      Generally. *See* **Landlord and tenant** (Recovery of possession).
      Order for possession. *See* **Landlord and tenant** (Recovery of possession—Order for possession).
      Protected tenancy. *See* **Rent restriction** (Possession).
  Lease—
    Forfeiture. *See* **Landlord and tenant** (Forfeiture of lease—Forfeiture—Action for possession by lessor).
    Parting with possession—
      Covenant. *See* **Landlord and tenant** (Covenant—Parting with possession).
  Local authority dwelling. *See* **Housing** (Local authority houses—Possession).
  Matrimonial home—
    Deserted wife's right to remain. *See* **Husband and wife** (Deserted wife's right to remain in matrimonial home—Possession).
  Mortgaged property—
    Action by mortgagee for possession. *See* **Mortgage** (Action by mortgagee for possession).
    Generally. *See* **Mortgage** (Possession of mortgaged property).
    Mortgagee's right to recover possession. *See* **Mortgage** (Possession of mortgaged property—Mortgagee's right to recover possession).
    Mortgagor not in occupation. *See* **Mortgage** (Possession of mortgaged property—Mortgagor not in occupation).
    Order for possession. *See* **Mortgage** (Order for possession of mortgaged property).
    Remedies of mortgagee. *See* **Mortgage** (Remedies of mortgagee—Possession proceedings).
  Parting with possession—
    Covenant—
      Lease. *See* **Landlord and tenant** (Covenant—Parting with possession).
  Protected tenancy—
    Recovery by landlord. *See* **Rent restriction** (Possession).
    Sale of land. *See* **Sale of land** (Protected tenancy).
  Recovery—
    Hire-purchase agreement. *See* **Hire-purchase** (Possession).
    Landlord, by—
      Generally. *See* **Landlord and tenant** (Recovery of possession).
      Illegal lease. *See* **Contract** (Illegality—Lease of land—Recovery of possession—Lease illegal).
      Protected tenancy. *See* **Rent restriction** (Possession).
    Landlord, by. *See* **Landlord and tenant** (Recovery of possession).
    Sale for purpose of administration of deceased's estate. *See* **Administration of estates** (Sale for purposes of administration—Recovery of possession for purposes of sale).
    Winding up of company. *See* **Company** (Winding up—Possession of property).
  Regulated tenancy—
    Recovery by landlord. *See* **Rent restriction** (Possession).
  Restitution order—
    Possession at time of apprehension. *See* **Sentence** (Restitution order—Safe deposit in accused's name—Money taken from safe deposit after arrest).
  Right of possession—
    Trover. *See* **Trover** (Right of possession).
  Salmon—
    Possession for sale during close season. *See* **Fish** (Salmon and trout—Restriction on sale or possession for sale of salmon during close season).
  Sheriff—
    Walking possession agreement. *See* **Execution** (Writ of fi fa—Seizure of goods—Walking possession agreement).
  Statutory tenancy—
    Recovery by landlord. *See* **Rent restriction** (Possession).
  Stolen goods—
    Receiving. *See* **Criminal law** (Receiving stolen property—Possession).
  Summary proceedings for possession of land. *See* **Land** (Summary proceedings for possession).
  Suspended order for—
    Costs—
      Agricultural worker. *See* **Agriculture** (Agricultural worker—Tied cottage—Possession—Suspended order for possession—Costs).
    Leave to issue execution. *See* **Execution** (Leave to issue execution—Application—Suspended order for possession).
  Tied cottage—
    Agricultural worker. *See* **Agriculture** (Agricultural worker—Tied cottage—Possession).
  Title deeds—
    Voluntary parting with possession—
      Lien—Solicitor—Preservation of lien. *See* **Solicitor** (Lien—Title deeds).
  Trespass to land. *See* **Trespass to land** (Possession sufficient to support trespass).
  Walking possession agreement—
    Distress for rent. *See* **Distress** (Distress for rent).
  Warrant—
    Jurisdiction to stay—
      County court. *See* **County court** (Execution—Warrant for possession of premises—Suspension of execution—Jurisdiction).

POSSESSION (cont)—
Writ of possession—
Execution—
Generally. *See* **Execution** (Possession—Writ of possession).
Resumption of possession by person evicted—Jurisdiction to commit for contempt person evicted.
See **Contempt of court** (Committal—Jurisdiction—Execution of writ of possession—Resumption of possession by person evicted—Jurisdiction to commit for contempt person evicted).
Leave to issue writ. *See* **Execution** (Possession—Leave to issue writ).
Wrongful and irregular execution. *See* **Execution** (Wrongful and irregular execution—Writ of possession).

POST
Admiralty practice. *See* **Admiralty** (Practice—Post).
Appearance by. *See* **Practice** (Appearance—Appearance by post).
Chambers proceedings—
Communications by post or telephone. *See* **Practice** (Chambers proceedings—Communications by post or telephone).
Companies Court—
Chambers proceedings. *See* **Practice** (Companies Court—Chambers—Postal transactions).
Contract—
Acceptance by post. *See* **Contract** (Offer and acceptance—Acceptance—Acceptance by post).
County court mail. *See* **County court** (Postal transactions).
Divorce—
Postal facilities in divorce registry. *See* **Divorce** (Practice—Postal facilities in divorce registry).
Indecent or obscene article sent by post—
Offence—
Meaning of obscene. *See* **Criminal law** (Obscene publications—Indecent or obscene—Obscene—Meaning—Items which are shocking or lewd—Sending postal packet enclosing indecent or obscene article).
Post Office. *See* **Post Office**.
Practice—
Generally. *See* **Practice** (Post).
Prisoner—
Letters to and from prisoner. *See* **Prison** (Letters—Prisoner's letters).
Probate citation—
Issue. *See* **Probate** (Citation—Application for issue).
Queen's Bench Division. *See* **Practice** (Post—Use of postal facilities—Queen's Bench Division).
Service by post—
Building preservation notice. *See* **Town and country planning** (Building of special architectural or historic interest—Building preservation order—Service of building preservation notice by post).
Date of service—
First and second class mail. *See* **Practice** (Post—First and second class mail—Affidavit of service).
Generally. *See* **Practice** (Service—Service by post).
Notice to treat—
Compulsory purchase. *See* **Compulsory purchase** (Notice to treat—Service—Post).
Registered post—
Enforcement notice. *See* **Town and country planning** (Enforcement notice—Service).
Notice of severance. *See* **Joint tenancy** (Notice of severance—Service—Registered post).
Summons—
County court. *See* **County court** (Practice—Service of summons—Service by post).
Writ—
Service on company. *See* **Writ** (Service on company—Service by post).
Use of postal facilities—
Admiralty Registry. *See* **Practice** (Post—Use of postal facilities—Queen's Bench Division—Admiralty Registry).
Issue of writs etc. *See* **Practice** (Post—Use of postal facilities—Issue of writs etc).
Taxation of costs. *See* **Costs** (Taxation—Procedure—Postal facilities).

POST OFFICE
County court instructions to—
Delivery of mail. *See* **County court** (Postal transactions—County court instructions to Post Office not to deliver mail on Saturdays).
First and second class mail—
Date of service etc. *See* **Practice** (Post—First and second class mail—Affidavit of service).
Registered postal packet—
Carriage overseas—
Carriage by air—Carriage of postal packet by agent of Post Office—Statutory immunity of Post Office and persons engaged in carriage of mail 'proceedings in tort' for loss or damage to post—Statutory liability imposed specifically on carriers of goods by air—Whether statutory liability prevailing over vicarious immunity of carrier—Whether 'proceedings in tort' including statutory liability—Carriage by Air Act 1961, Sch 1, art 18—Post Office Act 1969, s 29. **American Express Co v British Airways Board** [1983] 1 557, QBD.
Liability in bailment—Carriage of postal packet overseas by agent of Post Office—Packet stolen while in custody of agents—Statutory immunity of Post Office and persons engaged in carriage of mail from 'proceedings in tort' for loss or damage to post—Whether 'proceedings in tort' including action in bailment—Post Office Act 1969, s 29. **American Express Co v British Airways Board** [1983] **1** 557, QBD.
Whether contractual relationship between sender and Her Majesty's Postmaster-General—Post Office Act 1908, s 13—British Commonwealth and Foreign Post Warrant 1948 (SI 1948 No 590), reg 49 (as substituted by S I 1950 No 771), reg 61. **Triefus & Co Ltd v Post Office** [1957] **2** 387, CA.

POST OFFICE (cont)—
    Registered postal packet (cont)—
        Loss or damage to registered inland postal packet—
            Damages—Measure of damages—Market value—Crown Proceedings Act 1947, s 9(2), provisos (b),(c). **Building and Civil Engineering Holidays Scheme Management Ltd v Post Office** [1965] **1** 163, CA.
    Savings Bank—
        Deposit—
            Transfer on death of holder—Rights of transferee. **Note** [1954] **1** 519, .
        Dispute between Postmaster-General and creditor of depositor—
            Dispute—Claim by creditor of depositor—Refusal by Postmaster-General of creditor's request for payment out of depositor's account—Statutory propriety of Postmaster-General's refusal unchallenged—Reference by creditor to register of friendly societies—Jurisdiction of registrar—Whether there was a dispute between the Postmaster-General and a creditor of the depositor within Post Office Savings Bank Act 1954, s 8(1)(b). **Jones, Re** [1965] **2** 428, QBD.
    Trade union—
        Recognition—
            Withdrawal of recognition by Post Office—Whether breach of statutory duty. *See* **Trade union** (Recognition—Statutory duty—Withdrawal of recognition by Post Office).

POST-MORTEM EXAMINATION
    Coroner's power to direct. *See* **Coroner** (Post-mortem examination—Power of coroner to direct post-mortem examination).
    Post-mortem examination without inquest—
        Power of coroner to direct post-mortem examination without ordering inquest. *See* **Coroner** (Post-mortem examination—Post-mortem examination without inquest).

POST-NUPTIAL SETTLEMENT
    Variation—
        Divorce—
            Financial provision. *See* **Divorce** (Financial provision).
        Generally. *See* **Variation of Settlement (Matrimonial Causes)** (Post-nuptial settlement).

POSTDATED CHEQUE
    Obtaining property by deception. *See* **Criminal law** (Obtaining property by deception—Deception—Cheque—Postdated cheque).

POTATO MARKETING
    Charge on registered producers—
        Powers of Potato Marketing Board—
            Powers to enter and inspect and to demand information relating to potatoes—Whether entitled to enter and measure acreage—Whether entitled to demand information of arable acreage—Potato Marketing Scheme 1955 (SI 1955 No 690), paras 81(1), 82(1), 83(1)(a). **Potato Marketing Board v Merricks** [1958] **2** 538, QBD.
            Producers exceeding basic acreage—Uniform charge on all registered producers—Whether proper exercise of board's powers—Potato Marketing Scheme 1933 (SR & O 1933 No 1186). **Potato Marketing Board v Harlow** [1936] **1** 489, KBD.
    Potato Marketing Board—
        Disciplinary committee—
            Constitution—Chairman to be not a member of the Potato Marketing Board but an 'independent person'—Chairman paid a fee by the board—Whether 'independent person'—Agricultural Marketing Act 1949, s 8(1)—Arbitration Act 1950, s 22—Potato Marketing Scheme 1955 (SI 1955 No 690), para 83(2)(a), (3). **Potato Marketing Board v Merricks** [1958] **2** 538, QBD.
    Scheme—
        Substitutional scheme—
            Draft scheme laid by Minister before Parliament for approval—Draft scheme challenged as ultra vires—Agricultural Marketing Act 1931, s 1. **Merricks v Heathcoat-Amory** [1955] **2** 453, Ch D.

POULTRY
    Dealer—
        Keeping of records. *See* **Animal** (Poultry—Poultry dealer—Keeping of records).
    Owner—
        Right to kill dog chasing chickens. *See* **Animal** (Dog—Chasing chickens—Right of poultry-owner to kill).
    Poultry farm—
        Nuisance—
            Noise—Crowing of cocks. *See* **Nuisance** (Noise—Poultry farm—Crowing of cocks).
    Sale of feedings stuffs for use of. *See* **Agriculture** (Feeding stuffs—Sale for use as food for cattle or poultry).

POUND BREACH
    Breach. *See* **Distress** (Distress for rent—Impounding goods).

POURING AISLES
    Iron and steel foundries, in—
        Provisions as to. *See* **Factory** (Gangways and pouring aisles).

POVERTY
    Relief of—
        Charitable purpose. *See* **Charity** (Relief of poverty).

POWER
    Appointment, of. *See* **Power of appointment**.
    Attorney, of. *See* **Power of attorney**.

POWER (cont)—
    Implied release—
        Settlement—
            Power to revoke settlement—Release of power—Subsequent inconsistent dealing—Settlor having life interest—Trustees empowered to pay or apply trust property for settlor's benefit at settlor's request—Deed of release assigning settlor's life interest in property to trustees—Trustees to hold released property on trusts declared by the trust instrument as if the settlor were dead—Whether settlor having effectively extinguished trustees' power to make provision for his benefit—Income Tax Act 1952, s 404(2). **IRC v Cookson** [1977] **2** 331, CA.

POWER OF ADVANCEMENT
    Rule against perpetuities. *See* **Rule against perpetuities**.

POWER OF APPOINTMENT
    Adoption—
        Power to appoint among children or remoter issue—
            Whether benefitting adopted grandchildren. *See* Exercise by will—Special power—Objects, *below*.
    Bare power—
        Exercise of power. *See* Exercise of power—Bare power, *below*.
    Collateral power to make grants—
        No gift over in case of non-exercise—
            Validity. **Sayer Trust, Re** [1956] **3** 600, Ch D.
    Creation of power—
        Creation by will—
            Life interest in residuary estate bequeathed with full power to deal with capital as if donee's own—Gift over—Bequest effective to create general power of appointment. **Lawry's Estate, Re** [1937] **4** 1, Ch D.
    Deed for benefit of employees—
        Power or imperative trust. *See* **Settlement** (Power—Discretionary power—Discretion to make grants to 'dependants' and 'dependent relatives' of employees).
    Delegation of power—
        Power with consent to appoint generally except to named persons—
            Appointment to new trustees on discretionary trusts—Validity. **Triffitt's Settlement, Re** [1958] **2** 299, Ch D.
    Excessive execution—
        Appointment of absolute interest with gift over—
            Gift over infringing perpetuity rule—Whether whole appointment invalid. **Pratt's Settlement Trusts, Re** [1943] **2** 458, Ch D.
        Delegation of power—
            Intermediate power—Settlement giving trustees power to appoint to 'such persons' as they thought fit—Trustees executing deed of appointment empowering them to appoint to 'such persons' as they thought fit—Whether deed of appointment a valid exercise of power of appointment in settlement. **Hay's Settlement Trusts, Re** [1981] **3** 786, Ch D.
            Special power to appoint among children and issue—'In such manner in all respects' as appointor should appoint—Discretionary trusts after forfeiture of life interest under appointment. **Morris' Settlement Trusts, Re** [1951] **2** 528, CA.
            Special power to appoint among children or remoter issue—Power to appoint with such trusts for their respective benefit and such provisions for their respective advancement, maintenance and education at the discretion of the trustees or of any other person or persons as appointor should appoint—Validity of appointment directing immediately discretionary trusts by incorporation of, s 33(1)(ii)(b) of Trustee Act 1925. **Hunter's Will Trusts, Re** [1962] **3** 1050, Ch D.
        Genuine intention to benefit objects—
            Conditional gift of appointor's residue—Condition for appointees settling shares of appointed fund—Whether excessive exercise. **Burton's Settlement, Re** [1954] **3** 193, Ch D.
        Power to appoint £1,500—
            Appointment of £1,000 free of duty—Whether appointment in excess of power. **Lonsdale's Will Trusts, Re** [1959] **3** 679, CA.
        Power to appoint £25,000—
            Appointment of £15,000 clear of death duties—Total sum including duties exceeding £25,000. **Keele Estates, Re** [1952] **2** 164, CA.
        Power to appoint part of income not exceeding in whole stated annual sum—
            Whether appointment of that sum free of duty an excessive exercise of power. **Smith-Bosanquet, Re** [1940] **3** 519, Ch D.
        Special power to appoint among children—
            Appointment making appointees under doctrine of election bound to settle appointed shares—Validity. **Neave's Settlement Trusts, Re** [1938] **3** 220, Ch D.
    Exercise by will—
        General power—
            General and special powers of appointment conferred by settlement—Powers exercisable by deed or will—Testator devising and bequeathing all real and personal estate to future wife—Exercise of special power in will by appointing income of trust funds to future wife for life after testator's death—Residuary devise and bequest—General bequest of personalty operating as valid exercise of general power—Wills Act 1837, s 27. **Box's Settlement, Re** [1945] **1** 547, Ch D.
            Power given by English settlement—Exercise by will of testator domiciled abroad—Blending of settled funds with testator's free personalty—Whether settled funds subjected to restrictions on testamentary disposition imposed by testator's domiciliary law. **Khan's Settlement, Re** [1966] **1** 160, Ch D.
            Power given by English settlement—Residuary gift by will of testatrix domiciled abroad—Wills Act 1837, s 27. **Waite's Settlement Trusts, Re** [1957] **1** 629, Ch D.
            Power to allocate among such persons as trustees think fit—Whether rule against delegation of making of will—Whether power valid. **Beatty's Will Trusts, Re** [1990] **3** 844, Ch D.

POWER OF APPOINTMENT (cont)—
  Exercise by will (cont)—
    General power (cont)—
      Power to appoint 'in such manner ... expressly referring to this power as though it were a special power'—Whether a disposition 'including any property over which I may have any general power of appointment' a valid appointment. **Priestley's Will Trusts, Re** [1971] **2** 817, CA.
      Power to appoint on 'trust for such persons or person not being her husband' as daughter should appoint—Purported exercise of power by spinster daughter in favour of charity—Validity. **Harvey (decd), Re** [1950] **1** 491, Ch D.
      Residuary bequest—Express exercise by will of general powers arising under two different settlements—Will silent as to powers arising under third settlement—Whether contrary intention appeared by the will—Wills Act 1837, s 27. **Thirlwell's Will Trusts, Re** [1957] **3** 465, Ch D.
    Special power—
      Expression of intention to exercise—Gift, subject to payment of debts, of 'all my real and personal estate whatsoever and wheresoever and over which I shall have any disposing power at the time of my decease'—Gift to objects of the special power—'And'—Failure to use 'appoint'. **Welford's Will Trusts, Re** [1946] **1** 23, Ch D.
      Expression of intention to exercise—'I give devise and appoint all my property'—Non-objects of power named as substitutional beneficiaries. **Latta's Settlement, Re** [1949] **1** 665, Ch D.
      Expression of intention to exercise—Reference to property—Donee also possessing property of same description. **Waldron's Settlement, Re** [1940] **3** 442, Ch D.
      Expression of intention to exercise—Whether intention to exercise special powers expressed in will. **Holdford's Settlement, Re, Lloyds Bank Ltd v Holdford** [1944] **2** 462, Ch D.
      Gift subject to payments of debts of 'all the residue ... including any property over which I may have any power of disposition at the date of my death' to objects of power—Whether special power exercised by will. **Knight (decd), Re** [1957] **2** 252, CA.
      Objects—Testamentary power of appointment amongst children or remoter issue conferred in 1902—Son of donee of power adopted two children in 1950, then being childless—Exercise of power in favour of grandchildren of donee of power by will made in 1951—Donee of power died in October 1957—Child born to donee's son by his second wife in March 1958—Whether adopted grandchildren benefited under exercise of power—Whether exercise of power was a disposition within Adoption Act 1950, s 13(2). **Brinkley's Will Trusts, Re** [1967] **3** 805, Ch D.
      Personalty—Whether special power exercisable by nuncupative will, made by soldier on active service and admitted to probate—Wills Act 1837, ss 9, 10, 11, 27—Wills (Soldiers and Sailors) Act 1918, s 3(1). **Chichester's (Earl) Will Trusts, Re** [1946] **1** 722, Ch D.
      Power given by English will—Exercise in Scottish will—Relevant law. **McMorran (decd), Re** [1958] **1** 186, Ch D.
      Residuary gift—Direction to pay debts out of residue—'Appoint'—'Estate and effects of which I shall have power to dispose at my decease'. **Beresford's Will Trusts, Re** [1938] **3** 566, Ch D.
  Succession duty. *See* **Succession duty** (Incidence—Exercise by will of special power of appointment).
  Exercise of power—
    Bare power—
      Extent of interest to pass under power—Gift of residue to testatrix' brother and sister for their lives and at their deaths to go to charities which they may have selected—No intention to establish endowment—Whether power to appoint capital—Whether power exercisable by survivor of donees. **Beesty's Will Trusts, Re** [1964] **3** 82, Ch D.
    Exercise by will—
      Generally. *See* Exercise by will, *above*.
    Exercise of power out of time—
      Trustees executing deed of trust in purported exercise of power of appointment—Power expiring one day before execution of deed—Whether deed taking effect in equity. **Breadner v Granville-Grossman** [2000] **4** 705, Ch D.
    Life interest with power to resort to capital—
      Power to convert to own use—Gift over—Declaration of conversion. **Shuker's Estate, Re** [1937] **3** 25, Ch D.
    Requisites of valid exercise—
      Range of objects of power irrelevant—Same rule applicable to general, special and hybrid powers—Compliance with requirements of power—Sufficient indication of intention to exercise power—Bequest of income from estate to testator's wife and after her death to such person or persons not connected with her by marriage as she should by will or codicil appoint—Bequest by wife of 'all my estate ... over which I shall then have power of appointment or disposition' to friend—Whether sufficient intention to exercise power. **Lawrence's Will Trusts, Re** [1971] **3** 433, Ch D.
    Special power—
      Construction—Appointment offending rule against perpetuities—Clause containing saving words—Beneficiaries extending beyond lives in being—Whether saving words effective to validate gift clause. **IRC v Williams** [1969] **3** 614, Ch D.
      Power to tenant for life to appoint to issue—As well the capital as the income ... with such future or other trusts ... and such provisions for their respective advancement ... at the discretion of ... my trustees as the tenant for life should appoint—Whether by exercise of power trustees could be authorised to advance to issue. **Bainbridge (decd), Re** [1948] **2** 657, Ch D.
      Power to will trustees to appoint by way of settlement for benefit of testator's son his wife and children or remoter issue or for benefit of any such objects and with such ulterior or ultimate trusts as trustees should think fit—Meaning of 'ulterior or ultimate trusts'—Whether delegation of testator's power to make a will—Validity. **Abrahams' Will Trusts, Re** [1967] **2** 1175, Ch D.
      Trusts arising—Advancement. *See* **Trust and trustee** (Powers of trustee—Advancement—Trusts arising on exercise of special power of appointment).
    Validity—
      Settlement—Discretionary trusts in favour of specified class of beneficiaries—Power to appoint that capital should be held on trust for any one of specified class—Specified class including settlor's wife or widow—Appointment of capital to be held on settlement trusts subject to the exclusion of settlor's wife or widow from specified class—Validity of appointment. **Blausten v IRC** [1972] **1** 41, CA.

POWER OF APPOINTMENT (cont)—

Extinguishment of power of appointment. *See* **Variation of trusts** (Power of appointment—Extinguishment of power).

Failure to exercise—

Power of appointment by deed or will—

Trust implied in favour of objects of power—Class benefiting—Construction. **Arnold's Trusts, Re** [1946] **2** 579, Ch D.

Fiduciary relationship between donee and objects. *See* Release—Release as regards one particular object—Whether fiduciary relationship between donee and objects, *below*.

Fraud on a power—

Antecedent agreement to benefit non-objects—

Power to appoint in favour of one object only—Necessity for proof of antecedent agreement with appointee to benefit stranger. **Nicholson's Settlement, Re** [1938] **3** 532, CA.

Corrupt purpose—

Purchase of appointee's interest by appointor—Appointor and appointee in relationship of parent and child—In absence of intention by appointor to benefit himself or non-object, appointment by parent to child not invalidated merely because parent purchases child's interest. **Merton's Settlement, Re** [1953] **2** 707, Ch D.

Effect of fraud on a power—

Exercise of special power in favour of two appointees—Severance—Subsequent appointment to same appointees—Freedom from taint of second appointment—Onus of proof. **Chadwick's Trusts, Re** [1939] **1** 850, Ch D.

Exercise to further some purpose other than benefit of object—

Special power of appointment among children and remoter issue—Power, contained in appointor's marriage settlement, exercised by will in favour of appointor's surviving children—Condition directing forfeiture of appointee's share of appointor's residuary trust funds unless appointee's share under settlement settled as directed. **Simpson's Marriage Settlement, Re** [1952] **1** 963, Ch D.

Foreign purpose—

Intention to benefit non-object—Absence of moral suasion. **Dick, Re** [1953] **1** 559, CA.

Special power of appointment among nephews and nieces—

Power exercised in favour of a nephew—Agreement by appointee to benefit appointor's children. **Crawshay, Re** [1948] **1** 107, CA.

Variation of trust by the court. *See* **Variation of trusts** (Power of appointment—Fraud on power).

General power—

Exercise by will—

Foreign will. *See* **Conflict of laws** (Power of appointment—General power—Exercise of power—Foreign will).

Generally. *See* Exercise by will—General power, *above*.

Implied trust for objects—

No gift over in default of appointment—

Implication of gift to members of class—Power in nature of a trust. **Perowne (decd), Re** [1951] **2** 201, Ch D.

Intermediate power. *See* **Settlement** (Power—Intermediate power).

Joint power. *See* Special power—Joint power, *below*.

Omission of words—

Gift in default of appointment. *See* **Will** (Construction—Intention of testator—Words of will showing omission of words of power of appointment and gift in default of appointment).

Perpetuity—

Excessive execution of power. *See* Excessive execution—Appointment of absolute interest with gift over—Gift over infringing perpetuity rule, *above*.

Exercise of power. *See* Exercise of power—Special power—Construction—Appointment offending rule against perpetuities, *above*.

Rule against perpetuities—

Generally. *See* **Rule against perpetuities** (Power of appointment).

Release—

Power coupled with a duty or trust—

Factors affecting determination whether power was coupled with trust—Beneficial or vicarious powers—Trust deeds establishing school contained special power to revoke and re-appoint trusts and discretionary powers—Appointment amongst such of founder's issue as trustees of founder's will should appoint—Whether power was capable of release by trustees of founder's will. **Wills' Trust Deeds, Re** [1963] **1** 390, Ch D.

Power to capitalise income—

Exercise of power (conferred by a subsequent clause) to declare new trusts excluding power to capitalise income—No other material difference in new trusts—Whether exercise of power was valid. **Muir v IRC** [1966] **3** 38, CA.

Release as regards one particular object—

Whether fiduciary relationship between donee and objects—Whether distinction between release and covenant not to exercise power. **Brown's Settlement, Re** [1939] **3** 391, Ch D.

Revocation—

Power of appointment by deed or will—

Power exercised by will—Subsequent exercise by deed—No revocation of deed before death—Whether exercise of power by deed or will operative. **Butler's Settlement Trust, Re** [1942] **2** 191, Ch D.

Power to revoke appointment—

Exercise not by deed—No power of revocation reserved—Power to select charities as beneficiaries in residuary estate of testatrix—Power to joint donees and survivor—Whether joint appointment revocable by survivor. **Beesty's Will Trusts, Re** [1964] **3** 82, Ch D.

Special power of appointment—

Fraudulent exercise—Special power to appoint among children and issue—Appointor having life interest in income of trust fund—Revocable appointment to children and grandchildren—Revocation with intent to further scheme for distribution of part of capital of trust fund between appointor and adult children. **Greaves' Will Trusts, Re** [1954] **1** 771, CA.

POWER OF APPOINTMENT (cont)—

Revocation (cont)—

Special power of appointment (cont)—

Property subject to power to be divided equally amongst objects of power in default of appointment—Exercise of power by deed containing power of revocation—Subsequent release and discharge of power—No reference in release to previous appointment—Whether release effectual to revoke appointment. **Chatterton's Settlement, Re** [1946] **2** 211, Ch D.

Rule against perpetuities. *See* **Rule against perpetuities** (Power of appointment).

Scottish will—

Exercise in Scottish will of power given by English will. *See* Exercise by will—Special power—Power given by English will—Exercise in Scottish will, *above*.

Settlement. *See* **Settlement** (Power of appointment).

Soldier on active service—

Whether special power exercisable by nuncupative will. *See* Exercise by will—Special power—Personalty—Whether special power exercisable by nuncupative will, made by soldier on active service and admitted to probate, *above*.

Special power—

Appointment—

Validity—Marriage settlement dated before 1926—Power exercised by deed dated after 1926—'Trusts created by an instrument coming into operation after the commencement of' the Law of Property Act 1925—Law of Property Act 1925, s 161(2). **Leigh's Marriage Settlement, Re** [1952] **2** 57, Ch D.

Exercise of power—

Effect—When appointed trusts constituted. *See* **Trust and trustee** (Constitution of trust—Exercise of special power of appointment).

Exercise by will—Foreign will. *See* **Conflict of laws** (Power of appointment—Special power—Exercise of power—Power given by English will—Exercise by Scottish will).

Exercise by will—Generally. *See* Exercise by will—Special power, *above*.

Generally. *See* Exercise of power—Special power, *above*.

Joint power—

Exercise with consent. **Churston Settled Estates, Re** [1954] **1** 725, Ch D.

Power to appoint by deed a life interest to a wife who should survive the appointor—

Irrevocable appointment by deed—Subsequent dissolution of marriage—Whether deed effective to confer life interest on former wife. **Slaughter's Estate, Re** [1945] **2** 214, Ch D.

Power to appoint limited interest in contemplation of marriage to any surviving wife—

Power exercised by irrevocable deed—Marriage dissolved on wife's petition—Death of appointor—Whether appointment effective. **Allan (decd), Re** [1954] **1** 646, CA.

Revocation. *See* Revocation—Special power of appointment, *above*.

Survivorship of power—

Construction—

Will—Power to trustees or assigns—Public Trustee. **Symm's Will Trusts, Re** [1936] **3** 236, Ch D.

Trustee—

Whether general power enables trustee to appoint himself. *See* **Trust and trustee** (Powers of trustee—Power to appoint to himself).

Uncertainty—

Collateral power—

Description of objects—Power conferred by testator's will to appoint residuary estate to 'any of my old friends'. **Gibbard (decd), Re** [1966] **1** 273, Ch D.

Discretion to select income beneficiaries. *See* **Settlement** (Power—Discretionary power—Discretion to make grants to 'dependants' and 'dependent relatives' of employees—Power coupled with a duty and power collateral).

Executors directed to pay to 'such friend or friends' as nominated by widow—Validity. **Coates (decd), Re** [1955] **1** 26, Ch D.

Power coupled with a duty and power collateral—

Ascertainment of objects—Impossibility of ascertaining all members of a class. **Sayer Trust, Re** [1956] **3** 600, Ch D.

Settlement—

Objects—Power of selection. *See* **Settlement** (Power—Discretionary power—Discretion over income of trust fund).

Unascertainable class of objects—

Intermediate power vested in trustees—Discretionary power to appoint to anyone in the world except specified class—Whether power invalid as being too wide. **Hay's Settlement Trusts, Re** [1981] **3** 786, Ch D.

Validity of power. **Gestetner, Re** [1953] **1** 1150, Ch D; **Gresham's Settlement, Re** [1956] **2** 193, Ch D.

Variation of settlement. *See* **Variation of Settlement (Matrimonial Causes)** (Power of appointment upon petitioner's second marriage).

Variation of trust by the court—

Exercise of power. *See* **Variation of trusts** (Benefit—Exercise of special power).

Will—

Exercise by. *See* Exercise by will, *above*.

POWER OF ATTORNEY

Abrogation of power—

Outbreak of war—

Donor of power in neutral territory and donee in British territory occupied by enemy—Validity of acts done by donee under power. **Hangkam Kwingtong Woo v Liu Lan Fong** [1951] **2** 567, PC.

Conflict of laws. *See* **Conflict of laws** (Power of attorney).

Debenture—

Company. *See* **Company** (Debenture—Power of attorney).

POWER OF ATTORNEY (cont)—
Enduring power of attorney—
  Administration of estates—
    Grant of administration—Effect of enduring powers of attorney on existing grants and on applications for new grants—Limitation to be included in grants—Enduring Powers of Attorney Act 1985—Non-Contentious Probate Rules 1954, rr 30, 33. **Practice Direction** [1986] **2** 41, Fam D.
  Court of Protection—
    Applications prior to registration—Enduring Powers of Attorney Act 1985. **Practice Direction** [1986] **2** 42, Ct of Protection.
  Creation—
    Capacity of donor—Mental capacity of donor when power created—Burden of proof when registration of power opposed—Whether burden of proof on attorney to establish donor's capacity if objectors producing evidence that donor lacked capacity—Enduring Powers of Attorney Act 1985, s 6(6). **W, Re** [2001] **4** 88, CA.
    Capacity of donor—Mental capacity when power executed—Donor at time of execution fully understanding nature and effect of power but incapable by reason of mental disorder of managing and administering property and affairs—Whether purported power of attorney creating a valid power—Whether power should be registered—Enduring Powers of Attorney Act 1985, s 6(5)(a). **K, Re** [1988] **1** 358, Ch D.
  Disposal of property—
    Attorney having power to make provision for needs of any person if donor might have been expected to do so—Testatrix executing enduring power of attorney which was subsequently registered—Attorneys making payment towards education of testatrix's grandson—Whether valid exercise of power of attorney—Whether education of child constituting 'need'—Enduring Powers of Attorney Act 1985, s 3(4). **Cameron (decd), Re** [1999] **2** 924, Ch D.
    Power to give directions with respect to 'disposal by the attorney of [donor's] property'—Whether court empowered to direct attorney to make gift to third party in recognition of moral obligation owed by donor—Enduring Powers of Attorney Act 1985, s 8(2)(b)(i). **R (enduring power of attorney), Re** [1990] **2** 893, Ch D.
  Extent of power—
    Whether enduring power of attorney entitling holder to conduct litigation or provide advocacy services—Courts and Legal Services Act 1990, s 28(2)(d). **Gregory v Turner** [2003] **2** 1114, CA.
  Form—
    Explanatory information and marginal notes—Necessity for inclusion—Enduring Powers of Attorney Act 1985, s 2(6)—Enduring Powers of Attorney (Prescribed Form) Regulations 1987, reg 2(1), (2). **Practice Direction** [1989] **2** 64, Ct of Protection.
    Instrument appointing more than one person as attorney not creating enduring power unless instrument specifying whether attorneys appointed to act either jointly or jointly and severally—Instrument appointing W or alternatively A, B and C jointly and severally—Whether valid enduring power of attorney—Mental Capacity Act 2005, Sch 4, para 20(1). **J (enduring power of attorney), Re** [2009] **2** 1051, Ct of Protection.
  Procedural requirements. See Enduring power of attorney—Form, *above.*
  Registration—
    Objection—Unsuitability of attorney—Hostility between attorney and relative—Whether attorney unsuitable—Whether hostility impeding proper administration of estate or causing distress to donor of power—Enduring Powers of Attorney Act 1985, s 6(5)(e). **F, Re** [2004] **3** 277, Ch D.
  Revocation—
    Donor executing power of attorney appointing two of her three daughters as attorneys—Donor executing new power appointing all three daughters as attorneys—Whether later power revoking earlier power—Enduring Powers of Attorney Act 1985. **E, Re** [2000] **3** 1004, Ch D.
Exercise for agent's own purposes—
  Ratification by principal of act of agent—
    Estoppel by silence and delay. **Imperial Bank of Canada v Begley** [1936] **2** 367, PC.
General power—
  Extent of power—
    Execution of verifying affidavit—Order for discovery with verifying affidavit—Affidavit sworn by attorney—Whether affidavit complying with requirements of order—Whether attorney entitled to swear verifying affidavit—Powers of Attorney Act 1971, s 7(1)(b). **Clauss v Pir** [1987] **2** 752, Ch D.
  Sale of land—
    Vendor and purchaser—Co-proprietors—Proprietors agreeing to sell land—Transfer signed by one co-proprietor on behalf of another co-proprietor under general power of attorney—Transfer expressly stating that co-proprietors sold as beneficial owners—Whether co-proprietors holding land as trustees—Whether donee of power of attorney executing transfer as trustee—Whether co-proprietor entitled to execute transfer under general power of attorney—Trustee Act 1925, s 25—Powers of Attorney Act 1971, ss 9, 10. **Walia v Michael Naughton Ltd** [1985] **3** 673, Ch D.
Lasting power of attorney—
  Validity—
    Benefit of others—Public Guardian asked to register instruments expressing donor's intention that attorney(s) use funds to benefit someone other than donor—Whether provisions valid—Whether conflict where beneficiary also attorney—Guidance—Mental Capacity Act 2005, ss 4(4), 12, 23(2). **Various Lasting Powers of Attorney, Re** [2020] **3** 879, COP.
Non est factum. See **Document** (Non est factum—Power of attorney).
Revocation—
  Power of attorney prepared and executed abroad—
    Power intended to operate in England—Whether power coupled with an interest—Whether revocable. **Sinfra Aktiengesellschaft v Sinfra Ltd** [1939] **2** 675, KBD.
Stamp duty. See **Stamp duty** (Letter or power of attorney).

POWER STATION
Installation of equipment in—
  Application of Building Regulations. See **Building** (Building regulations—Application—Construction of a building—Operation in power station).

POWERED HAND-TOOL

Use in building operations—
    Duty to fence. *See* **Building** (Building operations—Fencing of machinery—Dangerous machinery—Powered hand-tool).

POWERS OF TRUSTEE

Discretionary trusts—
    Isle of Man—
        Distinctions between trusts and powers. **Schmidt v Rosewood Trust Ltd** [2003] **3** 76, PC.

PRACTICE

Absence of party—
    Commercial Court—
        Applicant failing to appear—Application challenging jurisdiction—Whether jurisdiction to proceed—CPR 23.11. **CHEP Equipment Pooling BV v ITS Ltd** [2022] **4** 856, Comm Ct.
    Court of Appeal—
        Appeal from Upper Tribunal—Appellant failing to appear—Whether jurisdiction to proceed—CPR 1.1, 52.20(1)—Tribunal Procedure (Upper Tribunal) Rules 2008, SI 2008/2698, rr 8, 38. **Leave.EU Group Ltd v Information Comrs** [2022] **3** 959, CA.
    Setting aside judgment. *See* **Judgment** (Setting aside—Judgment after trial in absence of party).
Abuse of process—
    Commencement of proceedings. *See* **Pleading** (Striking out—Abuse of process of the court—Claim form).
    Dismissal of action. *See* **Action** (Dismissal—Abuse of process of court).
    Stay of proceedings—
        Court-martial. *See* **Court-martial** (Trial—Stay of proceedings—Abuse of process).
        Criminal proceedings. *See* **Criminal law** (Trial—Stay of proceedings—Abuse of process).
        Proceedings for disqualification of company director. *See* **Company** (Director—Disqualification—Stay of proceedings—Abuse of process).
    Striking out—
        County court practice. *See* **County court** (Practice—Striking out—Defence—Abuse of process of court).
        Employment tribunal. *See* **Employment tribunal** (Striking out—Abuse of process).
        Generally. *See* Striking out—Abuse of process, *below*.
Acknowledgment of service—
    Admiralty practice. *See* **Admiralty** (Practice—Form of writs and acknowledgments of service).
    Notice of intention to contest proceedings—
        Oral agreement extending time for service of defence—Oral agreement not confirmed in writing until after expiry of time limit for service of defence—Defendant allowing time for service of defence to expire without issuing summons to set aside writ—Whether defendant irrevocably submitting to jurisdiction and waiving any irregularity in writ—Whether service of writ should be set aside—RSC Ord 3, r 5, Ord 12, r 8(1)(7). **Lawson v Midland Travellers Ltd** [1993] **1** 989, CA.
        Summons by defendant applying for order setting aside writ alleging court lacked jurisdiction—Non-compliance with rules for application—Failure to state 'grounds' of application in summons—Failure to serve supporting affidavit with summons—Failure to apply within prescribed time limit for extension of time for serving affidavit—Whether summons a nullity—Whether acknowledgment of service amounting to submission to jurisdiction—Whether court having discretion to treat failure to comply with rules as irregularities and to allow summons to proceed—Whether requirement of 'application to court' within prescribed period requiring only issue of summons within prescribed period—RSC Ord 2, r 1(1), (2), Ord 12, r 8(1), (2). **Carmel Exporters (Sales) Ltd v Sea-Land Services Inc** [1981] **1** 984, QBD.
Use of post—
    Chancery Division. *See* Chancery Division—Applications by post or telephone, *below*.
Action for annulment—
    Generally. *See* **European Union** (Action for annulment).
    Procedure. *See* **European Union** (Procedure—Action for annulment).
Actuarial evidence—
    Admissibility—
        Non-medical evidence. *See* Evidence—Expert evidence—Admissibility—Non-medical evidence—Actuarial evidence, *below*.
Adding defendant—
    Generally. *See* Parties—Adding defendant, *below*.
    Leave to add party—
        Writ issued before expiration of limitation period—Leave sought after expiration. *See* **Limitation of action** (Fatal accident—Material facts of decisive character unknown to deceased—Application for leave to join new defendant to action).
Adding persons as parties. *See* Parties—Adding persons as parties, *below*.
Adding plaintiff. *See* Parties—Adding plaintiff, *below*.
Address for service—
    Serviceman's address—
        Maintenance. *See* **Husband and wife** (Maintenance—Address—Husband's address for service).
Adjournment—
    Closure order application—
        Jurisdiction of magistrates. *See* **Magistrates** (Adjournment—Jurisdiction—Closure order).
    Adjournment of motions. *See* Motion—Adjournment, *below*.
    Adjournment of proceedings—
        Appeal in similar case being heard in superior court—
            Special circumstances—Variation of trusts of settlement—Settlor in poor health. **Yates' Settlement Trusts, Re** [1954] **1** 619, CA.
        Bankruptcy proceedings. *See* **Bankruptcy** (Practice—Adjournment of bankruptcy proceedings).
        Chambers proceedings. *See* Chambers proceedings—Adjournment to judge, *below*.
        Committal proceedings. *See* **Contempt of court** (Committal—Application—Adjournment).

PRACTICE (cont)—
  Adjournment of proceedings (cont)—
    Dealing with cases justly—
      Defendant applying for order setting aside interlocutory judgments before orders giving effect to judgments entered—Witness for defendant becoming seriously ill—Defendant standing down legal team and other witnesses, failing to lodge skeleton argument and seeking adjournment—Matters relevant to exercise of court's discretion to adjourn—CPR 1.1. **Albon (t/a NA Carriage Co) v Naza Motor Trading Sdn Bhd (No 5)** [2008] 1 995, Ch D; [2008] **2 Comm** 280, Ch D.
    Inherent power of court to adjourn proceedings—
      Adjournment for stated time—Direction under RSC Ord 55, r 5A. **Hinckley & South Leicestershire Permanent Building Society v Freeman** [1940] **4** 212, Ch D.
      Mortgagee's claim for possession—Arrears of instalments paid, but mortgagor unable to repay loan within reasonable period—RSC Ord 55, r 5A. **Robertson v Cilia** [1956] **3** 651, Ch D.
      Mortgagee's claim for possession—Principal sum not repayable by instalments. **Birmingham Citizens Permanent Building Society v Caunt** [1962] **1** 163, Ch D; **Braithwaite v Winwood** [1960] **3** 642, Ch D.
  Adjournment of summons—
    Chancery Division. *See* Summons—Chancery Division—Adjournment of summons, *below.*
    Masters' summonses—
      Generally. *See* Summons—Masters' summonses—Adjournment, *below.*
  Administration of deceased's estate—
    Generally. *See* **Administration of estates** (Practice).
    Grant of administration—
      Intestacy. *See* **Intestacy** (Grant of administration—Practice).
  Administration order—
    Company. *See* **Company** (Administration order).
  Administrative Court—
    Application for permission for judicial review—
      Costs—CPR 44.13. **Practice Note** [2004] **2** 994, QBD.
    Change of title to. *See* Crown Office list—Change of title to Administrative Court, *below.*
    Health care professionals—
      Appeals against decisions of Professional Conduct Committees—National Health Service Reform and Health Care Professions Act 2002. **Practice Statement** [2004] **1** 322, QBD.
    Late claim for asylum—
      Refusal of support—Interim relief—Extension of time for acknowledgment of service—Nationality, Immigration and Asylum Act 2002, s 55. **Practice Statement** [2004] **1** 923, QBD.
    Non-derogating control orders—
      Supervisory hearing—Subsequent supervisory hearings—Whether judge deciding issues arising on supervisory hearing disqualified from adjudicating in subsequent proceedings—Status of findings made by judge in supervisory hearing in subsequent proceedings—Prevention of Terrorism Act 2005, s 3(10). **Secretary of State for the Home Dept v AF (No 2)** [2008] **2** 67, QBD.
    Procedure for challenging decisions of Immigration Appeal Tribunal—
      Nationality Immigration and Asylum Act 2002. **Practice Statement** [2004] **1** 322, QBD.
    Procedure for urgent applications—
      Listing policy. **Practice Statement** [2002] **1** 633, Admin Ct.
    Proceeds of crime—
      Applications—Proceeds of Crime Act 2002. **Practice Statement** [2004] **1** 322, QBD.
  Admiralty—
    Assessors—
      Remuneration of nautical and other assessors. **Practice Direction (Remuneration of nautical and other assessors)** [2007] **2 Comm** 364, QBD.
  Admiralty. *See* **Admiralty** (Practice).
  Admiralty and Commercial Court Registry—
    Administrative arrangements—
      Court file—Issue of process—Filing of documents—Interlocutory applications—Orders, decrees and judgments—Judgment by default—Applications to masters—Listing—Setting down for trial—RSC Ord 35, r 10—RSC (Amendment) 1987. **Practice Note** [1987] **3** 616, QBD.
      Supply of documents from court records—Arbitration claim form—Whether successful claimant seeking to enforce award 'party to proceedings'—Whether claimant permitted to search as 'any other person'—Civil Procedure Rules, r 5.4. **Advance Specialist Treatment Engineering Ltd v Cleveland Structural Engineering (Hong Kong) Ltd** [2000] **2 Comm** 189, QBD.
    Postal facilities, use of. *See* Post—Use of postal facilities—Queen's Bench Division—Admiralty Registry, *below.*
    Setting down for trial—
      Time for setting down—Documents to be lodged—Time for delivery of skeleton arguments—RSC Ord 34, r 3(1)—Guide to Commercial Court Practice, para 6.5, App III, para (7), App V, para 5. **Practice Direction** [1998] **2** 672, QBD.
  Admission. *See* **Admission**.
  Adoption—
    Application—
      Generally. *See* **Adoption** (Application).
    Generally. *See* **Adoption** (Practice).
    Order. *See* **Adoption** (Order).
  Affidavit—
    Chambers proceedings—
      Affidavit evidence. *See* Chambers proceedings—Affidavit evidence, *below.*
    Court of Appeal and High Court—
      Marking—Binding—Sequence—Pagination—Copies—Bundles of documents generally—Effect of failure to comply with rules—RSC Ord 41. **Practice Direction** [1995] **2** 511, QBD; **Practice Note** [1983] **3** 33, CA.
    Court of Protection. *See* **Mental health** (Court of Protection—Practice—Evidence—Evidence by affidavit).

PRACTICE (cont)—
Affidavit (cont)—
    Generally. *See* **Affidavit**.
    Restrictive Practices Court. *See* **Restrictive trade practices** (Court—Evidence—Affidavits, exhibits, documents).
Affiliation proceedings—
    Appeal—
        Generally. *See* **Affiliation** (Affiliation order—Appeal).
    Application for order. *See* **Affiliation** (Application for order).
Agreed statement of facts—
    Admiralty practice. *See* **Admiralty** (Practice—Agreed statement of facts).
Alternative claims against two defendants—
    Election—
        Leave to sign judgment against one defendant—Whether bar to proceedings against other. **Christopher (C) (Hove) Ltd v Williams** [1936] **3** 68, CA.
Alternative dispute resolution—
    Commercial Court. *See* **Commercial Court** (Practice—Alternative dispute resolution).
Amendment—
    Indorsement on writ. *See* **Writ** (Indorsement).
    Judgment or order—
        Correction of accidental slip or omission. *See* **Judgment** (Order—Correction—Accidental slip or omission).
    Parties—
        Change of name of limited company after institution of proceedings. **Practice Direction** [1965] **1** 43, QBD.
    Pleading. *See* **Pleading** (Amendment).
    Statement of claim—
        Leave to amend. *See* **Statement of case** (Leave to amend).
    Writ—
        Generally. *See* **Writ** (Amendment).
Ancillary relief—
    Family Division. *See* Family Division—Ancillary relief, *below*.
    Family proceedings. *See* Family proceedings—Ancillary relief, *below*.
Answer—
    Divorce petition, to. *See* **Divorce** (Practice—Answer).
Anton Piller order—
    Disclosure. *See* **Disclosure and inspection of documents** (Search order).
    Generally. *See* Pre-trial or post-judgment relief—Search order, *below*.
Appeal—
    Absence of defendant. *See* **Criminal law** (Appeal—Leave to appeal—Application—Practice).
    Affiliation proceedings. *See* **Affiliation** (Affiliation order—Appeal).
    Anton Piller order—
        Ex parte refusal of order. *See* Pre-trial or post-judgment relief—Search order—Interlocutory motion—Ex parte application—Refusal—Appeal, *below*.
    Appeal from district judge—
        Queen's Bench Division matters—Appeals from district judges on circuits—Documents—Bundle of papers to be lodged in advance of hearing—Bundle to be paged and indexed—Notes of appeal—Pleadings—Affidavits—Order made in action—Notes of judge's reasons—Bundle to be agreed—Time of lodging bundle—Documents not lodged not be adduced in evidence or relied on without leave of judge—Skeleton argument or chronology in complex cases. **Practice Note** [1991] **1** 1056, QBD.
    Appeal from findings of fact—
        Approach to be taken by appellate court to conclusions of primary fact reached by trial judge. **Bahamasair Holdings Ltd v Messier Dowty Inc** [2019] **1** 285, PC.
        Review or rehearing—Guidance—CPR 52.11. **Assicurazioni Generali SpA v Arab Insurance Group (BSC)** [2003] **1 Comm** 140, CA.
    Appeal from master—
        Judge in chambers, to. *See* Chambers proceedings—Appeal from master, *below*.
    Appeal to Court of Appeal—
        Change of law after trial and before appeal—Duty of Court of Appeal—RSC Ord 58, rr 1, 4. **New Brunswick Rly Co v British and French Trust Corp Ltd** [1938] **4** 747, HL.
        Criminal cases. *See* **Criminal law** (Court of Appeal).
        Dismissal of appeal. *See* **Court of Appeal** (Appeal—Dismissal).
        Estimate of length of hearing. *See* **Court of Appeal** (Appeal—Estimate of length of hearing).
        Expedited hearing of appeal. *See* **Court of Appeal** (Appeal—Expedited appeal).
        Generally. *See* **Court of Appeal** (Practice).
        Powers of the court—Incompetent proceedings—Objection taken by court itself—Appeal from county court—Fact found upon sufficient evidence. **Westminster Bank Ltd v Edwards** [1942] **1** 470, HL.
        Presentation of appeal—Civil Division. *See* **Court of Appeal** (Practice—Civil Division—Presentation of appeals).
    Arbitration award. *See* **Arbitration** (Award—Appeal).
    Asylum and immigration. *See* **Immigration** (Practice—Asylum and Immigration Tribunal granting permission to appeal to Court of Appeal).
    Bankruptcy—
        Generally. *See* **Bankruptcy** (Appeal).
    Case stated. *See* **Case stated**.
    Certification of trade union as independent—
        Procedure on appeal. *See* **Trade union** (Certification as independent trade union—Appeal against issue of certificate—Procedure on appeal).

PRACTICE (cont)—
  Appeal (cont)—
    Conditions of appeal—
      Payment into court—Appellant ordered to make payment into court of judgment sum as condition of appeal—Whether condition stifling appeal—Whether and to what extent access to funds from third party to be taken into account—CPR 52.9. **Goldtrail Travel Ltd (in liq) v Onur Air Taimacilik AS** [2018] **1** 721, SC.
    Costs. *See* **Costs** (Appeal).
    Court of Appeal, to. *See* Appeal—Appeal to Court of Appeal, *above*.
    Court of Ecclesiastical Causes Reserved. *See* **Ecclesiastical law** (Court of Ecclesiastical Causes Reserved).
    Criminal cases—
      Court of Appeal. *See* **Criminal law** (Court of Appeal).
      Generally. *See* **Criminal law** (Appeal).
      Legal aid. *See* **Legal aid** (Criminal cases—Practice—Appeal).
    Death of party to appeal—
      House of Lords. *See* **House of Lords** (Parties to appeal—Death of party).
    Divorce—
      Generally. *See* **Divorce** (Appeal).
    Ecclesiastical courts—
      Faculty proceedings. *See* **Ecclesiastical law** (Faculty—Appeal).
    Employment Appeal Tribunal. *See* **Employment Appeal Tribunal** (Practice—Appeals).
    Employment Tribunal, from. *See* **Employment tribunal** (Appeal from tribunal).
    Family Division—
      Generally. *See* **Family Division** (Appeal).
    Filing of skeleton arguments and bundle of authorities—
      Guidance—CPR PD 52, paras 5.6, 5.7, 5.8, 7.6, 7.7, 15.11A. **Harvey Shopfitters Ltd v ADI Ltd** [2004] **2** 982, CA.
      Guidance—CPR PD 52, paras 5.9, 7.7, 15.11. **Haggis v DPP** [2004] **2** 382n, QBD.
    House of Lords. *See* **House of Lords** (Appeal).
    Immigration appeal. *See* **Immigration** (Appeal).
    Industrial tribunal, from—
      Generally. *See* **Employment tribunal** (Appeal from tribunal).
    Insolvency proceedings—
      Generally. *See* **Insolvency** (Appeal).
      Hearing on Northern or North Eastern Circuits. *See* Chancery Division—Northern Area—Appeals, *below*.
    Leave to appeal—
      Arbitration award. *See* **Arbitration** (Award—Leave to appeal against award).
      County court. *See* **County court** (Appeal—Leave).
      Court of Appeal. *See* **Court of Appeal** (Leave to appeal).
      Criminal proceedings. *See* **Criminal law** (Appeal—Leave to appeal—Practice).
      House of Lords. *See* **House of Lords** (Leave to appeal).
      Interlocutory proceedings. *See* **Court of Appeal** (Interlocutory appeal—Leave to appeal).
      Privy Council. *See* **Privy Council** (Leave to appeal).
    Mental health review tribunal—
      Appeal against decision of tribunal. *See* **Mental health** (Mental health review tribunal—Decision).
    New provisions governing civil appeals in private law matters—
      Explanation and guidance—Access to Justice Act 1999—Access to Justice Act 1999 (Destination of Appeals) Order 2000. **Tanfern Ltd v Cameron-MacDonald** [2000] **2** 801, CA.
      Refusal by High Court judge to grant extension of time to appeal from decision of lower court—Whether refusal appealable to Court of Appeal—Access to Justice Act 1999, s 54(4). **Foenander v Bond Lewis & Co** [2001] **2** 1019, CA.
    New provisions on second appeals from county court or High Court—
      Scope and effect—Access to Justice Act 1999, ss 54, 55—CPR Pt 52. **Clark (Inspector of Taxes) v Perks** [2000] **4** 1, CA.
    New provisions relating to appeals in civil proceedings—
      Dismissal on paper of applications for permission to appeal—Provision of transcripts at public expense to unrepresented appellants—Guidance—CPR Pt 52, Practice Direction. **Hyams v Plender** [2001] **2** 179, CA.
    Northern Area—
      Chancery Division practice. *See* Chancery Division—Northern Area—Appeals, *below*.
    Notice of appeal—
      Court of Appeal. *See* **Court of Appeal** (Notice of appeal).
    Pending appeal—
      No live issue—Publicly funded litigation—Event occurring which disposes of issue between parties—Duty of counsel and solicitors—Duty to ensure appeal is withdrawn or to seek directions. **Ainsbury v Millington** [1987] **1** 929, HL.
    Permission to appeal—
      Jurisdiction—Appeal from Upper Tribunal—Upper Tribunal refusing permission to appeal—Upper Tribunal refusing to review decision to refuse permission to appeal—Whether Court of Appeal having jurisdiction to grant permission to appeal against Upper Tribunal's refusal to review decision -Tribunals, Courts and Enforcement Act 2007, ss 10, 13. **Samuda v Secretary of State for Work and Pensions** [2014] **3** 201, CA.
    Power of appeal court to impose conditions on bringing of appeal where there was 'compelling reason' to do so—
      Whether availability to successful party of normal enforcement provisions in itself fatal to application for payment of security in respect of judgment sum—CPR 52.9. **Bell Electric Ltd v Aweco Appliance Systems GmbH & Co KG** [2003] **1** 344, CA.
    Preparatory hearing. *See* **Criminal law** (Trial—Preparatory hearing—Purposes of preparatory hearing).
    Privy Council—
      Leave to appeal. *See* **Privy Council** (Leave to appeal).

PRACTICE (cont)—
  Appeal (cont)—
    Privy Council (cont)—
      Statement of reasons. *See* **Privy Council** (Reasons for decision—Statement of reasons—Need for court from which appeal arises to state reasons for decision).
    Rates. *See* **Rates** (Appeal).
    Relisting after dismissal—
      Appeal dismissed by consent—Dismissal effected formally in listing office without reference to or approval of judge or other judicial officer—Appeal with respect to claim for repayment of tax—Revenue making repayment of tax—Appellants' solicitor consenting to dismissal of appeal without informing appellants of consequences of dismissal—Revenue claiming repayment made in error and making assessment for recovery of repayment—Appellants applying for relisting of appeal—Whether appellants' solicitor having authority to consent to dismissal of appeal—Whether parties entering into contract to abandon appeal—Whether appeal should be relisted. **Sheppard v IRC** [1992] **3** 58, Ch D.
    Reopening of appeal—
      Generally. *See* **Appeal** (Reopening of appeal).
      Jurisdiction of High Court. *See* **High Court** (Jurisdiction—Application to reopen appeal).
    Respondent's notice. *See* **Court of Appeal** (Respondent's notice).
    Search order—
      Ex parte refusal of order. *See* Pre-trial or post-judgment relief—Search order—Interlocutory motion—Ex parte application—Refusal—Appeal, *below.*
    Security for costs. *See* **Costs** (Security for costs—Appeal).
    Summary judgment. *See* Summary judgment—Appeal, *below.*
    Time for appeal—
      Court of Appeal. *See* **Court of Appeal** (Time for appeal).
    Withdrawal of appeal—
      Appeal from order of master—Appeal not to be withdrawn without leave of court—Application to judge necessary—Distinction between withdrawal of appeal and dismissal of appeal by consent. **Buckbod Investments Ltd v Nana-Otchere** [1985] **1** 283, Ch D.
  Appearance—
    Appearance after judgment—
      Fraud—Ex parte application for leave to enter—Defendant's claim based on allegation of fraud. **Stern v Friedmann** [1953] **2** 565, Ch D.
    Appearance by post—
      Appearance by post by defendants personally or by defendants' solicitors—London writs—District registry writs—Rules of the Supreme Court (No 1) 1960 (SI 1960 No 545). **Practice Note** [1960] **2** 109, QBD.
    Appearance not entered within prescribed time—
      Application for leave to enter judgment in default—Judgment entered notwithstanding defendant's appearance at hearing of application. **Redditch Benefit Building Society v Roberts** [1940] **1** 342, CA.
    Appearance on behalf of another—
      Application for authority to enter appearance on behalf of another person sui juris—Whether court having power to grant application. **Llewellyn v Carrickford** [1970] **2** 24, Ch D.
    Appearance out of time—
      Probate action—Appearance refused by Central Office after certificate of non-appearance issued—Practice of Central Office—RSC Ord 12 r 22. **Thomas, Re** [1940] **4** 145, CA.
    Authority to enter appearance—
      Whether conflict of interests of person authorised jeopardising authority. *See* **Solicitor** (Duty—Conflict of interest—Entry of appearance).
    Conditional appearance—
      Withdrawal. *See* Appearance—Withdrawal of appearance—Conditional appearance, *below.*
    Place for entering appearance—
      Writ issued in district registry against company—Company's head office and registered office in London, and factory in district of district registry—Appearance in London—RSC Ord 12, rr 4, 5. **Davies v British Geon Ltd** [1956] **3** 389, CA.
    Privy Council—
      Withdrawal of appearance. *See* **Privy Council** (Appearance—Withdrawal of appearance).
    Time limit for entry of appearance—
      Effect of disruption of postal deliveries on. *See* Post—Postal delay—Time limited for entry of appearance, *below.*
    Unconditional appearance by defendant—
      Right to plead that plaintiff has no cause of action—RSC Ord 25, r 2. **Wilkinson v Barking Corp** [1948] **1** 564, CA.
    Video link, by—
      Prisoner. *See* **Prison** (Prisoner—Powers of transfer—Transfer of prisoners for other judicial purposes).
    Withdrawal of appearance—
      Conditional appearance—Foreign company defendants—Defendants competently advised—Application by defendants to set aside writ refused—Appearance not entered by mistake—Defendants out of jurisdiction not allowed to resile from election made by entry of conditional appearance—Leave to withdraw appearance refusal—RSC Ord 21, r 1. **Somportex Ltd v Philadelphia Chewing Gum Corp** [1968] **3** 26, CA.
      Jurisdiction—Appearance entered by mistake—Unconditional appearance entered by party—Fact that limitation period had expired when party added to action overlooked—Whether jurisdiction to give leave to withdraw appearance and substitute conditional appearance—Whether jurisdiction limited to cases of mistakes of a particular kind in entering appearance—Whether if jurisdiction existed discretion properly exercised by allowing withdrawal of appearance and substitution of conditional appearance—RSC Ord 21, r 1. **Firth v John Mowlem & Co Ltd** [1978] **3** 331, CA.

PRACTICE (cont)—

Application for directions—
  Right to a fair and public hearing—
    Trustees of charity applying in private for directions relating to pending proceedings—Whether court entitled to pronounce judgment in private—Human Rights Act 1998, Sch 1, Pt I, art 6. **Trusts of X Charity, Re** [2003] **3** 860, Ch D.
Application for financial provision—
  Divorce. *See* **Divorce** (Financial provision—Application).
Application for leave to bring an action against a hospital board—
  Leave granted by a judge—
    Appeal against grant of leave—Jurisdiction of Court of Appeal to hear appeal—Mental Treatment Act 1930, s 16(2)—RSC Ord 54, r 23. **Shoesmith v Lancashire Mental Hospitals Board (Re an intended action)** [1938] **3** 186, CA.
Application of High Court practice—
  Case not expressly provided for—
    High Court practice applicable to matters of principle not expressly provided for in county court rules—Judgement or order—Finality—Judge setting aside order on terms to be complied with within specified time limit—Failure to comply with time limit—Judge having no power under county court rules to extend time limit after expiry—Whether provisions of Supreme Court rules applicable so as to give jurisdiction to extend time—County Courts Act 1959, ss 98, 103—RSC Ord 3, r 5(1)—CCR Ord 13, r(1). **R v Bloomsbury and Marylebone County Court, ex p Villerwest Ltd** [1976] **1** 897, CA.
Application relating to chambers proceedings. *See* Chambers proceedings—Applications, *below.*
Application to search for, inspect and copy documents—
  Access to documents on court file—
    Documents part of proceedings heard in private and in public—Court making order that non-parties might not obtain documents on court file—Non-party to proceedings applying for permission to have copies of consent order, defence and counterclaim and defendant's witness statement—Whether access to documents should be granted—CPR 5.4C. **ABC Ltd v Y** [2011] **4** 113, Ch D.
  Documents for which the court's permission required—
    Application by non-party newspaper publisher to have access to witness statements in advance of trial—Witness statements already referred to during pre-trial hearing—Whether court having power to grant non-party access to statements—CPR 5.4C(2), 32.12(2)(c), 32.13. **Blue v Ashley** [2018] **2** 284, QBD.
    Application by non-party to inspect documents on court file—Underlying proceedings began by claim form and subsequently stayed to arbitration—Whether appropriate to disclose documents to non-party to arbitration agreement—CPR 5.4. **Glidepath BV v Thompson** [2005] **2 Comm** 833, QBD.
    Application to inspect and copy documents in court record—Case having ended—Whether court capable of giving permission—CPR 5.4(5)(b). **Guardian Newspapers Ltd, Re** [2005] **3** 155, Ch D.
    Identification of documents sought—Criteria for allowing access—CPR 5.4(2)(c). **Dian AO v Davis Frankel & Mead (a firm)** [2005] **1 Comm** 482, QBD; [2005] **1** 1074, QBD.
Applications relating to children—
  Family Division. *See* **Child** (Practice—Matrimonial causes).
Apportionment of costs. *See* **Costs** (Apportionment).
Arbitration. *See* **Arbitration** (Practice).
Assessment of case. *See* Summons for directions—Assessment of case, *below.*
Assessor—
  Admiralty proceedings. *See* **Admiralty** (Practice—Assessors).
  Generally. *See* **Assessor**.
Associate—
  Certificate of associate—
    Postal despatch of copy certificate with pleadings. **Practice Direction** [1964] **2** 955, QBD.
Asylum and immigration—
  Appeal. *See* **Immigration** (Practice—Asylum and Immigration Tribunal granting permission to appeal to Court of Appeal).
Audience—
  Right of audience—
    High Court of Justice—Defendant a limited company—Right of managing director to appear in court on behalf of the company—RSC Ord 4, r 2. **Frinton and Walton UDC v Walton and District Sand and Mineral Co Ltd** [1938] **1** 649, Ch D.
    High Court of Justice—Solicitor—Formal and unopposed proceedings—Statement in open court in settlement of claim in defamation proceedings—Defendant seeking leave for solicitor to read agreed statement—Whether court having discretion to grant leave. **Abse v Smith** [1986] **1** 350, CA.
    Supreme Court—Solicitor—Formal and unopposed proceedings—Circumstances in which solicitor may represent his client in open court. **Practice Direction** [1986] **2** 226, SC Taxing Office.
Automatic directions—
  Striking out—
    County court practice. *See* **County court** (Practice—Striking out—Automatic directions).
Bankers' books—
  Evidence—
    Civil proceedings. *See* **Evidence** (Bankers' books).
    Criminal proceedings. *See* **Criminal evidence** (Bankers' books).
Bankruptcy—
  Generally. *See* **Bankruptcy** (Practice).
  Petition. *See* **Bankruptcy** (Petition).
Barrister—
  Appearance in court on own behalf. *See* **Counsel** (Appearance—Appearance in court on own behalf—Practice).
Birmingham Mercantile List. *See* Commercial cases—Midland and Oxford Circuit—Hearing of cases of commercial or business character—Birmingham Mercantile List, *below.*

PRACTICE (cont)—
  Blood tests—
    Procedure—
      Tests to determine paternity. *See* **Paternity** (Blood test—Procedure).
  Bristol—
    Commercial cases. *See* Commercial cases—Bristol, *below.*
  Capacity of parties. *See* Parties—Capacity, *below.*
  Cardiff—
    Mercantile lists. *See* Queen's Bench Division—Mercantile lists—Cardiff and Chester, *below.*
    Recorder—
      Mode of address. *See* **Judge** (Mode of address—Recorder).
  Case management—
    Civil proceedings. *See* Civil litigation—Case management, *below.*
    Criminal proceedings. *See* Criminal proceedings—Case management, *below.*
    Disclosure—
      Protocol on disclosure. **R v K** [2006] **2** 552n, CA.
    Technology and Construction Court. *See* Technology and Construction Court—Case management, *below.*
  Case management. *See* Civil litigation—Case management, *below.*
  Case stated—
    Generally. *See* **Case stated.**
    Income tax. *See* **Income tax** (Case stated).
  Certificate of associate. *See* Associate—Certificate of associate, *above.*
  Certiorari—
    Court of Appeal hearing motion. *See* **Court of Appeal** (Certiorari—Practice).
    Generally. *See* **Certiorari.**
  Chambers proceedings—
    Adjournment to judge—
      Chancery Division—Generally. *See* Chancery Division—Chambers proceedings—Adjournment to judge, *below.*
      Originating summons—Discretion of master to adjourn summons unheard or to hear it first—Parties informing master that whatever his decision adjournment to judge would be sought—Summons raising difficult point of law—Whether master should hear summons before adjourning it to judge—RSC Ord 32, r 14(1), (4). **Beaumont (decd), Re** [1980] **1** 266, Ch D.
      Right to adjournment—Right of any party to have adjournment to the judge in person—Party to summons applying to have summons adjourned to judge—Master refusing because party not a party to the action—Whether 'party' means party to action or party to summons—RSC Ord 32, r 14. **Gawthrop v Boulton** [1978] **3** 615, Ch D.
    Administrative arrangements—
      Chancery Division. *See* Chancery Division—Administrative arrangements—Chancery chambers, *below.*
    Affidavit evidence—
      Limitation on time for swearing further affidavits—Date of next hearing. **Practice Direction** [1970] **1** 11, Ch D.
      Service of copy affidavit—Time for service—Consideration whether time needed to answer—RSC Ord 28, r 3(3). **Practice Direction** [1970] **1** 11, Ch D.
    Appeal from master—
      Appeal to judge in chambers—Procedure—RSC Ord 58, r 1. **Practice Direction** [1983] **1** 131, Ch D.
      Grounds of appeal not required in notice of appeal. **Practice Direction** [1984] **1** 720, Ch D.
      Index of practice directions relating to. *See* Chancery Division—Practice direction, *below.*
    Applications—
      Powers of principal clerks—Ex parte applications—RSC Ord 12, r 7, Ord 15, r 7, Ord 48, r 1, Ord 49, rr 1, 2, Ord 65, r 4. **Practice Direction** [1974] **2** 211, CA.
      Summons—Date of hearing—Hearing 'on a day to be fixed'—Summons issued by landlord for interim rent—Whether summons required to specify return day—Whether summons issued for day and time to be fixed invalid—Whether summons must be served promptly—RSC Ord 32, r 3. **Coates Bros plc v General Accident Life Assurance Ltd** [1991] **3** 929, Ch D.
    Communications by post or telephone—
      Chancery Division—Classes of business which may be transacted without personal attendance. **Practice Direction** [1977] **2** 173, Ch D.
      Chancery Division—Generally. *See* Chancery Division—Applications by post or telephone, *below.*
    Companies Court. *See* Companies Court—Chambers, *below.*
    Costs—
      Assessment. *See* **Costs** (Assessment—Assessment in chambers).
    Family proceedings. *See* **Family proceedings** (Chambers hearings).
    Judgment—
      Chancery Division. *See* Chancery Division—Chambers proceedings—Judgment, *below.*
    Masters' appointments—
      Adjournment—Vacation of appointment other than where application settled. **Practice Direction** [1988] **3** 1085, Ch D.
    Master's powers—
      Monetary limit—Increase of limit. **Practice Direction** [1983] **1** 131, Ch D.
      Monetary limit—Limit for exercise of powers increased to £15,000 in certain cases—New limit applying to appointment of a trustee where a trustee being superseded without his consent, to approval of compromise on behalf of person under disability and to payment or transfer of funds out of court—Application of limit to payment or transfer of funds out of court. **Practice Direction** [1977] **3** 121, Ch D.
      Orders which may be made by Chancery masters—RSC (Chancery Provisions) 1954 (SI 1954 No 1728), r 7—RSC Ord 55, r 15. **Practice Note** [1955] **1** 913, Ch D; [1960] **3** 497, Ch D.
      Orders which may be made by Chancery masters—RSC Ord 32, r 14. **Practice Direction** [1970] **1** 1183, Ch D; [1971] **2** 215, Ch D; [1975] **1** 255, Ch D; [1975] **1** 640, Ch D; [1976] **2** 610, Ch D.

PRACTICE (cont)—
  Chambers proceedings (cont)—
    Master's powers (cont)—
      Orders which may not be made by Chancery masters—Exceptions—Land Registration Act
      1925—Landlord and Tenant Act 1927—Landlord and Tenant Act 1954, ss 24a, 38(4)—Variation of
      Trusts Act 1958, s 1(1)—Leasehold Reform Act 1967, s 19—Law of Property Act 1969, ss 21,
      25—Land Charges Act 1972—Solicitors Act 1974, Sch 1, Pt II, paras 10, 11—Inheritance (Provision
      for Family and Dependants) Act 1975—Administration of Justice Act 1985, s 48—RSC Ord 32,
      r 14(1)(i), Ord 104, r 2(1). **Practice Direction** [1990] **1** 255, Ch D.
    Masters' summonses—
      Advance hearing—Cases ready for hearing before return date—Procedure. **Practice Direction**
      [1975] **2** 1136, Ch D.
      Queen's Bench Division—Adjournment—Restoration—Vacation of appointments. **Practice Direction**
      [1979] **3** 222, QBD.
      Queen's Bench Division—Return dates—Expedition—New arrangements. **Practice Direction**
      [1977] **3** 943, QBD; [1979] **3** 185, QBD.
    Orders—
      Master's orders to be made in master's name only—Order under judge's name only if made by
      judge. **Practice Direction** [1975] **1** 576, Ch D.
    Party acting in person—
      Right to assistance—Right of friend to assist by attendance, note-taking and advice—Litigant in
      person making chambers application in family proceedings—Judge refusing applicant
      permission to act as litigant's McKenzie friend—Whether judge could refuse litigant's request for
      assistance of McKenzie friend—Whether judge ought to give reasons for refusing such a request.
      R v Bow County Court, ex p Pelling [1999] **2** 582, QBD; [1999] **4** 751, CA.
    Publication—
      Ward of court. *See* **Ward of court** (Publication of proceedings).
    Queen's Bench Division—
      Chambers applications and appeals—Inter partes applications and appeals and ex parte
      applications—Listing—General list—Special appointments—Procedure—Papers for perusal by
      judge—Affidavits in support of ex parte applications—RSC Ord 29, r 1. **Practice Note**
      [1983] **1** 1119, QBD.
      Chambers applications and appeals—Inter partes applications and appeals—Listing—General
      list—Chambers appeals list—Special appointments—Estimate of length of hearing—Papers for
      perusal by judge—Skeleton argument or chronology. **Practice Note** [1989] **1** 1120, QBD.
      Chambers applications and appeals—Inter partes applications and appeals—Listing—General
      list—Chambers warned list—Estimate of length of hearing—Papers for perusal by
      judge—Skeleton argument or chronology. **Practice Note** [1996] **4** 575, QBD.
      Chambers applications and appeals—Inter partes applications and appeals—Listing—General
      list—Special appointments—Procedure—Papers for perusal by judge—Affidavits. **Practice Note**
      [1993] **3** 846, QBD.
      Chambers applications—Hearing before judge in chambers—Sittings in chambers outside London
      wherever High Court sittings held—Issue of notice of appeal or summons in district
      registry—Applications for bail. **Practice Note** [1976] **1** 736, QBD.
      Chambers applications—Hearing before judges in chambers—Sittings in chambers at trial centres
      outside London. **Practice Direction** [1972] **1** 286, QBD; [1973] **1** 25, QBD.
      Lists—Application to judge in chambers estimated to last more than 30 minutes—Special
      appointment. **Practice Direction** [1965] **2** 28, QBD.
      Lists—Applications to judge in chambers to be published in daily cause list—Duration of hearing to
      be estimated and indorsed on filed copy—Special appointment for applications estimated to last
      more than 45 minutes. **Practice Direction** [1959] **3** 97, QBD.
      Report of proceedings—Judge permitting directions made in chambers to be released to press but
      ordering parties and their advisers not to make any comments to media—Whether judge right to
      do so. **Hodgson v Imperial Tobacco Ltd** [1998] **2** 673, CA.
      Report of proceedings—Power of court to prohibit publication of information relating to
      proceedings—Applications to strike out action and for judgment in default of defence—Order
      granting applications—Power to prohibit publication of report of proceedings—Administration of
      Justice Act 1960, s 12(1)(e)(2). **Wallersteiner v Moir** [1974] **3** 217, CA.
      Termination of proceedings—Notification. **Practice Direction** [1970] **1** 671, Ch D.
    Setting down for trial—
      Delay—Failure to set case down for trial by date specified in order—Effect—Review by master.
      Practice Direction [1975] **1** 576, Ch D.
    Telephone contact—
      Necessary information to be given by solicitors. **Practice Direction** [1970] **1** 11, Ch D.
    Termination of proceedings by agreement—
      Attendance and collection of papers. **Practice Direction** [1963] **1** 416, Ch D.
  Chancery Division—
    Adjournment of motions. *See* Motion—Adjournment, *below*.
    Administrative arrangements—
      Chancery chambers—Court file—Issue of process—Fees—Assignment of masters—Ex parte
      applications—Appeals—Filing of documents—Orders—Judgments by default—Agreed adjourn-
      ment of motions—Motions judge—Listing—Receivers' accounts—RSC (Amendment No 2) 1982.
      Practice Direction [1982] **3** 124, Ch D.
      Chancery chambers—Official referees' business—Location. **Practice Direction** [1989] **1** 896, Ch D.
    Affidavit—
      Affidavit supporting—Certificate of birth, marriage or death—Affidavit no longer required—
      Certificate admitted in evidence. **Practice Direction** [1969] **2** 639, Ch D.
      Affidavit sworn before proceedings commenced—Acceptance. **Practice Direction** [1969] **2** 639,
      Ch D.
      Binding in book form. **Practice Direction** [1969] **2** 639, Ch D.
      Cross-examination of deponent—Further proceedings between parties pending in foreign court.
      See Interlocutory proceedings—Cross-examination on affidavit—Further proceedings between
      parties pending in foreign court, *below*.

PRACTICE (cont)—
  Chancery Division (cont)—
    Affidavit (cont)—
      Cross-examination of deponent—Order for cross-examination—Procedure—RSC Ord 38, r 2(3). **Practice Direction** [1969] **2** 736, Ch D.
      Cross-examination of deponent—Service of notice—Deponent out of jurisdiction—RSC Ord 38, r 28. **Lucas (decd), Re** [1952] **1** 102, Ch D.
      Dates and sums of money to be in figures and not in words—Infringement of practice direction—Authority to masters to order affidavit to be taken off file on preliminary hearing—Costs of re-swearing and re-filing to be borne by solicitor. **Love v Pharaoh** [1954] **1** 120, Ch D.
      Filing. See **Affidavit** (Filing).
      Index of practice directions relating to. See Chancery Division—Practice direction, *below*.
      Office copies—Ex parte applications without summons—Mortgages—Orders nisi for foreclosure or redemption. **Practice Direction** [1954] **3** 364, Ch D; [1955] **1** 30, Ch D.
      Office copies—No longer required—Exceptions. **Practice Direction** [1969] **2** 639, Ch D.
      Office copies—Office copies of affidavits normally no longer required. **Practice Direction** [1983] **1** 131, Ch D.
    Appeal from order of master—
      Withdrawal of appeal. See Appeal—Withdrawal of appeal, *above*.
    Application under Inheritance Family Provision Act 1938—
      Evidence. See **Family provision** (Evidence—Practice).
    Applications by post or telephone—
      Applications which may be made by post or telephone—Issue of writ or originating process—Acknowledgment of service—Issue of summons—Agreed orders—Appeals from masters—Adjournment by consent—Legal aid taxation—Documents—Filing—Office copies—Drawing up of orders. **Practice Direction** [1983] **2** 541, Ch D.
    Bankruptcy—
      Lists—Appeals—Applications—Urgent ex parte applications—Insolvency Act 1986, s 268. **Practice Direction** [1988] **2** 511, Ch D.
    Case stated. See **Case stated** (Chancery Division).
    Chambers proceedings—
      Adjournment to judge—Adjournment within stated time. **Practice Direction** [1966] **3** 84, Ch D.
      Adjournment to judge—Application to master for adjournment—Application to be made before master's order drawn up and perfected. **Practice Direction** [1965] **3** 306, Ch D.
      Adjournment to judge—Application to master for adjournment—Time limit—Applications after order pronounced but before order perfected. **Practice Direction** [1975] **1** 232, Ch D.
      Adjournment to judge—Infants—Contested applications relating to infants in which witnesses are to be cross-examined—Fixing date for hearing—Counsel's certificate as to estimated length of hearing—Application to vary date fixed. **Practice Direction** [1966] **2** 1040, Ch D.
      Adjournment to judge—Master's order passed and entered—Motion to judge to set aside order—Whether judge having jurisdiction to set aside order when perfected. **Whiteoaks Clifton Property Services Ltd v Jackson** [1975] **2** 85, Ch D.
      Adjournment to judge—Matter which party considers suitable to refer to judge—Procedure for directions—RSC Ord 32, rr 12, 14(3). **Practice Direction** [1990] **1** 255, Ch D.
      Adjournment to judge—Right to adjournment—Plaintiff's solicitor declined master's invitation to adjourn matter to judge—Before order passed and entered plaintiffs applied for adjournment—Master then adjourned matter to judge—Whether plaintiffs had lost their right to such adjournment. **London Permanent Benefit Building Society v De Baer** [1968] **1** 372, Ch D.
      Adjournment to judge—Vendor and purchaser summons—Lists—Date for hearing. **Practice Direction** [1967] **1** 656, Ch D; [1970] **1** 671, Ch D.
      Administrative arrangements. See Chancery Division—Administrative arrangements—Chancery chambers, *above*.
      Appeal from master. See Chambers proceedings—Appeal from master, *above*.
      Date of hearing. See Chambers proceedings, *above*.
      Index of practice directions relating to. See Chancery Division—Practice direction, *below*.
      Judgment—Status of judgment—Whether judgment given in chambers secret document—Whether leave should be given to disseminate judgment. **Forbes v Smith** [1998] **1** 973, Ch D.
      Masters' appointments. See Chambers proceedings—Masters' appointments, *above*.
      Masters' powers. See Chambers proceedings—Master's powers, *above*.
    Chancery Guide—
      Guidance on conduct of complex cases—Use of information technology. **Morris v Bank of America National Trust** [2000] **1** 954, CA.
      Practice directions—Provisions of Chancery Guide to prevail in case of inconsistency with any previous direction. **Practice Note** [1995] **2** 512, Ch D.
    Companies Court—
      Generally. See Companies Court, *below*.
      Lists—Adjourned applications and petitions. **Practice Direction** [1988] **2** 511, Ch D.
    Consent order. See Consent order—Chancery Division, *below*.
    Contempt of court—
      Committal order—Application by litigant in person. See **Contempt of court** (Committal—Application—Litigant in person—Chancery Division).
    Costs—
      Assessment in chambers. See **Costs** (Assessment—Assessment in chambers—Chancery Division).
    Designation of persons of less than full age—
      Use of term 'minor'. **Practice Direction** [1970] **2** 280, Ch D.
    Directions in force. See Chancery Division—Practice direction—Index of directions in force, *below*.
    Directors' disqualification applications—
      Background—Public interest in early resolution—Court control over conduct of proceedings—Summary procedure—Agreements as to disqualification period. **Practice Note** [1996] **1** 442, Ch D.
      Procedure—First hearing of summons—Setting down for trial—Fixing date for trial—Pre-trial review—Trial—Summary procedure—Hearings outside London. **Practice Note** [1996] **1** 445, Ch D.

PRACTICE (cont)—
  Chancery Division (cont)—
    Documents—
      Arrangement in bundles. **Practice Direction** [1970] **1** 671, Ch D.
      Documents for use abroad. *See* Document—Document for use abroad, *below.*
      Filing by post. *See* Chancery Division—Applications by post or telephone, *above.*
      Originals to be exhibited—Exceptions. **Practice Direction** [1970] **1** 671, Ch D.
      Photographic copies—Legibility. **Practice Direction** [1970] **1** 671, Ch D.
    Early trial. *See* Trial—Order for early trial, *below.*
    Estimate of length of trial. *See* Trial—Estimate of length of trial, *below.*
    Ex parte applications to master and consent orders—
      File to be bespoken from registry—Masters normally to deal only with cases allocated to
        them—Procedure in emergencies—Minutes of orders to be made by consent. **Practice Direction**
        [1993] **1** 786, Ch D.
    Foreclosure—
      Affidavit—Affidavit of due execution. *See* **Mortgage** (Foreclosure—Application for foreclosure
        nisi—Affidavit of due execution).
      Redemption—Orders nisi. *See* **Mortgage** (Foreclosure—Redemption—Orders nisi).
    Hearing dates—
      Target dates—Parties and legal representatives to be ready and available for hearing within target
        dates—Interlocutory applications after proceedings set down to be made to motions judge if
        appointment before master would delay hearing of proceedings. **Practice Direction** [1994] **2** 384,
        Ch D.
    Hearings by judges outside London—
      Bristol—New arrangements—Weekly sittings for motions and other urgent business—Urgent
        applications at other times—Commencement of proceedings—Authorised jurisdiction. **Practice**
        Direction [1989] **1** 831, Ch D.
      Cardiff—New arrangements—Weekly sittings for motions and other urgent business—Urgent
        applications at other times—Commencement of proceedings—Authorised jurisdiction. **Practice**
        Direction [1989] **1** 832, Ch D.
      Causes or matters for hearing by High Court judge—Adjournment of certain causes or matters to
        circuit judges—Transfer of applications to London—Service of cross-notices of motion. **Practice**
        Direction [1988] **2** 509, Ch D.
      Circuit judges exercising powers of judge of Chancery Division. *See* Chancery Division—
        Proceedings outside London—Excepted Chancery jurisdiction, *below.*
      Court and chambers procedure. **Practice Direction** [1982] **3** 124, Ch D; **Practice Directions**
        [1972] **1** 103, Ch D.
      Interlocutory applications. *See* Chancery Division—Interlocutory applications—Causes or matters
        outside London, *below.*
    Infant's estate—
      Application for appointment of guardian—Property not worth more than £500—Straightforward
        application—Property to be paid into court—Jurisdiction of Chancery masters. **Practice Direction**
        [1970] **1** 885, Ch D.
    Injunction—
      Interlocutory. *See* **Injunction** (Interlocutory—Practice—Chancery Division).
    Inquiries for next-of-kin—
      Separate certificates. **Practice Direction** [1970] **2** 280, Ch D.
    Insolvency proceedings. *See* **Insolvency**.
    Interlocutory applications—
      Applications to be made by summons to master. **Practice Direction** [1984] **1** 720, Ch D.
      Causes or matters outside London. **Practice Direction** [1983] **3** 544, Ch D; [1984] **1** 750, Ch D.
      Interlocutory applications to master. **Morley v Woolfson** [1954] **3** 378, Ch D.
    Interlocutory procedure—
      Expedition—Judge's order—Form of order—Order on hearing motion for interlocutory
        relief—Order on giving leave to defend on summons for summary Judgment—RSC Ord 14,
        Ord 86. **Practice Direction** [1974] **1** 1039, Ch D.
    Interlocutory proceedings—
      Stay of proceedings. *See* Interlocutory proceedings—Stay of proceedings, *below.*
    Legal aid certificates—
      Lodgment of copies in chambers. *See* Chancery Division—Applications by post or telephone,
        above.
    Listing—
      Motions—Estimated length of hearing—Counsel's certificate. **Practice Direction** [1992] **1** 689, Ch D.
      Non-witness list. *See* Chancery Division—Non-witness list, *below.*
      Northern Area. *See* Chancery Division—Northern Area—Lists, *below.*
      Revenue list. *See* Chancery Division—Revenue list, *below.*
      Revision of system. *See* Chancery Division—Revision of system for listing causes and matters,
        below.
      Short causes list. *See* Chancery Division—Short Causes List, *below.*
      Summonses—Chambers summonses—Chambers summonses adjourned by master—Listing in
        non-witness list. **Practice Direction** [1992] **1** 689, Ch D.
      Unassigned cases. *See* Chancery Division—Unassigned cases, *below.*
      Warned List. *See* Chancery Division—Warned List, *below.*
      Witness list. *See* Chancery Division—Witness list, *below.*
    Lists—
      Revision of system for listing causes and matters—Appointment of clerk of lists. **Practice Direction**
        [1975] **1** 56, Ch D.
    Litigation. *See* Civil litigation—Litigation in Queen's Bench Division, Chancery Division and county
      courts other than family proceedings, *below.*
    Masters—
      Business before Chancery masters—Abolition of distinction between term time and vacation
        business—Hearings in Companies Court and before judges unaffected—RSC Ord 64, r 3. **Practice**
        Direction [1993] **1** 360, Ch D.

PRACTICE (cont)—
  Chancery Division (cont)—
    Masters (cont)—
      Masters' powers. *See* Chambers proceedings—Master's powers, *above.*
    Mortgaged property—
      Enquiry of prior mortgages before applying for possession. *See* **Mortgage** (Possession of mortgaged property—Second mortgagee—Subsequent encumbrances).
    Motion. *See* Motion, *below.*
    New practice and procedure. *See* Queen's Bench Division and Chancery Division—New practice and procedure, *below.*
    Non-witness list—
      New system. *See* Chancery Division—Revision of system for listing causes and matters, *below.*
      Publication of warned list—Applications to fix dates for hearing—Duty to give clerk of lists information relevant to length of hearing. **Practice Direction** [1975] **1** 56, Ch D.
      Warned List. *See* Chancery Division—Warned List—Causes and matters in Witness List Part 2 and Non-Witness List, *below.*
    Northern Area—
      Appeals—Insolvency and revenue appeals—Hearing of insolvency and revenue appeals on Northern or North Eastern Circuits—Requests for arrangements to be made for appeal to be heard on Northern or North Eastern Circuits—Insolvency Act 1986, s 375(2)—RSC Ord 59—Insolvency Rules 1986, rr 7.48(2), 7.49(1)(2). **Practice Note** [1995] **4** 129, Ch D.
      Appeals—Insolvency and revenue appeals—Hearing of insolvency and revenue appeals on Northern or North Eastern Circuits—Requests for arrangements to be made for appeal to be heard on Northern or North Eastern Circuits—Insolvency Act 1986, s 375(2)—RSC Ord 55, r 1(3), Ord 59, Ord 77, r 2(1), Ord 91—Insolvency Rules 1986, rr 7.47, 7.49. **Practice Note** [1991] **1** 608, Ch D.
      Lists—Fixed dates—Motion days—Papers for judge—Urgent matters. **Practice Note** [1985] **1** 190, Ch D.
      Lists—Fixed dates—Warned cases—Motion days—Papers for judge—Urgent matters. **Practice Note** [1986] **3** 63, Ch D.
      Sittings—Dates and venues of sittings—Cases not finishing within allocated period—Listing of Chancery business—Adjournment or transfer of cases to London. **Practice Direction** [1988] **2** 801, Ch D.
    Order—
      Drawing up—Bespeaking orders. *See* Order—Drawing-up—Bespeaking orders, *below.*
      Order on motion—Drawing up of order—Application that order be drawn up by solicitors—Procedure. **Practice Direction** [1970] **1** 281, Ch D.
      Order requiring execution of deed—Judgment in default of appearance—Form of order—Specific performance of agreement to execute lease—Judgment against lessor—Minutes of order providing that defendant execute lease containing 'the usual covenants' in form of a draft annexed—Defendant's right to object to proposed terms of lease even though in default of appearance—Appropriate order that defendant execute lease to be settled by judge if parties fail to agree—RSC Ord 44, r 8. **Charalambous v Ktori** [1972] **3** 701, Ch D.
    Order and Accounts Section—
      Merger of Accounts Section and Drafting Section. **Practice Direction** [1994] **1** 672, Ch D.
    Originating summons. *See* **Originating summons**.
    Parties—
      Change of name. *See* Parties—Change of name, *below.*
    Patent proceedings. *See* **Patent**.
    Practice direction—
      Index of directions in force. **Practice Direction** [1987] **1** 879, Ch D.
    Proceedings outside London—
      Excepted Chancery jurisdiction—Order for trial—Standard directions—Pleadings to be lodged—Transfer between district registries. **Practice Direction** [1985] **1** 256, Ch D.
    Reading lists. *See* Reading lists, *below.*
    References to European Court. *See* **European Union** (Reference to European Court—Practice—Chancery Division).
    Revenue list—
      Fixing date for hearing cases in revenue list. **Practice Direction** [1972] **1** 1055, Ch D.
      New listing procedure for revenue appeals—Abolition of Revenue Paper. **Practice Note** [1982] **3** 904, Ch D.
      Northern Area—Hearing of insolvency and revenue appeals. *See* Chancery Division—Northern Area—Appeals—Insolvency and revenue appeals, *above.*
    Revision of system for listing causes and matters—
      Consolidation of former directions. **Practice Direction** [1983] **1** 1145, Ch D.
    Sale of land by court. *See* **Sale of land** (Sale by court).
    Secret proceedings—
      Judgment—Reporting restrictions—Defendant being investigated by Swedish prosecutors—Claimant bringing summary judgment proceedings against defendant—Hearing taking place in secret and judge giving judgment adverse to defendant—Defendant fearing that judge's conclusions would encourage Swedish authorities to prosecute—Whether court should prohibit publication of judgment. **Trustor AB v Smallbone** [2000] **1** 811, Ch D.
    Setting down action. *See* Trial—Setting down action—Chancery Division, *below.*
    Short Causes List—
      Applications in regard to proceedings in short cause list. **Practice Direction** [1966] **2** 720, Ch D.
      Day of hearing in Chancery Division. **Practice Direction** [1965] **3** 641, Ch D.
      Short motions to be listed for hearing on any weekday. **Practice Direction** [1988] **2** 511, Ch D.
    Short Probate List—
      Applications for probate on affidavit evidence to be heard on any weekday. **Practice Direction** [1988] **2** 511, Ch D.
      New system. *See* Chancery Division—Revision of system for listing causes and matters, *above.*

PRACTICE (cont)—
  Chancery Division (cont)—
    Short summons list—
      Summonses unlikely to last more than five minutes—Arrangements for hearing. **Practice Direction** [1987] **2** 544, Ch D.
    Speedy trial. *See* Trial—Order for early trial, *below*.
    Stay of proceedings—
      Consent order without personal attendance—Parties represented by solicitors—Procedure. **Practice Direction** [1971] **1** 64, Ch D.
      Proceedings set down for hearing in court—Consent order—Application to be in person—Procedure. **Practice Direction** [1971] **1** 64, Ch D.
    Summary judgment. *See* Summary judgment—Chancery Division, *below*.
    Summons. *See* Summons—Chancery Division, *below*.
    Summons for directions. *See* Summons for directions—Chancery Division, *below*.
    Telephone—
      Applications by telephone. *See* Chancery Division—Applications by post or telephone, *above*.
    Title of proceedings. *See* Title of proceedings—Chancery Division, *below*.
    Transfer of cause or matter from one group of judges to another—
      Consent order without personal attendance—Letter explaining reasons for transfer. **Practice Direction** [1977] **2** 173, Ch D.
      Procedure. **Practice Direction** [1974] **1** 240, Ch D.
    Transfer of proceedings from High Court to county court. *See* **County court** (Transfer of action—Transfer from High Court—Chancery business).
    Transfer of proceedings to Queen's Bench Division—
      Allegation of fraud. *See* Transfer of proceedings between Divisions of High Court—Jury trial available as of right in action begun in Queen's Bench Division where fraud in issue—Action begun in Chancery Division including allegation of fraud, *below*.
    Trial—
      Adjournment to place not authorised for trial of proceedings—Power of court to adjourn trial for purpose of hearing testimony of witness too infirm to travel. *See* Trial—Place of trial—Adjournment of trial—Adjournment to such place as court thinks fit—Witness—Examination—Witness too infirm to travel to London—Witness fit to be examined at village where she lived—Village not a place authorised for trial of proceedings in Chancery Division, *below*.
      Speedy trial. *See* Trial—Order for early trial, *below*.
    Trustee—
      Proceedings under Trustee Act 1925—Vesting order—Land—Company—Dissolution—Freehold property vested in company before dissolution—Agreement by company to distribute property among shareholders—Failure to convey legal estate to shareholders—Company trustee for shareholders—Trustee Act 1925, s 44(ii)(c). **Strathblaine Estates Ltd, Re** [1948] **1** 162, Ch D.
    Trusts—
      Applications in relation to administration of trusts—Prospective costs orders—CPR Sch 1, RSC Ord 85. **Practice Note** [2001] **3** 574, Ch D.
    Unassigned cases—
      Cases not assigned to particular judge—Procedure for listing and hearing unassigned cases. **Practice Note** [1986] **2** 1002, QBD.
    Warned List—
      Causes and matters in Witness List Part 2 and Non-Witness List—Notice to solicitor of setting down for hearing. **Practice Note** [1978] **2** 645, Ch D.
    Witness action—
      Witness list. *See* Chancery Division—Witness list, *below*.
    Witness list—
      Applications in regard to actions in witness list, Parts 1 and 2. **Practice Direction** [1966] **2** 720, Ch D.
      Estimate of expected duration—Revision of estimate—Revision in light of supervening circumstances. **Forspan v Altmann** [1968] **2** 760, Ch D.
      Fixed dates. **Practice Direction** [1961] **1** 926, Ch D.
      Part 1 (fixed date) and Part 2 (not more than two days, no date fixed)—Counsel's certificate. **Practice Note** [1966] **1** 916, Ch D.
      Part 1—Actions to be tried on a fixed date—Intimation that parties willing to have case listed for earlier hearing—Period of notice of earlier hearing. **Practice Direction** [1972] **3** 254, Ch D.
      Part 1—Procedure for fixing date for trial. **Practice Direction** [1973] **1** 30, Ch D.
      Part 2—Actions estimated to last three days or less—Transfer of such actions from Part 1. **Practice Direction** [1973] **2** 422, Ch D.
      Part 2—New arrangements—Hearing at short notice—Estimated length of hearing. **Practice Note** [1969] **1** 787, Ch D.
      Part 2—Warned List. *See* Chancery Division—Warned List—Causes and matters in Witness List Part 2 and Non-Witness List, *above*.
      Reorganisation—Transitional arrangements. **Practice Direction** [1974] **3** 177, Ch D.
      Revision of system. *See* Chancery Division—Revision of system for listing causes and matters, *above*.
  Charging order. *See* **Execution** (Charging order).
  Charity proceedings—
    Generally. *See* **Charity** (Proceedings).
  Chester—
    Mercantile lists. *See* Queen's Bench Division—Mercantile lists—Cardiff and Chester, *below*.
  Children—
    Chancery Division—
      Chambers applications. *See* **Minor** (Practice—Chancery Division—Chambers applications relating to minors).
    Court proceedings in relation to children. *See* **Child** (Court proceedings in relation to child).
    Divorce proceedings. *See* **Divorce** (Practice—Children).
    Family Division—
      Applications relating to children. *See* **Child** (Practice—Matrimonial causes).

PRACTICE (cont)—
 Children (cont)—
  Welfare report. *See* **Child** (Welfare—Welfare report).
 Circuit judge—
  Mode of address. *See* **Judge** (Circuit judge—Deputy circuit judge—Mode of address).
 Citation of cases—
  Civil courts—
   Restrictions and rules—Categories of judgments citeable only if purporting to establish new principle or extend present law—Requirement for advocates to indicate proposition of law demonstrated by each authority cited. **Practice Note** [2001] **2** 510, Sup Ct.
  Court of Appeal, Civil Division—
   Generally. *See* **Court of Appeal** (Practice—Civil Division—Citation of authority).
  Reports—
   Court of Appeal, Civil Division. *See* **Court of Appeal** (Practice—Civil Division—Citation of cases—Reports).
   Report by person not member of the Bar. **Birtwistle v Tweedale** [1953] **2** 1598, CA.
   Revenue cases—Law Reports series or Reports of Tax Cases—Law Reports to be used when case there reported—Practice in revenue cases. **Westminster Bank Exor and Trustee Co (Channel Islands) Ltd v National Bank of Greece SA** [1970] **3** 656, HL.
   Revenue cases—Law Reports series or Reports of Tax Cases—Tax Cases may be used if counsel think it more convenient—References to Law Reports also to be given. **Bray (Inspector of Taxes) v Best** [1989] **1** 969, HL.
 Civil litigation—
  Case management—
   Allocation—Allocation of claim to multi-track by court—Requirements of case management conference—Requirement to file costs budget within prescribed time period—Claim treated as allocated to multi-track—Whether directions hearing case management conference—Whether party to litigation failing to file costs budget within prescribed time period—CPR Pt 8. **Kershaw v Roberts** [2015] **1** 734, Ch D.
   Allocation—Matters relevant to allocation to a track—Financial value of claim—Assessment of financial value by court—Disregard of any amount not in dispute—Admission of part of sum claimed—CPR 26.7(1), 26(8). **Akhtar v Boland** [2015] **1** 644, CA.
   Directions—Claim valued in excess of £18million—Whether the court had the power to order the filing and exchange of costs budgets in claim valued in excess of limit in CPR—CPR 3.13. **CIP Properties (AIPT) Ltd v Galliford Try Infrastructure Ltd** [2015] **1 Comm** 765, QBD.
   Directions—Clinical negligence actions—Published and unpublished literature upon which expert witness proposing to rely—Best practice in multi-track actions in county courts and High Court. **Wardlaw v Farrar** [2003] **4** 1358n, CA.
   Disclosure—Statement of truth to be signed personally—Party refusing to sign personally under protocol of Saudi Arabian royal family—Judgment entered against him—Whether case management decision within margin accorded—Whether appropriate for appellate court to interfere—Whether sanction disproportionate—Effect on case management decisions of underlying strength of a party's case on the merits. **Abdulaziz Bin Mishal Bin Abdulaziz Al Saud (Prince) v Apex Global Management Ltd** [2015] **2** 206, SC; [2015] **2** 1183, SC.
   Extension of time—Respondent's notice—Application for extension of time to file respondent's notice—Applicable principles—CPR 3.1(2)(a), 3.9, 52.5(2)(b). **Altomart Ltd v Salford Estates (No 2) Ltd** [2016] **2** 328, CA.
   Importance of reducing costs and delay of civil litigation. **Practice** [1995] **1** 586, Fam D; **Practice Note** [1995] **1** 385, QBD and Ch D.
   Powers of judge to vary procedural rules —Practice directions—Powers of judge to issue or vary practice directions—Civil Procedure Act 1997, ss 5, 9. **Bovale Ltd v Secretary of State for Communities and Local Government** [2009] **3** 340, CA.
   Relief from sanctions—Defendant's failure to file listing questionnaire by date specified in a directions order and subsequent 'unless' order—Judgment in default entered against defendant—Defendant granted relief from sanction—Default judgment set aside— Whether relief from sanction properly granted—CPR 3.9. **British Gas Trading Ltd v Oak Cash & Carry Ltd** [2015] **1 Comm** 1000, QBD; [2016] **2 Comm** 840, CA; [2016] **4** 129, CA.
   Relief from sanction—Claimant failing to serve further information with notice of commencement of detailed assessment proceedings - Whether further information being required at time detailed assessment proceedings being commenced—Whether 'all or nothing' sanction applying - CPR 3.9, 47.6, 44.3B. **Long v Value Properties Ltd** [2015] **3** 419, Ch D.
   Relief from sanction—Company filing further evidence after deadline stipulated by court—Judge refusing reliance on witness statements—Whether relief from sanctions required before admitting further evidence—Whether relevant principles correctly applied—Insolvency (England and Wales) Rules 2016, SI 2016/1024, r 7.16—CPR 3.9. **Wolf Rock (Cornwall) Ltd v Langhelle** [2021] **2 Comm** 625, Ch D.
   Relief from sanction—Defendant's failure to comply with court order made pursuant to case management hearing—No express sanction contained in order—Whether order containing implied sanction. **Djurberg v Richmond London BC** [2020] **2 Comm** 727, Ch D.
   Relief from sanction—Defendants' failure to comply with directions as to disclosure—Defence and counterclaims struck out—Whether decision to strike out based on misstatement of facts—Whether defendants' submissions a matter for appeal rather than application for relief from sanction—CPR 3.1(7). **Newland Shipping & Forwarding Ltd v Toba Trading FZC** [2015] **1 Comm** 735, QBD.
   Relief from sanction—Requirement for court to consider need for litigation to be conducted efficiently and at proportionate cost—Requirement for court to consider need to enforce compliance with rules, practice directions and orders—Defendant's application to set aside judgment in default of acknowledgement of service and judgment on assessment of damages—Applications lodged some eight months after judgment in default and some six weeks after judgment on assessment of damages—Whether court should exercise its discretion to set aside judgments—CPR 3.9(1). **Avanesov v Shymkentpivo** [2015] **1 Comm** 1260, QBD.

PRACTICE (cont)—
Commencement of proceedings (cont)—
Limitation of action—
When proceedings 'brought'. *See* **Limitation of action** (Period of limitation—Personal injury claim—When proceedings 'brought' for purposes of limitation period).
Commercial cases—
Bristol—
Bristol Mercantile Court—Designation of circuit judge or Queen's Counsel to act as judge of High Court to hear matter proceeding in Bristol Mercantile Court—Withdrawal of power of designation. **Practice Note** [1999] **2** 1024, QBD.
Hearing of cases of commercial or business character—Bristol Mercantile Court List—Actions which may be included in list—Commencement of actions—Circuit mercantile judges—Rules governing actions—Chronologies, lists, skeleton arguments and core bundles—Powers of circuit commercial judges—Transfer of actions to Queen's Bench Division or Chancery Division High Court judge sitting on circuit or to Commercial Court in London—Designation of circuit judge or Queen's Counsel to act as judge of High Court to hear matter proceeding in Bristol Mercantile Court—Supreme Court Act 1981, s 9—RSC Ord 72. **Practice Note** [1993] **4** 1023, QBD.
Midland and Oxford Circuit—
Hearing of cases of commercial or business character—Birmingham Mercantile List—Actions which may be included in list—Commencement of actions—Circuit commercial judges—Rules governing actions—Expeditious and economical disposal of actions—Chronologies, lists, skeleton arguments and core bundles—Powers of circuit commercial judges—Transfer of actions to Commercial Court or to High Court judge sitting on circuit—Supreme Court Act 1981, s 9—RSC Ord 72. **Practice Note** [1993] **4** 381, QBD.
Northern Circuit—
Hearing of cases of commercial or business character—Manchester and Liverpool Commercial Lists—Actions which may be included in lists—Commencement of actions—Circuit commercial judges—Rules governing actions—Expeditious and economical disposal of actions—Chronologies, lists, skeleton arguments and core bundles—Powers of circuit commercial judges—Transfer of actions to Commercial Court or to High Court judge sitting on circuit—Supreme Court Act 1981, s 9—RSC Ord 72. **Practice Note** [1990] **1** 528, QBD.
Renaming of Manchester and Liverpool Commercial Lists—Lists to be known as Mercantile Lists. **Practice Note** [1992] **3** 375, QBD.
Commercial Court—
Absence of party. *See* Absence of party—Commercial Court, *above.*
Admiralty and Commercial Court Registry—
Generally. *See* Admiralty and Commercial Court Registry, *above.*
Civil Procedure Rules—
General information. **Practice Direction** [1999] **2 Comm** 575, QBD; [1999] **4** 471, QBD.
Generally. *See* **Commercial Court** (Practice).
Harmonisation of Admiralty Court and Commercial Court practice. *See* **Admiralty** (Practice—Admiralty Court practice to harmonise with Commercial Court practice).
Pleading—
Particulars—Marine insurance. *See* **Pleading** (Particulars—Marine insurance).
Sittings in Long Vacation—
Hearing of commercial actions and summonses—Not necessary to establish that matter is 'Long Vacation business' but preference to be given to urgent matters, Special Cases and short cases—Applications to fix dates for hearings in vacation—RSC ord 64, r 4(1). **Practice Direction** [1977] **1** 912, Comm Ct.
Urgent matters—
Revised practice—Fridays to be devoted to dealing with summonses and other short but urgent matters—Tuesdays no longer to be summons days—New system to be operated flexibly to avoid difficulties—Parties to notify Commercial Court office of changes in estimated lengths of summonses etc—Counsels' clerks to notify office where counsel involved in more than one summons listed for a particular date—Existence of, and suggestions for dealing with, difficulties arising from new practice to be notified to Commercial Court Committee or Commercial Court office. **Practice Direction** [1981] **3** 864, QBD.
Companies Court—
Applications—
Applications which are to be made to judge in open court—Applications which are to be made to registrar—Applications which may be dealt with by chief clerk—Insolvency Act 1986, ss 5(3), 14(3), 18(3), 127—Insolvency Rules 1986, rr 4.3, 4.8(6), 4.15, 4.19, 4.22(2), 4.35, 4.47, 4.59, 4.74(4), 4.85, 4.102, 4.103, 4.111, 4.221, 7.11, 13.2(2). **Practice Direction** [1987] **1** 107, Companies Ct.
Applications in Long Vacation—
Applications for schemes of arrangement or reconstruction, for reduction of share capital or in respect of capital redemption reserve funds or share premium accounts—Applications restricted to cases of urgent need—Applications to sanction a scheme or for confirmation of reduction of capital, capital redemption reserve fund or share premium account—Circumstances in which applications will be heard—Applications to registrar for orders convening meetings to consider schemes and for directions on reduction applications—Companies Act 1948, ss 56, 58, 67, 206. **Practice Direction** [1977] **1** 688, Ch D.
Applications for schemes of arrangement or reconstruction, for reduction of share capital or in respect of capital redemption reserve funds or share premium accounts—Extension of existing arrangements. **Practice Direction** [1978] **1** 820, Companies Ct.
Applications for schemes of arrangement or reconstruction, for reduction of share capital or in respect of capital redemption reserve funds or share premium accounts—Modification of existing arrangements. **Practice Direction** [1982] **2** 454, Companies Ct.
Attendance before registrar—
Compulsory winding up. *See* **Company** (Compulsory winding up—Procedure—Attendance before registrar).

Companies Court (cont)—
Chambers—
Orders—Orders drafted in chambers normally to be engrossed without reference to parties' solicitors—Orders dismissing winding-up petitions not normally to be drawn up. **Practice Direction** [1984] **2** 736, Companies Ct.

Postal transactions—Companies (Winding-up) Rules 1949 (SI 1949 No 330)—RSC Ord 102. **Practice Direction** [1979] **3** 602, Ch D.

Chief clerk—
Applications and orders—Exercise of functions by chief clerk—Direction that certain petitions not to be advertised before first hearing—Companies (Winding-up) Rules 1949, r 28. **Practice Direction** [1982] **1** 846, Ch D.

Applications and orders—Exercise of functions by chief clerk—Hearing of applications by and adjournment to registrar. **Practice Direction** [1979] **3** 613, Ch D.

Compulsory winding up of company. See **Company** (Compulsory winding up—Procedure).
Insolvency proceedings—
Applications for appointment of provisional liquidator—Procedure. **Practice Note** [1996] **4** 1024, Ch D.

Lists. See Chancery Division—Companies Court—Lists, *above.*
Schemes of arrangement—
Creditor issues—Applicant's responsibilities—Companies Act 1985, s 425. **Practice Statement** [2002] **3** 96, Ch D.

Schemes of arrangement and reductions of capital—
Arrangements for hearing. **Practice Note** [1996] **4** 1022, Ch D.

Summons—
Summons to be returnable before 'the Companies Court judge'. **Practice Direction** [1992] **3** 736, Ch D.

Company—
Hearing. See Hearing—Company matters, *below.*
Compensation for goodwill in respect of business premises. See **Landlord and tenant** (Compensation for goodwill in respect of business premises—Practice).
Complaint—
Unfair industrial practice. See **Industrial relations** (Unfair industrial practice—Complaint).
Compromise of action—
Action to recover money loaned to borrower—
Borrower claiming loans unlawful moneylending transactions—Genuine dispute of fact whether lender a moneylender—Borrower and lender agreeing to compromise—Both parties legally advised—Borrower agreeing loans not moneylending transactions—Borrower agreeing to pay lender fixed sum by monthly instalments—Agreement providing that if action brought by lender for money due under agreement, not open to borrower to raise defence of unlawful moneylending—Subsequent action by lender to enforce compromise agreement—Borrower claiming agreement not binding—Effect of agreement. **Binder v Alachouzos** [1972] **2** 189, CA.

Approval of court—
Approval on behalf of infant—Agreement reached between parties on liability while claimant an infant—Approval of court not sought—Whether agreement binding—CPR 21.10. **Drinkall v Whitwood** [2004] **4** 378, CA.

Approval on behalf of infant—Compromise after infant attains age of 18—Whether order sanctioning compromise required. **Practice Direction** [1970] **1** 553, QBD.

Approval on behalf of infant—Costs—Claims brought solely for the purpose of obtaining court approval of settlement of personal injury claims —Whether costs subject to predictive costs regime—Whether small claims costs regime applicable—Whether fees of counsel for attending hearing recoverable as disbursement—CPR 8.9(c), 21.10(2), 27, 45, 44.5. **Dockerill v Tullett** [2012] **3** 359, CA.

Approval on behalf of infant—Court of Appeal—Claim by infant plaintiff for damages for personal injuries—Verdict for plaintiff—appeal by defendants—Action settled while appeal pending—Necessity for obtaining approval of Court of Appeal—RSC Ord 22, r 14. **Walsh v Kemp (George) Ltd** [1938] **2** 266, CA.

Approval on behalf of infant—Duties of guardian ad litem—Duty to consider whether terms of compromise in minor's interest—Duty to oppose terms he considers contrary to minor's interest—Trust and trustee—Minor beneficiary—Corporate trustee seeking approval of court for compromise of proceedings including term increasing trustee's fees. **Barbour's Settlement, Re** [1974] **1** 1188, Ch D.

Compromise by or on behalf of child or protected party—Parties in personal injury claim agreeing compromise—Claimant not known to be lacking capacity—Claimant subsequently found to have been lacking capacity at time of agreement—Whether compromise valid—Whether approval of court necessary—CPR 21.10. **Dunhill v Burgin** [2013] **1** 482, QBD; [2014] **2** 364, SC.

Settlement of claim under Fatal Accidents Acts involving widow as well as infant. See **Fatal accident** (Compromise—Approval by court).
Terms of order approving settlement—Payment into court within specified period—Procedure—Drawing up and serving order—Payment within specified time—Extension of time—Payment before order served—Supreme Court Funds Rules 1927 (SR & O 1927 No 1184), Appendix, Form 23. **Practice Direction** [1969] **3** 416, .

Compromise agreement—
Construction—Party to settlement agreement subsequently bringing claim alleging forgery involving other party—Whether claim covered by compromise agreement. **Satyam Computer Services Ltd v Upaid Systems Ltd** [2008] **1** Comm 737, QBD.

Consent order—
Breach of undertaking in recital to order—Cause of action—Whether breaches of undertakings actionable by way of proceedings for breach of contract. **Independiente Ltd v Music Trading On-Line (HK) Ltd** [2007] **4** 736, CA.

PRACTICE (cont)—
  Compromise of action (cont)—
    Consent order (cont)—
      Order in Tomlin form—Breach of terms of compromise—Schedule to Tomlin order included some but not all terms of deed of compromise—Plaintiff seeking to enforce order—Whether defendant entitled to rely on breach by plaintiff of terms of deed not included in order as defence to action. **Horizon Technologies International Ltd v Lucky Wealth Consultants Ltd** [1992] **1** 469, PC.
      Order in Tomlin form—Court not prepared to sanction undertaking to court—Order made more than 30 years previously—Whether undertaking enforceable by injunction. **Wilson & Whitworth Ltd v Express & Independent Newspapers Ltd** [1969] **1** 294, Ch D.
      Order in Tomlin form—Effect of agreement between parties—Defendant agreeing to sell property and divide proceeds with plaintiff—Whether compromise imposing immediate trust for sale of property. **Anders Utkilens Rederi A/S v O/Y Lovisa Stevedoring Co A/B** [1985] **2** 669, Ch D.
      Order in Tomlin form—Function of court—Interpleader proceedings—Terms agreed by counsel—Order within jurisdiction of court—Court under no duty to approve or disapprove agreed order—Court having no right to refuse to make agreed order. **Noel v Becker** [1971] **2** 1186, CA.
      Order in Tomlin form—Variation of terms of compromise—Whether court having general power to vary terms of compromise agreement in schedule to Tomlin order on grounds of material or unforeseen change of circumstances undermining basis of agreement. **Community Care North East (a partnership) v Durham CC** [2010] **4** 733, QBD.
      Uncertainty—Whether consent order could be void for uncertainty. **Scammell v Dicker** [2005] **3** 838, CA.
    Consent to order—
      Terms of settlement agreed on correspondence but no implied agreement to order staying proceedings—No jurisdiction to make Tomlin order without further consent, viz, to the order being made. **McCallum v Country Residences Ltd** [1965] **2** 264, CA.
    Costs. See **Costs** (Order for costs—Compromise).
    Discontinuance of action—
      Stay of action—Settlement agreed before hearing of action—Terms of settlement embodied in consent order staying action—Application by intervener for joinder after settlement concluded—Whether consent order staying action amounting to discontinuance of action—Whether action still in being when application made by intervener for joinder—RSC Ord 15, r 6(2). **ROFA Sport Management AG v DHL International (UK) Ltd** [1989] **2** 743, CA.
    Effect on third party proceedings. See Third party proceedings—Settlement between plaintiff and defendant—Effect, below.
    Infant—
      Entitlement of infant plaintiff on majority to moneys recovered. See **Damages** (Infant—Claim by infant plaintiff—Entitlement of infant on majority to money recovered—Compromise of action).
    Joint tortfeasors—
      Contribution—Settlement by one tortfeasor. See **Tort** (Contribution between joint tortfeasors—Settlement of action by one tortfeasor).
    Linked actions—
      Whether agreement settling action against one party precluding claimants from bringing fresh but related action against another party. **Heaton v Axa Equity and Law Life Assurance Society plc** [2000] **4** 673, CA.
    Settlement agreed before hearing of action—
      Terms of settlement not made an order of the court—No order for proceedings to be stayed—Breach of agreed terms—Jurisdiction of court to enforce settlement—Methods of disposing of action where terms of settlement agreed before or during hearing. **Green v Rozen** [1955] **2** 797, QBD.
    Settlement agreement—
      Construction —Party to settlement agreement subsequently bringing claim alleging forgery involving other party—Whether claim covered by settlement agreement. **Satyam Computer Services Ltd v Upaid Systems Ltd** [2008] **2 Comm** 465, CA.
    Tomlin order—
      Consent order in Tomlin form. See Compromise of action—Consent order—Order in Tomlin form, above.
      Enforcement—Motion to enforce terms of compromise going beyond scope of original action—Whether Tomlin order can be enforced by application in same action. **Phillips (E F) & Sons Ltd v Clarke** [1969] **3** 710, Ch D.
  Compulsory purchase—
    Notice to treat—
      Service. See **Compulsory purchase** (Notice to treat—Service).
  Conduct of proceedings—
    Access to confidential information—
      Plaintiffs applying for Anton Piller order against defendants—Judge given confidential information which was not revealed to defendants—Whether judge should be given information which could not be disclosed to defendants at a later stage—Whether defendants' solicitors can be excluded from access to information disclosed to court. **WEA Records Ltd v Visions Channel 4 Ltd** [1983] **2** 589, CA.
      Trustee in bankruptcy applying ex parte for oral examination of solicitors believed to have information relating to bankrupt's affairs—Court referring to undisclosed confidential information relied on by trustee—Whether court entitled to refer to confidential information not disclosed to solicitors—Insolvency Act 1986, s 366. **Murjani (a bankrupt), Re** [1996] **1** 65, Ch D.
    Disclosure—
      Production contrary to public interest—Emanations of the Crown or government seeking to rely on material whose disclosure contrary to public interest—Claim against Crown for damages in tort and for breach of statutory duty—Crown seeking 'closed material' procedure—Whether court having common law power to order closed material procedure in trial of civil claim. **Al Rawi v Security Service** [2010] **4** 559, CA; [2012] **1** 1, SC.

PRACTICE (cont)—
Conduct of proceedings (cont)—
Language—
Foreign litigant in person—Foreign litigant unable to speak or understand English—Litigant appearing in person—Discretion of court—Whether evidence should be translated—Whether foreign litigant should be allowed to address court through interpreter. **Fuld (decd), In the Estate of** [1965] **2** 653, Prob.
Foreign plaintiff wishing to conduct proceedings through interpreter—Discretion of court. **Trepca Mines Ltd, Re** [1960] **3** 304, CA.
Welsh language—When right to use in Welsh court—Welsh Courts Act 1942, s 1. **R v Merthyr Tydfil Justices, ex p Jenkins** [1967] **1** 636, QBD.
Confidential information—
Access to. *See* Conduct of proceedings—Access to confidential information, *above*.
Generally. *See* **Confidential information**.
Privilege—
Disclosure of documents. *See* **Disclosure and inspection of documents** (Privilege—Confidential documents).
Consent order—
Chancery Division—
Ex parte applications to master and consent orders. *See* Chancery Division—Ex parte applications to master and consent orders, *above*.
Order sought going outside relief claimed in notice of motion or writ—Procedure—Written consent required—Respondent's undertaking. **Practice Direction** [1985] **1** 1040, Ch D.
Stay of proceedings. *See* Chancery Division—Stay of proceedings—Proceedings set down for hearing in court—Consent order, *above*.
Claimant obtaining freezing order against defendant—
Debt owed to defendant by third party being paid into account held by parties' solicitors—Court discharging freezing order by consent on undertaking by defendant not to withdraw or dispose of money in account—Whether terms of consent order giving claimant charge over money in account. **Flightline Ltd v Edwards** [2003] **3** 1200, CA.
Compromise of action. *See* Compromise of action—Consent order, *above*.
Consent order made without personal attendance—
Chancery Division—Interlocutory orders—Final orders concluding, staying or discontinuing proceedings where all parties sui juris—Exceptions to procedure—Classes of applications in which personal attendance normally required. **Practice Direction** [1977] **2** 173, Ch D.
Extension of time for complying with order—
Jurisdiction of court to extend time limit where party to consent order in default—Meaning of 'consent' order—Whether order evidencing real contract between parties or merely one to which parties did not object—Whether court having jurisdiction to extend time for complying with order—RSC Ord 3, r 5. **Siebe Gorman & Co Ltd v Pneupac Ltd** [1982] **1** 377, CA.
Financial provision—
Divorce. *See* **Divorce** (Financial provision—Consent order).
Generally. *See* **Judgment** (Order—Consent order).
Interest on costs—
Date from which interest payable. *See* **Costs** (Interest on costs—Date from which interest payable—Consent order).
Summons issued and indorsed with consent—
Procedure for obtaining order—Postal facilities. **Practice Direction** [1969] **2** 1140, QBD.
Consistory court—
Representation of parties—
Numerous parties opposing petition. *See* **Ecclesiastical law** (Consistory court—Representation of parties—Numerous parties opposing petition).
Consolidation of actions—
Actions for damages for personal injuries—
Different plaintiffs represented by different solicitors—Consolidation up to determination of liability—Separate issues as to damages—Form of order—Eight plaintiffs and three defendants—Similar causes of action alleged—RSC Ord 49, r 8. **Healey v Waddington (A) & Sons Ltd** [1954] **1** 861, CA.
Libel actions—
Libel actions brought by different plaintiffs against same defendants—Plaintiffs in both actions represented by same solicitors—Defences in both actions not identical—Application by defendants on summons for directions in second action for consolidation of both actions—No summons issued in first action—Jurisdiction—Discretion—RSC Ord 49, r 8. **Daws v Daily Sketch & Sunday Graphic Ltd** [1960] **1** 397, CA.
Separate libels contained in one book—Probable embarrassment at trial—Difficulty of apportioning costs—RSC Ord 49, r 8. **Marchant v Ford** [1936] **3** 104, CA.
Order for consolidation and service out of jurisdiction—
Limitation period prolonged to advantage of plaintiff—Whether discretion to consolidate should be exercised if plaintiff gains limitation advantage. **Arab Monetary Fund v Hashim (No 4)** [1992] **4** 860, CA.
Payments into court—
Separate writs—Payments into court admitting liability by each of two defendants—One plaintiff recovering more and one less than amount paid in—Form of order. **English v Bloom and London Passenger Transport Board** [1936] **2** 1592, KBD.
Two or more causes pending in same Division—
Pending—Whether cause pending when writ issued—Whether cause pending only when writ served—RSC Ord 4, r 9(1). **Arab Monetary Fund v Hashim (No 4)** [1992] **4** 860, CA.
Construction of statute. *See* **Statute** (Construction).
Contempt of court—
Application for committal order—
County court. *See* **Contempt of court** (Committal—County court—Application).
Generally. *See* **Contempt of court** (Committal—Application).

PRACTICE (cont)—
    Contempt of court (cont)—
        Application for release of contemnor. *See* **Contempt of court** (Release of contemnor—Application for release of contemnor).
        Committal. *See* **Contempt of court** (Committal).
        Generally. *See* **Contempt of court**.
        Publications concerning legal proceedings—
            Copyright—Distribution of court business. *See* Distribution of business among High Court Divisions—Copyright matters, *below*.
            Copyright—Generally. *See* **Copyright**.
            Order for postponement of publication. *See* **Contempt of court** (Publications concerning legal proceedings—Postponement of publication).
    Contribution—
        Generally. *See* **Contribution**.
    Correction—
        Judgment or order—
            Accidental slip or omission. *See* **Judgment** (Order—Correction—Accidental slip or omission).
        Name of party after expiry of limitation period. *See* Parties—Correction of name after expiry of limitation period, *below*.
    Costs—
        Admiralty. *See* **Admiralty** (Costs).
        Arbitration proceedings. *See* **Arbitration** (Costs).
        Certiorari. *See* **Certiorari** (Costs).
        Contempt of court—
            Committal. *See* **Contempt of court** (Committal—Costs).
        Counsel—
            Payment of costs by counsel personally. *See* **Counsel** (Payment of costs by counsel personally).
        County court. *See* **County court** (Costs).
        Court of Protection. *See* **Mental health** (Court of Protection—Practice—Costs).
        Criminal cases—
            Generally. *See* **Criminal law** (Costs).
        Divorce. *See* **Divorce** (Costs).
        Ecclesiastical cases—
            Faculty proceedings. *See* **Ecclesiastical law** (Faculty—Costs).
        Family proceedings. *See* **Family proceedings** (Costs).
        Generally. *See* **Costs**.
        House of Lords. *See* **House of Lords** (Costs).
        Judicial review—
            Costs of application for judicial review. *See* **Judicial review** (Costs of application).
        Legal aid. *See* **Legal aid**.
        Mortgage—
            Litigation relating to mortgage security. *See* **Mortgage** (Costs).
        Reduction of costs—
            Case management. *See* Civil litigation—Case management—Importance of reducing costs and delay of civil litigation, *above*.
        Solicitor—
            Generally. *See* **Solicitor** (Costs).
            Payment of costs by solicitor personally. *See* **Solicitor** (Payment of costs by solicitor personally).
    Counsel—
        Appearance in court on own behalf. *See* **Counsel** (Appearance—Appearance in court on own behalf—Practice).
        Fees—
            Family Division. *See* Family Division—Counsel's fees, *below*.
            Legal aid cases—Generally. *See* **Legal aid** (Counsel's fees).
            Note of judgment. *See* **Counsel** (Fees—Note of judgment).
            Queen's Bench Division. *See* Queen's Bench Division—Counsel's fees, *below*.
            Taxation of costs—Legal aid cases—Generally. *See* **Legal aid** (Taxation of costs—Counsel's fee).
        Originating summons—
            Parties with same interest represented by separate counsel. *See* **Originating summons** (Parties—Construction summons—Parties with same interest represented by separate counsel).
    Counterclaim—
        Amendment. *See* **Pleading** (Amendment).
        Counterclaim against co-defendant—
            Whether defendant entitled to summary judgment against co-defendant. *See* Summary judgment—Counterclaim against co-defendant, *below*.
        Dismissal for want of prosecution. *See* Dismissal of counterclaim for want of prosecution, *below*.
    County court. *See* **County court**.
    Court of Appeal—
        Criminal appeal. *See* **Criminal law** (Court of Appeal).
        Generally. *See* **Court of Appeal**.
    Court of Ecclesiastical Causes Reserved. *See* **Ecclesiastical law** (Court of Ecclesiastical Causes Reserved).
    Court of Protection—
        Medical treatment—
            Applications—Guidance. **Practice Guidance: Applications relating to medical treatment** [2020] 3 873, COP.
    Court of Protection. *See* **Mental health** (Court of Protection—Practice).
    Court-martial. *See* **Court-martial**.
    Criminal injuries compensation claim—
        Generally. *See* **Compensation** (Criminal injuries).
        Ward of court. *See* **Ward of court** (Practice—Criminal injuries compensation claim).
    Criminal proceedings—
        Appeal. *See* **Criminal law** (Appeal).

PRACTICE (cont)—
  Criminal proceedings (cont)—
    Case management—
      Heavy fraud and other complex criminal proceedings—Criminal Procedure and Investigations Act 1996, ss 3(1), 28-34—Criminal Justice Act 2003, ss 33-39, 43—Criminal Procedure Rules 2005, SI 2005/384. **Protocol for the control and management of heavy fraud and other complex criminal cases** [2005] **2** 429, CA.
      Management of legal issues in complex cases—Preparatory hearing—Guidance—Criminal Justice Act 1987, s 7—Criminal Procedure and Investigations Act 1996, s 40. **R v Quillan** [2016] **2** 653, CA.
    Consolidation of existing practice directions, practice statements and practice notes— **Practice Direction** [2002] **3** 904, CA.
      Amendment—Appeals against sentence—Provision of notice to the prosecution. **Amendment to the Consolidated Criminal Practice Direction (Appeals against sentence-the provision of notice to the prosecution)** [2003] **4** 665, CA.
      Amendment—Case management. **Amendment to the Consolidated Criminal Practice Direction (Case management)** [2005] **3** 91, CA.
      Amendment—Excusal from jury service. **Amendment to the Consolidated Criminal Practice Direction (Jury service)** [2005] **3** 89, CA.
      Amendment—Forms for use in criminal proceedings. **Amendment to the Consolidated Criminal Practice Direction (Forms for use in criminal proceedings)** [2005] **2** 916, CA; [2006] **3** 484, CA.
    Court of Appeal. *See* **Criminal law** (Court of Appeal).
    Evidence. *See* **Criminal law** (Procedure—Evidence).
    Trial. *See* **Criminal law** (Trial).
    Victim personal statements—
      Consideration of statements before determining sentence—Procedure. **Practice Direction** [2001] **4** 640, CA.
  Cross-claim—
    Set-off. *See* **Set-off** (Cross-claim).
  Cross-examination—
    Bankruptcy—
      Debtor abroad—Cross-examination on affidavits. *See* **Bankruptcy** (Practice—Evidence—Debtor abroad—Cross-examination on affidavits).
    Committal proceedings—
      Magistrate refusing to allow cross-examination during committal proceedings—Prerogative order. *See* **Criminal law** (Committal—Preliminary hearing before justices—Prerogative order—Magistrate refusing to allow cross-examination during committal proceedings).
    Criminal proceedings, in. *See* **Criminal evidence**.
    Cross-examination on deponent's affidavit—
      Summoning of witness—Whether order necessary to summon witness for cross-examination—RSC Ord 37, r 20. **Debtor (No 472 of 1950), Re a** [1958] **1** 581, CA.
    Interlocutory proceedings. *See* Interlocutory proceedings—Cross-examination of defendant, *below.*
    Interventions by judge—
      Interventions by judge during examination and cross-examination of witnesses—Whether new trial should be granted. **Jones v National Coal Board** [1957] **2** 155, CA.
    Personal injury action—
      Video evidence—Claimant seeking damages for personal injury—Defendant possessing videotape evidence apparently undermining claimant's case on impact of injury—Defendant disclosing videos to claimant—Action being struck out because of oversight by both parties—Defendant not attending application for reinstatement—District Judge reinstating action and setting trial date—Defendant subsequently applying to rely on video evidence in claimant's cross-examination—Court dismissing application on grounds that use of video evidence would lead to loss of trial date—Principles governing use of video evidence for purposes of cross-examination in personal injury cases—CPR 1.1, 1.3, 1.4, 32.1. **Rall v Hume** [2001] **3** 248, CA.
    Right to cross-examine—
      Co-defendant's right in Chancery Division—Construction summons involving also disputed questions of fact—Witness's affidavit evidence, filed on behalf of trustees, favourable to first defendant—Other defendants cross-examining witness—Whether first defendant entitled to cross-examine witness in order to strengthen witness's evidence in his favour. **McPhail v Doulton** [1967] **3** 159, Ch D.
      Refusal of right—Discretion of court—Application to annul adjudication. *See* **Bankruptcy** (Annulment—Application to annul adjudication—Cross-examination of bankrupt—Affidavit of bankrupt used in court—Cross-examination on affidavit—Discretion of court to refuse to allow cross-examination).
      Refusal of right—Substantial wrong or miscarriage of justice occasioned—Possibility of effect on decision—Matrimonial Causes Rules 1957 (SI 1957 No 619), r 73(7)—RSC Ord 59, r 11(2). **Blaise v Blaise** [1969] **2** 1032, CA.
    Slander—
      Justification not pleaded—Notice given to call evidence in mitigation of damages—Whether cross-examination on specific instances of misconduct admissible—Evidence of general bad reputation only admissible—RSC Ord 36, r 37. **D & L Caterers Ltd v D'Anjou** [1945] **1** 563, CA.
    Two defendants—
      Distinct cases. **Dryden v Surrey CC and Stewart** [1936] **2** 535, KBD.
    Witness called by judge—
      Right to cross-examine witness—Witness recalled by judge—Recall for cross-examination—Right not personal to judge—Subsequent interlocutory reference to official referee to report on one matter in issue—Jurisdiction of official referee to order defendant to appear before him for cross-examination—RSC Ord 36A, r 7(1)(a). **Fallon v Calvert** [1960] **1** 281, CA.
    Witness cross-examined on statement signed by him and made to other party—
      Statement held by cross-examining counsel but not put in evidence—Statement privileged—Waiver of privilege—Right of party calling witness to inspection of statement and to have it put in evidence. **Burnell v British Transport Commission** [1955] **3** 822, CA.

PRACTICE (cont)—
  Cross-examination (cont)—
    Witness's aide-memoire—
      Cross-examination on witness's note—Whether note becoming evidence in the case. **R v Britton** [1987] **2** 412, CA.
  Crown Court. *See* **Crown Court**.
  Crown Office list—
    Applications outside London—
      Urgent matters—Proceedings to be continued in London. **Practice Note** [1983] **2** 1020, QBD.
    Arrangement of list—
      Cases not ready to be heard—Cases ready to be heard—Cases stood out—Expedited list—Cases listed for hearing. **Practice Note** [1987] **1** 368, QBD.
    Change of title to Administrative Court—
      Renaming of orders—Lead nominated judge. **Practice Note** [2000] **4** 1071, QBD.
    Estimated length of hearing—
      Notice of estimate—Duty of counsel's clerks. **Practice Note** [1987] **1** 1184, QBD.
    Judicial review—
      Application for leave to apply for judicial review—Documents to be lodged—Relevant legislative provisions and statutory instruments. **Practice Note** [1997] **1** 128, QBD.
    Striking out for want of prosecution—
      Confirmation by applicant or appellant of case being active—Cases to be listed to show cause why they should not be struck out where no confirmation received—Withdrawal of solicitors—Solicitor regarded as continuing to act where no order declaring he has ceased to act has been obtained—RSC Ord 67, rr 1, 6. **Practice Note** [1991] **1** 1055, QBD.
    Time estimates—
      Skeleton arguments and paginated bundles—Failure to observe time limits for lodging skeleton arguments and paginated bundles—Late Crown Office papers resulting in adjournment of hearing may be penalised in costs. **Practice Note** [1994] **4** 671, QBD.
      Skeleton arguments and paginated bundles—New time limits—Arrangements for transcription of proceedings. **Practice Direction** [2000] **2** 896, QBD.
    Uncontested proceedings. *See* Uncontested proceedings—Crown Office list, *below*.
  Custody proceedings—
    Divorce. *See* **Divorce** (Custody).
    Generally. *See* **Minor** (Custody).
    Judge—
      Interview with child. *See* **Divorce** (Custody—Application—Procedure—Child—Private interview with judge).
      Removal of proceedings instituted in court of summary jurisdiction to High Court. *See* **Minor** (Custody—Jurisdiction—Removal of proceedings to High Court).
    Ward of court. *See* **Ward of court** (Custody).
  Damages—
    Breach of contract—
      Generally. *See* **Contract** (Damages for breach).
    Defamation action—
      Exemplary or punitive damages. *See* **Libel and slander** (Exemplary or punitive damages).
      Generally. *See* **Libel and slander** (Damages).
    False imprisonment. *See* **False imprisonment** (Damages).
    Generally. *See* **Damages**.
  Death of party to appeal—
    House of Lords. *See* **House of Lords** (Parties to appeal—Death of party).
  Decimalisation. *See* **Decimalisation** (Practice).
  Declaration—
    Declaration on originating summons. *See* **Originating summons** (Declaration on originating summons).
    Generally. *See* **Declaration**.
    Restrictive Practices Court. *See* **Restrictive trade practices** (Court—Power to make declaration).
    Validity of marriage—
      Parties to proceedings. *See* **Marriage** (Validity—Declaration—Parties to proceedings).
  Deconsolidation of actions—
    Libel actions—
      Libel actions by each of two plaintiffs against each of two defendants—Each pair of actions against same defendants consolidated—New trials directed—Co-plaintiffs in consolidated actions becoming represented by different solicitors—Application by defendants for consolidation of the four actions—Application by one plaintiff for deconsolidation of all actions—Single question in issue—Consolidation of four actions—Separate representation of plaintiffs not appropriate. **Lewis v Daily Telegraph Ltd (No 2)** [1964] **1** 705, CA.
  Decree absolute of divorce. *See* **Divorce** (Decree absolute).
  Decree nisi—
    Divorce. *See* **Divorce** (Decree nisi).
    Nullity proceedings. *See* **Nullity** (Decree nisi).
  Defamation—
    Pleading—
      Particulars. *See* **Libel and slander** (Particulars).
      Statement in open court. *See* **Libel and slander** (Statement in open court).
    Trial by jury—
      Libel. *See* Trial—Trial by jury—Libel, *below*.
  Default of defence—
    Judgment. *See* **Judgment** (Default of defence).
  Delay—
    Dismissal of action for want of prosecution. *See* Dismissal of action for want of prosecution, *below*.
    Moves to reduce delay. *See* Civil litigation—Case management—Importance of reducing costs and delay of civil litigation, *above*.
  Deportation appeal. *See* **Immigration** (Appeal—Deportation).

PRACTICE (cont)—
  Devolution issues—
    Wales—
      Directions—Notice to Attorney General and Assembly—Reference of devolution issue by one court
        to another court—Reference of devolution issue to Judicial Committee of Privy Council—Judicial
        review proceedings—Family proceedings—Civil proceedings—Criminal proceedings—Appeals—
        Government of Wales Act 1998, Sch 8. **Practice Note** [1999] **3** 466, Sup Ct.
  Directions, application for. *See* Application for directions, *above*.
  Disclosure and inspection of documents. *See* **Disclosure and inspection of documents**.
  Discontinuance of action—
    Consent order staying action—
      Whether consent order staying action amounting to discontinuance of action. *See* Compromise of
        action—Discontinuance of action—Stay of action, *above*.
    Costs—
      Discretion. *See* **Costs** (Order for costs—Discretion—Discontinuance of action).
    County court practice. *See* **County court** (Practice—Discontinuance of action).
    Discontinuance by plaintiff—
      Action brought in England claiming damages for personal injuries—Defendant ordered to make
        interim payments on admitting liability—Plaintiff commencing action in America in hope of
        getting higher damages—Plaintiff purporting to discontinue English action—Defendant applying
        for order to strike out notice of discontinuance and for injunction to restrain plaintiff continuing
        proceedings in America and commencing other proceedings there or elsewhere—Whether notice
        of discontinuance should be struck out—Whether injunction should be granted—RSC Ord 21,
        r 2(1). **Castanho v Brown & Root (UK) Ltd** [1981] **1** 143, HL.
      Plaintiff obtaining judgment in default—Defendant applying to set aside—Affidavit in support
        exhibiting defence and counterclaim—Parties agreeing consent order setting aside default
        judgment with unconditional liberty to serve defence and counterclaim—Plaintiff's solicitors
        obtaining carriage of consent order—Plaintiff discontinuing action immediately—Whether
        defendant's counterclaim surviving discontinuance—Whether consent order excluding plaintiff's
        right to discontinue—Whether service of notice of discontinuance an abuse of process—RSC
        Ord 15, r 2(3). **Ernst & Young (a firm) v Butte Mining plc** [1996] **2** 623, Ch D.
      Written statement delivered by plaintiff after delivery of defence—Statement delivered pursuant to
        order made on interlocutory application by plaintiff—Delivery of statement a 'proceeding in the
        action'—Subsequent notice of discontinuance invalid—RSC Ord 26, r 1—RSC Ord 53A, r 21A.
        Barclay Davit Co Ltd v Samuel Taylor & Sons (Brierley Hill) Ltd [1946] **2** 41, Ch D.
    Fatal accident. *See* **Fatal accident** (Action—Right of action—Action for damages for personal injury
      negligently discontinued after claimant's death).
  Discovery. *See* **Disclosure and inspection of documents**.
  Dismissal of action as abuse of process of court. *See* **Action** (Dismissal—Abuse of process of court).
  Dismissal of action for failure to serve statement of claim. *See* **Action** (Dismissal—Failure to serve
    statement of claim).
  Dismissal of action for want of prosecution—
    Abuse of process of court—
      Libel action—Plaintiff's conduct warranting inference that not his intention to bring action to
        trial—Plaintiff director of company—Purpose of writ to gag criticism of his conduct of company's
        affairs. **Wallersteiner v Moir** [1974] **3** 217, CA.
    Appeal—
      Action dismissed—Notice of appeal served by plaintiff outside prescribed time limit—No
        explanation given of delay—Application for leave to appeal out of time—Whether court able to
        exercise discretion in plaintiff's favour—Whether prejudice to defendant material—RSC Ord 3,
        r 5. **Finnegan v Parkside Health Authority** [1998] **1** 595, CA.
    Applications to quash certain orders or decisions of a Minister or Government department—
      Applications affecting other parties as well as immediate parties to applications—Undesirability of
        leaving applications outstanding indefinitely—Applications to be entered in Special Paper
        List—Applications to be dismissed if not prosecuted without delay—RSC Ord 94. **Biggins v
        Secretary of State for the Environment** [1981] **1** 1200, QBD.
    Arbitration proceedings. *See* **Arbitration** (Practice—Want of prosecution).
    Conditional order—
      Extension of time limit for taking steps prescribed by order—Discretion of judge to extend time
        limit—Factors relevant to exercise of discretion—Delay—Prejudice to defendant—Jurisdiction of
        judge to refuse to extend time limit on ground of delay even though no likelihood of prejudice to
        defendant if extension granted. **Pryer v Smith** [1977] **1** 218, CA.
      Jurisdiction to make order—Order dismissing action in event of breach of time limits prescribed by
        order for taking further steps in action—Order made on grounds of inexcusable and inordinate
        delay—No evidence of likelihood of prejudice to defendant as a result of delay—Whether judge
        having jurisdiction to make conditional order. **Pryer v Smith** [1977] **1** 218, CA.
    County court—
      Jurisdiction. *See* **County court** (Jurisdiction—Dismissal of action for want of prosecution).
    Delay—
      Delay in delivering statement of claim—Plaintiff applying for interlocutory relief before serving
        statement of claim and obtaining undertakings from defendant until trial of action—Plaintiff
        failing to serve statement of claim within prescribed time—Defendant applying for order to
        dismiss action—Whether mere failure to observe time limit in rules equivalent to disobedience of
        peremptory order—Whether court can dismiss action for failure to serve statement of claim in
        time without considering nature of delay—Whether court should dismiss action where delay
        inordinate and inexcusable but not contumelious and plaintiff likely to issue fresh writ within
        limitation period—RSC Ord 18, r 1, Ord 19, r 1. **Greek City Co Ltd v Demetriou (t/a Spectron
        Electronics)** [1983] **2** 921, Ch D.
      Delay in delivering statement of claim—Whether plaintiff unlikely to recover from solicitor or trade
        union a relevant consideration—RSC Ord 19, r 1. **Rowe v Tregaskes** [1968] **3** 447, CA.
      Delay substantial but not inordinate—Failure of plaintiff to comply with order to give security for
        costs—Explanation of failure—Time for giving security extended. **Thomson v Times Newspapers
        Ltd** [1969] **3** 648, CA.

773

Dismissal of action for want of prosecution (cont)—

Delay (cont)—

Inordinate delay without excuse. *See* Dismissal of action for want of prosecution—Inordinate delay without excuse, *below.*

Prejudice to defendant—Delay before issue of writ—Delay after issue of writ—Action brought within limitation period—Delay in bringing action causing prejudice to defendant—Delay after issue of writ exceeding limits prescribed by rules of court—Delay after issue of writ inordinate and inexcusable—Whether necessary to show that prejudice to defendant significantly increased by delay after issue of writ. **Birkett v James** [1977] **2** 801, HL.

Prejudice to defendant—Delay before issue of writ—Delay after issue of writ—Delay before issue of writ permissible under limitation rules—Delay causing prejudice to defendant—Delay after issue of writ inordinate and inexcusable—Subsequent inexcusable delay causing no further prejudice to defendant—Whether court may take account of prejudice caused by earlier delay. **Parker (William C) Ltd v F J Ham & Son Ltd** [1972] **3** 1051, CA.

Prejudice to defendant—Delay before issue of writ—Delay causing prejudice to defendant—Significant increase in prejudice in consequence of delay after issue of writ—Threat of action hanging over defendant prejudicing conduct of his affairs—Action brought outside limitation period pursuant to leave of court—Delay in bringing action causing prejudice to defendant—Delay after issue of writ inordinate and inexcusable—Whether prejudice to defendant significantly increased by delay after issue of writ. **Biss v Lambeth, Southwark and Lewisham Health Authority** [1978] **2** 125, CA.

Prejudice to defendant—Inquiry as to damages under cross-undertaking—Delay in presenting inquiry—Application to strike out—Principles to be applied by court in considering application—Whether party had to show that he had been prejudiced by delay. **Barratt Manchester Ltd v Bolton Metropolitan BC** [1998] **1** 1, CA.

Discretion—

Inordinate delay and prejudice to defendant established—Refusal to dismiss action—Relevant considerations—Trial of action imminent—Limitation period unexpired—Open to plaintiff to bring fresh action in respect of claim if first action dismissed. **Dutton v Spink and Beeching (Sales) Ltd** [1977] **1** 287, CA.

Inordinate delay without excuse—Plaintiff's belief that action would proceed to trial—Defendant's conduct inducing plaintiff to believe that action would proceed to trial notwithstanding plaintiff's delay—Whether court having discretion to strike out action for want of prosecution. **Reynolds v British Leyland Ltd** [1991] **2** 243, CA.

Inordinate delay without excuse—

Abuse of process—No intention of proceeding with action—Whether commencement and continuation of proceedings with no intention of bringing them to conclusion sufficient to amount to abuse of process—Whether court entitled to dismiss action—Whether necessary to establish want of prosecution. **Grovit v Doctor** [1997] **2** 417, HL.

Action being statute-barred if struck out—Plaintiff having second possible cause of action subject to longer and unexpired limitation period—Plaintiff likely to commence second action if original action struck out—Whether appropriate to strike out original action. **Arbuthnot Latham Bank Ltd v Trafalgar Holdings Ltd** [1998] **2** 181, CA.

Admission of liability—Serious prejudice to trial of issue as to damages—Dismissal of action. **Gloria v Sokoloff** [1969] **1** 204, CA.

Delay after issue of writ but before expiry of limitation period—Whether delay after issue of writ but before expiry of limitation period can be relied on after expiry of limitation period to justify dismissal of action for want of prosecution. **Rath v C S Lawrence & Partners (a firm) (P J Cook & Co (a firm), third party)** [1991] **3** 679, CA.

Delay before and after issue of writ—Impairment of memory of witnesses—Prejudice to defendant—Whether specific evidence of prejudice to defendant required to justify dismissal of action—Whether prejudice to be inferred from circumstances. **Shtun v Zalejska** [1996] **3** 411, CA.

Delay before and after issue of writ—Writ issued six months before expiration of six-year limitation period—Writ not served until three months after expiration of limitation period—Fair trial of action still possible despite delay—Defendants suffering no prejudice from post-writ delay—Whether plaintiff should be penalised for delay occurring between accrual of cause of action and date of issue of writ within limitation period—Whether post-writ delay sufficient ground for striking out action—Whether prejudice justifying striking out confined to prejudice affecting conduct of trial or extending to prejudice to defendant's business interests—Whether anxiety accompanying litigation sufficient ground of prejudice justifying striking out action. **Dept of Transport v Chris Smaller (Transport) Ltd** [1989] **1** 897, HL.

Delay before issue of writ—Delay after issue of writ—Action brought within limitation period—Whether court may have regard to delay before issue of writ in determining whether delay after issue of writ inordinate and inexcusable. **Birkett v James** [1977] **2** 801, HL.

Delay before issue of writ—Writ claiming damages for personal injuries issued outside three year limitation period pursuant to leave of court—Whether inordinate and inexcusable delay before issue of writ sufficiently prejudicial to defendants to justify dismissal of action for want of prosecution. **Biss v Lambeth, Southwark and Lewisham Health Authority** [1978] **2** 125, CA.

Delay caused by both plaintiff and defendant—Whether appropriate to allocate prejudice to different periods of delay. **Hunter v Skingley** [1997] **3** 568, CA.

Delay in delivering statement of claim—Delay due to plaintiff's inaction due to mental condition, which partly caused by injury—No real dispute as to liability—No negligence by plaintiff's solicitor—Delay prejudicial to defendant on questions of damages and payment in. **Martin v Turner** [1970] **1** 256, CA.

Discretion. *See* Dismissal of action for want of prosecution—Discretion—Inordinate delay without excuse, *above.*

Dismissal before expiry of limitation period—Question whether limitation period had expired open to serious argument—Likelihood of plaintiff bringing fresh action if first action dismissed—Court having no power to prevent plaintiff bringing fresh action—Whether interests of justice would be best served if court dismissed action. **Barclays Bank plc v Miller (Frank, third party)** [1990] **1** 1040, CA.

Failure to deliver statement of claim. *See* **Action** (Dismissal—Failure to serve statement of claim).

PRACTICE (cont)—
Dismissal of action for want of prosecution (cont)—
Inordinate delay without excuse (cont)—

Grave injustice to one party or to both—Discretion to dismiss action without affording opportunity for default to be remedied—Plaintiff left to remedy against his solicitors for negligence—Factors for consideration in exercise of court's discretion. **Allen v Sir Alfred McAlpine & Sons Ltd** [1968] **1** 543, CA.

Limitation period not expired—Likelihood of plaintiff bringing second action if first action dismissed—Action by infant plaintiff—Plaintiff having right to bring second action within extended limitation period if first action dismissed—Whether right to bring second action within extended period precluding court from dismissing action for want of prosecution—Whether court can dismiss action if inaction in prosecuting action outrageous notwithstanding right to bring fresh action—Limitation Act 1939, s 22(1). **Tolley v Morris** [1979] **2** 561, HL.

Limitation period not expired—Likelihood of plaintiff bringing second action if first action dismissed—Court having no power to prevent plaintiff bringing second action—Whether court should refuse to dismiss pending action when likely that plaintiff would in that event bring fresh action. **Birkett v James** [1977] **2** 801, HL.

No steps taken by plaintiff for two years after close of pleadings—Summons to dismiss action for want of prosecution—Second action brought based on same cause of action—Summons to dismiss second action as abuse of process of court—Application of doctrine of laches—Burden of proof—Whether dismissal of first action futile in light of second action—Whether second action abuse of process of court. **Joyce v Joyce** [1979] **1** 175, Ch D.

Personal injury to infant plaintiff—No defence on liability—Defendants paid £500 into court—No prejudice to defendants—Action not to be dismissed. **Marlton (an infant) v Lee-Leviten** [1968] **2** 874, CA.

Plaintiff an infant at time cause of action arose—Delay due to inaction of plaintiff's father—Subsequent delay by plaintiff after coming of age and after death of father—Subsequent delay by plaintiff's solicitors—Liability of defendant admitted and substantial offer made in early stages of action—Overall delay of ten years on part of plaintiff following offer—Subsequent withdrawal of offer—Undertaking by plaintiff to limit claim to amount of original offer—Prejudice to defendant—Contemporaneous medical reports available—No opportunity to examine medical witnesses—Undertaking to limit claim impracticable. **Paxton v Allsopp** [1971] **3** 370, CA.

Plaintiff's claim virtually undisputed—Counterclaim not proceeded with—Limitation period not expired—Action not dismissed. **Instrumatic Ltd v Supabrase Ltd** [1969] **2** 131, CA.

Plaintiffs in default in not proceeding with action—Counterclaim by defendants—Defendants took no step to secure that counterclaim should be heard—No statutory time bar applicable—Cross-applications for dismissal of action and of counterclaim—Appropriate order—RSC Ord 25, r 1(5). **Zimmer Orthopaedic Ltd v Zimmer Manufacturing Co** [1968] **3** 449, CA.

Plaintiffs in default in not proceeding with action—Liquidators of defendants in default in not pursuing liabilities—No prejudice to defendants—Delay in moving to strike out—Limitation period not exhausted. **Austin Securities Ltd v Northgate and English Stores Ltd** [1969] **2** 753, CA.

Prejudice to defendant—Admission of liability—Size of claim increased by delay—Whether financial prejudice due to delay sufficient to justify striking out. **Hayes v Bowman** [1989] **2** 293, CA.

Prejudice to defendant—Defendant's conduct inducing plaintiff to believe action would proceed to trial—Correspondence between parties' solicitors after inordinate and inexcusable delay by plaintiff—Whether defendant estopped from relying on delay to have action struck out—Whether defendant's subsequent conduct causing plaintiff to incur further expense in pursuing action constituting absolute bar to striking out. **Roebuck v Mungovin** [1994] **1** 568, HL.

Prejudice to defendant—Personal injury claim—Delay before issue of writ permissible under limitation rules—Failure to deliver statement of claim within prescribed period or agreed extension—Delay inexcusable—Court entitled to have regard to overall period since date of accident in determining whether delay inordinate and prejudicial to defendant. **Sweeney v Sir Robert McAlpine & Sons Ltd** [1974] **1** 474, CA.

Prejudice to defendant—Size of claim increased by delay—Whether financial prejudice due to delay sufficient to justify striking out—Whether defendant having to bring into account value to him of having in hand money, but for period of delay, payable as damages to plaintiff. **Gahan v Szerelmey (UK) Ltd** [1996] **2** 291, CA.

Statement of claim delivered after summons for dismissal of action taken out before hearing of summons—Discretion of court—Action dismissed—RSC Ord 19, r 1. **Clough v Clough** [1968] **1** 1179, CA.

Three periods of delay after issue of writ—First two periods of delay occurring before expiry of limitation period—Third period of delay occurring after expiry of limitation period—Periods of delay amounting to three years in total out of a period of six years five months between issue of writ and application to dismiss action—Whether first two periods of delay relevant—Whether court entitled to take account of all three periods of delay on application to dismiss action for want of prosecution—Whether delay inordinate and inexcusable. **Trill v Sacher** [1993] **1** 961, CA.

Time limits prescribed by rules of court—Plaintiff not in breach of time limits—Plaintiff's overall delay inordinate and inexcusable—Whether court having jurisdiction to dismiss action for want of prosecution. **Thorpe v Alexander Fork Lift Trucks Ltd** [1975] **3** 579, CA.

Unexplained delay for 12 years—RSC Ord 27, r 1. **Krakauer v Katz** [1954] **1** 244, CA.

Writ issued February 1963—Negotiations breaking down March 1965—Plaintiff seeking to revive action in January 1967. **Fitzpatrick v Batger & Co Ltd** [1967] **2** 657, CA.

Order for costs in interlocutory proceedings. *See* **Costs** (Preliminary issue—Plaintiffs successful on trial of preliminary issue—Order for costs in favour of plaintiffs—Action subsequently dismissed for want of prosecution).

Originating summons—

Action commenced by originating summons—Plaintiff failing to prosecute action with due dispatch—Whether court having power to strike out summons—Whether defendant required to show inordinate and inexcusable delay and prejudice—RSC Ord 28, r 10. **United Bank Ltd v Maniar** [1988] **1** 229, Ch D.

Dismissal of action for want of prosecution (cont)—
    Remedy against plaintiff's solicitors—
        Delay caused by negligence of plaintiff's solicitors—Whether fact that plaintiff may have remedy against solicitors relevant consideration in deciding whether to dismiss action for want of prosecution. **Birkett v James** [1977] **2** 801, HL.
    Res judicata. *See* **Estoppel** (Res judicata—Want of prosecution—Dismissal of earlier action for want of prosecution).
    Third party proceedings. *See* Third party proceedings—Dismissal for want of prosecution, *below*.
    Without prejudice correspondence—
        Admissibility in application to strike out for want of prosecution. *See* **Evidence** (Without prejudice correspondence—Application to dismiss action for want of prosecution).
Dismissal of counterclaim for want of prosecution—
    Inordinate delay without excuse—
        Delay in prosecuting counterclaim—No steps taken by either party for over three years—Defendant by counterclaim obtaining order striking out counterclaim for want of prosecution—Whether court having power to strike out counterclaim for want of prosecution—If so, whether court dismissing counterclaim should also dismiss claim in main action. **Owen (t/a Max Owen Associates) v Pugh** [1995] **3** 345, QBD.
Dispensing with service—
    Claim form—
        Service out of jurisdiction. *See* **Claim form** (Service—Service out of the jurisdiction—Dispensing with service).
Distribution of business among High Court Divisions—
    Copyright matters—
        Writ in copyright action issued out of Queen's Bench Division—Judge in chambers making order for delivery up of printing plates and granting injunction restraining breach of copyright on ex parte application—Whether order made on false basis of law—Supreme Court Act 1981, s 61, Sch 1, para 1(i). **Apac Rowena Ltd v Norpol Packaging Ltd** [1991] **4** 516, Ch D.
District judge—
    Appeal from. *See* Appeal—Appeal from district judge, *above*.
Divorce—
    Custody. *See* **Divorce** (Custody).
    Decree absolute. *See* **Divorce** (Decree absolute).
    Decree nisi. *See* **Divorce** (Decree nisi).
    Financial provision. *See* **Divorce** (Financial provision).
    Generally. *See* **Divorce** (Practice).
Document—
    Application to search for, inspect and copy documents. *See* Application to search for, inspect and copy documents, *above*.
    Chancery Division. *See* Chancery Division—Documents, *above*.
    Court of Appeal—
        Generally. *See* **Court of Appeal** (Practice).
    Court of Appeal and High Court—
        Marking—Binding—Sequence—Pagination—Copies—Bundles of documents generally—Effect of failure to comply with rules—RSC Ord 41. **Practice Direction** [1995] **2** 511, QBD; **Practice Note** [1983] **3** 33, CA.
    Destruction. *See* **Document** (Destruction).
    Detention by court—
        Inherent jurisdiction—Document material to case—Interests of justice—Document not proved or put in evidence—Document submitted for inspection consequent on order of court—Document belonging to person not a party to proceedings—Power of court to order detention of document pending judgment in action or further order once document in court's hands. **Beck v Value Capital Ltd** [1974] **3** 437, Ch D.
    Disclosure. *See* **Disclosure and inspection of documents**.
    Document for use abroad—
        Certification—Judgments, orders and other filed documents for use in foreign or Commonwealth courts—Issue of—Authentication—Chancery Division—Queen's Bench Division. **Practice Direction** [1971] **2** 160, QBD.
    Filing. *See* Filing, *below*.
    Production in evidence—
        Leave to produce plan, photograph or model as evidence without giving other party opportunity to inspect it—Discretion of court to allow production—'Special reasons' for allowing production—Guidelines on how discretion should be exercised—RSC Ord 38, r 5. **McGuinness v Kellogg Co of GB Ltd** [1988] **2** 902, CA.
        Leave to produce video film as evidence without giving the other party opportunity to inspect it—Personal injury case—Video film showing plaintiff to be a deliberate malingerer—Whether order for non-disclosure pre-trial appropriate in the context of the 'cards-on-the-table' approach to litigation—RSC Ord 38, r 5. **Khan v Armaguard Ltd** [1994] **3** 545, CA.
    Restrictive Practices Court—
        Marking etc. *See* **Restrictive trade practices** (Court—Evidence—Affidavits, exhibits, documents).
Drawing-up orders. *See* Order—Drawing-up, *below*.
Early trial. *See* Trial—Order for early trial, *below*.
Ecclesiastical courts. *See* **Ecclesiastical law**.
Employment Appeal Tribunal. *See* **Employment Appeal Tribunal** (Practice).
Employment tribunal—
    Procedure. *See* **Employment tribunal** (Procedure).
    Striking out. *See* **Employment tribunal** (Striking out).
Employment tribunal. *See* **Employment tribunal**.
Enduring power of attorney—
    Court of Protection. *See* **Power of attorney** (Enduring power of attorney).
Error of procedure—
    Service by court. *See* **Claim form** (Service—Service by court—Error of procedure).

PRACTICE (cont)—
    Estate duty. *See* **Estate duty** (Practice).
    Estimate of length of trial. *See* Trial—Estimate of length of trial, *below*.
    Estoppel. *See* **Estoppel**.
    European Court—
        Generally. *See* **European Union** (European Court of Justice).
        Reference to. *See* **European Union** (Reference to European Court—Practice).
    European Union. *See* **European Union** (Procedure).
    Evidence—
        Arbitration appeal. *See* **Arbitration** (Award—Appeal—Evidence).
        Civil proceedings—
            Standard of proof. *See* **Evidence** (Standard of proof—Civil proceedings).
        Court of Appeal. *See* **Court of Appeal** (Evidence).
        Criminal proceedings. *See* **Criminal evidence**.
        Documentary evidence—
            Admissibility. *See* **Document** (Admissibility in evidence).
        Expert evidence—
            Admissibility—Investigation into aircraft accident—Death in aircraft accident—Proceedings in negligence brought against pilot—Air Accident Investigation Branch report—Whether report admissible in proceedings against pilot—Whether report excluded under common law rule—Whether report conforming to rules governing experts' reports—CPR 35. **Hoyle v Rogers** [2014] 3 550, CA.
            Admissibility—Non-medical evidence—Actuarial evidence—Application to master or registrar for leave to adduce non-medical oral expert evidence at trial—Whether master, registrar or judge in chambers having power to rule on admissibility of evidence when hearing application for leave to adduce evidence—RSC Ord 38, rr 36(1), 38(1). **Sullivan v West Yorkshire Passenger Transport Executive** [1985] 2 134, CA.
            Court expert. *See* **Evidence** (Expert evidence—Court expert).
            Disclosure to other parties—Action for medical negligence—Disclosure of experts' reports—Whether mutual pre-trial disclosure of reports appropriate in medical negligence cases—Whether directions should be made ordering such disclosure—RSC Ord 38, r 38. **Naylor v Preston Area Health Authority** [1987] 2 353, CA.
            Disclosure to other parties—Action for medical negligence—Disclosure of reports—Number of medical witnesses—Whether action for medical negligence an exception to general rule requiring disclosure of medical reports in personal injuries actions unless sufficient reason for non disclosure—Whether number of medical witnesses should be limited in action for medical negligence—RSC Ord 38, r 37(2). **Rahman v Kirklees Area Health Authority** [1980] 3 610, CA.
            Disclosure to other parties—Defendant wishing to give expert evidence on his own behalf—Whether rules of disclosure apply where expert witness is one of the parties. **Shell Pensions Trust Ltd v Pell Frischmann & Partners (a firm)** [1986] 2 911, QBD.
            Disclosure to other parties—Order made during case management conference giving permission to each party to instruct expert in named field—Defendant instructing one expert then deciding to rely on a second expert—Judge deciding permission limited to first expert—Judge giving permission for defendant to rely on second expert provided report of first expert disclosed—Whether original order identifying first expert—Whether imposing condition as to disclosure curtailing right to legal professional privilege—CPR 35.4. **Vasiliou v Hajigeorgiou** [2005] 3 17, CA.
            Disclosure to other parties—Substance of evidence in form of written report—RSC Ord 38, r 38(1). **Ollett v Bristol Aerojet Ltd** [1979] 3 544, QBD.
            Disclosure to other parties—Time for disclosure—Personal injuries action—Non-medical expert's reports—Court ordering disclosure of reports—Whether disclosure should be mutual—Whether court may order one party to disclose his expert's report first—RSC Ord 38, r 37. **Kirkup v British Rail Engineering Ltd** [1983] 3 147, CA.
            Exchange of experts' reports. *See* **Evidence** (Expert evidence—Experts' reports).
            Expert's responsibilities—Court ordering defendant's expert to provide details of matters referred to in practice direction—Expert failing to provide details and court debarring him from giving expert evidence—Whether appropriate to bar expert from giving evidence—Whether parties should be allowed to override by agreement judge's exercise of discretion—CPR Pt 35, practice direction, para 1. **Stevens v Gullis (Pile, third party)** [2000] 1 527, CA.
            Jointly-instructed sole expert—Whether permissible for party to have conference with jointly-instructed expert in other party's absence—CPR 35.7. **Peet v Mid-Kent Healthcare NHS Trust** [2002] 3 688, CA.
            Personal injuries action—Reports. *See* Personal injuries action—Experts' reports, *below*.
        Expert witness—
            Admissibility—Expert witness having long-standing friendship with party proposing to call him—Whether relationship between expert and party rendering expert's evidence inadmissible. **Liverpool Roman Catholic Archdiocese Trustees Incorporated v Goldberg (No 2)** [2001] 4 950, Ch D.
        Generally. *See* **Evidence**.
        Immigration appeal. *See* **Immigration** (Appeal—Evidence).
        Restrictive Practices Court. *See* **Restrictive trade practices** (Court—Evidence).
        Similar facts. *See* **Evidence** (Similar facts).
        Standard of proof. *See* **Evidence** (Standard of proof).
        Video link, by—
            Prisoner. *See* **Prison** (Prisoner—Powers of transfer—Transfer of prisoners for other judicial purposes).
        Without prejudice negotiations. *See* **Evidence** (Without prejudice negotiations).
    Ex parte application—
        Chancery Division. *See* Chancery Division—Ex parte applications to master and consent orders, *above*.
        Duty of applicant—
            Duty to be candid with court—Extent of duty. **Debtor (No 75N of 1982, Warrington), Re a, ex p the Debtor v National Westminster Bank plc** [1983] 3 545, Ch D.
        Leave on. *See* Leave on ex parte application, *below*.

PRACTICE (cont)—
  Ex parte application (cont)—
    Wardship proceedings. *See* **Ward of court** (Practice—Application in wardship proceedings—Ex parte application).
  Ex parte proceedings—
    Costs. *See* **Costs** (Order for costs—Ex parte proceedings).
  Exchange of witnesses' statements. *See* **Evidence** (Exchange of witnesses' statements).
  Execution. *See* **Execution**.
  Exhibits—
    County court. *See* **County court** (Practice—Exhibits).
    Court of Appeal and High Court—
      Marking—Binding—Sequence—Pagination—Copies—Bundles of documents generally—Effect of failure to comply with rules—RSC Ord 41. **Practice Direction** [1995] **2** 511, QBD; **Practice Note** [1983] **3** 33, CA.
    Generally. *See* **Evidence** (Exhibits).
    Restrictive Practices Court. *See* **Restrictive trade practices** (Court—Evidence—Affidavits, exhibits, documents).
  Expedited hearings—
    Divisional Court. *See* **Divisional Court** (Expedited hearings).
  Expert evidence—
    Admiralty action. *See* **Evidence** (Expert witness—Admiralty action).
    Criminal proceedings. *See* **Criminal evidence** (Expert evidence).
    Generally. *See* Evidence—Expert evidence, *above*.
    Legal aid case. *See* **Legal aid** (Expert evidence).
    Personal injuries action—
      Reports. *See* Personal injuries action—Experts' reports, *below*.
  Extension of time—
    Company—
      Registration of charge. *See* **Company** (Charge—Registration—Extension of time).
    Family provision application. *See* **Family provision** (Time for application—Extension).
    Generally. *See* **Time** (Extension of time).
  Extradition—
    Appeal—
      Appeal where case sent to Secretary of State—Skeleton arguments—Bundles—Extradition Act 2003, s 103—CPR PD 52, 54. **Mustafa Kamel Mustafa (otherwise Abu Hamza) v United States Government** [2008] **3** 1069n, QBD.
  Faculty—
    Ecclesiastical cases—
      Generally. *See* **Ecclesiastical law** (Faculty—Practice).
      Jurisdiction. *See* **Ecclesiastical law** (Faculty—Jurisdiction).
  Family court—
    Allocation of cases—
      Enforcement proceedings to be commenced in family court save for limited circumstances—Matrimonial and Family Proceedings Act 1984, s 31E(1)(a)—CPR 73.10C(3)—FPR 5.4, PD 40A, para 4.1. **S v E** [2018] **3** 938, Fam Ct.
    Proceedings and decisions—
      Fact-finding hearings—Proper approach to fact-finding where domestic abuse alleged—Whether focus on pattern of behaviour as opposed to specific incidents—Relevance of criminal law concepts—Guidance—Children Act 1989, s 1(3)(e)—FPR PD 12J. **H-N (children) (domestic abuse: finding of fact hearings), Re** [2022] **1** 475n, CA.
      Review—Reopening findings of fact—Proper approach. **CTD (a child) (care proceedings: rehearing), Re** [2021] **1** 803n, CA.
      Review—Whether family court having jurisdiction to review findings of fact—Whether review by trial court or appeal appropriate—Test to be applied—Matrimonial and Family Proceedings Act 1984, s 31F(6). **E (children: reopening findings of fact), Re** [2020] **2** 539, CA.
    Reporting—
      Guidance. **Practice Guidance: Reporting in the Family Courts** [2020] **2** 395, Fam D.
  Family Division—
    Affidavit—
      Filing. *See* **Affidavit** (Filing—Practice—Family Division).
    Allocation of cases to judiciary—
      District judges—Jurisdiction—Inheritance (Provision for Family and Defendants) Act 1975—Trusts of Land and Appointment of Trustees Act 1996, s 14—CPR Pt 2. **Practice Direction** [1999] **3** 192, Fam D.
    Ancillary relief—
      Arrangement involving acquisition, retention, use or control of criminal property—Guidance—Proceeds of Crime Act 2002, ss 328, 333, 335, 338, 342. **P v P (ancillary relief: proceeds of crime)** [2003] **4** 843, Fam D.
      Property adjustment and lump sum orders—Costs—Estimate of parties' costs to be made—Costs already incurred and expected costs of hearing to be differentiated. **Practice Direction** [1988] **2** 63, Fam D.
    Appeal from magistrates' court. *See* Family proceedings—Appeals—Appeals from magistrates' courts, *below*.
    Appeal from registrar. *See* **Family Division** (Appeal—Appeal from registrar).
    Applications relating to children. *See* **Child** (Practice—Matrimonial causes—Applications relating to children).
    Case stated. *See* **Case stated** (Family Division).
    Cases proceeding in Royal Courts of Justice—
      Judicial continuity—Allocated judge—Case management conference—Children Act 1989, Pt IV. **Practice Direction** [2002] **3** 603, Fam D.
    Counsel's fees—
      Interlocutory fees—Scale of fees to be allowed on taxation. **Practice Direction** [1980] **1** 496, Fam D; [1982] **1** 128, Fam D.

PRACTICE (cont)—
  Family Division (cont)—
    Divisional Court—
      Appeal to Divisional Court—Child—Child a party in court below and affected by appeal—Guardian ad litem—Continuation of appointment—Notice—Consent—Legal aid—RSC Ord 55, r 4(1)(a), Ord 80, r 3(8), Ord 90, rr 28, 29(4)(b)—Legal Aid (General) Regulations 1980, reg 47. **Practice Direction** [1986] **1** 896, Fam D.
    Estimated length of hearing—
      Notice of estimate. **Practice Direction** [1984] **1** 783, Fam D.
    Generally. *See* **Family Division**.
    Incapacitated adults—
      Declaratory proceedings—Commencement and determination. **Practice Direction** [2002] **1** 794, Fam D.
    Long Vacation. *See* Long Vacation—Family Division, *below*.
    Lump sum applications—
      Costs. *See* Family Division—Ancillary relief—Property adjustment and lump sum orders—Costs, *above*.
    Matrimonial causes—
      Generally. *See* Matrimonial causes, *below*.
      Matrimonial home—Generally. *See* **Husband and wife** (Matrimonial home).
    Minors—
      Removal outside jurisdiction. *See* **Minor** (Removal outside jurisdiction).
    Proceedings relating to children—
      Estimated length of hearing—Duty of parties to give time estimate—Revision of time estimate—Children Act 1989. **Practice Direction** [1994] **1** 155, Fam D.
    Reporting. *See* Family court, *above*.
    Sale of land by court. *See* **Sale of land** (Sale by court).
    Solicitor acting in matrimonial proceedings for petitioner—
      Notice of acting—Notice of change—Notice of acting required to be filed where solicitor acting for limited purpose—Notice of change required to be filed where solicitor instructed generally in proceedings—Consequence of failure to file notice. **Practice Direction** [1977] **1** 844, Fam D.
    Tape recorders—
      Use in court. *See* Tape recorders—Use of tape recorders in court, *below*.
    Video conferencing—
      Procedure—Facilities in Royal Courts of Justice. **Practice Direction** [2002] **1** 1024, Fam D.
    Welfare report on child. *See* **Child** (Welfare—Welfare report).
    Without notice orders—
      Disclosure obligations—Recital of evidence in order—Undertakings in damages—Guidance. **W v H (Family Division: without notice orders)** [2001] **1** 300, Fam D.
      Guidance. **Kelly v BBC** [2001] **1** 323, Fam D.
      Undertakings—Principles and guidance. **S (a child) (Family Division: without notice orders), Re** [2001] **1** 362, Fam D.
  Family proceedings—
    Ancillary relief—
      Conciliation—Financial dispute resolution appointment—Admissibility in evidence of things said during appointment—Court's expectations of parties and legal representatives. **Practice Direction** [1997] **3** 768, Fam D.
      Costs—Family Proceedings (Amendment) Rules 2006. **Practice Direction (Ancillary Relief: Costs)** [2006] **2** 643, Fam D.
      Pre-application protocol—Financial dispute resolution appointment—Expert evidence—Family Proceedings (Amendment No 2) Rules 1999. **Practice Direction** [2000] **3** 379, Fam D.
    Appeals—
      Appeals from magistrates' courts—Documents to be filed in care centre registry—Appeal to be heard by Family Division judge—Place of hearing—Domestic Proceedings and Magistrates' Courts Act 1978—Children Act 1989, s 94—Family Proceedings Rules 1991, rr 4.22, 8.2—Children (Allocation of Proceedings) Order 1991, Sch 2. **Practice Direction** [1992] **1** 864, Fam D.
    Chambers proceedings. *See* **Family proceedings** (Chambers hearings).
    Committal applications—
      Procedure. **Practice Direction** [2001] **2** 704, Fam D.
    Family court. *See* Family court, *above*.
    Generally. *See* **Family proceedings**.
    Hearings—
      Court bundles. **Practice Direction** [2000] **2** 287, Fam D.
    Human rights—
      Citation of authority—Claims for declaration of incompatibility—Claims in respect of judicial acts—Human Rights Act 1998, ss 2, 4. **Practice Direction** [2000] **4** 288, Fam D.
    Proceedings within jurisdiction of county courts—
      Allocation to specified judges or specified descriptions of judge—Pending proceedings—Judges of Family Division included in all descriptions of judge—Proceedings including more than one specified class of proceedings—Adjournment where unopposed proceedings becoming opposed during trial and no longer of description allocated to trial judge—Interim orders—Allocation of appeals—Adoption Act 1976, ss 14, 15, 18, 20, 21, 27, 28, 29, 55—Domestic Violence and Matrimonial Proceedings Act 1976, s 1—Supreme Court Act 1981, s 128—Matrimonial Homes Act 1983, ss 1, 9—Matrimonial Proceedings Act 1984, s 42—Children Act 1989, ss 4(1)(a), (3), 5(1), 6(7), 8, 10, 13(1), 16(6), 25, 31, 33(7), 34, 36(1), 38(1), 39(1), (2), (3), (4), 43, 44, 45(4), (8), 46(7), 48(9), 50, 91(14), (15), (17), Sch 2, para 19(1), Sch 3, paras 6, 15(2), 17(1), Sch 14, para 11(3)—Courts and Legal Services Act 1990, s 9—CCR Ord 37, r 6—Family Proceedings Rules 1991, r 8.1—Children (Allocation of Proceedings) Order 1991—Children (Allocation of Proceedings) (Appeals) Order 1991. **Practice Direction** [1991] **4** 764, Fam D.
  Review. *See* Family court—Proceedings and decisions—Review, *above*.
  Family provision. *See* **Family provision**.

PRACTICE (cont)—
    Fast track—
        District judge—
            Jurisdiction—Whether district judge having jurisdiction to continue to hear trial of liability on fast track if allowing amendment taking value of claim over fast track limit—Whether district judge should reallocate claim to multi-track if allowing such amendment—CPR 26.10. **Maguire v Molin** [2002] **4** 325, CA.
    Fax—
        Service by fax. See Service—Service by fax, *below*.
    Filing—
        Affidavit. *See* **Affidavit** (Filing).
        Filing of document at court—
            Whether delivery of document to court office constituting 'filing' if no one present to receive or authenticate it—CPR 2.3(1). **Van Aken v Camden London BC** [2003] **1** 552, CA.
    Financial provision—
        Divorce proceedings. *See* **Divorce** (Financial provision—Practice and procedure).
        Nullity proceedings. *See* **Nullity** (Financial provision).
    Fitness to plead—
        Criminal proceedings. *See* **Criminal law** (Trial—Fitness to plead).
    Foreclosure proceedings—
        Parties—
            Property subject to debentures issued in a series—All debenture holders to be made defendants—RSC Ord 16. **Westminster Bank Ltd v Residential Properties Improvement Co Ltd** [1938] **2** 374, Ch D.
    Foreign cause of action—
        Stay of proceedings. *See* Stay of proceedings—Foreign cause of action, *below*.
    Foreign child—
        Adoption. *See* **Adoption** (Practice—Foreign child).
    Foreign currency—
        Judgment. *See* **Judgment** (Payment of sum of money—Foreign currency).
    Foreign decree—
        Divorce—
            Generally. *See* **Divorce** (Foreign decree).
        Nullity suit—
            Recognition. *See* **Nullity** (Recognition of foreign decree).
    Foreign defendant—
        Adding as defendant. *See* Parties—Adding defendant—Foreign defendant, *below*.
    Foreign judgment—
        Enforcement or recognition. *See* **Conflict of laws** (Foreign judgment).
        Registration in England. *See* **Conflict of laws** (Foreign judgment—Registration in England).
    Foreign law—
        Conflict of laws. *See* **Conflict of laws** (Foreign law).
        Evidence. *See* **Evidence** (Foreign law).
    Foreign order—
        Enforcement. *See* **Conflict of laws** (Foreign order—Enforcement).
    Foreign party. *See* Parties—Foreign party, *below*.
    Foreign proceedings—
        Document for use in. *See* Document—Document for use abroad, *above*.
        Restraint of foreign proceedings. *See* **Conflict of laws** (Foreign proceedings—Restraint of foreign proceedings).
    Forfeiture—
        Relief against forfeiture—
            Time—Power to extend time—Liberty to apply. **Chandless-Chandless v Nicholson** [1942] **2** 315, CA.
    Fraud—
        Proceedings involving alternative allegation of fraud—
            Action begun by originating summons—Whether essential to be begun by writ or whether may continue as though commenced by writ—RSC Ord 5, r 2, Ord 28, r 8. **Green Lane (462), Ilford, Re** [1971] **1** 315, Ch D.
    Freeing child for adoption. *See* **Adoption** (Practice—Freeing child for adoption).
    Freezing order—
        Generally. *See* Pre-trial or post-judgment relief—Freezing order, *below*.
    Funds in court—
        Funds exceeding £7,500—
            Holding by Public Trustee out of court—Direction by court—Minors' funds—Powers of court extended to district registrars—Procedure—Fees. **Practice Direction** [1977] **3** 351, QBD.
            Holding by Public Trustee out of court—Procedure—Fees—RSC Ord 80, r 12. **Practice Direction** [1970] **1** 811, QBD.
        Investment of funds in court—
            Admiralty practice. *See* **Admiralty** (Practice—Investment of funds in court).
            Payments to be placed to deposit account and not short-term investment account—Deposit rate—Payment of deposit interest—Short-term investment account only available for money held in court for benefit of successful plaintiffs under disability—Payments to which new rules apply—Supreme Court Funds (Amendment) Rules 1983—County Court Funds (Amendment) Rules 1983. **Practice Direction** [1983] **1** 928, LC.
        Public trustee. *See* **Public Trustee** (Funds in court—Investment of).
        Payment out—
            Funds belonging to foreign state—Application by solicitors representing person claiming to represent government of foreign state—Duty of solicitors to obtain properly constituted authority to receive money—Court requiring confirmation that solicitors on record had properly constituted authority to receive money and that government instructing them was in fact government of foreign state. **Somalia (Republic) v Woodhouse Drake & Carey (Suisse) SA** [1993] **1** 371, QBD.

PRACTICE (cont)—
    Funds in court (cont)—
        Payment out (cont)—
            Funds belonging to foreign state—Application for payment out by person claiming to represent government of foreign state—Application opposed by former diplomatic representative of legitimate government overthrown in civil war—Whether former diplomatic representative having locus standi to be joined as party to proceedings. **Somalia (Republic) v Woodhouse Drake & Carey (Suisse) SA** [1993] **1** 371, QBD.
        Transfer to High Court from county court—
            Minors' funds—Procedure—County Courts Act 1959, s 174A—Supreme Court Funds Rules 1975, r 22(4). **Practice Direction** [1983] **1** 800, QBD.
        Transfer to short-term investment account—
            Procedure for obtaining order. **Practice Direction** [1970] **1** 1107, QBD.
            Revocation of earlier direction—Supreme Court Funds (Amendment) Rules 1983. **Practice Direction** [1983] **2** 35, QBD.
    Garnishee order—
        Generally. *See* **Execution** (Garnishee order).
    Grant of administration. *See* **Administration of estates** (Grant of administration—Practice).
    Group action—
        Costs. *See* **Costs** (Group action).
    Guardian ad litem—
        Adoption proceedings. *See* **Adoption** (Practice—Guardian ad litem).
        Official Solicitor. *See* **Official Solicitor** (Guardian ad litem).
        Wardship proceedings. *See* **Ward of court** (Guardian ad litem).
    Guardianship of minors—
        Appeals. *See* **Minor** (Guardianship—Appeals from county courts or courts of summary jurisdiction).
        Custody and access. *See* **Minor** (Practice—Wardship and guardianship proceedings—Custody and access).
        Evidence. *See* **Minor** (Guardianship—Evidence).
        Generally. *See* **Guardianship of minor** (Practice).
        Removal of minor outside jurisdiction. *See* **Minor** (Removal outside jurisdiction).
    Habeas corpus—
        Extradition. *See* **Extradition** (Habeas corpus).
        Generally. *See* **Habeas corpus**.
    Handed down judgment. *See* **Judgment** (Handed down judgments).
    Hansard—
        Reference to Hansard—
            Construction of statute. *See* **Statute** (Construction—Hansard—Reference to proceedings in Parliament as an aid to construction).
            Construction of statutory instrument. *See* **Statutory instrument** (Construction—Hansard—Reference to proceedings in Parliament as an aid to construction).
    Hear-by dates—
        Court of Appeal. *See* **Court of Appeal** (Practice—Hear-by dates).
    Hearing—
        Application for committal for contempt of court—
            Wardship proceedings. *See* **Contempt of court** (Committal—Application—Hearing—Contempt in relation to wardship proceedings).
        Chancery Division—
            Dates. *See* Chancery Division—Hearing dates, *above*.
            Hearings by judges outside London. *See* Chancery Division—Hearings by judges outside London, *above*.
        Company matters. **Practice Direction** [2000] **1** 928, Ch D.
        County court—
            Failure to request hearing date within time prescribed. *See* **County court** (Practice—Striking out—Failure to request hearing date within time prescribed).
        Court of Appeal, Civil Division. *See* **Court of Appeal** (Practice—Hearing).
        Expediting hearing—
            Undefended suit. **Practice Direction** [1965] **1** 340, Div.
        Family proceedings. *See* Family proceedings—Hearings, *above*.
        Hearing in private—
            Circumstances in which hearing will be conducted in camera. **R v Chief Registrar of Friendly Societies, ex p New Cross Building Society** [1984] **2** 27, CA.
            Confidential information—Disagreement between parties as to whether partial final (and confidential) arbitral award binding in court proceedings—Party making 'privity application' to resolve disagreement—At case management conference ('CMC') preceding hearing of privity application judge ordering that CMC be heard in private and that award not to become public until court having determined that it should—Whether judge failing to properly apply test for private hearing—Whether judge wrong to order that award not to become public until decision of court to that effect—Whether privity application should be heard in private—CPR 39.2, CPR 62.10. **CDE v NOP** [2022] **2 Comm** 691, CA.
            Legitimation case. *See* **Legitimation** (Practice—Hearing of petition in camera).
        Matrimonial causes—
            Royal Courts of Justice—Circuit judges sitting as judges of High Court—Circuit judges hearing shorter High Court applications and 'short' High Court matrimonial causes—High Court judges hearing longer applications in county court matrimonial causes—Rules as to right of audience—Costs—Courts Act 1971, ss 20(3), 23. **Practice Direction** [1973] **2** 288, Fam D.
    House of Lords. *See* **House of Lords**.
    Husband and wife—
        Injunction. *See* **Injunction** (Husband and wife).
        Maintenance. *See* **Husband and wife** (Maintenance).
        Summary proceedings. *See* **Husband and wife** (Property—Summary proceedings).
    Immigration—
        Appeal. *See* **Immigration** (Appeal).

PRACTICE (cont)—

Immigration (cont)—
   Application to Divisional Court. *See* **Immigration** (Practice—Application to Divisional Court).
   Generally. *See* **Immigration** (Practice).
   Successive applications for leave to enter UK. *See* **Immigration** (Leave to enter—Successive applications).
Immunity from civil action—
   Generally. *See* **Action** (Immunity from suit).
Indemnity costs—
   Order for costs. *See* **Costs** (Order for costs—Indemnity costs).
Indictment. *See* **Indictment**.
Indorsement—
   Judgment—
      Default of defence. *See* **Judgment** (Default of defence—Indorsement of court copy of judgment).
   Writ. *See* **Writ** (Indorsement).
Industrial relations. *See* **Industrial relations** (Practice).
Industrial tribunal—
   Generally. *See* **Employment tribunal**.
Injunction—
   Attachment of power of arrest to injunction—
      Husband and wife—Domestic violence. *See* **Injunction** (Husband and wife—Domestic violence—Attachment of power of arrest to injunction—Practice).
   Generally. *See* **Injunction**.
   Interlocutory—
      Freezing order. *See* Pre-trial or post-judgment relief—Freezing order, *below*.
      Standard forms of order—Provision of draft on disk. **Practice Direction** [1997] **1** 287, High Ct.
      Variation—Appeal—Leave to appeal—Freezing order—Application to vary freezing order—Order granting or refusing such variation—Whether leave to appeal from order required—Supreme Court Act 1981, s 18(1)(h). **Atlas Maritime Co SA v Avalon Maritime Ltd, The Coral Rose (No 2)** [1991] **4** 781, CA.
   Summary procedure. *See* **Injunction** (Summary procedure—Practice).
Inquest. *See* **Coroner** (Inquest—Practice and procedure).
Insolvency proceedings. *See* **Insolvency**.
Inspection by judge—
   Absence of parties—
      Action for nuisance—Purpose of inspection. **Halsey v Esso Petroleum Co Ltd** [1961] **2** 145, QBD.
      Scene of accident—No demonstration or reconstruction of circumstances of accident—No relevant change in circumstances—Propriety. **Salsbury v Woodland** [1969] **3** 863, CA.
   Discretion—
      Nature of inspection—Real evidence—Judge having power to inspect even though parties united in opposition—Application by one party for view—Proper approach to determine whether sufficient grounds for rejecting application—RSC Ord 35, r 8(1). **Tito v Waddell** [1975] **3** 997, Ch D.
   Function of view—
      Allegation of unsafe system of work—No rebutting evidence—Judge taking into consideration own opinion formed on inspection—Power of judge. **Buckingham v Daily News Ltd** [1956] **2** 904, CA.
   Inspection of any place with respect to which question arises—
      Place outside jurisdiction—Action relating to land outside jurisdiction—Whether judge having power to inspect land outside jurisdiction—RSC Ord 35, r 8(1). **Tito v Waddell** [1975] **3** 997, Ch D.
   Opinion formed on inspection—
      Allegation of unsafe system of work—No rebutting evidence—Judge taking into consideration own opinion formed on inspection. **Buckingham v Daily News Ltd** [1956] **2** 904, CA.
Inspection of goods—
   Non-compliance with order—
      Striking out defence—RSC Ord 31, r 21. **Oxford (Charles) Ltd v Gonshaw Ltd** [1948] **2** 229, CA.
Inspection of property—
   Document not subject-matter of action—
      Interlocutory motion—Ex parte application—Jurisdiction to make order—Plaintiff wishing to support claim by reference to books of account in defendant's custody—Plaintiff fearing that accounts would be destroyed—Whether discretion to order inspection and removal of accounts—Principles on which discretion to be exercised. **Yousif v Salama** [1980] **3** 405, CA.
   Joinder of parties. *See* Parties—Joinder of parties—Inspection of property, *below*.
   Property subject-matter of action or in respect of which question arising—
      Document—Document alleged to be defamatory—Application to inspect document before issue of writ for libel—Whether application to obtain discovery of 'document' or application to inspect 'property'—Supreme Court Act 1981, s 33(1)(a), (2). **Huddleston v Control Risks Information Services Ltd** [1987] **2** 1035, QBD.
      Document—Expert inspection of document as to which question arose in an action—Written agreement allegedly signed by testatrix—Execution by her in issue—Production of agreement and other documents bearing testatrix's signature, for examination and test by handwriting expert—Plaintiffs legally aided—Condition for communication of result to defendants—Condition wrongly imposed—RSC, Ord 50, r 3—Legal Aid and Advice Act 1949, s 1(7)(b). **Saxton (decd), Re** [1962] **3** 92, CA.
      House—Property not in possession of party to action—Order against party not in possession subject to consent of requisitioning local authority—RSC Ord 50, r 3. **Penfold v Pearlberg** [1955] **3** 120, Ch D.
   Pre-trial relief. *See* Pre-trial or post-judgment relief—Search order, *below*.
Insurance—
   Motor insurance—
      Motor Insurers' Bureau—Adding as defendant. *See* **Motor insurance** (Rights of third parties against insurers—Motor Insurers' Bureau—Adding as defendant).
Interest—
   Arbitration award. *See* **Arbitration** (Award—Interest).
   Damages. *See* **Interest** (Damages).

PRACTICE (cont)—
  Interest (cont)—
    Discretion of court to award—
      Inherent equitable jurisdiction—Whether jurisdiction to award interest in simple action for debt. **Lawrie (Alex) Factors Ltd v Modern Injection Moulds Ltd** [1981] **3** 658, QBD.
      Proceedings commenced before coming into force of Act—Law Reform (Miscellaneous Provisions) Act 1934, s 3(1). **Bank of Athens Société Anonyme v Royal Exchange Assurance** [1938] **1** 514, KBD.
    Interest on costs. *See* **Costs** (Interest on costs).
    Pleading—
      Claim—Debt or liquidated sum—Indorsements for interest—Contractual interest—Supreme Court Act 1981, s 35—Bills of Exchange Act 1882—RSC Ord 6, r 2(1)(b), Ord 13, r 1(2), Ord 18, r 8, Ord 22, r 1(8). **Practice Direction** [1983] **1** 934, QBD.
      Claim—Whether interest must be claimed in statement of claim—Law Reform (Miscellaneous Provisions) Act 1934, s 3—RSC Ord 20, r 6. **Riches v Westminster Bank Ltd** [1943] **2** 725, CA.
  Interim payments order—
    Generally. *See* Pre-trial or post-judgment relief—Interim payment, *below*.
    Landlord and tenant—
      Action for forfeiture of lease. *See* **Landlord and tenant** (Forfeiture of lease—Interim payments order).
  Interim remedy—
    Payment into court of specified fund where there was dispute over party's right to fund—
      Whether debt constituting 'specified fund' in action for repayment of debt—CPR 25.1(1)(I). **Myers v Design Inc (International) Ltd** [2003] **1** 1168, Ch D.
  Interlocutory injunction. *See* **Injunction** (Interlocutory).
  Interlocutory proceedings—
    Affidavit—
      Application to strike out. *See* **Affidavit** (Striking out—Hearsay—Exception—Interlocutory proceedings).
    Applications in Chancery Division. *See* Chancery Division—Interlocutory applications, *above*.
    Commercial Court. *See* **Commercial Court** (Practice—Interlocutory proceedings).
    Cross-examination of defendant—
      Cross-examination before service of statement of claim—Interlocutory order requiring defendant to disclose information to plaintiff—Defendant's answers not complying with order—Whether court having jurisdiction to order cross-examination of defendant before service of statement of claim. **Bayer AG v Winter (No 2)** [1986] **2** 43, Ch D.
    Cross-examination on affidavit—
      Further proceedings between parties pending in foreign court—Whether order would be made. **Pergamon Press Ltd v Maxwell** [1970] **2** 809, Ch D.
    Expedition of proceedings—
      Chancery Division. *See* Chancery Division—Interlocutory procedure—Expedition, *above*.
    Mandatory injunction. *See* **Injunction** (Interlocutory—Mandatory injunction).
    Stay of proceedings—
      Failure by applicant to pay costs of previous similar proceedings—Whether applicant should be allowed to proceed with subsequent proceedings for the same or equivalent relief. **Thames Investment and Securities plc v Benjamin** [1984] **3** 393, Ch D.
  Interpleader relief—
    Generally. *See* **Interpleader**.
    Service out of the jurisdiction. *See* Service out of the jurisdiction—Interpleader relief, *below*.
  Interpreter—
    Evidence—
      Defendant in criminal proceedings speaking only Bosnian Romany—Court unable to find interpreter competent in Bosnian Romany—Circumstances in which double interpretation permissible. **R v West London Youth Court, ex p N** [2000] **1** 823, QBD.
      Interpreter called to give evidence of religious customs—Propriety—Interpreter called by judge to give evidence of Sikh marriage customs—No express consent of parties—No evidence of interpreter's expertise or qualifications entitling him to give evidence. **Singh v Singh** [1971] **2** 828, CA.
  Interrogatories—
    Defamation actions. *See* **Libel and slander** (Interrogatory).
    Divorce. *See* **Divorce** (Practice—Interrogatories).
  Intervention—
    Admiralty action in rem. *See* **Admiralty** (Practice—Action in rem—Intervention).
  Investment of funds in court—
    Admiralty practice. *See* **Admiralty** (Practice—Investment of funds in court).
    Public trustee. *See* **Public Trustee** (Funds in court—Investment of).
  Irregularity—
    Irregularity in any proceeding—
      Application for leave for extension of time for personal injuries action—Application made to district registrar instead of by summons to judge in chambers—Order made by district registrar that s 2(1) of Limitation Act 1939, should not be a defence—Whether a nullity or whether order could be corrected and treated as valid—RSC Ord 2, r 1(1), Ord 128, r 1. **Harkness v Bell's Asbestos and Engineering Ltd** [1966] **3** 843, CA.
      Non-compliance with rules—Effect—Discretion of court—Discretion to set aside irregular proceeding or waive irregularity—Exercise of discretion—Whether proceeding to be treated as regular until application made to set it aside—Whether party in default entitled to rely on irregularity where no application by other party to set aside proceeding or no action taken on such application by court—Whether irregularity should be waived if defaulting party would receive unjustified benefit—RSC Ord 2, r 1. **Metroinvest Anstalt v Commercial Union Assurance Co plc** [1985] **2** 318, CA.

PRACTICE (cont)—
 Irregularity (cont)—
  Irregularity in any proceeding (cont)—
   Non-compliance with rules—Service of amended writs—Writs not reissued or resealed in accordance with rules of court—Writs subsequently resealed, reissued and served outside expiry of limitation period—Whether irregularity nullifying proceedings—RSC Ord 2, r 1, Ord 15, rr 6, 8—Limitation Act 1980, s 35. **Bank of America National Trust and Savings Association v Chrismas** [1994] **1** 401, QBD.
  Pleading—
   Application to set aside—Application to strike out—Reasonable time—Applicant taking fresh step in action—Application to strike out pleading on ground that it might prejudice, embarrass or delay fair trial—Statement of claim—Cause of action not mentioned in writ—New action statute-barred—Delivery of defence three months after service of statement of claim—Complexity of issues—Delay not unreasonable—Defence specifically keeping open objection to inclusion of new cause of action in statement of claim—Whether delivery of defence constituting a waiver of irregularity—Whether defendant entitled to apply to strike out new cause of action even though delivery of defence a 'fresh step'—RSC Ord 2, r 2(1), Ord 18, r 19. **Brickfield Properties Ltd v Newton** [1971] **3** 328, CA.
  Summons—
   Interested party not served with summons taken out by administrator—Party present at hearing but treated as not entitled to be present—No adjournment—Order made on summons set aside as being wholly irregular—RSC Ord 70, r 1. **Chettiar v Chettiar (No 2)** [1962] **2** 238, PC.
 Joinder of causes of action—
  Order for exclusion—
   Libel—Slander—Statement that plaintiff was person referred to in libel. **Bridgmont v Associated Newspapers Ltd** [1951] **2** 285, CA.
  Plaintiffs properly joined for one cause of action—
   Right to unite in same action a separate cause of action against same defendants—RSC Ord 16, r 1, Ord 18, r 1, r 6. **Harris v Ashworth** [1962] **1** 438, Ch D.
 Joinder of parties—
  Generally. *See* Parties—Joinder of parties, *below*.
  Joinder of defendants. *See* Parties—Adding defendant, *below*.
  Wardship and custody proceedings—
   Joinder of child as party. *See* **Minor** (Practice—Wardship and custody proceedings—Joinder of child as party).
 Joint tortfeasors—
  Contribution—
   Liability for damages—Action against two defendants—Action against second defendant stayed—First defendant claiming contribution from second defendant—Whether second defendant remaining 'a party to the action' after stay of action—Whether second defendant's 'liability' required to be procedurally enforceable as current and subsisting liability at time of claim for contribution—Civil Liability (Contribution) Act 1978, s 1—RSC Ord 16, r 8(1). **Lister (R A) & Co Ltd v E G Thomson (Shipping) Ltd (No 2)** [1987] **3** 1032, QBD.
   Settlement reached between plaintiff and some defendants—Remaining defendant issuing contribution notice against co-defendants—Whether prior settlement invalidating contribution notice—Whether subsequent discontinuance by plaintiff rendering new contribution notice necessary—RSC Ord 16, rr 1, 8. **Harper v Gray & Walker (a firm)** [1985] **2** 507, QBD.
  Interrogatories—
   Administration of interrogatories by one tortfeasor to another. *See* **Disclosure and inspection of documents** (Interrogatory—Examination of 'opposite parties'—Joint tortfeasors).
  Offer—
   Jurisdiction of master to allow one defendant to offer to pay a proportion of any liability—Law Reform (Married Women and Tortfeasors) Act 1935, s 6—RSC Ord 30, r 2. **Sigley v Hale** [1938] **3** 87, CA.
 Judge—
  Generally. *See* **Judge**.
 Judge's note—
  Appeal from county court. *See* **County court** (Appeal—Note of county court judgment).
  Appeal, for use on. *See* **Court of Appeal** (Judge's note—Practice).
 Judgment—
  Action on—
   Limitation period. *See* **Limitation of action** (Action—Action on judgment).
  Amendment—
   Correction of clerical mistakes or accidental slips or omissions. *See* **Judgment** (Order—Correction—Accidental slip or omission).
  Appeal from county court. *See* **County court** (Appeal—Note of county court judgment).
  Confidentiality. *See* **Judgment** (Handed down judgments—Judgments in advance of hearing—Draft judgments—Confidentiality).
  County court. *See* **County court** (Judgment or order).
  Court of Appeal. *See* **Court of Appeal** (Judgment).
  Default of defence. *See* **Judgment** (Default of defence).
  Execution. *See* **Execution**.
  Foreign judgment—
   Divorce. *See* **Divorce** (Foreign decree).
   Enforcement or recognition. *See* **Conflict of laws** (Foreign judgment).
  Generally. *See* **Judgment**.
  Issue estoppel. *See* **Estoppel** (Issue estoppel—Foreign judgment).
  Judgment in advance of hearing. *See* **Judgment** (Handed down judgments—Judgments in advance of hearing).
  Judgment in chambers—
   Chancery Division. *See* Chancery Division—Chambers proceedings—Judgment, *above*.
  Note of. *See* Note of judgment, *below*.
  Res judicata. *See* **Estoppel** (Res judicata—Foreign judgment).

PRACTICE (cont)—
    Judgment (cont)—
        Summary judgment. *See* Summary judgment, *below.*
    Judgment debtor—
        Examination. *See* **Execution** (Disclosure in aid of execution—Examination of judgment debtor—
        Practice).
    Judicial fees—
        House of Lords. *See* **House of Lords** (Judicial fees).
    Judicial review—
        Concurrent wardship and judicial review proceedings. *See* **Ward of court** (Practice—Judicial review).
        Crown Office list. *See* Crown Office list—Judicial review, *above.*
        Generally. *See* **Judicial review**.
    Judicial separation—
        Decree—
            Form. *See* **Husband and wife** (Judicial separation—Decree—Form of decree).
        Petition—
            Form. *See* **Husband and wife** (Judicial separation—Form of petition).
    Judicial trustee. *See* **Trust and trustee** (Judicial trustee).
    Jurisdiction—
        Court of Appeal—
            Appeal from Employment Appeal Tribunal. *See* **Court of Appeal** (Jurisdiction—Appeal from
            Employment Appeal Tribunal).
            Private litigation—Parties compromising action prior to hearing of appeal—Parties and interveners
            arguing appeal raising public interest issues relating to ambit of money laundering legislation
            and legal professionals—Whether Court of Appeal having jurisdiction to hear appeal—Whether
            legislation intended to cover ordinary conduct of litigation by legal professionals—Whether
            legislation intended to cover consensual resolution in litigious context—Proceeds of Crime
            Act 2002, s 328. **Bowman v Fels** [2005] **4** 609, CA.
    Jury. *See* **Jury**.
    Juvenile court. *See* **Magistrates** (Juvenile court—Procedure).
    Land—
        Limitation of action. *See* **Limitation of action** (Land).
    Land registration. *See* **Land registration**.
    Landlord and tenant—
        Generally. *See* **Landlord and tenant**.
        Notice to quit—
            Agricultural holding—Service of notice. *See* **Agricultural holding** (Notice to quit—Service).
    Language—
        Court proceedings. *See* Conduct of proceedings—Language, *above.*
    Law reports—
        Citation—
            Court of Appeal, Civil Division. *See* **Court of Appeal** (Practice—Civil Division—Citation of
            cases—Reports).
            Generally. *See* Citation of cases—Reports, *above.*
        Duty of advocates to keep up to date with recent reported authority. **Copeland v Smith** [2000] **1** 457, CA.
    Leave on ex parte application—
        Revocation of leave—
            Jurisdiction—Leave granted under misapprehension. **Becker v Noel** [1971] **2** 1248n, CA.
            Jurisdiction—Whether High Court judge having jurisdiction to vary or revoke ex parte order made
            by another High Court judge—Judicature (Civil Procedure Code) Law (Jamaica), s 686—RSC
            Ord 32, r 6. **Minister of Foreign Affairs Trade and Industry v Vehicles and Supplies Ltd** [1991] **4** 65,
            PC.
    Leave to appeal—
        Arbitration proceedings. *See* **Arbitration** (Award—Leave to appeal against award).
        County court, from. *See* **County court** (Appeal—Leave).
        Court of Appeal. *See* **Court of Appeal** (Leave to appeal).
        Criminal proceedings. *See* **Criminal law** (Appeal—Leave to appeal—Practice).
        House of Lords. *See* **House of Lords** (Leave to appeal).
        Immigration appeal. *See* **Immigration** (Appeal—Leave to appeal).
        Interlocutory proceedings. *See* **Court of Appeal** (Interlocutory appeal—Leave to appeal).
        Privy Council. *See* **Privy Council** (Leave to appeal).
    Leave to apply for judicial review. *See* **Judicial review** (Leave to apply for judicial review).
    Leave to begin proceedings—
        Insolvency legislation. *See* **Insolvency** (Jurisdiction—Leave to commence proceedings).
    Leave to enforce arbitration award. *See* **Arbitration** (Award—Enforcement—Leave).
    Leeds—
        Mercantile list. *See* **Queen's Bench Division**—Mercantile lists—Leeds and Newcastle upon Tyne, *below.*
    Legal aid. *See* **Legal aid**.
    Legal professional privilege—
        Generally. *See* **Privilege** (Legal professional privilege).
        New Zealand. *See* **New Zealand** (Legal professional privilege).
    Legitimation—
        Power of court to order hearing of petition in camera. *See* **Legitimation** (Practice—Hearing of petition
        in camera—Power of court to order hearing in camera).
    Letter box, service through. *See* Service—Service through letter box, *below.*
    Libel and slander—
        Pleading—
            Particulars. *See* **Libel and slander** (Particulars).
        Statement in open court. *See* **Libel and slander** (Statement in open court).
        Trial by jury—
            Libel. *See* Trial—Trial by jury—Libel, *below.*
    Liberty to apply—
        Family Division. *See* **Family Division** (Applications to the court—Liberty to apply).

PRACTICE (cont)—

Limitation of action. *See* **Limitation of action**.

Lis pendens—
  Stay of proceedings—
    Conflict of laws. *See* **Conflict of laws** (Stay of proceedings—Lis pendens).

List of authorities—
  Procedure—
    Queen's Bench Division—List of authorities to which counsel propose to refer to be handed in before hearing. **Practice Direction** [1961] **1** 541, QBD.

Listing causes and matters—
  Chancery Division. *See* Chancery Division—Revision of system for listing causes and matters, *above*.

Lists—
  Chancery Division—
    Northern Area. *See* Chancery Division—Northern Area—Lists, *above*.
    Unassigned cases. *See* Chancery Division—Unassigned cases, *above*.
  Court of Appeal. *See* **Court of Appeal** (Practice—Lists).
  Crown Office list. *See* Crown Office list, *above*.
  Queen's Bench Division. *See* Queen's Bench Division—Lists, *below*.

Litigant in person—
  Assistance. *See* Trial—Party acting in person—Right to assistance, *below*.
  Certiorari application—
    Right of audience. *See* **Certiorari** (Application—Right of audience—Litigant in person).
  Chambers proceedings—
    Assistance. *See* Chambers proceedings—Party acting in person—Right to assistance, *above*.
  Contempt of court—
    Application for committal by litigant in person. *See* **Contempt of court** (Committal—Application—Litigant in person).
  Costs—
    County court costs. *See* **County court** (Costs—Jurisdiction—Litigant in person).
    Review of taxation—Jurisdiction. *See* **Costs** (Taxation—Review of taxation—Jurisdiction—Litigant in person).
    Taxation. *See* **Costs** (Taxation—Litigant appearing in person).
  Court of Appeal—
    Right of audience. *See* **Court of Appeal** (Right of audience—Litigant in person).
  Vexatious proceedings. *See* **Vexatious proceedings** (Litigant in person).

Local authority—
  Promotion or protection of interests of inhabitants of their area—
    Expedient that authority institute proceedings—Whether question whether proceedings expedient for promotion or protection of interests of inhabitants a matter for authority to consider—Whether question whether proceedings expedient for promotion or protection of interests of inhabitants may be determined on striking-out application—Local Government Act 1972, s 222(1). **Derbyshire CC v Times Newspapers Ltd** [1992] **3** 65, CA.

Long Vacation—
  Commercial Court. *See* Commercial Court—Sittings in Long Vacation, *above*.
  Companies Court—
    Applications in Long Vacation. *See* Companies Court—Applications in Long Vacation, *above*.
  Court of Appeal. *See* **Court of Appeal** (Practice—Long Vacation).
  Family Division—
    Business to be taken in Long Vacation—Estimated length—Certificate of fitness for vacation business. **Practice Direction** [1984] **2** 320, Fam D.
  Hearing during vacation—
    Application for order to fix date for hearing—Urgent need—Merger of companies by scheme of arrangement—Order made conditionally—RSC Ord 64, r 4(2). **Showerings, Vine Products and Whiteways Ltd, Re** [1968] **3** 276, Ch D.
    Matters to be heard—Applications requiring to be immediately or promptly heard—Factors to be considered by judge in determining whether particular matter vacation business—Principles applicable—Mortgage of petrol station—Mortgagor to sell mortgagee's motor fuel only—Alleged breach of agreement—Interlocutory injunction sought by mortgagee in vacation—Whether 'vacation business' Ord 64, r 4(1), (2). **Esso Petroleum Co Ltd v Dawn Property Co Ltd** [1973] **3** 181, Ch D.
  Queen's Bench Division—
    Judge in chambers and masters—Service, filing and amendment of pleadings—Summonses issuable without leave returnable before master—Appeals—Marking of applications or appeals as fit for August or vacation—RSC Ord 3, r 3, Ord 18, r 5, Ord 64, r 3. **Practice Note** [1983] **1** 1098, QBD.

Magistrates. *See* **Magistrates**.

Magistrates' courts—
  Anti-social Behaviour Orders—
    Qualification of justices dealing with applications for ASBOs in respect of persons under 18—Guidance. **Practice Direction (Magistrates' Courts: Anti-Social Behaviour Orders: Composition of Benches)** [2006] **1** 886, QBD.

Maintenance—
  Generally. *See* **Husband and wife** (Maintenance).

Malicious falsehood—
  Special damage not pleaded. *See* **Malicious falsehood** (Damages—Pecuniary loss—Special damage not pleaded).

Mandatory injunction—
  Interlocutory proceedings. *See* **Injunction** (Interlocutory—Mandatory injunction).

Mareva injunction—
  Generally. *See* Pre-trial or post-judgment relief—Freezing order, *below*.

Marine insurance—
  Order for ship's papers. *See* **Disclosure and inspection of documents** (Marine insurance actions—Order for ship's papers).

PRACTICE (cont)—
  Master's certificate—
    Discharge or variation after expiration of time limited—
      Special circumstances—Change of solicitors—Illness of solicitor's managing clerk—RSC Ord 55, r 71. **Jacobson v Lee** [1949] **2** 517, Ch D.
  Masters' lists—
    Queen's Bench Division. *See* Queen's Bench Division—Lists—Masters' lists, *below*.
  Masters' powers—
    Chambers proceedings. *See* Chambers proceedings—Master's powers, *above*.
    Chancery Division. *See* Chambers proceedings—Master's powers, *above*.
  Masters' summonses—
    Chambers proceedings. *See* Chambers proceedings—Masters' summonses, *above*.
    Generally. *See* Summons—Masters' summonses, *below*.
  Matrimonial causes—
    Applications to the court—
      Liberty to apply. *See* **Family Division** (Applications to the court—Liberty to apply).
    Child—
      Applications relating to children. *See* **Child** (Practice—Matrimonial causes—Applications relating to children).
      Psychiatric examination. *See* **Minor** (Psychiatric examination—Wardship and matrimonial causes).
    Matrimonial causes list. *See* **Divorce** (Matrimonial causes list).
    Matrimonial home—
      Generally. *See* **Husband and wife** (Matrimonial home).
    Solicitor acting for petitioner. *See* Family Division—Solicitor acting in matrimonial proceedings for petitioner, *above*.
    Trial—
      Directions for trial—Applications for property adjustment and lump sums—Pre-trial review—Registrar to consider possibility of settlement of case or to clarify issues—Directions as to discovery. **Practice Direction (Matrimonial causes: Property adjustment and lump sums: Pre-trial review)** [1980] **1** 592, Fam D.
      Trial—Divorce proceedings. *See* **Divorce** (Practice—Trial).
  Matrimonial property—
    Related applications. *See* **Husband and wife** (Property—Summary proceedings—Related application in divorce proceedings).
  McKenzie friend—
    Litigant in person—
      Chambers proceedings—Right of litigant to assistance of McKenzie friend. *See* Chambers proceedings—Party acting in person—Right to assistance, *above*.
  Medical reports—
    Agreed report—
      Order for agreed medical reports—Form of order—One report only to be filed. **Harrison v Liverpool Corp** [1943] **2** 449, CA.
      Production of report by one party—Reciprocal action by other party—Contents of report. **Devine v British Transport Commission** [1954] **1** 1025, QBD.
      Trial of case on agreed medical report—When order for case to be so tried is proper. **Proctor v Peebles (Papermakers) Ltd** [1941] **2** 80, CA.
    Disclosure—
      Action for medical negligence. *See* Evidence—Expert evidence—Disclosure to other parties—Action for medical negligence, *above*.
      Privilege—Waiver of privilege. *See* **Disclosure and inspection of documents** (Privilege—Waiver of privilege—Medical reports).
      Stay of proceedings—Medical examination of plaintiff at defendant's request. *See* Stay of proceedings—Medical examination of plaintiff at defendant's request—Disclosure of medical reports to plaintiff, *below*.
    Order for exchange—
      Validity—RSC Ord 30, r 6(1),(4). **Worrall v Reich** [1955] **1** 363, CA.
  Medical treatment—
    Child. *See* **Minor** (Medical treatment).
    Insensate patient—
      Withdrawal of treatment. *See* **Medical treatment** (Withdrawal of treatment—Insensate patient).
    Ward of court—
      Jurisdiction of court. *See* **Ward of court** (Jurisdiction—Medical treatment).
  Mental health legislation—
    Proceedings under. *See* **Mental health**.
  Mental health review tribunal. *See* **Mental health** (Mental health review tribunal).
  Mental patient—
    Execution of will. *See* **Mental health** (Patient's property—Execution of will).
    Will. *See* **Mental health** (Patient's property—Will).
  Mercantile Court—
    Bristol. *See* Commercial cases—Bristol—Bristol Mercantile Court, *above*.
  Mercantile lists—
    Queen's Bench Division—
      Generally. *See* Queen's Bench Division—Mercantile lists, *below*.
  Midland and Oxford Circuit—
    Commercial cases. *See* Commercial cases—Midland and Oxford Circuit, *above*.
  Minors—
    Change of surname. *See* **Minor** (Change of surname).
    Control of damages recovered for personal injury. *See* **Minor** (Money recovered).
    Removal outside jurisdiction. *See* **Minor** (Removal outside jurisdiction).
    Wardship and custody proceedings. *See* **Minor** (Practice—Wardship and custody proceedings).
    Wardship and guardianship proceedings. *See* **Minor** (Practice—Wardship and guardianship proceedings).

PRACTICE (cont)—
Mortgaged property—
    Action by mortgagee for possession. *See* **Mortgage** (Action by mortgagee for possession).
    Enquiry of prior mortgagees before applying for possession. *See* **Mortgage** (Possession of mortgaged property—Second mortgagee—Subsequent encumbrances).
    Mortgage action—
        Generally. *See* **Mortgage** (Mortgage action).
    Order for possession. *See* **Mortgage** (Order for possession of mortgaged property).
    Originating summons—
        Adjournment into open court. *See* **Mortgage** (Possession of mortgaged property—Persons not parties to mortgage claiming to be entitled to possession).
    Parties—
        Proceedings by mortgagee for possession. *See* **Mortgage** (Action by mortgagee for possession—Parties).
Motion—
    Adjournment—
        Chancery Division—Agreed adjournment—Procedure. **Practice Direction** [1983] **1** 131, Ch D.
        Chancery Division—Agreed adjournment—Procedure—Consolidation of previous directions. **Practice Direction** [1988] **2** 510, Ch D.
        Chancery Division—Agreed adjournment—Successive adjournments—Optional procedure. **Practice Direction** [1976] **2** 198, Ch D; **Practice Note** [1977] **2** 540, Ch D.
    Ex parte motion—
        Chancery Division. **Practice Direction** [1980] **2** 750, Ch D.
    Hearing—
        Affidavit—Cross-examination on affidavit. *See* Interlocutory proceedings—Cross-examination on affidavit, *above.*
        Affidavit—Office copies. **Practice Direction** [1969] **2** 639, Ch D.
        Chancery Division. **Practice Direction** [1980] **2** 750, Ch D.
    Listing—
        Generally. *See* Chancery Division—Listing—Motions, *above.*
        Revision of system. *See* Chancery Division—Revision of system for listing causes and matters, *above.*
    Motion in respect of trade mark. *See* **Trade mark** (Motions in respect of trade marks).
    Northern Area—
        Listing. *See* Chancery Division—Northern Area—Lists—Fixed dates—Motion days, *above.*
    Notice of motion—
        Chancery Division. **Practice Direction** [1980] **2** 750, Ch D.
        Chancery Division—Chancery motions judge—Notice of motion need not state name of judge before whom motion will be moved—Companies Court summonses to be returnable before 'the Companies Court judge'—Exception in respect of Patents Court—Judge to be assigned to hear motions. **Practice Direction** [1992] **3** 736, Ch D.
        Lodging of notice of motion and other documents—Chancery Division—Change in procedure. **Practice Direction** [1985] **1** 384, Ch D.
        Service by post. *See* Post—Postal delay—Service by post of notice of motion, *below.*
        Service out of the jurisdiction—Bankruptcy proceedings. *See* **Bankruptcy** (Service—Service out of jurisdiction—Motion).
    Order on motion—
        Drawing-up of order—Procedure—Chancery Division. *See* Chancery Division—Order—Order on motion—Drawing up of order, *above.*
    Originating motion—
        Third party proceedings—Whether proceedings begun by originating motion can be treated as third party proceedings. *See* Third party proceedings—Originating motion, *below.*
    Power to stand motion over until trial—
        Evidence filed by defendants—Conflict of fact—Whether motion for injunction should be stood over to trial. **Pictograph Ltd v Lee-Smith Photomechanics Ltd** [1964] **1** 668, Ch D.
        Evidence filed on affidavits—Substantial dispute of fact—Facts incapable of being sufficiently determined on affidavit evidence—Whether court having power to stand motion over until trial. **Société Française d'Applications Commerciales et Industrielles SARL v Electronic Concepts Ltd** [1975] **3** 425, Ch D.
    Standing over and saving motions—
        Chancery Division. **Practice Direction** [1980] **2** 750, Ch D.
Name of parties—
    Change of. *See* Parties—Change of name, *below.*
Nearest relative—
    Mental health patient. *See* **Mental health** (Patient—Nearest relative).
Negligence—
    Judgment for plaintiff—
        Money taken out of court—Whether plaintiff can appeal on quantum of damages. **Mills v Duckworth** [1938] **1** 318, CA.
New trial—
    County court. *See* **County court** (New trial).
New Zealand—
    Service out of the jurisdiction. *See* Service out of the jurisdiction—New Zealand, *below.*
Next of kin—
    Inquiries for. *See* Chancery Division—Inquiries for next-of-kin, *above.*
No case to answer—
    Criminal trial. *See* **Criminal law** (Trial—No case to answer).
    Rejection of submission—
        Appeal against rejection of submission—Evidence to be considered on appeal where defendant elected to adduce evidence after rejection of submission—Appeal decided on whole evidence. **Payne v Harrison** [1961] **2** 873, CA.

PRACTICE (cont)—
  No case to answer (cont)—
    Time for ruling on submission—
      Defamation action—Words complained of not actionable without proof of special damage—No special damage alleged or proved—Whether judge's ruling necessary immediately after submission. **Cleghorn v Sadler** [1945] 1 544, KBD.
      Judge not bound to rule until conclusion of evidence—Whether judge has discretion to put defendant to election whether to call evidence or to stand on his submission. **Payne v Harrison** [1961] 2 873, CA.
      Time to make submission. *See* Trial—Submission of no case—Time to make submission, *below*.
    Trial by jury—
      Defendants not put to election whether to call evidence—Discretion of judge. **Young v Rank** [1950] 2 166, KBD.
  Nominal defendant—
    Accident to employee in government factory—
      Action for damages for negligence or breach of statutory duty—Superintendent of factory nominated by government as defendant—Jurisdiction of court to hear case against nominal defendant. **Royster v Cavey** [1946] 2 642, CA.
  Non-contentious probate. *See* **Probate** (Practice—Non-contentious probate).
  Non-party—
    Order for costs. *See* **Costs** (Order for costs—Payment of costs by non-party).
    Payment of costs. *See* **Costs** (Order for costs—Payment of costs by non-party).
  Nonsuit—
    County court practice. *See* **County court** (Practice—Nonsuit).
  Northern Circuit—
    Commercial cases. *See* Commercial cases—Northern Circuit, *above*.
  Note of judgment—
    Appeal from Chancery Division or Queen's Bench Division—
      Signed judgment handed down by judge—Direction that no official shorthand note or mechanical recording be taken—Copy of signed judgment to be lodged in lieu of official shorthand note—Duty of appellant's solicitor—RSC Ord 59, r 9(1)(f), Ord 68, r 1. **Practice Note** [1990] 2 1024, CA.
      Signed judgment handed down by judge—Official shorthand note of judgment—Copy of signed judgment to be lodged in lieu of official shorthand note—Duty of appellant's solicitor—RSC Ord 59, r 9(1)(f); Ord 68, r 1. **Practice Note** [1995] 3 850, CA.
    Counsel's fee for taking note of judgment. *See* **Counsel** (Fees—Note of judgment).
  Notice of appeal—
    Court of Appeal. *See* **Court of Appeal** (Notice of appeal).
  Notice of motion. *See* Motion—Notice of motion, *above*.
  Nuisance order—
    Terms. *See* **Nuisance** (Statutory nuisance—Nuisance order—Terms of order).
  Nullity suit—
    Foreign decree—
      Recognition. *See* **Nullity** (Recognition of foreign decree).
    Generally. *See* **Nullity** (Practice).
    Petition. *See* **Nullity** (Petition).
  Numbering of judgments. *See* **Judgment** (Numbering of judgments).
  Occupier's liability—
    Option to claim in contract or tort for breach of duty. *See* **Occupier's liability** (Common duty of care—Liability in contract—Option to claim in contract or tort for breach of duty).
  Offer of amends—
    Defamation cases. *See* **Libel and slander** (Offer of amends).
  Offer to settle—
    Acceptance of offer after expiry of 21 day period—
      Acceptance of offer needing permission of the court—Extent of judge's discretion—CPR Pt 36. **Capital Bank plc v Stickland** [2005] 2 544, CA.
    Costs. *See* **Costs** (Offers to settle).
    Costs. *See* **Costs** (Order for costs—Discretion—Offer to settle).
    CPR Pt 36 offer—
      Costs. *See* **Costs** (Offers to settle—CPR Pt 36 offer).
      Effect of offer—Withdrawal of offer—Whether Pt 36 offer subject to general law of offer and acceptance—CPR Pt 36. **Gibbon v Manchester City Council** [2011] 2 258, CA.
      Natural justice—Withdrawal of offer—Offeree accepting offer before expiry of 21 day period—Offeror withdrawing offer before expiry of 21 day period—Offeror applying without notice for permission to withdraw offer—Offeror receiving permission to withdraw—No information or evidence disclosed to offeree—Whether court could receive information or evidence not disclosed to offeree—Whether contrary to principles of open and natural justice—CPR 23.9(2), 36.3(5), 36.9(2). **Evans v Royal Wolverhampton Hospitals NHS Foundation Trust** [2015] 1 1091, QBD.
      Whether time-limited offer capable of being CPR Pt 36 offer—CPR Pt 36. **C v D** [2011] 2 404, Ch D.
    Offer including disposition of interest in land—
      Acceptance of offer—Statutory requirements for contract for sale or other disposition of interest in land—Whether CPR Pt 36 settlement agreement existing where statutory requirements not complied with—Whether settlement agreement enforceable by court—Law of Property (Miscellaneous Provisions) Act 1989, s 2—CPR Pt 36. **Orton v Collins** [2007] 3 863, Ch D.
    Technical error in CPR Pt 36 offer—
      Overriding objective of CPR—Defendants notifying claimants of existence of error in Pt 36 offer but failing to disclose its nature—Whether claimants entitled to rely on Pt 36 offer—CPR 1.3, 1.4, 36.21. **Hertsmere Primary Care Trust v Administrators of Balasubramanium's Estate** [2005] 3 274, Ch D.
  Official referee—
    Appeal—
      Generally. *See* **Appeal** (Official referee).

PRACTICE (cont)—
  Official referee (cont)—
    Appeal (cont)—
      Leave to appeal. *See* **Court of Appeal** (Leave to appeal—Requirement of leave—Official referee).
    Discretion of—
      Review of. *See* **Court of Appeal** (Discretion of Official Referee—Review of exercise of discretion).
    Reference to—
      Procedure. *See* Reference to referee, *below.*
  Official Solicitor—
    Costs. *See* **Costs** (Official Solicitor).
    Generally. *See* **Official Solicitor.**
    Guardian ad litem—
      Paternity—Blood test. *See* **Paternity** (Blood test—Divorce—Guardian ad litem—Official Solicitor).
  Order—
    Committal order—
      Contempt of court. *See* **Contempt of court** (Committal—Order).
    Consent order. *See* Consent order, *above.*
    Correction—
      Accidental slip or omission. *See* **Judgment** (Order—Correction—Accidental slip or omission).
    Costs—
      Generally. *See* **Costs** (Order for costs).
    County court—
      Enforcement. *See* **County court** (Judgment or order—Enforcement).
    Drawing-up—
      Bespeaking orders—Chancery Division—Necessity to bespeak order promptly—Where undue delay in bespeaking order application may be listed for hearing in open court—Order for costs may be made against solicitor personally—RSC Ord 42, r 7, Ord 62, r 8. **Practice Direction** [1980] **2** 400, Fam D.
      Drawing up procedural orders made in chambers—Chancery Division. **Practice Direction** [1960] **3** 415, Ch D.
      Interlocutory order made without personal attendance—Lodging of engrossments of proposed order. **Practice Direction** [1977] **2** 173, Ch D.
      Judgments and orders settled by Chancery registrars. **Practice Direction** [1961] **1** 159, Ch D.
      Minutes of order drawn by counsel—Consent orders—Chancery Division. **Practice Direction** [1960] **3** 416, Ch D.
      Need for order to be drawn up before application made in respect of order—Winding up of company. *See* **Company** (Voluntary winding up—Examination of officer of company etc—Application to discharge order—Need to have order formally drawn up before application).
      Order on motion—Chancery Division. *See* Chancery Division—Order—Order on motion—Drawing up of order, *above.*
    Final order—
      Power to vary or revoke orders—Effect of COVID-19 pandemic—Respondents ordered to buy out petitioner's minority shareholding—Court determining valuation date for purchase of minority shareholding—Value of company reduced by pandemic after valuation date—Whether order determining valuation date should be varied or replaced to take account of effect of pandemic—Companies Act 2006, s 996—CPR 3.1(7). **Dinglis Properties Ltd, Re** [2021] **1 Comm** 649, Ch D; [2021] **1** 685, Ch D.
      Power to vary or revoke orders—Judgment on admissions—Unadvised defendant admitting liability—Judge making final order—Defendant advised of existence of defence—Defendant seeking to withdraw admission, amend defence and plead counterclaim—Defendant seeking revocation of final order—Whether court having jurisdiction to revoke final order—CPR 3.1(7). **Kojima v HSBC Bank plc** [2011] **3** 359, Ch D; **Kojima v HSBC Bank plc (Note)** [2012] **1** 1392, CA.
    Postal despatch of copy order—
      Crown Office and Associates' Department. **Practice Direction** [1964] **2** 955, QBD.
    Power to vary or revoke orders—
      Costs—Allocation to particular track—Re-allocation—Case allocated to small claims track re-allocated to fast track—No provision for altering special rules about small claims track costs prior to re-allocation—Whether court having power to vary re-allocation order—Guidance—CPR 3.1(7), 44.11. **Tibbles v SIG plc (t/a Asphaltic Roofing Supplies)** [2012] **4** 259, CA.
    'Unless' orders and other peremptory orders—
      Form of order—Time limits—Meaning of 'unless by 7 days of order'—CPR 2.9—CPR PD 40B, para 8.2. **Poule Securities Ltd v Howe** [2022] **4** 887, CA.
      Unless order for provision of further information—Test for compliance—CPR. **Gravity Highway (owners) v Maritime Maisie (owners)** [2021] **2 Comm** 340, QBD.
    'Unless' orders and other peremptory orders—
      Disclosure requirements contained within freezing order—Respondents failing to comply with disclosure requirements—Respondents seeking to challenge jurisdiction of English court—Whether court having power to make unless order requiring compliance with disclosure element of freezing order—Whether appropriate to make such order. **JSC BTA Bank v Ablyazov (No 3)** [2011] **1 Comm** 1093, QBD.
      Form of order—Order required to make clear precise period within which act is to be done—Form of order where affected party is not present or represented—Form or order where affected party is present or represented—RSC Ord 42, r 2(1). **Practice Direction** [1986] **2** 576, QBD.
      Jurisdiction—Unless order debarring defence of claims. *See* **Contempt of court** (Committal—Breach of court order—Contemnor failing to surrender).
      Non-compliance with order striking out claim or defence unless act done within specified time—Application to extend time—Whether jurisdiction to extend time where failure to comply with 'unless' order—RSC Ord 3, r 5(1). **Samuels v Linzi Dresses Ltd** [1980] **1** 803, CA.
      Non-compliance with 'unless' order—Consequences—Guidance—CPR Pt 3. **Marcan Shipping (London) Ltd v Kefalas** [2007] **3** 365, CA.

PRACTICE (cont)—
   Order (cont)—
      'Unless' orders and other peremptory orders (cont)—
         Non-compliance with 'unless' order—Consequences—Non-compliance with order striking out
            claim or defence unless act done within specified time—Exercise of court's discretion to extend
            time for compliance with order—Whether defaults of defendant's solicitor severable from
            defendant's cause—Factors to be taken into account. **Pereira v Beanlands** [1996] **3** 528, Ch D.
         Non-compliance with 'unless' order—Consequences—Non-compliance with order striking out
            claim or defence unless act done within specified time—Whether pleading should be struck out if
            failure to comply with 'unless' order not contumacious. **Grand Metropolitan Nominee (No 2) Co
            Ltd v Evans** [1993] **1** 642, CA; **Jokai Tea Holdings Ltd, Re** [1993] **1** 630, CA.
         Power to vary or revoke orders—Appellants failing to comply with 'unless' order—First application
            to relief from sanctions refused—Second application for relief from sanctions—Whether material
            change in circumstances necessary in second application—Whether appellants establishing
            material change in circumstances by substantial compliance with unless order—CPR 3.1(7).
            Thevarajah v Riordan [2017] **1** 329, SC.
   Originating motion—
      Third party proceedings—
         Whether proceedings begun by originating motion can be treated as third party proceedings. See
            Third party proceedings—Originating motion, *below*.
   Originating summons—
      Dismissal of action commenced by—
         Dismissal for want of prosecution. See Dismissal of action for want of prosecution—Originating
            summons, *above*.
      Generally. See **Originating summons**.
      Mortgaged property—
         Action by mortgagee for possession. See **Mortgage** (Action by mortgagee for possession—
            Originating summons).
   Overriding objective, the. See Adjournment of proceedings—Dealing with cases justly, *above*.
   Oversea company—
      Service. See **Company** (Oversea company—Service on oversea company).
   Particulars—
      Defamation cases—
         Generally. See **Libel and slander** (Particulars).
      Generally. See **Pleading** (Particulars).
      Particulars of claim. See **Particulars of claim**.
   Parties—
      Absence of party. See Absence of party, *above*.
      Actions and proceedings by and against patients—
         Proceeding by next friend—Party said to be 'of unsound mind, not so found by
            inquisition'—Reasonable ground for thinking party capable of managing affairs—Dismissal of
            proceeding. **J (orse B) (by her next friend) v J** [1952] **2** 1129, Div.
      Adding defendant—
         Action to restrain infringement of trade mark—Alleged contract between plaintiffs and third party
            permitting user of trade mark by third party—Third party employed by defendants—Defendants
            applying for order to join third party as additional defendant—RSC Ord 16, r 11. **Bentley Motors
            (1931) Ltd v Lagonda Ltd** [1945] **2** 211, Ch D.
         Amendment of writ—Adding or substituting party as defendant—Amendment of writ to change
            defendant from H E Co (Leeds) Ltd to H E Co Ltd—Limitation period expired—Whether rule of
            court permitting amendment was ultra vires—Whether leave to amend was just—Supreme Court
            of Judicature (Consolidation) Act 1925, s 99(1)(a)—RSC Ord 20, r 5(2), (3). **Mitchell v Harris
            Engineering Co Ltd** [1967] **2** 682, CA.
         Amendment of writ—Amendment to change defendant 'E B (a firm)' to 'E B Ltd'—Whether a
            correction of a mere misnomer—Amendment sought after limitation period expired. **Davies v
            Elsby Bros Ltd** [1960] **3** 672, CA.
         Amendment of writ—Date from which added defendant becomes party to proceedings—Action
            against added defendant time-barred at date writ amended—Whether joinder taking effect from
            date of original writ or from date writ amended—Whether added defendant entitled to plead
            defence of limitation on basis that joinder takes effect from date writ amended. **Liff v Peasley**
            [1980] **1** 623, CA.
         Amendment of writ—Date from which added defendant becomes party to proceedings—Arguable
            but not clear that action against added defendant timebarred at date of amendment—Whether
            joinder taking effect from date of original writ or from date writ amended—Whether if former
            court nevertheless having power to allow amendment on terms that joinder taking effect from
            date of amendment—RSC Ord 15, r 6(2)(b)(ii). **Liptons Cash Registers and Business Equipment
            Ltd v Hugin (GB) Ltd** [1982] **1** 595, QBD.
         Amendment of writ—Date from which added defendant becomes party to proceedings—Claim
            against proposed defendant time-barred—Plaintiff claiming that he had not acquired knowledge
            of relevant facts until within limitation period—Procedure for determining issue of date of
            plaintiff's knowledge—Whether issue of date of plaintiff's knowledge can be determined on
            application in existing action to amend writ to add proposed defendant—Whether plaintiff
            required to issue fresh writ against proposed defendant—Limitation Act 1939, s 2A(4)(b), (8).
            Leadbitter v Hodge Finance Ltd [1982] **2** 167, QBD.
         Amendment of writ—Date from which added defendant becomes party to proceedings—Writ
            amended at central office on day with which limitation period expired—Service on added
            defendants effected subsequently—Action not statute-barred—Amendment effective on day
            when writ stamped as amended—RSC, Ord 15, r 6(2)(b), r 8(2), (4). **Seabridge v H Cox & Sons
            (Plant Hire) Ltd** [1968] **1** 570, CA.
         Amendment of writ—Date from which added defendant becomes party to proceedings—Writ not
            amended and re-served on added defendant until after expiry of limitation period—Whether
            defendant joined as party from date when amended writ served on him—Whether joinder
            relating back to date when writ first issued—RSC Ord 15, r 8(4)(a). **Ketteman v Hansel Properties
            Ltd** [1988] **1** 38, HL.

791

Amendment of writ—Defendant entering unconditional appearance to amended writ—Defendant serving defence that action time-barred—Defendant applying for order to strike out joinder—Whether entry of unconditional appearance precluding defendant from objecting to joinder—Whether defendant ceasing to be a party because he had improperly been made a party or because he had ceased to be a proper party on service of defence pleading statute of limitation—RSC Ord 15, r 6(2)(a). **Liff v Peasley** [1980] **1** 623, CA.

Defendants applying for order that plaintiffs should add further defendants—Proposed new parties unnecessary for determination of issues pleaded but intended to become plaintiffs on counterclaim—RSC Ord 16, r 11. **Atid Navigation Co Ltd v Fairplay Towage & Shipping Co Ltd** [1955] **1** 698, Ch D.

Defendants applying for order to join another defendant—Prima facie case that proposed defendant's rights might be legally affected by the result of the action—RSC Ord 16, r 11. **Amon v Raphael Tuck & Sons Ltd** [1956] **1** 273, QBD.

Failure to add defendant—Res judicata—Issue determined in earlier proceedings—Failure to add defendant as defendant in earlier proceedings—Striking out pleading. See **Pleading** (Striking out—Estoppel per rem judicatam—Issue determined in earlier action against different defendant—Failure of plaintiff to add defendant in second action as defendant in first action).

Foreign defendant—Action in tort—Plaintiffs applying to join foreign defendant for purpose of obtaining discovery—Prospective defendant alleged to be joint tortfeasor—Test to be applied in permitting joinder of defendant in cases within scope of European jurisdiction convention—Whether plaintiffs required to show good arguable case or merely that claim would not be struck out—Whether joinder to obtain discovery an abuse of process—Civil Jurisdiction and Judgments Act 1982, Sch 1, art 5(3)—RSC Ord 11, r 1, Ord 18, r 19. **Molnlycke AB v Procter & Gamble Ltd** [1992] **4** 47, CA.

Foreign government—Applicants not asserting title to property but claiming possession or control through bank as bailee—Invocation of doctrine of immunity of foreign sovereign States—Applicants not necessary parties at commencement of action—Action against Bank of England for delivery up of gold bars deposited with bank by governments of United Kingdom, United States of America, and France—Application by governments of United States and France to be added as defendants—RSC Ord 16, r 11. **Dollfus Mieg et Cie SA v Bank of England** [1950] **2** 605, Ch D.

Personal representatives—Action by testator's former wife—Former wife claiming as beneficiary of estate under maintenance order—Claim against testator's employers for payment of sums due under insurance policies into estate—Personal representatives unwilling to sue—Addition of personal representatives as formal defendants—Beneficiary as plaintiff—Special circumstances justifying form of action. **Field v Firmenich & Co** [1971] **1** 1104, Ch D.

Third party—Third party intending to dispute basis of plaintiff's claim and to counterclaim—Whether jurisdiction to join third party as co-defendant—RSC Ord 16, r 11. **Sanchez (Miguel) & Cia SL v Result (owners) (Nello Simoni Ltd, third party)** [1958] **1** 839, Admin Ct.

Adding defendant. See Parties—Adding defendant, *above.*

Consent to joinder—Necessary party—Whether consent necessary. **Vandervell Trustees Ltd v White** [1969] **3** 496, CA.

Consent to joinder—Unwilling party—Costs. **Vandervell Trustees Ltd v White** [1969] **3** 496, CA.

County court. See **County court** (Practice—Parties—Adding persons as parties).

Jurisdiction—Addition of company—Defendant holding majority of shares in company—Plaintiff having no cause of action against company—Whether company proper party to proceedings—Whether company could be joined as party to proceedings even though plaintiff having no cause against it—RSC Ord 15, r 6(2)(b)(ii). **TSB Private Bank International SA v Chabra** [1992] **2** 245, Ch D.

Jurisdiction—Addition of person with only a commercial interest in outcome of proceedings—Interest of creditor of party to action—Whether Mareva creditor of a party having sufficient interest to be joined as party to action—Whether necessary to have interest directly related to subject matter of proceedings—RSC Ord 15, r 6(2)(b)(ii). **Sanders Lead Co Inc v Entores Metal Brokers Ltd** [1984] **1** 857, CA.

Jurisdiction—Addition of person with only a commercial interest in subject-matter of proceedings—No power to add person having no legal interest in subject-matter—RSC Ord 16, r 11. **I G Farbenindustrie A G Agreement, Re** [1943] **2** 525, CA.

Jurisdiction—Group litigation order—Potential claimants applying for group litigation order—Potential Pt 20 defendants applying for issues in group litigation order to be broadened so as to include them in litigation from outset—Court having power to add persons as new parties to proceedings—Whether court having power to broaden issues in group litigation order sought before commencement of proceedings—CPR 19.2(2). **Davies v Dept of Trade and Industry** [2007] **1** 518, CA.

Limitation period. See **Limitation of action** (Leave to add party to proceedings).

Motor Insurers' Bureau—Action by insurers to avoid third party policy—Notice to third party—Motor Insurers' Bureau liable to satisfy judgment obtained by third party if that judgment not satisfied by insured or insurers—Liability arising under contract with Minister of Transport to which third party not privy—Whether bureau entitled to be joined in insurers' action—Road Traffic Act 1960, s 207(3)—RSC Ord 15, r 6(2)(b). **Fire, Auto and Marine Insurance Co Ltd v Greene** [1964] **2** 761, QBD.

Motor Insurers' Bureau—Action by pedestrian against motor cyclist—Defendant insured but insurance company unknown—Defendant unable to be traced—Whether Motor Insurers' Bureau should be added as a party—RSC Ord 15, r 6(2)(b). **Gurtner v Circuit** [1968] **1** 328, CA.

Motor Insurers' Bureau—Plaintiff claiming compensation against bureau for injuries caused by unidentified person—Bureau requiring plaintiff to bring action against identified party to accident—Bureau wishing to be joined as second defendants to action—Discretion of court—Whether joinder necessary to ensure effectual and complete determination of matters in dispute—RSC Ord 15, r 6(2)(b). **White v London Transport Executive** [1971] **3** 1, CA.

PRACTICE (cont)—
  Parties (cont)—
    Adding persons as parties (cont)—
      Necessary party—Inland Revenue Commissioners—Whether presence necessary to effectual and complete determination of matters—RSC Ord 15, r 6(2)(b). **Vandervell Trustees Ltd v White** [1970] **3** 16, HL.
      Necessary party—Party whose presence necessary to ensure all matters in dispute effectually and completely determined—RSC Ord 15, r 6(2)(b). **Settlement Corp v Hochschild (No 2)** [1970] **1** 60, Ch D.
    Adding plaintiff—
      Amendment of writ—Application to disapply limitation period—Personal injuries action—Whether leave to amend may be given after application to disapply limitation period granted—Whether application for leave to amend to add additional plaintiff should be made before or at same time as application to disapply limitation period—Limitation Act 1980, s 33(1)—RSC Ord 15, r 6(5), Ord 20, r 5(5). **Howe v David Brown Tractors (Retail) Ltd (Rustons Engineering Co Ltd, third party)** [1991] **4** 30, CA.
      Application by party added to be removed from proceedings—Second defendant joined as party to proceedings outside three-year limitation period—Second defendant applying to be removed from proceedings but not raising limitation as defence—Master dismissing application—Notice of appeal served ten months after decision of master—Judge refusing to grant extension of time for appealing on grounds of inexcusable delay only—Whether judge right to do so—RSC Ord 3, r 5, Ord 15, r 6, Ord 58, r 1. **Marshall v Gradon Construction Services Ltd** [1997] **4** 880, CA.
    Application for declaration—
      Locus standi of applicant. *See* **Declaration** (Jurisdiction—Locus standi of applicant).
    Application to Court of Protection under Mental Health Act 1959, s 103. *See* **Mental health** (Patient's property—Execution of will—Attestation).
    Assignment of cause of action—
      Co-directors and owners of company causing company to assign to them all rights arising out of its relationship with defendant bank—Plaintiff directors obtaining legal aid and commencing proceedings against bank—Legal aid not available to company—Whether assignment of rights valid—Whether assignment a device to enable director to bring proceedings with legal aid. **Norglen Ltd (in liq) v Reeds Rains Prudential Ltd** [1996] **1** 945, CA.
    Attorney General—
      Proceedings relating to charities. *See* Parties—Proceedings relating to charities—Attorney General, *below*.
    Capacity—
      Capacity to conduct proceedings—Test of capacity to make decisions likely to be required in course of proceedings—Whether test of capacity for claimant applying to claim as formulated or actual claim—CPR Pt 21. **Dunhill v Burgin** [2014] **2** 364, SC.
      Claimant suffering brain damage as result of road traffic accident—Claimant compromising action—Claimant seeking to sue solicitors advising him to compromise—Claimant seeking to re-open issue of capacity—Whether claimant a 'patient' under the rules of the court—Whether burden of proof on claimant to show inability of managing or administering his affairs—Test to be applied to determine whether capacity in issue—Time at which issue of capacity to be raised—RSC Ord 80, r 10—CPR Pt 21. **Masterman-Lister v Brutton & Co** [2003] **3** 162, CA.
      Local authority—Proceedings for statutory nuisance instituted before authorising resolution—Ratification by resolution 3 days later—Validity—Public Health Act 1936, s 100. **Warwick RDC v Miller-Mead** [1962] **1** 212, CA.
    Change of name—
      Company—Public company—Reregistration of name with words 'public limited company' or 'plc' or Welsh equivalent—Companies Act 1980, ss 2(2), 78(3)(b), (d). **Practice Direction** [1982] **1** 384, Fam D.
      Notice to be filed and copies served on other parties—New name to be substituted in title. **Practice Direction** [1984] **1** 720, Ch D.
      Proceedings by or against company—Practice. **Practice Direction** [1965] **1** 43, QBD.
      Surname. *See* Parties—Name—Change of surname, *below*.
    Change of parties—
      Application for order to carry on proceedings—Jurisdiction to grant leave after judgment at the trial—RSC Ord 17, r 4. **Tate's Will Trusts, Re** [1959] **2** 450, Ch D.
    Charity—
      Attorney General. *See* Parties—Proceedings relating to charities—Attorney General, *below*.
      Charity proceedings. *See* **Charity** (Proceedings—Parties).
    Co-plaintiffs—
      Striking out one plaintiff and adding that party as defendant—Copyright—Infringement—Licensees commencing infringement action and joining owners of copyright as co-plaintiffs—Copyright owners withdrawing retainer of solicitors for the co-plaintiffs and applying to be struck out as co-plaintiffs and to be added as defendants—Whether and on what terms order should be made—Copyright Act 1956, s 19(3)—RSC Ord 16, r 11. **Warwick Film Productions Ltd v Eisinger** [1963] **2** 892, Ch D.
    Copyright action—
      Co-owners of copyright. *See* **Copyright** (Co-ownership—Action—Parties).
    Correction of name after expiry of limitation period—
      Leave—Action begun in name of dissolved plaintiff companies—Trustee in bankruptcy applying to be substituted as plaintiff—Whether correction directed at name or identity of plaintiff—RSC Ord 20, r 5(3). **International Bulk Shipping and Services Ltd v Minerals and Metals Trading Corp of India** [1996] **1** 1017, CA.
      Leave—Application for leave to substitute name of new party—Whether leave to correct name of party should be given—RSC Ord 20, r 5—CCR Ord 15, r 3. **Evans Construction Co Ltd v Charrington & Co Ltd** [1983] **1** 310, CA.
    Defamation action. *See* **Libel and slander** (Parties).
    Defendants—
      Adding defendant. *See* Parties—Adding defendant, *above*.

PRACTICE (cont)—
  Parties (cont)—
    Description of parties—
      Corporate body. **Practice Direction** [1969] **2** 1130, QBD.

      Defendants sued as individual partners in Swiss general partnership—Partnership being separate entity but not a corporation under Swiss law—Whether defendants could be sued as individuals—Whether partnership should be named as defendant. **Oxnard Financing SA v Rahn** [1998] **3** 19, CA.

      Description sufficiently certain to identify defendant—Whether requirement that defendant be named—CPR PD 7, para 4.1(1)—CPR 3.10. **Bloomsbury Publishing Group Ltd v News Group Newspapers Ltd** [2003] **3** 736, Ch D.

      Doubt as to sex or description—Appropriate description in title of writ and memorandum of appearance. **Practice Direction** [1969] **2** 1130, QBD.

      Female plaintiff or defendant—Use of term 'feme sole'. **Ross v Collins** [1964] **1** 861, CA.

      Unincorporated body. **Practice Direction** [1969] **2** 1130, QBD.

    Discharge of ex parte injunction—
      Application by one defendant. *See* **Injunction** (Ex parte injunction—Discharge—Application by one defendant).

    Divorce proceedings. *See* **Divorce** (Parties).

    Existence of plaintiff—
      Plaintiff Panamanian company issuing writ against defendant in relation to an alleged contract—Plaintiff subsequently dissolved, but continuing to exist under Panamanian law for three years for certain limited purposes—Whether plaintiff remaining in existence beyond three-year period for purpose of resolving proceedings. **Phoenix Marine Inc v China Ocean Shipping Co** [1999] **1 Comm** 138, QBD.

    Family proceedings. *See* **Family proceedings** (Parties).

    Foreign party—
      Entitlement to sue in English courts—Foreign legal institution—Institution having no animate content—Hindu temple—Whether institution having sufficient legal personality entitling it to sue in English courts. **Bumper Development Corp Ltd v Comr of Police of the Metropolis (Union of India, claimants)** [1991] **4** 638, CA.

    Intervention by persons not parties—
      Attorney General—Intervention in private suit—Rights. **Adams v Adams (A-G intervening)** [1970] **3** 572, Div.

    Joinder of parties—
      Claim for negative declaration—Claim between insurer and assured—Insurer seeking declaration it was not liable to indemnify assured in respect of assured's liability under judgment in earlier proceedings—Judgment debt in favour of applicants—Applicants seeking to be joined to instant proceedings as second to fourth defendants—Whether applicants to be joined—CPR 19.2(2). **Chubb Insurance Co of Europe SA v Davies** [2004] **2 Comm** 827, QBD.

      Claim for negative declaration—Whether party properly joined—Whether claim should be set aside as against party—Whether negative declaration should be granted. **Messier-Dowty Ltd v Sabena SA (No 2)** [2000] **1 Comm** 833, CA; [2001] **1** 275, CA.

      Consent to joinder—Whether consent of all parties necessary. **Vandervell Trustees Ltd v White** [1970] **3** 16, HL.

      Crown—Joinder as party—Hypothetical question—Possible liability to estate duty. **Barnato (decd), Re** [1949] **1** 515, CA.

      Ecclesiastical law—Petition for faculty. *See* **Ecclesiastical law** (Faculty—Petition—Locus standi—Parties entitled to be joined as petitioners).

      Inspection of property—Joinder of defendant to enable property to be inspected—No rights to be adjusted between person joined and any other party to action—Whether jurisdiction to join person as party to action solely for purpose of obtaining order for inspection of his property—RSC Ord 29, r 2. **Douihech v Findlay** [1990] **3** 118, QBD.

      Joinder of defendants. *See* Parties—Adding defendant, *above*.

      Joinder of plaintiffs—Common questions of law or fact—One party Crown claiming bona vacantia—Judicial discretion—RSC Ord 16, r 1. **Banque des Marchands de Moscou (Koupetschesky) and A-G v Midland Bank Ltd** [1939] **2** 364, CA.

      Joinder of plaintiffs—Transaction or series of transactions—Action for interference with light—RSC Ord 16, r 1. **Bendir v Anson** [1936] **3** 326, CA.

      Joinder of plaintiff—Condition imposed on joinder—Assignment of company including claim against insurer to director—Company being subject to order to provide security for costs of action against insurer—Company being unable to provide security—Director applying to be added as plaintiff in action—Court ordering director to be joined as plaintiff subject to paying security for costs in same amount as order against company—Whether court having power to impose condition on joinder—Whether joinder should be set aside—CCR Ord 13, rr 1(8), 8(1). **Eurocross Sales Ltd v Cornhill Insurance plc** [1995] **4** 950, CA.

      Joint contractors—One joint contractor suing alone—Other joint contractor unwilling to sue—No offer of indemnity for costs made by plaintiff to his joint contractor—Joint contractor did not object to being added as defendant, but defendants objected—Absence of offer by plaintiff of indemnity for costs to his joint contractor did not constitute a ground on which defendants could maintain their objection. **Burnside v Harrison Marks Productions Ltd** [1968] **2** 286, CA.

      Party whose presence necessary to ensure all matters in dispute effectually and completely determined—Action seeking execution of trusts of will of testator dying domiciled in India—Beneficiaries seeking to prevent transmission of proceeds of redemption of savings bonds out of jurisdiction—Moneys to be used for payment of Indian estate duty—Application by Union of India to be joined as defendant—Whether a necessary party—RSC Ord 15, r 6. **Lord Cable (decd), Re** [1976] **3** 417, Ch D.

PRACTICE (cont)—
  Parties (cont)—
    Joinder of parties (cont)—
      Persons jointly entitled to a remedy—Container companies recovering sums under multi-layered
        excess of loss insurance programme—Insurers claiming rights of subrogation over sums
        recovered—Lead insurance company seeking permission to represent participating following
        insurers—Container companies contending insurers' subrogation action not properly constituted
        since non-participating following insurer with joint entitlement to remedies sought not joined to
        action—Concept of 'joint entitlement'—Whether action properly constituted—Whether to grant
        leading insurer permission to represent participating following insurers—CPR 19.3, 19.6. **Royal &
        Sun Alliance Insurance plc v Textainer Group Holdings Ltd** [2022] **2 Comm** 319, Comm Ct.
  Law Society—
    Proceedings in which court giving guidance to solicitors in performance of their duties. **Pearson v
      Pearson (Queen's Proctor showing cause)** [1969] **3** 323, Div.
  Libel and slander. *See* **Libel and slander** (Parties).
  Local authority—
    Assertion and protection of rights of public—Local authority instituting proceedings for injunction
      to prevent use of premises for Sunday market—Whether local authority bound to sue on relation
      of Attorney General—Whether authority entitled to sue in own name—Local Government Act
      1972, s 222(1)(a). **Solihull Metropolitan BC v Maxfern Ltd** [1977] **2** 177, Ch D.
    Assertion and protection of rights of public—Whether bound to sue on relation of Attorney
      General—Highways Act 1959, s 116(2), (5). **Hampshire CC v Shonleigh Nominees Ltd** [1970] **2** 144,
      Ch D.
    Condition precedent—Statutory nuisance—Proceedings in High Court instituted before resolution
      that remedy by summary proceedings inadequate—Resolution passed 3 days later—Whether
      action properly instituted—Public Health Act 1936, s 100. **Warwick RDC v Miller-Mead**
      [1962] **1** 212, CA.
    Promotion or protection of interests of inhabitants of their area—Local authority obtaining
      injunction to restrain breaches by defendant of tree preservation order—Local authority applying
      for committal of defendant for breaches of injunction—Whether local authority bound to sue on
      relation of Attorney General—Whether local authority entitled to obtain injunction in own
      name—Local Government Act 1972, s 222(1)(a). **Kent CC v Batchelor** [1978] **3** 980, QBD.
    Promotion or protection of interests of inhabitants of their area—Prevention of deliberate
      contravention of Sunday trading laws—Local authority seeking injunction to restrain trader from
      acting in contravention of law—Whether authority bound to sue on relation of Attorney
      General—Whether local authority entitled to obtain injunction in own name—Shops Act 1950,
      ss 47, 71(1)—Local Government Act 1972, s 222(1)(a). **Stoke-on-Trent City Council v B & Q (Retail)
      Ltd** [1984] **2** 332, HL.
    Promotion or protection of interests of inhabitants of their area—Whether bound to sue on relation
      of Attorney General—Public nuisance—Local Government Act 1933, s 276. **Prestatyn UDC v
      Prestatyn Raceway Ltd** [1969] **3** 1573, Ch D.
  Locus standi—
    Locus standi going to jurisdiction of court—Whether parties can consent to court hearing party with
      no locus standi. **R v Secretary of State for Social Services, ex p Child Poverty Action Group**
      [1989] **1** 1047, CA.
  Mandamus—
    Sufficiency of interest. *See* **Mandamus** (Applicant).
  Misnomer—
    Amendment—Plaintiffs a French trading firm—Wrongly described as corporate body—Addition of
      names of members of firm—RSC Ord 16, r 2, Ord 72, r 2. **Etablissement Baudelot v RS Graham
      and Co Ltd** [1953] **1** 149, CA.
    Solicitor—Warranty—Client's name—Proceedings entitled as having been brought by one
      company—Proceedings not brought by that company but by company succeeding to
      claim—Whether solicitor acting in proceedings providing warranty as to name of client. **SEB
      Trygg Liv Holding Aktiebolag v Manches** [2006] **1** 437, CA; [2006] **2 Comm** 38, CA.
  Name—
    Change of name—Generally. *See* Parties—Change of name, *above*.
    Change of surname. **Practice Direction** [1965] **1** 928, QBD.
  Necessary parties—
    Equitable assignment of part of debt—Assignor's action for whole debt—Whether assignee
      necessary party. **Walter & Sullivan Ltd v Murphy (J) & Sons Ltd** [1955] **1** 843, CA.
  Party acting in person—
    Assistance. *See* Trial—Party acting in person—Right to assistance, *below*.
  Party in contempt of court. *See* **Contempt of court** (Party in contempt).
  Plaintiffs—
    Co-plaintiffs should be represented by same solicitor unless separate representation authorised.
      Lewis v Daily Telegraph Ltd (No 2) [1964] **1** 705, CA.
    Substitution of. *See* Parties—Substitution—Substitution of plaintiff, *below*.
  Proceedings relating to charities—
    Attorney General—Appeal—Removal of trustee—Appeal against order of Charity Commissioners
      removing trustee—Charity Commissioners and Attorney General made defendants—Attorney
      General alone should be joined as defendant in first instance—RSC Ord 108, r 4(2). **Jones v A-G**
      [1972] **2** 637, Ch D.
    Attorney General—Attorney General appropriate party on behalf of Sovereign in execution of duty
      to protect property given to charity. **Belling (decd), Re, London Borough of Enfield v Public
      Trustee** [1967] **1** 105, Ch D.
    Attorney General—Substitution of Attorney General as party to proceedings brought by local
      authority. *See* Parties—Substitution—Charity—Attorney General—Local charity—Action by local
      inhabitants, *below*.
    Charity Commissioners—Attorney General—Whether Charity Commissioners or Attorney General
      necessary parties. **Neville Estates Ltd v Madden** [1961] **3** 769, Ch D.
    Local authority—Local authority not appropriate body to protect property given to charity. **Belling
      (decd), Re, London Borough of Enfield v Public Trustee** [1967] **1** 105, Ch D.

PRACTICE (cont)—
  Parties (cont)—
    Proceedings relating to charities (cont)—
      Meaning of 'charity proceedings'. *See* **Charity** (Proceedings—Parties).
      Permissible parties. *See* **Charity** (Proceedings—Parties—Permissible parties).
    Rectification proceedings. *See* **Deed** (Rectification—Parties to proceedings).
    Representation—
      Consistory court. *See* **Ecclesiastical law** (Consistory court—Representation of parties).
      Representation of deceased person interested in proceedings. *See* Representation of deceased person interested in proceedings, *below.*
    Representative proceedings—
      Action in tort—Suit by minority shareholder on behalf of itself and other shareholders—Shareholder seeking declaration of entitlement to damages for conspiracy against directors of company and seeking damages—Whether jurisdiction to entertain representative action where cause of action of each member of class a separate cause in tort for which proof of damage necessary—Whether court should exercise discretion to make representation order. **Prudential Assurance Co Ltd v Newman Industries Ltd** [1979] **3** 507, Ch D.
      Infringement of copyright—Claim for injunction and damages—Member of class which produced, made or distributed most of sound recordings in country suing on behalf of itself and the other members of the class—Sale of pirate recordings—Defendant admitting infringements of copyright and assertions as to members of class—Whether member of class entitled in representative capacity to injunction and to inquiry as to damages. **EMI Records Ltd v Riley** [1981] **2** 838, Ch D.
      Representation order—Members' club—Action in tort—Claim for damages by servant of club for injury on club premises—Assistant honorary secretary and chairman of house committee made defendants—Order authorising them to defend action in representative capacity—RSC Ord 16, r 9. **Campbell v Thompson** [1953] **1** 831, QBD.
      Representation order—Unincorporated association—Fluctuating membership—Action for goods supplied—RSC Ord 16, r 9. **Barker v Allanson** [1937] **1** 75, CA.
      'Same interest' in proceedings—Action against multiple insurers—Insurers from England and elsewhere dealing on Belgian insurance market—Substantial number of insurers contracting to provide liability insurance for charterers of vessel—Each insurer contracting on terms which included leading underwriter clause—Leading underwriter clause stipulating that each insurer liable for respective share for all decisions against leading underwriter—Writ issued in England by cargo owners against largest single insurer and leading underwriter as representing all insurers—Writ claiming damages against insurers severally—Prior action against all insurers commenced in Belgium—Whether English action properly constituted as representative action—Whether all insurers having 'same interest' in English action—Whether England appropriate forum for deciding claim—RSC Ord 15, r 12(1). **Irish Shipping Ltd v Commercial Union Assurance Co plc** [1989] **3** 853, CA.
      'Same interest' in proceedings—Claim for remedial relief on behalf of over 27,500 individuals and 457 villages following oil spill affecting large area—Whether claimants having 'same interest' in claim—Whether representative claim—CPR 19.6(1). **Jalla v Shell International Trading and Shipping Co Ltd** [2022] **2** 1056, CA.
      Substitution of party. *See* Parties—Substitution—Representative action, *below.*
      Suit on behalf of numerous persons having same interest—General principles—CPR 19.6(1). **Millharbour Management Ltd v Weston Homes Ltd** [2011] **3** 1027, QBD.
      Suit on behalf of numerous persons having same interest—Tenants of council houses—Proposed to increase rents of some tenants—Whether four council tenants to be allowed to sue in representative capacity on behalf of all other council tenants—RSC Ord 16, r 9. **Smith v Cardiff Corp** [1953] **2** 1373, CA.
      Suit on behalf of wine producers of Champagne district of France. **Bollinger (J) v Costa Brava Wine Co Ltd (No 2)** [1961] **1** 561, Ch D.
  Res judicata—
    Privy of party to proceedings. *See* **Estoppel** (Res judicata—Privity of party to proceedings).
  Separate actions by different plaintiffs against same defendant—
    Order that actions be listed and tried together—Effect—Whether there is jurisdiction to order unsuccessful plaintiff in one action to pay defendant's costs of both actions—RSC Ord 65, r 1. **Fairfax (John) & Sons Pty Ltd v E C De Witt & Co (Australia) Pty Ltd** [1957] **3** 410, CA.
  Specific performance. *See* **Specific performance** (Parties).
  Standing to bring proceedings—
    Human rights proceedings. *See* **Human rights** (Proceedings—Standing to bring proceedings for breach of convention rights).
  Striking out party—
    Action instituted without proper authority—Ratification on behalf of plaintiff—Action in name of company without authority—Liquidation of company—Adoption of proceedings by liquidator. **Danish Mercantile Co Ltd v Beaumont** [1951] **1** 925, CA.
    Defendant added after expiration of limitation period for bringing action against him—Defendant seeking order that he should cease to be a party—Test to be applied in deciding whether to grant order—RSC Ord 15, r 6(2)(a). **Leicester Wholesale Fruit Market Ltd v Grundy** [1990] **1** 442, CA.
  Substitution—
    Action against deceased person—Defendant dead at date of issue of writ—Substitution of executors—RSC Ord 2, r 1, Ord 15, r 6, Ord 20, r 5. **Dawson (Bradford) Ltd v Dove** [1971] **1** 554, QBD.
    Arbitration. *See* **Arbitration** (Practice—Substitution of party).
    Arbitration proceedings—Arbitration erroneously brought by defendant reinsureds whose rights under contract of reinsurance had been transferred under statutory scheme to a separate company—Arbitrator allowing substitution of reinsured upon discovery of error—Claimant reinsurers challenging validity of arbitrators appointment where proceedings no longer between original parties—Whether substitution properly made. **Harper Versicherungs AG v Indemnity Marine Assurance Co Ltd** [2006] **2** Comm 225, QBD.

Beneficiaries applying to be substituted for plaintiff trustees—Employee pension fund making payments to employer company after receiving legal advice—Company subsequently going into receivership—Pension fund having insufficient assets to fund pensioners entitlement—Trustees bringing action for negligence against legal advisers—Trustees wishing to abandon action because of risk of personal exposure to costs—Representative beneficiaries applying to be substituted as plaintiffs—Whether court having jurisdiction to order substitution. **Bradstock Trustee Services Ltd v Nabarro Nathanson (a firm)** [1995] **4** 888, Ch D.

Charity—Attorney General—Local charity—Action by local inhabitants—Action for declaration that park held by local authority subject to charitable trust—Plaintiffs having no locus standi—Whether power to substitute Attorney General as plaintiff—RSC Ord 15, r 6. **Hauxwell v Barton-upon-Humber UDC** [1973] **2** 1022, Ch D.

Date from when substituted party becomes party to proceedings—Action on bill of lading—Bill of lading subject to Hague Visby Rules for claims in respect of carriage of goods—Writ amended and re-served on substituted defendant outside one-year limitation period prescribed by Hague Visby Rules—Whether defendant joined as party from date when amended writ served on him—Whether joiner relating back to date when writ first issued—Whether Hague Visby Rules time limit substantive or procedural—Carriage of Goods by Sea Act 1971, Sch, art III, para 6—Limitation Act 1980, s 35—RSC Ord 20, r 5. **Payabi v Armstel Shipping Corp** [1992] **3** 329, QBD.

Representative action—Substitution of party as plaintiff—Withdrawal of named plaintiff from action—Power to substitute one of unnamed parties as plaintiff—RSC Ord 15, r 6—RSC Ord 20, r 5(1). **Moon v Atherton** [1972] **3** 145, CA.

Substitution after expiry of limitation period—Application to add claimants to libel proceedings—Whether addition of parties being substitution of parties for part of claim—Whether substitution should be permitted if amounting to adding new claims—CPR 17.4, 19.5. **Adelson v Associated Newspapers Ltd** [2007] **4** 330, CA.

Substitution after expiry of limitation period—Claim mistakenly brought against limited liability partnership instead of against former partnership—Limitation period for starting new action expiring before mistake recognised—Whether possible to substitute former partnership as defendant—Limitation Act 1980, s 35—CPR 19.5. **Insight Group Ltd v Kingston Smith (a firm)** [2013] **3** 518, QBD.

Substitution after expiry of limitation period—Party named in claim form in mistake for new party—Correct approach—CPR 19.5. **Morgan Est (Scotland) Ltd v Hanson Concrete Products Ltd** [2005] **3** 135, CA.

Substitution after expiry of limitation period—Plaintiff foreign company ceasing to exist as separate entity and incorporated into new company during course of proceedings—Whether rules permitting substitution of new company as plaintiff after expiry of limitation period—Limitation Act 1980, s 35—RSC Ord 15, r 7. **Industrie Chimiche Italia Centrale v Alexander Tsaviliris & Sons Maritime Co** [1996] **1** 114, QBD.

Substitution after expiry of limitation period—Plaintiff health authority ceasing to exist and replaced by National Health Service trust during course of proceedings—Whether rules permitting substitution of trust as plaintiff after expiry of limitation period—Limitation Act 1980, s 35—RSC Ord 15, r 7. **Yorkshire Regional Health Authority v Fairclough Building Ltd** [1996] **1** 519, CA.

Substitution after expiry of limitation period—Rule of procedure empowering court to permit change of parties after expiry of limitation period under any enactment allowing such a change or under which such a change was allowed—Whether rule only applying to enactments which expressly allowed change of parties after expiry of limitation period—CPR 19.5(1)(c). **Parsons v George** [2004] **3** 633, CA.

Substitution after judgment—Action by two companies against defendants—Agreement to compromise action—Consent judgment—Second plaintiff company merging before judgment with third company—Application after judgment to substitute third company as second plaintiff—Power of court to allow substitution—Circumstances in which exercisable—RSC Order 15, rr 6(2), 7(2). **Mercer Alloys Corp v Rolls Royce Ltd** [1972] **1** 211, CA.

Substitution of plaintiff—Action begun by plaintiff company—Application to substitute firm as plaintiff—Whether judge entitled to take merits into account in determining application. **Kings Quality Homes Ltd v AJ Paints Ltd** [1997] **3** 267, CA.

Substitution of plaintiff—Action begun in name of deceased—Plaintiff dying after issue of writ—Writ in name of deceased served on defendant—Deceased's widow and personal representative applying for substitution of her name as plaintiff after service—Whether proceedings a nullity—Law Reform (Miscellaneous Provisions) Act 1934, s 1—RSC Ord 2, r 1, Ord 15, r 7(1). **Fielding v Rigby** [1993] **4** 294, CA.

Substitution of plaintiff—Action begun in name of firm—Sole proprietor of firm dead—Substitution of proprietor's executrix as plaintiff—RSC Ord 16, r 2. **Alexander Mountain & Co v Rumere Ltd** [1948] **2** 482, CA.

Substitution of plaintiff—Company's cause of action assigned to individuals—Individuals applying to be substituted or joined as plaintiffs and obtaining legal aid to continue the action—Legal aid not available to company—Whether assignment valid. **Circuit Systems Ltd (in liq) v Zuken-Redac (UK) Ltd** [1998] **1** 218, HL.

Substitution of plaintiff—Plaintiff foreign company ceasing to exist during course of proceedings—Successor to plaintiff's rights and obligations applying to be substituted as plaintiff—Whether court having power in principle to substitute successor as plaintiff—If so, whether court should exercise that power after expiry of relevant limitation period—Whether court should allow substitution—Limitation Act 1980, s 35—RSC Ord 15, r 7(2). **Toprak Enerji Sanayi AS v Sale Tilney Technology plc** [1994] **3** 483, QBD.

PRACTICE (cont)—
Parties (cont)—
Substitution (cont)—
Trustee in bankruptcy—Bankrupt plaintiff companies bringing action in own names to enforce arbitration awards—Trustee in bankruptcy applying to be substituted as plaintiff and for leave to issue and serve new proceedings—Application made after expiry of limitation period—Whether rules permitting amendment—Whether action by non-existent company a nullity—RSC Ord 15, r 6. **International Bulk Shipping and Services Ltd v Minerals and Metals Trading Corp of India** [1996] **1** 1017, CA.
Unnamed defendant—
Bank holding items in safety deposit boxes—Bank unable to trace persons with interest in contents—Bank applying for order to inspect property before claims made—Whether application permitted where defendants unknown—Torts (Interference with Goods) Act 1977, ss 12, 13—Senior Courts Act 1981, s 33—CPR 25.1(1)(c)(ii), (i). **Crédit Agricole Corp and Investment Bank v Persons with or claiming an immediate right to possess goods contained in certain safety deposit boxes** [2022] **1 Comm** 239, Ch D; **Credit Agricole Corporate and Investment Bank v Persons with or claiming an immediate right to possess goods contained in certain safety deposit boxes** [2022] **1** 83, Ch D.
Injunction—Injunction against 'persons unknown'—Injunction to prevent unauthorised encampments on local authority land—Whether permissible to make final injunctions against persons unknown—Senior Courts Act 1981, s 37—Town and Country Planning Act 1990, s 187B. **Barking and Dagenham London BC v Persons unknown (London Gypsies and Travellers intervening)** [2022] **4** 51, CA.
Injunction—Injunctions against 'persons unknown'—Claimants granted interim injunction against 'persons unknown', being protesters against the sale of clothing containing animal products—Whether claim form properly served—Whether interim injunction to be discharged—Whether final injunction to be granted—CPR 6.15, 6.16, 40.12. **Canada Goose UK Retail Ltd v Persons unknown** [2020] **4** 575, CA.
Injunction—Injunctions granted against 'persons unknown' to restrain potentially unlawful acts of protest before they occurred—Whether judge in error—Requirements for grant—Human Rights Act 1998, s 12(3). **Ineos Upstream Ltd v Persons unknown** [2019] **4** 699, CA.
Road traffic accident—Unidentified driver—Claim for declaration vehicle insurer liable to satisfy judgment—Application to substitute 'person unknown' as defendant—Whether, and in what circumstances, permissible to sue unnamed defendant—Whether insurer liable—Road Traffic Act 1988, s 151—CPR 6.15—European Parliament and Council Directive 2009/103/EC, art 18. **Cameron v Liverpool Victoria Insurance Co Ltd** [2019] **2 Comm** 467, SC; [2019] **3** 1, SC.
Wardship proceedings. *See* **Ward of court** (Practice—Parties to proceedings).
Winding up of company—
Misfeasance action against director—Whether liquidator a necessary party. *See* **Company** (Winding up—Misfeasance—Director—Misfeasance action by company in liquidation against director—Whether liquidator necessary as co-plaintiff).
Partnership—
Service of writ on partnership. *See* **Writ** (Service on partnership).
Patent—
Appeal tribunal. *See* **Patent** (Appeal tribunal—Practice).
Generally. *See* **Patent** (Practice).
Patents Court. *See* **Patent** (Patents Court).
Payment into court—
Acceptance—
Acceptance in error—Mistaken interpretation of pleadings—Power of court to grant relief. **Kaprow (S) & Co Ltd v Maclelland & Co Ltd** [1948] **1** 264, CA.
Effect—Counterclaim and set-off—Acceptance by plaintiff of sum paid in by defendant as 'enough to satisfy plaintiff's claim'—Whether defendant free to pursue counterclaim—RSC Ord 22, r 1. **French (A Martin) (a firm) v Kingswood Hill Ltd** [1960] **2** 251, CA.
Statement in open court—Action for assault. *See* Statement in open court—Action for assault, *below.*
Time for acceptance—Extension of time—Whether court should extend time for acceptance where risks have changed appreciably—Whether change of plea amounting to appreciable change in risks—RSC Ord 22, rr 3(1)(a), 5. **Proetta v Times Newspapers Ltd** [1991] **4** 46, CA.
Withdrawal of acceptance—Procedure—RSC Ord 22, r 2(1)(2). **Derrick v Williams** [1939] **2** 559, CA.
Admission of liability—
Admission inconsistent with pleadings—Defendant not precluded from disputing liability—Duty of parties to regularise proceedings—RSC Ord 22. **Bonitto v Fuerst Bros & Co Ltd** [1944] **1** 91, HL.
Judgment should not be for less than amount paid in. **Harrison v Liverpool Corp** [1943] **2** 449, CA.
Withdrawal of admission—Defence subsequently amended by leave and admission of liability withdrawn—Money taken out by plaintiff—Defendant's right to withdraw notice admitting liability and to recover money paid in—RSC Ord 22, rr 3, 6. **Williams v Boag** [1940] **4** 246, CA.
Cheque—
Time at which payment into court made—Whether payment into court made when cheque received in Court Funds Office or only once funds have cleared—Court Funds Rules 1987, SI 1987/821, r 16. **ENE Kos 1 Ltd v Petroleo Brasileiro SA** [2010] **1 Comm** 656, CA; [2010] **1** 1099, CA.
Conditions of appeal. *See* Appeal—Conditions of appeal—Payment into court, *above.*
Consolidated actions. *See* Consolidation of actions—Payments into court, *above.*
Costs—
Generally. *See* **Costs** (Payment into court).
Interest on costs. *See* **Costs** (Interest on costs—Payment into court by defendant).
Order for costs—Discretion. *See* **Costs** (Order for costs—Discretion—Payment into court).
Sum awarded greater than sum paid in—Leave to amend particulars of special damage at trial—Sum awarded in respect of matters pleaded before amendment less than sum paid in—Defendant entitled to costs after payment in. **Cheeseman v Bowaters UK Paper Mills Ltd** [1971] **3** 513, CA.

Payment into court (cont)—
Costs (cont)—
Sum recovered no greater than sum paid in—Discretion as to costs after date of payment in—Award of costs to plaintiffs—Action for debt—Parties coming to agreement on amount of debt after issue of High Court writ—Defendants refusing to pay interest or costs on High Court scale—Defendants paying amount of debt into court—Plaintiffs subsequently obtaining judgment for interest and costs on High Court scale—Plaintiffs awarded costs after date of payment in. **Vehicle and General Insurance Co Ltd (in liq) v Christie Ltd** [1976] **1** 747, QBD.
Trial judge determining liability issue in favour of claimant—Disclosure to judge that payment in by defendants but not its amount—Judge awarding claimant its costs on issue of liability—Whether possible to disclose actual amount of payment in to judge—CPR 36.19, 44.3(4). **HSS Hire Services Group plc v BMB Builders Merchants Ltd** [2005] **3** 486, CA.
Costs. *See* **Costs** (Payment into court).
County court—
Generally. *See* **County court** (Practice—Payment into court).
Denial of liability—
Denial of liability in notice inconsistent with pleadings—Admissions of negligence and special damage in defence—RSC Ord 22, r 1. **Davies v Rustproof Metal Window Co Ltd** [1943] **1** 248, CA.
Interest—
Claimant under a disability—Defendants making payment into court—Payment in accepted on behalf of claimant—Acceptance requiring approval of court—Whether claimant entitled to receive interest on payment in from date of acceptance or from date of approval—CPR 21.10—CPR 36 PD 7.10. **Brennan v ECO Composting Ltd** [2007] **3** 67, QBD.
Payment to be made without regard to possible order for interest. **Jefford v Gee** [1970] **1** 1202, CA.
Interim remedy, as—
Specific fund. *See* Interim remedy—Payment into court of specified fund where there was dispute over party's right to fund, *above*.
Investment of money. *See* Funds in court—Investment of funds in court, *above*.
Joint or alternative claims—
Defendants sued jointly or in the alternative—Payment in by one of several defendants—Plaintiff bringing action against architect and builder for defective work—Mutual or overlapping items in claims against architect and builder—Payment in by builder accepted by plaintiff in satisfaction of claim against builder—Whether architect and builder 'sued jointly or in the alternative' in respect of mutual or overlapping items—Whether acceptance of payment in by builder barring claim against architect—RSC Ord 22, r 3(4). **Townsend v Stone Toms & Partners (a firm)** [1981] **2** 690, CA.
Legal aid—
Costs. *See* **Legal aid** (Costs—Payment into court).
Lodgment of money—
Money—Foreign currency—Payment into court without conversion into sterling—Jurisdiction of court to order that sum be placed in foreign currency deposit account—Treasury consent under exchange control regulations—Admiralty court—Proceeds of sale of ship—Sale for sum expressed in foreign currency—Circumstances in which court will order that proceeds of sale be paid into court and placed into deposit account without conversion—Administration of Justice Act 1965, s 4(1)—Supreme Court Funds Rules 1927 (SR & O 1927 No 1184), r 33(1). **Halcyon the Great, The** [1975] **1** 882, QBD.
Lump sum payment where several causes of action—
Discretion of court—Copyright—Damages for infringement and conversion—RSC Ord 22, r 1(1), (2). **Tallent v Coldwell and Tailor & Cutter Ltd** [1938] **2** 107, Ch D.
Discretion of court—Different classes of persons beneficially entitled—RSC Ord 22, r 1(1), (2). **Gears v Braley** [1940] **3** 376, CA.
Discretion of court—Libel action—RSC Ord 82, r 4(1). **Pedley v Cambridge Newspapers Ltd** [1964] **2** 794, CA.
Discretion of court—Three defendants sued severally—Damages for breach of confidence and infringement of copyright—RSC Ord 22, rr 1(2), 4. **Robertson v Aberdeen Journals Ltd** [1954] **2** 767, Ch D.
Payment in of lump sum—Apportionment—Salvage—RSC Ord 22, r 1(2). **Bosworth, The** [1960] **1** 146, Admin Ct.
Lump sum payment where several plaintiffs—
Payment in of single sum—Apportionment—Defendants refusing to apportion payment in between plaintiffs—Plaintiffs' claims not identical—Non-apportionment causing plaintiffs embarrassment—Whether defendants entitled to make single payment—Whether defendants should be ordered to apportion payment in—RSC Ord 22, r 1(1), (5). **Walker v Turpin** [1993] **4** 865, CA.
Money remaining in court—
Application for payment out—Copyright action—Inquiry as to damages or account of profits—Plaintiff electing to take account of profits—Whether court should order payment out—RSC Ord 22, r 5. **Braben v Emap Images Ltd** [1997] **2** 544, Ch D.
Non-disclosure of payment into court—
Application at trial for payment out—Application by plaintiff opposed by defendant—Application having effect of disclosing payment in—Application made by plaintiff after seeing prospects of success diminishing—Jurisdiction of judge to continue hearing following disclosure of payment in—Whether plaintiff entitled to make application at trial—Whether judge should order new trial following disclosure of payment in and refusal of plaintiff's application—RSC Ord 22, rr 5, 7. **Gaskins v British Aluminium Co Ltd** [1976] **1** 208, CA.
Communication to judge—Oral judgment giving damages—Disclosure of payment into court—Alteration of quantum of damages in formal judgment—Jurisdiction—RSC Ord 22, r 6. **Millensted v Grosvenor House (Park Lane) Ltd** [1937] **1** 736, CA.
Non-disclosure on appeal as to quantum of damages. *See* **Court of Appeal** (Practice—Payment into court—Non-disclosure—Appeal as to quantum of damages).

PRACTICE (cont)—
  Payment into court (cont)—
    Notice—
      Several causes of action—Causes of action not specified—Landlord's action sufficient—RSC forfeiture for non-payment of rent and breach of covenant to pay rates, etc—Notice of payment in referring to Common Law Procedure Act 1852, s 212—Whether notice sufficient—RSC Ord 22, r 1(2). **Standard Pattern Co Ltd v Ivey** [1962] **1** 452, Ch D.
    Offer of settlement—
      Effect of offer—Discretion—Trial judge's discretion to treat offer as payment in—Banker's bond—Defendant providing security for damages by way of banker's bond—Defendant offering amount secured to plaintiff in settlement of claim—Whether offer could be treated as equivalent to payment in for purposes of costs—Whether court could order in advance of trial that offer to be treated as payment in—Whether fetter on trial judge's discretion—RSC Ord 22, r 1. **Corby DC v Holst & Co Ltd** [1985] **1** 321, CA.
    Order for—
      Compromise of action—Procedure. See Compromise of action—Approval of court—Terms of order approving settlement—Payment into court within specified period—Procedure, *above*.
    Several causes of action—
      Payment in of lump sum. See Payment into court—Lump sum payment where several causes of action, *above*.
    Stay of proceedings—
      Issue of proceedings in second action—Jurisdiction of court to strike out second action as abuse of court's process—County court action—Action by plaintiff against defendant to recover uninsured loss arising from road accident—Plaintiff accepting defendant's payment into court—Plaintiff's insurers issuing proceedings in name of plaintiff in county court against defendant to recover amount paid to plaintiff—Whether payment into court barring claim by plaintiff's insurers—Whether insurer's action an abuse of process—CCR 1981, Ord 11, r 3(3). **Buckland v Palmer** [1984] **3** 554, CA.
      Removal of stay—Claimants' failure to provide further security as to costs by date specified in consent order—Security provided one day late—Defendants refusing to accept further security one day late—Whether short delay had material impact on the efficient conduct of litigation—Whether defendants' strict reliance on terms of consent order frustrated the requirement for proceedings to be conducted co-operatively and efficiently—CPR 3.9. **Summit Navigation Ltd v Generali Romani Asigurare Reasigurare SA** [2015] **1 Comm** 360, QBD.
      Removal of stay—Stay effected by payment into court of whole amount of claim—Jurisdiction of court to remove stay in proper case—County court action—Action by plaintiff against defendant to recover uninsured loss arising from road accident—Plaintiff having been paid by his insurers for his insured loss but no claim yet brought by him to recover amount of insured loss from defendant—Payment in by defendant's insurers of full amount of claim for uninsured loss—Payment in an attempt by defendant's insurers to bar claim by plaintiff for amount of insured loss—Whether court having jurisdiction to remove a stay effected by payment in—Whether proper case for exercise of discretion to remove stay—CCR Ord 11, r 7(2). **Lambert v Mainland Market Deliveries Ltd** [1977] **2** 826, CA.
    Two causes of action—
      No apportionment. **Emcee Ltd v Sunday Pictorial Newspapers (1920) Ltd** [1939] **2** 384, KBD.
    Withdrawal of payment in—
      Costs of action—Defendant withdrawing payment in on ground of change of circumstances—Plaintiff succeeding in action but recovering less than sum previously in court—Defendant seeking costs incurred after date of payment in—Whether fact of payment in should be taken into account in awarding costs of action. **Garner v Cleggs (a firm)** [1983] **2** 398, CA.
      Discretion of court to allow withdrawal—Circumstances in which discretion exercisable—Change in circumstances—Defendant company paying in sum representing difference between plaintiffs' claim and company's counterclaim—Receiver of company subsequently appointed and company later going into liquidation—Whether plaintiffs secured creditors to extent of payment in—Whether company's insolvency a change of circumstance justifying withdrawal of payment in—RSC Ord 22, r 1(3). **Sherratt (W A) Ltd v John Bromley (Church Stretton) Ltd** [1985] **1** 216, CA.
      Discretion of court to allow withdrawal—Circumstances in which discretion exercisable—Change in circumstances—Defendant company paying in sum representing difference between plaintiff's claim and counterclaim—Receiver appointed for defendant company—Defendants' counterclaim amended to increase amount of defendants' claim—Payment in likely in event of RSC defendants' insolvency to put plaintiff in position of secured creditor if plaintiff successful—Whether change in circumstances justifying withdrawal of payment in. Ord 22, r 1(3). **Peal Furniture Co Ltd v Adrian Share (Interiors) Ltd** [1977] **2** 211, CA.
      Discretion of court to allow withdrawal—Plaintiff foreign company ceasing to exist during course of proceedings—Defendant applying for leave to withdraw notices of payment in in respect of sums already paid into court—Whether payments into court available to successor to rights and obligations of plaintiff. **Toprak Enerji Sanayi AS v Sale Tilney Technology plc** [1994] **3** 483, QBD.
      Money not taken out within seven days—Application to vary amount paid in—Withdrawal of money paid in in whole or in part—Procedure—RSC Ord 22, rr 1, 2. **Cumper v Pothecary** [1941] **2** 516, CA.
    Withdrawal or reduction of payment in—
      Whether application for reduction of payment in operating as automatic stay on acceptance if issued within 21-day period for acceptance and before acceptance—CPR 36.6(5), 36.11(1). **Flynn v Scougall** [2004] **3** 609, CA.
  Payment out of court—
    Administration of estates—
      Payment out of court to creditors—Fund exceeding £1,000—No order for further consideration—Summons in chambers—Jurisdiction—RSC Ord 55, r 2(1). **Rothermere (Viscount) (decd), Re** [1948] **1** 709, Ch D.
    Admiralty practice. See **Admiralty** (Practice—Payment out of court).
    Affidavit of no settlement—
      Affidavit not longer required. **Practice Direction** [1958] **2** 785, Ch D.

PRACTICE (cont)—
　　Payment out of court (cont)—
　　　　Application—
　　　　　　Time for application—Application to take out money in court after final speeches, but before judgment—Indication by judge that he did not believe applicant's evidence—RSC Ord 22, r 3. **Millar v Building Contractors (Luton) Ltd** [1953] **2** 339, QBD.
　　　　Claims under Fatal Accidents Acts etc—
　　　　　　Damages recovered by widow paid into court—Re-marriage—Right of widow to payment out—RSC Ord 22, r 14(9). **Taylor (formerly Ryan) v Cheltenham & Hereford Breweries Ltd** [1952] **1** 1135, CA.
　　　　　　Damages recovered by widow paid into court—Transfer to county court—Whether widow entitled to payment out—County Courts Act 1934, s 164(2), (3). **Cross v Edey** [1958] **1** 170, CA.
　　　　　　Widow and infant daughter's damages paid into court—Payment out to bank trustees on trusts of a deed containing wide investment clause—RSC Ord 22, r 14(2). **Woodley v Tersons Ltd** [1958] **3** 305, QBD.
　　　　County court. *See* **County court** (Payment out of court).
　　　　Interest—
　　　　　　Defendant lodging money in court as condition of liberty to defend—Defendant giving notice of appropriation—Transfer of accrued interest to Paymaster General—Transfer limited to cases where plaintiff had accepted money paid in—Successful defendant entitled to accrued interest—Supreme Court Funds Rules 1975 (SI 1975 No 1803), r 27(1). **Schroeder v Accountant General** [1980] **2** 648, QBD.
　　　　　　Destination of interest accruing on money paid into court—Court Funds Rules 1987, r 28(1). **Practice Direction** [1988] **3** 896, QBD.
　　　　　　Payment to plaintiff in satisfaction of judgment debt—Judgment including order for payment out in part satisfaction of judgment debt—Interest on money in court—Whether order for payment out 'satisfied' judgment debt pro tanto—Whether judgment debt, pro tanto, ceased to exist on making order for payment out—Whether plaintiff entitled to interest on money in court from date of pronouncement of judgment until receipt of money paid out—Judgments Act 1838, s 17. **Parsons v Mather & Platt Ltd** [1977] **2** 715, QBD.
　　　　Mistake—
　　　　　　Payment into court—Jurisdiction of county court to order. *See* **County court** (Jurisdiction—Order for repayment of money paid out of court in error).
　　　　Payment to nominee—
　　　　　　Solicitors on behalf of client—Nominees of administrators—RSC Ord 55, r 2(1). **Woodhead v Bates** [1963] **2** 877, Ch D.
　　　　Wife, to—
　　　　　　Affidavit of no settlement. *See* **Husband and wife** (Payment out of court to wife—Affidavit of no settlement).
　　Pending appeal. *See* Appeal—Pending appeal, *above*.
　　Pending proceedings—
　　　　Interlocutory injunction. *See* **Injunction** (Interlocutory—Pending proceedings).
　　Peremptory order—
　　　　Form of order. *See* Order—'Unless' orders and other peremptory orders—Form of order, *above*.
　　Personal injuries action—
　　　　Damages—
　　　　　　Generally. *See* **Damages** (Personal injury).
　　　　　　Interest. *See* **Interest** (Damages—Personal injury).
　　　　　　Provisional damages—Default of notice of intention to defend claim or of defence—RSC Ord 12, r 6(2), Ord 13, Ord 19, Ord 25, r 1(7), Ord 37, r 8(5). **Practice Direction** [1988] **2** 102, QBD.
　　　　　　Provisional damages—Judgment after trial—Case file—Preservation—Orders without trial—Draft order—Duties of plaintiff's solicitor—Duties of Central Office—Supreme Court Act 1981, s 32A—RSC Ord 37, r 8. **Practice Direction** [1995] **2** 511, QBD; **Practice Note** [1985] **2** 895, QBD.
　　　　　　Provisional damages—Transfer of action from High Court to county court. *See* **County court** (Transfer of action—Transfer from High Court—Personal injuries action—Action in which provisional damages claimed).
　　　　Disclosure against persons not parties to proceedings. *See* **Disclosure and inspection of documents** (Disclosure against persons not parties to proceedings—Claim in respect of personal injuries or death).
　　　　Experts' reports—
　　　　　　Agreed reports—Reports to be lodged with proper officer after agreement or setting down for trial—RSC Ord 34, r 3. **Practice Direction** [1979] **1** 818, QBD.
　　　　　　Disclosure to other parties—Action for medical negligence. *See* Evidence—Expert evidence—Disclosure to other parties—Action for medical negligence, *above*.
　　　　　　Disclosure to other parties—Pre-action protocol requiring party to provide other party with names of proposed experts before instructing an expert—Protocol giving other party opportunity to object to any of named experts—Claimant instructing expert to whom defendant had taken no objection but refusing to disclose his report—Whether defendant's failure to object to expert nominated by claimant transforming expert into single joint expert whose report was available to both parties—Whether refusal to disclose report of expert to whom no objection made by other side constituting non-compliance with protocol—Pre-Action Protocol for Personal Injury Claims, paras 3.14, 3.16. **Carlson v Townsend** [2001] **3** 663, CA.
　　　　　　Group litigation—Medical report served with statement of claim—Reports prepared on basis of statement of facts prepared by plaintiffs' solicitors—Production of documents referred to in medical reports prepared for plaintiffs—Procedure for production of statement of facts prepared by plaintiffs' solicitors—RSC Ord 18, r 12(1A). **B v John Wyeth & Brother Ltd** [1992] **1** 443, CA.
　　　　　　Reports on which parties intend to rely—Reports to be lodged with proper officer after action set down for trial whether or not agreed—RSC Ord 34, r 3. **Practice Direction** [1989] **3** 926, QBD.
　　　　　　Road traffic accidents—Low velocity collisions—Claims for soft tissue injuries—Causation—Permission to adduce expert evidence—Guidance. **Casey v Cartwright** [2007] **2** 78, CA.
　　　　Fundamental dishonesty—
　　　　　　Application to dismiss claim—When application to be determined—Whether only after quantum assessment—Criminal Justice and Courts Act 2015, s 57. **Patel v Arriva Midlands Ltd** [2019] **3** 702, QBD.

PRACTICE (cont)—
Personal injuries action (cont)—
Limitation of action—
Commencement of proceedings. *See* **Limitation of action** (Period of limitation—Personal injury claim—When proceedings 'brought' for purposes of limitation period).
Generally. *See* **Limitation of action** (Personal injury claim).
When time begins to run. *See* **Limitation of action** (When time begins to run—Personal injury claim).
Medical examination of plaintiff—
Stay of proceedings. *See* Stay of proceedings—Medical examination of plaintiff at defendant's request, *below.*
Special damage—
Loss of earnings, future earning capacity or pension rights and medical expenses—Particulars of claim to be prepared and served on other parties. **Practice Direction** [1984] **3** 165, QBD.
Writ—
Indorsement—Value of action—Writs for issue by High Court—Indorsement with value of action—Actions in which indorsement cannot be put on writ to be commenced in county court—High Court and County Courts Jurisdiction Order 1991, arts 5, 9. **Practice Direction** [1991] **3** 352, QBD.
Personal representatives—
Adding as defendants. *See* Parties—Adding defendant—Personal representatives, *above.*
Persons under disability—
Minor—
Proceeding by next friend—Adoption of action on attaining majority—Title to subsequent proceedings. **Carberry v Davies** [1968] **2** 817, CA.
Settlement of action—
Assizes—Settlement—After entry for trial and before coming in day's list—Party under disability. **Practice Direction** [1953] **2** 1561, Assizes.
Petition—
Bankruptcy. *See* **Bankruptcy** (Petition).
Company—
Compulsory winding up—Generally. *See* **Company** (Compulsory winding up—Procedure).
Petition for relief under Companies Act 1948, s 210. *See* **Company** (Oppression—Petition—Practice).
Divorce. *See* **Divorce** (Petition).
Faculty, for. *See* **Ecclesiastical law** (Faculty—Petition).
House of Lords—
Leave to appeal—Costs. *See* **House of Lords** (Costs—Petition for leave to appeal).
Leave to appeal—Generally. *See* **House of Lords** (Leave to appeal—Petition for leave to appeal).
Petition of appeal. *See* **House of Lords** (Petition).
Insolvency. *See* **Insolvency** (Petition).
Judicial separation. *See* **Husband and wife** (Judicial separation—Form of petition).
Local government election. *See* **Elections** (Local government—Election petition).
Nullity. *See* **Nullity** (Petition).
Petition of right. *See* **Petition of right.**
Pleading. *See* **Pleading.**
Post—
Admiralty practice. *See* **Admiralty** (Practice—Post).
Appearance by. *See* Appearance—Appearance by post, *above.*
Companies Court—
Chambers proceedings. *See* Companies Court—Chambers—Postal transactions, *above.*
County court. *See* **County court** (Postal transactions).
Divorce registry—
Use of postal facilities. *See* **Divorce** (Practice—Postal facilities in divorce registry).
First and second class mail—
Affidavit of service—Interpretation Act 1978, s 7—RSC Ord 10, r 1(3). **Practice Direction** [1985] **1** 889, QBD.
Postal delay—
Period between service of notice of motion and hearing. **Practice Direction** [1969] **1** 304, Ch D.
Service by post of notice of motion—Temporary delay in delivery of mail. **Practice Direction** [1969] **1** 304, Ch D.
Time limited for entry of appearance—Entry of judgment in default of appearance—Temporary delay in delivery of mail—RSC Ord 12, r 5. **Practice Direction** [1969] **1** 346, QBD.
Service by post—
Generally. *See* Service—Service by post, *below.*
Notice to treat—Compulsory acquisition of land. *See* **Compulsory purchase** (Notice to treat—Service—Post).
Use of postal facilities—
Chancery Division. *See* Chancery Division—Applications by post or telephone, *above.*
Issue of writs etc—Changes in Central Office practice. **Practice Direction** [1980] **3** 822, QBD.
Queen's Bench Division—Admiralty Registry—Extension of use—Filing and lodgment of certain documents—Conditions to be complied with. **Practice Direction** [1976] **3** 224, QBD.
Queen's Bench Division—Admiralty Registry—Modifications of usual practice—Posting of orders. **Practice Direction** [1976] **2** 446, QBD.
Queen's Bench Division—Conditions to be complied with—Application by letter—Date of application—Rejection of application by post—Particular classes of business which may be dealt with by post. **Practice Direction** [1976] **2** 312, QBD.
Taxation of costs. *See* **Costs** (Taxation—Procedure—Postal facilities).
Writ—
Issue—Application by post. *See* **Writ** (Issue).
Power of attorney—
Enduring power of attorney—
Court of Protection. *See* **Power of attorney** (Enduring power of attorney).

PRACTICE (cont)—
    Pre-trial or post-judgment relief (cont)—
        Freezing order (cont)—
            Arbitration—Continuation application—Claimant applying ex parte for worldwide freezing order and 'Cargo Injunction' in support of arbitrations commenced previous day against defendant—Whether court having jurisdiction to entertain application for continuation—Whether material non-disclosure by claimant—Whether Cargo Injunction in effect specific performance of contract to sell commodities—Whether commodities on specific vessel to be sold by defendant (or its forwarding agent) and directions to be given for preservation of proceeds—Sale of Goods Act 1979, s 52—Arbitration Act 1996, s 44. **VTB Commodities Trading DAC v JSC Antipinsky Refinery (Petraco Oil Company SA intervening)** [2020] **2 Comm** 613, QBD.
            Arbitration—Order in support of arbitration proceedings—Dispute under charterparty containing English law and arbitration clause—Judgment creditor obtaining worldwide freezing injunction against judgment debtor's parent company—Parent company incorporated in Singapore and owing debts to judgment debtor—Whether worldwide freezing order should be continued—Whether grounds for serving parent company out of jurisdiction—CPR PD 6B, r 3.1. **Parbulk II AS v PT Humpuss Intermoda Transportasi TBK** [2012] **2 Comm** 513, QBD.
            Arbitration—Order in support of arbitration proceedings—Judgment creditor obtaining permission to serve claim form seeking worldwide freezing order on subsidiaries of judgment debtor—Subsidiaries not party to arbitration agreement or arbitration—Subsidiaries having no presence or business in the jurisdiction—Whether court had jurisdiction to make order against subsidiaries—Whether subsidiaries were necessary or proper party—CPR 62.5, PD 6B 3.1(3). **Cruz City 1 Mauritius Holdings v Unitech Ltd** [2015] **1 Comm** 305, QBD.
            Arbitration—Order in support of arbitration proceedings—Ship sale—Buyer obtaining worldwide freezing order on without notice application in Singapore prior to completion of sale—Singaporean court subsequently discharging order on basis of lack of jurisdiction—Buyer seeking worldwide freezing order in English court—Whether appropriate to grant order. **Swift-Fortune Ltd v Magnifica Marine SA** [2008] **1 Comm** 559, QBD.
            Assets—Assets covered by injunction—After-acquired assets—Life assurance policy maturing after grant of injunction—Whether proceeds of policy covered by injunction. **TDK Tape Distributor (UK) Ltd v Videochoice Ltd** [1985] **3** 345, QBD.
            Assets—Assets covered by injunction—Claimant obtaining Mareva injunction prohibiting defendants from disposing or dealing with 'their assets and/or funds'—Principal defendant transferring funds from accounts held in his name to accounts held in wife's name—Whether transfers breaching order if defendant having no beneficial interest in accounts. **Federal Bank of the Middle East Ltd v Hadkinson** [2000] **2** 395, CA.
            Assets—Assets covered by injunction—Order defining assets as including assets 'whether the Respondent is interested in them legally, beneficially or otherwise'—Whether injunction including assets that respondent held as trustee or nominee for third party and in which he had no beneficial interest. **JSC BTA Bank v Solodchenko** [2011] **2 Comm** 1063, CA; [2011] **4** 1240, CA.
            Assets—Assets not covered by injunction—Ordinary living expenses—Legal expenses—Ordinary living expenses excepted from ambit of injunction—Defendant employing Queen's Counsel to defend him in serious criminal proceedings—Whether Queen's Counsel's fee falling within 'ordinary living expenses'. **TDK Tape Distributor (UK) Ltd v Videochoice Ltd** [1985] **3** 345, QBD.
            Assets—Claimant obtaining freezing order prohibiting defendant from disposing of or dealing with assets—Reasonable legal expenses excepted from ambit of order provided defendant notifying claimant as to source of money prior to spending—Defendant entering into loan agreements—Defendant exercising right under loan agreements by directing lenders to pay proceeds of loan to third parties to meet legal expenses—Whether right to borrow constituting asset—Whether exercise of right constituting dealing and disposing of asset. **JSC BTA Bank v Ablyazov (No 5)** [2012] **2 Comm** 1243, QBD; [2014] **1 Comm** 700, CA; [2016] **1 Comm** 97, SC; [2016] **1** 608, SC.
            Assets—Dissipation of assets—World-wide freezing order discharged at inter partes hearing—Judge finding good arguable case that respondent engaged in wrongdoing against appellant but deciding no real risk of dissipation of assets—Correct approach in law to question of whether an inference of dissipation should be made. **Lakatamia Shipping Co Ltd v Morimoto** [2020] **2 Comm** 359, CA.
            Assets—Foreign corporation—Plaintiff shipowner having claims against defendant charterer—Defendant a Panamanian corporation with a London bank account—Bank account in overdraft—Whether defendant having assets within jurisdiction—Whether injunction to be granted merely because defendant a foreign corporation—Guidelines for applications for Mareva injunction. **Third Chandris Shipping Corp v Unimarine SA** [1979] **2** 972, QBD and CA.
            Assets—Supplementary benefit arrears—Benefit arrears owed to defendant whose assets frozen by injunction—Crown having notice of injunction—Probability that defendant would dispose of payment of arrears in breach of injunction—Crown applying to court for directions as to payment—Whether payment should be made directly to defendant or into bank account frozen by injunction—Crown Proceedings Act 1947, s 25(4)—Supplementary Benefits Act 1976, s 16(1). **Bank Mellat v Kazmi (Secretary of State for Social Services intervening)** [1989] **1** 925, CA.
            Bank's duty of care. See **Bank** (Duty of care—Freezing order).
            Claimant's interest in Bolivian company nationalised by Bolivian government—Claimant seeking to commence arbitral proceedings against Bolivia and the nationalised company—Claimant obtaining ex parte attachment order in New York—Claimant seeking freezing order in respect of assets in England—Whether English court having jurisdiction to grant freezing order in respect of New York attachment or arbitral proceedings—Whether defendants entitled to state immunity—Civil Jurisdiction and Judgments Act 1982, s 25—State Immunity Act 1978, ss 9, 13. **ETI Euro Telecom International NV v Republic of Bolivia** [2009] **2 Comm** 37, CA.
            Committal order—Disclosure—Power to make order requiring solicitors to disclose client's contact details—Client found to be in breach of asset disclosure order and in contempt of court—Party seeking disclosure of client's contact details and assets to aid enforcement of committal order—Whether court having jurisdiction to order disclosure—Whether discretion should be exercised in favour of disclosure—Senior Courts Act 1981, s 37(1). **JSC BTA Bank v Solodchenko** [2012] **1** 735, Ch D.
            Conflict of laws. See **Conflict of laws** (Foreign law—Enforcement—Penal law—Freezing order).

804

PRACTICE (cont)—
  Pre-trial or post-judgment relief (cont)—
    Freezing order (cont)—
      Costs of innocent third party—Variation of injunction—Innocent third party successfully seeking variation of injunction—Third party entitled to reasonable costs of application—Costs to be taxed on solicitor and own client basis—Burden of establishing reasonableness of costs on third party—RSC Ord 62, r 29(1). **Project Development Co Ltd SA v KMK Securities Ltd (Syndicate Bank intervening)** [1983] **1** 465, QBD.

      County court practice. *See* **County court** (Practice—Freezing order).

      Cross-undertaking in damages—Application for further fortification of claimant's cross-undertaking in damages—Whether applicant had to show a good arguable case for further fortification or prove causation and likely loss on the balance of probabilities. **Energy Venture Partners Ltd v Malabu Oil and Gas Ltd** [2015] **1 Comm** 97, CA.

      Cross-undertaking in damages—Securities and Investments Board—Worldwide freezing order granted to Securities and Investments Board against defendants—Whether board required to give cross-undertaking in damages—Financial Services Act 1986, ss 6(1), 61(1). **Securities and Investments Board v Lloyd-Wright** [1993] **4** 210, Ch D.

      Damages. *See* **Injunction** (Interlocutory—Undertaking as to damages—Discharge of injunction—Inquiry as to damages).

      Discharge of injunction for breach of duty not to mislead court—Inter partes hearing—Worldwide freezing and proprietary injunctions—Freezing injunction obtained in part on evidence of criminal conviction in foreign jurisdiction—Fact that evidence in support of conviction flawed concealed from court—Whether principles on duty of full and frank disclosure applicable by analogy—Whether court deliberately misled—Whether client should be relieved from normal consequences of breach where breach fault of solicitor. **Boreh v Republic of Djibouti** [2015] **2 Comm** 669, QBD; [2015] **3** 577, QBD.

      Discharge of injunction on grounds of non-disclosure of material facts. *See* Pre-trial or post-judgment relief—Ex parte application—Disclosure of material facts to court—Non-disclosure of material facts—Application to discharge Mareva injunction or Anton Piller order on grounds of material non-disclosure, *above*.

      Disclosure in aid of injunction—Arbitration award—Post-award injunction restraining removal of assets out of or disposal within jurisdiction—Worldwide disclosure order—Whether court having unlimited jurisdiction to order disclosure of assets to facilitate enforcement of award—Whether scope of disclosure order limited to extent of Mareva relief—Arbitration Act 1950, s 12(6)(f), (h)—Supreme Court Act 1981, s 37(1). **Gidrxslme Shipping Co Ltd v Tantomar-Transportes Maritimos Lda** [1994] **4** 507, QBD.

      Disclosure in aid of injunction—Privilege against self-incrimination—Defendants arguing information revealed could be used against them in criminal proceedings in Kazakhstan—Whether judge erring in ordering disclosure. **JSC BTA Bank v Ablyazov** [2010] **1 Comm** 1029, CA.

      Disclosure in aid of injunction—Privilege against self-incrimination—Plaintiffs alleging conspiracy to defraud—Order requiring disclosure of value and whereabouts of defendants' overseas assets—Whether defendants entitled to claim privilege against self-incrimination in respect of information—Theft Act 1968, s 31. **Sociedade Nacional de Combustiveis de Angola UEE v Lundqvist** [1990] **3** 283, CA.

      Disclosure in aid of injunction—Undertaking not to use information disclosed in committal proceedings without permission of court—Whether exceptional circumstances required for release from undertaking. **Dadourian Group International Inc v Simms (No 2)** [2007] **2** 329, CA; [2007] **2 Comm** 498, CA.

      Disclosure of assets and delivery up of particular assets in aid of Mareva injunction—Defendant involved in large scale infringement of plaintiffs' copyright—Inference that defendant spent money from his unlawful activities on goods easily disposed of—Motor vehicles—Delivery up of motor vehicles in defendant's possession pending trial—Guidelines for court to follow in ordering delivery up of chattels pending trial. **CBS UK Ltd v Lambert** [1982] **3** 237, CA.

      Disclosure or interrogatory in aid of injunction—Order to disclose assets within jurisdiction—Whether order can be extended to encompass disclosure of assets outside jurisdiction—Supreme Court Act 1981, s 37. **Allied Arab Bank Ltd v Hajjar** [1987] **3** 739, QBD.

      Disclosure or interrogatory in aid of injunction—Power to make order for discovery or interrogatories in aid of Mareva injunction—Discovery of amounts standing in defendant's bank account—Inspection of banker's books—Whether power to order discovery or interrogatories relating to defendant's bank account—Banker's Books Evidence Act 1879, s 7—Supreme Court of Judicature (Consolidation) Act 1925, s 45(1)—RSC Ord 24, r 7(1), Ord 26, r 1(1). **A v C** [1980] **2** 347, QBD.

      Disclosure or interrogatory in aid of injunction—Power to make order for discovery or interrogatories in aid of freezing order—Defendant possibly breaking terms of freezing order—Whether jurisdiction to order discovery or interrogatories in aid of freezing order—Whether jurisdiction to order discovery of past assets and their disposal to provide material for contempt proceedings—Supreme Court of Judicature (Consolidation) Act 1925, s 45(1)—RSC Ord 24, rr 1(1), 7(1), Ord 26, r 1(1). **Bekhor (A J) & Co Ltd v Bilton** [1981] **2** 565, CA.

      Disclosure or interrogatory in aid of injunction—Power to make order for discovery or interrogatories in aid of freezing order—Foreign assets—Whether power to order discovery of foreign assets ancillary to freezing order—Whether plaintiff required to give undertaking not to use information disclosed without consent of defendant or leave of court. **Ashtiani v Kashi** [1986] **2** 970, CA.

      Disclosure or interrogatory in aid of injunction—Power to make order for discovery or interrogatories in aid of freezing order—Freezing order made in support of Mareva injunction granted by Canadian court—Canadian action being a personal action for damages without any proprietary claim—Whether court having power to order delivery up of documents in support of freezing order on a personal action for damages without any proprietary claim. **Cinar Corp v Panju** [2007] **1 Comm** 373, QBD.

805

PRACTICE (cont)—
Pre-trial or post-judgment relief (cont)—
Freezing order (cont)—

Disclosure or interrogatory in aid of injunction—Privilege against self-incrimination—Foreign organisation obtaining order directing defendant accused of defrauding organisation to disclose details of assets wherever held—Defendant applying to set aside disclosure order on ground of risk of incriminating self and others under foreign law—Whether discretionary privilege against self-incrimination extending to criminal offences and penalties under foreign law—Whether court having power to take into account possibility that defendant might incriminate himself and/or others in exercising discretion to make or continue disclosure order—Whether court having jurisdiction to limit disclosure to plaintiff's solicitors—Civil Evidence Act 1968, s 14(1). **Arab Monetary Fund v Hashim** [1989] **3** 466, Ch D.

Domestic and worldwide freezing orders granted in support of application to register foreign judgment—Whether court having jurisdiction to grant worldwide freezing order—Whether imposition of undertakings on applicant in relation to domestic freezing order contrary to European law—Council Regulation (EC) 44/2001, art 47. **Banco Nacional de Comercio Exterior SNC v Empresa de Telecomunicaciones de Cuba SA** [2007] **2 Comm** 1093, CA.

Effect of injunction—Dispute between foreign shipowner and foreign charterer going to arbitration in London—Charterer having fund within jurisdiction—Shipowner obtaining injunction restraining charterer from removing assets up to stated amount out of jurisdiction—Receiver under debenture executed by charterer applying for discharge of injunction so fund could be removed out of jurisdiction—Whether shipowner having prior right in fund under injunction—Whether injunction operating as pre-trial attachment of fund—Whether receiver as charterer's agent bound by injunction—Whether debenture holder entitled to apply in shipowner's action for discharge of injunction. **Cretanor Maritime Co Ltd v Irish Marine Management Ltd** [1978] **3** 164, CA.

Effect of injunction—Whether Mareva creditor having sufficient interest in outcome of proceedings between third party and debtor to be joined as party to proceedings—RSC Ord 15, r 6(2)(b)(ii). **Sanders Lead Co Inc v Entores Metal Brokers Ltd** [1984] **1** 857, CA.

Enforcement—Writ ne exeat regno. *See* **Equity** (Ne exeat regno—Writ—Application for writ and freezing order).

Ex parte application—Duty of applicant to disclose material facts—Non-disclosure of material facts—Consequences of non-disclosure—Grant of fresh injunction—Plaintiff failing to disclose existence of proceedings in another jurisdiction when applying for injunction—Judge discharging injunction and immediately regranting fresh injunction in substantially same terms—Test to be applied in discharging and regranting freezing orders—Whether order should have been regranted. **Behbehani v Salem** [1989] **2** 143, CA.

Ex parte application—Duty of applicant to disclose material facts—Non-disclosure of material facts—Consequences of non-disclosure—Plaintiff company obtaining ex parte injunction against defendant alleging three instances of fraud—Plaintiff company and defendant engaging in complicated financial transactions over period of years—Plaintiff company not disclosing full extent of financial dealings between parties when applying for injunction—Plaintiff company applying inter partes for continuation of injunction until after trial—Whether injunction should be continued—Whether complaint of non-disclosure and issue of appropriate relief should be considered as soon as defendant able to show material non-disclosure. **Shobokshi (Ali & Fahd) Group Ltd v Moneim** [1989] **2** 404, Ch D.

Ex parte application—Duty of applicant to disclose material facts—Non-disclosure of material facts—Consequences of non-disclosure—Principles to be applied in determining whether there has been relevant non-disclosure—Whether injunction should be discharged. **Brink's-MAT Ltd v Elcombe** [1988] **3** 188, CA.

Ex parte application—Duty of applicant to disclose material facts—Non-disclosure of material facts—Consequences of non-disclosure—Whether injunction should be discharged because of material non-disclosure—Whether court having discretion to grant fresh injunction—Whether fresh injunction will be refused if applicant guilty of delay in pursuing action. **Lloyds Bowmaker Ltd v Britannia Arrow Holdings plc (Lavens, third party)** [1988] **3** 178, CA.

Ex parte application—Fire on board defendant's ship causing abandonment of planned voyage—Plaintiffs claiming to be owners of the ship's cargo—Defendant offering security for plaintiffs' claim—Plaintiffs applying ex parte for Mareva injunction—Plaintiffs failing to disclose defendant's offer of security—Defendant applying for discharge of injunction on grounds of material non-disclosure—Whether injunction should be discharged. **Gulf Interstate Oil Corp v ANT Trade and Transport Ltd of Malta** [1999] **1 Comm** 97, QBD.

Ex parte application—Whether order must contain express undertakings not to start proceedings overseas or use information obtained in United Kingdom for purpose of overseas proceedings. **Tate Access Floors Inc v Boswell** [1990] **3** 303, Ch D.

Injunction in support of foreign proceedings—Freezing orders sought against defendant resident abroad and non-cause of action defendant within jurisdiction—Whether jurisdiction to grant injunction in support of foreign proceedings—Whether jurisdiction to serve out where no personal jurisdiction over defendant—Whether foreign judgment enforceable within jurisdiction—Whether injunction necessary for enforcement—RSC Ord 11, r 1(1)(i)—Eastern Caribbean Supreme Court (Virgin Islands) Act, s 24(1)—Eastern Caribbean Supreme Court Civil Procedure Rules 2000, r 7.3. **Convoy Collateral Ltd v Broad Idea International Ltd (British Virgin Islands)** [2022] **1** 289, PC; [2022] **1 Comm** 633, PC.

Injunction in support of order for costs—Application for injunction made before taxation of costs—Whether court having jurisdiction to grant injunction in respect of untaxed costs. **Jet West Ltd v Haddican** [1992] **2** 545, CA.

Injunction restraining disposition of defendant's assets within jurisdiction—Whether court having jurisdiction to grant injunction in advance of judgment—Supreme Court of Judicature (Consolidation) Act 1925, s 45(1). **Mareva Cia Naviera SA v International Bulkcarriers SA (1975)** [1980] **1** 213, CA; **Nippon Yusen Kaisha v Karageorgis** [1975] **3** 282, CA.

PRACTICE (cont)—
  Pre-trial or post-judgment relief (cont)—
    Freezing order (cont)—
      Injunction restraining removal of assets out of jurisdiction—Variation of injunction—Defendant
      wishing to exclude Zambian bank notes ordered by it for issue in Zambia from scope of
      injunction—Defendant willing to pay considerable price to recover bank notes—Whether removal
      of bank notes from jurisdiction constituting dissipation of an asset available to satisfy judgment
      debt—Whether bank notes having value in open market to plaintiff—Whether maintaining
      injunction amounting to holding defendant to ransom—Whether application to vary empty
      application—Whether injunction should be varied in exercise of court's general equitable
      discretion. **Camdex International Ltd v Bank of Zambia (No 2)** [1997] **1** 728, CA.
      Injunction restraining removal of assets out of or disposal within jurisdiction—Ex parte
      application—Order representing serious restriction on rights of persons bound by its
      terms—Consistent approach to be adopted in relation to form and carrying out of order—New
      standard form of order—Guidelines. **Practice Direction** [1994] **4** 52, .
      Injunction restraining removal of assets out of or disposal within jurisdiction—Grant of injunction
      between final judgment and execution—Grant of injunction in aid of execution—Whether High
      Court having power to grant Mareva injunction in aid of execution—Supreme Court Act 1981,
      s 37(3)—RSC Ord 29, r 1(1). **Orwell Steel (Erection and Fabrication) Ltd v Asphalt and Tarmac
      (UK) Ltd** [1985] **3** 747, QBD.
      Injunction restraining removal of assets out of or disposal within jurisdiction—Injunction
      restraining removal of asets out of the jurisdiction. *See* Pre-trial or post-judgment relief—Freezing
      order—Injunction restraining removal of assets out of the jurisdiction, *below.*
      Injunction restraining removal of assets out of or disposal within jurisdiction—Prohibition including
      'any interest under any trust'—Defendant member of class of potential beneficiaries under
      discretionary trusts—Order requiring defendant to provide information about trusts—Whether
      jurisdiction to order disclosure. **JSC Mezhdunarodniy Promyshlenniy Bank v Pugachev** [2015] **2
      Comm** 816, CA.
      Injunction restraining removal of assets out of or disposal within jurisdiction—Protection of
      interests of innocent third parties—Imposition of terms to protect interests of third parties—Port
      authority—Injunction affecting movements of ship within port and thereby having adverse affect
      on port authority—Terms court will impose as condition of granting injunction to protect interests
      of port authority—Mode of representations to Commercial Court by third parties adversely
      affected by Mareva injunctions. **Clipper Maritime Co Ltd v Mineralimportexport** [1981] **3** 664,
      QBD.
      Injunction restraining removal of assets out of or disposal within jurisdiction—Protection of
      interests of third parties—Shipowner—Cargo belonging to defendant loaded on board
      shipowner's vessel pursuant to voyage charter between shipowner and defendant—Injunction
      preventing ship from sailing and therefore interfering with shipowner's trading activities and with
      crew's leave arrangements—Shipowner applying for discharge of injunction—Plaintiff offering
      shipowners indemnity against loss or damage resulting from grant of injunction—Whether
      shipowner entitled to have injunction discharged—Whether abuse of Mareva injunction to grant
      injunction if it interferes with innocent third party's general or trading rights—Whether offer of
      indemnity to shipowner entitling plaintiff to continuance of injunction. **Galaxia Maritime SA v
      Mineralimportexport** [1982] **1** 796, CA.
      Injunction restraining removal of assets out of or disposal within jurisdiction—Application to vary injunction to
      enable defendant to pay debts and legal expenses and meet reasonable living expenses—
      Whether injunction should be maintained to preserve trust fund and plaintiff's tracing rights if
      successful in action. **PCW (Underwriting Agencies) Ltd v Dixon** [1983] **2** 158, QBD.
      Injunction restraining removal of assets out of the jurisdiction—Bankruptcy proceedings against
      foreign company having assets in England—United States company's assets in England made
      subject to restraining order by United States bankruptcy court—Company's English creditors
      obtaining Mareva injunctions preventing removal of assets out of jurisdiction—Company
      applying to discharge or vary injunctions—Whether English court should recognise and give
      effect to United States restraining order—Whether English court should allow United States court
      to govern disposition of assets in England—Whether court should continue injunctions.
      Felixstowe Dock and Rly Co v US Lines Inc [1988] **2** 77, QBD.
      Injunction restraining removal of assets out of the jurisdiction—Debt payable outside jurisdiction
      by company residing within jurisdiction—Whether debt constituting asset within jurisdiction.
      Deutsche Schachtbau-und Tiefbohrgesellschaft mbH v Ras Al Khaimah National Oil Co
      [1987] **2** 769, CA.
      Injunction restraining removal of assets out of the jurisdiction—English defendant—Whether
      jurisdiction to grant Mareva injunction against English national domiciled in England—Whether
      Mareva jurisdiction restricted to preventing foreigners from removing assets out of jurisdiction.
      Barclay-Johnson v Yuill [1980] **3** 190, Ch D.
      Injunction restraining removal of assets out of the jurisdiction—English defendant—Whether
      jurisdiction to grant Mareva injunction against defendant resident in England—Whether Mareva
      jurisdiction restricted to preventing foreigners resident abroad from removing assets out of
      jurisdiction. **Prince Abdul Rahman Bin Turki Al Sudairy v Abu-Taha** [1980] **3** 409, CA.
      Injunction restraining removal of assets out of the jurisdiction—Injunction in advance of judgment
      on plaintiff's claim—Discretion to grant injunction when just and convenient to do so—Factors to
      be considered in exercise of discretion—Whether plaintiff required to show he has a good
      arguable case—Whether plaintiff required to show real risk of prejudice if injunction
      refused—Supreme Court Act 1981, s 37. **Ninemia Maritime Corp v Trave Schiffahrtsgesellschaft
      mbH & Co KG** [1984] **1** 398, QBD and CA.
      Injunction restraining removal of assets out of the jurisdiction—Injunction in advance of judgment
      on plaintiff's claim—Discretion to grant injunction when just and convenient to do so—Factors to
      be considered in exercising discretion—Injunction may be granted where plaintiff has a good
      arguable case on claim against defendant—Injunction may be granted in respect of goods as well
      as assets—Fact that grant of injunction might compel defendant to give security, making it just
      and convenient to grant injunction—Supreme Court of Judicature (Consolidation) Act 1925,
      s 45(1). **Rasu Maritima SA v Perusahaan Pertambangan Minyak Dan Gas Bumi Negara
      (Pertamina) and Government of Indonesia (as interveners)** [1977] **3** 324, CA.

PRACTICE (cont)—
Pre-trial or post-judgment relief (cont)—
Freezing order (cont)—

Injunction restraining removal of assets out of the jurisdiction—Injunction in advance of plaintiff's claim—Action alleging Lebanese husband and wife defrauding husband's creditors in Abu Dhabi—Husband transferring money to wife in Abu Dhabi instead of paying creditors—Wife transferring money from Abu Dhabi to her bank account in England—Wife present and owning house in England—Whether jurisdiction to grant Mareva injunction where defendant is temporarily within the jurisdiction and can be served here—Whether cause of action against husband in respect of which he could be served out of jurisdiction—Whether jurisdiction to grant injunction against him. **Chartered Bank v Daklouche** [1980] **1** 205, CA.

Injunction restraining removal of assets out of the jurisdiction—Personal injuries claim—Plaintiff legally aided and unable to give satisfactory undertaking in damages if action failed—Whether Mareva injunction able to be granted in personal injuries action—Whether injunction should be granted regardless of plaintiff's inability to give undertaking as to damages. **Allen v Jambo Holdings Ltd** [1980] **2** 502, CA.

Injunction restraining removal of assets out of the jurisdiction—Plaintiff seeking variation of injunction to include assets in name of third party—Whether injunction should be refused because third party asserting claim over part of assets—When the court will grant injunction to include assets which on their face belong to third party. **SCF Finance Co Ltd v Masri** [1985] **2** 747, CA.

Injunction restraining removal of assets out of the jurisdiction—Unidentified assets—Costs incurred by third party in ascertaining whether any assets to which injunction applies in his possession—Need for plaintiff to give undertaking to bear such costs. **Searose v Seatrain (UK) Ltd** [1981] **1** 806, QBD.

Injunction restraining removal of assets out of the jurisdiction—Variation of injunction—Intervener seeking variation to enable defendant to use proceeds of insurance to repay loan made by intervener—Proceeds of insurance sole asset of defendant—Defendant denuded of assets if proceeds of insurance used to repay loan—Plaintiff having large claim against defendant—Whether court should order variation of injunction to enable defendant to repay loan out of proceeds of insurance. **Iraqi Ministry of Defence v Arcepey Shipping Co SA (Gillespie Bros & Co Ltd intervening)** [1980] **1** 480, QBD.

Injunction restraining removal of assets out of the jurisdiction—Variation of injunction—Variation to increase defendant's allowance for living expenses, to meet outstanding debts and to pay defendant's legal costs—Whether injunction should be varied. **PCW (Underwriting Agencies) Ltd v Dixon** [1983] **2** 697, CA.

Injunction restraining removal of assets out of the jurisdiction—Variation of injunction—Variation to permit release of part of assets to pay defendant's legal costs of proceedings—Burden of proof on defendant to obtain release of assets—Defendant adducing evidence that he was likely to incur substantial legal costs but not that he had no other assets available to pay costs—Whether injunction should be varied. **A v C (No 2)** [1981] **2** 126, QBD.

Jurisdiction—Action against several defendants—Compromise of action on terms that first defendant admitting liability and undertaking to pay sums due and plaintiff abandoning causes of action against fourth defendant—First defendant not paying sums due and plaintiff entering judgment against first defendant—Court granting Mareva injuction against fourth defendant—Injunction incidental to and in aid of enforcement of judgment debt—Whether court having jurisdiction to grant injunction. **Mercantile Group (Europe) AG v Aiyela** [1994] **1** 110, CA.

Jurisdiction—Application by foreign State for injunction over assets connected to in rem forfeiture proceedings commenced in the United States of America—Defendants not party to U.S forfeiture proceedings—Whether it was expedient to grant injunction over defendant's assets in England—Whether injunction was ancillary to or, in support of proceedings in foreign state—Civil Jurisdiction and Judgments Act 1982, s 25. **Blue Holding (1) Pte Ltd v USA** [2015] **1 Comm** 1, CA; [2015] **2** 237, CA.

Jurisdiction—Claim for specific performance of option in share agreement—Action pending in Swiss courts to determine whether option validly exercised—Circumstances giving rise to valid exercise of option not yet arising—Whether threatened breach of term of contract sufficient cause of action to support freezing order. **Zucker v Tyndall Holdings plc** [1993] **1** 124, CA.

Jurisdiction—Customs and Excise claiming customs duty from defendant—Defendant intending to transfer its business to new company—Customs and Excise seeking Mareva injunction to restrain transfer—Whether appropriate to invoke Mareva jurisdiction where defendant proposing to effect a bona fide transfer—Whether appropriate to invoke Mareva jurisdiction to fill gap in insolvency law—Whether Customs and Excise should give cross-undertaking in damages—Insolvency Act 1986, ss 238, 423. **Customs and Excise Comrs v Anchor Foods Ltd** [1999] **3** 268, Ch D.

Jurisdiction—Judge making without notice freezing order in circumstances where no proceedings for substantive relief commenced or formulated—Whether court having jurisdiction—Whether proper for order to be made. **Fourie v Le Roux** [2007] **1 Comm** 571, HL; [2007] **1** 1087, HL.

Jurisdiction—Maintenance assessment by Child Support Agency—Arrears accumulating under assessment—Application for interim relief pending making of a liability order in magistrates' court—Application for freezing order in support of and as ancillary to statutory enforcement procedure for maintenance assessments—Whether High Court having jurisdiction to grant relief—Supreme Court Act 1981, s 37—Child Support Act 1991. **Dept of Social Security v Butler** [1995] **4** 193, CA.

Jurisdiction—Mareva injunction granted by Court of Appeal on appeal—Injunction giving parties 'liberty to apply' to discharge or vary order—Defendant applying to Court of Appeal to discharge order—Whether Court of Appeal having jurisdiction to entertain application—Whether application ancillary to exercise by Court of Appeal of its appellate jurisdiction—Supreme Court Act 1981, s 15(3), 16. **Ocean Software Ltd v Kay** [1992] **2** 673, CA.

PRACTICE (cont)—
   Pre-trial or post-judgment relief (cont)—
      Freezing order (cont)—
         Jurisdiction—Russian bank owed substantial sums by group of companies—Loan guaranteed by first defendant—First defendant being discretionary beneficiary of trusts—Trusts owning second and third defendants (non cause of action defendants)—Proceedings brought in Russia—Orders made ex parte in United Kingdom in support of Russian proceedings—Inter partes hearing—Whether jurisdiction for service out of jurisdiction present—Whether orders to be continued against defendants—Civil Jurisdiction and Judgments Act 1982, s 25—Civil Procedure Rules, Practice Direction 6B, para 3.1. **Joint Stock Company VTB Bank v Skurikhin** [2013] **2 Comm** 418, QBD.

         Land register—Registration of Mareva injunction—Whether plaintiff entitled to register Mareva injunction in land charges register—Land Charges Act 1972, s 6(1)(a). **Stockler v Fourways Estates Ltd** [1983] **3** 501, QBD.

         Living expenses—Payment of debts—Worldwide pre-judgment freezing order granted in support of non-proprietary claim—Judge limiting amount of 'ordinary living expenses' for first defendant under order—Judge refusing permission for first defendant to pay certain debts from frozen funds—Proper approach concerning 'ordinary living expenses'—Whether judge erring. **Vneshprombank LLC v Bedzhamov** [2020] **1 Comm** 911, CA.

         Notification injunction. *See* Pre-trial or post-judgment relief—Notification injunction, *below*.

         Plaintiff suspecting breach of order and applying to cross-examine defendant—Whether cross-examination should be allowed—Whether defendant entitled to rely on privilege against self-incrimination. **Den Norske Bank ASA v Antonatos** [1998] **3** 74, CA.

         Post-judgment injunction—Judge removing exception from freezing order that defendant not prohibited from dealing with or disposing of any assets in ordinary and proper course of business—Whether judge being entitled to exercise discretion to remove exception. **Emmott v Michael Wilson & Partners Ltd** [2019] **2 Comm** 761, CA; [2019] **4** 1054, CA.

         Post-judgment injunction—Meaning of 'real risk of dissipation'. **Les Ambassadeurs Club Ltd v Yu** [2022] **2 Comm** 283, CA; [2022] **2** 443, CA.

         Post-judgment injunction—Variation—Application for variation by administrative receivers appointed by debenture holder—Injunction applying to assets charged by debenture executed by company—Debenture holder appointing administrative receivers—Receivers applying for variation of injunction to allow disposition of charged assets—Whether receivers entitled to apply for variation—Whether receivers entitled to costs on indemnity basis. **Capital Cameras Ltd v Harold Lines Ltd (National Westminster Bank plc intervening)** [1991] **3** 389, Ch D.

         Proprietary injunction—Claimant applying for freezing injunction after long delay after giving notice to defendants—Claimant seeking interim proprietary injunction in claim for constructive trust and knowing receipt—Whether just and convenient to grant proprietary injunction—Whether risk of dissipation of assets—Whether claimant entitled to freezing injunction. **Madoff Securities International Ltd v Raven** [2012] **2 Comm** 634, QBD.

         Protection of interests of innocent third parties—Banks and other third parties holding bank accounts and other assets of defendant—Obligations of banks and other third parties—Guidelines on the issue of Mareva injunctions affecting bank accounts and other assets. **Z Ltd v A** [1982] **1** 556, CA.

         Protection of interests of innocent third parties—Banks—Assets covered by injunction held by bank—Variation of injunction to protect bank—Protection of bank's usual rights of set-off against a customers' funds—Bank making loans to defendant prior to injunction—Whether bank entitled to variation of injunction to enable it to exercise usual rights of set-off in respect of loans—Whether bank required to make disclosures regarding state of defendant's accounts with it and existence of other assets of defendant available to meet repayment of principle and interest under loans. **Oceanica Castelana Armadora SA v Mineralimportexport (Barclays Bank International Ltd intervening)** [1983] **2** 65, QBD.

         Service out of the jurisdiction. *See* Service out of the jurisdiction—Pre-trial or post-judgment relief—Freezing order, *below*.

         Specific performance order combined with freezing order—Sale of land. *See* **Specific performance** (Sale of land—Freezing order).

         Standard forms of order—Revision of forms. **Practice Direction** [1997] **1** 288, High Ct.

         Third parties. *See* **Injunction** (Freezing order—Third parties).

         Third party commencing proceedings in the Netherlands against plaintiffs—Whether court having jurisdiction to grant Mareva injunction in aid of Dutch proceedings—Civil Jurisdiction and Judgments Act 1982, s 25, Sch 1, art 24. **Alltrans Inc v Interdom Holdings Ltd (Johnson Stevens Agencies Ltd, third parties)** [1991] **4** 458, CA.

         Third party debt orders—Judicial discretion—Judge refusing to vary freezing order against defendant to permit him to repay loan made by daughter and granting claimant companies final third party debt order with respect to defendant's accounts—Whether judge in error. **Novoship (UK) Ltd v Mikhaylyuk** [2014] **1 Comm** 993, CA.

         Third party interests—Claimant obtaining judgment against wife—Claimant alleging wife trustee of husband's assets—Husband and wife resident overseas—Claimant applying for freezing order against husband's assets—Whether jurisdiction to make order—Civil Procedure Rules 1998, 19.2. **C Inc plc v L** [2001] **2 Comm** 446, QBD.

         Third party interests—Claimant seeking to enforce arbitral awards against defendant—Claimant seeking freezing orders against third parties—Third parties existing solely for purpose of transferring oil sale proceeds to defendant—Whether appropriate to grant freezing order. **Yukos Capital Sarl v OJSC Rosneft Oil Co** [2011] **1 Comm** 172, QBD.

         Third party interests—Injunction granted against bank—Effect of injunction on normal course of banking business—Whether bank should be subject of Mareva injunction—Whether other interlocutory relief should be granted with respect to funds claimed. **Polly Peck International plc v Nadir (No 2)** [1992] **4** 769, CA.

         Third party interests—Injunction granted against guarantor—Guarantor holding majority of shares in company—Plaintiff having no cause of action against company—Whether company proper party to proceedings—Whether court having jurisdiction to grant injunction against company. **TSB Private Bank International SA v Chabra** [1992] **2** 245, Ch D.

PRACTICE (cont)—
  Pre-trial or post-judgment relief (cont)—
    Freezing order (cont)—
      Third party interests—Plaintiff bank bringing proceedings against defendants for breach of trust
        and obtaining worldwide Mareva injunction—Proviso to injunction allowing for defendants'
        reasonable legal expenses—Whether expenditure of moneys under proviso could amount to
        further breach of trust—Whether recipient of moneys would be in breach of constructive trust as
        a result of knowing receipt or dishonest assistance. **United Mizrahi Bank Ltd v Doherty**
        [1998] **2** 230, Ch D.
      Undertaking as to damages—Aggravated and exemplary damages. *See* **Injunction** (Interlocutory—
        Undertaking as to damages—Discharge of injunction—Inquiry as to damages—Search and
        seizure order—Freezing order).
      Undertaking as to damages—Discharge of injunction—Whether inquiry as to damages should be
        ordered before trial. *See* **Injunction** (Interlocutory—Undertaking as to damages—Discharge of
        injunction—Inquiry as to damages—Mareva injunction).
      Variation—Application for release of Mareva funds—Defendant company having no assets apart
        from Mareva funds—Defendant applying for release of Mareva funds to enable it to meet legal
        expenses—Parent company exercising complete financial and management control over
        defendant—Whether variation should be granted—Whether court entitled to look behind
        corporate veil and take account of relationship between parent and subsidiary company—
        Whether court entitled to take into account funds to which defendant had no legal right. **Atlas
        Maritime Co SA v Avalon Maritime Ltd, The Coral Rose (No 3)** [1991] **4** 783, CA.
      Variation—Application for release of Mareva funds—Defendant company having no assets apart
        from Mareva funds—Defendant's operations entirely financed and managed by parent
        company—Defendant applying for release of Mareva funds to enable it to transfer those funds to
        parent company as business debt owing to creditor—Evidence of parent company exercising
        complete financial and management control over defendant—Whether variation should be
        granted—Whether relationship between companies one of debtor and creditor—Whether
        proposed transfer of funds amounting to repayment in ordinary course of business. **Atlas
        Maritime Co SA v Avalon Maritime Ltd, The Coral Rose (No 1)** [1991] **4** 769, CA.
      Winding up petition, related to. *See* **Company** (Compulsory winding up—Petition by
        creditor—Freezing order).
      Without notice application—Duty of applicant to disclose material facts—Claimants obtaining order
        in attempt to enforce arbitral award against Laos government—Order extending to assets within
        jurisdiction belonging to Laos central bank—Whether claimants failing to fulfil duty of
        disclosure—Whether order to be discharged as result of breach of duty. **Thai-Lao Lignite
        (Thailand) Co Ltd v Government of Lao People's Democratic Republic** [2013] **2 Comm** 883, QBD.
      Worldwide freezing order—Application for continuation of freezing order—Assets already subject
        to restraint order—Whether existence of restraint order meaning unable to show real risk of
        dissipation of assets—Proceeds of Crime Act 2002, s 41. **AA v BB** [2022] **1 Comm** 1352, CA.
      Worldwide freezing order—Application for discharge—Whether claimant satisfying 'good arguable
        case' test. **PJSC Tatneft v Bogolyubov** [2017] **1 Comm** 833, QBD.
      Worldwide freezing order—Application for worldwide freezing injunction—Application made before
        three different judges on substantially the same facts—Whether hearing before third judge abuse
        of process—Material factors in the exercise of discretion to grant renewed application.
        Laemthong International Lines Co Ltd v Artis [2004] **2 Comm** 797, QBD.
      Worldwide freezing order—Claimant seeking permission to enforce worldwide freezing order in
        foreign jurisdiction—Guidance. **Dadourian Group International Inc v Simms** [2005] **2 Comm** 224,
        Ch D; [2005] **2** 651, Ch D; [2006] **1 Comm** 709, CA; [2006] **3** 48, CA.
      Worldwide freezing order—Defendant commencing proceedings in Germany in relation to
        acknowledgment of debt to plaintiff company—High Court granting plaintiff 's ex parte
        application for worldwide Mareva injunction—Judge varying injunction at inter partes hearing by
        confining its effect to England on grounds that he was being asked to grant relief in support of
        another jurisdiction and circumstances were not exceptional—Whether judge right to do
        so—Civil Jurisdiction and Judgments Act 1982, s 25, Sch 1, art 50. **S & T Bautrading v Nordling**
        [1997] **3** 718, CA.
      Worldwide freezing order—Foreign judgment or arbitration award—Whether court will grant
        worldwide Mareva injunction in support of foreign judgment or arbitration award. **Rosseel NV v
        Oriental Commercial and Shipping (UK) Ltd** [1990] **3** 545, CA.
      Worldwide freezing order—Form of order—Assets abroad—Whether appropriate to permit
        defendants to deal with their assets only so long as value of their assets within England and
        Wales above maximum amount. **JSC BTA Bank v Ablyazov (No 2)** [2010] **1 Comm** 1040, QBD.
      Worldwide freezing order—Interim order in support of proposed foreign arbitral proceedings
        granted—Whether appropriate to continue order—Arbitration Act 1996, s 44. **Mobil Cerro Negro
        Ltd v Petroleos de Venezuela SA** [2008] **2 Comm** 1034, QBD.
      Worldwide freezing order—Jurisdiction—Claimants obtaining worldwide freezing order in support
        of Italian proceedings—Claimants seeking to extend order to defendants resident in
        Italy—Whether English court having jurisdiction—Civil Jurisdiction and Judgments Act 1982,
        s 25—CPR PD 6B, para 3.1(3), (5). **Belletti v Morici** [2010] **1 Comm** 412, QBD.
      Worldwide freezing order—Matrimonial proceedings—Mareva injunction pending appeal—
        Husband and wife living abroad and husband claiming domicile abroad—Wife petitioning for
        divorce on basis of domicile in England—Husband challenging jurisdiction of court—Court
        granting interim maintenance pending determination and worldwide injunction over all
        husband's assets—Wife's petition dismissed for want of jurisdiction—Wife appealing and seeking
        continuation of worldwide Mareva injunction pending determination of appeal—Whether grant of
        worldwide Mareva injunction appropriate. **Ghoth v Ghoth** [1992] **2** 920, CA.
      Worldwide freezing order—Order for disclosure of assets attached to freezing order—Defendants
        applying for discharge of freezing order—Defendants applying for stay of disclosure order
        pending hearing of application for discharge—Whether disclosure order should be stayed.
        Motorola Credit Corp v Uzan [2002] **2 Comm** 945, CA.

PRACTICE (cont)—
   Pre-trial or post-judgment relief (cont)—
      Freezing order (cont)—

        Worldwide freezing order—Order in aid of execution of arbitration award—Application pending by defendant to set aside permission to enforce award—Whether defendant to be considered as judgment debtor -Whether freezing order should contain exception permitting payments in ordinary and proper course of business. **Nomihold Securities Inc v Mobile Telesystems Finance SA** [2012] **1 Comm** 223, CA.

        Worldwide freezing order—Plaintiff commencing proceedings in Switzerland against defendant who was domiciled and resident in England—High Court granting plaintiff worldwide freezing order against defendant in aid of Swiss proceedings—Whether court right to do so—Whether exceptional circumstances required—Civil Jurisdiction and Judgments Act 1982, s 25. **Crédit Suisse Fides Trust SA v Cuoghi** [1997] 3 724, CA.

        Worldwide freezing order—Post-judgment injunction—Extra-territorial effect of injunction—Protection of third parties—Foreign defendant having foreign assets—Defendant likely to attempt to frustrate execution of judgment against him—Whether court having jurisdiction to grant freezing order over defendant's foreign assets before or after judgment—Whether worldwide injunction should be qualified by express proviso protecting third parties. **Babanaft International Co SA v Bassatne** [1989] **1** 433, CA.

        Worldwide freezing order—Post-judgment injunction—Whether injunction enforcement or protective measure—Whether court having jurisdiction to grant order—Whether power to name individual directors within order. **Masri v Consolidated Contractors International (UK) Ltd (No 2)** [2008] **1 Comm** 305, QBD.

        Worldwide freezing order—Pre-trial injunction—Consent order—Plaintiff obtaining interim relief in aid of substantive action proceeding in Irish court—Court discharging injunction by consent on failure of Irish action and directing inquiry into damages which plaintiff ought to pay—Whether court retaining discretion whether to order plaintiff to pay damages to defendants. **Balkanbank v Taher** [1995] **2** 904, CA.

        Worldwide freezing order—Pre-trial injunction—Counterclaim—Jurisdiction—Plaintiff obtaining interim relief in aid of substantive action proceeding in Irish court—Court discharging injunction by consent on failure of Irish action—Defendants seeking to advance counterclaims in respect of losses sustained by reason of the injunction—Whether court having jurisdiction to entertain counterclaims in respect of claim for interim relief—Whether originating summons seeking Mareva relief an 'action' for purposes of procedural rules—Civil Jurisdiction and Judgments Act 1982, s 25, Sch 1, art 24—RSC Ord 28, r 7(1). **Balkanbank v Taher** [1995] **2** 904, CA.

        Worldwide freezing order—Pre-trial injunction—Extra-territorial effect of injunction—Injunction restraining foreign defendants from disposing of assets outside jurisdiction—Defendants having no assets within jurisdiction and likely to dissipate their assets to frustrate judgment or order against them—Receiver of foreign assets being appointed in aid of injunction—Receivership assets held on joint account in Switzerland and including fiduciary deposits made by Swiss banks outside Switzerland—Receiver obtaining ex parte injunctions restraining removal from jurisdictions in which they were held of assets deposited with banks outside Switzerland—Whether injunctions should be continued—Whether court having power to order transfer or receivership assets from one jurisdiction to another. **Derby & Co Ltd v Weldon (No 6)** [1990] **3** 263, CA.

        Worldwide freezing order—Pre-trial injunction—Extra-territorial effect of injunction—Protection of third parties—Foreign defendant having foreign assets—Proceedings brought by Republic of Haiti in French court to recover money embezzled by former president—Defendant likely to attempt to frustrate execution of judgment against him—Whether court having jurisdiction to grant freezing order over defendant's foreign assets before judgment—Whether worldwide injunction should be qualified by express proviso protecting third parties—Civil Jurisdiction and Judgments Act 1982, s 25, Sch 1, art 24—RSC Ord 11, r 1(2). **Haiti (Republic) v Duvalier** [1989] **1** 456, CA.

        Worldwide freezing order—Pre-trial injunction—Extra-territorial effect of injunction—Protection of third parties—Foreign defendant having foreign assets—Proceedings brought by United States banking group against former directors of subsidiary alleging breach of contract, conspiracy and fraudulent breach of fiduciary duty over loans made to Far Eastern commodity dealer which collapsed owing over £35m to banking group—Defendants likely to attempt to frustrate execution of judgment against them—Whether court having jurisdiction to grant Mareva injunction over defendants' foreign assets before judgment—Whether worldwide injunction should be subject to undertakings by plaintiffs not to enforce order overseas or use in foreign proceedings information about overseas assets disclosed by defendants without leave of English court. **Derby & Co Ltd v Weldon (No 1)** [1989] **1** 469, CA.

        Worldwide freezing order—Pre-trial injunction—Extra-territorial effect of injunction—Protection of third parties—Injunction restraining foreign defendants from disposing of assets outside jurisdiction—Defendants having no assets within jurisdiction and likely to dissipate their assets to frustrate judgment or order against them—Whether pre-trial Mareva injunction should be granted against foreign defendant with no assets within jurisdiction—Whether receiver of foreign assets should be appointed—Whether defendants should be ordered to reveal the nature, value and whereabouts of foreign assets—Whether order should be made subject to proviso that third parties indirectly affected by it not bound by it until it is recognised or registered or enforced by foreign court. **Derby & Co Ltd v Weldon (No 2)** [1989] **1** 1002, CA.

        Worldwide freezing order—Pre-trial injunction—Injunction restraining disposal of assets outside jurisdiction—Ex parte application—Order representing serious restriction on rights of persons bound by its terms—Consistent approach to be adopted in relation to form and carrying out of order—New standard form of order—Guidelines. **Practice Direction** [1994] **4** 52, .

PRACTICE (cont)—
  Pre-trial or post-judgment relief (cont)—
    Freezing order (cont)—
      Worldwide freezing order—Pre-trial injunction—Liquidation of group of companies—Companies insolvent as result of frauds perpetrated by senior executives—Proceedings brought by liquidators against defendants alleging fraud—Liquidators seeking compensation from defendants for complicity in fraudulent conduct of senior executives—Multiplicity of suits in foreign jurisdictions—Undertaking by liquidators not without leave of the court to seek to enforce injunction in countries other than England and Wales—Whether liquidators should be required to give further undertaking not to commence new proceedings based on same or similar subject matter in foreign jurisdictions without leave—Whether liquidators should be restricted in aiding foreign criminal proceedings—Insolvency Act 1986, ss 212, 213, 214, 238, 426. **Bank of Credit and Commerce International SA, Re (No 9)** [1994] **3** 764, Ch D and CA.

      Worldwide freezing order—Pre-trial order—Cause of action not yet arising—Pt 20 claimant obtaining worldwide freezing order—Pt 20 defendant seeking to set aside order—Principles to be applied in determining whether claimant having arguable case—Whether freezing order should be set aside. **Papamichael v National Westminster Bank plc** [2002] **2 Comm** 60, QBD.

      Worldwide freezing order—Pre-trial order—Extra-territorial effect of order—Protection of third parties—Freezing order in standard form—Proviso protecting third parties in respect of assets outside the jurisdiction—Appropriate terms. **Bank of China v NBM LLC** [2001] **4** 954, QBD; [2002] **1 Comm** 472, CA; [2002] **1** 717, CA.

      Worldwide freezing order—Registration of foreign judgment—Worldwide freezing order granted to assist enforcement of foreign judgment—Whether court having jurisdiction to grant worldwide freezing order where used in enforcement of foreign judgment—Council Regulation (EC) 44/2001, art 47. **Banco Nacional de Comercio Exterior SNC v Empresa de Telecomunicaciones de Cuba SA** [2007] **2 Comm** 46, QBD.

      Writ containing claim for liquidated demand and injunction to restrain defendant from removing assets out of jurisdiction—Plaintiff granted injunction—Plaintiff applying for leave to enter judgment in default of appearance in claim for liquidated demand—Whether claim for injunction in writ precluding plaintiff from entering judgment in claim for liquidated demand in default of appearance by defendant—RSC Ord 13, r 6. **Stewart Chartering Ltd v C & O Managements SA** [1980] **1** 718, QBD.

  Injunction—
    Post-judgment—Generally. See **Injunction** (Post-judgment).
    Variation or discharge. See **Injunction** (Variation or discharge—Jurisdiction).

  Interim payment—
    Defendant having arguable defence of set-off or counterclaim exceeding claim—Whether court required to take into account likelihood of defence of set-off succeeding at trial when deciding whether plaintiff would obtain judgment for substantial sum—Whether set-off defence only to be taken into account when court deciding whether to exercise discretion to make interim payment—RSC Ord 29, rr 10, 12(c). **Shanning International Ltd v George Wimpey International Ltd** [1988] **3** 475, CA.

    Interest—Date from which interest payable—Rate at which interest payable—Whether interest running from date quantum identifiable or date cause of action accruing. **Kuwait Airways Corp v Kuwait Insurance Co SAK (No 2)** [2000] **1 Comm** 972, QBD.

    Jurisdiction to order interim payment—Alternative claims in debt and damages—Court satisfied plaintiff would succeed under one or other claim—Whether court having power to order interim payment to be made to plaintiff—RSC Ord 29, rr 11, 12. **Shearson Lehman Bros Inc v Maclaine Watson & Co Ltd** [1987] **2** 181, CA.

    Jurisdiction to order interim payment—Conditional leave to defend—Whether court having power to order interim payment where defendant given unconditional leave to defend—RSC Ord 29, r 11. **British and Commonwealth Holdings plc v Quadrex Holdings Inc** [1989] **3** 492, CA.

    Jurisdiction to order interim payment—Evidence of need or prejudice—Applicant obtaining joint and several orders for interim payments against defendants without producing evidence of need or prejudice—Whether court having power to order interim payments in absence of evidence of need or prejudice—Whether court having power to make joint and several orders for interim payments against a number of defendants—RSC Ord 29, rr 11, 12. **Schott Kem Ltd v Bentley** [1990] **3** 850, CA.

    Jurisdiction to order interim payment—Standard of proof—Application for interim payment made against more than one defendant—Court satisfied that plaintiffs would succeed in obtaining judgment against either one of two defendants—Defendants granted unconditional leave to defend—Whether court having power to order interim payment to be made to plaintiffs—Whether plaintiffs proving likelihood of success to necessary standard against particular defendant—Whether sufficient for plaintiffs to show that they were bound to succeed against one or other of defendants—Whether existence of unconditional leave to defend preventing court from making interim payment order—RSC Ord 29, r 11(1)(c). **Ricci Burns Ltd v Toole** [1989] **3** 478, CA.

    Jurisdiction to order interim payment—Taxpayer obtaining interim payment order against Revenue and Customs Commissioners—Conditions for grant of interim payment order—CPR 25.7. **GKN Group v Revenue and Customs Comrs** [2012] **3** 111, CA.

    Jurisdiction to order interim payment—Uninsured defendant—Plaintiff bringing action for negligence in relation to road traffic accident against uninsured defendant—Whether court having power to order interim payment to be made to plaintiff which Motor Insurers' Bureau would have to meet—RSC Ord 29, r 11(2). **Sharp v Pereria** [1998] **4** 145, CA.

    Labourer claiming damages against four entities for injuries suffered whilst working on building site—Interim payment sought—Judge making order on basis labourer would obtain judgment for substantial damages against one of two insured companies—Conditions of grant of interim payment—Whether conditions for interim payment satisfied—CPR 25.7(1)(c), (e). **Arshdeep v Buttar Construction Ltd** [2022] **1 Comm** 1277, CA.

    Repayment of interim payment—Interest—Jurisdiction to award interest—Whether court having power to order payment of interest when ordering repayment of interim payment—Supreme Court Act 1981, s 32—RSC Ord 29, r 17. **Mercers Co v New Hampshire Insurance Co** [1991] **4** 542, QBD; [1992] **3** 57, CA.

PRACTICE (cont)—
  Pre-trial or post-judgment relief (cont)—
    Mareva injunction. *See* Pre-trial or post-judgment relief—Freezing order, *above.*
    Notification injunction—
      Application made by claimants for notification injunction requiring defendants to give notice to them prior to disposing of any assets—Claimants not applying for full freezing injunction—Whether free-standing notification injunction may be granted in principle—Relevant threshold test—Meaning of 'good arguable case' in context of application—Whether risk of dissipation of assets—Senior Courts Act 1981, s 37. **Holyoake v Candy** [2016] **2 Comm** 711, Ch D.
      Defendants appealing interim notification injunction order—Whether correct test applied in imposing notification order—Whether sufficient evidence available to demonstrate requisite risk of dissipation. **Holyoake v Candy** [2017] **2 Comm** 513, CA.
    Receiver—
      Appointment of receiver in relation to defendants' receipts from oil concession situated abroad—Whether infringement of foreign court's territorial jurisdiction—Whether court having jurisdiction to grant order. **Masri v Consolidated Contractors International (UK) Ltd (No 2)** [2008] **1 Comm** 305, QBD.
      Appointment of receiver in relation to judgment debtor's receipts from oil concession situated abroad—Whether infringement of foreign court's territorial jurisdiction—Whether power to grant order in relation to future debts. **Masri v Consolidated Contractors International (UK) Ltd (No 2)** [2008] **2 Comm** 1099, CA.
    Requests for further information—
      Self-incrimination—Privilege—Withdrawal of privilege—Proceedings for infringement of rights pertaining to any intellectual property—Meaning of 'intellectual property' including 'technical or commercial information'—Meaning of 'technical or commercial information'—Senior Courts Act 1981, s 72(5). **Phillips v News Group Newspapers Ltd** [2011] **2** 725, Ch D; [2012] **4** 207, SC.
      Self-incrimination—Privilege—Withdrawal of privilege—Right to a fair trial—Proceedings for infringement of rights pertaining to any intellectual property—Meaning of 'intellectual property' including 'technical or commercial information'—Meaning of 'technical or commercial information'—Senior Courts Act 1981, s 72(5)—Human Rights Act 1998, Sch 1, Pt I, art 6. **Phillips v News Group Newspapers Ltd** [2012] **2** 74, CA.
    Search order—
      Aggravated and exemplary damages. *See* **Injunction** (Interlocutory—Undertaking as to damages—Discharge of injunction—Inquiry as to damages—Search and seizure order—Freezing order).
      Collateral use of information obtained under order—Undertaking not to use documents disclosed for collateral or ulterior purpose—Plaintiff executing search order—Plaintiff subsequently executing second search order in second action and discovering evidence of breaches of first search order—Whether plaintiff entitled to use documents discovered under second order to bring proceedings for contempt for breach of first order. **Crest Homes plc v Marks** [1987] **2** 1074, HL.
      Discharge of order on grounds of non-disclosure of material facts. *See* Pre-trial or post-judgment relief—Ex parte application—Disclosure of material facts to court—Non-disclosure of material facts, *above.*
      Discretion to make order—Principles on which discretion to be exercised—Plaintiff wishing to support claim by reference to books of account in defendant's custody—Books of account not forming subject matter of claim—Plaintiff fearing that accounts would be destroyed—Whether court having discretion to order inspection and removal of accounts. **Yousif v Salama** [1980] **3** 405, CA.
      Ex parte application for search order—Application after judgment—Judgment for liquidated sum—Whether court having jurisdiction to make search order in aid of execution of judgment already obtained. **Distributori Automatici Italia SpA v Holford General Trading Co Ltd** [1985] **3** 750, QBD.
      Ex parte application for search order—Cross-undertaking as to damages by plaintiff—Whether defendant entitled to raise actions by counterclaim founded on search order but not on plaintiff's cross-undertaking—Whether action for abuse of court's process still existing—Whether plaintiff seeking search order under duty of care to party affected by order to place full and frank evidence before court. **Digital Equipment Corp v Darkcrest Ltd** [1984] **3** 381, Ch D.
      Ex parte application for search order—Order requiring defendant to disclose information relating to counterfeit operation—Defendant admitting involvement but refusing to disclose information on ground that disclosure would jeopardise safety—Defendant applying to court to discharge order—Factors to be considered by court in weighing risk of violence against need for disclosure. **Coca-Cola Co v Gilbey** [1995] **4** 711, Ch D.
      Ex parte application—Order representing serious restriction on rights of persons bound by its terms—Consistent approach to be adopted in relation to form and carrying out of order—New standard form of order—Guidelines. **Practice Direction** [1994] **4** 52, .
      Execution of order—Safeguards relating to execution of orders. **Universal Thermosensors Ltd v Hibben** [1992] **3** 257, Ch D.
      Imaged digital data—Search and seizure orders granted allowing claimants to go first in inspecting and interrogating imaged digital data—Factors to consider when deciding which party to go first—Civil Procedure Act 1997, s 7. **A v B** [2020] **1 Comm** 1083, Ch D.
      Imaging order—Guidance—Civil Procedure Act 1997, s 7—CPR PD 25A. **TBD (Owen Holland) Ltd v Simons** [2021] **4** 889, CA.
      Interlocutory motion—Ex parte application—Appeal against order—Writ claiming injunctions to restrain defendants from producing or selling copies of films and video tapes—Judge granting injunctions—Defendants complying with order and then subsequently seeking to set aside order—Judge not making order on defendants' motion but granting leave to appeal to Court of Appeal—Whether appeal to Court of Appeal proper course where motion to set aside not heard and determined by judge at first instance—Whether Court of Appeal will hear appeal from ex parte order. **WEA Records Ltd v Visions Channel 4 Ltd** [1983] **2** 589, CA.

Pre-trial or post-judgment relief (cont)—
Search order (cont)—

Interlocutory motion—Ex parte application—Articles on premises controlled by respondent—Order requiring respondent to deliver up infringing articles for custody until trial of action—Action for infringement of copyright—Danger that infringing articles might disappear if respondent given notice—Preservation of respondent's rights—Circumstances in which ex parte order should be granted. **Universal City Studios Inc v Mukhtar & Sons** [1976] **2** 330, Ch D.

Interlocutory motion—Ex parte application—Documents and property on premises controlled by respondent—Order requiring respondent to permit applicants to enter premises for purpose of inspection etc—Circumstances in which order will be made ex parte—Danger that in default of an order applicants might be deprived of a remedy in the action—Danger that if notice of motion given documents and property might be destroyed—Action for infringement of copyright—Order requiring defendant to permit plaintiffs to enter defendant's premises for purposes of inspection, photographing of documents and property and removal of infringing copies—RSC Ord 29, r 2. **EMI Ltd v Pandit** [1975] **1** 418, Ch D.

Interlocutory motion—Ex parte application—Documents on premises controlled by respondents—Orders requiring respondents to permit applicants to enter premises for purpose of inspection etc—Circumstances in which order will be made ex parte—Nature of order—Danger that in default of order applicants might be deprived of a remedy in the action—Danger that if notice of motion given documents might be destroyed or taken out of the jurisdiction—Action for infringement of copyright—Order requiring respondents to permit applicants to enter respondents' premises for purposes of inspection and removal of documents. **Anton Piller KG v Manufacturing Processes Ltd** [1976] **1** 779, CA.

Interlocutory motion—Ex parte application—Foreign defendant—Order against foreign defendant in respect of foreign premises—Whether court having jurisdiction to grant order against foreign defendant in respect of foreign premises. **Altertext Inc v Advanced Data Communications Ltd** [1985] **1** 395, Ch D.

Interlocutory motion—Ex parte application—Jurisdiction to make order—Writ claiming injunctions to restrain defendant from producing and selling unauthorised recordings of live performances of musical works—Unauthorised recordings of live performances a criminal offence but not breach of copyright or a tort—Whether jurisdiction to issue ex parte order for inspection of unauthorised recordings if no breach of copyright or no tort committed—Dramatic and Musical Performers' Protection Act 1958, s 1. **Island Records Ltd, Ex p** [1978] **3** 824, CA.

Interlocutory motion—Ex parte application—Principles relating to grant of order—Duty of plaintiff's solicitor when executing order—Cross-undertaking as to damages by plaintiff—Award of damages for breach of undertaking—Aggravated damages awarded for excessive and oppressive manner in which order executed. **Columbia Picture Industries Inc v Robinson** [1986] **3** 338, Ch D.

Interlocutory motion—Ex parte application—Refusal—Appeal—Appeals normally to be heard in open court—Counsel to give written reasons where hearing in camera is sought. **Practice Note** [1982] **3** 924, CA.

Interlocutory motion—Ex parte application—Requirement that defendant permit execution of Anton Piller order 'forthwith'—Forthwith—Legal advice—Whether requirement of consent to execution 'forthwith' meaning at once or immediately—Whether defendant in contempt if after taking legal advice he declines to allow execution pending application to discharge or vary order—Factors to be taken into account by court in deciding whether contempt committed. **Bhimji v Chatwani** [1991] **1** 705, Ch D.

Privilege against self-incrimination—Action for damages for conspiracy—Risk of criminal prosecution—Order for disclosure of information and documents relating to alleged conspiracy—Order including proviso to safeguard defendant's right to claim privilege against self-incrimination—Defendant electing not to claim privilege—Whether proviso an effective safeguard of defendant's rights. **IBM UK Ltd v Prima Data International Ltd** [1994] **4** 748, Ch D.

Privilege against self-incrimination—Collateral use of information obtained under order—Undertaking not to use documents disclosed for collateral or ulterior purpose—Dominant purpose in seeking search order being to use its fruits in committal proceedings—Whether search order should be granted which included provisions likely to require the defendant to incriminate himself—Whether search order should be set aside. **Cobra Golf Ltd v Rata** [1997] **2** 150, Ch D.

Privilege against self-incrimination—Exception to rule against self-incrimination—Proceedings for infringement of copyright or passing off—Proceedings for apprehended infringement of copyright or apprehended passing off—Withdrawal of privilege against self-incrimination—Extent of withdrawal—Whether withdrawal extending to any offence or only to offences in connection with infringement of copyright or passing off—Supreme Court Act 1981, s 72(1), (2)(c), (5). **Universal City Studios Inc v Hubbard** [1984] **1** 661, CA.

Privilege against self-incrimination—Infringement of trade mark. See **Trade mark** (Infringement—Search order—Self-incrimination).

Privilege against self-incrimination—Interlocutory motion—Ex parte application—Order requiring disclosure of information—Defendants pirating films and selling unauthorised video cassettes—Defendants ordered to disclose information regarding pirating and selling cassettes—Information likely to result in defendants being prosecuted for conspiracy to defraud—Whether defendants entitled to claim privilege against self-incrimination in respect of disclosure of information. **Rank Film Distributors Ltd v Video Information Centre** [1981] **2** 76, HL.

Privilege against self-incrimination—Material constituting freestanding evidence which had not been created by respondent to search order under compulsion—Whether privilege against self-incrimination extending to freestanding evidence—Human Rights Act 1998, Sch 1. **C plc v P (Secretary of State for the Home Office and anor intervening)** [2006] **4** 311, Ch D; [2007] **3** 1034, CA.

PRACTICE (cont)—
  Pre-trial or post-judgment relief (cont)—
    Search order (cont)—
      Privilege against self-incrimination—Plaintiffs alleging conspiracy to defraud—Defendants reasonably apprehending that prosecution for conspiracy to defraud might be brought in United Kingdom and that documents produced or obtained under search order might tend to incriminate them—Whether defendants entitled to claim privilege against self-incrimination in respect of disclosure of information—Whether defendants entitled to claim privilege against self-incrimination in respect of order requiring them to permit plaintiffs to enter, search and seize documents—Whether individuals defendants entitled to claim privilege against self-incrimination on behalf of corporate defendants with whom they were connected. **Tate Access Floors Inc v Boswell** [1990] **3** 303, Ch D.
      Trade secrets—Injunction restraining disclosure. *See* **Employment** (Duty of servant—Confidential information—Injunction restraining disclosure—Search order).
      Undertaking as to damages—Aggravated and exemplary damages. *See* **Injunction** (Interlocutory—Undertaking as to damages—Discharge of injunction—Inquiry as to damages—Search and seizure order—Freezing order).
      Undertaking by plaintiffs' solicitors—Extent of undertaking—Customs and Excise Commissioners seeking access to documents and articles held by solicitors under search order—Commissioners acting in exercise of power to require furnishing of information or production of documents in connection with supplies of goods or services—Whether plaintiffs' solicitors requiring leave of court before allowing commissioners access to documents or articles—Finance Act 1972, s 35(2). **Customs and Excise Comrs v A E Hamlin & Co (a firm)** [1983] **3** 654, Ch D.
    Service. *See* Service—Pre-trial or post-judgment relief, *below*.
    Service out of the jurisdiction. *See* Service out of the jurisdiction—Pre-trial or post-judgment relief, *below*.
    Third party debt orders—
      Account held by bank on behalf of trustee where judgment debtor beneficial owner of funds—Whether funds belonging to judgment debtor—Whether funds capable of being subject to third party debt order—CPR 72.2(1)(a). **AIG Capital Partners Inc v Republic of Kazakhstan (National Bank of Kazakhstan intervening)** [2006] **1 Comm** 1, QBD; [2006] **1** 284, QBD.
      More than six years elapsing since judgment—Claimant applying for third party debt order in Singapore—Singaporean court seeking indication as to whether English court would grant application—Whether English court would issue third party debt orders more than six years after judgment—CPR Pt 72, RSC Ord 46, r 2. **Westacre Investments Inc v Yugoimport SDPR** [2009] **1 Comm** 780, QBD.
  Precedent. *See* **Precedent**.
  Preliminary point of law—
    Application for trial of preliminary issue on point of law—
      Hypothetical facts—Unsuitability of procedure. **Windsor Refrigerator Co Ltd v Branch Nominees Ltd** [1961] **1** 277, CA.
      Libel action—Investigation of facts requisite first—Point of law of great uncertainty on the extent or existence of absolute privilege for communications by serving officers of friendly foreign powers in England—Unsuitability of question for determination as a preliminary point. **Richards v Naum** [1966] **3** 812, CA.
      Libel action—Issue whether words complained of capable of defamatory meaning—Whether suitable to be tried as preliminary issue. **Keays v Murdoch Magazines (UK) Ltd** [1991] **4** 491, CA.
      Libel action—Issue whether words complained of capable of defamatory meaning—Whether suitable to be tried as preliminary issue—RSC Ord 25, r 2. **Morris v Sandess Universal Products** [1954] **1** 47, CA.
      Libel action—Newspaper defendants in libel action relying on defences of justification and qualified privilege—Judge ordering issues of privilege and malice to be determined before justification—Whether order inconsistent with test for qualified privilege—CPR 3.1(2), 32. **GKR Karate (UK) Ltd v Yorkshire Post Newspapers Ltd** [2000] **2** 931, CA.
      Test whether preliminary issue should be ordered—Decisive of litigation if point of law decided one way—Action by East German company against West German company—Claim by East German company against solicitors acting for West German company in respect of money for fees and disbursement received by solicitors in good faith from West German company—Preliminary issue ordered. **Carl-Zeiss-Stiftung v Herbert Smith & Co (a firm)** [1968] **2** 1002, CA.
    Arbitration proceedings. *See* **Arbitration** (Preliminary question of law).
    Matters appropriate to be considered as preliminary issues. **National Coal Board v Wm Neill & Son (St Helens) Ltd** [1984] **1** 555, QBD.
    Order for trial of preliminary point of law—
      Judge's control of proceedings—Trial judge ordering preliminary determination of certain issues—Whether parties entitled as of right to have case tried to conclusion after all evidence adduced—Whether appellate court should uphold judge's decision to order trial of preliminary issue unless decision plainly wrong. **Ashmore v Corp of Lloyd's** [1992] **2** 486, HL.
      Terms of order—Necessity to define point of law—RSC Ord 25, r 2. **National Real Estate and Finance Co Ltd v Hassan** [1939] **2** 154, CA.
    Question of far-reaching legal principle—
      Assumed facts—Unsuitability of procedure. **Attia v British Gas plc** [1987] **3** 455, CA.
    Security for costs—
      Person in position of plaintiff. *See* **Costs** (Security for costs—Person in position of plaintiff—Preliminary point of law).
    Trial of preliminary issue determining no duty of care arising in performance by local authority of its statutory duties to children—
      Whether exclusion of existence of duty of care as preliminary issue constituting breach of right to fair trial—Human Rights Act 1998, Sch 1, Pt I, art 6. **D v East Berkshire Community Health NHS Trust** [2003] **4** 796, CA.
  Preservation of subject-matter of cause of action—
    Inspection. *See* Pre-trial or post-judgment relief, *below*.
  Privilege—
    Arrest. *See* **Arrest** (Privilege from arrest).

PRACTICE (cont)—
  Privilege (cont)—
    Defamation cases. *See* **Libel and slander** (Privilege).
    Diplomatic privilege. *See* **Constitutional law** (Diplomatic privilege).
    Disclosure of documents—
      Generally. *See* **Disclosure and inspection of documents** (Privilege).
      Legal professional privilege. *See* **Disclosure and inspection of documents** (Legal professional
        privilege).
    Evidence. *See* **Evidence** (Privilege).
    Generally. *See* **Privilege**.
    Legal professional privilege—
      Generally. *See* **Privilege** (Legal professional privilege).
  Privy Council—
    Generally. *See* **Privy Council**.
  Probate. *See* **Probate**.
  Procedure summons—
    Date for hearing. *See* Chancery Division—Hearing dates, *above*.
    Setting down. *See* Summons—Chancery Division—Procedure summons—Setting down, *below*.
  Proceedings seeking relief by way of anti-suit injunction—
    Proceedings pending in Texas—
      Whether claimants entitled to leave to serve second defendant out of jurisdiction—RSC Ord 11, r 1.
        Amoco (UK) Exploration Co v British American Offshore Ltd [1999] **2 Comm** 201, QBD.
  Production of documents—
    Company documents—
      Inquiry into company's dealings. *See* **Company** (Administration—Inquiry into company's
        dealings—Production of documents).
    Generally. *See* **Disclosure and inspection of documents**.
    Income tax purposes, for. *See* **Income tax** (Information—Production of documents).
    Privilege—
      Generally. *See* **Disclosure and inspection of documents** (Privilege).
      Legal professional privilege. *See* **Disclosure and inspection of documents** (Legal professional
        privilege).
  Prohibition order—
    Financial Services Authority. *See* **Financial services** (Financial Services Authority (FSA)—Powers—
      Prohibition order).
  Property—
    Inspection of. *See* Inspection of property, *above*.
    Matrimonial property—
      Related applications. *See* **Husband and wife** (Property—Summary proceedings—Related
        application in divorce proceedings).
    Mortgage. *See* **Mortgage**.
  Psychiatric examination—
    Minor—
      Wardship and matrimonial causes. *See* **Minor** (Psychiatric examination—Wardship and
        matrimonial causes).
  Public trustee—
    Investment of funds in court. *See* **Public Trustee** (Funds in court—Investment of).
  Publication of information relating to proceedings in private—
    Contempt of court. *See* **Contempt of court** (Publications concerning legal proceedings—Court sitting in
      private).
  Queen's Bench Division—
    Appointments before Queen's Bench masters—
      Form of application. **Practice Direction** [1971] **3** 1024, QBD.
      Private room appointments—Form of application—Postal applications—RSC Ord 1, r 10. **Practice
        Direction** [1993] **4** 768, QBD.
    Certificate of associate. *See* Associate—Certificate of associate, *above*.
    Chambers proceedings—
      Generally. *See* Chambers proceedings—Queen's Bench Division, *above*.
    Commercial Court. *See* **Commercial Court** (Practice).
    Costs—
      Review of taxation. *See* **Costs** (Taxation—Review of taxation).
    Counsel's fees—
      Interlocutory fees—Accident cases—Scale of fees to be allowed on taxation. **Practice Direction**
        [1981] **3** 480, SC Taxing Office; [1984] **1** 848, SC Taxing Office.
    Damages awarded to mental patient—
      Transfer of damages to Court of Protection. *See* **Mental health** (Patient's property—Damages—
        Damages awarded in Queen's Bench Division action—Transfer of damages to Court of
        Protection).
    Jury trial—
      Cases where party entitled to trial by jury. *See* **Jury** (Trial by jury—Cases where party entitled to
        trial by jury—Queen's Bench Division).
    List of authorities. *See* List of authorities—Procedure—Queen's Bench Division, *above*.
    Lists—
      Masters' lists—Senior Master's list—Floating list—Cases which may be placed in lists—Other
        urgent applications. **Practice Direction** [1992] **1** 345, QBD.
      Masters' lists—Short notice list—Urgent applications lasting five minutes or less—Conditions for
        inclusion in list—Form of summons—Fee—Lodging—Indorsement of backsheet—Lodging party
        to hand original summons to master at hearing—RSC Ord 4, r 8(1), Ord 66. **Practice Direction**
        [1993] **1** 787, QBD.
      Mercantile lists. *See* Queen's Bench Division—Mercantile lists, *below*.
    Litigation. *See* Civil litigation—Litigation in Queen's Bench Division, Chancery Division and county
      courts other than family proceedings, *above*.
    Long Vacation. *See* Long Vacation—Queen's Bench Division, *above*.

PRACTICE (cont)—
Queen's Bench Division (cont)—
  Masters' summonses. *See* Summons—Masters' summonses, *below.*
  Mercantile lists—
    Cardiff and Chester. **Practice Direction** [2000] **1 Comm** 384, QBD; [2000] **2** 448, QBD.
    Leeds and Newcastle upon Tyne—Procedure. **Practice Direction** [1997] **2** 223, QBD.
    Liverpool and Manchester—Telephone summonses—When appropriate—Procedure. **Practice Direction** [1997] **1** 381, QBD.
  New practice and procedure. *See* Queen's Bench Division and Chancery Division—New practice and procedure, *below.*
  Personal injuries action—
    Generally. *See* Personal injuries action, *above.*
  Setting down action. *See* Trial—Setting down action, *below.*
  Summons for directions. *See* Summons for directions, *below.*
  Transfer of action—
    Transfer to county court. *See* **County court** (Transfer of action—Transfer from High Court—Transfer from Queen's Bench Division).
Queen's Bench Division and Chancery Division—
  New practice and procedure—
    Issue of writ—Postal facilities—Issue of originating summons—Service out of jurisdiction—Acknowledgment of service—Costs on default judgments—Appeal from district registrars—Evidence by deposition—Enforcing arbitration awards—RSC (Amendment No 2) 1982. **Practice Direction** [1982] **3** 639, Ch D and QBD.
Quia timet action—
  Defamation case—
    Particulars of pleading. *See* **Libel and slander** (Particulars—Quia timet injunction).
  Mandatory injunction. *See* **Injunction** (Mandatory injunction—Quia timet action).
Ratification of proceedings—
  Agent. *See* **Agent** (Ratification—Solicitor).
Re-examination—
  Previous contradictory statement of own witness—
    Written statement. **Cartwright v W Richardson & Co Ltd** [1955] **1** 742, QBD.
Reading lists—
  Estimated length of hearing. **Practice Direction** [2000] **1** 640, Ch D.
Recorder—
  Mode of address. *See* **Recorder** (Mode of address).
Reference to European Court. *See* **European Union** (Reference to European Court).
Reference to referee—
  Claim based on conspiracy to defraud—
    Some accounts involved—Supreme Court of Judicature (Consolidation) Act 1925, s 89. **Ullstrom v Naar** [1939] **1** 164, CA.
  Claim based on negligence of professional man—
    Appeal from decision of official referee—Finality of official referee's decision of fact—Supreme Court of Judicature (Consolidation) Act 1925, s 89(b)—Administration of Justice Act 1932, s 1. **Osenton (Charles) & Co v Johnston** [1941] **2** 245, HL.
  Inherent jurisdiction—
    Court expert's report—Irrelevant matter expurged—RSC Ord 37A. **Audley Land Co Ltd v Kendall** [1955] **2** 273, QBD.
  Inquiry and report—
    Attendance of witness—Jurisdiction of referee to order attendance of defendant—Purpose of attendance being to enable defendant to be cross-examined—RSC Ord 36A, r 7(1)(a). **Fallon v Calvert** [1960] **1** 281, CA.
  Order by district registrar—
    Jurisdiction of registrar—Registrar assigning business to circuit judge as official referee—Registrar reserving interlocutory applications to himself—Registrar subsequently making orders in respect of interlocutory matters—Extent of registrar's jurisdiction—Courts Act 1971, s 25(4). **Durston v O'Keeffe** [1974] **2** 1163, QBD.
  Power to order trial before official referee—
    Exercise of power—Absence of appeal from referee on questions of fact—Pleadings raising allegations of importance to party—Trial before judge providing opportunity for Court of Appeal to review findings of fact—Party entitled to trial before judge. **Simplicity Products Co (a firm) v Domestic Installations Co Ltd** [1973] **2** 619, CA.
  Procedure—
    Hearing of first summons—Delivery of pleadings—Solicitors to be ready to state nature of claim and defence—Directions and orders by referee—Date for trial of action—Expert evidence. **Practice Direction** [1968] **2** 1213, Official Referees.
  Report on reference—
    Form of report—Landlord and Tenant Act 1927—Supreme Court of Judicature (Consolidation) Act 1925, s 88(2). **Freeman v Dartford Brewery Co Ltd** [1938] **3** 120, KBD.
  Setting aside decision of referee—
    Decision given by a judge on principle—Amount referred to referee—Application to set aside referee's decision—Jurisdiction of single judge—Supreme Court of Judicature (Consolidation) Act 1925, ss 88, 89, 90(2)—RSC Ord 59A, r 1. **Telsen Electric Co Ltd v Eastick (J J) & Sons (No 2)** [1938] **2** 462, CA.
Registered designs—
  Actions and matters relating to. *See* **Design** (Practice—Motion—Actions and matters relating to registered designs).
Related claims—
  Procedure—
    Related claims made by many plaintiffs against same defendants—Court procedures to be applied and adapted flexibly so as to reach quick and economical decisions. **Davies (Joseph Owen) v Eli Lilly & Co** [1987] **3** 94, CA.

PRACTICE (cont)—
    Relator action—
        Generally. *See* **Attorney General** (Relator action).
        Injunction—
            Public right. *See* **Injunction** (Public right—Relator action).
        Local authority. *See* Parties—Local authority, *above*.
    Relief from sanction—
        Case management. *See* Civil litigation—Case management—Relief from sanction, *above*.
        'Unless' orders and other peremptory orders. *See* Order—'Unless' orders and other peremptory orders, *above*.
    Relief from sanction. *See* Civil litigation—Case management—Relief from sanction, *above*.
    Remission of action for personal injuries to county court—
        Grounds for exercise of discretion—
            Action against two defendants—Probability of plaintiffs' success in action—County Courts Act 1919, s 2. **Fawcett v Johnson's Service Garage** [1939] **3** 377, CA.
    Renewal of writ—
        Generally. *See* **Writ** (Extension of validity).
    Reopening of appeal. *See* **Appeal** (Reopening of appeal).
    Reporting restrictions—
        Anonymity order—
            Judicial review of housing accommodation decision—Proper approach to application for anonymisation—Housing Act 1996, s 166(4)—CPR 39.2. **XXX v Camden London BC** [2021] **3** 1034, CA.
    Representation of deceased person interested in proceedings—
        Appointment of person to represent estate—
            Joint tortfeasors—Contribution—No representative of deceased joint tortfeasor's estate—Power of court or judge to appoint representative—Law Reform (Married Women and Tortfeasors) Act 1935, s 6—RSC Ord 16, r 46. **Lean v Alston** [1947] **1** 261, CA.
            Necessity for consent—RSC Ord 16, r 46. **Pratt v London Passenger Transport Board** [1937] **1** 473, CA.
    Representation of parties—
        Local authority—
            Treasury Solicitor. *See* **Local authority** (Representation by Treasury Solicitor).
    Representative proceedings—
        Members club. *See* **Club** (Members' club—Parties to action—Representation order).
        Minority shareholder. *See* **Company** (Minority shareholder—Representative action).
        Parties. *See* Parties—Representative proceedings, *above*.
        Production of documents. *See* **Disclosure and inspection of documents** (Production of documents—Representative action).
        Substitution of unnamed party as plaintiff. *See* Parties—Substitution—Representative action—Substitution of party as plaintiff—Withdrawal of named plaintiff from action, *above*.
        Unincorporated body—
            Proceedings to determine who were its lawfully elected officers—Writ issued by purported president claiming to represent all members—Division of opinion between plaintiff and the members—Community of interest in determination of issue—Whether representative action appropriate—RSC Ord 15, r 12. **John v Rees** [1969] **2** 274, Ch D.
    Reserved judgment—
        Court of Appeal, Civil Division. *See* **Court of Appeal** (Practice—Civil Division—Reserved judgments).
    Residence order—
        Family proceedings—
            Generally. *See* **Family proceedings** (Orders in family proceedings—Residence order).
    Respondent's notice—
        Court of Appeal. *See* **Court of Appeal** (Respondent's notice).
    Restrictive Practices Court. *See* **Restrictive trade practices** (Court).
    Return date—
        Masters' summonses—
            Chambers proceedings—Queen's Bench Division. *See* Chambers proceedings—Masters' summonses—Queen's Bench Division—Return dates, *above*.
    Revenue appeal—
        Hearing on Northern or North Eastern Circuit. *See* Chancery Division—Northern Area—Appeals—Insolvency and revenue appeals, *above*.
    Revenue list. *See* Chancery Division—Revenue list, *above*.
    Review of taxation of costs—
        Generally. *See* **Costs** (Taxation—Review of taxation).
    Right of audience. *See* Audience—Right of audience, *above*.
    Rules of court—
        Effect of alteration of rules of court on proceedings. *See* **Statutory instrument** (Rules of court—Alteration).
    Sale of land—
        Sale by court. *See* **Sale of land** (Sale by court).
    Search order—
        Generally. *See* Pre-trial or post-judgment relief—Search order, *above*.
    Secure accommodation order—
        Family proceedings. *See* **Family proceedings** (Orders in family proceedings—Secure accommodation order).
    Security for costs—
        Arbitration proceedings. *See* **Arbitration** (Costs—Security for costs).
        Bankruptcy appeal. *See* **Bankruptcy** (Appeal—Security for costs).
        County court. *See* **County court** (Security for costs).
        Divorce—
            Security for wife's costs. *See* **Divorce** (Costs—Security for wife's costs).
        Generally. *See* **Costs** (Security for costs).
        House of Lords. *See* **House of Lords** (Costs—Security for costs).

PRACTICE (cont)—
 Security for costs (cont)—
  Legal aid. *See* **Legal aid** (Security for costs).
 Service—
  Acknowledgment of service—
   Admiralty practice. *See* **Admiralty** (Practice—Form of writs and acknowledgments of service).
   Generally. *See* Acknowledgment of service, *above*.
  Action for account. *See* **Account** (Action for—Service).
  Address for—Serviceman's address—Maintenance. *See* **Husband and wife** (Maintenance—Address—Husband's address for service).
  Application for service by an alternative method—
   Defendant company's last place of business not active—Service of proceedings upon lawyer acting for related company—Whether 'good reason' for service by alternative method—CPR 6.8(1). **Addax BV Geneva Branch v Coral Suki SA** [2005] **2 Comm** 137, QBD.
  Arbitration—
   Notice to refer dispute to. *See* **Arbitration** (Commencement—Service of notice to refer a dispute to arbitration).
  Bankruptcy notice. *See* **Bankruptcy** (Bankruptcy notice—Service).
  Billeting notice. *See* **Billeting** (Billeting notice—Service).
  Claim form. *See* **Claim form** (Service).
  Company—
   Application to restore company's name to register. *See* **Company** (Restoration to register—Application—Service of application).
   Generally. *See* Service—Service of document on company, *below*.
   Oversea company. *See* **Company** (Oversea company—Service on oversea company).
   Writ. *See* **Writ** (Service on company).
  County court summons. *See* **County court** (Practice—Service of summons).
  Deemed service—
   Service by post. *See* Service—Service by post—Deemed service, *below*.
   Writ—Acknowledgment of service—Acknowledgment of service filed in order to make payment into court—Writ not served—Whether right to make payment in 'at any time' restricted to any time after service of writ—Whether defendant estopped by acknowledgment of service from asserting that writ had not been duly served—RSC Ord 10, r 1(5), Ord 22, r 1(1). **Towers v Morley** [1992] **2** 762, CA.
   Writ—Writ deemed by acknowledgment of service to be served 'unless the contrary [is] shown'—Plaintiffs' solicitors sending copy of writ to defendants' solicitors for information only—Defendants acknowledging service of writ and requiring plaintiffs to serve statement of claim—Whether plaintiffs entitled to show that writ had not been duly served—Whether plaintiffs obliged to serve statement of claim—RSC Ord 10, r 1(5), Ord 18, r 1. **Abu Dhabi Helicopters Ltd v International Aeradio plc** [1986] **1** 395, CA.
  Document required to be served on defendant—
   Magistrates' court proceedings—Defendant and his solicitor not present in court—Document served on counsel for defendant—Validity—Whether counsel having authority to accept service on behalf of defendant—Road Traffic Act 1972, s 10(5). **Penman v Parker** [1986] **2** 862, QBD.
   Service of mandatory order—Order not properly served as penal notice not attached—Whether court having power to dispense with service of copy of order retrospectively—RSC Ord 45, r 7. **Davy International Ltd v Tazzyman** [1997] **3** 183, CA.
  E-mail, by—
   Arbitration proceedings. *See* **Arbitration** (Practice—Service—Service of notice by e-mail).
  Employment appeal tribunal. *See* **Employment Appeal Tribunal** (Practice).
  Extension of time for service—
   Claim form. *See* **Claim form** (Service—Extension of time for service).
  Extradition request and certificate. *See* **Extradition** (Extradition request and certificate).
  Fax, by. *See* Service—Service by fax, *below*.
  Hansard—
   Procedure for service, on parties, of extracts from Hansard as aid to construction of statute. *See* **Statute** (Construction—Hansard—Reference to proceedings in Parliament as an aid to construction).
  Insolvency proceedings. *See* **Insolvency** (Service).
  Letter box, through. *See* Service—Service through letter box, *below*.
  Notice of appeal—
   Appeal against committal for contempt of court. *See* **Contempt of court** (Committal—Appeal against committal—Notice of appeal—Service).
   Divorce. *See* **Divorce** (Practice—Service—Notice of appeal).
   Employment Appeal Tribunal. *See* **Employment Appeal Tribunal** (Practice—Service).
   Generally. *See* **Court of Appeal** (Notice of appeal—Service).
  Notice of motion—
   Appeal against committal by county court for contempt of court. *See* **Contempt of court** (Committal—Appeal against committal—Committal by county court—Motion for release pending appeal to Court of Appeal—Service of notice of motion).
   Bankruptcy proceedings—Service out of jurisdiction. *See* **Bankruptcy** (Service—Service out of jurisdiction—Motion).
  Notice of severance—
   Joint tenancy. *See* **Joint tenancy** (Notice of severance—Service).
  Notice to quit—
   Administration of estate. *See* **Administration of estates** (Practice—Service—Notice to quit).
   Agricultural holding. *See* **Agricultural holding** (Notice to quit—Service).
   Business premises. *See* **Landlord and tenant** (Notice to quit—Business premises—Service of notice).
   Estate vested in President of Family Division. *See* **Administration of estates** (Practice—Service—Notice to quit).
   Generally. *See* **Landlord and tenant** (Notice to quit).

PRACTICE (cont)—

Service (cont)—

Notice to treat—

Compulsory purchase. *See* **Compulsory purchase** (Notice to treat—Service).

Originating summons—

Generally. *See* **Originating summons** (Service).

Oversea company. *See* **Company** (Oversea company—Service on oversea company).

Particulars of claim. *See* **Particulars of claim** (Service).

Partnership—

Service of writ on partnership. *See* **Writ** (Service on partnership).

Personal service—

Manner of effecting personal service—Defective copy of writ served—No division of High Court specified—No district registry specified—Whether the service was the 'proceeding'—Whether service of writ void—RSC Ord 2, r 1, Ord 5, r 3, Ord 70, r 1. **Smalley v Robey & Co Ltd** [1962] **1** 133, CA.

Manner of effecting personal service—Share purchase agreement providing that written notice of any claim alleging breach of agreement to be served within two years of completion—Agreement providing for notice to be served personally or by recorded delivery—Agreement providing that proceedings in respect of claim must be issued and served within twelve months of date of notice—Whether contractual methods of service of notice exclusive—Whether personal service requiring personal delivery to party at address. **Ener-G Holdings plc v Hormell** [2012] **1 Comm** 466, QBD; [2013] **1 Comm** 1162, CA.

Petition—

Bankruptcy. *See* **Bankruptcy** (Petition—Service).

Divorce. *See* **Divorce** (Practice—Service—Petition).

Post, use of. *See* Service—Service by post, *below*.

Pre-trial or post-judgment relief—

Court permitting service of disclosure order on solicitors previously acting for defendants—Arbitration proceedings effectively concluded and claimant not relying on Arbitration Act 1996—Whether open to court to serve on solicitors—CPR 62.2. **Cruz City 1 Mauritius Holdings v Unitech Ltd** [2013] **2 Comm** 1137, QBD.

Proof of service—

Statutory demand—Bankruptcy. *See* **Insolvency** (Statutory demand—Service—Proof of service).

Reply to defence—

Time for service of reply—Failure to deliver reply to defence—Master's discretion—Interlocutory and final appeals—Jurisdiction of Divisional Court. **Kronstein v Korda** [1937] **1** 357, CA.

Respondent's notice—

Court of Appeal. *See* **Court of Appeal** (Respondent's notice—Service).

Service by alternative means. *See* **Claim form** (Service—Service by alternative means).

Service by electronic communication—

Third party surveyor's award emailed to parties' surveyors—Whether service of notice by email constituting good service—Party Wall etc Act 1996, ss 10, 15. **Knight v Goulandris** [2018] **3** 505, CA.

Service by fax—

Transmission—Whether reasonable time should be allowed between arrival of document at fax machine and communication to person concerned—RSC Ord 65, r 5(2B). **Anson (Lady Elizabeth) (t/a Party Planners) v Trump** [1998] **3** 331, CA.

Validity—List of documents required to be served by plaintiffs on defendant by specified date—Plaintiffs transmitting by fax legible list of documents on specified date—Whether document transmitted by fax validly served—Whether service by fax complying with rules of court—Whether quality of document produced by fax acceptable—RSC Ord 65, r 5(1), Ord 66, rr 1, 2. **Hastie & Jenkerson (a firm) v McMahon** [1991] **1** 255, CA.

Service by post—

County court summons. *See* **County court** (Practice—Service of summons—Service by post).

Date of service—First and second class mail. *See* Post—First and second class mail—Affidavit of service, *above*.

Deemed service—Signed for first class—Whether Royal Mail's 'Signed For 1st Class' service falling within deemed service provisions—CPR 6.26. **Diriye v Bojaj** [2021] **3** 1019, CA.

Deemed service—Writ—Writ served by post deemed to be served on seventh day after date on which writ sent 'unless the contrary is shown'—Writ sent five days before expiry and received by defendant two days later—Whether plaintiff entitled to show that service in fact effected while writ valid—Whether writ valid—RSC Ord 10, r 1(3)(a). **Hodgson v Hart DC** [1986] **1** 400, CA.

First class post. *See* Service—Service by post—Service by first class post at individual's last known residence, *below*.

Need for process to reach person to be served—Notice of date fixed for hearing adjourned appeal. **R v Appeal Committee of County of London Quarter Sessions, ex p Rossi** [1956] **1** 670, CA.

Notice to treat—Compulsory purchase. *See* **Compulsory purchase** (Notice to treat—Service—Post).

Registered post—Notice of date of hearing—Letter returned undelivered—Right to have judgment set aside. **R v Appeal Committee of County of London Quarter Sessions, ex p Rossi** [1956] **1** 670, CA.

Sending copy of writ by post—Send—Redirection by Post Office—Writ posted by plaintiff to defendant at old address—Writ redirected by Post Office to defendant's new address—Whether writ 'sent' to defendant—Whether writ validly served on defendant—RSC Ord 10, r 1(2). **Austin Rover Group Ltd v Crouch Butler Savage Associates (a firm)** [1986] **3** 50, CA.

Service by first class post at individual's last known residence—Defendant having no notice of proceedings—Whether order made at trial to be set aside—Whether breach of right to access to court—Human Rights Act 1998, Sch 1, Pt I, art 6—CPR 6.5(6). **Akram v Adam** [2005] **1** 741, CA.

Service by first class post at individual's last known residence—Whether such service establishing jurisdiction over defendant not domiciled or present in England at time of service—CPR 6.5(6). **Chellaram v Chellaram (No 2)** [2002] **3** 17, Ch D.

Service on partnership. *See* **Writ** (Service on partnership—Service by post).

PRACTICE (cont)—
 Service (cont)—
  Service by post (cont)—
   Writ for service within the jurisdiction—Whether defendant required to be physically present within jurisdiction at time when service is effected by post—RSC Ord 10, r 1(2). **Barclays Bank of Swaziland v Hahn** [1989] **1** 193, CA.
   Writ posted by plaintiff to defendant at the defendant's last known address and not returned undelivered—Defendant having changed employment and moved away from the area leaving no forwarding address—Defendant without notice of proceedings—Whether writ validly served on defendant—RSC Ord 10, r 1(2)(a). **Forward v West Sussex CC** [1995] **4** 207, CA.
   Writs purportedly served on three defendants by being put in single envelope addressed to first defendant and sent to embassy—Whether envelope properly addressed to each defendant—Whether service in single envelope addressed to each defendant permitted—RSC Ord 10, r 1(2). **Crescent Oil and Shipping Services Ltd v Importang UEE** [1997] **3** 428, QBD.
  Service of document on company—
   Misfeasance summons. *See* **Company** (Winding up—Misfeasance—Misfeasance summons).
   Oversea company. *See* **Company** (Oversea company—Service on oversea company).
   Service on London embassy—Whether service on diplomatic mission valid service on State of that mission—State Immunity Act 1978, s 12(1). **Kuwait Airways Corp v Iraqi Airways Co** [1995] **3** 694, HL.
   Service on 'secretary, treasurer or other similar officer'—Other similar officer—Person in charge of London office—Iraqi airline winding down United Kingdom operations and leaving cargo accounts officer in charge during Gulf War—Whether service of writ on junior employee left in charge valid service of writ on airline—RSC Ord 65, r 3(1). **Kuwait Airways Corp v Iraqi Airways Co** [1995] **3** 694, HL.
   Validity of service by registered post. **TO Supplies (London) Ltd v Jerry Creighton Ltd** [1951] **2** 992, KBD.
   Writ. *See* **Writ** (Service on company).
  Service on solicitor—
   Claim form. *See* **Claim form** (Service—Address for service—Service by means other than personal service—Service on solicitor).
  Service out of the jurisdiction. *See* Service out of the jurisdiction, *below*.
  Service through letter box—
   Affidavit of service—Defendant absent from jurisdiction—Plaintiff inserting copy writ through letter box—Defendant returning to jurisdiction some nine months later—Plaintiff unable to swear affidavit that writ would have come to defendant's knowledge within seven days of service—Whether writ validly served on defendant—Whether mandatory to swear affidavit that writ would have come to defendant's knowledge within seven days of service—RSC Ord 10, rr 1(2)(b), (3)(b)(i). **India Videogram Association Ltd v Patel** [1991] **1** 214, Ch D.
   Date of service—Deemed date of service—Writ served through letter box deemed to be served on seventh day after date on which letter inserted through letter box 'unless the contrary is shown'—Defendant absent from jurisdiction when copy writ inserted through letter box—Defendant arriving within jurisdiction two hours later—Defendant learning that special messenger had delivered envelope to his flat—Defendant leaving country next day without picking up envelope—Whether deemed date of service displaced—RSC Ord 10, r 1(3)(a). **Barclays Bank of Swaziland v Hahn** [1989] **2** 398, HL.
   Time of service—Writ served through letter box deemed to be served on seventh day after date on which writ inserted through letter box 'unless the contrary is shown'—Whether proof of date on which a copy writ inserted through letter box effecting good service on that date—Whether proof of earlier service can only be shown by proof that copy writ came to notice of partner before expiry of seven-day period—RSC Ord 10, r 1(3)(a). **Marsden v Kingswell Watts (a firm)** [1992] **2** 239, CA.
   Writ for service on defendant within jurisdiction—Defendant absent from jurisdiction when copy writ inserted through letter box—Defendant arriving within jurisdiction two hours later—Defendant learning that special messenger had delivered envelope to his flat—Defendant leaving country next day without picking up envelope—Whether defendant required to be within jurisdiction when service effected through letter box—RSC Ord 10, r 1(2)(b). **Barclays Bank of Swaziland v Hahn** [1989] **2** 398, HL.
  Statutory demand—
   Bankruptcy. *See* **Insolvency** (Statutory demand—Service).
  Subpoena ad testificandum. *See* Subpoena ad testificandum—Service, *below*.
  Substituted service—
   Bankruptcy notice. *See* **Bankruptcy** (Bankruptcy notice—Service—Substituted service).
   Bankruptcy petition. *See* **Bankruptcy** (Petition—Service—Substituted service).
   Defendant a prisoner of war in Germany—Whether alien enemy—Enemy—Trading with the Enemy Act 1939, s 2—RSC Ord 9, r 14B. **Vandyke v Adams** [1942] **1** 139, Ch D.
   Defendant solicitor's whereabouts unknown—Plaintiff granted leave to effect substituted service of writ by serving on Solicitors' Indemnity Fund—Whether power to order substituted service where no likelihood that such service would bring proceedings to notice of defendant—RSC Ord 65, r 4(3). **Abbey National plc v Frost (Solicitors' Indemnity Fund Ltd intervening)** [1998] **2** 321, Ch D.
   Judgment summons—Arrears of maintenance, for. *See* **Divorce** (Practice—Service—Substituted service—Judgment summons).
   Notice of writ—Court's discretion—Personal service 'impracticable'—Relief claimed in writ—Whether relief claimed in writ or terms of agreement sued on good reasons for permitting substituted service—RSC Ord 65, r 4. **Paragon Group Ltd v Burnell** [1991] **2** 388, CA.
   Notice of writ—Court's discretion—Personal service 'impracticable'—Whether power to order substituted service where plaintiff unable to effect prompt personal service—RSC Ord 65, r 4(1). **Conan Doyle's Will Trusts, Re** [1971] **2** 1377, Ch D.
   Order for substituted service in running down action—Appeal by insurers in own name to have order set aside—Insurers no parties to action—Policy giving insurers control of proceedings—Whether insurers entitled to apply to have order set aside. **Murfin v Ashbridge and Martin** [1941] **1** 231, CA.

PRACTICE (cont)—
  Service (cont)—
    Substituted service (cont)—
      Partnership with head office in enemy-occupied territory—Service on manager of London office—RSC Ord 48A, r 3. **Meyer v Dreyfus (Louis) et Cie** [1940] **4** 157, CA.
      Plaintiff issuing proceedings against solicitor whose whereabouts were unknown—Plaintiff seeking order for substituted service on Solicitors' Indemnity Fund—Whether such an order could be granted if no likelihood that it would bring proceedings to defendant's notice—RSC Ord 65, r 4. **Abbey National plc v Frost (Solicitors' Indemnity Fund Ltd intervening)** [1999] **2** 206, CA.
      Proposed action against alien in enemy-occupied country—Service by advertisement in newspaper published in neutral country and circulating in country where alien resides. **Churchill (VL) & Co Ltd, and Lonberg, Re an intended action between** [1941] **3** 137, CA.
      Service of concurrent writ out of jurisdiction—Misnomer of defendants—Conditional appearance—Summons to set aside order for service of writ, and all subsequent proceedings—Misnomer trivial—Validity of writ—Correct procedure to be adopted by defendants—RSC Ord 11, r 1—RSC Ord 12, r 30—RSC Ord 70, rr 1, 2, 3. **Alexander Korda Film Productions Ltd v Columbia Pictures Corp Ltd** [1946] **2** 424, Ch D.
      Statutory demand—Bankruptcy. *See* **Insolvency** (Statutory demand—Service—Substituted service).
      Substituted service within jurisdiction—Defendant outside jurisdiction at date of issue of writ—Defendant subsequently within the jurisdiction—Personal service of writ impracticable—Whether order for substituted service could be made—RSC Ord 65, r 4(1). **Myerson v Martin** [1979] **3** 667, CA.
      Substituted service within jurisdiction—Personal injury action arising out of road accident—Principles on which directed—Service on defendant c/o insurance company which had no authority from defendant—Defendant unable to be traced—Order for substituted service wrongly made. **Gurtner v Circuit** [1968] **1** 328, CA.
    Summons—
      Application for order that solicitor has ceased to act for party to litigation. *See* **Solicitor** (Withdrawal—Application for order that solicitor has ceased to act for party to litigation—Service of application).
      County court. *See* **County court** (Practice—Service of summons).
      Originating summons. *See* **Originating summons** (Service).
      Summons for judgment. *See* Summary judgment—Summons for judgment, *below*.
    Time for service of writ—
      Note on form inconsistent with rules—Time for service of writ prescribed by rules inconsistent with note on writ—Rules prevail—RSC, Ord 6, r 1, r 8(1), App A, Forms 1, 2. **Trow v Ind Coope (West Midlands) Ltd** [1967] **2** 900, CA.
      Service of writ more than 12 months from date of issue—Unconditional appearance by defendants—Effect—Waiver of irregularity—RSC Ord 8, r 1, Ord 64, r 7. **Sheldon v Brown Bayley's Steelworks Ltd** [1953] **2** 894, CA.
      Writ against two defendants—First defendant served within 12 months of issue of writ—Whether service on second defendant after expiry of 12 months valid—RSC Ord 6, r 8. **Jones v Jones** [1970] **3** 47, CA.
    Writ—
      Admiralty action in personam. *See* **Admiralty** (Practice—Action in personam—Writ—Service).
      Admiralty action in rem. *See* **Admiralty** (Practice—Action in rem—Writ—Service).
      Deemed service. *See* Service—Deemed service, *above*.
      Partnership. *See* **Writ** (Service on partnership).
      Service on company—Foreign company. *See* **Company** (Foreign company—Writ—Service of writ on company).
      Service on company—Oversea company. *See* **Company** (Oversea company—Service on oversea company).
      Service on company—Service by post. *See* **Writ** (Service on company—Service by post).
      Service out of jurisdiction—Generally. *See* Service out of the jurisdiction, *below*.
      Time for service of. *See* Service—Time for service of writ, *above*.
  Service out of the jurisdiction—
    Action by trustee in bankruptcy—
      Quasicontractual right—Recovery of money given by bankrupt to his children less than three months before date of presentation of petition in bankruptcy—RSC Ord 11, r 1(e). **Rousou (a bankrupt), Trustee of v Rousou** [1955] **2** 169, Ch D; [1955] **3** 486, Ch D.
    Action for breach of express trust—
      Whether applicable law or domicile of trust to be determined for jurisdiction purposes as at date when court seised of proceedings or when cause of action arose—Civil Jurisdiction and Judgments Act 1982, Sch 1, art 5(6)—CPR 6.20(11). **Chellaram v Chellaram (No 2)** [2002] **3** 17, Ch D.
    Action for fraudulent misrepresentation—
      Leave to serve notice of writ out of the jurisdiction—Defendant domiciled in Scotland—Whether claim for breach of warranty could be included in statement of claim—RSC Ord 11, r 1(e). **Waterhouse v Reid** [1938] **1** 235, CA.
    Action for rescission—
      Permission to serve out of jurisdiction—Merits threshold test—Strength of case on merits to be established to obtain leave to serve out of the jurisdiction—Relationship to strength of claim to be established to avoid being struck out—CPR 3.4(2), 6.20, 24.2. **De Molestina v Ponton** [2002] **1 Comm** 587, QBD.
    Action founded on tort committed within jurisdiction—
      Claim against joint tortfeasor for contribution—Defendants applying to set aside permission to serve out of jurisdiction—Whether contribution claim being 'claim ... in tort' for purposes of practice direction—Whether foreign courts more convenient forum—Meaning of 'claim ... in tort'—Civil Liability (Contribution) Act 1978, ss 1, 2—CPR PD 6B, para 3.1(9)—European Parliament and Council Directive 2014/104/EU. **Samsung Electronics Co Ltd v LG Display Co Ltd** [2022] **1 Comm** 619, Comm Ct; [2022] **1** 717, Comm Ct.

PRACTICE (cont)—
  Service out of the jurisdiction (cont)—
    Action founded on tort not committed within jurisdiction (cont)—
      Claim against joint tortfeasor for contribution—Defendants applying to set aside permission to
        serve out of jurisdiction—Whether foreign courts more convenient forum—Civil Liability
        (Contribution) Act 1978, ss 1, 2. **Samsung Electronics Co Ltd v LG Display Co Ltd** [2022] 2
        Comm 432, CA.

      Claim for compensation for breach of statutory data protection principles—Representative
        claim—Claim alleging defendant secretly collecting data about internet usage—Whether pleaded
        facts disclosing any basis for compensation—Whether court should permit claim to continue as
        representative claim—Whether service out of jurisdiction to be allowed—Meaning of
        'damage'—Data Protection Act 1998, s 13—CPR 19.6—European Parliament and Council Directive
        95/46/EC, art 23. **Lloyd v Google LLC** [2022] **1 Comm** 1107, SC; [2022] **2** 209, SC.

      Claim for compensation for breach of statutory data protection principles—Representative
        claim—Claim alleging defendant secretly collecting data about internet usage—Whether pleaded
        facts disclosing any basis for compensation—Whether court should permit claim to continue as
        representative claim—Whether service out of jurisdiction to be allowed—Data Protection Act
        1998, s 13—Human Rights Act 1998, Sch 1, Pt I, art 8—CPR 19.6—European Parliament and
        Council Directive 95/46/EC, art 23—Charter of Fundamental Rights of the European Union, art 8.
        Lloyd v Google LLC [2019] **1** 740, QBD; [2020] **2 Comm** 128, CA; [2020] **2** 676, CA.

      Claim for negligence—Alleged tort committed in America—Damages suffered within jurisdiction'—
        Whether 'tort committed within the jurisdiction—RSC Ord 11, r 1(ee). **Monro (George) Ltd v
        American Cyanamid and Chemical Corp** [1944] **1** 386, CA.

      Claim for negligence—Plaintiff employee injured in England through using defective machine made
        in Germany but purchased in England—Claim by plaintiff against defendant employers in
        negligence—Application by defendants for leave to serve third party notice on German
        manufacturers outside jurisdiction—Whether cause of action substantially arising in
        England—RSC Ord 11, r 1(1)(h). **Castree v E R Squibb & Sons Ltd** [1980] **2** 589, CA.

      Fraudulent or negligent misrepresentation—Misrepresentation made by telephone and telex from
        Bahamas to England—Misrepresentation received and acted on by plaintiff in England—Whether
        tort committed in England—RSC Ord 11, r 1(1)(h). **Diamond v Bank of London & Montreal Ltd**
        [1979] **1** 561, CA.

      Libel in foreign newspaper—Small circulation in England—Foreign plaintiff—No regulation in
        England—Substance of complaint—RSC Ord 11, r 1(ee). **Kroch v Rossell et Cie Société des
        Personnes à Responsibilité Limitée** [1937] **1** 725, CA.

      Matters to be considered by court in determining whether to grant leave to service writ out of
        jurisdiction—Locality of cause of action—Tortious acts committed outside jurisdiction—Damage
        suffered within jurisdiction—Plaintiffs bringing action for conspiracy against two United States
        companies who had combined to advance their own commercial interests—Conspirators' acts
        committed in New York—Plaintiffs suffering damage in London—Whether tort committed within
        jurisdiction—Whether plaintiffs entitled to leave to serve writ out of jurisdiction—RSC Ord 11,
        r 1(1)(f). **Metall und Rohstoff AG v Donaldson Lufkin & Jenrette Inc** [1989] **3** 14, CA.

      Negligent decisions by plaintiff company's directors outside jurisdiction—Decisions made on the
        basis of negligent financial information provided by its agent within jurisdiction—Whether action
        founded on tort committed within jurisdiction—RSC Ord 11, r 1(1)(h). **Multinational Gas and
        Petrochemical Co v Multinational Gas and Petrochemical Services Ltd** [1983] **2** 563, CA.

      Slander published in England—Allegations made by one Californian oil company about activities of
        another Californian oil company in Persian Gulf—Action already started in USA between the two
        companies—Allegations in that action similar to those made in England—US proceedings
        halted—Whether leave to serve writ out of jurisdiction should be given—RSC Ord 11, r 1(1)(h).
        Buttes Gas and Oil Co v Hammer [1971] **3** 1025, CA.

    Action in respect of breach of contract within jurisdiction—

      Action for account and payment of commission—Breach of contract committed within
        jurisdiction—English company acting as American company's agent in Europe—Commission
        payable in England—Duty to render account in England—Prima facie case—RSC Ord 11, r 1(e).
        International Corp Ltd v Besser Manufacturing Co [1950] **1** 355, CA.

      Breach committed within the jurisdiction—Contract to deliver cargo to one port in United Kingdom
        to be nominated by plaintiffs—Ship lost when outside jurisdiction and before port of delivery
        nominated—Whether breach committed within the jurisdiction—Whether evidence that plaintiffs
        would have nominated English port admissible—RSC Ord 11, r 1(e). **Cuban Atlantic Sugar Sales
        Corp v Cia de Vapores San Elefterio Limitada** [1960] **1** 141, CA.

      Breach—Proof of breach—Contracts to pay pension—Contract made in Czechoslovakia—Pension
        payable in England—RSC Ord 11, r 1(e), Ord 11, r 4. **Vitkovice Horni a Hutni Tezirstvo v Korner**
        [1951] **2** 334, HL.

      Contract—Need for prima facie evidence of contract with defendant—RSC, Ord 11, rr 1(e), 4. **Cromie
        v Moore** [1936] **2** 177, CA.

      Discretion to grant leave to serve out of jurisdiction—Factors to be considered—RSC Ord 11, r 1(e).
        Oppenheimer v Louis Rosenthal & Co, A-G v Oppenheimer [1937] **1** 23, CA.

      Leave to serve writ out of jurisdiction—Test for grant of leave—Whether plaintiff having to show
        good arguable case that court had jurisdiction—Whether plaintiff having to show that there was
        serious issue to be tried for exercise of discretion to grant leave. **Seaconsar Far East Ltd v Bank
        Markazi Jomhouri Islami Iran** [1993] **4** 456, HL.

      Necessity for evidence that breach occurred within jurisdiction—Leave on terms. **Malik v Narodni
        Banka Ceskoslovenska** [1946] **2** 663, CA.

PRACTICE (cont)—
  Service out of the jurisdiction (cont)—
    Action in which injunction sought—
      Injunction ordering defendant to do or refrain from doing anything within jurisdiction—Injunction not part of substantive relief to which plaintiff's cause of action entitled him—Need to establish that thing sought to be restrained invasion of right belonging to plaintiff in England—Plaintiff applying for leave to serve writ claiming damages and injunction restraining defendant doing something within jurisdiction—Claim for damages not within any of permissible grounds for grant of leave—Claim for injunction ancillary to claim for damages—Claim for injunction restraining defendant from disposing of assets within jurisdiction or removing them out of jurisdiction—Claim for interlocutory injunction—Whether claim for injunction sufficient to found jurisdiction—RSC Ord 11, r 1(1)(i). **Siskina (cargo owners) v Distos Cia Naviera SA** [1977] **3** 803, CA and HL.
    Action on contract governed by English law—
      Alternative foreign forum—Foreign defendant—Marine insurance policy issued in Kuwait providing for claims to be paid in Kuwait—Whether proper law of contract Kuwaiti law or English law—Whether plaintiff required to show that justice could not be obtained in alternative forum or that there would be excessive cost, delay or inconvenience—Whether leave to serve proceedings out of jurisdiction should be granted—RSC Ord 11, rr 1(1)(f)(iii), 4(2). **Amin Rasheed Shipping Corp v Kuwait Insurance Co, The Al Wahab** [1983] **2** 884, HL.
      Charterparty between English owners and Dutch charterers—Charterparty governed by English law—Charterers' residence and principal place of business in Holland—Charterers having no place of business or assets in England—Claim by owners based on exemption clause—Dutch law compelling Dutch courts to disregard exemption clause even though charterparty governed by English law—Leave to serve notice of writ out of jurisdiction—RSC Ord 11, r 1(f). **Coast Lines Ltd v Hudig & Veder Chartering NV** [1972] **1** 451, CA.
      Claim by creditor against defendants with foreign domicile—Order made for service out of proceedings on foreign defendants—Dispute arising as to jurisdiction of court—Whether order and service out of jurisdiction to be set aside—Insolvency Act 1986, s 423—CPR PD 6B, paras 3.1(3), (4A), (20)(a). **Orexim Trading Ltd v Mahavir Port and Terminal Private Ltd** [2018] **2** Comm 365, QBD.
      Claims alleging anti-competitive conduct made against defendants with foreign domicile—Order made for service out of proceedings on foreign defendants—Dispute arising as to jurisdiction of court—Whether foreign defendants necessary or proper parties to claims against local defendant—Whether damage within jurisdiction—Whether order and service out of jurisdiction to be set aside—CPR PD 6B, para 3.1(3), (9)(a). **Microsoft Mobile OY (Ltd) v Sony Europe Ltd** [2018] **1** Comm 419, Ch D.
      Disputed issue of fact—Proper approach to determination of putative proper law of contract—CPR 6.20(5)(c), (d). **Marubeni Hong Kong and South China Ltd v Mongolian Government** [2002] **2** Comm 873, QBD.
      Disputed issue of fact—Standard of proof—Contract for construction of cement plant in Pakistan by Romanian contractors for Cayman Island plaintiffs—Contract governed by English law—Contract containing obligation that contractors provide plaintiffs with performance bond—Plaintiffs bringing action against bank providing bond to enforce bond—Disputed oral agreement that performance bond subject to English law—Whether plaintiffs having good arguable case that performance bond subject to English law—Whether plaintiffs entitled to leave to serve writ out of jurisdiction—RSC Ord 11, r 1(1). **Attock Cement Co Ltd v Romanian Bank for Foreign Trade** [1989] **1** 1189, CA.
      Express provision and further conflicting provision—RSC Ord 11, r 1(e)(iii). **Ocean Steamship Co Ltd v Queensland State Wheat Board** [1941] **1** 158, CA.
      Governed by English law—Bill of lading—Contract not governed by English law—RSC Ord 11, r 1(e)(iii), (g). **Kadel Chajkin and Ce De Ltd v Mitchell Cotts & Co (Middle East) Ltd and A/S Motortramp** [1947] **2** 786, KBD.
      Inferred choice of law—Intention of parties—Contract of insurance—Contract concluded in America—Premiums and claims payable there—Contract part of wider cover—Scheme of cover that all policies should be uniform and be governed by English law—Contract incorporating 'Follow London' clause—Contract also incorporating New York Suable Clause—First sentence of that clause inapplicable to contract—Effect to be given to rest of clause by carrying out parties' intention—Inference of intention that contract should be governed by English law—Service out of jurisdiction of writ by assured against American claims—RSC Ord 11, r 1(1)(f)(iii). **Armadora Occidental SA v Horace Mann Insurance Co** [1978] **1** 407, CA.
      Insurance policy entered into in England—Defendant claiming to be insured injured in Ohio—Defendant bringing proceedings in Ohio—English insurer bringing action in England seeking declarations that policy subject to English law and jurisdiction—Defendant applying to stay English proceedings—Whether insurance policy governed by English law—Whether court should exercise discretion to stay English proceedings—CPR 6.20. **CGU International Insurance plc v Szabo** [2002] **1** Comm 83, QBD.
      Law with which transaction has closest and most real connection—Contract between oil company registered in London and defendant domiciled in Texas—Contract for exploitation by company of defendant's oil concession in Libya—Parties not intending contract to be governed by law of Libya—Whether contract 'governed by English law'—RSC Ord 11, r 1(1)(f)(iii). **BP Exploration Co (Libya) Ltd v Hunt** [1976] **3** 879, QBD.
      Proper law of contract—Time for determining proper law of contract—Claim in respect of general average contribution—Lloyd's average bond executed in Algeria between Cypriot shipowner and insurers of Algerian consignees—Bond not stating law governing contract and not incorporating terms of bill of lading—Parties having no connection with England—Bill of lading giving shipowner right to nominate venue for adjustment of general average—Shipowner arranging for adjustment in London—Shipowners claiming against insurers in England—Whether designation of London by shipowners under bill of lading making English law the proper law of the contract under the bond RSC Ord 11, r 1(1)(f)(iii). **Armar Shipping Co Ltd v Caisse Algérienne d'Assurance et de Réassurance** [1981] **1** 498, CA.

Service out of the jurisdiction (cont)—
Action on contract made by or through agent within jurisdiction on behalf of principal outside jurisdiction—
Foreign plaintiff entering into contract through London agents—Bermudan insurance company making reinsurance contract with Kenyan company through London brokers—Bermudan company issuing writ against Kenyan company and seeking leave to serve writ out of jurisdiction—Whether principal trading or residing out of the jurisdiction including plaintiff or limited to defendant—Whether court having jurisdiction to grant leave to serve writ out of jurisdiction—RSC Ord 11, 1(1)(d)(ii). **Union International Insurance Co Ltd v Jubilee Insurance Co Ltd** [1991] **1** 740, QBD.
Through—Non-delivery of cargo—Action against shipowners by consignees abroad—Charterparty between foreigners for carriage between foreign countries—Charterparty in English—Signature on behalf of shipowners by English agents—Bill of lading in English signed by master abroad—RSC Ord 11, r 1(e)(ii), (iii). **Metamorphosis, The** [1953] **1** 723, Admin Ct.
Action on contract made within the jurisdiction—
Loan agreement containing no express provision for interest—Claim for repayment of principal sum and interest—Whether single cause of action—Whether interest payable being implied term—CPR PD 6B, para 3.1. **Al Jaber v Al Ibrahim** [2019] **1 Comm** 1093, CA.
Written contract made in England—Contract subsequently amended by written agreement made abroad—Whether amended contract 'made within the jurisdiction'—RSC Ord 11, r 1(1)(f)(i). **BP Exploration Co (Libya) Ltd v Hunt** [1976] **3** 879, QBD.
Action properly brought against defendant within jurisdiction—
Person out of jurisdiction necessary or proper party—Action brought by consignees of cargo against shipowners and charterers—Shipowners not physically within the jurisdiction—Shipowners instructing solicitors within the jurisdiction to accept service of proceedings—Whether action 'properly brought' against shipowners—Whether it matters whether voluntary submission to jurisdiction occurring before or after issue of writ—RSC Ord 11, r 1(1)(j). **Amanuel v Alexandros Shipping Co** [1986] **1** 278, QBD.
Person out of jurisdiction necessary or proper party—Action by conservancy authority against shipowners and Minister of Supply as cargo owner to recover expenditure incurred in removing wreck—Shipowners outside jurisdiction—RSC Ord 11, r 1(g). **Tyne Improvement Comrs v Armement Anversois SA** [1949] **1** 294, HL.
Person out of jurisdiction necessary or proper party—Action not properly brought against defendant within jurisdiction—Duty of applicant to make full disclosure to court of all the facts within his knowledge—Court to consider all relevant matters without necessity of deciding disputed matters—RSC Ord 11, r 1(g). **Bloomfield v Serenyi** [1945] **2** 646, CA.
Person out of jurisdiction necessary or proper party—Application of power to permit service out of jurisdiction—Whether person requiring to be 'necessary and proper party' to be added or substituted as party—CPR 6.20, 19.1, 19.2. **United Film Distribution Ltd v Chhabria** [2001] **2 Comm** 865, CA.
Person out of jurisdiction necessary or proper party—First claimant sustaining personal injuries in road traffic accident in Costa Rica—Claimants obtaining permission to serve proceedings on defendants out of jurisdiction—Sixth defendant seeking to set aside order for service out and for declaration that English court having no jurisdiction over it—Claimants seeking to rely on 'necessary or proper party' gateway—Whether serious issue to be tried—Whether good arguable case—Whether English court appropriate forum—Whether permission for service outside jurisdiction to be set aside—Whether declaration that English court having no jurisdiction over sixth defendant should be granted—CPR PD 6B, paras 3.1(3), (9)(a). **Gunn (a protected party, by her litigation friend Gunn) v Diaz** [2017] **2 Comm** 129, QBD.
Person out of jurisdiction necessary or proper party—Real defendant to action—Discretion of court—Non-disclosure not amounting to attempt to deceive court—RSC Ord 11, r 1(g). **Ellinger v Guinness, Mahon & Co, Frankfurter Bank AG and Metall Gesellschaft AG** [1939] **4** 16, Ch D.
Properly brought—Predominant (but not sole reason) for suing English defendant to enable service of writ on foreign defendant—English defendant unlikely to have funds to satisfy judgment—Plaintiff having good arguable case against English defendant and bringing proceedings in good faith—Whether action properly brought against defendant within jurisdiction—RSC Ord 11, r 1(1)(j). **Multinational Gas and Petrochemical Co v Multinational Gas and Petrochemical Services Ltd** [1983] **2** 563, CA.
Action relating to English company—
Leave—English company operating exclusively in Argentina—Minority shareholder of company seeking buy-out order against majority shareholder on basis of unfair prejudice—Whether minority shareholder requiring leave to serve unfair prejudice petition out of jurisdiction—RSC Ord 11, r 1(2)(b)—Companies (Unfair Prejudice Applications) Proceedings Rules 1986, r 4(2). **Harrods (Buenos Aires) Ltd, Re (No 2)** [1991] **4** 348, CA.
Action to enforce, rescind, dissolve, annul or otherwise affect a contract—
Otherwise affect—Action for declaration that no contract between plaintiff and defendant—Agents of reinsurers issuing two reinsurance policies for defendant—Plaintiff insurer claiming reinsurance without authority and denying existence of contract of reinsurance with defendant—Plaintiff obtaining leave to serve writ out of jurisdiction on ground that its claim affected contract between reinsurers and their agents—Whether court having jurisdiction to uphold service of writ—Whether plaintiff required to show that his claim affected a contract between himself and defendant—Whether sufficient for plaintiff to show that his claim affected contract between himself and third party—RSC Ord 11, r 1(1)(d)(ii), (e). **Finnish Marine Insurance Co Ltd v Protective National Insurance Co** [1989] **2** 929, QBD.
Otherwise affect—Claim for moneys owing under frustrated contract—Whether a claim 'otherwise affecting' a contract—RSC Ord 11, r 1(1)(f). **BP Exploration Co (Libya) Ltd v Hunt** [1976] **3** 879, QBD.
Otherwise affect—Claim under foreign contract—Claim on dishonoured Greek cheque given as security for indebtedness incurred under English brokerage contract—Whether claim in respect of Greek cheque directly 'affecting' contract governed by English law—Whether good arguable case that rules for service out of jurisdiction complied with—RSC Ord 11, r 1(1)(a)(iii). **Hutton (EF) & Co (London) Ltd v Mofarrij** [1989] **2** 633, CA.

PRACTICE (cont)—
  Service out of the jurisdiction (cont)—
    Alternative forum available—
      Appropriate forum—England agreed or exclusive forum for resolution of disputes—Whether England proper place for claim to be tried—CPR 6.21(2A). **Marubeni Hong Kong and South China Ltd v Mongolian Government** [2002] **2 Comm** 873, QBD.
      Appropriate forum—Forum in which case can be tried more suitably for parties' interests and ends of justice—Burden of proof—Forum with which action has most real and substantial connection—Effect of deprivation of legitimate personal or juridical advantage—Effect of prior litigation involving similar parties and same issues, expert and lawyers—Principles to be applied—Factors to be considered—RSC Ord 11, r 1(1). **Spiliada Maritime Corp v Cansulex Ltd, The Spiliada** [1986] **3** 843, HL.
      Appropriate forum—Forum in which case can be tried more suitably for parties' interests and ends of justice—Plaintiffs seeking to avoid reinsurance contracts and obtaining leave to serve writ out of jurisdiction on reinsurers in Sweden—Reinsurers claiming Sweden more appropriate forum since focus of dispute was conduct of its affairs in Sweden—RSC Ord 11, r 1(1)(d)(i), (ii). **Trade Indemnity plc v Försäkringsaktiebølaget Njord (in liq)** [1995] **1** 796, QBD.
      Appropriate forum—Insurance contract made in England in respect of Jamaican power plant—Policy wording not finalised—Jurisdiction clause NMA 1483 included in slip conditions—Insurers issuing proceedings in England—Insured applying to set aside service out of the jurisdiction—Whether contract subject to Jamaican jurisdiction—Whether insurers having submitted to Jamaican jurisdiction in other proceedings. **Burrows v Jamaica Private Power Co Ltd** [2002] **1 Comm** 374, QBD.
      Loan agreements—Claimant bank alleging fraud by defendants—Related criminal proceedings already having concluded in Kazakhstan—Defendants applying to have service of proceedings against them set aside as England not appropriate forum—Judge finding claimant failing to establish England most appropriate forum for dispute—Whether England appropriate forum for proceedings—Whether judge erring—Civil Procedure Rules, Practice Direction 6B, para 3.1—CPR 6.37. **Alliance Bank JSC v Aquanta Corp** [2013] **1 Comm** 819, CA.
    Application to extend time for service—
      Defendant seeking to set aside ex parte order allowing extension of time for service—Whether order to be set aside—CPR 7.5, 7.6. **Euro-Asian Oil SA v Abilo (UK) Ltd** [2014] **1 Comm** 162, QBD.
    Appropriate forum—
      Charterparty providing for London arbitration—Claimant chartering vessel—Addendum to charterparty providing for Singapore arbitration—Claimant claiming for overpaid hire under charterparty—Claimant alleging first defendant being party to charterparty as disponent owner—Defendants maintaining second defendant being appropriate party—London arbitral tribunal holding first defendant as appropriate party and tribunal had jurisdiction to determine substantive dispute—Second defendant commencing Singapore arbitration against claimant—Claimant seeking enforcement of London arbitral award and declarations as to parties under charterparty—Whether claimant permitted to serve out of jurisdiction on defendants—Whether claimant entitled to interim injunction to restrain Singapore arbitration proceedings. **Golden Ocean Group Ltd v Humpuss Intermoda Transportasi Tbk Ltd** [2013] **2 Comm** 1025, QBD.
      Claimant company bringing claim in England against second defendant American company—Claimant being granted permission to serve claim on second defendant outside jurisdiction—Second defendant applying to set aside order permitting service out of jurisdiction—Whether England being appropriate forum for claim. **BAT Industries plc v Windward Prospects Ltd** [2014] **2 Comm** 757, QBD.
      English and American technology companies entering non-disclosure agreement—American company applying for patents—English company alleging American company using proprietary information in breach of agreement—English company bringing proceedings in England against American company—English company granted permission to serve claims out of jurisdiction—American company applying to set aside permission—Whether test for service out of jurisdiction being met—Whether England appropriate forum—CPR 6.36—CPR Practice Direction 6B, para 3.1. **Conductive Inkjet Technology Ltd v Uni-Pixel Displays Inc** [2014] **1 Comm** 654, Ch D.
      Forum in which case can be tried more suitably for parties' interests and ends of justice—Claim brought by English claimant alleging deceit and/or conspiracy in regard to loan to fund purchase of Russian companies—Whether applicable law English or Russian law—Whether England proper place in which to bring claim—Whether England clearly appropriate forum for trial of action—CPR Practice Direction 6B, para 3.1(9)(a). **VTB Capital plc v Nutritek International Corp** [2013] **1 Comm** 1009, SC; [2013] **1** 1296, SC.
  Bankruptcy—
    Bankruptcy petition. *See* **Bankruptcy** (Petition—Service—Service out of jurisdiction).
    Bankruptcy proceedings—Generally. *See* **Bankruptcy** (Service—Service out of jurisdiction).
    Inquiry into debtor's dealings and property—Summons to persons capable of giving information. *See* **Bankruptcy** (Inquiry as to debtor's dealings and property—Summons to persons capable of giving information—Service—Service out of jurisdiction).
    Statutory demand. *See* **Bankruptcy** (Service—Service out of jurisdiction).
  Bill of lading containing exclusive foreign jurisdiction clause—
    Time limit for bringing action in foreign court expiring—Service of English proceedings out of jurisdiction in breach of jurisdiction clause—Whether service of English proceedings to be set aside—Whether strong cause shown as to why English jurisdiction should be maintained—Reasonableness of plaintiffs' conduct in ignoring time bar in contractual forum—RSC Ord 11, r 4(2). **Citi-March Ltd v Neptune Orient Lines Ltd** [1996] **2** 545, QBD.
  Changes in Central Office practice—
    RSC Ord 11. **Practice Direction** [1980] **3** 822, QBD.
  Claim form. *See* **Claim form** (Service—Service out of the jurisdiction).
  Claim whose whole subject matter relates to property within the jurisdiction—
    Whether claim having to be claim to property within the jurisdiction or some interest in it—CPR 6.20(10). **Banca Carige SpA Cassa Di Risparmio Di Genova E Imperia v Banco Nacional De Cuba** [2001] **3** 923, Ch D.

PRACTICE (cont)—
  Service out of the jurisdiction (cont)—
    Contract containing English law and jurisdiction clause—
      Defendant claiming that contract entered into on its behalf but without its authority—Defendant
        disputing validity of contracts—Whether English law and jurisdiction clause severable from main
        contracts for purposes of permission to serve—Whether necessary to have good arguable case as
        to existence of contracts—CPR PD 6B, para 3.1. **Rimpacific Navigation Inc v Daehan Shipbuilding
        Co Ltd** [2010] **2 Comm** 814, QBD.
    Contract made within jurisdiction or governed by English law—
      Dispute between Jordanian buyer and Singaporean charterer concerning delivery of goods by sea
        to Jordan—Sub-charter and bills of lading governed by English law—Charterer obtaining
        permission to serve proceedings on buyer in Jordan—Buyer disputing jurisdiction of English
        court—Whether charterer entitled to serve claim for anti-suit injunction out of the
        jurisdiction—Whether charterer entitled to serve claims for negative declaratory relief out of the
        jurisdiction—CPR Practice Direction 6B, para 3.16). **Navig8 Pte Ltd v Al-Riyadh Co for Vegetable
        Oil Industry** [2013] **2 Comm** 145, QBD.
      English registered company carrying on business overseas—Allegation of irregularity in conduct of
        company's affairs—English registered company carrying on business in France—Company
        having French and American directors—Allegation that directors in breach of duty to
        company—Nature of relationship between director and company—Whether relationship between
        director and company contractual—Whether writ could be served on director outside
        jurisdiction—RSC Ord 11, r 1(1)(d)(i), (iii). **Newtherapeutics Ltd v Katz** [1991] **2** 151, Ch D.
    Customs and excise—
      Condemnation and forfeiture of goods seized by Commissioners of Customs and Excise—Whether
        writ can be served out of jurisdiction—RSC Ord 11, r 1. **Customs and Excise Comrs v I F S Irish
        Fully Fashioned Stockings Ltd** [1957] **1** 108, QBD.
    Defendant resident in EEC, Scotland or Northern Ireland—
      Leave to serve abroad not required—Indorsement of writ—Writs not indorsed not to be served out
        of jurisdiction without leave—Countries to which practice applies—Default judgments—Civil
        Jurisdiction and Judgments Act 1982—RSC Ord 6, r 7, Ord 11, r 1(1), (2)(a), Ord 13, r 7B. **Practice
        Direction** [1987] **1** 160, QBD.
    Defendant resident in Ireland—
      Resident in Eire—Whether 'resident in Ireland'—RSC Ord 11, rr 1, 2—Irish Free State (Consequential
        Adaptation of Enactments) Order 1923 (S R & O 1923 No 405). **Hume Pipe and Concrete
        Construction Co Ltd v Moracrete Ltd** [1942] **1** 74, CA.
    Discretion to give leave for service of writ out of jurisdiction—
      Good arguable case—Plaintiff giving insufficient particulars of damage suffered—Whether plaintiff
        had good arguable case—Whether leave for service of writ out of jurisdiction ought to be
        given—RSC Ord 11, r 1(1)(h). **Diamond v Bank of London & Montreal Ltd** [1979] **1** 561, CA.
    Discretion to give permission for service of claim form out of jurisdiction—
      Carriage of wheat by sea from Australia to Sri Lanka—Ship grounding off coast of Sri
        Lanka—Claimant owner not party to original charterparty—Claimant bringing action based on
        Lloyd's average bond—Defendant applying to set aside service of proceedings—Whether judge
        erring in refusing to set aside. **Galaxy Special Maritime Enterprise v Prima Ceylon Ltd** [2006] **2
        Comm** 902, CA.
    Extension of time for service. *See* Service out of the jurisdiction—Application to extend time for
      service, *above.*
    Foreign jurisdiction clause—
      Circumstances justifying service out of jurisdiction despite clause—Distributorship agreement—
        Plaintiffs having sole agency rights for distribution of first defendants' products in United
        Kingdom—First defendants a Spanish company—Agreement providing for 'law claims' to be
        submitted to Barcelona court—First defendants terminating agreement and appointing second
        defendants as agents—Second defendants an English company—Plaintiffs claiming injunctions
        and damages against both defendants for breach of contract, interference with contract and
        conspiracy—First defendants a proper and necessary party to proceedings against second
        defendants—RSC Ord 11, r 1. **Evans Marshall & Co Ltd v Bertola SA** [1973] **1** 992, CA.
      Exclusive Zambian law and jurisdiction clause in insurance contract between first claimant and
        Zambian insurers in relation to mine situated in Zambia—Separate insurance agreement relating
        to same mine entered into by claimants with other insurers—Claimants bringing proceedings in
        England and seeking to join Zambian insurers to English proceedings—Whether risk of
        fragmented proceedings sufficient to prevent enforcement of exclusive jurisdiction clause where
        party seeking service out ought to have been aware that risk of inconsistent decision possible.
        Konkola Copper Mines plc v Coromin Ltd (No 2) [2006] **2 Comm** 400, QBD.
      Insurance—Jewellers' block policy—Policy signed in England—Foreign companies as assured—
        Policy to be governed by Belgian law and disputes to be subject to Belgian jurisdiction—Loss of
        jewels in Naples—Alleged smuggling into Italy—Underwriters repudiated liability on ground of
        non-disclosure and illegality—Action by underwriters in England claiming declaration that policy
        void or voidable—Whether leave to serve notice of writ out of jurisdiction should be given—RSC
        Ord 11, r 1(f). **Mackender v Feldia AG** [1966] **3** 847, CA.
    Information of debt—
      Writ of subpoena—Party out of the jurisdiction—Applicability of RSC Ord 11—Crown Suits Act
        1865, s 37—Supreme Court of Judicature (Consolidation) Act 1925, s 99(1)(a), (g). **A-G v Prosser**
        [1938] **3** 32, CA.
    Insolvency proceedings. *See* **Insolvency** (Service—Service out of jurisdiction).
    International convention—
      Claimant serving proceedings on defendant in Czech Republic pursuant to bilateral international
        convention—States not notifying European Commission of bilateral convention as required by EC
        law—Whether bilateral convention having effect—Whether service valid—Council Regulation
        (EC) 1348/2000, art 20—European Parliament and Council Regulation 1393/2007, art 20—
        Convention between United Kingdom and Czechoslovakia on legal proceedings in civil and
        commercial matters 1924. **Debt Collection London Ltd v SK Slavia Praha-Fotbal AS** [2010] **1
        Comm** 902, QBD.

PRACTICE (cont)—
  Service out of the jurisdiction (cont)—
    Interpleader relief—
      Whether application for interpleader relief 'claim made in respect of a contract'—Whether court
        having power to serve application for interpleader relief out of jurisdiction—Civil Procedure Rules
        1998, r 6.20. **Cool Carriers AB v HSBC Bank USA** [2001] **2 Comm** 177, QBD.
    Isle of Man. *See* **Isle of Man** (Practice—Service out of the jurisdiction).
    Land within the jurisdiction—
      Action founded on contract and on trust—Settlor conveying land in England to Jersey
        company—Company undertaking undertaking under declaration of trust to hold land as bare
        nominee and to account to settlor for proceeds of sale if land sold—Company contracting to sell
        land—Settlor dying before completion of sale—At company's request bulk of proceeds of sale
        paid into its bank account in Jersey—Remainder of proceeds held in England—Official Solicitor
        appointed administrator ad colligenda bona—Action in England by Official Solicitor against
        company—Official Solicitor claiming declaration that proceeds of sale held in trust for settlor's
        estate—Whether Official Solicitor should be granted leave to serve proceedings on company out
        of jurisdiction—RSC Ord 11, r 1(1)(b), (e), (f). **Official Solicitor v Stype Investments (Jersey) Ltd**
        [1983] **1** 629, Ch D.
    Master and servant—
      Contract made in jurisdiction—Personal injuries to employee sustained abroad—Action framed in
        contract—Whether only remedy in tort—RSC Ord 11, r 1(e). **Matthews v Kuwait Bechtel Corp**
        [1959] **2** 345, CA.
    Method of service for foreign proceedings objected to by state where service to be effected—
      Whether service valid. **Habib Bank Ltd v Central Bank of Sudan** [2007] **1 Comm** 53, QBD.
      Whether service valid—Whether service could be treated as valid—Whether service could be
        dispensed with—Hague Convention on the Service Abroad of Judicial and Extrajudicial
        Documents in Civil or Commercial Matters 1965, arts 10, 15—CPR 3.10, 6.9, 12.3. **Shiblaq v**
        Sadikoglu [2004] **2 Comm** 596, QBD.
    Motion—
      Bankruptcy proceedings. *See* **Bankruptcy** (Service—Service out of jurisdiction—Motion).
    Necessary or proper party to action—
      Action properly brought against a person served in the jurisdiction—Person out of jurisdiction a
        necessary or proper party to action—Counterclaim—Foreign resident bringing action against
        English defendant—Plaintiff leaving address for service within jurisdiction as required by rules of
        court—Defendant serving defence and counterclaim on plaintiff—Defendant making another
        foreign resident second defendant to counterclaim—Whether counterclaim 'properly brought'
        against plaintiff—Whether court having jurisdiction to give leave to serve defence and
        counterclaim on second defendant to counterclaim out of the jurisdiction—RSC Ord 11, r 1(1)(j).
        Derby & Co Ltd v Larsson [1976] **1** 401, CA and HL.
      Action properly brought against a person served in the jurisdiction—Person out of jurisdiction a
        necessary or proper party to action—Foreign defendant having good defence—Action by
        liquidator against foreign shareholders and directors of company—Shareholders unanimously
        approving directors' acts—Whether shareholders owing duty of care to creditors—Whether
        directors' act becoming acts of company—Whether foreign defendants having good defence to
        action—RSC Ord 11, r 1(1)(f). **Multinational Gas and Petrochemical Co v Multinational Gas and**
        Petrochemical Services Ltd [1983] **2** 563, CA.
      Action properly brought against a person served in the jurisdiction—Person out of jurisdiction a
        necessary or proper party to action—Judge granting permission to serve out of
        jurisdiction—Guidelines for exercise of discretion in relation to contribution—Whether existence
        of right to recover in arbitration proceedings obviating potential prejudice—RSC Ord 11,
        r 1(1)(c)—CPR 6.20. **Petroleo Brasiliero SA v Mellitus Shipping Inc** [2001] **1 Comm** 993, CA.
      Claim against UK parent company and subsidiary—Application for permission to serve subsidiary
        out of jurisdiction—Whether parent company owing duty of care—Whether real issue to be
        tried—Approach to determining issue—Whether Court of Appeal erring by conducting mini trial
        of issues. **HRH Emere Godwin Bebe Okpabi v Royal Dutch Shell plc** [2021] **2 Comm** 465,
        SC; [2021] **3** 191, SC.
      Claimant bank seeking to recover funds loaned to first defendant Kuwaiti company under Islamic
        finance agreement—Bank also bringing claims against second and third defendants concerning
        role in first defendant—Whether serious issue to be tried—Whether English court appropriate
        forum—Whether permission for service outside jurisdiction to be set aside. **Standard Bank plc v**
        EFAD Real Estate Company WLL [2014] **2 Comm** 208, QBD.
    New practice and procedure—
      Queen's Bench Division and Chancery Division. *See* Queen's Bench Division and Chancery
        Division—New practice and procedure, *above*.
    New Zealand—
      Service of proceedings without leave—Appearance of defendant under protest—Whether court
        retaining inherent discretion to decline jurisdiction—Whether defendant's submission of forum
        non conveniens may be raised on application by defendant to set aside service—New Zealand
        High Court Rules, rr 219(a), (h), 131. **Kuwait Asia Bank EC v National Mutual Life Nominees Ltd**
        [1990] **3** 404, PC.
    Order for examination as to assets—
      Action against guarantor resident in Greece—Guarantee conferring exclusive jurisdiction on High
        Court—Writ claiming amount owing under guarantee served on guarantor's agent in
        England—Judgment entered in default of acknowledgement of service for amount
        claimed—Order made for defendant to attend before court to be examined as to assets—Order
        served on defendant outside jurisdiction—Whether order could be served on defendant outside
        jurisdiction without leave—Civil Jurisdiction and Judgments Act 1982, Sch 1, art 17—RSC Ord 11,
        r 9(4), Ord 48, r 1. **Union Bank of Finland Ltd v Lelakis** [1996] **4** 305, QBD and CA.
    Partnership—
      One partner out of jurisdiction—Action against partnership in firm's name—Service of writ on
        partners within jurisdiction—Service of concurrent writ on partner outside jurisdiction—RSC
        Ord 11, r 1(g), Ord 48A, rr 1, 3, 8. **West of England Steamship Owners Protection and Indemnity**
        Association Ltd v Holman (John) & Sons [1957] **3** 421, Ch D.

PRACTICE (cont)—
Service out of the jurisdiction (cont)—
Pre-trial or post-judgment relief—
Freezing order—Claimant seeking to enforce arbitral award against defendant—Claimant seeking worldwide freezing order against subsidiaries of defendant—Subsidiaries not party to arbitration agreement or arbitration—Subsidiaries having no presence in the jurisdiction—Whether court had jurisdiction to grant order allowing service of claim form on the subsidiaries out of the jurisdiction—Whether order sought was brought to enforce arbitral award—CPR 62.17, 62.2, 62.5—Arbitration Act 1996, s 44. **Cruz City 1 Mauritius Holdings v Unitech Ltd** [2015] **1 Comm** 305, QBD.
Freezing order—Defendant domiciled in non-convention country—Plaintiff seeking injunction in aid of foreign proceedings—Plaintiff obtaining injunction to restrain removal of defendant's assets from United Kingdom pending trial of action in France—Whether court having power to order service on defendant in non-convention country of proceedings for interim relief in aid of foreign substantive proceedings—Civil Jurisdiction and Judgments Act 1982, s 25(1), Sch 1, art 24—RSC Ord 11, r 1(1)(b). **X v Y** [1989] **3** 689, QBD.
Freezing order—Defendant resident abroad—Plaintiff seeking injunction in aid of foreign proceedings—Plaintiff suing defendant in Monaco—Defendant having assets in Hong Kong—No cause of action in Hong Kong—Plaintiff wishing to protect enforceability of judgment obtained in Monaco against defendant's assets in Hong Kong—Whether Hong Kong court having jurisdiction to grant worldwide Mareva injunction and leave to serve intended writ out of jurisdiction—Whether leave should be granted because injunction sought in action or claim was brought to enforce any judgment—RSC Ord 11, r 1(1)(b), (m). **Mercedes-Benz AG v Leiduck** [1995] **3** 929, PC.
Order requiring officer of judgment debtor company to attend court to provide information about judgment debtor's means—Company based overseas—Officer based overseas—Whether jurisdiction to make order against officer overseas—Whether power to serve such an order out of the jurisdiction—Civil Procedure Act 1997, s 1—CPR 6, 71.2. **Masri v Consolidated Contractors International Co SAL** [2009] **4** 847, HL; [2010] **1 Comm** 220, HL.
Service by alternative means—
Arbitration—Claimant serving arbitration claim form on defendant in Thailand—Defendant challenging service on basis that service not valid method permitted by Thai law—Claimant applying retrospectively for alternative service—Whether good reason for authorisation of alternative service shown—Whether arbitration proceedings being exceptional circumstances for permitting service by alternative means—CPR 6.15. **Bitumex (HK) Co Ltd v IRPC Public Co Ltd** [2012] **2 Comm** 1131, QBD.
Claimant seeking non-party costs order—Claimant instructing local agent to serve application notice at property in United Status owned by non-party- Non-party not resident in United Status—Judge giving permission to serve out of the jurisdiction by alternative means—Whether service in accordance with original order—Whether appropriate to order service out by alternative means at all—CPR 6.15(1), 6.37(5)(b), 6.36, PD 6B 3.1(18)—Commercial Court Guide, para 9, App 16. **Deutsche Bank AG v Sebastian Holdings Inc (No 2)** [2014] **1 Comm** 733, QBD.
Claimant serving German defendant via English solicitors—Whether service effective—Hague Convention 1965—Civil Procedure Rules 1998, 6.8. **Knauf UK GmbH v British Gypsum Ltd** [2001] **2 Comm** 332, QBD.
Company or corporation—Person holding a senior position within the company or corporation—Company incorporated under laws of India—Company holding occasional board meetings in England—Claimants serving claim form on director present in the jurisdiction—Whether company carrying on business within jurisdiction at time of service—Whether service on senior officer valid where company or corporation not carrying on business in jurisdiction. **SSL International plc v TTK LIG Ltd** [2012] **1 Comm** 429, CA.
E-mail—Claimant seeking information from three entities domiciled in the United States—Claimant seeking permission to serve proceedings by e-mail on basis that delay might defeat purpose for which relief sought—Whether court having power to order service by e-mail on defendants domiciled in the United States—CPR 6.15(1). **Bacon v Automattic Inc** [2011] **2 Comm** 852, QBD.
Subpoena ad testificandum. *See* Subpoena ad testificandum—Service—Service out of jurisdiction, *below*.
Writ—
Application for leave to serve writ out of jurisdiction—Application granted and later in day plaintiffs serving writ on first defendant inside jurisdiction—Thereafter plaintiffs serving writ on third defendant out of jurisdiction—Third defendant applying to set aside writ on ground that on date of application there was no other defendant who had been duly served—Whether service of writ valid—Whether judge could exercise his discretion retrospectively to validate service of writ—RSC Ord 11, r 1(1)(c). **Kuwait Oil Tanker Co SAK v Al Bader (No 2)** [1997] **2** 855, CA; [2000] **2 Comm** 271, CA.
Bankruptcy proceedings. *See* **Bankruptcy** (Service—Service out of jurisdiction—Writ and motion).
Leave—Service without leave—Validity of writ and limitation period for action expired—Whether failure to get leave for service out of jurisdiction rendering service of writ a nullity or merely an 'irregularity' which can be cured—Whether if irregularity court having power to cure by granting leave for service out of jurisdiction retroactively—Whether if court having that power it should exercise it—Whether improper for court to grant retroactive leave for service out of jurisdiction if improper for court to exercise discretion to renew writ because action statute-barred—RSC Ord 2, r 1, Ord 11, r 1, Ord 12, rr 7, 8. **Leal v Dunlop Bio-Processes International Ltd** [1984] **2** 207, CA.
Service permissible without leave—Methods of service available—RSC Ord 10, r 1(1), (4), (5), Ord 11, rr 1(1), (2), 5(1), (2), (3)(a), 6(2), (2A), Ord 65, r 4. **Practice Direction** [1989] **3** 562, QBD.
Writ or notice of writ—
Ghana—Fully responsible status accorded to part of Her Majesty's dominions—Subsequently became republic—Writ served on Ghanaian company—RSC Ord 11, r 6—Ghana (Consequential Provision) Act 1960, s 1(1). **Gohoho v Guinea Press Ltd** [1962] **3** 785, CA.
Serviceman—
Maintenance—
Address for service. *See* **Husband and wife** (Maintenance—Address—Husband's address for service).

PRACTICE (cont)—
    Set-off—
        Costs—
            County court. *See* **County court** (Costs—Set-off).
            Generally. *See* **Costs** (Set-off).
            Legal aid. *See* **Legal aid** (Costs—Set-off).
        Generally. *See* **Set-off**.
        Limitation period. *See* **Limitation of action** (Set-off or counterclaim).
    Setting aside arbitration award. *See* **Arbitration** (Award—Setting aside award).
    Setting aside consent order. *See* **Judgment** (Order—Consent order—Interlocutory order—Setting aside).
    Setting aside judgment. *See* **Judgment** (Setting aside).
    Setting aside order for extension of time limit. *See* **Limitation of action** (Extension of time limit—Order for
        extension—Application by defendants to set aside order).
    Setting aside subpoena ad testificandum. *See* Subpoena ad testificandum—Setting aside, *below*.
    Setting aside subpoena duces tecum. *See* Subpoena duces tecum—Setting aside, *below*.
    Setting down for trial—
        Generally. *See* Trial—Setting down action, *below*.
        Trial out of London. *See* Trial—Trial out of London—Setting down action, *below*.
    Settlement of action—
        Libel action—
            Statement in open court. *See* **Libel and slander** (Statement in open court).
    Sheriff's interpleader. *See* **Interpleader** (Sheriff's interpleader).
    Short cause list—
        Chancery Division. *See* Chancery Division—Short Causes List, *above*.
        Queens Bench Division. *See* Trial—Lists—Short cause list, *below*.
    Shorthand writer's notes—
        Application for transcript—
            Notes of discussion in judge's private room. **Vernazza v Barburriza & Co Ltd** [1937] **4** 364, CA.
        Costs—
            Costs payable by another or out of fund—Request by judge for transcript—Evidence of request for
                taxing master—Duty of counsel. **Griffiths v Howard** [1939] **3** 56, Ch D.
            Costs payable by another or out of fund—Right of judge to require transcript—Legal Aid (General)
                Regulations 1950 (SI 1950 No 1359), reg 14(3). **Theocharides v Joannou** [1953] **2** 52, Ch D.
        Evidence—
            Copies of notes for Court of Appeal—Provision at public expense—Discretion of judge executive
                function—No jurisdiction in Court of Appeal to entertain appeal. **Bradford Third Equitable Benefit
                Building Society v Borders (No 2)** [1939] **3** 29, CA.
    Similar fact evidence—
        Civil proceedings. *See* **Evidence** (Similar facts).
    Slander action. *See* **Libel and slander**.
    Slip rule—
        Judgment or order—
            Correction. *See* **Judgment** (Order—Correction—Accidental slip or omission).
    Solicitor—
        Costs—
            Generally. *See* **Solicitor** (Costs).
        Generally. *See* **Solicitor** (Practice).
        Payment of costs by solicitor personally. *See* **Solicitor** (Payment of costs by solicitor personally).
        Right of audience—
            Crown Court. *See* **Crown Court** (Practice—Solicitor—Right of audience).
    Special case—
        Form—
            Arbitration proceedings. *See* **Arbitration** (Special case—Form).
        Special case by order before trial—
            Special question in respect of question of law—Hypothetical facts—Questions of law stated for the
                opinion of court on basis of assumptions of fact—Unsuitability of procedure. **Sumner v
                Henderson (William) & Sons Ltd** [1963] **2** 712, CA.
    Specific performance—
        Summary procedure. *See* **Specific performance** (Summary procedure).
    Speeches. *See* Trial—Speeches, *below*.
    Speedy trial. *See* Trial—Order for early trial, *below*.
    Stakeholder claim—
        Charterparty—
            Arbitration awards obtained by head owners against disponent owners and by disponent owners
                against charterers—Settlement agreement between head and disponent owners allowing for
                sums paid by charterers to be either retained by disponent owners or assigned to head
                owners—Head owners obtaining US court order attaching debts of charterers to disponent
                owners—US order subsequently being vacated—Charterers serving stakeholder claim—Whether
                'competing claims' being made against charterers—CPR Pt 86. **ST Shipping and Transport Pte Ltd
                v Space Shipping Ltd (No 2)** [2018] **2 Comm** 658, QBD.
    Standing to bring proceedings—
        Human rights proceedings. *See* **Human rights** (Proceedings—Standing to bring proceedings for breach
        of convention rights).
    Statement in open court—
        Action for assault—
            Settlement of action—Acceptance of money paid into court in satisfaction of action for
                assault—Whether procedure for making statement in open court on acceptance of money paid
                into court in settlement of action for libel or slander, malicious prosecution or false imprisonment
                appropriate where plaintiff accepts money paid into court in satisfaction of claim for
                assault—Whether statement can be made in open court if claim is for assault and either malicious
                prosecution or false imprisonment—RSC Ord 82, r 5(1). **Smith v Comr of Police of the Metropolis**
                [1991] **1** 714, QBD.
        Defamation action. *See* **Libel and slander** (Statement in open court).

PRACTICE (cont)—
Statement of claim. *See* **Statement of case**.
Stay of execution. *See* **Execution** (Stay).
Stay of proceedings—
  Action against several defendants—
    Terms of compromise of action between plaintiff company and all defendants except defendant B
    were agreed—Whether second defendant who acted in person but was neither present in court
    not represented should attend to sign registrar's book—Second defendant agreeing to terms of
    compromise and signing copy of minutes of order expressing agreement with such modifications
    as court thought fit—Court's discretion. **Kota Tinggi (Johore) Rubber Co Ltd, The v Burden**
    [1970] **1** 388, Ch D.
  Action based on felony—
    Facts alleged in pleadings consistent with misdemeanour. **Clark (Jack) (Rainham) Ltd v Clark**
    [1946] **2** 683, CA.
  Action by several plaintiffs against one defendant—
    Present action based on negligence alone—Other actions based on negligence and breach of
    statutory duty—Whether present action should be stayed pending hearing of one test
    action—Supreme Court of Judicature (Consolidation) Act 1925, s 41(a)—RSC Ord 49, r 8. **Perry v**
    Croydon BC [1938] **3** 670, CA.
  Action to enforce defendant's statutory obligations—
    Bill before Parliament affecting rights of parties—Whether action should be stayed pending passing
    of Bill into law. **Willow Wren Canal Carrying Co Ltd v British Transport Commission** [1956] **1** 567,
    Ch D.
  Admiralty proceedings—
    Jurisdiction. *See* **Admiralty** (Jurisdiction—Action in rem—Stay of proceedings).
    Lis alibi pendens. *See* **Admiralty** (Practice—Lis alibi pendens—Stay of proceedings in England).
  Appropriate forum—
    Libel—American magazine accusing Russian plaintiffs of misconduct in Russia—Plaintiffs bringing
    libel actions in England in respect of publication in England—Whether actions should be stayed
    on grounds of forum non conveniens. **Berezovsky v Michaels** [2000] **2** 986, HL.
  Arbitration—
    Agreement providing for arbitration—Admiralty—Action in rem—Release of arrested ship. *See*
    Admiralty (Jurisdiction—Action in rem—Arrest of ship—Stay of proceedings).
    Agreement providing for arbitration—Arbitration subject to rules of International Chamber of
    Commerce—Order that parties pay shares of tribunal's advance costs prior to arbitration—
    Whether defendant's failure to pay share of advance costs a repudiatory breach of parties'
    arbitration agreement entitling claimant to bring proceedings in High Court—Whether arbitration
    agreement rendered inoperative—Arbitration Act 1996, s 9(4). **BDMS Ltd v Rafael Advanced**
    Defence Systems [2015] **1** Comm 627, QBD.
    Agreement providing for arbitration—Claims under series of guarantees governed by English
    law—Subsequent guarantees governed by Panamanian law and subject to ICC arbitration—
    Whether guarantees 'on demand'—Parallel judicial and arbitration proceedings—Whether claim
    in judicial proceedings 'in respect of a matter' subject to arbitration—Whether stay should be
    granted on case management grounds—Arbitration Act 1996, s 9. **Autoridad del Canal de**
    Panamá v Sacyr SA [2018] **1** Comm 916, QBD.
    Generally. *See* **Arbitration** (Stay of court proceedings).
  Automatic stay of proceedings under CPR transitional provisions—
    Lifting of stay—Considerations to be taken into account—CPR 3.9—CPR PD 51, para 19. **Woodhouse**
    v Consignia plc [2002] **2** 737, CA.
  Bankruptcy—
    Action by bankrupt—Minority shareholder's action—Whether action stayed. **Birch v Sullivan**
    [1958] **1** 56, Ch D.
    Action pending against bankrupt—Whether action stayed by his adjudication—Bankruptcy Act
    1914, s 9(1). **Realisations Industrielles et Commerciales SA v Loescher & Partners** [1957] **3** 241,
    QBD.
    Stay of committal proceedings for non-payment of rates—Jurisdiction of bankruptcy court to stay
    committal proceedings. *See* **Insolvency** (Jurisdiction—Stay of proceedings—Non-payment of
    rates).
  Chancery Division. *See* Chancery Division—Stay of proceedings, *above*.
  Company—
    Compulsory winding up—Stay pending appeal against winding up order. *See* **Company**
    (Compulsory winding up—Winding up order—Stay pending appeal).
    Creditors' voluntary winding up—Stay of winding up—Application. *See* **Company** (Voluntary
    winding up—Power to stay winding up—Creditors' voluntary winding up—Application for stay of
    winding up).
    Director—Disqualification proceedings. *See* **Company** (Director—Disqualification—Stay of proceed-
    ings).
    Winding up—Generally. *See* **Company** (Winding up—Stay or restraint of proceedings against
    company).
    Winding up—Stay of pending proceedings. *See* **Company** (Winding up—Stay of pending
    proceedings).
  Concurrent civil and criminal proceedings in respect of same subject-matter—
    Plaintiff in civil proceedings applying for summary judgment—Application by defendant for stay of
    civil proceedings until conclusion of criminal proceedings—Contention that affidavit in
    opposition to summons for summary judgment would disclose defence to criminal charges and
    prejudice trial—Whether court should grant stay. **Jefferson Ltd v Bhetcha** [1979] **2** 1108, CA.
    Proceedings pending in courts of co-ordinate jurisdiction—Assumption of jurisdiction. *See*
    Jurisdiction (Concurrent proceedings—Assumption of jurisdiction—Concurrent proceedings in
    same matter pending in courts of co-ordinate jurisdiction—Civil and criminal proceedings).

Stay of proceedings (cont)—
Concurrent proceedings before county court and High Court—
Issue of law in both sets of proceedings substantially the same—Landlord and tenant proceedings—Tenant applying in county court for new tenancy under Part II of Landlord and Tenant Act 1954—Landlord subsequently by summons seeking High Court declaration that tenancy not a business tenancy—Stay of High Court proceedings. **Royal Bank of Scotland Ltd v Citrusdal Investments Ltd** [1971] 3 558, Ch D.

Landlord and tenant—Tenant applying in county court for new tenancy—High Court action by tenant for declaration of invalidity of landlord's notice to terminate tenancy—Whether county court hearing should be adjourned until after High Court proceedings. **Airport Restaurants Ltd v Southend-on-Sea Corp** [1960] 2 888, CA.

Concurrent proceedings before distinct tribunals—
Election by plaintiffs held to be the appropriate course—Factors determining exercise of court's discretion—Material time at which to assess position—Appeal to Minister against planning decision—Application to High Court concurrently for declaration on validity of planning permission—Application for stay of High Court proceedings—Withdrawal of appeal to Minister after argument before High Court and before decision on staying proceedings in High Court—Duplication of proceedings in regard to issue raised in appeal to Minister—Whether abuse of process—Whether discretion to grant stay should be exercised—Supreme Court of Judicature (Consolidation) Act 1925, s 41. **Slough Estates Ltd v Slough BC** [1967] 2 270, Ch D.

Concurrent proceedings in England and abroad—
Defendant seeking order staying proceedings pending expert investigation ordered in French proceedings—Whether court should exercise discretion to stay proceedings. **Messier-Dowty Ltd v Sabena SA** [2000] 1 Comm 101, QBD.

Divorce petition presented in England—Proceedings against petitioner begun by respondent abroad—Advantage to petitioner from proceeding in England—Delay by respondent. **Sealey (orse Callan) v Callan** [1953] 1 942, Div.

Substantial reasons for letting English action continue. **Ionian Bank Ltd v Couvreur** [1969] 2 651, CA.

Conflict of laws—
Generally. See **Conflict of laws** (Stay of proceedings).

Jurisdiction—Civil and commercial matters. See **Conflict of laws** (Jurisdiction—Civil and commercial matters—Stay of proceedings).

Consent order staying action—
Whether amounting to discontinuance of action. See Compromise of action—Discontinuance of action—Stay of action, above.

Contempt of court—
Order of English court in 1955 for wife to deliver up documents to husband—Order made to preserve position pending decision of foreign court on community property—Order not personally served but wife informed of contents—Non-compliance with order—Order of foreign court in 1957 awarding bulk of community property and alimony to wife—Action by wife in 1963 claiming arrears of alimony under order of foreign court—Application by husband to stay proceedings on ground that wife in contempt of court—Whether wife precluded by contempt from pursuing action—Whether justice required stay of proceedings. **Bettinson v Bettinson** [1965] 1 102, Ch D.

Costs orders in earlier proceedings—
Lloyd's applying for summary judgment against names—Names relying on defence of fraud—Court holding that alleged fraud could not provide a defence—Lloyd's obtaining summary judgment and costs orders—Names relying on same fraud allegations in claims for damages against Lloyd's—Lloyd's applying for claims to be stayed pending payment of costs in summary judgment proceedings—Whether stay should be granted. **Society of Lloyd's v Jaffray** [1999] 1 Comm 354, QBD.

Court-martial. See **Court-martial** (Trial—Stay of proceedings).

Criminal proceedings. See **Criminal law** (Trial—Stay of proceedings).

Divorce. See **Divorce** (Practice—Stay of proceedings).

Exercise of discretion—
Appropriate forum—Forum with which action having most real and substantial connection—Balance of fairness and convenience—Action relating to English company—English company operating exclusively in Argentina—Minority shareholder of company seeking buy-out order against majority shareholder on basis of unfair prejudice—All economic and management considerations connected with Argentina—All witnesses and documents in Argentina—Buy-out remedy not available in Argentina—Minority shareholder entitled to damages in Argentina for loss caused by majority shareholder deceit or negligence—Whether absence of identical relief in foreign forum preventing plaintiff/petitioner from obtaining substantial justice in foreign forum—Whether English court proper forum to decide affairs of company incorporated in England. **Harrods (Buenos Aires) Ltd, Re (No 2)** [1991] 4 348, CA.

Concurrent proceedings in England and abroad—Appellant insurer of vessel lost in Philippines—Owners of cargo bringing claims against appellant in Philippines—Respondent reinsurers seeking declarations releasing them from liability to indemnify appellant—Judge refusing appellant stay pending outcome of proceedings in Philippines—Whether judge in error. **Amlin Corporate Member Ltd and others v Oriental Assurance Corporation, The Princess of the Stars** [2013] 1 Comm 495, CA.

Plaintiff purchasing shares in company in reliance on report prepared by defendant—Plaintiff referring claim against seller under sale agreement to foreign arbitration—Plaintiff commencing High Court proceedings for negligent misstatement against defendant—Whether court correctly exercising discretion to stay proceedings. **Reichhold Norway ASA v Goldman Sachs International** [1999] 2 Comm 174, CA; [2000] 2 679, CA.

Stay of proceedings (cont)—
Foreign cause of action—

Appropriate forum—Application by defendant and third party in English action for antisuit injunction to restrain foreign plaintiffs in English action from pursuing counterclaim as defendants in US action—Whether plaintiffs' counterclaim invading or threatening applicant's right to be sued in country of domicile or other contracting state under international convention—Whether convention applicable to proceedings for antisuit injunction—Whether England appropriate forum for determination of dispute—Civil Jurisdiction and Judgments Act 1982, Sch 1, art 6, Sch 3C, art 6. **Société Commerciale de Réassurance v Eras International Ltd (No 2)** [1995] **2** 278, QBD.

Appropriate forum—Forum in which case can be tried more suitably for parties' interests and ends of justice—Burden of proof—Forum with which action has most real and substantial connection. **Arab Monetary Fund v Hashim (No 3)** [1990] **1** 685, Ch D.

Appropriate forum—Forum in which case can be tried more suitably for parties' interests and ends of justice—Forum with which action has most real and substantial connection—Plaintiff's cause of action arising in Namibia—Plaintiff relying on legal aid to fund proceedings but ineligible for legal aid in Namibia—Plaintiff commencing proceedings in England—Whether availability of legal aid in competing jurisdictions relevant in determining whether English proceedings should be stayed—Legal Aid Act 1988, s 31(1). **Connelly v RTZ Corp plc** [1997] **4** 335, HL.

Appropriate forum—Forum in which case can be tried more suitably for parties' interests and ends of justice—Personal injury claims—Proceedings commenced in England—Whether foreign forum appropriate—Whether availability of legal aid in foreign forum relevant in determining whether English proceedings should be stayed. **Lubbe v Cape plc** [2000] **4** 268, HL.

Foreign court natural or appropriate forum—Factors to be considered in deciding whether stay should be granted—Dispute between Turkish company with English shareholders and Turkish bank—Whether court limited to considering only convenience and expense and plaintiff's personal or juridical advantage—Whether court entitled to consider other factors—Whether court entitled to grant stay even though it would be more inconvenient and expensive for plaintiff's to bring action in Turkey. **Muduroglu Ltd v TC Ziraat Bankasi** [1986] **3** 682, CA.

Grounds justifying stay—Burden of proving grounds on defendant—Proof that continuance of action would work injustice—Whether necessary to prove action oppressive or vexatious. **MacShannon v Rockware Glass Ltd** [1978] **1** 625, HL.

Interlocutory application—Defendant and third party in English proceedings applying for antisuit injunction to restrain foreign plaintiffs from bringing or pursuing counterclaim as defendants in US proceedings—Whether English court having jurisdiction to grant antisuit injunction against foreign plaintiffs—Principles to be applied by court when determining whether to grant injunction—RSC Ord 16, rr 8, 9, Ord 29, r 1. **Société Commerciale de Réassurance v Eras International Ltd (No 2)** [1995] **2** 278, QBD.

Public policy—Cumulative effect of other similar cases—Industrial injury suffered by plaintiff in Scotland—Plaintiff domiciled in Scotland—Defendant company having headquarters in England—Growing practice of litigating in England claims arising out of industrial accidents in Scotland—Defendant alleging that cumulative effect of similar cases rendering plaintiff's action an abuse of process of court—Whether what had happened in other cases relevant in determining whether plaintiff's action should be stayed. **MacShannon v Rockware Glass Ltd** [1977] **2** 449, CA.

Reasonable justification for bringing action in English court—What amounts to reasonable justification—Belief of plaintiff that proceedings would be quicker, damages higher and greater proportion of costs would be recovered in English proceedings—Industrial accident in Scotland—Plaintiff domiciled in Scotland—Defendant having head office in London—Evidence adduced by defendant that plaintiff would suffer none of supposed disadvantages by bringing action in Scotland—Whether plaintiff's belief that he would do better in English proceedings reasonable justification for bringing action in England. **MacShannon v Rockware Glass Ltd** [1977] **2** 449, CA; [1978] **1** 625, HL.

Foreign court—

Determination of disputes by. *See* **Conflict of laws** (Stay of proceedings—Agreement to refer to foreign court—Action commenced in England).

Foreign defendant—

Action in rem—Action by foreign plaintiff against defendant's vessel whilst vessel visiting English port—Grounds justifying stay—Balance of advantage to plaintiff and disadvantage to defendant of allowing action to proceed—Degree of relative advantage and disadvantage—Substantial advantage—Necessity of showing that disadvantage even more substantial—Collision between plaintiff's and defendant's vessels in foreign waters—Proceedings arising out of collision commenced by other parties against defendant in foreign court—Foreign court appropriate and convenient forum in which action to be tried—Plaintiff offered adequate security for foreign proceedings—Additional expense and delay of separate action in England—Whether sufficient grounds to justify a stay of proceedings. **Atlantic Star, The** [1973] **2** 175, HL.

Action in rem—Action by foreign plaintiff against defendants' vessel whilst vessel visiting English port—Grounds justifying stay—Proceedings pending in foreign court commenced by defendants—Whether existence of foreign proceedings sufficient ground for granting stay of proceedings—Whether existence of foreign proceedings a factor to be taken into account in weighing balance of convenience. **Abidin Daver, The** [1984] **1** 470, HL.

Appropriate forum—Forum in which case can be tried more suitably for parties' interests and ends of justice—Burden of proof—Forum with which action has most real and substantial connection—Effect of deprivation of legitimate personal or juridical advantage—Effect of prior litigation involving similar parties and same issues, experts and lawyers—Principles to be applied—Factors to be considered. **Spiliada Maritime Corp v Cansulex Ltd, The Spiliada** [1986] **3** 843, HL.

PRACTICE (cont)—
 Stay of proceedings (cont)—
  Foreign defendant (cont)—
   Appropriate forum—Insurance contract containing English jurisdiction clause—Plaintiffs properly serving proceedings in respect of insurance contract on foreign insurers at their London office—Insurers applying for stay of proceedings on ground of forum non conveniens—Whether jurisdiction clause imposing obligation on parties to sue in English courts—Whether court should stay English proceedings. **Berisford (S & W) plc v New Hampshire Insurance Co** [1990] **2** 321, QBD.
   Jurisdiction—Foreign defendant applying for stay of proceedings pending reference to arbitration—Whether application to stay amounting to voluntary submission to jurisdiction of court to decide merits—Whether court having jurisdiction to consider application to stay but no jurisdiction to decide merits—Arbitration Act 1975, s 1. **Finnish Marine Insurance Co Ltd v Protective National Insurance Co** [1989] **2** 929, QBD.
   Jurisdiction—Foreign defendant simultaneously disputing jurisdiction of court and applying for stay of proceedings pending outcome of proceedings abroad—Whether application to stay amounting to submission by defendant to jurisdiction of court—Whether court having jurisdiction to consider application to stay before considering question of jurisdiction to deal with merits—Whether court ought first to consider application to stay if decision on jurisdiction can only be reached by deciding issue which is subject of foreign proceedings. **Williams & Glyn's Bank plc v Astro Dinamico Cia Naviera SA** [1984] **1** 760, HL.
   Jurisdiction—Plaintiffs taking out insurance policy through London office of foreign insurers—Plaintiffs properly serving proceedings on insurers at their London office in respect of losses incurred by second plaintiff in New York—Insurers applying to stay proceedings on ground of forum non conveniens—Insurers and effective plaintiff both incorporated under United States law—Whether convention governing rules on jurisdiction of courts of European Communities applicable—Whether insurers 'deemed to be domiciled' in United Kingdom for purposes of convention—Whether English courts having jurisdiction under convention to stay proceedings—Civil Jurisdiction and Judgments Act 1982, Sch 1, arts 2, 8. **Berisford (S & W) plc v New Hampshire Insurance Co** [1990] **2** 321, QBD.
   Writ served on defendant whilst on short visit to England—Grounds justifying a stay—Burden of proving grounds on defendant—Proof that continuance of action would work an injustice to defendant as being oppressive or vexatious—Proof that stay would not work injustice to plaintiff—Plaintiff and defendant living in France—Sale of painting by defendant to plaintiff in France—Action for rescission of contract—Writ issued in England—Writ served on defendant while in England for Ascot races—Issue one of fact whether painting by named artist—Issue international in character—Parties' associations international and not only with France—No presumption that proceedings oppressive where defendant served whilst on brief visit to England—Defendant failing to show that trial in England would work injustice to himself and stay of action would not cause injustice to plaintiff. **Maharanee of Baroda v Wildenstein** [1972] **2** 689, CA.
  Foreign jurisdiction clause—
   Agreement made in Switzerland containing purported assignment by Swiss corporation to Swiss bank of its rights of action in England against another—Agreement providing that all disputes regarding it be determined by Swiss court—Bank selling rights of action to third party for large sum—Corporation bringing action in England against bank claiming assignment void—Application for stay of proceedings—Whether Switzerland appropriate forum for dispute—Whether application should be granted. **Trendtex Trading Corp v Crédit Suisse** [1981] **3** 520, HL.
  Foreign proceedings. See **Conflict of laws** (Foreign proceedings—Restraint of foreign proceedings).
  Interlocutory proceedings. See Interlocutory proceedings—Stay of proceedings, *above*.
  Jurisdiction—
   Appropriate forum—Company domiciled in England and Argentina—Company's issued share capital owned by two Swiss companies—Minority shareholder presenting petition in English courts for order that majority shareholder purchase its shares in company—Majority shareholder applying for stay of proceedings on ground of forum non conveniens—Whether English court having jurisdiction to stay proceedings—Whether domicile rule in Convention on Jurisdiction and the Enforcement of Civil and Commercial Judgments removing English court's discretion to stay action on ground of forum non conveniens—Civil Jurisdiction and Judgments Act 1982, s 49, Sch 1, art 2. **Harrods (Buenos Aires) Ltd, Re** [1991] **4** 334, CA.
   Appropriate forum—Litigation pending in foreign court—United States plaintiff taking out reinsurance policies on London market—Plaintiff properly serving proceedings on reinsurers in United Kingdom—Plaintiff also applying in New York to dismiss proceedings for negative declaratory relief commenced by reinsurers—Reinsurers applying to stay proceedings on grounds of forum non conveniens or lis alibi pendens—Reinsurers agreeing to be treated as domiciled in United Kingdom for purpose of their application—Whether domicile rule in convention governing rules on jurisdiction of courts of European Communities removing English court's discretion to stay action on grounds for forum non conveniens or lis alibi pendens—Whether English court having jurisdiction to stay proceedings—Civil Jurisdiction and Judgments Act 1982, Sch 1, arts 2, 21. **Arkwright Mutual Insurance Co Ltd v Bryanston Insurance Co Ltd** [1990] **2** 335, QBD.
   Claimants issuing claim in England against 13 defendants following Commission decision that certain commercial groups having operated cartel—Certain defendants bringing proceedings in Sweden against claimants—Defendants applying for stay of English proceedings—Whether extension of time needed to enable stay application to be made—Whether 'related actions'—Whether court should exercise its discretion to grant stay—Whether stay to be granted on case management grounds—CPR 3.1, 11—European Parliament and Council Regulation 1215/2012/EU, art 30. **Office Depot International BV v Holdham SA** [2020] **1 Comm** 772, Ch D.
   Clause in agreement providing for dispute resolution by way of expert determination—Court proceedings commenced claiming damages—Application for stay of court proceedings—Whether court having power to stay proceedings in absence of arbitration clause. **Cott UK Ltd v F E Barber Ltd** [1997] **3** 540, QBD.

PRACTICE (cont)—
   Stay of proceedings (cont)—
      Jurisdiction (cont)—
         Company—Company bringing action against defendant for sums allegedly due under contract—Company assigning right of action under various contracts to claimant—Claimant bringing action against defendant based on same contract as company's action—Court dismissing company's action for want of prosecution and ordering company to pay defendant's costs—Whether court having jurisdiction to stay claimant's action until payment of costs in company's action. **Sinclair v British Telecommunications plc** [2000] **2** 461, CA.
         Company—Compulsory winding up. *See* **Company** (Compulsory winding up—Stay of proceedings—Other proceedings against company—Jurisdiction of court).
         Contract to refer disputes to alternative dispute resolution—Whether court entitled to decline to enforce agreement. **Cable & Wireless plc v IBM UK Ltd** [2002] **2 Comm** 1041, QBD.
         Foreign defendant—Generally. *See* Stay of proceedings—Foreign defendant—Jurisdiction, *above*.
      Medical examination of plaintiff at defendant's request—
         Disclosure of medical reports to plaintiff—Refusal of plaintiff to submit to examination unless medical reports disclosed to him—Application by defendant for stay until plaintiff unconditionally submitted to examination—Whether stay should be granted—RSC Ord 38, r 37. **Megarity v DJ Ryan & Sons Ltd** [1980] **2** 832, CA.
         Disclosure of medical reports to plaintiff—Stay subject to condition that defendant undertakes to supply reports to plaintiff—Examination of plaintiff a privilege—Defendant not entitled to privilege unless he acts fairly by it by showing reports to plaintiff. **Clarke v Martlew** [1972] **3** 764, CA.
         Exchange of medical reports—Reciprocity—Plaintiff agreeing to submit to examination on condition defendant supplies copy of report—Plaintiff only entitled to insist on condition if willing to supply copies of own medical reports in exchange. **McGinley v Burke** [1973] **2** 1010, QBD.
         Refusal to submit to examination—Claim under Fatal Accidents Acts—Claim by widow in respect of husband's death—Widow's expectation of life relevant to compensation element in claim—No evidence that widow's health and expectation of life other than normal for her age—Whether stay of proceeding should be granted until widow submits to examination. **Baugh v Delta Water Fittings Ltd** [1971] **3** 258, .
         Refusal to submit to examination—Examination by medical practitioner of defendant's choice—Plaintiff refusing to submit to examination by defendant's chosen practitioner but willing to be examined by any other practitioner—Reasonableness of plaintiff's refusal—Plaintiff acting unreasonably if refusal would prevent just determination of the cause—Infringement of defendant's right to choose own expert witnesses. **Starr v National Coal Board** [1977] **1** 243, CA.
         Refusal to submit to examination—Examination involving discomfort and risk—Reasonableness of plaintiff's refusal to submit to examination—Reasonableness of refusal to be balanced against reasonableness of defendant's request—Reasonableness to be considered in light of information or advice received from parties' advisers—Matters to be considered—Plaintiff suffering from industrial deafness—Plaintiff alleging deafness noise-induced as a result of employer's negligence—Plaintiff's experts revealing that deafness in right ear not noise-induced—Employer seeking further examination to see if deafness in left ear having connection with deafness in right ear—Examination including tests involving running water into outer ear, X-raying inner ear and passing fine needle through ear-drum—Plaintiff contending tests would involve discomfort, radiation hazard and danger of infection—Whether proceedings should be stayed pending examination of plaintiff. **Prescott v Bulldog Tools Ltd** [1981] **3** 869, QBD.
         Refusal to submit to examination—Examination involving risk—Reasonableness of plaintiff's refusal to submit to examination—Plaintiff suffering from industrial dermatitis—Defendant seeking examination involving patch testing of plaintiff—Patch testing involving minimal but real risk of recrudescence of dermatitis—Whether plaintiff's objection reasonable—Whether plaintiff should give evidence of reasons for objection—Whether proceedings should be stayed pending patch testing of plaintiff. **Aspinall v Sterling Mansell Ltd** [1981] **3** 866, QBD.
         Refusal to submit to examination—Psychiatric examination. *See* Stay of proceedings—Medical examination of plaintiff at defendant's request—Refusal to submit to psychiatric examination, *below*.
         Refusal to submit to examination—Refusal to submit unless plaintiff's doctor present—Uneducated and unskilled plaintiff—Whether general rule that plaintiff need not submit to examination by defendant's doctor unless plaintiff's doctor present—Whether necessary to have reasonable grounds for having plaintiff's doctor present—Whether fact that plaintiff a woman in her fifties a reasonable ground. **Hall v Avon Area Health Authority (Teaching)** [1980] **1** 516, CA.
         Refusal to submit to examination—Refusal unreasonable. **Edmeades v Thames Board Mills Ltd** [1969] **2** 127, CA.
         Refusal to submit to psychiatric examination—Amendment of statement of claim substantially enlarging gravity of neurosis aspect of case as originally pleaded—Delay—Plaintiff's refusal unreasonable. **Lane v Willis** [1972] **1** 430, CA.
   Partnership—
      Dissolution. *See* **Partnership** (Dissolution—Arbitration—Stay of proceedings).
   Payment into court. *See* Payment into court—Stay of proceedings, *above*.
   Persons entitled to apply for stay—
      Applicant not a party to the action—Omnibus operator which had issued free pass on condition that operator and its servants should not be liable to holder of pass for injury, however caused—Pass-holder injured boarding omnibus—Action by pass-holder against servant of operator—Whether operator entitled to stay of proceedings—Supreme Court of Judicature (Consolidation) Act 1925, s 41, proviso(b). **Gore v Van der Lann (Liverpool Corp intervening)** [1967] **1** 360, CA.
   Proceedings against company—
      Company in liquidation sued by employee of company for damages for wrongful dismissal by liquidator. **Cook v 'X' Chair Patents Co Ltd** [1959] **3** 906, Ch D.

PRACTICE (cont)—
    Stay of proceedings (cont)—
        Proceedings in separate jurisdictions—
            Plaintiff initiating proceedings against same defendant in England and another jurisdiction in relation to same issue—Defendant serving counterclaim in English action—Plaintiff applying for stay of counterclaim in English action—Whether plaintiff required to elect which set of proceedings to pursue—Whether English claim should be discontinued—Whether counterclaim should be stayed. **Australian Commercial Research and Development Ltd v ANZ McCaughan Merchant Bank Ltd** [1989] **3** 65, Ch D.
        Proceedings in tort—
            Discretion to stay proceedings arising out of acts in respect of which proceedings have been, or could be, brought in Industrial Court. *See* **Industrial relations** (Proceedings—Duplication).
        Removal of stay—
            Action in respect of fatal accident—Action commenced by one dependant in personal capacity—Consent order embodying settlement—Application by another dependant to remove stay—Discretion of court to order removal. **Cooper v Williams** [1963] **2** 282, CA.
            Payment into court. *See* Payment into court—Stay of proceedings—Removal of stay, *above.*
        Serving soldier—
            Defendant's witnesses out of jurisdiction—Whether case must stand over until return of witnesses within the jurisdiction. **Coppin v Bush** [1942] **1** 518, CA.
            Usual order—RSC Ord 36, r 10. **Bell v Walker** [1941] **1** 307, CA.
        Summary judgment. *See* Summary judgment—Stay of proceedings, *below.*
        Winding up of company by court. *See* **Company** (Compulsory winding up—Stay of proceedings).
    Sterilisation—
        Child—
            Consent of High Court. *See* **Sterilisation** (Child—Consent).
        Mentally handicapped person—
            Consent of High Court. *See* **Sterilisation** (Mentally handicapped person—Consent).
    Striking out—
        Abuse of process—
            Ancillary relief. *See* **Divorce** (Financial provision—Application—Application to strike out).
            Claimant shareholder and director procuring grant of standby letter of credit to defendant bank as security for loan to company—Defendant failing to call on standby letter of credit and failing to procure its extension before its lapse—Claimant giving personal guarantee—Defendant bringing proceedings against claimant under personal guarantee—Judge setting aside guarantee for misrepresentation—Claimant bringing proceedings against defendant alleging breach of duty in failing to call on standby letter of credit—Judge striking out claim as abuse of process and granting summary judgment in favour of defendant—Whether proceedings abuse of process. **Kotonou v National Westminster Bank plc** [2017] **1 Comm** 350n, CA.
            Claimant shareholder and director procuring grant of standby letter of credit to defendant bank as security for loan to company—Defendant failing to call on standby letter of credit and failing to procure its extension before its lapse—Claimant giving personal guarantee—Defendant bringing proceedings against claimant under personal guarantee—Judge setting aside guarantee for misrepresentation—Claimant bringing proceedings against defendant alleging breach of duty in failing to call on standby letter of credit—Whether claimant's proceedings alleging facts contrary to findings of judge in earlier proceedings—Whether proceedings abuse of process. **Kotonou v National Westminster Bank plc** [2011] **1 Comm** 1164, Ch D.
            Claimants bringing claim against defendants—Claimants relying upon forged documents and perjured evidence—Defendants forging documents in support of defence—Whether court should strike out claim. **Masood v Zahoor** [2010] **1** 888, CA.
            Company commencing arbitral proceedings alleging that director/employee breached certain contractual and fiduciary duties—Arbitral tribunal holding that director/employee did not breach such duties—Company commencing court proceedings against third parties on basis they assisted and procured same alleged breaches—Third parties applying for proceedings to be struck out for abuse of process—Whether doctrine of abuse of process applicable where decision under collateral attack that of arbitral tribunal. **Michael Wilson & Partners Ltd v Sinclair** [2013] **1 Comm** 476, QBD.
            Company commencing arbitral proceedings alleging that director/employee breached certain contractual and fiduciary duties—Arbitral tribunal holding that director/employee did not breach such duties—Company commencing court proceedings against third parties on basis they assisted and procured same alleged breaches—Third parties applying for proceedings to be struck out for abuse of process—Whether abuse of process jurisdiction applying when prior determination arbitration award. **Michael Wilson & Partners Ltd v Sinclair** [2017] **2 Comm** 30, CA; [2017] **4** 216, CA.
            Employment tribunal. *See* **Employment tribunal** (Striking out—Abuse of process).
            Fraudulent claim—Defendant admitting liability for causing road traffic accident—Claimants suffering injuries—Claimants advancing genuine claims and fraudulent claim in respect of injuries—Claimants' conspiracy to advance fraudulent claim amounting to serious abuse of process of court—Whether court having power to strike out whole claim on ground of involvement in fraudulent claim—Whether court having power to strike out claim at end of trial—CPR 3.4(2)(b). **Ul-Haq v Shah** [2010] **1** 73, CA.
            Fraudulent claim—Defendant found liable in personal injury action—Defendant subjecting claimant to surveillance—Surveillance evidence showing exaggeration of effect of injury—At trial of quantum judge finding exaggerated claim fraudulent—Judge refusing to strike out statement of claim and awarding damages for actual loss—Whether court having power to strike out whole claim on ground of involvement in fraudulent claim—Whether court having power to strike out claim at end of trial—CPR 3.4(2). **Summers v Fairclough Homes Ltd** [2012] **4** 317, SC.
            Group litigation—Claimant bringing proceedings and making late application to join existing group action subject to group litigation order—Claimant's application refused—Whether claimant's existing parallel claim abuse of process. **Taylor v Nugent Care Society** [2004] **3** 671, CA.

PRACTICE (cont)—
  Striking out (cont)—
    Abuse of process (cont)—
      Warehousing—Liechtenstein foundation board member transferring asset to defendant—
      Foundation bringing proceedings to recover asset—Defendant bringing proceedings in
      Liechtenstein to remove foundation's board—Parties ceasing activity in domestic proceedings for
      ten months—Whether foundation's conduct in not pursuing domestic claim an abuse of
      process—Whether claim should be struck out. **Asturion Fondation v Alibrahim** [2020] **2
      Comm** 965, CA.
    Action—
      Action brought in wrong court—Action wrongly brought in High Court—Transfer of action to
      county court—Exercise of discretion—Whether High Court judge having discretion to transfer to
      county court action wrongly brought in High Court—Whether action required to be struck
      out—Exercise of discretion to strike out action wrongly brought in High Court—County Courts Act
      1984, s 40(1). **Restick v Crickmore** [1994] **2** 112, CA.
      Amendment—Draft consent order filed but not approved—No steps taken in action between 2013
      and 2018—Claimant presenting amended claim—Whether claimant entitled to amend particulars
      of claim—Whether claim to be struck out on ground of delay. **Djurberg v Richmond London BC**
      [2020] **2 Comm** 727, Ch D.
    Admiralty claims. *See* **Admiralty** (Practice—Striking out).
    Affidavit. *See* **Affidavit** (Striking out).
    Ancillary relief. *See* **Divorce** (Financial provision—Application—Application to strike out).
    Contempt of court proceedings—
      Committal application. *See* **Contempt of court** (Committal—Application—Striking out).
    County court practice. *See* **County court** (Practice—Striking out).
    Defence—
      Generally. *See* **Pleading** (Striking out—Defence).
      Jurisdiction of Court of Appeal. *See* **Court of Appeal** (Jurisdiction—Striking out defence).
    Insolvency proceedings—
      Ordinary application. *See* **Insolvency** (Application—Ordinary application—Striking out).
    Mid-trial—
      Application made to strike out part of counterclaim during trial—Whether court having jurisdiction
      to strike out—Approach to be taken to application to strike out mid-trial. **National Westminster
      Bank plc v Rabobank Nederland** [2007] **1 Comm** 975, QBD.
    Notice of appeal. *See* **Court of Appeal** (Notice of appeal—Striking out).
    Originating summons. *See* **Originating summons** (Striking out).
    Party. *See* Parties—Striking out party, *above*.
    Pleading—
      Action commenced in High Court—Jurisdiction of county court to strike out pleading. *See* **County
      court** (Jurisdiction—Striking out pleading—Action commenced in High Court).
      Divorce. *See* **Divorce** (Practice—Pleading—Striking out).
      Generally. *See* **Pleading** (Striking out).
      Statement of claim. *See* **Statement of case** (Striking out).
    Shareholder—
      Damage to company—Shareholder claiming loss—No reflective loss principle—Defendant claiming
      beneficial ownership of companies alleged to have made irrecoverable loans to third
      company—Whether defendant having standing to bring action to recover loans—Whether
      defendant's claim contrary to no reflective loss principle. **Barclay Pharmaceuticals Ltd v
      Waypharm LP** [2014] **2 Comm** 82, QBD.
  Submission of list of authorities—
    Queen's Bench Division. *See* List of authorities—Procedure—Queen's Bench Division, *above*.
  Subpoena ad testificandum—
    Issue—
      Discretion to refuse issue—Oppression—Application for financial provision in divorce
      proceedings—Inheritance—Wife applying for lump sum order—Wife only child of elderly
      widowed father—Likelihood of wife inheriting father's estate—Husband wanting to subpoena
      father to give evidence of his assets and testamentary intentions—Relevance of father's
      evidence—Whether father compellable witness—Matrimonial Causes Act 1973, s 25(1)(a).
      Morgan v Morgan [1977] **2** 515, Fam D.
      Issue by High Court to secure attendance of witness before tribunal. *See* **Witness**
      (Attendance—Tribunal—Power of High Court to aid tribunal by issuing subpoena ad
      testificandum).
    Service—
      Service out of jurisdiction—Revenue side—Need for leave of court. **A-G v Prosser** [1938] **3** 32, CA.
    Setting aside—
      Subpoena issued before pleadings closed or summons for directions issued—RSC Ord 37, r 34A.
      MacBryan v Brooke [1946] **2** 688, CA.
  Subpoena duces tecum—
    Company—
      Compelling production of documents. **Penn-Texas Corp v Murat Anstalt (No 2)** [1964] **2** 594, CA.
    Issue—
      Jurisdiction of Queen's Bench Division where powers of inferior tribunal incomplete—Whether
      leave to issue necessary—Documents need not be specified in subpoena before it is issued—RSC
      Ord 37, r 30. **Soul v IRC** [1963] **1** 68, CA.
    Setting aside—
      Application to set aside subpoena—Non-party required to produce documents on a date prior to
      main trial date—Absence of authority for new practice compelling early production of
      documents—Whether subpoena defective—Whether interlocutory practice flawed. **Khanna v
      Lovell White Durrant (a firm)** [1994] **4** 267, Ch D.

PRACTICE (cont)—
 Subpoena duces tecum (cont)—
  Setting aside (cont)—
   Locus standi—Time in which application may be made—Whether only respondent to subpoena
    having locus standi to apply to set subpoena aside—Whether person whose legal rights will be
    interfered with have locus standi to apply to set subpoena aside—Whether too late to apply to set
    subpoena aside once documents have been lodged with court but before respondent has proved
    them. **Marcel v Comr of Police of the Metropolis** [1991] **1** 845, Ch D.
 Substituted service—
  Bankruptcy notice. *See* **Bankruptcy** (Bankruptcy notice—Service—Substituted service).
  Bankruptcy petition. *See* **Bankruptcy** (Petition—Service—Substituted service).
  Generally. *See* Service—Substituted service, *above*.
  Statutory demand—
   Bankruptcy. *See* **Insolvency** (Statutory demand—Service—Substituted service).
 Substitution of parties. *See* Parties—Substitution, *above*.
 Summary assessment of costs—
  Court of Appeal, Civil Division. *See* **Court of Appeal** (Practice—Civil Division—Costs—Summary
   assessment of costs).
 Summary judgment—
  Action for damages for negligence—
   Manner in which application for summary judgment to be made—Affidavit stating deponent's
    belief no defence except as to amount of damages—Claim arising out of accident causing death
    or personal injury—Defence mere denial of negligence and damage—Tribunal to assess
    damages—RSC Ord 14, r 1. **Dummer v Brown** [1953] **1** 1158, CA.
  Action for recovery of debt or damages—
   Claimant seeking summary judgment in respect of unpaid invoices—Invoice rendered pursuant to
    agreement to provide consultancy services—Whether claimant entitled to summary judgment.
    E-Nik Ltd v Dept for Communities and Local Government [2013] **2 Comm** 868, QBD.
   Proceedings tried in Court of record for recovery of debt or damages—Tried—Proceedings
    concluded by summary judgment—Whether proceedings 'tried'—Law Reform (Miscellaneous
    Provisions) Act 1934, s 3(1)—RSC Ord 14. **Gardner Steel Ltd v Sheffield Bros (Profiles) Ltd**
    [1978] **3** 399, CA.
  Appeal—
   Further evidence—Admissibility—Evidence available at time of hearing application for summary
    judgment—Whether hearing application for summary judgment a hearing 'on the
    merits'—Whether further evidence admissible only on special grounds—RSC Ord 14, Ord 59,
    r 10(2), Ord 86. **Langdale v Danby** [1982] **3** 129, HL.
  Bill of exchange—
   Action between immediate parties—Holder in due course—Dishonoured bill returned to drawer by
    holder in due course. *See* **Bill of exchange** (Holder in due course—Drawer of bill discounting it to
    holder in due course—Bill dishonoured on presentation for payment—Dishonoured bill returned
    to drawer by holder in due course—Action on bill by drawer—Application for summary
    judgment).
  Chancery Division—
   Application including claim for injunction—Application to be heard on any weekday—Return date
    in summons—RSC Ords 14, 86. **Practice Direction** [1988] **2** 511, Ch D.
   Application including claim for injunction—Summons—Return date—Adjournment where hearing
    likely to be more than 30 minutes—RSC Ord 14. **Practice Direction** [1993] **1** 359, Ch D.
   Applications to be made by summons—Summons to be returnable before judge in
    chambers—Documents required—RSC Ords 14, 86. **Practice Direction** [1984] **1** 720, Ch D.
  Conditional leave to defend—
   Appeal—Grounds on which Court of Appeal may interfere with condition imposed by judge in
    exercise of his discretion under RSC Ord 14, r 6. **Gordon v Cradock** [1963] **2** 121, CA.
   Payment into court as condition of giving leave—Discretion—Sum which defendant not able to
    pay—Whether proper exercise of discretion—RSC Ord 14. **Yorke (M V) Motors (a firm) v Edwards**
    [1982] **1** 1024, HL.
   Payment into court as condition of giving leave—Need for foundation for imposing such
    condition—RSC Ord 14, r 1. **Fieldrank Ltd v Stein** [1961] **3** 681, CA.
   Payment into court as condition of giving leave—RSC Ord 14. **Ionian Bank Ltd v Couvreur**
    [1969] **2** 651, CA.
  Counterclaim against co-defendant—
   Whether defendant entitled to summary judgment against co-defendant—RSC Ord 16, rr 4(3), 8(1),
    (2), (3). **Heath (C E) plc v Ceram Holding Co** [1989] **1** 203, CA.
  Defamation case—
   Trial by jury. *See* **Jury** (Trial by jury—Defamation—Summary judgment).
  Defence. *See* **Pleading** (Defence—Filing a defence).
  Entitlement to summary judgment—
   Appellant bank claiming repayment of loan and relying on terms of promissory note—Respondent
    customer asserting that note a forgery—Customer producing alternative documents substantially
    in same terms as promissory note—Bank applying for summary judgment on grounds that
    customer's documentary evidence still entitling bank to relief sought—Whether summary
    judgment appropriate—Whether forgery allegation requiring determination at trial—Whether
    alternative defences giving rise to issues requiring trial—Supreme Court of Jamaica Civil
    Procedure Rules 2002, Pt 15.2. **Sagicor Bank Jamaica Ltd v Taylor-Wright** [2018] **3** 1039, PC.
   Claimant bank alleging to have suffered loss as result of fraud in relation to parcels of silver at
    Chinese warehouse—Judge granting first defendant summary judgment against claimant and
    setting aside service of claim form on second defendant—Judge finding on basis of contractual
    documentation no evidence of any agreement between claimant and defendants for storage
    services in relation to the parcels of silver—Whether appropriate to grant summary judgment to
    first defendant and set aside service on second defendant. **Standard Bank plc v Via Mat
    International Ltd** [2013] **2 Comm** 1222, CA.

Summary judgment (cont)—
Entitlement to summary judgment (cont)—
Conditional order on setting aside summary judgment—Claimant lenders obtaining summary judgment on its claims—Order for summary judgment having to be set aside—Judge refusing to impose conditional order of interim payment or payment into court for want of power to do so—Whether judge correct—Senior Courts Act 1981, s 32—CPR 3.1(3), 25.1(1)(k). **Deutsche Bank AG v Unitech Global Ltd** [2016] **2 Comm** 689, CA; [2017] **1** 570, CA.
Defence to claim—Counter-indemnity—Defendant providing counter-indemnity to bank in respect of performance bond issued by bank—Bank paying out under performance bond—Defendant declining to pay out under counter-indemnity—Bank seeking summary judgment—Appropriate test applicable on application for summary judgment under terms of counter-indemnity—Whether bank entitled to summary judgment. **Banque Saudi Fransi v Lear Siegler Services Inc** [2007] **1 Comm** 67, CA.
Defence to claim—Defence consisting of point of law—Plaintiff entitled to summary judgment only if point of law misconceived or plainly unsustainable—RSC Ord 14. **Home and Overseas Insurance Co Ltd v Mentor Insurance Co (UK) Ltd (in liq)** [1989] **3** 74, CA.
Fatal accident claim. *See* **Fatal accident** (Action—Summary judgment).
Injunction. *See* **Injunction** (Summary procedure—Practice—Summary judgment for injunction).
Interest—
Award of interest on summary judgment. *See* **Interest** (Damages—Jurisdiction to include interest in award of damages—Summary judgment).
Leave to defend—
Appeal—Judge giving plaintiffs leave to sign judgment in respect of part of claim but granting defendants unconditional leave to defend as to remainder of claim—Grounds on which Court of Appeal will interfere with exercise of judge's discretion—RSC Ord 14, rr 3, 4. **Lloyds Bank plc v Ellis-Fewster** [1983] **2** 424, CA.
Appeal—Triable issue of law—Circumstances in which issue of law should be decided then and there—Circumstances in which leave to defend should be granted to enable issue of law to be tried separately. **Carter (R G) Ltd v Clarke** [1990] **2** 209, CA.
Appeal—Whether appeal a rehearing—Whether Court of Appeal restricted to reviewing judge's exercise of discretion—RSC Ord 14, r 3(1). **European Asian Bank AG v Punjab and Sind Bank** [1983] **2** 508, CA.
Arguable point of law raised by defendant—Stay of proceedings pending arbitration—Circumstances in which court will give summary judgment—Whether court should give leave to defend—Arbitration Act 1975, s 1(1)—RSC Ord 14. **SL Sethia Liners Ltd v State Trading Corp of India Ltd** [1986] **2** 395, CA.
Bill of exchange—Action on bill of exchange by holder in due course—Defence of fraud affecting bill set up—Clear evidence of value given in good faith and no ground shown on which that evidence could be challenged—Defendant not entitled to leave to defend where such evidence but only if real issue raised whether bill was taken in good faith and for value—RSC Ord 14, r 3(1). **Bank für Gemeinwirtschaft v City of London Garages Ltd** [1971] **1** 541, CA.
Conditional leave to defend. *See* Summary judgment—Conditional leave to defend, *above.*
Defendants convicted in criminal trials of handling stolen goods—Plaintiffs bringing civil action for conversion—Plaintiffs applying for summary judgment—Whether plaintiffs' delay in bringing summary judgment application an abuse of process of court—Whether defendants seeking to relitigate same issues on same evidence as called in criminal trials—RSC Ord 14—Civil Evidence Act 1968, s 11. **Brinks Ltd v Abu-Saleh (No 1)** [1995] **4** 65, Ch D.
Factors to be considered—Question of amount of liability—Qualified admission—'£10,000 or thereabouts'—Condition on which leave granted. **Contract Discount Corp Ltd v Furlong** [1948] **1** 274, CA.
Parol agreement varying agreement within Statute of Frauds—Part performance—RSC Ord 14. **Knapp-Fisher v Crisp** [1936] **3** 560, CA.
Set-off and counterclaim—Equitable set-off—RSC Ord 14. **Morgan & Sons Ltd v Johnson (S Martin) & Co Ltd** [1948] **2** 196, CA.
Some other reason for a trial—Bill of exchange—Action on bill of exchange by holder in due course—Defence of fraud and illegality raised but no reasonable defence disclosed—RSC Ord 14, r 3(1). **Bank für Gemeinwirtschaft v City of London Garages Ltd** [1971] **1** 541, CA.
Some other reason for a trial—Sale of matrimonial home occupied by wife—Purchaser to be put to strict proof of his claim to evict wife—RSC Ord 14, r 3(1). **Miles v Bull** [1968] **3** 632, QBD.
Trial without further pleadings—Concurrent remedies—Application for alternative relief—Unconditional leave to defend—Appeal from judge—Right of appeal—Supreme Court of Judicature (Consolidation) Act 1925, s 31(1)(c)—RSC Ord 14, r 1(a), Ord 14B, r 1. **Customs and Excise Comrs v Anco Plant & Machinery Co Ltd** [1956] **3** 59, CA.
Unconditional leave to defend—Test of whether leave should be granted—Defendant seeking unconditional leave to defend—Defendant's affidavits giving conflicting evidence—Whether fair or reasonable probability of defendant having a real or bona fide defence—Whether defendant having credible defence—RSC Ord 14. **National Westminster Bank plc v Daniel** [1994] **1** 156, CA.
Leave to sign judgment—
Application in respect of one of several claims—Second application, in respect of remaining claims—Whether second application maintainable—RSC Ord 14, r 1(a). **Stainer v Tragett** [1955] **3** 742, CA.
Defective affidavit in support of summons—Whether further affidavits admissible—RSC Ord 14, rr 1(a), 2. **Les Fils Dreyfus et Cie Société Anonyme v Clarke** [1958] **1** 459, CA.
Payment into court of part of claim in full satisfaction with admission of liability—Application to sign final judgment for whole amount—Possible defence disclosed in plaintiff's affidavit—RSC Ord 14, r 4. **Shaerf (Recenia R) Ltd v Smyth (t/a G O Smyth & Co)** [1936] **2** 1622, CA.
Set-off and counterclaim—Bill of exchange given in pursuance of contract—Claim by defendants for damages for breach—RSC Ord 14, r 1. **Lamont (James) & Co Ltd v Hyland Ltd (No 2)** [1950] **1** 929, CA.

PRACTICE (cont)—
  Summary judgment (cont)—
    No defence to part of claim—
      Damages for breach of contract—Admission of liability but dispute as to quantum of damages—Substantial sum indisputably due to plaintiff—Amount unquantified—Whether court having power to give summary judgment for sum indisputably due to plaintiffs—RSC Ord 14, rr 1(1), 3(1). **Associated Bulk Carriers Ltd v Koch Shipping Inc** [1978] **2** 254, CA.
    Principles—
      CPR 24.2. **Swain v Hillman** [2001] **1** 91, CA.
    Set-off—
      Right of set-off. See **Set-off** (Right of set-off—Summary judgment).
    Setting aside judgment—
      Summons for judgment—No attendance by defendants—Judgment signed—Negotiations—Lapse of time for appealing—Unsuccessful application to extend time for appealing—Application to set aside judgment—Whether judgment obtained 'by default'—RSC Ord 14, r 1, Ord 27, r 15. **Spira v Spira** [1939] **3** 924, CA.
    Specific performance. See **Specific performance** (Summary procedure).
    Stay of judgment pending appeal—
      Security as condition of granting stay—Defendant furnishing banker's guarantee as security in lieu of bringing sum ordered into court—Whether banker's guarantee appropriate security—RSC Ord 14. **Rosengrens Ltd v Safe Deposit Centres Ltd** [1984] **3** 198, CA.
    Stay of proceedings—
      Circumstances in which application for summary judgment will be stayed—Arguable point of law—Summary procedure not appropriate where point of law involved requiring extensive argument—RSC Ord 14. **Home and Overseas Insurance Co Ltd v Mentor Insurance Co (UK) Ltd (in liq)** [1989] **3** 74, CA.
      Concurrent civil and criminal proceedings in respect of same subject-matter. See Stay of proceedings—Concurrent civil and criminal proceedings in respect of same subject-matter—Plaintiff in civil proceedings applying for summary judgment, above.
    Summons for judgment—
      Form—Amendment—Forms PF 11 and PF 12. **Practice Direction** [1970] **1** 343, Central Office.
      Service—Time—Ten clear days—RSC Ord 14, r 2(3) (amended by SI 1969 No 1894). **Practice Direction** [1970] **1** 343, Central Office.
  Summary procedure—
    Injunction. See **Injunction** (Summary procedure—Practice).
    Specific performance. See **Specific performance** (Summary procedure).
  Summary proceedings—
    Possession of land. See **Land** (Summary proceedings for possession).
  Summons—
    Bankruptcy proceedings—
      Inquiry into debtor's dealings and property—Summons to persons capable of giving information. See **Bankruptcy** (Inquiry as to debtor's dealings and property—Summons to persons capable of giving information).
    Chancery Division—
      Adjournment of summons to judge. See Chambers proceedings—Adjournment to judge—Originating summons, above.
      Adjournment of summons—Adjournment with witnesses—Certificate of length of trial. **Practice Direction** [1963] **1** 766, Ch D.
      Adjournment of summons—Application by post. See Chancery Division—Applications by post or telephone, above.
      Adjournment of summons—Consent to adjournment—Letter of consent signed by all parties received by master's summons clerk. **Practice Direction** [1969] **1** 490, Ch D.
      Adjournment of summons—Consent to adjournment—Letter of consent signed by all parties received by master's summons clerk—Refusal by master to consent to adjournment in cases of undue delay—Restoration of adjourned summons. **Practice Direction** [1977] **2** 173, Ch D.
      Adjournment of summons—Summons adjourned generally—Restoration by telephone. **Practice Direction** [1969] **1** 490, Ch D.
      Chambers summons adjourned to judge—New procedure. See Chancery Division—Revision of system for listing causes and matters, above.
      Listing. See Chancery Division—Listing, above.
      Papers not lodged when summons taken out—Procedure for sending papers to summons clerk by post. **Practice Direction** [1969] **1** 490, Ch D.
      Procedure summons—Setting down—Hearing. **Practice Direction** [1974] **3** 880, Ch D.
      Short summons list. See Chancery Division—Short summons list, above.
      Summons for hearing by a master—Application by post for issue of summons—Documents to be supplied to master. **Practice Direction** [1977] **2** 173, Ch D.
    Commercial action—
      Transfer of action to Commercial Court. See **Commercial Court** (Practice—Summons—Summons for transfer of action).
    Commercial Court—
      Generally. See **Commercial Court** (Practice—Summons).
    County court—
      Service of summons. See **County court** (Practice—Service of summons).
    Directions, for. See Summons for directions, below.
    Hearing—
      Short summonses and applications—List—Procedure. **Practice Direction** [1972] **2** 1168, QBD.
    Irregularity. See Irregularity—Summons, above.
    Issue before service of notice of change of solicitors—
      Waiver of irregularity—RSC Ord 7, r 2(1)(6). **Krakauer v Katz** [1954] **1** 244, CA.
    Magistrates. See **Magistrates** (Summons).

PRACTICE (cont)—
  Summons (cont)—
    Masters' summonses—
      Adjournment—Adjournment by consent—Application for adjournment made shortly before
        summons due to be heard—Date for hearing fixed by arrangement of parties' solicitors four
        months in advance—Adjournment sought because no evidence filed by defendants and plaintiff
        absent abroad—Necessity to keep fixed appointments—Effect of late cancellation of
        appointments—Costs—Liability of parties' legal advisers for costs where adjournment
        occasioned by lack of preparation. **Fowkes v Duthie** [1991] **1** 337, QBD.
      Chambers proceedings. *See* Chambers proceedings—Masters' summonses, *above*.
      Queen's Bench Division—Time summonses—Arrangement for issue. **Practice Direction** [1992] **1** 64,
        QBD.
      Queen's Bench Division—Time summonses—Arrangements for issue—RSC Ord 32, r 3. **Practice
        Direction** [1978] **1** 723, QBD; [1989] **2** 480, SC Taxing Office.
    New form of writ of summons. *See* **Writ** (New form of writ of summons).
    Originating. *See* **Originating summons**.
    Restoration of summons to list—
      Restoration without leave—Procedure. **Practice Direction** [1969] **2** 1140, QBD.
    Service—
      Application for order that solicitor has ceased to act for party to litigation. *See* **Solicitor**
        (Withdrawal—Application for order that solicitor has ceased to act for party to litigation).
    Summons for leave to proceed under Courts (Emergency Powers) Act 1939—
      Summons not served on judgment debtor—Distinction between nullity and irregularity in
        procedure—Inherent jurisdiction of court—RSC Ord 70, rr 1, 2. **Craig v Kanseen** [1943] **1** 108, CA.
    Telephone summons—
      Patent proceedings. *See* **Patent** (Practice—Telephone summonses).
    Witness summons—
      Generally. *See* Witness summons, *below*.
      Magistrates' court. *See* **Magistrates** (Witness summons).
  Summons for directions—
    Admiralty practice. *See* **Admiralty** (Practice—Directions—Summons for directions).
    Admission of written statement—
      Interlocutory applications—Application on summons for directions for admission of written
        statement under Evidence Act 1938, s 1(2)—Order by master allowing evidence—Jurisdiction—
        'Court'—Supreme Court of Judicature (Consolidation) Act 1925, s 99(1)(d)—Evidence Act 1938,
        s 1—RSC Ord 30, r 2(2)(d), Ord 54, r 12. **Friend v Wallman** [1946] **2** 237, CA.
    Assessment of case—
      Grading as to substance, difficulty or public importance—Duty of parties to furnish court with
        up-to-date details affecting assessment. **Practice Direction** [1972] **1** 288, QBD.
    Chancery Division—
      Exchange of witness statements—Order for exchange normally to be made at hearing of summons
        for directions—Order to specify day on which exchange to be made—Objections to order—RSC
        Ord 38, r 2A. **Practice Direction** [1989] **1** 764, LC.
      Pleadings—Complete set of pleadings to be lodged on issuing summons for directions. **Practice
        Direction** [1989] **1** 764, LC.
      Timetable—Hearing more than year after issue of originating process—Duty of master or district
        registrar—Timetable for completion of remaining proceedings and procedural steps. **Practice
        Direction** [1977] **1** 543, Ch D.
      Timetable—Timetable no longer required. **Practice Direction** [1983] **1** 131, Ch D.
      Use of postal facilities. *See* Chancery Division—Applications by post or telephone, *above*.
    Disclosure on. *See* **Disclosure and inspection of documents** (Disclosure on summons for directions).
    Entry of trial—
      Order for entry of trial—When necessary. **Southey-Roberts Estates Ltd v Roe** [1956] **2** 829, Ch D.
    Expert evidence—
      Application for leave to call expert evidence—Disclosure of reports—Procedure—RSC Ord 25 (as
        amended by the Rules of the Supreme Court (Amendment) 1974, SI 1974 No 295)—RSC Ord 38,
        rr 35-44 (as added by the Rules of the Supreme Court (Amendment) 1974, SI 1974 No 295).
        Practice Direction [1974] **2** 966, QBD.
    Issue—
      Defendant failing to serve defence—Jurisdiction of court to give directions for trial. **Austin v Wildig**
        [1969] **1** 99, Ch D.
    Order for early trial on. *See* Trial—Order for early trial—Order on summons for directions, *below*.
    Place and mode of trial—
      Order fixing place and mode of trial—When order should be made. **Southey-Roberts Estates Ltd v
        Roe** [1956] **2** 829, Ch D.
    Queen's Bench Division—
      Jury list—Summons for directions and applications prior to setting down to be made to
        master—Interlocutory applications after setting down to be made to judge—Reference of
        applications by master to judge. **Practice Direction** [1993] **4** 416, QBD.
    Speedy trial. *See* Trial—Order for early trial—Summons for directions adjourned from judge to master,
      below.
  Supplemental order. *See* **Judgment** (Order—Supplemental order).
  Supreme Court of the United Kingdom. *See* **Supreme court** (Supreme Court of the United
    Kingdom—Practice).
  Tape recorders—
    Use of tape recorders in court—
      Leave of court—Discretion—Factors relevant to exercise of court's discretion—Contempt of Court
        Act 1981, s 9. **Practice Direction** [1981] **3** 848, Sup Ct.
  Taxation of costs—
    Admiralty. *See* **Admiralty** (Costs—Taxation).
    Arbitration. *See* **Arbitration** (Costs—Taxation).
    Divorce. *See* **Divorce** (Costs—Taxation).
    Generally. *See* **Costs** (Taxation).

PRACTICE (cont)—
  Taxation of costs (cont)—
    House of Lords. *See* **House of Lords** (Costs—Taxation).
    Legal aid cases—
      Generally. *See* **Legal aid** (Taxation of costs).
    Privy Council. *See* **Privy Council** (Costs—Taxation).
  Technology and Construction Court—
    Case management—
      Case management conference—Whether it was appropriate to order a fixed term window before disclosure for the purpose of allowing the parties to engage in alternative dispute resolution. **CIP Properties (AIPT) Ltd v Galliford Try Infrastructure Ltd** [2015] **1 Comm** 765, QBD.
      High Court judge business—Low value claims—Guidance. **West Country Renovations Ltd v McDowell** [2012] **3** 106, QBD.
      Interim arrangements. **Technology and Construction Court: Statement by the Lord Chief Justice of England and Wales** [2005] **3** 289, QBD.
    Transfer of proceedings to or from. *See* Transfer of proceedings from or to the Technology and Construction Court, *below*.
  Telephone—
    Chambers proceedings—
      Communications by telephone. *See* Chambers proceedings—Communications by post or telephone, *above*.
    Summons—
      Patent proceedings. *See* **Patent** (Practice—Telephone summonses).
  Third party debt orders. *See* Pre-trial or post-judgment relief—Third party debt orders, *above*.
  Third party notice—
    Generally. *See* Third party procedure—Notice, *below*.
    Summons for third party directions—
      Power of court to refuse directions in special circumstances—Whether refusal to give third party directions putting an end to third party proceedings—RSC Ord 16, r 4. **Courtenay-Evans v Stuart Passey & Associates (a firm) (Greater London Council, third party)** [1986] **1** 932, QBD.
  Third party procedure—
    Action against third party domiciled within jurisdiction in respect of foreign tort—
      Fatal accident—Action in England for injury and death of deceased in Spain following accident and treatment in Spanish hospital—Third party notice claiming contribution or indemnity from surgeon and hospital—Whether court having jurisdiction to entertain third party proceedings—Right of third party to be sued separately in country of domicile—Application of domestic rules of procedure regarding third party proceedings—Appropriate jurisdiction for obtaining contribution from joint tortfeasor—Exercise of discretion to decline jurisdiction—Civil Jurisdiction and Judgments Act 1982, Sch 1, arts 6, 21—RSC Ord 16, r 1(1). **Kinnear v Falconfilms NV (Hospital Ruber Internacional and anor, third parties)** [1994] **3** 42, QBD.
    Application—
      Company—Winding up—Third party procedure not applicable—Court in winding up having no jurisdiction to settle disputes between persons outside winding up. **Singer (A) & Co (Hat Manufacturers) Ltd, Re** [1943] **1** 225, CA.
    Application by third party to join fifth party as additional fourth party—
      Procedure—RSC Ord 16A, r 11(1), Ord 16, r 11. **Piddock v Clifford Products Ltd (Industrial Guarding Equipment Ltd, third party, Baldwin Instrument Co Ltd, fourth party, BAL Ltd, fifth party)** [1960] **3** 805, CA.
    Claims and issues between defendant and another party—
      Counterclaim by third party, a defendant in the action—Third-party notice served by second defendants on third defendants claiming indemnity or contribution—Third-party notice treated as statement of claim—Defence and counterclaim by third defendants—Whether court had jurisdiction to entertain counterclaim—Counterclaim including claim for payment and set-off of alleged indebtedness for work done in relation to matters, some of which were not the subject of the plaintiffs' action—Exercise of court's discretion to strike out counterclaim or to direct separate trials—RSC Ord 15, rr 2, 5(2), Ord 16, rr 1(3), 8(3). **Normar, The** [1968] **1** 753, Admin Ct.
    Notice—
      Claim against third party—Discretion of court to allow—Effect of notice to involve plaintiff in costly litigation, which may otherwise be avoided. **Glasgow City Corp v Robertson or Cameron** [1936] **2** 173, HL.
      Claim against third party—Relief or remedy relating to or connected with original subject matter of action—Connection with 'original subject-matter of the action'—Specific performance of agreement to sell land to vendors sued for specific performance of their subsequent sale of land—Whether third party notice valid—RSC Ord 16, r 1(1)(b). **Standard Securities Ltd v Hubbard** [1967] **2** 622, Ch D.
      Claim against third party—Relief or remedy relating to or connected with original subject matter of action—Relief or remedy substantially the same as some relief or remedy claimed by the plaintiff—Substantially the same relief—Claim for damages by plaintiff and by defendants against third party—Damages claimed on different grounds—Purpose of third party claim to determine who should ultimately bear loss—Whether relief claimed 'substantially the same'—RSC Ord 16, r 1(1)(b). **Myers v N & J Sherick Ltd** [1974] **1** 81, Ch D.
      Insurer—Action for damages for personal injuries—Personal injuries caused by motor car—Trial by judge alone—Whether defendants can add insurance company as a defendant—Repudiation of liability under the policy by insurance company—RSC Ord 16A, r 1. **Harman v Crilly** [1943] **1** 140, CA.
      Insurer—Action for damages for personal injuries—Personal injuries caused by motor car—Whether plaintiff can add defendant's insurance company as a defendant—RSC Ord 19, r 27. **Carpenter v Ebblewhite** [1938] **4** 41, CA.

PRACTICE (cont)—
  Third party procedure (cont)—
    Notice (cont)—
      Setting aside—Specific performance action on agreement for sublease for 21 years of part of land
        on which plaintiffs were erecting multi-storey car park and filling station—Subsequent agreement
        by defendants for underlease to third parties of multi-storey car park—Defendants issued third
        party notice for specific performance of agreement for underlease to third parties—Whether relief
        claimed against third parties substantially the same as relief claimed by plaintiff against the
        defendants—Whether third party notice should be set aside—RSC Ord 16, r 1(1)(b). **Chatsworth**
        Investments Ltd v Amoco (UK) Ltd [1968] **3** 357, CA.
      Summons for third party directions. *See* Third party notice—Summons for third party directions,
      above.
  Third party proceedings—
    Contribution. *See* **Contribution** (Third party proceedings).
    Crown, against. *See* **Crown** (Proceedings against—Third party proceedings).
    Defence—
      Illegality—Action by plaintiff against defendant based on conspiracy and fraud—Defendant issuing
        third party notice against plaintiff's accountant alleging negligence and breach of contract and
        claiming contribution in respect of damages if payable—Third party applying to have notice
        struck out—Whether illegality a valid defence to claim for contribution—Civil Liability
        (Contribution) Act 1978, ss 1(1), 2(1), (2), 6(1). **K v P (J, third party)** [1993] **1** 521, Ch D.
    Dismissal for want of prosecution—
      Inordinate and inexcusable delay—Four years between third party notice and summons for
        directions—Delay arising from plaintiffs' delay—Delay in action also by defendants—Defendants'
        need to be able to apply to strike out plaintiffs' action. **Slade & Kempton (Jewellery) Ltd v**
        Kayman (N) Ltd (Leroy, third party) [1969] **3** 786, CA.
    Originating motion—
      Whether proceedings begun by originating motion can be treated as third party proceedings—RSC
        Ord 16. **Aiden Shipping Co Ltd v Interbulk Ltd** [1985] **3** 641, CA.
    Security for costs. *See* **Costs** (Security for costs—Third party proceedings).
    Settlement between plaintiff and defendant—
      Effect—Whether third party proceedings barred by settlement. **Stott v West Yorkshire Road Car Co**
        Ltd [1971] **3** 534, CA.
  Time—
    Generally. *See* **Time.**
    Overriding time limit—
      Personal injury or fatal accident claim. *See* **Limitation of action** (Court's power to override time
        limit in personal injury or fatal accident claim—Practice).
  Title of proceedings—
    Appeal to House of Lords. *See* **House of Lords** (Leave to appeal—Petition for leave to appeal—Case
      title).
    Application for injunction—
      Grant of injunction before issue of originating process. **N (infants), Re** [1967] **1** 161, Ch D.
    Bankruptcy. *See* **Bankruptcy** (Practice—Title of proceedings).
    Chancery Division—
      Approved methods. **Practice Note** [1959] **2** 629, Ch D.
      Multiple plaintiffs or defendants—Approved method. **Brickman's Settlement, Re** [1982] **1** 336, Ch D.
    General rule—
      Exceptions. **Practice Direction** [1983] **1** 131, Ch D.
    Trustees—
      Individuals' names. **Routh Trustees v Central Land Board** [1960] **2** 436, CA.
  Tomlin order. *See* Compromise of action—Consent order—Order in Tomlin form, *above.*
  Track allocation—
    Re-allocation order—
      Variation or revocation. *See* Order—Power to vary or revoke orders—Costs—Allocation to
        particular track—Re-allocation, *above.*
  Transcripts—
    Admissibility in evidence—
      Transcript of criminal proceedings—Whether admissible in subsequent civil proceedings. *See*
        Document (Admissibility in evidence—Transcript of criminal proceedings).
    Cost of—
      Appeal to Court of Appeal. *See* **Costs** (Appeal to Court of Appeal—Shorthand transcript of evidence
        at trial—Cost of transcript).
    Court of Appeal. *See* **Court of Appeal** (Practice—Transcripts).
    Legal aid. *See* **Legal aid** (Costs—Transcript).
  Transfer of action—
    Action assigned to Chancery Division—
      Whether action should be transferred to Court of Chancery of Lancaster—Court of Chancery of
        Lancaster Act 1952, s 1. **Fullerton v Ryman** [1956] **2** 232, Ch D.
    Commercial Court, to. *See* **Commercial Court** (Practice—Summons—Summons for transfer of action).
    County court. *See* **County court** (Transfer of action).
    Employment tribunal. *See* **Employment tribunal** (Jurisdiction—Case management).
    High Court to county court. *See* **County court** (Transfer of action—Transfer from High Court).
    Transfer of action commenced in district registry to London—
      Defendant's right to have proceedings removed to London—RSC Ord 5, rr 1, 2—RSC Ord 12, rr 4, 6,
        7, Ord 35, rr 13, 14, 15, 16, 17, Ord 36, rr 1, 10. **Pooley v Bryning** [1940] **2** 377, CA.
  Transfer of cause or matter—
    Chancery Division—
      Transfer from one group of judges to another. *See* Chancery Division—Transfer of cause or matter
        from one group of judges to another, *above.*
  Transfer of defence bond—
    Transfer on death of holder. *See* **Defence bond** (Transfer—Transfer on death of holder).

PRACTICE (cont)—

Transfer of proceedings between Divisions of High Court—

  Husband and wife—

    Action by wife in Queen's Bench Division for arrears under maintenance agreement—Divorce and related proceedings started by husband in Family Division—Divorce petition defended by wife—Application by wife for summary judgment in Queen's Bench action—No procedure for obtaining summary judgment in Family Division proceedings—Financial rights and obligations of parties in issue in Family Division proceedings—Whether Queen's Bench action should be transferred to Family Division to be tried with other issues. **Temple v Temple** [1976] **3** 12, CA.

  Jury trial available as of right in action begun in Queen's Bench Division where fraud in issue—

    Action begun in Chancery Division including allegation of fraud—Whether right to have action transferred to Queen's Bench Division to obtain jury trial—Whether fraud in issue—Whether court should exercise discretion to transfer action—Administration of Justice (Miscellaneous Provisions) Act 1933, s 6(1). **Stafford Winfield Cook & Partners Ltd v Winfield** [1980] **3** 759, Ch D.

  Transfer sought to obtain speedier trial—

    Procedure—What claimant for transfer must show—How transfer should be effected. **Barclays Bank plc v Bemister** [1989] **1** 10, CA.

Transfer of proceedings between High Court and county court—

  Bankruptcy. *See* **Bankruptcy** (Application—Service—Transfer of proceedings).

  Family business and family proceedings—

    Actions suitable for transfer—Cases involving issues of complexity, difficulty or gravity unless undue delay or hardship would result from transfer—Question whether undue delay or hardship would result to be decided by county court not High Court—Discretion of county court to remained siesed of case when issues straightforward, easy and lightweight—Matrimonial and Family Proceedings Act 1984, ss 37, 39. **N and L (minors) (adoption proceedings: venue), Re** [1987] **2** 732, CA.

    Proceedings which may and may not be transferred—Adoption Act 1968, s 6—Guardianship of Minors Act 1971, s 15(3)—Matrimonial Causes Act 1973, ss 1(2)(e), 5, 19, 45(1)—Domicile and Matrimonial Proceedings Act 1973, s 5(6)—Children Act 1975, ss 14, 24—Matrimonial and Family Proceedings Act 1984, Pt III (ss 12-27), ss 37, 38, 39. **Practice Direction** [1987] **1** 1087, Fam D.

    Proceedings which may and may not be transferred—Guardianship of Minors Act 1971, s 15(3)—Matrimonial Causes Act 1973, ss 1(2)(e), 5, 19, 45(1)—Domicile and Matrimonial Proceedings Act 1973, s 5(6)—Adoption Act 1976, ss 17, 18, 53—Matrimonial and Family Proceedings Act 1984, Pt III (ss 12-27), 37, 38, 39—Family Law Act 1986, Pt I (ss 1-43), Pt III (ss 55-63). **Practice Direction** [1988] **2** 103, Fam D.

    Proceedings which may and may not be transferred—Matrimonial Causes Act 1973, ss 1(2)(e), 5, 19—Domicile and Matrimonial Proceedings Act 1973, s 5(6)—Adoption Act 1976—Matrimonial and Family Proceedings Act 1984, Pt III (ss 12-27)—ss 37, 38, 39—Family Law Act 1986, Pt I (ss 1-43), Pt III (ss 55-63)—Children Act 1989—Children (Allocation of Proceedings) Order 1991. **Practice Direction** [1992] **3** 151, Fam D.

  Proceedings which must be in county court—

    Mortgagee possession actions—Possession summonses transferred from county court to High Court and consolidated with proceedings for repayment of loans—Possession orders made in consolidated proceedings—Whether High Court having jurisdiction to make possession orders—Whether proceedings should have been deconsolidated and possession actions transferred back to county court before possession orders made—Whether borrowers requiring leave to appeal to extend grounds of appeal in relation to money judgments—County Courts Act 1984, ss 21(3), 42—Courts and Legal Services Act 1990, s 1—High Court and County Courts Jurisdiction Order 1991. **Yorkshire Bank plc v Hall** [1999] **1** 879, CA.

    Proceedings which may be transferred to county court—Review by court after setting down—Objections—Choice of county court—Proceedings transferred to High Court—Criteria relevant to transfer—Suitability for High Court trial—Appeal—Hearing of action—Value of action—County Courts Act 1984, ss 40(1), (2), (3), (4), (8), 41(1), 42(2)—Courts and Legal Services Act 1990, s 2—RSC Ord 14—RSC (Amendment No 2) 1991—High Court and County Courts Jurisdiction Order 1991, art 7(1), (5). **Practice Direction** [1991] **3** 349, QBD.

Transfer of proceedings from or to the Technology and Construction Court—

  Case listed in Queen's Bench Division transferred to circuit judge authorised to hear cases in Technology and Construction Court but not general Queen's Bench cases—

    No order transferring case to Technology and Construction Court drawn up—Parties having no opportunity to be heard on transfer or consent to transfer—Whether lack of opportunity vitiating transfer—Whether fatal procedural error—CPR 3.10, PD 49C, para 2.2. **Fawdry & Co (a firm) v Murfitt (Lord Chancellor intervening)** [2003] **4** 60, CA.

Trial—

  Admiralty practice. *See* **Admiralty** (Practice).

  Cause list—

    Removal of case from cause list—Order obtained by defendants dismissing jury action against them for want of prosecution—Crown Office not notified of order so that case left in list and brought on for hearing—Duty of both parties' solicitors to notify Crown Office of order—Liability for costs thrown away—RSC Ord 36, r 29(6). **Williamson v British Boxing Board of Control (1929)** [1958] **2** 228, QBD.

    Short cause list. *See* Trial—Lists—Short cause list, *below.*

    Solicitor's duty—Information to clerk of lists—Watching lists—Attendance at trial—Payment by solicitor personally of costs thrown away by non-attendance. **Practice Note** [1962] **1** 768, QBD.

  Clergyman—

    Ecclesiastical offence. *See* **Ecclesiastical law** (Clergyman—Offence—Trial).

  Continuance of postponed hearing—

    Trial resumed before a different judge after two years' interval—No evidence called before second judge—Judgment given by reference to recorded notes of first judge—Trengganu Civil Procedure Code, s 75. **Chua Chee Chor v Chua Kim Yong** [1963] **1** 102, PC.

  Court-martial. *See* **Court-martial** (Trial).

  Criminal proceedings. *See* **Criminal law** (Trial).

  Date for trial—

    Altering fixed date for non-jury actions. **Practice Direction** [1958] **3** 678, QBD.

PRACTICE (cont)—
   Trial (cont)—
      Date for trial (cont)—
         Commercial Court. *See* **Commercial Court** (Practice—Date for hearing).
         Fixing date for non-jury actions. **Practice Direction** [1957] 2 97, QBD.
         Postponing date for trial—Unavoidable delay caused by case being only partially prepared—
            Plaintiffs and defendants agreeing to postpone hearing—Test to be applied in determining
            whether trial should be postponed—Orders for costs where delay due to failure of parties or their
            legal advisers. **Boyle v Ford Motor Co Ltd** [1992] 2 228, CA.
         Postponing date of trial of non-jury actions. **Practice Direction** [1957] 1 422, QBD.
      Departure from case originally pleaded—
         Employers' liability established on same ground of fault as alleged by pursuer, but on state of fact
            averred by defenders—No such radical departure from the case averred by pursuer as would
            justify absolving employers from liability—Breach of statutory duty under Mines and Quarries
            Act 1954, s 48(1). **Stein (John G) & Co Ltd v O'Hanlon** [1965] 1 547, HL.
         Particulars of negligence—Finding against plaintiff on facts pleaded—Finding in favour of plaintiff
            on facts not pleaded—Order for new trial. **Lloyde v West Midlands Gas Board** [1971] 2 1240, CA.
         Pleaded negligence irrelevant in view of facts established—Such radical departure from case
            averred by plaintiff as to justify absolving defendants from liability—No evidence satisfying court
            of defendants' negligence on facts established. **Waghorn v George Wimpey & Co Ltd**
            [1970] 1 474, QBD.
      Estimate of length of trial—
         Certificate of counsel—Northern area listing of Chancery cases—Necessity for case to be ready for
            date fixed—Procedure for vacating allotted dates. **Practice Direction** [1980] 3 831, Ch D.
         Certificate of counsel—Summons adjourned for hearing with witnesses. **Practice Direction**
            [1963] 1 766, Ch D.
         Duty of solicitors—Substantial error in estimate—Transfer of case from short non-jury list to long
            non-jury list—Solicitors of both parties ordered to pay costs thrown away—RSC Ord 36, r 29(6).
            Ibbs v Holloway Bros Ltd [1952] 1 220, KBD.
         Family Division. *See* Family Division—Estimated length of hearing, *above*.
         Joint responsibility of counsel, counsel's clerk and solicitors to tell Clerk of the List of estimated
            length of trial of case in warned list—RSC Ord 36, r 9(2). **Practice Note** [1959] 1 576, PDA.
         Jury trial—Civil actions—Need for estimate to be realistic. **Practice Direction** [1981] 2 775, QBD.
      Evidence—
         Evidence taken before court examiner prior to trial of action—Order by master that evidence of
            witness be so taken and filed and that copy may be read and given in evidence on the
            trial—Whether evidence so taken becomes per se evidence in the trial—RSC Ord 37, r 5(1), 18.
            Fisher v CHT Ltd [1965] 2 601, QBD.
         Power of court to order party to civil suit to attend to give evidence. **Fallon v Calvert** [1960] 1 281,
            CA.
      Jury trial—
         County court. *See* **County court** (Trial by jury).
         Generally. *See* Trial—Trial by jury, *below*.
      Lists—
         Procedure—Lists to be kept by Clerk of the Lists. **Practice Direction** [1957] 1 219, QBD.
         Short cause list—Cases suitable for. **Dott v Brown** [1936] 1 543, CA.
         Short cause list—Estimated time for hearing—Action for trial in London—Time estimated for trial
            not exceeding four hours. **Practice Direction** [1977] 3 122, Fam D.
      Matrimonial causes. *See* Matrimonial causes—Trial, *above*.
      Mode of trial—
         Application as to mode of trial—Time when application must be made—Discretion of court to vary
            mode of trial—Action against police for false imprisonment and malicious prosecution—Order on
            summons for directions that trial of action be by judge alone—Plaintiff subsequently applying for
            trial by a judge and jury—Whether mode of trial 'fixed' on summons for directions—Whether
            time for making application as to mode of trial can be extended—Whether court having discretion
            to order that action be tried with jury—Supreme Court Act 1981, s 69—RSC Ord 3, r 5—RSC
            Ord 33, rr 4(1), 5(1). **Cropper v Chief Constable of South Yorkshire Police** [1990] 2 1005, CA.
         Application as to mode of trial—Time when application must be made—Discretion of court to vary
            mode of trial—Libel action—Trial requiring prolonged examination of documents or
            accounts—Trial by judge alone—Application for trial by judge alone—When application should be
            made—Discretion of court to consider application after place and mode of trial has been
            fixed—Supreme Court Act 1981, s 69—RSC Ord 33, rr 4, 5. **Beta Construction Ltd v Channel Four
            Television Co Ltd** [1990] 2 1012, CA.
      No case to answer—
         Submission of. *See* No case to answer, *above*.
      Notice and entry of trial—
         Inspection of documents not completed. **Southey-Roberts Estates Ltd v Roe** [1956] 2 829, Ch D.
      Order for early trial—
         Date of trial in discretion of judge in charge of list—RSC Ord 36, r 1A(1)(c). **Baron v Baron**
            [1952] 2 689, CA.
         Order on summons for directions. **Practice Direction** [1958] 3 678, QBD.
         Pleadings not closed—Inherent jurisdiction—Order that action be set down for trial in Part 1 of list,
            fixing date, and certifying speedy trial—RSC Ord 34, r 2(1). **Austin v Wildig** [1969] 1 99, Ch D.
         Summons for directions adjourned from judge to master—Documents to be lodged with master's
            summons clerk. **Practice Direction** [1979] 1 364, Ch D.
      Party acting in person—
         Right to assistance—McKenzie friend—Scope of right to assistance—Guidance. **Practice Guidance:
            McKenzie Friends (Civil and Family Courts)** [2010] 4 272, JC.
         Right to assistance—Refusal of right—Effect of refusal. **McKenzie v McKenzie** [1970] 3 1034, CA.
         Right to assistance—Right of friend to assist by attendance, note-taking and advice. **McKenzie v
            McKenzie** [1970] 3 1034, CA.

PRACTICE (cont)—
Trial (cont)—
    Party acting in person (cont)—
        Right to assistance—Right of friend to assist by attendance, note-taking and advice—Refusal of right by justices—Whether defendant entitled to assistance of 'McKenzie friend' as of right—Whether justices having discretion to refuse assistance of 'McKenzie friend'. **R v Leicester City Justices, ex p Barrow** [1991] **2** 437, QBD.
        Right to assistance—Right of friend to assist by attendance, note-taking and advice—Refusal of right by justices—Whether litigant in person entitled to assistance of another member of public as of right—Whether justices having discretion to refuse assistance of another member of public to litigant in person. **R v Leicester City Justices, ex p Barrow** [1991] **3** 935, CA.
    Patent action—
        Preparation for trial. *See* **Patent** (Practice—Preparation for trial).
    Place of trial—
        Adjournment of trial—Adjournment to such place as court thinks fit—Witness—Examination—Witness too infirm to travel to London—Witness fit to be examined at village where she lived—Village not a place authorised for trial of proceedings in Chancery Division—Power of court to adjourn trial to village for purpose of hearing witness's testimony—RSC Ord 33, r 1, Ord 35, r 3. **St Edmundsbury and Ipswich Diocesan Board of Finance v Clark** [1973] **2** 1155, Ch D. London. **Practice Direction** [1965] **1** 899, QBD.
    Recovery of debt or damages—
        Summary judgment. *See* Summary judgment—Action for recovery of debt or damages—Proceedings tried in Court of record for recovery of debt or damages, *above*.
    Separate trials—
        Action begun by writ—Different questions—Trial of one or more questions before others—Liability and damages—Claim for personal injuries—Trial of issue of liability before trial of issue of damages—Circumstances in which order for separate trials should be made—Just and convenient—Time and expense involved in trying issue of damages—RSC Ord 33, r 4(2). **Coenen v Payne** [1974] **2** 1109, CA.
        Issues of liability and damages—Separation of issues—Action for damages for breach of contract—Trial of liability separated from questions of amount of damages—No clear division of issues on pleadings—RSC Ord 36, r 7. **Polskie Towarzystwo Handlu Zagranicznego Dla Elektrotechniki 'Elektrim' Spolka Z Ograniczona Odpowiadziolnoscia v Electric Furnace Co Ltd** [1956] **2** 306, CA.
        Third party's counterclaim. *See* Third party procedure—Claims and issues between defendant and another party—Counterclaim by third party, a defendant in the action, *above*.
    Setting down action—
        Chancery Division—Direction by master or district registrar—Direction to solicitor to supply timetable giving dates of steps taken in action and master or district registrar's estimate of length of trial. **Practice Direction** [1977] **1** 543, Ch D.
        Queen's Bench Division—Setting down action for new trial—Setting down after time ordered has expired—Leave of court or consent of defendant no longer required—RSC Ord 3, r 6, Ord 34, r 2. **Practice Direction** [1979] **3** 193, QBD.
        Setting down action for new trial—Jury action—Jury having disagreed at original hearing. **Davidson v Rodwell** [1955] **2** 499, QBD.
        Setting down action for new trial—Queen's Bench Division—Setting down after time ordered has expired. **Practice Direction** [1964] **3** 496, QBD.
        Setting down action for new trial—Queen's Bench Division—Setting down after time ordered has expired—Leave of court required—RSC Ord 3, r 6, Ord 25, r 8, Ord 34, r 2(1), (2). **Practice Direction** [1996] **4** 224, QBD.
        Setting down action for trial in London—Lists—Administrative provisions. **Practice Direction** [1981] **3** 61, QBD.
        Setting down action for trial in Middlesex—Lists—Applications concerning dates for trial. **Practice Direction** [1958] **3** 678, QBD.
        Trial out of London. *See* Trial—Trial out of London—Setting down action, *below*.
    Speeches—
        Criminal proceedings. *See* **Criminal law** (Trial—Speeches).
        Order of speeches—Party to begin—Discretion of judge to give special directions as to party to begin—Probate action—Discretion unfettered—No rule of practice that party setting up last will should begin—Defendant setting up last will—Whether there should be a special direction that the defendant should begin depending on the facts of the particular case—RSC Ord 35, r 7(1). **Parry (decd), Re the Estate of** [1977] **1** 309, Ch D.
        Order of speeches—Right to last speech—Defendant leading documentary evidence when cross-examining plaintiff's witnesses but calling no witnesses—Whether defendant has right to last speech. **Weller v O'Brien** [1962] **3** 65, QBD.
    Submission of no case—
        Election—Negligence—No case to answer—Whether defendant submitting no case should be put to his election. **Storey v Storey** [1960] **3** 279, CA.
        Rejection of submission—Appeal against rejection. *See* No case to answer—Rejection of submission—Appeal against rejection of submission, *above*.
        Time for ruling on submission. *See* No case to answer—Time for ruling on submission, *above*.
        Time to make submission—Power of judge to enter judgment on case as whole—RSC Ord 36, r 39. **Grinsted v Hadrill** [1953] **1** 1188, CA.
    Summary trial. *See* **Magistrates** (Summary trial).
    Trial by jury—
        County court. *See* **County court** (Trial by jury).
        Discretion of court—Factors to be considered—Action for damages against solicitor—Plaintiff making detailed allegations of professional negligence against solicitor—Solicitor denying allegations—Plaintiff seeking trial by judge and jury—Plaintiff fearing judges would be prejudiced in favour of lawyers and so biased against him—Extent to which issues of credibility, integrity and honour relevant in determining mode of trial—Whether court to take into account plaintiff's fears of possible bias—Administration of Justice (Miscellaneous Provisions) Act 1933, s 6(1). **Williams v Beesley** [1973] **3** 144, HL.

PRACTICE (cont)—
  Trial (cont)—
    Trial by jury (cont)—
      Fraud—Charge of fraud alleged to be in issue—Defendant convicted of robbery of bank—Action by
        bank against defendant for money had and received through robbery—Whether defendant
        entitled to trial with a jury—Whether robbery 'fraud'—Whether action should be directed to be
        tried with a jury as a matter of discretion—Administration of Justice (Miscellaneous Provisions)
        Act 1933, s 6(1)(a). **Barclays Bank Ltd v Cole** [1966] 3 948, CA.
      Libel—Generally. *See* **Jury** (Trial by jury—Libel).
      Libel—Trial of action requiring prolonged examination of documents or accounts—Trial by judge
        alone—Discretion of court to order trial by jury even if prolonged examination of documents
        likely—Libel alleging illegal share dealings by public figure—Prolonged examination of
        documents likely—Whether trial should be by jury or judge alone—Supreme Court Act 1981,
        s 69(1), (3). **Goldsmith v Pressdram Ltd (1984)** [1987] 3 485, CA.
      Libel—Trial of action requiring prolonged examination of documents or accounts—Trial by judge
        alone—Multiple plaintiffs—Split trial—Complexity of documents in case likely to add to length
        and cost of trial—Action brought by one plaintiff requiring prolonged examination of documents
        or accounts—Whether action brought by other plaintiff should be heard as separate
        action—Supreme Court Act 1981, s 69. **Beta Construction Ltd v Channel Four Television Co Ltd**
        [1990] 2 1012, CA.
      Libel—Trial of action requiring prolonged examination of documents or accounts—Whether
        administration of justice would suffer if trial was with a jury—Whether judge having discretion to
        order trial by judge alone—Supreme Court Act 1981, s 69(1), (3). **De L'Isle (Viscount) v Times**
        Newspapers Ltd [1987] 3 499, CA.
      Malicious prosecution, misfeasance in public office and conspiracy—Trial of action requiring
        prolonged examination of documents or accounts—Whether trial should be by jury or judge
        alone—Whether examination could 'conveniently' be made with a jury—Supreme Court Act 1981,
        s 69(1), (3). **Taylor v Anderton (Police Complaints Authority intervening)** [1995] 2 420, CA.
      Non-commercial case—Application for City of London special jury—Application to be made to
        master. **Hagen v National Provincial Bank Ltd** [1937] 3 617, CA.
      Personal injuries claim—Negligent medical treatment necessitating penectomy—Claim for
        compensatory damages—Defendant admitting liability—Whether case falling into exceptional
        category where jury trial appropriate—Supreme Court Act 1981, s 69(1), (3)—RSC Ord 33, r 5(1). **H**
        v Ministry of Defence [1991] 2 834, CA.
      Slander—Application for trial with jury—Second defendant added when action part heard without a
        jury—Application by second defendant for a jury—Administration of Justice (Miscellaneous
        Provisions) Act 1933 s 6—RSC Ord 36, r 1. **Salvalene Lubricants Ltd v Darby** [1938] 1 224, CA.
  Trial out of London—
    Date—Fixturey of date—Certificate of readiness for trial. **Practice Direction** [1972] 1 287, QBD.
    Setting down action—Readiness for trial—Statement to be lodged with pleadings—Trial
      dates—Adjournments etc—RSC Ord 34, rr 5(3), 8(2). **Practice Note** [1987] 2 1039, QBD.
  Trial without pleadings—
    Election to proceed—Procedure for summary judgment not a concurrent remedy—RSC Ord 14,
      r 1(a), Ord 14B, r 1. **Customs and Excise Comrs v Anco Plant & Machinery Co Ltd** [1956] 3 59, CA.
  Witnesses. *See* **Witness**.
  Tribunal. *See* **Tribunal**.
  Trust—
    Chancery Division—
      Generally. *See* Chancery Division—Trusts, *above*.
    Generally. *See* **Trust and trustee** (Practice).
    Variation of trust—
      Generally. *See* **Variation of trusts** (Practice).
  Trust corporation—
    Grant of probate. *See* **Probate** (Grant—Trust corporation).
    Probate. *See* **Probate** (Practice—Trust corporation).
  Trustees—
    Severing defence—
      Separate representation. *See* **Trust and trustee** (Trustee's costs—Reimbursement of trustee—
        Contractual right—Breach of trust—Action dismissed—Severance of defence by trustees).
    Title of proceedings—
      Individual's names. *See* Title of proceedings—Trustees—Individuals' names, *above*.
  Uncontested proceedings—
    Crown Office list—
      Civil proceedings and criminal causes or matters—Disposal—Disposal without attendance—
        Interlocutory orders—Withdrawal of proceedings. **Practice Note** [1997] 2 799, QBD.
      Civil proceedings—Judicial review, cases stated, statutory appeals etc—Disposal—Disposal without
        attendance. **Practice Direction** [1982] 2 704, QBD.
      Criminal causes or matters—Disposal—Disposal without attendance. **Practice Note** [1983] 2 1020,
        QBD.
  'Unless' order. *See* Order—'Unless' orders and other peremptory orders, *below*.
  Variation of trusts—
    Generally. *See* **Variation of trusts** (Practice).
  Vexatious proceedings. *See* **Vexatious proceedings**.
  Video conferencing—
    Family Division. *See* Family Division—Video conferencing, *above*.
  Video link—
    Evidence through video link. *See* **Evidence** (Mode of giving evidence—Video link).
  View. *See* Inspection by judge, *above*.
  Wales—
    Crown Court practice. *See* **Crown Court** (Practice—Wales).
    Devolution issues. *See* Devolution issues—Wales, *above*.
  Want of prosecution—
    Arbitration. *See* **Arbitration** (Practice—Want of prosecution).

PRACTICE (cont)—
    Want of prosecution (cont)—
        Dismissal of action for. *See* Dismissal of action for want of prosecution, *above.*
        Dismissal of counterclaim for. *See* Dismissal of counterclaim for want of prosecution, *above.*
        Striking out for want of prosecution. *See* Crown Office list—Striking out for want of prosecution, *above.*
    Wardship proceedings. *See* **Ward of court** (Practice).
    Welsh language—
        Use in Welsh court. *See* **Crown Court** (Practice—Wales—Use of Welsh language).
    West Africa—
        Leave to appeal from high native tribunal. *See* **West Africa** (Practice—Appeal from high native tribunal—Leave to appeal).
    Will—
        Generally. *See* **Will.**
        Mental patient. *See* **Mental health** (Patient's property—Will).
    Withdrawal of appearance. *See* Appearance—Withdrawal of appearance, *above.*
    Withdrawal of payment into court. *See* Payment into court—Withdrawal of payment in, *above.*
    Withdrawal of solicitor. *See* **Solicitor** (Withdrawal).
    Without notice orders—
        Family Division. *See* Family Division—Without notice orders, *above.*
    Witness—
        Exchange of witnesses' statements. *See* **Evidence** (Exchange of witnesses' statements).
        Fees of medical inspectors—
            Nullity suit. *See* **Nullity** (Medical inspection—Fees).
        Generally. *See* **Witness.**
    Witness summons—
        Summons to produce documents to the court—
            Identification of documents—CPR 34.2. **Tajik Aluminium Plant v Hydro Aluminium AS** [2005] **4** 1232, CA; [2006] **2 Comm** 295, CA.
    Writ—
        Admiralty—
            Relief sought in rem and in personam. *See* **Admiralty** (Practice—Writ—Relief sought in rem and in personam).
        Extension of validity—
            Generally. *See* **Writ** (Extension of validity).
            Overriding time limit—Personal injury or fatal accident claim. *See* **Limitation of action** (Court's power to override time limit in personal injury or fatal accident claim—Practice—Application to extend validity of writ).
        Fi fa. *See* **Execution** (Writ of fi fa).
        Generally. *See* **Writ.**
        Renewal—
            Admiralty action in rem. *See* **Admiralty** (Practice—Action in rem—Writ—Renewal).
            Generally. *See* **Writ** (Extension of validity).
        Service—
            Bankruptcy proceedings—Service out of the jurisdiction. *See* **Bankruptcy** (Service—Service out of jurisdiction—Writ and motion).
            Foreign company. *See* **Company** (Foreign company—Writ—Service of writ on company).
            Generally. *See* Service, *above.*
            Oversea company. *See* **Company** (Oversea company—Service on oversea company).
            Partnership. *See* **Writ** (Service on partnership).
            Service out of jurisdiction. *See* Service out of the jurisdiction, *above.*
        Title of. *See* Parties—Description of parties, *above.*
        Writ of possession—
            Execution. *See* **Execution** (Possession—Writ of possession).

PRACTICE
    See Parties, *below.*

PRACTICE NOTES
    Construction—
        Practice notes issued by public authority. *See* **Statute** (Construction—Practice notes issued by public authority).

PRACTISING CERTIFICATE
    Solicitor—
        Generally. *See* **Solicitor** (Practising certificate).
        Lapse of partner's certificate—
            Dissolution of partnership. *See* **Solicitor** (Partnership—Dissolution—Lapse of practising certificate).

PRE-EMPTION
    Creation of interest in land—
        Option to purchase land—
            Option granted subsequently to grant of right of pre-emption. *See* **Option** (Pre-emption—Creation of interest in land—Option to purchase land granted subsequently to grant of right of pre-emption).
    Right of pre-emption—
        Creation of—
            Generally. *See* **Option** (Pre-emption).
            Will, by. *See* **Will** (Option).
        Implication of prohibition of making gift to defeat right. *See* **Contract** (Implied term—First refusal—Right of pre-emption—Gift of land, the subject of the right of pre-emption, made subsequently by grantor of right).
        Registration as land charge—
            Obligation affecting land. *See* **Land charge** (Registration—Obligation affecting land).

PRE-EMPTION (cont)—
 Right of pre-emption (cont)—
  Stock-in-trade—
   Computation of profits for income tax. *See* **Income tax** (Computation of profits—Stock-in-trade—
   Right of pre-emption).

PRE-TRIAL RELIEF
 Practice—
  Civil proceedings—
   Generally. *See* **Practice** (Pre-trial or post-judgment relief).

PRE-TRIAL REVIEW
 Criminal proceedings—
  Generally. *See* **Criminal law** (Trial—Pre-trial review).
  Plea-bargaining. *See* **Criminal law** (Trial—Plea—Plea-bargaining—Pre-trial review).
 Matrimonial causes—
  Defended causes—
   Directions for trial. *See* **Divorce** (Practice—Trial—Directions for trial—Defended causes—Pre-trial
   review).

PREAMBLE
 Construction of statute. *See* **Statute** (Construction—Preamble).

PRECEDENT
 Alteration to judgment by judge—
  Conflicting versions in different series of law reports—
   Inference that alteration recorded in Law Reports made by judge. **Buccleuch (Duke) v IRC**
   [1967] **1** 129, HL.
 Change of circumstances—
  Abrogation of rule embodied in precedent—
   Cessante ratione cessat ipsa lex—Whether justifying abrogation of rule embodied in binding
   precedent on ground that changed circumstances have nullified reason for rule—Whether limited
   to distinguishing a case as an exception to general rule. **Miliangos v George Frank (Textiles) Ltd**
   [1975] **3** 801, HL.
 Co-ordinate courts—
  Conflicting decisions—
   Stare decisis—Conflicting decisions of High Court—Earlier decision fully considered but not
   followed in later decision—Later decision normally to be considered as settling law at first
   instance—Exception where third judge convinced second judge wrong not to follow first.
   Colchester Estates (Cardiff) v Carlton Industries plc [1984] **2** 601, Ch D.
   Stare decisis—Divisional Court—Application for judicial review—Whether Divisional Court bound
   to follow earlier decision of another Divisional Court. **R v Greater Manchester Coroner, ex p Tal**
   [1984] **3** 240, QBD.
 Commonwealth country—
  Policy of law settled—
   House of Lords decision—Sphere of law where policy of the law largely determined by judicial
   opinion in the particular country—Law settled in country concerned—Libel—Exemplary
   damages—Whether decision of House of Lords, establishing differing law in England should be
   applied in Commonwealth country. **Australian Consolidated Press Ltd v Uren** [1967] **3** 523, PC.
 Court of Appeal—
  Binding effect of previous decisions of court—
   Power of court of first instance to depart from decision of Court of Appeal—Recent Court of Appeal
   decision—Possibility that House of Lords might reverse Court of Appeal decision—Whether court
   of first instance bound on interlocutory motion to apply law as stated by Court of Appeal. **Derby
   & Co Ltd v Weldon (No 3)** [1989] **3** 118, Ch D.
   Power of court to depart from previous decision—Authority of European Patent Office Boards of
   Appeal decisions—Exceptional circumstances—Patents—Whether Court of Appeal free to depart
   from ratio decidendi of own earlier decision if satisfied that European Patent Office Boards of
   Appeal having formed settled view of European patent law inconsistent with earlier decision.
   Actavis UK Ltd v Merck & Co Inc [2009] **1** 196, CA.
   Power of court to depart from previous decision—Decision given in ignorance of inconsistent
   statutory provision—Decision followed by another division of Court of Appeal—Inconsistent
   statutory provision not considered by other division—Whether either decision binding on Court
   of Appeal. **Rakhit v Carty** [1990] **2** 202, CA.
   Power of court to depart from previous decision—Exceptional circumstances in which court will
   depart from previous decision—Case unlikely to reach House of Lords and concerning liberty of
   subject. **Williams v Fawcett** [1985] **1** 787, CA.
   Power of court to depart from previous decision—House of Lords deciding appeal on different
   ground from that argued below—Whether Court of Appeal's decision in that case binding on
   another division of the Court of Appeal. **Al-Mehdawi v Secretary of State for the Home Dept**
   [1989] **1** 777, CA.
   Power of court to depart from previous decision—Power to add exceptions to general rule of stare
   decisis—Whether Court of Appeal entitled to depart from previous decision. **Davis v Johnson**
   [1978] **1** 1132, HL.
   Power of court to override own decisions. **Gallie v Lee** [1969] **1** 1062, CA.
   Reason which is not essential and necessary to a decision—Dicta—Whether court bound by reason
   which is not essential and necessary to a decision—Whether court entitled to disregard dicta of
   court of co-ordinate jurisdiction. **Norway's (State of) Application (No 2), Re** [1989] **1** 701, CA.
   Two-judge Court of Appeal—Whether two-judge court having same authority as three-judge court.
   Langley v North West Water Authority [1991] **3** 610, CA.
  Composition of court—
   Court composed of two Lords Justices—Interlocutory decision—Ratio decidendi not binding on
   Court of Appeal if wrong. **Chaplin v Boys** [1968] **1** 283, CA.

PRECEDENT (cont)—
  Court of Appeal (cont)—
    Composition of court (cont)—
      Criminal Division—Direction by court of three on exercise of discretion in sentencing not binding on later court of five. **R v Newsome** [1970] 3 455, CA.
      Full court—Full Court of Appeal has no greater power than division of the court—Decisions given per incuriam. **Young v Bristol Aeroplane Co Ltd** [1946] 1 98, HL.
    Conflicting decisions—
      Court of Appeal decisions disapproved by Privy Council—Liberty to depart from previous decisions. **Worcester Works Finance Ltd v Cooden Engineering Co Ltd** [1971] 3 708, CA.
      Court of Appeal decisions inconsistent with decision of House of Lords. **Fitzsimons v Ford Motor Co Ltd (Aero Engines)** [1946] 1 429, CA.
      Court of Appeal decisions inconsistent with general principles laid down by House of Lords. **Wilson v Chatterton** [1946] 1 431, CA.
      Decision of House of Lords conflicting with subsequent Privy Council decision—Privy Council decision deciding House of Lords decision wrongly decided—Whether Court of Appeal bound to follow House of Lords decision. **R v James** [2006] 1 759, CA.
      Duty of Court of Appeal to choose between earlier conflicting decisions. **Tiverton Estates Ltd v Wearwell Ltd** [1974] 1 209, CA.
      House of Lords decisions—Two reasons given—Whether both binding if the House of Lords should subsequently find one to be wrong. **Holmden's Settlement Trusts, Re** [1966] 2 661, CA.
      Majority and unanimous decisions conflicting. **Ross Smith v Ross Smith (orse Radford)** [1962] 1 344, HL.
    Criminal Division—
      Doctrine of stare decisis not applied with same rigidity as in Civil Division of Court of Appeal—Extent of discretion. **R v Varma** [2011] 2 935, CA.
      Doctrine of stare decisis not applied with the same rigidity as in Civil Division of Court of Appeal. **R v Gould** [1968] 1 849, CA; **R v Simpson** [2003] 3 531, CA.
    Decision per incuriam—
      Application of doctrine—Circumstances in which doctrine applying—Whether doctrine applying where court in earlier case might have reached different conclusion if different arguments or material had been placed before it. **Duke v GEC Reliance Ltd** [1987] 2 858, CA.
      Court in previous case having construed statute in sense which words cannot bear—Words of statute capable of only one meaning—Whether Court of Appeal bound to follow previous decision even though plainly wrong. **Farrell v Alexander** [1976] 1 129, CA.
      Previous decision of Court of Appeal—Application of doctrine. **DN (Rwanda) v Secretary of State for the Home Dept** [2018] 3 772, CA.
      Previous decision of Court of Appeal—Authority not fully reported in law report cited to court in earlier case—Full report of authority cited—Whether decision in earlier case binding on Court of Appeal in subsequent case. **Industrial Properties (Barton Hill) Ltd v Associated Electrical Industries Ltd** [1977] 2 293, CA.
    Divisional Court interpreting statutory provisions—
      Repeal and re-enactment of provisions—Extent to which Court of Appeal bound by earlier interpretation. **Royal Crown Derby Porcelain Co Ltd v Russell** [1949] 1 749, CA.
    Ex parte decision—
      Whether ex parte decision of Court of Appeal binding on High Court. **Amanuel v Alexandros Shipping Co** [1986] 1 278, QBD.
    House of Lords decision misinterpreted—
      Binding effect—Whether later Court of Appeal bound by decision of first Court of Appeal. **Williams v Glasbrook Bros Ltd** [1947] 2 884, CA.
    House of Lords decision per incuriam—
      Whether Court of Appeal bound to follow decision. **Cassell & Co Ltd v Broome** [1972] 1 801, HL.
    House of Lords majority decision—
      No discernible ratio decidendi common to majority speeches—Reasoning of House of Lords not binding—Court of Appeal free to adopt reasoning which appears to it to be correct—Court of Appeal bound to adopt reasoning which supports House of Lords decision. **Harper v National Coal Board** [1974] 2 441, CA.
    New Zealand. *See* New Zealand Court of Appeal, *below.*
    West Indies Associated States. *See* West Indies Associated States Court of Appeal, *below.*
  Damages—
    Similar cases—
      Discretion of judge to consider. **Waldon v War Office** [1956] 1 108, CA.
  Decision per incuriam—
    Circumstances in which decision regarded as given per incuriam—
      Deficiency of parties. **Morelle Ltd v Wakeling** [1955] 1 708, CA.
      Not all relevant authorities cited—Only one party represented—Whether grounds for treating decision as having been given per incuriam. **Miliangos v George Frank (Textiles) Ltd** [1975] 1 1076, CA.
    Court of Appeal. *See* Court of Appeal—Decision per incuriam, *above.*
  High Court—
    Upper Tribunal—
      Stare decisis—Whether Upper Tribunal bound by decision of High Court. **Gilchrist (as trustee of the JP Gilchrist 1993 Settlement) v Revenue and Customs Comrs** [2014] 4 943, UT.
  House of Lords—
    Appeal Committee—
      Grant or refusal of leave to appeal—Effect—Grant or refusal not implying disapproval or approval of judgment below. **Wilson v Colchester Justices** [1985] 2 97, HL.
    Committee for Privileges—
      Claim to peerage—Findings—Whether findings of committee adopted by House in earlier claim binding on committee in later claim. **Annandale and Hartfell Peerage Claim** [1985] 3 577, HL.

PRECEDENT (cont)—
  House of Lords (cont)—
    Conflicting decisions—
      Successful argument in later case not considered in earlier case—House of Lords satisfied that earlier case would have been decided differently if successful argument in later case had been argued in earlier case—Whether House of Lords should ignore earlier decision and follow later decision. **Moodie v IRC** [1993] **2** 49, HL.
    Decision of European Court of Human Rights inconsistent with previous decision of the House—
      Whether appropriate for House of Lords to depart from previous decision of the House. **Lambeth London BC v Kay** [2006] **4** 128, HL.
    Freedom to depart from own decisions—
      Circumstances in which House will not review previous decision. **Food Corp of India v Antclizo Shipping Corp** [1988] **2** 513, HL.
      Claimant issuing proceedings in respect of personal injuries before ordinary time limit expiring—Claimant subsequently bringing second action after expiry of time limit—House of Lords authority precluding discretion to disapply time limit in such circumstances—Whether House of Lords to depart from previous authority. **Horton v Sadler** [2006] **3** 1177, HL.
      Construction of statute. **Jones v Secretary of State for Social Services** [1972] **1** 145, HL.
      Criminal law—Need for certainty as to criminal law—Previous decision establishing existence of offence—Not appropriate to reconsider decision where effect would be to abolish offence. **Knuller (Publishing, Printing and Promotions) Ltd v DPP** [1972] **2** 898, HL.
      Grounds on which proper to depart from previous decision—Appellant contending that previous decision wrong—Income tax appeal—Whether proper to depart from previous decision merely on ground differently constituted committee of House thinks it wrong—Whether necessary to show some other ground justifying departure from previous decision. **Fitzleet Estates Ltd v Cherry (Inspector of Taxes)** [1977] **3** 996, HL.
      Recent decision—Whether appropriate for House of Lords to depart from recent decision of the House. **R v Kansal (No 2)** [2002] **1** 257, HL.
      Stare decisis an indispensable foundation of decisions of law. **Practice Direction** [1966] **3** 77, HL.
    House of Lords' decisions—
      Misinterpretation—Effect. *See* Court of Appeal—House of Lords decision misinterpreted, *above.*
      Own decision indistinguishable on facts need not be followed. **Chancery Lane Safe Deposit and Offices Co Ltd v IRC** [1966] **1** 1, HL.
      Privy Council and. *See* Privy Council—House of Lords decision, *below.*
      Supreme Court. *See* Supreme Court—Freedom to depart from decisions of House of Lords, *below.*
      When ratio decidendi binding on House of Lords. **Scruttons Ltd v Midland Silicones Ltd** [1962] **1** 1, HL.
    Long standing decisions. *See* Long-standing decisions—Construction of statute—House of Lords, *below.*
  International law—
    Rules of international law which form part of English law—
      Doctrine of stare decisis. *See* **International law** (Enforcement by English courts—Rules of international law which form part of English law—Doctrine of stare decicis).
  Long-standing decisions—
    Construction of statute—
      Decisions of Divisional Court overruled after standing for substantial period of time. **Brownsea Haven Properties Ltd v Poole Corp** [1958] **1** 205, CA.
      Enactment subsequently repealed and replaced. **R v Bow Road Domestic Proceedings Court, ex p Adedigba** [1968] **2** 89, CA.
      House of Lords—Whether House should overrule decision on rating Act. **Campbell College Belfast (Governors) v Comr of Valuation for Northern Ireland** [1964] **2** 705, HL.
      Similar enactment—Whether Court of Appeal should follow decision on previous similar enactment if erroneous. **Yeovil Glove Co Ltd, Re** [1964] **2** 849, CA.
    Followed for many years—
      Whether House of Lords should overrule such a decision. **Ross Smith v Ross Smith (orse Radford)** [1962] **1** 344, HL.
    Public interest requiring that common law offence should be reasserted in its true form—
      Misconception standing for over a century corrected. **Button v DPP** [1965] **3** 587, HL.
  National Industrial Relations Court—
    Decisions binding on court—
      Decisions of the Queen's Bench Divisional Court—Previous decisions of Industrial Court itself—Whether binding. **Chapman v Goonvean & Rostowrack China Clay Co Ltd** [1973] **1** 218, NIRC; **Secretary of State for Employment v Atkins Auto Laundries Ltd** [1972] **1** 987, NIRC.
  New Zealand Court of Appeal—
    Departure from decision of English Court of Appeal—
      Whether New Zealand Court of Appeal free to review English Court of Appeal authority and to depart from it if considered wrong. **A-G for Hong Kong v Reid** [1994] **1** 1, PC.
    Development of common law—
      Negligence—Court of Appeal not following House of Lords—Whether New Zealand Court of Appeal entitled to develop common law according to local policy considerations. **Invercargill City Council v Hamlin** [1996] **1** 756, PC.
  Overruling of previous authority—
    Declaratory theory of law—
      Retrospective effect of overruling previous authority—Subsequent decision changing settled view of law. **Kleinwort Benson Ltd v Lincoln City Council** [1998] **4** 513, HL.
  Privy Council—
    Conflicting decisions—
      Stare decisis—Board having power to review decisions. **Hughes and Vale Pty Ltd v State of New South Wales (The Commonwealth of Australia, Intervener)** [1954] **3** 607, PC.

PRECEDENT (cont)—
  Privy Council (cont)—
    House of Lords decision—
      Decision on legislation common to England and a colony—Decision on common law applicable in
      colony—Hong Kong—House of Lords decision that no jurisdiction to re-open financial settlement
      between husband and wife achieved by consent order dismissing wife's application for
      relief—Whether decision binding on Hong Kong Court of Appeal—Whether House of Lords
      decision binding on Privy Council. **De Lasala v De Lasala** [1979] 2 1146, PC.
    Status of decisions in courts of England and Wales—
      House of Lords or Supreme Court decision conflicting with subsequent Privy Council
      decision—Whether Privy Council decision binding authority—Judicial Committee of the Privy
      Council Practice Direction, paras 3.1.3, 4.2.2. **Willers v Joyce (No 2)** [2017] 2 383, SC.
  Ratio decidendi—
    Binding effect of decision—
      Decision on alternative grounds—House of Lords decision on alternative claim for tort of causing
      loss by unlawful means—Whether binding precedent. **Secretary of State for Health v Servier
      Laboratories Ltd** [2020] 2 514, CA; [2022] 1 1, SC.
      Legal principles which are binding. **Ashville Investments Ltd v Elmer Contractors Ltd** [1988] 2 577,
      CA; **Hetherington (decd), Re** [1989] 2 129, Ch D.
      Matter necessary for decision only is binding. **Penn-Texas Corp v Murat Anstalt (No 2)** [1964] 2 594,
      CA.
    Decision on alternative grounds—
      Whether each ground constituting binding precedent. **Miliangos v George Frank (Textiles) Ltd**
      [1975] 1 1076, CA.
    Decision on more than one ground—
      Whether each ground binding. **Jacobs v London CC** [1950] 1 737, HL.
    Obiter dictum—
      Binding effect. **Behrens v Bertram Mills Circus Ltd** [1957] 1 583, QBD.
      Binding effect—Expression of general principle by Supreme Court—Whether binding on inferior
      courts. **R (on the application of Youngsam) v Parole Board** [2018] 1 800, QBD; [2019] 3 954, CA; **R
      v Lichniak** [2002] 4 1122, HL.
      Binding effect—Supreme Court—Obiter dicta with which all Supreme Court judges concurring—
      Supreme Court directing that otherwise binding authority of Court of Appeal should no longer be
      followed—Whether Court of Appeal bound by obiter dicta of Supreme Court or previous Court of
      Appeal decision. **R v Barton** [2020] 4 742, CA.
    Proposition of law forming part of ratio decidendi—
      Proposition assumed to be correct for purpose of disposing of case—Point of law not
      argued—Proposition forming part of decision. **Baker v R** [1975] 3 55, PC.
  Reasons for decision—
    Conclusions of fact—
      Reasons not propositions of law—Negligence—Reasons given by judge for coming to conclusions
      of fact not to be regarded as law. **Qualcast (Wolverhampton) Ltd v Haynes** [1959] 2 38, HL.
  Scottish decision—
    Conformity—
      Revenue and taxation matters—Practice to follow decisions of Scottish court. **Secretary of State for
      Employment and Productivity v Clarke Chapman & Co Ltd** [1971] 2 798, QBD.
      Road traffic decisions. **Daley v Hargreaves** [1961] 1 552, QBD.
    Scottish and English decisions conflicting—
      English decisions followed. **Kahn v Newberry** [1959] 2 202, QBD.
  Social security commissioners—
    Decisions binding on commissioners—
      Previous decision of High Court given when exercising jurisdiction subsequently conferred on
      commissioners—Whether such decision binding on commissioners—Tribunals and Inquiries Act
      1971, s 13—Tribunals and Inquiries (Supplementary Benefit Appeal Tribunals) Order
      1977—Tribunals and Inquiries (Supplementary Benefit Appeal Tribunals (Revocation)) Order 1980.
      Chief Supplementary Benefit Officer v Leary [1985] 1 1061, CA.
  Supreme Court—
    Freedom to depart from decisions of House of Lords—
      Appropriate date for calculation of damages for future loss in fatal accident claims—Whether
      departure from previous decisions appropriate. **Knauer v Ministry of Justice** [2016] 4 897, SC.
  West Indies Associated States Court of Appeal—
    Binding effect of previous decisions of court—
      Whether court bound by its previous decisions where appeal lies to Privy Council. **A-G of St
      Christopher, Nevis and Anguilla v Reynolds** [1979] 3 129, PC.

PRECIOUS METALS
  Hallmarking. *See* **Hallmarking**.

PREFERENTIAL PAYMENTS
  Company—
    Winding up. *See* **Company** (Winding up—Preferential payments).

PREGNANCY
  Abortion. *See* **Abortion**.
  Dismissal on grounds of pregnancy—
    Discrimination against a woman. *See* **Employment** (Discrimination against a woman—Dismissal
    because of pregnancy).
    European Community—
      Equality of treatment of men and women. *See* **European Union** (Equality of treatment of men and
      women—Equal working conditions—Dismissal—Dismissal because of pregnancy).
    Unfair dismissal. *See* **Unfair dismissal** (Dismissal—Pregnancy).

PREGNANCY (cont)—
  In vitro fertilisation—
    Dismissal—
      European Community. *See* **European Union** (Equality of treatment of men and women—Equal
        working conditions—Dismissal—Discriminatory dismissal—In vitro fertilisation).
  Nullity suit. *See* **Nullity** (Pregnancy at date of marriage by person other than petitioner).
  Termination—
    Legal abortion. *See* **Abortion** (Legal abortion).
    Offence. *See* **Criminal law** (Abortion).
  Unwanted pregnancy—
    Negligence—
      Damages. *See* **Damages** (Unwanted pregnancy—Negligence).
    Personal injury—
      Damages. *See* **Damages** (Personal injury—Unwanted pregnancy).
  Working conditions—
    Sex discrimination—
      European Community. *See* **European Union** (Equality of treatment of men and women—Working
        conditions—Pregnancy).

PREJUDICE
  Dismissal action for want of prosecution—
    Delay—
      Prejudice to defendant. *See* **Practice** (Dismissal of action for want of prosecution—Delay—Prejudice
        to defendant).
  Estoppel by representation—
    Prejudice suffered by party misled by representation. *See* **Estoppel** (Representation—Prejudice suffered
      by party misled by representation).
  Fraudulent conveyance—
    Setting aside conveyance on application of person prejudiced. *See* **Fraudulent conveyance** (Setting
      aside conveyance on application of person prejudiced).
  Termination—
    Abortion. *See* **Abortion**.

PRELIMINARY ENQUIRIES
  Sale of land—
    Generally. *See* **Sale of land** (Preliminary enquiries).
    Reply—
      Damages for breach of warranty. *See* **Sale of land** (Damages for breach of contract—Warranty—
        Reply to preliminary enquiry).

PRELIMINARY HEARING
  Magistrates. *See* **Criminal law** (Committal—Preliminary hearing before justices).

PRELIMINARY ISSUE
  Arbitration. *See* **Arbitration** (Preliminary question of law).
  Costs. *See* **Costs** (Preliminary issue).
  Generally. *See* **Practice** (Preliminary point of law).
  Matters appropriate to be considered as preliminary issue. *See* **Practice** (Preliminary point of law—Matters
    appropriate to be considered as preliminary issues).
  Rent tribunal—
    Jurisdiction. *See* **Rent tribunal** (Preliminary issue as to jurisdiction).

PRELIMINARY RULING
  European Community law—
    Interpretation. *See* **European Union** (Reference to European Court—Request for preliminary ruling
      concerning interpretation of Community law).

PREMIUM
  Clog on equity of redemption. *See* **Mortgage** (Collateral advantage—Premium).
  Illegal premium—
    Lease. *See* **Rent restriction** (Premium).
  Insurance—
    Generally. *See* **Insurance** (Premium).
    Income tax—
      Annual payment. *See* **Income tax** (Annual payment—Insurance premiums).
      Capital or income. *See* **Income tax** (Capital or income receipts—Insurance—Premiums).
    Life insurance. *See* **Insurance** (Life insurance—Premium).
    Reinsurance. *See* **Insurance** (Reinsurance—Premium).
  Lease—
    Agreement for lease. *See* **Landlord and tenant** (Agreement for lease—Premium).
    Rent restriction. *See* **Rent restriction** (Premium).
  Selective employment tax. *See* **Selective employment tax** (Premium).

PREMIUM TRUST DEED
  Society of Lloyd's. *See* **Insurance** (Society of Lloyd's—Premium trust deed).

PREPACKED GOODS
  Short weight and packaging. *See* **Weights and measures** (Prepacked goods—Short weight).

PREPARATORY HEARING
  Appeal—
    Disclosure of documents. *See* **Criminal law** (Trial—Preparatory hearing—Purposes of preparatory
      hearing—Powers of judge at preparatory hearing—Disclosure of prosecution documents).

PREPARATORY HEARING (cont)—
  Criminal trial—
    Generally. *See* **Criminal law** (Trial—Preparatory hearing).
    Generally. *See* **Criminal law** (Trial—Presence of accused).

PREROGATIVE
  Prerogative of mercy—
    Bahamas. *See* **Bahamas** (Prerogative of mercy).
    Judicial review—
      Availability of remedy. *See* **Judicial review** (Availability of remedy—Royal prerogative—Prerogative
      of mercy).
  Royal prerogative. *See* **Crown** (Prerogative).

PREROGATIVE ORDER
  Application for—
    Expedited hearing. *See* **Divisional Court** (Expedited hearings—Cases stated—Prerogative orders).
  Certiorari. *See* **Certiorari**.
  Control of committal proceedings. *See* **Criminal law** (Committal—Preliminary hearing before
    justices—Prerogative order).
  Mandamus. *See* **Mandamus**.
  Prohibition. *See* **Prohibition**.

PRESCRIPTION
  Drainage. *See* **Easement** (Drainage—Prescription).
  Foreshore—
    Custom of acquiring sea-borne coal. *See* **Foreshore** (Rights over foreshore—Acquiring sea-borne coal).
  Grazing rights. *See* **Easement** (Grazing—Right to graze—Prescription).
  Light—
    Degree of light acquired by prescriptive right. *See* **Easement** (Light—Degree of light acquired by
    prescriptive right).
  Profit à prendre. *See* **Profit à prendre** (Prescription).
  Right of common. *See* **Commons** (Right of common—Creation—Prescription).
  Right of way. *See* **Easement** (Right of way—Prescription).
  Water—
    Easement. *See* **Easement** (Water—Prescription).

PRESERVATION
  Ancient monuments. *See* **Ancient monuments** (Preservation order).
  Building of architectural or historic interest. *See* **Town and country planning** (Building of special
    architectural or historic interest—Building preservation order).
  Trees. *See* **Town and country planning** (Trees—Preservation order).

PRESS AND PRINTING
  Distribution of written matter—
    What constitutes distribution—
      Incitement to racial hatred. *See* **Criminal law** (Public order—Incitement to racial hatred—
      Distribution of written matter).
  Freedom of expression—
    Antigua. *See* **Antigua** (Fundamental rights and freedoms—Freedom of expression).
    Child—
      Protection of child—Children and young persons legislation. *See* **Children and young persons**
      (Court proceedings—Protection of child concerned in proceedings—Freedom of publication).
      Protection of child—Generally. *See* **Child** (Protection—Freedom of publication).
    Ward of court—
      Protection of ward—Publication of matter likely to be harmful to ward. *See* **Ward of court**
      (Jurisdiction—Protection of ward—Freedom of publication).
  Libel—
    Press conference—
      Qualified Privilege. *See* **Libel and slander** (Qualified privilege—Public meeting).
    Publication. *See* **Libel and slander** (Publication).
    Republication—
      Effect of issue of writ on—Contempt of court. *See* **Contempt of court** (Republication of alleged
      libel—Pending proceedings—Republication after issue of writ).
  Manuscript—
    Alteration—
      Licensee, by. *See* **Copyright** (Licence—Rights of licensee—Right to make alterations).
      Repudiation of contract. *See* **Contract** (Repudiation—Publisher and author—Alteration of
      manuscript).
  Printing press—
    Duty to fence. *See* **Factory** (Dangerous parts of machinery—Duty to fence—Fencing to be kept in
    position while machinery in motion or use—Printing press).
  Privilege—
    Evidence. *See* **Evidence** (Privilege—Press).

PRESSURE TO DISMISS UNFAIRLY
  See **Unfair dismissal** (Pressure on employer to dismiss unfairly).

PRESUMPTION
  Advancement—
    Generally. *See* **Gift** (Presumption of advancement).
    Husband and wife. *See* **Husband and wife** (Presumption of advancement).
  Charitable objects, of. *See* **Charity** (Charitable trust—Will—Gift to body not registered as charity—Animal
    sanctuary—Subsequent registration as a charity with written constitution).

PRESUMPTION (cont)—
Commorientes. *See* **Administration of estates** (Commorientes—Statutory presumption).
Continuance of life—
Nature of presumption—
Whether presumption of law. **Chard v Chard (orse Northcott)** [1955] **3** 721, Div.
Continuity of employment. *See* **Employment** (Continuity—Presumption as to continuity).
Corruption—
Criminal offence. *See* **Criminal law** (Corruption—Presumption of corruption).
Criminal capacity—
Child. *See* **Criminal law** (Criminal capacity—Child).
Dedication of highway. *See* **Highway** (Dedication—Presumption).
Doli incapax. *See* **Criminal law** (Criminal capacity—Child).
Fact affecting title. *See* **Sale of land** (Title—Vendor's obligation to prove—Presumption of fact affecting title).
Intention to create legal relations, against. *See* **Contract** (Intention to create legal relationship—Presumption against intention).
Legacies to same person—
Cumulative. *See* **Will** (Codicil—Cumulative or repetitive bequests—Presumption that legacies given by different instruments cumulative).
Legitimacy—
Generally. *See* **Legitimacy** (Presumption of legitimacy).
Paternity—
Onus of proof—Blood test. *See* **Paternity** (Blood test—Onus of proof—Presumption of legitimacy).
Loss or damage to goods—
Carriage of goods subject to special risks inherent in specified circumstances—
Presumption that loss or damage attributable to one or more of special risks. *See* **Carriers** (Loss or damage to goods—Special risks inherent in specified circumstances—Presumption that loss or damage attributable to one or more of special risks).
Marriage—
Cohabitation. *See* **Marriage** (Presumption of marriage from cohabitation).
Validity. *See* **Marriage** (Validity—Presumption of validity).
Occupation of premises—
Owner having legal possession—
Rateable occupation. *See* **Rates** (Rateable occupation—Owner having legal possession—Presumption of occupation).
Undue influence. *See* **Equity** (Undue influence—Presumption of undue influence).
Yearly hiring. *See* **Employment** (Contract of service—Presumption of yearly hiring).

PREVENTION OF CRIME
Criminal law. *See* **Criminal law** (Prevention of crime).
Use of force in prevention of crime—
Defence to action for assault. *See* **Trespass to the person** (Assault—Defence—Use of force in prevention of crime).

PREVENTION OF TERRORISM
Rights of detained person—
Access to solicitor—
Person arrested under prevention of terrorism provisions. *See* **Solicitor** (Access to—Right of person in custody—Presence of solicitor during interview—Suspect arrested under prevention of terrorism provisions).

PREVENTIVE DETENTION
Dangerous driving. *See* **Road traffic** (Dangerous driving—Sentence—Preventive detention).
Generally. *See* **Sentence** (Preventive detention).

PREVIOUS CONVICTIONS
Criminal trial. *See* **Criminal law** (Trial—Previous convictions).
Disqualification for holding driving licence—
Evidence of previous convictions. *See* **Road traffic** (Disqualification for holding licence—Evidence of previous convictions).
Evidence in criminal proceedings. *See* **Criminal evidence** (Character of accused—Previous conviction).

PRICE
Control. *See* **Price control**.
False indication as to. *See* **Trade description** (False or misleading indication as to price).
Marking—
Consumer protection. *See* **Consumer protection** (Price marking).
Misleading price indication. *See* **Consumer protection** (Misleading price indication).
Mistake as to price. *See* **Mistake** (Price of subject-matter of transaction).
Price fixing—
Cartel offence. *See* **Criminal law** (Cartel offence—Ingredients of offence—Dishonestly agreeing with one or more other persons to make price-fixing arrangements).
Whether extraditable offence. *See* **Extradition** (Hearing—Extradition offence—Conduct constituting an extradition offence—Conspiracy to fix prices).
Price maintenance. *See* **Restrictive trade practices** (Resale price maintenance).
Sale of goods. *See* **Sale of goods** (Price).

PRICE CONTROL
Sale of goods at price exceeding statutory maximum permitted price—
Agreement for sale before order in force—
Transfer of property after order in force—Whether sale within meaning of order—Sale of Goods Act 1893, s 1(3), (4)—Canned Sardines (Maximum Prices) Order 1941 (SR & O 1941 No 671). **Mischeff v Springett** [1942] **2** 349, KBD.

PRICE CONTROL (cont)—

Sale of goods at price exceeding statutory maximum permitted price (cont)—

Eggs—

Sale of eggs for purposes of hatching—Whether purchaser a 'consumer'—Eggs (Control and Prices) (Great Britain) Order 1946 (SR & O 1946 No 880), art 7(1)(c), Sch II, Part II(f). **Brierley v Phillips** [1947] **1** 269, KBD.

Feeding stuffs—

Sale for seed purposes—Home-grown beans—Feeding Stuffs (Maximum Prices) Order 1940 (SR & O 1940 No 11), art 2. **Gilbert (TP) & Son Ltd v Birkin** [1941] **2** 489, KBD.

Footwear—

Price in excess of controlled price—Whether price marked on box containing footwear constituting offer for sale at that price—Goods and Services (Price Control) Act 1941, ss 1, 20(4)(a)—General Footwear (Maximum Prices and Charges) Order 1946 (SR & O 1946 No 1413) (as amended), arts 1, 5. **Phillips v Dalziel** [1948] **2** 810, KBD.

Iron and steel—

Schedules not printed—Defence. **Defiant Cycle Co Ltd v Newell** [1953] **2** 38, QBD.

Meat—

Act preparatory to commission of offence—Meat priced and marked with customer's name, but not delivered to customer—Liability of master for act of servant. **Gardner v Akeroyd** [1952] **2** 306, QBD.

Attempt to sell at excessive price—Meat parcels prepared with correct price tickets—False price tickets, to be affixed later, kept separately—Meat (Prices) (Great Britain) Order 1952 (SI 1952 No 1122), art 3. **Hope v Brown** [1954] **1** 330, QBD.

Offer to supply—Meat priced and marked with customer's name but not delivered—Whether offer within meaning of the order—Rationing Order 1939 (SR & O 1939 No 1856), art 2—Meat (Maximum Retail Prices) Order 1940 (SR & O 1940 No 37), art 4. **Wiles v Maddison** [1943] **1** 315, KBD.

Penalty—

Minimum penalty—Offender to derive 'no benefit from the offence'—Deduction of tax paid on excessive profit—Defence (General) Regulations 1939, reg 55AB(4)(a). **Betteley, Addyman and Jalland Ltd v Sington** [1948] **2** 81, KBD.

Proof—

Knowledge—Whether necessary to show accused knew maximum permitted price—Prices of Goods Act 1939, ss 1, 10(1), (3), (5), 15—Goods and Services (Price Control) Act 1941, s 4—Price-Controlled Goods (Restriction of Resale)(No 2) Order 1942 (SR & O 1942 No 958). **R v Jacobs** [1944] **1** 485, CCA.

Prosecution—

Time within which summary proceedings may be brought—Supplies and Services (Transitional Powers) Act 1945, s 2(1), (3)—Defence (Price Control) Regulations 1945, reg 10(1). **Wallace v Clench** [1947] **1** 175, KBD.

Sale of imported motor cars—

New Zealand. *See* **New Zealand** (Price control—Sale of imported motor cars).

PRIEST

Gift for relief of infirm, sick and aged priests—

Charitable purpose. *See* **Charity** (Religion—Priests—Relief of infirm, sick and aged priests).

Neglect of duty—

Offence. *See* **Ecclesiastical law** (Clergyman—Offence—Neglect of duty).

PRINCIPAL AND AGENT

See **Agent**.

PRINCIPAL IN SECOND DEGREE

See **Criminal law** (Principal in second degree).

PRINTED FORM

Contract—

Insertions—

Construction. *See* **Contract** (Construction—Printed form—Typed or written insertions).

Modification—

Writing—

Inconsistency of printed form with writing—Writing dominant. **Neuchatel Asphalte Co Ltd v Barnett** [1957] **1** 362, CA; **Renton (GH) & Co Ltd v Palmyra Trading Corp of Panama** [1956] **3** 957, HL.

PRISON

Access to legal adviser—

Access to discuss commencement of proceedings—

Proposed civil proceedings against prison officer for assault—Proposed proceedings arising out of prison treatment—Governor refusing visit by legal advisor to discuss proposed litigation—Visit contrary to simultaneous ventilation rule in prison standing orders which requires prisoner to lodge written complaint with governor before discussing complaint with legal advisor—Whether simultaneous ventilation rule ultra vires—Whether rule impeding prisoner's right of access to courts—Whether unimpeded access to solicitor part of right of access to courts—Prison Act 1952, s 47(1)—Prison Rules 1964, rr 33(1), 34, 47(12). **R v Secretary of State for the Home Dept, ex p Anderson** [1984] **1** 920, QBD.

PRISON (cont)—
  Access to legal adviser (cont)—
    Reasonable facilities for legal adviser to interview prisoner in connection with proceedings to which he
      was a party—
      Right to a fair trial—'Legal adviser' defined as 'counsel or solicitor'—Prisoner instructing foreign
        lawyer—Whether foreign lawyer falling within definition of 'legal adviser'—Courts and Legal
        Services Act 1990, ss 27, 28—Human Rights Act 1998, Sch 1, Pt I, art 6(3)—European
        Communities (Services of Lawyers) Order 1978, SI 1978/1910, art 5—Prison Rules 1999,
        SI 1999/728, r 2(1). **R (on the application of Van Hoogstraten) v Governor of Belmarsh Prison**
        [2003] **4** 309, QBD.
  Adult prison—
    Detention of young offender. *See* **Children and young persons** (Detention—Adult prison).
  Board of visitors—
    Certiorari—
      Jurisdiction. *See* **Certiorari** (Jurisdiction—Prison board of visitors).
    Exercise of disciplinary powers—
      Generally. *See* Discipline—Board of visitors, *below.*
      Natural justice. *See* **Natural justice** (Prison board of visitors—Exercise of disciplinary powers).
  Control unit—
    Legality. *See* Prison conditions—Separate control unit, *below.*
    Natural justice. *See* **Natural justice** (Prison control unit).
  Death in prison—
    State's obligation to investigate death. *See* **Human rights** (Right to life—State's obligation to
      investigate death—Death in prison).
  Discharge from prison—
    Remission of part of sentence—
      Discretion of Prison Commissioners—Reduction of sentence on appeal—How far misconduct
        before the appeal was allowed should be taken into account—Prison Rules 1949 (SI 1949
        No 1073), r 37 (as substituted by Prison Rules 1952 (SI 1952 No 1405), r 3). **Hancock v Prison**
        Comrs [1959] **3** 513, Vacation Ct.
  Discipline—
    Board of visitors—
      Exercise of disciplinary powers—Certiorari. *See* **Certiorari** (Jurisdiction—Prison board of
        visitors—Exercise of disciplinary powers).
      Exercise of disciplinary powers—Greater and lesser offences—Prison board of visitors finding
        charge of gross personal violence not proved against prisoner—Board substituting lesser implicit
        offence of assault—Whether greater offence including lesser offence—Whether board having
        power to convict for lesser offence—Prison Rules 1964, r 47(2)(4). **R v Dartmoor Prison Board of**
        Visitors, ex p Smith [1986] **2** 651, CA.
      Exercise of disciplinary powers—Laying of charge as soon as possible—As soon as
        possible—Charge of assault laid against prisoner over ten weeks after assault occurring—
        Whether charge laid 'as soon as possible'—Whether requirement that charge be laid 'as soon as
        possible' mandatory or directory—Prison Rules 1964, r 48(1). **R v Dartmoor Prison Board of**
        Visitors, ex p Smith [1986] **2** 651, CA.
      Exercise of disciplinary powers—Natural justice. *See* **Natural justice** (Prison board of
        visitors—Exercise of disciplinary powers).
    Governor—
      Exercise of disciplinary powers—Offence against discipline—Offence of having unauthorised article
        in cell—Proof of offence—Whether necessary to show not only that prisoner had knowledge of
        article in cell but also had some control over it—Prison Rules 1964, r 47(7). **R v Deputy Governor**
        of Camphill Prison, ex p King [1984] **3** 897, CA.
      Exercise of disciplinary powers—Whether governor's exercise of disciplinary powers open to
        judicial review. **Leech v Parkhurst Prison Deputy Governor** [1988] **1** 485, HL; **R v Deputy**
        Governor of Camphill Prison, ex p King [1984] **3** 897, CA.
    Natural justice. *See* **Natural justice** (Prison—Discipline).
    Offence against discipline—
      Charge—Rights of prisoner charged—Legal representation—Hearing before board of visitors—
        Whether prisoner entitled as of right to legal representation—Prison Rules (Northern Ireland)
        1982, r 30(2)—Convention for the Protection of Human Rights and Fundamental Freedom (1950),
        art 6(3)(c). **Hone v Maze Prison Board of Visitors** [1988] **1** 321, HL.
      Charge—Rights of prisoner charged—Legal representation—Whether prisoner entitled as of right to
        legal representation—Prison Rules 1964 (SI 1964 No 388), r 49(2). **Fraser v Mudge** [1975] **3** 78, CA.
      Charge—Rights of prisoner charged—Right to fair trial—Adjudication by governor—Whether
        disciplinary proceedings determining civil right of association—Whether governor independent
        and impartial tribunal—Whether adjudication breaching right to fair trial—Whether adjudication
        lawful—Human Rights Act 1998, Sch 1, Pt I, arts 3, 6(1), 8. **R (on the application of King) v**
        Secretary of State for Justice [2011] **3** 776, DC; [2012] **4** 44, CA.
      Right to a fair trial—Determination of criminal charge—Prisoner charged with disciplinary
        offence—Prisoner refused legal representation for hearing—Prisoner found guilty—Additional
        days imposed as penalty—Secretary of State remitting penalty—Secretary of State refusing to
        quash finding of guilt—Whether breach of right to fair trial—Human Rights Act 1998, Sch 1, Pt I,
        art 6. **R (on the application of Napier) v Secretary of State for the Home Dept** [2005] **3** 76, QBD.
    Removal from association—
      Prison governor or competent operational manager authorising prisoner's continued removal from
        association for period of more than 72 hours—Whether decisions to continue segregation
        beyond 72 hours lawful—Whether procedural fairness requiring prisoner's representations and
        disclosure of information on basis of decision to order continued segregation—Prison Act 1952,
        s 47(1)—Human Rights Act 1998, Sch 1, Pt I, art 6—Prison Rules 1999, SI 1999/728, r 45(1), (2). **R**
        (on the application of King) v Secretary of State for Justice [2016] **1** 1033, SC.
  Escape from prison—
    Escape risk classification—
      Life sentence. *See* Life sentence—Mandatory life sentence—Category A prisoner—Escape risk
        classification, *below.*

PRISON (cont)—

Escape from prison (cont)—

Permitting escape from prison. See **Criminal law** (Prison breach—Permitting escape from lawful custody).

Expenses—

Expenses of producing prisoner in court in interests of justice—

Secretary of State allowing prisoner to go to court to conduct own case—Secretary of State imposing condition requiring prepayment by prisoner of expenses—Expenses debited by prison governor against moneys held on prisoner's behalf—Whether expenses to be borne by state—Whether prisoner entitled to recover expenses—Criminal Justice Act 1961, s 29(1)—Prison Act 1952, ss 51, 53(2). **Becker v Home Office** [1972] 2 676, CA.

Removal from prison for judicial purposes—

Production of prisoner in court for purposes of civil litigation—Expenses of producing prisoner in court in interests of justice—Expense of conveying prisoner from prison to court—Prisoner granted leave to apply for judicial review of decisions of prison governor and Secretary of State—Prisoner refused legal aid to bring judicial review proceedings and wishing to attend court to argue case in person—Secretary of State requiring prisoner to make formal application to be taken to court and to pay costs of production in court—Whether prisoner required to meet costs of his production in court—Procedure for arranging for prisoner to be produced in court or to give evidence by other means—Criminal Justice Act 1961, s 29(1). **Wynne v Secretary of State for the Home Dept** [1992] 2 301, CA; [1993] 1 574, HL.

False imprisonment. See **False imprisonment**.

Governor—

Disciplinary powers. See Discipline—Governor, above.

Duty in respect of writ of habeas corpus ad respondendum. See **Habeas corpus** (Writ of habeas corpus ad respondendum—Prison governor's duty in respect of writ).

Power to order transfer of prisoner to another prison and segregation there. See Prison conditions—Removal from association—Prison governor ordering transfer of prisoner to another prison, below.

Letters—

Prisoner's letters—

Correspondence with legal adviser—Governor, by order, introducing revised rules for cell searching—Prisoners removed from cells and strip searched—Cell searched in prisoner's absence—Search of cell including inspection of correspondence with legal advisers—Whether governor's order valid—Prison Act 1952, s 47(1)—Prison Rules 1964, r 37A. **R v Secretary of State for the Home Dept, ex p Simms** [1998] 2 491, CA.

Correspondence with legal adviser—Power of governor to read or stop correspondence—Extent of power—When contempt of court. See **Contempt of court** (Obstruction of legal proceedings—Obstruction of person's right of access to courts—Prisoner—Legal communications).

Correspondence with legal adviser—Power of governor to read or stop correspondence—Governor stopping prisoner's application to commit him for contempt—Whether contempt of court. **Raymond v Honey** [1981] 2 1084, QBD.

Correspondence with legal adviser—Power of governor to read or stop correspondence—Power curtailed where prisoner a party to legal proceedings and corresponding about them with legal adviser—Prisoner lodging petition with European Commission of Human Rights alleging interference with correspondence with legal adviser—Whether prisoner 'a party to ... legal proceedings' by reason of lodging petition with commission—Prison Rules 1964, r 37A(1). **Guilfoyle v Home Office** [1981] 1 943, CA.

Correspondence with legal adviser—Power of governor to read or stop correspondence—Prison rule enabling governor to read and stop prisoner's correspondence with legal adviser in respect of contemplated proceedings—Whether rule ultra vires—Prison Act 1952, s 47(1)—Prison Rules 1964, rr 33(3), 37A(1). **R v Secretary of State for the Home Dept, ex p Leech** [1993] 4 539, CA.

Correspondence with legal adviser—Secretary of State introducing new policy on searching of cells—Policy requiring prison officers to examine prisoner's legal correspondence in absence of prisoner—Whether policy unjustifiably infringing prisoners' common law right to confidentiality in legal correspondence and right to respect for correspondence under human rights convention—Prison Act 1952, s 47(1)—Human Rights Act 1998, Sch 1, Pt I, art 8(1). **R v Secretary of State for the Home Dept, ex p Daly** [2001] 3 433, HL.

Life sentence—

Discretionary life sentence—

Post-tariff category A prisoner—Whether categorisation review team obliged to follow view of Discretionary Lifer Panel on categorisation of such a prisoner—Human Rights Act 1998, Sch 1, Pt I, art 5(4). **R (on the application of Williams) v Secretary of State for the Home Dept** [2002] 4 872, CA.

Generally. See **Sentence** (Life imprisonment).

Mandatory life sentence—

Category A prisoner—Annual review of categorisation by category A section—Refusal to change category—Refusal to release reports—Whether prisoner entitled to disclosure of reports considered by committee—Whether prisoner entitled to be informed of reasons for decision. **R v Secretary of State for the Home Dept, ex p Duggan** [1994] 3 277, QBD.

Category A prisoner—Escape risk classification—Category A prisoner classified as having high escape risk—Review of prisoner's escape risk—Whether reasons for classification decision to be given to prisoner—Whether principles of procedural fairness applying to classification decision. **R (on the application of Ali) v Director of High Security Prisons** [2010] 2 82, QBD.

Whole life tariff—Applicant serving mandatory life sentences for murder—Secretary of State deciding whole life tariff appropriate in applicant's case—Whether imposition of whole life tariff unlawful—Murder (Abolition of Death Penalty) Act 1965, s 1. **R v Secretary of State for the Home Dept, ex p Hindley** [2000] 2 385, HL.

Release on licence. See Release on licence—Life sentence—Mandatory life sentence, below.

Management and treatment of prisoner—

Life sentence. See Release on licence—Life sentence—Indeterminate sentence, below.

PRISON (cont)—
Medical officer—
Consent to medical treatment by medical officer. *See* **Medical practitioner** (Trespass to the person—Consent to medical treatment—Prison).
Whether prison officers including medical officer—
Prison Act 1952, s 7(1). **Freeman v Home Office** [1983] **3** 589, QBD.
Negligence—
Prison authorities—
Duty to prisoner—Protection against injury—Attack on prisoner by fellow prisoner. **Ellis v Home Office** [1953] **2** 149, CA.
Prison hospital—
Duty to take care. *See* **Negligence** (Duty to take care—Prison hospital).
Offences —
Conveyance etc of prohibited articles into or out of prison—
Mens rea—Whether offence of bringing, throwing or otherwise conveying prohibited article into or out of prison an offence of strict liability—Prison Act 1952, s 40C(1)(a). **R v M** [2010] **4** 51, CA.
Parole. *See* Release on licence, *below*.
Prison conditions—
Cruel and unusual punishments—
Prisoner housed in psychiatric wing of prison hospital although not suffering any psychiatric illness—Prisoner disturbed at night by mentally disturbed patients—Prisoner complaining that conditions amounted to infliction of 'cruell and unusuall punishments' contrary to Bill of Rights—Whether governor's care of prisoner open to judicial review. **R v Secretary of State for the Home Dept, ex p Herbage (No 2)** [1987] **1** 324, CA.
Removal from association—
Prison governor ordering transfer of prisoner to another prison—Governor ordering prisoner to be segregated at other prison—Whether prison governor having power to order transfer and segregation—Prison Act 1952, s 12—Prison Rules 1964, r 43. **Hague v Deputy Governor of Parkhurst Prison** [1990] **3** 687, CA.
Scottish prisons—Prisoner kept in segregation for prolonged period for own safety—Whether prisoner's segregation contrary to prison rules—Whether prolonged segregation breaching prisoner's Convention rights—Whether prisoner entitled to damages by way of just satisfaction—Prisons and Young Offender Institutions (Scotland) Rules 2006, SSI 2006/94, r 94—Human Rights Act 1998, Sch 1, Pt I, arts 3, 8. **Shahid v Scottish Ministers** [2016] **4** 363, SC.
Separate control unit—
Legality—Unit established in ordinary prison to deal with troublemakers—Prisoners in unit not allowed to associate with one another—Strict regime imposed—Whether Secretary of State having power to set up control unit—Whether detention of prisoners in unit justifiable—Whether regime in unit a 'cruel and unusual punishment' and contrary to Bill of Rights—Prison Act 1952, s 12(1)—Prison Rules 1964 (SI 1964 No 388), r 43. **Williams v Home Office (No 2)** [1981] **1** 1211, QBD.
Smoking—
Whether ban on smoking in enclosed public places applying to prisons—Health Act 2006, Ch 1, Pt 1. **R (on the application of Black) v Secretary of State for Justice** [2015] **4** 790, QBD.
Whether ban on smoking in enclosed public places applying to prisons—Health Act 2006, s 23, Ch 1, Pt 1, Ch 1, Pt 3. **R (on the application of Black) v Secretary of State for Justice** [2016] **3** 30, CA.
Whether ban on smoking in enclosed public places applying to prisons—Whether statutory provision binding Crown—Health Act 2006, Pt 1, Ch 1. **R (on the application of Black) v Secretary of State for Justice** [2018] **2** 212, SC.
Prison hospital—
Duty to take care. *See* **Negligence** (Duty to take care—Prison hospital).
Officers and nurses—
Misconduct in public office. *See* **Criminal law** (Misconduct in public office—Persons to whom offence applying—Serving prison hospital officers and prison nurses).
Prison officer—
Dismissal—
Judicial review of dismissal—Availability of remedy. *See* **Judicial review** (Availability of remedy—Employment by public authority—Dismissal of employee—Dismissal of prison officer).
Misfeasance by. *See* **Public office** (Abuse of—Misfeasance by a public officer—Prison officer).
Prisoner—
False Imprisonment. *See* **False imprisonment** (Prisoner serving sentence).
Gender—
Right to respect for private and family life—Consequences of issue of gender recognition certificate—Prisoner serving mandatory life sentence suffering from gender dysphoria—Prisoner receiving gender recognition certificate—Prisoner requiring period of two years living 'in role' as female before gender reassignment surgery could be considered—Prisoner applying for transfer to prison for female offenders—Secretary of State refusing transfer—Whether breach of right to respect for private and family life—Whether decision unreasonable—Human Rights Act 1998, Sch 1, Pt I, art 8—Gender Recognition Act 2004, s 9. **R (on the application of AB) v Secretary of State for Justice** [2010] **2** 151, QBD.
Hunger strike—
Right to self-determination—Duty of Home Office, prison officials, physicians and nursing staff responsible for care of prisoner—Prisoner on hunger strike—Prisoner having capacity to understand consequences of his decision—Home Secretary seeking declaratory relief as to whether it was lawful to permit hunger strike and allow prisoner to die—Whether prison officials and medical staff having duty to force feed prisoner. **Secretary of State for the Home Dept v Robb** [1995] **1** 677, Fam D.
Management and treatment of prisoners—
Life sentence. *See* Release on licence—Life sentence—Indeterminate sentence, *below*.

PRISON (cont)—
　　Prisoner (cont)—
　　　　Powers of transfer—
　　　　　　Transfer of prisoners for other judicial purposes—Prison authorities refusing to transport prisoner to hearing of civil claim but instead facilitating attendance by video link—Whether failure to produce prisoner violating right to fair trial—Whether decision unlawful—Crime (Sentences) Act 1997, Sch 1, para 3(1)—Human Rights Act 1998, Sch 1, Pt I, art 6. **R (on the application of Michael) v Governor of HMP Whitemoor (County Court at Oxford, interested party)** [2020] **4** 190, CA.
　　　　Property of prisoner—
　　　　　　Cash of prisoner at prison—Prison rules providing that such cash to be paid into account under control of governor and prisoner to be credited with amount in prison books—Whether rule imposing trust on moneys paid into account under that rule—Prison Rules 1999, rr 43(3), 44. **Duggan v Governor of Full Sutton Prison** [2003] **2** 678, Ch D; [2004] **2** 966, CA.
　　　　　　Money sent by post—Disposal of money by prison governor—Prison rules—Failure to dispose of money in accordance with rules—Rules regulatory only—Failure to observe rules not giving rise to cause of action—Cheque sent to prisoner not accounted for by prison authorities—Prisoner not entitled to claim damages for wrongful detention of cheque—Prison Rules 1964 (SI 1964 No 388), r 42(3). **Becker v Home Office** [1972] **2** 676, CA.
　　　　　　Prisoner claiming relevant rules imposing trust on prison governor in relation to prisoner's cash—Whether rules compatible with right to peaceful enjoyment of possessions under human rights convention—Human Rights Act 1998, Sch 1, Pt II, art 1—Prison Rules 1999, r 43(3). **Duggan v Governor of Full Sutton Prison** [2003] **2** 678, Ch D.
　　　　Release on licence—
　　　　　　Determinate sentence—Right to liberty and security—Claimant's period in custody on remand exceeding determinate sentence of imprisonment—Claimant being released on licence—Claimant being subject to automatic recall—Whether procedure for recall breaching right to liberty and security—Whether exclusion of credit for time served on automatic recall arbitrary—Human Rights Act 1998, Sch 1, Pt I, art 5—Criminal Justice Act 2003, ss 240ZA, 255B. **R (on the application of Galiazia) v Governor of HMP Hewell** [2016] **1** 660, DC.
　　　　　　Determinate sentence—Right to liberty and security—Lawfulness of detention—Claimant challenging recall to prison for breach of licence—Delay in review by parole board—Whether breach of right to liberty and security—Human Rights Act 1998, Sch 1, Pt I, art 5. **R (on the application of Youngsam) v Parole Board** [2018] **1** 800, QBD; [2019] **3** 954, CA; **R v Lichniak** [2002] **4** 1122, HL.
　　　　　　Determinate sentence—Right to liberty and security—Lawfulness of detention—Power to release prisoners on licence before required to do so—Recall of prisoners released early—Home detention curfew—Curfew condition—Power of Secretary of State to revoke licence and recall person released on licence for failure to comply with licence conditions or if whereabouts of person released on licence could no longer be electronically monitored—Discretionary release on licence of determinate sentence prisoner subject to curfew condition—Person recalled while curfew condition in force because his whereabouts could no longer be electronically monitored—Person recalled having no right of review of recall by Parole Board—Whether breach of right to liberty and security—Human Rights Act 1998, Sch 1, Pt I, art 5(4)—Criminal Justice Act 2003, ss 246, 255. **R (on the application of Whiston) v Secretary of State for Justice** [2014] **4** 251, SC.
　　　　　　Determinate sentence—Right to liberty and security—Parole board delaying consideration of application by determinate sentence prisoner for parole—Whether breach of right to liberty and security—Human Rights Act 1998, Sch 1, Pt I, art 5(4). **R (on the application of Johnson) v Secretary of State for the Home Dept** [2007] **3** 532, CA.
　　　　　　Determinate sentence—Right to liberty and security—Power of Secretary of State to release prisoner on licence if so recommended by Parole Board—Parole Board recommending prisoner's release—Secretary of State declining to exercise power to release—Whether breach of right to liberty and security—Criminal Justice Act 1991, s 35(1)—Human Rights Act 1998, Sch 1, Pt I, art 5(1)(a), (4). **R (on the application of Black) v Secretary of State for the Home Dept** [2008] **4** 151, CA; [2009] **4** 1, HL.
　　　　　　Extended determinate sentence—Right to liberty and security—Discrimination on grounds of 'other status'—Extended determinate sentence regime providing prisoner not eligible for release until two-thirds of custodial term served—Whether extended determinate sentence prisoner having 'other status'—Whether effect of regime discriminatory compared to prisoners serving different types of sentence—Human Rights Act 1998, Sch 1, Pt I, arts 5, 14—Criminal Justice Act 2003, ss 226A, 246A. **R (on the application of Stott) v Secretary for State for Justice** [2019] **2** 351, SC.
　　　　　　Parole Board recommending revocation of licence of prisoner released on licence—Parole Board deciding not to order re-release of prisoner—Whether decision procedurally fair—Whether prisoner entitled to oral hearing—Whether decision breaching right to liberty and security—Whether decision breaching right to fair trial—Criminal Justice Act 1991, s 39—Human Rights Act 1998, Sch 1, Pt I, arts 5(1), (4), 6(1). **R (on the application of Smith) v Parole Board** [2005] **1** 755, HL.
　　　　　　Procedural fairness—Right to liberty and security—Oral hearing before Parole Board—Circumstances in which board should hold oral hearing. **Osborn v Parole Board** [2014] **1** 369, SC.
　　　　　　Revocation of licence—Bail—Inherent jurisdiction of High Court—Prisoner released on licence—Prisoner's licence revoked—Prisoner recalled to prison—Parole commissioners reviewing recall—Parole commissioners refusing to direct release—Prisoner applying for judicial review—High Court finding commissioners' decision unlawful—High Court granting prisoner bail pending reconsideration by commissioners—Whether High Court having jurisdiction to grant bail. **Corey, Re** [2014] **1** 863, SC.
　　　　Removal from association. *See* Prison conditions—Removal from association, *above*.
　　　　Security categorisation—
　　　　　　Category A prisoner—Parole Board recommending prisoner's transfer to open conditions—Secretary of State not accepting recommendation—Basis on which Secretary of State could depart from board's recommendation—Whether Secretary of State's decision inconsistent with factual findings of board or failing to give adequate weight to board's assessment. **R (on the application of John) v Secretary of State for Justice** [2022] **1** 650, QBD.

Release on licence—
Conviction of further offence—
Duty of Crown Court—Revocation of licence—Duty to consider whether any sentence of imprisonment for further offence should be concurrent or consecutive to sentence for offence in respect of which licence revoked—Criminal Justice Act 1967, ss 60, 62(1), (2), (7). **Practice Note** [1976] **1** 271, CA.

Duty of magistrates' court—Applicant convicted of summary offence while on release from custody on licence—Whether justices entitled to impose a sentence in respect of offence and commit applicant to Crown Court to determine whether he should be returned to prison—Criminal Justice Act 1991, s 40(3)(b). **R v Harrow Justices, ex p Jordan** [1997] **2** 344, QBD.

Revocation of licence—Appeal—Judge sentencing accused to term of imprisonment and revoking release on licence—Whether accused having right of appeal against revocation of licence—Whether order revoking licence a 'sentence'—Criminal Justice Act 1967, ss 60, 61, 62(7)—Criminal Appeal Act 1968, s 9. **R v Welch** [1982] **2** 824, CA.

Revocation of licence—Defendant committing more than one offence—Defendant released on parole—Defendant subsequently convicted of offence committed before offence in respect of which he was paroled—Parole licence revoked—Whether defendant ineligible for parole for 12 months in respect of any sentence passed on him—Whether defendant only ineligible in respect of sentence for which he was paroled—Criminal Justice Act 1967, s 62(7), (10). **R v McKinnon** [1987] **2** 21, CA.

Revocation of licence—Offender committing fresh offences while on licence and being administratively recalled to custody—Sentencing court ordering offender to serve unexpired portion of sentence for earlier offence—Whether court having power to order offender to serve unexpired portion of sentence if offender already in custody following administrative recall—Criminal Justice Act 1991, ss 39, 40. **R v Sharkey** [2000] **1** 15, CA.

Custodial sentence. *See* **Sentence** (Custodial sentence—Licence—Statutory scheme providing for release of offender on licence rather than unconditionally).

Determinate sentence. *See* Prisoner—Release on licence—Determinate sentence, *above*.

Early release of prisoners—
Home detention curfew—Right to liberty and security—Delay in considering release under home detention curfew policy—Whether delay unlawful—Whether breach of right to liberty and security—Criminal Justice Act 1991, Pt II—Human Rights Act 1998, Sch 1, Pt I, art 5(4). **Mason v Secretary of State for Justice** [2009] **1** 1128, QBD.

Terrorist offenders. *See* **Sentence** (Imprisonment—Early release—Introduction of restrictions on early release of terrorist offenders).

Extended sentence—
Detention during extended period of sentence—Whether obligation to provide real opportunity for rehabilitation—Whether breach of right to liberty and security—Human Rights Act 1998, Sch 1, Pt I, art 5(1). **Brown v Parole Board for Scotland** [2018] **1** 909, SC.

Further release after recall—
Prisoners serving determinate sentence—Direction of Parole Board—Parole Board guidance—Whether test to be applied by Parole Board limited to consideration of public protection—Whether Parole Board entitled to balance risk to public against benefits to public or prisoner—Criminal Justice Act 2003, ss 255B, 255C. **R (on the application of King) v Parole Board** [2017] **2** 176, CA.

Home detention curfew licence, eligibility for. *See* **Sentence** (Consecutive sentences—Release dates—Eligibility for home detention curfew or conditional release).

Home leave—
Secretary of State deciding to implement new scheme governing eligibility of prisoners to apply for home leave—Prisoners entitled to apply for home leave after serving one-third of sentence under old scheme but only after having served half their sentence under new scheme—New scheme deferring applicants' earliest date for eligibility by substantial period—Whether inmate compact signed by applicants at beginning of sentence giving rise to legitimate expectation overriding new scheme—Whether decision to apply new policy lawful—Test to be applied. **R v Secretary of State for the Home Dept, ex p Hargreaves** [1997] **1** 397, CA.

Indeterminate sentence—
Delay in decision of Parole Board—Human rights. *See* **Human rights** (Infringement of human rights—Damages—Right to liberty and security—Lawfulness of detention to be decided speedily).

Life sentence—
Automatic or discretionary life sentence—Determination by Parole Board whether prisoner should be released on licence—Board scheduling hearings only after expiry of tariff period—Whether procedure infringing prisoner's right to have lawfulness of detention decided speedily—Human Rights Act 1998, Sch 1, Pt I, art 5(4). **R (on the application of Noorkoiv) v Secretary of State for the Home Dept** [2002] **4** 515, .

Indeterminate sentence—Sentence of imprisonment for public protection—Minimum term— Provision for release on licence after expiry of minimum term after review by Parole Board -Public law duty to make reasonable provision to enable prisoners sentenced to imprisonment for public protection to demonstrate their safety for release to Parole Board—Whether public law duty affected by level of resources made available by Secretary of State—Whether breach of Convention rights—Human Rights Act 1998, Sch 1, Pt I, art 5. **Fletcher v Governor of HMP Whatton** [2015] **3** 558, QBD.

Indeterminate sentence—Sentence of imprisonment for public protection—Minimum term— Provision for release on licence after expiry of minimum term after review by Parole Board—Offender sentenced to imprisonment for public protection detained in prison with insufficient provision for offending behaviour work—Offender's ability to demonstrate progress to Parole Board reduced or eliminated—Whether Secretary of State's actions lawful—Whether opportunity for offending behaviour work necessary. **R (on the application of Walker) v Secretary of State for Justice (formerly Secretary of State for the Home Dept)** [2008] **3** 104, CA; **R (on the application of Wells) v Parole Board** [2008] **1** 138, DC.

PRISON (cont)—
  Release on licence (cont)—
    Life sentence (cont)—
      Indeterminate sentence—Sentence of imprisonment for public protection—Minimum term—
      Provision for release on licence after expiry of minimum term after review by Parole
      Board—Offenders sentenced to imprisonment for public protection detained in prison with
      insufficient provision for offending behaviour work—Secretary of State acknowledging breach of
      public law duty to make reasonable provision to enable prisoners sentenced to imprisonment for
      public protection to demonstrate their safety for release to Parole Board—Whether detention
      after expiry of minimum term unlawful at common law—Whether breach of right to liberty and
      security—Whether delay in determining safety for release breach of right to take proceedings by
      which court speedily deciding lawfulness of detention—Crime (Sentences) Act 1997,
      s 28—Human Rights Act 1998, Sch 1, Pt I, art 5(1), (4)—Criminal Justice Act 2003, s 225. **R (on the
      application of James) v Secretary of State for Justice** [2009] **4** 255, HL.

      Indeterminate sentence—Sentence of imprisonment for public protection—Minimum term—
      Provision for release on licence after expiry of minimum term after review by Parole
      Board—Offenders sentenced to indeterminate sentences detained in prison with delay in
      providing offending behaviour work to enable them to demonstrate their safety for release to
      Parole Board—Whether detention after expiry of minimum term breach of right to liberty and
      security—Whether delay in determining safety for release breach of right to take proceedings by
      which court speedily deciding lawfulness of detention—Human Rights Act 1998, Sch 1, Pt I,
      art 5(1), (4). **R (on the application of Haney) v Secretary of State for Justice** [2015] **2** 822, SC.

      Indeterminate sentence—Sentence of imprisonment for public protection—Minimum term—
      Provision for release on licence after expiry of minimum term after review by Parole
      Board—Release where no longer necessary for protection of public that prisoner
      confined—Whether test for release same as test for imposition of sentence of imprisonment for
      public protection—Crime (Sentences) Act 1997, s 28(6)(b)—Criminal Justice Act 2003, s 225(1)(b).
      R (on the application of Sturnham) v Parole Board of England and Wales (No 2) [2013] **4** 177, SC.

      Mandatory life sentence—Right to liberty and security—Secretary of State putting information
      about prisoner before Parole Board but not disclosing information to prisoner—Parole Board
      directing disclosure of information to specially appointed advocate—Whether Parole Board
      acting ultra vires—Whether breach of right to liberty and security—Criminal Justice Act 1991,
      s 32—Human Rights Act 1998, Sch 1, Pt I, art 5(4). **R (on the application of Roberts) v Parole
      Board** [2004] **2** 776, QBD; **Roberts v Parole Board** [2004] **4** 1136, CA; [2006] **1** 39, HL.

      Mandatory life sentence—Tariff period—Procedure for fixing tariff period—Judiciary invited to
      advise on period that should be served for purposes of retribution and deterrence—Secretary of
      State taking account of judicial recommendation in reaching decision on appropriate
      tariff—Whether Secretary of State entitled to set tariff period differing from that recommended by
      judiciary—Whether Secretary of State required to adopt judicial view of tariff—Criminal Justice
      Act 1967, s 35. **Doody v Secretary of State for the Home Dept** [1993] **3** 92, HL.

      Mandatory life sentence—Tariff period—Procedure for fixing tariff period—Secretary of State
      setting higher tariff period than that recommended by judiciary on basis of aggravating features
      of crime—Subsequent Secretary of State accepting that aggravating features absent but
      maintaining higher tariff period—Whether Secretary of State entitled to increase tariff
      retrospectively in absence of exceptional circumstances—Criminal Justice Act 1991, s 35. **Pierson
      v Secretary of State for the Home Dept** [1997] **3** 577, HL.

      Mandatory or discretionary life sentence—Detention in mental hospital—Secretary of State
      refusing to refer mandatory or discretionary life prisoners' cases to Parole Board—Whether life
      prisoner serving sentence while patient in mental hospital—Whether life prisoner who was a
      mental patient while under detention eligible for review by Parole Board—Mental Health Act
      1983, s 50(1)—Criminal Justice Act 1991, ss 34, 35(2), Sch 12, para 9. **R v Secretary of State for
      the Home Dept, ex p Hickey (No 1)** [1995] **1** 479, CA.

      Mandatory or discretionary life sentence—Tariff period—Principles of natural justice—Secretary of
      State deciding tariff period—Date for first review of prisoner's sentence set according to tariff
      period—Whether mandatory life prisoner entitled to make representations to Secretary of State
      before tariff period set—Whether Secretary of State required to inform prisoner of tariff period
      recommended by judiciary and other opinions expressed by judiciary relevant to decision on
      tariff—Whether Secretary of State required to give reasons if he departs from judicial view of
      tariff period. **Doody v Secretary of State for the Home Dept** [1993] **3** 92, HL.

      Mandatory or discretionary life sentence—Tariff period—Young person aged 17 convicted of
      manslaughter on grounds of diminished responsibility and sentenced to detention for life—Home
      Secretary setting tariff period of nine years, later reduced to seven years—Whether tariff
      correct—Children and Young Persons Act 1933, ss 44, 53(2). **R v Secretary of State for the Home
      Dept, ex p Furber** [1998] **1** 23, QBD.

      Right to liberty and security—Statutory scheme for recall of life prisoners while on
      licence—Whether statutory scheme compatible with right to liberty and security—Crime
      (Sentences) Act 1997, s 32—Human Rights Act 1998, Sch 1, Pt I, art 5. **R (on the application of
      Hirst) v Secretary of State for the Home Dept** [2006] **4** 639, CA.

  Mandatory sentence—
      Detention during Her Majesty's pleasure—Children aged ten convicted of murder—Tariff
      period—Home Secretary setting tariff period of 15 years—Whether policy in setting tariff
      lawful—Whether decision procedurally fair—Children and Young Persons Act 1933, ss 44(1),
      53(1)—Criminal Justice Act 1991, s 35. **R v Secretary of State for the Home Dept, ex p Venables**
      [1997] **3** 97, HL.

      Detention during Her Majesty's pleasure—Person under the age of 18 years at time offence
      committed convicted of murder—Tariff period—Right to a fair trial—Lord Chief Justice receiving
      written representations and reviewing tariff period—Whether breach of right to a fair
      trial—Whether oral hearing required—Human Rights Act 1998, Sch 1, Pt I, art 6(1). **R (on the
      application of Dudson) v Secretary of State for the Home Dept** [2006] **1** 421, HL.

PRISON (cont)—
Release on licence (cont)—
Mandatory sentence (cont)—
Detention during Her Majesty's pleasure—Person under the age of 18 years at time offence committed convicted of murder—Tariff period—Secretary of State for Home Department setting tariff period—Secretary of State reviewing period following establishment of duty to review—New policy applying to existing detainees after new legislative scheme coming into force by which Lord Chief Justice reviewing tariff period and making recommendation to Secretary of State—Lord Chief Justice reviewing tariff period under new policy but not reducing it—Whether tariff period remaining subject to continuing review by Secretary of State. **R (on the application of Smith) v Secretary of State for the Home Dept** [2006] **1** 407, HL.
Parole Board—
Duty of Parole Board in dealing with cases to consider documents given to it by Secretary of State—Whether Parole Board having power to decide documents given to it by Secretary of State be withheld from panel considering release on licence—Criminal Justice Act 2003, s 239(3). **R (on the application of McGetrick) v Parole Board** [2013] **3** 636, CA.
Prisoner convicted of serious sexual offences and indeterminate sentence imposed—Parole Board directing release following expiry of minimum term of imprisonment—Whether direction irrational—Whether parole board failing to take into account relevant considerations—Whether principle of open justice applying to parole board proceedings—Criminal Justice Act 2003, s 239—Parole Board Rules 2016, SI 2016/1041, r 25. **R (on the application of DSD) v Parole Board of England and Wales** [2018] **3** 417, DC.
Sponsorship by Ministry of Justice—Right to liberty and security—Whether Board having necessary objective independence—Whether Parole Board constituting a 'court' for convention purposes—Human Rights Act 1998, Sch 1, Pt I, art 5(4). **R (on the application of Brooke) v Parole Board** [2008] **3** 289, CA.
Refusal to release on licence—
Danger to public safety—Life Sentence Review Commissioners (Northern Ireland)—Standard of proof—Correct approach. **R (on the application of D) v Life Sentence Review Comrs** [2008] **4** 992, HL.
Danger to public safety—Prisoner serving mandatory life sentence—Prisoner having served tariff part of sentence—Home Secretary refusing to release prisoner on licence on ground that prisoner might commit serious non-violent offences—Whether Home Secretary's decision lawful—Criminal Justice Act 1991, s 35(2). **R v Secretary of State for the Home Dept, ex p Stafford** [1998] **4** 7, HL.
Danger to public safety—Test of dangerousness to the public to be applied by Parole Board—Prisoner serving discretionary life sentence—Prisoner having served period necessary to satisfy requirements of deterrence and rehabilitation—Parole Board refusing to recommend applicant for release because of risk to public—Whether Parole Board applying correct test of dangerousness in refusing to recommend prisoner for release—Whether correct test likelihood that prisoner would probably commit further serious offences. **R v Parole Board, ex p Bradley** [1990] **3** 828, QBD.
Post-tariff mandatory life prisoner—Right to liberty and security—Directions given by Secretary of State to Parole Board identifying matters to be taken into account by Parole Board—Whether legislation empowering Secretary of State to give directions applicable to Parole Board's judicial functions—Criminal Justice Act 1991, s 32(6)—Crime (Sentences) Act 1997, s 28(6)(b). **R (on the application of Girling) v Parole Board** [2006] **1** 11, QBD; [2007] **2** 688, CA.
Reasons for refusal—Prisoner serving discretionary life sentence—Whether Parole Board required to inform discretionary life prisoner of reasons for refusal to recommend release—Whether contrary to rules of natural justice not to inform prisoner of reasons. **R v Parole Board, ex p Bradley** [1990] **3** 828, QBD.
Reasons for refusal—Whether Parole Board or local review committee required to inform prisoner of reasons for refusal to recommend release—Whether contrary to rules of natural justice not to inform prisoner of reasons—Criminal Justice Act 1967, ss 59-62—Local Review Committee Rules 1967 (SI 1967 No 1462). **Payne v Lord Harris of Greenwich** [1981] **2** 842, CA.
Review by Parole Board—Prisoner serving discretionary life sentence released on licence—Secretary of State revoking licence and recalling prisoner—Parole Board giving extra-statutory confirmation of recall prior to formal review—Statutory review by Parole Board—Board refusing to order re-release of prisoner—Whether board's earlier confirmation resulting in procedural irregularity or bias—Whether board applying correct test on review—Criminal Justice Act 1991, ss 34(4), 39(2), (4). **R v Parole Board, ex p Watson** [1996] **2** 641, CA.
Review by Parole Board—Reports for presentation to Parole Board—Prisoner serving discretionary life sentence—Whether natural justice requiring disclosure to prisoner of reports to be presented to Parole Board on review of case. **R v Parole Board, ex p Wilson** [1992] **2** 576, CA.
Right to liberty and security—Prohibition of discrimination—Secretary of State having discretionary power to release on licence prisoners serving determinate sentences of 15 years or more when their release was recommended by Parole Board—Secretary of State having discretionary power to release on licence long-term prisoners liable to removal from United Kingdom—Secretary of State refusing to release on licence prisoner serving determinate sentence of 18 years whose release was recommended by Parole Board—Secretary of State refusing to release on licence long-term prisoners liable to removal from United Kingdom—Whether discriminatory breaches of right to liberty and security—Criminal Justice Act 1991, Pt II—Human Rights Act 1998, Sch 1, Pt I, arts 5, 14. **R (on the application of Clift) v Secretary of State for the Home Dept** [2007] **2** 1, HL.
Revocation of licence. *See* Prisoner—Release on licence—Revocation of licence, *above.*
Secretary of State deciding to change parole policy regarding certain categories of offences—
Policy formulated without prior consultation with Parole Board—Policy rendering prisoners within certain categories ineligible for parole save in exceptional circumstances—Whether Secretary of State under duty to consult Parole Board before changing parole policy—Whether policy lawful—Criminal Justice Act 1967, ss 59(3), (6), 60(1), 61(1). **Findlay v Secretary of State for the Home Dept** [1984] **3** 801, CA and HL.

PRISON (cont)—
  Release on licence (cont)—
    Secretary of State, power of—
      Right to liberty and security. *See* Prisoner—Release on licence—Determinate sentence—Right to liberty and security—Power of Secretary of State to release prisoner on licence if so recommended by Parole Board, *above*.
    Terrorist offenders. *See* **Sentence** (Imprisonment—Early release—Introduction of restrictions on early release of terrorist offenders).
    Unconditional release—
      Transitional provisions—Prisoner sentenced to long-term determinate sentence—Parole regime providing for unconditional release at three-quarter point of sentence—Change of parole regime—New regime providing only for release on licence—Prisoner released on licence, recalled and re-released on licence—Transitional provisions applying—Transitional provisions not providing for prisoner's re-release on licence—Whether drafting error—Whether error to be corrected by court—Criminal Justice Act 1991, ss 33(3), 37(1), (1A), 39(1), (2)—Criminal Justice Act 2003—Criminal Justice Act 2003 (Commencement No 8 and Transitional and Savings Provisions) Order 2005, SI 2005/950, Sch 2, paras 19, 23. **R (on the application of Kelly) v Secretary of State for Justice** [2008] **3** 844, CA.
      Transitional provisions—Prisoner sentenced to long-term determinate sentence following offending in 1998—Parole regime providing for unconditional release at three-quarter point of sentence—Prisoner released on licence—Change of parole regime—New regime providing only for release on licence—Prisoner recalled to prison—Effect of recall—Whether prisoner entitled to unconditional release at three-quarter point of sentence—Criminal Justice Act 1991, s 37—Criminal Justice Act 2003, ss 249, 254—Criminal Justice Act 2003 (Commencement No 8 and Transitional and Saving Provisions) Order 2005, SI 2005/950, paras 19, 23. **R (on the application of Stellato) v Secretary of State for the Home Dept** [2007] **2** 737, HL.
  Removal from association—
    Child. *See* **Children and young persons** (Detention—Removal from association).
  Removal of prisoner from one prison to another—
    Secretary of State's discretion—
      Decision to move prisoner from one prison to another—Category A prisoner remanded in London prison pending trial—Prisoner instructing London lawyers to prepare defence—Parents living in London and unable to travel due to ill health—Prisoner removed to a prison 60 miles outside London for operational and security reasons—Whether court could review Secretary of State's decision to move prisoner to another prison—Whether court would inquire into operational or security reasons for removal—Prison Act 1952, s 12(2). **R v Secretary of State for the Home Dept, ex p McAvoy** [1984] **3** 417, QBD.
  Repatriation of prisoner—
    Transfer into United Kingdom—
      Calculation of release date—Prisoner transferred to England to serve balance of sentence—Secretary of State applying early release provisions to balance of sentence rather than whole sentence—Whether Secretary of State's method for calculating release date lawful—Convention on the Transfer of Sentenced Persons 1983—Repatriation of Prisoners Act 1984. **R v Secretary of State for the Home Dept, ex p Oshin** [2000] **2** 955, QBD.
      Continued enforcement of sentence—Compatibility of sentence—Sentence incompatible with law of United Kingdom—Basis on which compatibility to be determined—Transfer of prisoner from Spain to England—Prisoner sentenced in Spain to 12 years' imprisonment for counterfeiting offence—Maximum sentence in England for similar offence 10 years' imprisonment—Sentence in England unlikely in practice to exceed 4 years' imprisonment—Whether compatibility of sentence to be determined by comparing maximum sentences or sentences likely to be imposed in practice—Repatriation of Prisoners Act 1984, s 1—Convention on the Transfer of Sentenced Persons 1983, art 10. **Read v Secretary of State for the Home Dept** [1988] **3** 993, HL.
      Continued enforcement of sentence—Remission of sentence—Basis on which remission to be determined—Whether basis for determining any remission earned by prisoner limited to period in custody in England—Whether remission can be granted in respect of period in foreign custody. **Read v Secretary of State for the Home Dept** [1988] **3** 993, HL.
      Pardon, amnesty, commutation—Review of judgment—Grant of pardon under Crown prerogative—Prisoner convicted and sentenced in Bulgaria—Prisoner exhausting appeal process and process of executive review in Bulgaria—Prisoner transferred into United Kingdom—International arrangements providing for grant of pardon, amnesty or commutation of sentence in accordance with constitution or other laws—International arrangements providing sentencing state alone having right to decide on application for review of judgment—Whether Secretary of State having power to grant pardon under Crown prerogative—Whether review of judgment—Repatriation of Prisoners Act 1984, ss 1, 3—Convention on the Transfer of Sentenced Persons 1983, arts 12, 13. **R (on the application of Shields) v Secretary of State for Justice** [2009] **3** 265, QBD.
  Security categorisation. *See* Prisoner—Security categorisation, *above*.
  Sentence of imprisonment. *See* **Sentence** (Imprisonment).
  Sex discrimination. *See* **Sex discrimination** (Prisons).
  Visits—
    Visits by journalists—
      Journalists seeking to visit prisoners who claimed to be victims of miscarriages of justice—Prison authorities only allowing visits to proceed if journalists signed undertaking not to use information gained for professional purposes—Journalists refusing to sign and visits not allowed to proceed—Whether complete ban on oral interviews between journalists and prisoners lawful—Prison Service Standing Order 5A, paras 37, 37A. **R v Secretary of State for the Home Dept, ex p Simms** [1998] **2** 491, CA; [1999] **3** 400, HL.

PRISON BREACH
  Autrefois convict—
    Disciplinary proceedings. *See* **Criminal law** (Autrefois convict—Escape from prison—Disciplinary proceedings before visiting justices—Punishment awarded by justices—Subsequent trial on indictment for prison breach).

PRISONER
Custody—
    Liability of custodian for acts of escaped prisoners. *See* **Negligence** (Duty to take care—Custody of prisoners—Liability for acts of prisoners).
Escaped prisoner—
    Harbouring escaped prisoner. *See* **Criminal law** (Harbouring escaped prisoner).
Existing prisoner—
    Mandatory life sentence—
        Tariff. *See* **Sentence** (Mandatory life sentence—Murder—Tariff—Existing prisoners).
False imprisonment—
    Prisoner serving sentence. *See* **False imprisonment** (Prisoner serving sentence).
Generally. *See* **Prison**.
Hunger strike. *See* **Prison** (Prisoner—Hunger strike).
Liability for acts of prisoner—
    Public authority. *See* **Vicarious liability** (Non-employment relationship—Public authority performing statutory functions for public benefit).
Mental health. *See* **Mental health** (Prisoner).
National insurance benefit—
    Disqualification from receipt. *See* **Social security** (Benefit—Disqualification—Persons undergoing penal servitude, imprisonment or detention in legal custody).
Prison. *See* **Prison**.
Property of prisoner. *See* **Prison** (Prisoner—Property of prisoner).
Remand prisoner—
    Access to solicitor. *See* **Solicitor** (Access to—Right of person in custody—Remand prisoner).
    Right to marry. *See* **Marriage** (Right to marry—Person in detention—Remand prisoner).

PRISONER OF WAR
Geneva Convention. *See* **War** (Prisoners of war—Privileges of prisoners protected by Geneva Convention—Nationals of detaining power not entitled to privileges of Geneva Convention as prisoners of war).
Habeas corpus—
    Jurisdiction. *See* **Habeas corpus** (Jurisdiction—Prisoner of war).
Malaysia. *See* **Malaysia** (Prisoner of war).

PRIVACY
Anonymity in court proceedings—
    Human rights. *See* **Human rights** (Right to respect for private and family life—Freedom of expression).
Breach of confidence. *See* **Equity** (Breach of confidence).
Child—
    Court proceedings—
        Private prosecution. *See* **Criminal law** (Trial—Stay of proceedings—Abuse of process—Private prosecution—Privacy for children involved in certain proceedings).
    Court proceedings. *See* **Child** (Court proceedings in relation to child—Proceedings in private).
Citizen's right of privacy—
    Police powers to tap telephone. *See* **Police** (Powers—Telephone tapping—Citizen's rights of property, privacy and confidentiality).
Confidential information. *See* **Confidential information**.
Data protection. *See* **Data protection**.
Freedom of expression, restriction on—
    Human rights. *See* **Human rights** (Freedom of expression—Restriction on freedom of expression).
Human rights legislation—
    Right to respect for private and family life. *See* **Human rights** (Right to respect for private and family life).
Invasion of—
    Cause of action. *See* **Tort** (Cause of action—Invasion of privacy).
Nuisance—
    Overlooking. *See* **Nuisance** (Overlooking—Privacy).
Police investigation—
    Right to private and family life. *See* **Human rights** (Right to respect for private and family life—Freedom of expression—Police investigation).
Will. *See* **Will** (Privacy).

PRIVATE ACT OF PARLIAMENT
Validity. *See* **Statute** (Validity—Private Act of Parliament).

PRIVATE CARRIER'S LICENCE
Goods vehicle. *See* **Road traffic** (Goods vehicle—Private carrier's licence).

PRIVATE CITIZEN
Arrest by private citizen—
    Breach of the peace. *See* **Arrest** (Arrest without warrant—Breach of the peace—Citizen's right to arrest another person breaking or threatening to break the peace).

PRIVATE COMPANY
See **Company** (Private company).

PRIVATE EXAMINATION
Bankruptcy proceedings—
    Inspection of file. *See* **Bankruptcy** (Record of proceedings—Private examination).

PRIVATE HIRE VEHICLE
Licence—
    Generally. *See* **Road traffic** (Private hire vehicle—Licence).

PRIVATE HIRE VEHICLE (cont)—
    Licence (cont)—
        London. *See* **Licensing** (Private hire vehicles—Passenger contract—Obligations of London operators).

PRIVATE INTERNATIONAL LAW
    See **Conflict of laws**.

PRIVATE LAW ACTION
    Public law defence—
        Statement of claim—
            Striking out. *See* **Statement of case** (Striking out—Private law action—Public law defence).

PRIVATE LOTTERY
    See **Gaming** (Lottery—Private lottery).

PRIVATE NUISANCE
    See **Nuisance**.

PRIVATE PARTY
    Express carriage—
        Special occasion. *See* **Road traffic** (Express carriage—Special occasion—Conveyance of private party).

PRIVATE PLACE
    Indecent exposure in—
        Offence. *See* **Criminal law** (Indecent exposure—Wilfully, openly, lewdly and obscenely exposing person—Openly—Exposure in private room).

PRIVATE PREMISES
    Breach of the peace. *See* **Criminal law** (Breach of the peace—Common law offence—Breach of the peace on private premises).

PRIVATE PROSECUTION
    Costs—
        Award out of central funds. *See* **Criminal law** (Costs—Power to award costs—Award out of central funds).
        Taxation—
            Appeal against taxation. *See* **Crown Court** (Appeal from Crown Court—Costs—Court of Appeal, Criminal Division—Jurisdiction—Costs of successful private prosecution).
    Crown Court—
        Trial. *See* **Criminal law** (Trial—Crown Court—Private prosecution).
    Director of Public Prosecutions' decision not to institute proceedings—
        Whether decision precluding private prosecution. *See* **Criminal law** (Proceedings—Duties of Director of Public Prosecutions—Institution of proceedings—Private prosecution).
    Director of Public Prosecutions undertaking conduct of proceedings—
        Scope of 'conduct' of proceedings. *See* **Criminal law** (Proceedings—Duties of Director of Public Prosecutions—Undertaking conduct of proceedings).
    Magistrates—
        Refusal to issue summons. *See* **Magistrates** (Summons—Refusal to issue summons—Private prosecution).
    Police—
        Property, retention of, for purpose of assisting private prosecution. *See* **Police** (Powers—Power to retain property relevant to criminal proceedings).
    Summons—
        Crown discontinuing prosecution—
            Refusal to issue summons. *See* **Magistrates** (Summons—Refusal to issue summons—Private prosecution).

PRIVATE RESIDENCE
    Capital gains tax—
        Exemption. *See* **Capital gains tax** (Exemptions and reliefs—Private residence).
    Income tax. *See* **Income tax** (Residence).
    Search and seizure of goods—
        Police. *See* **Police** (Right of search—Right of search and seizure—Entry to private premises).

PRIVATE RIGHT OF WAY
    Easement. *See* **Easement** (Right of way).

PRIVATE RIGHTS
    Loss of private rights without compensation. *See* **Statute** (Confiscatory statutory provision—Loss of private rights without compensation).

PRIVATE SECURITY
    Door supervisors—
        Licensing. *See* **Licensing** (Private Security—Licensing criteria).
    Licensing—
        Generally. *See* **Licensing** (Private Security).
    Security Industry Authority—
        Functions of. *See* **Licensing** (Private Security—Security Industry Authority—Functions of authority).

PRIVATE STREET WORKS
    See **Highway** (Private street works).

PRIVILEGE

Absolute privilege—
    Defamation cases. *See* **Libel and slander** (Privilege—Absolute privilege).
    Tribunal recognised by law—
        Communications with tribunal—Libel and slander. *See* **Libel and slander** (Privilege—Absolute privilege—Tribunal recognised by law).
Anton Piller order—
    Privilege against self-incrimination. *See* **Practice** (Pre-trial or post-judgment relief—Search order—Privilege against self-incrimination).
Arrest, from. *See* **Arrest** (Privilege from arrest).
Confidential relationships. *See* **Evidence** (Privilege—Confidential relationships).
Crown servant—
    Evidence—
        Foreign tribunal—Privilege of Crown servant from giving evidence before foreign tribunal. *See* **Evidence** (Foreign tribunal—Examination of witness in relation to matters pending before foreign tribunal—Privilege of witness from giving evidence before foreign tribunal—Privilege of Crown servant).
Defamation. *See* **Libel and slander** (Privilege).
Diplomatic. *See* **Constitutional law** (Diplomatic privilege).
Disclosure and inspection of documents. *See* **Disclosure and inspection of documents** (Privilege).
Divorce proceedings, in. *See* **Divorce** (Evidence—Privilege).
Document—
    Generally. *See* **Document** (Privilege).
Evidence. *See* **Evidence** (Privilege).
Family proceedings—
    Evidence. *See* **Family proceedings** (Evidence—Privilege).
    Legal professional privilege. *See* **Disclosure and inspection of documents** (Legal professional privilege—Family proceedings).
Inspection of property—
    Privilege against self-incrimination. *See* **Practice** (Pre-trial or post-judgment relief—Search order—Privilege against self-incrimination).
Judge—
    Immunity from suit. *See* **Judge** (Immunity from suit).
Legal advice privilege. *See* Legal professional privilege—Legal advice privilege, *below*.
Legal professional privilege—
    Care proceedings—
        Medical report concerning welfare of child—Whether court entitled to disclose report to police. *See* **Family proceedings** (Confidential information in care proceedings—Disclosure to police—Medical report concerning welfare of child—Privilege—Legal professional privilege).
    Company and its directors. *See* Legal professional privilege—Joint interest privilege, *below*.
    Disclosure and inspection of documents. *See* **Disclosure and inspection of documents** (Legal professional privilege).
    Documents—
        Copies—Copies made for purpose of obtaining legal advice—Copy of affidavit served on defendants in unrelated proceedings—Defendants sending photocopy of affidavit to their solicitors—Affidavit not privileged—Whether copy of affidavit privileged—Whether defendants' solicitors obliged to produce copy to plaintiff's solicitors. **Dubai Bank Ltd v Galadari** [1989] 3 769, CA.
        Copies—Copies made for purpose of obtaining legal advice—Documents containing information relevant to tax liability—Original documents not accessible to Revenue—Copy documents in possession of barrister—Revenue serving notice on barrister requiring him to make copies available for inspection—Whether barrister obliged to produce copies to Revenue—Whether barrister entitled to claim professional privilege in respect of copies—Taxes Management Act 1970, ss 20(3), 20B(8). **R v Board of Inland Revenue, ex p Goldberg** [1988] 3 248, QBD.
        Criminal proceedings—Documents in possession or control of accused's solicitor—Statement by accused's co-defendant that accused not involved in offence—Co-defendant giving evidence for Crown at accused's trial—Whether privilege attaching to statement made by co-defendant to solicitor. **R v Ataou** [1988] 2 321, CA.
        Criminal proceedings—Extent of privilege in criminal law—Police seizing documents submitted to solicitor for advice but not coming into existence for that purpose—Whether documents privileged. **Truman (Frank) Export Ltd v Metropolitan Police Comr** [1977] 3 431, QBD.
        Criminal proceedings—Items subject to legal privilege—Conveyancing transactions—Records of conveyancing transaction—Solicitors acting in connection with purchase of property for client suspected by police of armed robbery—Police seeking order requiring solicitor to produce records of conveyancing transaction—Whether records of conveyancing transaction privileged—Whether correspondence giving advice in connection with conveyance privileged—Police and Criminal Evidence Act 1984, s 10, Sch 1, para 1. **R v Crown Court at Inner London Sessions, ex p Baines & Baines (a firm)** [1987] 3 1025, QBD.
        Criminal proceedings—Witness summons—Material evidence—Committal proceedings—Documents likely to be material evidence—Witness having previously made inconsistent statement to his solicitor when he himself was charged with same crime with which accused charged—Whether legal professional privilege overriding public interest in securing that all relevant and admissible evidence made available to accused for his defence—Whether magistrate having jurisdiction to issue witness summons for production of witness's instructions to solicitor—Criminal Procedure Act 1865, ss 4, 5—Magistrates' Courts Act 1980, s 97. **R v Derby Magistrates' Court, ex p B** [1995] 4 526, HL.
    Disclosure and inspection of. *See* **Disclosure and inspection of documents** (Legal professional privilege).
    European Union. *See* **European Union** (Restrictive trade practices—Investigation of undertakings—Investigation into anti-competitive practices—Documents being seized—Documents containing communications between lawyer and client—Legal professional privilege being claimed in respect of documents).

PRIVILEGE (cont)—
    Legal professional privilege (cont)—
        Documents (cont)—
            Law society investigating complaint against law firm—Law firm voluntarily providing privileged documents to law society for limited purpose on express basis that privilege not waived—Whether privilege lost or waived by limited disclosure. **B v Auckland District Law Society** [2004] **4** 269, PC.
            Production—Criminal proceedings—Documents in possession or control of solicitor—Documents furthering defence of accused—Whether privilege attaching to documents. **R v Barton** [1972] **2** 1192, Lincoln Crown Ct.
            Production—Generally. *See* **Disclosure and inspection of documents** (Legal professional privilege).
            Translations—Whether translations of unprivileged documents in control of party claiming privilege to be treated differently from copies of such documents. **Sumitomo Corp v Credit Lyonnais Rouse Ltd** [2002] **4** 68, CA.
        Expert evidence—
            Criminal proceedings. *See* **Criminal evidence** (Expert evidence—Legal professional privilege).
        Forged documents or instruments—
            Search warrant—Documents in possession of solicitor. *See* **Police** (Search warrant—Forged documents or instruments—Lawful authority or excuse for possession of forged documents—Solicitor—Legal professional privilege).
        Interrogatory—
            Generally. *See* **Disclosure and inspection of documents** (Interrogatory—Privilege—Legal professional privilege).
        Joint interest privilege—
            Privilege arising where two or more persons having joint interest in subject matter of document—Company and its directors—Company enjoying legal professional privilege—Whether directors enjoying privilege in their capacity as individuals—Approach to application for joint interest privilege. **R (on the application of Ford) v Financial Services Authority (Johnson and another, interested parties)** [2012] **1** 1238, Admin Ct.
        Joint privilege—
            Data subject access request to solicitors by beneficiaries under Bahamian trusts—Whether data exempt from subject information provisions under legal professional privilege exemption—Whether beneficiary and trustee having joint privilege—Data Protection Act 1998, Sch 7, para 10. **Dawson-Damer v Taylor Wessing LLP** [2020] **2 Comm** 820, CA; [2020] **4** 600, CA.
        Legal advice privilege—
            Communication or document—Multi-addressee emails—Whether communication having to have dominant purpose of seeking or giving legal advice to fall within the scope of legal advice privilege—Correct approach to multi-addressee emails. **R (on the application of Jet2.com Ltd) v Civil Aviation Authority (Law Society of England and Wales intervening)** [2020] **4** 374, CA.
            Scope—Documents attached to email—Regulator requiring production of documents pursuant to its investigatory powers—Whether privilege applying to documents purely by virtue of their being attached to emails between respondent and its solicitors—Whether production of documents to regulator for purposes of investigation would infringe privilege—Statutory Auditors and Third Country Auditors Regulations 2016, SI 2016/649, Sch 2, para 1. **Financial Reporting Council Ltd v Sports Direct International plc** [2019] **2** 974, Ch D; [2020] **2 Comm** 1027, CA; [2020] **4** 552, CA.
            Scope—Foreign lawyer—Communications between foreign qualified in-house legal adviser and client—Whether legal advice privilege extending to foreign qualified lawyers. **PJSC Tatneft v Bogolyubov** [2021] **2** 224, QBD; [2021] **2 Comm** 450, QBD.
        Loss of privilege in connection with criminal proceedings—
            Test. **Butler v Board of Trade** [1970] **3** 593, Ch D.
        New Zealand. *See* **New Zealand** (Legal professional privilege).
        No defence against statutory inspection of solicitor's accounts. *See* **Solicitor** (Clients' account—Inspection of books of account, bank pass books, vouchers etc).
        Scope—
            Accountants legal advice on tax. *See* **Judicial review** (Information—Power to require information—Production of documents).
        Solicitor and client—
            Communications between legal adviser and client—Allegation that purpose of communication was furtherance of crime—Whether court entitled to look at document without requiring independent evidence of purpose of document. **R v Governor of Pentonville Prison, ex p Osman** [1989] **3** 701, QBD.
            Communications between legal adviser and client—Communications passing between solicitor and client in course of conveyancing transaction—Whether such communications privileged. **Balabel v Air-India** [1988] **2** 246, CA.
            Communications between legal adviser and client—Information received by solicitor from third party for onward transmission to client—Whether such communications privileged—Whether such communications separable from solicitor/client communications ordinarily privileged. **Getty (Sarah C) Trust, Re** [1985] **2** 809, QBD.
            Communications between legal adviser and client—Inspector of taxes exercising statutory investigatory power to investigate tax-related scheme—Whether provision authorising inspector to require disclosure of material subject to legal professional privilege—Taxes Management Act 1970, s 20(1), (7). **R (on the application of Morgan Grenfell & Co Ltd) v Special Comr of Income Tax** [2001] **1** 535, QBD; [2002] **1** 776, CA; [2002] **3** 1, HL.
            Communications between legal adviser and client—Judge ordering solicitors to produce to police any record or log recording applicant's arrival at their offices on a particular date, including appointment diaries and attendance notes—Documents likely to be material evidence—Whether documents privileged—Whether documents communications made for purposes of seeking or receiving legal advice—Police and Criminal Evidence Act 1984, s 9, Sch 1. **R v Crown Court at Manchester, ex p Rogers** [1999] **4** 35, QBD.

PRIVILEGE (cont)—
  Legal professional privilege (cont)—
    Solicitor and client (cont)—
      Communications between legal adviser and client—Party seeking disclosure of client's contact details and assets to aid enforcement of committal order—Whether court having jurisdiction to order disclosure—Whether discretion should be exercised in favour of disclosure. **JSC BTA Bank v Solodchenko** [2012] **1** 735, Ch D.
      Communications between legal adviser and joint clients—Application for disclosure—Joint retainer privilege ('JRP')—Insurer and insured jointly engaged solicitors and counsel to advise on claims made in group litigation—Insured assigning its professional negligence claims against said solicitors and counsel to third party by deed of assignment—Whether third party entitled to disclosure of files covered by JRP in principle—Whether any right to disclosure limited or lost by virtue of deed or factual background—Whether appropriate to give guidance on any categories of documents to be disclosed. **Travelers Insurance Co Ltd v Armstrong (joint administrators of Transform Medical Group (CS) Ltd)** [2022] **1 Comm** 1366, CA.
      Communications between legal advisor and joint clients—Husband and wife transferring property into sole ownership of wife—Communications passing between solicitor in joint capacity and husband and/or wife in course of transfer of property—Husband subsequently adjudicated bankrupt—Trustee in bankruptcy seeking to set aside transfer as being voluntary settlement and void against trustee—Wife seeking to assert privilege as ground for refusing to disclose to trustee communications relating to transfer—Whether wife entitled to assert privilege—Whether trustee standing in position of bankrupt or in position of third party for purposes of rule precluding joint clients from maintaining privilege against each other. **Konigsberg (a bankrupt), Re, ex p the trustee v Konigsberg** [1989] **3** 289, Ch D.
      Communications between legal advisor and joint clients—Insurers instructing solicitors to conduct defence of proceedings brought against insured—Solicitors instructing counsel to consider whether insurers entitled to repudiate liability—Insurers repudiating liability and insured bringing third party proceedings against insurers—Insurers' defence relying on statements made by insured at conference with counsel—Whether implied waiver of privilege between joint clients extending beyond emergence of actual conflict of interest. **TSB Bank plc v Robert Irving & Burns (a firm) (Colonia Baltica Insurance Ltd, third party)** [2000] **2** 826, CA.
      Loss of privilege—Defendant advised by solicitor to make no reply to police questions—Statement by solicitor as to grounds for advice adduced in evidence—Whether legal professional privilege waived—Whether questions could be asked about factual basis for advice. **R v Bowden** [1999] **4** 43, CA.
      Loss of privilege—Waiver—Costs assessment—Client seeking detailed assessment of former solicitors' bill of costs—Client applying for hearing to be held in private—Whether waiver of privilege absolute or limited—Whether application to be heard in public or in private—CPR 39.2(3). **Eurasian Natural Resources Corp Ltd v Dechert LLP** [2017] **3** 1084, CA.
      Loss of privilege—Waiver—Criminal proceedings—Defendant presenting statement to police through his solicitor during interview—Defendant contradicting statement at trial and alleging error by solicitor in preparing it—Prosecution commenting on absence from witness box of defendant's solicitor to confirm truth of evidence—Whether prosecution's comment permissible. **R v Seaton** [2011] **1** 932, CA.
      Loss of privilege—Waiver—Dissolution of company—Crown disclaiming all interest in property—Whether legal advice privilege attaching to communications between foreign company and lawyers lost upon dissolution of company. **Addlesee v Dentons Europe LLP** [2020] **1** 124, CA.
      Loss of privilege—Waiver—Mother of injured child in care proceedings claiming father did not hurt child—Mother subsequently filing witness statement identifying father as perpetrator—Mother disclosing contents of discussions with lawyers in witness statement—Whether mother waived legal professional privilege—Whether unfair to allow mother to not reveal whole of relevant information—Whether risk court and father would only have partial and potentially misleading understanding of material. **D (a child), Re** [2011] **4** 434, CA.
    Surveillance and covert human intelligence sources. *See* **Investigatory Powers** (Regulation of investigatory powers—Surveillance and covert human intelligence sources—Authorisation of surveillance and human intelligence sources—Lawful surveillance—Authorisation of directed surveillance—Legal professional privilege).
    Trustee in bankruptcy. *See* **Bankruptcy** (Trustee in bankruptcy—Legal professional privilege).
  Libel and slander. *See* **Libel and slander** (Privilege).
  Loss of privilege—
    Inadvertent disclosure of document on inspection—
      Whether privilege lost if document inadvertently disclosed as the result of obvious mistake. **Guinness Peat Properties Ltd v Fitzroy Robinson Partnership (a firm)** [1987] **2** 716, CA.
  Member of Parliament—
    Action against member of Parliament. *See* **Parliament** (Privilege—Action against member of Parliament).
  Newspaper reporter—
    Evidence. *See* **Evidence** (Privilege—Press—Newspaper reporter).
  Parliament—
    Generally. *See* **Parliament** (Privilege).
    New Zealand. *See* **New Zealand** (Parliament—Parliamentary privilege).
  Public interest immunity—
    Disclosure and inspection of documents. *See* **Disclosure and inspection of documents** (Privilege—Production contrary to public interest).
    Production contrary to public interest—
      Risk of serious harm to public security—Judgment—Principle of open justice—Judgment of court redacted to omit material obtained from intelligence sharing arrangements between United Kingdom and United States—Whether unredacted judgment should be published. **R (on the application of Mohamed) v Secretary of State for Foreign and Commonwealth Affairs** [2010] **4** 91, CA; **R (on the application of Mohamed) v Secretary of State for Foreign and Commonwealth Affairs (No 2)** [2010] **4** 177n, CA.

PRIVILEGE (cont)—
  Public interest immunity (cont)—
    Production contrary to public interest (cont)—
        Sentencing—Confiscation order—Judge ruling in favour of Crown on public interest immunity in relation to certain material—Judge subsequently making confiscation order—Whether special counsel required to be appointed. **R v May** [2005] **3** 523, CA.
        Use of privileged information in civil proceedings—Plaintiff commencing proceedings against police for payment for information leading to arrest and conviction of persons involved in serious crime—Police contending that plaintiff precluded from asserting in open court that he acted as informer on grounds of public interest immunity—Whether police informer precluded from bringing proceedings to recover moneys promised in exchange for information. **Savage v Chief Constable of Hampshire Constabulary** [1997] **2** 631, CA.
        Use of privileged information in civil proceedings—Police complaints and disciplinary files—Statements taken in investigation into complaints of police misconduct—Complainant bringing civil action against police—Police refusing to give undertaking not to use in civil proceedings information obtained in course of complaints investigation—Whether police prevented from using in civil proceedings information obtained in course of complaints investigation. **R v Chief Constable of West Midlands Police, ex p Wiley** [1994] **3** 420, HL.
        Use of privileged information in civil proceedings—Reports and working papers of investigating police officers—Plaintiff claiming malicious prosecution, misfeasance in public office and conspiracy by chief constable of police—Reports prepared by police following inquiries into matters connected with prosecution of plaintiff—Police claiming reports protected by public interest immunity—Whether reports belonging to class entitled to public interest immunity—Whether inspection of reports necessary for 'disposing fairly of the cause or matter or for saving costs'—RSC Ord 24, r 13(1). **Taylor v Anderton (Police Complaints Authority intervening)** [1995] **2** 420, CA.
  Qualified privilege—
    Libel and slander. *See* **Libel and slander** (Qualified privilege).
  Search order—
    Privilege against self-incrimination. *See* **Practice** (Pre-trial or post-judgment relief—Search order—Privilege against self-incrimination).
  Self-incrimination, against—
    Defence in proceedings for contempt of court. *See* **Contempt of court** (Defence—Self-incrimination).
    Defendant for purposes of disclosure only. *See* **Disclosure and inspection of documents** (Defendant for purposes of disclosure only—Norwich Pharmacal order).
    Department of Trade and Industry investigation of company's affairs—
        Whether common law privilege against self-incrimination available to persons questioned by inspectors. *See* **Company** (Investigation by Department of Trade and Industry—Affairs of company—Duty of officers and agents of company to give information—Privilege against self-incrimination).
    Freezing order—
        Discovery in aid of injunction. *See* **Practice** (Pre-trial or post-judgment relief—Freezing order—Disclosure in aid of injunction—Privilege against self-incrimination).
    Injunction—
        Discovery in aid of injunction—Generally. *See* **Practice** (Pre-trial or post-judgment relief—Disclosure in aid of injunction—Privilege against self-incrimination).
    Insolvency of company—
        Inquiry into company's affairs. *See* **Company** (Insolvency—Inquiry into company affairs—Examination of officers of company etc—Privilege against self-incrimination).
    Inspection of property which subject-matter of action. *See* **Practice** (Pre-trial or post-judgment relief—Search order—Privilege against self-incrimination).
    Intellectual property proceedings. *See* **Practice** (Pre-trial or post-judgment relief—Requests for further information—Self-incrimination—Privilege—Withdrawal of privilege—Proceedings for infringement of rights pertaining to any intellectual property).
    Provisional liquidator's inquiry into company's affairs. *See* **Company** (Provisional liquidation—Inquiry into company affairs—Examination of officers of company etc—Privilege against self-incrimination).
    Search order. *See* **Practice** (Pre-trial or post-judgment relief—Search order—Privilege against self-incrimination).
    Terrorist investigation—
        Disclosure of material. *See* **Criminal evidence** (Special procedure material—Terrorist investigation—Circuit judge making production order against journalist).
    Use in criminal proceedings of admissions made during ancillary relief proceedings. *See* **Evidence** (Admissibility—Criminal proceedings—Admissions made during ancillary relief proceedings).
  Solicitor and client—
    Legal advice privilege. *See* Legal professional privilege—Legal advice privilege, *above*.
  Special procedure material—
    Access to special procedure material—
        Legal privilege. *See* **Criminal evidence** (Special procedure material—Access to special procedure material—Legal privilege).
  Taxation of costs—
    Documents lodged with taxing master. *See* **Costs** (Taxation—Review of taxation—Right to see documents lodged with taxing master—Privileged documents).
  Will—
    Soldier's or mariner's privileged will. *See* **Will** (Soldier's or mariner's privileged will).
  Without prejudice correspondence—
    Privilege from admission in evidence. *See* **Evidence** (Without prejudice correspondence).
  Witness—
    Immunity from civil action. *See* **Action** (Immunity from suit—Witness).
    Statement—
        Exchange of witnesses' statements. *See* **Evidence** (Exchange of witnesses' statements—Statement of oral evidence—Privilege).

PRIVITY

Contract—
    Restitution. *See* **Contract** (Restitution—Contract for sale of hotel).
    Stranger to contract. *See* **Contract** (Stranger to contract).
Party to proceedings—
    Res judicata. *See* **Estoppel** (Res judicata—Privity of party to proceedings).

PRIVY COUNCIL

Abatement of appeal—
    Death of party—
        Death before appeal heard—Party not appearing and not represented—Appeal in divorce matter—Reserved judgment prepared—Discovery of death of party. **Hodge v Marsh** [1936] **1** 848, PC.
Abolition of right of appeal to—
    Canada. *See* **Canada** (Appeals to Privy Council—Abolition).
Appeal—
    Canada, from. *See* **Canada** (Appeals to Privy Council).
    Ceylon, from. *See* **Ceylon** (Appeal to Privy Council).
    Compromise of. *See* Compromise of appeal, *below*.
    Criminal appeal. *See* Criminal appeal, *below*.
    Damages. *See* Damages—Appeal, *below*.
    Exclusion of right of appeal. *See* Exclusion of right of appeal, *below*.
    Leave to appeal. *See* Leave to appeal, *below*.
    Limits inter se of constitutional powers of Commonwealth and State—
        Australia. *See* **Australia** (Appeal to Privy Council—Limits of constitutional powers).
    Pastoral scheme. *See* **Ecclesiastical law** (Appeal—Pastoral scheme).
    Right of appeal. *See* Right of appeal, *below*.
Appearance—
    Withdrawal of appearance—
        Withdrawal of appearance—Effect of withdrawal on appeal—Judicial Committee Rules 1957 (SI 1957 No 2224), r 34. **Khatijabai Jiwa Hasham v Zenab D/O Chandu Nansi, Widow and Exrx of Haji Gulam Hussein Harji (decd)** [1958] **3** 719, PC.
Australia—
    New South Wales—
        Negligence—Cause of action—Foreseeability—Wharf damaged by fire caused through careless-ness of charterers' servants in allowing bunkering oil to spill from ship into water—Whether damage could reasonably have been foreseen. **Wagon Mound, The (No 1)** [1961] **1** 404, PC.
Compromise of appeal—
    Minor's interest—
        Certificate of court below. **Shukrullah (Shaikh) v Musammat Zohra Bibi** [1936] **3** 1011, PC.
Concurrent findings of fact in courts below—
    Review of facts by Judicial Committee—
        Concurrent findings of High Court and Court of Appeal—Practice of the Judicial Committee regarding re-hearing—Practice not to review facts for third time unless exceptional circumstances—Dissentient judgment in Court of Appeal not justifying review. **Chua Chee Chor v Chua Kim Yong** [1963] **1** 102, PC.
Contempt of court—
    Penalty for contempt—
        Jurisdiction of Privy Council to entertain appeal—Order of overseas court of record imposing penalty for contempt. **Ambard v A-G for Trinidad and Tobago** [1936] **1** 704, PC.
Costs—
    Counsel's fees—
        Hong Kong appeal—Fees of overseas counsel. *See* Costs—Taxation—Hong Kong appeal—Fees of overseas counsel, *below*.
        Refresher fees. **Practice Note** [1959] **1** 733, PC.
    Printed record—
        Inclusion of matters not relevant to subject-matter of appeal—Cost of printing irrelevant matter deducted from costs. **Lim Siew Neo v Pang Keah Swee** [1958] **1** 313, PC.
    Taxation—
        Hong Kong appeal—Fees of overseas counsel—Work carried out overseas in connection with appeal to Privy Council—Travelling expenses and hotel bills of Hong Kong counsel—Counsel's fees for settling case—Jurisdiction of Privy Council registrar—Hong Kong (Appeal to Privy Council) Order in Council of 10 August 1909, r 25—Judicial Committee (General Appellate Jurisdiction) Rules Order 1982, Sch 2, r 76. **Tai Hing Cotton Mill Ltd v Liu Chong Hing Bank Ltd (No 2)** [1986] **1** 897, PC.
Criminal appeal—
    First review of summing-up—
        Duty of Judicial Committee. **Broadhurst v R** [1964] **1** 111, PC.
    Right of appeal—
        Appeal by special leave—Grounds for allowing appeal. **Renouf v A-G for Jersey** [1936] **1** 936, PC.
    Special leave to appeal—
        Misdirection—Burden of proof—Circumstances only within knowledge of prisoners—Ceylon Evidence Ordinance (No 14 of 1895), s 106. **Attygalle v R** [1936] **2** 116, PC.
Damages—
    Appeal—
        Erroneous assessment by trial judge—Substitution of Board's own assessment—Board's practice. **Selvanayagam v University of the West Indies** [1983] **1** 824, PC.
    Interest—
        Jurisdiction to award interest. *See* Jurisdiction—Interest—Interest on award of damages, *below*.

PRIVY COUNCIL (cont)—
    Exclusion of right of appeal—
        Power of Dominion legislature—
            Power to exclude appeals from dominion and provincial courts—British North America Act 1867, ss 91, 92, 101—Statute of Westminster 1931. **A-G of Ontario v A-G of Canada (A-G of Quebec intervening)** [1947] **1** 137, PC.
    Exercise of discretion—
        Review by Judicial Committee—
            Principle on which Judicial Committee may review discretion of Commonwealth court—Delay in making deposit required for purpose of appeal—Deposit not made 'forthwith'—Appeal dismissed for non-compliance with rules—Application to restore appeal refused—West African Court of Appeal Rules, r 23(3). **Short v A-G of Sierra Leone** [1964] **1** 125, PC.
    Fresh point—
        Fact and law—
            Evidence must be such as to establish that facts would support new plea—Fresh point of law not readily allowed even if facts beyond dispute. **United Marketing Co v Hasham Kara** [1963] **2** 553, PC.
        Trial before judge and jury—
            Fresh point raised which was not raised or considered by judge and jury. **Perkowski v Wellington Corp (City of)** [1958] **3** 368, PC.
        Trial before judge sitting without a jury—
            Defence raised which was not raised before or mentioned by trial judge—Defence of sudden fight to charge of murder—Defence required to be proved by defendant—Whether Privy Council entitled to consider defence—Whether real risk of failure of justice if defence not considered by Privy Council—Whether sufficient evidence on which a reasonable tribunal could find defence was made out—Singapore Penal Code, s 300(c), exception 4. **Kunjo v Public Prosecutor** [1978] **1** 1209, PC.
    General Medical Council—
        Powers of Privy Council. *See* **Medical practitioner** (Appeal against determination of disciplinary committee—Powers of Privy Council).
    Grant of Royal Charter—
        Decision of committee to recommend grant of charter to professional body—
            Guidance—Application for judicial review of decision to recommend—Whether decision to recommend amenable to judicial review—Whether decision made in accordance with published criteria—Whether decision tainted by apparent bias. **R (on the application of the Project Management Institute) v Minister for the Cabinet Office** [2016] **4** 334, CA.
    India—
        Income tax—
            Business—Expenditure—Annual payment made as part of consideration of purchase of business—Distinguished from one for the purpose of producing profits. **Tata Hydro-Electric Agencies Ltd (Bombay) v Income Tax Comr, Bombay Presidency and Aden** [1937] **2** 291, PC.
    Jurisdiction—
        Appeal from Ceylon. *See* **Ceylon** (Appeal to Privy Council—Jurisdiction—Right of Privy Council to entertain appeal from Ceylon).
        Effect of independence—
            Nature of Order in Council implementing report of Judicial Committee—Constitutional position of Judicial Committee in relation to appeals—Status of independence attained by former colony—Whether jurisdiction of Her Majesty in Council terminated by necessary implication. **Ibralebbe v R** [1964] **1** 251, PC.
        Finality of decision of colonial supreme court—
            Membership of a colonial legislative council—Order in Council providing for reference by legislative council of colony to supreme court—Finality of court's determination—Absence of jurisdiction over such questions save on reference from legislative council—Office as minister similarly outside jurisdiction—Trinidad and Tobago (Constitution) Order in Council 1950 (SI 1950 No 510), s 40(1) as substituted by Trinidad and Tobago (Constitution) (Amendment) Order in Council 1956 (SI 1956 No 835), s 27. **Patterson v Solomon** [1960] **2** 20, PC.
    Interest—
        Interest on award of damages—Jurisdiction to award interest—Determination of appropriate rate of interest. **Central Electricity Board of Mauritius v Bata Shoe Co (Mauritius) Ltd (note)** [1982] **3** 1149, PC.
    Leave to appeal—
        New Zealand—Governor-General's exercise of prerogative of mercy—Opinion of Court of Appeal—Petitioner convicted of murder and applying to Governor-General for exercise of prerogative of mercy—Governor-General seeking 'assistance' of Court of Appeal—Court of Appeal furnishing 'opinion' to Governor-General adverse to petitioner—Whether Court of Appeal's opinion a 'determination'—Whether petitioner having right to appeal to Privy Council against Court of Appeal's opinion—Judicial Committee Act 1833, s 3—Crimes Act 1961 (New Zealand), s 406(b). **Thomas (Arthur) v R** [1979] **2** 142, PC.
        Special leave. *See* Leave to appeal—Special leave—Jurisdiction, *below*.
    Leave to appeal granted—
        Objection to jurisdiction to hear appeal—No dissatisfaction with order of court from which leave to appeal sought—Ruling asked on law applicable to assessment of damages at new trial—Judicial Committee Act 1833, s 3. **Australian Consolidated Press Ltd v Uren** [1967] **3** 523, PC.
    Matter within competency of tribunal—
        Jurisdiction to hear appeal on matter—No intention that right of appeal to Crown should attach—Ceylon—Validity of Parliamentary election—Ceylon (Parliamentary Elections) Order in Council 1946, s 50, s 83. **Senanayake v Navaratne** [1954] **2** 805, PC.
    Original jurisdiction—
        No jurisdiction as court of first instance to hear appeal against mandatory sentence of death. **Walker v R** [1993] **4** 789, PC.

PRIVY COUNCIL (cont)—
    Leave to appeal—
        Appeal in forma pauperis—
            Certificate by counsel that in his view there was reasonable ground of appeal—Applications should not be granted automatically merely because counsel's certificate that there was reasonable ground of appeal has been furnished. **Nelson v East African Newspapers (Nation Series) Ltd** [1963] **3** 812, PC.
        Ceylon. See **Ceylon** (Appeal to Privy Council—Leave).
        Grant of special leave—
            Grant not disentitling appellant to contend that no appeal lay. **Patterson v Solomon** [1960] **2** 20, PC.
        Ground for refusing leave—
            Insufficient doubt to justify leave to appeal. **Thornton v The Police** [1962] **3** 88, PC.
        Jurisdiction—
            New Zealand. See Jurisdiction—Leave to appeal—New Zealand, above.
            Question as to jurisdiction to hear appeal—Decision on jurisdiction before advising grant of leave. **Dennis Hotels Pty Ltd v State of Victoria, A-G of the Commonwealth of Australia (intervener)** [1961] **2** 940, PC.
        Person aggrieved—
            Attorney General in colony—Attorney General responsible for bringing before judge any misconduct of barrister or solicitor of sufficient gravity to warrant disciplinary action—West African (Appeal to Privy Council) Order in Council 1949, s 34. **A-G of the Gambia v N'Jie** [1961] **2** 504, PC.
        Special leave—
            Discretionary—Special leave refused even though appeal lay as of right under territorial legislation. **Lopes v Valliappa Chettiar** [1968] **2** 136, PC.
            Grant—Effect. See Leave to appeal—Grant of special leave—Grant not disentitling appellant to contend that no appeal lay, above.
            Jurisdiction—Belize—Whether Privy Council having jurisdiction to hear petition for special leave after expiry of time limits laid down in proclamation providing for postponement of death sentence pending appeal—Whether Privy Council having jurisdiction to hear petition for special leave after petition for mercy has been refused—Judicial Committee (General Appellate Jurisdiction) Rules Order 1982, r 5. **Logan v R** [1996] **4** 190, PC.
            Prerogative. **Mahesh Prasad Singh (Raja Sarda) v Badri Lal Sahu** [1936] **1** 361, PC.
        Time within which to apply for leave—
            West Africa. See **West Africa** (Appeal to Privy Council—Leave to appeal—Application to be made to court within 21 days from date of judgment to be appealed from).
    Order in Council, on advice of—
        Judicial review—
            Jurisdiction. See **Crown** (Prerogative—Review of exercise of prerogative power by court).
    Precedent. See **Precedent** (Privy Council).
    Reasons for decision—
        Statement of reasons—
            Need for court from which appeal arises to state reasons for decision—Judicial Committee Rules 1925 (SR & O 1925, No 440), r 16. **Nana Osei Assibey III, Kokofuhene v Nana Kwasi Agyeman, Boagyaahene** [1952] **2** 1084, PC.
    Right of appeal—
        Appeal as of right dependent on amount of the matter in dispute—
            Amounts expressed in pounds sterling—Whether English pounds meant—Verdict of £500 damages given in New South Wales—Minimum amount for appeal as of right '£500 sterling'—Australian pound worth less than English pound—SR & O 1909 No 1521, r 2(a). **Skelton v Jones** [1962] **3** 85, PC.
            Appeal by taxpayer—Competency—Competency dependent on amount taxpayer been adjudged liable to pay being £500 or over—Constitution of Jamaica, s 110(1)(a). **Fletcher v Income Tax Comr** [1971] **3** 1185, PC.
        Criminal appeal. See Criminal appeal—Right of appeal, above.
        Decision of Court of Appeal—
            Jurisdiction conferred on Court of Appeal by special Act. **Hem Singh v Mahant Basant Das** [1936] **1** 356, PC.
        East Africa. See **East Africa** (Appeal to Privy Council—Appeal as of right).
        Exclusion of. See Exclusion of right of appeal, above.
        Ontario, from. See **Canada** (Appeals to Privy Council—Ontario—Appeal as of right).
        West Africa. See **West Africa** (Appeal to Privy Council—Appeal as of right).
    West Africa—
        Appeal as of right—
            Value of matter in dispute. See **West Africa** (Appeal to Privy Council—Appeal as of right—Value of matter in dispute).
        Estoppel. See **West Africa** (Estoppel).

PRIZE LAW
    Condemnation—
        Freight—
            Ship of neutral country carrying contraband—Seizure with hostile intent—Neutral country becoming belligerent enemy. **Sado Maru, Part Cargo ex SS** [1947] **1** 430, Admin Ct.
        Goods—
            Ownership of goods—Exchange of goods immediately before hostilities—Public policy. **Glenearn, The** [1941] **1** 371, Admin Ct.
        Ship—
            Anticipating embargo—Arrest of enemy merchant ship before outbreak of war—Whether immune from confiscation—Hague Convention VI, arts 1, 2. **Pomona, The** [1943] **1** 408, Admin Ct.
            Claims arising out of purported exercise of belligerent rights barred by peace treaty—Ships aground in port—Capture of port—Ships formally boarded and certificate of prize signed four years after armistice, but before signing of peace treaty—Naval Prize Act 1864, s 16. **Bellaman, The** [1948] **2** 679, Admin Ct.

PRIZE LAW (cont)—
Condemnation (cont)—
Ship (cont)—
Enemy flag—Duress—Ship built in Germany by German subsidiary of Dutch company under agreement with and subsidised by German government. **Unitas, The** [1950] **2** 219, PC.
Partly constructed ship not capable of floating—Ship under construction in building yard—Seizure at same time as capture of port—No intention by captors to seize as immediate prize—Seizure after surrender of belligerent. **Schiffahrt-Treuhand GmbH v Procurator-General** [1953] **1** 364, PC.
Seizure of ship of enemy-occupied country—Claim against ship for salvage—Condemnation delayed—Rights of salvors. **Prins Knud, The** [1941] **1** 443, Admin Ct.
Ship taken out of harbour when capture of harbour imminent—Scuttled in deep water about a mile and a half from shore—Formally seized as prize six years after capture of harbour. **Giuseppe Mazzini, The** [1949] **2** 1094, Admin Ct.
Ships scuttled in land-locked bay of enemy island—Subsequent capture of island—Ships formally seized in prize six years after capture of island. **Giuseppe Mazzini, The** [1949] **2** 1094, Admin Ct.
Costs—
Crown's immunity from costs—
Compensation in lieu of freight—Matter referred by agreement to registrar—Question of amount only. **Panaghiotis, The** [1942] **2** 525, Admin Ct.
Salvage—
Payment—
Jurisdiction to order payment. **France Fenwick Tyne and Wear Co Ltd v HM Procurator-General** [1942] **2** 453, PC.
Visit and search—
Neutral ship ordered to British port for better examination—
Reasonable suspicion. **Mim, The** [1947] **2** 476, Admin Ct.

PRIZES
Amusements with prizes. *See* **Gaming** (Amusements with prizes).
Distribution of prizes by chance—
Competition. *See* **Gaming** (Prize competition).
Lottery. *See* **Gaming** (Lottery—Scheme involving distribution of prizes by chance).

PROBATE
Action—
Compromise of action—
Form of order—Chancery Division. **Practice Direction** [1972] **3** 319, Ch D.
Terms of compromise not signed by party cited to see proceedings—Application that party cited should be bound by compromise—RSC Ord 16, r 9A. **Tame (decd), Re** [1956] **2** 293, Prob.
Continuance of action—
Corporate executor plaintiff—Amalgamation with another company—Whether corporate executor, having transferred business of acting as personal representative, should continue as plaintiff in the action. **Skinner (decd), Re** [1958] **3** 273, Prob.
Costs. *See* Costs, *below.*
Dismissal of action—
Delay in instituting action—Action commenced six years from grant of probate—Application to strike out—Whether delay alone a ground for striking out probate action—Whether action must also be shown to be frivolous, vexatious or abuse of process—RSC Ord 18, r 19(1)(d). **Flynn (decd), Re** [1982] **1** 882, Ch D.
No reasonable cause of action—Plea that testator did not know and approve contents of will—Plea of undue influence—Particulars pleading that beneficiary induced gravely ill testator to execute codicil benefitting beneficiary the day before he died—Codicil drawn up in accordance with testator's previous instructions—Whether pleading sufficiently specifying plea of want of knowledge and approval of contents of codicil—Whether pleading sufficiently supporting plea of undue influence and showing testator coerced into signing codicil—RSC Ord 18, r 19(1)(a), Ord 76, r 9(3). **Flynn (decd), Re** [1982] **1** 882, Ch D.
Evidence—
Conflict of laws—Knowledge and approval of contents of testamentary instrument—Rule whereby affirmative evidence required that disposition was by a free and capable testator—Burden of proof—Lex fori to be followed. **Fuld (decd), In the Estate of (No 3)** [1965] **3** 776, Prob.
Privilege—Witness whose evidence relates to execution of testamentary document—Court's witness on that matter—Legal professional privilege does not prevent the court requiring production of documents in order to reach truth as to execution. **Fuld (decd), In the Estate of (No 2)** [1965] **2** 657, Prob.
Interest in estate—
Claim form in probate action requiring statement of nature of interest of claimant in estate—Claimant having no interest under will or intestacy of deceased—Claimant having potential claim for financial provision—Claimant alleging will forged or obtained by undue influence and commencing probate action—Whether claimant having interest in estate—Inheritance (Provision for Family and Dependants) Act 1975—CPR 57.7(1). **O'Brien v Seagrave** [2007] **3** 633, Ch D.
Second action—
Dismissal—First action brought in personal capacity—Second action brought in representative capacity before judgment in first action—Grounds for dismissal of second action—Plaintiff cognisant of first action and not intervening. **Langton (decd), Re** [1964] **1** 749, CA.
Witness—
Status—Attesting witness called to give evidence as to due execution—Collateral issues of testamentary capacity and knowledge and approval—Whether attesting witness giving evidence on collateral issues witness of court. **Webster (decd), Re** [1974] **3** 822, Ch D.
Citation—
Application for issue—
Procedure—Non-contentious matter—Postal application—Non-Contentious Probate Rules 1954 (SI 1954 No 796), rr 45, 46, 47. **Practice Direction** [1969] **3** 192, Prob.

PROBATE (cont)—
  Citation (cont)—
    Citation to propound a will—
      Codicil—Citation by executor of will to beneficiary under codicil to propound codicil—Beneficiary
      not entering appearance to citation—No evidence of invalidity of codicil—Whether probate of will
      should be granted without codicil. **Muirhead (decd), Re** [1971] **1** 609, Prob.
  Claim form—
    Interest in estate. *See* Action—Interest in estate—Claim form in probate action requiring statement of
    nature of interest of claimant in estate, *above*.
  Contentious probate—
    Practice. *See* Practice—Contentious probate, *below*.
  Corporation—
    Grant to corporation. *See* Grant—Grant to corporation entitled to grant if an individual, *below*.
  Costs—
    Administrator pendente lite—
      Costs of administration and remuneration of administrator—Possible benefit of administration to
      estate—Apportionment between estate and party bringing proceedings. **Howlett (decd), Re**
      [1950] **1** 485, Prob.
    Discontinuance—
      Claimant commencing probate action—Claimant subsequently applying to discontinue action—
      Incidence of costs on discontinuance—CPR 57.11. **Wylde (decd), Re** [2006] **4** 345, Ch D.
    Incidence—
      Undue influence alleged but not proved—Whether litigation due to fault of testator or of beneficiary
      establishing will—Whether costs payable out of estate. **Cutcliffe (decd), Re** [1958] **3** 642, CA.
      Whether probate actions subject to special rules as to costs—Whether dispute over mutual wills
      analogous to probate actions—Whether costs to be ordered from the estate—Whether executors
      to be ordered to pay costs personally. **Shovelar v Lane** [2011] **4** 669, CA.
    Security for costs—
      Caveator—Contentious proceedings. *See* **Costs** (Security for costs—Person in position of
      plaintiff—Probate proceedings—Caveator).
    Taxation—
      Bill of costs—Item numbers to be shown—Rules of the Supreme Court (No 3) 1959 (SI 1959
      No 1958), Sch 2, App 2. **Practice Direction** [1960] **1** 347, PDA.
      Finality of taxation—Order for payment by defendant of plaintiff's costs—Subsequent taxation of
      costs of administrator pendente lite—Accounts of administrator—Right of plaintiff to further
      order for payment of administrator's costs and accounts. **Segalov (decd), In the Estate of**
      [1952] **2** 107, Prob.
      Non-contentious business—Fair and reasonable sum in circumstances. *See* **Costs** (Taxation—
      Solicitor—Non-contentious business—Fair and reasonable sum in circumstances).
      Objection to taxing officer's decision. **Practice Direction** [1955] **2** 326, PDA.
  County court—
    Jurisdiction—
      Power to pronounce for validity of will—County Courts Act 1934, ss 60(1), 61. **Thomas (decd), Re**
      [1949] **1** 1048, Prob.
  Dismissal of action. *See* Action—Dismissal of action, *above*.
  Document—
    Admission to probate—
      Considerations relevant—Difference between considerations admissible for the purpose of
      deciding on admissibility to probate and for determining construction of testamentary document
      admitted to probate. **Le Cras v Perpetual Trustee Co Ltd** [1967] **3** 915, PC.
      Document of no dispositive effect—Codicil the provisions of which as construed by court take effect
      only on testator surviving his wife—Duty of Probate Court to construe document—Surrounding
      circumstances. **Thomas, In the Estate of** [1939] **2** 567, Prob.
      Document of no dispositive effect—Document with no dispositive contents executed as will—Lists
      of bequests on separate papers found under same cover—Papers not referred to in
      will—Circumstantial evidence. **Saxton, In the Estate of** [1939] **2** 418, Prob.
      Holograph will attested but not signed—Will enclosed in envelope signed but not attested. **Mann, In**
      the Estate of [1942] **2** 193, Prob.
      Testator's intention regarding admission to probate—Relevance of testator's intention—Zavah in
      Hebrew language—Testator executing zavah in Hebrew alongside English will—Zavah intended
      to be binding in Jewish law and enforceable in rabbinical court—Testator expressing no intention
      whether it was to be enforceable in English court—English will invalid—Whether zavah should be
      admitted to probate as testator's last will. **Berger (decd), Re** [1989] **1** 591, CA.
      Will in foreign language—Evidence of foreign law to ascertain testator's intention—Whether
      permissible for court to refer questions on meaning or effect of foreign law to foreign court.
      Berger (decd), Re [1989] **1** 591, CA.
      Will in foreign language—Whether authenticated translation or text in foreign language document
      admissible to probate. **Berger (decd), Re** [1989] **1** 591, CA.
    Practice. *See* Practice—Documents, *below*.
  Domicile of deceased. *See* Grant—Domicile of deceased, *below*.
  Evidence—
    Admission of document. *See* Document—Admission to probate, *above*.
    Conflict of laws. *See* Action—Evidence—Conflict of laws, *above*.
    Foreign law. *See* Practice—Non-contentious probate—Evidence of foreign law, *below*.
    Lost will. *See* Lost will—Evidence, *below*.
    Parol evidence. *See* Lost will—Parol evidence of contents, *below*.
    Privilege. *See* Action—Evidence—Privilege, *above*.
  Exclusion of words in will. *See* Grant—Exclusion of words in will, *below*.
  Exclusive of matter—
    Signature of legatees not intending to witness will. *See* **Will** (Attestation—Attestation
    clause—Superfluous signature).
  Executors—
    Release from liability. *See* Renunciation—Release of executors from liability in respect of estate, *below*.

PROBATE (cont)—

Executors (cont)—

Restriction on number. *See* Grant—Restriction on number of executors to whom grant may issue in respect of same property, *below.*

Fees—

Court fees—

Impressed stamps. **Practice Note** [1957] **3** 298, Div.

Foreign will—

Jurisdiction. *See* Grant—No estate of deceased within jurisdiction—Power to make grant, *below.*

Validity—

Proof—Formal validity according to local law—Will made before notary—Properly authenticated copy issued by notary—Presumption of validity. **Practice Direction** [1972] **3** 1019, Fam D.

Grant—

Application—

Legitimation—Applicant's right dependent on a person's legitimation—Practice. **Practice Direction** [1965] **2** 560, Prob.

Postal applications—Principal Registry—Facilities for postal applications by solicitors. **Practice Direction** [1975] **2** 280, Fam D.

Practice where deceased dying domiciled abroad. **Practice Direction** [1953] **2** 1154, Prob.

Attorney—

Further grant to attorney administrator. **Practice Direction** [1957] **1** 602, Prob.

Confirmation—

Re-sealing—Provision of copies for deposit. **Practice Direction** [1954] **2** 534, Prob.

Death, as evidence of. *See* **Evidence** (Death—Evidence for procedural matters—Grant of probate or letters of administration).

Domicile of deceased—

Statement of domicile in grant—Non-Contentious Probate Rules, 1954 (SI 1954 No 796), r 6(5)—Non-Contentious Probate (Amendment) Rules 1961 (SI 1961 No 72), r 2. **Practice Direction** [1961] **1** 465, Prob.

Exclusion of words in will—

Carrying out intention of testator—Exclusion of words from codicil. **Swords, Re** [1952] **2** 281, Prob.

Carrying out intention of testator—Intention that codicil should revoke particular sub-clause of will—Slip by drafting solicitor in carrying out instructions—Codicil as drafted and executed revoking whole of relevant clause—Whether court required by any rule of evidence or law to hold that testator knew and approved of contents of codicil—Absence of power for court to add words to codicil—Omission of words as nearest way to give effect to intentions of testator. **Morris (decd), Re** [1970] **1** 1057, PDA.

Carrying out intention of testator—Testator wishing to benefit two persons—Testator executing will in their favour—Testator believing stocks and shares required to be dealt with in separate blocks in separate wills—Testator subsequently executing three further wills in favour of same beneficiaries—Each of the three wills concerned with different blocks of property—Each will containing revocation clause—Wills executed on same day—No indication which executed last—Power of court to authorise omission of words inserted inadvertently or by misunderstanding—Misunderstanding by testator as to what necessary to carry out his wishes. **Phelan (decd), Re** [1971] **3** 1256, Prob.

Offensive passages in will—Power of court—Scandalous and defamatory statements in will—No dispositive effect—Statements forming part of reasons for dispositions of property. **Hall, In the Estate of** [1943] **2** 159, Prob.

Power of court—Omission altering sense of what remains. **Horrocks, Re** [1939] **1** 579, CA.

Testator ignorant of gift effected by words—Testator intending different gift—Error in carrying out instructions of testator—Intention of testatrix that after life interests capital of residuary estate should devolve on M—Error in typing out engrossment of will—Will as executed omitting gift of capital to M and giving capital to M's wife and children—Whether parts of residuary clause dealing with capital should be omitted from probate on ground that testatrix did not know and approve of gift of capital to persons other than M. **Reynette-James (decd), Re** [1975] **3** 1037, Ch D.

Form—

Solemn form. *See* Grant—Solemn form, *below.*

Grant to corporation entitled to grant if an individual—

Grant to nominee. **Practice Direction** [1956] **1** 305, Prob.

Joint will—

Later will revoking joint will—Conditional will—Grant of administration with joint will annexed. **O'Connor (decd), In the Estate of** [1942] **1** 546, Prob.

Limited grant—

Will and two codicils—Second codicil disputed—Grant of probate limited to will and first codicil. **Day, In the Estate of** [1940] **2** 544, Prob.

No estate of deceased within jurisdiction—

Power to make grant—Foreign will disposing only of property abroad—Administration of Justice Act 1932, s 2(1). **Wayland, In the Estate of** [1951] **2** 1041, Prob.

Power to make grant—Whether grant to be made to alleged father to enable him thereby to establish paternity of deceased who died abroad—Administration of Estates Act 1932, s 2. **Aldrich v A-G (Rogers intervening)** [1968] **1** 345, Prob.

Non-contentious probate—

Grant of representation. *See* Practice—Non-contentious probate—Grant of representation, *below.*

Notice—

Standing search—Practice. *See* **Administration of estates** (Grant of administration—Standing search).

Opposition—

Want of knowledge and approval—Circumstances giving rise to suspicion—Need to be attendant on, or relevant to, preparation and execution of will—Allegation of immoral conduct between deceased and beneficiary struck out—Contentious Probate Rules, r 40A—RSC Ord 19, rr 25(a), 27. **R (decd), Re** [1950] **2** 117, Prob.

PROBATE (cont)—
Grant (cont)—
  Person incapable of managing his own affairs—
    Applicant not authorised by Court of Protection—Application for use and benefit of person not resident in institution—Evidence of incapacity such person. **Practice Direction** [1969] **1** 494, Prob.
    Applicant not authorised by Court of Protection—Evidence of incapacity of person for whose benefit grant required. **Practice Note** [1958] **2** 600, Prob; [1962] **2** 613, Prob.
  Resealing—
    Applications for resealing—Dispensing with advertisement of application—Colonial Probates Acts 1892 and 1927. **Practice Direction** [1954] **2** 552, Prob.
    Cessation of resealing in England of grants made in Rhodesia—Applications for grants of representation in case of persons dying domiciled in Rhodesia. **Practice Direction** [1970] **1** 1248, Prob.
    English grants in Northern Ireland. **Practice Direction** [1956] **2** 361, Prob.
    Grants made in Southern Rhodesia—Grants made in Zimbabwe—Colonial Probates Act 1892. **Practice Direction** [1980] **2** 324, Fam D.
    Scottish confirmation or Northern Irish or colonial grant—Application by post at Principal Probate Registry. **Practice Direction** [1959] **2** 560, Prob.
  Restriction on number of executors to whom grant may issue in respect of same property—
    Same property—Testator appointing four general executors and one literary executor in respect of certain manuscripts—Number to whom grant may issue—Supreme Court of Judicature (Consolidation) Act 1925, s 160(1). **Holland, In the Estate of** [1936] **3** 13, Prob.
  Revocation of grant—
    Executors incapable of performing duties. **Galbraith, In the Estate of** [1951] **2** 470, Prob.
    Swearing false Inland Revenue affidavit. **Cope, In the Estate of** [1954] **1** 698, Prob.
    Trial—Summing-up—Misdirection—Solicitor author of will and chief beneficiary—General direction to jury to regard with suspicion evidence of author of will—No sufficiently jealous scrutiny of evidence. **Wintle v Nye** [1959] **1** 552, HL.
  Second or subsequent grant through solicitor—
    Application by post at Principal Probate Registry—Non-Contentious Probate Rules 1954 (SI 1954 No 796), r 3(1). **Practice Direction** [1959] **2** 560, Prob.
  Solemn form—
    Procedure for compelling after grant in common form—Caveat and citation by party disputing—Citor's duty to issue writ—Motion for grant of letters of administration inapplicable—Whether 'contentious business'—Non-Contentious Probate Rules 1954 (SI 1954 No 796), r 47—Contentious Probate Business Rules, r 3. **Jolley (decd), In the Estate of** [1964] **1** 596, CA.
    Setting aside grant—Defendant not appearing at trial—Absence of defendant not due to mistake but to negotiation amounting to compromise—RSC Ord 36, r 33. **Barraclough (decd), Re** [1965] **2** 311, Prob.
  Solicitor's estate—
    Law Society's nominees—Nominees obtaining grant of representation to estate of solicitor practising on his own at his death—Procedure. **Practice Direction** [1965] **1** 923, Prob.
  Solicitor's office reference—
    Inclusion in grant. **Practice Direction** [1970] **3** 176, Prob; [1972] **1** 1056, Fam D.
  Trust corporation—
    Application for grant—Oath in support of application—Wording—Oath referring to Supreme Court of Judicature (Consolidation) Act 1925 instead of Supreme Court Act 1981—Acceptance of oath in support. **Practice Direction** [1982] **1** 512, Fam D.
    Corporation appointed executor on terms and conditions in existence at date of will—Terms and conditions not limiting corporation's power to take full grant—Production of terms and conditions not necessary where oath contains statement to that effect. **Practice Direction** [1981] **2** 1104, Fam D.
    Corporation entitled to act as custodian trustee—Bank of Ireland—Bank appointed executor of will of testatrix domiciled in Republic of Ireland—Bank entitled to grant of probate of will in England—Bank constituted under law of member state of European Economic Community—Bank empowered by statute to undertake trust business in England—Public Trustee Rules 1912 (SR & O 1912 No 348), r 30(b)(i), (ii)(as amended by Public Trustee (Custodian Trustee) Rules 1975 (SI 1975 No 1189), r 2). **Bigger (decd), Re** [1977] **2** 644, Fam D.
    Practice. *See* Practice—Trust corporation, *below*.
Incapacity. *See* Grant—Person incapable of managing his own affairs, *above*.
Inheritance tax—
  Inland Revenue accounts—
    Procedure—Presentation of receipted accounts to probate registries. **Practice Direction** [1989] **3** 938, Fam D.
Inland Revenue affidavit. *See* Grant—Revocation of grant—Swearing false Inland Revenue affidavit, *above*.
Intention of testator—
  Carrying out intention of testator. *See* Grant—Exclusion of words in will—Carrying out intention of testator, *above*.
Interest in estate. *See* Action—Interest in estate, *above*.
Joint will. *See* Grant—Joint will, *above*.
Jurisdiction—
  County court. *See* County court—Jurisdiction, *above*.
  Exclusion of words in will. *See* Grant—Exclusion of words in will, *above*.
Limited grant. *See* Grant—Limited grant, *above*.
Lost will—
  Evidence—
    Execution—Attestation—Completed draft will—Person shown as attesting witness in draft will unable to recollect execution—Omnia praesumuntur rite esse acta. **Webb (decd), Re** [1964] **2** 91, Prob.
  Ex parte application for probate of reconstructed contents—
    Application to be made to register—Non-Contentious Probate Rules 1954 (SI 1954 No 796), r 53(1). **Nuttall (decd), In the Estate of** [1955] **2** 921, Prob.

PROBATE (cont)—
Lost will (cont)—
Parol evidence of contents—
Standard of proof. **Wipperman, In the Estate of** [1953] **1** 764, Prob.
Soldier's or mariner's privileged will. *See* **Will** (Soldier's or mariner's privileged will—Lost will—Probate).
Mutual wills—
Costs, incidence of costs. *See* Costs—Incidence—Whether probate actions subject to special rules as to costs, *above.*
Non-contentious probate—
Practice. *See* Practice—Non-contentious probate, *below.*
Pleading—
Contents of pleading—
Plea of want of knowledge and approval—Plea of undue influence—Nature of case relied on required to be specified—Allegation which would be relevant in support of plea of undue influence—Party pleading that testator did not know and approve of contents of will when executing it—Party alleging in support of that plea matters which would also support plea of undue influence—Party precluded from doing so unless undue influence also pleaded—Whether party's allegations in support of plea of want of knowledge and approval an allegation which would be 'relevant in support of' plea of undue influence—RSC Ord 76, r 9(3). **Stott (decd), Re** [1980] **1** 259, Ch D.
Defence—
Defence that testatrix of unsound mind—Particulars—RSC Ord 19, r 25A. **Reynolds (decd), Re** [1955] **1** 18, CA.
Plaintiff alleged in defence to have feloniously caused death of deceased testator—Relevance—Defendant entitled to make allegation though plaintiff not prosecuted. **G (decd), In the Estate of** [1946] **1** 579, Prob.
Postal application—
Citation. *See* Citation—Application for issue, *above.*
Practice—
Attorney—
Further grant to attorney administrator. *See* Grant—Attorney, *above.*
Cause list—
Cases set down for hearing up to 31st December 1967—No date fixed—Removal from list—Restoration. **Practice Direction** [1968] **3** 871, Prob.
Citation—
Postal application for issue. *See* Citation—Application for issue, *above.*
Contentious probate—
Accounts of administrators pendente lite—Information as to unconverted assets—Exhibition of inventory—Frequency of accounts. **Practice Direction** [1973] **2** 334, Ch D.
Copies of scripts—Lodgment. **Practice Direction** [1973] **2** 334, Ch D.
Form of guarantee by administrators pendente lite. **Practice Direction** [1971] **3** 327, Ch D.
Short causes—Hearing. **Practice Direction** [1971] **3** 327, Ch D.
Trial of action outside London—Transmission of scripts—Procedure—RSC Ord 36, r 3. **Practice Direction** [1974] **3** 752, Ch D.
Trial on affidavit evidence—Verification of original will or codicil—RSC Ord 76, rr 10, 12. **Practice Direction** [1974] **3** 752, Ch D.
Copies of wills and grants—
Postal applications—Applications to be dealt with by York sub-registry—Applications direct to district registries or York sub-registry—Supreme Court Act 1981, ss 124, 125(c). **Practice Direction** [1990] **3** 734, Fam D.
Costs. *See* Costs, *above.*
Documents—
Size—RSC Ord 66, r 1. **Practice Direction** [1967] **3** 848, Prob.
Testamentary documents—Fiat copies—Photographic facsimiles. **Practice Direction** [1979] **3** 859, Fam D.
Non-contentious probate—
Application to the court—Liberty to apply—'Liberty to apply' not giving right to apply to the court without complying with the rules—Non-Contentious Probate Rules 1954 (SI 1954 No 796). **Practice Direction** [1980] **1** 1008, Fam D.
Evidence of foreign law—Persons qualified to give evidence—Particulars to be set out in affidavit—Civil Evidence Act 1972, s 4(1)—Non-Contentious Probate Rules 1954 (SI 1954 No 796), r 18. **Practice Direction** [1972] **3** 912, Fam D.
Executor—Appointment—Appointment of firm of solicitors—Appointment of firm without naming partners—Oath to lead grant—Form of oath—Notice of application—Non-Contentious Probate Rules 1987, r 27(1). **Practice Direction** [1990] **2** 576, Fam D.
Foreign divorce—Recognition. **Practice Direction** [1972] **1** 144, Fam D.
Grant of probate—Notice of application for grant—Notice to executor to whom power is reserved—Dispensing with notice—Preliminary inquiry whether registrar would be prepared to dispense with notice—Non-Contentious Probate Rules 1987, r 27. **Practice Direction** [1988] **1** 192, Fam D.
Grant of representation—Caveat—Extension for further six months—Application for extension to be made in month before expiry of caveat—Requirement for written application—Fees—Non-Contentious Probate Rules 1954 (SI 1954 No 796), r 44—Non-Contentious Probate Fees Order 1975 (SI 1975 No 1344), r 5—Non-Contentious Probate (Amendment) Rules 1976 (SI 1976 No 1362), r 44(4A). **Practice Direction** [1976] **3** 416, Fam D.
Grant of representation—Caveat—Warnings and appearances—Removal of caveats—Non-Contentious Probate Rules 1987, r 44(5), (6), (10), (12), Sch 1, Form 4. **Practice Direction** [1988] **3** 544, Fam D.
Grant of representation—Computer records—Annual calendar books—Supreme Court Act 1981, s 111. **Practice Direction** [1999] **1** 384, Fam D.

PROBATE (cont)—
  Practice (cont)—
    Non-contentious probate (cont)—
      Grant of representation—Entitlement to grant of representation—Construction of references to relationship between two persons—Presumptions as to survivorship—Oath in support of grant—Clearing off prior claims—Family Law Reform Act 1987, ss 1, 18, 21. **Practice Direction** [1988] **2** 308, Fam D.
      Grant of representation—Fee—Cases not requiring Inland Revenue Account—Value of estate—Oath required with application for grant—Non-Contentious Probate Fees Order 1981 (SI 1981 No 861)—Capital Transfer Tax (Delivery of Accounts) Regulations 1981 (SI 1981 No 880). **Practice Direction** [1981] **2** 832, Fam D.
      Grant of representation—Grant ad colligenda bona—Notice—Guidance—Non-Contentious Probate Rules 1987, SI 1987/202, rr 7(1)(b), 61(1), 66(1). **Ghafoor v Cliff** [2006] **2** 1079, Ch D.
      Grant of representation—Grant on behalf of minor—Evidence in support of application—Application by mother—Application by father having or who has acquired parental responsibility—Application by father not married to mother at time of birth of child but who has parental responsibility—Application by parent having parental responsibility by virtue of adoption order—Application by guardian having parental responsibility—Sexual Offences Act 1956—Guardianship of Minors Act 1971—Adoption Act 1976, s 12—Family Law Reform Act 1987, s 4(1)—Children Act 1989, ss 2(1), 4, 5, Sch 14, paras 4, 6, 12, 13—Non-Contentious Probate Rules 1987, r 32—Parental Responsibility Agreement Regulations 1991—Non-Contentious Probate (Amendment) Rules 1991. **Practice Direction** [1991] **4** 562, Fam D.
      Grant of representation—Oath in support of application—Oath to include name and dates of birth and death of deceased—Name and date of death of deceased to be included in notice for standing search or caveat. **Practice Direction** [1999] **1** 832, Fam D.
      Grant of representation—Probate records—Required information—Revision. **Practice Direction** [2002] **2** 640, Fam D.
    Omission of words from probate of will—
      Application—Copy of order to be annexed to will. **Practice Direction** [1968] **2** 592, Prob; **Practice Note** [1964] **1** 952, Prob.
    Receipt or certificate given by solicitor's clerk—
      Signature by clerk. **Practice Direction** [1953] **2** 1234, PDA.
    Resealing of grant. See Grant—Resealing, above.
    Short Probate List—
      New system. See **Practice** (Chancery Division—Revision of system for listing causes and matters).
    Solicitor's office reference—
      Inclusion in grant. See Grant—Solicitor's office reference—Inclusion in grant, above.
    Stamp duty—
      Deed or other instrument—Doubt whether instrument duly stamped—Submission of instrument to Controller of Stamps for preliminary noting and endorsement—Solicitor required to give undertaking to resubmit instrument for formal adjudication. **Practice Note** [1978] **1** 1046, Fam D.
    Summons—
      Counsel summonses—Place of hearing. **Practice Note** [1959] **2** 144, PDA.
    Summons for directions—
      Subsequent applications to be by notice—RSC Ord 30, r 7(3). **Practice Direction** [1963] **2** 483, Prob.
    Taxation of costs. See Costs—Taxation, above.
    Trial—
      Place of trial—London. **Practice Direction** [1965] **1** 1039, Prob.
      Speeches—Party to begin—Discretion of judge. See **Practice** (Trial—Speeches—Order of speeches—Party to begin—Discretion of judge to give special directions as to party to begin—Probate action).
    Trust corporation—
      Grant of probate to trust corporation. See Grant—Trust corporation, above.
      Public company—Reregistration of name with words 'public limited company' or 'plc' or Welsh equivalent—Companies Act 1980, ss 2(2), 78(3)(b), (d). **Practice Direction** [1982] **1** 384, Fam D.
    Writ—
      Issue of writ—Registrar acting in quasi-judicial capacity in relation to issue of writ—Discretion to refuse issue of writ where action would be abuse of process—Plaintiff's action for revocation, and for probate of earlier will, in personal capacity dismissed—Same relief sought on same issues by plaintiff in representative capacity in subsequent action—Issue of subsequent writ rightly refused—RSC Ord 76, r 2(3). **Langton (decd), Re** [1964] **1** 749, CA.
  Probate Division—
    Power of court to decide questions of construction—
      Motion to admit later of two wills to probate—Revocation of former will by later—Extent of powers of construction of Probate Division. **Fawcett, In the Estate of** [1941] **2** 341, Prob.
  Probate judge—
    Whether a trustee. See **Trust and trustee** (Probate judge—Vesting of estate of intestate—Whether probate judge a trustee).
  Procedure—
    Citation—
      Postal application. See Citation—Application for issue, above.
  Property abroad. See Grant—No estate of deceased within jurisdiction, above.
  Renunciation—
    Release of executors from liability in respect of estate—
      Right of executors to release from liability. **Tiger v Barclays Bank Ltd** [1951] **2** 262, KBD.
  Revocation of grant. See Grant—Revocation of grant, above.
  Signature on will. See **Will** (Execution—Place of testator's signature).
  Solemn form. See Grant—Solemn form, above.
  Solicitor's estate—
    Law Society's nominees. See Grant—Solicitor's estate, above.
  Status of witness. See Action—Witness—Status, above.
  Summons. See Practice—Summons, above.

PROBATE (cont)—
    Testamentary documents—
        Practice. *See* Practice—Documents—Testamentary documents, *above*.
    Two wills admitted—
        Construction. *See* **Will** (Construction—Two wills admitted to probate).
    Undue influence—
        Allegations in support of plea of want of knowledge and approval—
            Nature of case required to be specified. *See* Pleading—Contents of pleading—Plea of want of
                knowledge and approval—Plea of undue influence—Nature of case relied on required to be
                specified, *above*.
    Valuation—
        'Valuation agreed for probate'. *See* **Will** (Valuation of effects—Probate valuation—Direction to executors
        to transfer land at 'valuation agreed for probate').
    Will—
        Validity—
            Execution. *See* **Will** (Execution).
            Forgery—Evidence—Conviction—Admissibility. *See* **Evidence** (Conviction—Admission as evidence
                in civil proceedings—Subsisting conviction—Conviction subject to appeal—Adjournment of civil
                proceedings pending appeal—Probate—Will—Validity—Allegation that will a forgery).
            Knowledge and approval—Burden on propounder to establish 'righteousness of the
                transaction'—Judge finding testator having known and approved of part of will only—Whether
                judge misapplying doctrine of 'righteousness of the transaction'. **Fuller v Strum** [2002] **2** 87, CA.
    Will of person dying domiciled abroad—
        Will relating to English estate admitted to probate by court of deceased's domicile—Probate in
        England of duly authenticated copy. **Yahuda (decd), Re** [1956] **2** 262, Prob.
    Writ—
        Issue by registrar. *See* Practice—Writ—Issue of writ, *above*.

PROBATE JUDGE
    Whether probate judge a trustee. *See* **Trust and trustee** (Probate judge—Vesting of estate of
    intestate—Whether probate judge a trustee).

PROBATION
    Magistrates' jurisdiction. *See* **Magistrates** (Jurisdiction—Probation).
    Officer—
        Divorce—
            Reconciliation—Reference to probation officer. *See* **Divorce** (Reconciliation—Certificate with regard
              to—Names etc of persons qualified to help—Organisations and persons regarded as authorised
              to help).
        Extent of authority—
            Matrimonial proceedings—Whether authorised to make admissions or apply for adjournment on
            behalf of party. **Smith v Smith** [1957] **2** 397, Div.
    Order—
        Breach—
            Crown Court—Jurisdiction—Jurisdiction of section of Crown Court which made order. *See* **Crown**
            Court (Jurisdiction—Single indivisible court—Jurisdiction of sections of Crown Court—
            Jurisdiction to examine decision of other section of court—Probation order).
            Sentence. *See* **Sentence** (Breach of probation order).
        Criminal contempt of court—
            Jurisdiction to make probation order in respect of criminal contempt. *See* **Contempt of court**
            (Criminal contempt—Sentence—Probation).
        Generally. *See* **Sentence** (Probation order).

PROBATIONARY SOLICITOR'S REPRESENTATIVE
    Access to—
        Right of person in custody. *See* **Solicitor** (Access to—Right of person in custody—Access by
        probationary solicitor's representative (PSR)).

PROCEDURE
    See **Practice**.

PROCEEDS OF CRIME
    Bank, duty of. *See* **Bank** (Banker/client relationship—Duty of bank—Proceeds of crime).
    Civil recovery—
        Unlawful conduct. *See* Unlawful conduct—Civil recovery of proceeds of unlawful conduct, *below*.
    Confiscation order. *See* **Sentence** (Confiscation order—Proceeds of crime).
    Costs—
        Magistrates—
            Jurisdiction. *See* **Costs** (Order for costs—Jurisdiction—Magistrates—Power to award costs—
            Forfeiture of cash representing property obtained through unlawful conduct or intended to be
            used in unlawful conduct).
    Criminal conduct. *See* **Criminal law** (Proceeds of crime—Criminal conduct).
    Criminal law. *See* **Criminal law** (Proceeds of crime).
    Criminal lifestyle—
        Confiscation order. *See* **Sentence** (Confiscation order—Proceeds of crime—Criminal lifestyle).
    Criminal property—
        Benefit from criminal conduct. *See* **Criminal law** (Proceeds of crime—Criminal conduct—Criminal
        property—Money laundering—Property constituting or representing benefit from criminal conduct).

PROCEEDS OF CRIME (cont)—

Criminal property (cont)—

Knowledge or suspicion of arrangement facilitating acquisition, retention, use or control of criminal property—

Appropriate consent—Bank making authorised disclosure to Serious Organised Crime Agency in relation to trust accounts—Trust accounts held for claimant—Agency refusing appropriate consent—Claimant requesting review of decision—Agency refusing—Whether person making authorised disclosure only person capable of requesting review of decision—Proceeds of Crime Act 2002, ss 328, 335. **R (on the application of UMBS Online Ltd) v Serious Organised Crime Agency** [2008] **1** 465, CA.

Bank forming relevant suspicion in relation to customer's account—Bank delaying in carrying out customer's instructions while making authorised disclosure and receiving appropriate consent—Customer bringing claim for loss suffered consequent on bank's delay and refusal to give information—Bank applying to strike out claim—Whether bank required to prove relevant suspicion—Proceeds of Crime Act 2002, Pt 7. **Shah v HSBC Private Bank (UK) Ltd** [2010] **3** 477, CA; [2011] **1 Comm** 67, CA.

Bank forming relevant suspicion in relation to customer's account—Bank freezing account without explanation—Correctness of bank's action—Proceeds of Crime Act 2002, ss 328, 335, 338. **Squirrell Ltd v National Westminster Bank plc (Customs and Excise Comrs intervening)** [2005] **1 Comm** 749, Ch D; [2005] **2** 784, Ch D.

Bank forming relevant suspicion in relation to customer's account—Bank refusing to carry out customer's instructions—Whether customer entitled to mandatory injunction—Meaning of 'suspect'—Whether evidence of suspicion required to be adduced—Proceeds of Crime Act 2002, ss 328(1), 333(2)(c), (3)(b). **K Ltd v National Westminster Bank plc (Revenue and Customs Comrs and anor intervening)** [2006] **2 Comm** 655, CA; [2006] **4** 907, CA.

Defendant opening bank accounts on behalf of fraudster—Bank accounts receiving money paid in by victims via fraudulent website established by fraudster—Whether requirement for property to constitute criminal property prior to arrangement coming into operation—Whether requirement for property to exist at time of entering into or becoming concerned in arrangement—Proceeds of Crime Act 2002, s 328(1). **R v GH** [2015] **4** 274, SC.

Employee of bank's parent company forming relevant suspicion in relation to customer's account—Employee not formally appointed as nominated officer—Whether employee's suspicion should be attributed to bank—Whether employee being nominated officer—Whether bank having relevant suspicion—Proceeds of Crime Act 2002, ss 330, 331, 335, 336, 338. **Shah v HSBC Private Bank (UK) Ltd** [2013] **1 Comm** 72, QBD.

Relevant property. *See* Request by overseas authority in connection with criminal investigations or proceedings—Restraint order—Relevant property, *below*.

Declaratory relief—

Claimant informing police of suspect transactions—

Claimant seeking consent of police to transfer related moneys—Police refusing consent—Claimant seeking declaration that moneys not proceeds of crime—Whether appropriate for claimant to seek declaration—Criminal Justice Act 1988, s 93A. **Amalgamated Metal Trading Ltd v City of London Police Financial Investigation Unit** [2003] **1 Comm** 900, QBD; [2003] **4** 1225, QBD.

External requests and orders. *See* Request by overseas authority in connection with criminal investigations or proceedings, *below*.

Generally. *See* **Criminal law** (Proceeds of crime).

Interlocutory injunction to restrain dealings with proceeds of crime. *See* **Injunction** (Interlocutory—Preservation of proceeds of crime).

Investigations—

Unexplained wealth orders—

Politically exposed person—Unexplained wealth order made against Azerbaijani national whose husband had been convicted in Azerbaijan for fraud and embezzlement whilst chairman of Azerbaijani bank—Whether appellant a politically exposed person—Whether bank a state-owned enterprise—Whether income requirement met—Whether unexplained wealth order offending against rule against self-incrimination and/or spousal privilege—Civil Evidence Act 1968, s 14—Proceeds of Crime Act 2002, ss 362B, 362F. **Hajiyeva v National Crime Agency** [2020] **2 Comm** 741, CA; [2020] **4** 147, CA.

Isle of Man. *See* **Isle of Man** (Criminal law—Proceeds of crime).

Money laundering—

Criminal conduct. *See* **Criminal law** (Proceeds of crime—Criminal conduct).

Financial Services Authority, powers of. *See* **Financial services** (Financial Services Authority (FSA)—Powers—Prosecution of criminal offences).

Practice—

Administrative Court. *See* **Practice** (Administrative Court—Proceeds of crime).

Request by overseas authority in connection with criminal investigations or proceedings—

Restraint order—

Relevant property—Property in England or Wales—Whether court having power to make restraint order over property outside England or Wales— Proceeds of Crime Act 2002, s 447—Proceeds of Crime Act 2002 (External Requests and Orders) Order 2005, SI 2005/3181, arts 6, 7, 8. **Serious Fraud Office v King** [2008] **3** 830, CA; [2009] **2** 223, HL.

Restraint order—

Appointment of receiver—

Remuneration. *See* **Receiver** (Appointed by court—Remuneration).

Breach of—

Perverting course of justice. *See* **Criminal law** (Obstructing course of justice—Perverting course of justice—Breach of restraint order made under proceeds of crime legislation).

Legal expenses—

Criminal investigation into affairs of alleged offender—Alleged offender instructing solicitors in connection with investigation—Alleged offender paying moneys to solicitors on account—Restraint order obtained against alleged offender—Work done by solicitors exceeding moneys held for alleged offender on client account—Whether restraint order preventing solicitors presenting bill of costs to alleged offender and transferring moneys to office account—Proceeds of Crime Act 2002, ss 40, 41. **Revenue and Customs Prosecutions Office v Allad** [2009] **3** 530, CA.

PROCEEDS OF CRIME (cont)—

Restraint order (cont)—

Variation. *See* **Restraint order** (Variation of order prior to conviction).

Sentence—

Confiscation order. *See* **Sentence** (Confiscation order—Proceeds of crime).

Tainted gifts. *See* **Sentence** (Confiscation order—Proceeds of crime—Tainted gifts).

Unlawful conduct—

Civil recovery of proceeds of unlawful conduct—

Account freezing order—Application for account freezing order—Whether magistrates' court having power to hear application in private—Guidance—Human Rights Act 1998, Sch 1, Pt I, arts 8, 10—Proceeds of Crime Act 2002, s 303Z1(4). **R (on the application of Javadov) v Westminster Magistrates' Court (National Crime Agency, interested parties)** [2022] 1 730, DC.

Civil recovery order—Disclosure order—Whether civil recovery order available in relation to property situated outside England and Wales—Whether disclosure order having extraterritorial effect—Whether Serious Organised Crime Agency having authority to issue notices to persons outside jurisdiction—Proceeds of Crime Act 2002, Pt 5, s 357. **Perry v Serious Organised Crime Agency** [2012] 4 795, SC.

Civil recovery order—Whether order available in relation to property situated outside England and Wales—Proceeds of Crime Act 2002, Pt 5. **Perry v Serious Organised Crime Agency** [2011] 4 470, CA.

Conduct occurring in country outside the United Kingdom and unlawful under criminal law of that country which would be unlawful under criminal law of United Kingdom if occurring in United Kingdom—Defendant convicted in France of offences of people trafficking—Director of Assets Recovery Agency bringing proceedings for civil recovery order—Whether judgment of French court discharging burden of proving that unlawful conduct in country outside the United Kingdom had occurred—Proceeds of Crime Act 2002, s 241. **Director of the Assets Recovery Agency v Virtosu** [2008] 3 637, QBD.

Forfeiture—Seizure of cash on reasonable grounds for suspecting cash intended by any person for use in unlawful conduct—Provisions for forfeiture where cash intended for use in unlawful conduct—Meaning of 'use'—Proceeds of Crime Act 2002, s 298(2)(b). **Begum v West Midlands Police (Birmingham Magistrates' Court, interested party)** [2013] 1 1261, CA.

Property freezing order—Application to vary—Applicant previously failing to disclose assets—Burden of proof—Whether burden on applicant to prove non-existence of undisclosed assets—Whether burden of proof on Serious Organised Crime Agency to prove existence of assets as yet undisclosed—Proceeds of Crime Act 2002, ss 245A, 245C. **Serious Organised Crime Agency v Azam** [2014] 1 206, CA.

Recovery of assets from non-convicted persons—Right to a fair trial—Persons failing to show origin of assets—Enforcement authority granted order to recover assets on balance of probabilities—Whether burden of proof should be beyond reasonable doubt—Whether by finding on balance of probabilities breaching right to fair trial—Whether costs in proceedings should include costs of interim receiver's investigation and report—Senior Courts Act 1981, s 51(1)—Human Rights Act 1998, Sch 1, Pt I, art 6(2)—Proceeds of Crime Act 2002, ss 241, 246. **Serious Organised Crime Agency v Gale** [2012] 2 1, SC.

Restrictions on dealing with property —Recovery orders—Interim receiving order—Exclusion from interim receiving order—Exclusion for legal expenses—Property to which interim receiving order does not apply—Applicant seeking further exclusion from interim receiving order—Whether applicant having property to which interim receiving order not applying—Whether exclusion order regime applying to individual sued as trustee—Proceeds of Crime Act 2002, ss 252, 266(8A)—CPR Practice Direction on Civil Recovery Proceedings, para 7A. **Serious Organised Crime Agency v Szepietowski** [2009] 4 393, Ch D.

PROCEEDS OF SALE

Interest. *See* **Interest** (Proceeds of sale).

Sale of land—

Contract to divide proceeds. *See* **Land charge** (General equitable charge—Charge on land—Contract to divide proceeds of sale of land).

PROCESSION

Preservation of public order. *See* **Public order** (Preservation of public order on occasion of processions).

Public order. *See* **Public order** (Procession).

PROCURING

Abortion—

Procuring drugs or instrument. *See* **Criminal law** (Abortion—Procuring drugs or instrument with intent to effect abortion).

Breach of contract—

Tort. *See* **Tort** (Inducement to commit breach of contract).

Commission of offence. *See* **Criminal law** (Aiding and abetting—Procuring commission of offence).

Intent to commit crime. *See* **Criminal law** (Procuring with intent).

Mental defective. *See* **Criminal law** (Sexual intercourse—Mental defective—Procuring defective).

Procurement of violation of right. *See* **Tort** (Procurement of violation of right).

Prostitution. *See* **Criminal law** (Prostitution—Procuring woman to become a common prostitute).

PRODUCT LIABILITY

European Union. *See* **European Union** (Consumer protection—Product liability).

PRODUCT LICENCE

Medicine. *See* **Medicine** (Product licence).

PRODUCTION OF COAL

Regulation. *See* **Coal mining** (Regulation of production).

PRODUCTION OF DOCUMENTS
Company documents—
    Generally. *See* **Company** (Documents—Production of documents).
    Inquiry into company's dealings. *See* **Company** (Administration—Inquiry into company's dealings—Production of documents).
    Power of Department of Trade to require production of documents. *See* **Company** (Documents—Inspection—Power of Department of Trade to require production of documents).
Criminal cases—
    Witness summons. *See* **Criminal evidence** (Witness—Witness summons—Production of documents).
Crown Privilege—
    Power of Rules Committee to making rules relating to production and Crown Privilege. *See* **Statutory instrument** (Rules of court—Power of Rule Committees—Power to make rules relating to production of documents and Crown privilege).
Foreign tribunal, before—
    English company documents. *See* **Company** (Documents—Production of documents—Production before foreign tribunal).
    Evidence for purpose of civil proceedings. *See* **Evidence** (Foreign tribunal—Evidence for purpose of civil proceedings—Production of documents).
Generally. *See* **Disclosure and inspection of documents** (Production of documents).
Income tax purposes, for. *See* **Income tax** (Information—Production of documents).
Legal professional privilege—
    Disclosure and inspection of documents. *See* **Disclosure and inspection of documents** (Legal professional privilege).
    Generally. *See* **Privilege** (Legal professional privilege).

PROFESSIONAL BASKETBALL PLAYER
Freedom of movement—
    European Community. *See* **European Union** (Workers—Freedom of movement—Professional basketball players).

PROFESSIONAL CONDUCT COMMITTEE OF BAR COUNCIL
Judicial review of committee's decision—
    Availability of remedy. *See* **Judicial review** (Availability of remedy—Disciplinary proceedings—Professional Conduct Committee of Bar Council).

PROFESSIONAL FOOTBALLER
Freedom of movement—
    European Community. *See* **European Union** (Workers—Freedom of movement—Professional footballers).
Proceeds of benefit match—
    Income tax. *See* **Income tax** (Emoluments from office or employment—Voluntary payment—Payment arising in ordinary course of taxpayer's employment—Professional football players—Proceeds of benefit matches or payments in lieu thereof).
Signing-on fee—
    Income tax—Capital or income. *See* **Income tax** (Capital or income receipts—Professional sportsman).
Testimonial payment—
    Income tax. *See* **Income tax** (Emoluments from office or employment—Receipt 'from' employment—Testimonial).

PROFESSIONAL INDEMNITY INSURANCE
Generally. *See* **Insurance** (Liability insurance—Professional indemnity insurance).

PROFESSIONAL MISCONDUCT
Attorney at law—
    Trinidad and Tobago. *See* **Trinidad and Tobago** (Legal profession—Attorney at Law).
Counsel—
    Gambia. *See* **Gambia** (Counsel—Professional misconduct).
    Generally. *See* **Counsel** (Professional misconduct).
Dentist. *See* **Dentist** (Professional misconduct).
Disciplinary proceedings—
    Misconduct rendering convicted person unfit to be on register of society—
        Effect of conditional discharge. *See* **Tribunal** (Statutory tribunal—Disciplinary committee of professional society—Misconduct rendering convicted person unfit to be on register of society).
    Publications concerning—
        Contempt of court. *See* **Contempt of court** (Publications concerning disciplinary proceedings).
Medical practitioner—
    Disciplinary proceedings. *See* **Medical practitioner** (Disciplinary committee).
    Generally. *See* **Medical practitioner** (Professional misconduct).
Ophthalmic optician—
    Erasure of name from register. *See* **Ophthalmic optician** (Erasure of name from register—Infamous conduct in a professional respect).
Osteopath. *See* **Osteopath** (Professional conduct and fitness to practise).
Professional Conduct Committee—
    Interim suspension powers. *See* **Osteopath** (Professional conduct and fitness to practise—Professional Conduct Committee—Interim suspension powers).
Solicitor—
    Disciplinary proceedings. *See* **Solicitor** (Disciplinary proceedings).
    Negligence. *See* **Solicitor** (Negligence).
Veterinary surgeon. *See* **Veterinary surgeon** (Discipline—Professional misconduct).

PROFESSIONAL PERSON
Negligence—
    Counsel. *See* **Counsel** (Negligence).

PROFESSIONAL PERSON (cont)—
Negligence (cont)—
Generally. *See* **Negligence** (Professional person).
Information or advice. *See* **Negligence** (Information or advice).
Manslaughter. *See* **Criminal law** (Manslaughter—Negligence—Professional man).
Solicitor. *See* **Solicitor** (Negligence).

PROFESSIONAL PRIVILEGE
Legal profession—
Disclosure and inspection of documents. *See* **Disclosure and inspection of documents** (Legal professional privilege).
Generally. *See* **Privilege** (Legal professional privilege).

PROFESSIONAL SPORTSMAN
Income tax—
Collections for meritorious performances. *See* **Income tax** (Emoluments from office or employment—Voluntary payment—Payment arising in ordinary course of taxpayer's employment—Professional cricketer—Collections made for meritorious performances).
Proceeds of benefit match. *See* **Income tax** (Emoluments from office or employment—Voluntary payment—Payment arising in ordinary course of taxpayer's employment—Professional football players—Proceeds of benefit matches or payments in lieu thereof).
Signing-on fee—
Capital or income. *See* **Income tax** (Capital or income receipts—Professional sportsman).
Testimonial payment—
Footballer. *See* **Income tax** (Emoluments from office or employment—Receipt 'from' employment—Testimonial).

PROFESSIONAL TRUSTEE
Remuneration. *See* **Trust and trustee** (Remuneration of trustee—Professional trustee).

PROFIT À PRENDRE
Abandonment—
Right of common. *See* **Commons** (Right of common—Abandonment).
Coal—
Acquisition of sea-borne coal from foreshore. *See* **Foreshore** (Rights over foreshore—Acquiring sea-borne coal).
Contract of sale—
Illegality—
Enforceability of contract—Dishonest motive of vendor—Innocence of purchaser. *See* **Contract** (Illegality—Enforceability of contract—Dishonest motive of vendor—Innocence of purchaser—Sale of profit à prendre).
Easement distinguished. *See* **Easement** (Distinction from profit à prendre).
Extent of profit à prendre—
Profit appurtenant—
Extent of right related to nature of dominant tenement—Profit unlimited in scope—Express grant—Right of pasture—Sheep rights—Right to graze unlimited as to number of sheep and period of grazing—Right in severalty appurtenant to dominant tenement created by express grant—Whether right capable of subsisting as a profit appurtenant. **Anderson v Bostock** [1976] **1** 560, Ch D.
Oral grant—
No memorandum in writing—
Action in trespass by grantee—Possession and part performance by grantee—Whether grantee entitled to maintain action in trespass. **Mason v Clarke** [1955] **1** 914, HL.
Prescription—
Lost modern grant—
Right of common. *See* **Commons** (Right of common—Creation).
Right of pasturage—
Accommodation of dominant tenement—Whether test of real or appreciable benefit. **Polo Woods Foundation v Shelton-Agar** [2010] **1** 539, Ch D.
Sheep rights—
Right of pasture—Continuity of user—Evidence not showing sufficient continuity of user. **White v Taylor (No 2)** [1968] **1** 1015, Ch D.
Sheep rights—
Access—
Watering sheep—Water from well—Right to place troughs for watering sheep on waste land—Necessary access only, but with vehicles where necessary. **White v Taylor (No 2)** [1968] **1** 1015, Ch D.
Right of pasture—
Continuity of user. *See* Prescription—Sheep rights—Right of pasture—Continuity of user, *above*.
Extent of right. *See* Extent of profit à prendre, *above*.
Grant on sale by auction of lands in single ownership—Former waste land of manor—Construction of grants—Reference to particulars and conditions of sale—Extrinsic evidence where latent ambiguity in particular wording—Apportionment of sheep rights when lot sold at auction no longer held in single ownership—General words in conveyances—Conveyancing Act 1881, s 6. **White v Taylor (No 2)** [1968] **1** 1015, Ch D.

PROFITS
Account of profits—
Damages for breach of contract—
Whether account of profits available for breach of contract. *See* **Contract** (Damages for breach—Account of profits).
Trustee. *See* **Trust and trustee** (Profit from trust—Account of profits).

PROFITS (cont)—
    Corporation profits tax—
        Hong Kong. *See* **Hong Kong** (Corporation profits tax).
    Damages for loss of profits—
        Misrepresentation. *See* **Misrepresentation** (Damages—Deceit—Measure of damages—Loss of profits).
    Excess profits tax. *See* **Excess profits tax**.
    Income tax—
        Computation of profits. *See* **Income tax** (Computation of profits).
        Deduction in computing profits. *See* **Income tax** (Deduction in computing profits).
        Generally. *See* **Income tax** (Profits).
    Obtained by servant dishonestly. *See* **Employment** (Profits obtained by servant dishonestly by virtue of employment).
    Partnership—
        Dissolution. *See* **Partnership** (Dissolution—Profits).
    Profits tax. *See* **Profits tax**.
    Unjust enrichment—
        Restitution. *See* **Restitution** (Unjust enrichment—Investment profit).

PROFITS TAX
    Allowance—
        Industrial building or structure—
            Annual allowance for dwelling-house built for and occupied by men at colliery—Buildings likely to have no value at date when mine worked out—Buildings having substantial value if mining ceased at the time of assessment—Income Tax Act 1945, s 8(3), proviso. **National Coal Board v IRC** [1957] 2 461, HL.
    Appeal—
        Appeal by company against assessments to profits tax and excess profits tax—
            Order for rehearing of appeal of director against Sch E assessment—Success of director's appeal would destroy substructure of assessment on company—Appeals by company remitted to be heard by same panel of commissioners as director's appeal. **Rose v Humbles (Inspector of Taxes)** [1970] 2 519, Ch D.
        Case stated—
            Appeal from income tax commissioners—Dismissal of appeals by consent. **Practice Note** [1956] 1 880, Ch D.
    Chargeable accounting period—
        Determination by Inland Revenue Commissioners—
            Interval between company's old and new businesses—Commencement of business as investment company—Last chargeable accounting period—Period before interval—Finance Act 1937, ss 19(4), 20(2)(a), (b)—Finance Act 1947, s 35(1)(c). **EYL Trading Co Ltd v IRC** [1962] 3 303, CA.
        Last period of company—
            Investment company's voluntary winding-up—No longer investment company after winding-up resolution—Finance Act 1937, s 19(4). **IRC v Olive Mill Ltd (in liq)** [1963] 2 130, Ch D.
    Computation of profits—
        Accountancy method—
            Valuation of work in progress. **Ostime (Inspector of Taxes) v Duple Motor Bodies Ltd** [1961] 2 167, HL.
        Deduction—
            Capital expenditure—Payments under lease—Payments for right of entry and compensation for damage—Opencast coal mining—Transient and recurrent operation—Income Tax Act 1952, s 137. **Rorke (HJ) Ltd v IRC** [1960] 3 359, Ch D.
            Capital expenditure—Premiums on grant of leases—Oil company—Tied service stations—Lease of premies to oil company for premium—Sub-lease back to proprietor at nominal rent—Covenants binding proprietor to use company's oil—Deductibility of premium in computing company's profits—Income Tax Act 1952, s 137(f). **Regent Oil Co Ltd v Strick (Inspector of Taxes)** [1965] 3 174, HL.
            Director's remuneration—Controlling interest of directors—Directors not holding majority of shares—Majority of shares held by another company—Director owning majority of shares of that company—Effect of register of members—Finance Act 1937, Sch 4, para 11—Finance Act 1952, s 34. **Berendsen (S) Ltd v IRC** [1957] 2 612, CA.
            Director's remuneration—Controlling interest of directors—Shares registered in name of custodian trustee—Finance Act 1937, Sch IV, para 11. **IRC v Silverts Ltd** [1951] 1 703, CA.
            Interest payable out of the profits—Interest on cumulative income stock—Interest payable 'to the extent to which the net profits ... shall be sufficient'—Deficiency out of net profits of succeeding years 'if and so far as the same shall suffice'—Finance Act 1937, Sch IV, para 4. **IRC v Pullman Car Co Ltd** [1954] 2 491, Ch D.
            Money wholly and exclusively laid out or expended for the purposes of trade—Racecourse Betting Control Board—Whether payments made as working expenses or as statutory distributions of surplus deductible where board's business beneficial—Racecourse Betting Act 1928, s 3(6)—Income Tax Act 1952, s 137(a). **Racecourse Betting Control Board v Young (Inspector of Taxes)** [1959] 3 215, HL.
            Rentcharge—Whether income or capital payments—Rentcharges given as consideration for lessee's purchase of lessor's interest—Purchaser a property investment company—Whether rentcharges allowable deduction in computing lessee's profits for profits tax purposes—Income Tax Act 1952, s 177. **IRC v Land Securities Investment Trust Ltd** [1969] 2 430, HL.
            Rent—Company holding 88 year lease of premises—Scheme to acquire freehold—Subsidiary becoming freeholder—Freeholder becoming lessee for 22 years—Company becoming sub-lessee—Company's higher rent for shorter period—No deduction of increase of rent—Payment for acquisition of capital asset (freehold)—Income Tax Act 1952, s 137(a), (f). **Littlewoods Mail Order Stores Ltd v McGregor (Inspector of Taxes)** [1969] 3 855, CA.

PROFITS TAX (cont)—
  Computation of profits (cont)—
    Deduction (cont)—
      Trade expenses—Asset constituting stock-in-trade—Price or value at date of acquisition—Hotel bought by property developer—Negotiated price £72,000—Value at time £150,000—Conveyance direct to own company at £72,000—Finding of commercial acquisition by company—Not a gift by developer to company—Price not value deductible. **Jacgilden (Weston Hall) Ltd v Castle (Inspector of Taxes)** [1969] **3** 1110, Ch D.
    Franked investment income—
      Dividends from subsidiary company—'Functions' of company alleged to consist wholly of holding property—Colliery company's undertaking nationalised—Subsequent activities devoted to obtaining compensation pending liquidation—Whether company carrying on a trade or business—Finance Act 1937, s 19(4). **Briggs (Henry), Son & Co Ltd v IRC** [1961] **1** 220, HL.
    Income received from investments or other property—
      Income excluded from computation—Income received from dividends from 'a body corporate carrying on a trade or business' to which statutory provision applicable—Companies ceasing to trade before distributing dividends—Finance Act 1937, Sch 4, para 7(1)(a)—Finance Act 1947, s 32(1). **IRC v Clifforia Investments Ltd** [1963] **1** 159, Ch D.
    Profits of trade or business—
      Income received from investments or other property—Nationalisation of colliery undertaking—Interim income payments pending satisfaction of compensation—Cesser of colliery trade—Continuance of other separate trades—Finance Act 1937, Sch IV, para 7 (as amended by Finance Act 1947, s 32(1))—Coal Industry Nationalisation Act 1946, s 22(2), (3)—Coal Industry (No 2) Act 1949, s 1(2). **IRC v Butterley Co Ltd** [1956] **2** 197, HL.
    Property dealing company—
      War damage value payments—Whether to be included in computing profits of company. **London Investment and Mortgage Co Ltd v Worthington (Inspector of Taxes)** [1958] **2** 230, HL.
    Trading receipts—
      Insurance premiums—Return of excess of premiums—Share of surplus assets of mutual insurance company on winding-up—Whether income or capital receipt. **Stafford Coal and Iron Co Ltd v Brogan (Inspector of Taxes)** [1963] **3** 277, HL.
  Corporation profits tax—
    Hong Kong. *See* **Hong Kong** (Corporation profits tax).
  Distribution—
    Director-controlled company—
      Payments to a director for manufacture and sale of patented article under licence from the director, the patentee—Full consideration received by company—Whether payments were amounts applied by way of remuneration, loans or otherwise for the benefit of any person—Finance Act 1947, s 36(1). **IRC v H Dunning & Co (1946) Ltd** [1960] **3** 75, Ch D.
    Distribution charge—
      Reconstruction—Vendor company's business sold in 1950 in consideration of shares in purchasing company—Subsequent sale by vendor company of shares of purchasing company—Liquidation of vendor company in 1955—Liability to distribution charge—Finance Act 1947, ss 30, 36(4), 43(1). **IRC v JB Hodge & Co (Glasgow) Ltd** [1961] **3** 172, HL.
    Exclusion of sums applied in reducing share capital—
      Redemption of preference shares—Price equal to nominal amount of shares plus a premium—Whether 'sum applied in reducing share capital'—Finance Act 1947, s 36(1), proviso. **IRC v Universal Grinding Wheel Co Ltd** [1955] **2** 29, HL.
    Gross relevant distribution—
      Repayment or return of share capital—Exclusion of distribution of capital—Company in voluntary liquidation—Transfer of assets to new company—Balance less expenses paid to shareholders—Finance Act 1947, s 35(1)—Finance Act 1951, s 31(1), (5). **IRC v Pollock & Peel Ltd (in liq)** [1957] **2** 483, CA.
      Repayment or return of share capital—Exclusion of distribution of capital—Company in voluntary liquidation—Transfer of assets to new company—Direction that profits tax be computed as if capital not previously increased—Validity—Finance Act 1937, s 20(2)(b)—Finance Act 1947, ss 35(1)(c), 36(4)—Finance Act 1951, s 32(1), (3), (4). **Ackland & Prattern Ltd (in liq) v IRC** [1960] **3** 367, Ch D.
    Meaning—
      Capital profits dividend—Whether 'distribution' including capital profits dividend—Finance Act 1947, s 36(1). **IRC v Bell & Nicolson Ltd** [1952] **1** 428, Ch D.
    Net relevant distributions—
      Trading loss—Gross relevant distributions made—Franked investment income less than amount of trading loss but exceeding gross relevant distributions—Whether there were net relevant distributions liable to distribution charge—Finance Act 1947, s 34(2)—Finance Act 1937, Sch 4, para 7(1A) (substituted by Finance Act 1947, s 32(1)). **IRC v South Georgia Co Ltd** [1958] **1** 593, HL.
  Excess profits tax. *See* **Excess profits tax**.
  Exemption—
    Principal company subject to surtax direction—
      Notice requiring profits of subsidiary to be treated as profits of principal company—Exemption of subsidiary company—Finance Act 1937, s 22(1), (2). **Heelex Investments Ltd v IRC** [1955] **1** 641, CA.
    Statutory undertaker—
      Authorised person limited by enactment as regards charge for service—Carriage of passengers by road—Taxi-cab proprietors—Cabs licensed under statute—Maximum fares prescribed—Relationship between driver and company that of bailee and bailor of cab—Finance Act 1937, s 19(5). **London General Cab Co Ltd v IRC** [1950] **2** 566, Ch D.
  Hong Kong. *See* **Hong Kong** (Corporation profits tax).

PROFITS TAX (cont)—
Relief—
Double taxation agreements with other countries—
Allowance of overseas tax as credit against United Kingdom profits tax—Relief not to exceed amount of profits tax—Companies—Grouping notice—Effect—Principal company trading in United Kingdom—Subsidiary companies also trading in United Kingdom—Principal company making United Kingdom losses—Subsidiary companies making United Kingdom profits—Overseas dividends and trading income of principal company exceeding United Kingdom losses—Principal company giving 'grouping notice' in respect of all subsidiaries—Method of computing entitlement to relief for profits tax having regard to grouping notice—Whether relief computed by reference to profits tax on income of principal company and subsidiaries or of principal company only—Finance Act 1937, s 22—Income Tax Act 1952, s 347(2), Sch 16. **IRC v Babcock & Wilcox Ltd** [1971] **3** 1335, Ch D.
Non-distribution relief—
Company ordinarily resident both within and outside the United Kingdom—Finance Act 1947, s 39(1). **Union Corp Ltd v IRC** [1953] **1** 729, HL.
Subsidiary company—
Principal company's notice that subsiary's profits to be treated as principal's—
Determination by winding-up of principal company—Finance Act 1937, s 22(1). **IRC v Olive Mill Ltd (in liq)** [1963] **2** 130, Ch D.
Tax paid by virtue of notice—Whether whole tax paid by principal paid by virtue of the notice. **Chloride Batteries Ltd v Gahan (Inspector of Taxes)** [1956] **1** 828, HL.
Transitional relief on supersession of income tax and profits tax by corporation tax—
Existing companies with overseas trading income. *See* **Income tax** (Corporation tax—Transitional provisions—Transitional relief—Company with overseas trading income).

PROHIBITED GOODS
Importation. *See* **Customs and excise** (Importation of prohibited goods).

PROHIBITED STEPS ORDER
Family proceedings. *See* **Family proceedings** (Orders in family proceedings—Prohibited steps order).

PROHIBITION
Arbitrator—
Power of court to issue order directed to private arbitrator—
Circumstances in which power exercisable. **R v Disputes Committee of the National Joint Council for the Craft of Dental Technicians, ex p Neate** [1953] **1** 327, QBD.
Costs. *See* **Costs** (Prohibition).
Crown Court. *See* **Crown Court** (Supervisory jurisdiction of High Court—Orders of mandamus, prohibition or certiorari).
Grant—
Grant where right of appeal—
Co-existence of right of appeal and right to order of prohibition—Patents Act 1949, s 44(1). **Parke Davis & Co v Comptroller-General of Patents, Designs and Trade Marks** [1953] **1** 862, QBD.
Justices—
Right to issue—
Prohibition against proceeding in excess of jurisdiction—Right where case stated for opinion of High Court on question of jurisdiction. **R v Wimbledon Justices, ex p Derwent** [1953] **1** 390, QBD.
Locus standi of applicant—
Application to prevent local authority misusing powers—
Film censorship—Local authority permitting exhibtion of films contrary to law—Application by resident in area of local authority—Resident's wife a ratepayer—Whether resident having suffcient locus standi to apply for order of prohibition—Whether court having power to prevent local authority misusing powers. **R v Greater London Council, ex p Blackburn** [1976] **3** 184, CA.
Nuisance—
Statutory nuisance. *See* **Nuisance** (Statutory nuisance—Prohibition notice).
Prohibition order—
Jurisdiction of Financial Services Authority. *See* **Financial services** (Financial Services Authority (FSA)—Powers—Prohibition order).
Renaming of order of. *See* **Practice** (Crown Office list—Change of title to Administrative Court—Renaming of orders).
Rent tribunal—
Prohibition against proceeding in excess of jurisdiction—
Circumstances in which appropriate to apply for prohibition—When application for prohibition should be made. **R v Tottenham and District Rent Tribunal, ex p Northfield (Highgate) Ltd** [1956] **2** 863, QBD.

PROHIBITION NOTICE
Statutory nuisance. *See* **Nuisance** (Statutory nuisance—Prohibition notice).

PROHIBITION ORDER
FSA's powers as to. *See* **Financial services** (Financial Services Authority (FSA)—Powers—Prohibition order).

PROMISE
Enforcement—
Intention to create legal relationship. *See* **Contract** (Intention to create legal relationship—Promise—Enforcement).

PROMISSORY ESTOPPEL
See **Estoppel** (Promissory estoppel).

PROMISSORY NOTE

Generally. *See* **Bill of exchange** (Promissory note).
Implied indemnity. *See* **Indemnity** (Implied indemnity—Promissory note).
Income tax—
    Discount. *See* **Income tax** (Discounts—Bill of exchange or promissory note).
Liability—
    Payment made to third party. *See* **Money** (Promissory note).
Rate of exchange. *See* **Money** (Currency—Rate of exchange—Promissory notes payable in Turkish gold pounds).
Sale of land—
    Conditional contract. *See* **Sale of land** (Contract—Conditional contract—Promissory note).
Stamp duty. *See* **Stamp duty** (Promissory note).

PROPER LAW

Contract, of. *See* **Conflict of laws** (Contract—Proper law of contract).
Settlement, of. *See* **Conflict of laws** (Settlement—Proper law of settlement).

PROPERTY

Animals. *See* **Animal** (Property in animals).
Beneficial ownership—
    Damage to property—
        Negligence. *See* **Negligence** (Duty to take care—Economic loss—Damage to property—Consequential loss to beneficial owner of property).
Company—
    Winding up—
        Distribution of company's property. *See* **Company** (Winding up—Distribution of company's property).
Compulsory purchase. *See* **Compulsory purchase**.
Criminal property—
    Proceeds of crime. *See* **Proceeds of crime** (Criminal property).
Damage to property—
    Criminal. *See* **Criminal law** (Damage to property).
    Negligence. *See* **Negligence** (Damage—Damage to property).
Equity—
    Marshalling. *See* **Equity** (Marshalling).
    Proprietary estoppel. *See* **Estoppel** (Proprietary estoppel).
Family provision. *See* **Family provision** (Property).
Insurance. *See* **Insurance** (Property insurance).
Joint ownership—
    Bankruptcy. *See* **Bankruptcy** (Trustee in bankruptcy—Vesting of property in trustee—Bankrupt and spouse jointly owning and occupying property).
Marshalling. *See* **Equity** (Marshalling).
Mortgage. *See* **Mortgage**.
Option to purchase. *See* **Option** (Option to purchase).
Partnership property. *See* **Partnership** (Partnership property).
Passing of property—
    Sale of goods. *See* **Sale of goods** (Passing of property).
Police powers. *See* **Police** (Powers—Power to seize and retain property relevant to criminal proceedings).
Prisoner, of. *See* **Prison** (Prisoner—Property of prisoner).
Property adjustment order—
    Divorce. *See* **Divorce** (Property—Adjustment order).
Rates. *See* **Rates**.

PROPRIETARY ESTOPPEL

Acquisition of real property—
    Conduct leading representee to act to his detriment—
        Conduct leading representee to believe that property belonged to him. *See* **Estoppel** (Conduct—Conduct leading representee to act to his detriment—Acquisition of real property—Conduct leading representee to believe that property belonged to him).
Generally. *See* **Estoppel** (Proprietary estoppel).
Rates. *See* **Rates**.

PROSCRIBED ORGANISATION

Criminal proceedings. *See* **Criminal law** (Proscribed organisation).

PROSECUTION

Closing speech—
    Criminal trial. *See* **Criminal law** (Trial—Speeches—Prosecution—Closing speech).
Costs. *See* **Criminal law** (Costs—Prosecution costs).
Criminal law. *See* **Criminal law** (Prosecution).
Director of Public Prosecutions—
    Consent to institution of proceedings—
        Proceedings for gross indecency. *See* **Criminal law** (Gross indecency—Proceedings—Consent of Director of Public Prosecutions).
    Duties—
        Conduct of proceedings. *See* **Criminal law** (Proceedings—Duties of Director of Public Prosecutions).
Evidence—
    Committal proceedings. *See* **Criminal law** (Committal—Preliminary hearing before justices—Evidence for the prosecution).
    Generally. *See* **Criminal evidence** (Prosecution evidence).
    Prosecution not disclosing material evidence to defence—
        Certiorari. *See* **Certiorari** (Justices—Natural justice—Prosecution not disclosing material evidence to defence).

PROSECUTION (cont)—
Food and drugs offences. *See* **Food and drugs** (Offence—Prosecution).
Imputation on character of prosecutor or witness. *See* **Criminal evidence** (Character of accused—Imputation on character of prosecutor or witness).
Local authority's powers. *See* **Local authority** (Powers—Powers to prosecute).
Malicious prosecution. *See* **Malicious prosecution**.
Notice of intended prosecution—
　Motoring offences. *See* **Road traffic** (Notice of intended prosecution).
Road traffic offence. *See* **Road traffic** (Offence—Prosecution).
Security Industry Authority—
　Power to prosecute. *See* **Licensing** (Private Security—Security Industry Authority—Functions of authority).
Speeches. *See* **Criminal law** (Trial—Speeches—Prosecution).
Time limit—
　False trade description. *See* **Trade description** (False trade description—Time limit for prosecutions).
　Generally. *See* **Criminal law** (Time—Time limit for bringing prosecution).
　Illegal entry into United Kingdom. *See* **Immigration** (Illegal entry and other offences—Time limit for prosecution).
　Offence under factories legislation. *See* **Factory** (Offence—Prosecution—Time limit).
　Sale of goods at price exceeding statutory maximum permitted price. *See* **Price control** (Sale of goods at price exceeding statutory maximum permitted price—Prosecution—Time within which summary proceedings may be brought).
Trial. *See* **Criminal law** (Trial—Prosecution).
Want of prosecution—
　Dismissal of action. *See* **Practice** (Dismissal of action for want of prosecution).

PROSECUTOR
Character of—
　Evidence in criminal proceedings. *See* **Criminal evidence** (Character of prosecutor).
　Generally. *See* **Criminal law** (Prosecutor).

PROSPECTUS
Company—
　Criminal liability for false statement. *See* **Criminal law** (Company—False statement—Prospectus).
　Generally. *See* **Company** (Prospectus).

PROSTITUTION
Criminal offences relating to prostitution—
　Generally. *See* **Criminal law** (Prostitution).
　Keeping a brothel. *See* **Criminal law** (Brothel—Keeping a brothel).
Divorce—
　Adultery—
　　What amounts to adultery. *See* **Divorce** (Adultery—What constitutes—Prostitution).
Use of premises for—
　Nuisance. *See* **Nuisance** (Prostitution—Use of premises for prostitution).

PROTECTED BUILDING
Value added tax—
　Zero rating. *See* **Value added tax** (Zero-rating—Protected building).

PROTECTED DISCLOSURE
Victimisation, as a consequence of. *See* **Employment** (Victimisation—Protected disclosure).

PROTECTED LIFE INTEREST
Election against will—
　Effect. *See* **Equity** (Election—Election against will—Effect—Protected life interest).
Settlement. *See* **Settlement** (Protected life interest).

PROTECTED TENANCY
Generally. *See* **Rent restriction**.
Sale of land. *See* **Sale of land** (Protected tenancy).
Transfer on termination of marriage. *See* **Divorce** (Property—Protected or statutory tenancy—Transfer of protected or statutory tenancy on termination of marriage).

PROTECTION AGAINST WEATHER
Right to. *See* **Easement** (Protection against weather).

PROTECTION OF ANIMALS
See **Animal** (Protection).

PROTECTION OF CHILD
Generally. *See* **Child** (Protection).

PROTECTION OF ENVIRONMENT
See **Environment** (Protection).

PROTECTION OF SUBJECT
Duty of Crown. *See* **Crown** (Duty—Duty to protect subject).

PROTECTIVE APPLIANCE
Safe system of working. *See* **Safe system of working** (Duty to give information or advice—Protective appliance).

PROTECTIVE AWARD
Redundancy—
Failure to consult appropriate trade union. *See* **Redundancy** (Employer's duty to consult appropriate trade union—Failure to consult union—Protective award against employer).

PROTECTIVE TRUST
Beneficiaries resident in enemy territory—
Forfeiture. *See* **Trust and trustee** (Protective trust—All beneficiaries resident in enemy territory—Forfeiture).
Nullity decree—
Effect where protective trust to endure only while life tenant remained widower but widower remarried and second marriage was declared null. *See* **Will** (Gift—Gift during widowhood—Decree of nullity in respect of second marriage).
Protected life interest—
Forfeiture—
Election against will—Liability to compensate disappointed beneficiaries. *See* **Equity** (Election—Election against will—Effect—Protected life interest).
Variation by the court. *See* **Variation of trusts** (Protective trust).

PROTESTOR
Aerodromes—
Endangering safety at aerodromes. *See* **Criminal law** (Aerodromes—Endangering safety at aerodromes—Direct action by protesters to halt deportation flight).
Human rights. *See* **Human rights** (Freedom of expression—Freedom of assembly—Protestors).
Peaceful protestor—
Power of police to remove. *See* **Police** (Powers—Removal of peaceful protesters).
Police powers—
Power to stop, search and detain. *See* **Police** (Powers—Power to stop, search and detain—Protestors).
Stop, search and detention of—
Police powers. *See* **Police** (Powers—Power to stop, search and detain—Protestors).

PROVIDENT SOCIETIES
Industrial and provident societies. *See* **Industrial and provident societies**.

PROVISIONAL BID
Auction—
Conversion of goods—
Auctioneer's liability. *See* **Conversion** (Auctioneer's liability—Provisional bid).

PROVISIONAL DAMAGES
Personal injuries action—
Generally. *See* **Damages** (Personal injury—Provisional damages).
Practice—
Generally. *See* **Practice** (Personal injuries action—Damages—Provisional damages).

PROVISIONAL LICENCE
Driving licence—
Conditions attached. *See* **Road traffic** (Driving licence—Conditions attached to provisional licences).
Disqualification. *See* **Road traffic** (Disqualification for holding licence—Provisional licence).
Generally. *See* **Road traffic** (Driving licence—Provisional licence).

PROVISIONAL LIQUIDATOR
See **Company** (Compulsory winding up).

PROVISIONAL REGISTRATION
Common land. *See* **Commons** (Registration—Provisional registration).

PROVISIONAL WARRANT
Arrest—
Fugitive offender. *See* **Extradition** (Arrest—Provisional warrant).

PROVISO
Function of proviso. *See* **Statute** (Proviso).

PROVOCATION
Criminal charge—
Defence. *See* **Criminal law** (Provocation—Provocation as a defence).
Cruelty—
Divorce. *See* **Divorce** (Cruelty—Provocation).
Murder—
Belize. *See* **Belize** (Criminal law—Murder—Provocation).
Generally. *See* **Criminal law** (Murder—Provocation).

PROXY
Company meeting. *See* **Company** (Meeting—Proxy).
Stamp duty. *See* **Stamp duty** (Letter or power of attorney—Proxy).

PSYCHIATRIC DAMAGE
Damages for. *See* **Damages** (Personal injury—Psychiatric damage).

PSYCHIATRIC EXAMINATION
Minor, of. *See* **Minor** (Psychiatric examination).

PSYCHIATRIC INJURY
Whether psychiatric injury can amount to 'actual bodily harm'. *See* **Criminal law** (Assault—Assault occasioning actual bodily harm—Actual bodily harm—Psychiatric injury).

PSYCHIATRIST
Evidence as expert—
Criminal proceedings. *See* **Criminal evidence** (Expert evidence—Psychiatrist).

PSYCHOLOGIST
Educational psychologist—
Duty of care. *See* **Negligence** (Duty to take care—Existence of duty—Educational psychologist).

PSYCHOPATHIC DISORDER
Discharge from hospital. *See* **Mental health** (Patient—Discharge from hospital—Psychopathic disorder).

PUBLIC AUTHORITY
Act done in pursuance of public duty or authority—
Public duty or authority—
Local authority providing public swimming baths—Accident—Whether local authority in providing swimming bath acting 'in pursuance of any public duty or authority'—Solicitor and client costs—Public Authorities Protection Act 1893, s 1(b)—Public Health (London) Act 1936, s 167. **Clarke v Bethnal Green BC** [1939] 2 54, KBD.
Breach of statutory duty—
Damages. *See* **Damages** (Breach of statutory duty—Breach by public authority).
Challenge to validity of public authority's decision—
Judicial review. *See* **Judicial review** (Challenge to validity of public authority's decision).
Compulsory acquisition of land by—
Assessment of compensation. *See* **Compulsory purchase** (Compensation—Assessment—Land acquired by public authority).
Confidential information—
Disclosure. *See* **Confidential information** (Disclosure—Disclosure by public body).
Contract not to exercise statutory powers. *See* Statutory powers—Contract not to exercise, *below.*
Corruption of officer or employee. *See* **Criminal law** (Corruption).
Discretionary powers. *See* Statutory powers—Discretionary powers, *below.*
Employee of public authority—
Dismissal—
Judicial review—Availability of remedy. *See* **Judicial review** (Availability of remedy—Employment by public authority—Dismissal of employee).
Superannuation. *See* Staff—Superannuation, *below.*
Transfer of—
Compensation. *See* Transfer of officers—Compensation, *below.*
Excessive exercise of powers. *See* Statutory powers—Excessive exercise of statutory powers, *below.*
Human rights. *See* **Human rights** (Public authority).
India—
Act of State. *See* **India** (Public authorities—Acts of State).
Interlocutory injunction—
Generally. *See* **Injunction** (Interlocutory—Public authority).
Public authority exercising statutory duties as defendant. *See* **Injunction** (Interlocutory—Public authority performing statutory duties as defendant).
Judicial review—
Availability of remedy. *See* **Judicial review** (Availability of remedy—Public authority).
Decision of public authority—
Challenge to validity by way of application for judicial review. *See* **Judicial review** (Challenge to validity of public authority's decision).
Limitation of action—
Act done in execution of statute or of public duty or authority—
Act done by person—Bank of England—Register of securities—Act done in intended execution of an Act of Parliament—Removal of name from register—Refusal to restore—Date from which time runs—Limitation Act 1939, s 21(1). **Welch v Bank of England (Francis & Praed, third parties)** [1955] 1 811, Ch D.
Action for negligence against medical officers of county hospital—Writ issued more than six months after date when cause of action accruing—Whether medical officers entitled to protection of Act—Public Authorities Protection Act 1893, s 1. **Nelson v Cookson** [1939] 4 30, KBD.
Action for negligence against medical specialist at hospital administered by hospital board—Writ issued more than a year after date when cause of action accruing—Whether treatment given by specialist 'act done in execution of public duty'—Whether specialist entitled to protection of Limitation Act 1939, s 21(1). **Higgins v North West Metropolitan Hospital Board** [1954] 1 414, QBD.
Action for negligence against specialist at hospital administered under the National Health Service—Writ issued more than one year after date when cause of action accruing—Whether specialist acting in execution of statute—Whether within protection of—Limitation Act 1939, s 21(1). **Razzel v Snowball** [1954] 3 429, CA.
Commissioner of Metropolitan Police—Dismissal of police officer—Claim by officer that dismissal illegal—Claim in respect of acts done more than year before writ issued—Limitation Act 1939, s 21. **Hogg v Scott** [1947] 1 788, KBD.
Governors of grammar school—Pupil slipping on worn step on snowy day—Infancy of plaintiff—Action brought more than year from date cause of action accrued—Whether governor 'public authority' within protection of Public Authorities Protection Act 1893, s 1—Limitation Act 1939, ss 21, 22. **Woodward v Hastings (Mayor)** [1944] 2 565, CA.

891

PUBLIC AUTHORITY (cont)—
 Limitation of action (cont)—
  Act done in execution of statute or of public duty or authority (cont)—
   One year limitation period—Exception where act, neglect or default continuing one—Catchment board—Cleansing watercourse—Dredgings deposited on bank—Plaintiff's bridge destroyed three years later owing to diversion of flood waters—Date on which cause of action accrued—Limitation Act 1939, s 21(1). **Marriage v East Norfolk Rivers Catchment Board** [1949] **2** 1021, CA.
   Prisoner on remand provided with furnished cell in pursuance of contract with prison commissioners—Injury suffered through alleged defect in china chamber provided—Whether prison commissioners a public authority—Prison Act 1877, ss 6, 9, 39—Public Authorities Protection Act 1893, s 1—Prison Rules 1933 (SR & O 1933 No 809), r 122. **Jacoby v Prison Comrs** [1940] **3** 506, CA.
   Public authority—Railway company—Whether railway company a 'public authority'—Public Authorities Protection Act 1893, s 1. **Swain v Southern Rly Co** [1939] **2** 794, CA.
   Public duty or authority—Agreement to augment teachers' war service pay—Limitation Act 1939, s 21(1)—Local Government Staffs (War Service) Act 1939, s 1(1). **Turburville v West Ham Corp** [1950] **2** 54, CA.
   Public duty—School managers and headmistress—Injury to child through want of supervision—Writ issued more than six months later—Whether school managers and headmistress within protection of statute—Public Authorities Protection Act 1893, s 1—Education Act 1921, ss 29, 30, 31. **Greenwood v Atherton** [1938] **4** 686, CA.
   Public—Harbour board—Action under power to carry on trade of wharfingers and warehousemen—Trade not subsidiary to main purpose of managing and controlling harbour—Straits Settlements Public Authorities Protection Ordinance (Revised Laws 1936, s 2(2), as amended by Public Authorities Protection (Amendment) Ordinance 1939, s 2—Limitation Act 1939, s 21(1). **Firestone Tire and Rubber Co (SS) Ltd v Singapore Harbour Board** [1952] **2** 219, PC.
   Soldier on duty—Member of Canadian forces—Action for damages for personal injuries brought against him more than year after date when cause of action accrued—Whether member of Canadian forces in same position as member of home forces—Visiting Forces (British Commonwealth) Act 1933, s 2(3)(b)—Limitation Act 1939, s 21(1). **Reeves v Deane-Freeman** [1953] **1** 461, CA.
   Statute giving local authority power to erect pavilion—Entertainment pavilion erected and carried on by local authority—Plaintiff injured by falling poster-frame—Writ issued more than six months after accident—Whether local authority within protection of Public Authorities Protection Act 1893, s 1. **Hawkes v Torquay Corp** [1938] **4** 16, Exeter Summer Assizes.
   Steamship requisitioned by Minister of War Transport operating on charter—Loss of commercial cargo by fire—Alleged negligence of Minister's officers in loading and discharge of cargo—Whether acts done in execution of public duty or authority—Limitation Act 1939, s 21. **Western India Match Co Ltd v Lock** [1946] **2** 227, KBD.
  Claim for contribution by joint tortfeasor—
   Commencement of period of limitation—Length of period—Law Reform (Married Women and Tortfeasors) Act 1935, s 6(1)(c)—Limitation Act 1935, ss 6(1)(c), 21(1)—RSC Ord 16A, r 1. **Wimpey (George) & Co Ltd v British Overseas Airways Corp** [1954] **3** 661, HL.
  Justices' protection. See **Magistrates** (Civil liability).
  Neglect or default in execution of statutory public duty or authority—
   Failure to pay fees of registration officer—Action for fees as registration officer—Action brought more than one year after completion of register—Whether payment in execution of statute—Limitation Act 1939, s 21. **Mountain v Bermondsey BC** [1941] **3** 498, KBD.
  Wheat Commission—
   Recovery of quota payments made to Wheat Commission. See **Agriculture** (Wheat—Quota payments—Recovery of quota payments made to Wheat Commission—Payments made more than six months before commencement of action).
 Local authority. See **Local authority**.
 Meeting—
  Admission of public—
   Power to exclude public—Prevention of disorderly conduct—Whether public body having power to prevent public from entering meeting if public likely to disrupt meeting—Whether power exercisable only at meeting itself—Public Bodies (Admissions to Meetings) Act 1960, s 1(1), (8). **R v Brent Health Authority, ex p Francis** [1985] **1** 74, QBD.
   Power to exclude public—Whether police and local authorities having power to exclude and eject from council meetings—Whether use of force against claimants being reasonable - Human Rights Act 1998, Sch 1, Pt I, arts 10, 11. **Laporte v Metropolitan Police Comr** [2015] **3** 438, QBD.
   Resolution to exclude public—Reason for exclusion—Special reason arising from nature of business or of proceedings—Accommodation for public at place of meeting—Lack of accommodation—Reasonable provision made to accommodate public—Unexpectedly large numbers wishing to attend meeting—Resolution by body to exclude all members of public rather than select some to fill available seats—Whether a reason 'arising from the nature of [the] business or of the proceedings'—Whether resolution valid—Public Bodies (Admission to Meetings) Act 1960, s 1(2). **R v Liverpool City Council, ex p Liverpool Taxi Fleet Operators' Association** [1975] **1** 379, QBD.
   Resolution to exclude public—Reason for reason stated in the resolution—Failure of body to state reason in resolution—No-one suffering injury in consequence of failure—Whether requirement the reason be stated in resolution mandatory or directory—Whether resolution valid—Public Bodies (Admission to Meetings) Act 1960, s 1(2). **R v Liverpool City Council, ex p Liverpool Taxi Fleet Operators' Association** [1975] **1** 379, QBD.
 Minister—
  Exercise of statutory power—
   House of Commons approval—Minister's exercise of statutory power requiring House of Commons approval—Whether Minister's exercise of power reviewable by courts on grounds of unreasonableness. **Nottinghamshire CC v Secretary of State for the Environment** [1986] **1** 199, HL.
  Judicial control. See Statutory powers—Duty of Minister, *below.*

892

PUBLIC AUTHORITY (cont)—
Natural justice. *See* **Natural justice** (Public authority).
Operation of air and sea ports—
Discretion—
Discretion to ban export of live animals—Ban on lawful trade in response to unlawful protest by
animal rights protesters—Whether public authorities operating air and sea ports having general
discretion to ban lawful trade in live animals—If so, whether export of livestock could be banned
on ground of unlawful disruption by protesters—Harbours, Docks and Piers Clauses Act 1847,
ss 33, 40—Air Navigation Order 1989, art 78(3). **R v Coventry City Council, ex p Phoenix Aviation**
[1995] **3** 37, QBD.
Parochial church council. *See* **Ecclesiastical law** (Parochial church council—Public authority).
Staff—
Superannuation—
War bonus—Whether included in calculation of pension. **Tibbals v Port of London Authority**
[1937] **2** 413, HL.
Statutory duty—
Local authority. *See* **Local authority** (Statutory duty).
Statutory powers—
Alternative or overlapping powers—
Town and country planning—Exercise of power under one statute carrying right to
compensation—Exercise of power under another might not carrying compensation—Whether
power carrying right to compensation should be exercised. **Westminster Bank Ltd v Minister of
Housing and Local Government** [1970] **1** 734, HL.
Contract not to exercise—
Option to purchase property—Consideration for option included covenant by local planning
authority not to exercise statutory power of compulsory acquisition—Cricket field—Covenant
ineffective in law—Contract granting option not reasonable bargain without effective
covenant—Option unenforceable by local authority—Land charge in respect of option vacated.
Staines UDC's Agreement, Re [1968] **2** 1, Ch D.
Discretionary powers—
Liability for non-feasance—Land drainage. **Smith v Cawdle Fen, Ely (Cambridge), Comrs**
[1938] **4** 64, KBD.
Duty of Minister—
Duty to consult—Sufficient consultation—Minister under duty to consult relevant organisations
before amending regulations—Department giving applicant organisation 8 days and 5 days to
comment on proposed amendments—Wording of some amendments not sent to applicant—
Whether obligation to consult mandatory or directory—What amounts to sufficient
consultation—Whether for minister or court to decide whether consultation sufficient—Whether
inadequate consultation requiring amending regulations to be quashed—Social Security and
Housing Benefits Act 1982, s 36(1)—Housing Benefits Amendment (No 4) Regulations 1984. **R v
Secretary of State for Social Services, ex p Association of Metropolitan Authorities** [1986] **1** 164,
QBD.
Judicial control of executive discretion—Complaint by milk producers asking for reference to
committee investigation—Discretion of Minister not expressly limited to enactment—Minister
declining to refer complaint—Previous applications by producers to Milk Marketing Board
unavailing—Producers in a minority on board—Whether mandamus would lie—Agricultural
Marketing Act 1958, s 19(3). **Padfield v Minister of Agriculture Fisheries and Food** [1968] **1** 694,
HL.
Duty to take care. *See* **Negligence** (Duty to take care—Statutory powers).
Excessive exercise of statutory powers—
Greater London Council—Grant to Inner London Education Authority—Express statutory provisions
relating to funding of authority—Whether GLC's grant ultra vires—Local Government Act 1972,
s 111—Local Government Act 1985, s 97(1). **Westminster City Council v Greater London Council**
[1986] **2** 278, HL.
Greater London Council—Reduction of fares on London Transport—GLC requiring London
Transport to reduce fares by 25 per cent—Fare reduction likely to cause substantial operating
deficit by London Transport—GLC empowered to take necessary and appropriate action to enable
London Transport to balance accounts—GLC proposing to make grant to London Transport to
enable it to balance its accounts—GLC issuing supplementary rate precept to London boroughs
to finance grant—Whether GLC acting in excess of statutory powers—Transport (London) Act
1969, ss 5(1), 7(3)(b), 7(6). **Bromley London BC v Greater London Council** [1982] **1** 129, CA and HL.
Greater London Council—Reduction of fares on London Transport—GLC requiring London
Transport to reduce fares—London Transport required 'so far as practicable' to make up
operating deficits in subsequent years—Whether GLC entitled to make grant to London Transport
to reduce or eliminate deficit—Whether fact that London Transport only required to make up
deficit 'so far as practicable' enabling GLC to make grant to London Transport—Whether GLC
acting within legal powers in directing London Transport to reduce fares—Transport (London) Act
1969, ss 1, 5(1), 7(3)(b), (6). **R v London Transport Executive, ex p Greater London Council**
[1983] **2** 262, QBD.
Highway authority—Repair of road—Excessive exercise of statutory powers is not a ground for
saddling a statutory authority with permanent obligation to maintain a road. **Alsager UDC v
Barratt** [1965] **1** 889, QBD.
Local authority resolution appropriating land—Local authority having no power to appropriate part
of land—Whether resolution valid appropriation for balance of land—Whether whole resolution
invalid. **Thames Water Authority v Elmbridge BC** [1983] **1** 836, CA.
Fettering future exercise of statutory powers—
Exercise of existing powers fettering future exercise of powers—Alternative or overlapping
powers—Restriction of user—Restrictive covenant controlling future use of land held by
authority—Covenant by authority not to create lettings of flats on estate owned by authority
except by long leases at a premium—Whether covenant a fetter on authority's duty to provide
housing accommodation in its district—Housing Act 1957, s 104. **R v Hammersmith and Fulham
London BC, ex p Beddowes** [1987] **1** 369, CA.

PUBLIC AUTHORITY (cont)—
   Statutory powers (cont)—
      Fettering future exercise of statutory powers (cont)—
         Exercise of existing powers fettering future exercise of powers—Creation of right extending over period of years—Restrictive covenant controlling use of land owned by authority—Lease of premises adjoining airfield owned by local authority—Covenant by authority to maintain airfield as municipal aerodrome—Whether covenant invalid as fettering exercise of statutory powers—Local Government Act 1933, s 163(1). **Dowty Boulton Paul Ltd v Wolverhampton Corp** [1971] **2** 277, Ch D.
      Implied powers of local authority. *See* **Local authority** (Statutory powers—Implied power).
      Interference with private rights in exercise of powers—
         Damage to riparian owners—Possibility of alternative method—Onus of proof. **Provender Millers (Winchester) Ltd v Southampton CC** [1939] **4** 157, CA.
         Erection of barrier along pavement in front of plaintiff's building—Nuisance—Invasion of private rights of property—Newcastle-upon-Tyne Improvement Act 1865, ss 22, 65. **Dormer v Newcastle-upon-Tyne Corp** [1940] **2** 521, CA.
         Erection of bus-shelter—Interference with access to private premises—Permissive power—Authority acting reasonably—Swindon Corporation Act 1926, ss 21, 25. **Edgington, Bishop and Withy v Swindon BC** [1938] **4** 57, KBD.
      Licence granted under statutory power—
         Condition—Severability—Entertainment licence granted with condition attached—Condition invalid—Whether invalid condition capable of severance—Local Government (Miscellaneous Provisions) Act 1982, Sch 1, paras 3, 4. **R v North Hertfordshire DC, ex p Cobbold** [1985] **3** 486, QBD.
      Misuse of powers—
         Application for order of prohibition—Locus standi of applicant. *See* **Prohibition** (Locus standi of applicant—Application to prevent local authority misusing powers).
         Discretionary powers—Race relations—General statutory duty to promote good race relations—Open spaces—Power to ban persons from using open spaces—Football club having licence to use local authority's recreation ground—Members of club taking part in sporting tour of South Africa—Local authority passing resolution banning club from using recreation ground for 12 months—Whether local authority acting unreasonably or misusing power to promote good race relations—Race Relations Act 1976, s 71. **Wheeler v Leicester City Council** [1985] **2** 1106, HL.
         Duty to promote good race relations—Borough with multiracial population—Company belonging to group with interests in South Africa supplying goods to borough council—Council deciding to boycott company's goods and to campaign to persuade other local authorities to do likewise—Whether local authority acting unreasonably or misusing power to promote good race relations—Race Relations Act 1976, s 71. **R v Lewisham London BC, ex p Shell UK Ltd** [1988] **1** 938, QBD.
         Exercise of power for unlawful purpose—Validity—Licence—Power to revoke licence—Threat to exercise power for unlawful purpose—Wireless telegraphy—Broadcast receiving licence—Colour television—Licence holder obtaining new licence before expiry of current licence—Purpose to avoid payment of increased statutory fee coming into force on date of expiry of existing licence—Home Office threatening to revoke new licence unless licence holder pay additional sum representing difference between increased fee and former fee—Home Office having no lawful authority to demand payment of additional sum—Whether threatened revocation of licence valid—Wireless Telegraphy Act 1949, s 1(4). **Congreve v Home Office** [1976] **1** 697, QBD and CA.
         Irrelevant consideration—Irrelevant consideration taken into account in deciding to use statutory power—Power to publish information—Inner London Education Authority entitled to publish information on matters relating to local government—Authority conducting media campaign to inform public of proposed government cuts in education and persuade public opinion to oppose cuts—Whether purpose of persuading public opinion an irrelevant consideration—Whether decision to conduct media campaign valid—Local Government Act 1972, s 142(2). **R v Inner London Education Authority, ex p Westminster City Council** [1986] **1** 19, QBD.
         Power to fix wage rates for employees—Strike by employees causing crisis in local authority's administration—Local authority agreeing to substantial increase in wage rates for striking employees—Whether wage rates excessive and ultra vires—Whether councillors who approved settlement liable personally for extra expenditure—Local Government Act 1972, s 161. **Pickwell v Camden London BC** [1983] **1** 602, QBD.
      Order made under statutory power—
         Administrative order—Validity—Severance—Part of administrative order invalid—Severance of invalid part—Direction made to Greater London Council by Secretary of State pursuant to statutory powers—Part of direction invalid—Whether whole direction invalid—Whether invalid part severable leaving valid part to take effect—London Regional Transport Act 1984, s 49. **R v Secretary of State for Transport, ex p Greater London Council** [1985] **3** 300, QBD.
         Subsequent statute conferring power to make similar order but subject to confirmation by Minister—Order made within scope of subsequent power but under previous statute and without confirmation—Whether order valid—Town Police Clauses Act 1847, s 21—Road Traffic Act 1930, s 46(1), (2)—Road and Rail Traffic Act 1933, s 29(4). **Brownsea Haven Properties Ltd v Poole Corp** [1958] **1** 205, CA.
   Transfer of officers—
      Compensation—
         Loss of office—Limit of amount of compensation—Annuity or lump sum—Option of officer—Pensions Commutation Acts 1871-1882—London Passenger Transport Act 1933, s 73(6), Sch XIV. **Rich v London Passenger Transport Board** [1936] **1** 912, CA.
         Transfer of employee of London County Council tramways to London Passenger Transport Board—Weekly servant—Right to and assessment of compensation—Consideration of earnings since dismissal—London Passenger Transport Act 1933, s 73, Sch XIV, para 4(e). **Perry and London Passenger Transport Board, Re an abitration between** [1939] **2** 421, KBD.
   Unlawful act—
      Entitlement to damages. *See* **Damages** (Entitlement to damages—Relief or remedy for unlawful act of public authority).

PUBLIC AUTHORITY (cont)—
  Unreasonable exercise of functions—
    Power of Secretary of State to intervene—
      Local education authority. *See* **Education** (Local education authority—Power of Secretary of State to prevent unreasonable exercise of functions).

PUBLIC BENEFIT
  Charity. *See* **Charity** (Public benefit).

PUBLIC BODY
  Confidential information—
    Disclosure. *See* **Confidential information** (Disclosure—Disclosure by public body).
  Officer or employee—
    Corruption. *See* **Criminal law** (Corruption—Public body).

PUBLIC BUILDING
  Removal of article from building. *See* **Criminal law** (Removal of articles from public building).

PUBLIC CARRIER'S LICENCE
  Goods vehicle. *See* **Road traffic** (Goods vehicle—Public carrier's licence).

PUBLIC COMPANY
  Generally. *See* **Company**.
  Party to civil proceedings—
    Change of name—
      Practice. *See* **Practice** (Parties—Change of name—Company).

PUBLIC CONTRACTS
  Generally. *See* **Public procurement** (Public contracts).

PUBLIC DECENCY
  Act outraging public decency. *See* **Criminal law** (Public decency—Act outraging public decency).
  Conspiracy to outrage public decency. *See* **Criminal law** (Conspiracy—Outrage to public decency).

PUBLIC DISCLOSURE COMMISSION
  Bahamas—
    Natural justice—
      Duty to hear parties etc. *See* **Natural justice** (Hearing—Duty to hear parties etc—Bahamas Public Disclosure Commission).

PUBLIC DOCUMENT
  Evidence—
    Admissibility—
      Hearsay evidence. *See* **Evidence** (Hearsay—Public documents).

PUBLIC ELECTRONIC COMMUNICATIONS NETWORK
  Criminal proceedings. *See* **Criminal law** (Public electronic communications network).

PUBLIC ENTERTAINMENT
  Licensing. *See* **Entertainment** (Public entertainment—Entertainments licence).

PUBLIC EXAMINATION
  Bankruptcy. *See* **Bankruptcy** (Public examination).
  Company—
    Compulsory winding up. *See* **Company** (Compulsory winding up—Public examination).

PUBLIC GOOD
  Obscene publication—
    Defence to criminal charge. *See* **Criminal law** (Obscene publications—Defence of public good).

PUBLIC HEALTH
  Appeal to quarter sessions—
    Right of appeal—
      Person aggrieved—Costs not given to successful party before magistrates—Right of appeal against refusal of magistrates to grant costs—Public Health Act 1936, s 301. **R v Lancashire Quarter Sessions Appeal Committee, ex p Huyton-with-Roby UDC** [1954] 3 225, QBD.
  Buildings—
    Control of buildings—
      Regulations—Breach of regulations—Notice requiring removal of structures—Validity—'Owner' of premises—Statement as to right of appeal—Need to state right to apply for extension of time—Statutory extension of time limit—Form of notice to owner—Service on owner—Wrongful removal of structures—Damages—Public Health Act 1936, ss 65(1)(3), 300(3), 343(1)—Building Restrictions (War-Time Contraventions) Act 1946, s 3(1). **Nalder v Ilford Corp** [1950] 2 903, KBD.
      Restriction on erection of buildings—Buildings—Erection of advertisement hoarding near highway—Whether a 'building'—Surrey County Council Act 1931, s 67. **Super Sites Ltd v Keen** [1938] 2 471, KBD.
      Temporary buildings—Movable structure—Converted omnibus—Motor lorry—Whether 'temporary buildings'—Public Health Acts Amendment Act 1907, s 27. **Gumbrell v Swale RDC** [1936] 3 935, KBD.

PUBLIC HEALTH (cont)—
Buildings (cont)—
Dangerous buildings—
Emergency measures—Compensation for damage—Requirement person seeking compensation not in default—Local authority using emergency powers to prohibit public access to pier—Tenant of premises on pier seeking compensation—Whether tenant in default—Whether tenant entitled to compensation—Building Act 1984, ss 78, 106. **Hastings BC v Manolete Partners plc** [2017] **2** 611, SC.
Dangerous structures—
Metropolis—Notice to take down, repair, or otherwise secure—Discretion of magistrate to order one of the three courses to be pursued—London Building Acts (Amendment) Act 1939, s 64. **Bewley & Co Ltd v London CC** [1953] **2** 821, QBD.
Order to repair or demolish—Failure by owner to comply with order—Demolition carried out by local authority—Machinery removed from premises by local authority—Right to remove machinery—Whether 'rubbish resulting from the demolition' included machinery on the premises—Public Health Act 1936, s 58. **McVittie v Bolton Corp** [1945] **1** 379, CA.
Order to repair or demolish—Works of repair unspecified in order—Whether order defective—Public Health Act 1936, s 58. **R v Bolton Recorder, ex p McVittie** [1939] **4** 236, CA.
Paving and draining of yards and passages—
Passage giving access to a house—Path giving access to a house—Whether included in 'passage giving access to a house'—Public Health Act 1936, s 56(1). **Denton UDC v Bursted Properties Ltd** [1955] **1** 273, QBD.
Caravans. *See* Movable dwellings, *below*.
Common lodging-house—
Registration—
Application to register premises as common lodging-house—Duty of local authority on receipt of application—Obligation to register premises unless statutory grounds for refusing application—Local authority declining to entertain application—No statutory grounds of refusal given—Mandamus issued directing authority to entertain application in accordance with statute—Public Health Act 1936, s 238(1). **R v Hounslow London Borough, ex p Pizzey** [1977] **1** 305, QBD.
Application to register premises as common lodging-house—Refusal of application—Appeal—Local authority not complying with statutory duty in refusing application—Whether order of mandamus should be issued—Whether remedy by way of appeal to magistrates—Public Health Act 1936, ss 238(1), 239. **R v Hounslow London Borough, ex p Pizzey** [1977] **1** 305, QBD.
Letting at weekly rent in advance—Whether premises outside definition of common lodging-house—Public Health Act 1936, ss 235, 236. **People's Hostels Ltd v Turley** [1938] **4** 72, KBD.
Drainage—
New buildings—
Drainage of buildings in combination—Planning permission for new buildings subject to properties being connected to public sewer—Distance to main sewer more than one hundred feet—No resolution requiring connexion with main sewer passed—No undertaking given by local authority to bear cost of sewer beyond first hundred feet—Whether local authority liable to contribute to expenses of connexion—Public Health Act 1936, ss 37(1)(4), 38(1), (2). **Princes Investments Ltd v Frimley and Camberley UDC** [1962] **2** 104, QBD.
Satisfactory provision to be made for drainage of building—Drainage of the building—Drains of particular building—Public Health Act 1936, s 37(1). **Chesterton RDC v Ralph Thompson Ltd** [1947] **1** 273, KBD.
Sewerage. *See* Sewerage—Drainage, *below*.
Stopped-up drains—
Liability to clear stopped-up drains—Notice to remedy stopped-up drains—Validity of notice—Sewage overflowing onto landowner's land—Local authority serving notice requiring him to remedy defect within 48 hours—Local authority undertaking work and discovering that blockage was on highway land and not on landowner's land—Whether drain on landowner's land 'stopped up'—Whether landowner liable to pay cost of unstopping drain—Public Health Act 1961, s 17. **Rotherham Metropolitan BC v Dodds** [1986] **2** 867, CA.
Dustbin. *See* Refuse—Notice requiring owner or occupier to provide dustbin, *below*.
Emergency—
COVID-19—
Judicial review of regulations imposing restrictions in response to COVID-19 public health emergency—Whether power to make regulations—Whether regulations lawful—Public Health (Control of Disease) Act 1984, s 45C—Health Protection (Coronavirus, Restrictions) (England) Regulations 2020, SI 2020/350. **R (on the application of Dolan) v Secretary of State for Health and Social Care** [2021] **1** 780, CA.
Entry on premises—
Notice—
Twenty-four hours' notice of intended entry—Letter stating intention to 'proceed under s 290(6) of the Public Health Act 1936', sent to occupier four months before entry—Whether notice of intended entry—Public Health Act 1936, s 287(1), proviso. **Stroud v Bradbury** [1952] **2** 76, QBD.
European Union—
Generally. *See* **European Union** (Public health).
Sale of goods. *See* **European Union** (Freedom of movement—Goods—Quantitative restrictions and equivalent measures—Public health).
Expenses—
Recovery—
Expenses of maintenance of patient in hospital—Recovery from person legally liable to maintain patient—'If possessed of sufficient means'—Local Government Act 1929, s 16—Poor Law Act 1930, s 14. **Middlesex CC v Nathan** [1937] **3** 283, KBD.
Expenses of maintenance of patient in hospital—Right of action of local authority—Recovery of expenses—Claim against deceased's estate—Right of action in contract against deceased's husband—'Whether expenses not recoverable from any other source'—Public Health Act 1936, s 184(1). **Middlesex CC v Kiverstein** [1942] **1** 596, CA.

PUBLIC HEALTH (cont)—
Expenses (cont)—
Recovery (cont)—
Jurisdiction of county court—Public Health Act 1936, ss 24, 293. **Great Yarmouth Corp v Gibson** [1956] **1** 113, CA.
Litter—
Depositing and leaving litter—
Offence. *See* **Criminal law** (Litter—Depositing and leaving litter).
Movable dwellings—
Vans intended for use for human habitation—
Vans not to be placed on land without permission from corporation—Exception in favour of travelling showmen—Scope of exception—Owner of land permitted showmen to occupy land with vans in which they lived—No permission from corporation—Whether permission necessary—Birmingham Corporation Act 1935, s 43. **Drakeley v Manzoni** [1938] **1** 67, KBD Divl Ct.
Nuisance. *See* **Nuisance** (Statutory nuisance).
Offensive trades—
Consent by local authority to establishment of offensive trades—
Requirement that consent should be in writing—Whether requirement directory or mandatory— Company carrying on offensive trades without written consent but with knowledge and approval of local authority for 23 years—Whether local authority's course of conduct sufficient consent—Public Health Act 1936, ss 107(1), 283(1). **Epping Forest DC v Essex Rendering Ltd** [1983] **1** 359, HL.
Pharmacy—
Freedom of establishment—
European Community. *See* **European Union** (Freedom of establishment—Restriction on freedom to provide services—Public health—Pharmacies).
Public sewer. *See* Sewerage, *below.*
Rag collection—
Restriction on sales etc by persons collecting or dealing in rags etc—
Restriction on sale or delivery of article to person under fourteen—Article—Delivery of goldfish to person under age of 14 years—Whether an 'article'—Public Health Act 1936, s 154(1). **Daly v Cannon** [1954] **1** 315, QBD Divl Ct.
Recovery of expenses—
Maintenance of patient in hospital. *See* Expenses—Recovery—Expenses of maintenance of patient in hospital, *above.*
Refuse—
Collection—
Closure or obstruction of means of access—Refusal by householder to allow local authority's dustmen to use passageway through his house to collect refuse from adjoining houses—Whether council, relying on prior usage of passageway, had established a means of access—Means of access as an easement—Public Health Act 1936, s 55(2). **Coupe v Barrett** [1969] **3** 37, QBD.
House refuse—
Removal—Duty of local authority—Converted dwelling-house used as office by insurance company—Whether refuse emanating therefrom 'house refuse'—Public Health Act 1936, s 72(1)(2). **Iron Trades Mutual Employers Insurance Association Ltd v Sheffield Corp** [1974] **1** 182, QBD.
Notice requiring owner or occupier to provide dustbin—
Notice set aside by justices—Right of local authority to appeal to quarter sessions—Whether person aggrieved—Public Health Act 1936, s 301. **R v Nottingham Quarter Sessions, ex p Harlow** [1952] **2** 78, QBD.
Owner of building required by local authority to provide dustbin—House subject to Rent Restrictions Acts—Appeal by owner to justices—Copy of notice of appeal given to occupier—Court 'may' make such order as it thinks fit—Duty of court—Whether obliged to require owner or occupier to provide dustbin—Public Health Act 1936, s 75(1), (3)—Local Government (Miscellaneous Provisions) Act 1953, s 8(4)(b). **Peterborough Corp v Holdich** [1955] **3** 424, QBD.
Owner of building required by local authority to provide dustbin—House subject to Rent Restrictions Acts—Dustbin originally provided by owner—No contractual obligation to provide—Owner's appeal to justices allowed—Transfer of 'burden or liability' from landlord to tenant—Increase of Rent and Mortgage Interest (Restrictions) Act 1920, s 2(3)—Public Health Act 1936, s 75(1). **First National Housing Trust Ltd v Chesterfield RDC** [1948] **2** 658, KBD.
Owner of building required by local authority to provide dustbin—Right of appeal to justices—Public Health Act 1936, s 75. **Croydon Corp v Thomas** [1947] **1** 239, KBD.
Sewerage—
Adoption by local authority of sewers and sewage disposal works—
Sewer—Part of newly contructed sewer sealed off—Whether sealed off part remained a sewer—Public Health Act 1936, s 17, s 343. **Blackdown Properties Ltd v Ministry of Housing and Local Government** [1965] **2** 345, Ch D.
Conversion of natural watercourse into sewer—
Discharge of sewage into natural stream for over 20 years—Statute making discharge of sewage into stream illegal—Whether watercourse converted into 'sewer'—Public Health Act 1875, s 4—Rivers Pollution Prevention Act 1876, s 3. **Legge (George) & Son Ltd v Wenlock Corp** [1938] **1** 37, HL.
Discharge of trade effluent into public sewers—
Discharge from premises before 1937—New premises added in 1946—Effluent from both premises same in nature and amount as before 1937—Need for notice of discharge of effluent after 1946—Public Health (Drainage of Trade Premises) Act 1937, ss 2(1), 4(1), 14(1). **Yorkshire Dyeing and Proofing Co Ltd v Middleton BC** [1953] **1** 540, QBD.
Whether liquid containing mixture of trade product and surface water 'trade effluent'—Meaning of 'trade effluent'—Water Industry Act 1991, s 141(1). **Boots UK Ltd v Severn Trent Water Ltd** [2019] **3** 371, CA.

PUBLIC HEALTH (cont)—
  Sewerage (cont)—
    Drainage—
      Surface water—Whether sewerage undertakers having implied power to discharge water onto another's land or watercourse—Transfer of water authorities' functions to water undertakers and sewerage undertakers—Transfer scheme—Transfer of property, rights and liabilities—Whether transfer scheme transferring pre-existing implied power to discharge water—Water Act 1989, s 4, Sch 2, para 2—Water Industry Act 1991. **Manchester Ship Canal Co Ltd v United Utilities Water plc** [2013] **2** 642, CA; [2014] **4** 40, SC.
      Surface water—Whether sewerage undertakers having implied power to discharge water onto another's land or watercourse—Water Industry Act 1991, ss 94, 155, 159, 165. **British Waterways Board v Severn Trent Water Ltd** [2000] **1** 347, Ch D; [2001] **3** 673, CA.
    Overloading of sewers—
      Flooding of neighbouring premises—Nuisance—Liability of sanitary authority. *See* **Nuisance** (Creation of nuisance—Sewer—Overflow—Flooding of neighbouring premises—Overloading of sewers—Sanitary authority under statutory duty to allow occupiers of houses to discharge sewage into sewers—Liability of sanitary authority).
  Public sewer—
    Agreement to vest sewer in local authority—Sewer constructed by defendant in lane subsequently adopted at defendant's request by local authority as public highway—Defendant also requesting local authority to adopt sewer—Local authority recommended to adopt sewer but resolution therefor never passed—Sewer subsequently shown on statutory map as public sewer—Local authority in course of correspondence permitting plaintiff to connect his sewer to the 'public sewer'—Whether correspondence 'an agreement to acquire...sewer'—Whether 'acquired' limited to acquisitions by agreement or covering acquisitions by operation of law—Public Health Act 1936, ss 15(1)(iii), 18(1), 20(1)(b), (2). **Royco Homes Ltd v Eatonwill Construction Ltd** [1978] **2** 821, Ch D.
    Meaning—Pipe constructed to receive flood water from river—Pipe also constructed to drain surface water from buildings and road surfaces—Whether pipe a public sewer—Public Health Act 1936, s 15(1). **Hutton v Esher UDC** [1973] **2** 1123, CA.
    Provision of—Local authority—Power to construct sewer 'in, on or over' land on giving reasonable notice—Land—Proposal by local authority to construct sewer through site of plaintiff's bungalow—Construction of sewer involving demolition of bungalow—Whether 'land' including buildings—Whether authority entitled to demolish building in order to construct sewer—Interpretation Act 1889, s 3—Public Health Act 1936, s 15(1). **Hutton v Esher UDC** [1973] **2** 1123, CA.
    Provision of—Provision of public sewers otherwise than by requisition—Further duty to provide sewers—Statutory sewerage undertaker accepting duty to provide public sewer—Whether sewerage undertaker able to revoke or withhold decision to accept duty—Water Industry Act 1991, s 101A. **R (on the application of Dwr Cymru Cyf) v Environment Agency** [2009] **2** 919, QBD.
    Right to communicate with public sewers—Owner or occupier of premises entitled to have drains or sewer communicate with public sewer—Sewerage undertaker entitled to refuse to permit communication if mode of construction or condition of drain or sewer not satisfying standards reasonably required or making of communication would be prejudicial to sewerage system—Whether sewerage undertaker having right to refuse to permit communication to be made on ground proposed point of connection not suitable—Water Industry Act 1991, s 106. **Barratt Homes Ltd v Dwr Cymru Cyf (Welsh Water)** [2010] **1** 965, SC.
  Waste disposal—
    Environment. *See* **Environment** (Waste—Waste disposal).
    Prohibition on unlicensed disposal of waste—
      Controlled waste—Appellant operating waste management facility—Employee causing waste to be deposited in breach of appellant's licence—Whether appellant liable for breach—Whether appellant knowingly causing waste to be deposited in breach of licence—Environmental Protection Act 1990, s 33(1). **Shanks & McEwan (Teesside) Ltd v Environment Agency** [1997] **2** 332, QBD.
      Controlled waste—Waste temporarily deposited on unlicensed site pending removal elsewhere—Whether offence of depositing controlled waste committed—Control of Pollution Act 1974, s 3. **R v Metropolitan Stipendiary Magistrate, ex p London Waste Regulation Authority** [1993] **3** 113, QBD.
      Deposit of waste in breach of conditions of waste disposal licence—Whether necessary to prove knowledge of breach of condition or merely knowledge of deposit—Control of Pollution Act 1974, s 3(1). **Ashcroft v Cambro Waste Products Ltd** [1981] **3** 699, QBD.
      Environment. *See* **Environment** (Waste—Waste disposal—Prohibition on unlicensed disposal of waste).
      Proceeds of crime. *See* **Sentence** (Confiscation order—Proceeds of crime—Criminal lifestyle—Benefit—Conduct and benefit—Pecuniary advantage—Offence of depositing waste on land without license).
      Request for information—Local authority discovering waste on sites leased to company—Authority requesting information from company under statutory provision—Whether privilege against self-incrimination available in respect of such a request—Environmental Protection Act 1990, s 71(2)—European Convention for the Protection of Human Rights and Fundamental Freedoms 1950, art 6(1). **R v Hertfordshire CC, ex p Green Environmental Industries Ltd** [2000] **1** 773, HL.
    Radioactive waste—
      Statutory authorisation—Company authorised to discharge radioactive waste from premises—Company obtaining variation of authorisations to enable testing of operation of new plant—Whether variation of authorisations valid or justified—Radioactive Substances Act 1960, ss 6(1), 8(1), (4), (7)—Council Directive (Euratom) 80/836, art 6. **R v Inspectorate of Pollution, ex p Greenpeace Ltd (No 2)** [1994] **4** 329, QBD.
  Waste management licence—
    Disclaimer—Voluntry winding up of company. *See* **Company** (Voluntary winding up—Disclaimer of onerous property—Waste management licence).

PUBLIC HEALTH (cont)—
    Water—
        Works vesting in local authority. *See* **Water supply** (Local authority—Works used for gratuitous supply
        of water to inhabitants of district vested in local authority).

PUBLIC HOUSE
    Assault on police officer in execution of duty. *See* **Police** (Assault on constable in execution of
    duty—Execution of duty—Failure to leave licensed premises).
    Beer supply agreement—
        EC rules on competition. *See* **European Union** (Rules on competition—Agreements preventing,
        restricting or distorting competition—Beer supply agreements—Public house).
    Development value—
        Site of former public house. *See* **Town and country planning** (Development value—Site of former
        public house).
    Disorderly house. *See* **Criminal law** (Disorderly house).
    Licence—
        Sale of intoxicating liquor. *See* **Licensing**.
    Tied house covenants—
        European Community Competition Rules. *See* **European Union** (Rules on competition—Agreements
        preventing, restricting or distorting competition—Leasing of public houses).
        Restraint of trade. *See* **Restraint of trade by agreement** (Public house—Tied house covenants).

PUBLIC INQUIRY
    Natural justice. *See* **Natural justice** (Public inquiry).

PUBLIC INTEREST
    Criminal evidence—
        Disclosure of information to defence. *See* **Criminal evidence** (Prosecution evidence—Disclosure of
        information to defence—Public interest immunity).
    Disclosure of confidential information—
        Affidavit of means—
            Matrimonial proceedings—Financial provision. *See* **Divorce** (Financial provision—Affidavit of
            means—Confidentiality—Public interest in disclosure of information).
        Breach of confidence. *See* **Equity** (Breach of confidence—Defence—Public interest in disclosure).
        Doctor and patient. *See* **Medical practitioner** (Doctor and patient—Disclosure of confidential
        information—Public interest).
    Disclosure of documents—
        Confidence—
            Implied undertaking—Public interest in disclosure of information. *See* **Disclosure and inspection of**
            documents (Production of documents—Confidence—Implied undertaking—Public interest in
            disclosure of information).
        Production contrary to public interest—
            Generally. *See* **Disclosure and inspection of documents** (Production of documents—Production
            contrary to public interest).
            Inquest. *See* **Disclosure and inspection of documents** (Privilege—Production contrary to public
            interest—Inquest).
            Privilege. *See* **Disclosure and inspection of documents** (Privilege—Production contrary to public
            interest).
    Injunction—
        Nuisance—
            Conflict between public and private interest—Continuing threat of damage—Balance of conflicting
            interests. *See* **Injunction** (Nuisance—Continuing threat of damage—Balance of conflicting
            interests—Interest of public at large conflicting with interest of private individual).
    Landlord and tenant—
        Business premises. *See* **Landlord and tenant** (Business premises—Public interest).
    Libel and slander—
        Qualified privilege. *See* **Libel and slander** (Qualified privilege—Public interest).
    Privilege—
        Disclosure of documents—
            Production contrary to public interest. *See* **Disclosure and inspection of documents**
            (Privilege—Production contrary to public interest).
    Public interest immunity—
        Generally. *See* **Privilege** (Public interest immunity).
    Protection of—
        Electricity, supply of. *See* **Electricity** (Supply—Protection of public interest).
    Telegraphs and telephones—
        Placing of telegraphic lines across private land. *See* **Telegraphs etc** (Telegraphic lines—Placing of
        telegraph line across private land—Public interest).
    Value added tax—
        Public interest exemptions—
            European Community. *See* **European Union** (Value added tax—Exemptions—Public interest
            exemptions).

PUBLIC LAW DEFENCE
    Private law action—
        Statement of claim—
            Striking out. *See* **Statement of case** (Striking out—Private law action—Public law defence).

PUBLIC LIABILITY INSURANCE
    See **Insurance** (Liability insurance—Public liability insurance).

PUBLIC LIBRARY
    See **Library** (Public library).

PUBLIC MEETING
Newspaper report—
  Defamation—
    Qualified privilege. *See* **Libel and slander** (Qualified privilege—Public meeting—Meeting for furtherance or discussion of matter of public concern—Report of meeting in newspaper).
Public order—
  Offensive conduct conducive to breaches of peace—
    Public meeting. *See* **Public order** (Offensive conduct conducive to breaches of peace—Threatening, abusive or insulting words or behaviour—Public meeting).

PUBLIC MISCHIEF
Conspiracy. *See* **Criminal law** (Conspiracy—Public mischief).
Indictment. *See* **Indictment** (Joinder of charges—Charges founded on same facts—Sedition and effecting public mischief).

PUBLIC MORALS
Conspiracy to corrupt public morals. *See* **Criminal law** (Conspiracy—Corruption of public morals).

PUBLIC NUISANCE
Criminal proceedings. *See* **Criminal law** (Public nuisance).
Exemplary damages. *See* **Damages** (Exemplary damages—Nuisance).
Generally. *See* **Nuisance** (Public nuisance).
Highway. *See* **Highway** (Public nuisance).
Injunction. *See* **Injunction** (Nuisance—Public nuisance).
Interference with public right of navigation. *See* **Water and watercourses** (Navigation—Public right of navigation (PRN)—Public nuisance).

PUBLIC OFFICE
Abuse of—
  Misfeasance by a public officer—
    Exemplary damages. *See* **Damages** (Exemplary damages—Misfeasance in public office).
    Exercise of private contractual power—Council owning freehold premises—Plaintiff holding premises under agreement for lease made with council—Council refusing consent for change in use of premises—Plaintiff alleging council's action motivated by malice on part of majority councillors because of plaintiff's husband's political activities in opposition to majority—Whether plaintiff having good cause of action against council if malice on part of majority of councillors established. **Jones v Swansea City Council** [1990] 3 737, HL.
    Home Office—Delay—Home Office further delaying issue of European Economic Area residence card after giving undertaking in court that residence card would be issued—Whether misfeasance in public office—Remedy for breach of undertaking. **B v Home Office** [2012] 4 276, QBD.
    Ingredients of tort. **Three Rivers DC v Bank of England (No 3)** [1996] 3 558, QBD; [2000] 3 1, HL.
    Ingredients of tort—Special damage—Interference by prison officers with prisoner's confidential legal correspondence—Whether tort actionable per se. **Watkins v Secretary of State for the Home Dept** [2006] 2 353, HL.
    Ingredients of tort—Special damage—Interference by prison officers with prisoner's right of access to the court—Whether special damage necessary. **Watkins v Secretary of State for the Home Dept** [2004] 4 1158, CA.
    Ingredients of tort—Special damage—Whether loss of liberty damage—Whether prisoner moved from open conditions to closed conditions suffering loss of liberty. **Karagozlu v Metropolitan Police Comr** [2007] 2 1055, CA.
    Ingredients of tort—Whether action for misfeasance in public office excluded where predictable victim neither an identifiable individual nor an identifiable group of individuals. **Akenzua and anor (administrators of the estate of Laws (decd)) v Secretary of State for the Home Dept** [2003] 1 35, CA.
    Ingredients of tort—Whether necessary to prove that public officer acted in bad faith or without reasonable excuse in exercise of official power—Whether suspect in criminal or disciplinary proceedings having cause of action in tort for misfeasance in public office where investigating police officer making false and defamatory report to superior officer. **Calveley v Chief Constable of Merseyside Police** [1989] 1 1025, HL.
    Misfeasance a necessary element of tort of abuse of public office. **Dunlop v Woollahra Municipal Council** [1981] 1 1202, PC.
    Prison officer—Vicarious liability of Home Office—Whether Home Office can be vicariously liable for misfeasance in public office by prison officers. **Racz v Home Office** [1994] 1 97, HL.
    Whether misfeasance a necessary element of tort—Whether tort committed if public officer had knowledge that he had no power to act and that he would injure plaintiff. **Bourgoin SA v Ministry of Agriculture, Fisheries and Food** [1985] 3 585, QBD and CA.
Communication of restricted information. *See* **Criminal law** (Official secrets—Communication of information—Person holding office under His Majesty).
Income tax on emoluments. *See* **Income tax** (Emoluments from office or employment—Public office in United Kingdom).
Misbehaviour in. *See* **Criminal law** (Misbehaviour in public office).
Misconduct in. *See* **Criminal law** (Misconduct in public office).
Will—
  Condition—
    Specific condition—Forfeiture upon acceptance of public office. *See* **Will** (Condition—Specific conditions—Forfeiture upon acceptance of public office).

PUBLIC ORDER
Breach of the peace—
  False imprisonment. *See* **False imprisonment** (Necessity—Right to liberty and security—Breach of the peace taking place or reasonably thought to be imminent).
  Police powers. *See* **Police** (Power—Removal of peaceful protesters—Actual or threatened breach of peace).

900

PUBLIC ORDER (cont)—

Demonstration—

Statutory requirement for organiser of demonstration to apply to police for authorisation—
Whether requirement applying to demonstration started before commencement of provision—
Public Order Act 1986, s 14—Serious Organised Crime and Police Act 2005, s 132. **R (on the application of Haw) v Secretary of State for the Home Dept** [2006] **3** 428, DC and CA.

Football—

Designated football match—
Indecent or racialist chanting—Whether chanting including use of word 'Paki' of a racialist nature—Football (Offences) Act 1991, s 3(2)(b). **DPP v Stoke-on-Trent Magistrates' Court** [2003] **3** 1086, QBD.

Football banning order—
Whether football banning order constituting a penalty for purposes of human rights convention—Football Spectators Act 1989, ss 14A, 14B—Human Rights Act 1998, Sch 1, Pt I, art 7. **Gough v Chief Constable of Derbyshire Constabulary** [2001] **4** 289, QBD DC.

Whether scheme for imposition of football banning order contravening Community law on freedom of movement—Whether scheme contravening right to fair trial—Football Spectators Act 1989, s 14B—Human Rights Act 1998, Sch 1, Pt I, art 6—Council Directive (EEC) 73/148, art 2. **Gough v Chief Constable of Derbyshire Constabulary** [2001] **4** 289, QBD DC; [2002] **2** 985, CA.

Incitement to racial hatred. *See* **Criminal law** (Public order—Incitement to racial hatred).

Offensive conduct conducive to breaches of peace—

Public place. *See* Public place—Offensive conduct conducive to breaches of peace, *below*.

Threatening, abusive or insulting words or behaviour—
Information—Defective information—Belief that unlawful violence would be used or provoked—Relevant belief—Whether relevant belief that of person threatened, abused or insulted—Whether belief of any other person sufficient—Whether information referring to belief of 'another person' defective—Whether information misleading—Whether information valid—Public Order Act 1986, s 4(1)—Magistrates' Courts Rules 1981, r 100. **Loade v DPP** [1990] **1** 36, QBD.

Information—Duplicity—Information alleging 'threatening and insulting words and behaviour'—Allegation relating to single incident—Whether information bad for duplicity—Public Order Act 1936, s 5, as substituted by the Race Relations Act 1965, s 7. **Vernon v Paddon** [1973] **3** 302, QBD.

Insulting—Nature of insulting behaviour—Homosexual activity in public lavatory—Accused making homosexual advances to plain clothes police officer—Accused's behaviour not observed by anyone else—Whether accused indulging in 'insulting behaviour ... likely' to occasion breach of peace—Whether reaction of other persons who might have observed conduct to be taken into account—Whether likelihood of disturbance short of violence sufficient to constitute breach of peace—Public Order Act 1936, s 5. **Parkin v Norman** [1982] **2** 583, QBD.

Insulting—Nature of insulting behaviour—Homosexual activity in public place—Defendants engaged in overt homosexual behaviour at bus stop—Defendants' behaviour observed by passing couples—Defendants unaware of other persons in vicinity—Whether defendants using 'insulting ... behaviour ... whereby a breach of peace may be occasioned'—Whether necessary for conduct to be directed at another person in order to be insulting—Whether overt homosexual behaviour in public place insulting to member of public witnessing it—Metropolitan Police Act 1839, s 54(13). **Masterson v Holden** [1986] **3** 39, QBD.

Insulting—Question whether behaviour 'insulting' one of fact—Word 'insulting' having ordinary meaning—Behaviour affronting other people, or evidencing a disrespect of their rights so as to give rise to resentment or protest not necessarily insulting—Public Order Act 1936, s 5, as substituted by the Race Relations Act 1965, s 7. **Brutus v Cozens** [1972] **2** 1, QBD; [1972] **2** 1297, HL.

Overlapping offences—Affray—Fighting in public place—Actual violence and not merely threat of violence involved—Facts alleged sufficient to found charge of affray—Whether open to prosecution to proceed on charge of threatening behaviour—Public Order Act 1936, s 5. **R v Oakwell** [1978] **1** 1223, CA.

Person likely to be caused harassment, alarm or distress—Police officer—Whether police officer capable of being caused harassment, alarm or distress by threatening, abusive or insulting words or behaviour—Public Order Act 1986, s 5(1). **DPP v Orum** [1988] **3** 449, QBD.

Public meeting—Group of persons in audience intent on obstructing speaker—Words in fact insulting to them—Speaker must take his audience as he finds them—Whether contravention of Public Order Act 1936, s 5. **Jordan v Burgoyne** [1963] **2** 225, QBD.

Quarrel between neighbours taking place on highway—Whether contravention of Act—Public Order Act 1936, s 5. **Ward v Holman** [1964] **2** 729, QBD.

Parliament Square Garden and surrounding areas. *See* Public place—Authorisation of demonstrations in designated area—Demonstrations in vicinity of Parliament, *below*.

Police powers—

Power to stop, search and detain. *See* **Police** (Powers—Power to stop, search and detain).

Processions and assemblies. *See* **Police** (Powers—Processions and assemblies).

Political uniforms. *See* Uniforms in connection with political objects, *below*.

Preservation of public order on occasion of processions—

Order prohibiting processions—
Offence to organise public procession in contravention of order—Procession formed spontaneously—Subsequently led and directed by an individual—Whether 'organising' procession—Public Order Act 1936, s 3(4). **Flockhart v Robertson** [1950] **1** 1091, KBD.

Procession—

Advance notice of public processions—
Notice not required where procession commonly or customarily held—Mass cycle ride starting from same meeting point in London at same time monthly since 1994—Whether procession commonly or customarily held—Public Order Act 1986, s 11(1), (2). **Kay v Metropolitan Police Comr** [2007] **4** 31, CA; [2009] **2** 935, HL.

PUBLIC ORDER (cont)—
  Procession (cont)—
    Imposing conditions on public processions—
      Consideration of route or proposed route—Mass cycle ride starting from same meeting point in
      London at same time monthly with no fixed, settled or pre-determined route—Police imposing
      conditions as to route of procession—Whether route or proposed route of unnotified,
      spontaneous and unpredictable procession capable of being given consideration—Public Order
      Act 1986, ss 11, 12. **Powlesland v DPP** [2014] **3** 479, DC.
    Imposing conditions on public processions. *See* **Police** (Powers—Processions and assemblies).
  Public authority meeting—
    Admission of public. *See* **Public authority** (Meeting—Admission of public).
  Public place—
    Authorisation of demonstrations in designated area—
      Demonstrations in vicinity of Parliament—Right to fair trial—Freedom of expression—Freedom of
      assembly and association—Police commissioner authorising protestor's demonstration in
      designated area—Responsible authority deciding to direct protestor to cease prohibited activities
      in controlled area—Whether decision lawful—Whether breach of rights to fair trial and freedoms
      of expression and assembly—Human Rights Act 1998, Sch 1, Pt I, arts 6, 10, 11—Serious
      Organised Crime and Police Act 2005, s 134—Police Reform and Social Responsibility Act 2011,
      ss 143, 145. **R (on the application of Gallastegui) v Westminster City Council** [2012] **4** 401,
      DC; [2013] **2** 579, CA.
    Offensive conduct conducive to breaches of peace—
      Disturbance on railway station platform—Whether platform 'public place'—Public Order Act 1936,
      ss 5, 9. **Cooper v Shield** [1971] **2** 917, QBD.
      Open space to which public have access—Open space—Tennis club—Club grounds consisting of
      complex of tennis courts, administrative buildings and partly covered stands around one tennis
      court—Disruption of tennis match on one of courts—Whether court consisting an open
      space—Public Order Act 1936, s 9. **Brutus v Cozens** [1972] **2** 1, QBD.
    Premises or place to which public have or are permitted to have access—
      Public denied access to certain parts of premises—Football ground—Pitch surrounded by
      speedway track and spectator stands—Public admitted to stands but prohibited from entering
      track or pitch—Spectator arrested on track and charged with using threatening words or
      behaviour in a public place—Whether football ground as a whole, including pitch and tract, to be
      treated as a 'public place'—Public Order Act 1936, ss 5 (as substituted by the Race Relations Act
      1965, s 7), 9(1) (as substituted by the Criminal Justice Act 1972, s 33). **Cawley v Frost** [1976] **3** 743,
      QBD.
    Threatening, abusive or insulting words or behaviour. *See* Offensive conduct conducive to breaches of
    peace—Threatening, abusive or insulting words or behaviour, *above*.
  Racial hatred—
    Publishing or distributing written material. *See* **Criminal law** (Racial hatred—Publishing or distributing
    written material).
  Riot—
    Generally. *See* **Criminal law** (Riot).
  Trespass—
    Aggravated trespass. *See* **Criminal law** (Trespass—Aggravated trespass).
    Trespassory assembly. *See* **Criminal law** (Trespassory assembly).
  Uniforms in connection with political objects—
    Prohibition—
      Uniform—Meaning—Single article of clothing—Article worn by each member of group to indicate
      that they are together and in association—Black beret—Whether single article capable of
      constituting 'uniform'—Whether necessary that article should cover whole or most of
      body—Public Order Act 1936, s 1(1). **O'Moran v DPP** [1975] **1** 473, QBD.
      Wearing of uniform to signify wearer's association with political organisation or with promotion of
      political objects—Evidence that uniform signifies association with political organisation—
      Evidence that uniform used in past to signify such association—Evidence that group assembling
      together wore uniform to indicate such association—Public Order Act 1936, s 1(1). **O'Moran v DPP**
      [1975] **1** 473, QBD.
  Unlawful assembly. *See* **Criminal law** (Unlawful assembly).
  Violence—
    Provoking unlawful violence—
      Threatening, abusive or insulting writing. *See* **Criminal law** (Threatening, abusive or insulting
      writing—Provoking unlawful violence).
    Violent disorder. *See* **Criminal law** (Violent disorder).

PUBLIC PERFORMANCE
  Infringement of copyright. *See* **Copyright** (Conflict of laws—Public performance).

PUBLIC PLACE
  Affray. *See* **Criminal law** (Affray—Public place).
  Drunkenness. *See* **Intoxicating liquor** (Offences—Drunk and disorderly in a public place).
  Frequenting with intent. *See* **Criminal law** (Vagrancy—Frequenting public place with intent).
  Offences against public order. *See* **Public order** (Public place).
  Offensive weapons—
    Generally. *See* **Criminal law** (Offensive weapons—Having offensive weapon in public place).
    Possession in public place—
      Sentence. *See* **Sentence** (Possession of an offensive weapon in a public place).
  Premises open to public—
    Duty to institute crowd control. *See* **Negligence** (Duty to take care—Premises open to public—Danger
    from rush of people—Duty to institute crowd control).
  Removal of articles from public place. *See* **Criminal law** (Removal of articles from public building).
  Road traffic legislation. *See* **Road traffic**.

PUBLIC PLACE (cont)—
Unfitness to drive—
Being in charge of vehicle. *See* **Road traffic** (Being in charge of vehicle when unfit to drive through drink or drugs—Road or other public place).
Unlawful assembly. *See* **Criminal law** (Unlawful assembly—Public place).

PUBLIC POLICY
Birth certificate—
Refusal of application for certificate on public policy grounds. *See* **Registration** (Births, deaths and marriages—Application for birth certificate—Refusal on public policy grounds).
Contract—
Frustration. *See* **Contract** (Frustration—Public policy).
Illegality. *See* **Contract** (Illegality—Public policy).
Jurisdiction of the court—
Exclusion. *See* **Contract** (Illegality—Public policy—Jurisdiction of court—Exclusion).
Damages—
Assessment. *See* **Damages** (Assessment—Public policy).
Foreign judgment—
Enforcement. *See* **Conflict of laws** (Foreign judgment—Enforcement—Public policy).
Forum shopping—
Prevention of. *See* **Conflict of laws** (Tort—Actionability in England—Tort not justified by lex loci delicti—'Not justified'—Prevention of forum shopping as a matter of public policy).
Insurance—
Accident insurance—
Accidental death resulting from criminal acts of insured—Right of insured to indemnity for damages claimed in respect of death. *See* **Insurance** (Accident insurance—Perils insured against—Accident—Public policy).
Enforcement of policy contrary to public policy. *See* **Insurance** (Illegality—Enforcement of policy contrary to public policy).
Life insurance—
Death of assured resulting from criminal act of beneficiary under policy. *See* **Insurance** (Life insurance—Death of assured resulting from criminal act of beneficiary under policy—Public policy).
Intestate's estate—
Exclusion from benefit on grounds of public policy. *See* **Intestacy** (Succession—Exclusion from benefit—Public policy).
Loan index-linked to foreign currency—
Repayment—
Enforceability. *See* **Money** (Loan—Repayment of loan index-linked to foreign currency—Enforceability—Public policy).
Marriage—
Gift subject to condition encouraging separation. *See* **Will** (Condition—Family matters—Condition inducing future separation of spouses—Public policy).
National insurance—
Disqualification from benefit on grounds of public policy. *See* **Social security** (Benefit—Disqualification—Public policy).
Settlement—
Forfeiture clause—
Validity. *See* **Settlement** (Forfeiture—Validity of forfeiture clause—Public policy).
Stay of proceedings—
Foreign cause of action. *See* **Practice** (Stay of proceedings—Foreign cause of action—Public policy).
Succession on death—
Exclusion from benefit—
Intestacy—Murder of deceased. *See* **Intestacy** (Succession—Exclusion from benefit—Public policy—Murder of deceased).
Manslaughter of deceased. *See* **Will** (Benefit—Exclusion from benefit—Public policy—Manslaughter).
Will—
Exclusion from benefit—
Beneficiary convicted of manslaughter of testator. *See* **Will** (Benefit—Exclusion from benefit—Public policy—Manslaughter).

PUBLIC PROCUREMENT
European Union. *See* **European Union** (Public procurement).
Public contract—
Remedies—
Company pursuing claim against public body for damages for breaches of body's EU and UK obligations regarding award of contract—Whether Directive 89/665/EEC only requiring damages for 'sufficiently serious' breach of Directive 2004/18/EC—Whether acte clair—Whether UK regulations exceeding requirements of European law—Whether award of damages might be refused on ground that economic operator not issuing claim form before contracting authority entering into contract—Public Contracts Regulations 2006, SI 2006/5, regs 47D, 47J(2)(c)—Council Directive 89/665/EEC—European Parliament and Council Directive 2004/18/EC. **EnergySolutions EU Ltd v Nuclear Decommissioning Authority** [2017] **4** 1, SC.
Public contracts—
Equal treatment of service providers—
Transparency—Test of reasonably well-informed and normally diligent tenderer—Public tender process for medical services to health authorities—Tenderer complaining that criteria in invitation to tender insufficiently clear—Whether test of reasonably well-informed and normally diligent tenderer requiring evidence on what actual tenderer did or thought—Public Contracts (Scotland) Regulations 2006, SSI 2006/1—Council Directive (EC) 2004/18. **Healthcare at Home Ltd v Common Services Agency** [2014] **4** 210, SC.

PUBLIC PROCUREMENT (cont)—
  Public contracts (cont)—
    Equal treatment of service providers (cont)—
      Transparency—Unified contract for provision of publicly funded legal work—Contract providing Legal Services Commission with power to make unilateral amendments—Lawfulness of contract—Whether contract breaching requirements of transparency—Whether contract breaching requirement that technical specifications be sufficiently precise to allow subject of contract to be determined—Public Contracts Regulations 2006, SI 2006/5, regs 4(3), 9—Council Directive (EC) 2004/18. **R (on the application of the Law Society) v Legal Services Commission** [2008] **2** 148, CA.
    Modification of contracts—
      Whether proposed modifications 'substantial'—Public Contracts Regulations 2006, SI 2006/5—Public Contracts Regulations 2015, SI 2015/102, reg 72(1), (8)—European Parliament and Council Directive 2014/24/EU. **Edenred (UK Group) Ltd v HM Treasury** [2016] **1** 763, SC.
  Public services contracts—
    Public procurement exemption—Mutual insurer—Local authority entering into insurance contracts with mutual insurer without first conducting tender process in relation to award of such contracts—Scope of exemption—Whether exemption applying to insurance contracts—Whether exemption applying in circumstances arising—Public Contracts Regulations 2006, SI 2006/5—Council Directive (EC) 2004/18. **Risk Management Partners Ltd v Brent London BC** [2011] **2** 209, SC.
    Utilities contracts—Proper approach to interpretation of domestic legislation implementing Directives—Public tender process for high-speed passenger railway trains using Channel Tunnel—Status of rail service operator—Public Contracts Regulations 2006, SI 2006/5—Utilities Contracts Regulations 2006, SI 2006/6—Council Directive (EC) 2004/17—Council Directive (EC) 2004/18. **Alstom Transport v Eurostar International Ltd** [2012] **2 Comm** 869, Ch D; [2012] **3** 263, Ch D.

PUBLIC RECREATION GROUND
  Provision of—
    Charitable purpose. See **Charity** (Benefit to community—Health and welfare—Inhabitants of named parish—Provision of public recreation ground).

PUBLIC REVENUE
  Cheating the public revenue. See **Criminal law** (Cheating the public revenue).

PUBLIC REVENUE DIVIDEND
  Income tax. See **Income tax** (Public revenue dividends).

PUBLIC RIGHT
  Enforcement—
    Local authority—
      Assertion and protection of rights of public. See **Practice** (Parties—Local authority—Assertion and protection of rights of public).
    Refusal of Attorney General to consent to relator action—
      Right of member of public to sue in own name. See **Attorney General** (Relator action—Refusal of consent to relator action).
  Highway—
    Protection of rights of public to use and enjoy highway. See **Highway** (Protection of public rights).
  Injunction—
    Relator action. See **Injunction** (Public right—Relator action).

PUBLIC RIGHT OF WAY
  Generally. See **Highway**.
  Order as to—
    Judicial review—
      Availability of remedy. See **Judicial review** (Availability of remedy—Exclusion by statute—Public right of way order).

PUBLIC SAFETY
  Dangerous offenders—
    Sentence. See **Sentence** (Custodial sentence—Dangerous offenders).
  Prisoner—
    Release on licence. See **Prison** (Release on licence—Refusal to release on licence—Danger to public safety).

PUBLIC SECTOR HOUSING
  Security of tenure. See **Housing** (Local authority houses—Security of tenure).

PUBLIC SERVICE VEHICLE
  Generally. See **Road traffic** (Public service vehicle).
  Negligence—
    Exclusion of liability. See **Carriers** (Negligence—Exclusion of liability).

PUBLIC SUBSIDIES
  European Community—
    State aids. See **European Union** (State aids—Public subsidies).

PUBLIC TRANSPORT
  Air—
    Carriage of passengers. See **Carriage by air** (Private pilot's licence—Flight for the purpose of public transport).
  Local authority. See **Local authority** (Transport).

PUBLIC TRANSPORT (cont)—
London Passenger Transport Board. *See* **London Passenger Transport Board.**
London Transport Executive. *See* **London Transport Executive.**
Road traffic. *See* **Road traffic** (Public transport).
Stage carriage. *See* **Road traffic** (Stage carriage).
Value added tax—
Transport of passengers—
Zero-rating. *See* **Value added tax** (Zero-rating—Transport of passengers).

PUBLIC TRUSTEE
Directions of court—
Discretion of Public Trustee to apply to court for directions where beneficiary cannot be found—
Refusal by Public Trustee to pay sequestrator of life tenant's interest on ground that no sufficient evidence that life tenant still alive—Whether court should direct Public Trustee to exercise discretion to apply for directions—Public Trustee Act 1906, s 10—Public Trustee Rules 1912 (SR & O 1912 No 348), r 28. **Wilson (decd), Re** [1964] **1** 196, Ch D.
Funds in court—
Holding by. *See* **Practice** (Funds in court—Funds exceeding £7,500—Holding by Public Trustee out of court).
Investment of—
Common investment funds—Capital fund—Damages—Damages awarded to a minor—Principle governing investment in capital fund. **Practice Note** [1971] **1** 109, QBD.
Mental patient's property—
Appointment of Public Trustee as receiver. *See* **Mental health** (Patient's property—Receiver—Appointment of Public Trustee as receiver).
Notice to quit—
Service on Public Trustee—
Intestacy. *See* **Landlord and tenant** (Notice to quit—Service—Intestacy—Service on Public Trustee).
Powers—
Trust or settlement—
Appointment as sole trustee—Public Trustee appointed sole trustee of trust—Trust instrument providing that trustees' discretions and discretionary powers not exercisable by less than two trustees—Whether Public Trustee entitled to exercise discretions and discretionary powers conferred on trustees by trust instrument—Public Trustee Act 1906, s 5(1). **Duxbury's Settlement Trusts, Re** [1995] **3** 145, CA.
Remuneration. *See* **Trust and trustee** (Remuneration of trustee—Public Trustee).

PUBLIC UTILITY UNDERTAKING
Compulsory purchase—
Compensation—
Assessment. *See* **Compulsory purchase** (Compensation—Assessment—Public utility undertaking).
Limitation of action—
Statutory undertaker's right to recover expense of making good damage to apparatus—
Whether cause of action accruing when damage caused or when expense of making good incurred—Public Utilities Street Works Act 1950, s 26(6). **Yorkshire Electricity Board v British Telecommunications plc** [1986] **2** 961, HL.

PUBLIC WORKS CONTRACT
European Community. *See* **European Union** (Public procurement—Public works contracts).

PUBLICATION
Child—
Protection—
Children and young persons legislation. *See* **Children and young persons** (Court proceedings—Protection of child concerned in proceedings—Freedom of publication).
Generally. *See* **Child** (Protection—Freedom of publication).
Ward of court. *See* **Ward of court** (Jurisdiction—Protection of ward—Freedom of publication).
Committal proceedings—
Reports of proceedings—
Order lifting restrictions. *See* **Criminal law** (Committal—Preliminary hearing before justices—Publicity—Order lifting restrictions).
Contempt of court—
Publications concerning disciplinary proceedings. *See* **Contempt of court** (Publications concerning disciplinary proceedings).
Publications concerning legal proceedings. *See* **Contempt of court** (Publications concerning legal proceedings).
Copyright—
Infringement. *See* **Copyright**.
Elections—
Publications printed etc for purpose of promoting election of a candidate. *See* **Elections** (Publications).
Internet—
Defamation. *See* **Libel and slander** (Publication—Internet posting).
Legal proceedings, concerning—
Contempt of court. *See* **Contempt of court** (Publications concerning legal proceedings).
Libel. *See* **Libel and slander** (Publication).
Obscene. *See* **Criminal law** (Obscene publications).
Patent—
Invention. *See* **Patent** (Invention—Publication).
Spent conviction—
Rehabilitation of offenders. *See* **Rehabilitation** (Rehabilitation of offenders—Spent conviction—Publication referring to spent conviction).
Unsolicited publications—
Offences. *See* **Criminal law** (Unsolicited publications).

PUBLICATION (cont)—
    Ward of court—
        Protection—
            Publication of matter likely to be harmful to ward. *See* **Ward of court** (Jurisdiction—Protection of ward—Freedom of publication).

PUBLISHER
    Contempt of court. *See* **Contempt of court** (Publications concerning legal proceedings).
    Contract with author—
        Repudiation—
            Alteration of manuscript. *See* **Contract** (Repudiation—Publisher and author—Alteration of manuscript).
    Entertaining expenses—
        Deduction in computing profits for income tax purposes. *See* **Income tax** (Deduction in computing profits—Expenses wholly and exclusively laid out for purposes of trade—Entertaining expenses).

PUMPING STATION
    Water supply. *See* **Water supply** (Power to obtain water outside water district of corporation).

PUNISHMENT
    Retrospective punishment—
        Human rights legislation. *See* **Human rights** (Retrospective punishment).

PUNITIVE DAMAGES
    Defamation action. *See* **Libel and slander** (Exemplary or punitive damages).
    Generally. *See* **Damages** (Exemplary damages).

PUNITIVE FINE
    Fine in addition to imprisonment—
        Confiscation of criminal profits. *See* **Sentence** (Fine—Capacity to pay—Confiscation of criminal profits—Fine in addition to imprisonment).

PUPIL
    Education. *See* **Education** (Pupil).

PUPILLAGE
    Barrister. *See* **Barrister** (Pupillage).

PURCHASE NOTICE
    Confirmation. *See* **Town and country planning** (Purchase notice—Confirmation).

PURCHASE ORDER
    War damage. *See* **Town and country planning** (War damage).

PURCHASE TAX
    Certificate of registration—
        Condition—
            Requirement that representations as holder be made only in specified circumstances or in respect of specified goods—No directions issued as to circumstances or goods—Whether notice imposing condition valid—Purchase Tax Act 1963, s 6(4)(b). **Marsh (B) (Wholesale) Ltd v Customs and Excise Comrs** [1970] **1** 990, QBD.
    Chargeable goods—
        Admission of all facts pleaded—
            Objection in law—Whether evidence subsequently admissible. *See* **Evidence** (Point of law in issue on pleadings—Defence containing admission of facts alleged in statement of claim but raising objection in point of law—Claim for declaration that plastic closures for tins were not chargeable to purchase tax).
    Appliances and apparatus of a kind used for domestic purposes—
        Electric heating pads and blankets—Whether 'appliances and apparatus of a kind used for domestic purposes'—Finance (No 2) Act 1940, Sch VII, para 7. **A-G v Milliwatt Ltd** [1948] **1** 331, KBD.
    Chocolates, sweets and similar confectionery—
        'Butterkist'—Similar confectionery—Distribution mainly through cinemas and confectionery trade—Packaging suitable for confectionery—Whether confectionery similar to chocolates and sweets—Purchase Tax Act 1963, s 2, Sch 1, Part 1, Group 34. **Customs and Excise Comrs v Clark's Cereal Products Ltd** [1968] **3** 778, QBD.
        Sweetened popcorn—'Confectionery'—Whether confectionery similar to chocolates and sweets—Purchase Tax Act 1963, s 2, Sch 1, Part 1, Group 34. **Customs and Excise Comrs v Popcorn House Ltd** [1968] **3** 782, QBD.
        Toffee apples—Sale to wholesalers and distributors in fruit trade—Not sold through confectionery trade—Whether articles of confectionery similar to chocolates and sweets—Purchase Tax Act 1963, s 2, Sch 1, Part 1, Group 34. **Candy Maid Confections Ltd v Customs and Excise Comrs** [1968] **3** 773, Ch D.
    Drugs and medicines—
        Syrup of blackcurrant containing vitamin C—Ribena—Ribena on market principally as health drink for normally healthy persons—Predominant use as a refreshing drink which might also make good any vitamin C deficiency in diet—Use to increase vitamin C intake of expectant and nursing mothers—Occasional use to prevent recurrence of scurvy—Whether a 'drug or medicine'—Whether exempt from charge as a preparation consisting of a scheduled substance and a vehicle—Purchase Tax Act 1963, s 2(1), Sch 1, Part 1, r 1, Group 33—Purchase Tax (No 2) Order 1968 (SI 1968 No 1511), art 1, Sch, Head III. **Beecham Foods Ltd v Customs and Excise Comrs** [1972] **1** 498, HL.

PURCHASE TAX (cont)—

Chargeable goods (cont)—
Furniture—
Built-in dressing table units which were unstable unless fixed between other units of furniture and to walls—Units easily removable—Whether chargeable to tax as 'furniture'—Purchase Tax Act 1963, Sch 1, Part 1, Group 11. **Austin (F) (Leyton) Ltd v Customs and Excise Comrs** [1968] **2** 13, Ch D.
Kits of parts—Components for assembling backed storage units in tiers—Assembled units able to stand without having been affixed to wall—Whether kits were 'furniture' for the purposes of purchase tax—Finance Act 1958, s 1, Sch 2, Group 11(b). **Customs and Excise Comrs v HG Kewley Ltd** [1965] **1** 929, CA.
Kits of parts—Panels, and metal channels for joining them, sold in kits from which one or more of several different articles of furniture could be made—Whether 'furniture' for the purposes of purchase tax—Finance Act 1948, s 20, Sch 8, Part 1, Group 11(A). **Betterways Panels Ltd v Customs and Excise Comrs (1951)** [1964] **1** 948, KBD.
Hardware—
Kitchenware—Plastic lids supplied with coffee tins for resealing opened tins—Whether plastic lids were 'hardware' or 'kitchenware' within Group 11—Purchase Tax Act 1963, Sch 1, Part 1, Group 11. **Pioneer Plastic Containers Ltd v Customs and Excise Comrs** [1968] **1** 192, Ch D.
Manufactured beverages including fruit juices—
Including fruit juices—Orange juice freshly pressed from a single orange—Whether manufactured beverage—Purchase Tax Act 1963, s 2(1), (2), Sch 1, Part 1, Group 35(a). **Customs and Excise Comrs v Savoy Hotel Ltd** [1966] **2** 299, QBD.
Pictures, prints, engravings etc—
Goods produced in quantity for general sale—Sale—Consideration for supply of goods—Goods produced for distribution to customers purchasing specified other goods—Coins bearing likenesses of members of English World Cup soccer team—Coins produced by petrol suppliers for distribution by petrol stations to motorists purchasing specified quantity of suppliers' petrol—Whether coins supplied in consideration of money payments by motorists—Whether coins produced for 'sale' to motorists—Purchase Tax Act 1963, Sch 1, Group 25. **Esso Petroleum Ltd v Customs and Excise Comrs** [1976] **1** 117, HL.
Pictorial stamps—Stamps attached to goods sold by manufacturers to retailers for resale—Whether 'pictures'—Finance Act 1948, s 20(1), Sch VIII, Part I, Group 25. **Stephenson Bros Ltd v Customs and Excise Comrs** [1953] **1** 469, Ch D.
Chargeable process—
Conversion of vehicle—
Conversion of army wireless type vehicle into shooting brake—Whether 'chargeable process'—Finance Act 1946, s 16(1), (3). **Coleborn and Sons Ltd v Blond** [1950] **2** 351, CA.
Demand—
Signature—
Demand authorised by proper officer but signed by officer not so authorised—Customs and Excise Act 1952, s 4(1). **Customs and Excise Comrs v Cure & Deeley Ltd** [1961] **3** 641, QBD.
Discovery—
Summary application to High Court—
Power to order production of records and documents—Incrimination of tax-payer—Order where defendant not a 'registered person'—Finance Act 1946, s 20(2), (3)—Crown Proceedings Act 1947, s 14(2)(d). **Customs and Excise Comrs v Ingram** [1948] **1** 927, CA.
Discrimination—
European Union. *See* **European Union** (Taxation—Discrimination—Property purchase tax).
Double charge of tax—
Relief—
Tax chargeable on appropriation of goods by wholesaler—Tax paid on previous occasion on purchase by vendor to wholesaler—Finance Act 1944, s 15(1). **Customs and Excise Comrs v Rensop Drapers Ltd** [1951] **1** 450, CA.
Evasion—
Imported goods—
Evasion of purchase tax and evasion of customs duty—Whether one offence—Customs Consolidation Act 1876, s 186—Finance Act 1944, s 11(1). **Beck v Binks** [1948] **2** 1058, KBD.
False returns—
Company's liability—
False returns with intent to deceive made by servant of company in fraud of company—Whether company liable. **Moore v I Bresler Ltd** [1944] **2** 515, KBD.
Goods appropriated or applied by wholesalers and manufacturers—
Appropriated or applied—
Sale by manufacturer to private person—Date of appropriation of goods to contract—Finance (No 2) Act 1940, s 25. **Morris (B) Ltd v Lunzer** [1942] **1** 77, CA.
Incidence—
Contract price of goods agreed without reference to tax—
Tax to be borne by the seller—Finance (No 2) Act 1940, ss 18, 22, 23, 25, 27, 28. **Love v Norman Wright (Builders) Ltd** [1944] **1** 618, CA.
Information to be supplied to commissioners by person concerned with the purchase of goods—
Purchase—
Meaning—Information as to sales—Whether 'purchase'—Whether court has jurisdiction to specify form in which information to be given—Finance Act 1946, s 20(3). **Customs and Excise Comrs v Ingram** [1949] **1** 896, CA.
Manufacturer—
Goods for use in or in connection with business—
Production of diaries for distribution to church congregation—Costs and profits derived from advertising revenue—Delivery to minister without charge—Free distribution to members of congregation—Publishers made diaries for use in connection with business—Appropriation of diaries constituting chargeable purchase—Finance (No 2) Act 1940, s 25(1)—Finance Act 1962, s 6(3). **Warwickshire Publishing Co Ltd v Customs and Excise Comrs** [1970] **1** 291, CA.

PURCHASE TAX (cont)—
    Refund—
        Money paid under mistake of law—
            Payment made while liability sub judice. **Sebel Products Ltd v Customs and Excise Comrs** [1949] **1** 729, Ch D.
    Regulations—
        Validity—
            Power of Commissioners of Customs and Excise to make regulation which 'appears to them necessary' to enable them to discharge their functions—Whether commissioners sole judges of what was necessary—Ouster of court's jurisdiction—Finance (No 2) Act 1940, s 33—Purchase Tax Regulations 1945 (S R & O 1945 No 517), reg 12. **Customs and Excise Comrs v Cure & Deeley Ltd** [1961] **3** 641, QBD.
    Value added tax—
        Relief. *See* **Value added tax** (Relief—Goods held at commencement of April 1973—Goods on which purchase tax or other duty paid).
    Wholesale value—
        Calculation—
            Appropriation by manufacturer of chargeable goods for sale in retail department—Opinion of commissioners—Power of court to review—Finance (No 2) Act 1940, s 21(1). **A-G v A W Gamage Ltd** [1949] **2** 732, KBD.
            Stationery—Football coupons printed by subsidiary of pools promoters—Copyright material used in compilation of coupons—Royalties paid by pool promoters for non-exclusive licence to reproduce or authorise reproduction of copyright material—Whether a copyright element should be included in wholesale value—Finance (No 2) Act 1940, s 21, Sch 8, paras 3, 4, 5. **Customs and Excise Comrs v Moores (J & C) Ltd** [1964] **2** 983, HL.

PURCHASER
    Fiduciary duty to purchaser—
        Sale of land. *See* **Sale of land** (Vendor—Fiduciary duty to purchaser).

PURCHASER'S LIEN
    Sale of land. *See* **Sale of land** (Purchaser's lien).

PURPOSE TRUST
    See **Trust and trustee** (Purpose).

Q

QUALIFICATIONS
Mutual recognition—
European Community. *See* **European Union** (Freedom of establishment—Mutual recognition of qualifications).

QUALIFIED PRIVILEGE
Libel and slander. *See* **Libel and slander** (Qualified privilege).

QUANTUM MERUIT
Additional to salary—
Bonus. *See* **Employment** (Remuneration—Quantum meruit).
Contract—
Generally. *See* **Contract** (Quantum meruit).

QUARANTINE
Animal—
Importation of animal. *See* **Animal** (Importation of animal—Quarantine).

QUARRY
Management and control—
Supervision by quarry manager—
Safety—Avoidance of danger from falls—Duty of manager to avoid danger from falls—Inspection of quarry face—Quarry worked on single face system—Deceased working on floor of quarry near face—Manager and deputy manager unaware that deceased working there—Deceased killed by fall of rock from face—Whether sole manager had supervision over quarry operations in progress—Mines and Quarries Act 1954, ss 103(1), 108(1), 157. **Sanderson v Millom Hematite Ore & Iron Co Ltd** [1967] 3 1050, Assizes.
Minerals—
Right to work—
Refusal to grant rights over adjoining fields—Reasonable offer and refusal—Extent of jurisdiction—Mines (Working Facilities and Support) Act 1923, ss 1, 3, 6, 9. **West of England Road Metal Co Ltd, Re** [1936] 2 1607, Com.
Safe methods of working—
Statutory duty of manager—
Duty to ensure quarrying operations carried on so as to avoid danger—Duty to ensure inspection carried out by competent person—'Competent'—Mines and Quarries Act 1954, s 108(1)—Quarries (General) Regulations 1956 (SI 1956 No 1780) regs 2(1)(b), 41. **Brazier v Skipton Rock Co Ltd** [1962] 1 955, Assizes.

QUARTER SESSIONS
Abolition—
Replacement by Crown Court. *See* **Crown Court**.
Adjournment of hearing. *See* Appeal to—Hearing—Adjournment sine die, *below*.
Allocutus. *See* **Criminal law** (Trial—Allocutus—Quarter sessions).
Appeal from—
Statutory provision that judgment of quarter sessions final—
Right of appeal by way of case stated—Summary Jurisdiction Act 1879, s 40—Gaming Act 1968, Sch 7, para 11(4). **Tehrani v Rostron** [1971] 3 790, CA.
Appeal to—
Abandonment of appeal—
Application to withdraw notice of abandonment—Jurisdiction—No power to entertain application unless abandonment a nullity, as through mistake or fraud. **R v Essex Quarter Sessions, ex p Larkin** [1961] 3 930, QBD.
Appeal against approved school order—
Jurisdiction—Order against young person aged 16—Appeal by parent—Young person over 17 when appeal heard—Jurisdiction to hear appeal. **Rugman v Drover (sub nom Drover v Rugman)** [1950] 2 575, KBD.
Appeal against committal of offenders to quarter sessions for sentence—
Jurisdiction—Sentence—Order made on conviction—Committal for sentence—Appeal against committal—Competency—Criminal Justice Act 1948, s 36(2). **R v London Sessions Appeal Committee, ex p Rogers** [1951] 1 343, KBD.
Appeal against conviction—
Practice—Documents to be placed before the court. **R v Grimsby Borough Quarter Sessions, ex p Fuller** [1955] 3 300, QBD.
Practice—Documents to be sent to quarter sessions. **Practice Note** [1956] 1 448, QBD; **R v Dorset Quarter Sessions, ex p O'Brien** [1956] 1 449, QBD.
Right of person aggrieved by order or conviction to appeal—Plea of guilty at trial—Whether person unequivocally pleading guilty can be 'aggrieved' by conviction—Metropolitan Police Courts Act 1839, s 50. **R v Appeal Committee of County of London Quarter Sessions (Deputy Chairman), ex p Borg** [1957] 3 28, QBD.
Substitution of conviction of alternative offence—Conviction by justices for malicious wounding—On appeal conviction for common assault substituted—Whether quarter sessions had jurisdiction to substitute a conviction of the lesser offence—Offences against the Person Act 1861, s 20. **Lawrence v Lawrence** [1968] 1 1191, QBD.
Appeal against order for forfeiture of recognisance—
Jurisdiction where sum or penalty adjudged to be paid more than £3—Whether sum or penalty adjudged to be paid including estreating of recognisance—Metropolitan Police Courts Act 1839, s 50—Public Health Act 1875, s 269—Summary Jurisdiction Act 1879, ss 9(1), 13, 19—Criminal Justice Administration Act 1914, s 37—Criminal Justice Act 1925, s 25. **Cockhill v Davies** [1943] 1 638, KBD.

Appeal to (cont)—
Appeal against sentence—
Hearing solely on evidence given below—No objection by counsel—Whether confirmation of sentence valid—Amendment of notice of appeal to include appeal against conviction—Jurisdiction. **Paprika Ltd v Board of Trade** [1944] **1** 372, KBD.
Sentence—Order made on conviction—Order that defendant should enter into recognisance—Whether 'order made on conviction'—Criminal Justice Act 1948, s 36(2). **R v London Sessions Appeal Committee, ex p Beaumont** [1951] **1** 232, KBD.
Approved school order, against—
Jurisdiction. See Appeal to—Appeal against approved school order—Jurisdiction, above.
Betting and gaming appeal—
Appeal against refusal of permit for amusements with prizes—Jurisdiction on appeal—Betting, Gaming and Lotteries Act 1963, s 49(1), Sch 6, para 6. **Sagnata Investments Ltd v Norwich Corp** [1971] **2** 1441, CA.
Customs offence—
Condemnation of goods by magistrate—Claimants ordered to pay five guineas costs—Appeal by claimants to quarter sessions against order of condemnation—Competency. **R v London (County) Quarter Sessions, ex p Bowes** [1950] **2** 1043, KBD.
Hearing—
Adjournment sine die—Notice—Notice of adjourned hearing sent by registered letter—Letter returned—Hearing in absence of respondent—Irregularity—Summary Jurisdiction (Appeals) Act 1933, s 3(1)(as amended by Criminal Justice Act 1948, s 83(3), Sch X, and Magistrates' Courts Act 1952, s 131, s 132(1), Sch V, Sch VI)—Interpretation Act 1889, s 26. **R v Appeal Committee of County of London Quarter Sessions, ex p Rossi** [1956] **1** 670, CA.
Jurisdiction—
London—Power of one justice sitting alone to hear and determine appeal—Administration of Justice Act 1964, s 7(6). **R v Inner London Quarter Sessions, ex p D'Souza** [1970] **1** 481, QBD.
Jurisdiction of appeal committee—
Appeal abandoned—Application for costs to new committee—Quarter Sessions Act 1849, ss 5, 6—Summary Jurisdiction (Appeals) Act 1933, s 7—Administration of Justice (Miscellaneous Provisions) Act 1938, s 3. **R v Lincoln Justices (Parts of Lindsey), ex p Trafford** [1944] **1** 286, KBD.
Jurisdiction to amend summons—
Conviction by court of summary jurisdiction under repealed statute—Power of quarter sessions to amend summons—Summary Jurisdiction Act 1879, s 31(1)(vii), as substituted by Summary Jurisdiction (Appeals) Act 1933, s 1—Food and Drugs (Milk, Dairies and Artificial Cream) Act 1950, s 36(3). **Meek v Powell** [1952] **1** 347, KBD.
Jurisdiction to entertain question of exemption from penalty—
Information by employers against employees alleged to be actual offenders dismissed—Notice of appeal to be given to employees—Merchandise Marks Act 1926, s 6—Magistrates Courts Act 1952, s 84(1). **R v Epsom Justices, ex p Dawnier Motors Ltd** [1960] **3** 635, QBD.
Jurisdiction to entertain question of what plea should have been entered at trial—
Equivocal plea of guilty—Determination whether or not plea of guilty before magistrates was equivocal—Determination to be made only on basis of what happened before magistrates—Accused fully understanding charge—Nothing occurring before magistrates casting doubt on plea—Jurisdiction of quarter sessions to entertain application for change of plea excluded. **R v Marylebone Justices, ex p Westminster City Council** [1971] **1** 1025, QBD.
Plea of guilty accompanied by statement indicating innocence—Remission of case to court of summary jurisdiction—Order expressing the opinion of quarter sessions. **R v Tottenham Justices, ex p Rubens** [1970] **1** 879, QBD.
Plea of guilty accompanied by statement indicating innocence—Remission of case to court of summary jurisdiction—Summary Jurisdiction Act 1879, s 31(1)(as substituted by Summary Jurisdiction (Appeals) Act 1933, s 1). **R v Durham Quarter Sessions, ex p Virgo** [1952] **1** 466, QBD.
Plea of guilty at trial—Failure of accused to understand nature or gravity of offence—Whether accused having right of appeal—Criminal Justice Act 1948, s 36(1). **R v West Kent Quarter Sessions, ex p Files** [1951] **2** 728, KBD.
Leave—
Time for—Application for leave after sentence passed—Accused committed to quarter sessions for sentence. **R v Tottenham Justices, ex p Rubens** [1970] **1** 879, QBD.
Licensing appeal—
Intoxicating liquor. See **Licensing** (Appeal).
Licensing justices refusing to renew dancing and music licence. **R v East Riding Quarter Sessions, ex p Newton** [1967] **3** 118, CA.
Limited right of appeal under special Act—
General right of appeal under general Act—Generalia specialibus non derogant—Coal Mines Act 1911, s 104—Criminal Justice Administration Act 1914, s 37(1). **Walker v Hemmant** [1943] **2** 160, KBD.
Local authority, by. See **Local authority** (Appeal to quarter sessions).
Notice of appeal—
Persons to be served with notice—Summons against retailer under Food and Drugs Act 1938—Information laid by retailer against manufacturer under s 83—First summons dismissed—Conviction on second summons—Appeal against conviction—Whether notice of appeal required to be given to prosecutor of first summons—Summary Jurisdiction (Appeals) Act 1933, s 1—Food and Drugs Act 1938, ss 3, 83. **R v Derby Recorder, ex p Spalton** [1944] **1** 721, KBD.
Order made on determining complaint—
Whether dismissal of complaint in respect of refusal of fire certificate an order. See **Fire** (Certificate—Refusal to issue—Appeal from refusal to justices—Dismissal of complaint by justices—Appeal to quarter sessions—Jurisdiction to hear appeal—Order).
Variation of decision of court of summary jurisdiction—
Motoring offence—Licence suspended by magistrates—Disqualification removed by order on appeal—Jurisdiction—Desirability of stating special reasons—Road Traffic Act 1930, s 35—Summary Jurisdiction (Appeals) Act 1933, s 31(1)(vii). **R v Recorder of Leicester, ex p Gabbitas** [1946] **1** 615, KBD.

QUARTER SESSIONS (cont)—

Betting and gaming appeal. *See* Appeal to—Betting and gaming appeal, *above.*

Case stated. *See* **Case stated** (Quarter sessions).

Civil proceedings—

Costs. *See* Costs—Civil proceedings, *below.*

Committal of offender for sentence—

Appeal against committal. *See* Appeal to—Appeal against committal of offenders to quarter sessions for sentence, *above.*

Appeal against sentence—

Consecutive terms of detention at a detention centre for two offences—Sentence to such detention inappropriate after previous sentence to such detention—Sentence to one day's imprisonment and disqualification for driving ordered for third offence—Whether appeal lies since Act of 1967—Magistrates' Courts Act 1952, s 28(1)—Criminal Justice Act 1967, s 97(3)(a),(c)(ii),(6),(7). **R v Moore** [1968] **1** 790, CA.

Borstal training—

Prisoner sentenced to borstal training in Scotland and released on licence—Conviction in England while on licence—Committal to quarter sessions with a view to borstal training—Jurisdiction of quarter sessions to order return to borstal institution—Criminal Justice Act 1961, ss 12(1), 38(2)(a)—Criminal Justice Act 1948, s 29(3)(d), as amended. **R v Welsh** [1967] **3** 846, Vacation Ct, CA.

Procedure—Documents to be sent to quarter sessions—Criminal Justice Act 1948, ss 20, 29. **Practice Note** [1956] **1** 448, QBD.

Proof of age—Age admitted by accused—Sworn evidence not given of age or other matters required by statute—Validity of committal—Criminal Justice Act 1948, s 20(3). **R v Grimsby Recorder, ex p Purser** [1951] **2** 889, KBD.

Right of appeal to Court of Appeal against sentence. *See* **Sentence** (Appeal—Borstal training).

Road traffic offences—Disqualification—Powers of quarter sessions—Criminal Justice Act 1948, s 20(5)(a)—Magistrates' Courts Act 1952, s 28. **R v Dangerfield** [1959] **3** 88, CCA.

Road traffic offences—Disqualification—Variation—Disqualification imposed by committing justices—Whether quarter sessions had power to vary disqualification—Criminal Justice Act 1948, s 20(5)(a)(ii)—Magistrates' Courts Act 1952, s 28—Road Traffic Act 1962, s 5(1), (3), (5). **R v McNulty** [1964] **3** 713, CCA.

Character and antecedents—

Matters to be taken into consideration—Magistrates' Courts Act 1952, s 29. **R v King's Lynn Justices, ex p Carter** [1968] **3** 858, QBD.

Matters to be taken into consideration—Whether confined to previous convictions—Criminal Justice Act 1948, s 29(1). **R v Vallett** [1951] **1** 231, CCA.

Factors to be considered by quarter sessions before sentencing offender—

Duty of quarter sessions to ascertain whether appeal against conviction pending—Criminal Justice Act 1948, s 29(1). **R v Faithful** [1950] **2** 1251, CCA.

Jurisdiction of quarter sessions—

Issue of bench warrant—Offender failing to surrender to bail—Whether quarter sessions had jurisdiction to issue bench warrant—Criminal Justice Act 1948, s 29(3)(a)—Magistrates' Courts Act 1952, s 29. **R v Lloyd-Jones, ex p Thomas** [1958] **3** 425, QBD.

Sentence of less than 12 months' imprisonment on each of two charges—Sentences running consecutively—Whether the court has power to make an order under Criminal Justice Act 1948, s 22(1), as amended by Prison Act 1952, s 54, Sch 3. **R v Mordanam** [1959] **3** 875, CCA.

Practice—

Documents to be sent to quarter sessions—Criminal Justice Act 1948, s 29—Magistrates' Courts Act 1952, s 29. **Practice Note** [1956] **1** 448, QBD; **R v Dorset Quarter Sessions, ex p O'Brien** [1956] **1** 449, QBD.

Identification of prisoner—Criminal Justice Act 1948, s 29(1). **R v Barker** [1951] **1** 479, CCA.

Record—Particulars—Record should show sufficient to make clear with what charges quarter sessions were concerned—In case of a plea of guilty record to show dates of offences and sums involved. **R v Hooper** [1967] **1** 766, CA.

Sentence—

Orders for compensation in magistrates' court at same time as committal for sentence—Whether orders were a sentence or part of a sentence—Magistrates' Courts Act 1952, s 34. **R v Dorset Quarter Sessions, ex p Randall** [1966] **3** 952, QBD.

Summary trial of indictable offence—

Conviction by court of summary jurisdiction of indictable offence—Offence not triable at quarter sessions—No power to sentence at quarter sessions. **R v Middlesex Quarter Sessions, ex p DPP** [1950] **1** 916, KBD.

Gravity of offences apparent from nature of charges—Nothing emerging from proceedings to increase their gravity—Offender found to be of good character—Court previously troubled with several offences of similar nature—Power of court to commit for sentence—Magistrates' Courts Act 1952, s 29. **R v Tower Bridge Magistrate, ex p Osman** [1971] **2** 1018, QBD.

Costs—

Civil proceedings—

General rule—Costs following event—Proceedings by member of public as complainant against highway authority—Complainant having proprietary right directly affected by outcome of proceedings—Justices finding in complainant's favour—Absence of special circumstances—Complainant entitled to award of costs. **Riggall v Hereford CC** [1972] **1** 301, QBD.

Discretion of quarter sessions—

Exercise of discretion—Appeal from court of summary jurisdiction—Costs of successful appellant disallowed—Reason for disallowance stated by court—Decision based on conclusion of court on material issue—Appellant's evidence not heard. **Becker v Purchase** [1950] **2** 837, KBD.

Power to order prosecutor to pay costs—

Exercise of power—Appeal to quarter sessions—Sentence—Police appearing in order to inform court of facts on appeal against sentence—Sentence reduced—Costs should not be ordered to be paid by police. **David v Metropolitan Police Comr** [1962] **1** 491, QBD Divl Ct.

Forfeiture of recognisance. *See* Appeal to—Appeal against order for forfeiture of recognisance, *above.*

QUARTER SESSIONS (cont)—
    Highway—
        Determination whether public right of way. *See* **Highway** (Dedication—Evidence—Provisional map—Dispute—Determination of quarter sessions).
    Jurisdiction—
        Appeal—
            Appeal against approved school order. *See* Appeal to—Appeal against approved school order—Jurisdiction, *above*.
            Gaming—Appeal against refusal of permit for provision of amusements with prizes. *See* **Gaming** (Amusements with prizes—Permit for provision of amusements with prizes—Application—Refusal—Appeal—Quarter sessions—Jurisdiction of quarter sessions).
            Sentence—Conviction and sentence by magistrates' court—Committal by quarter sessions to themselves for sentence—Whether quarter sessions had jurisdiction to commit appellant to themselves for sentence—Summary Jurisdiction Act 1879, s 31, para (vii), para (viii), as substituted by Summary Jurisdiction (Appeals) Act 1933, s 1—Criminal Justice Act 1948, s 29(3)—Magistrates' Courts Act 1952, s 29. **R v Bullock** [1963] **3** 506, CCA, QBD.
        Autrefois acquit—
            Acquittal of offender at summary trial by justices—Summary trial a nullity for want of jurisdiction—Committal subsequently for trial by quarter sessions—Certificate of entry of acquittal in register of proceedings—Whether quarter sessions had jurisdiction to inquire into validity of acquittal—Magistrates' Courts Rules 1952 (SI 1952 No 2190), r 56. **R v West** [1962] **2** 624, CCA.
        Direction for trial at assizes—
            Jurisdiction under commission of the peace—Indictment first preferred at assizes—Accused lawfully indicted and tried—Criminal Justice Act 1925, s 14(2). **R v Wilson** [1967] **2** 1088, CA.
    Limited right of appeal to. *See* Appeal to—Limited right of appeal under special Act, *above*.
    Local authority—
        Appeal. *See* **Local authority** (Appeal to quarter sessions).
    Notice of appeal. *See* Appeal to—Notice of appeal, *above*.
    Recognisance—
        Forfeiture—
            Appeal—Jurisdiction. *See* Appeal to—Appeal against order for forfeiture of recognisance, *above*.
    Recorder—
        Custom for magistrates to sit with recorder—
            Validity of proceedings. **R v Burnley Recorder, ex p New Empire (Burnley) Ltd** [1940] **2** 412, KBD.
    Refusal to state case. *See* **Mandamus** (Quarter sessions—Refusal to state case).
    Replacement by Crown Court. *See* **Crown Court**.
    Sentence—
        Appeal against sentence. *See* Appeal to—Appeal against sentence, *above*.
        Borstal training. *See* **Sentence** (Borstal training).
        Committal to quarter sessions. *See* Committal of offender for sentence, *above*.
    Variation of magistrates' decision. *See* Appeal to—Variation of decision of court of summary jurisdiction, *above*.

QUASHING ORDER
    Renaming of certiorari as. *See* **Practice** (Crown Office list—Change of title to Administrative Court—Renaming of orders).

QUASI-CONTRACT
    Generally. *See* **Contract** (Quasi-contract).
    Money had and received. *See* **Money** (Money had and received).
    Restitution. *See* **Restitution** (Quasi-contract).

QUASI-JUDICIAL FUNCTION
    Acting in quasi-judicial capacity—
        Exercise of statutory power—
            Minister's order superseding municipal council for incompetence. *See* **Natural justice** (Quasi-judicial function—Exercise of statutory power).
        Minister. *See* **Natural justice** (Quasi-judicial function—Minister).

QUAY
    Generally. *See* **Harbour** (Quay).
    Licence to use. *See* **Licence** (Licence to use quay for business of repairing boats).
    Navigation—
        Right of public to use quay for purposes incidental to navigation. *See* **Water and watercourses** (Navigation—Public right of navigation (PRN)—Quay on foreshore—Quay within port—Right of public to use quay for purposes incidental to navigation on payment of reasonable charge).

QUEEN'S BENCH DIVISION
    Admiralty. *See* **Admiralty** (Practice).
    Associate's certificate. *See* **Practice** (Associate—Certificate of associate).
    Chambers proceedings—
        Generally. *See* **Practice** (Chambers proceedings—Queen's Bench Division).
        Masters' summonses. *See* **Practice** (Chambers proceedings—Masters' summonses).
    Commercial Court. *See* **Commercial Court**.
    Costs—
        Appeal from master. *See* **Costs** (Appeal—Appeal from master of Queen's Bench Division).
        Taxation—
            Jurisdiction. *See* **Court** (Jurisdiction—High Court of Justice—Divisions of High Court).
            Review of taxation. *See* **Costs** (Taxation—Review of taxation).
    Counsel's fees. *See* **Practice** (Queen's Bench Division—Counsel's fees).
    Crown Office list. *See* **Practice** (Crown Office list).

Divisional Court—
Appeal to Court of Appeal—
Jurisdiction of Court of Appeal. *See* **Court of Appeal** (Jurisdiction—Appeal from Divisional Court).
Funds in court—
Practice. *See* **Practice** (Funds in court).
Judgments—
Numbering of. *See* **Judgment** (Numbering of judgments).
Jurisdiction—
Generally. *See* **Court** (Jurisdiction—High Court of Justice—Divisions of High Court).
Grant of remedy or relief where proceedings for such remedy or relief assigned to another Division.
See **Court** (Jurisdiction—High Court of Justice—Divisions of High Court).
Subpoena duces tecum. *See* **Practice** (Subpoena duces tecum—Issue—Jurisdiction of Queen's Bench
Division where powers of inferior tribunal incomplete).
Jury trial—
Cases where party entitled to trial by jury. *See* **Jury** (Trial by jury—Cases where party entitled to trial by
jury—Queen's Bench Division).
Leeds and Newcastle upon Tyne. *See* **Practice** (Queen's Bench Division—Mercantile lists—Leeds and
Newcastle upon Tyne).
List of authorities—
Procedure. *See* **Practice** (List of authorities—Procedure—Queen's Bench Division).
Liverpool and Manchester. *See* **Practice** (Queen's Bench Division—Mercantile lists—Liverpool and
Manchester).
Long Vacation—
Practice. *See* **Practice** (Long Vacation—Queen's Bench Division).
Master—
Appeal against decision. *See* **Appeal** (Master of Queen's Bench Division).
Appointments before master. *See* **Practice** (Queen's Bench Division—Appointments before Queen's
Bench masters).
Lists. *See* **Practice** (Queen's Bench Division—Lists—Masters' lists).
Summons—
Practice—Masters' summonses. *See* **Practice** (Summons—Masters' summonses—Queen's Bench
Division).
Mental patient—
Damages awarded to mental patient—
Transfer of damages to Court of Protection. *See* **Mental health** (Patient's property—Damages—
Damages awarded in Queen's Bench Division action—Transfer of damages to Court of
Protection).
Note of judgment—
Practice—
Appeal from Chancery Division or Queen's Bench Division. *See* **Practice** (Note of
judgment—Appeal from Chancery Division or Queen's Bench Division).
Numbering of judgments. *See* **Judgment** (Numbering of judgments).
Postal facilities, use of. *See* **Practice** (Post—Use of postal facilities—Queen's Bench Division).
Setting down action. *See* **Practice** (Trial—Setting down action).
Summons for directions. *See* **Practice** (Summons for directions).
Tape recorders—
Use of tape recorders in court—
Practice. *See* **Practice** (Tape recorders—Use of tape recorders in court).
Transfer of action—
Transfer to county court. *See* **County court** (Transfer of action—Transfer from High Court—Transfer
from Queen's Bench Division).

QUEEN'S PROCTOR
Argument by—
Divorce. *See* **Divorce** (Practice—Queen's Proctor—Argument).
Intervention—
Costs—
Legal aid. *See* **Legal aid** (Costs—Divorce—Queen's Proctor's intervention).
Divorce proceedings. *See* **Divorce** (Intervention).

QUEENSLAND
Statute—
Powers of legislature—
Acts conferring authority on Commissioner for Transport to licence road services and to fix and
exact licence fees—Validity—Whether legislature thereby purported to delegate sovereign
powers, i e, of taxation, to commissioner—State Transport Facilities Acts 1946-1959—State
Transport Act 1960. **Cobb & Co Ltd v Kropp** [1966] **2** 913, PC.
Validating statute—
Retrospective effect—Acts previously held invalid validated in truncated form as from their
enactment—Licences and permits issued under Acts prior to validation validated—State
Transport Facilities Acts 1946 to 1959—State Transport Act 1960—Transport Laws Validation Act
1962 (No 24 of 1962), ss 3, 4. **Western Transport Pty Ltd v Kropp** [1964] **3** 722, PC.
Succession duty—
Administration duty—
Estate of deceased testator domiciled in New South Wales in course of administration—Death of
residuary legatee intestate—Estate not fully administered at time of intestate's death—Whether
intestate had 'beneficial interest' in testator's residuary estate so as to constitute taxable
succession—Administration to intestate's estate not taken out in Queensland—Possession of
property of testator not taken by any one as administrator of intestate—Whether administration
duty exigible—Succession and Probate Duties Acts 1892 to 1955, s 4—Succession and Probate
Duties Acts Declaratory and Admendment Act 1935, s 2. **Comr of Stamp Duties v Livingston**
[1964] **3** 692, PC.

QUESTION OF LAW
Appeal—
  Criminal cases—
    Jurisdiction of Court of Appeal. *See* **Criminal law** (Court of Appeal—Jurisdiction—Decision on question of law).
  Court-martial—
    Procedure on submission of question of law. *See* **Court-martial** (Procedure—Submission on question of law).

QUIA TIMET ACTION
Defamation case—
  Particulars of pleading. *See* **Libel and slander** (Particulars—Quia timet injunction).
Injunction. *See* **Injunction** (Quia timet action).
Mandatory injunction. *See* **Injunction** (Mandatory injunction—Quia timet action).

QUIET ENJOYMENT
Covenant—
  Lease. *See* **Landlord and tenant** (Covenant—Quiet enjoyment).

QUORUM
Meeting—
  Company. *See* **Company** (Meeting—Quorum).

QUOTA
Coal—
  Regulation of production by. *See* **Coal mining** (Regulation of production—Regulation by quota).
Dairy produce quotas. *See* **Agriculture** (Dairy farming—Dairy produce quotas).
Wheat—
  Quota payments. *See* **Agriculture** (Wheat—Quota payments).

RABBI
Judicial review of decision of Chief Rabbi—
Availability of remedy. *See* **Judicial review** (Availability of remedy—Chief Rabbi).

RACE RELATIONS
Advertisements and notices—
Unlawful discrimination. *See* Unlawful discrimination—Advertisements and notices, *below*.
Application of race relations legislation to Crown—
Discrimination by Crown in immigration control—
Race Relations Act 1976, s 75(1). **Home Office v Commission for Racial Equality** [1981] **1** 1042, QBD.
Army—
Investigation of complaint by soldier of racial abuse—
Duty of Army Board when investigating complaint—Applicant making complaint of racial discrimination—Applicant requesting disclosure of documents and oral hearing of complaint—Board refusing request and adjudicating on complaint without meeting—Whether members of board making decision required to meet and confer—Whether board required to give applicant access to documents—Whether board required to hold oral hearing and permit cross-examination—Army Act 1955, s 181—Race Relations Act 1976, s 75(8)(9). **R v Army Board of the Defence Council, ex p Anderson** [1991] **3** 375, QBD.
Commission for Racial Equality—
Duties—
Extent. *See* Discrimination—Duty of Commission for Racial Equality, *below*.
Investigation of complaint. *See* Investigation of complaint—Commission for Racial Equality, *below*.
Complaint—
Investigation of. *See* Investigation of complaint, *below*.
Criminal offences—
Racially or religiously aggravated offences. *See* **Criminal law** (Racially or religiously aggravated offences).
Discrimination—
Acts done under statutory authority etc—
Discriminatory act done 'in pursuance of any instrument made under any enactment by a Minister of the Crown'—In pursuance of—Employment—Applicant seeking qualified teacher status in United Kingdom—Applicant qualified in Hong Kong—Application refused on ground that Hong Kong training not comparable with approved English course—Whether requirement for comparability discriminatory—Whether requirement laid down 'in pursuance of' instrument made under statute—Race Relations Act 1976, ss 1(1), 12(1), 41—Education (Teachers) Regulations 1982, Sch 5, para 2(b). **Hampson v Dept of Education and Science** [1990] **2** 513, HL.
Discovery—
Proceedings before industrial tribunal. *See* **Employment tribunal** (Procedure—Disclosure of documents—Racial discrimination).
Discrimination against racial group—
Admissions policy of voluntary aided faith school—Child qualifying for admission to school if child's mother Jewish by descent or conversion—Whether discrimination on racial grounds—Race Relations Act 1976, ss 1, 3. **R (on the application of E) v Governing Body of JFS (Secretary of State for Children, School and Families and others, interested parties) (United Synagogue intervening)** [2009] **4** 375, CA; [2010] **1** 319, SC.
Gipsies—Racial group defined by reference to colour, race, nationality or ethnic or national origins—Ethnic origins—Travellers—Publican refusing to admit 'travellers' to public house—Whether unlawful discrimination against gipsies—Whether gipsies a racial group—Race Relations Act 1976, ss 1(1)(a)(b), 3(1), 29. **Commission for Racial Equality v Dutton** [1989] **1** 306, CA.
Sikhs—Racial group defined by reference to colour, race, nationality or ethnic or national origins—Ethnic or national origins—Ethnic—Headmaster refusing to admit Sikh boy to school unless he removed his turban and cut his hair—Headmaster desiring to minimise religious distinctions in school which wearing of turbans would accentuate—Whether unlawful discrimination—Whether Sikhs a 'racial group'—Whether Sikhs a group defined by reference to 'ethnic or national origins'—Whether discrimination justifiable—Race Relations Act 1976, ss 1(1)(b), 3(1). **Mandla v Dowell Lee** [1983] **1** 1062, HL.
Discrimination by victimisation. *See* Discrimination—Victimisation, *below*.
Discrimination on grounds of national origin—
Employment—Discovery of confidential documents—Employment tribunal. *See* **Employment tribunal** (Procedure—Disclosure of documents—Confidential documents—Complaint of discrimination in employment).
Housing accommodation—Exclusion of non-British subject from council's housing list—Whether discrimination on ground of national origins—Race Relations Act 1968, ss 1(1), 5(a), (c). **Ealing London Borough v Race Relations Board** [1971] **1** 424, QBD; [1972] **1** 105, HL.
Duty of Commission for Racial Equality—
Elimination of discrimination—Commission proposing to investigate immigration control with a view to eliminating discrimination against coloured immigrants—Whether investigation connected with commission's duties—Whether commission's duty limited to elimination of discrimination expressly made unlawful by legislation—Whether enforcement of immigration control provision of goods, facilities and services—Whether commission having power to conduct investigation—Race Relations Act 1976, ss 20(1), 43(1)(a). **Home Office v Commission for Racial Equality** [1981] **1** 1042, QBD.
Promotion of equality of opportunity and good race relations—Commission proposing to investigate immigration control—Whether promotion of equality of opportunity and good race relations restricted to areas where unlawful discrimination—Whether inquiry into immigration control would promote good race relations—Race Relations Act 1976, s 43(1)(b). **Home Office v Commission for Racial Equality** [1981] **1** 1042, QBD.

Discrimination (cont)—
Employment—
Applicant seeking qualified teacher status in United Kingdom—Applicant qualified in Hong Kong—Secretary of State refusing to recognise applicant on ground that Hong Kong training not comparable with approved English course—Whether requirement that applicant should have comparable qualification a 'condition or requirement'—Whether imposition of condition justifiable—Whether act of discrimination done 'in pursuance of any instrument made under any enactment by a Minister of the Crown'—Race Relations Act 1976, ss 1(1), 41. **Hampson v Dept of Education and Science** [1990] **2** 25, CA.

Complaint of discrimination—Burden of proof—Race Relations Act 1976, s 54A. **Wong v Igen Ltd (Equal Opportunities Commission and ors intervening)** [2005] **3** 812, CA.

Discrimination on racial grounds—Act of discrimination—Continuing act—Proper approach to determining whether act extended over period of time—Race Relations Act 1976, s 68. **Hendricks v Metropolitan Police Comr** [2003] **1** 654, CA.

Discrimination on racial grounds—Applicant dismissed from employment with local authority for alleged misconduct—Applicant contending that dismissal constituted racial discrimination—Whether fact that employer acted unreasonably in dismissing employee giving rise to presumption of 'less favourable treatment'—Whether absence of non-satisfactory explanation for less favourable treatment giving rise to presumption of racial discrimination—Race Relations Act 1976, s 1. **Glasgow City Council v Zafar** [1998] **2** 953, HL.

Discrimination on racial grounds—Asian bank employees treated less favourably as to pension entitlement than their European comparators—Asian employees commencing service in the 1970s with United Kingdom bank on terms that their service with banks in East Africa would not count towards their pension entitlement with United Kingdom bank—Whether term of contract 'a deliberate omission'—Whether term of contract extending throughout duration of employment—Employees making complaints of unlawful racial discrimination to industrial tribunal—Whether complaints brought within three months of when act complained of was done—Whether complaints time-barred—Whether tribunal having jurisdiction to entertain complaint—Race Relations Act 1976, ss 1(1)(a), 4(2), 54(1), 68(1), (7). **Barclays Bank plc v Kapur** [1991] **1** 646, HL.

Discrimination on racial grounds—Complainants employed by licensees in department store—Withdrawal of store approval of complainants thereby resulting in their consequent dismissal—Refusal of approval resulting in one complainant failing to obtain job with licensee—Complaints of unlawful discrimination—Whether store liable to complainants as contract workers employed by licensees—Race Relations Act 1976, s 7(1). **Harrods Ltd v Remick** [1998] **1** 52, CA.

Discrimination on racial grounds—Discrimination by qualifying bodies—Labour party not selecting complainant as electoral candidate—Whether discrimination on racial grounds—Whether Labour party qualifying body—Employment tribunal erroneously holding Labour party a qualifying body—Court of Appeal in unconnected proceedings holding Labour party not a qualifying body—Whether issue estoppel arising—Race Relations Act 1976, ss 12(1), 25(1). **Ahsan v Watt (formerly Carter) (sued on behalf of the Labour Party)** [2008] **1** 869, HL.

Discrimination on racial grounds—Employee subjected to severe verbal and physical racial abuse by fellow employees—Employee resigning as a result of treatment suffered—Whether employers liable for conduct of their employees—Whether employees acting in 'the course of [their] employment'—Race Relations Act 1976, s 32(1). **Jones v Tower Boot Co Ltd** [1997] **2** 406, CA.

Discrimination on racial grounds—Person who knowingly 'aids' another to do act of unlawful discrimination—Meaning of 'aids'—Race Relations Act 1976, s 33(1). **Anyanwu v South Bank Student Union (Commission for Racial Equality, interveners)** [2001] **2** 353, HL.

Discrimination on racial grounds—Statutory provision making it unlawful for employer to discriminate against employee on racial grounds by 'dismissing' him—Whether constructive dismissal falling within terms of provision—Race Relations Act 1976, s 4(2)(c). **Derby Specialist Fabrication Ltd v Burton** [2001] **2** 840, EAT.

Discrimination on racial grounds—University student union employing applicants—University expelling applicants and barring them from university premises—Student union dismissing applicants—Applicants bringing proceedings for racial discrimination—Whether university knowingly aiding union in discriminating against applicants—Race Relations Act 1976, s 33. **Anyanwu v South Bank Student Union (Commission for Racial Equality, interveners)** [2000] **1** 1, CA.

Discrimination on racial grounds—Whether claim for compensation for racial discrimination surviving death of complainant—Law Reform (Miscellaneous Provisions) Act 1934, s 1(1). **Harris (suing as personal representative of Andrews (decd)) v Lewisham and Guy's Mental Health NHS Trust** [2000] **3** 769, CA.

Dismissal. See **Employment** (Discrimination—Racial discrimination—Dismissal).

Generally. See **Employment** (Discrimination—Racial discrimination).

Illegality—Employee obtaining contract of employment by illegal conduct—Employer dismissing employee—Whether employee able to bring claim for race discrimination. **Vakante v Addey & Stanhope School** [2004] **4** 1056, CA.

Work permit—Non-EEC national—Immigrant having indefinite leave to enter—Employer requiring work permit or proof of employment status—British citizens and EEC nationals not required to produce proof of employment status—Whether immigrants having indefinite leave to enter treated less favourably by being required to produce proof of employment status—Whether unlawful discrimination on grounds of nationality—Race Relations Act 1976, ss 1(1)(a), 3(4). **Dhatt v McDonald's Hamburgers Ltd** [1991] **3** 692, CA.

Indirect discrimination—
Provision, criterion or practice—Congestion charging zone—Mayor of London removing exemption from congestion charge for minicabs unless designated wheelchair accessible—Exemption not removed for taxis—Vast majority of minicab drivers from black and minority ethnic backgrounds whereas majority of taxi drivers white—Whether measure discriminatory—Whether measure appropriate—Whether other less intrusive means available to achieve aim—Whether measure proportionate means of achieving legitimate aim—Standard of scrutiny required—Equality Act 2010, s 19. **R (on the application of Independent Workers Union of Great Britain) v Mayor of London (Transport for London, interested party)** [2021] **3** 334, CA.

RACE RELATIONS (cont)—
  Discrimination (cont)—
    Local authority—
      Whether prohibition of discrimination in provision of goods, facilities or services applying to local authority looking after children—Race Relations Act 1976, ss 20(1), 23(2). **Conwell v Newham London BC** [2000] **1** 696, EAT.
    Police—
      Dismissal of special constable. *See* **Police** (Dismissal—Constable—Special constable—Discrimination on grounds of race).
    Unlawful. *See* Unlawful discrimination, *below.*
    Victimisation—
      Burden of proof—Reverse burden of proof applying to complaints to employment tribunal of discrimination—Whether reverse burden of proof extending to complaints of victimisation—Race Relations Act 1976, ss 1, 2, 54A—Council Directive (EC) 2000/43, arts 8, 9. **Oyarce v Cheshire CC** [2008] **4** 907, CA.
      Circumstances relevant for purposes of legislation—Person victimised treated less favourably than others—Appellant belonging to taxi proprietor's organisation—Appellant alleging fee charged by organisation discriminatory—Appellant making complaint to industrial tribunal and making tape recordings of conversations with members to support his case—Appellant expelled from membership of organisation for making secret tape recordings—Whether appellant victimised in 'circumstances relevant for the purposes' of legislation—Race Relations Act 1976, s 2(1). **Aziz v Trinity Street Taxis Ltd** [1988] **2** 860, CA.
      Circumstances relevant for purposes of legislation—Person victimised treated less favourably than others—Job centre clerk employed to interview prospective employers and employees—Clerk required to treat information received as confidential—Clerk reporting prospective employers for alleged racial discrimination—Clerk moved to less interesting job—Clerk bringing complaint against his employers alleging victimisation—Whether clerk victimised in 'circumstances relevant for the purposes' of legislation—Whether clerk victimised because he gave information 'in connection with proceedings' against an employer practising racial discrimination or because his reports were something done 'under or by reference to' legislation—Race Relations Act 1976, s 2(1). **Kirby v Manpower Services Commission** [1980] **3** 334, EAT.
      Police sergeant bringing racial discrimination proceedings against chief constable in respect of rejection of application for promotion to inspector—Sergeant applying for similar post with another force while proceedings pending—Chief constable refusing to provide reference sought by other force for fear of prejudicing position in pending proceedings—Whether refusal constituting victimisation 'by reason that' sergeant had brought discrimination proceedings—Race Relations Act 1976, s 2(1)(a). **Khan v Chief Constable of West Yorkshire Police** [2001] **4** 834, HL.
      Respondent employer interviewing applicant for position—Interviewers being aware that applicant had brought proceedings for racial discrimination against respondent and rejecting application—Applicant bringing fresh proceedings for victimisation against respondent—Whether conscious motivation a prerequisite for victimisation—Whether employer liable only if person who made interview arrangements acted in discriminatory manner—Race Relations Act 1976, ss 2(1), 4(1)(a). **Lippiatt v South Gloucestershire Council** [1999] **4** 149, CA.
  Employment—
    Discrimination. *See* Discrimination—Employment, *above.*
    Employment tribunal—
      Whether employment tribunal having jurisdiction to hear complaint relating to benefit arising from employment relationship after termination of employment—Whether tribunal having jurisdiction to hear complaint of discrimination based on employer's failure to comply with reinstatement order—Race Relations Act 1976, s 4(2). **Relaxion Group plc v Rhys-Harper** [2003] **4** 1113, HL.
  European Community—
    Equal treatment between persons irrespective of racial or ethnic origin—
      Interpretation of Directive. *See* **European Union** (Reference to European Court—Reference for a preliminary ruling concerning interpretation of Community law—Interpretation of directive—Principle of equal treatment irrespective of racial or ethnic origin).
  Incitement—
    Incitement to racial hatred—
      Public order. *See* **Criminal law** (Public order—Incitement to racial hatred).
    Incitement to unlawful discrimination—
      Incitement not limited to advice, encouragement or persuasion—Incitement including threats and bringing of pressure—Pressure brought on foster parents of children in local authority care to accept white children only—Race Relations Act 1968, s 12. **Applin v Race Relations Board** [1974] **2** 73, HL.
  Investigation of complaint—
    Commission for Racial Equality—
      Duty to act fairly—Requirements of fairness—Parties entitled to fair hearing—Evidence of discrimination contained in report submitted by commission's officers—Witnesses not present before commission when person accused of discrimination given opportunity to make oral representations—No opportunity for accused person to cross-examine witnesses—Whether accused person entitled to cross-examine witnesses—Whether denial of opportunity to cross-examine witnesses a breach of natural justice. **R v Commission for Racial Equality, ex p Cottrell & Rothon (a firm)** [1980] **3** 265, QBD.
      Evidence—Hearsay. *See* **Evidence** (Hearsay—Race relations cases—Hearing before Commission for Racial Equality).
    Conciliation committee—
      Requirement to form an opinion whether 'any person' has been guilty of unlawful discrimination—Finding of committee—Finding that unlawful discrimination has taken place—Whether necessary to identify in finding person who has been guilty of discrimination—Race Relations Act 1968, s 15(3)(a). **Selvarajan v Race Relations Board** [1976] **1** 12, CA.

RACE RELATIONS (cont)—
Investigation of complaint (cont)—
Race Relations Board—

Duty to act fairly—Requirements of fairness—Parties entitled to be informed of substance of case against them—Duty of members of the board to consider all the evidence and papers in the case—Board delegating function of collecting information to officer of the board—Report of officer recommending board to form opinion that no discrimination had taken place—Three members of board only considering all the papers in case—Board concluding that no discrimination had taken place—Whether board having acted fairly. **Selvarajan v Race Relations Board** [1976] **1** 12, CA.

Reinvestigation of complaint after investigation by conciliation committee—Report of conciliation committee—Whether board limited to considering report only—Whether board entitled to consider all the evidence before conciliation committee—Race Relations Act 1968, s 15(5). **Selvarajan v Race Relations Board** [1976] **1** 12, CA.

Local authority—
General statutory duty—

Duty to promote good race relations—Misuse of power—Borough with multiracial population—Company belonging to group with interests in South Africa supplying goods to borough council—Council deciding to boycott company's goods—Whether council entitled to have regard to statutory duty to promote good race relations when exercising its discretion with respect to trading with a particular company—Race Relations Act 1976, s 71. **R v Lewisham London BC, ex p Shell UK Ltd** [1988] **1** 938, QBD.

Duty to promote good race relations—Misuse of power—Control of open spaces and public health—Whether local authority entitled to have regard to statutory duty to promote good race relations when exercising its discretion with respect to open spaces and public health—Race Relations Act 1976, s 71. **Wheeler v Leicester City Council** [1985] **2** 1106, HL.

Medical Practices Committee—
Appeal to Secretary of State—

Appeal raising complaint against committee of racial discrimination—Medical practitioner appealing against refusal to appoint him to vacancy—Appeal refused by Secretary of State without oral hearing—Whether Secretary of State required to deal with racial allegation as discrete issue—Whether Secretary of State required to hold oral hearing—Whether appellant entitled to disclosure of all material necessary to enable him to present appeal—Race Relations Act 1976, ss 12, 54(2)—National Health Service Act 1977, s 33(5)—National Health Service (General Medical and Pharmaceutical Services) Regulations 1974, reg 12(3). **R v Dept of Health, ex p Gandhi** [1991] **4** 547, QBD.

Non-discrimination notice—
Requirements of notice—

Appeal—Procedure—Race Relations Act 1976, s 59. **Commission for Racial Equality v Amari Plastics Ltd** [1982] **2** 499, CA.

Appeal—Scope of appeal—Whether appeal limited to appeal against reasonableness of requirements of the notice—Whether appellant entitled to challenge all findings of fact on which notice was based—Race Relations Act 1976, s 59. **Commission for Racial Equality v Amari Plastics Ltd** [1982] **2** 499, CA.

Proceedings—
Assessors—

Whether assessors in race relations cases having role in decision-making process—Whether views of such assessors to be disclosed to parties in course of hearing or judgment—Race Relations Act 1976, s 67(4). **Ahmed v Governing Body of the University of Oxford** [2003] **1** 915, CA.

Proceedings in pursuance of a determination by the Race Relations Board—

Declaration—Exclusion of jurisdiction to grant. *See* **Declaration** (Jurisdiction—Hypothetical question—Determination by Race Relations Board on unlawful act of discrimination).

Public order offences. *See* **Public order**.

Race Relations Board—

Investigation of complaint. *See* Investigation of complaint—Race Relations Board, *above*.

Racially aggravated offences. *See* **Criminal law** (Racially or religiously aggravated offences).

Sierra Leone—

Constitution of Sierra Leone. *See* **Sierra Leone** (Constitution—Discrimination—Race).

Unlawful discrimination—
Advertisements and notices—

Indication of intention to do an act of discrimination—Words which can reasonably be understood as indicating intention—Test to be applied—Natural and ordinary meaning of words used—Advertisement of posts for nurses and medical staff in South Africa—Advertisement containing words 'All white patients'—Whether words could reasonably be understood as indicating intention to employ only white nurses—Race Relations Act 1968, s 6(1). **Race Relations Board v Associated Newspapers Group Ltd** [1978] **3** 419, CA.

Damages—

Injury to feelings—Measure of damages. **Alexander v Home Office** [1988] **2** 118, CA.

Discrimination against complainant personally—

Less favourable treatment—Barmaid instructed not to serve coloured people—Barmaid dismissed for refusing to obey instruction and making complaint to industrial tribunal—Whether barmaid discriminated against personally on racial grounds—Whether industrial tribunal had jurisdiction to hear barmaid's complaint—Race Relations Act 1976, ss 1 (1)(a), 30, 60(3)(b). **Zarczynska v Levy** [1979] **1** 814, EAT.

Less favourable treatment—Manager instructed not to admit black people to amusement centre—Manager dismissed for refusing to obey instruction—Whether manager discriminated against personally on racial grounds—Race Relations Act 1976, ss 1(1)(a), 4(2)(c). **Showboat Entertainment Centre Ltd v Owens** [1984] **1** 836, EAT.

RACE RELATIONS (cont)—
  Unlawful discrimination (cont)—
    Discrimination by person concerned with provision of goods etc to a section of the public—
      Club—Associate members of club—Club one of 4,000 working men's clubs belonging to
        union—Members of the clubs eligible to become associates of union—Associates entitled to
        enter any club belonging to union and enjoy substantially all rights of full members—Some clubs
        operating colour bar—Others not operating colour bar—Club refusing to provide facilities and
        services to an associate on ground of colour—Whether club concerned in provision of facilities
        and services to a section of the public—Whether associates 'a section of the public'—Race
        Relations Act 1968, s 2(1). **Dockers' Labour Club and Institute Ltd v Race Relations Board**
        [1974] **3** 592, HL.
      Club—Members' club—Club providing facilities and services to members—Club rejecting
        application for membership on ground of applicant's colour—Conservative club—Adult male
        Conservatives eligible for membership—Club's rules providing for selection of members by
        process of nomination and election—Eligible applicants for membership always admitted in
        practice—No evidence that election process a facade—Whether members of club a 'section of the
        public'—Whether club providing facilities and services to a section of the public—Race Relations
        Act 1968, s 2(1). **Charter v Race Relations Board** [1973] **1** 512, HL.
      Persons seeking to obtain or use goods etc—Children in care of local authority—Local authority in
        exercise of statutory duty placing children with foster parents—Foster parents undertaking to
        care for each child and bring him up as they would a child of their own—Whether children in care
        a 'section of the public'—Whether children persons seeking to obtain or use facilities and services
        provided by foster parents—Whether unlawful for foster parents to refuse to accept coloured
        children—Race Relations Act 1968, s 2(1). **Applin v Race Relations Board** [1974] **2** 73, HL.
    Pleading—
      Particulars before defence. See **Pleading** (Particulars—Particulars before defence—Racial
        discrimination).
    Provision of goods, facilities or services—
      Services—Advice to taxpayer enabling him to claim tax relief to which he is entitled—Taxpayer
        originating from India entitled to tax relief in respect of child—Taxpayers claiming relief normally
        only required to produce short form of birth certificate relating to child—Taxpayer advised and
        required to produce full birth certificate because he came from India—Inland Revenue having
        policy that all persons from Indian sub-continent required to produce full certificate for child
        when first claiming tax relief—Whether unlawful discrimination—Whether Inland Revenue
        providing 'services' to public in disseminating and giving advice on entitlement to claim tax
        relief—Race Relations Act 1976, s 20(1). **Savjani v IRC** [1981] **1** 1121, CA.
      Services—Whether police providing services in assisting or protecting members of the
        public—Whether commissioner of police vicariously liable for actions of officers—Whether
        officers authorised agents of commissioner—Race Relations Act 1976, ss 20, 32(2), 53. **Farah v
        Comr of Police of the Metropolis** [1997] **1** 289, CA.
    Racial group—
      Non-EEC nationals—University fees—College charging non-residents of EEC higher fees than home
        students for reasons of economy—Whether discrimination justifiable irrespective of national
        origin—Whether discrimination unintentional—Whether student entitled to restitution of excess
        or damages—Race Relations Act 1976, ss 1(1)(b), 17(a), 57(3), 72. **Orphanos v Queen Mary
        College** [1985] **2** 233, HL.
    Statutory provision rendering it unlawful for organisation of workers to discriminate against member—
      Society providing advice and assistance to member medical professionals—Whether society an
        organisation of workers—Race Relations Act 1976, ss 11, 78(1). **Sadek v Medical Protection
        Society** [2004] **4** 118, CA.

RACEHORSE
  Sale of right to send mares to stallion—
    Consideration—
      Income tax—Capital or income. See **Income tax** (Capital or income receipts—Sale of
        property—Racehorse—Acquisition of right to send mares to stallion free of charge).

RACIAL DISCRIMINATION
  See **Race relations**.

RADAR
  Use of radar in fog—
    Collision regulations. See **Shipping** (Collision regulations—Use of radar in fog).

RADIO
  Generally. See **Wireless**.
  Government control over broadcasting. See **Broadcasting** (Government control over broadcasting).
  Political advertising—
    Ban by Radio Authority on political advertising—
      Judicial review of Radio Authority decision. See **Judicial review** (Radio Authority—Ban on political
        advertising).

RADIOACTIVE WASTE
  Disposal. See **Public health** (Waste disposal—Radioactive waste).

RADIOGRAPHER
  Negligence—
    Liability of hospital. See **Hospital** (Liability for negligence of members of staff—Radiographer).

RAILWAY
  Accident report—
    Disclosure of documents. See **Disclosure and inspection of documents** (Legal professional
      privilege—Accident report).

RAILWAY (cont)—

Accommodation works—

Accommodation crossing—

Extent of obligations of railway authority—Closing of gates—Provision of whistle-board—Driver of train failing to observe headlights of approaching car—Death of car driver—Liability of railway authority. **Lloyds Bank Ltd v British Transport Commission** [1956] **3** 291, CA.

Extent of obligations of railway authority—No obligation to employ watchman or keeper—Effect of propinquity to level crossing—Railways Clauses Consolidation Act 1845, s 47. **Liddiatt v Great Western Rly Co** [1946] **1** 731, CA.

Extent of obligations of railway authority—Whether engine-driver on approaching accommodation crossing in fog under duty to whistle, reduce speed or take special precautions. **Hazell v British Transport Commission** [1958] **1** 116, QBD; **Kemshead v British Transport Commission** [1958] **1** 119, CA; **Knight v Great Western Rly Co** [1942] **2** 286, KBD.

Duty of railway authority to maintain works—

Bridge over railway line—Owner of land adjoining railway conveying part of his land to railway authority for railway purposes—Railway authority covenanting to make and for ever maintain bridge over railway for owner's convenience—Adjoining land used for purposes of a brewery—Use of adjoining land altered after construction of bridge—Extent of railway authority's duty to maintain bridge thereafter—Whether bridge 'accommodation works'—Whether owner of adjoining land permitted to use bridge for purpose other than that contemplated by conveyance—Railway Clauses Consolidation Act 1845, s 68. **Sampson (TRH) Associates Ltd v British Railways Board** [1983] **1** 257, Ch D.

Fencing separating land acquired for railway from adjoining agricultural land—Railway authority required to maintain fencing 'at all times thereafter'—Railway closed down, track and railway equipment removed and land sold to third party—Fencing not maintained—Cattle straying from adjoining land through fencing onto site of disused railway—Whether railway authority under duty to maintain fencing in perpetuity—Whether cesser of use of land for railway terminating railway authority's obligation to maintain fence—Railways Clauses Consolidation Act 1845, s 68. **Walker (R) & Son (a firm) v British Railways Board (Lancashire CC, third party)** [1984] **2** 249, Ch D.

Gates on crossing over line—Crossing connecting land farmed by plaintiff on both sides of line—Railway line built under private Act passed before Railways Clauses Consolidation Act 1845—Private Act imposing duty on railway board's predecessors to maintain works 'made by them'—New line built after 1850—Crossing made by plaintiff's landlord—Board assuming duty of maintaining crossing—Defective gateway on to crossing—Plaintiff's cattle escaping on to crossing and hit by train—Whether railways board in breach of statutory duty—South Devon Railway Act 1844, s 318—Railways Clauses Consolidation Act 1845, ss 1, 68. **Short v British Railways Board** [1974] **3** 28, QBD.

Persons to whom duty owed—Accommodation bridge—Pedestrian injured by tripping over pot-hole on bridge—British Railways Board not responsible—Duty of local authority to maintain and repair bridge—Railways Clauses Consolidation Act 1845, s 68—Occupiers' Liability Act 1957, ss 1(2)(4), 2(6). **Greenhalgh v British Railways Board** [1969] **2** 114, CA.

Stile at crossing over line—Crossing a public footpath—Railway line built in 1861—No evidence that footpath existing at that time—Footpath in use before 1876—Stile in disrepair—Whether railway undertaker in breach of duty to 'maintain good and sufficient gates and stiles'—Railway Clauses Consolidation Act 1845, s 61. **Thomas v British Railways Board** [1976] **3** 15, CA.

Duty of railway authority to make and maintain fences—

Quality of fence required—Railways Clauses Consolidation Act 1845, s 68. **Cooper v Railway Executive (Southern Region)** [1953] **1** 477, Assizes.

Duty of railway authority to make and maintain such works—

Exception—Adjoining owners accepting compensation in lieu—Rights of occupiers—Railways Clauses Consolidation Act 1845, s 68. **Tudor v Great Western Rly Co** [1947] **2** 768, CA.

Amalgamation—

Compensation to existing officers and servants—

Dismissal of employee of company amalgamated—Dismissal in order to effect reduction in expenses—Evidence that dismissal would have occurred if no amalgamation—Right of employee to compensation—Whether necessary dismissal by reason of amalgamation—Railways Act 1921, Sch III, para (5). **Borman v London and North Eastern Rly Co** [1942] **1** 671, CA.

Employee's position worsened—Compensation from amalgamated company—Claim—Limitation—Date from which time runs—Railways Act 1921, Sch III, paras (3), (4)—Limitation Act 1939, ss 2(1), 27(1), (6). **Pegler v Railway Executive** [1948] **1** 559, HL.

Employee's position worsened—Practice of former company to retain employees after 60—Dismissal at 60 by amalgamated company—Right of employee to compensation—Railways Act 1921, Sch III, paras (3), (4), (5). **Parker and Great Western Rly Co's Arbitration, Re** [1944] **1** 400, CA.

Bridge—

Accommodation work—

Duty of railway authority to maintain bridge. *See* Accommodation works—Duty of railway authority to maintain works—Bridge over railway line, *above*.

British Railways Board—

Powers—

Acts and facilities incidental to provision of railway services—Manufacture for sale—Railway tank wagons—Whether Board had power to manufacture wagons for sale if required for use on Board's railways—Transport Act 1962, ss 3(1), 13(1), 14(1)(I). **Roberts (Charles) & Co Ltd v British Railways Board** [1964] **3** 651, Ch D.

Bye-law—

Validity—

Prohibition of transfer of ticket. **London, Midland and Scottish Rly Co v Greaver** [1936] **3** 333, KBD.

Carriage of animals by rail. *See* **Animal** (Carriage by sea, air, road or rail).

Carriage of goods by rail—

Standard terms and conditions. *See* **Carriers** (Contract—Carriage of goods—Standard terms and conditions of carriage by rail).

Carriage of passengers by rail—

Negligence. *See* **Negligence** (Railway—Duty to passengers and invitees).

RAILWAY (cont)—
    Charges—
        Carriage of merchandise—
            Exceptional rate—Consent of Railway Rates Tribunal—Right of audience before tribunal—Scope of tribunal's inquiry—Proposed exceptional rates likely to compete with coastwise shipping—Right of shippers to appear on application to Railway Rates Tribunal—Railways Act 1921, s 37(1). **Great Western Rly Co v UK Chamber of Shipping** [1937] 2 138, CA.
            Exceptional rate—Consent of Railway Rates Tribunal—Statutory requirements to be fulfilled before exceptional rate 'granted'—Fixed by tribunal—Entered in rate book—Railways Act 1921, s 37. **Great Western Rly Co v Henry R James & Sons Ltd** [1936] 2 660, CA.
    Closure of line—
        Consent of Minister—
            Condition that licence for adequate bus service obtained—Licence granted with effect when 'time of appeal expired'—Appeal lodged—Whether licence effective after appeal time had expired but before appeal decided. **Warwickshire CC v British Railways Board** [1969] 3 631, Ch D.
    Construction of railway—
        Execution of works connected therewith—
            Railway constructed under statutory authority above level of road—Inclined approaches to level of railway—Subsidence of railway and road—Railway restored to original level—Liability of railway authority to restore level of inclined planes—Railways Clauses Consolidation Act 1845, s 16—South Yorkshire, Doncaster and Goole Railway (Deviation and Extension of Elsecar Branch) Act 1850, s 3. **Railway Executive v Yorkshire (West Riding) CC** [1949] 1 836, CA.
    Crossing of roads—
        Bridge carrying road over railway—
            Immediate approaches of bridge—Extent of liability to repair road and embankment—Railways Clauses Consolidation Act 1845, s 46. **Monmouthshire CC v British Transport Commission** [1957] 3 384, CA.
            Repair of roadway—Liability of railway undertaker—Great North of England Railway Act 1837, ss 31, 33, 35. **London and North Eastern Rly Co v Yorkshire (North Riding) CC** [1936] 1 692, HL.
        Level crossing—
            Closing of gates—Statutory duty—Accommodation road converted into public highway—Railways Clauses Consolidation Act 1845, ss 47, 75. **Copps v Payne** [1950] 1 246, KBD.
            Closing of gates—Statutory duty—Gate not securely closed—Accident to engine driver—Accident partly due to negligence of motorist—Motorist liable for compensation to engine driver—Right to recover contribution from railway company—Brighton and Chichester Railway Act 1844, s 274—Law Reform (Married Women and Tortfeasors) Act 1935, s 6(1)(c). **Knapp v Railway Executive** [1949] 2 508, CA.
            Railway undertaker's duty to provide gate-keeper and lodge—Duty at crossing of public carriage road—Crossing originally accommodation crossing—Road taken over by local authority—Construction of additional line under private Act—No gatekeeper or lodge at crossing—Person killed—Whether railway undertaker in breach of statutory duty—Railways Clauses Consolidation Act 1845, s 47—Railways Clauses Act 1863, s 6. **Lloyds Bank Ltd v Railway Executive** [1952] 1 1248, CA.
    Duty of care to passengers. *See* **Negligence** (Railway—Duty to passengers and invitees).
    Easement—
        Level crossing—
            Right of crossing railway line excepted on conveyance of land to railway company—Right appurtenant to farm—Crossing providing only connexion between farm, other land and highway—Whether easement of way a general right for all purposes or limited to domestic and agricultural purposes—Railways Clauses Consolidation Act 1845, s 68. **British Railways Board v Glass** [1964] 3 418, CA.
    Employee—
        Superannuation. *See* Superannuation—Employees of railway company, *below*.
    Fire—
        Damage to crops—
            Loss of deficiency payment—Whether recoverable as damage—Railway Fires Act 1905, s 1, amended by Railway Fires Act (1905) Amendment Act 1923, s 1—Cereals (Deficiency Payments) Order 1955 (SI 1955 No 962). **Langlands (J) (Swanley) Ltd v British Transport Commission** [1956] 2 702, QBD.
    Ground lever working points—
        Safety precautions—
            Statutory duty—Positioning of points—Parallel to the adjacent lines or in such other position and be of such form as to cause as little obstruction as possible—Shunter caused to fall from step of locomotive by lever—Whether breach of statutory duty—Whether lever negligently sited—Contributory negligence—Prevention of Accidents Rules 1902 (S R & O 1902 No 616), r 5. **Hicks v British Transport Commission** [1958] 2 39, CA.
    Level crossing—
        Easement. *See* Easement—Level crossing, *above*.
    Light railway—
        Amending order. *See* **Light railway** (Amending order).
    Look-out—
        Statutory duty to appoint in circumstances in which danger is likely to arise—
            Ganger and two men sent to do three-man job—Line on which no train scheduled but on which engine or diverted train might come at any time—Ganger told no train scheduled—Work proving more difficult than anticipated and ganger having to stand near live line—Ganger did not send for look-out—Ganger struck by train diverted on to line—Breach of statutory duty by railway authority—Whether sole responsibility of ganger—Prevention of Accidents Rules 1902 (SR & O 1922 No 696), r 9. **Keaney v British Railways Board** [1968] 2 532, CA.
        Work for the purpose of relaying or repairing permanent way—
            Death of signal fitter on line—Signal fitter engaged on routine oiling of signal apparatus on permanent way—Whether oiling 'repairing the permanent way'—Railway Employment (Prevention of Accidents) Act 1900, s 1(1), schedule, cl 12—Prevention of Accidents Rules 1902 (SR & O 1902 No 616), r 9. **London and North Eastern Rly Co v Berriman** [1946] 1 255, HL.

RAILWAY (cont)—

Look-out (cont)—

Work for the purpose of relaying or repairing permanent way (cont)—

Injury to employee on line—Contributory negligence of workman—Whether circumstances in which 'danger is likely to arise'—Railway Employment (Prevention of Accidents) Act 1900, Sch, cl 12—Prevention of Accidents Rules 1902 (SR & O 1902 No 616), r 9. **Hutchinson v London and North Eastern Rly Co** [1942] **1** 330, CA.

Lengthmen engaged on tightening nose bolts on line—Work involving use of 'T' spanner—Whether 'danger ... likely to arise'—Railway Employment (Prevention of Accidents) Act 1900, s 1(1), Sch, cl 12—Prevention of Accidents Rules 1902 (SR & O 1902 No 616), r 9. **Reilly v British Transport Commission** [1956] **3** 857, QBD.

Provision of one look-out insufficient—Prevention of Accidents Rules 1902 (SR & O 1902 No 616), r 9. **Dyer v Southern Rly Co** [1948] **1** 516, KBD.

Re-layer inspecting line to determine lengths of metals later required for re-laying—Whether working 'for the purpose of relaying or repairing line'—Railway Employment (Prevention of Accidents) Act 1900, s 1(1), Sch, cl 12—Prevention of Accidents Rules 1902 (SR & O 1902 No 616), r 9. **Judson v British Transport Commission** [1954] **1** 624, CA.

Sub-ganger lengthman engaged on tightening loose fish-plates on goods line—Train going at slow speed—Whether 'danger ... likely to arise'—Prevention of Accidents Rules 1902 (S R & O 1902 No 616), r 9. **Cade v British Transport Commission** [1958] **2** 615, HL.

Mines—

Mines lying near railway—

Compensation for not working mines—Whether sum deductible for income tax and profits tax if profits had been earned—Railway Clauses Consolidation Act 1845, s 78 (as substituted by Mines (Working Facilities and Support) Act 1923, s 15). **McGhie (Thomas) & Sons Ltd v British Transport Commission** [1962] **2** 646, QBD.

Railway lines above ground at mines. *See* **Mine** (Railway lines above ground at mines).

Negligence—

Duty to take care. *See* **Negligence** (Duty to take care—Railway).

Generally. *See* **Negligence** (Railway).

Rescuer—

Duty to rescuer. *See* **Negligence** (Duty to take care—Rescuer—Railway).

Occupier's liability—

Carriage of passengers—

Safety of premises. *See* **Occupier's liability** (Carriage of passengers—Safety of premises).

Offence—

Travelling on railway with intent to avoid payment of fare—

Intent to avoid payment of fare of co-passenger—Whether co-passenger in process of 'travelling' when at ticket barrier after alighting from train—London Transport Board Bye-laws No 8(1) made under Transport Act 1962, s 67. **Murphy v Verati** [1967] **1** 861, QBD.

Intent to avoid payment of fare—Degree of intention required—Intention of passenger to pay only part of fare at time of travel—Intention of passenger to pay balance at later date if requested to do so—Whether 'intending to avoid payment of fare'—Whether intention permanently to avoid payment necessary—Regulation of Railways Act 1889, s 5(3)(a). **Corbyn v Saunders** [1978] **2** 697, QBD.

Time for formation of intent—Regulation of Railways Act 1889, s 5(3)(a). **Bremme v Dubery** [1964] **1** 193, QBD.

Use of partly used non-transferable ticket issued to another—Whether necessary to prove intent to defraud—Regulation of Railways Act 1889, s 5(3)(a). **Browning v Floyd** [1946] **2** 367, KBD.

Unlawful act endangering safety of person conveyed on a railway—

Danger—Whether actual danger must be established—Offences against the Person Act 1861, s 34. **R v Pearce** [1966] **3** 618, CA.

Passengers—

Duty of care to. *See* **Negligence** (Railway—Duty to passengers and invitees).

Occupier's liability—

Safety of passengers. *See* **Occupier's liability** (Carriage of passengers—Safety of premises).

Platform—

Whether 'public place' within meaning of Public Order Act 1936. *See* **Public order** (Public place—Offensive conduct conducive to breaches of peace—Disturbance on railway station platform).

Premises—

Safety of employees—

Breach of statutory duty. *See* **Employment** (Duty of master—Offices, shops and railway premises).

Public authority—

Private person performing functions of public nature. *See* **Human rights** (Public authority—Private person performing functions of public nature).

Railway and Canal Commission—

Jurisdiction—

Application for ancillary rights for working of a quarry. *See* **Mine** (Application for ancillary rights).

Coal—Removal of restrictions on working of coal. *See* **Coal mining** (Restrictions on working coal—Removal of restrictions—Jurisdiction—Railway and Canal Commission).

Diversion of highway. *See* **Highway** (Diversion—Order—Jurisdiction—Railway and Canal Commission).

Review of order—

Application—Time for application—Railway and Canal Traffic Act 1888, s 18(2)—Rules of Procedure 1924, r 69. **Railways (Valuation for Rating) Act 1930, Re, Re application by the Railway Assessment Authority** [1936] **2** 316, Ry, Can Com.

Rating—

Railway assessment authority—

Jurisdiction—Valuation roll—Estimated relative values—Adjustment—Time for objection expired—Railways (Valuation for Rating) Act 1930. **R v Railway Assessment Authority, ex p Southampton Corp** [1937] **1** 431, KBD.

RAILWAY (cont)—
Rating (cont)—
Railway hereditament—
Amendment of valuation list—Proposal for amendment of list—Railway valuation roll—Hereditament shown in railway valuation roll as railway hereditament—Meaning of 'railway valuation roll'—Rating and Valuation Act 1925, s 37—Railways (Valuation for Rating) Act 1930. **Worthing Corp v Southern Rly Co** [1943] **2** 331, HL.
Exclusion of premises occupied as a dwelling-house, hotel or place of public refreshment—Hostel and canteen for railway staff—Whether 'occupied as dwelling-house or hotel'—Railways (Valuation for Rating) Act 1930, s 1(3). **Railway Assessment Authority v Great Western Rly Co** [1947] **2** 794, HL.
Exclusion of premises so let out as to be capable of separate assessment—Premises let at railway stations—Whether capable of separate assessment—Railways (Valuation for Rating) Act 1930, s 1(3). **Westminster City Council v Southern Rly Co** [1936] **2** 322, HL.
Meaning and extent of term—Bridge constructed under statutory authority—Two decks—Upper deck carrying railway—Lower deck carrying roadway—Whether lower deck 'railway hereditament'—Railways (Valuation for Rating) Act 1930, s 1(3). **Newcastle-upon-Tyne Corp v Railway Assessment Authority** [1936] **3** 616, HL.
Occupancy by Crown—Inclusion in supplemental list as so occupied—Resumption of occupancy of railway company—Inclusion in provisional list after passing of Local Government Act 1948, and the coming into force of provisions exempting railway hereditaments from rating—Local Government Act 1948, ss 85, 89(5). **R v St Pancras Borough Assessment Committee, ex p Railway Executive** [1949] **2** 371, CA.
Principles of assessment—Fair and just division of the net receipts as between landlord and tenant—Railways (Valuation for Rating) Act 1930, s 4. **Railway Assessment Authority v Southern Rly Co** [1936] **1** 26, HL.
Repair of privately owned wagons on railway company's property—
Walking pass to repairing company's employees to enter on railway company's property—
Condition incorporated on pass relieving railway company of responsibility for injury by accident—No evidence of actual knowledge of condition—Reasonable notice of condition—Onus of proof. **Henson v London and North Eastern Rly Co** [1946] **1** 653, CA.
Report—
Accident report—
Disclosure of documents. *See* **Disclosure and inspection of documents** (Legal professional privilege—Accident report).
Retirement benefits—
Employees of railway company—
Discrimination against a woman. *See* **Employment** (Discrimination against a woman—Provision in relation to retirement).
Rolling stock—
Lease—
Proper law. *See* **Conflict of laws** (Contract—Proper law of contract—Lease of railway rolling stock).
Safe system of working. *See* **Safe system of working** (Safe place of work—Narrow walkway between rail tracks).
Siding—
Enclosed yard—
Vagrancy. *See* **Criminal law** (Vagrancy—Found in enclosed premises for an unlawful purpose—Enclosed area—Area—Railway siding).
Superannuation—
Employees of railway company—
Contributory scheme—Company contribution equal amount—Division of fund into classes—Contributions and pensions calculated by reference to annual wages—War bonus to be included for the purposes of contributions and pensions—Overtime and Sunday pay to be disregarded—Members' duty to make up deficiency in wages before participating in fund. **Picken v Bruce** [1945] **1** 73, CA.
Value added tax—
Zero-rating—
Transport of passengers—Student travel scheme—Sale of identity card for purpose of scheme. *See* **Value added tax** (Zero-rating—Transport of passengers—Supply of travel concession voucher—Student travel scheme—Sale of identity card for purpose of scheme—British Railways Board).

RAPE
Attempted rape—
Acts constituting offence. *See* **Criminal law** (Attempt—Acts preparatory to offence—Acts constituting offence—Rape—Attempted rape).
Custodial sentence—
Whether attempted rape a 'sexual offence' or a 'violent offence'. *See* **Sentence** (Custodial sentence—Sexual offence—Violent offence—Attempted rape).
Damages for rape. *See* **Trespass to the person** (Damages—General damages—Damages for rape and sexual assault).
Generally. *See* **Criminal law** (Rape).

RATE OF EXCHANGE
Currency. *See* **Money** (Currency—Rate of exchange).
Date at which calculated. *See* **Money** (Currency—Date at which rate of exchange calculated).

RATE SUPPORT GRANT
See **Rates** (Rate support grant).

RATES
Agricultural buildings—
Exemption from rates. *See* Exemption—Agricultural buildings, *below.*

RATES (cont)—
Appeal—
  Appeal to Crown Court—
    Jurisdiction—Refusal by rating authority to remit or reduce rates—Whether ratepayer entitled to appeal to Crown Court—General Rate Act 1967, s 7(1)(c). **Investors in Industry Commercial Properties Ltd v Norwich City Council** [1986] **2** 193, HL.
    Mode of appeal—Whether appeal by way of judicial review—General Rate Act 1967, s 7. **R v Rochdale Metropolitan BC, ex p Cromer Ring Mill Ltd** [1982] **3** 761, QBD.
  Lands Tribunal. *See* Lands Tribunal—Appeal, *below.*
  Local valuation court. *See* Local valuation court—Appeal, *below.*
  Practice—
    Appeal by case stated from tribunal—Form of order of Court of Appeal—RSC. Ord 58A, r 3(4)(5). **National Pig Progeny Testing Board v Greenall** [1960] **3** 556, CA.
Assessment—
  Assessment committee. *See* Assessment committee, *below.*
  Generally. *See* Valuation, *below.*
Assessment committee—
  Clerk—
    Appointment of officer of county borough council—Rating and Valuation Act 1925, s 55. **R v Salford Assessment Committee** [1937] **2** 98, CA.
  Meetings—
    Right of exclusion—County valuation committee officer—Rating and Valuation Act 1925, ss 17, 18. **Middlesex County Valuation Committee v West Middlesex Assessment Area Assessment Committee** [1937] **1** 403, CA.
  Powers and duties of committee—
    Objection to proposed assessment—Industrial property not previously rated—'Proposal' for gross assessment agreed between owners and the rating authority—Assessment committee fixing valuation in excess of 'proposal' in the absence of owners—Proceedings of assessment irregular—Application for order of certiorari—Committee bound to act judicially—Rating and Valuation Act 1925, ss 27, 37. **R v Newmarket Assessment Committee, ex p Allen Newport Ltd** [1945] **2** 371, KBD.
    Objection to proposed assessment—Judicial discretion of assessment committee—Report of competent valuer not seen by parties concerned—Committee's duty to make report known to parties—Rating and Valuation Act 1925, s 38, Sch IV, Part III, para 3. **R v Westminster Assessment Committee, ex p Grosvenor House (Park Lane) Ltd** [1940] **4** 132, CA.
  Procedure—
    Inspection of property—Appeal to quarter sessions—Jurisdiction of quarter sessions—Rating and Valuation Act 1925, ss 18(3), 31(1), (4). **Hulme v Bucklow Area Assessment Committee** [1940] **3** 79, KBD.
Building occupied in parts—
  Occupation. *See* Rateable occupation—Building occupied in parts, *below.*
Charges for levying distress. *See* Distress for rates—Charges for levying distress, *below.*
Charitable and other organisations—
  Amount of rates chargeable—
    Nil amount charged prior to the coming into force of new valuation list—Occupier formerly wholly exempt from rates but now becoming chargeable—Whether entitled to limitation of rates to nil—Rating and Valuation (Miscellaneous Provisions) Act 1955, s 8(2)(a). **Horace Plunkett Foundation v St Pancras BC** [1958] **1** 122, QBD.
  Hereditament consisting of playing field occupied for purposes of club—
    Friendly society's sports ground—Licence to use sports ground at specified times granted by occupier to club—Whether sports ground occupied for the purposes of the club—Rating and Valuation (Miscellaneous Provisions) Act 1955, s 8(1)(c), (2). **Parker v Ealing (Borough of)** [1961] **1** 147, Ch D.
  Hereditament occupied and used for purposes of organisation not established or conducted for profit—
    Established or conducted for profit—Whether conducted for profit—Whether charitable organisation, though not established for profit, was conducted for profit by reason of terms of trust—Rating and Valuation (Miscellaneous Provisions) Act 1955, s 8(1)(a). **Guinness Trust (London Fund) v West Ham Corp** [1959] **1** 482, CA.
    Main objects of organisation concerned with advancement of social welfare—Union of working men's clubs—Finding by quarter sessions what main objects were—Business of general advisers—Conclusiveness—Not concerned with the advancement of social welfare—Objects including to carry on the business of publishers, traders, manufacturers, etc—Whether established or conducted for profit—Rating and Valuation (Miscellaneous Provisions) Act 1955, s 8(1)(a). **Working Men's Club and Institute Union Ltd v Swansea Corp** [1959] **3** 769, CA.
    Zoo—Zoological society incorporated as company limited by guarantee—Main objects charitable—Organisation concerned with advancement of education—Whether organisation, though not established for profit, was conducted for profit—Rating and Valuation (Miscellaneous Provisions) Act 1955, s 8(1)(a), (2). **North of England Zoological Society v Chester RDC** [1959] **3** 116, CA.
  Hereditament occupied by charity—
    Armed forces' dependants charity—Charity owned seventy-eight flats in which dependants of deceased officers resided—Whether flats occupied by dependants or by charity—Whether charity entitled to rating relief—Rating and Valuation Act 1961, s 11(1)(a). **Soldiers', Sailors' and Airmen's Families Association v Merton Corp** [1966] **3** 780, CA.
    School—Charitable body—Houses occupied by masters on school premises rent free—Occupation by master not essential for efficient performance of duty but associated with extra-curricular activities—Occupation by vice-principal essential for purpose of his duties—Occupation under licence—Nature of obligation to reside—Whether express or implied term—Whether occupation exclusively charitable for purposes of exemption from rates—Valuation (Ireland) Amendment Act 1854, s 2—Valuation (Ireland) Act 1852, s 16. **Northern Ireland Comr of Valuation v Fermanagh Protestant Board of Education** [1969] **3** 352, HL.

RATES (cont)—
  Charitable and other organisations (cont)—
    Hereditament occupied for purposes of non-profit making organisation—
      Notice terminating limitation of rates chargeable—When notice may be given—Notice given before expiration of first year of new valuation list but after rate for second had been made—Rating and Valuation (Miscellaneous Provisions) Act 1955, s 8(2), (3). **Westminster City Council v University of London King's College** [1958] **3** 25, Ch D.
      Notice terminating limitation of rates chargeable—When notice may be given—Rating and Valuation (Miscellaneous Provisions) Act 1955, s 8(3). **St Pancras BC v University of London** [1957] **3** 673, CA.
    Hereditament occupied for purposes of organisation—
      Trade union war memorial convalescent home vested in trustees under trust deeds—Home conducted for benefit of union members and their wives—Trustees under strict union control—Whether trustees or union the organisation for whose purposes the home was occupied—Rating and Valuation (Miscellaneous Provisions) Act 1955, s 8(1)(a). **Isaacs v Market Bosworth RDC** [1960] **1** 433, QBD.
    Hereditament occupied for purposes of organisation whose main objects charitable—
      Royal College of Nursing—Organisation to promote the 'advance of nursing as a profession'—Rating and Valuation (Miscellaneous Provisions) Act 1955, s 8(1)(a). **Royal College of Nursing v St Marylebone Corp** [1959] **3** 663, CA.
    Hereditament occupied for purposes of organisation whose main objects concerned with advancement of education—
      Chartered Insurance Institute—Whether organisation for advancement of education or for enabling persons to practise insurance to greater advantage—Rating and Valuation (Miscellaneous Provisions) Act 1955, s 8(1). **Chartered Insurance Institute v London Corp** [1957] **2** 638, QBD.
    Hereditament occupied for purposes of organisation whose main objects concerned with advancement of religion—
      Freemasonry—Organisation mainly concerned with administrative work relating to Freemasonry—Whether main object of organisation concerned with advancement of religion—Whether objects of Freemasonry concerned with the advancement of religion—Rating and Valuation (Miscellaneous Provisions) Act 1955, s 8(1). **United Grand Lodge of Ancient Free and Accepted Masons of England v Holborn BC** [1957] **3** 281, QBD.
    Hereditament occupied for purposes of organisation whose main objects concerned with advancement of religion, education or social welfare—
      Theosophical Society of England—Rating and Valuation (Miscellaneous Provisions) Act 1955, s 8(1)(a). **Berry v St Marylebone Corp** [1957] **3** 677, CA.
    Hereditament occupied for purposes of organisation whose main objects concerned with advancement of social welfare—
      Ex-services association—Main object to promote comradeship between and improve conditions and welfare of all ranks of HM Forces—Organisation for the advancement of social welfare—Ascertainment of main object of organisation having written constitution—Rating and Valuation (Miscellaneous Provisions) Act 1955, s 8(1)(a). **Victory (Ex-Services) Association Ltd v Paddington BC** [1960] **1** 498, QBD.
      Friendly society's sports ground—Society not established or conducted for profit—Society's benefits payable to non-members—Whether an organisation whose main objects were concerned with the advancement of social welfare—Rating and Valuation (Miscellaneous Provisions) Act 1955, s 8(1)(a), (2). **Independent Order of Odd Fellows Manchester Unity Friendly Society v Manchester Corp** [1958] **3** 378, CA.
      Friendly society's sports ground—Whether society non-profit making organisation—Whether 'main objects are charitable or are otherwise concerned with the advancement of social welfare'—Rating and Valuation (Miscellaneous Provisions) Act 1955, s 8(1)(a). **National Deposit Friendly Society (Trustees) v Skegness UDC** [1958] **2** 601, HL.
      General Nursing Council for England and Wales—Organisation concerned with advancement of social welfare—Rating and Valuation (Miscellaneous Provisions) Act 1955, s 8(1)(a). **General Nursing Council for England and Wales v St Marylebone Corp** [1959] **1** 325, HL.
      Holiday camp for Derbyshire miners, their dependants and invitees—Camp established from compulsory contributions levied under statute—Accommodation and board at camp provided at cost—All Derbyshire miners employed by National Coal Board—Whether camp concerned with the advancement of 'social welfare'—Rating and Valuation (Miscellaneous Provisions) Act 1955, s 8(1). **Skegness UDC v Derbyshire Miners' Welfare Committee** [1959] **2** 258, HL.
      Industrial Orthopaedic Society—Society occupiers of hospital and other medical units—Objects of society to provide free medical treatment to its members—Membership of 400,000 nearly all of whom were industrial workers contributing minimum of 3d a week—Whether society concerned with advancement of social welfare—Rating and Valuation (Miscellaneous Provisions) Act 1955, s 8(1). **Waterson v Hendon BC** [1959] **2** 760, QBD.
  Hereditament wholly or mainly used for charitable purposes—
    Cremation society—Non-profit making company incorporated for promotion of cremation—Fees charged, but not with a view to profit—No religious basis—Whether society established for charitable purposes only—Local Government (Financial Provisions, etc) (Scotland) Act 1962, s 4(2), (10). **Scottish Burial Reform and Cremation Society Ltd v Glasgow City Corp** [1967] **3** 215, HL.
    Educational charity—Hereditaments used for administration and management of property of charity—Whether used for charitable purposes—Rating and Valuation Act 1961, s 11(1). **Aldous v Southwark Corp** [1968] **3** 498, CA.
    Fund raising activities—Charity for relief of poverty—Shops occupied by charity—Shops used for reception and sorting of articles given to charity and for subsequent sale—Whether shops 'used for charitable purposes'—General Rate Act 1967, s 40(1). **Oxfam v City of Birmingham DC** [1975] **2** 289, HL.

RATES (cont)—
  Charitable and other organisations (cont)—
    Hereditament wholly or mainly used for charitable purposes (cont)—
      Holiday centre for Derbyshire miners, their wives and families—Provision enabling trustees to admit members of public to surplus accommodation—Admission of public necessary to meet overheads and keep charges to an amount enabling qualified persons to attend and thus served purpose of charity—Registered charity—Whether hereditament 'wholly or mainly used for charitable purposes'—Charities Act 1960, s 5(1)—Rating and Valuation Act 1961, s 11(1). **Wynn v Skegness UDC** [1966] **3** 336, Ch D.
    Loss of right to relief—
      Change of identity—Charitable organisation occupying hereditament entitled to limitation of rates—Extensions and new building increasing floor area four times—Boundaries of unit of assessment unaltered—Whether hereditament lost identity owing to extensions of buildings—Rating and Valuation (Miscellaneous Provisions) Act 1955, s 8(2)—Rating and Valuation Act 1925, s 68(1). **Institute of Orthopaedics v Harrow Corp** [1962] **3** 964, Ch D.
    Right to claim relief—
      Full amount of rates without claiming relief paid in first year of new valuation list—Whether ratepayer loses right to claim relief in subsequent years—Rating and Valuation (Miscellaneous Provisions) Act 1955, s 8(2). **Waterson v Hendon BC** [1959] **2** 760, QBD.
  Completion notice—
    Validity of service—
      Indirect service—Local authority handing completion notice to building manager's receptionist—Receptionist emailing notice to building owner—Whether notice validly served where not directly delivered to owner—Whether notice validly served where received in electronic form—Local Government Finance Act 1988, Sch 4A—Electronic Communications Act 2000. **UKI (Kingsway) Ltd v Westminster City Council** [2019] **2** 421, SC.
  De-rating of freight transport hereditament—
    Hereditament occupied and used for dock purposes as part of dock undertaking—
      Undertaking whereof substantial volume of business concerned with unshipping of merchandise not intended for use of undertakers—Installations for unshipping and storing oil—Ratepayer selling agent for oil companies—Use of hereditament for dock purposes—Occupation and use of hereditament as part of a dock undertaking—Oil 'intended for the use of' the ratepayer—Rating and Valuation (Apportionment) Act 1928, s 5(1)(c), (3), s 6(3)(b). **Shell-Mex and BP Ltd v Clayton (Valuation Officer)** [1956] **3** 185, HL.
      Undertaking whereof substantial volume of business concerned with unshipping of merchandise not intended for use of undertakers—Wharf—Whether premises forming part of dock undertaking—Rating and Valuation (Apportionment) Act 1928, s 5(3). **Southern Essex Assessment Committee v Betty & Tom Ltd** [1937] **3** 441, CA.
  De-rating of industrial hereditaments—
    Apportionment of net annual value—
      Site used for gravel pit and for rubbish tip—Factory and Workshop Act 1901, s 149(4)—Rating and Valuation (Apportionment) Act 1928, s 4(2). **Ham River Grit Co Ltd v Richmond Rating Authority** [1949] **1** 286, KBD.
    Exclusion from relief of certain hereditaments. *See* Exclusion from relief of certain hereditaments occupied and used as factory or workshop, *below.*
    Hereditament occupied and used as factory or workshop. *See* Hereditament occupied and used as factory or workshop, *below.*
  Deduction—
    Tithe and tithe rentcharge. *See* **Tithe and tithe rentcharge** (Extinguishment—Compensation—Deduction in respect of rates).
  Distress for rates—
    Abatement of proceedings on payment of rates and costs—
      Cost of person for his attendance to make levy—Rates tendered before levy made—Whether costs of levy recoverable—Whether 'cost of ... person for his attendance to make levy' including costs payable if levy had been made—General Rate Act 1967, ss 101(1), 105(2). **Brintons Ltd v Wyre Forest DC** [1977] **1** 836, QBD.
      Whether debtor entitled to halt distress process during seizure by appropriate tender or payment—Non-Domestic Rating (Collection and Enforcement) (Local Lists) Regulations 1989, reg 14, Sch 3. **Wilson v South Kesteven DC** [2000] **4** 577, CA.
    Appeal—
      Appeal to Court of Appeal—Appeal from Divisional Court. *See* **Court of Appeal** (Jurisdiction—Appeal from Divisional Court—Distress for rates).
    Application for warrant—
      Defence of non-occupation of premises—Jurisdiction of magistrates to entertain defence. *See* **Magistrates** (Jurisdiction—Warrant for distress for non-payment of rates).
      Defence—Allegation that assessment increased on defective proposal. **East Barnet UDC v Allen Trenarry (Barnet) Ltd** [1948] **2** 583, KBD.
      Jurisdiction—Extent of jurisdiction—Defence by ratepayers' claiming partial relief from rate—No appeal by ratepayers to quarter sessions against the rate—Nothing due if ratepayers entitled to relief—Rating and Valuation (Miscellaneous Provisions) Act 1955, s 8(1)(c), (2). **Evans v Brook** [1959] **2** 399, QBD.
      Limitation period—Application more than six years after demand—Statutory bar to proceedings—Limitation Act 1939, ss 2(1)(d), 31(1). **China v Harrow UDC** [1953] **2** 1296, QBD.
    Charges for levying distress—
      Levying distress—Seizure of goods necessary—Bailiff attending premises to make levy—Rates paid before bailiff started on process of selecting goods for levy—Bailiff neither stating that goods were seized nor acting in manner amounting to taking possession of goods—Whether levying of a distress—Whether cost of levying distress recoverable by rating authority—Distress for Rates Order 1972 (SI 1972 No 820), para 3(1)(ii). **Brintons Ltd v Wyre Forest DC** [1977] **1** 836, QBD.
    Company—
      Generally. *See* **Company** (Distress—Rates).

RATES (cont)—
  Distress for rates (cont)—
    Imprisonment in default of distress—
      Warrant of commitment to prison—Inquiry as to means before issue of warrant of commitment—Rating authority applying for warrant of commitment—Magistrates inquiring into means of defaulting ratepayer and postponing issue of warrant subject to payment of arrears by instalments—Defaulting ratepayer not complying with condition as to payment—Magistrates issuing warrant without making further inquiry whether ratepayer's failure to pay instalments was due to wilful refusal or culpable neglect—Whether issue of warrant unlawful—General Rate Act 1967, s 103(1)(a). **R v Poole Justices, ex p Fleet** [1983] **2** 897, QBD.
    Issue of warrant—
      Persons against whom warrant may issue—Person entitled to receive the rent—Rent collected by rent collector—Warrant issued against rent collector—Middlesex County Council (General Powers) Act 1938, s 118(2). **Adams v Southall Rating Authority** [1943] **1** 491, KBD.
      Time for issue—Rating period not expired—Whether warrant could issue before period expired—Poor Relief Act 1601, s 2. **Thomson v Beckenham Rating Authority** [1947] **2** 274, KBD.
    Occupier of part of premises—Liability for whole rate. *See* Rateable occupation—Non-occupation of part of premises—Liability for rates for whole premises, *below*.
    Priority—
      Distress for rent and distress for rates. *See* **Distress** (Priority—Distress for rent and distress for rates).
    Rent in arrear—
      Claim by landlord for rent out of proceeds of distress—Whether distress an execution—Landlord and Tenant Act 1709, s 1. **Potts v Hickman** [1940] **4** 491, HL.
  Drainage rates. *See* **Land drainage** (Drainage rates).
  Exclusion from relief of certain hereditaments occupied and used as factory or workshop—
    Factory or workshop occupied and used for purposes of retail shop—
      Canteen situated apart from factory but exclusively for use of employees—Whether part of industrial hereditament—Rating and Valuation (Apportionment) Act 1928, s 3. **Simmonds Aerocessories (Western) Ltd v Assessment Committee** [1944] **1** 264, KBD.
    Factory or workshop primarily occupied and used for maintenance of occupier's road vehicles—
      Distinguished from reconditioning—Rating and Valuation (Apportionment) Act 1928, s 3(1), (2). **London Transport Executive v Betts (Valuation Officer)** [1958] **2** 636, HL.
      Purposes of user—Primary and substantial purposes—Reconditioning of parts of vehicles—Maintenance of occupier's road vehicles—Whether hereditament as a whole an industrial hereditament—Apportionment between industrial and other use—Rating and Valuation (Apportionment) Act 1928, ss 3(2)(b), 4. **East Yorkshire Motor Services Ltd v Clayton (Valuation Officer)** [1961] **3** 758, CA.
    Factory or workshop primarily occupied and used for non-factory or workshop purposes—
      Building close to but not attached to main factory—'Contiguous'—Building used for storage and distribution—Whether part of industrial hereditament—Rating and Valuation (Apportionment) Act 1928, s 3(1), (3). **Jobling (James A) & Co Ltd v Sunderland County Borough Assessment Committee** [1944] **1** 500, CA.
      Research establishment—Use for making and testing prototypes and parts of vehicles—Factory and Workshop Act 1901, s 149—Rating and Valuation (Apportionment) Act 1928, s 3(1) proviso(f). **Ferguson (Harry) Research Ltd v Warwick RDC** [1960] **2** 283, CA.
    Factory or workshop primarily occupied and used for purposes of retail shop—
      Canteen solely for use of employees—Whether part of industrial hereditament—Factory and Workshop Act 1901, s 149(4)—Rating and Valuation (Apportionment) Act 1928, s 3. **London Co-op Society Ltd v Southern Essex Assessment Committee** [1941] **3** 252, KBD.
      Cleaners and dyers—Work of the same nature as repair work—Articles received from and delivered to customers themselves—Whether 'retail shop'—Rating and Valuation (Apportionment) Act 1928, s 3. **Ritz Cleaners Ltd v West Middlesex Assessment Committee** [1937] **2** 368, CA.
      Laundry—Accommodation for public resort—Customers leaving articles in basket and collecting at office—Customers leaving and collecting articles on slab—Delivery by van—Whether laundry used primarily for purposes of retail shop—Rating and Valuation (Apportionment) Act 1928, s 3(1), (4). **Almond (Valuation Officer) v Heathfield Laundry (Birmingham) Ltd** [1960] **3** 700, CA.
      Motor service depot—Partly used as retail shop—Work done to the order of insurance companies—Whether retail repair work—Rating and Valuation (Apportionment) Act 1928, s 3(1), (4). **Meriden RDC v Standard Motor Co Ltd** [1957] **3** 222, CA.
      Printing works with shop—Whether excluded from relief—Rating and Valuation (Apportionment) Act 1928, s 3(1). **McGowan v Osgoldcross Area Assessment Committee, West Riding of Yorkshire** [1936] **2** 170, KBD.
      Sawmills, timberyard and office—Rating and Valuation (Apportionment) Act 1928, s 3(1), (4). **Dolton Bournes & Dolton Ltd v Osmond (Valuation Officer)** [1955] **2** 258, CA.
  Exemption—
    Agricultural buildings—
      Buildings occupied together with agricultural land and used solely in connection with agricultural operations thereon. *See* Exemption—Buildings occupied together with agricultural land and used solely in connection with agricultural operations thereon, *below*.
      Buildings used for keeping and breeding of livestock—Livestock—Thoroughbred racehorses—Whether thoroughbred horses 'livestock'—Rating Act 1971, s 2(1)(a). **Hemens (Valuation Officer) v Whitsbury Farm and Stud Ltd** [1988] **1** 72, HL.
      Buildings used for keeping or breeding of livestock—Livestock—Fish bred and kept in tanks for sale as food—Whether fish raised for food constituting livestock—General Rate Act 1967, s 26—Rating Act 1971, ss 1(3), 2(1)(a). **Cresswell (Valuation Officer) v BOC Ltd** [1980] **3** 443, CA.
      Buildings used for keeping or breeding of livestock—Poultry processing factory—Building occupied by 'persons' who are the 'occupiers' qualifying for rating relief—Whether 'persons' and 'occupiers' in plural also including singular—Whether a limited company qualifying for relief—General Rate Act 1967, s 26(4)(b)(i)—Rating Act 1971, s 4(2)(b)(ii). **Prior (Valuation Officer) v Sovereign Chicken Ltd** [1984] **2** 289, CA.

RATES (cont)—
  Exemption (cont)—
    Agricultural land—
      Exception—Land kept or preserved mainly or exclusively for purposes of sport or recreation—Land partly used for training racehorses—Whether separately rateable hereditament—Rating and Valuation (Apportionment) Act 1928, s 2. **Jarvis v Cambridgeshire Rural Assessment Area Assessment Committee** [1938] **4** 186, KBD.

      Exception—Land used as racecourse—Arable land used once a year as a racecourse—Whether user as a racecourse de minimis—Whether land qualifying for agricultural exemption from rating—General Rate Act 1967, s 26(3). **Hayes (Valuation Officer) v Loyd** [1985] **2** 313, HL.

      Exception—Land used as racecourse—Land partly used for purposes of motor cycle track racing but otherwise used as pasture land—Whether separately rateable hereditament—Rating and Valuation (Apportionment) Act 1928, s 2(2). **Wimborne and Cranborne RDC v East Dorset Assessment Committee** [1940] **3** 201, CA.

      Land used as arable meadow or pasture ground only—Field used for grazing and turf cutting—Whether exempt—Rating and Valuation (Apportionment) Act 1928, s 2(2)—Local Government Act 1929, s 67(1). **Meriden and Solihull Rating Authority v Tyacke** [1950] **1** 939, KBD.

      Nursery grounds—Area used for turf cutting—Whether 'nursery grounds'—Rating and Valuation (Apportionment) Act 1928, s 2(2)—Local Government Act 1929, s 67(1). **Butser Turf and Timber Co Ltd v Petersfield Rating Authority** [1950] **1** 288, KBD.

    Buildings occupied together with agricultural land and used solely in connection with agricultural operations thereon—
      Agricultural operations thereon—Dairy—Treatment of milk from neighbouring farm—Dairy buildings not entitled to exemption—Rating and Valuation (Apportionment) Act 1928, s 2(2). **Perrins v Draper** [1953] **2** 863, CA.

      Agricultural operations thereon—Pig progeny testing station—Ploughing of land unconnected with buildings—Whether buildings exempt—Rating and Valuation (Apportionment) Act 1928, s 2(2). **National Pig Progeny Testing Board v Greenall** [1960] **3** 556, CA.

      Buildings occupied together with buildings used for keeping and breeding of livestock—Occupied together with—Provender mill and poultry processing factory—Mill and factory providing feed and processing plant for broiler houses on 67 farms situated up to 120 miles away—Whether mill and factory 'occupied together with' broiler houses on farms—Whether distance relevant factor—General Rate Act 1967, s 26(1)—Rating Act 1971, ss 1(1), 2(1)(b). **Farmer (Valuation Officer) v Buxted Poultry Ltd** [1993] **1** 117, HL.

      Occupied together with agricultural land—Rating and Valuation (Apportionment) Act 1928, s 2(2). **Eastwood (W & J B) Ltd v Herrod (Valuation Officer)** [1970] **1** 774, HL.

      Occupied together with agricultural land—Used solely in connection with agricultural operations thereon—Broiler houses—Adjoining land used for isolation, sterilising equipment and storing litter but not for 'poultry farming'—Not agricultural land—Broiler houses on farm land—No interconnection of farming and broiler house operations—Rating and Valuation (Apportionment) Act 1928, s 2(2). **Gilmore (Valuation Officer) v Baker-Carr** [1962] **3** 230, CA.

      Occupied—Used solely in connection with—Grain drying plant—Provision by farmers' syndicate—Used to dry their grain—Controlled by management committee—Whether plant agricultural building within—Rating and Valuation (Apportionment) Act 1928, s 2(2). **Farmers' Machinery Syndicate (11th Hampshire) v Shaw (Valuation Officer)** [1961] **1** 285, CA.

      Thoroughbred racehorse stud—Thoroughbred stud consisting of stud buildings and grazing paddocks—Whether grazing of thoroughbred horses an 'agricultural operation'—Whether stud buildings used 'in connection with' agricultural operation—Whether stud buildings used 'solely' in connection with agricultural operation—General Rate Act 1967, s 26(3), (4)(a). **Hemens (Valuation Officer) v Whitsbury Farm and Stud Ltd** [1988] **1** 72, HL.

      Used solely in connection with agricultural operations thereon—Bull pens, stores, laboratory, offices—Artificial insemination of cattle—Collection of semen from bulls—Whether buildings 'agricultural buildings'—Rating and Valuation (Apportionment) Act 1928, s 2(2)—Local Government Act 1929, s 67(1). **Thompson v Milk Marketing Board** [1952] **2** 344, CA.

      Used solely in connection with agricultural operations thereon—Provender mill—Mill owned by company providing feed for broiler houses on company's farms—6% to 8% of mill's production delivered to other turkey farmers—Whether mill 'used solely in connection with' operations carried on in broiler houses on company's farms—General Rate Act 1967, s 26(1)—Rating Act 1971, ss 1(1), (2), 2(3)(a). **Farmer (Valuation Officer) v Buxted Poultry Ltd** [1992] **2** 70, CA.

      Used solely in connection with agricultural operations thereon—Shed used as garage—Car used partly for farm and partly for private purposes—Whether shed 'agricultural building'—Rating and Valuation (Apportionment) Act 1928, s 2(2)—Agricultural Rates Act 1929, s 1(1). **Parry v Anglesey Assessment Committee** [1948] **2** 1060, KBD.

      Used solely in connection with agricultural operations thereon—Test to be applied—Poultry houses—Layer houses, hatchery, broiler houses, packing station, mill—Use for production of broiler chickens—Hens not running on land—Cockerels running on land for 12 out of 64 weeks of life—Land growing four per cent of feeding ingredients—Use of litter for manure on land—Poultry houses used for different operation from land—Test not use of land and buildings for combined agricultural operation—Rating and Valuation (Apportionment) Act 1928, s 2(2). **Eastwood (W & J B) Ltd v Herrod (Valuation Officer)** [1970] **1** 774, HL.

  Charity—
    Northern Ireland. See **Northern Ireland** (Rates—Exemption—Charity).

  Land belonging to a vicarage—
    Exemption from parochial taxes under Inclosure Act—Exemption from general rate imposed by Rating and Valuation Act 1925, s 2—Rating and Valuation Act 1925, ss 2(1), (2), (3)(a), 64(1)(b), (2)(a), (b). **Wiltshire County Valuation Committee v Marlborough and Ramsbury Rating Authority** [1948] **1** 694, CA.

  Land owned by public hospital—
    New South Wales. See **New South Wales** (Rates—Exemption—Land owned by public hospital).

RATES (cont)—
Exemption (cont)—
Listed building—
Structure fixed to building—Hereditament included in list of buildings of architectural or historic interest—Unoccupied property—Hereditament comprising two buildings connected by a footbridge and tunnel—One building listed but the other not—Buildings used together as commercial unit—Buildings becoming unoccupied—Whether unlisted building part of listed building—Whether unlisted building a structure fixed to listed building—Whether exemption available if only part of hereditament listed—General Rate Act 1967, Sch 1, para 2(c)—Town and Country Planning Act 1971, s 54(9). **Debenhams plc v Westminster City Council** [1987] **1** 51, HL.
Palestine. See **Palestine** (Rating).
Place of public religious worship—
Mormon temple—Use for special ceremonies—Admission only of Mormons of good standing—Associated buildings, one of which used for public religious worship—Whether temple place of public religious worship—Whether associated buildings used in connection with place of public religious worship—Whether associated buildings used for carrying out administrative or other activities relating to the organisation of the conduct of public religious worship in place of public religious worship—Local Government Finance Act 1988, Sch 5, para 11. **Gallagher (Valuation Officer) v Church of Jesus Christ of Latter-Day Saints** [2008] **4** 640, HL.
Place 'exclusively appropriated to public religious worship'—Rooms adjoining gospel hall and used for children's educational, recreational and religious activities—Sunday school—Poor Rate Exemption Act 1833, ss 1, 2—Sunday and Ragged Schools (Exemption from Rating) Act 1869, s 2. **Rogers v Lewisham BC** [1951] **2** 718, CA.
Public—Mormon temple—Use for special ceremonies—Admission only of Mormons of good standing—Temple not a place of 'public' religious worship within—Rating and Valuation (Miscellaneous Provisions) Act 1955, s 7(2). **Church of Jesus Christ of Latter-Day Saints v Henning (Valuation Officer)** [1963] **2** 733, HL.
Public—Proper test of public religious worship—Private premises used by Christian sect for meetings of religious worship—Sect not advertising their activities—No notice board outside premises to advertise meetings—Sect prepared to admit properly disposed members of public who presented themselves for worship—Whether proper test that public at large invited by some outward indication to worship—General Rate Act 1967, s 39(2)(a). **Broxtowe BC v Birch** [1983] **1** 641, CA.
Scientific, literary or fine arts society—
Institute for the advancement of fuel technology—Object also to uphold the status of members—Authorised purposes—Whether exempt—Scientific Societies Act 1843, s 1. **Institute of Fuel v Morley (Valuation Officer)** [1955] **3** 843, HL.
Institution for 'promotion and advancement of naval and military science and science and literature'—Supported by Government grant and members' subscriptions—Whether instituted for the 'purposes of science, literature or the fine arts exclusively' and supported by voluntary contributions so as to be exempt from rating—Scientific Societies Act 1843, s 1. **Westminster City Council v Royal United Service Institution** [1938] **2** 545, KBD.
Institution of mechanical engineers—Development of mechanical engineering—Subscriptions of members—Advantages of membership of organisation of professional men—Whether institution for 'purposes of science exclusively'—Whether subscriptions were 'voluntary' contributions—Scientific Societies Act 1843, s 1. **Institution of Mechanical Engineers v Cane (Valuation Officer)** [1960] **3** 715, HL.
Laundries research association—Company limited by guarantee—Advice to members and courses for students—Government grant—Whether association instituted for 'purposes of science exclusively'—Whether supported by 'voluntary contributions'—Scientific Societies Act 1843, s 1. **British Launderers' Research Association v Central Middlesex Assessment Committee** [1949] **1** 21, CA.
Music college—Unconditional legacies benefactions for special purposes—Gift for scholarships and prizes at a college gifts in kind—Government grants—Percentage of total income—Whether society supported by 'annual voluntary contributions'—Scientific Societies Act 1843, s 1. **Cane (Valuation Officer) v Royal College of Music** [1961] **2** 12, CA.
School incorporated 'to further research in ... the languages of Eastern and African peoples'—Supported in part by annual voluntary contributions—Whether instituted for 'purposes of science, literature or the fine arts exclusively'—Scientific Societies Act 1843, s 1. **School of Oriental and African Studies v Westminster City Rating Authority** [1940] **2** 537, HL.
Society for preservation and promotion of folk dances, songs and music—Whether for purposes of 'fine arts' exclusively—Scientific Societies Act 1843, s 1. **O'Sullivan v English Folk Dance and Song Society** [1955] **2** 845, CA.
Subscription library—Benefit confined to members—Whether instituted for purposes of literature exclusively—What were annual voluntary contributions—What proportion sufficient to make society one supported in part by such contributions—Scientific Societies Act 1843, s 1. **London Library v Cane (Valuation Officer)** [1959] **3** 726, CA.
Surcharge, from. See Surcharge on unused commercial building—Exemption from surcharge, below.
Unoccupied property. See Non-domestic rates—Unoccupied property—Exemption where owner company being wound up, below.
Farmhouse. See **Income tax** (Deduction in computing profits—Domestic or private expenses—Farming).
Gas board—
Rate period beginning after 31st March 1952 and before 1st April 1956—
Adjustment to new basis of assessment for rate periods beginning after 31st March 1952 and before 1st April 1956—Estoppel of local authority—Gas undertaking of local authority nationalised—Gas showrooms and offices in town hall formerly used for gas undertaking of local authority let to gas board by local authority—Lease providing for payment of rates by board—No separate assessment of premises—Contributions to rates formerly made by gas committee of local authority—Payments made by board under lease on account of rates of amounts equal to rates on value on which gas committee's contributions had been computed—No formal demand of rates from board—Whether sums paid by board were 'rates actually levied' on board by local authority for purposes of Rating and Valuation (Miscellaneous Provisions) Act 1955, s 6, Sch 4, para 2(1). **North Western Gas Board v Manchester Corp** [1963] **3** 442, CA.

929

RATES (cont)—
Gas board (cont)—
Rate period beginning after 31st March 1952 and before 1st April 1956 (cont)—
Calculation of amount of rates leviable—Repayment or allowance of difference between amount leviable and amount actually levied—Rating and Valuation (Miscellaneous Provisions) Act 1955, Sch 4, para 2(1). **West Hartlepool Corp v Northern Gas Board** [1957] **1** 394, QBD.
General rate fund—
Payment out of fund. See **Local government** (Expenditure—Payment out of general rate fund).
Hereditament—
Hereditament occupied and used as factory or workshop. See Hereditament occupied and used as factory or workshop, *below.*
Separate hereditament. See Separate hereditament, *below.*
Hereditament occupied and used as factory or workshop—
Premises where adapting for sale of any article—
Cleaning and cooling of milk for transport—Factory and Workshop Act 1901, s 149(1)(c)(iii)—Rating and Valuation (Apportionment) Act 1928, s 3(1). **Wiltshire County Valuation Committee v London Co-op Society Ltd** [1950] **1** 937, KBD.
Collation of greetings cards—Rating and Valuation (Apportionment) Act 1928, s 3(1), (2)—Factory and Workshop Act 1901, s 149(1). **Hudson's Bay Co v Thompson (Valuation Officer)** [1958] **3** 243, CA.
Egg packing station—Rating and Valuation (Apportionment) Act 1928, s 3(1). **Richardson & Son v Middlesbrough Borough Assessment Committee** [1947] **1** 884, KBD.
Packaging process—Motor car parts made fit for use abroad—Protection against climatic conditions—Factory and Workshop Act 1901, s 149(1)(c)(iii)—Rating and Valuation (Apportionment) Act 1928, s 3(1). **Cockram v Tropical Preservation Co Ltd** [1951] **2** 520, CA.
Slaughtering—Treatment of carcases—Factory and Workshop Act 1901, s 149(1)—Rating and Valuation (Apportionment) Act 1928, s 3(1). **Fatstock Marketing Corp Ltd v Morgan (Valuation Officer)** [1958] **1** 646, CA.
Sorting grading and matching of skins—Whether an 'industrial hereditament'—Rating and Valuation (Apportionment) Act 1928, s 3(1), (2)—Factory and Workshop Act 1901, s 149(1). **Hudson's Bay Co v Thompson (Valuation Officer)** [1959] **3** 150, HL.
Timber—Natural drying of timber—Factory and Workshop Act 1901, s 149(1)—Rating and Valuation (Apportionment) Act 1928, s 3(1). **Buncombe (Valuation Officer) v Baltic Sawmills Co Ltd** [1961] **3** 272, CA.
Wholesale distributive business—Sorting, identification and arrangement of goods—Whether an industrial hereditament—Factory and Workshop Act 1901, s 149(1)(c)(iii)—Rating and Valuation (Apportionment) Act 1928, s 3(1). **Cohen (Davis) & Sons Ltd v Hall** [1952] **1** 157, CA.
Premises where making of an article—
Premises used for testing aeroplane propellers and correcting minor faults—Whether an industrial hereditament—Factory and Workshop Act 1901, s 149—Rating and Valuation (Apportionment) Act 1928, s 3(1). **Acton Corp v West Middlesex Assessment Committee** [1949] **1** 409, KBD Divl Ct.
Premises wherein manual labour exercised by way of trade—
Premises occupied by non-profit-making company—Company carrying on club—Services in connection with motoring provided for club members—Premises used by company for upkeep of its own road vehicles and their component parts—Whether work done 'by way of trade'—Factory and Workshop Act 1901, s 149(1)(c)—Rating and Valuation (Apportionment) Act 1928, s 3(1), (2)(b) (as amended by Local Government Act 1929, s 69). **Automobile Pty Ltd v Brown (Valuation Officer)** [1955] **2** 214, CA.
Husband and wife. See Rateable occupation—Occupation by relatives—Husband and wife, *below.*
Lands Tribunal—
Appeal—
Appeal from decision of local valuation court—Interim decision—Appeal lay only against final decision—Local Government Act 1948, ss 48(4), 49(1). **Oswestry Corp v Hudd (Valuation Officer)** [1966] **1** 490, CA.
Appeal from decision of local valuation court—Onus of proof—Tribunal requiring to be satisfied as to something wrong in findings below—Lands Tribunal Rules 1956 (SI 1956 No 1734), r 45(4). **Sole v Henning (Valuation Officer)** [1959] **3** 398, CA.
Jurisdiction—Jurisdiction to hear valuation officer—Appeal by ratepayer from decision of local valuation court—No cross-appeal by valuation officer—Notice by valuation officer of intention to appear on hearing of appeal—Application by valuation officer for assessment directed by local valuation court to be increased—Local Government Act 1948, ss 48(4), 49(1)—Lands Tribunal Act 1949, s 1(3)(e)—Lands Tribunal Rules 1949 (SI 1949 No 2263), rr 9(1), 38(4). **Ellerby v March (Valuation Officer)** [1954] **2** 375, CA.
Jurisdiction—Method of valuation agreed by parties—Evidence supporting value higher than that yielded by the agreed method—Power to fix higher figure—Local Government Act 1948, s 48(4). **Morecambe and Heysham Corp v Robinson (Valuation Officer)** [1961] **1** 721, CA.
Case stated—
Form—Title of case. **National Pig Progeny Testing Board v Greenall** [1960] **3** 556, CA.
Evidence—
Evidence after decision reserved—Discretion of tribunal to refuse to hear evidence that might have been adduced at hearing. **Wexler v Playle (Valuation Officer)** [1960] **1** 338, CA.
Local valuation court—
Appeal—
Jurisdiction—Direction giving effect to contention of appellant—Contention of appellant—Valuation officer and ratepayer agreeing figure lower than proposal figure—Rating authority not a party to agreement—Valuation court finding agreed figure correct and directing alteration of valuation list accordingly—Rating authority appealing to Lands Tribunal—Whether tribunal having jurisdiction to make higher assessment than that determined by valuation court—Whether 'the contention of the appellant' is the proposal figure or is limited to the agreed or a lower figure—General Rate Act 1967, s 76(5). **Ellesmere Port and Neston BC v Shell UK Ltd** [1980] **1** 383, CA.

RATES (cont)—
  Local valuation court (cont)—
    Appeal (cont)—
      Parties entitled to be heard—Rating authority—Valuation officer and ratepayer reaching agreement on figures—Rating authority not party to agreement—Rating officer and ratepayer putting forward agreed figures before valuation court and calling no other evidence—Rating authority wishing to contest agreed figures—Whether rating authority entitled to be heard on agreed figures—General Rate Act 1967, s 76(4). **Ellesmere Port and Neston BC v Shell UK Ltd** [1980] **1** 383, CA.
      Res judicata—Scientific society's claim for exemption—Claim upheld on appeal for previous valuation list—Decision not appealed—Circumstances admitted to be unchanged—Whether valuation officer estopped from opposing claim. **Society of Medical Officers of Health v Hope (Valuation Officer)** [1960] **1** 317, HL.
      Withdrawal of objection to proposal to alter valuation list—Effect—Valuation court not entitled to proceed with hearing of appeal—Local Government Act 1948, s 41(6). **R v East Norfolk Local Valuation Court, ex p Martin** [1951] **1** 743, KBD.
      Withdrawal of proposal by valuation officer after objection lodged—Rating authority intending to appear in support—Withdrawal valid—Local Government Act 1948, s 48(4). **Brixham UDC, Re applications by** [1954] **3** 561, QBD.
    Contempt of court—
      Publication concerning proceedings before court. See **Contempt of court** (Publications concerning legal proceedings—Court—Inferior court—Local valuation court).
  Matrimonial home—
    Occupation by wife after separation—
      Liability of husband for rates. See **Husband and wife** (Matrimonial home—Rates).
    Rateable occupation—
      Generally. See Rateable occupation—Occupation by relatives—Husband and wife, *below*.
  Metropolis—
    Assessment—
      Provisional list—Alteration in value of hereditament—Reduction in value of club premises due to war conditions—'General alteration in the values of all classes of hereditaments'—Rating and Valuation (Postponement of Valuations) Act 1940, s 1(2)(b). **Westminster Assessment Committee v Conservative Club** [1944] **1** 104, HL.
      Supplemental list—Alteration in value of hereditament—Dwelling-house let to one tenant changed into tenement house let to two tenants—Increased rent—Whether 'from any cause increased in value'—Valuation (Metropolis) Act 1869, s 47. **R v Camberwell Borough Assessment Committee, ex p Metropolitan Housing Corp Ltd** [1939] **2** 283, KBD.
  Net annual value of property for rating—
    Mortgagee's action for possession—
      Jurisdiction of High Court. See **Mortgage** (Action by mortgagee for possession—Jurisdiction of High Court—Net annual value of property for rating).
  New South Wales. See **New South Wales** (Rates).
  Non-domestic rates—
    Collection and enforcement—
      Company scheme of arrangement. See **Company** (Scheme of arrangement—Compromise with creditors or members—Company voluntary arrangements—Non-domestic rates).
    Unoccupied property—
      Exemption where owner company being wound up—Owners of unoccupied commercial properties seeking to avoid rates by granting leases to special purpose vehicle companies—SPVs then wound up voluntarily or allowed to be struck off—Whether SPV 'owner'—Whether corporate veil could be pierced—Local Government Finance Act 1988, ss 45(1), 65(1)—Non-Domestic Rating (Unoccupied Property) (England) Regulations 2008, SI 2008/386, reg 4(k). **Rossendale BC v Hurstwood Properties (A) Ltd** [2022] **1 Comm** 253, SC; [2022] **2** 113, SC.
  Non-payment of rates—
    Committal proceedings—
      Stay of proceedings by bankruptcy court—Whether bankruptcy court having jurisdiction to stay committal proceedings. See **Insolvency** (Jurisdiction—Stay of proceedings—Non-payment of rates).
    Distress. See Distress for rates, *above*.
  Overpayment—
    Refund—
      Discretion to refund overpayment—Extent of discretion—Rates paid by owner of unoccupied property under mistake of law—Refusal of rating authority to make refund—Principles to be applied by rating authority in exercising discretion to refund overpaid rates—Factors to be considered—General Rate Act 1967, s 9(1)(e). **Tower Hamlets London BC v Chetnik Developments Ltd** [1988] **1** 961, HL.
      Discretion to refund overpayment—Extent of discretion—Whether discretion complete and unfettered—General Rate Act 1967, s 9. **R v Rochdale Metropolitan BC, ex p Cromer Ring Mill Ltd** [1982] **3** 761, QBD.
  Owner's rate—
    Drainage rates. See **Land drainage** (Drainage rates—Owners's rate).
  Payment of rates—
    Full rate—
      Reduced to 'composition rates and rents' if paid within prescribed time—Second half of reduced amount due on a Sunday—Demand note stating Monday as day for payment—Cheque posted on Monday—Whether payment in time—Validity of demand note. **Joynson's Exors v Liverpool Corp** [1938] **4** 183, KBD.
    Overpayment. See Overpayment, *above*.
    Payment by instalments—
      Company scheme of arrangement. See **Company** (Scheme of arrangement—Compromise with creditors or members—Company voluntary arrangements—Non-domestic rates).

RATES (cont)—
  Plant and machinery deemed to be part of hereditament—
    Cotton-mill—
      Production discontinued—Occupation only for preservation of process machinery and plant—Beneficial occupation—Rating and Valuation Act 1925, s 24. **Townley Mill Co (1919) Ltd v Oldham Assessment Committee** [1937] **1** 11, HL.
    Plant used or intended to be used in connection with services mainly or exclusively as part of manufacturing operations or trade processes—
      Air handling system—Ratepayer operating retail premises—Premises requiring heavy-duty air handling system on account of large number of refrigerator cabinets—Whether air handling system to be taken into account in assessing rateable value—Valuation for Rating (Plant and Machinery) (England) Regulations 2000, SI 2000/540, reg 2. **Iceland Foods Ltd v Berry (Valuation Officer)** [2018] **3** 192, SC.
    Primary transformation of power—
      Motor generators used as transforming plant—Cells for electrolytic process—Rating and Valuation Act 1925, s 24, Sch III, Cases 1(a), 4—Plant and Machinery (Valuation for Rating) Order 1927 (SR & O 1927 No 480). **South Wales Aluminium Co Ltd v Neath Assessment Area Assessment Committee** [1943] **2** 587, KBD.
    Production and generation of power—
      Electric power converted into hydraulic and pneumatic power—Whether conversion plant 'pumping engines for hydraulic power' 'used in connection with ... the generation ... of power'—Rating and Valuation Act 1925, s 24(1), Sch 3—General Rate Act 1967, s 21(1), Sch 3—Plant and Machinery (Rating) Order 1960 (SI 1960 No 122), Class 1A. **Chesterfield Tube Co Ltd v Thomas (Valuation Officer)** [1970] **3** 733, CA.
    Such plant or combination of plant and machinery as is or is in nature of building or structure—
      Ovens—Chambers for conditioning or treatment—Trays attached to endless belt passing through oven—Whether in the nature of a structure—Plant and Machinery (Valuation for Rating) Order 1927 (S R & O 1927 No 480), Sch, Class 4—Rating and Valuation Act 1925, s 24(1). **Collier (W) Ltd v Fielding (Valuation Officer)** [1958] **1** 694, CA.
      Structure—Plant conveyed to site in one piece—Whether feat of engineering involved not a test—Catwalks and connecting pipes—Constituent parts of a process boiler separately rateable—Rating and Valuation Act 1925, s 24(1),(5)—Plant and Machinery (Valuation for Rating) Order 1927 (SR & O 1927 No 480), Sch, Class 4. **BP Refinery (Kent) Ltd v Walker (Valuation Officer)** [1957] **1** 700, CA.
      Tank—Underground petrol tank in brick and concrete compartment—Whether whole or container only constituted a tank within Plant and Machinery (Valuation for Rating) Order 1927, (S R & O 1927 No 480), Sch, Class 4—Rating and Valuation Act 1925, s 24(1). **Shell-Mex and BP Ltd v Holyoak (Valuation Officer)** [1959] **1** 391, HL.
      Unit basis—Contractor's theory—Blast and fixed melting furnaces and coke ovens—Tilting melting furnaces and gas and blast mains—'Structure'—'In nature of structure'—Movability—Rating and Valuation Act 1925, s 22(1)(b)—Plant and Machinery (Valuation for Rating) Order 1927 (S R & O 1927 No 480), Sch, Class (4). **Cardiff Rating Authority v Guest Keen Baldwins Iron and Steel Co Ltd** [1949] **1** 27, CA.
    Transformers and distribution boards—
      Main transmission of power—Rating and Valuation Act 1925, s 24, Sch III—Plant and Machinery (Valuation for Rating) Order 1927 (S R & O 1927 No 480). **Thomas (Richard) & Co Ltd v Monmouth County Valuation Committee and West Monmouthshire Assessment Committee** [1944] **1** 417, CA.
  Proposal for alteration of current valuation list—
    Alteration in value since commencement of rating year—
      Time at which value to be ascertained—Rating and Valuation Act 1925, s 37(1), (7), (10). **Barrett and Russell's Gravesend Brewery Ltd v Gravesend Assessment Committee** [1941] **2** 308, KBD.
    Appearance before assessment committee—
      County valuation committee—Officer authorised by general resolution of valuation committee—Rating and Valuation Act 1925, s 31(9). **R v Surrey (North Eastern Area) Assessment Committee, ex p Surrey County Valuation Committee** [1947] **2** 276, KBD.
    Electricity hereditament—
      Power to amend deleted assessment—Rating and Valuation Act 1925, s 20(1)—Local Government Act 1948, s 92(3),(4)—Rating and Valuation (Transitional) Regulations 1949 (SI 1949 No 2313), reg 3(1). **R v Cockram (Valuation Officer), ex p East Midlands Electricity Board** [1952] **2** 44, QBD.
    Large scale revaluation—
      Proposals by county valuation committee to increase large proportion of assessments in area—Systematic examination of all assessments with a view to revaluation—Validity of large scale revaluation—Quarter Sessions Act 1849, s 11—Rating and Valuation Act 1925, ss 18, 19, 21(2), 31(3), 37(1)—Rating and Valuation (Postponement of Valuations) Act 1938, s 1—Rating and Valuation (Postponement of Valuations) Act 1940, s 1(3). **Pratt v North West Norfolk Assessment Committee and Norfolk County Valuation Committee** [1947] **1** 920, HL.
    Notice of proposal to be given to occupier—
      Notice of proposal served on owner of premises and also on occupier of premises—Attendance of owner at hearing before the assessment committee—Whether owner had locus standi in the matter—Appeal to quarter sessions by owner from the committee's decision—Whether quarter sessions had jurisdiction to entertain appeal—Rating and Valuation Act 1925, s 37(1), (4), (5), (7), (8). **Upper Agbrigg Assessment Committee v Gartsides (Brookside Brewery) Ltd & Bents Brewery Co Ltd** [1945] **1** 338, CA.
      Occupier—Whether occupier of whole undivided hereditament entitled to notice of proposed amendment affecting notional hereditaments of parts of whole—Rating and Valuation Act 1925, s 37(1), (3), (7). **R v West Derby Assessment Committee, ex p Mersey Docks and Harbour Board and Liverpool Rating Authority** [1938] **4** 110, KBD.

RATES (cont)—
Proposal for alteration of current valuation list (cont)—
Person aggrieved—
Ratepayer in same rating or precepting area as hereditament to which proposal relates—
Hereditament underassessed—Ratepayer correctly assessed applying to have rateable value
increased—Ratepayer unable to show that he had suffered financial detriment in consequence of
under-assessment—Whether ratepayer a 'person ... who is aggrieved' by value ascribed to
hereditament—General Rate Act 1967, s 69(1). **Arsenal Football Club Ltd v Smith (Valuation
Officer)** [1977] **2** 267, HL.

Rating authority—Authority concluding that all properties of particular type were or might be under
valued—Whether authority a 'person aggrieved'—Rating and Valuation Act 1925, s 37(2). **R v
Surrey (Mid-Eastern Area) Assessment Committee, ex p Merton and Morden UDC** [1948] **1** 856,
KBD.

Power to make proposal—
Amendment of current valuation list by rating authority—Rating and Valuation Act 1925,
s 37—Rating and Valuation (Postponement of Valuations) Act 1940. **Murphy Radio Ltd v Welwyn
Garden City Rating Authority** [1943] **2** 16, KBD.

Numerous hereditaments wrongly valued in current list—No change in conditions effecting general
rise in values—Revaluation by rating authority—Whether new list—'Person aggrieved'—Rating
and Valuation Act 1925, s 37(1),(3). **R v Worthing BC and Horsham and Worthing Assessment
Committee, ex p Burgess** [1937] **2** 681, KBD.

Proposal for insertion of assessment in list—Rating authority's power to make—Local Government
Act 1948, s 40(1)(b). **Walsh (John) Ltd v Sheffield City Council** [1957] **3** 353, CA.

Proposal—
Meaning—Objection to assessments as 'unfair and incorrect'—Proposed amendment by valuation
committee—No grounds specified—Whether 'a proposal for the amendment of the list'—Person
aggrieved—Rating and Valuation Act 1925, s 37(1),(2). **R v Thanet and District Assessment
Committee and Kent County Valuation Committee, ex p Isle of Thanet Gas Light & Coke Co**
[1939] **2** 489, KBD.

Proposal based on accounts five years old—
Automatic percentage increase of previous value—Validity—Rating and Valuation Act 1925, s 37.
Norwich Rating Authority v Norwich Assessment Committee and Fountain [1941] **3** 225, KBD.

Proposal by rating authority—
Delegation of rating authority's powers to finance committee—Ratification of proposal by rating
authority—Validity of proposal—Rating and Valuation Act 1925, s 37(1). **R v Heston and Isleworth
Rating Area Authority and South Middlesex Assessment Committee, ex p Conti** [1941] **2** 116,
KBD.

Proposal by valuation officer—
Rating authority levying rates on proposed rateable value prior to amending rateable value on
valuation list—Whether rating authority empowered to levy rates on proposed rateable
value—General Rate Act 1967, ss 2(4), 6, 19(3), 67(6). **R v Hackney London BC, ex p S G Warburg
Group Management Ltd** [1988] **3** 1009, QBD.

Specification of grounds for proposal—
Amount of increase—Whether necessary to state on form amount of proposed increase—Rating
and Valuation Act 1925, s 37(2). **R v Surrey (Mid-Eastern Area) Assessment Committee, ex p
Merton and Morden UDC** [1948] **1** 856, KBD.

Grounds on which proposed amendment supported—Indication of extent to which existing
valuations incorrect and unfair—Form indicating proposed revised assessment—Whether
grounds of proposal sufficiently indicated—Rating and Valuation Act 1925, s 37(2)(b). **R v
Winchester Area Assessment Committee, ex p Wright** [1948] **2** 552, CA.

Need to indicate clearly what rating authority proposing—Rating and Valuation Act 1925, s 37(2). **R
v Reading Assessment Committee, ex p McCarthy E Fitt Ltd** [1948] **1** 194, KBD.

Rate support grant—
Grant-related expenditure—
Calculation of local authority expenditure limits—Secretary of State required to set limits by
reference to 'principles applicable to all local authorities'—Secretary of State's method for
calculating limits having different effect on high-spending and low-spending authorities—
Secretary of State adopting different baselines on which to calculate expenditure increases for
high-spending and low-spending authorities—Whether Secretary of State applying different
principles to different authorities—Whether Secretary entitled to adopt principle producing
different consequences for different authorities—Local Government, Planning and Land Act 1980,
s 59(11A). **Nottinghamshire CC v Secretary of State for the Environment** [1986] **1** 199, HL.

Reduction—
Statutory discretion of Secretary of State to reduce grant pending introduction of new
legislation—Secretary of State making decision pursuant to transitional provisions to reduce local
authority rate support grant—Decision quashed on local authority's application for judicial
review—Secretary of State making second decision after ending of year to which transitional
provisions applying—Whether such decision valid and effective—Local Government, Planning
and Land Act 1980, ss 48, 49, 50. **R v Secretary of State for the Environment, ex p Hackney
London BC** [1984] **1** 956, CA.

Statutory discretion of Secretary of State to reduce grant—Exercise of discretion—Secretary of
State hearing representations from rating authorities before he received statutory power to
reduce their grants—Secretary of State refusing to hear further representations from authorities
after receiving power and before exercising his discretion—Secretary of State applying formula
contained in order to determine amount of reduction—Whether order valid—Whether decision of
Secretary of State valid—Local Government, Planning and Land Act 1980, ss 48, 49, 50—Rate
Support Grant (Principles for Multipliers) Order 1980, para 3, Sch. **R v Secretary of State for the
Environment, ex p Brent London BC** [1983] **3** 321, QBD.

RATES (cont)—
    Rate support grant (cont)—
        Reduction (cont)—
            Statutory discretion of Secretary of State to reduce grant—Secretary of State notifying local authority of amounts to be paid and dates on which payment to be made—Secretary of State subsequently making decision to reduce amounts and notifying local authority accordingly—Decision quashed on local authority's application for judicial review—Local authority requesting payments in accordance with original notification—Secretary of State refusing and withholding payment pending making second decision—Whether local authority entitled to payment in accordance with original notification—Whether Secretary of State entitled to defer payment pending making second decision—Local Government Act 1974, s 2(2), Local Government, Planning and Land Act 1980, ss 48, 49, 50, Rate Support Grant Regulations 1979, reg 5. **R v Secretary of State for the Environment, ex p Hackney London BC** [1984] **1** 956, CA.

Rateable hereditament—
    Rateable occupation—
        Plant and machinery deemed to be part of hereditament—ATMs situated in retail premises—ATMs and retail premises in different ownership—Whether ATM site separate hereditament—Whether retailer or bank in rateable occupation—Valuation for Rating (Plant and Machinery) (England) Regulations 2000, SI 2000/540, reg 2(b). **Cardtronics UK Ltd v Sykes (Valuation Officers)** [2020] **4** 253, SC.

Rateable occupation—
    Building occupied in parts—
        Occupation by lodger or tenant—Owner occupying rest of house—Control by owner—Assessment of parts separately—Rating and Valuation Act 1925, s 23(1). **Helman v Horsham and Worthing Assessment Committee** [1949] **1** 776, CA.
        Treatment as single hereditament in occupation of person who receives the rents—Managing agent collecting rents from property, deducting outgoings including rates therefrom and paying balance to owners—Whether agent 'person who receives the rents'—Whether agent rateable occupier of property—General Rate Act 1967, s 24. **Arsenal Football Club Ltd v Smith (Valuation Officer)** [1977] **2** 267, HL.

    Chattels enjoyed with land—
        Disused colliery tip—No finding as to tip's constituting part of the land—Purchasers' (ratepayers') exclusive right to remove materials from tip except red ash, which was reserved to vendor—Tip, viewed as chattels, in rateable occupation—Purchasers' exclusive or paramount occupation. **Ryan Industrial Fuels Ltd v Morgan (Valuation Officer)** [1965] **3** 465, CA.
        Residential caravan—Pitch on caravan operators' site—Caravan in position more than a year—Rateability of caravan—Partial control by site operators—Paramount occupation—Separate occupation by caravan owner. **Field Place Caravan Park Ltd v Harding (Valuation Officer)** [1966] **3** 247, CA.

    Hereditaments owned by local authority—
        Used for public benefit—Swimming pool, concert hall and similar activities producing considerable income. **North Riding of Yorkshire County Valuation Committee v Guisborough Assessment Committee and Borough of Redcar** [1942] **2** 589, KBD.

    Ingredients of occupation—
        Benefit to possessor—Art gallery—Trust of gallery for enjoyment by the public in perpetuity—Gallery vested in local authority—Whether trusts allowed any potentiality of beneficial occupation by local authority. **Kingston-upon-Hull Corp v Clayton (Valuation Officer)** [1961] **3** 118, HL.
        Exclusive occupation—Common land—Golf course—Crown land subject to rights of common—Crown licence to golf clubs to maintain and use golf courses—No power to exclude commoners or public. **Peak (Valuation Officer) v Burley Golf Club** [1960] **2** 199, CA.
        Exclusive occupation—Yacht mooring—Whether occupation exclusive. **Bradshaw v Davey** [1952] **1** 350, KBD.
        Permanence of occupation—Temporary occupation—Occupation permanently affecting contours and appearance of site—Building contractors—Borrow pit—Purpose of occupation to remove earth from site for purpose of constructing motorway—Occupation for less than 12 months—Large quantities of soil removed within that period—Whether contractors in rateable occupation of site. **Dick Hampton (Earth Moving) Ltd v Lewis (Valuation Officer)** [1975] **3** 946, CA.

    Joint rateable occupation—
        Husband separated from wife—Wife remaining in actual occupation of matrimonial home—Husband remaining rateable occupier and paying wife interim alimony—Husband informing rating authority that future demands for rates to be served on wife—Whether rateable occupation could have changed from that of the husband to a joint rateable occupation. **Malden and Combe Corp v Bennett** [1963] **2** 527, QBD.

    Non-occupation of part of premises—
        Liability for rates for whole premises—Description in valuation list—Description of premises as 'workshop and store'—Premises consisting of three separate structures—House and two factories—Ratepayer occupying one factory and part of house—Whether ratepayer liable for rates for whole premises. **Camden London Borough v Herwald** [1978] **2** 880, CA.

    Non-occupation of premises—
        Liability for rates—Unoccupied hereditament—Description in valuation list—Description of premises as 'offices'—Use as offices prohibited by planning condition—Whether description of hereditament in valuation list essential element in identity of hereditament—Whether owner prohibited by law from occupying hereditament—Whether hereditament kept vacant by reason of action taken by local authority prohibiting occupation—General Rate Act 1967, Sch 1, paras 1(1), 2. **Hailbury Investments Ltd v Westminster City Council** [1986] **3** 440, HL.

    Occupation by master or servant—
        Rateable occupier—Test to identify. **Northern Ireland Comr of Valuation v Fermanagh Protestant Board of Education** [1969] **3** 352, HL.

RATES (cont)—
Rateable occupation (cont)—
Occupation by receiver—
Possession—Blocks of flats owned by companies—Tenants paying rent inclusive of rates—Rates in arrears—Order appointing receiver and manager—Receiver entered in rate-book of borough council as new rateable occupier—No appeal against entry—Whether change of occupation of premises—Liability to be rated—Poor Rate Assessment and Collection Act 1869, s 16. **Gyton v Palmour** [1944] 2 540, KBD.

Receiver appointed under debenture charging company's property—Debenture empowering receiver to take possession of property charged but not effecting transfer of possession to receiver or obliging him to take possession—Debenture and appointment of receiver containing usual agency provision deeming receiver to be company's agent—Whether receiver in rateable occupation of property—Whether rating authority having reasonable grounds for believing receiver in rateable occupation—Whether burden of proof on receiver to show that he was not in rateable occupation—General Rate Act 1967, s 97(1). **Ratford v Northavon DC** [1986] 3 193, CA.

Occupation by relatives—
Husband and wife—Former matrimonial home—Husband divorced from wife—Wife and children remaining in matrimonial home—Wife having equitable half share in house by virtue of court order—Whether husband deriving beneficial use and occupation of it by virtue of obligation to maintain—Whether husband liable for rates after decree absolute. **Routhan v Arun DC** [1981] 3 752, CA.

Husband and wife—Former matrimonial home—Husband leaving wife in home—Bankruptcy of husband—Wife remaining in home—Effect of bankruptcy—Husband's continuing obligation to provide for wife—Whether husband in rateable occupation. **Hounslow London Borough v Peake** [1974] 1 688, QBD.

Husband and wife—Former matrimonial home—Husband separated from wife—Wife and children remaining in matrimonial home—Home purchased by wife in her sole name—Husband having no interest in home—Whether husband in beneficial occupation—Whether husband deriving beneficial use from house because obligation to maintain wife partly discharged by wife's occupation of home. **Brown v Oxford City Council** [1978] 3 1113, QBD.

Husband and wife—Former matrimonial home—Wife in occupation by agreement—Husband agreeing to pay rates—Nature of wife's right to occupation—Licensor/licensee relationship—Actual and exclusive occupation. **Mourton v Hounslow London Borough** [1970] 2 564, QBD.

Husband and wife—Husband separated from wife—Wife allowed to live in husband's father's house rent free—Whether husband liable for rates. **Cardiff Corp v Robinson** [1956] 3 56, QBD.

Owner occupier removed to mental institution—Order of master in lunacy authorising wife to occupy house rent free on payment of rates—Wife not party to order, but continuing to occupy house with knowledge thereof. **Robinson v Taylor** [1948] 1 291, KBD.

Occupation by servant or agent—
Gas research station—Area gas board conducting research for Gas Council—Whether Gas Council were occupiers. **Solihull Corp v Gas Council** [1962] 1 898, HL.

Necessity for occupation by servant—Obligation of servant to reside on premises, and residence of material assistance to master, but no necessity for residence for doing the work of the employment—Church officer, employee of church board, responsible for looking after church building and performing duties in church, residing in house owned by church board adjacent to church and forming part of same building—Church board in rateable occupation of house for purpose of rating relief—House also 'wholly or mainly used for charitable purposes', although a residence only for church officer—Local Government (Financial Provisions etc) (Scotland) Act 1962, s 4(2). **Glasgow City Corp v Johnstone** [1965] 1 730, HL.

Occupation by trespassers—
Trespassers forming themselves into unincorporated association—Trespassers exercising exclusive joint occupation of premises—Whether member of group of trespassers exercising exclusive joint occupation of premises liable for rates—General Rate Act 1967, s 97(1). **Westminster City Council v Tomlin** [1990] 1 920, CA.

Occupation by unincorporated association—
Rates demanded from member of association—Whether membership of association making member the 'occupier' of premises used by association. **Verrall v Hackney London BC** [1983] 1 277, CA.

Owner having legal possession—
Presumption of occupation—Rebuttal—Occupation by another—Exclusion of owner from hereditament by trespassers in occupation—Former employees of company in liquidation taking over possession and control of factory—Liquidator prevented from gaining access to factory—Liquidator coming to arrangement with employees for completion of unfinished work in factory and for assistance in sale of factory—Liquidator choosing not to enforce legal right to possession of factory in order to avoid confrontation—Whether liquidator in occupation of factory—General Rate Act 1967, s 16. **Briant Colour Printing Co Ltd (in liq), Re** [1977] 3 968, CA.

Person liable for rates—
Occupier—Premises described in valuation list as single hereditament—Premises used by different legal entities at different times—Whether any one user liable for rates on whole of premises. **Verrall v Hackney London BC** [1983] 1 277, CA.

Occupier—Property of syndicate—Control by committee of syndicate. **A-G (ex rel Thomas Brownlee Paisley) v St Ives RDC** [1961] 1 265, CA.

Person named in valuation list—Onus of showing not in rateable occupation—Husband separated from wife—Wife continuing to occupy former matrimonial home—General Rate Act 1967, s 97(1). **Des Salles d'Epinoix v Kensington and Chelsea Royal Borough** [1970] 1 18, QBD.

Playing field vested in local authority—
Acquisition by deed—Trust for perpetual use by public—Restriction on user by public ancillary to management—Cricket and football pitches and tennis courts let to clubs—Temporary exclusion of public. **Burnell v Downham Market UDC** [1952] 1 601, CA.

Premises left empty—
Intention to occupy—Bungalows advertised to be let furnished or unfurnished—Whether owner in beneficial occupation—Liability to be rated. **Bayliss v Chatters** [1940] 1 620, KBD.

RATES (cont)—

Rateable occupation (cont)—

Premises left empty (cont)—

Intention to occupy—Charity—Ecclesiastical corporation—Accommodation held available to provide residence for minister of religion—House provided by church as official residence of minister—House vacated by retiring minister—Held available for successor—Successor not appointed until 11 months later—Whether house unoccupied during interim period—General Rate Act 1967, ss 17(1), 40(1),(9), Sch 1, para 2(f). **Bexley Congregational Church Treasurer v Bexley London Borough** [1972] **2** 662, CA.

Intention to occupy—Lease of unfurnished dwelling-houses taken in case of emergency—Houses empty and unused—Whether rateably occupied. **Associated Cinema Properties Ltd v Hampstead BC** [1944] **1** 436, CA.

Public park—

Absence of formal 'dedication' to the public—Acquisition for use as public walks and pleasure grounds—Powers of sale and leasing ancillary to use. **Blake (Valuation Officer) v Hendon Corp** [1961] **3** 601, CA.

Refreshment pavilion—Letting to ice-cream merchant—Refreshments for the use of persons resorting to the park only—Duty to keep open during specified hours—Occupation ancillary to that of the park. **Sheffield Corp v Tranter** [1957] **2** 583, CA.

Rateable hereditament—

Chattels enjoyed with land—Vessel used as floating nightclub—Vessel permanently secured to land—Vessel's owner licensed to use land for such purpose—Whether rateable. **Cinderella Rockerfellas Ltd v Rudd** [2003] **3** 219, CA.

Mobile telephone operator erecting aerial mast on hereditament located on highway—Operator occupying hereditament free of charge pursuant to statutory right—Whether any value to be attributed to the land for rating purposes—Telecommunications Act 1984, Sch 2, para 9(1). **Orange PCS Ltd v Bradford** [2004] **2** 651, CA.

Temporary structures—

Builders' huts assembled and used on building site—Whether part of rateable hereditament. **London CC v Wilkins (Valuation Officer)** [1956] **3** 38, HL.

Site occupied for purpose of carrying out works contract—Temporary structures erected, and used, by contractors on site of aerodrome under construction—Rating and Valuation Act 1925, s 37(10). **Laing (John) & Son Ltd v Kingswood Assessment Committee** [1949] **1** 224, CA.

Warehouse temporarily unused—

Alterations preparatory to intended use—Purchase of warehouse premises for use as a bonded store—Alterations to premises—No use of premises as bonded store until after alterations were completed—Whether premises 'unoccupied' during period of alteration—Local Government (Scotland) Act 1947, s 243(1) (as amended by Valuation and Rating (Scotland) Act 1956, s 44, Sch 7, Part 3), s 379(1). **Arbuckle Smith & Co Ltd v Greenock Corp** [1960] **1** 568, HL.

Rateable value—

House—

Leasehold enfranchisement. *See* **Landlord and tenant** (Leasehold enfranchisement—House— Rateable value).

Protected tenancy. *See* **Rent restriction** (Rateable value).

Ratepayer—

Action against local authority—

Ratepayer's locus standi. *See* **Local authority** (Action—Action against local authority—Action by ratepayer against local authority).

Recovery of rates—

Recovery otherwise than by distress—

Whether action lies. **Liverpool Corp v Hope** [1938] **1** 492, CA.

Refund—

Overpayment. *See* Overpayment—Refund, *above*.

Relief—

Air-raid protection works—

Reduction of area available for business purposes—Reduction in assessment—Rating and Valuation (Air-Raid Works) Act 1938, s 1(1). **Waterlow & Sons Ltd v Shoreditch Assessment Committee** [1942] **1** 669, KBD.

Charity. *See* Charitable and other organisations, *above*.

Dwelling-house—

Hereditament used wholly for the purpose of a private dwelling or private dwellings—House containing flats let to holiday makers—Rateable occupier carrying on business of letting flats—Whether house used wholly for purpose of a private dwelling—Whether occupier entitled to reduction in rate levied—General Rate Act 1967, ss 48(1), 115(1), Sch 13, paras 1, 2. **Skittrall v South Hams DC** [1976] **3** 1, Ch D.

Structures supplied for use of invalids, disabled or handicapped persons. *See* Structures supplied for use of invalids, disabled or handicapped persons, *below*.

Remission of rate—

Poverty of ratepayer—

War damage to property rated—Remission of Rates (London) Act 1940. **Stepney BC v Woolf** [1943] **1** 64, KBD.

Refusal—

Appeal to Crown Court—Jurisdiction of Crown Court. *See* Appeal—Appeal to Crown Court—Jurisdiction—Refusal by rating authority to remit or reduce rates, *above*.

Resolution to fix general rate—

Duty of councillor when voting on resolution. *See* **Local government** (Meeting—Voting—Duty of councillor when voting—Resolution to fix general rate).

936

RATES (cont)—
  Separate hereditament—
    Two properties in same occupation—
      Adjoining sites—Occupation of each in different capacity—Contractors engaged in building
      motorway—Contractors using site adjoining motorway as borrow pit to remove earth for
      construction of motorway—Site of borrow pit and motorway used as one and in appearance
      largely indistinguishable—Whether motorway and borrow pit separate hereditaments. **Dick
      Hampton (Earth Moving) Ltd v Lewis (Valuation Officer)** [1975] **3** 946, CA.
      Caravan sites—Two caravan sites in one occupation—Separation by quarry side—Valuation officer
      unaware of upper site when lower assessed—Proposal to assess upper site separately—
      Construction of entry in valuation list. **Sussex Caravan Parks Ltd v Richardson (Valuation Officer)**
      [1961] **1** 731, CA.
      Non-contiguous floors—Whether different storeys under common occupation in same block to be
      entered as single or separate hereditaments in rating list for purpose of non-domestic rating.
      Woolway (Valuation Officer) v Mazars LLP [2016] **1** 299, SC.
      Premises on opposite sides of highway—Bakery and repair depot—Whether one or two
      hereditaments. **Gilbert (Valuation Officer) v S Hickinbottom & Sons Ltd** [1956] **2** 101, CA.
      Works and offices—Separation by occupier's agricultural land—Connection by occupier's private
      road (150 yards long)—Private road serving other properties of occupier—Whether two
      properties separate hereditaments. **Butterley Co Ltd v Tasker (Valuation Officer)** [1961] **1** 574, CA.
  Structures supplied for use of invalids, disabled or handicapped persons—
    Structure—
      Blind persons' home—Principal building or only annexe or adjunct thereof—Institution with main
      two-storey building—Rating and Valuation (Miscellaneous Provisions) Act 1955, s 9(1). **Almond v
      Birmingham Royal Institution for the Blind** [1967] **2** 317, HL.
      Blind persons' home—Whether for prevention of, or care in, illness, mental defectiveness,
      etc—Whether welfare arrangements—Whether structure similar to those for such purposes—
      Rating and Valuation (Miscellaneous Provisions) Act 1955, s 9(1)—National Health Service Act
      1946, ss 28(1), 79(1)—National Assistance Act 1948, s 29(1). **Jewish Blind Society Trustees v
      Henning (Valuation Officer)** [1961] **1** 47, CA.
      Garage for disabled person's vehicle—'Structure' which is 'of a kind similar to' those supplied by
      Minister of Health—'Supplied' otherwise—Brick-built garage annexed to house—Minister's
      garages temporary prefabricated structures—Garage owned by disabled person—Rating and
      Valuation (Miscellaneous Provisions) Act 1955, s 9(1). **Walker (Valuation Officer) v Wood**
      [1962] **3** 188, CA.
  Structure supplied for use of person in pursuance of arrangements for after-care of any person
  suffering from illness—
      Structure of a kind similar to structures which could be provided by local authority or voluntary
      organisation—Flat acquired by disabled ratepayer—Ratepayer confined to wheelchair—Flat
      adapted for purpose of after-care—Ratepayer living in flat with wife—Whether flat a structure of a
      kind similar to one which local authority could supply for care or after-care of persons suffering
      from illness—General Rate Act 1967, s 45—Health Services and Public Health Act 1968, s 12(1).
      Vandyk v Oliver (Valuation Officer) [1976] **1** 466, HL.
  Structure supplied for use of person in pursuance of arrangements for handicapped persons—
      Structure of a kind which could be provided by local authority—School for deaf children—Claim by
      owners of school for relief—Local education authorities having power to provide such schools
      under Education Acts—Whether local authority having power to provide school under statutory
      powers to make arrangements for handicapped—National Assistance Act 1948, s 29—General
      Rate Act 1967, s 45. **Trustees of the Royal Cross School for the Deaf v Morton (Valuation Officer)**
      [1975] **2** 519, CA.
  Surcharge on unused commercial building—
    Exemption from surcharge—
      Hereditaments constructed as factories, mills or other premises of a similar character for use
      wholly or mainly for industrial purposes—Surcharge imposed in respect of a garage—Garage
      registered as factory under Factories Act 1961—Maintenance and repair work carried out at
      garage—Whether garage exempt from surcharge—General Rate Act 1967, s 17A (as inserted by
      the Local Government Act 1974, s 16)—Rating Surcharge (Exemption) Regulations 1974 (SI 1974
      No 1563), reg 3. **Post Office v Oxford City Council** [1980] **2** 439, CA.
  Unoccupied property—
      Liability for surcharge when no rates payable in respect of building—No resolution by rating
      authority that unoccupied property in area should be rated—Whether surcharge payable—
      Whether passing of resolution to rate unoccupied property a precondition of liability to
      surcharge—General Rate Act 1967, s 17A(1), (4) (added by the Local Government Act 1974, s 16).
      Dixon v Harding [1977] **2** 227, QBD.
  Unpaid surcharge constituting charge on land comprised in hereditament—
      Scope of charge—When charge imposed land subject to legal mortgage and owner's interest
      consisting merely of equity of redemption—Mortgagee exercising power of sale under mortgage
      and selling land to defendant—Whether defendant liable for surcharge—Whether charge for
      unpaid surcharge having priority over defendant's interest in land—Whether 'charge on land'
      imposing charge on all existing interests at time charge created including mortgagee's
      interest—Whether charge imposed only on owner's interest at that date consisting of equity of
      redemption—General Rate Act 1967, ss 17A(1), 17B(3). **Westminster City Council v Haymarket
      Publishing Ltd** [1981] **2** 555, CA.
  Unoccupied property—
    Newly erected building—
      Amendment of rate—Building unoccupied—Hereditament not entered in valuation list—Objection
      to valuation officer's proposed valuation—Whether local authority having power to amend rate
      notwithstanding unresolved objection—General Rate Act 1967, s 6, Sch 1, para 1. **Trendworthy
      Two Ltd v Islington London BC** [1988] **1** 953, HL.

RATES (cont)—
  Unoccupied property (cont)—
    Newly erected building (cont)—
      Completion—Completion notice—Appeal—Date of completion—Determination by court—
        Application—Evidence—Appeal not abandoned or dismissed—erection of building to be treated
        as having been completed on 'such date as the court shall determine'—Appeal against
        completion notice allowed—No application to fix a completion date made until after judgment
        delivered—No evidence as to likely date of completion—Whether court bound to fix completion
        date—General Rate Act 1967, Sch 1, para 8(5). **Ravenseft Properties Ltd v Newham London
        Borough** [1976] **1** 580, CA.
      Completion—Completion notice—Completion notice relating to whole of building—Hereditament
        entered in valuation list consisting of part only of building—Unoccupied property rate charged in
        respect of part only—Lessees of tower block sub-letting top 14 floors to ratepayers—Ratepayers
        leaving those floors unoccupied for nine months—Valuation list in respect of tower block
        containing only the hereditament comprising the 14 floors—Whether necessary that
        hereditament described in completion notice and hereditament in valuation list should be
        identical—Whether ratepayers liable for unoccupied property rate—General Rate Act 1967, Sch 1,
        paras 1, 8(1). **Camden London Borough v Post Office** [1977] **2** 795, CA.
      Completion—Date of completion—Development in two stages—First stage completed—Work
        customarily remaining to be done—Dispute over date when first stage completed—Principles to
        be applied in determining completion date—Principles to be applied in determining period
        reasonably required for completion of customary work—General Rate Act 1967, Sch 1, paras 8, 9.
        London Merchant Securities plc v Islington London BC [1987] **2** 961, HL.
      Completion—Liability to be rated from date of completion—Meaning of 'completion'—Building not
        capable of being occupied—Building lacking features necessary for occupation and which when
        provided would have to be taken into account for valuation purposes—Office block—Main
        structure completed—No internal partitioning on any of storeys to be occupied as
        offices—Whether erection of storeys completed—Whether rating authority having power to serve
        completion notices—General Rate Act 1967, Sch 1, paras 7, 8(1), (5), 10. **Ravenseft Properties Ltd
        v Newham London Borough** [1976] **1** 580, CA.
      Completion—Liability to be rated from date of completion—Meaning of 'completion'—Building not
        capable of being occupied—Building lacking features necessary for occupation—Telephone
        exchange—Work by building contractor finished—Building lacking equipment including
        telephone equipment—Building not capable of being occupied as a telephone exchange—
        Whether building completed—General Rate Act 1967, Sch 1, para 8(1). **Post Office v Nottingham
        City Council** [1976] **2** 831, CA.
    Resolution for rating of unoccupied property—
      Premises being modernised—Premises not only unoccupied but also incapable of occupation—
        Whether liable to rates—General Rate Act 1967, s 17(1), Sch 1. **Easiwork Homes Ltd v Redbridge
        London Borough** [1970] **2** 635, QBD.
      Rating provisions to come into operation on day specified in the resolution—Specified in the
        resolution—Date not expressly stated in resolution—Rating authority's intention that rating
        should start on 1st April 1974—All public announcements stating that rating to start on that
        date—Whether requirement that date should 'be specified in the resolution' complied
        with—General Rate Act 1967, s 17, Sch 1. **Sheffield City Council v Graingers Wines Ltd**
        [1978] **2** 70, CA.
    Surcharge on unused commercial building. See Surcharge on unused commercial building—
      Unoccupied property, above.
  Unoccupied property. See Non-domestic rates—Unoccupied property, above.
  Unused commercial building—
    Surcharge. See Surcharge on unused commercial building, above.
  Valuation—
    Advertising station—
      Rights let out by agreement hereditament for rating purposes—Neon sign—Grant of rights of fixing
        and exhibiting a flashing neon advertising sign to be erected by grantee—Sign erected—Basis of
        valuation—Local Government Act 1948, s 56. **Imperial Tobacco Co (of GB and Ireland) Ltd v
        Pierson (Valuation Officer)** [1960] **2** 780, HL.
    Agricultural dwelling-house—
      Limitation of value by amount in respect of the dwelling-house which may be deducted from
        wages—Agricultural Wages (Regulation) Acts 1924-1940—Local Government Act 1929, s 72.
        Bomford v South Worcestershire Area Assessment Committee [1947] **1** 299, CA.
    Agriculture worker's cottage. See **Agriculture** (Rating—Valuation).
    Airport fuel distribution depot—
      Rights appurtenant to hereditament—Additional rights of trading and access inseparable from
        installation—Rents basis—No deduction from rent for inseparable ancillary rights—Lease
        conferring right to supply fuel to aircraft over the airport—Bowser parking site—Rent covering
        manoeuvring area outside site. **Shell-Mex and BP Ltd v Langley (Valuation Officer)** [1962] **3** 433,
        CA.
    Burial ground—
      Limitation on value of hereditament—Land acquired under the provisions of the Burial Act
        1852—Crematorium—Whether entitled to limitation on value as burial ground—Burial Act 1852,
        s 26—Burial Act 1855, s 15—Cremation Act 1902, s 4. **Law (Valuation Officer) v Wandsworth BC**
        [1957] **3** 71, CA.
    Calculation—
      Factors to be taken into account—State of locality in which hereditament is situated at date of
        proposal—Whether effect of enterprise zone on value of nearby commercial and industrial
        premises to be taken into account—General Rate Act 1967, s 20(1)(b). **Clement (Valuation Officer)
        v Addis Ltd** [1988] **1** 593, HL.
    Caravan camping site—
      Evidence of value—Valuation by parties on profits basis and contractor's basis—Rejection of both
        methods by Lands Tribunal—Valuation on adjusted rent of site—Rejection of evidence
        erroneous—All classes of evidence admissible. **Garton v Hunter (Valuation Officer)** [1969] **1** 451,
        CA.

RATES (cont)—
  Valuation (cont)—
    Club—
      Member's club—Factors not to be taken into account—Profits from sale of liquor—Absence of alternative accommodation—Monopoly of club facilities. **Aberdare UDC v Pontypridd Area Assessment Committee** [1947] 2 877, KBD DC.
    Deduction from gross value—
      Rate, charge, or assessment made by commissioners of sewers 'or other like authority'—Sea defence rate levied by urban district council—Rating and Valuation Act 1925, s 22(1)(a). **Havant and Waterloo UDC v Payne (Valuation Officer)** [1953] 2 85, CA.
    Dock and harbour undertaking—
      Offices—Profits basis—Whether valuation as part of undertaking or at full commercial value—Rating and Valuation Act 1925, s 22(1)—Local Government Act 1948, s 89(6). **Clayton (Valuation Officer) v British Transport Commission** [1955] 2 274, CA.
      Power of Secretary of State to prescribe method of valuation—Validity of order prescribing method—Rateable value defined by order as percentage of 'relevant receipts' of undertaking—'Relevant receipts' including receipts originating outside rating area and receipts from leased property separately rated—Whether Secretary of State entitled to prescribe rateable value based on total receipts of undertaking—Whether order ultra vires—General Rate Act 1967, s 35—Docks and Harbours (Valuation) Order 1971 (SI 1971 No 561), arts 2(1), 3(2)—Docks and Harbours (Valuation)(Amendment) Order 1973 (SI 1973 No 654), art 4. **Milford Haven Conservancy Board v IRC** [1976] 3 263, CA.
    Dock undertaking—
      Profits basis—Nil assessment—Loss on dock undertaking—Part of British Transport Commission's undertaking—No obligation to adjust charges to cover costs—Stock and loan interest excluded from dock accounts—Whether departure from profits basis justified. **British Transport Commission v Hingley (Valuation Officer)** [1961] 1 837, CA.
    Dwelling-house—
      Disrepair—Landlord's liability to repair—Dwelling-house in poor state of repair—Disrepair disregarded in arriving at value—Valuation for Rating Act 1953, s 2(2), (3)(a). **Wexler v Playle (Valuation Officer)** [1960] 1 338, CA.
      Harassment by neighbours—First floor flat in house—Letting including right to use bathroom in ground floor flat and to pass through ground floor flat to garden—Ground floor flat illegally occupied by 13 persons—Ratepayer subjected to harassment by occupants of ground floor flat—Whether harassment ground for reduction of assessment of first floor flat—General Rate Act 1967, s 19(2), (6). **Black v Oliver (Valuation officer)** [1978] 3 408, CA.
      Letting of rooms singly for residential purposes—Premises where substantially the whole of available accommodation was so let excluded—Four rooms used by occupier, seven let—Whether four rooms part of available accommodation—Valuation for Rating Act 1953, s 3(2). **Walls v Peak (Valuation Officer)** [1960] 2 81, CA.
      Method of valuation—Interest on purchase price, etc—Valuation for Rating Act 1953, s 2(2). **Sole v Henning (Valuation Officer)** [1959] 3 398, CA.
      Nil valuation—Ratepayer in beneficial occupation—Flat in house—Flat in extreme state of disrepair—Ratepayer living in flat for 25 years and remaining there to retain Rent Act protection and qualify for rehousing when closing order on house made—Nobody other than ratepayer likely to pay rent for flat—Whether possible to have nil valuation where ratepayer in actual beneficial occupation. **Black v Oliver (Valuation officer)** [1978] 3 408, CA.
      Statutory restriction on occupation—Statutory restriction not making ratepayer's actual occupation illegal—First floor flat in house—House in extreme state of disrepair—Direction by local authority limiting occupation of house to one household—At date of direction ratepayer only occupant of house—At date of proposal to alter valuation list ground floor flat illegally occupied by another household—Whether direction to be taken into account in assessing rent hypothetical tenant would pay for ratepayer's flat on assumption flat vacant—Whether because of direction there should be a nil valuation of ratepayer's flat—General Rate Act 1967, s 19(2), (6). **Black v Oliver (Valuation officer)** [1978] 3 408, CA.
    Electricity undertaking—
      Aggregate rateable value of hereditaments occupied for the purpose of generating electricity—Order containing annual formula calculating value based on generating capacity—Whether order ultra vires—Local Government Finance Act 1988, Sch 6, para 3(2)—Electricity Supply Industry (Rateable Values) Order 1994, SI 1994/3282. **R (on the application of Edison First Power Ltd) v Central Valuation Officer** [2003] 4 209, HL.
      Profits basis—Calculation of profits—Deduction of excess profits tax. **Yeovil RDC v South Somerset and District Electricity Co Ltd** [1947] 1 669, CA.
      Profits basis—Limiting profits basis to accounts for year preceding date of assessment—Whether 'special circumstances' rendering profits basis inapplicable—Rating and Valuation Act 1925, s 31(5). **Barking Borough Rating Authority v Central Electricity Board** [1940] 3 477, CA.
      Special classes of property—Ring main—Apportionment of annual value between areas where tapped and not tapped. **Metropolitan Electric Supply Co Ltd v Buckingham County Valuation Committee** [1939] 1 36, KBD.
    Foreshore, esplanade and gardens—
      Profits basis yielding low value—Finding that occupying local authority would give higher rent. **Morecambe and Heysham Corp v Robinson (Valuation Officer)** [1961] 1 721, CA.
    Gas company—
      Computation on profits basis—Capital sum required for conduct of undertaking—Source from which, and price at which, capital obtainable irrelevant. **Croydon Gas Co v Croydon County Borough Rating Authority** [1946] 1 384, KBD.
    Hypothetical tenancy—
      Impending redevelopment—Part of factory required for road widening—Expectation of demolition in a year—Effect on value taken into account—Rating and Valuation Act 1925, s 22(1)(b). **Dawkins (Valuation Officer) v Ash Bros & Heaton Ltd** [1969] 2 246, HL.
    Land—
      New South Wales. *See* **New South Wales** (Rates—Valuation—Land).

RATES (cont)—
  Valuation (cont)—
    Licensed premises—
      Monopoly value—Capital value—Rent the hypothetical tenant would pay—Licensing (Consolidation) Act 1910, s 14(2). **Appenrodt v Central Middlesex Assessment Committee** [1937] **2** 325, CA.
      Profits basis—Direct method of assessing gross value—Notice calling for particulars of trade actually done during each of past three years—Whether such particulars 'reasonably required' by valuation officer—Local Government Act 1948, s 58(1), (2) (as amended)—Rating and Valuation Act 1925, s 68. **Watney Mann Ltd v Langley** [1963] **3** 967, QBD.
      Tied house. **Robinson Bros (Brewers) Ltd v Houghton and Chester-le-Street Assessment Committee** [1938] **2** 79, HL.
    List. *See* Valuation list, *below*.
    Market—
      Tolls—Rateability—Franchise tolls for admission to market—Distinction from stallage and pickage, tolls for particular use of soil—Cattle tolls—Charge for all cattle entering market—Franchise tolls not taken into consideration in ascertaining rateable value. **Oswestry Corp v Hudd (Valuation Officer)** [1966] **1** 490, CA.
    Non-industrial building—
      Gross value—Chain and anchor testing house—Hereditament was a factory—Whether used wholly or mainly for 'industrial purposes'—Rating and Valuation Act 1925, s 22(1)(a), 1(b), (4)—Rating and Valuation (Miscellaneous Provisions) Act 1955, s 5(1), (2), (3). **Crowe (Valuation Officer) v Lloyds British Testing Co Ltd** [1960] **1** 411, CA.
    Plant and machinery—
      Dry dock—Hereditament containing dry dock—Exclusion of plant from valuation of hereditament—Plant used in connection with dry dock—Dock as a functional entity—Dock consisting of excavated cavity and associated installations—Installations constituting plant—Whether dock as a whole to be regarded as plant—Whether walls and floor of dock to be regarded separately as forming part of hereditament—General Rate Act 1967, s 21(1). **Manchester Marine Ltd v Duckworth (Valuation Officer)** [1973] **3** 838, CA.
      Plant and machinery deemed to be part of hereditament. *See* Plant and machinery deemed to be part of hereditament, *above*.
    Racecourse—
      New South Wales. *See* **New South Wales** (Rates—Valuation—Racecourse).
      Premises used for operating totalisator—Racecourse Betting Act 1928, ss 1, 2, 3—Betting and Lotteries Act 1934, s 18(1). **Racecourse Betting Control Board v Brighton County Borough Rating Authority** [1942] **1** 611, CA.
    Uniformity—
      County valuation committee—Right to proceed by instalments. **R v Cornwall County Valuation Committee, ex p Falmouth BC** [1937] **2** 266, CA.
    Valuation by reference to rents—
      Assumption that hereditament in state of reasonable repair, excluding any repairs which a reasonable landlord would consider uneconomic—Office premises vacant and subject to construction works—Whether distinction between repairs and improvements—Whether works constituting repairs—Whether rateable value of premises nominal—Local Government Finance Act 1988, Sch 6, para 2. **Newbigin v SJ & J Monk (a firm)** [2015] **4** 1014, CA.
      Assumption that hereditament in state of reasonable repair, excluding any repairs which a reasonable landlord would consider uneconomic—Office premises vacant and subject to redevelopment works—Whether premises to be rated on basis they were offices in state of reasonable repair—Whether premises to be rated on basis they were undergoing reconstruction—Whether rateable value of premises nominal—Local Government Finance Act 1988, Sch 6, para 2. **Newbigin v SJ & J Monk (a firm)** [2017] **2** 971, SC.
      Flats—Provision of service and amenities by landlord—Ascertainment of gross rateable value—Valuation (Metropolis) Act 1869, s 4. **Bell Property Trust Ltd v Hampstead Borough Assessment Committee** [1940] **3** 640, CA.
      Vacant office building—No actual tenant willing to occupy property and pay positive price for doing so at valuation date—Comparable buildings in local area being let and occupied at valuation date—Whether valuation of rateable value to be determined by general demand in area for comparable office buildings—Local Government Finance Act 1988, Sch 6, para 2. **Telereal Trillium Ltd v Hewitt (Valuation Officer)** [2019] **4** 219, SC.
    Valuer. *See* **Valuer**.
    Waste incinerator and electricity generator—
      Ratepayer company owning and operating hereditament whose primary function was incineration of waste—Hereditament including generator producing electrical power and heat for sale—Whether hereditament's primary function was 'in connection with' scheme for production for sale of electrical power and heat—Electricity Generators (Rateable Values) Order 1989, art 3(2)(a)(ii). **Coventry and Solihull Waste Disposal Co Ltd v Russell (Valuation Officer)** [2000] **1** 97, HL.
    Water undertaking—
      Gross receipts—Revenue from precepts on board's constituent authorities—Precepts to meet cost of uncompleted works. **Mid-Northamptonshire Water Board v Lee (Valuation Officer)** [1957] **2** 143, HL.
      Profits basis—Gross receipts—Revenue from precepts on board's constituent authorities—Precepts to meet cost of uncompleted works. **Mid-Northamptonshire Water Board v Lee (Valuation Officer)** [1957] **2** 143, HL.
      Profits basis—Indirectly productive hereditament—Water intake—Departure from usual method of calculation on profits basis—Special circumstances—Altitude of hereditament—Rating and Valuation Act 1925, s 22(1)(b). **Metropolitan Water Board v Hertford Corp** [1953] **1** 1047, CA.
    Wireless relay service—
      Valuation on profits basis. **Amalgamated Relays Ltd v Burnley Rating Authority** [1950] **1** 253, KBD.
    Zoological gardens—
      Valuation on profits basis—Exceptional hereditament—Factors to be considered—Receipts from employment of tenant's capital—Gains from hiring out animals—Profits tax. **Surrey County Valuation Committee v Chessington Zoo Ltd** [1950] **1** 154, KBD.

RATES (cont)—
  Valuation list—
    Amendment—
      Amendment by assessment committee of its own motion—Union Assessment Committee Act 1862, s 26—Rating and Valuation Act 1925, s 30. **R v West Middlesex Assessment Committee, ex p Southall Rating Authority** [1942] **2** 280, KBD.
    Construction—
      Description—Evidence. **Sussex Caravan Parks Ltd v Richardson (Valuation Officer)** [1961] **1** 731, CA.
    Date of valuation—
      Common valuation date—Assessment of gross values of shop premises—Valuation officer estimating rent payable on 1 April 1973 when valuation list came into force—Estimate made in 1972 from information supplied to valuation officer in 1971—Whether 1 April 1973 common valuation date—General Rate Act 1967, s 68(1). **K Shoe Shops Ltd v Hardy (Valuation Officer)** [1983] **3** 609, HL.
    Description in valuation list—
      Premises partly occupied—Liability for rates for whole premises. *See* Rateable occupation—Non-occupation of part of premises—Liability for rates for whole premises—Description in valuation list, *above*.
    Preparation—
      Assessing gross values of dwellings—Errors not vitiating list as a whole—Whether prerogative remedy by certiorari or mandamus lies for fundamental error going to the root of list as a whole—Inconsistent treatment of classes of flats—Valuation officer assessing hypothetical rent in good faith—Rating and Valuation (Miscellaneous Provisions) Act 1955, s 1(2)—Rating and Valuation Act 1925, s 68 (as modified by Valuation for Rating Act 1953, s 2(1), (2))—Local Government Act 1948, s 57(1) (as amended by Rating and Valuation (Miscellaneous Provisions) Act 1955, s 15, Sch 7). **R v Paddington Valuation Officer, ex p Peachey Property Corp Ltd** [1965] **2** 836, CA.
    Proposal for alteration—
      Effective date of alteration—Local Government Finance Act 1988, ss 41(1), 55. **National Car Parks Ltd v Baird (Valuation Officer)** [2005] **1** 53, CA.
    Provisional list—
      Objection to proposed assessment—Alteration in value—Cause—Valuation (Metropolis) Act 1869, s 47. **R v Westminster Assessment Committee, ex p Junior Carlton Club (Trustees)** [1940] **3** 155, KBD.
  Valuer—
    Employment by rating authority—
      Inclusive remuneration—Claim by rating authority to all documents prepared by valuers in course of work—Right of valuers to retain documents—Rating and Valuation Act 1925, s 38. **Leicestershire CC v Michael Faraday & Partners Ltd** [1941] **2** 483, CA.
      Payment out of general rate fund. **Grainger v Liverpool Corp** [1954] **1** 333, QBD.
    Generally. *See* **Valuer**.
  Water rates—
    Generally. *See* **Water supply** (Water rates).
    Lands Tribunal—
      Transfer of jurisdiction from county court. *See* **Lands Tribunal** (Jurisdiction—Water rates—Transfer of jurisdiction from county court).
    Recovery—
      Dispute—Jurisdiction of county court. *See* **County court** (Jurisdiction—Rates—Recovery of water rates—Dispute).

RATIFICATION
  Authority—
    Agent. *See* **Agent** (Authority—Ostensible authority—Ratification).

RATIO DECIDENDI
  Precedent. *See* **Precedent** (Ratio decidendi).

RATIONING
  Acquiring rationed goods without coupons—
    Fine—
      Fine based on purchase price—Whether purchase tax properly included in purchase price. **Paprika Ltd v Board of Trade** [1944] **1** 372, KBD.
    Onus of proof—
      Burden of proof on person charged—Consumer Rationing (Consolidation) Order 1944 (SR & O 1944 No 800), arts 3, 4. **R v Sellars** [1946] **1** 82, CCA.
      Duty of prosecution to establish prima facie case—Consumer Rationing (Consolidation) Order 1944 (SR & O 1944 No 800), arts 1, 2(3), 4. **R v Putland and Sorrell** [1946] **1** 85, CCA.
  Clothing—
    Possession of false coupons—
      Knowledge of falsity—Defence (General) Regulations 1939, reg 82(1)(b). **R v Greenberg** [1942] **2** 344, CCA.
  Food—
    Catering establishment—
      Fats and cheese—Exceeding amounts which may be used in specified period—Used—Use, not for consumption by customers, but for manufacture of articles to be stored—Whether an offence—Fats, Cheese and Tea (Rationing) (No 2) Order 1946 (SR & O 1946 No 1116), arts 8, 10 (as amended by Fats, Cheese and Tea (Rationing) (No 2) (Amendment No 3) Order 1946 (SR & O 1946 No 2025). **Quaintways Restaurant Ltd v Budd** [1948] **1** 782, KBD.
    Charge of supplying unregistered customer with rationed food—
      Further charge of supplying rationed food without coupon—Whether two offences committed—Charge of supplying two different rationed foods—Whether information bad for duplicity—Rationing Order 1939 (SR & O 1939 No 1856), arts 2, 7(a),(c). **Kite v Brown** [1940] **4** 293, KBD.

RATIONING (cont)—
  Food (cont)—
    Offering an excessive quantity of meat at an excessive price—
      Meat priced and marked with customer's name but not delivered to customer—Whether offer within meaning of the order—Rationing Order 1939 (SR & O 1939 No 1856), art 2—Meat (Maximum Retail Prices) Order 1940 (SR & O 1940 No 37), art 4. **Wiles v Maddison** [1943] **1** 315, KBD.
    Prescribed amount for household consumption—
      Husband and wife—Customer with lawful use of own and husband's ration books—Whether customer may lump both rations together when ordering from retailer—Excessive charge—Rationing Order 1939 (SR & O 1939 No 1856), art 6—Food (Butter) Order 1941 (SR & O 1941 No 666), art 2. **Charman v Thomas** [1942] **2** 514, KBD.
    Returns understating number of registered customers—
      Returns false in a material particular and made recklessly—Rationing Order 1939 (SR & O 1939 No 1856), art 42. **Stevens & Steeds Ltd v King** [1943] **1** 314, KBD.
  Petrol—
    Application for petrol coupons—
      False returns with intent to deceive made by servants of company—Liability of company. **DPP v Kent and Sussex Contractors Ltd** [1944] **1** 119, KBD Divl Ct.
      False statement—Application by employee for allocation of petrol—Untrue statements—Letter by employers certifying accuracy of information furnished—Untrue statements not within knowledge of employers—Whether 'knows' to be interpreted as 'ought to have known'—Defence (General) Regulations 1939, reg 82(2). **London Computator Ltd v Seymour** [1944] **2** 11, KBD.

READINESS, NOTICE OF
  Arrived ship under port charterparty—
    Commencement of lay days. See **Shipping** (Commencement of lay days—Arrived ship under port charterparty—Notice of readiness).
  Waiver of defect. See **Shipping** (Commencement of lay days—Notice of readiness to load—Congestion at load port).

READING LIST
  Practice. See **Practice** (Reading lists).

REAL PROPERTY
  Estates or interests capable of subsisting in land. See **Land** (Estates or interests capable of subsisting at law).
  Generally. See **Land**.
  Option to purchase—
    Will. See **Will** (Option—Option to purchase realty).
  Owner—
    Negligence—
      Duty to take care. See **Negligence** (Duty to take care—Owner of realty).
  Restraint on alienation—
    Fee simple. See **Restraint on alienation** (Fee simple estate).
  Sale of land. See **Sale of land**.
  Tenants in common. See **Tenants in common** (Real property).
  Trust for sale. See **Trust and trustee** (Trust for sale—Realty).

REBATE
  Hydrocarbon oils—
    Duty. See **Customs and excise** (Hydrocarbon oils—Rebate).
  Redundancy payment—
    Rebate to employer. See **Redundancy** (Payment—Rebate to employer).

RECEIVER
  Action against receiver—
    Procedure—
      Action for breach of contract—Necessity for leave of court. **Botilbol (decd), Re** [1947] **1** 26, Ch D.
  Appointed by court—
    Company, in case of. See **Company** (Receiver—Appointment by court).
  Powers—
    Small repairs not exceeding £150. **Practice Direction** [1970] **1** 671, Ch D.
  Remuneration—
    Appellant charged with VAT and PAYE offences—Respondent seizing money from appellant's home—Seized sum being used to pay receiver's remuneration—Appellant acquitted of charges—Appellant seeking to recover receiver's remuneration by costs order against respondent in High Court proceedings—Whether receiver's remuneration costs of and incidental to proceedings. **Andrews, Re** [1999] **2** 751, CA.
    Confiscation order. See **Sentence** (Confiscation order—Receivership order—Satisfaction of confiscation order).
    Protection of property—Receiver appointed in respect of assets being realisable property to which restraint order applied—Assets not realisable property—Quashing of restraint order and receivership order—Receiver asserting lien over assets for remuneration and expenses during currency of receivership—Whether receiver entitled to remuneration and expenses out of assets—Whether breach of right to protection of property—Whether court having power to order payment of receiver's remuneration and expenses by Crown—Human Rights Act 1998, s 3, Sch 1, Pt II, art 1—Proceeds of Crime Act 2002, Pt 2. **CPS v Eastenders Group** [2013] **2** 437, CA; [2014] **3** 1, SC.

RECEIVER (cont)—
Appointed by court (cont)—
Remuneration (cont)—
Receiver appointed to preserve assets of defendant who might become subject to confiscation order—Whether receiver entitled to use assets of defendant to meet costs of receivership—Whether court having discretion to order payment of receiver's costs by Revenue and Customs Commissioners—Criminal Justice Act 1988, ss 76, 77—CPR 69.7. **Capewell v Revenue and Customs Comrs** [2007] **2** 370, HL.
Receiver appointed to preserve assets of defendant who might become subject to confiscation order—Whether receiver entitled to use assets of unconvicted or acquitted defendant to meet costs of receivership—Criminal Justice Act 1988—Drug Trafficking Act 1994—Human Rights Act 1998, Sch 1, Pt II, art 1. **Hughes v Customs and Excise Comrs** [2002] **4** 633, CA.
Receiver appointed to protect or preserve property—Remuneration and expenditure exceeding moneys received in getting in and dealing with property—Whether court having power to order parties to litigation to pay excess—Whether receiver's remuneration costs 'of and incidental to ... proceedings' in which receiver appointed by court—Supreme Court Act 1981, s 51(1). **Evans v Clayhope Properties Ltd** [1988] **1** 444, CA.
Receivership order in respect of criminal defendant subsequently discharged—Assets over which defendant having bare legal title—Whether receiver's lien for remuneration, costs and expenses extending to assets over which defendant having bare legal title—Criminal Justice Act 1988, ss 74, 77, 88, 89, 102. **Sinclair (former Receiver of Glatt) v Glatt** [2009] **4** 724, CA.
Restraint order—
Appointment of receiver to take possession of realisable property—Guidelines—Criminal Justice Act 1988, Pt VI. **Capewell v Customs and Excise Comrs** [2005] **1** 900n, CA.
Appointment—
Court, by—
Company, in case of. See **Company** (Receiver—Appointment by court).
Generally. See Appointed by court, *above*.
Debenture holder, by. See **Company** (Receiver—Appointment by debenture holder).
Dissolution of partnership—
Generally. See **Partnership** (Dissolution—Appointment of receiver).
Retirement of partner. See **Partnership** (Receiver—Appointment).
Equitable execution. See **Execution** (Equitable execution—Receiver—Appointment of receiver over power of revocation of trust).
Invalid appointment—
Conversion. See **Conversion** (Contractual rights—Invalid appointment of receivers).
Local authority under statutory duty to provide housing—
Failure to provide heating in breach of tenancy agreements—Whether appropriate for court to appoint receiver to restore heating services—Supreme Court Act 1981, s 37—Housing Act 1957, s 111. **Parker v Camden London BC** [1985] **2** 141, CA.
Protection or preservation of property—
Landlord failing to collect rents or to repair—Whether court will appoint receiver to collect rents and to effect repairs—Supreme Court Act 1981, s 37. **Hart v Emelkirk Ltd** [1983] **3** 15, Ch D.
Charging order—
Land. See **Execution** (Charging order—Land—Application for appointment of receiver to enforce charge).
Charity. See **Charity** (Receiver and manager).
Company—
Debenture. See **Company** (Debenture—Receiver).
Generally. See **Company** (Receiver).
Liability to tax. See **Income tax** (Receiver—Company—Liability of receiver to tax).
Petition in compulsory winding up. See **Company** (Compulsory winding up—Petition by receiver under debenture).
Debenture—
Ratification—
Whether subsequent receiver, appointed by debenture-holders, can ratify contract not authorised by former receiver. See **Agent** (Ratification—Validity—Receiver appointed by debenture-holders of first company).
Drug trafficking—
Appointment of receiver—
Powers of receiver. See **Drugs** (Drug trafficking).
Equitable execution. See **Execution** (Equitable execution—Receiver).
Foreign receiver—
Title to assets in England. See **Conflict of laws** (Receiver—Foreign receiver—Title to assets in England).
Mental patient's property. See **Mental health** (Patient's property—Receiver).
Mortgage. See **Mortgage** (Receiver).
Mortgaged property—
Appointment of receiver—
War time. See **Emergency legislation** (Mortgage—Appointment of receiver).
Generally. See **Mortgage** (Receiver).
Official Receiver—
Petition by—
Compulsory winding up of company. See **Company** (Compulsory winding up—Petition by Official Receiver).
Order appointing receiver—
Landlord and tenant cases—
Whether order registrable against landlord's title. See **Land charge** (Registration—Order appointing receiver—Receiver appointed by court to manage property—Tenanted property in disrepair).
Rateable occupation of premises. See **Rates** (Rateable occupation—Occupation by receiver).
Remuneration—
Court appointed receiver. See Appointed by court—Remuneration, *above*.

RECEIVING
Stolen property—
Generally. *See* **Criminal law** (Receiving stolen property).
Handling stolen goods. *See* **Criminal law** (Handling stolen goods).
Indictment. *See* **Indictment** (Joinder of two or more accused—Receiving stolen property).

RECEIVING ORDER
See **Bankruptcy** (Receiving order).

RECISSION
Misrepresentation. *See* **Misrepresentation**.

RECKLESS DRIVING
Duress as a defence. *See* **Criminal law** (Duress as a defence—Reckless driving).
Generally. *See* **Road traffic** (Reckless driving).

RECKLESSNESS
Assault—
Criminal liability. *See* **Criminal law** (Assault—Mens rea—Recklessness).
Criminal damage—
Recklessness whether property would be destroyed or damaged. *See* **Criminal law** (Damage to property—Recklessness whether property would be destroyed or damaged).
Inducement to invest money—
Criminal liability. *See* **Criminal law** (Inducement to invest money—Reckless making of statement or promise).
Manslaughter. *See* **Criminal law** (Manslaughter—Recklessness or gross negligence).

RECOGNISANCE
Acknowledgment in name of another. *See* **Criminal law** (Forgery—Acknowledging recognisance in name of another).
Arrest—
Breath test—
Arrest of motorist following test. *See* **Road traffic** (Breath test—Arrest following breath test—Recognisance).
Bail—
Generally. *See* **Criminal law** (Bail—Recognisance).
Case stated—
Magistrates' court. *See* **Case stated** (Magistrates' courts—Recognisance).
Forfeiture—
Appeal to quarter sessions against order for forfeiture. *See* **Quarter sessions** (Appeal to—Appeal against order for forfeiture of recognisance).
Binding-over. *See* **Magistrates** (Binding over—Forfeiture of recognisance).

RECOGNITION
Foreign divorce. *See* **Divorce** (Foreign decree—Recognition by English court).
Foreign government—
Conflict of laws. *See* **Conflict of laws** (Foreign government—Recognition).
Generally. *See* **International law** (Recognition of foreign government).
Foreign judgment. *See* **Conflict of laws** (Foreign judgment—Recognition and enforcement).
Foreign nullity decree. *See* **Nullity** (Recognition of foreign decree).
Foreign sovereign state. *See* **Constitutional law** (Foreign sovereign state—Recognition).
Trade union—
Generally. *See* **Trade union** (Recognition).
Redundancy. *See* **Redundancy** (Employer's duty to consult appropriate trade union—Recognition of trade union).

RECOMMENDATION TO MERCY
Criminal trial. *See* **Criminal law** (Trial—Recommendation to mercy).

RECONCILIATION
Divorce. *See* **Divorce** (Reconciliation).

RECONSTRUCTION
Church organ—
Faculty. *See* **Ecclesiastical law** (Faculty—Reconstruction of church organ).
Company—
Generally. *See* **Company** (Reconstruction).
Meaning—
Intention to reconstruct premises. *See* **Landlord and tenant** (Opposition to grant of new tenancy of business premises—Intention of landlord to demolish or reconstruct premises comprised in holding—Reconstruct—Meaning).

RECORD
Business—
Admissibility in evidence—
Criminal proceedings. *See* **Criminal evidence** (Record relating to trade or business).
Error of law on face of record—
Certiorari. *See* **Certiorari** (Error of law on face of record).
Estoppel by—
Issue estoppel. *See* **Estoppel** (Issue estoppel).
Res judicata. *See* **Estoppel** (Res judicata).

RECORD (cont)—
Evidence—
Admissibility in evidence. *See* **Document** (Admissibility in evidence—Record as evidence of facts stated therein).
Tape recorded conversation—
Admissibility in criminal proceedings. *See* **Criminal evidence** (Exclusion of evidence—Discretion—Tape recorded conversation).
Formal record—
Power of court in subsequent proceedings to go behind formal record. *See* **Estoppel** (Res judicata—Formal record—Power of court in subsequent proceedings to go behind formal record).
Goods vehicle. *See* **Road traffic** (Goods vehicle—Driver's records).
Trade or business—
Evidence in criminal proceedings. *See* **Criminal evidence** (Record relating to trade or business).

RECORDED DELIVERY SERVICE
Service of notice by. *See* **Joint tenancy** (Notice of severance—Service—Registered post).

RECORDER
Assistant recorder—
Mode of address—
Style of reference in court list. **Practice Direction** [1982] **1** 320, CA.
Crown Court—
Offences triable by recorder. *See* **Crown Court** (Distribution of court business—Classification of offences—Offences triable by High Court judge, circuit judge, recorder).
Mode of address—
Generally. *See* **Judge** (Mode of address—Recorder).
Style of reference in court list. **Practice Direction** [1982] **1** 320, CA.

RECORDS
Musical works, of—
Copyright—
Exception from protection of records made by manufacturer for sale by retail. *See* **Copyright** (Musical work—Exception from protection—Making of record by manufacturer for sale by retail).
Infringement by playing records in shop. *See* **Copyright** (Conflict of laws—Public performance—Shop).
Shop—
Playing of records in public—
Infringement of copyright. *See* **Copyright** (Conflict of laws—Public performance—Shop).

RECOURSE AGREEMENT
Hire-purchase. *See* **Hire-purchase** (Recourse agreement).

RECOVERY VEHICLE
Trade licence. *See* **Road traffic** (Trade licence—Motor trader—Recovery vehicle).

RECREATION
Charitable object—
Exhibition of agricultural and horticultural produce. *See* **Charity** (Benefit to community—Showground, park and recreation—Exhibition of agricultural and horticultural produce).

RECREATIONAL CHARITY
See **Charity** (Recreational charity).

RECTIFICATION
Articles of association—
Jurisdiction of court. *See* **Company** (Articles of association—Mistake—Rectification of mistake—Jurisdiction of court).
Contract. *See* **Contract** (Rectification).
Deed—
Estoppel. *See* **Estoppel** (Deed—Rectifiable deed).
Generally. *See* **Deed** (Rectification).
Land register. *See* **Land registration** (Rectification of register).
Lease. *See* **Landlord and tenant** (Lease—Rectification).
Life assurance policy. *See* **Insurance** (Life insurance—Policy—Rectification).
Mistake—
Generally. *See* **Mistake** (Rectification).
Magistrates' jurisdiction. *See* **Magistrates** (Jurisdiction—Reopening case to rectify mistake etc).
Patent register. *See* **Patent** (Rectification of register).
Register of charges—
Company. *See* **Company** (Charge—Registration—Rectification of register).
Share register. *See* **Company** (Shares—Register—Rectification).
Tenancy agreement. *See* **Landlord and tenant** (Tenancy agreement—Rectification).
Trade mark register. *See* **Trade mark** (Rectification of register).
Will. *See* **Will** (Rectification).

REDEMPTION
Compensation—
Redemption of weekly payment. *See* **Workmen's compensation** (Redemption of weekly payment).
Mortgage. *See* **Mortgage** (Redemption).
Tithe and tithe rentcharge. *See* **Tithe and tithe rentcharge** (Redemption).

REDISTRIBUTION OF SEATS
Parliamentary election. *See* **Elections** (Parliamentary—Redistribution of seats).

REDUCED EARNING ALLOWANCE
Equality of treatment of men and women—
European Community. *See* **European Union** (Equality of treatment of men and women—Social security—Reduced earning allowance).

REDUNDANCY
Academic staff—
University—
Dismissal for redundancy. *See* **University** (Academic staff—Dismissal—Redundancy).
Award—
Protective award—
Failure to consult appropriate trade union. *See* Employer's duty to consult appropriate trade union—Failure to consult union—Protective award against employer, *below*.
Calculation of amount of payment—
Employment for which no normal working hours—
Average weekly rate of remuneration—Meaning of 'remuneration'—Employee receiving each week from employees wages and expenses in respect of car—Employee dismissed by reason of redundancy—Assessment of redundancy payment—Whether car expenses to be included as part of employee's remuneration—Redundancy Payments Act 1965, s 1(1), Sch 1, para 5(1)—Contracts of Employment Act 1972, Sch 2, para 3(2). **S & U Stores Ltd v Wilkes** [1974] **3** 401, NIRC.
Employment for which normal working hours—
Amount of week's pay—Average hourly rate of remuneration—Remuneration varying with amount of work done—Incentive or productivity bonus built into wage structure—Bonus over and above basic hourly rate of remuneration paid for extra work done in normal working hours—Whether bonus part of average hourly rate of remuneration—Whether bonus payment for overtime—Distinction between employee whose remuneration varies with amount of work done and 'time' worker when calculating redundancy payment—Redundancy Payments Act 1965, Sch 1, para 5(1)—Contracts of Employment Act 1972, Sch 2, para 2(2), (3). **Ogden v Ardphalt Asphalt Ltd** [1977] **1** 267, EAT.
Amount of week's pay—Average hourly rate of remuneration—Voluntary overtime earnings—Payment of overtime premium—Whether overtime premium to be deducted from total actual remuneration for purpose of calculating hourly rate of remuneration—Employment Protection (Consolidation) Act 1978, Sch 14, paras 3(3), 5(2). **British Coal Corp v Cheesbrough** [1990] **1** 641, HL.
Amount of week's pay—Travel allowance paid to employees—Whether to be taken into account for assessing redundancy payment—Normal working hours—Contracts of Employment Act 1963, Sch 2, para 2(2)—Redundancy Payments Act 1965, s 1(1), Sch 1, para 5(1). **Bailey (N G) & Co Ltd v Preddy** [1971] **3** 225, QBD.
Express term of contract as to number of working hours—Consensual variation of term—Variation implied by conduct—Contracts of Employment Act 1963, Sch 2, para 1(1), (2). **Armstrong Whitworth Rolls Ltd v Mustard** [1971] **1** 598, QBD.
Normal working hours—Overtime—Statement of terms of employment referred normal working hours to works rules—Works rules stated normal working hours to be forty hour week—Overtime worked—Whether overtime obligatory under national agreements—Whether overtime working to be taken into account in assessing redundancy payment—Redundancy Payments Act 1965, s 1, Sch 1, para 5—Contracts of Employment Act 1963, Sch 2, paras 1(1), 3(1). **Pearson v Jones (William) Ltd** [1967] **2** 1062, QBD.
Overtime—Employee entitled to overtime pay—Contract fixing minimum number of working hours—Minimum number of working hours exceeding number of working hours without overtime—Contract guaranteeing employment for 40 hours a week at basic hourly rate—Contract obliging employee to work overtime when required by employer—Employer not obliged to provide overtime work—Employee regularly working 57 hour week—Whether contract 'fixing' minimum number of working hours in excess of number of hours without overtime—Whether normal working hours 57 hours a week—Contracts of Employment Act 1963, Sch 2, para 1(1), (2). **Tarmac Roadstone Holdings Ltd v Peacock** [1973] **2** 485, CA.
Claim for redundancy payment—
Notice of claim to employer—
Time at which notice to be given—Notice required to be given before the end of six months 'beginning with' date on which termination of employment takes effect—Notice of claim given by employee before dismissal took effect—Whether notice of claim could be given before commencement of prescribed period—Redundancy Payments Act 1965, s 21(b). **Watts v Rubery Owen Conveyancer Ltd** [1977] **2** 1, EAT.
Notice of claim to tribunal. *See* Notice of claim to tribunal, *below*.
Collective redundancy—
European Union. *See* **European Union** (Employment—Protection of employees following death of employer—Collective redundancy).
Continuity of employment. *See* **Employment** (Continuity).
Death of employer—
European Union. *See* **European Union** (Employment—Protection of employees following death of employer—Collective redundancy).
Discrimination against a woman—
Unfair dismissal and redundancy payments. *See* **Employment** (Discrimination against a woman—Unfair dismissal and redundancy payments).
Dismissal by reason of redundancy—
Cessation of or diminution in requirements of business for employees to carry out work of a particular kind—
Work of a particular kind—Slaughtering company employing applicants as meat plant operatives—Applicants normally working in slaughter hall but could be required to work elsewhere under their contracts—Company requiring fewer employees in slaughter hall and dismissing applicants—Whether applicants dismissed by reason of redundancy—Contracts of Employment and Redundancy Payments Act (Northern Ireland) 1965, s 11(2)(b). **Murray v Foyle Meats Ltd** [1999] **3** 769, HL.

946

REDUNDANCY (cont)—
  Dismissal by reason of redundancy (cont)—
    Cessation of or diminution in requirements of business for employees to carry out work of a particular kind—
      Dismissal attributable to diminution—Woodworker engaged in boatbuilding—Change from wood to fibreglass—Employee found uneconomic after study of costs—Employee not replaced—Redundancy Payments Act 1965, s 1(2)(b), 9(2)(b). **Hindle v Percival Boats Ltd** [1969] **1** 836, CA.
      Place where person employed—Steel erector employed in construction industry—Refusal of employee to work away from home—Dismissal—Whether implied term in contract of employment relating to place of work—Travelling an essential feature of employment in the industry. **Stevenson v Tees-side Bridge and Engineering Ltd** [1971] **1** 296, QBD.
      Test to be applied—Whether account to be taken of terms and conditions of employment of employee claiming redundancy payment—Employees brought to work from long distance at employers' expense—Provision of transport ceasing to be economic—Employers withdrawing transport—Employees dismissed by reason of employers' repudiation of contract—Employers engaging other men living nearby in place of dismissed employees—Whether employees dismissed by reason of redundancy—Redundancy Payments Act 1965, s 1(2)(b). **Chapman v Goonvean & Rostowrack China Clay Co Ltd** [1973] **2** 1063, CA.
      Work of a particular kind—Employee engaged to do clerical work from 9.30 am to 5.30 pm five days a week—Employer altering employee's days and hours of work—Employee's total number of working hours unaltered—Employee's actual work unchanged—Employee dismissed for refusing to accept alteration in hours of work—Employee replaced by person willing to work the new hours—Whether change of hours act constituting change in 'kind of work' required—Whether employee entitled to redundancy payment—Redundancy Payments Act 1965, s 1(2)(b). **Johnson v Nottinghamshire Combined Police Authority** [1974] **1** 1082, CA.
      Work of a particular kind—Fitter operating garage's emergency breakdown service—Fitter occupying flat rent-free in part of business premises connected with another side of employers' business—Sale by employers of that side of the business and of premises which contained flat—Notice given to fitter to terminate employment and vacate flat—Subsequent offer by employers of reemployment as fitter refused—Emergency breakdown service discontinued—Whether fitter entitled to redundancy payment—Redundancy Payments Act 1965, s 1(2). **Arnold v Harrington (Thomas) Ltd** [1967] **2** 866, QBD.
    Change of ownership of business—
      Business unchanged but employee's duties altered—Garage taken over by new company with different business methods—Re-organisation transferring rather different work to manager—Manager unable to adapt himself to new duties—Overall requirements of business unchanged—Manager dismissed and replaced by new manager—Whether old manager dismissed on account of redundancy and entitled to redundancy payment—Redundancy Payments Act 1965, s 1(2)(b). **North Riding Garages Ltd v Butterwick** [1967] **1** 644, QBD.
      Distinction between transfer of business or part of business and transfer of assets—Employer transferring one of two factories and plant therein to new owner—New owner taking over from employer contracts of employment of employees—Employees engaged in same sort of work as before transfer from employer—New owner guaranteed orders from employer for period of 7 months—Guaranteed orders constituting only two-thirds of new owner's business—Remaining third of business coming from new owner's own customers—Whether transfer of 'part of ... business'—Redundancy Payments Act 1965, s 13(1)(a). **Melon v Hector Powe Ltd** [1981] **1** 313, HL.
      No dismissal if new owner renews employee's contract or re-engages him—Owner farmer sold farm by public auction, and subsequently, by another public auction the live and dead stock—Incoming farmer bought only part of live and dead stock—Employee farm worker was re-employed by new owner without any break in employment and continued in similar work—Whether 'change of ownership of business'—Whether employee entitled to redundancy payment from vendor farmer—Redundancy Payments Act 1965, s 13(1)(a). **Lloyd v Brassey** [1969] **1** 382, CA.
      No dismissal if new owner renews employee's contract or re-engages him—Re-engagement—Offer in writing—Requirements of valid offer—Sale of part of business by vendor employers and re-engagement by purchasing employers—Circular letter not showing material differences between old and new terms of employment—Different terms as to notice overtime wages and insurance scheme—Position as if re-engagement on new contract by vendor employers—Whether re-engagement was in pursuance of an offer in writing within Redundancy Payments Act 1965, ss 3(2)(b), 13(2). **Havenhand v Black (Thomas) Ltd** [1968] **2** 1037, QBD.
      No dismissal if new owner renews employee's contract or re-engages him—Re-engagement—Sale of business by former employer—Condition that purchasers of business make written offer of re-engagement to all employees in business on same terms as in existing contracts—No written offer made—Employee working for purchasers for two weeks for same wages paid by former employer—Employee's wages then changed by purchasers—Employee subsequently dismissed by purchasers—Whether conduct of purchasers and employee amounting to offer and acceptance of re-engagement on terms not differing from previous contract—Whether employee entitled to redundancy payment from former employer—Redundancy Payments Act 1965, ss 3(2)(a), 13(2). **Ubsdell v Paterson** [1973] **1** 685, NIRC.
    Death of employer—
      Renewal of contract or re-engagement by deceased's personal representative—Implied agreement to renew contract or re-engage employee—Employee continuing to do same work as under previous contract of employment—Need to show that employee and personal representative had acted in such a way that they must be taken to have agreed that employment should continue—Redundancy Payments Act 1965, Sch 4, para 3 (as substituted by the Employment Protection Act 1975, Sch 16, para 23). **Ranger v Brown** [1978] **2** 726, EAT.
    Dismissal—
      Employer's offer of employment at reduced wages and inferior status—Employee commenced work at reduced wages and subsequently left employment for other work—Whether employee 'dismissed' or whether consensual variation of original contract—Whether employee entitled to redundancy payment—Redundancy Payments Act 1965, s 3(1)(a), (2)(b). **Marriott v Oxford and District Co-op Society Ltd** [1969] **1** 471, QBD.

REDUNDANCY (cont)—
  Dismissal by reason of redundancy (cont)—
    Dismissal (cont)—
      Notice to employee to terminate contract of employment—Employee verbally requesting termination of contract on date prior to expiry of notice—Employers agreeing to request—Employee leaving before expiry date—Whether employee 'dismissed' or whether consensual termination of contract—Redundancy Payments Act 1965, s 4(1), (2). **McAlwane v Boughton Estates Ltd** [1973] **2** 299, NIRC.
      Termination of contract of employment by employer—Event in accordance with enactment or rule of law affecting employer operating to terminate contract of employment of employee—Whether intervention by Law Society in solicitor's practice event affecting employer to terminate contract of employment of employee—Employment Rights Act 1996, s 136(5). **Rose v Dodd** [2006] **1** 464, CA.
      Termination of contract of employment by employer—Repudiation of contract by employer—Acceptance of repudiation by employee—Contract to employ at particular premises—Employee warned by employers that business was to be transferred to new premises—Employers insisting on right to require employee to work at new premises—Employee giving notice terminating contract before date of move fixed—Employee claiming redundancy payment from employers—Whether employee's contract repudiated by employers—Whether contract terminated by employers—Redundancy Payments Act 1965, s 3(1)(a). **Maher v Fram Gerrard Ltd** [1974] **1** 449, NIRC.
      Termination of contract of employment by employer—Repudiation of contract by employer—Circumstances in which employee will be taken to have accepted repudiation—Employee informed that work being transferred to new premises—Employee not indicating whether prepared to work at new premises—Employee directed to work at new premises—No renewal of contract or offer of new contract by employer—Employee working at new premises for short time and then giving week's notice—Whether employee having accepted employer's repudiation of contract—Whether contract terminated by employer alone or by mutual agreement between employer and employee. **Shields Furniture Ltd v Goff** [1973] **2** 653, NIRC.
  Employers' intention to cease to carry on business in place where employee employed—
    Place where employee employed—Notice that there would be no further work in Sussex and offer of employment in other areas—Whether dismissal by reason of redundancy—Redundancy Payments Act 1965, ss 1(2), 3(1). **McCulloch (R H) Ltd v Moore** [1967] **2** 290, QBD.
  Equality of treatment of men and women—
    European Community. *See* **European Union** (Equality of treatment of men and women—Equal working conditions—Dismissal—Dismissal by reason of redundancy).
  No dismissal on renewal of contract or re-engagement—
    Offer of alternative employment—Employer's offer of employment at reduced wages and inferior status—Employee commenced work at reduced wages and subsequently left employment for other work—Whether consensual variation of contract—Redundancy Payments Act 1965, s 3(1)(a). **Marriott v Oxford and District Co-op Society Ltd** [1969] **3** 1126, CA.
  Presumption that dismissal by reason of redundancy—
    Employee absent from work because of sickness for period of 18 months—Practice of employers to take back employees after period of absence through sickness—Employee not entitled to sick pay during absence—Employers closing down works—Employers giving employee notice to terminate contract—Whether dismissal by reason of redundancy—Redundancy Payments Act 1965, s 9(2). **Marshall v Harland & Wolff Ltd** [1972] **2** 715, NIRC.
  Employer's duty to consult appropriate trade union—
    Employer 'proposing to dismiss [employees] as redundant'—
      Proposing—Consultation with union required to take place 'at the earliest opportunity'—Company—Winding-up order—All employees automatically made redundant without union consultation when company wound up by court—Whether administrators under duty to consult union before making application to court which resulted in winding up—Whether administrators 'proposing to dismiss [employees] as redundant'—Whether administration order a 'special circumstance' relieving corporate employer from duty to consult union on proposed redundancies—Employment Protection Act 1975, ss 99, 100, 101—Insolvency Act 1986, s 130—Council Directive (EEC) 75/129. **Hartlebury Printers Ltd (in liq), Re** [1993] **1** 470, Ch D.
  Failure to consult union—
    Protective award against employer—Jurisdiction—Purpose of award—Factors to be considered in deciding to make award—Employees continuing in employment with purchasers of business—No hardship or loss of remuneration—Whether jurisdiction to make protective award—Whether purpose of award to compensate for lost renumeration or to punish employer for failing to consult union—Whether payments under contract of employment made by another employer during protected period discharging defaulting employer's liability under protective award—Employment Protection Act 1975, ss 101(3), (4), 102(3). **Spillers-French (Holdings) Ltd v Union of Shop, Distributive and Allied Workers** [1980] **1** 231, EAT.
    Protective award against employer—Period of award—Factors to be considered in assessing period—Seriousness of employer's default—Whether provision for calculation of period of award penal—Whether maximum period to be awarded where employer's default blatant—Employment Protection Act 1975, s 101(5). **Talke Fashions Ltd v Amalgamated Society of Textile Workers and Kindred Trades** [1978] **2** 649, EAT.
    Protective award against employer—Period of award—Factors to be considered in assessing period—Whether purpose of award compensatory—Trade Union and Labour Relations (Consolidation) Act 1992, ss 188, 189. **GMB v Susie Radin Ltd** [2004] **2** 279, CA.
  Recognition of trade union—
    Duty to consult trade union recognised by employer—Employees dismissed on ground of redundancy—Union not consulted before employees dismissed—No collective bargaining on wages between employer and union—National agreement between employers' association and union—Employer's factory manager and union representative discussing company's operations over a not insubstantial period of time—Whether union 'recognised by' employer—Employment Protection Act 1975, s 99(1). **National Union of Tailors and Garment Workers v Charles Ingram & Co Ltd** [1978] **1** 1271, EAT.

REDUNDANCY (cont)—
    Employer's duty to consult appropriate trade union (cont)—
        Recognition of trade union (cont)—
            Duty to consult trade union recognised by employer—Employees dismissed on ground of redundancy—Union not consulted before employees dismissed—No collective bargaining on wages between employer and union—Union representative allowed to put up notice and collect union dues on employer's premises—Employer consulting union representative on security matters and changes in employees' duties—Whether union 'recognised by' employer—Employment Protection Act 1975, s 99(1). **Wilson (Joshua) & Bros Ltd v Union of Shop Distributive and Allied Workers** [1978] **3 4**, EAT.
        Special circumstances rendering it not reasonably practicable to comply with duty—
            Genuine belief that no appropriate trade union to be consulted—Employer dismissing of employees as redundant—No consultation with trade union before employees dismissed—Employer genuinely believing that there was no appropriate trade union to be consulted—Whether genuine belief that no appropriate trade union to be consulted a 'special circumstance' rendering it not reasonably practicable for the employer to consult union—Whether belief that there was no appropriate trade union to be consulted must be reasonably held—Employment Protection Act 1975, s 99(8). **Wilson (Joshua) & Bros Ltd v Union of Shop Distributive and Allied Workers** [1978] **3 4**, EAT.
            Insolvency—Company deciding to cease trading because of insolvency—Dismissal of employees as redundant in consequence—No consultation with trade union representatives before decision made to cease trading—Company hoping to continue trading up to last minute—Whether circumstances of insolvency may amount to 'special circumstances' which render it not reasonably practicable for the employer to comply with the requirement to consult union representatives—Employment Protection Act 1975, s 99(8). **Clarks of Hove Ltd v Bakers' Union** [1979] **1** 152, CA.
    Employer's duty to consult appropriate trade union—
        Employer's duty to consult representatives. *See* Employer's duty to consult representatives, *below.*
        Fixed term contracts—
            University not including in collective consultation process employees on fixed term contracts where contract due to end during consultation period—Non-renewal of fixed term contracts constituting dismissal of employees—Whether 'dismissed as redundant'—Whether dismissal 'for a reason not related to the individual concerned'—Trade Union and Labour Relations (Consolidation) Act 1992, ss 188(1), 195(1). **University and College Union v University of Stirling** [2016] **1** 524, SC.
    Employer's duty to consult representatives—
        Failure to consult representatives—
            Foreign state—Validity of legislation—USA operating military base in UK—Collective redundancies being made upon closure of base—Employee representative bringing claim for failure to consult—Domestic legislation enacted pursuant to European law—Amendment made by secondary legislation—Whether foreign state having duty to consult representatives—Whether obligation to consult applying to employment by public administrative establishment—Whether amendment ultra vires—European Communities Act 1972, s 2(2)—Trade Union and Labour Relations (Consolidation) Act 1992, s 188—Collective Redundancies and Transfer of Undertakings (Protection of Employment) (Amendment) Regulations 1995, SI 1995/2587—Council Directive 98/59/EC. **USA v Nolan** [2016] **1** 857, SC.
    Entitlement to redundancy payment—
        Qualifying period of employment—
            Concurrent but separate contracts of employment—Number of hours worked each week—Employee employed under concurrent but separate contracts to teach three part-time courses—Employee not working more than six hours per week under any one contract—Aggregate of hours worked under all three contracts exceeding eight hours per week—Whether employee permitted to aggregate hours worked under separate contracts—Whether employee qualifying to claim redundancy payment—Employment Protection (Consolidation) Act 1978, Sch 13, paras 4, 6. **Surrey CC v Lewis** [1987] **3** 641, HL.
    Exclusion from right to redundancy payment—
        Avoidance of exclusion—
            Employee given notice to terminate contract—Employer entitled to dismiss employee without notice by reason of his taking part in strike—Employer dismissing him for that reason—Dismissal by reason of redundancy of employee taking part in strike—Employee not dismissed for taking part in strike—Whether exclusion from right to redundancy payment avoided—Redundancy Payments Act 1965, ss 2(2), 10(1). **Simmons v Hoover Ltd** [1977] **1** 775, EAT.
        Change of ownership of business—
            Unreasonable refusal of offer by new owner to renew contract of employment or re-engage employee—Meaning of 'change of ownership'—Tenant farmer terminating tenancy on retiring—Employee farm worker dismissed on termination of tenancy—Offered re-employment by in-coming tenant farmer refused it—No transfer of ownership of business—Employee dismissed on account of redundancy—Redundancy Payments Act 1965, s 13(1), (3), (4). **Bandey v Penn** [1968] **1** 1187, Div.
    Conduct entitling employer to terminate contract of employment without notice—
        Participation in strike—Repudiation of contract of employment—Whether participation in strike constituting breach of contract of employment—Whether breach of so fundamental kind as to entitle employer to terminate contract without notice—Redundancy Payments Act 1965, s 2(2). **Simmons v Hoover Ltd** [1977] **1** 775, EAT.
    Exclusion by agreement—
        Agreement by person employed under contract for fixed term of two years or more—Meaning of 'fixed term'—Contract for a definite term—Contract terminable before expiry of term by notice on either side—Whether a contract for a 'fixed term'—Redundancy Payments Act 1965, s 15(2). **BBC v Ioannou** [1975] **2** 999, CA.
    Refusal of offer of re-engagement. *See* Unreasonable refusal of offer of re-engagement, *below.*
    Local government officer—
        Compensation. *See* **Local government** (Officer—Compensation for loss of employment).

REDUNDANCY (cont)—

Notice of claim to tribunal—

Time within which notice to be given—

Notice to be referred to tribunal in accordance with regulations—Referred—Regulations requiring institution of proceedings by 'sending' notice—Notice posted within prescribed time but never received—Whether permissible to construe 'referred' by reference to language of regulations—Whether notice 'referred' if posted but not delivered within prescribed time—Redundancy Payments Act 1965, s 21(c)—Industrial Tribunals (Labour Relations) Regulations 1974 (SI 1974 No 1386), Sch, r 1. **Nash v Ryan Plant International Ltd** [1978] **1** 492, EAT.

Notice to employer of claim for redundancy payment. *See* Claim for redundancy payment—Notice of claim to employer, *above.*

Payment—

Calculation of amount. *See* Calculation of amount of payment, *above.*

Discrimination on grounds of age. *See* **Employment** (Discrimination—Discrimination on grounds of age—Redundancy benefits).

Entitlement to—

Generally. *See* Entitlement to redundancy payment, *above.*

Equality of treatment of men and women—

Discrimination against a woman—Generally. *See* **Employment** (Discrimination against a woman—Unfair dismissal and redundancy payments).

European Community. *See* **European Union** (Equality of treatment of men and women—Equal working conditions—Redundancy benefits).

Rebate to employer—

Entitlement—Liability of employer to make payment arising from agreement between employer and employee—Effect on liability of Secretary of State—Whether employer's liability to make payment under the agreement a liability to pay under the statute—Whether Secretary of State liable to make rebate to employer—Redundancy Payments Act 1965, s 30(1)(a). **Secretary of State for Employment v Globe Elastic Thread Co Ltd** [1979] **2** 1077, HL.

Entitlement—Liability of employer to make payment—Claim for payment submitted to employer out of time—Waiver by employer of possible statutory objection—Effect of waiver—Effect on rights of Secretary of State as trustee of the Redundancy Fund—Effect on right of employee to claim payment—Whether employer liable to make payment—Whether employer entitled to rebate—Redundancy Payments Act 1965, ss 21, 30(1)(a). **Secretary of State for Employment v Atkins Auto Laundries Ltd** [1972] **1** 987, NIRC.

Proceedings by Secretary of State to recover rebate—Proper mode of proceedings—Proceedings on ground employees not entitled to redundancy payment—Jurisdiction of industrial tribunal to determine question as to right of an employee to redundancy payment—Application by Secretary of State to tribunal for declaration that employees not dismissed by reason of redundancy—Jurisdiction of tribunal to entertain application—Whether application necessary before action in High Court for recovery of rebates as money paid under a mistake of fact—Whether High Court having jurisdiction to determine whether dismissals by reason of redundancy in action for recovery of rebates—Redundancy Payments Act 1965, s 9(1). **Secretary of State for Employment v Wellworthy Ltd** [1973] **3** 488, NIRC.

Period of continuous employment. *See* **Employment** (Continuity).

Pregnancy—

Dismissal for reason connected with pregnancy—

Unfair dismissal. *See* **Unfair dismissal** (Dismissal—Pregnancy—Reason connected with pregnancy—Redundancy).

Protective award—

Failure to consult appropriate trade union. *See* Employer's duty to consult appropriate trade union—Failure to consult union—Protective award against employer, *above.*

Recognition of union. *See* Employer's duty to consult appropriate trade union—Recognition of trade union, *above.*

Reference of questions to tribunal—

Appeal against determination of tribunal—

Right of appeal on point of law—Point of law—Meaning—Whether question whether term to be implied in contract of employment point of law. **O'Brien v Associated Fire Alarms Ltd** [1969] **1** 93, CA.

Right to redundancy payment by reason of lay-off or short-time—

Exclusion of right—

Reasonable expectation that within four weeks employee would enter on a period of employment of not less than 13 weeks—Period of employment—Meaning—Skilled employee laid off—Offer of inferior work by employer—Offer not accepted—Whether words 'period of employment' referring only to employment under existing contract of employment—Whether employee's right to redundancy payment excluded—Redundancy Payments Act 1965, s 6(4). **Neepsend Steel & Tool Corp Ltd v Vaughan** [1972] **3** 725, NIRC.

Unfair dismissal—

Claim for redundancy payment. *See* **Unfair dismissal** (Compensation—Redundancy payment).

Compensation—

Loss of accrued right to redundancy payment. *See* **Unfair dismissal** (Compensation—Loss of accrued right to redundancy payment).

Discrimination against a woman. *See* **Employment** (Discrimination against a woman—Unfair dismissal and redundancy payments).

Doubt as to which claim appropriate. *See* **Industrial relations** (Practice—Claim for redundancy payment or compensation for unfair dismissal).

Unreasonable refusal of offer of re-engagement—

Offer in writing—

Omission of term of offer from written offer—Effect—Whether omission invalidating offer—Redundancy Payments Act 1965, s 2(4). **Kaye v Cooke's (Finsbury) Ltd** [1973] **3** 434, NIRC.

REDUNDANCY (cont)—
Unreasonable refusal of offer of re-engagement (cont)—
Offer in writing (cont)—
Requirements of valid offer—Date of commencement of new employment—Need to specify date—Employers moving to new premises—Letter from employers to employees offering re-engagement at new premises on same terms and conditions as those currently in force—Letter not specifying precise date when new employment to start—New employment starting immediately after termination of existing employment—Whether necessary that offer should specify date—Redundancy Payments Act 1965, s 2(4). **Kaye v Cooke's (Finsbury) Ltd** [1973] **3** 434, NIRC.
Requirements of valid offer—Offer in writing—Requirements of valid offer—Notice posted on notice board addressed to all employees—Whether constituting an offer in writing—Redundancy Payments Act 1965, s 2(4). **McCreadie v Thomson & MacIntyre (Patternmakers) Ltd** [1971] **2** 1135, HL.
Specification of differences compared with previous contract—Whether necessary to specify points of similarity—Redundancy Payments Act 1965, s 2(4). **McCreadie v Thomson & MacIntyre (Patternmakers) Ltd** [1971] **2** 1135, HL.
Specification of differences compared with previous contract—Whether offer must conform to requirements of s 2(4)—Redundancy Payments Act 1965, s 2(4), s 3(2)(b). **Marriott v Oxford and District Co-op Society Ltd** [1969] **3** 1126, CA.
Offer of suitable employment—
Headmaster offered job in mobile pool of teachers—Same salary guaranteed—Necessity of moving house—Suitability of alternative offer of employment matter of degree and fact for Industrial Tribunal—Reasonableness of refusal of offer—'Suitable employment'—Redundancy Payments Act 1965, s 2(4). **Taylor v Kent CC** [1969] **2** 1080, QBD.
Reasonableness of refusal—
Offer of regular employment—Refusal on grounds that in employee's view alternative employment would not last more than limited period—Whether likely duration of alternative employment relevant in determining whether refusal unreasonable—Redundancy Payments Act 1965, s 2(4). **Morganite Crucible Co Ltd v Street** [1972] **2** 411, NIRC.

REDUNDANT CHURCH
See **Ecclesiastical law** (Redundant church).

REFERENCE
Character reference—
Reference by employer—
Duty of employer to take care. See **Negligence** (Duty to take care—Employer—Character reference given by employer on former employee).
Court of Appeal, Criminal Division—
Reference by Secretary of State. See **Criminal law** (Reference by Secretary of State).
Criminal appeal—
Reference by Home Secretary. See **Criminal law** (Appeal—Reference by Home Secretary).
European Court. See **European Union** (Reference to European Court).
Federal Supreme Court, Nigeria. See **Nigeria** (Reference—Interpretation of Constitution—Interpretation referred to Federal Supreme Court).
Point of law—
Reference following acquittal of accused. See **Criminal law** (Appeal—Reference of point of law following acquittal of accused).
Referee—
Practice. See **Practice** (Reference to referee).
Restrictive trade practices. See **Restrictive trade practices** (Reference).

REFERENDUMS
Elections. See **Elections** (Referendums).

REFERENTIAL TRUSTS
Will. See **Will** (Referential trusts).

REFINANCING ARRANGEMENTS
See **Hire-purchase** (Refinancing arrangements).

REFRESHING MEMORY
Witness in criminal proceedings. See **Criminal evidence** (Witness—Refreshing memory).

REFRESHMENT
Innkeeper—
Duty to provide. See **Inn** (Duty to supply refreshment and lodging to traveller).

REFRESHMENT HOUSE
Late night refreshment house—
Licence. See **Licensing** (Late night refreshment house).

REFUGE HOLES
Coal mine—
Statutory duty to provide. See **Coal mining** (Statutory duty—Provision of refuge holes).

REFUGEE
Asylum. See **Immigration** (Asylum—Refugee).
Immigration—
Deportation. See **Immigration** (Deportation—Refugee).
Generally. See **Immigration** (Refugee).
Leave to enter. See **Immigration** (Leave to enter—Refugee).

REFUGEE (cont)—
    Immunity from expulsion—
        Immunity by virtue of international convention. *See* **Lesotho** (Refugee—Expulsion—Refugee claiming immunity by virtue of international convention).

REFUND
    Deposit—
        Sale of land. *See* **Sale of land** (Recovery of deposit).
    Guarantee—
        Construction. *See* **Guarantee** (Construction—Refund guarantees).

REFUSE
    Accumulation or deposit—
        Statutory nuisance. *See* **Nuisance** (Statutory nuisance—Accumulation or deposit prejudicial to health or a nuisance).
    Generally. *See* **Public health** (Refuse).

REGIMENTAL RECORD
    Admissibility in evidence. *See* **Document** (Admissibility in evidence—Record as evidence of facts stated therein—Regimental record).

REGISTER
    Births, deaths and marriages. *See* **Registration** (Births, deaths and marriages).
    Child abuse register—
        Generally. *See* **Child** (Child abuse—Child abuse register).
        Judicial review of case conference decision to place alleged abuser's name on register—Availability of remedy. *See* **Judicial review** (Availability of remedy—Child abuse register).
    Company—
        Members of company. *See* **Company** (Register of members).
        Restoration to register. *See* **Company** (Restoration to register).
        Share register. *See* **Company** (Shares—Register).
    Court register—
        Magistrates' court—
            Practice. *See* **Magistrates** (Procedure—Court register).
    Land. *See* **Land registration**.
    Proprietorship register—
        Entry of purchase price—
            Whether evidence of receipt of purchase price. *See* **Land registration** (Transfer—Purchase price remaining unpaid—Deed of transfer containing acknowledgment of receipt of purchase price).

REGISTERED LAND
    Compulsory purchase—
        Costs—
            Promoter's liability. *See* **Compulsory purchase** (Costs—Promoter's liability—Registered land).
    Generally. *See* **Land registration**.
    Land charge—
        Registration. *See* **Land charge** (Registration—Registered land).
    Sale—
        Constructive trust. *See* **Trust and trustee** (Constructive trust—Sale of registered land).

REGISTERED OFFICE
    Company—
        Service—
            Writ. *See* **Writ** (Service on company—Registered office).
    Moneylender. *See* **Moneylender** (Licence—Address).

REGISTERED POST
    Generally. *See* **Post Office** (Registered postal packet).
    Service by registered post—
        Generally. *See* **Practice** (Service—Service by post—Registered post).
        Motoring offences—
            Notice of intended prosecution. *See* **Road traffic** (Notice of intended prosecution—Notice sent to defendant's residence by registered post).

REGISTERED TRADE UNION
    Dissolution. *See* **Trade union** (Dissolution—Registered trade union).

REGISTRAR
    Additional superintendent registrar of births, deaths and marriages—
        Corruption—
            Whether a 'person serving under the Crown'. *See* **Criminal law** (Corruption—Transactions with agents—Agent—Person serving under the Crown—Additional superintendent registrar of births, deaths and marriages).
    Appeal from registrar—
        Jurisdiction of Court of Appeal. *See* **Court of Appeal** (Jurisdiction—Appeal from registrar).
    Chief Registrar of Friendly Societies—
        Powers of control in relation to building societies. *See* **Building society** (Chief Registrar—Controls exercisable by Chief Registrar).
    County court—
        Appeal to judge—
            Divorce proceedings—Financial provision—Interlocutory appeal. *See* **Divorce** (Financial provision—Practice and procedure—County court—Interlocutory appeal in matrimonial proceedings—Appeal from registrar to county court judge).

REGISTRAR (cont)—
Court of Appeal—
  Civil Division—
    Functions of registrar. *See* **Court of Appeal** (Practice—New practice and procedure—Civil Division—Registrar).
  Criminal appeals—
    Registrar of criminal appeals—
      Disposal of groundless appeals. *See* **Criminal law** (Court of Appeal—Disposal of groundless appeal—Power of registrar of criminal appeals).
Divorce—
  Custody—
    Applications which may be made to registrar. *See* **Divorce** (Custody—Application—Applications which may be made to registrar).
Family Division—
  Appeal from—
    Practice. *See* **Family Division** (Appeal—Appeal from registrar).
Grant of administration. *See* **Administration of estates** (Grant of administration—Jurisdiction—Registrar).
Land registrar—
  Appeal—
    Procedure. *See* **Land registration** (Appeal—Procedure).
Powers—
  Application under s 17 of the Married Women's Property Act 1882. *See* **Husband and wife** (Property—Summary proceedings—Application—Procedure by originating summons—Absence of respondent—Powers of registrar).
  Reference to referee. *See* **Practice** (Reference to referee—Order by district registrar—Jurisdiction of registrar).
Superintendent registrar of births, deaths and marriages—
  Remuneration—
    Registrar paid by local authority—Powers of dismissal for failure to perform duties exercisable by Registrar General—Whether registrar employed by local authority—Whether office-holder or employee—Whether local authority bound to pay full salary despite registrar's failure to perform duties—Registration Service Act 1953, s 6(3), (4). **Miles v Wakefield Metropolitan DC** [1987] **1** 1089, HL.
Variation of settlement—
  Application for variation. *See* **Variation of Settlement (Matrimonial Causes)** (Application for variation—Practice—Made to registrar on affidavit).
Ward of court—
  Jurisdiction of registrar. *See* **Ward of court** (Jurisdiction—Registrar).

REGISTRATION
Accommodation. *See* **Housing** (Registration of living accommodation).
Adopted Children Register. *See* **Adoption** (Adopted Children Register).
Agreement—
  Restrictions on trade. *See* **Restrictive trade practices** (Registration of agreement).
Articles of clerkship. *See* **Solicitor** (Articled clerk).
Births, deaths and marriages—
  Application for birth certificate—
    Refusal on public policy grounds—Convicted murderer detained in secure mental hospital applying for birth certificate—Applicant adopted and unaware of natural mother's identity—Registrar General under statutory duty to supply details—Registrar General refusing application on public policy grounds because of possible threat to natural mother if applicant ever released—Whether Registrar General entitled to refuse application on public policy grounds—Whether public policy good ground for refusal if it relates to possible future criminal conduct—Adoption Act 1976, s 51. **R v Registrar General, ex p Smith** [1991] **2** 88, CA.
  Correction or erasure of entry in register—
    Bigamous marriage—Correction of register—Whether mandamus to correct register lies—Marriage Act 1836, s 23—Marriage Act 1949, s 61. **Dinizulu v A-G and Registrar-General** [1958] **3** 555, QBD.
    Surname of child—Child registered in surname of man mother was living with—Mother registering child in that name without father's consent—Mother intending that child be known by that name at date of registration—Father wanting child to be known by his surname—Whether father could require alteration of register—Whether error in register—Whether intention of one parent that child be known by name entered in register sufficient to establish that 'it is intended' that child should be so known—Births and Deaths Registration Act 1953, s 29(3)—Registration of Births, Deaths and Marriages Regulations 1968 (SI 1968 No 2049), reg 18(3). **D v B (orse D) (child: surname)** [1979] **1** 92, CA.
  Parental status—
    Gender—Transgender male conceiving and giving birth to child—Whether to be registered as 'mother', 'father' or 'parent' on child's birth certificate—Whether registration as 'mother' breaching human rights—Meaning of 'mother'—Human Rights Act 1998, Sch 1, Pt I, arts 8, 14—Gender Recognition Act 2004, ss 9, 12. **R (on the application of McConnell) v Registrar General for England and Wales** [2020] **2** 813, Fam D, CA.
Certificate—
  Building work, for. *See* **Building control** (Certificate of registration).
Charge—
  Charge created by company. *See* **Company** (Charge—Registration).
  Land charge. *See* **Land charge** (Registration).
  Minute of reduction of share capital of company—
    Form of minute for registration. *See* **Company** (Reduction of capital—Minute of reduction—Form of minute).
  Priority—
    Company debenture. *See* **Company** (Debenture—Priority—Competing charges—Order of registration).
Charity. *See* **Charity** (Registration).

REGISTRATION (cont)—
Child-minder. *See* **Child** (Registration of child-minders).
Club—
 Application for registration certificate. *See* **Licensing** (Club—Application for registration certificate).
 Registration for purpose of having gaming machines. *See* **Gaming** (Club—Registration).
Common land and rights of common. *See* **Commons** (Registration).
Common lodging-house. *See* **Public health** (Common lodging-house—Registration).
Company—
 Members of company. *See* **Company** (Register of members).
 Restoration of name to register. *See* **Company** (Restoration to register).
 Shares. *See* **Company** (Shares—Register).
Conditions imposed by building licence. *See* **Housing** (Registration of conditions imposed by building licence).
Correction or erasure of entry in register—
 Bigamous marriage—
  Correction of register—Whether mandamus to correct register lies—Marriage Act 1836, s 23—Marriage Act 1949, s 61. **Dinizulu v A-G and Registrar-General** [1958] 3 555, QBD.
Design. *See* **Design** (Registration).
Estate contract—
 Vacation of entry in register. *See* **Land charge** (Vacation of entry in register).
Film title. *See* **Cinema** (Film—Title—Registration).
Financial provision orders—
 Divorce. *See* **Divorce** (Financial provision—Registration of orders).
Fishing vessel—
 European Community. *See* **European Union** (Fishing rights—Common fishing policy—Fishing vessels—Registration).
Foreign judgment. *See* **Conflict of laws** (Foreign judgment—Registration in England).
Heavy motor car. *See* **Road traffic** (Heavy motor car—Registration).
Indian and Pakistani residents—
 Ceylon. *See* **Ceylon** (Registration of Indian and Pakistani residents).
Land—
 Common land. *See* **Commons** (Registration).
 Generally. *See* **Land registration**.
 Land charge—
  Generally. *See* **Land charge**.
  Matrimonial home. *See* **Husband and wife** (Matrimonial home—Land charge—Registration).
Living accommodation. *See* **Housing** (Registration of living accommodation).
Mentally disordered persons—
 Homes for. *See* **Mental health** (Registration of residential homes for mentally disordered persons).
Pending action. *See* **Land charge** (Pending action).
Premises—
 Place of meeting for religious worship. *See* **Ecclesiastical law** (Place of meeting for religious worship—Registration of premises).
Proprietary club—
 Registration for purposes of having gaming machines. *See* **Gaming** (Club—Registration—Registration for purpose of having gaming machines—Refusal to register or to renew registration—Proprietary club).
Restrictive trading agreement. *See* **Restrictive trade practices** (Registration of agreement).
Selective employment tax. *See* **Selective employment tax** (Registration).
Service mark. *See* **Trade mark** (Service mark—Registration).
Trade mark—
 European Community. *See* **European Union** (Trade marks—Registration).
 Generally. *See* **Trade mark** (Registration).
 Opposition to registration. *See* **Trade mark** (Opposition to registration).
 Service mark. *See* **Trade mark** (Service mark—Registration).
Value added tax. *See* **Value added tax** (Registration).

REGISTRY
Admiralty and Commercial Court Registry. *See* **Practice** (Admiralty and Commercial Court Registry).

REGULATED CONSUMER AGREEMENT
Generally. *See* **Consumer credit** (Agreement—Regulated consumer credit agreement).

REGULATED TENANCY
Possession—
 Recovery by landlord. *See* **Rent restriction** (Possession).
 Rent. *See* **Rent restriction** (Regulated tenancy).

REGULATIONS
European Union. *See* **European Union** (Regulations).
Generally. *See* **Statutory instrument**.
Validity—
 Challenging—
  Appeal or judicial review—Proper method of challenge on application for judicial review—RSC Ord 53. **Moss (Henry) of London v Customs and Excise Comrs** [1981] 2 86, CA.

REHABILITATION
Houses unfit for human habitation. *See* **Housing** (Clearance area—Rehabilitation of unfit houses).
Rehabilitation of offenders—
 Previous convictions—
  Reference at trial. *See* **Criminal law** (Trial—Previous convictions—Rehabilitation of offenders).

REHABILITATION (cont)—
Rehabilitation of offenders (cont)—
Spent conviction—
Disclosure of spent conviction—Disclosure in course of official duties—Official duties—Disclosure of spent convictions by London office of Interpol to foreign Interpol office in response to request about plaintiff's criminal activities—Plaintiff suspected of planning crimes abroad—Whether information disclosed by London Interpol office in course of 'official duties'—Whether duties of English police extending to suppression of crime abroad—Rehabilitation of Offenders Act 1974, s 9(2). **X v Comr of Police of the Metropolis** [1985] **1** 890, Ch D.

Prohibition on adducing evidence of spent conviction in proceedings before a judicial authority—Appeals against refusal and revocation of housing licences by local housing authority—Local authority relying on facts relating to forged gas safety certificates used in applications and in respect of which first appellant and husband convicted—Convictions spent at relevant time—Whether prohibition extending to evidence of conduct constituting spent convictions—Whether local authority 'judicial authority' when granting and revoking licences—Rehabilitation of Offenders Act 1974, ss 4(1)(a), (b), (6), 7—Housing Act 2004, s 66. **Hussain v Waltham Forest London BC** [2021] **4** 97, CA.

Publication referring to spent conviction—Grant of injunction restraining publication if publication is malicious—Rehabilitation of Offenders Act 1974, s 1(1). **Herbage v Pressdram Ltd** [1984] **2** 769, CA.

Reference to spent conviction in civil proceedings—Action against police for assault, damage to property, false imprisonment and malicious prosecution—Judge granting application to cross-examine plaintiff as to two previous spent convictions—Whether judge right to do so—Whether justice could be done without doing so—Whether substantial wrong or miscarriage had been occasioned—Rehabilitation of Offenders Act 1974, ss 4(1), 7(3). **Thomas v Comr of Police of the Metropolis** [1997] **1** 747, CA.

REHEARING
Divorce Division. *See* **Divorce—Rehearing**.
Evidence—
Answers to cross-examination on affidavits at first hearing—
Admissibility. *See* **Evidence** (Rehearing—Answers to cross-examination on affidavits at first hearing).

REINSTATEMENT
Covenant—
Lease—
Reinstatement of premises at end of term. *See* **Landlord and tenant** (Covenant—Reinstatement of premises at end of term).
Insurance—
Fire insurance. *See* **Insurance** (Fire insurance—Reinstatement).

REINSURANCE
Arbitration clause in reinsurance contract—
Validity—
Separability. *See* **Arbitration** (Agreement—Arbitration clause—Validity of arbitration clause—Separability—Reinsurance contracts containing arbitration clause).
Brokers—
Negligence—
Accrual of cause of action. *See* **Limitation of action** (Accrual of cause of action—Negligence—Brokers—Reinsurance).
Conflict of laws—
Jurisdiction—
Challenge to jurisdiction. *See* **Conflict of laws** (Jurisdiction—Challenge to jurisdiction).
Generally. *See* **Conflict of laws** (Jurisdiction—Civil and commercial matters—Reinsurance contract).
Reinsurance contract. *See* **Conflict of laws** (Jurisdiction—Challenge to jurisdiction—Reinsurance contract).
Proper law of contract. *See* **Conflict of laws** (Contract—Proper law of contract—Insurance and reinsurance policies).
Construction—
Claims co-operation clause. *See* **Insurance** (Reinsurance—Claims co-operation clause—Construction).
Damages—
Measure of damages—
Negligence. *See* **Damages** (Measure of damages—Negligence—Reinsurance).
Generally. *See* **Insurance** (Reinsurance).

REINTERMENT
Faculty—
Jurisdiction. *See* **Ecclesiastical law** (Faculty—Jurisdiction—Faculty for exhumation and reinterment of human remains).

RELATED ACTIONS
Conflict of laws—
Challenge to jurisdiction. *See* **Conflict of laws** (Jurisdiction—Challenge to jurisdiction—Civil and commercial matters—Related actions).
Stay of proceedings. *See* **Conflict of laws** (Stay of proceedings—Discretion).

RELATIVE
Nearest relative—
Mental health patient. *See* **Mental health** (Patient—Nearest relative).

RELATIVE (cont)—
    Relative of child—
        Adoption of child—
            Application for order—Practice. *See* **Adoption** (Order—Application for adoption order—Application
                by relative).
        Removal of child outside Great Britain—
            Removal for purposes of adoption. *See* **Adoption** (Removal of child outside Great Britain—Removal by
                relative).

RELATOR ACTION
    Generally. *See* **Attorney General** (Relator action).
    Injunction—
        Public right. *See* **Injunction** (Public right—Relator action).
    Local authority. *See* **Practice** (Parties—Local authority).

RELEASE
    Debt—
        Income tax—
            Deduction in computing profits. *See* **Income tax** (Deduction in computing profits—Debt—
                Subsequent release).
    Deed of release—
        Rectification. *See* **Deed** (Rectification—Deed of release).
    Employee—
        Enforceability of release. *See* **Equity** (Release—Enforceability of release).
    Power—
        Implied release. *See* **Power** (Implied release).
    Prisoner—
        Release on licence. *See* **Prison** (Release on licence).
    Vessel under arrest. *See* **Admiralty** (Arrest of vessel—Release).

RELIGION
    Adoption—
        Relevant consideration. *See* **Adoption** (Order—Application for adoption order—Considerations to be
            regarded—Religion).
    Blasphemy. *See* **Criminal law** (Blasphemy).
    Charitable purpose. *See* **Charity** (Religion).
    Child—
        Religious education. *See* **Minor** (Custody—Care and control—Religious education).
    Discrimination—
        Arbitrator. *See* **Arbitration** (Arbitrator—Appointment—Arbitrators required by arbitration clause in
            agreement between parties to be members of Ismaili community).
        Human rights—
            Protection of property. *See* **Human rights** (Freedom of thought, conscience and religion—Freedom
                to manifest religion or beliefs—Protection of property—Prohibition of discrimination).
        Teacher. *See* **Education** (Teacher—Religious discrimination).
    Ecclesiastical law. *See* **Ecclesiastical law**.
    Freedom of religion. *See* **Human rights and freedoms** (Freedom of religion).
    Fugitive offender—
        Extradition—
            Possibility, if returned, of punishment by reason of religion. *See* **Extradition** (Fugitive
                offender—Restrictions on return—Punishment by reason of race, religion, nationality or political
                opinions).
    Human rights—
        Freedom of thought, conscience and religion. *See* **Human rights** (Freedom of thought, conscience and
            religion).
    Place of meeting for religious worship—
        Registration as. *See* **Marriage** (Building registered for solemnisation of marriages—Place of meeting for
            religious worship).
    Places of public religious worship—
        Rates. *See* **Rates** (Exemption—Place of public religious worship).
    Public inquiry—
        Natural justice—
            Opportunity to be heard—Religion precluding party from attending on date set for hearing. *See*
                Natural justice (Public inquiry—Duty to hear parties—Opportunity to be heard—Religion
                prohibiting party from attending on date set for hearing).
    Religiously aggravated offence. *See* **Criminal law** (Racially or religiously aggravated offences).
    School—
        Freedom to manifest religion or belief. *See* **Education** (School—Freedom to manifest religion or belief).
    Ward of court—
        Care and control—
            Factors to be considered. *See* **Ward of court** (Care and control—Factors to be considered—
                Religion).
    Will—
        Condition. *See* **Will** (Condition—Religion).

RELIGIOUS BELIEF
    Refusal to join trade union on grounds of belief—
        Dismissal for refusing to join union—
            Unfair dismissal. *See* **Unfair dismissal** (Determination whether dismissal fair or unfair—Dismissal
              for refusing to join trade union in accordance with union membership agreement—Refusal to join
              on grounds of religious belief).

RELIGIOUS DISCRIMINATION
Teacher. *See* **Education** (Teacher—Religious discrimination).

RELIGIOUS EDUCATION
Child. *See* **Minor** (Custody—Care and control—Religious education).

RELIGIOUS ORGANISATION
Unincorporated association—
    Undue influence—
        Presumption of undue influence—Whether claim based on presumption of undue influence can be raised against unincorporated association. *See* **Equity** (Undue influence—Presumption of undue influence—Unincorporated association—Religious organisation).
    Vicarious liability for sexual abuse. *See* **Vicarious liability** (Non-employment relationship—Unincorporated association—Vicarious liability for sexual abuse).

RELIGIOUS SECT
Membership—
    Jury service—
        Whether membership of sect good reason for being excused from jury service. *See* **Jury** (Juror—Excuse—Grounds on which juror may be excused—Good reason for being excused jury service—Membership of religious sect).

RELIGIOUS WORSHIP
Place of meeting for—
    Rates—
        Exemption. *See* **Rates** (Exemption—Place of public religious worship).
    Registration. *See* **Ecclesiastical law** (Place of meeting for religious worship—Registration of premises).

REMAINDER
Will—
    Vesting—
        Bequest of residue and remainder. *See* **Will** (Gift—Vesting—Bequest of residue and remainder).

REMAND
Remand in custody—
    Access to solicitor—
        Right of person in custody. *See* **Solicitor** (Access to—Right of person in custody—Remand prisoner).
    Credit for periods of remand in custody. *See* **Sentence** (Custodial sentence—Credit for periods of remand in custody—Guidance).
    Generally. *See* **Criminal law** (Committal—Remand in custody).
Remand prisoner—
    Right to marry. *See* **Marriage** (Right to marry—Person in detention—Remand prisoner).
Remand to hospital for report on mental condition—
    Purpose of assessment. *See* **Mental health** (Admission of patient to hospital—Admission for assessment—Remand to hospital for report on accused's mental condition for purpose of obtaining evidence for use at trial by prosecution).
    Supervisory jurisdiction of High Court—
        Trial on indictment. *See* **Crown Court** (Supervisory jurisdiction of High Court—Trial on indictment—High Court having no supervisory jurisdiction in matters relating to trial on indictment—Remand to hospital for report on accused's mental condition for purpose of obtaining evidence for use at trial by prosecution).

REMARRIAGE
Divorced person—
    Application for financial provision. *See* **Divorce** (Financial provision—Application—Remarriage of party).
    Capacity to remarry immediately after decree absolute. *See* **Divorce** (Decree absolute—Remarriage—Capacity of divorced person to remarry immediately after grant of decree absolute).
Widow—
    Effect on damages under Fatal Accidents legislation. *See* **Fatal accident** (Damages—Remarriage of widow).
Will—
    Condition—
        Restraint of remarriage. *See* **Will** (Condition—Restraint of marriage—Remarriage).

REMOTENESS OF DAMAGE
Breach of contract—
    Damages—
        Foreseeable consequence of breach. *See* **Contract** (Damages for breach—Foreseeable consequence of breach).
    Generally. *See* **Damages** (Remoteness of damage).
    Negligence. *See* **Negligence** (Remoteness of damage).

REMUNERATION
Administrator—
    Power of court to authorise. *See* **Executor and administrator** (Administrator—Power of court to authorise remuneration).
Company director. *See* **Company** (Director—Remuneration).
Consultant—
    National Health Service. *See* **National Health Service** (Consultant—Remuneration).
Employee—
    Equality of treatment of men and women. *See* **Employment** (Equality of treatment of men and women).

REMUNERATION (cont)—
    Generally. *See* **Employment** (Remuneration).
    Income tax—
        Office or employment. *See* **Income tax** (Emoluments from office or employment).
    Judicial trustee. *See* **Trust and trustee** (Judicial trustee—Remuneration).
    Liquidator of company—
        Voluntary winding up. *See* **Company** (Voluntary winding up—Liquidator—Remuneration).
    Local government officer. *See* **Local government** (Officer—Remuneration).
    Medical practitioner—
        Failure to comply with terms of service. *See* **National Health Service** (Medical practitioner—Failure to
           comply with terms of service).
    Payment in current coin. *See* **Employment** (Remuneration—Artificer—Payment otherwise than in coin of
        realm).
    Payment in lieu of remuneration—
        Disqualification for unemployment benefit. *See* **Social security** (Unemployment benefit—
           Disqualification for benefit—Payment in lieu of remuneration which would have been received).
    Receiver—
        Company. *See* **Company** (Receiver—Remuneration).
        Receiver appointed by court—
           Generally. *See* **Receiver** (Appointed by court—Remuneration).
    Solicitor—
        Contingency fee. *See* **Solicitor** (Costs—Contingency fee).
        Generally. *See* **Solicitor** (Remuneration).
        Non-contentious business—
           Taxation of costs. *See* **Costs** (Taxation—Solicitor—Non-contentious business).
    Superintendent registrar of births, deaths and marriages. *See* **Registrar** (Superintendent registrar of births,
        deaths and marriages—Remuneration).
    Teacher. *See* **Education** (Teacher—Remuneration).
    Trustee. *See* **Trust and trustee** (Remuneration of trustee).

RENEWAL
    Lease—
        Covenant. *See* **Landlord and tenant** (Covenant—Renewal of lease).
    Writ—
        Admiralty action in personam. *See* **Admiralty** (Practice—Action in personam—Writ—Renewal).
        Admiralty action in rem. *See* **Admiralty** (Practice—Action in rem—Writ—Renewal).
        Principles on which renewal granted. *See* **Writ** (Extension of validity—Jurisdiction—Principles on which
           renewal granted).

RENT
    Acceptance by landlord—
        Waiver of forfeiture. *See* **Landlord and tenant** (Forfeiture of lease—Waiver of forfeiture—Acceptance of
           rent).
        Waiver of notice to quit. *See* **Landlord and tenant** (Notice to quit—Waiver—Acceptance of rent in
           respect of period after termination of tenancy).
    Administration of estates—
        Capital or income. *See* **Administration of estates** (Capital or income—Rent).
    Agricultural holding—
        Arbitration on terms of tenancies as to rent. *See* **Agricultural holding** (Arbitration—Rent).
    Arrears—
        Forfeiture of lease—
           Generally. *See* **Landlord and tenant** (Forfeiture of lease—Arrears of rent).
           Relief. *See* **Landlord and tenant** (Relief against forfeiture—Arrears of rent).
        Re-entry. *See* **Landlord and tenant** (Re-entry—Arrears of rent).
        Recovery—
           Limitation of action. *See* **Limitation of action** (Land—Action for recovery of arrears of rent).
    Assignment of lease—
        Obligation to pay rent. *See* **Landlord and tenant** (Assignment of lease—Obligation to pay rent).
    Best rent—
        Lease granted by mortgagor. *See* **Mortgage** (Power of leasing—Rent).
    Book—
        Failure to provide—
           Whether rent recoverable by action. *See* **Landlord and tenant** (Rent—Agreement for increase—Rent
               book required by law not supplied by landlord—Whether rent recoverable by action).
    Business premises. *See* **Landlord and tenant** (Rent—Business premises).
    Certainty—
        Rent review clause—
           Retrospective operation. *See* **Landlord and tenant** (Rent—Review—Retrospective operation—
               Certainty of rent).
    Claim for rent—
        Distress for rent—
           Set-off. *See* **Landlord and tenant** (Rent—Claim for rent—Distress for rent).
        Generally. *See* **Landlord and tenant** (Rent—Claim for rent).
        Set-off—
           Generally. *See* **Landlord and tenant** (Rent—Claim for rent—Set-off).
    Coal mining lease, under. *See* **Coal mining** (Mining lease—Rent).
    Company—
        Winding up—
           Liability for rent. *See* **Company** (Winding up—Proof and ranking of claims—Rent).
    Control. *See* **Rent control**.
    Corn rent. *See* **Corn rents**.

RENT (cont)—

Covenant to guarantee payment of rent—
   Whether covenant running with land. *See* **Landlord and tenant** (Covenant—Covenant running with
   land—Covenant to guarantee lessee's payment of rent).
Covenant to pay on gold basis. *See* **Landlord and tenant** (Rent—Covenant to pay on gold basis).
Covenant to pay rent—
   Assignment of benefit of covenant. *See* **Landlord and tenant** (Assignment of lease—Obligation to pay
   rent—Assignee—Express covenant with assignor to pay rent—Assignment of benefit of covenant).
Covenant to pay without deduction or set-off—
   Whether unfair contract term. *See* **Landlord and tenant** (Covenant—Payment of rent and service charge
   without deduction or set-off).
Deduction of tax—
   Failure to deduct. *See* **Income tax** (Annual payment—Deduction of tax—Failure to deduct—Rent on
   long lease).
Deficiency—
   Income tax—
     Deduction in computing profits. *See* **Income tax** (Deduction in computing profits—Deficiency in
     rent).
Demand—
   Waiver of forfeiture. *See* **Landlord and tenant** (Forfeiture of lease—Waiver of forfeiture—Demand for
   rent).
Distress. *See* **Distress** (Distress for rent).
Eviction for non-payment—
   Local authority dwelling. *See* **Housing** (Local authority houses—Management—Eviction—Non-payment
   of rent).
Excess rent—
   Income tax. *See* **Income tax** (Profits—Excess rent).
Fair rent—
   Determination of. *See* **Rent restriction** (Rent—Determination of fair rent).
   Generally. *See* **Rent restriction** (Fair rent).
   Local authority houses. *See* **Housing** (Local authority houses—Rent—Fair rent).
Fixing—
   Lease—
     Option to renew. *See* **Landlord and tenant** (Lease—Option to renew—Fixing of rent).
Furnished premises—
   Rent restriction. *See* **Rent restriction** (Furnished letting).
House constructed under building licence—
   Permitted rent. *See* **Housing** (House constructed under building licence—Permitted rent).
Housing benefit—
   Assessment. *See* **Social security** (Housing benefit—Assessment—Payment in respect of rent).
Income tax—
   Annual value of land. *See* **Income tax** (Land—Annual value—Rent).
   Damages in lieu of rent. *See* **Income tax** (Capital or income receipts—Damages—Loss of profit in
   respect of property—Damages awarded to landlord against tenant unlawfully remaining in
   occupation of property).
   Deduction in computing profits. *See* **Income tax** (Deduction in computing profits—Expenses wholly
   and exclusively laid out for purposes of trade—Rent).
   Excess rent. *See* **Income tax** (Profits—Excess rent).
   Expenditure to secure modification of rent obligation in lease—
     Deduction in computing profits—Capital or revenue expenditure. *See* **Income tax** (Deduction in
     computing profits—Capital or revenue expenditure—Payment to secure improvement in
     asset—Payment to secure modification of rent obligation in lease).
   Mining rents. *See* **Income tax** (Mining rents).
Increase—
   Agreement for increase—
     Failure to provide rent book—Whether rent recoverable by action. *See* **Landlord and tenant**
     (Rent—Agreement for increase—Rent book required by law not supplied by landlord—Whether
     rent recoverable by action).
   Notice—
     Local authority housing. *See* **Housing** (Local authority houses—Rent—Notice of increase).
   Regulated tenancy. *See* **Rent restriction** (Regulated tenancy—Increase of rent).
   Rent of agricultural worker. *See* **Agriculture** (Housing—Rural worker—Rent—Right to increase).
Interim rent—
   Business premises. *See* **Landlord and tenant** (Rent—Business premises—Interim rent).
Joint tenancy. *See* **Landlord and tenant** (Rent—Joint tenancy).
Limitation. *See* **Landlord and tenant** (Rent—Limitation).
Local authority housing. *See* **Housing** (Local authority houses—Rent).
Low—
   Tenancy at low rent—
     Continuation as statutory tenancy. *See* **Landlord and tenant** (Long tenancy at low rent).
     Leasehold enfranchisement. *See* **Landlord and tenant** (Leasehold enfranchisement—Tenancy at a
     low rent).
Mining rents—
   Income tax. *See* **Income tax** (Mining rents).
New tenancy—
   Business premises—
     Determination of rent. *See* **Landlord and tenant** (Rent—Business premises—New tenancy).
     Terms. *See* **Landlord and tenant** (Business premises—Terms of new tenancy—Rent).
Payment. *See* **Landlord and tenant** (Rent—Payment).
Permitted rent—
   House constructed under building licence. *See* **Housing** (House constructed under building
   licence—Permitted rent).

RENT (cont)—
    Protected tenancy—
        Amount of rent attributable to attendance forming substantial part of whole rent—
            Exclusion of tenancy from statutory protection. *See* **Rent restriction** (Protected tenancy—Excluded
            tenancies—Amount of rent attributable to attendance forming substantial part of whole rent).
    Quarterly—
        Time at which rent becomes due. *See* **Landlord and tenant** (Rent—Time at which rent becomes
        due—Quarterly rent).
    Rebate—
        Local authority houses. *See* **Housing** (Local authority houses—Rent—Rebate).
    Recovery—
        Arrears—
            Rent controlled premises. *See* **Rent restriction** (Possession—Procedure—Non-payment of rent).
        Limitation of action—
            Evacuation area. *See* **Emergency legislation** (Evacuation area—Recovery of rent—Limitation of
            action).
    Reduction. *See* **Landlord and tenant** (Rent—Reduction).
    Regulated. *See* **Rent restriction**.
    Reserved. *See* **Landlord and tenant** (Rent—Rent reserved).
    Restriction. *See* **Rent restriction**.
    Review. *See* **Landlord and tenant** (Rent—Review).
    Set-off against claim for rent—
        Equitable right of set-off—
            Cross-claim. *See* **Set-off** (Cross-claim—Equitable right of set-off—Claim for rent).
        Generally. *See* **Landlord and tenant** (Rent—Claim for rent—Set-off).
    Stamp duty—
        Lease—
            Consideration consisting of rent. *See* **Stamp duty** (Lease or tack—Consideration consisting of rent).
    Suspension of rent. *See* **Landlord and tenant** (Rent—Suspension of rent).
    Tenants in common—
        Real property—
            Occupation of whole property by one of tenants in common. *See* **Tenants in common** (Real
            property—Occupation of whole property by one of tenants in common—Rent).
    Underlease—
        Generally. *See* **Landlord and tenant** (Rent—Underlease).

RENT ASSESSMENT COMMITTEE
    Natural justice. *See* **Natural justice** (Rent assessment committee).
    Solicitor—
        Effect of membership of panel on practice of solicitor before committee or rent officer. *See* **Solicitor**
        (Practice—Rent assessment committee—Effect of membership of panel on practice of solicitor before
        committee or rent officer).

RENT CONTROL
    Application of Rent Control Act—
        Retrospective effect—
            Proceedings for possession commenced by landlord and case heard before coming into operation
            of Act—Judgment reserved—No order made until after Act in operation—Landlord and Tenant
            (Rent Control) Act 1949, s 10. **Jonas v Rosenberg** [1950] **1** 296, CA.
    Determination of reasonable rent for dwelling-house—
        Dwelling-house—
            Premises containing shop and dwelling accommodation—Covenant by tenant not to use premises
            save as shop for greengrocer's business—Whether a 'dwelling-house'—Rent and Mortgage
            Interest Restrictions Act 1939, s 3(3)—Landlord and Tenant (Rent Control) Act 1949, s 1(1). **R v
            Brighton and Area Rent Tribunal, ex p Slaughter** [1954] **1** 423, QBD.
            Premises containing shop and dwelling accommodation—Covenant by tenant to use premises for
            no business other than that of a tobacconist—Whether a 'dwelling-house'—Rent and Mortgage
            Interest Restrictions Act 1939, s 3(3)—Landlord and Tenant (Rent Control) Act 1949, s 1(1). **R v
            Folkestone Rent Tribunal, ex p Webb** [1954] **1** 427, QBD.
        Jurisdiction of tribunal—
            Determination of question on which jurisdiction depends—Unfurnished letting—Document signed
            by tenant describing letting as furnished alleged to be a sham—Proceedings before
            tribunal—Admissibility in evidence of unstamped documents—Landlord and Tenant (Rent
            Control) Act 1949, s 1(1). **R v Fulham, Hammersmith and Kensington Rent Tribunal, ex p Zerek**
            [1951] **1** 482, KBD.
            Exclusion of jurisdiction where limitation of rent in force under any enactment—Dwelling-house
            built under building licence—Maximum rent to be charged on letting stated in application for
            licence—No condition limiting rent attached to licence—Condition limiting rent and purporting to
            be condition 'attached to a building licence' registered as local land charge under Land Charges
            Act 1925, s 15, pursuant to Building Materials and Housing Act 1945, s 8(1)—Landlord and Tenant
            (Rent Control) Act 1949, s 1(7)(b). **R v Barnet Rent Tribunal, ex p Reeds Investments Ltd**
            [1950] **2** 848, KBD.
            Rectification of written tenancy agreement—Landlord and Tenant (Rent Control) Act 1949, s 1. **R v
            Hackney, Islington and Stoke Newington Rent Tribunal, ex p Keats** [1950] **2** 138, KBD.
            Reduction of rent—House converted into flats—Flat first rated as separate hereditament at £80—No
            appointment of assessment of dwelling-house—Landlord and Tenant (Rent Control) Act 1949,
            s 1(1). **R v Sidmouth Rent Tribunal, ex p Sellek** [1951] **1** 107, KBD.
            Rental equivalent—Determination—Premium—Payment to lessor for work done to premises—
            Payment to lessor of half profit on assignment of lease—Landlord and Tenant (Rent Control) Act
            1949, ss 1(5), 18(2), Sch I, Pt I, para 1. **R v Fulham, Hammersmith and Kensington Rent Tribunal,
            ex p Philippe** [1950] **2** 211, KBD.

RENT CONTROL (cont)—
Determination of reasonable rent for dwelling-house (cont)—
Procedure before tribunal—
Need to hear parties or evidence—Landlord and Tenant (Rent Control) Act 1949, s 1(1)—Landlord and Tenant (Rent Control) Regulations 1949 (SI 1949 No 1096), regs 4, 5, 8(1). **R v Brighton and Area Rent Tribunal, ex p Marine Parade Estates Ltd** [1950] **1** 946, KBD.
Right to make application—
Application by deserted wife in occupation of matrimonial home—Husband the tenant—No authority to act as husband's agent—Landlord and Tenant (Rent Control) Act 1949, s 1(1). **R v Twickenham Rent Tribunal, ex p Dunn** [1953] **2** 734, QBD.
Validity of application—
Misnomer of landlord—Landlord and Tenant (Rent Control) Regulations 1949 (SI 1949 No 1096), reg 3(2) (as amended by Landlord and Tenant (Rent Control) Amendment) Regulations 1950 (SI 1950 No 1763), reg 2). **Jackson (Francis) Developments Ltd v Hall** [1951] **2** 74, CA.
Withdrawal of application—
Jurisdiction of tribunal to proceed with hearing—Landlord and Tenant (Rent Control) Act 1949, s 1(1). **R v Hampstead and St Pancras Rent Tribunal, ex p Goodman** [1951] **1** 170, KBD.
Furnished letting—
Increase of rent—
Increase above contractual rent—Whether recoverable. **Villa D'Este Restaurant Ltd v Burton** [1957] **1** 862, CA.
Notice to quit—
Notice given after tenancy referred to tribunal—Validity and effect—Furnished Houses (Rent Control) Act 1946, s 5. **Alexander v Springate** [1951] **1** 351, KBD.
Reference to tribunal of contract for furnished letting. *See* Reference to tribunal of contract for furnished letting, *below.*
Rent in excess of registered rent—
Recovery—Amount recoverable—Payment of any sum in excess of the rent so entered—Furnished Houses (Rent Control) Act 1946, s 4(1)(a). **Henry v Taylor** [1954] **1** 721, CA.
Rent of premises fixed and registered—Subsequent letting of part of premises at rent exceeding that registered—Whether an offence—Furnished Houses (Rent Control) Act 1946, s 4(1)(a). **Gluchowska v Tottenham BC** [1954] **1** 408, QBD.
Requirement to pay—Rent under lease reduced—Option by deed to renew lease at original rent—Validity of option—Furnished Houses (Rent Control) Act 1946, s 4(1)(a). **Mauray v Durley Chine (Investments) Ltd** [1953] **2** 458, CA.
Right of tenant to recover excess rent—Rent of premises fixed and registered—Subsequent letting of premises to another tenant at rent exceeding that registered—Some money spent by landlord on repairs, etc, before the subsequent letting—Right of tenant, under subsequent letting, to recover excess rent—Furnished Houses (Rent Control) Act 1946, s 4(1)(a), (2). **De Jean v Fletcher** [1959] **1** 602, CA.
Premium—
Prohibition of premiums on grant or assignment of tenancy—
Excessive prices for furniture to be treated as premiums—Excessive price—Price exceeding 'reasonable price of articles'—Landlord and Tenant (Rent Control) Act 1949, s 3(1)(b). **Eales v Dale** [1954] **1** 717, CA.
Payment by tenants to builders for conversion of dwelling-houses into flats—Landlord and Tenant (Rent Control) Act 1949, ss 2(1), 18(2), Sch I, Pt I, para 1. **R v Birmingham (West) Rent Tribunal, ex p Edgbaston Investment Trust Ltd** [1951] **1** 198, KBD.
Purchase price of goodwill of business—Landlord and Tenant (Rent Control) Act 1949, ss 2(2), 18(2), Sch I, Pt I, para 1. **R v Barnet Rent Tribunal, ex p Millman** [1950] **2** 216, KBD.
Requirement of payment as condition of continuance of lease—Proviso for re-entry on breach of any of tenant's covenants—Agreement in 1948 to pay premium for grant of 14 years' lease—Premium payable by instalments over ten years—First annual instalment of premium falling due after 2 June 1949—Demand for payment of instalment—Instalments of premium not additional rent—Landlord and Tenant (Rent Control) Act 1949, s 2(1). **Regor Estates Ltd v Wright** [1951] **1** 219, CA.
Reference to tribunal of contract for furnished letting—
Contract under which lessee entitled to exclusive occupation of part of house—
Exclusive occupation—Meaning—Furnished room—Contract for 'paying guest' to occupy furnished room at a weekly charge—Landlady to have access to room at all times—Contract referred to rent tribunal—Jurisdiction—Furnished Houses (Rent Control) Act 1946, s 2(1). **R v Battersea, Wandsworth, Mitcham and Wimbledon Rent Tribunal, ex p Parikh** [1957] **1** 352, QBD.
Contract whereby lessee granted right to occupy house as residence in consideration of rent which includes payment for use of furniture or for services—
Furniture—Electric clock—Curtains—Gas cooker—Ascot water heater—Furnished Houses (Rent Control) Act 1946, s 2(1). **R v Blackpool Rent Tribunal, ex p Ashton** [1948] **1** 900, KBD.
Rent which includes payment for use of furniture or for services—Meaning—Need of contractual obligation of landlord—Breach of contract—Jurisdiction of tribunal—Furnished Houses (Rent Control) Act 1946, ss 2(1), 12(1). **R v Hampstead and St Pancras Rent Tribunal, ex p Ascot Lodge** [1947] **2** 12, KBD.
Residence—Use by tenant partly for business purposes and partly as residence—Boarding house—Whether occupation as a 'residence'—Furnished Houses (Rent Control) Act 1946, s 2(1). **R v York, Harrogate, Ripon and Northallerton Areas Rent Tribunal, ex p Ingle** [1954] **1** 440, QBD.
Jurisdiction of tribunal—
Determination of collateral question on which jurisdiction depends—Existence of tenancy at time of reference—Furnished Houses (Rent Control) Act 1946, s 2(1), (2). **R v City of London Rent Tribunal, ex p Honig** [1951] **1** 195, KBD.
Determination of question on which jurisdiction depends—Contract of tenancy—Identity of landlord—Circumstances of landlord—Furnished Houses (Rent Control) Act 1946, s 2(2). **R v Paddington and St Marylebone Rent Tribunal, ex p Haines** [1961] **3** 1047, QBD.
Increase of contractual rent—Whether increase recoverable—Furnished Houses (Rent Control) Act 1946, s 2(2), (3). **Villa D'Este Restaurant Ltd v Burton** [1957] **1** 862, CA.

RENT CONTROL (cont)—
  Reference to tribunal of contract for furnished letting (cont)—
    Jurisdiction of tribunal (cont)—
      New reference—Furnished house—Rent fixed on landlord's application—Further reference by new
      tenant—No change of circumstances—Jurisdiction to entertain new reference—Furnished
      Houses (Rent Control) Act 1946, s 2(2). **R v Fulham, Hammersmith and Kensington Rent Tribunal,**
      ex p Gormly [1951] **2** 1030, KBD.
      Re-consideration of registered rent—Change of circumstances—Receipt by landlord of war damage
      compensation—Furnished Houses (Rent Control) Act 1946, s 2(3). **R v Fulham, Hammersmith and**
      Kensington Rent Tribunal, ex p Hierowski [1953] **2** 4, QBD.
      Reference of lease to the tribunal by assignee of lease—Whether tribunal had jurisdiction to hear
      reference—Furnished Houses (Rent Control) Act 1946, s 2. **R v Tottenham and District Rent**
      Tribunal, ex p Northfield (Highgate) Ltd [1956] **2** 863, QBD.
      References to tribunal by local authority—Reference of 555 flats by local authority—Validity of
      reference—Taking into account by tribunal of matters not discussed at hearing—Powers and
      duties of tribunals—Furnished Houses (Rent Control) Act 1946, s 2(1). **R v Paddington and St**
      Marylebone Rent Tribunal, ex p Bell London and Provincial Properties Ltd [1949] **1** 720, KBD.
      Tenancy surrendered after reference to tribunal—Whether tribunal has jurisdiction—Furnished
      Houses (Rent Control) Act 1946, s 2(2). **R v West London Rent Tribunal, ex p Napper** [1965] **3** 734,
      QBD.
    Reduction of rent—
      Reduction below amount of standard rent—Attachment of rent to premises in rem—Reduction
      'affecting' Rent Restrictions Acts—Furnished Houses (Rent Control) Act 1946, ss 2(2), 3(2), 7. **R v**
      Fulham, Hammersmith and Kensington Rent Tribunal, ex p Marks [1951] **2** 465, KBD.
      Reduction below amount of standard rent—Furnished Houses (Rent Control) Act 1946, s 7. **R v**
      Paddington and St Marylebone Rent Tribunal, ex p Bedrock Investments Ltd [1948] **2** 528, CA.
  Rent—
    Determination of reasonable rent for dwelling-house. *See* Determination of reasonable rent for
    dwelling-house, *above.*
  Security of tenure—
    Application to tribunal—
      Validity—Misnomer of landlord—Landlord and Tenant (Rent Control) Act 1949, s 11—Landlord and
      Tenant (Rent Control) Regulations 1949 (SI 1949 No 1096), reg 3(2) (as amended by Landlord
      and Tenant (Rent Control) (Amendment) Regulations 1950 (SI 1950 No 1763), reg 2). **Jackson**
      (Francis) Developments Ltd v Hall [1951] **2** 74, CA.
    Power of tribunal to extend period—
      Notice to quit given more than three months after decision of tribunal—Furnished Houses (Rent
      Control) Act 1946, s 5—Landlord and Tenant (Rent Control) Act 1949, s 11(1), (2)(b). **Preston and**
      Area Rent Tribunal v Pickavance [1953] **2** 438, HL.
      Period extended—Application for further extension adjourned—Extended period expired—
      Jurisdiction of tribunal to grant further extension—Landlord and Tenant (Rent Control) Act 1949,
      s 11(2)(a), (b). **R v Paddington South Rent Tribunal, ex p Millard** [1955] **1** 691, QBD.
      Reference to tribunal after notice to quit—Furnished Houses (Rent Control) Act 1946, s 11(1). **R v Folkestone and Area Rent Tribunal, ex p Sharkey**
      [1951] **2** 921, KBD.
  Shared accommodation—
    Accommodation shared by tenant and sub-tenant—
      Vacation of premises by tenant—Landlord's right to possession against sub-tenant—Landlord and
      Tenant (Rent Control) Act 1949, s 7. **Solomon v Orwell** [1954] **1** 874, CA.

RENT OFFICER
  Functions of—
    Housing benefit. *See* **Social security** (Housing benefit—Assessment—Rent).
  Jurisdiction—
    Determination of fair rent. *See* **Rent restriction** (Rent—Determination of fair rent—Jurisdiction—Rent
    officer).

RENT RESTRICTION
  Abandonment of statutory tenancy—
    Acquisition of rights of mortgagee—
      Acquisition by tenant—Whether tenant's acquisition of rights of mortgagee amounted to
      abandonment. **Silsby v Holliman** [1955] **2** 373, Ch D.
  Agricultural worker—
    Agriculture—
      Livestock keeping—Animals kept for production of food—Keeping and rearing of pheasants for
      sport—Gamekeeper occupying cottage on agricultural holding—Gamekeeper employed to keep
      and rear pheasants for sport—Eighty per cent of birds killed sold—Whether gamekeeper
      employed to keep and rear livestock 'for the production of food'—Whether gamekeeper
      employed in 'agriculture'—Rent (Agriculture) Act 1976, s 1. **Glendyne (Lord) v Rapley**
      [1978] **2** 110, CA.
      Livestock keeping—Animals kept for production of food—Keeping and rearing of pheasants for
      sport—Gamekeeper occupying cottage on agricultural holding—Gamekeeper employed to keep
      and rear pheasants for sport—Majority of birds killed sold to butchers and game
      dealers—Whether pheasants 'livestock'—Whether gamekeeper keeping and breeding livestock—
      Whether gamekeeper employed in 'agriculture'—Rent (Agriculture) Act 1976, s 1. **Normanton**
      (Earl) v Giles [1980] **1** 106, HL.
    Dwelling-house required for his occupation—
      Death of farm worker referred to in certificate—Another farm worker engaged—No new certificate
      obtained—Rent and Mortgage Interest Restrictions (Amendment) Act 1933, Sch I, para (g) (ii).
      Harris v Rowley [1949] **2** 524, CA.
      Employee neither named nor described in certificate of agricultural committee—Sufficiency of
      certificate—Rent and Mortgage Interests Restrictions (Amendment) Act 1933, s 3, Sch I, para (g).
      Pickford v Mace [1943] **2** 321, CA.

Agricultural worker (cont)—
  Dwelling-house required for his occupation (cont)—
    Evidence—Certificate of War Agricultural Executive Committee—Whether certificate conclusive evidence that dwelling-house was 'reasonably' required—Other suitable accommodation on landlord's property—Rent and Mortgage Interest Restrictions (Amendment) Act 1933, Sch I, para (g), (ii). **Harris v Brent** [1945] **1** 386, CA.

Alterations—
  Combination of houses—
    Two controlled houses combined into one—Whether combined dwelling-house controlled—Rent and Mortgage Interest Restrictions (Amendment) Act 1933, ss 1(2), 16—Increase of Rent and Mortgage Interest (Restrictions) Act 1938, s 2. **R & P Properties v Baldwin** [1938] **4** 845, CA.

Alternative accommodation—
  Dwelling-house—
    Absence of garage irrelevant—Rent and Mortgage Interest Restrictions (Amendment) Act 1933, s 3(1), Sch I, para (h). **Briddon v George** [1946] **1** 609, CA.
    House let with café and used as boarding house—Rent and Mortgage Interest Restrictions (Amendment) Act 1933, ss 3(1)(b), (3)(a)—Rent and Mortgage Interest Restrictions Act 1939, s 3(3). **Luttrell v Addicott** [1946] **2** 625, CA.
    Two dwelling-houses under same roof but separated by third dwelling-house—Rent and Mortgage Interest Restrictions (Amendment) Act 1933, s 3(3)(b). **Selwyn v Hamill** [1948] **1** 70, CA.
  Part of premises as alternative to whole—
    Offer of share of house to tenant of whole house—Rent and Mortgage Interest Restrictions (Amendment) Act 1933, s 3(1)(b). **Barnard v Towers** [1953] **2** 877, CA.
    Offer to tenant of part of living accommodation presently let to him—Rent Act 1968, s 10(1)(a). **Mykolyshyn v Noah** [1971] **1** 48, CA.
    Sub-tenant of part of house purchasing reversion—Whether part of house occupied by tenant suitable alternative accommodation as compared with whole house—Rent and Mortgage Interest Restrictions (Amendment) Act 1933, s 3(1)(b). **Parmee v Mitchell** [1950] **1** 872, CA.
  Reasonable to make order—
    Consideration of need to house refugees and invalid—Rent and Mortgage Interest Restrictions (Amendment) Act 1933, s 3(1)(b). **Cumming v Danson** [1942] **2** 653, CA.
  Security of tenure—
    Offer of house owned by local authority—Rent and Mortgage Interest Restrictions (Amendment) Act 1933, s 3(2), (3). **Sills v Watkins** [1955] **3** 319, CA.
    Statutory tenant of whole house offered weekly tenancy of part of house—Proposal by landlord to convert house into two separate and self-contained premises—Converted premises decontrolled—Rent and Mortgage Interest Restrictions (Amendment) Act 1933, s 3(3)(b)—Housing Repairs and Rents Act 1954, s 35(1)(a). **Scrace v Windust** [1955] **2** 104, CA.
  Suitable to needs of tenant and family—
    Exclusion from family of housekeeper and her husband and child—Rent and Mortgage Interest Restrictions (Amendment) Act 1933, s 3(3)(ii). **Darnell v Millwood** [1951] **1** 88, CA.
    Inclusion in family of married sons and their wives living with tenant—Lodger—More than one house as alternative accommodation—Rent and Mortgage Interest Restrictions (Amendment) Act 1933, s 3(3). **Standingford v Probert** [1949] **2** 861, CA.
    Mother-in-law—Whether tenant's mother-in-law included in 'family'—Rent and Mortgage Interest Restrictions (Amendment) Act 1933, s 3(3). **Scrace v Windust** [1955] **2** 104, CA.
  Suitable to needs of tenant as regards extent and character—
    Character—Cultural interests and proximity of friends—Tenant living in London offered alternative accommodation in Luton—New accommodation suitable in all respects but removed from tenant's friends, mosque and cultural centre—Whether cultural interests and proximity of friends relevant to suitability to needs of tenant as regards 'character'—Rent Act 1977, s 98(1), Sch 15, Part IV, para 5(1)(b). **Siddiqui v Rashid** [1980] **3** 184, CA.
    Character—Tenant's life-style in old accommodation—Amenities incidental to accommodation—Tenant occupying large period country house in isolated position with outbuildings, stable and adjoining field—Tenants able to keep open house for family and friends and pony and numerous house pets—New accommodation consisting of detached modern house on estate near country village—New accommodation not having stable or field—Whether 'needs' of tenant restricted to housing needs—Whether tenant's personal life-style in old accommodation and enjoyment of incidental amenities relevant considerations—Rent Act 1977, s 98(1)(a), Sch 15, para 5(1)(b). **Hill v Rochard** [1983] **2** 21, CA.
    Environmental matters—Noise and smell—Tenant of small flat in quiet residential street—Claim for possession by landlords—Tenant offered more spacious flat by landlords—New flat in busy traffic thoroughfare subject to noise from traffic and other sources and to smell from nearby fish and chip shop—Whether noise and smell relevant matters in considering suitability of new flat to needs of tenant—Rent Act 1968, s 10(1), Sch 3, Part IV, para 3(1). **Redspring Ltd v Francis** [1973] **1** 640, CA.
    Insufficient room for all tenant's furniture—Whether suitable—Rent Act 1968, s 10(1)(a), Sch 3, Part IV, para 3(1)(b). **Mykolyshyn v Noah** [1971] **1** 48, CA.
    Tenant an artist—Three rooms for living and painting—Two of the three rooms offered as alternative accommodation—Rent Act 1968, s 10(1)(a), Sch 3, Part IV, para 3(1)(b). **MacDonnell v Daly** [1969] **3** 851, CA.

Business premises—
  Limit on increase of rent. *See* **Landlord and tenant** (Rent—Limitation—Prohibition on increase in rate of rent—Business premises).

Contractual tenancy—
  Notice increasing rent to standard rent—
    Notice invalid as out of time—Standard rent paid by tenant—Whether contractual tenancy ended—Estoppel. **Swanson's Agreement, Re** [1946] **2** 628, Ch D.

RENT RESTRICTION (cont)—
    Contractual tenancy (cont)—
        Notice to quit—
            Assignment by contractual tenant after notice but before its expiration—No prohibition in tenancy agreement against assignment—Assignee becoming statutory tenant—Whether landlord entitled to damages for failure of tenant to deliver up premises at end of term—Rent and Mortgage Interest Restrictions (Amendment) Act 1933, s 3(1), Sch 1, para (d). **Regional Properties Ltd v Frankenschwerth** [1951] **1** 178, CA.
    Costs—
        Action in county court—
            Action for possession—Landlord successful in establishing jurisdiction of court to grant relief—Order for possession refused as being too harsh in circumstances—Landlord awarded costs of action. **Ottway v Jones** [1955] **2** 585, CA.
        Action in High Court—
            Claim arising out of Acts raised in defence—Increase of Rent and Mortgage Interest (Restrictions) Act 1920, s 17(2). **Lee v Carter (K) Ltd** [1948] **2** 690, CA.
            Claim for possession and damages for breach of covenant—Joinder with claim for trespass—Trespass of trifling nature—Increase of Rent and Mortgage Interest (Restrictions) Act 1920, s 17(2)—County Courts Act 1934, ss 40(1), 47(1). **Tideway Investment and Property Holdings Ltd v Wellwood** [1952] **2** 514, CA.
            House within Rent Restrictions Acts—Acts not pleaded in defence—Increase of Rent and Mortgage Interest (Restrictions) Act 1920, s 17(2). **Jaslowitz v Burstein** [1948] **1** 40, KBD.
            Rent claimed £370—Whether claim arising out of Rent Restrictions Acts—Increase of Rent and Mortgage Interest (Restrictions) Act 1920, s 17(2). **Smith (AJ) & Co Ltd v Kirby** [1947] **1** 459, KBD.
    County court—
        Jurisdiction—
            Breach of covenant to repair in original tenancy agreement—Claim for £414 damages—Increase of Rent and Mortgage Interest (Restrictions) Act 1920, ss 15(1), 17(2). **Wolfe v Clarkson** [1950] **2** 529, CA.
            Declaration that tenant protected by Rent Acts. *See* Declaration that tenant protected by Rent Acts—Jurisdiction of county court, *below.*
            Furnished house—Whether apportionment provisions of Rent Restrictions Acts apply—County Courts Act 1934, s 48(1)—Increase of Rent and Mortgage Interest (Restrictions) Act 1920, s 12(2), proviso (i)—Rent and Mortgage Interest Restrictions Act 1923, s 10. **Soniershield v Robin** [1946] **1** 218, CA.
            Registered rent—Dwelling subject to regulated tenancy—County court's jurisdiction to 'determine any question ... as to the rent limit'—Scope of jurisdiction—Whether county court having jurisdiction to set aside or alter registered rent—Rent Act 1977, s 141(1)(b). **Tingey v Sutton** [1984] **3** 561, CA.
    Crown property—
        Flat owned by county Territorial Association—
            Exemption from Rent Restrictions Acts. **Territorial Forces Assn v Philpot** [1947] **2** 376, KBD.
        House owned by British Transport Commission—
            Application of Rent Restriction Acts. **Tamlin v Hannaford** [1949] **2** 327, CA.
        House owned by Territorial Association—
            Application of Rent Restriction Acts—Territorial Army Regulations 1936 (SR & O 1936 No 1166), reg 918. **London County Territorial and Auxiliary Forces Association v Nichols** [1948] **2** 432, CA.
    Death of tenant—
        Claim by adopted child to remain in possession—
            De facto adoption—Increase of Rent and Mortgage Interest (Restrictions) Act 1920, s 12(1)(g). **Brock v Wollams** [1949] **1** 715, CA.
        Claim by child to remain in possession—
            Alternative accommodation provided under statute before mother's death—Daughter claiming statutory tenancy of alternative accommodation—Increase of Rent and Mortgage Interest (Restrictions) Act 1920, s 12(1)(g). **Strutt v Panter** [1953] **1** 445, CA.
            Contractual tenancy—Premises let below standard rent—Increase of rent demanded by landlord and paid by tenant—No notice of increase served—Increase to a figure still below standard rent—Increase of Rent and Mortgage Interest (Restrictions) Act 1920, ss 3(2), 12(1)(g). **Mills v Bryce** [1951] **1** 111, CA.
            Conversion of statutory tenancy into contractual tenancy—Right of daughter of tenant to remain in possession—Increase of Rent and Mortgage Interest (Restrictions) Act 1920, s 12(1)(g). **Bungalows (Maidenhead) Ltd v Mason** [1954] **1** 1002, CA.
            Daughter sub-tenant. **Edmunds v Jones (1952)** [1957] **3** 23, CA.
            Tenancy protected by Rent Acts 1920—1939 coming to an end before commencement of Rent Act 1965—Widow succeeding as statutory tenant—Death of widow before commencement of Act of 1965—Claim for possession against child resident with widow for over six months before her death—Claim heard after commencement of Act of 1965—Whether child's occupation protected by Act of 1965—'Tenancy'—'Regulated tenancy'—Rent Act 1965, s 20(1). **Brown v Conway** [1967] **2** 793, CA.
            Vesting of tenancy in the probate judge—Notice to quit—Increase of Rent and Mortgage Interest (Restrictions) Act 1920, s 12(1)(g). **Smith v Mather** [1948] **1** 704, CA.
            Vesting of tenancy in the probate judge—Notice to quit—Subsequent grant of letters of administration to son—Doctrine of relation back—Increase of Rent and Mortgage Interest (Restrictions) Act 1920, s 12(1)(f). **Long (Fred) and Sons Ltd v Burgess** [1949] **2** 484, CA.
        Claim by first cousin to remain in possession—
            Consanguinity only relevant consideration—Increase of Rent and Mortgage Interest (Restrictions) Act 1920, s 12(1)(g). **Langdon v Horton** [1951] **1** 60, CA.
        Claim by friend to remain in possession—
            Defendant cohabiting with widow in widow's flat for 19 years—Both defendant and widow retaining own names—Defendant remaining married to wife but refusing reconciliation—Defendant remaining in flat after widow's death—Whether defendant entitled to succeed widow as statutory tenant—Whether defendant 'a member of the original tenant's family'—Rent Act 1977, Sch 1, para 3. **Watson v Lucas** [1980] **3** 647, CA.

Death of tenant (cont)—
Claim by friend to remain in possession (cont)—
Friend young man who had looked after elderly female tenant for many years—Platonic relationship between tenant and friend—Tenant treated friend as her nephew—No family relationship—Friend regarded by everyone as tenant's nephew—Whether friend could succeed to tenancy as statutory tenant—Whether friend 'a member of the original tenant's family'—Rent Act 1968, Sch 1, para 3. **Carega Properties SA (formerly Joram Developments Ltd) v Sharratt** [1979] **2** 1084, HL.

Tenant and lover having lived together for five years without holding themselves out as man and wife—Tenant desirous of retaining her independence and freedom as a single person—Lover remaining in house after tenant's death—Whether lover entitled to remain in possession—Whether lover 'a member of the tenant's family'—Rent Act 1977, Sch 1, para 3. **Helby v Rafferty** [1978] **3** 1016, CA.

Woman looking after and nursing tenant for many years—No family relationship—Increase of Rent and Mortgage Interest (Restrictions) Act 1920, s 12(1)(g). **Ross v Collins** [1964] **1** 861, CA.

Claim by mistress to remain in possession—
Parties and children living as a family—Increase of Rent and Mortgage Interest (Restrictions) Act 1920, s 12(1)(g). **Hawes v Evenden** [1953] **2** 737, CA.

Claim by niece to remain in possession—
Niece of tenant's wife—Nursing of tenant and wife for substantial period—Increase of Rent and Mortgage Interest (Restrictions) Act 1920, s 12(1)(g). **Jones v Whitehill** [1950] **1** 71, CA.

Claim by reputed spouse to remain in possession—
Child born to couple living in unmarried association—No de facto adoption of child by putative father—Increase of Rent and Mortgage Interest (Restrictions) Act 1920, s 12(1)(g). **Perry v Dembowski** [1951] **2** 50, CA.

No issue of couple living in unmarried association—Increase of Rent and Mortgage Interest (Restrictions) Act 1920, s 12(1)(g). **Gammans v Ekins** [1950] **2** 140, CA.

No issue of couple living in unmarried association—Rent Act 1968, Sch 1, para 3. **Dyson Holdings Ltd v Fox** [1975] **3** 1030, CA.

Claim by sister to remain in possession—
Contractual tenancy determined by notice to quit—Increase of Rent and Mortgage Interest (Restrictions) Act 1920, s 12(1)(g). **Thynne v Salmon** [1948] **1** 49, CA.

Claim by sole executrix to remain in possession—
Contractual tenancy terminated by notice to quit—Whether executrix 'tenant' within the meaning of the Rent Restrictions Acts—Increase of Rent and Mortgage Interest (Restrictions) Act 1920, s 12(1)(f)—Rent and Mortgage Interest Restrictions (Amendment) Act 1933, s 3(1). **Lawrance v Hartwell** [1946] **2** 257, CA.

Claim by widow to remain in possession—
Allegation that tenant a contractual tenant—Claim and acceptance by landlord from tenant of statutory increases of rent—No statutory notice of increase—Increase of Rent and Mortgage Interest (Restrictions) Act 1920, s 12(1)(g). **Baxter v Eckersley** [1950] **1** 139, CA.

Contractual tenancy determined by notice to quit—Increase of Rent and Mortgage Interest (Restrictions) Act 1920, s 12(1)(g). **Moodie v Hosegood** [1951] **2** 582, HL.

Disagreement between members of family regarding right to possession—
Action by one member to eject the other—No application made to county court under Increase of Rent and Mortgage Interest (Restrictions) Rules 1920 (S R & O 1920 No 1261), r 1(d), r 19—Increase of Rent and Mortgage Interest (Restrictions) Act 1920, s 12(1)(g). **Taylor v Willoughby** [1953] **2** 642, CA.

Competing claims of father and son—Son's claim more meritorious but father's need greater—Weighing competing factors—Tenancy granted to father—Rent Act 1968, Sch 1, para 3. **Williams v Williams** [1970] **3** 988, CA.

Wishes of deceased tenant—Whether wishes of deceased tenant relevant circumstances to be considered in deciding who should be statutory tenant—Increases of Rent and Mortgage Interest (Restrictions) Act 1920, s 12(1)(g). **Trayfoot v Lock** [1957] **1** 423, CA.

Family claim to possession—
Death of widow of tenant—No further statutory protection—Increase of Rent and Mortgage Interest (Restrictions) Act 1920, s 12(1)(g). **Summers v Donohue** [1945] **1** 599, CA.

Limitation to one succession only—Increase of Rent and Mortgage Interest (Restrictions) Act 1920, s 12(1)(g)—Interpretation Act 1889, s 1(1)(b). **Dealex Properties Ltd v Brooks** [1965] **1** 1080, CA.

Widow sole executrix—No probate taken out—Death of widow—Right of occupation of member of the family—Increase of Rent and Mortgage Interest (Restrictions) Act 1920, s 12(1)(g). **Whitmore v Lambert** [1955] **2** 147, CA.

Widow statutory tenant after death of tenant—Whether statutory tenancy passed to daughters on death of widow—Increase of Rent and Mortgage Interest (Restrictions) Act 1920, s 12(1)(g)—Rent Restrictions (Notices of Increase) Act 1923, s 1(1). **Phillips v Welton** [1948] **2** 845, CA.

Homosexual partner—
Family of original tenant—Claim by tenant's partner of same sex to remain in possession—Whether partner living with tenant as husband or wife—Whether partner a member of tenant's family—Rent Act 1977, Sch 1, paras 2, 3(1). **Fitzpatrick v Sterling Housing Association Ltd** [1999] **4** 705, HL.

Whether surviving same-sex partner entitled to succeed to deceased partner's statutory tenancy—Rent Act 1977, Sch 1, paras 2, 3(1)—Human Rights Act 1998, s 3, Sch 1, Pt I, arts 8, 14. **Ghaidan v Mendoza** [2002] **4** 1162, CA; [2004] **3** 411, HL.

Order for possession during tenant's lifetime—
Conditions on which order suspended not fulfilled by tenant—No enforcement of order by landlord—Effect on rights of member of tenant's family—Increase of Rent and Mortgage Interest (Restrictions) Act 1920, ss 5(2), 12(1)(g), 15(1)—County Court Rules 1936, Form 138. **Sherrin v Brand (orse Phelps)** [1956] **1** 194, CA.

Effect of conditional suspension of order on rights of member of tenant's family—Form of order—Increase of Rent and Mortgage Interest (Restrictions) Act 1920, s 12(1)(g). **Mills v Allen** [1953] **2** 534, CA.

RENT RESTRICTION (cont)—

Death of tenant (cont)—

Order for possession during tenant's lifetime (cont)—

Unconditional order suspended—Death of statutory tenant before date for possession—Increase of Rent and Mortgage Interest (Restrictions) Act 1920, s 12(1)(g). **American Economic Laundry Ltd v Little** [1950] **2** 1186, CA.

Residing with—

Grand-daughter and family having one room to themselves and sharing kitchen with tenant for weekly payment—Separate housekeeping arrangements and meals—Increase of Rent and Mortgage Interest (Restrictions) Act 1920, s 12(1)(g). **Collier v Stoneman** [1957] **3** 20, CA.

Son living in flat six months before death of mother in order to look after, clean and air it—Mother in hospital for some years before death—Whether 'residing with' his mother—Rent Act 1968, Sch 11, para 7. **Foreman v Beagley** [1969] **3** 838, CA.

Son returning to live with mother after deserting wife and children—Matrimonial home remaining in son's name—Death of mother seven months after son's return—Whether son entitled to succeed mother as statutory tenant—Rent Act 1968, Sch 1, para 7. **Morgon v Murch** [1970] **2** 100, CA.

Sole claimant—

Application for declaration—Application by landlord to vary order of registrar—Admission of fresh evidence—Increase of Rent and Mortgage Interest (Restrictions) Act 1920, s 12(1)(g)—Increase of Rent and Mortgage Interest (Restrictions) Rules 1920 (SR & O 1920 No 1261), rr 1(d), 7(b), 19. **Butler v Hudson** [1953] **2** 418, CA.

Tenant leaving no widow—

Implication of residence with tenant at time of his death—'Member of tenant's family'—Woman living in adultery with tenant—Increase of Rent and Mortgage Interest (Restrictions) Act 1920, s 12(1)(g). **Tinkham v Perry** [1951] **1** 249, CA.

Declaration that tenant protected by Rent Acts—

Jurisdiction of county court—

Ancillary to judgment for damages for breach of covenant for quiet enjoyment. **Kenny v Preen** [1962] **3** 814, CA.

Decontrol—

Actual possession by landlord—

Controlled rooms in a dwelling-house—Occupation by a trespasser—Subsequent letting to the trespasser—Whether landlord has regained actual possession—Rent and Mortgage Interest Restrictions Act 1923, s 2(1). **Holden v Howard** [1937] **4** 483, CA.

Key handed over to landlord's agent—Intention to decontrol—Rent and Mortgage Interest Restrictions Act 1923, s 2. **Goodier v Cooke** [1940] **2** 533, CA.

Key handed over to landlord's agent—Premises let to new tenant at increased rent—Application to register house as decontrolled—Error in filling in form—Wrong date inserted—Whether application valid—Rent and Mortgage Interest Restrictions Act 1923, s 2—Rent and Mortgage Interest Restrictions (Amendment) Act 1933, s 2(2). **Holt v Dawson** [1939] **3** 635, CA.

Key in landlord's letter-box—Rent and Mortgage Interest Restrictions Act 1923, s 2. **Thomas v Metropolitan Housing Corp Ltd** [1936] **1** 210, CA.

Step-daughter remaining in possession on death of tenant—Break in tenancy—Rent and Mortgage Interest Restrictions Act 1923, s 2(1). **Mouser v Major** [1941] **1** 180, CA.

Agreement to create new tenancy—

Notice—Whether prior notice in Form S necessary—Rent Act 1957, s 11(1), Sch 4, paras 2(2), 4. **King v Bristow** [1965] **2** 134, CA.

Class C dwelling-house—

Onus of proof of decontrol—Rent and Mortgage Interest Restrictions (Amendment) Act 1933, s 1(2). **Heginbottom v Watts** [1936] **2** 153, CA.

House let in two parts—

One part decontrolled—Subsequent letting of whole house—Whether subsequent letting within the Acts—Rent and Mortgage Interest Restrictions Act 1923, s 2(1). **Worthy v Lloyd** [1939] **1** 474, CA.

Recovery of possession by landlord in 1924—Portions united, but redivided in a different manner in 1928—No registration of house as decontrolled—Whether portion of house controlled—Rent and Mortgage Interest Restrictions Act 1923, s 2—Rent and Mortgage Interest Restrictions (Amendment) Act 1933, s 2(2). **Rynolds v Phillips** [1939] **3** 678, CA.

New tenancy—

Former tenancy of flat including right to use of garden—New tenancy of another flat with same right—Whether right part of the 'premises'—Rent Act 1957, s 11(2), proviso. **M & J S Properties Ltd v White** [1959] **2** 81, CA.

New tenancy of part of decontrolled premises granted while possession still protected—Whether person whose possession is so protected is a statutory tenant—Whether newly demised part of premises subject to Rent Acts—Rent Act 1957, s 11(2) proviso, (7), Sch 4, para 2. **Cheesman v Bagnall** [1962] **2** 195, QBD.

Possession—

Suspension of execution of order for possession—Costs—Landlord and Tenant (Temporary Provisions) Act 1958, s 4(2). **Spyropoulos v McClelland** [1959] **3** 319, CA.

Rateable value—

Flat and garage assessed for rates on Nov 7, 1956, as one hereditament—Division of assessment on tenant's proposal—Alteration having effect before Nov 7 effect before Nov 7, 1956—Whether alteration of rateable value effective for determining question of decontrol—Validity—Rent Act 1957, Sch 5, paras 1(a), (b), 2(1). **Holland v Ong** [1958] **1** 574, CA.

Recontrol—

House decontrolled before 1933, let again after 1933—Whether house recontrolled—Retrospective effect of statutes—Rent and Mortgage Interest Restrictions (Amendment) Act 1933, s 2. **Brooks v Brimecome** [1937] **2** 637, CA.

Registration of premises as decontrolled—

Effect of failure to register—Rent and Mortgage Interest Restrictions Act 1923, s 2—Rent and Mortgage Interest Restrictions (Amendment) Act 1933, s 2(2)—Rent and Mortgage Interest Restrictions Act 1939, s 9(3), Sch II. **Tibber v Upcott** [1940] **2** 159, CA.

RENT RESTRICTION (cont)—
  Decontrol (cont)—
    Separate and self-contained premises produced by conversion of other premises—
      Need for change of identity—Ground floor of house made into self-contained premises—Housing Repairs and Rents Act 1954, s 35(1)(a). **Higgins v Silverston** [1956] **2** 893, CA.
    Suspension of execution of order for possession—
      Landlord's proposal for grant of new tenancy not accepted by tenants—Tenants actuated by hope of future legislation more favourable to them—Reasonableness of refusal—Landlord and Tenant (Temporary Provisions) Act 1958, s 3(1)(a). **Sabey (Clifford) (Contractors) Ltd v Long** [1959] **2** 462, CA.
  Dwelling-house—
    Application of Acts to dwelling-house—
      Burden of proof—Payment of rent—Whether tenancy or service occupation—Increase of Rent and Mortgage Interest (Restrictions) Act 1938, s 7(1). **Ford v Langford** [1949] **1** 483, CA.
    Bed-sitting room in hotel—
      Provision of linen and cleaning services—Lessee staying for three years—Whether hotel a house—Whether lessee had exclusive occupation of a residence—Rent Act 1968, ss 70(1), 84(1). **Luganda v Service Hotels Ltd** [1969] **2** 692, CA.
    Dwelling-house let as a separate dwelling. *See* Protected tenancy—Tenancy under which a dwelling-house is let as a separate dwelling, *below.*
    Dwelling-house let together with land other than the site of the dwelling-house. *See* Dwelling-house let together with land other than the site of the dwelling-house, *below.*
    House destroyed by enemy action—
      Contractual tenancy not determined—House rebuilt—Tenant refused possession by landlord—Notice to tenant to quit—Claim by tenant for possession. **Denman v Brise** [1948] **2** 141, CA.
    House owned by local authority—
      Protection of sub-tenant—Rent and Mortgage Interest Restrictions Act 1939, s 3(2)(c). **Moore (Percy G) Ltd v Stretch** [1951] **1** 228, CA.
    House rendered uninhabitable by bomb—
      No loss of identity—Use by tenant for business purposes—Notice to quit served before repair. **Morleys (Birmingham) Ltd v Slater** [1950] **1** 331, CA.
      Notice to tenant to quit before rebuilding completed—Right of tenant to occupy rebuilt house—Rent and Mortgage Interest Restrictions Act 1939, s 3(3)—Landlord and Tenant (War Damage) (Amendment) Act 1941, s 1(6). **Ellis & Sons Amalgamated Properties Ltd v Sisman** [1948] **1** 44, CA.
    Improvement—
      Application by landlord for determination of new fair rent. *See* Rent—Determination of fair rent—Application—Change in condition of dwelling-house, *below.*
    Part of dwelling-house used for business purposes—
      Boarding house—Tenant living on premises—Business not incompatible with residence as tenant—Rent and Mortgage Interest Restrictions Act 1939, s 3(3). **Kitchen's Trustee v Madders** [1949] **2** 1079, CA.
      Tenant's removal to another house—One room still used as a dwelling—Onus of proof—Increase of Rent and Mortgage Interest (Restrictions) Act 1920, s 12(2), proviso (ii). **Green v Coggins** [1949] **2** 815, CA.
    Premises converted by tenant into two self-contained flats—
      Assignment of tenancy—Whether a tenancy of a dwelling-house for which a premium prohibited—Landlord and Tenant (Rent Control) Act 1949, s 2(2), (3). **Lower v Porter** [1956] **1** 150, CA.
    Reconstruction of war damaged dwelling-house—
      Question of fact whether premises so altered as to become a new dwelling—Garage not previously forming part of the demise included in the letting—Increase of Rent and Mortgage Interest (Restrictions) Act 1920, ss 1(1), 12(1)(a). **Solle v Butcher** [1949] **2** 1107, CA.
    Shop and dwelling accommodation—
      Covenant by tenant not to use shop save for specified business—Rent and Mortgage Interest Restrictions Act 1939 s 3(3)—Landlord and Tenant (Rent Control) Act 1949, s 1(1). **R v Brighton and Area Rent Tribunal, ex p Slaughter** [1954] **1** 423, QBD; **R v Folkestone Rent Tribunal, ex p Webb** [1954] **1** 427, QBD.
      Dominant purpose immaterial—Rent and Mortgage Interest Restrictions Act 1939, s 3(3). **Whiteley v Wilson** [1952] **2** 940, CA.
      Lease—Covenant by tenant to use premises for specified business purposes—Rent and Mortgage Interest Restrictions (Amendment) Act 1933, s 16(1)—Rent and Mortgage Interest Restrictions Act 1939, s 3(1), (3). **Levermore v Jobey** [1956] **2** 362, CA.
      Sub-tenancy of dwelling accommodation for residential purposes—New lease of premises subject to sub-tenancy—Whether letting subject to Rent Acts—Increase of Rent and Mortgage Interest (Restrictions) Act 1920, ss 1, 12(2)—Rent and Mortgage Interest Restrictions Act 1939, s 3(1), (3). **British Land Co Ltd v Herbert Silver (Menswear) Ltd** [1958] **1** 833, CA.
      Subsequently let separately to same tenant under two leases—Application of Rent Acts to shop—Rent and Mortgage Interest Restrictions Act 1939, s 3(3). **Cumbes v Robinson** [1951] **1** 661, CA.
    Two separated flats let together—
      Rateable value of the dwelling-house—Rent and Mortgage Interest Restrictions (Amendment) Act 1933, s 16(1)—Rent and Mortgage Interest Restrictions Act 1939, ss 3(1), 7(1). **Langford Property Co Ltd v Goldrich** [1949] **1** 402, CA.
    Use as private house—
      House and cottage contiguous but without internal communication—Covenant by tenant, in original tenancy agreement, to use 'the premises as a private dwelling-house only'—Cottage sub-let by tenant—Rent and Mortgage Interest Restrictions (Amendment) Act 1933, s 16(1)—Rent and Mortgage Interest Restrictions Act 1939, ss 3(1), 3(3). **Whitty v Scott-Russell** [1950] **1** 884, CA.

967

RENT RESTRICTION (cont)—
Dwelling-house (cont)—
Use for business purposes—
Premises let for business purposes—Tenant living on premises—No knowledge by landlord—Costs—County Court or High Court scale—Proceedings arising out of Rent Acts—Decision that Rent Acts did not apply—Increase of Rent and Mortgage Interest (Restrictions) Act, ss 12(2), 17(2). **Wolfe v Hogan** [1949] **1** 570, CA.
Test whether premises outside Rent Acts by reason of business use. **Vickery v Martin** [1944] **2** 167, CA.
Dwelling-house let together with land other than the site of the dwelling-house—
Camping site and bungalow—
Dominant purpose of lease the carrying on of business of letting out camping sites—Rent and Mortgage Interest Restrictions Act 1939, s 3(3). **Feyereisel v Parry** [1952] **1** 728, CA.
Garage business and dwelling-house—
Premises divisible into separate entities—Dominant purpose of letting the carrying on of business—Rent and Mortgage Interest Restrictions Act 1939, s 3(3). **Thompstone v Simpson** [1952] **1** 431, Assizes.
Excessive charge for furniture—
Dwelling-house to which the principal Act applies—
First letting under Rent and Mortgage Interest Restrictions Act 1939—Rent and Mortgage Interest Restrictions Act 1923, s 9(1). **Minns v Moore** [1949] **2** 800, CA.
Exclusion of Acts—
Registration of living accommodation—
Householder not in physical occupation of premises at date of registration—Relative dates of letting and registration. **Baldwin v Gurnsey** [1948] **2** 165, CA.
Extension of protection to furnished tenancies—
Transitional provisions—
Order for possession against tenant made but not executed at date Act coming into force—Court of opinion order would not have been made if Act had been in force when tenancy came to an end—Power of court to rescind or vary order—Rescission of order—Discretion—Principles governing exercise of discretion—Rent Act 1974, s 1, Sch 3, para 3(3). **Sainesbury (John) & Co (a firm) v Roberts** [1975] **2** 801, CA.
Extortionate rent—
Limitation of time—
Date from which time begins to run. **Stray v Docker** [1944] **1** 367, KBD.
Rent including right to use kitchen, bathroom and garden in common with other tenant—
Application of Acts—Increase of Rent and Mortgage Interest (Restrictions) Act 1920, s 10. **Banks v Cope-Brown** [1948] **2** 76, Div.
Fair rent—
Application for determination—
Application by unincorporated tenants' association—Amount of proposed rent not set out, but words used from which rent could be calculated with certainty—Whether sufficient—Whether tenant himself must put in application or sign it—Rent Regulation (Forms etc) (England and Wales) Regulations 1965 (SI 1965 No 1976), Sch 3, Form 4. **R v London Rent Assessment Panel, ex p Braq Investments Ltd** [1969] **2** 1012, QBD.
Failure to specify amount of rent sought to be registered—Whether fatal defect rendering application a nullity—Rent Act 1965, s 26(5), Sch 3, para 2—Rent Regulation (Forms, etc) (England and Wales) Regulations 1965 (SI 1965 No 1976), reg 7, Sch 3, Form 4, para 9. **Chapman v Earl** [1968] **2** 1214, QBD.
Calculation on basis of 1962 capital costs—
Deduction of scarcity value—Whether deduction properly made—Rent Act 1968, s 46(1). **Anglo-Italian Properties Ltd v London Rent Assessment Panel** [1969] **2** 1128, QBD.
Cost of services—
Management charge in respect of services—Selective employment tax in respect of staff—Rentals of residential staff's flats—Cost of central heating—Whether such management charge and SET allowable in calculating cost of services—Whether amount allowable in respect of rent of staff flats and of cost of central heating may be reduced below figure of actual costs, if smaller amount appropriate—Whether rent assessment committee bound to inspect staff flats—Rent Act 1965, s 27, Sch 3, para 12. **Metropolitan Properties Co Ltd v Noble** [1968] **2** 313, QBD.
Determination of fair rent. *See* Rent—Determination of fair rent, *below*.
Evidence—
Best evidence of fair rent—Fair rent fixed for comparable properties—Presumption that assessments correct in law until contrary is proved—Contractor's theory of valuation of little weight where comparable fair rents or market rents—Rent Act 1968, s 46. **Tormes Property Co Ltd v Landau** [1970] **3** 653, QBD.
Expert opinion—Whether rent assessment committee bound to accept expert opinion. **Metropolitan Properties Co (FGC) Ltd v Lannon** [1968] **1** 354, QBD.
Regard to be had to all the circumstances—
All the circumstances other than personal circumstances—Meaning of 'personal circumstances'—Tenant's right to remain in possession—Determination of rent having regard to capital value—Capital value of house with sitting tenant less than capital value with vacant possession—Whether tenant's right to remain in possession a personal circumstance to be disregarded—Whether regard to be had to capital value with vacant possession—Rent (Scotland) Act 1971, s 42(1). **Mason v Skilling** [1974] **3** 977, HL.
Locality of dwelling-house—Extent of 'locality'—Matter for decision of rent assessment tribunal—Rent Act 1968, s 46. **Palmer v Peabody Trust** [1974] **3** 355, QBD.
Security of tenure—Landlord housing trust—Tenant of housing trust having no statutory security of tenure—Tenant seeking reduction of sum fixed as fair rent on account of absence of security of tenure—Whether ground for reduction of sum fixed—Rent Act 1968, s 46(1). **Palmer v Peabody Trust** [1974] **3** 355, QBD.

RENT RESTRICTION (cont)—
  Furnished letting (cont)—
    Conversion to unfurnished letting (cont)—
      Invalid notice to quit to furnished sub-tenant expiring at midnight on 25th March—Removal of furniture by tenant earlier on 25 March—Cesser of tenant's interest at midnight on 25 March—Sub-tenant remaining in occupation—Subsequent valid notice to quit given by landlord to sub-tenant—Claims by sub-tenant that tenancy had become an unfurnished tenancy. **Chalcots Developments Ltd v De Gray** [1967] **2** 888, CA.
      Purchase of furniture by tenant—Effect on tenancy—Estoppel—Conduct of tenant leading to belief letting was unfurnished. **Welch v Nagy** [1949] **2** 868, CA.
      Tenant possessed of furniture, but willing to accept furnished tenancy to secure premises—Subsequent removal of furniture by landlord and use by tenant of his own—Rent and Mortgage Interest Restrictions Act 1923, s 10(1). **Seabrook v Mervyn** [1947] **1** 295, CA.
    Extension of protection to furnished tenancies—
      Rent payable—Rent of unfurnished flat registered as £400 per annum—Flat let furnished at £20 per week—Furnished letting becoming protected by the Rent Act 1974—Whether registered rent of unfurnished flat applicable to furnished letting—Whether registered rent or contractual rent recoverable by landlord—Rent Act 1974, s 1(1). **Metrobarn Ltd v Gehring** [1976] **3** 178, CA.
      Statutory exception—Furnished tenancies granted on or after commencement date protected except where resident landlord—Exception excluded where fixed term tenancy granted to person who immediately before it was granted was tenant under earlier tenancy which 'by virtue of this section' was not a protected tenancy—Transitional provision—Earlier tenancy granted before commencement date deemed to be granted on that date—Resident landlord granting tenant two successive fixed term tenancies of furnished premises—First tenancy unprotected when granted—Statute extending protection to furnished premises before termination of first tenancy and commencement of second—Whether second tenancy protected—Whether first tenancy not a protected tenancy 'by virtue of this section'—Rent Act 1968, s 5A(1), (5)—Rent Act 1974, Sch 3, para 1. **Stubbs v Assopardi** [1978] **2** 399, CA.
    Recovery of excess rent—
      Rent including payment for attendance as well as payment for furniture—Increase of Rent and Mortgage Interest (Restrictions) Act 1920, s 9(1), s 12(2)(i). **Lederer v Parker** [1949] **2** 443, CA.
  House constructed under building licence. *See* **Housing** (House constructed under building licence—Permitted rent).
  House or part of a house let—
    Application of Rent Restriction Acts—
      House not let at date of passing of Act—House let subsequently—Whether Act applicable—Increase of Rent and Mortgage Interest (Restrictions) Act 1920, s 12(2)—Rent and Mortgage Interest Restrictions Act 1923, s 2(1)—Increase of Rent and Mortgage Interest (Restrictions) Act 1938, s 4. **Schaffer v Ross** [1939] **4** 363, CA.
  House unfit for human habitation—
    Notice to execute works—
      Person having control—Receipt of rackrent—'Full net annual value' of house—House controlled under Rent Restriction Acts—Housing Act 1936, s 9(4). **Rawlence v Croydon Corp** [1952] **2** 535, CA.
  Illegal premium. *See* Premium, *below*.
  Implied condition of tenancy—
    Access by landlord to execute repairs—
      Not equivalent to express reservation of right of access and entry. **Mint v Good** [1950] **2** 1159, CA.
  Increase of rent—
    Notice of increase—
      Rates—Error in stating amounts of rates in notice—Error in using wrong prescribed form—Signed by landlord's agents without stating that they were his agents—Increase of weekly rent correctly stated—Errors in stating rates de minimis—Admission of facts as to rates given under misunderstanding as water rate not included—Appeal decided on true figures—Rent Restrictions Regulations 1940 (SR & O 1940 No 238), Sch 1—Increase of Rent and Mortgage Interest (Restrictions) Act 1920, s 3(2). **Fredco Estates Ltd v Bryant** [1961] **1** 34, CA.
    Regulated tenancy. *See* Regulated tenancy—Increase of rent, *below*.
  Land let together with house—
    At date of letting in 1937 house rated at £4 and land not rated—
      Land rated at £9 in 1953, rateable value of house not increased—Possession sought by landlord in 1954—Increase of Rent and Mortgage Interest (Restrictions) Act 1920, s 12(2)(iii), (6). **Davies v Gilbert** [1955] **1** 415, CA.
  Land originally let to tenant together with dwelling-house—
    Reversionary estate in land subsequently severed—Rent in respect of land apportioned between two new landlords—Effect of severance of reversion on tenancy—Whether severance terminating existing tenancy and creating two separate tenancies—Rent Act 1968, s 1(2). **Jelley v Buckman** [1973] **3** 853, CA.
  Landlord—
    Mortgagee seeking possession against tenant—
      Mortgage expressly excluding power to let premises—Default in payment of instalments due under mortgage—Increase of Rent and Mortgage Interest (Restrictions) Act 1920, s 12(1)(g)—Law of Property Act 1925, s 99(1)—Rent and Mortgage Interest Restrictions (Amendment) Act 1933, s 3(1), Sch 1. **Dudley and District Benefit Building Society v Emerson** [1949] **2** 252, CA.
    Protected tenancy—
      Recovery of possession. *See* Possession, *below*.
    Purchaser of landlord's interest—
      Purchaser in receipt of rent pending completion—Whether purchaser himself a landlord—Increase of Rent and Mortgage Interest (Restrictions) Act 1920, s 12(1)(f), (g). **Sheridan v Dickson** [1970] **3** 1049, CA.
  Letting at less than standard rent—
    No clause allowing deduction from standard rent—
      Right of landlord to increase rent to standard rent. **Capital & Counties Properties Ltd v Butler** [1944] **2** 223, CA.

RENT RESTRICTION (cont)—

Long tenancy at low rent—

Continuance on same terms as before—

Licence in 1931 to adapt dwelling-house for multiple occupation—Covenant by tenant to re-instate premises as private dwelling-house at expiration of the term granted by the lease—Tenant of whole house continuing in occupation beyond term date as statutory tenant—Whether tenant's liability to re-instate premises extinguished on his becoming a statutory tenant—Landlord and Tenant Act 1954, s 3(2)(a). **Byrne v Herbert** [1965] 3 705, QBD.

Continuation as statutory tenancy. *See* **Landlord and tenant** (Long tenancy at low rent—Continuation as statutory tenancy).

Separate dwelling—

Premises formerly let in two parts—Tenant intending to reconvert to one dwelling—Tenant's furniture in both parts—Active use of one part only by tenant—Whether tenant entitled to protection for whole premises—Whether let as separate dwelling—Landlord and Tenant Act 1954, ss 2(1), 22(3). **Haines v Herbert** [1963] 3 715, CA.

Tenant having purchased remainder of long lease—Premises consisting of penthouse comprising maisonette with self-contained flat attached—Premises originally used as family home—Tenant subletting maisonette for latter part of long lease—Sublease expiring day before expiry of long lease—Subtenant refusing to give up occupation of maisonette on expiry of sublease—Tenant in occupation of flat on expiry of long lease—Whether tenant entitled to protection under Rent Acts for whole of the penthouse—Whether penthouse let as one separate dwelling—Landlord and Tenant Act 1954, ss 1, 2(1), 3(2), 22(3). **Regalian Securities Ltd v Ramsden** [1981] 2 65, HL.

Tenant having purchased remainder of long lease—Tenant in occupation of part of house on expiry of lease—Remainder of house sub-let—Intention of tenant to make home in house—Whether whole house let as separate dwelling—Whether tenant in personal occupation—Landlord and Tenant Act 1954, ss 2(1), 22(3). **Herbert v Byrne** [1964] 1 882, CA.

Tenant having purchased remainder of long lease—Tenant in occupation of part of house on expiry of lease—Rest of house sub-let in furnished rooms—Rateable value of whole house above, part occupied by tenant below, rent restrictions limit—Whether part occupied by tenant let as a separate dwelling—Whether tenant protected by virtue of Landlord and Tenant Act 1954, ss 2(1), 22(3). **Crown Lodge (Surbiton) Investments Ltd v Nalecz** [1967] 1 489, CA.

Mortgaged property—

Loss of protection. *See* **Mortgage** (Possession of mortgaged property—Premises subject to Rent Restrictions Acts).

Unauthorised lease. *See* **Mortgage** (Action by mortgagee for possession—House subject to Rent Restrictions Acts).

Net rent—

Calculation—

Deduction of rates chargeable on the occupier—Increase of Rent and Mortgage Interest (Restrictions) Act 1920, ss 2(1), 12(1)(c). **Strood Estates Co Ltd v Gregory** [1937] 3 656, HL.

Obligation of the tenancy—

Employment—

Undertaking by tenant to remain in employment of third party—Rent and Mortgage Interest Restrictions (Amendment) Act 1933, Sch I, para (a). **RMR Housing Society Ltd v Combs** [1951] 1 16, CA.

Payment to tenant in return for giving up possession—

Statutory tenancy—

Agreement to make—Illegality—Unenforceability—Whether purchaser of landlord's interest in receipt of rent pending completion a landlord—Increase of Rent and Mortgage Interest (Restrictions) Act 1920, ss 12(1)(f), (g), 15(2). **Sheridan v Dickson** [1970] 3 1049, CA.

Tenant to receive sum of money in event of giving up possession on specified date—

Contract enforceable by tenant. **Rajbenbach v Mamon** [1955] 1 12, QBD.

Permitted increase in rent—

Improvement of house—

Covenant by landlord to provide services previously supplied voluntarily—Increase of Rent and Mortgage Interest (Restrictions) Act 1920, s 2(3). **Asher v Seaford Court Estates Ltd** [1950] 1 1018, HL.

Replacement of defective floor—Laying of additional concrete bed—Increase of Rent and Mortgage Interest (Restrictions) Act 1920, s 2(1)(a), (5). **Wates v Rowland** [1952] 1 470, CA.

Substitution of modern one-pipe for worn out two-pipe drainage system—Substitution of single large water tank for separate tanks in each flat—Raising of area—Increase of Rent and Mortgage Interest (Restrictions) Act 1920, s 2(1)(a). **Morcom v Campbell-Johnson** [1955] 3 264, CA.

Inclusive rent—

Transfer of liability for rates to tenant—'Corresponding reduction'—Intervening reduction of valuation for rates operating retrospectively from before 1939—Increase of Rent and Mortgage Interest (Restrictions) Act 1920, s 2(1)(b),(3), proviso—Rent and Mortgage Interest Restrictions Act 1939, s 3(1), Sch I. **Regis Property Co Ltd v Redman** [1956] 2 335, CA.

Landlords liable under lease to pay rates—

Statutory tenancy after end of lease—Statutory tenant's liability for increased rent—Increase in respect of rate-increase before statutory tenancy began—Increase of Rent and Mortgage Interest (Restrictions) Act 1920, ss 2(1)(b), (3), 15(1), as amended by Rent and Mortgage Interest Restrictions Act 1939. **Westminster & Kensington Freeholds Ltd v Holme** [1955] 1 581, CA.

Repairs increase—

Declaration that conditions justifying an increase were fulfilled—Certificate of disrepair granted by local authority—Revocation of certificate—Jurisdiction of court to determine whether conditions fulfilled—Housing Repairs and Rents Acts 1954, ss 23(1)(a), 25(1), 26. **London Hospital (Board of Governors) v Jacobs** [1956] 2 603, CA.

Landlord's declaration of having carried out repairs—No application by tenant to county court to determine if carried out—Whether entitled to defend action for increased rent on ground that declaration was fraudulent—Housing Repairs and Rents Act 1954, ss 23(1), 25(1), Sch II, para 4(1). **Lazarus Estates Ltd v Beasley** [1956] 1 341, CA.

Permitted increase in rent (cont)—
Repairs increase (cont)—
Landlord's election not to be liable for internal repairs—Effect on rent increase in case of old control dwelling-house—Increase of Rent and Mortgage Interest (Restrictions) Act 1920, s 2(1)(d)—Housing Repairs and Rents Act 1954, ss 23(1), 30(1), (3). **Jackson v Croucher** [1956] **1** 170, CA.
Notice of increase—Calculation not completed in the prescribed form of notice—Validity of notice—Amendment—Housing Repairs and Rents Act 1954, s 25(3), (4)—Housing Repairs (Increase of Rent) Regulations 1954 (SI 1954 No 1036), Sch I. **Jackson v Croucher** [1956] **1** 170, CA.
Services increase—
Services exemplified—Maintenance of lifts and boilers—Floor coverings to common parts—Housing Repairs and Rents Act 1954, s 40(1)(b). **R v Paddington North and St Marylebone Rent Tribunal, ex p Perry** [1955] **3** 391, QBD.
Transfer to landlord of liability to repair previously borne by tenant—
Covenant to provide services previously supplied voluntarily—Assessment of increase—Successive tenancies—Increase on successive tenancies in respect of same transfer—Date of assessment—Increase of Rent and Mortgage Interest (Restrictions) Act 1920, s 2(3). **Regis Property Co Ltd v Redman** [1956] **2** 335, CA.
Exception for fair wear and tear extinguished—Increase of Rent and Mortgage Interest (Restrictions) Act 1920, s 2(3). **Winchester Court Ltd v Miller** [1944] **2** 106, CA.
Transfer of liability previously borne by landlord as tenant—Right of appeal—Increase of Rent and Mortgage Interest (Restrictions) Act 1920, s 2(3)—Rent and Mortgage Interest Restrictions Act 1923, s 11(1). **Beck v Newbold** [1952] **2** 412, CA.
Persons protected—
Company—
Limitation of increase of rent—Increase of Rent and Mortgage Interest (Restrictions) Act 1920, s 1. **Carter v SU Carburetter Co Ltd** [1942] **2** 228, CA.
Deserted wife in occupation under letting to husband—
Adultery by wife—No step by husband to revoke wife's authority to occupy. **Wabe v Taylor** [1952] **2** 420, CA.
Separate actions against husband and wife—No statutory ground pleaded by landlord—Husband's consent to possession. **Middleton v Baldock** [1950] **1** 708, CA.
Licensee of tenant—
Letting to husband—Separation of husband and wife—Wife remaining in house—Furniture belonging to husband remaining on the premises—Right of landlord to recover possession—Rent and Mortgage Interest Restrictions (Amendment) Act 1933—Rent and Mortgage Interest Restrictions Act 1939. **Brown v Draper** [1944] **1** 246, CA.
Tenant sub-letting premises as furnished letting—
Sub-tenant acquiring statutory security of tenure—Landlord and Tenant (Rent Control) Act 1949, s 11(2)(a). **Jackson (Francis) Developments Ltd v Hall** [1951] **2** 74, CA.
Possession—
Action for possession—
Parties—Tenant's family—Husband and wife living in council flat but separated pending divorce—Council obtaining possession of flat by consent order made against husband—Council required to provide alternative accommodation for tenant and family—Whether wife entitled to separate alternative accommodation—Whether wife entitled to be joined as party to possession proceedings—Whether consent order void—Housing Act 1985, s 84(2)(b), Sch 2, Pt II, ground 10, Pt IV, para 1. **Wandsworth London BC v Fadayomi** [1987] **3** 474, CA.
Allowing premises to be used for immoral or illegal purposes—
Order for possession suspended indefinitely—Right of landlord to immediate possession—Increase of Rent and Mortgage Interest (Restrictions) Act 1920, s 5(2)—Rent and Mortgage Interest Restrictions (Amendment) Act 1933, s 3(1), Sch I, para (b). **Yates v Morris** [1950] **2** 577, CA.
Tenant convicted of being in possession of drug—Certificate of conviction bearing no reference to premises occupied by tenant—Necessity for landlord to establish link between conviction and premises—Overriding requirement of reasonableness of order for possession—Rent Act 1968, s 10, Sch 3, case 2. **Abrahams v Wilson** [1971] **2** 1114, CA.
Alternative accommodation to which tenant had moved—
Oral agreement as to security of tenure—Tenancy in equity. **Kingswood Estate Co Ltd v Anderson** [1962] **3** 593, CA.
Breach of covenant—
Assignment by sub-tenant without consent of both superior landlord and tenant—Assignment with consent of tenant only—Enforcement of covenant by superior landlord—Increase of Rent and Mortgage Interest (Restrictions) Act 1920, s 15(3)—Rent and Mortgage Interest Restrictions (Amendment) Act 1933, Sch I, paras (a), (d). **Drive Yourself Hire Co (London) Ltd v Strutt** [1953] **2** 1475, CA.
Avowed intention of continuing breach—Keeping dog in flat for medical reasons without landlord's permission—Whether reasonable to make order—Rent and Mortgage Interest Restrictions (Amendment) Act 1933, s 3(1), Sch I. **Bell London and Provincial Properties Ltd v Reuben** [1946] **2** 547, CA.
Breach during contractual tenancy—Failure to remedy before expiration of tenancy—Tenant continuing in possession. **Tideway Investment and Property Holdings Ltd v Wellwood** [1952] **2** 514, CA.
Consent of landlord to subletting otherwise in breach of covenant—Acceptance by landlord of rent from head lessee after knowledge of breach—Rent and Mortgage Interest Restrictions (Amendment) Act 1933, Sch I, para (d). **Hyde v Pimley** [1952] **2** 102, CA.
Covenant by tenant to repair—Whether material date at which to determine whether covenant broken was the day of hearing or a previous time—Rent and Mortgage Interest Restrictions (Amendment) Act 1933, s 3(1), Sch 1, para (a). **Brown v Davies** [1957] **3** 401, CA.
Covenant not to use premises for any business but only as a private dwelling-house—Tenants taking in paying guests—Reasonableness of order for possession—Rent and Mortgage Interest Restrictions (Amendment) Act 1933, s 3(1)(a), Sch I, para (a). **Tendler v Sproule** [1947] **1** 193, CA.
No subletting allowed—No breach by sub-letting part of premises. **Esdaile v Lewis** [1956] **2** 357, CA.

RENT RESTRICTION (cont)—
   Possession (cont)—
      Breach of covenant (cont)—
         Subletting of whole of premises without consent of landlord—No evidence of there being such subletting at commencement of proceedings—Jurisdiction to make order for possession—Rent and Mortgage Interest Restrictions (Amendment) Act 1933, Sch 1, para (d). **Finkle v Strzelczyk** [1961] **3** 409, CA.
         Subletting room without consent—Increase of Rent and Mortgage Interest (Restrictions) Act 1920, s 15(3). **Maley v Fearn** [1946] **2** 583, CA.
         Subletting without consent—Landlord aware of continuing breach—Rent restriction—Sale of premises—Claim for possession against sub-tenant—'Lawfully or unlawfully sub-let'—Increase of Rent and Mortgage Interest (Restrictions) Act 1920, ss 5(5), 15(3)—Rent and Mortgage Interest Restrictions Act 1923, s 7(1). **Norman v Simpson** [1946] **1** 74, CA.
         Waiver by landlord of breach of covenant against subletting—Date of institution of proceedings material date—Increase of Rent and Mortgage Interest (Restrictions) Act 1920, s 15(3). **Oak Property Co Ltd v Chapman** [1947] **2** 1, CA.
         Waiver—Statutory tenant unlawfully subletting premises—Landlord's agent knowing of unlawful subletting but sending demand for rent to statutory tenant—Whether rent demand amounting to waiver of landlord's right to seek possession for breach of covenant—Rent Act 1977, s 3(3). **Trustees of Henry Smith's Charity v Willson** [1983] **1** 73, CA.
      Breach of obligation—
         Bankruptcy of statutory tenant—Protected tenancy containing proviso for re-entry in event of tenant's bankruptcy—Statutory tenant becoming bankrupt—Landlords seeking possession on grounds of breach or non—performance of obligation of previous protected tenancy—Whether proviso for re-entry in event of bankruptcy constituting obligation not to become bankrupt—Rent Act 1977, Sch 15, Case 1. **Cadogan Estates Ltd v McMahon** [2000] **4** 897, HL.
      Closing order in force in respect of building—
         Dwelling-house subject to closing order—Order made under Public Health (London) Act 1936, Sch V, para 8—Housing Act 1936, s 156(1)(e). **Marela Ltd v Machorowski** [1953] **1** 960, CA.
      Conditional order—
         Subsequent conditional postponing order—Conditions ultimately fulfilled—Discharge of original order—Jurisdiction—Increase of Rent and Mortgage Interest (Restrictions) Act 1920, s 5(2)—County Courts Act 1934, s 180(1). **Haymills Houses Ltd v Blake** [1955] **1** 592, CA.
      Dwelling subject to protected or statutory tenancy—
         Effect on subtenancy of termination of superior tenancy—Dwelling house divided into flats subject to protected tenancies—Forfeiture of headlease—Whether subtenants holding as protected or statutory tenants of landlord—Rent Act 1977, s 137(2). **John Lyon Free Grammar School (Keepers and Governors) v James** [1995] **4** 740, CA.
         Effect on subtenancy of termination of superior tenancy—Subtenant to whom dwelling has been lawfully sublet—Extent of subtenant's right to remain in possession—Meaning of 'lawfully sublet'—Dwelling lawfully sublet without landlord's consent—Tenant's tenancy terminated—Landlord bringing proceedings for possession against subtenant—Whether subletting by original tenant without landlord's consent entitling landlord to possession order against subtenant—Rent Act 1977, ss 98(1)(b), 137, Sch 15, Case 6. **Leith Properties Ltd v Springer** [1982] **3** 731, CA.
      Dwelling-house let together with land comprising less than two acres—
         Additional adjoining land comprising over three and a half acres in extent let later—Original letting and subsequent letting to expire on the same date—Rateable value of house under £75—Claim for possession by landlord—'Land ... let together with a dwelling-house'—Date of letting immaterial—Land comprising over two acres at time of action for possession—Extent of land let at time of claim for possession relevant—Rent and Mortgage Interest Restrictions Act 1939, s 3(1), (3). **Mann v Merrill** [1945] **1** 708, CA.
      Form of order—
         Possession on failure of tenant to fulfil conditions—Tenant authorised to continue breach of covenant and trespass. **Tideway Investment and Property Holdings Ltd v Wellwood** [1952] **2** 514, CA.
      Hardship—
         Availability of defence after Rent Act 1957—Comparative hardship—Finality of decision of county court judge—Jurisdiction to reverse county court decision—Rent and Mortgage Interest Restrictions (Amendment) Act 1933, s 3(1)(a), Sch 1, para (h), proviso—Rent Act 1957, s 26, Sch 6, para 21. **Piper v Harvey** [1958] **1** 454, CA.
         Burden of proof—Discretion of judge—Rent and Mortgage Interest Restrictions (Amendment) Act 1933, s 3(1), (3), sch l, para (h). **Robinson v Donovan** [1946] **2** 731, CA.
         Comparative hardship—Finality of decision of county court judge—Change of circumstances pending appeal—Whether taken into consideration—Rent and Mortgage Interest Restrictions (Amendment) Act 1933, s 3(1), Sch l, para (h), proviso. **King v Taylor** [1954] **3** 373, CA.
         Comparative hardship—Finality of decision of county court judge—Rent and Mortgage Interest Restrictions (Amendment) Act 1933, Sch 1, para (h), proviso. **Coplans v King** [1947] **2** 393, CA.
         Financial position of tenant—Steps taken by tenant to obtain accommodation—Rent and Mortgage Interest Restrictions (Amendment) Act 1933, s 3(1), Sch l, para (h). **Kelley v Goodwin** [1947] **1** 810, CA.
         Future hardship—Possession postponed for 4 months—Rent and Mortgage Interest Restrictions (Amendment) Act 1933, Sch l, para (h), proviso. **Wheeler v Evans** [1947] **2** 740, CA.
         Hardship to landlord's relative—Reasonableness—Consideration of matters material to claims under specific paragraphs—Rent and Mortgage Interest Restrictions (Amendment) Act 1933, s 3(1)(b), Sch l, para (h), proviso. **Rhodes v Cornford** [1947] **2** 601, CA.
         Hardship to persons affected other than landlord or tenant—Rent and Mortgage Interest Restrictions (Amendment) Act 1933, Sch l, para (h), proviso. **Harte v Frampton** [1947] **2** 604, CA.
         How far question of fact—Matters for consideration—Rent and Mortgage Interest Restrictions (Amendment) Act 1933, s 3(1), Sch l, para (h). **Chandler v Strevett** [1947] **1** 164, CA.
         Matters to be considered—Sale or storage of furniture—'Future hardship—'Other accommodation'—Whether necessarily protected accommodation—Offer of accommodation in house whereof possession sought—Rent and Mortgage Interest Restrictions (Amendment) Act 1933, s 3(1), Sch l, para (h). **Sims v Wilson** [1946] **2** 261, CA.

RENT RESTRICTION (cont)—
  Possession (cont)—
    House required by landlord for employee—
      Dismissal of employee—Employee remaining in occupation and paying weekly rent—Claim for possession—New employee in whole-time employment at date of hearing—Date of hearing material—Increase of Rent and Mortgage Interest Restrictions (Amendment) Act 1933, s 3(1)(a), Sch 1, para (g). **Benninga (Mitcham) Ltd v Bijstra** [1945] **2** 433, CA.
      Employee under contract but unable to commence work owing to illness—Termination of contract shortly after order of county court—Rent and Mortgage Interest Restrictions (Amendment) Act 1933, Sch 1, para (g). **Fuggle (R F) Ltd v Gadsden** [1948] **2** 160, CA.
      Employment by former landlord—Occupation continued after death of former landlord under new agreement—Rent and Mortgage Interest Restrictions (Amendment) Act 1933, s 3(1), Sch 1, para(g), (i). **Read v Gordon** [1941] **1** 222, CA.
      House acquired by new landlord—Tenant continuing in changed employment with former landlord—No right of possession for new landlord's employee—Rent and Mortgage Interest Restrictions (Amendment) Act 1933, Sch 1, para (g). **Duncan v Hay** [1956] **3** 555, CA.
      Knowledge of tenant—Materiality—Rent and Mortgage Interest Restrictions (Amendment) Act 1933, Sch 1, para (g). **Royal Crown Derby Porcelain Co Ltd v Russell** [1949] **1** 749, CA.
      No evidence that house let in consequence of particular employment—Rent and Mortgage Interest Restrictions (Amendment) Act 1933, Sch 1, para (g), (i). **Munro v Daw** [1947] **2** 360, CA.
      Tenancy continued on termination of employment—Rent employment—Rent increased—Order for possession refused—Counterclaim for overpayment of rent allowed—Counterclaim satisfied and reduced rent subsequently accepted—'Rent payable in respect of tenancy' less than two-thirds of rateable value—Increase of Rent and Mortgage Interest Restrictions (Amendment) Act 1933, s 3, Sch 1, para (g). **Stone (J & F) Lighting & Radio Ltd v Levitt** [1946] **2** 653, HL.
      Tenant allowed to remain in possession on termination of employment—Whether fresh tenancy—Rent and Mortgage Interest Restrictions (Amendment) Act 1933, s 3(1)(a), Sch 1, para(g), (i). **Braithwaite & Co Ltd v Elliott** [1946] **2** 537, CA.
      Termination of employment—Employee in occupation of premises after notice to quit—Acceptance of rent for two weeks—Whether creation of new tenancy—Rent and Mortgage Interest Restrictions (Amendment) Act 1933, Sch 1, para(g)—Rent and Mortgage Interest Restrictions Act 1939, s 3. **Thompsons (Funeral Furnishers) Ltd v Phillips** [1945] **2** 49, CA.
    House required by landlord for own use—
      Claim by joint owners—House required for occupation as residence for only one owner—Whether both joint owners constituting 'the owner-occupier'—Whether necessary that house should be required as residence for both joint owners—Whether court having jurisdiction to grant possession if house required for only one joint owner—Rent Act 1968, Sch 3, Part 11, Case 10. **Tilling v Whiteman** [1979] **1** 737, HL.
      Claim by joint owners—'Landlord'—Rent and Mortgage Interest Restrictions (Amendment) Act 1933, s 3(1) Sch 1, para (h)—Interpretation Act 1889, s 1. **Baker v Lewis** [1946] **2** 592, CA.
      Claim by two joint owners—Dwelling-house required for occupation as residence for only one owner—Alternative accommodation—Accommodation for furniture—Rent and Mortgage Interest Restrictions (Amendment) Act 1933, s 3(1), (3), Sch I, para (h), (i). **McIntyre v Hardcastle** [1948] **1** 696, CA.
      Contract for sale of dwelling-house in June 1939—Letting by vendors in November 1939—Completion of purchase in September 1945—Whether landlord by purchase after 1st September 1939—Rent and Mortgage Interest Restrictions (Amendment) Act 1933, Sch 1, para (h) (as amended by Rent and Mortgage Interest Restrictions Act 1939, s 3(1) Sch 1). **Emberson v Robinson** [1953] **2** 755, CA.
      Death of landlord before execution of order—House devised to daughter—Claim by daughter to enforce order—Rent and Mortgage Interest Restrictions (Amendment) Act 1933, Sch 1, para (h). **Goldthorpe v Bain** [1952] **2** 23, CA.
      Death of landlord intestate—Widow suing as administratrix and personally—Whether widow landlord by purchase—Rent and Mortgage Interest Restrictions (Amendment) Act 1933, Sch I, para (h). **Littlechild v Holt** [1949] **1** 933, CA.
      Defendant becoming tenant after purchase—Whether landlord by purchase—Rent and Mortgage Interest Restrictions (Amendment) Act 1933, Sch I, para (h). **Fowle v Bell** [1946] **2** 668, CA.
      Expiry of contractual tenancy—Notice to quit—Tenant holding over—Acceptance of rent by landlord—Statutory tenancy—No necessity for notice to quit—Increase of Rent and Mortgage Interest (Restrictions) Act 1920, s 15(1)—Rent and Mortgage Interest Restrictions (Amendment) Act 1933, s 3, Sch I, para (h)—Rent and Mortgage Interest Restrictions Act 1939, s 3. **Morrison v Jacobs** [1945] **2** 430, CA.
      Grantee of head-lease subject to tenant's tenancy—Grantor a purchaser—Rent and Mortgage Interest Restrictions (Amendment) Act 1933, Sch I, para (h). **Lucas v Lineham** [1950] **1** 586, CA.
      House required for occupation as a residence—Required—Landlord having another residence and the right to use daughter's flat—Whether 'required' meant reasonably required—Whether sufficient for landlord to prove that he bona fide wanted, and genuinely intended, to occupy house as his residence—Rent Act 1968, Sch 3, Part II, Case 10, para (c)(as amended by the Rent Act 1974, Sch 1). **Kennealy v Dunne** [1977] **2** 16, CA.
      Intention to install married couple as tenants of the upper floor—Married couple looking after landlord in old age—Two households, not a single household—Whether dwelling-house reasonably required by landlord for his own occupation within Rent and Mortgage Interest Restrictions (Amendment) Act 1933, Sch 1, para (h). **Bloomfield v Westley** [1963] **2** 337, CA; **Richter v Wilson** [1963] **2** 335, CA.
      Landlord a beneficiary under will whereby house was devised on trust for sale—Trustees permitted beneficiary to use or let house—Beneficiary sole party to letting—Law of Property Act 1925, s 29(2)—Rent and Mortgage Interest Restrictions (Amendment) Act 1933, Sch 1, para (h). **Stratford v Syrett** [1957] **3** 363, CA.
      Landlord becoming landlord by taking lease at a rent—Whether landlord by purchase—Rent and Mortgage Interest Restrictions (Amendment) Act 1933, Sch I, para (h). **Powell v Cleland** [1947] **2** 672, CA.
      Landlord taking as beneficiary under will as varied by family arrangement—Whether landlord by purchase—Rent Act 1968, s 10, Sch 3, Case 8. **Thomas v Fryer** [1970] **2** 1, CA.

Possession (cont)—
House required by landlord for own use (cont)—
Plaintiffs claiming as personal representatives of beneficial owners—Administrators of deceased parents' estates letting house belonging to estates—Administrators also adopting deceaseds' infant children who were beneficial owners of house—Defendant holding over as statutory tenant—Administrators claiming possession as landlords—Administrators wishing to live in house with children—Whether personal representative having no beneficial interest in property can be 'the landlord' of premises for which possession claimed—Whether administrators entitled to claim possession as landlords requiring possession of house for their occupation—Rent Act 1977, s 98(1)(b), Sch 15, Case 9. **Patel v Patel** [1982] **1** 68, CA.
Plaintiffs claiming as personal representatives of deceased landlord—One of the plaintiffs deceased landlord's widow—Premises required by widow 'for her own occupation'—No evidence whether widow beneficially entitled to premises—Point not raised by defendant at trial—Whether point may be raised in Court of Appeal—Order by county court judge giving plaintiff possession 'subject to plaintiff allowing defendant a Rent Act protected tenancy' of part of house with joint use of kitchen and out-offices—Order not within power of judge to make—Order for new trial—Rent and Mortgage Interest Restrictions (Amendment) Act 1933, s 3(1), Sch I, para (h). **Sharpe v Nicholls** [1945] **2** 55, CA.
Purchase by sub-tenant in 1952—Surrender of tenancy of the whole house against grant of new tenancy of the part of the house occupied by tenant—Whether landlord by purchase—Rent and Mortgage Interest Restrictions (Amendment) Act 1933, Sch I, para (h). **Wright v Walford** [1955] **1** 207, CA.
Purchase in 1950—Order for possession of whole house against tenant in 1953—Action for possession against sub-tenant of upper floor—Landlords of sub-tenant, not by purchase, but through order against tenant—Rent and Mortgage Interest Restrictions (Amendment) Act 1933, Sch I, para (h). **Cairns v Piper** [1954] **2** 611, CA.
Purchase of house and granting of tenancy to vendor who remained in occupation—Whether landlord by purchase—Rent and Mortgage Interest Restrictions (Amendment) Act 1933, Sch I, para (h). **Newton v Biggs** [1953] **1** 99, CA.
Recovery of possession by landlord who occupied house as own residence at any time prior to grant of tenancy—Act enabling landlord to recover possession if he had occupied house himself at any time—Act coming into effect after order for possession refused but while appeal pending—Act expressed to have retrospective effect—Whether retrospective effect applying to pending appeal—Rent Act 1977, Sch 15, Case 11—Rent (Amendment) Act 1985, s 1(1), (4). **Hewitt v Lewis** [1986] **1** 927, CA.
Recovery of possession by person who 'occupied' house as own residence and 'let' it on regulated tenancy—Whether person who last occupied house several years before relevant tenancy an 'owner-occupier'—Whether occupation as residence must immediately precede relevant letting to qualify person as 'owner-occupier'—Rent Act 1977, Sch 15, Case 11. **Pocock v Steel** [1985] **1** 434, CA.
Trustees under will enabled to permit beneficiary use of house or to receive net rents and profits—Beneficiary not party to letting of house—Rent and Mortgage Interest Restrictions (Amendment) Act 1933, Sch I, para (h), (i). **Parker v Rosenberg** [1947] **1** 87, CA.
Unoccupied house purchased by plaintiff—Subsequent tenancy agreement—Whether plaintiff landlord by purchase—Rent and Mortgage Interest Restrictions (Amendment) Act 1933, Sch I, para (h)—Increase of Rent and Mortgage Interest (Restrictions) Act 1938, Sch II. **Epps v Rothnie** [1946] **1** 146, CA.
Use as family home—Landlord himself unable to reside in house—Rent and Mortgage Interest Restrictions (Amendment) Act 1933, Sch I, para (h), (i). **Smith v Penny** [1946] **2** 672, CA.
Necessary for convenient occupation—
Cottage in rectory grounds—Claim for possession by rector—Whether necessary for convenient occupation of rectory—Pluralities Act 1838, s 59. **Neale v Jennings** [1946] **1** 224, CA.
Non-payment of rent—
Arrears of rent—Landlord's right to forfeiture for non-payment of rent—Reasonableness of order for possession—Arrears due to illness—Form of order—County Courts Act 1959, s 191(1)(a)—Rent and Mortgage Interest Restrictions (Amendment) Act 1933, s 3—Rent Act 1965, s 32. **Wolmer Securities Ltd v Corne** [1966] **2** 691, CA.
Arrears paid into court before hearing—Jurisdiction to make order—Reasonableness—Rent and Mortgage Interest Restrictions (Amendment) Act 1933, s 3(1)(a), Sch I, para (a). **Dellenty v Pellow** [1951] **2** 716, CA.
Waiver of past irregularities in payment—Rent 'lawfully due'—Tender by tenant before proceedings commenced—Rent and Mortgage Interest Restrictions (Amendment) Act 1933, Sch I, para (a). **Bird v Hildage** [1947] **2** 7, CA.
Nuisance or annoyance to adjoining occupiers—
Adjoining—Whether neighbouring occupiers whose premises not physically contiguous to tenant's premises are 'adjoining' occupiers—Rent Act 1977, s 98(1), Sch 15, Case 2. **Cobstone Investments Ltd v Maxim** [1984] **2** 635, CA.
User of premises by tenant for immoral purpose—No evidence from adjoining occupiers of actual nuisance or annoyance—Right to draw inference from user of premises—Rent and Mortgage Interest Restrictions (Amendment) Act 1933, s 3(1)(a), Sch I, para (b). **Platts (Frederick) Co Ltd v Grigor** [1950] **1** 941, CA.
Order—
Application to set aside—Power to make—Application by wife—Matrimonial Homes Act 1967, s 1(1), (5)—Rent Act 1968, s 11(2). **Penn v Dunn** [1970] **2** 858, CA.
Order obtained by misrepresentation—
Compensation for damage or loss sustained by tenant—Misrepresentation by landlord that premises required for own occupation—Consent by tenant to order for possession—Immediate sale of premises with vacant possession—Compensation for damage or loss sustained as result of order—Increase of Rent and Mortgage Interest (Restrictions) Act 1920, s 5(6). **Thorne v Smith** [1947] **1** 39, CA.

Possession (cont)—
Overcharging on sublet part of premises—
Reasonableness of order for possession—Whether court ought to consider possibility of overcrowding—Rent and Mortgage Interest Restrictions (Amendment) Act 1933, ss 3, 4—Housing Act 1936, s 58, Sch V. **Boulton v Sutherland** [1938] **1** 488, CA.
Overcrowding—
Material date for determining whether dwelling-house overcrowded—Housing Act 1936, ss 59(3), 65(1). **Zbytniewski v Broughton** [1956] **3** 348, CA.
Premises not in reasonable state of repair—
Certificate of sanitary authority—Whether ipso facto bar to landlord's right of possession—Rent and Mortgage Interest Restrictions (Amendment) Act 1933, s 12, Sch I, para (b). **Peach v Lowe** [1947] **1** 441, CA.
Premises unfit for human habitation—
Closing order—Reliance on closing order by landlord claiming possession—Whether landlord entitled to rely on closing order whether premises unfit because of own breach of contractual or statutory duty to maintain premises—Housing Act 1957, s 27(5). **Buswell v Goodwin** [1971] **1** 418, CA.
Procedure—
County court to be preferred to High Court—Landlord electing to proceed in High Court—Need for court to be informed of facts—Rent in arrear—Reasonableness of order for possession—Duty of court—Rent and Mortgage Interest Restrictions (Amendment) Act 1933, s 3. **Smith v Poulter** [1947] **1** 216, KBD.
Court—Judgment for possession signed in High Court by landlord in default of appearance—Premises to which Rent Acts applied by Rent Act 1965—Invalidity of judgment for recovery of possession for want of determination whether reasonable to give judgment for possession—Jurisdiction of High Court to determine forfeiture of lease—Policy of legislature that proceedings for possession of rent restricted premises should be brought in county court—Rent and Mortgage Interest Restrictions (Amendment) Act 1933, s 3(1)—Rent Act 1965, ss 31, 35(1), (3). **Peachey Property Corpn Ltd v Robinson** [1966] **2** 981, CA.
Indorsement on writ of summons—Certificate of solicitor or plaintiff's affidavit—Increase in rateable values—New forms of indorsement—Rent Act 1968, s 1, as amended by Counter-Inflation Act 1973, s 14—RSC Ord 6, r 2(1)(c)—RSC Ord 13, r 4(2). **Practice Direction** [1973] **2** 336, QBD.
Non-payment of rent—Application by summons for leave to enter judgment for possession—Personal service of summons required—Arrears of rent and service charges and mesne profits claimed as well as possession, but judgment in respect of them to be entered without leave—Rent and Mortgage Interest Restrictions (Amendment) Act 1933, s 3(1)—RSC Ord 19, rr 5, 6. **Lircata Properties Ltd v Jones** [1967] **3** 386, Ch D.
Non-payment of rent—Motion for judgment in default of defence—Arrears of rent and service charges, and mesne profits claimed as well as possession—Leave to enter judgment for possession necessary—Such leave to be obtained on summons, not motion—Order for possession on the motion refused—Rent and Mortgage Interest Restrictions (Amendment) Act 1933, s 3(1)—RSC Ord 19, r 2, 3, 5, 6. **Peachey Property Corp Ltd v Morley** [1967] **3** 30, Ch D.
Protected tenancy—
Entitlement to protection—Tenant previously having applied for reduction in rent of furnished letting. **Thomas v Pascal** [1969] **3** 937, CA.
Occupation of dwelling house as residence—Occupation of two dwelling houses—Tenant occupying one room of flat for sleeping five days a week—Tenant occupying dwelling house elsewhere at all other times—Remainder of flat occupied by member of tenant's family—Whether tenant occupying flat as residence—Rent Act 1968, s 3(2)—Rent Act 1977, s 2(1)(a). **Hampstead Way Investments Ltd v Lewis-Weare** [1985] **1** 564, HL.
Occupation of dwelling house as residence—Occupation of two dwelling houses—Tenant using one house for sleeping in—Tenant using adjoining house for normal living purposes and meals—Whether tenant occupying adjoining house as residence—Whether tenant's user of adjoining house extending to all activities essential to exhibit characteristics of complete home—Rent Act 1977, s 2(1)(a). **Kavanagh v Lyroudias** [1985] **1** 560, CA.
Right to respect for private and family life—New protected tenancies restricted to special cases—New tenancy granted to person who immediately before grant was protected tenant by person who at that time was the landlord under the protected tenancy—Agreement for new tenancy made between protected tenant and landlord under protected tenancy—Agreement providing for determination of existing tenancy by tenant vacating property for 24 hours and delivering up keys—Agreement providing for grant of assured shorthold tenancy—Tenant resuming occupation after 24 hours as provided by agreement—Agreement not followed by grant of tenancy—Whether new tenancy a protected tenancy—Whether 'tenancy' including agreement for tenancy—Whether agreement for tenancy taking effect as tenancy—Whether loss of protected tenancy breach of right to respect for private and family life—Housing Act 1988, ss 34(1)(b), 45(1)—Human Rights Act 1998, Sch 1, Pt I, art 8. **Truro Diocesan Board of Finance Ltd v Foley** [2009] **1** 814, CA.
Purported surrender of premises—
Dwelling-house left by tenant—Wife remaining in occupation—Tenant's furniture remaining on premises—Purported surrender by tenant of premises by agreement. **Old Gate Estates Ltd v Alexander** [1949] **2** 822, CA.
Reasonableness—
Breach of covenant—Installation of gas water heater—Rent and Mortgage Interest Restrictions (Amendment) Act 1933, s 3(1), Sch I, para (a). **Tideway Investment and Property Holdings Ltd v Wellwood** [1952] **2** 514, CA.
Landlord giving untrue evidence that accommodation furnished—Whether a proper consideration in deciding reasonableness of order—Rent and Mortgage Interest Restrictions (Amendment) Act 1933, s 3(1). **Yelland v Taylor** [1957] **1** 627, CA.
Landlord's only motive financial gain—Landlord offering, as 'suitable alternative accommodation', new house at higher rent, so as to sell old house at greater profit—Rent and Mortgage Interest Restrictions (Amendment) Act 1933, s 3(1). **Cresswell v Hodgson** [1951] **1** 710, CA.

RENT RESTRICTION (cont)—
    Possession (cont)—
        Reasonableness (cont)—
            Lesser hardship to another tenant of landlord—Rent and Mortgage Interest Restrictions (Amendment) Act 1933, s 3(1). **Hardie v Frediani** [1958] **1** 529, CA.
            Overcrowding of landlord's family—Order for possession of sub-let portion of house but not of whole house let to tenant—Rent and Mortgage Interest Restrictions (Amendment) Act 1933, ss 3, 4—Housing Act 1936, s 58, Sch V. **Boulton v Sutherland** [1938] **1** 488, CA.
            Tenant taking paying guests to augment income—Use of gardens as playground for children—Rent and Mortgage Interest Restrictions (Amendment) Act 1933, s 3(1). **Warren v Austen** [1947] **2** 185, CA.
        Rescission or variation of order for possession made before Act of 1965—
            Consent order—Premises brought within Acts by Rent Act 1965—Power to rescind or vary unexecuted order—Discretion of court—Factors to be taken into consideration—Rent Act 1965, s 20(1). **Mouat-Balthasar v Murphy** [1966] **3** 477, CA.
        Tenant not in personal occupation—
            Manager—Tenant or his manager to reside on the premises—Residence by manager. **Dando (S L) Ltd v Hitchcock** [1954] **2** 335, CA.
            Occupation as home—House in county and flat in London—Occupation for sleeping five or six times a year. **Beck v Scholz** [1953] **1** 814, CA.
            Occupation by tenant's parents—Intention to return. **Cove v Flick** [1954] **2** 441, CA.
            Tenant living elsewhere and passing two nights a week in premises. **Langford Property Co Ltd v Athanassoglou** [1948] **2** 722, CA.
            Tenant unable to live in house owing to illness—Intention to return—House kept in readiness for return—Rent and Mortgage Interest Restrictions (Amendment) Act 1933, s 3(1). **Wigley v Leigh** [1950] **1** 73, CA.
        Unconditional order—
            Subsequent conditional order postponing date for possession and discharging original order on fulfilment of conditions—Increase of Rent and Mortgage Interest (Restrictions) Act 1920, s 5(2). **Payne v Cooper** [1957] **3** 335, CA.
    Practice—
        Separate actions for possession against husband and wife—
            Consolidating actions—Joinder of parties in one action. **Middleton v Baldock** [1950] **1** 708, CA.
    Premises not within Acts—
        Company tenancy—
            Flat let to company and occupied by company's nominee—Whether tenancy a sham—Whether occupier a protected tenant. **Hilton v Plustitle Ltd** [1988] **3** 1051, CA.
        Dwelling-house owned by housing trust—
            Trust for charitable purposes—Funds devoted to provision of housing for the working classes—Housing Act 1936, s 188(1)—Housing Repairs and Rents Act 1954, s 33(1), (9). **Guinness Trust (London Fund) v Green** [1955] **2** 871, CA.
        House originally not within 1939 Act—
            Subsequent damage by enemy action—Rateable value reduced—Whether brought within the protection of the Act—New house—Rent and Mortgage Interest Restrictions Act 1939, ss 3(1), 7(1). **Eyre v Haynes** [1946] **1** 225, CA.
        Lease of parsonage house—
            Applicability of Rent Restriction Acts—Pluralities Act 1838, ss 32, 33, 36, 43, 46, 59. **Gloucester (Bishop) v Cunnington** [1943] **1** 61, CA.
            Claim to possession for purpose of reletting—Whether Rent Restrictions Acts applicable. **Brandon v Grundy** [1943] **2** 208, CA.
        Rateable value—
            Flats let together and assessed together for rates—Rateable value of each flat ascertained by apportionment—Flats subsequently separately assessed—Such assessment not first assessment—Rent and Mortgage Interest Restrictions Act 1939, ss 3(1), 7(2), (3). **Temple v National Mutual Life Association of Australasia Ltd** [1955] **2** 758, CA.
        Rent less than two-thirds of rateable value—
            Extrinsic evidence—Tenancy for one year at such weekly rent 'in consideration of the payment by the tenant' of a stated sum, 'and thereafter (shguld the tenant be desirous of continuing his tenancy) on a monthly basis at the said rent'—Tenant remaining in occupation after expiry of year—Notice to quit served after expiry of initial year—Admission of extrinsic evidence to contradict written tenancy agreement—Increase of Rent and Mortgate Interest (Restrictions) Act 1920, s 12(7). **O'Connor v Hume** [1954] **2** 301, CA.
    Premises within Acts—
        Agricultural housing—
            Dwelling-house subject to the provisions of the Housing (Rural Workers) Acts—House not included among the dwelling-houses expressly excluded from scope of Rent Restrictions Acts—Rent and Mortgage Interest Restrictions Act 1939, s 3(2)(c). **Black Mill Ltd v Straker** [1949] **2** 919, CA.
        Boarding-house—
            Tenant reserving for own use certain rooms according to requirements—Whether subject to control—Rent and Mortgage Interest Restrictions Act 1939, s 3(3). **Vickery v Martin** [1944] **2** 167, CA.
        Change of identity—
            Premises originally not within 1939 Act—Damage by enemy action—Reduction of rateable value—Rent and Mortgage Interest Restrictions Act 1939, s 3(1)(a). **Hazell, Watson & Viney Ltd v Malvermi** [1953] **2** 58, QBD.
    Premium—
        Advance payment of rent—
            Rent paid for three years in advance—Whether payment constituted a premium—Whether tenancy rendered invalid by payment of premium—Landlord and Tenant (Rent Control) Act 1949, s 2. **Rymer (Grace) Investments Ltd v Waite** [1958] **2** 777, CA.

Premium (cont)—
Illegal premium—
Specific performance—Agreement to assign tenancy—Protected tenancy—Agreement conditional on payment of illegal premium—Purchasers agreeing to pay vendor substantial sum for chattels—Chattels worth much less to knowledge of parties—Amount of contract sum in excess of value of chattels an illegal premium—Purchasers refusing to pay contract sum—Purchasers offering to pay reasonable sum for chattels—Whether purchasers entitled to specific performance of agreement on payment of reasonable sum—Rent Act 1968, ss 86, 88, 89, 90(1). **Ailion v Spiekermann** [1976] **1** 497, Ch D.

Payment—
Requirement of payment as condition of lease. *See* Premium—Requirement of payment as condition of grant of lease, *below.*

Third party receiving benefit—Tenant required by landlord, as condition of grant of tenancy, to sell house, owned jointly by him and his wife, to third party at undervalue of £500—Whether sale at undervalue constituted payment of premium—'Pecuniary consideration'—Whether landlord liable to repay £500 to tenant—Landlord and Tenant (Rent Control) Act 1949, ss 2(1), (5), 18(2). **Elmdene Estates Ltd v White** [1960] **1** 306, HL.

Payment expressed as consideration for agreement to grant a lease for one year if tenant suitable—Recital that landlords unwilling to grant a lease within Rent Restrictions Acts—Rent stated in lease less than two-thirds of rateable value—Premium commuted rent—Total rent thus exceeding two-thirds of rateable value. **Samrose Properties Ltd v Gibbard** [1958] **1** 502, CA.

Recovery—
Agreement voidable at option of either party—Counterclaim for avoidance of lease and for possession—Premium paid and agreement executed—Landlord and Tenant (Rent Control) Act 1949, s 2(5). **Haberman v Westminster Permanent Building Society** [1950] **2** 16, CA.

Consideration nominally paid for goodwill. **Lower v Porter** [1956] **1** 150, CA.

Payment by sub-tenant for sub-tenancy—Tenant a statutory tenant—Inability to grant sub-tenancy—Action at common law—Failure of consideration. **Gray v Southouse** [1949] **2** 1019, KBD.

Premium paid by third party—Period of limitation for recovery—Increase of Rent and Mortgage Interest (Restrictions) Act 1920, s 14(1)—Rent and Mortgage Interest Restrictions Act 1923, s 8(2)—Landlord and Tenant (Rent Control) Act 1949, s 2(5). **Temple v Lewis** [1953] **2** 1130, CA.

Requirement of payment as condition of grant of lease—
Payment not required by landlord—Agreement between landlord and outgoing tenant for surrender of lease and grant of new lease to incoming tenant—Requirement of payment of premium by outgoing tenant from incoming tenant—Whether illegal premium—Rent Act 1968, s 85. **Zimmerman v Grossman** [1971] **1** 363, CA.

Requirement or receipt by any person of premium as condition of or in connection with grant of protected tenancy—Any person—Person other than landlord—Outgoing tenant—Tenant requiring and receiving premium from new tenant as condition of procuring grant by landlord of tenancy to new tenant—Whether premium required and received by outgoing tenant illegal—Rent Act 1968, s 85(1), (2). **Farrell v Alexander** [1976] **2** 721, HL.

Sum paid as commuted rent—Landlord and Tenant (Rent Control) Act 1949, ss 2(1), (5), 18(2). **Woods v Wise** [1955] **1** 767, CA.

Requirement of premium as condition of assignment of tenancy—
Proposed assignment—Agreement to assign tenancy in consideration of payment of premium—Landlord requiring surrender of tenancy in exercise of power contained in lease—Landlord agreeing to grant new lease to proposed assignee—Premium paid to outgoing tenant following grant of new tenancy—Whether premium recoverable as having been paid as a condition of or in connection with assignment of tenancy—Rent Act 1968, s 86(1), (2). **Farrell v Alexander** [1976] **1** 129, CA.

Protected tenancy—
Excluded tenancies—
Amount of rent attributable to attendance forming substantial part of whole rent—Substantial part of whole rent—Bedsittingroom let to tenant at rent of £7 per week—Landlord arranging for housekeeper to clean room daily and change linen weekly—Whether amount of rent attributable to attendance forming 'substantial part of the whole rent'—Rent Act 1968, s 2(1), (3) (as amended by the Rent Act 1974, ss 1(4)(a), 16(2), Sch 4, Part I). **Marchant v Charters** [1977] **3** 918, CA.

Holiday letting—Intention of parties—Tenancy agreement expressly stating that its purpose was to confer on tenant right to occupy house for purpose of holiday—Claim by tenant that purpose of tenancy not holiday letting—No allegation of misrepresentation or mistake or claim for rectification—Burden of proof on tenant to show that contract did not represent true intention of parties—Whether express words of agreement prevailed—Rent Act 1968, s 2(1) (as added by the Rent Act 1974, s 2(1)). **Buchmann v May** [1978] **2** 993, CA.

Rent including payments in respect of board or attendance—Board—Provision of continental breakfast—Whether provision of continental breakfast constituting 'board'—Rent Act 1977, s 7(1). **Otter v Norman** [1988] **2** 897, HL.

Furnished premises. *See* Furnished letting—Extension of protection to furnished tenancies, *above.*

Misrepresentation—
Fraudulent misrepresentation—Rescission—Effect of rescission—Landlord induced by fraudulent misrepresentation to grant tenant protected tenancy—Protected tenancy expiring by effluxion of time and statutory tenancy arising—Rescission of protected tenancy—Whether rescission of protected tenancy bringing statutory tenancy to an end—Rent Act 1977, ss 2(1)(a), 98(1). **Killick v Roberts** [1991] **4** 289, CA.

Loss through fraudulent misrepresentation. *See* **Misrepresentation** (Fraudulent misrepresentation—Loss of protected tenancy).

Recovery of possession. *See* Possession, *above.*

Tenancy or licence—
Occupant of single room—Test whether occupant tenant or licensee—Intention—Nature and quality of occupation—Need to determine whether intention that occupier should have stake in room or whether he only had permission to occupy—Rent Act 1968, s 1. **Marchant v Charters** [1977] **3** 918, CA.

RENT RESTRICTION (cont)—
Protected tenancy (cont)—
Tenancy under which a dwelling-house is let as a separate dwelling—
Premises let to educational institution—Covenant to use premises 'as private residence only in the occupation of one person per room'—Covenant to sublet only to person who is pursuing or intending to pursue course of study provided by institution—Five of institution's students each taking a room—Each student having exclusive use of own room—Students sharing cooking and washing facilities—Whether 'dwelling-house let as a separate dwelling'—Rent Act 1977, ss 1, 8. **St Catherine's College v Dorling** [1979] 3 250, CA.
Termination of. *See* Termination of protected tenancy, *below.*
Transfer on termination of marriage. *See* **Divorce** (Property—Protected or statutory tenancy—Transfer of protected or statutory tenancy on termination of marriage).
Rateable value—
Apportionment of rateable value—
Question arising in proceedings whether dwelling-house within limits of rateable value—Presumption that house within limits unless contrary shown—Meaning of 'proceedings'—Question arising as to proper apportionement—Determination by county court—Rent officer—Determination of fair rent—Ground floor flat—Flat not separately rated—Rateable value of whole house exceeding limits—Rent officer deciding that on apportionment of rateable value flat within limits—Landlord not objecting—Whether question as to rateable value arising in 'proceedings'—Whether 'question arising' as to proper apportionment of rateable value requiring reference to county court—Whether rent officer having power to determine apportionment so as to establish own jurisdiction—Rent Act 1968, ss 1(3), 6(2). **R v Westminster (City) London Borough Rent Officer, ex p Rendall** [1973] 3 119, CA.
Appropriate day—
Refund of rates in respect of period within which appropriate day fell—Refund calculated on basis of rateable value below £400 (Greater London)—Valuation list for relevant period showing rateable value in excess of £400—Whether protected tenancy—Rating and Valuation Act 1961, s 17—Rent Act 1965, s 43(4). **Rodwell v Gwynne Trusts Ltd** [1970] 1 314, HL.
Division into two dwelling-houses without structural alteration—
Rateable value of combined houses above limit prescribed for control—Rent and Mortgage Interest Restrictions Act 1923, s 2—Rent and Mortgage Interest Restrictions (Amendment) Act 1933, s 2. **Fox v Marshall** [1938] 4 773, CA.
Evidence—
Neighbouring premises. **Oscroft v Benabo** [1967] 2 548, CA.
Recovery of overpaid rent—
Bankruptcy of landlord—
Right of tenant to deduct amount of rent overpaid from rent payable to trustee. **Hole v Cuzen** [1953] 1 87, CA.
Overpayment by tenant—
Right of tenant's personal representative to recovery—Increase of Rent and Mortgage Interest (Restrictions) Act 1920, s 14(1). **Dean v Wiesengrund** [1955] 2 432, CA.
Time of application—
Tenant no longer tenant at time of application—Increase of Rent and Mortgage Interest (Restrictions) Act 1920, s 9(1). **Riordan v Minchin** [1948] 2 633, CA.
Registered rent—
County court jurisdiction. *See* County court—Jurisdiction—Registered rent, *above.*
Regulated tenancy—
Increase of rent—
Notice of increase—Date from which increase to take effect—Increase in 'rent payable for any statutory period'—Rent payable on specified date for each rental period—Notice specifying increase to take effect during course of rental period and for apportioned part of period—Validity—Whether notice must specify date on which rent for relevant period payable as date from which increase to take effect—Rent Act 1968, s 22(2)(b). **Avenue Properties (St John's Wood) Ltd v Aisinzon** [1976] 2 177, CA.
Tenancies excluded from being regulated tenancy. *See* Tenancies excluded from being regulated tenancies, *below.*
Rent—
Amount recoverable—
Premises previously let unfurnished and fair rent registered—Landlord subsequently letting premises furnished at substantially higher rent—Contractual tenancy terminating by effluxion of time and tenant holding over as statutory tenant—Whether amount of rent recoverable by landlord limited to registered rent—Rent Act 1977, ss 44, 67(3). **Rakhit v Carty** [1990] 2 202, CA.
Determination of fair rent—
Application—Change in condition of dwelling-house—Application before expiry of three years from date of registration of rent—Improvement effected by landlord—Application by landlord for mid-term review—Whether rent officer in determining fair rent to have regard to all circumstances of dwelling-house or only to change in condition due to improvement—Rent Act 1968, ss 44(3), 46(1). **London Housing and Commercial Properties v Cowan** [1976] 2 385, QBD.
Jurisdiction—Preliminary issue—County court—Reference to county court—Status of applicant—Landlord contending applicant not tenant of house—Jurisdiction of rent officer or rent assessment committee to consider and determine issue—Whether proper course to leave parties to refer issue to county court—Rent Act 1968, s 105(1). **R v Rent Officer for Brent London Borough, ex p Ganatra** [1976] 1 849, QBD.
Jurisdiction—Rent officer—Jurisdiction to determine whether there is a tenancy within the Rent Acts—Allegation by tenant that tenancy protected—Contention by landlord that tenancy was holiday let only—Rent officer satisfied that tenancy was protected tenancy—Whether rent officer under a duty to determine fair rent before court deciding whether there was a protected tenancy. **R v Rent Officer for Camden, ex p Ebiri** [1981] 1 950, QBD.

Rent (cont)—
Determination of fair rent (cont)—
Jurisdiction—Rent officer—Jurisdiction to determine whether there was a tenancy within the Rent Acts—Determination involving resolution of issue whether so-called licence was a device to avoid the Rent Acts—Exercise of jurisdiction—Issue as to licence determined on submissions of parties' solicitors—Oral evidence not given—Improper exercise of discretion—Determination of rent officer quashed—Rent Act 1968, s 105(1). **R v Rent Officer for Kensington and Chelsea, ex p Noel** [1977] **1** 356, QBD.
Ministers making order capping increase in rents of regulated tenancies—Whether order ultra vires enabling legislation—Landlord and Tenant Act 1985, s 31—Rent Acts (Maximum Fair Rent) Order 1999. **R v Secretary of State for the Environment, Transport and the Regions, ex p Spath Holme Ltd** [2001] **1** 195, HL.
Objection—Objection to rent determined by rent officer—Reference to rent assessment committee—Whether rent assessment committee entitled to have regard to registered fair rent comparables in determining a fair rent where close market rent comparables available—Whether rent assessment committee's reasons adequate—Rent Act 1977, s 70(1), (2), (3). **Curtis v London Rent Assessment Committee** [1997] **4** 842, CA.
Objection—Reference to rent assessment committee—Withdrawal of objection—Withdrawal after reference to committee and before hearing—Right of objector to withdraw objection after reference to committee—Rent Act 1968, Sch 6, para 6. **Hanson v Church Comrs for England** [1976] **1** 245, QBD; [1977] **3** 404, CA.
Rent assessment committee—Bias—Chairman living with father in other property of which associate company of landlords was landlord—Chairman advising father in dispute with his landlord—Chairman's firm acting for other tenants in that property on similar matters in dispute—Whether sufficient interest to disqualify him on account of bias. **Metropolitan Properties Co (FGC) v Lannon** [1968] **3** 304, CA.
Rent assessment committee—Jurisdiction—Appeal—Mid-term review—Improvement effected by landlord—Landlord applying for mid-term review—Rent officer reassessing rent—Landlord appealing against reassessment to committee—Whether committee having jurisdiction to hold that improvement insufficient to warrant mid-term review—Whether committee entitled to determine fair rent as original rent registered—Rent Act 1968, s 44(3), Sch 6, para 9. **London Housing and Commercial Properties v Cowan** [1976] **2** 385, QBD.
Rent assessment committee—Majority decision—Whether unanimous decision necessary. *See* **Tribunal** (Decision—Majority decision).
Secretary of State making order capping increase in rents of regulated tenancies—Whether order ultra vires enabling legislation—Landlord and Tenant Act 1985, s 31—Rent Acts (Maximum Fair Rent) Order 1999. **R v Secretary of State for the Environment, Transport and the Regions, ex p Spath Holme Ltd** [2000] **1** 884, CA.
Exclusive use of part of house given in return for services—
No money rent or monetary quantification of services—Whether performance of services constituting rent—Whether tenancy or licence to occupy—Whether protected tenancy. **Barnes v Barratt** [1970] **2** 483, CA.
Increase of rent—
Regulated tenancy. *See* Regulated tenancy—Increase of rent, *above*.
Limit. *See* Rent limit, *below*.
Registered rent—
Reconsideration—Applicant—Person gaining freehold after expiration of lease—No lease at time of application—Whether qualified to apply—Rent Act 1968, ss 75(1), 84(1). **R v East London Rent Tribunal, ex p Schryer** [1969] **3** 447, QBD.
Rent in form of services—
Dwelling-house let to caretaker of landlord's premises—Wages deducted from rent—Rent paid still exceeding two-thirds of rateable value—Subsequent extinction of rent by increase of wages. **Montague v Browning** [1954] **2** 601, CA.
Standard rent. *See* Standard rent, *below*.
Suspension of obligation to pay—
Premises not in reasonable state of repair—Certificate of sanitary authority—Whether obligation to pay suspended in toto—Rent Restrictions (Notice of Increase) Act 1923, s 3(3). **Peach v Lowe** [1947] **1** 441, CA.
Total of rent and rates paid by tenant—
Agreement under Poor Rate Assessment and Collection Act 1869, s 3, by landlords with rating authority to be liable for rates—Increase of Rent and Mortgage Interest (Restrictions) Act 1920, s 12(7)—Landlord and Tenant (Rent Control) Act 1949, s 2(1). **Sidney Trading Co Ltd v Finsbury BC** [1952] **1** 460, QBD.
Rent assessment committee—
Bias. *See* Rent—Determination of fair rent—Rent assessment committee—Bias, *above*.
Determination of fair rent. *See* Rent—Determination of fair rent—Rent assessment committee, *above*.
Rent limit—
Adjustment for repairs—
Appropriate factor—Basis of determination—Whether determination a decision of fact—Rent Act 1957, s 1(1), Sch 1, Pt I, para 1(2), (3). **Regis Property Co Ltd v Dudley** [1958] **1** 510, CA; [1958] **3** 491, HL.
Reasonable charge for services provided by landlord—
Depreciation of plant—Profit on services—Rent Act 1957, s 1(1)(b). **Regis Property Co Ltd v Dudley** [1958] **1** 510, CA.
Rent officer—
Jurisdiction—
Determination of fair rent. *See* Rent—Determination of fair rent—Jurisdiction—Rent officer, *above*.
Rent tribunal. *See* **Rent tribunal**.
Requisitioned property—
No tenancy created in favour of occupant—
Occupant not protected by Rent Restriction Acts. **Southgate BC v Watson** [1944] **1** 603, CA.

RENT RESTRICTION (cont)—
  Resident landlord—
    Death of resident landlord or transfer of landlord's interest inter vivos—
      Transitional period—Tenant having security of tenure during transitional period—Nature of tenancy at expiration of transitional period—Effect of notice to quit served and expiring during transitional period—Rent Act 1977, s 12(1), Sch 2, paras 1, 3. **Landau v Sloane** [1981] **1** 705, HL.
  Separate dwelling—
    Additional accommodation in same house—
      Separate tenancy agreements—Intention of parties—Treatment of both tenancies as one letting—Increase of Rent and Mortgage Interest (Restrictions) Act 1920, s 12(2). **Wimbush v Cibulia** [1949] **2** 432, CA.
    Common use of scullery between tenant and sub-tenant—
      Proceedings for possession commenced by landlord before June 2, 1949—Effect of Landlord and Tenant (Rent Control) Act 1949, ss 9, 10. **Hutchinson v Jauncey** [1950] **1** 165, CA.
    Exclusive letting of room with user, in common with other tenants, of other rooms, including kitchen—
      Whether letting a separate dwelling—Rent and Mortgage Interest Restrictions (Amendment) Act 1933, s 16(1). **Llewellyn v Hinson** [1948] **2** 95, CA.
    House let for the purpose of multiple residential occupation—
      Tenant subletting rooms in house for separate occupation—Tenant not himself occupying any part of house as his residence—Whether singular word 'dwelling' including plural—Whether house 'let as a ... dwelling'—Rent Act 1968, s 1(1). **Horford Investments Ltd v Lambert** [1974] **1** 131, CA.
    Letting of part of flat—
      Use of the kitchen and the bathroom together with the employees of the landlord—Understanding that employees shall use bathroom and kitchen for taking fresh water and washing purposes—Increase of Rent and Mortgage Interest (Restrictions) Act 1920, s 12(2). **Marsh Ltd v Cooper** [1969] **2** 498, CA.
    Letting of rooms—
      Letting of rooms with licence to use kitchen—Declaration in agreement that tenancy to be within Rent Acts. **Rogers v Hyde** [1951] **2** 79, CA.
      Use of extra bedroom in common with landlord—Increase of Rent and Mortgage Interest (Restrictions) Act 1920, s 12(2). **Goodrich v Paisner** [1956] **2** 176, HL.
    Part of a separate dwelling-house—
      Flat let as residence a separate dwelling-house—Additional room let to tenant of flat as servant's room—Distinct contracts of letting and different dates, terms and conditions—Single room not part of the dwelling-house that the flat constituted for the purposes of the Rent Acts. **Metropolitan Properties Co (FGC) Ltd v Barder** [1968] **1** 536, CA.
    Parts of dwelling-house sublet by tenant—
      Different parts sublet from time to time—Occupation by tenant of parts not sublet. **Berkeley v Papadoyannis** [1954] **2** 409, CA.
    Rooms in premises adjoining hotel—
      Rooms let for extra bedroom accommodation for hotel—Rooms usually occupied by hotel guests and on occasions by tenant's family and staff—Whether rooms 'separate dwelling'—Increase of Rent and Mortgage Interest (Restrictions) Act 1920, s 12(2). **Curl v Angelo** [1948] **2** 189, CA.
    Two floors sublet by contractual tenant—
      Not 'self-contained' flats—Expiration of contractual tenancy—Claim by landlord for possession of floors sublet—Increase of Rent and Mortgage Interest (Restrictions) Act 1920, s 15(1). **Crowhurst v Maidment** [1952] **2** 808, CA.
    Two self-contained flats—
      Tenant of house at all times resident in lower flat—Upper flat sub-let—Acquirement of freehold of house by former sub-tenant of upper flat—Recovery of possession. **Murgatroyd v Tresarden** [1946] **2** 723, CA.
    Unfurnished tenancy—
      Subletting of one room, furnished, with use, in common with tenant, of kitchen—Rent and Mortgage Interest Restrictions (Amendment) Act 1933, s 16(1), Sch I, para (d)—Rent and Mortgage Interest Restrictions Act 1939, s 3(2)(b). **Baker v Turner** [1950] **1** 834, HL.
  Shared accommodation—
    Kitchen shared by two tenants—
      One tenant landlord's son—Son becoming landlord—Right to possession against other tenant—Landlord and Tenant (Rent Control) Act 1949, s 8(1)(b). **Tovey v Tyack** [1954] **3** 210, CA.
      Premises vacated by one tenant—Right of landlord to possession as against remaining tenant—Landlord and Tenant (Rent Control) Act 1949, s 8(1)(b). **Isaacs v Titus** [1954] **1** 470, CA; **Lockwood v Lowe** [1954] **1** 472, CA.
    Living rooms let to tenant—
      Joint use of bathroom, boxroom, wc and kitchen—Not let as separate dwelling. **Kenyon v Walker** [1946] **2** 595, CA.
      Joint use of bathroom—Let as separate dwelling. **Cole v Harris** [1945] **2** 146, CA.
    Sole use of one living room—
      Scullery shared—Right to use scullery for cooking—Increase of Rent and Mortgage Interest (Restrictions) Act 1920, s 12(2). **Fredco Estates Ltd v Bryant** [1961] **1** 34, CA.
    Sole use of three unfurnished rooms and joint use of other rooms—
      Part of house let as a separate dwelling. **Krauss v Boyne** [1946] **1** 543, KBD.
    Sole use of two rooms—
      Kitchen and bathroom shared with landlord's employees—Employees to use kitchen and bathroom for taking water and washing purposes only—Whether dwelling-house. **Marsh Ltd v Cooper** [1969] **2** 498, CA.
    Sole use of unfurnished living rooms—
      Joint use of bathroom and kitchen—Sharing house. **Neale v Del Soto** [1945] **1** 191, CA.
    Sole use of unfurnished rooms—
      Sharing of other living rooms—Right to draw water and boil clothes in kitchen—Increase of Rent and Mortgage Interest (Restrictions) Act 1920, s 12(2). **Hayward v Marshall** [1952] **1** 663, CA.

RENT RESTRICTION (cont)—
  Standard rent—
    Application to ascertain—
      Flat let unfurnished during currency of furnished letting—Subsequent unfurnished letting at increased rent—Whether standard rent to be ascertained in relation to first or second unfurnished letting—Increase of Rent and Mortgage Interest (Restrictions) Act 1920, s 12(1)(a). **Anspach v Charlton Steam Shipping Co Ltd** [1955] 1 693, CA.
      Previous judgment—Previous judgment for possession and recovery of arrears of rent at a rate higher than the standard rent—No estoppel—Illegality—Rent and Mortgage Restrictions Act 1923, s 11. **Griffiths v Davies** [1943] 2 209, CA.
    Apportionment—
      Application by tenant of whole property—Property as a whole outside Rent Restrictions Acts—Property comprising principal dwelling-house and a lodge—Increase of Rent and Mortgage Interest (Restrictions) Act 1920, s 12(3). **Amphlett v Dorrell** [1948] 2 674, CA.
      County court decision final and conclusive—Increase of Rent and Mortgage Interest (Restrictions) Act 1920, s 12(3)—Increase of Rent and Mortgage Interest (Restrictions) Act 1938, s 5. **Gover v Field** [1944] 1 151, CA.
      Exclusive use of three rooms with use in common of combined bathroom and lavatory—Three rooms 'part of a house let as a separate dwelling'—Whole house itself not controlled—No apportionment of standard rent—Increase of Rent and Mortgage Interest (Restrictions) Act 1920, ss 12(1), (2), (3), 14(1)—Rent and Mortgage Interest Restrictions (Amendment) Act 1933, s 16(1)—Increase of Rent and Mortgage Interest (Restrictions) Act 1938, ss 5, 7(6)—Rent and Mortgage Interest Restrictions Act 1939, ss 3, 7(1). **Cole v Harris** [1945] 2 146, CA.
      Flat let with another flat—Whole dwelling outside Rent Acts—Flat first let as separate dwelling subsequently—Increase of Rent and Mortgage Interest (Restrictions) Act 1920, s 12(1), (3). **Capital & Provincial Property Trust Ltd v Rice** [1951] 2 600, HL.
      House converted into flats—Whole house outside Rent Acts—Increase of Rent and Mortgage Interest (Restrictions) Act 1920, s 12(3). **Lindop v Quaife** [1949] 1 456, CA.
      Let—First let—Flat originally in one lease of three separate premises—Subsequent separate letting of flat—Increase of Rent and Mortgage Interest (Restrictions) Act 1920, s 12(1), (3). **Upsons Ltd v Herne** [1946] 2 309, CA.
      Loss of identity of original dwelling-house—Substantial structural alterations—Alterations made to enable house to be let as two separate units—Separate gas and electricity meters fitted—Sink installed—Gas cooker substituted for gas fire—Increase of Rent and Mortgage Interest (Restrictions) Act 1920, s 12(3) (as amended by Rent and Mortgage Interest Restrictions (Amendment) Act 1933, s 17(2)). **Monk v Murphy, Same v Brock** [1949] 1 786, CA.
      Period of decontrol—Conversion of premises—House let for dwelling-house purposes from 1929 to 1935, but for business purposes from 1935 to 1946—Subsequent conversion into residential flats—Increase of Rent and Mortgage Interest (Restrictions) Act 1920, s 12(1)(a) (as amended by Rent and Mortgage Interest Restrictions Act 1939, s 3(1), Sch I), s 12(3). **Mitchell v Barnes** [1949] 2 719, CA.
      Refusal to determine application—Building comprising two flats—Letting after 1 September 1939—Standard rent fixed by rent tribunal—Alleged prior letting as one house before 1st September 1939—Subsequent application for apportionment—Duty to hear and determine application—Increase of Rent and Mortgage Interest (Restrictions) Act 1920, s 12(3)—Landlord and Tenant (Rent Control) Act 1949, s 1(1). **R v Pugh (Judge), ex p Graham** [1951] 2 307, KBD.
      Sole use of two unfurnished rooms and joint use of other rooms—'Part of a house let as a separate dwelling'—Increase of Rent and Mortgage Interest (Restrictions) Act 1920, s 12(2), (3), (8)—Rent and Mortgage Interest Restrictions (Amendment) Act 1933, s 16(1). **Neale v Del Soto** [1945] 1 191, CA.
  Contractual tenancy at rent lower than standard rent—
    Termination of contractual tenancy—Right of landlord to increase rent to amount of standard rent—Estoppel—Increase of Rent and Mortgage Interest (Restrictions) Act 1920, s 15(1). **Dean v Bruce** [1951] 2 926, CA.
  Cottage formerly decontrolled—
    Not let on 1 September 1939—Recontrolled by Rent and Mortgage Interest Restrictions Act 1939. **Davies v Warwick** [1943] 1 309, CA.
  Dwelling-house let in separate parts to two tenants—
    Subsequently whole house let to one tenant—Whether house originally let as a complete dwelling—Increase of Rent and Mortgage Interest (Restrictions) Act 1920, s 12(1)(a)—Rent and Mortgage Interest Restrictions (Amendment) Act 1933, s 16—Rent and Mortgage Interest Restrictions Act 1939, ss 3, 7(1). **Vaughan v Shaw** [1945] 2 52, CA.
  Dwelling-house owner-occupied from 1930 until 1936—
    Let before 1930 at 14s per week and after 1936 at 35s per week—Owner's occupation not registered—Whether house controlled immediately before the Act of 1938—Rent and Mortgage Interest Restrictions (Amendment) Act 1933, s 1(2). **Norton v White** [1949] 1 925, CA.
  First let—
    Dwelling-house first let furnished—Subsequently let unfurnished—Increase of Rent and Mortgage Interest (Restrictions) Act 1920, s 12(1)(a), (2)(i). **Signy v Abbey National Building Society** [1944] 1 448, CA.
    House within Housing (Rural Workers) Acts first let at rent of 7s. 6d. a week imposed under those Acts—House later freed from Housing (Rural Workers) Acts and let at rent of 17s. 6d. **Roberts v Jones** [1946] 2 678, CA.
  House divided into two flats—
    No evidence of letting of house or flats before 1928—Lower flat let in 1928 for one year at 25s. a week—Lower flat again let in 1937 at 17s. 6d. a week—Increase of Rent and Mortgage Interest (Restrictions) Act 1920, s 12(1)(a). **Stirling v Gilbert** [1952] 2 153, CA.
  House first let furnished—
    Purchase of furniture by tenant during occupation—Subsequent letting furnished—Increase of Rent and Mortgage Interest (Restrictions) Act 1920, s 12(1). **Stagg v Brickett** [1951] 1 152, CA.
  Lease reserving rent of £200—
    Agreement of same date reducing rent to £150. **White v Richmond Court Ltd** [1944] 1 689, CA.

RENT RESTRICTION (cont)—
Statutory tenant (cont)—
  Conversion into contractual tenant—
    Acceptance of new rent book containing new conditions of tenancy. **Bungalows (Maidenhead) Ltd v Mason** [1954] **1** 1002, CA.
  Death of resident landlord—
    Transitional period. *See* Resident landlord—Death of resident landlord or transfer of landlord's interest inter vivos—Transitional period, *above.*
  Estate or interest—
    Insufficient to maintain action for trespass—Non-occupying tenant—Licence to defendant to occupy—Defendant's occupation not to preserve premises for tenant's return—Increase of Rent and Mortgage Interest (Restrictions) Act 1920, s 15(1). **Thompson v Ward** [1953] **1** 1169, CA.
    None. **Harrington v Croydon Corp** [1967] **3** 929, CA.
    Right of occupation—No legal estate. **Solomon v Orwell** [1954] **1** 874, CA.
  Forfeiture for non-occupation—
    Lease of shop and dwelling-house—Dwelling-house sub-let—Expiration of lease—Tenant not then occupying dwelling-house—Subsequent resumption of possession—Increase of Rent and Mortgage Interest (Restrictions) Act 1920, s 15(1). **Brown (John M) Ltd v Bestwick** [1950] **2** 338, CA.
    Premises left owing to disrepair—Animus revertendi. **Bushford v Falco** [1954] **1** 957, CA.
    Tenant a patient in mental hospital for six years—No intention to abandon occupation—Daughter in occupation, with tenant's furniture—Tenant's condition improved, and becoming a voluntary patient—Slight possibility of return to premises—Whether sufficient hope and possibility of return to retain status of statutory tenant. **Tickner v Hearn** [1961] **1** 65, CA.
    Tenant leaving with intent to live elsewhere for three years—Animus revertendi. **Dixon v Tommis** [1952] **1** 725, CA.
    Tenant serving term of imprisonment—Animus possidendi—Corpus possessionis. **Brown v Brash & Ambrose** [1948] **1** 922, CA.
  Holding over—
    Contractual tenant holding over—Whether statutory tenant. **Murray, Bull & Co Ltd v Murray** [1952] **2** 1079, QBD.
  Licensee—
    Employee of company remaining, after his retirement, in occupation of flat belonging to company. **Murray, Bull & Co Ltd v Murray** [1952] **2** 1079, QBD.
    Occupation on behalf of tenant by mistress—Mistress having borne children to statutory tenant—Tenant leaving premises permanently—Mistress remaining in occupation—Tenant executing surrender—Whether mistress continuing to occupy premises on behalf of tenant—Whether mistress entitled to rely on statutory tenancy—Rent Act 1968, s 3(1). **Smith (Colin) Music Ltd v Ridge** [1975] **1** 290, CA.
  Termination of tenancy—
    Landlord obtaining order for possession—Tenant applying to set aside order—Landlord applying for warrant of execution and forcibly evicting tenant before warrant executed by court bailiff—Whether tenant a statutory tenant at time of eviction—Whether eviction unlawful—Rent Act 1977, s 2(1)(a)—Protection from Eviction Act 1977, ss 3(1), 8(1)—Housing Act 1988, s 27—CCR Ord 26, r 17(1). **Haniff v Robinson** [1993] **1** 185, CA.
Sub-tenancy—
  Cottage and ten acres with rateable value within Rent Restrictions Acts—
    Cottage and ten acres part of farm of seventy-four acres (including farmhouse) let to tenant—Surrender of tenancy of farm—Whether farm was 'premises' within Housing Repairs and Rents Act 1954, s 41. **Hobhouse v Wall** [1963] **1** 701, CA.
  Determination of superior tenancy—
    Business premises—Flat above shop—Subtenancy of flat forming part of property let as business premises—Whether property constituting 'premises'—Whether on determination of superior tenancy of business premises residential subtenancy of part of property continuing to qualify for statutory protection—Rent Act 1977, s 137(3). **Pittalis v Grant** [1989] **2** 622, CA.
    Business premises—Flats within premises—Sub-tenancy of flats forming part of property let for business purposes—Whether property constituting 'premises'—Whether on determination of superior tenancy of business premises residential sub-tenancy of part of property continuing to qualify for statutory protection—Rent Act 1977, ss 24(3), 137(3). **Wellcome Trust Ltd v Hammad** [1998] **1** 657, CA.
    Sub-tenancy of dwelling-house forming part of premises let as a whole on superior lettings—Premises—Meaning—Buildings used for residential purposes—Farm—Farm buildings including cottage—Tenant of farm subletting cottage—Sub-tenancy protected as between tenant and sub-tenant—Termination of tenancy of farm—Whether farm 'premises' of which cottage forming part—Rent Act 1968, s 18(5). **Maunsell v Olins** [1975] **1** 16, HL.
  Dwelling-house let at rent less than two-thirds of rateable value—
    Subletting at rent more than two-thirds of rateable value—Expiry of head lease—Right of landlords to possession—Increase of Rent and Mortgage Interest (Restrictions) Act 1920, ss 12(7), 15(3). **Knightsbridge Estates Trust Ltd v Deeley** [1950] **1** 577, CA.
  Exclusive use of part of flat—
    Kitchen shared with tenant—Order for possession against tenant—Landlord's right to possession against sub-tenant—Increase of Rent and Mortgage Interest (Restrictions) Act 1920, s 15(3)—Landlord and Tenant (Rent Control) Act 1949, s 8(1). **Stanley v Compton** [1951] **1** 859, CA.
  Exclusive use of part of house—
    Kitchen and other essential parts of house shared with tenant—Surrender of tenancy by tenant—Landlord's right to possession against sub-tenant—Landlord and Tenant (Rent Control) Act 1949, s 9. **Shackleton v Greenhalgh** [1950] **2** 1223, CA.
  Letting—
    Letting to intermediate landlord outside Acts as agricultural holding let to farmer—Sub-tenancy of cottage on farm—Cottage occupied as private dwelling, not in connection with farm work—Whether sub-tenant protected by Rent Restrictions Acts—Increase of Rent and Mortgage Interest (Restrictions) Act 1920, s 12(2), proviso (iii). **Critchley v Clifford** [1961] **3** 288, CA.

RENT RESTRICTION (cont)—
  Sub-tenancy (cont)—
    Paddock outside Rent Acts—
      Subletting with part of tenant's own dwelling-house subject to Acts—Right to landlord to recover possession of paddock—Rent and Mortgage Interest Restrictions (Amendment) Act 1933, s 3(1)—Increase of Rent and Mortgage Interest (Restrictions) Act 1920, s 15(3). **Knight v Olive** [1954] **1** 701, CA.
    Premises decontrolled—
      Possession of sublet part—Whether landlord entitled to possession of sublet part with rateable value below £40—Increase of Rent and Mortgage Interest (Restrictions) Act 1920, s 15(3)—Housing Repairs and Rents Act 1954, s 41—Rent Act 1957, s 11(1), (3), Sch 4—Landlord and Tenant (Temporary Provisions) Act 1958, s 3(1). **Legge v Matthews** [1960] **1** 595, CA.
      Unlawful sub-tenant of part of premises with rateable value below £40—Sub-tenancy becoming lawful by waiver of breach by landlord in 1958—Whether landlord entitled to recover possession from sub-tenant—Increase of Rent and Mortgage Interest (Restrictions) Act 1920, s 15(3). **Muspratt v Johnston** [1963] **2** 339, CA.
    Premises outside Rent Restrictions Acts—
      Notional separate subletting of part within Rent Restrictions Acts—Whether landlord entitled to recover possession—Increase of Rent and Mortgage Interest (Restrictions) Act 1920, s 15(3)—Housing Repairs and Rents Act 1954, s 41—Landlord and Tenant Act 1954, s 15. **Cadogan (Earl) v Henthorne** [1956] **3** 851, QBD.
      Surrender of lease of whole premises—Right of landlord to possession of part sub-let—Rent and Mortgage Interest Restrictions (Amendment) Act 1933, s 3(1)—Increase of Rent and Mortgage Interest (Restrictions) Act 1920, s 15(3). **Cow v Casey** [1949] **1** 197, CA.
    Sub-tenant deemed to become tenant—
      Acceptance by landlord of rent from head lessee after knowledge of breach of subletting convenant—Qualified acceptance—Question of fact whether such acceptance to be treated as unequivocal act of affirmation of tenancy—'Unlawful sub-letting'—No right of re-entry—Increase of Rent and Mortgage Interest (Restrictions) Act 1920, s 15(3). **Carter v Green** [1950] **1** 627, CA.
      Continued acceptance by landlord of rent from headlease after knowledge of breach of subletting convenant—Deemed to be dwelling-house to which Rent Acts apply—Increase of Rent and Mortgage Interest (Restrictions) Act 1920, s 15(3)—Increase of Rent and Mortgage Interest (Restrictions) Act 1938, s 7(1). **Wright v Arnold** [1946] **2** 616, CA.
      Part of premises sub-let by widow of statutory tenant—Death of widow—'Determination' of interest—Increase of Rent and Mortgage Interest (Restrictions) Act 1920, s 15(3). **Lewis v Reeves** [1951] **2** 855, CA.
    Unlawful sub-tenancy—
      Tenant covenanting not to let premises for more than six months without landlord's consent—Tenant subletting premises on periodic monthly tenancy—Whether subtenancy for a period exceeding six months—Whether landlord's consent required—Rent Act 1977, s 137. **Trustees of Henry Smith's Charity v Willson** [1983] **1** 73, CA.
  Surrender of tenancy—
    Acceptance of wife of statutory tenant as tenant—
      Whether equivalent to giving up possession. **Collins v Claughton** [1959] **1** 95, CA.
    Contract by statutory tenant to purchase house—
      Failure to complete—Rescission of contract by landlord—Tenant remaining in possession—Nature of occupation. **Nightingale v Courtney** [1954] **1** 362, CA.
    Contractual tenancy from year to year—
      Agreement to terminate and grant of licence to former tenant—Validity. **Foster v Robinson** [1950] **2** 342, CA.
  Tenancies excluded from being regulated tenancies—
    Housing association—
      Association becoming immediate reversioner of lease—Tenancy subsisting at date of acquisition—Rateable value of dwelling-house then above Rent Act limit—Tenancy expired in October, 1965—Rent then in arrear—Action for possession brought in November, 1965—Rent Act 1965 (operative Dec 8, 1965) extended to dwelling house—Whether housing association entitled to recover possession on ground that tenancy was free from Rent Acts under Housing Repairs and Rents Act 1954, s 33(1), (2)(b)—Rent Act 1965, ss 1(2), 20(1)(a). **Dolphin Square Trust Ltd v Hartman** [1967] **1** 624, CA.
    Premises described in lease as shop and premises—
      Parties comtemplating letting as a shop—Used as dwelling-house by sub-tenant—Whether tenancy within Rent Acts—Rent Act 1968, s 1(1). **Ponder v Hillman** [1969] **3** 694, Ch D.
  Tenancies within Rent Restrictions Acts—
    Agreement to purchase house—
      Possession as tenant at will pending completion—payment of sum representing interest on unpaid purchase money—Failure to complete—Statutory tenancy. **Jackson (Francis) Developments Ltd v Stemp** [1943] **2** 601, CA.
  Tenant—
    Adjudication of bankruptcy—
      No disclaimer of lease by trustee in bankruptcy—Bankrupt permitted by trustee to remain in residence—No statutory tenancy acquired. **Stafford v Levy** [1946] **2** 256, CA.
    Persons deriving title under original tenant—
      Administratrix of original tenant's estate—Increase of Rent and Mortgage Interest (Restrictions) Act 1920, s 12(1)(f). **Harrison v Hopkins** [1949] **2** 597, CA.
    Statutory tenant. *See* Statutory tenant, *above.*
  Termination of protected tenancy—
    Statutory tenant person who immediately before termination was protected tenant—
      Bankruptcy of protected tenant—Effect—Tenancy vesting in trustee in bankruptcy—Bankrupt remaining in occupation—Disclaimer of tenancy by trustee in bankruptcy—Action by landlord for possession—Whether bankrupt a person who immediately before termination of tenancy was a protected tenant—Whether bankrupt entitled to protection as statutory tenant—Rent Act 1968, s 3(1). **Smalley v Quarrier** [1975] **2** 688, CA.

RENT RESTRICTION (cont)—

Termination of statutory tenancy—

Landlord obtaining possession order—

Tenant applying to set aside order. *See* Statutory tenant—Termination of tenancy—Landlord obtaining order for possession, *above.*

Substitution of contractual tenancy—

Agreement that tenant should pay rates instead of landlord as theretofore—Corresponding decrease in rent. **Steel (M & H) (a firm) v Cockcroft** [1951] **2** 175, CA.

Terms in contractual tenancy—

Incorporation into statutory tenancy—

Agreement by contractual tenant to pay on expiration of tenancy '£40 towards re-decoration'—Increase of Rent and Mortgage Interest (Restrictions) Act 1920, s 15(1). **Boyer v Warbey** [1953] **1** 269, CA.

Landlord providing hot water, central heating and other services—Notice to quit—Tenant holding over as statutory tenant—Whether statutory tenant entitled to benefit of original terms of tenancy—'Attendance'—Increase of Rent and Mortgage Interest (Restrictions) Act 1920, ss 12, 15—Rent and Mortgage Interest Restrictions Act 1923, s 10. **Engvall v Ideal Flats Ltd** [1945] **1** 230, CA.

Terms allowing bonus on punctual payment of rent—Agreement terminated by notice from landlord increasing rent—Additional rent on account of statutory increase for rates—Statutory tenancy—Whether proviso for bonus imported into statutory tenancy—Increase of Rent and Mortgage Interest (Restrictions) Act 1920, ss 2, 15(1)—Rent Restrictions (Notice of Increase) Act 1923, s 1. **Regional Properties Ltd v Oxley** [1945] **2** 418, HL.

Transfer of burden—

Repair—

Tenant liable to repair under agreement—Repairs done by landlord for many years—Whether transfer of burden implied. **London Hospital (Board of Governors) v Jacobs** [1956] **2** 603, CA.

Transfer of liability for rates—

Corresponding reduction in rent—

Relevant date—Increase of Rent and Mortgage Interest (Restrictions) Act 1920, s 2(3), proviso. **Woodside House (Wimbledon) Ltd v Hutchinson** [1949] **2** 709, CA.

RENT TRIBUNAL

Certiorari to quash decision of tribunal—

Circumstances in which certiorari will lie—

Excess of jurisdiction—Jurisdiction under Housing Repairs and Rents Act 1954, s 40(1)(b), (2)(b), (5). **R v Paddington North and St Marylebone Rent Tribunal, ex p Perry** [1955] **3** 391, QBD.

Circumstances in which certiorari will not lie—

Decision good on its face and not outside jurisdiction of tribunal—Furnished Houses (Rent Control) Act 1946, s 2. **R v Paddington and St Marylebone Furnished Houses Rent Tribunal, ex p Kendal Hotels Ltd** [1947] **1** 448, KBD.

Costs—

Certiorari granted against tribunal—Payment of costs by tribunal. **R v Kingston-upon-Hull Rent Tribunal, ex p Black** [1949] **1** 260, KBD.

Preliminary issue as to jurisdiction—

County court's jurisdiction to determine issue—

Question as to application of statute to a contract of tenancy—Issue as to application of statute raised before tribunal—Application by tenant for determination of fair rent—Landlord contending statute had no application to contract of tenancy—Whether tribunal having jurisdiction to determine issue before considering tenant's application on its merits—Whether tribunal bound to refer issue for determination by county court—Rent Act 1968, s 105(1). **R v Croydon and South West London Rent Tribunal, ex p Ryzewska** [1977] **1** 312, QBD.

Proceedings before tribunal—

Refusal of tribunal to admit in evidence unstamped document—

Power of tribunal. **R v Fulham, Hammersmith and Kensington Rent Tribunal, ex p Zerek** [1951] **1** 482, KBD.

Prohibition. *See* **Prohibition** (Rent tribunal).

Reference of contract—

Jurisdiction—

Jurisdiction of tribunal to set aside its own order—Notice of hearing of reference sent to landlord and tenant—Tenant not appearing at hearing—Tribunal making order in absence of tenant—Tenant subsequently informing tribunal that he never received notice of hearing—Tenant applying to tribunal for hearing and re-instatement of reference—Whether tribunal having power to re-open reference. **R v Kensington and Chelsea Rent Tribunal, ex p MacFarlane** [1974] **3** 390, QBD.

Reference by local authority—Validity of reference—Test—Whether reference made mala fide or frivolously, capriciously or vexatiously—Relevance of factors taken into or left out of account—Views of tenants—Likelihood of reductions of rent—Block references without individual consideration—Court's power to review administrative decision—Rent Act 1968, s 72(1). **R v Barnet and Camden Rent Tribunal, ex p Frey Investments Ltd** [1972] **1** 1185, CA.

Reference otherwise than by local authority—Jurisdiction of tribunal to refuse to entertain reference if satisfied reference frivolous or vexatious—Extent of jurisdiction—Rent Act 1968, s 73(5). **R v Kensington and Chelsea Rent Tribunal, ex p MacFarlane** [1974] **3** 390, QBD.

Reference under Furnished Houses (Rent Control) Act 1946. *See* **Rent control** (Reference to tribunal of contract for furnished letting).

RENT TRIBUNAL (cont)—
 Reference of contract (cont)—
  Withdrawal of reference—
   Withdrawal before tribunal have 'entered upon consideration' of reference—Time when withdrawal effective—Time when tribunal enter on consideration of reference—Withdrawal effective when delivered to tribunal's offices in office hours or reasonable time thereafter for withdrawal to be seen by clerk to tribunal—Tribunal entering on consideration as soon as all members have read papers and before meeting—Notice of withdrawal delivered to tribunal's offices after office hours on Friday—Members of tribunal reading papers in reference at home over weekend—Notice of withdrawal communicated to clerk on Monday morning—Withdrawal ineffective—Rent ineffective—Rent Act 1968, s 73(1). **R v Tottenham District Rent Tribunal, ex p Fryer Bros (Properties) Ltd** [1971] **3** 563, CA.

RENTCHARGE
 Creation of rentcharges—
  Prohibition of creation of rentcharges—
   Exceptions—Estate rentcharge—Rentcharge created for purpose of meeting cost of performance by rent owner for provision of services for benefit of land affected by rent charge or for benefit of that and other land—Rentcharge representing payment for performance by rent owner of covenant by rent owner which is reasonable—Rentcharge created by transfer of registered land—Whether rentcharge for benefit of owner of land—Whether rentcharge reasonable—Meaning—Rentcharges Act 1977, s 2(4), (5). **Canwell Estate Co Ltd v Smith Brothers Farm Ltd** [2012] **2** 1159, CA.
 Income tax—
  Capital or income receipts—
   Rentcharge payable for fixed period as consideration for transfer of property. *See* **Income tax** (Capital or income receipts—Transfer of capital asset—Cash payments of fixed amounts over fixed period as consideration for transfer—Rentcharges).
 Rule against perpetuities. *See* **Rule against perpetuities** (Remoteness—Rentcharge).
 Settlement—
  Jointure rentcharge. *See* **Settlement** (Jointure rentcharge).
 Tithe. *See* **Tithe and tithe rentcharge.**

REOPENING OF APPEAL
 Generally. *See* **Appeal** (Reopening of appeal).

REPAIR
 Agricultural holding. *See* **Agricultural holding** (Repairs).
 Bailed goods, of. *See* **Bailment** (Bailment for reward—Liability of bailee—Repair of goods bailed).
 Breach of covenant—
  Forfeiture of lease. *See* **Landlord and tenant** (Forfeiture of lease—Breach of repairing covenant).
 Building—
  Damages—
   Assessment of damages. *See* **Damages** (Assessment—Date at which damages assessed—Repairs to buildings).
   Measure of damages. *See* **Damages** (Measure of damages—Repairs to building).
   Nuisance. *See* **Nuisance** (Damages—Repairs to building).
  Defect in building—
   Negligence—Economic loss—Cost of repair—Builder's liability. *See* **Negligence** (Duty to take care—Economic loss—Building—Defect in building—Cost of repair).
  Inherent defect—
   Covenant to repair. *See* **Landlord and tenant** (Repair—Construction of covenant—Covenant 'to repair'—Covenant to repay landlord cost of repairs—Inherent defect).
  Value added tax—
   Zero-rating. *See* **Value added tax** (Zero-rating—Building works—Alteration of building—Work of repair or maintenance).
 Car—
  Contract—
   Implied term—Implication necessary to give business efficacy to contract. *See* **Contract** (Implied term—Implication necessary to give business efficacy to contract—Car repair).
   Implied term—Performance within reasonable time. *See* **Contract** (Implied term—Performance within reasonable time—Repair of motor car at request of car owner).
 Chancel—
  Liability to repair. *See* **Ecclesiastical law** (Chancel—Liability to repair chancel).
 Church. *See* **Ecclesiastical law** (Church—Repairs and maintenance).
 Cost of repairs—
  Lease. *See* **Landlord and tenant** (Repair—Cost of repairs).
 Dangerous thing—
  Repairer's liability in negligence. *See* **Negligence** (Dangerous things—Repairer's liability).
 Drains. *See* **Land drainage** (Drainage board—Maintenance and repair of drains).
 Dyke. *See* **Land drainage** (Drainage board—Maintenance and repair of dyke).
 Hedge—
  Boundary. *See* **Boundary** (Hedge—Repair).
 Highway—
  Scope of duty to maintain—
   Duty to repair and keep in repair. *See* **Highway** (Maintenance—Scope of duty to maintain—Duty to repair and keep in repair).
 Housing—
  Local authority notice to execute works. *See* **Housing** (House in disrepair—Notice to execute works).
  Unfit for human habitation—
   House capable at reasonable expense of being rendered fit. *See* **Housing** (House unfit for human habitation—Notice to execute works—House capable at reasonable expense of being rendered fit—Factors to be considered—Cost of repairs compared to value of house).

REPAIR (cont)—
  Housing (cont)—
    Unfit for human habitation (cont)—
      Notice to execute works. *See* **Housing** (House unfit for human habitation—Notice to execute works).
      Premises beyond repair at reasonable cost. *See* **Housing** (House unfit for human habitation—Premises beyond repair at reasonable cost).
  Implied covenant in lease. *See* **Landlord and tenant** (Implied covenant to repair).
  Income tax—
    Capital or revenue expenditure. *See* **Income tax** (Deduction in computing profits—Capital or revenue expenditure—Repairs).
  Inherent defect—
    Building—
      Covenant to repair. *See* **Landlord and tenant** (Repair—Construction of covenant—Covenant 'to repair'—Covenant to repay landlord cost of repairs—Inherent defect).
  Land drainage—
    Commutation of obligation to repair by catchment board. *See* **Land drainage** (Catchment board—Commutation of obligation to repair).
  Lease—
    Covenant in lease—
      Breach of covenant. *See* **Landlord and tenant** (Breach of covenant to repair).
      Damages for breach of covenant to repair. *See* **Landlord and tenant** (Damages for failure to repair).
      Generally. *See* **Landlord and tenant** (Repair).
      Implied covenant. *See* **Landlord and tenant** (Implied covenant to repair).
  Lien—
    Repairer's lien. *See* **Lien** (Repairer's lien).
    Ship repairs, as to. *See* **Shipping** (Maritime lien—Liens recognised by English law—Lien for repairs to ship).
  Listed building—
    Notice. *See* **Town and country planning** (Building of special architectural or historic interest—Repairs notice).
  Premises—
    Damages for breach of covenant to repair. *See* **Landlord and tenant** (Damages for failure to repair).
  River bank. *See* **Land drainage** (Drainage board—Maintenance and repair of river bank).
  River wall. *See* **Land drainage** (Drainage board—Maintenance and repair of river wall).
  Sea wall. *See* **Land drainage** (Sea wall—Negligence—Duty of catchment board to repair).
  Ship—
    Dry dock—
      Statutory regulations. *See* **Dock** (Repair of ship in dry dock).
    Execution of repairs prior to sale—
      Admiralty proceedings. *See* **Admiralty** (Appraisement and sale—Execution of repairs prior to sale).
    General average contribution. *See* **Shipping** (General average—General average expenditure—Temporary repairs).
    Lien for repairs to ship—
      Priority. *See* **Shipping** (Maritime lien—Liens recognised by English law—Lien for repairs to ship).
    Restriction on. *See* **Dock** (Shiprepairs and alterations—Licence).
  Tramway—
    Repair of road. *See* **Tramway** (Repair of road).

REPATRIATION
  Prisoner. *See* **Prison** (Repatriation of prisoner).

REPEAL
  Provisions brought into operation on different dates. *See* **Statute** (Commencement—Repeals—Different provisions brought into operation on different dates).
  Retrospective operation of repeal. *See* **Statute** (Retrospective operation—Repeal).
  Statute. *See* **Statute** (Repeal).

REPETITIVE STRAIN INJURY
  Employment—
    Employer's duty of care. *See* **Negligence** (Duty to take care—Employer—Employee developing symptoms of repetitive strain injury).

REPORT
  Adoption proceedings—
    Disclosure of confidential reports. *See* **Adoption** (Practice—Reports—Disclosure).
  Chambers proceedings, of. *See* **Practice** (Chambers proceedings—Queen's Bench Division—Report of proceedings).
  Citation—
    Court of Appeal, Civil Division. *See* **Court of Appeal** (Practice—Civil Division—Citation of cases—Reports).
    Generally. *See* **Practice** (Citation of cases—Reports).
  Committal proceedings—
    Generally. *See* **Criminal law** (Committal—Preliminary hearing before justices—Publicity).
  Court welfare officer's report—
    Divorce proceedings—
      Practice. *See* **Divorce** (Practice—Children—Report of court welfare officer).
  Expert evidence—
    Disclosure of substance of evidence to other parties—
      Written report. *See* **Practice** (Evidence—Expert evidence—Disclosure to other parties—Substance of evidence in form of written report).
  Experts' reports—
    Personal injuries action. *See* **Practice** (Personal injuries action—Experts' reports).

REPORT (cont)—
Law report—
  Citation—
    Court of Appeal. *See* **Court of Appeal** (Practice—Civil Division—Citation of cases).
    Generally. *See* **Practice** (Citation of cases—Reports).
  Newspaper—
    Committal proceedings. *See* **Criminal law** (Committal—Preliminary hearing before justices—Newspaper report).
    Contempt of court—
      Publications concerning legal proceedings. *See* **Contempt of court** (Publications concerning legal proceedings).
  Official Referee—
    Reference, report on. *See* **Practice** (Reference to referee—Report on reference).
  Official Solicitor—
    Wardship proceedings—
      Disclosure. *See* **Ward of court** (Practice—Official Solicitor—Official Solicitor' report—Disclosure).
  Reporting restrictions—
    Contempt of court. *See* **Contempt of court** (Publications concerning legal proceedings).
    Criminal trial. *See* **Criminal law** (Trial—Reporting restrictions).
    Family courts. *See* **Practice** (Family court—Reporting).
    Generally. *See* **Practice** (Reporting restrictions).
  Select committee—
    Privilege. *See* **Parliament** (Privilege—Report of select committee).

REPORTER
  Children and family reporter. *See* **Family proceedings** (Confidential information in children proceedings—Children and family reporter (CFR)).

REPRESENTATION
  Co-plaintiffs. *See* **Practice** (Parties—Plaintiffs—Co-plaintiffs should be represented by same solicitor unless separate representation authorised).
  Company—
    Meeting. *See* **Company** (Meeting—Representation).
  Criminal trial—
    Counsel, duties of. *See* **Criminal law** (Trial—Counsel—Solicitor—Duties).
    Defendant. *See* **Criminal law** (Trial—Defendant—Representation).
    Solicitor, duties of. *See* **Criminal law** (Trial—Counsel—Solicitor—Duties).
  Deceased person—
    Representation in proceedings where no personal representative. *See* **Practice** (Representation of deceased person interested in proceedings).
  Deceit. *See* **Deceit** (Representation).
  Estoppel by representation. *See* **Estoppel** (Representation).
  Grant—
    Practice. *See* **Probate** (Practice—Non-contentious probate—Grant of representation).
  Misrepresentation. *See* **Misrepresentation**.
  Solicitor—
    Negligence. *See* **Solicitor** (Negligence—Negligent misrepresentation).
  Trade union—
    Legal proceedings. *See* **Trade union** (Legal proceedings).
  Warranty—
    Pre-contract negotiations. *See* **Contract** (Warranty—Representation—Pre-contract negotiations).

REPRESENTATIVE ACTION
  Club. *See* **Club** (Members' club—Parties to action—Representation order).
  Minority shareholder. *See* **Company** (Minority shareholder—Representative action).
  Parties. *See* **Practice** (Parties—Representative proceedings).
  Production of documents. *See* **Disclosure and inspection of documents** (Production of documents—Representative action).
  Shareholder. *See* **Company** (Shareholder—Minority shareholder—Representative action).

REPUDIATION
  Agreement for lease. *See* **Landlord and tenant** (Agreement for lease—Repudiation).
  Contract—
    Anticipatory breach. *See* **Contract** (Repudiation—Anticipatory breach).
    Charterparty—
      Anticipatory breach. *See* **Contract** (Repudiation—Anticipatory breach—Charterparty).
      Generally. *See* **Contract** (Repudiation—Charterparty).
    Generally. *See* **Contract** (Repudiation).
  Sale of goods—
    Breach constituting repudiation. *See* **Sale of goods** (Rescission of contract—Ground for treating contract as repudiated).
    Generally. *See* **Sale of goods** (Repudiation of contract).
  Sale of land—
    Generally. *See* **Sale of land** (Repudiation of contract).
    Repudiation by vendor—Damages. *See* **Sale of land** (Damages for breach of contract—Repudiation by vendor).
  Service contract—
    Recovery of contract price. *See* **Contract** (Repudiation—Contract for services).
    Unilateral repudiation by servant. *See* **Employment** (Contract of service—Breach of contract—Unilateral repudiation of contract by servant).
  Insurance claim—
    Burglary insurance. *See* **Insurance** (Burglary insurance—Claim—Repudiation of claim without repudiation of policy by insurance company).

REPUDIATION (cont)—

Lease. *See* **Landlord and tenant** (Lease—Repudiation).

Partnership, dissolution of. *See* **Partnership** (Dissolution—Dissolution by the court).

REPUTATION

Conspiracy—

Tort—

Whether damages for injury to reputation or business reputation recoverable when defamation not alleged. *See* **Tort** (Conspiracy—Ingredients of tort—Damages).

Libel and slander. *See* **Libel and slander**.

REQUISITION

Chattel already subject of hiring agreement—

Hiring agreement subject to determination forthwith on notice—

Requisition notice sufficient to determine hiring agreement—Defence (General) Regulations 1939, reg 53(2). **Lane v Minister of War Transport** [1942] **2** 28, CA.

Compensation—

Agreement—

Disclaimer—Effect—House requisitioned by military authorities—Agreement with tenant—Compensation payable in respect of house and in respect of storage of furniture—Disclaimer of lease by tenant—Whether tenant still entitled to compensation in respect of storage of furniture—Construction of agreement—Compensation (Defence) Act 1939, s 2—Landlord and Tenant (Requisitioned Land) Act 1942, ss 1, 2. **Looker v R** [1944] **2** 513, KBD.

Application of compensation—

Deprivation of enjoyment of easement—Compensation for requisition—Compensation for dilapidations—Compensation (Defence) Act 1939, s 2(2). **Ellenborough Park, Re** [1955] **2** 38, Ch D.

Land subject to mortgage—Land leased to company—Covenant by lessee to insure against fire—Insurance money to be laid out in re-building—Mortgage by lessee—Property destroyed by fire while requisitioned—Insurance policy not kept up—Whether compensation to be applied in same manner as money receivable under policy—Compensation (Defence) Act 1939, s 2(1)(b), s 14. **Radnor (Earl) v Folkestone Pier and Lift Co** [1950] **2** 690, Ch D.

Person entitled to compensation—

Requisition of ship—Purchase of ship subject to time charterparty—Whether charterer entitled to compensation paid to purchaser—Compensation (Defence) Act 1939, ss 4, 15. **Port Line Ltd v Ben Line Steamers Ltd** [1958] **1** 787, QBD.

Sale of requisitioned land—Derequisitioned before completion—Entitlement of purchaser to compensation—Compensation (Defence) Act 1939, s 2(1)(b), (3). **Hamilton-Snowball's Conveyance, Re** [1958] **2** 319, Ch D.

Release from requisition—

Compensation to owner for accepting licensee as statutory tenant—Date when compensation becomes payable—Requisitioned Houses and Housing (Amendment) Act 1955, s 4(2)(c). **East Ham Corp v Ministry of Housing and Local Government** [1959] **3** 508, Ch D.

Right of owner to compensation—

Owner—Receiver of rackrent—Formal claim made by lessee—Right of lessor to claim as 'owner'—Computation of rackrent—Regard to restrictive covenants in lease—Date at which rackrent to be computed—Compensation (Defence) Act 1939, ss 2(3), 11, 17(1)—Public Health Act 1936, s 343(1). **Borthwick-Norton v Collier** [1950] **2** 204, CA.

Ship—

Cargo—Ship ordered by Minister of Shipping to proceed from Belfast to Manchester to discharge requisitioned cargo—Whether requisitioning of cargo amounts to requisitioning of ship—Compensation (Defence) Act 1939, ss 4, 7—Defence (General) Regulations 1939, reg 53(2). **Minister of War Transport and N G Nicolaou, Re a Dispute between** [1944] **2** 322, KBD.

Sums included—

Expenses—Legal costs—Property requisitioned by military authorities—Compensation fixed by negotiation—Claimant's solicitors' costs of negotiation—Inclusion of such costs in compensation—Compensation (Defence) Act 1939, ss 2(1)(d), 7, 9. **Rhodes v Secretary of State for War** [1941] **3** 407, KBD.

Work done on land—

Exclusion of damage to land while possession retained—Damage to land—Air-raid shelter erected during possession by Crown—Shelter removed after possession yielded up—Right to compensation for period between return of possession and restoration to original condition—Compensation (Defence) Act 1939, s 3(2)—Requisitioned Land and War Works Act 1948, s 11(2). **Lyons (J) & Co Ltd v Secretary of State for Home Affairs** [1950] **1** 280, KBD.

Duration—

Confirmation of requisition by Minister—

Extension of period of requisition. **Acton Corp v Morris** [1953] **2** 932, CA.

Land—

Land comprised in a lease—

Damage to land—Protection against breach of covenant to repair—'Land'—Electric Plant—Storage battery—Whether 'fixture'—Landlord and Tenant (Requisitioned Land) Act 1944, s 1(1). **Jordan v May** [1947] **1** 231, CA.

Use of land while in possession of competent authority—

Discretion of authority—Exclusion of court's jurisdiction—Defence (General) Regulations 1939, reg 51(2). **Demetriades v Glasgow Corp** [1951] **1** 457, HL.

Powers of competent authority—Agreement purporting to grant tenancy—Whether lease or licence—Defence (General) Regulations 1939, reg 51(1), (2). **Ministry of Agriculture and Fisheries v Matthews** [1949] **2** 724, KBD.

Powers of competent authority—Extent of powers—Whether including power to transfer requisition—Defence (General) Regulations 1939, reg 51(1), (2). **Blount v War Office** [1953] **1** 1071, Assizes.

Powers of competent authority—Extent of powers—Whether including power to transfer requisition—Defence (General) Regulations 1939, regs 49, 51. **Progress Building Ltd v Westminster City Corp** [1947] **1** 684, KBD.

REQUISITION (cont)—
Premises—
Delegation of power—
Delegation to local authority—Exercise of power by authority—Conditions in circulars issued by Minister of Health—Purported ratification and adoption by Minister—Defence (General) Regulations 1939, reg 51(1), (5)—Supplies and Services (Transitional Powers) Act 1945, s 1(1). **Blackpool Corp v Locker** [1948] **1** 85, CA.
Effect of delegation—Power to take possession delegated to local authority—Possession taken for the purpose of providing accommodation for refugees from enemy attack—Local authority directed to retain possession for different purposes—Powers of requisitioning authority—Emergency Powers (Defence) Act 1939, s 1—Requisitioned Land and War Works Act 1945, s 28(2)—Defence (General) Regulations 1939, reg 51(1), (5). **Gordon, Dadds & Co v Morris** [1945] **2** 616, Ch D.
Letter of authority from official of Ministry of Health to town clerk—Right of local authority to sue for possession—Requisition 'necessary or expedient'—Defence (General) Regulations 1939, reg 51(1), (2)(a), (5) (as amended)—Emergency Powers (Defence) Act 1939, s 7. **Lewisham BC v Roberts** [1949] **1** 815, CA.
Sufficiency of letter from Minister—Requisition of part of premises—Need for part to be specified in delegation—Defence (General) Regulations 1939, reg 51(1), (5)—Emergency Powers (Defence) Act 1939, s 7. **Carlish v East Ham Corp** [1948] **2** 550, KBD.
Discretion of competent authority—
No jurisdiction of court to interfere with bona fide exercise of discretion—Defence (General) Regulations 1939, reg 51(1). **Carltona Ltd v Comrs of Works** [1943] **2** 560, CA.
Purchase of requisitioned premises—
Right of purchaser to possession—Defence (General) Regulations 1939, reg 51(1). **Erith Corp v Holder** [1949] **1** 389, CA.
Tenancy agreement—
Frustration. *See* **Landlord and tenant** (Determination of lease—Requisition of premises—Frustration of tenancy agreement).
Registration as land charge—
Equitable easement. *See* **Land charge** (Equitable easement—Right or privilege over or affecting land being an equitable interest).

REQUISITIONED LAND
Sale of land. *See* **Sale of land** (Requisitioned land).

REQUISITIONS ON TITLE
Sale of land. *See* **Sale of land** (Requisitions on title).

RES GESTAE
Evidence—
Civil proceedings. *See* **Evidence** (Res gestae).
Criminal proceedings. *See* **Criminal evidence** (Res gestae).

RES IPSA LOQUITUR
Negligence. *See* **Negligence** (Res ipsa loquitur).

RES JUDICATA
Arbitration. *See* **Arbitration** (Res judicata).
Divorce—
Custody proceedings. *See* **Divorce** (Custody—Custody proceedings—Evidence not given at hearing of divorce suit—Estoppel).
Maintenance proceedings. *See* **Divorce** (Financial provision—Estoppel in maintenance proceedings).
Employment tribunal—
Decision of tribunal. *See* **Employment tribunal** (Procedure—Decision—Res judicata).
Estoppel—
Admission of evidence. *See* **Estoppel** (Res judicata—Admission of evidence).
Criminal law. *See* **Criminal law** (Estoppel).
Generally. *See* **Estoppel** (Res judicata).
Issue estoppel. *See* **Estoppel** (Issue estoppel).
Striking out pleading. *See* **Pleading** (Striking out—Estoppel per rem judicatam).
Foreign judgment—
Conclusiveness in English proceedings. *See* **Conflict of laws** (Foreign judgment—Conclusiveness in English proceedings).
Generally. *See* **Estoppel** (Res judicata).
Income tax assessment. *See* **Income tax** (Assessment—Res judicata).
Issue—
Criminal proceedings. *See* **Criminal law** (Estoppel—Issue estoppel).
Unfair dismissal—
Dismissal procedure. *See* **Unfair dismissal** (Determination whether dismissal fair or unfair—Procedure relating to dismissal—Unfair procedure—Res judicata).

RESALE PRICE MAINTENANCE
See **Restrictive trade practices** (Resale price maintenance).

RESCISSION
Agreement for lease—
Balance of premium not paid. *See* **Landlord and tenant** (Agreement for lease—Premium—Balance of premium not paid).
Contract—
Fraud—
Undisclosed principal. *See* **Agent** (Contract—Undisclosed principal—Fraud of principal—Rescission of contract made with innocent agent for fraud of undisclosed principal).

RESCISSION (cont)—
    Contract (cont)—
        Generally. *See* **Contract** (Rescission).
        Sale of goods. *See* **Sale of goods** (Rescission of contract).
        Sale of land. *See* **Sale of land** (Rescission of contract).
        Shipbuilding contract—
            Default in payment. *See* **Contract** (Shipbuilding contract—Default in payment—Rescission).
    Decree nisi—
        Divorce. *See* **Divorce** (Decree nisi—Rescission).
    Insolvency order. *See* **Insolvency** (Order—Rescission).
    Misrepresentation. *See* **Misrepresentation**.
    Protected tenancy—
        Grant of tenancy induced by fraudulent misrepresentation. *See* **Rent restriction** (Protected tenancy—Misrepresentation—Fraudulent misrepresentation—Rescission).
    Receiving order. *See* **Bankruptcy** (Receiving order—Rescission).
    Sale of goods—
        Generally. *See* **Sale of goods** (Rescission of contract).
        Resale by unpaid seller. *See* **Sale of goods** (Unpaid seller—Resale—Effect as rescission of contract of sale).
    Winding up order. *See* **Company** (Compulsory winding up—Winding up order—Rescission).

RESCUE
    Contributory negligence—
        Rescue of child—
            Emergency act. *See* **Negligence** (Contributory negligence—Emergency act—Rescue of child).
    Negligence—
        Coastguard—
            Duty to take care. *See* **Negligence** (Duty to take care—Coastguard—Negligence in rescue operation).
            Duty to rescuer. *See* **Negligence** (Duty to take care—Rescuer).

RESERVATION
    Easement—
        Right of way—
            Reservation in conveyance. *See* **Easement** (Right of way—Reservation in conveyance).
    Sale of goods—
        Reservation of title. *See* **Sale of goods** (Passing of property—Vendor retaining property in goods).
    Sale of land—
        Conveyance. *See* **Sale of land** (Conveyance—Exception and reservation).

RESERVED JUDGMENT
    Court of Appeal, Civil Division—
        Practice. *See* **Court of Appeal** (Practice—Civil Division—Reserved judgments).

RESERVOIR
    Navigation. *See* **Water and watercourses** (Navigation—Reservoir).
    Water draining into reservoir—
        Right of owner of reservoir. *See* **Water and watercourses** (Reservoir—Surface water collected in reservoir on owner's land).

RESETTLEMENT COMPENSATION
    Local government officer—
        Loss of employment. *See* **Local government** (Officer—Compensation for loss of employment—Resettlement compensation).

RESIDENCE
    Bankruptcy—
        Petition—
            Conditions for presentation—Debtor ordinarily residing in England. *See* **Bankruptcy** (Petition—Conditions for presentation—Debtor carrying on business in England).
    Capital gains tax—
        Exemption. *See* **Capital gains tax** (Exemptions and reliefs—Private residence).
    Council tax purposes, for. *See* **Local government** (Council tax—Sole or main residence).
    Divorce—
        Foreign decree—
            Recognition based on residence. *See* **Divorce** (Foreign decree—Recognition by English court—Basis of recognition—Residence).
        Habitual residence. *See* **Divorce** (Jurisdiction—Habitual residence).
    Domicile—
        Acquisition of domicile of choice—
            Generally. *See* **Domicile** (Acquisition of domicile of choice—Residence).
            Income tax. *See* **Income tax** (Domicile—Acquisition of domicile of choice in England).
    Elections—
        Parliamentary—
            Qualification to vote. *See* **Elections** (Parliamentary—Qualification to vote—Residence).
    European Community—
        Citizenship and. *See* **European Union** (Citizenship—Freedom to reside and move freely within territory of member states).
        Right of residence—
            Workers. *See* **European Union** (Workers—Freedom of movement—Right of residence).
    Immigration. *See* **Immigration** (Residence).
    Income tax. *See* **Income tax** (Residence).

RESIDENCE (cont)—
Nullity of marriage—
Jurisdiction. *See* **Nullity** (Jurisdiction—Residence).
Ordinarily resident out of jurisdiction—
Plaintiff—
Security for costs. *See* **Costs** (Security for costs—Plaintiff ordinarily resident out of the jurisdiction).
Place of residence—
Determination for purposes of approved school order. *See* **Children and young persons** (Approved school order—Insertion of name of local authority in whose district child or young person resident—Determination of place of residence).
Will—
Condition of residence. *See* **Will** (Condition—Residence).

RESIDENCE ORDER
Family proceedings—
Generally. *See* **Family proceedings** (Orders in family proceedings—Residence order).
Residence or contact order. *See* **Family proceedings** (Orders in family proceedings—Residence or contact orders).
Shared residence order. *See* **Family proceedings** (Orders in family proceedings—Residence order—Shared residence order).

RESIDENT LANDLORD
Rent restriction. *See* **Rent restriction** (Resident landlord).

RESIDENTIAL ACCOMMODATION
Agreement to share—
Licence distinguished from tenancy. *See* **Licence** (Licence to occupy premises—Licence distinguished from tenancy—Agreement to share residential accommodation).
Non-exclusive occupation—
Licence to occupy premises. *See* **Licence** (Licence to occupy premises—Description in document—Terms of agreement indicating licence—Terms appearing to make occupation non-exclusive—Two agreements to share residential accommodation).
Local authority residential care home. *See* **Local authority** (Residential care home).
Person in need of care and attention—
Attendance allowance. *See* **Social security** (Attendance allowance—Entitlement—Person in need of care and attention—Person in residential accommodation provided by local authority).
Income support. *See* **Social security** (Income support—Person in need of care and attention—Person in residential accommodation provided by local authority).

RESIDENTIAL PROPERTY
Landlord and tenant—
Generally. *See* **Landlord and tenant** (Residential property).
Trespass—
Damages. *See* **Damages** (Trespass to land—Residential property).

RESIDUARY ESTATE
Income from residuary estate—
Distribution of property as an intestacy. *See* **Will** (Distribution of property as on intestacy—Income from residuary estate).

RESIDUE
Will—
Generally. *See* **Will** (Residue).
Payment of death duties out of residue. *See* **Will** (Payment of death duties—Payment out of residue).
Secret trust—
Standard of proof. *See* **Trust and trustee** (Secret trust—Expressed orally—Standard of proof required—Gift of residue by will).
Vesting—
Bequest of residue and remainder. *See* **Will** (Gift—Vesting—Bequest of residue and remainder).
Bequest of residue—Trust for specified purpose—Expression of purpose construed as mere indication of motive for gifts—Overriding intention to benefit donee. *See* **Will** (Gift—Absolute gift—Trust for specified purpose—Expression of purpose construed as mere indication of motive for gift—Overriding intention to benefit donee—Bequest of residue to wife on trust to be used for maintenance of wife and mother and education of daughter up to university grade).

RESIGNATION
Company director. *See* **Company** (Director—Resignation).
Unincorporated association—
Resignation of member. *See* **Unincorporated association** (Resignation of member).

RESOLUTION
Company. *See* **Company** (Resolution).

RESPONDENT'S NOTICE
Court of Appeal. *See* **Court of Appeal** (Respondent's notice).

RESTAURANT
Capital allowances—
Income tax—
Ship used as floating restaurant—Whether ship plant. *See* **Capital allowances** (Plant—Apparatus used by taxpayer for purpose of business—Ship used as floating restaurant).

RESTITUTION

Claims for repayment of sums unduly levied or benefits unduly claimed—
    Demand—
        Statutory requirement to pay tax without lawful authority—Whether restitutionary claim for repayment of unlawful tax available only where paid in response to official demand. **Test Claimants in the Franked Investment Income Group Litigation v Revenue and Customs Comrs** [2012] **3** 909, SC.

Common law claims—
    Recovery of sums not due—
        Statutory regime—Common law restitution claim brought to recover allegedly overpaid income tax—Whether statutory regime for recovery of overpayments excluding common law claims—Taxes Management Act 1970, s 33, Sch 1AB. **Wallace v Revenue and Customs Comrs** [2018] **2** 833, Ch D.

Conflict of laws—
    Jurisdiction. *See* **Conflict of laws** (Jurisdiction—Challenge to jurisdiction—Restitution).
Conjugal rights. *See* **Husband and wife** (Restitution of conjugal rights).
Contract. *See* **Contract** (Restitution).
Counter-restitution—
    Duress. *See* **Contract** (Duress—Rescission—Counter-restitution).
Defence—
    Estoppel by representation—
        Prejudice suffered by party misled by representation making it inequitable to require him to make restitution. *See* **Estoppel** (Representation—Prejudice suffered by party misled by representation—Prejudice making it inequitable to require party misled to make restitution).
Investment business—
    Generally. *See* **Investment business** (Restitution).
    Restitution order. *See* **Investment business** (Restitution—Restitution order).
Money had and received—
    Defence—
        Change of position—Claimants victims of fraud—Claimants paying moneys into bank account on instruction of fraudsters—Bank paying moneys out—Bank having suspicion that account used for money laundering but not having suspicions about particular transactions—Whether bank entitled to defence of change of position. **Abou-Rahmah v Abacha** [2007] **1 Comm** 827, CA.

Money paid to Crown—
    Payment of unlawful demand for tax—
        Payment under mistake of law—Time limit within which claims to be made—Time limit reduced from six years from date mistake discovered to six years from date paid with no transitional arrangements—Time limit further restricted by retrospectively applying new limit to all claims brought before 8 September 2003 with no transitional arrangements—Whether EU law requiring reasonable transitional arrangements—Whether reduced time limits breaching EU law—Whether open to Revenue to rely on reduced time limits as defences to test claims—Finance Act 2004, s 320—Finance Act 2007, s 107. **Test Claimants in the Franked Investment Income Group Litigation v Revenue and Customs Comrs** [2012] **3** 909, SC.
        Recovery of money paid and interest—Building society paying tax in response to demand made under ultra vires regulations—Whether society immediately acquiring prima facie right to be repaid the amount paid—Whether interest payable from date of payment—Whether general restitutionary principle that if subject pays in response to unlawful demand for tax he immediately acquires right to be repaid. **Woolwich Building Society v IRC (No 2)** [1992] **3** 737, HL.

Money paid under mistake of fact—
    Defence—
        Customer authorising bank to make interbank transfer in discharge of debt owed to third party—Bank making transfer under mistake of fact—Whether money recoverable from payee. **Lloyds Bank plc v Independent Insurance Co Ltd** [1999] **1 Comm** 8, CA.

Payment under mistake of law—
    Limitation—
        Stamp duty reserve tax charge at higher rate of 1.5% declared incompatible with EU law—Claimant seeking restitution of tax paid under a mistake—Extension to limitation period applying in case of mistake—Retrospective legislation removing benefit of extension to limitation period in relation to claims in tax—Whether retrospective legislation compatible with EU law—Limitation Act 1980, s 32(1)(c)—Finance Act 2004, s 320. **Jazztel plc v Revenue and Customs Comrs** [2017] **4** 470, Ch D; [2022] **3** 911, CA.
    Postponement of limitation period—
        Action for relief from consequences of mistake—Whether mistake must be part of legal foundation of claim—Whether extended limitation period applicable not based on mistake but where mistake part of circumstances giving rise to action—Limitation Act 1980, s 32(1)(c). **Test Claimants in the Franked Investment Income Group Litigation v Revenue and Customs Comrs** [2012] **3** 909, SC.

Quasi-contract—
    Money had and received—
        Mortgage application—Express condition of mortgage offer that property to be used solely for residential purposes—Purchaser using property for commercial purpose—Mortgagor defaulting—Mortgagee obtaining possession of property and selling property at substantial loss—Mortgagee seeking to recover loss from solicitors acting for mortgagor and mortgagee, claiming by way of restitution account in quasi-contract for money had and received—Whether claim disclosing reasonable cause of action. **Portman Building Society v Hamlyn Taylor Neck (a firm)** [1998] **4** 202, CA.
    Wasted costs—
        Costs incurred in preparation for intended contract—Tender for residential development of land subject to contract—Property developer incurring substantial expenses in preparation for intended contract—Delays to proposed development as developers attempted to satisfy landowner's requirements—Contract never concluded because parties unable to agree price due to fluctuations in residential property market values—Whether property developer entitled to recover costs wasted in preparation for contract. **Regalian Properties plc v London Dockland Development Corp** [1995] **1** 1005, Ch D.

RESTITUTION (cont)—

Restitution order. *See* **Sentence** (Restitution order).

Social security—

Recovery of overpayment. *See* **Social security** (Benefit—Overpayment—Recovery).

Theft—

Intent to make restitution. *See* **Criminal law** (Theft—Dishonesty—Intention to make restitution).

Unjust enrichment—

Company—

Winding up—Distribution of assets. *See* **Company** (Winding up—Power to exclude creditors not proving in time—Exclusion of creditor from benefit of distribution of assets—Unjust enrichment).

Compensation—

Letters of credit opened in respect of contracts of sale of quantity of steel scrap—Bank failing to honour letters of credit—Seller incurring costs in respect of port storage and container demurrage—Whether seller entitled to restitutionary remedy against bank in respect of such costs. **Fortis Bank SA/NV v Indian Overseas Bank (No 2)** [2012] **1 Comm** 41, QBD.

Money paid under mistake of law—Simple or compound interest—United Kingdom resident subsidiary company with non-resident parent company paying advance corporation tax early—Company claiming interest for period of pre-payment—Whether compound interest payable. **Sempra Metals Ltd (formerly Metallgesellschaft Ltd) v IRC** [2007] **4** 657, HL.

Money paid under quashed legislation—Mobile network operators seeking restitution for annual licence fees paid under quashed regulations—Whether counterfactual analysis needed in determining extent of restitution—Wireless Telegraphy Act 2006—Wireless Telegraphy (Licence Charges) Regulations 2011, SI 2011/1128—Wireless Telegraphy (Licence Charges for the 900 MHz frequency band and the 1800 MHz frequency band) (Amendment and Further Provisions) Regulations 2015, SI 2015/1709. **Vodafone Ltd v Office of Communications** [2020] **4** 415, CA.

Oral agreement—Agreement for payment of introduction fee to agent if property sold for £6.5m—Property sold to introduced purchaser for £6m—Introduction fee withheld and appellant bringing claims in contract and unjust enrichment—Whether agreement excluding claim for reasonable sum in respect of benefit conferred—Value of benefit conferred. **Barton v Gwyn-Jones** [2020] **2 Comm** 652, CA.

Quantum meruit—Services rendered—Market value—Whether permissible to have regard to defendant's subjective opinion of value of services rendered in order to reduce or increase amount payable. **Benedetti v Sawiris** [2013] **2 Comm** 801, SC; [2013] **4** 253, SC.

Services rendered under contract between claimant and third party—Individual defendants wishing to develop land—Individual defendants sole shareholders and directors of corporate defendant—Corporate defendant contracting with claimant builders to develop land—Builders leaving site and corporate defendant refusing to pay outstanding invoices—Recorder finding corporate defendant liable in contract—Recorder holding individual defendants jointly and severally liable in restitution for unjust enrichment—Whether individual defendants could be held liable in restitution for unjust enrichment when services from which they benefited were given pursuant to contract between builders and corporate defendant. **MacDonald v Costello** [2012] **1 Comm** 357, CA.

Work done on property of another—Work done by party in honest belief property belonging to him—Recovery of property by true owner—Liability of true owner to pay compensation for work done—Sale of motor vehicle—Sale by thief—Purchase by buyer acting in good faith and without notice of defect in title—Buyer effecting extensive repairs to vehicle—Vehicle recovered by police—Interpleader proceedings—Vehicle to be returned to person from whom stolen—Claim by buyer for cost of repairs—Whether recoverable. **Greenwood v Bennett** [1972] **3** 586, CA.

Defence—

Change of position—Claimant bank making money placement available to defendant bank—Defendant transferring part of placement to third party bank to satisfy debt owed to that bank—Defendant admitting payment for its benefit—Defendant alleging change of position—Whether defendant entitled to rely on defence of change of position. **National Bank of Egypt International Ltd v Oman Housing Bank SAOC** [2003] **1 Comm** 246, QBD.

Change of position—Claimant overpaying royalties to defendants over six-year period—Defendants increasing outgoings by reference to sums paid—Claimant seeking to set off overpayments against future royalties—Whether payment constituting representation for purposes of estoppel by representation—Whether defendants establishing defence of change of position. **Philip Collins Ltd v Davis** [2000] **3** 808, Ch D.

Change of position—Defendant encountering funding difficulties in obtaining goods to sell to claimant—Defendant arranging for false bill of lading to be presented to obtain funding for transaction—Bank disposing of warrants for goods—Claimant not informed of disposal—Bank paying away money remitted in settlement on instructions of defendant—Whether judge correct to acquit bank of deceit and dishonesty—Whether bank entitled to rely on defence of change of position. **Niru Battery Manufacturing Co v Milestone Trading Ltd** [2002] **2 Comm** 705, QBD; [2004] **1 Comm** 193, CA.

Change of position—Illegality—Whether innocent recipient precluded from relying on change of position defence if change illegal. **Barros Mattos Jnr v MacDaniels Ltd** [2004] **2 Comm** 501, Ch D; [2004] **3** 299, Ch D.

Change of position—Life assurance company mistakenly making overpayment to policyholder—Policyholder using bulk of overpayment to acquire other pension policy and reduce mortgage—Whether policyholder entitled to rely on defence of change of position. **Scottish Equitable plc v Derby** [2001] **2 Comm** 274, CA; [2001] **3** 818, CA.

Change of position—Whether defence to claim for restitution based on unjust enrichment that defendant has changed position in good faith and inequitable to require defendant to make restitution. **Lipkin Gorman (a firm) v Karpnale Ltd (1986)** [1992] **4** 512, HL.

Failure of consideration—

Recovery of money paid—Company advancing funds for fixed term to plaintiffs secured by mortgage over their property—Mortgage instrument altered without knowledge or consent of mortgagors—Defendants making interest repayments but failing to repay capital sum—Whether company entitled to recover advance from plaintiffs—Whether failure of consideration. **Goss v Chilcott** [1997] **2** 110, PC.

RESTITUTION (cont)—
Unjust enrichment (cont)—
Investment profit—
Entitlement to profit—Firm committing act of bankruptcy—Defendant obtaining funds from partners' joint account before firm adjudicated bankrupt—Defendant investing money and making considerable profit—Trustee in bankruptcy claiming entitlement to original sum and profit—Whether trustee in bankruptcy entitled to trace investment profit. **Jones (FC) & Sons (a firm) (trustee of the property of) v Jones** [1996] **4** 721, CA.
Proprietary restitutionary claim—
Compensation—Chose in action and other intangible property—Defendant receiving carbon emission allowances (EUAs) from claimant occasioned by third party fraud—Classification of EUAs as property—Whether third party fraudster becoming a constructive trustee of the EUAs so that a claim in unconscionable receipt of trust property available—If claimant retaining full legal title whether correct basis for common law proprietary restitutionary claim—Whether proprietary restitutionary claim distinct from claim for restitution on grounds of unjust enrichment -Requisite state of knowledge of defendant. **Armstrong DLW GmbH v Winnington Networks Ltd** [2012] **3** 425, Ch D.
Subrogation—
Unpaid vendor's lien—Sale of family home subject to charges in favour of bank—Bank agreeing to release of charges and purchase of second property on basis charge granted over new property—Second property registered in name of appellant daughter—Charge void as invalidly executed—Whether appellant unjustly enriched at bank's expense—Whether appropriate remedy to subrogate bank to unpaid vendor's lien. **Bank of Cyprus UK Ltd v Menelaou** [2016] **2 Comm** 259, SC; [2016] **2** 913, SC.
Writ of—
Land—
Execution of possession order. See **Land** (Summary proceedings for possession—Execution of possession order—Writ of restitution).

RESTITUTION ORDER
See **Sentence** (Restitution order).

RESTRAINT OF FOREIGN PROCEEDINGS
Generally. See **Conflict of laws** (Foreign proceedings—Restraint of foreign proceedings).

RESTRAINT OF MARRIAGE
Will—
Condition. See **Will** (Condition—Restraint of marriage).

RESTRAINT OF TRADE
Agreement, by. See **Restraint of trade by agreement**.
Auction—
Knock-out agreement. See **Auction** (Knock-out agreement).
Mortgaged property—
Clog on equity of redemption. See **Mortgage** (Clog on equity of redemption—Restraint of trade).
Payment in consideration of covenant—
Income tax—
Capital or revenue expenditure. See **Income tax** (Deduction in computing profits—Capital or revenue expenditure—Covenants in restraint of trade).
Professional code of conduct—
Arbitrators' Code of Conduct rules. See **Arbitration** (Arbitrator—Arbitrators' Code of Conduct of the International Cotton Association (ICA)).
Resolution of society. See **Restraint of trade by agreement** (Professional society—Resolution of members restricting trading activities of members).
Trade union rules. See **Trade union** (Rules—Validity).

RESTRAINT OF TRADE BY AGREEMENT
Arbitration award—
Award restricting area within which a co-operative society might trade—
Society member of registered co-operative union—Society ceasing to be member of union—Validity of award—Industrial and Provident Societies Act 1893, s 22. **Birtley District Co-op Society Ltd v Windy Nook and District Industrial Co-op Society Ltd** [1959] **1** 623, QBD.
Boxer and manager—
Conflict of interest—
Agreement between professional boxer and manager/promoter—Agreement obliging boxer to fight in contests in which manager/promoter financially interested and on terms unilaterally imposed on boxer—Boxer achieving championship status and manager/promoter exercising option to extend agreement for further term—Boxer seeking to establish he was no longer bound by agreement on restraint of trade grounds—Whether agreement in restraint of trade—If so, whether terms of agreement nevertheless reasonable—Whether agreement unenforceable. **Watson v Prager** [1991] **3** 487, Ch D.
Damages for breach. See **Restrictive trade practices** (Restrictions accepted by parties to agreement—Damages for breach).
Employer and employee—
Articled clerk—
Covenant not to practise within 15 miles of town where employer's business situated during whole life of employee—Reasonableness. **Dickson v Jones** [1939] **3** 182, Ch D.
Butcher's shop—
Manager—Scope of restrictions on service—Radius agreement—Radius of five miles—Trade proved not to exceed one mile—Validity. **Empire Meat Co Ltd v Patrick** [1939] **2** 85, CA.

Employer and employee (cont)—
Calendered sheeting business—
World-wide restriction—Employers manufacturing PVC calendered sheeting—Employers having large percentage of UK market for PVC calendered sheeting for adhesive tape but much smaller percentage of total PVC calendered sheeting market—Defendant employed mainly in relation to production of PVC calendered sheeting for adhesive tape—Agreement that defendant not to seek employment with any of employers' 'competitors' in PVC calendering field for at least one year after leaving employers—Reasonableness. **Commercial Plastics Ltd v Vincent** [1964] **3** 546, CA.
Clause not expressed to be in restraint of trade—
Provision for payment of money—Duty of court to have regard to likely effect of provision—Provision clearly operating in restraint of trade—Provision to be treated as being in restraint of trade. **Stenhouse Australia Ltd v Phillips** [1974] **1** 117, PC.
Collector and salesman in credit drapery trade—
Covenant for period of five years after termination of employment not to canvass or solicit orders from customers in employers' books during last three years of employment—Employment terminable at two weeks' notice—Covenant unreasonable. **M & S Drapers (a firm) v Reynolds** [1956] **3** 814, CA.
Companies each agreeing not to employ persons employed by the other within previous five years—Reasonableness—Restriction on employees' freedom of choice of employment—Public policy. **Kores Manufacturing Co Ltd v Kolok Manufacturing Co Ltd** [1958] **2** 65, CA.
Consideration for agreement—
Agreement entered into at termination of employment—Transfer of shares in limited company—Consideration paid by company—Severability—Companies Act 1929, s 45. **Spink (Bournemouth) Ltd v Spink** [1936] **1** 597, Ch D.
Construction of covenant—
Covenant capable of being construed without alteration of words in sense that would render it reasonable—Employers carrying on mail order business in United Kingdom—Rival mail order company in United Kingdom having subsidiary companies carrying on various businesses throughout the world—Employee responsible for planning catalogue on which employers' mail order business based—Agreement that employee would not seek employment with rival company or any of its subsidiaries within year after leaving employers—Reasonable for employers to seek protection of confidential information relating to mail order business—Whether covenant should be construed as applying only to rival company's mail order business in United Kingdom and not to whole range of business throughout world. **Littlewoods Organisation Ltd v Harris** [1978] **1** 1026, CA.
Post-employment non-competition covenant—Covenant not to 'directly or indirectly engage or be concerned or interested in' any competing business—Whether covenant in unreasonable restraint of trade—Whether provision severable. **Tillman v Egon Zehnder Ltd** [2020] **1** 477, SC.
Credit betting business—
Defendant employed as manager by firm of bookmakers and commission agents in Cheltenham—Clause in contract of service that for three years after cessation of service the defendant would not carry on business of commission agents in or within 12 miles of Cheltenham—New terms of service superseding original service agreement—Defendant later dismissed and started commission agent business within area—Whether restriction is illegal restraint of trade—Whether restriction binding on defendant under new terms of service. **Strange (S W) Ltd v Mann** [1965] **1** 1069, Ch D.
Dairyman and milk roundsman—
Agreement not for one year after termination of employment to serve or sell milk or dairy produce to customers served by employee during last six months of employment—Validity. **Home Counties Dairies Ltd v Skilton** [1970] **1** 1227, CA.
Employee of partnership—
Solicitor—Solicitor employed by partnership consisting of two partners—One partner owning goodwill of firm—Solicitor's contract of employment containing five-mile and five-year restraint of trade clause—Partnership dissolving—Solicitor setting up practice with one partner 120 yards from firm's offices—Whether solicitor employed by partners or by proprietor firm—Whether dissolution of partnership constituting breach and termination of solicitor's contract of employment—Whether solicitor entitled to set up practice in competition with firm notwithstanding restraint of trade clause. **Briggs v Oates** [1991] **1** 407, Ch D.
Estate agents' clerk and negotiator in charge of branch office—
Business having recurring customers—Covenant not to carry on or work in similar business within five miles radius of branch and main offices for three years after end of employment—Severability of restrictions as to branch and as to main offices—Employee unqualified—Relevance to reasonableness of restriction in the public interest. **Scorer v Seymour-Johns** [1966] **3** 347, CA.
Hairdressing salon—
Standard form of contract—Qualified hairdressing assistant—Agreement not for one year after termination of employment to be in any way engaged in business of ladies' hairdresser in any capacity—Validity. **White (Marion) Ltd v Francis** [1972] **3** 857, CA.
Insurance broker—
Period of restraint—Reasonableness—Restraint for five years after termination of employment—Insurance brokers—Prohibition on employee soliciting former employer's clients—'Clients' narrowly defined—Test for determining whether period reasonable—Question to be determined by judge—Determination by judge after informing himself of all relevant circumstances. **Stenhouse Australia Ltd v Phillips** [1974] **1** 117, PC.
Mail order business—
Confidentiality of information—Employers' mail order business based on catalogue—Employee responsible for planning catalogue—Agreement that employee would not seek employment with rival company within a year after leaving employers—Whether employers possessing confidential information requiring protection. **Littlewoods Organisation Ltd v Harris** [1978] **1** 1026, CA.

RESTRAINT OF TRADE BY AGREEMENT (cont)—

Employer and employee (cont)—

Medical practice—

Covenant by doctor in 'assistantship' agreement—Covenantees general practitioners—Covenant not to 'practise ... in any department of medicine surgery or midwifery nor accept nor fill any professional appointment' within ten miles for five years—Reasonableness—Onus of proof—Special circumstances justifying restraint. **Routh v Jones** [1947] **1** 758, CA.

Scope—Limits of time and space—Covenant not to practise 'as physician surgeon or apothecary at any time within five miles or professionally visit or consult with patients of practice'. **Jenkins v Reid** [1948] **1** 471, Ch D.

Period of restraint—

Restraint for two years after termination of employment—Covenant by employee not to solicit employer's clients—Employees leaving employer and setting up new business—New business purporting to accept contract from clients of employer before expiry of two-year period—Clients no longer intending to do further business with employer—Whether covenant enforceable against new business. **John Michael Design plc v Cooke** [1987] **2** 332, CA.

Restrictive covenants in contract of employment to take effect on termination of contract 'howsoever arising' or 'howsoever occasioned'—

Whether unreasonable and in unlawful restraint of trade. **Rock Refrigeration Ltd v Jones** [1997] **1** 1, CA.

Sales representative—

Covenant not for two years after end of employment to canvass etc any person who shall at any time during employment have been a customer of the employer—Restraint might apply to customers unknown to employee, and to customers who might have ceased to be customers before end of employment—Validity. **Plowman (G W) & Son Ltd v Ash** [1964] **2** 10, CA.

Covenant not to deal in allocated district in similar goods for one year after termination of employment—Same clause of agreement also requiring representative not to solicit orders or supply goods to customers in district supplied by company in last 12 months of employment—Allocated district covering Manchester area—Restriction on dealing invalid as being too wide—Whether restriction on soliciting and supplying severable as a matter of construction—Whether incumbent on court to consider as a matter of policy whether restriction should be treated as severable. **Lucas (T) & Co Ltd v Mitchell** [1972] **3** 689, CA.

Covenant not to solicit orders etc in area in which he worked for employers—Sales representative for spare parts for motor car lighting systems—Reasonableness of covenant—Covenant applicable to many persons not customers of employers nor called on during employment—Validity. **Gledhow Autoparts Ltd v Delaney** [1965] **3** 288, CA.

Transfer of trade, business and undertaking—

Continuity of employment—Employee employed by transferor immediately before transfer—Transferee of business dismissing employee and seeking to enforce restraint of trade clause in employee's contract of employment—Whether transferee can enforce restraint of trade clause in contract of employment made between transferor and employee—Whether restraint of trade clause only applying to transferor's business and not to business transferred—Transfer of Undertakings (Protection of Employment) Regulations 1981, reg 5(1)—Council Directive (EEC) 77/187. **Morris Angel & Son Ltd v Hollande** [1993] **3** 569, CA.

European Community rules. *See* **European Union** (Rules on competition).

Exclusive agent and principal—

Image rights representation agreement—

Claimant engaged by professional footballer as agent to negotiate contracts with third parties to exploit image rights under written agreement—Written agreement providing for commission on gross sum payable under any contract or arrangement made for exploitation of image rights—Claimant also providing same service to footballer's wife but without written agreement—Whether on true construction of agreement commission to be paid on sums payable after termination of agreement—Whether agreement unreasonable restraint of trade—Whether claimant able to recover commission or limited to quantum meruit for services provided—Whether amount payable on quantum meruit determined by written agreement—Whether services provided to footballer's wife pursuant to implied contract on same terms as written agreement. **Proactive Sports Management Ltd v Rooney** [2012] **2 Comm** 815, CA.

Self-employed sales agent—

Agents right to payment of accrued commission after termination of agency conditional on agent not working for competitor organisation within one year of termination—Plaintiff agent resigning to work for competitor and claiming accrued commission—Defendant company refusing to pay—Whether condition a restraint of trade—If so, whether restraint of trade condition severable from entitlement to receive commission after termination. **Marshall v NM Financial Management Ltd** [1995] **4** 785, Ch D.

Exclusive distribution agreement—

Right to renewal expressed to be 'as long as permitted by law'—

Whether words capable of being enforced—Whether contract rendered in restraint of trade—Whether contract contrary to community law—Whether English common law to be disapplied where corresponding community law not applying—EC Treaty, art 81. **Days Medical Aids Ltd v Pihsiang Machinery Manufacturing Co Ltd** [2004] **1 Comm** 991, QBD.

Exclusive management agreement—

Repudiation of agreement—

Claimant seeking damages from first defendant for repudiation of management contract—Alternative claim made in restitution (quantum meruit) for services provided to first defendant and financial investment in his career—First defendant applying to strike out claim or for summary judgment to be entered in his favour—Whether contract in restraint of trade—Reasonableness of any restraints—CPR 3.4(2)(a). **CJ Motorsport Consulting Ltd v Bird** [2020] **1 Comm** 279, QBD.

Exclusive services agreement—
  Standard form agreement—
    Restrictions during continuance of agreement—Agreement between song-writer and music publishers—Writer undertaking to provide exclusive services to publishers—Writer assigning to publishers copyright in existing works and works to be composed during period of years—Publishers under no obligation to publish writer's works—Writer entitled to £50 advance on royalties and further advances of £50 on recoupment of previous advance from royalties received—Publishers alone entitled to terminate agrment by notice—Whether doctrine of restraint of trade applicable to agreement—Whether agreement in unreasonable restraint of trade. **Schroeder (A) Music Publishing Co Ltd v Macaulay** [1974] **3** 616, HL.
Football Association and Football League—
  Retention and transfer system in respect of professional players—
    Whether in unjustifiable restraint of trade—Whether player registered with and formerly employed by football club could maintain action against Football Association and Football League for declaration of invalidity of their relevant rules and regulations in the absence of direct contractual relation with Association and League. **Eastham v Newcastle United Football Club Ltd** [1963] **3** 139, Ch D.
Interlocutory injunction. *See* **Injunction** (Interlocutory—Restraint of trade).
Lessor and lessee—
  Election—
    Lease containing covenant in restraint of trade—Covenant by lessee—Election between observing covenant and surrendering lease—Whether lessee should be put to election. **Amoco Australia Pty Ltd v Rocca Bros Motor Engineering Co Pty Ltd** [1975] **1** 968, PC.
  Enforceability of covenant—
    Developer granting lease to anchor tenant at shopping centre—Lease containing restrictive covenant not to lease to other shops in competition with anchor tenant—Whether doctrine against restraint of trade engaged—Proper criterion for engagement of doctrine. **Peninsula Securities Ltd v Dunnes Stores (Bangor) Ltd** [2021] **1** 1, SC; [2021] **1 Comm** 395, SC.
Licensor and licensee—
  Reasonableness as between parties—
    Public interest—Licence to make and use patented material—Compensation payable to licensors on licensees using or selling more than stated amount—Continued operation of provision after expiration of patents. **Tool Metal Manufacturing Co Ltd v Tungsten Electric Co Ltd** [1955] **2** 657, HL.
Non-disclosure agreement—
  Solicitors—
    Law firms entering into non-disclosure agreement in order to collaborate on group litigation—Agreement containing non-compete undertaking—Promisor recruiting its own clients and collaborating with another law firm—Whether non-compete undertaking enforceable—Whether promisor in breach of non-compete undertaking. **Harcus Sinclair LLP v Your Lawyers Ltd** [2022] **1** 673, SC; [2022] **1 Comm** 869, SC.
Partnership—
  Medical partnership—
    National Health Service practice—Covenant by outgoing partner not to practise within a prescribed area—Covenant by outgoing partner not to attend patients of the partnership—Whether covenants valid—National Health Service Act 1946, s 35. **Macfarlane v Kent** [1965] **2** 376, Ch D.
    National Health Service practice—Mutual covenants by partners under which retiring or expelled partner would not practice within a prescribed area for two years—Whether covenant contrary to public policy—Whether covenant unlawful as infringing prohibition against sale of goodwill of national health service practice—National Health Service Act 1977, s 54(1), Sch 10, para 2(4), (5). **Kerr v Morris** [1986] **3** 217, CA.
    Restriction on practice in event of dissolution of partnership—Construction of restraint of trade clause—Undertaking 'not to practise in the practice area'—Whether restraint unreasonably wide—Whether undertaking to be construed as undertaking by defendant not to practise as a general medical practitioner—Whether undertaking enforceable. **Clarke v Newland** [1991] **1** 397, CA.
    Restriction on practice in event of dissolution of partnership—Prohibition on professionally advising, attending, prescribing for or treating any patient or former patient of partnership for period of five years—Whether restraint general so as to preclude practice as a consultant—Whether restraint too wide. **Peyton v Mindham** [1971] **3** 1215, Ch D.
    Retiring partner prohibited from 'directly or indirectly carrying on or being interested or concerned in carrying on the business or profession of medicine ... within a radius of ten miles'—Reasonableness. **Whitehill v Bradford** [1952] **1** 115, CA.
    Retiring partner prohibited from engaging in practice within a radius of ten miles of partnership surgery—Whether restraint general so as to preclude practice as a consultant—Whether reasonable. **Lyne-Pirkis v Jones** [1969] **3** 738, CA.
  Newspaper partnership—
    Outgoing partner 'not ... directly or indirectly [to] carry on or be engaged or interested in any business similar to or competing with the business of the partnership'—Publication of weekly newspaper dealing with sport and entertainment—Purchase by one partner of other partner's share—Contract of service with competing newspaper—Severability of covenant. **Ronbar Enterprises Ltd v Green** [1954] **2** 266, CA.
  Solicitors—
    Restriction on practice in event of partner ceasing to be a partner—Deed of partnership providing that outgoing partner not to solicit or act for clients of firm except for 'any client introduced to the firm' by him—Defendant partner joining sole practioner practising under name of firm—Other partner dying leaving defendant in sole practice—Defendant later joined by other partners—Whether clients for whom defendant acted in sole practice clients 'introduced to the firm' by defendant—Whether defendant entitled to continue to act for clients for whom he had acted while in sole practice. **Oswald Hickson Collier & Co (a firm) v Carter-Ruck** [1984] **2** 15, CA.

RESTRAINT OF TRADE BY AGREEMENT (cont)—
  Partnership (cont)—
    Solicitors (cont)—
      Restriction on practice in event of partner ceasing to be partner—Firm of solicitors divided into self-contained departments—Partnership agreement containing restrictive covenant preventing partner from acting for any client of firm if he ceased to be a partner—Goodwill put in at nominal figure in partnership agreement—Whether restrictive covenant too wide—Whether covenant should only apply to department of firm in which outgoing partner employed—Whether firm entitled to protect goodwill when only nominal amount paid for it. **Deacons (a firm) v Bridge** [1984] **2** 19, PC.
  Pension scheme—
    Trust—
      Forfeiture provision—Obligatory pension scheme—Rule that benefits of retired employees who entered employment with competing firms would be liable to be forfeited—Whether rule unenforceable and void for restraint of trade. **Bull v Pitney-Bowes Ltd** [1966] **3** 384, QBD.
  Petrol filling station—
    Solus agreement—
      Agreement between owner of garage and petrol supplier for purchase and sale exclusively of supplier's products—Obligation on garage owner to carry on filling station while agreement in force—Duration of agreement 12 years if 600,000 gallons of petrol then sold—Validity of agreement. **Petrofina (GB) Ltd v Martin** [1966] **1** 126, CA.
      Agreement between owner of garage and petrol supplier for purchase and sale exclusively of supplier's products—Obligation on garage owner to carry on filling station while agreement in force—Obligation to keep station open—Obligations to be undertaken by successor—Duration of two agreements, for four years and five months and twenty-one years respectively—One agreement supported by and partly repealed in mortgage—Whether doctrine of restraint of trade applied to agreements and to mortgage—Whether agreements in unreasonable restraint of trade. **Esso Petroleum Co Ltd v Harper's Garage (Stourport) Ltd** [1967] **1** 699, HL.
      Agreement between owner of garage and petrol supplier for purchase and sale exclusively of supplier's products—Obligation to be undertaken by successor—Duration of agreement seven and a half years—Injunction by consent until trial restraining garage owner from purchasing motor fuel from other suppliers—Subsequent decisions of Court of Appeal that doctrine of restraint of trade applied to such agreements—Motion to discharge injunction on ground that agreement was in restraint of trade. **Regent Oil Co Ltd v Leavesley (JT) (Lichfield) Ltd** [1966] **2** 454, Ch D.
      Agreement between owner of garage and petrol supplier for purchase and sale exclusively of supplier's products—Restraint also regarding lubricating oils—Obligation on garage owner to carry on filling station while agreement in force—Duration of agreement twelve years if six hundred thousand gallons of petrol then sold—Agreement not part of lease or mortgage—Whether doctrine of restraint of trade applied to agreement—Whether agreement in unreasonable restraint of trade. **Petrofina (GB) Ltd v Martin** [1966] **1** 126, CA.
      Lease by garage owner to petrol supplier—Underlease to company to operate service station—Covenant in underlease for exclusive sale of supplier's products—Assignment of underlease by licence granted by supplier—Interim injunction to restrain breach of covenant. **Cleveland Petroleum Co Ltd v Dartstone Ltd** [1969] **1** 201, CA.
      Legal charge—Agreement in legal charge between owner of garage and petrol supplier to purchase, resell and advertise exclusively supplier's products—Reasonableness of restraints—Limitation of tie to five years—Loan at low rate of interest repayable during period of tie—Reasonableness in reference to interests of parties—Reasonableness in interests of public—General considerations of economic and social policy—Relevance—No evidence that restraints severely and arbitrarily restricting freedom to trade. **Texaco Ltd v Mulberry Filling Station Ltd** [1972] **1** 513, Ch D.
      Legal charge—Loan by supplier to dealer on legal charge—Advance of rebates under solus agreement that dealer should purchase from suppliers and sell exclusively their petrol products—Arrangements terminable by dealer on notice if profit margin not maintained—Profit margin defined as difference between wholesale and retail prices published from time to time in the eetroleum Times—Validity of arrangements—Whether affected by Resale Prices Act 1964, s 1(2), (4). **Regent Oil Co Ltd v Aldon Motors Ltd** [1965] **2** 644, CA.
      Mortgage—Agreement between owner of garage and petrol supplier for exclusive purchase and resale of supplier's products—Company which owned filling station facing insolvency—Company agreeing to solus agreement in lease and lease-back transaction designed to raise finance from supplier to prevent company's insolvency—Company leasing garage to supplier for 51 years in return for premium—Supplier immediately leasing back garage to proprietor of company—Whether tie in lease-back void as being in unreasonable restraint of trade. **Alec Lobb (Garages) Ltd v Total Oil GB Ltd** [1985] **1** 303, CA.
      Mortgage—Agreement between owner of garage and petrol supplier for purchase and resale exclusively of supplier's products—Duration of longest agreement 21 years—Obligation to keep garage open and conduct its business—Implication of term—Continuance and enforcement of obligation in regard to resale price maintenance not necessary for business efficacy—Injunction granted to enforce negative obligation. **Esso Petroleum Co Ltd v Harper's Garage (Stourport) Ltd** [1966] **1** 725, CA.
  Pleading—
    Defence—
      Justifying circumstances to be pleaded in defence. **Pharmaceutical Society of GB v Dickson** [1968] **2** 686, HL.
  Professional society—
    Resolution of members restricting trading activities of members—
      Part of code of professional conduct, binding in honour but enforceable only through disciplinary statutory committee—Justiciable issue—Member entitled to court's determination of validity of resolution—No evidence of reasonableness of restriction in public interest—Whether restriction in unreasonable restraint of trade—Whether ultra vires the society as not sufficiently related to relevant main object of society. **Pharmaceutical Society of GB v Dickson** [1968] **2** 686, HL.

RESTRAINT OF TRADE BY AGREEMENT (cont)—
Public house—
  Tied house covenants—
    Applicability of doctrine of restraint of trade—Validity of ordinary tied house covenants with brewers. **Petrofina (GB) Ltd v Martin** [1966] **1** 126, CA.
Reasonableness—
  Contractual term—
    Reasonableness of restraint on trade. **Società Esplosivi Industriali SpA v Ordnance Technologies (UK) Ltd (formerly SEI (UK) Ltd)** [2004] **1 Comm** 619, Ch D.
Right to work—
  Monopoly control—
    Exclusion from work—Public policy. **Nagle v Feilden** [1966] **1** 689, CA.
Separate agreements—
  Lease and underlease—
    Single transaction—Estoppel—Underlease unenforceable as containing covenants in restraint of trade—Enforceability of lease—Provision in lease asserting that it was independent of any other contract, lease or agreement between parties—Lease by dealer of site of petrol filling station to petrol company—Underlease by petrol company to dealer—Underlease unenforceable as containing petrol tie in restraint of trade—Whether lease unenforceable—Whether dealer estopped from asserting that lease unenforceable. **Amoco Australia Pty Ltd v Rocca Bros Motor Engineering Co Pty Ltd** [1975] **1** 968, PC.
    Single transaction—Void covenant in underlease—Whether void covenant severable—Whether sufficient consideration to support agreement apart from void covenant. **Alec Lobb (Garages) Ltd v Total Oil GB Ltd** [1985] **1** 303, CA.
Services agreement—
  Business reorganisation—
    Covenants preventing defendant from soliciting or enticing claimant's clients, dealing with clients, or undertaking any services in relation to defined business—Covenants to apply throughout 99-year duration of services agreement—Whether covenants in restraint of trade—Whether covenants reasonable—Proper criterion for engagement of doctrine. **Quantum Actuarial LLP v Quantum Advisory Ltd** [2022] **1 Comm** 473, CA.
Shareholders' agreement—
  Employee shareholders—
    Proper construction of restrictive covenants in shareholders' agreement—Shareholders' agreement prohibiting employee shareholders from competing with company during employment and for period of 12 months after ceasing to be shareholder—Whether covenants in shareholders' agreement enforceable once respondent ceasing to be company's agent. **Guest Services Worldwide Ltd v Shelmerdine** [2020] **2 Comm** 455, CA.
Sporting association—
  International Cricket Conference and Test and County Cricket Board—
    Monopoly control of official cricket—Change of rules to ban players who had contracted to play for private promoter—Retrospective ban—Whether change of rules in unreasonable restraint of trade. **Greig v Insole** [1978] **3** 449, Ch D.
Supplier and buyer—
  Solus agreement—
    Enforcement of agreement—Injunction to restrain breach of tie—Unjust and inequitable to enforce tie—Supplier operating scheme causing hardship to buyer—Scheme subsidising other buyers tied to supplier—Defendant buyer excluded from scheme—Exclusion causing hardship—Injunction restraining defendant from breach of tie refused whilst scheme operating. **Shell UK Ltd v Lostock Garage Ltd** [1977] **1** 481, CA.
    Reasonableness of tie—Time at which reasonableness to be tested—Tie reasonable when contract made—Afterwards tie found to be operating unreasonably—Garage owner 'tied' to Shell for supplies of petrol—Subsequently Shell operating scheme to subsidise neighbouring Shell garages—Garage owner excluded from scheme—Hardship thereby suffered—Whether tie unenforceable whilst scheme operating. **Shell UK Ltd v Lostock Garage Ltd** [1977] **1** 481, CA.
Vendor and purchaser—
  Sale of business—
    Accountant—Covenant by vendor not to carry on accountancy business within 15 mile radius for 15 years—Reasonableness. **Bates (D) & Co v Dale** [1937] **3** 650, Ch D.
    Covenant by vendor of business not to compete—Gift by vendor to sons of capital to establish competing business—Breach of covenant—Procuring breach. **Batts Combe Quarry Ltd v Ford** [1942] **2** 639, CA.
  Sale of controlling interest in company—
    Covenant not directly or indirectly to engage in sardine business in Canada—Covenant entered into by managing director of company on sale of controlling interest in company—Injury to public—How far covenantor prevented from holding shares in competing company—Declaration as to validity of covenants. **Connors Bros Ltd v Connors** [1940] **4** 179, PC.
  Sale of motor car—
    Covenant not to resell motor car within two years—Breach—Measure of damages. **British Motor Trade Association v Gilbert** [1951] **2** 641, Ch D.

RESTRAINT ON ALIENATION
Fee simple estate—
  Condition—
    Repugnancy—Condition in restraint of alienation—Covenant not to sell land separately from adjoining land—Purchaser acquiring plot of land adjoining land already owned by purchaser—Covenant by purchaser not to sell plot separately from adjoining land—Whether covenant void as being unlawful restraint on alienation. **Caldy Manor Estate Ltd v Farrell** [1974] **3** 753, CA.

RESTRAINT ON ANTICIPATION
See **Husband and wife** (Restraint on anticipation).

RESTRAINT ORDER
Breach of—
Perverting course of justice. *See* **Criminal law** (Obstructing course of justice—Perverting course of justice—Breach of restraint order made under proceeds of crime legislation).
Drug trafficking. *See* **Drugs** (Drug trafficking—Restraint order).
Generally. *See* **Sentence** (Restraint order).
Harassment. *See* **Criminal law** (Harassment—Restraining order).
Receiver—
Appointment. *See* **Receiver** (Appointed by court—Restraint order).
Remuneration. *See* **Receiver** (Appointed by court—Remuneration).
Variation of order prior to conviction—
Whether order variable on application of general creditor—
Criminal Justice Act 1988, ss 77(1), (2), 82(2), (4), (6). **X (restraint order), Re** [2004] **3** 1077, QBD.
Proceeds of Crime Act 2002, s 69(2)(c). **Serious Fraud Office v Lexi Holdings plc** [2009] **1** 586, CA.

RESTRICTION ORDER
Mentally disordered prisoner. *See* **Sentence** (Hospital order—Restriction order).

RESTRICTIONS ON PAY INCREASES
Statutory restriction. *See* **Employment** (Remuneration—Restrictions on pay increases).

RESTRICTIVE COVENANT
Compensation for accepting covenant—
Company director—
Income tax. *See* **Income tax** (Emoluments from office or employment—Compensation—Restrictive covenant).
Consideration for grant of covenant—
Income tax—
Capital or income. *See* **Income tax** (Capital or income receipts—Restrictive covenant).
Undertaking in connection with future employment. *See* **Income tax** (Surtax—Restrictive covenant—Consideration for restrictive covenant—Future employment—Undertaking in connection with the employment).
Injunction—
County court—
Jurisdiction—Claim for injunction ancillary to claim for specific relief—Claim for £1 damages and injunction. *See* **County court** (Jurisdiction—Injunction—Jurisdiction to grant injunction if claim for injunction ancillary to claim for specific relief—Plaintiffs alleging breach of restrictive covenant in contract and claiming £1 damages and injunction).
Land—
Covenant affecting land. *See* **Restrictive covenant affecting land**.
Landlord and tenant. *See* **Landlord and tenant** (Restrictive covenant).
Restraint of trade. *See* **Restraint of trade by agreement**.

RESTRICTIVE COVENANT AFFECTING LAND
Annexation of benefit—
Annexation by statute—
Covenant not to ensure for benefit of covenantee's successors in title unless expressly assigned—Covenant not expressly assigned on transfer of land—Covenant not to build more than one house on plot—Covenantor's successor in title proposing to build additional house on plot—Action by covenantee's successors in title to enforce covenant—Whether benefit of covenant annexed by statute—Whether covenant a 'right appertaining or reputed to appertain to the land'—Law of Property Act 1925, ss 62(1), 78. **Roake v Chadha** [1983] **3** 503, Ch D.
Covenant relating to or touching and concerning covenantee's land—Sufficient description of covenantee's land for purpose of annexation—Conveyance containing covenant not expressly or impliedly annexing benefit of covenant—Whether benefit of covenant annexed and running with covenantee's land under statute—Whether covenant annexed to land enuring only for benefit of land as a whole or for benefit of every part of it—Law of Property Act 1925, s 78(1). **Federated Homes Ltd v Mill Lodge Properties Ltd** [1980] **1** 371, CA.
Covenant expressed to be for benefit of remainder of vendor's estate—
Whether benefit annexed to every part of estate retained. **Jeffs' Transfer, Re (No 2)** [1966] **1** 937, Ch D.
Covenant expressed to be for benefit of 'vendor's adjoining and neighbouring land'—
Defendant engaged in trade and business on her land—Vendor sold some of land in neighbourhood to plaintiffs—Whether plaintiffs entitled to enforce covenant—Whether annexation of covenant was to whole of vendor's adjoining and neighbouring land or to each and every part of it—Planning authority for use of land in manner in fact constituting breach of restrictive covenant—No bar to enforcement of restrictive covenant. **Russell v Archdale** [1962] **2** 305, Ch D.
Covenant to 'enure for the protection of the adjoining or neighbouring land part of or lately part of the Selwyn estate'—
Certainty of description of land and meaning of 'lately'—Whether benefit of covenant annexed to parts of Selwyn estate. **Selwyn's Conveyance, Re** [1967] **1** 339, Ch D.
Description of land to be benefited—
Insufficient description. **Heywood's Conveyance, Re** [1938] **2** 230, Ch D.
Retained land—
Acts detrimental to adjoining land—Benefit of whole or any parts of retained land. **Zetland (Marquess) v Driver** [1938] **2** 158, CA.
Intention that benefit of purchaser's covenants be annexed to retained land—Restrictive covenant in conveyance preventing purchasers or their successors using land for building purposes other than houses or for trade or business—No reference in conveyance to retained land or to vendor's successors in title—Vendor not living on retained land—Whether benefit of purchaser's covenants annexed to retained land—Conveyancing and Law of Property Act 1881, s 58(1). **Sainsbury (J) plc v Enfield London BC** [1989] **2** 817, Ch D.

RESTRICTIVE COVENANT AFFECTING LAND (cont)—
Assignment of benefit—
Benefit of restrictive covenant annexed to whole of land retained by vendor—
Express assignment of benefit to subsequent purchaser of the retained land to whom benefit of restrictive covenant would pass automatically—Whether benefit assignable a question of construction. **Stilwell v Blackman** [1967] **3** 514, Ch D.
Enforcement of covenant by assignee—
Covenant to protect covenantee's business—No identification of land to be benefited so as to annex covenant to land—Death of covenantee—No assent to vesting of benefit in beneficiary entitled—Power of beneficiary to assign benefit—Open to court to look at attendant circumstances to see if land to be benefited shown with sufficient certainty. **Newton Abbot Co-op Society Ltd v Williamson & Treadgold Ltd** [1952] **1** 279, Ch D.
Benefit of covenant—
Assignment. *See* Assignment of benefit, *above*.
Capacity of retained land to be benefited by enforcement of covenants—
Private roadway—plaintiffs intending purchasers of land to which access given by a private roadway—Defendants owners of soil of roadway—Defendants assignees of restrictive covenants affecting land to be purchased by plaintiffs—Restrictions limited user of land—Increase of buildings on land, if restrictions were not binding, would increase use of roadway and might lead to greater costs of repairing road and reduce defendants' chance of selling roadway—Restrictions therefore sensibly affecting roadway—Defendants entitled to enforce restrictions. **Gadd's Land Transfer, Re** [1965] **2** 800, Ch D.
Conveyance, in—
Mandatory injunction. *See* **Injunction** (Mandatory injunction—Discretion over grant of remedy—Breach of covenant in conveyance).
Inducement to commit—
Tort. *See* **Tort** (Inducement to commit breach of contract—Restrictive covenant).
Land benefited—
Conflicting clauses in deed—Land too extensive to be benefited. **Ballard's Conveyance, Re** [1937] **2** 691, Ch D.
No building scheme—
Devolution of benefit of covenants—Subsequent purchaser of part of land retained. **Drake v Gray** [1936] **1** 363, CA.
Persons not parties to covenant—
Assigns of purchasers from common vendor—Person not party to nor referred to in deed containing covenant—Law of Property Act 1925, s 56(1). **White v Bijou Mansions Ltd** [1938] **1** 546, CA.
Settled land—
Right of tenant for life to enforce covenant—Original covenantee tenant for life—Death of covenantee—Trustees of settlement as special executors executing vesting assent in favour of plaintiff as tenant for life—Vesting assent containing no express reference to benefit of covenant—Special executors bare trustees of benefit of covenant for plaintiff—Plaintiff entitled to sue on covenant in equity without making special executors parties—Settled Land Act 1925, s 7(1). **Leicester (Earl) v Wells-next-the-Sea UDC** [1972] **3** 77, Ch D.
Building scheme—
Community of interests—
Reciprocity of obligation—Estate laid out in lots—Division into sublots—Action by purchaser of one sublot against another. **Lawrence v South County Freeholds Ltd** [1939] **2** 503, Ch D.
Reciprocity of obligation—Scheme restrictions relating to original plot—Division into sub-plots—No covenants between sub-purchasers inter se or with sub-vendor—Whether benefit of covenants enforceable by sub-purchasers inter se. **Brunner v Greenslade** [1970] **3** 833, Ch D.
Criteria necessary to establish existence of scheme—
Effect of omission of restrictions from minority of transfers—Provision that covenants should enure for benefit of 'remainder of estate of vendor'—Whether 'remainder' meant unsold part. **Eagling v Gardner** [1970] **2** 838, Ch D.
Deed of mutual covenant—
Estate of common vendor not laid out in plots before conveyances to purchasers—All conveyances contained covenants in substantially the same terms—Covenants included one not to use dwellinghouse or other building otherwise than as a private residence—Plaintiffs, owners of four houses on property, entitled to benefit of covenant—Defendants purchased house on property with knowledge of covenants—Demolished house and erected instead a building containing nine residential flats—Whether building scheme established notwithstanding estate not laid out in lots before sale—Remedy—Injunction or damages. **Baxter v Four Oaks Properties Ltd** [1965] **1** 906, Ch D.
Defined area—
Reservation of right to vendor to sell unsold land free from restrictions—Existence of defined area a matter of conjecture—Whether building scheme would be implied. **Wembley Park Estate Co Ltd's Transfer, Re** [1968] **1** 457, Ch D.
Discharge or modification. *See* Discharge or modification—Building scheme, *below*.
Division into lots—
Common ownership of subsequent purchaser—Land subject to scheme divided into lots—Lots conveyed subject to restrictions imposed by scheme—Certain lots subsequently coming into common ownership—Common owner subsequently conveying lots to different purchasers—Conveyances expressed to be subject to restrictions imposed by scheme—Whether purchasers of lots previously in common ownernhip and successors in title entitled to enforce restrictions inter se. **Texaco Antilles Ltd v Kernochan** [1973] **2** 118, PC.
Provision in conveyance of lot that scheme for roads, buildings, lands etc shown on plan attached to conveyance and building and other restrictions imposed on purchaser 'not binding on vendor and vendor entitled to alter or vary same'—Whether provision inconsistent with a building scheme—Whether provision establishing intention by vendor not to create a building scheme. **Elm Avenue (6, 8, 10 and 12), New Milton, Re, ex p New Forest DC** [1984] **3** 632, Ch D.

RESTRICTIVE COVENANT AFFECTING LAND (cont)—
  Building scheme (cont)—
    Termination—
      Superseding covenants—Purchasers mutually release covenants and enter into superseding covenants—Whether building scheme terminated—Joint restrictive covenant by tenants in common in deed of 1899—Whether covenant effective to give rise to equitable restriction binding successors in title. **Pinewood Estate, Farnborough, Re** [1957] **2** 517, Ch D.
  Construction of covenant—
    Amusement arcade—
      Covenant prohibiting use of land as an amusement arcade—Coin-operated amusement machines for children installed on land—Whether an 'amusement arcade'—Whether amusement arcade limited to premises containing gaming machines—Whether age of patrons relevant. **Shaw v Applegate** [1978] **1** 123, CA.
    Erection of building—
      Covenant against erecting a building—Moving shed erected on free land to land subject to covenant—Breach. **Gardiner v Walsh** [1936] **3** 870, Ch D.
    Permit—
      Covenant not to permit land to be used for other than specified purpose—Sale of land by covenantee—Covenant by purchaser T Ltd not to 'cause or permit' land to be used otherwise than for horse-racing, etc—Covenant limited so that T Ltd not liable for breach after parting with land—Contract for sale by T Ltd to third party with intention of using land for development—Intention known to T Ltd—Whether by completing sale purchaser would permit land to be used in breach of covenant. **Tophams Ltd v Earl of Sefton** [1966] **1** 1039, HL.
      Implication as to implying control of use of land by covenantor—Covenant by purchaser not to 'use or permit the use of' property conveyed for purpose other than smallholdings and allotments—Purchaser local authority—Land no longer required for allotments—Land appropriated for housing—Condition of sale by local authority that purchasers build houses on land—Whether by completing sale local authority 'permitting' purchasers to use land in breach of covenant. **Leicester (Earl) v Wells-next-the-Sea UDC** [1972] **3** 77, Ch D.
    Remainder of estate—
      Provision that covenant should enure for benefit of 'remainder of estate of vendor—Covenant not to erect buildings on property 'except a private dwelling-house'—Dwelling-house already on property at date of purchase—Whether covenant contemplated additional dwelling-house. **Eagling v Gardner** [1970] **2** 838, Ch D.
  Use as a dwelling-house—
    Covenant by purchaser not to use burdened property 'for any purpose other than that of a single private dwelling-house'—Dwelling-house already on property at date of purchase—Purchaser obtaining planning permission to erect a second dwelling-house on part of burdened property—Whether covenant preventing erection of second private dwelling-house on burdened land. **Endericks' Conveyance, Re** [1973] **1** 843, CA.
    Covenant not to use burdened property 'for any purpose other than those of or in connection with a private dwellinghouse' (first covenant)—Covenant not to erect dwelling house or other building on land conveyed unless plans and drawings approved by vendor company (second covenant)—Whether first covenant preventing erection of more than one dwelling house on plot—Whether dissolution of vendor company discharging second covenant or rendering it absolute in effect. **Crest Nicholson Residential (South) Ltd v McAllister** [2003] **1** 46, Ch D; [2004] **2** 991n, CA.
    Covenant not to use house for any purpose other than as private dwelling house—Covenant not to carry on activity which might become detrimental to transferor—Secretary of State purchasing two houses on residential estate subject to covenants as to user—Houses intended for use to provide supervised housing for former mental patients as part of 'care in the community' policy—Whether user in breach of covenants—Whether user constituting ordinary use of private dwelling house—Whether user detrimental to transferor—Whether financial loss suffered in exploiting retained land recoverable. **C & G Homes Ltd v Secretary of State for Health** [1991] **2** 841, CA.
  Covenant prohibiting or restricting conversion of single dwelling house into two or more separate dwelling houses—
    Variation—
      Power of court to vary covenant where planning permission granted for use of premises as converted—Exercise of power—Matters to be taken into account—Guidance—Housing Act 1985, s 610. **Lawntown Ltd v Camenzuli** [2008] **1** 446, CA.
  Damages in lieu of injunction. *See* **Injunction** (Damages in lieu of injunction—Breach of restrictive covenant affecting land).
  Declaration whether covenant affecting land unenforceable—
    Burden of proof on owner seeking declaration—
      Law of Property Act 1925, s 84(2). **Elm Avenue (6, 8, 10 and 12), New Milton, Re, ex p New Forest DC** [1984] **3** 632, Ch D.
    Costs of High Court application—
      Declaration that land not affected by restrictions—No prior application to Lands Tribunal for modification or discharge—Defendants' costs to date of adjournment to judge to be paid by the plaintiffs on common fund basis—Law of Property Act 1925, s 84(2). **Wembley Park Estate Co Ltd's Transfer, Re** [1968] **1** 457, Ch D.
      Incidence of costs—Law of Property Act 1925, s 84(2). **Jeffkins' Indenture, Re** [1965] **1** 608, Ch D.
      Incidence of costs—Pre-CPR rule of practice—Whether consistent with CPR—Law of Property Act 1925, s 84(2)—CPR 44.3(2). **University of East London Higher Education Corp v Barking and Dagenham London BC (No 2)** [2005] **3** 416, Ch D.
      Prior application to Lands Tribunal—Hostile litigation between objectors and plaintiff—Modification of covenant—Costs in High Court—Law of Property Act 1925, s 84(2). **Jeffs' Transfer, Re (No 2)** [1966] **1** 937, Ch D.

RESTRICTIVE COVENANT AFFECTING LAND (cont)—

Declaration whether covenant affecting land unenforceable (cont)—

Costs of High Court application (cont)—

Prior application to Lands Tribunal—Objection raised before Lands Tribunal to modification of restrictive covenant—Application to High Court necessitated by objection—Objectors consenting, when High Court proceedings instituted, to order that they were not entitled to enforce covenant—Objectors not entitled to costs in High Court—Law of Property Act 1925, s 84(2). **Jeffs' Transfer, Re** [1965] **2** 798, Ch D.

Covenants not to build or to fell trees—

Nobody legally entitled to enforce them—Small part of land subject to covenants intended as school site—No appearance of persons interested—Discretion whether to make declaration—Law of Property Act 1925, s 84(2). **Freeman-Thomas Indenture, Re** [1957] **1** 532, Ch D.

Discretion—

Permission for development not yet obtained—Whether court should make declaration that restrictions did not affect land, although permission for development might not be obtained—Law of Property Act 1925, s 84(2). **Wembley Park Estate Co Ltd's Transfer, Re** [1968] **1** 457, Ch D.

Form of declaration—

Covenants imposed by the same deeds affected also other land not belonging to applicant—Proper form of declaration. **Jeffkins' Indenture, Re** [1965] **1** 608, Ch D.

Future covenant—

Application to determine enforceability of restrictions if contract completed—Future question—No jurisdiction under statute to decide future question—Jurisdiction of court to entertain matter under general jurisdiction—Law of Property Act 1925, s 84(2). **Gadd's Land Transfer, Re** [1965] **2** 800, Ch D.

Discharge or modification—

Acquisition of land by defendant for statutory purposes—

Acquisition by agreement rather than by compulsory purchase—Whether persons entitled to benefit of restrictive covenants can prevent use of land for statutory purposes—Whether acquisition of land by local authority automatically discharging restrictive covenants—Whether persons entitled to restrictive covenants can claim compensation for injurious affection—Compulsory Purchase Act 1965, s 10(2). **Elm Avenue (6, 8, 10 and 12), New Milton, Re, ex p New Forest DC** [1984] **3** 632, Ch D.

Defendant having responsibility for persons suffering from mental health disability—Defendant proposing to use acquired property for purpose of housing five patients—Restrictive covenant requiring property to be used as private dwelling house—Whether statutory body, having acquired land for purpose of carrying out statutory functions, can be restrained by injunction from making use of land for purpose for which it was acquired. **Brown v Heathlands Mental Health National Health Service Trust** [1996] **1** 133, Ch D.

Application for leave to apply to Lands Tribunal—

Proceedings to enforce covenant—Circumstances in which leave to apply and stay of proceedings should be granted—Law of Property Act 1925, s 84(9). **Richardson v Jackson** [1954] **1** 437, Ch D.

Building scheme—

Whether building scheme creating increased presumption against modification of restrictive covenant—Law of Property Act 1925, s 84. **Dobbin v Redpath** [2007] **4** 465, CA.

Change of circumstances—

Covenant imposed in February 1963—Application to modify in February 1965—No change of circumstances affecting land—Applicants covenantors, respondents covenantees—Modification refused—Law of Property Act 1925, s 84(1). **Cresswell (Trustees of the Cobbett Settlement) v Proctor (Trustees of the Convent of The Holy Family)** [1968] **2** 682, CA.

Condition as to compensation—

Delay in enforcing covenants—Adjoining owners bringing action on covenants more than year after building operations begun in breach of covenants—Application for modification granted on condition compensation paid to adjoining owners—Whether delay having effect of wiping out loss consequent on modification—Law of Property Act 1925, s 84. **Spencer Flats Ltd, Re** [1936] **2** 1392, Ch D.

Conditions to be satisfied—

Persons entitled to benefit of restriction agreeing to their discharge—Application for discharge or modification of restrictions—Persons entitled to benefit of restrictions failing to respond to notice of application—Whether failure to respond sufficient evidence of agreement to discharge—Law of Property Act 1925, s 84(1). **University of Westminster, Re** [1998] **3** 1014, CA.

Restriction contrary to public interest—Discretion—Cynical breach of covenant—Developer building homes on land contrary to restrictive covenant—Developer applying to modify covenant after construction work completed—Tribunal granting application subject to payment of compensation—Whether cynical breach material to issue of whether restriction contrary to public interest—Whether tribunal erring in exercise of its discretion—Law of Property Act 1925, s 84. **Alexander Devine Children's Cancer Trust v Housing Solutions Ltd** [2021] **2** 871, SC.

Restriction not securing to persons entitled to benefit of it any practical benefits of substantial value or advantage—Benefits—Whether landscape view not visible from land itself but visible from land close by capable of being a 'practical benefit'—Whether evidence that persons entitled to benefit actually taking advantage of it essential—Law of Property Act 1925, s 84(1), (1A). **Gilbert v Spoor** [1982] **2** 576, CA.

Jurisdiction—

Applicant a party to covenant—Law of Property Act 1925, s 84(1), (12)—Landlord and Tenant Act 1954, s 52. **Ridley v Taylor** [1965] **2** 51, CA.

Determining objectors' title to restrictions—Jurisdiction of tribunal—Title based on building scheme—Finding that no building scheme—Propriety of determination—Law of Property Act 1925, s 84(1), (2). **Purkiss' Application, Re** [1962] **2** 690, CA.

RESTRICTIVE COVENANT AFFECTING LAND (cont)—
Discharge or modification (cont)—
Land affected by any restriction arising under covenant—
Application by original covenantor—Covenant not running with land—Covenant merely binding covenantor personally—Covenant with vendor of plot of land not to erect any fence around covenantor's front garden—Whether restriction under covenant affecting land—Law of Property Act 1925, s 84(1) (as amended by the Law of Property Act 1969, s 28). **Shepherd Homes Ltd v Sandham (No 2)** [1971] **2** 1267, Ch D.
Leasehold—
Injury to landlord—Loss of power to exact rent in return for modification—Restrictive covenant re-imposed on grant of licence (but subject thereto) less than 25 years before application—Law of Property Act 1925, s 84(1)(c), (12)—Landlord and Tenant Act 1954, s 52. **Ridley v Taylor** [1965] **2** 51, CA.
Term of more than seventy years, after the expiration of fifty years of the term—How calculated—Date of lease or date from which term expressed to run—Law of Property Act 1925, s 84(12). **Cadogan (Earl) v Guinness** [1936] **2** 29, Ch D.
Preliminary issue—
Costs application to modify restrictive covenant—Preliminary issue as to whether objectors to be admitted—Incidence of costs—Law of Property Act 1925, s 84—Lands Tribunal Practice Directions, para 22.4. **Winter v Traditional & Contemporary Contracts Ltd** [2007] **2** 343, CA.
Question of law arising on application—
Adjournment to court—Award conditional on objectors establishing right to sue—Law of Property Act 1925, s 84. **Spencer Flats Ltd, Re** [1936] **2** 1392, Ch D.
Jurisdiction of tribunal—Difficult point of law—No general rule that tribunal should refrain from resolving difficult points of law—Decision of tribunal open to challenge in courts. **Shepherd Homes Ltd v Sandham (No 2)** [1971] **2** 1267, Ch D.
Status of covenantee—
National Trust—National Trust not possessed of land in locality—Statutory power of enforcement—Nature of deemed capacity of National Trust as if covenant for benefit of adjacent land—Custodians of natural beauty of land—Whether other grounds of opposing modification sufficient—National Trust Act 1937, s 8. **Gee v National Trust for Places of Historic Interest or Natural Beauty** [1966] **1** 954, CA.
Stay of proceedings in action to enforce covenant by injunction—
Conditions of granting stay—Undertaking by defendants—Cross-undertaking by plaintiffs—Building scheme limiting density of building on neighbouring land—Development of land by defendants exceeding permitted density—Law of Property Act 1925, s 84(9). **Hanning v Gable-Jeffreys Properties Ltd** [1965] **1** 924, Ch D.
What must be shown—
Change in character of property or neighbourhood—Private owners—High class residential neighbourhood—Law of Property Act 1925, s 84—RSC Ord 54D, rr 1, 2, 3, 8. **Henderson's Conveyance, Re** [1940] **4** 1, Ch D.
Obsolete restrictions—Building estate—Covenants inposed in 1898 with object of preserving estate as residential area—Covenant prohibiting trade of innkeeper to be carried on on the land—Some change in character of part of estate—Serious injury to persons entitled to benefit of covenant, if covenant discharged—Whether covenant 'obsolete'—Law of Property Act 1925, s 84(1)(a). **Truman, Hanbury, Buxton & Co Ltd's Application, Re** [1955] **3** 559, CA.
Obsolete restrictions—Impeding reasonable user of land—Large houses to be used only as private dwelling-houses save with written consent of lessor—Most houses in district converted into flats or guest houses—Lessor willing to consent to change of user subject to preserving residential character of neighbourhood—Discretion of Lands Tribunal—Law of Property Act 1925, s 84(1). **Driscoll v Church Comrs for England** [1956] **3** 802, CA.
Residential area—Covenants imposed in 1908 and 1945 to use premises as private dwelling-house only—No change of character of neighbourhood—Proposed use as convalescent home for employees of owner—Law of Property Act 1925, s 84(1)(a), (6c). **Ghey and Galton's Application, Re** [1957] **3** 164, CA.
Enforceability—
Conveyances of estate to purchasers in parcels—
Covenants by purchasers to observe restrictions designed to maintain nature of estate—Covenant by vendor in each conveyance that same restrictions would be imposed on future purchasers—Common interest and common benefit—Conveyances equivalent to deeds of mutual covenant—Whether covenants enforceable by and against successors in title to original purchasers. **Dolphin's Conveyance, Re** [1970] **2** 664, Ch D.
Covenant capable of benefiting land—
Estate owner reasonably taking view that covenant for benefit of his land—Others reasonably taking view that benefit of covenant spent—Whether covenant enforceable. **Wrotham Park Estate Co v Parkside Homes Ltd** [1974] **2** 321, Ch D.
Enforceability against vendor's successors in title—
Repairing covenant—Positive covenant to repair demised property—Owner of house and contiguous cottage selling cottage and covenanting to maintain common roof in good repair—Whether covenant binding vendor's successors in title—Whether rule that positive covenants not running with freehold still applying—Law of Property Act 1925, s 79. **Rhone v Stephens** [1994] **2** 65, HL.
Requisitioned land at date of covenant by purchaser—
Compulsory purchase of land by government department subsequently, subject to restrictive covenant—Restrictive covenant limiting use to agricultural use—Land acquired as reserve airfield in emergency—Occupation of land meanwhile by industrial company, under licence from Air Ministry—Land preserved by company as an airfield but used by company for industrial activities as well as for purposes of Air Ministry—Whether restrictive covenant enforceable. **Marten v Flight Refuelling Ltd** [1961] **2** 696, Ch D.

RESTRICTIVE COVENANT AFFECTING LAND (cont)—

Extinguishment—

Freehold—

Common ownership of burdened and benefited land—Local authority owning benefited land as housing authority and burdened land as education authority—Whether unity of seisin extinguishing covenant. **University of East London Higher Education Corp v Barking and Dagenham London BC** [2005] **3** 398, Ch D.

Common ownership of burdened and benefited land—Owner in fee simple of benefited land purchasing part of burdened land—Subsequent sale by common owner of benefited and burdened land to different purchasers—Whether burdened land remaining subject to covenant—Whether unity of seisin of burdened and benefited land extinguishing covenant or merely suspending it until revival on sale of benefited land—Law of Property Act 1925, s 84(2)(a). **Tiltwood, Sussex, Re** [1978] **2** 1091, Ch D.

Leasehold—

Merger of term—Covenant by lessor in lease binding land other than that demised—Lessees' successors in title acquired freehold reversion and merged term—Present owner of land burdened by covenant was not party to the merger but acquired land with knowledge of the covenant—Whether restrictive covenant still binding in equity notwithstanding merger. **Golden Lion Hotel (Hunstanton) Ltd v Carter** [1965] **3** 506, Ch D.

Implication of covenant—

Restrictions referred to in habendum but no covenant taken—

Subsequent conveyance without reference to covenants—No certainty as to parties to covenant or as to land to be benefited. **Rutherford's Conveyance, Re** [1938] **1** 495, Ch D.

Inducement to commit breach of covenant—

Tort. See **Tort** (Inducement to commit breach of contract—Restrictive covenant).

Injunction to restrain breach of covenant. See **Injunction** (Discretion—Acquiescence by plaintiff in activities constituting breach of plaintiff's rights—Restrictive covenant affecting land).

Land charge—

Registration as. See **Land charge** (Registration—Restrictive covenant).

Landlord and tenant. See **Landlord and tenant** (Restrictive covenant).

Notice—

Registered land. See **Land registration** (Notice—Notice of restrictive covenant).

Tenants precluded from inquiring into lessor's title. See **Landlord and tenant** (Covenant—Notice of covenant—Tenant precluded from inquiring into lessor's title—Notice of restrictive covenants).

Registered land—

Notice. See **Land registration** (Notice—Notice of restrictive covenant).

Rectification of register—

Date from which rectification effective. See **Land registration** (Rectification of register—Date from which rectification effective—Effect on dispositions before date of rectification—Restrictive covenant).

Registration as land charge. See **Land charge** (Registration—Restrictive covenant).

Trade—

Covenant against trade—

Jobbing builder. **Westripp v Baldock** [1939] **1** 279, CA.

Uncertainty—

Limits of prohibition in covenant impossible to ascertain—

Restriction of matters 'which shall injure prejudice affect or destroy the natural aspect and condition of the land'—Whether covenant void for uncertainty. **National Trust for Places of Historic Interest or Natural Beauty v Midlands Electricity Board** [1952] **1** 298, Ch D.

Variation. See Covenant prohibiting or restricting conversion of single dwelling house into two or more separate dwelling houses, above.

RESTRICTIVE PRACTICES COURT

See **Restrictive trade practices** (Court).

RESTRICTIVE TRADE PRACTICES

Agreement—

New agreement—

Test whether new agreement is 'to the like effect' to another agreement in respect of restrictions declared to be contrary to the public interest—Effect—Test to be applied where court has given reasoned judgment on reference of original agreement—Restrictive Trade Practices Act 1956, s 20(3). **Black Bolt and Nut Association of GB's Agreement, Re (No 2)** [1962] **1** 139, CA.

Test whether new agreement is 'to the like effect' to another agreement in respect of restrictions declared to be contrary to the public interest—Original agreement compelled preponderant purchaser of large transformers to pay prices dictated by suppliers—New agreement to effect bargain between preponderant customer for large transformers and manufacturers thereof as to allocation of orders and prices to be paid—Restrictive Trade Practices Act 1956, s 20(3)(b). **Associated Transformer Manufacturers' Agreement (No 2), Re** [1971] **1** 409, RPC.

Registration. See Registration of agreement, below.

Appeal to Court of Appeal by way of case stated—

Application after judgment for judgment to be amplified or amended—

Application for judgment to be amplified to include reference to evidence before court—Refusal. **National Federation of Retail Newsagents, Booksellers and Stationers v Registrar of Restrictive Trading Agreements (Nos 3 & 4)** [1971] **2** 493, RPC; **National Federation of Retail Newsagents, Booksellers and Stationers v Registrar of Restrictive Trading Agreements (Nos 3 & 4)** [1971] **2** 514, CA.

Nature of application—Whether application interlocutory—Restrictive Trade Practices Act 1956, Schedule, paras 7 and 8—Restrictive Practices Court Rules 1957 (SI 1957 No 603) rr 48, 81. **National Federation of Retail Newsagents, Booksellers and Stationers' Agreement, Re (No 4)** [1970] **1** 289, RPC.

RESTRICTIVE TRADE PRACTICES (cont)—
Appeal to Court of Appeal by way of case stated (cont)—
Jurisdiction of Court of Appeal—
Documents—Whether court entitled to look at documents before Restrictive Practices Court but not referred to in judgment. **National Federation of Retail Newsagents, Booksellers and Stationers v Registrar of Restrictive Trading Agreements (Nos 3 & 4)** [1971] 2 514, CA.
Committal order—
Execution. *See* **Contempt of court** (Committal—Order—Execution).
Contempt of court—
Acts amounting to contempt of court—
Proceedings no longer pending—Subsequent victimisation of witness—Witness removed from office—Whether removal constituted a contempt of court. **A-G v Butterworth** [1962] 3 326, CA.
Publication of matter tending to interfere with due course of justice in proceedings before court. **Cement Makers' Federation's Agreement, Re** [1961] 2 75, RPC.
Breach of undertaking given to court—
Company giving undertaking to court in respect of agreement declared contrary to public interest—Company subsequently becoming wholly-owned subsidary of publicly-owned corporation—All assets, liabilities and obligations of company transferred by vesting order to corporation—Corporation entering into agreements in breach of undertaking given by company—Whether undertaking given to court forming part of obligations transferred to corporation—Whether corporation in contempt of court—Iron and Steel Act 1969, s 8(1)—Steel Companies (Vesting) Order 1970, art 3. **British Concrete Pipe Association, Re** [1983] 1 203, CA.
Concerted action with regard to prices and discounts—Exchanges of advance information as to price changes—Statements of fact on behalf of respondents, including statements by way of mitigation, to be supported by evidence—Nature of punishment. **Galvanized Tank Manufacturers' Association's Agreement, Re** [1965] 2 1003, RPC.
Undertaking not to enter into any arrangement to the like effect as former agreement in respect of restrictions rendered void with reference to court—Former agreement superseded by new rate notification scheme, which was in part permissive—No agreement amongst member companies that they would all operate the new scheme, but each soon aware that others were doing so—Whether an 'arrangement'—Whether to 'the like effect' as original agreement—Whether contempt of court—Legal advice as mitigation of contempt. **Agreement of Mileage Conference Group of Tyre Manufacturers' Conference Ltd, Re** [1966] 2 849, RPC.
Committal order—
Execution. *See* **Contempt of court** (Committal—Order—Execution—Restrictive Practices Court).
Court—
Contempt of court—
Committal—Appeal against committal—Notice of appeal—Service. *See* **Contempt of court** (Committal—Appeal against committal—Notice of appeal—Service—Restrictive Practices Court).
Committal—Order—Execution. *See* **Contempt of court** (Committal—Order—Execution—Restrictive Practices Court).
Generally. *See* Contempt of court, *above*.
Court of Appeal—
Appeal to. *See* Appeal to Court of Appeal by way of case stated, *above*.
Evidence—
Affidavits, exhibits, documents—Marking—Binding—Sequence—Pagination—Copies—Bundles of documents generally—Effect of failure to comply with rules—RSC Ord 41. **Practice Direction** [1984] 3 126, RPC.
Answers to questionnaire sent out by trade association—Discretion of court to admit as evidence. **Cement Makers' Federation's Agreement, Re** [1961] 2 75, RPC.
Cross-examination of witnesses—When proofs of witnesses to be treated as evidence in the case. **Yarn Spinners' Agreement, Re** [1959] 1 299, RPC.
Evidence of opinion by trade witnesses. **Chemists' Federation, Re the agreement between the members of** [1958] 3 448, RPC.
Exchange of proofs—Supply of proofs for court—Confirmation in evidence-in-chief—Additions to proofs. **Associated Transformer Manufacturers' Agreement, Re** [1961] 2 233, RPC.
Exchange of proofs—Time. **Permanent Magnet Association's Agreement, Re** [1962] 2 775, RPC.
Hearing in camera. **British Bottle Association's Agreement, Re** [1961] 2 208, RPC.
Interlocutory applications—
Consent orders. **Practice Direction** [1958] 3 681, RPC.
Discovery. **Chemists' Federation, Re the agreement between the members of** [1958] 3 448, RPC.
Documentary evidence in lieu of calling witnesses. **Chemists' Federation, Re the agreement between the members of** [1958] 3 448, RPC.
Exchange of statements of witnesses etc. **Chemists' Federation, Re the agreement between the members of** [1958] 3 448, RPC.
Particulars. **Chemists' Federation, Re the agreement between the members of** [1958] 3 448, RPC.
Time—Applications for extension or abridgment of time—Restrictive Practices Court Rules 1957 (SI 1957 No 603), r 49. **Practice Direction** [1957] 3 439, RPC.
Jurisdiction—
Alteration after date of reference—Overseas trading restrictions severed from home trading restrictions and embodied in new document—Discretion of court to deal with overseas trading restrictions—Restrictive Trade Practices Act 1956, ss 8(8), 20. **Federation of British Carpet Manufacturers' Agreement, Re** [1960] 1 356, RPC.
Discovery—Purpose of discovery to show existence of suspected unwritten arrangement—Jurisdiction of court on a reference was to consider written agreement referred to it—Original agreement admitted to contain a restriction but subsequently varied—Variation prohibiting arrangement that constituted restriction but otherwise bearing similarity to former clause containing restriction—Whether discovery should be granted. **Crane Makers' Association's Agreement, Re** [1965] 2 561, CA.
Termination of agreement before reference—Restrictive Trade Practices Act 1956, ss 1(2), 20(1), (3), (5). **Associated Newspapers Ltd v Registrar of Restrictive Trading Agreements** [1964] 1 55, HL.

Court (cont)—
Power to make declaration—
Admission of registrable restriction—Whether declaration made on admissions. **Birmingham Association of Building Trades Employers Agreement, Re** [1963] 2 361, RPC.
No other relief sought—Discretion. **Associated Transformer Manufacturers' Agreement (No 2), Re** [1971] **1** 409, RPC.
Power where agreement terminated or varied—Past restrictions—Whether declaration as to past restrictions would be made—Restrictive Trade Practices Act 1956, s 20(5). **Bakers' (Federation of Wholesale and Multiple) Agreement, Re** [1960] **1** 227, RPC.
Power to order examination on oath—
Examination of directors, manager, secretary or other officer of body corporate—Manager—Other officer—Whether including local managers of nation-wide organisations—Restrictive Trade Practices Act 1956, s 15(3). **Registrar of Restrictive Trading Agreements v WH Smith & Son Ltd** [1969] **3** 1065, CA.
Examination of directors, manager, secretary or other officer of body corporate—Reasonable cause to believe restrictive agreement made—Restrictive Trade Practices Act 1956, s 15(3). **Registrar of Restrictive Trading Agreements v WH Smith & Son Ltd** [1969] **3** 1065, CA.
Practice—
Agreed statement defining main issues. **Distant Water Vessels Development Scheme, Re** [1966] **3** 897, RPC.
Appearance—Body corporate—Solicitor—Restrictive Practices Court Rules 1957 (SI 1957 No 603), r 90—Restrictive Practices Court (Resale Prices) Rules 1965 (SI 1965 No 236), rr 16, 37. **Practice Direction** [1966] **1** 581, RPC.
Costs—Wasted costs. See **Costs** (Wasted costs—Restrictive trade practices).
Definition of real issue with a view to reducing the volume of evidence. **Locked Coil Ropemakers' Association's Agreement, Re** [1965] **1** 382, RPC.
Interlocutory applications. See Court—Interlocutory applications, *above*.
Pleading—Facts and matters in relation to foreign countries—Issue intended to be raised should be shown on pleadings. **Chocolate and Sugar Confectionery Resale Price Reference, Re** [1967] **3** 261, RPC.
Representation order—Applications for representation orders by members of trade associations—Restrictive Practices Court Rules 1957 (SI 1957 No 603), r 49. **Practice Direction** [1957] **2** 843, RPC.
Service of order—Service of order by post and not by personal service—Recorded delivery service. **Wholesale Confectioners' Alliance of GB and Northern Ireland's Agreement, Re (No 2)** [1961] **2** 8, RPC.
Statement of case. See Court—Statement of case, *below*.
Uncontested case—Notification by respondents that they will not contest proceedings—Declaration by court that restrictions contrary to public interest—Restrictive Practices Court Rules 1957 (SI 1957 No 603), as amended by Restrictive Practices Court (Amendment) Rules 1965 (SI 1965 No 22), r 64A. **Coventry Newspapers Ltd, Birmingham Post and Mail Ltd's Agreement, Re** [1965] **1** 963, RPC.
Undertaking—Variation—Proposed recommendations by trade associations to members of terms and conditions of home trade—Recommendation by Registrar to Board of Trade that terms and conditions are of no substantial economic significance—Release from undertakings to extent necessary to make recommendations of terms, etc, to traders—Restrictive Trade Practices Act 1956, ss 12, 20(3). **Yarn Spinners' Agreement, Re (No 2)** [1960] **3** 809, RPC.
Variation of decision—Application—Contents of affidavit—Listing of proceedings—Evidence—Information to be provided to court—Restrictive Trade Practices Act 1976, s 4. **Practice Direction** [1987] **1** 602, RPC.
Reference to. See Reference, *below*.
Statement of case—
Agreed amendment—Procedure. **Reinforcement Conference, Re agreement between Members of** [1961] **2** 820, RPC.
Late delivery—Unreasonable delay—Costs—Restrictive Practices Court Rules 1957 (SI 1957 No 603), rr 76, 77. **Wire Nails Manufacturers' Agreement, Re** [1961] **2** 342, RPC.
Need for statement of case to identify admitted restrictions and give particulars—Answer should identify and further alleged restrictions—Reply should give particulars of any such further restrictions admitted—Restrictive Practices Court Rules 1957 (SI 1957 No 603), r 18—Restrictive Trade Practices Act 1956, s 20(1). **Practice Direction** [1958] **3** 520, RPC.
Declaration as to. See Court—Power to make declaration, *above*.
European Union—
Generally. See **European Union** (Restrictive trade practices).
Restriction on freedom to provide services. See **European Union** (Freedom of establishment—Restriction on freedom to provide services).
Rules on competition. See **European Union** (Rules on competition).
Interference with trade—
Tort. See **Tort** (Interference with trade—Unlawful means—Restrictive trade practice).
Jurisdiction. See Court—Jurisdiction, *above*.
Justification of restriction—
Maintenance of another restriction—
Black Bolt and Nut Association of Great Britain—Price list for ordinary users upheld but separate price fixing machinery for large users condemned on earlier reference—Maintenance of approved ordinary user restriction impossible without supplementation—New agreement applying to large users—Whether new restriction for large users was reasonably required for maintenance of ordinary user restrictions—Restrictive Trade Practices Act 1956, s 21(1)(g). **Black Bolt and Nut Association of GB's Agreement, Re (No 3)** [1966] **1** 220, RPC.
Necessity to negotiate fair terms—
Lack of proof that existing terms unfair—Boycotts by retail newsagents of daily newspaper—Whether reasonably necessary to negotiate fair terms—Restrictive Trade Practices Act 1956, s 21(1)(d). **National Federation of Retail Newsagents, Booksellers and Stationers v Registrar of Restrictive Trading Agreements (Nos 3 & 4)** [1971] **2** 514, CA.

RESTRICTIVE TRADE PRACTICES (cont)—
Justification of restriction (cont)—
Necessity to negotiate fair terms (cont)—
Maintenance of exports—Wire Rope Associations—Division of 'goods' for purposes of negotiating fair terms with preponderant buyer—Agreements to charge common prices—Whether division of 'goods' or of 'trade or business' commercially sensible—Reduction in export business—Restrictive Trade Practices Act 1956, s 21(1)(b), (d), (f). **Locked Coil Ropemakers' Association's Agreement, Re** [1965] 1 382, RPC.

Supply of goods—National Federation of Retail Newsagents, Booksellers and Stationers—Category of 'goods' for purposes of negotiating fair terms with preponderant seller—New periodical brought out by publishers—Recommendations by federation that members should not buy on terms proposed by publishers—Whether periodical was a distinct category of 'goods' differing from others for a similar public published by the same publishers—Restrictive Trade Practices Act 1956, s 21(1)(d). **National Federation of Retail Newsagents, Booksellers and Stationers' Agreement, Re** [1965] 2 417, RPC.

Supply of goods—Sulphuric Acid Association—Common buying and shipping pool—Preponderant foreign supplier—Common prices imposed by pool—Restrictions on purchase from other sources—Restrictions on use and re-sale—Need of combination for negotiating 'fair terms' for the supply of goods—Foreign combine controlling 'preponderant part' of business of supply—Restrictive Trade Practices Act 1956, s 21(1)(d), (g). **National Sulphuric Acid Association Ltd's Agreement, Re** [1963] 3 73, RPC.

Trade or business—Preponderant part—Whether certain daily newspaper controlled a preponderant part of the trade or business—Restrictive Trade Practices Act 1956, s 21(1)(d). **National Federation of Retail Newsagents, Booksellers and Stationers v Registrar of Restrictive Trading Agreements (Nos 3 & 4)** [1971] 2 514, CA.

Protection of public against injury—
Specific and substantial benefit to public. *See* Justification of restriction—Specific and substantial benefit to public, *below.*

Specific and substantial benefit to public—
Blanket Manufacturers' Association—Minimum price scheme—Minimum substance restriction—Restrictions as to terms of sale—Whether removal of restrictions would deny public substantial benefit—Restrictive Trade Practices Act 1956, s 21(1)(b). **Blanket Manufacturers' Association's Agreement, Re** [1959] 2 1, RPC.

Bread price restriction—Scottish Bakers' Associations—Agreements not to sell except at prices recommended by Associations—Whether removal of restriction would deny public substantial benefit—Restrictive Trade Practices Act 1956, s 21(1)(b). **Scottish Association of Master Bakers' Agreement, Re** [1959] 3 98, RPC.

Bread price restriction—Wholesale and Multiple Bakers (Great Britain and Northern Ireland) Federation—Agreement not to sell at retail prices higher than those recommended by Federation—Whether removal of restriction would deny public substantial benefit—Restrictive Trade Practices Act 1956, s 21(1)(b). **Bakers' (Federation of Wholesale and Multiple) Agreement, Re** [1960] 1 227, RPC.

British Bottle Association—Minimum price scheme—Apprehended 'price war'—Ancillary restriction involving exemption from liability to purchasers for injury from goods sold—Whether removal of restrictions would deny public as purchasers substantial benefit—Whether purchasers of filled bottles or only wholesalers or purchasers of bottles for filling were included in that public—Restrictive Trade Practices Act 1956, s 21(1)b). **British Bottle Association's Agreement, Re** [1961] 2 208, RPC.

Building trades' association—Standard forms of contract—Bills of quantities—Daywork charges—Recommendations and rules of association concerning use of forms, against tendering for contracts without bills of quantities, against submitting priced bills of quantities with tenders, and for use of standard schedules of daywork charges—Whether removal of restrictions would deny public substantial benefit—Restrictive Trade Practices Act 1956, s 21(1)(b). **Birmingham Association of Building Trades Employers Agreement, Re** [1963] 2 361, RPC.

Cement price fixing scheme—Merchants' margins—Rebates to user-purchasers and merchant-purchasers—Special rebates to cement asbestos manufacturers—Delivery of cement to be on a day-to-day basis of price—Quotations and contracts for supply of cement other than for specific job not to be made for period exceeding twelve months—Undertaking by merchants to re-sell at prices and on standard conditions as notified—Whether removal of main price fixing restriction would deny public substantial benefit—Whether other restrictions validated by validity of main restriction—Restrictive Trade Practices Act 1956, s 21(1)(b). **Cement Makers' Federation's Agreement, Re** [1961] 2 75, RPC.

Chemist's Federation—Restriction on sale of medicines except through retail chemists—Code of Standards worked by federation—Another code of advertising standards in existence—Whether restriction 'reasonably necessary'—Whether removal of restriction would deny public substantial benefit—Restrictive Trade Practices Act 1956, s 21(1)(a)(b). **Chemists' Federation, Re the agreement between the members of** [1958] 3 448, RPC.

Co-operative societies—Boundary agreement—Agreement by two societies not to canvass or solicit customers or deal in or supply goods or open any shop on other side of demarcation line—Whether removal of restrictions would deny public substantial benefit—Restrictive Trade Practices Act 1956, s 21(1)(b). **Doncaster Co-op Society Ltd's and Retford Co-op Society Ltd's Agreement, Re** [1960] 3 541, RPC.

Distant water fishermen—Fixing of reserve prices at port auctions—Whether necessary to prevent fall in prices and consequent reduction in catching capacity—Whether specific and substantial benefit to public as purchasers of white fish—Restrictive Trade Practices Act 1956, s 21(1)(b). **Distant Water Vessels Development Scheme, Re** [1966] 3 897, RPC.

Finance Houses Association—Hire-purchase of motor vehicles—Restriction of interest rates, commission to dealers, minimum down-payments, maximum hiring periods—Restrictive Trade Practices Act 1956, s 21(1)(b). **Finance Houses Association Ltd's Agreement, Re** [1965] 3 509, RPC.

RESTRICTIVE TRADE PRACTICES (cont)—
   Justification of restriction (cont)—
      Specific and substantial benefit to public (cont)—
         Maintenance of another restriction—Black Bolt and Nut Association of Great Britain—Minimum fixed price scheme—Discounts—Inter-trading between members—Obligation not to supply goods to government departments, railways, harbour boards or other large users at prices lower than lowest proposed quotation reported by any member to secretary of Association—Whether removal of restrictions would deny public substantial benefit—Whether restrictions reasonably required for purposes connected with maintenance of other restrictions accepted by parties—Restrictive Trade Practices Act 1956, s 21(1)(b), (g). **Black Bolt and Nut Association of GB's Agreement, Re** [1960] **3** 122, RPC.

         Maintenance of another restriction—Maintenance of exports—Permanent magnets—Minimum price fixing scheme—Technical pooling agreement—Research organisation established for all members—Benefit derived from research and price reductions passed to consumer—Whether removal of restrictions would 'deny' public substantial benefit 'resulting from' restrictions—Whether removal of restrictions would be likely to cause substantial reduction in volume of earnings of permanent magnet export business in relation to whole business of permanent magnet industry—Discounts to large buyers—New magnetic material not to be marketed except subject to approved terms—Whether restrictions reasonably required for purposes connected with maintenance of other restrictions accepted by parties—Restrictive Trade Practices Act 1956, s 21(1)(b), (f), (g). **Permanent Magnet Association's Agreement, Re** [1962] **2** 775, RPC.

         Maintenance of another restriction—Standard metal windows—Minimum price-fixing scheme—Exchange of information as to costing and technical efficiency—Whether restrictions resulted in lower costs and in lower prices to the public—Whether removal of restrictions would deny public substantial benefit—Whether restrictions reasonably required for purposes connected with maintenance of other restrictions accepted by parties—Restrictive Trade Practices Act 1956, s 21(1)(b), (g). **Standard Metal Window Group's Agreement, Re** [1962] **3** 210, RPC.

         Maintenance of exports—Carpet manufacturers—Price cum quality restriction—Wholesale dealings restrictions—Overseas trading restrictions—No sales to be made direct to consumer buyers other than buying agencies—Whether removal of restrictions would deny public substantial benefit—Whether removal of restrictions would be likely to cause substantial reduction in volume of earnings of carpet trade export business in relation to whole business of carpet trade—Restrictive Trade Practices Act 1956, s 21(1)(b), (f). **Federation of British Carpet Manufacturers' Agreement, Re** [1960] **1** 356, RPC.

         Maintenance of exports—Linoleum manufacturers—Minimum price and discount scheme—Whether removal of restrictions would deny public substantial benefit—Whether removal of restrictions would be likely to cause substantial reduction in volume or earnings of linoleum export business in relation to whole business of linoleum industry—Restrictive Trade Practices Act 1956, s 21(1)(b), (f). **Linoleum Manufacturers' Association's Agreement, Re** [1961] **2** 897, RPC.

         Motor vehicles distribution scheme—Price fixing scheme—Fixed retail prices—Condition as to appointing distributors of vehicles—Fixed discounts—Introductory commission—Sales to fleet users—Whether restrictions 'reasonably necessary'—Whether removal of restrictions would deny public substantial benefit—Restrictive Trade Practices Act 1956, s 21(1)(a), (b). **Motor Vehicles Distribution Scheme Agreement, Re** [1961] **1** 161, RPC.

         Net Book Agreement—Retail price maintenance without collective price fixing—Whether removal of restrictions would deny public 'specific' and 'substantial' benefits which they would otherwise enjoy 'by virtue of' the restrictions—Direct or remoter cause—Removal of restrictions conceded to end price maintenance—Consequences on book prices by reason of effect on stockholding booksellers—Probable increase in difficulty of obtaining publication of cultural works—Restrictive Trade Practices Act 1956, s 21(1)(b), (f), (g). **Net Book Agreement 1957, Re** [1962] **3** 751, RPC.

         Newspaper supplies—London daily newspapers—Newsagents' permits—Agreement not to supply newspapers to wholesale newsagents except on terms that newspapers supplied only to retail newsagents holding permits—Permits issued by association of newspaper proprietors—Whether removal of restriction would deny public substantial benefit—Restrictive Trade Practices Act 1956, s 21(1)(b). **Newspaper Proprietors' Association Ltd and National Federation of Retail Newsagents, Booksellers and Stationers, Agreement between, Re** [1961] **3** 428, RPC.

         Phenol Producers' Association—Agreement not to sell except at prices fixed by Association—Whether removal of restriction would deny public substantial benefit—Restrictive Trade Practices Act 1956, s 21(1)(b). **Phenol Producers' Associations' Agreement, Re** [1960] **2** 128, RPC.

         Prevention of unemployment—Yarn Spinners' Agreement—Minimum price scheme—Whether removal of restriction would deny public substantial benefit—Whether removal of restriction would be likely to have serious and persistent adverse effect on general level of unemployment in area—Restrictive Trade Practices Act 1956, s 21(1)(b), (e). **Yarn Spinners' Agreement, Re** [1959] **1** 299, RPC.

         Reasonably necessary to counteract monopoly—Maintenance of exports—Transformers—Price restrictions—Whether all restrictions could be grouped together for purposes of one paragraph of s 21(1) while one restriction was taken severally for purposes of another paragraph—'Earnings' of export business meant gross earnings—Quantitative standard of preponderance of preponderant buyer based on United Kingdom market—Whether removal of restrictions would deny public substantial benefit—Whether restriction reasonably necessary to enable members to negotiate fair terms for supply of goods to preponderant buyer—Whether removal of restrictions would be likely to cause substantial reduction in volume or earnings of export business—Restrictive Trade Practices Act 1956, s 21(1)(b), (d), (f). **Associated Transformer Manufacturers' Agreement, Re** [1961] **2** 233, RPC.

         Reasonably necessary to counteract monopoly—Maintenance of exports—Water-Tube Boilermakers' Association—Scheme for allotting contracts among members—Whether removal of restriction would deny public substantial benefit—Whether restriction reasonably necessary to enable members to negotiate fair terms for supply of goods to preponderant buyer—Whether removal of restriction would be likely to cause substantial reduction in the volume or earnings of the export business—Restrictive Trade Practices Act 1956, s 21(1)(b), (d), (f). **Water-Tube Boilermaker's Association's Agreement, Re** [1959] **3** 257, RPC.

RESTRICTIVE TRADE PRACTICES (cont)—
  Justification of restriction (cont)—
    Specific and substantial benefit to public (cont)—
      Steel—Heavy steel—Maximum prices of heavy steel products fixed by statutory board—
      Recommendations that maximum prices should normally be selling prices—Whether ending of
      recommendations would deny public substantial benefit—Restrictive Trade Practices Act 1956,
      s 21(1)(b), (f), (g). **British Heavy Steel Makers' Agreement, Re** [1964] **2** 916, RPC.
      Tyre trade—Car tyres and giant tyres supplied as replacements—Register of traders providing
      specified facilities for the fitting of tyres—Agreement not to offer or supply tyres at price reduced
      by trade terms to non-registered traders—Agreement not to offer or supply tyres at price reduced
      by trade terms to registered traders except in respect of types of tyre for which
      registered—Whether restriction reasonably necessary to protect public against injury by
      accidents resulting from tyre failures—Restrictive Trade Practices Act 1956, s 21(1)(a). **Tyre Trade**
      Register Agreement, Re [1963] **1** 890, RPC.
      Waste paper—Purchase from local authorities—Recommended minimum price guarantee—
      Whether removal of restriction would deny public substantial benefit—Restrictive Trade Practices
      Act 1956, s 21(1)(b). **British Paper and Board Makers' Association (Inc), Re an agreement between**
      the members of [1963] **2** 417, RPC.
      Wholesale Confectioners' Alliance of Great Britain and Northern Ireland—Recommendations as to
      price fixing schemes—Recommendation as to maximum prices to be paid by wholesalers to
      manufacturers—Comparable trade re-selling price rates by wholesalers to retailers—Whether
      removal of restrictions would deny public substantial benefit—Restrictive Trade Practices Act
      1956, s 21(1)(b). **Wholesale Confectioners' Alliance of GB and Northern Ireland's Agreement, Re**
      [1961] **1** 116, RPC.
  Presumption as to the public interest—
    Justification of restriction. *See* Justification of restriction, *above.*
  Reference—
    Burden of proof—
      Trade association recommendation, not clause in agreement, constituting restriction—Restrictive
      Trade Practices Act 1956, ss 6(7), 21(1). **Bakers' (Federation of Wholesale and Multiple)**
      Agreement, Re [1960] **1** 227, RPC.
    Costs—
      Discovery—Suppression of documents—Lump sum awarded—Restrictive Practices Court Rules
      1957 (SI 1957 No 603), rr 76, 77. **Motor Vehicles Distribution Scheme Agreement, Re** [1961] **1** 161,
      RPC.
      Refusal of registrar to make representation to Board of Trade that particulars of agreement of no
      substantial economic significance while proceedings pending—Whether unreasonable conduct—
      Restrictive Practices Rules 1957 (SI 1957 No 603), r 76. **British Waste Paper Association and**
      British Paper and Board Makers Association (Inc), Re, Agreement between [1963] **2** 424, RPC.
    Exemption, for—
      Resale price maintenance. *See* Resale price maintenance—Reference for exemption, *below.*
  Registration of agreement—
    Agreement between members of association not to consent to cancellation or variation of contracts
    without consent—
      Whether registrable—Restrictive Trade Practices Act 1956, s 6(1)(a)(c). **Blanket Manufacturers'**
      Association's Agreement, Re [1959] **2** 630, CA.
    Agreement confirming privileges or benefits only on parties complying with restrictive conditions—
      Agreement imposing obligations on parties not complying with such conditions—Parties—
      Agreement conferring privilege or benefit or imposing obligation only on one party—Whether
      registrable agreement—Restrictive Trade Practices Act 1956, s 6(4). **Cadbury Schweppes Ltd's**
      Agreement, Re [1975] **2** 307, RPC.
    Agreement imposing obligation to make payments calculated by reference to quantity of goods
    supplied—
      Profits pooling scheme—Obligation on members to pay into pool excess of levy over share of
      pool—Levy imposed on goods supplied by members to government departments—Amount of
      levy a fixed percentage of the weighted marginal cost of goods supplied by all members
      multiplied by the quantity of goods supplied by the member—Each member entitled to fixed
      share of pool—Whether registrable agreement—Restrictive Trade Practices Act 1956, s 6(5).
      Linoleum Manufacturers' Association's Agreement, Re [1963] **3** 221, Ch D.
    Agreement related to Crown agreement—
      Telephone manufacturers' agreement for equal division of business offered by the
      Postmaster-General—Manufacturers' agreement consequent on a Crown agreement between the
      manufacturers and the Postmaster-General—Postmaster-General agreeing by Crown agreement
      to order from manufacturer notified by committee appointed by the manufacturers—
      Manufacturers' agreement providing for allocation of orders and the putting forward of the
      selected manufacturer's name—Whether manufacturers' agreement contained new restrictions
      not in Crown agreement—Whether two agreements complementary and manufacturers'
      agreement outside scope of Act, as Crown not bound by Act—Restrictive Trade Practices Act
      1956, ss 6(1), 9(1). **Automatic Telephone & Electric Co Ltd's Application, Re** [1963] **2** 302, CA.
    Agreement relating to services—
      Agreement—Trading nexus between parties—Leases—Lease of business premises—Covenants in
      underleases containing restrictions on use, transfer and assignment of premises—Covenant to
      pay service charge to lessor—Lessor providing services of maintenance and cleaning for
      lessees—No trading nexus between lessor and lessees—Whether leases 'agreements'—Whether
      registrable agreements—Fair Trading Act 1973, s 107(1)—Restrictive Trade Practices (Services)
      Order 1976 (SI 1976 No 98), art 3(1). **Ravenseft Properties Ltd v Director General of Fair Trading**
      [1977] **1** 47, QBD.
    Arrangement—
      Marketing company owned by eight steel manufacturers—Separate similar agreements by
      manufacturers with company for marketing through company—Arrangement between steel
      manufacturers presumed from communications before the separate agreements were
      sealed—Restrictive Trade Practices Act 1956, s 6(1)(3). **British Basic Slag Ltd's Agreements, Re**
      [1963] **2** 807, CA.

RESTRICTIVE TRADE PRACTICES (cont)—
    Registration of agreement (cont)—
        Boundary agreement—
            Agreement by two co-operative societies not to accept members on other side of demarcation line—Whether a restriction—Restrictive Trade Practices Act 1956, s 6(1). **Doncaster Co-op Society Ltd's and Retford Co-op Society Ltd's Agreement, Re** [1960] 3 541, RPC.
        Excepted agreements—
            Agreement between two manufacturers to market citrus fruit drink concentrates through subsidiary of one of them—Agreement including supply and user agreements—Supply agreement between manufacturers and subsidiary—Whether manufacturers and its subsidiary 'single person' as 'inter-connected bodies corporate'—Whether permissible to extract supply and user parts of agreement and apply respective exemptions—Restrictive Trade Practices Act 1956, ss 7(2), 8(3), (7), (9). **Schweppes Ltd's Agreement, Re (No 2)** [1971] 2 1473, Ch D.
            Agreement for the supply of goods—Agreements between motor manufacturers and dealers—Bipartite agreements substituted for former multipartite agreements—Whether former agreements to be taken into consideration in interpreting new agreements—Restrictive Trade Practices Act 1956, ss 6(3), 7(2), 8(3). **Austin Motor Co Ltd's Agreements, Re** [1957] 3 62, Ch D.
            Agreement for the supply of goods—Exclusive supply agreement containing non-competition clause—Party undertaking not to sell goods by way of retail to supplier's customers—Party breaching agreement by obtaining supplies elsewhere but claiming agreement void because it had not been registered—Whether non-competition clause relating exclusively to goods supplied in pursuance of agreement—Whether agreement containing restrictions in respect of sale, or acquisition for sale, of other goods of same description—Whether agreement exempted from registration—Restrictive Trade Practices Act 1976, ss 6(1), 9(3)(7), Sch 3, para 2. **MD Foods plc (formerly Associated Dairies Ltd) v Baines** [1997] 1 833, HL.
            Agreement for the supply of goods—Whether including agreement containing agreements on other related or unrelated matters—Restrictive Trade Practices Act 1956, s 7(2). **Schweppes Ltd's Agreement, Re (No 2)** [1971] 2 1473, Ch D.
            Agreement for the supply of goods—Whether including agreement whereby other purposes also achieved—Restrictive Trade Practices Act 1956, ss 7(2), 8(3). **Cadbury Schweppes Ltd's Agreement, Re** [1975] 2 307, RPC.
        Restriction in respect of description of goods to be produced—
            Agreement not to produce copy of existing design—Whether restriction on descriptions of goods to be produced—Restrictive Trade Practices Act 1956, s 6(1)(c). **British Furniture Manufacturers Federated Associations' Agreement, Re** [1967] 1 465, RPC.
            Waste paper suppliers—Schedule of standard descriptions—Standard descriptions not to preclude special arrangements for any special quality or description of waste paper—'Descriptions'—Waste paper to be free from waxed paper or waxed board and from all unsuitable contraries except by special arrangement—Whether restrictions—Whether removal of restrictions would deny public substantial benefit—Restrictive Trade Practices Act 1956, ss 6(1)(b)(c), 21(1)(b). **British Waste Paper Association and British Paper and Board Makers Association (Inc), Re, Agreement between** [1963] 2 424, RPC.
        Restriction on prices to be charged—
            Agreement not to offer to supply goods in response to an invitation to tender until after discussions with other persons invited to tender—Whether a restriction in respect of the prices to be quoted—Whether a registrable agreement—Restrictive Trade Practices Act 1956, s 6(1)(a). **Electrical Installations at Exeter Hospital Agreement, Re** [1971] 1 347, RPC.
        Restriction on production—
            Exception—Restriction relating exclusively to goods supplied—Agreement by producer of citrus fruit drink concentrates to buy from another producer specified percentage of concentrates each year—Purchasing producer agreeing to compensate other producer if less than specified percentage ordered—Whether producer accepting restriction on production—Whether restriction relating exclusively to goods supplied—Restrictive Trade Practices Act 1956, ss 6(1)(3)(4), 7(2), 8(3). **Cadbury Schweppes Ltd's Agreement, Re** [1975] 2 307, RPC.
        Restriction on production, supply or acquisition of goods—
            Negative obligation implied from positive clause—Marketing company owned by eight steel manufacturers—Agreements with own members—Undertaking by marketing company to acquire members' basic slag and apportion sales fairly between them—No obligation on marketing company to acquire more basic slag than it could dispose of—Implied restriction on purchase from other members—Restrictive Trade Practices Act 1956, s 6(1)(c). **British Basic Slag Ltd's Agreements, Re** [1963] 2 807, CA.
        Time for registration—
            Failure to register within prescribed time—Consequences—Members of company operating from 1957 registrable agreement without registering it—Members failing to comply with later statutory requirement to register within prescribed time—Company subsequently voluntarily furnishing registrar with particulars of agreement—Agreement registered—One of members then taking steps to uncover and register any other restrictive agreement to which a party—Registrar seeking injunction restraining members from giving effect to or enforcing other unregistered registrable agreements—Necessity for injunction—Restrictive Trade Practices Act 1968, ss 6, 7. **Flushing Cistern Makers Ltd's Agreement, Re** [1973] 3 817, RPC.
        Trade association recommendation—
            Building traders' association—Standard forms of contract—Bills of quantities—Daywork charges—Recommendations and rules of association concerning use of forms, against tendering for contracts without bills of quantities, against submitting priced bills of quantities with tenders, and for use of standard schedules of daywork charges—Whether restrictions within Restrictive Trade Practices Act 1956, s 6(1)(5). **Birmingham Association of Building Trades Employers Agreement, Re** [1963] 2 361, RPC.
            Continuance of terms of trading—Resolution after date of reference for continuance by individual arrangements—Whether resolution a recommendation within Restrictive Trade Practices Act 1956, s 6(7). **Federation of British Carpet Manufacturers' Agreement, Re** [1960] 1 356, RPC.
            Recommendation by trade association requiring indemnity to be taken—Terms of indemnity left to individual members—Whether a specific restriction—Restrictive Trade Practices Act 1956, s 6(7). **Finance Houses Association Ltd's Agreement, Re** [1965] 3 509, RPC.

RESTRICTIVE TRADE PRACTICES (cont)—
Registration of agreement (cont)—
Trade association recommendation (cont)—
Specific recommendation—Action in relation to particular class of goods—Recommendation by newsagents' federation—Recommendation to boycott particular newspaper to make stand against reduction of profit margins by proprietors—Class of goods to which recommendation related—Matter in respect of which specific recommendation made—Form of order of court—Factors to be considered—Restrictive Practices Act 1956, ss 6(7), 20(3)(4). **National Federation of Retail Newsagents, Booksellers and Stationers' Agreement, Re (No 5)** [1973] **3** 283, RPC.
Specific recommendation—Action in relation to particular class of goods—Recommendation by newsagents' federation—Recommendation to boycott particular newspaper to make stand against reduction of profit margins by proprietors—Whether recommendation in relation to 'particular class of goods' wider than the class of goods directly affected—Restrictive Trade Practices Act 1956, s 6(7). **National Federation of Retail Newsagents, Booksellers and Stationers v Registrar of Restrictive Trading Agreements (Nos 3 & 4)** [1972] **2** 1269, HL.
Specific recommendation—Number of specific recommendations—Recommendations by newsagents' federation to boycott various publications—Whether recommendations capable of being considered collectively—Restrictive Trade Practices Act 1956, s 6(7). **National Federation of Retail Newsagents, Booksellers and Stationers v Registrar of Restrictive Trading Agreements (Nos 3 & 4)** [1972] **2** 1269, HL.
Removal of particulars from register of agreements of no economic significance—
Effect—
British Steel Founders' Association—Determination of certain restrictions before reference—Guidance prices restrictions declared contrary to policy interest, and undertaking given—Ancillary restrictions removed from register in pursuance of directions of Board of Trade—Whether court should make order as regards the ancillary restrictions—Restrictive Trade Practices Act 1956, ss 12(1), 20(1). **British Steel Founders' Association's Agreement, Re** [1963] **2** 530, RPC.
Powers of Board of Trade—
British Constructional Steelwork Association—Determination of price fixing scheme after reference by registrar—Remainder of agreement of no substantial economic significance—Representation by registrar to Board of Trade—Removal from register—Restrictive Trade Practices Act 1956, s 12(1). **British Constructional Steelwork Association's Agreement, Re** [1959] **1** 428, RPC.
Resale price maintenance—
Individual enforcement by legal proceedings of conditions as to resale prices—
Exceptions to individual enforcement—Acquisition of goods otherwise than for purpose of resale in course of business—Goods obtained by retailer from liquidator of purchasing company and sold below current list price of manufacturer—Whether resale within exemption from enforceability of condition—Meaning of 'acquire'—Restrictive Trade Practices Act 1956, s 25(2). **Mackintosh (John) & Sons Ltd v Baker's Bargain Stores (Seaford) Ltd** [1965] **3** 412, Vacation Ct.
Injunction against sale by retailer below fixed price—Notice of the condition relating to price—What constitutes notice—Restrictive Trade Practices Act 1956, s 25(1). **Goodyear Tyre and Rubber Co (GB) Ltd v Lancashire Batteries Ltd** [1958] **3** 7, CA.
Injunction against sale by retailer below fixed price—Purchase of article by retailer before operation of statute—Whether statute having retrospective effect—Restrictive Trade Practices Act 1956, s 25(1). **Dunlop Rubber Co Ltd v Longlife Battery Depot (a firm)** [1958] **3** 197, Ch D.
Injunction against sale by retailer below fixed price—Retail price of soft drink listed as '2s6d plus 3d' charge, refundable, on bottle—Property in bottle not intended to pass to customer—Correct retail price of drink in bottle, 2s6d, and 3d charge for hire of bottle—Restrictive Trade Practices Act 1956, s 25(1). **Beecham Foods Ltd v North Supplies (Edmonton) Ltd** [1959] **2** 336, Ch D.
Injunction against sale by retailer below fixed price—Whether goods acquired with notice of the condition—Restrictive Trade Practices Act 1956, s 25(1), (4). **County Laboratories Ltd v Mindel (J) Ltd** [1957] **1** 806, Ch D.
Injunction—Exemption pending reference under Resale Prices Act 1964—Whether injunction would be granted—Restrictive Trade Practices Act 1956, s 25(2)—Resale Prices Act 1964, s 6(3). **EMI Records Ltd v Morris** [1965] **2** 781, Ch D.
Interlocutory injunction—
Mandatory in form. *See* **Injunction** (Interlocutory—Mandatory injunction—Injunction mandatory in substance—Injunction to restrain unlawful withholding of supplies under Resale Prices Act 1964).
Proceedings before Restrictive Practices Court—
Practice—Directions—Preliminary application—Affidavit evidence—Restrictive Practices Court (Resale Prices) Rules 1965 (SI 1965 No 236), rr 9, 10, 12. **Practice Direction** [1966] **1** 544, RPC.
Reference for exemption—
Chocolate and sugar confectionery—Prospective price increase—Prospective disappearance of outlets for retail sales—Burden and standard of proof—Whether case for exemption of goods established—Resale Prices Act 1964, s 5(2)(a), (b), (c) and (e). **Chocolate and Sugar Confectionery Resale Price Reference, Re** [1967] **3** 261, RPC.
Footwear—Power of court to exempt classes of goods—Resale Prices Act 1964, s 5(1). **Footwear Reference, Re** [1965] **2** 858, RPC.
Footwear—Price cutting—Possible increases in retailers margins leading to increased prices—Resale Prices Act 1964, s 5(2)(c). **Footwear Resale Price Reference, Re** [1968] **3** 129, RPC.
Medicaments—Ethical products obtained on prescription—Proprietary medicines sold over the counter—Chemists dependent on wholesalers for frequent deliveries—Market for ethical products not affected by commercial considerations—Price of ethicals fixed by voluntary price regulation scheme—Profits on fast-moving ethicals partially subsidising sales of slower-moving ethicals—Fear of chemists being put out of business—Ethicals within power of exemption only to extent of supply under private prescription—Resale Prices Act 1964, s 5(2)(a), (b), (e). **Medicaments Reference, Re (No 2)** [1971] **1** 12, RPC.
Withholding of supplies—
Presumption that supplies withheld by supplier because of price cutting by dealer—Whether supplier entitled to show other grounds for withholding supplies—Resale Prices Act 1964, ss 2(4), 4(4). **Oxford Printing Co Ltd v Letraset Ltd** [1970] **2** 815, Ch D.

RESTRICTIVE TRADE PRACTICES (cont)—
Resale price maintenance (cont)—
Withholding of supplies (cont)—
Withholding on ground that dealer likely to sell goods below resale price—Whether withholding by suppliers on ground that dealer had advertised goods at 'cut prices' unlawful—Resale Prices Act 1964, s 2(1)(b). **Comet Radiovision Services Ltd v Farnell-Tandberg Ltd** [1971] **3** 230, Ch D.
Restraint of trade by agreement. See **Restraint of trade by agreement.**
Restriction declared contrary to public interest—
Order restraining persons giving effect to restriction or making other agreement to like effect—
Certain members of association refusing to be so represented or to take part in the proceedings—Undertaking by consent from members represented and appearing—Whether registrar entitled to injunction against dissenting members—Restrictive Trade Practices Act 1956, s 20(3)(a), (b)—Restrictive Practices Court Rules 1957 (SI 1957 No 603), r 23. **Inc National Association of British and Irish Millers Ltd's Scheme, Re** [1959] **2** 780, RPC.
Form of order—Whether trade association should be included in order restraining the enforcing of the restrictions or making new agreement with like restrictions—Whether trade association 'carrying on business'—Restrictive Trade Practices Act 1956, ss 6(1), 20(3). **Wholesale Confectioners' Alliance of GB and Northern Ireland's Agreement, Re (No 2)** [1961] **2** 8, RPC.
Grant of injunction—Whether injunction granted as of course where restrictions declared contrary to public interest—Restrictive Trade Practices Act 1956, s 20(3). **Chemists' Federation, Re the agreement between the members of** [1958] **3** 448, RPC.
New agreement to like effect—Whether members of trade associations should be restrained from enforcing restrictions or making new agreement with like effect—Restrictive Trade Practices Act 1956, s 20(3). **Tyre Trade Register Agreement, Re** [1963] **1** 890, RPC.
Party enjoined—Whether trade federation should be included in order restraining the enforcing of the restrictions or making new agreement with like restrictions—Whether Federation, a registered trade union whose members were retail newsagents, was 'carrying on business'—Restrictive Trade Practices Act 1956, s 20(3). **Newspaper Proprietors' Association Ltd and National Federation of Retail Newsagents, Booksellers and Stationers, Agreement between, Re** [1961] **3** 428, RPC.
Persons not represented—Whether injunction should be granted. **Birmingham Association of Building Trades Employers Agreement, Re** [1963] **2** 361, RPC.
Order restraining trade association or members making recommendation—
Form of order—Scope of recommendations restrained—Restrictive Trade Practices Act 1956, ss 6(7), 20(4). **Wholesale Confectioners' Alliance of GB and Northern Ireland's Agreement, Re (No 2)** [1961] **2** 8, RPC.
Restriction of agreement—
Excepted agreements—
Discovery—Proceedings for declarations that agreements not registrable—Application by registrar for discovery of documents relating to question for what purpose agreements made—Restrictive Trade Practices Act 1956, ss 8(3)(4), 13(2). **Automatic Telephone and Electric Co Ltd's Agreement, Re** [1965] **1** 206, CA.
Restrictions accepted by parties to agreement—
Damages for breach—
Parties entering agreement containing restrictive covenants as to competition, solicitation and use of confidential information—Judge finding defendants in breach and giving claimant option to elect for damages based on reasonable amount for release—Court of Appeal dismissing defendants' appeal—Whether judge and Court of Appeal in error. **One Step (Support) Ltd v Morris-Garner** [2018] **2 Comm** 769, SC; [2018] **3** 659, SC.
Parties entering agreement containing restrictive covenants as to competition, solicitation and use of confidential information—Judge finding defendants in breach and giving claimant option to elect for damages based on reasonable amount for release—Whether judge in error. **One Step (Support) Ltd v Morris-Garner** [2017] **2** 262, CA.
Restrictions—
Covenants in lease—Covenants negative in form—Covenants not requiring lessee to give up any right or freedom which he had before going into possession of premises—Whether covenants containing 'restrictions'—Fair Trading Act 1973, s 107(1)—Restrictive Trade Practices (Services) Order 1976 (SI 1976 No 98), art 3(1). **Ravenseft Properties Ltd v Director General of Fair Trading** [1977] **1** 47, QBD.
Undertaking—
Breach of undertaking—
Contempt of court. See Contempt of court—Breach of undertaking given to court, above.
Waste paper—Report of government working party recommending that waste paper contracts be a matter for individual negotiation and that an advisory organisation be set up—Whether implementation of report would involve breach of undertakings. **British Waste Paper Association and British Paper and Board Makers' Association (Inc) Agreement Re, (No 2)** [1966] **3** 836, RPC.
Form—
Adaptation to each particular case—Incorporation in formal order—Example of undertaking for, among other purposes, facilitating the Registrar's duties under Restrictive Trade Practices Act 1956, s 22. **Permanent Magnet Association's Agreement, Re** [1963] **1** 130, RPC.
Restrictions agreed to be contrary to the public interest—Application by registrar for injunction—Form of undertaking by respondents—Restrictive Trade Practices Act 1956, s 20(3). **British Constructional Steelwork Association's Agreement, Re** [1959] **1** 428, RPC.
Variation of decision of court—
Leave to make application—
Leave granted where prima facie evidence of a material change in the relevant circumstances—Evidence—Applicant making submission as to economic consequences of course of action—Applicant not adducing evidence of economist—Whether evidence of economist essential—Restrictive Trade Practices Act 1956, s 22(4). **Cement Makers' Federation's Agreement, Re** [1974] **2** 219, RPC.

RESULTING TRUST
Generally. See **Trust and trustee** (Resulting trust).

RESULTING TRUST (cont)—
Settlement—
Disposition—
Absolute gift or resulting trust. *See* **Settlement** (Disposition—Resulting trust).

RETAIL PRICE MAINTENANCE
Petrol filling station—
Solus agreement—
Implied term. *See* **Contract** (Implied term—Retail price maintenance—Petrol filling station—Solus agreement).

RETAINER
Right of—
Executor and administrator. *See* **Executor and administrator** (Retainer).
Solicitor. *See* **Solicitor** (Retainer).

RETAINING FEE
Availability for work. *See* **Employment** (Contract of service—Retaining fee).

RETAINING LIEN
Solicitor. *See* **Solicitor** (Lien—Retaining lien).

RETENTION OF PROPERTY
Property relevant to criminal proceedings—
Police powers. *See* **Police** (Powers—Power to retain property relevant to criminal proceedings).

RETIREMENT
Benefit, loss of—
Damages under Fatal Accidents Acts. *See* **Fatal accident** (Damages—Dependency—Widow—Loss of retirement benefit).
Compensation—
London government employee. *See* **London** (Local government—Employee—Retirement compensation).
Discrimination against a woman—
Provision in relation to retirement. *See* **Employment** (Discrimination against a woman—Provision in relation to retirement).
Discrimination on grounds of age—
European Union. *See* **European Union** (Employment—Equal treatment in employment and occupation—Dismissal—Discrimination on grounds of age).
Disposal of business—
Capital gains tax—
Relief. *See* **Capital gains tax** (Exemptions and reliefs—Disposal of business on retirement).
Pension—
Generally. *See* **Pension**.
State pension—
Generally. *See* **Social security** (Retirement pension).
Overpayment—Recovery. *See* **Social security** (Benefit—Overpayment—Recovery—Pension).
Unfair dismissal—
Restriction on right not to be unfairly dismissed—
Employee reaching normal retiring age or specified age. *See* **Unfair dismissal** (Right not to be unfairly dismissed—Restriction on right where employee reaches normal retiring age or specified age).

RETRIAL
Criminal proceedings—
Appeal—
No miscarriage of justice. *See* **Criminal law** (Appeal—No miscarriage of justice—Retrial).
Generally. *See* **Criminal law** (Trial—Retrial).
Indictment—
Amendment. *See* **Indictment** (Amendment—Retrial).

RETROSPECTIVE OPERATION
Confirmatory faculty—
Ecclesiastical law. *See* **Ecclesiastical law** (Faculty—Confirmatory faculty—Effect—Retrospective effect).
Maintenance order—
Power of court to vary order retrospectively. *See* **Husband and wife** (Variation or discharge of maintenance order—Power of court—Power to order retrospective variation).
Rent review. *See* **Landlord and tenant** (Rent—Review—Retrospective operation).
Statute—
Generally. *See* **Statute** (Retrospective operation).
Income tax. *See* **Income tax** (Statute—Retrospective operation).

RETROSPECTIVE PUNISHMENT
Human rights legislation. *See* **Human rights** (Retrospective punishment).

RETURN
Habeas corpus. *See* **Habeas corpus** (Return to writ).
Income tax. *See* **Income tax** (Return).
Value added tax—
Assessment in default of proper returns by taxpayer. *See* **Value added tax** (Assessment in default of proper returns by taxpayer).
Responsibility for making return. *See* **Value added tax** (Return).

RETURN DATE
    Masters' summonses—
        Chambers proceedings—
            Queen's Bench Division. *See* **Practice** (Chambers proceedings—Masters' summonses—Queen's Bench Division—Return dates).

RETURNING OFFICER
    Local government election—
        Determination of returning officer—
            Validity of nomination papers. *See* **Elections** (Local government—Nomination papers—Particulars to be given on nomination paper—Duty of returning officer to declare paper invalid where particulars not as required by law).
        Rejection of nomination papers—
            Particulars not as required by law—Names of candidates. *See* **Elections** (Local government—Nomination papers—Names of candidates—Particulars not as required by law—Rejection of papers by returning officer).

REUNIFICATION
    Family—
        European Community. *See* **European Union** (Immigration—Family reunification of minor children of third country nationals—Directive on right to family reunification).

REVENUE
    Appeal—
        Hearing on Northern or North Eastern Circuit—
            Practice. *See* **Practice** (Chancery Division—Northern Area—Appeals—Insolvency and revenue appeals).
    Business tax—
        Canada. *See* **Canada** (Business tax).
    Capital gains tax. *See* **Capital gains tax**.
    Capital transfer tax. *See* **Capital transfer tax**.
    Cheating the public revenue. *See* **Criminal law** (Cheating the public revenue).
    Contract of service—
        Contract calculated to deceive revenue authorities. *See* **Employment** (Contract of service—Legality).
    Corporation profits tax—
        Hong Kong. *See* **Hong Kong** (Corporation profits tax).
    Customs. *See* **Customs and excise**.
    Death duty—
        New South Wales. *See* **New South Wales** (Death duty).
        Payment of. *See* **Will** (Payment of death duties).
    Entertainment duty. *See* **Entertainment duty**.
    Estate duty—
        Australia. *See* **Australia** (Estate duty).
        Generally. *See* **Estate duty**.
        New Zealand. *See* **New Zealand** (Estate duty).
    Excess profits tax. *See* **Excess profits tax**.
    Excise duty—
        Generally. *See* **Customs and excise**.
        Motor vehicle. *See* **Road traffic** (Excise licence—Rate of duty).
    Foreign law—
        Enforcement. *See* **Conflict of laws** (Foreign law—Revenue law—Enforcement).
        Recognition. *See* **Conflict of laws** (Foreign law—Recognition—Revenue law).
    Gaming licence. *See* **Gaming** (Gaming licence).
    Income tax—
        Australia. *See* **Australia** (Income tax).
        Canada. *See* **Canada** (Income tax).
        Ceylon. *See* **Ceylon** (Income tax).
        Generally. *See* **Income tax**.
        New Zealand. *See* **New Zealand** (Income tax).
    Inheritance tax—
        Generally. *See* **Inheritance tax**.
        Probate. *See* **Probate** (Inheritance tax).
    Legacy duty—
        New South Wales. *See* **New South Wales** (Legacy duty).
    Local taxation licences. *See* **Local government** (Local taxation licences).
    National defence contribution. *See* **National defence contribution**.
    National savings. *See* **National savings**.
    Pool betting duty. *See* **Gaming** (Pool betting).
    Profits tax. *See* **Profits tax**.
    Purchase tax. *See* **Purchase tax**.
    Rates. *See* **Rates**.
    Receipt in full settlement—
        Re-opening of accounts. *See* **Mistake** (Payment subject to deduction of tax—Receipt in full settlement).
    Reports of cases—
        Citation. *See* **Practice** (Citation of cases—Reports—Revenue cases).
    Sales tax—
        Canada. *See* **Canada** (Sales tax).
    Scottish decision—
        Conformity. *See* **Precedent** (Scottish decision—Conformity—Revenue and taxation matters).
    Selective employment tax. *See* **Selective employment tax**.
    Stamp duty. *See* **Stamp duty**.
    Succession duty—
        Canada. *See* **Canada** (Succession duty).

REVENUE (cont)—
    Succession duty (cont)—
        Generally. *See* **Succession duty**.
    Value added tax—
        European Community. *See* **European Union** (Value added tax).
        Generally. *See* **Value added tax**.

REVENUE LIST
    See **Practice** (Chancery Division—Revenue list).

REVERSION
    Assignment—
        Breach of covenant to repair—
            Persons entitled to sue tenant. *See* **Landlord and tenant** (Repair—Landlord's covenant—Breach of covenant—Assignment of lease).
    Failure to repair premises—
        Diminution in value of reversion—
            Damages. *See* **Landlord and tenant** (Damages for failure to repair—Diminution in value of reversion).
    Flats—
        Disposal by landlord—
            Tenants' right to acquire reversion. *See* **Landlord and tenant** (Flats—Tenants' right to acquire landlord's reversion).
    Land—
        Generally. *See* **Land** (Reverter).
    Option to purchase—
        Enforcement—
            Option to purchase leasehold reversion. *See* **Option** (Option to purchase—Enforcement—Option to purchase leasehold reversion).
        Landlord and tenant. *See* **Landlord and tenant** (Lease—Reversion).
        Sale of land. *See* **Sale of land** (Leasehold interest—Option to purchase reversion).
    Sale—
        New South Wales. *See* **New South Wales** (Sale of reversion).
        Trustee, by. *See* **Variation of trusts** (Variation by the court—Administrative power—Sale of reversionary interest by trustees).
    School site—
        Conveyance under School Sites Acts. *See* **Education** (School—Conveyance under School Sites Acts—Reverter).
    Severance—
        Effect—
            Tenancy of business premises. *See* **Landlord and tenant** (Business premises—Continuation of tenancy—Severance of reversion).
        Notice to quit—
            Validity. *See* **Landlord and tenant** (Validity of notice to quit—Reversion severed—Notice as to severed part by owner of that part).
    Variation of settlement—
        Power of appointment upon petitioner's second marriage—
            Children's reversionary interest affected. *See* **Variation of Settlement (Matrimonial Causes)** (Power of appointment upon petitioner's second marriage—Children's reversionary interests affected).

REVIEW
    Benefits—
        National insurance—
            Review by Secretary of State. *See* **Social security** (Rates of benefit—Review by Secretary of State).
    Pre-trial review—
        Matrimonial causes—
            Defended causes—Directions for trial. *See* **Divorce** (Practice—Trial—Directions for trial—Defended causes—Pre-trial review).
    Rent. *See* **Landlord and tenant** (Rent—Review).
    Taxation of costs—
        Generally. *See* **Costs** (Taxation—Review of taxation).
        Legal aid proceedings. *See* **Legal aid** (Taxation of costs—Review of taxation).

REVOCABLE SETTLEMENT
    Income tax. *See* **Income tax** (Settlement—Revocable settlement).

REVOCATION
    Arbitrator's authority. *See* **Arbitration** (Arbitrator—Authority—Revocation).
    Committal order—
        Non-payment of judgment debt. *See* **Debt** (Non-payment of judgment debt—Committal—Order—Revocation).
    Destruction of will. *See* **Will** (Revocation—Destruction).
    Firearms certificate. *See* **Firearms** (Certificate—Revocation).
    Grant of administration—
        Intestacy. *See* **Intestacy** (Grant of administration—Revocation of grant).
    Leave to issue writ. *See* **Practice** (Leave on ex parte application—Revocation of leave).
    Licence—
        Hackney carriage. *See* **Road traffic** (Hackney carriage—Licence—Revocation of licence).
        Licence to enter premises. *See* **Licence** (Entry—Revocation of licence—Licence to enter premises).
        Licence to occupy premises. *See* **Licence** (Licence to occupy premises—Revocation).
    Maintenance order. *See* **Husband and wife** (Maintenance—Revocation of order).
    Planning permission. *See* **Town and country planning** (Permission for development—Revocation).

REVOCATION (cont)—

Power of appointment—
    Generally. *See* **Power of appointment** (Revocation).
    Rule against perpetuities. *See* **Rule against perpetuities** (Power of appointment—Power of revocation and new appointment).
Settlement—
    Power to revoke settlement—
        Implied release of power. *See* **Power** (Implied release—Settlement—Power to revoke settlement—Release of power).
Street trading licence. *See* **Street trading** (Licence—Revocation).
Will—
    Codicil—
        Revocation of bequest in will. *See* **Will** (Codicil—Revocation of bequest in will).
    Generally. *See* **Will** (Revocation).
    Revocation of English will by foreign will—
        Validity. *See* **Conflict of laws** (Will—Revocation—Validity).
    Revocatory clause—
        Construction. *See* **Will** (Construction—Revocatory clause).

REWARD

Bailment for reward—
    Generally. *See* **Bailment** (Bailment for reward).
    Sub-bailment for reward. *See* **Bailment** (Sub-bailment for reward).
Corruption—
    Offer of gift etc. *See* **Criminal law** (Corruption—Offer of gift, loan, fee etc—Reward).

RHODESIA

Northern Rhodesia. *See* **Rhodesia and Nyasaland**.
Southern Rhodesia. *See* **Southern Rhodesia**.
Stock transfer—
    Right to unpaid interest. *See* **Stock** (Transfer of stock—Rights transferred—Right to unpaid interest).

RHODESIA AND NYASALAND

Northern Rhodesia—
    Emergency legislation—
        Detention order—Regulation authorising governor to delegate 'powers' under emergency regulations—Whether regulation enabled governor to delegate duty of being satisfied of necessity to exercise power—Northern Rhodesia Emergency Power Regulations 1956, regs 16(1), 47. **Mungoni v A-G of Northern Rhodesia** [1960] **1** 446, PC.

RIFLE

Firearms certificate—
    Exemption—
        Shot gun—Smooth-bore gun with barrel not less than 24 inches in length—Rifle altered by removing rifling from barrel. *See* **Firearms** (Certificate—Exemption—Shot gun—Smooth-bore gun with barrel not less than 24 inches in length—Rifle altered by removing rifling from barrel).
    Extent of certificate—
        Whether covering telescopic sight. *See* **Firearms** (Certificate—Extent of certificate—Certificate for rifle).

RIGHT OF ACTION

Assignment—
    Equitable assignment. *See* **Chose in action** (Assignment—Equitable assignment—Right of action).
    Generally. *See* **Chose in action** (Assignment—Right of action).
    Trustee in bankruptcy—
        Power to assign right of action to bankrupt. *See* **Bankruptcy** (Trustee in bankruptcy—Power to assign right of action to bankrupt).
Concealment—
    Limitation of action. *See* **Limitation of action** (Concealment of right of action).
Fatal accident—
    Discontinuance. *See* **Fatal accident** (Action—Right of action—Action for damages for personal injury negligently discontinued after claimant's death).

RIGHT OF APPEAL

Criminal cases. *See* **Criminal law** (Appeal—Right of appeal).
Generally. *See* **Appeal** (Right of appeal).

RIGHT OF AUDIENCE

Court of Appeal. *See* **Court of Appeal** (Right of audience).
Generally. *See* **Practice** (Audience—Right of audience).
House of Lords. *See* **House of Lords** (Right of audience).
Litigant in person—
    Application for certiorari. *See* **Certiorari** (Application—Right of audience—Litigant in person).
    Court of Appeal. *See* **Court of Appeal** (Right of audience—Litigant in person).
Solicitor—
    Crown Court. *See* **Crown Court** (Practice—Solicitor—Right of audience).
    Generally. *See* **Practice** (Audience—Right of audience).
    Patent proceedings. *See* **Patent** (Practice—Telephone summonses).
Trade union official. *See* **Trade union** (Legal proceedings—Right of audience in High Court and Court of Appeal—Appearance by trade union official).

RIGHT OF COMMON

Generally. *See* **Commons** (Right of common).

RIGHT OF COMMON (cont)—
    Registration. *See* **Commons** (Registration).

RIGHT OF ENTRY
    Constable—
        Licensed premises. *See* **Intoxicating liquor** (Licensed premises—Constable—Right of entry).
    Drainage board—
        Generally. *See* **Land drainage** (Drainage board—Right of entry on land).
        Right of appeal. *See* **Appeal** (Right of appeal).
    Enforcement notice. *See* **Town and country planning** (Enforcement notice—Entry consequent on steps required by notice not being taken).
    Execution of civil process by bailiff. *See* **County court** (Execution—Bailiff—Entry).
    Forcible entry. *See* **Criminal law** (Forcible entry and detainer).
    Gas board. *See* **Gas** (Gas board—Powers of entry for purposes of inspection).
    Immigrant—
        Generally. *See* **Immigration**.
    Land—
        Breach of covenant. *See* **Land** (Estates or interests capable of subsisting at law—Rights of entry exercisable over or in respect of a legal term of years absolute—Right of entry on breach of covenant).
    National insurance inspector. *See* **Social security** (Inspector—Power to enter premises liable to inspection).
    Police—
        Power to enter private premises and remove instrument of crime. *See* **Police** (Right of search—Right of search and seizure—Entry to private premises).
        Power to enter private premises to effect arrest. *See* **Arrest** (Arrest without warrant—Constable—Power to enter (if need be by force) place to effect arrest).

RIGHT OF RE-ENTRY
    Generally. *See* **Landlord and tenant** (Relief against forfeiture—Right of re-entry).
    Lease—
        Assignment. *See* **Sale of land** (Leasehold interest—Right of re-entry).
        Generally. *See* **Landlord and tenant** (Relief against forfeiture—Right of re-entry).

RIGHT OF WAY
    Highway. *See* **Highway.**
    Occupier's liability. *See* **Occupier's liability** (Right of way).
    Private right of way. *See* **Easement** (Right of way).
    Public right of way—
        Order as to—
            Judicial review—Availability of remedy. *See* **Judicial review** (Availability of remedy—Exclusion by statute—Public right of way order).
    Public right of way. *See* **Highway.**
    Road traffic—
        Accident—
            Case management. *See* **Practice** (Civil litigation—Case management—Road traffic accidents).
    Sale of land—
        Duty of purchaser to satisfy himself as to incumbrances etc. *See* **Sale of land** (Incumbrances, easements, rights of way etc—Duty of purchaser to satisfy himself as to incumbrances).
    Unconsecrated curtilage of church—
        Faculty. *See* **Ecclesiastical law** (Faculty—Unconsecrated curtilage of church—Right of way).

RIGHT TO BUY
    Local authority houses—
        Enforcement of right to buy. *See* **Housing** (Local authority houses—Tenant's right to buy—Enforcement of right).
    Local authority housing—
        Generally. *See* **Housing** (Local authority houses—Tenant's right to buy).

RIGHT TO FAIR TRIAL
    Foreign sovereign state—
        Immunity from suit. *See* **Constitutional law** (Foreign sovereign state—Immunity from suit—Right to a fair trial).
    Medical practitioner—
        Fair conduct. *See* **Medical practitioner** (Professional misconduct—Suspension—Right to a fair trial).

RIGHT TO LIFE
    Coroner's inquest and. *See* **Coroner** (Inquest—Right to life).
    Damages for infringement of human rights. *See* **Human rights** (Infringement of human rights—Damages).
    Human rights legislation. *See* **Human rights** (Right to life).

RIGHT TO VOTE
    Elections for European Parliament. *See* **European Union** (European Parliament—Elections—Right to vote).

RIGHT TO WORK
    Trade union. *See* **Trade union** (Rules—Validity).

RIOT
    Damage—
        Compensation—
            Contract of insurance. *See* **Insurance** (Contract of insurance—Construction of terms—Public liability insurance).

RIOT (cont)—

Damage (cont)—

Compensation (cont)—

Four robbers entering shop and threatening occupants—Incident not attracting the attention of anyone outside the shop—Whether assembly 'tumultuous' as well as riotous—Whether police authority liable to pay compensation—Riot (Damages) Act 1886, s 2. **Dwyer (JW) Ltd v Receiver for the Metropolitan Police District** [1967] **2** 1051, QBD.

Invasion of private property by crowd wishing to see football match—Riot (Damage) Act 1886, s 2(1). **Munday v Metropolitan Police District Receiver** [1949] **1** 337, KBD.

Persons riotously and tumultuously assembled together—Whether amount of compensation payable including compensation for consequential loss—Riot (Damages) Act 1886, s 2. **Mitsui Sumitomo Insurance Co (Europe) Ltd v Mayor's Office for Policing and Crime** [2014] **1 Comm** 225, QBD; [2014] **1** 422, QBD; [2014] **2 Comm** 785, CA; [2014] **4** 540, CA; [2016] **2 Comm** 483, SC; [2016] **4** 283, SC.

Police authority—Liability—Statutory scheme for contracted-out immigration detention centres for persons detained and held by Secretary of State—Duty of police authority to keep law and order—Riot at contracted-out detention centre damaging premises—Whether police authority liable to pay compensation—Riot (Damages) Act 1886. **Yarl's Wood Immigration Ltd v Bedfordshire Police Authority** [2009] **1** 886, QBD; [2010] **2** 221, CA.

Generally. *See* **Criminal law** (Riot).

Police equipment. *See* **Police** (Equipment—Riot equipment).

RIPARIAN OWNERS

Liability for flooding. *See* **Water and watercourses** (Flooding—Protection of land from flooding).

Rights. *See* **Water and watercourses** (Pollution of river—Discharge of untreated sewage matter—Action by riparian owner and fishery owner against local authority).

RIPARIAN RIGHTS

See **Water and watercourses** (Riparian rights).

RIPON CATHEDRAL

Divine service—

Dispute as to form of service—

Jurisdiction of High Court. *See* **Ecclesiastical law** (Divine service—Obligation to hold services—Dispute as to form of service—Jurisdiction of High Court—Divine service—Ripon Cathedral).

RISK

Consent to risk of injury—

Defence to action for negligence. *See* **Negligence** (Volenti non fit injuria—Consent to risk of injury).

Insurance—

All risks. *See* **Insurance** (All risks insurance).

Motor insurance. *See* **Motor insurance** (Risk).

Reinsurance. *See* **Insurance** (Reinsurance—Risks insured).

Sale of goods—

Passing of risk. *See* **Sale of goods** (Passing of risk).

RIVER

Covenant—

Sale of land—

Contract with catchment board to widen, deepen and make good banks of river. *See* **Sale of land** (Covenant running with land—Benefit of covenant—Successor in title—Contract with catchment board to widen, deepen and make good banks of river).

Pollution. *See* **Water and watercourses** (Pollution of river).

River bank—

Maintenance—

Generally. *See* **Water and watercourses** (River bank—Maintenance).

Land drainage broad's duties. *See* **Land drainage** (Drainage board—Maintenance and repair of river bank).

River wall—

Maintenance and repair. *See* **Land drainage** (Drainage board—Maintenance and repair of river wall).

ROAD

Carriage of animals by road. *See* **Animal** (Carriage by sea, air, road or rail).

Carriage of goods by road—

Conflict of laws. *See* **Conflict of laws** (Jurisdiction—Civil and commercial matters—Special contractual jurisdiction).

Generally. *See* **Carriers**.

Coal mine—

Statutory duty. *See* **Coal mining** (Statutory duty—Road).

Development—

Beginning of development before expiry of planning permission—

Specified operation comprised in the development—Operation in the course of constructing a road. *See* **Town and country planning** (Duration of planning permission—Beginning of development before expiry date—Specified operation comprised in the development—Operation in the course of constructing a road).

Generally. *See* **Highway**.

Negligence on highway. *See* **Negligence** (Highway).

Street trading. *See* **Street trading**.

Traffic. *See* **Road traffic**.

ROAD ACCIDENT

Contributory negligence. *See* **Negligence** (Contributory negligence—Road accident).

ROAD ACCIDENT (cont)—
  Generally. *See* **Road traffic** (Accident).
  Negligence—
    Defence—
      Sudden event or affliction. *See* **Negligence** (Defence—Sudden event or affliction—Malfunction of mind—Road accident).
      Res ipsa loquitur. *See* **Negligence** (Res ipsa loquitur—Road accident).

ROAD CHARGES
  Covenant—
    Lease—
      Payment of all assessments, impositions and outgoings whatsoever. *See* **Landlord and tenant** (Covenant—Payment of all assessments, impositions and outgoings whatsoever—Road charges).

ROAD SERVICE LICENCE
  Public service vehicle. *See* **Road traffic** (Public service vehicle—Road service licence).

ROAD TRAFFIC
  Accident—
    Apportionment of liability. *See* **Negligence** (Contributory negligence—Apportionment of liability—Road traffic accident).
    Breath test—
      Accident owing to presence of motor vehicle on the road. *See* Breath test—Accident owing to presence of motor vehicle on road, *below.*
    Conflict of laws—
      Jurisdiction. *See* **Conflict of laws** (Jurisdiction—Challenge to jurisdiction—Civil and commercial matters—Insurance—Road traffic accident occurring in Germany).
    Contributory negligence—
      Passenger in car. *See* **Negligence** (Contributory negligence—Road accident—Passenger in car).
    Contributory negligence. *See* **Negligence** (Contributory negligence—Road accident).
    County court claim for cost of repairs—
      Availability of defence of tender. *See* **County court** (Payment into court—Tender—Unliquidated claim—Cost of repairs in road accident case).
      Payment of legal costs. *See* **County court** (Unliquidated claim—Legal costs—Cost of repairs in road accident case).
    Damage due to accident arising out of presence of vehicle on road—
      Criminal proceedings—Compensation. *See* **Sentence** (Compensation—Damage due to accident arising out of presence of vehicle on road).
    Damages—
      Generally. *See* **Damages** (Measure of damages).
      Hire of alternative vehicle. *See* **Damages** (Mitigation of loss—Motor car damaged in collision—Claimant hiring car whilst his own car being repaired).
      Loss of use of motor vehicle. *See* **Damages** (Measure of damages—Loss of use of motor vehicle).
      Mitigation of loss. *See* **Damages** (Mitigation of loss—Motor car damaged in collision).
    Duty to stop and furnish particulars—
      Accident owing to presence of vehicle on road—Passenger falling from omnibus—Omnibus not at authorised stopping place—Whether an accident 'owing to the presence of a motor vehicle on a road'—Road Traffic Act 1930, s 22(1). **Quelch v Phipps** [1955] **2** 302, QBD.
      Damage to stone wall and to vehicle—Whether damage or injury to any person, vehicle or animal—Road Traffic Act 1930, s 22. **Paget v Mayo** [1939] **2** 362, KBD.
      Driver's obligation to remain where he has stopped—Accident causing damage to another vehicle—For what period of time driver should remain where he has stopped—Duty personally to give information that may be required—Road Traffic Act 1960, s 77(1). **Lee v Knapp** [1966] **3** 961, QBD.
      Driver—Vehicle stationary at time of accident—Driver person who takes vehicle out—Remaining driver until journey finished—Road Traffic Act 1930, s 22(2). **Jones v Prothero** [1952] **1** 434, QBD.
      Ignorance of driver that accident has occurred—Whether mens rea essential to offence of failing to stop—Road Traffic Act 1930, s 22(2). **Harding v Price** [1948] **1** 283, KBD.
      Report to police—Motor car struck by motor cycle—Driver of car giving name and address to driver of motor cycle—Whether driver under obligation to report to police—Road Traffic Act 1930, s 22(1),(2). **Green v Dunn** [1953] **1** 550, QBD.
      Request by authorised person—Duty to report to police—Child injured—No request by authorised person for driver's name and address at time of accident—Obligation on driver to report to police within 24 hours—Road Traffic Act 1930, s 22(1),(2). **Peek v Towle** [1945] **2** 611, KBD.
    Intoxication—
      Contributory negligence. *See* **Negligence** (Contributory negligence—Road accident—Passenger in car).
    Negligence—
      Contributory negligence. *See* **Negligence** (Contributory negligence—Road accident).
      Contributory negligence—Apportionment of liability. *See* **Negligence** (Contributory negligence—Apportionment of liability—Road traffic accident).
      Res ipsa loquitur. *See* **Negligence** (Res ipsa loquitur—Road accident).
    Personal injuries action—
      Damages. *See* **Damages** (Personal injury).
      Experts' reports. *See* **Practice** (Personal injuries action—Experts' reports—Road traffic accidents).
  Age—
    Driving under age. *See* Driving under age, *below.*
  Agricultural vehicle—
    Driver's records—
      Exemption. *See* Goods vehicle—Driver's records—Agricultural vehicle exempt, *below.*
  Arrest—
    Breath test. *See* Breath test—Arrest following breath test, *below.*

Arrest (cont)—
Driving while unfit to drive through drink or drugs. *See* Driving while unfit to drive through drink or drugs—Arrest without warrant, *below.*
Obstruction—
London. *See* Obstruction—London—Arrest, *below.*
Request for specimen for laboratory test—
Conditions precedent to request. *See* Specimen for laboratory test to determine driver's blood-alcohol proportion—Conditions precedent to request for specimen—Arrest, *below.*
Requirement to provide specimen for laboratory test—
Validity of requirement—Lawfulness of arrest. *See* Specimen for laboratory test to determine driver's blood-alcohol proportion—Requirement that person arrested under provisions of statute should provide specimen—Lawfulness of arrest, *below.*
Articulated vehicle—
Normally—
Length exceeding 15 metres—Exception where vehicle constructed and normally used for conveyance of indivisible loads of exceptional length—Indivisible load—Vehicle normally used to convey pre-loaded container—Container itself indivisible—Contents of container not indivisible—Whether 'load' refers to container or to contents of container—Motor Vehicles (Construction and Use) Regulations 1973 (SI 1973 No 24), regs 3(1), 9(1). **Patterson v Redpath Bros Ltd** [1979] **2** 108, QBD.
Overall length—
Articulated vehicle with two platforms for carrying cars—When three cars carried on upper platform, lifting gear not raised to vertical position and permitted overall length exceeded—Road Traffic Act 1960, s 64(2)—Motor Vehicles (Construction and Use) Regulations 1955 (SI 1955 No 482), reg 6(1). **Bason v Robson** [1962] **1** 520, QBD.
Length exceeding thirteen metres—Whether normally used for conveying indivisible loads of exceptional length—Meaning of 'normally used'—Forty-six out of 177 loads carried in a period of twelve months not indivisible loads of exceptional length—Motor Vehicles (Contruction and Use) Regulations 1963 (SI 1953 No 1646), reg 7(1), as amended by the Motor Vehicles (Construction and Use) (Amendment) (No 2) Regulations 1964 (SI 1964 No 1169), reg 4. **Peak Trailer & Chassis Ltd v Jackson** [1967] **1** 172, QBD.
Trailer superimposed on towing vehicle—
Breakdown vehicle towing lorry—Weight taken by jib of crane on towing vehicle—No contact between breakdown vehicle and lorry—Whether an 'articulated vehicle'—Road Traffic Act 1930, s 17(2)—Motor Vehicles (Construction and Use) Regulations 1947 (SR & O 1947 No 670), reg 3. **Hunter v Towers** [1951] **1** 349, KBD.
Use for unsuitable purpose—
Trailer bearing forklifts—Collision with bridge—Height of trailer and load greater than height of bridge—Whether trailer used for unsuitable purpose—Factors to be considered in determining suitability—Motor Vehicles (Construction and Use) Regulations 1969 (SI 1969 No 321), reg 76(3). **British Road Services Ltd v Owen** [1971] **2** 999, QBD.
Being in charge of motor vehicle with blood-alcohol proportion above prescribed limit—
Accused incapable of driving at time of arrest—
No likelihood of driving so long as any probability of blood-alcohol proportion exceeding prescribed limit—Onus of proof—Road Safety Act 1967 (c 30), s 1(3). **Northfield v Pinder** [1968] **3** 854, QBD.
Being in charge of vehicle when unfit to drive through drink or drugs—
Circumstances such that no likelihood of driving while unfit—
Condition of vehicle—Relevance—Driver involved in collision—Vehicle damaged—Driver subsequently consuming alcohol—Driver charged with being in charge while unfit through drink—Jury directed to disregard fact that driver's vehicle might not have been capable of being driven following accident—Whether a misdirection—Road Traffic Act 1960, s 6(2)—Road Safety Act 1967, s 1(4). **R v Lawrence (Paul Anthony)** [1973] **1** 364, CA.
In charge—
Defendant in car holding ignition key—Defendant's blood-alcohol level above prescribed limit—Defendant not owner of vehicle—Engine not running—No evidence that ignition key capable of starting car—Whether defendant 'in charge' of motor vehicle—Road Traffic Act 1972, ss 5, 6. **DPP v Watkins** [1989] **1** 1126, QBD.
Driver walking towards vehicle with intention of driving—Whether 'in charge' of vehicle—Road Traffic Act 1930, s 15(1). **Leach v Evans** [1952] **2** 264, QBD.
Vehicle left in public place away from home—Person leaving vehicle—Whether 'in charge' after leaving vehicle—Road Traffic Act 1930, s 15(1). **Haines v Roberts** [1953] **1** 344, QBD.
No intention of driving until fit to do so—
Burden of proof—Burden on defendant of showing no likelihood of driving while he remained unfit—Road Traffic Act 1960, s 6(2)(i). **Morton v Confer** [1963] **2** 765, QBD.
Road or other public place—
Public place—Parking enclosure at rear of inn—Road Traffic Act 1930, ss 15(1), 121. **Elkins v Cartlidge** [1947] **1** 829, KBD.
Validity of conviction—
Having charge of vehicle 'when under the influence of drink or drug'—Whether void for uncertainty. **Thomson v Knights** [1947] **1** 112, KBD.
Bicycle—
Auxiliary engine fitted. *See* Motor vehicle—Dual-purpose vehicle—Bicycle fitted with auxiliary engine, *below.*
Blood—
Specimen—
Determination of driver's blood-alcohol proportion. *See* Specimen for laboratory test to determine driver's blood-alcohol proportion—Blood, *below.*
Driving while unfit through drink or drugs. *See* Driving while unfit to drive through drink or drugs—Specimen of blood or urine, *below.*
Blood-alcohol proportion—
Breath test. *See* Breath test, *below.*

ROAD TRAFFIC (cont)—

Blood-alcohol proportion (cont)—
  In charge of vehicle. *See* Being in charge of motor vehicle with blood-alcohol proportion above prescribed limit, *above.*
Brakes—
  Efficient braking system. *See* Motor vehicle—Efficient braking system, *below.*
  Heavy motor car. *See* Heavy motor car—Braking system, *below.*
Breach of statutory duty—
  Civil action. *See* **Statutory duty** (Breach of duty imposed under sanction of penalty—Competence of civil action at suit of person aggrieved).
Breath test—
  Accident owing to presence of motor vehicle on road—
    Accident—Unintended occurrence having an adverse physical result—Broken down car being pushed by second car—Bumpers of two cars becoming interlocked—Both vehicles slightly damaged and could not be separated—Whether an 'accident'—Road Safety Act 1967, s 2(2). **R v Morris** [1972] **1** 384, CA.
    Accident—Untoward occurrence having adverse physical results—One event in chain of events leading to untoward occurrence a deliberate act—Car parked on slope deliberately released to roll down slope—Car suffering damage—Whether damage resulting from an 'accident'—Road Traffic Act 1972, s 8(2). **Chief Constable of West Midlands Police v Billingham** [1979] **2** 182, QBD.
    Issue whether accident occurred to be left to jury—Road Safety Act 1967, s 2(2). **R v Seward** [1970] **1** 329, CA.
  Arrest—
    Arrest for failure to provide specimen of breath—Validity—Constable a trespasser at time of request for specimen of breath—Request for breath specimen made at defendant's home after police unlawfully entering house—Whether defendant's non-compliance with request an offence—Whether defendant's subsequent arrest lawful—Road Traffic Act 1972, s 7(4), (6). **Fox v Chief Constable of Gwent** [1985] **1** 230, QBD.
    Arrest for failure to provide specimen of breath—Validity—Constable a trespasser at time of request for specimen of breath—Statutory conditions precedent for request of specimen complied with—Whether evidence of events subsequent to time when constable became a trespasser admissible in proceedings for failure to provide specimen—Road Traffic Act 1975, s 8(2), (5). **Morris v Beardmore** [1980] **2** 753, HL.
    Arrest for failure to provide specimen of breath—Validity—Constable entering private premises to effect arrest without invitation and as a trespasser following refusal of lawful request to provide specimen of breath—Whether arrest lawful—Road Traffic Act 1972, s 8(5). **Finnigan v Sandiford** [1981] **2** 267, HL.
  Arrest following breath test—
    Accused to be told under what powers arrest made—Road Traffic Act 1960, s 6(4)—Road Safety Act 1967, s 2(1). **R v Wall** [1969] **1** 968, CA.
    Form of words to be used. **Alderson v Booth** [1969] **2** 271, QBD.
    Necessary preliminary to provision of specimen—Road Traffic Act 1960, s 6(4)—Road Safety Act 1967, s 2(1). **Campbell v Tormey** [1969] **1** 961, QBD.
    Opportunity to provide further specimen—Right of person arrested to have opportunity of providing a further specimen of breath for a breath test while at police station—Whether person arrested must be taken to police station and given opportunity of providing a further specimen for breath test—Road Safety Act 1967, s 2(7). **Bourlet v Porter** [1973] **2** 800, HL.
    Powers under different Acts—Road Traffic Act 1960, s 6(4)—Road Safety Act 1967, s 2(4). **DPP v Carey** [1969] **3** 1662, HL.
    Recognisance—Power of police to require accused to enter into recognisance before release from police station—Road Safety Act 1967, s 4. **R v McKenzie** [1971] **1** 729, Assizes.
  Device—
    Analysis of breath specimen by approved device—Whether print-out produced by device at conclusion of analysis admissible evidence of failure to provide proper specimen—Whether print-out product of a mechanical device constituting real evidence at common law—Road Traffic Act 1972, s 8(7). **Castle v Cross** [1985] **1** 87, QBD.
    Evidence of approval by Secretary of State—Consignment note relating to delivery of device to police—Note not a record relating to a trade or business—Criminal Evidence Act 1965, s 1(1)(a)—Road Safety Act 1967, s 7(1). **R v Gwilliam** [1968] **3** 821, CA.
    Evidence of approval by Secretary of State—No evidence of approval—Effect—Road Safety Act 1967, ss 3(3), 7(1). **R v Withecombe** [1969] **1** 157, CA.
    Evidence of approval by Secretary of State—Oral evidence of Secretary of State's approval of breath test device—Judicial notice that device approved by Secretary of State—Formal proof no longer necessary—Road Safety Act 1967, s 7. **R v Jones (Rld)** [1969] **3** 1559, CA.
    Evidence of approval by Secretary of State—Written statement signifying Secretary of State's approval of a breath test device—Oral evidence unnecessary—Criminal Justice Act 1967, s 2(1),(7). **R v Holt** [1968] **3** 802, CA.
    Evidence of malfunctioning of device—What evidence admissible—Whether admissible evidence restricted to direct evidence of malfunctioning of device—Whether evidence of amount of alcohol consumed prior to taking test admissible for purposes of attacking reliability of device. **Cracknell v Willis** [1987] **3** 801, HL.
    Instructions for assembly—Compliance. **DPP v Carey** [1969] **3** 1662, HL.
    Instructions for use—Strict compliance with instructions not essential to validity of test—Mouth alcohol—Smoking—Inflation of bag—Road Safety Act 1967, s 7(1). **DPP v Carey** [1969] **3** 1662, HL.
    Instructions for use—Strict compliance with instructions not essential to validity of test—Smoking—High concentration of tobacco smoke liable to affect result of test—Instructions stating that smoking should not be permitted immediately before test—Defendant having been smoking shortly before test—No evidence that smoking affected result of test—Validity of test. **Watkinson v Barley** [1975] **1** 316, QBD.

ROAD TRAFFIC (cont)—
  Breath test (cont)—
    Device (cont)—
      Instructions for use—Strict compliance with instructions not essential to validity of test—Smoking—High concentration of tobacco smoke liable to affect result of test—Instructions stating that smoking should not be permitted immediately prior to test—Meaning of 'immediately prior to'—High concentration only likely if driver inhales through cigarette and at once exhales into bag—Sufficient compliance with instructions if driver had adequately cleared tobacco smoke from lungs before taking test. **A-G's Reference (No 2 of 1974)** [1975] **1** 658, CA.
      Order signifying approval by Secretary of State—Production of order signifying Secretary of State's approval of a breath test device—Order—Breath Test Device Approval (No 1) Order 1968 (dated 9th February 1968)—Documentary Evidence Act 1868, s 2 (as amended by Documentary Evidence Act 1882, s 2—Road Safety Act 1967, s 7(1). **R v Clarke (J F)** [1969] **1** 924, CA.
      Personal approval by Secretary of State—Whether personal approval of Secretary of State necessary—Road Safety Act 1967, s 7(1). **R v Skinner** [1968] **3** 124, CA.
      Presumption as to approval by Secretary of State—Whether maxim omnia praesumuntur rite esse acta sufficient to establish prima facie case—Road Safety Act 1967, ss 1(1), 2(4),(7), 7(1). **Scott v Baker** [1968] **2** 993, QBD.
      Print-out produced by device—Admissibility as evidence—Lion Intoximeter 3000 device—Whether print-out contains a 'statement' admissible as evidence—Road Traffic Act 1972, s 10(3)(a). **Gaimster v Marlow** [1985] **1** 82, QBD.
      Print-out produced by device—Inaccuracy of device—Malfunctioning of computer in way which was not relevant to accuracy of contents of print-out—Clock attached to computer producing print-out from device inaccurate—Whether print-out inadmissible in evidence of drink-driving charge—Police and Criminal Evidence Act 1984, s 69(1)—Road Traffic Offenders Act 1988, s 16. **DPP v McKeown** [1997] **1** 737, HL.
      Print-out produced by device—Validity—Challenge to validity—Evidence that device is defective—Acceptable evidence—Evidence acceptable only if directly proving device itself is defective—Inference drawn from condition of defendant before and after test not acceptable to prove device is defective—Road Traffic Act 1972, s 10(3)(a). **Hughes v McConnell** [1986] **1** 268, QBD.
      Proof of identity of device—Road Safety Act 1967, s 7(1). **Miller v Howe** [1969] **3** 451, QBD.
      Roadside device—Preliminary breath test—Provision of specimens for analysis—Use of specimens in proceedings—Whether prosecution required to adduce in evidence result in figures of roadside breath test—Road Traffic Act 1988, ss 5(1)(a), 6, 7(1)(a)—Road Traffic Offenders Act 1988, s 15(2). **Smith v DPP** [2007] **4** 1135, DC.
    Duty of constable to act bona fide to obtain true indication of proportion of alcohol in blood—
      Belief or knowledge thst suspect had consumed alcohol in previous 20 minutes. **DPP v Carey** [1969] **3** 1662, HL.
      Manufacturers' instructions attached to device—Constable ignorant of instructions—Failure to comply with instructions liable to affect result of test—Constable acting bona fide—Validity of test. **A-G's Reference (No 2 of 1974)** [1975] **1** 658, CA.
    Failure to provide specimen—
      Defective equipment—Failure to give specimen owing to defective equipment—Arrest—Provision of specimen of blood at police station—Conviction for driving with blood-alcohol proportion above prescribed limit—Validity of arrest—Road Safety Act 1967, s 2(5). **Hoyle v Walsh** [1969] **1** 38, QBD.
      Medical condition—Failure to give specimen of breath by reason of medical condition—Medical condition amounting to reasonable excuse for failure—Arrest—Road Safety Act 1967, s 2(3),(5). **Hirst v Wilson** [1969] **3** 1566, QBD.
      Reasonable excuse—Bronchitic condition—Road Safety Act 1967, s 2(3). **Hirst v Wilson** [1969] **3** 1566, QBD.
      Reasonable excuse—Generally. *See* Specimen—Failure to provide specimen—Reasonable excuse, *below*.
      Specimen for analysis or laboratory test. *See* Failure to provide specimen for analysis or laboratory test, *below*.
      Specimens for analysis on approved device—Failure to provide second specimen—Whether person can be convicted of failing to provide specimen if after providing one specimen he refuses to provide second specimen—Whether evidence of result of analysis of one specimen admissible for purposes of assessing penalty for failing to provide second specimen—Road Traffic Act 1972, ss 8(7), 10(2). **Cracknell v Willis** [1987] **3** 801, HL.
      Validity of arrest—Belief that driver had failed to supply specimen—Reasonable ground for belief—Driver failing to inflate bag fully—Sufficient quantity of breath to produce positive reading—Constable failing to check crystals before effecting arrest—Constable believing failure to inflate bag fully constituting failure to provide specimen—Whether arrest valid—Road Traffic Act 1972, s 8(5). **Walker v Lovell** [1975] **3** 107, HL.
    Hospital patient—
      Evidence of no objection by medical practitioner—Road Safety Act 1967, ss 2(2), 3(2)(a),(b). **R v Chapman** [1969] **2** 321, CA.
    Inflation of bag in requisite manner—
      Failure to inflate at one breath in accordance with manufacturer's instructions—Whether test valid—Road Safety Act 1967, ss 2(4), (5), 7(3). **Rendell v Hooper** [1970] **2** 72, QBD.
      Provision of specimen of breath in sufficient quantity to enable test to be carried out—Failure to inflate bag fully—Sufficient quantity of breath to produce positive reading—Whether failure to provide specimen of breath—Road Safety Act 1967, ss 2(5), 7(3). **R v Holah** [1973] **1** 106, CA.
      Provision of specimen of breath in sufficient quantity to enable test to be carried out—Failure to inflate bag fully—Sufficient quantity of breath to produce specimen of breath—Road Traffic Act 1972, ss 8(1), (3), 12(3). **Walker v Lovell** [1975] **3** 107, HL.
      Provision of specimen of breath in sufficient quantity to enable test to be carried out—Provision of specimen in more than one breath—Specimen so provided not of quality required to give reliable indication of proportion of alcohol in blood—Whether failure to provide specimen of breath—Road Traffic Act 1972, s 12(1), (3). **R v Littell** [1981] **3** 1, CA.

ROAD TRAFFIC (cont)—
  Breath test (cont)—
    Inflation of bag in requisite time—
      Failure to inflate as required—Whether subsequent attempt should be made—Whether offence of failing to supply specimen of breath—Road Safety Act 1967, s 2(3). **DPP v Carey** [1969] 3 1662, HL.
      Instructions to suspect. **DPP v Carey** [1969] 3 1662, HL.
    Mouth alcohol—
      Delay on account of mouth alcohol—Suspect refusing to wait—Power of arrest—Whether guilty of failing to supply specimen for breath test—Road Safety Act 1967, s 2(3),(5). **DPP v Carey** [1969] 3 1662, HL.
    Obstructing police—
      Positive act not per se unlawful. *See* **Criminal law** (Obstructing constable in execution of duty—Obstruction—Positive act constituting obstruction—Act not per se unlawful—Accused suspected by constable of driving with excessive quantity of alcohol in blood—Accused required to take a breath test).
    Person driving or attempting to drive—
      Driver committing traffic offence whilst vehicle in motion—Fresh pursuit culminating in requirement to provide specimen of breath for breath test off road—Whether one single transaction—Whether as soon as reasonably practicable—Road Safety Act 1967, s 2(1)(a),(b). **Sasson v Taverner** [1970] 1 215, QBD.
      Driver having stopped vehicle and got out—Driver stopped and questioned by police constable in connection with suspected offence—Suspicion of alcohol formed by constable during questioning—Whether accused driving or attempting to drive when suspicion formed—Road Safety Act 1967, s 2(1). **R v Reid (Philip)** [1973] 3 1020, CA.
      Driver stopped car voluntarily—Left driving seat to make a telephone call unconnected with driving—Questioned on matter unconnected with driving—Only then asked to take breath test—Whether then driving or attempting to drive—Road Safety Act 1967, s 2(1)(a). **R v Kelly** [1970] 2 198, CA.
      Issue whether accused driving or attempting to drive at relevant time—Issue of fact for jury—Proper direction to jury in clear cases—Road Safety Act 1967, s 2(1). **R v Bates** [1973] 2 509, CA.
      Issue whether accused was or was not driving—Primary facts not in dispute—When issue an issue of law—Road Safety Act 1967, s 2(1)(a). **R v Kelly** [1970] 2 198, CA.
      Meaning—Road Safety Act 1967, s 2(1). **Pinner v Everett** [1969] 3 257, HL.
      Person in driving seat—Remaining in driving seat for 20 minutes after driving ceased for discussion with passengers—Road safety Act 1967, s 2(1)(a). **Stevens v Thornborrow** [1969] 3 1487, QBD.
      Question of fact for jury—Road Safety Act 1967, s 2(1)(a). **R v Jones (EJM)** [1970] 1 209, CA.
      Requirement to take test—Requirement after person ceasing to drive—Requirement need not be contemporaneous with driving or attempting to drive—Requirement to be made as soon as possible thereafter—Driving and requirement must form part of continuous sequence of events—Road Safety Act 1967, s 2(1). **Sakhuja v Allen** [1972] 2 311, HL.
      Suspicion of alcohol or of commission of moving traffic offence—Suspicion arising after person has ceased driving—Whether necessary that suspicion should arise at time person driving—Considerations to be taken into account in determining whether person driving at relevant time—Road Safety Act 1967, s 2(1). **Edkins v Knowles** [1973] 2 503, QBD.
      Suspicion of alcohol—Reasonable cause to suspect alcohol—Suspicion arising when person driving or attempting to drive—Road Safety Act 1967, s 2(1)(a). **Pinner v Everett** [1969] 3 257, HL.
      Suspicion of alcohol—Reasonable cause to suspect person has alcohol in body—Suspicion arising after person has ceased driving—Whether necessary that suspicion should be contemporaneous with driving or attempted driving—Road Traffic Act 1967, s 2(1). **Sakhuja v Allen** [1972] 2 311, HL.
    Requirement to take test—
      As soon as reasonably practicable after commission of offence—Matter of degree and fact for justices—Road Safety Act 1967, s 2(1). **Arnold v Chief Constable of Kingston-upon-Hull** [1969] 3 646, QBD.
      As soon as reasonably practicable after commission of offence—Person driving a motor vehicle—Road Safety Act 1967, s 2(1). **R v Price** [1968] 3 814, CA.
      As soon as reasonably practicable after commission of offence—Person no longer driving a motor vehicle. **Campbell v Tormey** [1969] 1 961, QBD.
      Communication of requirement—Words constituting requirement spoken by constable in honest and reasonable belief that they were being heard and understood by driver—Whether prosecution must prove that driver understood requirement—Road Safety Act 1967, s 3(2)(b). **R v Nicholls** [1972] 2 186, CA.
      Hospital patient—Person at a hospital as a patient—At a hospital—Person attending hospital for treatment as out-patient—Request for breath test made in hospital car park after day's treatment finished—Whether suspect 'at a hospital'—Road Traffic Act 1972, s 8(2). **A-G's Reference (No 1 of 1976)** [1977] 3 557, CA.
      Hospital patient—Person at hospital as a patient—Patient—Person at hospital for purpose of being treated—Person attending hospital for treatment as out-patient—Request for breath test made at hospital after day's treatment completed—Whether person at hospital 'as a patient'—Road Traffic Act 1972, s 8(2). **A-G's Reference (No 1 of 1976)** [1977] 3 557, CA.
      Person driving or attempting to drive. *See* Breath test—Person driving or attempting to drive—Requirement to take test, *above.*
      Prerequisite of test—'Reasonable cause to suspect' driver has consumed alcohol above prescribed limit—Police forming suspicion after person ceased driving—Whether necessary that suspicion should arise at time person was driving—Road Traffic Act 1972, ss 6(1), 7(1)(b). **Blake v Pope** [1986] 3 185, QBD.
      Prerequisite of test—Whether lawful arrest an essential prerequisite of test—Road Traffic Act 1972, s 8(1). **Fox v Chief Constable of Gwent** [1985] 3 392, HL.
      Provision of specimen there or nearby—Matter of degree and fact for justices—Road Safety Act 1967, s 2(1). **Arnold v Chief Constable of Kingston-upon-Hull** [1969] 3 646, QBD; **Donegani v Ward** [1969] 3 636, QBD.

ROAD TRAFFIC (cont)—
  Breath test (cont)—
    Requirement to take test (cont)—
      Requirement made on defendant's property after defendant protesting that constable a trespasser—Whether requirement to take breath test lawful—Whether constable's implied licence to go on to defendant's property revoked—Road Traffic Act 1972, s 8(1). **Lambert v Roberts** [1981] **2** 15, QBD.

      What constitutes requirement—Road Safety Act 1967, s 2(1). **R v Clarke** [1969] **2** 1008, CA.

      When requirement may be made off road—Road Safety Act 1967, s 2(1)(b). **R v Jones (EJM)** [1970] **1** 209, CA.
    Second breath test—
      Suspect taking first breath test at police station—Whether suspect entitled to insist on second breath test at same station—Road Safety Act 1967, s 2(7). **Rooney v Haughton** [1970] **1** 1001, QBD.
    Smoking before or during test—
      Delay on account of smoking. **DPP v Carey** [1969] **3** 1662, HL.
    Suspicion of alcohol. *See* Breath test—Person driving or attempting to drive—Suspicion of alcohol, *above.*
    Validity—
      Failure to provide specimen for laboratory test. *See* Failure to provide specimen for laboratory test—Validity of breath test, *below.*
  Breathalyser. *See* Breath test—Device, *above.*
  Built-up area—
    Speeding. *See* Excessive speed—Built-up area, *below.*
  Bus—
    Stage carriage. *See* Stage carriage, *below.*
  Cab—
    Hackney carriage. *See* Hackney carriage, *below.*
  Car park—
    Road. *See* Road—Car park, *below.*
  Careless driving—
    Causing death by careless driving when under influence of drink or drugs—
      Failure to provide specimen—Use of specimens in proceedings—Crown seeking to admit evidence of hospital blood sample as relevant to defendant's refusal to provide specimen—Road Traffic Act 1988, s 3A—Road Traffic Offenders Act 1988, s 15. **R v Coe** [2010] **3** 83n, CA.
    Due consideration for other persons using road—
      Passengers in vehicle—Whether passengers are 'other persons using the road'—Road Traffic Act 1960, s 3(1). **Pawley v Wharldall** [1965] **2** 757, QBD.
    Error of judgment—
      Lack of care caused by error of judgment—Whether driving without due care and attention—Road Traffic Act 1930, s 12(1). **Simpson v Peat** [1952] **1** 447, QBD.
    Evidence—
      Identification of lorry causing accident between two cars—Number of lorry reported to police by independent witness—Independent witness unable at trial to remember number of lorry—Police evidence identifying accused as driver of lorry of a particular number but inadmissible as hearsay to identify lorry of that number as having caused the accident. **Jones v Metcalfe** [1967] **3** 205, QBD.
      Identity of driver—Circumstantial evidence sufficient to identify defendant as driver of vehicle involved in accident. **Hampson v Powell** [1970] **1** 929, QBD.
    Inexperience—
      Lack of skill due to inexperience—Driver exercising all the skill and attention to be expected from person with his short experience—Road Traffic Act 1930, s 12. **McCrone v Riding** [1938] **1** 157, KBD.
    Sentencing guidelines. *See* Causing death by careless or dangerous driving, *below.*
  Carriage of goods—
    Hire or reward—
      Goods vehicle. *See* Goods vehicle—Carriage of goods for hire or reward, *below.*
    Licence—
      Goods vehicle. *See* Goods vehicle—Carrier's licence, *below.*
    Passengers and goods. *See* Carriage of goods and passengers, *below.*
  Carriage of goods and passengers—
    Tachograph charts—
      Whether authorised officer empowered to require removal of tachograph charts from licensed transport operator's premises without prior written notice—Transport Act 1968, s 99(1)—Council Regulation (EEC) 3821/85, art 14(2). **Cantabrica Coach Holdings Ltd v Vehicle Inspectorate** [2002] **1** 595, HL.
  Causing dangerous vehicle to be on road. *See* Dangerous vehicle—Causing dangerous vehicle to be on road, *below.*
  Causing death by careless or dangerous driving—
    Sentence—
      Guidelines—Aggravating features—Careless driving when under influence of drink or drugs—Road Traffic Act 1988, ss 1, 3A—Criminal Justice Act 1993, s 67. **R v Shepherd** [1994] **2** 242, CA.
  Causing death by dangerous driving. *See* Dangerous driving—Causing death by dangerous driving, *below.*
  Causing death by driving—
    Unlicensed, disqualified or uninsured drivers. *See* Unlicensed, disqualified or uninsured drivers—Causing death by driving, *below.*
  Causing death by driving when unlicensed, disqualified or uninsured. *See* Unlicensed, disqualified or uninsured drivers—Causing death by driving, *below.*
  Causing death by reckless driving. *See* Reckless driving—Causing death by reckless driving, *below.*
  Causing vehicle to be used on road in breach of regulations. *See* Motor vehicle—Causing vehicle to be used on road in breach of regulations, *below.*
  Chassis—
    Motor tractor. *See* Motor tractor—Chassis, *below.*

ROAD TRAFFIC (cont)—
Collision between vehicles—
Contributory negligence. *See* **Negligence** (Contributory negligence—Collision between vehicles on road).
Proof of negligence. *See* **Negligence** (Proof of negligence—Collision between vehicles on road).
Conductor—
Stage carriage—
Offence. *See* Stage carriage—Offence by driver or conductor, *below*.
Conflict of laws—
Damages. *See* **Conflict of laws** (Tort—Proper law of tort—Damages—Road traffic accident in Spain).
Consent—
Specimen of blood or urine—
Driving while unfit through drink or drugs. *See* Driving while unfit to drive through drink or drugs—Specimen of blood or urine—Consent to, *below*.
Contributory negligence—
Collision between vehicles. *See* **Negligence** (Contributory negligence—Collision between vehicles on road).
Passenger in car. *See* **Negligence** (Contributory negligence—Road accident—Passenger in car).
Crash helmet—
Failure to wear—
Contributory negligence. *See* **Negligence** (Contributory negligence—Road accident—Crash helmet).
Dangerous driving—
Acquittal on charge of manslaughter—
Jurisdiction to try charge of dangerous driving—Whether quarter sessions having jurisdiction to try issue of dangerous driving after jury at assizes found accused not guilty of manslaughter—Road Traffic Act 1934, s 34. **R v Shipton, ex p DPP** [1957] **1** 206, QBD.
Autrefois acquit—
Acquittal of manslaughter. *See* **Criminal law** (Autrefois acquit—Manslaughter—Acquittal—Dangerous driving).
Causing death by dangerous driving—
Careless or dangerous driving. *See* Causing death by careless or dangerous driving, *above*.
Causing death by dangerous driving or by careless driving when under influence of drink or drugs—Sentence—Guidelines. **R v Cooksley** [2003] **3** 40, CA.
Causing death by dangerous driving or by careless driving when under influence of drink or drugs—Sentence—Increase in maximum sentence—Guidelines—Criminal Justice Act 2003, s 285. **R v Richardson** [2007] **2** 601, CA, C-MAC.
Causing—Substantial cause—Dangerous driving must be a substantial cause, but not necessarily the sole substantial cause, of death—Road Traffic Act 1960, s 1. **R v Gould** [1963] **2** 847, Assizes.
Causing—Substantial cause—Sufficient to show that dangerous driving was a cause of the accident and something more than de minimis—Road Traffic Act 1960, s 1. **R v Hennigan** [1971] **3** 133, CA.
Driving when current state of vehicle obviously dangerous—Specially authorised agricultural vehicle to which offence of using vehicle in a dangerous condition not applying—Whether abuse of process to bring prosecution for causing death by dangerous driving by driving when current state of vehicle obviously dangerous where vehicle specially authorised—Whether 'current state' implying difference from original manufactured condition—Road Traffic Act 1988, ss 1, 2, 2A, 40A, 44—Motor Vehicles (Authorisation of Special Types) General Order 1979. **R v Marchant** [2004] **1** 1187, CA.
Evidence of alcohol consumption by driver—Admissibility—Evidence of blood-alcohol concentration exceeding prescribed limit under the Road Safety Act 1967—Road Traffic Act 1960, s 1. **R v Thorpe** [1972] **1** 929, CA.
Evidence of alcohol consumption by driver—Admissibility—Whether evidence of amount of consumption necessary to establish actual or potential adverse affect on driver—Whether sufficient evidence before jury—Whether jury misdirected as to relevance of alcohol evidence—Road Traffic Act 1988, s 1. **R v Woodward** [1995] **3** 79, CA.
Indictment—Duplicity—Indictment charging driving at a speed and in a manner dangerous to the public—Whether bad for duplicity—Road Traffic Act 1960, s 1(1). **R v Clow** [1963] **2** 216, CCA.
Negligence—Manslaughter. *See* **Criminal law** (Manslaughter—Negligence—Degree of negligence—Dangerous driving of motor car).
Objective test—Degree of recklessness or carelessness immaterial—Road Traffic Act 1960, s 1(1). **R v Evans** [1962] **3** 1086, CCA.
Objective test—Evidence of drink taken—Admissibility—Road Traffic Act 1960, s 1. **R v McBride** [1961] **3** 6, CCA.
Scottish company charged with aiding etc offence committed in England. *See* **Criminal law** (Jurisdiction—Aiding and abetting—Causing death by dangerous driving).
Sentence—Disqualification for driving—Principles of sentencing—Categories of offences and offenders—Conviction because of momentary inattention or misjudgment—Relevance of driving record to period of disqualification—Cases in which custodial sentence appropriate. **R v Guilfoyle** [1973] **2** 844, CA.
Special reasons for not disqualifying. *See* Special reasons for not disqualifying—Causing death by dangerous driving, *below*.
Defence—
Ground that offence amounted to careless driving only likely to confuse jury—Defence—Right of trial judge to stop argument directed to establishing that defence. **R v Scammell** [1967] **3** 97, CA.
Mechanical defect—Knowledge—Brakes on car recently purchased then stated to have been overhauled—Brakes in fact defective—Defect known to driver—Whether defence of mechanical defect available where driver knew of defect—Road Traffic Act 1930, s 11(1). **R v Spurge** [1961] **2** 688, CCA.
Self-defence—Whether self-defence available as defence to charge of dangerous driving. **R v Riddell** [2018] **1** 62, CA.

Dangerous driving (cont)—
Driving dangerously—
Driving below standard of competent and careful driver—Obvious to competent and careful driver that driving dangerous—Circumstances shown to have been within knowledge of accused to be taken into regard in relation to dangerousness—Accused police driver with special skills—Whether circumstance within knowledge of accused to be taken into regard—Road Traffic Act 1988, ss 2, 2A(1), (3). **Milton v DPP** [2007] **4** 1026, DC; **R v Bannister** [2010] **2** 841, CA.
Excessive speed—
Potential danger—Driving not in fact dangerous to the public—Whether dangerous driving—Road Traffic Act 1930, s 11(1). **Bracegirdle v Oxley** [1947] **1** 126, KBD.
Information—
Two offences in one information—Dangerous driving and driving without due care and attention—Duty of justices to see that information amended—Charge of dangerous driving only—Road Traffic Act 1930, ss 11, 12(1)—Road Traffic Act 1934, s 35. **Edwards v Jones** [1947] **1** 830, KBD.
Joinder of charges. *See* **Indictment** (Joinder of charges—Road traffic offences—Dangerous driving).
Mens rea—
Automatism—Driving without awareness—Whether 'driving without awareness' capable of founding defence of automatism—Whether good defence to charge of dangerous driving. **A-G's Reference (No 2 of 1992)** [1993] **4** 683, CA.
Automatism—Inference of automatism—Diabetic driver overcome during part of journey by effect of insulin for reasons unknown to himself—Car proceeding for five miles along road which was not straight—Car proceeding dangerously—Whether defence of automatism made out—Road Traffic Act 1960, ss 2(1), 3(1). **Watmore v Jenkins** [1962] **2** 868, QBD.
Automatism—Onus of proving automatism—Whether mens rea an element of the offence—Road Traffic Act 1930, s 11(1). **Hill v Baxter** [1958] **1** 193, QBD.
Fault—Offence not absolute—Fault of driver causing dangerous situation sufficient to constitute offence—Meaning of 'fault'—Failure to achieve standard of experienced and competent driver—Fault must be a cause of dangerous situation—Inference of fault from facts of situation—Driver entitled to prove special facts avoiding inference of fault—Road Traffic Act 1960, s 2(1). **R v Gosney** [1971] **3** 220, CA.
Police driver. *See* Dangerous driving—Driving dangerously—Driving below standard of competent and careful driver, *above*.
Sentence—
Guidelines. *See* Causing death by careless or dangerous driving—Sentence, *above*.
Preventive detention—Circumstances which justify such a sentence—Protection of public. **R v Higginbotham** [1961] **3** 616, CCA.
What amounts to dangerous driving—
Circumstances of case—Vehicle dangerous to public having regard to traffic which might reasonably be expected to be on road—Whether offence of dangerous driving proved—Road Traffic Act 1930, s 11(1). **Durnell v Scott** [1939] **1** 183, KBD.
Motorist bumping another car while attempting to get into parking space in cul-de-sac—No evidence of danger to public—Whether motorist properly convicted of dangerous driving—Road Traffic Act 1972, s 2. **R v Jones (Yvonne)** [1978] **3** 1098, CA.
Dangerous vehicle—
Causing dangerous vehicle to be on road—
Repair to vehicle by garage—Owner driving vehicle after repair—Accident due to negligence of garage proprietor's workman—Liability of garage proprietor—Motor Vehicles (Construction and Use) Regulations 1951 (SI 1951 No 2101), reg 101. **Shave v Rosner** [1954] **2** 280, QBD.
Defective tyres. *See* Tyres—Defective tyre, *below*.
Device for breath test. *See* Breath test—Device, *above*.
Directions—
Failure to comply with direction—
Direction by constable engaged in regulation of traffic—Direction given by constable in execution of duty—Obstruction of constable. *See* **Criminal law** (Obstructing constable in execution of duty—Execution of duty—Direction to motorist to disobey traffic regulations).
Direction by constable engaged in regulation of traffic—Direction given by constable in execution of duty—Power at common law of constable to direct traffic derived from duty to protect life and property—Accused driving car on motorway—Constable directing accused to leave carriageway in order to take part in traffic census—Accused refusing to comply with constable's direction—Whether direction given by constable in execution of duty—Road Traffic Act 1972, s 22(1). **Hoffman v Thomas** [1974] **2** 233, QBD.
Disqualification for holding licence—
Adjournment in order to enable disqualification to be imposed—
Magistrates' court—Plea of guilty notified in writing—Adjournment of case for purpose of enabling disqualification to be imposed—Notice of adjournment to give reason therefor—Magistrates' Courts Act 1952, s 14(2)—Magistrates' Courts Act 1957, ss 1(2), proviso(iii), 1(3). **R v Mason** [1965] **2** 308, Crown Ct Liverpool.
Committal of offender to Crown Court—
Power to disqualify in addition to imposing sentence of Borstal training. *See* **Crown Court** (Committal of offender to Crown Court for sentence—Borstal training—Road traffic offence—Disqualification).
Consecutive periods—
Driving whilst uninsured—Whether period of disqualification for driving whilst uninsured can be made consecutive to previous period of disqualification—Road Traffic Act 1960, s 201—Road Traffic Act 1962, s 5(5). **Jones v Powell** [1965] **1** 674, QBD.
Express statement—Duty of court to state expressly that period of disqualification is consecutive—Road Traffic Act 1962, s 5(3),(5). **R v Sixsmith (Stipendiary Magistrate), ex p Morris** [1966] **3** 473, QBD.

ROAD TRAFFIC (cont)—
  Disqualification for holding licence (cont)—
    Disqualification after repeated offences—
      Mitigating grounds justifying non-disqualification or disqualification for less than prescribed period—Motorist convicted and sent to prison for driving while disqualified—Motorist incapable of keeping away from motor vehicles—Sentencing policy not to impose disqualification extending for substantial period after release of such an offender from prison—Whether sentencing policy a 'ground for mitigating the normal consequences of the conviction'—Transport Act 1981, s 19(2). **R v Thomas** [1983] **3** 756, CA.
    Driving while disqualified. *See* Driving while disqualified for holding licence, *below.*
    Evidence of previous convictions—
      Appeal to Crown Court—Appeal against sentence only—Offence involving obligatory endorsement—Driving licence endorsed by justices—Duty of Crown Court to order production of driving licence for endorsement—Duty of court to examine licence for purpose of determining whether disqualification should be ordered—Road Traffic Act 1972, ss 93(3), 101(4). **Dyson v Ellison** [1975] **1** 276, QBD.
      Certificate of disqualification—Certificate should be limited to that fact—Prevention of Crimes Act 1871, s 18. **Stone v Bastick** [1965] **3** 713, QBD.
      Certificate of disqualification—Proof of person named in certificate being person whose conviction to be proved—Police and Criminal Evidence Act 1984, s 73(1). **Pattison v DPP** [2006] **2** 317, QBD.
      Production of driving licence—Proof of previous conviction resulting in disqualification—Whether proof should be by producing driving licence with endorsement of particulars of disqualification—Road Traffic Act 1962, s 7(1). **Stone v Bastick** [1965] **3** 713, QBD.
    Mitigating grounds justifying non-disqualification following previous endorsements—
      Circumstances attending previous convictions—Whether evidence of circumstances attending previous convictions admissible—Road Traffic Act 1962, s 5(3). **Lambie v Woodage** [1972] **2** 462, HL.
      Disqualification imposed on third offence—Whether the fact that the two previous convictions had been taken into consideration on disqualification for the third offence could be a mitigating ground on fourth offence—Road Traffic Act 1962, s 5(3). **Fearon v Sydney** [1966] **2** 694, QBD.
      Reasons for non-disqualifying—Circumstances which may be taken into account in determining whether or not to disqualify—Road Traffic Act 1962, s 5(3). **Baker v Cole** [1971] **3** 680, QBD.
    Penalty points. *See* Penalty points—Disqualification, *below.*
    Period of disqualification—
      Indefinite period—Life disqualification—Whether permissible as disqualification for certain period—Road Traffic Act 1962, s 5. **R v Tunde-Olarinde** [1967] **2** 491, CA.
      Indefinite period—No power to disqualify for indefinite period—Road Traffic Act 1930, s 15. **R v Fowler** [1937] **2** 380, CCA.
      Life disqualification—Propriety—Offender aged 28—Previous disqualifications extending for some 12 years—Disqualifications not for bad driving—Whether life disqualification depriving offender of all future opportunity for driving, should stand—Road Traffic Act 1962, s 5. **R v Bond** [1968] **2** 1040, CA.
      Long period—Considerations to be taken into account. **R v Shirley** [1969] **3** 678, CA.
      Sentence of imprisonment and disqualification—Period of disqualification should exceed term of imprisonment—Road Traffic Act 1930, ss 6(1)(a), 7(4). **R v Phillips** [1955] **3** 273, CCA.
    Plea of guilty in accused's absence—
      Adjournment of proceedings before ordering disqualification. *See* **Magistrates** (Plea of guilty—Absence of accused—Adjournment of proceedings before ordering disqualification).
    Power to impose disqualification—
      Conviction of stealing motor car—No conviction of taking and driving away without owner's consent—Offences of taking away motor cars without owner's consent taken into consideration—Whether power to impose disqualification—Road Traffic Act 1930, s 6(1)—Road Traffic Act 1956, s 26(1), Sch 4, para 8. **R v Williams** [1962] **3** 639, CCA.
    Provisional licence—
      Breach of condition—Offence—Driving while disqualified—No defence that accused entitled to hold provisional licence and drive in accordance with conditions of licence—Driver failing to exhibit L plates—Road Traffic Act 1960, ss 104(3), 109(3), 110. **Hunter v Coombs** [1962] **1** 904, QBD.
    Removal—
      Application to remove disqualification after disqualification removed in part—Jurisdiction of justices to hear application—Road Traffic Act 1930, s 7(3). **R v Manchester Justices, ex p Gaynor** [1956] **1** 610, QBD.
      Removal in part—Disqualification for driving motor vehicles of all classes for five years—Whether disqualification removable in part on subsequent good behaviour—Road Traffic Act 1930, s 7(3). **R v Cottrell** [1955] **3** 817, Assizes.
      Removal in part—Good behaviour—Whether disqualification removable in part on subsequent good behaviour—Road Traffic Act 1930, ss 6(1), 7(3). **R v Cottrell (No 2)** [1956] **1** 751, CA.
      When application for removal may be made—Road Traffic Act 1960, s 106(2), as amended by Road Traffic Act 1962, s 6(1). **R v Lambeth Metropolitan Magistrate, ex p Everett** [1967] **3** 648, QBD.
    Sentence—
      Appeal—Disqualification a sentence for purpose of appeal to Court of Criminal Appeal—Court having jurisdiction to vary sentence of disqualification—Criminal Appeal Act 1907, s 21. **R v McNulty** [1964] **3** 713, CCA.
      Order of disqualification—Whether order of disqualification a sentence—Magistrates' Courts Act 1952, s 83(3)(d)—Road Traffic Act 1960, ss 104(1), 105(1). **R v Surrey Quarter Sessions, ex p Comr of Police of the Metropolis** [1962] **1** 825, QBD.
    Separate periods of disqualification—
      Periods running concurrently—Whether court having Power to impose consecutive periods of disqualification. **R v Meese** [1973] **2** 1103, CA.
    Severable from conviction—
      Excess of jurisdiction—Disqualification severable from conviction—Order of certiorari quashing disqualification not having effect of quashing conviction and fine—Road Traffic Act 1930, s 12(2) (as substituted by Road Traffic Act 1934, s 5(2), as amended by Road Traffic Act 1956, s 55, Sch 9). **R v Arundel Justices, ex p Jackson** [1959] **2** 407, QBD.

ROAD TRAFFIC (cont)—
  Disqualification for holding licence (cont)—
    Special reasons for not disqualifying—
      Driving while unfit through drink or drugs. *See* Driving while unfit to drive through drink or drugs—Special reasons for not disqualifying, *below.*
      Generally. *See* Special reasons for not disqualifying, *below.*
    Subsequent conviction for driving whilst disqualified—
      Original disqualification quashed—Whether certiorari available to give ancillary relief. *See* **Certiorari** (Jurisdiction—Ancillary relief—Applicant convicted of motoring offence and disqualified from holding driving licence).
    Test of competence to drive—
      Disqualification until driving test retaken—Circumstances not disclosing lack of competence by driver—Whether test should be ordered—Road Traffic Act 1972, s 93(7). **R v Donnelly** [1975] **1** 785, CA.
    Using vehicle on road without insurance policy being in force. *See* **Motor insurance** (Disqualification for using etc vehicle on road without policy being in force).
  Drink—
    Blood-alcohol proportion of driver—
      Breath test. *See* Breath test, *above.*
      Special reasons for not disqualifying. *See* Special reasons for not disqualifying—Driving with blood-alcohol proportion above prescribed limit, *below.*
      Specimen for laboratory test. *See* Specimen for laboratory test to determine driver's blood-alcohol proportion, *below.*
    Driving while unfit. *See* Driving while unfit to drive through drink or drugs, *below.*
    Unfitness to drive—
      In charge of vehicle. *See* Being in charge of vehicle when unfit to drive through drink or drugs, *above.*
  Driver—
    Contributory negligence—
      Learner driver and instructor. *See* **Negligence** (Contributory negligence—Road accident—Learner-driver and instructor).
    Duty to stop and furnish particulars of accident. *See* Accident—Duty to stop and furnish particulars—Driver, *above.*
    Duty to take care. *See* **Negligence** (Duty to take care—Driver of motor vehicle).
    Offence—
      Generally. *See* Driving, *below.*
      Identity of driver—Information. *See* Offence—Duty to give information—Duty of any person to give information which it is in his power to give and may lead to identification of driver, *below.*
    Pedestrian crossing—
      Duty of driver. *See* Pedestrian crossing—Duty of driver, *below.*
    Stage carriage—
      Offence by driver or conductor. *See* Stage carriage—Offence by driver or conductor, *below.*
    Using vehicle on road in breach of regulations. *See* Motor vehicle—Using vehicle on road in breach of regulations—Driver of vehicle, *below.*
  Driver's records—
    Goods vehicle. *See* Goods vehicle—Driver's records, *below.*
  Driving—
    Breath test—
      Person driving or attempting to drive. *See* Breath test—Person driving or attempting to drive, *above.*
    Careless driving. *See* Careless driving, *above.*
    Control of vehicle—
      Learner being taught to drive—Sitting in driver's seat and using accelerator and footbrake—Instructor holding steering wheel and handbrake—Road Traffic Act 1930, s 4(1). **Langman v Valentine** [1952] **2** 803, QBD.
    Dangerous driving. *See* Dangerous driving, *above.*
    Driving while disqualified for holding licence. *See* Driving while disqualified for holding licence, *below.*
    Excessive speed. *See* Excessive speed, *below.*
    Reckless driving. *See* Reckless driving, *below.*
    Steering vehicle down incline—
      Engine not running—Accused releasing handbrake and steering vehicle 100 yards to garage—Whether accused 'driving'—Road Traffic Act 1930, s 7(4). **Saycell v Bool** [1948] **2** 83, KBD.
    Towed vehicle—
      Steersman of towed broken-down vehicle—Whether 'driving'—Road Traffic Act 1930, ss 1, 4(1), 11(1), 121—Road Traffic (Driving Licences) Act 1936, s 1(1)—Motor Vehicles (Construction and Use) Regulations 1941 (SR & O 1941 No 398), reg 82(2). **Wallace v Major** [1946] **2** 87, KBD.
    Using driver's controls for purpose of directing movement of car—
      Accused pushing car with both feet on road and occasionally adjusting steering wheel—Whether accused 'driving'—Road Traffic Act 1972, s 99(b). **R v MacDonagh** [1974] **2** 257, CA.
  Driving examiner—
    Duty of care. *See* **Negligence** (Duty to take care—Driving examiner).
  Driving licence—
    Community driving licence—
      Mutual recognition of driving licences issued by member states—Member state cancelling driver's right to drive—Driver obtaining new licence in another member state after expiry of cancellation period—Whether member state permitted to refuse to recognise driving licence issued by another member state where licence holder failing to meet requirement as to residence in issuing member state at date of issue—Whether member state permitted to reserve to itself right to issue new driving licence to person in respect of whom member state had cancelled right to drive—Council Directive (EEC) 91/439, arts 1(2), 7(1)(b), 8(4), 9. **Kapper (Criminal proceedings against) (Case C-476/01)** [2005] **EC** 257, ECJ.

    Driving licence (cont)—
        Conditions attached to provisional licences—
            Motor bicycle not having sidecar attached—Sidecar—Tubular steel framework without structure—Passenger could not safely be carried on framework—Motor Vehicles (Driving Licences) Regulations 1963 (SI 1963 No 1026), reg 7(1)(d). **Cox v Harrison** [1968] **3** 811, QBD.
            Offence of using motor vehicle on road without supervision of qualified driver—Bond mini-car—Second seat able to be fitted to transverse bars—Whether vehicle constructed to carry only one person—Motor Vehicles (Driving Licences) Regulations 1963 (SI 1963 No 1026), reg 7(2)(b). **Vincent v Whitehead** [1966] **1** 917, QBD.
        Disqualification. *See* Disqualification for holding licence, *above.*
        Driving without licence. *See* Driving without licence, *below.*
        Endorsement—
            Common law misdemeanour—Attempt to commit offence of taking and driving away motor vehicle without consent of owner or other lawful authority—No power to order endorsement of offender's driving licence—Road Traffic Act 1960, s 217—Road Traffic Act 1962, s 7—Magistrates' Courts Act 1952, s 19(9). **Bell v Ingham** [1968] **2** 333, QBD.
            Obligatory endorsement—Offence of failing to secure load on vehicle—Motor Vehicles (Construction and Use) Regulations 1963 (SI 1963 No 1646), reg 73(2)—Road Traffic Act 1960, s 64(2), as amended—Road Traffic Act 1962, ss 7, 8, Sch 1, Pt 2, para 19(a). **Beighton v Brown** [1965] **1** 793, QBD.
            Penalty points. *See* Penalty points—Disqualification—Endorsement of licence, *below.*
        Groups of vehicles for which licence granted—
            Means of reversing—Three-wheeled motor vehicle constructed with means of reversing which not immediately usable by reason of reversing equipment being blanked off—Whether vehicle within group A or group G—Motor Vehicles (Driving Licences) Regulations 1950 (SI 1950 No 333), Sch 2. **Baldwin v Worsman** [1963] **2** 8, Div.
        Heavy goods vehicle. *See* Heavy goods vehicle driver's licence, *below.*
        Obtained by false pretence—
            Motor insurance—Extent of cover. *See* **Motor insurance** (Compulsory insurance against third party risks—Extent of cover—Driver under age of 16—Licence obtained by false pretence).
        Possession—
            Burden of proof in criminal proceedings. *See* **Criminal evidence** (Burden of proof—Facts peculiarly within knowledge of accused—Licence—Charge of driving without licence).
        Provisional licence—
            Conditions attached to provisional licences—Motor bicycle not having sidecar attached—Sidecar—Structure attached to motor bicycle for purpose of carrying goods—Whether sidecar limited to structure for safe carriage of passenger—Motor Vehicle (Driving Licences) Regulations 1971 (SI 1971 No 451), reg 6(1)(d), (2)(e). **Keen v Parker** [1976] **1** 203, QBD.
        Disqualification. *See* Disqualification for holding licence—Provisional licence, *above.*
        Refusal to grant—
            Appeal—Person aggrieved—Refusal by licensing authority to grant, being satisfied on inquiry that applicant suffering from prescribed disease—Whether applicant 'person aggrieved'—Right of appeal—Road Traffic Act 1960, ss 100(2), 103. **R v Cardiff City Justices, ex p Cardiff City Council** [1962] **1** 751, QBD.
            Prescribed disease—Refusal by licensing authority to grant licence being satisfied on inquiry that applicant suffering from prescribed disease—Applicant suffering from epilepsy which did not show itself while controlled by drugs—Whether applicant suffering from prescribed disease—Road Traffic Act 1960, s 100(2). **Devon CC v Hawkins** [1967] **1** 235, QBD.
        Supervision of learner driver—
            Bubble car—Three-wheeled motor vehicle with seats for driver and passenger—Whether driver holding provisional licence required to drive under supervision of qualified driver—Motor Vehicles (Driving Licences) Regulations 1963 (SI 1963 No 1026), reg 7(2)(e). **Brown v Anderson** [1965] **2** 1, QBD.
            L sign on vehicle—Duty of supervisor—Road Traffic Act 1930, s 5(3)—Motor Vehicles (Driving Licences) Regulations 1937 (SR & O 1937 No 438), reg 16(3)(a), (c). **Rubie v Faulkner** [1940] **1** 285, KBD.
            Visiting force permit—Holder of permit—Whether holder of such permit entitled to supervise learner driver holding provisional driving licence—Permit was not a licence within Part 2 of Road Traffic Act 1960, not equated with such a licence for this purpose—Motor Vehicles (International Circulation) Act 1952, s 1(2)(b)—Road Traffic Act 1960, s 102—Motor Vehicles (Driving Licences) Regulations 1950 (SI 1950 No 333), reg 16(3)(a)—Motor Vehicles (International Circulation) Order 1957 (SI 1957 No 1074), art 3(1)(a). **Urey v Lummis** [1962] **2** 463, QBD.
        Test conducted in accordance with regulations—
            Jurisdiction of magistrate—Power to question findings of examiner—Whether jurisdiction limited to determining whether test conducted in accordance with regulations—Road Traffic Act 1934, s 6(6). **Geraghty v Morris** [1939] **2** 269, KBD.
    Driving test—
        Conduct of test. *See* Driving licence—Test conducted in accordance with regulations, *above.*
        Disqualified driver. *See* Disqualification for holding licence—Test of competence to drive, *above.*
        Test taken in uninsured car. *See* **Motor insurance** (Driving school—Implied duty to insure against third party risks).
    Driving under age—
        Heavy motor car—
            Driver under 21 years of age—Election as to appropriate statutory offence—Offence of under age or offence of driving while disqualified—Whether prosecution may elect to proceed under s 110 rather than s 5—Road Traffic Act 1960, ss 5, 97(1), 110(b), as amended by Road Traffic Act 1962, s 8 and Sch 1. **R v Saddleworth Justices, ex p Staples** [1968] **1** 1189, QBD.
    Driving while disqualified for holding licence—
        Absolute prohibition—
            Knowledge of defendant—Defendant having no knowledge that he had been disqualified—Road Traffic Act 1930, s 7(4). **Taylor v Kenyon** [1952] **2** 726, QBD.

ROAD TRAFFIC (cont)—
Driving while disqualified for holding licence (cont)—
Disqualification—
Disqualification for an additional period under totting up procedure—Application for removal of disqualification—Power of justices' to remove disqualification—Circumstances in which justices may remove disqualification—Road Traffic Act 1960, s 110(b)—Road Traffic Act 1962, s 5(3), (5)—Road Traffic (Disqualification) Act 1970, s 2(1). **R v Bradfield and Sonning Justices, ex p Holdsworth** [1971] **3** 755, QBD.
Driving—
Meaning—Using driver's controls for purpose of directing movement of car—Accused sitting in driver's seat of car and controlling it while it was being towed—Whether accused 'driving' towed car—Road Traffic Act 1972, s 99(b). **McQuaid v Anderton** [1980] **3** 540, QBD.
Fine instead of imprisonment—
Special circumstances—Circumstances justifying fine rather than imprisonment—Sudden emergency—No other means of transport—Road Traffic Act 1930, s 7(4). **Aichroth v Cottee** [1954] **2** 856, QBD.
Special circumstances—Test to be applied—Circumstances of special rather than general character relating to offence and not offender—Road Traffic Act 1930, s 7(4). **Lines v Hersom** [1951] **2** 650, KBD.
Forfeiture of car used for driving while disqualified—
Jurisdiction to make forfeiture order. *See* **Sentence** (Forfeiture order—Forfeiture of property—Property—Property used for committing any offence—Car used for driving while disqualified).
Imprisonment—
Fine instead of imprisonment. *See* Driving while disqualified for holding licence—Fine instead of imprisonment, *above*.
Young offender—Offender under 21 of age—Sentence—When sentence of imprisonment may be imposed—Road Traffic Act 1930, s 7(4)—Criminal Justice Act 1948, s 17(2). **Davidson-Houston v Lanning** [1955] **2** 737, QBD.
Mens rea—
Mistake—Driving on a road—Defendant driving in mistaken belief that place where he is driving is not a road—Whether guilty of offence of driving on a road while disqualified—Road Traffic Act 1972, s 99. **R v Miller** [1975] **2** 974, CA.
Original disqualification quashed—
Whether certiorari available to give ancillary relief. *See* **Certiorari** (Jurisdiction—Ancillary relief—Applicant convicted of motoring offence and disqualified from holding driving licence).
Driving while unfit to drive through drink or drugs—
Arrest without warrant—
Power of constable to arrest on reasonable suspicion that offence committed—Road Traffic Act 1960, s 6(4). **Wiltshire v Barrett** [1965] **2** 271, CA.
Burden of proof—
Consumption of alcohol after ceasing to drive but before breath test—Evidence before court that defendant had consumed alcohol after ceasing to drive but before breath test—Whether prosecution under burden to negative such evidence—Road Traffic Act 1972, s 6. **R v Newcastle-upon-Tyne Justices, ex p Hindle** [1984] **1** 770, QBD.
Drug—
Insulin—Overaction of insulin properly taken by a diabetic—Whether insulin a 'drug'—Road Traffic Act 1930, s 15(1). **Armstrong v Clark** [1957] **1** 433, QBD.
Drunk in charge of carriage—
Carriage—Bicycle—Whether bicycle a 'carriage'—Licensing Act 1872, s 12. **Corkery v Carpenter** [1950] **2** 745, KBD.
Evidence—
Amount of liquor consumed—Conversion of proportion of alcohol in blood as certified in analyst's certificates into quantity of liquor consumed—Tables of destruction rate and conversion rates accepted by medical profession—Whether evidence of medical practitioner on quantity of liquor consumed computed by reference to table admissible—Road Traffic Act 1962, s 2(2). **R v Somers** [1963] **3** 808, CCA.
Back-calculation—Specimen to determine driver's blood-alcohol level taken some hours after driving—Specimen showing blood-alcohol level below prescribed limit—Whether evidence of calculation of amount of alcohol eliminated between driving and providing specimen admissible—Road Traffic Act 1972, s 6(1). **Gumbley v Cunningham** [1989] **1** 5, HL.
Medical evidence—Consent—Accused having consented to being examined after having been told that it was no part of doctor's duty to examine him in order to give opinion as to unfitness to drive through drink—Evidence of doctor ought not to have been received—Road Traffic Act 1960, s 6. **R v Payne** [1963] **1** 848, CCA.
Medical evidence—No evidence called from doctor taking specimen of blood at police station—Whether requirement for doctor to give evidence mandatory—Road Traffic Offenders Act 1988, s 16(2). **Steward v DPP** [2003] **4** 1105, DC.
Non-expert medical evidence—Whether non-expert medical witness can testify as to his impression whether accused had taken drink—Whether such witness can give his opinion whether, as result of such drink, accused fit to drive—Road Traffic Act 1960, s 6(1). **R v Davies** [1962] **3** 97, C-MAC.
Police doctor—Independent professional man—Evidence to be accepted as that of professional man under duty to advise court—Road Traffic Act 1930, s 15(1). **R v Nowell** [1948] **1** 794, CCA.
Mens rea—
Effect of drug—Diabetic—Effect of insulin—Diabetic driver overcome by effect of Insulin for reasons unknown to himself—Whether guilty of offence—Road Traffic Act 1960, s 6(1). **Watmore v Jenkins** [1962] **2** 868, QBD.
Sentence—
Preventive detention—Whether appropriate. **R v Smith** [1961] **2** 743, CCA.

ROAD TRAFFIC (cont)—
Driving while unfit to drive through drink or drugs (cont)—
  Special reasons for not disqualifying—
    Criteria for special reasons—Respondent unfit to drive through drink—Car in which respondent was
    a passenger leaving road and ending up in field—Respondent driving car for a few yards from
    field to highway and parking it—Respondent intending only to park car and not to drive
    it—Respondent convicted of driving while unfit to drive through drink—Whether circumstances
    constituting special reasons for not disqualifying respondent—Road Traffic Act 1972, s 93(1).
    Chatters v Burke [1986] **3** 168, QBD.
    Driver fit when commencing journey—Stopping car on feeling effects of drink—Road Traffic Act
    1930, s 15(2). **Duck v Peacock** [1949] **1** 318, KBD.
    Failure to provide specimen—Reasonable excuse. *See* Specimen—Failure to provide specimen—
    Reasonable excuse, *below.*
    Ignorance of combined effect of drink and drugs—Road Traffic Act 1930, s 15(2). **Chapman v**
    O'Hagan [1949] **2** 690, KBD.
    No attempt to drive and no intention to drive—Road Traffic Act 1930, s 15(2). **Jowett-Shooter v**
    Franklin [1949] **2** 730, KBD.
  Specimen of blood or urine—
    Analyst's certificate as to proportion of alcohol in specimen—Certificate as evidence of matters
    certified—Admissibility—Failure to serve copy on accused not less than seven days before
    hearing or trial—Waiver of objection to admission by accused—Failure by accused to object to
    admission before close of prosecution case constituting waiver—Road Traffic Act 1962, s 2(2). **R v**
    Banks [1972] **1** 1041, CA.
    Blood-alcohol concentration as ascertained from laboratory test—Specimen provided for
    laboratory test for purpose of charge of driving with blood-alcohol concentration above
    prescribed limit—Defendant having consumed alcohol after driving and before test—Whether
    result of test admissible as evidence of unfitness to drive—Road Traffic Act 1972, ss 5(1), 7(1). **R v**
    Richards (Stanley) [1974] **3** 696, CA.
    Consent to—Lack of consent established—Discretion to exclude evidence—Road Traffic Act 1962,
    s 2(1). **R v Palfrey, R v Sadler** [1970] **2** 12, CA.
    Consent to—Specimen provided after warning required by statutory provisions relating driving
    with blood-alcohol proportion above prescribed limit—Whether specimen may be used to
    support charge of driving while unfit—Road Traffic Act 1962, s 2(1)—Road Safety Act 1967,
    s 3(10). **R v Palfrey, R v Sadler** [1970] **2** 12, CA.
    Failure to provide specimen—Reasonable excuse. *See* Specimen—Failure to provide specimen—
    Reasonable excuse, *below.*
    Offer to supply part of specimen to accused—Necessity for constable, requesting specimen for
    analysis, simultaneously to offer to supply part of specimen to accused—Discretion of trial judge
    to admit evidence of request or specimen if no prejudice to accused where no offer made until
    after specimen provided—Road Traffic Act 1962, s 2(5). **R v Mitten** [1965] **2** 59, CCA.
    Offer to supply part of specimen to accused—Time when offer should be made—Necessity for
    constable requesting specimen of urine for analysis at same time to offer to supply part of
    specimen in suitable container—Road Traffic Act 1962, s 2(5). **R v Price** [1963] **3** 938, CCA.
    Procedure to be followed in requiring driver to provide specimen of blood or urine—Road Traffic
    Act 1988, ss 7(3), (4), 8(2). **DPP v Jackson** [1998] **3** 769, HL; **DPP v Warren** [1992] **4** 865, HL.
    Specimen provided to a medical practitioner—No request by accused to be supplied with such a
    specimen—Whether certificate of authorised analyst admissible in evidence—Road Traffic Act
    1962, s 2(1), (4), (5). **R v Dooley** [1964] **1** 178, Crown Ct Liverpool.
    Supply of specimen to accused—Specimen of urine to be supplied to accused within a reasonable
    time after specimen is taken—Ordinarily, though not necessarily, before accused leaves police
    station—Road Traffic Act 1962, s 2(4)(b). **R v Sharp** [1968] **3** 182, CA.
    Urine test—Practice—Disputes as to admissibility of evidence—Road Traffic Act 1962, s 2(5). **R v**
    Mitten [1965] **2** 59, CCA.
  Specimens of breath—
    Specimens for analysis on approved device—Failure to provide second specimen—Whether
    evidence of single specimen admissible on charge of driving with excess alcohol—Whether
    person can be convicted of driving with excess alcohol on evidence of only one specimen of
    breath—Road Traffic Act 1972, ss 6(1), 10(2). **Cracknell v Willis** [1987] **3** 801, HL.
Driving with blood-alcohol proportion above prescribed limit—
  Breath test. *See* Breath test, *above.*
  Special reasons for not disqualifying. *See* Special reasons for not disqualifying—Driving with
  blood-alcohol proportion above prescribed limit, *below.*
  Specimen for laboratory test. *See* Specimen for laboratory test to determine driver's blood-alcohol
  proportion, *below.*
Driving with excess alcohol—
  Driving after consuming so much alcohol that proportion in breath exceeds prescribed limit—
    Respondent having a month earlier been injected by doctor with pain-relieving drug containing
    benzyl alcohol—Whether 'consuming' restricted to act of drinking—Road Traffic Act 1988,
    s 5(1)(a). **DPP v Johnson** [1995] **4** 53, QBD.
Driving without licence—
  Onus of proof—
    Possession of licence—Onus on accused of proving he has licence—Road Traffic Act 1930, s 4(1).
    John v Humphreys [1955] **1** 793, QBD.
Drugs—
  Driving while unfit. *See* Driving while unfit to drive through drink or drugs, *above.*
  Unfitness to drive—
    In charge of vehicle. *See* Being in charge of vehicle when unfit to drive through drink or drugs,
    above.
Dual-purpose vehicle—
  Bicycle fitted with auxiliary engine. *See* Motor vehicle—Dual-purpose vehicle—Bicycle fitted with
  auxiliary engine, *below.*
  Speeding. *See* Excessive speed—Dual-purpose vehicle, *below.*

ROAD TRAFFIC (cont)—
Dumper—
Vehicle intended or adapted for use on road. *See* Motor vehicle—Intended or adapted for use on road—Dumpers, *below.*
Emergency—
Driving with blood-alcohol proportion above prescribed limit—
Special reason for not disqualifying. *See* Special reasons for not disqualifying—Driving with blood-alcohol proportion above prescribed limit—Emergency, *below.*
Stopping on motorway. *See* Motorway—Restrictions on stopping—Emergency, *below.*
Excessive speed—
Built-up area—
Road with no lighting by lamps—Speed limit signs erected by local authority—Prima facie proof that road to be deemed to be in built up area—Road Traffic Act 1934, s 1(1)(b). **Boyd-Gibbins v Skinner** [1951] **1** 1049, KBD.
Corroboration of evidence—
Evidence of two witnesses each relating to a different time and place on the road—Whether corroboration—Road Traffic Act 1930, s 10(3)—Road Traffic Act 1934, s 2(3), sch 1. **Brighty v Pearson** [1938] **4** 127, KBD.
Speedometer reading—Evidence as to accuracy—Evidence by two police officers of speedometer reading—Whether sufficient without evidence as to accuracy of speedometer—Road Traffic Act 1934, s 2(3). **Melhuish v Morris** [1938] **4** 98, KBD.
Speedometer reading—Evidence of one police officer of speedometer reading—No evidence as to accuracy of speedometer—Road Traffic Act 1930, s 10(3) (as substituted by Road Traffic Act 1934, s 2(3). **Penny v Nicholas** [1950] **2** 89, KBD.
Speedometer reading—Sufficiency—Corroboration by another witness—Whether necessary—Road Traffic Act 1934, s 2(3). **Russell v Beesley** [1937] **1** 527, KBD.
Dangerous driving. *See* Dangerous driving—Excessive speed, *above.*
Dual-purpose vehicle—
Van with transverse seats and with windows fitted on each side—Side windows covered by painted panels of wood screwed into windows—Whether van goods vehicle or dual-purpose vehicle—Road Traffic Act 1960, Sch 1, para 14(2)(b)(ii), as substituted by Motor Vehicles (Variation of Speed Limits) Regulations 1962 (SI 1962 No 204), reg 3. **Popperwell v Cockerton** [1968] **1** 1038, QBD.
Evidence—
Opinion of one witness—Police officer's evidence of excessive speed on inspection of damage to vehicle and skid marks—Whether police officer's evidence merely an opinion of excessive speed—Whether accused properly convicted soley on police officer's evidence—Road Traffic Regulation Act 1984, s 89(2). **Crossland v DPP** [1988] **3** 712, QBD.
Exemption—
Police—Use of vehicle for police purposes—Police officer driving vehicle in course of duties to give evidence at court—Speed limit exceeded—Whether vehicle being used for police purposes—Road Traffic Act 1960, s 25. **Aitken v Yarwood** [1964] **2** 537, QBD.
Goods vehicle—
Motor van with pneumatic tyres—No carrier's licence issued in respect of vehicle—Road Traffic Act 1930, Sch I, para 2(1)(a), as substituted by Road Traffic Act 1934, s 2(1), Sch I—Motor Vehicles (Variation of Speed Limit) Regulations 1950 (SI 1950 No 1705), reg 2. **Manning v Hammond** [1951] **2** 815, KBD.
Shooting brake with C licence—Use solely for carrying passengers—Road and Rail Traffic Act 1933, s 9(2). **Blenkin v Bell** [1952] **1** 1258, QBD.
Utility car—Whether subject to speed limit—Road Traffic Act 1934, s 2, Sch I. **Hubbard v Messenger** [1937] **4** 48, KBD.
Vehicle capable of carrying passengers—Use solely for carrying passengers—Road Traffic Act 1934, Sch I, para 2(1)(a). **Woolley v Moore** [1952] **2** 797, QBD.
Vehicle not being used for carrying goods—Road Traffic Act 1934, Sch I, para 2(1)(a), as amended by Motor Vehicles (Variation of Speed Limit) Regulations 1955 (SI 1955 No 1880), reg 2. **Bryson v Rogers** [1956] **2** 826, QBD.
Negligence. *See* **Negligence** (Vehicles—Speed).
Passenger vehicle—
Vehicle adapted to carry more than seven passengers exclusive of driver—Adapted—Vehicle originally so constructed and not since altered—Road Traffic Act 1960, ss 24(1), 117(1)(b), Sch 1, para 1(1), (2). **Maddox v Storer** [1962] **1** 831, QBD.
Excise licence—
Altered condition of vehicle—
Goods vehicle—Saloon car fitted with rails to carry samples of clothing for commercial traveller—When no samples being carried passengers could continue to use and sit in rear seats—Whether a goods vehicle—Vehicles (Excise) Act 1949, s 27(1). **Taylor v Mead** [1961] **1** 626, QBD.
Exhibition of licence on vehicle—
Offence—Failure to exhibit licence—Defendant not in possession of licence—Defendant convicted of not having licence in force for vehicle—Whether fact that defendant has no licence defence to charge of failing to exhibit it—Vehicles (Excise) Act 1971, ss 8(1), 12(4). **Pilgram v Dean** [1974] **2** 751, QBD.
Fraudulent use of licence—
Intention to defraud—Essentiality of intent to avoid paying duty—Motor vehicle licence placed on another vehicle so broken down that it was uncertain whether it was any longer mechanically propelled—Intent to avoid enquiries by police—No direction whether vehicle was mechanically propelled—Whether fraudulent intention shown—Vehicles (Excise) Act 1962, s 17(1). **R v Manners-Astley** [1967] **3** 899, CA.
Intention to defraud—Intent—What intent must be proved—Whether necessary to prove intent to avoid paying proper licence fee—Whether sufficient merely to prove intent to deceive person performing public duty—Vehicles (Excise) Act 1971, s 26(1). **R v Terry** [1984] **1** 65, HL.

Excise licence (cont)—
Rate of duty—
Alteration of vehicle or its use—Lorry licensed as farmer's goods vehicle—Farmer's goods vehicle carrying produce of agricultural land which vehicle owner 'occupies'—Lorry owners engaged in grass-drying business—Lorry used for transporting grass clippings to their premises—Lorry carrying clippings from farm not owned by lorry owners—Agreement between lorry owners and farmer—Farmer allowing lorry owners unrestricted access to his field to cut grass and remove clippings—Operation lasting 3 1/2 days—Whether lorry owners 'occupiers' of the land—Whether lorry entitled to carry farmer's goods vehicle licence—Vehicles (Excise) Act 1971, s 18, Sch 4, para 9. **Howard v Grass Products Ltd** [1972] 3 530, QBD.
Altered condition of vehicle—Loose equipment—Removable boards fitted to sides of lorry—Whether 'loose equipment'—Finance Act 1922, s 14(1)(2)—Road Traffic Act s 26. **Lowe v Stone** [1948] 2 1076, KBD.
Goods vehicle—Agricultural engine—Mechanically propelled lime-spreading vehicle—Carriage of lime—Vehicles (Excise) Act 1949, s 4(2)(a) (as amended by Finance Act 1950, s 13(2), s 5(1)). **R v Berkshire CC, ex p Berkshire Lime Co (Childrey) Ltd** [1953] 2 779, QBD.
Goods vehicle—Estate car delivery van used for carrying photographic equipment in connection with business of photographer—Vehicles (Excise) Act 1949, ss 13(1), 27(1)—Finance Act 1952, s 7(2). **Taylor v Thompson** [1956] 1 352, QBD.
Goods vehicle—Used for conveyance of goods—Vehicle containing no goods—Trailer containing goods—Vehicles (Excise) Act 1949, s 27(1). **James v Davies** [1952] 2 758, QBD.
Goods vehicle—Utility van towing unladen caravan—Vehicles (Excise) Act 1949, s 27(1). **Pearson v Boyes** [1953] 1 492, QBD.
Haulage vehicle—Tractor used for hauling timber loaded on trailer—Equipment fitted to tractor for loading felled timber on to trailer—Whether goods vehicle or haulage vehicle—Vehicles (Excise) Act 1949, s 4(2)(f) (as amended by Finance Act 1950, ss 13(2)(d), 5(1)(2), 27(1)). **Worgan (TK) & Son Ltd v Gloucestershire CC** [1961] 2 301, CA.
Haulage vehicle—Unladen weight—Ballast block—Loose equipment—Tractor carrying tools and ballast—Road Traffic Act 1930, s 26—Finance Act 1933, s 25, Sch VII, Pt II, para 4(e)(ii). **London CC v Hays Wharf Cartage Co Ltd** [1953] 2 34, QBD.
Unlicensed vehicle—
Keeping vehicle on road without a licence—Unlicensed vehicle bought for sale by garage owner and placed in roadway during re-arrangement of showroom—Whether keeping vehicle on road—Vehicles (Excise) Act 1962, s 7. **Dudley v Holland** [1963] 3 732, QBD.
Minimum penalty—Amount of duty chargeable—Rebuttal of presumption—Vehicles (Excise) Act 1949, s 15(1). **Holland v Perry** [1952] 2 720, QBD.
User attracting higher rate of duty—Not a summary offence—Liability to excise penalty—Vehicles (Excise) Act 1949, s 13(2). **Brown v Allweather Mechanical Grouting Co Ltd** [1953] 1 474, QBD.
Express carriage—
Road service licence—
Backing of licence—Conditions—Conditions affecting licence in area in which it is granted—Jurisdiction of Traffic Commissioners—Jurisdiction of Minister of Transport on appeal—Road Traffic Act 1930, ss 72, 73, 81—Road Traffic Act 1934, s 40. **R v Minister of Transport, ex p Valliant Direct Coaches Ltd** [1937] 1 264, KBD.
Separate fares—
Carriage in consideration of separate payments—Carrying friends of owner-driver—Payment for oil and petrol used—Road Traffic Act 1930, s 61. **East Midland Traffic Area Traffic Comrs v Tyler** [1938] 3 39, KBD.
Employees of company—Payment by company—Conveyance, by owner-driver of bus, of passengers employees of company at fixed weekly sum paid by company—Payments by employees to company towards that sum—No payment by employees direct to owner—Knowledge of bus driver that unlawful to carry employees if they in fact contributing to sum paid by company—Whether passengers carried for hire or reward at separate fares—Whether bus driver caused vehicle to be used as express carriage—Road Traffic Act 1960, ss 117(1)(a), 118(3)(b), 134(3). **Wurzal v Wilson** [1965] 1 26, QBD.
Lump sum payment—Car used to take owner's fellow workmen home from work—Owner paid lump sum a week—Each passenger contributing equal amount to lump sum payment whether travelling or not—Road Traffic Act 1930, s 61(1). **Lyons v Denscombe** [1949] 1 977, KBD.
Special occasion—
Conveyance of private party—Conveyance of members of club to football matches on six separate occasions—Conveyance of persons not members of club—No knowledge by owners of carriage—Vicarious liability—Road Traffic Act 1930, s 61(2)—Road Traffic Act 1934, s 25(1). **Browning v Watson (JWH) (Rochester) Ltd** [1953] 2 775, QBD.
Conveyance of private party—Journey advertised by organisers—Coach-owners' ignorance of advertisement—Road Traffic Act 1934, s 25(1)(b). **Reynolds v Austin (G H) & Sons Ltd** [1951] 1 606, KBD.
Conveyance of private party—Members of club conveyed on fishing trips on seven consecutive Sundays—Need to prove occasion special to locality in which journey made—Road Traffic Act 1930, s 61(2)—Road Traffic Act 1934, s 25(1). **Wurzal v Dowker** [1953] 2 88, QBD.
Conveyance of private party—Necessity for driver's work ticket—Belief of coach owner that party a private party—Road Traffic Act 1930, s 72—Road Traffic Act 1930, s 72—Road Traffic Act 1934, s 25. **Evans v Hassan** [1936] 2 107, KBD.
Event continuing over lengthy period—Motor car used to convey passengers to see Blackpool illuminations—Illuminations continued 49 days—Whether a 'special occasion'—Road Traffic Act 1930, s 61(1). **Nelson v Blackford** [1936] 2 109, KBD.
Passengers travelling frequently—Members of club—Conveyance to football ground when team playing at home—Whether passengers travelling 'frequently'—Road Traffic Act 1930, ss 61(2), 72(1), (10)—Road Traffic Act 1934, s 25(1)(e). **Sidery v Evans and Peters** [1938] 4 137, KBD.
Use of hackney carriage as an express carriage—
Sharing of fare by passengers—Owner permitting such use—Road Traffic Act 1930, ss 61, 72(10). **Newell v Cross** [1936] 2 203, KBD.

ROAD TRAFFIC (cont)—

Failure to provide specimen for laboratory test (cont)—
  Reasonable excuse (cont)—
    Physical or mental inability to provide specimen—Risk to health in providing specimen—Consumption of alcohol by accused after ceasing to drive and before requirement—Whether a reasonable excuse—Road Safety Act 1967, s 3(3). **R v Lennard** [1973] **2** 831, CA.
    Religious belief—Belief precluding motorist from supplying specimen of blood—Whether belief capable in law of amounting to reasonable excuse—Road Safety Act 1967, s 3(3). **R v John (Graham)** [1974] **2** 561, CA.
  Refusal to supply specimen—
    What constitutes refusal—Road Safety Act 1967, s 3(3), (6). **R v Clarke** [1969] **2** 1008, CA.
  Urine—
    Request—Request to supply specimen not in accordance with statutory provisions—Effect—Road Safety Act 1967, s 3(6)(b). **R v Pursehouse** [1970] **3** 218, CA.
  Validity of breath test—
    Approved device—Prosecution failing to prove breath test device approved by Secretary of State—Conviction quashed—Road Safety Act 1967, ss 3(3), 7(1). **R v Withecombe** [1969] **1** 157, CA.
  Warning—
    Failure to give warning—Effect—Whether failure to give warning as to consequences of failure to provide specimen prevents specimen being one provided under statute—Whether, on failure to give warning, prejudice is suffered by accused and is relevant in directing jury whether to acquit or not—Road Safety Act 1967, ss 1(1), (2), 3(1), (3), (10). **R v Brush** [1968] **3** 467, CA.
Fare—
  Hackney carriage. See Hackney carriage—Fare, *below*.
  Separate fares—
    Express carriage. See Express carriage—Separate fares, *above*.
  Stage carriage. See Stage carriage—Fare, *below*.
Fixed penalty offences—
  Causing or permitting vehicle to be parked with one or more wheels on any part of urban road other than carriageway. See Urban road—Parking—Criminal offence, *below*.
Giving way—
  Priority to vehicles coming on driver's right. See **Negligence** (Highway—Traffic—Giving way).
Go-Kart—
  Whether intended or adapted for use on road. See Motor vehicle—Intended or adapted for use on road—Go-Kart, *below*.
Goods vehicle—
  Adapted for use for the conveyance of goods—
    Vehicle purchased as passenger-carrying vehicle—After purchase vehicle fitted with large roof rack for purpose of carrying goods for hire or reward—Rack capable of being removed or replaced within few minutes—Whether vehicle goods vehicle requiring C licence—Road Traffic Act 1960, ss 164(1)(a), 191(1). **Flower Freight Co Ltd v Hammond** [1962] **3** 950, QBD.
  Carriage of goods for hire or reward—
    Carriers paid to carry spoil from building site to carriers' gravel and sand pit—Spoil used in the course of carriers' business to fill in worked out parts of pit—Whether carriage of spoil for hire or reward in breach of condition of licence—Road Traffic Act 1960, ss 164(5)(a), 168(3). **Hammond v Hall and Ham River Ltd** [1965] **2** 811, HL.
    Effluent from septic tanks which carrier cleansed for inclusive charge—Carriage of effluent by motor vehicle to farm—Disinfectant added to effluent—No separate charge for removing effluent from premises, or for delivering it to farm—Whether carriage for reward—Whether carriage of own goods—Road and Rail Traffic Act 1933, ss 1(1),(5)(b), 2(4). **Sweetway Sanitary Cleansers Ltd v Bradley** [1961] **2** 821, QBD.
    Goods subjected to process or treatment in course of trade or business—Open-cast coal mining—Carriage of coal from site to and from screening plant—Road and Rail Traffic Act 1933, s 1(5)(b). **Wimpey (George) & Co Ltd v John** [1951] **1** 307, KBD.
    Goods subjected to process or treatment in course of trade or business—Racehorse trainer—Carriage of horse in horsebox—Whether training of racehorses treatment in the course of trade or business—Road and Rail Traffic Act 1933, ss 1(5)(b), 9(1). **Nugent v Phillips** [1939] **4** 57, KBD.
    Rubbish from building site—Vehicle use to carry away rubbish—Whether vehicle used for carriage of goods for hire or reward—Road and Rail Traffic Act 1933, ss 1(5)(a), 9(1). **Spittle v Thames Grit and Aggregates Ltd** [1937] **4** 101, KBD.
    Window cleaner's equipment—Carriage of ladders, buckets, and articles for cleaning—Road and Rail Traffic Act 1933, ss 1(1)(b), 2(4), 36(1). **Clarke v Cherry** [1953] **1** 267, QBD.
  Carrier's licence—
    Licence holder owner driver of vehicle—Contract with appellants to carry concrete for hire or reward—Owner driver falling ill—Employee of appellants sent to drive vehicle—Appellants possessing no carrier's licence—Employee's wages and insurance paid by appellants while he drove vehicle but small sum deducted from contract payments—Arrangement continued only until appellants' contracts carried out—Whether employee servant of owner or appellants—Road Traffic Act 1960, s 164(1),(3). **Ready Mixed Concrete (East Midlands) Ltd v Yorkshire Traffic Area Licensing Authority** [1970] **1** 890, QBD Divl Ct.
    Limited carrier's licence. See Goods vehicle—Limited carrier's licence, *below*.
    Private carrier's licence. See Goods vehicle—Private carrier's licence, *below*.
    Public carrier's licence. See Goods vehicle—Public carrier's licence, *below*.
  Driver's records—
    Agricultural vehicle exempt—Lorry moving agricultural implements from one farm to another—Whether vehicle being used 'in the business of agriculture'—Goods Vehicles (Keeping of Records) Regulations 1935 (SR & O 1935 No 314), reg 6(3)(a). **Flatman v Poole** [1937] **1** 495, KBD.

ROAD TRAFFIC (cont)—
 Goods vehicle (cont)—
  Driver's records (cont)—
   Agricultural vehicle exempt—Vehicle conveying farm produce to retail customer—Whether being 'used in the business of agriculture'—Road and Rail Traffic Act 1933, s 16(1)—Goods Vehicles (Keeping of Records) Regulations 1935 (SR & O 1935 No 314), reg 6(3)(a). **Manley v Dabson** [1949] **2** 578, KBD.
   Driver failing to keep proper record—Due diligence by holder of licence to secure compliance with regulations—Warning on back of daily record sheets supplied to drivers as to filling in records accurately—No system of checking records and informing drivers that records must be filled up used by holder of licence—Due diligence not exercised—Road Traffic Act 1960, s 186(1)—Road Traffic Act 1962, s 20—Goods Vehicles (Keeping of Records) Regulations 1935 (SR & O 1935 No 314), reg 6. **Wurzal v WGA Robinson (Express Haulage) Ltd** [1969] **2** 1021, QBD.
   Duty of driver to keep records—Information as to periods of driving, rest etc—Journey to destination outside Great Britain—Return journey to Great Britain—Whether duty to record information as to periods of driving, rest, etc whilst outside Great Britain—Drivers' Hours (Goods Vehicles) (Keeping of Records) Regulations 1970 (SI 1970 No 123), reg 3(1). **Lawson v Fox** [1973] **2** 309, QBD.
   Holder of licence delegating checking of records to secretary—Failure by secretary to cause records to be maintained—Reasonable belief by holder of licence that secretary competent—Liability of holder of licence—Road Trafic Act 1960 s 186(1)—Road Traffic Act 1962, s 20—Goods Vehicles (Keeping of Records) Regulations 1935, (S R & O 1935 No 314), reg 6. **Series v Poole** [1967] **3** 849, QBD.
   Part-time driver—Salesman provided by employer with authorised vehicle—No obligation to use vehicle for work—Whether record of hours of work, etc, to be kept when salesman actually using vehicle—Whether salesman was a 'part-time driver'—Road Traffic Act 1960, s 186(1)—Goods Vehicles (Keeping of Records) Regulations 1935 (SR & O 1935 No 314), reg 5. **Gross Cash Registers Ltd v Vogt** [1965] **3** 832, QBD.
  Excise duty—
   Rate. See Excise licence—Rate of duty—Goods vehicle, above.
  Goods or burden of any description—
   Conveyance of burden—Sound-recording van—Apparatus an essentially permanent fixture—Whether a 'burden' conveyed by van—Road Traffic Act 1930, ss 2(4)(b), 10(1), Sch I. **Burmingham v Lindsell** [1936] **2** 159, KBD.
  Heavy goods vehicle—
   Driver's licence. See Heavy goods vehicle driver's licence, below.
   Prohibition of night-time use of heavy goods vehicles in residential areas of London without permit—Condition of permit requiring vehicles to be fitted with air brake noise suppressors—EEC regulations regarding brakes and permissible sound levels not requiring installation of air brake noise suppressors—Whether requirement to fit air brake noise suppressor as condition for grant of permit for night-time use in London unlawful—Whether condition contrary to Community law—Road Traffic Regulation Act 1984, s 6—Council Directives (EEC) 70/157, 71/320. **Freight Transport Association Ltd v London Boroughs Transport Committee** [1991] **3** 915, HL.
  Large goods vehicle—
   Large goods vehicle driver's licence—Revocation or suspension of licences—Referral of matters of conduct to traffic commissioners—Conduct—Road Traffic Act 1988, ss 116, 121. **Meredith v Traffic Comr for the Western Traffic Area** [2011] **1** 1010, QBD.
  Limitation of driver's time on duty—
   Break and rest periods—Weekly rest period—Day—Whether 'day' meaning any 24-hour period commencing at midnight—Whether driver guilty of breaking weekly rest period requirement if he works six consecutive driving periods in less than six days—Transport Act 1968, s 96(11A)—EC Council Regulation 3820/85, arts 6(1), 8(3). **Kelly v Shulman** [1989] **1** 106, QBD.
   Company providing road maintenance services and using lorry to transport road planing machine for use at another site—Driver failing to keep tachograph record—Whether company's use of lorry was use 'in connection with' highway maintenance and control—Transport Act 1968, s 97—Council Regulation (EEC) 3820/85, art 4(6). **Vehicle Inspectorate v Bruce Cook Road Planing Ltd** [1999] **4** 761, HL.
   Evidence—Driver's records—Prosecution of employers for permitting driver to exceed permitted hours—Only evidence records of hours kept by driver—Records required to be kept by statute—Whether records admissible in evidence—Road Traffic Act 1930, s 19—Road and Rail Traffic Act 1933, s 16. **Beer v WH Clench (1930) Ltd** [1936] **1** 449, KBD.
   Evidence—Evidence of bad character—Causing or permitting failure without reasonable excuse to make relevant record or entry—Defendant charged with permitting failure to make relevant records or entries during certain period—Prosecution seeking to rely on evidence of failures in earlier period—Whether evidence of bad character—Whether evidence which had to do with alleged facts of offence charged—Transport Act 1968, s 99ZE—Criminal Justice Act 2003, s 98. **Vehicle and Operator Services Agency v Ace Crane and Transport Ltd** [2010] **2** 791, DC.
   Journey home—Car provided by employer—Whether time spent on journey home by private car provided by employer constitutes hours for rest—Road Traffic Act 1960, s 73(1), 4—Goods Vehicles (Keeping of Records) Regulations 1935 (SR & O 1935 No 314), reg 6(1). **Witchell v Abbott** [1966] **2** 657, QBD.
   Length of working day—Periods of duty, driving and rest—Computation of periods—Journey to destination outside Great Britain—Return journey to Great Britain—Whether account to be taken of driver's activities outside Great Britain in computing periods of duty, driving and rest—Transport Act 1968, ss 96(1), (3)(a), 103(1). **Lawson v Fox** [1974] **1** 783, HL.
   Other work in connection with vehicle—Watching vehicle being loaded—Driver standing by and watching loading—Driver responsible for vehicle but taking no part in actual work of loading—Whether driver engaged in 'other work in connection with' the vehicle—Road Traffic Act 1930, s 19. **Wells & Son Ltd v Sidery** [1939] **4** 54, KBD.
   Permitting driver to drive for more than allowed continuous period—Actual knowledge or knowledge of circumstances on part of employers necessary to constitute offence—Road Traffic Act 1960, s 73(1)(c)(ii). **Grays Haulage Co Ltd v Arnold** [1966] **1** 896, QBD.

ROAD TRAFFIC (cont)—
  Goods vehicle (cont)—
    Limitation of driver's time on duty (cont)—
      Time spent on other work in connexion with a vehicle or the load carried thereby—Assisting at depot after period of driving—Unloading vans and sorting parcels—Road Traffic Act 1930, s 19(1)(i),(2)(b). **Parkinson v Axon** [1951] **2** 647, KBD.
      Voluntary overtime in employers' scrapyard—Whether time when driver bound by terms of employment—Road Traffic Act 1960, s 73(4). **Potter v Gorbould** [1969] **3** 828, QBD.
    Limited carrier's licence—
      Failure to comply with conditions of B licence—Aiding and abetting—Liability of hirer—Road and Rail Traffic Act 1933, s 9(1). **Carter v Mace** [1949] **2** 714, KBD.
      Use of vehicle—Person by whom vehicle used—Vehicle hired by owner to another person—Driver paid by owner—Vehicle used to carry goods for hire or reward for greater distance than permitted by owner's licence—Road and Rail Traffic Act 1933, s 1(3). **Sykes v Millington** [1953] **1** 1098, QBD.
    Mirrors—
      Vehicle properly equipped with mirrors for normal use—Vehicle carrying load of such dimensions that mirrors were ineffective—Whether contravention of regulations—Motor Vehicles (Construction and Use) Regulations 1963 (SI 1963 No 1646), reg 17(1)(a). **Mawdsley v Walter Cox (Transport) Ltd** [1965] **3** 728, QBD.
    Operator's licence—
      Exemption—Cases in which licence not required—Tower wagon—Vehicle on which only goods carried are those required in connection with work on which tower wagon ordinarily used as such—Meaning of 'tower wagon'—Vehicle used solely as mobile tower enabling overhead work to be done—Transport Act 1968, s 60(1)(2)—Goods Vehicles (Operators' Licences) Regulations 1969 (SI 1969 No 1636), reg 3, Sch 1, para 20. **Anderson and Heeley Ltd v Paterson** [1975] **1** 523, QBD.
    Plating and test certificates. *See* Plating and test certificates for goods vehicles, *below*.
    Private carrier's licence—
      Carriage for hire or reward—Whether breach of terms of licence—Road and Rail Traffic Act 1933, s 2(1). **Wurzal v Houghton Main Home Coal Delivery Service Ltd** [1936] **3** 311, KBD.
      Transfer—Whether licensing authority can hold an inquiry—Road and Rail Traffic Act 1933, s 11. **Woodward, Re application by** [1937] **4** 656, Ch D.
      Vehicle used to carry goods for hire or reward by person other than licence holder—No identification certificate affixed—Road and Rail Traffic Act 1933, ss 2(4), 9(1)—Goods Vehicles (Licences and Prohibitions) Regulations 1936 (SR & O 1936 No 269), reg 12(2). **Lloyd v Lee (E) Ltd** [1951] **1** 589, KBD.
    Public carrier's licence—
      Application—Contract A licence existing—Proposed substitution of A licence—Owner of goods carried under contract supporting application—Question whether proposed change in his best interests irrelevant to the grant of application. **Merchandise Transport Ltd v British Transport Commission** [1961] **3** 495, CA.
      Condition to use vehicle for hauling goods of one firm—Use for haulage for other firms—Permit to use outside 25 miles radius—Effect of permit on conditions of licence—Road and Rail Traffic Act 1933, s 9(1)—Transport Act 1947, s 52(1). **Barham v Castell** [1951] **2** 809, KBD.
      Failure to comply with conditions of A licence—Aiding and abetting—Hirer making reasonable inquiries—Road and Rail Traffic Act 1933, s 9(1). **Davies, Turner & Co Ltd v Brodie** [1954] **3** 283, QBD.
      Form of application—Form—Vires—Whether question on application form as to proposed facilities were ultra vires—Whether answers by applicant as to normal user to be taken into account on subsequent application for additional vehicles—Road Traffic Act 1960, s 172(2)(a)—Goods Vehicles (Licences and Prohibitions) Regulations 1960 (SI 1960 No 1505), reg 4(4), Sch 2, Form G V 1A, para 7(a). **Munson v British Railways Board** [1965] **3** 441, CA.
      Restriction on area of operation—Application to licensing authority to specify new 'operating centre'—Desire to carry goods more than 25 miles from true centre—Transport Act 1947, ss 52(1), 58(4). **R v Licensing Authority for Goods Vehicles for the Metropolitan Traffic Area, ex p B E Barrett Ltd** [1949] **1** 656, KBD.
      Restriction on area of operation—Exception—Carriage of meat—Fish not included—Transport Act 1947, ss 52(1)(a), 125(1). **Wardhaugh (A F) Ltd v Mace** [1952] **2** 28, QBD.
      Restriction on area of operation—Permit to carry agricultural produce outside twenty-five miles limit—Imported unprocessed hides—Transport Act 1947, s 52(1). **Scarr v Wurzal** [1951] **1** 1014, KBD.
      Subsidiary company's application—Undertaking to carry only parent company's goods on outward journeys—Uneconomic competition for return loads—Parent company already having C licence—Conditional B licence appropriate—Whether relationship between subsidiary and parent company could be considered. **Merchandise Transport Ltd v British Transport Commission** [1961] **3** 495, CA.
      Transport tribunal—Appellate jurisdiction—Objection—Whether tribunal limited to objection—Precedent—Previous decisions not to inhibit tribunal examining the merits of each case. **Merchandise Transport Ltd v British Transport Commission** [1961] **3** 495, CA.
    Right to licence—
      Agreement for use of name and tonnage—Illegality—Road and Rail Traffic Act 1933, ss 1(1),(3),(8), 7, 8, 16, 21. **Nash v Stevenson Transport Ltd** [1936] **1** 906, CA.
    Speed limit. *See* Excessive speed—Goods vehicle, *above*.
    Suspension of licence—
      Overloading goods vehicles—Carrier convicted and fined—Jurisdiction of licensing authority also to suspend licences for same offences—Road Traffic Act 1960, s 178(1)(b). **Hampton (R) & Sons, Re** [1965] **3** 106, CA.
  Hackney carriage—
    Carriage of person with consent of hirer—
      Express consent—Acquiescence of hirer insufficient—Town Police Clauses Act 1847, s 59. **Yates v Gates** [1970] **1** 754, QBD.

ROAD TRAFFIC (cont)—
Hackney carriage (cont)—
Fare—
Agreement to pay more than legal fare—Booking fee—Telephone booking service—Booking fee charged for use of telephone service—Hirer told of fee during negotiations—Fee collected by taxi driver at same time as payment for journey—Payment for journey charged at rate prescribed by byelaws—Whether agreement to pay booking fee an 'agreement for payment of more than the fare allowed' by byelaws—Town Police Clauses Act 1847, s 55. **House v Reynolds** [1977] **1** 689, QBD.
Metropolitan police area—Journey exceeding six miles—Agreed fare in excess of prescribed rates—London Hackney Carriage Act 1853, s 17(1),(2)—Metropolitan Public Carriages Act 1869, s 9(3), restriction (2)—London Cab Order 1934, (SR & O 1934 No 1346). **Goodman v Serle** [1947] **2** 318, KBD.
Overcharging—Taking as a fare a greater sum than that authorised by byelaws—Booking fee—Telephone booking service—Booking fee charged for use of telephone service—Hirer told of fee during negotiations—Fee collected by taxi driver at same time as payment for journey—Payment for journey charged at rate prescribed by byelaws—Whether booking fee part of fare—Whether driver guilty of 'taking as a fare' a greater sum than that authorised by byelaws—Town Police Clauses Act 1847, s 58. **House v Reynolds** [1977] **1** 689, QBD.
Hiring—
Conflict between statute and byelaw—Validity of byelaw. *See* **Byelaw** (Validity—Repugnant to statute—Hackney carriage).
Licence—
Application for licence—Evidence—Spent convictions—Authority admitting evidence relating to applicant's spent convictions to decide whether applicant fit and proper person—Whether authority right to do so—Whether authority having to identify issues to which spent convictions must relate before considering their admissibility—Rehabilitation of Offenders Act 1974, s 7(3). **Adamson v Waveney DC** [1997] **2** 898, QBD.
Change of ownership of licensed hackney carriage—New owner's right to amendment of licence and register—Town Police Clauses Act 1847, s 37. **R v Weymouth Corp, ex p Teletax (Weymouth) Ltd** [1947] **1** 779, KBD.
Driver required to have licence whether or not hackney carriage plying for hire—Town Police Clauses Act 1847, s 46. **Yates v Gates** [1970] **1** 754, QBD.
Grant of licence—Natural justice—Duty of licensing authority to act fairly—Duty to give a hearing to all those affected by decision to grant or refuse applications for licences—Council as licensing authority resolving to increase total number of licences for taxi cabs within area—Resolution made without giving taxi cab owners' association an opportunity to be heard—Association previously assured that they would be given opportunity to make representations—Resolution also disregarding previous undertaking to association that no further licences would be issued until proposed legislation controlling private hire cars in force—Council not at liberty to disregard undertaking—Undertaking compatible with council's statutory duties—Order prohibiting council from acting on resolution until representations by interested persons heard and other matters, including undertaking, considered—Town Police Clauses Act 1847, s 37. **Liverpool Taxi Owners' Association, Re** [1972] **2** 589, CA.
Inspection—Whether district council entitled to charge fees for inspection of vehicles at time inspection carried out—Local Government (Miscellaneous Provisions) Act 1976, s 70(1)(2). **Kelly v Liverpool City Council** [2003] **2** 772, CA.
Revocation of licence—Power to revoke licence on second conviction for any offence against Town Police Clauses Act 1847, or bye-laws—Whether there must be second conviction for same offence—Town Police Clauses Act 1847, s 50. **Bowers v Gloucester Corp** [1963] **1** 437, QBD.
Suspension or revocation—Appeal—Appeal to Crown Court—Right of appeal—Person aggrieved—Local authority—Local authority revoking hackney carriage licences—Licence-holder appealing to magistrates' court—Magistrates allowing appeal and making order for costs against local authority—Whether local authority having right to appeal to Crown Court—Whether local authority 'person aggrieved' by magistrates' decision—Public Health Act 1936, s 301—Local Government (Miscellaneous Provisions) Act 1976, ss 60, 61, 77. **Cook v Southend BC** [1990] **1** 243, CA.
Plying for hire—
Mini-cab—Advertisements and telephone number on vehicle—Radio aerial on roof providing two-way communication—Notice reading 'Mini-cab booking' on sun vizor—Metropolitan Public Carriage Act 1869, s 7. **Newman v Vincent** [1962] **2** 806, QBD.
Mini-cab—Advertisements and telephone number on vehicle—Radio aerial on roof providing two-way communication—Vehicle parked in bus stand-by—Metropolitan Public Carriage Act 1869, s 7. **Rose v Welbeck Motors Ltd** [1962] **2** 801, QBD.
Motor cars—Plying for hire without being licensed—Vehicles standing in public street—Hire and payment made in adjacent street—No contract with, and no payment to, driver of vehicle—Metropolitan Public Carriage Act 1869, s 7. **Gilbert v McKay** [1946] **1** 458, KBD.
Obligation to accept fare while travelling along street—London Hackney Carriage Act 1853, ss 7, 17(2). **Hunt v Morgan** [1948] **2** 1065, KBD.
Private hire service—Service advertised but vehicles to be hired not marked or exhibited as such—Hire arranged at office—Metropolitan Public Carriage Act 1869, s 7. **Cogley v Sherwood** [1959] **2** 313, QBD.
Standing in any street or place—Standing—Meaning—Something akin to waiting or parking—London Hackney Carriage Act 1831, s 35. **Eldridge v British Airports Authority** [1970] **2** 92, QBD.
Standing or place appointed—Plying for hire 'elsewhere than at some standing or place appointed'—Plying for hire in private place—London Hackney Carriages Act 1843, s 33—London Passenger Transport Act 1934, s 112. **Benjamin v Cooper** [1951] **2** 907, KBD.
Sign indicating vehicle is a hackney carriage—
What amounts to—Sign complying with bye-laws—Vehicle carrying sign 'M Mosley Wakefield 19'—Whether a distinctive sign indicating vehicle a hackney carriage—Roads Act 1920, s 11(1)—Road Vehicles (Registration and Licensing) Regulations 1941 (SR & O 1941 No 1149), reg 31, Sch V. **Eccles v Kirke** [1949] **1** 428, KBD.

ROAD TRAFFIC (cont)—
Hackney carriage (cont)—
Use as express carriage. *See* Express carriage—Use of hackney carriage as an express carriage, *above.*
Hand signal—
Stopping of vehicle—
Failure to give signal. *See* Stopping of vehicle—Failure to give hand signal, *below.*
Heavy goods vehicle driver's licence—
Application—
Appeal against refusal—Applicant not having driving experience for qualifying period—Licensing authority bound to refuse application—Appeal to justices—Licensing authority ordered to grant licence—Application for certiorari to quash order—Whether applicant 'person aggrieved'—Whether justices having power to make order—Road Traffic Act 1960, s 195(2), Sch 15, para 1. **R v Ipswich Justices, ex p Robson** [1971] **2** 1395, QBD.
Heavy motor car—
Abnormal indivisible load—
Notification to highway and bridge authority—Failure to notify—Whether power to dispense wholly with notice—Motor Vehicles (Authorisation of Special Types) General Order 1969 (SI 1969 No 344), art 28(2). **Cohen (George) 600 Group Ltd v Hird** [1970] **2** 650, QBD.
Undue expense or risk of damage—Expense or risk in dividing the load only to be considered—Load consisting of two separate entities, loaded together to strengthen each other during carriage—Motor Vehicles (Authorisation of Special Types) General Order 1955 (SI 1955 No 1038), art 13. **Sunter Bros Ltd v Arlidge** [1962] **1** 510, QBD.
Braking system—
Six-wheeled lorry with four front wheels—Hand-brake operating only on the two rear wheels—Road Traffic Act 1930, s 3—Motor Vehicles (Construction and Use) Regulations 1955 (SI 1955 No 482), reg 39(1),(7)(a)(i). **Langton v Johnson** [1956] **3** 474, QBD.
Driving under age. *See* Driving under age—Heavy motor car, *above.*
Overall length—
Heavy goods motor lorry with container affixed to platform—Container enabling vehicle to carry livestock—Length of vehicle without container thirty feet—Length of vehicle with container thirty-five feet—Whether contravention of Road Traffic Act 1960, s 64(2), and Motor Vehicles (Construction and Use) Regulations 1955 (SI 1955 No 482), reg 6(3), as amended by Motor Vehicles (Construction and Use) (Amendment) Regulations 1961 (SI 1961 No 1313), reg 2(1). **Hughes (Claude) & Co (Carlisle) Ltd v Hyde** [1963] **1** 598, QBD.
Overhang—
Overall length—Pantechnicon with movable tailboard—Permitted overhang exceeded when tailboard down—Road Traffic Act 1930, s 3(1)—Motor Vehicles (Construction and Use) Regulations 1947 (SR & O 1947 No 670), reg 33. **Andrews v Kershaw (HE) Ltd** [1951] **2** 764, KBD.
Overall length—Pantechnicon with movable tailboard—Tailboard constructed to increase carrying capacity—Permitted overhang exceeded when tailboard down—Whether offence under regulations relating to overall length and overhang—Motor Vehicles (Construction and Use) Regulations 1963 (SI 1963 No 1646), regs 3(1), 41 (as amended by Motor Vehicles (Construction and Use) (Amendment) (No 2) Regulations 1964 (SI 1964 No 1169)). **Guest Scottish Carriers Ltd v Trend** [1967] **3** 52, QBD.
Overall length—Permitted overhang exceeded when container clipped on to vehicle—Container acting as body of vehicle—Container easily detachable and transferable to other vehicles—Whether vehicle exceeding permitted overhang—Whether container part of vehicle—Motor Vehicles (Construction and Use) Regulations 1978, reg 58. **Hawkins v Harold A Russett Ltd** [1983] **1** 215, QBD.
Registration—
Date of registration—Provisions applicable to vehicles 'registered on or after 1st January, 1932'—Motor Vehicles (Construction and Use) (Amendment) Provisional Regulations 1931, reg 10(ii). **Mackinnon v Peate** [1936] **2** 240, KBD.
Weight transmitted to road surface—
Ascertainment of weight—Motor Vehicles (Construction and Use) Regulations 1931 (SR & O 1931 No 4), reg 59. **Prosser v Richings** [1936] **2** 1627, KBD.
Highway Code—
Breach of code—
Contributory negligence. *See* **Negligence** (Contributory negligence—Breach of Highway Code).
Hire or reward—
Carriage of goods—
Goods vehicle. *See* Goods vehicle—Carriage of goods for hire or reward, *above.*
Hospital patient—
Breath test. *See* Breath test—Hospital patient, *above.*
Failure to provide specimen for laboratory test. *See* Failure to provide specimen for laboratory test—Hospital patient, *above.*
Specimen for laboratory test to determine blood-alcohol proportion. *See* Specimen for laboratory test to determine driver's blood-alcohol proportion—Hospital patient, *below.*
Hours of duty—
Goods vehicle driver. *See* Goods vehicle—Limitation of driver's time on duty, *above.*
Indictment—
Joinder of charges. *See* **Indictment** (Joinder of charges—Road traffic).
Insurance—
Motor insurance—
Generally. *See* **Motor insurance**.
Using vehicle on road without policy of insurance being in force—Accused not driver. *See* **Motor insurance** (Using vehicle or causing or permitting vehicle to be used on road without policy being in force—Accused not the driver).
Using of motor vehicle while uninsured. *See* **Motor insurance** (Compulsory insurance against third party risks—Breach of statutory duty—Owner uninsured).
Laboratory test—
Failure to provide specimen. *See* Failure to provide specimen for laboratory test, *above.*

ROAD TRAFFIC (cont)—

Laboratory test (cont)—

Specimen to determine driver's blood-alcohol proportion. *See* Specimen for laboratory test to determine driver's blood-alcohol proportion, *below*.

Land implement—

Trailer. *See* Trailer—Land implement, *below*.

Learner driver—

Examiner—

Duty of care. *See* **Negligence** (Duty to take care—Driving examiner).

Instructor—

Contributory negligence—Accident. *See* **Negligence** (Contributory negligence—Road accident—Learner-driver and instructor).

Supervision. *See* Driving licence—Supervision of learner driver, *above*.

Licence—

Driving licence. *See* Driving licence, *above*.

Excise licence. *See* Excise licence, *above*.

Goods vehicle—

Carrier's licence. *See* Goods vehicle—Carrier's licence, *above*.

Heavy goods vehicle driver's licence. *See* Heavy goods vehicle driver's licence, *above*.

Operator's licence. *See* Goods vehicle—Operator's licence, *above*.

Hackney carriage. *See* Hackney carriage—Licence, *above*.

Road service licence—

Express carriage. *See* Express carriage—Road service licence, *above*.

Public service vehicle. *See* Public service vehicle—Road service licence, *below*.

Trade licence. *See* Trade licence, *below*.

Light locomotive—

Construction—

Relevant date—Lorry converted to carry generating plant—Offence—Drawing trailers—Whether date of conversion relevant date of 'construction'—Road Traffic Act 1930, s 2(1)(b). **Keeble v Miller** [1950] **1** 261, KBD.

Light signals. *See* Traffic sign—Light signals, *below*.

Lighting of vehicles—

Civil liability for breach of duty—

Duty imposed under sanction of penalty—Failure to carry rear light on car during hours of darkness—Whether separate remedy available to person aggrieved—Road Transport Lighting Act 1927, ss 1, 10. **Clark v Brims** [1947] **1** 242, KBD.

Road—

Forecourt of shop adjoining highway—Forecourt used only by customers—No wall between forecourt and highway—Road Transport Lighting Act 1927, ss 1(1), 15. **Thomas v Dando** [1951] **1** 1010, KBD.

Limitation of time on duty—

Goods vehicle driver. *See* Goods vehicle—Limitation of driver's time on duty, *above*.

Loading of vehicles—

Restrictions on waiting and loading. *See* Waiting and loading restrictions, *below*.

London—

London Passenger Transport Board. *See* **London Passenger Transport Board**.

London Transport Executive. *See* **London Transport Executive**.

Waiting and loading restrictions. *See* Waiting and loading restrictions—London, *below*.

Lorry—

Heavy motor vehicle. *See* Heavy motor car, *above*.

Mechanically propelled vehicle. *See* Motor vehicle—Mechanically propelled vehicle, *below*.

Mini-cab—

Plying for hire. *See* Hackney carriage—Plying for hire—Mini-cab, *above*.

Mirror—

Goods vehicle. *See* Goods vehicle—Mirrors, *above*.

Motor bicycle—

Provisional licence—

Conditions attached to licence—Bicycle not having sidecar attached. *See* Driving licence—Conditions attached to provisional licences—Motor bicycle not having sidecar attached, *above*.

Sidecar—

Provisional licence—Conditions. *See* Driving licence—Provisional licence—Conditions attached to provisional licences—Motor bicycle not having sidecar attached, *above*.

Motor cycle—

Crash helmet—

Failure to wear. *See* **Negligence** (Contributory negligence—Road accident—Crash helmet).

Modified motor cycle—

Whether a 'motor vehicle'. *See* Motor vehicle—Motor cycle, *below*.

Motor insurance. *See* **Motor insurance**.

Motor tractor—

Chassis—

Chassis capable of being used for various types of vehicle—Chassis destined to be fitted with fire engine body—Whether chassis a motor tractor—Road Traffic Act 1960, s 253(1),(6). **Millard v Turvey** [1968] **2** 7, QBD.

Overall width—

Motor tractor towing land implement on road—Whether one vehicle—Motor Vehicles (Construction and Use) Regulations 1955 (SI 1955 No 482), reg 33—Motor Vehicles (Authorisation of Special Types) General Order 1955 (SI 1955 No 1038), art 10, as amended by Motor Vehicles (Authorisation of Special Types) Order 1956 (SI 1956 No 1265), art 3(2). **Gwennap (William) (Agricultural) Ltd v Amphlett** [1957] **2** 605, QBD.

Motor vehicle—
Abandoned or broken down vehicle on road—
Removal—Police powers of removal—Police power to arrange for removal—Whether police vicariously liable for negligence of independent contractor engaged to remove abandoned vehicle—Removal and Disposal of Vehicles Regulations 1968 reg 4. **Rivers v Cutting** [1982] 3 69, CA.
Articulated vehicle. *See* Articulated vehicle, *above.*
Carriage of passengers for hire or reward—
Insurance. *See* **Motor insurance** (Compulsory insurance against third party risks—Passengers carried for hire or reward in private vehicle).
Causing vehicle to be used on road in breach of regulations—
Mens rea of offence—Driver employed by company overloading one of company's vehicles—Company having forbidden drivers to overload vehicles—Knowledge of overloading—Knowledge of company required to be that of someone exercising control over company's affairs—Company having no knowledge of overloading—Whether company having 'caused' vehicle to be used in contravention of regulations—Whether offence absolute—Road Traffic Act 1972, s 40(5)(b). **Ross Hillman Ltd v Bond** [1974] 2 287, QBD.
Collision—
Negligence—Contributory negligence. *See* **Negligence** (Contributory negligence—Collision between vehicles on road).
Damage due to accident arising out of presence of vehicle on road—
Criminal proceedings—Compensation. *See* **Sentence** (Compensation—Damage due to accident arising out of presence of vehicle on road).
Dangerous vehicle. *See* Dangerous vehicle, *above.*
Driving. *See* Driving, *above.*
Dual-purpose vehicle—
Bicycle fitted with auxiliary engine—Use as pedal cycle—No removal of essential parts of engine—Need of third party insurance and driving licence—Road Traffic Act 1930, ss 1, 4(1), 35(1). **Floyd v Bush** [1953] 1 265, QBD.
Bicycle fitted with auxiliary engine—Use as pedal cycle after removal of essential parts of engine—Need for third-party insurance—Road Traffic Act 1930, ss 1, 35(1). **Lawrence v Howlett** [1952] 2 74, QBD.
Duty of driver to take care. *See* **Negligence** (Duty to take care—Driver of motor vehicle).
Efficient braking system—
Maintenance—Brakes not maintained in good and efficient working order—Accident caused thereby—Whether car 'equipped with efficient braking system'—Motor Vehicles (Construction and Use) Regulations 1937 (SR & O 1937 No 229), reg 34(1). **Cole v Young** [1938] 4 39, KBD.
Efficient working order—
Trailer—Trailer insecurely attached but vehicle trailer and coupling in good repair—Whether in such condition that no danger likely to be caused—Whether in efficient working order—Motor Vehicles (Construction and Use) Regulations 1955 (SI 1955 No 482), reg 73(1). **O'Neill v Brown** [1961] 1 571, QBD.
Excise licence. *See* Excise licence, *above.*
Goods vehicle. *See* Goods vehicle, *above.*
Heavy motor car. *See* Heavy motor car, *above.*
Insurance. *See* **Motor insurance**.
Intended or adapted for use on road—
Dumpers—Use of dumpers on road in housing estate in course of construction—Dumpers not equipped with horns and did not display identity certificate—Whether dumpers intended or adapted for use on roads—Road and Rail Traffic Act 1933, s 36—Road Traffic Act 1930, s 1. **Daley v Hargreaves** [1961] 1 552, QBD.
Go-Kart—Mechanically propelled vehicle with engine at rear—Tubular frame mounted on four small wheels and equipped with seat, steering-wheel and column, and silencer—Brakes operating on rear wheels only—Whether vehicle intended or adapted for use on roads—'Intended'—'Adapted'—Road Traffic Act 1960, s 253(1). **Burns v Currell** [1963] 2 297, QBD.
Land implement—
Trailer. *See* Trailer—Land implement, *below.*
Latent defect—
Defence. *See* **Negligence** (Defence—Latent defect—Motor vehicle).
Leaving vehicle in parking place otherwise than as authorised. *See* Parking place—Leaving vehicle otherwise than as authorised, *below.*
Light locomotive. *See* Light locomotive, *above.*
Lighting. *See* Lighting of vehicles, *above.*
Mechanically propelled vehicle—
Car with no engine—Possibility that engine might shortly be replaced and motive power restored—Vehicles (Excise) Act 1949, ss 1, 15. **Newberry v Simmonds** [1961] 2 318, QBD.
Incapable of being driven—Car with incomplete engine, no batteries, no gearbox, three flat tyres and one tyre missing, incapable of movement under its own power—Repairs necessary to put car into running order out of all proportion to its value—Vehicles (Excise) Act 1949, s 15(1), as amended by Finance Act 1959, s 10(1), Sch 3, para 1(1), (6)—Road Traffic Act 1960, ss 201(1), 253(1). **Smart v Allan** [1962] 3 893, QBD.
Motor cycle—
Motor cycle manufactured for road use but adapted for use in scrambling on private land—Whether motor cycle a 'motor vehicle'—Road Traffic Act 1972, s 190. **Chief Constable of Avon and Somerset v Fleming** [1987] 1 318, QBD.
Motor tractor. *See* Motor tractor, *above.*
Negligence. *See* **Negligence** (Vehicles).
Overall length—
Articulated vehicle. *See* Articulated vehicle—Overall length, *above.*
Heavy motor car. *See* Heavy motor car—Overall length, *above.*
Overall width—
Motor tractor. *See* Motor tractor—Overall width, *above.*

ROAD TRAFFIC (cont)—
  Motor vehicle (cont)—
    Overhang—
      Heavy motor car. *See* Heavy motor car—Overhang, *above.*
    Permitting vehicle to be used on road in breach of regulations—
      Knowledge of user—Limited company—Trailer used with defective brake—Need to prove knowledge before permitting user could be established—Motor Vehicles (Construction and Use) Regulations 1951 (SI 1951 No 2101), reg 75, reg 101. **James & Son Ltd v Smee** [1954] 3 273, QBD.
    Public service vehicle. *See* Public service vehicle, *below.*
    Registration mark—
      Assignment. *See* **Chose in action** (Assignment—Vehicle registration mark).
    Sale by thief—
      Purchaser effecting extensive repairs to vehicle—Court order that vehicle to be returned to true owner—Liability of true owner to compensate purchaser for work done. *See* **Restitution** (Unjust enrichment—Compensation—Work done on property of another).
    Sale in unroadworthy condition—
      Information—Information alleging more than one breach of regulations. *See* **Magistrates** (Information—Duplicity—Information alleging more than one breach of regulations—Sale of motor vehicle in unroadworthy condition in breach of regulations).
      Offer to sell—Offence—Sale of vehicle by auction—Auctioneer inviting bids for vehicle—Whether auctioneer 'offering to sell' vehicle—Road Traffic Act 1960, s 68(1) (as amended by the Road Traffic Act 1962, s 51(1), Sch 4, Part I). **British Car Auctions Ltd v Wright** [1972] 3 462, QBD.
      Right of action for breach of statutory requirements—Car sold with defective brakes—Accident caused thereby—Statutory liability of vendor—Penalty prescribed by statute—No right of action to purchaser for vendor's statutory offence—Road Traffic Act 1930, ss 3, 59, 113(2)—Road Traffic Act 1934, s 8—Motor Vehicles (Construction and Use) Regulations 1937, (SR & O 1937 No 229), regs 39(1), 68—Motor Vehicles (Construction and Use) (Amendment No 2) Provisional Regulations 1938, reg 7. **Badham v Lambs Ltd** [1945] 2 295, KBD.
    Seat belt—
      Failure to wear—Contributory negligence. *See* **Negligence** (Contributory negligence—Road accident—Seat belt).
    Special type—
      Two tractors carrying abnormal indivisible load—Whether one vehicle—How many attendants necessary—Road Traffic Act 1930, s 17(1)—Motor Vehicles (Authorisation of Special Types) General Order 1955 (SI 1955 No 1038), art 18. **Dixon v BRS (Pickfords) Ltd** [1959] 1 449, QBD.
      Two trailers drawn by one locomotive carrying abnormal indivisible load with another locomotive in attendance—Maximum total weight of trailers and load over forty tons—Overall width exceeding nine feet six inches—Total of four persons in attendance—Whether effect of non-compliance as to number of attendants contravened condition as to maximum total weight—Motor Vehicles (Construction and Use) Regulations 1955 (SI 1955 No 482), reg 66—Motor Vehicles (Authorisation of Special Types) General Order 1955 (SI 1955 No 1038), art 14—Road Traffic Act 1960, s 64(1),(4). **Cook (Siddle C) Ltd v Holden** [1962] 3 984, QBD.
    Stage carriage. *See* Stage carriage, *below.*
    Stopping at school crossings. *See* School crossing—Stopping of motor vehicles, *below.*
    Taking vehicle without authority. *See* Taking vehicle without authority, *below.*
    Test. *See* Vehicle test, *below.*
    Tyres. *See* Tyres, *below.*
    Unladen weight—
      Wooden container attached to base of lorry—Whether 'alternative body'—Road Traffic Act 1930, s 26—Motor Vehicles (Construction and Use) Regulations 1951 (SI 1951 No 2101), regs 61, 63(2), 101. **Cording v Halse** [1954] 3 287, QBD.
    Unlicensed vehicle. *See* Excise licence—Unlicensed vehicle, *above.*
    Using vehicle on road in breach of regulations—
      Driver of vehicle—Accident due to improper loading—Whether driver liable as user of vehicle—Motor Vehicles (Construction and Use) Regulations 1937 (SR & O 1937 No 229), regs 67(2), 94. **Gifford v Whittaker** [1942] 1 604, KBD.
      Hire of vehicle—Lorry hired with driver from haulage contractors by quarry owners—Lorry loaded with tarmac at quarry owners' works—Quarry owners responsible for correct weight of lorry leaving works—Lorry overloaded and driven on road by haulage contractors' driver—Whether quarry owners were 'using' lorry at the time—Whether contravention by them of Road Traffic Act 1960 s 64(2), as amended by Road Traffic Act 1962, s 8, Sch 1, Pt 2, para 19—Motor Vehicles (Construction and Use) Regulations 1966 (SI 1966 No 1288), reg 70(1). **Windle v Dunning & Son Ltd** [1968] 2 46, QBD.
      Mens rea—Motor van driven with defective brake—Absolute offence—Motor Vehicles (Constructions and Use) Regulations 1951 (SI 1951 No 2101), regs 75, 101. **James & Son Ltd v Smee** [1954] 3 273, QBD.
      Owner of vehicle—Liability—Vehicle being driven on road by third party at owner's request—Whether owner using vehicle—Road Traffic Act 1960, s 64(2), as substituted by the Road Traffic (Amendment) Act 1967, s 6(1). **Crawford v Haughton** [1972] 1 535, QBD.
  Motorway—
    Restrictions on stopping—
      Emergency—Stopping on verge—Stopping by reason of any accident, illness or other emergency—Meaning of emergency—Sudden occurrence not essential—Necessity of showing that danger alleged to constitute emergency not foreseeable before proceeding on to motorway—Driver overcome by drowsiness—Motorways Traffic Regulations 1959 (SI 1959 No 1147), regs 7(2), 9. **Higgins v Bernard** [1972] 1 1037, QBD.
      Remaining at rest on carriageway—Carriageway—Vehicle parked on hard shoulder of motorway—Hard shoulder part of 'verge' not carriageway—Hard should distinguished from 'marginal strip'—Marginal strip part of carriageway—Motorways Traffic Regulations 1959 (SI 1959 No 1147), regs 3(1)(a),(d),(h), 7(1). **Wallwork v Rowland** [1972] 1 53, QBD.
  Negligence—
    Contributory negligence—
      Child. *See* **Child** (Negligence—Contributory negligence).

ROAD TRAFFIC (cont)—
Negligence (cont)—
Contributory negligence (cont)—
Road accident. *See* **Negligence** (Contributory negligence—Road accident).
Damages—
Loss of consortium. *See* **Damages** (Personal injury—Consortium—Impairment of consortium—Wife injured in accident for which defendant liable).
Nervous shock. *See* **Damages** (Personal injury—Nervous shock—Wife witnessing accident in which husband killed and children injured).
Driving of motor vehicle—
Vicarious liability—Principal and agent. *See* **Vicarious liability** (Principal and agent).
Exclusion of liability—
Public service vehicle. *See* **Carriers** (Negligence—Exclusion of liability).
Highway. *See* **Negligence** (Highway).
Vehicles. *See* **Negligence** (Vehicles).
Notice of intended prosecution—
Contravention of pedestrian crossing regulations—
Obligation to give notice—Whether requirement to give notice need be complied with—Road Traffic Act 1960, ss 14(1), 241—Road Traffic Regulation Act 1967, s 23(1)(5)—'Pelican' Pedestrian Crossings Regulations and General Directions 1969, (SI 1969 No 888). **Sulston v Hammond** [1970] **2** 830, QBD.
Limited company—
Name of company in notice—Inaccuracy—Company registered as owner of vehicle—Omission of 'Limited' from company's name in notice—Validity of notice—Road Traffic Act 1930, s 21(c). **Springate v Questier** [1952] **2** 21, QBD.
Notice sent to defendant's residence by registered post—
Defendant away on holiday unknown to police—Notice received by person in defendant's employ—Road Traffic Act 1930, s 21(c)—Interpretation Act 1889, s 26. **Layton v Shires** [1959] **3** 587, QBD.
Defendant away on holiday unknown to police—Notice returned to police undelivered—Defendant bus driver employed by London Transport Executive—Not warned of prosecution at the time offence committed—No notice served on London Transport Executive as registered owners of vehicle—Whether notice served on defendant—Whether case within exemption from requirement of service—Road Traffic Act 1889, s 26. **Beer v Davies** [1958] **2** 255, QBD.
Defendant in hospital to knowledge of police—Notice received by defendant's wife—Notice not communicated to defendant—Road Traffic Act 1960, s 241(2)(c)(i). **Hosier v Goodall** [1962] **1** 30, QBD.
Defendant in hospital to knowledge of police—Notice returned marked 'unable to deliver'—Fresh notice served personally out of time—Whether adequate notice—Road Traffic Act 1930, s 21. **Stanley v Thomas** [1939] **2** 636, KBD.
Defendant known to be in hospital at time as result of accident—Defendant's wife living at defendant's residence—Road Traffic Act 1930, s 21(c)—Interpretation Act 1889, s 26. **Sandland v Neale** [1955] **3** 571, BD.
Notice sent eleven days after commission of the offence—Defendant known to be then seriously ill in hospital—Road Traffic Act 1930, s 21(c). **Holt v Dyson** [1950] **2** 840, KBD.
Notice to firm instead of individual—
Driver of car unknown to police—Inaccurate information regarding owner of car given to police by local taxation officer—Notice of intended prosecution sent to firm of which owner was member instead of to owner—Notice to firm not notice to individual member of firm—Reasonable diligence shown by police—Road Traffic Act 1930, ss 11, 21. **Clarke v Mould** [1945] **2** 551, KBD.
Objection that notice not given—
Alternatives of service on driver or registered owner—Non-compliance with both alternatives must be proved in order to establish defence—Road Traffic Act 1960, s 241(2),(3). **Sanders v Scott** [1961] **2** 403, QBD.
Procedure—Whether issue must be raised as preliminary point—Road Traffic Act 1930, s 21. **R v Edmonton Justices, ex p Brooks** [1960] **2** 475, QBD.
Service of notice—
Notice deemed to have been served—Receipt after more than 14 days—Road Traffic Act 1960, s 241(2)(c), as amended by Road Traffic Act 1962, s 51 and Sch 4. **Groome v Driscoll** [1969] **3** 1638, QBD.
Notice handed to defendant's wife at defendant's home when defendant not in house—Defendant's wife authorised to accept letters for him—Notice handed by defendant's wife to him within 14 days—Whether compliance with statute—Road Traffic Act 1960, s 241(2)(c)(ii), as amended by Road Traffic Act 1962, s 51(1) and Sch 4, Pt 1. **Burt v Kirkcaldy** [1965] **1** 741, QBD.
Notice sent to defendant's residence by registered post. *See* Notice of intended prosecution—Notice sent to defendant's residence by registered post, *above*.
Service by post—Delivery in ordinary course of post—Deeming provisions—Notice of intended prosecution sent by first class post delivered after specified period—Whether notice deemed served within specified period—Interpretation Act 1978, s 7—Road Traffic Offenders Act 1988, s 1. **Gidden v Chief Constable of Humberside** [2010] **2** 75, DC.
Service within 14 days—Computation of time—'Within fourteen days' of commission of alleged offence—Computation of time for service—Offence committed on 11th January—Notice sent by registered post on 24th January, and delivered on 25th January—Road Traffic Act 1930, s 21(c). **Stewart v Chapman** [1951] **2** 613, KBD.
Service within 14 days—Notice sent by recorded delivery service—Notice despatched on 14th day—Notice not capable of being delivered within 14 day period in ordinary course of post—Validity—Road Traffic Act 1960, s 241(2), as amended by the Road Traffic Act 1962, s 51 and Sch 4. **Nicholson v Tapp** [1972] **3** 245, QBD.
Specification of nature of alleged offence—
Sufficiency—Notice referring to 'offence against s 12 of Road Traffic Act 1930'—No reference to driving without due care and attention or without due consideration—Road Traffic Act 1930, ss 12(1), 21(c). **Venn v Morgan** [1949] **2** 562, KBD.

ROAD TRAFFIC (cont)—
  Notice of intended prosecution (cont)—
    Specification of time of alleged offence—
      Time of alleged offence wrongly stated—Validity of notice—Road Traffic Act 1930, s 21(c). **Pope v Clarke** [1953] **2** 704, QBD.
    Warning at time offence committed—
      Time—Warning given one and a half hours after the alleged offence was committed—Whether it was given at the time the offence was committed—Road Traffic Act 1930, s 21. **Jollye v Dale** [1960] **2** 369, QBD.
    Withdrawal—
      Intimation by police, subsequent to notice, stating that no further action would be taken—Further subsequent intimation that a prosecution would be instituted—Whether original notice still effective to enable court to convict—Road Traffic Act 1930, s 21. **Lund v Thompson** [1958] **3** 356, QBD.
  Obstruction—
    London—
      Arrest—Motor car left in thoroughfare—Persistent refusal by owner to remove car after repeated requests by police officer—Power of police officer to arrest owner without warrant—Metropolitan Police Act 1839, s 54, para 6—Prevention of Crimes Amendment Act 1885, s 2. **Gelberg v Miller** [1961] **1** 291, QBD.
    Parking place—
      Part of road designated by local authority as parking place within certain hours—Garage proprietors using parking place during permitted hours for parking vehicles from garage—Whether vehicles an unnecessary obstruction in contravention of Motor Vehicles (Construction and Use) Regulations 1955 (SI 1955 No 482), reg 89. **Anderson (W R) (Motors) Ltd v Hargreaves** [1962] **1** 129, QBD.
    Prevention of obstruction of streets. *See* Regulation of traffic—Prevention of obstruction of streets, *below*.
    Public service vehicle left in thoroughfare—
      Causing vehicle to stand on road so as unnecessarily to obstruct road—Driver's spell of duty finished—Left vehicle at bus stop—Relief driver late—Traffic held up in interval before relief driver arrived—Whether driver who left vehicle remained person in charge of vehicle until relief driver took over—Public Service Vehicles (Conduct of Drivers, Conductors and Passengers) Regulations 1936 (S R & O 1936 No 619), reg 7—Motor Vehicles (Construction and Use) Regulations 1955 (SI 1955 No 482), reg 89. **Ellis v Smith** [1962] **3** 954, QBD.
  Offence—
    Aiding and abetting—
      Acquittal of principal—Motor omnibus driver charged with driving without due care and attention and charge dismissed—Conductor of same vehicle charged with aiding and abetting offence alleged against driver—Conductor convicted—Validity of conviction—Road Traffic Act 1930, s 12(1). **Thornton v Mitchell** [1940] **1** 339, KBD.
    Duty to give information—
      Duty of any person to give information which it is in his power to give and may lead to identification of driver—Doctor—Information obtained by doctor in professional capacity—Whether 'any ... person' to be construed restrictively so as not to include doctor under professional duty of confidence—Whether 'in (doctor's) power' to disclose information—Road Traffic Act 1972, s 168(2)(b). **Hunter v Mann** [1974] **2** 414, QBD.
      Offence against regulations made under repealed statute—Whether regulations became part of replacing statute—Whether offence against regulations an offence against the statute—Road Traffic Act 1930, s 30—Road Traffic Act 1960, ss 64, 232(2)(a)—Motor Vehicles (Construction and Use) Regulations 1955 (SI 1955 No 482), regs 89, 104. **Rathbone v Bundock** [1962] **2** 257, QBD.
      Owner—Request to give name and address of driver—Right of owner to be told nature of offence before giving information—Road Traffic Act 1930, s 113(3)(b). **Pulton v Leader** [1949] **2** 747, KBD.
      Request signed by police inspector—Authority to sign notice given orally to inspector by superintendent of police—Whether delegation of authority from chief of police—Exception to maxim delegatus non potest delegare—Road Traffic Act 1960, s 232(2)(a). **Nelms v Roe** [1969] **3** 1379, QBD.
      Request signed by police sergeant—Delegation of authority from a chief officer of police—Road Traffic Act 1960, s 232. **Record Tower Cranes Ltd v Gisbey** [1969] **1** 418, QBD.
      Self-incrimination—Driver of vehicle—Whether driver under obligation to give information to incriminate himself—Road Traffic Act 1960, s 232(2)(b). **Bingham v Bruce** [1962] **1** 136, QBD.
      Vehicle owner's obligation—Whether vehicle involved in alleged offence—Burden of proof—Road Traffic Act 1960, s 232(3). **Neal v Fior** [1968] **3** 865, QBD.
    Prosecution—
      Driver and owner—Goods vehicle—Licence—Prosecution of driver as well as owner—Undesirability—Road and Rail Traffic Act 1933, s 1(1)—Vehicles (Excise) Act 1949, s 13(1). **Carpenter v Campbell** [1953] **1** 280, QBD.
    Self-incrimination—
      Driver of vehicle—Statutory provision requiring defendant to identify driver of car—Defendant admitting that she was driver and being charged with driving car after consuming excessive alcohol—Whether use of admission in evidence by prosecution infringing defendant's right to fair hearing—Road Traffic Act 1988, s 172(2)(a)—Human Rights Act 1998, Sch 1, Pt I, art 6(1). **Brown v Stott (Procurator Fiscal, Dunfermline)** [2001] **2** 97, PC.
    Separate offences—
      Convictions of two separate offences on same facts—Obstruction—Contravention of waiting regulations—One conviction quashed—Motor Vehicles (Construction and Use) Regulations 1955 (SI 1955 No 482), reg 89—London Traffic (Restriction of Waiting) (Station Parade, Gerrards Cross) Regulations 1952 (SI 1952 No 1294), reg 3. **R v Burnham Justices, ex p Ansorge** [1959] **3** 505, QBD.

ROAD TRAFFIC (cont)—
Offence (cont)—
    Summary offence—
        Conspiracy—Goods vehicle—Driver—Limitation of time on duty—Record of hours worked—
        Offences triable summarily—Whether conspiracy to commit offences can be made subject of
        indictment—Road Traffic Act 1960, ss 73(1), (3), 186(1), (6)—Goods Vehicles (Keeping of Records)
        Regulations 1935 (SR & O 1935 No 314), reg 6. **R v Blamires Transport Services Ltd** [1963] **3** 170,
        CA.
    Summary proceedings—
        Attempt to take and drive away vehicle without consent—Attempt to commit indictable
        offence—Whether attempt triable summarily—Road Traffic Act 1930, s 28(1)—Criminal Justice
        Act 1925, s 24(1) Sch 11 para 17. **R v Fussell** [1951] **2** 761, CCA.
    Summons or information—
        Discretion of prosecutor—Application for summons for careless driving—Refusal on ground
        information for dangerous driving should be laid—Mandamus to issue summons. **R v Nuneaton
        Justices, ex p Parker** [1954] **3** 251, QBD.
    Taking vehicle without authority—
        Aggravated vehicle-taking—Accident causing injury to person—Whether offence requiring element
        of fault in driving of defendant—Theft Act 1968, s 12A(1), (2)(b). **R v Taylor** [2016] **4** 617, CA.
Omnibus—
    Injury to passenger while alighting. *See* **Negligence** (Vehicles—Passenger injured while alighting from
    omnibus).
    Stage carriage. *See* Stage carriage, *below.*
Omnibus service—
    Alteration of London service. *See* **London Transport Executive** (Duty to consult with local authorities
    before altering bus services).
Operator's licence—
    Goods vehicle. *See* Goods vehicle—Operator's licence, *above.*
Overall length—
    Articulated vehicle. *See* Articulated vehicle—Overall length, *above.*
    Heavy motor car. *See* Heavy motor car—Overall length, *above.*
Overall width—
    Motor tractor. *See* Motor tractor—Overall width, *above.*
Overhang—
    Heavy motor car. *See* Heavy motor car—Overhang, *above.*
Overtaking—
    Zebra crossing. *See* Pedestrian crossing—Zebra crossing—Overtaking, *below.*
Parking—
    Blood-alcohol proportion above prescribed limit—
        Special reason for not disqualifying. *See* Special reasons for not disqualifying—Driving with
        blood-alcohol proportion above prescribed limit—Parking, *below.*
    Controlled parking zone—
        Road markings. *See* Traffic sign—Road markings—Controlled parking zone, *below.*
    Negligence—
        Parking on highway. *See* **Negligence** (Highway—Parking of vehicle).
    Parking place. *See* Parking place, *below.*
    Right to park cars—
        Easement. *See* **Easement** (Right to park cars).
    Traffic sign. *See* Traffic sign—Parking, *below.*
    Unlighted vehicle—
        Nuisance. *See* **Nuisance** (Highway—Unlighted vehicle on highway).
    Waiting and loading restrictions. *See* Waiting and loading restrictions, *below.*
Parking place—
    Leaving vehicle otherwise than as authorised—
        Meter charge payable on leaving vehicle in parking place—Driver leaving vehicle for a few minutes
        while obtaining change to enable him to put coin in meter—Returned at once to pay the
        charge—Whether driver guilty of offence of failing to pay initial charge—Parking Places
        (Westminster) (No 1) Order 1959, art 8(1)—Road Traffic Act 1956 s 22(1). **Strong v Dawtry**
        [1961] **1** 926, QBD.
        Waiting in parking place for permitted purpose—Use of parking place suspended—Effect of
        suspension—Parking place provided with parking bays controlled by meters—Suspension of use
        of bay—Vehicle left in bay suspended from use—Vehicle being used to deliver goods at premises
        adjacent to bay—Whether leaving vehicle in bay unauthorised—Whether bay remained a 'parking
        place'—Whether permissible to 'wait' in bay although use of bay suspended—Road Traffic
        Regulation Act 1967, s 42(1)(a)—Parking Places and Restriction of Waiting and Loading
        (Luton)(No 1) Order 1964 (SI 1964 No 1753), arts 4, 23(1), 26(1)(i). **Wilson v Arnott** [1977] **2** 5, QBD.
    Local authority powers. *See* **Local authority** (Powers—Designation of paying parking places on
    highways).
    Obstruction. *See* Obstruction—Parking place, *above.*
Particulars of accident—
    Duty to stop and furnish particulars. *See* Accident—Duty to stop and furnish particulars, *above.*
Passenger—
    Due consideration—
        Careless driving. *See* Careless driving—Due consideration for other persons using road—
        Passengers in vehicle, *above.*
    Duty of driver to take care. *See* **Negligence** (Duty to take care—Driver of motor vehicle—Duty to
    passenger in vehicle).
    Exclusion of liability to passenger. *See* **Negligence** (Volenti non fit injuria—Consent to risk of
    injury—Agreement to exclude liability—Passenger in vehicle).
    Express carriage. *See* Express carriage, *above.*
    Omnibus—
        Injury while alighting from bus. *See* **Negligence** (Vehicles—Passenger injured while alighting from
        omnibus).

ROAD TRAFFIC (cont)—
  Passenger (cont)—
    Stage carriage—
      Excess of prescribed maximum. *See* Stage carriage—Number of standing passengers in excess of prescribed maximum, *below.*
    Volenti non fit injuria—
      Knowledge of risk. *See* **Negligence** (Volenti non fit injuria—Knowledge of risk—Passenger in car).
  Passenger vehicle—
    Limitation of driver's time on duty under Community rules—
      Offence for employer to permit driver to contravene rules—Meaning of permit—Requisite mens rea—Effect of employer's failure to examine tachograph charts—Transport Act 1968, s 96(11A). **Vehicle Inspectorate v Nuttall** [1999] 3 833, HL.
  Pedestrian crossing—
    Accident—
      Failure of motorist to stop before reaching crossing—Contributory negligence—Whether duty of pedestrian altered by reason of black-out—Pedestrian Crossing Places (Traffic) Provisional Regulations 1939, regs 3, 4, 7. **Knight v Sampson** [1938] 3 309, KBD; **Sparks v Edward Ash Ltd** [1943] 1 1, CA.
      Failure of motorist to stop before reaching crossing—Contributory negligence of pedestrian—Availability of defence—Pedestrian Crossing Places (Traffic) Provisional Regulations 1935, regs 3, 4. **Bailey v Geddes** [1937] 3 671, CA.
    Contravention of regulations—
      Notice of intended prosecution. *See* Notice of intended prosecution—Contravention of pedestrian crossing regulations, *above.*
    Controlled crossing—
      Applicability of regulations—Pedestrian Crossing Places (Traffic) Provisional Regulations 1935, regs 3, 4, 5. **Chisholm v London Passenger Transport Board** [1938] 4 850, CA.
      Crossing with refuge—Whether refuge part of crossing—Pedestrian stepping from refuge—Contributory negligence—Pedestrian Crossing Places (Traffic) Provisional Regulations 1935, regs 2, 3, 4, 5. **Wilkinson v Chetham-Strode** [1940] 2 643, CA.
      Duty of approaching driver—Interrupted view of crossing—Injury to foot passenger thereon—Pedestrian Crossing Places (Traffic) Regulations 1941 (S R 20 1941 No 397), reg 3. **London Passenger Transport Board v Upson** [1949] 1 60, HL.
    Duty of driver—
      Controlled crossing. *See* Pedestrian crossing—Controlled crossing—Duty of approaching driver, *above.*
      Right to proceed when satisfied that persons crossing are out of danger. **Kayser v London Passenger Transport Board** [1950] 1 231, KBD.
    School crossing. *See* School crossing, *below.*
    Uncontrolled crossing—
      Failure of motorist to stop before reaching crossing—Limits of crossing—Approach studs—Whether motor car is within limits of crossing when it has crossed approach studs—Pedestrian Crossings Regulations 1954 (SI 1954 No 370), reg 4. **Hughes v Hall** [1960] 2 504, QBD.
      Failure to accord precedence to foot-passenger—Latent mechanical defect—Control of vehicle taken from driver by occurence of event outside his possible or reasonable control and in respect of which he is not at fault—Whether breach of obligation to afford precedence—Pedestrian Crossing Regulations 1954 (SI 1954 No 370), reg 4. **Burns v Bidder** [1966] 3 29, QBD.
      Failure to accord precedence to foot-passenger—Waiver of precedence—Whether pedestrian had waived precedence—Pedestrian Crossing Regulations 1954 (SI 1954 No 370), reg 4. **Neal v Bedford** [1965] 3 250, QBD.
      Precedence to foot-passenger—Failure of motorist to stop before reaching crossing—Interrupted view of crossing—Liability of motorist—Pedestrian Crossings Regulations 1954 (SI 1954 No 370), reg 4. **Gibbons v Kahl** [1955] 3 345, QBD.
      Precedence to foot-passenger—Precedence not accorded—Driver not negligent—Liability of driver—Pedestrian Crossings (London) Regulations 1951 (SI 1951 No 1193), reg 4. **Leicester v Pearson** [1952] 2 71, QBD.
    Zebra crossing—
      Overtaking—Prohibition—Stationary vehicle stopped for purpose of complying with regulations—Regulations requiring vehicle driver to give precedence to pedestrian on carriageway within limits of controlled zebra crossing—Pedestrians for whom stationary vehicle stopped having left crossing at time of overtaking—Whether offence committed by overtaking stationary vehicle—Whether a stationary vehicle which had initially stopped to give precedence to pedestrians and had not moved off, a vehicle which 'is stopped for the purpose of complying with' regulation giving precedence to pedestrians—'Zebra' Pedestrian Crossings Regulations 1971 (SI 1971 No 1524), reg 10(b). **Connor v Paterson** [1977] 3 516, QBD.
      Overtaking—Prohibition—Stationary vehicle stopped for purpose of complying with regulations—Regulations requiring vehicle driver to give precedence to pedestrian on carriageway within limits of uncontrolled zebra crossing—Offence to overtake stationary vehicle—Pedestrian on pavement adjacent to crossing—Vehicle stopping to allow pedestrian to cross—Defendant overtaking stationary vehicle before pedestrian having stepped on to crossing—Whether stationary vehicle stopped 'for purpose of complying with' regulations—Whether an offence to overtake vehicle before pedestrian on crossing—'Zebra' Pedestrian Crossings Regulations 1971 (SI 1971 No 1524), regs 8, 10(b). **Gullen v Ford** [1975] 2 24, QBD.
  Penalty points—
    Disqualification—
      Disqualification after repeated offences. *See* Disqualification for holding licence—Disqualification after repeated offences, *above.*
      Endorsement of licence—Endorsement with penalty points—General guidance on disqualification and endorsement of licence. **R v Kent** [1983] 3 1, CA.
      Endorsement of licence—Endorsement with penalty points—Whether endorsement of penalty points can be ordered at same time as disqualification from driving imposed—Road Traffic Act 1972, s 101(1)—Transport Act 1981, s 19(1), Sch 7. **R v Kent** [1983] 3 1, CA.

ROAD TRAFFIC (cont)—
  Penalty points (cont)—
    Disqualification (cont)—
      Endorsement of licence—Endorsement with penalty points—Whether endorsement of penalty points can be ordered at same time as disqualification imposed—Road Traffic Offenders Act 1988, s 44(1). **R v Usaceva** [2016] **1** 741, CA.
  Permitting vehicle to be used on road in breach of regulations. *See* Motor vehicle—Permitting vehicle to be used on road in breach of regulations, *above*.
  Plating and test certificates for goods vehicles—
    Exemption—
      Tower wagon—Meaning—Vehicle into which there is built any expanding or extensible contrivance—Contrivance designed for facilitating erection, inspection, repair or maintenance of overhead structures or equipment—Vehicle not constructed or adapted for use nor used for conveyance of loads except contrivance and articles used in connection therewith—Vehicle used for erection of street lighting—Converted goods vehicle—Body removed from chassis—Extensible contrivance fitted behind car with platform for carrying tools and equipment—Vehicle used to carry concrete pillars intended to form part of street lights—Whether vehicle a 'tower wagon'—Vehicles (Excise) Act 1971, Sch 4, para 9(1)—Goods Vehicles (Plating and Testing) Regulations 1971 (SI 1971 No 352), reg 4(2), Sch 2, Item 6. **Anderson and Heeley Ltd v Paterson** [1975] **1** 523, QBD.
      Trailer temporarily in Great Britain—Trailer owned by United Kingdom company—Trailer used for carrying goods between England and Continent—Presence in England intermittent, but regular and repeated—Whether 'temporarily in Great Britain'—Road Safety Act 1967, ss 9, 14(1),(2)—Goods Vehicles (Plating and Testing) Regulations 1968 (SI 1968 No 601), reg 3(2), Sch 2, class 27. **British Road Services Ltd v Wurzal** [1971] **3** 480, QBD.
  Plying for hire—
    Hackney carriage. *See* Hackney carriage—Plying for hire, *above*.
  Police—
    Exemption from speed limits. *See* Excessive speed—Exemption—Police, *above*.
    Power to stop vehicles—
      Whether including power to detain vehicle. *See* **Police** (Powers—Power to detain stopped vehicle).
    Report to police—
      Accident. *See* Accident—Duty to stop and furnish particulars—Report to police, *above*.
  Private carrier's licence—
    Goods vehicle. *See* Goods vehicle—Private carrier's licence, *above*.
  Private hire vehicle—
    Licence—
      Grant of licence—Appellant applying for licence after being acquitted of indecent assault—Local authority refusing application on ground appellant not a fit and proper person to hold a licence—Appeal to magistrates—Magistrates dismissing appeal after admitting hearsay evidence and applying civil standard of proof—Whether magistrates right to do so—Local Government (Miscellaneous Provisions) Act 1976, s 51(1). **McCool v Rushcliffe BC** [1998] **3** 889, QBD.
  Prosecution—
    Offence. *See* Offence—Prosecution, *above*.
  Provisional licence—
    Conditions attached. *See* Driving licence—Conditions attached to provisional licences, *above*.
    Disqualification. *See* Disqualification for holding licence—Provisional licence, *above*.
    Generally. *See* Driving licence—Provisional licence, *above*.
  Public carrier's licence—
    Goods vehicle. *See* Goods vehicle—Public carrier's licence, *above*.
  Public service vehicle—
    Negligence—
      Exclusion of liability—Free pass. *See* **Carriers** (Negligence—Exclusion of liability—Passengers—Free pass).
      Generally. *See* **Negligence** (Vehicles—Public service vehicle).
    Obstruction—
      Vehicle left in thoroughfare. *See* Obstruction—Public service vehicle left in thoroughfare, *above*.
    Road service licence—
      Breach of condition—Wilful breach by servant of condition attached to licence—Liability of employer—Road Traffic Act 1960, ss 134(3), 136(1). **Newton (G) Ltd v Smith** [1962] **2** 19, QBD.
    Stage carriage. *See* Stage carriage, *below*.
    Suspension of licence—
      Power of commissioners—Suspension for a fixed period—Power to suspend licence if operator appears not to be a fit person—Maintenance of vehicles below standard—Commissioners expressing view that operator ought to be penalised for past failures in respect of maintenance—No power to impose suspension by way of penalty—Appeal to Secretary of State—Power of Secretary of State to confirm suspension on basis that facts found showing operator not a fit person—Propriety of suspension for a fixed period—Road Traffic Act 1960, s 127(7) (as amended by the Transport Act 1968, s 35(1)). **Robinson v Secretary of State for the Environment** [1973] **3** 1045, QBD.
  Public transport—
    British Transport Commission—
      Delegation of powers to transport executive—Extent of powers and validity of delegation—Road Traffic Act 1930, s 72(1)—Transport Act 1947, ss 2(1)(a),(3), 3(1), 12(1), 14(2),(4), 65(1). **Smith v London Transport Executive** [1951] **1** 667, HL.
    Local authority—
      Authority operating omnibus undertaking under local Act—Revenue to be applied in maintaining omnibuses, garages etc—New omnibuses required for replacement or as additions—Purchase out of capital or revenue—Mynyddislwyn Urban District Council Act 1926, ss 90, 91. **A-G v West Monmouthshire Omnibus Board** [1947] **1** 248, Ch D.
    Generally. *See* **Local authority** (Transport).
    London Passenger Transport Board. *See* **London Passenger Transport Board**.
    London Transport Executive. *See* **London Transport Executive**.

ROAD TRAFFIC (cont)—
    Public transport (cont)—
        Service provided by commission or agent of commission—
            Share capital of company actually providing service acquired by British Transport Commission—Services of company—Whether provided by commission—Transport Act 1947, s 65(1). **R v South Wales Traffic Licensing Authority, ex p Ebbw Vale UDC** [1951] **1** 806, CA.
    Reasonable excuse—
        Failure to provide specimen for laboratory test. *See* Failure to provide specimen for laboratory test—Reasonable excuse, *above*.
    Reckless driving—
        Causing death by reckless driving—
            Charge of manslaughter—Proper direction to jury. **R v Seymour** [1983] **2** 1058, HL.
            Reckless—Mens rea—Mens rea lying in accused's mental attitude to obligation to drive with due care and attention—Whether prosecution required to prove accused foresaw the risk of an accident and deliberately decided to take that risk—Road Traffic Act 1972, ss 1, 2 (as substituted by the Criminal Law Act 1977, s 50). **R v Murphy (William)** [1980] **2** 325, CA.
            Reckless—Mens rea—Proper direction to be given to jury—Defendant suffering from mental illness short of insanity—Whether such condition relevant to defendant's state of mind on charge of reckless driving—Road Traffic Act 1972, s 2. **R v Bell** [1984] **3** 842, CA.
            Reckless—Mens rea—Proper direction to be given to jury—Road Traffic Act 1972, ss 1, 2 (as substituted by the Criminal Law Act 1977, s 50(1)). **R v Lawrence** [1981] **1** 974, HL.
            Reckless—Mens rea—Proper direction to be given to jury—Road Traffic Act 1988, s 1. **R v Reid** [1992] **3** 673, HL.
            Sentence—Principles of sentencing—Circumstances aggravating offence—Circumstances mitigating offence—Cases in which custodial sentence appropriate—Road Traffic Act 1972, s 1. **R v Boswell** [1984] **3** 353, CA.
        Defence—
            Driver committing reckless acts in order lawfully to arrest offender—Whether reasonable use of force in lawfully arresting offender defence to charge of reckless driving—Criminal Law Act 1967, s 3(1)—Road Traffic Act 1972, s 2. **R v Renouf** [1986] **2** 449, CA.
            Duress. *See* **Criminal law** (Duress as a defence—Reckless driving).
    Recovery vehicle—
        Trade licence. *See* Trade licence—Motor trader—Recovery vehicle, *below*.
    Registration—
        Heavy motor car. *See* Heavy motor car—Registration, *above*.
    Regulation of traffic—
        Prevention of obstruction of streets—
            Any occasion when streets thronged or liable to be obstructed—One-way traffic system for all vehicles in two streets—Order by local authority—For six months' holiday season—'Route' to be observed—Town Police Clauses Act 1847, s 21. **Brownsea Haven Properties Ltd v Poole Corp** [1958] **1** 205, CA.
            Order restricting sale of confectionery, etc—Restricted hours not specified—Validity—Town Police Clauses Act 1847, s 21. **Etherington v Carter** [1937] **2** 528, KBD.
            Streets in neighbourhood of Parliament. *See* **Parliament** (Prevention of obstruction of streets in neighbourhood of Parliament).
    Removal of disqualification. *See* Disqualification for holding licence—Removal, *above*.
    Requirement to take breath test. *See* Breath test—Requirement to take test, *above*.
    Road—
        Car park—
            Private footpath leading from car park—Footpath used by members of bowling club and holders of allotment gardens but not by general public—Whether car park itself, or as part of private footpath, a 'road'—Road Traffic Act 1930, s 121. **Griffin v Squires** [1958] **3** 468, QBD.
        Caravan park—
            Public access—Admittance to caravan park restricted to persons registering at reception area and obtaining vehicle pass—Admittance granted to any person satisfying conditions for admission—Admittance not restricted to persons having characteristics personal to themselves—Whether users of park constituting special class distinct from members of general public—Whether caravan park a 'public place'—Road Traffic Act 1988, s 5(1)(a). **DPP v Vivier** [1991] **4** 18, QBD.
        Driving motor vehicle elsewhere than on roads—
            Statutory provision prohibiting driving without lawful authority onto or upon 'any common land, moorland or land of any other description not being land forming part of a road'—Statute defining 'road' as any road to which public had access—Whether 'land of any other description' to be construed ejusdem generis with 'common land' and 'moorland'—Whether definition of road satisfied only if public having access to it in sense of using it as road—Road Traffic Act 1988, ss 34(1)(a), 192. **Massey v Boulden** [2003] **2** 87, CA.
        Lighting of vehicles. *See* Lighting of vehicles—Road, *above*.
        Public access—
            Road within premises of Port of London Authority—Passes required to enter dock area—Unauthorised persons refused admission—Whether a 'road to which the public has access'—Road Traffic Act 1930, s 121(1). **Buchanan v Motor Insurers' Bureau** [1955] **1** 607, QBD.
        Using vehicle on road without insurance policy being in force. *See* **Motor insurance** (Compulsory insurance against third party risks).
        Vehicle intended or adapted for use on road. *See* Motor vehicle—Intended or adapted for use on road, *above*.
    Road service licence—
        Express carriage. *See* Express carriage—Road service licence, *above*.
        Public service vehicle. *See* Public service vehicle—Road service licence, *above*.
    Sale of car in dangerous condition—
        Negligence—
            Defect discoverable by reasonable diligence. *See* **Negligence** (Dangerous things—Defect discoverable by reasonable diligence—Car in dangerous condition).
    Sale of vehicle in unroadworthy condition. *See* Motor vehicle—Sale in unroadworthy condition, *above*.

ROAD TRAFFIC (cont)—
  School crossing—
    Stopping of motor vehicles—
      Motorist's obligation to stop where prescribed sign exhibited—Vehicle to be stopped 'so as not to stop or impede (children) crossing'—Motorist proceeding while sign exhibited but after children past his side of the road—Whether an offence—Road Traffic Regulation Act 1967, s 25(1),(2). **Franklin v Langdown** [1971] **3** 662, QBD.
      Necessity for patrol to exhibit stop sign to view of oncoming traffic—Road Traffic Act 1960, s 48(1),(2). **Hoy v Smith** [1964] **3** 670, QBD.
  Seat belt—
    Failure to wear—
      Contributory negligence. *See* **Negligence** (Contributory negligence—Road accident—Seat belt).
  Sign—
    Traffic sign. *See* Traffic sign, *below*.
  Signal—
    Stopping of vehicle—
      Failure to give hand signal. *See* Stopping of vehicle—Failure to give hand signal, *below*.
  Skid—
    Negligence. *See* **Negligence** (Vehicles—Skid).
  Special occasion—
    Express carriage. *See* Express carriage—Special occasion, *above*.
    Stage carriage. *See* Stage carriage—Special occasion, *below*.
  Special reasons for not disqualifying—
    Causing death by dangerous driving—
      Ambulance driver taking urgent case to hospital—Driver told to hurry—Life of unborn baby and mother depending on speed at which hospital reached—Driver crossing traffic lights at red—Collision with motor scooter killing rider—Plea of guilty to causing death by dangerous driving—Special reasons why driver should not be disqualified—Road Traffic Act 1962, s 5(1). **R v Lundt-Smith** [1964] **3** 225, Assizes.
    Driving while unfit through drink or drugs. *See* Driving while unfit to drive through drink or drugs—Special reasons for not disqualifying, *above*.
    Driving with blood-alcohol proportion above prescribed limit—
      Addition to driver's drink without his knowledge—Proof that addition accounted for excess over prescribed limit—Onus of proof—Onus on driver to prove on balance of probabilities that addition accounted for excess—Circumstances in which necessary for driver to adduce medical evidence—Road Traffic Act 1962, s 5(1)—Road Safety Act 1967, s 1(1). **Pugsley v Hunter** [1973] **2** 10, QBD.
      Amount of excess—Whether amount of excess a special reason for not disqualifying—Road Traffic Act 1962, s 5(1)—Road Safety Act 1967, ss 1(1), 5(2)(a). **Delaroy-Hall v Tadman** [1969] **1** 25, QBD.
      Driver's ability impaired through also taking drugs—No knowledge of potential risk—Road Traffic Act 1962, s 5(1)—Road Safety Act 1967, s 1(1). **R v Scott** [1969] **2** 450, CA.
      Emergency—Reasons of emergency compelling driver to drive with too much alcohol in blood—Factors to be considered in determining whether driver should not be disqualified—Road Traffic Act 1972, s 93(1). **Taylor v Rajan** [1974] **1** 1087, QBD.
      Ignorance of combined effect of small consumption of alcohol with inhalation of fumes with alcoholic content—Road Traffic Act 1960, s 6(1)—Road Traffic Act 1962, s 5(1). **Brewer v Metropolitan Police Comr** [1969] **1** 513, QBD.
      Non-impairment of driving ability—Accident not the fault of accused—Road Safety Act 1967, s 1(1). **Taylor v Austin** [1969] **1** 544, QBD.
      Non-impairment of driving ability—Liver condition unknown to driver—Road Traffic Act 1962, s 5(1)—Road Safety Act 1967, ss 1(1), 3(3)(a). **R v Jackson** [1969] **2** 453, CA.
      Non-impairment of driving ability—Medical emergency—Evidence to support plea not to disqualify—Grounds for finding special reasons to be stated—Road Traffic Act 1962, ss 5(1), 9. **Brown v Dyerson** [1968] **3** 39, QBD.
      Parking—Driving vehicle from one parking place to another—Driving vehicle 200 yards along busy street—Potential danger to other road users—Road Traffic Act 1962, s 5(1)—Road Safety Act 1967, s 1(1). **Coombs v Kehoe** [1972] **2** 55, QBD.
      Parking—Driving vehicle from one parking place to another—Driving vehicle few yards from highway on to private drive—Road Traffic Act 1962, s 5(1)—Road Safety Act 1967, s 1(1). **James v Hall** [1972] **2** 59, QBD.
    Evidence—
      Plea of guilty—Duty of justices to hear evidence as to matters said to constitute special reasons—Road Traffic Act 1930, s 15(2). **Jones v English** [1951] **2** 853, KBD.
    Using vehicle on road without insurance policy being in force. *See* **Motor insurance** (Disqualification for using etc vehicle on road without policy being in force).
    What are special reasons—
      Reasons special to facts of case—Mitigating or extenuating circumstances—Circumstances peculiar to offender not special reason—Hardship to offender on first offence not special reasons—Road Traffic Act 1930, s 15(2). **Whittall v Kirby** [1946] **2** 552, KBD.
  Special road—
    Failure by prosecution to prove notices and regulations—
      Discretion of magistrates to grant adjournment—Road Traffic Act 1960, 9 Eliz ss 20(5), 37(5)—Special Roads (Notice of Opening) Regulations 1962, (SI 1962 No 1320), reg 1. **Royal v Prescott-Clarke** [1966] **2** 366, QBD.
  Special types of vehicle. *See* Motor vehicle—Special type, *above*.
  Specimen—
    Breath test. *See* Breath test, *above*.
    Driving while unfit through drink or drugs—
      Blood or urine. *See* Driving while unfit to drive through drink or drugs—Specimen of blood or urine, *above*.
    Failure to provide specimen—
      Breath test. *See* Breath test—Failure to provide specimen, *above*.

ROAD TRAFFIC (cont)—
    Specimen (cont)—
        Failure to provide specimen (cont)—
           Careless driving. *See* Careless driving—Causing death by careless driving when under influence of drink or drugs—Failure to provide specimen, *above.*
           Reasonable excuse—Requirement to provide specimen at police station—Suspect refusing to provide specimen until he has exercised right to consult solicitor—Whether amounting to reasonable excuse—Road Traffic Act 1972, s 8(7)—Police and Criminal Evidence Act 1984, s 58. **DPP v Billington** [1988] **1** 435, QBD.
        Specimen for laboratory test to determine driver's blood-alcohol proportion. *See* Specimen for laboratory test to determine driver's blood-alcohol proportion, *below.*
    Specimen for laboratory test to determine driver's blood-alcohol proportion—
        Blood—
           Division of specimen into parts—Analysis by ordinary equipment and ordinary skill—Analysis by gas chromatography. **Smith v Cole** [1971] **1** 200, QBD.
           Division of specimen into parts—Onus of proving part sufficient for and capable of analysis—Analysis by ordinary equipment and ordinary skill—Road Traffic Act 1962, s 2(4). **R v Nixon** [1969] **2** 688, CA.
           Division of specimen into parts—Part must be capable of analysis—Part congealing before analysis—Road Traffic Act 1962, s 2(4). **Earl v Roy** [1969] **2** 684, QBD.
           Site from which specimen to be taken—Selection of site by doctor—Road Safety Act 1967, s 3(3). **Solesbury v Pugh** [1969] **2** 1171, QBD.
           Specimen divided into three parts instead of two—Whether proper divisions for purpose of analysis—Specimen offered to driver and accepted by him—Whether he asked for it—Road Traffic Act 1962, s 2(4)(a). **Ley v Donegani** [1968] **3** 226, QBD.
        Conditions precedent to request for specimen—
           Arrest—Lawful arrest—Necessity of informing driver of reason for arrest—Driver giving specimen of breath sufficient to give positive reading—Driver informed that arrest for failing to provide specimen of breath—Whether arrest lawful—Road Safety Act 1967, s 2(4)(5). **R v Holah** [1973] **1** 106, CA.
           Arrest—Lawfulness of arrest not material to validity of request for specimen—Road Safety Act 1967, s 3(1). **R v Palfrey, R v Sadler** [1970] **2** 12, CA.
           Arrest—Person who has been arrested under provisions of Road Traffic Acts—Defendant under arrest for theft of car—Defendant not arrested or informed that he was under arrest under Road Traffic Acts—Whether request for specimen validly made—Road Safety Act 1967, s 3(1). **R v Weir** [1972] **3** 906, Crown Ct.
           Request for specimen—Whether specimen must be provided at same police station at which request for specimen made—Road Traffic Act 1972, s 9(1). **Pascoe v Nicholson** [1981] **2** 769, HL.
        Failure to provide specimen. *See* Failure to provide specimen for laboratory test, *above.*
        Hospital patient—
           Failure to notify medical practitioner of proposal to warn before patient required to supply specimen—Road Safety Act 1967, s 3(2),(10). **R v Knightley** [1971] **2** 1041, CA.
           Requirement to provide specimen—Requirement made while motorist a patient at hospital—Motorist subsequently discharging himself—Motorist providing specimen at hospital following discharge—Whether necessary that motorist should be a patient at hospital when specimen provided there—Road Safety Act 1967, s 3(2). **Bourlet v Porter** [1973] **2** 800, HL.
           Requirement to provide specimen—Warning of effect of failure to comply with requirement—Duty of constable to notify medical practitioner in charge of patient of 'proposal to make the requirement'—Whether constable obliged to notify medical practitioner of intention to warn patient of possible penal consequences of failure to comply with requirement—Road Traffic Act 1972, s 9(2), (7). **Baker v Foulkes** [1975] **3** 651, HL.
           Right of medical practitioner to object—Continuing right—Road Safety Act 1967, s 3(2). **Bosley v Long** [1970] **3** 286, QBD.
           Right of medical practitioner to object—Right a condition precedent to requirement to provide specimen—Right to object to provision of specimen not continuing after requirement made—Road Safety Act 1967, s 3(2). **Bourlet v Porter** [1973] **2** 800, HL.
           Specimen to be provided at hospital—Road Safety Act 1967, s 3(2). **Bosley v Long** [1970] **3** 286, QBD.
        Requirement that person arrested under provisions of statute should provide specimen—
           Lawfulness of arrest—Unlawful arrest of driver following alleged failure to provide specimen for breath test—Subsequent laboratory test showing blood-alcohol proportion above prescribed limit—Whether driver a 'person arrested under' provisions of statute—Whether result of laboratory test admissible for purpose of proving commission of offence—Road Traffic Act 1972, ss 6(1), 9(1). **Spicer v Holt** [1976] **3** 71, HL.
        Specimen of blood or urine—
           Two specimens of urine provided by motorist—Specimens considered by police officer to be inadequate—Subsequent request for specimen of blood by police officer—Specimens of urine in fact adequate—Whether permissible for police officer to request specimen of blood when proper specimen already provided—Road Safety Act 1967, s 3(6). **R v Hyams** [1972] **3** 651, CA.
        Test relating to proportion of alcohol at time of driving—
           Drink consumed after driving ceased before specimen provided—Evidence as to result of test if adjusted to take account of alcohol consumed after driving ceased—Whether evidence admissible—Road Safety Act 1967, s 1(1). **Rowlands v Hamilton** [1971] **1** 1089, HL.
           Drink consumed after driving ceased before specimen provided—Road Safety Act 1967, s 1(1). **R v Durrant** [1969] **3** 1357, CA.
           Suspect drinking before administration of breath test—Test subsequently proving positive—Laboratory test positive—Whether offence made out—Road Safety Act 1967, s 1(1). **DPP v Carey** [1969] **3** 1662, HL.
    Speeding. *See* Excessive speed, *above.*

ROAD TRAFFIC (cont)—
  Stage carriage—
    Fare—
      Intent to avoid payment of fare—Fare from the place whence passenger started—Bus passenger buying a ticket and travelling beyond fare stage for which ticket valid—Whether additional fare an excess fare from the place to which ticket valid or the full fare from the start less the amount paid—Whether dishonest intent necessary—London Passenger Transport Act 1936, s 91(1)(2)(a). **Covington v Wright** [1963] **2** 212, QBD.
    Number of standing passengers in excess of prescribed maximum—
      Conductor charged with permitting excess number of passengers to be carried—Whether conductor the wrong person to be charged as a principal offender—Public Service Vehicles and Trolley Vehicles (Carrying Capacity) Regulations 1954 (SI 1954 No 1612), reg 3, reg 4. **Spires v Smith** [1956] **2** 277, QBD.
    Offence by driver or conductor—
      Endangering safety of passenger by negligence—Conductor—Duty of care of conductor—Injury to passenger through driver not stopping at compulsory stop—Conductor collecting fares on top of car—No negligence on part of conductor—Stage Carriages Act 1832, s 48. **Askew v Bowtell** [1947] **1** 883, KBD.
      Injuring property of owner through negligence or by wanton and furious driving—Proof of negligence—Whether necessary to prove in addition 'wanton and furious driving'—Stage Carriages Act 1832, s 48. **Chapman v Kirke** [1948] **2** 556, KBD.
    Special occasion—
      Conveyance of guests once a week from holiday camp to railway station—Road Traffic Act 1930, s 61(2)—Road Traffic Act 1934, s 25(1). **Victoria Motors (Scarborough) Ltd v Wurzal** [1951] **1** 1016, KBD.
      Separate payments by passengers—Owner's ignorance of use to which vehicle put—Road Traffic Act 1930, ss 61, 72(1), (10)—Road Traffic Act 1934, s 25. **Evans v Dell** [1937] **1** 349, KBD.
  Stolen vehicle—
    Travelling in vehicle known to have been stolen. *See* Taking vehicle without authority—Travelling in vehicle known to have been stolen, *below.*
  Stopping of vehicle—
    Failure to give hand signal—
      Stop-light automatically operated by brakes—Accident—Negligence—Failure of defendant to give hand signal—Whether defendant entitled to rely on stop-light—Road Traffic Act 1930, ss 30(1)(h), 45—Motor Vehicles (Direction Indicator and Stop Light) Regulations 1935 (SR & O 1935 No 897). **Croston v Vaughan** [1937] **4** 249, CA.
    Motorway, on. *See* Motorway—Restrictions on stopping, *above.*
    School crossing. *See* School crossing—Stopping of motor vehicles, *above.*
  Supervision of learner driver. *See* Driving licence—Supervision of learner driver, *above.*
  Suspension of licence—
    Goods vehicle. *See* Goods vehicle—Suspension of licence, *above.*
    Public service vehicle. *See* Public service vehicle—Suspension of licence, *above.*
  Suspension of use of parking place—
    Leaving vehicle otherwise than as authorised—
      Waiting in parking place for permitted purpose. *See* Parking place—Leaving vehicle otherwise than as authorised—Waiting in parking place for permitted purpose—Use of parking place suspended, *above.*
  Suspicion of alcohol—
    Breath test. *See* Breath test—Person driving or attempting to drive—Suspicion of alcohol, *above.*
  Tachograph charts. *See* Carriage of goods and passengers—Tachograph charts, *above.*
  Taking vehicle without authority—
    Accused not the driver—
      Evidence that occupants of motor vehicle were acting in concert—Sufficiency of evidence—Road Traffic Act 1930, s 28. **Ross v Rivenall** [1959] **2** 376, QBD.
    Attempt—
      Sentence—Not to exceed that which may be imposed for full offence. **R v Pearce** [1952] **2** 718, CCA.
    Compensation order—
      Damage due to accident arising out of presence of vehicle on road—Limitation of compensation to damage to property recovered. *See* **Sentence** (Compensation—Damage due to accident arising out of presence of vehicle on road—Limitation of compensation to damage to property recovered in case of offence under Theft Act 1968—Taking motor vehicle without consent).
    Consent—
      Taking and driving away without owner's consent—Consent obtained by false pretence—Whether consent vitiated—Theft Act 1968, s 12(1). **R v Peart** [1970] **2** 823, CA.
      Taking and driving away without owner's consent—Consent obtained by fraudulent misrepresentation—Whether consent vitiated—Theft Act 1968, s 12(1). **Whittaker v Campbell** [1983] **3** 582, QBD.
    Driving away—
      What amounts to—Releasing handbrake—Vehicle running away on own—Need to establish that accused was in control of steering—Road Traffic Act 1960, s 217(1). **R v Roberts** [1964] **2** 541, CCA.
    Employer's vehicle—
      Driver using employer's van for own purpose—Driver in lawful possession of van before using it for unauthorised purpose—Road Traffic Act 1930, s 28(1). **Mowe v Perraton** [1952] **1** 423, QBD.
      Driver using employer's van for own purpose—Use outside working hours—Road Traffic Act 1960, s 217. **R v Wibberley** [1965] **3** 718, CCA.
    Liability of passengers—
      Knowledge of theft—Passengers allowing themselves to be carried in vehicle knowing it to have been stolen by driver—Whether passengers guilty of taking and driving away vehicle without consent or authority—Road Traffic Act 1960, s 217(1), (as amended by Road Traffic Act 1962, s 44). **Tolley v Giddings** [1964] **1** 201, QBD.
    Taking—
      Unauthorised assumption of possession coupled with some movement of vehicle—Theft Act 1968, s 12(1). **R v Bogacki** [1973] **2** 864, CA.

ROAD TRAFFIC (cont)—
Taking vehicle without authority (cont)—
Taking and driving away—
What amounts to—Causing vehicle to move from where it stands—Motor vehicle pushed a few yards by two defendants, while a third steered—Road Traffic Act 1930, s 28(1). **Shimmell v Fisher** [1951] **2** 672, KBD.
Travelling in vehicle known to have been stolen—
Accused not present when vehicle wrongfully taken by another person—Motor cycle—Accused aged 15—Not present when motor cycle wrongfully taken by another boy of same age—Whether riding on cycle, some hours later, as pillion passenger, sufficient to constitute offence—Road Traffic Act 1930, s 28(1). **D (an infant) v Parsons** [1960] **2** 493, QBD Divl Ct.
Accused not present when vehicle wrongfully taken by another person—Whether travelling in the vehicle subsequently, knowing it to have been taken without lawful authority, sufficient to constitute offence—Road Traffic Act 1930, s 28(1). **R v Stally** [1959] **3** 814, CCA.
Taxi—
Hackney carriage. *See* Hackney carriage, *above*.
Test certificate—
Day of issue—
Implicit in certificate that condition of vehicle at time of examination remains the same on day of issue—Certificate false in a material particular if condition of vehicle defective at date of issue—Road Traffic Act 1960, ss 65(2), 236. **R v Evans (Stanley)** [1964] **3** 666, CCA.
False in material particular—
Back-dated certificate—Car owner found to be without test certificate—Two days later back-dated certificate issued by garage proprietor—Whether certificate false in a material particular—Road Traffic Act 1960, s 236. **Murphy v Griffiths** [1967] **1** 424, QBD.
Goods vehicle. *See* Plating and test certificates for goods vehicles, *above*.
Test of competence to drive—
Conduct of test. *See* Driving licence—Test conducted in accordance with regulations, *above*.
Disqualified driver. *See* Disqualification for holding licence—Test of competence to drive, *above*.
Time on duty—
Limitation—
Goods vehicle driver. *See* Goods vehicle—Limitation of driver's time on duty, *above*.
Tower wagon—
Exemption from requirement of plating and test certificates. *See* Plating and test certificates for goods vehicles—Exemption—Tower wagon, *above*.
Trade licence—
General trade licence—
Break-down van used by repairer and dealer for towing for hire—Road Vehicles (Registration and Licensing) Regulations 1949 (SI 1949 No 1618), reg 29, art D(1). **Carey v Heath** [1951] **2** 774, KBD.
Lorry used by dealers in new and second-hand motor cars and motor car repairers in connexion with building operations at their garage—Road Vehicles (Registration and Licensing) Regulations 1955 (SI 1955 No 1664), reg 29, art D(1). **James v Evans Motors (County Garages) Ltd** [1963] **1** 7, QBD.
Motor ambulance—Used for towing trailer laden with motor-boat—Whether vehicle used for unauthorised purpose—Roads Act 1920, s 12—Road Vehicles (Registration and Licensing) Regulations 1924 (S R & O 1924 1462), reg 29D. **Dark v Western Motor & Carriage Co (Bristol) Ltd** [1939] **1** 143, KBD.
Motor car used for towing caravan—Caravan not a mechanically propelled vehicle—Road Vehicles (Registration and Licensing) Regulations 1949 (SI 1949 No 1618), reg 29, art D(4). **Jelliff v Harrington** [1951] **1** 384, KBD.
Limited trade licence—
Tractor towing loaded trailer—Road Vehicles (Registration and Licensing) Regulations 1941 (SR & O 1941 No 1149), reg 30, art B(1), provisos (b), (i). **Carrimore Six Wheelers Ltd v Arnold** [1949] **2** 416, KBD.
Misuse of general trade licence—
Proceedings—Power of county council to institute proceedings in respect of offence committed in their county—Licence issued by another county council—Vehicles (Excise) Act 1949, s 8—Road Vehicles (Registration and Licensing) Regulations 1953 (SI 1953 No 231), reg 35. **R v Reigate Justices, ex p Holland** [1956] **2** 289, QBD.
Motor trader—
Recovery vehicle—Use of recovery vehicle on a public road by virtue of a trade licence—Vehicle equipped for raising but not for drawing disabled vehicle—Whether a 'recovery vehicle'—Vehicles (Excise) Act 1971, s 16(8)—Road Vehicles (Registration and Licensing) Regulations 1971 (SI 1971 No 450), reg 35(3). **Pearson (E) & Son (Teesside) Ltd v Richardson** [1972] **3** 277, QBD.
Traffic lights—
Collision—
Contributory negligence. *See* **Negligence** (Contributory negligence—Collision between vehicles on road—Traffic lights).
Duty of driver to take care. *See* **Negligence** (Duty to take care—Driver of motor vehicle—Traffic lights).
Negligence—
Police—Malfunctioning of lights. *See* **Police** (Negligence—Duty to take care—Malfunctioning of traffic lights).
Vehicles. *See* **Negligence** (Vehicles—Traffic lights).
Traffic sign—
Failure to conform to traffic sign—
Mens rea—Automatism—Whether mens rea an element of the offence of failing to conform to a traffic sign—Road Traffic Act 1930, s 49(b). **Hill v Baxter** [1958] **1** 193, QBD.
Halt at major road ahead—
Compliance—Whether essential to come to a standstill. **Tolhurst v Webster** [1936] **3** 1020, KBD.
Part of sign only seen by motorist—Obedience to order as seen—Failure to comply with whole order. **Brooks v Jefferies** [1936] **3** 232, KBD.

ROAD TRAFFIC (cont)—
  Traffic sign (cont)—
    Light signals—
      Fire engine—Disobedience to traffic-lights—Traffic Signs (Size, Colour and Type) Provisional Regulations 1933, reg 28. **Ward v London CC** [1938] **2** 341, KBD.
      Stop line at road junction—Vehicle crossing stop line when traffic light green—Vehicle stopped when half of vehicle had crossed stop line—Waited for traffic to cross in front of it—Moved forward across road when light signal had changed to red—Only rear half of vehicle crossed stop line when traffic light was red—Whether contravention of Traffic Signs Regulations and General Directions 1964, reg 34(1)(a)—Road Traffic Act 1960, s 14, as amended by Road Traffic Act 1962, s 8 and Sch 1, Pt 2, para 13. **Ryan v Smith** [1967] **1** 611, QBD.
      Vehicles approaching light-controlled crossing—Speed of approach—Disobedience to traffic-lights—Highway Code—Road Traffic Act 1930, s 45(4). **Eva (Joseph) Ltd v Reeves** [1938] **2** 115, CA.
    Parking—
      London—Restricted street—No yellow line on road to indicate that street was restricted—Car parked in restricted street during prescribed hours—Whether offence committed—Parking Zones (Waiting and Loading Restriction) Order 1966, arts 3(1), 5(1)—London Government Act 1963, s 9—Road Traffic Act 1960, ss 34, 51(3), 52(1), (2)—Traffic Signs Regulations and General Directions 1964 (SI 1964 No 1857) directions 6, 26, as amended by Traffic Signs General Directions 1966 (SI 1966 No 489). **Cooper v Hall** [1968] **1** 185, QBD.
      Unilateral waiting—Parking prohibited on east side of road from 9 am on Monday falling on odd day in month—Appellant parking car on east side of road at 6 am on such Monday—Car remaining until after 9 am—No traffic signs erected in road to indicate that the prohibition depended on whether Monday fell on odd day in month—Whether offence committed—Traffic Regulation Orders (Procedure) (England and Wales) Regulations 1961 (SI 1961 No 485), reg 15(c)—Brighton Corporation (Various Roads) (No 3) (Unilateral Waiting) Order 1965. **James v Cavey** [1967] **1** 1048, QBD.
    Portable sign—
      Regulation of movement of traffic—Sign put up by road traffic officer requiring traffic to stop—Validity of authorisation by Minister of Transport—Road Traffic Act 1930, ss 48, 49. **Langley Cartage Co Ltd v Jenks** [1937] **2** 525, KBD.
    Road markings—
      Cause of action for contravention of regulation—Vehicle parked in contravention of regulation having causative effect on accident—No negligence at common law—Traffic Signs Regulations and General Directions 1964 (SI 1964 No 1857), reg 23(2)(a). **Kelly v WRN Contracting Ltd (Burke, third party)** [1968] **1** 369, Assizes.
      Controlled parking zone—Irregularities in signage and road markings within controlled parking zone—Whether controlled parking zone valid—Traffic Signs Regulations and General Directions 2002, SI 2002/3113, reg 4. **R (on the application of Herron) v Parking Adjudicator (Sunderland City Council and Secretary of State for Transport, interested parties)** [2012] **1** 709, CA.
    Siting—
      Duty of Ministry. See **Highway** (Traffic sign—Siting—Duty of Ministry).
    Slow—
      Duty of driver—Duty to reduce speed so that he can pull up quickly should other vehicle approach. **Buffel v Cardox (Gt Britain) Ltd** [1950] **2** 878, CA.
    White line on road—
      Driving on wrong side of line—Whether white line a traffic sign—Whether driver 'failing to conform to an indication given by a traffic sign'—Road Traffic Act 1930, ss 48(9), 49. **Evans v Cross** [1938] **1** 751, KBD.
  Traffic signal—
    Duty to take care. See **Negligence** (Duty to take care—Traffic signal).
  Trailer—
    Anything on four wheels drawn by vehicle—
      Poultry shed drawn on road by tractor—'Land Implement'—Road Traffic Act 1930, s 1—Motor Vehicles (Construction and Use) Regulations 1947, reg 3(1). **Garner v Burr** [1950] **2** 683, KBD.
    Efficient working order—
      Vehicle and trailer. See Motor vehicle—Efficient working order—Trailer, above.
    Indivisible load of exceptional length—
      Distribution of load dangerous to persons on trailer or highway—Trailer constructed and normally used for conveyance of exceptional length—Not exempt where distribution of load dangerous—Motor Vehicles (Construction and Use) Regulations 1931 (SR & O 1931 No 4), regs 62, 85. **Cripps v Cooper** [1936] **2** 48, KBD.
    Land implement—
      Scraper—Scraper used for civil engineering work in levelling land, excavating and removing earth—Whether scraper a land implement—Motor Vehicles (Construction and Use) Regulations 1966 (SI 1966 No 1288), reg 3. **Markham v Stacey** [1968] **3** 758, QBD.
      Two wheeled trailer—Trailer comprising hopper mounted on chassis designed to distribute lime, slag, salt, fertilisers, etc, on agricultural land—Mechanism operated by means of power derived from towing tractor through power shaft drive—Whether 'land implement'—Motor Vehicles (Construction and Use) Regulations 1955 (SI 1955 No 482), reg 3(1). **Amalgamated Roadstone Corp Ltd v Bond** [1963] **1** 682, QBD.
    Person in attendance—
      Exemption—Closed trailer constructed and used for carrying meat—Trailer carrying tiles—Trailer constructed and generally used for carrying meat—Whether exempt—Road Traffic Act 1930, s 17—Motor Vehicles (Construction and Use) Regulations 1931, reg 77. **Union Cartage Co Ltd v Heamon** [1937] **1** 538, KBD.
      Exemption—Trailer with not more than two wheels—Towing of four-wheeled vehicle—Two wheels only on road—Whether exempt as a two wheel trailer—Road Traffic Act 1930, s 17(1)—Motor Vehicles (Construction and Use) Regulations 1947 (SR & O 1947 No 670), reg 85(iii). **Carey v Heath** [1951] **2** 774, KBD.
    Special type of vehicle—
      Two trailers carrying abnormal indivisible load. See Motor vehicle—Special type, above.

ROAD TRAFFIC (cont)—
   Trailer (cont)—
      Superimposed on towing vehicle. *See* Articulated vehicle—Trailer superimposed on towing vehicle, *above*.
   Tramcar—
      Stage carriage. *See* Stage carriage, *above*.
   Transport—
      Road transport—
         European Community. *See* **European Union** (Road transport).
      Value added tax—
         Zero-rating. *See* **Value added tax** (Zero-rating—Transport of passengers).
   Travel concessions—
      Local authority. *See* **Local authority** (Transport—Travel concessions).
   Travelling in vehicle known to have been stolen. *See* Taking vehicle without authority—Travelling in vehicle known to have been stolen, *above*.
   Tyres—
      Defective tyre—
         Separate offences—Single user on road with two defective tyres—Whether separate information required in respect of each wheel used with defective tyre—Road Traffic Act 1960, s 64—Motor Vehicles (Construction and Use) Regulations 1969 (SI 1969 No 321), reg 83(1)(a), (f), (4). **Saines v Woodhouse** [1970] **2** 388, QBD.
   Unfitness to drive—
      In charge of vehicle. *See* Being in charge of vehicle when unfit to drive through drink or drugs, *above*.
   Unladen weight—
      Motor vehicle. *See* Motor vehicle—Unladen weight, *above*.
   Unlicensed vehicle. *See* Excise licence—Unlicensed vehicle, *above*.
   Unlicensed, disqualified or uninsured drivers—
      Causing death by driving—
         Whether offence requiring fault or blameworthy conduct—Whether offence requiring that driving be substantial or major cause of death—Road Traffic Act 1988, s 3ZB. **Prosecution Appeal, R v H** [2011] **4** 761, CA; **R v Hughes** [2013] **4** 613, SC; **R v Williams** [2011] **3** 969, CA.
   Unlighted vehicle on highway—
      Negligence. *See* **Negligence** (Highway—Unlighted vehicle).
   Urban road—
      Parking—
         Criminal offence—Causing or permitting vehicle to be parked with one or more wheels on any part of urban road other than carriageway—Whether rider of motorcycle parked with one or both wheels raised above pavement committing offence—Greater London Council (General Powers) Act 1974, s 15. **Wolman v Islington London BC** [2008] **1** 1259, CA.
   Urine—
      Specimen—
         Driving while unfit through drink or drugs. *See* Driving while unfit to drive through drink or drugs—Specimen of blood or urine, *above*.
         Specimen for laboratory test—
            Determination of driver's blood-alcohol proportion. *See* Specimen for laboratory test to determine driver's blood-alcohol proportion—Specimen of blood or urine, *above*.
   Using vehicle on road in breach of regulations. *See* Motor vehicle—Using vehicle on road in breach of regulations, *above*.
   Using vehicle or causing or permitting vehicle to be used on road without policy being in force. *See* **Motor insurance** (Using vehicle or causing or permitting vehicle to be used on road without policy being in force).
   Vehicle—
      Motor vehicle. *See* Motor vehicle, *above*.
   Vehicle test—
      Authorised examiner—
         Withdrawal of authorisation—Discretion of Minister of Transport—Motor Vehicles (Tests) Regulations 1968 (SI 1968 No 1714), reg 26(3), Sch 3, para 2. **R v Minister of Transport, ex p Males** [1970] **3** 434, QBD.
      Test certificate. *See* Test certificate, *above*.
   Waiting and loading restrictions—
      Leaving vehicle in parking place otherwise than as authorised. *See* Parking place—Leaving vehicle otherwise than as authorised—Waiting in parking place for permitted purpose, *above*.
      London—
         Prohibition of waiting longer than necessary to enable any person to board or alight—Accused getting out of car and taking parcel into nearby flat—Whether 'alighting' while taking parcel into flat—London Parking Zones (Waiting and Loading) (Restriction) Regulations 1960 (SI 1960 No 594), reg 4(a). **Clifford-Turner v Waterman** [1961] **3** 974, QBD.
         Taxi—Driver left taxi unattended in prohibited street to deliver parcel at house in street—Vehicles on hire for purpose of delivering unaccompanied parcel—Whether hackney carriage a goods vehicle—Contravention of art 5(1), (2) of Order of 1966—Whether ultra vires—Parking Zones (Waiting and Loading Restriction) Order 1966, arts 3(1), 5(1), (2) and 9(3)—London Hackney Carriage Act 1853, s 7—London Government Act 1963, s 10(1). **Levinson v Powell** [1967] **3** 796, QBD.
      Waiting prohibited subject to exemption for loading and unloading—
         Prohibition of waiting in restricted road—Distinction between vehicle delivering or collecting goods and driver using vehicle to deliver or collect goods himself—Need to show that use of vehicle reasonably necessary because goods cannot conveniently be carried by hand—Goods including cash in case from bank—Driver parking car in restricted road and collecting cash from bank—Driver placing cash in pocket and returning to car—Whether car parked 'for purpose of ... collecting' cash—Whether car exempt from prohibition on waiting—Parking Places and Controlled Parking Zone (Manchester) Order 1971, arts 27, 29(1). **Richards v McKnight** [1977] **3** 625, QBD.

ROAD TRAFFIC (cont)—
  Waiting and loading restrictions (cont)—
    Waiting prohibited subject to exemption for loading and unloading (cont)—
      Respondent delivering goods—Goods offloaded and left at entrance to premises and van driven to
      another prohibited street by respondent—Whether van being unloaded in second street—County
      of Dorset (Various Roads, Swanage) (Prohibition and Restriction of Waiting) Order 1967. **Pratt v
      Hayward** [1969] 3 1094, QBD.
  Weight—
    Heavy motor car—
      Weight transmitted to road surface. *See* Heavy motor car—Weight transmitted to road surface,
      above.
    Unladen weight of vehicle. *See* Motor vehicle—Unladen weight, *above*.
  Wheelclamping—
    Wrongful interference with goods. *See* **Tort** (Wrongful interference with goods—Cause of
    action—Plaintiff parking vehicle on private property without authority).
  Zebra crossing. *See* Pedestrian crossing—Zebra crossing, *above*.

ROAD TRANSPORT
  Carriage by road. *See* **Carriers**.
  European Community. *See* **European Union** (Road transport).

ROADS AND SEWERS
  Covenant—
    Upkeep of common roads and sewers. *See* **Sale of land** (Covenant running with land—Burden of
    covenant).

ROADWORTHINESS
  Motor insurance policy—
    Condition. *See* **Motor insurance** (Conditions—Roadworthiness).

ROBBERY
  See **Criminal law** (Robbery).

ROOF
  Building regulations—
    Roof work. *See* **Building** (Roof work).
  Working place—
    Place on which workman requried to work for appreciable period of time. *See* **Building** (Working
    places—Meaning—Place on which workman required to work for appreciable period of
    time—Work on flat roof for period of 10 to 15 minutes).

ROULETTE
  Lawfulness. *See* **Gaming** (Lawful and unlawful gaming—Roulette).

ROYAL ARMS
  Display in church to signify royal supremacy—
    Faculty—
      Jurisdiction. *See* **Ecclesiastical law** (Faculty—Jurisdiction—Royal arms—Display in church to
      signify royal supremacy).

ROYAL CHARTER
  Privy Council—
    Decision to recommend grant—
      Judicial review. *See* **Privy Council** (Grant of Royal Charter—Decision of committee to recommend
      grant of charter to professional body).

ROYAL COLLEGE OF SURGEONS
  Gift to—
    Charitable object. *See* **Charity** (Benefit to community—Surgery—Promotion of surgery—Incidental
    benefits to individuals—Gift to Royal College of Surgeons).

ROYAL COMMISSION
  Natural justice. *See* **Natural justice** (Royal Commission).

ROYAL FORCES
  Court-martial. *See* **Court-martial**.
  Generally. *See* **Armed forces**.
  Property of member of—
    Exemption from estate duty—
      Death on war service. *See* **Estate duty** (Exemption—Death on war service).

ROYAL PALACE
  Nigeria—
    Title to. *See* **Nigeria** (Title to property—Royal palace at Lagos).

ROYAL PREROGATIVE
  Generally. *See* **Crown** (Prerogative).
  Mercy—
    Judicial review of Home Secretary's decision—
      Availability of remedy. *See* **Judicial review** (Availability of remedy—Royal prerogative—Prerogative
      of mercy).
  Right to legislate in colonies. *See* **Malta** (Right to legislate in colonies).

ROYALTIES

Capital gains tax—
  Exemption—
    Disposal of right to annual payments due under personal covenant not secured on property—Royalty or other sum paid in respect of user of a patent. *See* **Capital gains tax** (Exemptions and reliefs—Disposal of right to annual payments due under personal covenant not secured on property—Annual payment—Royalty or other sum paid in respect of the user of a patent).
Deduction of tax—
  Acceptance of deduction under mistake of law—
    Accord and satisfaction. *See* **Accord and satisfaction** (Royalties—Deduction of tax).
  Generally. *See* **Income tax** (Annual payment—Payment out of profits etc already taxed—Inference that payment made net of tax—Royalties).
Income tax. *See* **Income tax** (Royalties).

RUBBISH

Accumulation or deposit—
  Statutory nuisance. *See* **Nuisance** (Statutory nuisance—Accumulation or deposit prejudicial to health or a nuisance).
Public health legislation. *See* **Public health** (Refuse).

RULE AGAINST PERPETUITIES

Accumulation of income. *See* **Accumulation** (Excessive period).
Alternative disposition—
  Primary trust for non-charitable purpose—
    Gift over on refusal of bequest—Gift over to charity—Gift over on future uncertain event void. **Spensley's Will Trusts, Re** [1954] 1 178, CA.
  Two distinct events—
    Whichever shall last happen—Gift to take effect on death of last surviving child or widow or widower of children whichever shall last happen—Whether adequate expression of alternative events. **Curryer's Will Trusts, Re** [1938] 3 574, Ch D.
Alternative independent limitation—
  Failure of prior limitation—
    Will—Residue given on trust for sale—Settled share—Discretionary trust for any widow donee may leave—Void limitation—Effect upon subsequent limitation—Alternative independent limitation. **Coleman's Will Trusts, Re** [1936] 2 225, Ch D.
Application of rule—
  Objects of trust capable of taking outside perpetuity period—
    Gift by way of remainder to 'issue' of beneficiary—Settlement—Date on which interests vest—Gift to issue on attaining 21—Whether issue limited to children—Whether issue limited to those in being at date of death of beneficiary or at date of death of child of beneficiary—Whether gift void for remoteness. **Drummond's Settlement, Re** [1988] 1 449, CA.
    Gift for education of children of named families—Children to be 'the lawful descendants' of three named individuals—Money to be invested by trustees 'under a trust for ever to be called' after testatrix and her mother—Trust void for perpetuity. **Compton (No 2), Re** [1946] 1 117, Ch D.
    Will—Power to distribute residue—Discretion of trustees—Among such of the descendants of testator's brothers and sisters in such shares and at such proper times as the trustees should determine. **Symm's Will Trusts, Re** [1936] 3 236, Ch D.
Charitable gift—
  Dependent on future uncertain event—
    Trustees directed to retain fund until such time as a candidate for the priesthood comes forward from a certain church. **Mander (decd), Re** [1950] 2 191, Ch D.
  Gift over for non-charitable purposes—
    Gift to named charities—On amalgamation gift over for purposes of charity or benevolence—Gift over void. **Bawdens Settlement, Re** [1953] 2 1235, Ch D.
  Gift over from one charity to another—
    Second charity incorporated by royal charter. **Royal College of Surgeons of England v National Provincial Bank Ltd** [1952] 1 984, HL.
  Validation where gift partly non-charitable—
    Purposes partly charitable and partly non-charitable—Power of selection amongst orders of nuns which were charitable and orders of nuns which were not charitable—No express indication of alternative purposes—Conveyancing Act 1919-1954 (New South Wales), s 37D. **Leahy v A-G of New South Wales** [1959] 2 300, PC.
Children—
  Presumption that woman past age of child-bearing—
    Presumption inapplicable for purpose of rule against perpetuities. **IRC v Bernstein** [1960] 1 697, Ch D.
Conditional gift—
  Specified event to happen during life in being—
    Gift to son—Gift taking effect when the present 'war with Germany shall terminate' and 'peace be declared'—Gift to take effect during lifetime of son. **Grotrian (decd), Re** [1955] 1 788, Ch D.
Distribution—
  Life in being—
    Date of distribution—Not date when distribution first possible but date when distribution actually effected. **Luck, Re** [1940] 3 307, CA.
Express limitation by reference to rule—
  Discretionary trust for children and grandchildren—
    Within the limitations prescribed by law—Validity. **Vaux, Re, Nicholson v Vaux** [1938] 4 297, CA.
Gift over after uncertain period—
  Duration of war—
    Gift over taking effect 'after the termination of the present war'—Validity. **Engels, Re** [1943] 1 506, Ch D.

RULE AGAINST PERPETUITIES (cont)—
Gift over after uncertain period (cont)—
Fulfilment of condition—
Gift rendering capital inalienable—Gift of income to non-charitable association 'until vivisection shall be made a punishable offence'—Gift over to Royal Society for Prevention of Cruelty to Animals—Validity of gift and gift over—Contingency. **Wightwick's Will Trusts, Re** [1950] **1** 689, Ch D.
Impossibility of infringing rule—
Age of lawful marriage—
Gift to the grandchildren of named person living at testatrix's death or born within five years therefrom and attaining 21—Impossibility of child of named person being born after death of testatrix lawfully marrying and having children within five years of death. **Gaite's Will Trusts, Re** [1949] **1** 459, Ch D.
Lease—
Land, options relating to. *See* **Landlord and tenant** (Lease—Options relating to land—Rule against perpetuities).
Lives in being—
Choice of lives in being—
Difficulty of ascertainment—Descendants of Queen Victoria—Validity. **Leverhulme (No 2), Re** [1943] **2** 274, Ch D.
Trustees—
Objects of trust not limited to lives in being—Single indivisible trust—Original trustees and trustees for time being—Trust fund distributable 'at such time or times' as the trustees think fit—Trustees defined as 'the first trustees and ... the trustees or trustee for the time being'—Trust not capable of being construed as two distinct trusts, one to original trustees and one to trustees for time being. **Innes (Inspector of Taxes) v Harrison** [1954] **1** 884, Ch D.
Pension scheme—
Register of pensionable employees—
Entries on register annually—Powers of committee to apply moneys on failure of employees to qualify for pension—Power to determine scheme—Whether powers void for perpetuity—Application of Perpetuities and Accumulations Act 1964, ss 3, 15. **Meadows (Thomas) & Co Ltd and Subsidiary Companies (1960) Staff Pension Scheme Rules, Re** [1971] **1** 239, Ch D.
Possibility of gift vesting outside perpetuity period—
Delay in vesting involving breach of trust—
Trust for sale—Vesting of gift on completion of sale—Devise in will of life interest in real property—Trust to sell farm on death of life tenant—Proceeds of sale to be divided among class of beneficiaries living at date of completion of sale—No express or implied power to postpone sale—Duty of trustees to sell property within year of life tenant's death—Possibility that trustees might delay completing sale for more than 21 years—Whether possibility to be taken into account. **Atkin's Will Trusts, Re** [1974] **2** 1, Ch D.
Power of advancement—
Effect of rule on power—
Fiduciary power under former settlement being exercised. **Pilkington v IRC** [1962] **3** 622, HL.
Power arising under will—
Time as at which application of rule to be considered. **Pilkington v IRC** [1962] **3** 622, HL.
Power extending to 'vested' share—
Construction—Power exercisable in anticipation of absolute vesting not in defeasance—Power admittedly invalid for remoteness in relation to some interests—Whether power void. **Wills' Will Trusts, Re** [1958] **2** 472, Ch D.
Power of appointment—
Appointment on trust to pay income during their joint lives to two grandchildren in equal shares as tenants in common—
After death of either grandchild to pay whole income to survivor—Neither grandchild alive at date of deed conferring power of appointment—Reversionary interest of survivor contingent and therefore void. **Legh's Resettlement Trusts, Re** [1937] **3** 823, CA.
Direction to apply capital if income falls below certain sum—
Contingent interest—Gift over to other appointees if share of appointee fails to vest absolutely in her child on her death—Appointees not born at date of settlement. **Johnson's Settlement Trusts, Re** [1943] **2** 499, Ch D.
Discretion to select beneficiaries—
Single decision—Implication that decision to be reached within reasonable time—Pension provision for managing director of company. **Leek (decd), Re** [1968] **1** 793, CA.
Excessive execution. *See* **Power of appointment** (Excessive execution—Appointment of absolute interest with gift over—Gift over infringing perpetuity rule).
Exercise of power of advancement—
Creation of special power of appointment—Power of advancement conferred by settlement and exercised by subsequent settlement—Special power of appointment contained in subsequent settlement—Read back into will under which original settlement made—Special power to be exercised 'without transgressing the rule against perpetuities'—Invalidity of exercise of power of advancement and of 1957 settlement. **Abrahams' Will Trusts, Re** [1967] **2** 1175, Ch D.
Joint power—
General or special power—Effect in relation to rule against perpetuities—Settlement conferring joint power of appointment on donees—Second settlement—Donees exercising power of appointment by re-settling property on trusts of second settlement—Period of second settlement exceeding perpetuity period for first settlement—Whether limitations of second settlement to be read back into first settlement—Whether donees of power of appointment to be treated as having equivalent of absolute interest in property subject of power. **Earl of Coventry's Indentures, Re** [1973] **3** 1, Ch D.
Power of revocation and new appointment—
Possibility of exercise beyond period. **Watson's Settlement Trusts, Re** [1959] **2** 676, Ch D.
Power of selection—
Discretion to select beneficiaries. *See* **Trust and trustee** (Discretionary trust—Uncertainty—Power of selection).

RULE AGAINST PERPETUITIES (cont)—
    Reference to rule—
        Meaning—
            Reference to 'rule against perpetuities' in instrument—Reference to be taken as a reference to the true rule in absence of a sufficient expression to the contrary. **IRC v Williams** [1969] **3** 614, Ch D.
    Remoteness—
        Limitation by reference to statutes of distribution—
            Gift over on failure of trusts—Limitation by reference to 'the statutes for the distribution of' personal estate of intestates—Possibility of existence of persons having contingent interests at longest time allowed by rule against perpetuities—Persons under 21 or not having married—Administration of Estates Act 1925, s 47(1). **Hart's Will Trusts, Re** [1949] **2** 898, Ch D.
        Rentcharge—
            Amount of charge ascertainable by reference to gross rateable value from time to time—Charge immediately vesting on creation—Whether validly created. **Beachway Management Ltd v Wisewell** [1971] **1** 1, Ch D.
        Scheme for administration of fund for benefit of employees of company—
            Uncertainty in description of persons to benefit—Whether validated by Superannuation and Other Trust Funds (Validation) Act 1927, ss 1, 2. **Flavel's Will Trusts, Re** [1969] **2** 232, Ch D.
    Rule prohibiting limitations to issue of unborn persons—
        Abolition of rule by statute—
            Marriage settlement dated before coming into force of statute—Power of appointment under marriage settlement exercised by deed after coming into force—Application of rule—Law of Property Act 1925, s 161(2). **Leigh's Marriage Settlement, Re** [1952] **2** 57, Ch D.
    Settlement—
        Dependent limitations—
            Clause in will contained two distinct provisions—First provision dependent on exhaustion of objects of preceding trust—Preceding trust infringed rule against perpetuities—First provision of clause also thereby invalidated—Second provision of clause not dependent on exhaustion of objects of prior trust—Second provision did not fail for perpetuity. **Hubbard's Will Trusts, Re** [1962] **2** 917, Ch D.
            Limitation dependent on void limitation—Accord with previous valid limitations—Dependent limitation void. **Mill's Declaration of Trust, Re** [1950] **2** 292, CA.
            Residue of testator's estate given on first for sale—Settled shares—Discretionary trusts during life of any widow of named person—Void limitation—Effect on subsequent gifts of capital. **Allan's Will Trusts, Re** [1958] **1** 401, Ch D.
            Successive interests each taking effect on termination of antecedent interests—If one interest void for perpetuity ulterior interests void—Whether provision in event of 'failure of trusts hereinbefore declared' covered nullity for infringing rule against perpetuities. **Buckton's Declaration of Trust, Re** [1964] **2** 487, Ch D.
        Gift to children—
            Provisions for substitution and cross-remainders—Income of trust fund to be paid to settlor's children from death of settlor's widow to death of last surviving child with provisions for substitution and cross-remainders—Provisions for substitution and cross-remainders to be read as separation directions—Settlor's children born before date of settlement—No breach of rule against perpetuities. **Hey's Settlement Trusts and Will Trusts, Re, Hey v Nickel-Lean** [1945] **1** 618, Ch D.
        Limitation to a class—
            Introduction of new members into original class of takers—Gift to children who should attain 25—Proviso that, if any son should die under the age of 25 leaving any children who should attain 21, such children should take the share to which the parent would have been entitled, had he attained 25. **Hooper's Settlement Trusts, Re** [1948] **2** 261, Ch D.
            Introduction of new members into original class of takers—Gift to composite class of children and grandchildren who should attain 21. **Lord's Settlement, Re** [1947] **2** 685, Ch D.
        Provision for taking by substitution—
            Gift of income of trust fund to children of settlor on youngest child attaining 21—Vesting of interest on each child's attaining 21—Proviso that, if any child should die before 'attaining a vested interest' leaving any children who should attain 21, such children should take parents' share 'by substitution'—Introduction of new members into original class of takers—Words 'by substitution' not having genuine substitutionary effect—Gift invalid. **Lord's Settlement, Re** [1947] **2** 685, Ch D.
    Statutory perpetuity period—
        Instrument taking effect after commencement of Act—
            Variation of trusts—Arrangement approved by court under Variation of Trusts Act—Arrangement approved after commencement of Act—Trust established before commencement—Whether arrangement coupled with court's order constituting an 'instrument'—Variation of Trusts Act 1958, s 1—Perpetuities and Accumulations Act 1964, s 15(5). **Holt's Settlement, Re** [1968] **1** 470, Ch D.
        Specified number of years—
            Specified—Codicil of will providing that for purpose of trusts perpetuity period to be from date of testatrix's death to 1 January 2020—Testatrix dying on 1 February 1976—Whether number of years 'specified'—Whether period unambiguously identified—Perpetuities and Accumulations Act 1964, s 1(1). **Green's Will Trusts, Re** [1985] **3** 455, Ch D.
    Uncertain period before vesting—
        Realisation of estate—
            Executor's year—Residuary bequest—Direction to realise and divide residue of estate—Legatee to be existing at time of realisation of residuary estate—No express power to postpone realisation—Whether gift referred to end of executor's year—Validity. **Petrie (decd), Re** [1961] **3** 1067, CA.
    Unincorporated association—
        Gift to association—
            Absolute gift to members on trust for association—Bequest in will—Gift to committee of local political party—Whether bequest a gift to members of association—Whether gift imposing a trust on association—Whether gift void for perpetuity. **Grant's Will Trusts, Re** [1979] **3** 359, Ch D.

RULE AGAINST PERPETUITIES (cont)—
   Unincorporated association (cont)—
      Gift to association (cont)—
         Absolute gift to members or trust for association as continuing body—Bequest in will—Whether bequest valid as absolute gift to existing members or invalid as an endowment tending to perpetuity. **Leahy v A-G of New South Wales** [1959] **2** 300, PC.
   Vendor and purchaser—
      Option to purchase land—
         No time limit for exercise—Specific performance against original grantee of option—Foundation of jurisdiction to grant decree. **Hutton v Watling** [1948] **1** 803, CA.
   Void restriction on valid limitation—
      Forfeiture clause—
         Interests of children or grandchildren—Forfeiture in event of child or grandchild forsaking Jewish faith or marrying outside faith—Event to be proved to the satisfaction of trustees—Forfeiture clause void. **Spitzel's Will Trusts, Re** [1939] **2** 266, Ch D.

RULE IN ANDREWS V PARTINGTON
   Settlement—
      Class gift—
         Distribution date. *See* **Settlement** (Class gift—Distribution date).

RULE IN BAIN V FOTHERGILL
   Breach of contract for sale of land—
      Vendor's inability to show good title—
         Limitation of damages. *See* **Sale of land** (Damages for breach of contract—Vendor's inability to show good title—Damages limited to cost of investigating title).

RULE IN LASSENCE V TIERNEY
   Settlement—
      Disposition—
         Absolute gift or resulting trust. *See* **Settlement** (Disposition—Resulting trust).

RULE IN RYLANDS V FLETCHER
   See **Nuisance** (Escape in consequence of non-natural use of land).

RULE IN SHELLEY'S CASE
   Heirlooms—
      Descent—
         Will. *See* **Will** (Heirloom—Descent—Rule in Shelley v Shelley).

RULE OF LAW
   Separation of powers. *See* **Constitutional law** (Separation of powers).

RULES
   Charity. *See* **Charity** (Unincorporated association—Rules).
   Immigration. *See* **Immigration** (Rules).
   National rules—
      European Community. *See* **European Union** (National rules).
   Statutory instrument. *See* **Statutory instrument**.
   Trade union. *See* **Trade union** (Rules).
   Unincorporated association. *See* **Unincorporated association** (Rules).

RULES OF COURT
   Generally. *See* **Statutory instrument** (Rules of court).
   Practice. *See* **Practice**.

RULES OF PROCEDURE
   Non-compliance—
      Whether proceedings a nullity. *See* **Practice** (Irregularity).

RURAL DISTRICT COUNCIL
   Election of councillors. *See* **Elections** (Local government—Election of rural district councillors).

RURAL WORKER
   Housing. *See* **Agriculture** (Housing—Rural worker).

RYLANDS V FLETCHER
   Principle of. *See* **Nuisance** (Escape in consequence of non-natural use of land).

S

SACRAMENT HOUSE
Church. *See* **Ecclesiastical law** (Ornaments—Sacrament house).

SAFE MEANS OF ACCESS
Dock—
    Loading and unloading operations. *See* **Dock** (Loading and unloading—Safe means of access).
    Repair of ship in dry dock—
        Safe means of access to workplace. *See* **Dock** (Repair of ship in dry dock—Statutory duty to provide safe means of access to work place).
Place of work—
    Factory. *See* **Factory** (Safe means of access to place of work).
Working places—
    Building regulations. *See* **Building** (Working places—Safe means of access).

SAFE PORT
Charterparty. *See* **Shipping** (Charterparty—Safe port).

SAFE SYSTEM OF WORKING
Child—
    Dangerous machinery. *See* Dangerous machinery—Child, *below*.
Contributory negligence—
    Unsafe system. *See* **Negligence** (Contributory negligence—Unsafe system of work).
Dangerous employment—
    Duty of master—
        Duty to ensure that danger is minimised. **Naismith v London Film Productions Ltd** [1939] 1 794, CA.
    Employment only possible at some risk to health of servant—
        Servant wishing to engage or continue in employment—No duty on master to refuse to employ or to dismiss servant. **Withers v Perry Chain Co Ltd** [1961] 3 676, CA.
Dangerous machinery—
    Child—
        Child of ten invited to help with threshing—Injury by dangerous machine—Allurement. **Holdman v Hamlyn** [1943] 2 137, CA.
    Circular saw—
        Duty to instruct and supervise—Apprentice on farm aged 18—No experience of circular saws—Misrepresentation as to experience—Consequent lack of supervision—Negligent operation of saw—Injury. **Kerry v Carter** [1969] 3 723, CA.
    Common law duty—
        Exemption from particular fencing provision of regulations—Whether common law duty to require workman to work cutters of horizontal milling machine with guard provided or provide alternative guard. **Quinn v Horsfall & Bickham Ltd** [1956] 2 467, CA.
    Oiling of machinery—
        Factory containing many machines of which a few were dangerous to oil when in motion—Whether employers owed duty to give instructions not to oil dangerous machines when in motion. **Lewis v High Duty Alloys Ltd** [1957] 1 740, Assizes.
    Young person under 18—
        Exposure to risk of injury—Machine with moving part—Bacon slicing machine—No locking device on cutting blade—Young person injured while cleaning cutting blade in different manner to that instructed—Defence of due diligence—Offices, Shops and Railway Premises Act 1963, ss 18(1), 67. **Dewhurst (JH) Ltd v Coventry Corp** [1969] 3 1225, QBD.
Delegation of duty to servant—
    Precautions—
        Duty to instruct workmen—Whether the devising of precautions should be left to workmen or whether employer should instruct workmen. **Gibb v United Steel Companies Ltd** [1957] 2 110, Assizes.
    Servant's attention drawn to statutory regulations—
        Contributory negligence—Electricity (Factories Act) Special Regulations 1908 (SR & O 1908 No 1312), reg 18(d) (as amended by Electricity (Factories Act) Special Regulations 1944 (SR & O 1944 No 739)). **Barcock v Brighton Corp** [1949] 1 251, KBD.
Duty to give information or advice—
    Health and Safety at Work etc Act. *See* **Health and safety at work** (Employer's duties).
    Protective appliance—
        Availability of protective clothing—Foundry—Injury to experienced moulder. **Qualcast (Wolverhampton) Ltd v Haynes** [1959] 2 38, HL.
        Availability of protective clothing—Notice advising workman of availability and advising him to wear it—Workman unable to read, but master unaware of this—Foundry—Injury from molten metal—Probability that protective clothing would not have been used. **James v Hepworth & Grandage Ltd** [1967] 2 829, CA.
        Conflicting medical opinions whether appliance would be effective protection—Barrier cream not provided by employer—Burden of proof of failure to take reasonable care. **Brown v Rolls Royce Ltd** [1960] 1 577, HL.
        Duty to provide masks and to persuade workmen to wear them—Risk of silicosis in steel foundry—Measure of damages. **Crookall v Vickers-Armstrong Ltd** [1955] 2 12, Assizes.
        Notice of precautionary measures posted up—Instructions given to workman—Protective cream and washing facilities provided—Workman's failure to take precautions unknown to employer. **Woods v Durable Suites Ltd** [1953] 2 391, CA.
        Protection of eyes—Grinding machine—Goggles in office 30 feet away—No notice on machine that goggles should be used—Men left to ask for goggles if they wanted them. **Finch v Telegraph Construction and Maintenance Co Ltd** [1949] 1 452, KBD.

SAFE SYSTEM OF WORKING (cont)—
Duty to give information or advice (cont)—
Protective appliance (cont)—
Protection of eyes—Grinding machine—Goggles not provided—Probability that toolsetter would not have used goggles, if provided, unless compelled to do so—Duty not only to provide safety appliances but also to ensure their use by means of orders and supervision. **Nolan v Dental Manufacturing Co Ltd** [1958] **2** 449, Assizes.
Protection of eyes—Special risk of injury—One-eyed workman—Need to provide goggles—Injury to other eye. **Paris v Stepney BC** [1951] **1** 42, HL.
Protective cream kept in store but not in workshop—No insistence by foreman on its use. **Clifford v Charles H Challen & Sons Ltd** [1951] **1** 72, CA.
Warning—
Duty of master to warn servant of danger—Extent—Overhead travelling cable-way low above roof to which servant had access and might be expected to go. **Quintas v National Smelting Co Ltd** [1961] **1** 630, CA.
When duty arises—
Omission to give instructions—Defect in system or breach of duty to take reasonable steps for safety of employees. **Winter v Cardiff RDC** [1950] **1** 819, HL.
Mine—
Support of roof. *See* **Mine** (Support—Support of roof—Duty of master to servant to provide safe system of work).
Permitting unsafe system to be in operation—
Burden of proof—
Alternative system—Whether workman required to plead and prove alternative system of work which would have been safe. **Dixon v Cementation Co Ltd** [1960] **3** 417, CA.
Plant—
Provision of proper plant and appliances—
Staging in wet dock. **Lovell v Blundells and T Albert Crompton & Co Ltd** [1944] **2** 53, KBD.
Safety of plant—
Onus of proof—Railway wagon in dangerous condition—Knowledge of state of wagon—Contributory negligence. **McDonald v British Transport Commission** [1955] **3** 789, Assizes.
Pleading—
Whether plaintiff need plead a particular system which would be safe. *See* **Statement of case** (Personal injuries action—Allegation of failure to provide safe system of working).
Reasonable care not to expose employee to unnecessary risk—
Acts of independent contractors—
Modernisation of store premises—Business of store continuing during modernisation—Responsibility of employers, owners and occupiers of store, for negligence of contractors, engineers or architects in carrying out or supervising such modernisation—Fire—Death of employee due to fire—Alleged fault in electrical cable—Whether employers liable for any negligence of cable manufacturers. **Sumner v Henderson (William) & Sons Ltd** [1963] **1** 408, QBD.
Cleaning floor made slippery by escape of viscous fluid before work began—
Escape of fluid due to negligence of servant of master—Fluid not dangerous in itself—Plaintiff employee instructed to clear up mess and supplied with necessary equipment but not given detailed instructions—Floor occupied by pallets standing on short legs and used as platforms for heavy bags of pipeclay stored on them—Plaintiff injured through slipping on floor—Liability of master. **Vinnyey v Star Paper Mills Ltd** [1965] **1** 175, Assizes.
Expert advice—
Reliance by employer on expert advice as to safety—Mining—Support for roof—Advice of mine owner followed by tunnelling contractor—Accident to contractor's employee due to fall of stone from roof of mine—Insufficient support to roof—Whether contractor liable to employee. **Szumczyk v Associated Tunnelling Co Ltd** [1956] **1** 126, Assizes.
Extent of master's duty—
Defence—Good practice of trade followed—Whether conclusive that there was no evidence of negligence to go to jury. **Cavanagh v Ulster Weaving Co Ltd** [1959] **2** 745, HL.
Employee at place where it was not his duty to go after work had ceased. **Brophy v JC Bradfield & Co Ltd** [1955] **3** 286, CA.
Reasonable care not absolute duty—Following advice of expert. **Szumczyk v Associated Tunnelling Co Ltd** [1956] **1** 126, Assizes.
System to be modified to meet circumstances of particular job—Unloading of cargo—Change over from discharging by means of a derrick to hauling up by straight lift—Breaking of rope. **Porter v Port of Liverpool Stevedoring Co Ltd** [1944] **2** 411, Assizes.
System to be modified to meet circumstances of particular job—Unloading of cargo—Use of married gear. **Speed v Thomas Swift & Co** [1943] **1** 539, CA.
Farming—
Fierce bull owned by master—No order by master to servant not to enter stall—Servant entered stall and injured by bull—Liability of master. **Rands v McNeil** [1954] **3** 593, CA.
Fencing of hatches on ship—
Seaman falling down an open hatch in grain ship while at sea—General practice of grain ships not to fence hatches while at sea—Whether danger reasonably foreseeable. **Morris v West Hartlepool Steam Navigation Co Ltd** [1956] **1** 385, HL.
Knowledge of risk—
Duty to keep knowledge up to date. **Graham v Co-op Wholesale Society Ltd** [1957] **1** 654, QBD.
Lighting—
Inadequate lighting in wet dock. **Garcia v Harland & Wolff Ltd** [1943] **2** 477, KBD.
Scalding water from shower—
Breach of statutory duty—Whether servant should have tested water before entering shower—Merchant Shipping (Crew Accommodation) Regulations 1953 (SI 1953 No 1036), reg 24(3). **Foulder v Canadian Pacific Steamships Ltd** [1969] **1** 283, Liverpool Summer Assizes.
Servant provided with unmanageable horse—
Injured by horse running away—Volenti non fit injuria—Whether risk incidental to employment. **Bowater v Rowley Regis Corp** [1944] **1** 465, CA.

SAFE SYSTEM OF WORKING (cont)—

Reasonable care not to expose employee to unnecessary risk (cont)—

Slippery duckboard—
Servant injured while washing teacup for her own use—Course of emgployment—Acts reasonably incidental to daily work. **Davidson v Handley Page Ltd** [1945] **1** 235, CA; **Paine v Colne Valley Electricity Supply Co Ltd** [1938] **4** 803, KBD.

Steps—
Handrail—Set of three steel steps leading to platform—Duty to provide handrail. **Kimpton v Steel Co of Wales Ltd** [1960] **2** 274, CA.

Untrained foreign labourer with poor knowledge of English—
Labourer employed to carry molten metal—Iron and Steel Foundries Regulations 1953 (SI 1953 No 1464), reg 6(2)(a). **Hawkins v Ian Ross (Castings) Ltd** [1970] **1** 180, QBD.

Window cleaner—
Best system possible in the circumstances—Defective window sash—No safety appliances provided. **General Cleaning Contractors Ltd v Christmas** [1952] **2** 1110, HL.

Instructions—Instructions to be given even if likely to be ignored. **Drummond v British Building Cleaners Ltd** [1954] **3** 507, CA.

Practice of trade—Inspection—No practice in trade of inspecting premises for danger—Duty of master. **Wilson v Tyneside Window Cleaning Co** [1958] **2** 265, CA.

Safe place of work—
Common law duty to protect employee from foreseeable risk of danger to health. *See* **Employment** (Duty of master—Safety of employees—Common law duty to protect employee from foreseeable risk of danger to health).

Dry dock—
Re-concreting of wall—Employee working on ledge two feet six inches wide with back to well—Failure to provide fence. **Bath v British Transport Commission** [1954] **2** 542, CA.

Servant employed to paint ship from altar courses—No safety precautions. **Hurley v J Sanders & Co Ltd** [1955] **1** 833, Assizes.

Electrical station—
Kiosk housing transformer. **Paine v Colne Valley Electricity Supply Co Ltd** [1938] **4** 803, KBD.

Narrow walkway between rail tracks—
One track belonging to master and another track belonging to British Transport Commission—Servant injured by traffic on British Transport Commission's track. **Braithwaite v South Durham Steel Co Ltd** [1958] **3** 161, Assizes.

Occupation of master—
Work on premises not occupied by master. **Cilia v James (H M) & Sons, Spark (third party)** [1954] **2** 9, QBD.

Rainwater on floor of passage leading to canteen—
Workman slipping and suffering injury. **Davies v De Havilland Aircraft Co Ltd** [1950] **2** 582, KBD.

Scaffolding—
Workman employed by sub-contractors killed by pipe falling from platform of scaffolding—Scaffolding erected by other sub-contractors—Gaps between boards of platform and no toe boards to platform. **Hughes v McGoff and Vickers Ltd** [1955] **2** 291, Assizes.

Ship under repair—
Defective staging—Accident to workman employed by sub-contractors engaged for the electric arc welding—Staging provided by contractors—Sub-contractors for specialised work not responsible for staging erected by contractors. **Hodgson v British Arc Welding Co Ltd** [1946] **1** 95, KBD.

Well—
Clearing well of water—Petrol pump used on platform down well—Danger from carbon monoxide—Employees told not to go down well—Danger of death not indicated—Liability of master to servants and to doctor attempting rescue. **Baker v T E Hopkins & Son Ltd** [1959] **3** 225, CA.

Safety of equipment—
Allowing servant to borrow equipment—
Trestles and planks—Employee borrowing equipment from contractors—Equipment collapsing owing to latent defect—Whether master guilty of negligence. **Quinn v Green (JW) (Painters) Ltd** [1965] **3** 785, CA.

Delegation of duty—
Selection of equipment—Whether duty sufficiently discharged by relying solely on experienced workman to select equipment—Yard foreman using inadequate shackles for lifting load—Contrast between common law and statutory duties. **Richardson v Stephenson Clarke Ltd** [1969] **3** 705, Assizes.

Loading ship—
Rope-sling breaking and contents falling on workman below—Rope changed without knowledge of employers. **O'Melia v Freight Conveyors Ltd, and Rederiaktiebolaget Svenska Lloyd** [1940] **4** 516, Assizes.

Secondhand machine—
Latent defect—Duty to exercise reasonable care when acquiring machine—Burden of proof. **Pearce v Round Oak Steel Works Ltd** [1969] **3** 680, CA.

Tool bought from reputable manufacturers—
Defect in tool due to work done by manufacturers' independent contractors—Previous accident to another servant from same tool of which employers had knowledge—Whether manufacturers were liable to servant. **Taylor v Rover Co Ltd (Richard W Carr & Co Ltd, third party)** [1966] **2** 181, Assizes.

Latent defect—Whether duty to examine tools—Dangerous goods—Negligence—Liability of manufacturers—Tools supplied for use in trade—Burden of proof. **Mason v Williams & Williams Ltd** [1955] **1** 808, Assizes.

Tool bought from reputable supplier who had bought it from reputable manufacturers—
Defect due to negligence in manufacture—Defect not discoverable by employers, but patent to manufacturers. **Davie v New Merton Board Mills Ltd** [1959] **1** 346, HL.

Steel foundry—
Pouring aisle. *See* **Factory** (Gangways and pouring aisles).

SAFETY

Access—
  Means of access—
    Factory. *See* **Factory** (Safe means of access to place of work).
    Working places. *See* **Building** (Working places—Safe means of access).
Building—
  Access to working places. *See* **Building** (Working places—Safe means of access).
  Building operations. *See* **Building** (Building operations).
  Regulations relating to. *See* **Building** (Building regulations).
Club. *See* **Club** (Members' club—Safety of premises).
Consumer protection regulations. *See* **Consumer protection** (Safety regulations).
Dock. *See* **Dock**.
Employees—
  Defective equipment—
    Liability of employer. *See* **Employment** (Liability of master—Defective equipment).
  Discrimination against a woman in interests of safety. *See* **Employment** (Discrimination against a woman—Act of discrimination—Discrimination in the interests of safety).
  Duty of employer under Health and Safety at Work etc Act. *See* **Health and safety at work** (Employer's duties).
  Generally. *See* **Employment** (Duty of master—Safety of employees).
Factory—
  Safe means of access to place of work. *See* **Factory** (Safe means of access to place of work).
  Safe place of work. *See* **Factory** (Safe place of work).
Food. *See* **Food and drugs** (Food safety).
Health and safety at work—
  Generally. *See* **Health and safety at work**.
Inn. *See* **Inn** (Safety of premises).
Members' club. *See* **Club** (Members' club—Safety of premises).
Mines—
  Roads and working places. *See* **Mine** (Safety of roads and working places).
Non-domestic premises—
  Premises made available as place of work—
    Statutory duty of persons having control of such premises. *See* **Health and safety at work** (Non-domestic premises).
Offices, shops and railway premises—
  Liability of employer for breach of statutory duty. *See* **Employment** (Duty of master—Offices, shops and railway premises—Safety of employees).
Place of work—
  Factory. *See* **Factory** (Safe place of work).
  Safe system of working. *See* **Safe system of working**.
School premises—
  Statutory duty of local education authority. *See* **Education** (Local education authority—Statutory duty in respect of school premises).
Ship—
  Offence—
    Failure to operate ship in safe manner. *See* **Shipping** (Offence—Failure to operate ship in safe manner).
System of working. *See* **Safe system of working**.
Working places—
  Building. *See* **Building** (Working places).
  Coal mine. *See* **Coal mining** (Statutory duty—Security of road and working place).

SAFETY BELTS

Building operations. *See* **Building** (Building operations—Safety nets, sheets and belts).
Seat belts in car—
  Failure to wear—
    Contributory negligence. *See* **Negligence** (Contributory negligence—Road accident—Seat belt).

SAFETY NETS

Building operations. *See* **Building** (Building operations—Safety nets, sheets and belts).

SAILOR

Will. *See* **Will** (Soldier's or mariner's privileged will).

SAINT VINCENT AND THE GRENADINES

Parliament—
  Parliamentary privilege—
    Bill of Rights—Right of access to court—Claim against government for constitutional relief in respect of alleged discriminatory and/or illegitimate expropriation of property—Proposed use in court of statement made by Prime Minister during parliamentary debate—Statutory provision against admissibility of evidence relating to parliamentary proceedings without permission of the Speaker—Whether statement admissible in evidence in support of claim—Bill of Rights (1688), art 9—House of Assembly (Privileges, Immunities and Powers) Act 1966 (Saint Vincent and the Grenadines), s 16—Constitution of Saint Vincent and the Grenadines 1979, ss 6, 16. **Toussaint v A-G of Saint Vincent and the Grenadines** [2008] **1** 1, PC.

SALARY

Generally. *See* **Employment** (Remuneration).
Income tax—
  Office or employment. *See* **Income tax** (Emoluments from office or employment).

SALE OF GOODS

Acceptance—
Act inconsistent with ownership of seller—
Constructive delivery—Delivery by seller direct to sub-purchaser at request of purchaser—Goods not in accordance with sample—Right of subsequent rejection—Sale of Goods Act 1893, s 35. **Ruben (E & S) Ltd v Faire Bros & Co Ltd** [1949] **1** 215, KBD.
Delivery to employee of purchaser—
Act of purchaser—Goods remaining on premises for three weeks—No act by purchaser in relation to goods—Whether goods accepted by purchaser—Sale of Goods Act 1893, ss 4(3), 35. **Debtor (No 38 of 1938), Re a** [1938] **4** 308, Ch D.
Lapse of reasonable time—
New car—Major breakdown after three weeks and 140 miles—Buyer purporting to reject car—Whether lapse of reasonable time—Sale of Goods Act 1979, ss 11(4), 35(1). **Bernstein v Pamson Motors (Golders Green) Ltd** [1987] **2** 220, QBD.
New yacht—Yacht supplied with overweight keel—Parties corresponding on possible remedial work—Buyer purporting to reject yacht—Whether lapse of reasonable time—Sale of Goods Act 1979, ss 11(4), 35. **Clegg v Olle Andersson (t/a Nordic Marine)** [2003] **1 Comm** 721, CA.
Specialist part fitted to vehicle—Installation not carried out in accordance with guarantee—Vehicle intended for subsequent resale—Buyer rejecting part after six months on information of potential sub-buyer—Whether lapse of reasonable time—Sale of Goods Act 1979, s 35. **Truk (UK) Ltd v Tokmakidis GmbH** [2000] **2 Comm** 594, Bristol Mercantile Ct.
Agent—
Authority. *See* **Agent** (Authority).
Commission. *See* **Agent** (Commission).
Sale by agent—
Goods in possession of agent. *See* Disposition by seller in possession after sale—Possession of agent, *below.*
Sale by person in course of business as agent on behalf of undisclosed principal—Implied conditions as to merchantable quality and fitness for purpose—Buyer purchasing boat thinking it was owned by agents—Buyer not informed that agents acting as agents nor name of owner nor that owner was not selling in course of business—Boat unseaworthy—Whether buyer entitled to sue owner—Whether buyer restricted to suing agent—Sale of Goods Act 1979, s 14(2), (3), (5). **Boyter v Thomson** [1995] **3** 135, HL.
Signature to contract 'for account of our [disclosed] principal'—Liability of principal for defect in goods sold. **Lester v Balfour Williamson Merchant Shippers Ltd** [1953] **1** 1146, QBD.
Arbitration—
Reference—
Time limit. *See* Breach of contract—Time limit for reference to arbitration, *below.*
Auction—
Auctioneer's rights against purchaser—
Action for price. *See* **Auctioneer** (Rights against purchaser—Action for price).
Generally. *See* **Auction**.
Bailee—
Damages—
Conversion. *See* **Conversion** (Damages—Measure of damages—Sale of goods by bailee).
Bailment—
Agency of necessity. *See* **Agent** (Agency of necessity—Gratuitous bailee—Sale of bailed goods).
Bargain offers—
Consumer protection. *See* **Consumer protection** (Price marking—Bargain offers relating to goods).
Bill of lading—
C and f contract. *See* C and f contract—Bill of lading, *below.*
C i f contract. *See* C i f contract—Bill of lading, *below.*
Delivery order—
Contract of carriage—Parties—Contract between shipowners and importer—Contract in terms of bill of lading—Freight payable at destination—Bill of lading presented to shipowners' agents in exchange for delivery orders—Delivery orders in same terms as bill of lading—Delivery order in respect of part of cargo endorsed by importer to third party—Whether contract between third party and shipowner. **Cremer v General Carriers SA** [1974] **1** 1, QBD.
Generally. *See* **Shipping** (Bill of lading).
Payment against bill of lading—
Passing of property. *See* Passing of property—Payment against bill of lading, *below.*
Breach of contract—
Damages for breach of contract—
Anticipatory breach. *See* **Contract** (Damages for breach—Anticipatory breach—Sale of goods).
Date at which damages assessed. *See* **Contract** (Damages for breach—Date at which damages assessed).
Foreseeability. *See* **Contract** (Damages for breach—Foreseeable consequence of breach).
Generally. *See* **Contract** (Damages for breach—Sale of goods).
Indemnity against claims by sub-purchaser. *See* **Contract** (Damages for breach—Sale of goods—Indemnity against claims by sub-purchaser).
Loss directly and naturally resulting from breach of warranty. *See* **Contract** (Damages for breach—Sale of goods—Loss directly and naturally resulting from breach of warranty).
Loss of profit on resale. *See* **Contract** (Damages for breach—Sale of goods—Loss of profit on resale).
Measure of damages. *See* **Contract** (Damages for breach—Measure of damages).
Mitigation of loss. *See* **Contract** (Damages for breach—Mitigation of loss).
Special damage—Need to plead. *See* **Pleading** (Damage—Special damage—Need to plead).
Time limit for reference to arbitration—
Fundamental breach—Time limit not applicable—Sale of mahogany logs—Delivery of mahogany logs, but short measure and substantially undergrade—Whether breach of fundamental term—Whether time limit applicable. **Smeaton Hanscomb & Co Ltd v Sassoon I Setty, Son & Co (No 1)** [1953] **2** 1471, QBD.

SALE OF GOODS (cont)—
Buyer—
Right to reject goods. *See* Rejection of goods—Right to reject, *below.*
Right to sell. *See* Vendor retaining property in goods—Contract reserving property in goods to vendor until payment of all debts due to vendor, *below.*
C and f contract—
Bill of lading—
Payment to be made against clean bill of lading—Bill of lading stating that goods shipped in apparent good order and condition—Bill also stating that goods subsequently discharged on account of fire damage—Bill tendered to buyers—Bill rejected by buyers on ground that it was not a clean bill of lading—Whether bill 'clean'—Whether buyers entitled to reject bill. **Golodetz (M) & Co Inc v Czarnikow-Rionda Co Inc** [1980] **1** 501, CA.
Passing of property. *See* Passing of property, *below.*
C i f contract—
Bill of lading—
From port of transhipment—Dated as from port of loading—Custom of trade. **Meyer (NV Arnold Otto) v Aune** [1939] **3** 168, KBD.
Cargo sold to cargo owners by charterers of ship—
Freight to be payable by cargo owners on arrival of ship—Bills of lading provided for freight to be payable at destination—Ship ran aground before reaching destination but was salved with cargo—Apportionment of liability to pay salvage reward in respect of ship and cargo—Whether freight element in price of cargo at risk of charterers or cargo owners. **Pantanassa, The** [1970] **1** 848, Admin Ct.
Contract in common form—
Special clause as to service of notices added—Compliance with special clause condition precedent. **Luis de Ridder Ltd v André & Cie SA, Lausanne** [1941] **1** 380, KBD.
Damages for breach of contract. *See* Breach of contract, *above.*
Delivery to named port—
Right of vendor to insist on delivery at named port. **Fibrosa Spolka Akcyjna v Fairbairn Lawson Combe Barbour Ltd** [1942] **2** 122, HL.
Documents to be tendered—
Bill of lading referring to charterparty—Whether charterparty necessary document—Inclusion of war risks clause in bill of lading—Reasonable and customary clause. **Finska Cellulosaföreningen v Westfield Paper Co Ltd** [1940] **4** 473, KBD.
Documents not sighted on vessel's arrival—Buyer refusing to accept delivery of cargo on ground that it was infested—Documents tendered after arrival of vessel—Buyer rejecting documents but not on ground of late tender—Whether buyer estopped from relying on late tender at subsequent arbitration for damages—GAFTA form 61, cl 13. **Cerealmangimi SpA v Alfred C Toepfer** [1981] **3** 533, QBD.
Force majeure clause. *See* Force majeure (Sale of goods—Force majeure clause).
Frustration—
Performance possible by route which was not customary—Closing of Suez Canal. **Tsakiroglou & Co Ltd v Noblee & Thorl GmbH** [1960] **2** 160, CA; [1961] **2** 179, HL.
Insurance—
Increased premium due to war risk—Goods shipped on ship of belligerent state. **Oulu Osakayetio of Oulu, Finland v Laver & Co Ltd** [1940] **2** 243, CA.
Obligation of sellers to ship by customary route—
Frustration—Closing of Suez Canal. **Carapanayoti & Co Ltd v ET Green Ltd** [1958] **3** 115, QBD.
Passing of property—
Reservation of right of disposal. *See* Passing of property—Reservation of right of disposal—C i f contract, *below.*
Unascertained goods. *See* Passing of property—Unascertained goods—Ascertainment—Cif contract, *below.*
Passing of risk. *See* Passing of risk—C i f contracts for sale of goods that in fact were to come from bulk cargo afloat, *below.*
Sale by sample—
Certificate of quality—Conclusive evidence clause—Contract for sale by sample providing that trade association's certificate of quality was to be final—Goods discharged at port of discharge in two instalments—Sellers obtaining certificate of quality in respect of first instalment only—Certificate later proved to be inaccurate—Buyers' bank wrongly rejecting conforming documents tendered by sellers—Sellers electing to treat contract as repudiated—Whether buyers entitled to reject whole consignment because second instalment not conforming with contract description—Whether buyers' right to reject goods for nonconformity surviving sellers' rescission of contract—Sale of Goods Act 1893, s 30(1), (3). **Gill & Duffus SA v Berger & Co Inc** [1984] **1** 438, HL.
Car—
Conditional sale agreement. *See* Conditional sale agreement—Agreement for sale of car, *below.*
Contract—
Mistake as to identity of party—Deception. *See* **Contract** (Mistake—Identity of party—Deception as to identity—Oral offer of car for sale).
New car. *See* Motor car—New car, *below.*
Chain of purchases—
Whether circle of contracts genuine transactions. *See* **Agent** (Creation of agency—Agency for entering into contract).
Computer software. *See* **Agent** (Commercial agent—Meaning—Agent promoting software supplied to principal's customers electronically and not on any tangible medium).
Condition—
Means of delivery—
Specified steamer—Sale of potatoes—Offer for 'Saturday's steamer'—Acceptance of offer—Condition that goods to be shipped on that steamer—Delay due to failure to load by shipowner—Whether buyer entitled to reject goods. **Wilson v Wright** [1937] **4** 371, CA.

SALE OF GOODS (cont)—
 Default by seller (cont)—
  Notice of default—
   Contract for sale on GAFTA terms—Buyers serving notice of default before end of shipment period—Sellers treating notice of default as repudiatory breach and accepting repudiation—Whether party incorrectly serving notice of default under GAFTA default clause thereby committing repudiatory breach of contract. **Gulf Agri Trade FZCO v Aston Agro Industrial AG** [2009] **1 Comm** 991, QBD.
 Defective goods—
  Principal and agent—
   Liability of principal. *See* **Agent** (Liability of principal—Defective goods).
 Deferred payment—
  Passing of property. *See* Passing of property—Payment of purchase price—Property passing when contract made—Different intention—Deferred purchase price, *below.*
 Del credere agent. *See* **Agent** (Del credere agent).
 Delivery—
  Conditions inhibiting delivery imposed by vendor's supplier—
   Dealer to use his 'best endeavours to secure delivery' within reasonable time or by specified date—Conditions in regard to sale by dealer imposed by manufacturer after date of contract between dealer and customer—Customer required to enter into covenant against re-sale—Refusal by customer to enter into covenant—Refusal by manufacturer to deliver car to dealer for appropriation to customer—Liability of dealer. **Monkland v Jack Barclay Ltd** [1951] **1** 714, CA.
   Delivery to be within reasonable time—Refusal by manufacturer to supply dealer except subject to conditions regarding sale by dealer unacceptable by purchaser—Liability of dealer. **Hartwells of Oxford Ltd v British Motor Trade Association** [1950] **2** 705, CA.
  Constructive delivery—
   Sale and leaseback transaction—Unauthorised sale by original owner—Two sale and leaseback agreements made in relation to same goods—Position of buyers—Conversion—Whether making of agreement for sale and entering into the lease constituting 'delivery'—Whether buyers liable in conversion—Sale of Goods Act 1979, ss 24, 25. **Michael Gerson (Leasing) Ltd v Wilkinson** [2000] **2 Comm** 890, CA; [2001] **1** 148, CA.
  Defence to action for failure to deliver—
   Purported compliance with control order—Sale of timber—Government order prohibiting disposal of timber coming into force after contract—Order not prohibiting delivery under contract already made. **Rappaport v London Plywood and Timber Co Ltd** [1940] **1** 576, KBD.
  F o t contract—
   Contract allowing for delivery at a range of places in country of destination—Whether right and duty to nominate place for delivery lying with sellers or buyers. **Zenziper Grains and Feed Stuffs v Bulk Trading Corp Ltd** [2001] **1 Comm** 385, CA.
  Implied condition—
   Contract for sale of future goods—Contract for sale of about 275 tons of barley to be grown on seller's land—Crop yielding only 140 tons—Seller failing to deliver 140 tons to buyer—Whether implied condition of contract that seller released from obligation to deliver any barley if unable to deliver full amount—Sale of Goods Act 1893, ss 5(2), 61(2). **Sainsbury (HR & S) Ltd v Street** [1972] **3** 1127, Assizes.
  Insolvency of seller—
   Clause providing for insolvency—Notice condition precedent—Clause providing for default—Voluntary default—General Produce Brokers' Association contract. **Adair (J F) & Co Ltd v Birnbaum** [1938] **4** 775, CA.
  Partial failure to deliver—
   Delivery of lesser quantity—Rights of purchaser—Prescribed and non-prescribed conditions—Inconsistency—Control of Timber (No 21) Order 1941 (SR & O 1941 No 2088), arts 1(1), (2), 6, Sch III. **Wilkinson v Barclay** [1946] **2** 337, CA.
  Separate consignments—
   Short delivery—Rejection of goods—Contract for sale of suits—Delivery by instalments at sellers' discretion—Short delivery of one suit on one instalment—Whether contract divisible—Whether short delivery of one suit going to root of contract—Whether buyers entitled to reject delivery of entire contract—Sale of Goods Act 1893, ss 30(1), 31(2). **Regent OHG Aisenstadt und Barig v Francesco of Jermyn St Ltd** [1981] **3** 327, QBD.
  Wrong quantity—
   Printed words—Compensation for undershipment—Typewritten words—'Sold subject to shipment'—Short delivery—Liability of sellers. **Hollis Bros & Co Ltd v White Sea Timber Trust Ltd** [1936] **3** 895, KBD.
 Deposit—
  Sale of plant and machinery—
   Contract requiring deposit amounting to nearly 60 per cent of sale price of factory plus plant and machinery—Whether deposits permissible in respect of contracts for sale of plant and machinery—Whether arguable that deposit unreasonable—Whether unreasonable deposit recoverable as penalty or only subject to relief against forfeiture. **Amble Assets LLP (in administration) v Longbenton Foods Ltd (in administration)** [2012] **1 Comm** 764, Ch D.
 Description—
  False trade description. *See* **Trade description** (False trade description).
  Implied condition as to merchantable quality. *See* Implied condition as to merchantable quality—Goods bought by description, *below.*
  Implied condition goods correspond with description. *See* Implied condition goods correspond with description, *below.*
  Shipment of goods—
   Contract containing clause 'Shipment and destination: Afloat per ss Morton Bay due London approximately June 8'—Whether condition of contract that goods shipped on a ship which at date of contract due to arrive approximately on that date. **MacPherson Train & Co Ltd v Howard Ross & Co Ltd** [1955] **2** 445, QBD.

SALE OF GOODS (cont)—
Description (cont)—
Trade description—
Mutual ignorance as to deficiency in quality—Goods of contract description supplied—Validity of contract. **Harrison & Jones Ltd v Bunten & Lancaster Ltd** [1953] **1** 903, QBD.
Detention by purchaser—
Passing of property—
Detention beyond reasonable time. See Passing of property—Detention beyond reasonable time, below.
Disposition by seller in possession after sale—
Delivery of the goods under any disposition—
Disposition—Seller in possession having purchased car from previous sellers—Seller remaining in possession after subsequent sale of car to finance company—Seller's cheque to previous sellers dishonoured—Retaking of car by previous sellers from seller's custody with his acquiescence—Previous sellers unaware at time of retaking of subsequent sale to finance company—Whether retaking a delivery of the car under a disposition thereof—Sale of Goods Act 1893, s 25(1). **Worcester Works Finance Ltd v Cooden Engineering Co Ltd** [1971] **3** 708, CA.
Goods bought by finance company from motor car dealer for purpose of hire-purchase transactions—Motor car dealer continuing in possession with authority to resell in own name and retain purchase money—Authority subject only to obligation to account to finance company—Sale by dealer to third party—Title of third party to goods purchased from dealer. **Pacific Motor Auctions Pty Ltd v Motor Credits (Hire Finance) Ltd** [1965] **2** 105, PC.
Goods sold to finance company in hire-purchase transaction—
Subsequently seized by shopkeeper—Resale for cash—Title of second purchaser—Bills of Sale Act 1878—Bills of Sale Act (1878) Amendment Act 1882—Sale of Goods Act 1893, s 25(1). **Olds Discount Co Ltd v Krett and Krett** [1940] **3** 36, KBD.
Hire of goods by vendor under hire-purchase agreement—
Goods remaining in possession of vendor—Subsequent sale by vendor—Whether subsequent sale effective to transfer title—Factors Act 1889, s 8. **Union Transport Finance Ltd v Ballardie** [1937] **1** 420, Assizes.
Possession of agent—
Pledge by vendor in possession—Warehouseman—Whether goods in possession of vendor when in possession of agent—Sale of Goods Act 1893, s 25(1). **City Fur Manufacturing Co Ltd v Fureenbond (Brokers) London Ltd** [1937] **1** 799, KBD.
Seller continuing in possession—
Unlawful possession—Sale of car to finance company—Finance company hiring car to third party on hire-purchase terms—Seller remaining in possession of car without knowledge of finance company—Subsequent disposition of car by seller—Whether relevant that seller's continued possession wrongful—Whether disposition passing a good title—Sale of Goods Act 1893, s 25(1). **Worcester Works Finance Ltd v Cooden Engineering Co Ltd** [1971] **3** 708, CA.
Drugs. See **Drugs** (Sale of drugs).
Duty of seller—
Export licence—
Absolute or qualified duty—Force majeure—Government ban on all exports—Seller responsible for 'obtaining any necessary export licence'—Failure to obtain such licence not providing ground for claim of force majeure if at time contract made regulations requiring licence in force—Seller obtaining export licence—Export of sugar from Poland—Polish government imposing ban on all exports of sugar due to crop failure and revoking licences already granted—Whether seller under absolute duty to obtain licence which would remain valid until shipment—Rules of London Refined Sugar Association, rr 18(a), 21. **Czarnikow (C) Ltd v Centrala Handlu Zagranicznego 'Rolimpex'** [1978] **2** 1043, HL.
Absolute or qualified duty—Force majeure—Quota restrictions on export—Contracts requiring seller to obtain export licences—Contracts providing for incorporation of GAFTA form 78 including force majeure clause—Seller unable to obtain export licence—Whether force majeure clause overridden by terms of contracts requiring seller to obtain export licences—Whether force majeure clause applying to events of total export ban only—Whether force majeure clause applying to events restricting or partially restricting export—GAFTA form 78, cl 17. **Public Company Rise v Nibulon SA** [2015] **2 Comm** 778, QBD.
Absolute or qualified duty—Force majeure—Quota restrictions on export—Sellers required to 'provide for export certificate'—Quota exhausted and sellers unable to obtain certificate—Whether sellers under absolute obligation to provide export certificate—Whether sellers merely required to use best endeavours to obtain export certificate. **Pagnan SpA v Tradax Ocean Transportation SA** [1987] **3** 565, CA.
Licence for export from Finland necessary—Contract provided for delivery as soon as export licence granted—Licences granted only to members of Finnish exporters' association—Sellers not members of association—Whether sellers liable in damages for failure to deliver goods. **Cassidy (Peter) Seed Co Ltd v Osuustukkukauppa IL** [1957] **1** 484, QBD.
Enforcement—
Contract of sale—
Distinction from contract for work and labour done and materials supplied. See Contract—Distinguished from contract for work and labour done and materials supplied, above.
Exception clause—
Latent defects. See Implied condition as to fitness—Exception clause for latent defects, below.
Exclusion of implied terms—
Implied condition as to merchantable quality. See Implied condition as to merchantable quality—Exclusion of implied term, below.
Export—
Payment—
Exchange control. See **Currency control** (Exchange control—Payment for exports—Export of goods to destination outside scheduled territories).

SALE OF GOODS (cont)—
Export licence—
    Duty to obtain licence—
        Buyer or seller's duty—Licence necessary for export—English contract—Export licences granted only to Portuguese suppliers. **Pound (A V) & Co Ltd v M W Hardy & Co Inc** [1956] **1** 639, HL.
        Duty of seller. *See* Duty of seller—Export licence, *above*.
F o b contract—
    Credit. *See* Payment—Confirmed letter of credit—F o b contract, *below*.
    Passing of property—
        Reservation of right of disposal. *See* Passing of property—Reservation of right of disposal—F o b contract, *below*.
    Payment—
        Confirmed letter of credit. *See* Payment—Confirmed letter of credit—F o b contract, *below*.
False trade description. *See* **Trade description** (False trade description).
Feeding stuffs. *See* **Agriculture** (Feeding stuffs—Sale for use as food for cattle or poultry).
Fertiliser—
    Analysis of sample. *See* **Agriculture** (Fertiliser—Analysis of sample).
Firearms—
    Restrictions on sale. *See* **Firearms** (Restrictions on sale).
Fitness for purpose—
    Implied condition. *See* Implied condition as to fitness, *below*.
Food and drugs. *See* **Food and drugs**.
Force majeure—
    Frustration. *See* **Contract** (Frustration—Force majeure).
    Generally. *See* **Force majeure** (Sale of goods).
Fraud—
    Election of seller to avoid contract for fraud. *See* Voidable title—Fraud—Election of seller to avoid contract for fraud, *below*.
Frustration—
    C i f contract. *See* C i f contract—Frustration, *above*.
    Force majeure. *See* **Contract** (Frustration—Force majeure—Sale of goods).
Goods made by blind or otherwise disabled person—
    Sale from house to house by person registered for sale of such goods—
        Whether person requiring licence for house to house collections. *See* **House to house collection** (Collection—Sale of goods—Sale of goods made by blind or otherwise disabled person).
Hire-purchase. *See* **Hire-purchase**.
House to house—
    Licence for house to house collections. *See* **House to house collection** (Collection—Sale of goods).
Identity of party—
    Deception as to identity of purchaser. *See* **Contract** (Mistake—Identity of party—Deception as to identity).
Implied condition—
    Description—
        Correspondence with. *See* Implied condition goods correspond with description, *below*.
    Fitness, as to. *See* Implied condition as to fitness, *below*.
    Merchantable quality, as to. *See* Implied condition as to merchantable quality, *below*.
    Vendor's right to sell. *See* Title—Implied condition of vendor's right to sell, *below*.
Implied condition as to fitness—
    Abnormal circumstances—
        Idiosyncrasy in circumstances of use of goods by buyer—Idiosyncrasy unknown to either buyer or seller—Installation of new type of camshaft in engine of plaintiffs' fishing vessel—Vessel having abnormal tendency to produce excessive torsional resonance when fitted with new type of camshaft—Excessive torsional resonance causing excessive wear on camshaft—Whether sellers of camshaft in breach of implied condition as to reasonable fitness for purpose—Sale of Goods Act 1979, s 14(3). **Slater v Finning Ltd** [1996] **3** 398, HL.
        Idiosyncrasy of buyer—Idiosyncracy not made known to seller—Sale of tweed coat specially made for buyer—Dermatitis—Buyer having abnormally sensitive skin—Whether seller liable for breach of implied condition of fitness—Sale of Goods Act 1893, s 14(1). **Griffiths v Peter Conway Ltd** [1939] **1** 685, CA.
    Contract for sale of bespoke staircase—
        Purchasers rejecting staircase on delivery—Staircase designed for installation into a dwelling house—Staircase as designed and supplied not complying with building regulations—Non-compliance with building regulations possible to remedy by modifying design of staircase—Whether breach of implied term entitling purchaser to reject staircase. **Lowe v W Machell Joinery Ltd** [2012] **1 Comm** 153, CA.
    Contract for work and materials. *See* **Building contract** (Warranty—Implied warranty—Fitness or quality of materials).
    Contract partly for the sale of goods and partly for rendering of services—
        Dangerous hair dye. **Ingham v Emes** [1955] **2** 740, CA; **Watson v Buckley, Osborne, Garrett & Co Ltd and Wyrovoys Products Ltd** [1940] **1** 174, Assizes.
    Dealing as consumer—
        Express term of conditional sale agreement excluding liability for fitness where purchaser 'dealing as consumer'—Whether agreement containing implied condition that car was reasonably fit for purposes for which it was purchased—Whether implied condition excluded by express term of agreement—Unfair Contract Terms Act 1977, s 6(2)—Sale of Goods Act 1979, s 14(3). **R & B Customs Brokers Co Ltd v United Dominions Trust Ltd (Saunders Abbott (1980) Ltd, third party)** [1988] **1** 847, CA.

SALE OF GOODS (cont)—
Implied condition as to fitness (cont)—
Defective trailer coupling supplied by garage to vehicle owner for use with trailer—
Coupling unsafe for purpose for which it was designed by manufacturer—Continued use of coupling by user after he ought to have known of defective condition—Defective coupling causing trailer to break loose from vehicle and cause damage to another vehicle resulting in death and injury to occupants—Whether continued use of defective coupling by owner in contemplation of parties at time of sale—Whether conduct of owner broke chain of causation between suppliers breach of warranty in supplying defective coupling and the accident—Liability of owner, supplier and manufacturer inter se. **Lambert v Lewis** [1980] **1** 978, CA.
Exception clause for latent defects—
Incorporation of clause inferred from course of bargaining—Buyers and sellers members of London Cattle Food Association—Whether inference that buyers relied on sellers' skill and judgment should be made—Condition of fitness of ground nut extracts for re-sale for use for food for cattle or poultry—Unfit for food for poultry—Whether implied condition broken—Compounded food fed to pheasants—Remoteness of damage—Sale of Goods Act 1893, s 14(1), (2). **Kendall (Henry) & Sons (a firm) v William Lillico & Sons Ltd** [1968] **2** 444, HL.
Fitness for human consumption—
Food poisoning—Husband and wife lunching in hotel—Husband paying for meal—Wife taken ill by food poisoning—Whether wife entitled to sue in contract. **Lockett v Charles (A & M) Ltd** [1938] **4** 170, KBD.
Foreign undisclosed principal as purchaser—
Purpose for which goods required made known to sellers—Sale of Goods Act 1893, s 14(1). **Teheran-Europe Co Ltd v ST Belton (Tractors) Ltd** [1968] **1** 585, QBD.
Goods of a description which it is in course of the seller's business to supply—
Description—Seller compounder of animal feeding stuffs—Contract to supply food for mink—Seller having no previous experience in dealing with mink food—Whether mink food goods of a description which is in course of business to supply—Mink food compounded according to buyer's formula—In course of seller's business to supply ingredients—Mink food goods 'of a kind' which in course of business to supply—Contract for sale of mink food made in way of business—Sale of Goods Act 1893, s 14(1), (2). **Ashington Piggeries Ltd v Christopher Hill Ltd** [1971] **1** 847, HL.
Goods within general description though taking special form or designed for special use—Sale of Goods Act 1893, s 14(1). **Spencer Trading Co Ltd v Devon (Fixol and Stickphast Ltd, third parties)** [1947] **1** 284, KBD.
Implied condition as to satisfactory quality. *See* Implied condition as to satisfactory quality, *below.*
Instructions—
Recommendation for use—Warning against use after stated time—Farmer purchasing herbicide to kill wild oats infesting crops—Instructions containing warning that use after specified growth stage of crops not recommended—Herbicide ineffective after specified growth stage of crops—Farmer misunderstanding warning—Farmer understanding warning to mean only that late use might cause damage to crops—Whether herbicide fit for purpose for which supplied—Sale of Goods Act 1979, s 14(3). **Wormell v RHM Agriculture (East) Ltd** [1987] **3** 75, CA.
Particular purpose made known to seller—
Disclosure of purpose by agent—Motor tractor sold for road construction purposes—Disclosure of purpose made by gratuitous agent of purchaser—Whether buyer showing reliance on seller's skill or judgment—New South Wales Sale of Goods Act 1923—53, s 19(1). **Ashford Shire Council v Dependable Motors Pty Ltd** [1961] **1** 96, PC.
General purpose known to seller—Herring meal—Use in compounding mink food—Knowledge of seller that herring meal required for compounding animal feeding stuffs—Knowledge that herring meal had been used for preparing mink food—Sellers unaware that particular consignment required for mink food—Herring meal contaminated by DMNA—DMNA toxic to mink—Whether use for compounding animal feeding stuffs sufficiently definite to constitute particular purpose—Sale of Goods Act 1893, s 14(1). **Ashington Piggeries Ltd v Christopher Hill Ltd** [1971] **1** 847, HL.
Nature of buyer's business known to seller's agents—Potatoes for human consumption in England shipped from Cyprus—Deterioration of potatoes in transit—Sale of Goods Act 1893, s 14(1)(2). **Mash & Murrell Ltd v Joseph I Emanuel Ltd** [1962] **1** 77, CA.
Resale in foreign country—Air compressors—Purpose of resale in Persia made known to seller—Buyers a Persian company undisclosed principals—Buyers relied on own skill and judgment—No warranty of fitness for resale in Persia implied—Sale of Goods Act 1893, ss 13(1), 14(1). **Teheran-Europe Co Ltd v ST Belton (Tractors) Ltd** [1968] **2** 886, CA.
Vehicle—Fitness to be driven on road—Secondhand motor car—Engine seizing up after 2,300 miles—Replacement engine necessary—Whether car reasonably fit for purpose of being driven on road at time of sale—Sale of Goods Act 1893, s 14(1). **Crowther v Shannon Motor Co (a firm)** [1975] **1** 139, CA.
Warning of hazard—Chemical sold in glass ampoules for use in manufacturing process—Choice of chemical made by purchaser—Danger of explosion if in contact with water—Warning by seller only of harmful vapour—Course of previous dealing between parties reasonably causing reliance on seller to give adequate warning of dangerous hazard—Explosion causing death and extensive damage when ampoules broken while being washed—Whether goods fit for purpose if not adequately labelled with warning of explosion hazard—Sale of Goods Act 1893, s 14(1). **Vacwell Engineering Co Ltd v BDH Chemicals Ltd** [1969] **3** 1681, QBD.
Reasonably fit—
Secondhand motor car—Buyer told of defect in clutch—Car driven for four weeks without trouble—Defect in clutch then found to be serious—Whether breach of implied condition that car reasonably fit for purpose—Sale of Goods Act 1893, s 14(1)(2). **Bartlett v Sidney Marcus Ltd** [1965] **2** 753, CA.

SALE OF GOODS (cont)—
  Implied condition as to fitness (cont)—
    Reliance on seller's skill and judgment—
      Partial reliance—Idiosyncrasy of purchaser outside seller's sphere of expertise—Onus of proof—Seller compounder of animal feeding stuffs—Buyer requiring food for mink—Seller having no experience of mink food—Contract to supply mink food according to buyer's formula—Reliance on seller to supply ingredients suitable for feeding to animals generally—Herring meal in mink food contaminated by DMNA—DMNA toxic to mink—Evidence whether DMNA harmful to animals generally—Onus on sellers to prove affirmatively that DMNA harmless to animals other than mink—Sale of Goods Act 1893, s 14(1). **Ashington Piggeries Ltd v Christopher Hill Ltd** [1971] **1** 847, HL.
      Stated purpose not materially different from purpose for which the goods commonly bought—Whether condition as to fitness for purpose different from condition as to merchantable quality—Sale of Goods Act 1979, s 14(3). **Aswan Engineering Establishment Co v Lupdine Ltd (Thurgar Bolle Ltd, third party)** [1987] **1** 135, CA.
  Implied condition as to merchantable quality—
    Exclusion of implied term—
      Deterioration of perishable goods—Express condition that seller take reasonable care to protect goods and notify any deterioration—Sale of potatoes—Deterioration of potatoes—Whether breach of implied condition as to merchantable quality—Sale of Goods Act 1893, ss 14(2), 55. **Horn v Minister of Food** [1948] **2** 1036, KBD.
      Unfair contract term—Whether fair and reasonable for seller to rely on clause limiting liability for supplying goods not of merchantable quality—Sale of Goods Act 1979, s 55. **Mitchell (George) (Chesterhall) Ltd v Finney Lock Seeds Ltd** [1983] **2** 737, HL.
    Goods—
      Container or packaging—Farmer purchasing herbicide to kill wild oats—Misleading instructions by manufacturer as to use of herbicide—Herbicide failing to produce expected result—Whether herbicide of unmerchantable quality—Whether 'goods' meaning container, packaging and any instructions supplied with goods as well as goods themselves—Sale of Goods Act 1979, s 14(2), (3). **Wormell v RHM Agriculture (East) Ltd** [1986] **1** 769, QBD.
    Goods bought by description—
      Lemonade—Sale of lemonade containing poison—Liability of retailer—Whether goods bought by description—Sale of Goods Act 1893, s 14(1)(2). **Daniels and Daniels v White (R) & Sons Ltd and Tarbard** [1938] **4** 258, KBD.
      Sale over counter—Catapult—Purchaser boy aged six—Catapult displayed in shop window where seen by boy who then purchased it in shop—Reliance on seller's skill or judgment—Whether sale by description—Sale of Goods Act 1893, s 14(2). **Perry v Godley (Burton & Sons (Bermondsey) Ltd, third party, Graham, fourth party)** [1960] **1** 36, QBD.
      Unsuitable for contract purposes—Goods sold for lower price for another purpose—Whether abatement of price indicative that goods not of merchantable quality—Sale of Goods Act 1893, s 14(2). **Brown (BS) & Son Ltd v Craiks Ltd** [1970] **1** 823, HL.
    Goods manufactured to precise specification—
      Unsuitable for contract purpose—Suitable for other purposes—No evidence that goods manufactured to specification used for other purposes—Sale of Goods Act 1983, s 14(2). **Brown (BS) & Son Ltd v Craiks Ltd** [1970] **1** 823, HL.
  Implied terms as to quality and fitness for purpose—
    F o b contract—Defendant contracting to sell gasoil to claimant—Contract containing specifications of gasoil at time of loading—Clause excluding 'guarantees, warranties or representations' concerning merchantability, fitness or suitability for purpose of gasoil—Gasoil subsequently rejected by receivers—Buyer alleging gasoil off specification at destination—Whether implied statutory term as to fitness for purpose—Whether implied term at common law that gasoil capable of remaining during voyage and for a reasonable time thereafter of satisfactory quality and/or on specification—Whether any implied terms excluded by express term of contract—Sale of Goods Act 1979, s 14(2), (3). **KG Bominflot Bunkergesellschaft für Mineralole mbh & Co KG v Petroplus Marketing AG** [2011] **2 Comm** 522, CA.
    F o b contract—Defendant contracting to sell gasoil to claimant—Contract containing specifications of gasoil at time of shipment—Clause excluding 'guarantees, warranties or representations' concerning merchantability, fitness or suitability for purpose of oil—Claimant alleging that gasoil not conforming to contract specifications at destination—Whether implied term that goods to be of satisfactory quality upon arrival at destination—Whether implied term that goods reasonably fit for purpose during voyage and for reasonable time thereafter—Whether proposed implied terms inconsistent with express terms—Whether implied terms excluded by clause—Sale of Goods Act 1979, s 14(2), (3). **KG Bominflot Bunkergesellschaft für Mineralole mbh & Co KG v Petroplus Marketing AG** [2009] **2 Comm** 827, QBD.
    Fob contract—Defendant contracting to sell gasoil to claimant—Contract containing specification for gasoil at time of loading on vessel—Gasoil being on specification at time of loading but off specification at destination—Gasoil being rejected by third party—Claimant bringing proceedings for breach of contract—High Court holding as preliminary issue that there being implied term that gasoil of satisfactory quality on delivery—Whether express terms as to specification of gasoil at time of loading excluding implied term as to satisfactory quality—Sale of Goods Act 1979, s 14(2). **KG Bominflot Bunkergesellschaft fur Mineralole mbH & Co v Petroplus Marketing AG (No 2), The Mercini Lady** [2013] **1 Comm** 610, QBD.
    Misrepresentation—Contract to supply integrated software system—'Entire agreement' clause—Whether terms implied into contract for supply of software system—Whether 'entire agreement' clause subject to statutory test of reasonableness—Misrepresentation Act 1967, s 3—Unfair Contract Terms Act 1977, s 3(2)—Sale of Goods Act 1979, s 14—Supply of Goods and Services Act 1982, ss 9, 13. **Watford Electronics Ltd v Sanderson CFL Ltd** [2000] **2 Comm** 984, QBD.
  Merchantable quality—
    Matters to be considered—Purchaser's reasonable expectations about goods at time of sale as well as their condition—Whether secondhand car enthusiast's car of merchantable quality—Whether court may interfere where award of damages is manifestly unjust due to incorrect decision on issue of merchantable quality—Sale of Goods Act 1979, s 14(2). **Shine v General Guarantee Corp Ltd (Reeds Motor Co (a firm), third party)** [1988] **1** 911, CA.

SALE OF GOODS (cont)—
  Implied condition as to merchantable quality (cont)—
    Merchantable quality (cont)—
      New car—Car suffering from series of defects—Car repaired under manufacturers' warranty—Car still rejected by purchaser after five months' use and 5,500 miles—Whether car of merchantable quality—Whether existence of manufacturers' warranty relevant—Unfair Contract Terms Act 1977, s 6(2)—Sale of Goods Act 1979, s 14(2)(6). **Rogers v Parish (Scarborough) Ltd** [1987] **2** 232, CA.
      New car—Major breakdown after three weeks and 140 miles—Car repaired as 'good as new' under manufacturers' warranty—Buyer refusing to accept return of car—Whether car when originally delivered of merchantable quality—Sale of Goods Act 1979, s 14(2)(6). **Bernstein v Pamson Motors (Golders Green) Ltd** [1987] **2** 220, QBD.
      Painting—Painting forged—Whether painting of merchantable quality—Sale of Goods Act 1979, s 14(2)(6). **Harlingdon & Leinster Enterprises Ltd v Christopher Hull Fine Art Ltd** [1990] **1** 737, CA.
      Words to be construed in commercial sense—Goods of merchantable quality if saleable for ordinary use for which goods of that description bought and sold—Price—Relevance—Goods suitable for ordinary use but because of poor condition only saleable at price substantially below contract price—Whether goods 'of merchantable quality'—Sale of Goods Act 1893, s 14(2). **Cehave NV v Bremer Handelsgesellschaft mbH** [1975] **3** 739, CA.
    Part of goods only not merchantable—
      Unfit goods in consignment—Explosive substance in consignment of fuel—Whether whole consignment unmerchantable—Sale of Goods Act 1893, s 14(2). **Wilson v Rickett, Cockerell & Co Ltd** [1954] **1** 868, CA.
    Sale in the course of a business—
      Meaning—Sale of fishing vessel used exclusively for purposes of fishing business—Condition that vessel of merchantable quality only implied if sale 'in the course of a business'—Sale of vessel incidental to business—Whether sale made in the course of a business—Whether condition implied as to merchantable quality—Sale of Goods Act 1979, s 14(2). **Stevenson v Rogers** [1999] **1** 613, CA.
    Suitability for purpose—
      Purpose for which goods might reasonably be expected to be used—Whether goods required to be suitable for every purpose for which they were normally bought—Sale of Goods Act 1979, s 14(6). **Aswan Engineering Establishment Co v Lupdine Ltd (Thurgar Bolle Ltd, third party)** [1987] **1** 135, CA.
  Implied condition as to satisfactory quality—
    Exclusion of implied terms—
      Contract for supply of carbon dioxide—Contract warranting purity of carbon dioxide no less than that laid down in relevant British Standard—Contract excluding all other implied warranties—Carbon dioxide contaminated with benzene—Whether contractual reference to British Standard establishing undertaking of suitability—Whether exclusion clause reasonable—Unfair Contract Terms Act 1977, Sch 2. **Britvic Soft Drinks v Messer UK Ltd** [2002] **2 Comm** 321, CA.
      Contract for supply of carbon dioxide—Contract warranting purity of carbon dioxide no less than that laid down in relevant British Standard—Contract excluding all other implied warranties—Contract limiting liability in respect of direct physical damage to property—Carbon dioxide contaminated with benzene—Contaminated carbon dioxide mixed with alcoholic concentrate and water to produce final product—Whether damage to final product direct physical damage—Whether limitation clause applicable—Whether exclusion clause reasonable—Unfair Contract Terms Act 1977, s 6. **Bacardi-Martini Beverages Ltd v Thomas Hardy Packaging Ltd** [2002] **2 Comm** 335, CA.
    Satisfactory quality—
      New yacht—Yacht supplied with overweight keel—Buyer refusing to accept yacht—Whether yacht when originally delivered of satisfactory quality—Sale of Goods Act 1979, s 14(2). **Clegg v Olle Andersson (t/a Nordic Marine)** [2003] **1 Comm** 721, CA.
  Implied condition goods correspond with description—
    Correspondence with description—
      Contamination of goods—Herring meal—Herring meal a constituent of mink food—Contamination of herring meal by DMNA—Formation from chemical reaction of sodium nitrite—Sodium nitrite used as preservative of herring—Contamination by DMNA not resulting in different substance to herring meal—Defect a matter of quality or condition rather than of description—Sale of Goods Act 1893, s 13. **Ashington Piggeries Ltd v Christopher Hill Ltd** [1971] **1** 847, HL.
      Goods to be loaded on deck—Stipulation in contract that timber 'to be loaded on deck one-third'—More than one-third loaded on deck—Whether buyers entitled to reject on ground of failure to correspond with description. **Messers Ltd v Morrison's Export Co Ltd** [1939] **1** 92, KBD.
    Identification of goods—
      Stipulation as to quality distinguished—Herring meal—Contract for sale of 'Norwegian herring meal fair average quality of the season'—Fair average quality of season not part of description—Stipulation as to quality only and not for purpose of identifying goods. **Ashington Piggeries Ltd v Christopher Hill Ltd** [1971] **1** 847, HL.
    Sale by description—
      Car advertised as 1961 model—Car in fact made up of rear of 1961 car and front of earlier model—Car examined by buyer before sale—Deviation from description in advertisement not apparent on reasonable examination and not known to either buyer or seller—Whether a sale of goods by description—Sale of Goods Act 1893, s 13. **Beale v Taylor** [1967] **3** 253, CA.
      Painting—Seller attributing painting to recognised artist—Seller having no expertise in works by that artist—Painting forged—Buyer buying painting without questioning painting's provenance—Whether buyer relying on seller's attribution—Whether sale of painting by description—Sale of Goods Act 1979, s 13(1). **Harlingdon & Leinster Enterprises Ltd v Christopher Hull Fine Art Ltd** [1990] **1** 737, CA.
    Words of description—
      Safety glass—Laminated glass—Words 'safety glass' generally understood to mean laminated glass—Whether warranty of absolute safety—Sale of Goods Act 1893, ss 13, 14(2). **Grenfell v EB Meyrowitz Ltd** [1936] **2** 1313, CA.

SALE OF GOODS (cont)—
Implied condition of right to sell—
Implied condition of quiet possession—
Vessel detained by authorities after loading—Whether breach of implied right to sell—Whether breach of implied right to quiet possession—Whether implied rights excluded by entire agreement clause—Sale of Goods Act 1979, s 12(1), (2)(b). **Great Elephant Corp v Trafigura Beheer BV, The Crudesky** [2013] **1 Comm** 415, QBD.
Implied conditions as to satisfactory quality—
Exclusion of implied terms—
Contract for sale of ship on Norwegian Saleform 1993—Contract providing that vessel be delivered and taken over 'as she was at the time of inspection' and delivered 'with her class maintained'—Whether contract excluding implied condition as to satisfactory quality—Sale of Goods Act 1979, ss 14, 55. **Dalmare SpA v Union Maritime Ltd** [2013] **2 Comm** 70, QBD; [2013] **2** 870, QBD.
Transfer of property—
Food—Claimants falling ill after consuming food at hotel arranged by defendant holiday provider—Whether defendant in breach of implied condition as to satisfactory quality of goods—Whether consumption of food and drink involving transfer of property—Supply of Goods and Services Act 1982, s 4(2). **Wood v TUI Travel plc (t/a First Choice)** [2017] **2 Comm** 734, CA.
Implied terms as to quality and fitness for purpose—
Goods—
Computer disk—Whether computer disk 'goods'—Sale of Goods Act 1979, ss 14, 61—Supply of Goods and Services Act 1982, ss 9, 18. **St Albans City and District Council v International Computers Ltd** [1996] **4** 481, CA.
Implied warranty—
Quiet possession—
Interference with possession by title paramount—Exception to implied warranty in case of disturbance by title paramount—Sale of stolen property—Whether implied exception to warranty as to quiet possession in case of disturbance by title paramount—Sale of Goods Act 1893, s 12(2). **Mason v Burningham** [1949] **2** 134, CA.
Title paramount not in existence at date of sale—Sale of machinery—Application by third party for patent—Complete specification published after sale of machinery—Patentee's rights having retrospective effect—Seller and buyer unaware of patent at date of sale—Action by patentee against buyer for infringement of patent by using machinery—Action constituting interference with buyer's possession—Whether seller in breach of warranty as to quiet possession—Sale of Goods Act 1893, s 12(2). **Microbeads AC v Vinhurst Road Markings Ltd** [1975] **1** 529, CA.
Reconditioned goods—
Certificate by third party. *See* Condition—Reconditioned goods—Certificate by third party, *above*.
Injunction—
Form of order. *See* **Injunction** (Form of order—Sale of goods).
Generally. *See* **Injunction** (Sale of goods).
Insolvency of seller—
Delivery of goods. *See* Delivery—Insolvency of seller—Clause providing for insolvency, *above*.
Intoxicating liquor—
Licensing. *See* **Licensing**.
Offence—
Sale without licence. *See* **Licensing** (Sale of liquor by retail without licence).
Market overt—
Market constituted by charter or statute—
Private sale—Goods offered by auction in public market—Subsequent private sale in same market—Sale of Goods Act 1893, s 22(1). **Bishopsgate Motor Finance Corp Ltd v Transport Brakes Ltd** [1949] **1** 37, CA.
Sale between sunrise and sunset—
Buyer acquiring good title—Necessity of showing that sale took place between sunrise and sunset—Sale of Goods Act 1893, s 22(1). **Reid v Comr of Police of the Metropolis** [1973] **2** 97, CA.
Medicine. *See* **Medicine** (Sale by retail).
Mercantile agent. *See* **Agent** (Mercantile agent).
Merchantable quality—
Implied condition. *See* Implied condition as to merchantable quality, *above*.
Misrepresentation—
Fraudulent misrepresentation. *See* **Misrepresentation** (Fraudulent misrepresentation—Sale of goods).
Innocent misrepresentation. *See* **Misrepresentation** (Innocent misrepresentation—Sale of goods).
Warranty distinguished. *See* Warranty—Misrepresentation distinguished, *below*.
Mistake—
Identity of party—
Deception as to. *See* **Contract** (Mistake—Identity of party—Deception as to identity).
Price. *See* **Mistake** (Price of subject-matter of transaction).
Rectification. *See* **Mistake** (Rectification—Sale of goods).
Motor car—
New car—
Acceptance. *See* Acceptance—Lapse of reasonable time—New car, *above*.
Injunction against selling as new a car that was not new. **Morris Motors Ltd v Phelan** [1960] **2** 208, Ch D.
When a car ceases to be new. **Morris Motors Ltd v Lilley (t/a G & L Motors)** [1959] **3** 737, Ch D.
Motor vehicle—
Displaying for sale notice in vehicle. *See* **Street trading** (Offence—Displaying for sale notice in private vehicle).
Motor car. *See* Motor car, *above*.
Protection of private purchaser without notice of hire-purchase agreement. *See* **Hire-purchase** (Motor vehicle—Protection of private purchaser without notice of hire-purchase agreement).
Sale in unroadworthy condition. *See* **Road traffic** (Motor vehicle—Sale in unroadworthy condition).

SALE OF GOODS (cont)—
  Nature of transaction—
    Consideration—
      Goods produced 'for general sale'—Purchase tax. *See* **Purchase tax** (Chargeable goods—Pictures, prints, engravings etc—Goods produced in quantity for general sale).
  Non-acceptance—
    Damages. *See* **Contract** (Damages for breach—Sale of goods—Non-acceptance).
  Note or memorandum in writing—
    Particulars of transaction in document not signed by party to be charged—
      Letter signed by that party to third person referring to transaction—Sale of Goods Act 1893, s 4(1). **Turner (LD) Ltd v Hatton (RS) (Bradford) Ltd** [1952] **1** 1286, Assizes.
    Signature of auctioneers' employee on behalf of purchaser—
      Action by auctioneer—Whether signature sufficient to bind purchaser in action by auctioneer—Sale of Goods Act 1893, s 4(1). **Wilson v Pike** [1948] **2** 267, CA.
    Sufficiency—
      Omission of vendor's name—Deficiency supplied by purchaser's admission—Omission of term as to delivery—Sale of Goods Act 1893, s 4(1). **Walford v Narin** [1948] **2** 85, KBD.
  Obtaining credit by fraud—
    Credit. *See* **Criminal law** (Obtaining credit by fraud—Credit—Sale of goods).
  Offer for sale or invitation to treat—
    Advertisement of Bramblefinch hens at 25s each in periodical under classified advertisements. *See* **Animal** (Protection—Bird—Restriction on sale or offer for sale of live wild bird—'Offer for sale').
  Part exchange. *See* **Price**—Sale for cash and part exchange, *below.*
  Passing of property—
    Acceptance of goods. *See* Acceptance, *above.*
    Appropriation of goods to contract—
      Intention of parties—Unascertained goods—Presumption that property not passing until goods appropriated to contract—Parties intending that property should pass before appropriation—Whether property passing according to parties' intention—Sale of Goods Act 1893, s 18, r 5(1). **Karlshamns Oljefabriker v Eastport Navigation Corp** [1982] **1** 208, QBD.
    Approval of sample—
      Import of goods—Failure to obtain import licence—Acceptance of shipping documents by buyers—Whether approval of sample condition precedent to payment—Whether condition operative where it cannot be fulfilled owing to buyer's default. **Mitchell Cotts & Co (Middle East) Ltd v Hairco Ltd** [1943] **2** 552, CA.
    Ascertained goods—
      Goods held by seller segregated from trade stock—Other goods included with trade stock—Whether goods sufficiently ascertained for property in them to have passed to customers—Sale of Goods Act 1979, ss 16-18. **Stapylton Fletcher Ltd (in administrative receivership), Re** [1995] **1** 192, Ch D.
      Purchase price provided by auctioneers—Bankruptcy of purchaser—Whether property in goods in purchaser or auctioneers—Sale of Goods Act 1893, s 17(1). **Capon, Re** [1940] **2** 135, CA.
    Auction. *See* **Auction** (Passing of property).
    Bargain to give contents of house in return for services—
      Common establishment—Housekeeper undertaking to look after children permanently—Sale of Goods Act 1893, s 18, r 1. **Koppel v Koppel (Wide claimant)** [1966] **2** 187, CA.
    Delivery of goods on sale or return—
      Notice of rejection—Requirements—Notice of rejection given without specifying rejected goods and goods not available for collection at date of notice—Whether notice valid—Sale of Goods Act 1979, s 18. **Atari Corp (UK) Ltd v Electronics Boutique Stores (UK) Ltd** [1998] **1** 1010, CA.
    Detention beyond reasonable time—
      Reasonable time a question of fact depending on circumstances—Car delivered on sale or return in summer holiday period—Judicial notice of decline of secondhand car market in autumn—Car not returned by mid-November—Sale of Goods Act 1893, s 18, r 4(b). **Poole v Smith's Car Sales (Balham) Ltd** [1962] **2** 482, CA.
    Goods to be collected—
      Agreement to collect scrap metal from artillery ranges—Collector entitled to retain as his property goods 'collected therefrom'—Metal collected in a dump but not removed from the ranges—Whether collector having acquired ownership of metal. **Gale v New** [1937] **4** 645, CA.
  No set-off clause—
    Action for price—Claimant company selling goods to defendant company on credit—Defendant being unable to pay invoices and negotiating repayments with claimant—Claimant seeking payment for goods and services—Defendant commencing proceedings against claimant for breach of exclusivity obligation—Defendant contending claimant breaching repayment agreement and seeking set-off—Claimant relying on no set-off clause in standard terms and conditions—Parties disputing due date for payments—Claimant seeking summary judgment—Whether claimant being able to maintain action on price—Effect of retention of title clause—Whether defendant having arguable claim for damages for breach of repayment agreement—Whether contracts incorporating no set-off clause—Sale of Goods Act 1979, s 49. **FG Wilson (Engineering) Ltd v John Holt & Co (Liverpool) Ltd** [2014] **1 Comm** 393, CA; [2014] **1** 785, CA.
    Action for price—Claimant company selling goods to defendant company on credit—Defendant being unable to pay invoices and negotiating repayments with claimant—Claimant seeking payment for goods and services—Defendant commencing proceedings against claimant for breach of exclusivity obligation—Defendant contending claimant breaching repayment agreement and seeking set-off—Claimant relying on no set-off clause in standard terms and conditions—Parties disputing due date for payments—Court ordering determination of reasonableness of no set-off clause as preliminary point—Claimant seeking summary judgment—Whether claimant being able to maintain action on price—Whether defendant having arguable claim for damages for breach of repayment agreement—Whether contracts incorporating no set-off clause—Whether no set-off clause applying and being reasonable—Unfair Contract Terms Act 1977—Sale of Goods Act 1979, s 49. **FG Wilson (Engineering) Ltd v John Holt & Co (Liverpool) Ltd** [2013] **1 Comm** 223, QBD.

SALE OF GOODS (cont)—
Passing of property (cont)—
Payment against bill of lading—
Payment required to be by bill of exchange indorsed by buyer's bank—Reservation of right of disposal—Buyers unable to obtain indorsed bill of exchange—Parties agreeing that goods held 'to the order of' or 'at the disposal of' sellers pending resale by buyers—Buyers taking delivery of goods from carriers—Whether property in goods passing from sellers to buyers—Whether implied contract between buyers and carriers on terms of bill of lading—Whether buyers entitled to sue carriers for damage to goods occurring during carriage—Bills of Lading Act 1855, s 1—Sale of Goods Act 1979, s 19(1). **Leigh & Sillavan Ltd v Aliakmon Shipping Co Ltd** [1985] **2** 44, CA.

Payment against delivery order—
Payment on receipt of delivery order containing undertaking and guarantee by sellers' agent—Delivery rendered impossible owing to enemy occupation of place of delivery—Whether total failure of consideration—Whether buyer entitled to recover payment. **Comptoir D'Achat et de Vente du Boerenbond Belge SA v Luis de Ridder Ltda** [1949] **1** 269, HL.

Payment by instalments—
Effect of clause that property should pass on payment of first instalment—Contract to build yacht—No evidence that on payment of first instalment construction of yacht had begun—Purchaser not bound to accept delivery if he was not reasonably satisfied with the performance of the craft on its trial run—Whether performance covered defective workmanship and materials and non-compliance with specification. **McDougall v Aeromarine of Emsworth Ltd** [1958] **3** 431, QBD.

Payment of purchase price—
Property passing when contract made—Different intention—Deferred purchase price—Agreement giving use subject to payment of interest and depreciation—Whether sale with provision for instalments or agreement to sell—Sale of Goods Act 1893, s 18, r 1. **Anchor Line (Henderson Bros) Ltd, Re** [1936] **2** 941, CA.

Reservation of right of disposal—
C f r contract—Payment by letter of credit including term allowing buyer to cancel payment if cargo rejected—Buyer entering into on-sale contract with another company—On-sale agreement not containing rejection clause—Cargo rejected—On-sale buyer selling cargo as salvage—Whether on-sale buyer entitled to sue cargo operator—Whether property passing with bill of lading—Whether on-sale buyer owner of goods—Whether breaches by cargo operator causing on-sale buyer's loss—Sale of Goods Act 1979, s 25(1). **Carlos Soto SAU v AP Møller-Maersk AS** [2015] **2 Comm** 382, QBD.

C i f contract—Presumption that property not passing until presentation of documents and payment of price—Contrary intention appearing from circumstances—Conduct and relationship of parties—Contract between associated companies—Bill of lading—Goods deliverable to order of seller—Goods delivered to carrier for shipment—Payment against documents not required—Seller's agents despatching endorsed bill of lading to buyer by post during voyage—Seller having power to divert goods before despatch of bill of lading—Whether property passing on date bill of lading posted. **Owners of the cargo lately laden on board the ship or vessel Albacruz v Owners of the ship or vessel Albazero** [1975] **3** 21, CA.

F o b contract—Payment by instalments—Bill of lading stating that goods deliverable to sellers' order—Part payment by buyers—Goods found to be damaged on discharge—Whether property passing to buyers on shipment—Whether buyers having title to sue for damage—Sale of Goods Act 1979, s 19. **Mitsui & Co Ltd v Flota Mercante Grancolombiana SA** [1989] **1** 951, CA.

Theft—
Property belonging to another. *See* **Criminal law** (Theft—Property belonging to another—Sale of goods—Passing of property).

Unascertained goods—
Ascertainment—Cif contract—Purchase of goods in bulk under separate contracts—Purchaser entitled to all remaining goods after prior deliveries—Goods damaged after prior deliveries but before delivery to purchaser—Whether goods not ascertained until physically allocated to separate contracts—Whether goods ascertained by process of exhaustion—Sale of Goods Act 1893, s 16. **Karlshamns Oljefabriker v Eastport Navigation Corp** [1982] **1** 208, QBD.

Unascertained goods in possession of third party—Passing of risk—Buyers' carrier given delivery note addressed to warehouseman—Goods for carrier put out on pavement from bulk by warehouseman before carrier's arrival—Delivery note accepted by warehouseman—Goods thereafter loaded by carrier—Goods at buyers' risk from time of acceptance of delivery note by warehouseman and indication by him to carrier of goods for transport to buyers—Sale of Goods Act 1893, ss 18, r 5, 29(3). **Wardar's (Import & Export) Co Ltd v Norwood (W) & Sons Ltd** [1968] **2** 602, CA.

Vendor retaining property in goods—
Bunkers on board time-chartered vessel—Contract for supply of bunkers to charterer reserving vendor's title until bunkers paid for—Charterer not paying for bunkers—Shipowner terminating charterparty for non-payment of hire and thereby obtaining possession of bunkers not paid for by charterer—Shipowner subsequently consuming bunkers—Whether possession of bunkers obtained by charterers with consent of vendors—Whether bunkers delivered by charterers to shipowners—Whether shipowners deriving good title to bunkers—Factors Act 1889, s 1(2)—Sale of Goods Act 1979, ss 25(1), 61(1). **Forsythe International (UK) Ltd v Silver Shipping Co Ltd** [1994] **1** 851, QBD.

Contract reserving property in goods to vendor after delivery until payment made in full—Vendor supplying leather used by buyers in manufacture of handbags—Leather becoming inseparable part of handbags—Purchaser becoming insolvent—Whether vendor retaining property in unused leather—Whether vendor having property in unsold handbags—Whether fiduciary relationship existing between vendor and purchaser—Whether vendor entitled to trace and recover debt from proceeds of sale of handbags—Whether vendor limited to a charge over the goods—Whether the charge void for non-registration—Companies Act 1948, s 95. **Peachdart Ltd, Re** [1983] **3** 204, Ch D.

SALE OF GOODS (cont)—
Passing of property (cont)—
Vendor retaining property in goods (cont)—
Contract reserving property in goods to vendor until payment of all debts due to vendor—Purchaser becoming insolvent—Goods transferred to purchaser pursuant to contract of sale—Whether property in goods remaining property of vendor or forming part of assets of purchaser—Whether reservation of property clause effective to create right of security over goods without transfer of possession—Sale of Goods Act 1979, ss 19(2), 62(4). **Armour v Thyssen Edelstahlwerke AG** [1990] 3 481, HL.

Disposition by buyer after sale—Buyer never in possession of goods—Buyer selling goods on to sub-purchaser—Seller delivering goods to sub-purchaser at request of buyer—Contract for sale of car—Contract reserving seller's title to car until car paid for—Buyer reselling car to sub-purchaser—Seller delivering car direct to sub-purchaser—Buyer going into liquidation before paying seller for car—Whether seller entitled to recover vehicle under reservation of title clause in contract—Whether reservation of title clause preventing passing of title to bona fide sub-purchaser—Whether delivery of goods direct to sub-purchaser by seller passing good title to sub-purchaser—Whether seller delivering car to sub-purchaser as deemed agent of buyer—Sale of Goods Act 1979, s 25. **Four Point Garage Ltd v Carter** [1985] 3 12, QBD.

Equitable charge—Floating charge—Goods supplied on credit terms—Contract reserving 'equitable and beneficial ownership' in goods to vendor until full payment made—Purchaser free to use goods as he pleased in ordinary course of his business—Purchaser becoming insolvent—Whether vendor's retention of title creating a trust or merely an equitable charge—Whether charge a floating charge—Whether charge 'created by' vendor or purchaser—Whether charge void against other creditors for want of registration—Companies Act 1948, s 95(1). **Bond Worth Ltd, Re** [1979] 3 919, Ch D.

Goods supplied on credit terms—Clause reserving vendor's title to bunkers until paid for in full but permitting vessel owner to use bunkers from moment of delivery—Whether property in bunkers passing—Whether terms giving rise to contract for sale of goods—Sale of Goods Act 1979, ss 2, 49(1). **PST Energy 7 Shipping LLC v OW Bunker Malta Ltd** [2016] 1 Comm 503, CA.

Goods supplied on credit terms—Clause reserving vendor's title to bunkers until paid for in full but permitting vessel owner to use bunkers from moment of delivery—Whether terms giving rise to contract for sale of goods—Whether implied term—Sale of Goods Act 1979, ss 2, 49. **PST Energy 7 Shipping LLC v OW Bunker Malta Ltd** [2017] 1 Comm 1, SC.

Goods supplied on credit terms—Contract reserving property in goods to vendor after delivery—Property reserved to vendor until full payment made for goods and all other goods supplied—Vendor supplying resin used by buyers in manufacture of chipboard—Resin becoming inseparable component of chipboard—Purchaser becoming insolvent—Whether vendor having charge on chipboard manufactured from resin or on proceeds of sale of chipboard—Whether fiduciary relationship existing between vendor and purchaser—Whether vendor entitled to trace and recover debt from proceeds of sale of chipboard—Whether any charge arising would be void—Companies Act 1948, s 95. **Borden (UK) Ltd v Scottish Timber Products Ltd** [1979] 3 961, CA.

Goods supplied to company on credit terms—Clause reserving vendor's title to goods until goods paid for—Company becoming insolvent before goods paid for—Receiver appointed by debenture holders—Effect of retention of title clause—Whether clause giving rise to 'charge created by ... company' in favour of vendor—Whether charge void against receiver for non-registration—Whether vendor retaining title to unused goods in company's possession—Companies Act 1948, s 95. **Clough Mill Ltd v Martin** [1984] 3 982, CA.

Goods supplied to company on credit terms—Clause reserving vendor's title to goods until goods paid for—Company going into receivership before goods paid for—Goods sold on to company's customers but not paid for at time of receivership—Effect of retention of title clause. **Andrabell Ltd (in liq), Re** [1984] 3 407, Ch D.

Goods supplied to company on credit terms—Clause reserving vendor's title to goods until goods paid for—Company going into receivership before goods paid for—Goods sold on to company's customers but not paid for at time of receivership—Effect of reservation of title clause. **Hendy Lennox (Industrial Engines) Ltd v Grahame Puttick Ltd** [1984] 2 152, QBD.

Passing of risk—
C i f contracts for sale of goods that in fact were to come from bulk cargo afloat—
Bills of lading issue by sub-time charterers—Delivery orders issue by sellers, without option to do so under contracts—Time when risk passed. **Margarine Union GmbH v Cambay Prince Steamship Co Ltd** [1967] 3 775, QBD.

Delivery delayed through fault of buyer—
Buyer's liability for loss—Sale of Goods Act 1893, s 20. **Demby Hamilton & Co Ltd v Barden (Endeavour Wines Ltd, third party)** [1949] 1 435, KBD.

Passing off—
Get-up of goods. *See* **Passing off** (Get-up of goods).

Pawned articles—
Interest. *See* **Interest** (Sale of pawned articles).

Payment—
Bank guarantee or letter of credit—
Time for issuing. **Sinason-Teicher Inter-American Grain Corp v Oilcakes and Oilseeds Trading Co Ltd** [1954] 3 468, CA.

Confirmed credit—
Credit available on presentation inter alia of bills of lading—Bills presented must normally be clean bills of lading—Condition on back of bills of lading absolving shippers from liability if goods not marked and secured in accordance with condition—Whether acknowledgment of compliance with condition must be tendered before payment under letter of credit—Validity of condition—Carriage of Goods by Sea Act 1924, Sch, art IV, r 2(n), (o), art III, r 8. **British Imex Industries Ltd v Midland Bank Ltd** [1958] 1 264, QBD.

Time for opening credit. **Pavia & Co SPA v Thurmann-Neilson** [1952] 1 492, CA.

SALE OF GOODS (cont)—
  Payment (cont)—
    Confirmed letter of credit—
      Confirmed irrevocable letter of credit established—Effect—Whether constituting absolute or conditional payment—Construction of contract—Letter of credit ordinarily operating as conditional payment—Payment absolute and buyer discharged from liability when letter of credit honoured by confirming bank. **Alan (W J) & Co Ltd v El Nasr Export & Import Co** [1972] **2** 127, CA.
      F o b contract—Freight pre-paid bills of lading—Whether buyers entitled to require sellers to present 'freight pre-paid' bills of lading in order to obtain payment. **Glencore Grain Rotterdam BV v Lebanese Organisation for International Commerce** [1997] **4** 514, CA.
      F o b contract—Time when credit should be opened. **Stach (Ian) Ltd v Baker Bosly Ltd** [1958] **1** 542, QBD.
      Injunction—Application for injunction restraining sellers dealing with second of two letters of credit—Dispute regarding quality of goods sold. **Malas (t/a Hamzeh Malas & Sons) v British Imex Industries Ltd** [1958] **1** 262, CA.
    Credit card—
      Nature of credit card transaction—Effect of credit card company's liquidation—Company operating credit card system for purchase of petrol at garages—Company going into liquidation—Debts outstanding from cardholders not paid by company to garages—Whether cardholders' debts due to company or to garages—Whether liquidator bound to pay garages from money collected from cardholders before company had paid garages. **Charge Card Services Ltd, Re** [1988] **3** 702, CA.
      Processing of credit card payments—Card payments—Merchant entering into merchant services agreement with merchant acquirer—Merchant processing credit card transactions for supply of prohibited goods or services by third parties—Merchant acquirer terminating agreement—Merchant acquirer retaining moneys otherwise payable to merchant—Whether merchant entitled to retain moneys—Whether card payments within merchant services agreement—Whether retention of moneys a penalty. **Lancore Services Ltd v Barclays Bank plc** [2010] **1** 763, CA; [2010] **2 Comm** 273, CA.
    Currency of payment—
      Variation—Waiver. *See* **Contract** (Breach—Waiver—Conduct amounting to waiver—Contract for sale of goods—Stipulation as to payment—Currency of account).
    Instalments—
      One instalment on delivery of specified articles—Balance of original sum to become due on default—Admissibility of evidence of value of specified articles—Penalty clause. **Latter v Colwill** [1937] **1** 442, CA.
      Passing of property. *See* Passing of property—Payment by instalments, *above.*
    Letter of credit—
      Bank—Duty—Irrevocable credit. *See* **Bank** (Documentary credit—Irrevocable credit).
      Confirmed letter of credit. *See* Payment—Confirmed letter of credit, *above.*
  Performance bond—
    Documentary credit—
      Generally. *See* **Bank** (Documentary credit—Performance bond).
  Plant and machinery—
    Deposit. *See* Deposit—Sale of plant and machinery, *above.*
  Pre-packed goods—
    Food etc. *See* **Weights and measures** (Prepacked goods).
  Precious metals—
    Hallmarking. *See* **Hallmarking**.
  Price—
    Bargain offers—
      Consumer protection. *See* **Consumer protection** (Price marking—Bargain offers relating to goods).
    False or misleading indication as to price. *See* **Trade description** (False or misleading indication as to price).
    Price control. *See* **Price control** (Sale of goods at price exceeding statutory maximum permitted price).
    Price maintenance—
      Exemption of goods from abolition of resale price maintenace. *See* **Restrictive trade practices** (Resale price maintenance—Reference for exemption).
    Sale for cash and part exchange—
      Sale of vehicle for specified price—Part of price to be satisfied by exchange of vehicles within stipulated time—Failure of exchange—Whether seller entitled to sue for whole price. **Dawson (GJ) (Clapham) Ltd v Dutfield (H & G)** [1936] **2** 232, KBD.
  Quality—
    Clause regulating buyer's claim for inferior quality—
      Application to deterioration owing to defective packing. **Minister of Materials v Steel Bros & Co Ltd** [1952] **1** 522, CA.
    Merchantable quality. *See* Implied condition as to merchantable quality, *above.*
    Sample. *See* Sale by sample, *below.*
    Satisfactory quality. *See* Implied condition as to satisfactory quality, *above.*
  Quantity—
    Total requirements—
      Construction of clause—Sale of steel—Quantity expressed as 'Buyer's requirements up to 8,000 tons'—Whether mere option to purchase any quantity up to 8,000 tons—Whether buyer only entitled to demand steel actually required for business. **Kier (JL) & Co Ltd v Whitehead Iron and Steel Co Ltd** [1938] **1** 591, KBD.
  Quiet possession—
    Implied warranty. *See* Implied warranty—Quiet possession, *above.*
  Rejection of goods—
    Exclusion of rejection for faults and defects—
      Strict construction—Not excluding liability for damages. **Ashington Piggeries Ltd v Christopher Hill Ltd** [1971] **1** 847, HL.

SALE OF GOODS (cont)—
    Rejection of goods (cont)—
        Restriction on right to reject—
            Notice within time limit in respect of claims for quality or condition—Sale of marked goods—Whether restrictions on rejection applying to unmarked goods—Whether buyer entitled to reject unmarked goods—Timber not properly seasoned—Faulty manufacture. **Vsesojwzoje Objedinenije 'Exportles' v Allen (TW) & Sons Ltd** [1938] **3** 375, KBD.

            Variation from specification greater than that permitted by contract—Restriction on rejection of 'the goods herein named nor any part of them'. **Wilensko Slaski Towarzystwo Drewno v Fenwick & Co (West Hartlepool) Ltd** [1938] **3** 429, KBD.

        Right to reject—
            Bill of lading—Date forged—Shipment after contract date—Right to reject—Goods retained by buyer after knowledge of breach of contract—Measure of damage—'Delivery' of goods—Effect of dealings with documents by buyer—Sale of Goods Act 1893, s 35. **Chao (t/a Zung Fu Co) v British Traders and Shippers Ltd (NV Handelsmaatschappij J Smits Import-Export, third party)** [1954] **1** 779, QBD.

            FOB contract for supply of bulk quantity of wheat—Contract incorporating terms of contract for onward sale to Egyptian state wheat procurement body—Contract also incorporating GAFTA 49 terms insofar as they did not conflict with terms of contract—Buyer's supervisor at loading port nominated in compliance with contract but not GAFTA terms—Cargo deemed not acceptable—Certificate of analysis provided by supervisor not compliant with contractual documentary requirements—Whether free on board buyer entitled to reject goods on basis of deficient documentary requirements—Whether buyer entitled to reject cargo having failed to nominate a GAFTA-approved supervisor pursuant to GAFTA terms—GAFTA 49 Terms—GAFTA Sampling Rules No 124. **Aston FFI (Suisse) SA v Louis Dreyfus Commodities Suisse SA** [2015] **1 Comm** 985, QBD.

            Faulty equipment returned by buyer to seller for inspection and repair—Seller repairing equipment—Seller refusing to reveal extent of fault or nature of repair—Whether buyer entitled to reject equipment—Sale of Goods Act 1979, s 35(2)(a), (6)(a). **Ritchie (J & H) Ltd v Lloyd Ltd** [2007] **1 Comm** 987, HL; [2007] **2** 353, HL.

            Restriction on right to reject. *See* Rejection of goods—Restriction on right to reject, *above.*

            'Ship's delivery order'—Request to ship to deliver goods to buyers—Order addressed by shipowner to dock master porter—Shipment of goods to named port—Shipment to different port and transhipment to named port—Buyer's right to reject. **Colin & Shields v W Weddel & Co Ltd** [1952] **2** 337, CA.

        Sale of 15,000 units of corn—
            Separate documents for each 1,000 units and each 1,000 units to be considered a separate contract—Notice of appropriation for about 15,444 units—First provisional invoice for 15,444 units—Amended provisional invoice for 15,000 units—Validity of first tender—Whether withdrawn by amended provisional invoice—Validity of second tender—Sale of Goods Act 1893, ss 17-19, 30-32. **Smyth (Ross T) & Co Ltd v Bailey (T D) Son & Co** [1940] **3** 60, HL.

        Severability of contract—
            Separate consignments—Rejection of second consignment of goods following acceptance of first—Seller having option to perform contract by making one or more shipments—Each shipment to be deemed a separate contract—Goods shipped in two consignments in one ship on same date under separate bills of lading—Whether more than one shipment and thus separate contracts entitling buyer who had accepted one consignment to reject the other—Sale of Goods Act 1893, s 11(1)(c). **Rosenthal (J) & Sons Ltd v Esmail (t/a H M H Esmail & Sons)** [1965] **2** 860, HL.

Repudiation of contract—
    Acceptance of repudiation—
        Need to establish acceptance—Determination whether term has been repudiation a question of fact. **Household Machines Ltd v Cosmos Exporters Ltd** [1946] **2** 622, KBD.

    Notice of default by seller. *See* Default by seller—Notice of default—Contract for sale on GAFTA terms, *above.*

Repurchase—
    Power of repurchase. *See* Default by seller—Express power of repurchase—Special procedure under power, *above.*

Rescission of contract—
    Ground for treating contract as repudiated—
        Conditions and warranties—Breach of stipulation other than condition—Breach going to the root of the contract—Breach of term that goods should be shipped in good condition—Part of cargo found damaged on delivery—Whether term a stipulation other than a condition—Whether buyers entitled to reject entire cargo—Sale of Goods Act 1893, ss 11(1), 61(2). **Cehave NV v Bremer Handelsgesellschaft mbH** [1975] **3** 739, CA.

    Resale by unpaid seller. *See* Unpaid seller—Resale—Effect as rescission of contract of sale, *below.*

Reservation of right of disposal. *See* Passing of property—Reservation of right of disposal, *above.*

Reservation of title. *See* Passing of property—Vendor retaining property in goods, *above.*

Sale by sample—
    Breach of condition as to quality—
        Offer by defendants to accept return of undisposed stock—Offer rejected—Damages—Mitigation—Duty of plaintiffs to ascertain precise meaning of offer—Sale of Goods Act 1893, ss 35, 56. **Houndsditch Warehouse Co Ltd v Waltex Ltd** [1944] **2** 518, KBD.

    C i f contract. *See* C i f contract—Sale by sample, *above.*

    Goods not in accordance with sample—
        Simple process necessary to make goods correspond with sample—Whether right of rejection on ground goods not in accordance with sample. **Ruben (E & S) Ltd v Faire Bros & Co Ltd** [1949] **1** 215, KBD.

    Goods sold 'with all faults and imperfections'—
        Goods not corresponding with sample—Liability of vendor. **Champanhac & Co Ltd v Waller & Co Ltd** [1948] **2** 724, KBD.

SALE OF GOODS (cont)—
  Sale by sample (cont)—
    Reasonable examination of sample—
      Sale between wholesalers—Defect not apparent on examination—Sale of Goods Act 1893, s 15(2)(c). **Perry v Godley (Burton & Sons (Bermondsey) Ltd, third party, Graham, fourth party)** [1960] **1** 36, QBD.
  Sample. *See* Sale by sample, *above.*
  Seller—
    Disposition by seller in possession after sale. *See* Disposition by seller in possession after sale, *above.*
  Separate consignments—
    Rejection of goods. *See* Rejection of goods—Severability of contract—Separate consignments, *above.*
    Short delivery. *See* Delivery—Separate consignments—Short delivery, *above.*
  Ship—
    Contract. *See* **Ship** (Sale—Contract).
  Shipment of goods—
    Description. *See* Description—Shipment of goods, *above.*
    Fob stowed contract—
      Construction of shipment period provision—Clause providing for 'One vessel only presenting October 2006 Shipment at Buyer's option, with 10 days pre-advise of vessel arrival'—Whether loading to be completed by 31 October 2006. **Cereal Investments Co SA v ED&F Man Sugar Ltd** [2008] **2 Comm** 873, QBD.
  Specific performance. *See* **Specific performance** (Sale of goods).
  Stolen property—
    Warranty as to quiet possession. *See* Implied warranty—Quiet possession—Interference with possession by title paramount—Exception to implied warranty in case of disturbance by title paramount—Sale of stolen property, *above.*
  Stoppage in transit—
    Free house, London—
      Termination of transit. **Plischke (Johann) & Sohne GmbH v Allison Bros Ltd** [1936] **2** 1009, KBD.
  Supply—
    Distinguished from sale—
      Supply of medicine or drug. *See* **National Health Service** (Pharmaceutical services—Supply of medicine or drug—Contractual relationship between chemist and National Health Service Executive Council that of contract for services).
  Theft—
    Identification of property stolen—
      Charge of stealing part only of certain items—Proof that whole of each item stolen. *See* **Criminal law** (Theft—Property belonging to another—Identification of property stolen—Charge of stealing part only of certain items—Proof that whole of each item stolen—Sale of goods).
    Property belonging to another—
      Passing of property. *See* **Criminal law** (Theft—Property belonging to another—Sale of goods—Passing of property).
  Time of delivery—
    Conditions inhibiting delivery imposed by vendor's supplier. *See* Delivery—Conditions inhibiting delivery imposed by vendor's supplier, *above.*
  Time of performance—
    Shipbuilding contract—
      Yacht required for use in 1957 yachting season—Fixed delivery date but delivery on that date not guaranteed—Reasonable time—Whether a condition of the contract—Sale of Goods Act 1893, s 10(1). **McDougall v Aeromarine of Emsworth Ltd** [1958] **3** 431, QBD.
    Time of the essence—
      Original condition in regard to time waived—Subsequent notice fixing time for completion—Reasonableness—Conduct amounting to waiver. **Rickards (Charles) Ltd v Oppenheim** [1950] **1** 420, CA.
  Title—
    Illegality of related agreement—
      Finance company purchasing motor car outright with intention to let it under hire-purchase agreement—Hire-purchase agreement illegal by reason of non-payment of initial deposit required by statutory regulations—Whether finance company's title under original sale vitiated by illegality of hire-purchase agreement so as to preclude later claim in action for conversion of motor car. **Belvoir Finance Co Ltd v Harold G Cole & Co Ltd** [1969] **2** 904, QBD.
    Implied condition of vendor's right to sell—
      Breach—Total failure of consideration—Recovery of purchase price—Motor car sold by hirer in breach of hire-purchase agreement—Re-sold in good faith—Contract of sale rescinded by purchaser—Damages—Sale of Goods Act 1893, s 12(1). **Butterworth v Kingsway Motors Ltd, Hayton (third party), Kennedy (fourth party), Rudolph (fifth party)** [1954] **2** 694, Assizes.
    Motor vehicle subject to hire-purchase agreement—
      Acquisition of good title by private purchaser without notice. *See* **Hire-purchase** (Motor vehicle—Protection of private purchaser without notice of hire-purchase agreement).
    Passing of property. *See* Passing of property, *above.*
    Sale by hirer—
      Sale before goods purchased—Hirer having option to purchase goods sold—Re-sale by purchaser—Hirer subsequently exercising option—Whether title of subsequent purchasers made good on hirer acquiring title. **Butterworth v Kingsway Motors Ltd, Hayton (third party), Kennedy (fourth party), Rudolph (fifth party)** [1954] **2** 694, Assizes.
    Sale of car by dealer to finance company under illegal contract—
      Car let out by finance company to hirer under illegal hire-purchase agreement—Car delivered by dealer straight to hirer—Car sold to third party by hirer's salesman—Whether hirer's salesman liable in conversion. **Belvoir Finance Co Ltd v Stapleton** [1970] **3** 664, CA.
    Transfer. *See* Transfer of title, *below.*

SALE OF GOODS (cont)—
  Title (cont)—
    Unascertained goods—
      Claimants selling oil to oil trader—Oil trader mixing oil and on-selling—Whether claimants able to establish title against subsequent purchasers. **Glencore International AG v Metro Trading Inc** [2001] **1 Comm** 103, QBD.
      Generic goods—Purchasers buying gold bullion for future delivery from company dealing in bullion—Dealer holding non-allocated stocks of bullion for customers—Company becoming insolvent and having insufficient stocks of bullion to satisfy debt owed to secured creditor—Non-allocated claimants asserting proprietary interest in bullion held by company—Whether non-allocated claimants entitled to proprietary interest in company's bullion stocks in priority to secured creditor—Whether contract for sale of unascertained goods conferring equitable title to goods. **Goldcorp Exchange Ltd (in receivership), Re** [1994] **2** 806, PC.
      Voidable title. *See* Voidable title, *below*.
  Trade description—
    False trade description. *See* **Trade description**.
    Generally. *See* Description—Trade description, *above*.
    Offences due to fault of another person. *See* **Trade description** (Offences due to fault of another person).
  Transfer of title—
    Agent put in possession of goods and authorised to sell as principal—
      Irrelevance of whether sale was or was not in ordinary course of business. **Lloyds and Scottish Finance Ltd v Williamson** [1965] **1** 641, CA.
    Conflict of laws. *See* **Conflict of laws** (Movables—Title to goods).
    Mercantile agent—
      Power to transfer title. *See* **Agent** (Mercantile agent—Power to transfer title).
    Owner giving seller documents enabling seller to represent himself as owner—
      No authority to sell—Seller an apparently reputable motor dealer—Owner not precluded by negligence from denying seller's authority to sell—Title of owner against bona fide purchaser for value from seller—Sale of Goods Act 1893, s 21(1). **Mercantile Credit Co Ltd v Hamblin** [1964] **3** 592, CA.
      Seller agreeing to sell car to plaintiffs—Plaintiffs paying by banker's draft—Bank refusing to cash draft—Seller disappearing—Bank reimbursing plaintiffs—Plaintiffs claiming title to car—Whether seller had bought or agreed to buy car from owner—Whether owner precluded by conduct from denying seller's authority to sell if merely an agreement to sell and no actual sale—Sale of Goods Act 1979, ss 2(5), 21, 25. **Shaw v Comr of Police of the Metropolis (Natalegawa, claimant)** [1987] **3** 405, CA.
  Transit, stoppage in. *See* Stoppage in transit, *above*.
  Unpaid seller—
    Assent to other sale or disposition—
      Seller to be paid out of cash received from buyer's customers—Goods lying in warehouse—Delivery order by seller to buyer sent by buyer to warehousemen—Fresh delivery order by buyer to purchasers from him—Original seller not paid by buyer—Whether unpaid seller's right of lien on goods lost—Whether purchaser from buyer protected—Sale of Goods Act 1893, ss 47, 25(2). **Mount (DF) Ltd v Jay & Jay (Provisions) Co Ltd** [1959] **3** 307, QBD.
    Resale—
      Effect as rescission of contract of sale—Resale of part of goods sold—Right to retain proceeds of resale—Right to sue buyer for damages for non-acceptance, but not for price—Measure of damages—Sale of Goods Act 1893, s 48(3). **Ward (R V) Ltd v Bignall** [1967] **2** 449, CA.
      Exercise by seller of right of resale on failure of buyer to pay price—Buyer's right to recover deposit—Sale of Goods Act 1893, s 48(3). **Gallagher v Shilcock** [1949] **1** 921, KBD.
  Variation of contract. *See* **Contract** (Variation—Contract for sale of goods).
  Vendor retaining property in goods—
    Contract reserving property in goods to vendor until payment of all debts due to vendor—
      Retention of title clause—Whether buyer having authority to sell goods prior to payment of all debts due to vendor. **Fairfax Gerrard Holdings Ltd v Capital Bank plc** [2008] **1 Comm** 632, CA.
  Voidable title—
    Acquisition of voidable title—
      Hire-purchase transaction—Dealer with notice of defect in title to goods acting as general agent for finance company—Whether finance company obtained a good title to the goods—Sale of Goods Act 1893, s 23. **Car and Universal Finance Co Ltd v Caldwell** [1964] **1** 290, CA.
    Fraud—
      Election of seller to avoid contract for fraud—Whether seller must communicate election to purchaser if purchaser's title is to be avoided. **Car and Universal Finance Co Ltd v Caldwell** [1964] **1** 290, CA.
    Sale under voidable title—
      Sale before avoidance—Voidable contract—Fraud—Hire-purchase of motor car—Hirer selling car for cash and another car—Resale of second car before title avoided—Whether resale effective to transfer title—Sale of Goods Act 1893, ss 12(1), 23. **Robin and Rambler Coaches Ltd v Turner** [1947] **2** 284, KBD.
  Warranty—
    Auction—
      Conditions in catalogue excluding warranty unless specially mentioned and appearing in account—Oral guarantee. **Harling v Eddy** [1951] **2** 212, CA.
      Stipulations in catalogue and conditions of sale excluding auctioneer from responsibility for misdescription—Verbal assurance of condition—Breach—Right of buyer to damages. **Couchman v Hill** [1947] **1** 103, CA.
    Feeding stuffs. *See* **Agriculture** (Feeding stuffs—Sale for use as food for cattle or poultry—Implied warranty suitable for use as such).
    Fertilizers and Feeding Stuffs Act 1926—
      Whether warranty limited to sales in the United Kingdom. *See* **Statute** (Territorial operation).
    Implied—
      Generally. *See* Implied warranty, *above*.

SALE OF GOODS (cont)—
  Warranty (cont)—
    Implied (cont)—
      Reconditioned goods—Certificate by third party. *See* Condition—Reconditioned goods—Certificate by third party, *above.*
      Misrepresentation distinguished—
        Inference that representation intended to be a warranty—Representation made for purpose of inducing person to enter into contract—Representation acted on—Sale of secondhand motor car—Misrepresentation as to mileage—Purchaser thereby induced to buy car—Whether warranty or innocent misrepresentation. **Bentley (Dick) Productions Ltd v Harold Smith (Motors) Ltd** [1965] **2** 65, CA.
        Sale of motor car to dealers—Vendor honestly believing car 1948 model—Car in fact 1939 model—Whether vendor having warranted that car 1948 model—Whether innocent misrepresentation. **Chess (Oscar) Ltd v Williams** [1957] **1** 325, CA.
        Sale of motor vehicle—Wrong entry in registration book—Seller having bought vehicle after entry made—Seller not responsible for wrong entry—Memorandum of agreement for sale not referring to date of model—Whether wrong entry a representation or a warranty. **Routledge v McKay** [1954] **1** 855, CA.
    Quiet possession—
      Implied warranty. *See* Implied warranty—Quiet possession, *above.*
  Weights and measures. *See* **Weights and measures.**

SALE OF LAND
  Abatement of purchase price—
    Damages in addition. *See* Damages for breach of contract—Damages in addition to specific performance and abatement of purchase price, *below.*
  Abstract of title. *See* Title—Abstract, *below.*
  Acceptance of tender—
    Effect of qualification 'subject to contract'—
      Letter communicating acceptance containing qualification by mistake—Tender documents containing full particulars of contract and nothing further to be negotiated—Words 'subject to contract' meaningless—Whether words should be expunged—Whether acceptance constituting a contract. **Richards (Michael) Properties Ltd v Corp of Wardens of St Saviour's Parish, Southwark** [1975] **3** 416, Ch D.
  Advertisement—
    Display without consent of local authority. *See* **Town and country planning** (Advertisement—Display without consent).
  Agreement—
    Agreement subject to contract—
      Exchange of contracts. *See* Exchange of contracts—Agreement subject to contract, *below.*
    Equitable interest—
      Priority. *See* **Mortgage** (Equitable interest—Priority—Agreement for sale of land).
  Agricultural holding. *See* **Agricultural holding** (Sale).
  Apportionment of outgoings. *See* Condition—Apportionment of outgoings, *below.*
  Assignment—
    Leasehold interest. *See* Leasehold interest—Assignment, *below.*
  Assignment of contract for—
    Benefit and burden. *See* **Contract** (Stranger to contract—Benefit and burden—Vendor and purchaser entering into contract for sale of land).
  Auctioneer—
    Memorandum of contract—
      Signature. *See* Memorandum of contract—Signature of party to be charged—Auctioneer's signature, *below.*
    Remuneration. *See* Sale by court—Auctioneer, *below.*
  Bankruptcy—
    Purchaser committing act of bankruptcy before completion—
      Rescission of contract. *See* Rescission of contract—Bankruptcy, *below.*
    Sale by trustee in bankruptcy—
      Title of trustee. *See* **Bankruptcy** (Trustee in bankruptcy—Title of trustee—Property—Trustee contracting to sell property).
  Boundary—
    Conveyance—
      Parcels vague. *See* **Boundary** (Conveyance—Conveyance of plot of land—Parcels vague).
  Breach of contract—
    Damages. *See* Damages for breach of contract, *below.*
    Election whether to affirm or rescind—
      Generally. *See* **Contract** (Breach—Election whether to affirm or rescind).
    Evidence of possession—
      Special condition of sale stipulating for statutory declaration of twenty years' undisputed possession of part of the land—Vendors unable to show undisputed possession for that period—Vendors offered proof of twelve years' adverse possession—Purchasers required the land in question to enable them to effect development—Whether contract enforceable. **Wimpey (George) & Co Ltd v Sohn** [1966] **1** 232, CA.
    Remedy—
      Damages or specific performance—Election providing that vendor permitted to resell land if purchaser failed to complete—Provision that if vendor resold at a loss purchaser to pay difference as liquidated damages—Vendors seeking specific performance of contract—Purchaser not complying with decree of specific performance—Vendors seeking to repudiate contract and resell land—Whether vendors entitled to claim damages for any loss on resale. **Capital and Suburban Properties Ltd v Swycher** [1976] **1** 881, CA.

SALE OF LAND (cont)—
    Builder—
        Warranty—
            Damages for breach. *See* Damages for breach of contract—Warranty—Newly constructed
                house—Builder, *below*.
    Building plots—
        Parcels. *See* Conveyance—Parcels—Building plots, *below*.
    Capital gains tax—
        Exemptions—
            Private residence. *See* **Capital gains tax** (Exemptions and reliefs—Private residence).
    Charity—
        Consent to sale. *See* Condition—Consent to sale required by statute—Sale by charity, *below*.
        Sale of charity estate. *See* **Charity** (Sale of charity estate—Land held by charity).
    Charity estate. *See* **Charity** (Sale of charity estate).
    Church—
        Unconsecrated curtilage—
            Faculty jurisdiction. *See* **Ecclesiastical law** (Faculty—Unconsecrated curtilage of church—Sale—
                Power to authorise sale).
    Commission—
        Estate agent. *See* **Estate agent** (Commission).
    Company—
        Liquidator—
            Duty. *See* **Company** (Compulsory winding up—Liquidator—Duty—Sale of land).
        Memorandum of contract. *See* Memorandum of contract—Company, *below*.
    Completion—
        Completion statement defective—
            Completion statement received two hours before notice to complete due to expire—Completion
                statement failing to specify correct purchase price—No tender of purchase price by
                purchaser—Whether purchaser in breach of contract. **Carne v Debono** [1988] 3 485, CA.
        Delay in completion—
            Forfeiture of deposit—Unreasonable delay—Vendor rescinding contract 22 days after expiry of
                notice to complete. *See* Deposit—Forfeiture—Purchaser's failure to complete—Vendor serving
                ineffective notice to complete—Vendor rescinding contract 22 days after expiry of notice to
                complete, *below*.
            Unreasonable delay—Rescission—Whether unreasonable delay by purchaser entitling vendor to
                rescind contract without serving notice to complete. **Graham v Pitkin** [1992] 2 235, PC.
        Failure to complete purchase—
            Damages—Damages in substitution for specific performance. *See* Damages for breach of
                contract—Damages in substitution for specific performance—Damages at common law for
                repudiation of contract—Purchaser failing to complete in time, *below*.
            Forfeiture of deposit. *See* Deposit—Forfeiture—Purchaser's failure to complete, *below*.
            Time not initially of the essence—Vendor subsequently purporting to make time of essence—No
                impropriety on part of purchaser—Request for delay—Right of vendor to forfeit deposit and
                resell—Damages when property wrongfully resold. **Smith v Hamilton** [1950] 2 928, Ch D.
        Failure to complete purchase or perform intermediate obligation by date stipulated in contract—
            Time not of essence—Service of notice making time of essence—Vendor's obligation to prove
                title—Contract specifying date for performance of obligation—Vendor failing to perform
                obligation within time fixed by contract—Whether purchaser entitled to serve notice making time
                of essence immediately on failure to perform intermediate obligation—Whether purchaser
                required to wait until unreasonable delay in performing obligation before serving notice. **Behzadi
                v Shaftesbury Hotels Ltd** [1991] 2 477, CA.
        Notice to complete. *See* Notice to complete, *below*.
        Possession before completion—
            Conveyance on completion of payment of instalments. *See* Possession before completion—
                Conveyance on completion of payment of instalments, *below*.
            Interest on unpaid purchase money. *See* Interest on unpaid purchase money—Possession before
                completion, *below*.
    Condition—
        Apportionment of outgoings—
            War damage contribution—Whether instalment of contribution 'outgoings'—War Damage Act 1941,
                ss 18, 20, 23, 82—Law Society's Conditions of Sale, cl 5(3)(b). **Jacobs and Stedman's Contract, Re**
                [1942] 2 104, Ch D.
        Condition precedent—
            Deposit. *See* Deposit—Condition precedent, *below*.
        Condition to which effect not given by conveyance but capable of taking effect after completion—
            Condition requiring vacant possession on completion—Failure to give vacant possession—Breach
                of contract for sale—Law Society's Conditions of Sale 1953, condition 33. **Hissett v Reading
                Roofing Co Ltd** [1970] 1 122, Ch D.
        Consent to sale required by statute—
            Contract expressed to be subject to obtaining consent—Consent not having been obtained when
                contract made—Consent obtained subsequently—Vendors a charity—Consent to sale by Charity
                Commissioners—Whether contract invalid because of failure to obtain prior consent—Charities
                Act 1960, s 29(1). **Richards (Michael) Properties Ltd v Corp of Wardens of St Saviour's Parish,
                Southwark** [1975] 3 416, Ch D.
            Sale by charity—Consent of Charity Commissioners—Absence of consent at date of
                contract—When sale is made—Charitable Trusts Amendment Act 1855, s 29. **Milner v
                Staffordshire Congregational Union (Inc)** [1956] 1 494, Ch D.
        Implied condition—
            Notice of requisition order served pending completion—Possession not taken by government
                before actual completion—Incumbrance. **Winslow Hall Estates Co and United Glass Bottle
                Manufacturers Ltd's Contract, Re** [1941] 3 124, Ch D.

SALE OF LAND (cont)—
Condition (cont)—
Indemnification of vendor against tenant's claim—
Option to renew conferred by underlease—Option not registered as estate contract—Contract to sell reversion incorporating condition that purchaser should indemnify vendor against claims by tenant—Assignment of reversion—Notice by tenant exercising option—Refusal by purchaser to grant new lease—Whether original lessors entitled to indemnity from purchaser against claim by tenant for breach of covenant to renew—National Conditions of Sale (17th Edn), condition 18(3). **Eagon v Dent** [1965] **3** 334, Ch Ct, County Palatine of Lanc.
Misleading condition—
Land charged with annuity—Time for answer to requisition—Waiver—Law Society's General Conditions of Sale, cll 9(4), 31. **Ossemsley Estates Ltd, Re** [1937] **3** 774, CA.
Planning permission to be obtained—
Contract 'conditional upon planning consent being granted for use ... as a hotel'—Planning consent granted subject to conditions requiring provision of adequate visibility splay and 'No Entry' sign—Consent relating only to town planning legislation. **West (Richard) and Partners (Inverness) Ltd v Dick** [1969] **1** 943, CA.
Deposit paid and balance payable on completion—Outline planning permission given—Detailed plans rejected—Rescission of contract by purchasers—Whether planning permission in contract meant outline permission—Whether reasonable steps taken by purchasers to get approval of detailed plans. **Hargreaves Transport Ltd v Lynch** [1969] **1** 455, CA.
Reasonable time for satisfying condition—
Agreement subject to planning permission and approval of title—No provision as to time for satisfying conditions—Planning permission not obtained more than three years after agreement—Condition to be satisfied within reasonable time—Time must be reasonable as at date of contract and reasonable to both parties. **Longlands Farm, Long Common, Botley, Hants, Re** [1968] **3** 552, Ch D.
Time for performance—
Purchase conditional on vendor's obtaining renewal of leases—Recovery of deposit. **Aberfoyle Plantations Ltd v Cheng** [1959] **3** 910, PC.
Waiver of condition—
Condition for benefit of one party—Waiver by that party—Right to waive condition only where by its terms or by necessary implication exclusively for benefit of party waiving it—Purchaser intending to develop site—Contract for sale of site conditional on purchaser obtaining planning consent within specified period—Purchaser failing to obtain planning consent—Whether purchaser entitled to waive condition and enforce contract. **Heron Garage Properties Ltd v Moss** [1974] **1** 421, Ch D.
Consent—
Assignment of leasehold interest. See Leasehold interest—Consent to assignment, below.
Contract—
Agent authorised to make contract—
Registration as land charge. See **Land charge** (Estate contract—Contract to convey or create a legal estate—Contract appointing and authorising agent to make contract for sale of land).
Agreement contemplating execution of formal document—
Agreement to purchase 'subject to formal contract to be prepared by the vendor's solicitors if the vendor shall so require'—Whether agreement enforceable. **Riley v Troll** [1953] **1** 966, Assizes.
Agreement to discharge debt—
Conditional on transfer of land by debtor to creditor—Whether a contract for sale of land—Law of Property Act 1925, s 205(1)(xxiv). **Simpson v Connolly** [1953] **2** 474, QBD.
Breach—
Damages—Generally. See Damages for breach of contract, below.
Damages—Mitigation. See **Damages** (Mitigation of loss—Sale of land).
Waiver of breach. See **Contract** (Breach—Waiver—Conduct amounting to waiver—Contract for sale of residue of lease).
Completion—
Notice to complete. See Notice to complete, below.
Conditional contract—
Promissory note—Promise to pay sum of money on certain date or in default to convey certain land to promisee—Promise for 'value received'—Whether relationship of vendor and purchaser established—Whether ascertainable price or consideration to support contract. **Savage v Uwechia** [1961] **1** 830, PC.
Contract by correspondence—
Whether contract resulting from acceptance by letter of an oral offer referring to written document not itself a letter constituting a 'contract by correspondence'—Law of Property Act 1925, s 46. **Stearn v Twitchell** [1985] **1** 631, Ch D.
Whether offer and acceptance in course of correspondence constituting exchange of contracts—Whether sufficient writing to fulfil statutory requirements—Law of Property (Miscellaneous Provisions) Act 1989, s 2(1). **Commission for the New Towns v Cooper (GB) Ltd** [1995] **2** 929, CA.
Exchange of contracts. See Exchange of contracts, below.
Form of contract—
Necessity for writing—Incorporation of terms—Agreement for sale of land—Prior to exchange of contracts parties agreeing by letter that exchange subject to vendor showing good title—Purchaser failing to pay on completion—Vendor seeking specific performance of contract—Whether letter part of original contract—Whether letter a collateral contract outside statutory provisions governing sale of land—Whether collateral contract enforceable by specific performance—Law of Property (Miscellaneous Provisions) Act 1989, s 2. **Record v Bell** [1991] **4** 471, Ch D.

SALE OF LAND (cont)—
  Contract (cont)—
    Form of contract (cont)—
      Necessity for writing—Incorporation of terms—Agreement for sale of land—Sale by developers of property development—Parties agreeing for finder's fee on exchange of contracts—Contracts assignable to sub-purchasers—Provision for finder's fee not assignable—Developers bringing proceedings for specific performance—Whether contracts incorporating all terms expressly agreed—Law of Property (Miscellaneous Provisions) Act 1989, s 2(1). **North Eastern Properties v Coleman** [2010] **2 Comm** 494, CA; [2010] **3** 528, CA.
      Necessity for writing—Requirement to set contract out in writing—Meaning of 'set out'—Requirement to identify purchaser—Claimant bringing claim based on agreement for sale of land—Whether agreement identifying purchaser—Whether contract complying with relevant requirements. **Francis v F Berndes Ltd** [2012] **1 Comm** 735, Ch D.
      Two documents—Agreement for sale of land—Letter referring to and enclosing plan prepared by purchaser and showing his name as addressee—Signature of purchaser on plan only—Whether letter and plan constituting a single document—Whether purchaser causing name to be typed on letter as addressee constituting signature—Law of Property (Miscellaneous Provisions) Act 1989, s 2. **Firstpost Homes Ltd v Johnson** [1995] **4** 355, CA.
      Variation—Formalities required—Whether variation of contract for sale of land requiring same formalities applying to formation of contract—Whether alteration of completion date required to be incorporated in one document signed by or on behalf of both parties—Law of Property (Miscellaneous Provisions) Act 1989, s 2. **McCausland v Duncan Lawrie Ltd** [1996] **4** 995, CA.
    Formation—
      Certainty of terms. See **Contract** (Enforceability—Certainty of terms—Sale of land).
      Exchange of contracts—Necessity for exchange—Concluded contract before exchange—Intention of parties—Offer by council by letter to sell council house to sitting tenant—Form of agreement for sale enclosed with letter—Agreement devised with object of dispensing with legal formalities—Agreement signed by tenant and returned to council—Date when tenancy ceased and mortgage repayments began left blank on agreement—Contract concluded by offer and acceptance—Contract binding on council though not signed by them and contracts not exchanged—Letter containing offer constituting sufficient note or memorandum of contract. **Storer v Manchester City Council** [1974] **3** 824, CA.
      Offer and acceptance. See **Contract** (Offer and acceptance—Offer—Sale of land).
      Subject to contract—Agreement to offer land to purchaser if vendor wishing to sell—Agreement setting out steps to be taken by parties if vendor giving notice of willingness to sell—Agreement 'subject to contract'—Vendor giving notice of wish to sell and purchaser accepting—Whether agreement constituting a binding contract—Whether words 'subject to contract' having prima facie meaning—Whether exceptional circumstances displacing prima facie meaning. **Alpenstow Ltd v Regalian Properties plc** [1985] **2** 545, Ch D.
    Frustration—
      Change of circumstances—Building sold for development. See **Contract** (Frustration—Change of circumstances—Building sold for development).
      Change of circumstances—Generally. See **Contract** (Frustration—Change of circumstances—Sale of land).
    Generally. See **Contract** (Sale of land).
    Incorporation of terms. See Contract—Form of contract—Necessity for writing—Incorporation of terms, above.
    Memorandum—
      Evidence of contract. See Memorandum of contract, below.
    Mistake—
      Existence of mistake at date of contract—Building sold for deveopment. See **Contract** (Mistake—Common mistake—Existence of mistake at date of contract—Building sold for development).
    Penalty—
      Relief against penalty. See **Equity** (Penalty—Relief against penalty—Contract for sale of land).
    Registration as land charge—
      Registration in name of estate owner. See **Land charge** (Registration—Registration in name of estate owner).
    Rescission. See Rescission of contract, below.
    Specific performance. See **Specific performance** (Sale of land).
    Time of the essence—
      Hong Kong. See **Contract** (Time—Time of the essence—Hong Kong—Sale of land).
    Uncertainty. See Uncertainty of contract, below.
    Waiver of breach. See **Contract** (Breach—Waiver—Conduct amounting to waiver—Contract for sale of residue of lease).
  Conveyance—
    Boundary. See **Boundary** (Conveyance).
    Construction—
      Burden of proof—Whether burden of proof on plaintiff. **Scott v Martin** [1987] **2** 813, CA.
      Conduct of parties—Contemporanea expositio—Applicability of doctrine—Boundaries and parcels—Application of doctrine to determine boundaries of parcels included in conveyance—Way crossing land conveyed—Way not expressly included in conveyance—Parties treating way as part of land conveyed—Period of limitation not expired—Whether conduct of parties reason for construing conveyance so as to include way. **St Edmundsbury and Ipswich Diocesan Board of Finance v Clark (No 2)** [1973] **3** 902, Ch D.
      Evidence of circumstances surrounding conveyance—Admissibility as an aid to construction—Admissibility to contradict plain words of conveyance—Dwelling-house—Meaning—Conveyance of 'All that dwellinghouse and premises'—Cellar or space under ground floor of house conveyed—Cellar connected by steps to adjoining house retained by vendor—No access to cellar from house conveyed—Whether 'dwellinghouse' apt to include inaccessible space under ground floor of house—Whether evidence of observable facts on ground admissible to show that cellar excepted from conveyance. **Grigsby v Melville** [1973] **3** 455, CA.

SALE OF LAND (cont)—
  Conveyance (cont)—
    Construction (cont)—
      Rights of pasture—Reference to particulars at auction sale—Words in conveyance referring to equitable rights. **White v Taylor (No 2)** [1968] **1** 1015, Ch D.
    Escrow—
      Delivery of conveyance as escrow—Implied condition. *See* **Deed** (Escrow—Condition—Implied condition—Conveyance executed in anticipation of sale).
    Exception and reservation—
      Implied exception—General words of exception and reservation—Exception from conveyance of part of underlying structure of premises conveyed—Adjoining shop and cottage premises in common ownership—Cellar under cottage premises—Access to cellar only from shop—Sale of cottage—Conveyance excepting and reserving 'such rights and easements...as may be enjoyed in connection with' shop—Whether cellar excepted from conveyance—Whether fee simple in cellar reserved to vendor. **Grigsby v Melville** [1973] **1** 385, Ch D.
      Mines and minerals. *See* **Mine** (Minerals).
    Fraudulent conveyance. *See* **Fraudulent conveyance**.
    General words—
      Creation of easement. *See* **Easement** (Repair—Right to enter on land to maintain outside wall of house—Non-continuous easement—Creation—Severance of land from common ownership—General words in conveyance).
      Erections—Greenhouses resting on concrete—Law of Property Act 1925, s 62(1). **Dibble (HE) Ltd (t/a Mill Lane Nurseries) v Moore (West, third party)** [1969] **3** 1465, CA.
    Merger of contract in conveyance. *See* Merger of contract in conveyance, *below*.
    Parcels—
      Building plots—Boundary between two plots not stated—Subsequent conveyances with similar parcels—Boundary deemed straight—Building operations on one plot before ultimate conveyances of other plot—Building encroached—Effect of ultimate conveyance of plot encroached on. **Hopgood v Brown** [1955] **1** 550, CA.
      Reference to plan—Conveyance of dwelling-house—Footings and eaves projecting beyond area conveyed as depicted by plan—Whether footings conveyed. **Truckell v Stock** [1957] **1** 74, CA.
      Reference to plan—Conveyance of land and building in separate lots—Large building divided into two halves—Transfer deeds not defining boundary but referring to plan—Scale of plan too small to show precise boundary—Transfer deeds referring to dividing wall as party wall—Whether boundary insufficiently identified—Whether extrinsic evidence admissible to determine boundary. **Scarfe v Adams** [1981] **1** 843, CA.
      Reference to plan—Conveyance of land edged with red on plan—Land edged red mistakenly including land to which vendor had no title—Inference to be drawn from plan—Whether conveyance including land to which vendor had no title. **Dunning (A J) & Sons (Shopfitters) Ltd v Sykes & Son (Poole) Ltd** [1987] **1** 700, CA.
      Reference to plan—Large scale plan necessary if plan alone to be used to describe boundary. **Scarfe v Adams** [1981] **1** 843, CA.
      Reference to plan—Parcels stated to be delineated on plan 'by way of identification only'—Boundary of property conveyed not clear from description of parcels—Whether court entitled to refer to plan in order to ascertain boundary. **Wigginton & Milner Ltd v Winster Engineering Ltd** [1978] **3** 436, CA.
      Reference to plan—Right of way—Way over and along 'private road'—Road not defined in conveyance—Road constructed pursuant to planning permission—Planning permission requiring road to consist of 13-foot carriageway and 3-foot verges—Whether court entitled to refer to plan and planning permission in construing conveyance—Whether road including carriageway and verges. **Scott v Martin** [1987] **2** 813, CA.
      Right of purchaser to insist on plan—Draft conveyance identifying property by reference to plan to be annexed—Whether identification by reference to certain number in certain street sufficient. **Sharman and Meade's Contract, Re** [1936] **2** 1547, Ch D.
      Substratum—Inclusion—Parcels defined by reference to boundaries on surface—Parcels including substratum to centre of earth in absence of words to contrary—Conveyance of 'All that dwellinghouse and premises'—Cellar or space under ground floor of house conveyed—Cellar connected by steps to adjoining house retained by vendor—No access to cellar from house conveyed—Whether conveyed—Whether conveyance effective to include cellar in parcels of property conveyed. **Grigsby v Melville** [1973] **3** 455, CA.
      Way crossing land—Way not expressly included in parcels—Grass verges between way and parcels of land expressly conveyed—Presumption that way included in conveyance ad medium filum—Conveyance expressed to be subject to right of way—Whether existence of grass verges precluding application of presumption. **St Edmundsbury and Ipswich Diocesan Board of Finance v Clark (No 2)** [1973] **3** 902, Ch D.
    Plan—
      Admissibility. **Leachman v L & K Richardson Ltd** [1969] **3** 20, Ch D.
    Preparation—
      Unqualified person. *See* **Solicitor** (Unqualified person—Preparation of documents etc).
    Rectification. *See* **Deed** (Rectification—Conveyance).
    Registered land—
      Canada. *See* **Canada** (Registered land—Conveyance).
    Restrictive covenant. *See* **Restrictive covenant affecting land**.
    Stamp duty. *See* **Stamp duty** (Conveyance on sale).
  Costs—
    Purchaser's lien. *See* Purchaser's lien—Costs of suit, *below*.
    Specific performance. *See* **Specific performance** (Sale of land—Costs of action).
    Transfer of registered land—
      Scale fee. *See* **Land registration** (Costs—Transfer of registered land on sale—Scale fee).
  Court, sale by. *See* Sale by court, *below*.
  Covenant—
    Covenant running with land. *See* Covenant running with land, *below*.

SALE OF LAND (cont)—
  Covenant (cont)—
    Implied covenant—
      Assignment of leasehold interest. *See* Leasehold interest—Assignment—Implied covenant, *below.*
    Purchaser's covenant—
      Erection and maintenance of bridge. *See* **Bridge** (Maintenance—Covenant to maintain—Covenant
        by purchaser of land to erect and maintain bridge).
    Restraint of trade. *See* **Restraint of trade by agreement** (Vendor and purchaser).
    Title, for. *See* Covenants for title, *below.*
  Covenant running with land—
    Benefit of covenant—
      Successor in title—Contract with catchment board to widen, deepen and make good banks of
        river—Bursting of banks—Flooding of adjoining land owned by successor in title to party to
        contract—Liability of board—Law of Property Act 1925, s 78(1). **Smith v River Douglas Catchment
        Board** [1949] 2 179, CA.
    Burden of covenant—
      Covenants by owners to contribute to upkeep of common roads and sewers—Deed declaring trusts
        of roads and sewers for benefit of owners of plots of successors in title of owners to make
        contribution—Acceptance of benefit of covenants. **Halsall v Brizell** [1957] 1 371, Ch D.
  Covenants for title—
    Impropriate rectory—
      Sale of rectorial land—Liability under implied covenants—Liability to repair or contribute to repair
        of chancel—Vendor not deriving title otherwise than by purchase for value—Liability to repair
        attached to owner of land—No breach of implied covenant by purchaser—Law of Property Act
        1925, Sch II, Part I. **Chivers & Sons Ltd v Secretary of State for Air (Queens' College, Cambridge,
        third party)** [1955] 2 607, Ch D.
  Damages—
    Breach of contract. *See* Damages for breach of contract, *below.*
    Misrepresentation. *See* Misrepresentation—Damages, *below.*
    Mitigation of loss. *See* **Damages** (Mitigation of loss—Benefit accruing to plaintiff—Sale of land).
    Negligence of solicitor. *See* **Solicitor** (Negligence—Damages—Sale of land).
    Rescission of contract. *See* Rescission of contract—Damages, *below.*
  Damages for breach of contract—
    Breach of covenant to carry out remedial work prior to sale—
      Remedial work required by covenant not sufficient to prevent damage—Vendor contracting to sell
        house with patio on top of cellar—Water penetrating cellar from patio and surrounding
        ground—Vendor covenanting to waterproof patio—Vendor failing to carry out work—
        Waterproofing patio only capable of preventing 70 per cent of water penetrating cellar—Whether
        purchaser entitled to substantial or merely nominal damages. **Dean v Ainley** [1987] 3 748, CA.
    Claim for rescission and damages for breach of contract—
      Order for rescission and enquiry as to damages—Plaintiff not entitled to more than nominal
        damages where contract rescinded—Plaintiff entitled to payment of such sums as would restore
        him to position in which he would have been if contract had not been made—Reference in order
        to 'damages' to be construed accordingly. **Horsler v Zorro** [1975] 1 584, Ch D.
    Damages in addition to specific performance—
      Damages for delay in completing contract—Cause of action in damages accruing after issue of writ
        claiming specific performance and damages in addition thereto—Claim for specific performance
        not pursued at hearing because by then land conveyed to plaintiff—Plaintiff continuing to claim
        damages for delay in completion—Completion date occurring after date of writ—Whether
        damages for delay in completion recoverable in specific performance action although cause of
        action accruing after issue of writ. **Oakacre Ltd v Claire Cleaners (Holdings) Ltd** [1981] 3 667,
        Ch D.
    Damages in addition to specific performance and abatement of purchase price—
      Date for assessment of damages—Contract for sale of land free from incumbrances—Land subject
        to mortgages—Cost of redeeming mortgages exceeding purchase price—Purchaser entitled to
        conveyance of property subject to mortgages—Compensation for cost of redeeming
        mortgages—Abatement of purchase price—Damages in respect of excess of cost of redeeming
        mortgages over purchase price—Damages limited to amount by which value of property
        exceeding purchase price—Date for assessing value of property—Date of breach or date of
        completion—Appreciation in value of property—Chancery Amendment Act 1858, s 2. **Grant v
        Dawkins** [1973] 3 897, Ch D.
    Damages in substitution for specific performance—
      Damages at common law for repudiation of contract—Purchaser failing to complete in
        time—Vendor choosing to pursue remedy of specific performance—Specific performance
        rendered impossible—Land sold by mortgagees because vendor defaulting on mortgages—
        Purchaser's failure to complete preventing vendor from redeeming mortgages and being able to
        convey land to purchaser—Whether vendor entitled to seek alternative remedy of common law
        damages for repudiation of contract performance aborted. **Johnson v Agnew** [1979] 1 883, HL.
      Damages for loss of bargain—Date for assessment—Date of breach or date of hearing of action for
        specific performance—Increase in value of property between date of breach and date of
        hearing—Chancery Amendment Act 1858, s 2. **Wroth v Tyler** [1973] 1 897, Ch D.
      Date of assessment—Purchaser claiming specific performance of contract for sale of
        house—Purchaser then buying another house—Purchaser subsequently electing to claim
        damages in lieu of specific performance—Date at which damages should be assessed—Whether
        damages should be assessed at date of purchase of other house or date of election to claim
        damages. **Domb v Isoz** [1980] 1 942, CA.
      Date of assessment—Whether damages to be assessed as at date of hearing of action—Effect of
        plaintiff's delay in bringing proceedings. **Malhotra v Choudhury** [1979] 1 186, CA.
      Generally. *See* **Specific performance** (Damages in substitution for specific performance).
      Vendor obtaining order for specific performance against purchaser—Purchaser failing to carry out
        order for specific performance—Whether vendor entitled to damages in lieu of specific
        performance—Chancery Amendment Act 1858, s 2. **Biggin v Minton** [1977] 2 647, Ch D.

SALE OF LAND (cont)—
  Damages for breach of contract (cont)—
    Date at which damages assessed. See **Contract** (Damages for breach—Date at which damages assessed—Date of breach or date of hearing—Sale of land).
    Loss of bargain—
      Defect in vendor's title—Vendor unable without any fault to show good title—Nominal damages for loss of bargain—Defect in title—Wife's right to occupy matrimonial home—Wife entering in charges register a notice of right of occupation after exchange of contracts—Vendor unable to persuade wife to remove notice—Vendor withdrawing from contract—Whether purchaser limited to nominal damages for loss of bargain. **Wroth v Tyler** [1973] **1** 897, Ch D.
      Vendors agreeing to sell property to purchasers—Purchasers entering into sub-contract with third party to resell property at profit—Vendors unaware of sub-contract at time of entering into contract with purchasers—Vendors refusing to complete when learning of resale—Purchasers unable to complete resale and selling at loss—Whether purchasers entitled to damages for loss on resale caused by vendors' breach of contract. **Seven Seas Properties Ltd v Al-Essa (No 2)** [1993] **3** 577, Ch D.
    Measure of damages—
      Breach of contract caused by agent's want of authority—Vendors' solicitor signing contract for sale of house on behalf of clients—Solicitor having no authority to sign for vendors—Purchaser unable to obtain specific performance against vendors—Purchaser suing solicitor—Whether damages should be assessed as at date of completion or at date of judgment. **Suleman v Shahsavari** [1989] **2** 460, Ch D.
      Breach of covenant—Breach not causing damage—Damages serving no useful purpose—Water penetrating cellar from patio and surrounding earth—Vendor covenanting to waterproof patio—Vendor failing to carry out work—Waterproofing patio only capable of preventing 70 per cent of water penetrating cellar—Whether award of damages serving any useful purpose—Whether purchaser entitled to damages—Whether purchaser required to expend any damages awarded on remedial work. **Dean v Ainley** [1987] **3** 748, CA.
    Misrepresentation—
      Title of vendor—Representation by vendor that he has title to sell—Representation false—Vendor having no reasonable grounds for believing representation to be true—Claim by purchaser for damages for loss of bargain—Whether in absence of fraud purchaser limited to damages measured by expenses incurred in consequence of misrepresentation—Misrepresentation Act 1967, s 2(1). **Watts v Spence** [1975] **2** 528, Ch D.
    No loss of bargain—
      Damages recoverable—Failure of vendor to complete for reason other than defect of title—Damages for loss of use of deposit and for costs of approving and executing contract. **Wallington v Townsend** [1939] **2** 225, Ch D.
    Repudiation by purchaser—
      Deposit. See **Contract** (Damages for breach—Deposit—Sale of land—Purchaser in repudiatory breach of contract for sale of property).
      Interest—Claim for interest on purchase money from completion date to date of purchaser's repudiation of contract—Contract entitling vendor to interest at specified rate from date fixed for completion until purchase actually completed—Whether vendor entitled to interest at contractual rate where contract repudiated. **Janred Properties Ltd v Ente Nazionale Italiano per il Turismo** [1989] **2** 444, CA.
    Repudiation by vendor—
      Costs incurred by purchaser prior to execution of contract—Performance of act required to be done by contract—Improvements effected to property by purchaser prior to completion—What costs recoverable. **Lloyd v Stanbury** [1971] **2** 267, Ch D.
      Intention of purchaser to convert property—Purchaser a dealer in real estate—Whether knowledge of those matters to be imputed to vendor. **Diamond v Campbell-Jones** [1960] **1** 583, Ch D.
    Vendor's inability to show good title—
      Damages limited to cost of investigating title—Limitation on damages if vendor's inability to show good title not attributable to his default—Bad faith constituting default—Unwillingness to use best endeavours to obtain good title amounting to bad faith—Vendor and wife holding property as joint tenants—Vendor granting purchaser option to purchase house—Vendor's wife refusing to consent to sale to plaintiff—Vendor unable to make good title—Vendor not attempting to persuade wife to consent to sale—Whether vendor's failure to attempt to persuade wife to consent amounting to bad faith—Whether vendor's inability to show good title attributable to his default—Whether damages for vendor's breach of contract should be limited to costs of investigating title. **Malhotra v Choudhury** [1979] **1** 186, CA.
      Damages limited to cost of investigating title—Limitation on damages if vendor's inability to show good title not attributable to his default—Conveyances by vendor many years before contract giving rise to claims affecting vendor's ability to make good title—Adverse claims only made at time of contract—Purchaser aware of adverse claims when entering into contract—Vendor unable to make good title—Purchaser claiming damages—Whether vendor voluntarily creating situation in which he was unable to make good title—Whether purchaser's damages limited to his expenses. **Ray v Druce** [1985] **2** 482, Ch D.
      Limitation on damages if vendor's inability to show good title not attributable to his default—Contract for purchase of farm with vacant possession on completion—Farm occupied by persons as business tenants—Vendor failing to serve notice terminating tenancy—Vendor failing to take proceedings against tenants—Whether vendor doing all he reasonably could to get vacant possession—Whether damages to be assessed in accordance with general law—Whether purchaser entitled to damages for loss of profits—Whether purchaser's damages limited to expenses incurred in abortive sale. **Sharneyford Supplies Ltd v Edge (Barrington Black Austin & Co (a firm), third party)** [1987] **1** 588, CA.

SALE OF LAND (cont)—
  Damages for breach of contract (cont)—
    Vendor's inability to show good title (cont)—
      Limitation on damages if vendor's inability to show good title not attributable to his default—Sale and sub-sale—Vendor failing to complete in sale to purchaser—Purchaser unable to complete sub-sale to sub-purchaser—Sub-purchaser rescinding contract on day notice to complete sale expired—Sub-purchaser bringing action against purchaser for breach of contract of sub-sale—Purchaser given no chance to use best endeavours to obtain good title—Whether sub-purchaser's damages limited to its expenses. **Seven Seas Properties Ltd v Al-Essa** [1989] 1 164, Ch D.
    Warranty—
      Information given by vendor before sale—Estimated income from estate inaccurate—Absence of fraud—Reliance on information by purchaser—Whether purchaser entitled to damages for breach of warranty. **Terrene Ltd v Nelson** [1937] 3 739, Ch D.
      Newly constructed house—Builder vendor of house—Purchaser informing vendor that she desired to be assured house well built—Assurance given—Sale completed—Fall of ceiling—Whether vendor liable to purchaser for breach of warranty. **Otto (M) & E Otto v Bolton & Norris** [1936] 1 960, KBD.
      Reply to preliminary enquiry—Reply affirming that property had not suffered war damage—Reply untrue—Reply confirmed in answer to requisitions on title—Whether vendor liable for breach of warranty. **Mahon v Ainscough** [1952] 1 337, CA.
      Reply to preliminary enquiry—Representation as to promptitude of payment of rents—Representation untrue but not fraudulent—Whether a breach of warranty. **London County Freehold and Leasehold Properties Ltd v Berkeley Property and Investment Co** [1936] 2 1039, CA.
  Deed—
    Insufficiently stamped deed—
    Title. See Title—Insufficiently stamped deed, below.
  Defective property—
    Damages—
      Mitigation of loss. See **Damages** (Mitigation of loss—Benefit accruing to plaintiff—Sale of land).
  Delay through fault of vendor—
    Interest on unpaid purchase money. See Interest on unpaid purchase money—Delay through fault of vendor, below.
  Deposit—
    Auction—
      Auctioneer's lien on deposit for commission and disbursements. See **Auctioneer** (Lien—Lien on deposit for commission and disbursements).
    Condition precedent—
      Failure to pay deposit—Provision for payment of deposit by purchaser on or before signing of contract—Purchaser delivering cheque to vendor on signing of contract—Cheque subsequently dishonoured—Whether payment of deposit condition precedent to contract taking effect—Whether vendor bound by contract. **Myton Ltd v Schwab-Morris** [1974] 1 326, Ch D.
    Estate agent—
      Capacity in which deposit prior to contract received by estate agent. See **Estate agent** (Deposit—Deposit prior to contract—Capacity in which deposit received by estate agent).
    Forfeiture—
      Application for leave to forfeit deposit and re-enter—Emergency legislation. See **Emergency legislation** (Sale of land—Failure to complete—Application for leave to forfeit deposit and to re-enter).
      Penalty—Relief against forfeiture—Purchaser's failure to complete—Contract providing for payment of deposit of 25% of contract price—Purchaser failing to complete within stipulated time—Vendor forfeiting deposit—Whether amount of deposit required to be reasonable—Whether deposit of more than 10% unreasonable—Whether deposit of 25% of contract price a penalty—Whether deposit to be repaid in full. **Workers Trust and Merchant Bank Ltd v Dojap Investments Ltd** [1993] 2 370, PC.
      Purchaser's failure to complete—Purchaser unable to complete because purchaser's bank not arranging transfer of funds in time—Vendor rescinding contract and forfeiting deposit—Purchaser able to complete 14 days after rescission—Purchaser claiming return of deposit—Whether contract frustrated by failure of purchaser's bank to transfer funds in time—Whether court having jurisdiction to order return of deposit if it thought fit—Whether if court having jurisdiction it should exercise discretion to order return of deposit—Law of Property Act 1925, s 49(2). **Universal Corp v Five Ways Properties Ltd** [1979] 1 552, CA.
      Purchaser's failure to complete—Vendor rescinding contract and forfeiting deposit—Contract excluding court's discretion to order repayment of deposit—Vendor in breach of contract—Whether purchaser entitled to return of deposit—Law of Property Act 1925, s 49(2). **Country and Metropolitan Homes Surrey Ltd v Topclaim Ltd** [1997] 1 254, Ch D.
      Purchaser's failure to complete—Vendor rescinding contract and forfeiting deposit—Vendor subsequently selling land to other purchaser at higher price—Whether original purchaser entitled to refund of deposit—Law of Property Act 1925, s 49(2). **Aribisala v St James Homes (Grosvenor Dock) Ltd** [2008] 3 762, Ch D.
      Purchaser's failure to complete—Vendor serving ineffective notice to complete—Vendor rescinding contract 22 days after expiry of notice to complete—Vendor rescinding because of advent of new buyer—Whether purchaser guilty of unreasonably long delay in completing—Whether vendor entitled to forfeit deposit. **Cole v Rose** [1978] 3 1121, Ch D.
      Purchaser's failure to complete—Vendor serving notice to complete within specified period—Vendor rescinding contract and forfeiting deposit—Purchaser claiming return of deposit on basis vendor itself not ready, able and willing to complete during period of notice to complete—Whether court should exercise its discretion to order return of deposit in circumstances where vendor subsequently sold property at a profit—Exercise of court's discretion—Law of Property Act 1925, s 49(2). **Midill (97PL) Ltd v Park Lane Estates Ltd** [2009] 2 Comm 561, Ch D and CA; [2009] 2 1067, Ch D and CA.

SALE OF LAND (cont)—
  Deposit (cont)—
    Part of deposit paid—
      Purchaser failing to complete—Vendor electing to rescind—Whether also entitled to payment of outstanding part of deposit. **Lowe v Hope** [1969] **3** 605, Ch D.
    Payment—
      Exercise of option to purchase. *See* **Option** (Option to purchase—Exercise of option—Deposit).
      Failure to pay deposit on time under contract—Vendor entering into contract for sale of property to purchaser—Contract being conditional on purchaser obtaining planning permission and consent of certain committee—Deposit being due within 60 working days from later of those two dates—Purchaser obtaining planning permission other than that envisaged and parties renegotiating—Supplemental agreement providing that reduced deposit due 60 working days after grant of original planning permission—Purchaser failing to pay deposit on due date—Vendor's solicitors agreeing to specified extension and purporting to make time of the essence—Purchaser failing to make payment and vendor writing to terminate contract—Vendor seeking declaration that contract validly terminated—Summary judgment being granted in vendor's favour—Purchaser appealing—Whether failure to pay deposit on time under contract for sale of land necessarily constituting repudiatory breach of contract entitling vendor to terminate contract. **Samarenko v Dawn Hill House Ltd** [2012] **2 Comm** 240, CA; [2012] **2** 476, CA.
    Purchaser's lien. *See* Purchaser's lien—Deposit, *below*.
    Recovery—
      Generally. *See* Recovery of deposit, *below*.
      War time. *See* **Emergency legislation** (Sale of land—Recovery of deposit).
    Stakeholder, payment to. *See* Stakeholder—Deposit paid to stakeholder, *below*.
  Disclosure—
    Rents of properties sold specified in particulars of sale—
      Premises subject to Rent Acts—Certificate of disrepair—Abatement of rent under certificate of disrepair as from future date until repairs carried out—Non-disclosure by vendor of certificate of disrepair—Whether vendor could require performance of contract without regard to abatement of rent. **Englefield Holdings Ltd and Sinclair's Contract, Re** [1962] **3** 503, Ch D.
    Vendor's duty to disclose defect in title—
      Leasehold. *See* Title—Leasehold—Disclosure, *below*.
  Easements—
    Registration—
      Sale of registered land with benefit of easements over unregistered land—Right of way and drainage rights—Whether vendor could be required by purchaser to procure registration of easements at Land Registry before completion—Land Registration Act 1925, s 110(5). **Evans's Contract, Re** [1970] **1** 1236, Ch D.
  Enquiries—
    Preliminary enquiries. *See* Preliminary enquiries, *below*.
  Equitable burden on land. *See* **Acquiescence** (Estoppel—Acquiescence in expenditure being made in reliance on right over land of another).
  Estate agent—
    Authority. *See* **Estate agent** (Authority).
    Commission. *See* **Estate agent** (Commission).
    Deposit. *See* **Estate agent** (Deposit).
    Remuneration—
      Generally. *See* Sale by court—Estate agents and auctioneers, *below*.
  Estate contract—
    Registration as land charge. *See* **Land charge** (Estate contract).
  Estate duty liability—
    Defect in title—
      Rescission of contract. *See* Rescission of contract—Defect in title—Contingent liability to estate duty, *below*.
  Estoppel—
    Constructive trust. *See* **Estoppel** (Proprietary estoppel—Constructive trust—Sale of land).
    Rescission of contract. *See* Rescission of contract—Estoppel, *below*.
  Evidence—
    Construction of conveyance. *See* Conveyance—Construction—Evidence of circumstances surrounding conveyance, *above*.
    Memorandum of contract. *See* Memorandum of contract, *below*.
    Possession—
      Breach of contract—Evidence of possession. *See* Breach of contract—Evidence of possession, *above*.
  Exception and reservation. *See* Conveyance—Exception and reservation, *above*.
  Exchange of contracts—
    Agreement subject to contract—
      Parts exchanged required to be in identical terms—Agreement to vary draft contract by altering amount of deposit payable—Purchaser's part amended—Vendor's part by mistake not amended—Exchange of parts not resulting in concluded contract. **Harrison v Battye** [1974] **3** 830, CA.
      Parts exchanged required to be in identical terms—Purchase price of house to include fittings and fixtures—Purchase price apportioned in vendor's part of contract—Purchase price not apportioned in purchaser's part of contract—Whether contract could be rectified—Whether exchange of parts resulting in concluded contract. **Domb v Isoz** [1980] **1** 942, CA.
    Authority of solicitor—
      Exchange by telephone—Vendor's solicitor holding vendor's and purchaser's parts of contract duly signed—Vendor's and purchaser's solicitors agreeing to exchange contracts by telephone—Whether such exchange resulting in binding contract. **Domb v Isoz** [1980] **1** 942, CA.
    Constructive exchange—
      Purchasers' part returned by vendor to purchasers in mistake for vendor's part—Whether binding contract created. **Harrison v Battye** [1974] **3** 830, CA.

SALE OF LAND (cont)—
Exchange of contracts (cont)—
Duplicate contracts—
Need of actual physical exchange—Ordinary method by which contract brought into existence—Contract not binding until signed parts of contracts exchanged. **Eccles v Bryant** [1947] **2** 865, CA.
Necessity for exchange—
Concluded contract before exchange—Intention of parties—Offer by council by letter to sell council house to sitting tenant—Form of agreement for sale enclosed with letter—Agreement devised with object of dispensing with legal formalities—Agreement signed by tenant and returned to council—Date when tenancy ceased and mortgage repayments began left blank on agreement—Contract concluded by offer and acceptance—Contract binding on council though not signed by them and contracts not exchanged—Letter containing offer constituting sufficient note or memorandum of contract. **Storer v Manchester City Council** [1974] **3** 824, CA.

Concluded contract before exchange—Intention of parties—Offer by council in printed form to sell council house to sitting tenant—Tenant completing and returning application to purchase but asking for reduction of purchase price on account of repairs required—Council advising that state of property taken into account in establishing purchase price—Tenant asking council to continue with sale in accordance with application—Council refusing to proceed with application following change in policy—Whether offer made by council and accepted by tenant—Whether conduct of parties and correspondence between them disclosed a contract for purchase by tenant—Whether parties ad idem—Whether contract binding on council although not reduced to formal written document. **Gibson v Manchester City Council** [1978] **2** 583, CA.
Same solicitor acting for both parties—
Exchange unnecessary—Parties bound when complete contract signed and nothing more remains to be done. **Smith v Mansi** [1962] **3** 857, CA.
Fiduciary duty—
Vendor's duty to purchaser. See Vendor—Fiduciary duty to purchaser, *below*.
Forfeiture—
Deposit. See Deposit—Forfeiture, *above*.
Forgery—
Letter to deceive prospective purchaser. See **Criminal law** (Forgery—Intent to defraud—Fraud distinguished from deceit—Intent to deceive insufficient—Sale of land).
Liability of solicitors and estate agents—
Whether vendors' solicitors acting in breach of warranty of authority—Whether vendors' solicitors and agents owing duty of care to purchaser—Whether vendors' solicitors acting in breach of trust releasing purchase money to client—Whether relief to be granted—Whether undertaking to be enforced—Trustee Act 1925, s 61—Money Laundering Regulations 2007, SI 2007/2157. **P&P Property Ltd v Owen White & Catlin LLP** [2018] **4** 277, CA.
Formation of contract—
Acceptance of tender. See Acceptance of tender, *above*.
Consensus ad idem—
Uncommunicated reservation of vendor—Formal contract signed by both parties and handed to their solicitor with day and month of completion date left blank—Date later completed by solicitor—Time for completion alternatively provided by conditions of sale—Intention of vendor not to bind himself by signature not communicated to purchaser—Whether evidence of such intention admissible—National Conditions of Sale (17th Edn), condition 4. **Smith v Mansi** [1962] **3** 857, CA.
Electronic communications—
Option to purchase. See **Contract** (Signature—Real property—Option to purchase).
Exchange of contracts. See Exchange of contracts, *above*.
Generally. See Contract—Formation, *above*.
Incorporation of terms. See Contract—Form of contract—Necessity for writing—Incorporation of terms, *above*.
Necessity for writing. See Contract—Form of contract—Necessity for writing, *above*.
Offer and acceptance. See **Contract** (Offer and acceptance).
Provisional agreement—
Agreement provisional 'until' formal agreement executed—Whether immediately binding. **Branca v Cobarro** [1947] **2** 101, CA.
Fraudulent conveyance. See **Fraudulent conveyance**.
House—
Fitness for habitation—
Warranty in contract—Construction. See **Contract** (Construction—Warranty—Fitness of house for habitation).
House completed at date of sale—
Implied warranty—
Fitness for habitation—Sale by builder of new house—Whether implied warranty house fit for human habitation. **Hoskins v Woodham** [1938] **1** 692, KBD.
House in course of erection—
Implied warranty as to workmanship etc—
Express term for completing house in proper manner—Whether warranty of fitness of materials should also be implied—Whether defective work done before contract of sale was within clause for properly completing house—Defects clause not taking away rights under warranty clause—National Conditions of Sale (16th Edn), condition 12(3). **Hancock v BW Brazier (Anerley) Ltd** [1966] **2** 901, CA.

Express terms as to the way in which the house was to be completed—Whether warranty of fitness excluded by express terms. **Lynch v Thorne** [1956] **1** 744, CA.

Foundations of house—Cracks in walls due to settlement caused by roots of poplar trees—Whether implied warranty extending to foundations below ground. **Jennings v Tavener** [1955] **2** 769, QBD.

Sale of house by builder—Certain fittings not fixed and plastering still to be done—Whether sale of complete house or house in course of erection. **Perry v Sharon Development Co Ltd** [1937] **4** 390, CA.

SALE OF LAND (cont)—
House in course of erection (cont)—
Implied warranty as to workmanship etc (cont)—
Supply of good and proper materials—Whether implied warranty applicable to materials used before contract signed. **Hancock v BW Brazier (Anerley) Ltd** [1966] **2** 901, CA.
Implied condition. *See* Condition—Implied condition, *above.*
Implied covenant—
Assignment of leasehold interest. *See* Leasehold interest—Assignment—Implied covenant, *below.*
Implied warranty—
House completed at date of sale. *See* House completed at date of sale—Implied warranty, *above.*
House in course of erection—
Warranty as to workmanship etc. *See* House in course of erection—Implied warranty as to workmanship etc, *above.*
Incumbrances, easements, rights of way etc—
Duty of purchaser to satisfy himself as to incumbrances—
Whether principle of caveat emptor applying—National Conditions of Sale (20th edn), condition 14. **Celsteel Ltd v Alton House Holdings Ltd (No 2)** [1986] **1** 598, Ch D.
Innocent misrepresentation—
Damages. *See* **Misrepresentation** (Innocent misrepresentation—Sale of land—Damages).
Interest on unpaid purchase money—
Delay through fault of vendor—
Provision that interest to be paid from date fixed for completion—Contract incorporating Law Society's General Conditions so far as not varied by agreement or inconsistent—Whether Law Society's General Conditions excluded as inconsistent—Whether purchaser liable to pay interest where delay due to vendor's default—Law Society's General Conditions of Sale (1934 Edn), cl 7. **Debenham and Mercer's Contract, Re** [1944] **1** 364, Ch D.
Option to take income of property in lieu—
Condition entitling vendor to interest if completion delayed, except where delay attributable to default of vendor—Condition granting vendor option to take income of property instead of interest—Vendor electing to take income—Completion delayed by circumstances foreseeable by vendor, not connected with question of title—Whether delay attributable to 'default' of vendor—Whether vendor entitled to interest or to take income—National Conditions of Sale (17th Edn), condition 6. **Hewitt's Contract, Re** [1963] **3** 419, Ch D.
Possession before completion—
Delay in completion through vendor's default in deducing title—Purchaser taking possession on date fixed for completion—Special conditions incorporating Law Society's Conditions of Sale 'so far as not varied or inconsistent'—Clause providing for payment of interest from date of taking possession omitted—Whether purchaser liable for interest from date of taking possession—Law Society's Conditions of Sale, cll 6, 7. **Priestley's Contract, Re** [1947] **1** 716, Ch D.
Failure to complete—Payment of purchase money into court—Liability of purchaser to pay interest from date of lodgment until completion. **Pearlberg v May** [1951] **1** 1001, CA.
Investigation of title. *See* Title—Investigation, *below.*
Joint tenants—
Settled land—
Power of sale. *See* **Settlement** (Powers of tenant for life—Joint tenants—Power of sale).
Leasehold interest—
Assignment—
Consent. *See* Leasehold interest—Consent to assignment, *below.*
Construction—Rent—Liability to pay—Liability pending completion—Date for completion agreed—Rent payable from that date even if consent to assignment of lease not forthcoming—Purchaser to be allowed to enter on that date—Consent to assignment not forthcoming—Entry by purchaser delayed—Whether purchaser liable for rent after agreed date and before entry. **Cantor Art Services Ltd v Kenneth Bieber Photography Ltd** [1969] **3** 843, CA.
Implied covenant—Conveyance by assignors as 'beneficial owners'—Implied covenants that lease not void or voidable and that all covenants performed up to time of conveyance—Covenant to repair not performed—Condition of sale that property taken with full notice of state of repair—Liability of assignors—Rectification of lease—Law of Property Act 1925, s 76(1)(b), Sch II, Part II. **Butler v Mountview Estates Ltd** [1951] **1** 693, KBD.
Consent to assignment—
Consent to assignment to be obtained 'where necessary'—Necessary—Tenant contracting to sell residue of term of lease—Landlord's consent required under lease—Consent withheld—Tenant seeking rescission of contract—What facts tenant required to prove—National Conditions of Sale (20th edn), condition 11(5). **Bickel v Courtenay Investments (Nominees) Ltd** [1984] **1** 657, Ch D.
Vendors' duty—Sub-lease—Consent refused by immediate landlord—Ground of refusal that assignees' user would contravene covenant in head-lease—Whether vendors under a duty to approach freeholders for a licence or to afford purchasers opportunity to do so. **Lipmans Wallpaper Ltd v Mason & Hodghton Ltd** [1968] **1** 1123, Ch D.
Contract—
Condition—Subject to landlords' consent to assignment being obtained by vendor. **Property and Bloodstock Ltd v Emerton** [1967] **3** 321, CA.
Disclosure. *See* Title—Leasehold—Disclosure, *below.*
General words implied—
Flats supplied with hot water and central heating by landlords—No covenant to supply—Whether right conferred on tenant by general words—Law of Property Act 1925, s 62. **Regis Property Co Ltd v Redman** [1956] **2** 335, CA.
Option to purchase reversion—
Assignment to assignee of lease—Option in lease to purchase freehold reversion expectant on term of years granted by lease—Assignment of lease—Subsequent assignment of option to assignee of lease—Whether option enforceable by assignee. **Griffith v Pelton** [1957] **3** 75, CA.

SALE OF LAND (cont)—
Leasehold interest (cont)—
Right of re-entry—
Assignment of leasehold interest in part of premises—Covenant to perform and observe stipulations for benefit of retained premises—Right of re-entry on breach of covenant—Covenant by purchaser that successors in title would observe stipulations—Purchaser relieved from liability for non-performance of covenant after parting with interest—Covenant not directly enforceable against successor in title—Failure by successor in title to perform or observe stipulations—Whether right of re-entry effective although no one liable to be sued for breach of covenant. **Shiloh Spinners Ltd v Harding** [1973] **1** 90, HL.
Sub-underlease of flat described by vendor in contract of sale as 'underlease'—
Flat comprised in head lease which included other flats in same former house—Enforceability of contract of sale. **Becker v Partridge** [1966] **2** 266, CA.
Liquidator—
Compulsory winding up of company. *See* **Company** (Compulsory winding up—Liquidator—Duty—Sale of land).
Local authority—
Power to sell land. *See* **Local authority** (Land—Power to sell land).
Sale of local authority house to tenant. *See* **Housing** (Local authority houses—Tenant's right to buy).
Lock-out agreement—
Oral agreement that seller would not negotiate with other prospective purchasers for two weeks after buyer receiving draft contract—
Whether lock-out agreement a contract for sale of interests in land—Whether agreement required to be in writing and signed by parties—Law of Property (Miscellaneous Provisions) Act 1989, s 2(1). **Pitt v PHH Asset Management Ltd** [1993] **4** 961, CA.
Loss of bargain—
Damages. *See* Damages for breach of contract—Loss of bargain, *above.*
Matrimonial home—
Sale under trust for sale—
Bankruptcy. *See* **Bankruptcy** (Property available for distribution—Matrimonial home—Sale under trust for sale).
Generally. *See* **Husband and wife** (Matrimonial home—Sale under trust for sale).
Memorandum of contract—
Admission of existence of contract—
Evidence—Admissibility to prove real bargain different from that contained in document—Law of Property Act 1925, s 40(1). **Beckett v Nurse** [1948] **1** 81, CA.
Auction—
Whether auctioneer owes duty to purchaser to sign on behalf of vendor. *See* **Auctioneer** (Memorandum—Signature—Duty to purchaser).
Circumstances in which memorandum must evidence existence of contract—
Effect of qualification 'subject to contract'—Waiver of qualification—Waiver by subsequent oral agreement—Solicitors' letters—Oral contract concluded by parties prior to solicitors' correspondence—Vendor's solicitors' letter referring to 'proposed purchase ... subject to contract'—Vendor's solicitors forwarding draft contract—Parties subsequently entering into new oral agreement based on increased purchase price—Vendor's solicitors' letter acknowledging 'increase in purchase price has been mutually agreed'—Letter not expressed to be subject to contract—Whether qualification in earlier letter waived by new oral agreement—Whether subsequent letter read with earlier correspondence and draft contract constituting a note or memorandum of new agreement—Law of Property Act 1925, s 40(1). **Law v Jones** [1973] **2** 437, CA.
Company—
Minutes of company meeting sufficient memorandum—Law of Property Act 1925, s 53(1)(a). **Strathblaine Estates Ltd, Re** [1948] **1** 162, Ch D.
Compromise of pending legal proceedings—
Applicability of requirement of note or memorandum of agreement in writing—Compromise including provision for transfer of interest in land—Compromise not evidenced in writing—Whether compromise enforceable—Law of Property Act 1925, s 40(1). **Steadman v Steadman** [1973] **3** 977, CA.
Compulsory purchase—
Service of notice to treat by acquiring authority—Agreement on price to be paid by authority—Whether agreement to be evidenced by note or memorandum in writing—Law of Property Act 1925, s 40(1). **Munton v Greater London Council** [1976] **2** 815, CA.
Contract for disposition of land—
Oral contract for disposition of land—Oral contract for surrender of lease—Reliance on oral contract by way of defence—Landlord refusing to accept surrender and claiming rent beyond surrender date—Whether tenant entitled to rely on oral contract for surrender of lease as defence to landlord's claim—Whether tenant in substance seeking to enforce oral contract—Conveyancing and Property Ordinance (Hong Kong), s 3. **Take Harvest Ltd v Liu** [1993] **2** 459, PC.
Contract for the disposition of an interest in land—
Oral contract to enter into formal written contract for sale of land—Vendor refusing to complete—No note or memorandum evidencing oral contract—Whether purchaser able to sue on oral contract—Whether oral contract a 'contract for the...disposition of...[an] interest in land'—Law of Property Act 1925, s 40(1). **Daulia Ltd v Four Millbank Nominees Ltd** [1978] **2** 557, CA.
Deficiency in document signed by party to be charged—
Reference to other document—No reference in document so signed to second document or to other transaction than that effected by first document—Cheque for deposit on sale signed by purchaser and receipt for cheque prepared and signed by vendor on same occasion but subsequently to the signing of the cheque—Cheque drawn in favour of vendor's solicitors, not vendor—Whether cheque and receipt sufficient to satisfy Law of Property Act 1925, s 40. **Timmins v Moreland Street Property Co Ltd** [1957] **3** 265, CA.

SALE OF LAND (cont)—
  Memorandum of contract (cont)—
    Deficiency in memorandum supplied by second document—

      No reference in second document to memorandum—Omission of material term in alleged memorandum—Concession by plaintiff of term in favour of defendant to render contract enforceable—Law of Property Act 1925, s 40(1). **Burgess v Cox** [1950] **2** 1212, Ch D.

    Description of parties—

      Agent of purchaser contracting in own name—Knowledge of agency by vendor—Right of purchaser to maintain action for specific performance—Vendors tenants in common—One vendor having no power to convey interest—Right of purchaser to order against other vendors in respect of their shares. **Basma (Abdul Karim) v Weekes** [1950] **2** 146, PC.

      Agent of vendor contracting in own name—Agent having authority to enter into contract on behalf of vendor—Right of purchaser to maintain action for specific performance—Whether vendor sufficiently described—Law of Property Act 1925, s 40(1). **Davies v Sweet** [1962] **1** 92, CA.

      Vendor not named in record of contract—Condition of sale—Vendor will convey as personal representative—Whether memorandum sufficient. **Fay v Miller, Wilkins & Co** [1941] **2** 18, CA.

    Interest in land—

      Undivided share—Joint ownership of freehold premises—Sale by one co-owner to the other—Whether a sale of an 'interest in land'—Law of Property Act 1925, s 40(1). **Cooper v Critchley** [1955] **1** 520, CA.

    Memorandum as evidence of existence of contract—

      Effect of qualification 'subject to contract'—Effect of letter setting out terms of contract but not recognising existence of contract—Oral agreement for purchase of property—Letter from purchaser's solicitor referring to 'proposed sale ... subject to contract' and requesting draft contract—Letter from vendor's solicitors acknowledging letter and enclosing draft contract for approval—Whether letter enclosing draft contract a sufficient memorandum of contract—Law of Property Act 1925, s 40(1). **Tiverton Estates Ltd v Wearwell Ltd** [1974] **1** 209, CA.

    Omission of material term from memorandum—

      Balance of purchase money 'to be paid immediately on possession'—When possession to be given not stated—Verbal agreement that possession should be given only when vendor had found other accommodation—Insufficiency of memorandum—No enforceable contract—Law of Property Act 1925, s 40. **Johnson v Humphrey** [1946] **1** 460, Ch D.

      Purchaser seeking to enforce contract—Receipt for deposit signed by vendor—Receipt omitting term that purchaser would pay half defendant's costs of sale—Purchaser's submission to performance of missing term—Whether purchaser entitled to specific performance—Law of Property Act 1925, s 40(1). **Scott v Bradley** [1971] **1** 583, Ch D.

      Term exclusively for benefit of one party—Right to waive and proceed on agreement as evidenced by memorandum—Term specifying date of vacant possession—Law of Property Act 1925, s 40(1). **Hawkins v Price** [1947] **1** 689, Ch D.

      Term orally agreed—Letter of solicitors acting for both parties stating the material term and note of confirmation by client by telephone—Whether documents sufficient memorandum—Authority of solicitor—Law of Property Act 1925, s 40(1). **Gavaghan v Edwards** [1961] **2** 477, CA.

    Option to purchase—

      Contract for sale or other disposition of interest in land—Vendor granting purchaser option to purchase land—Agreement executed in two exchanged parts containing agreed terms and signed by both parties—Option exercised by purchaser giving notice in writing—Whether contract of sale formed by executed agreement or by exercise of option—Law of Property (Miscellaneous Provisions) Act 1989, s 2. **Spiro v Glencrown Properties Ltd** [1991] **1** 600, Ch D.

    Signature of party to be charged—

      Alteration to memorandum after signature—Memorandum not signed again following alteration—Alteration modifying terms of agreement—Modification agreed to by parties—Party to be charged not signing memorandum afresh or expressly reviving existing signature by appropriate words or gestures—Whether agreement enforceable—Law of Property Act 1925, s 40(1). **New Hart Builders Ltd v Brindley** [1975] **1** 1007, Ch D.

      Auctioneer's signature—Incorporation of conditions of sale in memorandum—Memorandum containing receipt for deposit—Memorandum signed by auctioneer and purchaser before payment of deposit—Authority of auctioneer to sign memorandum irrevocable—Law of Property Act 1925, s 40. **Phillips v Butler** [1945] **2** 258, Ch D.

      Sale by public auction—Agreement signed only by purchaser—Vendor's name and initials inserted at head of agreement by auctioneer before auction—Admissibility of evidence of intention of parties that document should be final written record of contract—Law of Property Act 1925, s 40(1). **Leeman v Stocks** [1951] **1** 1043, Ch D.

      Vendor's lawyer giving receipt for deposit received—Vendor's lawyer receiving deposit as stakeholder—Whether stakeholder having authority to sign memorandum on behalf of vendor—Statute of Frauds 1762 (Barbados), s 2. **Elias v George Sahely & Co (Barbados) Ltd** [1982] **3** 801, PC.

    Sufficient memorandum—

      Contents of memorandum—Material terms—Purchase price—Payment by instalments—Memorandum recording existence of agreement and amount of purchase price—Memorandum omitting term that payment of price to be by instalments—Whether material term of agreement—Whether sufficient memorandum—Law of Property Act 1925, s 40(1). **Tweddell v Henderson** [1975] **2** 1096, Ch D.

    Two documents—

      Letter by purchaser's solicitors—Terms of agreement 'subject to contract'—Amendment to make offer unconditional—Letter of acceptance by vendor's solicitors—Letter incorporated reference to letter by vendor's solicitors—Whether letters sufficient memorandum of agreement—Effect of 'subject to contract'—Law of Property Act 1925, s 40(1). **Griffiths v Young** [1970] **3** 601, CA.

SALE OF LAND (cont)—
  Memorandum of contract (cont)—
    Two documents (cont)—
      Oral agreement for sale of land—Letter from purchaser's lawyer containing terms of contract and enclosing deposit—Vendor's lawyer giving receipt for deposit—Receipt containing neither contractual terms nor reference to letter—Parol evidence admitted to explain transaction referred to in receipt and to identify letter as relating to transaction—Whether parol evidence rightly admitted—Whether letter and receipt together constituting sufficient note or memorandum evidencing oral contract—Statute of Frauds 1762 (Barbados), s 2. **Elias v George Sahely & Co (Barbados) Ltd** [1982] **3** 801, PC.
  Merger of contract in conveyance—
    Registered land—
      Transfer—No document which is conveyance—Whether doctrine of merger applicable to transfer of registered land. **Knight Sugar Co Ltd v Alberta Rly and Irrigation Co** [1938] **1** 266, PC.
  Misdescription—
    Freehold decontrolled properties—
      Small part controlled—Recovery of deposit—Increase of Rent and Mortgage Interest (Restrictions) Act 1920, s 12(2)(i)—Rent and Mortgage Interest Restrictions Act 1923, s 10. **Ridley v Oster** [1939] **1** 618, KBD.
    Rescission of contract. See Rescission of contract—Misdescription, *below*.
  Misrepresentation—
    Damages for breach of contract—
      Concealment of incumbrance—Fraud—Need to prove intention to defraud—Law of Property Act 1925, s 183(2). **District Bank Ltd v Luigi Grill Ltd** [1943] **1** 136, Ch D.
      Generally. See Damages for breach of contract—Misrepresentation, *above*.
    Fraudulent misrepresentation—
      Dimensions of garden. See **Misrepresentation** (Fraudulent misrepresentation—Dimensions of garden).
    Innocent misrepresentation. See **Misrepresentation** (Innocent misrepresentation—Sale of land).
    Negligent misrepresentation—
      Solicitor—Scope of duty of care. See **Solicitor** (Negligence—Duty of care—Negligent misrepresentation—Sale of land).
    Particulars of sale—
      Particulars stating that property connected to main drainage—Vendors' agents informing purchasers' solicitors that statement erroneous—Purchasers' solicitors failing to inform purchasers—Subsequent repetition of misrepresentation by vendors—Whether knowledge of purchasers' solicitors to be imputed to purchasers—Whether purchasers entitled to rely on misrepresentation. **Strover v Harrington** [1988] **1** 769, Ch D.
    Rescission of contract. See Rescission of contract—Misrepresentation, *below*.
  Mortgage—
    Discharge of mortgage. See Title—Discharge of mortgage, *below*.
    Generally. See **Mortgage** (Sale).
    Redemption—
      Order for sale. See **Mortgage** (Redemption—Order for sale).
  Mortgage. See **Mortgage** (Sale).
  Necessity for writing. See Contract—Form of contract—Necessity for writing, *above*.
  Negligence—
    Solicitor. See **Solicitor** (Negligence—Sale of land).
  Notice—
    Notice to complete. See Notice to complete, *below*.
    Tenant in occupation—
      Purchaser bound by equities tenant can enforce against vendor—Applicability to equity for rectification—No constructive notice of equity for rectification of tenancy agreement—Law of Property Act 1925, s 199(1)(ii)(a). **Smith v Jones** [1954] **2** 823, Ch D.
  Notice of actual state and condition of property—
    Building work—
      House in course of erection—Provision that purchaser takes written notice of state and condition applicable only in regard to obligation as to conveyance of land—Inapplicable to building work of new house—National Conditions of Sale (16th Edn), condition 12(3). **Hancock v BW Brazier (Anerley) Ltd** [1966] **2** 901, CA.
  Notice to complete—
    Failure of purchaser to complete on date fixed for completion—
      Power of vendor to resell after notice—Rights of vendor conditional on giving notice—Whether failure of purchaser to complete capable of amounting to fundamental breach entitling vendor to rescind contract—The Statutory Form of Conditions of Sale 1925 (S R & O 1925 No 779), condition 9. **Rightside Properties Ltd v Gray** [1974] **2** 1169, Ch D.
    Failure of vendor to complete on date fixed for completion—
      Vendor completing within reasonable time after service on him of notice to complete—Effect of notice to complete on contractual date for completion—Failure of third party to complete contract resulting in defendant being in breach of contract with plaintiff—Time not essence of contract between third party and defendant—Defendant liable in damages to plaintiff—Defendant claiming indemnity from third party—Whether third party in breach where contract completed in reasonable time of date of completion if time not essence—Whether service of notice to complete depriving defendant of any remedy accruing to him on original failure of third party to complete—Whether third party liable to indemnify defendant against claim by plaintiff—Law of Property Act 1925, s 41—Law Society's Conditions of Sale (1973 Revision), condition 19. **Raineri v Miles (Wiejski and anor, third parties)** [1980] **2** 145, HL.

SALE OF LAND (cont)—
  Notice to complete (cont)—
    Notice making time of the essence—
      Condition empowering either party to serve notice to complete on or after completion date—Notice to require completion 'in conformity with this condition'—Failure to complete within period specified in notice a breach of contract—Letter from purchasers to vendors—Request that letter be treated as 'Notice to complete the contract in accordance with its terms'—Vendors failing to complete within prescribed time—Terms of contract not making time of essence—Whether letter an effective notice to complete—National Conditions of Sale (18th Edn), condition 22. **Babacomp Ltd v Rightside Properties Ltd** [1974] **1** 142, CA.

      Notice to complete served by vendor—Purchaser willing and able to complete on date fixed—Vendor unable to do so—Vendor subsequently able to complete—Claim by vendor for specific performance—Right of purchaser to rescission and return of deposit—Law of Property Act 1925, s 49(2). **Finkielkraut v Monohan** [1949] **2** 234, Ch D.

    Order for specific performance of contract—
      Order for specific performance with consequential directions—Failure of party obtaining order to comply with order—Whether completion notice under contract served after order for specific performance valid—Whether order for specific performance superseding provisions of contract—Law Society's Conditions of Sale (1970 Edn), general condition 19(4). **Singh (Sudagar) v Nazeer** [1978] **3** 817, Ch D.

    Period of notice—
      Right of vendor to give to purchaser 'at least twenty-one days' notice'—Vendor giving notice to complete 'within 21 days'—Whether notice valid—The Statutory Form of Conditions of Sale 1925 (SR & O 1925 No 779), condition 9. **Rightside Properties Ltd v Gray** [1974] **2** 1169, Ch D.

    Provision for notice—
      Effect of provision on contractual obligation to complete on date fixed for completion or within reasonable time thereafter—Provision entitling plaintiffs to serve notice to complete in event of defendant's failure to complete on date fixed—Defective notice making time essence of contract—Defendant failing to complete within reasonable time of completion date—No valid notice served by plaintiffs—Whether defendant in breach of contract—Law Society's Conditions of Sale (1973 Revision), condition 19. **Woods v Mackenzie Hill Ltd** [1975] **2** 170, Ch D.

    Reasonable notice—
      Time not of the essence of contract—Failure of expected sub-sale—Notice to complete within 28 days—Whether reasonable in all the circumstances—National Conditions of Sale (16th Edn), cl 23(1). **Barr's Contract, Re** [1956] **2** 853, Ch D.

      Time not of the essence of the contract—Notice making time of the essence—Contract specifying date for performance of obligation to deliver abstract of title—Failure to deliver abstract by specified date—Purchaser serving notice making time of the essence and giving vendor seven days to perform obligation—Whether time for performance reasonable. **Behzadi v Shaftesbury Hotels Ltd** [1991] **2** 477, CA.

    Term that party to whom notice given shall complete within specified period—
      Purchaser giving notice to vendor—Purchaser failing to complete within prescribed period—Whether notice binding on purchaser—Whether vendor entitled to rescind contract—National Conditions of Sale (18th Edn), condition 22. **Quadrangle Development and Construction Co Ltd v Jenner** [1974] **1** 729, CA.

    Validity—
      Material misdescription of area in conditions of sale—Whether vendors ready and willing to fulfil own outstanding obligations—Whether notice to complete valid—National Conditions of Sale (20th edn), condition 22. **Bechal v Kitsford Holdings Ltd** [1988] **3** 985, Ch D.

      Notice requiring completion in conformity with conditions in contract—Contract requiring completion within 15 working days of service of notice to complete—Notice going on to state consequences of failure to complete within 28 days of service—Whether notice ambiguous—Whether notice to complete valid—Law Society's General Conditions of Sale (1984 revision), condition 23. **Delta Vale Properties Ltd v Mills** [1990] **2** 176, CA.

      Party giving notice ready and willing to fulfil own outstanding obligations—Dispute as to terms of contract—Vendors claiming contracts varied to increase price—Vendors giving notice on basis of increased price—Court subsequently finding no price increase—Whether notice relating to contracts between parties—Whether vendors ready and willing to fulfil own outstanding obligations—Whether notice valid—RICS Common Auction Conditions (2002), condition 7. **Dhand v Oakglade Investments Ltd** [2013] **1 Comm** 22, CA.

      Party giving notice ready and willing to fulfil own outstanding obligations—Notice by vendor—Sale of freehold property—Duty of vendor to make available to purchaser particulars of leases—Purchaser's solicitors discovering existence of undisclosed lease on final date stipulated by notice to complete—Solicitor refusing to complete without further instructions—Contract providing that omissions etc not having effect of annulling sale or entitling party to compensation unless materially affecting value of property—Purchaser subsequently agreeing to complete at agreed price—Vendor purporting to call off sale and forfeit deposit—Whether entitled to give notice to complete—National Conditions of Sale (18th Edn), conditions 17, 18, 22. **Pagebar Properties Ltd v Derby Investment Holdings Ltd** [1973] **1** 65, Ch D.

      Party giving notice ready and willing to fulfil own outstanding obligations—Notice by vendor—Vendor not deducing title on date set for completion—Vendor eventually deducing title on day notice to complete issued—Contract requiring ten working days' notice to complete—Vendor giving one working day to complete from date of notice—Purchaser not in breach—Purchaser not complying with notice—Vendor rescinding contract—Whether notice to complete ineffective under contract and general law—Whether vendor in breach of contract—Standard Conditions of Sale (2nd edn), condition 6.8. **Country and Metropolitan Homes Surrey Ltd v Topclaim Ltd** [1997] **1** 254, Ch D.

SALE OF LAND (cont)—
  Notice to complete (cont)—
    Validity (cont)—
      Party giving notice ready and willing to fulfil own outstanding obligations—Purchaser failing to complete on due date—Purchaser's solicitor requesting details of charges on land—Vendor's notice to complete accompanied by letter that details of charges would be sent later—Vendor subsequently purporting to rescind contract and forfeit deposit—Whether vendor's solicitor prepared at time of notice to undertake charges would be discharged—Whether vendor willing and ready to complete at time of notice—Whether notice valid—Law Society's Conditions of Sale (1970 Edn), condition 19. **Cole v Rose** [1978] 3 1121, Ch D.
    Waiver—
      Effect of negotiations by vendor with third party—Vendor serving notice on purchaser making time essence of contract—Before completion date purchaser negotiating with third party to take over contract—Purchaser failing to complete in time—Third party negotiating direct with vendor and obtaining two extensions of time—Whether purchaser entitled to benefit of extensions given to third party—Whether giving extensions of time to third party amounted to waiver by vendor of condition that time of the essence for purchaser. **Buckland v Farmer & Moody (a firm)** [1978] 3 929, CA.
  Offer and acceptance—
    Letter by proposed vendor—
      Whether constituting an offer. See **Contract** (Offer and acceptance—Offer—Sale of land—Letter by proposed vendor).
    Offer. See **Contract** (Offer and acceptance—Offer—Sale of land).
    Tender. See Acceptance of tender, above.
  Option to purchase land or interest therein—
    Exercise of option—
      Notice in writing to vendor—Service by post. See **Contract** (Offer and acceptance—Acceptance—Acceptance by post—Mode of acceptance prescribed—Notice in writing to offeror—Option—Option to purchase freehold property—Notice).
      Notice in writing to vendor—Whether notice a contract for sale of interest in land. See Memorandum of contract—Option to purchase—Contract for sale or other disposition of interest in land, above.
    Generally. See **Option** (Option to purchase).
    Specific performance. See **Specific performance** (Option to purchase land).
    Testamentary option. See **Will** (Option—Option to purchase realty).
  Outgoings—
    Rights of parties pending completion—
      War damage contribution—Contract of sale providing for payment by instalments and conveyance when instalments fully paid—Incidence of contribution. **Watford Corp and Ware, Re a contract between** [1943] 1 54, Ch D.
  Parcels. See Conveyance—Parcels, above.
  Part performance of contract—
    Acts constituting part performance—
      Acts as evidence of existence of contract—Acts as evidence of nature of contract—Payment of sum of money—Circumstances in which payment capable of constituting part performance—Compromise of proceedings—Husband and wife—Agreement to variation of maintenance order—Husband to pay lump sum in respect of arrears—Balance of arrears to be discharged—Wife to transfer interest in matrimonial home for agreed sum—Agreement approved by justices—Sum in respect of arrears paid by husband—Form of transfer prepared by husband's solicitors and sent to wife for signature—Whether sufficient acts of part performance—Law of Property Act 1925, s 40. **Steadman v Steadman** [1974] 2 977, HL.
      Acts must be referable to some contract and consistent with contract alleged—Acts need not be referable only to contract alleged. **Kingswood Estate Co Ltd v Anderson** [1962] 3 593, CA.
      Expenditure of money as part performance—Expenditure on alterations—Mental weakness of vendor—Capacity to contract—Onus of proof—Law of Property Act 1925, s 40. **Broughton v Snook** [1938] 1 411, Ch D.
    Generally. See **Contract** (Part performance).
  Planning permission. See Condition—Planning permission to be obtained, above.
  Possession before completion—
    Conveyance on completion of payment of instalments—
      Instalments based on outgoings—Whether instalments 'rent'—Purchaser let into possession as tenant at will—Default in payment of instalments—Right of vendor to possession. **Dunthorne & Shore v Wiggins** [1943] 2 678, CA.
    Interest on unpaid purchase money. See Interest on unpaid purchase money—Possession before completion, above.
  Power of attorney—
    General power. See **Power of attorney** (General power—Sale of land).
  Pre-emption—
    Right of first refusal—
      Implication of prohibition of making gift to defeat right. See **Contract** (Implied term—First refusal—Right of pre-emption—Gift of land, the subject of the right of pre-emption, made subsequently by grantor of right).
  Preliminary enquiries—
    Tenancies within Rent Restrictions Acts—
      Solicitor's duty in relation to ascertaining recoverable rents—Rents being paid—Duty to ascertain whether rents being paid recoverable rents. **Goody v Baring** [1956] 2 11, Ch D.
  Preparation of documents—
    Unqualified person. See **Solicitor** (Unqualified person—Preparation of documents etc).
  Price—
    Cost of making up roads—
      Price to include 'cost of roads, sewers and other services'—Cost of making up roads to satisfaction of local authority not included—Public Health Act 1875, s 150. **Smith v Jones** [1952] 2 907, QBD.

SALE OF LAND (cont)—
Proceeds—
    Contract to divide. *See* **Land charge** (General equitable charge—Charge on land—Contract to divide proceeds of sale of land).
Promissory note—
    Conditional contract. *See* Contract—Conditional contract—Promissory note, *above.*
Protected tenancy—
    Possession—
        Order for possession—Protected tenant signing contract for sale providing for purchaser to be given vacant possession—Tenant refusing to give up possession—Whether purchaser entitled to order for possession—Rent Act 1977, s 98(1). **Appleton v Aspin** [1988] **1** 904, CA.
Purchase price—
    Income tax—
        Capital or income receipt. *See* **Income tax** (Capital or income receipts—Sale of property—Land).
Purchaser—
    Fiduciary duty to vendor—
        Purchaser assuming position of self-appointed agent of vendor—Duty to disclose acts done as vendor's purported agent—Duty to account for profit made in course of purported agency in event of non—disclosure—Agreement to purchase property for sum which was less than sum obtainable by vendor if planning permission to develop property were granted—Before exchange of contracts purchaser making planning application for development of part of property—Application made without vendor's knowledge or authority—Application in name of vendor and signed by purchaser's employee as 'agent' for vendor—Certificate under town and country planning legislation accompanying application in form appropriate to an application by vendor as owner of land—Vendor completing sale without disclosure by purchaser that planning application made and granted—Whether purchaser liable to account to vendor for profit accruing as result of planning permission—Whether fiduciary relationship existing between purchaser and vendor at date of application for planning permission. **English v Dedham Vale Properties Ltd** [1978] **1** 382, Ch D.
    Lien. *See* Purchaser's lien, *below.*
    Purchaser in possession—
        Order that purchaser relinquish possession—Acceptance of title—Order to make payment into court—Whether defendant should have option to go out of possession. **Maskell v Ivory** [1970] **1** 488, Ch D.
        Order that purchaser relinquish possession—Substantial proportion of purchase price paid—Sale including goodwill and stock-in-trade—Contract specifically regulating rights of parties—Whether vendor entitled to order that purchaser pay outstanding balance into court or relinquish possession of property—National Conditions of Sale (20th edn), condition 8. **Attfield v D J Plant Hire and General Contractors Co Ltd** [1986] **3** 273, Ch D.
Purchaser's lien—
    Costs of suit—
        Deposit paid to stakeholder—Contract broken off otherwise than by default of purchaser—Action to compel performance of contract—Whether purchaser's lien covering costs of suit. **Combe v Swaythling** [1947] **1** 838, Ch D.
    Deposit—
        Entry by purchaser into possession pending completion—Deposit paid on purchase price—Subsequent mortgage of property by vendor—Claim for possession by mortgagee—Contract unenforceable against mortgagee—Rights of purchaser—Whether entitled to lien in respect of deposit. **Lee-Parker v Izzet** [1971] **3** 1099, Ch D.
Recovery of deposit—
    Forfeiture. *See* Deposit—Forfeiture—Purchaser's failure to complete, *above.*
    Requisitioning of property—
        Service of requisition notice—Negotiation by vendor for withdrawal of notice on ground of hardship—Statement by vendor to requisitioning authority that he intended to reside on the property—Whether requisition notice effective for the purpose of exercising power to enter into possession of property—Repudiation of contract by purchaser—Whether purchaser entitled to recover deposit—Law of Property Act 1925, s 49(2)—Defence (General) Regulations 1939, reg 51. **Macara (James) Ltd v Barclay** [1944] **2** 589, CA.
Registered land—
    Constructive trust. *See* **Trust and trustee** (Constructive trust—Sale of registered land).
Rentcharge—
    Rule against perpetuities. *See* **Rule against perpetuities** (Remoteness—Rentcharge).
Repudiation of contract—
    Damages—
        Damages in substitution for specific performance. *See* Damages for breach of contract—Damages in substitution for specific performance—Damages at common law for repudiation of contract, *above.*
    Deposit, failure to pay. *See* Deposit—Payment—Failure to pay deposit on time under contract, *above.*
    Effect—
        Other party in default—Failure to complete on date fixed for completion—Time not of essence—Other party not in unreasonable delay—Need for other party to prove ability to complete as condition of claim for damages for wrongful repudiation—Failure by purchaser to complete on date fixed—Vendor purporting to terminate contract—Purchaser not in unreasonable delay—Right of purchaser to treat purported termination as wrongful repudiation—Whether purchaser required to fulfil obligations under contract following repudiation in order to bring action based on repudiation—Whether purchaser required to prove he is ready willing and able to complete—Law of Property Act 1925, s 41. **Rightside Properties Ltd v Gray** [1974] **2** 1169, Ch D.
    Lack of title. *See* Title—Lack of title—Repudiation by purchaser, *below.*
    Payment of purchase price by instalments—
        Conveyance of portion of land as each instalment paid—Failure to pay instalments. **Thorpe v Fasey** [1949] **2** 393, Ch D.

SALE OF LAND (cont)—
  Repudiation of contract (cont)—
    Repudiation by vendor—
      Damages. *See* Damages for breach of contract—Repudiation by vendor, *above.*
      Rescission—
        Attempted rescission amounting to repudiation—Purchaser wishing to get out of contract with vendor for sale of land—Purchaser purporting to rely on term of contract to rescind—Judge holding that purchaser not entitled to rescind—Whether purchaser's erroneous attempt to rescind amounting to repudiation entitling vendor to damages. **Woodar Investment Development Ltd v Wimpey Construction UK Ltd** [1980] **1** 571, HL.
        Purchaser failing to complete on contractual completion date—Vendor serving notices to complete—Vendor sending notices of rescission before final date for completion under notices to complete—Purchasers treating notices of rescission as repudiatory breach and accepting that breach—Whether premature service of notices of rescission by vendor amounting to repudiatory breach of contracts of sale. **Eminence Property Developments Ltd v Heaney** [2011] **2 Comm** 223, CA.
  Requisitioned land—
    Compensation in respect of the taking possession of land—
      Land derequisitioned after date of contract but before conveyance—Whether compensation comprehended in sale—Compensation (Defence) Act 1939, s 2(1)(b)(3). **Hamilton-Snowball's Conveyance, Re** [1958] **2** 319, Ch D.
  Requisitions on title—
    Duty of purchaser's solicitor—
      Complete enquiries before contract—Duty of solicitor to deliver requisitions even though enquiries so complete that only necessary to ask whether answers still complete and accurate. **Goody v Baring** [1956] **2** 11, Ch D.
    Time limit—
      Abstract of title imperfect—Effect—Duty of purchaser—Abstract deficient only in unimportant respects—Duty to raise requisitions so far as possible on information supplied within prescribed time limit—Right to raise further requisitions when new material received—Purchaser not entitled to delay making any requisitions until abstract complete—Law Society's General Conditions of Sale (1973 Revision), condition 10(1)(3). **Ogilvy v Hope-Davies** [1976] **1** 683, Ch D.
  Rescission—
    Fraudulent misrepresentation. *See* **Misrepresentation** (Fraudulent misrepresentation—Dimensions of garden).
    Generally. *See* Rescission of contract, *below.*
    Innocent misrepresentation. *See* **Misrepresentation** (Innocent misrepresentation—Sale of land).
  Rescission of contract—
    Attempted rescission amounting to repudiation. *See* Repudiation of contract—Rescission, *above.*
    Bankruptcy—
      Purchaser committing act of bankruptcy before completion—Right of vendor to rescind. **Jennings' (a bankrupt) Trustee v King** [1952] **2** 608, Ch D.
    Completion statement—
      Completion statement received two hours before notice to complete due to expire—Completion statement failing to specify correct purchase price—No tender of purchase price by purchaser—Whether purchaser in breach of contract. **Carne v Debono** [1988] **3** 485, CA.
    Contract for sale of leasehold interest—
      Purchaser entitled to rescind if reversioner's licence to assign 'cannot be obtained'—Vendor unable to obtain licence because of purchaser's fault—Vendor purporting to rescind contract—Whether right to rescind arising on contractual date for completion—Whether question whether licence 'cannot be obtained' a question of fact—National Conditions of Sale (20th edn), condition 11(5). **Practice Direction** [1987] **1** 107, Companies Ct.
    Damages—
      Decree of specific performance—Failure of purchaser to complete—Forfeiture of deposit—Election by vendor to rescind contract—Right to recover damages or mesne profits as damages barred by election—Occupation rent not payable by purchaser. **Barber v Wolfe** [1945] **1** 399, Ch D.
    Defect in title—
      Common mistake—Misrepresentation—Contract for purchase of development land incorporating National Conditions of Sale—Vendor disclosing incumbrances of which it had knowledge or means of knowledge—Discovery of undisclosed sewer buried under land—Purchaser claiming rescission for mistake and misrepresentation—Whether contract precluding rescission for mistake—Whether misrepresentation by vendor—Whether damages to be awarded in lieu of rescission—Misrepresentation Act 1967, s 2(2)—National Conditions of Sale (20th edn), conditions 14, 17(e). **Sindall (William) plc v Cambridgeshire CC** [1994] **3** 932, CA.
      Contingent liability to estate duty—Right of purchaser to require vendor to obtain policy of indemnity—Gift of property to vendor one year before contract of sale—Donor still living—Right of purchaser to rescind contract on failure of vendor to obtain policy of indemnity. **Manning v Turner** [1956] **3** 641, Ch Ct County Palatine of Lanca.
      Election whether to affirm or rescind contract. *See* **Contract** (Breach—Election whether to affirm or rescind—Contract for sale of leasehold property—Vendor having defective title).
    Effect of order for specific performance—
      Purchaser failing to complete in time—Vendor choosing to pursue remedy of specific performance—Whether contract rescinded ab initio. **Johnson v Agnew** [1979] **1** 883, HL.
    Estoppel—
      Failure of vendor to answer requisition—Requisition on restrictive covenant on sale of land by open contract—No notice by purchaser fixing time within which to answer requisition—Notice to complete served by vendor—Rescission by purchaser—Issue of vendor and purchaser summons by purchaser—Whether purchaser estopped from alleging rescission of contract. **Stone and Saville's Contract, Re** [1963] **1** 353, CA.

SALE OF LAND (cont)—

Rescission of contract (cont)—

Forfeiture of right to rescind by recklessness—

Condition for vendor's rescinding for objection with which unable to comply—Mortgaged property sold free from incumbrances—No inquiry made before contract whether mortgagees would join in conveyance—Refusal of mortgagees to join in conveyance—Whether vendor lost right to rescind by reason of recklessness in signing contract—Law Society's Conditions of Sale (1953), cl 10(1). **Baines v Tweddle** [1959] **2** 724, CA.

Innocent misrepresentation. *See* **Misrepresentation** (Innocent misrepresentation—Sale of land).

Misdescription—

Size of site area erroneously stated—Law Society's Conditions of Sale 1953, condition 35. **Watson v Burton** [1956] **3** 929, Ch D.

Misrepresentation—

Assignee's right to rescind—A induced to enter into contract by vendor's misrepresentation—Benefit of contract given by A to B—Completion by conveyance to B—Whether B can rescind. **Gross v Lewis Hillman Ltd** [1969] **3** 1476, CA.

Fraudulent. *See* **Misrepresentation** (Fraudulent misrepresentation—Dimensions of garden).

Innocent. *See* **Misrepresentation** (Innocent misrepresentation—Sale of land).

Notice—

Validity—National Conditions of Sale (17th Edn) condition 10(5)—Whether notice of rescission could be given validly without first giving notice under condition 8(6). **Lipmans Wallpaper Ltd v Mason & Hodghton Ltd** [1968] **1** 1123, Ch D.

Purchaser entitled to rescind contract if property destroyed by enemy action 'prior to the date fixed for completion'—

Completion date 27th November—Purchase money paid to vendor and purchaser let into possession of part of property on 23rd November—Property destroyed by enemy action on 25th November—Whether purchaser entitled to rescind contract. **Killner v France** [1946] **2** 83, KBD.

Repudiation. *See* Repudiation of contract—Rescission, *above*.

Rescission—

Vendor making time essence of contract—Vendor 'rescinding contract on purchaser's failure to complete'—Annullment ab initio or acceptance of breach as repudiation discharging contract—Vendor rescinding contract while reserving right to cover 'full losses'—Whether rescission annulled contract ab initio—Whether vendor lost right to damages. **Buckland v Farmer & Moody (a firm)** [1978] **3** 929, CA.

Unreasonable exercise of right to rescind—

Condition for vendor's rescinding for requisition with which unable to comply—Inability of vendor to comply with requisition—Vendor had previously accepted title on information offered to purchaser—Defect in title not disclosed to purchaser before contract—Whether there was recklessness in entering into contract—Whether exercise of power of rescission arbitrary or capricious or unreasonable. **Selkirk v Romar Investments Ltd** [1963] **3** 994, PC.

Waiver of right of rescission—

Action for specific performance still on file when notice of rescission served—Validity of notice. **Public Trustee v Pearlberg** [1940] **2** 270, CA.

Vendor and purchaser summons—Whether issue of summons constituting a waiver of rescission. **Stone and Saville's Contract, Re** [1963] **1** 353, CA.

Restrictive covenant affecting land. *See* **Restrictive covenant affecting land**.

Right of re-entry. *See* Leasehold interest—Right of re-entry, *above*.

Rule against perpetuities. *See* **Rule against perpetuities** (Vendor and purchaser—Option to purchase land).

Sale by court—

Administration of estate. *See* **Administration of estates** (Practice—Sale by court).

Auctioneer—

Commission—Sale by court in administering estate—Auctioneer's commission—Sale at more than £25,000. **Wolfe (decd), Re** [1952] **2** 545, Ch D.

Remuneration. **Practice Direction** [1957] **3** 540, Ch D; [1958] **3** 534, Ch D.

Estate agents and auctioneers—

Scale of remuneration—Sales pursuant to orders of Chancery Division, Family Division, Court of Protection or divorce county courts. **Practice Direction** [1983] **1** 160, Fam D.

Resale on setting aside executor's purchase of land forming part of estate—

Form of relief. **Holder v Holder** [1968] **1** 665, CA.

Sale of registered land held on trust for sale—

Lodging of caution by person interested in proceeds of sale—

Locus standi of cautioner. *See* **Land registration** (Caution against dealings—Lodging of caution by person interested in land—Sale of land held on trust for sale by registered proprietor).

Sale to company—

Vendor's lien—

Whether registrable as charge. *See* **Company** (Charge—Registration—Unpaid vendor's lien—Property sold to company).

Search—

Land charge—

Conclusiveness of official certificate of search. *See* **Land charge** (Search—Official certificate of search—Conclusiveness).

Settled land—

Sale to tenant for life. *See* **Settlement** (Powers of tenant for life—Sale of settled land to tenant for life).

Solicitor—

Acting for vendor and purchaser—

Danger of so acting. *See* **Solicitor** (Sale of land—Acting for vendor and purchaser—Danger of so acting).

Exchange of contracts. *See* Exchange of contracts—Same solicitor acting for both parties, *above*.

Costs. *See* **Costs** (Taxation—Solicitor—Non-contentious business—Fair and reasonable sum in circumstances—Factors to be considered—Conveyancing).

Generally. *See* **Solicitor** (Sale of land).

Negligence—

Damages. *See* **Solicitor** (Negligence—Damages—Sale of land).

SALE OF LAND (cont)—
  Solicitor (cont)—
    Negligence (cont)—
      Generally. *See* **Solicitor** (Negligence—Sale of land).
    Specific performance—
      Damages in addition to specific performance. *See* Damages for breach of contract—Damages in addition to specific performance and abatement of purchase price, *above*.
      Damages in substitution for specific performance. *See* Damages for breach of contract—Damages in substitution for specific performance, *above*.
      Doubtful title. *See* **Specific performance** (Title—Doubtful title).
      Generally. *See* **Specific performance** (Sale of land).
      Notice to complete—
        Validity of completion notice under contract served after order for specific performance obtained. *See* Notice to complete—Order for specific performance of contract—Order for specific performance with consequential directions—Failure of party obtaining order to comply with order—Whether completion notice under contract served after order for specific performance valid, *above*.
      Rescission of contract—
        Damages. *See* Rescission of contract—Damages—Decree of specific performance, *above*.
  Stakeholder—
    Deposit paid to stakeholder—
      Payment over of deposit on instructions of vendor and purchaser—Solicitor stakeholder—Vendor owing fees to solicitor—Vendor assigning interest in land to plaintiff—Plaintiff and purchaser requiring solicitor to transfer deposit to new stakeholder—Whether solicitor holding deposit in contract or quasi-contract or as trustee—Whether solicitor required to comply with request—Whether solicitor entitled to retain amount of fees owing. **Rockeagle Ltd v Alsop Wilkinson (a firm)** [1991] 4 659, CA.
      Purchaser's lien—Costs of suit. *See* Purchaser's lien—Costs of suit—Deposit paid to stakeholder, *above*.
  Stamp duty—
    Conveyance on sale. *See* **Stamp duty** (Conveyance on sale).
    Inadequate consideration. *See* **Stamp duty** (Voluntary disposition inter vivos—Inadequate consideration—Conveyance or transfer operating as a voluntary disposition).
  Subject to contract—
    Exchange of contracts. *See* Exchange of contracts—Agreement subject to contract, *above*.
    Memorandum of contract. *See* Memorandum of contract—Circumstances in which memorandum must evidence existence of contract—Effect of qualification 'subject to contract', *above*.
  Subrogation—
    Vendor's lien. *See* Vendor's lien—Subrogation, *below*.
  Telephonic exchange of contracts. *See* Exchange of contracts—Authority of solicitor—Exchange by telephone, *above*.
  Tender—
    Acceptance. *See* Acceptance of tender, *above*.
  Time for performance—
    Condition. *See* Condition—Time for performance, *above*.
  Time of the essence. *See* Notice to complete—Notice making time of the essence, *above*.
  Title—
    Abstract—
      Deed over 30 years old—Execution under power of attorney—Abstract of power of attorney. **Copelin's Contract, Re** [1937] 4 447, Ch D.
    Defect—
      Assent used where conveyance required—Assent executed as a deed—Effectiveness to convey legal estate—Whether purchaser entitled to have formal defect cured—Law of Property Act 1925, ss 52(1), 63(1), 205(i)(ii). **Stirrup's Contract, Re** [1961] 1 805, Ch D.
      Contingent liability to estate duty on death of living donor of property within five years of gift—Purchaser's right to insurance policy of indemnity—Right to rescind contract on vendor's failure to obtain policy. **Manning v Turner** [1956] 3 641, Ch Ct County Palatine of Lanca.
      Disclosure of defect—Local land charge—Notice of charge—Purchaser deemed to have made searches and inquiries—Contract at auction for purchase of freehold property—Property subject to local land charge—Contract containing condition that purchaser deemed to have searched local land charges register—Purchaser failing to make search and unaware of local land charge—Vendor serving notice to complete—Whether vendor able to show good title—Whether vendor required to make full and frank disclosure of incumbrance—Whether purchaser deemed to have notice of land charge—Law of Property Act 1925, s 198(1)—National Conditions of Sale (20th edn), condition 11. **Rignall Developments Ltd v Halil** [1987] 3 170, Ch D.
      Rescission of contract. *See* Rescission of contract—Defect in title, *above*.
      Vendor to obtain release of restrictive covenant against building—Local authority passing town planning resolution whereby land to be left as open space—Whether condition still binding on vendors. **Cleadon Trust Ltd v Davis** [1940] 3 648, CA.
      Vendor unable to make good title—Estate agent's entitlement to commission. *See* **Estate agent** (Commission—Agent instructed to introduce purchaser for property at specified price or obtain offer—Inability of vendor to make title after agreement for sale executed).
    Discharge of mortgage—
      Discharge of charge by way of legal mortgage by receipt indorsed—Receipt dated two days after conveyance to vendor's predecessor in title—Notice served by vendor requiring completion within twenty-eight days—Time made the essence of the contract by condition of sale—Whether receipt indorsed operating as a transfer—Whether receipt operating as an estoppel against charge—Whether vendor able and ready to complete—National Conditions of Sale (17th Edn), condition 22—Law of Property Act 1925, ss 87, 115(3). **Cumberland Court (Brighton) Ltd v Taylor** [1963] 2 536, Ch D.
    Doubtful title—
      Whether to be forced on purchaser. *See* **Specific performance** (Title—Doubtful title).

SALE OF LAND (cont)—
Title (cont)—
Equitable owner—
Vendor having firm contract to purchase property—Right to describe himself as owner—Vendor unable to complete because of rescission of contract to purchase by original vendors—Claim by proposed purchaser for damages for fraud—Right of person having firm contract to purchase to offer property for sale as owner. **Gordon Hill Trust Ltd v Segall** [1941] **2** 379, CA.
Exercise of power a link in title—
Exercise of power unchallenged for 21 years—No assumption of validity. **Holmes (W & R) and Cosmopolitan Press Ltd's Contract, Re** [1943] **2** 716, Ch D.
Insufficiently stamped deed—
Statutory declaration—Declaration contradicting prima facie title—Deed not shown by abstract to be stamped—Production by vendor. **Spollon and Long's Contract, Re** [1936] **2** 711, Ch D.
Investigation—
Assent—Assent not in accordance with title disclosed—Conclusiveness—'Sufficient evidence'—Administration of Estates Act 1925, s 36(7). **Duce and Boots Cash Chemists (Southern) Ltd's Contract, Re** [1937] **3** 788, Ch D.
Lack of title—
Repudiation by purchaser—Vendor having leasehold title—Ability to compel assurance by freeholder—Sale of freehold land and business assets—Vendor only leaseholder—Whether purchaser entitled to repudiate on ground of lack of title. **Elliott v Pierson** [1948] **1** 939, Ch D.
Leasehold—
Disclosure—Contractual provision that vendor's title accepted—Vendor's duty to disclose any defect of which he knows or ought to know—Vendor's sub-underlease granted in breach of covenant in underlease which was thus liable to forfeiture—Underlease not inspected by vendor's solicitor on occasion of sub-letting to vendor—Whether purchaser entitled to rescission. **Becker v Partridge** [1966] **2** 266, CA.
Requisitions on title. *See* Requisitions on title, *above*.
Underlease—
Headlease disclaimed on bankruptcy of lessee—Sale of underlease—Whether underlease properly described as such after disclaimer. **Cottrell and Thompson's Contract, Re** [1943] **1** 169, Ch D.
Vendor's inability to show good title—
Damages for breach of contract. *See* Damages for breach of contract—Vendor's inability to show good title, *above*.
Vendor's obligation to prove—
Adverse claim after contract of sale but before completion—Refusal by purchaser to complete—Service by vendor of completion notice—Validity—Duty of vendor to clear title—Vendor not 'able to complete' until title cleared—National Conditions of Sale (17th Edn), condition 22. **Horton v Kurzke** [1971] **2** 577, Ch D.
Presumption of fact affecting title—When court entitled to make presumption—Will of testator dying in 1911 giving son option to purchase property—Deed of family arrangement made in 1912 reciting contract for sale of property to son at stated sum—Further deed made in 1930 reciting that contract for sale not yet performed and performance suspended by consent of all interested parties—Recital not making clear whether suspension to be indefinite—Contract not remaining in existence—Son dying in 1942 without completing contract—Trustees in 1973 entering into contract for sale of property to purchasers—Whether trustees showing good title—Whether court entitled to presume abandonment of 1912 contract. **MEPC Ltd v Christian-Edwards** [1978] **1** 295, Ch D; [1979] **3** 752, HL.
Trading for tax purposes. *See* **Income tax** (Trade—Adventure in nature of trade—Isolated transaction—Sale of land).
Trading transaction—
Income tax. *See* **Income tax** (Profits—Trading receipts—Land—Disposal).
Trust for sale—
Generally. *See* **Trust and trustee** (Trust for sale).
Matrimonial home. *See* **Husband and wife** (Matrimonial home—Sale under trust for sale).
Trustee—
Vendor as trustee for purchaser. *See* Vendor—Fiduciary duty to purchaser, *below*.
Uncertainty of contract—
Special condition—
Sale 'subject to the purchaser obtaining a satisfactory mortgage'—Effect of condition making vendor's and purchaser's obligations conditional on obtaining satisfactory mortgage—Condition void for uncertainty—Amount of loan and terms of repayment left at large. **Lee-Parker v Izzet (No 2)** [1972] **2** 800, Ch D.
Vacant possession—
Condition of contract. *See* Condition—Condition to which effect not given by conveyance but capable of taking effect after completion—Condition requiring vacant possession on completion, *above*.
Position of parties pending completion—
Maintenance of property—State and condition of property sold—Breach of undertaking to deliver vacant possession. **Cumberland Consolidated Holdings Ltd v Ireland** [1946] **1** 284, CA.
Property vacant when inspected by purchaser—
Sold with vacant possession—No reference in particulars to tenancies—Whether vacant possession a condition of the contract—Notice of requisition served pending completion—Keys handed to requisitioning authority before date for completion. **Cook v Taylor** [1942] **2** 85, Ch D.
Specific performance. *See* **Specific performance** (Sale of land—Sale with vacant possession).
Vacant possession by certain date—
Failure by vendor to give possession—Purchaser's right to recover stamp duty and legal costs of purchase of second house. **Beard v Porter** [1947] **2** 407, CA.
Vendor—
Fiduciary duty to purchaser—
Vendor as trustee for purchaser—Trust of property pending completion—Sale of property by vendor to third party before completion—Whether vendor holding proceeds of sale on trust for original purchaser. **Lake v Bayliss** [1974] **2** 1114, Ch D.

SALE OF LAND (cont)—
 Vendor (cont)—
  Fiduciary duty to purchaser (cont)—
   Vendor as trustee for purchaser—Whether scope of fiduciary duty extending beyond land the subject of sale. **Englewood Properties Ltd v Patel** [2005] **3** 307, Ch D.
   Lien. *See* Vendor's lien, *below.*
   Obligation to prove title. *See* Title—Vendor's obligation to prove, *above.*
 Vendor and purchaser summons—
  Lists. *See* **Practice** (Chancery Division—Chambers proceedings—Adjournment to judge—Vendor and purchaser summons—Lists).
 Vendor's lien—
  Agreement by vendor to leave part of purchase price on mortgage—
   Equitable charge created forthwith—Exclusion of vendor's lien—Sequence of execution of conveyance and mortgage. **Cityfield Properties Ltd, Re** [1968] **3** 625, CA.
  Exclusion—
   Contractual right of resale in case of non-completion—Whether lien excluded. **Birmingham (decd), Re** [1958] **2** 397, Ch D.
  Property sold to company—
   Registration of lien. *See* **Company** (Charge—Registration—Unpaid vendor's lien—Property sold to company).
  Registered land—
   Overriding interest. *See* **Land registration** (Overriding interest—Rights of person in actual occupation of land—Unpaid vendor's lien).
  Subrogation—
   Circumstances in which doctrine applicable. *See* **Subrogation** (Circumstances in which doctrine applicable).
   Creditor providing purchase money—Charge to secure loan—Charge constituting abandonment of vendor's lien—Charge invalid—Charge valid at inception—Subsequent invalidity—Effect—Creditor advancing sum to purchaser—Creditor obtaining first legal charge on property purchased as condition of loan—Purchaser limited company—Charge becoming void against liquidator and other creditors of company for want of registration within prescribed period—Whether creditor entitled by subrogation to vendor's lien—Companies Act 1948, s 95. **Burston Finance Ltd v Speirway Ltd** [1974] **3** 735, Ch D.
   Creditor providing purchase money—Contrary intention excluding doctrine of subrogation—Unsecured loan—Creditor taking shares in company and providing loan to company for purchase of property—Loan used by company to buy property—Company in liquidation—Whether creditor entitled by subrogation to vendor's lien. **Paul v Speirway Ltd (in liq)** [1976] **2** 587, Ch D.
   Mortgagee's lien—Mortgage unenforceable—Money borrowed used in purchase of security for loan—Subrogation of vendor's lien—Moneylenders Act 1927, s 6. **Congresbury Motors Ltd v Anglo-Belge Finance Co Ltd** [1970] **3** 385, CA.
   Mortgage—Provision of purchase money by mortgagee—Execution of valid charge in favour of mortgagee—Remortgage of property to second mortgagee—Sum advanced by second mortgagee used to discharge debt to first mortgagee—Second mortgage invalid and unenforceable—Whether vendor's lien extinguished on execution of valid charge in favour of first mortgagee—Whether second mortgagee entitled by subrogation to vendor's lien. **Coptic Ltd v Bailey** [1972] **1** 1242, Ch D.
 Waiver of condition. *See* Condition—Waiver of condition, *above.*
 Waiver of notice to complete. *See* Notice to complete—Waiver, *above.*
 Waiver of right of rescission. *See* Rescission of contract—Waiver of right of rescission, *above.*
 Warranty—
  Damages for breach. *See* Damages for breach of contract—Warranty, *above.*
  Implied warranty—
   House completed at date of sale. *See* House completed at date of sale—Implied warranty, *above.*
   House in course of erection—Warranty as to workmanship etc. *See* House in course of erection—Implied warranty as to workmanship etc, *above.*
  Solicitor—
   Warranty of authority. *See* **Solicitor** (Sale of land—Warranty of authority).
 Water supply—
  Contemporaneous agreement for supply of water. *See* **Water supply** (Sale of land—Contemporaneous agreement for supply of water).

SALMON AND FRESHWATER FISHERIES
 See **Fish** (Salmon and trout).

SALVAGE
 Admiralty jurisdiction—
  Action in rem—
   Claim arising out of use or hire of ship—Salvage agreement. *See* **Admiralty** (Jurisdiction—Action in rem—Claim arising out of agreement relating to use or hire of ship—Salvage agreement).
   Claim in the nature of salvage. *See* **Admiralty** (Jurisdiction—Action in rem—Claim in nature of salvage).
 Agreement—
  Arbitration—
   Extent of arbitrator's jurisdiction. *See* **Arbitration** (Arbitrator—Jurisdiction—Salvage arbitration).
   Scope of arbitration clause. *See* **Arbitration** (Agreement—Arbitration clause—Scope—Salvage agreement).
  Arbitration. *See* **Arbitration** (Salvage arbitration).
 Cargo—
  Apportionment of liability to pay salvage reward. *See* **Sale of goods** (C and f contract).
  Storage expenses. *See* **Shipping** (Salvage—Cargo—Storage expenses).
 Costs—
  County court jurisdiction. *See* **Admiralty** (Costs—Jurisdiction—County court—Salvage action).

SALVAGE (cont)—
    Crown acting as salvor—
        Claim against Crown—
            Petition of right. *See* **Petition of right** (Salvage—Crown acting as salvor).
    Crown entitled by statute to claim for salvage services. *See* **Statute** (Crown—Crown entitled by statute to
        claim for salvage services).
    Generally. *See* **Shipping** (Salvage).
    Jurisdiction to order payment. *See* **Prize law** (Salvage).
    Salvage services—
        Statement of claim—
            Application to amend to plead further services. *See* **Admiralty** (Practice—Action in
                rem—Writ—Amendment—Application to amend statement of claim to plead further salvage
                services rendered to same ship).
    Shipping. *See* **Shipping** (Salvage).

SAMPLE
    Evidence of criminal proceedings. *See* **Criminal evidence** (Sample).
    Fertilisers and feeding stuffs. *See* **Agriculture** (Fertiliser—Analysis of sample).
    Food and drugs. *See* **Food and drugs** (Samples).
    Intimate sample taken from defendant—
        Use of sample as evidence in criminal proceedings. *See* **Criminal evidence** (Intimate sample taken from
        defendant).
    Sale of goods. *See* **Sale of goods** (Sale by sample).

SANCTIONS
    Southern Rhodesia—
        Criminal offence. *See* **Criminal law** (Sanctions relating to Southern Rhodesia).
    Terrorism. *See* **Terrorism** (Sanctions).
    Terrorism, prevention of. *See* **Terrorism** (Prevention of—Sanctions).

SAND
    Sand bin—
        Unlit on pavement. *See* **Lighting restriction** (Obstructions on highway—Lighting obstructions—
        Sandbag-barrier on pavement).
    Sand blasting—
        Factory—
            Removal of dust. *See* **Factory** (Removal of dust—Sand blasting).

SANDBAG
    Barrier on pavement—
        Obstructing highway—
            Pedestrian injured. *See* **Lighting restriction** (Obstructions on highway—Lighting obstructions—
            Sandbag-barrier on pavement).

SANDERSON ORDER
    See **Costs** (Sanderson order).

SASKATCHEWAN
    Business tax. *See* **Canada** (Business tax—Saskatchewan).

SATELLITE DISH
    Direct tax—
        European Community—
            Freedom of movement of services. *See* **European Union** (Freedom of movement—Services—
            Television broadcasting—Satellite dishes).

SAVINGS
    National development bonds. *See* **National savings** (National development bonds).
    National savings. *See* **National savings**.
    Trustee savings bank. *See* **Trustee savings bank**.

SCAFFOLDING
    See **Building** (Scaffolding).

SCALE FEES
    Solicitor. *See* **Solicitor** (Remuneration—Charging below scale fee).

SCALE OF COSTS
    County court—
        Discretion. *See* **County court** (Costs—Discretion—Scale of costs).
    House of Lords—
        Taxation of costs—
            Increase to scale. *See* **House of Lords** (Costs—Taxation—Increase to scale of costs).

SCHEME OF ARRANGEMENT
    Companies Court—
        Practice. *See* **Practice** (Companies Court—Schemes of arrangement).
    Company. *See* **Company** (Scheme of arrangement).

SCHEME OF MANAGEMENT
    Municipal cemetery. *See* **Ecclesiastical law** (Cemetery—Municipal cemetery—Scheme of management).

SCHIZOPHRENIA
Damage to property—
  Arson—
    Recklessness whether property would be destroyed or damaged. *See* **Criminal law** (Damage to property—Recklessness whether property would be destroyed or damaged—Recklessness—Arson—Schizophrenic sheltering in straw stack lighting fire in stack to keep warm).
Ground of divorce—
  Cruelty. *See* **Divorce** (Cruelty—Mental disorder—Schizophrenia).

SCHOLARSHIP
Income—
  Exemption from tax. *See* **Income tax** (Exemption—Scholarship income).

SCHOOL
Anti-social behaviour. *See* **Education** (School—Anti-social behaviour).
Attendance. *See* **Education** (School attendance).
Child unable to attend school—
  Local education authority's duty. *See* **Education** (Local education authority—Statutory duty to make arrangements for provision of suitable education for children unable to attend school).
Choice of—
  Parental wishes—
    Regard to, by local education authority. *See* **Education** (Local education authority—Regard to wishes of parents).
Community school. *See* **Education** (Community school).
Comprehensive—
  Development plan—
    Revision. *See* **Education** (Development plan—Revision—Alteration of development plan by introduction of scheme for converting existing secondary schools into comprehensive schools).
  Proposals for introducing comprehensive schools—
    Local education authority modifying proposals—Unreasonable exercise of functions—Power of Secretary of State to intervene. *See* **Education** (Local education authority—Power of Secretary of State to prevent unreasonable exercise of functions—Unreasonable—Conduct in which no reasonable authority would engage—Modification of proposals approved by previous members of authority—Proposals for introducing comprehensive system of education).
Conveyance under School Sites Acts. *See* **Education** (School—Conveyance under School Sites Acts).
Corporal punishment—
  Independent school. *See* **Education** (School—Independent school—Corporal punishment).
Crossing. *See* **Road traffic** (School crossing).
Disabled children—
  Rates—
    Relief. *See* **Rates** (Structures supplied for use of invalids, disabled or handicapped persons—Structure supplied for use of person in pursuance of arrangements for handicapped persons—Structure of a kind which could be provided by local authority—School for deaf children).
Duty to provide schools. *See* **Education** (Statutory duty to make schools available for full-time education).
Education of pupil. *See* **Education** (Pupil).
Establishment or discontinuance. *See* **Education** (School—Establishment or discontinuance of school).
Fees—
  Maintenance order. *See* **Minor** (Maintenance—Education or training—Maintenance order including element in respect of school fees).
Generally. *See* **Education** (School).
Governors—
  Act done in pursuance of public duty or authority—
    Limitation of action. *See* **Public authority** (Limitation of action).
  Removal by local education authority. *See* **Education** (Local education authority—Removal of governor).
Independent school. *See* **Education** (School—Independent school).
Meals. *See* **Education** (School meals).
Negligence. *See* **Negligence** (School).
Premises—
  Statutory duty of local education authority. *See* **Education** (Local education authority—Statutory duty in respect of school premises).
School chapel consecrated to divine worship—
  Lease. *See* **Ecclesiastical law** (Consecrated ground—Lease—Chapel—School chapel consecrated to divine worship).
  Whether chapel subject to faculty jurisdiction in respect of building works. *See* **Ecclesiastical law** (Faculty—Consecrated school chapel—Planning and listed building controls).
Special educational needs—
  Generally. *See* **Education** (Special educational needs).
Sport—
  Charity—
    Promotion and encouragement of sport—Trust to promote association football in schools and universities. *See* **Charity** (Education—Educational purposes—Sport—Promotion and encouragement of sport—Trust to promote, encourage and provide facilities for pupils of schools and universities to play association football and other games).
  Negligence—
    Duty of care. *See* **Negligence** (School—Duty of care—Sport).
Transport to and from school—
  Provision by local education authority. *See* **Education** (Local education authority—Provision of transport for pupils—Transport to and from school).

SCIENTIFIC ADVISER
Patents Appeal Tribunal—
Appointment of adviser—
Practice. *See* **Patent** (Appeal tribunal—Practice—Appointment of scientific adviser).

SCIENTIFIC INTEREST
Site of special scientific interest—
Loss of use of land—
Compensation—Arbitration. *See* **Compensation** (Measure of compensation—Arbitration—Appeal against award—Site of special scientific interest).
Protection. *See* **Environment** (Protection—Site of special scientific interest).

SCIENTOLOGY
Chapel of Church of Scientology—
Registration. *See* **Ecclesiastical law** (Place of meeting for religious worship—Registration of premises—Duty of Registrar General—Duty to be satisfied that premises qualify for registration—Chapel of Church of Scientology).
Confidence—
Information acquired on course of Scientology. *See* **Equity** (Breach of confidence—Defence—Public interest in publication—Scientology—Courses of instruction in cult of Scientology).
Employment—
Foreign national—
National of member state of EEC—Right of national to enter UK to take up employment with Church of Scientology. *See* **Immigration** (Workers—Freedom of movement—Nationals of member states of European Community—Restrictions imposed by member states on freedom of movement—Public policy—Measures imposing restrictions to be based exclusively on personal conduct of individual concerned—Personal conduct—Meaning—Membership of socially harmful organisation—Voluntary a).

SCOTLAND
Cause of action arising in Scotland—
Stay of proceedings. *See* **Practice** (Stay of proceedings—Foreign cause of action).
Devolution—
Constitutional law. *See* **Constitutional law** (Devolution—Scotland).
Health board—
Proceedings against board—
Whether a proceeding against the Crown. *See* **Crown** (Proceedings against—Health authority—Scottish Health Board).
Land—
Contract for sale—Specific performance. *See* **Specific performance** (Sale of land—Land outside jurisdiction—Contract for sale of land in Scotland).
Public authority—
Education authority—
Dismissal of teacher—Appointment during authority's pleasure—Natural justice. *See* **Natural justice** (Public authority—Dismissal of employee).
Scottish decision—
Precedent. *See* **Precedent** (Scottish decision).
Scottish warrant—
Jurisdiction of English court over execution of Scottish warrant in England. *See* **Judicial review** (Jurisdiction—Jurisdiction of Divisional Court—Jurisdiction of English court over execution of Scottish warrant in England).
Supreme Court of the United Kingdom—
Jurisdiction. *See* **Supreme court** (Supreme Court of the United Kingdom—Practice—Jurisdiction—Scotland).

SCRAP MATERIAL
Use of land—
Town and country planning—
Discontinuance order. *See* **Town and country planning** (Discontinuance order—Use of land—Jurisdiction to make order—Operations carried out on land—Exclusion of operations carried out on land from definition of use of land—Discontinuance order made in respect of use of land for storing and sorting scrap material).

SCRAP METAL
Change of use for planning purposes—
Recovery of scrap metal. *See* **Town and country planning** (Development—Material change of use—Recovery of scrap metal).
Dealer—
Record of dealings—
Particulars—Description of scrap metal—Fair description required—Abbreviated description recognised by trade—Scrap Metal Dealers Act 1964, s 2. **Jenkins v A Cohen & Co Ltd** [1971] 2 1384, QBD.
Meaning—
Metal included within term—
Scrap produced by new metal—Whether included in term 'scrap metal'—Scrap Metal Dealers Act 1964, s 9. **Jenkins v A Cohen & Co Ltd** [1971] 2 1384, QBD.

SCRIPT
Copyright—
Dramatic or musical performance. *See* **Copyright** (Dramatic or musical performance—Script).

SCULPTURE
   Church, in—
      Faculty. *See* **Ecclesiastical law** (Faculty—Sculpture).

SEA
   Carriage of animals by sea. *See* **Animal** (Carriage by sea, air, road or rail).
   Collision at sea—
      Contributory negligence. *See* **Negligence** (Contributory negligence—Collision at sea).
      Generally. *See* **Shipping** (Collision).
   Fishing. *See* **Fish** (Seafishing).
   Fishing rights—
      European Community. *See* **European Union** (Fishing rights).
   Foreshore. *See* **Foreshore**.
   Recession—
      Gradual and imperceptible—
         Accretion of land—Boundary—Seashore—Accretion to land adjoining seashore. *See* **Boundary**
         (Seashore—Conveyance of land—Natural feature or right line boundary—Sea beach—Recession
         of sea).
   Sea-bed—
      Possession—
         Possession sufficient to support trespass. *See* **Trespass to land** (Possession sufficient to support
         trespass—Sea-bed).
      Recovery of possession. *See* **Limitation of action** (Land—Recovery—Sea-bed).
   Seashore—
      Boundary. *See* **Boundary** (Seashore).
   Shipping. *See* **Shipping**.

SEA WALL
   Repair—
      Duty of catchment board to repair—
         Negligence. *See* **Land drainage** (Sea wall—Negligence—Duty of catchment board to repair).

SEAL
   Contract—
      Local authority. *See* **Local authority** (Contract—Seal).
   Deed—
      Company. *See* **Deed** (Sealing—Company).
      Execution. *See* **Deed** (Execution—Sealing).

SEALED BIDS
   Invitation to make sealed bids for shares—
      Implied term. *See* **Contract** (Implied term—Bids—Sealed bids—Contract for sale of shares).
      Whether an offer or invitation to treat. *See* **Contract** (Offer and acceptance—Invitation to
      treat—Contract for sale of shares).

SEAMAN
   Wages—
      Claim for wages—
         Admiralty jurisdiction. *See* **Admiralty** (Jurisdiction—Action in rem—Claim for wages).
         Ranking of claim by master. *See* **Shipping** (Crew—Master—Wages—Claim for wages—Lien for
         wages—Whether claim for wages by master ranking pari passu with claim of crew).
      Maritime lien. *See* **Shipping** (Maritime lien—Wages—Seaman).
   Will—
      Privilege. *See* **Will** (Soldier's or mariner's privileged will).

SEARCH
   Commons register—
      Sale of land—
         Solicitor—Negligence. *See* **Solicitor** (Negligence—Sale of land—Search of commons register).
   Customs and excise. *See* **Customs and excise** (Duties—Imported goods—Search and seizure).
   Grant of administration—
      Standing search. *See* **Administration of estates** (Grant of administration—Standing search).
   Income tax—
      Suspected offence—
         Warrant to enter premises and seize documents. *See* **Income tax** (Offence—Fraud—Suspected
         offence—Warrant to enter and seize documents).
   Land charge. *See* **Land charge** (Search).
   Police—
      Power to stop, search and detain. *See* **Police** (Powers—Power to stop, search and detain).
      Right of search. *See* **Police** (Right of search).
   Right of search. *See* **Police** (Right of search).
   Search warrant—
      Competition investigation. *See* **Competition** (Investigation and enforcement—Search warrant).
   Unlawful search—
      Admissibility of evidence obtained in search. *See* **Criminal evidence** (Illegally obtained
      evidence—Unlawful search).

SEARCH ORDER
   Generally. *See* **Practice** (Pre-trial or post-judgment relief—Search order).

SEARCH WARRANT
   Club—
      Search of licensed premises. *See* **Licensing** (Club—Search warrant—Search of licensed premises).

SEARCH WARRANT (cont)—
 Income tax offence—
  Suspected fraud. *See* **Income tax** (Offence—Fraud—Suspected offence—Warrant to enter and seize documents).
 Obscene publications—
  Validity. *See* **Criminal law** (Obscene publications—Power of search and seizure—Validity of warrant).
 Police. *See* **Police** (Search warrant).

SEASHORE
 Boundary. *See* **Boundary** (Seashore).

SEAT BELT
 Motor vehicle—
  Failure to wear seat belt—
   Contributory negligence. *See* **Negligence** (Contributory negligence—Road accident—Seat belt).

SECLUSION
 Mental health patient. *See* **Mental health** (Patient—Seclusion).

SECONDARY EVIDENCE
 Contents of document—
  Admissibility in criminal proceedings. *See* **Criminal evidence** (Document—Secondary evidence as to contents).

SECONDHAND CAR
 Sale—
  Damages for non-acceptance—
   Estimated loss resulting from breach—Available market. *See* **Contract** (Damages for breach—Sale of goods—Non-acceptance—Estimated loss directly and naturally resulting from breach—Available market—Secondhand car).

SECRET COMMISSION
 Agent. *See* **Agent** (Secret commission).

SECRET PROCEEDINGS
 Chancery Division—
  Practice. *See* **Practice** (Chancery Division—Secret proceedings).

SECRET PROCESS
 Pleading—
  Particulars. *See* **Pleading** (Particulars—Secret process).

SECRET TRUST
 See **Trust and trustee** (Secret trust).

SECRETARY
 Company. *See* **Company** (Secretary).

SECRETARY OF STATE
 Civil Aviation Authority—
  Power to give guidance to authority. *See* **Air traffic** (Civil Aviation Authority—Powers of Secretary of State—Guidance to authority).
 Reference to court—
  Criminal appeal. *See* **Criminal law** (Appeal—Reference by Home Secretary).
 Social security—
  Rates of benefit—
   Review. *See* **Social security** (Rates of benefit—Review by Secretary of State).

SECRETS
 Confidential information—
  Bank—
   Banker/client relationship. *See* **Bank** (Banker/client relationship—Duty of bank—Duty of confidentiality).
  Generally. *See* **Confidential information**.
 Official secrets—
  Offences. *See* **Criminal law** (Official secrets).
 Trade secrets—
  Generally. *See* **Trade secrets**.
  Injunction against disclosure of information—
   Interlocutory injunction. *See* **Injunction** (Interlocutory—Confidential information—Trade secrets).

SECULAR USE
 Consecrated ground—
  Faculty. *See* **Ecclesiastical law** (Faculty—Secular use of consecrated ground).
 Unconsecrated curtilage of church—
  Faculty. *See* **Ecclesiastical law** (Faculty—Unconsecrated curtilage of church).

SECURE ACCOMMODATION ORDER
 Family proceedings. *See* **Family proceedings** (Orders in family proceedings—Secure accommodation order).

SECURE TENANCY
Forfeiture of lease—
Breach of covenant prohibiting assignment. *See* **Landlord and tenant** (Forfeiture of lease—Breach of covenant prohibiting assignment—Secure tenancy).
Homeless person—
Temporary housing accommodation. *See* **Housing** (Homeless person—Security of tenure).
Local authority houses. *See* **Housing** (Local authority houses—Security of tenure—Secure tenancy).
Possession. *See* **Rent restriction** (Possession).
Succession on death of secure tenant. *See* **Housing** (Local authority houses—Security of tenure—Secure tenancy—Succession on death of secure tenant).

SECURED CREDITOR
Bankruptcy petition. *See* **Bankruptcy** (Petition—Creditor's petition—Secured creditor).

SECURITIES
Bank. *See* **Bank** (Securities).
Dealing without licence. *See* **Criminal law** (Dealing in securities without a licence).
Deposit—
Bank. *See* **Bank** (Securities—Deposit of securities).
Exchange control—
Generally. *See* **Currency control**.
Issue of security to person resident outside scheduled territories—
Issue without Treasury permission—Rectification of share register. *See* **Company** (Shares—Register—Rectification—Issue of security in breach of exchange control legislation—Shares issued to person resident outside scheduled territories without Treasury permission).
Foreign securities—
Income tax. *See* **Income tax** (Foreign securities).
Insider dealing. *See* **Company** (Insider dealing).
Marshalling. *See* **Equity** (Marshalling).
Transaction in securities—
Tax advantage. *See* **Income tax** (Tax advantage—Transaction in securities).
Will—
Gift—
Specific bequests. *See* **Will** (Gift—Specific bequests—My securities).

SECURITIES AND INVESTMENTS BOARD
Freezing order—
Cross-undertaking in damages. *See* **Practice** (Pre-trial or post-judgment relief—Freezing order—Cross-undertaking in damages).

SECURITISATION OF DEBT
Trust deed—
Construction. *See* **Trust and trustee** (Trust deed and deed of charge—Construction—Securitisation of debt).

SECURITY
Border security—
Philippines—
European Commission Decision. *See* **European Union** (Commission—Decision—Annulment—Commission approving project giving assistance to the Philippines to improve their border security).
Building society advances. *See* **Building society** (Advances—Security on which advances may be made).
Debt on a security—
Capital gains tax—
Disposal of assets. *See* **Capital gains tax** (Disposal of assets—Debt—Debt on a security).
Injunction—
Cross-undertaking. *See* **Injunction** (Interlocutory—Condition of relief—Security for fulfilment of cross-undertaking).
Internal security—
Malaysia. *See* **Malaysia** (Internal security).
Loan—
Power to give—
Parochial church council. *See* **Ecclesiastical law** (Parochial church council—Conduct of financial affairs of church—Borrowing powers).
Moneylender's contract. *See* **Moneylender** (Security).
Mortgage debt. *See* **Mortgage** (Debt—Security).
National security—
Deportation of alien—
Natural justice—Validity of order. *See* **Alien** (Deportation—Order—Validity—Natural justice—Deportation in the interest of national security).
Generally. *See* **National security**.
Procuring execution of valuable security by deception. *See* **Criminal law** (Procuring execution of valuable security by deception).
Vessel under arrest—
Release following provision of security. *See* **Admiralty** (Arrest of vessel—Release—Release following provision of security).

SECURITY BILLS OF SALE
See **Bill of sale** (Security bills of sale).

SECURITY COUNCIL
United Nations—
> Peace-keeping force. *See* **United Nations** (Peace-keeping force established pursuant to resolution of Security Council).

SECURITY FOR COSTS
Appeal—
> Appeal by third party. *See* **Court of Appeal** (Third party—Appeal against judgment in favour of plaintiff in main action—Leave—Circumstances in which leave will be granted—Whether defendant a necessary party—Security for costs).
> Bankruptcy. *See* **Bankruptcy** (Appeal—Security for costs).
> Generally. *See* **Costs** (Security for costs—Appeal).
Arbitration. *See* **Arbitration** (Costs—Security for costs).
Company—
> Appeal against winding up order. *See* **Company** (Compulsory winding up—Security for costs—Appeal by company against winding up order).
> Generally. *See* **Costs** (Security for costs—Company).
County court. *See* **County court** (Security for costs).
Divorce—
> Poor person. *See* **Divorce** (Costs—Poor person—Security for costs).
> Security for wife's costs. *See* **Divorce** (Costs—Security for wife's costs).
European Community. *See* **European Union** (Costs—Security for costs).
Generally. *See* **Costs** (Security for costs).
House of Lords. *See* **House of Lords** (Costs—Security for costs).
Legal aid. *See* **Legal aid** (Security for costs).

SECURITY OF TENURE
Agricultural worker. *See* **Rent restriction** (Agricultural worker).
Business premises—
> Contracting out of statutory provisions governing security of tenure. *See* **Landlord and tenant** (Business premises—Contracting out).
Caravan site—
> Protected site—
>> Gipsies occupying caravans on site seasonally as main or only residence—Whether site 'protected site'—Whether occupants entitled to security of tenure. *See* **Local authority** (Caravan sites—Provision of caravan sites—Duty of local authority—Duty to provide accommodation for gipsies).
Council house tenant—
> Action for possession. *See* **Housing** (Local authority houses—Possession—Security of tenure).
> Generally. *See* **Housing** (Local authority houses—Security of tenure).
Homeless person—
> Temporary housing accommodation. *See* **Housing** (Local authority houses—Security of tenure).
Residential property. *See* **Landlord and tenant** (Residential property—Security of tenure).

SECURITY SERVICE
Powers—
> Undercover agents—
>> Whether Security Service having legal power to authorise agents' participation in criminality—Whether guidance on use of agents participating in criminality lawful—Security Service Act 1989, ss 1, 2. **Privacy International v Secretary of State for Foreign and Commonwealth Affairs** [2022] **1** 25, CA.
Protection of security service—
> Prevention of disclosure of confidential information—
>> Interlocutory injunction—Whether protection of security service a ground for granting interlocutory injunction. *See* **Injunction** (Interlocutory—Preservation of position pending trial—Prevention of disclosure of confidential information—Protection of security service).
>> Permanent injunction against disclosure of information. *See* **Confidential information** (Injunction against disclosure of information—Information relating to security service).

SEDITION
Crime. *See* **Criminal law** (Sedition).

SEDUCTION
Action by female seduced—
> Evidence—
>> No evidence necessary of disability for service consequent on seduction—Seduction Act 1922 (Alberta), ss 1-5. **Brownlee v MacMillan** [1940] **3** 384, PC.
Daughter—
> Father and mother not married—
>> Effect on action by father—Master of the house. **Beetham v James** [1937] **1** 580, KBD.
Rape—
> Availability of action—
>> Whether action can be brought if rape proved. **Mattouk v Massad** [1943] **2** 517, PC.

SEEDS
Sale—
> Statement of prescribed particulars—
>> Failure to deliver statement—Misrepresentation as to type of seed—Buyer's right to sue for breach of warranty—Seeds Act 1920, ss 1(1), 8(1). **Marles v Phillip Trant & Sons Ltd (Mackinnon, third party) (No 1)** [1953] **1** 645, Assizes.
>> Presumption of correctness—Proof by purchaser that goods supplied not in accordance with particulars—Seeds Act 1920, s 6(1). **Marles v Phillip Trant & Sons Ltd (Mackinnon, third party) (No 2)** [1953] **1** 651, CA.

SEINE NET
Prohibition—
Seafishing. *See* **Fish** (Seafishing—Prohibition by byelaw of fishing with seine net within three-mile limit).

SEIZURE OF PROPERTY
Foreign law—
Recognition. *See* **Conflict of laws** (Foreign law—Recognition—Seizure of property).
Writ of fi fa. *See* **Execution** (Writ of fi fa—Seizure of goods).

SELECTIVE EMPLOYMENT TAX
Appeal—
Decision of tribunal on question of proper industrial classification—
When tribunal's decision may be interfered with. **Fisher-Bendix Ltd v Secretary of State for Employment and Productivity** [1970] 2 286, CA.
When tribunal's decision may be interfered with—Tribunal's decision not to be interfered with, if it could reasonably have been reached. **Secretary of State for Employment and Productivity v C Maurice & Co Ltd** [1969] 2 37, HL.
Time for appealing—
Decision of Industrial Tribunal given orally—Notice of appeal to be served and appeal entered within 28 days of decision—Reasons for decision to be recorded in document signed by chairman and entered in register of applications—Copy of decision to be transmitted to applicant and Minister—Decision given on Jan 12 and copy decision sent to Minister 12 days later when recorded—Notice of appeal given by Minister 26 days after decision received by him—Whether notice of appeal and entering of appeal was within time—RSC Ord 55, r 4(4). **Minister of Labour v Genner Iron & Steel Co (Wollescote) Ltd** [1967] 3 278, QBD.
Premium—
Activity in which establishment engaged—
Designing—Employers prepared designs of metal-working machine tools for other companies who made the tools and used them to manufacture other products—Whether employers carried on an activity within heading 332 of the classification, viz, manufacturing metal-working machine tools—Selective Employment Payments Act 1966, ss 1(2)(a)(i), 10(5). **Lord Advocate v Reliant Tool Co** [1968] 1 162, HL.
Firms whose business consisted in buying steel sheets which they cut into various shapes according to requirements of customers—Whether businesses fell within Ord III to Ord VI of Standard Industrial Classification—Selective Employment Payments Act 1966, s 1(2)(a). **Minister of Labour v Genner Iron & Steel Co (Wollescote) Ltd** [1967] 3 278, QBD.
Publishing—Three journalists employed in London by Canadian publishers to collect news for newspapers published in Canada—Whether activities carried on in London fell within heading 486—Smaller activity not shown to be part of a larger activity of publishers—Whether editorial staff of publishers within heading 486—Selective Employment Payments Act 1966, s 1(2). **Minister of Labour v Southam News Services of Canada** [1968] 1 310, QBD.
Refrigeration of plant—Employers' main business activity was to plan cooling installations for abattoirs, supermarkets, hospitals, etc, and to install cooling equipment—Employers manufactured the coolers, but obtained other components from other manufacturers—Whether their main activity constituted manufacturing of refrigerators, etc within heading 339.3 and Ord VI of the Standard Industrial Classification—Whether employers' establishment satisfied Selective Employment Payments Act 1966, s 1(2)(a)(i). **Prestcold (Central) Ltd v Minister of Labour** [1969] 1 69, CA.
Repair of washing machines—Repair by manufacturers from after-sales establishments—Standard Industrial Classification—Whether repair properly classified under heading 820(5), heading 349(3) or heading 365—Selective Employment Payments Act 1966, s 1(2). **Fisher-Bendix Ltd v Secretary of State for Employment and Productivity** [1970] 2 286, CA.
Waste paper dealers—Activities consisted in collecting, cleaning, sorting and separating waste paper, before sale to paper and board mills—Whether activity was part of the manufacture of waste paper—Whether manufacturing—Whether within heading 481 or 499.2 of the Standard Industrial Classification, having regard to heading 832.6, which included dealers in waste paper—Selective Employment Payments Act 1966, ss 1(2)(a), 10(5). **Carfax Waste Paper Co Ltd v Minister of Labour** [1968] 1 1041, QBD.
Payment of premium in respect of employment in or carried out from an establishment—
Establishment—Meaning—Degree of permanence—Relevance of degree of control of activities on site—Supply of electrical generators by company on site—Installation of generators at site over period of five years—Offices, canteen and general accommodation of temporary character erected at site—Effective administrative control over activities at site exercised from company's head office—Whether site an establishment—Selective Employment Payments Act 1966, s 1(2). **Secretary of State for Employment and Productivity v Clarke Chapman & Co Ltd** [1971] 2 798, QBD.
Head office of employers constituting an establishment—Employers carrying out work on sites scattered all over United Kingdom—Site qualifying as an establishment—Central planning carried out at headquarters—Employees on site hired through headquarters where individually taken on and documents kept—Gross weekly pay calculated on site—Net pay calculated at headquarters—Whether employees on site in employment 'carried out from' headquarters—Selective Employment Payments Act 1966, s 1(2). **Lord Advocate v Babcock & Wilcox (Operations) Ltd** [1972] 1 1130, HL.
Supply of electrical generators by company—Installation of generators at site by employees of company—Site qualifying as 'establishment'—Effective control over activities at site from company's head office at different establishment—Employees recruited in locality of site—Appointment of employees subject to approval of head office—Whether employment of employees 'carried out from' establishment where head office situated—Selective Employment Payments Act 1966, s 1(2). **Secretary of State for Employment and Productivity v Clarke Chapman & Co Ltd** [1971] 2 798, QBD.

SELECTIVE EMPLOYMENT TAX (cont)—
Refund—
Right to refund—
Activities falling within statutory definition of agriculture—Breeding cats and dogs for sale for research—Whether within definition of 'agriculture' as extended by definition of 'livestock'—Selective Employment Payments Act 1966, s 10(1). **Minister of Agriculture, Fisheries and Food v Appleton** [1969] **3** 1051, QBD.
Aircraft refuelling depot at airport—Depot held by petrol company under lease—Essential service for operation of airport—Whether employees of petrol company at depot, engaged in re-fuelling aircraft, were employed wholly or mainly in non-qualifying activities by way of the sale of goods—Standard Industrial Classification, heading 706, heading 810(6)—Selective Employment Payments Act 1966, ss 2(2)(3), 10(1). **Esso Petroleum Co Ltd v Minister of Labour** [1968] **3** 425, CA.
Business and private activities—Horticulture—Gardener employed full-time but working for ten to fifteen per cent of his time on produce for sale—No entitlement to refund unless employment wholly or mainly in connexion with activity by way of business—Registration of establishment a condition precedent to obtaining refund but not conferring a right thereto—Selective Employment Payments Act 1966, s 2(2)(b), s 7. **Minister of Agriculture, Fisheries and Food v Mason** [1968] **3** 76, QBD.
Electrical industry—Laying and jointing cable—Whether distribution of electricity for public supply—Standard Industrial Classification, heading 500, heading 602—Selective Employment Payments Act 1966, s 2(2), (3). **Secretary of State for Employment and Productivity v C Maurice & Co Ltd** [1969] **2** 37, HL.
Sub-postmaster employing two women wholly in the handling of money and clerical work—Whether employees engaged in non-qualifying activities carried on for office purposes—Offices, Shops and Railway Premises Act 1963, s 1(2)—Selective Employment Payment Act 1966, ss 2(2)(b)(ii), 10(1). **Minister of Labour v Morgan** [1967] **2** 732, QBD.
Registration—
Refund—
Registration of establishment not conferring of itself entitlement to refund. **Minister of Agriculture, Fisheries and Food v Mason** [1968] **3** 76, QBD.
Standard Industrial Classification—
Construction—
Introduction to classification. **Fisher-Bendix Ltd v Secretary of State for Employment and Productivity** [1970] **2** 286, CA.
Minimum list headings—
Comparison with construction of legal documents. **Secretary of State for Employment and Productivity v C Maurice & Co Ltd** [1969] **2** 37, HL.
Mutual exclusiveness—Whether headings mutually exclusive. **Central Press Photos Ltd v Dept of Employment and Productivity** [1970] **3** 775, CA.
Trade meaning not dictionary meaning. **Central Press Photos Ltd v Dept of Employment and Productivity** [1970] **3** 775, CA.

SELF-CONTROL
Murder—
Provocation—
Self-control of reasonable man. *See* **Criminal law** (Murder—Provocation—Self-control of reasonable man).

SELF-DEFENCE
Assault. *See* **Criminal law** (Assault—Self-defence).
Criminal proceedings—
Burden of proof. *See* **Criminal evidence** (Burden of proof—Defence—Self-defence).
Generally. *See* **Criminal law** (Self-defence).
Direction to jury. *See* **Jury** (Direction to jury—Self-defence).
Murder. *See* **Criminal law** (Murder—Self-defence).
Trespass to the person—
Battery. *See* **Trespass to the person** (Battery—Defence —Self-defence).
Wounding. *See* **Criminal law** (Wounding—Self-defence).

SELF-EMPLOYED PERSON
Determination of question whether person employed or self employed. *See* **Social security** (Determination of claims and questions—Determination of question whether persons employed or self-employed).
Employment under contract for services—
Dismissal—
Unfair dismissal. *See* **Unfair dismissal** (Excluded classes of employment—Employment under contract for services—Employer and manager agreeing for tax purposes that manager to be self-employed in the future).

SELF-INCRIMINATION
Family proceedings. *See* **Family proceedings** (Disclosure—Self-incrimination).
Privilege against self-incrimination—
Bank requiring person suspected of contravening banking legislation to disclose information required for purpose of investigation—
Suspect claiming privilege against self-incrimination—Whether entitled to rely on privilege. *See* **Bank** (Deposit-taking business—Control by Bank of England—Bank's power to require person suspected of contravening banking legislation to disclose information required for purpose of investigation—Privilege against self-incrimination).
Defence in proceedings for contempt of court. *See* **Contempt of court** (Defence—Self-incrimination).
Department of Trade and Industry investigation of company's affairs—
Whether common law privilege against self-incrimination available to persons questioned by inspectors. *See* **Company** (Investigation by Department of Trade and Industry—Affairs of company—Duty of officers and agents of company to give information—Privilege against self-incrimination).

SELF-INCRIMINATION (cont)—
    Privilege against self-incrimination (cont)—
        Disclosure of documents. *See* **Disclosure and inspection of documents** (Privilege—Self-incrimination).
        Injunction—
            Disclosure in aid of injunction—Generally. *See* **Practice** (Pre-trial or post-judgment relief—
            Disclosure in aid of injunction—Privilege against self-incrimination).
        Insolvency of company—
            Inquiry into company's affairs. *See* **Company** (Insolvency—Inquiry into company affairs—
            Examination of officers of company etc—Privilege against self-incrimination).
            Provisional liquidator's inquiry into company's affairs. *See* **Company** (Provisional liquidation—Inquiry
            into company affairs—Examination of officers of company etc—Privilege against self-incrimination).
        Search order. *See* **Practice** (Pre-trial or post-judgment relief—Search order—Privilege against
        self-incrimination).
        Witness. *See* **Evidence** (Privilege—Incrimination of witness or spouse).
    Right against self-incrimination. *See* **Human rights** (Right to a fair hearing—Right against
    self-incrimination).
    Road traffic offence. *See* **Road traffic** (Offence—Self-incrimination).

SELF-INDUCED AUTOMATISM
    Defence to criminal charge. *See* **Criminal law** (Automatism—Self-induced automatism).

SELF-REDRESS
    Trespass to land—
        Remedy. *See* **Trespass to land** (Remedy—Self-redress).

SENATE OF THE INNS OF COURT
    Disciplinary jurisdiction. *See* **Counsel** (Disciplinary jurisdiction—Senate of the Inns of Court and the Bar).

SENTENCE
    Age of offender—
        Borstal training. *See* Borstal training—Age within limits of qualification for borstal training, *below*.
        Extreme old age—
            Mitigation. *See* Factors in assessing sentence—Mitigation—Extreme old age, *below*.
        Imposition of penalty prohibited in case of 'person under' specified age—
            Relevant date for determining age—Date of offence or of conviction—Death penalty—Jamaica—
            Imposition of death penalty on 'persons under the age of eighteen' prohibited—Accused
            convicted of murder—Accused under eighteen on date of offence and over eighteen on date of
            conviction—Juveniles Law (Jamaica), s 29(1). **Baker v R** [1975] **3** 55, PC.
        Preventive detention. *See* Preventive detention—Age of offender, *below*.
    Aggravating features—
        Offence committed on bail—
            Whether fact that offence committed on bail may be taken into account in determining sentence. **R
            v Baverstock** [1993] **2** 32, CA.
    Aiding and abetting—
        Murder. *See* Murder—Life imprisonment—Minimum term—Determination of minimum term in relation
        to mandatory life sentence, *below*.
    Appeal—
        Application for leave to appeal against sentence—
            Bail pending appeal—Whether applicant released on bail should be returned to prison. **R v Cullis**
            [1969] **1** 593, CA.
            Powers exercisable by single judge—Whether single judge entitled to grant leave to appeal on
            limited grounds only—Criminal Appeal Act 1968, ss 11, 31. **R v Hyde** [2017] **3** 580, CA.
        Binding-over order—
            Right of appeal against order—Whether binding-over order a 'sentence'—Criminal Appeal Act 1968,
            ss 9, 50(1). **R v Williams (Carl)** [1982] **3** 1092, CA.
        Borstal training—
            Accused on licence from borstal—Tried summarily and committed to quarter sessions for
            sentence—Ordered to be returned to borstal—Whether right of appeal to the Court of Appeal
            against sentence—Criminal Justice Act 1961, s 12(1)(a). **R v Bebbington** [1969] **3** 426, CA.
            Reports to be made available to court—Necessity for court to have up-to-date probation report and
            report from borstal institution. **R v Weekes** [1969] **1** 947, CA.
        Breach of probation order—
            Matters to be before court—Probation order together with statement of breach in respect of which
            charge brought to be before court. **R v Maber** [1954] **1** 666, CCA.
        Commencement of sentence—
            Application for leave to appeal—Special treatment of appellant—Time counting as part of
            sentence—Application for leave to appeal—Refusal by judge in chambers—Appeal to full
            court—Dismissal of appeal—Criminal Justice Act 1948, s 38(2). **R v Bedford** [1948] **2** 766, CCA.
        Committal for sentence a nullity—
            Conviction by court of summary jurisdiction of hybrid offence—Committal to quarter sessions for
            sentence—Committal a nullity—Right of offender to appeal against sentence—Magistrates'
            Courts Act 1952, ss 18(1), 29. **R v Jones (Gwyn)** [1969] **1** 325, CA.
        Conditional discharge—
            Right of appeal against order—Defective order—Jurisdiction of court to entertain appeal on ground
            that order a nullity. **R v Wehner** [1977] **3** 553, CA.
        Conviction quashed on one count of indictment—
            Increase of sentences on other count—Power of Court of Appeal to increase sentence on other part
            of indictment in substitution for sentence passed at trial—Criminal Appeal Act 1907, s 5(1) (as
            amended by Criminal Appeal Act 1966, s 4(2)). **R v Craig** [1967] **1** 1052, CA.
            Sentence on another count varied—Criminal Appeal Act 1907, s 5(1). **R v Lovelock** [1956] **3** 223,
            CCA.

SENTENCE (cont)—
 Appeal (cont)—
  Conviction quashed on one count of indictment (cont)—
   Sentences on other counts—Whether court has power to pass sentence on other counts of indictment on which trial judge has not passed sentence—Ceylon Court of Criminal Appeal Ordinance (No 23 of 1938), s 6(1). **R v Edirimanasingham** [1961] **1** 376, PC.
  Costs—
   Legal aid costs—Contribution order—Order that accused charged on indictment should contribute to his legal aid costs—Whether order a 'sentence'—Whether right of appeal against order—Criminal Appeal Act 1968, ss 9, 50(1). **R v Hayden** [1975] **2** 558, CA.
   Order as to costs—Accused convicted on indictment—Accused ordered to contribute to prosecution costs—Whether order a 'sentence'—Whether right of appeal against order—Criminal Appeal Act 1968, ss 9, 50(1)—Costs in Criminal Cases Act 1973, s 4(1). **R v Hayden** [1975] **2** 558, CA.
   Penal or other sum—Defendant acquitted—Order that defendant pay costs—Right of appeal—Order for payment of 'penal or other sum'—Whether defendant entitled to appeal—Summary Jurisdiction and Criminal Justice Act (Northern Ireland) 1935, s 24(1). **Benson v Northern Ireland Road Transport Board** [1942] **1** 465, HL.
  Crown Court—
   Power of court on appeal—Generally. *See* **Crown Court** (Appeal to Crown Court—Power of court on appeal—Sentence).
  Dangerous offenders—
   Mandatory sentence—Crown court failing to apply mandatory sentence—Whether Court of Appeal bound to impose mandatory sentence where mandatory sentence more severe than sentence actually imposed—Criminal Appeal Act 1968, s 11(3)—Criminal Justice Act 2003, Pt 12, Ch 5. **R v Reynolds** [2007] **4** 369, CA.
  Fresh evidence. *See* **Criminal law** (Appeal—Fresh evidence—Appeal against sentence).
  Handling stolen goods—
   Relation of sentence to facts of particular charge—Disparity of sentence between co-offenders. **R v Parker** [1970] **2** 458, CA.
  Imprisonment—
   Application for leave to appeal. *See* **Criminal law** (Appeal—Leave to appeal—Application—Sentence of imprisonment).
  Increase of sentence—
   Power to increase sentence. **Practice Note** [1961] **3** 522, CCA.
  Magistrates' court, from—Practice. *See* **Magistrates** (Review of justices' decision—Sentence—Appeal to Divisional Court).
  Probation order—
   Breach of. *See* Appeal—Breach of probation order, *above*.
   Right of appeal against order—Order invalid. **R v Marquis** [1974] **2** 1216, CA.
   Right of appeal against order—Whether offender against whom order made having right of appeal—Criminal Justice Act 1948, s 12(1). **R v Tucker** [1974] **2** 639, CA.
  Quashing of sentence on appeal—
   Substitution of a shorter term of imprisonment—Original sentence rendered null only for the future—Criminal Appeal Act 1907, s 4(3). **Hancock v Prison Comrs** [1959] **3** 513, Vacation Ct.
  Right of appeal—
   Breach of recognisance. *See* Binding-over—Breach of recognisance—Right of appeal, *below*.
   Compensation order—Theft Act 1968, s 28(1), (5)—Criminal Appeal Act 1968, s 30(4). **R v Parker** [1970] **2** 458, CA.
   Discretionary life sentence—Judge stipulating 'the relevant part' of the sentence to be served before defendant eligible for parole—Defendant appealing against excessive 'relevant part' of sentence—Whether period specified as 'relevant part' of sentence was a matter which could be the subject of an appeal—Criminal Appeal Act 1968, s 9(1)—Criminal Justice Act 1991, s 34. **R v Dalton** [1995] **2** 349, CA.
   Probation order. *See* Appeal—Probation order—Right of appeal against order, *above*.
   Sentence not one which court of summary jurisdiction had power to impose—Order to return to borstal institution—Offender sentenced to borstal training in Scotland—Released on licence—Conviction in England while on licence—Committal to quarter sessions with a view to borstal training—Order by quarter sessions that he be returned to borstal institution—Whether order lawful and one which quarter sessions had power to impose—Whether right of appeal to Court of Appeal—Criminal Justice Act 1948, s 29(3)(d)—Criminal Justice Act 1961, ss 12(1), 38(2)(a). **R v Welsh** [1967] **3** 846, Vacation Ct, CA.
  Sentence fixed by law—
   Right of appeal—No appeal against sentence of life imprisonment fixed by law—Criminal Appeal Act 1907, s 3—Homicide Act 1957, s 9(1). **Practice Note** [1957] **2** 378, CCA.
  Sentence passed on conviction—
   Recognisance estreated and in default of payment further six months' imprisonment—Appeal against further six months' imprisonment—Order made 'on' conviction—Criminal Appeal Act 1907, ss 3(c), 21. **R v Harman** [1959] **2** 738, CCA.
   Recognisance estreated and in default of payment further six months' imprisonment—Order not made for the offence—Criminal Appeal Act 1968, s 9. **R v Thayne** [1969] **3** 652, CA.
  Suspended sentence—
   Allowance for period in custody pending appeal—Practice—Criminal Justice Act 1967, s 67(1). **Practice Note** [1970] **1** 273, CA.
  Validity of sentence—
   Jurisdiction of Court of Appeal. *See* **Criminal law** (Court of Appeal—Jurisdiction—Validity of sentence).

SENTENCE (cont)—

Causing or allowing death of child or vulnerable adult. *See* Imprisonment—Length of sentence—Causing or allowing death of child or vulnerable adult, *below.*

Commencement—

Crown Court. *See* **Crown Court** (Sentence—Commencement).

Committal for sentence—

Crown Court. *See* **Crown Court** (Committal of offender to Crown Court for sentence).

Magistrates. *See* **Magistrates** (Committal for sentence).

Quarter sessions. *See* **Quarter sessions** (Committal of offender for sentence).

Common law offence—

Attempt—

Duration of imprisonment—Sentence not to exceed that imposable for full offence—Road Traffic Act 1930, s 28(1)(b)—Criminal Justice Act 1948, s 21(1)(a). **R v Pearce** [1952] 2 718, CCA.

Duration of imprisonment—Term should not exceed maximum that may be awarded for completed offence. **Verrier v DPP** [1966] 3 568, HL.

Imprisonment for longer than two years. **R v Higgins** [1951] 2 758, .

Conspiracy—

Duration—Conspiracy to commit a statutory offence—Whether sentence limited to maximum period that could be imposed for the substantive offence. **Verrier v DPP** [1966] 3 568, HL.

Period longer than maximum for substantive offence—Circumstances in which sentence may exceed maximum for substantive offence. **R v Morris** [1950] 2 965, CCA.

Limit on sentence for common law misdemeanour—

Sentence of imprisonment for longer than two years. **R v Morris** [1950] 2 965, CCA.

Community order—

Breach of requirement of order—

Failure without reasonable excuse to comply with requirement of order—Whether pending appeal a reasonable excuse for failure to comply—Criminal Justice Act 2003, Sch 8, para 9. **West Midlands Probation Board v Sutton Coldfield Magistrates' Court** [2008] 3 1193, DC.

Community requirement. *See* Suspended sentence—Community requirement , *below.*

Community service order—

Consecutive orders—

Orders in respect of person already subject to a community service order made by another court—Power to impose an order to run consecutively to first order—Maximum aggregate period of consecutive orders—Powers of Criminal Courts Act 1973, s 14(1). **R v Evans** [1977] 1 228, CA.

Company director—

Disqualification—

Fraudulent trading and fraudulent conversion when director—Sentence of imprisonment and disqualification for being a director for five years—Date from which disqualification should run—Companies Act 1948, s 188. **R v Bradley** [1961] 1 669, CCA.

Compensation—

Damage due to accident arising out of presence of vehicle on road—

Limitation of compensation to damage to property recovered in case of offence under Theft Act 1968—Taking motor vehicle without consent—Vehicle taken without consent in collision with other cars—Whether compensation order could be made in respect of damage caused to other cars—Whether compensation order limited to damage caused to vehicle taken without consent—Powers of Criminal Courts Act 1973, s 35(2), (3). **Quigley v Stokes** [1977] 2 317, QBD.

Loss or damage resulting from offence—

Costs incurred in civil proceedings against accused—Civil proceedings taken by victim in respect of matters constituting offence—Victim not recovering costs of civil proceedings—Whether victim entitled to compensation in respect of costs following conviction of accused—Criminal Justice Act 1972, s 1(1). **Hammertons Cars Ltd v Redbridge London Borough** [1974] 2 216, QBD.

Proof of amount of damage. *See* Compensation—Order—Principles applicable in making order—Compensation order not to be made unless the sum claimed by the victim for the damage is agreed or proved, *below.*

Means and prospect of rehabilitation—

Irrelevant—Forfeiture Act 1870, s 4 (as amended). **R v Ironfield** [1971] 1 202, CA.

Relevance—No order to be made where liable to be self-defeating—Circumstances in which order liable to be self-defeating—Offender unlikely to have sufficient means to comply with order—Temptation to resort to crime in order to make necessary payment—Criminal Justice Act 1972, s 1(1), (4). **R v Oddy** [1974] 2 666, CA.

Means of convicted person—

Regard to be had to means in determining whether to make order—Order to be made only in simple cases—Order involving weekly payment over period of years not appropriate—Criminal Justice Act 1972, s 1(1), (4). **R v Daly** [1974] 1 290, CA.

Order—

Amount of compensation—Determination of amount of order—Evidence and representations—Whether compensation order can be based simply on prosecutor's representations without evidence regarding amount claimed as compensation—Whether some evidence of amount claimed as compensation always required—Powers of Criminal Courts Act 1973, s 35(1)(1A). **R v Horsham Justices, ex p Richards** [1985] 2 1114, QBD.

Compensation for personal injury, loss or damage resulting from the offence—Anxiety and distress directly caused by offence—Defendant throwing stone through window of house—Magistrates awarding compensation to occupier for his distress and anxiety—Whether distress and anxiety amounting to 'personal injury ... or damage' resulting from offence—Powers of Criminal Courts Act 1973, s 35(1). **Bond v Chief Constable of Kent** [1983] 1 456, QBD.

Compensation for personal injury, loss or damage resulting from the offence—Loss—Financial loss—Power of court to include amount by way of interest in order—When appropriate for court to include interest in order—Powers of Criminal Courts Act 1973, s 35(1). **R v Schofield** [1978] 2 705, CA.

Determination of amount of order in respect of bereavement—Whether amount of order unlimited or limited to sums which could be awarded by way of damages in civil proceedings—Powers of Criminal Courts Act 1973, s 35(3D). **R v Gateway Foodmarkets Ltd** [1997] 3 78, CA.

Form of order—Criminal Justice Act 1972, s 1(1). **R v Oddy** [1974] 2 666, CA.

SENTENCE (cont)—
  Compensation (cont)—
    Order (cont)—
      Inability of convicted person to meet all claims in full—How assets should be apportioned. **R v Amey** [1983] **1** 865, CA.
      Indictable offence—No application by person aggrieved—Validity of order—Magistrates' court—Forfeiture Act 1870, s 4, as amended. **R v Forest Justices, ex p Coppin** [1969] **2** 668, QBD.
      Indictable offence—No application by person aggrieved—Validity of order—Quarter sessions—Forfeiture Act 1870, s 4 (as amended). **R v Taylor** [1969] **2** 662, CA.
      Joint and several order—Power to make joint and several order against joint offenders—Circumstances in which power should be exercised—Criminal Justice Act 1972, s 1(1). **R v Grundy** [1974] **1** 292, CA.
      Judicial review. *See* **Crown Court** (Supervisory jurisdiction of High Court—Trial on indictment).
      Order for payment of compensation and costs resulting from conviction for offence—Magistrate authorising clerk to issue garnishee proceedings to secure payment—Garnishee order nisi made against convicted person's bank account—Garnishee order nisi discharged and clerk taking fresh proceedings for garnishee order—Whether clerk 'authorised' by court to take further garnishee proceedings—Magistrates' Court Act 1980, s 87(3). **Gooch v Ewing (Allied Irish Bank Ltd, garnishee)** [1985] **3** 654, CA.
      Order for payment of compensation and costs resulting from conviction for offence—Petition for leave to appeal against conviction to House of Lords pending—Suspension of order—Magistrate authorising clerk to issue garnishee proceedings to attach convicted person's bank account in respect of sums due—Whether sums referred to in authorisation 'sums adjudged to be paid'—Whether authorisation valid—Criminal Appeal Act 1968, s 42—Powers of Criminal Courts Act 1973, s 36—Magistrates' Courts Act 1980, s 87(3). **Gooch v Ewing (Allied Irish Bank Ltd, garnishee)** [1985] **3** 654, CA.
      Order made on conviction—Whether compensation order a sentence—Whether justices entitled to impose compensation order and commit offender with a view to borstal training. **R v Dorset Quarter Sessions, ex p Randall** [1966] **3** 952, QBD.
      Persons jointly convicted—Principles applicable in making order. **R v Amey** [1983] **1** 865, CA.
      Principles applicable in making order—Compensation order not to be made unless the sum claimed by the victim for the damage is agreed or proved—Powers of Criminal Courts Act 1973, s 35(1). **R v Vivian** [1979] **1** 48, CA.
      Principles applicable in making order—Compensation order not to be made unless the sum claimed by victim is agreed or proved—Degree of proof required—Necessity for amount of loss to be proved by evidence. **R v Amey** [1983] **1** 865, CA.
      Retention of property in anticipation of making of order—Police powers. *See* **Police** (Powers—Power to retain property relevant to criminal proceedings—Retention in respect of anticipated restitution, compensation or forfeiture order).
  Parent or guardian's liability—
    Local authority as guardian—Young person placed in care of local authority pursuant to care order—Local authority allowing young person to be under charge and control of parents—Young person committing offences while residing with parents—Whether local authority having 'charge of or control over' young person when offences committed—Children and Young Persons Act 1933, s 55(1) (as amended by the Children and Young Persons Act 1969, s 72(3), Sch 5, para 5, and the Criminal Justice Act 1972, s 64(1), Sch 5), s 107(1)—Children Act 1948, s 13(2) (as substituted by the Children and Young Persons Act 1969, s 49). **Lincoln Corp v Parker** [1974] **2** 949, QBD.
    Local authority as guardian—Young person placed in care of local authority pursuant to care order—Local authority allowing young person to be under charge and control of parent—Young person committing offences while residing with parent—Whether local authority having 'charge of or control over' young person when offences committed—Children and Young Persons Act 1933, s 55(1)(as amended by the Children and Young Persons Act 1969, s 72(3), Sch 5, para 5, and the Powers of Criminal Courts Act 1973, s 56(1), Sch 5, para 1), s 107(1)—Children Act 1948, s 13(2)(as substituted by the Children and Young Persons Act 1969, s 49). **Leicestershire CC v Cross** [1976] **2** 491, QBD.
    Local authority as guardian—Young person placed in care of local authority pursuant to care order—Local authority placing young person in community home—Community home not controlled by local authority—Young person absconding from community home and committing offence—Compensation order against local authority—Whether local authority 'guardian' of young person—Children and Young Persons Act 1933 (as amended by the Criminal Justice Act 1972, s 64(1), Sch 5), 107. **Somerset CC v Brice** [1973] **3** 438, QBD.
    Local authority as guardian—Young persons remanded in local authority accommodation—Youths in local authority accommodation committing offences—Justices imposing compensation order on local authority—Whether local authority having 'parental responsibility' for youths—Children and Young Persons Act 1933, s 55(5)—Children and Young Persons Act 1969, s 23—Children Act 1989, ss 3, 33, 44. **North Yorkshire CC v Selby Youth Court Justices** [1994] **1** 991, QBD.
    Neglect of control—Parent or guardian conducing to commission of offence by neglecting to exercise due care or control over child or young person—Local authority guardian of child—Test for determining whether local authority guilty of neglect conducing to commission of offence—Child placed in care of local authority pursuant to care order—Authority placing child in community home—Home not a secure penal institution—Purpose of home to rehabilitate children—Child absconding from home and committing offence—Whether authority having conduced to commission of offence by neglecting to exercise due care or control of child—Children and Young Persons Act 1933, s 55 (as amended by the Criminal Justice Act 1972, s 64(1), Sch 5). **Somerset CC v Kingscott** [1975] **1** 326, QBD.
  Stolen goods—
    Not recovered—Plea of guilty to burglary—Indictment specifying items stolen—Most items recovered—Accused subsequently denying that remaining items stolen—No application for compensation order—Whether court should make compensation order in respect of unrecovered items—Criminal Justice Act 1972, s 1(1). **R v Kneeshaw** [1974] **1** 896, CA.
    Recovered—Goods in respect of which accused convicted all recovered—Order made in respect of other goods not subject of charge—Annulment of order—Theft Act 1968, s 28(1)—Criminal Appeal Act 1968, s 30(4). **R v Parker** [1970] **2** 458, CA.

SENTENCE (cont)—
Concurrent or consecutive sentences—
Further convictions—
Bad record of accused—Second conviction for similar offence as first conviction—Bad record taken into account on both convictions—Whether subsequent sentence should be concurrent with or consecutive to first. **R v Ames** [1938] **1** 515, CCA.
Life imprisonment minimum term. *See* Life imprisonment—Minimum period of imprisonment, *below.*
Concurrent sentences—
Convictions on two counts arising out of the same facts and involving same criminality—Consecutive sentences not appropriate. **R v Torr** [1966] **1** 178, CCA.
Preventive detention. *See* Preventive detention—Concurrent sentences, *below.*
Reduction—
Period spent in custody. *See* Reduction—Period spent in custody—Concurrent sentences, *below.*
Conditional discharge—
Appeal. *See* Conditional discharge, *above.*
Breach of condition—
Not to be taken into consideration on subsequent conviction—Sentence to be passed for original offence. **R v Webb** [1953] **1** 1156, CCA.
Sentence of borstal training for first offence—Need for nominal sentence in respect of breach of condition. **R v Fry** [1955] **1** 21, CCA.
Confiscation order. *See* Confiscation order—Crown Court—Jurisdiction—Defendant convicted of concealing criminal property, *below.*
Conviction deemed not to be conviction for purpose of other proceedings—
Whether finding of guilt can be taken into account in other proceedings. *See* **Conviction** (Discharge—Conditional discharge—Discharge having effect that conviction deemed not to be conviction for purpose of other proceedings).
Explanation of effect of order—
Judge not explaining effect of order to defendant—Judge obtaining undertaking from defendant's counsel to explain effect of order to defendant—Explanation given before order made—Whether court prohibited from delegating function of explanation—Whether order valid—Powers of Criminal Courts Act 1973, s 7(3). **R v Wehner** [1977] **3** 553, CA.
Fine imposed—
Order of conditional discharge not to be made if fine also imposed—Criminal Justice Act 1948, ss 7(1), 13. **R v McClelland** [1951] **1** 557, CCA.
Confiscation order—
Application for confiscation order—
Duty to disclose intention to institute civil proceedings—Revenue prosecuting offender for fraudulent evasion of tax and duty—Offender convicted—Revenue applying for confiscation order—Confiscation order made—Revenue subsequently serving statutory demand for unpaid duty and penalties and petioning for bankruptcy order against offender—Whether Revenue having had duty to disclose intention to institute civil proceedings—Whether bankruptcy order should be made—Criminal Justice Act 1988, s 71. **Revenue and Customs Comrs v Crossman** [2008] **1** 483, Ch D.
Prosecutions instituted and conducted otherwise than by the Crown Prosecution Service—Private prosecution resulting in conviction for conspiracy to defraud—Whether private prosecutor entitled to bring confiscation proceedings—Prosecution of Offences Act 1985, s 6—Proceeds of Crime Act 2002, ss 6, 40(9). **R v Zinga** [2014] **3** 90, CA.
Time limit—Defendants pleading guilty but sentencing taking place more than six months later—Prosecution applying for confiscation orders—Defendants contending that application made more than six months since their convictions and therefore outside time limit—Whether conviction was date when offender was found or pleaded guilty or date of sentence—Criminal Justice Act 1988, ss 71, 72AA, 72A. **R v Shergill** [1999] **2** 485, CA.
Whether non-compliance with statutory procedural requirements going to court's jurisdiction—Criminal Justice Act 1988, ss 71, 72—Proceeds of Crime Act 1995, s 16(5). **R v Simpson** [2003] **3** 531, CA.
Burden of proof—
Whether assumptions made in assessing proceeds of drug trafficking compatible with presumption of innocence under human rights convention—Proceeds of Crime (Scotland) Act 1995, s 3(2)—Human Rights Act 1998, Sch 1, Pt I, art 6(2). **McIntosh v Lord Advocate** [2001] **2** 638, PC.
Whether statutory provisions governing confiscation orders compatible with presumption of innocence and right to peaceful enjoyment of possessions under human rights convention—Criminal Justice Act 1988, s 72AA—Drug Trafficking Act 1994, s 4—Human Rights Act 1998, Sch 1, Pt I, art 6, Pt II, art 1. **R v Benjafield** [2001] **2** 609, CA; **R v Rezvi** [2001] **2** 609, CA.
Civil proceedings instituted by victim. *See* Confiscation order—Proceeds of crime—Benefit—Duty of court to make confiscation order—Power of court to make confiscation order where victim of offence instituting civil proceedings, *below.*
Crown Court—
Jurisdiction—Defendant convicted of concealing criminal property—Defendant conditionally discharged—Crown Court making confiscation order—Whether Crown Court having power to make confiscation order against defendant following conditional discharge—Powers of Criminal Courts (Sentencing) Act 2000, ss 12, 14—Proceeds of Crime Act 2002, s 6. **R v Clarke** [2009] **4** 298, CA.
Jurisdiction—Defendant convicted of concealing criminal property—Defendant conditionally discharged—Crown Court making confiscation order—Whether Crown Court having power to make confiscation order against defendant following conditional discharge—Powers of Criminal Courts (Sentencing) Act 2000, s 12—Proceeds of Crime Act 2002, s 6. **R v Varma** [2011] **2** 935, CA.
Jurisdiction—Defendant convicted of fraudulent evasion of duty—Defendant conditionally discharged—Crown Court making confiscation order—Whether Crown Court having power to make confiscation order against defendant following conditional discharge—Powers of Criminal Courts (Sentencing) Act 2000, s 12—Proceeds of Crime Act 2002, s 6. **R v Varma** [2013] **1** 129, SC.

SENTENCE (cont)—
  Confiscation order (cont)—
    Crown Court (cont)—
      Jurisdiction—Defendants convicted of series of benefit fraud offences—Some offences predating commencement date of current legislation—Court making confiscation orders under current legislation in respect only of offences occurring after commencement date of legislation—Whether court having jurisdiction to make orders—Proceeds of Crime Act 2002, s 156—Proceeds of Crime Act 2002 (Commencement No 5, Transitional Provisions, Savings and Amendment) Order 2003, SI 2003/333, art 4. **R v McCool (Northern Ireland)** [2018] 3 849, SC.

      Jurisdiction—Whether Crown Court having jurisdiction to make confiscation order on committal for sentence from a magistrates' court in respect of offences committed before 30 September 1998—Powers of Criminal Courts Act 1973, s 42(1)—Magistrates' Courts Act 1980, s 38—Criminal Justice Act 1988, s 71. **R v Pope** [2002] 3 889, HL.

    Drug trafficking—
      Benefit from drug trafficking—Standard of proof—Presumption of innocence—Right to fair trial—Defendant convicted of drugs offence but deriving no benefit—Judge in confiscation proceedings finding other drug trafficking proved to criminal standard during trial—Judge not applying statutory assumptions as to defendant's property—Whether confiscation order valid—Whether statutory assumptions mandatory—Whether finding based on other drug trafficking amounting to fresh charge—Whether presumption of innocence applying—Whether breach of right to fair trial—Drug Trafficking Act 1994, ss 2(8)(a), 4—Human Rights Act 1998, Sch 1, Pt I, art 6(1)(2). **R v Briggs-Price** [2009] 4 594, HL.

      Generally. *See* **Drugs** (Drug trafficking—Confiscation order).

      Realisable property. *See* **Drugs** (Drug trafficking—Confiscation order—Satisfaction of order—Realisable property).

      Warrant of commitment to enforce order. *See* **Drugs** (Drug trafficking—Confiscation order—Warrant of commitment to enforce order).

      Whether for purposes of calculating proceeds of drug trafficking each defendant to be regarded as having received whole of money or property received by one defendant on behalf of defendants jointly—Drug Trafficking Act 1994, s 2. **R v Green** [2007] 3 751, CA; [2008] 4 119, HL.

      Whether statutory provisions governing confiscation orders compatible with human rights—Drug Trafficking Act 1994, s 4(3)—Human Rights Act 1998, Sch 1, Pt I, art 6, Pt II, art 1. **R v Benjafield** [2002] 1 815, HL.

    Enforcement —
      Right to a fair hearing—Delay in enforcement of confiscation order—Whether breach of right to a fair hearing—Whether proceedings for enforcement of confiscation order other than by sanction of imprisonment proceedings determining civil rights and obligations or criminal charge—Human Rights Act 1998, Sch 1, Pt I, art 6(1). **R (on the application of Minshall) v Marylebone Magistrates' Court (Revenue and Customs Prosecutions Office interested party)** [2009] 2 806, QBD.

    Fraudulent evasion of excise duty—
      Pecuniary advantage—Defendant fraudulently evading excise duty on imported goods—Customs officers seizing goods before sale—Whether defendant obtaining pecuniary advantage from failure to pay duty—Criminal Justice Act 1988, ss 71, 74. **R v Smith (David)** [2002] 1 366, HL.

    Order for costs—
      Judge making costs order before determination of amount payable under confiscation order—Whether order for costs lawful—Criminal Justice Act 1988, s 72. **R v Threapleton** [2003] 3 458, CA.

    Postponement of confiscation proceedings—
      Effect on power of court to award costs—Defendant sentenced in respect of offences of applying false trade descriptions to second-hand vehicles—Confiscation proceedings postponed—No order for costs made at sentencing hearing—Costs awarded after conclusion of confiscation proceedings—Powers of court to postpone costs order relating to costs of case as a whole until conclusion of confiscation proceedings—Proceeds of Crime Act 2002, ss 13-15. **R v Constantine** [2011] 3 767, CA.

      Judge making forfeiture order—Prosecution failing to comply with procedural requirements—Whether substantial non-compliance with statutory procedural requirements for postponement of confiscation proceedings going to court's jurisdiction—Whether technical breaches of statutory requirements sufficient to render confiscation order invalid—Proceeds of Crime Act 2002, ss 13(3), 14(11), (12), 15(2). **R v Guraj** [2017] 4 848, SC.

      Judge making forfeiture order—Prosecution failing to comply with procedural requirements—Whether substantial non-compliance with statutory procedural requirements for postponement of confiscation proceedings going to court's jurisdiction—Whether technical breaches of statutory requirements sufficient to render confiscation order invalid—Misuse of Drugs Act 1971, s 27(1)—Proceeds of Crime Act 2002, ss 6, 14, 15(2). **R v Guraj** [2016] 2 13, CA.

      Whether non-compliance with statutory procedural requirements for postponement of confiscation proceedings going to court's jurisdiction—Criminal Justice Act 1988, s 72A(3). **R v Soneji** [2005] 4 321, HL.

      Whether non-compliance with statutory procedural requirements for postponement of confiscation proceedings going to court's jurisdiction—Whether court having to specify period of postponement when deciding to postpone confiscation proceedings—Criminal Justice Act 1988, s 72A. **R v Knights** [2005] 4 347, HL; **R v Sekhon** [2003] 3 508, CA.

    Postponement of determination for period not exceeding six months beginning with date of conviction—
      Exceptional circumstances allowing court to specify longer period—Whether substantive hearing started within six month period being within period not exceeding six months—Whether listing difficulties capable of being exceptional circumstances—Criminal Justice Act 1988, s 72A(3). **R v Young** [2004] 2 63, CA.

SENTENCE (cont)—
    Confiscation order (cont)—
        Proceeds of crime—

        Appellants being convicted of conspiracy to cheat public revenue—Missing trader fraud causing loss to public revenue in excess of £12m—Judge finding prosecution proving on balance of probabilities each appellant benefited from fraud in sum of £72m—Judge finding appellants had hidden assets—Whether total amount of money received into bank account controlled by appellants in furtherance of fraud being property obtained by appellant as result of or in connection with commission of offence as defined by Criminal Justice Act 1988 s 71(4)—Whether court bound to reject appellants' case that current realisable assets less than full amount of benefit given conclusion that appellants had not revealed their true extent or value—Criminal Justice Act 1988, s 71. **R v Ahmad** [2012] **2** 1137, CA.

        Appellants being convicted of conspiracy to cheat public revenue—Missing trader fraud causing loss to public revenue in excess of £35m—Agreed benefit to appellants of £3,668,990—Appellants submitting no assets to pay criminal benefit attributable—Judge finding appellants did not tell truth about realisable assets—Judge making confiscation order in full amount of benefit in each case—Proper approach to determining realisable amounts—Criminal Justice Act 1988, s 71(4). **R v McIntosh** [2011] **4** 917, CA.

        Available amount—Value—Property held on trust for defendant and siblings beneficially as tenants in common—Prohibition against sale of property without consent of other tenants and consent not forthcoming—Whether value of defendant's beneficial interest nil in calculating available amount recoverable under confiscation order—Trusts of Land and Appointment of Trustees Act 1996, s 14—Proceeds of Crime Act 2002, ss 9(1), 79(3). **R v Modjiri** [2010] **4** 837, CA.

        Benefit—Calculation of benefit—Appellant convicted of handling stolen goods and confiscation order made—Calculation of appellant's benefit from criminal conduct—Whether VAT accounted for and/or paid to HMRC to be included in turnover figure for calculation—Whether double recovery by HMRC violating right to property—Human Rights Act 1998, Sch 1, Pt II, art 1—Proceeds of Crime Act 2002, ss 6, 76. **R v Harvey** [2016] **4** 521, SC.

        Benefit—Calculation of benefit—Interest in property—Defendants in separate appeals being convicted of carousel fraud and conspiracy to defraud respectively—Confiscation orders being made—Whether each defendant separately liable for whole amount of benefit—Whether amount of confiscation order to be apportioned to avoid disproportionate outcome—Whether confiscation orders infringing defendants' right to protection of property—Human Rights Act 1998, Sch 1, Pt II, art 1—Proceeds of Crime Act 2002, s 76(4), 79(1), (2). **R v Ahmad** [2014] **4** 767, SC; **R v Fields** [2014] **4** 767, SC.

        Benefit—Calculation of benefit—Interest in property—Market value of property obtained by thief or handler—Relevance of previous legislative scheme and authorities—Proceeds of Crime Act 2002, ss 79, 80. **R v Rose** [2008] **3** 315, CA.

        Benefit—Calculation of benefit—Interest in property—Right to protection of property—Defendant purchasing property using fraudulently obtained mortgage loan—Loan constituting 60% of purchase price with balance consisting of defendant's untainted funds—Loan redeemed and property remortgaged to different lender—Defendant convicted of obtaining money transfer by deception in relation to first mortgage—Judge making confiscation order in value of property less untainted funds—Order reduced on appeal to 60% of property's market value—Nature of defendant's benefit—Whether application of rules for calculation of benefit compatible with right to protection of property—Human Rights Act 1998, Sch 1, Pt II, art 1—Proceeds of Crime Act 2002, ss 6(5), 76(4), 79(3), 80(2), (3). **R v Waya** [2013] **1** 889, SC.

        Benefit—Co-principal conspirators jointly obtaining benefit of proceeds of conspiracy—Whether benefit obtained by each equalling full amount of proceeds—Whether amount of confiscation order to be apportioned to avoid disproportionate outcome—Proceeds of Crime Act 2002, s 79(3). **R v Fields** [2014] **2** 811, CA.

        Benefit—Conduct and benefit—Pecuniary advantage—Person obtaining pecuniary advantage as result of conduct to be taken to obtain sum of money equal to value of pecuniary advantage—Defendant involved in value added tax fraud conspiracy—Amount of confiscation order—Proceeds of Crime Act 2002, s 76(5). **R v Takkar** [2011] **3** 340, CA.

        Benefit—Crown applying for confiscation order—Whether proceedings could be stayed where results of statutory criteria oppressive—Proceeds of Crime Act 2002, s 6. **R v Nelson** [2010] **4** 666, CA.

        Benefit—Defendants playing active role in physical handling of contraband goods so as to assist in their commercial realisation -Confiscation orders made by consent on basis that benefit was the evasion of duty and value added tax—Defendants consenting to confiscation orders on basis of mistake of law—Defendants not liable for excise duty and value added tax on contraband—Whether defendants precluded from appealing against confiscation orders made by consent—Whether defendants obtaining benefit from criminal conduct—Proceeds of Crime Act 2002, ss 156, 158, 224—Proceeds of Crime (Northern Ireland) Order 1996, SI 1996/1299—Tobacco Products Regulations 2001, SI 2001/1712, reg 13. **R v Mackle** [2014] **2** 170, SC.

        Benefit—Duty of court to make confiscation order—Power of court to make confiscation order where victim of offence instituting civil proceedings—Whether court having discretion to make confiscation order where offender having repaid or standing ready to repay victim but no civil proceedings instituted—Whether making confiscation order abuse of process where offender required to pay sum greater than would have been recoverable in civil proceedings—Criminal Justice Act 1988, ss 71, 72—Proceeds of Crime Act 2002, ss 6, 13. **R v Morgan** [2008] **4** 890, CA.

        Benefit—Person benefiting from offence if he obtained property—Companies obtaining property fraudulently—Companies jointly controlled by offenders—Whether each offender obtaining benefit of whole of property obtained—Criminal Justice Act 1988, s 71(4). **R v May** [2005] **3** 523, CA; [2008] **4** 97, HL.

        Benefit—Person benefiting from offence if he obtained property—Obtaining property—Criminal Justice Act 1988, s 71(4). **Jennings v CPS** [2008] **4** 113, HL.

SENTENCE (cont)—
  Confiscation order (cont)—
    Proceeds of crime (cont)—
      Benefit—Proceedings—Defendant convicted of an offence or offences in proceedings before Crown Court—Defendant pleading guilty on same day to two indictments with offences pre-dating and post-dating change in confiscation order regime—Judge making two confiscation orders at single confiscation hearing—Whether 'proceedings' covering all matters dealt with on single occasion—Criminal Justice Act 1988, s 72AA(1)(c)(i)—Proceeds of Crime Act 2002, s 6—Proceeds of Crime Act 2002 (Commencement No 5, Transitional Provisions, Savings and Amendment) Order 2003, SI 2003/333, art 3(1). **R v Moulden** [2009] **2** 912, CA.
      Benefit—Value of property—Market value—Whether goods of illegal nature obtained by defendant to be treated as having no value for purpose of calculation of benefit—Proceeds of Crime Act 2002, s 79(2). **R v Islam** [2010] **1** 493, HL.
      Company directors—Directors conspiring to make secret profit—Directors convicted of cheating the public revenue—Confiscation orders made against directors—Whether company having proprietary interest over assets of directors in priority to confiscation orders—Proceeds of Crime Act 2002. **Crown Prosecution Service v Aquila Advisory Ltd** [2022] **2** 864, SC.
      Criminal lifestyle—Benefit—Conduct and benefit—Pecuniary advantage—Offence of conspiracy to fraudulently evade excise duty—Offence committed over period of at least six months being condition of defendant having criminal lifestyle—Pecuniary advantage obtained as a result of or in connection with conduct—Whether condition fulfilled where offence of conspiracy committed over period of at least six months—Whether pecuniary advantage obtained—Whether defendant liable to pay excise duty—Proceeds of Crime Act 2002, ss 6(4), 75(2)(c), 76(4), (5). **R v Bajwa** [2012] **1** 348, CA.
      Criminal lifestyle—Benefit—Conduct and benefit—Pecuniary advantage—Offence of depositing waste on land without license—Offence of knowlingly permitting operation of regulated facility—Offence of knowingly causing controlled waste to be submitted to listed operation without permit—Defendant permitting waste deposits by others on land without receiving payment —Whether defendant benefiting from criminal conduct by obtaining pecuniary advantage—Whether confiscation order disproportionate—Human Rights Act 1998, Sch 1, Pt II, art 1—Proceeds of Crime Act 2002, ss 6(4)(b), (5)(b), 10(3), (6)(a), (6)(b), 76(4). **R v Morgan** [2014] **1** 1208, CA.
      Drug trafficking. *See* Confiscation order—Drug trafficking, *above*.
      Postponement of confiscation proceedings. *See* Confiscation order—Postponement of confiscation proceedings, *above*.
      Property likely to be realised or used to satisfy confiscation order—Third-party interest—Representations—Whether court required to give third party opportunity to make representations before making confiscation order—Proceeds of Crime Act 2002, ss 156, 160A, 199. **R v Hilton (Northern Ireland)** [2021] **1** 109, SC.
      Tainted gifts—Proportionality—Enforcement receiver—Defendant convicted of money laundering—Defendant having given partner money to fund purchase of council house—Money being 'tainted gift'—Whether disproportionate to include tainted gift in amount of order—Whether possible to appoint enforcement receiver—Proceeds of Crime Act 2002, ss 6(5)(b), 10A. **R v Morrison** [2019] **4** 181, CA.
      Whether statutory provisions governing confiscation orders compatible with human rights—Criminal Justice Act 1988, s 72AA—Human Rights Act 1998, Sch 1, Pt I, art 6, Pt II, art 1. **R v Rezvi** [2001] **2** 609, CA; [2002] **1** 801, HL.
    Qualifying offences—
      Benefit from offence—Defendant convicted of trade mark offences of possession of items with a view to gain—Whether defendant benefiting from offences—Criminal Justice Act 1988, ss 71(4), 72AA—Trade Marks Act 1994, s 92(1)(c), (3)(b). **R v Davies (Derrick)** [2004] **2** 706, CA.
    Realisable property—
      Appellant corruptly accepting loan to buy property—Loan secured by legal charge in favour of third party—Appellant convicted of conspiracy to corrupt—Trial judge satisfied that loan was gift and legal charge unlikely to be enforced—Whether trial judge entitled to ignore legal charge when calculating amount of appellant's realisable property—Whether exercise of trial judge's discretion to make confiscation order unreasonable—Criminal Justice Act 1988, ss 71(6), 74(4). **R v Harvey** [1999] **1** 710, CA.
      Claims of third parties—Defendant convicted of conspiracy to cheat the public revenue—Confiscation order made—Whether defendant having interest in property registered in name of third party—Criminal Justice Act 1988, s 102(7). **Revenue and Customs Prosecutions Office v May** [2010] **3** 1173, CA.
      Defendants obtaining property fraudulently—Defendants benefiting from criminal conduct—Realisable property including assets available to them jointly—Whether value of each defendant's realisable property including value of jointly-held assets—Criminal Justice Act 1988, ss 71, 74. **R v Gangar** [2012] **4** 972, CA.
      Pensions—Criminal Justice Act 1988, ss 74, 80, 102. **Ahmed v Crown Prosecution Service** [2019] **1** 1003, CA.
      Right to respect for private and family life—Value of offender's beneficial share in matrimonial home—Whether judge making confiscation order having discretion to exclude value of offender's beneficial share in computing realisable property—Whether breach of right to respect for private and family life—Criminal Justice Act 1988, ss 71(6)(b), 74—Human Rights Act 1998, Sch 1, Pt I, art 8. **R v Ahmed** [2005] **1** 128, CA.
    Receiver's costs. *See* **Receiver** (Appointed by court—Remuneration—Receivership order in respect of criminal defendant subsequently discharged).
    Receivership order—
      Satisfaction of consfiscation order—Application of proceeds—Interest—Receiver retaining sums in respect of remuneration and disbursements—Whether receiver required to pay all proceeds to magistrates' court—Whether court having discretion as to interest on sums unpaid—Criminal Justice Act 1988, ss 75A, 81. **Hansford v Southampton Magistrates' Court** [2008] **4** 432, DC.
  Consecutive sentences—
    Community service order. *See* Community service order—Consecutive orders, *above*.
    Concurrent or consecutive sentences. *See* Concurrent or consecutive sentences, *above*.

SENTENCE (cont)—

Consecutive sentences (cont)—

Corrective training. *See* Corrective training—Consecutive sentences, *below*.

Dangerous offenders. *See* Custodial sentence—Dangerous offenders—Extended sentences—Consecutive sentences, *below*.

Discretion to impose—

Maximum sentences for like offences—Whether maximum sentences imposed on several convictions each for a separate like offence can be directed to run consecutively—Official Secrets Act 1911, s 1(1)(c)—Official Secrets Act 1920, s 8(1). **R v Blake** [1961] **3** 125, CCA.

Extended term of imprisonment. *See* Extended term of imprisonment—Consecutive terms, *below*.

Further sentence—

Form of further sentence where prisoner already subject to consecutive sentences—Note whether prisoner subject to consecutive sentences to be added to list of previous convictions. **Practice Note** [1959] **2** 144, PDA.

Hard labour—

Consecutive sentences of imprisonment with hard labour amounting to three years—Penal servitude for three years substituted—Penal Servitude Act 1926, s 1. **R v Darry** [1945] **2** 454, CCA.

Life imprisonment—

Consecutive to term being served—Whether sentence of life imprisonment to run consecutively with sentence of imprisonment then being served permissible and desirable. **Jones v DPP** [1962] **1** 569, HL.

Subsequent sentence of imprisonment to run consecutively—Subsequent sentence invalid. **R v Foy** [1962] **2** 246, CCA.

Magistrates' court—

Consecutive terms of imprisonment. *See* Imprisonment—Magistrates' court—Consecutive terms, *below*.

Prison sentence made consecutive to existing detention centre sentence—

Wrong in principle—Sentence should be concurrent with detention so that accused goes straight to prison. **R v Raisis** [1969] **3** 455, CA.

Proportion of sentence—

Separate indictment—Undesirability of proportion of sentence on one indictment being made to run consecutively to sentence imposed on second indictment. **R v Gregory and Mills** [1969] **2** 174, CA.

Release dates—

Eligibility for home detention curfew or conditional release—Prisoners serving sentences of imprisonment of less than 12 months—Transitional provisions—Sentences of longer than 12 months—Criminal Justice Act 1991—Criminal Justice Act 2003—Criminal Justice Act 2003 (Commencement No 8 and Transitional and Saving Provisions) Order 2005, SI 2005/950, Sch 2, para 14. **R (on the application of Noone) v Governor of Drake Hall Prison** [2009] **1** 494, CA; [2010] **4** 463, SC.

Series of offences—

Separate and distinct offences—Spying—Whether sentences to run concurrently—Official Secrets Act 1911, s 1(1)(c)—Official Secrets Act 1920, s 8(1). **R v Britten** [1969] **1** 517, CA.

Subsequent offence—

Prisoner already serving sentence—Sentence to commence at expiration of previous sentence—Subsequent offence meaning subsequent conviction for offence—Criminal Law Act 1928, s 10. **R v Greenberg** [1943] **1** 504, CCA.

Suspended sentence. *See* Suspended sentence—Consecutive sentences, *below*.

Consecutive terms—

Conviction following release on licence. *See* Custodial sentence—Imposition of custodial sentence longer than that commensurate with seriousness of offence—Restriction on consecutive sentences for released prisoners, *below*.

Offender committing offence while released on licence from sentence imposed for earlier offence—

Offender ordered to be returned to prison to serve unexpired part of sentence for earlier offence—Whether court could impose sentence for new offence to run consecutively to period of return to prison—Criminal Justice Act 1991, s 40—Crime and Disorder Act 1998, s 102. **R v Lowe** [1999] **3** 762, CA.

Contempt of court—

Breach of injunction. *See* **Contempt of court** (Committal—Breach of injunction—Maximum sentence).

Committal. *See* **Contempt of court** (Committal).

Criminal contempt. *See* **Contempt of court** (Criminal contempt—Sentence).

Corrective training—

Adverse report by Prison Commissioners—

Accused unsuitable for corrective training—Duty of court to have regard to report. **R v Murray** [1950] **2** 925, CCA.

Appropriate term—

Corrective training a form of imprisonment—Whether sentence of three years' corrective training appropriate—Petty offence but previous convictions. **R v McCarthy** [1955] **2** 927, CCA.

Concurrent with term of imprisonment—

Not to run concurrently with imprisonment—Criminal Justice Act 1948, s 21(1). **R v Heritage** [1951] **1** 1013, CCA.

Sentence of imprisonment to run concurrently with corrective training—Sentence of imprisonment not to take effect at conclusion of period of corrective training—Criminal Justice Act 1948, s 21(1). **R v Talbot** [1953] **1** 340, CCA.

Consecutive sentences—

Power of the court to pass consecutive sentences—Criminal Justice Act 1948, s 21(1). **R v Albury** [1951] **1** 491, CCA.

Duration. *See* Corrective training—Length of sentence, *below*.

Further sentence on offender already serving sentence of corrective training—

Further offence committed while offender released on licence. **R v Wilsher** [1953] **2** 326, CCA.

Imprisonment—

Difference between imprisonment and corrective training—Criminal Justice Act 1948, s 21(1). **R v Ledger** [1950] **1** 1104, CCA.

SENTENCE (cont)—
 Corrective training (cont)—
  Length of sentence—
   Term long enough for real reform to be attempted—Criminal Justice Act 1948, s 21(1). **R v Barrett** [1949] **2** 689, CCA.
   Two years permissible if adequate for the individual case—Criminal Justice Act 1948, s 21(1). **Practice Direction** [1961] **1** 619, CCA.
  Notice of previous convictions—
   Cases where notice need not be served—Criminal Justice Act 1948, s 23. **Practice Note** [1966] **2** 905, CCA.
   Committal for sentence—Service of notice three days before sentence by quarter sessions—Criminal Justice Act 1948, s 23(1). **R v Grant** [1951] **1** 28, CCA.
   Proof of service—Averment of convictions in indictment—Sentence set aside—Criminal Justice Act 1948, s 23(1). **R v Allen** [1949] **2** 808, CCA.
  Preventive detention—
   Need for date of prisoner's birth in police reports and prison reports. **R v Rossi** [1955] **1** 368, CCA.
   Notice of intention to prove previous convictions—Contents of notice—Criminal Justice Act 1948, ss 21(1)(2), 23(1)(2). **R v Evans** [1956] **3** 750, CCA.
   Notice of intention to prove previous convictions—Proof of service—Admission of convictions by offender—Attachment of notice to indictment—Criminal Justice Act 1948, ss 21(1)(2), 23(1). **R v Dickson** [1949] **2** 810, Assizes.
   Previous convictions—Conviction in Northern Ireland—Convictions in Scotland and abroad—Criminal Justice Act 1948, ss 21(1)(2), 23(1). **R v Murphy** [1949] **2** 867, CCA.
   Supervision—Previous convictions—Previous occasions—Criminal Justice Act 1948, ss 21(1)(b), 21(2)(b), 22(1)(a). **R v Rogers** [1953] **1** 206, CCA.
  Previous convictions—
   Probation order not previous conviction for purpose of sentence of corrective training—Criminal Justice Act 1948, ss 12(1), 21(1). **R v Stobbart** [1951] **2** 753, CCA.
   Scottish previous convictions—No evidence that previous convictions punishable by law of Scotland on indictment with imprisonment for two years or more—Whether sentence of corrective training should stand—Criminal Justice Act 1948, s 21(1)(b). **R v Cavan** [1961] **1** 560, CCA.
  Prison Commissioners' report—
   Copy to be given to offender—Proof—Criminal Justice Act 1948, ss 20(8), 21(5). **Practice Note** [1959] **2** 734, CCA.
   Purpose of corrective training—Duties of Prison Commissioners when reporting on prisoners eligible for corrective training. **Practice Note** [1962] **1** 671, CCA.
  Purpose—
   When an appropriate sentence. **R v Chipchase** [1962] **1** 647, CCA.
  When appropriate sentence—
   Fulfilment of statutory conditions not sufficient to justify sentence—Duty of court to consider facts and circumstances of the case—Criminal Justice Act 1948, s 21(1). **R v Apicella** [1949] **2** 813, CCA.
 Costs of appeal. *See* Appeal—Costs, *above*.
 Court-martial. *See* **Court-martial** (Sentence).
 Criminal bankruptcy order—
  Amendment—
   Jurisdiction of Crown Court. *See* **Crown Court** (Order—Amendment—Jurisdiction—Criminal bankruptcy order—Criminal bankruptcy order in respect of several offences).
  Generally. *See* **Criminal law** (Bankruptcy order).
 Criminal contempt—
  Generally. *See* **Contempt of court** (Criminal contempt—Sentence).
  Summary committal. *See* **Contempt of court** (Criminal contempt—Jurisdiction—Summary committal).
 Crown Court—
  Confiscation order. *See* Confiscation order—Crown Court, *above*.
  Generally. *See* **Crown Court** (Sentence).
 Custodial sentence—
  Credit for periods of remand in custody—
   Guidance—Criminal Justice Act 1967, s 67—Powers of Criminal Courts (Sentencing) Act 2000, ss 84, 116, 155—Criminal Justice Act 2003, ss 240, 265. **R v Gordon** [2007] **2** 768, CA.
   'Time served'—Claimant's period in custody on remand exceeding determinate sentence of imprisonment—Claimant being released on licence—Claimant claiming credit for licence period of sentence—Whether credit allowable for custodial part of sentence only—Criminal Justice Act 2003, s 240ZA. **R (on the application of Galiazia) v Governor of HMP Hewell** [2016] **1** 660, DC.
  Dangerous offenders—
   Extended sentences—Consecutive sentences—Consecutive sentences involving extended sentences—Guidance—Criminal Justice Act 2003, ss 227, 228. **R v C** [2007] **3** 735, CA.
   Extended sentences—Risk of serious harm—Meaning of 'members of the public'—Whether including members of public outside United Kingdom—Criminal Justice Act 2003, s 226A(1)(b). **R v Abdallah** [2017] **2** 795n, CA.
   Indeterminate sentence of imprisonment for public protection—Whether preservation of sentence of imprisonment for public protection after scheme abolished unlawful—Whether sentence imposed contrary to principle of lex mitior—Criminal Justice Act 2003—Legal Aid, Sentencing and Punishment of Offenders Act 2012, s 123—Legal Aid, Sentencing and Punishment of Offenders Act 2012 (Commencement No 4 and Saving Provisions) Order 2012, SI 2012/2906, art 6(a). **R v Docherty** [2017] **4** 263, SC.
   Specified offence—Assessment of dangerousness—Assessment of significant risk to members of public of serious harm occasioned by commission of further such offences—Guidance—Criminal Justice Act 2003, s 229. **R v Johnson** [2007] **1** 1237, CA.
   Specified offence—Assessment of dangerousness—Consideration of outstanding offences—Criminal Justice Act 2003, s 229. **R v Lavery** [2009] **3** 295, CA.
   Specified offence—Serious offence—Advance indication of sentence—Guidance—Criminal Justice Act 2003, Pt 12, Ch 5. **R v Kulah** [2008] **1** 16, CA.

SENTENCE (cont)—
  Custodial sentence (cont)—
    Dangerous offenders (cont)—
      Specified offence—Serious offence—Assessment of dangerousness—Imprisonment for public protection for serious offences—Information to be taken into account by court in assessment of dangerousness—Criminal Justice Act 2003, s 229. **R v Considine** [2007] **3** 621, CA.

      Specified offence—Serious offence—Assessment of dangerousness—Imprisonment for public protection for serious offences—Making indecent photographs of a child—Significant risk of re-offending—Necessary link between re-offending and causing serious harm—Effect of sexual offences prevention order on criteria for imposition of sentence of imprisonment for public protection—Criminal Justice Act 2003, ss 225, 229—Sexual Offences Act 2003, s 104. **R v Terrell** [2008] **2** 1065, CA.

      Specified offence—Serious offence—Assessment of dangerousness—Imprisonment for public protection—Extended sentences—Guidance on amendments—Criminal Justice Act 2003, ss 225(3), (3A), (3B), 227, 229. **A-G's Reference (No 55 of 2008)** [2009] **2** 867, CA.

      Specified offence—Serious offence—Extended sentences—Guidance—Criminal Justice Act 2003, ss 224, 225, 226, 227, 228, 229. **R v Lang** [2006] **2** 410, CA.

      Specified offence—Serious offence—Imprisonment for public protection for serious offences—Minimum term—Minimum term where sentence of imprisonment for public protection imposed on offender already serving determinate sentence—Credit for days spent on remand—Guidance—Criminal Justice Act 2003, Pt 12, Ch 5, s 240—Remand in Custody (Effect of Concurrent and Consecutive Sentences of Imprisonment) Rules 2005, SI 2005/2054, r 2. **R v Ashes** [2008] **1** 113, CA.

      Specified offence—Serious offence—Imprisonment for public protection for serious offences—Minimum term—Notional determinate sentence—Guidance—Criminal Justice Act 2003, s 225. **R v Delucca** [2010] **4** 290, CA.

      Specified offence—Serious offence—Imprisonment for public protection for serious offences—Sentence of imprisonment for public protection to be imposed where offender previously convicted of specified offence—Specified offence of robbery where offender had in his possession a firearm or imitation firearm—Offender previously convicted of offence of robbery where accomplice had in his possession a firearm—Whether offender could be sentenced to imprisonment for public protection—Criminal Justice Act 2003, s 225, Sch 15A, para 10. **R v Gore** [2010] **3** 743, CA.

      Specified offence—Serious offence—Imprisonment for public protection for serious offences—Whether sentence of imprisonment for public protection capable of being ordered to run consecutively to another sentence of imprisonment for public protection—Whether sentence of imprisonment for public protection capable of being ordered to run consecutively to period of return to prison where offence committed during original sentence—Guidance—Powers of Criminal Courts (Sentencing) Act 2000, s 116—Criminal Justice Act 2003, s 225. **R v O'Brien** [2006] **4** 1012, CA.

      Specified offence—Serious offence—Imprisonment for public protection—Offender serving sentence of life imprisonment—Offender released on licence—Offender arrested—Offender recalled under terms of licence—Sentencing judge finding significant risk to members of public of serious harm occasioned by commission by offender of further specified offences—Offender sentenced to imprisonment for public protection—Whether sentence of imprisonment for public protection could be imposed where offender recalled under life sentence—Whether sentence of imprisonment for public protection should be imposed where offender recalled under life sentence—Criminal Justice Act 2003, s 225. **R v Smith** [2011] **4** 661, SC.

  Imposition of custodial sentence longer than that commensurate with seriousness of offence—
    Lawfulness of detention—Whether convention right requiring periodic review of lawfulness of continued detention of offender who had served commensurate element of sentence—Criminal Justice Act 1991, s 2(2)(b)—Powers of Criminal Courts (Sentencing) Act 2000, s 80(2)(b)—Human Rights Act 1998, Sch 1, Pt I, art 5(1)(a), (4). **R (on the application of Giles) v Parole Board** [2002] **3** 1123, CA; [2003] **4** 429, HL.

  Restriction on consecutive sentences for released prisoners—Further release after recall—Offender released on licence—Offender convicted of fresh offence—Whether sentence for fresh offence to be lengthened to create period of custody longer than remaining period of original sentence—Criminal Justice Act 2003, ss 153(2), 255A, 255B, 255C, 255D, 256, 265—Powers of Criminal Courts (Sentencing) Act 2000, s 116. **R v Costello** [2010] **3** 490, CA.

  Licence—
    Claimant committing rapes before 1983 when maximum sentence was life imprisonment—Court sentencing claimant in 1995 to 12 years' imprisonment for those offences—Release regime applicable in 1995 providing for release on licence at two-thirds point of sentence whereas regime applicable in 1983 providing for unconditional release at same point—Whether release on licence infringing claimant's convention right not to be subjected to penalty heavier than that applicable at time offence committed—Criminal Justice Act 1991, ss 33(2), 37(4)(a), 39—Human Rights Act 1998, Sch 1, Pt I, art 7(1). **R (on the application of Uttley) v Secretary of State for the Home Dept** [2003] **4** 891, CA; [2004] **4** 1, HL.

    Statutory scheme providing for release of offender on licence rather than unconditionally—Whether scheme incompatible with convention prohibition on heavier retrospective penalties when applying to offences committed before scheme's implementation—Criminal Justice Act 1991, ss 33(2), 37, 39—Human Rights Act 1998, Sch 1, Pt I, art 7. **R (on the application of Uttley) v Secretary of State for the Home Dept** [2003] **4** 891, CA.

  Offences meriting custodial sentence and offences not meriting custodial sentence—
    Whether court having jurisdiction to pass custodial sentence in respect of offences which by themselves do not merit custodial sentence. **R v Oliver** [1993] **2** 9, CA.

  Practical effect of sentence—
    Explanation of effect of sentence to be given when sentence passed—Model form of words. **Practice Note** [1998] **1** 733, CA.

SENTENCE (cont)—
  Custodial sentence (cont)—
    Purpose of custodial sentence—
      Punishment and deterrence—Sentence commensurate with seriousness of offence—Sentence commensurate with punishment and deterrence—Prevalence of type of offence may be taken into account—Length of sentence not to be increased to make special example of defendant—Criminal Justice Act 1991, s 2(2). **R v Cunningham** [1993] **2** 15, CA.
    Reasons for imposing custodial sentence—
      Reasons to be explained to offender in ordinary language—Criminal Justice Act 1991, s 1(2), (4). **R v Baverstock** [1993] **2** 32, CA.
    Seriousness of offence—
      Offence so serious that only custodial sentence can be justified—Guidelines—Criminal Justice Act 1991, s 1(2)(a). **R v Howells** [1999] **1** 50, CA.
      Offence so serious that only custodial sentence can be justified—Test of whether offence sufficiently serious to justify custodial sentence—Mitigating factors to be taken into account—Criminal Justice Act 1991, ss 1(2)(a), 28(1). **R v Cox** [1993] **2** 19, CA.
    Sexual offence—
      Extended licence—Statutory provision empowering court to extend until end of sentence licence period in respect of sexual offences—Whether provision applying to sentence imposed for offence committed before its implementation—Criminal Justice Act 1991, s 44 (as originally enacted)—Human Rights Act 1998, s 3, Sch 1, Pt I, art 7—Powers of Criminal Courts (Sentencing) Act 2000, s 86. **R v T** [2003] **4** 877, CA.
      Extended licence—Statutory provision empowering court to extend until end of sentence licence period in respect of sexual offences—Whether such extension violating convention prohibition on heavier retrospective penalties if imposed in respect of offence committed before provision implemented—Criminal Justice Act 1991, s 32(6)—Human Rights Act 1998, Sch 1, Pt I, art 7—Powers of Criminal Courts (Sentencing) Act 2000, s 86. **R v R** [2003] **4** 882, CA.
      Violent offence—Attempted rape—Whether attempted rape a 'sexual offence'—Whether attempted rape a 'violent offence'—Criminal Justice Act 1991, ss 1(2), 31(1). **R v Robinson** [1993] 2 1, CA.
    Warning to counsel—
      Judge contemplating longer sentence than is commensurate with seriousness of offence—Whether judge under duty to warn counsel that he is contemplating custodial sentence—Whether judge under duty to warn counsel that he is contemplating longer sentence than is commensurate with seriousness of offence—Criminal Justice Act 1991, s 2(2). **R v Baverstock** [1993] **2** 32, CA.
  Dangerous driving. *See* **Road traffic** (Dangerous driving—Sentence).
  Dangerous offenders. *See* Custodial sentence—Dangerous offenders, *above*.
  Death sentence—
    Execution—
      Trinidad and Tobago. *See* **Trinidad and Tobago** (Criminal law—Execution of death penalty).
    Review—
      Gibraltar. *See* **Gibraltar** (Criminal law—Special courts—Death sentence—Special provision for review of death sentence).
  Deferment of sentence—
    Consent of accused—
      Counsel for accused inviting court to defer sentence—Court deciding to adopt that course—Accused not specifically asked to give his consent to deferment—Whether counsel's invitation equivalent to expression of consent by accused—Whether deferment valid—Powers of Criminal Courts Act 1973, s 1(3). **R v Fairhead** [1975] **2** 737, CA.
    Custodial sentence following deferment—
      Report to court on conduct of accused and change of circumstances following deferment—Report not unfavourable to accused—Whether substantial custodial sentence wrong in principle—Powers of Criminal Courts Act 1973, s 1(1). **R v Gilby** [1975] **2** 743, CA.
    Exercise of power of deferment—
      Matters to be considered by court before exercising power—Duty of court once it has decided to exercise power—Circumstances in which exercise of power appropriate—Powers of Criminal Courts Act 1973, s 1(1). **R v George** [1984] **3** 13, CA.
    Magistrates—
      Powers following deferment of sentence—Power to commit offender to Crown Court for sentence—Power to make such ancillary orders as may be appropriate on final disposal of case—Magistrates' Courts Act 1952, ss 28, 29—Powers of Criminal Courts Act 1973, s 1(1). **R v Gilby** [1975] **2** 743, CA.
    Practice—
      Desirability of asking accused personally to give consent—Desirability of court stating expressly that sentence to be deferred under relevant statutory provisions—Powers of Criminal Courts Act 1973, s 1. **R v Fairhead** [1975] **2** 737, CA.
    Sentencing of offender after expiration of period of deferment—
      Duties of court before passing sentence. **R v George** [1984] **3** 13, CA.
      Jurisdiction—Court deferring sentencing offender for six months—Offender charged with further offences during that period—Offender returning to court for sentencing after expiry of six months' period—Court 'deferring' sentencing offender until result of additional charges known—Jurisdiction of court to sentence offender after period of deferment has expired—Jurisdiction of court further to postpone sentencing offender—Criminal Justice Act 1972, s 22. **R v Ingle** [1974] **3** 811, CA.
  Deferred sentence—
    Conviction of further offence before different location of Crown Court. *See* **Crown Court** (Transfer of proceedings between locations—Sentence—Deferred sentence passed on offender—Conviction of further offence before different location of court during period of deferment).
    Review of sentence by Court of Appeal—
      Review on ground sentence unduly lenient—Whether deferred sentence a 'sentence' which can be reviewed by Court of Appeal—Criminal Appeal Act 1968, s 50(1)—Criminal Justice Act 1988, s 36(1). **A-G's Reference (No 22 of 1992)** [1994] **1** 105, CA.

SENTENCE (cont)—
    Deportation—
        Recommendation—
            Detention pending making of deportation order—Detention of person released on bail—Release on bail by any court having power to release person bailed—Applicant admitted to bail pending trial on one offence—Applicant later convicted of second offence by another court and recommended for deportation—On completion of imprisonment for second offence applicant detained in prison pending making of deportation order—Whether applicant 'for the time being released on bail by any court having power so to release [her]'—Whether applicant entitled to invoke grant of bail in respect of first offence as rendering invalid her detention pending deportation for second offence—Immigration Act 1981, Sch 3, para 2(1). **R v Governor of Holloway Prison, ex p Giambi** [1982] **1** 434, QBD.
            EEC national—Recommendation for deportation of EEC national following conviction of criminal offence—Need for court to give reasons for recommendation—Mode of giving reasons—Crown Court—Magistrates' Court—EEC Council Directive 64/221, arts 6, 9(1). **R v Secretary of State for the Home Dept, ex p Dannenberg** [1984] **2** 481, CA.
            Guidelines on making order recommending deportation. **R v Nazari** [1980] **3** 880, CA.
            Judge passing sentences of imprisonment on defendants but adjourning question of deportation at their request—Judge making deportation recommendation three months after imposing prison sentences—Whether judge having power to adjourn question of deportation beyond seven days—Whether judge having power to make recommendation for deportation outside 28-day time limit for varying sentence—Immigration Act 1971, s 6(2). **R v Tuegel** [2000] **2** 872, CA.
            Stateless aliens—Recommendation made for other purposes. **R v Goldfarb** [1936] **1** 169, CCA.
    Detention—
        Age of offender—
            Committal for sentence—Specified offence—Serious offence—Offender under eighteen at date of conviction and over eighteen at date of sentencing—Applicable sentencing regime—Criminal Justice Act 2003, ss 225, 226, 227, 228. **R v Robson** [2007] **1** 506, CA.
            Committal for sentence—Youthful offender under seventeen at date of conviction, over seventeen at date of sentencing—No notification that detention centre available for persons under seventeen—Court of summary jurisdiction therefore without jurisdiction to impose sentence of detention—Sentence of borstal training imposed by quarter sessions—Whether quarter sessions had jurisdiction to impose sentence of detention—Criminal Justice Act, 1948, s 20(5). **R v Hammond** [1963] **2** 475, CCA.
        Children and young persons—
            Generally. *See* **Children and young persons** (Detention).
        Juvenile offenders—
            Generally. *See* **Children and young persons** (Detention).
        Preventive detention. *See* Preventive detention, *below.*
        Right to challenge lawfulness of detention. *See* **Prison** (Prisoner—Release on licence—Determinate sentence—Right to liberty and security).
    Detention and training order—
        Sexual offences—
            Notification requirements—Length of notification period for adult offender specified by reference to term of imprisonment—Length of notification period for young offender specified by reference to period of detention young offender liable to serve under detention and training order—Whether 12-month detention and training order equivalent to 12-month sentence of imprisonment—Sexual Offences Act 2003, s 131(a). **R v Slocombe** [2006] **1** 670, CA.
    Determinate sentence—
        Release on licence. *See* **Prison** (Prisoner—Release on licence—Determinate sentence).
    Disciplinary proceedings—
        Misconduct—
            Barrister. *See* **Counsel** (Disciplinary proceedings—Sentence).
    Disqualification—
        Criminal contempt. *See* **Contempt of court** (Criminal contempt—Sentence).
        Driving licence. *See* **Road traffic** (Disqualification for holding licence).
        Order disqualifying individual from working with children—
            Whether such an order could be made in respect of offence committed before implementation of statutory provisions creating order—Criminal Justice and Court Services Act 2000, s 28—Human Rights Act 1998, Sch 1, Pt I, art 7. **R v Field** [2003] **3** 769, CA.
    Driving while unfit through drink or drugs. *See* **Road traffic** (Driving while unfit to drive through drink or drugs).
    Drug offence—
        Illegal possession of heroin. *See* **Drugs** (Dangerous drugs—Heroin—Illegal possession—Sentence).
    Ecclesiastical offence. *See* **Ecclesiastical law** (Censure).
    Electronic monitoring (tag)—
        Sexual offences prevention order. *See* Sexual offences prevention order—Terms—Requirement to wear location monitoring device (tag) added to order, *below.*
    Enforcement—
        Community requirement. *See* Suspended sentence—Community requirement , *below.*
    Evidence—
        Accused's history—
            Evidence before sentence—Details to be communicated to defending counsel. **R v Crabtree** [1952] **2** 974, CCA.
        Similar offences—
            Plea of guilty to charge in respect of single incident—Evidence of other similar incidents forming course of conduct—Incest—Admission of single act of incest with daughter—Allegations by daughter of regular intercourse over long period—Denial of other acts of incest by accused—Judge hearing evidence of accused and daughter before passing sentence—Judge not believing accused and sentencing him on basis that incest committed by accused as regular course of conduct—Effect to deprive accused of right to trial by jury—Propriety of course followed by judge. **R v Huchison** [1972] **1** 936, CA.

SENTENCE (cont)—
  Exceptional sentence—
    Gravity of offence—
      Conspiracy to stop mail—Exceptional sentence for exceptional crime—Post Office Act 1953, s 54. **R v Boal** [1964] **3** 269, CCA.
  Existing prisoner—
    Dangerous offenders. *See* Custodial sentence—Dangerous offenders, *above*.
  Extended term of imprisonment—
    Appropriate sentence for existing offences to be imposed—
      Concurrent instead of consecutive terms of imprisonment imposed with a view to qualifying offender for an extended term if offence committed in future—Wrong in principle—Criminal Justice Act 1967, s 37. **R v Lycett** [1968] **2** 1021, CA.
    Conditions to be satisfied—
      Previous convictions—Qualifying sentences—Sentence of imprisonment for a term of three years or more—Two sentences of imprisonment each for a term of two years or more—Sentence of imprisonment—Whether including a sentence of corrective training—Criminal Justice Act 1967, s 37(2), (4)(c)(ii). **R v Newton** [1973] **1** 758, CA.
      Three year period from previous conviction—Offence committed before expiration of three years from previous conviction or from release from prison—Offence committed before release from prison—Defendant absconding shortly before end of five year term of imprisonment and committing further offence—Whether jurisdiction to impose extended term of imprisonment on conviction of further offence—Criminal Justice Act 1967, s 37(4)(a). **R v Johnson** [1976] **1** 869, CA.
    Consecutive terms—
      Extended term consecutive to an existing term—Propriety. **R v Stewart** [1971] **2** 905, CA.
      Non-extended term to run consecutively to extended term—Non-extended term ordered to run consecutively to unexpired portion of extended term imposed on different occasion—Propriety—Criminal Justice Act 1967, s 37(2). **R v Jackson** [1974] **1** 640, CA.
      Terms imposed in respect of separate offences—Terms certified as an extended term—Propriety—Whether extended term may only be imposed in respect of single offence—Criminal Justice Act 1967, s 37(2). **R v McKenna** [1974] **1** 637, CA.
    Consecutive terms. *See* Custodial sentence—Dangerous offenders—Extended sentences—Consecutive sentences, *above*.
    Notice of previous conviction or sentence—
      Procedure—Criminal Justice Act 1967, s 38(3). **R v Concannon** [1970] **3** 198, CA.
    Principles to be applied when imposing an extended sentence—
      Definition of violent offence—Whether threat to kill constituting violent offence—Criminal Justice Act 1991, ss 2(2)(b), 31(1). **R v Ragg** [1995] **4** 155, CA.
      Protection of public—Object of extended term not only length of sentence but licensing provisions—Term of nine years reduced to seven on appeal—Criminal Justice Act 1967, ss 37(2), (4), 59. **R v Goody** [1970] **2** 385, CA.
    Purpose of extended term to protect public from persistent offender—
      Extended term not exceeding maximum term for particular offence—Whether extended term properly given for totality of sentences—Criminal Justice Act 1967, ss 37(2), (3), (5), 60. **DPP v Ottewell** [1968] **3** 153, HL.
    Release on licence. *See* **Prison** (Release on licence—Extended sentence).
    Suspended sentence—
      Extended term not applicable to a suspended sentence—Criminal Justice Act 1967, s 37. **R v Barrett** [1969] **3** 272, CA; **R v Roberts** [1971] **2** 529, CA.
  Factors in assessing sentence—
    Criminal conduct on other occasions—
      Defendant indicted and convicted on specimen count charging him with criminal conduct of specified kind on specified occasion—Whether court entitled to take into account other offences when passing sentence, where defendant not admitting commission of those offences and not asking court to take them into account—Criminal Justice Act 1991, ss 2, 3(3), 31. **R v Kidd** [1998] **1** 42, CA.
    Mitigation—
      Extreme old age—Appropriate allowance to be made for extreme old age in sentencing process. **R v Clarke** [2018] **2** 333, CA.
      Plea of guilty—Plea as factor in mitigation of sentence. **R v de Haan** [1967] **3** 618, CA.
    Plea of not guilty—
      Conduct of defence—Whether proper factors in assessing sentence. **R v Harper (note)** [1967] **3** 619, CA.
    Seriousness of offence—
      Harm caused—Severe psychological harm—Assessment—Evidence required—Guidance—Criminal Justice Act 2003, s 143. **R v Chall** [2019] **4** 497n, CA.
  Financial reporting order. *See* **Criminal law** (Court of Appeal—Jurisdiction—Financial reporting order).
  Fine—
    Bankruptcy of accused—
      Accused adjudicated bankrupt after sentence imposed—Crown not proving in bankruptcy proceedings for fine as a debt—Imprisonment in default of payment of fine—Whether failure of Crown to prove in bankruptcy releasing accused from obligation to pay fine—Whether imprisonment in default of payment unlawful—Bankruptcy Act 1914, Sch 2, r 1. **Savundra, Re** [1973] **3** 406, QBD.
    Capacity to pay—
      Amount of fine should be within offender's capacity to pay. **Churchill v Walton** [1966] **2** 215, CCA.
      Confiscation of criminal profits—Fine in addition to imprisonment—Principles on which fine should be imposed—Powers of Criminal Courts Act 1973, ss 30, 31(2). **R v Garner** [1986] **1** 78, CA.
    Child or young person. *See* **Children and young persons** (Fine).
    Criminal bankruptcy order—
      Fine in addition to criminal bankruptcy order—Principles on which fine should be imposed—Powers of Criminal Courts Act 1973, ss 35(4A), 39(1). **R v Garner** [1986] **1** 78, CA.
    Driving while disqualified. *See* **Road traffic** (Driving while disqualified for holding licence—Fine instead of imprisonment).

SENTENCE (cont)—
  Hospital order (cont)—
    Order for admission to hospital within 28 days—
      Order amended to provide for transfer to different hospital—Patient admitted more than 28 days after date of original order—Whether admisssion and detention in hospital lawful—Mental Health Act 1983, ss 37, 40. **R (on the application of DB) v Nottinghamshire Healthcare NHS Trust** [2009] **2** 792, CA.
    Order in lieu of imprisonment—
      When proper to make hospital order in lieu of sentence of imprisonment. **R v Morris** [1961] **2** 672, CCA.
    Order restricting discharge—
      Accused charged with murder but convicted of manslaughter on ground of diminished responsibility—Punishment not merited owing to mental disorder—Secure hospital available—Whether proper to make hospital order coupled with order restricting discharge—Mental Health Act 1959, ss 60, 65. **R v Cox (Maurice)** [1968] **1** 386, CA.
    Power of court to make hospital order—
      Magistrates' court—Accused charged with offence and asked whether he elected for summary trial—Accused not understanding what was meant—Accused making no reply—Evidence clearly showing accused had committed offence—Whether justices bound to act as examing magistrates because accused had not consented to summary trial—Whether justices could make hospital order without trying accused—Mental Health Act 1959, s 60(2)—Magistrates' Courts Act 1980, ss 18, 20(3)(b). **R v Lincolnshire (Kesteven) Justices, ex p O'Connor** [1983] **1** 901, QBD.
    Restriction order—
      Enquiry as to facilities for legal custody—Mental Health Act 1959, ss 60, 65. **R v Higginbotham** [1961] **3** 616, CCA.
      Secretary of State's powers—Administrative matters—Court of Appeal only concerned that order valid—Mental Health Act 1959, s 65. **R v McNaney** [1969] **2** 35, CA.
      Secretary of State's powers—Mentally sub-normal person—Indecency—Conviction—Three years' imprisonment—Transfer to mental hospital and restriction imposed for period of sentence—Guidance in regard to convicted prisoners suffering from mental disorder—Mental Health Act 1959, ss 60, 65, 72. **R v Gardiner** [1967] **1** 895, CA.
  Imprisonment—
    Breach of enforcement notice. *See* **Town and country planning** (Enforcement notice—Persistent breach of notice).
    Dangerous offenders. *See* Custodial sentence—Dangerous offenders, *above*.
    Driving while disqualified. *See* **Road traffic** (Driving while disqualified for holding licence—Imprisonment).
    Early release—
      Introduction of restrictions on early release of terrorist offenders—New regime applying to prisoners already serving sentences of imprisonment—Whether regime discriminatory on ground of 'other status'—Whether regime offending principle of non-retroactivity of criminal law—Whether regime contrary to right to liberty—Human Rights Act 1998, Sch 1, Pt I, arts 5, 7, 14—Criminal Justice Act 2003, s 247A—Terrorist Offenders (Restriction of Early Release) Act 2020. **R (on the application of Khan) v Secretary of State for the Justice Dept** [2021] **2** 1033, DC.
    Extended term. *See* Extended term of imprisonment, *above*.
    Fine and imprisonment—
      Further term of imprisonment in default of payment—Death of felon while serving sentence for felony and before fine paid—Whether Crown entitled to recover fine from felon's personal representatives—Criminal Justice Act 1948, ss 14(1), 15. **Treasury (H M) v Harris** [1957] **2** 455, QBD.
      Maximum sentence of imprisonment and also fine—Further term of imprisonment in default of payment—Validity—Criminal Justice Act 1948, s 14(1). **R v Carver** [1955] **1** 413, CCA.
    Generally. *See* Custodial sentence, *above*.
    Length of sentence—
      Buggery—Commission of buggery by man with boy under age of sixteen—Appropriate term of imprisonment—Factors to be taken into account—Aggravating and mitigating factors. **R v Willis** [1975] **1** 620, CA.
      Causing or allowing death of child or vulnerable adult—Levels of culpability—Comparison to general principles to be applied in manslaughter cases—Domestic Violence, Crime and Victims Act 2004, s 5. **R v Ikram** [2008] **4** 253, CA.
      Forgery—Possessing and uttering forged bank notes—Appropriate sentence. **R v Caughie** [1969] **3** 950, CA.
      Fraudulent evasion of duty chargeable on goods—Aggravating and mitigating factors—Appropriate sentence—Guidelines—Customs and Excise Management Act 1979, s 170. **R v Czyzewski** [2004] **3** 135, CA; **R v Dosanjh** [1998] **3** 618, CA.
      Misprision of felony. **Sykes v DPP** [1961] **3** 33, HL.
      Power to impose heavier sentence where greater deterrent required—Power exercisable even though stage not reached where extended term of imprisonment justified. **DPP v Ottewell** [1968] **2** 593, CA; [1968] **3** 153, HL.
      Sentencing guidelines—Violent personal robberies in the home. **R v Roe** [2011] **4** 773, CA.
    Life imprisonment. *See* Life imprisonment, *below*.
    Magistrates' court—
      Consecutive terms—Aggregate of terms imposed by court not to exceed 12 months—Court imposing a term of imprisonment of 12 months for several offences—Court subsequently imposing sentence of imprisonment of 144 days for default in payment of fines—Terms to run consecutively—Whether prescribed maximum period of 12 months exceeded—Magistrates' Courts Act 1952, s 108(1). **Forrest v Brighton Justices** [1981] **2** 711, HL.

SENTENCE (cont)—
 Imprisonment (cont)—
  Magistrates' court (cont)—
   Consecutive terms—Aggregate of terms imposed by court not to exceed six months—Court
    imposing a term of imprisonment and two fines for three separate offences—Court subsequently
    fixing terms of imprisonment in default of payment of fines—Terms to run consecutively to each
    other and to original term of imprisonment—Aggregate of terms fixed in default of payment of
    fines not exceeding six months—Aggregate of all three terms exceeding six months—Whether
    order fixing terms in default of payment of fines valid—Magistrates' Courts Act 1952, s 108(1). **R
    v Metropolitan Stipendiary Magistrate for South Westminster, ex p Green** [1977] 1 353, QBD.
   Consecutive terms—Committal to custody for breach of injunction in domestic proceedings—
    Whether committal to custody in domestic proceedings the same as imprisonment—Whether
    magistrates having power to order consecutive periods of custody for separate breaches of
    injunction—Magistrates' Courts Act 1980, ss 63(3), 133(1). **Head v Head** [1982] 3 14, Fam D.
   Non-payment of fine. See **Magistrates** (Fine—Committal to prison in default of payment).
   Person not legally represented—Appeal—Power of court on appeal—Sentence of imprisonment by
    justices invalid as defendant not legally represented—Appeal by way of rehearing—Defendant
    legally represented on appeal—Whether Crown Court having power to confirm sentence of
    imprisonment on appeal—Courts Act 1971, s 9(4)—Powers of Criminal Courts Act 1973, s 21(1). **R
    v Birmingham Justices, ex p Wyatt** [1975] 3 897, QBD.
  Period of imprisonment—
   Minimum period of—Murder. See Murder—Minimum period of imprisonment, *below.*
   Unlawfully at large—Escape of prisoner while serving sentence in England—Committal to prison in
    Trinidad pursuant to warrant for arrest issued in England—Return to English prison—Whether
    period between committal to prison in Trinidad and return to English prison to be taken into
    account in calculating period for which prisoner liable to be detained—Prison Act 1952, s 49(2) (as
    amended by Criminal Justice Act 1961, s 30(4)). **R v Leeds Prison Governor, ex p Stafford**
    [1964] 1 610, QBD.
  Preventive detention. See Preventive detention, *below.*
  Public protection, for—
   Dangerous offenders. See Custodial sentence—Dangerous offenders—Specified offence—Serious
    offence—Imprisonment for public protection for serious offences, *above.*
  Release of prisoner on licence. See **Prison** (Release on licence).
  Sexual intercourse with girl under 16. See **Criminal law** (Sexual intercourse—Girl under
   16—Sentence—Imprisonment or fine).
  Youthful offender. See Youthful offender—Imprisonment, *below.*
 Incest. See **Criminal law** (Incest—Sentence).
 Incorrigible rogue—
  Binding-over—
   Nigerian offender—Offender sentenced to twelve months' imprisonment—Order binding offender
    over at end of imprisonment to return to Nigeria—Whether binding-over order valid—Justices of
    the Peace Act 1361. **R v Ayu** [1958] 3 636, CCA.
  Generally. See **Criminal law** (Incorrigible rogue—Sentence).
 Indeterminate sentence—
  Delay in decision of Parole Board—
   Human rights. See **Human rights** (Infringement of human rights—Damages—Right to liberty and
    security—Lawfulness of detention to be decided speedily).
  Release in licence. See **Prison** (Release on licence—Life sentence—Indeterminate sentence).
 Indictable offence tried summarily—
  Committal for sentence—
   Jurisdiction of quarter sessions—Offence not triable on indictment at quarter sessions—No power
    to sentence at quarter sessions—Prevention of Corruption Act 1906, ss 1, 2—Criminal Justice Act
    1948, s 29(3)(a). **R v Middlesex Quarter Sessions, ex p DPP** [1950] 1 916, KBD.
  Election by accused at summary trial for trial by jury—
   Graver offences added on indictment to those charged for summary trial—Sentence not limited to
    maximum that justices could pass—Children and Young Persons Act 1933, s 1(1)—Offences
    against the Person Act 1861, ss 18, 20. **R v Roe** [1967] 1 492, CA.
 Jurisdiction—
  Magistrates—
   Excess or absence of jurisdiction—Civil liability of magistrates. See **Magistrates** (Civil
    liability—Excess or absence of jurisdiction—Sentence).
 Juvenile—
  Detention—
   Generally. See **Children and young persons** (Detention).
 Life imprisonment—
  Category A prisoner—
   Annual review of categorisation by Category A section. See **Prison** (Life sentence—Mandatory life
    sentence—Category A prisoner—Annual review of categorisation by category A section).
  Commonwealth citizen—
   Power to make recommendation for deportation. See **Commonwealth immigrant** (Deportation—
    Recommendation for deportation—Sentence of life imprisonment—Whether recommendation
    for deportation appropriate in case of fixed sentence of life imprisonment).
  Deportation—
   Recommendation for deportation inappropriate. **R v Assa Singh** [1965] 1 938, CCA.
  Discretionary life sentence—
   Adult defendant committing a 'serious offence'—Defendant having previous conviction for another
    'serious offence'—Whether exceptional circumstances justifying court in not imposing life
    sentence—Crime (Sentences) Act 1997, ss 2, 28. **R v Kelly** [1999] 2 13, CA.
   Appeal. See Appeal—Right of appeal—Discretionary life sentence, *above.*

SENTENCE (cont)—
  Life imprisonment (cont)—
    Discretionary life sentence (cont)—
      Minimum period of imprisonment—Guidelines—Requirement that court have regard to guidelines—Discount for guilty plea—Maximum discount where offender indicating willingness to admit guilt at first reasonable opportunity—Whether maximum discount applicable where offender having no alternative but to plead guilty—Whether double jeopardy principle applying to minimum period of imprisonment within discretionary life sentence—Criminal Justice Act 2003, s 172. **A-G's References (No 14 and 15 of 2006)** [2007] **1** 718, CA.
      Part of sentence to be served before case referred to Parole Board—Relevant part—Practice—Judge not obliged to specify relevant part of sentence but should do so save in exceptional cases—Duty of judge when specifying relevant part—Order to be made in open court—Counsel for defendant to be permitted to address court—Judge to give reasons—Judge no longer to make written report to Secretary of State—Criminal Justice Act 1991, s 34. **Practice Note** [1993] **1** 747, CA.
      Sentence of detention for life—Part of sentence to be served before case referred to Parole Board—Exercise of discretion in determining that part—Part to be served in case of young offender—Criminal Justice 1991, s 34—Crime (Sentences) Act 1997, s 28. **R v M** [1998] **2** 939, CA.
    Life imprisonment for second serious offence—
      Defendant being arrested while staging incompetent and unaggressive bank robbery—Defendant being convicted of attempted robbery and possessing imitation firearm on arrest—Defendant having previous conviction for having imitation firearm with intent to resist arrest—Judge holding that he was bound to impose life sentences for second serious offence—Whether judge correct in so holding—Whether exceptional circumstances existing to justify court in not imposing life sentence—Firearms Act 1968, ss 17, 18—Crime (Sentences) Act 1997, s 2. **R v Buckland** [2000] **1** 907, CA.
      Whether buggery serious offence for purposes of automatic life sentences—Sexual Offences Act 1956, s 1—Crime (Sentences) Act 1997, s 2(5)(e). **R v Wood** [2000] **3** 561, CA.
      Whether imposition of automatic life sentence for second serious offence compatible with provisions of human rights convention—Crime (Sentences) Act 1997, s 2—Human Rights Act 1998, s 3, Sch 1, Pt I, arts 3, 5, 7. **R v Offen** [2001] **2** 154, CA.
      Whether imposition on mentally ill offender of automatic life sentence for second serious offence compatible with provisions of human rights convention—Mental Health Act 1983, s 37—Crime (Sentences) Act 2000, s 109—Human Rights Act 1998, Sch 1, Pt I, art 3. **R v Drew** [2003] **4** 557, HL.
    Life sentence for second listed offence—
      Life sentence for serious offences—Extended sentence for certain violent or sexual offences—Guidance—Criminal Justice Act 2003, ss 224A, 225, 226A. **A-G's Reference (No 27 of 2013)** [2015] **1** 93, CA.
    Mandatory life sentence—
      Whole life tariff. *See* **Prison** (Life sentence—Mandatory life sentence—Whole life tariff).
    Mandatory life sentence. *See* Mandatory life sentence, *below.*
    Manslaughter—
      Principle to be applied in deciding whether to impose life imprisonment. **R v Picker** [1970] **2** 226, CA.
    Minimum period of imprisonment—
      Manslaughter—Power of court to recommend minimum period of imprisonment—Murder (Abolition of Death Penalty) Act 1965, s 1(2). **R v Flemming** [1973] **2** 401, CA.
    Minimum term—
      Discretionary life sentence for manslaughter—Defendant pleading guilty in 2014 to manslaughter committed in 2000—Recorder sentencing defendant to life imprisonment with specified minimum term—Whether minimum term should be no longer than minimum term which would have been imposed at time of commission of offence—Human Rights Act 1998, Sch 1, Pt I, art 7(1)—Criminal Justice Act 2003, Sch 21. **R v Bell** [2016] **3** 284, CA.
      Prisoner serving sentence of life imprisonment with minimum term—Prisoner committing offences while serving minimum term—Prisoner sentenced to further imprisonment commencing at expiration of minimum term—Whether lawful to impose determinate sentence consecutively to minimum period under life sentence—Crime (Sentences) Act 1997 s 28(7). **R v Taylor** [2012] **1** 443, CA.
    Release of prisoner on licence. *See* **Prison** (Release on licence—Life sentence).
  Magistrates' court—
    Appeal from—
      Practice. *See* **Magistrates** (Review of justices' decision—Sentence—Appeal to Divisional Court).
    Imprisonment—
      Sentence of. *See* Imprisonment—Magistrates' court, *above.*
  Mandatory life sentence—
    Murder—
      Minimum term—Statutory starting point—Offences where the offender 'took a knife or other weapon to the scene'—Guidance—Criminal Justice Act 2003, Sch 21, para 5A. **R v Kelly** [2011] **4** 687, CA.
      Minimum term—Whole life order—Prohibition of inhuman or degrading treatment or punishment—Whether mandatory life sentence with whole life order breach of prohibition of inhuman or degrading treatment or punishment—Crime (Sentences) Act 1997, s 30—Human Rights Act 1998, Sch 1, Pt I, art 3—Criminal Justice Act 2003, s 269. **A-G's Reference (No 69 of 2013)** [2014] **3** 73, CA.
      Minimum term—Whole life order—Prohibition of inhuman or degrading treatment or punishment—Whether mandatory life sentence with whole life order breach of prohibition of inhuman or degrading treatment or punishment—Human Rights Act 1998, Sch 1, Pt I, art 3—Criminal Justice Act 2003, Sch 21, para 4. **R v Oakes** [2013] **2** 30, CA.
      Minimum term—Whole life order—Prohibition of inhuman or degrading treatment or punishment—Whether mandatory life sentence with whole life order breach of prohibition of inhuman or degrading treatment or punishment—Whether mandatory life sentence with whole life order irreducible life sentence—Crime (Sentences) Act 1997, s 30—Human Rights Act 1998, Sch 1, Pt I, art 3—Criminal Justice Act 2003, s 269, Sch 21. **R v Bieber** [2009] **1** 295, CA.

SENTENCE (cont)—
  Murder (cont)—
    Life imprisonment—
      Minimum term—Determination of minimum term in relation to mandatory life sentence—Duty to
        give reasons—Aiding and abetting murder—Statutory starting point—Offender convicted of
        murder as aider or abettor—Offender sentenced to life imprisonment with minimum term of
        three years—Judge departing from statutory starting point—Whether sentence unduly
        lenient—Criminal Justice Act 1988, s 36(3A)—Criminal Justice Act 2003, s 270, Sch 21. **A-G's**
        Reference (No 24 of 2008) [2009] 3 839, CA.
      Minimum term—Setting of minimum terms of imprisonment for adults convicted of
        murder—Guidance. **Practice Statement** [2002] **3** 412, CA.
    Mandatory life sentence. *See* Mandatory life sentence, *above.*
    Minimum period of imprisonment—
      Recommendation of minimum period to be served under sentence of life imprisonment—Whether
        appeal lies—Murder (Abolition of Death Penalty) Act 1965, s 1(2). **R v Aitken** [1966] **2** 453, CCA.
    Minimum term—
      Review of. *See* Principles of sentencing—Mandatory life sentence—Murder—Minimum term,
        below.
    Tariff—
      Existing prisoners. *See* Mandatory life sentence—Murder—Tariff—Existing prisoners, *above.*
    Young person. *See* Young person—Serious criminal offence—Murder, *below.*
  Notification and orders—
    Notification requirements—
      Notification period —Indefinite period—Right to respect for private and family life—Sexual
        offences—Offenders subject to notification requirements for indefinite period—Whether
        interference with right to respect for private and family life—Whether notification requirements
        proportionate—Human Rights Act 1998, Sch 1, Pt I, art 8—Sexual Offences Act 2003, s 82(1). **R (on**
        the application of JF (by his litigation friend OF)) v Secretary of State for the Home Dept
        [2010] **1** 1024, CA; [2010] **2** 707, SC.
  Offence triable summarily but election by accused for trial by jury—
    Consecutive sentences—
      Conviction at quarter sessions on three counts of driving while disqualified—Consecutive
        sentences each of maximum allowable on summary conviction—Whether such sentences
        permissible—Magistrates' Courts Act 1952, ss 25(1), (6), 108(1). **R v Furlong** [1962] **1** 656, CCA.
    Maximum sentence—
      Conviction at quarter sessions—Sentence of nine months' imprisonment imposed—Maximum of
        six months' imprisonment allowable on summary conviction, but twelve months' on conviction
        on indictment—Whether sentence imposed by quarter sessions valid—Road Traffic Act 1960,
        s 110, as amended by Road Traffic Act 1962, s 8, Sch 1, Pt 1, para 6. **R v Gibbs** [1964] **3** 776, CCA.
  Other offences taken into consideration. *See* **Criminal law** (Trial—Other offences taken into consideration).
  Parole. *See* **Prison** (Release on licence).
  Pollution offences—
    Polluting controlled waters—
      Fine —Sentencing principles—Water and sewerage undertaker allowing escape of bleach into
        river—Approach to be taken to determining level of fine—Water Resources Act 1991, s 85(1). **R v**
        Thames Water Utilities Ltd [2010] **3** 47, CA.
  Possession of an offensive weapon in a public place—
    Guidance—
      Prevention of Crime Act 1953, s 1. **R v Poulton** [2003] **4** 869, CA.
  Postponement—
    Crown Court—
      Jurisdiction—Postponement of part of sentence—Postponement for period in excess of 28
        days—Road traffic offences—Custodial sentences and periods of disqualification imposed—
        Defendant's licence not available when sentences imposed—Subsequent research showing that
        defendant had two previous convictions carrying disqualification—Defendant brought back to
        court seven weeks later and further period of disqualification imposed under totting-up
        procedure—Whether court having jurisdiction to order disqualification after lapse of seven
        weeks—Courts Act 1971, s 11(2)—Road Traffic Act 1972, s 93(3). **R v Annesley** [1976] **1** 589, CA.
  Pre-sentence report—
    Adequacy of report—
      Trial judge to determine adequacy of pre-sentence report—Criminal Justice Act 1991, s 3(1), (2). **R v**
        Okinikan [1993] **2** 5, CA.
  Preventive detention—
    Age of offender—
      Prisoner aged under thirty when offence committed, but aged thirty when sentenced—Criminal
        Justice Act 1948, s 21(2). **R v Fallows** [1954] **1** 623, CCA.
    Circumstances to be taken into consideration—
      Circumstances to be taken into consideration before imposing such a sentence. **Practice Note**
        [1962] **1** 671, CCA.
    Concurrent sentences—
      Second sentence while first still current—Second sentence to date from conviction and absorb
        unexpired portion of first sentence. **R v Lake** [1961] **1** 587, CCA.
    Driving while unfit through drink or drugs. *See* **Road traffic** (Driving while unfit to drive through drink
      or drugs—Sentence—Preventive detention).
    Length of sentence—
      Normal period of eight years—Criminal Justice Act 1948, s 21(2). **R v Sedgwick** [1950] **2** 397, CCA.
    Notice of previous convictions—
      Cases where notices need not be served—Criminal Justice Act 1948, s 23. **Practice Note**
        [1966] **2** 905, CCA.
      Three clear days' notice—Criminal Justice Act 1948, s 23(1). **R v Long** [1959] **3** 559, CCA.

SENTENCE (cont)—
    Preventive detention (cont)—
        Offence out of character with previous offences—
            Offence for which sentenced to preventive detention out of character with previous offences—Fourteen previous convictions for offences of dishonesty—Fifteenth offence unlawful sexual intercourse with girl aged fifteen—Whether preventive detention proper sentence for the last offence. **R v Crehan** [1962] 1 608, CCA.
        Previous convictions—
            Notice of. *See* Preventive detention—Notice of previous convictions, *above*.
            Scottish previous convictions—No evidence that previous offences punishable by law of Scotland on indictment with imprisonment for two years or more—Whether sentence of preventive detention valid—Criminal Justice Act 1948, s 21(2)(b). **R v Cameron (1952)** [1961] 1 558, CCA; **R v Clarkson** [1961] 1 557, CCA.
        Prison Commissioners' report—
            Copy to be given to offender—Proof—Criminal Justice Act 1948, ss 20(8), 21(5). **Practice Note** [1959] 2 734, CCA.
            Copy to be given to offender—Whether condition precedent to passing of sentence—Criminal Justice Act 1948, s 21(5). **Philpot, Re** [1960] 1 165, QBD.
        When an appropriate sentence—
            Length of sentence—Criminal Justice Act 1948, s 21(2). **R v Askew** [1949] 2 687, CCA.
            Prisoner over 30 years of age and having three previous convictions—Not necessarily rendering him liable to sentence of preventive detention. **R v Powell** [1953] 2 1202, CCA.
    Previous convictions—
        Circumstances of other offences—
            Seriousness of offence or its combination with another offence—Previous convictions not to be taken into account—Sentencing judge entitled to take into account circumstances of previous offences or offences presently before court in determining seriousness of instant offence—Criminal Justice Act 1991, s 29. **R v Bexley** [1993] 2 23, CA.
        Generally. *See* **Criminal law** (Trial—Previous convictions).
        Preventive detention—
            Notice of previous convictions. *See* Preventive detention—Notice of previous convictions, *above*.
        Previous convictions of offender to be supplied to trial judge—
            Criminal Justice Act 1991, s 29. **R v Baverstock** [1993] 2 32, CA.
        Proof—
            Certificate of previous conviction—Certificate signed by clerk of peace—Conviction by magistrates' court and committal to quarter sessions for sentence—Whether certificate properly signed by clerk of peace. **Stone v Bastick** [1965] 3 713, QBD.
    Principles of sentencing—
        Co-accused—
            Disparity—Principles to be applied—Whether grounds for reduction. **R v Coe** [1969] 1 65, CA.
        Curative element—
            Alcoholism—Activation of suspended sentence to be decided before considering cure. **R v Moylan** [1969] 3 783, CA.
            Alcoholism—Whether consideration of cure should be taken into account. **R v Ford** [1969] 3 782, CA.
        Mandatory life sentence—
            Murder—Minimum term—Tariff—Existing prisoners—Transitional provisions providing for applications or references to High Court judge—Jurisdiction of Court of Appeal to conduct 'review of sentence' on basis of exceptional progress in prison—Correct approach to reviews of sentences—Criminal Justice Act 2003, Sch 22, paras 3, 6. **R v Gill** [2012] 2 456, CA.
    Probation order—
        Breach. *See* Breach of probation order, *above*.
        Concurrent sentences—
            Detention—Concurrent sentence of detention in detention centre for three months and probation order for two years imposed separately on two counts—Whether probation order valid—Criminal Justice Act 1948, ss 3(1), 18(2). **R v Evans** [1958] 3 673, CCA.
        Currency control—
            Export—Deliberate offence. **Pickett v Fesq** [1949] 2 705, KBD.
        Fine—
            Power of court to impose fine in addition to probation order—Criminal Justice Act 1948, ss 3(1), 13. **R v Parry** [1950] 2 1179, CCA.
        Good character and antecedents—
            Deliberate refusal to comply with statutory obligation—Conscientious objector refusing to undergo medical examination—Probation of Offenders Act 1907—Criminal Justice Administration Act 1914, s 8. **Eversfield v Story** [1942] 1 268, KBD.
        Incorrigible rogue. *See* **Criminal law** (Incorrigible rogue—Sentence—Probation).
        Order—
            Activation of suspended sentence. *See* Suspended sentence—Activation—Fresh offence committed in respect of which probation order imposed, *below*.
        Terms of order—
            Additional requirements—Attendance at day training centre—Non-statutory day centre—Whether conditions for attendance at statutory centres also applicable to non-statutory centres—Powers of Criminal Courts Act 1973, ss 2(3), 4. **Cullen v Rogers** [1982] 2 570, HL.
            Additional requirements—Limitations on additional requirements—Custodial or other element amounting to a sentence not to be imposed—Discretion conferred on probation officer to be well defined—Powers of Criminal Courts Act 1973, s 2(3). **Cullen v Rogers** [1982] 2 570, HL.
            Offender a citizen of Northern Ireland—Whether offender can be required, as term of probation order, to return to Ireland and stay there—Criminal Justice Act 1948, s 3(1), (2). **R v McCartan** [1958] 3 140, CCA.
        Willingness of offender to comply with order—
            Jurisdiction of court—Willingness of offender to comply with order not giving court jurisdiction to impose conditions not authorised by legislation—Powers of Criminal Courts Act 1973, s 2(6). **Cullen v Rogers** [1982] 2 570, HL.

SENTENCE (cont)—
  Probation order (cont)—
    Willingness of offender to comply with order (cont)—
      Probation order ineffective unless offender expresses his willingness to comply—Offender to be
      given a fair opportunity to make choice whether to be bound by order—Offender given
      impression custodial sentence only alternative to order—Whether order valid—Criminal Justice
      Act 1948, s 3(5)(as amended by the Children and Young Persons Act 1969, s 72(4), Sch 6). **R v
      Marquis** [1974] **2** 1216, CA.
  Prohibition of inhuman or degrading treatment or punishment—
    Mandatory life sentence. *See* Mandatory life sentence—Murder—Minimum term—Whole life order,
    above.
  Public protection, for—
    Dangerous offenders. *See* Custodial sentence—Dangerous offenders, *above*.
    Life imprisonment—
      Release on licence. *See* **Prison** (Release on licence—Life sentence—Indeterminate sentence—
      Sentence of imprisonment for public protection).
  Quarter sessions—
    Appeal against sentence to quarter sessions. *See* **Quarter sessions** (Appeal to—Appeal against
    sentence).
  Rape. *See* **Criminal law** (Rape—Sentence).
  Recall of prisoner to increase or decrease sentence—
    Accused pleading guilty—
      Plea in mitigation—Accused giving evidence against co-accused—Whether power to recall if
      evidence differs from plea in mitigation. **R v Stone** [1970] **2** 594, CA.
  Reckless driving—
    Causing death by reckless driving. *See* **Road traffic** (Reckless driving—Causing death by reckless
    driving—Sentence).
  Reduction—
    Guilty plea—
      Stage in proceedings at which offender indicating intention to plead guilty—Defendant
      apprehended in stolen car fleeing scene of burglary—Defendant refusing to co-operate with
      police or to be interviewed—Defendant subsequently pleading guilty on arraignment—
      Sentencing judge refusing to give full credit for plea—Whether failure to indicate plea in police
      interview or prior to arraignment entitling judge to reduce credit—Whether fact defendant caught
      'red-handed' entitling judge to reduce credit—Meaning of 'proceedings for the offence'—Criminal
      Justice (Northern Ireland) Order 1996, SI 1996/3160, art 33. **R v Maughan (Northern Ireland)**
      [2022] **4** 873, SC.
    Period spent in custody—
      Concurrent sentences—Defendant spending separate periods in custody pending sentence for
      separate offences—Defendant sentenced to concurrent periods of imprisonment—Period of
      custody by which sentence to be reduced—Criminal Justice Act 1967, s 67(1), (1A)(b)(i). **R v
      Governor of Brockhill Prison, ex p Evans** [1997] **1** 439, QBD.
      Concurrent sentences—Defendant spending separate periods in custody pending sentence for
      separate offences—Defendant sentenced to concurrent periods of imprisonment—Whether
      defendant's sentence should be reduced by both periods spent in custody pending
      sentence—Criminal Justice Act 1967, s 67(1). **R v Governor of Blundeston Prison, ex p Gaffney**
      [1982] **2** 492, QBD.
      Consecutive sentences—Defendant remanded in custody in respect of two separate
      offences—Defendant sentenced at trial to 18 months' imprisonment on each offence—Whether
      time spent on remand should be deducted from each sentence or from total sentence when
      calculating release date—Criminal Justice Act 1967, ss 67(1), 104(2). **R v Secretary of State for the
      Home Dept, ex p Naughton** [1997] **1** 426, QBD.
      Credit for. *See* Custodial sentence—Credit for periods of remand in custody, *above*.
    Period spent in local authority accommodation—
      Young offender being remanded to local authority accommodation—Magistrate imposing curfew
      condition on remand but not imposing security requirement—Local authority placing offender in
      children's home which had not been approved by Secretary of State for purpose of restricting
      liberty—Offender being sentenced to detention and claiming automatic deduction for period
      spent on remand in children's home—Whether offender entitled to automatic deduction—
      Criminal Justice Act 1967, s 67(1A)(c). **R v Secretary of State for the Home Dept, ex p A**
      [2000] **1** 651, HL.
    Review—
      Offenders assisting investigations and prosecutions—Assistance by defendant—Reduction in
      sentence—Review of sentence—Guidance—Serious Organised Crime and Police Act 2005, ss 73,
      74. **R v P** [2008] **2** 684, CA.
      Offenders assisting investigations and prosecutions—Assistance by defendants—Reduction in
      sentence—Review of sentence—Interests of justice—Judicial review of decision not to refer
      sentence back to original sentencing court—Whether sentence should be referred back to original
      sentencing court—Serious Organised Crime and Police Act 2005, s 74. **Loughlin's Application for
      Judicial Review (Northern Ireland), Re** [2018] **1** 361, SC.
    Short-term or long-term prisoner—
      Consecutive sentences—Defendant sentenced to separate consecutive terms of imprisonment by
      different courts—Defendant serving short-term and long-term sentences—Whether sentences to
      be treated separately or as single term for purpose of calculating defendant's release
      date—Criminal Justice Act 1991, ss 33, 51(2). **R v Secretary of State for the Home Dept, ex p
      François** [1998] **1** 929, HL.
  Release on licence—
    Conviction following release on licence—
      Consecutive terms. *See* Custodial sentence—Imposition of custodial sentence longer than that
      commensurate with seriousness of offence—Restriction on consecutive sentences for released
      prisoners, *above*.
      Credit for periods of remand in custody. *See* Custodial sentence—Credit for periods of remand in
      custody—'Time served', *above*.

SENTENCE (cont)—
  Release on licence (cont)—
    Life sentence. *See* **Prison** (Release on licence—Life sentence).
    Prison. *See* **Prison** (Prisoner—Release on licence).
  Remission—
    Abolition of remission—
      Matters to be taken into account when imposing sentence of less than four years. *See* Matters to be
        taken into account—Early release of prisoners—Abolition of remission, *above*.
    Discretion of Prison Commissioners. *See* **Prison** (Discharge from prison—Remission of part of
      sentence—Discretion of Prison Commissioners).
    Prospect of remission—
      Relevance to sentence—Regard not had to the earning of remission when awarding sentence. **R v
        Blake** [1961] **3** 125, CCA.
    Repatriation of prisoner—
      Transfer into United Kingdom. *See* **Prison** (Repatriation of prisoner—Transfer into United
        Kingdom—Continued enforcement of sentence—Remission of sentence).
  Restitution order—
    Choses in action—
      Enforcement of order—Stolen money deposited in bank accounts—Rights to recover deposits
        constituted choses in action which could be the subject of a restitution order—Restitution order
        not directed expressly to any named person—Whether order binding and enforceable by civil
        action—Larceny Act 1916, ss 45, 46(1). **Barclays Bank Ltd v Milne** [1963] **3** 663, QBD.
    Discretion—
      Circumstances in which discretionary power might or should not be exercised by a criminal
        court—Competing claim by third party—Magistrates' Courts Act 1952, s 33(1)—Larceny Act 1916,
        s 45(1). **Stamp v United Dominion Trust (Commercial) Ltd** [1967] **1** 251, QBD.
      Statement by accused at trial that money belonged to a third party—No evidence or documents
        before court to prove that money belonged to accused—Whether order should be made—Theft
        Act 1968, s 28(1)(c), (4). **R v Ferguson** [1970] **2** 820, CA.
    Jurisdiction—
      Order not made on day of conviction—Possession of property by third party no bar—Magistrates'
        Courts Act 1952, s 33—Larceny Act 1916, s 45(1). **Stamp v United Dominion Trust (Commercial)
        Ltd** [1967] **1** 251, QBD.
    Magistrates—
      Committal of accused to Crown Court for sentence—Whether magistrates having jurisdiction to
        make restitution order against accused after committal—Magistrates' Courts Act 1952,
        s 29—Criminal Justice Act 1967, s 56(5). **R v Blackpool Justices, ex p Charlson and Gregory**
        [1972] **3** 854, QBD.
    Retention of property in anticipation of making of order—
      Police powers. *See* **Police** (Powers—Power to retain property relevant to criminal proceedings—
        Retention in respect of anticipated restitution, compensation or forfeiture order).
    Safe deposit in accused's name—
      Money taken from safe deposit after arrest—Whether money taken out of his possession on his
        apprehension—Theft Act 1968, s 28(1)(c). **R v Ferguson** [1970] **2** 820, CA.
  Restraint order—
    Contempt of court—
      Jurisdiction. *See* **Contempt of court** (Appeal—Jurisdiction—Restraint order).
    Power to make restraint order—
      Restraint order for purpose of aiding enforcememt of external confiscation order—External
        confiscation order—United States court ordering shares in company to be forfeited following
        criminal proceedings—Defendant failing to forfeit shares—United States court later valuing
        shares by adopting notional interest and increasing sum to be paid—Whether such an order an
        external confiscation order—Criminal Justice Act 1988 (Designated Countries and Territories)
        Order 1991, Sch 3, s 71(1). **United States Government v Montgomery (Montgomery, third party)**
        [1999] **1** 84, CA.
      Restraint order for purpose of aiding enforcement of external confiscation order—External
        confiscation order—United States court ordering shares in company to be forfeited following
        criminal proceedings—Defendant failing to forfeit shares and United States court adding interest
        to sum outstanding—United States government seeking to enforce confiscation order in United
        Kingdom—Relevant legislation not applying to United States confiscation orders when first
        confiscation order made—Whether legislation applying retrospectively to United States
        confiscation orders—Whether confiscation order to which interest subsequently added an
        external confiscation order—Criminal Justice Act 1988, ss 76(1), 77, 96, 102(4)—Criminal Justice
        Act 1988 (Designated Countries and Territories) Order 1991. **United States Government v
        Montgomery (Montgomery, third party)** [2001] **1** 815, HL.
    Risk of dissipation of assets—
      Duty of disclosure—Delay in making application—Guidance—Criminal Justice Act 1988, s 77.
        Jennings v CPS [2005] **4** 391, CA.
  Review. *See* Reduction—Review, *above*.
  Serious crime prevention order—
    Crown Court. *See* **Crown Court** (Sentence—Serious crime prevention order).
  Serious offences—
    Life sentence. *See* Life imprisonment, *above*.
  Serious organised crime—
    Review. *See* Reduction—Review, *above*.
  Seriousness of offence, assessment of. *See* Factors in assessing sentence—Seriousness of offence, *above*.
  Several offences—
    Form of sentence—
      Concurrent sentences or general sentence—Indictment containing five counts—No sentence on
        individual counts—Conviction on one count quashed—Validity of sentence. **Hastings, Re**
        [1958] **1** 707, QBD.

SENTENCE (cont)—
  Several offences (cont)—
    Separate sentences—
      Consecutive or concurrent—Sentence imposed for each offence to be stated and whether sentence concurrent or consecutive. **Practice Direction** [1962] **1** 417, CCA.
  Several prisoners charged—
    One prisoner pleading guilty—
      Other prisoners tried later—All prisoners to be sentenced together. **R v Payne** [1950] **1** 102, CCA.
  Sexual intercourse with girl under 16. *See* **Criminal law** (Sexual intercourse—Girl under 16—Sentence).
  Sexual offences—
    Life sentence. *See* Life imprisonment, *above.*
    Prevention orders. *See* Custodial sentence—Dangerous offenders—Specified offence, *above.*
    Principles of sentencing—
      Historic sexual crime—Correct approach to sen-tencing in cases of historic abuse. **R v Hall** [2012] **2** 340, CA.
  Sexual offences against children—
    Sentencing principles—
      Cases where no sexual activity in fact occurring—Proper approach to assessing seriousness of offence—Sexual Offences Act 2003, s 14—Sentencing Act 2020, s 63. **R v Reed** [2022] **1** 60, CA.
      Relevant considerations. **A-G's References (No 120, 91 and 119 of 2002)** [2003] **2** 955, CA.
  Sexual offences prevention order—
    Protection from serious physical or psychological harm—
      Order relating to child of defendant—Nature of harm to child of defendant—Whether interests of child to be protected by invoking jurisdiction of family court—Sexual Offences Act 2003, ss 104, 106(3). **R v D** [2006] **2** 726, CA.
      Requirements of necessity, proportionality and clarity—Guidance—Criminal Justice Act 2003, s 104. **R v Smith** [2012] **1** 451, CA.
    Terms—
      Prohibitions necessary for purpose of protecting public from serious harm—Guidance—Sexual Offences Act 2003, ss 104, 107(2). **R v Hemsley** [2010] **3** 965, CA.
      Requirement to wear location monitoring device (tag) added to order—Whether absence of express words in statute permitting electronic monitoring precluding court from imposing wearing of tag—Whether order requiring person to wear tag substantively a prohibitive order—Whether disputed parts of order 'in accordance with the law'—Human Rights Act 1998, Sch 1, Pt I, art 8—Sexual Offences Act 2003, ss 107(2), 108(5). **R (on the application of Richards) v Teesside Magistrates' Court** [2016] **2** 950, CA.
    Variation, renewal and discharge—
      Appeals—Person subject to sexual offences prevention order applying to Crown Court for variation of order—Crown Court refusing to vary order—Whether Court of Appeal having jurisdiction on appeal—Guidance—Sexual Offences Act 2003, ss 108, 110(3)(a). **R v Hoath, R v Standage** [2011] **4** 306, CA.
  Social security offence—
    Obtaining welfare benefits by fraud. *See* Fraud on the public purse—Obtaining welfare benefits by fraud, *above.*
  Solicitor—
    Disciplinary proceedings. *See* **Solicitor** (Disciplinary proceedings—Sentence).
  Supervision order—
    Conviction on indictment—
      Conviction by justices and committal for sentence—Whether offender to be treated as having been 'convicted on indictment'—Whether court having power to make supervision order—Criminal Justice Act 1948, ss 22(1), (2), 29(1). **R v Browes** [1949] **2** 449, CCA.
    Discharged prisoner—
      Registration of address—Person having no fixed abode—Trial by jury, on offender's election—Maximum sentence—Prison Act 1952, s 29(1)(b), Sch 1, paras 1(1), 2(1), 4(1). **R v Bishop** [1959] **2** 787, CCA.
    Duty of court to make order in absence of special reasons—
      Special reasons for not making order to be stated—Criminal Justice Act 1948, s 22(1). **R v Keeler** [1949] **2** 805, CCA.
    Order not made by court of trial per incuriam—
      Inclusion in sentence by Court of Criminal Appeal. **R v Rogers** [1953] **1** 206, CCA.
    Power of court to make order—
      Sentence of corrective training—Criminal Justice Act 1948, s 22(1), (2). **R v Speakman** [1949] **2** 807, CCA.
    Previous convictions—
      Admission—Need to caution prisoner—Notice of intention to prove conviction—Need to give notice to produce notice—Criminal Justice Act 1948, ss 21(1), 22(1), 23(1). **Practice Note** [1950] **1** 37, CCA.
      Need for sentences as well as convictions on two 'previous occasions'—Breach of probation order—Sentence for original offence and for second offence during probation passed on same occasion—Criminal Justice Act 1948, s 22(1)(a). **R v Perfect** [1957] **2** 250, CCA.
      Sentence of imprisonment—Imprisonment for non-payment of fine—Whether 'sentenced to imprisonment'—Criminal Justice Act 1948, s 22(1). **R v Driscoll** [1955] **2** 113, CCA.
  Suspended sentence—
    Activation—
      Fresh offence committed in respect of which conditional discharge imposed—Appellant within operational period of suspended sentence—Justices giving notice to Crown Court of conviction—Whether conditional discharge a conviction enabling activation of suspended sentence—Whether statutory amendments giving effect to Parliamentary intention—Powers of Criminal Courts Act 1973, ss 1C, 23, 24, 25—Criminal Justice Act 1991, s 8. **R v Moore** [1995] **4** 843, CA.
      Fresh offence committed in respect of which probation order imposed—Whether probation order a conviction such as to enable suspended sentence to be activated—Criminal Justice Act 1948, s 12—Criminal Justice Act 1967, ss 39(1), 40(1). **R v Tarry** [1970] **2** 185, CA.

SENTENCE (cont)—
  Suspended sentence (cont)—
    Activation (cont)—
      Subsequent offence of different character from offence in respect of which suspended sentence was imposed—Whether suspended sentence should be brought into effect—Criminal Justice Act 1967, s 40(1)(a). **R v Griffiths** [1969] **2** 805, CA.
      Unjust—Trivial offence in respect of which suspended sentence was imposed—Criminal Justice Act 1967, s 40(1). **R v Moylan** [1969] **3** 783, CA.
    Community requirement —
      Unpaid work requirement—Obligations of person subject to unpaid work requirement—Breach of community requirement—Extension of unpaid work requirement—Enforcement—Criminal Justice Act 2003, s 200(2), (4), Sch 12, paras 7(2), 18(1). **West Yorkshire Probation Board v Cruickshanks** [2010] **4** 1110, DC.
    Consecutive sentences—
      Sentences not consecutive to period of imprisonment then being served—Criminal Justice Act 1967, s 39(3), s 104(2). **R v Flanders** [1968] **3** 534, CA.
      Totality of consecutive sentences exceeding two years—Validity of suspended sentence—Criminal Justice Act 1967, ss 39(1), 104(2). **R v Coleman** [1969] **2** 1074, CA.
      Two sentences of six months consecutive—Mandatory requirement that sentences be suspended—Court on appeal against sentence not entitled to deal with appellant more severely than he was dealt with by court below—Order that sentences stand but be suspended—Criminal Justice Act 1967, s 39(3)—Criminal Appeal Act 1968, s 11(3). **R v March** [1970] **2** 536, CA.
    Conviction of prisoner of capital murder and of offence on another count—
      Sentence on latter count should be suspended. **Practice Direction** [1964] **3** 509, CCA.
    Criminal contempt—
      Application of provisions relating to suspended sentences. *See* **Contempt of court** (Criminal contempt—Power to commit instantly to prison—Provisions relating to suspended sentences not applicable to criminal contempt).
    Emergency legislation—
      Statute requiring that convicted person 'be sentenced to imprisonment for not less than' minimum period specified during period of emergency—Whether power of court to suspend sentence taken away—Criminal Justice (Temporary Provisions) Act (Northern Ireland) 1970, s 1—Treatment of Offenders Act (Northern Ireland) 1968, s 18. **Kennedy v Spratt** [1971] **1** 805, HL.
    Fine—
      Imprisonment in default of payment of fine—Whether court imposing suspended sentence can also impose fine—Need for care to see that fine imposed in addition to suspended sentence is well within convicted person's means. **R v King** [1970] **2** 249, CA.
    Fresh offence committed during period of suspension—
      Court dealing with fresh offence making no order regarding suspended sentence—Whether subsequent court has power to activate suspended sentence for same breach—Powers of Criminal Courts Act 1973, s 23(1)(d). **R v Folan** [1980] **1** 217, CA.
      Extended term ordered for fresh offence—Exception to rule that suspended sentence should be consecutive to sentence for fresh offence. **R v Wilkinson** [1969] **3** 1263, CA.
      Extended term ordered for fresh offence—Matters to be considered in determining extended sentence—Criminal Justice Act 1967, s 37. **R v Roberts** [1971] **2** 529, CA.
      Extended term ordered for fresh offence—Sentence for fresh offence to be dealt with first—Matters to be considered in determining extended sentence. **R v Wilkinson** [1969] **3** 1263, CA.
      Extended term ordered for fresh offence—Suspended sentence concurrent to extended sentence—Criminal Justice Act 1967, s 37. **R v Roberts** [1971] **2** 529, CA.
      Extension of period of suspended sentence—Imposition of immediate sentence of imprisonment for fresh offence—Undesirability of subjecting accused to immediate and suspended sentences at same time—Criminal Justice Act 1967, s 40(1)(c). **R v Goodlad** [1973] **2** 1200, CA.
      Magistrates wishing to make order of probation or discharge—Duty to commit to assizes or quarter sessions for sentence—Criminal Justice Act 1967, s 56. **R v Tarry** [1970] **2** 185, CA.
      Sentence for fresh offence to be dealt with first—Suspended sentence to take effect consecutively to sentence for current offence. **R v Ithell** [1969] **2** 449, CA.
    Initial sentence attracting mandatory suspension—
      Variation of initial sentence to impose immediate custodial sentence—Whether court has power to vary inital sentence—Criminal Justice Act 1967, s 39(3). **R v Newsome** [1970] **3** 455, CA.
    Partial suspension—
      Matters to be considered by court before ordering partial suspension of sentence—Circumstances in which partially suspended sentence appropriate—Whether court can order partial suspension of sentence for offence committed before court given power to order partial suspension—Criminal Law Act 1977, s 47(1), (8), Sch 14, para 5. **R v Clarke (Linda)** [1982] **3** 232, CA.
    Suitability as alternative to probation—
      Necessity of eliminating prison sentence—Alternative sentences. **R v O'Keefe** [1969] **1** 426, CA.
    Suspended sentence only to be imposed in 'exceptional circumstances'—
      Whether good character, youth or early plea of guilty are exceptional circumstances—Powers of Criminal Courts Act 1973, s 22(2). **R v Okinikan** [1993] **2** 5, CA.
    Two or more suspended sentences—
      Sentences imposed on different occasions—Time for deciding whether suspended sentence should be concurrent with or consecutive to an earlier suspended sentence is the time when the sentences are implemented—Criminal Justice Act 1967, s 40. **R v Blakeway** [1969] **2** 1133, CA.
      Sentences on same occasion—Decision whether sentences should run concurrently or consecutively to be made at time sentences imposed—Criminal Justice Act 1967, s 104(2). **R v Wilkinson** [1970] **3** 439, CA.
    Youthful offender. *See* Youthful offender—Suspended sentence, *below*.
  Terrorism—
    Terrorist offences—
      Dissemination of terrorist publications—Seriousness of offence—Guidance—Terrorism Act 2006, s 2. **R v Rahman** [2008] **4** 661, CA.
      Preparation of terrorist acts—Case comparison—Terrorism Act 2006, s 5. **R v Abdallah** [2017] **2** 795n, CA.

SENTENCE (cont)—
    Terrorism (cont)—
        Terrorist offences (cont)—
            Preparation of terrorist acts—Guidance—Terrorism Act 2006, s 5. **R v Kahar** [2017] **2** 782n, CA.
    Validity—
        Appeal—
            Jurisdiction of Court of Appeal. *See* **Criminal law** (Court of Appeal—Jurisdiction—Validity of sentence).
    Variation of sentence—
        Court of Appeal. *See* Appeal—Variation, *above*.
        Criminal bankruptcy order. *See* **Crown Court** (Order—Amendment—Jurisdiction—Criminal bankruptcy order—Criminal bankruptcy order in respect of several offences).
        Crown Court. *See* **Crown Court** (Sentence—Power to vary sentence or other order).
        Divisional Court. *See* **Divisional Court** (Jurisdiction—Variation of sentence).
    Victim personal statement—
        Consideration of. *See* **Practice** (Criminal proceedings—Victim personal statements).
    Young offender—
        Custodial sentence—
            Applicant aged 16 sentenced to six months' detention for one offence and one month each for other offences—Whether one-month sentences lawful—Criminal Justice Act 1982, s 1A. **R v Dover Youth Court, ex p K** [1998] **4** 24, QBD.
            Burglary—Whether burglary of dwelling house automatically qualifying young offender for custodial sentence—Criminal Justice Act 1982, s 1(4), (4A)(c). **R v Mussell** [1991] **2** 609, CA.
            Restriction on imposing custodial sentence on young offender—Criteria for deciding whether young offender qualifies for custodial sentence—Whether criteria mutually exclusive—Whether offences may be aggregated when considering seriousness of offence—Criminal Justice Act 1982, ss 1(4), (4A), 2(4). **R v Davison** [1990] **2** 976, CA.
            Restriction on imposing custodial sentence on young offender—Young offender convicted of a number of offences—Young offender qualifying for custodial sentence in respect of one offence—Appropriate sentence for other offences—Whether court can impose custodial sentences for offences which did not cause young offender to qualify for custodial sentence—Criminal Justice Act 1982, s 1(4), (4A). **R v Mussell** [1991] **2** 609, CA.
        Offender attaining age of 21 between conviction and sentence—
            Whether accused should be sentenced as juvenile or adult—Criminal Justice Act 1982, s 1(3A). **R v Danga** [1992] **1** 624, CA.
    Young person—
        Serious criminal offence—
            Appropriate period of detention—Relevant factors in determining period of detention—Gravity of offence—Attempted murder, grievous bodily harm and robbery—Safety of public—Power of Home Secretary to release offender before expiration of period—Period of detention in effect maximum period offender liable to be detained—Necessity of ensuring that offender not released whilst activities still likely to be a source of danger—Children and Young Persons Act 1933, s 53(2)(as amended by the Criminal Justice Act 1948, s 83(3), Sch 10 and the Criminal Justice Act 1961, ss 2(1), 41(1), Sch 4). **R v Storey** [1973] **3** 562, CA.
            Detention for such period as may be specified in the sentence—Life imprisonment—Whether life imprisonment 'a period which may be specified in the sentence'—Children and Young Persons Act 1933, s 53(2). **R v Abbott** [1963] **1** 738, CCA.
            Minimum term—Setting of minimum terms for juveniles sentenced to detention during Her Majesty's pleasure—Guidance. **Practice Statement** [2002] **3** 412, CA.
            Murder—Minimum term—Determination of minimum term where offender aged under 18 at time of offence sentenced to detention during Her Majesty's pleasure—Criminal Justice Act 2003, Sch 21, para 7. **A-G's Reference (No 126 of 2006)** [2007] **1** 1254, CA.
            Murder—Young offenders sentenced to be detained during Her Majesty's pleasure—Recommendations as to tariff. **Thompson, Re** [2001] **1** 737, CA.
            Setting of tariffs for juveniles sentenced to detention during Her Majesty's pleasure—Review of existing tariffs—Principles and practice. **Practice Note** [2000] **4** 831, CA.
            Tariff period—Eleven-year-old boy being convicted of murder and being sentenced to detention during Her Majesty's pleasure—Secretary of State fixing tariff period—Whether fixing of tariff by Secretary of State violating convention right—Whether detention during Her Majesty's pleasure breaching right to liberty—Convention for the Protection of Human Rights and Fundamental Freedoms 1950, arts 5, 6. **T v United Kingdom (note)** [2000] **2** 1024, ECt HR.
    Youthful offender—
        Borstal training. *See* Borstal training, *above*.
        Driving while disqualified—
            Imprisonment. *See* **Road traffic** (Driving while disqualified for holding licence—Imprisonment—Young offender).
        Imprisonment—
            No other method of dealing with offender appropriate—Statutory provision that youthful offender not to be imprisoned unless court of opinion no other method of dealing with him appropriate—Contempt in face of court—Whether statutory provision mandatory or directory—Whether sentence of imprisonment for contempt proper—Criminal Justice Act 1948, s 17(2). **Morris v The Crown Office** [1970] **1** 1079, CA.
            Restriction on imposing imprisonment—Imprisonment not to be imposed on person under 21 unless court of opinion no other method of dealing with him appropriate—Fine and imprisonment—Validity—Imposition of fine indicating that imprisonment not only appropriate method of dealing with offender—Whether imposition of fine and imprisonment justifiable in principle—Powers of Criminal Courts Act 1973, s 19(2). **R v Genese** [1976] **2** 600, QBD.
            Restriction on imposing imprisonment—Restriction not applying to person serving sentence of imprisonment when sentence passed—Offence committed and sentence passed when defendant released from prison on licence subject to supervision in place of remission—Whether 'serving a sentence of imprisonment' while released on licence—Whether restriction on sentence applicable to him—Criminal Justice Act 1961, s 3(2). **R v Orpwood** [1981] **2** 1053, .

SENTENCE (cont)—
  Youthful offender (cont)—
    Imprisonment (cont)—
      Restriction on imposing imprisonment—Restriction not applying to person serving sentence of imprisonment when sentence passed—Offences committed and sentence passed while defendant released on parole following sentence of imprisonment for earlier offence—Whether defendant 'serving a sentence of imprisonment' while on parole—Whether restriction on sentencing applicable to defendant—Criminal Justice Act 1961, s 3(1), (2)—Criminal Justice Act 1967, s 60. **R v Mellor** [1981] **2** 1049, CA.
      Statement of reason why no other sentence appropriate—Offender twice sentenced to borstal training—Criminal Justice Act 1948, s 17(3)—Criminal Justice Act 1961, s 3(3). **R v Jackson (alias Rintoul)** [1966] **2** 346, CCA.
    Suspended sentence—
      Conviction for subsequent offence and sentence to six months' imprisonment—Subsequently suspended sentence of six months ordered to take effect consecutively after six months' term then current—Whether order activating suspended sentence was a passing of sentence within s 3 of Act of 1961 or was a dealing with offender within s 40(1) of the Act of 1967—Whether s 3(1) was contravened—Criminal Justice Act 1961, s 3(1), (2)—Criminal Justice Act 1967, s 40(1). **R v Lamb (Alan)** [1968] **3** 206, CA.

SENTENCING
  See **Sentence**.

SEPARATION
  Husband and wife—
    Agreement. See **Husband and wife** (Separation agreement).
    Divorce. See **Divorce** (Separation).
    Order. See **Husband and wife** (Separation order).
    Rape. See **Criminal law** (Rape—Husband and wife—Separation order in force).

SEPARATION OF POWERS
  Constitutional law—
    Generally. See **Constitutional law** (Constitution—Separation of powers).
    Jamaica. See **Jamaica** (Constitutional law—Separation of powers).

SEQUESTRATION
  Contempt of court. See **Contempt of court** (Sequestration).
  Enforcement of judgment by. See **Execution** (Sequestration).

SERIOUS FRAUD OFFICE
  Company investigation. See **Company** (Investigation by Serious Fraud Office).
  Investigation—
    Decision to cease investigation—
      Rule of law. See **Constitutional law** (Separation of powers—Separation of judicial and executive power—Rule of law—Serious Fraud Office).
    Disclosure of documents—
      Right to respect for correspondence—Serious Fraud Office executing search warrants and obtaining documents—Director of Serious Fraud Office exercising discretion to disclose documents to government department—Whether breach of right to respect for correspondence—Whether Serious Fraud Office required to notify owner of documents before disclosure—Whether disclosure fair—Criminal Justice Act 1987, s 3(5)(a)—Human Rights Act 1998, Sch 1, Pt I, art 8(2). **R (on the application of Kent Pharmaceuticals Ltd) v Director of Serious Fraud Office (Secretary of State for the Home Dept and anor, interested parties)** [2005] **1** 449, CA.
    Investigation of suspected offence involving serious or complex fraud—
      Duty of public authority to act in a way compatible with a convention right—Whether Director of Serious Fraud Office having duty to investigate in United Kingdom where convention right might be violated by trial of suspected person outside United Kingdom—Criminal Justice Act 1987, s 1(3)—Human Rights Act 1998, s 6(1). **R (on the application of Bermingham) v Director of Serious Fraud Office** [2006] **3** 239, DC.
    Jurisdiction. See **Fraud** (Investigation—Jurisdiction).
    Seizure of documents—
      Issue of warrants where not practicable to serve notice requiring person under investigation or any other person to produce specified documents or where service of notice might seriously prejudice investigation—Serious Fraud Office applying for warrant following request for mutual legal assistance from abroad—District judge issuing warrant in respect of material held by claimant—Police executing warrant and seizing documents—Whether issue and execution of warrant lawful—Guidance as to principles to be applied—Criminal Justice Act 1987, s 2(3), (4). **R (on the application of Energy Financing Team Ltd) v Bow Street Magistrates' Court** [2005] **4** 285, DC.
  Use of defence case statements—
    Re-interviewing witnesses after service of defence statements. See **Criminal evidence** (Prosecution evidence—Use of defence case statements—Re-interviewing witnesses—Re-interviewing witnesses after service of defence case statements—Serious Fraud Office).

SERIOUS ORGANISED CRIME AGENCY
  Authorised disclosure to. See **Proceeds of crime** (Criminal property—Knowledge or suspicion of arrangement facilitating acquisition, retention, use or control of criminal property).

SERVANT
  Agreement—
    Restraint of trade. See **Restraint of trade by agreement** (Employer and employee).

SERVANT (cont)—
  Company—
    Criminal liability of company for acts of servant. *See* **Criminal law** (Company—Criminal liability—Act of servant).
  Contract of service—
    Breach of undertaking—
      Injunction. *See* **Injunction** (Breach of covenant—Breach of undertaking—Contract of service).
    Capital gains tax—
      Employer's rights under service agreement—Payment to employer by employee to secure release from service agreement. *See* **Capital gains tax** (Disposal of assets—Employer's rights under service agreement with employee—Payment to company by employee to secure release from service agreement).
    Continuous employment. *See* **Employment** (Continuity).
    Generally. *See* **Employment** (Contract of service).
    Income tax—
      Employment—Emoluments from employment. *See* **Income tax** (Emoluments from office or employment—Employment—Contract of service).
  Crown servant. *See* **Crown** (Crown servant).
  Dismissal—
    Award of damages after. *See* **Damages** (Personal injury—Dismissal from work in consequence of injury—Dismissal following award at trial).
    Redundancy. *See* **Redundancy** (Dismissal by reason of redundancy).
  Larceny as a servant. *See* **Criminal law** (Larceny—Servant).
  Loss of services—
    Crown servant. *See* **Crown** (Crown servant—Loss of services).
  Master and servant. *See* **Employment**.
  Vicarious liability—
    Loan of servant. *See* **Vicarious liability** (Loan of servant).

SERVICE
  Acknowledgment of service—
    Admiralty practice. *See* **Admiralty** (Practice—Form of writs and acknowledgments of service).
    Generally. *See* **Practice** (Acknowledgment of service).
  Action for account. *See* **Account** (Action for—Service).
  Affidavit of service—
    Admiralty proceedings. *See* **Admiralty** (Practice—Post—First and second class mail—Affidavit of service).
  Alternative means, by—
    Service out of the jurisdiction—
      Claim form. *See* **Claim form** (Service—Service out of the jurisdiction—Service of claim form by alternative method or at alternative place).
      Generally. *See* **Practice** (Service out of the jurisdiction—Service by alternative means).
  Bankruptcy—
    Application. *See* **Bankruptcy** (Application—Service).
    Bankruptcy notice. *See* **Bankruptcy** (Bankruptcy notice—Service).
    Bankruptcy petition—
      Evidence. *See* **Bankruptcy** (Appeal—Appeal against adjudication—Allegation that petition not served on debtor).
      Generally. *See* **Bankruptcy** (Petition—Service).
    Statutory demand. *See* **Insolvency** (Statutory demand—Service).
  Billeting notice. *See* **Billeting** (Billeting notice—Service).
  Claim form—
    Extension of time for service. *See* **Claim form** (Extension of time for service).
    Generally. *See* **Claim form** (Service).
    Residence. *See* **Claim form** (Service—Domicile—Residence).
  Company—
    Overseas company. *See* **Company** (Oversea company—Service on oversea company).
  County court—
    Service of documents relating to application for new tenancy of business premises. *See* **County court** (Practice—Service of documents relating to application for new tenancy of business premises).
    Summons. *See* **County court** (Practice—Service of summons).
  Divorce—
    Notice of appeal. *See* **Divorce** (Practice—Service—Notice of appeal).
    Petition. *See* **Divorce** (Practice—Service—Petition).
  Electronic communication, by—
    Arbitration proceedings. *See* **Arbitration** (Practice—Service—Service of notice by e-mail).
    Claim form. *See* **Claim form** (Service—Methods of service—Electronic communication).
    Practice. *See* **Practice** (Service—Service by electronic communication).
    Rates completion notice. *See* **Rates** (Completion notice—Validity of service).
    Service out of the jurisdiction. *See* **Practice** (Service out of the jurisdiction—Service by alternative means—E-mail).
  Employment Appeal Tribunal. *See* **Employment Appeal Tribunal** (Practice—Service).
  Enforcement notice. *See* **Town and country planning** (Enforcement notice—Service).
  Extradition—
    Appeal—
      Notice of appeal, service of. *See* **Extradition** (Extradition order—Appeal—Notice of appeal).
    Extradition request and certificate. *See* **Extradition** (Extradition request and certificate—Service).
  Fax, by—
    Claim form. *See* **Claim form** (Service—Service on defendant's solicitors—Service by fax).
  Foreign judgment—
    Criminal law. *See* **Criminal law** (International co-operation in respect of criminal proceedings and investigation—Service of overseas process).
    Generally. *See* **Practice** (Service).

SERVICE (cont)—
Writ—
    Action for possession—
        Effect of service. *See* **Landlord and tenant** (Forfeiture of lease—Forfeiture—Action for possession by lessor—Issue of writ not sufficient to bring about forfeiture).
    Admiralty action in personam. *See* **Admiralty** (Practice—Action in personam—Writ—Service).
    Admiralty action in rem. *See* **Admiralty** (Practice—Action in rem—Writ—Service).
    Extension of validity—
        Cause of action statute barred. *See* **Writ** (Extension of validity—Action statute-barred—Writ not served).
    Generally. *See* **Practice** (Service).
    Oversea company. *See* **Company** (Oversea company—Service on oversea company).
    Partnership. *See* **Writ** (Service on partnership).
    Service on company. *See* **Writ** (Service on company).
    Service on foreign company. *See* **Company** (Foreign company—Writ—Service of writ on company).
    Service out of the jurisdiction. *See* **Practice** (Service out of the jurisdiction).

SERVICE CHARGE
Business premises—
    Inclusion in terms of new tenancy. *See* **Landlord and tenant** (Business premises—Terms of new tenancy—Inclusion of service charge over and above reserved rent).
Covenant to pay without deduction or set-off—
    Whether unfair contract term. *See* **Landlord and tenant** (Covenant—Payment of rent and service charge without deduction or set-off).
Flat. *See* **Landlord and tenant** (Service charge).
Landlord and tenant. *See* **Landlord and tenant** (Service charge).
Local authority houses—
    Reasonable of covenant as to service charge. *See* **Housing** (Local authority houses—Tenant's right to buy—Service charge).

SERVICE CONTRACT
Generally. *See* **Employment** (Contract of service).
Repudiation. *See* **Contract** (Repudiation—Contract for services).

SERVICE MARK
See **Trade mark** (Service mark).

SERVICE OCCUPANCY
Small tenement—
    Recovery of possession. *See* **Landlord and tenant** (Small tenement—Recovery of possession—Service occupancy).
Termination of service—
    Failure to deliver up. *See* **Emergency legislation** (Re-entry of property—Leave to re-enter property—Service occupier—Failure to deliver up on termination of employment).

SERVICEMAN
Negligence—
    Duty to take care. *See* **Negligence** (Duty to take care—Serviceman).

SERVICES
European Community, within—
    Freedom of movement. *See* **European Union** (Freedom of movement—Services).
European Community, within. *See* **European Union** (Freedom of movement—Services).
Fire brigade—
    Payment for. *See* **Fire brigade** (Payment for services).
Racial discrimination—
    Provision of services. *See* **Race relations** (Unlawful discrimination—Provision of goods, facilities or services).
Restrictive trading agreement—
    Registration. *See* **Restrictive trade practices** (Registration of agreement—Agreement relating to services).
Sexual discrimination—
    Provision of services. *See* **Sex discrimination** (Provision of goods, facilities or services).
Trade or business—
    False or misleading statement as to services. *See* **Trade description** (False or misleading statement as to services etc).
Value added tax—
    Club or association—
        Supply of services for a consideration. *See* **Value added tax** (Club or association—Supply of services for consideration).
    European Community. *See* **European Union** (Value added tax—Supply of goods or services).
    Generally. *See* **Value added tax** (Supply of goods or services).

SET-OFF
Assignment of debt—
    Right of debtor to set off against assignee sums owed by assignor to debtor. *See* **Chose in action** (Assignment—Debt—Set-off—Right of debtor to set off against assignee sums owed by assignor to debtor).
Bank account—
    Separate accounts. *See* **Bank** (Account—Separate accounts—Right to combine or set-off).
Bankruptcy—
    Generally. *See* **Bankruptcy** (Set-off).
    Proof. *See* **Bankruptcy** (Proof—Set-off).

SET-OFF (cont)—

Breach of trust. *See* **Trust and trustee** (Breach of trust—Set-off).

Charterparty—

    Hire—

        Equitable set-off. *See* **Shipping** (Time charterparty—Hire—Equitable set-off).

Community aid—

    European Community. *See* **European Union** (Set-off—Community aid).

Companies winding up—

    Application of bankruptcy rules in winding up of insolvent English companies. *See* **Company** (Winding up—Application of bankruptcy rules—Set-off).

    Compulsory winding up—

        Mutual credits, debts and dealings between company and debtor. *See* **Company** (Compulsory winding up—Debtor—Mutual credits, debts and dealings between company and debtor—Set-off).

    Generally. *See* **Company** (Winding up—Set-off).

    Secured debt. *See* **Company** (Winding up—Proof of debts—Set-off—Mutual dealings—Secured debt).

Contract—

    No set-off clause. *See* **Sale of goods** (Passing of property—No set-off clause).

Costs—

    County court. *See* **County court** (Costs—Set-off).

    Generally. *See* **Costs** (Set-off).

    Legal aid—

        Charge on property recovered for deficiency of costs. *See* **Legal aid** (Costs—Set-off).

        Generally. *See* **Legal aid** (Costs—Set-off).

Cross-claim—

    Equitable right of set-off— **Geldof Metaalconstructie NV v Simon Carves Ltd** [2010] **4** 847n, CA.

        Circumstances in which cross-claim can be regarded as a set-off. **Hanak v Green** [1958] **2** 141, CA.

        Claim for rent—Cross-claim for damages arising out of landlord's defective construction of premises—Landlord's claim for rent arising out of breach of lease—Tenant's claim for damages arising out of prior agreement to build and lease premises to tenant—Whether sufficient connection between transactions on which claim and counterclaim based to give rise to equitable set-off—Whether equitable set-off available in action for rent—Whether unliquidated demand can be set off in equity against claim for debt. **British Anzani (Felixstowe) Ltd v International Marine Management (UK) Ltd** [1979] **2** 1063, QBD.

        Contract of employment—Teacher—Claim for salary—Teacher refusing to provide cover for absent colleague in breach of contract of employment—Employer deducting appropriate sum by way of damages from teacher's monthly salary—Teacher bringing action against employer for full salary—Whether equitable right of set-off available in action for salary under contract of employment. **Sim v Rotherham Metropolitan BC** [1986] **3** 387, Ch D.

        Counterclaim by owners of salved vessel for damage done by salvers' diver—Right of limitation restricting amount of counterclaim. **Tojo Maru, The** [1969] **3** 1179, CA.

        Garnishee proceedings. **Hale v Victoria Plumbing Co Ltd and En-Tout-Cas Co Ltd** [1966] **2** 672, CA.

        Licence agreement in respect of garage—Provision for payment for fuel deliveries by direct debit—Defendant cancelling direct debit arrangement before paying for past fuel deliveries—Plaintiff commencing proceedings to recover amount owing and applying for summary judgment—Defendant alleging repudiatory breach of contract, counterclaiming for damages for future losses and seeking to set off those damages to extinguish admitted debt—Whether defence of equitable set-off available when direct debit cancelled after delivery of goods or services—Whether direct debit same as cheque—Whether counterclaim for future loss sufficiently connected with claim for payment for past deliveries to allow for an equitable set-off. **Esso Petroleum Co Ltd v Milton** [1997] **2** 593, CA.

        When doctrine of equitable set-off applicable—Claim by shipowners for freight—Cross-claim by charterers for short delivery of cargo—Mere existence of cross-claim not a ground for intervention of equity. **Aries Tanker Corp v Total Transport Ltd** [1977] **1** 398, HL.

    Legal right of set-off—

        Applications to enforce two GAFTA arbitration awards—Applicant seeking to set off against liability under arbitration award debts due under washout agreement—Whether washout debt enforceable so as to allow set-off against liability under arbitration award—GAFTA form 64, cll 11, 29. **Glencore Grain Ltd v Agros Trading Co Ltd** [1999] **2 Comm** 288, CA.

        Claim and cross-claim—Independent transactions—Cross-claim subject of pending arbitration proceedings—Whether cross-claim capable of being set off against claim pleaded in court. **Aectra Refining and Marketing Inc v Exmar NV** [1995] **1** 641, CA.

        Claim for specific performance—Plaintiff having right to require defendant to assign patent rights for non-payment of fees—Defendant not paying fees—Plaintiff owing defendant more than outstanding fees in respect of other transactions—Whether plaintiff entitled to specific performance of assignment because of defendant's non-payment—Whether right of set-off available against claim for equitable relief based on money claim. **BICC plc v Burndy Corp** [1985] **1** 417, CA.

        Claim under charterparty for stipulated daily rate of hire of vessel over off-hire periods—Quantum of claim subject to dispute—Whether claim constituting legal set-off—Whether claim sufficiently ascertainable. **Aectra Refining and Marketing Inc v Exmar NV** [1995] **1** 641, CA.

Distress for rent. *See* **Landlord and tenant** (Rent—Claim for rent—Distress for rent—Set-off).

Freight—

    Claim for freight. *See* **Shipping** (Freight—Claim for freight—Set-off).

    Domestic carriage of goods by road—

        Claim for freight. *See* **Carriers** (Contract—Carriage of goods—Freight—Claim for freight—Set-off).

Insolvency and. *See* **Insolvency** (Set-off).

Legal aid—

    Costs—

        Charge on property recovered for deficiency of costs—Set-off. *See* **Legal aid** (Charge on property recovered for deficiency of costs).

        Generally. *See* **Legal aid** (Costs—Set-off).

Limitation period. *See* **Limitation of action** (Set-off or counterclaim).

SET-OFF (cont)—
  Rent—
    Claim for rent. *See* **Landlord and tenant** (Rent—Claim for rent—Set-off).
  Right of set-off—
    Contracting out—
      Bank providing facilities to defendant company to finance oil purchases—Defendant undertaking to repay bank without any deduction, set-off or counterclaim—Bank claiming amount owing—Defendant making counterclaim and seeking to set off amount of counterclaim—Whether parties to contract can contract out of right of set-off—Whether defendant precluded by contract from claiming right of set-off against bank. **Hongkong and Shanghai Banking Corp v Kloeckner & Co AG** [1989] **3** 513, QBD.
      Plaintiff selling company—Contract providing that payment was 'absolute and unconditional' and 'shall not be affected ... by any other matter whatsoever'—Whether purchaser's right of set-off excluded. **BOC Group plc v Centeon LLC** [1999] **1 Comm** 970, CA.
      Whether exception to general contractual bar to set-off or counterclaim preventing set-off under an affiliated company's contract. **Sinochem International Oil (London) Co Ltd v Mobil Sales and Supply Corp (Sinochem International Oil Co Ltd, third party)** [1999] **2 Comm** 522, QBD; [2000] **1 Comm** 474, CA.
  Exclusion—
    Unfair contract term. *See* **Contract** (Unfair terms—Term excluding right of set-off).
  Summary judgment—
    Counterclaim—Set-off at law—Plaintiffs claiming demurrage in respect of contract of sale under joint venture arrangement—Claim for liquidated amount—Defendants counterclaiming for short payment under earlier contract—Payment fixed by reference to contract price paid by defendants to suppliers—Whether counterclaim for liquidated sum—Whether defendants entitled to set off counterclaim—Whether defendants' right to recover on counterclaim a triable issue—Whether defendants entitled to unconditional leave to defend. **Axel Johnson Petroleum AB v MG Mineral Group AG** [1992] **2** 163, CA.

SETTING ASIDE
  Judgment. *See* **Judgment** (Setting aside).

SETTING DOWN ACTION
  See **Practice** (Trial—Setting down action).

SETTLED ESTATES
  Variation of trust by the court. *See* **Variation of trusts** (Benefit—Settled estates).

SETTLED LAND
  Application of capital money—
    Payment for improvements—
      Payment for money expended and costs incurred incidental to improvements—Agricultural holdings subject to trusts under settlement—Landlord paying to outgoing tenants compensation for improvements—Whether compensation recoverable from capital moneys—Settled Land Act 1925, s 73(1)(iii), (iv)—Agricultural Holdings Act 1948, ss 47, 48, 82. **King v Wellesley** [1971] **2** 1140, Ch D.
    Payment of money expended and costs incurred by landlord in execution of improvement—
      Landlord—Meaning—Application by tenant for life for order that trustees meet cost of works out of capital money—Tenant for life bankrupt—Whether 'landlord' within Settled Land Act 1925, s 73(1)(iv) (as amended by Agricultural Holdings Act 1948, s 96(1))—Agricultural Holdings Act 1948, s 81(1), Sch III, para 23. **Brougham and Vaux's (Lord) Settled Estates, Re** [1953] **2** 655, Ch D.
    Money expended under statute or under custom or agreement or otherwise—Meaning of 'or otherwise'—Expenditure on improvements by assign of tenant for life—Repairs to agricultural property executed before 1st March 1948—Settled Land Act 1925, s 73(1)(iv)(as amended by Agricultural Holdings Act 1948, s 96(1)). **Sutherland Settlement Trusts, Re** [1953] **2** 27, Ch D.
    Redemption of improvement rentcharge—
      'Redemption'—Tithe annuity—'Discharge'—Payment by tenant for life of periodical instalments under rentcharge, representing capital and interest, and of annuities—Right to recoupment, in respect of such part of payments as represented capital, out of capital moneys subject to settlement—Settled Land Act 1925, s 73(1)(xiii), (xvi). **Sandbach (decd), Re** [1951] **1** 971, CA.
  Capital money—
    Application. *See* Application of capital money, *above*.
    Investment—
      Power of tenant for life to direct change of investment—Settled Land Act 1925, s 73. **St Aubyn (L M) v A-G (No 2)** [1951] **2** 473, HL.
  Improvements—
    Expenditure payable out of capital—
      Additions and alterations to buildings to enable them to be let—Additions and alterations—Meaning—Additions and alterations not confined to structural alterations and additions—Settled Land Act 1925, Sch III, Part I, para xxiii. **Lindsay's Settlement (No 2), Re** [1941] **1** 143, Ch D.
      Additions and alterations to buildings to enable them to be let—Conversion of dwelling-house into shops and flats—Whether expenditure to be borne by capital—Settled Land Act 1925, Sch III, Part I, para xxiii. **Swanwick House, Prestbury, Re** [1939] **3** 531, Ch D.
      Drainage—Compliance with order under Housing Act—New drainage—Inclusion of subsidiary repairs in sum payable out of capital—Settled Land Act 1925, s 83, Sch III, Part I, para xxi. **Lindsay's Settlement (No 2), Re** [1941] **1** 143, Ch D.
      Structural additions to building—Erection of garages, chauffeur's flat etc short distance from mansion house—Whether additions near enough to house to be part of buildings of mansion house—Settled Land Act 1925, Sch III, Part II, para v. **Insole's Settlement, Re** [1938] **3** 406, CA.
    Income tax allowances in respect of improvements—
      Allowances received by tenant for life—Whether tenant for life accountable to settlement trustees for allowances—Settled Land Act 1925, ss 73(1)(iii), (iv), 75(2), 107(1). **Pelly (decd), Re** [1956] **2** 326, CA.

SETTLED LAND (cont)—

Land held on trust for persons entitled in undivided shares—
  Persons entitled in undivided shares on death of tenant for life—
    Right of trustee of settlement to call for legal estate—Personal representative of testator as trustee of settlement—Settled Land Act 1925, ss 30(3), 36(1). **Thomas, Re** [1939] **1** 379, Ch D.
Leasing powers of tenant for life. *See* **Settlement** (Powers of tenant for life—Leasing).
Name and arms clause in will. *See* **Will** (Condition—Name and arms clause).
Settlement—
  Statutory meaning—
    Agreement for settlement—Consent order after divorce decree—Husband to secure house jointly held to wife 'for her life occupation'—Whether an 'agreement' within Settled Land Act 1925, s 1(1). **Bacon v Bacon** [1947] **2** 327, Div.
    Exclusion of land held on trust for sale—Land subject to equitable interests and then held on trust for sale—Legal estate vested in the persons who are the trustees for sale but not as such trustees—Compound settlement—Deeds forming compound settlement—Trustees of compound settlement—Settled Land Act 1925, s 1(1)(v), (7)—Law of Property Amendment Act 1926, Sch. **Sharpe's Deed of Release, Re** [1938] **3** 449, Ch D.
Transaction affecting settled land—
  Act of Parliament constituting settlement—
    Entrenching section in Act—Settled land of national artistic and historical importance—Tenant in tail in remainder irresponsible—Proposed conveyance by tenant in tail in possession of settled land to trustees of new trust to be held on trust for sale to detriment of tenant in tail in remainder—Whether court having jurisdiction to authorise proposed conveyance—Effect of entrenching section—Settled Land Act 1925, s 64. **Hambro v Duke of Marlborough** [1994] **3** 332, Ch D.
  Power of court to order unauthorised transaction to be effected—
    Transaction for benefit of settled land—Purchase of furniture and chattels to re-equip mansion house destroyed by enemy action—Settled Land Act 1925, s 64. **Mount Edgcumbe Settled Estates, Re** [1950] **2** 242, Ch D.
    Transaction for benefit of settled land—Trustees empowered to effect transaction for benefit of property—Trustees wishing to transfer part of trust property to maintenance fund—Persons not beneficiaries under settlement likely to become beneficiaries under maintenance fund—Whether trustees empowered to establish maintenance fund—Settled Land Act 1925, s 64. **Raikes v Lygon** [1988] **1** 884, Ch D.
Will—
  Will made abroad—
    Whether proceeds of sale of settled land personalty. *See* **Will** (Will made abroad—Proceeds of sale of settled land—Whether personalty).

SETTLEMENT

Absolute gift—
  Restrictions on enjoyment—
    Failure of trusts—Destination of trust fund. **Gatti's Voluntary Settlement Trusts, Re** [1936] **2** 1489, Ch D.
Acceleration—
  'After the death of'—
    Wife's interest in income not accruing on husband's death as she was not then his widow—Potential interest of wife in income—Context required to make doctrine of acceleration applicable—Interest in default of appointment accelerated notwithstanding continuance of power of appointment—Contingent interest accelerated. **Dawson's Settlement, Re** [1966] **3** 68, Ch D.
  Assignment of life interest—
    Assignment with intent to merge it in contingent reversionary absolute interest—No acceleration. **Bellville's Settlement, Re** [1963] **3** 270, Ch D.
  Derivative settlement—
    Income for 21 year period subjected by deed and order of the court to the same trusts as would arise on the expiration of that period—Intervening trust for accumulation which did not arise as events happened—Whether interests arising on the expiration of the year period were accelerated. **Midland Bank Exor and Trustee Co Ltd v IRC** [1959] **1** 180, CA.
  Disclaimer by life tenant—
    Annuities subject to life interest—Whether annuities accelerated. **Hodge, Re** [1943] **2** 304, Ch D.
    Distribution 'upon the determination or failure of the last surviving life interest'—Whether disclaimer can alter vested interests in possession. **Young's Settlement Trusts, Re** [1959] **2** 74, Ch D.
    Fund held in trust for son and daughter of testatrix and after death for either of his or her children at 21—Son released his life interest—Acceleration to bring children into possession—Class of children remaining open for after-born children of former life tenant—Rule in Andrews v Partington not applicable. **Kean v Harker** [1969] **3** 1, Ch D.
    Interests in remainder vested subject to defeasance. **Taylor (decd), Re** [1957] **3** 56, Ch D.
    Intermediate income—Devise of land to A for life with remainder to his sons in tail male, with remainder to B in fee simple—Disclaimer by A having as yet no son—Destination of intermediate income—Whether income expressly disposed of—Law of Property Act 1925, s 175(1). **Hatfeild (decd), Re** [1957] **2** 261, Ch D.
    Life interest in share of residue—Share to be equally divided between issue on death of life tenant—Whether existing issue take to the exclusion of those subsequently born. **Davies (decd), Re** [1957] **3** 52, Ch D.
    Residuary gift of life interest to A and B with remainder to unborn children of B on attaining specified age—Gift over to named charities in event of no child being born or attaining specified age—Disclaimer of life interests by A and B—B alive at death of testatrix but no children born—Destination of income pending death of B or birth of child—Whether doctrine of acceleration applicable in case of alternative contingent gifts—Whether acceleration of income in favour of charities. **Scott (decd), Re** [1975] **2** 1033, Ch D.
  Doctrine of acceleration—
    General statement of doctrine. **Kebty-Fletcher's Will Trusts, Re** [1967] **3** 1076, Ch D.

SETTLEMENT (cont)—
Acceleration (cont)—
Forfeiture of life interest—
'Any event whereby any [person] entitled to any life interest would if such life interest belonged to him absolutely be deprived of the personal enjoyment thereof'—Beneficiary in German occupied territory against his will—Whether an 'enemy'—Operation of defeasance clause—Trading with the Enemy Act 1939, s 2(1)(b). **Hatch, Re** [1948] **2** 288, Ch D.
Gift to C for life with remainder to first and other sons in tail male, and remainders over—Forfeiture of C's life interest, while C a bachelor—Acceleration of second life estate—Accelerated life estate not determined by birth of son to C. **Blathwayt's Will Trusts, Re** [1950] **1** 582, Ch D.
Invalidity of primary trust—
Resulting trust to settlor or acceleration of secondary trust. **Flower's Settlement Trusts, Re** [1957] **1** 462, CA.
Accruer clause—
Accruer to funds which had not 'failed or determined'—
Fund paid absolutely to beneficiary in accordance with trusts of the settlement. **Huntington's Settlement Trusts, Re** [1949] **1** 674, Ch D.
Trusts for children and grandchildren in unequal shares—
Accruing share accrues to other beneficiaries equally. **Bower's Settlement Trusts, Re** [1942] **1** 278, Ch D.
Accumulation of income—
Generally. See **Accumulation**.
Total income for tax purposes. See **Income tax** (Total income—Trust income—Accumulation).
Adoption. See Beneficial interest—Ultimate trust for statutory next-of-kin, below.
Advancement—
Consent of wife—
Wife resident in enemy country—Power of court to dispense with consent—No power in Custodian of Enemy Property to give consent. **Forster's Settlement, Re** [1942] **1** 180, Ch D.
Express trust to accumulate income during settlor's lifetime—
Trusts for settlor's grandchildren—Express powers of advancement and maintenance—Whether powers applicable during accumulation period. **Henderson's Trusts, Re** [1969] **3** 769, CA.
Power to advance proportion of trust fund—
Power to advance half of trust fund to tenant for life—Whether advances up to prescribed limit at date of advancement exhausting power of advancement—Whether if balance retained by trustees increasing in value, trustees having power to make further advances to bring aggregate or advances up to prescribed limit. **Abergavenny's (Marquess) Estate Act Trusts, Re** [1981] **2** 643, Ch D.
Power to raise capital to establish life tenant in business or otherwise for his benefit or advancement—
Settlement on tenant for life and his wife and children—'Benefit'. **Halsted's Will Trusts, Re** [1937] **2** 570, Ch D.
Purchase of business or share in a business—
Deposit with Lloyd's trustees to become underwriter—Whether included—Expediency—Trustee Act 1925, s 57(1). **Craven's Estate, Re** [1937] **3** 33, Ch D.
Trustees failing to have proper understanding of effect of advancement—
Advancement of funds of settlement to son of life tenant—Advanced funds to be held on trusts of sub-settlement—Trust for son for life with certain other powers and trusts—All powers and trusts other than life interest void for perpetuity—Whether advancement for benefit of son—Whether advancement effective to create a life interest in possession in son. **Hastings-Bass (decd), Re** [1974] **2** 193, CA.
Capital gains tax—Trust gains not able to be set off against beneficiaries' losses—Scope of rule of equity requiring trustees to take into account all relevant considerations and not take into account any irrelevant considerations when exercising power—Whether advancement to be set aside. **Pitt v Holt** [2011] **2** 450, CA; [2013] **3** 429, SC.
After-acquired property—
Covenant to settle—
Children of marriage to attain vested interest at 21—Death of only child to attain a vested interest—Child's property left to mother—Whether property brought into settlement after death of child to be held for benefit of child or on ultimate trusts in default of issue attaining vested interest. **Benett-Stanford's Settlement Trusts, Re** [1947] **1** 888, Ch D.
Coalescence of accreted property—Whether accreted property coalesced with wife's trust fund—Appointment by will of wife's trust fund. **Rydon Marriage Settlement, Re** [1954] **3** 1, CA.
Covenant by beneficiary—Property acquired more than thirty years later—Received by trustees and held on trusts of settlement—Claim by beneficiary to recover property from trustees. **Adlard's Settlement Trust, Re** [1953] **2** 1437, Ch D.
Covenant to settle on trusts of a will—Covenantor acquiring absolute interest (i) under the settlement and (ii) under the will—Application of covenant. **Rogers' Settlement, Re** [1951] **1** 236, Ch D.
Enforcement of covenant by beneficiaries—Voluntary settlement—Assignment of defeasible interest—Enforcement of covenant for further assurance. **Kay's Settlement, Re** [1939] **1** 245, Ch D.
Exclusion of property where intention expressed—Appointment of property—Power of appointor to express intention to exclude property. **De la Bere's Marriage Settlement Trusts, Re** [1941] **2** 533, Ch D.
Hotchpot clause—Appointment of the 'wife's trust fund'—Whether accretion to original fund caught by appointment. **Rydon Marriage Settlement, Re** [1954] **3** 1, CA.
Property to which the wife may become entitled in possession or reversion—Property vested in reversion before marriage falling into possession during marriage—Property appointed to wife during marriage. **Maltby Marriage Settlement, Re** [1953] **2** 220, Ch D.
Property to which the wife might 'after the marriage become entitled in possession or reversion'—At date of settlement wife entitled to vested but defeasible interest and indefeasibly vested interest—These not caught by covenant—At date of settlement wife entitled to contingent interest which would be caught by covenant if it vested during marriage—Doubtful whether covenant would be effective after marriage. **Peel's Settlement, Re** [1964] **3** 567, Ch D.

SETTLEMENT (cont)—
  After-acquired property (cont)—
    Covenant to settle (cont)—
      Separate provision that all property comprised within covenant subject to trusts of settlement—Settlor entitled to reversionary interest under will—Death of settlor without having assigned reversionary interest to trustees of settlement—Same trustee both of will and of settlement—Beneficiaries under settlement volunteers—Whether investments standing in trustee's name representing reversionary interest formed part of settlor's estate or were held on trusts of settlement. **Ralli's Will Trusts, Re** [1963] **3** 940, Ch D.
  Agreement to permit rent free occupation of property for life—
    Agreement by employer to allow widow of employee to occupy house rent free for life or so long as she may desire—
      Agreement making widow a tenant for life—Property held by landlords in trust for widow for life and subject thereto in trust for them—Purchaser of landlord's interest with notice of trust—Trust binding on purchaser. **Binions v Evans** [1972] **2** 70, CA.
  Father surrendering life interest in settled land in favour of son—
    Undertakings by son to allow father and stepmother and the survivor of them to occupy house rent-free for life or so long as they might desire—Whether undertaking constituting grant of life interest creating settlement of land—Settled Land Act 1925, s 1(1). **Dent v Dent** [1996] **1** 659, Ch D.
  Appeal—
    Income tax. *See* **Income tax** (Appeal—Settlement).
  Appointed period—
    Period of income trust—
      Certainty in years relevant to surtax assessments—Possible uncertainty in later years—Validity. **Muir v IRC** [1966] **3** 38, CA.
  Apportionment—
    Capital or income. *See* Capital or income—Apportionment, *below*.
  Arbitration—
    Jurisdiction of arbitrator following settlement. *See* **Arbitration** (Arbitrator—Jurisdiction—Settlement).
  Bankruptcy—
    Avoidance of settlement. *See* **Bankruptcy** (Avoidance of settlement).
  Beneficial interest—
    Ultimate trust for statutory next-of-kin—
      Distribution—Right to respect for private and family life—Prohibition of discrimination—Settlement made when legislation not including adopted children in definition of next-of-kin—Legislation subsequently granting inheritance rights to adopted children—Whether adopted children taking under ultimate trust—Effect of rights to respect for private and family life and prohibition of discrimination—Administration of Estates Act 1925, s 50(1)—Adoption of Children Act 1926, s 5—Human Rights Act 1998, Sch 1, Pt I, arts 8, 14. **Erskine 1948 Trust, Re** [2012] **3** 532, Ch D.
  Beneficial interests—
    Absolute beneficial interest—
      Division of trust fund—Accruer clause—Trustees directed to divide the trust fund or without actual division to treat the same as divided into two equal parts and to appropriate one of such parts as the share of each of settlor's two daughters—Daughter's share not to vest absolutely in her—Life interest to daughter with remainder to issue—Both daughters dying without issue—Destination of trust fund. **Burton's Settlement Trusts, Re** [1955] **1** 433, CA.
    Exclusion from participation—
      Exclusion on death of life tenant of 'an eldest son entitled for the time being under my will to my real estates for his life'—Exclusion of deceased eldest son who had been life tenant under will. **Gunter's Settlement Trusts, Re** [1949] **1** 680, Ch D.
    Gap in limitations—
      No provision for events that happened—Whether gap remediable by construction. **Cochrane's Settlement Trusts, Re** [1955] **1** 222, Ch D.
    Information—
      Duty of trustees to inform beneficiary of his interest—Duty to pay share of income to joint tenant of income and capital. **Hawksley v May** [1955] **3** 353, QBD.
    Life interest—
      Power to surrender determinable life interest in vested share of child or issue in favour of child or issue—Appointment by life tenant to grandchildren 'upon attaining' thirty or surviving twenty-one years from date of appointment—Proviso creating gifts over—Whether interests appointed were vested subject to being divested or were contingent interests—Rule in Phipps v Ackers—Surrender of life interest to trustees to intent that it be extinguished and funds held on trust as if life tenant were dead—Whether surrender was within the power to surrender or whether the life interest was forfeited. **Penton's Settlements, Re** [1968] **1** 36, Ch D.
    Limitation dependent on void limitation—
      Accord with previous valid limitations—'Issue'. **Mill's Declaration of Trust, Re** [1950] **2** 292, CA.
    Male issue and male descendants—
      Line of descent—Whether restricted to the male line of descent. **Du Cros' Settlement, Re** [1961] **3** 193, Ch D.
    Settlement of personalty—
      Implication of cross remainders. **Bickerton's Settlement, Re** [1942] **1** 217, Ch D; **Hey's Settlement Trusts and Will Trusts, Re, Hey v Nickel-Lean** [1945] **1** 618, Ch D.
    Strict settlement—
      Limitation of tenancy in tail—Remainder to first and other sons of younger daughters in tail male—Whether entitled successively as tenants in tail male. **Gosset's Settlement, Re** [1943] **2** 515, Ch D.
    Trusts for issue—
      Females attaining 21 or marrying under that age—Omitted words supplied. **Hargraves' Trusts, Re** [1937] **2** 545, Ch D.
    Ultimate trust for statutory next-of-kin—
      Distribution—Whether rules before 1926 or after 1925 applicable—Contrary intention—Administration of Estates Act 1925, s 50(2). **Hooper's Settlement Trusts, Re** [1943] **1** 173, CA.

SETTLEMENT (cont)—
  Beneficial interests (cont)—
    Without leaving issue—
      Life interest to daughter and then to the issue on attaining 21—Gift over if she should die married without leaving issue—Daughter died having had two sons who attained 21 but pre-deceased her—Whether interests of issue defeated. **Milling's Settlement, Re** [1944] **1** 541, Ch D.
  Capital gains tax—
    Beneficiary becoming absolutely entitled to settled property. *See* **Capital gains tax** (Settlement—Beneficiary becoming absolutely entitled to settled property).
    Generally. *See* **Capital gains tax** (Settlement).
    Person becoming absolutely entitled as against trustee—
      Disposal of assets. *See* **Capital gains tax** (Disposal of assets—Person becoming absolutely entitled as against trustee).
  Capital or income—
    Absolute interest in settled funds—
      Income from funds temporarily charged in favour of third party. **Holliday's Will Trusts, Re** [1947] **1** 695, Ch D.
    Apportionment—
      Dividends—Dividends of company paid out of capital assets. **Doughty, Re** [1947] **1** 207, CA.
      Dividends—Paid out of past profits—Year to which dividends attributable—Call on shares—Satisfied out of dividends. **Joel, Re** [1936] **2** 962, Ch D.
      Fixed investment trust—Sub-units held by trustees—Nature of sums distributed by investment trust. **Whitehead's Will Trusts, Re** [1959] **2** 497, Ch D.
      Investments sold after death of tenant for life—Dividends partly accrued due during lifetime of tenant for life—Payment of apportioned part out of purchase money to the estate of tenant for life. **Firth, Re** [1938] **2** 217, Ch D.
      Power to trustees to determine apportionment in 'cases of doubt'. **Fenwick, Re** [1936] **2** 1096, Ch D.
      Profit on sale of company's assets—Application of dividend with other funds in purchase of house—Right of tenant for life to equitable charge on house. **Maclaren's Settlement Trusts, Re** [1951] **2** 414, Ch D.
      Profit on sale of company's assets—Company to continue as investment and holding company. **Kleinwort's Settlement Trusts, Re** [1951] **2** 328, Ch D; **Sechiari, Re** [1950] **1** 417, Ch D.
      Profit on sale of company's assets—Notice by company of intention to declare dividend—Duty of trustees to sell cum dividend. **Rudd's Will Trusts, Re** [1952] **1** 254, Ch D.
      Profit on sale of part of company's interests—Sale during testator's lifetime—Dividend payable in respect of date during testator's lifetime, but not paid until after his death. **Winder's Will Trusts, Re** [1951] **2** 362, Ch D.
      Sale of land—Purchase price quantified under Town and Country Planning Act 1954 and including unexpended balance of established development value—Whether the additional one-seventh involved in computing that balance to be regarded as interest—Town and Country Planning Act 1954, s 17(2). **Hasluck (decd), Re** [1957] **3** 371, Ch D.
      Sale of larch trees—Right of tenant for life to purchase money—Sale in proper course of management. **Harker's Will Trust, Re** [1938] **1** 145, Ch D.
      Scheme of arrangement—Cancellation of all unpaid interest on allotment of new securities and payment of cash—Apportionment of securities and cash—Companies Act 1948, s 206. **Morris's Will Trusts, Re** [1960] **3** 548, Ch D.
      Securities sold after death of tenant for life—Dividends partly accrued due during lifetime of tenant for life—Payment of apportioned part out of purchase money to the estate of tenant for life. **Winterstoke's Will Trusts, Re** [1937] **4** 63, Ch D.
      Settled share of residue—Ordinary and preference shares appropriated thereto—Payment of past preference dividend by transfer of ordinary shares. **National Carbonising Co Ltd v British Coal Distillation Ltd** [1936] **2** 1012, CA.
      Tithe redemption annuities—Tithe Act 1925—Tithe Act 1936. **Leicester's Settled Estates, Re** [1938] **3** 553, Ch D.
    Business profits and losses—
      Business owned and carried on by testator—Business sold as a going concern after testator's death—Whether profit made before death and loss made after death in business was attributable to capital or income—Whether rule excluded by the terms of will. **Berry (decd), Re** [1961] **1** 529, Ch D.
    Capital distribution by company in respect of shares—
      Trust of dividends, interest and annual income from certain shares—Destination of sum distributed. **Ward, Re** [1936] **2** 773, Ch D.
    Casual profit—
      Compensation for damage to house during military occupation. **Pomfret's Settlement, Re** [1951] **2** 951, Ch D.
      Compensation in nature of gratuity—Compensation for malicious damage. **Macnamara, Re** [1936] **1** 602, Ch D.
      Damages—Injury to land by improvements by river conservators—Agreement apart from arbitration. **Lindsay's Settlement (No 1), Re** [1941] **1** 104, Ch D.
    Conversion of dwelling-house into shops and flats—
      Expenditure to enable buildings to be let. **Swanwick House, Prestbury, Re** [1939] **3** 531, Ch D.
    Discretionary trust—
      Accumulation of income as part of capital fund. *See* Power of appointment—Transfer of assets to trustees to hold on discretionary trusts—Trustees directed to accumulate income as part of capital fund, *below.*
    Family settlement—
      Permanent improvements charged to income or corpus—Trustees' power to recoup income out of corpus—Accumulations Act 1800. **Syed Omar Bin Shaikh Alkaff v Syed Abdulrahman Bin Shaikh Alkaff** [1941] **2** 346, PC.
    Jointure and interest on portions—
      Charged primarily on income—Charged also on capital—Deficiency of income—Paid voluntarily by tenant for life—Recoupment from capital. **Warwick's Settlement Trusts, Re** [1938] **1** 639, CA.

SETTLEMENT (cont)—
    Capital or income (cont)—
        Release of life interest—
            Income of settled funds under resulting trust during life of settlor's wife—Income becoming subject to settlor's will after release of life interest—Whether capital or income of settlor's residuary estate. **Guinness's Settlement, Re** [1966] 2 497, Ch D.
        Shares in limited company—
            Capitalisation of company's reserved capital profits by bonus issue of loan stock—Whether loan stock capital or income in hands of trustee shareholders for beneficiaries entitled in succession. **Outen's Will Trust, Re** [1962] 3 478, Ch D.
            Payments to shareholders out of share premium account—Companies Act 1948, s 56(1)(2)(3). **Duff's Settlements Trusts, Re** [1951] 2 534, CA.
    Capital transfer tax—
        Distribution of settled property—
            Excluded property. *See* **Capital transfer tax** (Exemptions and reliefs—Excluded property).
        Generally. *See* **Capital transfer tax** (Settlement).
    Children—
        Adopted children—
            Children adopted in Union of South Africa—Adopting parents domiciled in Southern Rhodesia where this adoption was said not to be recognised—Trust in default of appointment for children of adopting father—Settlement subject to law of England—Whether adopted children entitled to benefit under trust for children. **Valentine's Settlement, Re** [1965] 2 226, CA.
        Divorce of parents. *See* **Divorce** (Financial provision—Child—Settlement).
        Income tax. *See* **Income tax** (Settlement—Children).
    Class gift—
        Accumulation of surplus income—
            Destination. *See* **Accumulation** (Excessive period—Destination of income accruing after statutory period—Accumulation directed for the benefit of a class).
        Distribution date—
            Attainment of specified age—Payment of income to beneficiary over twenty-one—Trustee Act 1925, s 31(1)(ii). **Watt's Will Trusts, Re** [1936] 2 1555, Ch D.
            Compound gift—Trust for children of settlor's son who before expiration of 21 years from death of survivor of settlor or son attain age of 25 and other children of son living at expiration of that period—Whether class closing on eldest child attaining age of 25—Whether gift to compound class—Whether fact that class closing rule could not apply to one part of compound class precluding it from operating on other part—Whether fact that application of rule would reduce scope of one limb of gift to improbable but not impossible circumstances sufficient to exclude application of rule. **Clifford's Settlement Trusts, Re** [1980] 1 1013, Ch D.
            Defined closing date—Deed of appointment providing for fund to be held for beneficiaries reaching 18 before 'vesting day' and those living at vesting day—Deed further providing for fund income to be distributed on 'closing date'—Closing date defined as earlier of vesting day or 25 years from date of appointment—Whether class closing rule applying—Whether class closing when eldest beneficiary reaching 18. **Tom's Settlement, Re** [1987] 1 1081, Ch D.
            Fund held in trust for nephew and after death of nephew in trust for his children at 21—Nephew released his life interest—Nephew's eldest child attained 21—Class of children of nephew remaining open for afterborn children of nephew—No acceleration of interests. **Kebty-Fletcher's Will Trusts, Re** [1967] 3 1076, Ch D.
            Gift by way of remainder to 'issue' of life tenant—'Issue' including all generations—Date for ascertainment of class entitled to take—Gift to beneficiary for life 'and thereafter for the issue of the [beneficiary] as and when they attain the age of twenty one years' in equal shares if more than one—Class limited to those in being at the date of death of life tenant—Class excluding issue born after life tenant—Whether class including issue attaining age of 21 and predeceasing life tenant. **Deeley's Settlement, Re** [1973] 3 1127, Ch D.
            Gift of share of residue to 'my grandchildren (the children of my son [EJM]),'—Distribution postponed until the youngest is twenty-one years of age—Whether grandchildren born after testator's death included in class. **Manners (decd), Re** [1955] 3 83, Ch D.
            Gift to children of grandson living on the attainment of the age of twenty-one by the youngest of such children—Only one such child living at date of death of testatrix—Possibility of birth of further children—Rights of existing child. **Ransome's Will Trusts, Re** [1957] 1 690, Ch D.
            Gift to children on attaining specified age—Gift in futuro subject to life interest—No member of class existing at cesser of life interest—Closing of class on attainment of specified age by one member of class. **Bleckly (decd), Re** [1951] 1 1064, CA.
            Gift to wife for life with remainder to relations of testator and wife—Date for ascertaining relations—Shares—Gift to be 'shared to my relations also my wife's relations'—Whether testator's relations and wife's relations to be ascertained at testator's death or wife's death—Whether testator contemplated single class of his own and wife's relations amongst whom gift to be shared equally. **Shield's Will Trusts, Re** [1974] 2 274, Ch D.
            Income gift—Rule of convenience as to closing of class at date of distribution inapplicable. **Ward's Will Trusts, Re** [1964] 3 442, Ch D.
            Joint tenancy or tenancy in common—Gift of residue to 'relations' of testator and his wife subject to wife's life interest. **Gansloser's Will Trusts, Re** [1951] 2 936, CA.
            Settlement of land—Trust for sale—Power of trustees to postpone sale—Trust for children of settlor's two sons 'who shall attain the age of twenty one years' etc—Eldest grandchild attaining age of 21—Sons still living—Grandchild having no power to compel sale of land on attaining vested interest—Whether fact that at the time of the settlement the property settled was solely land excluding the operation of the rule in Andrews v Partington. **Edmondson's Will Trusts, Re** [1972] 1 444, CA.
            Substituted gift for children of member of class dying during life of tenant for life—Death of member without issue during life of tenant for life—Vesting. **Greenwood v Greenwood** [1939] 2 150, PC.
            Substituted gift for children of member of class dying during life of tenant for life—Vesting of gift on testator's death—Children of member living at date of will, but not children of member then dead, entitled to share as joint tenants. **Brooke's Will Trusts, Re** [1953] 1 668, Ch D.

SETTLEMENT (cont)—
Class gift (cont)—
Distribution date (cont)—
Trust for children of settlor's four named children who should attain the age of 21 or being female marry—Trust for accumulation during settlor's lifetime—Express powers of maintenance and advancement in regard to vested or contingent absolute or presumptive share of any grandchild—Death of settlor—Whether class closed on attainment of vested interest by eldest grandchild. **Henderson's Trusts, Re** [1969] **3** 769, CA.
Trust for girl aged four at testator's death, for life and after her death for her issue at 21 etc—Proviso that issue of deceased child of life tenant should take per stirpes—Four children born to life tenant and a number of grandchildren born in her lifetime—Issue in existence at life tenant's death intended to take beneficially but not those born afterwards—Rule in Andrews v Partington not applicable—Gift not void for remoteness nor for uncertainty. **Cockle's Will Trusts, Re** [1967] **1** 391, Ch D.
Trust for grandchildren of settlor who attain vesting age—Grandchildren 'now born or who shall be born hereafter'—Vesting age defined as age of 25 or in case of grandchild born less than four years before death of survivor of settlor's sons the age he would be if he lived for 21 years after that death—Settlor's sons still living on eldest grandchild attaining vesting age—Whether class closed on attainment of vesting age by eldest grandchild. **Chapman's Settlement Trusts, Re** [1978] **1** 1122, CA.
Trust for settlor's children then living or thereafter to be born who should attain the age of 21 or, being female, marry—Attainment of 21 years by settlor's three children—Settlor still living—Whether trust fund distributable. **Wernher's Settlement Trusts, Re** [1961] **1** 184, Ch D.
Exclusion—
Member of class precluded from taking by felonious killing of testator—Destination of share of excluded member. **Peacock (decd), Re** [1957] **2** 98, Ch D.
Condition—
Income of trust funds to be paid to TS after transfer by her of certain shares in settlor's name—Trust funds held on other trusts until execution of transfers and after TS's death—Failure to execute transfers during settlor's lifetime—Whether transfer to settlor's executors sufficient compliance with conditions. **Sage's Settlement Trusts, Re** [1946] **2** 298, Ch D.
Conflict of laws. *See* **Conflict of laws** (Settlement).
Consent judgment—
Indemnity. *See* **Indemnity** (Extent of liability under indemnity—Settlement of proceedings against principal).
Contingent interest—
Contingent interest distinguished from interest dependent on event bound to happen—
Interest subject to condition that beneficiary survive designated person—Designated person described by reference to newspaper announcement of his death—Whether interest dependent on designated person's death or on survival for specified period. **IRC v Trustees of Sir John Aird's Settlement** [1983] **3** 481, CA.
Contingent interest distinguished from vested interest liable to be divested—
Interest subject to condition precedent or subsequent—Gift over on failure of condition—Appointment—Appointed funds to be held on trust for beneficiary 'if she shall attain the age of 21-years and subject as aforesaid' for two other persons—Whether beneficiary having vested interest liable to be divested. **Mallinson Consolidated Trusts, Re** [1974] **2** 530, Ch D.
Ownership of income from trust fund—Trustees to hold trust fund until beneficiary attained age of 30—Direction to accumulate up to age of 22—Beneficiary between age of 22 and 25 not entitled to direct trustees to pay income—Gift over on failure or determination of the trust—Contrary intention—Whether beneficiary's interest vested or contingent. **Brotherton v IRC** [1978] **2** 267, CA.
Costs—
Conditional fee agreement—
Termination. *See* **Costs** (Order for costs—Conditional fee agreement—Termination).
CPR Pt 36 offer. *See* **Costs** (Offers to settle—CPR Pt 36 offer).
Covenant—
Enforceability—
Contract with covenantor's father and trustees to settle proceeds of sale of pictures—Enforceability by volunteers not parties thereto—Covenant not to sell pictures without giving written notice to trustees and 'in case any pictures shall be sold' the net proceeds to be held on trusts of settlement—Consideration given by covenantor's father—Children of covenantor to be beneficially entitled in default of appointment—Whether covenant was enforceable in favour of children. **Cook's Settlement Trusts, Re** [1964] **3** 898, Ch D.
CPR Pt 36 offer—
Costs. *See* **Costs** (Offers to settle—CPR Pt 36 offer).
Discretionary trust—
Capital transfer tax. *See* **Capital transfer tax**.
Estate duty. *See* **Estate duty** (Passing of property—Discretionary trust).
Generally. *See* **Trust and trustee** (Discretionary trust).
Income tax. *See* **Income tax** (Settlement—Discretionary trust).
Disposition—
Resulting trust—
Settlor making separate settlements in favour of each of his children as principal beneficiary—Trusts in favour of principal beneficiary not exhaustive—Gift to children other than principal beneficiary inconsistent with trusts in favour of principal beneficiary—Whether absolute gift in favour of principal beneficiary—Whether resulting trust for taxpayer—Income and Corporation Taxes Act 1970, s 457. **Watson v Holland (Inspector of Taxes)** [1985] **1** 290, Ch D.
Distribution—
Per stirpes or per capita—
Class gift—Substitutional gift—Gift over to children of settlor—In event of any child being dead leaving issue who attain 21 such issue to take deceased parent's share—Whether distribution to issue per stirpes or per capita. **Manly's Will Trusts, Re (No 2)** [1976] **1** 673, Ch D.

1154

SETTLEMENT (cont)—
Distribution (cont)—
Presumption of death—
Marriage settlement—Husband's disappearance in 1917—Last heard of in 1920—Liberty for settled property to be distributed as if husband were dead. **Newson-Smith's Settlement, Re** [1962] **3** 963, Ch D.
Divorce—
Variation of settlement—
Financial provision. *See* **Divorce** (Financial provision).
Entailed interest—
Entailed interest in personalty—
Disposal of income pending birth of person entitled—Accumulation—Subsequent gift to carry intermediate income—Law of Property Act 1925, s 130(1). **Crossley's Settlement Trusts, Re** [1955] **2** 801, Ch D.
Will—
Revocatory clause. *See* **Will** (Construction—Revocatory clause—Entailed interest).
Estate duty—
Exemption—
Marriage settlement. *See* **Estate duty** (Exemption—Marriage settlement).
Investments in England representing proceeds of sale of land in Eire—
Purpose of devolution. **Midleton (Earl) v Cottesloe** [1949] **1** 841, HL.
Property comprised in settlement. *See* **Estate duty** (Property passing on death—Property comprised in a settlement).
Estate tail—
Contingent interest in tail in remainder—
Disentailing assuranc—Devise to person who should become Duke of St. Albans in tail mal—Disentailing assurance executed by presumed heir to dukedo—Effect of disentailing assurance-Fines and Recoveries Act 1833, s 15. **St Albans' (Duke) Will Trusts, Re** [1962] **2** 402, Ch D.
Rule in Shelley's case. *See* Rule in Shelley's case—Future interests—Estate tail, *below.*
Tenant in tail in remainder wishing to bar entail—
Estate subsisting in same lands prior to estate tail—Owner of prior estate not protector of settlement—Whether Court of Chancery protector of settlement—Whether consent of court to disentail necessary—Fines and Recoveries Act 1833, ss 22, 33. **Darnley's Will Trusts, Re** [1970] **1** 319, Ch D.
Foreign adoption—
Succession. *See* **Adoption** (Foreign adoption—Settlement—Beneficial succession).
Foreign settlement—
Variation. *See* **Variation of trusts** (Jurisdiction—Trust containing foreign element).
Forfeiture—
Effect—
Interest to be determined 'as if dead'—Remainder over to eldest son of tenant for life—Eldest son born after forfeiture—Acceleration of subsequent life interest on forfeiture—Whether eldest son excluded from any interest in settled property by reason of parent's forfeiture. **Blathwayt v Lord Cawley** [1975] **3** 625, HL.
Express advancement clause—
Consent to advancement. **Shaw's Settlement Trusts, Re** [1951] **1** 656, Ch D.
Forfeiture only for acts done without consent—
Forfeiture by reason of legislation—No consent given or possible—Trading with the Enemy Act 1939—Trading with the Enemy (Specified Areas) Order 1940 (SR & O 1940 No 1219). **Furness, Re** [1944] **1** 575, CA.
Income becoming payable to another—
Beneficiary becoming enemy—Payment of further sums to Custodian of Enemy Property—Trading with the Enemy Act 1939, s 7(1)(a),(b)—Trading with the Enemy (Custodian) Order 1939 (SR & O 1939 No 1198), art 1(i),(ii)(e). **Fraenkel v Whitty** [1947] **2** 646, Ch D.
Variation of settlement—Principal beneficiary given contingent interest in part of income—Whether 'any part of the income becomes vested in any other person'. **Dennis's Settlement Trusts, Re** [1942] **1** 520, Ch D.
Writ of sequestration—Income payable to sequestrators. **Baring's Settlement Trusts, Re** [1940] **3** 20, Ch D.
Interest determinable on bankruptcy—
Breach of trust—Unauthorised advances by trustee to tenant for life—Income taken to replace capital. **Balfour's Settlement, Re** [1938] **3** 259, Ch D.
Protected life interest—
Receiver appointed under Lunacy Act—Fees payable to percentage account—Charge on income of life tenant—Discretionary trusts brought into operation—Lunacy Act 1890, s 148(1),(3)—Lunacy Act 1891, s 27(3)—Supreme Court Funds Rules 1927, r 67(3)—Management of Patients Estates Rules 1934 (SR & O 1934 No 269), rr 148, 152, 154, 156. **Custance's Settlements, Re** [1945] **2** 441, Ch D.
Rentcharge to secure instalments in respect of improvements—Some improvements not within Settled Land Act 1925, Sch III, Part II—Settled Land Act 1925, s 85. **Liberty's Will Trusts, Re** [1937] **1** 399, Ch D.
Receiver in lunacy of life tenant's property appointed—
Percentage charged on estate of lunatic—Lunacy Act 1890, s 148(3). **Westby's Settlement, Re** [1950] **1** 479, CA.
Validity of forfeiture clause—
Certainty—Provision for reference of questions of doubt for determination by specified authority—Effect—Forfeiture in event of departure 'from the Jewish faith', marriage to a person who is not an 'approved wife' or separation from an 'approved wife'—Approved wife defined as wife who is 'of Jewish blood' by both parents and who practices 'the Jewish faith'—In case of dispute or doubt question to be determined by a chief rabbi—Whether provision for reference to chief rabbi rendering forfeiture clause sufficiently certain. **Tuck's Settlement Trusts, Re** [1976] **1** 545, Ch D.

SETTLEMENT (cont)—
  Forfeiture (cont)—
    Validity of forfeiture clause (cont)—
      Public policy—Person entitled being or becoming a Roman Catholic—Whether clause void on
        grounds of impermissible discrimination or as being likely to influence manner in which child is
        brought up. **Blathwayt v Lord Cawley** [1975] **3** 625, HL.
  Hotchpot—
    Life interest—
      Basis of valuation—Actual or actuarial value—Interest on actuarial value. **Finnegan v Cementation
        Co Ltd** [1953] **1** 1130, CA.
  Human rights—
    Right to respect for private and family life—
      Adoption. *See* Beneficial interest—Ultimate trust for statutory next-of-kin, *above.*
  Husband and wife—
    Injunction. *See* **Injunction** (Husband and wife—Settlement of property).
  Income tax—
    Annual payment. *See* **Income tax** (Annual payment—Settlement).
    Generally. *See* **Income tax** (Settlement).
  Infant's estate—
    Appointment of guardian—
      Application. *See* **Practice** (Chancery Division—Infant's estate—Application for appointment of
        guardian).
  Investment—
    Power of investment—
      'Ordinary preferred stock or shares'. **Powell-Cotton's Re-Settlement, Re** [1957] **1** 404, Ch D.
      Shares of companies in any British 'colony or dependency'—Companies in Canada—Statute of
        Westminster 1931, s 7. **Brassey's Settlement, Re** [1955] **1** 577, Ch D.
      Such investments 'as to [the trustee] may seem fit'—Whether power limited to trustee securities.
        Harari's Settlement Trusts, Re [1949] **1** 430, Ch D.
  Irrevocable settlement—
    Children—
      Income tax. *See* **Income tax** (Settlement—Children—Irrevocable settlement).
  Issue—
    Substitutional gift—
      Meaning of 'issue'—Gift over to children of settlor—In event of any child being then dead leaving
        issue who attain 21, such issue to take deceased parent's share—Whether 'issue' meaning
        children of deceased child or issue of all degrees. **Manly's Will Trusts, Re (No 2)** [1976] **1** 673,
        Ch D.
  Jointure rentcharge—
    Annual sums in arrears—
      Income subsequently available for payment of arrears—Deduction of income-tax—Rate of tax to be
        deducted—'Standard rate for the year in which the amount payable becomes due'—Payment of
        jointures 'without any deduction'—Exoneration from succession and estate duties—Income Tax
        Act 1918, All Schedules Rules, r 19—Finance Act 1927, s 39(1). **Sebright, Re** [1944] **2** 547, Ch D.
  Land—
    Settled land. *See* **Settled land.**
  Legacy duty—
    Incidence. *See* **Legacy duty** (Incidence).
  Life interest—
    Protected life interest—
      Determinable on re-marriage—Nullity decree in respect of re-marriage. *See* **Will** (Gift—Gift during
        widowhood—Decree of nullity in respect of second marriage).
      Forfeiture—Election against will—Liability to compensate disappointed beneficiaries. *See* **Equity**
        (Election—Election against will—Effect—Protected life interest).
  Life tenant—
    Income tax. *See* **Income tax** (Persons chargeable—Life tenant).
  Maintenance—
    Statutory power—
      Exclusion of power by contrary direction. *See* **Trust and trustee** (Maintenance—Statutory
        power—Exclusion of power by contrary direction).
  Mansion house—
    Damaged by fire—
      Insurance moneys received by trustees as capital moneys under Settled Land Act 1925—Mansion
        house on lease—No express obligation in lease to apply moneys to reinstating property—Notice
        of claim by tenant for moneys to be applied in reinstating property not given for some
        months—Application of part of insurance moneys meanwhile—Extent of Settled Land Act
        trustees' obligation to apply insurance moneys in reinstatement. **Mumford Hotels Ltd v Wheler**
        [1963] **3** 250, Ch D.
    Maintenance and repair—
      Application by tenant for life to raise sum to enable him to maintain mansion house as family
        residence—Jurisdiction of the court to sanction—Settled Land Act 1925, s 64—Settled Land and
        Trustee Acts (Court's General Powers) Act 1943, s 1. **Scarisbrick Settled Estates, Re** [1944] **1** 404,
        Ch D.
      Income of settled estates insufficient—Sums allowed by order of court out of testator's estate to
        meet expenses—Whether charged against income of other property given by testator's will on
        trusts corresponding to those of settled estates—Whether ordered to be paid out of such income
        in priority to annuities ranking first by the will. **Berkeley (decd), Re** [1968] **3** 364, CA.
    Property regarded as—
      Original principal mansion house let—Smaller house used as residence by tenant for life.
        Feversham Settled Estate, Re [1938] **2** 210, Ch D.

1156

SETTLEMENT (cont)—
  Marriage settlement—
    Accumulation of income—
      Property settled comprising inter alia shares in a particular company—Direction for accumulation of dividends on shares after settlor's death—Issue of bonus shares—Conversion of total shares into stock—Bonus shares accretion to original shares—Direction to accumulate applicable to bonus shares forming part of whole stock. **Wright's Settlement Trusts, Re** [1945] **1** 587, Ch D.
    Additional gift—
      Gift of £20,000 by will to be held on trusts of daughter's marriage settlement—Covenant by testator in settlement to bring £10,000 into the settlement—£20,000 declared to be 'in addition' to the £10,000—Settlement trust fund vested in daughter's son—Death of son before death of testator—Destination of £20,000 on daughter's death. **Hickman's Will Trusts, Re** [1950] **2** 285, Ch D.
    Covenant to pay if marriage 'solemnised'—
      Ultimate trust for husband's next-of-kin—Marriage subsequently annulled—Total failure of consideration—Rights of beneficiaries defeated—Trust fund to be repaid to settlor's estate. **Ames' Settlement, Re** [1946] **1** 689, Ch D.
    Estate duty—
      Exemption. See **Estate duty** (Exemption—Marriage settlement).
    Gift to issue—
      'For my said daughter's benefit and that of any children she may have'—Settlement including trust for children of first marriage—Children of second marriage excluded—Whether settlement in conformity with direction in will. **Potter's Will Trusts, Re** [1943] **2** 805, CA.
      Substitutional or original gift—Life interests to husband, then to wife—Husband and wife dying without issue—Gift to uncles and aunts of husband and the issue of any who may have predeceased the husband—Gift over to issue of uncles and aunts substitutional—Gift to issue through all degrees—Gift contingent—Issue entitled to take—Time for substitution death of husband—Issue taking who survive parent and living at death of husband. **Earle's Settlement Trusts, Re** [1971] **2** 1188, Ch D.
    Lost settlement—
      Implication of provisions. **Knapp's Settlement, Re** [1952] **1** 458, Ch D.
    Proper law of settlement. See **Conflict of laws** (Settlement—Proper law of settlement—Marriage settlement).
    Protected life interest of husband—
      Divorce—Variation of settlement by order of Divorce Court—Whether forfeiture—Trustee Act 1925, s 33—Supreme Court of Judicature (Consolidation) Act 1925, s 192. **General Accident, Fire and Life Assurance Corp Ltd v IRC** [1963] **3** 259, CA.
  Meaning for tax purposes. See **Income tax** (Settlement—Meaning).
  Mental patient. See **Mental health** (Patient's property—Settlement).
  Mining leases—
    Capitalisation of rent—
      Resettlement subject to overriding interests not compound settlement for this purpose—Extension of term—Whether surrender and regrant—Right of tenant for life to retain whole rent—Settled Estates Act 1877, s 4—Settled Land Act 1882, ss 7(1), 11—Settled Land Act 1925, ss 52, 59(1). **Arkwright's Settlement, Re** [1945] **1** 404, Ch D.
      Tenant for life not unimpeachable for waste—Leases granted by predecessor—Proportion of rents tenant for life entitled to retain—Settled Land Act 1925, s 47. **Fitzwalter, Re** [1943] **2** 328, CA.
  Offer to settle. See **Practice** (Offer to settle).
  Personalty—
    Personalty settled to devolve with realty—
      Beneficial interest in personalty—Personalty to be used and enjoyed by person 'actually entitled to possession or receipt of rents and profits' of settled land—Actually entitled to possession— Beneficiary entitled to interest in settled land subject to prior life interest—Beneficiary predeceasing life tenant—Whether beneficiary 'actually entitled to possession' of settled land—Whether beneficiary's interest in personalty dependent on surviving life tenant. **Morrison's Settlement, Re** [1973] **3** 1094, Ch D.
  Portions—
    Children entitled—
      Trust for children other than first or only son entitled for first estate in tail male—Disentail and resettlement by son entitled in remainder to estate tail—Death before life tenant—Whether entitled to portion. **Leeke's Settlement Trusts, Re** [1937] **2** 563, Ch D.
  Post-nuptial settlement—
    Life assurance policy effected for benefit of 'widow or children'—
      Jurisdiction to vary settlement—Matrimonial Causes Act 1950, s 125. **Lort-Williams v Lort-Williams** [1951] **2** 241, CA.
    Variation—
      Generally. See **Variation of Settlement (Matrimonial Causes)** (Post-nuptial settlement).
  Power—
    Appointment as respects expectant interests—
      Meaning of 'expectant interests'. **Dowie's Will Trusts, Re** [1949] **1** 968, Ch D.
    Discretionary power—
      Discretion over income of trust fund—Particular beneficiaries could in fact be ascertained with certainty—Power not void for uncertainty. **Whishaw v Stephens** [1968] **3** 785, HL.
      Discretion to make grants to 'dependants' and 'dependent relatives' of employees—Power coupled with a duty and power collateral—Impossibility of ascertaining all members of class of beneficiaries—Uncertainty. **Sayer Trust, Re** [1956] **3** 600, Ch D.
    Intermediate power—
      Power conferred on trustees to nominate and add to a class of beneficiaries—Power exercisable in favour of anyone with certain exceptions—Whether valid. **Manisty's Settlement, Re** [1973] **2** 1203, Ch D.

SETTLEMENT (cont)—
Power (cont)—
Intermediate power (cont)—
Validity—Settlement giving trustees power to appoint to 'such persons' as they thought fit—Trustees executing deed of appointment empowering them to appoint to 'such persons' as they thought fit—Whether deed of appointment valid. **Hay's Settlement Trusts, Re** [1981] **3** 786, Ch D.
Power of appointment. *See* Power of appointment, *below.*
Power of sale—
Trustees having power of sale with consent of annuitant—Trustees also statutory owners—Inconsistency of two powers of sale—Statutory powers only exercisable—Settled Land Act 1925, s 108(1). **Jefferys, Re** [1938] **4** 120, Ch D.
Revocation—
Power to revoke settlement—Release of power—Implied release. *See* **Power** (Implied release—Settlement—Power to revoke settlement).
Power of appointment—
Transfer of assets to trustees to hold on discretionary trusts—
Trustees directed to accumulate income as part of capital fund—Trustees required to pay capital as directed among a class of beneficiaries—Person giving directions entitled to act as he thought proper—Whether payments made to appointees distributions of capital or income—Whether potential appointees had a right to be paid and power to enjoy income of trust fund—Income Tax Act 1952, s 412(1). **Vestey v IRC (No 2)** [1979] **2** 225, Ch D.
Powers of tenant for life—
Bankrupt tenant for life—
Order giving powers to trustee of settlement—Jurisdiction of court—Settled Land Act 1925, s 24(1). **Thornhill's Settlement, Re** [1940] **4** 249, CA.
By whom exercisable—
Compound settlement—Person named in last deed of compound settlement as tenant for life of that settlement—Settled Land Act 1925, s 23(1)(a). **Beaumont Settled Estates, Re** [1937] **2** 353, Ch D.
Discretion given to trustees to pay income to all or any of a class of persons—Settled Land Act 1925, s 20(1)(viii). **Gallenga Will Trusts, Re** [1938] **1** 106, Ch D.
Limitations to A with life remainder to his sons in tail with remainder to B for life—Assignment by A of life interest to trustee for benefit of 'the persons beneficially interested in the premises' under the settlement—A aged 80 and unlikely to have son—Whether B 'the person next entitled in remainder'—Settled Land Act 1925, s 105(1). **Maryon-Wilson's Settlements, Re** [1969] **3** 558, Ch D.
Joint tenants—
Power of sale—Disagreement as to exercise of power—No evidence of mala fides in refusing to concur in sale—Whether court could order sale—Whether court should do so—Settled Land Act 1925, s 93. **Barker v Addiscott** [1969] **3** 685, Ch D.
Leasing—
Reservation of 'best rent'—Onus of proof—Lease for less than three years—Need for condition of re-entry—Settled Land Act 1925, ss 42(1)(ii), 42(5)(ii), 110(1). **Davies v Hall** [1954] **2** 330, CA.
Settled and unsettled property comprised in one lease—Contract to grant lease in consideration of redevelopment—Whether 'agreement for a lease'—Lease to take effect after twelve years—Property leased in lots—Agregate rent exceeding one-fifth of aggregate annual values—Settled Land Act 1925, ss 42(1)(i), 44(3)(iii), 90(1)(iii), 117(1)(x). **Rycroft's Settlements, Re** [1961] **3** 581, Ch D.
Limitation tending to discourage exercise of powers—
Application of income under personalty settlement for benefit of settled land—Limitation over on land ceasing to be settled—Sale of settled land—Settled Land Act 1925, s 106(1)(b). **Aberconway's Settlement Trusts, Re** [1953] **2** 350, CA.
Bequest of fund upon trust to apply part of income, at trustee's discretion, for outgoings of real estate settled under same will—Income not so required to be paid to tenant for life of the settled land—Gift over of whole fund on sale of settled land—Settled land sold under statutory powers—Gift over of fund void—Tenant for life to continue to receive income—Settled Land Act 1925, s 106. **Herbert, Re** [1946] **1** 421, Ch D.
Sale of settled land to tenant for life—
Unauthorised sale by Settled Land Act trustees—Whether transaction voidable—Whether Settled Land Act powers applicable—Settled Land Act 1925, s 68(2). **Pennant's Will Trusts, Re** [1969] **2** 862, Ch D.
Proceeds of sale of settled land—
Option to son to purchase after death of tenant for life—
Sale by tenant for life—Whether son entitled to proceeds of sale on tenant for life's death. **Armstrong's Will Trusts, Re** [1943] **2** 537, Ch D.
Realty or personalty—
Whether proceeds realty or personalty—Settled Land Act 1925, s 75(5). **Cartwright, Re** [1938] **4** 209, CA.
Proper law. *See* **Conflict of laws** (Settlement—Proper law of settlement).
Protected life interest—
Power of trustees to waive statutory protective trust—
Implied limitations on exercise of power—Intention of settlor—Election by beneficiary against will under equitable doctrine of election—Availability of trust fund subject to protected life interest to compensate disappointed beneficiaries—Election effecting forfeiture of protected life interest and thereby rendering fund unavailable—Power of trustees to determine protected life interest in order to make trust fund available to compensate disappointed beneficiaries—Whether trustees under a duty to exercise power for that purpose. **Gordon's Will Trusts, Re** [1976] **2** 577, Ch D.
Public Trustee—
Generally. *See* **Public Trustee**.

SETTLEMENT (cont)—
Purchaser dealing in good faith with tenant for life—
    Protection of purchaser—
        Agreement for lease with option to renew—Lessee unaware that tenant for life not absolute owner—Notice served exercising option—Order for specific performance sought—Whether executory contract for a lease a 'lease or other disposition'—Whether lessee 'purchaser dealing in good faith with a tenant for life'—Whether option rent best rent—Settled Land Act 1925, s 110(1). **Morgan's Lease, Re** [1971] **2** 235, Ch D.
Rectification—
    Voluntary settlement. See **Deed** (Rectification—Voluntary settlement).
Resulting trust—
    Absolute gift or resulting trust. See Disposition—Resulting trust, *above*.
    Generally. See **Trust and trustee** (Resulting trust).
Right to take interest under settlement—
    Legitimated person. See **Legitimation** (Right of legitimated persons to take interests in property—Disposition coming into operation after date of legitimation—Settlement).
Rule against perpetuities. See **Rule against perpetuities**.
Rule in Howe v Earl of Dartmouth—
    Exclusion—
        Residuary bequest including leasehold property held for more than sixty years unexpired at testator's death—Successive life interests and gift over of 'my property'—Whether leasehold property settled land or held on trust for sale—Settled Land Act 1925, s 73(1)(xi). **Gough (decd), Re** [1957] **2** 193, Ch D.
Rule in Shelley's case—
    Future interests—
        Estate tail. **Routledge, Re** [1942] **2** 418, Ch D.
    Strict settlement in common form—
        Limitation to W for life, with remainder to his sons in tail male and remainders over. **Williams' Will Trusts, Re** [1952] **2** 502, Ch D.
Settled land. See **Settled land**.
Tenant for life—
    Powers. See Powers of tenant for life, *above*.
    Sale of heirloom by. See **Limitation of action** (Concealment of right of action by fraud—Conversion—Action based on fraud—Right of action concealed by fraud—Sale of heirloom by tenant for life to defendants).
Trust—
    Discretionary trust—
        Uncertainty—Perpetuity. See **Trust and trustee** (Discretionary trust—Uncertainty—Power of selection).
    Trust to pay legacies mentioned in will—
        Death of legatees before death of settlor—Rights of legatees. **Hall's Settlement Trusts, Re** [1937] **1** 571, Ch D.
    Uncertainty—
        Condition precedent—Conditions qualifying beneficiary to receive income—Provision for reference of questions of doubt for determination by specified authority—Marriage to an 'approved wife'—Approved wife defined as wife who is 'of Jewish blood' by both parents and who practices 'the Jewish faith'—Income payable to beneficiary so long as he is married to an approved wife—In case of dispute or doubt question whether wife an 'approved wife' to be determined by a chief rabbi—Whether provision for reference to chief rabbi an ouster of the court's jurisdiction—Whether provision rendering qualification sufficiently certain. **Tuck's Settlement Trusts, Re** [1976] **1** 545, Ch D.
Trustees—
    De facto trustees. See **Capital gains tax** (Settlement—Trustees of the settlement—Whether de facto trustees 'trustees of the settlement').
    Notice—
        Settled Land Act trustee's notice of terms of lease by knowledge of tenant for life—Tenant for life the only other trustee. **Mumford Hotels Ltd v Wheler** [1963] **3** 250, Ch D.
    Power to appoint new trustees—
        Extension of statutory powers—Will provided 'person entitled to possession or receipts of rents and profits' should have power to appoint new trustees—Whether power 'any power relating to the settled land'—A tenant for life, but B in possession of rents and profits—Whether power exercisable by A or B—Settled Land Act 1925, s 108(2). **Maryon-Wilson's Settlements, Re** [1969] **3** 558, Ch D.
        New trustees resident abroad—Validity of appointment—No absolute bar against appointment of trustees resident abroad—Power to appoint in exceptional circumstances—Beneficiaries under settlement resident abroad—Trustee Act 1925, s 36(1). **Whitehead's Will Trusts, Re** [1971] **2** 1334, Ch D.
    Removal of trustees—
        Jurisdiction. See **Trust and trustee** (Removal of trustee—Jurisdiction—Settlement).
    Remuneration. See **Trust and trustee** (Remuneration of trustee).
Uncertainty—
    Conceptual uncertainty—
        Conditions qualifying beneficiary to receive income—Marriage to an 'approved wife'—Approved wife defined as wife who is 'of Jewish blood' by one or both parents and brought up in and practising 'Jewish faith'—Income payable to beneficiary so long as married to an approved wife—Provision that doubt whether a person qualifying as an approved wife to be decided by a third person—Provision that doubt to be decided by a chief rabbi—Whether provisions as to 'Jewish blood' and 'Jewish faith' sufficiently certain—Whether provision that doubt to be decided by a chief rabbi cured uncertainty—Whether provision for determination by chief rabbi ouster of court's jurisdiction. **Tuck's Settlement Trusts, Re** [1978] **1** 1047, CA.

SETTLEMENT (cont)—
Uncertainty (cont)—
Determination of matters of doubt or difficulty as to meaning of settlement—
Provision for reference of questions of doubt to specified third party for determination—Validity—
Ouster of court's jurisdiction—Power of third party or trustees to apply to court for directions to
assist third party—Whether provision for reference to third party an ouster of court's jurisdiction.
Tuck's Settlement Trusts, Re [1978] **1** 1047, CA.
Variation of settlement. *See* **Variation of Settlement (Matrimonial Causes).**
Variation of trusts—
Compromise of dispute—
Infants' interests—Ambiguity in investment clause—Proposed substitution of new investment
clause—Jurisdiction. **Powell-Cotton's Re-Settlement, Re** [1956] **1** 60, CA.
Infants possibly interested. **Hylton's (Lord) Settlement, Re** [1954] **2** 647, CA.
Court order for benefit of settled land—
Land held by trustees of settlement on trust for sale—Settled Land Act 1925, s 64—Law of Property
Act 1925, s 28(1). **Simmons' Trust, Re** [1955] **3** 818, Ch D.
No administrative problem—Settled Land Act 1925, s 64(1)—Trustee Act 1925, s 57(1). **Chapman v
Chapman** [1954] **1** 798, HL.
Sale or mortgage—To raise money for payment of debts of tenant for life—Repayment secured by
life policy—Jurisdiction of court to sanction—Settled Land Act 1925, s 64. **White-Popham Settled
Estates, Re** [1936] **2** 1486, CA.
Generally. *See* **Variation of trusts.**
Mentally disordered patient's beneficial interest varied. *See* **Mental health** (Patient's property—
Variation of trusts).
Variation for benefit of minor—
Sale of minor's reversionary interest—Whether court could sanction sale. **Heyworth's Settlements,
Re** [1956] **2** 21, Ch D.
Voluntary settlement—
Rectification of deed. *See* **Deed** (Rectification—Voluntary settlement).
Revocation—
Power to revoke with consent of a judge of the Chancery Division—Validity. **Hooker's Settlement,
Re** [1954] **3** 321, Ch D.
Validity—
Undue influence—Settlement by unmarried girl shortly after coming of age—No independent
advice—Laches—Costs of trustee. **Bullock v Lloyds Bank Ltd** [1954] **3** 726, Ch D.
Will—
Generally. *See* **Will.**
Referential trusts—
Incorporation of trusts of even date—Disposal of residue by reference to settlement of even date.
See **Will** (Referential trusts—Incorporation of trusts of even date—Disposal of residue by
reference to settlement of even date).
Words of limitation absent—
Succeeding clause with gift over and resulting trust to settlor—
Rectification—No evidence extraneous to settlement available—Power of court to rectify. **Banks v
Ripley** [1940] **3** 49, Ch D.

SEVERANCE
Administrative order—
Public authority—
Order made under statutory power—Part of order invalid—Severability of invalid part. *See* **Public
authority** (Statutory powers—Order made under statutory power—Administrative order).
Contract—
Illegal term. *See* **Contract** (Illegality—Severability of illegal term).
Indictment—
Severance of counts. *See* **Indictment** (Count—Severance of counts).
Joint tenancy—
Generally. *See* **Joint tenancy** (Severance).
Notice of severance. *See* **Joint tenancy** (Notice of severance).
Licence—
Condition attached to licence—
Licence granted under statutory power. *See* **Public authority** (Statutory powers—Licence granted
under statutory power—Condition—Severability).
Statutory instrument—
Severance of invalid part. *See* **Statutory instrument** (Validity—Part of instrument invalid—Severance of
invalid part).

SEVERE DISABLEMENT ALLOWANCE
Equality of treatment of men and women—
European Community. *See* **European Union** (Equality of treatment of men and women—Social
security—Severe disablement allowance).

SEWAGE
Discharge—
Causing sewage effluent to be discharged into river—
Pollution of river. *See* **Water and watercourses** (Pollution of river—Causing sewage effluent to be
discharged into controlled waters).
Pollution of river. *See* **Water and watercourses** (Pollution of river—Discharge of untreated sewage
matter).
Pollution—
Offences. *See* **Environment** (Protection—Pollution—Waste management).

SEWER
Discharge of effluent into—
  Regulation by contract—
    Duration of contract—Whether terminable on notice. *See* **Contract** (Time—Duration of contract—Whether determinable by reasonable notice—Contract regulating the discharge of trade effluent into the public sewer).
Nuisance—
  Creation of nuisance. *See* **Nuisance** (Creation of nuisance—Sewer).
  Generally. *See* **Nuisance** (Sewer).
  Obstruction by sewer pipe in river bed. *See* **Nuisance** (Failure to remedy—Creation of nuisance by lapse of time—Pipe in river bed—Sewer—Obstruction to flow of river caused by pipe of sewer constructed by local authority beneath river bed not becoming exposed as river bed washed away).
  Overflow—
    Flooding of neighbouring premises. *See* **Nuisance** (Creation of nuisance—Sewer—Overflow—Flooding of neighbouring premises).
    Generally. *See* **Nuisance** (Sewer—Overflow).
Public sewer—
  Agreement to vest sewer in local authority. *See* **Public health** (Sewerage—Public sewer—Agreement to vest sewer in local authority).
Trespass—
  Discharge of effluent through sewer. *See* **Trespass to land** (Sewer).
Water and watercourses—
  Generally. *See* **Water and watercourses** (Flow of water—Natural watercourse—Sewer).

SEWERAGE
Charges—
  Liability of person not in receipt of sewerage services. *See* **Water supply** (Charges—Power of water authority to make charges—Charges for services performed—Liability of person who has not received services).
Public health. *See* **Public health** (Sewerage).

SEX DISCRIMINATION
Discrimination—
  Discrimination on ground of sexual orientation—
    Civil partnership. *See* **Marriage** (Civil partnership—Opposite-sex couple).
    Harassment on grounds of sexual orientation—Unwanted conduct with purpose or effect of violating person's dignity or creating intimidating, hostile, degrading, humiliating or offensive environment—Whether homophobic banter directed by other employees toward employee who is not homosexual, not perceived or assumed to be homosexual by other employees, and who accepts that other employees do not believe him to be homosexual harassment on grounds of sexual orientation—Employment Equality (Sexual Orientation) Regulations 2003, SI 2003/1661, reg 5—Council Directive (EC) 2000/78. **English v Thomas Sanderson Blinds Ltd** [2009] **2** 468, CA.
    Provision of goods, facilities or services—Adoption agencies—Charity providing adoption agency services to heterosexual couples—Regulations making it unlawful to discriminate on grounds of sexual orientation in the provision of goods, facilities or services to the public or a section of the public—Charity seeking to amend its objects clause to take advantage of exception to regulations—Whether amendment permissible—Human Rights Act 1998, Sch 1, Pt I, art 14—Equality Act (Sexual Orientation) Regulations 2007, SI 2007/1263, reg 18. **Catholic Care (Diocese of Leeds) v Charity Commission for England and Wales** [2010] **4** 1041, Ch D.
    Whether sex discrimination—Sex Discrimination Act 1975, ss 1(1)(a), 5(3). **MacDonald v Advocate General for Scotland** [2004] **1** 339, HL.
  Discrimination on grounds of sexual orientation—
    Freedom of thought, conscience and religion—Goods, facilities and services—Policy of hoteliers restricting provision of double-bedded rooms in hotel to married couples for religious reasons—Homosexual couple refused double-bedded room—Whether discrimination on grounds of sexual orientation—Whether finding of discrimination compatible with hoteliers' rights to freedom of thought, conscience and religion—Human Rights Act 1998, Sch 1, Pt I, art 9—Equality Act (Sexual Orientation) Regulations 2007, SI 2007/1263, regs 3, 4. **Bull v Hall** [2012] **2** 1017, CA; [2014] **1** 919, SC.
    General exceptions—Charities—Exception where person acting in pursuance of charitable instrument—Proportionate means of achieving legitimate aim—Charity providing adoption services wishing to restrict services to heterosexual potential adoptive parents—Whether proportionate means of achieving legitimate aim—Equality Act 2010, s 193. **Catholic Care (Diocese of Leeds) v Charity Commission for England and Wales** [2013] **2** 1114, UT.
    Goods, facilities and services—Accommodation in hotel, boarding house or similar establishment—Policy of owner of bed and breakfast accommodation restricting provision of double-bedded rooms to heterosexual married couples for religious reasons—Homosexual couple refused double-bedded room—Whether discrimination on grounds of sexual orientation—Whether bed and breakfast accommodation a boarding house or similar establishment—Whether bed and breakfast accommodation arrangement under which persons treated as members of family—Equality Act (Sexual Orientation) Regulations 2007, SI 2007/1263, regs 3, 4(2), 6(1). **Black v Wilkinson** [2013] **4** 1053, CA.
    Pension. *See* **Pension** (Equal treatment in employment and occupation—Sexual orientation).
  Requirement or condition such that proportion of people of one sex who can comply with it considerably smaller than proportion of people of other sex—
    Can comply—Theoretical or practical possibility—Age limits for employment—Upper age limit of 28 as requirement of candidate for employment—Large proportion of women in twenties engaged in bringing up children—Not in practice possible for many women in twenties to take on full-time work—Theoretically possible for any woman under 28 to apply for employment—Whether proportion of women who 'can comply' with age limit considerably smaller than proportion of men—Whether age limit constituting discrimination against women—Sex Discrimination Act 1975, s 1(1)(b)(i). **Price v Civil Service Commission** [1978] **1** 1228, EAT.

SEX DISCRIMINATION (cont)—
Discrimination (cont)—
Requirement or condition such that proportion of people of one sex who can comply with it considerably smaller than proportion of people of other sex (cont)—
Justifiable requirement irrespective of sex—Employment—Onus on employer of showing that requirement justifiable—Need to show requirement necessary and not merely convenient—Need for requirement to be weighed against discriminatory effect—Sex Discrimination Act 1975, s 1(1)(b)(ii). **Steel v Union of Post Office Workers** [1978] **2** 504, EAT.
Requirement or condition of full-time service—Woman employee employed on full-time basis—Employee applying to change to work on part-time basis in order to look after baby—Employer refusing application because all employees within grade employed on full-time basis—Whether obligation of full-time service a 'requirement or condition'—Whether proportion of women capable of complying with requirement of full-time service smaller than proportion of men—Whether requirement of full-time service justifiable irrespective of sex of person to whom it applied—Sex Discrimination Act 1975, ss 1(1), 6(2). **Home Office v Holmes** [1984] **3** 549, EAT.
Victimisation—
Female employees bringing equal pay proceedings—Employer sending letters to all employees setting out consequences of successful proceedings—Whether employees bringing equal pay proceedings less favourably treated by reason of their bringing proceedings—Whether employer discriminating against employees bringing equal pay proceedings by subjecting them to detriment—Sex Discrimination Act 1975, ss 4(1), 6(2)(b). **Derbyshire v St Helens Metropolitan BC** [2007] **3** 81, HL.
Discrimination on grounds of sexual orientation—
Provision of goods, facilities or services. *See* **Discrimination** (Provision of goods, facilities or services—Discrimination on grounds of sexual orientation, religious belief or political opinion).
Education—
Local education authority. *See* **Education** (Local education authority—Sex discrimination).
Employment—
Complaint of discrimination—
Burden of proof—Sex Discrimination Act 1975, s 63A. **Wong v Igen Ltd (Equal Opportunities Commission and ors intervening)** [2005] **3** 812, CA.
Discovery of confidential documents—
Industrial tribunal. *See* **Employment tribunal** (Procedure—Disclosure of documents—Confidential documents—Complaint of discrimination in employment).
Discrimination against a man. *See* **Employment** (Discrimination against a man).
Discrimination against a woman—
Generally. *See* **Employment** (Discrimination against a woman).
Northern Ireland. *See* **Northern Ireland** (Employment—Discrimination against a woman).
Equality of treatment—
European Community. *See* **European Union** (Equality of treatment of men and women).
Generally. *See* **Employment** (Equality of treatment of men and women).
Generally. *See* **Employment** (Discrimination).
Jurisdiction of employment tribunal. *See* **Employment** (Sex discrimination—Jurisdiction of employment tribunal).
Northern Ireland—
Discrimination against a woman. *See* **Northern Ireland** (Employment—Discrimination against a woman).
Equal treatment—
Public sector equality duty—
Provision of separate services—Single-sex approved premises for prisoners released on licence—Fewer places required for women—Limited number and geographical distribution of approved premises for women making it less likely for women to be accommodated near their homes—Whether direct discrimination—Whether indirect discrimination—Whether discrimination justified—Equality Act 2010, ss 13, 19, Sch 3, para 26. **R (on the application of Coll) v Secretary of State for Justice** [2018] **1** 31, SC.
European Community. *See* **European Union** (Equality of treatment of men and women).
Immigration—
Removal of Commonwealth immigrant married to woman student—
Wife of male student entitled to remain while husband a student. *See* **Commonwealth immigrant** (Admission—Refusal of admission—Removal of immigrant—Sex discrimination—Removal of immigrant married to woman student having permission to stay in United Kingdom for limited period).
Special voucher scheme for Commonwealth citizens. *See* **Commonwealth immigrant** (Special voucher scheme—Sex discrimination).
Pension—
Equality of treatment—
Generally. *See* **Pension** (Equality of treatment of men and women).
Prisons—
Deductions from prisoners' earnings for work for private employer outside prison except in exceptional circumstances—
Money raised to be paid to victim support group—Whether excessive and disproportionate detrimental effect on female prisoners—Whether indirect discrimination—Human Rights Act 1998, Sch 1, Pt I, art 14. **R (on the application of S) v Secretary of State for Justice** [2013] **1** 66, QBD.
Provision of goods, facilities or services—
Entry to swimming pool—
Pensioners admitted free to pool—Plaintiff and his wife both aged 61—Wife admitted free because she had reached pensionable age for women of 60—Plaintiff required to pay because he had not reached pensionable age for men of 65—Whether plaintiff unlawfully discriminated against on grounds of sex—Sex Discrimination Act 1975, ss 1(1)(a), 29. **James v Eastleigh BC** [1990] **2** 607, HL.

SEX DISCRIMINATION (cont)—
Provision of goods, facilities or services (cont)—
  Serving drinks at wine bar—
    Men permitted to stand and drink in bar area—Women served only while seated away from bar area—Women complaining of less favourable treatment—Whether unlawful discrimination of women on ground of sex—Sex Discrimination Act 1975, ss 1(1)(a), 29(1). **Gill v El Vino Co Ltd** [1983] **1** 398, CA.
Sexual orientation, discrimination on ground of. *See* Discrimination—Discrimination on grounds of sexual orientation, *above*.
Social security—
  European Community. *See* **European Union** (Equality of treatment of men and women—Social security).
  Invalid care allowance. *See* **Social security** (Invalid care allowance—Sex discrimination).

SEX EDUCATION
Justification for publishing obscene publication—
  Article in interest of learning—
    Defence of public good. *See* **Criminal law** (Obscene publications—Defence of public good—Publication justified on ground that article in interests of science, literature, art or learning or other objects of general concern—Interests of learning—Sex education).

SEX ESTABLISHMENT
Control—
  Licensing—
    Licensing authority levying fee for management of licensing regime—Fee refundable if application for licence unsuccessful—Whether fee authorised under domestic and EU law—Local Government (Miscellaneous Provisions) Act 1982, Sch 3, para 19—Provision of Services Regulations 2009, SI 2009/2999, reg 18—European Parliament and Council Directive 2006/123/EC, art 13(2). **R (on the application of Hemming (t/a Simply Pleasure Ltd)) v Westminster City Council** [2015] **4** 471, SC.
    Offence—Knowingly using or causing or permitting use of premises as sex establishment except under and in accordance with terms of licence—Knowingly—What knowledge must be proved—Whether sufficient to prove knowledge of use of premises as sex establishment—Whether prosecution must prove that defendant knew premises were used other than under and in accordance with terms of a licence—Local Government (Miscellaneous Provisions) Act 1982, Sch 3, paras 6(1), 20(1)(a). **Westminster City Council v Croyalgrange Ltd** [1986] **2** 353, HL.
    Offence—Knowingly using or causing or permitting use of premises as sex establishment except under and in accordance with terms of licence—Sex encounter establishment—Premises at which performances, services or entertainments 'which are not unlawful' are carried on—Which are not unlawful—Whether defence to charge of knowingly using premises as sex establishment without licence to show that activities carried on are unlawful—Whether prosecution required to prove activities are not unlawful—Local Government (Miscellaneous Provisions) Act 1982, Sch 3, paras 3a, 20. **McMonagle v Westminster City Council** [1990] **1** 993, HL.
    Offence—Validity of licensing authority's decision to refuse licence—Whether validity of decision can be challenged in criminal proceedings for operating without licence—Local Government (Miscellaneous Provisions) Act 1982, Sch 3, paras 20(1), 28(1). **Plymouth City Council v Quietlynn Ltd** [1987] **2** 1040, QBD.
    Renewal of licence—No change in character of locality or use to which premises in vicinity are put—Whether licensing authority entitled to refuse application for renewal of licence if no change in character of locality or use to which premises in vicinity are put—Local Government (Miscellaneous Provisions) Act 1982, Sch 3, para 12(3)(d). **R v Birmingham City Council, ex p Sheptonhurst Ltd** [1990] **1** 1026, CA.
    Right to freedom of expression—Right to protection of property—Licensing authority refusing to grant sex establishment licence—Licensing authority taking into account representations received after expiry of relevant period—Whether authority's decision lawful—Whether decision in breach of rights to freedom of expression and protection of property—Human Rights Act 1998, Sch 1, Pt I, art 10, Pt II, art 1—Local Government (Miscellaneous Provisions) (Northern Ireland) Order 1985, SI 1985/1208. **Miss Behavin' Ltd v Belfast City Council** [2007] **3** 1007, HL.

SEX OFFENDER ORDER
See **Magistrates** (Order—Sex offender order).

SEX SHOP
Nuisance—
  Interlocutory injunction. *See* **Injunction** (Nuisance—Interlocutory injunction—Sex shop).

SEXUAL ABUSE
Child—
  Generally. *See* **Child** (Child abuse).
  Matrimonial proceedings—
    Allegation of sexual abuse in access proceedings—Hearsay evidence—Admissibility. *See* **Minor** (Custody—Access—Allegation of sexual abuse—Evidence—Hearsay).
    Allegation of sexual abuse in access proceedings—Standard of proof. *See* **Minor** (Custody—Access—Allegation of sexual abuse—Standard of proof).
  Ward of court—
    Protection. *See* **Ward of court** (Care and control—Protection of ward—Child sex abuse).
  Family proceedings—
    Care order. *See* **Family proceedings** (Orders in family proceedings—Care order—Conditions to be satisfied before making care order—Child likely to suffer significant harm if order not made).
  Vicarious liability—
    Unincorporated association. *See* **Vicarious liability** (Non-employment relationship—Unincorporated association—Vicarious liability for sexual abuse).

SEXUAL ASSAULT
    Criminal proceedings. *See* **Criminal law** (Sexual assault).

SEXUAL CONDUCT
    Confidential information relating to sexual conduct—
        Disclosure—
            Equitable relief. *See* **Equity** (Breach of confidence—Confidential information—Information relating to sexual conduct).

SEXUAL DEVIANCY
    Mental disorder by reason of sexual deviancy—
        Scope of mental health legislation. *See* **Mental health** (Mental disorder—Person not suffering from mental disorder by reason only of sexual deviancy).

SEXUAL INTERCOURSE
    Abduction of unmarried girl—
        Intention to have unlawful sexual intercourse. *See* **Criminal law** (Abduction—Unmarried girl under 18—Intention to have unlawful sexual intercourse).
    Boy under age of 14—
        Whether irrebuttable presumption of criminal law that boy under 14 incapable of having sexual intercourse applying in civil law. *See* **Affiliation** (Putative father—Boy under age of 14).
    Offences involving intercourse. *See* **Criminal law** (Sexual intercourse).

SEXUAL OFFENCES
    Abuse of process. *See* **Criminal law** (Trial—Stay of proceedings—Abuse of process).
    Attempt—
        Impossible offence. *See* **Criminal law** (Attempt—Impossible offence).
    Buggery. *See* **Criminal law** (Buggery).
    Character of accused—
        Evidence. *See* **Criminal evidence** (Character of accused—Sexual offence).
    Character of prosecutor—
        Evidence. *See* **Criminal evidence** (Character of prosecutor—Sexual offence).
    Children, against—
        Sentence. *See* **Sentence** (Sexual offences against children).
    Complaint—
        Criminal evidence. *See* **Criminal evidence** (Complaints in sexual cases).
        Sexual cases, in. *See* **Criminal evidence** (Complaints in sexual cases).
    Corroboration of evidence—
        Generally. *See* **Criminal evidence** (Corroboration—Sexual offence).
        Similar fact evidence. *See* **Criminal evidence** (Corroboration—Similar fact evidence—Sexual offences).
    Cross-examination of complainant about previous sexual experience with men. *See* **Criminal evidence** (Sexual offence—Cross-examination of complainant about previous sexual experience).
    Custodial sentence. *See* **Sentence** (Custodial sentence—Sexual offence).
    Detention and training order. *See* **Sentence** (Detention and training order—Sexual offences).
    Entrapment. *See* **Criminal law** (Trial—Stay of proceedings—Abuse of process—Entrapment).
    Evidence—
        Generally. *See* **Criminal evidence** (Sexual offence).
    Generally. *See* **Criminal law** (Sexual offences).
    Historic sexual crime—
        Sentence. *See* **Sentence** (Sexual offences—Principles of sentencing—Historic sexual crime).
    Incest. *See* **Criminal law** (Incest).
    Indecent assault. *See* **Criminal law** (Indecent assault).
    Indecent offences between males—
        Time limit for bringing prosecution. *See* **Criminal law** (Time—Time limit for bringing prosecution—Indecent offences between males).
    Intercourse, involving. *See* **Criminal law** (Sexual intercourse).
    Prostitution. *See* **Criminal law** (Prostitution).
    Rape. *See* **Criminal law** (Rape).
    Reporting restrictions—
        Jurisdiction of Crown Court. *See* **Crown Court** (Jurisdiction—Sexual offences—Anonymity of victims of certain offences—Contemporary reports of proceedings).
    Sentence—
        Sexual offences against children. *See* **Sentence** (Sexual offences against children).
        Sexual offences prevention order. *See* **Sentence** (Sexual offences prevention order).
    Sentence. *See* **Sentence** (Sexual offences).
    Sexual assault—
        Generally. *See* **Criminal law** (Sexual assault).
        Intoxication as a defence. *See* **Criminal law** (Intoxication as a defence—Capacity to form intent—Sexual assault).
    Soliciting for immoral purposes. *See* **Criminal law** (Soliciting for immoral purposes).
    Statement by victim. *See* **Criminal evidence** (Sexual offence—Statement by victim).

SEXUAL ORIENTATION
    Equal treatment in employment and occupation—
        Pension. *See* **Pension** (Equal treatment in employment and occupation—Sexual orientation).

SEXUAL RELATIONS
    Consent—
        Capacity. *See* **Mental health** (Persons who lack capacity—Mental capacity—Inability to make decisions—Capacity to consent to sexual relations).

SHAFT
  Coal mine—
    Safety precautions at entrance to shaft. *See* **Coal mining** (Statutory duty—Safety precautions at entrance to shafts).

SHARE CAPITAL
  Company—
    Generally. *See* **Company** (Capital—Share capital).

SHARE FISHERMEN
  Contract of service. *See* **Employment** (Contract of service—Share fishermen).

SHARE PREMIUM ACCOUNT
  See **Company** (Share premium account).

SHARE REGISTER
  See **Company** (Shares—Register).

SHAREHOLDER
  Generally. *See* **Company** (Shareholder).
  Minority shareholder. *See* **Company** (Minority shareholder).

SHARES
  Charging order. *See* **Execution** (Charging order—Stock or shares).
  Conflict of laws. *See* **Conflict of laws** (Shares).
  Constructive trust. *See* **Trust and trustee** (Constructive trust—Shares in company).
  Employee—
    Preferential right to apply for shares—
      Income tax—Emoluments from employment. *See* **Income tax** (Emoluments from office or employment—Causal nexus between employment and benefit received—Preferential right to apply for shares).
  Exchange—
    Company amalgamation—
      Capital gains tax. *See* **Capital gains tax** (Disposal of assets—Company amalgamation—Exchange of shares or debentures).
  Generally. *See* **Company** (Shares).
  Lien on shares. *See* **Lien** (Equitable lien—Purchase of shares).
  Offer for subscription or sale—
    Criminal proceedings. *See* **Criminal law** (Company—Offer of shares for subscription or sale).
  Option to purchase—
    Construction of scheme rules. *See* **Option** (Option to purchase—Shares—Construction of scheme rules).
    Generally. *See* **Option** (Option to purchase—Shares).
    Option available to employees of company and its subsidiaries—
      Whether option lapsing on sale of subsidiary. *See* **Contract** (Condition subsequent—Company—Share option).
  Will—
    Donee assigning benefit of option and dying without exercising it. *See* **Will** (Option—Option to purchase shares—Donee assigning benefit of option and dying without exercising it).
  Purchase—
    Warranty—
      Construction. *See* **Contract** (Construction—Warranty—Share purchase).
  Register. *See* **Company** (Shares—Register).
  Restriction on transfer etc of shares—
    Investigation by Board of Trade. *See* **Company** (Investigation by Board of Trade—Restrictions on transfer etc of shares).
  Sale—
    Contract—
      Condition precedent—Waiver. *See* **Contract** (Condition precedent—Waiver—Contract for sale of a holding of shares).
    Fraudulent misrepresentation. *See* **Misrepresentation** (Fraudulent misrepresentation—Sale of shares).
  Setting aside valuation—
    Shares of private company. *See* **Valuer** (Valuation—Setting aside valuation—Shares of private company).
  Share option agreement—
    Construction. *See* **Contract** (Construction—Share option agreement).
  Shareholder—
    Company. *See* **Company** (Shareholder).
  Situs. *See* **Company** (Shares—Situs of shares).
  Specific performance—
    Sale of shares in company. *See* **Specific performance** (Sale of shares in company).
  Transaction in securities—
    Tax advantage. *See* **Income tax** (Tax advantage—Transaction in securities).
  Transfer of shares—
    Generally. *See* **Company** (Transfer of shares).
  Trust—
    Constructive trust. *See* **Trust and trustee** (Constructive trust—Shares in company).
    Generally. *See* **Trust and trustee** (Shares in company).
  Valuation—
    Capital gains tax. *See* **Capital gains tax** (Assets—Valuation—Market value—Shares).
    Estate duty. *See* **Estate duty** (Valuation—Shares in company).

SHARES (cont)—
Valuation (cont)—
Shares in private company—
Setting aside valuation. *See* **Valuer** (Valuation—Setting aside valuation—Shares of private company).
Will—
Gift—
Bequest to a company of shares in the company. *See* **Will** (Gift—Shares in company—Bequest to a company of shares in the company).

SHEEP RIGHTS
Profit à prendre. *See* **Profit à prendre** (Sheep rights).

SHERIFF
Bankruptcy proceedings—
Restriction on right of execution creditor—
Money paid to sheriff to avoid sale of goods. *See* **Bankruptcy** (Execution—Restriction on right of execution creditor—Money paid to sheriff to avoid sale of goods).
Duties—
Execution against company. *See* **Execution** (Winding up of company—Creditors' rights—Duties of sheriff).
Interpleader. *See* **Interpleader** (Sheriff's interpleader).
Possession—
Walking possession. *See* **Execution** (Writ of fi fa—Seizure of goods—Walking possession agreement).
Protection of. *See* **Execution** (Sheriff—Protection).

SHIP
Admiralty. *See* **Admiralty**.
Appraisement and sale. *See* **Admiralty** (Appraisement and sale).
Arrest. *See* **Admiralty** (Arrest of vessel).
Beneficial ownership—
Admiralty action in rem—
Jurisdiction. *See* **Admiralty** (Jurisdiction—Action in rem—Beneficial ownership).
Construction—
Insurance. *See* **Insurance** (Shipbuilders' all risks policy—Shipyard).
Custody of Admiralty Marshal—
Interference—
Contempt of court. *See* **Contempt of court** (Admiralty—Interference with ship in custody of Admiralty Marshal).
Floating restaurant—
Plant—
Capital allowances—Income tax. *See* **Capital allowances** (Plant—Apparatus used by taxpayer for purpose of business—Ship used as floating restaurant).
Foreign ship—
Offences on board—
Jurisdiction. *See* **Criminal law** (Jurisdiction—Ship).
Forfeiture—
Ship used in importation of prohibited goods. *See* **Customs and excise** (Forfeiture—Ship—Ship having had on board prohibited spirit—Ship used in importation of prohibited goods).
Forfeiture or condemnation—
Claim for customs duty. *See* **Admiralty** (Jurisdiction—Action in rem—Claim for forfeiture or condemnation of ship—Customs duty).
Generally. *See* **Shipping**.
Health and safety—
Detention —
Detention notice—Detention notices issued in respect of cruise ship following outbreaks of gastrointestinal virus on successive cruises—Whether notices valid—Whether facts pleaded in defence constituting sufficient grounds for detention of vessel—Whether defendants wrongfully interfering with vessel—Merchant Shipping Act 1995, ss 94, 95—Merchant Shipping and Fishing Vessels (Health and Safety at Work) Regulations 1997, SI 1997/2962, reg 28. **Club Cruise Entertainment and Travelling Services Europe BV v Dept for Transport** [2009] **1 Comm** 955, QBD.
Importation of goods—
Prohibited goods—
Forfeiture of ship. *See* **Customs and excise** (Forfeiture—Ship—Ship having had on board prohibited spirit—Ship used in importation of prohibited goods).
Negligence—
Fencing of hatches—
General practice not to fence hatches—Obvious risk of injury to seamen. *See* **Negligence** (Duty to take care—Foreseeable harm—General practice not to take precautionary measures—Ship—Open unfenced hatch).
Offences on board—
Jurisdiction. *See* **Criminal law** (Jurisdiction—Ship).
Open hatches—
Safe system of working. *See* **Safe system of working** (Reasonable care not to expose employee to unnecessary risk—Fencing of hatches on ship).
Ownership—
Beneficial ownership. *See* **Admiralty** (Jurisdiction—Action in rem—Beneficial ownership—Ship chartered on demise).
Repair—
Dry dock—
Regulations. *See* **Dock** (Repair of ship in dry dock).
Safe system of working. *See* **Safe system of working** (Safe place of work—Ship under repair).

SHIP (cont)—
Sale—
Appraisement and sale. *See* **Admiralty** (Appraisement and sale).
Contract—
Contract stated to be 'sub details'—Whether binding contract created. **Thoresen & Co (Bangkok) Ltd v Fathom Marine Co Ltd [2004] 1 Comm 935,** QBD.
Injunction. *See* **Injunction** (Breach of contract—Breach of restrictive covenant).
Place of payment—Contract on Norwegian sale form—Seller nominating bank in Singapore for lodging of deposit and bank in Greece for payment—Whether same bank to be used for payment and deposit under contract—Whether place of payment to be the same as place of closing—Whether buyer obliged to pay full price at Greek bank—Whether buyer able to effect part payment by releasing deposit in Singaporean bank account. **PT Berlian Laju Tanker TBK v Nuse Shipping Ltd [2008] 2 Comm 784,** QBD.
Provision of certificates—Contract on Norwegian Saleform—Contract requiring delivery of vessel with national/international trading certificates as well as other certificates held by vessel at time of inspection—Contract allowing buyers to cancel contract if seller not ready to complete legal transfer provided that seller having three days after giving notice of readiness to make arrangements for documentation—Whether Saleform requiring seller to deliver vessel with all certificates required by law as at date of delivery or as at date of inspection—Whether Saleform permitting seller three days to procure that it was ready and able to deliver the bill of sale—Norwegian Saleform 1993, cll 8, 11, 14. **Polestar Maritime Ltd v YHM Shipping Co Ltd [2012] 2 Comm 447,** CA; **Polestar Maritime Ltd v YHM Shipping Co Ltd, The Rewa [2011] 2 Comm 864,** QBD.
Seller's warranty and indemnity—Sellers of vessels warranting that they were free from all encumbrances, mortgages and maritime liens—Sellers indemnifying buyers against consequences of claims made against vessels 'incurred prior to the time of delivery'—Defendant guaranteeing sellers' obligations under indemnity subject to specified limits per vessel 'in respect of any claim'—Scope of indemnity and guarantee—Norwegian sale form, cl 9. **Rank Enterprises Ltd v Gerard [2000] 1 Comm 449,** CA.
Damages for breach of contract—
Recovery of deposit. *See* **Contract** (Damages for breach—Deposit—Sale of ships).
Implied conditions as to satisfactory quality. *See* **Sale of goods** (Implied conditions as to satisfactory quality—Exclusion of implied terms—Contract for sale of ship on Norwegian Saleform 1993).
Mortgage—
Duty of mortgagee. *See* **Mortgage** (Sale—Duty of mortgagee—Ship).
Proper law of contract. *See* **Conflict of laws** (Contract—Proper law of contract—Contract for sale of ship).
Sale by Admiralty Marshal. *See* **Admiralty** (Appraisement and sale—Currency of sale—Jurisdiction of Admiralty marshal).
Waste—
Pollution—
European Community. *See* **European Union** (Environment—Ship-source pollution—Waste).
Withdrawal from charterparty—
Time charter—
Non-payment of hire. *See* **Shipping** (Time charterparty—Withdrawal of vessel for non-payment of hire).

SHIPBUILDING CONTRACT
See **Contract** (Shipbuilding contract).

SHIPBUILDING YARD
Insurance. *See* **Insurance** (Shipbuilders' all risks policy—Shipyard).
Regulations concerning. *See* **Dock** (Shipbuilding yard).

SHIPPING
Admiralty—
Generally. *See* **Admiralty**.
Jurisdiction. *See* **Admiralty** (Jurisdiction).
Practice. *See* **Admiralty** (Practice).
Admiralty. *See* **Admiralty**.
Arbitration clause—
Charterparty—
Centrocon arbitration clause. *See* Charterparty—Incorporation of amended Centrocon arbitration clause, *below.*
Commencement of arbitration. *See* **Arbitration** (Commencement—Charterparty).
Incorporation in bill of lading. *See* Bill of lading—Incorporation of terms of charterparty—Arbitration clause, *below.*
Time for bringing claims under arbitration clause. *See* Charterparty—Time for bringing claims under arbitration clause, *below.*
Arrest of vessel—
Generally. *See* **Admiralty** (Arrest of vessel).
Jurisdiction. *See* **Admiralty** (Jurisdiction—Action in rem—Arrest of ship).
Arrived ship—
Arrived ship under berth charterparty. *See* Commencement of lay days—Arrived ship under berth charterparty, *below.*
Arrived ship under port charterparty. *See* Commencement of lay days—Arrived ship under port charterparty, *below.*
Demurrage—
Generally. *See* Demurrage—Arrived ship, *below.*
Availability of port—
Arrived ship under port charterparty. *See* Commencement of lay days—Arrived ship under port charterparty, *below.*

SHIPPING (cont)—
Baltime charterparty—
Time charterparty—
Exceptions. *See* Time charterparty—Exceptions—Baltime charterparty, *below.*
Bareboat charterparty. *See* Charterparty—Bareboat charterparty, *below.*
Berth charterparty—
Arrived ship under berth charterparty—
Commencement of lay days. *See* Commencement of lay days—Arrived ship under berth charterparty, *below.*
Bill of lading—
Action on bill of lading subject to Hague Visby Rules—
Substitution of parties—Date from when substituted party becomes party to proceedings. *See* **Practice** (Parties—Substitution—Date from when substituted party becomes party to proceedings—Action on bill of lading).
C and f contract. *See* Sale of goods (C and f contract—Bill of lading).
C i f contract. *See* Sale of goods (C i f contract—Bill of lading).
Care of cargo—
Bill of lading incorporating Hague Rules—Bill of lading incorporating voyage charterparty on Synacomex 90 form—Contracts of carriage of bags of rice from Pakistan to Abidjan—Cargo claimants alleging cargo damage and short delivery—Charterparty purporting to transfer responsibility for loading and stowage of goods from carrier to charterer/cargo interests—Preliminary issue arising for determination—Whether incorporated charterparty transferring responsibility for loading and stowage from carrier to charterer/cargo interests. **Societe de Distribution de Toutes Merchandises en Cote D'Ivoire (trading as 'SDTM-CI') v Continental Lines NV** [2016] **1 Comm** 1016, QBD.
Bill of lading incorporating Hague Rules—Clause for discharge of cargo in the event of strike—Strike at port of delivery—Delivery at port other than that named in bill of lading—Carriage of Goods by Sea Act 1924, Sch, art III, rr 2, 8, art IV, r 4—Water Carriage of Goods Act 1936 (RSC 1952 c 291), Sch, art III, rr 2, 8, art IV, r 4. **Renton (GH) & Co Ltd v Palmyra Trading Corp of Panama** [1956] **3** 957, HL.
Bill of lading incorporating Hague-Visby Rules—Goods damaged in course of loading—Bill of lading incorporating voyage charterparty—Charterparty purporting to transfer responsibility for loading, stowage and discharge of cargo to cargo owners—Whether rules precluding transfer of responsibility—Hague-Visby Rules, art III, rr 2, 8. **Jindal Iron and Steel Co Ltd v Islamic Solidarity Shipping Co Jordan Inc** [2002] **2 Comm** 364, QBD; [2003] **1 Comm** 747, CA; [2005] **1 Comm** 1, HL; [2005] **1** 175, HL.
Exclusion clause—Exclusion of carrier's liability for loss or damage to cargo—Damage occurring to cargo—Claimant alleging carrier in breach of duty—Carrier seeking to rely on exclusion clause—Claimant arguing exclusion clause unenforceable as incompatible with and repugnant to commercial purpose of contract—Whether exclusion clause enforceable. **Mitsubishi Corp v Eastwind Transport Ltd** [2005] **1 Comm** 328, QBD.
Carriage of goods by sea—
Cargo to be delivered via electronic release system ('ERS') in operation at discharge port—Carrier providing release note containing pin code to shipper's local port agent in exchange for original bill of lading—Cargo being misappropriated by unauthorised use of pin code—Shipper claiming damages for breach of contract—Whether provision of pin code itself amounting in law to delivery of possession of goods—Whether release note containing pin code itself delivery order for purposes of bill of lading—Whether release note with pin code contained in it ship's delivery order—Whether shipper estopped from claiming breach of contract. **MSC Mediterranean Shipping Co SA v Glencore International AG** [2017] **2 Comm** 881, CA.
Hague Rules—Straight bill of lading—Rules applying to contracts 'covered by a bill of lading or any similar document of title'—Status of straight bill of lading—Carriage of Goods By Sea Act 1971, s 1(4)—Hague Rules, art I(b). **MacWilliam (JI) Co Inc v Mediterranean Shipping Co SA** [2003] **2 Comm** 219, CA; [2003] **3** 369, CA; [2005] **1 Comm** 393, HL; [2005] **2** 86, HL.
Holder of bill of lading—Bank refusing to accept presentation of bill of lading against letter of credit in respect of cargo of gasoil—Cargo discharged on arrival at destination pursuant to letter of indemnity provided by seller—Bank subsequently agreeing to pay seller in full under letter of credit following claim brought against it by seller—Whether bank had acquired title to sue vessel's owner for mis-delivery—Whether bank had become holder of bill of lading having refused to accept presentation—Whether bank had become holder of bill of lading having subsequently paid out under letter of credit—Whether claim brought by seller against bank a claim for the repayment of a debt or for damages for breach of contract—Carriage of Goods by Sea Act 1992, ss 2, 5(2). **Standard Chartered Bank v Dorchester LNG (2) Ltd** [2015] **2 Comm** 362, CA; [2015] **2** 395, CA.
Holder of bill of lading—Rights of suit in respect of loss suffered by others—Whether holder of bill of lading's right of suit in respect of loss suffered by others a separate cause of action to right of action for loss suffered by holder of bill of lading—Carriage of Goods by Sea Act 1992, s 2(4). **Pace Shipping Co Ltd of Malta v Churchgate Nigeria Ltd of Nigeria** [2011] **1 Comm** 939, QBD.
Holder of bill of lading—Vessel and cargo lost following explosion on board vessel—Claimant intermediate buyer of cargo not party to bills of lading—Claimant acquiring bills of lading for purposes of insurance claim—Whether claimant holder of bills for purposes of acquiring right of suit and liability under bills—Carriage of Goods by Sea Act 1992, ss 3(1)(b), 5(2). **Primetrade AG v Ythan Ltd** [2006] **1 Comm** 157, QBD; [2006] **1** 367, QBD.
Title to cargoes passing to claimants after commencement of voyage—Cargoes carried on vessel owned by defendants but chartered to another company—Bills of lading signed on charterers' form—Demise clause describing owners as carrier but bills signed on behalf of charterers as carrier—Bills containing limitation clause protecting carrier's independent contractors—Cargo damaged due to defective stowage and claimants bringing claims in contract and tort against defendants—Whether bills of lading owner's or charterers' bills—Whether defendants owing claimants duty of care in tort—Whether shipowner entitled to protection of Himalaya clause. **Homburg Houtimport BV v Agrosin Private Ltd** [2001] **1 Comm** 455, CA.
Casualty. *See* Shipping casualty, *below.*

SHIPPING (cont)—
Bill of lading (cont)—
Condition of cargo—
Defendant charterer letting vessel to claimant voyage charterer for carriage of cargo—When discharging some cargo found to be damaged—Defendant settling claim by shipowner relating to damaged cargo—Defendant making indemnity claim against claimant—Claimant (by its agent) found to have warranted cargo shipped in apparent good order condition—Bill of lading held to be inaccurate as matter of fact—Whether words 'Clean on Board' and 'Shipped at the Port of Loading in apparent good order and condition' in draft bill of lading amounting to representation or warranty as to apparent condition of cargo or invitation to master to make representation of fact in accordance with own assessment—Whether statement in bill of lading inaccurate as a matter of law—Whether claimant obliged to indemnify defendant for inaccurate statement by implied indemnity or implied contractual warranty or term—Carriage of Goods by Sea Act 1971, Sch, art III. **Priminds Shipping (HK) Co Ltd v Noble Chartering Inc** [2021] **1 Comm** 166, Comm Ct; [2021] **2 Comm** 866, CA.
Dangerous cargo—
Liability of shipper—Cargo of groundnuts infected with Khapra beetle—Shippers and carriers unaware of infestation at time of shipment—Carriers required to dump whole of cargo at sea although no danger of beetle infestation spreading to other cargo—Vessel detained and delayed—Whether groundnut cargo being goods of a 'dangerous nature'—Whether shipper's liability excluded or qualified under Hague Rules—Whether shippers' liability divested by virtue of indorsement of bill of lading—Bills of Lading Act 1855, s 1—Hague Rules, art IV, rr 3, 6. **Effort Shipping Co Ltd v Linden Management SA** [1998] **1** 495, HL.
Deck cargo—
Scope of contract of carriage. *See* Bill of lading—Scope of contract of carriage—Deck cargo, *below*.
Delivery of cargo—
Apportionment of cargo—Port of Liverpool—Master porter—Duty to consignees—Cargo damaged during voyage—Part of different consignments of chestnuts intermixed—Duty to apportion loose chestnuts—Duty to weigh—Mersey Docks (Corporation Purchase) Act 1861, ss 23, 24. **Gill and Duffus (Liverpool) Ltd v Scruttons Ltd** [1953] **2** 977, Assizes.
Delay—Measure of damages—Delay on voyage due to unseaworthiness—Outbreak of war—Diversion of ship by Admiralty—Transhipment of cargo to neutral ships for completion of voyage—Damages—Cost of transhipment. **Monarch Steamship Co Ltd v Karlshamns Oljefabriker (AB)** [1949] **1** 1, HL.
Delay—Measure of damages—Shipper taking delivery and paying freight—Right to recover increase in import duty and loss of profit. **Ardennes (owner of cargo), The v The Ardennes (owners)** [1950] **2** 517, KBD.
Misdelivery on forged bill of lading—Claimant shipping goods on defendants' vessels—Defendants delivering goods on forged bill of lading—Claimant suing defendants for breach of duty and conversion—Bill of lading excluding liability for loss or damage to goods after discharge—Whether defendants' liability excluded. **Motis Exports Ltd v Dampskibsselskabet AF 1912, A/S** [2000] **1 Comm** 91, CA.
Misdelivery on forged bill of lading—Plaintiff shipping goods on defendants' vessels—Defendants delivering goods on forged bill of lading—Plaintiffs suing defendants for breach of duty and conversion—Whether defendants' ignorance of forgery provided a defence. **Motis Exports Ltd v Dampskibsselskabet AF 1912, A/S** [1999] **1 Comm** 571, QBD.
Over-delivery by shipowners to consignees—Whether consignees to be charged with goods over-delivered. **Nordborg, The** [1939] **1** 70, CA.
Production of bill of lading—Delivery of cargo without production of bill of lading—Bills of lading transferred by claimants to banks—Defendant carrier delivering goods without presentation of original bill of lading—Whether claimants retaining title to sue in contract—Carriage of Goods by Sea Act 1992, ss 2, 5. **East West Corp v DKBS 1912** [2003] **1 Comm** 525, CA; [2003] **2** 700, CA.
Production of bill of lading—Delivery of cargo without production of bill of lading—Exemption clause—Cesser of liability of carrier on goods being discharged—Construction. **Sze Hai Tong Bank Ltd v Rambler Cycle Co Ltd** [1959] **3** 182, PC.
Production of bill of lading—Delivery of cargo without production of bill of lading—Title to sue—Bills of lading transferred by claimants to banks—Defendant carrier delivering goods without presentation of original bill of lading—Whether claimants retaining title to sue—Whether implied term in bill of lading permitting carrier to deliver goods when reasonable explanation for absence of bills of lading given—Carriage of Goods by Sea Act 1992, ss 2(1), 5(2)(a). **East West Corp v DKBS 1912** [2002] **1 Comm** 676, QBD.
Deviation—
Ships to go to loading ports as ordered—Orders not received by master owing to non-delivery of cablegram—Lien of shipowners—Freight—Deviation—Claim for return of deposit contributed in general average. **Hain Steamship Co Ltd v Tate and Lyle Ltd** [1936] **2** 597, HL.
Evidence in criminal proceedings—
Record relating to trade or business—Degree of permanence of record—Bill of lading and cargo manifest relating to container shipped to United Kingdom. *See* **Criminal evidence** (Record relating to trade or business—Record—Relevance of degree of permanence of record—Documents prepared for purpose of single transaction—Bill of lading and cargo manifest relating to container shipped from overseas to United Kingdom).
Evidence of the contract—
Inclusion of term at variance with contract between parties—Admissibility of evidence as to true contract. **Ardennes (owner of cargo), The v The Ardennes (owners)** [1950] **2** 517, KBD.
Exceptions—
Cause arising without actual fault or neglect of agents or servants of carrier—Damage to cargo—Theft of cover-plate of storm valve by stevedore when loading—Ship thereby rendered unseaworthy—Cargo damaged by water entering through hole left uncovered—Whether damage due to cause arising 'without the fault or neglect of the agents or servants of the carrier'—Whether thief was agent of the shipowners when stealing the cover-plate—Carriage of Goods by Sea Act 1924, Sch, art IV, r 2(q). **Leesh River Tea Co Ltd v British India Steam Navigation Co Ltd** [1966] **3** 593, CA.

SHIPPING (cont)—
Bill of lading (cont)—
Exceptions (cont)—
Panama Canal Zone—Clause paramount incorporating United States Carriage of Goods by Sea Act 1936 with respect to shipments from United States ports—Whether clause applicable to shipment from a port in the Panama Canal Zone. **Stafford Allen & Sons Ltd v Pacific Steam Navigation Co Ltd** [1956] **2** 716, CA.
Perils of the sea—Charterers' risk—Unexplained heeling of ship and loss of cargo when loading. **Stranna, The** [1938] **1** 458, CA.
Goods sold on c and f terms—
Freight to be payable at destination—Whether freight at risk of sellers or buyers. *See* **Sale of goods** (C and f contract).
Immunities of shipowner—
Neglect in management of ship—Soundings—Failure to take proper soundings—Whether shipowner liable for damage resulting from failure—Whether 'neglect in management of ship'—Australian Sea Carriage of Goods Act 1924 (No 22 of 1924), Sch, art III, r 1, art IV, r 2(a). **Riverstone Meat Co Pty Ltd v Lancashire Shipping Co Ltd** [1960] **1** 193, CA.
Implied undertaking to use due diligence to make ship seaworthy—
Contract incorporating Hague Rules—Goods lost as result of fire after loading completed but before ship sailed—Whether carrier entitled to immunity—Water Carriage of Goods Act 1936 (RSC 1952, c 29), Sch, art III, r 1, art IV, rr 1, 2(a)(b). **Maxine Footwear Co Ltd v Canadian Government Merchant Marine Ltd** [1959] **2** 740, PC.
Due diligence before and at beginning of voyage—Voyage in stages—Sufficiency of coal—Water Carriage of Goods Act 1910 (RSC 1927, c 207), ss 6, 7. **Northumbrian Shipping Co Ltd v Timm (E) & Son Ltd** [1939] **2** 648, HL.
Lloyd's Register and load line surveys—Work entrusted to competent independent contractors—Unseaworthiness due to negligence of contractors' employee—Negligence not discoverable—Whether due diligence exercised by shipowners—Australian Sea Carriage of Goods Act 1924 (No 22 of 1924), Sch, art III, r 1, art IV, rr 1, 2(a). **Riverstone Meat Co Pty Ltd v Lancashire Shipping Co Ltd** [1961] **1** 495, HL.
Voyage—Bunkering—Obligation of shipowner—Canadian Water Carriage of Goods Act 1936 (RSC 1952, c29), Sch, art III, r 1, art IV, r 1. **Makedonia, The** [1962] **2** 614, Admin Ct.
Incorporation of terms of charterparty—
Arbitration clause—Bill of lading providing for 'all other conditions ... as per [the] charterparty'—Charterparty providing for bill of lading to incorporate arbitration clause-Whether arbitration clause a 'condition' incorporated in bill of lading—Whether reference to charterparty permissible to ascertain terms incorporated in bill of lading. **Astro Valiente Cia Naviera SA v Pakistan Ministry of Food and Agriculture (No 2)** [1982] **1** 823, QBD.
Arbitration clause—Bill of lading providing that 'all conditions and exceptions of [the] charterparty' deemed to be incorporated in bill of lading—Charterparty providing for bill of lading to incorporate 'all terms and conditions of [the] charter including ... the arbitration clause'—Whether arbitration clause a 'condition' incorporated in bill of lading—Whether arbitration clause incorporated in bill of lading by charterparty or bill of lading. **Skips A/S Nordheim v Syrian Petroleum Co Ltd** [1983] **2** 375, QBD.
Arbitration clause—First bills of lading providing for incorporation of 'all terms and conditions of the charterparty ... including the Law and Arbitration clause'—Second bills of lading providing for incorporation of 'all the terms whatsoever of the said Charter'—Charterparty not providing for bills of lading to incorporate arbitration clause—Whether arbitration clause incorporated in bills of lading. **Delos (cargo owners) v Delos Shipping Ltd** [2001] **1 Comm** 763, QBD.
Arbitration clause—General clause incorporating terms and conditions of charterparty and specifically incorporating arbitration clause—Arbitration clause providing that any dispute arising under charterparty to be referred to arbitration—Dispute arising under bills of lading—Whether dispute one which parties had agreed to refer to arbitration. **Rena K, The** [1979] **1** 397, QBD.
Arbitration clause—General clause incorporating terms and conditions of charterparty and specifically incorporating cl 30—Arbitration clause was cl 32—Wrong number stated in error—Falsa demonstratio—Paramount clause in bill of lading incorporating Hague Rules—Arbitration clause imposed time limit for appointing arbitrator, being one year from date of final discharge of cargo—Whether arbitration clause in charterparty incorporated in bill of lading contract—Meaning of 'suit'—Carriage of Goods by Sea Act 1924, Sch, art 3, rr 6, 8. **Merak, The** [1965] **1** 230, CA.
Arbitration clause—General words of incorporation—Test of incorporation—Defendant owners bringing arbitration proceedings in London—Defendants relying on terms of recap telex as constituting charterparty for purposes of bill of lading—Consignees contending no charterparty in existence—Whether contract contained in or evidenced by recap telex reduced to writing. **Welex AG v Rosa Maritime Ltd** [2002] **1 Comm** 939, QBD.
Bills of lading providing that freight payable as per charterparty—Bills of lading referring to application of Hague Rules—Defendants commencing proceedings in Morocco where cargo was partially discharged—Moroccan proceedings governed by Hamburg Rules—Claimant commencing proceedings in England and given permission to serve claim form on defendants out of jurisdiction—Defendant applying to set aside order permitting service out—Whether English courts having jurisdiction—Whether claimant entitled to final anti-suit injunction in respect of Moroccan proceedings—Whether order permitting service out of the jurisdiction to be set aside. **Golden Endurance Shipping SA v RMA Watanya SA** [2015] **2 Comm** 435, QBD.
Bills of lading providing that freight payable as per charterparty—Whether owner could require freight to be paid directly to it by sub-sub-sub-charterer. **Dry Bulk Handy Holding Inc v Fayette International Holdings Ltd** [2013] **1 Comm** 177, QBD.
Demurrage—Liability of holder of bill of lading. **Roland-Linie Schiffahrt GmbH v Spillers Ltd** [1956] **3** 383, QBD.
Evidence of contract of carriage—Express incorporation of terms, conditions and exceptions of charterparty—Plaintiffs suing for non-delivery of cargo as consignees, not as charterers. **Metamorphosis, The** [1953] **1** 723, Admin Ct.

SHIPPING (cont)—
  Bill of lading (cont)—
    Incorporation of terms of charterparty (cont)—
      General words of incorporation—Test of incorporation—Arbitration clause—Arbitration clause
        referring to all disputes 'under this contract'—Arbitration clause not directly germane to
        subject-matter of bill of lading. **Annefield, The** [1971] **1** 394, CA, Admin Ct.
      Inter-club agreement—Charterparty providing cargo claims to be apportioned in accordance with
        inter-club agreement—Bills of lading being ante-dated by charterers and not in accordance with
        mate's receipts contrary to charterparty—Damage occurring to cargo resulting from
        unseaworthiness—Cargo interests bringing claim against owners—Owners settling cargo
        action—Owners bringing action against charterers—Whether inter-club agreement rendered
        inapplicable by ante-dated and 'clean' bills of lading. **Transpacific Discovery SA v Cargill
        International SA** [2001] **1 Comm** 937, QBD.
      Term excluding liability—Charterparty providing that captain should sign bills of lading as
        presented and excepting any act, neglect, default or error of judgment in the management and/or
        navigation of vessel—Charterers requiring master to sign bill of lading which incorporated all the
        terms, conditions and exceptions of the charterparty 'dated as overleaf ', but date of charterparty
        not in fact filled in on front of bill—Vessel subsequently causing damage to consignee's crane
        and consignee suing shipowners—Whether shipowners entitled to indemnity or damages from
        charterers—Whether bill of lading incorporating terms of charterparty—Whether bill of lading
        proper and contractual bill—Whether master required to sign bill. **Orinoco Navigation Ltd v
        Ecotrade SpA** [1999] **2 Comm** 257, QBD.
      Terms relating to shipment, carriage or delivery of cargo and imposing obligations on
        'charterer'—Whether incorporation rendering consignees of cargo as holders of bill of lading
        when cargo discharged personally liable for obligations of 'charterer'. **Miramar Maritime Corp v
        Holborn Oil Trading Ltd** [1984] **2** 326, HL.
    Issued to shippers without production of mate's receipts—
      Sellers to have vendor's lien so long as they held mate's receipts—Indorsement of bills of
        lading—Rights of sellers in conversion. **Nippon Yusen Kaisha v Ramjiban Serowgee** [1938] **2** 285,
        PC.
    Limitation of liability—
      Loss of or damage to goods—Bill of lading incorporating Hague-Visby Rules—Cargo-owner
        claiming that some goods damaged whilst on carrier's vessel and value of rest of cargo
        consequently depreciated—Whether liability limited by reference to gross weight of goods
        physically damaged or gross weight of whole cargo—Carriage of Goods by Sea Act 1971, Sch,
        art IV, r 5. **Serena Navigation Ltd v Dera Commercial Establishment** [2008] **2 Comm** 1005, QBD.
      Loss of or damage to goods—Package limitation—Cargo-owners and shipowners entering into
        contracts of carriage for shipment of cargo from Belgium to Yemen—Bills of lading containing
        common form paramount clause providing for 'Hague Rules ... dated ... 1924 as enacted in
        country of shipment' to apply—Cargo damaged during carriage—Claim commenced to recover
        loss agreed to be subject to English law and jurisdiction—Cargo-owners seeking to rely on higher
        package limitation provided for by (old) Hague Rules—Judge finding Hague-Visby Rules
        applying—Whether Hague or Hague-Visby Rules applying—Carriage of Goods by Sea Act 1971,
        s 1, Schedule. **Yemgas FZCO v Superior Pescadores SA** [2016] **2 Comm** 104, CA.
    Rights of stranger to contract—Bill of lading extending benefit of defences and liabilities conferred
        thereby to independent contractors employed by carrier—Bill of lading also providing that
        carrier's responsibility terminating as soon as goods left ship's tackle—Goods discharged and
        stored by stevedore employed by carrier—Goods stolen from stevedore's store—Whether
        stevedore entitled to benefit of contractual provisions of bill of lading. **Port Jackson Stevedoring
        Pty Ltd v Salmond & Spraggon (Australia) Pty Ltd** [1980] **3** 257, PC.
    Rights of stranger to contract—Himalaya clause—Exclusive jurisdiction clause—Bill of lading
        issued by charterers containing both Himalaya clause protecting sub-contractors and exclusive
        jurisdiction clause for resolution of all disputes in Indonesia—Cargo owners bringing action in
        Hong Kong against shipowners in respect of damage to cargo—Shipowners applying for stay of
        Hong Kong proceedings under exclusive jurisdiction clause—Whether shipowners entitled to
        benefit of Himalaya clause to claim protection of exclusive jurisdiction clause—Whether exclusive
        jurisdiction clause an exception, limitation, provision, condition or liberty benefiting the carrier
        within the meaning of Himalaya clause. **Mahkutai, The** [1996] **3** 502, PC.
    Rights of stranger to contract—Whether stevedores entitled to rely on contract contained in bill of
        lading as limiting their liability to cargo-owner—Whether 'carrier' in United States Act, and in bill
        of lading, included stevedores—Whether carrier contracted as agent for stevedores—Whether
        implied contract between cargo-owner and stevedores entitling stevedores to have benefit of
        immunity from liability in contract of carriage—United States Carriage of Goods by Sea Act 1936,
        s 4(5). **Scruttons Ltd v Midland Silicones Ltd** [1962] **1** 1, HL.
    Stowage—Package—Compliance with Harter Act. **Studebaker Distributors Ltd v Charlton Steam
        Shipping Co Ltd** [1937] **4** 304, KBD.
    Negligent issue of bill of lading—
      Failure to despatch goods to ship—Discovery delayed by negligent issue of bill of
        lading—Shipper's resultant liability in damages to purchaser for failure to deliver
        goods—Measure of damages. **Heskell v Continental Express Ltd** [1950] **1** 1033, KBD.
      Goods not received at dock—Liability of loading broker. **Heskell v Continental Express Ltd**
        [1950] **1** 1033, KBD.
    Omission to incorporate Hague Rules—
      Act of country of port of shipment requiring incorporation—Consignees and ship of another
        country—Illegality—Law governing contract—Newfoundland Carriage of Goods by Sea Act 1932,
        ss 1, 3. **Vita Food Products Inc v Unus Shipping Co Ltd (in liq)** [1939] **1** 513, PC.
    Payment against bill of lading—
      Passing of property. *See* **Sale of goods** (Passing of property—Payment against bill of lading).
    Quantity of cargo—
      Receipt as to. *See* Bill of lading—Receipt as to quantity of cargo, *below.*

1171

SHIPPING (cont)—
  Bill of lading (cont)—
    Receipt as to condition of cargo—
      Duty of master—Master issuing claused bill of lading—Claimants contending master having no
        basis to clause bills—Whether master entitled to act on honest belief—Whether master required
        to sign only bills accurately stating order and condition—Carriage of Goods by Sea Act 1971,
        s 1(4), Schedule, art III, r 3. **David Agmashenebeli (cargo owners), The v The David
        Agmashenebeli (owners)** [2002] **2 Comm** 806, QBD.
      Estoppel—Representation in bill of lading—Reliance on representation—Representee acting to his
        detriment—Statement in bill of lading that goods shipped in good order and condition—
        Representee purchaser of goods under contract with shipper—Contract providing that certificate
        as to quality to be final—Certificate issued by inspector—Goods shipped in unsatisfactory
        condition—Bill of lading not claused to take account of condition of goods—Action by
        representee against shipowner for damage to goods—Whether representee would have been
        bound under contract with shipper to take up bills of lading even if claused—Whether
        representee having acted to his detriment in taking up clean bills of lading—Whether shipowner
        estopped from relying on fact that damage due to pre-shipment condition of goods. **Cremer v
        General Carriers SA** [1974] **1** 1, QBD.
      Goods shipped in defective condition—Clean bill of lading issued by shipowner in consideration of
        letter of indemnity from shipper—Compensation for loss to consignee owing to defective
        condition paid by shipowner—Claim by shipowner against shipper on letter of indemnity
        unenforceable—Ex turpi causa non oritur actio. **Brown, Jenkinson & Co Ltd v Percy Dalton
        (London) Ltd** [1957] **2** 844, CA.
    Receipt as to quantity of cargo—
      Short delivery—Bills of lading stating number of bags shipped but containing condition that
        weight, contents and value unknown—Mode of proof of contents and weight of missing bags by
        consignee—Indian Carriage of Goods by Sea Act 1925, Sch, art III, rr 3, 4—Carriage of Goods by
        Sea Act 1924, Sch, art III, rr 3, 4. **A-G of Ceylon v Scindia Steam Navigation Co Ltd** [1961] **3** 684,
        PC.
    Scope of contract of carriage—
      Deck cargo—Cargo 'stated' as being carried on deck—Clause in bill of lading giving liberty to carry
        goods as deck cargo—Carriage subject to obligation properly and carefully to carry—Carriage of
        Goods by Sea Act 1924, s 3, Sch, arts I(c), III, r 2. **Svenska Traktor Aktiebolaget v Maritime Agencies
        (Southampton) Ltd** [1953] **2** 570, QBD.
      Goods damaged in course of loading—Limitation of ship's liability—Carriage of Goods by Sea Act
        1924, s 3, Sch, arts I(b)(e), II, IV, r (5). **Pyrene Co Ltd v Scindia Steam Navigation Co Ltd**
        [1954] **2** 158, QBD.
    Sea waybill —
      Bill of lading containing English exclusive jurisdiction clause—Second defendant bringing
        proceedings in Benin relying on photocopy of bill—Second defendant not original party to
        contract of carriage—Whether bill constituting sea waybill—Whether rights of suit under contract
        transferring to second defendant—Carriage of Goods by Sea Act 1992, ss 1, 2. **AP Moller-Maersk
        A/S (t/a Maersk Line) v Sonaec Villas Cen Sad Fadoul** [2010] **2 Comm** 1159, QBD.
      Diversion of goods by shipper—Cancellation of original bill—Whether shipper entitled to divert
        goods even though rights under sea waybill transferred to consignee named in bill—Carriage of
        Goods by Sea Act 1992, ss 1, 2. **AP Moller-Maersk A/S (t/a Maersk Line) v Sonaec Villas Cen Sad
        Fadoul** [2010] **2 Comm** 1159, QBD.
    Seaworthiness of ship—
      Implied undertaking. *See* Bill of lading—Implied undertaking to use due diligence to make ship
        seaworthy, *above.*
    Time for bringing claims—
      Suit barred unless brought within one year after delivery of goods—Action brought in New York
        within one year, but by wrong plaintiff—Further action brought in England after one year by right
        plaintiff—Whether action in England statute-barred—Carriage of Goods by Sea Act 1924, s 1, Sch,
        art III, r 6. **Cia Colombiana de Seguros v Pacific Steam Navigation Co** [1964] **1** 216, QBD.
      Suit barred unless brought within one year after delivery of goods—Action brought overseas within
        one year but stayed because of arbitration clause—Arbitration action brought in England after
        one year—Whether action in England time-barred—Whether extension of time appropriate—
        Carriage of Goods by Sea Act 1924, s 1, Schedule, art III, r 6. **Thyssen Inc v Calypso Shipping Corp
        SA** [2000] **2 Comm** 97, QBD.
      Suit barred unless brought within one year after delivery of goods—Arbitral tribunal striking out
        cargo claim made within one-year time limit where inordinate and inexcusable delay
        found—Whether apparent bias on part of tribunal—Whether claim particularised within six-year
        limitation period applicable to contractual claims could be struck out for 'inordinate delay'
        because parties had contracted for shorter limitation period—Whether geographic deviation
        precluding carrier from relying on one-year time bar—Whether, where one-year time bar
        applying, period between cause of action arising and expiry of contractual time limit to be taken
        into account when assessing whether delay 'inordinate'—Proper order, burden and/or standard of
        proof applicable to assessment of whether delay 'inexcusable'—Carriage of Goods by Sea Act
        1924, Schedule, art III, r 6—Arbitration Act 1996, ss 41(3), 68, 69. **Dera Commercial Estate v Derya
        Inc** [2019] **1 Comm** 448, QBD; [2019] **1** 1147, QBD.
      Suit barred unless brought within one year after delivery of goods—Counterclaim based on delay
        in shipment—Whether claim having sufficiently close association with cargo intended to be
        shipped—Whether one-year time limit applicable—Carriage of Goods by Sea Act 1924, s 1, Sch,
        art III, r 6. **Linea Naviera Paramaconi SA v Abnormal Load Engineering Ltd** [2001] **1 Comm** 946,
        QBD.
      Suit barred unless brought within one year after delivery of goods—Fundamental breach of
        contract—Loss or misdelivery of consignee's goods—Effect on time bar clause—Whether
        fundamental breach depriving party in breach of benefit of time bar clause—Water Carriage of
        Goods Act 1936 (Canada), Sch (Hague Rules), art III, r 6. **Port Jackson Stevedoring Pty Ltd v
        Salmond & Spraggon (Australia) Pty Ltd** [1980] **3** 257, PC.

SHIPPING (cont)—
  Cargo (cont)—
    Readiness to discharge (cont)—
      Lay days—Commencement. *See* Commencement of lay days—Readiness to discharge, *below*.
    Salvage. *See* Salvage—Cargo, *below*.
  Carriage by sea—
    Bill of lading. *See* Bill of lading—Carriage of goods by sea, *above*.
    Breach of condition of contract—
      Laycan—Implied term as to shipment period—Force majeure clause—Duty to give ETAs honestly and on reasonable grounds—Defendant cancelling contract on basis claimant in breach—Meaning of laycan in CIF contract—Whether defendant entitled to cancel contract. **SHV Gas Supply and Trading SAS v Naftomar Shipping and Trading Co Ltd Inc** [2006] 2 Comm 515, QBD.
      Right of other party to terminate contract—Stipulation as to time—Contract incorporating rule requiring sellers to have cargo ready for delivery at any time within contract period. *See* **Contract** (Condition—Breach—Effect—Right of other party to terminate contract—Stipulation as to time—Shipping contract incorporating rule requiring sellers to have cargo ready for delivery at any time within contract period).
    Cif contract—
      Notice of readiness—Discharge port—Vessel arriving at discharge port and unable to berth because berth occupied and because of tidal conditions—Master tendering notice of readiness at usual waiting place—Whether under terms of contract master entitled to tender notice of readiness. **Suek AG v Glencore International AG, The Hang Ta** [2011] 2 Comm 1154, QBD.
    cip contract —
      Buyer purchasing vehicles on cip terms Tripoli—Seller contracting with freight forwarders to arrange carriage and insurance—Freight forwarders contracting with carrier—Freight forwarders warranting that vehicles shipped under deck for insurance purposes—Vehicles shipped on deck and washed overboard during voyage—Insurers refusing to pay out on basis of breach of warranty—Whether shipping of vehicles on deck amounting to a breach of contract of carriage—Whether freight forwarders negligent in giving warranty—Whether negligence giving rise to any loss. **Geofizika DD v MMB International Ltd (Greenshields Cowie & Co Ltd, Part 20 defendant)** [2011] 1 Comm 492, CA.
      Claimant entering cip contract with defendant for purchase of vehicles to be delivered at Libya—Defendant contracting with Pt 20 defendant for freight forwarding—Part 20 defendant contracting with carrier—Vehicles stored on deck and washed overboard during voyage—Whether defendant in breach of contract by failing to secure contract requiring below-deck carriage—Whether defendant in breach of contract in failing to secure appropriate insurance cover—Whether Pt 20 defendant in breach of duty to exercise reasonable skill and care in relation to freight forwarding arrangements. **Geofizika DD v MMB International Ltd (Greenshields Cowie & Co Ltd, Part 20 defendant)** [2009] 2 Comm 1034, QBD.
    Claim arising out of agreement relating to carriage of goods—
      Admiralty jurisdiction. *See* **Admiralty** (Jurisdiction—Action in rem—Claim arising out of agreement relating to carriage of goods).
  Conflict of laws—
    Carriage of goods by sea. *See* **Conflict of laws** (Shipping—Carriage of goods by sea).
  Damages for breach of contract—
    Assessment of damages—Charterers failing to declare laycans—Disponent owners accepting failure as repudiatory breach—Whether disponent owners required to be able to show they could have performed contract had breach not occurred. **Flame SA v Glory Wealth Shipping PTE Ltd, The Glory Wealth** [2014] 1 Comm 1043, QBD.
    Charterparty providing for ship-to-ship transfers subject to owners' prior approval of transfer vessels which not to be unreasonably withheld—Owners withholding consent for ship-to-ship transfer between two very large crude carriers of identical size—Whether withholding of approval reasonable. **Falkonera Shipping Co v Arcadia Energy Pte Ltd** [2015] 2 Comm 401, CA.
    Contract to sell cargo of fuel oil—Cargo rejected by discharge port authorities in Pakistan—Buyer refusing to open letter of credit for further shipments—Whether buyer in breach of contract. **Mena Energy DMCC v Hascol Petroleum Ltd** [2017] 2 Comm 1058, QBD.
    Late redelivery under time charterparty. *See* Time charterparty—Last voyage—Late redelivery, *below*.
    Loss of or damage to goods—Bill of lading holder receiving damaged cargo from carrier—Arbitrators finding carrier liable and awarding full damages—Whether bill of lading holder entitled to full damages irrespective of earlier recovery from intermediate cargo seller—Carriage of Goods by Sea Act 1992, s 2(1), (4). **Sevylor Shipping and Trading Corp v Altfadul Company for Foods, Fruits & Livestock** [2018] 2 Comm 847, QBD.
    Loss of or damage to goods—Bills of lading incorporating Hague-Visby Rules—Barratry—Exemption for fire unless caused by actual fault or privity of carrier—Exemption for loss or damage arising from any cause without actual fault or privity of the carrier or without fault or neglect of agents or servants of carrier—Whether barratry requiring intentionally committed crime or fraud—Whether exemption for fire applying if loss arising from barratry—Whether exemption for loss or damage arising from any cause applying—Carriage of Goods by Sea Act 1971, Schedule, art IV, r 2(b) and (q). **Glencore Energy UK Ltd v Freeport Holdings Ltd** [2018] 2 Comm 219, QBD.
    Loss of or damage to goods—Cargo shipped from English port—Cargo owners entitled under Hague-Visby Rules to bring action in England—Bill of lading providing for Dutch court to have exclusive jurisdiction—Carrier's liability limited under bill of lading to £250—Hague-Visby Rules extending carrier's liability to £11,500—Damage to cargo during carriage estimated at £22,000—Whether Hague-Visby Rules ousting proper law of contract—Whether exclusive jurisdiction and limitation of liability provisions in bill of lading null and void—Carriage of Goods by Sea Act 1971, Sch, art III, para 8, art X. **Hollandia, The** [1982] 3 1141, HL.

SHIPPING (cont)—
Carriage by sea (cont)—
Damages for breach of contract (cont)—

Loss of or damage to goods—Cargo shipped from English port—Cargo owners entitled under Hague-Visby Rules to bring action in England—Bill of lading providing for Indonesian court to have exclusive jurisdiction—Carriers entitled to invoke tonnage limitation under Indonesian law—Tonnage limitation providing for lower liability than Hague-Visby Rules—Whether Hague-Visby Rules restricted to package limitation—Whether Hague-Visby Rules applying to contract—Whether exclusive jurisdiction and limitation of liability clauses in bill of lading valid—Carriage of Goods by Sea Act 1971, Sch, art III, para 8, art VIII. **Benarty, The** [1984] **3** 961, CA.

Loss of or damage to goods—Cargo shipped from Italian port—English law being proper law of contract—Bill of lading providing for Hague Rules as enacted in country of shipment to apply and for arts I-VIII of Hague Rules to apply where no such enactment in force—Bill of lading providing for Hague-Visby Rules to apply where compulsorily applicable—Hague Rules not enacted in Italy—Goods damaged during loading process—Whether contract incorporating terms of bill of lading—Whether Hague or Hague-Visby Rules applying to contract of carriage—Carriage of Goods by Sea Act 1971, s 1(4). **Parsons Corp v CV Scheepvaartonderneming Happy Ranger** [2002] **1 Comm** 176, QBD.

Loss of or damage to goods—Carrier's obligations—Bill of lading incorporating Hague Rules—Carriage on LCL/FCL terms—Cargo of coffee beans found to have condensate damage on outturn—Claimants contending defendant carrier having failed to properly and carefully care for and carry cargo—Carrier relying on various defences including inherent vice and inevitability of damage—Judge rejecting defences and entering judgment for claimants—Burden of proof in cargo claims governed by Hague Rules—Whether judge erring in law—Carriage of Goods by Sea Act 1971, Schedule, arts III, r 2, IV, r 2(m). **Volcafe Ltd v Compania Sud Americana De Vapores SA (t/a CSAV)** [2017] **1 Comm** 751, CA.

Loss of or damage to goods—Carrier's obligations—Bill of lading incorporating Hague Rules—Carriage on LCL/FCL terms—Cargo of coffee beans found to have condensate damage on outturn—Claimants contending defendant carrier having failed to properly and carefully care for and carry cargo—Carrier relying on various defences including inherent vice—Judge rejecting defences—Court of Appeal allowing carrier's appeal—Burden of proof in cargo claims governed by Hague Rules—Whether Court of Appeal erring—Carriage of Goods by Sea Act 1924, Schedule, arts III, r 2, IV, r 2(m). **Volcafe Ltd v Compania Sud Americana De Vapores SA (t/a CSAV)** [2019] **1 Comm** 397, SC; [2019] **2** 81, SC.

Loss of or damage to goods—Carrier's obligations—Bill of lading incorporating Hague Rules—Carriage on LCL/FCL terms—Cargo of coffee beans found to have condensate damage on outturn—Whether carrier correct that 'stuffing' of cargo into containers before loading on vessel not part of 'loading' process such that Hague Rules not applying—Res ipsa loquitur—Whether damage inevitable—Whether 'sound system' employed by carrier—Carriage of Goods by Sea Act 1971, Sch 1, arts I(e), III(2). **Volcafe Ltd v Compania Sud Americana De Vapores SA (t/a CSAV)** [2016] **1 Comm** 657, QBD.

Loss of or damage to goods—Damage to cargoes of gasoil and mogas—Nature and extent of obligations imposed by charterparty—Whether failure to care for cargo—Whether owners' counterclaim for demurrage time-barred. **Petroleum Oil and Gas Corporation of South Africa (Pty) Ltd v FR8 Singapore Pte Ltd** [2009] **1 Comm** 556, QBD.

Loss of or damage to goods—Limitation of liability—Cargo carried on deck in breach of contract of carriage—Whether owners entitled to rely on limitation provisions when goods carried in breach of contract—Hague Rules, art IV, r 5. **Daewoo Heavy Industries Ltd v Klipriver Shipping** [2002] **2 Comm** 560, QBD; [2003] **1 Comm** 801, CA.

Loss of or damage to goods—Limitation of liability—Liability determined by reference to gold value—Shipowners admitting liability in respect of damage to goods—Provisions of bill of lading limiting liability to £100—Cargo owners claiming damages of £100 expressed as a gold value figure—Whether shipowners' liability limited to '£100' or '£100 sterling gold value'—Hague Rules, art IV, r 5, art IX. **Rosa S, The** [1989] **1** 489, QBD.

Loss of or damage to goods—Limitation of liability—Package limitation—Charterparty incorporating Hague Rules—Parties contracting to transport cargo of fish oil in bulk—Cargo suffering damage and charterer claiming damages—Owner seeking to limit liability pursuant to Hague Rules package limitation—Meaning of 'unit'—Whether package limitation applying to bulk cargo—Hague Rules, art IV, r 5. **Sea Tank Shipping AS (formerly known as Tank Invest AS) v Vinnlustodin HF** [2018] **2 Comm** 191, CA; [2018] **3** 981, CA.

Loss of or damage to goods—Limitation of liability—Package limitation—Contract of carriage for shipment of three container loads of unpackaged tuna loins and bags of frozen tuna parts from Spain to Japan—Contract providing for bills of lading but waybills being issued instead—Receiver claiming cargo suffered damage during carriage—Whether Hague or Hague-Visby Rules applying—Whether limitation applying to all three containers collectively or to each container individually—Whether relevant 'package or unit' container or individual tuna loins or bag—Carriage of Goods by Sea Act 1971, Schedule, art IV, r 5. **Kyokuyo Co Ltd v AP Møller-Maersk A/S (t/a 'Maersk Line')** [2017] **2 Comm** 922, QBD; [2018] **2 Comm** 503, CA; [2018] **3** 1009, CA.

Loss of or damage to goods—Limitation of liability—'Package'—Meaning—Cargo loaded in containers—Bills of lading stating containers 'said to contain' specified number of items such as bales, parcels, bags, crates, cartons, or pallets—Liability to be calculated by reference to package—Whether containers or bales etc to be treated as package—Hague Rules, art IV, r 5. **River Gurara (cargo owners) v Nigerian National Shipping Line Ltd** [1997] **4** 498, CA.

Loss of or damage to goods—Limitation of liability—Terms limiting liability to £100 Sterling, lawful money of the United Kingdom per package or unit as per Hague Rules—Whether carrier's liability determined by reference to gold value or nominal or paper value—Hague Rules, art IV, r 5, art IX. **Dairy Containers Ltd v Tasman Orient Line CV** [2004] **2 Comm** 667, PC.

Carriage by sea (cont)—
Damages for breach of contract (cont)—
Loss of or damage to goods—Proprietary interest in goods as a prerequisite of right to claim substantial damages—Action by consignor against carrier for loss or of damage to cargo—Consignor having no interest in cargo at date of loss or damage—Agreement between consignor and carrier contemplating further contract of carriage between carrier and consignee—Charterparty providing for issue of bill of lading—Action by charterer against shipowner for loss of cargo—Property in cargo having passed to endorsees of bill of lading at time of loss—Whether charterers as consignors entitled to substantial damages for loss. **Albazero, The, Albacruz (cargo owners) v Alazero (owners)** [1976] 3 129, HL.

Loss of or damage to goods—Right to claim substantial damages—Passing of property—Property in goods having passed from charterer to consignee at date of damage—Whether charterer entitled to claim substantial damages. **Gardano & Giampari v Greek Petroleum George Mamidakis & Co** [1961] 3 919, QBD.

Repudiation of charterparty following failure by charterers to acquire cargo—Whether liability for damages could be avoided—Whether demurrage could be claimed as part of owners' damages. **Odfjfell Seachem A/S v Continentale des Petroles et d'Investissements** [2005] 1 Comm 421, QBD.

Repudiation of time charterparty by sub-charterers—Sub-charterers in repudiatory breach of charterparty by early redelivery of vessel to disponent owners—Disponent owners redelivering vessel early under head charterparty—Whether damages for repudiatory breach to be assessed taking account of savings made by disponent owners by early redelivery under head charterparty. **Glory Wealth Shipping Pte Ltd v North China Shipping Ltd** [2011] 1 Comm 641, QBD.

Time limit for bringing action—Misdelivery of cargo—Cargo interests bringing action against carrier claiming damages for misdelivery of part of cargo—Cargo interests alleging theft by carrier—Action brought outside one-year limitation period prescribed by Hague Visby Rules for claims in respect of carriage of goods—Whether claim for misdelivery subject to one-year limitation period—Carriage of Goods by Sea Act 1971, Sch, art II, art III, para 6. **Cia Portorafti Commerciale SA v Ultramar Panama Inc** [1990] 3 967, CA.

Time limit for bringing action—Wrong or misdelivery of cargo—Cargo interests bringing action against carrier claiming damages for short delivery of cargo—Cargo interests alleging theft by carrier—Action brought outside one-year limitation period prescribed by Hague Visby Rules for claims in respect of carriage of goods—Whether claim subject to one-year limitation period—Carriage of Goods by Sea Act 1971, Sch, art II, art III, para 6. **Cia Portorafti Commerciale SA v Ultramar Panama Inc** [1990] 3 967, CA.

Damages for conversion—
Measure of damages—Parties entering into contract for carriage of cargo of copper cathodes—Fraudsters attempting to acquire delivery of cargo—Shipowners preventing goods from being released—Consignees seeking damages for conversion—Whether damages limited by operation of Hague Rules or Hague-Visby Rules—Whether consignee entitled to claim consequential losses including hedging losses—Whether damages to be assessed at time of conversion or at time of judgment. **Trafigura Beheer BV v Mediterranean Shipping Co SA** [2007] 2 Comm 149, QBD.

Measure of damages—Parties entering into contract for carriage of cargo of copper cathodes—Fraudsters attempting to acquire delivery of cargo—Shipowners preventing goods from being released—Consignees seeking damages for conversion—Whether Hague Rules or Hague-Visby Rules applicable to bill of lading—Meaning of 'compulsorily applicable'. **Trafigura Beheer BV v Mediterranean Shipping Co SA** [2008] 1 Comm 385, CA.

Insurance. *See* **Marine insurance**.

Mixture of goods. *See* **Carriers** (Contract—Carriage of goods—Mixture of goods).

Passengers. *See* Passengers—Carriage by sea, *below*.

Seaworthiness of vessel—
Charterparty incorporating Hague Rules. *See* Charterparty—Seaworthiness of vessel, *below*.

Charterparty—
Anticipatory breach—
Repudiation. *See* **Contract** (Repudiation—Anticipatory breach—Charterparty).
Arbitration—
Arbitration clause. *See* Charterparty—Arbitration clause, *below*.
Award—Generally. *See* **Arbitration** (Award).
Commencement. *See* **Arbitration** (Commencement—Charterparty).
Error on face of award—Setting aside award. *See* **Arbitration** (Award—Setting aside award—Error on face of award—Construction of clause in charterparty).

Identity of parties—First claimant signing charterparty as vessel's owner without qualification—Arbitration carried on between defendant and second claimant as owner—Whether first or second claimant or both party to charterparty and arbitration—Whether arbitrators having power to substitute name of second claimant for that of first claimant. **Internaut Shipping GmbH v Fercometal SARL** [2003] 2 Comm 760, CA.

Arbitration clause—
Charterparties providing for payment of commission to broker—Whether broker entitled to refer disputes to arbitration—Contracts (Rights of Third Parties) Act 1999, ss 1, 8. **Nisshin Shipping Co Ltd v Cleaves & Co Ltd** [2004] 1 Comm 481, QBD.

Construction—Charterparty providing for arbitration to be 'held in Hong Kong' and 'English law to be applied'—Claimant referring dispute to arbitration in England—Arbitrator determining he had jurisdiction to determine dispute—Defendant's application to set aside final arbitral award and for declaration tribunal had not been properly constituted—Whether arbitration subject to English or Hong Kong curial law—Whether seat of arbitration linked to governing procedure of arbitration. **Shagang South-Asia (Hong Kong) Trading Co Ltd v Daewoo Logistics** [2015] 1 Comm 545, QBD.

Construction—Head charter providing for Japanese law and jurisdiction—Sub-charter providing for English law and jurisdiction in disputes not involving head charterer—Dispute arising under sub-charter—Whether choice of law clause void for uncertainty—Whether jurisdiction clause void for uncertainty. **Sonatrach Petroleum Corp v Ferrell International Ltd** [2002] 1 Comm 627, QBD.

SHIPPING (cont)—
    Charterparty (cont)—
        Arbitration clause (cont)—
            Construction—Owners claiming demurrage from charterers—Charterers admitting claim but failing to make payment in full—Charterparty providing for 'any dispute' to be referred to arbitration—Whether failure to pay admitted claim constituting dispute within meaning of charterparty. **Exfin Shipping (India) Ltd Mumbai v Tolani Shipping Co Ltd Mumbai** [2006] **2 Comm** 938, QBD.

            Construction—Shelltime form—Owners purporting to rescind charterparty for fraud and bribery—Whether dispute arising 'under' charterparty—Whether arbitration clause surviving rescission of charterparty—Arbitration Act 1996, s 7. **Fiona Trust & Holding Corp v Privalov** [2007] **1 Comm** 81, QBD; [2007] **1 Comm** 891, CA; [2007] **2 Comm** 1053, HL; [2007] **4** 951, HL.

            Construction—Whether Hague-Visby Rules incorporated by 'paramount clause'—Whether fax sent to potential arbitrator and copied to owners constituting notice commencing arbitration—Arbitration Act 1996, s 14(4). **Seabridge Shipping AB v AC Orssleff's Eftf's A/S** [2000] **1 Comm** 415, QBD.

            Incorporation in bill of lading. *See* Bill of lading—Incorporation of terms of charterparty—Arbitration clause, *above.*

            Scope—All disputes arising during execution of the charterparty—Discharge of vessel stopped by shipowners—Vessel twice arrested by charterers—Claim by shipowners for wrongful arrest—Award by umpires in favour of shipowners—Jurisdiction of umpire to make award. **Astro Valiente Cia Naviera SA v Mabanaft GmbH** [1971] **2** 1301, QBD and CA.

            Scope—Whether dispute governed by charterparty or bill of lading. *See* **Arbitration** (Agreement—Arbitration clause—Scope—Clause in charterparty).

            Time for bringing claims under. *See* Charterparty—Time for bringing claims under arbitration clause, *above.*

    Arrived ship. *See* Commencement of lay days, *below.*

    Bareboat charterparty—
        Description of vessel—Bareboat charter of new vessel—Charterparty providing vessel to be constructed in accordance with its building contract and specifications—Charterer alleging vessel not supplied with buyer's supplies—Buyer's supplies defined in building contract as items buyer was to provide—Whether terms of charter obliging disponent owner to supply vessel to disponent charterer with buyer's supplies. **BW Gas AS v JAS Shipping Ltd** [2011] **1 Comm** 236, CA.

        Termination—Withdrawal of vessel for non-payment of hire—Waiver of right to terminate—Owner making demands for hire in respect of successive periods of hire—Owner terminating charterparty and withdrawing vessel—Notice of termination referring to earlier demands for hire but not last two demands—Whether last demands for hire constituting waiver of right to terminate for non-payment of hire in respect of earlier periods of charter. **Parbulk II A/S v Heritage Maritime Ltd SA** [2012] **2 Comm** 418, QBD.

    Berth charterparty—
        Arrived ship under berth charterparty. *See* Commencement of lay days—Arrived ship under berth charterparty, *below.*

    Breach—
        Repudiation. *See* **Contract** (Repudiation—Anticipatory breach—Charterparty).

    Conditions and warranties—
        Appellant chartering vessel from respondent—Clause of charterparty requiring owners to exercise due diligence in maintaining and restoring certain defects—Whether clause applied to defects existing when vessel delivered—Shelltime 4 charterparty, cl 3(i). **Poseidon Schiffahrt GmbH v Nomadic Navigation Co Ltd** [1999] **1 Comm** 454, CA.

        Misrepresentation—Reliance—Shipowner's circular containing unrealistic performance data relating to vessel provided to charterer in pre-contract negotiations—Charterparty containing performance warranty and compensation payable for over-consumption of fuel—High fuel consumption leading to purported rescission of charterparty by charterer—Whether representation as to expected performance implicit in representation as to actual performance in past—Whether shipowner's willingness to contract on terms eventually agreed amounting to repetition of misrepresentations previously made—Whether representation on fuel consumption inducing charterer to enter charterparty. **SK Shipping Europe Ltd v Capital VLCC 3 Corp** [2022] **2 Comm** 784, CA.

        Obligation to provide cargo—Obligation to nominate berth—Obligation to load—Time in which to be performed—Whether warranties or conditions. **Universal Cargo Carriers Corp v Citati** [1957] **3** 234, CA.

    Consecutive voyage charterparty—
        Charterparty to remain in force for two consecutive voyages—Deviation in first voyage—Whether charterers bound to make second voyage. **Cie Primera de Navagaziona de Panama and Cia Arrendataria de Monopolis de Petroleos SA, Re Arbitration between** [1939] **4** 81, CA.

        Frustration. *See* Charterparty—Frustration—Delay—Consecutive voyage charterparty, *above.*

        Right to substitute vessel—Construction—Charterparty for series of voyages by named ship—Clause giving owners liberty to substitute another ship—Right of owners to make more than one substitution. **Maritime et Commerciale of Geneva (SA) v Anglo-Iranian Oil Co Ltd** [1954] **1** 529, CA.

        Unseaworthiness of vessel—Damages—Incompetence of engine room staff—Whether damages assessed solely in relation to the voyage in which breach occurred. **Adamastos Shipping Co Ltd v Anglo-Saxon Petroleum Co Ltd** [1958] **1** 725, HL.

    Construction—
        BIMCO Non-Payment of Hire Clause for Time Charter Parties incorporated into charterparty—Charterers underpaying fourth hire instalment—Owners relying on BIMCO Clause to withdraw vessel after fifth and sixth hire instalments not making up shortfall—Arbitral tribunal ruling BIMCO Clause not engaged and owners in breach of charterparty—Whether possible to withdraw vessel under BIMCO Clause when breach relating to non-payment for earlier period of hire. **Quiana Navigation SA v Pacific Gulf Shipping (Singapore) Pte Ltd** [2020] **2 Comm** 252, QBD.

SHIPPING (cont)—
    Charterparty (cont)—
        Construction (cont)—

Charterparty and sub-charterparties containing BIMCO clause providing for reimbursement of US gross transport tax—Owner of vessel paying tax—Charterer reimbursing owner and seeking reimbursement from sub-charterer—Whether liability to reimburse cascading down chain of charterers. **Global Maritime Investments Ltd v STX Pan Ocean Co Ltd, The Dimitiris L** [2013] **1 Comm** 645, QBD.

Charterparty clause obliging charterers to pay for bunkers on board at time of redelivery at the 'price actually paid'—Charterers sub-chartering vessel to third party—Sub-charter requiring fixed prices payment for bunkers on delivery and redelivery—Charterers paying third party fixed price for bunkers on redelivery—Charterers sub-chartering vessel to owners—Fall in market rate for bunker prices—Owners paying lower market rate for bunkers during sub-charter—Vessel redelivered to charterers—Charterers claiming clause requiring owners to pay bunker prices as paid under sub-charter with third party—Whether 'price actually paid' meaning price paid by party seeking reimbursement or price paid when bunkers stemmed. **Eitzen Bulk A/S v TTMI Sarl** [2012] **2 Comm** 100, Comm Ct.

Charterparty on amended BIMCO SupplyTime 2017 Charter Party for Offshore Support Vessels form—Non-payment of invoices for hire of vessel and other services—Arbitral tribunal construing payments clause in owners' favour—Proper construction of payments clause—Arbitration Act 1996, s 69. **Boskalis Offshore Marine Contracting BV v Atlantic Marine and Aviation LLP** [2020] **1 Comm** 323, QBD.

Charterparty on amended Gencon 94 form—Fixture recap providing for notice of readiness to be tendered within 'port limits'—Vessel proceeding to congested loading port—Vessel unable to proceed straight to berth and anchoring at location directed by port authority—Whether vessel within 'Port limits'. **Navalmar UK Ltd v Kale Maden Hammaddeler Sanayi Ve Ticart AS** [2017] **2 Comm** 1033, QBD.

Claimant owners chartering vessel to respondent charterers—Charterparty providing that owners having right to withdraw vessel in default of payment after giving notice to charterers—Charterparty providing that owners entitled to suspend performance of obligations while payment remaining due—Charterers not paying hire—Owners purporting to suspend performance—Arbitrators finding as matter of construction that owners required to give notice before suspending performance of obligations—Owners appealing—Whether owners required to give charterers notice before suspending performance of obligations due to non-payment of hire. **Greatship (India) Ltd v Oceanografia SA de CV, The Greatship Dhriti** [2013] **1 Comm** 1244, QBD.

Demurrage—Clause providing for payment of increased demurrage rates in specified event—Delay in discharging cargo caused by charterers—Owners claiming demurrage at escalated rate, and bunkers consumed, for period during which vessel waiting to discharge—Whether demurrage payable at ordinary contractual rate or escalated rate—Whether term should be implied into charterparty allowing owners to claim demurrage at escalated rate. **Gard Shipping AS v Clearlake Shipping Pte Ltd** [2017] **2 Comm** 179, QBD.

Demurrage—Determination of date of discharge—Claim under charterparty requiring notification to charterer within 30 days of discharge—Whether date of completion of discharge to be determined by local time at place of discharge or according to time zone of recipient of notice. **Euronav NV v Repsol Trading SA** [2022] **2 Comm** 65, Comm Ct.

Identity of parties—Claimant charterers of four vessels claiming damages for breach of charterparties by first to fourth defendants as registered owners of vessels—Charterers contending charterparties fixed by fifth defendant as agent of owners—Proper approach to question of identity of parties to charters—Whether owners coming within phrase 'disponent owner' in charterparties—Whether fifth defendant having authority to act on behalf of owners—Whether defendants liable to charterers. **Navig8 Inc v South Vigour Shipping Inc** [2016] **2 Comm** 159, QBD.

Implied term. *See* **Contract** (Construction—Implied term—Charterparty).

In-transit loss (ITL) clause—Hague-Visby exceptions—Charter on amended BPVOY3 form—Loss of cargo of oil by piracy—Charterer claiming shipowner liable for loss pursuant to ITL clause in charterparty—Judge finding lost cargo not ITL or 'cargo loss' within meaning of clause—Judge further finding clause imposing liability on shipowner subject to Hague-Visby exceptions—Whether judge erring—BPVOY3, cl 46. **Trafigura Beheer BV v Navigazione Montanari SpA** [2016] **2 Comm** 119, CA.

Nature and status of classification obligation in charterparty—Claimant owners applying for final injunction against defendant charterers requiring delivery up of vessel—Arbitral tribunal construing classification obligation to be qualified rather than absolute—Tribunal holding classification obligation not to be condition of charterparty rather an intermediate term—Whether tribunal correct—Arbitration Act 1996, s 69. **Silverburn Shipping (IoM) Ltd v Ark Shipping Co LLC** [2019] **2 Comm** 914, QBD.

Signing subject clause—Charter on amended Supplytime 89 form—Defendant signing every page of charterparty—Claimant not signing every page—Whether both parties required to sign every term of charterparty—Whether claimant waiving signing requirement. **Oceanografia SA de CV v DSND Subsea AS** [2007] **1 Comm** 28, QBD.

'Subjects'—Arbitration clause contained in voyage charterparty—Fixture said to be subject to shippers/receivers' approval—Charterers freeing vessel after inspection failing to take place—Whether subjects lifted—Whether binding arbitration agreement entered into—Arbitration Act 1996, s 67. **DHL Project & Chartering Ltd v Gemini Ocean Shipping Co Ltd** [2022] **2 Comm** 732, Comm Ct.

'Subjects'—Suppliers' approval subject—Parties reaching in principle agreement for charter of vessel subject to Stem/Suppliers/Receivers/Management approval—Charterers lifting all subjects other than suppliers' approval subject—Charterers subsequently purporting to pull out of fixture—Whether binding charterparty concluded. **Nautica Marine Ltd v Trafigura Trading LLC** [2021] **1 Comm** 1157, Comm Ct.

Time charterparty. *See* Time charterparty—One time charter trip, *below.*

Charterparty (cont)—
Construction (cont)—
Voyage charterparty—Obligation to proceed with all convenient speed to loading port—Owners providing no estimated time of arrival at port of loading—Whether absolute obligation to commence approach voyage to port of loading at reasonable date. **CSSA Chartering and Shipping Services SA v Mitsui OSK Lines Ltd** [2018] **2 Comm** 62, QBD; [2019] **1 Comm** 875, CA.
Damage to harbour—
Chartered vessel damaging jetty—Owner of vessel liable to undertakers of harbour—Whether bareboat demise charterer of vessel constituting 'owner'—Harbours, Docks and Piers Clauses Act 1847, s 74—Zetland County Council Act 1974, s 4. **BP Exploration Operating Co Ltd v Chevron Transport (Scotland)** [2002] **1 Comm** 1, HL.
Dangerous cargo—
Duty of charterer not to ship dangerous goods—Exclusion of 'acids, explosives, arms, ammunition, or other dangerous cargo'—Turpentine—Ejusdem generis rule—Acceptance of cargo by master—Breach of charterparty by charterer—Liability to damages—Delay in unloading—Amount of damages—Limitation by terms of demurrage clause—USA Carriage of Goods Act 1936, s 4(6) (Carriage of Goods by Sea Act 1924, Sch, art IV, r 6). **Chandris v Isbrandtsen-Moller Co Inc** [1950] **1** 768, KBD.
Rats introduced with cargo of soyabean meal pellets—Whether dangerous cargo—Carriage of Goods by Sea Act 1971, Sch 1, art IV, r 6. **Bunge SA v Adm Do Brasil Ltd** [2010] **1 Comm** 784, QBD.
Deadfreight claim—
Minimum cargo above which charterers not liable for deadfreight claim—Conditions of load port such that vessel unable to load minimum cargo—Master informing charterers of restricted amount of cargo which vessel actually able to load at berth—Whether charterers entitled to bring deadfreight claim. **AIC Ltd v Marine Pilot Ltd** [2008] **2 Comm** 545, CA.
Delivery of cargo—
Delay—Measure of damages—Late delivery of goods due to deliberate breach of charterparty by deviation—Charterparty containing no liberty to deviate—Fall in market price of cargo between date ship should have arrived and date of actual arrival. **Heron II, The** [1967] **3** 686, HL.
Delay—Port authority ordering vessel off-berth and refusing to allow discharge of cargo unless provided with guarantee—Whether vessel 'detained' by reason of order of port authority—Whether charterers or owners responsible for providing security. **Nippon Yusen Kaisha Ltd v Scindia Steam Navigation Co Ltd** [2000] **1 Comm** 700, CA.
Letters of indemnity (LOI) issued in favour of disponent owners by charterers—Voyage charter containing time limit on validity of letter of indemnity—Whether LOI subject to time limit. **Navig8 Chemicals Pool Inc v Glencore Agriculture BV** [2019] **1 Comm** 1085, CA.
Owner requested to deliver cargo to named party without bills of lading—Letter of indemnity provided by each charterer to disponent owner—Holder of bills of lading arresting vessel—Owner providing security to secure release of vessel and seeking substitute security under letters of indemnity—Whether obligation under letters of indemnity discharged when vessel released—Whether charterers' undertakings conditional on delivery to named party. **Farenco Shipping Co Ltd v Daebo Shipping Co Ltd** [2009] **1 Comm** 423, QBD.
Short delivery—Damages—Loss and damage to cargo due to breaches of contract by both parties—Burden of proof—Onus on claimant to establish what part of loss was caused otherwise than by his breach of contract. **Government of Ceylon v Chandris** [1965] **3** 48, QBD.
Demise charter—
Beneficial ownership—Admiralty proceedings. *See* **Admiralty** (Jurisdiction—Action in rem—Beneficial ownership—Ship chartered on demise).
Demurrage—
Charterparty on amended Norgrain form—Application to court to determine preliminary question of law—Nature of demurrage payable under voyage charter when charterer failing to discharge vessel within laytime allowed—Whether owners entitled to damages in addition to demurrage for charterers' breach of contract. **K Line PTE Ltd v Priminds Shipping (HK) Co Ltd** [2021] **2 Comm** 719, Comm Ct.
Description of vessel—
Vessel not in existence at date of charterparty—Vessel identified by yard number and name of builders—Vessel built by different builders with different yard number under sub-contract—Original yard number used on export papers—Sub-contract builders a a subsidiary by builders named in charterparty—Whether words identifying vessel by reference to yard number and builders part of contractual description—Whether charterers entitled to refuse to take delivery of vessel on ground it failed to comply with description. **Reardon Smith Line Ltd v Hansen-Tangen** [1976] **3** 570, HL.
Exceptions—
Barratry—Vessel requisitioned by Spanish Republican Government—Refusal of crew to discharge vessel—Whether such conduct barratrous. **Cia Naviera Bachi v Hosegood (Henry) & Co Ltd** [1938] **2** 189, KBD.
Ice clause—Vessel damaged by ice—Notice of claim clause—Sufficiency of notice—Agency. **Rendal (A/S) v Arcos Ltd** [1937] **3** 577, HL.
Strikes. *See* Demurrage—Exceptions clause—Strikes, *below*.
War risks clause—Deviation and discharge of cargo by order of a 'Government'—Order of authorities not recognised as a government by United Kingdom government. **Luigi Monta of Genoa v Cechofracht Co Ltd** [1956] **2** 769, QBD.
Fire damaging cargo but not vessel—
Fire started by stevedores—Whether stevedores' fault transferring liability to charterers—Whether vessel off-hire—Whether failure of charterers to obtain dangerous cargo certificate transferring liability. **Macieo Shipping Ltd v Clipper Shipping Lines Ltd** [2000] **1 Comm** 920, QBD.
Fitness of vessel—
Tanker—Tanker classified as partially double-sided—Tanker not legally fit to carry permitted cargo of fuel oil—Charterparty requiring tanker to be in every way fit to carry cargo and in every way fit for service—Whether breach of terms of charterparty. **Golden Fleece Maritime Inc v ST Shipping and Transport Inc** [2008] **1 Comm** 497, QBD.

Charterparty (cont)—
Fitness of vessel (cont)—
Tanker—Vessel required to have on board documents and certificates required by applicable law—Vessel required to comply with all applicable conventions—International regulations coming into force during currency of charterparty requiring vessels carrying dirty petroleum products to be double sided—Vessels not fully double sided—Whether breach of terms of charterparty. **Golden Fleece Maritime Inc v ST Shipping and Transport Inc** [2009] **1 Comm** 908, CA.
Frustration—
Arbitration—Special case—Issue whether charterparty frustrated—Whether question of fact or question of law. **Angelia, The** [1973] **2** 144, QBD.
Delay—Charterer unable to load within lay days—Length of delay entitling owner to rescind—Delay must be long enough to frustrate charterparty—Assessment of length of delay question of fact. **Universal Cargo Carriers Corp v Citati** [1957] **3** 234, CA.
Delay—Consecutive voyage charterparty—Shipowners chartering vessel to charterers for six or seven consecutive voyages in 1979 season—Strike starting after completion of first voyage—Only two more voyages likely to be possible before end of 1979 season—Agreement by shipowners to charter vessel to charterers for seven voyages in 1980 season—Whether charterparty frustrated in whole or only in part. **Pioneer Shipping Ltd v BTP Tioxide Ltd** [1981] **2** 1030, HL.
Delay—Exception clause—Delay in loading cargo—Excepted cause in existence and ascertainable when charter made—Exception for unavoidable hindrances and causes or hindrances happening without the fault of the charterers—Delay in transporting cargo to port—Lack of transport—Consequent delay in loading frustrating charter—Lack of transport existing at time charter made—Lack of transport unknown to charterers and owners—Fact readily ascertainable by charterers on making enquiry—Whether exception clause giving protection when delay frustrating contract—Whether delay due to unavoidable hindrances in loading. **Angelia, The** [1973] **2** 144, QBD.
Delay—Unreasonable delay—Delay not necessarily constituting frustration. *See* **Contract** (Frustration—Delay—Unreasonable delay—Delay not necessarily constituting frustration—Charterparty).
Force majeure. *See* **Contract** (Frustration—Force majeure—Charterparty).
Liberty clause—Vegoilvoy standard form of Tanker Voyage Charterparty—Charterers cancelling charter before cargo made available on basis of ban on importation of vegetable oil at discharge port—Whether liberty clause excluding reliance on doctrine of frustration. **Select Commodities Ltd v Valdo SA** [2006] **2 Comm** 493, QBD.
War—Vessel under charterparty trapped in Shatt al-Arab river by war between Iran and Iraq—Whether declaration of war between Iran and Iraq automatically frustrating charterparty. **Finelvet AG v Vinava Shipping Co Ltd** [1983] **2** 658, QBD.
Hire—
Off-hire clause. *See* Charterparty—Off-hire clause, *below.*
Implied term—
Arrival of ship under port charterparty—Commencement of lay days. *See* Commencement of lay days—Arrived ship under port charterparty—Implied term, *below.*
Indemnity—Bill of lading—Clause paramount—Charterparty containing clause exempting shipowners from liability for cargo damage—Charterparty also containing bill of lading clause providing for liability under the Hague Rules—Cargo owners claiming against shipowners for damage to cargo—Shipowners settling cargo owners' claim and claiming indemnity from charterers—Whether clause exempting shipowners from liability or bill of lading clause prevailing—Whether implied term of charterparty that charterers bound to indemnify shipowners for liability incurred to cargo owners. **Ben Shipping Co (Pte) Ltd v An Bord Bainne** [1986] **2** 177, QBD.
Indemnity—Limitation of action. *See* **Limitation of action** (Indemnity—Accrual of cause of action—Charterparty).
Incorporation of amended Centrocon arbitration clause—
Whether applicable between owners and charterers. **Tradax Export SA v Volkswagenwerk AG** [1969] **2** 144, QBD.
Incorporation of bill of lading—
Incorporation of United States Paramount clause—Application to charterparty of United States Carriage of Goods by Sea Act 1936—Whether paramount clause must be rejected as insensible—Whether loss or damage excepted by s 4(2)(a) of the Act includes loss of services of vessel—Whether damages assessed solely in relation to the voyage in which the breach occurred—United States Carriage of Goods by Sea Act 1936 (Public Statutes No 521), preamble, ss 3(1), 4(1), (2), 5, 13. **Adamastos Shipping Co Ltd v Anglo-Saxon Petroleum Co Ltd** [1958] **1** 725, HL.
Incorporation of Hague Rules. *See* **Arbitration** (Commencement—Charterparty—Time-bar—Incorporation of Hague Rules).
Incorporation of paramount clause—
No qualifying words included—Whether Hague Rules incorporated into charterparty—Carriage of Goods by Sea Act 1924, Sch, art III, r 6. **Nea Agrex SA v Baltic Shipping Co Ltd** [1976] **2** 842, CA.
Paramountcy of Hague Rules—Charter warranting for vessel to perform laden passage at specific speed—Vessel unable to maintain speed—Whether warranty conflicting with Hague Rules incorporated by clause paramount. **Bayoil SA v Seawind Tankers Corp** [2001] **1 Comm** 392, QBD.
Incorporation of pro forma terms—
Fixture recap providing for discharging on Sundays and holidays—Pro forma terms including Sundays and holidays but excluding super holidays—Whether inconsistency between fixture recap and pro forma terms. **Cobelfret Bulk Carriers NV v Swissmarine Services SA** [2010] **2 Comm** 128, QBD.
Incorporation of terms in bill of lading. *See* Bill of lading—Incorporation of terms of charterparty, *above.*
Indemnity—
Implied term. *See* Charterparty—Implied term—Indemnity, *above.*

SHIPPING (cont)—
  Charterparty (cont)—
    Injunction—
      Anti-suit injunction. *See* **Injunction** (Anti-suit injunction—Charterparties containing English law and arbitration clauses).
    Loading—
      Laycan—Term of charterparty narrowing spread of laycan—Whether condition precedent to nomination of vessel—Whether breach of charterparty repudiatory. **Universal Bulk Carriers Ltd v Andre et Cie SA** [2001] **2 Comm** 510, CA.
      Unseaworthiness—Charterers failing to ensure proper lashing of timber cargo—Cargo falling overboard and damaging vessel—Whether owners under obligation to intervene to prevent vessel sailing in unseaworthy condition. **Transocean Liners Reederei GmbH v Euxine Shipping Co Ltd** [1999] **1 Comm** 724, QBD.
      Vessel chartered on New York Product Exchange (1946) form—Cargo exploding leading to damage to vessel—Whether owners owing charterers duty to intervene in loading to prevent vessel sailing in unseaworthy condition. **Compania Sud American Vapores v Hamburg** [2006] **2 Comm** 1, QBD.
    Loading of cargo—
      New York Produce Exchange (1981) form—Obligation on master to reject any cargo subject to clausing of bills of lading—Master refusing to accept cargo on that basis—What circumstances entitling master to reject cargo. **Sea Success Maritime Inc v African Maritime Carriers Ltd** [2005] **2 Comm** 441, QBD.
      Vessel unable to complete loading owing to adverse weather conditions—Whether absolute obligation on owner to load full and complete cargo. **China Offshore Oil (Singapore) International Pte Ltd v Giant Shipping Ltd** [2001] **1 Comm** 429, QBD.
    Negligence exception clause—
      Clause providing that captain shall prosecute his voyages with utmost dispatch—Breach—Claim for damages—No finding of negligence—Liability of shipowners. **Suzuki & Co Ltd v T Beynon & Co Ltd** [1926] **Rep** 536, HL.
    Nomination of berth—
      Port charterparty. *See* Port charterparty—Nomination of berth, *below.*
    Off-hire clause—
      Charterparty containing off-hire clause in event vessel 'captured or seized or detained or arrested by any authority or by any legal process'—Vessel—Clause permitting transit through 'Gulf of Aden' with suspension of hire in event of piracy—Vessel captured by pirates in Arabian Sea—Meaning of 'captured or seized or detained or arrested by any authority or by any legal process'—Meaning of 'Gulf of Aden' in time charter—Arbitration Act 1996, s 69. **Eleni Shipping Ltd v Transgrain Shipping BV** [2019] **2 Comm** 667, QBD.
      Charterparty containing off-hire clause in the event of 'capture/seizure, or detention or threatened detention by any authority'—Vessel sailing off coast of Somalia when hijacked by pirates—Vessel released after owners paying ransom—Charterers claiming vessel being off-hire whilst subject to hijacking—Owners arguing capture required to be by an authority and pirates not constituting 'authority' so that vessel not off-hire during period of hijacking—Whether capture required to be by an authority in order to constitute off-hire event. **Osmium Shipping Corp v Cargill International SA** [2012] **2 Comm** 197, QBD.
      Head owners of vessel chartering vessel to disponent owners—Disponent owners entering into charterparty with charterers—Clauses in charterparty providing for drydocking and cancellation of charterparty where more than 30 days delay—Permission sought from charterers by owners on behalf of headowners to use vessel for short voyage before drydocking—Total delay including drydocking exceeding 30 days—Whether charterers entitled to cancel balance of charterparty. **HBC Hamburg Bulk Carriers GmbH & Co KG v Tangshan Haixing Shipping Co Ltd** [2007] **1 Comm** 1127, QBD.
      Loss of time from default of the master—Cargo rejected at initial discharge port—Vessel proceeding to international waters where instructed to proceed to new discharge port—Issues arising with bills of lading—Vessel drifting in international waters whilst issues with bills of lading resolved—Whether vessel off-hire during drifting period. **Minerva Navigation Inc v Oceana Shipping AG, The Athena** [2013] **2 Comm** 28, QBD.
      Vessel chartered to sub-charterer—Charterparty providing for termination by sub-charterer where vessel off-hire for more than 20 consecutive days—Vessel bound for Shanghai—Vessel suffering damage and proceeding to Hong Kong instead—Vessel's new route identical to sub-charterer's route for one-and-a-half days before deviation—Whether vessel off-hire for 20 consecutive days. **TS Lines Ltd v Delphis NV** [2010] **1 Comm** 434, QBD.
    Payment in foreign currency—
      Date at which rate of exchange calculated—Demurrage payable in dollars. *See* **Money** (Currency—Date at which rate of exchange calculated—Charterparty providing for demurrage to be calculated in dollars).
    Port charterparty. *See* Port charterparty, *below.*
    Pre-trial or post-judgment relief. *See* **Practice** (Pre-trial or post-judgment relief—Disclosure in aid of enforcement—Dispute under charterparty containing English law and litigation clause).
    Proper law. *See* **Conflict of laws** (Contract—Proper law of contract—Charterparty).
    Repudiation—
      Anticipatory breach. *See* **Contract** (Repudiation—Anticipatory breach).
      Election whether to accept repudiation. *See* **Contract** (Repudiation—Election whether to accept repudiation—Charterparty).
      Generally. *See* **Contract** (Repudiation—Charterparty).
      Renunciation of breach—Owners of vessel claiming charterers renouncing charterparty—Owners purporting to terminate charterparty on account of renunciation—Arbitral tribunal finding owners not entitled to damages because owners affirming charterparty before termination and owners themselves repudiating charterparty after affirming charterparty—Whether tribunal erring. **White Rosebay Shipping SA v Hong Kong Chain Glory Shipping Ltd, The Fortune Plum** [2013] **2 Comm** 449, QBD.

Berth charter—Charterparty specifying loading port but not loading berth—Berth to be nominated by charterers—No express warranty of safety of loading port or berth—Owners warranting that satisfied with port specifications—Vessel sustaining damage as result of contact with underwater projection at loading berth—Arbitrators finding charterers not obliged to nominate safe berth—Whether charterers having implied obligation to nominate safe loading berth—Whether error of law in arbitrators' decision. **Mediterranean Salvage and Towage Ltd v Seamar Trading and Commerce Inc** [2009] **1 Comm** 411, QBD.

Berth charter—Implied term—Charterparty specifying loading port but not loading berth—Berth to be nominated by charterers—No express warranty of safety of loading port or berth—Vessel sustaining damage as result of contact with hidden underwater projection at loading berth—Whether charterparty containing implied warranty of safety of nominated berth. **Mediterranean Salvage and Towage Ltd v Seamar Trading and Commerce Inc** [2010] **1 Comm** 1, CA.

Warranty that berth 'always accessible'—Whether 'always accessible' including departure as well as entry. **Seatrade Group NV v Hakan Agro DMCC** [2018] **2 Comm** 843, QBD.

Safe port—
Charterparty providing for loading 'one safe port Ventspils'—Whether clause amounting to warranty by charterers as to safety of load port. **AIC Ltd v Marine Pilot Ltd** [2008] **2 Comm** 545, CA.

Deadfreight claim—Master of vessel indicating weight vessel able to carry due to draft restrictions caused by silting of channel leading to loading port—Weight below minimum contractual weight specified in order to avoid deadfreight claim—Charterer giving notice of minimum weight to be carried but agreeing to reduced amount—Owners bringing deadfreight claim and seeking damages for breach of safe port clause in alternative—Whether notice given by charterer of legal effect—Whether charterer warranting safety of loading port. **AIC Ltd v Marine Pilot Ltd** [2007] **2 Comm** 189, QBD.

Insurance—Owner's right to insure vessel against risks of unsafety arising from breach of charterer's duty with respect to safety of vessel—Whether owner's right to insure freeing charterer from liability for risks of unsafety arising after vessel's arrival at port which was prospectively safe at date of nomination. **Kodros Shipping Corp v Empresa Cubana de Fletes** [1982] **3** 350, HL.

Obligation of charterer to nominate safe port—Prospective safety—Unexpected and abnormal event—Port becoming unsafe after nomination and after arrival—Whether charterer in breach of obligation to nominate safe port—Whether charterer's obligation to nominate safe port amounting to a warranty. **Kodros Shipping Corp v Empresa Cubana de Fletes** [1982] **3** 350, HL.

Obligation of charterer to nominate safe port—Vessel delayed at port nominated by charterers—Delay caused by grounding of vessels due to misalignment of buoys—Owners claiming loss arising from delay—Whether charterers in breach of safe port clause. **Independent Petroleum Group Ltd v Seacarriers Count Pte Ltd** [2007] **1 Comm** 882, QBD.

Obligation of charterer to nominate safe port—Vessel discharging cargo at port nominated by charterer—Vessel leaving berth due to heavy seas and severe winds—Vessel colliding with breakwater whilst attempting to navigate to open sea—Whether port unsafe. **Gard Marine & Energy Ltd v China National Chartering Co Ltd** [2013] **2 Comm** 1058, QBD, CA; [2015] **2 Comm** 894, QBD, CA; [2018] **1 Comm** 1, SC; [2018] **1** 832, SC.

Obligation of charterer to nominate safe port—Vessel discharging cargo at port nominated by charterer—Vessel leaving berth due to heavy seas and severe winds—Vessel colliding with breakwater whilst attempting to navigate to open sea—Whether port unsafe—Whether causal link between unsafe port and casualty. **Gard Marine & Energy Ltd v China National Chartering Co Ltd** [2013] **2 Comm** 1058, QBD, CA; [2015] **2 Comm** 894, QBD, CA.

Whether port must be politically safe as well as physically safe. **Kodros Shipping Corp v Empresa Cubana de Fletes** [1982] **3** 350, HL.

Sale of chartered ship—
Purchase with notice of charterparty—Ship subsequently requisitioned—Whether purchaser bound by charterparty—Whether owners received compensation as trustees for charterers—Compensation (Defence) Act 1939, ss 4, 15. **Port Line Ltd v Ben Line Steamers Ltd** [1958] **1** 787, QBD.

Seaworthiness of vessel—
Due diligence—Loss due to act, neglect or default of the master—Ship unseaworthy at commencement of voyage—Unskilful loading of bunkers during voyage—Claim for general average. **Smith Hogg & Co Ltd v Black Sea and Baltic General Insurance Co Ltd** [1940] **3** 405, HL.

Due diligence—Obligation of owners to make vessel seaworthy—Whether obligation absolute—Failure of engine part—Owners delegating obligation and subsequent investigation to independent contractor—Whether owners establishing exercise of due diligence in absence of evidence regarding independent contractor. **Eridania SpA v Oetker** [2000] **2 Comm** 108, CA.

Implied warranty—Vessel in need of special permission to load cargo from authorities at stipulated port of loading—Whether need of permission breach of implied warranty of seaworthiness—Whether additional warranty by shipowners to use reasonably diligence to obtain permission, and to obtain it within a reasonable time, to be implied. **Cie Algerienne de Meunerie v Katana Soc di Navigatione Maritima Spa** [1960] **2** 55, CA.

Obligation of owners to make vessel seaworthy—Ship carrying too much cargo to pass through Panama Canal—Ship fully efficient in all other respects—Whether ship unseaworthy—Carriage of Goods by Sea Act 1936 (USA), Sch (Hague Rules), art III, r 1 (a). **Actis Co Ltd v Sanko Steamship Co Ltd** [1982] **1** 390, CA.

Owners' obligation to obtain and retain necessary certificates, documents etc—Vessel operating in coal and iron ore markets—Ship vetting system known as 'RightShip' used in coal and iron ore markets—Whether owners required under terms of an amended New York Produce Exchange charterparty to obtain and retain RightShip approval for vessel. **Seagate Shipping Ltd v Glencore International AG** [2009] **1 Comm** 148, QBD.

Termination—
Notice. See **Contract** (Termination—Notice).

SHIPPING (cont)—
  Charterparty (cont)—
    Time charter—
      Freight—Implied terms—Owners' right to freight due under bills of lading—Whether charterparty
        containing implied obligation owners would not revoke charterers' authority to collect from
        sub-charterers freight payable under bills of lading unless hire and/or sums were due to owners
        under charterparty. **Alpha Marine Corp v Minmetals Logistics Zhejiang Co Ltd** [2022] **1
        Comm** 974, QBD.
      Generally. *See* Time charterparty, *below.*
      Loss of freight—Insurance claim—Exemption clause—Claim consequent on loss of time. *See*
        Marine insurance (Freight—Exemption clause—Claim consequent on loss of time—Time charter).
      Withdrawal—Waiver—Act of agent constituting waiver—Default in payment of hire—Right of
        withdrawal arising on default—Payment tendered before right of withdrawal exercised—Payment
        received by owner's bank—Owner instructing bank to refuse payment on being informed of
        payment by bank—Whether act of bank in receiving payment constituting a waiver of owner's
        right of withdrawal by acceptance of payment. **Mardorf Peach & Co Ltd v Attica Sea Carriers Corp
        of Liberia** [1976] **2** 249, CA.
    Time for bringing claims—
      Arbitration clause. *See* Charterparty—Time for bringing claims under arbitration clause, *below.*
      Charterparty discharging charterers from liability unless owners brought claim within 90 days of
        vessel's discharge—Charterparty requiring owners to provide 'signed copy' of charterparty within
        90-day limit—Charterers providing owners with unsigned copy of charterparty within time limit—Owners claiming
        demurrage but failing to provide signed copy of charterparty within time limit—Whether owners'
        demurrage claim time-barred—Whether charterparty required to be signed by both owners and
        charterers. **Mira Oil Resources of Tortola v Bocimar NV** [1999] **1 Comm** 732, QBD.
      Suit barred unless brought within one year after delivery of goods or date on which goods should
        have been delivered—Consignee alleging goods contaminated and refusing delivery—Charterers
        ordering vessel to deliver cargo elsewhere—Action brought within one year of delivery at second
        port but more than one year from notice of readiness at original discharge port—Whether action
        time-barred—Carriage of Goods by Sea Act 1971, Schedule, art III, r 6. **Trafigura Beheer BV v
        Golden Stavraetos Maritime Inc** [2002] **2 Comm** 984, QBD; [2003] **2 Comm** 347, CA; [2003] **4** 746,
        CA.
    Time for bringing claims under arbitration clause—
      Application of clause—'All disputes ... arising out of this contract'—General average
        claim—Charterparty making special provision for general average—Arbitration clause providing
        time limit for claims—General average act occurring during voyage—Claim by owners for
        general average—Charterers disputing liability to make general average contribution—Whether a
        dispute 'arising out of' contract—Whether time limit applicable. **Union of India v EB Aaby's Rederi
        A/S** [1974] **2** 874, HL.
      Generally. *See* **Arbitration** (Commencement).
      Head charterparty containing Centrocon arbitration clause providing for cargo claims to be brought
        within 12 months of final discharge of cargo—Charterparty further stating that cargo claims be
        settled as per Inter-Club Agreement 1996 terms providing for written notification of claims to be
        given within 24 months of delivery of cargo—Sub-charterers settling claim in respect of carriage
        of cargo and bringing claim against charterers—Charterers bringing claim against
        owners—Neither claim brought within 12 months of final discharge of cargo—Whether 12-month
        or 24-month time limit applicable. **MH Progress Lines SA v Orient Shipping Rotterdam BV**
        [2012] **1 Comm** 1230, QBD.
      Incorporation of amended Centrocon arbitration clause—Whether applicable between owners and
        charterers. **Tradax Export SA v Volkswagenwerk AG** [1969] **2** 144, QBD.
      Waiver—New contract—Arbitration clause stipulating time limit for claims—Claim by owners for
        general average—Charterparty giving vessel lien on cargo for average—General average act
        occurring during voyage—Claim submitted by owners—Charterers giving undertaking to pay
        general average 'legally due' and requesting release of cargo—Owners acknowledging
        undertaking and releasing cargo—Charterers subsequently disputing liability for general
        average—Whether owners' claim under new contract—Whether time limit stipulated in
        arbitration clause applicable. **Union of India v EB Aaby's Rederi A/S** [1974] **2** 874, HL.
    War risks—
      Agreement to pay demurrage and/or dead freight if ship detained by any cause—Ship damaged
        beyond repair—Frustration. **D/SA/S Gulnes v Imperial Chemical Industries Ltd** [1938] **1** 24, KBD.
      Charterparty containing Conwartime clause preventing vessel from sailing where vessel, crew or
        cargo exposed to war risks—War risks including acts of piracy—Charterparty trading limits clause
        expressly excluding countries including Eritrea, Ethiopia, and Somalia but not Kenya—Trading
        limits clause permitting passing of Gulf of Aden where naval system present to reduce risk of
        piracy—Charterers instructing vessel to proceed to Mombasa, Kenya—Owner refusing
        instructions due to risk of piracy in Indian Ocean—No material increase in risk of piracy occurring
        since date of charterparty—Whether Conwartime clause requiring material increase in war risk
        after date of charterparty before owner's liberty to refuse to obey exercisable—Whether owner
        accepting risk of piracy in trading to Mombasa. **Taokas Navigation SA v Komrowski Bulk
        Shipping KG (GmbH & Co)** [2013] **1 Comm** 564, QBD.
      Charterparty containing Conwartime clause preventing vessel from sailing without written consent
        of owners where in reasonable judgment of master or owners vessel, crew or cargo 'may be'
        exposed to war risks—War risks including acts of piracy—Charterers instructing vessel to proceed
        through area where risk of piracy—Owners refusing to do so and claiming extra cost of
        proceeding via safe route—Meaning of words 'may be or are likely to be, exposed to War
        Risks'—Whether master or owner under duty to make reasonable enquiries to assess risk in
        exercise of discretion to withhold consent. **Pacific Basin IHX Ltd v Bulkhandling Handymax AS**
        [2012] **1 Comm** 639, QBD.
  Cif contract—
    Carriage by sea. *See* Carriage by sea—Cif contract, *above.*
    Sale of goods. *See* **Sale of goods** (C i f contract).

SHIPPING (cont)—
  Collision—
    Appeal—
      Whether appropriate for court to ask its own assessors questions not addressed by the court below. **Selat Arjuna, The (owners) v The Contship Success (owners)** [2000] **1 Comm** 905, CA.
    Causation—
      Novus actus interveniens—Refusal by plaintiffs of defendants' offer to tow—Plaintiffs' ship subsequently sinking and becoming a total loss—Reasonableness of refusal. **Guildford, The** [1956] **2** 915, Admin Ct.
      Novus actus interveniens—Salvage assistance declined until too late—Ship sinking in port of refuge some twenty hours after collision—Sinking not a direct result of collision. **Fritz Thyssen, The** [1967] **3** 117, CA.
    Collision regulations. See Collision regulations, below.
    Consequential damage—
      Beaching—Negligence by damaged vessel—Aggravation of damage. **Grainton (owners) v Genua (owners)** [1936] **2** 798, Admin Ct.
    Contributory negligence. See **Negligence** (Contributory negligence—Collision at sea).
    Costs—
      Both ships equally to blame—Costs should follow apportionment of blameworthiness. **Lucile Bloomfield, The** [1967] **2** 633, CA.
      Discretion of wreck commissioner—Reasons for exercise of discretion—Motor tanker and motor vessel colliding—Investigation ordered by Department of Trade—Master of tanker separately represented at hearing—Commissioner exonerating master of all blame—Master applying for costs of £3,600—Department not challenging amount of master's costs—Commissioner awarding £1,500 'in exercise of discretion as a contribution'—Commissioner giving no reasons for award—Whether commissioner having exercised his discretion judicially—Whether commissioner should state reasons for exercise of discretion—Merchant Shipping Act 1894, s 466(8). **R v Wreck Comr, ex p Knight** [1976] **3** 8, QBD.
    Court of formal investigation—
      Findings of court of formal investigation—Whether findings binding in subsequent collision action. See **Estoppel** (Issue estoppel—Shipping—Collision—Court of formal investigation).
    Damages—
      Generally. See Damages in collision cases, below.
      Interest. See **Interest** (Damages—Collision at sea).
    Limitation of action—
      Claimant ship owners bringing collision claims—Claimants being refused extension of time for issuing actions in personam—Whether claims time-barred—Whether extension of time required for bringing separate in personam proceedings—Merchant Shipping Act 1995, s 190. **Stolt Kestrel BV v Sener Petrol Denizcilik Ticaret AS** [2016] **1 Comm** 843, CA.
      Loss of life—Action by administratrix of deceased member of crew against owners of vessel—Action brought more than two years after collision in which deceased was injured—Whether two-year period applied to action brought against owners of ship on which deceased was carried as distinct from one brought against owners of the other vessel involved in the collision—Maritime Conventions Act 1911, s 8. **Niceto de Larrinaga, The** [1965] **2** 930, Admin Ct.
      Loss of life—Action for damages for loss of life—Action brought more than two years after casualty—Whether two-year period applied although ship sued was not in collision—Whether two-year period was affected by enactment of three-year period in relation to fatal accidents by s 3 of the Act of 1954—Discretion to extend two-year period—Maritime Conventions Act 1911, s 8—Law Reform (Limitation of Actions &c) Act 1954, s 3. **Alnwick, The** [1965] **2** 569, CA.
      Loss or damage to vessel—Collision between vessels—Parties agreeing mutual unlimited extension of time to commence proceedings subject to one month's notice—Claimant giving notice of intention to commence proceedings—Claimant issuing claim form—Defendant giving notice and issuing claim form for counterclaim more than one month after claimant's notice—Whether counterclaim out-of-time on true construction of agreement to extend time—Whether counterclaim subject to statutory limitation period—Whether time to be extended in favour of defendant—Merchant Shipping Act 1990, s 190. **Gold Shipping Navigation Co SA v Lulu Maritime Ltd** [2010] **2 Comm** 64, QBD.
      Loss or damage to vessel—Loss or damage caused by fault of another vessel—Loss or damage caused by collision or by fault of navigation without actual collision—Fault other than fault of navigation—Fault of management—Damage caused to vessel by fault of management of other vessel without collision—Whether action therefore subject to two year limitation period—Maritime Conventions Act 1911, s 8. **Norwhale, The** [1975] **2** 501, QBD.
    Negligence. See **Negligence** in collision cases, below.
    Ship leaving dock—
      Order of dock master—Liability of dock authority—Maritime Conventions Act 1911, s 1. **King Orry (owners) v Rockabill (owners)** [1937] **1** 191, CA.
    Towage—
      Negligent navigation—Collision between tug and passing vessel—No signal by tow to tug to warn her of on-coming vessel—Whether tug-owners or tow-owners liable for negligence of officer-in-charge of tug. **Panther, The, and The Ericbank** [1957] **1** 641, Admin Ct.
  Collision regulations—
    Crossing vessels—
      Convoys meeting on a crossing course—Crossing rule—Duties and obligations—Regulations for Preventing Collisions at Sea, rr 19, 21, 22. **A-G v Anglo-American Oil Co Ltd** [1946] **1** 359, CA.
      Crossing rule—Collision between two vessels just outside narrow channel at port of Jebel Ali in United Arab Emirates—One vessel disembarking her pilot during course of passage along narrow channel and another vessel waiting to embark same pilot—Liability in dispute between owners of vessels—Whether crossing rules applicable—Whether give-way vessel having to be on a steady course for crossing rules to apply—Apportionment of liability—International Regulations for Preventing Collisions at Sea 1972, rr 9, 15, 16, 17. **Nautical Challenge Ltd v Evergreen Marine (UK) Ltd** [2018] **1 Comm** 775, QBD; [2019] **1 Comm** 303, CA; [2021] **2 Comm** 907, SC; [2021] **4** 1113, SC.

Collision regulations (cont)—
Crossing vessels (cont)—
Give-way vessel failing to take appropriate action—Failure of stand-on vessel to take action avoiding collision by her manoeuvre alone—Apportionment—International Regulations for the Prevention of Collisions at Sea 1972, r 17. **Sitarem (owners) v Spirit (owners and/or demise charterers)** [2001] **2 Comm** 837, QBD.

Narrow channel rule—Apportionment of liability where multiple vessels at fault—Collision between two vessels in narrow channel outside port of Mumbai—Whether narrow channel in question being dredged channel marked on relevant admiralty chart—Whether narrow channel rule applying where vessel navigating outside dredged channel—Whether allegations of navigational fault made by parties substantiated—Whether degree of fault of non-parties to be taken into account upon apportioning liability—Merchant Shipping Act 1995, s 187—International Regulations for Preventing Collisions at Sea 1972, rr 5, 6, 9(a). **Nordlake, The** [2016] **2 Comm** 449, QBD.

Restricted visibility—Whether cause of collision failure of one vessel to take correct avoiding action—Use of VHF communications—Discretion of stand-on vessel to take avoiding action—International Regulations for the Prevention of Collisions at Sea 1972, r 17. **Mineral Dampier (owners and/or demise charterers of the) v Hanjin Madras (owners and/or demise charterers of the)** [2001] **2 Comm** 805, CA; **Mineral Dampier (owners and/or demise charterers) v Hanjin Madras (owners and/or demise charterers)** [2000] **1 Comm** 870, QBD.

Fog—
Use of radar. See Collision regulations—Use of radar in fog, *below*.

Lights—
'Vessel from any accident under command—Accident—Vessel towed and tugs under command—Standard of lighting—Regulations for Preventing Collisions at Sea (Sea Regulations 1910 (SR & O 1910 No 1113)), art 4(a), art 29—Merchant Shipping Act 1894, s 419(1). **Albion, The** [1953] **1** 978, CA.

Narrow channel—
Waiting at bend rule—Entrance to harbour—Harwich Harbour Conservancy Board (1929) Bye-laws, No 8. **Prinses Juliana, The** [1936] **1** 685, Admin Ct.

Observance—
Liability for infringement—Liability of master—Navigation of ship delegated to duly certificated officer of the watch—Infringement of collision regulations caused by act or omission of officer of the watch—Master not present on bridge at time of infringement and having no knowledge of infringement—Whether infringement of collision regulations an offence of strict liability—Whether master guilty of an offence—Merchant Shipping Act 1894, s 419(2). **Bradshaw v Ewart-James** [1983] **1** 12, QBD.

Overtaking vessel—
Vessel coming up with another vessel more than two points abaft her beam—Coming up with—Risk of collision—Degree of proximity required—Need to establish risk of collision exists before overtaking rule applies—Overtaking vessel ceasing to be more than two points abaft overtaken vessel's beam before risk of collision arising—Vessels on converging courses—Whether overtaking vessel to be regarded as 'coming up with' other vessel before risk of collision had arisen—Whether overtaking rule or crossing rule applicable—Whether overtaking or overtaken vessel under duty to give way—Collision Regulations (Ships and Seaplanes on the Water) and Signals of Distress (Ships) Order 1965 (SI 1965 No 1525), rr 19, 24. **Nowy Sacz, The** [1978] **2** 297, CA.

Radar—
Evidence—Radar echoes recorded mechanically—Real evidence—Radar not monitored by human agency—Whether photographic record admissible in evidence in collision action. **Statue of Liberty, The** [1968] **2** 195, Admin Ct.

Use in fog. See Collision regulations—Use of radar in fog, *below*.

Signals—
Manoeuvring signals relate not only to vessel sounding but also to the vessel for whose benefit they are sounded—Failure to sound a manoeuvring signal may constitute contributory negligence—Collision Regulations 1948 (SI 1953 No 1557), Sch 1, r 28(a). **Dayspring, The** [1965] **1** 297, Admin Ct.

Use of radar in fog—
Ascertainment of position of vessel—Immoderate speed—Necessity to use radar properly with seamanlike prudence—Collision Regulations 1948 (SI 1953 No 1557), Sch 1, r 16(b). **Sitala, The** [1963] **2** 290, Admin Ct.

Excessive speed in fog—Failure to use radar equipment—Negligence. **Chusan, The** [1956] **1** 178, Admin Ct.

Ship equipped with radar—Excessive speed—Use of equipment. **Chusan, The** [1956] **1** 178, Admin Ct.

Use as aid to safety as well as aid to navigation—Collision Regulations 1948 (SI 1953 No 1557), Sch 1), r 16(a). **Kurt Arlt, The** [1962] **2** 27, Admin Ct.

Use by vessels at sea in foggy conditions—Ascertainment of position of vessel—Collision Regulations 1948 (SI 1953 No 1557, Sch 1), r 16(b). **Gunnar Knudsen, The** [1962] **1** 315, Admin Ct.

Commencement of lay days—
Arrived ship under berth charterparty—
Notice of readiness—Charterparty providing that notice of readiness could be given 'whether in berth or not'—Vessel arriving at port but unable to berth because of fog although berth available—Notice of readiness given on arrival—Whether 'whether in berth or not' clause converting berth charter into port charter—Whether notice of readiness could be given on arrival if berth available but unable to be reached because of weather. **Bulk Transport Group Shipping Co Ltd v Seacrystal Shipping Ltd** [1988] **3** 745, HL.

When ship 'arrived'—Ship 'to proceed to one or two safe ports East Canada or Newfoundland, place or places as ordered by charterers'—'Place'—Berth in port. **Stag Line Ltd v Board of Trade** [1950] **1** 1105, CA.

SHIPPING (cont)—
Commencement of lay days (cont)—
Arrived ship under port charterparty—

Arrival at only and usual waiting place for ships awaiting berth at nominated port—Waiting place outside legal, fiscal and administrative limits of nominated port—Ship at charterer's disposition at waiting place—Waiting place near open sea 40 miles from port—Whether ship an arrived ship on arrival at waiting place. **Federal Commerce and Navigation Co Ltd v Tradax Export SA** [1977] **2** 849, HL.

Arrival at position in port where within immediate and effective disposition of charterer—Ship kept waiting because berth not available—Ship anchoring at usual waiting place for ships coming to port—Anchorage within geographical, fiscal, legal and administrative area of port—Anchorage 17 miles from docks—Whether ship an 'arrived ship' on anchoring at usual waiting place. **Johanna Oldendorff, The** [1973] **3** 148, HL.

Charterers' duty to nominate 'place reachable on arrival'—Delay in entering port—All berths occupied—Vessel waiting outside breakwater but within roads for 4 days until berth available—Whether vessel 'arrived ship'—Whether charterers liable for damages for delay when delay within lay days. **Delian Spirit, The** [1971] **2** 1060, QBD and CA.

Implied term—Clause in charterparty that notice could be given 'whether in berth or not'—Port of destination one of ports on River Weser—Arrival of ship at Weser Lightship—Lightship usual and only waiting place for ships awaiting berth at named port—Lightship outside legal, fiscal and administrative limits of port—Whether an implied term of charterparty that ship became an arrived ship on reaching lightship. **Federal Commerce and Navigation Co Ltd v Tradax Export SA** [1977] **2** 849, HL.

Notice of readiness—Clause in port charterparty that notice could be given 'whether in berth or not'—Charterparty on form appropriate to berth charterparty—Arrival of ship at usual and only waiting place for ships awaiting berth at nominated port—Waiting place outside legal, fiscal and administrative limits of port—Whether ship an arrived ship on arrival at waiting place. **Federal Commerce and Navigation Co Ltd v Tradax Export SA** [1977] **2** 849, HL.

Notice of readiness—Ship having to anchor at waiting place outside legal, fiscal and administrative limits of nominated port—Waiting place lightship 40 miles from nominated port—Shipowners undertaking voyage of convenience up river to port and back to lightship to give notice of readiness and constitute vessel an arrived ship—Whether notice of readiness given in course of voyage of convenience constituting ship an arrived ship. **Federal Commerce and Navigation Co Ltd v Tradax Export SA** [1977] **2** 849, HL.

Ship kept waiting because discharging place not immediately available—Liability of holders of bills of lading. **Roland-Linie Schiffahrt GmbH v Spillers Ltd** [1956] **3** 383, QBD.

Time lost waiting for berth—Delay due to cargo not being available—No berthing permit until cargo available—Ship kept lying in roads—Whether ship an arrived ship. **Sociedad Financiera de Bienes Raices SA v Agrimpex Hungarian Trading Co for Agricultural Products** [1960] **2** 578, HL.

Loading—

Conflict of provisions in charterparty—Provision that ship to load in customary manner in regular turn—Special provision that time for loading to commence at specified time after ship reported and ready—Special provision overriding reference to loading in regular turn. **Moor Line Ltd v Manganexport GmbH** [1936] **2** 404, KBD.

Loading range nominated by buyer 'subject to terminal acceptance'—Seller declining to make inquiries as to whether terminal accepted nomination of loading range—Loading delayed because of port congestion—Price of cargo rising during period of delay—Whether buyer entitled to demurrage—Whether buyer entitled to recover for increased costs of purchase. **SK Shipping Co Ltd v BB Energy (Asia) Pte Ltd** [2000] **1 Comm** 810, QBD.

Time lost in waiting for berth to count as loading time—Ship waiting for berth but ready to load—No notice of readiness sent by master—When loading time began to run. **North River Freighters Ltd v President of India** [1956] **1** 50, CA.

Notice of readiness to load—

Anticipated readiness—Vessel actually ready to load at time of notice of anticipated readiness—Whether sufficient for notice of actual readiness. **Christensen v Hindustan Steel Ltd** [1971] **2** 811, QBD.

Congestion at load port—Vessel tendering notice of readiness at outer anchorage and waiting there for berth—Vessel not proceeding to inner anchorage to wait although possible to do so—Load port authorities accepting notice of readiness—Whether notice of readiness valid under terms of charterparty—Whether waiver of defect in notice of readiness by load port authorities capable of binding charterer—Whether disponent owners entitled to demurrage. **Ocean Pride Maritime Ltd Partnership v Qingdao Ocean Shipping Co** [2008] **2 Comm** 330, QBD.

Invalid notice—Owners claiming demurrage—Charterers claiming despatch—Whether laytime commencing when no valid notice of readiness served. **Glencore Grain Ltd v Flacker Shipping Ltd** [2001] **1 Comm** 659, QBD; [2002] **2 Comm** 896, CA.

Notice of readiness given in advance of earliest lay day—Whether charterers decision to commence loading on receipt of notice amounting to sanctioning early commencement of laycan period. **Tidebrook Maritime Corp v Vitol SA of Geneva** [2006] **2 Comm** 813, CA.

Premature notice—Duty of owner to secure that vessel ready to load when notice given—Complete readiness in all holds to receive cargo subject to normal preliminaries or mere formalities—Master of vessel giving notice—Holds infested with pests—Holds requiring fumigation before loading could take place—Whether fumigation a normal preliminary or mere formality—Whether laytime commencing when notice given or when fumigation completed. **Tres Flores, The** [1973] **3** 967, CA.

Vessel tendering notice of readiness at anchorage—Free pratique granted more than six hours after tender of notice of readiness—Free pratique given before vessel arriving at berth—Master sending e-mail after grant of free pratique confirming readiness to load—Whether failure to secure free pratique within six hours rendering notice of readiness invalid—Whether master's e-mail constituting fresh notice of readiness—Whether alternative demurrage claim based on e-mail extinguished. **AET Inc Ltd v Arcadia Petroleum Ltd** [2011] **1 Comm** 153, CA.

SHIPPING (cont)—
  Commencement of lay days (cont)—
    Notice of readiness to load (cont)—
      Vessel tendering notice of readiness at anchorage—Free pratique granted more than six hours after tender of notice of readiness—Free pratique given before vessel arriving at berth—Whether failure to secure free pratique within six hours rendering notice of readiness invalid. **AET Inc Ltd v Arcadia Petroleum Ltd** [2010] **1 Comm** 23, QBD.
    Obstructions preventing loading of cargo—
      Time for loading not to count during continuance of obstructions. *See* Demurrage—Exceptions clause—Obstructions—Obstructions preventing loading of cargo—Time for loading not to count during continuance of obstructions, *below.*
    Readiness to discharge—
      Accessibility of cargo—Vessel chartered to carry part cargo of flour—Option to owners to complete cargo en route to discharging port—Flour cargo overstowed by other cargo loaded en route—Lay days commencing only when all flour cargo accessible for discharge. **Government of Ceylon v Société Franco-Tunisienne D'Armement-Tunis** [1960] **3** 797, QBD.
      Ship kept waiting because discharging berth not available—During waiting period ship not in physical condition to discharge cargo because of overstowage but ready in all other respects—Whether time spent waiting to count as discharging time. **Government of Ceylon v Société Franco-Tunisienne D'Armement-Tunis** [1960] **3** 797, QBD.
    Sale contract—
      Provision of letter of credit—Buyer tendering notice of readiness—Letter of credit opened some days thereafter—Whether laytime commencing after tendering of notice of readiness or after provision of letter of credit. **Kronos Worldwide Ltd v Sempra Oil Trading SARL** [2004] **1 Comm** 915, CA.
    Unloading—
      Unloading begun before notice of readiness given. **Pteroti Cia Naviera SA v National Coal Board** [1958] **1** 603, QBD.
  Compulsory pilotage. *See* **Harbour** (Pilotage district—Compulsory pilotage).
  Conflict of laws. *See* **Conflict of laws** (Shipping).
  Contract of affreightment—
    Construction—
      Damages for breach—Exceptions clause—Shipowner claiming damages against charterer for failing to make shipments of iron ore pellets following accident at mine—Whether charterer entitled to rely on exceptions clause to excuse liability—Whether shipowner entitled to substantial damages. **Classic Maritime Inc v Limbungan Makmur Sdn Bhd** [2019] **1 Comm** 647, QBD; [2019] **2** 622, QBD.
      Damages for breach—Loss of right to freight—Whether claimant suffering loss by reason of defendant's non-performance of contract where claimant would have directed defendant to make payment to third party had contract been performed. **Glory Wealth Shipping Pte Ltd v Flame SA** [2016] **2 Comm** 151, QBD.
      Nominated vessel—Relationship between disponent owner and nominated vessel—Whether contractual control by disponent owner over nominated vessel an essential characteristic of contractual nomination. **Flame SA v Glory Wealth Shipping PTE Ltd, The Glory Wealth** [2014] **1 Comm** 1043, QBD.
  Contract of carriage—
    cip contract. *See* Carriage by sea—cip contract , *above.*
    Scope of contract—
      Bill of lading. *See* Bill of lading—Scope of contract of carriage, *above.*
  Conversion—
    Damages. *See* Carriage by sea—Damages for conversion, *above.*
  Crew—
    Crew management agreement —
      BIMCO crew management agreement—Claimant demise charterer engaging crew management agency under standard crew management agreement—Crew management agency providing crew for claimant's vessel—Chief officer dying on board during loading operations—Claimant seeking to recover compensation and repatriation costs from defendant harbour authority under stevedoring agreement—Whether crewman employed by claimant or crew management agency—Whether claimant suffering loss 'of an indirect or consequential nature'. **Ferryways NV v Associated British Ports** [2008] **2 Comm** 504, QBD.
      Parties entering into crew management agreements on 'lump sum' basis—Claimant to receive half of monthly lump sum on termination of agreement by defendant—Parties amending agreements to be on 'costs plus fees' basis—Claimant to receive annual fees in 12 monthly instalments—Termination provisions amended so that reference to monthly lump sum deemed to be reference to fees—Whether on termination claimant entitled to half of annual fees or half of monthly instalment. **Bernhard Schulte Shipmanagement (Bermuda) Ltd Partnership v BP Shipping Ltd** [2009] **1 Comm** 601, QBD; [2010] **2 Comm** 795, CA.
    Master—
      Wages—Claim for wages—Lien for wages—Whether claim for wages by master ranking pari passu with claim of crew—Merchant Shipping Act 1970, s 18. **Royal Wells, The** [1984] **3** 193, QBD.
    Wages—
      Claim for wages—Lien for wages—Crew claiming maritime lien in respect of unpaid wages—Allotted part of wages paid to third party—Whether crew entitled to maritime lien in respect of allotted part of wages. **Cil v Turiddu (owners) (First National Bank of Maryland intervening)** [1999] **2 Comm** 161, CA.
  Damages for breach of contract—
    Carriage by sea. *See* Carriage by sea—Damages for breach of contract, *above.*
    Generally. *See* Carriage by sea—Damages for breach of contract, *above.*
  Damages in collision cases—
    Damaged vessel on time charter—
      Right of charterer to recover for pecuniary loss for damage caused to vessel by third party. **World Harmony, The** [1965] **2** 139, Admin Ct.

SHIPPING (cont)—
  Damages in collision cases (cont)—
    Detention—
      Detention in port to repair collision damage—No charterparty lost—Profits of subsequent voyages not to be taken into account. **Soya, The** [1956] **2** 393, CA.
      Detention in port to repair collision damage—Ship rendered unseaworthy by weather damage while proceeding to port for repair. **Carslogie, The** [1952] **1** 20, HL.
      Loss of earnings during period of detention—Repair not urgent—New charterparty entered into after collision—Ship late in arriving at loading port owing to detention for repair—Shipowners' failure to make timely arrangements for repair—Whether loss for breach of charterparty by late arrival at loading port recoverable in addition to damages for detention. **Pacific Concord, The** [1961] **1** 106, Admin Ct.
      Mitigation—Vessel on charter—Subsequent charter arranged before collision—Substitution of slower ship with smaller carrying capacity under current charter—Vessel becoming free before time when current charter would have ended—Subsequent charter brought forward to begin at earlier date—Assessment of value to owners of vessel of advancement of commencement of subsequent charter—Amount so computed allowed in mitigation of damages. **World Beauty, The** [1969] **3** 158, CA.
      No specific vessel chartered as replacement tonnage—Interest on capital value. **Hebridean Coast, The** [1961] **1** 82, HL.
    Interest—
      Collision during war between British ship and ship belonging to enemy alien—Damages awarded to alien at end of hostilities—Time from which interest accrues. **Berwickshire, The** [1950] **1** 699, Admin Ct.
      Right to deduct income tax on interest—Notification to payee of deduction—Income Tax Act 1952, ss 169, 170. **Norseman, The** [1957] **2** 660, Admin Ct.
    Loss of profits—
      Loss of claimants' fixture—Whether loss of profits from lost fixture recoverable only on ballast/laden basis—Whether loss of profits subject to discount as loss of chance. **Owners of the Ship 'Front Ace' v Owners of the Ship 'Vicky 1'** [2008] **2** Comm 42, CA.
      Pleasure vessel let on hire—Motor cruiser owned by plaintiffs for letting out on hire on the Broads—Loss of prospective profits of next season—Cruiser of distinctive design characteristic of plaintiffs' fleet—Fixed engagements at date of sinking for part of next season. **Fortunity, The** [1960] **2** 64, Admin Ct.
  Deadfreight claim. See Charterparty—Safe port—Deadfreight claim, *above.*
  Defective equipment—
    Employer's liability. See **Employment** (Liability of master—Defective equipment—Shipping).
  Delay—
    Damages. See Time charterparty—Last voyage—Late redelivery, *below.*
    Delivery of cargo—
      Bill of lading. See Bill of lading—Delivery of cargo—Delay, *above.*
    Frustration—
      Charterparty. See Charterparty—Frustration—Delay, *above.*
      Time charterparty. See Time charterparty—Frustration—Delay, *below.*
    Loading and discharging. See Loading and discharging—Delay, *below.*
  Delivery of cargo—
    Bill of lading. See Bill of lading—Delivery of cargo, *above.*
    Charterparty. See Charterparty—Delivery of cargo, *above.*
  Demurrage—
    Admiralty jurisdiction. See **Admiralty** (Jurisdiction—Claim for demurrage).
    Arrived ship—
      Place reachable on arrival—Breakdown of equipment—Vessel ordered off berth during repairs to defective sealine—Whether delay caused by breakdown of equipment—Asbatankvoy 1977 form, cl 8. **Portolana Cia Naviera Ltd v Vitol SA Inc** [2004] **2** Comm 578, CA.
      Place reachable on arrival—Delay after arrival of vessel at port—Delay due to all berths being occupied—Charterers not responsible for delay—Charterparty providing that delay in getting into berth for any reason outside charterers' control not to count as used laytime—Vessel detained for over nine days before getting a berth—Whether delay over which charterer had no control—Whether charterers in breach of warranty to designate and procure berth reachable on arrival of vessel—Whether charterer exempted from liability for demurrage for delay—Exxonvoy 1969 charterparty, cll 6, 8, 9. **Nereide SpA di Navigazione v Bulk Oil International Ltd** [1981] **3** 737, HL.
      Place reachable on arrival—Delay in entering port—Delay due to non-physical obstruction—Charterparty providing for discharge at place reachable on arrival designated and procured by charterer—Discharge delayed because of port regulations requiring compulsory pilotage and prohibiting night pilotage—Whether owners entitled to demurrage—Whether any distinction between physical and non-physical causes of obstruction rendering designated place unreachable. **K/S Arnt J Moerland v Kuwait Petroleum Corp** [1988] **2** 714, QBD.
      Place reachable on arrival—Vessel ordered off berth during repairs to defective sealine—Whether delay getting into berth—Whether delay constituting time consumed by vessel moving from port anchorage to discharging berth—Whether delay caused by breakdown of equipment—Asbatankvoy 1977 form, cll 6-8. **Portolana Cia Naviera Ltd v Vitol SA Inc** [2004] **1** Comm 269, QBD.
    Charterparty. See Charterparty—Demurrage, *above.*
    Charterparty on amended Norgrain form—
      Nature of demurrage payable under voyage charter when charterer failing to discharge vessel within laytime allowed—Whether demurrage liquidated damages for all consequences of charterer's failure to load or unload within laytime, or only some—Whether owners entitled to damages in addition to demurrage for charterers' breach of contract—Meaning of 'demurrage'. **K Line PTE Ltd v Priminds Shipping (HK) Co Ltd** [2022] **2** Comm 1044, CA; [2022] **3** 396, CA.

Container demurrage—Shipper contracting with carrier to carry goods in containers—Buyers refusing to take delivery of goods at port of discharge—Customs authorities refusing to allow unloading of containers without court order—Carrier claiming container demurrage against shipper—Whether demurrage payable—Whether contract frustrated—Whether carrier entitled to continuing demurrage. **MSC Mediterranean Shipping Company SA v Cottonex Anstalt** [2017] **1 Comm** 483, CA.

Container demurrage—Shipper contracting with carrier to carry goods in containers—Buyers refusing to take delivery of goods at port of discharge—Customs authorities refusing to allow unloading of containers without court order—Carrier claiming container demurrage against shipper—Whether demurrage beginning to run—Whether demurrage ceasing. **MSC Mediterranean Shipping Company SA v Cottonex Anstalt** [2015] **2 Comm** 614, QBD.

Discharge stopping on discovery of cargo contamination—Dispute arising as to responsibility for contamination—Owners, charterers and cargo purchasers entering into tripartite agreement providing for demurrage upon owners being found by arbitration tribunal not to be liable for contamination—Charterers not being party to owners' arbitration claim against purchasers—Tribunal declaring purchasers not liable—Owners claiming demurrage in accordance with tripartite agreement—Whether award binding charterers. **Seaglance Maritime v Casillo Commodities Italia SpA** [2016] **1 Comm** 206, QBD.

Time bar—Charter providing for documents to accompany demurrage claim within 90 days from completion of discharge of cargo—Defendant owners of vessel bringing demurrage claim against claimant charterers—Tribunal finding owners' claim time-barred save with respect to one discharge port due to re-labelling as claim for time lost waiting for orders—Whether re-labelled claim a demurrage claim—Whether any commercial considerations or consequences pointing to claim not being a demurrage claim for purposes of engaging provision. **Lukoil Asia Pacific Pte Ltd v Ocean Tankers (Pte) Ltd** [2018] **2 Comm** 108, QBD.

Time bar—Charterparty on amended BPVOY4 form providing that demurrage claim be presented with all supporting documentation within 90 days of completion of discharge—Owners disclosing documents to charterers in support of claim for demurrage under charterparty—Charterer arguing demurrage claim time-barred on basis claimant not having attached all necessary documents in support of claim within time period provided in charterparty—Whether claim time-barred—BPVOY4 form, cl 19.7, 20.1. **Kassiopi Maritime Co Ltd v FAL Shipping Co Ltd** [2016] **2 Comm** 243, QBD.

Time bar—Owners required to make demurrage claim together with all supporting documentation within 90 days of discharge of cargo—Charterparty containing warranty as to discharge time and/or average pumping pressure—Additional time beyond warranted time/average pumping pressure not counting as demurrage—Discharge not being completed within warranted time—Whether supporting documentation for purposes of demurrage claim including documentation required for additional time claim. **Waterfront Shipping Co Ltd v Trafigura AG** [2008] **1 Comm** 958, QBD.

Time bar—Owners required to make demurrage claim with all supporting documents within 90 days of discharge of cargo—Charterparty on amended Asbatankvoy forms—Demurrage to be calculated by reference to bill of lading quantities—Whether 'all supporting documents' including bill of lading. **Tricon Energy Ltd v MTM Trading LLC** [2020] **2 Comm** 543, Comm Ct.

Commencement of lay days. *See* Commencement of lay days, *above*.

Completion of loading—

Cargo of wheat put on board in bulk and requiring to be bagged before stowing—Loading not completed until grain bagged and stowed. **Argonaut Navigation Co Ltd v Ministry of Food** [1949] **1** 160, CA.

Right of charterers to detain ship for loading until expiry of lay-days. **Margaronis Navigation Agency Ltd v Henry W Peabody & Co of London Ltd** [1964] **3** 333, CA.

Contract to sell cargo of gas oil—

Construction of demurrage provisions—Seller claiming demurrage from buyer—Buyer having sold cargo on—Whether buyer liable to seller—Whether interest payable. **Galaxy Energy International Ltd v Bayoil SA** [2001] **1 Comm** 289, CA.

Deliberate delay—

Demurrage clause a stipulation for agreed damages, not an exception clause inserted for the benefit of one party—Demurrage clause continuing applicable after assumed fundamental breach of charterparty by wilful delay. **Suisse Atlantique Société d'Armement Maritime SA v NV Rotterdamsche Kolen Centrale** [1966] **2** 61, HL.

Determination of date of discharge. *See* Charterparty—Construction—Demurrage—Determination of date of discharge, *above*.

Exceptions clause—

Delay due to circumstances unknown to parties—Intervention of constituted authorities—Any cause beyond control of charterers—Order prohibiting night work—Inability to discharge cargo without working at night. **Steamship 'Induna' Co Ltd v British Phosphate Comrs** [1949] **1** 522, KBD.

Laytime not counting during period of strike—Meaning of 'strike'—Concerted stoppage of work by men to improve conditions or vent a grievance—Necessity for continuous stoppage—Dockers at discharging port accustomed to work in shifts 24 hours each day—Dockers not contractually obliged to work 24 hours—Dockers refusing to work during night in order to bring pressure on employers to improve terms and conditions of work—Whether refusal of dockers to work at night a 'strike'. **Tramp Shipping Corp v Greenwich Marine Inc** [1975] **2** 989, CA.

Obstructions—Berths requisitioned by government—Undertaking to provide berth as soon as possible—Whether absolute undertaking. **Reardon Smith Line Ltd v East Asiatic Co Ltd** [1938] **4** 107, KBD.

SHIPPING (cont)—
  Demurrage (cont)—
    Exceptions clause (cont)—
      Obstructions—Obstructions preventing loading of cargo—Time for loading not to count during
        continuance of obstructions—Nomination of berth—Failure to nominate before arrival of
        ship—Effect—Charterers having made arrangement to load at customary berths—Berths
        congested on arrival of ship—Alternative berth available—Not commercially practicable to load
        at alternative berth—Whether charterers entitled to rely on congestion as 'obstruction' preventing
        loading. **Prometheus, The** [1974] **1** 597, QBD.
      Obstructions—Obstructions preventing loading of cargo—Time for loading not to count during
        continuance of obstructions—Nomination of berth—Nomination before arrival of ship—Berth
        occupied by another vessel on arrival of ship—Effect of nomination—Port charterparty—
        Nomination amounting to an election which charterers could not thereafter change
        unilaterally—Congestion of berth amounting to an 'obstruction' preventing loading of cargo
        within meaning of charterparty. **Prometheus, The** [1974] **1** 597, QBD.
      Strike occurring while vessel on demurrage—Discharge prevented—Centrocon strike clause
        incorporated in Baltimore Form C charterparty—Whether demurrage payable during strike
        period. **Cia Naviera Aeolus SA v Union of India** [1962] **3** 670, HL.
      Strikes—Discharge delayed due to strike—Owners making claim for demurrage—Exception
        applying to 'strikes … or any other causes or accidents beyond the control of the
        consignee'—Whether strike having to be beyond control of consignee—Construction of
        charterparty. **Frontier International Shipping Corp v Swissmarine Corp Inc** [2005] **1 Comm** 528,
        QBD.
      Strikes—Discharge of four vessels delayed due to congestion at port caused by strikes—Strikes
        finished when vessels berthed—Vessels arriving before and after end of strikes—Owner making
        claim for demurrage—Exception applying to strikes beyond the control of the charterers
        preventing or delaying discharge—Whether exception applying where discharge delayed by
        after-effects of strike—Whether exception applying where vessel arriving after end of
        strike—Whether exception applying where vessel unable to berth due to berth congestion caused
        by strike. **Carboex SA v Louis Dreyfus Commodities Suisse SA** [2011] **2 Comm** 365, QBD; [2012] **2
        Comm** 1039, CA.
    Expiry of laytime—
      Cargo fumigated after expiry of laytime while vessel waiting in roads—Clause in charterparty that
        'time so used to not count'—Voyage charterparty—Whether charterers liable to pay demurrage in
        respect of period while fumigation being carried out—General principles applicable. **Dias Cia
        Naviera SA v Louis Dreyfus Corp** [1978] **1** 724, HL.
      F o b contract for sale of gasoline—Seller neither completing nor even commencing loading prior
        to end of laycan period—Whether seller in repudiatory breach entitling buyer to treat contract as
        terminated. **ERG Raffinerie Mediterranee SpA v Chevron USA Inc (t/a Chevron Texaco Global
        Trading)** [2006] **2 Comm** 913, QBD; [2007] **2 Comm** 548, CA.
      Strike occurring while vessel on laytime—Whether laytime extended by strike—Sugar Charterparty
        1969, cl 28. **Cero Navigation Corp v Jean Lion & Cie** [2000] **1 Comm** 214, QBD.
    Incorporation of terms of charterparty—
      Bill of lading. See Bill of lading—Incorporation of terms of charterparty—Demurrage, *above.*
    Late payment—
      Payment in sterling—Currency exchange loss—Damages arising from late payment of
        demurrage—Charterparty providing for demurrage to be calculated in US dollars but paid in
        sterling—Dispute over demurrage resolved by arbitration—Sterling exchange rate falling
        between date demurrage due and date of arbitration award—Whether currency exchange loss
        arising from late payment of demurrage recoverable. **President of India v Lips Maritime Corp**
        [1987] **3** 110, HL.
    Number of lay days. See Number of lay days, *below.*
    Payment in foreign currency—
      Date at which rate of exchange calculated. See **Money** (Currency—Date at which rate of exchange
        calculated—Charterparty providing for demurrage to be calculated in dollars).
    Rate of demurrage—
      Arrest and restraint of princes—Vessel detained by authorities until payment of fine—Whether
        conduct of authorities unlawful—Whether half demurrage payable during period of detention.
        Great Elephant Corp v Trafigura Beheer BV, The Crudesky [2013] **1 Comm** 415, QBD; [2013] **2
        Comm** 992, CA.
      Strike—Charterparty in Gencon form—General strike clause—Vessel delayed by strike—Whether
        half demurrage payable after strike ended until discharge completed. **Onisilos, The** [1971] **2** 497,
        CA.
    Sale contract—
      Relationship with demurrage provisions in charterparty—Sale contracts providing for demurrage
        'as per charterparty terms and conditions'—Sale contracts containing laytime provisions differing
        from laytime provisions in charterparty—Whether demurrage provisions in sale contracts
        operating by way of indemnity or giving rise to independent obligations. **Glencore Energy (UK)
        Ltd v Sonol Israel Ltd** [2012] **1 Comm** 101, QBD.
      Relationship with demurrage provisions in charterparty—Whether demurrage provisions in sale
        contract operating by way of indemnity or giving rise to independent obligations—Principles to
        be applied. **Fal Oil Ltd v Petronas Trading Corp SDN BHD** [2004] **2 Comm** 537, CA.
    Time lost waiting for berth—
      Computation of time—Port charterparty—Arrived ship—Charterparty in Gencon form—Time lost
        waiting for berth to count as laytime—Computation—Fridays and holidays excluded from
        computation of laytime—Whether time lost to be calculated on same basis as laytime—Whether
        Fridays and holidays should be excluded from computation of time lost. **Aldebaran Cia Maritima
        SA Panama v Aussenhandel AG Zurich** [1976] **2** 963, HL.
      Port charterparty—Arrived ship—Time at which ship becomes an arrived ship—Time at which ship
        begins waiting for berth within area of port—Ship required to wait at anchorage outside port
        because of congestion—Ship sailing to port and returning immediately to anchorage—Whether
        ship having arrived on entering area of port before returning to anchorage. **Federal Commerce
        and Navigation Co Ltd v Tradax Export SA** [1976] **1** 293, QBD.

SHIPPING (cont)—
  Despatch money—
    Charterers to have the right to average the days allowed for loading and discharging—
      Time allowed for loading exceeded—Time saved on discharge—Method of 'averaging'. **Alma
      Shipping Co SA v Salgaoucar E Irmaos (VM) Ltd** [1954] **2** 92, QBD.
  Deviation—
    Bill of lading. *See* Bill of lading—Deviation, *above.*
  Discharge—
    Custom of port—
      Term of charterparty that shipowners' stevedores be employed in discharging grain
      cargo—Receivers' right by custom to fill into bags or buckets before discharge—Consistency—
      Debit of half cost to shipowners. **Sameiling (A/S) v Grain Importers (Eire) Ltd** [1952] **2** 315, QBD.
    Discharge of cargo under arrest—
      Admiralty practice. *See* **Admiralty** (Practice—Discharge of cargo under arrest).
    Expenses of discharging cargo—
      Liability of charterers for expenses of off-loading and reloading occurring during voyage. *See*
      Loading and discharging—Expenses, *below.*
      Maximum charge—Charge not to exceed what other steamers pay (at London according to the
      tariff in force on 1st January 1935) maximum charges—Right of charterers to retain rebate
      allowed by stevedores. **Murrell SS Co Ltd v Nordenfjeldske SS Services Ltd** [1940] **1** 580, CA.
    Naming discharge berth—
      Delivery of cargo to safe berth—Nomination by charterer of discharge berth—Ship diverted to
      another berth—Consequent loss of freight—Right of shipowner to recover—Measure of
      damages. **Anglo-Danubian Transport Co Ltd v Ministry of Food** [1949] **2** 1068, KBD.
    Naming port of discharge—
      Ship to 'proceed (as ordered on signing bills of lading) direct to one safe port'—Option to discharge
      at two safe ports for small additional freight charge—Option exercised before bills of lading
      signed but by mistake not communicated to master or charterers' factors at loading port—Master
      signing bills of lading for one port only—Meaning of words 'on signing bills of
      lading'—Mistake—Estoppel. **A/S Tank of Oslo and Agence Maritime L Strauss of Paris, Re an
      arbitration between** [1940] **1** 40, CA.
    Notice of readiness to discharge. *See* Carriage by sea—Cif contract—Notice of readiness, *above.*
    Safe berth—
      Option to charterers to load and discharge at two safe berths in one port without extra charge.
      Radcliffe (WI) Steamship Co Ltd v Exportkhleb of Moscow [1939] **3** 528, KBD.
    Safe port—
      Obligation of charterer to nominate safe port. *See* Charterparty—Safe port—Obligation of charterer
      to nominate safe port, *above.*
    Seaworthy trim clause—
      Expense incurred in shifting cargo to trim ship—Overtime in moving ship and looking after
      stowage—Loss of time—Meaning of 'homogenous cargo'—What expenses recoverable from
      charterers. **Chandis v Union of India** [1956] **1** 358, CA.
  Dock—
    Loading and unloading in—
      Statutory regulation of. *See* **Dock** (Loading and unloading).
  Documentation—
    Seaworthiness of vessel. *See* Charterparty—Seaworthiness of vessel—Owners' obligation to obtain
    and retain necessary certificates, documents etc, *above.*
  Employment—
    Crew. *See* Crew—Crew management agreement , *above.*
  Entry by master in ship's log-book—
    Defamation—
      Qualified privilege. *See* **Libel and slander** (Qualified privilege—Duty and interest—Ship's log).
  Equipment—
    Defective equipment—
      Employer's liability. *See* **Employment** (Liability of master—Defective equipment—Shipping).
  Estoppel—
    Bill of lading—
      Condition of cargo—Receipt as to. *See* Bill of lading—Receipt as to condition of cargo—Estoppel,
      above.
  Exceptions—
    Bill of lading. *See* Bill of lading—Exceptions, *above.*
    Charterparty. *See* Charterparty—Exceptions, *above.*
  Expenses—
    Loading and discharging. *See* Loading and discharging—Expenses, *below.*
  Expenses of raising wreck—
    Removal of wreck—
      Limitation of liability. *See* Limitation of liability—Wreck removal—Wreck-raising expenses, *below.*
  Expiry of lay days—
    Detention of vessel—
      Completion of loading—Demurrage. *See* Demurrage—Completion of loading—Right of charterers
      to detain ship for loading until expiry of lay-days, *above.*
  F o b contract—
    Credit—
      Sale of goods. *See* Sale of goods (Payment—Confirmed letter of credit—F o b contract).
    Sale of goods—
      Construction of shipment period provision. *See* **Sale of goods** (Shipment of goods—Fob stowed
      contract—Construction of shipment period provision).
      Passing of property. *See* **Sale of goods** (Passing of property—Reservation of right of disposal—F o
      b contract).
  Failure to operate ship in safe manner. *See* Offence—Failure to operate ship in safe manner, *below.*
  Fishing rights—
    European Community. *See* **European Union** (Fishing rights).

SHIPPING (cont)—
Foreign sovereign state—
Immunity from suit—
Impleading foreign state. *See* **Constitutional law** (Foreign sovereign state—Immunity from suit—Impleading foreign sovereign state—Shipping).
Freight—
Amount of freight—
Computation—Carriage of contemplated cargo—Option to charterer to ship other lawful merchandise—Freight to be paid at rate agreed for contemplated cargo—Vessel completely loaded partly with contemplated cargo and partly with optional cargo. **Hain Steamship Co Ltd v Minister of Food** [1949] **1** 444, CA.
Claim for freight—
Defence—Cross-claim—Limitation period for cross-claim—Cross-claim for damage to cargo—Defence or counterclaim—Defence not subject to limitation period—Whether cross-claim a defence pro tanto to claim for freight—Whether cross-claim must be subject of cross-action to which limitation period applicable. **Henriksens Rederi A/S v PHZ Rolimpex** [1973] **3** 589, CA.
Defence—Cross-claim—Loss of cargo—Limitation period for bringing action for loss of cargo having expired—Whether charterers entitled to assert claim by way of defence to claim for freight. **Aries Tanker Corp v Total Transport Ltd** [1977] **1** 398, HL.
Freight payable on delivery—Cargo contaminated on delivery—Shipment of Bachaquero Crude Oil—Special quality of Bachaquero crude that free from paraffin—Oil contaminated with paraffin on discharge—Whether 'the cargo' delivered—Whether contamination making description 'Bachaquero Crude' commerically inapplicable or merely qualifying that description. **Montedison SpA v Icroma SpA** [1979] **3** 378, QBD.
Head charter providing for owner's lien upon any amounts due under charter—Sub-charterer failing to pay instalments of hire and entering liquidation—Shipowner sending notices of lien to sub-charterer further down chain requiring payment of freight directly to shipowner—Shipowner withdrawing vessel from first sub-charterer's service—Second sub-charterer requesting shipowners resume voyage—Whether shipowner entitled to demand payment to itself of freight from second sub-charterer—Whether notices effective to require payment—Whether request to shipowners to complete voyage generating obligation to pay reasonable remuneration to shipowners for so doing. **Dry Bulk Handy Holding Inc v Fayette International Holdings Ltd** [2013] **2 Comm** 295, CA.
Set-off—Freight forwarding agreements—Claimant making claim for storage of goods and applying for summary judgment—Defendant claiming set-off—Claimant contending contract relating to freight and not subject to set-off—Whether claimant entitled to summary judgment. **Globalink Transportation and Logistics Worldwide LLP v DHL Project & Chartering Ltd** [2019] **2 Comm** 393, QBD.
Set-off—Shipowner's failure to complete contract—Failure to complete voyage—Damages for shipowner's repudiation—Voyage charterparty providing for payment of lump sum freight within five days of signing bills of lading—Freight assigned to bank—Vessel arrested and impounded during voyage because of owner's insolvency—Bank claiming payment of freight—Whether owner's right to freight accruing before termination of charterparty—Whether charterers entitled to set off claim for damages for owner's wrongful repudiation against claim for freight—Whether charterers entitled to maintain set-off against bank claiming as assignees—Law of Property Act 1925, s 136(1). **Bank of Boston Connecticut v European Grain and Shipping Ltd** [1989] **1** 545, HL.
Set-off—Sub-charter providing for mode of payment of freight—Bill of lading incorporating charterparty provisions on payment of freight—Charterers agreeing that sub-charterers could deduct certain payments from freight payment although charterparty making no provision for such deductions—Owners claiming unpaid freight from shippers—Whether deducted payments went to discharge shippers' liability for freight—Whether bill of lading containing implied term that vessel would be discharged within a reasonable time. **Tradigrain SA v King Diamond Marine Ltd** [2000] **2 Comm** 542, CA.
Sub-charter providing for mode of payment of freight—Bill of lading incorporating charterparty provisions on payment of freight—Charterers agreeing that sub-charterers could deduct certain payments from freight payment, but charterparty making no provision for such deductions—Owners claiming unpaid freight from shippers and also claiming for delay in unloading vessel—Whether deducted payments went to discharge shippers' liability for freight—Whether bill of lading contained implied term that vessel would be discharged within a reasonable time. **Tradigrain SA v King Diamond Marine Ltd** [1999] **1 Comm** 837, QBD.
Freight payable in sterling—
Demurrage payable in foreign currency—Date at which rate of exchange calculated. *See* **Money** (Currency—Date at which rate of exchange calculated—Charterparty providing for demurrage to be calculated in dollars—No provision for payment in sterling—Freight payable in sterling in London at rate of exchange on bill of lading date).
Freight payable on delivery—
Load line submerged—Whether freight recoverable—Merchant Shipping (Safety and Load Line Conventions) Act 1932, ss 44, 57. **St John Shipping Corp v Joseph Rank Ltd** [1956] **3** 683, QBD.
Lien—
Moneys held in charterers' solicitors' client account pursuant to freezing order—Shipowners seeking to exercise lien over moneys in respect of freight—Arbitrator declaring valid exercise of lien by shipowner—Whether shipowner entitled to rely on purported lien and arbitrator's declaration as against third party claiming entitlement to moneys. **Samsun Logix Corp v Oceantrade Corp** [2008] **1 Comm** 673, QBD.
Vessel chartered on NYPE charter containing lien clause on 'all cargoes, sub-freights, hire and sub hire'—Vessel sub-chartered on same terms including lien—Vessel sub-sub-chartered—Whether lien taking effect as equitable assignment or contractual right—Whether owner acquiring charterer's claims for unpaid hire against sub-charterer as security for owner's claim against charterer—Whether owner acquiring sub-charterer's claim against sub-sub-charterer as security for owner's claim against charterer—Whether freezing injunctions against sub-charterer and sub-sub-charterer should be continued. **Western Bulk Shipowning III A/S v Carbofer Maritime Trading ApS** [2012] **2 Comm** 1140, QBD.

SHIPPING (cont)—
Frustration—
Charterparty. *See* Charterparty—Frustration, *above.*
Time charterparty. *See* Time charterparty—Frustration, *below.*
General average—
Contribution by cargo owner—
Ransom—Vessel detained by pirates in Gulf of Aden and ransom paid—Charterparty on amended BPVOY4 form—Charterparty including Gulf of Aden and war risk clauses—Whether relevant terms of charterparty incorporated into bills of lading—Whether shipowners could only look to their insurers or whether entitled to general average contribution from cargo interests. **Herculito Maritime Ltd v Gunvor International BV** [2021] **2 Comm** 1278, Comm Ct; [2022] **2 Comm** 1061, CA.
Contribution by cargo owners—
Accrual of cause of action for contribution—Action by ship managers against consignees of cargo and insurers claiming contribution—Writ issued within six years of first general average act and execution of average bonds in usual Lloyd's form secured by guarantee given by cargo insurers—Application to join shipowners as plaintiffs in action made more than six years after execution of bonds and guarantee—Application made within six years of publication of average adjustment statement—Whether shipowners' claim against consignees and insurers time-barred. **Castle Insurance Co Ltd v Hong Kong Islands Shipping Co Ltd** [1983] **3** 706, PC.
Bigham clause—Underwriters insuring claimants' vessel for its proportion of general average—Vessel suffering damage during voyage and claimants making non-separation agreement with cargo owners—Agreement including Bigham clause capping cargo owners' contribution—Whether underwriters liable to claimants for general average in excess of Bigham cap. **Comatra Ltd v Various Underwriters** [1999] **2 Comm** 1002, QBD; [2000] **2 Comm** 609, CA.
Enforcement—Lien—Shipowners seeking general average bond from cargo owners, backed by insurers' general average guarantee or cash deposit—Cargo owners refusing to provide bond but insurers providing guarantee—Shipowners refusing to deliver cargo in exercise of lien—Whether acceptance of insurers' guarantee inconsistent with lien—Whether shipowners entitled to exercise lien—Whether shipowners entitled to recover storage costs incurred in exercising lien—Whether shipowners entitled to recover storage costs as damages for breach or in substitution for damages for detention. **Metall Market OOO v Vitorio Shipping Co Ltd** [2012] **2 Comm** 577, QBD; [2013] **2 Comm** 585, CA.
Insurers—Ship owner bringing claim against defendant insurers for full and unqualified recovery of general average under relevant guarantees—Whether insurers having same defence as cargo interests to liability under general average guarantee if casualty event caused by owner's breach of Hague-Visby rules—Meaning of 'properly due'—Carriage of Goods by Sea Act 1971, Sch, art III, r 1—York-Antwerp Rules 1974, Rule D. **Navalmar UK Ltd v Ergo Versicherung AG** [2020] **2 Comm** 795, Comm Ct.
General average expenditure—
General average contribution paid by cargo owners to carrying ship—Right of cargo owners to recover contribution from owners of offending ship—Right of carrying ship to claim from offending ship whole amount of general average expenditure. **Morrison Steamship Co Ltd v Greystoke Castle (cargo owners)** [1946] **2** 696, HL.
Hijacked vessel—Negotiation period expenses—Whether negotiation period expenses allowable in general average—York-Antwerp Rules 1974, Rule F. **Mitsui & Co Ltd v Beteiligungsgesellschaft LPG Tankerflotte MBH and Co KG** [2018] **1** 545, SC; [2018] **1 Comm** 815, SC.
Hijacked vessel—Negotiation period expenses—Whether negotiation period expenses allowable in general average—York-Antwerp Rules 1974, rr A, F. **Mitsui & Co Ltd v Beteiligungsgesellschaft LPG Tankerflotte MBH and Co KG** [2017] **1 Comm** 264, CA.
Temporary repairs—Vessel damaged shortly after commencing voyage—Owners carrying out temporary repairs to enable vessel to continue voyage—Temporary repairs costing much less than permanent repairs—Owners claiming cost of temporary repairs as general average—Whether shipowner entitled to claim general average contribution in respect of temporary repairs—York-Antwerp Rules 1974, rules X(b), XIV. **Marida Ltd v Oswal Steel** [1994] **2** 289, HL.
Towage charges—Fire on ship in port of discharge—Towage to anchorage—Whether ship 'detained' in port—Whether towage charges 'port charges'—York-Antwerp Rules 1974, r XI. **Trade Green Shipping Inc v Securitas Bremer Allgemeine Versicherungs AG** [2001] **1 Comm** 1097, QBD.
Unseaworthiness—Expenditure incurred through ship-owners' fault—Ship unseaworthy and failure to exercise due diligence—Whether right to claim contribution from cargo owner—Remedies open to cargo owner—Whether remedies barred—York-Antwerp Rules 1950, r D—Carriage of Goods by Sea Act 1924, Sch, art III, r 6, para 3. **Goulandris Bros Ltd v Goldman (B) & Sons Ltd** [1957] **3** 100, QBD.
Unseaworthiness—Owners making general average claim against cargo interests for salvage costs after vessel ran aground—Cargo interests claiming vessel unseaworthy—Whether defective passage plans rendering vessel unseaworthy—Whether actions of master and crew carried out qua navigation to be treated as attempted performance by carrier of its duty qua carrier to exercise due diligence to make vessel seaworthy—Carriage of Goods by Sea Act 1971, Sch, art III, r 1. **Alize 1954 v Allianz Elementar Versicherungs AG** [2019] **2 Comm** 679, QBD; [2020] **2 Comm** 1072, CA.
Unseaworthiness—Owners making general average claim against cargo interests for salvage costs after vessel ran aground—Cargo interests claiming vessel unseaworthy—Whether defective passage plans rendering vessel unseaworthy—Whether actions of master and crew carried out qua navigation to be treated as attempted performance by carrier of its duty qua carrier to exercise due diligence to make vessel seaworthy—Whether failure of crew to exercise reasonable skill and care constituting want of due diligence on part of carrier—Carriage of Goods by Sea Act 1971, Schedule, art III, r 1, art IV, r 2(a). **Alize 1954 v Allianz Elementar Versicherungs AG** [2022] **1 Comm** 1315, SC; [2022] **2** 479, SC.

General average (cont)—
General average expenditure (cont)—
Unseaworthiness—Vessel's main engine breaking down at sea—Owners of vessel bringing claim against defendant under guarantee provided on behalf of cargo interests whereby promise made to pay contribution to general average which may be ascertained to be properly due—Cause of damage to vessel—Whether owners able to discharge burden to prove exercise of due diligence to make vessel seaworthy. **MT 'Cape Bonny' Tankschiffahrts GmbH & Co KG v Ping An Property and Casualty Insurance Company of China Ltd** [2018] **2 Comm** 437, QBD.

Vessel and cargo in position of peril—Towage contract on UK Standard Towage Conditions giving wide indemnity to tug owners—Contract a general average act—Expenditure reasonably incurred by shipowners defending actions on indemnity in Australian courts—Whether general average expenditure as being direct consequence of general average act—Risk of damage to tug at least a possibility at time of contract—York-Antwerp Rules 1950, rules A, C. **Australian Coastal Shipping Commission v Green** [1971] **1** 353, CA.

General average loss—
Contribution—Deviation—Whether indorsees of bill of lading bound to contribute in general average. **Hain Steamship Co Ltd v Tate and Lyle Ltd** [1936] **2** 597, HL.

Hague Rules—
Incorporation in charterparty. *See* **Arbitration** (Commencement—Charterparty—Time-bar—Incorporation of Hague Rules).

Harbour—
Dues—
Priority. *See* **Admiralty** (Appraisement and sale—Payment out of proceeds of sale—Priorities—Harbour dues).
Generally. *See* **Harbour**.

Harter Act—
Compliance with Act—
Limitation of liability—Bill of lading. *See* Bill of lading—Limitation of liability—Stowage—Package—Compliance with Harter Act, *above*.

Hijack—
General average expenditure. *See* General average—General average expenditure—Hijacked vessel, *above*.

Hire, payment of—
Time charterparty. *See* Time charterparty—Payment of hire, *below*.

Insurance. *See* **Marine insurance**.

Interest—
Right to deduct income tax on interest—
Damages in collision cases. *See* Damages in collision cases—Interest—Right to deduct income tax on interest, *above*.

International maritime transport—
EC rules on competition—
Abuse of dominant position. *See* **European Union** (Rules on competition—Abuse of dominant position—Collective dominant position—International maritime transport).

Lay days—
Commencement. *See* Commencement of lay days, *above*.
Expiry. *See* Demurrage—Expiry of laytime, *above*.
Number of lay days. *See* Number of lay days, *below*.

Laytime—
Commencement of laytime following notice of readiness. *See* Commencement of lay days—Notice of readiness to load, *above*.
Number of lay days. *See* Number of lay days, *below*.

Lighterage—
Unseaworthiness—
Exception clause—London Lighterage Clause—Unseaworthiness—Exemption from liability if loss or damage occasioned by unseaworthiness of craft—Whether unseaworthiness to be construed as at commencement of service or after—Exemption excluded if unseaworthy barge supplied recklessly—Meaning of 'recklessly'. **Shawinigan Ltd v Vokins & Co Ltd** [1961] **3** 396, QBD.

Limitation of liability—
Actual fault or privity of owner—
Actual fault of privity of owner who was also master—Collision—Whether entitled to limit liability—Merchant Shipping Act 1894, s 503(1) (as amended)—Merchant Shipping (Liability of Shipowners and Others) Act 1958, s 3(2). **Annie Hay, The** [1968] **1** 657, Admin Ct.
Collision—Fog—Control of owners of ship delegated to shipping department under ultimate supervision of director—Ship equipped with radar—Problems of navigation with radar in fog not impressed on master—Master's addiction to speed known to traffic department—Collision caused by inadequate use of radar and excessive speed in fog—Director alter ego of owners—Whether collision took place without owners' actual fault or privity—Merchant Shipping Act 1894, s 503(1) (as amended by Merchant Shipping (Liability of Shipowners and Others) Act 1958, s 2(1)). **Lady Gwendolen, The** [1965] **2** 283, CA.
Collision—HM ship—Failure of submarine to comply with rules concerning lights—'Actual fault or privity' of Board of Admiralty. **Truculent (HMS)** [1951] **2** 968, Admin Ct.
Collision—Insufficient complement of certificated officers—Breach of merchant shipping ordinance—Merchant Shipping Act 1894, s 503(1). **Empire Jamaica, The** [1956] **3** 144, HL.
Collision—Local traffic signals ignored—Compulsory pilot on board. **Hans Hoth, The** [1953] **1** 218, Admin Ct.
Collision—Owner conceding that navigation of vessel in breach of collision regulations and reckless—Owner seeking decree of limitation—Whether owner entitled to limitation of liability—Whether defendants having real prospect at trial of successfully defending claim for limitation decree—Merchant Shipping Act 1995, s 185, Sch 7, Pt I, art 4. **Margolle v Delta Maritime Co Ltd** [2003] **1 Comm** 102, QBD.

Limitation of liability (cont)—
Actual fault or privity of owner (cont)—
Collision—Owner or charterer by demise—Merchant Shipping Act 1894, s 503(i), (ii)—Merchant Shipping (Liability of Shipowners and Others) Act 1900, s 1—Merchant Shipping Act 1906, s 71—Merchant Shipping Act 1921, s 1(2). **Cory (William) & Son Ltd v Dorman Long & Co Ltd** [1936] **2** 386, CA.

Collision—Radar—If duty arises for owners to take action in respect of master's application of the Collision Regulations the duty is absolute and cannot be divested by delegation—Merchant Shipping Act 1894, s 419—Collision Regulations 1948 (SI 1953 No 1557, Sch 1), r 16(a). **Lady Gwendolen, The** [1965] **2** 283, CA.

Damage caused by master's negligence in using obsolete chart—Ship's managers failing to ensure that master having up-to-date charts—Vessel damaging pipeline not shown on obsolete chart—Whether actual fault of owners—Whether owners under obligation to ensure efficient management of ship in return for benefits conferred by statutory right to limitation—Whether owners entitled to leave navigation matters to discretion of master—Whether owners under duty to ensure master having up-to-date and corrected charts—Whether owners entitled to limitation of liability. **Grand Champion Tankers Ltd v Norpipe A/S** [1984] **2** 343, HL.

Loss of life—Negligence of shipowners' servants—Failure to provide safe system of work—Merchant Shipping Act 1894, s 503(1). **Beauchamp v Turrell** [1952] **1** 719, QBD.

Wreck removal—Expenses of removing barge sunk in canal—Canal undertakers' statutory right of recovery—Barge sunk through improper navigation of owners' servants—No fault or privity in owners—Injury or damage to the canal—Loss or damage caused to property or rights of any kind—Manchester Ship Canal Act 1897, s 9—Merchant Shipping Act 1894, s 503(1)—Merchant Shipping (Liability of Shipowners and Others) Act 1900, ss 1, 3—Manchester Ship Canal Act 1936, s 32(2). **Stonedale No 1, The** [1955] **2** 689, HL.

Bill of lading. *See* Bill of lading—Limitation of liability, *above.*

Collision—
Actual fault or privity of owner. *See* Limitation of liability—Actual fault or privity of owner, *above.*

Government owned ship—HMC ship—Canada Shipping Act 1934, s 649(1), s 712. **Nisbet Shipping Co Ltd v R** [1955] **3** 161, PC.

Contracting out or waiver of statutory right to limit liability—
Vessel colliding with sea berth—Whether permissible to contract out of or waive statutory right of limitation—Whether parties agreeing to exclude statutory right of limitation—Merchant Shipping (Maritime Claims Limitation of Liability) Act 1989—Convention on Limitation of Liability for Maritime Claims 1976. **Bahamas Oil Refining Co International Ltd v Owners of the Cape Bari Tankschiffahrts GMBH & Co KG** [2017] **1 Comm** 189, PC.

Conversion rate—
Rate prevailing at the date of decree—Devaluation of pound sterling after date of collision but before decree of limitation made—Rate for conversion of gold francs mentioned in s 1 of the Act of 1958 varied after devaluation—Whether new conversion rate applicable—Interest on amount fixed as limit of liability—What rate of interest applicable—Merchant Shipping (Liability of Shipowners and Others) Act 1958, s 1(3)—Merchant Shipping (Limitation of Liability) (Sterling Equivalents) Order 1967 (SI 1967 No 1725), art 2. **Abadesa, The** [1968] **2** 726, Admin Ct.

Rate prevailing at the date of decree—Devaluation of pound sterling after date of collision but before decree of limitation made—Rate for conversion of gold francs mentioned in s 1 of the Act of 1958 varied after devaluation—Whether new conversion rate applicable—Interest on amount fixed as limit of liability—What rate of interest applicable—Merchant Shipping (Liability of Shipowners and Others) Act 1958, s 1(3), (4)—Merchant Shipping (Limitation of Liability) (Sterling Equivalents) Order 1967 (SI 1967 No 1725), art 2. **Mecca, The** [1968] **2** 731, Admin Ct.

Costs of limitation action—
Appeal to Court of Appeal—Ordinary rules as to incidence of costs of appeals to be followed in limitation actions. **Bramley Moore, The** [1964] **1** 105, CA.

Appeal to Court of Appeal—Practice. **Empire Jamaica, The** [1955] **3** 60, CA.

Contested action—Plaintiffs to limitation action to pay normal costs of obtaining uncontested decree of limitation—Costs to follow event in contested action—Merchant Shipping Act 1894, s 503, as amended. **Alletta, The, (No 2)** [1972] **2** 414, QBD.

Limitation of liability under Convention on Limitation of Liability for Maritime Claims 1976—Whether costs should follow event where shipowner seeks to limit liability under convention—Merchant Shipping Act 1979, Sch 4, arts 1, 2, 4. **Capitan San Luis, The** [1994] **1** 1016, QBD.

Crown. *See* **Crown** (Crown ship—Collision—Limitation of liability of Crown).

Damage caused by act in 'management or navigation' of ship—
Damage caused by person 'on board' ship—Salvage work—Damage to salved ship caused by diver from salvor's tug—Diver under water firing bolt gun into salved ship—Firing of bolt gun before adjoining tank freed from gas causing explosion—Whether act of diver in 'management or navigation' of tug—Whether act of diver 'on board' tug—Merchant Shipping Act 1894, s 503(1)(d) (as amended by Merchant Shipping (Liability of Shipowners and Others) Act 1958, s 2(1)). **Tojo Maru, The** [1971] **1** 1110, HL.

Decree—
Form—Harbour board claiming in respect of removal of ship sunk in collision—RSC App Q, Form No 2. **Liverpool, The** [1959] **1** 492, Admin Ct.

Liability fund—
Jurisdiction to hear limitation claim—Whether ability to constitute limitation fund pre-condition to jurisdiction—Whether appropriate to grant anti-suit injunction—Merchant Shipping Act 1995, Sch 7, arts 10, 11. **Western Regent (Owners), The v Western Regent (Charterers), The** [2005] **2 Comm** 51, QBD; **Western Regent, The** [2005] **2 Comm** 515, CA.

Jurisdiction to hear limitation claim—Whether entitlement of owner to bring limitation claim limited to circumstances where claim already brought in jurisdiction—Merchant Shipping Act 1995, Sch 7, art 11. **Denise (Owners), The v Denise (Charterers), The** [2005] **2 Comm** 47, QBD.

SHIPPING (cont)—
Limitation of liability (cont)—
Limitation by reference to tonnage of ship—
Charterer—Ability of charterer to limit liability—Whether charterer's right to limit restricted to acts qua shipowner or purely by reference to type of claim—Merchant Shipping Act 1995—1976 Convention on Limitation of Liability for Maritime Claims, arts 1, 2. **CMA CGM SA v Classica Shipping Co Ltd** [2004] **1 Comm** 865, CA.

Limitation fund—
Establishment of fund by guarantee—Vessel lost as result of fire onboard—Owners seeking to establish limitation fund by means of guarantee in form of letter of undertaking provided by protection and indemnity club—Whether possible to establish limitation fund by means of guarantee—Merchant Shipping Act 1995, Sch 7, Pt I, art 11(2). **Kairos Shipping Ltd and another v Enka & Co LLC, The Atlantik Confidence** [2014] **1 Comm** 909, CA.

Interest—Rate of interest applicable. **Funabashi, The** [1972] **2** 181, QBD.

Interest—Shipowner paying into court at commencement of limitation action the limitation figure as at date of payment in plus interest thereon from date of collision to date of payment in—Fund invested—Right of shipowner to limit liability to amount of fund in court established in limitation action—Interest accruing on fund—Whether Admiralty Court having discretion to order payment out of accrued interest on fund in addition to fund itself—Merchant Shipping Act 1894, ss 503(1), 504—Merchant Shipping (Liability of Shipowners and Others) Act 1958, s 1—Supreme Court Act 1981, s 35A(1). **Polish Steam Ship Co v Atlantic Maritime Co** [1984] **3** 59, CA.

Jurisdiction—Cargo owners claiming damages for loss of cargo and arresting vessel in Singapore—Shipowners commencing limitation proceedings in English court—Claim for loss of cargo referred to London arbitration—Limitation convention providing for establishment of limitation fund in state in which 'legal proceedings' instituted—Whether 'legal proceedings' including arbitration proceedings—Whether English court having jurisdiction in relation to security in Singapore—Merchant Shipping Act 1995, Sch 7, arts 11(1), 13(2). **ICL Shipping Ltd v Chin Tai Steel Enterprise Co Ltd** [2004] **1 Comm** 246, QBD.

Notice of limitation fund—Prevention of arrest of other vessels—Notice of limitation fund to be filed in Admiralty Registry—Merchant Shipping Act 1979, Sch 4, Pt I, art 13(1). **Bowbelle, The** [1990] **3** 476, QBD.

Slot charterers—Vessel suffering damage during heavy weather—Shipowner constituting limitation fund for resulting claims—Claims made against slot charterers following accident—Slot charterers seeking to limit liability under fund—Whether charterers being 'shipowners' for purposes of limitation fund—Whether limitation fund deemed constituted by slot charterers as 'shipowners'—Merchant Shipping Act 1995, Sch 7, arts 1, 9, 11. **Metvale Ltd v Monsanto International Sarl** [2009] **1 Comm** 1158, QBD.

Persons entitled to limit liability—
Manager or operator of ship—Dumb barge—Purchaser of cargo undertaking activities on board barge at destination including anchoring vessel and ballasting—Barge dragging anchor during severe weather and damaging undersea cable—Whether purchaser of cargo 'operator' of barge—Whether purchaser entitled to limit liability—Merchant Shipping Act 1995, s 185, Sch 7, Pt I, art 1. **Splitt Chartering APS v Saga Shipholding Norway AS** [2021] **1 Comm** 257, QBD; [2022] **2 Comm** 873, CA.

Storm damaging craft moored in marina—Owner of marina seeking limitation of liability—Whether 'dock' including marina—Meaning of 'dock'—Merchant Shipping Act 1995, s 191. **Holyhead Marina Ltd v Farrer** [2022] **2 Comm** 979, CA.

Servant of person whose liability would not be excluded—
Employer engaged in joint enterprise with third party—Employee injured while on third party's tug under control of third party's employee—Whether third party's employee servant of employer—Whether employer entitled to limit liability—Merchant Shipping (Liability of Shipowners and Others) Act 1958, s 3(2)(a). **McDermid v Nash Dredging and Reclamation Co Ltd** [1987] **2** 878, HL.

Towage—
Collision between ship and dumb barge in tow by tug—Tug and tow in different ownership—Loss of dumb barge—Ship and tug found equally to blame—Tow found free from blame—Whether tug owners entitled to limit liability by sums calculated by reference to tonnage of tug alone—Merchant Shipping Act 1894, s 503(1)(d)(ii) (as amended by Merchant Shipping (Liability of Shipowners and Others) Act 1958, s 2(1)). **Bramley Moore, The** [1964] **1** 105, CA.

Indemnity clause in towage contract—Collision between trawler in tow and tug—Loss of tug and of lives of members of crew—Negligent navigation of trawler—Agreement to indemnify tug-owners against all loss and damage—Standard towage conditions—Claims by dependants of deceased and by owners of tug for negligent navigation—Claim by owners of tug for contractual indemnity—Whether owners of trawler entitled to limit liability—Merchant Shipping Act 1894, s 503(1). **Alsey Steam Fishing Co Ltd v Hillman (owners)** [1957] **1** 97, Admin Ct.

Limitation of liability on basis of tonnage of tug—Collision between ship and tug and barge in tow—Tug and barge in same ownership—Loss of ship—Ship and tug found to blame—Tow free from blame—Whether owner of tug and barge entitled to limit liability by reference to tonnage of tug alone—Merchant Shipping Act 1894, s 503(1)(d)(ii) (as amended by Merchant Shipping (Liability of Shipowners and Others) Act 1958, s 2(1)). **Sir Joseph Rawlinson, The** [1972] **3** 590, QBD.

Wreck removal—
Duty to mitigate loss—Fund paid into court—Claims—Claim by harbour board for expenses of raising wreck, etc—Claim by owners of wreck for liability to harbour board for excess of expenses over proceeds of sale of wreck, etc—Double proof—Duty of harbour board to mitigate loss—Whether owner could claim against fund—Whether harbour board should give credit for amount of owners' claim—Mersey Docks and Harbour Board Act 1954, s 3(3). **Liverpool, The (No 2)** [1960] **3** 307, CA.

Wreck-raising expenses incurred abroad. *See* **Admiralty** (Arrest of vessel—Release—Release following provision of security—Order of foreign court limiting liability and for payment into court).

SHIPPING (cont)—
  Limitation of liability (cont)—
    Wreck removal (cont)—
      Wreck-raising expenses—Removal of wreck by harbour authority under statutory powers—Wreck of vessel sunk in collision in which other ship solely to blame—Claim by owners of ship at fault to limit their liability in respect of wreck-raising expenses—Whether wreck-raising expenses were damage to vessel within Merchant Shipping Act 1894, s 503(1)—Whether wreck-raising expenses were damage caused to property or rights within Merchant Shipping (Liability of Shipowners and Others) Act 1900, s 1. **Arabert, The** [1961] **2** 385, Admin Ct.
  Limitation period—
    Claim for freight—
      Defence not subject to limitation period. *See* Freight—Claim for freight—Defence, *above*.
  Load line—
    Submersion—
      Jurisdiction—Additional fine—Earning capacity increased, but no evidence as to extent of increase—No jurisdiction to impose additional fine—Merchant Shipping (Safety and Load Line Conventions) Act 1932, s 44. **Rutberg v Williams** [1961] **2** 649, QBD.
  Loading—
    Alternative cargo—
      Exception—Strikes, 'Force majeure' or 'hindrance ... beyond charterers' control'—Nomination of loading port where five out of seven grain elevators strike-bound—Wheat intended cargo, but alternative cargo options—Decision of Wheat Board to load only liners and not tramps at port during strike—Sufficient wheat in non-strike bound elevators to load tramps concerned—Delay in loading tramps—Whether nomination of strike-bound loading port valid—Whether charterers protected from demurrage claims by exceptions clause—Whether charterers bound to ship alternative cargoes—Whether, on berth charterparty, charterers in breach for not acquiring cargo until congestion of shipping after strike would allow ship to berth. **Reardon Smith Line Ltd v Ministry of Agriculture, Fisheries and Food** [1963] **1** 545, HL.
      Strike—Charterers not responsible for delay if intended cargo cannot be provided—Alternative cargoes—Duty of charterers to provide alternative cargo—Reasonable time allowable for its provision—Whether cargo intended for shipment must be identifiable. **South African Despatch Line v Panamanian Steamship Niki (owners)** [1960] **1** 285, CA.
    Capacity of vessel—
      Full and complete cargo within maximum and minimum limits—Shipowners' option to declare quantity within those limits—'Approximative cargo' declared by master—Cargo loaded 3.18 per cent short of quantity declared—Whether shipowners in breach of contract—Gencon form charterparty. **Dreyfus (Louis) et Cie v Parnaso Cia Naviera SA** [1960] **1** 759, CA.
    Charterparty terms. *See* Charterparty—Loading, *above*.
    Dock, in—
      Statutory regulation of. *See* **Dock** (Loading and unloading).
    Full and complete cargo—
      De minimis rule. **Margaronis Navigation Agency Ltd v Henry W Peabody & Co of London Ltd** [1964] **3** 333, CA.
      Full cargo of wheat in bulk—Cost of bagging extra cargo—Ownership of bags—Bill of lading in form indorsed on charterparty—Indemnity to shipowner—Additional expense by reason of form of bill of lading. **Thomson v Dreyfus (Louis) & Co** [1936] **3** 687, CA.
      Inability of vessel to load full cargo—Gencon form of charterparty—Whether owners exempted from liability for expense incurred by charterers in sending balance of cargo elsewhere. **Dreyfus (Louis) et Cie v Parnaso Cia Naviera SA** [1960] **1** 759, CA.
      Lawful merchandise—Cargo not capable of being lawfully discharged at destination. **Leolga Cia de Navigacion v John Glynn & Son Ltd** [1953] **2** 327, QBD.
      Primary cargo wheat—Options to ship mixed cargo—No overriding obligation on charterers to exercise options in order to ship full substituted cargo if loading of wheat in bulk delayed by strike—Charterers protected by strike clause from liability for demurrage. **Reardon Smith Line Ltd v Ministry of Agriculture, Fisheries and Food** [1963] **1** 545, HL.
      Timber shipped in bundles—Custom to bundle—Stowage place completely filled but cargo short of carrying capacity—Dead freight. **Ångfartygs A/B Halfdan v Price & Pierce Ltd** [1939] **3** 672, CA.
    Lay days—
      Commencement. *See* Commencement of lay days—Loading, *above*.
    Loading and discharging. *See* Loading and discharging, *below*.
    Loading and stowage of cargo—
      Supervision of master—Master responsible for proper stowage and dunnaging of cargo—Stowage and dunnage instructions given by charterer—Damage to cargo—Improper stowage—Master having followed charterer's stowage instructions—Whether master liable for damage to cargo resulting from improper stowage. **Ismail v Polish Ocean Lines** [1976] **1** 902, CA.
    Nomination of berth—
      Effect of nomination—Selection of berth notified to owners or master—Whether amounting to an election which charterers thereafter unable to change unilaterally. **Prometheus, The** [1974] **1** 597, QBD.
    Nomination of loading port—
      Expenses. *See* Loading and discharging—Expenses—Nomination of loading ports, *below*.
    Number of lay days. *See* Number of lay days—Loading, *below*.
    Provision of cargo—
      Breach of duty—Whether matter of defence or counterclaim. **Sociedad Financiera de Bienes Raices SA v Agrimpex Hungarian Trading Co for Agricultural Products** [1960] **2** 578, HL.
    Readiness to load—
      Expected ready to load—Impossible date. **Jensen v Hollis Bros & Co Ltd** [1936] **1** 140, KBD.
      Fob contract incorporating GAFTA terms —Contract requiring buyers to have vessel presented at loading port in readiness to load within delivery period—Seller refusing to load contending that holds unclean—Whether degree of readiness required in sale agreement similar to that required for shipowners' notice of readiness under charterparty. **Soufflet Nagoce v Bunge SA** [2010] **1 Comm** 1023, QBD; [2011] **2 Comm** 435, CA.

    Loading (cont)—
        Readiness to load (cont)—
            Stowage space occupied by bunkers—Mainmast and after derricks not in position. **Noemijulia Steamship Co Ltd v Minister of Food** [1950] **2** 699, CA.
        Subject to supervision of captain—
            Shipowners to give benefit of insurance 'as far as club rules allow'—Rule giving insurers rights against third parties and rule restraining assignment. **Canadian Transport Co Ltd v Court Line Ltd** [1940] **3** 112, HL.
        Time for loading—
            Obstructions. *See* Demurrage—Exceptions clause—Obstructions—Obstructions preventing loading of cargo—Time for loading not to count during continuance of obstructions, *above*.
        Use of safe ports only—
            Damage caused by entering unsafe port—Safe port—Approved loading place—Warranty of safety of berth—Right of charterers to order loading at two safe loading places—Ship grounded at unsafe loading place—Liability of charterers—Volenti non fit injuria. **Cia Naviera Maropan SA v Bowaters Lloyd Pulp and Paper Mills Ltd** [1955] **2** 241, CA.
            Damage caused by entering unsafe port—Ship damaged at unsafe port or wharf nominated by charterer—Liability of charterer. **Reardon Smith Line Ltd v Australian Wheat Board** [1956] **1** 456, PC.
    Loading and discharging—
        Delay—
            Delay to discharge caused by 'government interferences' not counting as laytime or time on demurrage under charterparty—Whether seizure of cargo by local customs authorities at discharge port constituting 'government interferences'—Sugar Charter Party 1999, cl 28. **Sucden Middle-East v Yagci Denizcilik Ve Ticaret Ltd Sirketi** [2019] **2 Comm** 349, QBD.
            Vessel held in waiting area before being able to berth at discharge port—Claimant seller of crude oil bringing claim against defendant buyer on basis of implied contract—Compensation sought for 'detention' of vessel in waiting area before being able to berth at discharge port and for bunkers consumed whilst waiting—Whether implied contract—Whether claim one for demurrage—Whether claim time-barred. **Glencore Energy UK Ltd v OMV Supply & Trading Ltd** [2018] **2 Comm** 876, QBD.
        Expenses—
            Charterers required to load and discharge cargo at their expense—Ship carrying too much cargo to pass through Panama Canal—Part of cargo off-loaded to enable ship to pass through canal and then reloaded—Whether charterers liable for expenses of off-loading and reloading occurring during voyage. **Actis Co Ltd v Sanko Steamship Co Ltd** [1982] **1** 390, CA.
            Failure to discharge cargo at intended port—Port of discharge changing by agreement between charterers and disponent owners—Charterers agreeing to indemnify disponent owners in respect of all losses, expenses and damages arising from charterers' failure to discharge cargo—Whether disponent owners entitled to indemnity from charterers in respect of cost of traversing Suez Canal notwithstanding terms of a head charter requiring disponent owners to traverse Suez Canal in any event. **HBC Hamburg Bulk Carriers GmbH & Co KG v Huyton Inc** [2016] **1 Comm** 595, QBD.
            Nomination of loading ports—Vessel chartered on Asbatankvoy form—Extra expense incurred following change in nominated loading ports—Owner incurring extra bunkering costs as a result of change—Whether charterer bound to indemnify owner in respect of extra bunkering costs. **Antiparos ENE v SK Shipping Co Ltd** [2009] **1 Comm** 1004, QBD.
        Ship's chief officer injured whilst hatch being closed by ship's crew and charterers' stevedores during temporary loading and discharging of cargo—
            Stevedores participation in hatch closure pursuant to agreement between parties—Whether in the circumstances hatch operation to be regarded as part of act of loading and discharging. **CV Scheepvaartonderneming Flintermar v Sea Malta Co Ltd** [2005] **1 Comm** 497, CA.
    Loss of life—
        Limitation of action—
            Collision. *See* Collision—Limitation of action—Loss of life, *above*.
    Loss of or damage to goods—
        Breach of contract—
            Carriage by sea. *See* Carriage by sea—Damages for breach of contract—Loss of or damage to goods, *above*.
    Loss of profits, assessment of. *See* Damages in collision cases—Loss of profits, *above*.
    Loss or damage to vessel—
        Limitation of action—
            Collision. *See* Collision—Limitation of action—Loss or damage to vessel, *above*.
    Marine insurance. *See* **Marine insurance**.
    Maritime lien—
        Crew—
            Wages. *See* Crew—Wages—Claim for wages—Lien for wages, *above*.
        Enforcement—
            Arrest of ship in action for necessaries—Status of plaintiffs as secured creditors—Administration of Justice Act 1956, s 1(1)(m), (p). **Zafiro, The** [1959] **2** 537, Admin Ct.
        Extent—
            Repairs—Owners' repairs to particular vessel—Possessory lien but not maritime lien. **St Merriel, The** [1963] **1** 537, Admin Ct.
            Wages and disbursements—National insurance contributions—Agreement by employer to pay—Inclusion in wages. **Gee-Whiz, The** [1951] **1** 876, Admin Ct.
        Foreign state-owned vessel—
            Vessel outside territorial jurisdiction—Claim for possession by owners—Motion to set aside writ—Impleading a foreign government. **Cia Naviera Vascongada v Cristina, The Cristina** [1938] **1** 719, HL.

SHIPPING (cont)—
  Maritime lien (cont)—
    Liens recognised by English law—
      Lien for repairs to ship—Lien given by United States law—Lien not recognised as maritime lien by English or Singapore law—Priority—Mortgage having priority under law of Singapore over claim of repairer in distribution of proceeds of sale of ship—Claimant with maritime lien under Singapore law having priority over morgage—Ranking of claims. **Bankers Trust International Ltd v Todd Shipyard Corp** [1980] **3** 197, PC.
      Lien for unpaid national insurance contributions—Italian law—Not recognised maritime lien in English law. **Acrux, The** [1965] **2** 323, Admin Ct.
  Wages—
    Crew—Master. See Crew—Master—Wages—Claim for wages—Lien for wages, above.
    Seaman—Special contract—Wages payable under a special contract—Pension fund contributions—Employer's and employee's contributions—Failure of employer to pay contributions to fund—Lien on ship—Whether seaman entitled to maritime lien in respect of unpaid contributions—Administration of Justice Act 1956, ss 1(1)(o), 3(3). **Halcyon Skies, The** [1976] **1** 856, QBD.
  Maritime transport—
    European Union—
      Freedom of movement. See **European Union** (Freedom of movement—Services—Maritime transport).
  Mate's receipt—
    Production—
      Issue of bill of lading. See Bill of lading—Issued to shippers without production of mate's receipts, above.
  Misdelivery of cargo—
    Time limit for bringing action. See Carriage by sea—Damages for breach of contract—Time limit for bringing action—Misdelivery of cargo, above.
  Navigation—
    Combining to impede navigation. See Seamen—Offence—Combining to impede navigation, below.
  Merchant shipping—
    Demurrage—Liability for demurrage. **Triton Navigation Ltd v Vitol SA** [2004] **1** Comm 698, CA.
  Negligent navigation—
    Exemption clause in time charter. See Time charterparty—Exceptions—Negligent navigation, below.
  Public right of navigation—
    Generally. See **Water and watercourses** (Navigation—Public right of navigation (PRN)).
  Reservoir. See **Water and watercourses** (Navigation—Reservoir).
  Rules. See Navigation rules, below.
  Navigation rules—
    River Thames—
      Barge—Barge dropping down river on her anchor—Port of London River Bye-laws 1914-1934, bye-laws 5, 14. **Union Lighterage Co Ltd v Curlew (owners), The Curlew** [1936] **3** 676, Admin Ct.
      Waiting at bend—Risk of collision when approaching or rounding a point—Port of London River Bye-Laws 1938, bye-law 42(a). **Timandra, The** [1956] **2** 531, Admin Ct.
  Negligence—
    Carriage by sea—
      Passengers. See Passengers—Carriage by sea—Negligence, below.
    Collision cases. See Negligence in collision cases, below.
    Navigation—
      Exemption clause in time charter. See Time charterparty—Exceptions—Negligent navigation, below.
    Towage—Collision. See Collision—Towage—Negligent navigation, above.
    Salvage. See Salvage—Negligence of salvor, below.
    Survey of ship. See **Negligence** (Duty to take care—Survey of ship).
  Negligence in collision cases—
    Apportionment of liability—
      Apportionment equally if 'not possible to establish different degrees of fault'—Meaning—Maritime Conventions Act 1911, s 1(1). **Anneliese, The** [1970] **2** 29, CA.
      Collision between container vessel and array being towed by seismic survey vessel—Whether and extent to which seismic survey vessel at fault. **Western Neptune (owners, demise charterers and time charterers) v Philadelphia Express (owners and demise charterers)** [2010] **2** Comm 154, QBD.
      Collision regulations. See Collision regulations—Crossing vessels—Narrow channel rule, above.
      Contribution—Damages for loss of life or personal injuries—Plaintiffs one-third and defendants two-thirds to blame—Declaration of plaintiff's right to contribution—Scope of Maritime Conventions Act 1911, ss 2, 3. **Abadesa, The** [1966] **1** 190, Admin Ct.
      Defendants' ship grounding but refloated after collision with plaintiffs' ship for which defendants' ship 55 per cent to blame—Grounding of defendants' ship and collision with salvage tug following day while executing turning manoeuvre—Second grounding partly caused by negligence of defendants' ship's officer—Whether damage to defendants' ship by second grounding too remote to be recoverable or whether later negligence and original collision both causative—Whether further sub-apportionment of liability for second grounding permissible—Maritime Conventions Act 1911, s 1(1). **Calliope, The** [1970] **1** 624, PDA.
      Differentiation between vessels involved not possible—Whether appellate court would interfere with decision. **Lucile Bloomfield, The** [1967] **2** 633, CA.
      Ship in canal under tow—Collision between steam tug and passing vessel—No signal by tow to tug to warn her of on-coming vessel—Officer-in-charge of tug negligent in not stopping her port propeller revolving on seeing on-coming vessel—Whether tug-owners or tow-owners liable for negligence of officer-in-charge of tug—Maritime Conventions Act 1911, s 1(1). **Panther, The, and The Ericbank** [1957] **1** 641, Admin Ct.

Negligence in collision cases (cont)—
 Apportionment of liability (cont)—
  Ship in convoy, escorted by naval escort, and vessel on crossing course—Escort vessels equipped
   with radar and linked with convoy by radio-telephone communication—Failure of senior officer to
   warn convoy—Liability for contributory negligence—Application of Maritime Conventions Act
   1911, s 1(1). **Sobieski, The** [1949] **1** 701, CA.
  Two ships in collision—Third ship damaged trying to avoid colliding ships—Contribution to
   damage suffered by third ship—Method of apportionment of liability—Maritime Conventions Act
   1911, s 1(1). **Miraflores, The, and the Abadesa** [1967] **1** 672, HL.
  Vessel improperly moored athwart fairway—Insufficient look-out. **Corstar (owners) v Eurymedon**
   (owners) [1938] **1** 122, CA.
 Subrogation—
  Collision with jetty—Berthing of oil tanker at oil terminal—Tanker colliding with jetty and escaping
   oil polluting foreshore—Shipowners making payments to occupiers of foreshore in respect of
   pollution damage under voluntary agreement between major oil companies—Shipowners also
   making payments under arbitration award to operators of oil terminal for work done to clear up
   pollution—Whether shipowners entitled to sue tortfeasor in own name—Whether shipowners
   entitled to recover sums paid from tortfeasor as economic loss directly resulting from damage to
   their tanker. **Esso Petroleum Co Ltd v Hall Russell & Co Ltd (Shetland Islands Council, third party)**
   [1989] **1** 37, HL.
Notice of readiness—
 Arrived ship under port charterparty. *See* Commencement of lay days—Arrived ship under port
  charterparty—Notice of readiness, *above.*
Number of lay days—
 Loading—
  Excepted perils preventing time from counting as laytime—Mechanical breakdowns at mechanical
   loading port—Government interferences—Ship arriving off loading port and giving notice of
   readiness—Intended loading terminal unusable due to fire—Ship spending significant time
   waiting and making arrangements to berth at alternative terminal—Whether charterers required
   to have nominated berth in order for excepted perils clause to apply to prevent laytime from
   running—Whether fire at loading terminal mounting to 'mechanical breakdown'—Whether a
   refusal by port authority to allow vessels from loading at damaged terminal amounting to
   government interference. **ED&F Man Sugar Ltd v Unicargo Transportgesellschaft mbH** [2013] **1**
   Comm 955, QBD.
  Method of calculating lay days—Rate of loading. **Cia de Navigacion Zita, SA v Louis Dreyfus et Cie**
   [1953] **2** 1359, QBD; **Salgaoncar E Irmaos (VM) of Vasco de Gama v Goulandris Bros Ltd**
   [1954] **1** 563, QBD.
 Method of computation—
  Saturdays. **Reardon Smith Line Ltd v Ministry of Agriculture, Fisheries and Food** [1963] **1** 545, HL.
 Weather working days—
  Part of day unusable because of weather—Apportionment of usable and non-usable time in
   calculating weather working days. **Reardon Smith Line Ltd v Ministry of Agriculture, Fisheries**
   and Food [1963] **1** 545, HL.
  Regard to be had to working hours—Need to deduct number of hours during which work
   suspended because of weather. **Alvion Steamship Corp of Panama v Galban Lobo Trading Co SA**
   of Havana [1955] **1** 457, CA.
  Ship ordered by harbour master from berth for six days due to threat of bore tide—Illegality of
   loading—Whether time when ship absent from berth to be included in assessment of lay-time.
   Cia Crystal de Vapores of Panama v Herman & Mohatta (India) Ltd [1958] **2** 508, QBD.
  Weather such as to justify work being stopped—Work not interrupted, or not intended to be done,
   at that time—Whether times excluded in computing lay time. **Cia Naviera Azuero SA v British Oil**
   and Cake Mills Ltd [1957] **2** 241, QBD.
  Working days not unavailable for work because of weather—Expression not including non-working
   days on which weather would have permitted working. **Reardon Smith Line Ltd v Ministry of**
   Agriculture, Fisheries and Food [1963] **1** 545, HL.
  Working days—Overtime—Whether overtime included. **Maatschappij Zeevart (NV) v Friesacher (M)**
   Soehne [1962] **2** 511, QBD.
Obstructions—
 Exceptions clause—
  Demurrage. *See* Demurrage—Exceptions clause—Obstructions, *above.*
Off-hire clause. *See* Charterparty—Off-hire clause, *above.*
Offence—
 Act of master of ship causing death or serious injury—
  Rider of jet ski causing serious injury—Whether jet ski 'ship'—Whether jet ski 'vessel used in
   navigation'—Merchant Shipping Act 1995, ss 58, 313(1). **R v Goodwin** [2006] **2 Comm** 281,
   CA; [2006] **2** 519, CA.
 Failure to operate ship in safe manner—
  Shipowner's liability—Company chartering ship—Engine failure on ship—Failure due to fault by
   someone in company—Whether company vicariously liable for all acts of its employees—Nature
   of offence—Merchant Shipping Act 1988, s 31. **Seaboard Offshore Ltd v Secretary of State for**
   Transport [1994] **2** 99, HL.
 Seamen. *See* Seamen—Offence, *below.*
Oil in navigable waters—
 Discharge of oil into navigable waters—
  Damage to adjoining land. *See* **Trespass to land** (Oil—Discharge of oil into public navigable
   waters—Damage to adjoining land).
 Discharge of oil into prohibited sea area—
  Owner or master guilty of offence—Whether 'or' used in alternative and exclusionary
   sense—Whether owner and master may both be convicted of offence in respect of same
   discharge—Oil in Navigable Waters Act 1955, s 1(1), as amended by the Oil in Navigable Waters
   Act 1963, s 3, Schs 1, 2. **Federal Steam Navigation Co Ltd v Dept of Trade and Industry**
   [1974] **2** 97, HL.

SHIPPING (cont)—
Oil in navigable waters (cont)—
Discharge of oil into United Kingdom waters—
Waters navigable by sea-going ships—Dry dock—Vessel in dock—Dock navigable by sea-going ships when full of water—Discharge of oil from vessel when water partially pumped out of dock—Water no longer navigable at that stage—Whether oil discharged into 'waters...navigable by sea-going ships'—Prevention of Oil Pollution Act 1971, s 2(2)(b). **Rankin v De Coster** [1975] **2** 303, QBD.
Passenger steamer—
Certificate—
Fishing vessel used for pleasure trip—Need for certificate as to survey—Merchant Shipping Act 1894, s 267, s 271(1). **Graham v Duncan** [1950] **2** 534, KBD.
Meaning of 'passenger' for purpose of statutory requirements. *See* Passengers—Ship carrying more than 12 passengers required to have certificate of survey, *below*.
Passengers—
Carriage by sea—
Limitation of action—Personal injury action by passenger—Court's discretion to extend or exclude time limit. *See* **Limitation of action** (Court's power to override time limit in personal injury or fatal accident claim—Exercise of discretion—Carriage of passengers by sea).
Limitation of action—Personal injury action by passenger—Passenger bringing claim against appellant for personal injuries sustained whilst on board rigid inflatable boat—Appellant claiming contribution from sea carrier in respect of liability to passenger—Whether Athens Convention extending to contribution claims against carrier—Whether Athens Convention time bar for bringing claim against carrier applying—Civil Liability (Contribution) Act 1978, s 1—Merchant Shipping Act 1995, Sch 6, Pt I, arts 14, 16. **Feest v South West Strategic Health Authority (Bay Island Voyages, Part 20 defendant)** [2016] **1 Comm** 821, CA; [2016] **4** 107, CA.
Negligence—Exclusion of liability in contract of carriage—Conditions of passenger ticket—Exclusion of liability for loss or damage in certain circumstances—'From any other cause whatsoever'—Passenger slipping on floor being washed. **Beaumont-Thomas v Blue Star Line Ltd** [1939] **3** 127, CA.
Negligence—Exclusion of liability in contract of carriage—Protection of independent contractors and others not parties to the contract—Distinction between carriage of goods and carriage of passengers. **Adler v Dickson** [1954] **3** 397, CA.
Ship carrying more than 12 passengers required to have certificate of survey—
Ship used for sail training excursions for groups of people—Groups participating in sailing vessel—Whether people in groups 'passengers'—Whether people in groups 'engaged ... on the business of the ship'—Merchant Shipping Act 1894, s 271—Merchant Shipping (Safety Convention) Act 1949, s 26(1)(a). **Secretary of State for Trade and Industry v Booth** [1984] **1** 464, QBD.
Pilotage district. *See* **Harbour** (Pilotage district).
Port charterparty—
Arrived ship under port charterparty—
Commencement of laytime. *See* Commencement of lay days—Arrived ship under port charterparty, *above*.
Nomination of berth—
Effect of nomination—Selection of berth notified to owners or master—Whether amounting to an election which charterers thereafter unable to change unilaterally. **Prometheus, The** [1974] **1** 597, QBD.
Obstructions preventing loading of cargo—
Time for loading not to count during continuance of obstructions. *See* Demurrage—Exceptions clause—Obstructions—Obstructions preventing loading of cargo—Time for loading not to count during continuance of obstructions, *above*.
Prize law. *See* **Prize law**.
Production of bill of lading—
Delivery of cargo. *See* Bill of lading—Delivery of cargo—Production of bill of lading, *above*.
Repairs—
General average contribution. *See* General average—General average expenditure—Temporary repairs, *above*.
Safe berth—
Charterparty. *See* Charterparty—Safe berth, *above*.
Safe port—
Charterparty. *See* Charterparty—Safe port, *above*.
Safety convention—
Deck cargo—
Height—Timber carried on deck—Permitted height exceeded in two places—Whether more than one offence—Timber Cargo Regulations 1932 (SR & O 1932 No 110)—Merchant Shipping (Safety and Load Line Conventions) Act 1932, s 61(4), (6). **R v Campbell, ex p Nomikos** [1956] **2** 280, QBD.
Sale contract—
Demurrage. *See* Demurrage—Sale contract, *above*.
Sale of goods—
Implied terms as to merchantable quality and quality and fitness for purpose. *See* **Sale of goods** (Implied condition as to merchantable quality—Implied terms as to quality and fitness for purpose—F o b contract).
Sale of ship. *See* Sale of ship, *below*.
Sale of ship—
Chartered ship. *See* Charterparty—Sale of chartered ship, *above*.
Generally. *See* **Ship** (Sale).
Implied conditions as to satisfactory quality. *See* **Sale of goods** (Implied conditions as to satisfactory quality—Exclusion of implied terms—Contract for sale of ship on Norwegian Saleform 1993).

SHIPPING (cont)—
Sale of ship (cont)—
Seller's warranty and indemnity—
Sellers of vessels warranting that they were free from all encumbrances, mortgages and maritime liens—Sellers indemnifying buyers against consequences of claims made against vessels 'incurred prior to the time of delivery'—Defendant guaranteeing sellers' obligations under indemnity subject to specified limits per vessel 'in respect of any claim'—Guarantee remaining in force for one year—Scope of indemnity and guarantee—Norwegian sale form, cl 9. **Rank Enterprises Ltd v Gerard** [1999] **2 Comm** 749, QBD.

Salvage—
Admiralty jurisdiction—
Action in rem. *See* **Admiralty** (Jurisdiction—Action in rem—Claim in nature of salvage).
Agreement—
Admiralty jurisdiction. *See* **Admiralty** (Jurisdiction—Action in rem—Claim arising out of agreement relating to use or hire of ship—Salvage agreement).
Arbitration—Jurisdiction of arbitrator. *See* **Arbitration** (Arbitrator—Jurisdiction—Salvage arbitration).
Arbitration. *See* **Arbitration** (Salvage arbitration).
Cargo—
Storage expenses—Agreement—Vessel stranding—Master signing Lloyd's standard salvage agreement on behalf of shipowner and cargo owner—Arrangements made by salvors for storage of cargo ashore—Voyage abandoned by shipowner—Whether shipowner or cargo owner liable for storage expenses ashore—Whether salvors' authority limited to salving cargo—Whether cargo owner entitled to benefit of storage without paying for it. **China-Pacific SA v Food Corp of India** [1981] **3** 688, HL.
Costs—
County court jurisdiction. *See* **Admiralty** (Costs—Jurisdiction—County court—Salvage action).
Definition—
Distinction between towage and salvage—Ship losing propeller—Towed to place of temporary safety—Towed to home port via ports at which repairs could be effected and alternative service available—Whether salvage or towage. **Troilus, The** [1951] **2** 40, HL.
Disqualification from claiming salvage—
Salvage services by ship in same ownership as ship in collision—Remuneration—Circuity of action. **Kafiristan, The** [1937] **3** 747, HL.
Salving vessel and colliding vessel under control of different departments of Crown—Circuity of action. **Susan v Luckenbach, The** [1951] **1** 753, CA.
Evidence—
Ship's log—Admissibility—Admissions in pleadings—Inferences from admissions. **Finland (owners) v Cornish Rose (owners)** [1936] **2** 805, Admin Ct.
Negligence of salvor—
Damage to salved vessel—Successful salvage—Liability of salvor for negligence—Claim by salvor to award—Counterclaim by shipowner for damages—Damages exceeding remuneration to which salvor entitled—Whether shipowner restricted to right of set-off against salvage award—Whether shipowner entitled to maintain action for amount of actual loss. **Tojo Maru, The** [1971] **1** 1110, HL.
Degree of care and skill—Salvage department of navy. **Anglo-Saxon Petroleum Co Ltd v Damant** [1947] **2** 465, CA.
Payment into court—
Two sums paid into court—Two vessels belonging to same owner salvaged by five tugs and four tugs respectively also belonging to one owner—Payment into court of two separate sums in respect of each salved vessel—Separate causes of action by owners, master and crew of each tug joined in one action—Whether separate sums should be allocated in respect of each tug rendering salvage services—RSC Ord 22, r 1(5). **Talamba, The, and The Troll** [1965] **2** 775, Admin Ct.
Right to claim salvage—
Limitation—Limitation period of two years commencing on day 'salvage operations are terminated'—Claimant diver being refused salvage award—Whether salvage operations terminating when everything raised from seabed—Whether claim to salvage time-barred—International Convention on Salvage 1989, art 23(1). **R (on the application of Knight) v Secretary of State for Transport (Huzzey, interested parties)** [2018] **1 Comm** 1082, QBD.
Plaintiffs' tug providing assistance to defendants' vessel—Plaintiffs claiming salvage—Defendants contending that their vessel was not in danger—Whether views of those on board defendants' vessel relevant in assessing whether there was salvage danger—Whether award should include element to encourage plaintiffs to invest in salvage. **Hamtun, The, (owners) v The St John (owners)** [1999] **1 Comm** 587, QBD.
Port authority and employees—Exercise of statutory powers—Port authority and employees removing ship blocking harbour—Whether port authority and employees entitled to claim salvage—Merchant Shipping Act 1894, s 530—Boston Corporation Act 1935, s 26(1). **Gregerso, The** [1971] **1** 961, Admin Ct.
Salvage award—
Agreement as to amount—His Majesty's ships—Special agreement—Public policy—Merchant Shipping Act 1894, s 557—Merchant Shipping (Salvage) Act 1916, s 1. **Admiralty Comrs v Valverda (owners)** [1938] **1** 162, HL.
Apportionment among crew—Basis—Basic pay—Exclusion of war bonus. **Wilkinson v Barking Corp** [1948] **1** 564, CA.
Apportionment between owners, masters and crew. **Nestor (owners) v Mungana (owners)** [1936] **3** 670, Admin Ct.
Apportionment between two sets of salvors—Payment into court—One sum—Two salvors—Two causes of action consolidated—Whether sum paid need be apportioned between two salvors—RSC Ord 22, r 1(2). **Bosworth, The** [1960] **1** 146, Admin Ct.
Assessment of amount of award—Devaluation—Devaluation of pound sterling between termination of salvage services and award—Lloyd's standard form of salvage agreement—Whether devaluation relevant factor in fixing amount of award. **Teh Hu, The** [1969] **3** 1200, CA.

SHIPPING (cont)—
  Salvage (cont)—
    Salvage award (cont)—
      Assessment of amount of award—Disparity principle—Principle that sum awarded in 'straightforward towage cases' should not be wholly out of line with commercial towage rates—Whether disparity principle flawed—Whether commercial towage rates relevant to assessment. **Owners of the vessel 'Voutakos' v Tsavliris Salvage (International) Ltd** [2009] **1 Comm** 1067, QBD.

      Assessment of amount of award—Encouragement—Relevance of amount of salved fund—Whether permissible to take difficult future economic conditions into account to enhance award—Whether principle that although value of property salved to be considered in assessment of remuneration it must not be allowed to raise quantum to an amount altogether out of proportion to the services actually rendered applicable to complex and comprehensive cases. **Ocean Crown (owners) v Five Oceans Salvage Consultants** [2010] **2 Comm** 931, QBD.

      Assessment of amount of award—Tax liability—Award for personal services—Award liable to taxation in hands of salvors—Whether taxation taken into account in assessing amount of award. **Telemachus, The** [1957] **1** 72, Admin Ct.

      Assessment of amount of award—Tax liability—Award liable to taxation in hands of salvors—Whether taxation to be taken into account in assessing amount of award. **Island Tug & Barge Ltd v Makedonia Owners** [1958] **1** 236, QBD.

      Contribution—Value of ship. **Eisenach, The** [1936] **1** 855, Admin Ct.

      Interest—Admiralty Court—Power to award interest on salvage award—Proceedings for recovery of debt—Salvage services not rendered under any special form of salvage agreement—Whether proceedings for the recovery of salvage remuneration proceedings for recovery of debt—Whether Admiralty Court having jurisdiction to award interest—Law Reform (Miscellaneous Provisions) Act 1934, s 3(1). **Aldora, The** [1975] **2** 69, QBD.

      Special compensation for preventing or minimising damage to environment—Salvor entitled to special compensation of proportion of out-of-pocket expenses reasonably incurred in salvage operation and fair rate for equipment and personnel actually and reasonably used in salvage operation—Expenses—Fair rate—Whether fair rate should include profit element—International Convention on Salvage 1989, arts 13, 14. **Semco Salvage and Marine Pte Ltd v Lancer Navigation Co Ltd** [1997] **1** 502, HL.

    Statement of claim—
      Application to amend to plead further services. *See* **Admiralty** (Practice—Action in rem—Writ—Amendment—Application to amend statement of claim to plead further salvage services rendered to same ship).

  Seamen—
    Offence—
      Absence without leave—Seaman lawfully engaged to serve in fishing boat—Substitute—Oral engagement—Fishing boat's running agreement not signed—Refusal to proceed to sea—Merchant Shipping Act 1894, ss 376(1)(b), (d), 401(3). **Crawley v Parsons** [1952] **2** 488, QBD.

      Combining to impede navigation—Contract for service for commercial voyage—Refusal to load cargo of nitrate for war zone—Whether offence committed of combining to impede navigation of ship—Merchant Shipping Act 1894, s 225(1)(e). **Robson v Sykes** [1938] **2** 612, KBD.

      Continued wilful disobedience to lawful command—Seaman lawfully engaged to serve in fishing boat—Absence of seaman on shore without leave—Several commands by persons in authority to return on board wilfully disobeyed—Whether continued wilful disobedience to single command sufficient to constitute offence under Merchant Shipping Act 1894, s 376(1)(e). **Page v Williams** [1965] **1** 30, QBD.

      Desertion—Contract for service for two years—Seaman dissatisfied with treatment by ship's doctor—Advice by shore doctor that operation immediately necessary—Master not informed by seaman—Seaman going to hospital disobeying master's order to stay aboard pending inquiries—Whether desertion—Merchant Shipping Act 1894, ss 221, 228—Merchant Shipping Act 1906, s 36(1). **Moore v Canadian Pacific Steamship Co** [1945] **1** 128, Assizes.

      Evidence—Admissibility—Charges under Defence (General) Regulations—Ship's log-book—Entry not brought to man's notice as provided by the Merchant Shipping Act 1894—Whether log-book admissible as evidence of charge—Defence (General) Regulations 1939, reg 47A—Merchant Shipping Act 1894, ss 228, 239, 695. **Robinson v Robson** [1943] **1** 511, KBD.

    Wages—
      Claim by master. *See* Crew—Master—Wages—Claim for wages, *above*.

      Deduction from wages of fines—Statutory bar to further proceedings under Merchant Shipping Acts—Absentee punished by master by forfeiture of wages—Subsequent charge under Defence (General) Regulations—Whether seaman entitled to plead autrefois convict—Merchant Shipping Act 1894, ss 159, 221—Merchant Shipping Act 1906, s 44(5)—Defence (General) Regulations 1939, reg 47A. **Lewis v Mogan** [1943] **2** 272, KBD.

      Entitlement—When right to wages ends—Whether contract of service terminated by issue of writ—Whether judgment in action can be given for wages accruing after issue of writ. **Fairport, The** [1966] **2** 1026, Admin Ct.

      Entitlement—Wreck or loss of ship—Ship abandoned some time after original injury—Date of wreck—Merchant Shipping (International Labour Conventions) Act 1925, s 1(1). **Terneuzen, The** [1938] **2** 348, Admin Ct.

  Seaport—
    Public authority's discretion to ban export of live animals. *See* **Public authority** (Operation of air and sea ports—Discretion—Discretion to ban export of live animals).

  Seaworthiness of vessel—
    Charterparty incorporating Hague Rules. *See* Charterparty—Seaworthiness of vessel, *above*.
    General average. *See* General average—General average expenditure—Unseaworthiness, *above*.
    Implied term—
      Bill of lading. *See* Bill of lading—Implied undertaking to use due diligence to make ship seaworthy, *above*.
      Charterparty. *See* Charterparty—Seaworthiness, *above*.
    Terms of charterparty. *See* Charterparty—Seaworthiness of vessel, *above*.

SHIPPING (cont)—
Shipbuilding contract—
    Construction. *See* **Contract** (Construction—Shipbuilding contract).
    Generally. *See* **Contract** (Shipbuilding contract).
Shipment of goods—
    Description. *See* **Sale of goods** (Description—Shipment of goods).
Shipowners—
    Immunities of shipowners—
        Bill of lading. *See* Bill of lading—Immunities of shipowner, *above*.
        Limitation of liability. *See* Limitation of liability, *above*.
Shipping casualty—
    Formal investigation—
        Findings of formal investigation—Whether findings binding in subsequent collision or limitation action. *See* **Estoppel** (Issue estoppel—Shipping—Collision—Court of formal investigation).
        Procedure—Report—Rider by one assessor censuring chief engineer—No charge against chief engineer—Irregularity. **Seistan, The** [1960] **1** 32, Admin Ct.
        Rehearing of formal investigation—Costs—Principles to be applied. **MV Derbyshire, Rehearing of the Formal Investigation into the Loss of the** [2003] **1 Comm** 784, QBD.
        Suspension of master's certificate—Court of formal investigation—Report and annex read out in open court—Report subsequently altered—Altered report to be disregarded—Report recommending suspension of certificate—No clear decision to suspend—Whether suspension valid—Merchant Shipping Act 1894, s 470(1)(a), (2), (3). **Corchester, The** [1956] **3** 878, Admin Ct.
Slot charter—
    Arrest of vessel—
        Admiralty jurisdiction. *See* **Admiralty** (Jurisdiction—Action in rem—Arrest of ship—Slot charter).
    Limitation of liability. *See* Limitation of liability—Limitation fund—Slot charterers, *above*.
Stowage—
    Limitation of liability—
        Bill of lading. *See* Bill of lading—Limitation of liability—Stowage, *above*.
Stranding of vessel—
    Negligence—
        Pleading. *See* **Negligence** (Pleading—Stranding of vessel).
Strike—
    Demurrage—
        Exceptions clause. *See* Demurrage—Exceptions clause—Strike occurring while vessel on demurrage, *above*.
        Rate of demurrage. *See* Demurrage—Rate of demurrage—Strike, *above*.
    Laytime not counting during period of strike—
        Exceptions clause—Demurrage. *See* Demurrage—Exceptions clause—Laytime not counting during period of strike, *above*.
    Strike occurring while vessel on demurrage—
        Exceptions clause—Demurrage. *See* Demurrage—Exceptions clause—Strike occurring while vessel on demurrage, *above*.
Survey of ship—
    Negligence. *See* **Negligence** (Duty to take care—Survey of ship).
Time bar—
    Demurrage. *See* Demurrage—Claim—Time bar, *above*.
Time charterparty—
    Cancelling clause—
        Liberty to cancel if 'war breaks out involving Japan'—Meaning of 'war'. **Kawasaki Kisen Kabushiki Kaisha of Kobe v Bantham Steamship Co Ltd** [1939] **1** 819, CA.
        Liberty to cancel should certain powers become engaged in war with one another—Time within which option should be exercised—Implied term—Reasonable time. **Kawasaki Kisen Kabushiki Kaisha and Belships Co Ltd, Skibsaksjeselskap, Re an arbitration between** [1939] **2** 108, KBD.
    Cancelling date—
        Charterers at liberty to cancel charterparty if vessel not delivered at port in charterers' option by cancelling date—Vessel not delivered by cancelling date—Vessel not within range of potential delivery ports by cancelling date—Charterers not nominating delivery port—Charterers cancelling charterparty—Whether charterers entitled to cancel charterparty without having nominated delivery port. **Mansel Oil Ltd v Troon Storage Tankers SA** [2008] **2 Comm** 898, QBD; [2009] **2 Comm** 495, CA.
    Cargo—
        Time charterparty on New York Product Exchange Form incorporating Inter-Club Agreement 1996 (ICA)—ICA apportioning full liability to charterers for cargo claims where claim arising out of act of charterer—Damage to cargo caused by charterers' order to vessel to wait off discharge port—Whether fault or culpability required for charterers to bear full liability—Inter-Club Agreement 1996, cl 8(d). **Transgrain Shipping (Singapore) Pte Ltd v Yangtze Navigation (Hong Kong) Co Ltd** [2018] **2 Comm** 99, CA.
    Cesser of hire—
        Baltime charterparty—Damage hindering discharge—Additional costs of discharge. **Tynedale Steam Shipping Co Ltd v Anglo-Soviet Shipping Co Ltd** [1936] **1** 389, CA.
        Hire not payable if time lost from 'cause preventing full working of vessel'—Ship carrying too much cargo to pass through Panama Canal—Time lost while ship lightened to enable it to pass through canal—Whether overloading preventing full working of vessel. **Actis Co Ltd v Sanko Steamship Co Ltd** [1982] **1** 390, CA.
        Hire not payable in event of damage to hull or other accident hindering efficient working of vessel—Accident—Something unexpected or out of ordinary course of things—Vessel's hull becoming encrusted with thick coat of molluscs in fresh water port—Molluscs normally preferring salt water—Encrustation on vessel's hull resulting in material reduction in her speed—Whether encrustation an 'accident'—Whether charterers entitled not to pay hire for time lost as a result of vessel's reduction in speed. **Cosmos Bulk Transport Inc v China National Foreign Trade Transportation Corp** [1978] **1** 322, QBD.

SHIPPING (cont)—
Time charterparty (cont)—
Cesser of hire (cont)—
Hire not payable in respect of time lost owing to 'deficiency of men...or other accident'—Refusal of
officers and men to sail during war except in convoy. **Greek Government v Minister of Transport**
[1949] 1 171, CA.
Period occupied in fitting degaussing apparatus. **Sea and Land Securities Ltd and William
Dickinson & Co Ltd, Re an arbitration between** [1942] 1 503, CA.
Ship torpedoed but not sinking until 14 days later—When hire ceases to be payable—Actual total
loss—Constructive total loss—Abandonment—Marine Insurance Act 1906, ss 57(1), 60, 61, 62(1),
63. **Court Line Ltd v R** [1945] 2 357, CA.
Damages for breach—
Early termination—At time of termination shipping market having collapsed and no available
market for period charter corresponding to balance of charterparty—Market subsequently
reviving at later date but prior to contractual expiry date of charter—Appropriate measure of
damages. **Glory Wealth Shipping Pte Ltd v Korea Line Corp** [2012] 1 Comm 402, QBD.
Early termination—Whether damages should be based on hire which would have been earned by
replacing the charters with timecharter employment or by reference to owner's actual earnings
for unexpired term. **Spar Shipping AS v Grand China Logistics Holding (Group) Co Ltd** [2015] 1
Comm 879, QBD.
Damages for breach. *See* Time charterparty—Last voyage—Late redelivery—Charterers giving notice of
redelivery for last possible date under charterparty, *below*.
Duration of charterparty—
Extension of period to complete voyage—Days more or less at the charterers' option
clause—Whether charterers entitled to begin new voyage during days more at charterers' option
period—Whether period of charter including days more at charterers' option period for purposes
of clause permitting charterers to have use of vessel for extended time if vessel on voyage at time
of expiry of charter. **Petroleo Brasileiro SA v Kriti Akti Shipping Co SA** [2004] 2 Comm 396, CA.
Extension of period to complete voyage—Exercise of option on charter period extension—When
period of charter ended—Whether hire after charter period ended payable at charter rate or
market rate—Meaning of 'will be exceeded'. **Hector Steamship Co Ltd v VO Sovfracht, Moscow**
[1945] 1 540, KBD.
Extension of period to complete voyage—Voyage continuing after specified period because of dock
strikes—Whether hire for excess period payable at charter rate, or market rate. **Timber Shipping
Co SA v London and Overseas Freighters Ltd** [1971] 2 599, HL.
Employment and indemnity clause—
Master to be under orders of charterers—Charterers to indemnify owners against all liabilities
arising from compliance with orders—Charterers responsible for loss or damage caused to
owners by improper or negligent act by them or their servants—'Servants'—Independent
contractors engaged by charterers to load vessel—Stevedore injured—Owners paid sum to
stevedore in settlement of potential liability—Whether sum recoverable from charterers. **White
Rose, The** [1969] 3 374, QBD.
Master to follow orders of charterers—Charterers instructing master to follow shorter
route—Master taking longer route for safety of vessel—Whether routeing instructions orders as
to employment or navigation of vessel—Whether charterers entitled to deduct hire for additional
days at sea and cost of extra bunkers consumed. **Whistler International Ltd v Kawasaki Kisen
Kaisha Ltd** [1998] 4 286, QBD.
Master to obey order of charterer 'as regards employment'—Ship stranded while returning home in
ballast after discharging cargo at War Base—Ship ordered to leave port by charterer's
representative—Chief officer's request to postpone sailing owing to bad weather refused by sea
transport officer—Stranding of ship not consequence of order—Charterer not liable for Naval
Orders. **Larrinaga Steamship Co Ltd v R** [1945] 1 329, HL.
Employment clause—
Charterparty requiring master to follow orders of charterers and to prosecute voyage with utmost
despatch—Charterparty incorporating provision exempting owners from liability for any act,
neglect or default of master in navigation—Charterers instructing master to follow shorter
route—Master deciding to take longer route before commencement of voyage—Whether
instructions as to route orders as to employment or navigation of vessel—Carriage of Goods by
Sea Act 1971, Sch, art IV, r 2(a). **Whistler International Ltd v Kawasaki Kisen Kaisha Ltd** [1999] 2
Comm 1, CA; [1999] 4 199, CA; [2001] 1 Comm 76, HL; [2001] 1 403, HL.
Exceptions—
Baltime charterparty—Damage—Clause exempting owners from liability for 'damage ... whatsover
and howsoever caused'—Whether clause exempting owners from liability for financial damage
caused to charterers. **Tor Line AB v Alltrans Group of Canada Ltd** [1984] 1 103, HL.
Baltime charterparty—Damage—Second sentence of clause exempting owners from liability for
'damage...whatsoever and howsoever caused'—'Damage' in this part of clause to be widely
construed—Not limited to physical loss but covering financial loss—Claims by charterers for loss
of time and for expenses resulting from master's wrongful refusal to enter a port—'Damage' wide
enough to cover both heads of claim—Owners exempt from liability. **Nippon Yusen Kaisha v
Acme Shipping Corp** [1972] 1 35, CA.
Loss or damage arising from negligent navigation—Vessel chartered for lightening operations—
Charterparty purporting to incorporate US Carriage of Goods by Sea Act—US Act exempting
owners of chartered vessel from liability for 'loss or damage arising or resulting from ... neglect ...
in navigation'—Chartered vessel causing damage to charterers' vessel because of negligent
navigation—Whether owners of chartered vessel liable for damage—Whether US Act applying to
charterparties—Whether US Act only applying in respect of carriage to or from US
ports—Whether US Act applying to exempt owners from liability for damage—Carriage of Goods
by Sea Act 1936 (US), § 4(2)(a). **Seven Seas Transportation Ltd v Pacifico Union Marina Corp**
[1984] 2 140, CA.
Negligent navigation—Errors of navigation—Charterparty exempting shipowners from liability for
'errors of navigation'—Whether 'errors of navigation' including negligent navigation. **Seven Seas
Transportation Ltd v Pacifico Union Marina Corp** [1984] 2 140, CA.

SHIPPING (cont)—
  Time charterparty (cont)—
    Exceptions (cont)—
      Negligent navigation—Errors of navigation—Exemption clause in charterparty exempting owners from liability for 'errors of navigation'—Whether 'errors of navigation' including negligent navigation. **Industrie Chimiche Italia Centrale SpA v Nea Ninemia Shipping Co SA** [1983] **1** 686, QBD.
    Frustration—
      Delay—Salvage operation—Delay in redelivery of vessel due to failure of port authority to grant port clearance for vessel—Whether charterparty frustrated. **Edwinton Commercial Corp v Tsavliris Russ (Worldwide Salvage and Towage) Ltd** [2007] **1 Comm** 407, QBD; [2007] **2 Comm** 634, CA.
    Guarantee—
      Variation of charterparty terms—Owners letting ship to charterers for single time charter of 57.5 days minimum duration via Black Sea to Far East—Defendant guaranteeing charterers' obligations for time charter trip via Black Sea to Far East—Guarantee providing that defendant not exempted from liability by any variation in terms of charterparty—Owners and charterers agreeing addendum providing for about six/about eight months worldwide time charter—Whether addendum within scope of guarantee. **Melvin International SA v Poseidon Schiffahrt GmbH** [1999] **2 Comm** 761, QBD.
    Hire—
      Alternative rates of hire—Rate varying according to whether ship trading neutral or trading belligerent—Ship proceeding to neutral port—Whether calling at belligerent port to bunker was belligerent trading—Bills of lading—Duty of master to sign within reasonable time. **Halcyon SS Co Ltd v Continental Grain Co** [1943] **1** 558, CA.
      Cesser of hire. *See* Time charterparty—Cesser of hire, *above*.
      Equitable set-off—Charterer's contractual right to deduct from hire claims for bunkers on redelivery and slow speed—Whether deduction required to be precise and accurate—Whether deduction of amount subsequently proved to be excessive constituting non-payment of hire—Whether reasonable assessment made in good faith sufficient—Whether absence of express finding in special case that deductions were reasonable and made in good faith invalidating deductions. **Santiren Shipping Ltd v Unimarine SA** [1981] **1** 340, QBD.
      Equitable set-off—Whether charterers entitled to deduct from hire other claims against shipowners. **Federal Commerce and Navigation Ltd v Molena Alpha Inc** [1978] **3** 1066, CA.
      Lien for non-payment of hire—Exercise of lien—Charterparty entitling owner to exercise lien on cargo for amounts due under charter—Uncertainty whether cargo belonging to charterer or to third party—Bill of lading incorporating charterparty—Charterer ordering vessel to port of discharge to discharge—Owner threatening to withdraw vessel for non-payment of hire but ordering her to anchor off port of discharge—Owner purporting to exercise lien while vessel at anchorage—Whether lien properly exercised—Whether lien applicable to cargo—Whether denial of possession—Whether lien exercisable at anchorage or only at place of discharge in port. **Santiren Shipping Ltd v Unimarine SA** [1981] **1** 340, QBD.
      Lien for non-payment of hire—Sub-freights -Charterparty giving shipowners lien on sub-freights for any amounts due under charter—Nature of notice requirements under lien clause—Whether lien extending to sub-hire—Whether right to sub-freight assigned before it fell due—New York Product Exchange form, cl 18. **Dry Bulk Handy Holding Inc v Fayette International Holdings Ltd** [2013] **1 Comm** 177, QBD.
      Lien for non-payment of hire—Sub-freights—Charterparty giving owner lien on 'all sub-freights' for non-payment—Whether owner having lien over hire payable by sub-sub-charterer under time charter—Whether owner's lien limited to sub-freight payable under voyage charter. **Care Shipping Corp v Latin American Shipping Corp** [1983] **1** 1121, QBD.
      Lien for non-payment of hire—Sub-freights—Charterparty giving shipowners lien on 'all sub-freights' for non-payment of amounts due under its terms—Whether owners having lien over hire payable by sub-sub-charterers under time charter—Whether owners' lien limited to sub-freight payable under voyage charter—New York Produce Exchange form of charterparty, cl 18. **Care Shipping Corp v Itex Itagrani Export SA** [1992] **1** 91, QBD.
      Non-payment of hire—Lien. *See* Time charterparty—Hire—Lien for non-payment of hire, *above*.
      Non-payment of hire—Method of payment agreed between parties—Extrinsic evidence to prove method. **A/S Tankexpress v Cie Financiere Belge des Petroles SA** [1948] **2** 939, HL.
      Non-payment of hire—Withdrawal of vessel. *See* Time charterparty—Withdrawal of vessel for non-payment of hire, *below*.
      Off-hire clause. *See* Charterparty—Off-hire clause, *above*.
      Repayment of advance hire while vessel off hire—Assignment of receivables due under charterparty including hire—Owners of chartered vessel assigning receivables due under the charterparty including hire—Charterers paying hire in advance to assignees of receivables—Vessel off hire throughout period for which advance hire paid—Charterers unable to recover advance hire from owners—Whether charterers entitled to recover advance hire from assignees. **Pan Ocean Shipping Ltd v Creditcorp Ltd** [1994] **1** 470, HL.
      Substitution—Charterparty permitting owner to substitute vessel—Charterparty providing that substitute vessel coming on hire when in same position in relation to next loading port and when in same state of readiness as previously chartered vessel—Owner purporting to substitute vessel—Charterer disputing substitution—Charterer not specifying next loading port—Whether substitute vessel having to be delivered at place where previously chartered vessel withdrawn—Whether substitute vessel coming on hire. **Gas Natural Aprovisionamientos SDG SA v Methane Services Ltd** [2010] **2 Comm** 541, QBD.
    Indemnity—
      Implied term—Shipowners incurring loss in complying with charterers' orders as to employment of vessel—Shipowners claiming implied right to be indemnified by charterers in respect of loss—Whether shipowners entitled to an indemnity—Whether claim to an indemnity an implied term of charterparty. **Triad Shipping Co v Stellar Chartering and Brokerage Inc** [1995] **1** 595, CA.

SHIPPING (cont)—
   Time charterparty (cont)—
      Last voyage—
         Late redelivery—Charterers giving notice of redelivery for last possible date under charterparty—Owners fixing vessel for new charter—Vessel redelivered late after expiry of laycan period under new charter—Owners negotiating extension of cancellation date with new charterers on basis of reduction of daily rate under new charter—Whether charterers liable for owners' loss calculated on basis of difference between original and reduced daily rate under new charter. **Transfield Shipping Inc v Mercator Shipping Inc** [2007] **1 Comm** 379, QBD; [2008] **2 Comm** 753, HL; [2008] **4** 159, HL.

         Late redelivery—Charterparty providing for extra thirty days' hire at market rate payable on charterer not meeting obligation to redeliver on time—Last voyage overrunning by six days—Charterer paying market rate for overrun period only—Whether clause providing for extra hire to be paid being penalty. **Lansat Shipping Co Ltd v Glencore Grain BV** [2009] **2 Comm** 12, QBD; [2010] **1 Comm** 459, CA.

         Late redelivery—Charters giving notice of redelivery for last possible date under charterparty—Owners fixing vessel for new charter—Vessel redelivered late after expiry of laycan period under new charter—Owners negotiating extension of cancellation date with new charterers on basis of reduction of daily rate under new charter—Whether charterers liable for owners' loss calculated on basis of difference between original and reduced daily rate for duration of new charter. **Transfield Shipping Inc v Mercator Shipping Inc of Monrovia** [2008] **1 Comm** 685, CA.

         Late redelivery—Repudiation—Repudiation by late delivery—Charterers' order preventing redelivery on time—Time at which validity of charterers' order for final voyage prior to redelivery to be judged—Whether owners entitled to treat order as repudiatory breach of contract—Whether validity of charterers' order for final voyage to be determined when order given or when order to be performed. **Torvald Klaveness A/S v Arni Maritime Corp** [1994] **4** 998, HL.

         Whether period of charter including extension at charterers' option. **Petroleo Brasileiro SA v Kriti Akti Shipping Co SA** [2003] **2 Comm** 654, QBD.

      Notice of redelivery—
         Promissory estoppel. *See* Time charterparty—Redelivery—Notice of approximate date of redelivery, *below*.

      One time charter trip—
         Vessel chartered for one trip—Vessel carrying and discharging cargo—Whether charterparty permitting charterers to load further cargo after initial cargo having been discharged. **SBT Star Bulk & Tankers (Germany) GmbH & Co KG v Cosmotrade SA** [2017] **1 Comm** 231, QBD.

      Owners threatening to withdraw vessels—
         Relief—Parties referring dispute to arbitration—Charterer applying to court for interim injunctive relief—Whether charterer entitled to relief preventing owners from acting inconsistently with time charter. **LauritzenCool AB v Lady Navigation Inc** [2005] **1 Comm** 77, QBD; [2005] **2 Comm** 183, CA; [2006] **1** 866, CA.

      Parties—
         Claimant instructing shipbrokers to sub-charter vessel—Shipbrokers negotiating with defendants—Recap e-mails wrongly referring to claimant's ultimate parent company as time-chartering owner—No written charterparty concluded—Voyage going ahead and cargo discharged—Defendant paying freight to claimant—Claimant bringing arbitral claim against defendant for demurrage—Arbitrator striking out claim on basis no contract concluded between claimant and defendant—Claimant challenging arbitrator's decision—Whether recap e-mails forming charterparty between claimant and defendant—Whether charterparty coming into existence by reason of conduct of parties. **TTMI Sarl v Statoil ASA** [2011] **2 Comm** 647, QBD.

      Payment of hire—
         Off-hire clause—Time charter providing vessel off-hire until release if detained by any authority or legal process—Off-hire clause not applying if detention occasioned by any personal act or omission or default of the charterers or their agents—Vessel arrested due to demurrage dispute between sellers and buyers of cargo—Charterers withholding payment of hire to owners during arrest period—Whether sellers or buyers 'agents' of charterers. **NYK Bulkship (Atlantic) NV v Cargill International SA** [2016] **2 Comm** 587, SC; [2016] **4** 298, SC.

         Off-hire clause—Trip time charter providing that vessel off-hire until release if detained by any authority or legal process during currency of charterparty—Off-hire provision not applying if such detention had been occasioned by reason of 'calling port of trading' under charter—Charterers instructing vessel to proceed to New Orleans to load cargo—New Orleans port authorities detaining vessel under anti-terrorism legislation because vessel on first trip to United States—Whether vessel off-hire during period of detention. **Hyundai Merchant Marine Co Ltd v Furnace Withy (Australia) Pty** [2006] **2 Comm** 188, CA.

         Punctual payment—Anti-technicality clause—Owners to give 48 hours' notice to rectify default of payment before exercising right to withdraw ship—Payment not made on due date—Owners purporting to give conditional notice to rectify if payment not received—Notice of withdrawal given at end of banking hours on due date of payment—Whether default occurring at end of banking hours or at midnight on due date—Whether owners' notice to rectify valid—Whether terms of notice sufficiently clear. **Afovos Shipping Co SA v Pagnan** [1982] **3** 18, CA.

         Punctual payment—Unconditional right to immediate use of payment of hire—Charterers paying hire on due date by irrevocable transfer to owners' bank—Payment received by owners' bank on due date but not attracting interest for four days—Owners entitled on due date to withdraw amount paid subject to payment of four days' interest—Whether owners having unconditional right to immediate use of amount paid—Whether owners receiving equivalent of cash—Whether charterers making 'punctual payment'. **A/S Awilco v Fulvia SpA di Navigazione** [1981] **1** 652, HL.

      Printed and typed clauses in conflict—
         Construction—Baltime charterparty with added typed clause—Exception clause (printed) limiting shipowners' responsibility—Typed clause imposing positive obligation on shipowners specific to charterers' voyage—Conflict between clauses—Whether type clause prevailed over printed clause—Construction of printed exception clause (cl 13). **Gesellschaft Burgerlichen Rechts v Stockholms Rederiaktiebolag Svea** [1966] **1** 961, QBD.

SHIPPING (cont)—
  Time charterparty (cont)—
    Redelivery—
      Notice of approximate date of redelivery—Charterers giving 30 days' approximate notice of
        redelivery—Charterers subsequently fixing vessel for extra voyage and giving revised notice of
        approximate redelivery at later date within charter period partly on without prejudice
        basis—Meaning of 'without prejudice'—Whether implied term that where charterers giving an
        approximate date of redelivery, charterers obliged not to do anything deliberately that prevented
        that date from being met—Whether giving of notice of approximate redelivery giving rise to
        promissory estoppel. **IMT Shipping and Chartering GmbH v Chansung Shipping Co Ltd** [2009] 2
        Comm 177, QBD.
    Safe port. See Charterparty—Safe port, *above.*
    Speed and consumption warranty—
      Terms of charterparty contained in amended Shelltime 3 form, additional clauses and Gas Form
        C—Disputes arising as to whether vessel failing to perform in accordance with speed and
        consumption provisions—Whether speed and consumption warranty in Gas Form C incorporated
        into or prevailing over charterparty—Whether charterparty containing all weather warranty or
        qualified weather warranty. **Hyundai Merchant Marine Co Ltd v Daelim Corporation (Trafigura
        Beheer BV, Part 20 defendant)** [2012] 2 **Comm** 209, QBD.
    Speed warranty—
      Date at which warranty applies—Vessel at date of charterparty capable of steaming at speed
        warranted—Vessel at date of delivery to charterers incapable of steaming at speed
        warranted—Whether warranty applying at date of delivery of vessel—Whether owners in breach
        of warranty. **Cosmos Bulk Transport Inc v China National Foreign Trade Transportation Corp**
        [1978] 1 322, QBD.
    Unseaworthiness of vessel—
      Incompetent and inadequate engine-room staff—Whether charterers entitled to repudiate charter.
        Hong Kong Fir Shipping Co Ltd v Kawasaki Kisen Kaisha Ltd [1962] 1 474, CA.
    Use of safe ports only—
      Good and safe port—Ship damaged by ice—Extraordinary risk—Liability of charterers. **Grace & Co
        Ltd v General Steam Navigation Co Ltd** [1950] 1 201, KBD.
    Withdrawal of vessel for non-payment of hire—
      Breach of obligation to pay instalment of hire in advance—Effect of late payment before right of
        withdrawal exercised—Charter providing that payment to be made 'semi-monthly in
        advance'—Provision that 'failing the punctual and regular payment of the hire' owners at liberty
        to withdraw vessel—Charterers tendering payment a day late—Whether owners entitled to
        exercise right of withdrawal after payment tendered. **Mardorf Peach & Co Ltd v Attica Sea
        Carriers Corp of Liberia** [1977] 1 545, HL.
      Exercise of right to withdraw vessel—Owner hitherto accepting late payments—Whether owner
        estopped from exercising contractual right of withdrawal. **Scandinavian Trading Tanker Co AB v
        Flota Petrolera Ecuatoriana** [1983] 1 301, CA.
      Notice of withdrawal—Clause providing that owners to give to charterers 48 hours' notice before
        withdrawal of vessel for non-payment of hire—Charterers notifying owners of claim to set off
        certain payments and disbursements against cost of hire—Owners withdrawing vessel without
        giving notice—Whether charterers waiving right to notice by refusal to pay hire—Whether
        notification of claim to set off giving rise to promissory estoppel—Whether implied clear and
        unequivocal representation that owners did not need to give notice. **Italmare Shipping Co v
        Ocean Tanker Co Inc (No 2)** [1982] 3 273, QBD.
      Owners withdrawing vessel from charterers' service whilst vessel at port and charterers' cargo on
        board—Owners requiring charterers to arrange for discharge of cargo from vessel—Whether
        owners entitled to remuneration and expenses incurred until cargo discharged. **ENE Kos 1 Ltd v
        Petroleo Brasileiro SA (No 2)** [2012] 4 1, SC; [2013] 1 **Comm** 32, SC.
      Owners withdrawing vessel from intermediate charterer's service while vessel in service of
        sub-charterers—Sub-charterer requiring vessel to proceed to port to discharge cargo before
        vessel redelivered to owners—Whether sub-charterer liable to pay owners in respect of period
        after withdrawal of vessel. **Dry Bulk Handy Holding Inc v Fayette International Holdings Ltd**
        [2013] 1 **Comm** 177, QBD.
      Ownership of bunkers on board at time of withdrawal—Charterparty providing that on redelivery
        'whether ... at the end of the charter period or on earlier termination' shipowners to accept and
        pay for all bunkers on board—Charterparty also providing that charterers would pay for certain
        quantities of bunkers on delivery and 'about same quantities and prices [would apply] on
        redelivery'—Whether property in bunkers passing to shipowners on termination of charterparty.
        Forsythe International (UK) Ltd v Silver Shipping Co Ltd [1994] 1 851, QBD.
      Punctual payment—Anti-technicality clause—Charterers failing to pay hire on due date—Owners
        withdrawing vessel without serving charterers with notice to rectify failure—Owners not required
        to serve notice where 'intention to fail to make payment as set out'—Arbitral tribunal finding that
        failure to make payment by due date due to recklessness on part of charterers—Whether owners
        obliged to serve notice where non-payment due to recklessness—Whether charterers having
        intention to fail to make payment as set out. **Owneast Shipping Ltd v Qatar Navigation QSC**
        [2011] 2 **Comm** 76, QBD.
      Punctual payment—Anti-technicality clause—Charterparty proving for owners to withdraw vessel
        upon failure of charterers to make punctual payment of hire—Charterers repeatedly seeking
        reduced rate of hire and threatening bankruptcy—Owners and charterers entering compromise
        agreements for reduced rate—Compensation clauses reserving right to claim for future loss of
        earnings—Charterers failing to pay hire—Owners serving anti-technicality notice—Charterers
        failing to make payment—Owners withdrawing vessel and claiming damages—Whether
        obligation to make punctual payment of hire under payment, anti-technicality and/or
        compensation clauses being condition(s) of contract entitling owners to claim damages for loss
        of bargain—Whether compensation clauses penal. **Kuwait Rocks Co v AMN Bulkcarriers Inc, The
        Astra** [2013] 2 **Comm** 689, QBD.

SHIPPING (cont)—
  Time charterparty (cont)—
    Withdrawal of vessel for non-payment of hire (cont)—
      Punctual payment—Anti-technicality clause—Owners to give 48 hours' notice to rectify default of
        payment before exercising right to withdraw ship—Payment not made on due date—Owners
        giving notice at end of banking hours on due date of payment—Whether default occurring at end
        of banking hours or at midnight on due date—Whether owners' notice to rectify valid. **Afovos
        Shipping Co SA v Pagnan** [1983] **1** 449, HL.

      Punctual payment—Right to withdraw ship 'failing punctual payment'—Late payment made before
        right of withdrawal exercised—Whether shipowners entitled to withdraw in any event once
        payment overdue. **Brimnes, The** [1974] **3** 88, CA.

      Relief against forfeiture—Default in payment of hire—Right of withdrawal exercised—Whether
        court having jurisdiction to grant relief against forfeiture. **Scandinavian Trading Tanker Co AB v
        Flota Petrolera Ecuatoriana** [1983] **2** 763, HL.

      Tender of hire curing default—Instalment of hire due on a Saturday when banks were
        closed—Charterers mistakenly thinking that payment on the following Monday would
        do—Payment of hire tendered on Monday afternoon—Charterers in default of payment—Before
        payment tendered, notice sent by owners to the master withdrawing ship—Notice of withdrawal
        not sent to charterers until after payment tendered—Default in payment cured by
        tender—Owners not entitled to withdraw ship unless notice given to charterers—Whether
        sufficient tender of hire. **Empresa Cubana de Fletes v Lagonisi Shipping Co Ltd** [1971] **1** 193, CA.

      Vessel at port holding charterers' cargo at time of notice of withdrawal—Vessel remaining at port
        and cargo discharged approximately two-and-a-half days after notice of withdrawal—Owners
        obtaining bank guarantee at request of charterers as security for wrongful withdrawal
        claim—Owners subsequently obtaining summary judgment holding that withdrawal legitimate—
        Owners seeking compensation for use or detention of vessel after notice of withdrawal—Whether
        charterers liable under charterparty—Whether owners entitled to compensation as bailees of
        cargo—Whether owners entitled to recover expenses of obtaining and maintaining bank
        guarantee—Supreme Court Act 1981, s 51. **ENE Kos 1 Ltd v Petroleo Brasileiro SA (No 2)** [2010] **1
        Comm** 669, QBD.

      Waiver of right to withdraw—Acceptance of late payment—Evidence necessary to establish that
        late payment had been accepted by owners—Receipt of payment by owners' bank—Payment
        order delivered to owners' bank—Internal processing of order begun as soon as
        received—Owners instructing bank to refuse money and return it to charterers' bank as soon as
        informed of receipt of payment—Whether receipt of order and internal processing of payment
        order constituting acceptance on owners' behalf of late payment. **Mardorf Peach & Co Ltd v
        Attica Sea Carriers Corp of Liberia** [1977] **1** 545, HL.

      Waiver of right to withdraw—Hire payable in advance—Late payment—Acceptance by shipowner's
        bank—Hire relating in part to period after right of withdrawal has arisen—Shipowner's
        knowledge at time payment accepted that right of withdrawal has arisen—Shipowner's bank
        bound to accept payments tendered by charterers—Whether acceptance of hire accrued due
        before right of withdrawal arising constituting waiver—Whether acceptance by bank amounting
        to waiver. **Brimnes, The** [1974] **3** 88, CA.

      Waiver of right to withdraw—Underpayment of hire—Request by owner for explanation of
        under-payment and demand for balance of hire—Failure of charterer to comply with request or
        demand within reasonable time—Whether by reason of request and demand owner having
        waived right to withdraw vessel. **China National Foreign Trade Transportation Corp v Evlogia
        Shipping Co SA of Panama** [1979] **2** 1044, HL.

      Waiver of right to withdraw—Underpayment of hire—Underpayment in time—Acceptance of
        underpayment—Whether waiver of owner's right to withdraw vessel in event of failure to pay full
        hire. **China National Foreign Trade Transportation Corp v Evlogia Shipping Co SA of Panama**
        [1979] **2** 1044, HL.

    Withdrawal of vessels for non-payment of hire—

      Punctual payment—Anti-technicality clause—Charterparties providing for owners to withdraw
        vessel upon failure of charterers to make punctual payment of hire—Charterparties guaranteed
        by charterers' parent company—Charterers falling into arrears of hire—Owners serving
        anti-technicality notices—Charterers failing to make payment—Owners withdrawing vessels and
        claiming damages against charterers' parent under guarantees—Whether obligation to make
        punctual payment of hire under anti-technicality clauses being condition of contract entitling
        owners to claim damages for loss of bargain—Whether conduct of charterers amounting to
        renunciation of charterparties. **Spar Shipping AS v Grand China Logistics Holding (Group) Co Ltd**
        [2017] **2 Comm** 701, CA; [2017] **4** 124, CA.

      Punctual payment—Anti-technicality clause—Charterparties providing for owners to withdraw
        vessel upon failure of charterers to make punctual payment of hire—Charterparties guaranteed
        by charterers' parent company—Charterers falling into arrears of hire—Owners serving
        anti-technicality notices—Charterers failing to make payment—Owners withdrawing vessels and
        claiming damages against charterers' parent under guarantees—Whether obligation to make
        punctual payment of hire under anti-technicality clauses being condition of contract entitling
        owners to claim damages for loss of bargain. **Spar Shipping AS v Grand China Logistics Holding
        (Group) Co Ltd** [2015] **1 Comm** 879, QBD.

  Time for bringing claims—

    Construction of charterparty. *See* Charterparty—Time for bringing claims, *above.*

  Towage contract—

    Clause relieving tug of liability—

      Claim to indemnity by tug owners when in breach of terms of contract—Whether tug owner
        precluded from relying on exception clause. **Albion, The** [1953] **2** 679, CA.

1209

SHOCK
    Compensation—
        War injury—
            Civil defence volunteer. *See* **War injury** (Compensation—Civil defence volunteer—Physical injury—Shock).
    Mental shock—
        Damages. *See* **Damages** (Remoteness of damage—Mental shock).
    Nervous shock—
        Damages. *See* **Damages** (Personal injury—Nervous shock).
        Duty to take care—
            Generally. *See* **Negligence** (Duty to take care—Nervous shock).

SHOOTING AND SPORTING RIGHTS
    Game. *See* **Game** (Shooting and sporting rights).

SHOP
    Conditions of employment—
        Statutory half-holiday for shop assistants—
            Hotel—Dining-room open to non-residents—Waiter—Whether 'shop assistant'—Whether entitled to statutory weekly half-holiday—Shops Act 1912, ss 1, 19(1). **George Hotel (Colchester) Ltd v Ball** [1938] **3** 790, KBD.
    Copyright—
        Infringement—
            Playing of records in public. *See* **Copyright** (Conflict of laws—Public performance—Shop).
    Early closing. *See* Hours of closing—Early closing day, *below.*
    Fire certificate. *See* **Fire** (Certificate).
    Half holiday. *See* Conditions of employment—Statutory half-holiday for shop assistants, *above.*
    Hours of closing—
        Early closing day—
            Jewish shop—Order made by local authority in 1912—No special provision for Jewish registered shopkeepers—Subsequent legislation providing alternative early closing day for Jewish shops—Effect of order—Shops Act 1950, ss 1(2), 53(13), 76(2). **Miller's Cash Stores Ltd v West Ham Corp** [1955] **3** 282, QBD.
            Mixed shop—Closing order for different days for different trades—Shops Act 1950, s 1(2). **Fine-Fare Ltd v Brighton County BC** [1959] **1** 476, QBD.
            Mixed shop—Supermarket—Exemption order exempting shop of specified classes from early closing—Commodities sold by supermarket included some of those sold by shops of classes specified in order—Whether supermarket was entitled to exemption from early closing in respect of the sale of commodities sold by shops within the exemption order—Shops Act 1950, ss 1, 13(1). **Redbridge London Borough v Wests (Ilford) Ltd** [1968] **1** 277, QBD.
        Exemption—
            Sale of newly-cooked provisions for consumption off the premises—Sale of newly-baked bread after permitted hours—Whether newly-baked bread within the exemption of 'newly-cooked provisions'—Shops (Hours of Closing) Act 1928, ss 1, 8, Sch I, para 1(b). **London CC v Davis** [1938] **2** 764, KBD.
        Mixed shop—
            Early closing days. *See* Hours of closing—Early closing day—Mixed shop, *above.*
            Supermarket—Closing order referring to specified classes of shops and specified trades—Multiplicity of supermarket's trades included some of trades specified in closing order—Whether closing order applied to supermarket—Shops Act 1950, ss 8, 13(3). **Fine Fare Ltd v Aberdare UDC** [1965] **1** 679, QBD.
        Retail trading elsewhere than in shop—
            Place where retail trade or business carried on—Costermonger's barrow—Sale of goods in street from barrow after closing hour—Whether retail trade or business carried on in barrow or on piece of ground where barrow stood—Shops Act 1950, s 12. **Kahn v Newberry** [1959] **2** 202, QBD.
    Jewish shop—
        Early closing day. *See* Hours of closing—Early closing day, *above.*
        Sunday closing—
            Exemption. *See* Sunday closing—Exemption—Jewish shop, *below.*
    Launderette—
        Coin operated—
            Sunday closing. *See* Sunday closing—Premises to be closed for the serving of customers—Serving of customers—Coin-operated launderette, *below.*
    Lawful opening. *See* Sunday closing—Garage—Lawful opening for sale of petrol, oil and motor accessories, *below.*
    Medicine—
        Sale. *See* **Medicine** (Sale by retail—Shop).
    Mixed shop—
        Early closing day. *See* Hours of closing—Early closing day—Mixed shop, *above.*
        Hours of closing. *See* Hours of closing—Mixed shop, *above.*
    Mobile van equipped as shop—
        Sunday closing. *See* Sunday closing—Retail trading elsewhere than in shop—Mobile van equipped as shop, *below.*
    New tenancy. *See* **Landlord and tenant** (New tenancy—Shop).
    Notice—
        Display of notice stating purpose for which shop open on Sunday. *See* Sunday closing—Shop where several trades or businesses carried on—Display of notice stating purpose for which shop open, *below.*
    Premises—
        Safety of employees—
            Breach of statutory duty. *See* **Employment** (Duty of master—Offices, shops and railway premises).

SHOP (cont)—
Records—
Playing of records in public—
Infringement of copyright. *See* **Copyright** (Conflict of laws—Public performance—Shop).
Serving of customers—
Sunday. *See* Sunday closing—Premises to be closed for the serving of customers—Serving of customers, *below*.
Sex shop—
Nuisance—
Interlocutory injunction. *See* **Injunction** (Nuisance—Interlocutory injunction—Sex shop).
Stall—
Whether a shop. *See* **Medicine** (Sale by retail—Shop).
Sunday closing—
EEC Treaty—
Compatibility—Whether prohibition on Sunday trading constituting 'measures' having equivalent effect to quantitative restrictions on imports. *See* **European Union** (Imports—Reduction in volume of imports—Quantitative restrictions on imports from other member states—Measures having equivalent effect—Prohibition on Sunday trading).
Enforcement by local authority—
Promotion or protection of interests of inhabitants of its area—Trader in local authority's area deliberately and flagrantly flouting Sunday closing laws—Fines not acting as deterrent—Local authority applying for injunction to restrain trader from acting in contravention of law—Whether local authority proper plaintiff—Whether proceedings required to be brought by Attorney General—Whether local authority acting to protect interests of inhabitants—Shops Act 1950, ss 47, 71(1)—Local Government Act 1972, s 222(1)(a). **Stoke-on-Trent City Council v B & Q (Retail) Ltd** [1984] **2** 332, HL.
Exemption—
Jewish shop—Place where any retail trade is carried on—Market held in field—Jewish occupier of field—Occupier of field organising market and providing refreshments to people visiting market—Other traders occupying individual stalls—Other traders not of Jewish religion and not therefore individually entitled to exemption from restrictions on Sunday trading—Whether field as a whole to be treated as a 'shop'—Whether occupier of field able to obtain exemption extending to occupiers of individual stalls—Shops Act 1950, ss 53, 58. **Thanet DC v Ninedrive Ltd** [1978] **1** 703, Ch D.
Sale of meals or refreshments—Sale of bread on Sunday—'Meals or refreshments'—Shops (Sunday Trading Restriction) Act 1936, ss 1, 2, Schs I, para 1(b), II. **Wardale v Binns** [1946] **2** 100, KBD.
Sale of meals or refreshments—Sale of chocolate éclairs, cream buns, jam tarts, fruit cake, swiss roll and veal-and-ham pies—Whether 'meal or refreshment'—Shops (Sunday Trading Restriction) Act 1936, s 1, Schs I, II. **London CC v Lees** [1939] **1** 191, KBD.
Garage—
Lawful opening for sale of motor or cycle supplies or accessories—Information given about motor cars to potential customer—Isolated transaction—Whether garage open in contravention of Shops Act 1950, s 47. **Monaco Garage Ltd v Watford BC** [1967] **2** 1291, QBD.
Lawful opening for sale of petrol, oil and motor accessories—Information given about motor cars—Trial run in car—Whether garage open in contravention of Shops Act 1950, s 47. **Waterman v Wallasey Corp** [1954] **2** 187, QBD.
Premises to be closed for the serving of customers—
Serving of customers—Coin-operated launderette—Open on Sunday—Cleaner employed by business owners to clean launderette—Wife of director restocked general vending machine—No other person present on behalf of owners—Whether there was a 'serving of customers' on Sunday—Serving of customers meant personal serving of customers—Shops Act 1950, ss 47, 74(1). **Ilford Corp v Betterclean (Seven Kings) Ltd** [1965] **1** 900, QBD.
Retail trading elsewhere than in shop—
Exhibition stalls—Stalls forming part of exhibition to which public having access—Primary purpose of exhibition to enable stallholders to exhibit wares to those interested—Public admitted to exhibition on payment of entrance fee—Exhibition open on Sundays—Stallholders selling goods from stalls on Sundays—Whether stalls 'places' where retail trade or business carried on—Shops Act 1950, ss 47, 58. **Randall v D Turner (Garages) Ltd** [1973] **3** 369, QBD Divl Ct.
Market stalls—Degree of permanency—Market held on Sundays only—Stalls erected each Saturday and dismantled after trading on Sunday—Components of stalls not necessarily same each week—No space marked out on market site where stall to be erected each week—Whether stalls having sufficient degree of permanency to constitute places where any retail trade or business carried on—Shops Act 1950, ss 47, 58. **Maby v Warwick BC** [1972] **2** 1198, QBD.
Mobile van equipped as shop—Sale of goods in street from van—Whether van a shop—Whether retail trade or business carried on in van—Whether portion of street at which van stationary a 'place' where retail trade or business is carried on—Shops Act 1950, ss 58, 74(1). **Stone v Boreham** [1958] **2** 715, QBD.
Warehouse—Whether warehouse a 'shop' for retail trade or business—Whether warehouse a 'place' for retail trade—Whether box-tricycle a 'place' for retail sale of ice-cream—Shops (Sunday Trading Restriction) Act 1936, ss 11, 12, 13. **Eldorado Ice Cream Co Ltd v Clark** [1938] **1** 330, KBD.
Shop where several trades or businesses carried on—
Display of notice stating purpose for which shop open—Whether failure to display notice stating purpose for which shop is open is offence under Shops Act 1950, s 50 or s 47—Shops Act 1950, ss 47, 50, 53, 55, 57. **Tonkin v Raven** [1958] **3** 374, QBD.
Warehouse—
Whether a 'shop'. *See* Sunday closing—Retail trading elsewhere than in shop—Warehouse, *above*.

SHOP STEWARD
Election—
District committee of union—
Discretion to refuse member's election as shop steward. *See* **Natural justice** (Trade union—District committee of union—Discretion to refuse member's election as shop steward).

SHOP STEWARD (cont)—
Trade union—
Liability for wrongful acts of shop stewards. *See* **Trade union** (Official—Wrongful acts—Liability of union).

SHORT CAUSES LIST
Chancery Division. *See* **Practice** (Chancery Division—Short Causes List).
Queen's Bench Division. *See* **Practice** (Trial—Lists—Short cause list).

SHORT MEASURE
See **Weights and measures**.

SHORT PROBATE LIST
Practice—
Generally. *See* **Practice** (Chancery Division—Short Probate List).

SHORT SUMMONS LIST
Chancery Division. *See* **Practice** (Chancery Division—Short summons list).

SHORT WEIGHT
See **Weights and measures**.

SHORT-TERM GAINS
Taxation of. *See* **Capital gains tax** (Short-term gains).

SHORTHAND NOTE
Book containing account of trial based on shorthand note—
Copyright—
Ownership. *See* **Copyright** (Ownership—Presumption of ownership of copyright—Literary work—Selection of copied material and original matter—Books including accounts of the trials of Oscar Wilde—One book published anonymously in 1911 or 1912, much of it based on a shorthand note of the proceedings).
Civil proceedings—
Generally. *See* **Practice** (Shorthand writer's notes).
Matrimonial causes. *See* **Divorce** (Practice—Trial—Shorthand note of proceedings).
Costs of. *See* **Practice** (Shorthand writer's notes—Costs).
Criminal trial—
Revision by judge. *See* **Criminal law** (Trial—Shorthand note—Summing up—Transcript—Revision of transcript by judge).
Matrimonial causes. *See* **Divorce** (Practice—Trial—Shorthand note of proceedings).

SHORTHAND WRITER
Magistrates' court—
Presence in retiring room with magistrates. *See* **Magistrates** (Clerk—Presence in retiring room while justices consider decision—Shorthand writer also present).

SHOT-FIRING
Coal mine, in. *See* **Coal mining** (Statutory duty—Shot-firing).

SHOTGUN
Certificate—
Revocation. *See* **Firearms** (Certificate—Revocation—Shot gun certificate).

SHOWGROUND
Exhibition of agricultural and horticultural produce—
Charitable object. *See* **Charity** (Benefit to community—Showground, park and recreation—Exhibition of agricultural and horticultural produce).

SICK AND BENEVOLENT FUND
Dissolution—
Loss of substratum. *See* **Unincorporated association** (Dissolution—Loss of substratum—Sick and benevolent fund).

SICK PERSON
Social security services—
Generally. *See* **Social security** (Services for sick and disabled persons).

SICKNESS BENEFIT
Damages for personal injuries—
Deduction of sickness benefit—
Generally. *See* **Damages** (Personal injury—Loss of earnings—Deduction of industrial injury, disablement, sickness or invalidity benefit accruing to injured person).
Long-term sickness benefit payable under contract of employment. *See* **Damages** (Personal injury—Loss of earnings—Deduction of long-term sickness benefit payable under contract of employment).
Disqualification. *See* **Social security** (Benefit—Disqualification—Sickness benefit).

SICKNESS INSURANCE
European Community—
Equality of treatment of men and women. *See* **European Union** (Equality of treatment of men and women—Social security—Sickness insurance).
Freedom of movement of services. *See* **European Union** (Freedom of movement—Services—Medical care).

SICKNESS PAY

Reduction—
>Disability discrimination. *See* **Employment** (Disability—Discrimination—Reduction in sickness pay).

SIDECAR

Motor cycle—
>Provisional licence—
>>Conditions. *See* **Road traffic** (Driving licence—Provisional licence—Conditions attached to provisional licences—Motor bicycle not having sidecar attached).

SIDENOTE

Statute—
>Aid to construction. *See* **Statute** (Construction—Headings and marginal notes).

SIERRA LEONE

Colony and protectorate—
>Independent state created by Sierra Leone Independence Act 1961, s 1—
>>Prior Order in Council establishing constitution—Independent state combining Crown colony and protectorate—Colony a settlement within British Settlements Act 1887—Protectorate subject to jurisdiction under Foreign Jurisdiction Act 1890, s 1—Validity of Order in Council as within power to establish laws and institutions for peace, order and good government—British Settlements Act 1887, s 2. **Buck v A-G** [1965] **1** 882, CA.

Constitution—
>Discrimination—
>>Race—Person not of negro African descent born in Sierra Leone acquiring citizenship at time of independence—Amendment of Constitution retrospectively to limit citizenship to persons of negro African descent—Discrimination on ground of race—Sierra Leone (Constitution) Order in Council 1961 (SI 1961 No 741), Sch 2, ss 1, 23, 43. **Akar v A-G of Sierra Leone** [1969] **3** 384, PC.

Legislation—
>Special manner and form—Endorsement on Act by Clerk of House of Representatives—Act endorsed that it had been passed but no reference made to special manner and form—Whether to be inferred that not passed in accordance with special manner and form. **Akar v A-G of Sierra Leone** [1969] **3** 384, PC.

Legislation—
>Validity—
>>Reference in Act to provisions of earlier void Act—Effect. **Akar v A-G of Sierra Leone** [1969] **3** 384, PC.

Race—
>Discrimination. *See* Constitution—Discrimination—Race, *above*.

SIGNATURE

Acknowledgment—
>Limitation of action. *See* **Limitation of action** (Acknowledgment).

Company. *See* **Company** (Signature).

Contract—
>Package of agreements to be signed at same time. *See* **Contract** (Signature—Package of agreements to be executed at same time).

Depositions. *See* **Criminal evidence** (Committal for trial—Depositions—Signature).

Disputed signature—
>Evidence of handwriting—
>>Criminal proceedings. *See* **Criminal evidence** (Handwriting—Signature disputed).

Document—
>Mistake as to nature of document—
>>Non est factum. *See* **Document** (Non est factum—Reasonable care—Form signed in blank).

False signature—
>Driving certificate. *See* **Criminal law** (Forgery—Making false document—Signature on driving certificate).

Guarantee—
>Note or memorandum in writing. *See* **Guarantee** (Note or memorandum of agreement in writing—Signature).

Local authority—
>Document. *See* **Local government** (Documents—Signature).

Nomination paper, on—
>Local government election. *See* **Elections** (Local government—Nomination papers—Signature).

Notice to quit—
>Validity of notice. *See* **Landlord and tenant** (Validity of notice to quit—Signature).

Sale of land—
>Memorandum of contract. *See* **Sale of land** (Memorandum of contract—Signature of party to be charged).

Summons—
>Magistrates—
>>Summons issued by magistrates. *See* **Magistrates** (Summons—Form of summons—Signature).

Will—
>Signature of testator—
>>Attestation. *See* **Will** (Attestation).

Writ—
>Specially indorsed writ. *See* **Writ** (Indorsement—Signature—Specially indorsed writ).

SIGNING-ON FORM

Construction of form. *See* **Employment** (Contract of service—Signing-on form).

SIKH

Racial discrimination. *See* **Race relations** (Discrimination—Discrimination against racial group—Sikhs).

SIKH MARRIAGE
Arranged marriage—
  Consent—
    Absence—Duress. See **Nullity** (Consent to marriage—Duress).

SILENCE
Acceptance of contract by silence. See **Contract** (Offer and acceptance—Acceptance by silence).
Accused—
  Adverse comment by judge. See **Criminal law** (Trial—Summing up—Adverse comment—Silence of accused).
  Evidence—
    Admissibility. See **Criminal evidence** (Admissions and confessions—Silence of accused).
  Estoppel by conduct. See **Estoppel** (Conduct—Silence or inactivity).

SILVER
Hallmarking. See **Hallmarking**.

SILVER ALLOY COINS
Freedom of movement—
  European Community. See **European Union** (Freedom of movement—Goods—Coins—Silver alloy coins and gold coins).

SILVER COINS
Treasure trove—
  Crown's rights. See **Treasure trove** (Crown's right to treasure trove—Coins—Silver coins).

SILVER PLATE
See **Plate**.

SIMILAR FACTS
Evidence—
  Civil proceedings. See **Evidence** (Similar facts).
  Criminal proceedings. See **Criminal evidence** (Similar facts).

SIMILAR OFFENCES
Evidence in criminal proceedings. See **Criminal evidence** (Improper conduct of accused on other occasions—Similar offences).

SINGAPORE
Advocate and solicitor—
  Disciplinary proceedings—
    Conviction of criminal offence implying defect of character making person unfit for profession—Solicitor convicted of criminal offences—Solicitor struck off—Convictions vitiated by errors of law—Whether striking off should be revoked—Legal Profession Act (Singapore), ss 80, 95(6). **Jeyaretnam v Law Society of Singapore** [1989] 2 193, PC.
    Matters capable of being subject of disciplinary proceedings—Comment offensively critical of court—Conduct not within matters specified in legislation relating to conduct of legal practitioners—Whether conduct which may be subject to disciplinary action limited to matters specified in legislation—Whether comment offensively critical of court conduct subject to disciplinary action—Legal Profession Act (Singapore), ss 84(2), 88(1)(b), 89(1). **Hilborne v Law Society of Singapore** [1978] 2 757, PC.
Appeal—
  Court of Appeal. See Court of Appeal, below.
  High Court—
    Appeal from district court—Function of appellate judge—Appellate judge deciding that evidence accepted by district court judge untrue—Appellate judge refusing to reserve questions of law to Court of Appeal—Whether appellate judge exceeding proper function—Supreme Court of Judicature Act (Singapore), s 60. **Jeyaretnam v Law Society of Singapore** [1989] 2 193, PC.
Court of Appeal—
  Appeal—
    Right of appeal—Appeal against decision of judge of High Court—Application to High Court to have penalty imposed in disciplinary proceedings against advocate and solicitor set aside—Whether appeal lies to Court of Appeal against decision of judge of High Court—Supreme Court of Judicature Act (Singapore), s 29. **Hilborne v Law Society of Singapore** [1978] 2 757, PC.
Criminal law—
  Evidence—
    Statement by accused—Cross-examination on statement. See **Criminal evidence** (Statement by accused—Cross-examination on statement—Singapore).
  False statutory declaration—
    Declaration as evidence of fact—Accused signing statement which omitted words of solemn declaration—Statement exhibited to affidavit filed by official—Affidavit filed with court—Whether statement admissible as evidence of facts stated—Whether statement a declaration which court bound to receive as evidence of any fact—Penal Code (Singapore), s 199. **Jeyaretnam v Law Society of Singapore** [1989] 2 193, PC.
  Fraudulent disposal of property to prevent distribution to creditor—
    Cheque—Donation by way of cheque to political party—Receiver of party's assets appointed—Party officials diverting donation cheques with donors' approval before cheques paid into party's bank account—Whether officials guilty of fraudulent disposal of property to prevent distribution to party's creditor—Penal Code (Singapore), s 421. **Jeyaretnam v Law Society of Singapore** [1989] 2 193, PC.

SINGAPORE (cont)—
  Criminal law (cont)—
    Mens rea—
      Immigration—Entry—Order prohibiting individual entering Singapore—Ordinance silent on whether order should be served—No evidence that order served or individual notified of it—Contravention of order—Whether mens rea an essential element of offence—Whether ignorance of the law no excuse—Immigration Ordinance 1952 (as amended by Ordinance 1959 (No 22)). **Lim Chin Aik v R** [1963] 1 223, PC.
  Public authority—
    Limitation of action—
      Harbour board—Action under power to carry on trade of wharfingers and warehousemen—Trade not subsidiary to main purpose of managing and controlling harbour—Straits Settlements Public Authorities Protection Ordinance (Revised Laws 1936, s 2(2)(as amended by Public Authorities Protection (Amendment) Ordinance 1939, s 2)—Limitation Act 1939, s 21(1). **Firestone Tire and Rubber Co (SS) Ltd v Singapore Harbour Board** [1952] 2 219, PC.
  Straits Settlement. See **Straits Settlement**.

SINGLE JUDGE
  Refusal of leave to appeal—
    Criminal proceedings. See **Criminal law** (Appeal—Leave to appeal—Refusal—Single judge).

SINGLE ROOM
  Occupier—
    Tenant or licensee—
      Protected tenancy. See **Rent restriction** (Protected tenancy—Tenancy or licence—Occupant of single room).

SINGLE WOMAN
  Affiliation proceedings by. See **Affiliation** (Application for order—Single woman).

SISTER SHIP
  Admiralty action in rem—
    Invocation of Admiralty jurisdiction—
      When jurisdiction invoked—Concurrent proceedings against ship and sister ships. See **Admiralty** (Jurisdiction—Action in rem—Invocation of jurisdiction—When jurisdiction invoked—Plaintiff issuing concurrent proceedings against ship in connection with which claim arose and all her sister ships).

SITE OF SPECIAL SCIENTIFIC INTEREST
  Protection of. See **Environment** (Protection—Site of special scientific interest).

SKID
  Motor vehicle—
    Negligence. See **Negligence** (Vehicles—Skid).

SKULL
  Fracture—
    Damages. See **Damages** (Personal injury—Skull—Fracture).

SLANDER
  Costs—
    Conditional fee agreement. See **Costs** (Order for costs—Conditional fee agreement—Defamation).
  Counterclaim for slander—
    Jurisdiction of county court. See **County court** (Jurisdiction—Counterclaim—Counterclaim for slander).
  Generally. See **Libel and slander**.
  Goods, of. See **Slander of goods**.
  Title, of. See **Slander of title**.

SLANDER OF GOODS
  Disparagement of trader's goods—
    Puff—
      Rival traders—Statement by one trader disparaging rival trader's goods—Distinction between mere puff and actionable disparagement—Test to be applied—Intention that statement should be taken seriously—Right of trader to claim that his goods are superior to those of rivals—Defendants publishing report stating that laboratory experiments had shown that defendants' goods were superior to plaintiff's goods—Report intended to be taken seriously and not mere idle puff—Whether report founding a reasonable cause of action. **De Beers Abrasive Products Ltd v International General Electric Co of New York Ltd** [1975] 2 599, Ch D.

SLANDER OF TITLE
  No proof of malice or damage—
    Power of court to declare right to title—
      RSC Ord 25, r 5. **Lewis's Declaration of Trust, Re** [1953] 1 1005, Ch D.
  Professional description—
    Boxing title—
      Defendant represented as holding title held by plaintiff—Whether action for slander of title would lie if malice proved. **Serville v Constance** [1954] 1 662, Ch D.

SLAUGHTERHOUSE
  Licensing. See **Food and drugs** (Slaughterhouse—Licensing).

SLAVERY
  Trafficking people for exploitation. See **Criminal law** (Trafficking people for exploitation).

SLEEPWALKING
Automatism or insanity. *See* **Criminal law** (Automatism—Insanity distinguished—Sleepwalking).

SLIP RULE
Judgment—
Amending. *See* **Judgment** (Order—Correction—Accidental slip or omission).

SLOGAN
Advertising—
Passing off. *See* **Passing off** (Descriptive material—Imitation of advertising campaign).

SLOT CHARTER
Arrest of vessel—
Admiralty jurisdiction. *See* **Admiralty** (Jurisdiction—Action in rem—Arrest of ship—Slot charter).

SMALL DWELLINGS
See **Housing** (Small dwellings).

SMALL TENEMENT
Recovery of possession. *See* **Landlord and tenant** (Small tenement—Recovery of possession).

SMALLHOLDING
Death of tenant—
Succession. *See* **Agricultural holding** (Tenancy—Death of tenant—Smallholding).

SMELL
Nuisance. *See* **Nuisance** (Smell).

SMOKING
Ban in enclosed public places—
Prison. *See* **Prison** (Prison conditions—Smoking).
Contributory negligence. *See* **Negligence** (Contributory negligence—Lack of reasonable care by claimant for own safety—Smoking).
Motoring—
Breath test. *See* **Road traffic** (Breath test—Smoking before or during test).
Smokefree premises—
Licensing. *See* **Licensing** (Licensing objectives—Prevention of crime and disorder—Revocation of licence—Licensee convicted of offence of failing to comply with statutory duty to cause person smoking in smokefree premises to stop smoking).

SMUGGLING
Armed with offensive weapon. *See* **Customs and excise** (Armed with offensive weapon).
Money—
Export—
Prohibition of export of money. *See* **Currency control** (Exchange control—Prohibition of export of money—Smuggling money, Bank of England notes, out of the country).

SNOW
Highway—
Obstruction—
Civil liability for failure to remove obstruction. *See* **Highway** (Obstruction—Removal—Civil liability for failure to remove obstruction—Snow and ice on highway).

SNUFF
Oral snuff—
Ban on supply of—
Safety regulations—Duty to consult affected parties before making regulations. *See* **Consumer protection** (Safety regulations—Duty to consult affected parties before making regulations—Prohibition on supply of product—Oral snuff).

SOCIAL MEDIA
Data protection—
Transfer of data from European Union to third country. *See* **European Union** (Data protection—Processing and free movement of personal data—Transfer of data to third country by data controller).

SOCIAL SECURITY
Absence abroad—
Contributions. *See* Employed person—Absent abroad—Payment of contributions in respect of periods abroad, *below*.
Adjudication officer—
Negligence—
Duty to take care. *See* **Negligence** (Duty to take care—Existence of duty—Adjudication officer).
Administration of claims—
Supplementary benefit. *See* Supplementary benefit—Administration of claims, *below*.

Appeal—
  Decision of Minister—

    Employed person—Determination that employee engaged under contract of service—Appeal on question of law to High Court—Question whether person engaged under contract of service or for services mixed question of law and fact—Grounds on which court may interfere with Minister's decision—Driver engaged by company to drive earth moving machines—Features of contract with company pointing both to contract of service and contract for services—Decision of Minister one on which person properly instructed in relevant law could have come—Evidence to support decision—Decision containing no ex facie false proposition of law—No error of law established on appeal—National Insurance Act 1965, ss 1(2)(a), 65. **Global Plant Ltd v Secretary of State for Health and Social Security** [1971] 3 385, QBD.

  Decision of social security commissioner—

    Decision to refuse leave to appeal—No reasons given for decision—Judicial review of decision—Onus on applicant for judicial review—Attendance allowance—Applicant seeking to appeal from decision of Attendance Allowance Board—Social security commissioner refusing leave to appeal without giving reasons—Whether commissioner required to give reasons in the interests of justice—Whether court entitled to invite commissioner to state reasons in special cases—What applicant must show before court will grant judicial review—Tribunals and Inquiries (Social Security Commissioners) Order 1980, reg 2. **R v Secretary of State for Social Services, ex p Connolly** [1986] 1 998, CA.

  Social security commissioner, to. *See* Social security commissioners—Appeal to social security commissioner, *below.*

  Supplementary benefit—

    Appeal tribunal. *See* Supplementary benefit—Appeal tribunal, *below.*

Arrears of contributions—
  Recovery—

    Agreement by employer to pay contributions—Action by employee to recover wages from employer—Whether arrears of contributions part of employee's wages. **Gee-Whiz, The** [1951] 1 876, Admin Ct.

    Arrears payable under National Health Insurance Act 1936—Debt due to Crown—Whether assets of National Insurance Fund—National Insurance Act 1946, s 54(1), s 66(1)(a). **Ministry of National Insurance v Barrs** [1951] 1 532, CA.

    Conviction for failing to pay contributions—Liability on conviction to pay amount equal to unpaid contributions—Order for payment by court on conviction—Power to recover sums by civil proceedings—Whether court which enters conviction bound to make order for payment—National Insurance Act 1965, s 95(1), (3), (9). **Morgan v Quality Tools & Engineering (Stourbridge) Ltd** [1972] 1 744, QBD.

    Limitation—Revenue seeking to prevent time from running while liability appeals ongoing by seeking acknowledgment of claim or part payment from employers—Schemes not effective to prevent time from running—Whether contracts coming into effect under which employers promising not to rely on limitation defence—Whether employers estopped from relying on limitation defence. **Revenue and Customs Comrs v Benchdollar Ltd** [2010] 1 174, Ch D.

    Order for payment of arrears—Fine imposed—Whether sum enforceable as a civil debt or purpose of fixing maximum period of committal in default of payment—National Insurance Act 1946, s 54(1)—Magistrates' Courts Act 1952, s 64(3), Sch 3, para 4—National Insurance (Contributions) Regulations 1948 (SI 1948 No 1417), reg 19(5). **R v Marlow (Bucks) Justices, ex p Schiller** [1957] 2 783, QBD.

    Recoverable as a penalty—National Insurance Act 1946, s 8—National Insurance (Contributions) Regulations 1948 (SI 1948 No 1417), reg 19(1), (3), (5). **Shilvock v Booth** [1956] 1 382, QBD.

    Recoverable as a penalty—Whether a penalty—Whether magistrates' court has jurisdiction to remit arrears—National Insurance Act 1946, s 8—National Insurance (Contributions) Regulations 1948 (SI 1948 No 1417), reg 19(5)—Magistrates' Courts Act 1952, ss 27(1), 126(1), (3). **Leach v Litchfield** [1960] 3 739, QBD.

    Recovery following prosecution—Payment to National Insurance and Industrial Injuries Funds—Liability of directors in event of company failing to pay—Liability of person ceasing to be director before order for payment made but after period in which contributions should have been paid—National Insurance Act 1965, ss 8(2), 95(8). **Dept of Health and Social Security v Wayte** [1972] 1 255, CA.

Attendance allowance—
  Entitlement—

    Cooking of meals—Social Security Act 1975, s 35(1)(a). **R v National Insurance Comr, ex p Secretary of State for Social Services** [1981] 2 738, CA.

    Cooking of meals—Whether preparation of meals for disabled person constituting 'attention ... in connection with bodily functions'—Social Security Act 1975, s 35(1)(a). **Woodling v Secretary of State for Social Services** [1984] 1 593, HL.

    Person in need of care and attention—Person in residential accommodation provided by local authority—Accommodation transferred to voluntary organisation—Status of accommodation changed to residential care home—Applicant staying in accommodation but claiming attendance allowance—Whether applicant entitled to attendance allowance—Whether cost of applicant's accommodation could be borne out of public or local funds—National Assistance Act 1948, ss 21(1), 26—National Health Service Act 1977, Sch 8, para 2(1)—Social Security (Attendance Allowance) Amendment (No 3) Regulations 1983, reg 4(1)—Social Security (Attendance Allowance) Regulations 1991, reg 7(3). **Steane v Chief Adjudication Officer** [1996] 4 83, HL.

    Person requiring prolonged or repeated attendance during the night—Meaning of 'night'—Sunrise and sunset irrelevant—Domestic routine of household relevant fact—Period of inactivity beginning with time when household closes down for night—National Insurance (Old Persons' and Widows' Pension and Attendance Allowance) Act 1970, s 4(2). **R v National Insurance Comr, ex p Secretary of State for Social Services** [1974] 3 522, QBD.

SOCIAL SECURITY (cont)—
Attendance allowance (cont)—
Frequent attention throughout day in connection with bodily functions—
Attention—Blind man requiring assistance in bathing, eating and walking in unfamiliar surroundings—Whether assistance in walking in unfamiliar surroundings 'attention required in connection with ... bodily functions'—Social Security Act 1975, s 35(1)(a)(i). **Mallinson v Secretary of State for Social Security** [1994] 2 295, HL.
Attention—Claimant suffering from arthritis and incontinence—Incontinence causing extra laundry—Claimant unable to do laundry—Whether taking laundry away to be washed constituting 'attention ... in connection with' bodily functions—Social Security Contributions and Benefits Act 1992, s 64(2)(a). **Cockburn v Chief Adjudication Officer** [1997] 3 844, HL.
Attention—Deaf claimant requiring interpreter to use sign language to communicate with others—Whether provision of interpreter 'attention ... in connection with' bodily functions—Social Security Contributions and Benefits Act 1992, s 72(1)(b)(i). **Cockburn v Chief Adjudication Officer** [1997] 3 844, HL.
Benefit—
Asylum seekers—
Asylum seeker granted asylum many years after initial application—Domestic legislation precluding successful asylum seeker from claiming back dated payments of income support for period since date of asylum application—Whether entitlement to back payments under international conventions—Whether breach of Convention rights—United Nations Convention relating to the Status of Refugees 1951, art 28—Council Directive 2004/83/EC, art 28—Human Rights Act 1998, Sch 1, Pt 1, art 14. **Blakesley v Secretary of State for Work and Pensions** [2015] 4 529, CA.
Entitlement to asylum support—Failure to make claim as soon as reasonably possible upon arrival to United Kingdom—Disentitlement to asylum support—Legality of decision—Compliance with convention rights—Nationality, Immigration and Asylum Act 2002, s 55—Human Rights Act 1998, Sch 1, Pt I, arts 3, 6, 8. **R (on the application of Q) v Secretary of State for the Home Dept** [2003] 2 905, CA.
Benefit cap—
Cap on welfare benefits received by those in non-working households, equivalent to the net median earnings of working households—Differential treatment of men and women because of greater impact on single parents—International treaty on rights of children not part of domestic law—Whether differential treatment objectively justified—Whether human rights convention to be interpreted in light of international treaty—Whether breach of human rights—Human Rights Act 1998, Sch 1, art 14, First Protocol, art 1—Benefit Cap (Housing Benefit) Regulations 2012, SI 2012/2994. **R (on the application of SG) v Secretary of State for Work and Pensions** [2015] 4 939, SC.
Reduction of cap on welfare benefits—Whether unlawful—Whether discriminating against lone parents of young children, and young children of lone parents—Whether breaching human rights—Whether justified—Human Rights Act 1998, Sch 1, Pt I, arts 8, 14—Welfare Reform Act 2012, s 96(5A)—Housing Benefit Regulations 2006, SI 2006/213, reg 75CA—Benefit Cap (Housing Benefit and Universal Credit) (Amendment) Regulations 2016, SI 2016/909, reg 2(3)—United Nations Convention on the Rights of the Child, art 3(1). **R (on the application of DA) v Secretary of State for Work and Pensions** [2020] 1 573, SC.
Disqualification—
European Union law. *See* **European Union** (Reference to European Court—Reference for preliminary ruling concerning interpretation of European Union law—Interpretation of regulation).
European Union law. *See* **European Union** (Rules on competition).
Persons undergoing penal servitude, imprisonment or detention in legal custody—Convicted persons detained as of unsound mind and as mental defectives—Whether 'detention in legal custody'—National Insurance Act 1946, s 29(1)(b)—Criminal Justice Act 1948, s 66. **R v National Insurance Comr, ex p Timmis** [1954] 3 292, QBD.
Public policy—Widow's allowance—Claim by widow convicted of husband's manslaughter by stabbing—Jury's verdict showing killing to be deliberate and intentional act—Probation order only sentence passed on widow—Widow fulfilling conditions in social security legislation for claiming allowance—Whether widow entitled to allowance—Whether public policy applicable to claim for widow's allowance—Whether nature of crime such that entitlement to allowance not precluded by public policy—Social Security Act 1975, s 24(1). **R v National Insurance Comr, ex p Connor** [1981] 1 769, QBD.
Sickness benefit—Benefit in respect of period in prison or detention in legal custody—Claim for benefit while claimant serving prison sentence in Irish Republic—Whether claimant disqualified from receiving benefit while imprisoned abroad—National Insurance Act 1965, s 49(1)(b). **R v National Insurance Comr, ex p Warry** [1981] 1 229, QBD.
Earnings-related supplement—
Reckonable earnings—Emoluments assessable to income tax under Sch E from which tax is deductible—Casual employments in addition to regular employment—Tax deduction by casual employers impracticable—Effect on earnings-related supplementary benefit—Income Tax Act 1952, s 157—Income Tax (Employments) Regulations 1965 (SI 1965 No 516), reg 51(1)—National Insurance Act 1965, s 4(2)—National Insurance Act 1966, s 2(1), (5)(b). **Baker v Minister of Social Security** [1969] 2 836, QBD.
Income support—
Housing benefit—Council tax benefit—Pension credit—Entitlement—Person from abroad—Person from abroad not entitled to benefit—Person from abroad person not having right to reside in United Kingdom—Person lawfully present in United Kingdom claiming benefit—Whether lawful presence equated with right to reside—Income Support (General) Regulations 1987, SI 1987/1967, reg 21(3G)—Housing Benefit (General) Regulations 1987, SI 1987/1971, reg 7A—Council Tax Benefit (General) Regulations 1992, SI 1992/1814, reg 4A—State Pension Credit Regulations 2002, SI 2002/1792—EC Treaty, arts 12, 18. **Abdirahman v Secretary of State for Work and Pensions** [2007] 4 882, CA.

SOCIAL SECURITY (cont)—
  Benefit (cont)—
    Non-contributory benefits—
      Income-related benefits—Social assistance—Hybrid benefits—State pension credit—Entitlement—
        European Community national—Entitlement subject to right to reside test—Claimant not having
        right to reside—Claimant being refused state pension credit—Whether right to reside test overt
        discrimination—Whether covert discrimination justified—State Pension Credit Act 2002,
        s 1—State Pension Credit Regulations 2002, SI 2002/1792, reg 2—Council Regulation (EEC)
        1408/71, art 3. **Patmalniece v Secretary of State for Work and Pensions** [2009] **4** 738,
        CA; [2011] **3** 1, SC.
    Obtaining benefit by false statement etc—
      Meaning of benefit—National Insurance Act 1965, s 93(1)(c). **Tolfree v Florence** [1971] **1** 125, QBD.
    Obtaining benefit by fraud—
      Sentence. See **Sentence** (Fraud on the public purse—Obtaining welfare benefits by fraud).
    Overpayment—
      Insolvency. See **Insolvency** (Debt relief order—Discharge—Overpayment of benefit).
      Recovery—Claimant failing to declare receipt of unemployment benefit when claiming income
        support—Claimant signing declaration that he had correctly reported any facts which could affect
        amount of payment—Whether misrepresentation of material fact—Social Security Act 1986, s 53.
        Jones v Chief Adjudication Officer [1994] **1** 225, CA.
      Recovery—Claimant stating that neither he nor partner had any life insurances or endowment
        policies—Claimant unaware that partner had inherited policies from her father—Whether
        misrepresentation of material fact—Social Security Act 1986, s 53. **Jones v Chief Adjudication
        Officer** [1994] **1** 225, CA.
      Recovery—Pension—Legislation providing for recovery repealed and replaced—New legislation
        creating entirely new obligation—Whether new provision retrospective—Social Security Act
        1975, s 119—Supplementary Benefits Act 1976, s 20—Social Security Act 1986, s 53. **Plewa v
        Chief Adjudication Officer** [1994] **3** 323, HL.
      Recovery—Retrospective recovery of benefits paid in consequence of misrepresentation or failure
        to disclose material fact—Legislation providing that recovery of overpaid benefit could not be
        required if person receiving benefit had used due care and diligence—Legislation repealed and
        new legislation enacted conferring power on Secretary of State to recover overpaid benefit if
        payment made in consequence of misrepresentation or failure to disclose material fact—Whether
        new legislation retrospective—Social Security Act 1975, s 119—Social Security Act 1986, s 53.
        Secretary of State for Social Security v Tunnicliffe [1991] **2** 712, CA.
      Recovery—Statutory provision for recovery of benefit from person misrepresenting or failing to
        disclose relevant fact—Whether Secretary of State retaining common law remedies for mistake
        and restitution—Social Security Administration Act 1992, s 71. **R (on the application of the Child
        Poverty Action Group) v Secretary of State for Work and Pensions** [2009] **3** 633,
        QBD; [2010] **2** 113, CA; [2011] **1** 729, SC.
    Rates of benefit. See Rates of benefit, below.
    Widows' benefits—
      Bereavement payment—Widowed parent's allowance—Claimant marrying husband in Pakistan
        when husband still married to first wife under English law—Husband subsequently divorcing first
        wife—Whether claimant entitled to bereavement payment and widowed parent's allowance on
        death of husband as his 'spouse'—Whether refusal of benefits unjustified discrimination—
        Meaning of 'spouse'—Social Security Contributions and Benefits Act 1992, ss 36, 39A—Human
        Rights Act 1998, Sch 1, Pt I, art 14, Pt II, art 1—Social Security and Family Allowances
        (Polygamous Marriages) Regulations 1975, SI 1975/561, reg 2. **Akhtar v Secretary of State for
        Work and Pensions** [2022] **2** 937, CA.
      Widows' benefits not available to widowers—Prohibition of discrimination—Contributions and
        Benefits Act 1992, ss 36-38—Human Rights Act 1998, ss 3, 6, 8, Sch 1, Pt I, arts 8, 14, Pt II, art 1. **R
        (on the application of Hooper) v Secretary of State for Work and Pensions** [2003] **3** 673,
        CA; [2006] **1** 487, HL.
  Child benefit—
    Entitlement to benefit—
      European Community—Overlapping of rights. See **European Union** (Social security—Family
        benefits and family allowances—Overlapping of rights—Entitlement to benefit—Child benefit).
  Child tax credit—
    Entitlement—
      Claimant granted refugee status applying for backdated child tax credits—HMRC rejecting claim on
        grounds claimant receiving universal credit and therefore prevented from applying for
        pre-universal credit 'legacy benefits'—Whether claim for backdated tax credit valid for period of
        time before person recognised as refugee—Tax Credit (Immigration) Regulations 2003, SI
        2003/653, reg 3—Welfare Reform Act 2012 (Commencement No 23 and Transitional and
        Transitory Provisions) Order 2015, SI 2015/634, art 7. **R (on the application of DK) v Revenue and
        Customs Comrs (Secretary of State for Work and Pensions, interested party)** [2022] **3** 1025, CA.
      Discrimination—Sex—Father separated from mother of children—Father caring for children for
        significant length of time each week—Father's claim for child tax credit being refused on grounds
        of not having 'main responsibility' for children's care—Regulations making no provision for
        splitting of benefit payment between separated parents—Whether government decision to
        maintain no splitting rule unreasonable—Tax Credits Act 2002, ss 3, 8, 9(7)—Child Tax Credit
        Regulations 2002, SI 2002/2007, reg 3(1)—Human Rights Act 1998, Sch 1, Pt I, art 14,
        First Protocol, art 1. **Humphreys v Revenue and Customs Comrs** [2012] **4** 27, SC.
      Two child limit—Right to private and family life—Prohibition on discrimination—Whether limit
        breaching human rights—Whether exception perverse—Human Rights Act 1998, s 4, Sch 1, Pt I,
        arts 8, 9, 12, 14, Pt II, art 1—Tax Credits Act 2002, s 9—Welfare Reform Act 2012, s 10—Welfare
        Reform and Work Act 2016, ss 13, 14—United Nations Convention on the Rights of the Child. **SC
        v Secretary of State for Work and Pensions (Equality and Human Rights Commission
        intervening)** [2018] **3** 785, QBD.

Child tax credit (cont)—
Entitlement (cont)—
Two child limit—Right to private and family life—Right to marry and found a family—Right to peaceful enjoyment of possessions—Prohibition on discrimination—Whether limit breaching human rights—Human Rights Act 1998, Sch 1, Pt I, arts 8, 12, 14, Pt II, art 1—Welfare Reform and Work Act 2016—United Nations Convention on the Rights of the Child. **SC v Secretary of State for Work and Pensions (Equality and Human Rights Commission intervening)** [2019] 4 787, CA.

Two child limit—Right to private and family life—Right to marry and found a family—Right to peaceful enjoyment of possessions—Prohibition on discrimination—Whether limit breaching human rights—Whether provisions of unincorporated treaties relevant to interpretation of Convention rights—Approach to proportionality on issues of social and economic policy—Relevance of parliamentary material in determining compatibility of primary legislation with Convention rights—Human Rights Act 1998, Sch 1, Pt I, arts 8, 12, 14—Tax Credits Act 2002, s 9(3A), (3B)—Welfare Reform and Work Act 2016—United Nations Convention on the Rights of the Child. **R (on the application of SC) v Secretary of State for Work and Pensions** [2022] 3 95, SC.

Commissioner. *See* Social security commissioners, *below*.

Contract of service. *See* Employed person—Contract of service, *below*.

Contributions—
Agreement by employer to pay. *See* **Employment** (Remuneration—National insurance contributions).

Arrears. *See* Arrears of contributions, *above*.

Contribution conditions—
Determination of claims and questions—Whether Secretary of State having exclusive jurisdiction to decide what constitutes contribution conditions for particular claimant—Whether social security commissioner having jurisdiction to determine claimant's contribution conditions for entitlement to benefit—Social Security Administration Act 1992, s 17(1)(b)—Social Security Contributions and Benefits Act 1992, Sch 3, para 2(6)(b). **Secretary of State for Social Security v Scully** [1992] 4 1, CA.

Employer's contributions—
Liability to pay—No services rendered by employee in contribution week—Employee incapable of work and would but for that incapacity have been working—Incapacity of work—Employer a football club—Employee a professional footballer—Employee incapable of playing football in consequence of injury—Employee capable of doing other work—Whether employer liable to pay contributions where employee incapable of following his regular occupation—National Insurance Act 1965, s 8(5)—National Insurance (Industrial Injuries) Act 1965, s 3(2)(b). **Chesterfield Football Club Ltd v Secretary of State for Social Services** [1973] 1 679, QBD.

Employer's contributions—
Earnings paid to or for benefit of earner—Company making contribution to funded unapproved retirements benefit scheme—Employee entitled to benefits subject to contingency—Whether company liable to class 1 national insurance contributions on sums paid into scheme—Whether contributions earnings paid to or for benefit of earner—Social Security Contributions and Benefits Act 1992, s 6(1). **Forde and McHugh Ltd v Revenue and Customs Comrs** [2012] 3 1256, CA; [2014] 2 356, SC.

Exception from liability to pay contributions—
Persons not in receipt of income exceeding prescribed amount—Meaning of 'income'—National Insurance Act 1946, s 5(1)(a)(iii). **Longsdon v Minister of Pensions and National Insurance** [1956] 1 83, QBD.

Minister's decision conclusive and mandatory on questions involving payment of contributions under the Acts—
Ouster of the court's jurisdiction—National Insurance Act 1965, ss 64(1)(a), 97(1), (2)—National Insurance (Industrial Injuries) Act 1965, ss 35(1)(c), 70 (1), (2). **Dept of Health and Social Security v Walker Dean Walker Ltd** [1970] 1 757, QBD.

Recovery—
Recovery following prosecution—Company convicted for failure to make payment—Liability of directors—Whether director 'could reasonably be expected to have known' of failure to pay contributions—Social Security Act 1975, s 152(4). **Dept of Health and Social Security v Evans** [1985] 2 471, QBD.

Whether to be taken into account in assessing damages for personal injuries. *See* **Damages** (Personal injury—Loss of future earnings—National insurance contributions).

Determination of claims and questions—
Determination of question whether persons employed or self-employed—
Jurisdiction—Reference by court for determination by Minister—National Insurance Act 1965, ss 64(1)(a), (c), 97(2)—National Insurance (Industrial Injuries) Act 1965, ss 35(1), 70(2). **Ministry of Social Security v John Bryant & Co (Bristol) Ltd** [1968] 3 175, QBD.

Finality of decision of National Insurance Commissioner—
Determination in law on construction of enactment—Findings of fact—Claim to unemployment benefit—Whether originating summons to High Court lies to determine whether commissioner's decision bad in law—Commissioner's findings of fact final—National Insurance Act 1946, ss 13(1), proviso (a), 43(1). **Punton v Ministry of Pensions and National Insurance** [1963] 1 275, CA.

Jurisdiction of High Court on originating summons to determine whether commissioner's decision wrong in law—Exercise of court's discretion—Unemployment benefit—National Insurance Act 1946, s 43(1)—RSC Ord 54A, rr 1A, 4—National Insurance (Claims and Payments) Regulations 1948 (SI 1948 No 1041), reg 9—National Insurance (Determination of Claims and Questions) Regulations 1948 (SI 1948 No 1144), regs 10, 11, 15,19—Tribunals and Inquiries Act 1958, s 11(1). **Punton v Ministry of Pensions and National Insurance (No 2)** [1964] 1 448, CA.

Disability living allowance—
Care component—
'Cooking test'—Social Security Contributions and Benefits Act 1992, s 72(1)(a)(ii), (2). **Moyna v Secretary of State for Work and Pensions** [2003] 4 162, HL.

SOCIAL SECURITY (cont)—
Disability living allowance (cont)—
Care component (cont)—
Residence requirement—Whether United Kingdom precluded by EU law from imposing residence requirement as condition of entitlement to disability living allowance—Council Regulation 1408/71/EEC—Social Security Contributions and Benefits Act 1992, s 71(6)—Social Security (Disability Living Allowance) Regulations 1991, SI 1991/2890, reg 2(1). **Secretary of State for Work and Pensions v Tolley (as personal representative of Tolley (decd))** [2016] **1** 40n, SC.
Hospitalisation—
Child—Prohibition of discrimination—Child being in-patient at NHS hospital for period exceeding 84 days—Parents remaining primary carers throughout that period—Secretary of State suspending allowance after 84 days' hospitalisation in accordance with regulations—Whether regulations discriminatory and in breach of Convention rights—Human Rights Act 1998, Sch 1, Pt I, art 14, Pt II, art 1—Social Security (Disability Living Allowance) Regulations 1991, SI 1991/2890, regs 8, 10, 12A, 12B. **Mathieson v Secretary of State for Work and Pensions** [2016] **1** 779, SC.
Disabled person—
Social security services for. See Services for sick and disabled persons, *below.*
Disablement benefit—
Accident arising out of and in course of employment—
Accident occurring while claimant travelling from home to place where work to be undertaken—Relevant considerations—Whether injury 'arising out of and in course of employment'—Social Security Act 1975, s 50(1). **Nancollas v Insurance Officer** [1985] **1** 833, CA.
Activity out of which accident arose reasonably incidental to employment—Recreational activities—Employee expected to take part in activities but under no duty to do so—Police constable injured in football match—Football match organised by Police Athletic Association—Constable representing his force in match—Match played during constable's off-duty time—Whether injury 'arising out of and in the course of his employment'—National Insurance (Industrial Injuries) Act 1965, s 5(1). **R v National Insurance Comr, ex p Michael** [1976] **1** 566, QBD.
Burden of proof—Burden of proof whether accident arose out of employment—National Insurance (Industrial Injuries) Act 1946, s 7(4). **R v National Insurance (Industrial Injuries) Comr, ex p Richardson** [1958] **2** 689, QBD.
Permanent injury benefit—Permanent loss of earning ability—Nurse suffering neck and lower back injury—Injury wholly or mainly attributable to employment—Pre-existing degenerative spinal condition—Whether entitled to permanent injury benefit—Whether earning ability permanently reduced 'by reason of' the injury—Whether appropriate to ask what impact injury would have had on someone of similar age not suffering from degenerative spine condition—National Health Service (Injury Benefits) Regulations 1995, SI 1995/866, regs 3, 4. **NHS Business Services Authority v Young** [2018] **1** 131, CA.
Recreational activities—Employee expected to take part in activities but under no duty to do so—Police constable injured in football match—Constable representing his force in match—Match played during constable's off-duty time—Whether injury 'arising ... in the course of his employment'—Whether injury suffered whilst doing act reasonably incidental to his employment—National Insurance (Industrial Injuries) Act 1965, s 5(1). **R v National Insurance Comr, ex p Michael** [1977] **2** 420, CA.
Tea-break—Worker injured on factory premises at a time when he was overstaying the tea-break—Whether course of employment had been interrupted—National Insurance (Industrial Injuries) Act 1946, s 7(1),(4). **R v Industrial Injuries Comr, ex p Amalgamated Engineering Union** [1966] **1** 97, CA.
Assessment of degree of disability—
Greater disability than normal by reason of physical condition at date of assessment—Combination of causes—Loss of left eye due to accident and defect of vision in right eye due to disease, not to accident—Whether defect of vision in right eye was to be taken into consideration to increase assessment—National Insurance (Industrial Injuries) Act 1965, Sch 4, para 1(b)—National Insurance (Industrial Injuries) (Benefit) Regulations 1964, (SI 1964 No 504), reg 2(3)(a). **R v Industrial Injuries Comr, ex p Cable** [1968] **1** 9, CA.
Injury to organ of the body—One of two similar organs, the functions of which would be interchangeable or complementary—Injury to finger—Previous injury to finger of other hand—Whether hands were two similar organs, the functions of which would be interchangeable or complementary—National Insurance (Industrial Injuries) (Benefit) Regulations 1948, (SI 1948 No 1372), reg 2(5). **R v Medical Appeal Tribunal, ex p Burpitt** [1957] **2** 704, QBD.
Injury to organ of the body—One of two similar organs, the functions of which would be interchangeable or complementary—Injury to leg—Previous injury to other leg—Whether legs were two similar organs, the functions of which would be interchangeable or complementary—National Insurance (Industrial Injuries) (Benefit) Regulations 1948, (SI 1948 No 1372), reg 2(5). **R v Medical Appeal Tribunal (South Wales District), ex p Griffiths** [1958] **2** 227, QBD.
Claim—
Medical appeal tribunal. See **Industrial injury** (Medical appeal tribunal—Claim for disablement benefit).
Nature of proceedings—Medical appeal tribunal—Onus of proof—Discharge of assessment—Assessment made by medical board—Appeal tribunal suspicious that claimant malingering—Report of consultant before tribunal—Report suggesting claimant malingering—Whether tribunal bound to make positive finding of malingering before discharging assessment. **R v National Insurance Comr, ex p Viscusi** [1974] **2** 724, CA.
Entitlement—
Accident arising out of and in course of employment. See Disablement benefit—Accident arising out of and in course of employment, *above.*
Disability living allowance—Transitional provisions—Appellant awarded disability living allowance for fixed period—New regulations imposing additional condition on entitlement—Appellant unable to satisfy new condition when making further claim for allowance—Regulations containing transitional provision—Whether transitional provision extending duration of claimant's entitlement to benefit beyond term for which it had been awarded—Social Security (Persons From Abroad) Miscellaneous Amendments Regulations 1996, reg 12(3). **M (a minor) v Secretary of State for Social Security** [2001] **4** 41, HL.

SOCIAL SECURITY (cont)—
Disablement benefit (cont)—
Special hardship allowance—
Calculation of amount—Standard of remuneration—Pre-accident and post-accident occupation—
Comparison of remuneration in pre-accident and post-accident occupations—Whether
comparison should take account of difference in weekly number of hours worked in each
occupation—National Insurance (Industrial Injuries) Act 1965, s 14(b). **R v National Insurance
Comr, ex p Mellors** [1971] **1** 740, CA.
Incapacity to follow regular occupation or equivalent employment as result of relevant loss of
faculty—Regular occupation—Coal miner—Coal miner developing pneumoconiosis—Miner
advised that he could continue work provided done in approved dust conditions—Miner
returning to work under approved dust conditions—Miner subsequently giving up work due to
hypertension—Whether entitled to special hardship allowance—Whether incapable of following
employment of equivalent standard as a result of relevant loss of faculty—Social Security Act
1975, s 60(1). **R v National Insurance Comrs, ex p Steel** [1978] **3** 78, QBD.
Incapacity to follow regular occupation or equivalent employment as result of relevant loss of
faculty—Standards of comparison of probable remuneration and employments—Localities where
standards to be ascertained—National Insurance (Industrial Injuries) Act 1946, s 14(1)(a),(b),(4), as
amended by National Insurance (Industrial Injuries) Act 1948, s 1 and National Insurance &c, Act
1964, s 2(2), Sch 5, para 5. **R v National Injuries Comr, ex p Humphreys** [1965] **3** 885, .
Incapacity to follow regular occupation or equivalent employment as result of relevant loss of
faculty—Whether finding of medical board for purposes of disablement benefit (s 12) of
claimant's state at time of examination after accident on subsequent application for
special hardship increase (s 14)—National Insurance (Industrial Injuries) Act 1946, ss 12, 14(1). **R v
Industrial Injuries Comr, ex p Ward** [1964] **3** 907, QBD.
Discrimination on grounds of nationality—
European Union. *See* **European Union** (Discrimination—Discrimination on grounds of nationality—
Right of residence).
Disqualification from benefit. *See* Benefit—Disqualification, *above.*
Earnings-related supplement. *See* Benefit—Earnings-related supplement, *above.*
Employed person—
Absent abroad—
Payment of contributions in respect of periods abroad—Employment outside Great Britain—
Employment in continuation of employed contributor's employment in Great Britain—'In
continuation of'—Period of non-employment intervening between termination of employment in
Great Britain and subsequent employment outside Great Britain—Whether subsequent
employment must be continuous in point of time with employment in Great Britain—National
Insurance (Residence and Persons Abroad) Regulations 1948 (SI 1948 No 1275), reg 3(1). **East
African Airways Corp v Secretary of State for Social Services** [1973] **1** 165, QBD.
Contract of service—
Employments to be treated as employment under contract of service—Employment where dental
practitioner remunerated by salary—Dentist employed by local authority—Employment for
indefinite period until terminated by notice—Attendance obligatory on fixed number of occasions
per week—Payment at fixed rate for each session worked—Whether dentist in receipt of salary or
fees—National Insurance (Classification) Regulations 1948 (SI 1948 No 1425), Sch 1, Part 1, para
2(b)—National Insurance (Industrial Injuries)(Insurable and Excepted Employments) Regulations
1948 (SI 1948 No 1456), Sch 2, Part 1, para 2(b). **Greater London Council v Minister of Social
Security** [1971] **2** 285, QBD.
Music-hall artist—Whether employed under 'contract of service'—National Insurance Act 1946,
s 1(2)(a),(b). **Gould v Minister of National Insurance** [1951] **1** 368, KBD.
Owner drivers employed by manufacturers of concrete to deliver concrete—Whether contracts of
carriage with independent contractors or contracts of service. **Ready Mixed Concrete (South
East) Ltd v Minister of Pensions and National Insurance** [1968] **1** 433, QBD.
Part-time teacher at drama school—Payment by the hour or fixed fee—Absences to undertake
occasional theatrical engagements—No syllabus imposed by school—No administrative
duties—Whether contract of service—National Insurance Act 1965, s 1(2)(a). **Argent v Minister of
Social Security** [1968] **3** 208, QBD.
Series of contracts of employment—Interviewer working for market research company—Extent and
degree of control—Nature and provisions of contracts—Whether contract of service or for
services—National Insurance Act 1965, s 1(2)—National Insurance (Industrial Injuries) Act 1965,
s 1(2), Sch 1, Pt 1, para 1. **Market Investigations Ltd v Minister of Social Security** [1968] **3** 732,
QBD.
Person gainfully occupied in employment under contract of service—
Gainfully occupied—Research assistant incapacitated by poliomyelitis—Cost of travelling to and
from work exceeding remuneration—Whether 'gainfully occupied in employment'—National
Insurance Act 1946, s 1(2)(a),(b). **Vandyk v Minister of Pensions and National Insurance**
[1954] **2** 723, QBD.
Solicitor's articled clerk—Articles in usual form, not providing for any remuneration—£100 given to
clerk, in one year, in four equal payments—Clerk told to spend the money on holidays—Whether
'gainfully occupied in employment under a contract of service'—National Insurance Act 1946,
s 1(2)(a). **Benjamin v Minister of Pensions and National Insurance** [1960] **2** 851, QBD.
Employer's contributions. *See* Contributions—Employer's contributions, *above.*
Employment and support allowance—
Disability—
Discrimination—Persons with impaired mental, cognitive or intellectual difficulties—Duty to make
reasonable adjustments—Provision, criterion or practice putting disabled person at substantial
disadvantage—Equality Act 2010, s 21, Sch 2, para 2(5)(a),(b). **R (on the application of MM) v
Secretary of State for Work and Pensions** [2014] **2** 289, CA.
Equality of treatment of men and women—
Retirement pension. *See* Retirement pension—Equality of treatment of men and women, *below.*
European Union—
Citizenship. *See* **European Union** (Citizenship—Person holding nationality of a member state).

SOCIAL SECURITY (cont)—
European Union (cont)—
  Equality of treatment of men and women. *See* **European Union** (Equality of treatment of men and women—Social security).
  Freedom of movement of workers—
    Generally. *See* **European Union** (Workers—Freedom of movement—Social security).
    Income support. *See* **European Union** (Workers—Freedom of movement—Social security—Income support).
  Freedom of movement of workers. *See* **European Union** (Workers—Freedom of movement—Social security—Income support).
  Funeral payment. *See* **European Union** (Workers—Freedom of movement—Social security—Funeral payment).
  Generally. *See* **European Union** (Social security).
Family benefits and family allowances—
  European Community. *See* **European Union** (Social security—Family benefits and family allowances).
Family income supplement—
  Entitlement—
    Person engaged in remunerative full-time work—Whether claimant absent from work because of illness 'engaged in remunerative full-time work' at date of claim—Whether claimant required to be actually working at date of claim—Family Income Supplement Act 1976, s 1(1)(a). **R v Supplementary Benefits Commission, ex p Lewis** [1982] **1** 680, CA.
Funeral payment—
  Process of determination of claim—
    Necessary information relating to conditions of entitlement or exceptions to entitlement not known—Whether claim payable—Social Security (Maternity and Funeral Expenses) (General) Regulations (Northern Ireland) 1987, SR 1987/150, reg 6. **Kerr v Dept for Social Development** [2004] **4** 385, HL.
Gender recognition—
  Retirement pension. *See* Retirement pension—Equality of treatment of men and women, *below*.
Guardian's allowance—
  Persons entitled to allowance—
    Parent of child not entitled to allowance—Meaning of 'parent'—Illegitimate child adopted by grandmother—Child subsequently looked after by natural mother on death of grandmother—Natural mother claiming guardian's allowance—Whether natural mother ceasing to be a 'parent' once child adopted—Whether natural mother entitled to guardian's allowance—Social Security Act 1975, s 38(1), (2), (6)—Children Act 1975, Sch 1, para 3(2), (5). **Secretary of State for Social Services v S** [1983] **3** 173, CA.
Healthcare services—
  European Union—
    Treaty provisions. *See* **European Union** (Treaty provisions—Obligations under treaty—Failure to fulfil obligations—Social security—Hospital care).
Housing benefit—
  Assessment—
    Assessment of amount by which eligible rent to be reduced when rent payable by claimant unreasonably high in comparison with suitable alternative accommodation—Whether claimant's personal circumstances relevant in assessing amount of reduction—Housing Benefit (General) Regulations 1987, reg 11(2). **R v City of Westminster Housing Benefit Review Board, ex p Mehanne** [1999] **2** 317, CA; [2001] **2** 690, HL.
    Imposition of cap in cases of deemed under-occupation of social sector housing—'Bedroom tax'—Claimant living with severely disabled partner in two-bedroomed property—Regulations requiring discount to housing benefit for deemed under-occupancy—Whether deduction to housing benefit applying where would breach claimant's Convention rights—Whether account to be taken of discretionary housing payments received—Human Rights Act 1998, ss 3, 6, Sch 1, Pt I, arts 8, 14—Housing Benefit Regulations 2006, SI 2006/213, reg B13. **RR v Secretary of State for Work and Pensions (Equality and Human Rights Commission and others intervening)** [2020] **2** 477, SC.
    Imposition of cap in cases of deemed under-occupation of social sector housing—'Bedroom tax'—Effect of cap on persons with disabilities—Effect of cap on women living in sanctuary schemes—Whether breach of convention rights—Whether breach of public sector equality duty—Human Rights Act 1998, Sch 1, Pt I, arts 8, 14, Pt II, art 1—Equality Act 2010, s 149—Housing Benefit Regulations 2006, SI 2006/213, reg B13. **R (on the application of MA) v Secretary of State for Work and Pensions** [2017] **1** 869, SC.
    Payment in respect of rent—Local authority's financial situation—Whether local authority entitled to take its own financial situation into account when assessing amount of benefit payable to claimant in respect of rent—Housing Benefit (General) Regulations 1987, regs 10, 11(2). **R v Brent London BC, ex p Connery** [1990] **2** 353, QBD.
    Rent —Local reference rent—Locality—Meaning of 'locality'—Rent Officers (Housing Benefit Functions) Order 1997, SI 1997/1984, Sch 1, para 4(6). **R (on the application of Heffernan) v Rent Service** [2009] **1** 173, HL.
  Entitlement—
    Church members occupying church-owned property communally for religious reasons under agreements creating legally enforceable liability for rent and providing for specified form of lifestyle—Whether agreements pursuant to which church members occupying property on a commercial basis—Whether taking into account factors manifesting church members' religious beliefs breaching right to freedom of thought, conscience and religion—Human Rights Act 1998, Sch 1, Pt I, art 9—Housing Benefit (General) Regulations 1987, SI 1987/1971, reg 7. **Campbell v South Northamptonshire DC** [2004] **3** 387, CA.
    Determination of maximum rent—Meaning of 'bedroom'—Housing Benefit Regulations 2006, SI 2006/213, reg B13(5). **Hockley v Secretary of State for Work and Pensions** [2020] **2** 20, CA.

SOCIAL SECURITY (cont)—
    Housing benefit (cont)—
        Entitlement (cont)—
            Husband claiming housing benefit—Husband living with wife—Wife not fulfilling statutory
            condition for benefit—Whether husband making claim 'in respect of' wife—Whether wife making
            application for national insurance number—Meaning of 'in respect of'—Social Security
            Administration Act 1992, s 1(1A), (1B). **Secretary of State for Work and Pensions v Wilson**
            [2007] **1** 281, CA.

            Periodical payments—Service charges—Sheltered accommodation—Communal areas—
            Entitlement to housing benefit excluding payments for service charge for cleaning and fuel in
            respect of rooms in common use—Service charge for cleaning and fuel in respect of rooms in
            common use included in 'sheltered accommodation'—Meaning and construction of 'sheltered
            accommodation'—Social Security Contributions and Benefits Act 1992, Pt VII—Housing Benefit
            Regulations 2006, SI 2006/213, Sch 1. **Oxford City Council v Basey (by May, his litigation friend)**
            [2012] **3** 71, CA.

            Vires—Proposed amendments to housing benefit regulations referred to independent advisory
            committee informally for decision as to whether proposed amendments be referred to it
            formally—Whether amendments ultra vires—Whether committee misled—Whether amendments
            impliedly presented as neutral in effect—Housing Benefit (General) Regulations 1987,
            SI 1987/1971, reg 7. **Campbell v South Northamptonshire DC** [2004] **3** 387, CA.

    Incapacity benefit—
        Residence in member state. *See* **European Union** (Workers—Freedom of movement—Social
        security—Incapacity benefit to disabled young people).

    Income support—
        Assessment of needs—
            Capital administered by Court of Protection. *See* **Community care services** (Assessment of
            needs—Recovery of charges—Capital—Award of damages for personal injury—Sum of capital
            administered on behalf of person by Court of Protection).

        Capital limit—
            Calculation of capital—Income support claimant and another sharing beneficial interest in property
            as tenants in common in unequal shares—Whether claimant should be treated in calculating
            value of her capital assets as entitled to beneficial half share in property—Income Support
            (General) Regulations 1987, reg 52. **Hourigan v Secretary of State for Work and Pensions**
            [2003] **3** 924, CA.

        Disability premium—
            Calculation of amount—Entitlement to severe disability premium—Circumstances in which persons
            to be treated as being severely disabled—Secretary of State having power to make regulations
            specifying circumstances in which persons to be treated as being severely disabled—Disabled
            person entitled to disability premium if no non-dependants living with him—Claimant disabled
            and living with parents—Secretary of State making regulations providing that parents classed as
            non-dependants—Claimant no longer entitled to severe disability premium—Whether regulations
            ultra vires—Social Security Act 1986, s 22(4)—Income Support (General) Regulations 1987,
            reg 17(1), Sch 2, para 13(2)(a)(ii), (iii). **Chief Adjudication Officer v Foster** [1993] **1** 705, HL.

            Entitlement to severe disability premium—Claimant being denied premium on basis of residence
            with parents in their house—Subsequent decision granting premium to other claimants in same
            circumstances—Claimant seeking review—Effect of subsequent decision on earlier decision—
            Whether earlier decision reviewable as erroneous in law—Whether claimant 'residing with'
            parents—Whether claimant in 'joint occupation' with parents—Social Security Act 1975,
            s 104(1A)(7), (8)—Income Support (General) Regulations 1987, reg 3, Sch 2, para 13(2)(a)(ii). **Bate
            v Chief Adjudication Officer** [1996] **2** 790, HL.

            Protection of property—Peaceful enjoyment of possessions—Prohibition of discrimination—
            Statutory provision disentitling disabled persons from disability premium if 'without
            accommodation'—Person receiving income support including disability premium becoming
            homeless—Withdrawing of disability premium—Whether discriminatory—Whether within ambit
            of right to peaceful enjoyment of possessions—Whether discrimination justified—Social Security
            Contributions and Benefits Act 1992—Human Rights Act 1998, Sch 1, Pt I, art 14, Pt II,
            art 1—Income Support (General) Regulations 1987, SI 1987/1967, Sch 7, para 6. **R (on the
            application of RJM) v Secretary of State for Work and Pensions** [2009] **2** 556, HL.

        Entitlement—
            Claimant enrolled on university course of variable character—Claimant classified as part-time
            during second year of course—Whether claimant at material time 'student' for purposes of
            income support—Income Support (General) Regulations 1987, reg 61. **Chief Adjudication Officer
            v Webber** [1997] **4** 274, CA.

            Nationals of specified states subject to immigration control not excluded from entitlement to
            income support if lawfully present in United Kingdom—National of specified state temporarily
            admitted—Statutory provision deeming those temporarily admitted not to have entered United
            Kingdom—Whether national of specified state entitled to income support—Whether lawfully
            present in United Kingdom—Immigration Act 1971, s 11, Sch 2—Social Security (Immigration and
            Asylum) Consequential Amendments Regulations 2000, SI 2000/636, Schedule Pt I, para 4. **Szoma
            v Secretary of State for Work and Pensions** [2006] **1** 1, HL.

            Person from abroad only entitled to income support if habitually resident in United
            Kingdom—Meaning of habitually resident—Social security appeal tribunal finding claimant from
            Bangladesh habitually resident on date of arrival in United Kingdom—Tribunal considering only
            whether claimant had come to United Kingdom and for settled purposes—Whether tribunal right
            to do so—Income Support (General) Regulations 1987, reg 21(3), Sch 7, para 17. **Nessa v Chief
            Adjudication Officer** [1998] **2** 728, CA; [1999] **4** 677, HL.

        European Community—
            Freedom of movement of workers. *See* **European Union** (Workers—Freedom of movement—Social
            security—Income support).

SOCIAL SECURITY (cont)—
Income support (cont)—
Jobseeker's allowance—
Entitlement—Capital disregards—Dwelling occupied as the home—Claimant's large family living in two houses—Whether both houses one dwelling occupied as the home—Jobseeker's Allowance Regulations 1996, Sch 8, para 1. **Miah v Secretary of State for Work and Pensions** [2003] **4** 702, CA.
Entitlement—Method of calculating average weekly number of hours of remunerative work for persons in one-year cycle of work—Whether unpaid holiday periods to be taken into account for purpose of averaging exercise—Income Support (General) Regulations 1987, reg 5—Jobseeker's Allowance Regulations 1996, reg 51. **Banks v Chief Adjudication Officer** [2001] **4** 62, HL; **Stafford v Chief Adjudication Officer** [2000] **1** 686, CA.
Entitlement—Schemes for assisting persons to obtain employment—Statutory power for regulations to make provision for imposing on claimants of jobseeker's allowance in prescribed circumstances a requirement to participate in schemes of any prescribed description designed to assist them to obtain employment—Meaning of 'any prescribed description'—Regulations naming scheme—Regulations not describing scheme—Whether regulations lawful—Jobseekers Act 1995, s 17A—Jobseeker's Allowance (Employment and Enterprise) Regulations 2011, SI 2011/917. **R (on the application of Reilly) v Secretary of State for Work and Pensions** [2013] **3** 67, CA; [2014] **1** 505, SC.
Jobseeker's allowance—
Entitlement—Schemes for assisting persons to obtain employment—Prohibition of slavery and forced labour—Forced or compulsory labour—Whether requirement to participate in scheme assisting claimants of jobseeker's allowance to obtain employment a requirement to perform forced or compulsory labour—Human Rights Act 1998, Sch 1, Pt I, art 4—Jobseeker's Allowance (Employment and Enterprise) Regulations 2011, SI 2011/917. **R (on the application of Reilly) v Secretary of State for Work and Pensions** [2014] **1** 505, SC.
Overpayment—
Recovery—Income support including care component of disability living allowance for fixed period—Award of disability living allowance not renewed—Award continuing to be paid—Secretary of State seeking to recover overpayment—Whether Secretary of State entitled to rely on claimant's non-disclosure—Social Security Administration Act 1992, s 71—Social Security (Claims and Payments) Regulations 1987, SI 1987/1968, reg 32. **Hinchy v Secretary of State for Work and Pensions** [2003] **2** 289, CA; [2005] **2** 129, HL.
Person from abroad. See Benefit—Income support—Housing benefit—Council tax benefit—Pension credit—Entitlement—Person from abroad, *above*.
Person in need of care and attention—
Person in residential accommodation provided by local authority—Accommodation transferred to voluntary organisation—Status of accommodation changed to residential care home—Applicants staying in accommodation but claiming income support—Whether applicants entitled to income support at higher rate applicable to persons in residential care homes—National Assistance Act 1948, ss 21(1), 26—Income Support (General) Regulations 1987, reg 21, Sch 4, para 6(1). **Chief Adjudication Officer v Quinn** [1996] **4** 72, HL.
Urgent cases payments—
Asylum seekers—Claimant asylum seeker entitled to benefit until date claim for asylum recorded by Secretary of State as having been determined—Secretary of State recording determination of claim for asylum—Deliberate delay in notifying claimant—Whether claimant entitled to benefit until date of actual notification—Income Support (General) Regulations 1987, reg 70(3A)(b)(i). **R (on the application of Anufrijeva) v Secretary of State for the Home Dept** [2003] **3** 827, HL.
Asylum seekers—Entitlement of asylum seekers to urgent cases payments—Secretary of State making regulations removing entitlement to urgent cases payments from those seeking asylum otherwise than immediately on arrival in United Kingdom and from all claimants pending appeal from an adverse determination by Home Secretary—Whether regulations ultra vires—Social Security Contributions and Benefits Act 1992, ss 135(1), (2), 137(2)(a), 175(3)(a)—Social Security (Persons From Abroad) Miscellaneous Amendments Regulations 1996, reg 8. **R v Secretary of State for Social Security, ex p Joint Council for the Welfare of Immigrants** [1996] **4** 385, CA.
Industrial injury—
Disablement benefit. See Disablement benefit, *above*.
Generally. See **Industrial injury**.
Inflation—
Uprating of retirement pension. See Retirement pension—Inflation uprating, *below*.
Inspector—
Power to enter premises liable to inspection—
Exception—Inspector having no power to enter private dwelling-house not used for trade or business—Burden of proof—Inspector attempting to enter premises built as dwelling-house and once used as such—Accused refusing to allow inspector to enter premises—Accused relying on exception—Onus on accused to prove premises within exception—Magistrates' Courts Act 1952, s 81—National Insurance Act 1965, s 90. **Stott v Hefferon** [1974] **3** 673, QBD.
Exception—Inspector having no power to enter private dwelling-house not used for trade or business—Meaning of 'private dwelling-house'—Premises built as dwelling-house but no longer used as such—Whether 'private dwelling-house'—National Insurance Act 1965, s 90. **Stott v Hefferon** [1974] **3** 673, QBD.
Power to require information for the purpose of ascertaining whether contributions payable—
Employed person—Failure of employer to pay contributions—Refusal of employee to furnish information to inspector—Whether inspector having power to require employee to disclose name and address of employer—National Insurance Act 1965, s 90(3), (4). **Smith v Hawkins** [1972] **1** 910, QBD.
Institution of proceedings. See Offence—Institution of proceedings, *below*.
Invalid care allowance—
Entitlement—
Right to allowance dependent on disabled person being entitled to attendance allowance—Social Security Act 1973, ss 35, 37. **Woodling v Secretary of State for Social Services** [1984] **1** 593, HL.

SOCIAL SECURITY (cont)—
Invalid care allowance (cont)—
European Community—
Equality of treatment of men and women. *See* **European Union** (Equality of treatment of men and women—Social security—Severe disablement allowance—Invalid care allowance).
Sex discrimination—
Allowance not payable to married woman living with or maintained by husband or woman living with man as husband and wife—Allowance paid to man in corresponding circumstances—Whether United Kingdom scheme of invalid care allowance outside statutory schemes referred to in European Communities directive on equal treatment for men and women in matters of social security—Whether scheme contrary to principle of equal treatment—Whether conditions in scheme constituting discrimination on grounds of sex—Social Security Act 1975, s 37(3)(a)(i)—EC Council Directive 79/7, arts 1, 3(1)(a), 4. **Drake v Chief Adjudication Officer (Case 150/85)** [1986] **3** 65, ECJ.
Invalidity benefit—
EC workers. *See* **European Union** (Workers—Freedom of movement—Social security—Invalidity benefits).
Invalidity pension—
Non-contributory invalidity pension. *See* Non-contributory invalidity pension, *below.*
Jobseeker's allowance—
Age-related amount—
Highest age-related amount applicable to persons who had attained age of 25 years—Claimant aged 24 years old receiving contributions-based jobseeker's allowance calculated by reference to age-related amount for persons aged between 18 and 24 years—Whether receipt of lesser age-related amount infringing her human rights—Human Rights Act 1998, Sch 1, Pt I, art 14, Pt II, art 1. **R (on the application of Carson) v Secretary of State for Work and Pensions** [2003] **3** 577, CA; [2005] **4** 545, HL.
European Community. *See* **European Union** (Workers—Freedom of movement—Social security).
Income support. *See* Income support—Jobseeker's allowance, *above.*
Judicature (Appellate Jurisdiction) Law 1962—
Calculation of benefit—
Adjustment of exceptional circumstances—Award of amount exceeding basic allowance—Regard to be had to provisions for additional requirements—Additional requirements—Entitlement of recipient of allowance to further sum after two years—Sum awarded for additional requirements exceeding sum awarded for exceptional circumstances—Whether sum awarded for additional requirements to be reduced by amount of sum paid for exceptional circumstances—Ministry of Social Security Act 1966, Sch 2, paras 4, 12. **R v Greater Birmingham Appeal Tribunal, ex p Simper** [1973] **2** 461, QBD.
Local authority powers. *See* **Local authority** (Social services—Powers).
Maternity grant—
Entitlement—
Discrimination—Persons with parental responsibility for child pursuant to adoption order entitled to claim maternity grant—Whether refusal of grant to person with parental responsibility for child pursuant to residence order discriminatory—Human Rights Act 1998, Sch 1, Pt I, art 14—Social Fund Maternity and Funeral Expenses (General) Regulations 1987, SI 1987/481, reg 5. **Francis v Secretary of State for Work and Pensions** [2006] **1** 748, CA.
Mobility allowance—
Entitlement—
Inability to walk—National insurance—Blind person—Blind person unable to walk without guide—Whether such person entitled to mobility allowance—Whether inability to walk meaning inability to move on foot or inability to direct movement towards desired destination—Social Security Act 1975, s 37A. **Lees v Secretary of State for Social Services** [1985] **2** 203, HL.
Residence—Residence in Great Britain—Change of residence outside Great Britain after decision to pay allowance given—Whether continued residence in Great Britain throughout period allowance payable a condition for payment of allowance—Whether power to review decision to pay allowance where change of residence after date of decision to pay allowance—Social Security Act 1975, ss 37A(1)(7), 104 (1)(b). **Insurance Officer v Hemmant** [1984] **2** 533, CA.
Music-hall artist. *See* Employed person—Contract of service—Music-hall artist, *above.*
National insurance commissioner—
Certiorari—
Jurisdiction. *See* **Certiorari** (Jurisdiction—National insurance commissioners).
Finality of decision. *See* Determination of claims and questions—Finality of decision of National Insurance Commissioner, *above.*
National insurance stamps. *See* Stamp, *below.*
Non-contributory invalidity pension—
Entitlement—
Whether claim a necessary precondition to entitlement—Social Security (Northern Ireland) Act 1975, ss 36(1), 79(1). **Insurance Officer v McCaffrey** [1985] **1** 5, HL.
Offence—
Institution of proceedings—
Authorisation—Institution of proceedings by or with the consent of the Minister or by an inspector or other officer authorised in that behalf—Whether prosecution have to prove authorisation—National Insurance Act 1946, s 53(1). **Price v Humphries** [1958] **2** 725, QBD.
Knowingly making false statement or representation for purpose of obtaining benefit—
Ingredients of offence—Claimant knowingly making false statement in claim form—Claimant's purpose in making false statement merely to deceive his employer—Claimant unaware that his statement would affect amount of benefit payable—Whether offence committed—Whether necessary to prove that false statement made with intention of obtaining benefit—Social Security Act 1975, s 146(3). **Barrass v Reeve** [1980] **3** 705, QBD.
Overpayment of benefit—
Generally. *See* Benefit—Overpayment, *above.*
Unemployment benefit. *See* Unemployment benefit—Overpayment, *below.*

SOCIAL SECURITY (cont)—

Part-time employment. *See* Employed person—Contract of service—Part-time teacher at drama school, *above.*

Person from abroad. *See* Benefit—Income support—Housing benefit—Council tax benefit—Pension credit—Entitlement—Person from abroad, *above.*

Personal independence payment ('PIP')—
Daily living component—
Ability to carry out daily living activities—'Engaging with other people face to face'—Meaning of 'social support'—Welfare Reform Act 2012, s 78—Social Security (Personal Independence Payment) Regulations 2013, SI 2013/377, Sch 2, Pt 2, Activity 9, descriptors b, c. **MM v Secretary of State for Work and Pensions** [2020] **1** 829, SC.

Rates of benefit—
Review by Secretary of State—
Duty to review in each tax year rates of certain benefits to determine whether they have retained their value in relation to the general level of earnings or prices—Period to which Secretary of State must have regard for purposes of review—Social Security Act 1975, s 125. **Metzger v Dept of Health and Social Security** [1978] **3** 753, CA.

Recovery of arrears of contributions. *See* Arrears of contributions—Recovery, *above.*

Registered care homes—
Owners of care homes seeking deregistration—
Tribunal refusing deregistration on basis homes 'establishments' within meaning of statute—Meaning of 'establishment'—Whether homes establishments where occupants assured tenants—Care Standards Act 2000, s 3. **R (on the application of Moore) v Care Standards Tribunal** [2005] **3** 428, CA.

Retirement pension—
Entitlement—
Social Security Contributions and Benefits Act 1992, s 45(3)—Social Security Administration Act 1992, s 1(1)(a). **Secretary of State for Work and Pensions v Nelligan** [2003] **4** 171, CA.

Equality of treatment of men and women—
Qualifying age for pension different for men and women—Consequences of issue of gender recognition certificate—Male-to-female gender reassignment—Pension being refused to woman at qualifying age—Whether woman having right to be recognised as female for purposes of state pension without full gender recognition certificate—Whether refusal of pension discriminatory—Gender Recognition Act 2004, ss 4, 9—Council Directive 79/7/EEC, arts 4, 7(1)(a). **MB v Secretary of State for Work and Pensions** [2017] **1** 338n, SC.

Qualifying age for pension different for men and women—Consequences of issue of gender recognition certificate—Male-to-female gender reassignment—Pension being refused to woman at qualifying age—Woman without full gender recognition certificate—Full gender recognition certificate not to be issued to married person—Woman not wishing to have marriage annulled—Whether woman entitled to state pension at qualifying age for women—Whether woman having right to be recognised as female for purposes of state pension without full gender recognition certificate—Whether refusal of pension discriminatory—Gender Recognition Act 2004, ss 4, 9—Equality Act 2010—Council Directive (EEC) 79/7, arts 3, 4. **MB v Secretary of State for Work and Pensions** [2015] **1** 920, CA.

European Community—
Freedom of movement of workers. *See* **European Union** (Workers—Freedom of movement—Social security).

Inflation uprating—
Claimant not entitled to inflation uprating of state pension because of residence in South Africa—Whether freeze on claimant's pension infringing her human rights—Human Rights Act 1998, Sch 1, Pt I, art 14, Pt II, art 1. **R (on the application of Carson) v Secretary of State for Work and Pensions** [2002] **3** 994, QBD; [2003] **3** 577, CA; [2005] **4** 545, HL.

Public sector pensions—
Annual up-rating of benefits—Public sector pensions to be increased at same rate benefits increased—Duty of Secretary of State to review annual values in relation to general level of prices—Secretary of State deciding to use Consumer Price Index rather than Retail Price Index—Whether decision unlawful —Social Security Administration Act 1992, s 150. **R (on the application of FDA) v Secretary of State for Work and Pensions** [2012] **3** 301, DC and CA.

Schemes for assisting persons to obtain employment—
Jobseeker's allowance. *See* Income support—Jobseeker's allowance, *above.*

Services for sick and disabled persons—
Assessment of needs of sick and disabled persons—
Duty of local authority to assess needs of sick and disabled persons and to provide services to meet such needs—Whether local authority entitled to take into account effect on its resources in assessing and reassessing needs—Chronically Sick and Disabled Persons Act 1970, s 2(1). **R v Gloucestershire CC, ex p Barry** [1997] **2** 1, HL.

Recovery of charge for services—
Minor severely mentally and physically handicapped at birth as a result of negligence of hospital—Local authority paying for maintenance of minor at special home—Health authority indemnifying minor and his estate against any liability to local authority in respect of claim to recover its costs in providing services—Local authority several years later seeking to charge for those services—Whether charge had to be made at time services provided—Whether right to indemnity amounted to sufficient means to pay charge—Health and Social Services and Social Security Adjudications Act 1983, s 17. **Avon CC v Hooper** [1997] **1** 532, CA.

Severe disablement allowance—
Equality of treatment of men and women—
European Community. *See* **European Union** (Equality of treatment of men and women—Social security—Severe disablement allowance).

Sex discrimination—
European Community. *See* **European Union** (Equality of treatment of men and women—Social security).

Invalid care allowance. *See* Invalid care allowance—Sex discrimination, *above.*

1228

Sheltered accommodation—
  Housing benefit—
    Service charges. *See* Housing benefit—Entitlement—Periodical payments—Service charges—Sheltered accommodation, *above.*
Sickness benefit—
  Damages for personal injuries—
    Deduction of sickness benefit. *See* **Damages** (Personal injury—Loss of earnings—Deduction of industrial injury, disablement, sickness or invalidity benefit accruing to injured person).
  Disqualification. *See* Benefit—Disqualification—Sickness benefit, *above.*
Social fund—
  Repayments—
    Insolvency. *See* **Insolvency** (Debt relief order—Discharge—Overpayment of benefit).
Social security commissioners—
  Appeal to social security commissioner—
    Appeal from any decision of an appeal tribunal—Appeal tribunal dismissing application for extension of time beyond specified period—Appeal tribunal striking out appeal against 'out of jurisdiction' appeal—Social security commissioner granting permission to appeal but dismissing appeals—Secretary of State appealing—Whether commissioner having jurisdiction to entertain appeal from appeal tribunal—Whether appropriate court having jurisdiction to entertain appeal from Secretary of State as successful party—Social Security Act 1998, ss 12, 14(1), 15(1)—Social Security and Child Support (Decisions and Appeal) Regulations 1999, SI 1999/991, regs 31, 32, 46, 47. **Morina v Secretary of State for Work and Pensions** [2008] 1 718, CA.
    Appeal from commissioner's refusal of leave to appeal from decision of supplementary benefit appeal tribunal—Whether refusal of leave a 'decision' by commissioner—Whether Court of Appeal having jurisdiction to entertain appeal from commissioner's refusal of leave—Social Security Act 1980, s 14(2). **Bland v Chief Supplementary Benefit Officer** [1983] 1 537, CA.
    Appeal from commissioner's refusal of leave to appeal from decision of supplementary benefit appeal tribunal—Whether refusal of leave a 'decision' by commissioner—Whether Court of Appeal having jurisdiction to entertain appeal from commissioner's refusal of leave—Social Security Act 1980, s 14(2)—Social Security (Adjudication) Regulations 1984, regs 3(3), 9, Sch 2. **White v Chief Adjudication Officer** [1986] 2 905, CA.
    Jurisdiction of commissioner—Whether commissioner having jurisdiction to determine whether social security regulations ultra vires—Social Security Act 1975, s 101. **Chief Adjudication Officer v Foster** [1991] 3 846, CA; [1993] 1 705, HL.
  Decisions binding on commissioners. *See* **Precedent** (Social security commissioners).
Stamp—
  Forgery. *See* **Criminal law** (Forgery—Valuable security—National insurance stamp).
  Possession of fictitious stamp—
    Lawful excuse—Purchase in good faith from person not authorised to sell—Post Office Act 1908, s 65(1)(b)(as applied by the National Insurance and Industrial Injuries (Stamps) Regulations 1948 (SI 1948 No 1443), reg 1). **Winkle v Wiltshire** [1951] 1 479, KBD.
State pension credit—
  Entitlement. *See* Benefit—Non-contributory benefits—Income-related benefits—Social assistance—Hybrid benefits—State pension credit—Entitlement, *above.*
Supplementary benefit—
  Administration of claims—
    Statutory requirements for administration—Delay in determination of claims—Duties of adjudication officers—Time limit for consideration and determination of claims—Duty of Secretary of State to submit claims to adjudication officers 'forthwith'—Forthwith—Duty of adjudication officer to consider claim and so far as practicable dispose of it within 14 days—Whether Secretary of State under duty to ensure claims considered immediately on receipt—Social Security Act 1975, ss 98, 99(1). **R v Secretary of State for Social Services, ex p Child Poverty Action Group** [1989] 1 1047, CA.
  Appeal tribunal—
    Reasons for decision—Duty of tribunal to give adequate reasons—Consequence of giving inadequate reasons—Whether decision vitiated due to error of law—Tribunals and Inquiries Act 1971, s 12—Supplementary Benefits (Appeal Tribunal) Rules 1971, r 12(1). **Crake v Supplementary Benefits Commission** [1982] 1 498, QBD.
  Benefit paid for requirements of person whom another person is liable to maintain—
    Recovery of expenditure from relative liable for maintenance—Complaint against father for order requiring him to pay sums in respect of benefit paid to mother for children—Father divorced from mother—When divorce granted consent order made by court providing that father should not pay any maintenance to mother for children but should transfer his half-share in the matrimonial home to the mother—Father's resources sufficient to pay maintenance for children—Whether commission entitled to recover expenditure for children from father—Whether father a person 'liable to maintain' children notwithstanding terms of consent order—Supplementary Benefits Act 1976, ss 17(1), 18(1). **Hulley v Thompson** [1981] 1 1128, QBD.
  Calculation of benefit—
    Adjustment for exceptional circumstances—Availability for employment for limited period—Student applying for supplementary benefit for vacation period—Student registering for employment during vacation period—Student available for employment for limited period only—Whether availability for employment for limited period only an 'exceptional circumstance'—Whether 'exceptional circumstance' justifying reduction of benefit during period of limited availability—Supplementary Benefit Act 1966, Sch 2, para 4(1). **R v Barnsley Supplementary Benefits Appeal Tribunal, ex p Atkinson** [1977] 3 1031, CA.
    Adjustment of exceptional circumstances—Exceptional category of claimants—Student applying for supplementary benefit for vacation period—Commission treating all students as exceptional claimants without reference to particular circumstances of individual cases—Whether commission entitled to treat claimant's membership of whole category of claimants as 'exceptional circumstance'—Supplementary Benefit Act 1966, Sch 2, para 4(1). **R v Barnsley Supplementary Benefits Appeal Tribunal, ex p Atkinson** [1977] 3 1031, CA.

SOCIAL SECURITY (cont)—
Supplementary benefit (cont)—
Calculation of benefit (cont)—

Adjustment of exceptional circumstances—Resources available from public funds—Student applying for supplementary benefit for vacation period—Student awarded educational grant—Grant covering period of vacation—Grant paid out of public funds—Supplementary benefit payable out of public funds—Whether receipt of provision from two different funds an 'exceptional circumstance'—Supplementary Benefit Act 1966, Sch 2, para 4(1). **R v Barnsley Supplementary Benefits Appeal Tribunal, ex p Atkinson** [1977] 3 1031, CA.

Deduction of resources from requirements—Calculation of requirements—Requirements of 'householder'—Meaning of 'householder'—Joint tenants of flat—Whether each tenant a 'householder'—Supplementary Benefit Act 1966, Sch 2, para 9(b). **R v Preston Supplementary Benefits Appeal Tribunal, ex p Moore** [1975] 2 807, CA.

Deduction of resources from requirements—Calculation of requirements—Monthly salary paid in middle of each month, half in arrear half in advance—On date of November payment applicant on strike until following January—That part of payment constituting payment in advance covering period on strike—Employer informing applicant he would have to repay that part of payment at some future date—Applicant applying for benefit for wife and children for period 1st to 15th December—Whether entitled to benefit—Whether 'resources' to 15th December included the payment in advance liable to be repaid—Supplementary Benefits Act 1976, Sch 1, Part III. **R v Bolton Supplementary Benefits Appeal Tribunal, ex p Fordham** [1981] 1 50, CA.

Deduction of resources from requirements—Income resources—Gross earnings—Expenses—Whether expenses incurred wholly and necessarily in course of employment deductible in ascertaining gross earnings—Family Income Supplements (General) Regulations 1980, reg 2(3). **Parsons v Hogg** [1985] 2 897, CA.

Deduction of resources from requirements—Income resources—Lump sum—Accrued arrears of income—Recovery of arrears of weekly payments due under court order—Arrears having accrued during period prior to claim for supplementary benefit—Commission entitled to determine that lump sum income rather than capital resource—Whether as income sum to be attributed to period in past during which arrears accrued and therefore irrelevant for determining entitlement to future benefit—Supplementary Benefit Act 1966, s 4(1), Sch 2, para 1. **R v West London Supplementary Benefits Appeal Tribunal, ex p Taylor** [1975] 2 790, QBD.

Deduction of resources from requirements—Income resources—Normal gross income—Claimant on strike—Whether period when claimant on strike to be disregarded for purpose of calculating his family's 'normal gross income'—Family Income Supplements Act 1970, s 4—Family Income Supplements (General) Regulations 1980, reg 2. **Lowe v Rigby** [1985] 2 903, CA.

Deduction of resources from requirements—Income resources—Wages paid in arrear at termination of employment—Benefit claimed for two weeks following termination of employment—Amount of wages paid exceeding amount of benefit requirement—Whether last week's wages to be treated as income resources for period following termination of employment—Whether applicant entitled to benefit—Supplementary Benefits Act 1976, Sch 1, Part III—Supplementary Benefits (General) Regulations 1977 (SI 1977 no 1141), reg 3. **R v Manchester Supplementary Benefits Appeal Tribunal, ex p Riley** [1979] 2 1, QBD.

Deduction of resources from requirements—Notional or actual resources—Maintenance—Undertaking by son-in-law to maintain applicant—Applicant given permission to enter United Kingdom on strength of undertaking—Son-in-law later refusing to maintain applicant—Whether applicant's resources including notional sum for maintenance by son-in-law—Whether son-in-law under duty to maintain applicant—Supplementary Benefit Act 1966, s 4(1). **R v West London Supplementary Benefits Appeal Tribunal, ex p Clarke** [1975] 3 513, QBD.

Deduction of resources from requirements—Notional or actual resources—Student awarded educational grant—Grant covering period of vacation—Parental contribution—Parental contribution in form of maintenance in family home during vacation—Student applying for supplementary benefit for vacation period—Commission deducting portion of grant for vacation maintenance from requirements—Deduction greater than grant received by student—Student presumed to have received additional contribution to maintenance from parent—Commission treating presumption as inflexible rule—Whether parent's contribution should be taken into consideration in calculating student's resources—Supplementary Benefit Act 1966, Sch 2, para 1. **R v Barnsley Supplementary Benefits Appeal Tribunal, ex p Atkinson** [1977] 3 1031, CA.

Deduction of resources from requirements—Notional or actual resources—Student awarded grant—Grant covering period of vacation—Student having spent grant before start of vacation—Student applying for supplementary benefit for vacation period—Whether appropriate portion of grant for vacation period to be included in calculation of 'resources'—Supplementary Benefit Act 1966, Sch 2, para 1. **R v Preston Supplementary Benefits Appeal Tribunal, ex p Moore** [1975] 2 807, CA.

Reduction of amount of supplementary allowance—Claim for unemployment benefit not yet determined—Right to reduce allowance where commission of opinion applicant would be disqualified from receiving unemployment benefit—Failure of commission to form opinion whether applicant would be so disqualified—Whether reduction in allowance validly made—Supplementary Benefits Act 1976, Sch 1, para 9. **R v Greater Birmingham Supplementary Benefit Appeal Tribunal, ex p Khan** [1979] 3 759, QBD.

Damages for personal injuries—

Deduction of supplementary allowance paid after unemployment benefit ceasing. *See* **Damages** (Personal injury—Loss of earnings—Deduction of supplementary allowance paid after unemployment benefit ceasing).

Deduction of supplementary benefit—Special damages. *See* **Damages** (Personal injury—Special damage—Deductions—Supplementary benefit).

Supplementary benefit (cont)—
Entitlement—
Aggregation of requirements and resources—Person having to provide for requirements of another person—Meaning of 'requirements'—Other person child under age of 16—Mother providing for children—Children having sufficient independent means to provide for necessities of life—Mother not having to provide for children's necessities—Whether 'requirements' limited to payments for necessities of life—Whether mother having to provide for children's 'requirements'—Whether children's resources to be aggregated with mother's for purpose of determining her entitlement to supplementary benefit—Ministry of Social Security Act 1966, Sch 2, para 3(2). **K v JMP Co Ltd** [1975] **1** 1030, CA.

Aggregation of requirements and resources—Person having to provide for requirements of another person—Meaning of 'requirements'—Other person child under age of 16—Mother providing for child—Mother receiving money for support of child from father under court order—Amount payable exceeding normal requirements of child—Whether mother having to provide for 'requirements'—Whether child's resources to be aggregated with mother's for the purpose of determining her entitlement to supplementary benefit—Supplementary Benefits Act 1976, s 1, Sch 1, para 3(2). **Supplementary Benefits Commission v Jull** [1980] **3** 65, HL.

Aggregation of requirements and resources—Persons not married to each other who are living together as husband and wife—Factors necessary to establish man and woman living together as husband and wife—Whether sufficient to show man and woman living together in same household—Supplementary Benefits Act 1976, Sch 1, para 3(1)(b). **Crake v Supplementary Benefits Commission** [1982] **1** 498, QBD.

Exclusion of right to benefit—Full-time remunerative work—Remunerative work—Claimant running business from home at a loss and claiming benefit—Whether 'remunerative work' meaning profitable work or merely paid work—Whether claimant entitled to benefit—Supplementary Benefits Act 1976, s 6. **Perrot v Supplementary Benefits Commission** [1980] **3** 110, CA.

Exclusion of right to benefit—Medical or surgical requirements—Claimant undergoing osteopathic treatment on advice of doctors—Whether such treatment 'medical' or 'surgical' requirement—Whether claimant entitled to benefit—Supplementary Benefit Act 1966, s 6. **R v Peterborough Supplementary Benefits Appeal Tribunal, ex p Supplementary Benefits Commission** [1978] **3** 887, QBD.

Requirements—Requirements excluding medical, surgical, optical, aural or dental requirements—Medical requirements—Electrically operated special aids—Whether cost of electricity to operate special aids a 'medical ... requirement'—Whether cost an 'exceptional circumstance' for which benefit may be awarded—Supplementary Benefits Act 1976, ss 1(3), 3(1), Sch 1, para 4(1). **R v West London Supplementary Benefits Appeal Tribunal, ex p Wyatt** [1978] **2** 315, QBD.
Exceptional need—
Statute conferring on Supplementary Benefits Commission power to make single payment to meet exceptional need—Statute also excluding right to benefit in respect of medical or surgical requirements—Application for benefit in respect of such requirements to meet exceptional need—Jurisdiction of commission to make single payment in respect of medical or surgical requirements in case of exceptional need—Supplementary Benefit Act 1966, ss 6, 7. **R v Peterborough Supplementary Benefits Appeal Tribunal, ex p Supplementary Benefits Commission** [1978] **3** 887, QBD.
Fatal accident—
Deduction from damages. See **Fatal accident** (Damages—Deduction from damages—Supplementary benefit).
Husband and wife—
Effect on maintenance order of receipt of benefit by both spouses. See **Husband and wife** (Maintenance—Amount—Supplementary benefit).
Overpayment—
Recovery—Misrepresentation or non-disclosure—Recovery after death of claimant—Calculation of sums overpaid—Sum of cash and moneys in bank account discovered after death of claimant—Whether such sums are 'capital resources'—Whether such sums more properly 'resources not specified [elsewhere] in ... provisions'—Supplementary Benefits Act 1976, Sch 1, paras 20, 27. **Chief Supplementary Benefit Officer v Leary** [1985] **1** 1061, CA.

Recovery—Misrepresentation or non-disclosure—Recovery after death of claimant—Proceedings by Secretary of State against executor—Reference to appeal tribunal—Determination by tribunal of amount recoverable—Proceedings in High Court for recovery of amount determined by tribunal—Whether Secretary of State entitled to refer matter to tribunal after claimant's death—Whether proceedings for recovery of amount determined by tribunal maintainable against executor—Ministry of Social Security Act 1966, s 26(1), (2). **Secretary of State for Social Services v Solly** [1974] **3** 922, CA.
Payment—
Mareva injunction—Benefit arrears owing to defendant with assets frozen by injunction—Whether order for payment into bank account frozen by injunction an 'assignment of, or charge on, any supplementary benefit'—Whether court prevented from making order—Supplementary Benefits Act 1976, s 16(1). **Bank Mellat v Kazmi (Secretary of State for Social Services intervening)** [1989] **1** 925, CA.
Regulations—
Validity. See **Statutory instrument** (Power to make instrument—Regulations required to be placed before Parliament—Supplementary benefit regulations).
Unemployment benefit—
Disqualification for benefit—
Days of unemployment—Days not to be treated as days of unemployment—Employment to full extent normal—Claimant's pattern of work—Pattern of work normal in his case—Part-time employment—Claimant employed full-time for seven years—Claimant unemployed for five months—Claimant employed part-time working two days a week—Whether claimant employed 'to the full extent normal in his case'—Whether claimant disqualified for claiming unemployment benefit for three days a week when not working—Social Security (Unemployment, Sickness and Invalidity Benefit) Regulations 1975, reg 7(1)(e). **Riley v Chief Adjudication Officer (1985)** [1988] **1** 457, CA.

SOCIAL SECURITY (cont)—
  Unemployment benefit (cont)—
    Disqualification for benefit (cont)—
      Days of unemployment—Days not to be treated as days of unemployment—Employment to full extent normal—Claimant's pattern of work—Pattern of work normal in his case—Part-time employment—Part-time employment for fixed temporary period—Claimant unemployed for 21 months—Claimant employed part-time working two and a half days a week—Employment limited to maximum of 52 weeks—Whether claimant employed 'to the full extent normal in his case'—Whether claimant disqualified for claiming unemployment benefit for days when not working—Social Security (Unemployment, Sickness and Invalidity Benefit) Regulations 1983, reg 7(1)(e). **Chief Adjudication Officer v Brunt** [1988] 1 754, HL.
      Loss of employment due to stoppage of work—Persons not directly interested in dispute—Not belonging to grade or class of workers any of whom directly interested in dispute—National Insurance Act 1946, s 13(1), proviso (a), proviso(b). **Punton v Ministry of Pensions and National Insurance (No 2)** [1964] 1 448, CA.
      Loss of employment due to stoppage of work—Stoppage of work due to trade dispute—Person directly interested in trade dispute—Different groups of workers belonging to different unions employed by same employer—Claimant belonging to union not participating in dispute—Claimant laid off work because of dispute—Whether claimant 'directly interested in the trade dispute'—Whether claimant disqualified for unemployment benefit—Social Security Act 1975, s 19(1). **Presho v Insurance Officer** [1984] 1 97, HL.
      Payment in lieu of remuneration which would have been received—Royal Air Force officer made redundant—Officer receiving capital sum on redundancy under special government scheme—Capital sum assessed on loss of prospects, loss of higher pension etc and including unspecified element for loss of remuneration—Whether capital sum a 'payment ... in lieu ... of the remuneration which he would have received'—Whether officer entitled to unemployment benefit—Social Security (Unemployment, Sickness and Invalidity Benefit) Regulations 1975 (SI 1975 No 564), reg 7(1) (d). **R v National Insurance Comr, ex p Stratton** [1979] 2 278, CA.
      Voluntarily leaving employment without just cause—Just cause—Teacher voluntarily leaving employment pursuant to scheme for premature retirement of older teachers—Scheme containing financial inducements for voluntary early retirement—Whether teacher voluntarily retiring early under scheme having 'just cause' for leaving employment—Whether teacher entitled to receive benefit for first six weeks after retirement—Social Security Act 1975, s 20(1)(a). **Crewe v Social Security Comr** [1982] 2 745, CA.
  Overpayment—
    Benefits out of which recovery may be made—Legislation not permitting recovery out of supplementary benefit—Legislation repealed and new legislation enacted conferring power on Secretary of State to make transitional provision by regulations—Regulation specifying supplementary benefit among benefits from which overpayments may be deducted—Regulation providing for recovery of overpayments under previous legislation by deduction from supplementary benefit—Whether regulation ultra vires—Whether overpayment of unemployment benefit recoverable out of supplementary benefit—Social Security Act 1986, ss 53, 89(1)—Social Security (Payments on account, Overpayments and Recovery) Regulations 1987, regs 16(2)(e), 20(2). **Britnell v Secretary of State for Social Security** [1991] 2 726, HL.
  Widowed parent's allowance—
    Unmarried partner—
      Legislative requirement claimant married or civil partner of deceased—Whether requirement unjustifiably discriminating against survivor and/or children on basis of marital or birth status—Social Security Contributions and Benefits (Northern Ireland) Act 1992, s 39A—Human Rights Act 1998, Sch 1, Pt I, arts 8, 14, Pt II, art 1. **McLaughlin's Application for Judicial Review (Northern Ireland), Re** [2019] 1 471, SC.
  Widows' benefit. See Benefit—Widows' benefits, *above*.

SOCIAL SECURITY COMMISSIONERS
  Generally. See **Social security** (Social security commissioners).

SOCIAL SERVICES
  Local authority—
    Residential care home. See **Local authority** (Residential care home).

SOCIAL WELFARE
  Charitable trust—
    Recreational charity—
      Provision of facilities in interests of social welfare. See **Charity** (Recreational charity—Provision of facilities in interests of social welfare).

SOCIAL WORKER
  Affiliation proceedings—
    Admissibility of evidence. See **Affiliation** (Evidence—Admissibility—Evidence of welfare worker).

SOCIETY
  Building society. See **Building society**.
  Friendly society. See **Friendly society**.
  Industrial and provident societies. See **Industrial and provident societies**.

SOCIETY OF LLOYD'S
  Insurance. See **Insurance** (Society of Lloyd's).
  Responsibilities—
    Negotiation—
      Implied contractual obligation. See **Contract** (Implied term—Duty to negotiate—Responsibilities of Society of Lloyd's).

SODOMY
Divorce—
Ground for. *See* **Divorce** (Sodomy).
Robbery—
Accusation of sodomitical practices. *See* **Criminal law** (Robbery—Threat—Common law offence—Offence still in existence—Robbery by threat of accusation of sodomitical practices).

SOLDIER
Boy soldier—
Wardship jurisdiction. *See* **Ward of court** (Jurisdiction—Boy soldier).
Criminal injuries compensation—
Entitlement to compensation. *See* **Compensation** (Criminal injuries—Entitlement to compensation—Armed forces).
Negligence—
Duty to take care. *See* **Negligence** (Duty to take care—Serviceman).
Will. *See* **Will** (Soldier's or mariner's privileged will).

SOLE AGENCY
See **Agent** (Sole agency).

SOLE BARGAINING AGENT
Collective bargaining. *See* **Industrial relations** (Collective bargaining—Sole bargaining agent).

SOLICITING
Immoral purposes. *See* **Criminal law** (Soliciting for immoral purposes).
Prostitution—
Loitering or soliciting for purposes of prostitution. *See* **Criminal law** (Prostitution—Loitering or soliciting for purposes of prostitution).

SOLICITOR
Access to—
Right of person in custody—
Access by probationary solicitor's representative (PSR)—Applicant being dismissed by police for alleged misconduct but lodging appeal—Applicant obtaining employment as PSR—Deputy chief constable barring applicant as PSR from entering any police station in his force's area—Whether imposition of blanket ban on a PSR permissible—Police and Criminal Evidence Act 1984—Code of Practice for the Detention, Treatment and Questioning of Persons by Police Officers, paras 6.12, 6.13. **R (on the application of Thompson) v Chief Constable of Northumbria Constabulary** [2001] 4 354, CA.
Access by solicitor's clerk—A solicitor employing unqualified clerks to visit clients held in police custody—Chief constable issuing instructions that presence of such clerks at police interviews with suspects undesirable—Instructions leaving decision on access by clerks in particular cases to individual custody officers—Whether chief constable's instructions contrary to code of practice for detention of suspects—Code of Practice for the Detention, Treatment and Questioning of Persons by Police Officers, para 6.9. **R v Chief Constable of Avon and Somerset Constabulary, ex p Robinson** [1989] 2 15, QBD.
Delay in complying with request to consult solicitor—Road traffic offence—Person suspected of committing drink-driving offence arrested and held in custody—Suspect requesting to consult solicitor—Police requiring specimen of suspect's breath—Whether police required to delay taking specimen of breath until after suspect has consulted solicitor—Road Traffic Act 1972, ss 5, 6, 8—Police and Criminal Evidence Act 1984, s 58. **DPP v Billington** [1988] 1 435, QBD.
Police breaching statutory duty allowing person in custody access to solicitor—Whether actionable breach of duty—Whether damages recoverable—Northern Ireland (Emergency Provisions) Act 1987, s 15. **Cullen v Chief Constable of Royal Ulster Constabulary** [2004] 2 237, HL.
Presence of solicitor during interview—Suspect arrested under prevention of terrorism provisions—No statutory right to have solicitor present—Whether common law right—Whether House of Lords powerless to infer such right—Prevention of Terrorism (Temporary Provisions) Act 1989, s 14(1). **R v Chief Constable of Royal Ulster Constabulary, ex p Begley** [1997] 4 833, HL.
Remand prisoner—Validity of police policy to regulate access by solicitors to remand cells—Applicant held in cells at magistrates' court—Police policy to deny access by solicitors to cells after 10 a m—Applicant's solicitor seeking access at 3.15 pm—Whether applicant having right to see solicitor—Whether policy lawful—Police and Criminal Evidence Act 1984, s 58. **R v Chief Constable of South Wales, ex p Merrick** [1994] 2 560, QBD.
Right to be informed of right to communicate with legal adviser—Mode of communicating right to arrested person. **A-G of Trinidad and Tobago v Whiteman** [1992] 2 924, PC.
Right of prisoner. *See* **Prison** (Access to legal adviser).
Suspected person—
Right to consult solicitor—Delaying access to solicitor—Authority to delay access—Police officer's belief—Police officer required to have reasonable belief that suspect's access to solicitor will lead to other suspects being alerted—Nature of belief required—Police and Criminal Evidence Act 1984, s 58(8)(b). **R v Samuel** [1988] 2 135, CA.
Right to consult solicitor—Delaying access to solicitor—Suspect charged with offence—Whether police entitled to delay suspect's access to solicitor once he is charged with any offence—Whether confession obtained after access to solicitor wrongly delayed should be admitted—Police and Criminal Evidence Act 1984, s 78(1)—Code of Practice for Detention, Treatment and Questioning of Persons by Police Officers, Annex B, para 1. **R v Samuel** [1988] 2 135, CA.
Account—
Client's account. *See* Clients' account, *below*.
Information—
Solicitor acting as attorney for client in prison—Bankruptcy of client—Denial by solicitor of receipt of money on particular transactions—Procedure for enquiry—RSC Ord 52, r 25—Bankruptcy Act 1914, s 25(c). **Debtor (No 472 of 1950), Re a** [1958] 1 581, CA.

SOLICITOR (cont)—
  Account (cont)—
    Profits from trust. *See* **Trust and trustee** (Profit from trust—Account of profits—Agents for trust).
  Administration of estates—
    Grant of administration—
      Solicitor's office reference. *See* **Administration of estates** (Grant of administration—Practice—Solicitor's office reference).
  Administrator—
    Costs. *See* Costs—Solicitor administrator, *below*.
  Advice—
    Advice to partnership—
      Duty of solicitor. *See* Duty—Advice to partnership, *below*.
    Counsel's advice explained to client—
      Mitigation of contempt of court by acts based on mistaken belief of legality. *See* **Contempt of court** (Mitigation—Legal advice that a course of conduct would not amount to breach of undertaking).
    Inadequate advice. *See* Negligence—Inadequate advice, *below*.
    Legal aid. *See* **Legal aid** (Advice and assistance).
    Negligent advice—
      Cause of action. *See* Negligence—Cause of action—Negligent advice, *below*.
      Inadequate advice. *See* Negligence—Inadequate advice, *below*.
  Advocate—
    Liability in negligence. *See* Practice—Advocate—Liability in negligence, *below*.
  Appeal—
    Authority—
      Application for leave to appeal made without instructions. *See* **Criminal law** (Appeal—Leave to appeal—Application—Application by solicitor on behalf of client—Solicitor having no express instructions to appeal—Whether solicitor having implied authority to appeal on behalf of client).
    Disciplinary proceedings. *See* Disciplinary proceedings—Appeal, *below*.
  Articled clerk—
    Employment—
      Clerk articled to partner in firm but doing work for benefit of firm as a whole—Whether clerk employed by firm—Whether clerk can be articled to partner and employed by firm at same time. **Oliver v J P Malnick & Co (a firm)** [1983] 3 795, EAT.
    Qualification for solicitor to take—
      Continuous practice for five years—Solicitor in practice for more than five years but taking out practising certificate after Dec. 15 on four occasions in the five years—Whether solicitor had been in continuous practice for five years—Solicitors Act 1957, s 41(1). **Adlam v Law Society** [1968] **1** 17, Ch D.
  Audience—
    Client's right to be legally represented. *See* **Natural justice** (Domestic tribunal—Legal representation).
    Right of audience—
      Crown Court. *See* **Crown Court** (Practice—Solicitor—Right of audience).
      High Court. *See* **Practice** (Audience—Right of audience—High Court of Justice—Solicitor).
      Patent proceedings. *See* **Patent** (Practice—Telephone summonses).
  Authority—
    Acknowledgment for Limitation Act purposes—
      Recovery of land—Acknowledgment of plaintiff's title by defendant's solicitor. **Wright v Pepin** [1954] **2** 52, Ch D.
    Action begun without authority—
      Ratification by or on behalf of plaintiff. **Danish Mercantile Co Ltd v Beaumont** [1951] **1** 925, CA.
      Ratification by or on behalf of plaintiff—Expiration of limitation period applicable to cause of action—Whether plaintiff entitled to adopt action after expiry of limitation period. **Presentaciones Musicales SA v Secunda** [1994] **2** 737, CA.
    Criminal appeal—
      Application for leave to appeal without instructions. *See* **Criminal law** (Appeal—Leave to appeal—Application—Application by solicitor on behalf of client—Solicitor having no express instructions to appeal—Whether solicitor having implied authority to appeal on behalf of client).
    Notices—
      Receipt of notices on behalf of client—Solicitor having no authority to receive notices on behalf of client in absence of express authority. **Singer v Trustee of the property of Munro and anor (bankrupts)** [1981] 3 215, Ch D.
    Ostensible authority—
      Compromise of action—Solicitor's ostensible authority to compromise action—Action by buyer of house against builder for damages for defective construction of house—Builder's solicitor purporting to agree compromise of action on terms that builder was to purchase house from buyer at current value in proper condition—Builder expressly instructing his solicitor not to enter into such a compromise—Whether compromise within solicitor's ostensible authority vis-a-vis buyer—Whether distinction between solicitor's implied authority vis-a-vis own client and his ostensible authority vis-a-vis opposing litigant to compromise action—Whether solicitor having ostensible authority when he did not have implied authority—Whether repurchase of house at agreed valuation constituting matter collateral to action. **Waugh v H B Clifford & Sons Ltd** [1982] **1** 1095, CA.
      Solicitor giving false undertaking on behalf of firm as security for loan—Whether solicitor having ostensible authority to act for firm—Whether undertaking given in usual course of a solicitor's business—Whether undertaking enforceable against firm—Partnership Act 1890, s 5. **United Bank of Kuwait Ltd v Hammoud** [1988] 3 418, CA.
    Sale of land—
      Authority to sign memorandum. **Gavaghan v Edwards** [1961] **2** 477, CA.
      Exchange of contracts. *See* **Sale of land** (Exchange of contracts—Authority of solicitor).
  Bankruptcy of solicitor. *See* Clients' account—Bankruptcy of solicitor, *below*.
  Bill for lump sum. *See* Costs—Bill for lump sum—Client insisting on taxation, *below*.

SOLICITOR (cont)—
  Bill of costs—
    Taxation—
      Generally. *See* **Costs** (Taxation—Solicitor).
  Breach of duty—
    Client's action founded in contract—
      Measure of damages. **Bailey v Bullock** [1950] **2** 1167, KBD.
    Loan to client—
      Loan to repay amount due under agreement with registered moneylender—Original agreement illegal to knowledge of solicitor by reason of provision for compound interest—Alterations made to memorandum of original agreement after execution—Alterations made by solicitor when acting for moneylender—Material alteration to detriment of borrowers—Agreement void by reason of alterations—Solicitor failing to disclose defects in original agreement when making loan to borrowers for purpose of discharging obligation thereunder. **Spector v Ageda** [1971] **3** 417, Ch D.
    Purchase from client of shares in company—
      Failure to disclose negotiations for sale of controlling interest in company. **McMaster v Byrne** [1952] **1** 1362, PC.
    Solicitor acting for both building society and lender in mortgage transactions—
      Solicitor failing to communicate information to society—Borrowers defaulting and proceeds of sale of repossessed property insufficient to clear mortgage debt—Society bringing actions for damages against solicitors claiming damages for breach of duty at common law—Whether solicitor in breach of duty to society—Damages recoverable by society. **Bristol and West Building Society v Fancy & Jackson (a firm)** [1997] **4** 582, Ch D.
    Solicitor acting for both lender and borrower in remortgage transaction—
      Lender requesting specific advice concerning title and security but not concerning state of current mortgage account—Solicitor receiving information relating to arrears on current mortgage account and threat of legal proceedings prior to completion—Solicitor failing to pass on information to lender—Whether solicitor in breach of duty to lender. **National Home Loans Corp plc v Giffen Couch & Archer (a firm)** [1997] **3** 808, CA.
    Solicitor acting for both purchaser and mortgagee in conveyancing transaction—
      Solicitor receiving information that vendor buying the property in simultaneous transaction—Vendor paying price much lower either than price being paid by purchaser or valuation of property—Solicitor communicating information to purchaser but not to mortgagee—Whether solicitor in breach of duty to mortgagee. **Mortgage Express Ltd v Bowerman & Partners (a firm)** [1996] **2** 836, CA.
  Breach of trust—
    Duty. *See* Duty—Breach of trust, *below.*
  Cause list—
    Failure to watch cause list. *See* Payment of costs by solicitor personally—Failure to watch cause list, *below.*
  Change of solicitor—
    Effect on solicitor's retaining lien on documents. *See* Lien—Retaining lien—Solicitor discharging himself in course of action, *below.*
  Charging order—
    Fund recovered or preserved through solicitor's instrumentality—
      Fund lodged to await trial of action before solicitor retained—Charge limited to client's share of fund—Priority of charge to mortgage of fund arranged by solicitor, but subject to partnership debts—Effect of compromise of action—Solicitors Act 1932, s 69. **Wimbourne v Fine** [1952] **2** 681, Ch D.
  Money in client account—
    Lien. *See* Lien—Money in client account—Charging order, *below.*
  Taxation—
    Special circumstances need not be shown—Solicitors Act 1957, ss 69(2)(b), proviso (i), 72. **Harris v Yarm** [1959] **3** 618, Ch D.
  Client—
    Account of. *See* Clients' account, *below.*
    Application to court on behalf of client—
      Application to have dissolution of company declared void—Whether solicitor a 'person interested'. *See* **Company** (Dissolution—Application to have dissolution declared void—Application by solicitor for client having unsatisfied claim).
    Communication with client—
      Legal professional privilege. *See* **Privilege** (Legal professional privilege).
    Compensation. *See* Compensation fund, *below.*
    Duty to. *See* Duty—Client, *below.*
    Fiduciary relationship—
      Entitlement to act for client—Clause in partnership deed precluding outgoing partner of firm acting for client in future—Whether clause contrary to public policy. **Oswald Hickson Collier & Co (a firm) v Carter-Ruck** [1984] **2** 15, CA.
    Gift to solicitor. *See* Gift by client to solicitor, *below.*
    Lease—
      Option to determine—No duty to warn client of date for giving notice to determine. **Yager v Fishman & Co and Teff and Teff** [1944] **1** 552, CA.
    Legally assisted client—
      Duty to. **Francis v Francis and Dickerson** [1955] **3** 836, Div; **Kelly v London Transport Executive** [1982] **2** 842, CA.
    Negotiation of grant of underlease to architects—
      Unusual covenants in underlease restricting user—Omission of solicitor to advise and/or warn client on effect—Whether solicitor negligent. **Sykes v Midland Bank Executor and Trustee Co Ltd** [1970] **2** 471, CA.
    Solicitor's duty of confidentiality to client. *See* Duty—Client—Duty of confidentiality to client, *below.*
    Solicitor's lien over money in client account. *See* Lien—Money in client account, *below.*

SOLICITOR (cont)—
Clients' account—
  Bankruptcy of solicitor—
    Account not to vest in trustee in bankruptcy—Removal of solicitor from trusteeship of account—Appointment of new trustees—Bankruptcy Act 1914, ss 18(1), 38(1)—Trustee Act 1925, s 41(1). **Solicitor, (1951 M No 234), Re a** [1952] **1** 133, Ch D.
    Remuneration of trustee. *See* **Bankruptcy** (Trustee in bankruptcy—Remuneration—Expenses).
  Information—
    Bankruptcy of client. *See* Account—Information—Solicitor acting as attorney for client in prison—Bankruptcy of client, *above*.
  Inspection of books of account—
    Intervention by Law Society in solicitor's practice—Intervention by Law Society in solicitor's practice—Whether availability of statutory remedy precluding solicitor from bringing private law claim for negligence against Law Society arising from conduct of investigation leading to intervention—Solicitors Act 1974, Sch 1, para 6(4)—Solicitors' Accounts Rules 1991, r 27. **Miller v Law Society** [2002] **4** 312, Ch D.
  Inspection of books of account, bank pass books, vouchers etc—
    Law Society's power to require solicitor to produce books for inspection—Legal professional privilege—Solicitors' Accounts Rules 1945 (SR & O 1944 No 781), r 11(1), (2)—Solicitors Act 1957, s 29(1), (2). **Parry-Jones v Law Society** [1968] **1** 177, CA.
  Lien over money in clients' account. *See* Lien—Money in client account, *below*.
Company—
  Director—
    Disqualification. *See* **Company** (Director—Disqualification).
  Liquidator—
    Appointment of solicitor. *See* **Company** (Compulsory winding up—Liquidator—Appointment of solicitor).
Compensation—
  Compensation fund. *See* Compensation fund, *below*.
  Goodwill attaching to office premises. *See* Goodwill attaching to office premises—Compensation, *below*.
Compensation fund—
  Grant from fund to relieve loss or hardship suffered in consequence of solicitor's dishonesty—
    Law Society's policy in relation to grants from fund—Applicant depositing large sum of money with solicitor to facilitate loan arrangement—Solicitor dishonestly appropriating applicant's money—Law Society refusing to compensate applicant on grounds that applicant's recklessness justifying 100% reduction in compensation otherwise payable—Whether Law Society's decision lawful—Solicitors Act 1974, s 36. **R v Law Society, ex p Ingman Foods Oy AB** [1997] **2** 666, QBD.
    Law Society's policy in relation to grants from fund—Exclusion of grants in respect of damages or consequential loss—Claim for consequential loss on property deal caused by dishonesty of client's solicitor—Claim rejected in accordance with Law Society's policy not to authorise grants in respect of damages or consequential losses—Whether Law Society entitled to adopt policy not to authorise grants in respect of damages or consequential losses—Solicitors Act 1974, s 36. **R v Law Society, ex p Reigate Projects Ltd** [1992] **3** 232, QBD.
    Law Society's policy in relation to grants from fund—Lenders advancing funds on security of real property in consequence of solicitors' dishonest failure to disclose true circumstances of transactions—Lenders obtaining security but suffering loss when property repossessed because of initial overvaluation, intervening decline in property prices and additional costs incurred in perfecting and obtaining security—Law Society rejecting lenders' applications for compensation from fund on grounds that solicitors' dishonesty not principal cause of loss—Whether applicants entitled to compensation. **R v Law Society, ex p Mortgage Express Ltd** [1997] **2** 348, CA.
Compromise of action—
  Authority. *See* Authority—Ostensible authority—Compromise of action, *above*.
Concealment of right of action—
  Failure to commence action within statutory period. *See* **Limitation of action** (Concealment of right of action by fraud—Negligence—Failure by solicitor to commence an action on behalf of client within statutory period).
Conditional fee agreement—
  Costs. *See* Costs—Conditional fee agreement, *below*.
Confidential information—
  Solicitor's duty of confidentiality to client. *See* Duty—Client—Duty of confidentiality to client, *below*.
Conflict of interest. *See* Duty—Conflict of interest, *below*.
Constructive trustee—
  Liability. *See* Liability—Constructive trustee, *below*.
Contempt of court—
  Action prohibited by statute—
    Feigned issue raised by indorsement of writ—Gaming debt—Claim for account stated—Liability of solicitor. **R v Weisz, ex p Hector MacDonald Ltd** [1951] **2** 408, KBD.
  Criminal contempt—
    Intention to interfere with course of justice. *See* **Contempt of court** (Criminal contempt—Intention to interfere with course of justice—Solicitor).
Contentious business—
  Costs. *See* Costs—Contentious business, *below*.
  Taxation of bill of costs. *See* Costs (Taxation—Solicitor—Bill of costs for contentious business).
Contingency fee. *See* Costs—Contingency fee, *below*.
Conveyance of building—
  Negligence. *See* Negligence—Damages—Conveyance of building, *below*.
Conviction. *See* Disciplinary proceedings—Sentence—Conduct unbefitting a solicitor, not being professional misconduct, *below*.

SOLICITOR (cont)—
  Costs—
    Alleged want of authority on part of foreign defendant corporation to instruct solicitors in England—
      Claim that solicitors accountable to plaintiff for money received from defendant on account of
      costs—Action still pending—Preliminary issue directed. **Carl-Zeiss-Stiftung v Herbert Smith & Co
      (a firm)** [1968] 2 1002, CA.
    Bill for lump sum—
      Client insisting on taxation—Detailed bill taxed at sum greater than lump sum—Right of solicitor to
      recover amount of taxed bill—Solicitor's Remuneration (Gross Sum) Order 1934 (SR & O 1934
      No 548). **Solicitors, Re, Re Taxation of Costs** [1942] 2 499, CA.
    Bill of costs for contentious business—
      Taxation. *See* **Costs** (Taxation—Solicitor—Bill of costs for contentious business).
    Champerty—
      Champertous agreement between intending appellant and T in France in the French
      language—Solicitor employed in England to conduct appeal—Solicitor aware of champertous
      agreement—Appeal successfully prosecuted—Charging order made by consent for costs—
      Taxation of solicitor's bill of costs pursuant to charging order—Objection by appellant on ground
      of champerty—Contract of retainer under champertous agreement void and unenforceable, and
      solicitor not entitled to recover profit costs—Solicitor entitled to recover out of pocket expenses.
      Trepca Mines Ltd, Re [1962] 3 351, CA.
    Conditional fee agreement—
      Agreement with person providing advocacy or litigation services which provides for his fees and
      expenses to be payable only in specified circumstances—Meaning of 'expenses'—Solicitor and
      own client disbursements—Whether expenses—Courts and Legal Services Act 1990, s 58(2)(a).
      Flatman v Germany [2013] 4 349, CA.
      Client entering into conditional fee agreement with firm of solicitors—Solicitor acting on behalf of
      client moving to new firm and taking client with her—Whether conditional fee agreement capable
      of being assigned. **Jenkins v Young Brothers Transport Ltd** [2006] 2 798, QBD.
      Clients entering into retainer agreement providing for solicitors to charge percentage of monies
      recovered—Solicitors providing assistance to another firm of solicitors on record in related
      proceedings—Whether clients' solicitors providing litigation services—Whether agreement
      conditional fee agreement and unenforceable—Courts and Legal Services Act 1990, ss 58(2)(a),
      119(1). **Rees v Gateley Wareing (a firm)** [2015] 2 Comm 117, CA; [2015] 3 403, CA.
      Enforceability of agreement. *See* **Costs** (Order for costs—Conditional fee agreement—
      Enforceability of agreement).
      Generic costs—Conditional fee agreement covering basic costs—Solicitor incurring generic costs
      for group of clients with similar claims—Whether generic costs recoverable. **Brown v Russell
      Young & Co** [2007] 2 453, CA.
      Litigation services—Retainer providing for no charge to client if claim disputed and client deciding
      not to pursue claim—Whether retainer a conditional fee agreement—Whether work done by
      solicitor before client deciding not to pursue claim amounting to litigation services—Courts and
      Legal Services Act 1990, ss 58(1), (2)(a), 119(1). **Gaynor v Central West London Buses Ltd**
      [2007] 1 84, CA.
      Statutory provision requiring 'the legal representative' to provide client with certain information
      before making conditional fee agreement—Whether 'the legal representative' having to be
      individual who conducts the litigation—Whether duty of 'the legal representative' delegable—
      Whether duty delegable only to person capable of being 'the legal representative' if instructed as
      principal—Courts and Legal Services Act 1990, s 27(9)—Conditional Fee Agreements Regulations
      2000, regs 1(3), 4. **Sharratt v London Central Bus Co Ltd** [2003] 1 353, Sup Ct.
      Success fee uplift—After-the-event (ATE) insurance premium—Nuisance claim—Judge allowing
      claim and ordering defendants to pay 60% of costs including success fee and ATE
      premium—Whether success fee and ATE premium recoverable—Whether costs scheme
      compatible with convention rights—Courts and Legal Services Act 1990, s 58A(6), (7)—CPR
      43.2—Human Rights Act 1998, Sch 1, Pt I, art 6, Pt II, art 1—Access to Justice Act 1999, ss 27, 29.
      Lawrence v Fen Tigers Ltd (No 3) [2016] 2 97, SC.
      Success fee uplift—After-the-event (ATE) insurance premium—Personal injury claims—Modest and
      straightforward claims for personal injuries arising from road traffic accidents—Claimant entering
      into conditional fee agreement with success uplift—Claimant taking out ATE cover at outset for
      premium of £350—Court of Appeal allowing success fee of 20% and recovery of ATE premium in
      full—Whether ATE insurance premium recoverable from defendant as reasonable disbursement
      if claimant paying premium at outset—Whether amount of success fee and premium reasonable.
      Callery v Gray [2001] 3 833, CA; **Callery v Gray (Nos 1 and 2)** [2002] 3 417, HL.
      Success fee uplift—Conditional fee agreement made between solicitor and client after defendant
      had admitted liability—Assessment of risk in success fee—Whether reasonable. **C v W**
      [2009] 4 1129, CA.
      Success fee uplift—Personal injury claims—Modest and straightforward claims for personal injury
      arising from road traffic accidents—Appropriate level of success fee in such cases—Revised
      guidance. **Halloran v Delaney** [2003] 1 775, CA.
      Success fee uplift—Whether Law Society model conditional fee agreement applying to costs-only
      proceedings—Whether success fee recoverable in such proceedings. **Halloran v Delaney**
      [2003] 1 775, CA.
    Contentious business—
      Action to recover costs—Action on cheque—Client giving solicitor cheque which was dishonoured
      on presentation—Solicitor suing on cheque—Whether action on cheque circumventing statutory
      requirements and therefore barred—Solicitors Act 1974, ss 59, 69. **Martin Boston & Co (a firm) v
      Levy** [1982] 3 193, Ch D.
      Action to recover costs—Whether client's knowledge relevant in determining sufficiency of gross
      sum bill in contentious business—Solicitors Act 1974, s 69(2). **Ralph Hume Garry (a firm) v
      Gwillim** [2003] 1 1038, CA.
      Alleged agreement—Receipt of sum due thereunder—No submission of agreement to taxing
      officer—Whether solicitors entitled to immunity from taxation—Solicitors Act 1932, ss 60(5), 62.
      Simmons (Ernest) & Politzer (Eric B), Re [1954] 2 811, CA.

Contentious business (cont)—
Alleged agreement—Solicitors stating by letter that charges to be made on the basis of hourly rates applicable to partners or associates involved—Client replying by letter enclosing advance payment but not expressly assenting to rates proposed—Whether letters constituting a 'contentious business agreement'—Solicitors Act 1974, s 59. **Chamberlain v Boodle & King (a firm)** [1982] **3** 188, CA.

Oral agreement extending to both contentious and non-contentious business—Retainer of solicitor by trade union at a salary—Solicitor employed for union's accident cases and some other legal work—Solicitor later acted for union in their own contentious business—Money in hands of solicitor when his retainer terminated—Whether solicitor liable to account for profit costs received from opponents in accident cases—Whether solicitor entitled to profit costs for union's own litigation—Whether union could rely on oral agreement—Solicitors Act 1957, ss 34, 57, 59—Solicitors' Practice Rules 1936 (SR & O 1936 No 1005), r 3. **Electrical Trades Union v Tarlo** [1964] **2** 1, Ch D.

Taxation. See **Costs** (Taxation—Solicitor—Bill of costs for contentious business).
Contingency fee—
Arbitration—Conditional fee agreement between solicitors and client that fee payable only if client succeeded in arbitration—Whether agreement champertous—Courts and Legal Services Act 1990, s 58. **Bevan Ashford (a firm) v Geoff Yeandle (Contractors) Ltd (in liq)** [1998] **3** 238, Ch D.

Fee payable only in event of party being successful in action—Agreement between solicitor husband and wife that if action lost no fee payable—Whether agreement champertous—Whether husband entitled to profit costs—Solicitors Act 1974, s 59(2). **Thai Trading Co (a firm) v Taylor** [1998] **3** 65, CA.

Fee payable only in event of party being successful in action—Complaint of statutory nuisance—Nuisance remedied prior to trial and proceedings withdrawn—Complainant applying for costs—Solicitors never intending to pursue claim for costs against complainant—Whether complainant entitled to recover costs—Solicitors Practice Rules 1990. **Hughes v Kingston upon Hull City Council** [1999] **2** 49, QBD.

Fee payable only in event of party being successful in action—Contingency fees in general unlawful as being contrary to public policy—Exceptions—Company—Minority shareholder's action—Action in shareholder's own name—Action to redress wrongs against company committed by majority shareholder—Action in substance a representative action—Liability of minority shareholder to heavy costs—Right of indemnity against company—Whether contingency fee agreement between minority shareholder and legal advisers permissible. **Wallersteiner v Moir (No 2)** [1975] **1** 849, CA.

Fee payable only in event of party being successful in action—Solicitor agreeing to charge plaintiff in libel proceedings at full rate only if successful and to charge at lower rate if not—Whether agreement lawful or enforceable—Solicitors' Practice Rules 1990, r 8(1). **Awwad v Geraghty & Co (a firm)** [2000] **1** 608, CA.
Criminal cases—
Award of costs against solicitor. See **Criminal law** (Costs—Power to award costs).
Damages-based agreement—
Contract of retainer also providing for payment of costs if retainer terminated prematurely by client—Whether existence of clause invalidating whole contract—Courts and Legal Services Act 1990, s 58AA—Damages-Based Agreements Regulations 2013, SI 2013/609, regs 1, 4, 8. **Lexlaw Ltd v Zuberi (Bar Council intervening)** [2021] **4** 494, CA.
Determination whether business contentious or non-contentious—
Lump sum bill submitted for costs incurred before commencement of proceedings—Solicitors' Remuneration Order 1883, art 2(c) and Sch II. **Solicitor, Re a** [1955] **2** 283, CA.

Solicitor instructed by liquidator of company to obtain counsel's opinion whether certain proceedings should be taken—No proceedings taken—Lump sum bill delivered—Supreme Court of Judicature (Consolidation) Act 1925, s 225—Solicitors Act 1957, s 86(1)—Solicitors' Remuneration Order 1883, art 2, Sch 2. **Simpkin Marshall Ltd, Re** [1958] **3** 611, Ch D.
Disbursements—
Proportionality. See **Costs** (Assessment—Standard basis—Proportionality).
Estimate of costs—
Assessment. See **Costs** (Assessment—Estimate of costs).
Retainer. See Retainer—Termination of retainer—Solicitor exceeding costs estimate supplied to client at time of engagement, below.
Insurance. See **Insurance** (Legal expenses insurance).
Legal proceedings between husband and wife—
Title to property—Liability of husband for wife's costs—Married Women's Property Act 1882, s 17. **Nabarro (JN) & Sons v Kennedy** [1954] **2** 605, QBD.
Misconduct or neglect—
Medical report—Refusal to disclose. **Vose v Barr** [1966] **2** 226, Assizes.
Non-contentious business—
Agreement for payment of gross sum—Mistaken statement by solicitor as to basis on which remuneration could be calculated—Right of client to an order for delivery of itemised bill and taxation of bill—Solicitors Act 1957, s 57(4). **Rutter v Sheridan-Young** [1958] **2** 13, CA.

Application for taxation six years after payment—Discretion of court to order delivery of bill—Solicitors Renumeration Act General Order 1882, cl 2(a), cl 2 (c)—Solicitors Act 1932, ss 64, 66—Solicitors' Remuneration (Gross Sum) Order 1934 (S R & O 1934 No 548), art 1. **Solicitor, Re a** [1947] **1** 369, Ch D.

Application to transfer taxation of bill of costs to district registry—Jurisdiction of court to order transfer—Jurisdiction of district registrar to act as taxing master—RSC Ord 35, rr 6A, 17. **Solicitor, Re a, Re Taxation of Costs** [1944] **1** 523, Ch D.

Fair and reasonable sum in circumstances. See **Costs** (Taxation—Solicitor—Non-contentious business—Fair and reasonable sum in circumstances).

Gross sum—Charge of gross sum including disbursements—Discretion of court to order delivery of detailed bill—Solicitors Act 1932, ss 64, 66—Solicitors' Remuneration (Gross Sum) Order 1934 (SR & O 1934 No 548), art 1. **Solicitor, Re a, Re Taxation of Costs** [1953] **2** 23, CA.

SOLICITOR (cont)—
  Costs (cont)—
    Non-contentious business (cont)—
      Interest—Right to charge interest on bill of costs—Date from which interest runs—Solicitor serving notice required under remuneration rules on client some months after delivery of bill—Bill unpaid and solicitor bringing action to recover principal sum and interest—Whether solicitor entitled to interest from one month after delivery of bill or only from service of notice—Solicitors' Remuneration Order 1972 (SI 1972 No 1139), arts 3(2), 5. **Walton v Egan** [1982] **3** 849, QBD.
      Interest—Special agreement as to remuneration—Solicitor and client making agreement as to principal sum and interest—Action by solicitor to recover unpaid interest—Whether statutory provisions as to special agreements covering agreement as to interest—Whether special agreements subject to restrictions in rules regarding interest—Solicitors Act 1974, s 57—Solicitors' Remuneration Order 1972 (SI 1972 No 1139) arts 3, 5. **Walton v Egan** [1982] **3** 849, QBD.
      Oral agreement to charge less than scale fees—Solicitors Act 1932, s 57(3). **Solicitor, Re a** [1955] **3** 305, QBD.
      Recovery—Proceedings to recover costs for non-contentious business—Whether winding-up proceedings in respect of debt for costs for non-contentious business constituting 'proceedings to recover costs on bill for non-contentious business'—Solicitors' Remuneration Order 1972 (SI 1972 No 1139), art 3(2). **Lacaward Ltd, Re** [1981] **1** 254, Ch D.
    Paid bill—
      Taxation. See **Costs** (Taxation—Solicitor—Paid bill).
    Payment by solicitor personally. See Payment of costs by solicitor personally, *below*.
    Payment of costs by non-party. See **Costs** (Order for costs—Payment of costs by non-party).
    Professional conduct—
      Petitioner's solicitor interviewing respondent to obtain confession of adultery—Exclusion of these costs from order for costs on granting decree nisi—Whether a judicial exercise of discretion—Need to show that costs unnecessarily incurred—RSC Order 65, r 11. **Davies v Davies** [1960] **3** 248, CA.
    Recovery—
      Action to recover—Letter accompanying bill 'signed by solicitor'—Use of rubber stamps—Signature in name of firm by sole member—Solicitors Act 1932, s 65(2)(i). **Goodman v J Eban Ltd** [1954] **1** 763, CA.
      Charging order over client's property—Litigation culminating in order for costs in favour of solicitors' client—Order for costs making no provision for taxation—Subsequent proceedings on same dispute compromised by agreement—Compromise agreement extinguishing parties' rights and liabilities under contracts giving rise to dispute—Dormant client company failing to pay solicitors' fees—Client's only remaining asset being order for costs—Solicitors applying for charging order over order for costs—Whether order for untaxed costs constituting 'property' over which charging order could be made—Whether court having jurisdiction to make charging order to secure solicitors' untaxed costs—Whether compromise agreement extinguishing client's right to enforce order for costs—Solicitors Act 1974, s 73(1)(a), (b). **Fairfold Properties Ltd v Exmouth Docks Co Ltd (No 2)** [1992] **4** 289, Ch D.
      Contentious business—Action on cheque. See **Costs**—Contentious business—Action to recover costs—Action on cheque, *above*.
      Lien—Compromise—Defendant settling claim brought by claimant—Defendant agreeing to pay claimant's costs—Claimant withdrawing instructions to solicitors and personally reaching compromise with defendant of amount payable in costs—Solicitors giving notice to defendant of their claim for unpaid fees—Solicitors' claim for judicial review struck out—Defendant subsequently paying amount of costs agreed with claimant directly to claimant—Solicitors' fees remaining unpaid—Whether compromise of costs valid—Whether defendant could be compelled to pay solicitors' fees. **Khans Solicitors (a firm) v Chifuntwe** [2013] **4** 367, CA.
      Service of statutory demand—Setting aside statutory demand—Action to recover solicitors' costs—Solicitors serving statutory demand within one month of delivering bill of costs—Whether service of statutory demand constituting bringing of action—Whether solicitors barred from serving statutory demand within one month of delivering bill of costs—Solicitors Act 1974, s 69(1). **Debtor (No 88 of 1991), Re a** [1992] **4** 301, Ch D.
      Service of statutory demand—Unassessed bill—Debt capable of founding bankruptcy petition—Solicitor serving statutory demand—Period for taxation of bill other than in special circumstances expiring—Solicitor presenting bankruptcy petition—Whether debt liquidated sum—Whether client sufficiently acknowledging bill—Solicitors Act 1974, s 70(3)(a)—Insolvency Act 1986, s 267. **Truex v Toll** [2009] **4** 419, Ch D.
      Unqualified person—Client requesting advice from a solicitor—Receptionist referring client to non-solicitor member of firm but failing to inform him that adviser not a solicitor—Firm not sending client a client care letter and client not discovering adviser's status until after performance of legal services—Whether firm entitled to recover its costs from client. **Pilbrow v Pearless De Rougemont & Co** [1999] **3** 355, CA.
      Unqualified person—Partnership—Partner allowing practising certificate to lapse—Costs incurred in respect of work done by another partner during period of disqualification—Action to recover costs—Whether by virtue of partnership work to be treated as work done by disqualified partner—Whether other partner precluded from recovering costs in respect of work done—Solicitors Act 1957, s 18(2)(b). **Hudgell Yeates & Co v Watson** [1978] **2** 363, CA.
  Solicitor. See **Costs** (Taxation—Solicitor).
  Solicitor administrator—
    Sole administrator—Insolvent estate—Profit costs of preparing petition for administration in bankruptcy and of preparing and lodging accounts. **Worthington (decd), Re** [1954] **1** 677, Ch D.
  Taxation—
    Allowance in excess of statutory maximum. See **Costs** (Taxation—Discretion—Allowance of amount in excess of maximum prescribed by scale of costs—Preparation of case by solicitors).
    Generally. See **Costs** (Taxation).
    Legal aid. See **Legal aid** (Taxation of costs—Solicitor's fees and expenses).
    Review of taxation—Jurisdiction. See **Costs** (Taxation—Review of taxation—Jurisdiction—Solicitor).

SOLICITOR (cont)—
  Costs (cont)—
    Taxation (cont)—
      Taxation in Family Division—Telephone calls. *See* **Costs** (Taxation—Family Division—Solicitor—Telephone calls).
      Value added tax. *See* **Costs** (Taxation—Value added tax).
    Taxation. *See* **Costs** (Taxation—Solicitor).
    Transfer of registered land on sale. *See* **Land registration** (Costs—Transfer of registered land).
    Unqualified person. *See* Unqualified person—Costs, *below*.
    Withdrawal of delivered bill—
      Jurisdiction to permit. **Polak v Winchester (Marchioness)** [1956] **2** 660, CA.
      Redelivery—Jurisdiction to permit. *See* **Costs** (Taxation—Solicitor—Withdrawal and redelivery of bill).
  Criminal proceedings—
    Legal aid—
      Legal representation for the accused. *See* **Legal aid** (Criminal cases).
    Withdrawal. *See* Withdrawal—Criminal proceedings, *below*.
  Crown Court—
    Costs—
      Payment by solicitor personally. *See* Payment of costs by solicitor personally—Crown Court, *below*.
    Right of audience. *See* **Crown Court** (Practice—Solicitor—Right of audience).
  Damages—
    Liability—
      Breach of contract—Mental distress. *See* **Contract** (Damages for breach—Mental distress—Solicitor).
    Measure of damages against solicitor. *See* Breach of duty—Client's action founded in contract—Measure of damages, *above*.
    Mental distress—
      Breach of contract. *See* **Contract** (Damages for breach—Mental distress).
    Negligence. *See* Negligence—Damages, *below*.
  Defamation—
    Privilege against liability for defamation. *See* Disciplinary proceedings—Disciplinary committee—Privilege against liability for defamation, *below*.
  Delegation of responsibility—
    Professional misconduct. *See* Disciplinary proceedings—Professional misconduct—Delegation of responsibility, *below*.
  Disciplinary proceedings—
    Appeal—
      Grounds for variation of order by Divisional Court—Conduct unbefitting a solicitor—Indecent assault—Solicitor's name ordered to be struck off roll—Solicitors Act 1932, s 8—Solicitors (Disciplinary Appeals) Rules 1942 (SR & O 1942 No 1832), r 8. **Solicitor, Re a** [1956] **3** 516, QBD.
      Order to strike name off roll—Refusal of Disciplinary Committee to suspend publication of findings pending appeal—Provision under rules for suspending order—Whether court has inherent jurisdiction or prevent publication—Solicitors (Disciplinary Proceedings) Rules 1942 (SR & O 1942 No 1831), r 29(1). **Solicitor, Re a** [1944] **2** 432, KBD.
      Power of appellate court to lift suspension order when purpose accomplished—Failure of solicitor to keep account books in proper form—Solicitor ordered by disciplinary committee to be suspended from practice for six months—Purpose of order to enable submission of accountant's report covering relevant period—Appeal to Court of Appeal—Accountant's certificate for relevant period before Court of Appeal—Certificate showing that no deficiency on clients' account—Court of Appeal entitled to lift suspension order although order by disciplinary committee justified—Court instead ordering solicitor to pay all Law Society's costs in proceedings. **Solicitor, Re a** [1972] **2** 811, CA.
      Rehearing on appeal—New evidence by way of mitigation—Whether court would interfere with penalty imposed. **Lindsay Bowman Ltd, Re** [1969] **3** 601, Ch D.
      Restoration of name to roll of solicitors—Application for restoration of name to roll of solicitors—Application granted by Solicitors Disciplinary Tribunal—Whether Law Society having locus standi to appeal against tribunal's order to restore struck-off solicitor's name to roll—Solicitors Act 1974, ss 47(1)(b), 49(1)(a). **R v Master of the Rolls, ex p McKinnell** [1993] **1** 193, QBD.
    Applicant in person—
      Allegations of professional impropriety—Applicant not present before committee—Order by committee dismissing application—Appeal to the Divisional Court—Appellant not represented by counsel—Refusal by Divisional Court to hear the appeal—Solicitors Act 1932, s 8. **Two Solicitors, Re** [1937] **4** 451, CA.
      Application to strike solicitor's name off roll—Jurisdiction—Whether court having jurisdiction to entertain application by litigant in person—Whether application to strike solicitor's name off roll must be made by counsel—Solicitors Act 1974, ss 50(2), 51—RSC Ord 5, r 6. **Solicitors, Re, ex p Peasegood** [1994] **1** 298, QBD.
    Disciplinary committee—
      Privilege against liability for defamation—Solicitors Act 1957, s 46—Solicitors (Disciplinary Proceedings) Rules 1957 (SI 1957 No 2240), r 21. **Addis v Crocker** [1960] **2** 629, CA.
    Disciplinary tribunal—
      Admissible evidence—Standard of proof—English solicitor struck off roll of practitioners in Western Australia for unprofessional conduct—Complaint to Solicitors Disciplinary Tribunal that same conduct unbefitting a solicitor—Tribunal upholding complaint after considering decision of Western Australian disciplinary board—Whether decision of Western Australian board admissible—Whether tribunal required to adopt criminal standard of proof—Civil Evidence Act 1968, s 1(1)—Solicitors (Disciplinary Proceedings) Rules 1985, rr 39(a), 41. **Solicitor, Re a** [1992] **2** 335, QBD.
      Disciplinary tribunal finding allegations of dishonesty against solicitor proved and striking him from Roll of Solicitors—Whether abuse of process of court for solicitor in proceedings for damages against him to put in issue facts found by tribunal. **Conlon v Simms** [2007] **3** 802, CA.

SOLICITOR (cont)—
  Disciplinary proceedings (cont)—
   Disciplinary tribunal (cont)—
    Power of tribunal to impose conditions on practice—Whether tribunal should exercise power—Solicitors' Act 1974, s 47. **R (on the application of Camacho) v Law Society** [2004] **4** 126, DC.
    Power to refer case to Office for the Supervision of Solicitors —Applicant making complaint against solicitors to Solicitors Disciplinary Tribunal—Tribunal declining to determine whether prima facie case made out and referring case to Office for the Supervision of Solicitors—Whether tribunal having power to refer case before certifying that prima facie case established—Solicitors (Disciplinary Proceedings) Rules 1994, rr 4, 28. **R (on the application of Toth) v Solicitors Disciplinary Tribunal** [2001] **3** 180, QBD.
    Powers—Costs—Whether costs following event in disciplinary proceedings—Solicitors Act 1974, s 47(2). **Baxendale-Walker v Law Society** [2006] **3** 675, DC; [2007] **3** 330, CA.
    Powers—Power of tribunal to regulate its own procedure—Clerk retiring with tribunal members—Whether tribunal having power to permit clerk to retire with tribunal members—Solicitors (Disciplinary Proceedings) Rules 1994, SI 1994/288, r 31(a). **Virdi v Law Society (Solicitors Disciplinary Tribunal intervening)** [2010] **3** 653, CA.
  Evidence—
    Admissibility—Disciplinary tribunal finding allegations of dishonesty against solicitor proved and striking him from Roll of Solicitors—Whether findings of fact made in disciplinary proceedings admissible in proceedings for damages against solicitor as evidence of facts so found. **Conlon v Simms** [2006] **2** 1024, Ch D; [2007] **3** 802, CA.
  Inadequate professional services—
    Solicitor applying to Office for the Supervision of Solicitors (OSS) for oral hearing of complaint of inadequate professional services—OSS refusing oral hearing and directing reprimand, compensation and refunding of costs—Whether solicitor entitled to oral hearing—Whether determination of solicitor's civil rights and obligations—Solicitors Act 1974, Sch 1A, para 5(1)—Human Rights Act 1998, Sch 1, Pt I, art 6, Pt II, art 1. **R (on the application of Thompson) v Law Society** [2004] **2** 113, CA.
  Jurisdiction of court—
    Extent of court's jurisdiction—Exercise of court's jurisdiction—Jurisdiction of court to order solicitor to pay costs—Nature of conduct justifying court in exercising jurisdiction—Conduct required to be inexcusable and such as to merit reproof—Mistake, error of judgment or mere negligence insufficient—Solicitors Act 1974, s 50. **Thew (R & T) Ltd v Reeves (No 2)** [1982] **3** 1086, CA.
  Order for suspension—
    Name remaining on roll of solicitors—Use of description 'solicitor' while no practising certificate in force—Whether intention to imply that qualified to act as solicitor—Solicitors Act 1932, s 46. **Taylor v Richardson** [1938] **2** 681, KBD.
  Professional misconduct—
    Accident cases—Instructions from organisation making claims in accident cases—Failure of solicitor to make reasonable inquiry before accepting instructions—Suspension of solicitor from practice for two years—Solicitors Act 1932, s 8—Solicitors Act 1933, s 1—Solicitors' Practice Rules 1936 (SR & O 1936 No 1005), r 4(c). **Solicitor, Re a** [1945] **1** 445, CA.
    Delegation of responsibility—Failure to keep clients' account books properly written up—No misuse of clients' funds—No money missing from clients' funds—Accountant employed by solicitor failing to write up books—Accountant wrongly certifying that accounts rules complied with—Inspection by Law Society's accounts rules complied with—Inspection by Law Society's accountant in 1970 revealing books not written up since 1967—Solicitor failing to put books in order thereafter or when proceedings taken against him before disciplinary committee—Solicitor guilty of professional misconduct because of reprehensible failure and delay—Solicitor not entitled to escape responsibility for breach of accounts rules because books were handed over to accountant—Solicitors' Accounts Rules 1967, r 11. **Solicitor, Re a** [1972] **2** 811, CA.
    Dishonesty—Exceptional circumstances—Suspended suspension—Tribunal making findings solicitors suffering from mental health problems—Whether exceptional circumstances—Whether sanctions imposed unduly lenient. **Solicitors Regulation Authority v James** [2019] **2** 527, DC.
    Matter not appropriate for consideration by trial judge—Divorce—Petitioner's solicitor interviewing respondent and taking written confession of matrimonial misconduct—Whether conduct unprofessional. **Davies v Davies** [1960] **3** 248, CA.
  Sentence—
    Conduct unbefitting a solicitor, not being professional misconduct—Insulting behaviour—Previous convictions for indecent assault—Solicitor's name struck off the roll—Suitability of sentence. **Solicitor, Re a** [1960] **2** 621, QBD.
    Right to fair trial—Right to respect for private and family life—Solicitor convicted of obtaining money transfer by deception—Solicitor admitting before disciplinary tribunal conduct unbefitting a solicitor—Disciplinary tribunal striking solicitor from roll—Divisional Court substituting order for suspension—Applicable principles—Effect of European Convention for the Protection of Human Rights and Fundamental Freedoms 1950—Human Rights Act 1998, Sch 1, Pt I, arts 6, 8. **Salsbury v Law Society** [2009] **2** 487, CA.
    Solicitor improperly disbursing client funds instead of placing them in client account—Solicitor subsequently making good shortage in client account—Solicitor an honest man who had not stolen client's moneys in a premeditated fashion or embarked on a deliberate course of dishonest conduct—Solicitors Disciplinary Tribunal suspending solicitor from practice for two years—Divisional Court quashing order for suspension and substituting fine—Whether court right to do so. **Bolton v Law Society** [1994] **2** 486, CA.
  Singapore. *See* **Singapore** (Advocate and solicitor—Disciplinary proceedings).
  Solicitor taking gift under will of client—
    Client not separately advised before making will—Solicitor charged with conduct unbefitting solicitor—Solicitor struck off by disciplinary committee on ground that he was bound to forego benefit unless client separately advised—Whether standard imposed by committee too strict—Whether penalty too severe. **Solicitor, Re a** [1974] **3** 853, QBD.

SOLICITOR (cont)—
Dishonesty—
Intervention by Law Society in solicitor's practice—
Disclosure of documents—Law Society suspecting solicitor of being dishonest and failing to comply with accounting rules—Council of Law Society passing resolution vesting in Society moneys held by solicitor—Notice of resolution served on solicitor—Solicitor applying by originating summons for withdrawal of notice—Solicitor applying for discovery of Law Society's internal documents relating to its resolution—Whether order for discovery should be made—Solicitors Act 1974, Sch 1, paras 1(2), 6(4), (5)—RSC Ord 24, r 7, Ord 106, r 6(1). **Buckley v Law Society** [1983] **2** 1039, Ch D.

Disclosure of documents—Privilege—Production contrary to public interest—Identity of informants to Law Society regarding solicitor's dishonesty—Whether Law Society immune from disclosure of informants' identity. **Buckley v Law Society (No 2)** [1984] **3** 313, Ch D.

Nomination or appointment of solicitor to act as agent of Law Society in intervention—Nominated solicitor submitting bills to Law Society in respect of costs of acting in intervention—Law Society seeking under statutory provision reimbursement from solicitor in whose practice it had intervened—Solicitor seeking taxation of bills—Whether bills submitted to Law Society solicitor's bills—Whether solicitor's right to seek taxation of bills excluded by provision rendering him liable for Law Society's costs of intervention—Solicitors Act 1974, ss 70, 71, Sch 1, Pt II, para 13. **Pine v The Law Society** [2002] **2** 658, CA.

Resolution and notice vesting in Law Society moneys held by solicitor—Automatic suspension of practising certificate—Solicitor applying for withdrawal of notice—Whether court having power to terminate suspension of practising certificate without withdrawal of notice—Solicitors Act 1974, Sch 1, paras 6, 9. **Sritharan v Law Society** [2005] **4** 1105, CA.

Resolution and notice vesting in Law Society moneys held by solicitor—Withdrawal of notice—Whether court having implied power to order withdrawal of notice—Whether when considering withdrawal of notice court confined to considering material available to Law Society when passing resolution—Whether parties free to adduce evidence of matters occurring after date of resolution—Solicitors Act 1974, Sch 1, para 6. **Buckley v Law Society (No 2)** [1984] **3** 313, Ch D.

Solicitor applying for withdrawal of intervention—Nature of the court's jurisdiction. **Sheikh v Law Society** [2005] **4** 717, Ch D; [2007] **3** 183, CA.

Misappropriation of means—
Intention to repay—Fees received by solicitor for counsel and shorthand-writers misappropriated by him for his own benefit and use—Gross dishonesty admitted but intention ultimately to pay asserted—Whether an offence under Larceny Act 1916, s 20(1)(iv)(b)—Solicitors Act 1957, s 66—Solicitors' Accounts Rules 1945 (SR & O 1944 No 781), r 9(2). **R v Yule** [1963] **2** 780, CCA.

Divorce suit—
Lien. See Lien—Retaining lien—Divorce suit, *below.*
Documents—
Preparation by unqualified person. See Unqualified person—Preparation of documents etc, *below.*
Duty—
Advice to partnership—
Duty only to advise partner who has matter in hand on behalf of partnership. **Sykes v Midland Bank Executor and Trustee Co Ltd** [1970] **2** 471, CA.
Appeal from county court—
Provision of note of county court judgment. See **County court** (Appeal—Note of county court judgment—Provision of note).
Breach of duty. See Breach of duty, *above.*
Breach of trust—
Mortgage transaction—Solicitor acting for both borrower and society—Advance paid to solicitor to enable completion of purchase of property—Borrower required to pay indemnity premium in respect of additional security (mortgage indemnity guarantee) which society proposed to take from third party—Borrower in default—Insurance company liable to pay society sum computed by reference to amount by which proceeds falling short of outstanding debt due on mortgage—Society paying advance cheque to solicitor on basis of warranty or representation which solicitor knew or ought to have known was misleading—Society entitled to judgment for full amount of loss—Computation of loss—Whether society obliged to give credit for sums recovered or recoverable by it under mortgage indemnity guarantee. **Bristol and West Building Society v May May & Merrimans (a firm) (No 2)** [1997] **3** 206, Ch D.

Mortgage transaction—Solicitor acting for both borrower and society—Advance paid to solicitor to enable completion of purchase of property—Solicitor's obligation to disclose facts not relevant to title—Solicitor's obligation as a fiduciary—Payment away in breach of instructions—Misrepresentation in breach of fiduciary duty—Evidence required on application for summary judgment—Whether necessary to establish that if lender had known of undisclosed fact advance could not have been made. **Bristol and West Building Society v May May & Merrimans (a firm)** [1996] **2** 801, Ch D.

Mortgage transaction—Solicitors holding mortgage loan money on trust until completion—Fraudulent transaction—Solicitors remitting mortgage loan money to fraudsters—Whether solicitors in breach of trust—Whether completion taking place. **Lloyds TSB Bank plc v Markandan & Uddin (a firm)** [2012] **2** 884, CA.

Mortgage transaction—Compensation to lender. See **Trust and trustee** (Breach of trust—Compensation for breach—Trustee's duty to compensate beneficiary for losses—Re-mortgage).
Cause list. See **Practice** (Trial—Cause list—Solicitor's duty).
Client—
Duty of confidentiality to client—Conflict of interest. See Duty—Conflict of interest—Duty of confidentiality to client, *below.*
Duty of confidentiality to client—Fraud—Solicitors as trustees holding funds for client—Solicitors discovering strong evidence that funds acquired by client's fraud—Solicitors seeking directions of court—Whether solicitors' duty of confidence to client overridden by evidence of fraud—Whether solicitors should be directed to inform liquidator of company allegedly defrauded by client of proceedings—RSC Ord 85, r 2. **Finers (a firm) v Miro** [1991] **1** 182, CA.

SOLICITOR (cont)—
Duty (cont)—
Conflict of duty and interest—
Solicitor trustee—Breach of trust—Preference to own interest at expense of beneficiary—Non-disclosure of interest—Duty to illiterate persons. **Grahame v A-G of Fiji** [1936] **2** 992, PC.

Solicitors executors of their mother's will—Whether under duty to impeach extension of lease of her freehold property to them directed by her will—Reversion devised to their sisters—Lease on advantageous terms. **Wells (decd), Re** [1967] **3** 908, Ch D.

Conflict of interest—
Acting for both parties in transaction—Bankruptcy—Trustee in bankruptcy appointing petitioning creditor's solicitors to advise on administration of bankrupt's estate—Outstanding matters in relation to earlier proceedings involving bankrupt and petitioning creditor and its solicitors—Whether retention of petitioning creditor's solicitors by trustee creating conflict of interest—Whether outstanding matters giving rise to conflict of interest. **Schuppan (a bankrupt), Re** [1996] **2** 664, Ch D.

Acting for both parties in transaction—Liability of solicitor when assuming irreconcilable duties to different clients. **Hilton v Barker Booth and Eastwood (a firm)** [2005] **1** 651, HL.

Acting for both parties in transaction—Mortgage—Whether solicitor ought to refuse to act for both parties where interests may conflict—Whether solicitor can act for both parties if he obtains informed consent of both parties—What amounts to informed consent—Whether solicitor under duty to go beyond instructions by proffering unsought advice on wisdom of transaction. **Clark Boyce v Mouat** [1993] **4** 268, PC.

Acting for both parties in transaction—Whether conflict arising only when solicitor acting for both parties in same transaction. **Marks & Spencer plc v Freshfields Bruckhaus Deringer** [2004] **3** 773, Ch D.

Conflict of duty and interest. See Duty—Conflict of duty and interest, *above*.

Duty of confidentiality to client. **Conway v Ratiu** [2006] **1** 571n, CA.

Duty of confidentiality to client—Former client—Plaintiffs retaining firm of solicitors to act in patent litigation—Defendant a partner in firm but not engaged in the litigation—Partner joining new firm of solicitors—New firm retained by defendant in patent litigation—Plaintiffs seeking to restrain partner from acting as solicitor for defendant in patent litigation—Whether partner in possession of relevant confidential information—Test to be applied—Burden of proof. **Solicitors, Re a Firm of** [1995] **3** 482, Ch D.

Duty of confidentiality to client—Former client—Solicitor acting for client against former client—Large City firm instructed to act for client against former client—Firm previously receiving confidential information from former client relevant to subsequent litigation—Firm proposing to erect 'Chinese wall' to prevent leakage of confidential information received from former client—Former client seeking to restrain firm from acting for other client—Whether reasonable man informed of facts including proposed Chinese wall would anticipate danger of firm breaching duty of confidence to former client—Whether firm should be restrained from acting against former client. **Solicitors, Re a Firm of** [1992] **1** 353, CA.

Duty of confidentiality to client—Former client—Solicitor acting for defendant to arbitration proceedings—Solicitor moving to firm acting for claimant in arbitration proceedings—Defendant to arbitration proceedings seeking injunction preventing firm from acting in arbitration action—Whether real risk of inadvertent disclosure of information. **Koch Shipping Inc v Richards Butler (a firm)** [2002] **2 Comm** 957, CA.

Entry of appearance—Authority to enter appearance not affected by alleged conflict of interests. **Keys v Boulter** [1971] **1** 289, CA.

Merger of firms of solicitors—Merging firms acting for opposing sides in litigation—Plaintiff companies, acting by liquidators, making serious allegations of dishonesty against professional firms—Solicitors acting for liquidators merging with firm which had formerly advised professional defendants—Defendants refusing to consent to merged firm continuing to act for liquidators—Whether merged firm could properly continue to act for liquidators—Whether mischief or real prejudice to former client could be rightly anticipated—Whether merged firm able to satisfy court that sensitive information relating to respective cases would remain separate and confidential. **Supasave Retail Ltd v Coward Chance (a firm)** [1991] **1** 668, Ch D.

Solicitor advocate—Libel action—Solicitor advocate advising defendants that proposed article not defamatory—Plaintiff bringing action for libel and second defendant instructing solicitor advocate to represent him—Plaintiff applying to court to bar him from doing so—Whether breach of Law Society's Code for Advocacy for solicitor advocate to appear as advocate—Law Society's Code for Advocacy 1993, r 4.1(e). **Christie v Wilson** [1999] **1** 545, CA.

Solicitors acting for both lender and borrowers on further mortgage of matrimonial home—Husband and wife informing lender that loan required for their joint benefit—Husband informing solicitors that purpose of loan for his sole benefit—Solicitors subsequently being instructed also to act for lender—Whether lender fixed with constructive notice of husband's purpose—Whether knowledge coming to solicitors as solicitors for lender—Law of Property Act 1925, s 199. **Halifax Mortgage Services Ltd (formerly BNP Mortgages Ltd) v Stepsky** [1996] **2** 277, CA.

Termination of retainer—Criminal proceedings—Co-defendants—Cut-throat defence—Solicitor acting for one co-defendant where co-defendants blaming each other—Retainer terminated—Impropriety of solicitor afterwards acting for other co-defendant. **Saminadhen v Khan (note)** [1992] **1** 963, CA.

Criminal trial. See **Criminal law** (Trial—Counsel—Solicitor—Duties).

Disclosure of documents—
Ensuring that client understands obligation to give discovery. See **Disclosure and inspection of documents** (Duty of solicitor—Ensuring that clients appreciate their duty in regard to disclosure).

Divorce—
Disclosure of adultery by petitioner. See **Divorce** (Disclosure of documents—Adultery by petitioner—Duty of solicitor).

Duty to court—
Negotiating settlement of claims to damages, etc. **Jakeman v Jakeman and Turner** [1963] **3** 889, Div.

SOLICITOR (cont)—
  Duty (cont)—
    Duty to court (cont)—
      Solicitors Regulation Authority—Referral—Immigration and asylum—Guidance. **R (on the application of Sathivel) v Secretary of State for the Home Dept** [2018] **3** 79n, DC.
    Duty to third party—
      Sale of land. *See* **Sale of land** (Forgery—Liability of solicitors and estate agents).
    Knowledge—
      Case not reported in any major series of law reports. **Pearson v Pearson (Queen's Proctor showing cause)** [1969] **3** 323, Div.
    Litigation—
      Action arising out of car accident—No duty on defendants' solicitor to interview passenger in plaintiff's car, presumably friend of plaintiff and possibly potential claimant against defendants. **Roe v Robert McGregor & Sons Ltd** [1968] **2** 636, CA.
    Performance—
      Guidance by courts—Locus standi of Law Society. *See* **Practice** (Parties—Law Society— Proceedings in which court giving guidance to solicitors in performance of their duties).
    Will—
      Negligence. *See* Negligence—Will—Duty of care, *below*.
  Entry of appearance—
    Authority—
      Conflict of interests. *See* Duty—Conflict of interest—Entry of appearance, *above*.
  Exchange of contracts—
    Same solicitor acting for both parties. *See* **Sale of land** (Exchange of contracts—Same solicitor acting for both parties).
  Fees—
    Conditional fee agreement. *See* Costs—Conditional fee agreement, *above*.
    Legal aid—
      Criminal cases. *See* **Legal aid** (Criminal cases—Solicitors' fees).
      Taxation of costs. *See* **Legal aid** (Taxation of costs).
  Forged documents or instruments—
    Police—
      Search warrant—Lawful authority or excuse for possession of forged documents. *See* **Police** (Search warrant—Forged documents or instruments—Lawful authority or excuse for possession of forged documents—Solicitor).
  Fraudulent conversion. *See* **Criminal law** (Fraudulent conversion—Solicitor).
  Gift by client to solicitor—
    Residuary bequest by testatrix to her solicitor in will prepared by him—
      Knowledge and approval of testatrix—Burden of proof on solicitor to prove that testatrix knew and approved the contents of the will in so far as it benefited him—No independent advice to client—Duty of judge in summing-up to scrutinise vigilantly to the jury the evidence supporting the bequest. **Wintle v Nye** [1959] **1** 552, HL.
  Goodwill attaching to office premises—
    Compensation—
      Trade or business—Agencies for insurance companies and building societies—Relevant goodwill. **Stuchbery & Son v General Accident, Fire and Life Assurance Corp Ltd** [1949] **1** 1026, CA.
  Guarantees—
    Ordinary activity of practice. *See* Practice—Guarantees—Ordinary activity of practice, *below*.
  Indemnity insurance. *See* **Insurance** (Liability insurance—Professional indemnity insurance—Solicitor).
  Inspection of books of account, bank pass books, vouchers etc—
    Law society's power to require solicitor to produce books for inspection. *See* Clients' account—Inspection of books of account, bank pass books, vouchers etc—Law Society's power to require solicitor to produce books for inspection, *above*.
  Insurance—
    Professional indemnity insurance. *See* **Insurance** (Liability insurance—Professional indemnity insurance—Solicitor).
  Interrogation of suspect—
    Admissibility in criminal proceedings of answers and statements to police—
      Right of suspect to consult solicitor. *See* **Criminal evidence** (Admissions and confessions—Answers and statements to police—Right to consult solicitor).
  Intestacy—
    Administration of solicitor's estate. *See* **Intestacy** (Grant of administration—Solicitor's estate).
  Land registry official searches—
    Unqualified person. *See* Unqualified person—Preparation of documents etc—Land registry official searches, *below*.
  Law Society—
    Injunction—
      Law Society applying for injunction prohibiting struck-off solicitor from holding himself out as solicitor, or undertaking activities which would breach, or cause others to breach, the regulatory regime—Whether Law Society could rely on court's inherent or supervisory jurisdiction to obtain injunction—Whether injunction could be granted under specific statutory provision—Legal Services Act 2007, s 14. **Law Society of England & Wales v Shah** [2015] **3** 522, Ch D.
    Intervention—
      Compliance of Law Society's intervention procedure with human rights legislation—Human Rights Act 1998, Sch 1, Pt II, art 1. **Holder v Law Society** [2003] **3** 62, CA.
  Leave to appeal—
    Authority—
      Application made without instructions. *See* **Criminal law** (Appeal—Leave to appeal—Application— Application by solicitor on behalf of client—Solicitor having no express instructions to appeal—Whether solicitor having implied authority to appeal on behalf of client).
  Legal aid—
    Duty of solicitor to legally assisted client. *See* Client—Legally assisted client, *above*.

SOLICITOR (cont)—
  Legal aid (cont)—
    Failure to give notice of legal aid certificate. *See* Payment of costs by solicitor personally—Failure to give notice of legal aid certificate, *below*.
    Taxation of costs—
      Solicitor's fees and expenses. *See* **Legal aid** (Taxation of costs).
  Legal expenses insurance—
    Generally. *See* **Insurance** (Legal expenses insurance).
  Legal professional privilege—
    Disclosure of documents. *See* **Disclosure and inspection of documents** (Legal professional privilege).
    Generally. *See* **Privilege** (Legal professional privilege).
  Liability—
    Constructive trustee—
      Misappropriation of trust money—Liability of solicitor's partner for misappropriation—Money paid into firm's client account in name of express trustees—Money misappropriated by express trustees with solicitor's knowledge—Partner not having actual knowledge of misappropriation and acting throughout honestly and reasonably in regard to firm's affairs but having access to documents inspection of which might have revealed breach of trust—Solicitor liable to replace money as constructive trustee—Whether partner also liable as constructive trustee or under implied terms of partnership. **Bell's Indenture, Re** [1980] **3** 425, Ch D.
      Moneys on account of costs come to hands of defendant's solicitors for conduct of defence in action—Claim by plaintiff in that action that defendant trustee of all its assets for plaintiff—Separate action by plaintiff claiming that solicitor accountable to it for moneys received on account of costs from defendant in main action—Solicitors' knowledge of claim in main action—Liability of solicitors to account as constructive trustees to plaintiff. **Carl-Zeiss-Stiftung v Herbert Smith & Co (a firm) (No 2)** [1969] **2** 367, CA.
  Liability insurance—
    Professional indemnity insurance. *See* **Insurance** (Liability insurance—Professional indemnity insurance—Solicitor).
  Libel of solicitor—
    Letters by member of Parliament sent to Law Society and Lord Chancellor—
      Qualified privilege. *See* **Libel and slander** (Qualified privilege—Duty and interest—Member of Parliament).
  Lien—
    Equitable lien—
      Solicitors handling flight delay compensation claims—Majority of claims settled without dispute—Airline paying compensation direct to solicitors' clients—Solicitors losing opportunity to deduct fees from compensation paid—Whether solicitors entitled to equitable lien over compensation payments. **Bott & Co Solicitors Ltd v Ryanair DAC** [2022] **2 Comm** 475, SC; [2022] **4** 255, SC.
    Money in client account—
      Charging order—Plaintiff awarded decree of specific performance subject to payment of money to defendant—'Property recovered or preserved' through solicitor's instrumentality—Solicitors Act 1932, s 69. **Loescher v Dean** [1950] **2** 124, Ch D.
      Client's assets subject to Mareva injunction—Whether solicitor having lien over money in client account—Whether solicitor entitled to payment of costs out of money in client account. **Prekookeanska Plovidba v LNT Lines Srl** [1988] **3** 897, QBD.
    Money payable on compromise of actions—
      No application for charging order—Garnishee order nisi made in favour of client's judgment creditor—Creditor's right to have order made absolute—Solicitors Act 1932, s 69—RSC Ord 45, r 5. **Bibby (James) Ltd v Woods (Howard, Garnishee)** [1949] **2** 1, KBD.
      Personal injury claims in road traffic accidents—Clients entering conditional fee agreement (CFA) with solicitors—Notification of claims on online portal—Insurers settling claims direct with clients on terms not including solicitors' charges—Whether clients having contractual liability to pay solicitors' charges—Whether settlement debts owing creation to solicitors' services to clients under CFAs—Whether insurer having notice or knowledge of solicitors' interest in settlement debts. **Gavin Edmondson Solicitors Ltd v Haven Insurance Co Ltd** [2018] **3** 273, SC.
    Mortgage—
      Solicitor acting for mortgagor and mortgagee—Title deeds in custody and control of solicitor—Mortgagor owing to solicitor costs of transaction—Death of mortgagee—Solicitor one of the executors—Redemption action—Claim for lien raised by solicitor—Jus tertii—Order asked for premature. **Barratt v Gough-Thomas** [1945] **2** 650, CA.
    Property recovered or preserved in action—
      Property paid into joint account held in names of parties' solicitors—Defendants given leave to defend on condition they paid amount in dispute into joint account—Plaintiffs changing solicitors—Whether plaintiffs' new solicitors could be substituted for their former solicitors as holders of joint account—Whether plaintiffs' former solicitors having lien over fund in joint account. **Halvanon Insurance Co Ltd v Central Reinsurance Corp** [1988] **3** 857, QBD.
    Retaining lien—
      Divorce suit—Whether petitioner's solicitor entitled to absolute or qualified lien. **Hughes v Hughes** [1958] **3** 179, CA.
      Jurisdiction of court to grant relief in equity against exercise of solicitor's lien—Whether jurisdiction superseded by rules of court—RSC Ord 29, r 6. **Ismail v Richards Butler (a firm)** [1996] **2** 506, QBD.
      Lien over documents in respect of unpaid costs—Receiver of company requesting documents held by company's solicitors—Whether solicitors able to assert lien as against receiver. **Aveling Barford Ltd, Re** [1988] **3** 1019, Ch D.
      Lien over documents in respect of unpaid costs—Solicitor discharged during course of action—Client instructing new solicitor—First solicitor handing documents over to second solicitor—Second solicitor undertaking to hold documents to first solicitor's order in respect of outstanding fees and disbursements—Second solicitor photocopying documents and transmitting copies to client—Undertaking containing no express embargo on photocopying—Whether second solicitor in breach of undertaking. **Bentley v Gaisford** [1997] **1** 842, CA.

SOLICITOR (cont)—
  Lien (cont)—
    Retaining lien (cont)—
      Moneys in client account—Moneys held in professional capacity as solicitors—Moneys held for particular purpose. **Withers LLP (a firm) v Rybak (sun nom Withers LLP v Langbar International Ltd)** [2011] **3** 842n, Ch D; [2012] **2** 616, CA.

      Solicitor discharging himself in course of action—Non-payment of costs—Client instructing new solicitor—Client applying for order that papers in action be handed over to new solicitor—Whether solicitor who discharges himself required to hand over papers to new solicitor against undertaking to preserve his lien on the papers—Whether solicitor entitled to retain papers until court determines whether he had good cause to withdraw from action—Whether solicitor remaining client's solicitor until order made declaring that he has ceased to be client's solicitor—RSC Ord 67, r 6(1). **Gamlen Chemical Co (UK) Ltd v Rochem Ltd** [1980] **1** 1049, CA.

      Solicitor discharging himself in course of action—Non-payment of costs—Solicitor entering default judgment for amount of unpaid costs—Solicitor arresting client's vessel to secure payment of costs—Client applying for order that papers in action be handed over to new solicitor instructed by client—Whether arrest of vessel providing alternative security to lien—Whether solicitor waiving lien—Whether exceptional circumstances existing justifying court in refusing to order solicitor to hand over papers to new solicitor. **A v B** [1984] **1** 265, QBD.

      Solicitor discharging himself in course of action—Non-payment of costs—Solicitor instructed in respect of several matters some of which had previously been concluded—Solicitor having concurrent lien over live and dead cases—Whether client having general right to order that solicitor hand over papers to new solicitor against undertaking to preserve lien without providing further security—Whether exceptional circumstances existing justifying conditions as to provision of security in return for papers being handed over. **Ismail v Richards Butler (a firm)** [1996] **2** 506, QBD.

    Statutory lien or charging order—
      Charge on property recovered or preserved through solicitor's instrumentality—Solicitor taking security for costs—Whether waiver of right to charge on property recovered or preserved—Solicitors Act 1974, s 73. **Clifford Harris & Co v Solland International Ltd** [2005] **2** 334, Ch D.

      Funds in court to credit of partnership action—Extent of charge—Form of order—Solicitors Act 1932, s 69. **Kay v Lovell** [1940] **3** 89, Ch D.

      Order for costs only 'property recovered'—No distinction between order made on originating summons and any other order—Discretion of court to refuse order—Solicitors Act 1932, s 69. **Blake, Re** [1945] **1** 1, CA.

      Property sold in administration action—Proceeds paid into court—Extent of charge—Whether order limited to costs incurred in recovery of property—Solicitors Act 1932, s 69. **Clayton, Re** [1940] **2** 233, Ch D.

    Title deed and mortgage deed—
      Solicitor acting for mortgagor and mortgagee—Deeds in custody of solicitor—Death of mortgagee—Solicitor co-executor—Transfer of mortgage to solicitor—Redemption—Right of solicitor to retain deeds. **Barratt v Gough-Thomas** [1950] **2** 1048, .

    Title deeds—
      Preservation of lien after voluntary parting with possession of deeds—Deeds originally deposited with solicitors instructed by vendor to act in sale of property—Vendor changing solicitors—New solicitors asking original solicitors for deeds—Original solicitors' charges unpaid—Original solicitors handing over deeds subject to reservation that deeds held to their order pending payment of the outstanding charges—New solicitors refusing to accept reservation—Whether unilateral reservation sufficient to preserve original solicitors' lien. **Caldwell v Sumpters (a firm)** [1972] **1** 567, CA.

  Litigation—
    Delay in issuing and serving writ—
      Prejudice to client's claim to interest on damages—Liability of solicitor to client. **Jones v Jones** [1970] **3** 47, CA.

    Negligence. See Negligence—Litigation, *below*.
    Production of documents—
      Documents relating to action brought in name of applicant—Agreement giving insurance company absolute conduct and control of proceedings. **Crocker, Re** [1936] **2** 899, Ch D.

  Managing clerk—
    Conduct of case left to managing clerk—
      Payment of costs by solicitor personally. See Payment of costs by solicitor personally—Conduct of case left to managing clerk, *below*.

  Matrimonial proceedings—
    Acting for petitioner—
      Practice. See **Practice** (Family Division—Solicitor acting in matrimonial proceedings for petitioner).
    Decree granted in absence of party—
      Personal liability of solicitor for costs. See Payment of costs by solicitor personally—Matrimonial proceedings—Decree granted in absence of party, *below*.

  Medical report—
    Refusal to disclose—
      Misconduct or neglect—Costs. See Costs—Misconduct or neglect—Medical report—Refusal to disclose, *above*.

  Merger of firms of solicitors—
    Conflict of interest—
      Merging firms acting for opposing sides in litigation. See Duty—Conflict of interest—Merger of firms of solicitors, *above*.

  Misappropriation of means. See Dishonesty—Misappropriation of means, *above*.
  Mortgage—
    Lien on title deeds. See Lien—Mortgage, *above*.

SOLICITOR (cont)—
  Negligence—
    Action on motor insurance policy—
      Solicitor giving effect to pooling arrangement among insurance companies. **Groom v Crocker** [1938] **2** 394, CA.
    Causation—
      Damages—Negligent advice—Substantial property transaction involving company directors—Failure to advise board of plaintiff company on requirement for member approval—Members later rejecting transaction and demanding rescission—Company incurring loss—Whether solicitors' negligence effective cause of loss—Recovery of professional fees incurred in mitigating loss—Whether fees should be subject to some form of inquiry or taxation—Companies Act 1985, s 320. **British Racing Drivers' Club Ltd v Hextall Erskine & Co (a firm)** [1996] **3** 667, Ch D.
      Generally. See **Negligence** (Professional person—Causation).
    Cause of action—
      Accrual of cause of action. See **Limitation of action** (Accrual of cause of action—Negligence—Solicitor).
      Negligent advice—Accrual of action—Whether cause of action against solicitor complete when client acts on solicitor's negligent advice or when loss or damage occurs. **Forster v Outred & Co (a firm)** [1982] **2** 753, CA.
      Parallel claims in tort and contract. **Clark v Kirby-Smith** [1964] **2** 835, Ch D.
      Parallel claims in tort and contract—Limitation of action—Accrual of cause of action—Divorce—Matrimonial home in joint names of husband and wife—Property transferred into sole name of wife under agreement entitling husband to share of proceeds on sale—Solicitors failing to prepare declaration of trust or mortgage or register caution to protect husband's interest—Wife selling property eight years later and spending proceeds—Husband losing share in proceeds of sale and suing solicitors—When cause of action against solicitors accruing in contract and tort—Whether husband's cause of action time-barred. **Bell v Peter Browne & Co (a firm)** [1990] **3** 124, CA.
      Parallel claims in tort and contract—Solicitor drawing up option to purchase land—Solicitor acting for both grantor and grantee of option—Solicitor omitting to register option as estate contract—Grantor selling land to third party and defeating option—Grantee suing solicitor for negligence—Solicitor pleading that cause of action lay in contract only and consequently outside limitation period—Whether solicitor's duty to client under his retainer confined to contractual duty alone—Whether claim in tort for breach of duty to use reasonable care and skill precluded if there was a parallel contractual duty of care—Whether grantee able to sue solicitor in negligence. **Midland Bank Trust Co Ltd v Hett Stubbs & Kemp (a firm)** [1978] **3** 571, Ch D.
      Prejudice to client—Writ issued outside limitation period—Failure of application to override time limit—Personal injury or fatal accident claim. See **Limitation of action** (Court's power to override time limit in personal injury or fatal accident claim—Matters to which court may have regard—Prejudice to plaintiff—Remedy against solicitor—Plaintiff having remedy against solicitor for negligence if application to override time limit refused).
    Damages—
      Action not brought within limitation period—Action under Fatal Accidents Acts. **Kitchen v Royal Air Forces Association** [1958] **2** 241, CA.
      Action struck out for want of prosecution—Assessment of damages against solicitors where action struck out because delay on their part had rendered impossible fair trial of action—Approach to be adopted. **Sharif v Garrett & Co (a firm)** [2002] **3** 195, CA.
      Assessment of damages—Cost of cure. **Fulham Leisure Holdings Ltd v Nicholson Graham & Jones (a firm) (No 2)** [2006] **4** 1397n, Ch D.
      Assessment of damages—Date of assessment—Solicitor's negligence causing client to enter into unfavourable lease—Client unable to sell lease and surrendering it on payment of premium—Diminution in value principle not appropriate in assessing client's damages—Whether court could make general assessment of damages—Whether damages required to be assessed as at date of breach. **County Personnel (Employment Agency) Ltd v Alan R Pulver & Co (a firm)** [1987] **1** 289, CA.
      Cause of loss. See Negligence—Causation—Damages, *above*.
      Claimant bringing claim for personal injuries—Liability being admitted but claim struck out due to negligence of claimant's solicitors—Claimant bringing action for negligence against solicitors—Claimant diagnosed as having particular injury affecting earning capacity—After notional trial date claimant proving not to have particular injury—Whether court should take medical evidence subsequent to notional trial date into account in assessing damages. **Dudarec v Andrews** [2006] **2** 856, CA.
      Claimant bringing claim for personal injuries—Liability being admitted but claim struck out due to negligence of claimant's solicitors—Claimant bringing action for negligence against solicitors—Judge taking into account medical evidence subsequent to notional trial date in assessing damages—Whether judge entitled to do so—Whether judge should have made deduction for risks attendant on personal injury litigation. **Charles v Hugh James Jones & Jenkins (a firm)** [2000] **1** 289, CA.
      Client's action founded in contract—Measure of damages. **Bailey v Bullock** [1950] **2** 1167, KBD.
      Conveyance of building—Vendor's solicitor retained by purchaser—Discovery that plans of building not approved by local authority—Purchaser not informed. **Lake v Bushby** [1949] **2** 964, KBD.
      Loss of a chance—Claim against solicitors for lost opportunity to bring claim under government compensation scheme—Medical evidence post-dating settlement—Whether relevant to issue of loss. **Edwards v Hugh James Ford Simey Solicitors** [2020] **1** 749, SC.
      Measure of damages. See **Damages** (Measure of damages—Negligence—Solicitor).
      Mitigation of loss. See **Damages** (Mitigation of loss—Reasonable steps to mitigate damage—Professional negligence).
      New tenancy of business premises—Landlord's notice to quit stated intention not to oppose new tenancy—Solicitor instructed to apply for new tenancy—Failure to give notice of tenant's unwillingness to give up possession—No evidence from which value of any new tenancy granted could be estimated—Nominal damages only. **Clark v Kirby-Smith** [1964] **2** 835, Ch D.
      Purchase of freehold property by client—Defect in title—Damages recoverable by client—Duty to minimise loss. **Pilkington v Wood** [1953] **2** 810, Ch D.

SOLICITOR (cont)—
 Negligence (cont)—
  Damages (cont)—
   Sale of land—Delay in completion of sub-sale—Interest on mortgage and loss of interest on profit on sub-sale—Purchaser's solicitor failing to ensure title free from encumbrances—Failure to search commons register—Purchaser ignorant that land subject to registration in commons register—Purchaser having effected purchase by means of a loan on mortgage—Purchaser having secured sub-sale at substantial profit—Registration as common land made by mistake—Delay in completion of sub-sale caused by need to secure removal of entry from commons register—Whether purchaser entitled to claim as damages from solicitor interest paid on mortgage and interest lost on profit on sub-sale during period of delay. **G & K Ladenbau (UK) Ltd v Crawley & de Reya (a firm)** [1978] **1** 682, QBD.

   Sale of land—Exchange of contracts by purchasers' solicitors without sufficiently satisfying themselves that there were no building restrictions on land purchased—Vacant land in fact subject to such restrictions—Market value of land subject to restrictions equivalent to price paid by purchasers—Whether damages nil. **Ford v White & Co** [1964] **2** 755, Ch D.

   Sale of land—Requisition answered in accordance with general conveyancing practice—Purchaser thereby enabled to refuse to complete and to recover deposit—Opportunity for re-sale pending trial of action for return of deposit—Advice against re-sale—Premises subsequently damaged by fire—Remoteness of damage. **Simmons v Pennington & Son (a firm)** [1955] **1** 240, CA.

   Tenant in tail—Failure to advise disentailment—Death of tenant in tail—Diminution of estate—Damages recoverable by personal representative of tenant in tail. **Otter v Church, Adams, Tatham & Co (a firm)** [1953] **1** 168, Ch D.

   Will—Solicitor instructed to draft wills for two clients, man and woman, wishing to confer benefits on each other—Failure to advise clients in regard to revocation of wills on marriage—Marriage of clients after wills executed—Damage suffered by wife on death of husband intestate—Remoteness of damage—Measure of damages. **Hall v Meyrick** [1957] **2** 722, CA.

  Discontinuance of action—
   Fatal accident. See **Fatal accident** (Action—Right of action—Action for damages for personal injury negligently discontinued after claimant's death).

  Dismissal of action for want of prosecution—
   Remedy against plaintiff's solicitors. See **Practice** (Dismissal of action for want of prosecution—Remedy against plaintiff's solicitors—Delay caused by negligence of plaintiff's solicitors).

  Duty of care—
   Defendant solicitors advising claimant companies on acquisition and post-acquisition restructuring plans—Advice resulting in claimants 'pushing down' debt to its foreign subsidiary to obtain tax relief on interest payments in foreign jurisdiction—Foreign tax authorities determining interest payments being dividends not eligible for tax relief—Whether solicitors negligent. **Symrise AG v Baker & McKenzie (a firm)** [2016] **1 Comm** 603, QBD.

   Existence of duty. See **Negligence** (Duty to take care—Existence of duty).

   Instructions—Solicitors instructed by company to prepare draft contract of service for executive director—Executive director instructing solicitors as to terms of contract—Solicitors providing draft contract to company for approval—Whether draft contract requiring explanation—Whether solicitors in breach of duty of care. **Newcastle International Airport Ltd v Eversheds LLP** [2014] **2** 728, CA.

   Mortgage business—Solicitor acting for both lender and borrower—Scope of duty to borrower—Whilst carrying out searches solicitors coming across information suggesting property over-valued—Solicitors not informing lender—Lender making loan and subsequently suffering loss—Whether solicitors under duty to disclose information—Whether failure to disclose information a cause of lender's loss. **Goldsmith Williams Solicitors v E.Surv Ltd** [2016] **4** 229, CA.

   Negligent misrepresentation—Damages for breach of duty of care—Defence of contributory negligence. See **Misrepresentation** (Negligent misrepresentation—Damages for breach of duty of care—Contributory negligence).

   Negligent misrepresentation—Duty owed to third party—Solicitor acting for borrower—Whether solicitor assuming responsibility to commercial lender. **NRAM Ltd (formerly NRAM plc) v Steel (Scotland)** [2018] **3** 81, SC.

   Negligent misrepresentation—Sale of land—Duty owed to third party dealing with client—Inquiries before contract—Plaintiff acquiring underlease of premises from defendant—Headlease containing redevelopment break clause—Defendant's solicitors stating in answer to inquiries that there were no rights in headlease affecting plaintiff's enjoyment of property—Whether solicitor acting for vendor owing duty of care to purchaser when answering inquiries before contract—Whether defendant's solicitors liable to plaintiff for misrepresentation. **Gran Gelato Ltd v Richcliff (Group) Ltd** [1992] **1** 865, Ch D.

  Duty to exercise reasonable skill and care—
   Generally. See **Negligence** (Professional person—Duty to exercise reasonable skill and care).

   Unusual clause in lease—Duty to explain clause to client and alert client to risk of entering into unusual lease. **County Personnel (Employment Agency) Ltd v Alan R Pulver & Co (a firm)** [1987] **1** 289, CA.

  Immunity—
   Extent of immunity—Plaintiff's conviction quashed on appeal—Plaintiff suing solicitors for negligence in conduct of his defence in criminal proceedings—Whether solicitors immune from suit—Whether relitigating criminal trial contrary to public policy. **Acton v Graham Pearce & Co (a firm)** [1997] **3** 909, Ch D.

   Immunity when acting as an advocate—Advice as to plea in criminal proceedings—Extent of immunity. **Somasundaram v M Julius Melchior & Co (a firm)** [1989] **1** 129, CA.

SOLICITOR (cont)—
Negligence (cont)—
Inadequate advice—
Duty where solicitor advising individual as to intended provision of security in transaction for sole financial benefit of another in close personal relationship with individual—Client seeking independent advice as to transaction giving substantial assets to husband to avoid criminal prosecution of husband—Solicitor simply advising client not to proceed—Another solicitor in firm subsequently witnessing signatures to documents containing statement that client had taken advice and certifying client's free agreement and consent to mortgage—Extent of solicitors' duty to client. **Padden v Bevan Ashford (a firm)** [2012] **2** 718, CA.
Solicitor consulted by injured workman in respect of accident—Advice as to workmen's compensation—Failure to advise in respect of common law rights. **Griffiths v Evans** [1953] **2** 1364, CA.
Inter vivos gift—
Duty of care—Instructions to draft document giving effect to present right to future payment of gift—Solicitor drafting document and informing intended recipient that it was akin to a trust—Document not giving intended recipient of gift any enforceable rights—Donor subsequently refusing to fulfil promise—Whether solicitor owing duty of care to intended recipient—Whether solicitor liable for negligent misrepresentation. **Hemmens v Wilson Browne (a firm)** [1993] **4** 826, Ch D.
Litigation—
Acts or omissions in conduct of litigation—Whether an action for negligence can lie against a solicitor in regard to acts or omissions in litigation which, if counsel had been engaged, would have been within the province of counsel. **Rondel v Worsley** [1967] **3** 993, HL.
Measure of damages. *See* **Damages** (Measure of damages—Negligence—Solicitor).
Negligent misrepresentation—
Mortgage transaction—Solicitor acting for both borrower and building society—Solicitor incorrectly reporting to society that borrower having no other indebtedness and that no second charge contemplated—Society relying on representations in report and making mortgage advance—Borrower subsequently defaulting on mortgage and society suffering loss when realising its security—Whether solicitor liable in negligence to society for net loss arising from borrower's subsequent default—Whether solicitor in breach of trust or fiduciary duty to society. **Bristol and West Building Society v Mothew (t/a Stapley & Co)** [1996] **4** 698, CA.
Partnership—
Liability of solicitor for acts of partner—Plaintiff bringing action against partnership for negligence—Second defendant contending that he was not a partner in firm, but was merely held out as a partner—Whether second defendant liable on basis that he was held out as a partner. **Nationwide Building Society v Lewis** [1998] **3** 143, CA.
Registration of club—
Failure to notify client of refusal of registration. **Ashton v Wainwright** [1936] **1** 805, KBD.
Sale of dwelling-house—
Solicitor acting both for vendor and for purchaser—Duty to ascertain standard rent. **Goody v Baring** [1956] **2** 11, Ch D.
Sale of land—
Search of commons register—Circumstances in which purchaser's solicitor under a duty to client to search commons register—Land vacant and unbuilt on—Earlier conveyance indicating that part of land had until recently belonged to lord of the manor—Client intending to develop land—Importance to client of obtaining title free from encumbrances. **G & K Ladenbau (UK) Ltd v Crawley & de Reya (a firm)** [1978] **1** 682, QBD.
Sub-lease—
Duty of potential sub-lessee's solicitor to inspect head lease to ascertain covenants affecting premises. **Hill v Harris** [1965] **2** 358, CA.
Undertaking—
Breach of undertaking—Duty owed to third party—Husband's solicitors giving implied undertaking to wife's solicitors not to release husband's passport—Husband obtaining passport because of his solicitors' negligence and using it to leave United Kingdom with his children contrary to court order—Whether husband's solicitors owing duty to wife—Whether husband's solicitors in breach of that duty—Whether damage caused to wife too remote. **Al-Kandari v J R Brown & Co (a firm)** [1988] **1** 833, CA.
Breach of undertaking—Remedy—Solicitors acting for vendor in conveyancing transaction undertaking to redeem and discharge first and second charges—Solicitors remitting net proceeds of sale to vendor's account at first chargee bank—First chargee bank demanding payment from vendor of all indebtedness—First chargee bank appointing receiver—Appointment of receiver entitling second chargee to demand repayment of all sums outstanding—Solicitors breaching undertaking to redeem and discharge second charge—Whether performance of undertaking impossible. **Clark v Lucas Solicitors LLP** [2010] **2** 955, Ch D.
Will—
Duty of care—Instructions to draw up will conferring benefit on identified beneficiary—Defendant solicitors failing to execute valid will giving effect to testatrix's testamentary intentions—Court ordering costs of proceedings challenging validity of will to be paid out of estate—Solicitors paying disappointed residuary beneficiaries sum amounting to full value of residuary estate undiminished by costs of will action—Testatrix's personal representative bringing proceedings against solicitors seeking recovery of costs of will action—Whether negligent solicitors having liability to testatrix's estate for costs of proceedings challenging validity of will. **Corbett v Bond Pearce (a firm)** [2001] **3** 769, CA.
Duty of care—Instructions to draw up will conferring benefit on identified beneficiary—Solicitor failing to draw up will—Testator dying before will prepared or executed—Whether solicitor owing duty of care to intended beneficiary. **White v Jones** [1995] **1** 691, HL.
Duty of care—Instructions to draw up will conferring benefit on identified beneficiary—Solicitor failing to ensure that testatrix severed her joint tenancy in property disposed of by will—Property passing by survivorship and gift to beneficiary ineffective—Whether solicitor owing duty of care to intended beneficiary—Whether solicitor liable in negligence to beneficiary. **Carr-Glynn v Frearsons (a firm)** [1997] **2** 614, Ch D; [1998] **4** 225, CA.

Duty of care—Instructions to draw up will conferring benefit on identified beneficiary—Solicitor failing to warn testator that attestation by beneficiary's spouse would invalidate gift—Beneficiary's husband attesting will—Solicitor failing to notice attestation by him—Gift to beneficiary void—Whether solicitor owing duty of care to beneficiary—Whether solicitor liable in negligence to beneficiary—Whether fact a loss purely financial precluding claim in negligence—Whether beneficiary entitled to damages for legal expenses of investigating claim up to date of issue of writ. **Ross v Caunters (a firm)** [1979] **3** 580, Ch D.

Duty of care—Instructions to draw up will conferring bequest on beneficiary—Solicitor subsequently acting for testator in transaction concerning asset included in bequest—Transaction adversely affecting beneficiary's interest in bequest—Solicitor failing to advise testator of effect of transaction on beneficiary's interest—Whether solicitor owing duty of care to beneficiary. **Clarke v Bruce Lance & Co (a firm)** [1988] **1** 364, CA.

Duty of care—Testatrix leaving properties to beneficiary—Solicitors allegedly failing to progress administration of estate for five years—Executrix suing to recover loss of income on properties during five-year period—Whether executrix having cause of action. **Chappell v Somers & Blake (a firm)** [2003] **3** 1076, Ch D.

Duty of care—Will executed—Disappointed beneficiary claiming will failing to record testatrix's instructions—Whether beneficiary having remedy in negligence—Whether beneficiary should apply for rectification. **Walker v Geo H Medlicott & Son (a firm)** [1999] **1** 685, CA.

Non-contentious business—
Costs. *See* Costs—Non-contentious business, *above*.
Retainer. *See* Retainer—Termination of retainer—Non-contentious business, *below*.

Note—
Hearing before official referee—
Appeal—Substitution of note taken by solicitors for official referee's note. *See* **Court of Appeal** (Judge's note—Substitution of note taken by solicitors—Appeal from official referee).

Notice—
Signature—
Sufficiency of solicitor's signature to notice to terminate a licence on behalf of company, which itself was an agent. *See* **Licence** (Notice to terminate occupation).

Official Solicitor—
Costs. *See* **Costs** (Official Solicitor).
Generally. *See* **Official Solicitor**.

Parties—
Misnomer. *See* **Practice** (Parties—Misnomer—Solicitor).

Partnership—
Dissolution—
Lapse of practising certificate—Unlawful for person to act as a solicitor without a practising certificate—Partner inadvertently allowing practising certificate to lapse—Whether partnership dissolved by operation of law—Whether partnership reconstituted between remaining partners—Partnership Act 1890, s 34. **Hudgell Yeates & Co v Watson** [1978] **2** 363, CA.

Negligence. *See* Negligence—Partnership, *above*.

Restraint of trade by agreement—
Generally. *See* **Restraint of trade by agreement** (Partnership—Solicitors).

Solicitor employed by partnership—
Restraint of trade by agreement. *See* **Restraint of trade by agreement** (Employer and employee—Employee of partnership—Solicitor).

Payment of costs by solicitor personally—
Appeal against order that solicitor be personally liable—
Jurisdiction of Court of Appeal. *See* **Court of Appeal** (Jurisdiction—Appeal from order for costs—Order that solicitor be personally liable for costs).

Application for solicitor to pay costs personally—
Solicitors instructed by undischarged bankrupt in property claim—Solicitors unaware of client's bankruptcy—Solicitors not acting improperly, unreasonably or negligently—Solicitors commencing action and obtaining Mareva injunction—Injunction discharged on client admitting he was a bankrupt—Judge ordering solicitors to pay costs of proceedings—Whether proper exercise of discretion. **Nelson v Nelson** [1997] **1** 970, CA.

Summary jurisdiction—Solicitor ceasing to be on the record—Form of application—Solicitors Act 1932, s 5(1). **Brendon v Spiro** [1937] **2** 496, CA.

Trial judge criticising conduct of solicitor in his judgment—Trial judge referring findings to Law Society—Whether trial judge should hear and determine application—Whether trial judge disqualified from hearing application because of bias—RSC Ord 62, r 8. **Bahai v Rashidian** [1985] **3** 385, CA.

Conduct of case left to managing clerk—
Inadequate affidavits of documents—False to knowledge of clerk—Whether solicitor can be made personally responsible for costs. **Myers v Elman** [1939] **4** 484, HL.

Costs incurred by failure to conduct proceedings with reasonable competence and expedition—
Failure to comply with local practice direction of county court—Whether court having jurisdiction to order payment of costs by solicitor personally—RSC Ord 62, r 1(1)—CCR Ord 38, r 1. **Langley v North West Water Authority** [1991] **3** 610, CA.

Costs incurred unreasonably or improperly—
Application for leave to apply for judicial review withdrawn at hearing attended by prospective respondent—Whether wasted costs order appropriate—Whether prospective respondent a 'party' to proceedings—Whether court having jurisdiction to make wasted costs order in favour of prospective respondent—Supreme Court Act 1981, ss 51, 151. **R v Camden London BC, ex p Martin** [1997] **1** 307, QBD.

Defendant in criminal proceedings deliberately absenting himself from trial—Solicitor withdrawing—Judge making wasted costs order against solicitor—Whether solicitor's conduct unreasonable—Prosecution of Offences Act 1985, s 19A. **Boodhoo (wasted costs order), Re** [2007] **4** 762n, CA.

SOLICITOR (cont)—
Payment of costs by solicitor personally (cont)—
Costs incurred unreasonably or improperly (cont)—
Jurisdiction to order solicitor to pay wasted costs—Exercise of jurisdiction—Legal representatives ordered to pay personally opponents' costs—Whether conduct complained of 'improper, unreasonable or negligent'—Whether advocate immune in respect of conduct of litigation—Whether wasted costs order appropriate—Guidance on exercise of jurisdiction to impose wasted costs orders—Supreme Court Act 1981, s 51(6), (7)—Courts and Legal Services Act 1990, s 62. **Ridehalgh v Horsefield** [1994] **3** 848, CA.

Jurisdiction to order solicitor to pay wasted costs—Solicitors ordered to pay personally opponent's costs—Whether solicitors' conduct unreasonable—Whether wasted costs order appropriate—Supreme Court Act 1981, s 51(1), (3), (6), (7). **Tolstoy-Miloslavsky (Count) v Lord Aldington** [1996] **2** 556, CA.

Solicitor for defendant responsible for costs thrown away in civil proceedings—Conduct of solicitor not amounting to serious misconduct—Whether court having jurisdiction to order payment of costs by solicitor personally—Whether necessary that conduct of solicitor amounting serious dereliction of duty—RSC Ord 62, r 11(1). **Gupta v Comer** [1991] **1** 289, CA.

Solicitor swearing affidavit in support of petition to wind up company as insolvent—Solicitor having no grounds for believing company to be insolvent—Solicitor knowing petition bound to fail if fought on merits—Whether solicitor acting improperly or unreasonably—Whether order for wasted costs appropriate—Supreme Court Act 1981, s 51(6). **Company (No 006798 of 1995), Re a** [1996] **2** 417, Ch D.

Solicitors for defendant failing to apply promptly to set aside judgment entered against defendant in default and failing to inform plaintiff promptly that defendant had been granted legal aid and would be applying to set aside judgment—Plaintiff seeking order that defendant's solicitors pay the costs personally—Whether sufficient cause for order for costs to be made—RSC Ord 62, r 11. **Sinclair-Jones v Kay** [1988] **2** 611, CA.

Solicitors for defendants responsible for omissions in conduct of criminal proceedings—Courts ordering fresh trials or adjournments as a result of solicitors' omissions—Courts also ordering solicitors to pay personally whole or part of wasted costs—Whether solicitors' omissions amounting to serious dereliction of duty—Whether sufficient cause for orders for costs to be made against solicitors personally—Whether different considerations applying to civil and criminal cases. **Holden & Co (a firm) v CPS** [1990] **1** 368, CA.

Crown Court—
Jurisdiction to order solicitor personally to pay costs occasioned by his negligence. **R v Smith (Martin)** [1974] **1** 651, CA.

Delay by solicitor—
Payment into court—Defendant prevented from making payment into court because of delay by plaintiff's solicitors in providing particulars of damages claimed—Whether plaintiff's solicitors personally liable for costs for preventing defendant from making effective payment in—Whether late payment into court by defendant effective—RSC Ord 62, r 11, Ord 22, r 3. **King v Weston-Howell** [1989] **2** 375, CA.

Disclosure of privileged documents in application for solicitor to pay costs personally—
Defendants making admission shortly before trial contradicting initial defence—Plaintiff contending that defendants' solicitors knowingly conducted defence on false basis and applying for wasted costs order—Solicitors seeking disclosure of privileged documents containing statements made to them by defendants—Whether rule of court on disclosure of privileged documents in wasted costs applications ultra vires—Civil Procedure Act 1997, Sch 1, para 4—Civil Procedure Rules 1998, r 48.7(3). **General Mediterranean Holdings SA v Patel** [1999] **3** 673, QBD.

Divorce—
Intervention by Queen's Proctor. *See* **Divorce** (Intervention—Queen's Proctor showing cause why a decree nisi should not be made absolute—Costs—Fault by solicitors).

Error in estimate of length of trial—
Transfer of case from short non-jury list to long non-jury list—RSC Ord 36, r 29(6). **Ibbs v Holloway Bros Ltd** [1952] **1** 220, KBD.

Failure to give notice of legal aid certificate—
Failure due to mere oversight—Judgment in favour of unassisted party—Liability of solicitors for costs—Whether costs improper or wasted—Legal Aid (General) Regulations 1962 (SI 1962 No 148) reg 16(2)—RSC Ord 62, r 8. **Mauroux v Sociedade Comercial Abel Pereira da Fonseca SARL** [1972] **2** 1085, Ch D.

Failure to watch cause list—
No attendance in court, personally or by counsel, when case called on. **Practice Note** [1962] **1** 768, QBD.

Improper continuance of proceedings—
Change of position on discovery—Irrelevance of civil aid certificate—RSC Ord 65, r 11—Legal Aid and Advice Act 1949, s 1(7)(b). **Edwards v Edwards** [1958] **2** 179, Div.

Legal aid—
Legally-aided plaintiff bringing unsuccessful action against defendants—Defendants seeking order for costs against solicitor personally on ground that plaintiff's claim so hopeless that solicitor by inference guilty of serious misconduct in allowing action to continue—Plaintiff not waiving client's privilege—Whether order for costs against solicitor appropriate—RSC Ord 62, r 8(1). **Orchard v South Eastern Electricity Board** [1987] **1** 95, CA.

Matrimonial proceedings—
Decree granted in absence of party. **Wilkinson v Wilkinson** [1962] **1** 922, CA.

Disregard of client's instructions to contest damages—Costs wasted by default—Supreme Court Costs Rules 1959, r 8(1). **Jakeman v Jakeman and Turner** [1963] **3** 889, Div.

Letters sent to wrong address—Costs wasted by default—Supreme Court Costs Rules 1959, r 8(1). **D v D** [1963] **1** 602, Div.

Maintenance order made in husband's absence. **Kaye v Kaye** [1964] **1** 620, PDA.

SOLICITOR (cont)—
　Payment of costs by solicitor personally (cont)—
　　Reliance on counsel's advice—
　　　Legal aid—Legal aid certificate granted on basis of counsel's advice—Counsel subsequently
　　　reconsidering advice—Solicitor relying completely on counsel's advice—Solicitor failing to
　　　inform legal aid committee of change of circumstances of litigation—Application not granted by
　　　court-Law Society applying for costs of both parties to be paid by solicitor personally—Whether
　　　solicitor having duty to inform legal aid committee of change of circumstances—Whether
　　　reliance on advice of properly instructed counsel absolving solicitor from being guilty of
　　　dereliction of duty—Legal Aid Act 1974, s 13(1)—RSC Ord 62, r 8(1). **Davy-Chiesman v
　　　Davy-Chiesman** [1984] **1** 321, CA.
　Removal of case from cause list—
　　Failure to notify Crown Office of order involving removal of case from cause list. **Williamson v
　　British Boxing Board of Control (1929)** [1958] **2** 228, QBD.
　Setting aside order—
　　Order set aside in absence of notice of complaint and opportunity to answer it—Supreme Court
　　Costs Rules 1959, r 8(1) (c), (2). **Abraham v Jutsun** [1963] **2** 402, CA.
　Solicitor acting for legally-aided client. See Payment of costs by solicitor personally—Legal aid, *above*.
　Want of authority to institute action—
　　Action in name of foreign corporation—Corporation domiciled in Eastern Zone of Germany—Law
　　applicable to determine authority to sue. **Carl-Zeiss-Stiftung v Rayner & Keeler Ltd (No 2)**
　　[1966] **2** 536, HL.
Practice—
　Advocate—
　　Duty in regard to taking doubtful points of law. **Abraham v Jutsun** [1963] **2** 402, CA.
　　Liability in negligence—Whether an action for negligence as an advocate can lie against a solicitor.
　　Rondel v Worsley [1967] **3** 993, HL.
　　Right of audience—Crown Court. See **Crown Court** (Practice—Solicitor—Right of audience).
　Costs—
　　Before-the-event (BTE) insurance—Steps to be taken by solicitor to discover whether BTE insurance
　　available to client—Guidance. **Sarwar v Alam** [2001] **4** 541, CA.
　　Generally. See Costs, *above*.
　　Payment of costs by solicitor personally. See Payment of costs by solicitor personally, *above*.
　Defence certificate—
　　Right to undertake necessary work in giving notice of appeal or application for leave to appeal after
　　conviction recorded—Poor Prisoners' Defence (Defence Certificate) Regulations 1960 (SI 1960
　　No 260), reg 6. **R v Mullins** [1962] **3** 237, CCA.
　Guarantees—
　　Ordinary activity of practice—Whether giving of temporary guarantees to clients was ordinary
　　activity of practice of solicitor. **Jennings (Inspector of Taxes) v Barfield & Barfield** [1962] **2** 957,
　　Ch D.
　Rent assessment committee—
　　Effect of membership of panel on practice of solicitor before committee or rent officer.
　　Metropolitan Properties Co (FGC) v Lannon [1968] **3** 304, CA.
　Withdrawal. See Withdrawal, *below*.
Practising certificate—
　Articled clerk. See Articled clerk—Qualification for solicitor to take, *above*.
　Lapse—
　　Dissolution of partnership. See Partnership—Dissolution—Lapse of practising certificate, *above*.
　Retrospective effect to 16th November where taken out before 16th December—
　　Lack of qualification to practise during interval between 16th November and date of issue if
　　certificate issued after 15th December. **Adlam v Law Society** [1968] **1** 17, Ch D.
Prisoner's correspondence with. See **Prison** (Letters—Prisoner's letters—Correspondence with legal
　adviser).
Privilege—
　Legal professional privilege—
　　Disclosure and inspection of documents. See **Disclosure and inspection of documents** (Legal
　　professional privilege).
　　Generally. See **Privilege** (Legal professional privilege).
　Privilege against liability for defamation. See Disciplinary proceedings—Disciplinary committee—
　　Privilege against liability for defamation, *above*.
Production of documents. See Litigation—Production of documents, *above*.
Professional indemnity insurance. See **Insurance** (Liability insurance—Professional indemnity insurance—
　Solicitor).
Recovery of costs. See Costs—Recovery—Action to recover, *above*.
Remuneration—
　Charging below scale fee—
　　Solicitor acting for both mortgagor purchaser and mortgagee—Purchaser charged less than scale
　　fee—Solicitors' Remuneration Act General Order 1882, Sch I, Part I, r 6—Solicitors' Practice Rules
　　1936 (SR & O 1936 No 1005), rr 1, 2(A). **Solicitor, Re a** [1951] **2** 108, KBD.
　Legal aid—
　　Taxation of costs—Solicitor's fees and expenses—Criminal proceedings—Fair remuneration. See
　　Legal aid (Taxation of costs—Solicitor's fees and expenses—Criminal proceedings—Fair
　　remuneration).
　Non-contentious business—
　　Taxation of costs. See **Costs** (Taxation—Solicitor—Non-contentious business).

SOLICITOR (cont)—
Remuneration (cont)—
Order prescribing and regulating remuneration for non-contentious business—
Statutory committee—Duty to act fairly—Proposals for major change in method of remuneration—Preparation of draft order—Consultation with outside bodies—Draft required to be sent to the Council of the Law Society—Observations of council to be submitted to statutory committee within one month of receipt—Draft of order abolishing scale fees—Whether when major change proposed period should be extended and representative bodies other than council consulted—Whether draft sent to council should be first approved by committee—Solicitors Act 1957, s 56. **Practice Direction** [1972] 3 1019, Fam D.
Recovery. See Costs—Recovery, *above.*
Taxation of solicitor's bill of costs—
Procedure—Originating summons—Drawing up of order—Appeals—Appeal to judge in chambers—Fees payable—Applications to which direction applies—Solicitors Act 1974, Pt III, ss 57(5), 61(1), (3), (5), 62, 63, 64(3), 68, 69, 70(1), (2), (3), 73—RSC Ord 28, r 1A(1), Ord 32, Ord 42, rr 4, 5, Ord 58, Ord 106, r 3(1), (2), App A. **Practice Direction** [1990] 3 474, SC Taxing Office.
Rent assessment committee—
Effect of membership of panel on practice of solicitor before committee or rent officer. *See* Practice—Rent assessment committee, *above.*
Reputation—
Slander. *See* **Libel and slander** (Slander actionable per se—Official, professional or business reputation of plaintiff—Solicitor).
Retainer—
Novation of retainer—
Executor instructing solicitor in sole practice in administration of estate—Solicitor entering into partnership—Solicitor informing executor beforehand of change—Whether novation of retainer taking place. **Burton Marsden Douglas (a firm), Re** [2004] 3 222, Ch D.
Retainer to prosecute a succession of matters—
Entire contract—Termination—Costs. **Warmington v McMurray** [1937] 1 562, CA.
Termination of retainer—
Champerty—Champertous agreement—Differential fee contingent on outcome of litigation—Dispute over unpaid fees under the retainer—Whether retainer void or unenforceable against client—Whether client obliged to pay outstanding fees. **Aratra Potato Co Ltd v Taylor Joynson Garrett (a firm)** [1995] 4 695, QBD.
Mental incapacity of client—Solicitor instructed in personal injury claim under conditional fee arrangement—Client losing mental capacity—Whether mental incapacity of client terminating retainer. **Blankley v Central Manchester and Manchester Children's University Hospitals NHS Trust** [2014] 2 1104, QBD; [2016] 3 382, CA.
Non-contentious business—Legal work in connection with a property development and likely to extend over years—Whether entire contract—Whether retainer terminable by client on notice. **Milner (JH) & Son v Percy Bilton Ltd** [1966] 2 894, QBD.
Solicitor exceeding costs estimate supplied to client at time of engagement—Client refusing to pay fees in excess of costs estimate -Solicitor refusing to provide services until bill paid—Whether client having reasonable justification for withholding payment—Whether solicitor wrongfully terminating or suspending retainer. **Minkin v Cawdery Kaye Fireman & Taylor (a firm) (t/a CKFT)** [2012] 3 1117, CA.
Termination for good reason—Client retaining solicitors to advise and prosecute statutory planning appeal—Client instructing solicitors to advance points solicitors considering not properly arguable—Solicitors terminating retainer—Whether termination for good reason—Whether solicitors not able to terminate retainer unless advancing client's claim involving impropriety or misleading the court. **Richard Buxton (a firm) v Mills-Owens** [2010] 4 405, CA.
Terms and limits of solicitor's retainer—
Solicitor drawing up option to purchase land—Solicitor acting for both grantor and grantee of option—Solicitor omitting to register option as estate contract—Grantee consulting solicitor from time to time concerning exercise of option—Whether solicitor under duty to consider registration and enforceability of option when consulted about its exercise—Whether solicitor under general retainer to consider all aspects of client's interests when consulted by client on a specific problem. **Midland Bank Trust Co Ltd v Hett Stubbs & Kemp (a firm)** [1978] 3 571, Ch D.
Retaining lien. *See* Lien—Retaining lien, *above.*
Right of audience—
Crown Court. *See* **Crown Court** (Practice—Solicitor—Right of audience).
High Court. *See* **Practice** (Audience—Right of audience—High Court of Justice—Solicitor).
Patent proceedings. *See* **Patent** (Practice—Telephone summonses).
Sale of land—
Acting for vendor and purchaser—
Danger of so acting. **Smith v Mansi** [1962] 3 857, CA.
Exchange of contracts—
Authority of solicitor. *See* **Sale of land** (Exchange of contracts—Authority of solicitor).
Negligence—
Damages. *See* Negligence—Damages—Sale of land, *above.*
Negligent misrepresentation—Scope of solicitor's duty of care. *See* Negligence—Duty of care—Negligent misrepresentation—Sale of land, *above.*
Requisitions on title—
Duty of purchaser's solicitor. *See* **Sale of land** (Requisitions on title—Duty of purchaser's solicitor).
Warranty of authority—
Solicitor mistakenly believing that he was representing vendor and negotiating on vendor's behalf with purchaser's solicitor whom he knew to be acting for building society—Whether solicitor giving warranty of authority to both purchaser and building society—Whether building society's loss caused by solicitor's breach of warranty. **Penn v Bristol and West Building Society** [1997] 3 470, CA.
Scale fees—
Charging below scale fee. *See* Remuneration—Charging below scale fee, *above.*
Singapore. *See* **Singapore** (Advocate and solicitor).

SOLICITOR (cont)—
Solicitor advocate—
    Conflict of interest. *See* Duty—Conflict of interest—Solicitor advocate, *above.*
Solicitor's clerk—
    Access to persons in police custody. *See* Access to—Right of person in custody—Access by solicitor's clerk, *above.*
    Generally. *See* **Solicitor's clerk**.
Solicitor's estate—
    Law Society's nominees. *See* **Probate** (Grant—Solicitor's estate).
Solicitor's practice—
    Gift in will. *See* **Will** (Gift—Business—Solicitor's practice).
Stakeholder—
    Deposit paid to solicitor as stakeholder—
        Solicitor paying out deposit to one party on happening of specified event—Other party objecting to payment out—Whether stakeholder required to retain deposit pending arbitration of dispute between parties—Whether stakeholder's position affected by his position as solicitor for one of the parties. **Hastingwood Property Ltd v Saunders Bearman Anselm (a firm)** [1990] **3** 107, Ch D.
Suspension from practice. *See* Disciplinary proceedings, *above.*
Taxation of bill of costs—
    Generally. *See* **Costs** (Taxation—Solicitor).
    Legal aid cases. *See* **Legal aid** (Taxation of costs).
    Procedure. *See* Remuneration—Taxation of solicitor's bill of costs—Procedure, *above.*
    Solicitor acting on his own behalf—
        Value added tax. *See* **Costs** (Taxation—Value added tax—Solicitor acting on his own behalf).
    Telephone calls—
        Family Division. *See* **Costs** (Taxation—Family Division—Solicitor—Telephone calls).
Telephone calls—
    Taxation of bill of costs—
        Family Division. *See* **Costs** (Taxation—Family Division—Solicitor—Telephone calls).
Tenant in tail—
    Negligence. *See* Negligence—Damages—Tenant in tail, *above.*
Title deeds—
    Lien. *See* Lien—Title deeds, *above.*
Trial—
    Error in estimate of length of trial—
        Payment of costs by solicitor personally. *See* Payment of costs by solicitor personally—Error in estimate of length of trial, *above.*
Tribunal—
    Whether party entitled to be legally represented before domestic tribunal. *See* **Natural justice** (Domestic tribunal—Legal representation).
Trust—
    Trust documents—
        Inspection—Letter of trust's solicitors to the trustees. **Londonderry's Settlement, Re** [1964] **3** 855, CA.
Trustee—
    Remuneration—
        Professional charging clause. *See* **Trust and trustee** (Remuneration of trustee—Professional trustee—Charging clause).
    Solicitor acting on instructions of trustees—
        Breach of trust. *See* **Trust and trustee** (Breach of trust—Action by beneficiary—Constructive trustee—Solicitor acting for trustees).
    Solicitor trustee. *See* Duty—Conflict of duty and interest—Solicitor trustee, *above.*
    Will. *See* Will—Trustee, *below.*
Trustee in bankruptcy—
    Clients' account—
        Bankruptcy of solicitor—Account not to vest in trustee in bankruptcy. *See* Clients' account—Bankruptcy of solicitor—Account not to vest in trustee in bankruptcy, *above.*
    Employment of solicitor by trustee. *See* **Bankruptcy** (Trustee in bankruptcy—Employment of solicitor by trustee).
Undertaking—
    False undertaking given on behalf of firm as security for loan—
        Whether solicitor having ostensible authority to act for firm. *See* Authority—Ostensible authority—Solicitor giving false undertaking on behalf of firm as security for loan, *above.*
    Negligence. *See* Negligence—Undertaking, *above.*
    Non-compete undertaking given to another firm in course of collaborating with that firm—
        Whether non-compete undertaking a solicitor's undertaking. **Harcus Sinclair LLP v Your Lawyers Ltd** [2022] **1** 673, SC; [2022] **1 Comm** 869, SC.
    Summary jurisdiction—
        Extent of jurisdiction—Whether court's summary jurisdiction over solicitors exercisable whenever solicitor has accepted obligation in capacity as solicitor. **Hastingwood Property Ltd v Saunders Bearman Anselm (a firm)** [1990] **3** 107, Ch D.
        Material facts in issue to be resolved by court—Whether summary jurisdiction appropriate. **Fox (John) (a firm) v Bannister King & Rigbeys (a firm)** [1987] **1** 737, CA.
    Undertaking given by one solicitor to another—
        Statement that defendants would retain sum in client account until plaintiffs had 'sorted everything out'—Defendants paying sum to client on his demand—Whether statement amounting to undertaking to plaintiffs—Whether payment to client breaching undertaking—Whether court would order defendants to compensate plaintiffs for their loss. **Fox (John) (a firm) v Bannister King & Rigbeys (a firm)** [1987] **1** 737, CA.

SOLICITOR (cont)—
Undertaking (cont)—
  Undertaking given by one solicitor to another (cont)—
    Undertaking by one solicitor to pay another solicitor's costs of transaction—Enforceability of undertaking—Solicitor's client entering into transaction with fraudulent intention—Whether client's fraudulent intention in entering into transaction vitiating solicitor's undertaking—Whether undertaking enforceable by solicitor to whom undertaking given. **Rooks Rider (a firm) v Steel** [1993] **4** 716, Ch D.
  Undertaking to apply sums lent solely for purpose of acquiring good marketable title to property—
    Meaning of good marketable title—Whether solicitor's obligation absolute or qualified—Whether solicitor liable on undertaking. **Barclays Bank plc v Weeks Legg & Dean (a firm)** [1998] **3** 213, CA.
  Undertaking to hold leases to order of bank advancing money to client—
    Contracts by client for sale of leaseholds—Undertaking by solicitor to hold leases to bank's order and to pay over proceeds of sale to bank—Sales not completed—Deposits received by client—No order on solicitor to pay over deposits—One lease lost and another in possession of mortgagee—No order on solicitor to hand over lost lease—Solicitor ordered to obtain other lease from mortgagee and to deliver it to bank. **Solicitor, Re a** [1966] **3** 52, Ch D.
  Undertaking to procure execution of charge by client—
    Client not executing charge—Performance of undertaking becoming impossible—Whether solicitor guilty of professional misconduct in failing to perform undertaking—Whether court should exercise supervisory jurisdiction if performance of undertaking impossible—Whether solicitor should be ordered to compensate persons suffering loss because undertaking not performed. **Udall v Capri Lighting Ltd** [1987] **3** 262, CA.
  Undertaking to repay money lent for benefit of client by another solicitor—
    No undertaking to apply money in particular way—Solicitor not holding money in own hands—Whether undertaking given in capacity as a solicitor. **Silver (Geoffrey) & Drake v Thomas Anthony Baines** [1971] **1** 473, CA.
Unqualified person—
  Costs—
    Arbitration—Advocate not qualified as barrister or solicitor acting for party in arbitration proceedings—Whether person acting as barrister or solicitor—Whether unqualified advocate in arbitration proceedings entitled to payment of costs—Solicitors Act 1974, s 25. **Piper Double Glazing Ltd v DC Contracts (1992) Ltd** [1994] **1** 177, QBD.
  Preparation of documents etc—
    Clerk to local authority—Mortgage deeds for advances under Small Dwellings Acquisition Act 1899, s 1(1)—Right of authority to charge mortgagors—'Fee, gain or reward'—'Public officer'—Solicitors Act 1932, s 47(1), (3)(a)—Local Government Act 1933, s 188(1). **Beeston and Stapleford UDC v Smith** [1949] **1** 394, KBD.
    Directly or indirectly drawing or preparing instruments of transfer or charge—Directly or indirectly preparing—Meaning—Unqualified person carrying out all preparatory work for conveyance—Drafting of transfer or conveyance done by different person—Whether preparatory work amounting to preparation of transfer—Whether preparatory work indirectly preparing transfer—Solicitors Act 1957, s 20(1). **Green v Hoyle** [1976] **2** 633, QBD.
    Estate agent—Lease for fourteen years determinable by tenant at end of any year—Solicitors Act 1932, s 47(1), (4)(b). **Kushner v Law Society** [1952] **1** 404, KBD.
    Land registry official searches—Whether unqualified person can make an application for an official search or for an office copy of a document in relation to land registered under the Land Registration Act 1925—Solicitors Act 1957, s 20(1)(a)—Land Registration Rules (S R & O 1925 No 1093), rr 292, 296—Land Registration Rules 1930 (S R & O 1930 No 211), r 2. **Carter v Butcher** [1965] **1** 994, QBD.
    Preparation for or in expectation of fee etc—Unqualified person not himself receiving fee etc—Whether identity of person who receives fee relevant—Solicitors Act 1957, s 20(1). **Reynolds v Hoyle** [1975] **3** 934, QBD.
    Rent collector—Particulars of claim in county court actions for arrears of rent—Commission received in respect of all moneys recovered—No specific fee for drawing instrument—Solicitors Act 1932, s 47(1) (as amended by Solicitors Act 1941, s 23(1)). **Pacey v Atkinson** [1950] **1** 320, KBD.
  Pretending to be a solicitor—
    Advertisement containing representation by someone of being recognised by law and qualified to act as solicitor—Advertisement inserted by person intending to carry out the work—Whether wilful pretence—Solicitors Act 1957, s 19. **Carter v Butcher** [1965] **1** 994, QBD.
    Dismissal of information under Probation of Offenders Act 1907—Probation of Offenders Act 1907, s 1(1)—Solicitors Act 1932, s 46—Solicitors Act 1941, s 22, Sch III. **Hall v Jordan** [1947] **1** 826, KBD.
  Recovery of costs. *See* Costs—Recovery—Unqualified person, *above.*
Wardship proceedings—
  Notice of hearing—
    Notice sent to mother of ward and not to solicitor on record. *See* **Ward of court** (Practice—Hearing—Notice of hearing—Notice sent to mother of minor and not to solicitors on record).
Will—
  Attestation—
    Witness. *See* **Will** (Attestation—Witness—Solicitor).
  Negligence—
    Damages. *See* Negligence—Damages—Will, *above.*
    Duty of care. *See* Negligence—Will—Duty of care, *above.*
  Trustee—
    Solicitor who drafted will appointed sole executor and trustee—Whether entitled beneficially to residuary estate where trust void for uncertainty. **Pugh's Will Trusts, Re** [1967] **3** 337, Ch D.
Withdrawal—
  Application for order that solicitor has ceased to act for party to litigation—
    Service of application—Whether application must be served on every party to the litigation or merely on party for whom solicitor acted—Whether if improper motive suspected on part of litigant in withdrawing instructions court may insist on solicitor remaining on record to provide convenient postbox—RSC Ord 32, r 3, Ord 67, r 6(2). **Creehouse Ltd, Re** [1982] **3** 659, CA.

SOLICITOR (cont)—
  Withdrawal (cont)—
    Application for order where no notice of change given—
      Appeal to Court of Appeal pending—Practice—RSC Ord 7, r 4(1). **Practice Direction** [1961] **3** 64, Ch D.
    Criminal proceedings—
      Defence of prisoner legally aided. **R v Sowden** [1964] **3** 770, CCA.
  Writ—
    Delay in issuing and serving writ. See Litigation—Delay in issuing and serving writ, *above*.

SOLICITOR'S CLERK
  Disciplinary committee of Law Society—
    Power to make order restricting employment of unadmitted clerk—
      Clerk party to filing of misleading affidavit—No finding of misconduct on part of principal—Order made excluding clerk from employment without consent—Jurisdiction of committee to make order—Solicitors Act 1941, s 16(1)(b). **Solicitor's Clerk, Re a** [1956] **2** 242, QBD.
      Order excluding clerk from employment without consent—Order made after extension of committee's jurisdiction in respect of conduct before it—Whether disciplinary committee had jurisdiction to make order—Solicitors Act 1941, s 16(1) (as substituted by Solicitors (Amendment) Act 1956, s 11). **Solicitor's Clerk, Re a** [1957] **3** 617, QBD.

SOLICITOR'S PRACTICE
  Gift—
    Will. See **Will** (Gift—Business—Solicitor's practice).

SOLUS AGREEMENT
  Enforceability of tying covenant. See **Restraint of trade by agreement** (Petrol filling station—Solus agreement).
  Implied term—
    Circumstances in which term should be implied—
      Agreement between supplier and buyer. See **Contract** (Implied term—Circumstances in which term should be implied—Solus agreement between supplier and buyer).
  Lease of petrol filling station—
    Repudiation by landlord—
      Acceptance by tenant—Effect—Purchase of supplies elsewhere. See **Landlord and tenant** (Lease—Repudiation—Acceptance of repudiation—Effect—Continuance of lease—Solus agreement).
  Mortgaged property. See **Mortgage** (Clog on equity of redemption—Restraint of trade).
  Supplier and buyer. See **Restraint of trade by agreement** (Supplier and buyer).

SOLVENT ABUSE
  Death by solvent abuse—
    Coroner's verdict. See **Coroner** (Inquest—Verdict—Solvent abuse).

SOMALIA
  Interim government of Republic of Somalia—
    Locus standi to sue and be sued in English court. See **Conflict of laws** (Foreign government—Recognition—Locus standi to sue and be sued in English court).

SOMALILAND
  Criminal law—
    Representation by counsel—
      Appeal—Hearing without counsel—Counsel retained by government to appear for defendants—Unavoidable absence of counsel on appeal—Appeal not effectively heard—Poor Persons Defence Ordinance 1939 (Ordinance 1939 No 26), s 3(2). **Hirad (Galos) v R** [1944] **2** 50, PC.

SON
  Dependant—
    Family provision. See **Family provision** (Son).

SONG
  Copyright—
    Infringement—
      Film—Screen credit. See **Copyright** (Infringement—Film—Song—Screen credit).
    Title—
      Copyright. See **Copyright** (Title of song).

SOUND RECORDINGS
  Copyright. See **Copyright** (Sound recordings).

SOUNDNESS OF MIND
  Testator. See **Will** (Testator—Soundness of mind).

SOUTH AFRICA
  Income tax—
    Assessment—
      Capital appreciation—Sale of whole undertaking at profit—Place of assessment—Mining claims in Southern Rhodesia acquired and developed by English company—Ordinance of Southern Rhodesia (No 20 of 1918), ss 4(1), 5, 10. **Rhodesia Metals Ltd (in liq) v Taxes Comr** [1940] **3** 422, PC.

1256

SOUTH AUSTRALIA
Statute—
    Validity—
        Inconsistency of federal and state legislation—Validity of the Metropolitan and Export Abattoirs Act 1936-1952 (SA), s 52A—Validity of the Commonwealth Commerce (Meat Export) Regulations—Customs Act 1901-1951, ss 112, 270(1)(c). **O'Sullivan v Noarlunga Meat Ltd, Commonwealth of Australia (Interveners)** [1956] **3** 177, PC.

SOUTHERN RHODESIA
Commonwealth preference. *See* **Customs and excise** (Duties—Commonwealth preference—Goods consigned to United Kingdom from place in Commonwealth preference area—Southern Rhodesia).
Constitution—
    Unilateral declaration of independence by government—
        Dismissal of Ministers by Sovereign—Reversion of legislative function to Sovereign in Council—Ministers continuing in effective control of country—Status of government in control—Doctrine of necessity—Implied mandate—Regulations made by government in control—Validity of detention orders made under regulations. **Madzimbamuto v Lardner-Burke** [1968] **3** 561, PC.
        High Court of Rhodesia—Bankruptcy proceedings—Jurisdiction of English court to act in aid of another British court—Whether High Court of Rhodesia a 'British court'. *See* **Bankruptcy** (Jurisdiction—Jurisdiction to act in aid of another British court—British court—Court which is by its constitution British—Court in British colony—Necessity for court to recognise authority of British Crown—High Court of Rhodesia).
Criminal law—
    Punishment—
        Socius criminis—Capital punishment—Fixed penalty for arson—Applicable also to attempted arson—Whether statute ultra vires constitution as imposing inhuman or degrading punishment—Law and Order (Maintenance) Act No 53 of 1960, s 33A(1)—Southern Rhodesia (Constitution) Order in Council 1961 (SI 1961 No 2314), Constitution, s 60. **Runyowa v R** [1966] **1** 633, PC.
Sanctions relating to Southern Rhodesia. *See* **Criminal law** (Sanctions relating to Southern Rhodesia).
Divorce—
    Decree—
        Recognition by English courts. *See* **Divorce** (Foreign decree—Recognition by English court—Competence of court granting decree—Competence according to municipal law—Court irregularly constituted—Judge not fulfilling conditions precedent to entry on office—Decree of divorce pronounced in Southern Rhodesia).
Exports to—
    Payment for. *See* **Currency control** (Exchange control—Payment for exports—Export of goods to destination outside scheduled territories—Prerequisite as to prior payment not fulfilled—Ultimate destination of goods Southern Rhodesia).
Income tax—
    South Africa—
        Mining claims in Southern Rhodesia. *See* **South Africa** (Income tax—Assessment).
Probate—
    Resealing of grants made in Southern Rhodesia. *See* **Probate** (Grant—Resealing—Grants made in Southern Rhodesia).
Stock transfer—
    Right to unpaid interest. *See* **Stock** (Transfer of stock—Rights transferred—Right to unpaid interest).
Unilateral declaration of independence—
    Divorce granted by judge appointed after UDI—
        Judge appointed under invalid Constitution—Recognition of divorce decree. *See* **Divorce** (Foreign decree—Recognition by English court—Competence of court granting decree—Competence according to municipal law—Court irregularly constituted—Judge not fulfilling conditions precedent to entry on office—Decree of divorce pronounced in Southern Rhodesia).
    Judge appointed before UDI continuing to sit afterwards—
        Status. *See* **Conflict of laws** (Foreign judgment—Recognition by English courts—Competence of court giving judgment—Competence according to municipal law—Judges validly appointed under Constitution—Whether subsequent declaration can affect validity of continuation in office).

SOVEREIGN (PERSON)
Foreign—
    Immunity from suit. *See* **Constitutional law** (Foreign sovereign state—Immunity from suit).
Peerage—
    Creation. *See* **Peerage** (Creation).
Royal family—
    Will. *See* **Will** (Privacy—Senior royalty).

SPASTIC
Damages for personal injury. *See* **Damages** (Personal injury—Tetraplegia).

SPECIAL CASE
Arbitration. *See* **Arbitration** (Special case).
Order of court, by, before trial. *See* **Practice** (Special case—Special case by order before trial).

SPECIAL COMMISSIONER
Income tax—
    Appeal to commissioner. *See* **Income tax** (Appeal—Special commissioners).
    Judicial review of decision of commissioner—
        Availability of remedy. *See* **Judicial review** (Availability of remedy—Special Commissioner).

SPECIAL CONSTABLE
Dismissal. *See* **Police** (Dismissal—Constable—Special constable).

SPECIAL CONTRIBUTION
Additional assessment—
    Limitation on time for making—
        Assessment on executors of taxpayer—Finance Act 1948, s 55(1), (6)—Income Tax Act 1918, ss 67(2), 125(2)—Finance Act 1923, s 29(1), (3)—Special Contribution Regulations 1948 (SI 1948 No 2029), regs 4, 5, Sch. **Beauchamp's Exors v IRC** [1957] **1** 788, Ch D.
Investment income—
    Dividends on shares—
        Dividends on shares acquirable only by employees—Whether investment income within Income Tax Act 1918, s 14(3)(b)—Finance Act 1948, s 49(1). **Recknell v IRC** [1952] **2** 147, Ch D.
    Exclusion of income arising to persons carrying on a trade from property occupied by them for the purposes thereof—
        Land let to farmer by his wife—Farmer's land occupied by him in partnership—Whether wife's income from the rent to be excluded from investment income—Finance Act 1948, s 49(2)(b). **Worth v IRC** [1953] **1** 930, CA.
    Trustee—
        Annuity to trustee conditional on his acting as such—Whether investment income—Income Tax Act 1918, s 14(3)(a), (b)—Finance Act 1948, s 47(1). **Dale v IRC** [1953] **2** 671, HL.
Relief—
    Income received representing more than income attributable to a full year if income accrued from day to day—
        A full year's income—Discretion of commissioners in selecting relevant year—Finance Act 1948, s 61(1). **Fenwick v IRC** [1953] **2** 666, HL.

SPECIAL DAMAGE
Pleading. *See* **Pleading** (Damage—Special damage).

SPECIAL DAMAGES
Interest—
    Personal injury cases. *See* **Interest** (Damages—Personal injury—Special damages).

SPECIAL EDUCATIONAL NEEDS
Generally. *See* **Education** (Special educational needs).

SPECIAL HARDSHIP ALLOWANCE
Industrial injury. *See* **Social security** (Disablement benefit—Special hardship allowance).

SPECIAL HOURS CERTIFICATE
See **Licensing** (Permitted hours—Special hours certificate).

SPECIAL IMMIGRATION APPEALS COMMISSION
Admissibility of evidence. *See* **Evidence** (Admissibility—Special Immigration Appeals Commission).
Appeal—
    Generally. *See* **Immigration** (Appeal).
    Judicial review. *See* **Judicial review** (Special Immigration Appeals Commission).

SPECIAL MANAGER
Company—
    Compulsory winding up. *See* **Company** (Compulsory winding up—Special manager).

SPECIAL MESSENGER
Service of writ through letter box by—
    Practice. *See* **Practice** (Service—Service through letter box).

SPECIAL POLICE SERVICES
See **Police** (Special police services).

SPECIAL PROCEDURE LIST
See **Divorce** (Practice—Undefended causes).

SPECIAL PROCEDURE MATERIAL
Appeal against order for production of—
    Whether order for production of special procedure material an order in a 'criminal cause or matter'—Whether appeal against order lying to Court of Appeal. *See* **Criminal law** (Appeal—Criminal cause or matter—Order of Crown Court—Order for production of special procedure material).
Generally. *See* **Criminal evidence** (Special procedure material).

SPECIAL RESOLUTION
Company. *See* **Company** (Resolution—Special resolution).

SPECIAL ROAD
Generally. *See* **Road traffic** (Special road).
Motorway. *See* **Road traffic** (Motorway).

SPECIAL VOUCHER SCHEME
Commonwealth immigration—
    Appeal against refusal to issue special voucher. *See* **Commonwealth immigrant** (Appeal—Special voucher scheme).

SPECIALIST ANAESTHETIST
Negligence—
    Liability of hospital. *See* **Hospital** (Liability for negligence of members of staff—Specialist anaesthetist).

SPECIALLY INDORSED WRIT
See **Writ** (Indorsement—Signature—Specially indorsed writ).

SPECIALTY
Action on specialty—
Extortionate credit bargain. See **Limitation of action** (Action—Action on statute—Action based on Consumer Credit Act 1974—Action on specialty).
Limitation of action. See **Limitation of action** (Action—Action on statute—Action based on Consumer Credit Act 1974—Action on specialty—Appropriate period of limitation).
Right of action conferred by statute—
Period of limitation. See **Limitation of action** (Specialty—Right of action conferred by statute—Period of limitation).
Rule as to—
Extradition order and. See **Extradition** (Extradition order—Specialty rule).

SPECIFIC EDUCATIONAL NEEDS
Local authority's statutory duty to provide special education. See **Education** (Local education authority—Statutory duty to provide special education).

SPECIFIC ISSUE ORDER
Family proceedings. See **Family proceedings** (Orders in family proceedings—Specific issue order).

SPECIFIC PERFORMANCE
Action in rem—
Jurisdiction of Admiralty Court to grant relief. See **Admiralty** (Jurisdiction—Action in rem—Claim for equitable relief—Specific performance).
Agreement for lease. See Lease—Agreement for lease, *below*.
Agreement to erect fence—
Jurisdiction of county court. See **County court** (Jurisdiction—Specific performance—Agreement to erect fence).
Benefit of contract conferred on third party—
Enforcement by third party as personal representative of original party—
Original party entitled to nominal damages only—Contract for sale of business—Agreement to pay annuity to widow of seller—Widow not party to contract—Business transferred—Death of seller—Widow obtained letters of administration—Whether widow entitled to enforce payment of annuity specifically. **Beswick v Beswick** [1967] **2** 1197, HL.
Building contract—
Contract to make sewers and roads—
Sale of land for development—Covenant by defendant vendor to make sewers and roads on retained land—Retained land in possession of defendant—Whether fact that defendant undertaking work had not thereby obtained possession a bar to specific performance—Whether defendant must by the contract obtain possession of land. **Carpenters Estates Ltd v Davies** [1940] **1** 13, Ch D.
Conditional contract. See Sale of land—Conditional contract, *below*.
Contract for sale of land—
Generally. See Sale of land, *below*.
Costs—
Generally. See **Costs** (Specific performance).
Specific performance of contract for sale of land. See Sale of land—Costs of action, *below*.
County court jurisdiction—
Agreement for lease—
Rateable value of property not exceeding £500—Value of property exceeding £500. **Cornish v Brook Green Laundry Ltd** [1959] **1** 373, CA.
Agreements for sale, purchase or lease of property—
Agreement to erect fence—Agreement made as compromise of legal proceedings—Whether county court having jurisdiction to enforce agreement—County Courts Act 1934, ss 40, 52(1)(d), 71. **Bourne v McDonald** [1950] **2** 183, CA.
Equitable defence—
Defence based on right to specific performance—Value of property such as to exclude county court jurisdiction if plea raised by way of claim—Action for recovery of possession by landlord—Defence of agreement for oral tenancy for life—No counterclaim for specific performance—County Courts Act 1959, ss 52(1)(d), 74. **Kingswood Estate Co Ltd v Anderson** [1962] **3** 593, CA.
Damages in addition to specific performance—
Contract for sale of land. See **Sale of land** (Damages for breach of contract—Damages in addition to specific performance).
Damages in substitution for specific performance—
Election to accept remedy—
Estoppel. See **Estoppel** (Election—Litigation—Election to accept particular remedy—Action by purchaser for specific performance of contract—Purchaser awarded damages instead).
Jurisdiction to award damages where court having jurisdiction to entertain application for specific performance—
Want of mutuality precluding court in exercise of discretion from granting decree of specific performance—Specific performance of oral agreement for underlease—Consideration for agreement promise by underlessee to execute repairs—Repairs executed—Underlessor refusing to grant underlease—Underlessee applying for order for specific performance of agreement—Whether court deprived of jurisdiction to entertain application by lack of mutuality at date of contract—Whether court having jurisdiction to enforce contract for execution of repair works—Whether court having jurisdiction to award damages in substitution for specific performance—Chancery Amendment Act 1858, s 2. **Price v Strange** [1977] **3** 371, CA.
Sale of land. See **Sale of land** (Damages for breach of contract—Damages in substitution for specific performance).

SPECIFIC PERFORMANCE (cont)—
Defence to action—
    Breach of conditions of contract by plaintiff—
        Agreement for the operation of a sawmill—Option of purchase in agreement—Option exercised after breaches of agreement and after notice by defendant determining agreement on ground of breaches—Whether specific performance of term of agreement to request transfer of occupation permit and sawmill licence would be granted. **Australian Hardwoods Pty Ltd v Railways Comr** [1961] **1** 737, PC.
    Licence—
        Contract to let hall to political party—Wrongful repudiation of contract—Political party claiming specific performance of contract—Defence that licence to use hall was of short duration—Defence that repudiation occurred before licensee entered into possession—Defence that public disorder might result if contract performed—Whether specific performance could and should be ordered. **Verrall v Great Yarmouth BC** [1980] **1** 839, CA.
    Reprehensible conduct—
        Defendant contending that fraudulent misrepresentation by plaintiff induced it to enter into agreement—Defendant losing right to rescind contract—Whether defendant could rely on misrepresentation as defence to plaintiff's application for specific performance. **Geest plc v Fyffes plc** [1999] **1 Comm** 672, QBD.
    Set-off—
        Availability of set-off as a defence. *See* **Set-off** (Cross-claim—Legal right of set-off—Claim for specific performance).
Delay—
    Action not brought to trial quickly—
        Right of pre-emption offered but not exercised—Twenty-one year option exercised subsequently—Whether specific performance would be granted or plaintiff left to remedy in damages. **Du Sautoy v Symes** [1967] **1** 25, Ch D.
    Laches—
        Carriage of goods—Purchaser refusing to take delivery of goods—Goods stored at shipper's yard for some years—Shipper seeking order for specific performance requiring purchaser to accept delivery of goods—Whether defence of laches available. **P & O Nedlloyd BV v Arab Metals Co** [2007] **2 Comm** 401, CA.
Illegal contract—
    Lease—
        Illegal premium. *See* **Rent restriction** (Premium—Illegal premium—Specific performance).
Judgment in default of defence—
    Terms of order—
        Interest—Vendor's action—Conveyance and purchase money to be handed over simultaneously. **Palmer v Lark** [1945] **1** 355, Ch D.
Lapse of time—
    Contract for sale of building land—
        Purchase to be completed within two years—Plots to be conveyed to purchaser as buildings erected—Purchaser having entered on two plots, no building completed on them for many years—Delay attributable partly to antagonistic conduct of vendor—Action by purchaser for specific performance after ten years—No abandonment of contract. **Williams v Greatrex** [1956] **3** 705, CA.
Lease—
    Agreement for lease—
        Trustees agreeing to take long leases of properties held by subsidiary of development company—Director of development company also one of trustees. **Lindgren v L & P Estates Co Ltd** [1968] **1** 917, CA.
    Underlease—
        Underlease—Execution of underlease breach of covenant in lessor's head lease—Whether lessee entitled to specific performance of agreement to execute underlease. **Warmington v Miller** [1973] **2** 372, CA.
    Covenant to repair. *See* **Landlord and tenant** (Breach of covenant to repair—Specific performance).
    Option to renew—
        Settled land. *See* **Settlement** (Purchaser dealing in good faith with tenant for life—Protection of purchaser—Agreement for lease with option to renew).
    Service agreement in lease. *See* **Personal services**—Service agreement in lease, *below*.
Matrimonial home. *See* Sale of land—Sale with vacant possession—Duty of vendor to bring proceedings to obtain possession, *below*.
Mutual availability of remedy—
    Date at which defence of want of mutuality should be considered—
        Date of contract or date of trial—Plaintiff's obligations under contract not specifically enforceable—Plaintiff's obligations performed at date of trial—Application for specific performance of agreement for underlease—Underlessee agreeing to do repairs to underlessor's property in exchange for grant of new underlease—Repairs executed—Underlessor refusing to grant underlease—Whether underlessee entitled to decree of specific performance—Whether necessary that remedy of specific performance should have been mutually available at date of agreement. **Price v Strange** [1977] **3** 371, CA.
Option to purchase land—
    Agreement conferring option on third party—
        Exercise of option by third party—Right of third party to order of specific performance of agreement constituted by exercise of option. **Stromdale & Ball Ltd v Burden** [1952] **1** 59, Ch D.
    Document purporting to confer option on plaintiff—
        Contractual nature of document—Evidence to prove otherwise inadmissible. **Hutton v Watling** [1948] **1** 803, CA.
    No time limit for exercise—
        Decree against original grantee of option. **Hutton v Watling** [1948] **1** 803, CA.

SPECIFIC PERFORMANCE (cont)—
Option to purchase land (cont)—
Option granted gratuitously or for token consideration—
Equity will not assist a volunteer—Exercise of option by purchaser—Exercise of option constituting
contract of sale for agreed sum—Sum constituting adequate consideration—Refusal of vendor to
complete—Whether purchaser entitled to specific performance or confined to remedy in
damages. **Mountford v Scott** [1975] **1** 198, CA.
Order—
Delay in enforcing order—
Summons to proceed on order—Extension of time for proceeding where long period elapsing from
date of order—Refusal of extension of time—Purchaser obtaining order for specific performance
for sale of property with vacant possession—Purchaser intending to redevelop property—Order
not enforced for nearly eight years because vendor's former wife in occupation of
property—Purchaser reaching agreement with wife to provide her with alternative
accommodation—Purchaser applying for leave to issue summons to proceed on specific
performance order—Purchaser having reasonable explanation for delay—Whether detriment to
vendor justifying refusal of extension of time for enforcing order—Whether extension of time to
be refused only if both insufficient explanation for delay and detriment to vendor—Whether
purchaser entitled to supplemental order for inquiry as to damage suffered after date of specific
performance order by reason of vendor's delay—RSC Ord 3, r 5(1), Ord 44, r 2(1). **Easton v Brown**
[1981] **3** 278, Ch D.
Form of order—
Interested parties not all before court. *See* Parties—Interested parties not all before court—Form of
order, *below.*
Judgment in default of appearance. *See* **Practice** (Chancery Division—Order—Order requiring
execution of deed—Judgment in default of appearance—Form of order—Specific performance of
agreement to execute lease).
Parties—
Interested parties not all before court—
Form of order—Attempt to cure defect—Form of order leaving views of absent parties to be
ascertained—Whether damages a more appropriate remedy. **Tito v Waddell (No 2)** [1977] **3** 129,
Ch D.
Patent licence. *See* **Patent** (Licence—Specific performance of agreement to grant).
Personal services—
Service agreement in lease—
Covenant in lease to execute service agreement—Landlord covenanting to employ resident porter
to carry out specified duties—Landlord employing part-time non-resident porter—Whether
landlord in breach of covenant—Whether covenant capable of being enforced by specific
performance. **Posner v Scott-Lewis** [1986] **3** 513, Ch D.
Promise or representation—
Promise acted on by plaintiff—
Promise to make settlement—Agreement that as consideration promisor should be made trustee of
existing settlement—Promisor tenant for life under existing settlement—Promisor appointed
trustee by existing trustee—Appointment an innocent breach of trust—Whether promise
enforceable on behalf of beneficiaries under proposed settlement. **Briggs v Parsloe** [1937] **3** 831,
Ch D.
Publishing agreement—
Contract to publish signed article—
Article not written at date of contract—Refusal of publisher to print article as submitted. **Joseph v
National Magazine Co Ltd** [1958] **3** 52, Ch D.
Sale of goods—
Goods not specific or ascertained—
Power of court to order specific performance—Circumstances in which power exercisable. **Sky
Petroleum Ltd v VIP Petroleum Ltd** [1974] **1** 954, Ch D.
Sale of land—
Acceptance of title—
Order to make payment into court—Whether defendant should have option to go out of
possession. **Maskell v Ivory** [1970] **1** 488, Ch D.
Conditional contract—
Promissory note—Document promising to pay money for 'value received' or in default to convey
property—Whether conditional contract for sale of land of which specific performance would be
decreed. **Savage v Uwechia** [1961] **1** 830, PC.
Waiver of conditions—Subject to contract—Parties negotiating sale and purchase of lease subject
to contract—Tenant breaking off negotiations in May—Parties reaching oral agreement in
November—Letter from vendor confirming terms of oral agreement but stated to be subject to
contract—Whether oral agreement in November subject to contract—Whether subject to contract
qualification of previous negotiations continuing and applying to oral agreement—Whether oral
agreement the result of new negotiations or the resumption of existing negotiations. **Cohen v
Nessdale Ltd** [1982] **2** 97, CA.
Costs of action—
Accrual of equitable right to specific performance—Writ issued by purchaser—Accrual before date
of issue of writ—Time not made essence of contract—Completion week after date writ
issued—Whether purchaser entitled to costs. **Marks v Lilley** [1959] **2** 647, Ch D.
Purchaser's costs of suit—Completion of contract after issue of writ—Whether purchaser entitled to
costs. **Horton v Kurzke** [1971] **2** 577, Ch D.
Purchaser's costs of suit—Lien on property—Deposit paid to stakeholder. **Combe v Swaythling**
[1947] **1** 838, Ch D.
Damages in substitution for specific performance. *See* **Sale of land** (Damages for breach of
contract—Damages in substitution for specific performance).
Delay in completion—
Building land—Contract not completed for ten years—Time not made essence of the
contract—Specific performance granted. **Williams v Greatrex** [1956] **3** 705, CA.

SPECIFIC PERFORMANCE (cont)—
   Sale of land (cont)—
      Entry into possession as waiver of objection to title—
         Assignment of lease—Default by assignor to repair in compliance with covenant in lease—Entry into possession by assignee—Undertaking by assignor to effect repairs at later date—Assignee refusing to accept undertaking and vacating premises—Whether assignor entitled to specific performance. **Rellie v Pyke** [1936] **1** 345, Ch D.
      Freezing order—
         Specific performance order combined with freezing order—Whether jurisdiction to make combined order. **Seven Seas Properties Ltd v Al-Essa** [1989] **1** 164, Ch D.
      Land belonging to company—
         Vendor company inaccurately described in conveyance—Characteristics of company for purpose of identification—Whether vendor sufficiently identifiable. **Goldsmith (F) (Sicklesmere) Ltd v Baxter** [1969] **3** 733, Ch D.
         Vendor company placed in receivership by debenture holder before completion of contract for sale of land—Whether appointment of receiver destroying purchaser's equitable interest in land under contract for sale—Whether appointment of receiver affording vendor company defence to claim for specific performance of contract. **Freevale Ltd v Metrostore (Holdings) Ltd** [1984] **1** 495, Ch D.
      Land outside jurisdiction—
         Contract for sale of land in Scotland—Vendor and purchaser domiciled in England—Vendor seeking specific performance of agreement to buy land in Scotland—Whether court can decree specific performance of contract regarding land outside jurisdiction. **West (Richard) and Partners (Inverness) Ltd v Dick** [1969] **1** 943, CA.
      Notice to complete—
         Validity of completion notice under contract served after order for specific performance obtained. *See* **Sale of land** (Notice to complete—Order for specific performance of contract—Order for specific performance with consequential directions—Failure of party obtaining order to comply with order—Whether completion notice under contract served after order for specific performance valid).
      Refusal of specific performance—
         Hardship—Hardship to defendant—Unforeseen change in defendant's circumstances subsequent to date of contract—Unavoidable delay in completing contract not due to either party's fault—Defendant a young married woman with three young children contracting bone cancer resulting in amputation of leg subsequent to date of contract—Defendant becoming dependent on assistance from family and friends living in neighbourhood of house contracted to be sold—Removal to another home elsewhere likely to deprive her of that assistance—Whether hardship entitling court to refuse specific performance of contract. **Patel v Ali** [1984] **1** 978, Ch D.
      Rescission of contract—
         Damages. *See* **Sale of land** (Rescission of contract—Damages—Decree of specific performance).
      Right of purchaser to maintain action—
         Agent of purchaser contracting in own name—Knowledge of agency by vendor—Vendors tenants in common—One vendor having no power to convey interest—Right of purchaser to order against other vendors in respect of their shares. **Basma (Abdul Karim) v Weekes** [1950] **2** 146, PC.
      Sale with vacant possession—
         Duty of vendor to bring proceedings to obtain possession—Matrimonial home—Vendor's spouse's right of occupation—Right registered as a charge—Husband owner of home—Husband contracting to sell home—Wife subsequently registering right of occupation as a charge—Husband and wife living together—Wife unwilling to leave home—Wife's right of occupation personal to herself—Husband attempting without success to persuade wife short of litigation to remove notice of charge—Purchasers having alternative remedy in damages—Whether husband should be compelled to take proceedings to terminate wife's right of occupation—Whether purchasers entitled to specific performance subject to wife's right of occupation—Matrimonial Homes Act 1967, ss 1, 2. **Wroth v Tyler** [1973] **1** 897, Ch D.
         Vacant possession—House advertised for sale, subject to tenancy of first floor, with vacant possession of ground floor—Particulars in advertisement incorporated into contract—Condition stating that purchaser not entitled to compensation for any discrepancy in description—Further condition that purchaser bought subject to any notices—Purchaser signing contract—Purchaser then discovering existence of Housing Act direction precluding occupation of ground floor—Purchaser applying for specific performance of contract with abatement in purchase price—Effect of conditions—Whether purchaser entitled to abatement in purchase price—Whether 'vacant possession' meant merely that ground floor empty. **Topfell Ltd v Galley Properties Ltd** [1979] **2** 388, Ch D.
      Tenants in common—
         Sale by tenants in common—One vendor having no power to convey—Whether specific performance granted against others. **Basma (Abdul Karim) v Weekes** [1950] **2** 146, PC.
      Title. *See* Title, *below*.
      Vendor contracting to grant greater interest than he is competent to grant—
         Purchaser seeking to compel vendor to grant such lesser interest as he is competent to grant—Land held on trust for sale—Severance of joint tenancy—Joint tenant purporting to create charge on land without consent of other joint tenant—Matrimonial home held on trust for sale—Husband creating charge without consent of wife—Mortgagee seeking specific performance to extent of husband's true interest—Specific performance prejudicing wife's interest in matrimonial home—Whether court should order specific performance. **Cedar Holdings Ltd v Green** [1979] **3** 117, CA.
   Sale of shares in company—
      Winding up order—
         Vendor and purchaser entering into contract before commencement of winding up of company—Vendor claiming specific performance of contract after winding-up order made—Whether contract enforceable—Companies Act 1948, s 227. **Sullivan v Henderson** [1973] **1** 48, Ch D.

SPECIFIC PERFORMANCE (cont)—
  Service agreement—
    Contract to execute service agreement—
      Service agreement not specifically enforceable—Contract containing provision requiring defendants to appoint third party managing director of company for five years—Contract requiring only the performance of single act, ie execution of service agreement—Contract specifically enforceable—Immaterial that service agreement as a contract for personal services not specifically enforceable. **Giles (CH) & Co Ltd v Morris** [1972] **1** 960, Ch D.
  Summary procedure—
    Agreement for the sale, purchase or exchange of any property—
      Agreement to grant long lease of flat to be erected and to sell residue of term to lessee—Whether agreement for sale or purchase of property—RSC Ord 86, r 1(1). **Young v Markworth Properties Ltd** [1965] **1** 834, Ch D.
      Construction of house—Contract for the sale of house and land for £10,750—Contract conditional on purchaser fulfilling obligations under second contract—Purchaser under second contract agreeing to erect new house for vendor in accordance with plans and specifications—Payment for construction of new house to be satisfied by vendor completing sale under first contract—Vendor refusing to complete sale after new house erected—Whether agreement for the sale or exchange of any property—Whether purchaser entitled on summary judgment to specific performance—RSC Ord 86. **Doyle v East** [1972] **2** 1013, Ch D.
      Money consideration—Sale or purchase—Contract to transfer leasehold property—Absence of money consideration—RSC Ord 14A, r 1. **Robshaw Bros Ltd v Mayer** [1956] **3** 833, Ch D.
    Claim for specific performance or damages in lieu—
      Plaintiff electing to claim damages—Agreement to purchase or find a purchaser of shares at a fixed price—RSC Ord 14A (SI 1954 No 1728), r 1(1). **Woodlands v Hind** [1955] **2** 604, Ch D.
    Construction of documents—
      Question whether contract concluded by exchange of letters—No possibility of further facts emerging if case going formally for trial—Power of judge to determine point of construction on summary application—RSC Ord 86. **Bigg v Boyd Gibbins Ltd** [1971] **2** 183, CA.
    Leave to defend—
      Order for examination on oath—Circumstances in which such an order should be made—RSC Ord 86. **Sullivan v Henderson** [1973] **1** 48, Ch D.
    Masters' powers—
      Conditions to be satisfied before master gives summary judgment in specific performance action—Formal written agreement—Default of appearance by defendant or no appearance at hearing or clearly no defence—RSC Ord 14A. **Practice Note** [1955] **1** 913, Ch D.
    Purchaser's action—
      Transfer of land by vendor to company controlled by him—Transfer a sham—Decree granted against vendor and company—Whether summary procedure appropriate—RSC Ord 14A, r 1. **Jones v Lipman** [1962] **1** 442, Ch D.
    Summary judgment for specific performance—
      Issue be tried—Interest on purchase money—RSC Ord 14A. **Upjohn v Simmons** [1936] **1** 615, Ch D.
    Summons—
      Summons normally returnable before master—RSC Ord 86. **Practice Direction** [1993] **1** 359, Ch D.
  Title—
    Contract of sale of freehold land and business assets—
      Vendor only leaseholder—Ability to compel assurance by freeholder. **Elliott v Pierson** [1948] **1** 939, Ch D.
    Doubtful title—
      Contract for sale of land in 1912 between trustees of will and testator's son—Son never completing contract—Son dying in 1942—Representation to his estate not taken out—Trustees contracting to sell property to purchasers in 1973—Whether good title shown—Whether reasonably conceivable circumstances in which specific performance could be obtained. **MEPC Ltd v Christian-Edwards** [1978] **3** 795, CA.
      Latent ambiguity of description of beneficiaries in will—Deed of family arrangement to resolve ambiguity—Sale of reversionary interest subject to special conditions—Whether title too doubtful to be forced on purchaser. **Wilson v Thomas** [1958] **1** 871, Ch D.
  Uncertainty as to terms—
    Agreement not to bid at auction—
      Agreement to convey land bought at auction if plaintiff did not bid—Formula agreed on price payable within certain limits—Failure of defendant to convey—Whether agreement enforceable. **Pallant v Morgan** [1952] **2** 951, Ch D.
  Underlease. *See* Lease—Agreement for lease—Underlease, *above*.
  Vendor's lien—
    Transfer of shares—
      Preservation of lien. *See* **Lien** (Vendor's lien—Specific performance).

SPECIMEN
  Laboratory test—
    Driving with blood-alcohol proportion above permitted limit. *See* **Road traffic** (Specimen for laboratory test to determine driver's blood-alcohol proportion).

SPECTACLES
  European Community—
    Freedom of movement of goods. *See* **European Union** (Freedom of movement—Goods—Spectacles).

SPECTATOR
  Negligence—
    Duty to spectator at game or competion. *See* **Negligence** (Duty to take care—Spectator at game or competition).
  Risk of injury—
    Voluntary assumption of risk. *See* **Negligence** (Volenti non fit injuria—Spectator at game or competition).

SPEECH, FREEDOM OF
  University. *See* **University** (Freedom of speech).

SPEECHES
  Trial—
    Civil action—
      Order of speeches. *See* **Practice** (Trial—Speeches—Order of speeches).
    Criminal proceedings. *See* **Criminal law** (Trial—Speeches).

SPEEDING
  Motor vehicle—
    Negligence. *See* **Negligence** (Vehicles—Speed).
    Road traffic offence. *See* **Road traffic** (Excessive speed).

SPEEDY TRIAL
  Practice. *See* **Practice** (Trial—Order for early trial).

SPENT CONVICTION
  Rehabilitation of offenders. *See* **Rehabilitation** (Rehabilitation of offenders—Spent conviction).

SPERM
  Human fertilisation. *See* **Medical treatment** (Human fertilisation).

SPIRE
  Removal of church spire—
    Faculty—
      Jurisdiction. *See* **Ecclesiastical law** (Faculty—Jurisdiction—Removal of spire).

SPORT
  Assault—
    Defence. *See* **Criminal law** (Assault—Defence—Consent).
  Charity—
    Educational purposes. *See* **Charity** (Education—Educational purposes—Sport).
  Football—
    Police attendance at football matches. *See* **Police** (Special police services—Police attendance at football matches).
    Public order. *See* **Public order** (Football).
  International competition—
    European Community—
      Free movement of services. *See* **European Union** (Freedom of movement—Services—International sports competition).
  Negligence—
    Participant in sporting event—
      Duty to take care. *See* **Negligence** (Duty to take care—Participants in sporting event).
    School—
      Duty of care. *See* **Negligence** (School—Duty of care—Sport).
  Sporting and recreational facilities—
    Easement. *See* **Easement** (Sporting and recreational facilities).

SPORTING RIGHTS
  Game—
    Generally. *See* **Game** (Shooting and sporting rights).
  Lease—
    Reservation. *See* **Landlord and tenant** (Lease—Reservation—Sporting rights).

SPORTSMAN
  Foreign sportsman—
    Profits—
      Income tax. *See* **Income tax** (Profits—Foreign entertainers and sportsmen).
    Signing-on fee—
      Income tax—
        Capital or income. *See* **Income tax** (Capital or income receipts—Professional sportsman).

SPOT-BALL
  Newspaper competition—
    Restriction on. *See* **Gaming** (Prize competition—Forecast of result of future event—Future event—Newspaper competition—Spot-ball).

SPOUSE
  Communications between spouses—
    Evidence in criminal proceedings. *See* **Criminal evidence** (Spouse—Communication between spouses).
  Former spouse—
    Family provision. *See* **Family provision** (Former spouse).
  Injunction—
    Exclusion of spouse from matrimonial home. *See* **Injunction** (Exclusion of party from matrimonial home).
  Will—
    Mutual will. *See* **Will** (Mutual wills—Identical terms—Husband and wife).
  Witness for prosecution—
    Compellability. *See* **Criminal evidence** (Compellability as witness—Spouse as witness for prosecution).
    Competence. *See* **Criminal evidence** (Competence as witness—Spouse as witness for prosecution).

SPOUSE (cont)—
    Witness for prosecution (cont)—
        Divorced spouse—
            Competence as witness. *See* **Criminal evidence** (Competence as witness—Divorced spouse as witness for prosecution).

SPRAY IRRIGATION
    See **Water and watercourses** (Riparian rights—User—Extraordinary purpose—Spray-irrigation).

SPYING
    Criminal offence. *See* **Criminal law** (Official secrets).

SQUATTER
    Acquisition of title—
        Limitation of action. *See* **Limitation of action** (Land—Acquisition of title by squatter).
    Forcible entry on to premises—
        Criminal offence. *See* **Criminal law** (Forcible entry and detainer).
    Summary proceedings for possession of land. *See* **Land** (Summary proceedings for possession—Suspension of possession order).

ST CHRISTOPHER, NEVIS AND ANGUILLA
    Constitution—
        Fundamental rights and freedoms—
            Freedom of expression—Freedom to communicate ideas and information without interference—Law reasonably required in interests of public order not inconsistent with freedom—Public meeting—Use of loudspeaker—Statute making it offence to use 'noisy instrument' during course of public meeting without obtaining written permission of Chief of Police—Whether statute contravening provision in Constitution protecting freedom of expression—St Christopher, Nevis and Anguilla Constitution Order 1967 (S1 1967 No 228), Sch 2, s 10(1)(2)—Public Meetings and Processions Act 1969 (St Christopher, Nevis and Anguilla), s 5(1). **Francis v Chief of Police** [1973] 2 251, PC.
    Constitutional law—
        Governor's powers—
            State of emergency—Discretion to detain persons in time of emergency—If the Governor is satisfied—Governor having power to detain persons if satisfied that it was necessary to do so—Whether Governor's power unrestricted—Whether Governor required to be satisfied on reasonable grounds that detention of person reasonably justifiable and necessary—Consitution of St Christopher, Nevis and Anguilla (SI 1967 No 228, Sch 2), ss 3(6), 14, 103, 108—Leeward Islands (Emergency Powers) Order in Council 1959 (SI 1959 No 2206), s 3(1)—Emergency Powers Regulations 1967 (St Christopher, Nevis and Anguilla), reg 3(1). **A-G of St Christopher, Nevis and Anguilla v Reynolds** [1979] 3 129, PC.

STAG
    Protection of stags in captivity or confinement. *See* **Animal** (Protection—Animal in captivity or confinement—Stag).

STAGE CARRIAGE
    See **Road traffic** (Stage carriage).

STAIRCASE
    Guardrail—
        Building operations. *See* **Building** (Building operations—Stairs).
        Factory. *See* **Factory** (Staircase—Handrail).

STAKEHOLDER
    Sale of land—
        Deposit paid to stakeholder—
            Generally. *See* **Sale of land** (Stakeholder—Deposit paid to stakeholder).
            Purchaser's lien. *See* **Sale of land** (Purchaser's lien—Costs of suit—Deposit paid to stakeholder).
    Solicitor—
        Generally. *See* **Solicitor** (Stakeholder).

STALL
    Exhibition—
        Sunday trading. *See* **Shop** (Sunday closing—Retail trading elsewhere than in shop—Exhibition stalls).
    Highway, on. *See* **Highway** (Obstruction—Pitching stall on highway).
    Market—
        Right of stallholder. *See* **Markets and fairs** (Right of public to attend market—Stallholder).
        Stallage. *See* **Markets and fairs** (Stallage).
    Shop—
        Whether stall a 'shop'. *See* **Medicine** (Sale by retail—Shop).

STAMP COLLECTION
    Will—
        Gift—
            Personal chattels. *See* **Will** (Gift—Personal chattels—Articles of personal use).

STAMP DUTY

Adjudication—

Effect of adjudication—

Opinion given by commissioners that document not chargeable with duty—Previous reliance by party on invalidity of document on basis it had not been stamped—Document in fact chargeable with duty—Proxy forms—Forms unstamped—Company meeting—Rejection of proxy forms for want of stamp—Subsequent adjudication that forms not chargeable—Forms in fact chargeable—Whether compnay entitled to reject forms—Stamp Act 1891, s 12(1). **Marx v Estates and General Investments Ltd** [1975] **3** 1064, Ch D.

Voluntary disposition inter vivos—

Conveyance to trustees for sale. *See* Voluntary disposition inter vivos—Conveyance to trustees for sale—Necessity for adjudication, *below.*

Advances made to company—

Issue of loan capital. *See* Issue of loan capital—Issue—Advances made to company, *below.*

Annuity—

Sale of annuity—

Allotment of shares—Deed of covenant—Covenantor agreeing to pay nine-tenths of his professional income to company in consideration of allotment of shares—Whether deed chargeable with ad valorem duty—Valuation of shares—Stamp Act 1891, ss 14(4), 60. **Faber v IRC** [1936] **1** 617, KBD.

Policy securing half-yearly payments for 11 years on payment of a lump sum—Whether sale of annuity or security for annuity—Stamp Act 1891, s 87(2), Sch 1. **Commercial Union Assurance Co Ltd v IRC** [1937] **4** 159, KBD.

Assent. *See* Conveyance on sale—Instrument whereby property or estate or interest in property on sale thereof transferred to or vested in purchaser—Assent, *below.*

Bond, covenant or instrument—

Deed varying rent reserved by a lease—

Deed not itself a lease or tack for the purposes of charge to stamp duty—Chargeable as bond, covenant etc—Amount chargeable nevertheless limited to what would be chargeable if deed of variation were a lease or tack—Stamp Act 1891, s 77(5), Sch 1. **Gable Construction Co Ltd v IRC** [1968] **2** 968, Ch D.

Security—

Executory agreement creating obligation—Agreement providing for services—Total amount ultimately payable ascertainable—Specified sum subject to increase or decrease in certain eventualities—Stamp Act 1891, Sch 1. **Independent Television Authority v IRC** [1960] **2** 481, HL.

Capital—

Issue of loan capital. *See* Issue of loan capital, *below.*

Charity. *See* **Charity** (Stamp duty).

Conveyance on sale—

Contracts chargeable as conveyances on sale—

Agreement for sale of goodwill—Conditional agreement—Aqreement to pay a sum of money upon the transfer of licences relating to a motor coach business and covenant not to compete—Whether chargeable with ad valorem duty as agreement to sell goodwill—Stamp Act 1891, s 59(1). **Eastern National Omnibus Co Ltd v IRC** [1938] **3** 526, KBD.

Instrument whereby property or estate or interest in property on sale thereof transferred to or vested in purchaser—

Appropriation of stocks and shares in satisfaction of pecuniary legacy—Transfer of stock by executor—Whether instrument of transfer chargeable as 'conveyance on sale'—Administration of Estates Act 1925, s 41. **Jopling v IRC** [1940] **3** 279, KBD.

Assent giving effect to sale—Whether chargeable with ad valorem duty as conveyance on sale—Stamp Act 1891, s 54—Administration of Estates Act 1925, s 36(1), (4), (11). **GHR Co v IRC** [1943] **1** 424, KBD.

Conveyance of licensed premises—Amalgamation of companies—Shares of brewery company acquired by purchasing company from shareholders—Liquidation of brewery company—Conveyance of brewery company's land to purchasing company—Conveyance by liquidator of brewery company on authority of shareholders—Transfers of shares by vendor shareholders not registered—No evidence whether transfers stamped—Whether conveyance attracted stamp duty as a conveyance on sale—Stamp Act 1891, s 54, Sch 1. **Henty & Constable (Brewers) Ltd v IRC** [1961] **3** 1146, CA.

Deed of exchange—Freehold estate exchanged for leasehold interest in same land—Whether deed chargeable with ad valorem duty as conveyance on sale—Stamp Act 1891, s 54, Sch 1. **IRC v Littlewoods Mail Order Stores Ltd** [1962] **2** 279, HL.

Option to purchase land—Agreement in writing whereby for a consideration option granted to purchase land—Whether option 'property'—Whether agreement 'conveyance on sale'—Stamp Act 1891, s 54. **Wimpey (George) & Co Ltd v IRC** [1975] **2** 45, CA.

Transfer of shares—Agreement granting option to purchase shares and requiring immediate transfer of shares to potential purchaser in trust for vendors pending exercise of option—No transfer of beneficial interest—Subsequent oral exercise of option—Whether transfers chargeable as conveyances on sale—Whether option agreement chargeable as agreement for sale of beneficial interest—Stamp Act 1891, ss 54, 59, Sch 1. **Cory (William) & Sons Ltd v IRC** [1965] **1** 917, HL.

Transfer of shares—Shares subject to settlement—Oral agreement to exchange reversionary interest in settled shares for shares owned by life tenants—Trustees' subsequent transfer of shares to life tenants—Whether conveyance of beneficial interest—Stamp Act 1891, s 54, Sch 1—Law of Property Act 1925, s 53(1), (2). **Oughtred v IRC** [1959] **3** 623, HL.

Transfer of shares—Transfers executed in blank—Share certificates and transfers delivered to company acquiring the capital on a take-over bid—Shares then devalued by creation of prior ranking shares—Sub-sale to subsidiary company at the low value of devalued shares—Duty charged on the substantial consideration given to the share-holders to whom the take-over bid was made—Stamp Act 1891, s 58(4), Sch 1. **Fitch Lovell Ltd v IRC** [1962] **3** 685, Ch D.

1266

STAMP DUTY (cont)—
  Conveyance on sale (cont)—
    Instrument whereby property or estate or interest in property on sale thereof transferred to or vested in purchaser (cont)—
      Transfer of stock—Compulsory transfer under statutory provision—Company acquiring nine-tenths of other company's stock—Transfers of dissenting shareholder's stock executed by nominee—Whether transfer chargeable with ad valorem duty as conveyance on sale—Whether transfer on sale—Stamp Act 1891, s 54, Sch 1—Companies Act 1948, s 209. **Ridge Nominees Ltd v IRC** [1961] **3** 1108, CA.
    Periodical payments—
      Payments for a definite period exceeding 20 years—Provision for payment of all instalments on default in paying any instalment in due time—Whether charge for stamp duty limited to the aggregate of instalments for 20 years—Stamp Act 1891, s 56(2). **Western United Investment Co Ltd v IRC** [1958] **1** 257, Ch D.
      Separate instrument securing payments—Execution of separate instrument prior to conveyance on sale—Whether ad valorem duty chargeable on separate instrument—Stamp Act 1891, s 56(4). **Western United Investment Co Ltd v IRC** [1958] **1** 257, Ch D.
    Statement certifying transaction effected not forming part of series of transactions—
      Series of transactions—Finance (1909-10) Act 1910, s 73. **A-G v Cohen** [1937] **1** 27, CA.
    Transfer of shares—
      Court order whereby property or estate or interest in property on sale thereof transferred to or vested in purchaser—Scheme of arrangement—Court order—Whether ad valorem stamp duty payable on court order as conveyance or transfer on sale—Stamp Act 1891, s 54, Sch 1. **Sun Alliance Insurance Ltd v IRC** [1971] **1** 135, Ch D.
  Debt—
    Funded debt. See Issue of loan capital—Funded debt, *below*.
  Declaration of trust. See Voluntary disposition inter vivos—Declaration of trust, *below*.
  Deed of exchange. See Conveyance on sale—Instrument whereby property or estate or interest in property on sale thereof transferred to or vested in purchaser—Deed of exchange, *above*.
  Evasion—
    Fraud—
      Contract—Illegility. See **Contract** (Illegality—Deception of revenue authorities—Evasion of stamp duty).
  Gift—
    Voluntary disposition inter vivos. See Voluntary disposition inter vivos, *below*.
  Guarantee—
    Sale agreement. See Mortgage, bond, debenture or covenant—Principal or primary security for the payment or repayment of money—Guarantee of sale agreement, *below*.
  Insurance policy—
    Assignment of policy to secure overdraft from bank—
      Sufficiency of stamp—Amount recoverable by assignee—Stamp Act 1891, ss 88(2), 118(1). **Waterhouse's Policy, Re** [1937] **2** 91, Ch D.
  Interest—
    Overpaid duty. See Repayment—Interest on overpaid duty, *below*.
  Issue of loan capital—
    Ad valorem stamp duty payable on amount proposed to be secured by issue—
      Company having unsecured loan stocks protected by trust deeds—Issue by company of equivalent amounts of debenture stocks in place of unsecured loan stocks—New trust deeds protecting debenture stocks—Covenants to repay principal and interest in original trust deeds repeated or reproduced in new trust deed—Provision in new trust deed that covenants for repayment to continue to have effect but other covenants to cease to have effect—Debenture stocks secured by floating charges on assets of company and its subsidiaries and guarantees by subsidiaries—Whether 1967 conversion constituting an issue of loan capital liable to ad valorem duty—Finance Act 1899, s 8. **Associated British Maltsters Ltd v IRC** [1972] **3** 192, Ch D.
    Funded debt—
      Characteristics of funded debt—Debt having some degree of permanence or long-term character—Unnecessary for debt to be supported by some fund or transferable in separate amounts—Unnecessary for debt to have been created by conversion of existing short-term debt—Company reducing capital by cancelling shares held by another company—Consideration for cancellation creation of debt in favour of other company—Debt of long duration bearing interest at regular intervals—Whether debt a 'funded debt'—Finance Act 1899, s 8(5). **Reed International Ltd v IRC** [1975] **3** 218, HL.
    Issue—
      Advances made to company—Advances made in accordance with agreement between creditor and company—Advances accepted by company—No issue to creditor of certificate or other documentary evidence of title—Acceptance conferring right on creditor to participate in benefit of obligations imposed on company by virtue of terms under which sums advanced—Whether acceptance constituting an 'issue' of loan capital—Finance Act 1899, s 8(1). **Agricultural Mortgage Corp Ltd v IRC** [1978] **1** 248, CA.
    Loan capital—
      Capital raised which has character of borrowed money—Capital—Loan to company for strictly limited purpose—Sums advanced to enable company to carry on business more efficiently and economically—Loan available to meet claims of all creditors in event of winding—up—Whether money borrowed constituting 'capital' of company—Finance Act 1899, s 8(1)(5). **Agricultural Mortgage Corp Ltd v IRC** [1978] **1** 248, CA.
      Capital raised which has character of borrowed money—Raising of capital—Company reducing capital by cancelling shares held by other company—Consideration for cancellation creation of debt in favour of other company—Whether creation of debt constituting raising of capital—Finance Act 1899, s 8(1)(5). **Reed International Ltd v IRC** [1975] **1** 484, CA.

STAMP DUTY (cont)—
  Lease or tack—
    Consideration consisting of rent—
      Rent reserved by lease—Contingent or conditional rent—Rent to be a percentage of development expenditure up to a fixed maximum amount—Whether duty chargeable by reference to maximum amount of rent—Whether contingent or conditional rent constituting rent 'reserved' by lease—Whether contingent rent to be taken into account in assessing duty—Stamp Act 1891, Sch 1. **Coventry City Council v IRC** [1978] **1** 1107, Ch D.
  Letter or power of attorney—
    Proxy—
      Document authorising proxy to vote at any one meeting—Document not liable to duty—Document authorising proxy to vote at adjourned meeting or any new meeting dealing with specified matters—Whether document authorising proxy to vote 'at any one meeting'—Whether document liable to stamp duty—Stamp Act 1891, Sch 1 (as amended by the Finance Act 1949, s 35, Sch 8, para 17). **Marx v Estates and General Investments Ltd** [1975] **3** 1064, Ch D.
  Licensed premises—
    Conveyance. See Conveyance on sale—Instrument whereby property or estate or interest in property on sale thereof transferred to or vested in purchaser—Conveyance of licensed premises, *above.*
  Life insurance—
    Assignment. See **Insurance** (Life insurance—Assignment—Stamp duty).
  Loan capital—
    Issue. See Issue of loan capital, *above.*
  Mortgage, bond, debenture or covenant—
    Principal or primary security for the payment or repayment of money—
      Guarantee of sale agreement—Agreement to purchase stock of company—Purchase price payable in two instalments—Agreement by purchasers to procure that sum payable as second instalment guaranteed by bank—Whether guarantee 'principal or primary security'—Stamp Act 1891, Sch 1. **IRC v Henry Ansbacher & Co** [1962] **3** 843, HL.
    Transfer of mortgage by way of gift. See Voluntary disposition inter vivos—Mortgage—Transfer of mortgage by way of gift, *below.*
  Offence—
    Giving receipt liable to duty and not duly stamped—
      Gives a receipt—Electricity prepayment meter card—Entry by collector—Card property of company—Receipt not given within Stamp Act 1891, s 103(1). **A-G v Northwood Electric Light & Power Co Ltd** [1947] **1** 483, .
  Overpaid duty—
    Interest. See Repayment—Interest on overpaid duty, *below.*
  Payment under mistake of law—
    Restitution. See **Restitution** (Payment under mistake of law—Limitation—Stamp duty reserve tax charge at higher rate of 1.5% declared incompatible with EU law).
  Pecuniary legacy—
    Appropriation of stocks and shares in satisfaction of legacy. See Conveyance on sale—Instrument whereby property or estate or interest in property on sale thereof transferred to or vested in purchaser—Appropriation of stocks and shares in satisfaction of pecuniary legacy, *above.*
  Periodical payments. See Conveyance on sale—Periodical payments, *above.*
  Power of attorney. See Letter or power of attorney, *above.*
  Probate—
    Practice. See **Probate** (Practice—Stamp duty).
  Promissory note—
    Documents deemed to be promissory notes—
      Note promising payment of money out of fund which may or may not be available or on condition or contingency which may or may not be performed—Letter described as guarantee containing irrevocable undertaking to pay—Whether agreement or promissory note for purposes of stamping—Stamp Act 1891, ss 33(2), 38(1). **Wirth v Weigel Leygonie & Co Ltd** [1939] **3** 712, KBD.
  Proxy. See Letter or power of attorney—Proxy, *above.*
  Rate of duty—
    Rate in force on date instrument executed—
      Execution of deed—Delivery as an escrow—Deed signed, sealed and delivered as an escrow—Deed subsequently becoming effective on fulfilment of conditions of escrow—Whether deed 'executed' when delivered as an escrow or when conditions of escrow fulfilled—Stamp Act 1891, s 14(4). **Terrapin International Ltd v IRC** [1976] **2** 461, Ch D.
  Receipt—
    Offence. See Offence—Giving receipt liable to duty and not duly stamped, *above.*
  Reconstruction or amalgamation of companies—
    Acquisition of shares in existing company—
      Acquisition of not less than 90 per cent of issued share capital—Part of 90 per cent of issued share capital previously acquired for cash—Finance Act 1927, s 55. **Lever Bros Ltd v IRC** [1938] **2** 808, CA.
      Acquisition of not less than 90 per cent of issued share capital—Part of undertaking only acquired—Relation of relief to that part—Proportion borne by its value to 'the whole value of the undertaking'—Whether gross value of assets or net value (less liabilities)—Finance Act 1927, s 55(1)(c) (A)(i). **Gomme (E) Ltd v IRC** [1964] **3** 497, Ch D.
      Consideration for acquisition consisting as to not less than 90 per cent in the issue of shares in transferee company—Part consideration in form of shares—Part not less than 90 per cent of whole consideration—Price fixed—Addition for excess value of certain assets over value included—Reverse payment of profits pending completion—No deduction of latter payment in computing consideration—Finance Act 1927, s 55(1)(i). **Metal Box Plastic Films Ltd v IRC** [1969] **3** 1001, Ch D.

STAMP DUTY (cont)—

Reconstruction or amalgamation of companies (cont)—

Acquisition of shares in existing company (cont)—

Consideration for acquisition issue of shares in transferee company in exchange for shares in existing company—Consideration consisting as to not less than 90 per cent in issue of shares in transferee company—Issue of shares—Meaning—Shares issued subject to a condition requiring shareholders in existing company to transfer them to third party in exchange for cash—Whether consideration consisting in the issue of shares to shareholders in existing company—Whether necessary that shares should be issued to shareholders in existing company unconditionally—Finance Act 1927, s 55(1) (as amended by the Finance Act 1928, s 31). **Crane Fruehauf Ltd v IRC** [1975] **1** 429, CA.

Increase of capital to acquire shares in Northern Ireland company—Existing company—Finance Act 1927, s 55(1). **Nestlé Co Ltd v IRC** [1953] **1** 877, CA.

Particular existing company—Existing company an unlimited company—Relief from capital duty and from transfer stamp duty sought—Whether necessary that particular existing company should be a limited liability company to obtain relief claimed—Whether transferee company entitled to relief claimed—Finance Act 1927, s 55(1)(b)—Finance Act 1930, s 41. **Chelsea Land & Investment Co Ltd v IRC** [1978] **2** 113, CA.

Relief where 90 per cent of consideration in shares—Subsidiary company acquiring parent company's shares—Intermediate acquisition of subsidiary company's ordinary shares by a third company—Third company's offer of low priced option over subsidiary company's ordinary shares as inducement to preference shareholders of parent company to exchange their shares—Whether offer so made by third company was part of the consideration for the acquisition of the parent company's preference shares within Finance Act 1927, s 55(1). **Central and District Properties Ltd v IRC** [1966] **2** 433, HL.

Exclusion of relief—

Transferee company within two years of incorporation or authority for increase of capital ceasing to be beneficial owner of shares acquired—Ceasing to be beneficial owner—Conditional contract for disposal of shares—Contract signed before expiry of two year period—Condition fulfilled after expiry—Transferee company incorporated on 18th April 1969 and on same day acquiring whole of issued share capital of existing company—Revenue allowing claim for exemption from duty on transfer of shares—Chairman of transferee company signing agreement on 10th March 1971 for sale of existing company's shares to foreign company—Agreement expressed to be conditional on approval of transferee company in general meeting or on delivery at completion of minute of board meeting authorising sale—Board meeting resolution dated 1st April authorising sale delivered to foreign company on completion on 4th May—Whether contract of 10th March 1971 a conditional or binding contract—Whether transferee company having 'ceased...to be beneficial owner' of existing company's shares on 10th March 1971—Finance Act 1927, s 55(6)(c). **IRC v Ufitec Group Ltd** [1977] **3** 924, QBD.

Transferee company within two years of incorporation or authority for increase of capital ceasing to be beneficial owner of shares acquired—Ceasing to be beneficial owner otherwise than in consequence of reconstruction, amalgamation or liquidation—Amalgamation—Acquisition of more than 90 per cent of share capital—Need to show business substantially in same hands as before relevant transactions took place—Sale by transferee company of share capital in existing company to third company—Amalgamation of existing company and third company—Whether transferee company ceasing to be beneficial owner of shares in existing company 'in consequence of...amalgamation'—Finance Act 1927, s 55(6)(c). **IRC v Ufitec Group Ltd** [1977] **3** 924, QBD.

Issue of loan capital—

Relief where issue in connection with scheme for reconstruction or amalgamation and in exchange for holdings of loan capital of existing company—Meaning of 'in connection with'—Finance Act 1927, s 55(1)—Finance Act 1967, s 28(5). **Clarke Chapman-John Thompson Ltd v IRC** [1975] **3** 701, CA.

Transfer of property from one associated company to another—

Increase of nominal share capital—Transfer on sale—Reconstruction—Transfer of 'undertaking'—Issue of shares in transferee company to existing company—Existing company not taking as beneficial owner—Holding company with assets consisting of shares in subsidiary companies—Transfer of certain trade investments to subsidiary company—Increase in capital of subsidiary and issue of new shares to holding company—Creation of new subsidiary company—Agreement by holding company to transfer shares in first subsidiary company and surplus cash to new company—Increase in capital of new company and issue of shares to shareholders of holding company—Whether scheme for reconstruction of holding company—Whether property transferred to subsidiary company and to new company part of undertaking—Whether holding company taking shares in subsidiary and new company as 'beneficial owner'—Finance Act 1927, s 55—Finance Act 1930, s 42. **Baytrust Holdings Ltd v IRC** [1971] **3** 76, Ch D.

Partial take-over of first company by second company—Second company majority shareholder—Differences between second company and minority shareholders in first company—Formation of third company with share capital of £100 held by first company—Agreement between first company and third company—Scheme of arrangement—Approval by court—Purchase by third company of part of estates and shareholdings of first company—Shares of third company allotted direct to minority shareholders of first company by way of consideration—Claim to reliefs—Whether arrangement 'reconstruction'—Whether acquisition of 'not less than 90 per cent of issued share capital'—Whether first company 'beneficial owner' of not less than 90 per cent of issued share capital of third company—Finance Act 1927, s 55—Finance Act 1930, s 42. **Brooklands Selangor Holdings Ltd v IRC** [1970] **2** 76, Ch D.

Transfer of undertaking in return for shares in transferee company—

Sale by 'existing' company of part of shareholding within two years of amalgamation—Finance Act 1927, s 55(6)(b). **A-G v London Stadiums Ltd** [1949] **2** 1007, CA.

Relief from duty—

Reconstruction or amalgamation of companies. *See* Reconstruction or amalgamation of companies, *above*.

STAMP DUTY (cont)—
Relief from duty (cont)—
Transfer between associated companies. *See* Transfer of property from one associated company to another, *below*.
Repayment—
Interest on overpaid duty—
Amount of duty refunded to Revenue pending appeal to House of Lords—Appeal allowed—Interest five per cent—No retroactive operation of enactment—Finance Act 1965, s 91. **Shop and Store Developments Ltd v IRC** [1967] **1** 42, HL.
Jurisdiction of court to order payment of interest—Stamp Act 1891 s 13(1)(4)—Law Reform (Miscellaneous Provisions) Act 1934, s 3. **Western United Investment Co Ltd v IRC** [1958] **1** 257, Ch D.
Series of transactions. *See* Conveyance on sale—Statement certifying transaction effected not forming part of series of transactions, *above*.
Stamp duty land tax. *See* **Stamp duty land tax**.
Sufficiency of stamp. *See* Insurance policy—Assignment of policy to secure overdraft from bank—Sufficiency of stamp, *above*.
Transfer of property from one associated company to another—
Associated companies—
One company beneficial owner of more more than 90 per cent of issued share capital of the other—Meaning of issued share capital—Canadian company having two classes of share—American company owning less than 90 per cent of nominal issued share capital of Canadian company but more than 90 per cent in value of issued share capital of Canadian company—Transfer of shares held by American company in English company to Canadian company—Whether American company beneficial owner at time of not less than 90 per cent of issued share capital of Canadian company—Whether issued share capital meaning nominal issued share capital or value of issued share capital—Whether American and Canadian companies associated companies—Finance Act 1930, s 42 (as amended by Finance Act 1967, s 27). **Canada Safeway Ltd v IRC** [1972] **1** 666, Ch D.
Beneficial ownership—
Parent company having two wholly-owned subsidiaries—Transfer by one subsidiary to a company that was the wholly-owned subsidiary of the other subsidiary of the parent company—Share capital of transferee not in the beneficial ownership of the parent company—Parent company could be said to have 'controlling interest'—Finance Act 1930, s 42(2). **Rodwell Securities Ltd v IRC** [1968] **1** 257, Ch D.
Consideration for transfer—
Consideration 'provided directly or indirectly by' a person other than associated company—Arrangement necessarily involving provision of consideration by such person—Merger of business interests—First company setting up subsidiary—Transfer of business and assets to subsidiary—Subsidiary subsequently issuing shares to second company in return for transfer of business and assets—Subsidiary thereby becoming subsidiary of second company—Duty on instruments of transfer from first company to subsidiary—Whether arrangement whereunder consideration for transfer to be provided indirectly by second company—Finance Act 1930, s 42—Finance Act 1938, s 50. **Times Newspapers Ltd v IRC** [1971] **3** 98, Ch D.
Transfer of leasehold property from one associated company to another—Purchase price provided by mortgage to bank—Repayment of purchase price guaranteed by third company—Share capital of transferee company acquired by third company—Whether consideration for transfer indirectly provided by third company—Finance Act 1930, s 42—Finance Act 1938, s 50. **Curzon Offices Ltd v IRC** [1944] **1** 606, CA.
Transfer to associated company in return for allotment of shares—Sale of shares by associated company to issuing house which was not an associated company—Payment for allotment made out of proceeds of public issue—Whether the phrase 'consideration for the transfer' extended to include cash obtained for shares sold to issuing house—Finance Act 1930, s 42(1)—Finance Act 1938, s 50(1)(a). **Shop and Store Developments Ltd v IRC** [1967] **1** 42, HL.
Effect of instrument—
Contract by original owner to sell freehold and leasehold properties to a company—Purchase price received but no conveyance or transfer executed by owner—Death of owner—Subsequent sale by company to associated company—Conveyance, transfer and assignment executed by deceased's personal representatives—Whether exempt from ad valorem stamp duty—Stamp Act 1891, ss 54, 58(4)—Finance Act 1930, s 42—Finance Act 1938 s 50(1)(b). **Escoigne Properties Ltd v IRC** [1958] **1** 406, HL.
Transfer of stock. *See* Conveyance on sale—Instrument whereby property or estate or interest in property on sale thereof transferred to or vested in purchaser—Transfer of stock, *above*.
Trusts—
Order for varying—
Practice. *See* **Variation of trusts** (Practice—Stamp duty).
Unstamped documents—
Notice by court of omission—
Court of Appeal—Matter not raised in court below—'Agreement or memorandum relating to sale of goods'—Stamp Act 1891, s 14(1), Sch 1, Agreement or Memorandum, Exemption (3). **Routledge v McKay** [1954] **1** 855, CA.
Voluntary disposition inter vivos—
Conveyance to trustees for sale—
Necessity for adjudication—Finance (1909—10) Act 1910, s 74. **Robb's Contract, Re** [1941] **3** 186, CA.
Declaration of trust—
Deed of declaration of trust made under power in earlier deed to vary trusts—Whether chargeable with ad valorem stamp duty—Stamp Act 1891, s 62—Finance (1909—10) Act 1910, s 74(1). **Fuller v IRC** [1950] **2** 976, Ch D.

STAMP DUTY (cont)—
  Voluntary disposition inter vivos (cont)—
    Disposition by declaring new trusts—
      Transfer of shares—Transfer by settlor to trustees of settlement—Subsequent oral direction to
        trustees on what trusts shares to be held—Deed of declaration by trustees subsequently
        confirming trusts—Whether direction a 'disposition' of settlor's interest—Whether deed liable to
        ad valorem stamp duty—Stamp Act 1891, Sch 1 Finance (1909—10) Act 1910, s 74(1)—Law of
        Property Act 1925, ss 53(1)(c), 205(1)(ii). **Grey v IRC** [1959] **3** 603, HL.
    Inadequate consideration—
      Conveyance or transfer operating as a voluntary disposition—Adequacy of consideration—Family
        arrangement—Variation of trust—Surrender of reversionary life interest—Variation eliminating
        reversionary life interest and including beneficiary among class of beneficiaries under
        discretionary trusts—Whether reversionary life interest voluntarily disposed of—Finance
        (1909-1910) Act 1910, s 74(5). **Thorn v IRC** [1976] **2** 622, Ch D.
      Conveyance or transfer operating as a voluntary disposition—Intention of transferor—Relevance—
        Conveyance by reason of inadequacy of consideration conferring substantial benefit on
        transferee—Bargain at arm's length—No intention on part of transferor to confer any benefit on
        transferee—Whether open to collector to charge stamp duty on value of property conveyed
        rather than amount of consideration—Stamp Ordinance (Hong Kong)(c 117), s 27(1), (4). **Lap
        Shun Textiles Industrial Co Ltd v Collector of Stamp Revenue** [1976] **1** 833, PC.
    Mortgage—
      Transfer of mortgage by way of gift—Whether liable to ad valorem duty as voluntary disposition
        inter vivos or as mortgage—Finance (1909-10) Act 1910, s 74(1). **Anderson (Sir Alan Garrett) v IRC**
        [1938] **4** 491, KBD.
    Transfer of shares—
      Transfer by company in pursuance of resolution declaring capital bonus partly in specie and partly
        in cash—Whether transfer passing beneficial interest—Whether transfer liable to ad valorem
        duty—Finance (1909-10) Act 1910, s 74(6). **Associated British Engineering Ltd v IRC** [1940] **4** 278,
        KBD.
      Transfer by company in pursuance of special resolutions dividing amongst members part of
        company's assets in specie or in kind—Transfer by company of shares owned in another
        company—Whether transfer liable to ad valorem duty—Finance (1909-10) Act 1910, s 74(1), (5),
        (6). **Wigan Coal and Iron Co Ltd v IRC** [1945] **1** 392, KBD.
      Transfer stamped but bearing no adjudication stamp—Necessity for adjudication. **Conybear v
        British Briquettes Ltd** [1937] **4** 191, Ch D.
    Value of property conveyed or transferred—
      Variation of trust—Surrender of protected life interest—Elimination of prospective reversionary
        interests of unborn unascertained persons—Individual interests eliminated having no or only
        nominal market value—Variation of trusts effected by order of court—Whether property
        transferred by order having more than nominal value for purpose of stamp duty—Finance
        (1909-1910) Act 1910, s 74(1). **Thorn v IRC** [1976] **2** 622, Ch D.

STAMP DUTY LAND TAX
  Charity—
    Relief. *See* Relief—Charities relief, *below*.
  Liability—
    Alternative property finance—
      Shari'a compliant Ijara transaction—Taxpayer purchasing land and entering into contemporaneous
        sub-sale and leaseback arrangement with third-party bank in order to fund land purchase in
        manner compliant with Islamic finance principles—Whether taxpayer as opposed to third-party
        bank liable for stamp duty land tax on transaction—Finance Act 2003, ss 45(3), 71A, 75A. **Project
        Blue Ltd (formerly Project Blue (Guernsey) Ltd) v Revenue and Customs Comrs** [2017] **2** 549, CA.
  Relief—
    Charities relief—
      Interest in land acquired by bare trustee on behalf of charity and other non-charitable joint
        purchaser—Whether partial relief from stamp duty land tax available—Finance Act 2003, ss 43,
        103, Sch 8, Sch 16, para 3. **Pollen Estate Trustee Co Ltd v Revenue and Customs Comrs**
        [2013] **3** 742, CA.
  Transfer of rights—
    Effect of transfer of rights—
      Taxpayer entering into agreement to buy land—Purchase financed using Shari'a compliant funding
        arrangement involving sub-sale and leaseback—Taxpayer contending no liability to SDLT arising
        on transactions—Whether taxpayer liable to SDLT—Whether liability to SDLT arising on purchase
        price or consideration due from taxpayer to financier—Whether statutory scheme
        discriminatory—Human Rights Act 1998, Sch 1, Pt I, art 9—Finance Act 2003, ss 45(3), 71A, 75A,
        75B. **Project Blue Ltd (formerly Project Blue (Guernsey) Ltd) v Revenue and Customs Comrs**
        [2018] **3** 943, SC.

STAND-PIPES
  Right to charge water rates. *See* **Water supply** (Water rates—Right to charge—Water board's main in village
    street—Ancient right to water from stand-pipes free of charge).

STANDARD INDUSTRIAL CLASSIFICATION
  Selective employment tax. *See* **Selective employment tax** (Standard Industrial Classification).

STANDARD OF PROOF
  Criminal trial—
    Direction to jury. *See* **Criminal law** (Trial—Direction to jury—Standard of proof).
    Generally. *See* **Evidence** (Standard of proof).

STANDING ORDER
  Local authority. *See* **Local authority** (Standing orders).

STANNARIES AREA
  Cornwall—
    Offence committed by tinner—
      Jurisdiction of magistrates. *See* **Magistrates** (Jurisdiction—Summary offence—Offence committed by tinner in stannaries area of Cornwall).

STANNARIES COURT
  Abolition—
    Transfer of jurisdiction to county court—
      Jurisdiction of magistrates over summary offences. *See* **Magistrates** (Jurisdiction—Summary offence—Offence committed by tinner in stannaries area of Cornwall—Ancient right of tinners to be tried only by Stannaries Court—Abolition of Stannaries Court in 1896—Transfer of jurisdiction to county court).

STARE DECISIS
  International law—
    Rules of international law which form part of English law—
      Effect of doctrine of stare decisis. *See* **International law** (Enforcement by English courts—Rules of international law which form part of English law—Doctrine of stare decisis).
  Precedent. *See* **Precedent**.

STATE
  Act of—
    Constitutional law. *See* **Constitutional law** (Act of State).
  Acts for purpose prejudicial to State. *See* **Criminal law** (Official secrets—Acts for purpose prejudicial to safety or interests of State).
  Contract—
    Succession—
      Contract with predecessor state—Arbitration. *See* **Arbitration** (Award—Setting aside award—Jurisdiction—Jurisdiction to make award—Claimant state claiming not to be party to contract containing arbitration clause on basis that contract entered into with predecessor state).
  Foreign sovereign state—
    Immunity from suit. *See* **Constitutional law** (Foreign sovereign state—Immunity from suit).
    Redundancy. *See* **Redundancy** (Employer's duty to consult representatives—Failure to consult representatives—Foreign state).
  Heads of state—
    Applicability of EU law to. *See* **European Union** (Treaty provisions—Obligations under treaty—Failure to fulfil obligations—Right of EU citizens to move within territory of member states).
    Immunity from suit. *See* **Constitutional law** (Heads of foreign states—Immunity from suit).
  Obligation to investigate—
    Coroner. *See* **Coroner** (Inquest—Right to life—Duty to investigate certain deaths).
    Prohibition of torture. *See* **Human rights** (Inhuman or degrading treatment—Prohibition of torture—State's duty to investigate potential violations).
    Right to liberty and security. *See* **Human rights** (Right to liberty and security—Persons detained by British troops in Iraq—Investigative obligation).
    Right to life. *See* **Human rights** (Right to life—State's obligation to investigate death).
  Obligation to prevent inhuman or degrading treatment—
    Human rights. *See* **Human rights** (Inhuman or degrading treatment—State's obligation to prevent inhuman or degrading treatment).
  Operational duty to protect life. *See* **Human rights** (Right to life—State's operational duty to protect life).
  State aids—
    European Community. *See* **European Union** (State aids).
  State benefits—
    Damages—
      Fatal accident. *See* **Fatal accident** (Damages—State benefits).
  State immunity—
    Arbitration—
      Enforcement of award. *See* **Arbitration** (Award—Enforcement—UNCITRAL award against defendant state oil marketing board of Iraq).
    Foreign sovereign state. *See* **Constitutional law** (Foreign sovereign state—Immunity from suit).
    Heads of foreign states. *See* **Constitutional law** (Heads of foreign states—Immunity from suit).
  State liability—
    European Community. *See* **European Union** (State liability—Infringement of Community law attributable to state).

STATE AIDS
  European Union. *See* **European Union** (State aids).

STATE LIABILITY
  European Community—
    Damage caused to individuals. *See* **European Union** (State liability—Infringement of Community law attributable to state—Damage caused to individuals by infringements of Community law).

STATE OF EMERGENCY
  India. *See* **India** (State of emergency).
  St Christopher, Nevis and Anguilla—
    Governor's powers. *See* **St Christopher, Nevis and Anguilla** (Constitutional law—Governor's powers—State of emergency).

STATE PENSION
  Generally. *See* **Social security** (Retirement pension).

STATEMENT

False statement—
Furnishing false information—
False statement in hire-purchase agreement. *See* **Criminal law** (Furnishing false information—Falsifying document made or required for accounting purposes—False in a material particular—Material particular—Statement in hire-purchase agreement produced to finance company that hirer had been a company director for eight years—Statement false).
Negligence—
Careless statement causing damage to person or property. *See* **Negligence** (Duty to take care—Statement—Careless statement causing damage to person or property).
Information or advice. *See* **Negligence** (Information or advice).
Out of court—
Admissibility in evidence. *See* **Document** (Admissibility in evidence—Out-of-court statement).
Statement of claim. *See* **Statement of case**.
Statement to police—
Admissibility in criminal proceedings. *See* **Criminal evidence** (Admissions and confessions—Answers and statements to police).

STATEMENT OF CASE

Amendment—
Leave to amend. *See* Leave to amend, *below*.
Limitation of action—
Action alleging negligence in the conduct of a hospital—Allegation in statement of claim that authority responsible for negligence of house surgeon and surgeon—Amendment to include responsibility for pharmacist—New particular and not new cause of action—Public Authorities Protection Act 1893, s 1—Limitation Act 1939, s 21. **Collins v Hertfordshire CC** [1947] **1** 633, KBD.
Amendment creating new cause of action—Running-down action against authority also highway authority—Adding neglect to repair highway to negligent driving—Writ—Particularity of indorsement. **Marshall v London Passenger Transport Board** [1936] **3** 83, CA.
Amendment stating new cause of action—Period of limitation extended after expiration of period allowed by earlier Act—Public Authorities Protection Act 1893, s 1—Limitation Act 1939, ss 21, 33(a). **Batting v London Passenger Transport Board** [1941] **1** 228, CA.
Right to amend—
Claimant making demand under bond—Defendant refusing to pay—Claimant issuing proceedings for non-payment under bond—Defendant serving defence alleging demand incorrectly made—Claimant correcting demand—Claimant serving reply to defence alleging either original or later demand good for payment—Particulars of claim not being amended until after expiration of contractual limitation period—Whether amendment taking place at law within contractual limitation period—CPR 3.10, CPR PD 16, para 10.2 (now 9.2). **Maridive & Oil Services (SAE) v CNA Insurance Co (Europe) Ltd** [2002] **1 Comm** 653, CA.
Right to amend statement of claim after leave given to amend without proposed amendment first being formulated in writing—RSC Ord 28, r 12. **Busch v Stevens** [1962] **1** 412, QBD.
Salvage action—
Application to amend to plead further services. *See* **Admiralty** (Practice—Action in rem—Writ—Amendment—Application to amend statement of claim to plead further salvage services rendered to same ship).
Statement of claim amended by plaintiff but not in red—
Order to 'deliver amended statement of claim in proper form'—Dismissal of action for want of prosecution by failing to comply with order—Whether jurisdiction to order delivery of amended statement of claim. **Langton (decd), Re** [1960] **1** 657, CA.
Commercial Court—
Guidance. *See* **Commercial Court** (Practice—Revised guide to Commercial Court practice—Statements of case).
Declaration. *See* Specifying relief or remedy claimed—Declaration, *below*.
Delivery—
Delay—
Dismissal of action for want of prosecution. *See* **Practice** (Dismissal of action for want of prosecution—Delay—Delay in delivering statement of claim).
Failure to deliver statement of claim—
Dismissal of action. *See* **Action** (Dismissal—Failure to serve statement of claim).
Failure to deliver statement of claim—
Dismissal of action. *See* **Action** (Dismissal—Failure to serve statement of claim).
Leave to amend—
Amendment after expiry of limitation period. *See* **Pleading** (Amendment—Leave to amend after expiry of limitation period).
Amendment creating new cause of action—
Claim introduced by amendment statute-barred at date of amendment. **National Provincial Bank Ltd v Gaunt** [1942] **2** 112, CA.
Conspiracy to slander—
No nexus between alleged slander and special damage. **Ward v Lewis** [1955] **1** 55, CA.
Leave to amend after close of case—
Application for leave to amend after close of case but before judgment. **Loutfi v C Czarnikow Ltd** [1952] **2** 823, QBD.
Leave to amend after trial of action. *See* **Pleading** (Amendment—Leave to amend after trial of action—Statement of claim).
Statements made in 'without prejudice' discussions inconsistent with statements made in affidavit—Whether within 'unambiguous impropriety' exception to 'without prejudice' rule. **Savings and Investment Bank Ltd v Fincken** [2003] **3** 1091, Ch D.
Limitation of action. *See* Amendment—Limitation of action, *above*.
New cause of action. *See* Striking out—New cause of action, *below*.

STATEMENT OF CASE (cont)—
Personal injuries action—
  Allegation of failure to provide safe system of working—
    Whether plaintiff need plead a particular system which would be safe. **Dixon v Cementation Co Ltd** [1960] **3** 417, CA.
Power to strike out. *See* Striking out—No reasonable cause of action—Power to strike out exercisable only in clear and obvious case, *below*.
Safe system of working. *See* Personal injuries action—Allegation of failure to provide safe system of working, *above*.
Specifying relief or remedy claimed—
  Declaration—
    Statement of claim should set out declaration sought—Whether plaintiff should be allowed to ask for declaration in respect of such area of land as court after inquiry should think fit. **Biss v Smallburgh RDC** [1964] **2** 543, CA.
Striking out—
  Abuse of process—
    Action dismissed for want of prosecution—Second action in respect of same cause—Second action within limitation period—Second action not per se an abuse of process of court—Circumstances in which second action may be struck out—Prejudice to defendant. **Dept of Health and Social Security v Ereira** [1973] **3** 421, CA.
    Claim not bound to fail—Action brought to discredit defendant—Whether claim an abuse of process—Whether claim should be struck out. **Lonrho plc v Fayed (No 2)** [1991] **4** 961, Ch D.
    Forgery of documents. *See* **Practice** (Striking out—Abuse of process—Claimants bringing claim against defendants—Claimants relying upon forged documents and perjured evidence).
    Proceedings issued before introduction of Civil Procedure Rules—Appeal against striking out heard after introduction of Civil Procedure Rules—Whether reference to earlier authorities relevant—Alternatives to striking out—Civil Procedure Rules 1998. **Biguzzi v Rank Leisure plc** [1999] **4** 934, CA.
  Action against heads of government department—
    Action in respect of tort committed by subordinates—RSC Ord 19, r 27—RSC Ord 25, r 4. **Arbon v Anderson** [1942] **1** 264, CA.
  Action for false imprisonment brought by enemy aliens against Home Secretary—
    Statement of claim containing arguable point—Question whether acts done in pretended exercise of statutory powers, if not justifiable under such powers, justifiable in alternative and ex post facto under royal prerogative. **Hirsch v Somervell** [1946] **2** 430, CA.
  Action for permanent injunction—
    Refusal to give cross-undertaking in damages—Plaintiff refusing to apply for interlocutory injunction to avoid giving cross-undertaking in damages—Plaintiff acquiescing in defendant's course of conduct before applying for injunction—Whether plaintiff's claim vexatious—Whether claim for injunction should be struck out—Whether plaintiff should be ordered to apply for interlocutory injunction and give cross-undertaking in damages. **Blue Town Investments Ltd v Higgs & Hill plc** [1990] **2** 897, Ch D.
    Refusal to give cross-undertaking in damages—Plaintiff unwilling to seek interlocutory injunction because of risk attached to cross-undertaking in damages—Defendant left in state of uncertainty and subject to potential financial loss pending hearing of plaintiff's claim—Whether court having jurisdiction to order plaintiff to apply for interlocutory injunction and give cross-undertaking in damages backed by security. **Oxy Electric Ltd v Zainuddin** [1990] **2** 902, Ch D.
  Change of story by party seeking amendment—
    Amendment many years after events—Whether statement of claim should be struck out RSC Ord 20, r 5. **Rondel v Worsley** [1967] **3** 993, HL.
  Frivolous and vexatious—
    Account stated arising out of betting transactions—RSC Ord 25, r 4. **Gugenheim v Ladbroke & Co Ltd** [1947] **1** 292, CA.
    Conspiracy—Allegation that purpose unlawful—Subsequent action alleging that means unlawful. **Greenhalgh v Mallard** [1947] **2** 255, CA.
    First action alleging fraudulent misrepresentation and negligence—Second action alleging fraudulent conspiracy based on substantially same facts—Res judicata. **Wright v Bennett** [1948] **1** 227, CA.
  Limitation period—
    Statement of claim showing cause of action accruing before statutory period—Whether defendant can have statement of claim struck out—Possibility of plaintiff pleading exceptions to statute—Limitation Act 1623, s 7—RSC Ord 25, r 4. **Dismore v Milton** [1938] **3** 762, CA.
  New cause of action—
    Cause of action not in writ—Amendment of writ—Jurisdiction of court to allow amendment of writ—Discretion—New action statute-barred—Cause of action arising out of substantially the same facts as action in writ—Architect employed on construction of buildings—Writ alleging negligence in superintending work—Statement of claim alleging negligence in design and superintendence—Power to amend writ—Exercise of discretion—RSC Ord 18, r 15(2), Ord 20, r 5(1), (5). **Brickfield Properties Ltd v Newton** [1971] **3** 328, CA.
    Claim in writ for damages for wrongfully taking away the support of the plaintiffs' land and houses—Allegation in statement of claim of negligence in not preventing support being withdrawn—Whether allegation in statement of claim setting up new cause of action—RSC Ord 2, r 1, Ord 3, r 2. **Graff Bros Estates Ltd v Rimrose Brook Joint Sewerage Board** [1953] **2** 631, CA.
  No reasonable cause of action—
    Action to restrain Home Secretary from deporting enemy alien—Whether claim should be struck out—RSC Ord 25, r 4. **Netz v Rt Hon Chuter Ede PC, H M Secretary of State for Home Affairs** [1946] **1** 628, Ch D.
    Affidavit evidence—On ground for allegation that action unlikely to succeed—Whether affidavit evidence admissible on application—RSC Ord 18, r 19. **Wenlock v Moloney** [1965] **2** 871, CA.
    Inherent jurisdiction—Statement of claim disclosing cause of action—Application on which many affidavits were filed really on the ground that action was unlikely to succeed—Not a plain and obvious case—Trial in chambers on affidavit evidence—Improper exercise of jurisdiction—RSC Ord 18, r 19. **Wenlock v Moloney** [1965] **2** 871, CA.

STATEMENT OF CASE (cont)—
  Striking out (cont)—
    No reasonable cause of action (cont)—
      Limitation of action—Cause of action accruing before limitation period—Power of court to strike out
        statement of claim—Defendant proposing to rely on Statute of Limitations—Nothing before court
        to suggest that plaintiff having any escape from statute—RSC Ord 18, r 19. **Riches v DPP**
        [1973] **2** 935, CA.
      Negligence—Pile of lime mortar left in gutter outside defendant's house—Piece thrown by boy
        injuring plaintiff—Whether evidence of negligence by defendant. **Prince v Gregory** [1959] **1** 133,
        CA.
      Power to strike out exercisable only in clear and obvious case—Action with some chance of success
        on consideration of pleadings only—Libel action—Alleged libel in scientific paper criticising
        plaintiff's technique of dental anaesthesia—Plaintiff a practising dental surgeon—Words capable
        of bearing meaning defamatory of plaintiff in his profession—RSC Ord 18, r 19(1)(a).
        Drummond-Jackson v British Medical Association [1970] **1** 1094, CA.
      Rights vested in Custodian of Enemy Property—Custodian not a party. **Maerkle v British &
        Continental Fur Co Ltd** [1954] **3** 50, CA.
      Striking out part of claim—Libel—Claim against printer of advertising wrapper of book containing
        alleged libel—Assisting to publish—RSC Ord 25, r 4. **Marchant v Ford** [1936] **2** 1510, CA.
      Striking out part of claim—RSC Ord 19, 27—RSC Ord 25, r 4. **Willoughby v Eckstein** [1936] **1** 650,
        CA.
    Private law action—
      Public law defence—Institute of Chartered Accountants having express power to create byelaws for
        purpose of regulating affairs—Former member challenging validity of byelaw and bringing action
        alleging breach of implied term in membership—Whether power to create byelaws subject to
        implied term requiring it to be exercised reasonably—Whether public nature of institute
        excluding private law remedy—Whether action should be struck out as an abuse of process.
        Andreou v Institute of Chartered Accountants in England and Wales [1998] **1** 14, CA.
      Public law defence—Plaintiff bringing action against public authority for breach of
        contract—Authority claiming contract ultra vires—Whether plaintiff obliged to proceed by judicial
        review—Whether plaintiff's action should be struck out. **Doyle v Northumbria Probation
        Committee** [1991] **4** 294, QBD.
      Public law defence—Plaintiffs bringing action against local authority to recover sums due under
        improvement grants in respect of work to be carried out to houses to render them fit for human
        habitation—Local authority applying to strike out claims—Whether plaintiffs should have
        proceeded by way of judicial review—Whether claims should be struck out as an abuse of
        process—Housing Act 1985, s 189—Local Government and Housing Act 1989, s 117(3). **Trustees
        of the Dennis Rye Pension Fund v Sheffield City Council** [1997] **4** 747, CA.
      Public law defence—Rule that issues dependent on existence of public law rights should be
        determined by judicial review—Family practitioner committee abating doctor's basic practice
        allowance—Doctor bringing action claiming full allowance and alleging breach of contract by
        committee—Committee applying to strike out action—Whether doctor required to proceed by
        judicial review to assert entitlement to full allowance—Whether doctor entitled to establish
        private law right to full allowance by action—National Health Service (General Medical and
        Pharmaceutical Services) Regulations 1974, reg 24. **Roy v Kensington and Chelsea and
        Westminster Family Practitioner Committee** [1992] **1** 705, HL.
    Scandalous, frivolous or vexatious—
      Affidavit evidence—RSC Ord 25, r 4. **Day v Hill (William) (Park Lane) Ltd** [1949] **1** 219, CA.
    Vexatious proceedings—
      Attempt to relitigate issue determined in earlier proceedings—Parties—Different parties in
        subsequent proceedings—Local authority—Extraordinary audit—Secretary of State directing
        audit—Auditor surcharging amount of deficiency in accounts on councillors—Appeal of
        councillors to High Court dismissed—Secretary of State not party to appeal—Subsequent
        proceedings by councillors against Secretary of State and auditor—Allegation that direction to
        hold audit invalid—Whether allegation could have been raised in earlier proceedings. **Asher v
        Secretary of State for the Environment** [1974] **2** 156, CA.
  Sufficiency. See **Practice** (Trial—Departure from case originally pleaded).

STATUS
  Foreign law as to—
    Recognition. See **Conflict of laws** (Foreign law—Recognition—Status).
  Marital status—
    Declaration as to. See **Declaration** (Jurisdiction—Declaration as to marital status).
    Decree of nullity. See **Nullity** (Decree—Status).

STATUTE
  Action on—
    Limitation period. See **Limitation of action** (Action—Action on statute).
  Amendment—
    Amendment of primary legislation by subordinate legislation made under power contained in primary
      legislation—
      Whether such a power could only lawfully be exercised in relation to Acts on statute book when
        power enacted. **Thoburn v Sunderland City Council** [2002] **4** 156, QBD.
    Appeal pending—
      Taxation of costs—Legal aid in criminal proceedings—Appeal to High Court against review of
        taxation—Amendment of provision for awarding costs taking place between review and appeal.
        See **Legal aid** (Taxation of costs—Criminal proceedings—Appeal to High Court against review of
        taxation—Amendment of provision for awarding costs taking place between review and appeal).
    Construction. See Construction—Amendment, *below*.
    Retrospective operation. See Retrospective operation—Amendment, *below*.

STATUTE (cont)—
Breach—
Injunction—
Alternative remedies not exhausted—Power of court to grant relief. *See* **Injunction** (Alternative remedies—Alternative remedies not exhausted—Power of court to grant relief—Breach of statute).
Unwitting contravention of statute—
Exchange control legislation. *See* **Tort** (Fraud—Defence of illegality—Unwitting contravention of statute by plaintiff—Exchange control legislation).
Colonial legislation—
Criminal law—
Seditious writing concerning government—Words themselves not likely to incite to violence—No extrinsic evidence of seditious intention—Effect of English decisions on construction—Criminal Code of Gold Coast Colony, s 330. **Wallace-Johnson v R** [1940] **1** 241, PC.
Incorporation of English law—
Statute law—Whether statute law included. **Bashir v Comr of Lands** [1960] **1** 117, PC.
Repugnancy—
Deportation—Colonial Laws Validity Act 1865, s 2. **Thornton v The Police** [1962] **3** 88, PC.
Commencement—
Act coming into force on date subsequent to its enactment—
Discretionary power of court—Statutory provision affecting exercise of discretion—Whether court may take statutory provision into account although not yet brought into force—Children Act 1975, s 10(3). **S (infants) (adoption by parent), Re** [1977] **3** 671, CA.
Judgment giving effect after enactment but prior to coming into force—Fatal accident—Action by widow—Assessment of damages—Act abolishing rule that widow's prospects of remarriage to be taken into account—Judgment delivered six days prior to Act coming into force—Possibility of postponing judgment until after Act coming into force—No power to give effect to Act prior to coming into force—Law Reform (Miscellaneous Provisions) Act 1971, ss 4(1), 6(2). **Wilson v Dagnall** [1972] **2** 44, CA.
Promulgation—
Secretary of State making decision under new Act affecting asylum-seekers' rights before Act's promulgation—Whether unfairness cured by availability of judicial review—Nationality, Immigration and Asylum Act 2002, s 115. **R (on the application of L) v Secretary of State for the Home Dept** [2003] **1** 1062, CA.
Repeals—
Different provisions brought into operation on different dates—Construction of order appointing days. **Osgerby v Rushton** [1968] **2** 1196, QBD.
Statute having extra-territorial operation—
Statute brought into force on designated date—Whether brought into force in all territories at the moment when it came into force in England. **R v Logan** [1957] **2** 688, C-MAC.
Time—
Expiration of a period of one month beginning with the date on which it was passed—Caravan Sites and Control of Development Act 1960, s 50(4). **Hare v Gocher** [1962] **2** 763, QBD.
Comprehensive statutory code—
Power of court to go beyond provisions of code—
Application of principles of private law—Application of principles of private law permissible only where statutory code makes no provision for problem before court. **Pioneer Aggregates (UK) Ltd v Secretary of State for the Environment** [1984] **2** 358, HL.
Confiscatory statutory provision—
Loss of private rights without compensation—
Alternative procedure available by which the objective could be achieved—Liability to pay compensation under alternative procedure—Caravan Sites and Control of Development Act 1960, s 17(2). **Minister of Housing and Local Government v Hartnell** [1965] **1** 490, HL.
General control of development under town planning legislation—Special control available in regard to road widening under highways legislation—Liability under special control to pay compensation, but not under general control—Whether general control exercisable in regard to matters within special control—Highways Act 1959, s 72—Town and Country Planning Act 1962, ss 12, 23. **Westminster Bank Ltd v Minister of Housing and Local Government** [1968] **2** 1199, CA.
Loss of right to compensation—
Construction of words in context—Intention of legislature—Regard to statutes containing similar provisions—Reference to preamble and marginal note. **Limb & Co (Stevedores) (a firm) v British Transport Docks Board** [1971] **1** 828, QBD.
Conflict with international convention. *See* **Conflict of laws** (International convention—Ratified by executive—Implemented by statute—Conflict between convention and statute).
Consolidation Act—
Construction. *See* Construction—Consolidation Act, *below.*
Effecting no change in law—
Definition 'Unless the context otherwise requires'—Exclusion of application of definition which would effect alteration of the law consolidated—Law of Property Act 1925, s 205(1)(xx). **Beswick v Beswick** [1967] **2** 1197, HL.
New wording—
Recent amending legislation included in the consolidation—Meaning of 'disposition' in a section of the consolidating statute not limited to the meaning of corresponding words in the original statute thereby superseded as altered by the intervening legislation—Law of Property Act 1925, ss 53(1)(c), 205(1)(ii). **Grey v IRC** [1959] **3** 603, HL.
Reference to predecessor—
History of statutory provision—Reference to Act from which derived. **Merak, The** [1964] **3** 638, PDA.
Same word bearing different meanings in different sections—
Derivation of sections from different legislation. **R v Burt, ex p Presburg** [1960] **1** 424, QBD.
Construction—
Act implementing EEC directive. *See* **European Union** (National legislation—Construction).

STATUTE (cont)—
Construction (cont)—
Acts to be construed as one—
Ambiguity in earlier Act—Whether later Act affects construction of earlier Act. **Kirkness (Inspector of Taxes) v John Hudson & Co Ltd** [1955] **2** 345, HL.
Amendment of earlier Act by subsequent Act. **Crowe (Valuation Officer) v Lloyds British Testing Co Ltd** [1960] **1** 411, CA.
Ambiguous provision—
Principles applicable where enacting provision leaves scope of statutory right unclear. **Ashworth (Oliver) (Holdings) Ltd v Ballard (Kent) Ltd** [1999] **2** 791, CA.
Void for uncertainty. **Fawcett Properties Ltd v Buckingham CC** [1960] **3** 503, HL.
Amendment—
Assumption by later enactment not an amendment. **IRC v Butterley Co Ltd** [1956] **2** 197, HL.
Construction of earlier statute by reference to later amending statute. *See* Construction—Construction by reference to other statute—Definition in later amending Act, *below.*
Extension of court's jurisdiction in matrimonial causes by new enactment—Former statutory provisions thereafter read with new enactment as a new whole and not limited to former interpretation. **Tursi v Tursi** [1957] **2** 828, Div.
Minor and consequential amendments. **Woolley v Woolley (by her guardian)** [1966] **3** 855, Assizes.
Proviso applying only to one paragraph of schedule but expressed as proviso to schedule—Substitution of new paragraph without reference to proviso—Whether proviso applicable to substituted paragraph—Rent and Mortgage Interest Restrictions (Amendment) Act 1933, s 3(1)(a), Sch 1, para(h), proviso—Rent Act 1957, s 26, Sch 6, para 21. **Piper v Harvey** [1958] **1** 454, CA.
Statute of limitation. *See* **Limitation of action** (Statute—Amendment—Construction).
Anomalies—
Correction of obvious drafting error—Conditions for giving rectifying construction to statutory provision. **Inco Europe Ltd v First Choice Distribution (a firm)** [2000] **1 Comm** 674, HL; [2000] **2** 109, HL.
Correction of obvious drafting error—International co-operation with other countries in respect of criminal proceedings and investigations—Omission of reference to production order—Whether omission an error—Whether court could rectify error—Crime (International Co-operation) Act 2003, s 13(1)(b). **R (on the application of the Secretary of State for the Home Dept) v Southwark Crown Court** [2014] **3** 354, DC.
Correction of obvious drafting error—Statute abolishing sections containing offence in previous statute before implementing sections in new statute recreating repealed offences—Whether permissible for court to use interpretive powers to achieve clear intention of legislation—Forgery and Counterfeiting Act 1981, s 5(5)(f), (fa)—Identity Cards Act 2006, s 44(2), (3). **R (on the application of the CPS) v Bow Street Magistrates' Court (James and ors, interested parties)** [2006] **4** 1342, DC.
Words of statute leading to anomalous results—Words of statute plain—Circumstances in which court justified in departing from plain meaning of words of statute. **Stock v Frank Jones (Tipton) Ltd** [1978] **1** 948, HL.
Avoidance of absurdity etc—
No reason to believe party to be living—Construction to avoid absurdity or inconvenience or hardship—Matrimonial Causes Act 1950, s 16(2). **Thompson v Thompson** [1956] **1** 603, Div.
Strict sense of statutory provision ignored—Administration of Estates Act 1925, s 47(5), added by Intestates' Estates Act 1952, ss 1, 4, Sch 1. **Lockwood, Re** [1957] **3** 520, Ch D.
Bad faith—
Whether general words construed as not covering fraudulent acts. **Smith v East Elloe RDC** [1956] **1** 855, HL.
Code of Practice—
Code of Practice not issued contemporaneously with Act—Whether Code of Practice to be used as aid to interpreting Act. **R (on the application of CXF (by his mother, his litigation friend)) v Central Bedfordshire Council** [2019] **3** 20, CA.
Colonial statute—
Criminal law. *See* **West Africa** (Statute—Construction of colonial statute—Criminal law).
Conflict between enactments—
Double taxation relief agreement—Ceylon and United Kingdom—Subsequent taxing Act. *See* **Ceylon** (Income tax—Double taxation relief—Agreement with United Kingdom for relief—Subsequent Act taxing non-resident companies—Conflict between Act and agreement).
Conflict between provisions of statute—
Provision expressed to be 'subject to' other provision—Whether phrase 'subject to' implying that provisions should be construed so as to conflict. **Clark (C & J) Ltd v IRC** [1973] **2** 513, Ch D.
Whether rule that later provision prevails over former provision compatible with purposive interpretation of statutes. **Marr and anor (bankrupts), Re** [1990] **2** 880, CA.
Consolidation Act—
Reference to repealed legislation—Construction of consolidation Act not involving any point of difficulty or ambiguity—Whether reference to repealed legislation permissible for purpose of construing consolidation Act. **Farrell v Alexander** [1976] **2** 721, HL.
Constitution. *See* **Constitutional law** (Constitution—Construction).
Construction by reference to other statute—
Definition in earlier Act—Earlier Act dealing with same subject-matter—Definition omitted from subsequent Act—Whether permissible to construe expression by reference to definition in earlier repealed Act. **Richards v Curwen** [1977] **3** 426, QBD.
Definition in later amending Act—Later Act not to affect claims made before its commencement—Whether permissible in construing earlier Act to have regard to later Act in deciding claim arising before its commencement—Carriage by Air Act 1961, Sch 1, art 26(2)—Carriage by Air and Road Act 1979, s 2. **Fothergill v Monarch Airlines Ltd** [1979] **3** 445, CA.
Other statute directed to different subject-matter. **Soniershield v Robin** [1946] **1** 218, CA.
Parliamentary materials—Proper approach. **R (on the application of the Project for the Registration of Children as British Citizens) v Secretary of State for the Home Dept** [2022] **4** 95, SC.

STATUTE (cont)—
  Construction (cont)—
    Construction by reference to other statute (cont)—
      Whether court entitled to consider legislative history in determining scope of power. **R v Secretary of State for the Environment, Transport and the Regions, ex p Spath Holme Ltd** [2000] **1** 884, CA.
    Construction in accord with administrative practice—
      Construction preferred at first instance but overruled on appeal—Land Registration Act 1925, s 64(1)(a). **Strand Securities Ltd v Caswell** [1965] **1** 820, CA.
    Construction involving least alteration to law—
      Words not calculated to fit events. **Wimpey (George) & Co Ltd v British Overseas Airways Corp** [1954] **3** 661, HL.
    Construction of words within context—
      Application of proviso to one subsection to operation of another subsection—Civil Authorities (Special Powers) Act (Northern Ireland) 1922, s 1(1), (3). **McEldowney v Forde** [1969] **2** 1039, CA and HL.
    Contemporanea expositio—
      Example of inapplicability of doctrine. **Campbell College Belfast (Governors) v Comr of Valuation for Northern Ireland** [1964] **2** 705, HL.
    Contrary intention—
      Implication—Exclusion of statutory power. See **Trust and trustee** (Powers of trustee—Exclusion of power of advancement—Exclusion by contrary intention implied on construction of settlement).
    Convention—
      Convention given effect by legislation. See Construction—Convention given effect by legislation, *below.*
    Convention given effect by legislation—
      Effect to be given to plain words notwithstanding international treaty. **Collco Dealings Ltd v IRC** [1961] **1** 762, HL.
      No reference to convention—Whether convention can be referred to if not mentioned or incorporated in statute. **Salomon v Customs and Excise Comrs** [1966] **3** 871, CA.
      Principles to be applied in construing United Kingdom statute giving effect to international convention—Broad principles of general acceptation to be applied—European convention given effect by statute—Carriage of Goods by Road Act 1965, Sch. **Buchanan (James) & Co Ltd v Babco Forwarding and Shipping (UK) Ltd** [1977] **3** 1048, HL.
      Reference to French text in construing enactment giving effect to protocol. **Merak, The** [1964] **3** 638, PDA.
      Reference to foreign language text in construing English enactment giving effect to international convention—English text of convention incorporated in statute—Convention stating that English and foreign language texts equally authentic—Whether reference to foreign text permissible—Whether necessary to show English text ambiguous. **Buchanan (James) & Co Ltd v Babco Forwarding and Shipping (UK) Ltd** [1977] **3** 1048, HL.
      References to travaux préparatoires—Text of convention incorporated in statute—Circumstances in which reference to travaux préparatoires permissible—Plain meaning of text of convention—Minutes of negotiations preceding convention showing that text to be understood in sense other than plain meaning—Whether resort to minutes permissible to override plain meaning of text—Carriage by Air Act 1961, Sch 1, art 26(2). **Fothergill v Monarch Airlines Ltd** [1980] **2** 696, HL.
      Wording of statute in plain and ordinary meaning extending to cases not provided for in convention—Whether permissible to refer to convention to cut down scope of statute. **Norwhale, The** [1975] **2** 501, QBD.
    Convention impinging on English law—
      Convention guaranteeing certain human rights for all people—Convention adopted by United Kingdom—Statute making provision for depriving people of their liberty in certain circumstances—Statute not referring to convention—Whether terms of statute subject to convention—Immigration Act 1971, Sch 2, para 21(1)—Convention for the Protection of Human Rights and Fundamental Freedoms 1950, arts 5(1), 12(1). **R v Secretary of State for Home Affairs, ex p Bhajan Singh** [1975] **2** 1081, CA.
    Convention providing basis for English law—
      Reference to convention—Statute unambiguous. **Warwick Film Productions Ltd v Eisinger** [1967] **3** 367, Ch D.
    Correction of obvious drafting error—
      Release from prison on licence. See **Prison** (Release on licence—Unconditional release—Transitional provisions).
    Costs. See **Costs** (Order for costs—Action concerned with construction of legislation).
    Ejusdem generis rule—
      Rule applied to a phrase that did not include the word 'other'—'And in any case'—Town Police Clauses Act 1847, s 21. **Brownsea Haven Properties Ltd v Poole Corp** [1958] **1** 205, CA.
    European Community—
      National legislation. See **European Union** (National legislation—Construction).
    European Union legislation, in light of. See **European Union** (National legislation—Construction—Construction in light of Community legislation).
    Expressio unius, exclusio alterius—
      Recovery by executor of overpayments under Rent Restrictions Acts. **Dean v Wiesengrund** [1955] **2** 432, CA.
    General words—
      General words not to be so construed as to alter the previous policy of the law. **Chertsey UDC v Mixnam's Properties Ltd** [1964] **2** 627, HL.
    Generalia specialibus non derogant—
      Statute containing two prohibitions—Wide and limited prohibitions—Limited prohibition subject to exception—Limited prohibition wholly within wide prohibition—Whether wide prohibition to be treated as applying to cases within limited prohibition. **Number 20 Cannon Street Ltd v Singer & Friedlander Ltd** [1974] **2** 577, Ch D.

STATUTE (cont)—
  Construction (cont)—
    Hansard—
      Reference to proceedings in Parliament as an aid to construction—Ambiguous or obscure legislation—Final and interlocutory hearings—Procedure for service of extracts from Hansard on parties. **Practice Note** [1995] **1** 234, Sup Ct.
      Reference to proceedings in Parliament as an aid to construction—Ambiguous or obscure legislation—Whether court may look at parliamentary history of legislation or Hansard as aid to interpretation—Whether use of Hansard contravening Bill of Rights—Whether use of Hansard breach of parliamentary privilege—Bill of Rights (1688), s 1, art 9. **Pepper (Inspector of Taxes) v Hart** [1993] **1** 42, HL.
      Reference to proceedings in Parliament as an aid to construction—Whether court permitted to refer to Hansard to ascertain intention of Parliament. **Davis v Johnson** [1978] **1** 1132, HL.
      Reference to proceedings in Parliament as an aid to construction—Whether reference to Hansard permissible in determining scope of statutory power. **R v Secretary of State for the Environment, Transport and the Regions, ex p Spath Holme Ltd** [2001] **1** 195, HL.
    Headings and marginal notes—
      Central headings—Reference to. **Dsane v Hagan** [1961] **3** 380, Ch D.
      Cross-headings—Reference to. **DPP v Schildkamp** [1969] **3** 1640, HL.
      Marginal notes—Inaccuracy—No assistance on interpretation. **Britt v Buckinghamshire CC** [1963] **2** 175, CA.
      Marginal notes—Indication of scope of section—No assistance in distinguishing scope of section. **R v Kelt** [1977] **3** 1099, CA.
      Marginal notes—Subject-matter wider than suggested by note. **R v Surrey (North Eastern Area) Assessment Committee, ex p Surrey County Valuation Committee** [1947] **2** 276, KBD.
      Marginal notes—Use of marginal notes for interpretation of enactment. **DPP v Schildkamp** [1969] **3** 1640, HL; **Parsons v BNM Laboratories Ltd** [1963] **2** 658, CA; **Stephens v Cuckfield RDC** [1960] **2** 716, CA.
    Implication of words—
      No necessity to imply words. **Meux's Will Trusts, Re** [1957] **2** 630, Ch D.
      No sufficient reason to imply words—Justices Protection Act 1848, s 2. **O'Connor v Isaacs** [1956] **2** 417, CA.
    'In any place'. See **Trinidad and Tobago** (Statute—Construction—Power to arrest without warrant a person having in his possession 'in any place' articles reasonably suspected of being stolen).
    In pari materia—
      Conveyance—Series of statutes—Whether same meaning in latter statute of series—Stamp Act 1891, Sch 1—Finance Act 1938, s 50(1)(b). **IRC v Littlewoods Mail Order Stores Ltd** [1962] **2** 279, HL.
      Words interpreted in accordance with prior judicial interpretation of words in pari materia—Rent Act 1957, s 16. **Thompson v Stimpson** [1960] **3** 500, QBD.
    Inclusio unius exclusio alterius—
      Application of maxim—Choice between two named persons or objects—Road Traffic Act 1962, s 2(1). **R v Palfrey, R v Sadler** [1970] **2** 12, CA.
    Interpretation of word by tribunal—
      Appeal on point of law. See **Tribunal** (Appeal on point of law—Interpretation of word in statute).
    Interpretation section—
      Limiting effect—Whether interpretation section limits effect of substantive provisions. **Jobbins v Middlesex CC** [1948] **2** 610, CA.
    Later Act as aid to construction of earlier Act—
      Effect of subsequent enactment in pari materia with, but not amending Act to be construed—Resolution of ambiguity. **Camille and Henry Dreyfus Foundation Inc v IRC** [1954] **2** 466, CA.
      Effect of subsequent enactment passed on basis of construction of prior Act later called in question. **Davies Jenkins & Co Ltd v Davies (Inspector of Taxes)** [1967] **1** 913, HL.
    Long title—
      Reference to—When permissible to look to long title to control words of Act. **Ward v Holman** [1964] **2** 729, QBD.
      Reference to—Whether title may be referred to to resolve ambiguity in statute—Whether title may be used to restrict plain meaning of statute. **R v Galvin** [1987] **2** 851, CA.
    Long-standing practice—
      Stare decisis—Effect where court is asked to correct long-standing error. **Campbell College Belfast (Governors) v Comr of Valuation for Northern Ireland** [1964] **2** 705, HL.
    New Zealand. See **New Zealand** (Statute—Interpretation).
    Number—
      Words in singular to include words in plural—Selective reading of words in plural—Whether permissible—Interpretation Act 1889, s 1(1)(b). **Number 20 Cannon Street Ltd v Singer & Friedlander Ltd** [1974] **2** 577, Ch D.
    Parliamentary materials—
      Speeches of ministers proposing Bills for second reading—Reference to proceedings in Parliament as an aid to construction—Whether court may look at parliamentary history of legislation as aid to interpretation. **Three Rivers DC v Bank of England (No 2)** [1996] **2** 363, QBD.
    Penal statute. See Penal statute, *below.*
    Practice notes issued by public authority—
      Relevance—Whether admissible for consideration in determining a question of the construction of the statute. **London CC v Central Land Board** [1958] **3** 676, CA.
    Preamble—
      Acts in pari materia—Ex post facto inconvenience or absurdity—Whether clear enacting words restricted—4 & 5 Anne c 16. **A-G v HRH Prince Ernest Augustus of Hanover** [1957] **1** 49, HL.
      Preamble limiting general language in enacting provisions—4 & 5 Anne c 16. **A-G v HRH Prince Ernest Augustus of Hanover** [1957] **1** 49, HL.
    Punctuation—
      Reference to. **DPP v Schildkamp** [1969] **3** 1640, HL.

STATUTE (cont)—
   Construction (cont)—
      Purposive interpretation—
         Rates. *See* Rates (Non-domestic rates—Unoccupied property—Exemption where owner company
            being wound up).
      Repeal and re-enactment of provision—
         Extent to which Court of Appeal bound by earlier interpretation of Divisional Court. **Royal Crown
            Derby Porcelain Co Ltd v Russell** [1949] 1 749, CA.
         Scope of enactment determined by court in 1849—Enactment subsequently repealed and replaced
            in similar terms by successive statutes—Changed social conditions—Whether intention of
            Parliament that determination of 1849 should still apply—Affiliation proceedings brought by
            monther of child born abroad when mother domiciled abroad—Doctrine of stare decisis
            inapplicable. **R v Bow Road Domestic Proceedings Court, ex p Adedigba** [1968] 2 89, CA.
         Specific words re-enacted—Presumption that words intended to have meaning put on them by
            courts in earlier use—Rent Act 1968, s 85(1). **Zimmerman v Grossman** [1971] 1 363, CA.
      Report of committee—
         Report leading to the passing of the statute—Purpose for which permissible to look at report in
            relation to construction of statute. **Letang v Cooper** [1964] 2 929, CA.
         Report presented to Parliament—Committee recommending legislation—Report giving statement
            of existing law—Draft bill appended to report—Report containing commentary on draft
            bill—Commentary indicating that clause in draft bill intended to state but not alter common
            law—Draft bill enacted without alteration—Whether reference may be made to report to
            determine mischief which statute intended to cure—Whether reference may be made to report
            for a direct statement as to meaning of statute—Foreign Judgments (Reciprocal Enforcement) Act
            1933, s 8(1). **Black-Clawson International Ltd v Papierwerke Waldhof-Aschaffenburg AG**
            [1975] 1 810, HL.
      Singular including plural—
         Commissioners including sole commissioner—Whether contrary intention in enactment—
            Procedural section drafted to suit commissioners in plural—Commissioners Powers Ordinance
            1886 (Laws of Hong Kong, revised edition 1950), ss 2, 3(a)—Interpretation Ordinance (Laws of
            Hong Kong, revised edition 1950), ss 2(1), 3(5)(b). **Sin Poh Amalgamated (HK) Ltd v A-G of Hong
            Kong** [1965] 1 225, PC.
         Transferee company including companies—Whether contrary intention in enactment—Companies
            Act 1961 (NSW) s 185—Interpretation Act 1897 (NSW), s 2 (b). **Blue Metal Industries Ltd v RW
            Dilley** [1969] 3 437, PC.
         Wife—Widow—Marriage Ordinance (Laws of the Gold Coast 1951), s 48(1)—Courts Ordinance
            (Laws of the Gold Coast 1951), s 83—Interpretation Ordinance (Laws of the Gold Coast 1951),
            s 3(31),(45)—Statute 21 Henry 8 (1529), s 2—Statute of Distribution (1670), s 3. **Coleman v Shang
            alias Quartey** [1961] 2 406, PC.
      Singular not including plural—
         Contrary intention—Interpretation Act 1889, s 1(1)(b). **Dealex Properties Ltd v Brooks** [1965] 1 1080,
            CA.
      Specific terms—
         Accident—Liability for injury from water from any 'accident'—Peak Forest Canal Act 1794, s 15.
            Makin (J & J) Ltd v London & North Eastern Ry Co [1943] 1 645, CA.
         Assessment—Taxing Act—Machinery provision read as reference to charge of tax—Finance Act
            1940, Sch V, Pt 1. **English Sewing Cotton Co Ltd v IRC** [1947] 1 679, CA.
         Dependant—Limited to legitimate dependant. **Makein (decd), Re** [1955] 1 57, Ch D.
         Express provision—Repealing enactment not to affect things pending in the absence of express
            provision to that effect. **Shanmugan v Comr for the Registration of Indian and Pakistani
            Residents** [1962] 2 609, PC.
         Including—Definition. **Customs and Excise Comrs v Savoy Hotel Ltd** [1966] 2 299, QBD.
         May construed as meaning 'shall'. **Shuter, Re (No 2)** [1959] 3 481, QBD.
         Must—Imperative or directory requirement—Procedural provision—Rent Act 1965, Sch 3, para 2.
            Chapman v Earl [1968] 2 1214, QBD.
         Or—Conjunctive or disjunctive—'Or' not construed 'and'—Army Act 1955, s 70(2). **Cox v Army
            Council** [1962] 1 880, HL.
         Person appointed—Body of persons—Committee. **R v Minister of Agriculture and Fisheries, ex p
            Graham** [1955] 2 129, CA.
         Territorial waters—United Kingdom or its 'territorial waters'—Reference to be construed prima facie
            as including areas from time to time declared by Crown to be within jurisdiction—Area claimed
            by Crown at time of alleged offence than at time of passing of statute—Wireless
            Telegraphy Act 1949, s 6(1). **Post Office v Estuary Radio Ltd** [1967] 3 663, QBD and CA.
      Standard Industrial Classification—
         Reference to heading of industrial classification—Whether introduction to document containing
            classification could be taken into account. **Lord Advocate v Reliant Tool Co** [1968] 1 162, HL.
      Statutory instrument—
         Regulation in same terms as statute—Application of Interpretation Act 1889—Interpretation Act
            1889, s 1. **Potts or Riddell v Reid** [1942] 2 161, HL.
         Use of regulations for interpretation of section of statute. **Britt v Buckinghamshire CC** [1963] 2 175,
            CA; **Stephens v Cuckfield RDC** [1960] 2 716, CA.
         Use of rules made by Lord Chancellor for interpretation of section of statute. **Jackson v Hall**
            [1980] 1 177, HL.
      Temporal connotation—
         Use of historic present—'Applies'—Finance Act 1937, Sch 4, para 7(1)(a)—Finance Act 1947, s 32(1).
            IRC v Clifforia Investments Ltd [1963] 1 159, Ch D.
         Use of historic present—Where any such resumption is made—Words descriptive of purpose—Not
            stipulating that resumption should have been made—New South Wales Closer Settlement
            (Amendment) Act 1907 (No 12 of 1907), s 4(4)(b), proviso (as amended). **Pye v Minister for Lands
            for New South Wales** [1954] 3 514, PC.
      Transposition or addition of words—
         Necessity for transposing or adding words to construe statute—Landlord and Tenant Act 1927,
            s 18(1). **Salisbury v Gilmore & Marcel** [1942] 1 457, CA.

STATUTE (cont)—
    Construction (cont)—
        White Paper—
            Admissibility—Whether admissible for construing a document having the force of statute. **Katikiro of Buganda v A-G** [1960] **3** 849, PC.
        Word—
            Word occurring more than once in enactment—Consistency in meaning—Contrary intention—Rule that word should be given consistent meaning—Rule to give way where contrary intention indicated—Land—Finance Act 1976, Sch 5, para 29(2)(b)(3)—Interpretation Act 1978, Sch 2, para 5(b). **Payne (Inspector of Taxes) v Barratt Developments (Luton) Ltd** [1985] **1** 257, HL.
    Contract—
        Agreement confirmed by statute—
            Binding effect—Whether agreement binding by statutory force or binding in contract—Malvern Hills Act 1924, s 54, Sch 4. **Pyx Granite Co Ltd v Ministry of Housing and Local Government** [1959] **3** 1, HL.
        Contractual rights taken away—
            Words must not be ambiguous. **Allen v Thorn Electrical Industries Ltd** [1967] **2** 1137, CA.
    Convention—
        Application without statutory enactment. *See* **International law** (Convention—Enforcement by English courts—Provisions of convention not given force by Act of Parliament).
    Crown—
        Crown entitled by statute to claim for salvage services—
            Vicarious liability for negligence—Whether Crown vicariously liable for negligence of officers and servants. **Anglo-Saxon Petroleum Co Ltd v Damant** [1947] **2** 465, CA.
        Minister as representative of—
            Minister's laying scheme before Parliament. **Merricks v Heathcoat-Amory** [1955] **2** 453, Ch D.
        Parens patriae jurisdiction as to infants—
            Education of children—Education Act 1944. **Baker (infants), Re** [1961] **3** 276, CA.
            Effect of statutory powers and duties of local authorities—Children Act 1948. **M (an infant), Re** [1961] **1** 788, CA.
        Taxing Act—
            Liability of Crown servant for income tax. **Bank Voor Handel en Scheepvaart NV v Administrator of Hungarian Property** [1954] **1** 969, HL.
        Whether bound by statute—
            Emergency powers—Courts (Emergency Powers) Act 1939, s 1(1). **A-G v Hancock** [1940] **1** 32, KBD.
            Emergency powers—Courts (Emergency Powers) Act 1939—Possession of Mortgaged Land (Emergency Provisions) Act 1939. **Hutley's Legal Charge, Re** [1941] **2** 141, Ch D.
            Planning and highway legislation—Contractors employed by Crown encroaching on highway while carrying out work on adjoining Crown land—Highway and planning authorities serving removal, enforcement and stop notices on Crown in respect of encroachment—Whether notices valid—Whether Crown bound by planning and highway legislation—Principles applicable for determining whether Crown bound by particular statute—Town and Country Planning (Scotland) Act 1972, ss 84, 87—Roads (Scotland) Act 1984, ss 59, 87, 141(1). **Lord Advocate v Dumbarton DC** [1990] **1** 1, HL.
            Town and country planning legislation. **Ministry of Agriculture, Fisheries and Food v Jenkins** [1963] **2** 147, CA.
            United Kingdom Act imported into law of colony by ordinance. **Premchand Nathu & Co Ltd v Land Officer** [1963] **1** 216, PC.
    Definition—
        Definition in earlier statute—
            Construction of later statute by reference to definition. *See* Construction—Construction by reference to other statute—Definition in earlier Act, *above*.
        Statute defining term differently from ordinary meaning—
            Whether term as defined governing what is proposed, authorised or done under or by reference to statute. **Wyre Forest DC v Secretary of State for the Environment** [1990] **1** 780, HL.
    Ejusdem generis rule. *See* Construction—Ejusdem generis rule, *above*.
    Enforcement—
        Duty—
            Whether absolute. **Brown v National Coal Board** [1962] **1** 81, HL; **Hamilton v National Coal Board** [1960] **1** 76, HL.
        Non-observance of 'recognised terms and conditions'—
            Private remedies. **Hulland v William Saunders & Son** [1944] **2** 568, CA.
    European Union—
        National legislation. *See* **European Union** (National legislation—Construction).
        Withdrawal. *See* **European Union** (Withdrawal—Retained EU law).
    Expressio unius, exclusio alterius. *See* Construction—Expressio unius, exclusio alterius, *above*.
    Foreign—
        Construction—
            Opinion of expert witness—Rejection—Whether court can reject opinion of witness tendered as expert on foreign law. **Sharif v Azad** [1966] **3** 785, CA.
    Headings and marginal notes. *See* Construction—Headings and marginal notes, *above*.
    Inclusio unius exclusio alterius. *See* Construction—Inclusio unius exclusio alterius, *above*.
    Inconsistency with constitution—
        Ceylon—
            Validity of statute—Amendment of constitution. *See* **Ceylon** (Constitutional law—Amendment of constitution—Amending statute inconsistent with constitution).
    Interpretation section. *See* Construction—Interpretation section, *above*.
    Long title. *See* Construction—Long title, *above*.
    Mandatory statutory provision—
        Coast protection—
            Works scheme providing for coast protection charges—Whether time limit within which coast protection authority to levy charges was mandatory or directory—Coast Protection Act 1949, s 7(4)(b). **Cullimore v Lyme Regis Corp** [1961] **3** 1008, QBD.

STATUTE (cont)—
Mandatory statutory provision (cont)—
Waiver—
Concession invalid unless obtained in accordance with procedure laid down by statute—Whether waiver possible. **Ramia (Edward) Ltd v African Woods Ltd** [1960] **1** 627, PC.
Marginal note—
Aid to construction. *See* Construction—Headings and marginal notes, *above.*
Mischief Act designed to prevent. *See* Penal statute—Mischief Act designed to prevent, *below.*
New Zealand. *See* **New Zealand** (Statute).
No certiorari clause—
Jurisdiction to issue certiorari. *See* **Certiorari** (Jurisdiction—Statutory tribunal's decision—No certiorari provision in statute).
Obsolescence—
Naturalisation—
Statute deeming lineal descendants of Princess Sophia to be natural born subjects—4 & 5 Anne c 16. **A-G v HRH Prince Ernest Augustus of Hanover** [1957] **1** 49, HL.
Offence—
Absolute offence—
Interpretation of enactment—Road Traffic Act 1960, s 235(2). **R v Cummerson** [1968] **2** 863, CA.
Conviction under repealed statute—
Power of quarter sessions to amend summons on appeal from court of summary jurisdiction. **Meek v Powell** [1952] **1** 347, KBD.
Duplicity—
One or more offences—Whether enactment creating one or several offences. **Newton (G) Ltd v Smith** [1962] **2** 19, QBD.
Illegality not constituting an offence—
Enactment declaring lotteries unlawful—Betting and Lotteries Act 1934, s 21. **Sales-Matic Ltd v Hinchliffe** [1959] **3** 401, QBD.
Mens rea—
Intention to deprive accused of defence by way of absence of mens rea not to be imputed to Parliament. **Warner v Metropolitan Police Comr** [1968] **2** 356, HL.
Offences under this Act—
Offence against regulations—Whether offence under Act—Food and Drugs Act 1955, s 113(1). **United Dairies (London) Ltd v Beckenham Corp** [1961] **1** 579, QBD.
Regulations—
Contravention of regulation amounting to offence under Act. **Rathbone v Bundock** [1962] **2** 257, QBD.
Section of Act conferring power to make regulations and making non-compliance with regulations punishable—Whether such non-compliance an offence under the Part of the Act in which the section falls, for the purpose of a subsequent enactment of the Act—Road Traffic Act 1960, ss 35, 232(2)(b). **Bingham v Bruce** [1962] **1** 136, QBD.
Order made under repealed statutory power—
Scope of order limited by scope of power—
Superseding enactment conferring similar power not so limited—Original order saved—Scope of original order not extended. **Solicitor, Re a** [1955] **1** 257, QBD.
Superseding enactment containing similar power but limited in scope by narrower definition—Effect on scope of order. **Simpkin Marshall Ltd, Re** [1958] **3** 611, Ch D.
Ouster of jurisdiction by statute—
Certiorari. *See* **Certiorari** (Jurisdiction—Exclusion by statute).
Exclusion of right of appeal to Court of Appeal. *See* **Court of Appeal** (Appeal—Right of appeal—Exclusion of right of appeal).
Parens patriae jurisdiction. *See* Crown—Parens patriae jurisdiction, *above.*
Parliament—
Erroneous view of the law—
Effect. **Birmingham City Corp v West Midland Baptist (Trust) Association (Inc)** [1969] **3** 172, HL; **County of London (Devons Road, Poplar) Housing Confirmation Order 1945, Re** [1956] **1** 818, Ch D.
Penal statute—
Abolition of offence—
Offence committed before abolition—Indictment signed after abolition—Whether conviction valid—Interpretation Act 1889, s 38(2)—Criminal Law Act 1967, s 12. **R v Fisher** [1969] **1** 100, CA.
Offence committed before abolition—Prosecution for offence after abolition—Frequenting or loitering with intent—Whether person may be prosecuted after abolition for offence committed before abolition—Whether repealing statute showing contrary intention—Vagrancy Act 1824, s 4—Interpretation Act 1978, s 16—Criminal Attempts Act 1981, ss 8, 10, Sched, Part II. **Comr of Police of the Metropolis v Simeon** [1982] **2** 813, HL.
Avoidance of absurdity etc—
Substitution of 'or' for 'and', although result less favourable to accused—Official Secrets Act 1920, s 7. **R v Oakes** [1959] **2** 92, CCA.
Construction more favourable to accused—
Two possible meanings—Adoption of more lenient meaning—Rent Act 1968, s 85. **Zimmerman v Grossman** [1971] **1** 363, CA.
Two reasonable interpretations—Where there are two reasonable interpretations, the more lenient one should be adopted—Exchange Control Act 1947, s 1(1). **HPC Productions Ltd, Re** [1962] **1** 37, Ch D.
Mischief Act designed to prevent—
Ascertaining meaning by construing statute as a whole—Long title—Express savings. **Kennedy v Spratt** [1971] **1** 805, HL.
Implication against admission of self-incriminating evidence—Legislation designed to facilitate detection of fraud—Companies Act 1948, s 167(2), (4). **R v Harris (Richard)** [1970] **3** 746, CCC.
Ordinary rules of construction—
Wide and comprehensive language—Contemporaneous circumstances—Judicial notice. **Elderton v UK Totalisator Co Ltd** [1945] **2** 624, CA.

STATUTE (cont)—
  Penal statute (cont)—
    Retrospective operation. *See* Retrospective operation—Penal statute, *below.*
    Strict construction—
      Failure to comply with any of the provisions of a Part of an Act—One section in that Part an exempting provision—Failure to comply with requirement of exempting enactment—Whether an offence—Pharmacy and Poisons Act 1933, ss 18, 19, 24. **R v Staincross Justices, ex p Teasdale** [1960] **3** 572, QBD.
      Strict construction not extending beyond clear meaning. **Liew Sai Wah v Public Prosecutor** [1968] **2** 738, PC.
  Practice—
    Construction. *See* Construction—Construction in accord with administrative practice, *above.*
    Preamble. *See* Construction—Preamble, *above.*
  Private Act of Parliament—
    Validity. *See* Validity—Private Act of Parliament, *below.*
  Proviso—
    Function of proviso to limit or qualify substantive provision—
      Circumstances in which proviso may be construed as adding to and not merely qualifying what goes before—Stamp Duties Act 1920-1964 (New South Wales), s 102(2)(a). **Comr of Stamp Duties v Atwill** [1973] **1** 576, PC.
  Rectification—
    Obvious drafting error. *See* Construction—Anomalies—Correction of obvious drafting error, *above.*
  Repeal—
    Implication—
      Alteration of penalties—Metropolitan Paving Act 1817, s 75—Metropolis Management Act 1855, ss 122, 123. **Smith v Benabo** [1937] **1** 523, KBD.
      Right of entry on land by drainage board—Land Drainage Act 1930, s 34(4)—Land Drainage Act 1961, s 40(1). **Pattinson v Finningley Internal Drainage Board** [1970] **1** 790, QBD.
    Retrospective operation. *See* Retrospective operation—Repeal, *below.*
    Savings—
      Accrued right or privilege—Anything done—Landlord and Tenant Ordinance (Laws of Hong Kong, revised edition 1950, as amended), s 3A-s, 3E—Interpretation Ordinance (Laws of Hong Kong, revised edition 1950), s 10(b)(c). **Director of Public Works v Ho Po Sang** [1961] **2** 721, PC.
      Accrued right—Inchoate right—Motor insurance—Third-party's right against insurers—Ceylon Interpretation Ordinance 1900, s 6(3)(b). **Free Lanka Insurance Co Ltd v Ranasinghe** [1964] **1** 457, PC.
      Acquired right—Claimant having right to allowance under enactment—Claimant making claim within prescribed period but after repeal of enactment—Whether claimant's failure to claim before repeal precluded him from having acquired right under repealed enactment—Interpretation Act 1978, s 16(1)(c). **Chief Adjudication Officer v Maguire** [1999] **2** 859, CA.
    Subordinate legislation—
      Implied repeal—Whether enactment of statute repealed by implication by subordinate legislation. **Ridge v Baldwin** [1963] **2** 66, HL.
  Retrospective operation—
    Alteration in substantive law—
      Enactment not expressly nor by necessary implication retroactive—Matrimonial Causes Act 1963, s 3. **Carson v Carson and Stoyek** [1964] **1** 681, Div.
    Amendment affecting right acquired or accrued under previous enactment—
      Defence given by previous enactment—Defence given by previous enactment—Amendment taking away defence—Copyright—Design—Statute precluding right of action for breach of copyright where design not registered—Amendment enabling plaintiff to maintain action where design not registered—Failure to register design prior to amendment coming into force—Whether defendants' right to infringe copyright prior to amendment a right acquired or accrued—Copyright Act 1956, s 10 (as amended by the Design Copyright Act 1968)—Interpretation Act 1889, s 38(2)(a). **Sifam Electrical Instrument Co Ltd v Sangamo Weston Ltd** [1971] **2** 1074, Ch D.
    Amendment extending disciplinary jurisdiction—
      Amendment not expressly stated to be retroactive—Whether jurisdiction conferred in relation to conduct before date of amendment. **Solicitor's Clerk, Re a** [1957] **3** 617, QBD.
    Amendment increasing penalty—
      Increase in penalty by reference to date of conviction—Interpretation Act 1889, s 38(c), (d). **DPP v Lamb** [1941] **2** 499, KBD.
      Increase in penalty by reference to date of information. **Buckman v Button** [1943] **2** 82, KBD.
    Amendment of statute of limitation—
      Extension of limitation period. *See* **Limitation of action** (Statute—Amendment—Construction—Extension of limitation period).
    Divorce—
      Financial provision—Property adjustment. *See* **Divorce** (Financial provision—Lump sum order—Property adjustment order—Statutory powers—Retrospective operation).
    Immigration rules. *See* **Immigration** (Rules—Statement of changes in immigration rules—Presumption against retrospectivity).
    Implication of retrospective operation—
      Provision affecting substantive law—Divorce—Financial provision—Statutory provision empowering court to grant relief—Petition for divorce by wife filed prior to January 1971—Claim for maintenance—New statutory provision empowering court to order transfer of matrimonial home coming into force in January 1971—Provision not expressed to have retrospective effect—Provision affecting substantive law by creating new rights and obligations—Provision having retrospective effect by necessary implication—Matrimonial Proceedings and Property Act 1970, s 4(1), Sch 1, para 1. **Williams v Williams** [1971] **2** 764, Div.
    Income tax. *See* **Income tax** (Statute—Retrospective operation).
    Motor insurance—
      Rights of third parties against insurers. *See* **Motor insurance** (Rights of third parties against insurers—Rights under statute—Retrospective operation of statute).

STATUTE (cont)—
Retrospective operation (cont)—
Penal statute—
Principle that penal statute may not have retroactive effect—Whether principle will be enforced by Court of Justice of European Communities—Sea Fish (Specified United Kingdom Waters) (Prohibition of Fishing) Order 1982. **R v Kirk** [1985] **1** 453, ECJ.
Pending proceedings—
Alteration of law after judgment and before appeal—Dismissal of police constable by chief police officer—Dismissal held to be in contravention of statute—Amendment of statute after judgment and before appeal—Amendment validating dismissal of constables by chief police officers—Whether amendment affecting pending proceedings—Whether dismissal of constable validated retrospectively by amendment—Federal Constitution of Malaysia, art 135(1) proviso. **Zainal bin Hashim v Government of Malaysia** [1979] **3** 241, PC.
Alteration of law after judgment and before appeal—Duty of Court of Appeal—Vested substantive right not to be interfered with—Distinction for matters of procedure—Supreme Court of Judicature (Consolidation) Act 1925, s 27(1)—Supreme Court of Judicature (Amendment) Act 1959, s 1(1)—RSC Ord 58, r 9(3). **A-G v Vernazza** [1960] **3** 97, HL.
Disturbance of existing rights. **Hutchinson v Jauncey** [1950] **1** 165, CA.
Enactment empowering husband to give evidence rebutting condonation—Sexual intercourse before statute, trial after—No provision in Act excluding pending proceedings—Matrimonial Causes Act 1963, s 1. **Blyth v Blyth** [1966] **1** 524, HL.
Enactment providing for relief notwithstanding temporary cohabitation with a view to reconciliation—Cohabitation before statute, trial after—Matrimonial Causes Act 1963, s 2(1). **Herridge v Herridge (orse Harridge)** [1966] **1** 93, CA.
Statute coming into force after hearing of action but before judgment—Landlord and Tenant (Rent Control) Act 1949, s 10. **Jonas v Rosenberg** [1950] **1** 296, CA.
Supreme Court Rule Committee making rules purporting to apply Act to proceedings begun prior to its commencement date—Act expressly excluding such proceedings unless provided for by Lord Chancellor's order—Whether Act applying to proceedings begun before commencement date—Civil Evidence Act 1995, s 16. **Bairstow v Queens Moat Houses plc** [1998] **1** 343, CA.
Taxing Act repealing previous Act—Provisions of new Act applicable as if incorporated in previous Act—Proviso that no party to any 'legal proceedings' pending on certain date to be prejudiced—Appeal by taxpayer lodged on following day—Notice of objection to assessments and of refusal of Commissioner to amend assessments had been previously given—Statutory discretion of judge on appeal to reduce assessment had not been re-enacted in the new Act—Whether legal proceedings were pending on the relevant date—Whether court's discretion under the previous Act remained applicable to the appeal—Income Tax (Management) Act 1952, s 78(6)—Income Tax (Management) Act 1958, s 152, Sch 5, para 1. **Rattan Singh v Comr of Income Tax** [1967] **1** 999, PC.
Procedural provisions—
Amendment—Landlord and tenant legislation—Business premises—Compensation where court precluded from granting application for new tenancy—Amendment extinguishing necessity for application to court in order to establish right to compensation—Whether amendment a procedural provision—Whether amendment having retrospective operation—Landlord and Tenant Act 1954, s 37(1) (as amended by Law of Property Act 1969, s 11). **Grafton Street (14), London W1, Re** [1971] **2** 1, Ch D.
Evidence taken at investigation before enactment passed—Whether evidence admissible, by virtue of enactment, in action against a witness after enactment passed—Companies Act 1967, s 50. **Selangor United Rubber Estates Ltd v Cradock (a bankrupt) (No 2)** [1968] **1** 567, Ch D.
Limitation period—Statute introducing limitation period—Whether provision retrospective in operation—Contracts of Employment Act 1972, s 8(8). **Grimes v Sutton London Borough** [1973] **2** 448, NIRC.
Receiving—
Offence extended to persons assisting—Facts constituting alleged offence took place before enactment brought into force—Arraignment, trial and conviction thereafter—Whether enactment retroactive in operation—Criminal Law Act 1967, ss 4(7), 12(1). **R v Reah** [1968] **3** 269, CA.
Repeal—
Defence of no sufficient memorandum of sale of goods—Writ issued and defence delivered before repeal—Sale of Goods Act 1893, s 4—Law Reform (Enforcement of Contracts) Act 1954, s 2. **Craxfords (Ramsgate) Ltd v Williams & Steer Manufacturing Co Ltd** [1954] **3** 17, QBD.
Specific enactments—
Recovery of rent—Landlord and tenant (War Damage) (Amendment) Act 1941, s 13. **London Fan & Motor Co Ltd v Silverman** [1942] **1** 307, KBD.
Rights of way—Procedural enactment—Rights of Way Act 1932, s 1(2) (6). **A-G and Newton Abbot RDC v Dyer** [1946] **2** 252, Ch D.
Taxing Act—
Ceylon. See **Ceylon** (Statute—Retrospective operation—Taxing Act).
Validating statute—
Queensland. See **Queensland** (Statute—Validating statute—Retrospective effect).
Workmen's compensation—
Injury before amending Act passed—Disease first noticed many years later—Worker never in employment after amendment passed. **Sunshine Porcelain Potteries Pty Ltd v Nash** [1961] **3** 203, PC.
Royal prerogative—
Ouster by statute. See **Crown** (Prerogative—Ouster by statute).
Rules of court. See **Statutory instrument** (Rules of court).
Sidenote—
Aid to construction. See Construction—Headings and marginal notes, *above.*
Statutory authority—
Defence to action for nuisance. See **Nuisance** (Defence—Statutory authority).
Statutory duty. See **Statutory duty**.
Statutory instrument—
Aid to construction of statute. See Construction—Statutory instrument, *above.*

STATUTE (cont)—
Statutory powers of public authority. *See* **Public authority** (Statutory powers).
Statutory requirement—
    Procedural requirement—
        Non-compliance—Principles applicable for determining consequences of non-compliance with
        procedural requirement. **R v Immigration Appeal Tribunal, ex p Jeyeanthan** [1999] **3** 231, CA.
Taxing Act—
    Construction to avoid inequitable results—
        Estate duty. **Fry v IRC** [1958] **3** 90, CA.
    Retrospective operation—
        Ceylon. *See* **Ceylon** (Statute—Retrospective operation—Taxing Act).
    Vagueness—
        When court will say that subject has not been taxed in view of vagueness. **Customs and Excise
        Comrs v Top Ten Promotions Ltd** [1969] **3** 39, HL, QBD and HL.
Temporary offence—
    Expiry of statute. *See* **Criminal law** (Temporary statutory offence—Expiry of statute).
Temporary statute—
    Expiry—
        Effect of expiry on operation 'as respects things previously done'. **Wicks v DPP** [1947] **1** 205, HL.
Territorial operation—
    Territorial waters—
        Warranty—Whether warranty limited to sales in the United Kingdom—Fertilisers and Feeding
        Stuffs Act 1926, s 2(2). **Kendall (Henry) & Sons (a firm) v William Lillico & Sons Ltd** [1968] **2** 444,
        HL.
    United Kingdom—
        Warranty limited to sales in United Kingdom—Fertilisers and Feeding Stuffs Act 1926, s 2(2). **Draper
        (C E B) & Son Ltd v Turner (Edward) & Son Ltd** [1964] **3** 148, CA.
University—
    Officer—
        Refusal to perform duty imposed by university statute. *See* **University** (Officer—Refusal to perform
        duty imposed by university statute).
Validity—
    Constitution of independent sovereign state—
        Jurisdiction of court—Pleadings challenging validity of properly passed Act—Canada Act passed by
        United Kingdom Parliament to repatriate Canadian constitution to Canada—Allegation that Act
        ultra vires because 'consent' of dominion not properly obtained—Whether court having
        jurisdiction to inquire into validity of Act—Whether declaration in Act that dominion has
        requested and consented to legislation conclusive—Canada Act 1982. **Manuel v A-G** [1982] **3** 822,
        CA.
    Inconsistency between federal and state legislation—
        South Australia. *See* **South Australia** (Statute—Validity—Inconsistency of federal and state
        legislation).
    Private Act of Parliament—
        Passage of Act secured by improper means—Jurisdiction of court—Pleadings challenging validity
        of private Act—Allegation that Act obtained by false and misleading recitals in
        preamble—Application to strike out pleadings—Whether court having jurisdiction in
        circumstances to disregard provisions of Act—Whether court having jurisdiction to enquire into
        proceedings in Parliament—Whether pleadings raising triable issue. **British Railways Board v
        Pickin** [1974] **1** 609, HL.
    Public general Act—
        Parliament Act providing for enactment of Acts of Parliament without consent of House of
        Lords—House of Commons using Parliament Act procedure to amend Parliament Act—House of
        Commons using amended Parliament Act procedure to enact Hunting Act—Whether Hunting Act
        valid—Whether amended Parliament Act procedure valid—Parliament Act 1911, s 2(1)—
        Parliament Act 1949, s 1—Hunting Act 2004. **R (on the application of Jackson) v A-G**
        [2005] **4** 1253, HL.
    Reference in Act to provisions of earlier void Act. *See* **Sierra Leone** (Legislation—Validity—Reference in
    Act to provisions of earlier void Act).
Waiver—
    Mandatory statutory provision. *See* Mandatory statutory provision—Waiver, *above*.
White Paper—
    Admissibility as aid to construction of document having force of statute. *See* Construction—White
    Paper—Admissibility, *above*.

STATUTORY AUTHORITY
Acts done under statutory authority etc—
    Racial discrimination. *See* **Race relations** (Discrimination—Acts done under statutory authority etc).
Defence to action for nuisance. *See* **Nuisance** (Defence—Statutory authority).
Estoppel. *See* **Estoppel** (Statutory body).

STATUTORY BODY
Injunction—
    Illegal act. *See* **Injunction** (Illegal act of statutory body).

STATUTORY COMPANY
See **Company** (Statutory company).

STATUTORY DUTY
Accommodation—
    Duty of housing authority to provide accommodation—
        Homeless person. *See* **Housing** (Homeless person—Duty of housing authority to provide
        accommodation).

STATUTORY DUTY (cont)—

Bankruptcy—
Petition. See **Bankruptcy** (Petition—Statutory duty).
Bookmaker. See Breach of duty imposed under sanction of penalty—Competence of civil action at suit of person aggrieved—Bookmaker, *below.*
Breach—
Bankruptcy. See **Bankruptcy** (Petition—Statutory duty—Breach).
Breach by employers and employee—
Apportionment of responsibility where faults not co-extensive—Building regulations. See **Building** (Building regulations—Breach—Breach by employers and employee—Apportionment of responsibility where faults not co-extensive).
Breach of duty imposed under sanction of penalty. See Breach of duty imposed under sanction of penalty, *below.*
Cause of action—
Bankruptcy. See **Bankruptcy** (Petition—Statutory duty—Breach—Cause of action).
Traffic regulations—Road markings. See **Road traffic** (Traffic sign—Road markings—Cause of action for contravention of regulation).
Civil liability—
Landlord and tenant—Harassment—Residential occupier—Acts calculated to interfere with peace or comfort of occupier—Acts done with intent to cause occupier to give up occupation—Criminal offence—Whether commission of offence giving rise to civil liability at suit of occupier—Rent Act 1965, s 30(2), (4). **McCall v Abelesz** [1976] **1** 727, CA.
Lighting of vehicles. See **Road traffic** (Lighting of vehicles—Civil liability for breach of duty).
Coal mining. See **Coal mining** (Statutory duty—Breach).
Contributory negligence—
Workman and fellow employee. See **Negligence** (Contributory negligence—Workman and fellow employee—Breach of statutory duty).
Damages—
Generally. See **Damages** (Breach of statutory duty).
Measure of damages. See **Damages** (Measure of damages—Breach of statutory duty).
Factory—
Fencing of dangerous machinery. See **Factory** (Dangerous parts of machinery—Breach of duty to fence).
Failure to maintain motor vehicle in proper condition—
Malaysia. See **Malaysia** (Statutory duty—Breach—Failure to maintain motor vehicle in proper condition).
Highway—
Maintenance. See **Highway** (Maintenance—Statutory duty of highway authority—Breach of duty).
Indemnity. See **Indemnity** (Breach of statutory duty).
Independent Broadcasting Authority—
Content of programmes—Whether breach of statutory duty by Authority indictable as criminal offence. See **Broadcasting** (Content of programmes).
Insurance—
Motor insurance. See **Motor insurance** (Using vehicle or causing or permitting vehicle to be used on road without policy being in force—Cause or permit—Breach of statutory duty).
Land drainage—
Whether right of action for damages. See **Land drainage** (Embankment—Statutory duty to maintain under local Act—Transfer of obligation to river board—Breach of duty—Whether right of action for damages conferred).
Limitation—
Period of limitation. See **Limitation of action** (Period of limitation—Breach of statutory duty).
When time begins to run. See **Limitation of action** (When time begins to run—Action for damages for breach of statutory duty).
Motor insurance. See **Motor insurance** (Compulsory insurance against third party risks—Breach of statutory duty).
National Enterprise Board. See **Originating summons** (Striking out—Declaration—Breach of statutory duty—Public corporation).
National health insurance—
Failure to insure. See **National health insurance** (Failure to insure—Breach of statutory duty).
Offices, shops and railway premises—
Safety of employees. See **Employment** (Duty of master—Offices, shops and railway premises—Safety of employees).
Personal injury—
Damages. See **Damages** (Personal injury).
Limitation of action. See **Limitation of action** (Fatal accident—Material facts of decisive character unknown to deceased).
Right of action—
Sale of vehicle in unroadworthy condition. See **Road traffic** (Motor vehicle—Sale in unroadworthy condition—Right of action for breach of statutory requirements).
Schools—
Provision of schools for full-time education. See **Education** (Statutory duty to make schools available for full-time education—Failure to comply with duty).
Breach of duty imposed under sanction of penalty—
Competence of civil action at suit of person aggrieved—
Action for damages by person aggrieved—Clearway—Regulation forbidding parking on clearway—Plaintiff's car colliding with car parked on clearway—Whether plaintiff entitled to claim damages for breach of statutory duty—Road Traffic Act 1960, s 26—Various Trunk Roads (Prohibition of Waiting) (Clearways) Order 1963 (S1 1963 No 1172), art 4. **Coote v Stone** [1971] **1** 657, CA.

STATUTORY DUTY (cont)—
Breach of duty imposed under sanction of penalty (cont)—
Competence of civil action at suit of person aggrieved (cont)—
Action for damages by person aggrieved—Statutory duty to ensure compliance of lifeboat launching gear with safety requirements—Whether breach of duty resulting in civil liability—Merchant Shipping (Life Saving Appliances) Regulations 1980, reg 43(10), Sch 16, Pt II, para 1(c)—Merchant Shipping Act 1995, s 85. **Ziemniak v ETPM Deep Sea Ltd** [2003] **2 Comm** 283, CA.
Action for damages by person aggrieved—Statutory duty to ensure stability of fishing vessels in all foreseeable operating conditions—Whether breach of duty resulting in civil liability—Fishing Vessels (Safety Provisions) Rules 1975, SI 1975/330, r 16—Merchant Shipping Act 1995, ss 121, 185. **Todd v Adam** [2002] **2 Comm** 97, CA.
Action for damages by person aggrieved—Whether right of action if statutory duty not imposed for benefit or protection of particular class of persons. **Lonrho Ltd v Shell Petroleum Co Ltd** [1981] **2** 456, HL.
Bookmaker—Breach by occupier of dog racing track of duty to provide space for bookmaking—Whether bookmaker having right of civil action against occupier—Betting and Lotteries Act 1934, ss 11(2), 30(1). **Cutler v Wandsworth Stadium Ltd (in liq)** [1949] **1** 544, HL.
Failure to carry rear light on car during hours of darkness—Collision with another car—Person injured—Whether separate remedy available to person aggrieved—Road Transport Lighting Act 1927, ss 1, 10. **Clark v Brims** [1947] **1** 242, KBD.
Failure to maintain fire escape in good order—Employee on premises injured in fire—London Building Act 1930, s 5—London Building Acts (Amendment) Act 1939 ss 33(1), 133(2). **Solomons v Gertzenstein Ltd** [1954] **2** 625, CA.
Building legislation, under. See **Building** (Building regulations).
Coal mining. See **Coal mining** (Statutory duty).
Common law duty of care—
Relationship. See **Negligence** (Duty to take care—Statutory duty—Relation of statutory duty to common law duty).
Dangerous machinery—
Building operations. See **Building** (Building operations—Fencing of machinery—Dangerous machinery).
Coal mine. See **Coal mining** (Statutory duty—Machinery—Dangerous machinery).
Factory. See **Factory** (Dangerous parts of machinery).
Threshing machine. See **Agriculture** (Threshing machine—Fencing of dangerous parts).
Delegation—
Delegation to employee—
What constitutes delegation. **Manwaring v Billington** [1952] **2** 747, CA.
Doctrine of delegation—
Applicability of doctrine—Doctrine inapplicable where duty on both employer and employee and question was whose was the fault as between them. **Ginty v Belmont Building Supplies Ltd** [1959] **1** 414, QBD.
Distinguished from absolute liability. **R v Winson** [1968] **1** 197, CA.
Docks legislation. See **Dock**.
Education—
Provision of schools. See **Education** (Statutory duty to make schools available for full-time education).
Electricity—
Supply. See **Electricity** (Supply—Statutory duty).
Employer's breach of duty to workman—
Breach causing or materially contributing to workman's injury—
Onus of proof. **Bonnington Castings Ltd v Wardlaw** [1956] **1** 615, HL; **Nolan v Dental Manufacturing Co Ltd** [1958] **2** 449, Assizes.
Onus of proof—No duty to order or to exhort experienced employees to use safety belts, which there might be a duty to make available, where there was reasonable and widespread practice not to use them. **McWilliams v Sir William Arrol & Co Ltd** [1962] **1** 623, HL.
Contributory negligence—
Apportionment of liability—Employer in breach of statutory duty to workman—Negligence of workman contributing to accident—Safety regulations for protection of workmen—Standard by which employer's duty to be judged in apportioning liability—Flagrant and continuous breach of statutory obligations—Momentary error on part of workman. **Mullard v Ben Line Steamers Ltd** [1971] **2** 424, CA.
Employer's liability—
No apparent danger—Duty to ensure workman familiar with regulations—Whether absence of common law negligence relevant. **Boyle v Kodak Ltd** [1969] **2** 439, HL.
Enforcement—
Local authority. See **Local authority** (Statutory duty—Enforcement).
Factory legislation—
Generally. See **Factory**.
Highway—
Maintenance. See **Highway** (Maintenance—Statutory duty of highway authority).
Housing authority—
Duty to provide accommodation—
Homeless person. See **Housing** (Homeless person—Duty of housing authority to provide accommodation).
Limitation of action—
Period of limitation for breach of statutory duty. See **Limitation of action** (Period of limitation—Breach of statutory duty).
Local authority—
Education authority—
Generally. See **Education** (Local education authority).
Generally. See **Local authority** (Statutory duty).

STATUTORY DUTY (cont)—
    Local education authority—
        Duty in respect of school premises. *See* **Education** (Local education authority—Statutory duty in respect of school premises).
        Duty to ascertain what children mentally defective. *See* **Education** (Local education authority—Statutory duty to ascertain what children mentally defective).
    Mines—
        Safety of roads and working places. *See* **Mine** (Safety of roads and working places—Statutory duty to secure safety of roads and working places).
    Quarry manager. *See* **Quarry** (Safe methods of working).
    Railway—
        Look-out—
            Duty to appoint look-out. *See* **Railway** (Look-out—Statutory duty to appoint in circumstances in which danger is likely to arise).
    Recognition of trade union. *See* **Trade union** (Recognition—Statutory duty).
    Road traffic—
        Civil action. *See* Breach of duty imposed under sanction of penalty—Competence of civil action at suit of person aggrieved, *above*.

STATUTORY INSTRUMENT
    Aid to construction of statute. *See* **Statute** (Construction—Statutory instrument—Use of regulations for interpretation of section of statute).
    Construction—
        Anomaly—
            Correction of obvious drafting error—Conditions for giving rectifying construction to provision—Use of extraneous material—Humber Bridge (Revision of Tolls Vehicle Classification) Order 1997 (SI 1997/150)—Humber Bridge (Revision) Order 2000 (SI 2000/204)—Humber Bridge (Revision of Tolls) Order 2002 (SI 2002/786). **R (on the application of the Confederation of Passenger Transport UK) v Humber Bridge Board** [2004] 4 533, CA.
        Appeal—
            Right of appeal conferred—Implicit that only against adverse decisions. *See* **National Health Service** (Medical practitioner—Failure to comply with terms of service—Recommendation by executive council to Minister of Health to withhold sum from practitioner's remuneration).
        Convention—
            Order in Council effecting international convention—Court bound by meaning of Order in Council—Ambiguity—Reference to convention admissible to resolve ambiguity—Differences in wording between Order in Council and corresponding provision of convention—Territorial Waters Order in Council 1964, art 5(1). **Post Office v Estuary Radio Ltd** [1967] 3 663, QBD and CA.
        Enabling words in preamble. *See* Power to make instrument—Preamble—General enabling words in preamble, *below*.
        Evidence—
            Recondite subject-matter—Expert evidence admitted as to meaning attributed to words used in Order in Council—Territorial Waters Order in Council 1964. **Post Office v Estuary Radio Ltd** [1967] 3 663, QBD and CA.
        Hansard—
            Reference to proceedings in Parliament as an aid to construction—Regulations introduced to give effect to ruling by Court of Justice of European Communities that United Kingdom failed to fulfil obligations under EEC Treaty—Regulations not subject to parliamentary process of consideration and amendment—Whether legitimate to refer to Hansard to ascertain intention of Parliament with respect to regulations. **Pickstone v Freemans plc** [1988] 2 803, HL.
        Purposes of enabling statute—
            Purpose of regulations determined by regard to purpose of statutory enactment under which regulation was made—Statutory power to make regulations for the protection of the public health—Regulation prohibiting the placing of food so as to involve risk of contamination—Whether contamination included contamination of such a nature as not to be injurious to public health—Food and Drugs Act 1955, s 13—Food Hygiene Regulations 1955 (SI 1955 No 1906), reg 8. **MacFisheries (Wholesale & Retail) Ltd v Coventry Corp** [1957] 3 299, QBD.
        Vagueness—
            Any like organisation howsoever described—Whether too vague—Whether ambiguous—Civil Authorities (Special Powers) Act (Amending) (No 1) Regulations (Northern Ireland) 1967, (SR & O 1967 No 42). **McEldowney v Forde** [1969] 2 1039, CA and HL.
    Draft statutory instrument—
        Draft Order in Council—
            Draft of order required to be approved by Parliament—Applicant seeking judicial review of validity of draft order—Applicant contending that order would be ultra vires—Whether court having jurisdiction to grant relief before draft of order approved by Parliament. **R v HM Treasury, ex p Smedley** [1985] 1 589, CA.
    Effect of subsequent legislation on—
        Subsequent legislation modifying enactment under which instrument made—
            Instrument not in terms amended—Effect of instrument after modifying enactment in force—Statutes subsequently repealed and consolidated—Subordinate legislation continued by consolidating Act—Effect of instrument after the consolidation—Shops Act 1950, ss 1(2), 53(13), 76(2). **Miller's Cash Stores Ltd v West Ham Corp** [1955] 3 282, QBD.
        Subsequent legislation repealing enactment under which statutory instrument made—
            Saving for instruments made under repealed statute—Effect on instrument of doubtful validity—Former rule continued by superseding Act as if made under that Act—New rule in terms identical with former rule replacing rule intra vires—Bankruptcy Act 1914, ss 132(1), (2), 168(3)—Bankruptcy Rules 1952 (SI 1952 No 2113), r 219. **Fletcher, Re, ex p Fletcher v Official Receiver** [1955] 2 592, CA.

Effect of subsequent legislation on (cont)—
Subsequent legislation replacing enactment under which instrument made—
Subsequent legislation amended—Statutory instrument not modified in terms—Whether class of persons intended to be protected by instrument ascertained by reference to terms of repealed or subsisting legislation—Shipbuilding Regulations 1931 (SR & O 1931 No 133), preamble, reg 10—Factories Act 1937, s 60 (as amended by Factories Act 1948, s 12(1), Sch 1). **Canadian Pacific Steamships Ltd v Bryers** [1957] **3** 572, HL.
Power to make instrument—
Condition for making instrument that authority should 'satisfy himself'—
Subjective or objective test—Validity of regulations imposing fine—Emergency Powers Order in Council 1939, s 6(1)—Cyprus Emergency Powers (Collective Punishment) Regulations 1955, reg 3(g), (i), reg 5(1), (2). **Ross-Clunis v Papadopoullos** [1958] **2** 23, PC.
Instrument made under one subsection of Act—
Other subsection of enabling section limiting powers—Whether other subsection limiting powers to make instrument—Whether instrument ultra vires—Civil Authorities (Special Powers) Act (Amending)(No 1) Regulations (Northern Ireland) 1967 (SR & O 1967 No 42)—Civil Authorities (Special Powers) Act (Northern Ireland) 1922, s 1(1), (3). **McEldowney v Forde** [1969] **2** 1039, CA and HL.
Preamble—
General enabling words in preamble—Interpretation and effect of general enabling words—Whether general enabling words could be interpreted as referring to enabling power not expressly invoked—Health and Safety at Work etc Act 1974, ss 15(1), 47(2)—Supply of Machinery (Safety) Regulations 1992, SI 1992/3073. **Vibixa Ltd v Komori UK Ltd** [2006] **4** 294, CA.
Regulations required to be placed before Parliament—
Supplementary benefit regulations—Amount of supplementary benefit to be 'specified in or determined in accordance with regulations'—Secretary of State laying draft regulations before Parliament—Regulations referring to directory in which amount of benefit specified—Directory not laid before Parliament—Whether regulations valid—Statutory Instruments Act 1946, s 1(1)—Supplementary Benefits Act 1976, ss 33(1)(3), 34(1), Sch 1, para 2—Supplementary Benefit (Requirements and Resources) Miscellaneous Provisions (No 2) Regulations 1985. **R v Secretary of State for Social Services, ex p Camden London BC** [1987] **2** 560, CA.
Printing of statutory instruments—
Exemption from statutory requirements—
Certificate of exemption—Certificate—Letter from Ministry of Supply stating that price schedules 'have been certified to be exempted from printing'—Defence of failure to print instrument—Defence of absence of publication—Statutory Instruments Act 1946, ss 2(1), 3(2)—Statutory Instruments Regulations 1947 (SI 1948 No 1), reg 7. **Defiant Cycle Co Ltd v Newell** [1953] **2** 38, QBD.
Failure to comply with statutory requirements—
Effect on statutory instrument—Order made by Minister of Supply and laid before Parliament—Schedules forming part of order not printed, and not certified by Minister as not requiring to be printed—Validity of order—Statutory Instruments Act 1946, ss 2(1), 3(2)—Statutory Instruments Regulations 1947 (SI 1948 No 1), reg 7. **R v Sheer Metalcraft Ltd** [1954] **1** 542, Assizes.
Regulations—
European Community. *See* **European Union** (Regulations).
Repeal of statute under which instrument made—
Saving for instruments made under repealed statute—
Effect on instrument of doubtful validity. *See* Effect of subsequent legislation on—Subsequent legislation repealing enactment under which statutory instrument made, *above*.
Rules of court—
Alteration—
Effect on proceedings—Rules applicable to proceedings those in operation at date of proceedings—Alteration between date of divorce petition and date of application for maintenance. **Pachner v Parker** [1960] **1** 159, Div.
Power of Rule Committees—
Power to make rules giving Act retrospective effect—Supreme Court Rule Committee making rules purporting to apply Civil Evidence Act 1995 to proceedings begun prior to its commencement date—Act expressly excluding such proceedings unless provided for by Lord Chancellor's order—Whether Rule Committees having jurisdiction to amend Act so as to apply retrospectively—Supreme Court Act 1981, s 87—Civil Evidence Act 1995, s 16—Rules of the Supreme Court (Amendment) 1996, rr 8, 9. **Bairstow v Queens Moat Houses plc** [1998] **1** 343, CA.
Power to make rules relating to production of documents and Crown privilege—No power to alter substantive law—Crown privilege a matter of substantive law, not of practice and procedure—Supreme Court of Judicature (Consolidation) Act 1925, s 99(1)—RSC Ord 24, r 15. **Grosvenor Hotel, London, Re (No 2)** [1964] **3** 354, CA.
Power to make rules of court—
No express power—Statute conferring new jurisdiction on court—Statute not to come into force until rules of court made—Statute conferring no express power to make necessary rules of court—Express powers of court's rules committee limited to other statutory provisions—Whether committee having power to make rules of court for purpose of new statute—Interpretation Act 1889, s 14—Northern Ireland Act 1962, s 7(1)—Criminal Appeal (Northern Ireland) Act 1968, ss 48A (as inserted by the Criminal Justice Act 1972, s 63(3), Sch 4), 49—Criminal Justice Act 1972, s 66(6), proviso (b). **Reference under s 48A of the Criminal Appeal (Northern Ireland) Act 1968 (No 1 of 1975)** [1976] **2** 937, HL.
Validity—
Method of challenging—
Regulations. *See* **Regulations** (Validity—Challenging).
Order in Council to give effect to United Nations Resolution. *See* **Criminal law** (Offence created under power to make Order in Council giving effect to United Nations Resolution).

STATUTORY INSTRUMENT (cont)—
   Validity (cont)—
      Part of instrument invalid—
         Severance of invalid part—Effect of severance—Validity of remaining part—Test—Alteration of
            substance of remaining part—Taxing regulation—Invalid part specifying rate of tax—Severance
            of invalid part resulting in remaining part providing for different rate of tax from that
            contemplated by taxing authority—Whether whole provision invalid—Income Tax (Building
            Societies) Regulations 1986, reg 11. **Woolwich Equitable Building Society v IRC** [1991] **4** 92, HL.
         Severance of invalid part—Invalid part not inextricably interconnected with valid part—Whether
            whole instrument invalid—Whether invalid part may be severed leaving valid part in force—West
            Coast Herring (Prohibition of Fishing) Order 1978 (SI 1978 No 930). **Dunkley v Evans** [1981] **3** 285,
            QBD.
         Statutory requirements regarding printing of statutory instruments not complied with. *See* Printing of
            statutory instruments—Failure to comply with statutory requirements, *above*.

STATUTORY MARKET
   Disturbance—
      Levying of rival market—
         Availability of common law remedy. *See* **Markets and fairs** (Disturbance—Levying of rival
            market—Common law remedy—Disturbance of statutory market by levying of rival market).
   Generally. *See* **Markets and fairs** (Statutory market).

STATUTORY NUISANCE
   See **Nuisance** (Statutory nuisance).

STATUTORY OFFENCE
   Absolute liability. *See* **Criminal law** (Absolute liability—Statutory offence).
   Conspiracy to commit statutory offence. *See* **Criminal law** (Conspiracy—Statutory offence).

STATUTORY POWER
   Company incorporated by special Act—
      Public utility—
         Powers not transferable. **Salisbury Rly & Market House Co Ltd, Re** [1967] **1** 813, Ch D.
   Direction by Secretary of State in respect of other statutory duties—
      Telecommunications. *See* **Telecommunications** (Office of communications—Networks and spectrum
         functions—Direction given by Secretary of State).
   Duty of care in exercising statutory powers. *See* **Negligence** (Duty to take care—Statutory powers).
   Guidance—
      Civil Aviation Authority—
         Power of Secretary of State to give guidance to authority. *See* **Air traffic** (Civil Aviation
            Authority—Powers of Secretary of State—Guidance to authority).
   Local authority. *See* **Local authority** (Statutory powers).
   Mental patient's property—
      Management. *See* **Mental health** (Patient's property—Statutory powers).
   Negligence—
      Damage caused by exercise of powers. *See* **Negligence** (Statutory powers—Damage caused by
         exercise of powers).
      Duty to take care. *See* **Negligence** (Duty to take care—Statutory powers).
   Public authority. *See* **Public authority** (Statutory powers).

STATUTORY PROTECTION
   Tenancy of business premises—
      Exclusion of statutory protection. *See* **Landlord and tenant** (Business premises—Tenancy—Exclusion of
         statutory protection).

STATUTORY TENANCY
   Creation—
      Death of resident landlord. *See* **Rent restriction** (Resident landlord—Death of resident landlord or
         transfer of landlord's interest inter vivos).
   Generally. *See* **Rent restriction** (Statutory tenancy).
   Possession—
      Recovery by landlord. *See* **Rent restriction** (Possession).
   Termination of tenancy. *See* **Rent restriction** (Statutory tenant—Termination of tenancy).
   Terms of tenancy—
      Terms on termination of contractual long tenancy at low rent. *See* **Landlord and tenant** (Long tenancy
         at low rent—Continuation as statutory tenancy—Terms of statutory tenancy).
      Transfer on termination of marriage. *See* **Divorce** (Property—Protected or statutory tenancy—Transfer of
         protected or statutory tenancy on termination of marriage).

STATUTORY TENANT
   Death—
      Implied grant of lease. *See* **Landlord and tenant** (Implied grant of lease—Death of statutory tenant).
      Succession to tenancy. *See* **Rent restriction** (Death of tenant).

STATUTORY TRIBUNAL
   Agricultural Land Tribunal. *See* **Agricultural Land Tribunal**.
   Amendment of decision. *See* **Tribunal** (Decision—Amendment of decision—Power of statutory tribunal to
      amend own decision).
   Certiorari. *See* **Certiorari** (Statutory tribunal).
   Delegation of judicial duty. *See* **Tribunal** (Statutory tribunal—Delegation of judicial duty).
   Generally. *See* **Tribunal** (Statutory tribunal).

STATUTORY TRIBUNAL (cont)—
Jurisdiction of court—
Declaration on originating summons. *See* **Originating summons** (Declaration on originating summons—Jurisdiction—Statutory tribunal's decision final by statute).

STATUTORY TRUSTS
Intestacy. *See* **Intestacy** (Statutory trusts).

STATUTORY UNDERTAKERS
Land vested in—
Town and country planning. *See* **Town and country planning** (Statutory undertakers).
Nuisance—
Defence—
Statutory authority. *See* **Nuisance** (Defence—Statutory authority).

STAY OF EXECUTION
Generally. *See* **Execution** (Stay).
Possession—
Jurisdiction to order stay of warrant. *See* **County court** (Execution—Warrant for possession of premises—Suspension of execution—Jurisdiction).

STAY OF PROCEEDINGS
Admiralty proceedings—
Jurisdiction—
Action in rem. *See* **Admiralty** (Jurisdiction—Action in rem—Stay of proceedings).
Lis alibi pendens. *See* **Admiralty** (Practice—Lis alibi pendens—Stay of proceedings in England).
Agreement to refer to foreign court. *See* **Conflict of laws** (Stay of proceedings—Agreement to refer to foreign court).
Arbitration. *See* **Arbitration** (Stay of court proceedings).
Bankruptcy—
Stay of committal proceedings for non-payment of rates—
Jurisdiction of bankruptcy court to stay committal proceedings. *See* **Insolvency** (Jurisdiction—Stay of proceedings—Non-payment of rates).
Chancery Division. *See* **Practice** (Chancery Division—Stay of proceedings).
Company—
Director—
Disqualification proceedings. *See* **Company** (Director—Disqualification—Stay of proceedings).
Winding up—
Compulsory winding up. *See* **Company** (Compulsory winding up—Stay of proceedings).
Creditor's voluntary winding up. *See* **Company** (Voluntary winding up—Power to stay winding up—Creditors' voluntary winding up).
Generally. *See* **Company** (Winding up—Stay or restraint of proceedings against company).
Conflict of laws—
Generally. *See* **Conflict of laws** (Stay of proceedings).
Jurisdiction—
Civil and commercial matters. *See* **Conflict of laws** (Jurisdiction—Civil and commercial matters—Stay of proceedings).
Proceedings involving same cause of motion between same parties in courts of different member states. *See* **Conflict of laws** (Civil and commercial matters—Proceedings involving same cause of motion and between same parties in courts of different member states).
Court-martial. *See* **Court-martial** (Trial—Stay of proceedings).
Criminal proceedings. *See* **Criminal law** (Trial—Stay of proceedings).
Divorce. *See* **Divorce** (Practice—Stay of proceedings).
Foreign court—
Determination of disputes by. *See* **Conflict of laws** (Stay of proceedings—Agreement to refer to foreign court—Action commenced in England).
Foreign judgment—
Stay of enforcement proceedings pending appeal. *See* **Conflict of laws** (Foreign judgment—Enforcement—Stay of enforcement proceedings pending appeal).
Foreign proceedings—
Generally. *See* **Conflict of laws** (Foreign proceedings—Restraint of foreign proceedings).
Generally. *See* **Practice** (Stay of proceedings).
Interlocutory proceedings. *See* **Practice** (Interlocutory proceedings—Stay of proceedings).
Judicial review—
Concurrent complaint to independent adjudicator. *See* **Judicial review** (University—Stay of proceedings—Concurrent complaint to Office of the Independent Adjudicator).
Grant of leave to apply for judicial review—
Grant of leave operating as stay of proceedings to which application relates—Whether Secretary of State's decision 'proceedings'. *See* **Judicial review** (Application for judicial review—Application for leave to apply for judicial review—Stay of proceedings).
Lis alibi pendens—
Admiralty proceedings. *See* **Admiralty** (Practice—Lis alibi pendens—Stay of proceedings in England).
Order—
Stay of order pending appeal—
Access to minor—Order for access. *See* **Minor** (Custody—Access—Stay of order—Appeal).
Partnership—
Dissolution. *See* **Partnership** (Dissolution—Arbitration—Stay of proceedings).
Payment into court. *See* **Practice** (Payment into court—Stay of proceedings).
Summary judgment. *See* **Practice** (Summary judgment—Stay of proceedings).

STEALING
Child-stealing. *See* **Criminal law** (Child-stealing).
Generally. *See* **Criminal law** (Theft).

STEALING (cont)—
Going equipped for stealing. *See* **Criminal law** (Going equipped for stealing).

STEP-PARENT
Adoption of child—
    Application by parent and step-parent. *See* **Adoption** (Application—Married couple—Parent and step-parent of child).

STEPCHILD
Family provision. *See* **Family provision** (Stepchild).

STERILISATION
Child—
    Consent—
        Consent of High Court—Procedure—Application in Family Division—Form of order to be sought—Inherent jurisdiction—Specific issue order—Parties—Official Solicitor—Next friend or guardian ad litem—Summons for directions—Purpose of proceedings—Medical, psychological and social evaluations of child—Children Act 1989, s 8(1). **Practice Note** [1993] **3** 222, .
        Consent required—Sterilisation operation on child under 18 only to be carried out with consent of court exercising wardship jurisdiction—Liability of doctor carrying out sterilisation operation on child without consent of court. **B (a minor) (wardship: sterilisation), Re** [1987] **2** 206, Fam D, CA & HL.
        Mentally handicapped person. *See* Mentally handicapped person—Consent, *below*.
    Wardship proceedings—
        Fundamental rights of child. *See* **Ward of court** (Jurisdiction—Protection of ward—Fundamental rights of ward—Right of woman to reproduce—Sterilisation operation).
        Jurisdiction of court to authorise sterilisation. *See* **Ward of court** (Jurisdiction—Sterilisation).
Female patient—
    Negligence—
        Surgery. *See* **Medical practitioner** (Negligence—Surgery—Sterilisation of female patient).
Mentally handicapped person—
    Consent—
        Consent of High Court—Procedure—Originating summons issued out of Family Division—Form of order to be sought—Parties—Official Solicitor—Next friend or guardian ad litem—Summons for directions—Purpose of proceedings—Medical, psychological and social evaluations of patient. **Practice Note** [1993] **3** 222, .
        Female voluntary in-patient at mental health hospital—Patient having sexual relations with male patient and operation required to be performed on her in her best interests—Whether operation can lawfully be carried out despite inability of patient to consent—Whether court having jurisdiction to give or withhold consent to operation—Appropriate procedure to be adopted. **F v West Berkshire Health Authority (Mental Health Act Commission intervening)** [1989] **2** 545, HL.
    Consent to abortion and sterlisation. *See* **Abortion** (Legal abortion—Consent—Mentally handicapped person—Consent to abortion and sterilisation).
    Declaration as to lawfulness of proposed treatment—
        Procedure. *See* **Declaration** (Procedure—Declaration as to lawfulness of proposed conduct—Proposed medical treatment—Medical treatment of person unable to consent thereto—Mentally handicapped person—Sterilisation).

STOCK
Charging order. *See* **Execution** (Charging order—Stock or shares).
Colonial stock—
    Petition of right. *See* **Petition of right** (Colonial stock).
Gas stock—
    Issue for purpose of satisfying rights to compensation on nationalisation of gas. *See* **Gas** (Nationalisation—Compensation—Issue of gas stock for purpose of satisfying rights to compensation).
Stock Exchange. *See* **Stock Exchange**.
Stockholder—
    Stock transferred by statutory authority to Crown—
        Rectification of register. *See* **Petition of right** (Stockholder—Stock transferred by statutory authority to Crown).
Transfer of stock—
    Rights transferred—
        Right to unpaid interest—Transfer by procedure of Stock Exchange and by other methods—Transfer of colonial stock—Government of Southern Rhodesia trustee stock—No interest paid on stock or capital repaid after unilateral declaration of independence by government of Southern Rhodesia—Whether transferees of stock only entitled to claim interest and repayment of capital as to which there had been default after acquiring stock—Whether mode of acquisition of stock material. **Barclays Bank Ltd v R** [1974] **1** 305, QBD.
    Transfer by statutory authority to Crown—
        Petition of right by stockholder. *See* **Petition of right** (Stockholder—Stock transferred by statutory authority to Crown).
Valuation—
    Income tax—
        Computation of profits—Accountancy principles. *See* **Income tax** (Computation of profits—Accountancy principles—Stock).

STOCK EXCHANGE
Broker and client—
    Broker's right to indemnity—
        Vendor repudiating contract—Broker replacing stock—Broker's claim to indemnity—Principal's duty to broker—London Stock Exchange Rules, r 20. **Hichens Harrison Woolsten & Co v Jackson & Sons** [1943] **1** 128, HL.

STOCK EXCHANGE (cont)—
  Course of business—
    Continuation on agreed cover—
      Implied agreement—Right to close account—Length of notice. **Samson v Frazier, Jelke & Co** [1937] 2 588, KBD.
  Listing of shares. *See* **Company** (Shares—Listing of shares by stock exchange).
  Options—
    Cum all usage—
      Put options—Offer by American corporation to acquire half of each shareholder's holding of shares in an English company—Offer made after options over English company's shares entered into, and acceptable after last date for exercising options—Brokers liable as principals on option contracts—Client, option-holder, unwilling to submit to adjudication of the Council of The Stock Exchange on delivery of shares and payment of cash to fulfil options—Options exercised by letter of plaintiff's solicitors, not by member of The Stock Exchange—Whether options validly exercised. **Cunliffe-Owen v Teather & Greenwood** [1967] 3 561, Ch D.
  Shares quoted on—
    Valuation for capital gains tax. *See* **Capital gains tax** (Assets—Valuation—Market value—Shares—Shares quoted on London Stock Exchange).
  Trade association—
    Income tax. *See* **Income tax** (Trade—Trade association—Stock exchange).

STOCK-IN-TRADE
  Income tax—
    Computation of profits. *See* **Income tax** (Computation of profits—Stock-in-trade).

STOCKBROKER
  Right to indemnity. *See* **Stock Exchange** (Broker and client—Broker's right to indemnity).

STOLEN GOODS
  Handling. *See* **Criminal law** (Handling stolen goods).
  Receiving. *See* **Criminal law** (Receiving stolen property).
  Seizure—
    Police. *See* **Police** (Search warrant—Seizure of goods believed on reasonable grounds to be stolen goods).
  Value added tax—
    Supply of goods—
      Sale of stolen goods. *See* **Value added tax** (Supply of goods or services—Supply—Second-hand car dealer selling stolen cars at public auction).

STOP ORDER
  Bankruptcy proceedings. *See* **Bankruptcy** (Record of proceedings—Private examination—Stop order).

STOP, SEARCH AND DETENTION
  Police powers. *See* **Police** (Powers—Power to stop, search and detain).

STOP-LOSS INSURANCE
  Subrogation. *See* **Insurance** (Subrogation—Stop-loss insurance).

STOPPAGE IN TRANSITU
  Sale of goods. *See* **Sale of goods** (Stoppage in transit).

STORAGE
  Easement. *See* **Easement** (Storage).
  Expenses—
    Salvaged cargo. *See* **Shipping** (Salvage—Cargo—Storage expenses).
  Film, of. *See* **Cinema** (Film—Storage).

STRAITS SETTLEMENT
  Family settlement—
    Construction—
      Permanent improvements charged to income or corpus—Trustees' power to recoup income out of corpus—Accumulations Act 1800. **Syed Omar Bin Shaikh Alkaff v Syed Abdulrahman Bin Shaikh Alkaff** [1941] 2 346, PC.
  Public health—
    Housing—
      Dwelling-house declared to be insanitary—Declaration submitted to Governor-in-Council—Prohibition of further proceedings in respect of declaration—Quasi-judicial functions—Duties still remaining to be discharged—Singapore Improvement Ordinance (No 10 of 1927), ss 4, 57, 59-61. **Estate and Trust Agencies (1927) Ltd v Singapore Improvement Trust** [1937] 3 324, PC.

STRANGER
  Contract. *See* **Contract** (Stranger to contract).

STREET
  Betting—
    Prohibition of betting in streets. *See* **Gaming** (Betting—Prohibition of betting in streets and public places).
  Highway. *See* **Highway**.
  Loudspeaker—
    Use in street for advertising purposes. *See* **Advertisement** (Trade or business—Use of loudspeaker for advertising purposes).
  Prevention of obstruction—
    Regulation of traffic. *See* **Road traffic** (Regulation of traffic—Prevention of obstruction of streets).

STREET (cont)—
Prostitution—
Soliciting or loitering in street. *See* **Criminal law** (Prostitution—Loitering or soliciting for purposes of prostitution—In a street).
Street trading. *See* **Street trading**.
Traffic. *See* **Road traffic**.
Waterworks—
Duty of undertakers to reinstate street after execution of works. *See* **Water supply** (Waterworks—Duty of undertakers to reinstate streets etc after execution of work).

STREET BETTING
Prohibition of. *See* **Gaming** (Betting—Prohibition of betting in streets and public places).

STREET REFUGE
Lighting. *See* **Highway** (Obstruction—Lighting of obstruction—Street refuge).

STREET TRADING
Application to designate street as trading street—
Redesignation—
Earlier designation resolution rescinded—Right to apply anew—London County Council (General Powers) Act 1947, s 16. **R v Bermondsey BC, ex p Leonard** [1950] **1** 1069, KBD.
Licence—
Application—
Competing applications—Discretion of borough council to choose between competing applications—Adoption of waiting list—Power of borough council to give preference to applicants not already holding licence for another pitch in area—London County Council (General Powers) Act 1947, s 21(1) (as substituted by the London County Council (General Powers) Act 1962, s 33). **R v Tower Hamlets London Borough, ex p Kayne-Levenson** [1975] **1** 641, CA.
Nominated relative—Relative nominated by licence holder as person to whom he desires licence to be granted in event of licence holder's death—Timeous application by relative following death of licence holder—Duty of council to grant licence to relative unless grounds for refusal specified in statute—London County Council (General Powers) Act 1947, s 21(2A) (as inserted by the London County Council (General Powers) Act 1962, s 33). **R v Tower Hamlets London Borough, ex p Kayne-Levenson** [1975] **1** 641, CA.
Requirement that application should state 'street or streets' in which applicant intends to sell—Application specifying named market area comprising a number of streets—Necessary to specify particular street or streets—'Petticoat Lane' market area comprising ten streets—Application to trade in 'Any vacant position Petticoat Lane' invalid—London County Council (General Powers) Act 1947, s 21(1) (as amended by the London County Council (General Powers) Act 1962, s 33). **Perilly v Tower Hamlets BC** [1972] **3** 513, CA.
Cancellation—
Appeal—Right of person aggrieved to appeal to quarter sessions—Reversal of council's decision by magistrate—Right of council to appeal to quarter sessions—'Person aggrieved'—London County Council (General Powers) Act 1947, s 64. **R v London Sessions Appeal Committee, ex p Westminster City Council** [1951] **1** 1032, KBD.
Exemption—
Trader carrying on business with persons residing or employed in premises in a street—Street trading in course of that business—Ice cream vendor selling from stationary vehicle in street to residents in street—Vendor having no regular course of business with customers residing in street—Whether vendor exempt from requirement of having a street trading licence—London County Council (General Powers) Act 1947, ss 29, 30(c). **Islington London Borough v Panico** [1973] **3** 485, QBD.
Trader selling articles from receptacle which he ordinarily moves from place to place in pursuit of trade—Trader selling ice-cream from tricycle—Trader moving tricycle from street to street but stationary outside school when children entering or leaving—Whether exempt from requirement to hold licence—London County Council (General Powers) Act 1927, s 30. **Taylor v Townend** [1938] **1** 336, KBD.
Grant—
Borough council—Duty to grant licence as soon as reasonably practicable after receipt of application—Council receiving applications from two applicants—One application received day before the other—Only one available pitch—Whether council bound to grant application received first regardless of merits—London County Council (General Powers) Act 1947, s 21(2). **Perilly v Tower Hamlets BC** [1972] **3** 513, CA.
Power to grant one-day licence—London County Council (General Powers) Act 1927, s 39. **Dennis v Willmore** [1936] **2** 407, KBD Divl Ct.
Qualification to hold licence—
Person already holding licence for another pitch—Whether trader entitled to apply for licence for another pitch—Whether borough council having power to grant trader licences to operate separate pitches at the same time—London County Council (General Powers) Act 1947, s 21(1) (as substituted by the London County Council (General Powers) Act 1962, s 33). **R v Tower Hamlets London Borough, ex p Kayne-Levenson** [1975] **1** 641, CA.
Refusal—
Grounds for refusal—Applicant unsuitable to hold a licence—Unsuitability—Applicant holding licence for another pitch in same area—Whether rendering applicant 'unsuitable' to hold licence—London County Council (General Powers) Act 1947, s 21(3)(a). **R v Tower Hamlets London Borough, ex p Kayne-Levenson** [1975] **1** 641, CA.
Right of appeal—What constitutes refusal—Competing applications for licence—Council deciding to put application on waiting list—Council unable to accede to application because of lack of available space—Decision to place applicant on waiting list constituting a refusal—Duty of council to issue notice of refusal and to inform applicant of right of appeal—London County Council (General Powers) Act 1947, ss 21(3)(b), 25(1). **R v Tower Hamlets London Borough, ex p Kayne-Levenson** [1975] **1** 641, CA.

STREET TRADING (cont)—
  Licence (cont)—
    Revocation—
      Appeal—Powers of magistrate—London County Council (General Powers) Act 1947, s 25(1). **Stepney BC v Joffe** [1949] **1** 256, KBD.
      Natural justice—Application of the rules of natural justice. *See* **Natural justice** (Local authority—Street trading—Revocation of licence).
      Suitability of person to continue to be registered as licence holder—Manchester Corporation Act 1950, s 61(4)(b). **Manchester Corp v Penson** [1970] **1** 646, QBD.
  Offence—
    Displaying for sale notice in private vehicle—
      Private vehicle parked in road—Test for determining whether statutory defence satisfied—London Local Authorities Act 1990, s 38(2). **Onasanya v Newham London BC** [2006] **4** 459, DC.
    Trading from stationary position in street without licence—
      Street photographer taking photographs of persons in street and receiving deposit—Photographer not holding licence—Photographs sent to customers by post—Whether photographer guilty of offence—London County Council (General Powers) Act 1947, s 17(2). **Newman v Lipman** [1950] **2** 832, KBD.
  Pedlar—
    Definition—
      Person travelling and trading on foot—Salesman travelling in motor van to street and there going from house to house on foot—Whether acting as a 'pedlar'—Pedlars Act 1871, s 3. **Sample v Hulme** [1956] **3** 447, QBD.
    Trading as pedlar—
      Street trader travelling from place to place to trade from portable stand—Whether trading as a 'pedlar'—Pedlars Act 1871, s 3. **Watson v Malloy** [1988] **3** 459, QBD.
      Trading—Whether person must derive entire living or substantial part thereof from peddling to be a 'pedlar'—Whether person who regularly devotes part of his time to peddling requires a pedlar's certificate—Pedlars Act 1871, ss 3, 4. **Murphy v Duke** [1985] **2** 274, QBD.

STREET WORKS
  Damage to apparatus owned by statutory undertaker—
    Statutory undertaker's right to recover expense of making good damage to apparatus—
      Limitation of action. *See* **Public utility undertaking** (Limitation of action—Statutory undertaker's right to recover expense of making good damage to apparatus).
  Income tax—
    Cost of works payable in instalments. *See* **Income tax** (Annual payment—Deduction of tax—Street works).
  Liability for damage caused—
    Interruption of gas supply. *See* **Gas** (Supply of gas—Failure to supply—Interruption of gas supply caused by discharge of water from pipes owned by water undertaking).
    Negligence. *See* **Highway** (Maintenance—Negligence—Street works).
    Private. *See* **Highway** (Private street works).
    Public. *See* **Highway** (Street—Street works).
  Waterworks—
    Duty of undertakers to reinstate streets etc after execution of work. *See* **Water supply** (Waterworks—Duty of undertakers to reinstate streets etc after execution of work).

STRICT LIABILITY
  Absolute offences. *See* **Criminal law** (Absolute liability).
  Criminal law. *See* **Criminal law** (Strict liability).

STRIKE
  Dismissal in connection with strike—
    Unfair dismissal. *See* **Unfair dismissal** (Dismissal in connection with strike or other industrial action).
  Dismissal without notice—
    Conduct entitling employer to terminate contract without notice—
      Participation in strike—Exclusion from right to redundancy payment. *See* **Redundancy** (Exclusion from right to redundancy payment—Conduct entitling employer to terminate contract of employment without notice—Participation in strike).
  Illegal strike—
    Acts committed before commencement. *See* **Trade dispute** (Acts done in contemplation or furtherance of trade dispute—In contemplation or furtherance of—Acts committed before commencement of illegal strike).
  Irregular industrial action short of a strike—
    Emergency procedures. *See* **Industrial relations** (Industrial action—Emergency procedure).
  Prison officers, by—
    Prisoner's action for false imprisonment. *See* **False imprisonment** (Prisoner serving sentence—Strike by prison officers in breach of contract).
  Shipping—
    Demurrage—
      Exceptions clause. *See* **Shipping** (Demurrage—Exceptions clause—Strikes).
      Rate. *See* **Shipping** (Demurrage—Rate of demurrage—Strike).

STRIKING OUT
  Abuse of process. *See* **Practice** (Striking out—Abuse of process).
  Action. *See* **Practice** (Striking out—Action).
  Admiralty claims. *See* **Admiralty** (Practice—Striking out).
  Affidavit. *See* **Affidavit** (Striking out).
  Ancillary relief. *See* **Divorce** (Financial provision—Application—Application to strike out).
  Contempt of court proceedings—
    Committal application. *See* **Contempt of court** (Committal—Application—Striking out).
  County court practice. *See* **County court** (Practice—Striking out).

STRIKING OUT (cont)—
  Defence—
    Generally. *See* **Pleading** (Striking out—Defence).
    Jurisdiction of Court of Appeal. *See* **Court of Appeal** (Jurisdiction—Striking out defence).
  Employment tribunal. *See* **Employment tribunal** (Striking out).
  Immunity from legal process—
    Diplomatic privilege—
      Divorce proceedings by wife of diplomatic agent—Removal of immunity. *See* **Constitutional law**
        (Diplomatic privilege—Immunity from legal process—Removal of immunity on cessation of
        diplomatic function—Divorce proceedings by wife of diplomatic agent—Summons by husband to
        strike out petition on ground of diplomatic immunity).
  Industrial tribunal by. *See* **Employment tribunal** (Striking out).
  Insolvency proceedings—
    Ordinary application. *See* **Insolvency** (Application—Ordinary application—Striking out).
  Mid-trial. *See* **Practice** (Striking out—Mid-trial—Application made to strike out part of counterclaim during
    trial).
  Mid-trial. *See* **Practice** (Striking out—Mid-trial).
  Notice of appeal—
    Jurisdiction—
      Court of Appeal. *See* **Court of Appeal** (Notice of appeal—Striking out—Jurisdiction of court).
  Originating summons. *See* **Originating summons** (Striking out).
  Party. *See* **Practice** (Parties—Striking out party).
  Pleading—
    County court. *See* **County court** (Pleadings—Striking out).
    Divorce. *See* **Divorce** (Practice—Pleading—Striking out).
    Generally. *See* **Pleading** (Striking out).
    Statement of claim. *See* **Statement of case** (Striking out).

STRUCTURAL ALTERATION
  House—
    Improvement—
      Reduction in rateable value—Leasehold enfranchisement. *See* **Landlord and tenant** (Leasehold
        enfranchisement—House—Rateable value—Reduction—Improvement by execution of works
        amounting to structural alteration, extension or addition).

STUD POKER
  Lawfulness. *See* **Gaming** (Lawful and unlawful gaming—Card games—Stud poker).

STUDENT
  College—
    Dismissal—
      Governing body. *See* **Education** (College—Governing body).
  Hostel—
    Classes of use. *See* **Town and country planning** (Development—Use classes—Students' hostel).
  Immigrant—
    Leave to enter. *See* **Immigration** (Leave to enter—Non-patrial—Student).
  Lettings to students—
    Premises let to educational institution—
      Protected tenancy. *See* **Rent restriction** (Protected tenancy—Tenancy under which a dwelling-house
        is let as a separate dwelling—Premises let to educational institution).
  Loan—
    Higher education. *See* **Education** (Higher education—Student loans).
  Post-study work—
    Immigration. *See* **Immigration** (Leave to remain—Points-based system for skilled workers—Post-study
      work).
  Supplementary benefit—
    Calculation of benefit—
      Deduction of resources from requirements—Student awarded educational grant. *See* **Social**
        security (Supplementary benefit—Calculation of benefit—Deduction of resources from
        requirements—Notional or actual resources—Student awarded educational grant).
  Travel scheme—
    Value added tax—
      Zero-rating—Supply of travel concession voucher. *See* **Value added tax** (Zero-rating—Transport of
        passengers—Supply of travel concession voucher—Student travel scheme).
  University—
    Generally. *See* **University** (Student).
    Grant for study. *See* **University** (Grant for study).
    Suspension—
      Power to suspend students—Duty to hear parties etc. *See* **Natural justice** (Educational
        establishment—Suspension of student—Duty to hear parties etc).

STUDENTS' UNION
  Charitable purposes—
    Educational purposes—
      Generally. *See* **Charity** (Education—Educational purposes—Students' union).

SUB-BAILMENT FOR REWARD
  See **Bailment** (Sub-bailment for reward).

SUB-CONTRACT
  Generally. *See* **Contract** (Sub-contract).
  Incorporation of terms from head contract—
    Building contract. *See* **Building contract** (Sub-contract—Incorporation of clauses from head contract).

SUB-CONTRACT (cont)—
Personal contract, of. *See* **Contract** (Personal contract—Right to sub-contract).

SUB-CONTRACTOR
Building contract—
 Generally. *See* **Building contract** (Sub-contractors).
 Performance bond. *See* **Building contract** (Bond—Performance bond—Sub-contractor).
Construction industry—
 Income tax—
  Jurisdiction of General Commissioners. *See* **Income tax** (General Commissioners—Jurisdiction—Sub-contractors in the construction industry).
Negligence—
 Builder's liability for acts of sub-contractor. *See* **Negligence** (Duty to take care—Builder—Extent of duty—Liability for acts of sub-contractor).
Defective work or product—
 Duty to take care. *See* **Negligence** (Duty to take care—Defective work or product).
Performance bond—
 Building contract. *See* **Building contract** (Bond—Performance bond—Sub-contractor).

SUB-TENANCY
Covenant against sub-letting without consent. *See* **Landlord and tenant** (Covenant against underletting without consent).
Protected tenancy. *See* **Rent restriction** (Sub-tenancy).
Statutory tenancy. *See* **Rent restriction** (Sub-tenancy).

SUBJECT OF THE CROWN
Right to protection of Crown. *See* **Crown** (Duty—Duty to protect subject).

SUBJECT TO CONTRACT
Sale of land—
 Effect of qualification 'subject to contract'—
  Acceptance of tender. *See* **Sale of land** (Acceptance of tender—Effect of qualification 'subject to contract').
  Exchange of contracts. *See* **Sale of land** (Exchange of contracts—Agreement subject to contract).
  Memorandum of contract. *See* **Sale of land** (Memorandum of contract—Circumstances in which memorandum must evidence existence of contract—Effect of qualification 'subject to contract').

SUBLETTING
Subletting without consent. *See* **Landlord and tenant** (Covenant against underletting without consent).

SUBORDINATE LEGISLATION
Byelaw. *See* **Byelaw**.
Regulations. *See* **Regulations**.
Statutory instrument. *See* **Statutory instrument**.

SUBPOENA
Subpoena ad testificandum. *See* **Practice** (Subpoena ad testificandum).
Subpoena duces tecum. *See* **Practice** (Subpoena duces tecum).

SUBROGATION
Circumstances in which doctrine applicable—
 Loan used to pay off existing debt to third party—
  Bank paying debtor of company without authorisation or ratification—Company bringing action to recover unauthorised payment—Whether bank's honest but unreasonable belief of authority raising defence—Whether discharge of debt sufficient for equitable subrogation. **Crantrave Ltd v Lloyds Bank plc** [2000] **2 Comm** 89, CA; [2000] **4** 473, CA.
  No express contractual term that moneys advanced should be applied in any particular manner—Common intention of parties that moneys advanced should be used to pay off existing debt—Moneys in fact used for that purpose—Whether sufficient to entitled lender to be subrogated to charge in favour of third party. **Orakpo v Manson Investments Ltd** [1977] **3** 1, HL.
 Mortgage—
  Banks mortgage advance to purchaser paid to vendors solicitors pending completion—Money applied before completion towards discharge of vendors prior mortgage—Mortgage discharged partly by vendors own payments—Sale falling through—Whether bank entitled to charge by way of subrogation. **Boscawen v Bajwa** [1995] **4** 769, CA.
 Unenforceable loan contract—
  Charge executed pursuant to contract unenforceable—Moneylender's contract—Sum advanced pursuant to contract used to pay off existing charge—Moneylender's contract failing to comply with statutory requirements—Contract and charge executed pursuant thereto valid but unenforceable—Common intention of parties that sum advanced should be used to pay off existing charge—Whether, having acquired valid but unenforceable charge, moneylender entitled to be subrogated to security represented by existing charge. **Orakpo v Manson Investments Ltd** [1977] **3** 1, HL.
 Unjust enrichment—
  Lender advancing sum of money under unsecured loan, containing express condition that borrower's creditors would postpone repayment of loans—Condition postponing repayment unenforceable against borrower—Whether unenforceable condition 'defective security'—Whether lender entitled to be subrogated to charge of creditor if security defective. **Banque Financière de la Cité v Parc (Battersea) Ltd** [1998] **1** 737, HL.

SUBROGATION (cont)—
Circumstances in which doctrine applicable (cont)—
Unjust enrichment (cont)—
Recipient in restitution claim paying money away other than in good faith—Judgment entered jointly and severally against recipient and negligent tortfeasor—Negligent tortfeasor paying judgment debt—Whether negligent tortfeasor entitled to be subrogated to claimant's claim in restitution against recipient. **Niru Battery Manufacturing Co v Milestone Trading Ltd (No 2)** [2004] **2 Comm** 289, CA.
Registered charge—Lender advancing sum of money to borrower to redeem existing registered legal charge—Lender receiving charge capable of being registered but failing to register it—Second lender registering equitable charge—Whether lender entitled to be subrogated to existing legal charge. **Anfield (UK) Ltd v Bank of Scotland plc** [2011] **1** 708, Ch D; [2011] **1 Comm** 929, Ch D.
Tortfeasor seeking subrogation of claim in restitution—Whether tortfeasor having right to subrogate. **Niru Battery Manufacturing Co v Milestone Trading Ltd (No 2)** [2003] **2 Comm** 365, QBD.
Collision at sea—
Negligence—
Pollution damage. *See* **Shipping** (Negligence in collision cases—Subrogation).
Company—
Winding up—
Retention of possession of lease after winding up—Rights of landlord. *See* **Company** (Winding up—Proof and ranking of claims—Rent—Retention of possession after winding up—Rights of landlord—Subrogation of rights).
Effect of operation of doctrine—
Assignment of creditor's rights—
Doctrine not effecting assignment—Lender treated in equity as assignee of paid off creditor's rights—Lender treated as assignee to extent necessary to enable him to exercise paid off creditor's rights against borrower—Enforcement of rights by lender—Unnecessary to show cause of action based on contract. **Orakpo v Manson Investments Ltd** [1977] **1** 666, CA.
Indemnity. *See* **Indemnity** (Subrogation).
Insurance—
Generally. *See* **Insurance** (Subrogation).
Marine insurance. *See* **Marine insurance** (Subrogation).
Unjust enrichment. *See* **Restitution** (Unjust enrichment—Subrogation).
Vendor's lien. *See* **Sale of land** (Vendor's lien—Subrogation).

SUBSCRIPTION
Deduction from emoluments for assessment to income tax. *See* **Income tax** (Emoluments from office or employment—Expenses wholly, exclusively and necessarily incurred—Subscription).
Unincorporated association—
Failure of member to pay subscription—
Resignation by conduct. *See* **Unincorporated association** (Resignation of member—Resignation by conduct—Failure to pay subscription over number of years).
Value added tax—
Exemption—
Club or association—Rights of members over land. *See* **Value added tax** (Exemptions—Grant of right over or licence to occupy land—Members' club—Subscriptions).

SUBSIDENCE
Building—
Insurance. *See* **Insurance** (Accident insurance—Perils insured against—Subsidence or collapse of building).
Coal mining activities. *See* **Coal mining** (Subsidence).
Land. *See* **Land** (Support).

SUBSIDIARY COMPANY
Generally. *See* **Company** (Subsidiary company).

SUBSIDY
Income tax—
Government subsidy—
Trading receipt. *See* **Income tax** (Profits—Trading receipts—Government subsidy).
Public subsidy—
European Community. *See* **European Union** (State aids—Public subsidies).

SUBSTITUTE ARBITRATOR
Appointment. *See* **Arbitration** (Arbitrator—Appointment—Appointment of substitute arbitrator).

SUBSTITUTED SERVICE
Bankruptcy—
Bankruptcy notice. *See* **Bankruptcy** (Bankruptcy notice—Service—Substituted service).
Bankruptcy petition. *See* **Bankruptcy** (Petition—Service—Substituted service).
Generally. *See* **Practice** (Service—Substituted service).

SUBSTITUTION OF PARTY
Generally. *See* **Practice** (Parties—Substitution).

SUBSTITUTION OF VERDICT
Criminal appeal—
Alternative offence. *See* **Criminal law** (Appeal—Substitution of verdict—Alternative offence).

SUBSTITUTIONAL GIFT
Settlement—
Issue. *See* **Settlement** (Issue—Substitutional gift).
Will. *See* **Will** (Gift—Substitutional gift).

SUBTERRANEAN WATER
See **Water and watercourses** (Underground water).

SUBVENTION PAYMENTS
Income tax. *See* **Income tax** (Deduction in computing profits—Subvention payments).

SUCCESSION
Agricultural holding—
Tenancy. *See* **Agricultural holding** (Tenancy—Death of tenant).
Conflict of laws—
Generally. *See* **Conflict of laws** (Succession).
Windward and Leeward Islands. *See* **Windward and Leeward Islands** (Conflict of laws—Succession).
Family provision. *See* **Family provision**.
Foreign adoption. *See* **Adoption** (Foreign adoption—Death—Devolution of property).
Intestacy—
Generally. *See* **Intestacy** (Succession).
Palestine. *See* **Palestine** (Intestacy—Succession).
Secure tenancy—
Death of council house tenant. *See* **Housing** (Local authority houses—Security of tenure—Secure tenancy—Succession on death of secure tenant).
Statutory tenancy. *See* **Rent restriction** (Death of tenant).
Succession duty. *See* **Succession duty**.
Trade—
Income tax. *See* **Income tax** (Succession to trade).
Will—
Generally. *See* **Will**.
Legitimacy—
Succession to personal property in England. *See* **Will** (Legitimacy—Succession to personal property in England).

SUCCESSION DUTY
Canada. *See* **Canada** (Succession duty).
Incidence—
Exercise by will of special power of appointment—
Appointment of life interests in settled fund—Direction in will to pay all duties 'payable on my death under the terms of this my will'—Succession duty payable on death of testatrix in respect of life interests under appointment and duties to become payable on death of appointees not within direction for payment of duties. **Edwards, Re** [1946] **2** 408, Ch D.
Predecessor—
Settlement by party with defeasible estate and party with contingent interest subject thereto—Joint predecessors—Necessity for both parties to join in settlement to create interest of successor—Succession Duty Act 1853, s 2. **Drake's Settlement Trusts, Re** [1937] **4** 171, CA.
Queensland. *See* **Queensland** (Succession duty).
Succession—
Person beneficially entitled to property or income thereof under disposition—
Meaning of beneficially entitled—Pension granted to employee's widow—No enforceable right to pension—No succession duty payable—Succession Duty Act 1853, s 2. **Bibby (J) & Sons Ltd, Pensions Trust Deed, Re** [1952] **2** 483, Ch D.
Private Act of Parliament avoiding restraint upon alienation—
Whether succession destroyed—Succession Duty Act 1853, ss 2, 12, 15. **A-G v Glyn Mills & Co** [1940] **2** 103, HL.

SUGAR
European Community—
Export licence—
Failure to apply for licence within time limit—Penalty—Whether penalty breaching principle of proportionality. *See* **European Union** (Proportionality—Penalty).

SUGAR MARKET
EC Competition Rules. *See* **European Union** (Rules on competition—Agreements preventing, restricting or distorting competition—Sugar market).

SUICIDE
Assisting suicide—
Criminal law. *See* **Criminal law** (Suicide—Liability for complicity in another's suicide).
Causation—
Damages. *See* **Damages** (Remoteness of damage—Suicide).
Criminal liability for complicity in another's suicide. *See* **Criminal law** (Suicide—Liability for complicity in another's suicide).
Criminal proceedings—
Generally. *See* **Criminal law** (Suicide).
Death in prison—
State's obligation to investigate death. *See* **Human rights** (Right to life—State's obligation to investigate death—Death in prison).
Inquest. *See* **Coroner** (Inquest—Suicide).
Life insurance—
Exception. *See* **Insurance** (Life insurance—Exception—Suicide).

SUICIDE (cont)—
  Pact—
    Murder—
      Accessory before the fact. *See* **Criminal law** (Murder—Accessory before the fact—Suicide pact).
  Suicide risk—
    Mentally ill prisoner—
      Prison hospital—Negligence—Duty to take care. *See* **Negligence** (Duty to take care—Prison hospital—Mentally ill prisoner—Suicide risk).
    Person in police custody—
      Police—Negligence—Duty to take care. *See* **Police** (Negligence—Duty to take care—Person in custody—Suicide risk).
  War service injury—
    Widow's pension. *See* **War pension—Attributability**.

SUING AND LABOURING CLAUSE
  Marine insurance—
    Loss—
      Indemnity. *See* **Marine insurance** (Loss—Indemnity—Suing and labouring clause).
      Measure of indemnity. *See* **Marine insurance** (Measure of indemnity—Suing and labouring clause).

SUMMARY COMMITTAL
  Criminal contempt. *See* **Contempt of court** (Criminal contempt—Jurisdiction—Summary committal).

SUMMARY DISMISSAL
  Generally. *See* **Employment** (Dismissal—Summary dismissal).
  Unfair dismissal—
    Date of dismissal. *See* **Unfair dismissal** (Date of dismissal—Summary dismissal).

SUMMARY JUDGMENT
  Bill of exchange—
    Action between immediate parties—
      Holder in due course—Dishonoured bill returned to drawer by holder in due course. *See* **Bill of exchange** (Holder in due course—Drawer of bill discounting it to holder in due course—Bill dishonoured on presentation for payment—Dishonoured bill returned to drawer by holder in due course—Action on bill by drawer—Application for summary judgment).
  Costs—
    Discretion to award costs—
      Plaintiff obtaining leave to enter summary judgment against defendant for damages to be assessed. *See* **Costs** (Order for costs—Discretion—Plaintiff obtaining leave to enter summary judgment against defendant for damages to be assessed).
  Defamation cases—
    Trial by jury. *See* **Jury** (Trial by jury—Defamation—Summary judgment).
  Fatal accident claim. *See* **Fatal accident** (Action—Summary judgment).
  Generally. *See* **Practice** (Summary judgment).
  Injunction. *See* **Injunction** (Summary procedure—Practice—Summary judgment for injunction).
  Interest—
    Award of interest on summary judgment. *See* **Interest** (Damages—Jurisdiction to include interest in award of damages—Summary judgment).
  Mortgagee's action to recover principal moneys and interest under second mortgage. *See* **Mortgage** (Payment—Summary judgment—Leave).
  Set-off—
    Right of set-off. *See* **Set-off** (Right of set-off—Summary judgment).
  Specific performance. *See* **Specific performance** (Summary procedure).

SUMMARY OFFENCE
  Addition of counts to indictment. *See* **Indictment** (Addition of new counts—Summary offence).
  Committal for trial at Crown Court—
    Magistrates' jurisdiction. *See* **Crown Court** (Committal to Crown Court for trial—Jurisdiction—Summary offence).
  Conspiracy to commit summary offence. *See* **Criminal law** (Conspiracy—Indictment—Conspiracy to commit offence triable only summarily).
  Incitement to commit summary offence—
    Indictment. *See* **Criminal law** (Incitement—Indictable offence—Incitement to commit summary offence).
  Magistrates—
    Jurisdiction. *See* **Magistrates** (Jurisdiction—Summary offence).
  Perjury. *See* **Criminal law** (Perjury—Summary offence).
  Right of accused to claim trial by jury for summary offence. *See* **Magistrates** (Right of accused to claim trial by jury for summary offence).
  Road traffic offence. *See* **Road traffic** (Offence—Summary offence).

SUMMARY PROCEEDINGS
  Abatement of nuisance—
    Noise—
      Summary proceedings by local authority to abate, prohibit or restrict nuisance). *See* **Nuisance** (Noise—Summary proceedings by local authority to abate, prohibit or restrict nuisance).
  Byelaw—
    Challenge to validity of byelaw—
      Jurisdiction of magistrates to determine issue of validity. *See* **Byelaw** (Validity—Summary proceedings).
  Husband and wife. *See* **Husband and wife** (Summary proceedings).
  Possession of land. *See* **Land** (Summary proceedings for possession).

SUMMARY TRIAL
Arson. *See* **Criminal law** (Damage to property—Arson—Trial—Summary trial).
Attempt to commit crime—
Full offence committed—
Merger. *See* **Criminal law** (Attempt—Full offence committed—Merger—Summary proceedings).
Committal proceedings distinguished. *See* **Criminal law** (Committal—Preliminary hearing before justices—Summary trial distinguished).
Costs. *See* **Criminal law** (Costs—Magistrates' court).
Generally. *See* **Magistrates** (Summary trial).
Prosecution evidence—
Disclosure of information to defence. *See* **Criminal evidence** (Prosecution evidence—Disclosure of information to defence—Summary trial).
Summary trial of indictable offence—
Committal to quarter sessions for sentence. *See* **Quarter sessions** (Committal of offender for sentence—Summary trial of indictable offence).
Generally. *See* **Magistrates** (Summary trial for indictable offence).

SUMMING UP
Criminal trial—
Direction to jury—
Burden of proof. *See* **Jury** (Direction to jury—Burden of proof).
Generally. *See* **Criminal law** (Trial—Direction to jury).
Generally. *See* **Criminal law** (Trial—Summing up).

SUMMONS
Adjournment to judge—
Originating summons—
Chambers proceedings. *See* **Practice** (Chambers proceedings—Adjournment to judge—Originating summons).
Right to adjournment—
Chambers proceedings. *See* **Practice** (Chambers proceedings—Adjournment to judge—Right to adjournment—Right of any party to have adjournment to the judge in person).
Bankruptcy proceedings—
Inquiry into debtor's dealings and property—
Summons to persons capable of giving information. *See* **Bankruptcy** (Inquiry as to debtor's dealings and property—Summons to persons capable of giving information).
Chancery Division—
Generally. *See* **Practice** (Summons—Chancery Division).
Masters' summonses. *See* **Practice** (Chambers proceedings—Masters' summonses).
Commercial action—
Summons for transfer of action to commercial list. *See* **Commercial Court** (Practice—Summons—Summons for transfer of action).
Commercial Court—
Practice—
Generally. *See* **Commercial Court** (Practice—Summons).
County court—
Service of summons. *See* **County court** (Practice—Service of summons).
Family Division—
Consent summons—
Divorce. *See* **Divorce** (Consent applications).
Form—
Amendment—
Summons for judgment. *See* **Practice** (Summary judgment—Summons for judgment—Form—Amendment).
Generally. *See* **Practice** (Summons).
Information or summons—
Road traffic offence. *See* **Road traffic** (Offence—Summons or information).
Interpleader summons—
Issue of summons. *See* **Interpleader** (Issue of interpleader summons).
Irregularity. *See* **Practice** (Irregularity—Summons).
Judgment, for. *See* **Practice** (Summary judgment—Summons for judgment).
Leave to proceed under Courts (Emergency Powers) Act 1939, for. *See* **Practice** (Summons—Summons for leave to proceed under Courts (Emergency Powers) Act 1939).
Listing—
Chancery Division. *See* **Practice** (Chancery Division—Listing—Summonses).
Short summons. *See* **Practice** (Summons—Hearing—Short summonses and applications—List).
Magistrates. *See* **Magistrates** (Summons).
Masters' summonses—
Chambers proceedings. *See* **Practice** (Chambers proceedings—Masters' summonses).
Generally. *See* **Practice** (Summons—Masters' summonses).
Misfeasance summons—
Service on officer etc of company. *See* **Company** (Winding up—Misfeasance—Misfeasance summons—Service).
Originating. *See* **Originating summons**.
Procedure summons—
Chancery Division. *See* **Practice** (Summons—Chancery Division—Procedure summons).
Restoration to list. *See* **Practice** (Summons—Restoration of summons to list).
Telephone summons—
Patent proceedings. *See* **Patent** (Practice—Telephone summonses).
Two summonses for one offence—
Autrefois acquit. *See* **Criminal law** (Autrefois acquit—Same offence—Two summonses).
Witness summons—
County court. *See* **County court** (Witness summons).

SUMMONS (cont)—
Witness summons (cont)—
Criminal proceedings, generally. *See* **Criminal evidence** (Witness—Witness summons).
Generally. *See* **Practice** (Summons).
Magistrates' court. *See* **Magistrates** (Witness summons).
Practice—
Generally. *See* **Practice** (Witness summons).

SUMMONS FOR DIRECTIONS
Admiralty action. *See* **Admiralty** (Practice—Directions—Summons for directions).
Discovery on. *See* **Disclosure and inspection of documents** (Disclosure on summons for directions).
Dismissal of action for failure to take out. *See* **Practice** (Dismissal of action for want of prosecution—Inordinate delay without excuse—Plaintiffs in default in not proceeding with action).
Generally. *See* **Practice** (Summons for directions).

SUNDAY
Dies non juridicus—
Injunction. *See* **Injunction** (Sunday—Dies non juridicus).

SUNDAY CLOSING
Shop. *See* **Shop** (Sunday closing).

SUNDAY ENTERTAINMENT
Licence—
Cinema. *See* **Cinema** (Licence—Sunday performance).
Music and dancing. *See* **Entertainment** (Music and dancing licence—Application for Sunday licence).
Restrictions on—
Generally. *See* **Sunday observance** (Restrictions on Sunday entertainment).

SUNDAY OBSERVANCE
Prohibition on transaction of business by tradesmen etc on Sunday—
Sunday Observance Act—
Company transacting business on Sunday—Liability to penalty. **Houghton-Le Touzel v Mecca Ltd** [1950] **1** 638, KBD.
Tradesman—
Estate agent—Contract to effect sale of land on commission entered into on Sunday—Whether estate agent 'tradesman'—Sunday Observance Act 1677, s 1. **Gregory v Fearn** [1953] **2** 559, CA.
Transaction of business—
Contract between limited companies made on Sunday—Validity—Sunday Observance Act 1677, s 1—Interpretation Act 1889, s 2(1). **Rolloswin Investments Ltd v Chromolit Portugal Cutelarias e Produtos Metalicos SARL** [1970] **2** 673, QBD.
Restrictions on Sunday entertainment—
Advertising public entertainment for Sunday to which persons admitted by payment of money an offence—
'Admitted'—Advertisement for all-in wrestling—Charge for seat—Whether free admission—Sunday Observance Act 1780, ss 1, 3. **Kitchener v Evening Standard Co Ltd** [1936] **1** 48, KBD.
Announcement of boxing contest in periodical—Whether 'advertisement'—Whether manager who absent from contest 'keeper'—Whether announcer of fights 'master of ceremonies'—Sunday Observance Act 1780, ss 1, 2, 3. **Green v Berliner** [1936] **1** 199, KBD.
Newspaper—Advertisment that gardens open on Sunday and dancing there—Informer claiming penalties against printers and publishers of advertisements for advertising Sunday entertainments—Whether 'advertiser'—Whether advertisement of entertainment—Sunday Observance Act 1780, s 3. **Green v Kursaal (Southend-on-Sea) Estates Ltd** [1937] **1** 732, KBD.
Opening place for public entertainment on Sunday to which persons admitted by payment of money an offence—
Persons liable—Limited company—Evidence against company—Sunday Observance Act 1780, ss 1, 2. **Houghton-Le Touzel v Mecca Ltd** [1950] **1** 638, KBD.
Place used for public entertainment—Part of large park enclosed for purpose of motor cycle competition—Whether 'place'—Sunday Observance Act 1780, s 1. **Culley v Harrison** [1956] **2** 254, QBD.
Shop—
Closing. *See* **Shop** (Sunday closing).

SUNDAY TRADING
Prohibition on Sunday trading—
Generally. *See* **Sunday observance** (Prohibition on transaction of business by tradesmen etc on Sunday).
Whether prohibition constituting 'trading rule' having equivalent effect to quantitative restriction on imports—
Whether prohibition contravening European Community law. *See* **European Union** (Imports—Reduction in volume of imports—Quantitative restrictions on imports from other member states—Measures having equivalent effect—Prohibition on Sunday trading).

SUNLIGHT
Right to sunlight—
Degree of light acquired by prescriptive right—
Obstruction of sunlight to greenhouse. *See* **Easement** (Light—Degree of light acquired by prescriptive right—Ordinary amount of light—Obstruction of sunlight to greenhouse).

SUPER LEGALITE
Lawfulness. *See* **Gaming** (Lawful and unlawful gaming—Super Legalite).

SUPERANNUATION
Contribution—
Exemption from income tax. *See* **Income tax** (Exemption—Superannuation contribution).
Local government. *See* **Local government** (Superannuation).
Pension. *See* **Pension**.
Public authorities—
War bonus. *See* **Employment** (Superannuation).

SUPERINTENDENT REGISTRAR OF BIRTHS, DEATHS AND MARRIAGES
Generally. *See* **Registrar** (Superintendent registrar of births, deaths and marriages).

SUPERIOR ORDERS
Acting in obedience to superior orders—
Availability as a defence—
Criminal proceedings. **R v Clegg** [1995] **1** 334, HL.
Defence—
Criminal proceedings. *See* **Criminal law** (Defence—Defence of superior orders or Crown or Executive fiat).

SUPERMARKET
Hours of closing. *See* **Shop** (Hours of closing—Mixed shop—Supermarket).

SUPERVISION
Access to minor. *See* **Minor** (Custody—Access—Supervised access).
Demolition of a building. *See* **Building** (Demolition—Supervision).
Scaffolding, of. *See* **Building** (Scaffolding—Erection or alteration of scaffolding—Supervision).

SUPERVISION ORDER
Agricultural holding. *See* **Agricultural holding** (Supervision order).
Family proceedings—
Care order or supervision order. *See* **Family proceedings** (Orders in family proceedings—Care or supervision order).
Magistrates' court. *See* **Magistrates** (Fine—Supervision order).

SUPPER HOUR
Extension. *See* **Licensing** (Permitted hours—Extension—Supper-hour).

SUPPLEMENTARY BENEFIT
Generally. *See* **Social security** (Supplementary benefit).

SUPPLY
Controlled drug. *See* **Drugs** (Dangerous drugs—Supply).
Dangerous drugs—
Prohibition on. *See* **Drugs** (Dangerous drugs—Prohibition on supplying dangerous drugs).
Electricity. *See* **Electricity** (Supply).
Gas. *See* **Gas** (Supply of gas).
Value added tax—
Supply of goods or services. *See* **Value added tax** (Supply of goods or services).
Video recording—
Supply in breach of classification. *See* **Video recording** (Offence—Supply in breach of classification).

SUPPORT
Easement. *See* **Easement** (Support).
Electricity pylons—
Right of support. *See* **Electricity** (Pylons—Support).
Gas mains—
Right of support. *See* **Gas** (Support of gas mains—Right of support).
Land—
Generally. *See* **Land** (Support).
Mine—
Support of roof. *See* **Mine** (Support—Support of roof).
Semi-detached houses—
Support of adjoining semi-detached houses—
Compulsory purchase of one—Failure to notify owner of other house of order—Necessity of notifying owner of other house. *See* **Compulsory purchase** (Compulsory purchase order—Application to quash order—Notification of owner of land comprised in order—Failure to notify owner of semi-detached house adjoining house subject to order).

SUPREME COURT
Canada. *See* **Canada** (Supreme Court of Canada).
Costs—
Jurisdiction. *See* **Costs** (Jurisdiction—Costs of and incidental to all proceedings in Supreme Court).
Practice—
Generally. *See* **Practice**.
Precedent. *See* **Precedent** (Supreme Court).
Supreme Court of the United Kingdom—
Practice—
Appeal—Power of intervener to continue conduct of appeal where appellant seeking to withdraw. **MS (Pakistan) v Secretary of State for the Home Dept (Equality and Human Rights Commission and others intervening)** [2020] **3** 733, SC.

SUPREME COURT (cont)—
Supreme Court of the United Kingdom (cont)—
Practice (cont)—
Jurisdiction—Application for directions in pending appeal—Costs—Bankrupt ordered to pay costs in Court of Appeal and High Court before bankruptcy—Trustee in bankruptcy applying for directions as to personal liability in costs if he adopts pending appeal to Supreme Court—Whether jurisdiction to decide issue before appeal. **Gabriel v BPE Solicitors** [2015] **4** 672, SC.
Jurisdiction—Contempt of court—Appeal—Whether Supreme Court having jurisdiction to hear appeal against finding of contempt by differently constituted panel of Supreme Court justices—Administration of Justice Act 1960, s 13. **A-G v Crosland** [2022] **2** 401, SC.
Jurisdiction—Court of Appeal in Northern Ireland—Appeal by way of case stated—Attorney General's reference on devolution issue—Request for reference after judgment but before order drawn up—Whether jurisdiction to determine appeal—Whether Court of Appeal required to make reference—Judicature (Northern Ireland) Act 1978, s 42(6)—Northern Ireland Act 1998, Sch 10, paras 33, 34—County Courts (Northern Ireland) Order 1980, SI 1980/397, art 61(7). **Lee v Ashers Baking Co Ltd (Northern Ireland)** [2019] **1** 1, SC.
Jurisdiction—Enactment restricting appeal to Supreme Court—Recognition and enforcement of European member state parental responsibility order—Council Regulation providing judgment on appeal may be contested only by notified proceedings—UK notification listing 'single further appeal ... to the Court of Appeal'—Whether Supreme Court having jurisdiction to entertain further appeal—Constitutional Reform Act 2005, s 40(2), (6)—Council Regulation 2201/2003/EC, arts 34, 68. **D (a child) (No 2) (recognition and enforcement of judgment: Supreme Court jurisdiction), Re** [2016] **4** 95, SC.
Jurisdiction—Jurisdiction, relation to other courts etc—Financial restrictions proceedings—Appeal—Closed material procedure—Whether Supreme Court having power to adopt closed material procedure on appeal in financial restrictions proceedings—Constitutional Reform Act 2005, s 40—Counter-Terrorism Act 2008, s 63. **Bank Mellat v HM Treasury** [2013] **4** 495, SC.
Jurisdiction—Scotland—Compatibility issue appeal—Appeal from High Court of Justiciary—Nature of jurisdiction—High Court having identified correct test to apply—Whether open to Supreme Court to consider whether High Court's application of correct test so manifestly wrong that in effect it had applied wrong test—Criminal Procedure (Scotland) Act 1995, ss 288AA, 288ZA. **Macklin v HM Advocate (Scotland)** [2017] **1** 32, SC.
Live text-based communications—Policy. **Practice Statement** [2011] **1** 604, SC.

SURCHARGE
Local government audit. *See* **Local government** (Audit—Surcharge).
Rates—
Unused commercial building. *See* **Rates** (Surcharge on unused commercial building).
Surtax rate for previous year—
Retrospective operation of statute. *See* **Income tax** (Statute—Retrospective operation—Surcharge on surtax rate for previous year).

SURETY
Administration bond. *See* **Administration of estates** (Administration bond—Sureties).
Bankruptcy—
Forfeiture of lease—
Breach of covenant—Notice of breach—Bankruptcy of surety. *See* **Landlord and tenant** (Forfeiture of lease—Notice of breach—Failure to give notice—Breach of condition complained of—Bankruptcy of surety).
Proceedings for declaration of fraudulent preference in respect of debt guaranteed—
Joinder of surety. *See* **Bankruptcy** (Fraudulent preference—Joinder of parties—Bankrupt's account guaranteed by surety).
Co-sureties—
Guarantee. *See* **Guarantee** (Co-sureties).
Criminal law. *See* **Criminal law** (Bail).
Guarantee—
Generally. *See* **Guarantee** (Surety).
Landlord and tenant—
Covenant by surety to accept new lease if tenant becoming insolvent and disclaiming lease—
Whether surety's covenant running with land. *See* **Landlord and tenant** (Covenant—Covenant running with land—Covenant by surety to accept new lease if tenant becoming insolvent and disclaiming lease).

SURGEON
Negligence—
Operation. *See* **Negligence** (Professional person—Surgeon—Operation).
Vicarious liability—
Liability for acts of resident hospital staff. *See* **Vicarious liability** (Principal and agent—Surgeon).

SURGERY
Minor, on. *See* **Minor** (Medical treatment).
Negligence—
Medical practitioner. *See* **Medical practitioner** (Negligence—Surgery).
Promotion of—
Charitable object. *See* **Charity** (Benefit to community—Surgery—Promotion of surgery).
Surgeon's contract with patient—
Collateral warranty—
Breach. *See* **Contract** (Warranty—Collateral warranty—Breach—Surgery).
Nature of contract. *See* **Contract** (Surgery—Nature of contract).

SURNAME
    Divorce—
        Custody—
            Change of surname. *See* **Divorce** (Custody—Change of surname).
    Election—
        Local government election—
            Nomination papers—Particulars not as required by law—Rejection of papers by returning officer—Surname of candidate to be placed first in list of names. *See* **Elections** (Local government—Nomination papers—Names of candidates—Particulars not as required by law—Rejection of papers by returning officer—Surname of candidate to be placed first in list of names).
    Minor—
        Change of surname. *See* **Minor** (Change of surname).
    Registration—
        European Community trade mark. *See* **European Union** (Trade marks—Registration—Distinctiveness).

SURPLUS ASSETS
    Unincorporated association—
        Distribution of surplus assets on dissolution. *See* **Unincorporated association** (Dissolution—Distribution of surplus assets among members).

SURPLUS INCOME
    Accumulation. *See* **Accumulation** (Surplus income).

SURROGACY ARRANGEMENT
    Child born under surrogacy arrangement—
        Adoption—
            Payment for adoption. *See* **Adoption** (Payment for adoption—Payment or reward—Surrogacy arrangement).
            Parenthood. *See* **Family proceedings** (Orders in family proceedings—Parenthood in cases involving assisted reproduction—Parental orders—Child born under surrogacy arrangement).
    Child born under surrogacy arrangement in United States—
        Parental order—
            Single applicant—Father obtaining declaratory judgment from United States court relieving surrogate mother of any legal rights or responsibilities for child and establishing father's sole parentage—Father and child returning to United Kingdom—Father having no parental responsibility for child in United Kingdom—Father applying for parental order—Whether open to court to make parental order on application of single applicant—Whether possible to 'read down' relevant statutory provision to enable court to make order—Human Fertilisation and Embryology Act 1990, s 30—Human Rights Act 1998, s 3(1)—Human Fertilisation and Embryology Act 2008, s 54(1). **Z (a child) (surrogacy: parental order), Re** [2016] 2 83, Fam Ct.

SURTAX
    Avoidance. *See* **Income tax** (Avoidance—Surtax).
    Income tax—
        Generally. *See* **Income tax** (Surtax).
        Including surtax. *See* **Income tax** (Meaning of 'income tax'—Surtax).
    Surcharge on rate for previous year—
        Retrospective operation of statute. *See* **Income tax** (Statute—Retrospective operation—Surcharge on surtax rate for previous year).

SURVEY
    Negligence—
        Survey of ship. *See* **Negligence** (Duty to take care—Survey of ship).

SURVEYOR
    Negligence—
        Building society, report for—
            Jurisdiction of building societies ombudsman to investigate complaint. *See* **Building society** (Maladministration—Breach of contractual obligations—Negligent valuation report—Complaint to building societies ombudsman).
        Exclusion of liability—
            Unfair term of contract. *See* **Contract** (Unfair terms—Exclusion of liability for negligence—Surveyor).
        Generally. *See* **Negligence** (Surveyor).
        Immunity from suit. *See* **Negligence** (Immunity from suit—Surveyor).
        Information or advice. *See* **Negligence** (Information or advice—Knowledge third party might rely on information—Surveyor and valuer).
    Report—
        Negligence—
            Assessment of damages. *See* **Damages** (Assessment—Date at which damages assessed—Surveyor's report to purchaser negligently failing to disclose defects in building).
            Report for building society. *See* **Building society** (Maladministration—Breach of contractual obligations—Negligent valuation report).
    Valuation report—
        Obligation to inspect. *See* **Contract** (Construction—Contractual term—Valuation report).

SUSPECTED OFFENCE
    Income tax—
        Fraud. *See* **Income tax** (Offence—Fraud—Suspected offence).

SUSPECTED PERSON

Detention and questioning—
    Admissions and confessions. *See* **Criminal evidence** (Admissions and confessions).
    Right of access to solicitor. *See* **Solicitor** (Access to—Right of person in custody).
Vagrancy offence—
    Frequenting or loitering with intent. *See* **Criminal law** (Vagrancy—Frequenting or loitering with intent).
    Generally. *See* **Criminal law** (Vagrancy—Suspected person).
Ward of court—
    Police wishing to interview suspect who is a ward of court—
        Whether leave of court required. *See* **Criminal evidence** (Child—Ward of court—Suspect or victim of crime).

SUSPENDED ORDER

Committal—
    Non-payment of judgment debt. *See* **Debt** (Non-payment of judgment debt—Committal—Order—Suspension).
Possession—
    Costs—
        Special reasons—Agricultural worker—Tied cottage. *See* **Agriculture** (Agricultural worker—Tied cottage—Possession—Suspended order for possession—Costs).
    Discretion to suspend order. *See* **Landlord and tenant** (Recovery of possession—Order for possession—Suspension of order—Discretion).
    Leave to issue execution. *See* **Execution** (Leave to issue execution—Application—Suspended order for possession).
    Mortgaged property. *See* **Mortgage** (Possession of mortgaged property—Suspension of execution of order for possession).

SUSPENDED SENTENCE

See **Sentence** (Suspended sentence).

SWAP AGREEMENT

Interest rate swap agreement—
    Restitution. *See* **Contract** (Restitution—Interest rate swap agreement).
    Termination of contract. *See* **Contract** (Termination—Swap agreement).

SWAZILAND

Murder—
    Procedure—
        Native assessor—Opinion not given in public—Swaziland High Court Proclamation 1938, ss 8, 10(1). **Mahlikilili Dhalamini v R** [1943] **1** 463, PC.

SWIMMING POOL

Entry to swimming pool—
    Sex discrimination. *See* **Sex discrimination** (Provision of goods, facilities or services—Entry to swimming pool).

T

TABLE
Holy table. *See* **Ecclesiastical law** (Holy table).
Newspaper table used in conjunction with promotional game—
    Copyright—
        Whether table a 'literary work'. *See* **Copyright** (Literary work—Original literary work—Table).

TABLET
Memorial tablet within church—
    Ecclesiastical law. *See* **Ecclesiastical law** (Monument—Memorial tablet within church).

TACHOGRAPH CHART
Carriage of goods and passengers. *See* **Road traffic** (Carriage of goods and passengers—Tachograph charts).

TAKE-OVER
Capital gains tax—
    Effect of undisclosed take-over negotiations on valuation of shares—
        Market value—Shares quoted on London Stock Exchange. *See* **Capital gains tax** (Assets—Valuation—Market value—Shares—Shares quoted on London Stock Exchange—Quoted price as proper measure of market value—Special circumstances displacing quoted price as proper measure—Take-over).
City Code on Take-overs and Mergers—
    Construction. *See* **Document** (Construction—City Code on Take-overs and Mergers).
Company. *See* **Company** (Take-over bid).
Negligence—
    Information or advice—
        Knowledge third party might rely on information. *See* **Negligence** (Information or advice—Knowledge third party might rely on information—Company—Take-over bid).
Panel on Take-overs and Mergers—
    Judicial review of panel's decision—
        Whether panel's decision subject to judicial review. *See* **Judicial review** (Availability of remedy—Take-over Panel).
Reference to Monopolies and Mergers Commission. *See* **Monopolies and mergers**.

TAKING
Larceny. *See* **Criminal law** (Larceny—Taking).

TANGANYIKA
Land—
    Occupancy—
        Right of occupancy under certificate of occupancy—Interest in land distinct from lease—Conditions of occupancy not complied with—Revocation of certificate for failure to comply with conditions—Whether revocation valid if given without notice of breach—Tanganyika Land Ordinance 1923—Tanganyika Land (Law of Property and Conveyancing) Ordinance 1923—Conveyancing Act 1881, s 14(1). **Premchand Nathu & Co Ltd v Land Officer** [1963] **1** 216, PC.

TAPE RECORDING
Disclosure—
    Whether tape recording a 'document'. *See* **Disclosure and inspection of documents** (Production of documents—Document—Meaning—Tape recording).
Evidence in civil proceedings. *See* **Document** (Admissibility in evidence—Out-of-court statement—Out-of-court statement made 'orally' admissible only if proved by direct oral evidence by speaker—Statements recorded on tape recordings).
Evidence in criminal proceedings—
    Best evidence. *See* **Criminal evidence** (Best evidence—Tape recording).
    Discretion to exclude tape recording. *See* **Criminal evidence** (Exclusion of evidence—Discretion—Tape recorded conversation).
    Generally. *See* **Criminal evidence** (Tape recording).
    Refreshing memory. *See* **Criminal evidence** (Witness—Refreshing memory—Tape recording).
    Translation—
        Tape recording in criminal proceedings. *See* **Criminal evidence** (Best evidence—Tape recording—Translations).
Use of tape recorders in court—
    Practice. *See* **Practice** (Tape recorders—Use of tape recorders in court).

TAPPING
Telephone tapping—
    Powers of police to tap telephone. *See* **Police** (Powers—Telephone tapping).
    Use of telephone intercepts as evidence—
        Criminal trial. *See* **Criminal evidence** (Interception of communications—Telephone intercepts).
        Extradition proceedings. *See* **Extradition** (Committal—Evidence—Telephone intercept).

TAX
Advance corporation tax—
    Generally. *See* **Income tax** (Corporation tax—Advance corporation tax).
Advantage—
    Generally. *See* **Income tax** (Tax advantage).

TAX (cont)—
    Advantage (cont)—
        Rectification of deed—
            Deed of release—Deed not giving effect to parties' common intention. *See* **Deed**
            (Rectification—Deed of release—Deed not giving effect to parties' common intention—Deed
            giving tax advantage if rectified).
    Alcohol—
        European Community—
            Discrimination. *See* **European Union** (Taxation—Discrimination—Higher internal taxes being
            imposed on products from other member states—Different tax treatment of beer and wine).
    Appeal—
        Commissioners—
            Jurisdiction to hear appeal—Appeal against closure notice—During course of hearing Revenue
            seeking to rely on additional grounds to defend closure notice not stated in closure
            notice—Whether Special Commissioner having jurisdiction to permit Revenue to raise and rely
            on additional grounds to support the closure notices—Taxes Management Act 1970, ss 28B(1),
            31(1)(b). **Tower MCashback LLP 1 v Revenue and Customs Comrs** [2011] **3** 171, SC.
        High Court jurisdiction. *See* **High Court** (Jurisdiction—Tax appeals).
    Avoidance—
        Capital gains tax. *See* **Capital gains tax** (Tax avoidance scheme).
        Development land tax. *See* **Development land tax** (Tax avoidance scheme).
        Income tax. *See* **Income tax** (Avoidance).
        Value added tax. *See* **Value added tax** (Tax avoidance scheme).
    Business tax—
        Canada. *See* **Canada** (Business tax).
    Capital allowances—
        Income tax. *See* **Capital allowances**.
    Capital gains tax. *See* **Capital gains tax**.
    Capital transfer tax. *See* **Capital transfer tax**.
    Child tax credit. *See* **Social security** (Child tax credit).
    Citation of cases—
        Practice. *See* **Practice** (Citation of cases—Reports—Revenue cases).
    Closure notice—
        Appeal against. *See* Appeal—Commissioners—Jurisdiction to hear appeal—Appeal against closure
        notice, *above*.
        Validity—
            HMRC sending tax computational documents and covering letter to taxpayer—Documents omitting
            to charge taxpayer's interest rate swap transactions—HMRC subsequently issuing further
            documents with different conclusions—Whether first set of documents amounting to valid
            closure notice—Finance Act 1998, Sch 18, para 32(1). **Bristol & West plc v Revenue and Customs
            Comrs** [2017] **1** 480, CA.
    Corporation profits tax—
        Hong Kong. *See* **Hong Kong** (Corporation profits tax).
    Corporation tax—
        Company—
            Compulsory winding up. *See* **Company** (Compulsory winding up—Corporation tax on chargeable
            gains).
            European Community—Discrimination on grounds of nationality. *See* **European Union** (Freedom of
            establishment—Discrimination on grounds of nationality—Corporation tax).
        Direct internal taxation—
            European Community. *See* **European Union** (Freedom of establishment—Principle of non-
            discrimination—Direct internal taxation—Corporation tax).
        Generally. *See* **Corporation tax**.
        Group relief. *See* **Income tax** (Company—Group relief).
    Costs—
        Costs-sharing order. *See* **Costs** (Order for costs—Costs-sharing order—First-tier Tribunal).
    Council tax. *See* **Local government** (Council tax).
    Customs and excise—
        European Union. *See* **European Union** (Customs and excise).
    Damages—
        Effect on—
            Fatal accident. *See* **Fatal accident** (Damages—Taxation—Effect on award of incidence to tax).
        Lost future earnings—
            Allowance for incidence of tax. *See* **Damages** (Personal injury—Loss of future earnings—Income
            tax).
        Mitigation of loss—
            Tax benefit. *See* **Damages** (Mitigation of loss—Tax benefit).
        Wrongful dismissal. *See* **Contract** (Damages for breach—Wrongful dismissal—Taxation).
    Death duty—
        Generally. *See* **Estate duty**.
        New South Wales. *See* **New South Wales** (Death duty).
    Development land tax. *See* **Development land tax**.
    Discrimination—
        European Union. *See* **European Union** (Taxation—Discrimination).
    Divorce—
        Financial provision—
            Effect of order sought. *See* **Divorce** (Financial provision—Evidence—Effect of order sought—Tax).
            Tax implications. *See* **Divorce** (Financial provision—Tax implications).
    Entertainment duty. *See* **Entertainment duty**.
    Estate duty—
        Australia. *See* **Australia** (Estate duty).
        Generally. *See* **Estate duty**.
        New Zealand. *See* **New Zealand** (Estate duty).

TAX (cont)—
    European Union—
        Principle of non-discrimination. *See* **European Union** (Freedom of establishment—Principle of non-discrimination—Direct internal taxation).
        Workers tax exemptions. *See* **European Union** (Workers—Freedom of movement—Tax exemptions).
    European Union. *See* **European Union** (Taxation).
    Evasion—
        Confiscation order. *See* **Criminal law** (Confiscation order—Tax evasion).
        Offence arising out of tax evasion—
            Decision to prosecute—Judicial review of decision—Availability of remedy. *See* **Judicial review** (Availability of remedy—Decision to prosecute—Offence in connection with tax evasion).
            Whether ordinary offence arising out of tax evasion an extradition crime. *See* **Extradition** (Committal—Extradition crime—Offence arising out of tax evasion).
    Excess profits tax. *See* **Excess profits tax**.
    Exchange of information relating to tax matters—
        Human rights. *See* **Human rights** (Right to a fair hearing—Right against self-incrimination—Exchange of information relating to tax matters).
    Foreign revenue laws—
        Enforcement—
            Indirect enforcement—Danish tax authority bringing private law claims in relation to wrongful refunds of withholding tax—Authority alleging fraud in relation to refunds—Whether claims inadmissible as attempts to enforce foreign revenue laws. **Skatteforvaltningen (Danish Customs and Tax Administration) v Solo Capital Partners LLP (in special admin)** [2022] **2** 563, CA.
    Foreign tax tribunal—
        Evidence requested by tribunal—
            Examination of witnesses in relation to matters pending before tribunal. *See* **Evidence** (Foreign tribunal—Examination of witness in relation to matters pending before foreign tribunal—Evidence for purpose of civil proceedings—Proceedings in civil or commercial matter—Evidence requested by foreign tax tribunal).
    Gaming duty—
        Banker's profits—
            Gross gaming yield—Operator of casinos providing free bet vouchers and non-negotiable chips to selected customers—Whether free bet vouchers and non-negotiable chips having value in money or money's worth when staked or in relation to prizes—Betting and Gaming Duties Act 1981, s 20(3)—Finance Act 1997, s 11(10). **London Clubs Management Ltd v Revenue and Customs Comrs** [2021] **2** 333, SC.
    Immunity—
        Foreign sovereign state. *See* **Constitutional law** (Foreign sovereign state—Immunity from taxation).
    Income tax—
        Australia. *See* **Australia** (Income tax).
        Canada. *See* **Canada** (Income tax).
        Ceylon. *See* **Ceylon** (Income tax).
        Damages—
            Measure of damages. *See* **Damages** (Measure of damages—Income tax).
        European Community. *See* **European Union** (Freedom of movement—Principle of non-discrimination—Income tax).
        Generally. *See* **Income tax**.
        New Zealand. *See* **New Zealand** (Income tax).
        School fees—
            European Community. *See* **European Union** (Freedom of movement—Principle of non-discrimination—Income tax—National legislation providing for a proportion of fees paid to private school in Germany to be tax-deductible).
    Inheritance tax—
        Generally. *See* **Inheritance tax**.
        Probate. *See* **Probate** (Inheritance tax).
    Insurance premium tax—
        State aid—
            European Community. *See* **European Union** (State aids—Concept of state aid—Insurance premium tax).
        Value added tax—
            European Community. *See* **European Union** (Value added tax—Supply of goods or services—Insurance premium tax).
    Jurisdiction—
        High Court. *See* **High Court** (Jurisdiction—Tax).
    Landfill tax. *See* **Landfill tax**.
    Legacy duty—
        New South Wales. *See* **New South Wales** (Legacy duty).
    Local taxation licences. *See* **Local government** (Local taxation licences).
    Motor vehicle—
        Rate of duty. *See* **Road traffic** (Excise licence—Rate of duty).
    National defence contribution. *See* **National defence contribution**.
    Northern Ireland—
        Powers of Government of Northern Ireland. *See* **Northern Ireland** (Reference—Taxation—Powers of Government of Northern Ireland).
    Production of documents—
        Exchange of information relating to tax matters—
            Human rights. *See* **Human rights** (Right to a fair hearing—Right against self-incrimination—Exchange of information relating to tax matters).
    Profits tax—
        Generally. *See* **Profits tax**.
        Hong Kong. *See* **Hong Kong** (Profits tax).
    Purchase tax. *See* **Purchase tax**.
    Rates. *See* **Rates**.

TAX (cont)—
    Repayment of sums unduly levied or benefits unduly claimed—
        European Union. *See* **European Union** (Taxation—Claims for repayment of sums unduly levied or benefits unduly claimed).
        Restitution. *See* **Restitution** (Claims for repayment of sums unduly levied or benefits unduly claimed).
        Value added tax. *See* **Value added tax** (Overpayment of tax—Repayment).
    Reserve certificate—
        Interest in certificate. *See* **Income tax** (Interest—Tax reserve certificates).
    Sales tax—
        Canada. *See* **Canada** (Sales tax).
    School fees—
        European Community. *See* **European Union** (Freedom of movement—Principle of non-discrimination—Income tax—National legislation providing for a proportion of fees paid to private school in Germany to be tax-deductible).
    Scottish decision on taxation matters—
        Conformity. *See* **Precedent** (Scottish decision—Conformity—Revenue and taxation matters).
    Selective employment tax. *See* **Selective employment tax**.
    Stamp duty—
        Stamp duty land tax. *See* **Stamp duty land tax**.
    Stamp duty. *See* **Stamp duty**.
    Stamp duty land tax. *See* **Stamp duty land tax**.
    Succession duty—
        Canada—
            Canada. *See* **Canada** (Succession duty).
        Generally. *See* **Succession duty**.
    Tax credits—
        Powers of Inland Revenue Commissioners. *See* **Income tax** (Commissioners of Inland Revenue—Administration and management of taxation system—Tax credits).
    Taxing Act. *See* **Statute** (Taxing Act).
    Transport—
        Private air and boat transport—
            European Union. *See* **European Union** (Freedom of movement—Services—Private air and boat transport).
    Tribunal—
        Procedure—
            First-tier Tribunal. *See* **Tribunal** (First-tier Tribunal—Procedure).
        Upper tribunal. *See* **Tribunal** (Upper tribunal).
    Unlawful demand for tax—
        Repayment of money paid. *See* **Restitution** (Money paid to Crown—Payment of unlawful demand for tax).
    Value added tax—
        Costs—
            Taxation. *See* **Costs** (Taxation—Value added tax).
        European Community. *See* **European Union** (Value added tax).
        Generally. *See* **Value added tax**.
    Variation of settlement—
        Result of variation reduction in tax payable. *See* **Variation of Settlement (Matrimonial Causes)** (Jurisdiction—Divorce Division—Result of variation reduction in tax payable).
    Will—
        Income—
            Gift of income free of all taxes (including income tax) and duties. *See* **Will** (Gift—Income—Income free of all taxes (including income tax) and duties).

TAXATION OF COSTS
    Admiralty. *See* **Admiralty** (Costs—Taxation).
    Arbitration. *See* **Arbitration** (Costs—Taxation).
    Crown Court—
        Value added tax. *See* **Costs** (Taxation—Value added tax—Crown Court).
    Divorce. *See* **Divorce** (Costs—Taxation).
    Generally. *See* **Costs** (Taxation).
    House of Lords. *See* **House of Lords** (Costs—Taxation).
    Legal aid proceedings. *See* **Legal aid** (Taxation of costs).
    Privy Council. *See* **Privy Council** (Costs—Taxation).
    Vouching bills of costs. *See* **Costs** (Vouching bills of costs).
    Winding up—
        Company—Compulsory winding up. *See* **Company** (Compulsory winding up—Costs—Taxation).

TAXI
    Driver—
        Tips—
            Income tax. *See* **Income tax** (Emoluments from office or employment—Voluntary payment—Payment arising in ordinary course of taxpayers employment—Taxi-cab driver—Tips).
    Hackney carriage. *See* **Road traffic** (Hackney carriage).
    Waiting and loading restrictions—
        London. *See* **Road traffic** (Waiting and loading restrictions—London—Taxi).

TAXING ACT
    See **Statute** (Taxing Act).

TAXING MASTER
Costs—
  Taxation—
    Criminal proceedings—Appeal from decision—Legal aid. See **Legal aid** (Taxation of costs—Criminal proceedings—Appeal from decision of taxing master).
    Generally. See **Costs** (Taxation).

TEACHER
Dismissal—
  Appointment during pleasure—
    Natural justice. See **Natural justice** (Public authority—Dismissal of employee).
  Bias of tribunal inquiring into dismissal of teacher. See **Tribunal** (Membership—Bias—Inquiry into dismissal).
  Generally. See **Education** (Teacher).
  Negligence—
    Liability of local education authority. See **Education** (Local education authority—Negligence—Teacher).
  Suspension—
    Suspension pending determination of charges against teacher—
      Right of teacher to be heard prior to suspension. See **Natural justice** (Educational establishment—Complaint against teacher—Duty to hear parties etc).
  University. See **University** (Academic staff).

TECHNOLOGY
Electronic database—
  Lien. See **Lien** (Common law lien—Possession—Electronic database).
Mobile telephone networks. See **Telecommunications** (Mobile telephone networks).
Telecommunications. See **Telecommunications**.

TECHNOLOGY AND CONSTRUCTION COURT
Appeal to Court of Appeal—
  Application for leave to appeal—
    Test to be applied—Guidance—CPR 52.6. **Wheeldon Brothers Waste Ltd v Millennium Insurance Co Ltd** [2019] **1 Comm** 292n, CA; [2019] **1** 297n, CA.
Case management. See **Practice** (Technology and Construction Court—Case management).
Costs management scheme. See **Costs** (Assessment—Detailed assessment—Mercantile Courts and Technology and Construction Courts costs management scheme).
Numbering of judgments. See **Judgment** (Numbering of judgments).
Practice—
  Generally. See **Practice** (Technology and Construction Court).
Transfer of proceedings from or to. See **Practice** (Transfer of proceedings from or to the Technology and Construction Court).

TELECOMMUNICATIONS
Broadband connection services—
  Competition—
    European Union. See **European Union** (Rules on competition—Abuse of dominant position—Undertaking owning network for high-speed broadband connection).
EC Directive—
  Transposition into national law. See **European Union** (Directives—Transposition into national law—Telecommunications).
Electronic Communications Code—
  Conferral of code rights and their exercise—
    Electronic communications apparatus ('ECA') installed on land not owned by operator—Whether and how an operator who has already installed ECA on site can acquire new or better code rights from site owner—Meaning of 'occupier'—Communications Act 2003, Sch 3A, paras 9, 20, 105. **Cornerstone Telecommunications Infrastructure Ltd v Compton Beauchamp Estates Ltd** [2022] **4** 967, SC.
Interception of communications—
  Criminal law. See **Criminal law** (Interception of communications).
  Directions in the interests of national security—
    Bulk personal datasets—Bulk communications data—Use of data by security and intelligence agencies—Whether obtaining of bulk communications data in accordance with domestic law—Whether use of bulk data in accordance with the law for convention purposes—Telecommunications Act 1984, ss 45, 94—Human Rights Act 1998, Sch 1, Pt I, art 8. **Privacy International v Secretary of State for Foreign and Commonwealth Affairs** [2017] **3** 647, IPT.
    Bulk personal datasets—Bulk communications data—Use of data by security and intelligence agencies—Whether obtaining of bulk communications data in accordance with European law—Telecommunications Act 1984, s 94—Treaty on European Union, art 4—European Parliament and Council Directive 2002/58/EC, arts 1(3), 15(1). **Privacy International v Secretary of State for Foreign and Commonwealth Affairs (No 2)** [2018] **2** 166n, IPT.
    Bulk personal datasets—Bulk communications data—Use of data by security and intelligence agencies—Whether obtaining of bulk communications data in accordance with law—Telecommunications Act 1984, s 94—Human Rights Act 1998, Sch 1, Pt I, art 8. **Privacy International v Secretary of State for Foreign and Commonwealth Affairs (No 3)** [2018] **4** 275n, IPT.
Mobile telephone networks—
  Legal basis of regulation. See **European Union** (Regulations—Legal basis of regulation—Telecommunications—Roaming on public mobile telephone networks within European Union).
  Wireless telegraphy licence—
    Management of radio spectrum—Spectrum trading—Transfer of telegraphy licences to other persons—Principles to be applied—Wireless Telegraphy Act 2006, s 30—Council Directive (EC) 2002/20—Council Directive (EC) 2002/21. **Arqiva Ltd v Everything Everywhere Ltd (formerly T-Mobile (UK) Ltd)** [2012] **1** 607, TCC.

TELECOMMUNICATIONS (cont)—
 Office of communications—
  Networks and spectrum functions—
   Direction given by Secretary of State—Secretary of State directing Ofcom not to make it lawful to operate certain species of GSM gateway—Direction made on basis of national security and public safety concerns—Whether direction ultra vires—Communications Act 2003, s 5(2)—Wireless Telegraphy Act 2006, s 8(4). **R (on the application of VIP Communications Ltd (in liq)) v Secretary of State for the Home Dept (Office of Communications, interested party)** [2021] **3** 575, CA.

TELEGRAPHS ETC
 Broadcasting. *See* **Broadcasting**.
 Telegraphic lines—
  Injury to telegraphic line—
   Absolute liability—Liability of undertaker injuring telegraphic line—Defence—Undertaker relying on information given on site by Post Office engineer indicating position of underground telegraphic cable—Information inaccurate—Cable injured during course of digging to drain away flood water—Whether undertaker absolutely liable for injury to cable—Whether Post Office negligent in giving inaccurate information—Whether undertaker able to rely on negligence of Post Office as a defence to claim by Post Office against him—Telegraph Act 1878, s 8. **Post Office v Hampshire CC** [1979] **2** 818, CA.
   Absolute liability—Liability of undertaker injuring telegraphic line—Defence—Undertaker relying on plan prepared by Post Office showing position of underground telegraphic cable—Plan inaccurate—Cable injured during course of excavations in place where plan indicating no cable—Whether undertaker absolutely liable for injury to cable—Whether Post Office under duty to supply accurate plan—Whether undertaker able to counterclaim for negligence of Post Office to set off against his liability—Telegraphic Act 1878, s 8. **Post Office v Mears Construction Ltd** [1979] **2** 813, QBD.
  Placing of telegraph line across private land—
   Public interest—Consent of land owner sought by Post Office—Failure to give consent—'Amenities' not impaired—Two farming households in neighbourhood thereby deprived of telephone service—Whether failure to give consent was contrary to public interest—Wayleave—Telegraph (Construction) Act 1916, s 1. **Cartwright v Post Office** [1969] **1** 421, CA.
 Wireless—
  Licence—
   Block of flats—Wireless receiving set installed by landlord—Loud-speaker in tenant's flat—Liability of tenant for wireless licence—Wireless Telegraphy Act 1904, s 1(3). **King v Bull** [1937] **1** 585, KBD Divl Ct.

TELEPHONE
 Account—
  Certified account—
   Whether conclusive evidence of amount owing—Telegraph Act 1885, s 2—Telephone Regulations 1936 (SR & O 1936 No 173), reg 18(2). **Postmaster-General v Wadsworth** [1939] **4** 1, CA.
 Calls by solicitor—
  Taxation of costs in Family Division. *See* **Costs** (Taxation—Family Division—Solicitor—Telephone calls).
 Chambers proceedings—
  Communications by post or telephone. *See* **Practice** (Chambers proceedings—Communications by post or telephone).
 Contact by master in Chancery Division. *See* **Practice** (Chambers proceedings—Telephone contact).
 Interception of telephone calls—
  Powers of police. *See* **Police** (Powers—Telephone tapping).
  Publication of information obtained—
   Breach of confidence—Injunction. *See* **Equity** (Breach of confidence—Injunction—Information obtained by illegal telephone tapping).
  Use of telephone intercepts as evidence—
   Criminal trial. *See* **Criminal evidence** (Interception of communications—Telephone intercepts).
   Extradition proceedings. *See* **Extradition** (Committal—Evidence—Telephone intercept).
   Privilege against self-incrimination. *See* **Practice** (Pre-trial or post-judgment relief—Requests for further information—Self-incrimination).
  Warrant to intercept telephone calls—
   Judicial review of decision to issue warrant. *See* **Judicial review** (Availability of remedy—National security—Warrant to intercept telephone calls issued by Secretary of State).
 Mobile telephone—
  Telecommunications network. *See* **Telecommunications** (Mobile telephone networks).
 Patent proceedings—
  Telephone summons. *See* **Patent** (Practice—Telephone summonses).
 Sale of land—
  Exchange of contracts by telephone. *See* **Sale of land** (Exchange of contracts—Authority of solicitor—Exchange by telephone).

TELEVISION
 Authority—
  Privilege—
   Evidence. *See* **Evidence** (Privilege—Press—Television authority).
 Broadcast receiving licence—
  Revocation—
   Statutory power to revoke licence—Misuse of power. *See* **Public authority** (Statutory powers—Misuse of powers—Exercise of power for unlawful purpose—Validity—Licence—Power to revoke licence—Threat to exercise power for unlawful purpose—Wireless telegraphy—Broadcast receiving licence).

TELEVISION (cont)—
   Broadcasting—
      Broadcast receiving licence—
         Revocation—Statutory power to revoke licence—Misuse of power. *See* **Public authority** (Statutory powers—Misuse of powers—Exercise of power for unlawful purpose—Validity—Licence—Power to revoke licence—Threat to exercise power for unlawful purpose—Wireless telegraphy—Broadcast receiving licence).
      European Community—
         Freedom of movement of services. *See* **European Union** (Freedom of movement—Services—Television broadcasting).
      Generally. *See* **Broadcasting**.
   Examination of witness by television link—
      Witness in foreign jurisdiction. *See* **Evidence** (Witness—Witness in foreign jurisdiction—Examination of witness by live television link).
   Interference with reception—
      Nuisance. *See* **Nuisance** (Television—Interference with reception).
   Interview—
      Pending legal proceedings—
         Contempt of court. *See* **Contempt of court** (Publications concerning legal proceedings—Pending proceedings—Television interview at time when obvious that person interviewed about to be arrested and tried on charge of gross fraud).
   Nuisance. *See* **Nuisance** (Television).

TELEVISION FILM
   Document—
      Production in court—
         County court. *See* **County court** (Production of document—Meaning of 'document'—Cinematograph film).

TELEX
   Contract—
      Acceptance of offer by telex. *See* **Contract** (Offer and acceptance—Acceptance—Acceptance by telex).

TEMPORARY ACCOMMODATION
   Acquisition of land for—
      Authorisation by Minister. *See* **Housing** (Temporary accommodation—Acquisition of land—Authorisation by Minister).

TEMPORARY STATUTE
   See **Statute** (Temporary statute).

TEMPORARY STATUTORY OFFENCE
   See **Criminal law** (Temporary statutory offence).

TEMPORARY STRUCTURES
   Construction of—
      Building operations in. *See* **Building** (Construction of temporary structures for purposes of building operations etc).

TENANCY
   Adverse possession—
      Granted by. *See* **Limitation of action** (Land—Adverse possession—Seasonal tenancy).
   Agreement—
      Generally. *See* **Landlord and tenant** (Tenancy agreement).
      Indemnity. *See* **Indemnity** (Tenancy agreement).
      Registration as estate contract—
         Effect on subsequent mortgage. *See* **Land charge** (Estate contract—Tenancy agreement—Effect of registration on subsequent mortgages).
   Agricultural holding. *See* **Agricultural holding**.
   Allotment. *See* **Allotment**.
   Assured tenancy—
      Recovery of possession. *See* **Landlord and tenant** (Recovery of possession—Assured tenancy).
   At will—
      Business premises. *See* **Landlord and tenant** (Business premises—Tenancy—Tenancy at will).
      Characteristics. *See* **Landlord and tenant** (Tenancy—Tenancy at will).
      Licence distinguished. *See* **Licence** (Licence to occupy premises—Licence distinguished from tenancy at will).
   Business premises—
      Generally. *See* **Landlord and tenant** (Business premises).
      New tenancy. *See* **Landlord and tenant** (Business premises—Application for new tenancy).
      Opposition to grant of new tenancy. *See* **Landlord and tenant** (Opposition to grant of new tenancy of business premises).
   Company—
      Rent restriction—
         Premises not within Acts. *See* **Rent restriction** (Premises not within Acts—Company tenancy).
   Covenant—
      Generally. *See* **Landlord and tenant** (Covenant).
   Creation—
      Estate agent—
         Authority to create tenancy. *See* **Estate agent** (Authority—Authority to create tenancy).
   Demoted tenancy. *See* **Housing** (Local authority houses—Possession—Demoted tenancy).
   Encroachment by tenant. *See* **Landlord and tenant** (Encroachment by tenant).
   Enfranchisement. *See* **Landlord and tenant** (Leasehold enfranchisement).

TENANCY (cont)—

Entitlement—
   Permission for development. *See* **Town and country planning** (Permission for development—Certificate
   that applicant owner of fee simple or entitled to tenancy of land).
Estoppel—
   Tenancy by estoppel. *See* **Landlord and tenant** (Tenancy—Tenancy by estoppel).
Flat—
   Tenant's right to acquire landlord's reversion. *See* **Landlord and tenant** (Flats—Tenants' right to acquire
   landlord's reversion).
Furnished—
   Protected tenancy. *See* **Rent restriction** (Furnished letting).
Generally. *See* **Landlord and tenant.**
Grant. *See* **Landlord and tenant** (Tenancy—Grant).
Joint tenancy—
   Determination—
      Generally. *See* **Landlord and tenant** (Tenancy—Joint tenancy—Determination).
   Equitable charge—
      Creation of charge. *See* **Equity** (Charge—Creation of equitable charge—Joint tenancy).
   Generally. *See* **Joint tenancy.**
Lease. *See* **Landlord and tenant** (Lease).
Licence distinguished from—
   Generally. *See* **Landlord and tenant** (Tenancy—Tenancy distinguished from licence).
   Occupation of land. *See* **Licence** (Licence to occupy land).
   Occupation of premises. *See* **Licence** (Licence to occupy premises).
   Protected tenancy. *See* **Rent restriction** (Protected tenancy—Tenancy or licence).
Life tenant—
   Continuance of life—
      Burden of proof. *See* **Trust and trustee** (Life interest—Continuance of life of life tenant—Burden of
      proof).
Local authority tenancy—
   Divorce—
      Property adjustment order. *See* **Divorce** (Property—Adjustment order—Meaning of property—Local
      authority tenancy).
   Generally. *See* **Housing** (Local authority houses—Tenancy).
   Sale of house to tenant. *See* **Housing** (Local authority houses—Tenant's right to buy).
   Security of tenure—
      Action for possession. *See* **Housing** (Local authority houses—Possession—Security of tenure).
      Generally. *See* **Housing** (Local authority houses—Security of tenure).
   Tenant's right to buy premises. *See* **Housing** (Local authority houses—Tenant's right to buy).
   Transfer of tenancy. *See* **Housing** (Local authority houses—Transfer of tenancy).
Long tenancy—
   Long tenancy at low rent—
      Generally. *See* **Landlord and tenant** (Long tenancy at low rent).
      Protection. *See* **Rent restriction** (Long tenancy at low rent).
   Tenant having right to acquire freehold or extended lease. *See* **Landlord and tenant** (Leasehold
   enfranchisement—Long tenancy).
Mortgage—
   Receiver. *See* **Mortgage** (Receiver—Tenancy).
New tenancy—
   Business premises—
      Opposition to grant of new tenancy. *See* **Landlord and tenant** (Opposition to grant of new tenancy
      of business premises).
      Rent. *See* **Landlord and tenant** (Rent—Business premises—New tenancy).
   Shop. *See* **Landlord and tenant** (New tenancy).
Notice to quit. *See* **Landlord and tenant** (Notice to quit).
Notice to terminate—
   Business premises. *See* **Landlord and tenant** (Business premises—Notice by landlord to terminate
   tenancy).
Periodic—
   Creation. *See* **Landlord and tenant** (Tenancy—Periodic tenancy—Creation).
   Notice to quit—
      Validity. *See* **Landlord and tenant** (Validity of notice to quit—Periodic tenancy).
Protected—
   Generally. *See* **Rent restriction** (Protected tenancy).
   Possession. *See* **Rent restriction** (Possession).
   Sale of land. *See* **Sale of land** (Protected tenancy).
   Transfer on termination of marriage. *See* **Divorce** (Property—Protected or statutory tenancy—Transfer
   of protected or statutory tenancy on termination of marriage).
Regulated. *See* **Rent restriction** (Regulated tenancy).
Rent. *See* **Landlord and tenant** (Rent).
Rent restriction. *See* **Rent restriction.**
Residue under will—
   Division—
      Joint tenancy or tenancy in common. *See* **Will** (Residue—Division—Joint tenancy or tenancy in
      common).
Resulting trust. *See* **Trust and trustee** (Constructive trust—Tenancy agreement).
Secure tenancy—
   Forfeiture of lease—
      Breach of covenant prohibiting assignment. *See* **Landlord and tenant** (Forfeiture of lease—Breach
      of covenant prohibiting assignment—Secure tenancy).
   Public sector housing. *See* **Housing** (Local authority houses—Security of tenure).
Statutory—
   Generally. *See* **Rent restriction** (Statutory tenancy).

TENANCY (cont)—
 Statutory (cont)—
  Possession. *See* **Rent restriction** (Possession).
  Succession to tenancy on death of original tenant. *See* **Rent restriction** (Death of tenant).
  Transfer on termination of marriage. *See* **Divorce** (Property—Protected or statutory tenancy—Transfer of protected or statutory tenancy on termination of marriage).
  Transmission on death of tenant. *See* **Landlord and tenant** (Tenancy—Tenancy by estoppel—Transmission of statutory tenancy on death of tenant).
 Surrender. *See* **Landlord and tenant** (Surrender of tenancy).
 Unincorporated association—
  Status. *See* **Unincorporated association** (Status—Separate entity—Landlord's opposition to grant of new tenancy).
 Wartime—
  Creation. *See* **Landlord and tenant** (Tenancy—Creation—Wartime).
 Weekly—
  Divorce—
   Property adjustment order. *See* **Divorce** (Property—Adjustment order—Meaning of property—Tenancy—Weekly contractual tenancy).
 Yearly—
  Presumption of. *See* **Landlord and tenant** (Tenancy—Duration—Presumption of yearly tenancy).

TENANT
 Generally. *See* **Landlord and tenant**.
 Local authority tenant—
  Sale of house to tenant. *See* **Housing** (Local authority houses—Tenant's right to buy).

TENANT FOR LIFE
 Powers. *See* **Settlement** (Powers of tenant for life).

TENANT IN TAIL
 Infant—
  Sale of infant's entailed interest to tenant for life. *See* **Variation of trusts** (Variation by the court—Infant's interests—Tenant in tail in remainder).

TENANTS' ASSOCIATION
 Inducement to commit breach of contract—
  Tort—
   Justification. *See* **Tort** (Inducement to commit breach of contract—Justification—Tenants' association).

TENANTS IN COMMON
 Gift—
  Will—
   Gift over on death of all tenants in common. *See* **Will** (Gift—Gift over—Gift to tenants in common for life).
 Real property—
  Occupation of whole property by one of tenants in common—
   Rent—Family home purchased in joint names on trust for sale by man and woman living together—Relationship breaking down and woman leaving home because of man's violence—Some of children of family living with man in home—Whether man liable to pay occupation rent to woman—Whether rent to be assessed on basis of open market rent value or half the fair rent of a protected tenancy of house—Law of Property Act 1925, s 70. **Dennis v McDonald** [1982] 1 590, CA.
   Rent—Whether other tenant in common entitled to claim rent. **Jones (A E) v Jones (F W)** [1977] **2** 231, CA.
 Trust for sale. *See* **Trust and trustee** (Trust for sale—Realty—Tenancy in common).
 Sale of land—
  Specific performance. *See* **Specific performance** (Sale of land—Tenants in common).
 Will—
  Forfeiture clause—
   Alienation of interest. *See* **Will** (Forfeiture clause—Alienation of interest—Absolute gift of property to four sons as tenants in common).

TENDENCY TO DEPRAVE OR CORRUPT
 Obscene publications. *See* **Criminal law** (Obscene publications—Tendency to deprave or corrupt).

TENDER
 Acceptance of tender—
  Sale of land. *See* **Sale of land** (Acceptance of tender).
 Defence of tender—
  Payment into court—
   County court. *See* **County court** (Payment into court—Tender).
 Invitation to tender. *See* **Contract** (Invitation to tender).

TERRIER
 Pit bull terrier—
  Dangerous dog. *See* **Animal** (Dog—Dangerous dog—Pit bull terrier).

TERRITORIAL WATERS
 Magistrates' jurisdiction—
  Broadcasting. *See* **Magistrates** (Jurisdiction—Implied jurisdiction from enactment creating offence—Territorial waters).

TERRITORIAL WATERS (cont)—
 Petroleum rights—
  Crown. *See* **Petroleum rights** (Crown—Rights vested in Crown—Petroleum and natural gas situated inside and outside territorial waters).
 Seafishing—
  Prohibition of seine net. *See* **Fish** (Seafishing—Prohibition by byelaw of fishing with seine net within three-mile limit).

TERRORISM
 Act of terrorism—
  Use or threat of action designed to influence government or intimidate public. *See* **Criminal law** (Terrorism—Act of terrorism—Use or threat of action designed to influence government or intimidate public).
 Anonymity orders in proceedings—
  Human rights. *See* **Human rights** (Right to respect for private and family life—Freedom of expression—Persons suspected of being persons facilitating acts of terrorism).
 Arrest—
  Judicial review. *See* **Judicial review** (Terrorism—Arrest).
  Suspicion of being a terrorist. *See* **Arrest** (Terrorist —Suspicion of being a terrorist).
 Control order. *See* Prevention of—Control order, *below*.
 European Union—
  Action for annulment of Council decision. *See* **European Union** (Procedure—Action for annulment—Council decision).
  Police and judicial cooperation in criminal matters. *See* **European Union** (Police and judicial co-operation in criminal matters).
 Financing—
  Prevention of use of financial system for purposes of—
   European Union. *See* **European Union** (Freedom of movement—Services—Restriction on freedom—Prevention of use of financial system for purposes of money laundering and terrorist financing).
 Generally. *See* **Criminal law** (Terrorism).
 Human rights—
  Right to a fair hearing. *See* **Human rights** (Right to a fair hearing—Prevention of terrorism).
  Right to liberty and security. *See* **Human rights** (Right to liberty and security—Prevention of terrorism).
 Immigration—
  Assisting terrorist organisation. *See* **Immigration** (Leave to enter—Refugee—Asylum—Exclusion from provisions of Refugee Convention—Acts contrary to purpose and principles of United Nations).
 Prevention of—
  Control order—
   Anonymity of controlled person—Secretary of State making non-derogating control order against individual suspected of involvement in terrorism-related activity—Anonymity order made at commencement of proceedings—Appeal—Judgment—Whether anonymity order should be continued. **Secretary of State for the Home Dept v AP (No 2)** [2010] **4** 259, SC.
   Non-derogating control order—Modification, notification and proof of orders—Appeals relating to non-derogating control orders—Non-derogating control orders made with permission of court—Court giving directions for supervisory hearing—Controlled persons applying for modification of obligations imposed by orders—Secretary of State agreeing to certain modifications and refusing others—Controlled persons seeking to appeal—Whether changed circumstances necessary—Powers of court on appeal—Prevention of Terrorism Act 2005, ss 7(2), 10(3)(b). **AV v Secretary of State for the Home Dept** [2009] **1** 439, QBD.
   Power to make control orders—Requirements in control order—Requirement that controlled person submit to any search of his person required for purposes of monitoring compliance with other requirements of control order—Whether requirement to submit to search lawful—Prevention of Terrorism Act 2005, s 1(3), (4). **GG v Secretary of State for the Home Dept** [2010] **1** 721, CA.
   Right to a fair hearing. *See* **Human rights** (Right to a fair hearing—Prevention of terrorism—Control order).
   Right to liberty and security. *See* **Human rights** (Right to liberty and security—Prevention of terrorism—Control order).
   Terrorism prevention and investigation measure—Procedural fairness—Abuse of process— Requirement of disclosure of gist of allegations—Persons subject to control orders and terrorism prevention and investigation measures making allegations of abuse of process—Whether Secretary of State required to disclose gist of case on abuse of process. **Mohamed v Secretary of State for the Home Dept** [2014] 3 760, CA.
  Financial restrictions proceedings—
   Supreme Court of the United Kingdom, jurisdiction of. *See* **Supreme court** (Supreme Court of the United Kingdom—Practice—Jurisdiction—Jurisdiction, relation to other courts etc—Financial restrictions proceedings).
  Notification order—
   Metropolitan Police Commissioner applying for order imposing notification requirements on defendant on basis of conviction of corresponding foreign offence—Whether defendant being convicted of corresponding foreign offence—Whether Commissioner failing to consider relevant factors—Whether notification order in breach of defendant's right not to be subjected to inhuman or degrading treatment—Whether notification order in breach of defendant's right to respect for private and family life—Counter-Terrorism Act 2008, s 57, Sch 4, para 2—Human Rights Act 1998, Sch 1, Pt I, arts 3, 8. **Metropolitan Police Comr v Ahsan** [2016] 3 160, QBD.
  Port and border controls—
   Examination powers—Claimant British national being deported to United Kingdom from Somaliland—Claimant alleging ill-treatment by Somali authorities—Claimant being subject to control order issued by Secretary of State—Security service requesting ports duty officers to exercise powers under Terrorism Act 2000 Sch 7 to gain intelligence about time spent by claimant in Somaliland—Officers conducting examination pursuant to Sch 7—Claimant challenging exercise of those powers—Scope and extent of powers—Terrorism Act 2000, Sch 7. **CC v Comr of Police of the Metropolis** [2012] 2 1004, QBD.

TERRORISM (cont)—
  Prevention of (cont)—
    Port and border controls (cont)—
      Power to stop, question and detain—Determining whether person in port or border area concerned in commission, preparation or instigation of acts of terrorism—Freedom of expression—Whether exercise of power lawful—Whether exercise of power proportionate—Whether exercise of power incompatible with right to freedom of expression—Human Rights Act 1998, Sch 1, Pt I, art 10—Terrorism Act 2000, ss 1, 40, Sch 7. **R (on the application of Miranda) v Secretary of State for the Home Dept** [2014] **3** 447, DC.
      Power to stop, question and detain—Determining whether person in port or border area concerned in commission, preparation or instigation of acts of terrorism—Right to liberty and security—Right to a fair trial—Right to respect for private and family life—Whether exercise of power to stop, question and detain breach of convention rights—Human Rights Act 1998, Sch 1, Pt I, arts 5, 6, 8—Terrorism Act 2000, Sch 7. **Beghal v DPP** [2014] **1** 529, DC; [2016] **1** 483, SC.
  Sanctions—
    Financial restrictions—Claimant Iranian bank suspected of having been involved in transactions related to financing Iran's nuclear and ballistic missile programme—Treasury making order restricting United Kingdom financial sector from entering into or continuing with any business relationship or transaction with bank—Bank seeking to set order aside—Supreme Court finding order unlawful—Bank claiming damages for loss and damage caused by order—Whether open to Treasury to contend it had not acted unlawfully or in manner incompatible with Convention right—Whether open to Treasury to contend loss caused to bank by diminution in earnings before taxation irrecoverable as reflective loss—Whether recoverable damages limited to loss of 'possessions' themselves or whether recoverable damages including all losses flowing from unlawful interference with those 'possessions'—Human Rights Act 1998, ss 6(1), 7, 8, Sch 1, Pt II, art 1—Counter-Terrorism Act 2008, ss 62, 63, Sch 7—Financial Restrictions (Iran) Order 2009, SI 2009/2725—European Convention for the Protection of Human Rights and Fundamental Freedoms 1950. **Bank Mellat v HM Treasury** [2016] **1 Comm** 766, QBD.
    Financial restrictions—Claimant Iranian bank suspected of having been involved in transactions related to financing Iran's nuclear and ballistic missile programme—Treasury making order restricting United Kingdom financial sector from entering into or continuing with any business relationship or transaction with bank—Bank seeking to set order aside—Supreme Court finding order unlawful—Bank claiming damages for loss and damage caused by order—Whether bank entitled to claim loss of 60% of earnings before tax of English bank in which it held 60% of shares—Whether English bank having right to bring claim—Whether English bank a 'victim' of the order—Whether bank able to claim loss of future business—Human Rights Act 1998, ss 7, 8, Sch 1, Pt II, art 1—Counter-Terrorism Act 2008, ss 62, 63, Sch 7—Financial Restrictions (Iran) Order 2009, SI 2009/2725. **Bank Mellat v HM Treasury (No 3)** [2017] **1 Comm** 807, CA; [2017] **2** 139, CA.
    Financial restrictions—Treasury making order restricting United Kingdom financial sector from entering into or continuing with any business relationship or transaction with Iranian bank—Bank suspected of having been involved in transactions related to financing Iran's nuclear and ballistic missile programme—Bank challenging order on substantive and procedural grounds—Whether order proportionate—Whether order procedurally deficient—Counter-Terrorism Act 2008, ss 62, 63, Sch 7—Financial Restrictions (Iran) Order 2009, SI 2009/2725. **Bank Mellat v HM Treasury** [2011] **2** 802, CA; **Bank Mellat v HM Treasury (No 2)** [2013] **4** 533, SC.
  Proscribed organisation. *See* **Criminal law** (Proscribed organisation).
  Public electronic communications network, use of—
    Criminal law. *See* **Criminal law** (Public electronic communications network).
  Restrictive measures—
    Persons and entities associated with Usama bin Laden, the Al Qa'ida network and the Taliban—
      Social Security—Interpretation of European Union law. *See* **European Union** (Reference to European Court—Reference for preliminary ruling concerning interpretation of European Union law—Interpretation of regulation).
  Sanctions—
    European Union. *See* **European Union** (Regulations—Legal basis of regulation—Community foreign and security policy—Restrictive measures taken against certain persons and entities with view to combating terrorism).
    Financial restrictions. *See* Prevention of—Sanctions—Financial restrictions, *above*.
  Freezing of funds and economic resources—
    European Community Regulation implementing United Nations resolution—Regulation transposed into United Kingdom law—Funds not to be made to or for the benefit of listed person—Meaning of 'for the benefit of'—Al-Qa'ida and Taliban (United Nations Measures) Order 2002, SI 2002/111, art 7—Council Regulation (EC) 881/2002, art 2. **R (on the application of M) v HM Treasury** [2008] **2** 1097n, HL.
    United Nations Resolutions requiring freezing of funds and economic resources of terrorists—Resolutions given effect by Orders in Council—Orders unlawful—Whether order of court to be suspended. **Ahmed v HM Treasury (No 2)** [2010] **4** 829n, SC.
    United Nations Resolutions requiring freezing of funds and economic resources of terrorists—Resolutions given effect by Orders in Council—Whether Orders lawful—United Nations Act 1946, s 1—Terrorism (United Nations Measures) Order 2006, SI 2006/2657—Al-Qaida and Taliban (United Nations Measures) Order 2006, SI 2006/2952. **A v HM Treasury** [2008] **3** 361, QBD; [2009] **2** 747, CA; **Ahmed v HM Treasury** [2010] **4** 745, SC.
    United Nations Security Council maintaining list of persons associated with terrorism subject to sanctions—Secretary of State removing hold on appellant's designation on list—Appellant seeking judicial review—Whether Secretary of State under obligation to withhold support to committee decision on ground evidence obtained under torture—Whether interference with property rights requiring statutory authority—Standard of proof for designation—Whether full merits review of decision appropriate. **R (on the application of Youssef) v Secretary of State for Foreign and Commonwealth Affairs** [2016] **3** 261, SC.
  Sentence. *See* **Sentence** (Terrorism).
  Terrorist investigation—
    Criminal evidence. *See* **Criminal evidence** (Special procedure material—Terrorist investigation).

TERRORISM (cont)—
Terrorist offences—
Dissemination of terrorist publications—
Sentence. *See* **Sentence** (Terrorism—Terrorist offences—Dissemination of terrorist publications).
Possession for terrorist offences. *See* **Criminal law** (Terrorism—Terrorist offences—Possession for terrorist purposes).

TERRORIST
Access to solicitor—
Right of person arrested under prevention of terrorism provisions. *See* **Solicitor** (Access to—Right of person in custody—Presence of solicitor during interview—Suspect arrested under prevention of terrorism provisions).
Arrest without warrant. *See* **Arrest** (Arrest without warrant—Terrorist).
European Community—
Procedure—
Specific restrictive measures being directed against certain persons and entities with a view to combating terrorism. *See* **European Union** (Procedure—Action for annulment—Admissibility— Specific restrictive measures being directed against certain persons and entities with a view to combating terrorism).
Terrorist investigation—
Order for production of special procedure material. *See* **Criminal evidence** (Special procedure material—Terrorist investigation).
Power to stop, search and detain. *See* **Police** (Powers—Power to stop, search and detain—Searching for articles of a kind which could be used in connection with terrorism).

TEST CASE
Industrial tribunal—
Procedure. *See* **Employment tribunal** (Procedure—Test case).

TEST CERTIFICATE
Vehicle. *See* **Road traffic** (Test certificate).

TESTAMENTARY DISPOSITION
See **Will** (Testamentary disposition).

TESTAMENTARY DOCUMENT
Probate practice. *See* **Probate** (Practice—Documents—Testamentary documents).

TESTATOR
Alteration of will—
Expressed intention to alter will—
Delay in carrying out intention—Conditional revocation. *See* **Will** (Revocation—Conditional revocation—Expressed intention to alter will—Delay in carrying out intention).
Generally. *See* **Will** (Alteration).
Domicile. *See* **Will** (Testator—Domicile).
Execution of will—
Place of testator's signature. *See* **Will** (Execution—Place of testator's signature).
Family provision. *See* **Family provision**.
Generally. *See* **Will** (Testator).
Intention of testator—
Construction of will. *See* **Will** (Construction—Intention of testator).
Legacy to hospital. *See* **National Health Service** (Legacy to hospital).
Signature of will—
Attestation. *See* **Will** (Attestation—Acknowledgment of signature).
Soldier or mariner. *See* **Will** (Soldier's or mariner's privileged will).
Soundness of mind. *See* **Will** (Testator—Soundness of mind).
Testamentary capacity. *See* **Will** (Testator—Testamentary capacity).

TESTIMONIAL
Income tax on testimonial payment. *See* **Income tax** (Emoluments from office or employment—Receipt 'from' employment—Testimonial—Payment by way of testimonial to mark exceptional achievement in performance of services).
Negligence—
Character reference by employer. *See* **Negligence** (Duty to take care—Employer—Character reference given by employer on former employee).

TETRAPLEGIA
Damages. *See* **Damages** (Personal injury—Tetraplegia).

THALIDOMIDE
Personal injury—
Damages. *See* **Damages** (Personal injury—Thalidomide children).

THEATRE
Actor—
Part-time teacher at drama school—
National insurance. *See* **Social security** (Employed person—Contract of service—Part-time teacher at drama school).
Cinema. *See* **Cinema**.
Licence for sale and consumption of intoxicating liquor—
Exemption from need for justices' licence—
Special hours certificate—Application. *See* **Licensing** (Permitted hours—Special hours certificate— Application—Who may apply).

THEATRE (cont)—
Licence for the performance of stage plays—
Renewal—
Condition attached prohibiting theatre from selling intoxicating liquor or tobacco—Rules for ensuring order and decency—Proximity to theatre of a licensed house—Unconditional licence held for many years without complaint—Neighbouring theatre with conditional licence refused unconditional licence—Matters to be considered by and procedure of licensing authority on application to renew licence—Theatres Act 1843, s 9. **R v County Licensing (Stage Plays) Committee of Flint CC, ex p Barrett** [1957] **1** 112, CA.
Producer—
Negligence—
Prevention of theft. *See* **Negligence** (Duty to take care—Prevention of theft—Theatrical producer).
Stage play—
Causing presentation of unlicensed play or part of play—
Cause—Disobedience to stage directions by actor, contrary to orders of licensee of theatre—Liability of licensee—Theatres Act 1843, s 15. **Lovelace v DPP** [1954] **3** 481, QBD.
Substantial addition to script as licensed—Liability of absent producer—Theatres Act 1843, s 15. **Grade v DPP** [1942] **2** 118, KBD.
Sunday—
Restrictions. *See* **Sunday observance** (Restrictions on Sunday entertainment).
Video recording. *See* **Video recording**.

THEFT
Attempted theft—
When attempt begins. *See* **Criminal law** (Attempt—Acts preparatory to offence—When attempt begins).
Burglary. *See* **Criminal law** (Burglary).
Evasion of liability by deception. *See* **Criminal law** (Evasion of liability by deception).
Generally. *See* **Criminal law** (Theft).
Handling stolen goods. *See* **Criminal law** (Handling stolen goods).
Indictment. *See* **Indictment** (Theft-related offences).
Information—
Specified articles. *See* **Magistrates** (Information—Theft—Information charging accused with stealing specified articles).
Insurance against theft—
Scope of perils insured against. *See* **Insurance** (Property insurance—Perils insured against—Theft).
Murder in course of theft. *See* **Criminal law** (Murder—Capital murder—Murder in course or furtherance of theft).
Obtaining pecuniary advantage by deception. *See* **Criminal law** (Obtaining pecuniary advantage by deception).
Obtaining property by deception. *See* **Criminal law** (Obtaining property by deception).
Old law. *See* **Criminal law** (Larceny).
Prevention—
Duty of care to prevent theft. *See* **Negligence** (Duty to take care—Prevention of theft).
Taking vehicle without authority. *See* **Road traffic** (Taking vehicle without authority).
Traveller's cheque—
Reimbursement by bank. *See* **Bank** (Cheque—Traveller's cheque—Loss or theft—Reimbursement).

THIRD PARTY
Appeal—
Appeal by third party in main action. *See* **Court of Appeal** (Third party—Appeal against judgment in favour of plaintiff in main action).
Contract—
Right of third party to enforce contractual term. *See* **Contract** (Stranger to contract—Right of third party to enforce contractual term).
Contribution. *See* **Contribution** (Third party proceedings).
Costs—
Generally. *See* **Costs** (Third party).
Security for costs. *See* **Costs** (Security for costs—Third party proceedings).
Successful third party—
Discretion. *See* **Costs** (Order for costs—Discretion—Successful third party).
Custody application—
Divorce proceedings, in. *See* **Divorce** (Custody—Application—Application by third party for custody).
Damages—
Breach of contract. *See* **Contract** (Damages for breach—Third party).
Expenses of third party. *See* **Damages** (Expenses of third party).
Duty of care for acts of. *See* **Negligence** (Duty to take care—Act of third party).
Employer's liability insurance—
Third party rights against insurer. *See* **Insurance** (Employer's liability insurance—Third party's rights against insurers).
Food and drugs proceedings—
Defence—
Act or default of third party. *See* **Food and drugs** (Defence to proceedings—Contravention due to act or default of third party).
Libel—
Publication of libel to third party. *See* **Libel and slander** (Publication—Third party).
Third party debt order—
Practice. *See* **Practice** (Pre-trial or post-judgment relief—Third party debt orders).
Third party debt order. *See* **Execution** (Third party debt order).

THIRD PARTY INSURANCE
Employer's liability insurance—
Third party rights against insurers. *See* **Insurance** (Employer's liability insurance—Third party's rights against insurers).

THIRD PARTY INSURANCE (cont)—

Liability insurance—
Rights of third parties against insurers. *See* **Insurance** (Liability insurance—Third party's rights against insurers).

Motor insurance—
Compulsory third party insurance. *See* **Motor insurance** (Compulsory insurance against third party risks).
Rights of third parties against insurers. *See* **Motor insurance** (Rights of third parties against insurers).

Rights against insurer—
Generally. *See* **Insurance** (Third party's rights against insurer).

THIRD PARTY PROCEDURE

Appeal—
Respondent's notice—
Service on third party. *See* **Court of Appeal** (Respondent's notice—Service—Service on third party).
Generally. *See* **Practice** (Third party procedure).
Third party notice. *See* **Practice** (Third party notice).

THIRD PARTY PROCEEDINGS

Contribution. *See* **Contribution** (Third party proceedings).

Costs—
Security for costs. *See* **Costs** (Security for costs—Third party proceedings).
Crown, against. *See* **Crown** (Proceedings against—Third party proceedings).
Practice. *See* **Practice** (Third party proceedings).

THIRD PARTY RISKS

Motor insurance. *See* **Motor insurance** (Compulsory insurance against third party risks).

THREAT

Admission or confession obtained by threat—
Admissibility in criminal proceedings. *See* **Criminal evidence** (Admissions and confessions—Threat).

Breach of contract—
Duress—
Economic duress by threat to break contract. *See* **Contract** (Duress—Economic duress—Economic duress by threat to break contract).

Groundless threat of infringement proceedings—
Action under Registered Designs Act 1949 to restrain threat of proceedings. *See* **Design** (Action to restrain threat of proceedings for infringement).

Jury—
Intimidating or threatening jury. *See* **Jury** (Intimidating or threatening jury).

Robbery. *See* **Criminal law** (Robbery—Threat).

Threat to kill. *See* **Criminal law** (Threat to kill).

Witness—
Obstructing course of justice. *See* **Criminal law** (Obstructing course of justice—Witness—Intimidation).

THREATENING LETTER

See **Criminal law** (Threatening letters).

THREATENING WORDS OR BEHAVIOUR

Offensive conduct conducive to breaches of peace. *See* **Public order** (Offensive conduct conducive to breaches of peace—Threatening, abusive or insulting words or behaviour).

THREATENING, ABUSIVE OR INSULTING WRITING

Provoking violence. *See* **Criminal law** (Threatening, abusive or insulting writing—Provoking unlawful violence).

THRESHING MACHINE

Duty to fence dangerous parts. *See* **Agriculture** (Threshing machine—Fencing of dangerous parts).

TIDAL LANDS

Drainage rates—
Exemption. *See* **Land drainage** (Drainage rates—Exemption—Tidal lands).

TIDAL WATERS

Navigation—
Public right to navigate. *See* **Water and watercourses** (Navigation—Public right of navigation (PRN)).

Salvage services—
Admiralty jurisdiction—
Action in rem—Claim in the nature of salvage. *See* **Admiralty** (Jurisdiction—Action in rem—Claim in nature of salvage—Tidal waters).

TIMBER

Contract for sale of. *See* **Agriculture** (Timber—Contract for sale).

Rights—
Concession—
Gold Coast. *See* **West Africa** (Gold Coast—Concession of timber rights).
Timber control. *See* **Timber control**.

TIMBER CONTROL

    Application of restrictions—
        Application to purchaser to whom property in timber had passed before restrictions passed—
            Delivery after restrictions in force—Whether restrictions apply—Control of Timber (No 1) Order 1939 (SR & O 1939 No 1031), art 1—Control of Timber (No 5) Order 1939 (SR & O 1939 No 1329), arts 1-3. **Rappaport v London Plywood and Timber Co Ltd** [1940] **1** 576, KBD.

TIME

    Abridgement of time—
        Summary proceedings for possession of land. See **Land** (Summary proceedings for possession—Abridgement of time for making order).
    Advertisement of petition—
        Compulsory winding up of company. See **Company** (Compulsory winding up—Advertisement of petition—Time).
    Affiliation order—
        Application for. See **Affiliation** (Application for order—Time for application).
    Appeal—
        Court of Appeal. See **Court of Appeal** (Time for appeal).
        Courts-Martial Appeal Court. See **Court-martial** (Appeal—Application for leave to appeal—Time limit).
        Employment Appeal Tribunal. See **Employment Appeal Tribunal** (Practice—Appeals—Appeals out of time).
        House of Lords—
            Presentation of petition out of time. See **House of Lords** (Petition—Presentation out of time).
        Kenya—
            Need for judgment to be drawn up in formal decree before appeal—Time limit. See **Kenya** (Appeal—Judgment to be drawn up in formal decree before appeal—Time limit).
    Arbitration—
        Agreement—
            Limitation clause. See **Arbitration** (Agreement—Limitation clause).
        Commencement. See **Arbitration** (Commencement).
        Conflict of laws. See **Conflict of laws** (Contract—Arbitration—Time-bar).
        Setting aside award. See **Arbitration** (Award—Setting aside award—Time limit for application).
        Time limit for reference—
            Breach of contract—Sale of goods. See **Sale of goods** (Breach of contract—Time limit for reference to arbitration).
            Extension of time. See **Arbitration** (Reference to arbitration—Extension of time).
    Bill of exchange—
        Notice of dishonour. See **Bill of exchange** (Notice of dishonour—Time).
    Bill of lading—
        Time for bringing claims. See **Shipping** (Bill of lading—Time for bringing claims).
    Bingo club licence—
        Application for. See **Gaming** (Licensing of premises—Application for licence—Time limit).
    Business premises—
        Application for new tenancy out of time. See **Landlord and tenant** (Business premises—Application for new tenancy—Application out of time).
        Notice to terminate tenancy. See **Landlord and tenant** (Business premises—Notice by landlord to terminate tenancy—Time).
    Capital gains tax—
        Time limit. See **Capital gains tax** (Time limit for assessment).
    Charterparty—
        Generally. See **Shipping** (Time charterparty).
        Time for bringing claims. See **Shipping** (Charterparty—Time for bringing claims).
    Cheque, payment by—
        Payment into court. See **Practice** (Payment into court—Cheque—Time at which payment into court made).
    Claim for resettlement compensation—
        Local government officer—
            Time for making claim. See **Local government** (Officer—Compensation for loss of employment—Resettlement compensation—Local government—Officer—Compensation for loss of employment—Resettlement compensation—Time for making claim for compensation).
    Commission of offence—
        Difference between standard local time and Greenwich mean time—
            Charge under Army Act 1955. See **Court-martial** (Civil offence—Time of commission of offence—Charge under statute commencing Jan 1, 1957—Difference between standard local time and Greenwich mean time).
    Compensation for compulsory acquisition—
        Time for assessment. See **Compulsory purchase** (Compensation—Assessment—Time for assessment).
    Compulsory purchase order—
        Time limit for application to quash order. See **Compulsory purchase** (Compulsory purchase order—Application to quash order—Time limit).
    Computation—
        Divorce—
            Separation—Period of separation. See **Divorce** (Separation—Period of separation).
        Duration of specified period—
            Four months—Business premises—Application for new tenancy. See **Landlord and tenant** (Business premises—Application for new tenancy—Time—Computation of time).
            Limitation period—Arbitrations. See **Arbitration** (Commencement—Period of limitation—Date from which time runs).
            Limitation period—Day on which cause of action arising or offence committed excluded. **Marren v Dawson Bentley & Co Ltd** [1961] **2** 270, Assizes.
            Month—Devise of house to wife if she should be living at the expiration of a period of three months from the testator's death—Calendar months—Period reckoned in complete days—Date of testator's death excluded—Law of Property Act 1925, s 61. **Figgis (decd), Re** [1968] **1** 999, Ch D.

TIME (cont)—
    Computation (cont)—
        Duration of specified period (cont)—
            Motor insurance cover note—Commencement 11.45 am on 2nd December 1959—Cover note expressed to be valid for 15 days from the commencement date of risk—Period of cover was 15 days from midnight on 2nd December 1959. **Cartwright v MacCormack** [1963] **1** 11, CA.
            Period 'beginning with the date of'—Writ of summons issued on 10th September 1965 and served on 10th September 1966—Validity of writ for the purpose of service for 12 months beginning with the date of its issue—Whether service out of time—RSC Ord 6, r 8(1). **Trow v Ind Coope (West Midlands) Ltd** [1967] **2** 900, CA.
            Seven clear days—Company—Compulsory winding up—Advertisement of petition. *See* **Company** (Compulsory winding up—Advertisement of petition—Time—Seven clear days before hearing).
            Six weeks—Compulsory purchase order. *See* **Compulsory purchase** (Compulsory purchase order—Application to quash order—Time limit—Application to be made within six-week period).
            Three weeks—Company—Compulsory winding-up—Inability of company to pay debts. *See* **Company** (Compulsory winding up—Inability of company to pay debts—Neglect to pay sum due to creditor for three weeks after sum demanded—Time—Computation of period of three weeks).
        Medical termination of pregnancy—
            Statute providing abortion legally performed where 'pregnancy has not exceeded its twenty-fourth week'—When week 'exceeded'—Abortion Act 1967, s 1(1)(a). **R (on the application of British Pregnancy Advisory Service) v Secretary of State for Health and Social Care** [2019] **4** 661, QBD; [2020] **4** 1082, CA.
        Period of 'not less than four weeks before the date on which'—
            Weekly tenancy determinable by notice. *See* **Landlord and tenant** (Validity of notice to quit—Periodic tenancy—Certainty of duration—Weekly tenancy).
        Period of 'not less than two months after' giving of notice—
            Application for new tenancy of business premises. *See* **Landlord and tenant** (Business premises—Application for new tenancy—Time—Computation of time).
        Period within which an act may be done—
            New tenancy of business premises for three years 'from' 1st May 1963—Rent payable in advance—First payment on 1st May 1963—Notice terminating tenancy on 30th April 1966—Validity of notice—Landlord and Tenant Act 1954, s 25(4). **Ladyman v Wirral Estates Ltd** [1968] **2** 197, Assizes.
            Not less than four weeks before the date on which—Exclusive of both first and last days—Rent Act 1957, s 16. **Thompson v Stimpson** [1960] **3** 500, QBD.
        Service of notice—
            Motoring offence—Notice of intended prosecution—Service within 14 days. *See* **Road traffic** (Notice of intended prosecution—Service of notice—Service within 14 days—Computation of time).
    Confiscation order—
        Application for confiscation order—
            Time limit. *See* **Sentence** (Confiscation order—Application for confiscation order—Time limit).
    Consumer credit—
        Enforcement—
            Extension of time. *See* **Consumer credit** (Enforcement—Extension of time).
    Contract—
        Duration of contract. *See* **Contract** (Time—Duration of contract).
        Sale of goods. *See* **Sale of goods** (Time of performance).
        Time of the essence. *See* **Contract** (Time—Time of the essence).
    Conveyance—
        Notice to complete. *See* **Sale of land** (Notice to complete—Notice making time of the essence).
    County court action—
        Commencement. *See* **County court** (Action—Commencement of action—Time).
    Crime—
        Time limit for commencement of trial. *See* **Criminal law** (Trial—Commencement of trial—Time limit).
        Time limit for prosecution—
            Court-martial—Civil offence—Indecent offences between males. *See* **Court-martial** (Civil offence—Time limit—Sexual offences between males).
            Indecent offences between males. *See* **Criminal law** (Time—Time limit for bringing prosecution—Indecent offences between males).
        Time of commission of offence—
            Difference between standard local time and Greenwich mean time—Charge under Army Act 1955. *See* **Court-martial** (Civil offence—Time of commission of offence—Charge under statute commencing Jan 1, 1957—Difference between standard local time and Greenwich mean time).
    Crown Office list—
        Estimate of time. *See* **Practice** (Crown Office list—Time estimates).
    Customs—
        Time limit for institution of proceedings for offences. *See* **Customs and excise** (Insurance—Institution of proceedings for offences—Time limit).
    Decree absolute—
        Time limit for appeal against decree absolute—
            Nullity. *See* **Nullity** (Appeal—Time).
    Delay—
        Dismissal of action for. *See* **Practice** (Dismissal of action for want of prosecution—Delay).
    Delivery—
        Sale of goods—
            Conditions inhibiting delivery imposed by vendor's supplier. *See* **Sale of goods** (Delivery—Conditions inhibiting delivery imposed by vendor's supplier).
    Directions for removal of Commonwealth immigrant—
        Immigrant refused admission to United Kingdom. *See* **Commonwealth immigrant** (Admission—Refusal of admission—Removal of immigrant—Directions for removal—Time for giving directions).

TIME (cont)—
  Divorce—
    Answer—
      Leave to file answer out of time. *See* **Divorce** (Practice—Answer—Time—Leave to file answer out of time).
    Rehearing—
      Application for. *See* **Divorce** (Rehearing—Application for).
  Duration of specified period. *See* Computation—Duration of specified period, *above*.
  Employment—
    Period of continuous employment. *See* **Employment** (Continuity—Period of continuous employment).
  Essence of the contract—
    Generally. *See* **Contract** (Time—Time of the essence).
    Notice to complete—
      Sale of land. *See* **Sale of land** (Notice to complete—Notice making time of the essence).
  Extension of time—
    Answer—
      Divorce. *See* **Divorce** (Practice—Answer—Time—Leave to file answer out of time).
    Appeal—
      Court of Appeal. *See* **Court of Appeal** (Time for appeal—Extension of time for appeal).
      Courts-Martial Appeal Court. *See* **Court-martial** (Appeal—Application for leave to appeal—Time limit—Extension of time).
      House of Lords—Application for leave to appeal from High Court. *See* **House of Lords** (Appeal from High Court—Application for leave to appeal—Time—Extension of time).
      Immigration. *See* **Immigration** (Appeal—Time limit for appealing—Notice not given within limitation period).
      Licensing appeal. *See* **Licensing** (Appeal—Notice of appeal—Service—Time for service—Extension of time).
      Matrimonial proceedings—Appeal from magistrates' courts to Divisional Court. *See* **Husband and wife** (Summary proceedings—Appeal to Divisional Court—Extension of time).
      Statutory power necessary to enable time to be extended beyond statutory limit. *See* **Licensing** (Appeal—Notice of appeal—Service—Time for service—Extension of time).
    Application to state a case. *See* **Case stated** (Limitation of time—Need to comply with statutory requirements—Application to state a case—Time limit for application—Extension of time limit).
    Arbitration—
      Commencement. *See* **Arbitration** (Commencement).
      Conflict of laws. *See* **Conflict of laws** (Contract—Arbitration—Time-bar—Extension of time).
      Reference to arbitration. *See* **Arbitration** (Reference to arbitration—Extension of time).
    Bankruptcy—
      Appeal against adjudication. *See* **Bankruptcy** (Appeal—Appeal against adjudication—Extension of time for appealing).
    Building contract. *See* **Building contract** (Extension of time).
    Case management. *See* **Practice** (Civil litigation—Case management—Extension of time).
    Case stated. *See* **Case stated** (Limitation of time—Application for extension of time).
    Certiorari—
      Application for. *See* **Certiorari** (Time for application—Extension of time).
    Company—
      Registration of charge. *See* **Company** (Charge—Registration—Extension of time).
    Compulsory purchase order—
      Submission under Housing Acts for confirmation. *See* **Housing** (Compulsory purchase—Confirmation of order by Minister—Time for submission—Extension of time).
    Conditional leave to defend after judgment entered—
      Condition not fulfilled within time specified—Application to extend time—RSC Ord 64, r 7. **Manley Estates Ltd v Benedek** [1941] **1** 248, CA.
    Consent order. *See* **Practice** (Consent order—Extension of time for complying with order).
    County court—
      Jurisdiction. *See* **County court** (Jurisdiction—Inherent jurisdiction—Jurisdiction to amend order—Extension of time).
      Service of default summons. *See* **County court** (Practice—Service of summons—Time for service of default summons—Extension of time).
    Dismissal of action for want of prosecution—
      Conditional order—Extension of time limit for taking steps prescribed by order. *See* **Practice** (Dismissal of action for want of prosecution—Conditional order—Extension of time limit for taking steps prescribed by order).
    Divorce—
      Application for rehearing. *See* **Divorce** (Rehearing—Time—Extension of time for applying for rehearing).
    Family provision application. *See* **Family provision** (Time for application—Extension).
    Immigration. *See* **Immigration** (Illegal entry and other offences—Time limit for prosecution).
    Legal aid certificate. *See* **Legal aid** (Certificate—Extension of time for issue of full certificate).
    Limitation of actions. *See* **Limitation of action** (Extension of time limit).
    Maintenance application—
      Surviving spouse, by. *See* **Divorce** (Financial provision—Deceased former spouse—Maintenance for surviving spouse out of deceased's estate—Application—Interim order—Extension of time for applying).
    Patent appeal. *See* **Patent** (Appeal to Court of Appeal—Application for leave to appeal—Time for application—Extension of time for service of notice of appeal).
    Registration of company charge. *See* **Company** (Charge—Registration—Extension of time).
    Renewal of writ—
      Admiralty action in rem. *See* **Admiralty** (Practice—Action in rem—Writ—Renewal—Extension of time).
    Retrospective extension of time—
      Building contract. *See* **Building contract** (Extension of time—Retrospective extension of time).

TIME (cont)—
    Extension of time (cont)—
        Specific performance—
            Delay in enforcing order for specific performance. *See* **Specific performance** (Order—Delay in enforcing order—Summons to proceed on order—Extension of time for proceeding where long period elapsing from date of order).
        Taxation of costs. *See* **Costs** (Taxation—Time limit).
        Variation of maintenance agreement—
            Application by surviving spouse. *See* **Husband and wife** (Variation of maintenance agreement—Death of party—Application by surviving party after the death of the other party to the agreement).
        Writ. *See* **Writ** (Extension of validity).
    Family provision—
        Application. *See* **Family provision** (Time for application).
    Fatal accident claim. *See* **Fatal accident** (Action—Time).
    Guarantee—
        Issue of guarantee—
            Contract silent as to time when guarantee to be issued. *See* **Guarantee** (Time for issue of guarantee—Contract silent as to time when guarantee to be issued).
        Payment under. *See* **Guarantee** (Payment under—Period of limitation).
    Income tax—
        Additional assessment—
            Time limit. *See* **Income tax** (Additional assessment—Time limit).
        Recovery of penalty—
            Time limit. *See* **Income tax** (Penalty—Recovery—Time limit).
        Special contribution. *See* **Special contribution** (Additional assessment—Limitation on time for making).
    Injunction—
        Exclusion of party from matrimonial home—
            Time limit on operation of injunction. *See* **Injunction** (Exclusion of party from matrimonial home—County court—Time limit on operation of injunction).
    Interlocutory appeal—
        Extension of time. *See* **Court of Appeal** (Interlocutory appeal—Time for appeal—Leave to extend time to appeal).
    Interpleader—
        Summons. *See* **Interpleader** (Application—Time).
    Judicial acts—
        Relation back to earliest moment of day on which done—
            Divorce proceedings—Notice of application to make decree nisi absolute received by registrar on same day as, but after, respondent spouse's death—Purported filing of notice on that day—Whether doctrine of relation back had application to give effect to decree absolute as from the earliest moment of the day on which notice was filed. **Seaford (decd), Re** [1968] **1** 482, CA.
    Landlord and tenant—
        Business premises—
            Application for new tenancy. *See* **Landlord and tenant** (Business premises—Application for new tenancy—Time).
            Notice by landlord to terminate tenancy. *See* **Landlord and tenant** (Business premises—Notice by landlord to terminate tenancy—Time).
        Rent review clause—
            Failure to comply with time limits. *See* **Landlord and tenant** (Rent—Review—Failure to comply with time limits).
    Lapse of time—
        Amounting to lapse of offer. *See* **Contract** (Offer and acceptance—Offer—Lapse of offer—Lapse by reason of time).
    Lease—
        Option to renew. *See* **Landlord and tenant** (Lease—Option to renew—Time for exercise of option).
    Licence—
        Hearing of application for. *See* **Licensing** (Justices—Hearing of application for licence—Time).
    Limitation—
        Arbitration—
            Agreement. *See* **Arbitration** (Agreement—Limitation clause).
            Commencement—Charterparty. *See* **Arbitration** (Commencement—Charterparty—Time-bar).
        Carriage by air—
            Damage to baggage or cargo—Complaint within prescribed period. *See* **Carriage by air** (Damage to baggage or cargo—Complaint to carrier within prescribed period after discovery of damage).
        Carriage of goods by road—
            Action arising from contract of carriage. *See* **Carriers** (Contract—Carriage of goods—Action arising out of carriage—Limitation period).
        Carriage of goods by sea—
            Damages for breach of contract. *See* **Shipping** (Carriage by sea—Damages for breach of contract—Time limit for bringing action).
        Case stated—
            Generally. *See* **Case stated** (Limitation of time).
            Income tax appeal. *See* **Income tax** (Case stated—Transmission of case to High Court—Time limit).
        Destruction of obscene publications. *See* **Criminal law** (Obscene publications—Destruction—Limitation of time).
        European Community—
            Action for annulment. *See* **European Union** (Procedure—Action for annulment—Time limit).
            Claim for breach of rules relating to public supply contracts. *See* **European Union** (Procedure—Claim for breach of rules relating to public supply contracts—Time limit).

TIME (cont)—
Renewal of lease—
  Option—
    Exercise of option. *See* **Landlord and tenant** (Lease—Option to renew—Time for exercise of option).
Rent—
  Review—
    Failure to comply with time limits. *See* **Landlord and tenant** (Rent—Review—Failure to comply with time limits).
  Time at which rent becomes due—
    Quarterly rent. *See* **Landlord and tenant** (Rent—Time at which rent becomes due—Quarterly rent).
Repair—
  Landlord and tenant—
    Time when obligation to repair arises. *See* **Landlord and tenant** (Repair—Landlord's covenant—Time when obligation to repair arises).
Rescission of winding up order—
  Application for. *See* **Company** (Compulsory winding up—Winding up order—Rescission—Application for rescission).
Rules of court—
  Period of time fixed by rules or by order etc for doing any act—
    Period to be reckoned in accordance with rule—Period of time for doing act—Meaning—Applicability to non-mandatory rules or orders—Rule or order prescribing a time within which person must do specified act if he wishes to do so—Whether period of time to be reckoned in accordance with rule—RSC Ord 3, r 2. **Tanglecroft Ltd v The Hemdale Group Ltd** [1975] 3 599, CA.
Sale of land—
  Condition—
    Performance of contract. *See* **Sale of land** (Condition—Time for performance).
  Time limit for requisitions on title. *See* **Sale of land** (Requisitions on title—Time limit).
Sentence—
  Variation of sentence or other order—
    Power of Crown Court—Time limit for exercise of power. *See* **Crown Court** (Sentence—Power to vary sentence or other order—Time limit for exercise of such power).
Service—
  Claim form—
    Extension of time for service. *See* **Claim form** (Service—Extension of time for service).
  Default summons. *See* **County court** (Practice—Service of summons—Time for service of default summons).
  Notice to quit. *See* **Landlord and tenant** (Validity of notice to quit—Time for service).
  Writ. *See* **Practice** (Service—Time for service of writ).
Summons—
  Queen's Bench Division—
    Practice—Masters' summonses. *See* **Practice** (Summons—Masters' summonses—Queen's Bench Division—Time summonses).
Sunday—
  Injunction. *See* **Injunction** (Sunday).
Taxation of costs—
  Review of taxation—
    Review after issue of certificate of taxation. *See* **Costs** (Taxation—Review of taxation—Certificate of taxation).
  Time limit. *See* **Costs** (Taxation—Time limit).
Time charterparty—
  Generally. *See* **Shipping** (Time charterparty).
Town and country planning—
  Enforcement notice. *See* **Town and country planning** (Enforcement notice—Time limit).
Trial—
  Commencement—
    Criminal trial. *See* **Criminal law** (Trial—Commencement of trial—Time limit).
Unfair industrial practice—
  Complaint—
    Time limit. *See* **Industrial relations** (Unfair industrial practice—Complaint—Time limit).
Variation of sentence or other order—
  Power of Crown Court—
    Time limit for exercise of power. *See* **Crown Court** (Sentence—Power to vary sentence or other order—Time limit for exercise of such power).
Variation of settlement—
  Application for variation—
    Application out of time. *See* **Variation of Settlement (Matrimonial Causes)** (Application for variation—Application out of time).
Working time—
  Organisation of. *See* **Health and safety at work** (Organisation of working time).
Writ—
  Issue—
    Limitation period—Extension of limitation period. *See* **Writ** (Issue—Time).
  Service. *See* **Practice** (Service—Time for service of writ).

TIME CHARTER
See **Shipping** (Time charterparty).

TIN MINING
Stannaries area of Cornwall—
  Offence committed by tinner—
    Jurisdiction of magistrates. *See* **Magistrates** (Jurisdiction—Summary offence—Offence committed by tinner in stannaries area of Cornwall).

TIP
Taxi-cab driver—
Income tax. *See* **Income tax** (Emoluments from office or employment—Voluntary payment—Payment arising in ordinary course of taxpayers employment—Taxi-cab driver—Tips).

TISSUE TYPING
Embryo—
Human reproduction. *See* **Medical treatment**.

TITHE AND TITHE RENTCHARGE
Annuity—
Apportionment—
Owner of land—Highway authority—Liability to bear apportioned part of redemption annuity in respect of land occupied by highway—Tithe Act 1936, ss 10(1), 17(1)—Law of Property Act 1925, s 7(1) (as amended by Law of Property (Amendment) Act 1926, s 7, Sch). **Tithe Redemption Commission v Runcorn UDC** [1954] **1** 653, CA.
Enforcement—
Recovery by action—Tithe Act 1918, s 4—Law of Property Act 1925, s 121. **Public Trustee v Scarr** [1939] **1** 188, KBD.
Redemption. *See* Redemption—Annuity, *below.*
Arrears—
Recovery—
Limitation of time for recovery—Excluded period—Limitation period expiring before the commencement of excluded period—Tithe Act 1936, ss 1, 4(1), 20. **Queen Anne's Bounty (Governors) v Tithe Redemption Commission** [1938] **4** 368, CA; **Queen Anne's Bounty v Tithe Redemption Commission** [1937] **3** 515, Ch D.
Order of county court for recovery before appointed day—Whether 'arrears' order for costs—Tithe Act 1891, s 2—Tithe Act 1936, s 20. **Queen Anne's Bounty v Tithe Redemption Commission** [1937] **3** 515, Ch D.
Extinguishment—
Compensation—
Deduction in respect of rates—No deduction to be made 'in the case of a rentcharge created in lieu of any corn rent which was free from rates, or a rentcharge which was otherwise free from rates'—'Was'—'Free from rates'—Only rentcharges free from legal liability to be rated at the time they were created to be free from deduction for rates—Tithe Act 1936, Sch I, Pt I, paras 3(a), 4. **Tithe Redemption Commission v Queen Anne's Bounty (Governors)** [1946] **1** 148, Ch D.
Officer—Substantial detriment to his livelihood—Expectation of continuance in office—City of London (Tithes) Act 1947, s 16(1). **Price v City of London Corp** [1949] **2** 642, CA.
Officer—Substantial detriment to his livelihood—Right to enquire into total income of office holder—City of London (Tithes) Act 1947, s 16(1). **Langham v City of London Corp** [1948] **2** 1018, CA.
Right of devisee under will of testator dying in 1902—Tithe rentcharge included in bequest of life interest—Tithe Act 1936, s 7(1), Sch I, Pt I, para 5. **Lory's Will Trusts, Re** [1950] **1** 349, Ch D.
Recovery of tithe rentcharge—
Application to county court—
No notice of opposition by landowner—Right of landowner to be heard—Tithe Act 1891, ss 2(1), (7), 3(1)—Tithe Rentcharge Recovery Rules 1891-1933, rr 5, 8. **Queen Anne's Bounty (Governors) v Pitt-Rivers** [1936] **2** 161, KBD.
Redemption—
Annuity—
Land held by several owners—No apportionment of annuity—Liability of owner of part of land for annuity in respect of whole—Tithe Act 1936, ss 3(1), 16(1). **Tithe Redemption Commission v Brown** [1948] **1** 752, CA.
Remission—Agricultural holding—'Annual value'—Inclusion of value of house—Income Tax Act 1918, Sch B, r 1(a)—Tithe Act 1936, s 14(2). **R v Jordan, ex p Lutring** [1947] **2** 875, KBD.
Tithe document—
Admissibility in evidence. *See* **Document** (Admissibility in evidence—Tithe document).
Tithe Redemption Commission—
Jurisdiction—
Annuity—Annuity substituted for tithe rentcharge—Whether commission have jurisdiction to decide whether land was subject to tithe rentcharge before the 'appointed day'—Tithe Act 1936, ss 3(1), 4(1), (2), 9, 39(3). **Tithe Redemption Commission v Wynne** [1943] **2** 370, CA.

TITHE REDEMPTION COMMISSION
Tithe and tithe rentcharge. *See* **Tithe and tithe rentcharge** (Tithe Redemption Commission).

TITLE
Boxing title—
Slander of title. *See* **Slander of title** (Professional description—Boxing title—Defendant represented as holding title held by plaintiff).
Covenants for title—
Sale of land. *See* **Sale of land** (Covenants for title).
Deeds—
Solicitor's lien. *See* **Solicitor** (Lien—Title deeds).
Denial of landlord's title—
Forfeiture of lease. *See* **Landlord and tenant** (Forfeiture of lease—Denial of landlord's title).
Documents of title—
Deposit—
Charge—Common law retaining lien. *See* **Lien** (Deposit of documents of title).
Film—
Registration. *See* **Cinema** (Film—Title—Registration).
Foreign immovables—
Conflict of laws. *See* **Conflict of laws** (Jurisdiction—Title to foreign immovables).

TITLE (cont)—
Hire-purchase agreement—
    Generally. *See* **Hire-purchase** (Title).
    Illegality of agreement—
        Sale of goods. *See* **Sale of goods** (Title—Illegality of related agreement).
Honour—
    Succession—
        Binding effect of declaration of legitimacy of claimant on Crown. *See* **Legitimation** (Declaration of
           legitimacy—Binding effect—Crown—Peerage claim).
        Paternity—Evidence—Presumption of legitimacy—DNA evidence—Rival claimants to Baronetcy—
           Whether DNA evidence admissible in determining entitlement to Baronetcy. **Baronetcy of Pringle
           of Stichill, Re** [2017] **1** 106, PC.
Land—
    Acknowledgment. *See* **Limitation of action** (Acknowledgment—Title to land).
    Adverse possession. *See* **Limitation of action** (Land—Adverse possession).
    Landlord. *See* **Landlord and tenant** (Title).
    Rectification of land register affecting title of proprietor in possession. *See* **Land registration**
        (Rectification of register—Rectification affecting title of proprietor in possession).
    Registration. *See* **Land registration**.
    Royal palace at Lagos. *See* **Nigeria** (Title to property—Royal palace at Lagos).
Landlord and tenant—
    Defective title of landlord—
        Tenancy by estoppel. *See* **Landlord and tenant** (Tenancy—Tenancy by estoppel).
    Right of tenant to question landlord's title. *See* **Landlord and tenant** (Title—Right of tenant to question
        landlord's title).
Legal proceedings—
    Appeal to House of Lords. *See* **House of Lords** (Leave to appeal—Petition for leave to appeal—Case
        title).
    Bankruptcy. *See* **Bankruptcy** (Practice—Title of proceedings).
    Generally. *See* **Practice** (Title of proceedings).
Long title—
    Statute—
        Construction of statute—Reference to title. *See* **Statute** (Construction—Long title).
Motor vehicle—
    Private purchaser without notice of hire purchase agreement. *See* **Hire-purchase** (Title—Motor
        vehicle—Private purchaser without notice of hire-purchase agreement under which owner reclaiming
        vehicle).
Movables—
    Conflict of laws—
        Generally. *See* **Conflict of laws** (Movables—Title to goods).
Obligation binding on successors in title—
    Right of pre-emption—
        Registration as land charge. *See* **Land charge** (Registration—Obligation affecting land—Obligation
           binding on successors in title).
Possessory title—
    Acquisition by statutory tenant—
        Acquisition against mesne landlord. *See* **Rent restriction** (Statutory tenant—Acquisition of
           possessory title against mesne landlord).
Property—
    Defect in title—
        Negligence of solicitor. *See* **Solicitor** (Negligence—Damages—Purchase of freehold property by
           client—Defect in title).
Sale of goods—
    Generally. *See* **Sale of goods** (Title).
    Transfer of title—Sale of goods. *See* **Sale of goods** (Transfer of title).
    Voidable title. *See* **Sale of goods** (Voidable title).
Sale of land—
    Damages for breach of contract—
        Vendor's inability to show good title. *See* **Sale of land** (Damages for breach of contract—Vendor's
           inability to show good title).
    Delay in completion through vendor's default in deducing title—
        Interest on unpaid purchase money. *See* **Sale of land** (Interest on unpaid purchase
           money—Possession before completion—Delay in completion through vendor's default in
           deducing title).
    Generally. *See* **Sale of land** (Title).
    Requisition on title. *See* **Sale of land** (Requisitions on title).
Slander. *See* **Slander of title**.
Specific performance. *See* **Specific performance** (Title).
Title deeds—
    Solicitor—
        Lien. *See* **Solicitor** (Lien—Title deeds).
Title of proceedings—
    Appeal to House of Lords. *See* **House of Lords** (Leave to appeal—Petition for leave to appeal—Case
        title).
    Bankruptcy. *See* **Bankruptcy** (Practice—Title of proceedings).
    Generally. *See* **Practice** (Title of proceedings).
Trustee in bankruptcy. *See* **Bankruptcy** (Trustee in bankruptcy—Title of trustee).
Writ—
    Defect—
        Amendment. *See* **Writ** (Amendment—Defect in title).

TOBACCO

European Directive concerning advertising and sponsorship of tobacco products—
Legal basis of directive. *See* **European Union** (Directives—Legal basis of directive).
Sale by unlicensed person—
Aiding and abetting of sale by purchaser—
Purchaser buying tobacco from unlicensed person—Purchaser subsequently finding tobacco intended only for use outside United Kingdom—Seller agreeing to take tobacco back—Purchaser failing to return tobacco—Tobacco Act 1842, s 13. **Sayce v Coupe** [1952] **2** 715, QBD.

TOBAGO

Trinidad and Tobago. *See* **Trinidad and Tobago**.

TOLLS

Ancient demesne—
Privileges of tenants in manor of ancient demesne—
Exemption from toll for use of quay—Limits of privileges—Manor of Bosham—Who was entitled to privileges—Whether tenant of manor entitled to use quay and foreshore free of charge either for private purposes or in the course of his business of repairing boats. **Iveagh (Earl) v Martin** [1960] **2** 668, QBD.
Franchise tolls—
Bridge—
Crown franchise and exemption—Kenya Protectorate. **Nyali Ltd v A-G** [1956] **2** 689, HL.
Market—
Rating. *See* **Rates** (Valuation—Market—Tolls).

TOMB

Funeral accoutrement associated with tomb—
Sale—
Faculty jurisdiction. *See* **Ecclesiastical law** (Faculty—Sale of chattel—Monument—Funeral accoutrement associated with tomb).

TOMBSTONE

Inscription on—
Charge for—
Burial board, by. *See* **Burial** (Burial ground—Charge for monumental inscription—Right of burial board to charge for permission to cut inscriptions on gravestone).

TOMLIN ORDER

See **Practice** (Compromise of action—Consent order—Order in Tomlin form).

TONNAGE

Limitation of liability by reference to. *See* **Shipping** (Limitation of liability—Limitation by reference to tonnage of ship).

TOOL

Powered hand-tool—
Use in building operations—
Duty to fence. *See* **Building** (Building operations—Fencing of machinery—Dangerous machinery—Powered hand-tool).

TORT

Abroad—
Damages—
Assessment. *See* **Conflict of laws** (Tort—Damages—Assessment).
Abuse of process—
Actionable abuse of process—
Elements of tort—Abuse of process distinguished from malicious prosecution. **Speed Seal Products Ltd v Paddington** [1986] **1** 91, CA.
Judicial review proceedings—Defendants bringing judicial review proceedings against grant by local planning authority of planning permission to claimants—Claimants seeking damages in tort for abuse of process arising out of judicial review proceedings—Whether claimants having arguable claim in tort of abuse of process. **Land Securities Ltd v Fladgate Fielder (a firm)** [2010] **2** 741, CA.
Ingredients of tort—
Adduction of false evidence or submission of false case to sustain claim or defeat other party's claim—Whether giving rise to tort of abuse of process of court. **Metall und Rohstoff AG v Donaldson Lufkin & Jenrette Inc** [1989] **3** 14, CA.
Abuse of public office. *See* **Public office** (Abuse of).
Action founded on—
County court jurisdiction. *See* **County court** (Jurisdiction—Action founded in contract or tort).
Limitation of action. *See* **Limitation of action** (When time begins to run—Actions in tort).
Representative proceedings—
Parties. *See* **Practice** (Parties—Representative proceedings—Action in tort).
Service out of the jurisdiction. *See* **Practice** (Service out of the jurisdiction—Action founded on tort committed within jurisdiction).
Action on the case—
Unlawful act—
Action for loss or harm suffered as inevitable consequence of an unlawful, intentional and positive act—Whether including loss or harm suffered as result of invalid act. **Dunlop v Woollahra Municipal Council** [1981] **1** 1202, PC.
Agent—
Liability of principal. *See* **Agent** (Liability of principal—Tort).
Animal. *See* **Animal**.

TORT (cont)—
Assault and battery—
  Contributory negligence—
    Damages—Altercation taking place between employee and manager—Employee bringing claim for damages claiming employer vicariously liable for manager's assault—Employer raising defence of employee's contributory negligence—Trial judge rejecting psychiatric report on causation of employee's psychological problems—Whether employer could assert contributory negligence on part of employee in order to reduce damages—Whether trial judge failing to give proper reasons for rejecting psychiatric report—Law Reform (Contributory Negligence) Act 1945. **Co-operative Group (CWS) Ltd v Pritchard** [2012] **1** 205, CA.
  Availability of defence—
    Criminal conviction of defendant—
      Judgment on admission of facts—Assault resulting in death—Defendant having pleaded guilty to manslaughter—Action by deceased's widow—Defendant admitting assault and conviction but alleging defences to action—Whether defendant's admissions debarring him from raising defences—Whether widow entitled to judgment on pleadings—RSC Ord 27, r 3. **Murphy v Culhane** [1976] **3** 533, CA.
Cause of action—
  Contempt of court—
    Exercise of contractual right—Service of notice to quit by landlord on tenant—Malicious service in circumstances amounting to contempt of court—Whether valid exercise of contractual right—Whether contempt founding cause of action in tort. **Chapman v Honig** [1963] **2** 513, CA.
  Contribution between joint tortfeasors—
    Claim for contribution—Whether statutory claim for contribution between joint tortfeasors is a cause of action in tort. **Harvey v R G O'Dell Ltd (Galway, third party)** [1958] **1** 657, QBD.
  Invasion of privacy—
    Emotional distress—Whether there was a general common law tort of invasion of privacy—Whether damages were recoverable for intentionally causing emotional distress which did not constitute psychiatric injury—Human Rights Act 1998, Sch 1, Pt I, art 8. **Wainwright v Home Office** [2003] **4** 969, HL.
    Whether claimant children of celebrity having reasonable expectation of privacy—Whether claimants' right to privacy outweighing defendant newspaper's freedom of expression—Whether injunction restraining publication of claimants' photographs properly imposed—Human Rights Act 1998, Sch 1, Pt I, arts 8, 10. **Weller v Associated Newspapers Ltd** [2016] **3** 357, CA.
  Wrongful interference with goods. *See* Wrongful interference with goods—Cause of action, *below*.
Causing loss by unlawful means—
  Relationship between third party and claimant—
    Claim alleging patent for drug obtained by deceit on European Patent Office and English courts, delaying introduction of generic drug and causing loss to national health services—Whether interference with liberty of third party to 'deal' with claimant required. **Secretary of State for Health v Servier Laboratories Ltd** [2020] **2** 514, CA; [2022] **1** 1, SC.
Company—
  Liability of director for tort committed by company. *See* **Company** (Director—Liability—Tort—Tort committed by company).
Concurrent tortfeasors—
  Discharge of cause of action by settlement of claim—
    Deceased agreeing before his death to accept sum in 'full and final settlement and satisfaction' of personal injury claim—Sum accepted less than full value of claim—Executors bringing dependency claim against concurrent tortfeasor under Fatal Accidents Act 1976—Whether payment made in full satisfaction of claim—Whether action against concurrent tortfeasor barred. **Jameson and anor (exors of Jameson (decd)) v Central Electricity Generating Board (Babcock Energy Ltd, third party)** [1997] **4** 38, CA; [1999] **1** 193, HL.
Conflict of laws. *See* **Conflict of laws** (Tort).
Conspiracy—
  Conspiracy to commit tort—
    Criminal liability. *See* **Criminal law** (Conspiracy—Unlawful act—Tort).
  Damages—
    Competition Appeal Tribunal. *See* **Competition** (Competition Appeal Tribunal—Monetary claims before tribunal—Claim for loss or damage suffered as result of infringement of relevant prohibition).
  Defence—
    Contributory negligence—Claim based on alleged bribery of plaintiff's employee by defendants—Whether defendants' liability falling to be extinguished or reduced if plaintiff had opportunity to investigate and failed to take it—Whether contributory negligence a defence to a claim based on bribery. **Corporacion Nacional del Cobre de Chile v Sogemin Metals Ltd** [1997] **2** 917, Ch D.
  Husband and wife—
    Whether conspiracy between husband and wife capable of giving rise to tortious liability—Whether immunity of husband and wife from indictment for crime of conspiracy conferring immunity from tortious liability—Whether public policy requiring immunity from tortious liability. **Midland Bank Trust Co Ltd v Green (No 3)** [1981] **3** 744, CA.
  Ingredients of tort—
    Damages—Actual pecuniary loss—Whether damages for injury to reputation or business reputation recoverable when defamation not alleged—Whether damages for injury to business reputation recoverable as a form of injury to property—Whether damages for injury to feelings recoverable when defamation not alleged. **Lonrho plc v Fayed (No 5)** [1994] **1** 188, CA.
    Purpose—Predominant purpose of conspirators to protect their own legitimate interest—Conspirators also intending to injure plaintiff's trade or business—Defendants making false statements to third party to enable their own take-over bid to proceed and to prevent plaintiff's take-over bid proceeding—No predominant purpose to injure plaintiff—Whether tort established either if predominant purpose of conspirators was to injure plaintiff or if means used were unlawful. **Lonrho plc v Fayed** [1991] **3** 303, HL.

TORT (cont)—
  Conspiracy (cont)—
    Ingredients of tort (cont)—
      Purpose—Predominant purpose—Predominant purpose of defendants' agreement not to injure plaintiff but to benefit defendants' own interests—Whether tort restricted to acts done in execution of agreement where predominant purpose is to injure plaintiff—Whether viable cause of action in conspiracy if defendants' agreement combines unlawful means with a purpose to injure which is not predominant. **Allied Arab Bank Ltd v Hajjar (No 2)** [1988] **3** 103, QBD.

      Purpose—Predominant purpose—Scope of tort—Predominant purpose of conspirators' agreement not to injure plaintiff but to benefit conspirators' own interests—Whether tort extending to acts done in execution of agreement where predominant purpose was not to injure plaintiff but to benefit conspirators' interests. **Metall und Rohstoff AG v Donaldson Lufkin & Jenrette Inc** [1989] **3** 14, CA.

      Purpose—Predominant purpose—Scope of tort—Whether unlawful means conspiracy confined to trade and industrial disputes—Whether predominant intention to injure claimant necessary for unlawful means conspiracy—Whether intention to injure claimant could be inferred from acts themselves—Whether conspiracy merged in torts where unlawful means tortious. **Kuwait Oil Tanker Co SAK v Al Bader (No 2)** [1997] **2** 855, CA; [2000] **2 Comm** 271, CA.

      Unlawful means conspiracy—Agreement with racecourse owners for claimant to collect and distribute horseracing data to off-course bookmakers—Defendant collecting raceday data through agreement with pool betting service and distributing to off-course bookmakers—Claim for conspiracy to injure by unlawful means—Whether knowledge of unlawfulness of means employed required. **Racing Partnership Ltd v Sports Information Services Ltd** [2021] **2 Comm** 1184, CA; [2021] **3** 739, CA.

      Unlawful means conspiracy—Alleged unlawful means being serial contempts of court—Whether contempt of court constituting unlawful means. **JSC BTA Bank v Ablyazov** [2017] **2 Comm** 1, CA; [2017] **2** 918, CA; **JSC BTA Bank v Khrapunov** [2018] **2 Comm** 479, SC; [2018] **3** 293, SC.

      Unlawful means conspiracy—Alleged unlawful means being serial contempts of court—Whether contempt of court constituting unlawful means—Whether contempt actionable in damages. **JSC BTA Bank v Ablyazov** [2016] **2 Comm** 218, QBD.

      Unlawful means conspiracy—Claimant bringing action for damages for unlawful means conspiracy based on breach of statutory duty—Breach of statutory duty not sounding in damages—Whether wrongful act grounding action for unlawful means conspiracy if act not itself actionable. **Michaels v Taylor Woodrow Developments Ltd** [2000] **4** 645, Ch D.

      Whether tort requiring unlawful act relied on to be actionable at suit of plaintiff—Whether injury to plaintiff having to be predominant purpose of conspirators. **Yu Kong Line Ltd of Korea v Rendsburg Investments Corp of Liberia (No 2)** [1998] **4** 82, QBD.

    Master and servant. See **Employment** (Conspiracy).
  Contribution between joint tortfeasors—
    Action against two defendants—
      Action against second defendant not commenced within statutory period—First defendant's right to contribution from second defendant—Law Reform (Married Women and Tortfeasors) Act 1935, s 6(1)(c). **Morgan v Ashmore, Benson, Pease & Co Ltd** [1953] **1** 328, Assizes; **Wimpey (George) & Co Ltd v British Overseas Airways Corp** [1954] **3** 661, HL.

      Action against second defendants dismissed for want of prosecution—First defendants entitled to contribution from second defendants—Law Reform (Married Women and Tortfeasors) Act 1935, s 6(1)(c). **Hart v Hall & Pickles Ltd** [1968] **3** 291, CA.

      One defendant found not liable—Engineers sued by sewerage authority for breach of contract and negligence—Engineers claiming contribution and/or indemnity from sub-contractors engaged by main contractors—Sub-contractors found to be not liable to sewerage authority—Whether sub-contractors liable to indemnify engineers—Whether sub-contractors 'other tortfeasor who ... would if sued have been liable'—Law Reform (Married Women and Tortfeasors) Act 1935, s 6(1)(c). **Southern Water Authority v Carey** [1985] **2** 1077, QBD.

      One defendant found not negligent—Not a tortfeasor—No basis for claim for contribution by other defendant—Law Reform (Married Women and Tortfeasors) Act 1935, s 6(1)(c). **Johnson v Cartledge and Matthews (Matthews, third party)** [1939] **3** 654, Assizes.
    Apportionment —
      First defendant liable in deceit—Second defendant liable for breach of duty—Effect of contributory negligence and contractual limitation on apportionment—Civil Liability (Contribution) Act 1978. **Nationwide Building Society v Dunlop Haywards (DHL) Ltd** [2009] **2 Comm** 715, QBD.
    Assessment—
      Absence of party—Assessment in absence of party possibly liable for contributory negligence—Law Reform (Married Women and Tortfeasors) Act 1935, s 6(2). **Maxfield v Llewellyn** [1961] **3** 95, CA.
    Claim by defendant against third party—
      Assessment of contribution by third party—Law Reform (Married Women and Tortfeasors) Act 1935, s 6. **Burnham v Boyer and Brown** [1936] **2** 1165, KBD.

      Damage not occurring until after repeal of statute giving right to contribution and substitution of new rights—Person not entitled to recover contribution under later statute in respect of an obligation 'assumed by him' in respect of damage occurring before commencement of Act—Whether defendant's obligation to plaintiff based on 'obligation assumed by' defendant before coming into force of later statute—Whether defendant having right to contribution—Law Reform (Married Women and Tortfeasors) Act 1935, s 6—Interpretation Act 1978, s 16(1)(c), (e)—Civil Liability (Contribution) Act 1978, s 7(2). **Lampitt v Poole BC (Taylor and anor, third parties)** [1990] **2** 887, CA.

      Whether statutory regime having extra-territorial effect—Civil Liability (Contribution) Act 1978, ss 1, 2(3), 6(1), 7(3). **Roberts v Soldiers, Sailors, Airmen and Families Association - Forces Help** [2021] **2** 449, CA; [2021] **2 Comm** 497, CA.

TORT (cont)—
 Contribution between joint tortfeasors (cont)—
  Husband administrator of wife's estate—
   Claim by third person against husband for contribution in respect of liability arising out of wife's death—Loss of expectation of life—Right of wife to sue husband in tort—Married Women's Property Act 1882, s 12—Law Reform (Miscellaneous Provisions) Act 1934, s 1—Law Reform (Married Women and Tortfeasors) Act 1935, s 6—RSC Ord 25, rr 2-4. **Chant v Read** [1939] **2** 286, KBD.
  Jurisdiction to apportion blame without special application—
   Acquiescence in apportionment—Law Reform (Married Women and Tortfeasors) Act 1935, s 6(2). **Bell v Holmes** [1956] **3** 449, Assizes.
   Plaintiff's claims against both defendants settled in full by second defendant before trial—One plaintiff's name left on record—No evidence offered by plaintiff at trial—Jurisdiction of court to try issue between defendants as to contribution. **Calvert v Pick** [1954] **1** 566, QBD.
   Proceedings—Jurisdiction of Court of Appeal to vary proportions fixed by judge—Law Reform (Married Women and Tortfeasors) Act 1935, s 6(1)(c), (2). **Croston v Vaughan** [1937] **4** 249, CA.
  Master and servant joint tortfeasors—
   Common law exemption—Servant not immune from contribution to master—Law Reform (Married Women and Tortfeasors) Act 1935, s 6(2). **Lister v Romford Ice and Cold Storage Co Ltd** [1957] **1** 125, HL.
   Negligence of servant resulting in servant's death and injury to another person—Action by injured person against master commenced nearly two years after grant of adminstration of deceased servant's estate—Third-party notice served by master on administratrix—Law Reform (Miscellaneous Provisions) Act 1934, s 1(1), (3), (4)—Law Reform (Married Women and Tortfeasors) Act 1935, s 6(1)(c). **Harvey v R G O'Dell Ltd (Galway, third party)** [1958] **1** 657, QBD.
  Master's right to contribution by servant—
   Complete indemnity—Negligence of servant—No negligence on part of master or other servants—Law Reform (Married Women and Tortfeasors) Act 1935, ss 6(1)(c), (2). **Semtex Ltd v Gladstone** [1954] **2** 206, Assizes.
   Master himself responsible for damage—Liability of hospital board for negligence of doctor—Law Reform (Married Women and Tortfeasors) Act 1935, s 6(2). **Jones v Manchester Corp** [1952] **2** 125, CA.
  Negligence—
   Generally. *See* **Negligence** (Joint tortfeasors—Contribution).
  No appeal against one tortfeasor—
   Duty of Court of Appeal—Law Reform (Married Women and Tortfeasors) Act 1935, s 6. **Hanson v Wearmouth Coal Co Ltd and Sunderland Gas Co** [1939] **3** 47, CA.
  No representative of dead joint tortfeasor's estate—
   Power of court to appoint representative. **Lean v Alston** [1947] **1** 261, CA.
  Occupiers of public dry dock—
   Breaches of statutory duty—Law Reform (Married Women and Tortfeasors) Act 1935, s 6(2). **Rippon v Port of London Authority and J Russell & Co (Port of London Authority, third party)** [1940] **1** 637, KBD.
  Practice—
   Generally. *See* **Practice** (Joint tortfeasors—Contribution).
  Settlement of action by one tortfeasor—
   No admission of liability for damage by tortfeasor in settling action—Whether tortfeasor 'liable in respect of that damage'—Whether debarred from recovering contribution from second tortfeasor—Law Reform (Married Women and Tortfeasors) Act 1935, s 6(1)(c). **Stott v West Yorkshire Road Car Co Ltd** [1971] **3** 534, CA.
  Survival of claim for contribution on death of one joint tortfeasor—
   Joint tortfeasor's liability to plaintiff in main action not established or admitted at date of death—Joint tortfeasor not having subsisting cause of action for contribution at date of death—Whether joint tortfeasor's claim for contribution a defined inchoate right at date of death—Whether claim for contribution dying with claimant's death—Whether rule that a cause of action in tort dies with the person in whom cause vested applying to joint tortfeasor's claim—Whether claim for contribution preserved for benefit of claimant's estate under statute—Law Reform (Miscellaneous Provisions) Act 1934, s 1(1)—Law Reform (Married Women and Tortfeasors) Act 1935, s 6(1). **Ronex Properties Ltd v John Laing Construction Ltd (Clarke, Nicholls & Marcel (a firm), third parties)** [1982] **3** 961, CA.
 Conversion—
  Cheque—
   Bank. *See* **Bank** (Cheque—Conversion).
   Generally. *See* **Conversion**.
  Wrongful interference with goods. *See* Wrongful interference with goods—Conversion, *below*.
 County court jurisdiction—
  Action founded in contract or tort. *See* **County court** (Jurisdiction—Action founded in contract or tort).
 Crown—
  Exemption from liability. *See* **Crown** (Exemption from liability in tort).
 Damages—
  Contract and tort. *See* **Damages** (Contract and tort).
  County court—
   Transfer of action to High Court. *See* **County court** (Transfer of action—Transfer to High Court—Action founded on contract or tort).
  Exemplary damages. *See* **Damages** (Exemplary damages).
  Foreign currency—
   Jurisdiction to order payment of sum expressed in foreign currency. *See* **Judgment** (Foreign currency—Jurisdiction to order payment of sum expressed in foreign currency—Damages for tort).
  Generally. *See* **Damages**.
  Recoverability independent of claim against third party. *See* **Damages** (Contract and tort—Recoverability independent of claim against third party).

TORT (cont)—
Dangerous animal—
Liability for damage caused by animal. *See* **Animal** (Dangerous animal—Exceptions from liability).
Deceit—
Company director—
Liability. *See* **Company** (Director—Liability—Tort—Deceit).
Defence—
Contributory negligence. *See* **Negligence** (Contributory negligence—Apportionment of liability—Deceit).
Defamation. *See* **Libel and slander**.
Detinue. *See* **Detinue**.
Economic torts—
Causing loss by unlawful means. *See* Causing loss by unlawful means, *above*.
Exemplary damages. *See* **Damages** (Exemplary damages).
Exemption from liability in tort—
Crown. *See* **Crown** (Exemption from liability in tort).
False imprisonment. *See* **False imprisonment**.
Fatal accident. *See* **Fatal accident**.
Fraud—
Defence of illegality—
Claim in tort arising out of contract tainted with illegality—Defendant selling flat to plaintiffs fraudulently misrepresenting that it included a roof terrace—Value of flat and chattels falsely apportioned in contract to enable plaintiffs to avoid stamp duty—Plaintiffs claiming damages against defendant for fraudulent misrepresentation—Whether court should have regard to parties' conduct and relative moral culpability in determining whether illegality relevant—Whether plaintiffs' claim defeated by illegality in contract. **Saunders v Edwards** [1987] 2 651, CA.
Unwitting contravention of statute by plaintiff—Exchange control legislation—Payment made by plaintiff to defendant in consequence of defendant's fraud—Contract for sale to plaintiff of house outside scheduled territories—Defendant having no title or authority to sell house—Plaintiff's payment made without necessary Treasury permission—Plaintiff ignorant of exchange control legislation and unaware that payment illegal—Action by plaintiff for damages for fraud—Whether defendant entitled to raise defence of illegality. **Shelley v Paddock** [1980] 1 1009, CA.
Friendly society, by—
Action against trustees—
Competence. *See* **Friendly society** (Action against trustees—Tort).
Harassment—
Cause of action—
Trustee in bankruptcy. *See* **Insolvency** (Bankrupt's estate—Vesting in trustee—Cause of action—Harassment).
Civil remedy—
Cause of action—Non-targeted victim—First respondent pursuing course of conduct against husband amounting to harassment—Husband and wife bringing claim for damages—Judge dismissing wife's claim on basis conduct not targeted at wife—Whether judge in error—Meaning of 'victim of the course of conduct'—Protection from Harassment Act 1997, ss 1, 3, 7. **Levi v Bates** [2016] 1 625, CA.
Defence—
Course of conduct pursued for the purpose of preventing or detecting crime—Defendant carrying out campaign of correspondence with authorities making allegations against claimant of fraud, embezzlement and tax evasion—Authorities finding allegations groundless after investigation—Defendant continuing campaign and intruding into claimant's privacy—Whether purpose of course of conduct should be assessed by subjective test—Protection from Harassment Act 1997, s 1. **Hayes v Willoughby** [2013] 2 405, SC.
Injunction—
Defendant harassing plaintiff by unwanted telephone calls—Interference with ordinary use and enjoyment of premises—Order restraining defendant from using violence to, harassing, pestering or communicating with plaintiff in any way—Whether court having jurisdiction in private nuisance to restrain harassment by unwanted telephone calls—Whether jurisdiction can be exercised if no relationship between parties and recipient having no proprietary interest in premises where calls received—Whether injunction should be expressed in words which person restrained could readily understand. **Khorasandjian v Bush** [1993] 3 669, CA.
Prohibition of harassment—
Damages—Damages for anxiety and financial loss caused by harassment—Whether loss required to be reasonably foreseeable—Protection from Harassment Act 1997, s 3. **Jones v Ruth** [2012] 1 490, CA.
Offence of harassment—Civil remedy—Course of conduct amounting to harassment—Gravity of course of conduct—Protection from Harassment Act 1997, ss 1, 2, 3. **Ferguson v British Gas Trading Ltd** [2009] 3 304, CA.
Offence of harassment—Civil remedy—Course of conduct amounting to harassment—Right to respect for private and family life—Freedom of expression—Repeated publication of offensive or insulting words about a person's appearance or sexuality—Whether course of conduct amounting to harassment—Protection from Harassment Act 1997, s 1—Human Rights Act 1998, Sch 1, Pt I, arts 8, 10. **Trimingham v Associated Newspapers Ltd** [2012] 4 717, QBD.
Whether intentional infliction of harassment tort at common law. **Wong v Parkside Health NHS Trust** [2003] 3 932, CA.
High Court action—
Costs. *See* **Costs** (Tort—High Court action).
Husband's liability for wife's tort. *See* **Husband and wife** (Tort—Husband's liability for wife's tort).
Inducement to commit breach of contract—
Bona fide acts—
Defendant's actual or constructive knowledge of breach—Former servant of plaintiffs revealing secret process to defendants in breach of leaving agreement with plaintiffs—Belief of defendants that if process patentable it could not be secret. **British Industrial Plastics Ltd v Ferguson** [1940] 1 479, HL.

Inducement to commit breach of contract (cont)—

Conflict of laws. *See* **Conflict of laws** (Jurisdiction—Challenge to jurisdiction—Civil and commercial matters—Procuring or inducing a breach of contract).

Direct inducement—

Cricket authorities changing rules to ban players who had contracted to play for private promoter—Ban not to apply to players who withdrew from contracts by a stated date—Whether direct interference with contracts between players and private promoter—Whether ban intended to apply pressure on players—Whether cricket authorities justified in imposing ban. **Greig v Insole** [1978] **3** 449, Ch D.

Indirect inducement—

Interference with performance of contract—Shipbuilding contracts—Parent company contracting with service company to keep subsidiary in funds—Subsidiary contracting for construction of ships—Parent company failing to keep subsidiary in funds—Subsidiary defaulting on contractual payments to claimant shipyard—Whether parent company's conduct directed against shipyard—Test of intentional conduct required by tort of indirect inducement by unlawful means. **Stocznia Gdanska SA v Latvian Shipping Co (No 3)** [2002] **2 Comm** 768, CA.

Interference with performance of contract—Whether interference with performance of contract giving rise to cause of action at common law—Preconditions for cause of action. **Merkur Island Shipping Corp v Laughton** [1983] **2** 189, HL.

Recommendation of federation of newsagents, a trade association of retailers, to members to stop sale of newspaper—Federation seeking to induce breach of contract between wholesalers and newspaper proprietors—Ignorance of terms of contracts between proprietors and wholesalers no defence where act done without caring whether breach of contract caused—Balance of convenience—Interlocutory injunction granted. **Daily Mirror Newspapers Ltd v Gardner** [1968] **2** 163, CA.

Inference of intention—

Trade union—Officers of trade union knew of existence of labour only sub-contract but not its precise terms—Industrial action by union to get sub-contract terminated by main contractors—Irreparable damage to sub-contractor—Interlocutory injunction granted. **Emerald Construction Co Ltd v Lowthian** [1966] **1** 1013, CA.

Interference with contractual relations. *See* Interference with contractual relations, *below.*

Justification—

Tenants' association—Association inducing tenants to withhold rent—Alleged failure of common landlord to fulfil obligations under tenancy agreements—Remedy available at law—No justification for withholding rent. **Camden Nominees Ltd v Slack** [1940] **2** 1, Ch D.

Restrictive covenant—

Purchase of land for use in breach of restrictive covenant not building on land—Vendor had covenanted, as purchaser knew, not to cause or permit land to be used otherwise than for horse-racing etc—Vendor approached purchaser with a view to sale of land to purchaser for development for housing—Covenant would not be enforceable against purchaser after completion of sale—Whether purchaser had committed tort of inducing vendor to commit breach of covenant—Whether injunction would be granted. **Tophams Ltd v Earl of Sefton** [1966] **1** 1039, HL.

Unlawful means—

Absence of justification—Trade union instructing members not to handle appellants' barges—Breach pro tanto of members' contracts of employment when allocated under dock workers employment scheme—Customers of appellants caused thereby to break their contracts of hiring with appellants—No member of union employed by appellants—No trade dispute—Whether interlocutory injunction should be granted—Dock Workers (Regulation of Employment) Scheme 1947 (S R & O 1947 No 1189), Sch, para 8(4)(b)—Trade Disputes Act 1906, ss 3, 5(3). **Stratford (J T) & Son Ltd v Lindley** [1964] **3** 102, HL.

Intentional infliction of harm—

Claimant having brought private prosecution for assault—

Whether claimant entitled to rely on assault to found claim for intentional infliction of harm—Offences Against the Person Act 1861, s 45. **Wong v Parkside Health NHS Trust** [2003] **3** 932, CA.

Invasion of privacy—

Visitors to prison who were strip searched suffering distress and humiliation—Whether intentional infliction of harm—Whether invasion of privacy—Whether human rights legislation applicable despite events taking place before implementation of legislation—Human Rights Act 1998, s 3(1). **Wainwright v Home Office** [2003] **3** 943, CA.

Restrictions on publication—

Freedom of speech—Injunction—Father proposing to publish biography including details of sexual abuse suffered as a child and its psychological effects—Child seeking to restrain publication on grounds publication likely to cause him psychological harm—Elements of tort—Whether cause of action established. **OPO v Rhodes** [2015] **4** 1, SC.

Interference with contractual relations—

Inducement to commit breach of contract—

Employees diverting purchase of development land to own joint venture in breach of contractual duties to company—Defendant facilitating employees' business venture by providing finance—Whether tortious interference with contractual relations. **OBG Ltd v Allan** [2007] **4** 545, HL; [2008] **1 Comm** 1, HL.

Employer receiving legal advice that restrictive covenants in prospective employee's contract with previous employer more likely than not unenforceable—Covenants subsequently deemed enforceable and employee in breach of covenants—Whether tortious interference with contractual relations—State of mind required for inducing breach of contract. **Allen (t/a David Allen Chartered Accountants) v Dodd & Co Ltd** [2020] **4** 162, CA; [2021] **1 Comm** 229, CA.

TORT (cont)—
  Interference with contractual relations (cont)—
    Inducement to commit breach of contract (cont)—
      Japanese shipping line entering into joint venture in relation to its container liner service—Claimant carrying on container road haulage business under service agreement with indirect subsidiary of shipping line—Effect of joint venture that subsidiary having no haulage work to offer claimant—Whether real prospect of success in establishing claim against shipping line for inducement to commit breach of contract. **Kawasaki Kisen Kaisha Ltd v James Kemball Ltd** [2021] **2 Comm** 1102, CA; [2021] **3** 978, CA.
    Inducing or procuring a breach of contract—
      Administrators of company selling steel-making equipment to first defendant pursuant to hive-down arrangement in breach of company's contract with claimant—First defendant being company formed and controlled by administrators—First defendant then sold to second defendant—Whether breach of contract merely foreseeable consequence of hive-down arrangement—Whether first defendant's participation in hive-down arrangement sufficient to constitute inducement or procurement of breach of contract—Whether administrators able to be personally liable for inducement or procurement of breach of contract—Whether administrators able to be personally liable for conspiracy to injure by unlawful means—Whether first defendant lacking intention to cause loss by unlawful means—Whether first defendant able to rely on defence of justification based on administration's statutory purpose. **Lictor Anstalt v MIR Steel UK Ltd** [2012] **1 Comm** 592, Ch D.
      Contract with a minor—Footballer entering representation contract with claimant—Footballer being minor at time of contract—Footballer giving notice of termination of contract—Claimant alleging defendants inducing breach of contract—Defendants seeking summary judgment on ground that contract voidable—Whether liability for inducing or facilitating the breach of a voidable contract existing. **Proform Sports Management Ltd v Proactive Sports Management Ltd** [2007] **1 Comm** 356, Ch D; [2007] **1** 542, Ch D.
      Liechtenstein anstalt agreeing to provide equipment to fourth defendant—Agreement providing anstalt retaining ownership of equipment—Fourth defendant entering administration—First to third defendants appointed as administrators—Cypriot company agreeing to acquire assets of fourth defendant through appellant special purpose vehicle—Appellant, administrators and fourth defendant entering hive-down agreement—All parties aware of Liechtenstein anstalt's claim to ownership of equipment—Agreement stating appellant responsible for settling any claim by anstalt in respect of equipment—Hive-down agreement completed—Anstalt issuing proceedings against appellant alleging torts of conspiracy and inducement to breach contract—Appellant seeking to add administrators and fourth defendant as defendants—Judge dismissing application on ground of no real prospect of success—Whether hive-down agreement excluding anstalt's claims of conspiracy and inducement to breach contract against administrators and fourth defendant—Whether judge entitled to dismiss appellant's applications to add administrators and insolvent fourth defendant as defendants. **Lictor Anstalt v MIR Steel UK Ltd** [2013] **2 Comm** 54, CA.
  Interference with business—
    Conspiracy to injure by unlawful means—State of mind—Knowledge—Whether defendants having intention to injure. **Meretz Investments NV v ACP Ltd** [2006] **3** 1029, Ch D.
  Invalid appointment of receivers—
    Receivers acting as validly appointed receivers in relation to existing contracts—Whether tortious interference with contractual relations. **OBG Ltd v Allan** [2005] **2** 602, CA; **OBG Ltd v Allan** [2007] **4** 545, HL; [2008] **1 Comm** 1, HL.
  Justification—
    Equal or superior right—Mortgagee entering into arrangement with mortgagor for development of property—Mortgagee requiring mortgagor to terminate contract with architect as condition of development—Whether mortgagee justified in interfering with contract between mortgagor and architect. **Hill (Edwin) & Partners (a firm) v First National Finance Corp plc** [1988] **3** 801, CA.
  Knowledge—
    Pub tie—Brewery landlord providing lists of tied houses to beer seller—Beer seller supplying beer and other beverages to tied house—Landlord seeking injunctive relief—Whether beer seller having knowledge of contractual relations. **Unique Pub Properties Ltd v Beer Barrels & Minerals (Wales) Ltd** [2005] **1 Comm** 181, CA.
  Picketing—
    Trade dispute. *See* **Trade dispute** (Picketing—Interference with contract).
  Procurement of violation of a right. *See* Procurement of violation of right—Interference with contract, *below*.
  Unlawful means—
    Recommendation by trade association to members to stop orders of newspaper—Recommendation deemed a restriction presumed contrary to public policy—Restrictive Trade Practices Act 1956, ss 6(7), 21(1). **Daily Mirror Newspapers Ltd v Gardner** [1968] **2** 163, CA.
  Interference with parental rights—
    Right of action in tort. *See* **Parent** (Rights in respect of child—Unlawful interference with parental rights—Tort).
  Interference with trade—
    Unlawful means—
      Restrictive trade practice—Resolution of trade association to restrict transport of goods to nominated transport contractor—Particulars of resolution furnished to Registrar of Restrictive Trading Agreements—Notice to restrain implementation of resolution—Whether resolution illegal as being contrary to public policy—Whether court entitled to make order in advance of declaration by Restrictive Practices Court that resolution void—Restrictive Trade Practices Act 1956, s 21(1) (as amended by Restrictive Trade Practices Act 1968, s 10(1)). **Brekkes Ltd v Cattel** [1971] **1** 1031, Ch D.
  Interference with trade or business—
    Take-over bid—
      False statements made to third party to prevent rival's take-over bid succeeding—No predominant purpose to injure rival—No complete tort vis-à-vis third party—Whether false statements giving rise to cause of action. **Lonrho plc v Fayed** [1989] **2** 65, CA.

TORT (cont)—
  Intimidation—
    Picketing—
      Trade dispute. *See* **Trade dispute** (Picketing—Intimidation).
    Unlawful act—
      Threat to break contract—Threat an unlawful act for purpose of establishing tort—Threat against person other than plaintiff—Threat made in order to cause damage to plaintiff—Trade unionists threatening strike action against employers unless plaintiff dismissed—Whether threat to break contract sufficient to constitute unlawful element in tort of intimidation. **Rookes v Barnard** [1964] **1** 367, HL; **Stratford (J T) & Son Ltd v Lindley** [1964] **3** 102, HL.
  Joint tortfeasors—
    Apportionment of liability—
      Variation of apportionment by Court of Appeal. **Ceramic SS (owners) v Testbank SS (owners)** [1942] **1** 281, CA.
      Variation of apportionment on appeal—Limitation of jurisdiction. **British Fame (owners) v Macgregor (owners)** [1943] **1** 33, HL.
      Variation of apportionment on appeal—Limitation of jurisdiction—Same rule applicable to road collisions as to sea collisions. **Ingram v United Automobile Services Ltd** [1943] **2** 71, CA.
    Common design—
      Actions in furtherance of common design—Foreign conservation charity taking direct action against claimant's fishing vessels—Claimant bringing proceedings for trespass and conversion against United Kingdom charity associated with foreign conservation charity—Whether common design between defendants to carry out direct action involving violent intervention against property—Whether requirement that actions in furtherance of common design having to be essential part of commission of tort. **Fish & Fish Ltd v Sea Shepherd UK** [2013] **3** 867, CA.
      Actions in furtherance of common design—Foreign conservation charity taking direct action against claimant's fishing vessels—Claimant bringing proceedings for trespass and conversion against United Kingdom charity associated with foreign conservation charity—Whether United Kingdom charity liable as joint tortfeasor for damage suffered by claimant. **Fish & Fish Ltd v Sea Shepherd UK** [2015] **2 Comm** 867, SC; [2015] **4** 247, SC.
    Contribution. *See* Contribution between joint tortfeasors, *above.*
    Costs. *See* **Costs** (Joint tortfeasors).
    Discharge—
      Agreement not to sue one joint tortfeasor—Operation as discharge of other tortfeasors. **Apley Estates Co v de Bernales** [1947] **1** 213, CA.
    Interrogatories—
      Administration of interrogatories by one tortfeasor to another—Necessity of notice. **Clayson v Rolls Royce Ltd** [1950] **2** 884, CA.
    Judgment against one tortfeasor no bar to action against another person who would if sued have been held liable—
      If sued—Action against two defendants—Judgment entered against first defendant—Issue of second defendant's liability remitted for new trial—Judgment against first defendant unsatisfied—Whether second defendant immune from judgment as person who has been sued—Civil Law Act (Singapore), s 11(1)(a). **Wah Tat Bank Ltd v Chan Cheng Kum** [1975] **2** 257, PC.
      Satisfaction of judgment a bar to proceedings—Evidence of satisfaction—Single action against joint tortfeasors—One tortfeasor submitting to judgment for agreed sum of damages—Plaintiff refusing to disclose whether judgment satisfied—Smaller sum of damages awarded against second tortfeasor—Whether plaintiff barred from executing judgment against second tortfeasor—Law Reform (Married Women and Tortfeasors) Act 1935, s 6(1). **Bryanston Finance Ltd v De Vries** [1975] **2** 609, CA.
    Jurisdiction of master—
      Payment of proportion of liability—Jurisdiction of master to allow one defendant to offer to pay a proportion of any liability—Law Reform (Miscellaneous Provisions) Act 1935, s 6—RSC Ord 30, r 2. **Sigley v Hale** [1938] **3** 87, CA.
    Liability of one for act of other—
      Each joint tortfeasor also separate tortfeasor—No liability for act of another save under doctrine of respondeat superior—Malice of master not imputed to servant. **Egger v Viscount of Chelmsford** [1964] **3** 406, CA.
    Offer. *See* **Practice** (Joint tortfeasors—Offer).
    Practice—
      Generally. *See* **Practice** (Joint tortfeasors).
    Release or covenant not to sue—
      Cause of action for libel. *See* **Libel and slander** (Joint tortfeasors—Release or covenant not to sue).
  Jurisdiction. *See* **Conflict of laws** (Jurisdiction—Challenge to jurisdiction—Matters relating to tort).
  Limitation of action—
    Concealment of right of action—
      Breach of duty. *See* **Limitation of action** (Concealment of right of action—Breach of duty).
    Court's power to override time limit in personal injury or fatal accident claim. *See* **Limitation of action** (Court's power to override time limit in personal injury or fatal accident claim).
    When time begins to run. *See* **Limitation of action** (When time begins to run—Actions in tort).
  Malicious civil proceedings—
    Conflict of laws. *See* **Conflict of laws** (Tort—Proper law of tort—Malicious civil proceedings).
  Malicious falsehood. *See* **Malicious falsehood.**
  Malicious prosecution. *See* **Malicious prosecution.**
  Mentally disordered person—
    Knowledge of nature and quality of act—
      Assault—No knowledge that act wrongful—Whether a defence to action. **Morriss v Marsden** [1952] **1** 925, QBD.
  Misfeasance in public office. *See* **Public office** (Abuse of—Misfeasance by a public officer).
  Misrepresentation. *See* **Misrepresentation.**
  Negligence. *See* **Negligence.**
  Nuisance. *See* **Nuisance.**

TORT (cont)—
Occupier's liability. *See* **Occupier's liability**.
Partnership—
Liability of firm. *See* **Partnership** (Tort).
Passing off. *See* **Passing off**.
Perjury—
Civil action. *See* **Criminal law** (Perjury—Civil action).
Personal injuries—
Master and servant—
Liability to servant in contract or tort. *See* **Employment** (Liability of master—Contract or tort).
Procurement of breach of contract—
Injunction to restrain. *See* **Injunction** (Breach of contract—Procuring breach of contract).
Trade union—
Right to sue. *See* **Trade union** (Legal proceedings—Right of union to sue—Right to sue for procurement of breach of contract).
Procurement of violation of right—
Interference with contract—
Violation of plaintiff's secondary right to remedy for breach of contract—Interference with remedies for breach of contract—Defendant knowingly accepting transfer of shares in breach of covenant—Transfer of shares to defendant not restrained by injunction—Defendant having no contractual connection with plaintiff—Whether tort limited to interference with plaintiff's primary right to performance—Whether acceptance of shares by defendant actionable wrong. **Law Debenture Trust Corp plc v Ural Caspian Oil Corp Ltd** [1995] **1** 157, CA.
Representative proceedings—
Parties. *See* **Practice** (Parties—Representative proceedings—Action in tort).
Service out of the jurisdiction. *See* **Practice** (Service out of the jurisdiction—Action founded on tort committed within jurisdiction).
Solicitor—
Action for negligence—
Cause of action. *See* **Solicitor** (Negligence—Cause of action—Parallel claims in tort and contract).
Trespass to land—
Animal, by. *See* **Animal** (Trespass).
Generally. *See* **Trespass to land**.
Trespass to the person—
Generally. *See* **Trespass to the person**.
Medical practitioner. *See* **Medical practitioner** (Trespass to the person).
Trustee savings bank—
Action against bank. *See* **Trustee savings bank** (Action—Tort).
Vicarious immunity—
Immunity from tort—
Whether authority for the doctrine of vicarious immunity from tort. **Scruttons Ltd v Midland Silicones Ltd** [1962] **1** 1, HL.
Vicarious liability. *See* **Vicarious liability**.
Waiver—
Action on same facts based on contract—
Action not proceeding to judgment—Subsequent action against bank for conversion—Whether initiation of proceedings based on contract constituting waiver of tort. **United Australia Ltd v Barclays Bank Ltd** [1940] **4** 20, HL.
Watching and besetting premises. *See* **Nuisance** (Watching and besetting premises).
Wife's right to sue husband in tort. *See* **Husband and wife** (Tort—Right of wife to sue husband in tort).
Wrongful interference with goods—
Cause of action—
Claimant parking vehicle in parking bay on private property—Notice by adjacent bay prohibiting parking and warning that unattended vehicles risked clamping—Claimant in distressed state and failing to see notice—Whether claimant consenting to or willingly assuming risk of car being clamped. **Vine v Waltham Forest London BC** [2000] **4** 169, CA.
Plaintiff parking vehicle on private property without authority—Defendants immobilising vehicle—Whether defendants' action lawful. **Arthur v Anker** [1996] **3** 783, CA.
Conversion—
Denial of rights of ownership—Claimant's aircraft taken by sovereign government—Defendant not having taken or disposed of aircraft—Defendant treating aircraft as its own—Defendant registering aircraft in its own name—Whether tort of conversion established. **Kuwait Airways Corp v Iraqi Airways Co** [2002] **1** Comm 843, HL; [2002] **3** 209, HL; **Kuwait Airways Corp v Iraqi Airways Co (No 3)** [2001] **1** Comm 557, CA.
Denial of rights of ownership—Denial for indefinite period—Plaintiffs goods lying in defendant's depot—Defendant refusing to deliver goods to plaintiff or to allow plaintiff to enter depot to collect them himself—Defendant's refusal arising out of fears of industrial disruption affecting his business—Whether defendant's refusal amounting to conversion—Tort (Interference with Goods) Act 1977, s 1. **Perry (Howard E) & Co Ltd v British Railways Board** [1980] **2** 579, Ch D.
Generally. *See* **Conversion**.
Interlocutory relief—
Delivery up of goods—Exercise of court's powers—Discretion—Whether interlocutory relief only available in cases where goods in real and imminent danger of loss or destruction—Whether damages adequate remedy where goods' equivalent obtainable on market only with great difficulty—Whether defendant's fear of threats of unpleasant consequences if he complied with order a reason for refusing to make order—Torts (Interference with Goods) Act 1977, s 4(2)—RSC Ord 29, r 2A. **Perry (Howard E) & Co Ltd v British Railways Board** [1980] **2** 579, Ch D.
Trespass to goods. *See* **Trespass to goods**.
Trover. *See* **Trover**.

TORTURE
Criminal law. *See* **Criminal law** (Torture).

TORTURE (cont)—
Evidence obtained by—
  Admissibility. *See* **Evidence** (Admissibility—Hearsay—Confession).
Victims of—
  Immigration detention. *See* **Immigration** (Detention—Victims of torture).

TOTALISATOR
Dog racecourse. *See* **Gaming** (Totalisators on dog racecourses).

TOUTING
Street, in. *See* **Highway** (Street—Touting).

TOWAGE
Collision at sea. *See* **Shipping** (Collision—Towage).
Limitation of liability. *See* **Shipping** (Limitation of liability—Towage).
Salvage distinguished. *See* **Shipping** (Salvage—Definition—Distinction between towage and salvage).
Towage contract. *See* **Shipping** (Towage contract).

TOWER WAGON
Exemption from requirement of plating and test certificates. *See* **Road traffic** (Plating and test certificates for goods vehicles—Exemption—Tower wagon).

TOWN AND COUNTRY PLANNING
Access to highway—
  Street—
    Minimum width in local planning scheme—Carriageway giving access to building behind buildings fronting on highway—Whether a 'street'—Public Health Act 1875, s 4. **Cowan v Hendon BC** [1939] **3** 366, Ch D.
Advertisement—
  Advertisement in area to which planning scheme under Town and Country Planning Act 1932 applied—Display before 1st August 1948—Validity of enforcement notice under Town and Country Planning (Control of Advertisements) Regulations 1948 (SI 1948 No 1613), reg 23. **Dominant Sites Ltd v Hendon BC** [1952] **2** 899, QBD.
  Display without consent—
    Business premises, on. *See* Advertisement—Display without express consent on business premises, *below*.
    For sale boards—Estate agent displaying for sale board at property—Subsequently another estate agent displaying second board at property—Whether first estate agent committing offence of displaying for sale board without consent having been granted—Town and Country Planning Act 1971, s 109(2) Town and Country Planning (Control of Advertisements) Regulations 1984, regs 6, 14, class III(a)—Town and Country Planning (Control of Advertisements) (Amendment No 2) Regulations 1987. **Porter v Honey** [1988] **3** 1045, HL.
  Display without express consent on business premises—
    Business premises—Building normally used for specified purposes—'Business premises' not including forecourt or other land forming part of curtilage of building—Petrol service station—Station consisting of sales office, petrol pumps and concrete apron—Advertisements displayed on concrete apron in open air—Whether concrete apron part of building or whether forecourt forming part of curtilage of building—Town and Country Planning (Control of Advertisements) Regulations 1969 (SI 1969 No 1532), reg 14(1), (3)(a). **Heron Service Stations Ltd v Coupe** [1973] **2** 110, HL.
    Restrictions on advertisements containing letters, figures, symbols, emblems or devices over certain height—Advertisements on public houses showing cigarette packet, man holding up glass of beer and beer glass—Objects depicted all in excess of permitted height—Whether objects depicted 'figures, symbols, emblems or devices'—Town and Country Planning (Control of Advertisements) Regulations 1969 (SI 1969 No 1532), reg 14(2)(a). **McDonald v Howard Cook Advertising Ltd** [1971] **3** 1249, QBD.
  Hoarding—
    Land specified in planning scheme as 'land to be protected in respect of advertisements'—Notice to remove hoarding—Other hoardings already on site prior to date of scheme—Notices already served in regard to other hoardings—Conditions to be considered in determining whether hoarding 'seriously injures' amenity of land—Town and Country Planning Act 1932, s 47. **O'Ferrall (More) Ltd v Harrow UDC** [1946] **2** 489, KBD.
    Restriction on height of advertisement hoarding—Hoardings erected without submitting plans and sections to local authority—Advertisement separated into number of smaller pieces—Whether constituted 'hoarding'—Advertisements Regulation Act 1907, s 2(1). **Horlicks Ltd v Garvie** [1939] **1** 335, KBD.
    Structure—Advertising sign of sheet metal fixed to wall of old theatre—Manchester Corporation Act 1891, s 18(1). **Borough Billposting Co Ltd v Manchester Corp** [1948] **1** 807, KBD.
    Structure—Power of local authority to prohibit the use of a wall of dwelling-house for advertising purposes—Town and Country Planning Act 1932, s 47(5), (8)—Town and Country Planning (Interim Development) Act 1943, ss 5, 15, Sch I. **Mills and Rockleys Ltd v Leicester City Council** [1946] **1** 424, KBD.
  Licence—
    Right of local authority to charge fee for grant of licence—'Under and subject to such terms and conditions to be therein prescribed as the corporation may deem proper'—Liverpool Corporation (General Powers) Act 1930, s 29. **Liverpool Corp v Maiden (Arthur) Ltd** [1938] **4** 200, Assizes.
  Powers of local authority to control advertisements—
    Byelaws—Power to regulate exhibition of advertisements so as to affect injuriously amenities of public park—Byelaw prohibiting exhibition of advertisements near park—No reference to amenities—Validity of byelaw—Advertisements Regulation Act 1907, s 2. **Twickenham Corp v Solosigns Ltd** [1939] **3** 246, KBD.

TOWN AND COUNTRY PLANNING (cont)—

Agreement regulating development or use of land—

Caravan site—

Existing user rights—Agreement by site owner to limit number of structures on site to twenty-five—Proviso to agreement preserving 'any rights of whatever nature which the owner has or may have in the future' under the Act of 1947 or amending Acts 'or otherwise howsoever'—Subsequently planning permission granted on basis of existing user rights—Site licence granted for thirty-three caravans—Whether site could be used for twenty-five caravans only despite site licence for thirty-three caravans—Town and Country Planning Act 1947, s 25—Caravan Sites and Control of Development Act 1960, s 17(5). **Crittenden (Warren Park) Ltd v Surrey CC** [1965] **3** 917, Ch D.

Permission for development—

Condition—Agreement containing covenant which could not have been imposed as condition on grant of planning permission—Whether local planning authority entitled to require land owner to enter into agreement containing covenant which could not have been imposed as condition on grant of planning permission—Town and Country Planning Act 1971, ss 29(1), 52(1). **Good v Epping Forest DC** [1994] **2** 156, CA.

Agreement restricting planning in lieu of scheme—

Agreement alleged to have been with a committee of local authority—

Power of local authority to delegate to committee—Agreement relating to planning, development or user, but alleged to be more favourable to landowner than draft scheme—Whether interim development order required—Town and Country Planning Act 1932, ss 34, 48, 54—Local Government Act 1933, s 85. **A-G v Barnes BC and Ranelagh Club Ltd** [1938] **3** 711, Ch D.

Agricultural land—

Refusal to permit construction of a sports stadium—

Overriding need of agriculture—Town and Country Planning Act 1932, s 10(5). **R v East Kesteven RDC, ex p Sleaford and District White City Sports Stadium Co** [1947] **1** 310, KBD.

Amenity—

Notice to abate injury to amenity by condition of vacant site or other open land—

Building and surrounding yard used for business of car-breaking—Whether 'open land' included land within the curtilage of a building—Town and Country Planning Act 1947, s 33(1). **Stephens v Cuckfield RDC** [1960] **2** 716, CA.

Use of land in agricultural area as car dump—Established use since before 1947 but no express planning permission granted—Validity of notice—Town and Country Planning Act 1947, s 33(1). **Britt v Buckinghamshire CC** [1963] **2** 175, CA.

Ancient monuments. *See* **Ancient monuments**.

Appeal—

Appeal against enforcement notice. *See* Enforcement notice—Appeal against notice, *below*.

Appeal against refusal of permission for development. *See* Appeal to Minister against refusal of permission for development, *below*.

Costs—

Order for costs—Several parties. *See* **Costs** (Order for costs—Discretion—Several parties—Multiple representation in planning appeals).

Issue estoppel—

Appeal against planning decision—Appeal against enforcement notice—Whether issue estoppel applies to appeals against planning decisions or enforcement notices—Town and Country Planning Act 1971, s 88. **Thrasyvoulou v Secretary of State for the Environment** [1990] **1** 65, HL.

Appeal to Minister against refusal of permission for development—

Challenge to decision of inspector—

Appeal by local planning authority against grant of planning permission by inspector—Whether party challenging inspector's decision in planning permission appeal precluded from raising argument not advanced at inquiry. **South Oxfordshire DC v Secretary of State for the Environment, Transport and the Regions** [2000] **2** 667, QBD.

Findings of fact by inspector accepted by Minister but not inspector's 'conclusions' or recommendation—

No opportunity afforded to applicant to make further representations—Appeal dismissed by Minister—Application to quash Minister's decision—Whether inspector's conclusions were also findings of fact—Town and Country Planning Appeals (Inquiries Procedure) Rules 1965 (SI 1965 No 453), r 12(2). **Pavenham (Lord Luke of) v Minister of Housing and Local Government** [1967] **2** 1066, CA.

Findings of fact by inspector accepted by Minister but not inspector's recommendation—

Minister taking into consideration new evidence after close of inquiry—No opportunity afforded to applicant to make further representations—Appeal dismissed by Minister—Application to quash Minister's decision—Minister attaching weight to evidence disregarded by inspector—Inspector disregarding evidence because not proved before him—Consideration by Minister of material having no evidential value—Town and Country Planning (Inquiries Procedure) Rules (SI 1974 No 419), r 12(2)(b). **French Kier Developments Ltd v Secretary of State for the Environment** [1977] **1** 296, QBD.

Local inquiry—

Adjournment—Application for adjournment to allow applicant to prepare case and instruct counsel—Secretary of State refusing adjournment—Whether judge having jurisdiction to quash Secretary of State's decision—Whether Secretary of State's decision a 'decision ... on an appeal'—Town and Country Planning Act 1971, ss 36, 242(3)(b). **Co-op Retail Services Ltd v Secretary of State for the Environment** [1980] **1** 449, CA.

Inspector's power to award costs—Whether inspector precluded from taking into account pre-appeal conduct in determining whether to award costs—Local Government Act 1972, s 250(5)—Town and Country Planning Act 1990, s 320(2). **R v Secretary of State for the Environment, ex p Rochford DC** [2000] **3** 1018, QBD.

TOWN AND COUNTRY PLANNING (cont)—
Appeal to Minister against refusal of permission for development (cont)—
Local planning authority binding itself by agreement to resist development in area of Jodrell Bank—
Authority's decision refusing permission for development in the area void because of failure to comply with Act—Whether Minister properly seised of appeal—Minister entitled to deal with application de novo, or on footing that the authority had failed to notify applicant of an effective decision—Town and Country Planning Act 1962, ss 17(1), 23(4), 24. **Stringer v Minister of Housing and Local Government** [1971] **1** 65, QBD.

Natural justice—
Appeal against refusal to allow development near to radio telescope at Jodrell Bank—Minister having general policy of discouraging development interfering with the efficient working of the radio telescope—Refusal of permission by Minister because development might interfere with the working of telescope—Minister entitled to have general policy on matters relevant to planning decisions provided policy did not preclude him from fairly judging the relevant issues in each case—Policy did not preclude fair consideration of appeal—No ground for quashing decision. **Stringer v Minister of Housing and Local Government** [1971] **1** 65, QBD.

Notification of decision—
Decision in accordance with stated policy—Failure by Minister to exercise discretion properly in determination of appeal—Quasi-judicial function—Delegatus non potest delegare—Town and Country Planning Act 1962, ss 23, 179. **Lavender (H) and Son Ltd v Minister of Housing and Local Government** [1970] **3** 871, QBD.

Notification by letter—Challenge to minister's decision—Time limit for making application to High Court to quash decision—Time limit six weeks from date on which 'action' is taken—Whether time limit running from date letter signed and dated or from when notification received by applicant—Town and Country Planning Act 1971, ss 242, 245. **Griffiths v Secretary of State for the Environment** [1983] **1** 439, HL.

Reasons for decision—Reasons so obscurely stated as not to be good and sufficient reasons—Minister's decision dismissing appeal quashed—Town and Country Planning (Inquiries Procedure) Rules 1962 (SI 1962 No 1425), r 11(1). **Givaudan & Co Ltd v Minister of Housing and Local Government** [1966] **3** 696, QBD.

Reasons for decision—Reasons so obscurely stated as not to be good and sufficient reasons—Minister's decision dismissing appeal quashed—Town and Country Planning (Inquiries Procedure) Rules 1974 (SI 1974 No 419), r 13(1). **French Kier Developments Ltd v Secretary of State for the Environment** [1977] **1** 296, QBD.

Reasons for decision—Secretary of State identifying landmark points from inspector's report in his decision letter and stating his agreement therewith—Whether Secretary of State incorporating inspector's reasoning as his own—Whether Secretary of State complying with duty to give reasons for decision—Whether Secretary of State giving adequate reasons for decision—Test of whether Secretary of State's reasons adequate—Whether interests of applicant substantially prejudiced by deficiency of reasons—Town and Country Planning Act 1971, s 245—Town and Country Planning (Inquiries Procedure) Rules 1988, r 17(1). **Save Britain's Heritage v Secretary of State for the Environment** [1991] **2** 10, HL.

Reasons for decision—Special circumstances for inappropriate development—Whether reasons for decision adequate—Whether prior unlawful development material. **South Bucks DC v Porter** [2004] **4** 775, HL.

Validity of application for permission—
Company applying for planning permission and listed building consent—Planning authority taking view that applications were invalid—Company appealing to Secretary of State—Whether Secretary of State having jurisdiction to hear appeal—Whether planning authority sole arbiter of validity of application for planning permission—Town and Country Planning Act 1990, s 78—Planning (Listed Buildings and Conservation Areas) Act 1990, s 20. **R v Secretary of State for the Environment, Transport and the Regions, ex p Bath and North East Somerset DC** [1999] **4** 418, CA.

Validity of Minister's action—
Application to High Court to challenge validity—Person aggrieved—Refusal by local planning authority of permission to develop land by digging chalk—Appeal to Minister against refusal under s 16 of Town and Country Planning Act 1947—Local inquiry held at which objections made and evidence given by four adjoining landowners—Inspector's recommendation to minister that appeal be dismissed on ground of detriment to adjoining landowners—Appeal allowed by Minister—Whether landowners persons aggrieved by Minister's action—Town and Country Planning Act 1959, s 31(1)(b). **Buxton v Minister of Housing and Local Government** [1960] **3** 408, QBD.

Appropriation of land for planning purposes—
Local authority—
Power to appropriate land. *See* **Local authority** (Land—Power to appropriate land).

Breach of condition notice—
Validity—
Challenge to validity—Criminal proceedings for failure to comply with breach of condition notice—Whether defendant entitled to challenge validity of notice and validity of planning condition in criminal proceedings—Town and Country Planning Act 1990, ss 171B, 187A. **Dilieto v Ealing London BC** [1998] **2** 885, QBD.

Building of special architectural or historic interest—
Building preservation order—
Date on which order made—Town and Country Planning Act 1959, s 31(3)(d). **Iveagh (Earl) v Minister of Housing and Local Government** [1963] **3** 817, CA.

Neighbouring buildings—Whether architectural or historic interest of neighbouring buildings may be taken into account—Town and Country Planning Act 1947, s 29(1). **Iveagh (Earl) v Minister of Housing and Local Government** [1963] **3** 817, CA.

Building of special architectural or historic interest (cont)—
  Building preservation order (cont)—
    Service of building preservation notice by post—Notice coming into force as soon as served—Service on company—Company owner of building—Notice sent to company's registered office by recorded delivery service—Company failing to put name on door of registered office—Postman unable to find office at which to deliver letter containing notice—Letter returned to planning authority—Demolition taking place after attempted delivery of notice on company—Whether notice validly served—Whether demolition in breach of preservation order—Interpretation Act 1889, s 26—Town and Country Planning Act 1962, s 214—Town and Country Planning Act 1968, s 48. **Maltglade Ltd v St Albans RDC** [1972] 3 129, QBD.
  Demolition, alteration or extension—
    Offence—Offence of demolishing, altering or extending except as authorised—Whether offence of strict liability—Town and Country Planning Act 1971, s 55(1). **R v Wells Street Metropolitan Stipendiary Magistrate, ex p Westminster City Council** [1986] 3 4, QBD.
  Ecclesiastical building—
    Building for the time being used for ecclesiastical purposes—Building which would be so used but for works of demolition etc—Use of building discontinued because of proposed demolition—Proposal to demolish whole building—Whether exemption limited to cases where use discontinued because of actual demolition—Whether exemption applicable where whole building being demolished and therefore use incapable of being resumed—Town and Country Planning Act 1971, s 56(1)(a). **A-G (ex rel Bedfordshire CC) v Trustees of the Howard United Reformed Church, Bedford** [1975] 2 337, HL.
    Building for the time being used for ecclesiastical purposes—For the time being—Relevant time—Time when proposed works of demolition or alteration carried out—Town and Country Planning Act 1971, ss 55(1), 56(1)(a). **A-G (ex rel Bedfordshire CC) v Trustees of the Howard United Reformed Church, Bedford** [1975] 2 337, HL.
    Building owned by a church—Building having been used for ecclesiastical purposes only—Building having fallen into disuse—Building belonging to church other than Church of England—Whether an 'ecclesiastical building'—Town and Country Planning Act 1971, s 56(1)(a). **A-G (ex rel Bedfordshire CC) v Trustees of the Howard United Reformed Church, Bedford** [1975] 2 337, HL.
    Rectory—Whether rectory is within exemption for ecclesiastical buildings enacted in Town and Country Planning Act 1962, s 30(2)(a). **Phillips v Minister of Housing and Local Government** [1964] 2 824, CA.
  Listed building—
    Alteration works—Works involving demolition of part of listed building—Refusal of consent—Whether works amounting to alteration or demolition—Whether building owner entitled to compensation for refusal of consent by Secretary of State—Town and Country Planning Act 1990, s 336(1)—Planning (Listed Buildings and Conservation Areas) Act 1990, s 27(1). **Shimizu (UK) Ltd v Westminster City Council** [1997] 1 481, HL.
    Appeal against listed building enforcement notice—Pair of valuable urns on pedestals designated as listed buildings—Owner arranging removal—Owner appealing against enforcement order and refusal of listed building consent on ground urns not 'buildings'—Whether planning inspector permitted to consider status of items as 'buildings'—Criteria for identifying 'building'—Planning (Listed Buildings and Conservation Areas) Act 1990, ss 7, 8, 20, 39. **Dill v Secretary of State for Housing, Communities and Local Government** [2020] 4 631, SC.
    Consent for demolition—Presumption in favour of preservation of listed buildings—Special circumstances in which demolition may be authorised—Owners wishing to demolish eight listed buildings and erect single modern building in conservation area in City of London—Secretary of State accepting recommendation of inspector following planning inquiry that planning permission, listed building consent and conservation area consent be given for demolition and redevelopment—Whether Secretary of State entitled to depart from declared policy on demolition of listed buildings—Department of the Environment Circular 8/87. **Save Britain's Heritage v Secretary of State for the Environment** [1991] 2 10, HL.
    Consent for demolition—Whether building listed—Construction of list compiled by Secretary of State—Town and Country Planning (Scotland) Act 1972, s 52. **City of Edinburgh Council v Secretary of State for Scotland** [1998] 1 174, HL.
  Repairs notice—
    Compulsory acquisition of listed building requiring repair—Service of notice specifying works 'reasonably necessary for proper preservation' of building—Whether 'preservation' including restoration—Whether inclusion in notice of excessive items invalidating notice—Whether 'preservation' referring to features existing when building first listed or features existing at date of notice—Town and Country Planning Act 1971, ss 114, 115. **Robbins v Secretary of State for the Environment** [1989] 1 878, HL.
Caravan site licence—
  Caravan site—
    Meaning—Refers to the land forming the site independent of the number of caravans on it—Caravan Sites and Control of Development Act 1960, s 1(4). **Minister of Housing and Local Government v Hartnell** [1965] 1 490, HL.
  Condition—
    Appeal—Licence granted subject to conditions—No appeal against conditions—Application by licensee to alter conditions—Refusal by local authority—Whether licence holder had right of appeal against refusal of application—Caravan Sites and Control of Development Act 1960, s 8(2). **Peters v Yiewsley and West Drayton UDC** [1963] 1 843, QBD.
    Validity. *See* Caravan site licence—Validity of condition, *below*.
  Exemption from licensing requirements. *See* **Caravan site** (Licence—Exemption from licensing requirements).
  Existing site application—
    Application for site licence treated as application for planning permission—Conditions imposed derogating from existing user rights—Whether conditions ultra vires—Whether existing user rights limited to placing on site the maximum number of caravans previously using it—Caravan Sites and Control of Development Act 1960, s 17(2). **Minister of Housing and Local Government v Hartnell** [1965] 1 490, HL.

Caravan site licence (cont)—
  Existing site application (cont)—
    Construction as being made in respect of existing sites—Planning permission—Whether extending to whole area or part only—Whether deemed permission excluded—Whether initial application abandoned by making subsequent application—Caravan Sites and Control of Development Act 1960, s 17(1), (3). **James v Secretary of State for Wales** [1965] **3** 602, CA; [1966] **3** 964, HL.
    Exemption if application for licence made within two months beginning with commencement of Act—Commencement of Act at expiration of one month beginning with date on which it was passed—Computation of time—Caravan Sites and Control of Development Act 1960, ss 1(1), 14, 50(4). **Hare v Gocher** [1962] **2** 763, QBD.
    Extent of site—More than four years user by one caravan—Extent of site not specified—Enforcement notice covering whole area of land served out of time and quashed by Minister on appeal—Minister referred to two and a half acres as existing site—Site licence issued restricted to part of site on which one caravan stood and small area round—Whether applicant entitled to licence for two and a half acres—Whether Minister's decision raised res judicata—Caravan Sites and Control of Development Act 1960, ss 1(4), 17(1), (3). **R v Axbridge RDC, ex p Wormald** [1964] **1** 571, CA.
    Form—Letter 'I am making application for fifty...[caravans] as under the new Act'—Whether application for site licence—Caravan Sites and Control of Development Act 1960, ss 13, 17(1), (3). **Chelmsford RDC v Powell** [1963] **1** 150, QBD.
    Use of land—Waste land being developed as caravan site on 9th March 1960, but no caravan on site on that date—Previous intermittent use of land for caravans—Caravan user discontinued each year but no change of user—Caravan user constituting development without planning permission—Time for serving enforcement notice expired—Whether land 'used' or 'in use' as caravan site on 9th March 1960—Caravan Sites and Control of Development Act 1960, ss 1(4), 13(a). **Biss v Smallburgh RDC** [1964] **2** 543, CA.
  Validity of condition—
    Condition as to number of caravans on site imposed by local planning authority—Whether local authority issuing site licence can impose condition beyond scope of planning condition—Caravan Sites and Control of Development Act 1960, ss 3(3), 29(4). **R v Kent Justices, ex p Crittenden** [1963] **2** 245, QBD.
    Conditions not relating to physical use of land—Relating to control of rents, of contracts with caravan owners, of security of tenure and of normal terms of a tenancy—Uncertainty—Whether ultra vires and void—Caravan Sites and Control of Development Act 1960, s 5(1). **Chertsey UDC v Mixnam's Properties Ltd** [1964] **2** 627, HL.
    No action taken by planning authority on application for site licence—Deemed planning permission unrestricted as to number of caravans—Subsequent issue by local authority of licence with condition limiting number of caravans—Whether planning considerations may be taken into account in determining whether site licence conditions were unduly burdensome—Caravan Sites and Control of Development Act 1960, ss 5(1), 7(1), 17(3). **Esdell Caravan Parks Ltd v Hemel Hempstead RDC** [1965] **3** 737, CA.
Change of use—
  Condition attached to permission for change of use—
    Permission for temporary change of use of existing building—Condition attached that building be removed at the end of period of permission—Whether condition valid—Town and Country Planning Act 1971, s 29(1). **Newbury DC v Secretary of State for the Environment** [1980] **1** 731, HL.
    Planning permission granted with conditions limiting use to sale of specified categories—Categories subsequently extended—Decision notice extending categories not setting out conditions—Whether planning permission permitting use of store for food sales—Correct approach to interpretation—'Reasonable reader' test—Town and Country Planning Act 1990, s 73. **London Borough of Lambeth v Secretary of State for Housing, Communities and Local Government** [2019] **4** 981, SC.
  Time limits—
    Certificate of lawful use or development—Planning authority granting permission for erection of hay barn—Dwellinghouse built disguised as hay barn—Authority refusing certificate of lawful use—Whether breach of planning control consisting in 'change of use'—Whether deceit by owner precluding him from obtaining certificate—Town and Country Planning Act 1990, ss 171B, 191(1). **Welwyn Hatfield BC v Secretary of State for Communities and Local Government** [2011] **4** 851, SC.
Classes of use. *See* Development—Use classes, *below*.
Coast protection. *See* **Coast protection**.
Common land. *See* **Commons** (Registration—Town or village green).
Compensation—
  Compulsory purchase. *See* **Compulsory purchase** (Compensation).
  Depreciation of land values—
    Interest on compensation—Interest computed by reference to the period 1st July 1948 to 30th June 1955—Received in 1956-1959 by trustees in respect of sales of settled land during lives of two successive tenants for life and after death of second tenant for life—Whether interest apportionable over period by reference to which it was calculated and payable to personal representatives of tenants for life—Whether it should be treated as income accrued after death of second tenant for life—Town and Country Planning Act 1947, s 65(3)—Town and Country Planning Act 1953, s 2(1)—Town and Country Planning Act 1954, s 14(1)—Apportionment Act 1870, s 2. **Sneyd (decd), Re** [1961] **1** 744, Ch D.
    Principal and interest received by trustees—Apportionment between capital and income—Rule in Re Earl of Chesterfield's Trusts applied—Town and Country Planning Act 1954, ss 1, 14(1). **Chance (decd), Re** [1962] **1** 942, Ch D.
  Development restricted by statute—
    Compensation for injury to estate or interest—Whether development proposals practicable at date of claim for compensation—Proposals abandoned or amended—Restriction of Ribbon Development Act 1935, s 9(1)(a). **Melksham UDC v Wiltshire CC** [1937] **4** 142, KBD.

TOWN AND COUNTRY PLANNING (cont)—
  Compensation (cont)—
    Development restricted by statute (cont)—
      Ribbon development—Compensation for injury to estate or interest—Assessment of compensation—Decrease in market value—Expense of release from onerous agreement—Restriction of Ribbon Development Act 1935, s 9(1), (4). **Gibson v Norfolk CC** [1941] **1** 252, KBD.
      Ribbon development—Injurious affection of land—Claim for compensation—Date at which compensation should be assessed—Date of claim—Restriction of Ribbon Development Act 1935, s 9. **Huckle v Lowestoft Corp** [1942] **2** 688, KBD.
    Discontinuance order. *See* Discontinuance order—Compensation, *below*.
    Land scheduled as open space—
      Basis of computation—Whether loss of building profits also recoverable—Acquisition of Land (Assessment of Compensation) Act 1919, s 2(2)—Town and Country Planning Act 1932, s 10(6). **Collins v Feltham UDC** [1937] **4** 189, KBD.
    Land settled on trust for sale—
      Compensation was capital but not proceeds of sale arising under the trust for sale—Law of Property Act 1925, s 28(1)—Town and Country Planning Act 1954, s 66(1)—Town and Country Planning (Mortgages, Rentcharges, etc) Regulations 1955 (SI 1955 No 38), reg 10. **Meux's Will Trusts, Re** [1957] **2** 630, Ch D.
    Modification of planning permission—
      Permission for erection of agricultural cottage—Subsequent modification order—Condition restricting use to agricultural worker—Use limited by virtue of original permission—Town and Country Planning Act 1947, ss 18(3), 22(1). **Wilson v West Sussex CC** [1963] **1** 751, CA.
    Notice—
      Registration—Certificate of registrar of local land charges—Conclusiveness—Error—Omission of compensation notice—Whether certificate conclusive. **Ministry of Housing and Local Government v Sharp** [1970] **1** 1009, CA.
      Registration—Rules—Ultra vires—Whether power to make certificates issued by local land registrar conclusive as to existence of compensation notice—Town and Country Planning Act 1954, s 28(5)—Land Charges Act 1925, s 17(3)—Local Land Charges Rules 1934 (SR & O 1934 No 285), r 15—Local Land Charges (Amendment) Rules 1954 (SI 1954 No 1677), r 2. **Ministry of Housing and Local Government v Sharp** [1970] **1** 1009, CA.
    Purchase notice, on. *See* **Compulsory purchase** (Compensation—Purchase notice).
    Refusal of permission to develop—
      Generally. *See* Permission for development—Refusal—Compensation, *below*.
      Northern Ireland. *See* **Northern Ireland** (Town and country planning—Compensation—Refusal of permission to develop).
    Revocation of permission for development. *See* Permission for development—Revocation—Compensation, *below*.
    When right to compensation accrues—
      Date when scheme comes into operation—Town and Country Planning Act 1932, s 18. **Bury v Epping RDC and Essex CC** [1940] **4** 377, KBD.
  Compulsory purchase. *See* **Compulsory purchase.**
  Conservation area—
    Control of demolition—
      Agreement between planning authority and developer allowing development of land in conservation area—Agreement not specifically prohibiting demolition of buildings on land—Development not capable of being carried out without demolition of buildings—Developer demolishing buildings without consent of planning authority—Whether consent of authority necessary for demolition of buildings—Whether agreement containing implied consent of authority to demolition—Whether authority able to prohibit demolition in spite of implied consent in agreement—Town and Country Planning Act 1971, ss 52(3), 277A. **Windsor and Maidenhead Royal BC v Brandrose Investments Ltd** [1983] **1** 818, CA.
    Planning permission—
      Preservation and enhancement of area—Outline planning permission given before site designated part of conservation area—Development not preserving or enhancing area—Whether permission for development should be granted—Town and Country Planning Act 1971, s 277(8). **Bath Society v Secretary of State for the Environment** [1992] **1** 28, CA.
      Preservation and enhancement of area—Preserving area—Whether proposed development must positively preserve character or appearance of conservation area in question—Whether character or appearance of area would be preserved if development left character or appearance unharmed—Town and Country Planning Act 1971, s 277(8). **South Lakeland DC v Secretary of State for the Environment** [1992] **1** 573, HL.
  Crown—
    Whether bound by statute. *See* **Statute** (Crown—Whether bound by statute).
  Designation of area as site for proposed new town. *See* **New town** (Order designating area as site for proposed new town).
  Development—
    Beginning of development before expiry of permission. *See* Duration of planning permission—Beginning of development before expiry date, *below*.
    Building—
      Building operations in, on, over or under land—Large coal-hopper and conveyor, each on own wheels, installed in coal-yard—Town and Country Planning Act 1947, ss 12(2), 119(1). **Cheshire CC v Woodward** [1962] **1** 517, QBD.
      Works on land—Construction of model village, railway and racecourse—Town and Country Planning Act 1947, ss 12(2), 75(9), 119(1). **Buckinghamshire CC v Callingham** [1952] **1** 1166, CA.
    Building, engineering or other operations—
      Removal of soil banked against blast walls of explosives stores and magazines—Demolition of walls—Alteration of building—Development requiring planning permission—Whether error of law by Minister—Town and Country Planning Act 1962, s 12(1). **Coleshill and District Investment Co Ltd v Minister of Housing and Local Government** [1969] **2** 525, HL.

TOWN AND COUNTRY PLANNING (cont)—
    Development (cont)—
        Caravan site—
            Caravan—Chalet structure—Chalet structure falling within statutory definition but not ordinary
                meaning of caravan—Whether 'caravan' and 'caravan site' having statutory meaning or ordinary
                meaning in planning applications and planning permission—Caravan Sites and Control of
                Development Act 1960, s 29(1). **Wyre Forest DC v Secretary of State for the Environment**
                [1990] **1** 780, HL.
            Meaning—Caravan site licence. See Caravan site licence—Caravan site—Meaning, *above.*
        Compulsory purchase. See **Compulsory purchase** (Development).
        Development charge. See Development charge, *below.*
        Development consent—
            Environmental impact assessment—Environmental impact assessment development—Agriculture
                and aquaculture—Projects for use of uncultivated land or semi-natural areas for intensive
                agricultural purposes—Farm situated in area of outstanding natural beauty—Farm applying for
                permission for use of polythene coverings in cultivation of soft fruit—Whether environmental
                impact assessment required—Whether use of semi-natural area for intensive agricultural
                purpose—Meaning of 'semi-natural'—Town and Country Planning (Environmental Impact
                Assessment) (England and Wales) Regulations 1999, SI 1999/293, Sch 2. **R (on the application of**
                Wye Valley Action Association Ltd) v Herefordshire Council [2010] **2** 863, QBD.
        Development value. See Development value, *below.*
        Extinction of use—
            Open site used for market trading—Permission for erection of building over whole of site—Ground
                floor area beneath building left open—Permission expressly permitting use of area for trading on
                Sundays—Absence of express prohibition on weekday trading—Trading carried on on
                weekdays—Whether permission for development extinguishing right to use site for weekday
                trading. **Petticoat Lane Rentals Ltd v Secretary of State for the Environment** [1971] **2** 793, QBD.
        Green Belt land—
            Inappropriate development—Material change of use—Competing applications for permission to
                develop cemeteries on Green Belt land—Council granting planning permission—Whether
                material change of use to use as cemetery 'inappropriate development'—National Planning
                Policy Framework, paras 81, 87, 88, 89, 90. **R (on the application of Timmins) v Gedling BC**
                [2016] **1** 895, CA.
        Interim development. See Interim development, *below.*
        Material change of use—
            Council granting conditional planning permission for conversion of premises into flats—Permission
                prohibiting use of premises as temporary sleeping accommodation ie accommodation occupied
                by same person for less than 90 consecutive nights provided for a consideration arising by
                reason of occupant's employment—Company using flats to provide free holiday accommodation
                for employees—Whether accommodation provided for a consideration arising by reason of
                occupant's employment—Whether premises used as temporary sleeping accommodation—
                Greater London Council (General Powers) Act 1973, s 25(a). **R v Kensington and Chelsea Royal**
                London BC, ex p Lawrie Plantation Services Ltd [1999] **3** 929, HL.
            Dwelling-house—Planning unit—Permitted use of premises—Use since before appointed
                day—Addition built on to premises—Agricultural smallholding—Permitted use of farmhouse for
                sale of homegrown and imported produce—Conservatory built on to farmhouse—Conservatory
                used thereafter for sale of produce—Enforcement notice requiring discontinuance of use of
                conservatory as retail shop—Whether conservatory to be regarded as separate planning
                unit—Whether use permitted for farmhouse permitted for conservatory. **Wood v Secretary of**
                State for the Environment [1973] **2** 404, QBD.
            Dwelling-house—Private residences subsequently used for multiple occupation for gain—Whether
                material change in use necessitating planning permission—Question of fact and degree—Use as
                separate dwelling-house—Whether Rent Act decisions applicable—Town and Country Planning
                Act 1947, s 12(2), (3)(a). **Birmingham Corp v Minister of Housing and Local Government and**
                Habib Ullah [1963] **3** 668, QBD.
            Dwelling-house—Two or more separate dwelling-houses—Building previously used as a single
                dwelling-house used for multiple occupation for gain—Whether material change of use requiring
                planning permission—Dwelling-houses must in truth be separate—Question of fact and
                degree—Town and Country Planning Act 1962, s 12(3). **Ealing BC v Ryan** [1965] **1** 137,
                QBD Divl Ct.
            Intensification of use—Intensification of use capable of constituting a material change of
                use—Question whether it constitutes a material change of use a question of degree to be
                determined by Secretary of State. **Brooks and Burton Ltd v Secretary of State for the**
                Environment [1978] **1** 733, CA.
            Petrol filling station with land attached used also for the display and sale of cars—Discontinuance
                of use for the display and sale of cars—Whether resumption of use constitutes material change of
                use—Town and Country Planning Act 1962, s 12(1). **Hartley v Minister of Housing and Local**
                Government [1969] **3** 1658, CA.
            Planning unit—Determination of what constitutes appropriate unit—Factors to be considered—
                Planning unit to be taken as whole unit of occupation unless smaller unit recognisable as site of
                activities amounting to a separate use physically and functionally. **Burdle v Secretary of State for**
                the Environment [1972] **3** 240, QBD.
            Planning unit—Determination of what constitutes appropriate unit—New chapter in planning
                history—Extinction of existing use rights—Industrial site having existing use rights for repair and
                maintenance of vehicles—Old workshop on site replaced by new workshop without planning
                permission—Workshop covering only small portion of site—Whether new workshop a new
                planning unit starting with nil use—Whether new chapter in planning history commencing—
                Whether new workshop falling within existing use right attaching to whole site. **Jennings Motors**
                Ltd v Secretary of State for the Environment [1982] **1** 471, CA.
            Question of fact and degree. **Bendles Motors Ltd v Bristol Corp** [1963] **1** 578, QBD.

  Development (cont)—
    Material change of use (cont)—
      Recovery of scrap metal—Whether a material change of use from recovering 'metal' from scrap—Former use involved smelting of raw materials and production of foundry and basic pig iron—Proposed use involved receiving scrap for the processing and storage of ferrous and non-ferrous metals and ancillary uses connected therewith—Whether the proposed use was a special industrial use within Town and Country Planning (Use Classes) Order 1950 (SI 1950 No 1131), Sch, class 5, para(iv) or, having regard to art 3(3), was a class 4 use. **Cohen (George) 600 Group Ltd v Minister of Housing and Local Government** [1961] 2 682, QBD.

      Revival of commercial use but for sale of caravans instead of portable garden buildings etc—Use for sale only in place of former manufacture and sale—Hut on land used, both before and after revival of commercial use, as office in which sales conducted—Whether revival of commercial use and different nature of article sold a material change in the use of the land—Hut a 'shop'—Use of hut and other land for sale of caravans not development—Town and Country Planning (Use Classes) Order 1950 (SI 1950 No 1131), arts 2(2), 3(1), Sch. **Marshall v Nottingham City Corp** [1960] 1 659, QBD.

      Seasonal use—Normal use for two different purposes seasonally. **Webber v Minister of Housing and Local Government** [1967] 3 981, CA.

      Use for stationing residential caravans—Caravan—Structure designed or adapted for human habitation—Adapted for human habitation—Motor vehicle—Motor vehicle not designed for human habitation—Whether to be 'adapted' for human habitation vehicle requires physical alteration—Whether sufficient to constitute vehicle a caravan as being 'adapted' for human habitation if vehicle furnished to make it suitable for human habitation—Caravan Sites and Control of Development Act 1960, s 29(1). **Backer v Secretary of State for the Environment** [1983] 2 1021, QBD.

  National planning policy—
    Policy guidance—National Planning Policy Framework (NPPF) providing policies for supply of housing should not be considered up-to-date if local planning authority not demonstrating five-year supply of deliverable housing sites—Proper interpretation and application of policy. **Hopkins Homes Ltd v Secretary of State for Communities and Local Government** [2017] 1 1011, CA.

    Policy guidance—National Planning Policy Framework (NPPF) providing policies for supply of housing should not be considered up-to-date if local planning authority not demonstrating five-year supply of deliverable housing sites—Proper interpretation and application of policy—Meaning of 'for the supply of housing'. **Hopkins Homes Ltd v Secretary of State for Communities and Local Government** [2017] 4 938, SC.

    Policy guidance—National Planning Policy Framework (NPPF) providing presumption in favour of sustainable development where no relevant development planning policies or policies out-of-date—Environmental policy in time-expired development plan—Whether policy out of date—Whether presumption to be applied—Meaning of 'out-of-date'. **Peel Investments (North) Ltd v Secretary of State for Housing, Communities and Local Government** [2021] 2 581, CA.

  Neighbourhood development plan—
    Judicial review of neighbourhood development plan on basis of failure to follow examiner's recommendation—Whether claim brought in time—Whether time running from final step of making plan or from earlier step of considering examiner's report—Town and Country Planning Act 1990, s 61N. **R (on the application of Fylde Coast Farms Ltd (formerly Oyston Estates Ltd)) v Fylde BC** [2021] 4 381, SC.

  Permission—
    Condition—Certiorari to quash. *See* **Certiorari** (Jurisdiction—Planning authority—Decision of authority—Permission for development—Grant of permission subject to conditions).

    Generally. *See* Permission for development, *below.*

    Permission for development subject to time limit and for particular purpose only—Registration as local land charge. *See* **Land charge** (Local land charge—Registration—Town planning).

    Refusal of permission—Compensation—Northern Ireland. *See* **Northern Ireland** (Town and country planning—Compensation—Refusal of permission to develop).

  Permitted development—
    Development by mineral undertakers—Erection alteration or extension of building plant or machinery—Development on land in or adjacent to and belonging to a quarry or mine—Mine—Site on which mining operations are carried out—Mining operations—Winning and working of minerals—Adjacent—Belonging to—Meaning—Plaintiffs engaged in production of china clay—Crude slurry extracted from ground and partly treated on site—Slurry conveyed by pipeline to second site two miles distant—Process of drying clay completed on second site—Whether second site part of larger site on which 'mining operations are carried on'—Whether second site 'land in or adjacent to and belonging to a mine'—Town and Country Planning General Development Order 1963 (SI 1963 No 709), arts 2, 3, Sch 1, class XVIII, para 2. **English Clays Lovering Pochin & Co Ltd v Plymouth Corp** [1974] 2 239, CA.

    Development by telecommunications code system operators—Erection of mobile phone mast—Claimant objecting—Local planning authority resolving to refuse prior approval—Local planning authority failing to notify operator within time limit—Local planning authority serving enforcement notices—Operator appealing against notices—Inspector not dealing with claimant's objections on appeal—Whether claimant's convention rights infringed— Whether claimant having remedy—Town and Country Planning Act 1990, s 174(2)(a), (c)—Human Rights Act 1998, s 3, Sch 1, Pt 1, art 6—Town and Country Planning (General Permitted Development) Order 1995, SI 1995/418, Sch 2, Pt 24, art 3(1), Classes A(1)(a), A2(4) and A3(3), (5), (6) and (7). **R (on the application of Nunn) v First Secretary of State (Leeds City Council and anor, interested parties)** [2005] 2 987, CA.

Development for industrial purposes—Land used for carrying out industrial process otherwise than in contravention of planning control or without planning permission—Use in contravention of planning control and without permission at its inception but no longer liable to enforcement action by reason of lapse of time—Whether land used 'otherwise than (i) in contravention of previous planning control or (ii) without planning permission'—Whether owner of land entitled to carry out development constituting permitted development for industrial purposes—Town and Country Planning General Development Order 1973 (SI 1973 No 31), art 3(1), Sch 1, class VIII. **Brooks and Burton Ltd v Secretary of State for the Environment** [1978] **1** 733, CA.

Direction restricting permitted development—Approval of Secretary of State—Direction relating only to development in any particular area of any of specified classes not requiring Secretary of State's approval—Planning authority making direction restricting particular development—Whether a direction relating to 'development in [a] particular area'—Whether approval of Secretary of State required—Town and Country Planning General Development Order 1977 (SI 1977 No 289), art 4(3)(b). **Thanet DC v Ninedrive Ltd** [1978] **1** 703, Ch D.

Resumption of normal use—

Disused golf course—Land used for agricultural purposes since 1946—Whether land could be regarded as still temporarily so used and whether use as a golf course could still be regarded as the normal use—Whether planning permission required—Town and Country Planning Act 1962, s 13(2). **Kingdon v Minister of Housing and Local Government** [1967] **3** 614, QBD.

Unauthorised—

Enforcement of planning control. See Enforcement of planning control, below.

Use classes—

Building—Reference to building including land occupied therewith and used for same purpose—Use as general industrial building for any purpose—Test for determining whether land used as 'industrial building'—Land occupied with building and used for same purpose—Unnecessary to show that process carried out on land dependent on building or that land ancillary to building—Sufficient to show that land used for same purpose as building—Town and Country Planning (Use Classes) Order 1972 (SI 1972 No 1385), art 2(3), Sch, class IV. **Brooks and Burton Ltd v Secretary of State for the Environment** [1978] **1** 733, CA.

Industrial building—Basement used in connection with business of horticulture carried on in shop opposite—In summer basement used for storing plants and bulbs and for sorting and grading bulbs for display in the shop and in winter for making and repairing boxes and trays which were used for displaying goods in the shop—In 1955 use of basement changed to that of printers' engineers' workshop which was user as a light industrial building—Whether material change in user—Whether on appointed day basement used as 'industrial building', 'shop' or 'repository'—Town and Country Planning (Use Classes) Order 1950 (SI 1950 No 1131), art 2(2), Sch, classes I, III, X. **Horwitz v Rowson** [1960] **2** 881, QBD.

Industrial building—Light industrial building—Building previously used by local authority as a cooking centre for provision of school meals—Subsequent uses for purpose of making shirts—Whether use by local authority was for the purpose of a 'trade or business' within definition of 'industrial building'—Town and Country Planning (Use Classes) Order 1950 (SI 1950 No 1131)—Town and Country Planning (Use Classes) Order 1963 (SI 1963 No 708), arts 2(2), 3(1), Sch, class III. **Rael-Brook Ltd v Minister of Housing and Local Government** [1967] **1** 262, QBD.

Repository—Use of building to store civil defence vehicles and synthetic rubber—Whether used as a 'repository'—Town and Country Planning (Use Classes) Order 1972 (SI 1972 No 1385), Sch, Class X. **Newbury DC v Secretary of State for the Environment** [1980] **1** 731, HL.

Students' hostel—Subsequent use as residential hotel—Whether change of use requiring planning permission—Town and Country Planning (Use Classes) Order 1963 (SI 1963 No 708), art 3(1), Sch, class XI. **Mornford Investments Ltd v Minister of Housing and Local Government** [1970] **2** 253, QBD.

Unit for consideration in applying Use Classes Order—Whole of area used for particular purpose, including uses ancillary thereto, to be considered as single unit—Town and Country Planning (Use Classes) Order 1963 (SI 1963 No 708)—Town and Country Planning Act 1962, s 12(2)(f). **Trentham (G Percy) Ltd v Gloucestershire CC** [1966] **1** 701, CA.

Warehouse—Use as a wholesale warehouse or repository for any purpose—Meaning of wholesale warehouse—Meaning a question of fact—Open to Secretary of State to conclude that warehouse a building used primarily for storage—Cash and carry establishment used primarily for sale of goods not a warehouse—Town and Country Planning (Use Classes) Order 1972 (SI 1972 No 1385), Sch, Class X. **LTSS Print and Supply Services Ltd v Hackney London Borough** [1976] **1** 311, CA.

Validity of enforcement notice—

Development before 1st July 1948. See Enforcement notice—Validity—Development prior to 1st July 1948, below.

Value. See Development value, below.

Development charge—

Determination—

Land subject to development viewed as a whole—Estate acquired for building purposes—Heavy expenditure to make part of land suitable—Expenditure exceeding value of whole land for building purposes—Whether development charge exigible—Town and Country Planning Act 1947, s 70(2). **London CC v Central Land Board** [1958] **3** 676, CA.

Development consent—

Environmental impact assessment—

Agriculture and aquaculture. See Development—Development consent—Environmental impact assessment, above.

European Union. See **European Union** (Environment—Protection—Assessment of effects of certain plans and programmes on the environment).

  Development consent (cont)—
    Environmental impact assessment (cont)—
      Old mining permission—Local mineral authority determining conditions for continuation of operations under old mining permission without carrying out environmental impact assessment—Whether mineral authority required to carry out environmental impact assessment before determining conditions for continuation of operations under old mining permission—Planning and Compensation Act 1991, s 22, Sch 2—Council Directive (EEC) 85/337, arts 1.2, 2.1. **R v North Yorkshire CC, ex p Brown** [1999] **1** 969, HL.

      Permission for development—Outline permission—Reserved matters—Regulations providing for environmental impact assessment on grant of planning permission—Whether regulations correctly transposing Community law—Whether grant of outline permission and approval of reserved matters multi-stage development consent—Town and Country Planning (Assessment of Environmental Effects) Regulations 1988, SI 1988/1199, reg 4(2)—Council Directive (EEC) 85/337, arts 2(1), 4(2). **R (on the application of Barker) v Bromley London BC** [2007] **1** 1183, HL.

      Permission for development—Permission granted by local planning authority without amendment to development scheme against recommendations of planning officers—Whether authority having duty to give reasons—Appropriate remedy for breach—Town and Country Planning (Environmental Impact Assessment) Regulations 2011, SI 2011/1824, regs 3(4), 24(1)(c). **R (on the application of CPRE Kent) v Dover DC** [2018] **2** 121, SC.

      Permission for development—Planning permission for development already carried out—Whether development requiring environmental impact assessment capable of being given retrospective planning permission—Town and Country Planning Act 1990, s 73A—Town and Country Planning (Environmental Impact Assessment) (England and Wales) Regulations 1999, SI 1999/293—Council Directive (EEC) 85/337, art 2(3). **R (on the application of Ardagh Glass Ltd) v Chester City Council** [2011] **1** 476, CA.

      Permission for development—Screening—Correct approach towards timing of screening for need for environmental impact assessment and appropriate assessment in planning applications—Whether or extent to which 'mitigation measures' may be taken into account in environmental impact assessment screening—Whether discretion to refuse quashing of permission could and should be exercised if local authority's decision found to be unlawful—Town and Country Planning (Environmental Impact Assessment) Regulations 2011, SI 2011/1824—Conservation of Habitats and Species Regulations 2010, SI 2010/490. **R (on the application of Champion) v North Norfolk DC** [2015] **4** 169, SC.

  Development plan—
    Schools—
      Revision of development plan. *See* **Education** (Development plan—Revision—Alteration of development plan by introduction of scheme for converting existing secondary schools into comprehensive schools).

  Development value—
    Determination—
      Appeal to Lands Tribunal—Evidence—Admissibility—Values agreed in cases of comparable land—Town and Country Planning Act 1947, s 60(1)—Lands Tribunal Act 1949, s 1(3)(d). **Stockbridge Mill Co Ltd v Central Land Board** [1954] **2** 360, CA.

      Land requisitioned at relevant date—Whether requisition an incident relevant to calculation of value—Town and Country Planning Act 1947, ss 61(5), 89(1). **Routh Trustees v Central Land Board** [1960] **2** 436, CA.

    Site of former public house—
      Public house selling alcoholic and non-alcoholic drinks and light refreshments—Right to use as shop—Town and Country Planning Act 1947, s 61(2)—Town and Country Planning (Use Classes for Third Schedule Purposes) Order 1948 (SI 1948 No 955), Sch, para 2(2)—Town and Country Planning (Use Classes) Order 1948 (SI 1948 No 954), Sch, para 2(2). **Central Land Board v Saxone Shoe Co Ltd** [1955] **3** 415, CA.

    Unexpended balance of established development value—
      Interest—Whether additional one-seventh to be regarded as interest—Town and Country Planning Act 1954, s 17(2). **Hasluck (decd), Re** [1957] **3** 371, Ch D.

  Discontinuance order—
    Compensation—
      Factors to be taken into consideration—Offer by district valuer on behalf of compensating authority in course of negotiations—Offer originally made 'without prejudice' but 'without prejudice' lifted during hearing—Risks affecting purchaser's mind, in particular, his doubts as to the extent of existing user rights. **Blow v Norfolk CC** [1966] **3** 579, CA.

    Use of land—
      Jurisdiction to make order—Operations carried out on land—Exclusion of operations carried out on land from definition of use of land—Discontinuance order made in respect of use of land for storing and sorting scrap material—Whether storing and sorting of scrap material a 'use' of land or an 'operation' on it—Town and Country Planning Act 1971, ss 51(1)(a), 290. **Parkes v Secretary of State for the Environment** [1979] **1** 211, CA.

  District plan—
    Planning purpose—
      Character and vitality of area—Special uses adding to character and vitality—Plan incorporating planning authority's policy to protect and maintain industrial activities which added to character and vitality of area—Whether policy concerned with protection of individual users rather than development and use of land—Whether authority's policy a genuine planning purpose—Whether personal circumstances of occupiers, personal hardship etc required to be considered as specific exceptions to general policy. **Great Portland Estates plc v Westminster City Council** [1984] **3** 744, HL.

TOWN AND COUNTRY PLANNING (cont)—
District plan (cont)—
Planning purpose (cont)—
Office development—Plan incorporating authority's policy of prohibiting office development outside central zone except in special or exceptional cases—Criteria for special or exceptional circumstances to be outlined in non-statutory guidelines and not in plan—Public inquiry held into objection to policy and inspector making recommendations—Council not accepting recommendations—Whether planning authority's reasons for rejecting recommendations adequate and proper—Whether planning authority's omission of proposals from plan and inclusion of criteria in guidelines contrary to statutory duty to formulate its proposals in plan—Town and Country Planning Act 1971, Sch 4, para 11(2)—Town and Country (Local Plans for Greater London) Regulations 1974, reg 17(1). **Great Portland Estates plc v Westminster City Council** [1984] 3 744, HL.
Duration of planning permission—
Beginning of development before expiry date—
Specified operation comprised in the development—Construction of soakaway and trench for proposed house—Soakaway and trench not in accordance with approved plan—Whether construction of soakaway and trench colourable operation or to be regarded as relating to the implementation of the approved plan—Whether a 'specified operation'—Town and Country Planning Act 1971, s 43(1), (2)(c). **Spackman v Secretary of State for the Environment** [1977] **1** 257, QBD.
Specified operation comprised in the development—Operation in the course of constructing a road—Road—Private drive—Construction of short section of drive giving access from public road to proposed house—Whether private access drive a 'road'—Town and Country Planning Act 1971, s 43(1), (2)(d). **Spackman v Secretary of State for the Environment** [1977] **1** 257, QBD.
Extent of duration—
Whether permission can be abandoned—Whether permission can be extinguished merely by conduct—Whether commercial decision to terminate permitted operations on land extinguishing permission in absence of term in permission to that effect—Town and Country Planning Act 1971, s 33(1). **Pioneer Aggregates (UK) Ltd v Secretary of State for the Environment** [1984] 2 358, HL.
Electricity—
Overhead lines. *See* **Electricity** (Overhead lines—Consent required for overhead lines).
Enforcement notice—
Amendment—
District council serving enforcement notice requiring appellant to cease using site for car parking—Appellant unsuccessfully challenging enforcement notice—County council serving enforcement notice requiring appellant to cease using site for dumping—Inspector adding car parking use to county council's enforcement notice but failing to specify any steps to remedy such use—Whether amendment had effect of granting planning permission in respect of car parking use—Town and Country Planning Act 1990, ss 173(11), 176(1). **Tandridge DC v Verrechia** [1999] **3** 247, CA.
Misrecital. **James v Secretary of State for Wales** [1965] 3 602, CA.
Appeal against notice—
Caravan site—Amendment of grounds of appeal to Minister—Whether proper for new ground of appeal not stated in original notice of appeal to be considered by Minister—Caravan Sites and Control of Development Act 1960, s 33(1)(a), (b), (g), (4). **Chelmsford RDC v Powell** [1963] **1** 150, QBD.
Caravan site—Increase of caravans from eight to twenty-seven—'Development'—Whether decision of justices that there had been no development was a decision of fact—Town and Country Planning Act 1947, ss 12(2), 23(4). **Guildford RDC v Penny** [1959] **2** 111, CA.
Description of development—Sufficiency of description—Grounds on which court can quash notice—Town and Country Planning Act 1947, s 23(4). **Keats v London CC** [1954] 3 303, QBD.
Estoppel—Previous statement by officer of local planning authority that land had existing user right and that planning permission for this use was not needed—Purchase of land on faith of this statement—Notice requiring cesser of use—Town and Country Planning Act 1947, s 23(1). **Southend-on-Sea Corp v Hodgson (Wickford) Ltd** [1961] 2 46, QBD.
Grounds—Ground not raised in notice of appeal—Planning permission for twenty-eight days under general development order—Whether ground open to appellant before Minister or on appeal to Supreme Court—Caravan Sites and Control of Development Act 1960, s 33(1)(b)—Town and Country Planning General Development Order 1950 (SI 1950 No 728), art 3(1), Sch 1, Class IV, para 2. **Miller-Mead v Minister of Housing and Local Government** [1963] **1** 459, CA.
Grounds—Local authority agreeing not to enforce notice for three years if plaintiff not appealing against notice—Plaintiff agreeing on advice of local authority—Time for appeal elapsing—Plaintiff bringing action for damages for negligent advice of local authority in respect to plaintiff's right under notice—Local authority seeking to strike out claim on ground that claim for damages involving challenge to validity of enforcement notice and accordingly statute barred—Whether enforcement notice could be challenged on grounds not specified in statute—Town and Country Planning Act 1971, ss 88, 243. **Davy v Spelthorne BC** [1983] 3 278, HL.
Inquiry by inspector appointed by minister—Whether Minister in deciding appeal bound by inspector's report—Caravan Sites and Control of Development Act 1960, s 33(1). **Nelsovil Ltd v Minister of Housing and Local Government** [1962] **1** 423, QBD.
Issue estoppel. *See* **Appeal**—Issue estoppel—Appeal against planning decision—Appeal against enforcement notice, *above*.
Jurisdiction of justices to determine whether or not matters referred to in notice constituted development—Town and Country Planning Act 1947, s 17(2), proviso, s 23(4). **Eastbourne Corp v Fortes Ice Cream Parlour (1955) Ltd** [1959] 2 102, CA.
Leave—Procedure—Notice of application to be in writing—Supporting documents—Proposed respondent entitled to submit written response—Time for application—Town and Country Planning Act 1990, s 289(6)—Planning (Listed Buildings and Conservation Areas) Act 1990, s 65(5)—Planning and Compensation Act 1991, s 6(5), Sch 3, para 8(3)—RSC Ord 55. **Practice Note** [1992] **1** 448, QBD.

TOWN AND COUNTRY PLANNING (cont)—
Enforcement notice (cont)—
Appeal against notice (cont)—

Notice founded on breach of condition of grant of planning permission—Whether appellant could maintain that there had been no development and that no permission had been necessary—Development more than four years before notice—Town and Country Planning Act 1947, s 23(1), (4). **Mounsdon v Weymouth & Melcombe Regis Corp** [1960] **1** 538, QBD.

Notice of appeal to Minister—Notice in writing—Notice specifying grounds of appeal and facts on which based—Notice of appeal failing to comply with requirement to specify grounds and facts—Further notice complying with requirement served after expiry of time limited for appeal—Whether requirement to specify grounds and facts imperative—Whether first notice of appeal valid—Town and Country Planning Act 1968, s 16(1), (2). **Howard v Secretary of State for the Environment** [1974] **1** 644, CA.

Notice of no effect pending determination of appeal—Final determination of appeal—Whether appeal finally determined when Secretary of State makes decision—Whether appeal not finally determined until appeal on point of law disposed of—Town and Country Planning Act 1971, ss 88(10), 246. **R v Kuxhaus** [1988] **2** 705, CA.

Notice of no effect pending determination of appeal—Rejection of appeal by Secretary of State—Validity of rejection—Time limit for appeal against Secretary of State's decision expiring—Appellant prosecuted for failure to comply with enforcement notice—Appellant contending Secretary of State's rejection of appeal invalid and therefore effect of notice suspended—Whether appeal against enforcement notice finally determined—Town and Country Planning Act 1971, s 88(2), (3). **Button v Jenkins** [1975] **3** 585, QBD.

Person aggrieved—Whether local planning authority can be aggrieved—Town and Country Planning Act 1947, s 23(4), (5). **Ealing BC v Jones** [1959] **1** 286, QBD; **R v Dorset Sessions Appeal Committee, ex p Weymouth Corp** [1960] **2** 410, QBD.

Remission of matter for rehearing—Whether Secretary of State obliged to consider whole notice appeal de novo—Town and Country Planning Act 1990, ss 174, 289. **R (on the application of Perrett) v Secretary of State for Communities and Local Government** [2010] **2** 578, CA.

Renewal of previous use of land after 1st July 1948—Whether appeal should be allowed on the ground that there was no development of land—Town and Country Planning Act 1947, s 23(4). **Fyson v Buckinghamshire CC** [1958] **2** 286, QBD.

Variation—No existing use as to all caravans alleged in enforcement notice—Existing use for storage caravans, but not for residential caravans—Power of Minister to vary terms by restricting notice to residential caravans—Town and Country Planning Act 1947, s 23(1), (2)—Caravan Sites and Control of Development Act 1960, s 33(5), (6). **Miller-Mead v Minister of Housing and Local Government** [1963] **1** 459, CA.

Appeal from Minister to High Court—

Breach of condition of planning permission—Reasons for imposition of condition not stated in written notice of permission—Whether condition null—Whether enforcement notice null—Town and Country Planning General Development Order 1950 (SI 1950 No 728), art 5(9)(a)—Town and Country Planning Act 1947, s 23(1). **Brayhead (Ascot) Ltd v Berkshire CC** [1964] **1** 149, QBD.

Burden of proof of grounds of appeal to Minister—Exercise of discretion by Minister not a ground of appeal in point of law—Caravan Sites and Control of Development Act 1960, s 33(1)(a), (c), (g). **Nelsovil Ltd v Minister of Housing and Local Government** [1962] **1** 423, QBD.

Caravan site—Intensification of use—Reference back to Minister to determine whether material change of use. **James v Secretary of State for Wales** [1966] **3** 964, HL.

Evidence—Further evidence—To what extent fresh evidence may be adduced—Whether new rules of court permit rehearing of case on primary facts—Town and Country Planning Act 1962, s 180(1), (4)—RSC (Rev) Ord 55, rr 1(4), 7(2). **Green v Minister of Housing and Local Government** [1966] **3** 942, QBD.

Materiality of change of use—Question of fact and degree—Court will not interfere with Minister's decision, if no error in law, unless perverse in the sense of being unsupported by any evidence—Free standing egg vending machine at petrol filling station—Whether change of use of part of premises amounted to material change of use of whole premises—Caravan Sites and Control of Development Act 1960, s 34(1). **Bendles Motors Ltd v Bristol Corp** [1963] **1** 578, QBD.

Procedure—Alternative procedures laid down by statute 'according as' rules of court may provide—Rules of court providing for appeal by one alternative only—Whether appellant has right of election to pursue other alternative procedure—Appeal only as prescribed by rules of court—Caravan Sites and Control of Development Act 1960, s 34—RSC Ord 59A, r 6. **Hoser v Ministry of Housing and Local Government** [1962] **3** 945, Ch D.

Contents of notice—

Specification of matters alleged to constitute breach of planning control—Necessity for making clear whether development without permission or failure to comply with condition subject to which permission granted—Unnecessary to use actual words of Act—Notice alleging that recipient 'contravening the provisions of' the Planning Acts—Notice referring to specific section of Act—Notice requiring recipient to restore land to condition before 'unauthorised development' took place—Whether notice making it sufficiently clear that development without grant of planning permission alleged to have taken place—Town and Country Planning Act 1968, s 15(2), (5). **Eldon Garages Ltd v Kingston-upon-Hull County BC** [1974] **1** 358, Ch D.

Specification of steps required to remedy breach of planning control—Steps for restoring land to its condition before development took place—Breach of planning control—Discretion of planning authority to decide on steps required to remedy breach—Owner of site demolishing existing buildings and erecting new buildings without planning permission—Notice requiring demolition of new buildings only—Whether necessary for notice to require re-erection of previously existing buildings—Town and Country Planning Act 1968, s 15(5)(b). **Iddenden v Secretary of State for the Environment** [1972] **3** 883, CA.

Contravention—

Information—Information alleging contravention 'on and since' certain date—Whether a continuing offence—Whether information bad for duplicity—Town and Country Planning Act 1971, s 89(5). **Chiltern DC v Hodgetts** [1983] **1** 1057, HL.

TOWN AND COUNTRY PLANNING (cont)—
  Enforcement notice (cont)—
    Contravention (cont)—
      Information—Third offence—Fine imposed computed at £3 daily for a period extending more than
        six months before the date of the information—Town and Country Planning Act 1947,
        s 24(3)—Magistrates' Courts Act 1952, s 104. **R v Chertsey Justices, ex p Franks** [1961] **1** 825,
        QBD.
      Use of land in contravention of enforcement notice—Whether absolute offence or whether proof of
        knowledge of enforcement notice required—Town and Country Planning Act 1990, ss 179(6),
        285(2). **R v Collett** [1994] **2** 372, CA.
  Correction of informality, defect or error—
    Development of a type different from that alleged in the notice—Matter not raised at
      inquiry—Minister's discretion properly exercised by refusing to amend notice—Caravan Sites and
      Control of Development Act 1960, s 33(5). **Birmingham Corp v Minister of Housing and Local
      Government and Habib Ullah** [1963] **3** 668, QBD.
  Delay—
    Use of machinery of Town and Country Planning Act for purpose of delay—Injunction—Town and
      Country Planning Act 1947, s 12. **A-G (ex rel Egham UDC) v Smith** [1958] **2** 557, QBD.
  Effect—
    Reversion to earlier lawful use—Purpose for which land may be used without planning
      permission—Purpose for which land could lawfully have been used if development enforced
      against had not been carried out—Established use—Use unlawful at its inception but no longer
      liable to enforcement action by reason of lapse of time—Whether permission required for a
      resumption of that use after service of enforcement notice—Town and Country Planning Act 1971,
      s 23(9). **LTSS Print and Supply Services Ltd v Hackney London Borough** [1976] **1** 311, CA.
    Reversion to earlier lawful use—Purpose for which land may be used without planning
      permission—Purpose for which land could lawfully have been used if development enforced
      against had not been carried out—Use immediately preceding that enforced against
      unlawful—Whether person on whom enforcement notice served can follow planning history back
      to earlier lawful uses in order to revert to use which land lawfully used—Whether person on
      whom enforcement notice served only able to revert to use immediately preceding that enforced
      against provided that use was lawful—Town and Country Planning Act 1971, s 23(9). **Young v
      Secretary of State for the Environment** [1983] **2** 1105, HL.
  Entry consequent on steps required by notice not being taken—
    Power of local planning authority to enter land and take those steps—Whether authority entitled to
      enter for purpose of taking some only of the steps required by the notice—Town and Country
      Planning Act 1947, s 24(1)—Town and Country Planning Act 1962, s 48. **Arcam Demolition and
      Construction Co Ltd v Worcestershire CC** [1964] **2** 286, Ch D.
  Invalid notice—
    Application by occupier for continuance of user—Appeal to Minister—Estoppel from denying
      invalidity—Town and Country Planning Act 1947, ss 16(1), 23(1). **Swallow & Pearson (a firm) v
      Middlesex CC** [1953] **1** 580, QBD.
  Material change of use—
    Intensity of use amounting to a change of use—Notice restricting use to intensity before specified
      date—Separate notices—Notices relating to different areas of same site—Effect of notices unduly
      restrictive—Authority only permitted to restrict intensity of use in relation to site as a whole. **De
      Mulder v Secretary of State for the Environment** [1974] **1** 776, QBD.
  No appeal against notice—
    Subsequent summons for contravention—Matter not raised by appeal cannot be raised as defence
      to prosecution—Town and Country Planning Act 1947, ss 23(4), 24(1), (3). **Norris v Edmonton
      Corp** [1957] **2** 801, QBD.
    Subsequent summons for contravention—No power to question validity of notice—Town and
      Country Planning Act 1947, s 24(3). **Perrins v Perrins** [1951] **1** 1075, KBD.
  Notice founded on breach of condition of grant of planning permission—
    Comprehensive condition applying to land other than that to which permission truly related—Land
      used by railway company for emergency coal stacking ground and by coal merchants as coal
      depot—User of land as transit depot for handling and storage of crated motor vehicles carried by
      rail—Whether 'development'—Development permitted by General Development Orders—
      Permission not needed—Town and Country Planning Act 1932, s 53—Town and Country Planning
      Act 1947, s 12(2)—Town and Country Planning General Development Order 1948 (SI 1948
      No 958), art 3(1), Sch 1, class XVIII A—Town and Country Planning General Development Order
      1950 (SI 1950 No 728), art 3(1), Sch 1, class XVIII A. **East Barnet UDC v British Transport
      Commission** [1961] **3** 878, QBD.
  Persistent breach of notice—
    Convictions resulting in imprisonment in default of payment of fines—Injunction sought by
      Attorney General to restrain breach—Jurisdiction—Town and Country Planning Act 1947, s 24(3).
      A-G (ex rel Hornchurch UDC) v Bastow [1957] **1** 497, QBD.
  Reversion to earlier lawful use—
    Purpose for which land may be used without planning permission—Purpose for which land could
      lawfully have been used if development enforced against had not been carried out—Established
      use—Use unlawful at its inception but no longer liable to enforcement action by reason of lapse
      of time—Whether permission required for that use after service of enforcement notice—Town
      and Country Planning Act 1971, s 23(9). **LTSS Print and Supply Services Ltd v Hackney London
      Borough** [1975] **1** 374, QBD.
    Purpose for which land may be used without planning permission—Purpose for which land could
      lawfully have been used if development enforced against had not been carried out—Lawful
      use—Meaning—Previous use established without planning permission—Whether a 'lawful'
      use—Whether permission required to revert to that use—Town and Country Planning Act 1971,
      s 23(9). **Lamb (WT) & Sons Ltd v Secretary of State for the Environment** [1975] **2** 1117, QBD.

Enforcement notice (cont)—
Service—
Owner of land—Notice served on husband of freeholder—Land used for parking cars—Business of parking cars carried on by husband and wife jointly—Control of business in hands of husband—Husband described himself as owner when applying for planning permission—Whether service on husband sufficient—Whether enforcement notice enforceable—Town and Country Planning Act 1962, ss 45(3), 47(5), 221. **Courtney-Southan v Crawley UDC** [1967] 2 246, QBD.

Period for service—Four-year period—Seasonal use—Two different uses annually—Whether material change of use in each year from one to the other—Whether land normally used for one purpose also used on occasions for another—Town and Country Planning Act 1962, ss 13(3), 45(2). **Webber v Minister of Housing and Local Government** [1967] 3 981, CA.

Period for service—Mining operations—Development—Four year period from carrying out of development—Initial working of area more than four years previously—Whether subsequent working of area within four year period new development or continuation of original development—Whether power to serve enforcement notice in relation to excavations being carried out within area of initial cut—Town and Country Planning Act 1962, ss 12(1), 45(2). **David (Thomas) (Porthcawl) Ltd v Penybont RDC** [1972] 3 1092, CA.

Posting by prepaid registered post addressed to owner of caravan site—Certificate of delivery produced purporting to be signed by owner—Denial of receipt by owner not challenged in cross-examination—Whether service proved—Interpretation Act 1889, s 26—Town and Country Planning Act 1962, s 214(1)(c). **Moody v Godstone RDC** [1966] 2 696, QBD.

Time limit—
Building operations—Substantial completion—Date on which operations substantially completed—Town and Country Planning Act 1990, s 171B(1). **Sage v Secretary of State for the Environment, Transport and the Regions** [2003] 2 689, HL.

Validity—
Application by originating summons for declaration that notice invalid—Town and Country Planning Act 1947, s 23—RSC Ord 54A, rr 1, 1A. **Rigden v Whitstable UDC** [1958] 2 730, Ch D.

Breach of condition of planning permission—Permission as to use for limited period—Planning permission for use of field as site for travelling circus for period in 1952 subject to discontinuance at end of period—Use without planning permission for periods in subsequent years—Whether use discontinued in 1952—Whether use in subsequent years breach of condition of earlier planning permission—Town and Country Planning Act 1947, s 23(4)(a). **Postill v East Riding CC** [1956] 2 685, QBD.

Challenge to validity—Criminal proceedings for failure to comply with enforcement notice—Whether defendant entitled to challenge validity of notice in criminal proceedings—Town and Country Planning Act 1990, s 179(1). **R v Wicks** [1997] 2 801, HL.

Challenge to validity—Judicial review—Enforcement notice not served on claimant in time causing claimant to issue appeal out of time—Claimant challenging validity of notices in judicial review proceedings on ground that notices not served in compliance with statutory requirements—Whether validity of enforcement notices could only be challenged on ground of late service by way of statutory appeal—Whether breach of Convention rights—Whether enforcement notices should be quashed—Town and Country Planning Act 1990, ss 172, 174, 285—Human Rights Act 1998, Sch 1, Pt I, art 6. **R (on the application of Stern) v Horsham DC** [2013] 3 798, QBD.

Declaration—Whether proceedings barred by prior criminal proceedings. *See* **Declaration** (Jurisdiction—Discretion—Issue open in criminal proceedings where plaintiff convicted—Caravan site—Owner of site previously convicted for non-compliance with enforcement notice).

Development prior to 1st July 1948—No appeal to Minister—Bar to challenging validity of notice in other proceedings—Town and Country Planning Act 1947, s 23(1)—Caravan Sites and Control of Development Act 1960, s 33(1)(c), (8). **Findlow v Lewis** [1962] 3 7, QBD.

Development prior to 1st July 1948—Town and Country Planning Act 1947, ss 23(1), (2), (4), 75(1). **East Riding CC v Park Estate (Bridlington) Ltd** [1956] 2 669, HL.

Development prior to 1st July 1948—Town and Country Planning Act 1947, ss 23(1), 75(1). **Lincoln CC (Parts of Lindsey) v Henshall** [1953] 1 1143, QBD.

Erroneous recital—Development alleged to have been carried out without planning permission—Permission for twenty-eight days under general order—Caravan Sites and Control of Development Act 1960, s 33(6)—Town and Country Planning General Development Order 1950 (SI 1950 No 728), art 3(1), Sch 1, class IV. **Miller-Mead v Minister of Housing and Local Government** [1963] 1 459, CA.

Heritage asset—Inspector appointed by Secretary of State quashing rebuilding order over unlisted buildings in conservation area on basis demolition doing more good than harm—Council challenging inspector's decision—Whether inspector permitted to have regard to non-specific, but likely, future development proposals which, if implemented, would deliver public benefit that could outweigh harm to significance of designated heritage asset—National Planning Policy Framework, paras 193, 196. **Tower Hamlets London BC v Secretary of State for Housing, Communities and Local Government** [2020] 2 909, QBD.

Mining operations—Planning unit in relation to development—Area specified in enforcement notice—Actual working having occurred only within two smaller areas within area specified—Validity of notice in relation to larger area—Power of planning authority to determine that larger area planning unit for purposes of development in question—Town and Country Planning Act 1962, s 45(1). **David (Thomas) (Porthcawl) Ltd v Penybont RDC** [1972] 3 1092, CA.

Need to specify both date on which notice takes effect and period within which it must be complied with—Town and Country Planning Act 1947, s 23(2), (3). **Burgess v Jarvis** [1952] 1 592, CA; **Godstone RDC v Brazil** [1953] 2 763, QBD.

Need to specify date on which notice takes effect—Notice invalid—No appeal to justices against notice—Right to question validity on subsequent summons for contravention—Town and Country Planning Act 1947, ss 23(3), (4), 24(1), (3). **Mead v Plumtree** [1952] 2 723, QBD.

Notice served at time when appeal to the Minister against condition in planning permission pending—Whether invalid—Town and Country Planning Act 1947, s 23. **Davis v Miller** [1956] 3 109, QBD Divl Ct.

TOWN AND COUNTRY PLANNING (cont)—
  Enforcement notice (cont)—
    Validity (cont)—
      Owner and occupier—Occupier—Licensee as occupier—Owner of caravan site—Caravan dweller
        residing in caravan as permanent home—Weekly payments by caravan dweller to site owner for
        use of pitch—Caravan dweller licensee of pitch—Copies of notice served on site owner and
        caravan dweller on different dates—Whether caravan dweller occupier of part of site—Town and
        Country Planning Act 1962, s 45(3)(a). **Stevens v Bromley London Borough** [1972] **1** 712, CA.
      Owner and occupier—Occupier—Tenant of caravan site permitting companies in which he had
        interest to occupy parts of site for displaying and parking caravans and trailers—Site not sub-let
        to companies—One company making money payment to tenant—Enforcement notice served on
        one company as occupier of site—Town and Country Planning Act 1947, s 23(1). **Caravans and
        Automobiles Ltd v Southall BC** [1963] **2** 533, QBD.
      Owner and occupier—Owner and occupier notices coming into effect at different dates—Notices
        served on owner and occupiers, being different persons, on different dates—Each notice to come
        into effect twenty-eight days after service—Appeal by occupiers to Minister—Consequently
        notices could not take effect until final determination of appeal, and would then take effect at the
        same time—Whether notices valid—Town and Country Planning Act 1962, ss 45(3)(a), 46(1), (3),
        (4). **Bambury v Hounslow London Borough** [1966] **2** 532, QBD.
      Proceedings questioning validity of notice—Restriction on proceedings other than by statutory
        right of appeal—Proceedings begun before service of enforcement notice—Proceedings begun in
        anticipation of service of enforcement notice in order to challenge its validity when
        served—Originating summons seeking declaration that proposed use of premises within existing
        planning permission—Service of enforcement notice imminent—Summons taken out to
        challenge validity of notice when served—Whether proceedings begun before service of notice
        proceedings questioning validity of notice—Whether proceedings on originating summons
        should be stayed—Town and Country Planning Act 1971, s 243(1)(a). **Square Meals Frozen Foods
        Ltd v Dunstable BC** [1974] **1** 441, CA.
      Sufficient indication of the objection and of what was required to be done—Caravan site—Service
        of notice on caravan dwellers as occupiers as well as on owners of site—Town and Country
        Planning Act 1947, s 23(1)—Caravan Sites and Control of Development Act 1960, s 17(3)(b).
        Munnich v Godstone RDC [1966] **1** 930, CA.
      Wrong factual basis—Development alleged to have been carried out without planning
        permission—Permission for twenty-eight days under general order—Town and Country Planning
        Act 1947, s 23(1)—Town and Country Planning General Development Order 1950 (SI 1950
        No 728), art 3(1), Sch 1, class IV, para 2. **Cater v Essex CC** [1959] **2** 213, QBD.
      Wrong factual basis—Development alleged to have been carried out without planning
        permission—Permission originally granted for a limited period, since expired—No appeal to
        justices against notice—Right to question validity in High Court—Town and Country Planning Act
        1947, s 23(2), (4). **Francis v Yiewsley and West Drayton UDC** [1957] **3** 529, CA.
      Wrong factual basis—Misconception as to use to which land had been put—Notice alleging that
        land had been used as light industrial building—Land in fact used as general industrial
        building—Notice directed against intensification of use constituting material change of
        use—Notice making clear to recipient that it required reversion to former use—Whether notice
        valid. **Brooks and Burton Ltd v Secretary of State for the Environment** [1978] **1** 733, CA.
  Enforcement of planning control—
    Civil remedy—
      Trust operating faith centre on site of major strategic importance for housing and economic
        development—Trust granted temporary planning permission—Trust undertaking to submit
        planning application in accordance with criteria specified by local authority within period of
        temporary planning permission—Application submitted out of time and failing to meet
        criteria—Local authority being granted mandatory injunction—Whether court having discretion to
        refuse to grant injunction—Whether judge erring in failing to exercise discretion—Whether judge
        erring in refusing to suspend injunction pending outcome of appeal—Town and Country Planning
        Act 1990, s 106. **Newham London BC v Ali** [2015] **1** 63, CA.
      Unauthorised development—Caravan site—Development carried out without planning permission
        and in disregard of enforcement and stop notices—Dismissal of planning applications and
        criminal proceedings failing to secure compliance with notices—Defendants claiming no other
        site suitable for caravans—Whether planning authority entitled to injunction requiring use of
        caravan site to cease—Local Government Act 1972, s 222. **Waverley BC v Hilden** [1988] **1** 807,
        Ch D.
      Unauthorised development—Caravan site—Development carried out without planning permission
        and in disregard of enforcement notices and stop orders—Planning authority not instituting
        criminal proceedings but seeking injunction—Whether injunction should be granted in
        circumstances—Whether planning authority required to exhaust criminal remedies before
        applying for civil remedy—Local Government Act 1972, s 222. **Runnymede BC v Ball** [1986] **1** 629,
        CA.
    Enforcement notice. *See* Enforcement notice, *above.*
    Land subject to resolution to prepare planning scheme—
      Development carried out without permission before interim development order made—Town and
        Country Planning Act 1947, s 75(9). **Buckinghamshire CC v Callingham** [1952] **1** 1166, CA.
    Unauthorised development—
      Civil remedy. *See* Enforcement of planning control—Civil remedy—Unauthorised development,
        above.
      Deemed to comply with planning control until 31st December 1949, and no longer, by
        determination under Building Restrictions (War-Time Contraventions) Act 1946, s 2(8)—Power to
        enforce control thereafter—Town and Country Planning Act 1947, ss 75(2)(a), 76(5). **D'Alessio v
        Enfield UDC** [1951] **2** 754, KBD Divl Ct.
      Power of court to grant injunction restraining breach of planning control—Whether court required
        to exercise independent judgment on planning issues and hardship when considering whether to
        grant injunction—Guidance on exercise of power—Town and Country Planning Act 1990, s 187B.
        South Bucks DC v Porter [2002] **1** 425, CA; [2003] **3** 1, HL.

TOWN AND COUNTRY PLANNING (cont)—
Overhead lines—
Electricity. *See* **Electricity** (Overhead lines—Consent required for overhead lines).
Permission for development—
Agreement regulating development or use of land. *See* Agreement regulating development or use of land—Permission for development, *above.*
Alternative site—
Materiality of the availability of alternative sites to the consideration of the granting of planning permission—Application for planning permission to use land as airport—Reference of application to minister—Local inquiry—Inspector's report recommending permission be withheld on ground that alternative sites not fully investigated—Minister's letter granting planning permission but not showing whether he had considered question of alternative sites—On whom burden of showing the existence of suitable alternative sites rested—Whether Minister under any duty to seek out alternative sites—Town and Country Planning Act 1947, s 14(1). **Rhodes v Minister of Housing and Local Government** [1963] **1** 300, QBD.
Appeal to Minister against refusal of permission. *See* Appeal to Minister against refusal of permission for development, *above.*
Application for permission—
Advertisement of application—Proposed development representing departure from area development plan—Proposed departure not stated in advertisement—Effect of omission—Whether compliance with regulations concerning advertisements mandatory or directory—Town and Country Planning (Development Plans) (England) Direction 1981. **R v St Edmundsbury BC, ex p Investors in Industry Commercial Properties Ltd** [1985] **3** 234, QBD.
Certificate that applicant owner of fee simple or entitled to tenancy of land—
Error in certificate—Whether planning authority loses jurisdiction to deal with application if factual error in certificate—Town and Country Planning Act 1959, s 37(1)(a). **R v Bradford-on-Avon UDC, ex p Boulton** [1964] **2** 492, QBD.
Change of use—
Competing needs of existing use and proposed new use—Change of existing use—Test to be applied in deciding whether planning permission should be granted—Whether competing needs test applicable in determining application for planning permission—Town and Country Planning Act 1971, s 29(1). **London Residuary Body v Lambeth London BC** [1990] **2** 309, HL.
Condition attached to permission for change of use. *See* Change of use—Condition attached to permission for change of use, *above.*
Generally. *See* Development—Material change of use, *above.*
Compensation for modification. *See* Compensation—Modification of planning permission, *above.*
Condition—
Abrogation of existing use rights without compensation—Whether condition ultra vires—Town and Country Planning Act 1971, s 30(1). **Kingston-upon-Thames Royal London BC v Secretary of State for the Environment** [1974] **1** 193, QBD.
Application to develop land without compliance with conditions previously attached—Whether change of description of permitted development permitted—Town and Country Planning Act 1990, s 73. **Finney v Welsh Ministers** [2020] **1** 1034, CA.
Change of use—Condition attached to permission for change of use. *See* Change of use—Condition attached to permission for change of use, *above.*
Conditions as to land not included in application for permission—Validity—Town and Country Planning Act 1947, ss 14(2), 17(1). **Pyx Granite Co Ltd v Ministry of Housing and Local Government** [1959] **3** 1, HL.
Maximum floor area of new development—Developer required to retain listed buildings—Whether condition as to maximum floor area applying only to new buildings or including listed buildings. **Heron Corp Ltd v Manchester City Council** [1978] **3** 1240, CA.
Permission to build cottages on condition that occupants employed in agriculture etc—Validity—Town and Country Planning Act 1947, ss 14(1), 36. **Fawcett Properties Ltd v Buckingham CC** [1960] **3** 503, HL.
Planning obligation—Offered planning obligation not directly related to proposed development—Refusal of application accompanied by offered planning obligation—Validity of refusal—Developer offering to fund new link road if application for superstore granted—New road having only tenuous connection with proposed development—Secretary of State refusing application—Whether developer's offer of funding a material consideration—Whether Secretary of State's refusal valid—Town and Country Planning Act 1990, s 70(2). **Tesco Stores Ltd v Secretary of State for the Environment** [1995] **2** 636, HL.
Reasonableness—Ulterior purpose—Grant of permission for development of land as a supermarket—Condition attached that three independent retail units be provided—Whether condition fairly and reasonably relating to development—Whether condition within general ambit of permission sought. **R v St Edmundsbury BC, ex p Investors in Industry Commercial Properties Ltd** [1985] **3** 234, QBD.
Reasonableness—Ultra vires—Outline planning permission to lapse if detailed plans not submitted and approved within three years—Whether unreasonable or ultra vires—Whether severable—Town and Country Planning Act 1947, s 14(1). **Kent CC v Kingsway Investments (Kent) Ltd** [1970] **1** 70, HL.
Reasonableness—Ultra vires—Severability—Permission granted to private developer—Permission subject to conditions—Conditions requiring developer to make dwellings suitable for local authority tenants—Conditions requiring dwellings to be occupied by local authority tenants—Whether conditions ultra vires—Whether conditions severable. **R v Hillingdon London Borough, ex p Royco Homes Ltd** [1974] **2** 643, QBD.
Reasonableness—Ultra vires—Uncertainty—Severability—Permission granted subject to condition requiring developer to build road on his land and in effect to dedicate it as public highway without compensation—Validity of condition—Whether permission valid with condition struck out—Whether parts of condition severable—Town and Country Planning Act 1947, s 14(1), (2). **Hall & Co Ltd v Shoreham-by-Sea UDC** [1964] **1** 1, CA.

Permission for development (cont)—
Consent agreement under statute—
New Act coming into force—Whether consent agreement avoiding need to obtain planning permission—Town and Country Planning Act 1932, s 34(1)—Town and Country Planning Act 1947, s 12(1). **Thackray v Central Land Board** [1952] 1 1374, Ch D.
Construction—
Construction of permission with incorporated plan—Permission relating to land shown uncoloured on plan—Plan proposing development only of land shown coloured—Whether discrepancy between permission and plan reconcilable—Whether meaning of permission ascertainable. **Slough Estates Ltd v Slough BC (No 2)** [1970] 2 216, HL.
Incorporation of application etc by words of planning permission—Permission for erection of 'agricultural cottage'—Functional description—Purposes or design specified within s 18(3) and use limited accordingly—Town and Country Planning Act 1947, s 18(3). **Wilson v West Sussex CC** [1963] 1 751, CA.
Determination whether permission needed—
Application for determination—Implicit in application for planning permission—Letter of local planning authority that proposed erection of plant could be regarded as permitted development sufficient determination—Bye-law consent granted subsequently for larger plant—Warning against acting on bye-law consent before planning approval deleted from consent form—Whether deletion on bye-law consent amounted to determination that planning permission not required—Town and Country Planning Act 1962, s 43(1). **Wells v Minister of Housing and Local Government** [1967] 2 1041, CA.
Application refused by local planning authority and refusal confirmed by Minister—Further application approved and adopted by local planning committee—Whether Minister had jurisdiction to decide whether planning permission had been validly granted—Town and Country Planning Act 1947, s 17(1). **Edgwarebury Park Investments Ltd v Minister of Housing and Local Government** [1963] 1 124, QBD Divl Ct.
Development by local authority—
Development by local authority of land owned by it or in respect of which it is local planning authority—Application for permission—Procedure to be followed—Town and Country Planning Act 1971, ss 26, 270—Town and Country Planning General Regulations 1976, reg 4. **Steeples v Derbyshire CC** [1984] 3 468, QBD.
Duty to act fairly—Application to district council for planning permission for proposed development—Prior to application being considered majority group on council adopting policy of supporting proposed development—Whether council's decision on application pre-empted by policy—Whether council's decision would be vitiated by bias—Whether council should be prohibited from hearing application—Town and Country Planning Act 1971, s 29(2). **R v Amber Valley DC, ex p Jackson** [1984] 3 501, QBD.
Duty to act fairly—Local authority accepting developer's offer for development of authority's land—Local authority subsequently granting planning permission to developer—Local authority and developer then entering into binding agreement—Whether acceptance of developer's offer fettering local authority's discretion to grant or refuse planning permission—Whether local authority biased. **R v Sevenoaks DC, ex p Terry** [1985] 3 226, QBD.
Duty to act fairly—Local authority entering into contract with company for development of authority's land—Authority granting itself planning permission—Whether decision to grant planning permission could be seen to be fairly made—Whether decision made in breach of rules of natural justice. **Steeples v Derbyshire CC** [1984] 3 468, QBD.
Duty to act fairly—Test of whether local authority acting fairly—Local authority entering into contract with company for development of authority's land—Authority granting company planning permission—Whether decision to grant planning permission fairly made—Whether local authority's decision resulting from genuine and impartial exercise of discretion—Whether appearance or real likelihood of bias relevant. **R v St Edmundsbury BC, ex p Investors in Industry Commercial Properties Ltd** [1985] 3 234, QBD.
Duration of planning permission. See Duration of planning permission, *above.*
Electricity generating stations, construction of. See **Electricity** (Supply—Generating stations—Consent required for construction etc).
Environmental impact assessment development—
Statement required in decision to grant planning permission that environmental information taken into consideration—Whether statement of main reasons and considerations on which decision to grant planning permission based containing statement that environmental information taken into consideration—Town and Country Planning (Environmental Impact Assessment) (England and Wales) Regulations 1999, regs 3(2), 21(1). **R (on the application of Richardson) v North Yorkshire CC** [2004] 2 31, CA.
Interim development. See Interim development—Conditional permission, *above.*
Land unoccupied on appointed day—
Last use of land in contravention of local planning scheme—Whether permission required—Town and Country Planning Act 1947, s 12(5), proviso (i). **Glamorgan CC v Carter** [1962] 3 866, QBD.
Material consideration—
Cost of development—Whether cost of developing site a material consideration to be taken into account by planning authority when considering application for permission—Town and Country Planning Act 1971, s 29(1). **Murphy (J) & Sons Ltd v Secretary of State for the Environment** [1973] 2 26, QBD.
Council granting permission for change of use of land to erect wind turbine—Council taking into account community fund donation—Whether donation material consideration—Whether lawful—Town and Country Planning Act 1990, s 70(2)—Planning and Compulsory Purchase Act 2004, s 38(6). **R (on the application of Wright) v Resilient Energy Severndale Ltd** [2020] 2 1, SC.
Development likely to interfere with Jodrell Bank radio telescope—Such interference a material consideration to which the Minister, on appeal against the refusal of permission, was entitled to have regard—Material considerations not limited to matters of amenity but covering any consideration, in regard to public or private interests, which related to the use and development of land—Town and Country Planning Act 1962, s 17(1). **Stringer v Minister of Housing and Local Government** [1971] 1 65, QBD.

Permission for development (cont)—
Material consideration (cont)—
Existence of valid planning permission—Existing permission to build dwelling-house—Second application for permission to build dwelling-house on modified scale—Existence of valid permission a material consideration in determining whether to grant second application. **Spackman v Secretary of State for the Environment** [1977] **1** 257, QBD.

Financial considerations—Planning proposal combining improvements to opera house and substantial office accommodation—Commercial development undesirable but necessary to finance improvements to opera house—Whether financial considerations of planning proposal a material consideration—Whether planning authority entitled to take into account that undesirable development would benefit desirable development—Whether planning authority entitled to take into account that commercial development would fund improvements to opera house—Town and Country Planning Act 1971, s 29(1). **R v Westminster City Council, ex p Monahan** [1989] **2** 74, QBD and CA.

Green Belt land—Permission granted to extend operational face of quarry—Whether local planning authority correctly understanding meaning of 'openness' in national planning policies applying to mineral working in Green Belt—Whether visual effects 'material consideration' to be regarded in determining application—Town and Country Planning Act 1990—National Planning Policy Framework, para 90. **R (on the application of Samuel Smith Old Brewery (Tadcaster)) v North Yorkshire CC** [2020] **3** 527, SC.

Local authority's purpose in granting planning permission—Planning proposal for substantial residential development in industrial area—Companies carrying on 'offensive trades' objecting to proposal because nuisance claims against them could force them to relocate—Council granting permission—Council hoping that grant of permission would cause offensive trades to relocate without payment of compensation—Whether permission invalid or unreasonable or granted for ulterior purpose—Town and Country Planning Act 1971, ss 29(1), 51(1), 170. **R v Exeter City Council, ex p J L Thomas & Co Ltd** [1990] **1** 413, QBD.

Recommendation of local plan inspector—Recommendation that site be designated as open space on local plan—Whether recommendation material consideration when determining application for development on site—Town and Country Planning Act 1971, s 29(1). **Bath Society v Secretary of State for the Environment** [1992] **1** 28, CA.

Time expired permission—New application—Whether time expired permission a material consideration to be taken into account—Town and Country Planning Act 1971, s 29(1). **South Oxfordshire DC v Secretary of State for the Environment** [1981] **1** 954, QBD.
Metropolitan open land—
Appropriate development—Limited extension, alteration or replacement of existing dwellings not inappropriate providing new dwelling not materially larger—Planning authority granting permission for replacement dwelling double the size of original although with little alteration in visual impact—Whether replacement building 'materially larger'. **R (on the application of the Heath & Hampstead Society) v Vlachos** [2008] **3** 80, CA.
Multiple permissions in respect of same piece of land—
Permissions inconsistent with each other—Planning authority bound to consider application without regard to other permissions granted but not implemented—Implementation of permission rendering impossible implementation of earlier inconsistent permission. **Pilkington v Secretary of State for the Environment** [1974] **1** 283, QBD.
Necessity for permission—
Agreement between quarry-owners and local authority as to quarrying areas scheduled to Act of Parliament—Whether agreed quarrying was development 'authorised' by any local or private Act—Town and Country Planning General Development Order 1950 (SI 1950 No 728), art 3(1), Sch 1, class XII—Malvern Hills Act 1924, s 54, Sch 4. **Pyx Granite Co Ltd v Ministry of Housing and Local Government** [1959] **3** 1, HL.
Notification—
Error—Effect—Planning authority resolving to refuse permission—Applicant notified by planning officer in prescribed form that permission granted—Whether notice amounting to permission—Whether planning authority estopped from denying validity of notice. **Norfolk CC v Secretary of State for the Environment** [1973] **3** 673, QBD.

Notice of grant of limited permission not given within time laid down in General Development Order—Whether permission void or voidable—Town and Country Planning Act 1947, s 23(3)—Town and Country Planning General Development Order 1950 (SI 1950 No 728), art 5(8). **James v Secretary of State for Wales** [1965] **3** 602, CA.

Notice of refusal not given within time laid down in General Development Order—Mandatory requirement—Notice void—Enforcement notice given before application for development permission also invalidated—Town and Country Planning Act 1947, s 23(3)—Town and Country Planning General Development Order 1950 (SI 1950 No 728), art 5(8). **Edwick v Sunbury-on-Thames UDC** [1961] **3** 10, QBD.

Person hoping to acquire interest in the land—Obligation of authority to notify owner of application—Town and Country Planning Act 1947, s 14(1). **Hanily v Minister of Local Government and Planning** [1952] **1** 1293, QBD.

Reasons—Factors taken into account should be identified—Town and Country Planning (Inquiries Procedure) Rules 1965 (SI 1965 No 473), r 13(1). **Westminster Bank Ltd v Minister of Housing and Local Government** [1968] **2** 1199, CA.
Outline permission—
Approval of details—Whether an application for planning approval of details in outline permission is an application for planning permission—Town and Country Planning General Development Order 1950 (SI 1950 No 728), art 5. **R v Bradford-on-Avon UDC, ex p Boulton** [1964] **2** 492, QBD.

Design and siting reserved for subsequent approval—Subsequent application for approval on reserved matters refused on ground that development contrary to planning authority's proposals for the area—Whether outline permission a sufficient valid permission for development—Town and Country Planning General Development Order and Development Charge Applications Regulations 1950 (SI 1950 No 728), art 5(2). **Hamilton v West Sussex CC** [1958] **2** 174, QBD.

TOWN AND COUNTRY PLANNING (cont)—
  Permission for development (cont)—
    Outline permission (cont)—
      Reserved matters—Subsequent events affecting whole scheme—Developer obtaining outline
        planning permission on basis that all buildings on site would be demolished—Certain buildings
        subsequently listed as of special architectural importance and required to be retained—Whether
        planning authority entitled to refuse approval of reserved matters because character of whole
        scheme changed by retention of listed buildings. **Heron Corp Ltd v Manchester City Council**
        [1978] **3** 1240, CA.
      Reserved matters—Variation or revision of reserved matters once approval of them
        obtained—Developer obtaining outline planning permission in which certain matters
        reserved—Developer obtaining approval of reserved matters—Developer wishing to revise or
        vary matters for which approval obtained—Whether developer entitled to submit further
        application for approval of reserved matters—Whether fresh application for outline planning
        permission required. **Heron Corp Ltd v Manchester City Council** [1978] **3** 1240, CA.
    Permission to use land for any purpose on not more than 28 days in total in any calendar year—
      Information charging unlawful use on 12th January 1953, and on two dates in December
        1952—Town and Country Planning General Development Order 1950 (SI 1950 No 728), art 3(1),
        Sch I, Part I, class IV, para 2. **Godstone RDC v Brazil** [1953] **2** 763, QBD.
    Permissions before and after appointed day—
      Permission granted in 1945 under previous planning control for seven years determinable by notice
        thereafter—Second permission in 1947 for seven years only—Extension of permission in 1951
        under new planning control conditional on discontinuance at end of March 1960—User of
        premises begun in war period deemed to comply with previous planning control—No notice of
        discontinuance under permission of 1945—Permission of 1945 not registered as local land
        charge—Whether local planning authority entitled to serve enforcement notice after March
        1960—Building Restrictions (War-Time Contraventions) Act 1946, s 4(1)—Town and Country
        Planning Act 1947, s 76(2), (3). **Rose v Leeds Corp** [1964] **3** 618, CA.
    Power to revoke or modify planning permission—
      Compensation where planning permission revoked or modified—Whether open to planning
        authority to have regard to compensation payable when considering whether expedient to
        revoke or modify planning permission—Town and Country Planning Act 1990, ss 97, 107. **R (on
        the application of the Health and Safety Executive) v Wolverhampton City Council** [2012] **4** 429,
        SC.
    Refusal—
      Agricultural land—Refusal to permit construction of sports stadium—Overriding need of
        agriculture—Town and Country Planning Act 1932, s 10(5). **R v East Kesteven RDC, ex p Sleaford
        and District White City Sports Stadium Co** [1947] **1** 310, KBD.
      Alternative to exercising statutory power under Highways Act to prescribe improvement line with a
        view to road widening—Exercise of power under s 72 would carry right to compensation, but
        refusal of development permission might not or might carry less compensation—Dismissal by
        Minister of appeal from refusal of permission—Whether Minister's decision valid—Highways Act
        1959, s 72—Town and Country Planning Act 1962, ss 17, 23. **Westminster Bank Ltd v Minister of
        Housing and Local Government** [1970] **1** 734, HL.
      Appeal. *See* Appeal to Minister against refusal of permission for development, *above.*
      Compensation—Reasons relating to radio telescope at Jodrell Bank—No right to compensation for
        refusal on those grounds—Planning authority entitled to refuse permission on such grounds
        despite absence of compensation. **Stringer v Minister of Housing and Local Government**
        [1971] **1** 65, QBD.
      Material considerations—Desirability of retaining existing use—Permission for change of
        use—Permission for change from housing to office use—Refusal of permission on ground of
        need to retain housing use in area—Whether desirability of retaining existing use a material
        consideration—Town and Country Planning Act 1971, s 29(1). **Clyde & Co v Secretary of State for
        the Environment** [1977] **3** 1123, CA.
    Revocation—
      Compensation—Depreciation of value of interest in land—Statutory assumption that planning
        permission would be granted for development—Permission granted for demolition of house and
        erection of new dwelling—House demolished but no new dwelling erected—Permission for
        erection of new dwelling revoked—Compensation sought for revocation of planning
        permission—Whether planning permission assumed to be still subsisting was same as revoked
        permission—Whether assumption must be made that planning permission would be granted
        even though permission incapable of being implemented—Town and Country Planning Act 1971,
        s 164(4). **Canterbury City Council v Colley** [1993] **1** 591, HL.
      Compensation—Expenditure in carrying out work which is rendered abortive by order—
        Expenditure incurred by person interested in the land—Meaning of 'person interested in the
        land'—Whether meaning limited to person having a legal interest in the land—Whether a licensee
        capable of being a person interested in the land—Town and Country Planning Act 1971, s 164(1).
        Pennine Raceway Ltd v Kirklees Metropolitan Council [1982] **3** 628, CA.
      Compensation—Expenditure in carrying out work which is rendered abortive by order—Plans
        prepared but no building operations carried out—Plans prepared before permission obtained for
        building—Town and Country Planning (Interim Development) Act 1943, s 7(2), (3). **Holmes v
        Bradfield RDC** [1949] **1** 381, KBD.
      Direction that development of permitted class inexpedient—Whether direction valid in relation to
        development already carried out—Town and Country Planning General Development Order and
        Development Charge Applications Regulations 1950 (SI I 1950 No 728), art 4(1). **Cole v Somerset
        CC** [1956] **3** 531, QBD.
    Sale of land—
      Condition. *See* Sale of land (Condition—Planning permission to be obtained).
    Secretary of State's powers—
      Reference of applications to Secretary of State—Whether duty to give reasons not to 'call in'
        application—Whether legitimate expectation arising—Town and Country Planning Act 1990, s 77.
        **R (on the application of Save Britain's Heritage) v Secretary of State for Communities and Local
        Government** [2019] **1** 1117, CA.

TOWN AND COUNTRY PLANNING (cont)—

Permission for development (cont)—

Statutory presumption in favour of development plan—

Whether presumption displaced by other material considerations in particular circumstances—Town and Country Planning (Scotland) Act 1972, s 18A. **City of Edinburgh Council v Secretary of State for Scotland** [1998] **1** 174, HL.

Stopping up or diversion of highway—

Power to authorise diversion—Development obstructing footpath completed or partly completed before diversion authorised—Whether power to authorise diversion where development already completed or partly completed—Whether authority to divert highway then 'is necessary ... to enable development to be carried out'—Town and Country Planning Act 1971, s 209(1). **Ashby v Secretary of State for the Environment** [1980] **1** 508, CA.

Ultra vires—

Declaration—Applicant must show injuria as well as damnum—No legal right of applicant infringed by development on adjoining land to which planning permission related—No locus standi to maintain action against planning authority for declaration that permission ultra vires. **Gregory v Camden London Borough** [1966] **2** 196, QBD.

Environmental impact assessment—European Community directive requiring developer to submit environmental impact assessment in certain circumstances—Developer failing to submit environmental statement—Planning authority's report incorporating information required in such a statement—Developer submitting statement of case in public inquiry incorporating information by cross-reference—Whether developer's statement of case equivalent to environmental assessment—Town and Country Planning Act 1990, s 288—Council Directive (EEC) 85/337, Annex III—Town and Country Planning (Assessment of Environmental Effects) Regulations 1988, Sch 3. **Berkeley v Secretary of State for the Environment** [2000] **3** 897, HL.

Variation of detailed planning permission—

Variation allowed by planning authority's officer as being immaterial and not requiring further permission—Practice of planning authorities to allow their officers to decide on materiality of minor modifications to an approved plan—Matter within officer's ostensible authority and his decision, acted on by developers, binding on planning authority—Delegation of function of determining applications—Variation in site of house—Town and Country Planning Act 1968, s 64. **Lever (Finance) Ltd v Westminster Corp** [1970] **3** 496, CA.

Permitted development. *See* Development—Permitted development, *above.*

Planning authority—

Estoppel—

Whether private law concept of estoppel applicable to planning law. **R v East Sussex CC, ex p Reprotech (Pebsham) Ltd** [2002] **4** 58, HL.

Exercise of discretion—

Estoppel. *See* **Estoppel** (Statutory body—Local planning authority—Exercise of discretion).

Urban development corporation—

Bias—Judicial review—Decisions of urban development corporation granting planning permission for development—Participation in decisions by members and officer of corporation having disqualifying personal or pecuniary interests—Whether corporation's decisions indicating apparent bias—Test of bias—Whether same test applicable for non-judicial bodies as for judicial or quasi-judicial bodies—Whether apparent bias vitiating decisions. **R v Secretary of State for the Environment, ex p Kirkstall Valley Campaign Ltd** [1996] **3** 304, QBD.

Planning permission—

Judicial review of grant of planning permission—

Local authority granting planning permission for development on site inhabited by protected species of bats—Whether development constituting 'disturbance' of species—Meaning of 'disturbance'—Whether local planning authority acting lawfully in granting planning permission—Council Directive (EEC) 92/43, art 12(1)(b)—Conservation (Natural Habitats, &c) Regulations 1994, SI 1994/2716, regs 3(4), 39. **R (on the application of Morge) v Hampshire CC** [2011] **1** 744, SC.

Relief—Local authority granting planning permission for development without conducting assessment required by EU law implemented in UK—Relief refused on basis highly likely outcome not substantially different had assessment been carried out—Whether test to be applied in deciding whether to grant relief different where breach of EU law—Whether outcome would have been different had assessment been carried out—Senior Courts Act 1981, s 31(2A). **R (on the application of Hudson) v Windsor and Maidenhead Royal BC** [2022] **1** 948, CA.

Planning unit—

Determination of unit. *See* Development—Material change of use—Planning unit, *above.*

Protected species, site inhabited by—

Planning permission—

Judicial review. *See* Planning permission—Judicial review of grant of planning permission—Local authority granting planning permission for development on site inhabited by protected species of bats, *above.*

Purchase notice—

Compensation. *See* **Compulsory purchase** (Compensation—Purchase notice).

Confirmation—

Land incapable of reasonably beneficial use—Land incapable of reasonably beneficial use because of development on land in breach of planning control—No enforcement notice served within statutory period in respect of unlawful development—Whether unlawful development to be disregarded in deciding whether land capable of reasonably beneficial use in existing state—Whether purchase notice relating to land should be confirmed—Town and Country Planning Act 1971, s 180. **Balco Transport Services Ltd v Secretary of State for the Environment** [1985] **3** 689, CA.

Quashing of confirmation—Speaking decision for confirmation stating a sole ground—Invalidity of that ground—Town and Country Planning Act 1947, s 19(1)(a). **R v Minister of Housing and Local Government, ex p Chichester RDC** [1960] **2** 407, QBD.

TOWN AND COUNTRY PLANNING (cont)—
Purchase notice (cont)—
Confirmation (cont)—
Refusal of confirmation—Permission for other development in lieu of confirmation—Development contemplated by decision not development within Sch 3 to the Town and Country Planning Act 1947—Whether decision ultra vires—Town and Country Planning Act 1947, ss 19(2), 19(2A)(added by Town and Country Planning Act 1954, s 70). **R v Minister of Housing and Local Government, ex p Rank Organisation Ltd** [1958] **3** 322, QBD.
Refusal of confirmation—Power of Secretary of State to refuse confirmation—Land incapable of reasonably beneficial use—Land having a restricted use by virtue of previous planning permission—Power to refuse confirmation where appearing to Secretary of State that land ought, in accordance with previous planning permission, to remain undeveloped—Part only of land to which purchase notice relating having been subject of previous planning permission—Secretary of State having power to refuse confirmation only where whole of land to which purchase notice relating subject of previous planning permission—Town and Country Planning Act 1962, ss 129(1), 132(1)—Town and Country Planning Act 1968, s 32. **Plymouth City Corp v Secretary of State for the Environment** [1972] **3** 225, QBD.
Service of notice on borough council—Minister's notice of proposed action to confirm purchase notice without modification—No hearing before person appointed by Minister—Informal meeting between Minister, planning authority, and borough council—Substitution of planning authority for borough council as acquiring authority in purported confirmation of purchase notice—Town and Country Planning Act 1947, s 19(3)(5). **Ealing BC v Minister of Housing and Local Government** [1952] **2** 639, Ch D.
Jurisdiction of Lands Tribunal. *See* **Lands Tribunal** (Jurisdiction—Consent—Statutory tribunal).
Owner of land—
Person entitled to receive rackrent—Grant by freeholders of long lease—Confirmation of purchase notice—Town and Country Planning Act 1947, ss 19(1), (2), 119(1). **London Corp v Cusack-Smith** [1955] **1** 302, HL.
Qualifying interest—
Hereditament exempt from rating and specified as exempt in valuation list—Whether interest in such a hereditament a qualifying interest—Whether annual value did not exceed £250 for the purposes of Town and Country Planning Act 1959, s 39(4)(a). **Essex CC v Essex Incorporated Congregational Church Union** [1963] **1** 326, HL.
Validity—
Allocation—Land 'allocated' by a development plan—Allocation for purposes of functions of a local authority—Plan showing redevelopment area in residential area—Proposal to clear and redevelop—No specific exercise of power or duty by authority—Capability of redevelopment in part by private enterprise—Town and Country Planning Act 1959, ss 39(1), (2), 41(2), 57(1). **Bolton Corp v Owen** [1962] **1** 101, CA.
Owner serving successive purchase notices—Planning authority serving response notice to final purchase notice—Whether initial purchase notices valid—Whether statute limiting owner to one notice at a time—Whether statute permitting amendment of purchase notice by implication—Effect of service of concurrent purchase notices—Town and Country Planning Act 1990, ss 137, 139. **White v Herefordshire Council** [2008] **2** 852, CA.
Ribbon development—
Compensation. *See* Compensation—Development restricted by statute—Ribbon development, *above*.
Statutory review—
Costs. *See* **Costs** (Order for costs—Statutory review).
Statutory undertakers—
Operational land—
Land vested in statutory undertakers but not yet used by them for the purpose of their undertaking—Land not contiguous to land used for the purpose of a statutory undertaking—Town and Country Planning Act 1947, s 119(1). **R v Minister of Fuel and Power, ex p Warwickshire CC** [1957] **2** 731, QBD.
Stop notice—
Using land in contravention of stop notice—
Criminal prosecution—Defence that notice invalid—Whether validity of stop notice can be challenged in criminal proceedings—Town and Country Planning Act 1971, s 90(1), (2), (7). **R v Jenner** [1983] **2** 46, CA.
Time limits—
Change of use. *See* Change of use—Time limits, *above*.
Town planning scheme—
Industrial building—
Factory—Premises used for testing concrete—Town and Country Planning Act 1932, s 13(1)(c)—Factories Act 1937, s 151(1). **Hendon Corp v Stanger** [1948] **1** 377, CA.
Resolution to prepare scheme—
Scheme to include prohibition of use of land for certain purposes without consent of local authority—Validity—Town and Country Planning Act 1932, ss 1, 11. **Taylor v Brighton BC** [1947] **1** 864, CA.
Trees—
Preservation order—
Exemption to application of order—Cutting down, uprooting, topping or lopping of trees so far as necessary for prevention or abatement of nuisance—Scope of exemption—Town and Country Planning Act 1990, s 198(6)(b). **Perrin v Northampton BC** [2007] **1** 929, TCC; [2008] **4** 673, CA.
Prohibition of wilful destruction of trees—Destruction—Meaning—Damage to root system of tree—Damage reducing life expectancy of tree and rendering it less stable—Whether tree destroyed—Town and Country Planning Act 1962, s 29(1)(a). **Barnet London BC v Eastern Electricity Board** [1973] **2** 319, QBD.
Prohibition of wilful destruction of trees—Offence—Mens rea—Whether knowledge of preservation order a necessary ingredient of offence—Town and Country Planning Act 1971, s 102(1). **Maidstone BC v Mortimer** [1980] **3** 552, QBD.

TOWN AND COUNTRY PLANNING (cont)—
Unfinished buildings—
Works for the erection of a building—
Completion of clearance of site—Erection of new building not begun—Separate contracts for clearance and building—Town and Country Planning Act 1947, s 78(1). **London CC v Marks & Spencer Ltd** [1953] **1** 1095, HL.
Use of land—
Change of use—
Condition attached to permission for change of use. *See* Change of use—Condition attached to permission for change of use, *above.*
Discontinuance order. *See* Discontinuance order—Use of land, *above.*
District plan. *See* District plan, *above.*
Established use. *See* Established use, *above.*
Use classes. *See* Development—Use classes, *above.*
War damage—
Compulsory purchase order—
Direction by Minister that application for order under 1944 Act be continued after 1947 Act came into force—Direction given before 1947 Act came into force—Validity—Interpretation Act 1889, s 37—Town and Country Planning Act 1944, s 1(1)—Town and Country Planning Act 1947, s 113(2), (5), Sch X, para 16. **R v Minister of Town and Country Planning, ex p Montague Burton Ltd** [1950] **2** 282, CA.
Redevelopment of land—
Compulsory purchase—Order by Minister—Powers of Minister—Town and Country Planning Act 1944, s 1(1). **Phoenix Assurance Co Ltd v Minister of Town and Country Planning** [1947] **1** 454, KBD; **Robinson v Minister of Town and Country Planning** [1947] **1** 851, CA.
Works for the erection of a building—
Demolition of existing buildings and clearance of site—
Erection of new building not begun—Separate contracts for clearance and building—Town and Country Planning Act 1947, s 78(1). **London CC v Marks & Spencer Ltd** [1953] **1** 1095, HL.

TOWN OR VILLAGE GREEN
Registration. *See* **Commons** (Registration—Town or village green).

TRACING
Banker's books—
Power to make interlocutory order for disclosure of banker's books to show amount standing in defendant's account. *See* **Money** (Following money—Plaintiff seeking to trace money paid under mistake of fact induced by fraud—Power to make interlocutory order for disclosure of banker's books to show amount standing in defendant's account).
Disclosure—
Order for disclosure—
Order obtained in aid of tracing claim—Use of information obtained for allied purposes. *See* **Disclosure and inspection of documents** (Order for disclosure—Order for disclosure against bank in aid of tracing claim).
Equity. *See* **Equity** (Tracing).
Money—
Money had and received—
Right to trace funds at common law. *See* **Money** (Money had and received—Right to trace funds at common law).
Money paid under mistake of fact. *See* **Mistake** (Mistake of fact—Money paid under mistake of fact—Equitable right to trace money paid under mistake of fact).
Pension funds—
Improper application of pension funds—
Availability of equitable tracing remedy. *See* **Pension** (Pension scheme—Company pension scheme—Improper application of pension funds).

TRACK
Licensed track—
Charges to bookmakers. *See* **Gaming** (Betting—Licensed track—Charges to bookmakers).

TRADE
Advertising. *See* **Advertisement** (Trade or business).
Business premises—
Occupation for business purposes—
Residential property. *See* **Landlord and tenant** (Business premises—Occupied for business purposes—Residential flat used by tenant for his business).
Discontinuance—
Income tax. *See* **Income tax** (Discontinuance of trade).
Value added tax—
Taxpayer remaining registered—Responsibility for making return. *See* **Value added tax** (Return—Responsibility for making return—Taxpayer registered for value added tax—Taxpayer ceasing to trade but remaining registered).
Effluent—
Discharge into river. *See* **Water and watercourses** (Pollution of river—Discharge of trade effluent).
European Community—
Rules on competition. *See* **European Union** (Rules on competition).
Expenses—
Income tax. *See* **Income tax** (Deduction in computing profits).
Export control—
Control powers. *See* **Export control** (Control powers).
False trade description. *See* **Trade description.**

TRADE (cont)—
  Fraudulent trading—
    Company—
      Winding up. *See* **Company** (Winding up—Fraudulent trading).
  Income tax—
    Deduction in computing profits. *See* **Income tax** (Deduction in computing profits).
    Discontinuance of trade. *See* **Income tax** (Discontinuance of trade).
    Generally. *See* **Income tax** (Trade).
    Loss relief. *See* **Income tax** (Loss relief—Trade).
    Receipts. *See* **Income tax** (Profits—Trading receipts).
  Inter-state trade—
    Freedom of—
      Australia. *See* **Australia** (Freedom of inter-state trade).
  Interference with trade—
    Nuisance—
      Damages. *See* **Nuisance** (Damages—Interference with trade).
    Tort. *See* **Tort** (Interference with trade).
  Investment grants. *See* **Investment grant**.
  Mission—
    Representative of foreign country on—
      Whether entitled to diplomatic immunity. *See* **Constitutional law** (Diplomatic privilege—Immunity
        from legal process—Acceptance of diplomat by receiving country—Member of permanent
        mission).
  Occupation of premises for business purposes—
    Residential flat. *See* **Landlord and tenant** (Business premises—Occupied for business purposes—
      Residential flat used by tenant for his business).
  Offensive trade. *See* **Public health** (Offensive trades).
  Practice of trade—
    Defence to action for negligence. *See* **Negligence** (Defence—Practice of trade).
  Price maintenance—
    Resale price maintenance. *See* **Restrictive trade practices** (Resale price maintenance).
  Prize competition in connection with trade or business. *See* **Gaming** (Prize competition).
  Protection of trading interests—
    Damage to United Kingdom trading interests—
      Conflict of laws—Foreign measures which threaten to damage United Kingdom trading
        interests—Conditions under which Secretary of State may make order or direction prohibiting
        compliance with foreign measures—Measures—What constitutes foreign 'measures' which
        threaten to damage United Kingdom trading interests—Protection of Trading Interests Act 1980,
        ss 1, 2(1)—Protection of Trading Interests (US Antitrust Measures) Order 1983. **British Airways
        Board v Laker Airways Ltd** [1984] 3 39, HL.
  Receipts—
    Income tax. *See* **Income tax** (Profits—Trading receipts).
  Record relating to trade or business—
    Evidence in criminal proceedings. *See* **Criminal evidence** (Record relating to trade or business).
  Restraint of trade—
    Auction—
      Knock-out agreement. *See* **Auction** (Knock-out agreement).
    Expulsion from trade union—
      Unfettered power to expel in union rules. *See* **Trade union** (Rules—Validity—Rules giving
        unfettered power of expulsion from membership).
    Injunction—
      Interlocutory injunction. *See* **Injunction** (Interlocutory—Restraint of trade).
    Restraint of trade by agreement. *See* **Restraint of trade by agreement**.
  Restrictive practices—
    European Community. *See* **European Union** (Restrictive trade practices).
    Generally. *See* **Restrictive trade practices**.
  Street trading. *See* **Street trading**.
  Trade description. *See* **Trade description**.
  Trade dispute. *See* **Trade dispute**.
  Trade mark. *See* **Trade mark**.
  Trade secrets—
    Disclosure—
      Interlocutory injunction. *See* **Injunction** (Interlocutory—Confidential information—Trade secrets).
    Generally. *See* **Trade secrets**.
  Trade union—
    Generally. *See* **Trade union**.
    Redundancy—
      Employers' duty to consult appropriate trade union. *See* **Redundancy** (Employer's duty to consult
        appropriate trade union).
  Transfer of—
    Continuity of employment. *See* **Employment** (Continuity—Transfer of trade, business or undertaking).
  Weights and measures. *See* **Weights and measures**.

TRADE DESCRIPTION
  Accommodation—
    Hotel. *See* False or misleading statement as to services etc—Statement made recklessly—Hotel
      accommodation, *below*.
  Airline—
    Overbooking of seats. *See* False or misleading statement as to services etc—Promise in regard to
      future—Statement of fact distinguished from promise—Statement of existing intention—Booking and
      reservation of seat, *below*.
  Car—
    New car. *See* False trade description—False description—New car, *below*.

TRADE DESCRIPTION (cont)—

Civil action, right of. *See* False trade description—Civil right of action, *below.*

Defence to proceedings—

Act or default of another person—

Company—Exercise of supervisory function by employee of company—Failure by employee to exercise supervisory function properly—Whether employee to be identified with company— Whether employee 'another person'—Trade Descriptions Act 1968, s 24(1). **Tesco Supermarkets Ltd v Nattrass** [1971] **2** 127, HL.

Shop manager's failure to carry out accused's instructions—Whether manager 'another person' within Trade Descriptions Act 1968, s 24(1). **Beckett v Kingston Bros (Butchers) Ltd** [1970] **1** 715, QBD.

Mistake—

Mistake by person other than person charged—Mistake by servant or agent—Trade Descriptions Act 1968, s 24(1). **Birkenhead and District Co-op Society Ltd v Roberts** [1970] **3** 391, QBD.

Reasonable precautions and due diligence to avoid commission of offence—

Company—Large-scale business—Exercise of supervisory functions by employee—Exercise of due diligence by company a question of fact—Failure by employee to exercise supervisory function properly—Liability of company—Trade Descriptions Act 1968, s 24(1). **Tesco Supermarkets Ltd v Nattrass** [1971] **2** 127, HL.

Nature of defence—Short measure given by servant—Liability of master—No finding of inadvertence or mistake—Merchandise Marks Act 1887, s 2(2)(a), (b), (c). **Slatcher v George Mence Smith Ltd** [1951] **2** 388, KBD.

Sale of car by motor dealer—False mileage indicated on odometer—Dealer ignorant that odometer had been tampered with—Dealer not having received log book at time of sale—Car examined by servant of dealer and independent expert—Condition of car consistent with mileage shown on odometer—Whether dealer having taken all reasonable precautions and exercised due diligence—Whether dealer bound to acquire log book before sale in order to check mileage with previous owner—Trade Descriptions Act 1968, ss 1(1)(b), 24(1), (3). **Naish v Gore** [1971] **3** 737, QBD.

Disclaimer. *See* False trade description—Application in course of trade or business—Disclaimer of false trade description, *below.*

Document—

Interpretation—

False trade description or statement—Statement in document alleged to be false—Meaning of statement—Whether interpretation of document matter for judge or jury. **R v Sunair Holidays Ltd** [1973] **2** 1233, CA.

False or misleading indication as to price—

Contract to supply goods at price calculated according to agreed formula as and when purchaser calling for delivery—

Purchaser calling for delivery of goods and vendor appropriating those goods to contract and delivering them—Delivery accompanied by invoice charging higher price than contract price—Whether vendor 'supplying' or 'offering to supply' goods—Whether separate offences—Whether vendor 'offering to supply' goods and giving 'indication' in contract that goods were offered at price lower than that charged—Whether vendor 'supplying goods' and merely stating wrong price in invoice—Trade Descriptions Act 1968, s 1(1)(b), 6, 11(2). **Miller v Sadd (FA) & Son Ltd** [1981] **3** 265, QBD.

Counter-indication—

Self-service store—Goods displayed on stalls with misleading indication as to price—Stalls situated some distance away from cash till—Notice on cash till serving to give correct indication as to price—Whether defence that customer's false impression as to price subsequently corrected by notice on cash till—Trade Descriptions Act 1968, s 11(2). **Doble v David Greig Ltd** [1972] **2** 195, QBD.

Indication likely to be taken as an indication that goods being offered at price less than that at which in fact being offered—

Statements as to price susceptible of two possible meanings—One of meanings accurate—Whether statements 'likely to be taken' as indicating that goods offered at lower price—Trade Descriptions Act 1968, s 11(2). **Doble v David Greig Ltd** [1972] **2** 195, QBD.

Indication of previous offer at higher price—

Goods not offered for sale at higher price at shop indicated in advertisement—Goods previously offered for sale at higher price at another shop belonging to defendant—Whether false trade description if goods not previously offered at higher price at shop indicated at in advertisement—Trade Descriptions Act 1968, s 11(1)(b). **Westminster City Council v Ray Alan (Manshops) Ltd** [1982] **1** 771, QBD.

Offer at higher price for continuous period of 28 days within preceding six months—Necessity for prosecution to establish that no such offer made during full six month period—Trade Descriptions Act 1968, s 11(1), (3). **House of Holland Ltd v Brent London Borough** [1971] **2** 296, QBD.

Scope of offence—

Offence committed only in relation to trade or business—No application to transactions with members in members clubs—Trade Descriptions Act 1968, s 11. **John v Matthews** [1970] **2** 643, QBD.

False or misleading statement as to services etc—

False statement as to provision in the course of trade or business of services—

Qualification to provide services—Statement made by person that he is properly qualified to provide services—Whether 'statement ... as to ... provision ... of services'—Trade Descriptions Act 1968, s 14(1)(i). **R v Breeze** [1973] **2** 1141, CA.

Statement that services available under guarantee—Trade Descriptions Act 1968, s 14(1)(i). **Breed v Cluett** [1970] **2** 662, QBD.

False statement as to provision of facilities in course of trade or business—

Facility—Sign outside shop advertising closing down sale—Defendant continuing to trade at shop—Whether sign amounting to representation that a 'facility' was being provided in course of the trade or business—Trade Descriptions Act 1968, s 14(1)(b)(ii). **Westminster City Council v Ray Alan (Manshops) Ltd** [1982] **1** 771, QBD.

TRADE DESCRIPTION (cont)—

False or misleading statement as to services etc (cont)—

Making a statement—

Statement made after contract and after payment—Whether a 'statement' within Trade Descriptions Act 1968, s 14(1). **Breed v Cluett** [1970] 2 662, QBD.

When offence committed—Statement contained in brochure—Copies of brochure circulated to public—Separate complaints made independently by different readers—Separate prosecutions—Conviction on first prosecution—Whether single offence committed when brochure printed and published or separate offences committed each time contents of brochure communicated to a reader—Whether accused entitled to plead autrefois convict on second prosecution—Trade Descriptions Act 1968, s 14(1). **R v Thomson Holidays Ltd** [1974] 1 823, CA.

When offence committed—Statement contained in defendant's travel brochure—Defendant unaware that statement false at date of publication of brochure—Defendant subsequently learning of falsity—Steps taken to rectify mistake before statement read by complainant—Whether offence committed—Trade Descriptions Act 1968, s 14(1)(a). **Wings Ltd v Ellis** [1984] 3 577, HL.

Promise in regard to future—

Building of garage—Statements made before building started—Statement as to the date on which garage would be completed—Statement incapable of being true or false at time when made—Trade Descriptions Act 1968, s 14(1). **Beckett v Cohen** [1973] 1 120, QBD.

Prediction as to future facts—Statements incapable of being true or false at time made—Holiday brochure—Brochure issued in winter for following summer season—Brochure stating hotel had swimming pool—Swimming pool being built for summer season—Swimming pool not in fact completed by summer—Need to prove that statement meant hotel had swimming pool at time brochure issued—Trade Descriptions Act 1968, s 14(1). **R v Sunair Holidays Ltd** [1973] 2 1233, CA.

Statement of fact distinguished from promise—Statement of existing intention—Booking and reservation of seat—Airline—Customer booking seat on particular flight—Airline writing letter confirming reservation for flight—Policy of airline to overbook flights—Seats available at time of customer's booking—Airline subsequently overbooking flight—Customer in consequence unable to travel on flight—Customer travelling on following day—Whether letter from airline containing statement of fact as opposed to promise of future conduct—Trade Descriptions Act 1968, s 14(1). **British Airways Board v Taylor** [1976] 1 65, HL.

Statement in the course of any trade or business—

Trade or business—Profession—Statement made by professional man in course of providing professional services—Whether 'trade or business' including profession—Trade Descriptions Act 1968, s 14(1). **R v Breeze** [1973] 2 1141, CA.

Statement made recklessly—

Hotel accommodation—Description in travel agent's brochure—Rooms with terraces—Contract in existence by travel agents with hotel to keep such rooms for their clients—Acceptance of offer contained in brochure by holidaymakers—Holidaymakers given rooms without terrace—Alleged default of travel agents in checking accommodation—Any such default of travel agents subsequent to booking—Whether offence committed—Trade Descriptions Act 1968, s 14(1)(b), (2). **Sunair Holidays Ltd v Dodd** [1970] 2 410, QBD.

Statement made regardless of whether it is true or false—Statement in trade advertisement—Advertiser failing to appreciate that advertisement reasonably capable of being understood in sense different to that intended—Whether statement made regardless of truth or falsity—Trade Descriptions Act 1968, s 14(1), (2). **MFI Warehouses Ltd v Nattrass** [1973] 1 762, QBD.

False trade description—

Application in course of trade or business—

Disclaimer of false trade description—Circumstances in which inference that false trade description applied will be negatived—Bold, precise and compelling evidence of disclaimer required—Sale by dealers of used car with false mileometer reading—Dealers supplying printed document to customer stating, inter alia, that they were not answerable for mileage shown on mileometer—Whether sufficient to negative inference that false trade description applied to goods—Trade Descriptions Act 1968, s 1(1)(b). **R v Hammertons Cars Ltd** [1976] 3 758, CA.

Disclaimer of false trade description—Secondhand car—Car dealer reducing mileage on odometer—Dealer displaying notices disclaiming odometer's accuracy—Whether dealer protected from liability by disclaimer—Trade Descriptions Act 1968, s 1(1)(a). **R v Southwood** [1987] 3 556, CA.

Disclaimer of false trade description—Secondhand car—Dealers attaching disclaimer to car stating that mileage reading was incorrect—Dealers knowing true mileage of car but not disclosing it—Whether dealer having obligation to disclose true mileage of car if knowing that odometer materially understating mileage—Trade Descriptions Act 1968, s 1(1)(b). **Farrand v Lazarus** [2002] 3 175, QBD.

Disclaimer of false trade description—What constitutes effective disclaimer—Trade Descriptions Act 1968, s 1. **Norman v Bennett** [1974] 3 351, QBD.

Sale of car by car-hire firm—Car sold in accordance with usual practice when hire cars over certain age—Whether sale 'in course of trade or business' of car-hire firm—Trade Descriptions Act 1968, s 1(1)(b). **Havering London Borough v Stevenson** [1970] 3 609, QBD.

Secondhand car—Zeroing odometer—Whether reducing odometer of secondhand car to zero is applying false trade description—Trade Descriptions Act 1968, s 1(1)(a). **R v Southwood** [1987] 3 556, CA.

Self-employed courier using car almost exclusively for purpose of his business—Car traded in with false description—Whether car traded in 'in course of a trade or business'—Trade Descriptions Act 1968, s 1(1). **Davies v Sumner** [1984] 3 831, HL.

Application to goods—

Application of false trade description to goods by buyer—Application in course of trade or business carried on by buyer—Whether an offence—Trade Descriptions Act 1968, s 1(1)(a). **Fletcher v Budgen** [1974] 2 1243, QBD.

Package of goods—Item supplied with goods—Gas cooker—Brochure stating that battery torch supplied with cooker—Battery torch not in fact supplied with cooker—Whether 'goods' including torch or confined to cooker—Whether description applied to goods—Trade Descriptions Act 1968, s 1(1)(a). **British Gas Corp Ltd v Lubbock** [1974] 1 188, QBD.

TRADE DESCRIPTION (cont)—
    False trade description (cont)—
        Civil right of action—
            Rival trader—Whether action for damages lies for breach of statutory duty under Merchandise Marks Acts 1887 to 1953—Merchandise Marks Act 1887, s 2(2)—Merchandise Marks Act 1953, s 4. **Bollinger (J) v Costa Brava Wine Co Ltd** [1959] 3 800, Ch D.
        False description—
            New car—Damage and repair—Car damaged after leaving factory on way to dealers for supply to customer—Car repaired by someone other than manufacturers—Circumstances in which car may still be properly described as a 'new' car—Trade Descriptions Act 1968, s 1(1). **R v Ford Motor Co Ltd** [1974] 3 489, CA.
        Falsity of description—
            Application of trade description to contents rather than container—Milk bottle embossed with other than retailer's name—Foil cap on bottle embossed with retailer's name—Trade Descriptions Act 1968, ss 1(1)(b), 3(1). **Donnelly v Rowlands** [1971] 1 9, QBD.
            Description false but recognised by trade—Non-brewed vinegar—Intent to defraud—Whether offence against statute—Merchandise Marks Act 1887, s 2(1)(d). **Kat v Diment** [1950] 2 657, KBD Divl Ct.
            Description recognised by trade—Rolled gold cuff-links—Front only of links rolled gold—Description equivocal, but not false bearing in mind cost of article and usages of trade—Description not likely to mislead public—Whether a false trade description for purposes of Merchandise Marks Act 1887, s 2(2) as substituted by Merchandise Marks Act 1953, s 4. **Kingston-upon-Thames Corp v Woolworth (F W) & Co Ltd** [1968] 1 401, QBD.
            Jurisdiction of court to fix standard for commodity—Merchandise Marks Act 1887, s 2. **Stott v Green** [1936] 2 354, KBD.
        Meaning of trade description—
            Indication of composition of goods—Indication of physical characteristics—Gas cooker—False statement that battery torch supplied with cooker—Whether 'composition' including components—Whether indication of physical characteristics of goods—Trade Descriptions Act 1968, s 2. **British Gas Corp Ltd v Lubbock** [1974] 1 188, QBD.
            Indication of history including previous ownership or use—Previous use—Motor car—Mileage—Mileage recorded on mileometer substantially less than actual mileage—Whether reading on mileometer a trade description—Trade Descriptions Act 1968, ss 1(1), 2(1)(j). **R v Hammertons Cars Ltd** [1976] 3 758, CA; **Tarleton Engineering Co Ltd v Nattrass** [1973] 3 699, QBD.
            Indication of history including previous ownership or use—Previous use—Motor car—Mileage—Mileage recorded on odometer substantially less than actual mileage—Trader unaware of true mileage—Estimated mileage included by him in contract of sale—Estimated mileage substantially less than actual mileage—Whether estimate a false trade description—Trade Descriptions Act 1968, ss 2(1), 3(3). **Holloway v Cross** [1981] 1 1012, QBD.
            Indication of specified matters—Matters truth or falsity of which can be established as a matter of fact—Indication as to value—Goods contained in wrapper bearing words 'extra value'—Whether words a trade description—Trade Descriptions Act 1968, s 2(1). **Cadbury Ltd v Halliday** [1975] 2 226, QBD.
            Statement of nature of article sold—Egg substitute—'Equivalent in use to 12 eggs'—Whole description to be considered—Merchandise Marks Act 1887, s 3. **Evans v British Doughnut Co Ltd** [1944] 1 158, KBD.
        Passing off—
            Descriptive name. *See* **Passing off** (Descriptive name).
            Geographical name. *See* **Passing off** (Geographical name—False trade description).
        Possession of goods to which false trade description is applied—
            Possession—Goods of appellant company deposited in cold store of cold storage company—Weight of goods wrongly stated by producer on wrapped goods—Whether goods were in the possession of the appellant company while in cold store—Merchandise Marks Act 1887, s 2(2) (as amended by Merchandise Marks Act 1953, s 4). **Towers & Co Ltd v Gray** [1961] 2 68, QBD.
        Prosecution—
            Procedure—Sampling—Sample purchased by officer of local authority—Procedure prescribed by Food and Drugs Act 1938, not applied—Whether procedure applicable—Merchandise Marks Act 1887, s 2(1)(d)—Food and Drugs Act 1938, s 70(1). **Evans v Clinical Products Ltd** [1943] 1 222, KBD.
            Time limit for. *See* False trade description—Time limit for prosecutions, *below*.
        Scope of prohibition—
            Description attached to goods provided in course of trade or business—Motor vehicle—Vehicle brought to accused's garage for MOT test—Examiner giving notification of refusal of test certificate—Notification containing statement that tyres suffering from specified defect and unsafe—Tyres not suffering from defect specified—Statement a false description of vehicle—False description not attached to vehicle provided in course of trade—Statement not in breach of prohibition on false trade descriptions—Trade Descriptions Act 1968, s 1. **Wycombe Marsh Garages Ltd v Fowler** [1972] 3 248, QBD.
        Selling goods to which false trade description is applied—
            Sells—Whether person sells who appropriates or transfers goods under agreement for sale of unascertained goods—Merchandise Marks Act 1887, s 2(2) (as amended by Merchandise Marks Act 1953, s 4). **Preston v Albuery** [1963] 3 897, QBD.
        Supplying goods to which false trade description is applied. *See* Supplying goods to which false trade description is applied, *below*.
        Time at which false description applied—
            Cause to apply false trade description to goods—Manufacturer sold goods to retailer in August—Goods displayed by retailer in December and sold—Goods then short in volume or weight—Falsity of trade description at time when manufacturer applied it not proved—Whether false trade description applied at time of sale by retailer—Whether manufacturer caused retailer to apply false trade description—Merchandise Marks Act 1887, s 2(1). **Shulton (GB) Ltd v Slough BC** [1967] 2 137, QBD.
            Description applied to goods by seller after sale completed—Whether an offence—Trade Descriptions Act 1968, s 1(1)(a). **Wickens Motors (Gloucester) Ltd v Hall** [1972] 3 759, QBD.

False trade description (cont)—
    Time at which false description applied (cont)—
        Short deliveries of milk—Customer subsequently overcharged in monthly account—Overcharge not made at time of delivery, no application of a false trade description—Merchandise Marks Act 1887, s 2(2). **Stoodley (GT) v Thomas (HD) & Sons Ltd and G Cooksey** [1945] **2** 89, KBD.
        Supply of goods to which false trade description is applied—Meaning of 'is applied'—Trade Descriptions Act 1968, s 1(1)(b). **Norman v Bennett** [1974] **3** 351, QBD.
    Time limit for prosecutions—
        Time limit 12 months—Exception where time limit six months—Exception applying where offence supplying goods to which false trade description applied by oral statement—Car dealer advertising Bedford goods vehicle for sale—Advertisement giving false description of vehicle—Car dealer only having one Bedford goods vehicle in possession at time of advertisement—Prospective purchaser later visiting dealer and seeing several vehicles—Dealer informing purchaser that a particular vehicle the one referred to in advertisement—Purchaser buying that vehicle—Dealer charged more than six months afterwards with supplying vehicle to which false trade description applied—Whether trade descriptions' applied by oral statement—Whether prosecution brought within time limit—Magistrates' Courts Act 1952, s 104—Trade Descriptions Act 1968, ss 1(1)(b), 19(2), (4). **Rees v Munday** [1974] **3** 506, QBD.
Hotel. *See* False or misleading statement as to services etc—Statement made recklessly—Hotel accommodation, *above.*
Indication of origin on imported goods—
    Breach of statutory duty—
        Civil proceedings—Whether civil action available—Plaintiffs importers of foreign goods only—Merchandise Marks Act 1926, s 1. **London Armoury Co Ltd v Ever Ready Co (GB) Ltd** [1941] **1** 364, KBD.
    Umbrellas—
        Ribs and tubes made of iron or steel wire—Imported from Hong Kong as complete umbrellas—Whether necessary for ribs and tubes to be marked with an indication of origin—Merchandise Marks Act 1926, s 5(3)—Merchandise Marks (Imported Goods) No 10 Order, 1933 (S R & O 1933 No 491), art 1. **Littlewoods Mail Order Stores Ltd v Storey** [1962] **2** 865, QBD.
Manufacturer. *See* Offences due to fault of another person—Manufacturer and retailer, *below.*
Members' club—
    Transactions with members—
        Application of Trade Descriptions Act 1968. *See* **Club** (Members' club—Transactions with members—Application of Trade Descriptions Act 1968).
Milk bottle. *See* False trade description—Falsity of description—Application of trade description to contents rather than container, *above.*
Mistake. *See* Defence to proceedings—Mistake, *above.*
Offences due to fault of another person—
    Liability of other person for offence—
        Causal connection between act or default and commission of offence—Need to prove causal connection—Car dealers entering car for auction—Mileage of car in excess of nr figure recorded on mileometer evidence that car dealers having tampered with mileometer—Car purchased by car sales firm—Sales firm offering car for sale without checking mileage or adjusting mileometer—Whether commission of offence by sale firm due to act or default of car dealers—Trade Descriptions Act 1968, s 23. **Tarleton Engineering Co Ltd v Nattrass** [1973] **3** 699, QBD.
        Other person not acting in course of trade or business—Whether other person can properly be convicted—Trade Descriptions Act 1968, ss 1(1)(b), 23. **Olgeirsson v Kitching** [1986] **1** 746, QBD.
    Liability of other person to be charged with offence—
        Proof of commission of offence necessary to establish liability of other person—False or misleading statements as to services—Statement made recklessly by manager of business—Proprietor of business charged with offence—Proprietor having no knowledge of statement—Proprietor acquitted because of absence of mens rea—Manager also charged on ground that commission of offence due to his default—Whether manager entitled to acquittal if proprietor acquitted—Trade Descriptions Act 1968, ss 14(1)(b), 23. **Coupe v Guyett** [1973] **2** 1058, QBD.
    Manufacturer and retailer—
        Goods supplied by manufacturer bearing false indication as to value—Goods also bearing sufficient information to indicate falsity to retailer—Goods offered for sale by retailer—Whether commission of offence by retailer due to act or default of manufacturer—Trade Descriptions Act 1968, s 23. **Cadbury Ltd v Halliday** [1975] **2** 226, QBD.
Profession. *See* False or misleading statement as to services etc—Statement in the course of any trade or business, *above.*
Sale of goods by description. *See* **Sale of goods** (Description—Trade description).
Supplying goods to which false trade description is applied—
    Knowledge of false description—
        Knowledge on part of supplier that description false—Whether necessary to prove that supplier had actual or constructive knowledge that description false—Trade Descriptions Act 1968, s 1(1)(b). **Cottee v Douglas Seaton (Used Cars) Ltd** [1972] **3** 750, QBD.
        Knowledge on part of supplier that description has been applied a prerequisite of offence—Car suffering from rust damage—Damage filled in by owner with plastic filling and painted roughly—Sale by owner to car dealer—Filling repainted by dealer to conceal damage—Sale to second dealer—No knowledge by second dealer of repainting—Sale by second dealer to subsequent purchaser—Whether second dealer guilty of offence—Trade Descriptions Act 1968, s 1(1)(b). **Cottee v Douglas Seaton (Used Cars) Ltd** [1972] **3** 750, QBD.
        Partners—Partners in firm selling secondhand cars—First partner's function to sell cars—Second partner's function to deal with administrative work—First partner selling car to which false trade description applied—Second partner having no knowledge or means of knowledge of false representation—Partners jointly charged with offence—Whether second partner, in absence of statutory defence, vicariously liable for application of false trade description—Trade Descriptions Act 1968, s 1(1). **Clode v Barnes** [1974] **1** 1166, QBD.

TRADE DESCRIPTION (cont)—
Supplying goods to which false trade description is applied (cont)—
Supply—
Contract for sale of goods—Whether goods supplied when contract made or when goods delivered to purchaser—Trade Descriptions Act 1968, s 1(1)(b). **Rees v Munday** [1974] **3** 506, QBD.
Time limit for prosecutions. *See* False trade description—Time limit for prosecutions, *above*.
Trade usage. *See* False trade description—Falsity of description, *above*.

TRADE DISPUTE
Acts done in contemplation or furtherance of trade dispute—
Ballot before industrial action—
Conduct of ballot—Union plan telling postal worker members to intercept ballot papers at delivery office workplace, open immediately and vote at workplace—Whether union's plan amounting to 'interference' with conduct of ballot—Trade Union and Labour Relations (Consolidation) Act 1992, s 230—Human Rights Act 1998, Sch 1, Pt I, art 11. **Royal Mail Group Ltd v Communication Workers Union** [2020] **3** 1030, CA.
Industrial action authorised or endorsed by ballot—Whether action required to continue without substantial interruption if authority or endorsement of ballot to be relied on—Whether change in workforce over period of action rendering ballot ineffective—Trade Union 1984. **Post Office v Union of Communication Workers** [1990] **3** 199, CA.
Industrial action lacking support of ballot if person entitled to vote not accorded such entitlement—Circumstances in which failure to send person ballot paper not constituting denial of entitlement to vote—Trade Union and Labour Relations (Consolidation) Act 1992, ss 227(1), 230(2), 232A(c), 232B. **P v National Association of Schoolmasters/Union of Women Teachers** [2003] **1** 993, HL.
Notification to employer—Union providing information about employees potentially involved in strike action—Employer alleging information provided inadequate and inaccurate—Scope of duty to provide information about balloting process to employer—Trade Union and Labour Relations (Consolidation) Act 1992, ss 226A, 232B. **Serco Ltd (t/a Serco Docklands) v National Union of Rail, Maritime and Transport Workers** [2011] **3** 913, CA.
Question on voting paper—Union seeking authorisation of action up to and including strike—Whether question asking voter whether he is prepared to take part in industrial action up to and including strike satisfying legislative requirements—Whether voting paper required to ask voter both whether he is prepared to take part in strike and whether he is prepared to take part in action short of strike—Trade Union Act 1984, s 11(4). **Post Office v Union of Communication Workers** [1990] **3** 199, CA.
Immunity from civil action—
Inducement of breach of contract of employment—Employee-managers of on-licensed premises—Questionnaire of trade union seeking information of managers' terms of employment—Managers asked inter alia to state weekly sales and total wages bill—Express or implied terms of employment not to disclose confidential information—Inducement to disclose information—Interference with existing contractual obligations—Incitement to commit breach of contract of service—Whether questionnaire issued in contemplation or furtherance of a trade dispute—Trade Disputes Act 1906, s 3. **Bents Brewery Co Ltd v Hogan** [1945] **2** 570, Assizes.
Inducement of breach of statutory duty—Unlawful interference with employers' business—Statutory scheme regulating registered dock workers—Scheme providing that dock workers 'shall ... work for such periods as are reasonable'—Proposed abolition of scheme by legislation—Union balloting registered dock workers for authority to take industrial action—Dock workers in favour of strike—Whether threatened strike unlawful—Dock Workers (Regulation of Employment) (Amendment) Order 1967, Sch 2, cl 8(5)(b). **Associated British Ports v Transport and General Workers' Union** [1989] **3** 822, HL.
In contemplation or furtherance of—
Acts committed before commencement of illegal strike—Whether acts 'in furtherance of' strike—Trade Disputes and Trade Unions Act 1927, s 1. **R v Tearse, Lee, Haston and Keen** [1944] **2** 403, CCA.
Claim by party that he has acted in furtherance of trade dispute—Union in dispute with British Steel Corporation deciding to extend strike action to private steel sector—Union hoping that private steel companies would put pressure on government to allow British Steel to increase pay offer—Extension of strike not having immediate adverse trade or industrial effect on British Steel—Union honestly and sincerely believing that extension of strike to private sector would advance their cause in their dispute with British Steel—Whether union officers acting 'in ... furtherance of trade dispute'—Trade Union and Labour Relations Act 1974, s 13(1)(as substituted by the Trade Union and Labour Relations (Amendment) Act 1976, s 3(2)). **Duport Steels Ltd v Sirs** [1980] **1** 529, HL, QBD CA.
Industrial action taken as result of union ballot—Suspension of industrial action pending negotiations—Negotiations unsuccessful—Resumption of industrial action—Whether industrial action in furtherance of continuing dispute or fresh dispute—Whether fresh ballot required—Trade Union Act 1984, s 10. **Monsanto plc v Transport and General Workers' Union** [1987] **1** 358, CA.
Secondary action in furtherance of dispute—Claim by party that he had acted in furtherance of trade dispute—Employees of national newspaper company instructed by their union to black copy from Press Association—Union genuinely believing that blacking of copy would advance cause of provincial members involved in pay dispute with provincial newspaper proprietors—Whether union officers acting 'in...furtherance of' trade dispute—Trade Union and Labour Relations Act 1974, s 13(1) (as substituted by the Trade Union and Labour Relations (Amendment) Act 1976, s 3(2)). **Express Newspapers Ltd v MacShane** [1980] **1** 65, HL.
Secondary action in furtherance of dispute—Claim by party that he had acted in furtherance of trade dispute—Policy of television technicians' union that television stations should not buy in ready-made programmes from outside—Plaintiffs making programmes and agreeing to sell them to television station—Union blacking programmes—Whether union acting in contemplation or furtherance of 'trade dispute'—Whether union's action amounting to interference with plaintiffs' trade or business by unlawful means—Trade Union and Labour Relations Act 1974, ss 13, 29—Employment Act 1980, s 17. **Hadmor Productions Ltd v Hamilton** [1982] **1** 1042, HL.

TRADE DISPUTE (cont)—
Acts done in contemplation or furtherance of trade dispute (cont)—
In contemplation or furtherance of (cont)—
Secondary action in furtherance of dispute—Immunity of secondary action from suit in tort—Contract for supply of services between employer who is party to dispute and employer to whom secondary action relates—Vessel let on time charter by owners to charterers and sub-let to sub-charterers—Sub-charterers contracting with tug company for towage services to enable vessel to leave port—Vessel blacked while in port—Employees of tug company persuaded by seamen's union to take secondary action to prevent vessel leaving port—Whether contract for supply of services between shipowners and tug company—Whether secondary action directly preventing supply of services by shipowner under time charter—Whether secondary action by seamen's union actionable in tort—Trade Union and Labour Relations Act 1974, s 13(1)—Employment Act 1980, s 17(3), (6). **Merkur Island Shipping Corp v Laughton** [1983] 2 189, HL.
Secondary action in furtherance of dispute—Validity of secondary action—Contract for supply of goods or services between employer who is party to dispute and employer to whom secondary action relates—Goods or services supplied to associated company of employer who was party to dispute—Union action aimed at disrupting supply of goods or services to associated company—Whether secondary action by union immune from action in tort—Trade Union and Labour Relations Act 1974, s 13(2)—Employment Act 1980, s 17(3). **Dimbleby & Sons Ltd v National Union of Journalists** [1984] 1 751, HL.
Secondary action in furtherance of dispute—Validity of secondary action—Contract for supply of services between employer who is party to dispute and employer to whom secondary action relates—Vessel let on time charter by owners to charterers—Charterers engaging shipping agents to arrange harbour services with port authority—Vessel blacked while in port—Port authority's employees taking secondary action to prevent vessel leaving port—Whether contract for supply of services between owners and port authority—Whether secondary action by port authority's employees unlawful—Employment Act 1980, s 17(3),(6). **Marina Shipping Ltd v Laughton** [1982] 1 481, CA.
Secondary picketing—Union co-ordinating secondary picketing organised by branch unions—Whether union acting in furtherance or continuation of trade dispute—Whether inducing or encouraging branch unions to breach its rules and act ultra vires inducing or encouraging breach of contract by branch unions—Trade Union and Labour Relations Act 1974, s 13(1)—Employment Act 1980, s 17. **Thomas v National Union of Mineworkers (South Wales Area)** [1985] 2 1, Ch D.
Inducement to commit breach of contract of employment—
Evidence of knowledge of contract. **Thomson (DC) & Co Ltd v Deakin** [1952] 2 361, CA.
Non-unionist's contract of employment—Union's threat to call strike—No express exclusion of strike action in contract of employment—Notice of sufficient length to terminate contracts of employment of prospective strikers—Purpose to procure dismissal of plaintiff who formed breakaway union—Plaintiff dismissed as result—Strike notice lawful—Tort of intimidation not established—Protection under Trade Disputes Act 1906, s 3. **Morgan v Fry** [1968] 3 452, CA.
Sub-contract by main building contractors for labour only—Whether sub-contract a contract of employment—Trade Disputes Act 1906, s 3—Trade Disputes Act 1965, s 1. **Emerald Construction Co Ltd v Lowthian** [1966] 1 1013, CA.
Threat to induce employees to break contracts of employment—Overtime dispute—Trade dispute—Whether immunity conferred by statute—Trade Disputes Act 1906, s 3. **Camden Exhibition and Display Ltd v Lynott** [1965] 3 28, CA.
Threat to induce employees to break contracts of employment—Purpose of threat to secure recognition of union—Employers resisting threat—Whether immunity conferred—Trade Disputes Act 1906, s 3. **Stratford (J T) & Son Ltd v Lindley** [1964] 3 102, HL.
Injunction. *See* **Injunction** (Interlocutory—Trade dispute—Claim by party against whom injunction sought that he had acted in furtherance of trade dispute).
Interference with trade, business or employment—
Overriding purpose advancement of defendant union in rivalry with another union—No trade dispute—Picketing—Interference and threatened interference with fuel oil supplied to plaintiff company's hotel—Injunction—Whether injunction would be granted against threatened tort—Trade Disputes Act 1906, ss 3, 4, 5(3). **Torquay Hotel Co Ltd v Cousins** [1969] 1 522, CA.
Threat to strike in breach of contract with employers—Purpose of threat to secure dismissal of employee—Whether authors of threats liable for tort of intimidation—Whether immunity conferred—Conspiracy, and Protection of Property Act 1875, s 3 (as amended by Trade Disputes Act 1906, s 1)—Trade Disputes Act 1906, s 3. **Rookes v Barnard** [1964] 1 367, HL.
Meaning of trade dispute—
Acts of local committee after ineffective resolution for expulsion of member—Local committee preventing member from obtaining employment—Whether dispute between member and committee a 'trade dispute'—Whether committee's acts 'in furtherance of a trade dispute'—Trade Disputes Act 1906, ss 3, 5(3). **Huntley v Thornton** [1957] 1 234, Ch D.
Dispute between employers and workers—Dispute between shipowners and union—Attempts by union to induce port workers in England and elsewhere to break their contracts of employment and withdraw services from ship unless owners agreeing with union terms and conditions of employment of crew—Policy of union to compel owners by industrial action to employ crews on standard terms at union rates—Ship's crew not in dispute with owners—Whether dispute between owners and union a trade dispute—Whether acts done in contemplation or furtherance of trade dispute—Trade Union and Labour Relations Act 1974, s 13(1) (as amended by the Trade Union and Labour Relations (Amendment) Act 1976, s 3(2)), 29(1). **NWL Ltd v Woods** [1979] 3 614, HL.
Dispute relating 'wholly or mainly' to termination of employment—Union campaigning against privatisation of Post Office telecommunications and licensing of private telecommunications systems—Plaintiff granted licence to operate private system—Union instructing members not to interconnect plaintiff's system to Post Office system—Whether a dispute between Post Office and employees—Whether dispute relating wholly or mainly to termination of employees' employment—Trade Union and Labour Relations Act 1974, ss 13(1), 29(1)—Employment Act 1982, s 18(1). **Mercury Communications Ltd v Scott-Garner** [1984] 1 179, Ch D and CA.
Picketing. *See* Picketing, *below.*

TRADE DISPUTE (cont)—

Ballot before industrial action. *See* Acts done in contemplation ot furtherance of trade dispute—Ballot before industrial action, *above*.

Breach of peace. *See* Picketing—Breach of peace anticipated, *below*.

Conspiracy—
    Motive—
        Furtherance of trade dispute—Burden of proof—Trade Disputes Act 1906, s 1. **Stratford (J T) & Son Ltd v Lindley** [1964] **3** 102, HL.
        Legitimate protection of interests of trade union—Furtherance of trade dispute—Trade Disputes Act 1906, s 5. **Morgan v Fry** [1968] **3** 452, CA.

Dispute between employers and workmen or workmen and workmen—
    Claim by union for recognition—
        Claim made after refusal of company to negotiate over dismissal of employees—Whether trade dispute—Trade Disputes (Arbitration and Inquiry) Ordinance (Laws of Trinidad and Tobago 1950) s 2(1). **Beetham v Trinidad Cement Co Ltd** [1960] **1** 274, PC.

Dispute connected with employment or terms or conditions of employment—
    Controversy between two unions—No controversy as to employment by company—Union instructing members not to handle company's barges—Whether trade dispute—Trade Disputes Act 1906, ss 3, 5(3). **Stratford (J T) & Son Ltd v Lindley** [1964] **3** 102, HL.

Dispute as to agreement restricting embargoes or overtime working—Whether dispute as to terms and conditions of employment—Whether 'trade dispute'—Trade Disputes Act 1906, s 5(3). **Camden Exhibition and Display Ltd v Lynott** [1965] **3** 28, CA.

Dispute connected with terms and conditions of employment—
    Coercive interference with conduct of employer's business distinguished—
        Actions of employers not having reached stage involving dispute connected with terms and conditions of employment—Broadcasting corporation—Transmission of television programme to South Africa—Employees' trade union objecting to South African government's racial policy—Employees' union threatening industrial action to prevent transmission unless corporation stopped programme being transmitted to South Africa—Corporation refusing to do so—Employees required by contracts of employment to perform any duties that might reasonably be required of them—Whether dispute between union and corporation 'connected with terms and conditions of employment'—Trade Union and Labour Relations Act 1974, s 29(1). **BBC v Hearn** [1978] **1** 111, CA.

Meaning of 'terms and conditions of employment'—
    Trade Union and Labour Relations (Consolidation) Act 1992, s 244(1)(a). **P v National Association of Schoolmasters/Union of Women Teachers** [2003] **1** 993, HL.

Terms and conditions of employment—
    Terms and conditions understood and applied by parties but not incorporated in contract—Dispute connected with terms and conditions not incorporated in contract—Whether a 'trade dispute'—Trade Union and Labour Relations Act 1974, s 29(1). **BBC v Hearn** [1978] **1** 111, CA.

Duress—
    Economic duress—
        Threat to black ship—International trade union federation threatening to black ship berthed in Sweden until shipowners entered into contracts with federation and crew—Contracts requiring shipowners to pay compensation to federation in respect of crew's past wages and enter into fresh contracts of employment with crew on terms approved by federation—Shipowners complying with demands and signing required documents on threat of blacking—Shipowners seeking to avoid contracts with federation on ground of economic duress and claiming restitution of sums paid—Proper law of contracts English law—Economic pressure lawful under Swedish law—Whether legitimacy of economic duress to be determined by local law of place where industrial action occurred or by law governing contract—Whether shipowners entitled to avoid contracts and recover sums paid and losses. **Dimskal Shipping Co SA v International Transport Workers Federation** [1991] **4** 871, HL.
        Threat to black vessel unless payment made by shipowners to international seafarers welfare fund on behalf of crew members—Whether money recoverable by shipowners on basis of a resulting trust or as money paid under duress—Whether pressure legitimate so as to exclude restitutional remedy in an action for money had and received—Whether dispute as to payment to fund 'connected with terms and conditions of employment'—Trade Union and Labour Relations Act 1974, s 13 (as amended by the Trade Union and Labour Relations (Amendment) Act 1976, s 3(2)), 29(1). **Universe Tankships Inc of Monrovia v International Transport Workers' Federation** [1982] **2** 67, HL.

Illegal strike. *See* Acts done in contemplation or furtherance of trade dispute—In contemplation or furtherance of—Acts committed before commencement of illegal strike, *above*.

Immunity from civil action—
    Acts done in contemplation or furtherance of trade dispute. *See* Acts done in contemplation or furtherance of trade dispute—Immunity from civil action, *above*.

Inducement of breach of contract. *See* Acts done in contemplation or furtherance of trade dispute—Inducement to commit breach of contract of employment, *above*.

Industrial dispute. *See* **Industrial relations** (Industrial dispute).

Industrial tribunal. *See* **Employment tribunal**.

Injunction—
    Interlocutory. *See* **Injunction** (Interlocutory—Trade dispute).

Interference with trade, business or employment. *See* Acts done in contemplation or furtherance of trade dispute—Interference with trade, business or employment, *above*.

Master and servant. *See* **Employment** (Trade dispute).

Meaning of. *See* Acts done in contemplation or furtherance of trade dispute—Meaning of trade dispute, *above*.

National Arbitration Tribunal. *See* **Employment** (National Arbitration Tribunal).

Nuisance—
    Picketing. *See* Picketing—Nuisance, *below*.

TRADE DISPUTE (cont)—
Picketing—
Assault—
Obstruction of highway—Interference with contract—Intimidation—Nuisance—Picketing by union in course of trade dispute—Large numbers of pickets at collieries during miners' strike—Union organising secondary picketing of collieries and other industrial premises within and outside union's area—Whether picketing tortious—Whether mass picketing tortious and criminal—Whether injunction would be granted restraining picketing—Conspiracy and Protection of Property Act 1875, s 7. **Thomas v National Union of Mineworkers (South Wales Area)** [1985] 2 1, Ch D.
Breach of peace anticipated—
Obstruction of police—Right of police to take steps to prevent anticipated breach of peace—Whether police justified in limiting number of pickets—Discretion of police officer to take steps that he thought proper—Prevention of Crimes Amendment Act 1885, s 2. **Piddington v Bates** [1960] 3 660, QBD.
Interference with contract—
Picketing by union in course of trade dispute—Large numbers of pickets at collieries during miners' strike—Union organising secondary picketing of collieries and other industrial premises within and outside union's area—Whether picketing tortious—Whether injunction would be granted restraining picketing. **Thomas v National Union of Mineworkers (South Wales Area)** [1985] 2 1, Ch D.
Intimidation—
Picketing by union in cause of trade dispute—Large numbers of pickets at collieries during miners' strike—Union organising secondary picketing within and outside union's area—Whether picketing tortious—Whether injunction would be granted restraining picketing. **Thomas v National Union of Mineworkers (South Wales Area)** [1985] 2 1, Ch D.
Nuisance—
Interference with convenience must be substantial to constitute nuisance actionable at law—Injunction nevertheless able to be granted quia timet. **Torquay Hotel Co Ltd v Cousins** [1968] 3 43, Ch D.
Obstruction of highway—
Picketing by union in course of trade dispute—Large numbers of pickets at collieries during miners' strike—Union organising secondary picketing of collieries and other industrial premises within and outside union's area—Whether picketing tortious—Whether injunction would be granted restarting picketing. **Thomas v National Union of Mineworkers (South Wales Area)** [1985] 2 1, Ch D.
Right of peaceful picketing—Attendance at specified place for purpose of peaceful picketing—Attendance only for purpose of peaceful communication or persuasion—Attendance for that purpose not of itself an offence—Right to stop vehicle on highway for purpose of peaceful persuasion—Vehicle attempting to drive on to building site during building workers' strike—Driver stopping vehicle at picketer's request—Picketer failing to persuade driver not to drive on to site—Picketer then standing in front of vehicle to prevent it moving—Whether an implied right to stop and detain vehicles on highway for purpose of peaceful persuasion—Whether picketer attending on highway only for purpose of peaceful persuasion—Highways Act 1959, s 121—Industrial Relations Act 1971, s 134(1), (2). **Broome v DPP** [1974] 1 314, HL.
Right of peaceful picketing—Attendance at specified place for purpose of peaceful picketing—Obstruction of police—Intimidation—40 pickets moving in continuous circle on highway outside main entrance to factory—Approaching vehicles caused to halt temporarily and foot passengers impeded—No breach of peace anticipated—Whether intimidation—Whether conduct justified—Trade Disputes Act 1906, s 2(1). **Tynan v Balmer** [1966] 2 133, QBD.
Right of peaceful picketing—
Nature of right—Immunity from prosecution or civil action in certain circumstances—Picketer asserting right to communicate with driver of vehicle—Picketer one of large crowd—Police apprehending likelihood of disorder—Police forming cordon to enable vehicle to pass freely—Effect of cordon to prevent picketer communicating with driver—Picketer assaulting constable in attempt to break through cordon—Whether police infringing right of picketer to communicate with driver—Whether constable assaulted in execution of his duty—Industrial Relations Act 1971, s 134(1), (2). **Kavanagh v Hiscock** [1974] 2 177, QBD Divl Ct.
Obstruction of highway. *See* Picketing—Obstruction of highway—Right of peaceful picketing, *above*.
Picketing 'at or near' place of work—At or near—Premises on trading estate—Picket established at entrance to trading estate—Entrance to trading estate 0.7 mile from employers' premises—Whether picket taking place 'at or near' employees' place of work—Whether picketing lawful—Trade Union and Labour Relations Act 1974, s 15(1). **Rayware Ltd v Transport and General Workers' Union** [1989] 3 583, CA.
Whether right exercisable against will of owner of land and regardless of byelaws affecting land—Trade Union and Labour Relations Act 1974, s 15. **British Airports Authority v Ashton** [1983] 3 6, QBD.
Reference—
Fair Wages Resolution—
Condition of contract for reference by Minister of Labour of dispute whether Fair Wages Resolution being complied with to independent tribunal—Reference by Minister to Industrial Court—Validity—Jurisdiction of Industrial Court to hear reference—Whether mandamus to hear reference would lie—Industrial Courts Act 1919, s 2(3)—Standard Conditions of Government Contracts for Stores Purchases, Edition of September, 1962, condition 17, cl 3. **R v Industrial Court, ex p ASSET** [1964] 3 130, QBD.
Unemployment benefit—
Disqualification of persons losing employment because of stoppage of work—
Exception. *See* **Social security** (Unemployment benefit—Disqualification for benefit—Loss of employment due to stoppage of work).

TRADE EFFLUENT
Discharge into river. *See* **Water and watercourses** (Pollution of river—Discharge of trade effluent).
Discharge into sewer—
Contract regulating—
Duration of contract. *See* **Contract** (Time—Duration of contract—Whether determinable by reasonable notice—Contract regulating the discharge of trade effluent into the public sewer).

TRADE LICENCE
Vehicle. *See* **Road traffic** (Trade licence).

TRADE MARK
Assignment—
Restriction on assignment—
Exclusive rights—Enemy property—Assignment of trade marks with goodwill by Custodian of Enemy Property—Retention by former owner of right to use mark at common law—'Exclusive rights'—Effectiveness of assignment—Failure to advertise assignment—Trade Marks Act 1938, s 22(1), (4), (7). **Reuter (R J) Co Ltd v Mulhens (Ferd)** [1953] **2** 1160, CA.
Correction of register—
Entry of memorandum relating to a trade mark—
Agreement between registered proprietor and registered user imposing restrictions on statutory right of registered proprietor—Discretion of registrar—Whether entry of memorandum would be a proper exercise of discretion—Trade Marks Act 1938, s 34(1)(e)—Trade Marks Rules 1938 (SR & O 1938 No 661), r 85. **Svenska Aktiebolaget Gasaccumulator's Application, Re** [1962] **1** 886, CA.
Enemy property—
Trade marks vested in custodian. *See* **Trading with the enemy** (Custody of enemy property—Vesting of property in custodian of enemy property—Trade marks).
European Community—
Freedom of movement of goods. *See* **European Union** (Freedom of movement—Goods—Trade mark exhaustion).
European Union—
Freedom of movement of goods. *See* **European Union** (Freedom of movement—Goods—Trade mark exhaustion).
European Union. *See* **European Union** (Trade marks).
Exhaustion—
European Union—
Freedom of movement of goods. *See* **European Union** (Freedom of movement—Goods—Trade mark exhaustion).
Hallmark. *See* **Hallmarking.**
Infringement—
Advertisement—
Use of plaintiff's mark to describe plaintiff's goods in list advertising defendant's goods—Use to show that defendant's goods identical in substance but cheaper—Whether use was 'in relation to defendant's goods'—Trade Marks Act 1938, ss 4, 68(1), 71(2). **Bismag Ltd v Amblins (Chemists) Ltd** [1940] **2** 608, CA.
Effect of infringement—
Whether infringement of trade mark in itself constituting wrongdoing of sufficient depravity to engage doctrine of ex turpi causa. **Inter Lotto (UK) Ltd v Camelot Group plc** [2003] **3** 191, Ch D.
European Union. *See* **European Union** (Trade marks—Infringement).
Evidence—
Admissibility—Surveys—Reasonably well-informed and reasonably observant internet user— Whether evidence of witnesses selected from survey of internet users admissible. **Interflora Inc v Marks & Spencer plc** [2013] **2** 663, CA.
Internet—
European Union. *See* **European Union** (Trade marks—Infringement—Internet).
Injunction against internet service providers (ISPs)—Costs—Costs of implementing website-blocking orders—Whether ISPs or right-holders to bear costs—European Parliament and Council Directive 2000/31/EC—European Parliament and Council Directive 2001/29/EC—European Parliament and Council Directive 2004/48/EC. **Cartier International AG v British Sky Broadcasting Ltd** [2018] **2 Comm** 1057, SC; [2018] **2 Comm** 1057, SC; [2018] **4** 373, SC; [2018] **4** 373, SC.
Injunction against internet service providers (ISPs)—Injunction to prevent access to target websites on basis of third party infringement of trade mark—Form of order—'Unlawful activity'—Approval of court. **Cartier International AG v British Sky Broadcasting Ltd (No 2)** [2015] **1 Comm** 714n, Ch D; [2015] **1** 1023n, Ch D.
Injunction against internet service providers (ISPs)—Injunction to prevent access to target websites on basis of third party infringement of trade mark—Further application for injunctions against new websites. **Cartier International AG v British Sky Broadcasting Ltd (No 3)** [2015] **1 Comm** 718n, Ch D; [2015] **1** 1027n, Ch D.
Injunction against internet service providers (ISPs)—Jurisdiction—Applicable principles— Proportionality—Injunction sought against internet service providers to prevent access to websites on basis of third party infringement of trade mark—Whether orders proportionate— Costs—Senior Courts Act 1981, s 37(1)—Copyright, Designs and Patents Act 1988, s 97A—European Parliament and Council Directive 2000/31/EC—European Parliament and Council Directive 2001/29/EC, art 8(3)—European Parliament and Council Directive 2004/48/EC, art 11. **Cartier International AG v British Sky Broadcasting Ltd** [2017] **1 Comm** 507, CA; [2017] **1** 700, CA; **Cartier International AG v British Sky Broadcasting Ltd (No 3)** [2015] **1 Comm** 718n, Ch D; [2015] **1** 1027n, Ch D.
Injunction against service providers (ISPs)—Jurisdiction—Applicable principles—Proportionality— Injunction sought against internet service providers to prevent access to websites on basis of third party infringement of trade mark—Whether orders proportionate—Senior Courts Act 1981, s 37(1)—EP and Council Directive 2000/31/EC—EP and Council Directive 2004/48/EC, arts 3(1), (2), 11, 52(1). **Cartier International AG v British Sky Broadcasting Ltd** [2015] **1 Comm** 641, Ch D; [2015] **1** 949, Ch D.

TRADE MARK (cont)—
  Infringement (cont)—
    Likelihood of confusion—
      Similarity of mark and sign—Claimants proprietors of Community trade marks SCRABBLE and SCRAMBLE—Defendants selling electronic game 'SCRAMBLE' and 'SCRAMBLE WITH FRIENDS'—Whether threshold test of similarity—Whether similarity of mark and sign—Whether likelihood of confusion—Council Regulation 207/2009/EC, art 9(1)(a), (b), (c). **JW Spear & Sons Ltd v Zynga Inc (No 2)** [2016] **1** 226, CA.
    Mistake—
      Directory of trade marks—Ownership of plaintiff's trade mark attributed to another company—Mistake by publishers—Publication of inaccurate statement not a 'use' of the trade mark—Trade Marks Act 1938, ss 4(1), 68(2). **Ravok (M) (Weatherwear) Ltd v National Trade Press Ltd** [1955] **1** 621, QBD.
    Name—
      Defence—Bona fide use by person of own name—'Bona fide'—Maker's name—Confusion in the course of trade—Trade Marks Act 1938, ss 4(1), 8(1). **Baume & Co Ltd v A H Moore Ltd** [1958] **2** 113, CA.
      Internet domain names—Registration of company trade marks as Internet domain names—Registration of names carried out by dealer in domain names—Judge granting injunction against dealer—Whether judge right to do so—Whether infringement of trade mark—Trade Marks Act 1994, s 10(3). **British Telecommunications plc v One In A Million Ltd** [1998] **4** 476, CA.
    Sale of reconditioned goods—
      Reconditioned goods including parts not manufactured by registered proprietors—Trade Marks Act 1905, s 39. **Hoover Ltd v Air-Way Ltd** [1936] **1** 466, Ch D.
    Search order—
      Self-incrimination—Civil proceedings pertaining to infringement of intellectual property rights—Whether defendant's right to assert privilege against self-incrimination removed by statutory provision—Supreme Court Act 1981, s 72. **Cobra Golf Ltd v Rata** [1997] **2** 150, Ch D.
    Unauthorised use of registered trade mark—
      Criminal offence—Manufacture of goods authorised by registered trade mark holder but sale not authorised—Whether sale or possession of such goods by appellants constituting unauthorised use of trade marks—Whether disproportionate breach of appellants' property rights—Trade Marks Act 1994, s 92—Human Rights Act 1998, Sch 1, Pt II, art 1. **R v M** [2018] **1** 304, SC.
      Criminal offence—Whether essential ingredient of offence use of registered trade mark as indication of trade origin—Whether reasonable belief no relevant trade mark registered a defence—Trade Marks Act 1994, s 92. **R v Johnstone** [2003] **3** 884, HL.
    Use of identical trade mark—
      Long period of honest concurrent use—Level of confusion—First Council Directive (EEC) 89/104, art 4. **Budejovicky Budvar Narodni Podnik v Anheuser-Busch Inc** [2012] **3** 1405n, CA.
      Non-trade mark use—Whether use affected function of trademark—Trade Marks Act 1994, s 10—First Council Directive (EEC) 89/104, art 5(1). **Arsenal Football Club plc v Reed** [2003] **1** 137, Ch D; [2003] **3** 865, CA.
    Use of similar trade mark—
      Similar—Coca-Cola and Pepsi-Cola—Unfair Competition Act (Canada) 1932, ss 2(k), 3(c), 23(5)(b). **Coca-Cola Co of Canada Ltd v Pepsi-Cola Co of Canada Ltd** [1942] **1** 615, PC.
    Validity—
      Passing off—Revocation for non-use—Claimants proprietors of Community trade mark 'Assos' in respect of clothing—Defendant operating global online fashion company under brand name 'ASOS'—Defendant proprietor of UK trade mark 'ASOS' in respect of clothing—Scope of registration—Whether infringement of CTM—Whether likelihood of confusion—Whether UK trade mark valid—Trade Marks Act 1994, ss 5(2)(b), (3), (4)(a), 47(2)—Council Regulation 207/2009/EC, arts 8(4), 9(1)(b), (c), 12, 51. **Maier v Asos plc** [2016] **2** 738, CA.
  Licensing agreement—
    Inspection of account. *See* **Accounts** (Inspection—Scope of obligation—Licence agreement—Agreement in relation to patents and trade marks).
    Termination—
      Licensor terminating agreement on non-payment of minimum royalties—Payment being made within 14 days of due date—Whether termination provisional—Whether termination rendered ineffective by late payment. **Hay & Robertson plc v Kangol Ltd** [2004] **2 Comm** 185, .
  'Likelihood of confusion'—
    European Community. *See* **European Union** (Trade marks—'Likelihood of confusion').
  Mark—
    Container—
      Bottle—Whether distinctively shaped bottle can be registered as a trade mark—Trade Marks Act 1938. **Coca-Cola Co's Applications, Re** [1986] **2** 274, HL.
    Representation or description of external appearance of goods—
      Colour scheme—Scheme a complete representation of goods as appearing to eye—Capsules containing drugs—Colour scheme for complete capsule—Whether external appearances of goods capable of constituting a 'mark'. **Smith Kline & French Laboratories Ltd v Sterling-Winthrop Group Ltd** [1975] **2** 578, HL.
  Motions in respect of trade marks—
    Practice—
      Chancery Division. **Practice Direction** [1980] **2** 750, Ch D.
  Opposition to registration—
    Confusion—
      Contrary to morality—Mark formerly used by opponent in connection with his business in Czechoslovakia and Central Europe—Business nationalised in 1948 by Czechoslovakian law—No compensation paid—Opponent migrated to Canada—Nationalised business began exporting to United Kingdom—Such exporting continued thereafter—Opponent having established similar business in Canada began exporting to United Kingdom in 1960—Canadian exports small in comparison with exports from Czechoslovakian business—Whether Czechoslovakian business entitled to registration of mark—Trade Marks Act 1938, s 11. **Stredoceska Fruta Narodni Podnik's Application No B 836429, Re** [1968] **2** 913, Ch D.

TRADE MARK (cont)—
  Opposition to registration (cont)—
    Confusion (cont)—
      Use of mark alleged to be contrary to Merchandise Marks Act 1887—Forging trade mark—Foreign mark protected by law in Convention country—Discretion over registration of trade mark—Possibility of confusion as result of foreign advertisements reaching England—Trade Marks Act 1938, ss 11, 17, 52—Merchandise Marks Act 1887, ss 2(1), 3(1), 4. **Vitamins Ltd, Re application of** [1955] 3 827, Ch D.

      Use of mark on repaired stockings—Application to register mark for use on manufactured stockings—Opposition by manufacturers who owned another mark on ground of similarity—Trade mark generally limited to indication of origin—Use 'in relation' to goods—Connection in the course of trade—Trade Marks Act 1938, ss 3, 4(1), 9, 11, 12, 17(1), 28, 62, 65, 68. **Aristoc Ltd v Rysta Ltd** [1945] 1 34, HL.

  Owner of mark sole agent in United Kingdom of manufacturer of German calculating machine under agreement—
    Agreement terminated—Whether original registration in owner's name valid—Whether retention of mark by owner likely to cause deception or confusion to public—Whether court would exercise discretion and expunge mark—Trade Marks Act 1938, s 32. **Diehl KG's Application, Re** [1969] 3 338, Ch D.

  Passing off proceedings—
    Estoppel. *See* **Estoppel** (Res judicata—Issue estoppel—Trade mark proceedings—Passing off).

  Rectification of register—
    Mark by reason of its being likely to deceive or cause confusion disentitled to protection in a court of justice—
      Mark not likely to deceive or cause confusion at date of original registration—Mark subsequently becoming likely to cause confusion—Likelihood of confusion not arising from any blameworthy conduct on the part of the registered proprietor—Whether court having power to rectify register by expunging entry—Trade Marks Act 1938, ss 11, 32(1). **General Electric Co v The General Electric Co Ltd** [1972] 2 507, HL.

    Phonetic similarity to mark already in use—Application for removal from register more than seven years after registration—What must be established to show mark disentitled to protection—Discretion to remove registration—Trade Marks Act 1938, ss 11, 32. **Berlei (UK) Ltd v Bali Brassiere Co Inc** [1969] 2 812, HL.

  Registered users—
    Trafficking in trade mark—
      Application for registration of trade mark and registration of person as registered user—Proprietor not using or proposing to use mark in connection with goods similar to those to be marketed by licensees—Licence agreements including quality control provisions exercisable by proprietor over licensees' goods—Whether grant of proprietor's applications tending to facilitate 'trafficking' in trade mark—Trade Marks Act 1938, s 28(6). **American Greetings Corp's Application, Re** [1983] 2 609, Ch D and CA.

  Registration—
    Defensive registration of well-known trade marks—
      Use of mark in relation to other goods likely to be taken as indicating connection in course of trade—Character of evidence required—Trade Marks Act 1938, s 27(1). **Ferodo Ltd's Application, Re** [1945] 2 95, Ch D.

    Discretion—
      Circumstances which may be considered in exercise of discretion—No intention to use mark unless free publicity attached from name of television film feature—Series of 'Western' films shown in USA under title 'Rawhide'—Application by toy manufacturers to register 'Rawhide' in anticipation of series being shown in this country—Merchandising rights of film assigned to company other than applicants—Numerous such applications by applicants in respect of similar marks. **Cheryl Playthings Ltd's Application, Re** [1962] 2 86, Ch D.

    Distinctiveness—
      Acquired distinctiveness—KIT KAT—Three-dimensional sign in shape of KIT KAT chocolate bar—Whether mark having acquired distinctive character—Whether association sufficient—Whether reliance upon mark as indicating origin of goods required—Trade Marks Act 1994, s 3(1)—European Parliament and Council Directive 2008/95/EC, art 3(1), (3). **Société des Produits Nestlé SA v Cadbury UK Ltd** [2018] 2 39, CA.

      Acquired distinctiveness—KIT KAT—Three-dimensional sign in shape of KIT KAT chocolate bar—Whether mark having acquired distinctive character—Whether association sufficient—Whether reliance upon mark as indicating origin of goods required—Trade Marks Act 1994, s 3(1)—European Parliament and Council Directive 2008/95/EC, art 3(1), (3)—Council Regulation 207/2009/EC, art 7(1), (3). **Société des Produits Nestlé SA v Cadbury UK Ltd** [2016] 4 1081, Ch D.

      Colouring scheme—Mark adapted to distinguish goods with which applicant connected—Mark inherently adapted to distinguish—Combination of colours—Scheme in fact distinctive of applicant's goods—No motive for other proprietor to adopt scheme except to benefit from applicant's established goodwill—Whether scheme of colouring 'inherently adapted to distinguish' applicant's goods—Whether a 'distinctive mark'—Trade Marks Act 1938, s 9(1)(e), (2), (3)(a). **Smith Kline & French Laboratories Ltd v Sterling-Winthrop Group Ltd** [1975] 2 578, HL.

      Descriptive or distinctive words—'Shredded Wheat'—Capability of registration—Distinctive or merely descriptive words—Secondary meaning—Passing off—Product similar in shape but not in size—Carton quite different in make-up—Trade Mark and Design Act (RSC 1927, ss 5(1), 13. **Canadian Shredded Wheat Co Ltd v Kellogg Co of Canada Ltd** [1938] 1 618, PC.

      Geographical name—'Glastonburys'—Whether mark adapted to distinguish goods with which applicant connected—Rectification of register—Trade Marks Act 1905—1919, ss 3, 9(4), (5), 11, 19, 44. **Clark, Son & Morland Ltd's Trade Mark, Re** [1938] 2 377, HL.

      Geographical name—'Livron'—Invented word—Discretion to refuse registration—Mark calculated to deceive—Trade Marks Acts 1905-1919, ss 9, 11, 35—Trade Marks Act 1919, s 9. **Société des Usines Chimiques Rhone-Poulenc, Re the application of** [1937] 4 23, CA.

TRADE MARK (cont)—
Registration (cont)—
Distinctiveness (cont)—
Geographical name—'Yorkshire'—Solid drawn tubes and capillary fittings—Whether mark adapted to distinguish goods with which applicant connected—Whether mark inherently adapted to distinguish—'Adapted to distinguish'—Trade Marks Act 1938, s 9(1)(e)(3). **Yorkshire Copper Works Ltd v Trade Marks Registrar** [1954] **1** 570, HL.
Geographical name—'York'—Inherent capability of distinguishing—Mark factually distinctive of proprietor's goods and those of no-one else—Proprietor using mark on substantial scale and for long period—Whether past user and factual distinctiveness conclusive to show mark 'inherently capable of distinguishing'—Whether in relation to geographical name trader may obtain monopoly in its user to detriment of future traders—Trade Marks Act 1938, s 10(2)(a). **York Trailer Holdings Ltd v Registrar of Trade Marks** [1982] **1** 257, HL.
Invented word—Slang term—'Oomphies'—American slang term—Whether invented word—Trade Marks Act 1938, s 9(1)(c), (d), (11). **La Marquise Footwear's Application, Re** [1946] **2** 497, Ch D.
Machine twist—'Sheen'—Registrar consulting about desirability of registering word—Whether word 'Sheen' sufficiently distinctive—Whether consultation irregular—Trade Marks Acts 1905—1919, ss 9(5), 64(14). **Coats (J & P) Ltd's, Application, Re** [1936] **2** 975, CA.
Mark registered for roses—Intended user as variety name—Trade Marks Act 1938, s 9(1)(d), s 11. **Wheatcroft Bros Ltd, Re** [1954] **1** 110, Ch D.
Sign—Sign capable of being represented graphically—Conditions of registration—Colour—Purple—Company seeking to register the colour purple as 'applied to the whole visible surface' or being 'the predominant colour applied to the whole visible surface' of packaging of chocolate goods—Meaning of 'a sign' capable of being 'represented graphically'—Whether mark sufficiently clear, precise, self-contained, durable and objective—EP and Council Directive (EC) 2008/95, art 2. **Société des Produits Nestlé SA v Cadbury UK Ltd** [2014] **1** 1079, CA.
Sign—Sign capable of being represented graphically—Conditions of registration—Registered trade mark, the tile mark, relating to word game SCRABBLE—Challenge to validity of tile mark on ground mark not 'a sign'—Meaning of 'a sign' capable of being 'represented graphically'—Relevance of distinctiveness of mark to conditions of registration—Whether mark sufficiently clear, precise, self-contained, durable and objective—EP and Council Directive (EC) 2008/95, art 2. **Spear (JW) & Son Ltd v Zynga Inc** [2014] **1** 1093, CA.
Effect of registration—
Regulations standardising packaging and restricting branding on tobacco and related products—Whether registration conferring positive right to use trade mark—Whether unlawful interference with property rights—Human Rights Act 1998, Sch 1, Pt II, art 1—Standardised Packaging of Tobacco Products Regulations 2015, SI 2015/829—Charter of Fundamental Rights of the European Union, art 17. **R (on the application of British American Tobacco UK Ltd) v Secretary of State for Health** [2017] **2** 691, CA.
Whether owner of registered trade mark having statutory right to use mark overriding another person's common law passing off rights—Trade Marks Act 1994, s 9(1). **Inter Lotto (UK) Ltd v Camelot Group plc** [2003] **3** 191, Ch D.
Whether owner of registered trade mark having statutory right to use mark overriding another person's common law passing off rights—Trade Marks Act 1994, ss 2, 5(4), 9(1). **Inter Lotto (UK) Ltd v Camelot Group plc** [2003] **4** 575, CA.
Opposition. See Opposition to registration, *above.*
Phonetic equivalent of unregistrable word—
Whether registrable—Trade Marks Act 1938, s 9(1). **Electrix Ltd v Electrolux Ltd** [1959] **3** 170, HL.
Prohibition of registration of identical and resembling trade marks—
Application to register 'Vivicillin'—Three trade marks consisting of 'Cyllin' with or without additions already registered—Comparison of marks—No probability of confusion—Trade Marks Act 1938, ss 9(1)(c), 12(1), 17(2), 18(1). **Enoch, Re an application by** [1945] **2** 637, Ch D.
Mark likely to deceive or cause confusion with mark already on register—Defensive registration—Notional user—Trade Marks Act 1938, ss 12, 27(1), (6). **Eastex Manufacturing Co Ltd's Application, Re** [1947] **2** 55, Ch D.
Mark likely to deceive or cause confusion—Mark in respect of sulphadiazine preparations—Scheduled poison supplied only under statutory regulations—Trade Marks Act 1938, s 12(1). **Bayer Products Ltd's Application, Re** [1947] **2** 188, CA.
Service mark. See Service mark—Registration, *below.*
Removal from register—
Non-user—
Special circumstances in the trade—Foreign manufacturing company—War conditions preventing importation of goods—Trade Marks Act 1938, s 26(1)(b), (3). **Aktiebolaget Manus v Fullwood (R J) & Bland Ltd** [1949] **1** 205, CA.
Service mark—
Registration—
Provision of services—Provision—Retail services—Services provided in course of retailing goods—Services provided incidentally to or as adjunct of applicants' business of retailing goods—Applicants seeking to register mark as 'service mark' in respect of retail services—Whether mark registrable as services mark—Trade Marks Act 1938, s 68(1)—Trade Marks (Amendment) Act 1984, s 1(7). **Dee Corp plc, Re** [1989] **3** 948, CA.
Trust—
Whether trade mark in trust for manufacturer. See **Trust and trustee** (Constructive trust—Trade mark).
Validity—
Descriptive character—
Common name in trade—Claimants proprietors of Community trade mark SCRAMBLE—Whether mark designating character of goods—Whether mark customary in language or bona fide practices of, or common name in, trade—Council Regulation 207/2009/EC, arts 7(1), 51(1)(b). **JW Spear & Sons Ltd v Zynga Inc (No 2)** [2016] **1** 226, CA.

TRADE NAME
Passing off. See **Passing off** (Trade name).

TRADE NAME (cont)—
Registration—
Default in registration—
Disability of persons in default—Relief against disability—Grounds of relief—Belief that relief granted on request no 'sufficient cause' for failing to register—Effect of interpleading on plea of default under Act—Registration of Business Names Act 1916, s 8(1)(a). **Watson v Park Royal (Caterers) Ltd** [1961] **2** 346, QBD.

TRADE PROTECTION ASSOCIATION
Non-trading body—
Conspiracy to procure breach of contract—
Right of association to bring action. **British Motor Trade Association v Salvadori** [1949] **1** 208, Ch D.
Price maintenance—
Stop list—
Attempted purchase by person on stop list—Purchase money paid—Refusal to deliver—Recovery of price—Illegality. **Berg v Sadler & Moore** [1937] **1** 637, .
Rule providing for placing on stop list unless fine within limits to be fixed by association paid—Validity. **Thorne v Motor Trade Association** [1937] **3** 157, HL.

TRADE SECRETS
Disclosure—
Injunction. *See* **Employment** (Duty of servant—Confidential information—Injunction restraining disclosure).
Interlocutory injunction. *See* **Injunction** (Interlocutory—Confidential information—Trade secrets).
What constitutes trade secrets—
Whether restricted to secret formulae for manufacture of products—
Whether extending to non-technical or non-scientific information disclosure of which to competitor would cause owner real or significant harm. **Lansing Linde Ltd v Kerr** [1991] **1** 418, CA.

TRADE UNION
Action by member against union—
Matter of substance tinctured with oppression—
Invasion of members' individual rights. **Edwards v Halliwell** [1950] **2** 1064, CA.
Agreement—
Enforceability—
Agreement to provide benefits—Superannuation benefit—Union illegal at common law—Trade Union Act 1871, s 4. **Miller v Amalgamated Engineering Union** [1938] **2** 517, Ch D.
Breach of contract—
Inducement to commit—
Tort. *See* **Tort** (Inducement to commit breach of contract—Inference of intention—Trade union).
Breach of rules—
Complaint to industrial tribunal. *See* **Industrial relations** (Organisation of workers—Breach of rules—Complaint by member against organisation).
Certification as independent trade union—
Appeal—
Locus standi of appellant—Appeal to Employment Appeal Tribunal—Other union objecting to issue of certificate—Right of appeal expressly conferred on union refused certificate—Whether general right of appeal against decision of certification officer—Whether union objecting to issue of certificate to another union having right of appeal—Employment Protection Act 1975, ss 8(6), (9), 88(3). **General and Municipal Workers Union v Certification Officer** [1977] **1** 771, EAT.
Appeal against issue of certificate—
Procedure on appeal—Employment Protection Act 1975, s 8(9). **Blue Circle Staff Association v Certification Officer** [1977] **2** 145, EAT.
Appeal against refusal to issue certificate—
Procedure on appeal—Certification officer called as witness at appeal against his decision—Position of certification officer—Certification officer in judicial position and not to be cross-examined on validity of reasons for his decision—Desirability of Treasury Solicitor being made party to appeal as friend of appeal tribunal to protect public interest—Employment Protection Act 1975, s 8(9). **Squibb UK Staff Association v Certification Officer** [1979] **2** 452, CA.
Independence—
Freedom from domination or control of employer—Freedom from interference of employer—Factors to be considered in determining whether organisation independent of employer—Staff association—Certification officer refusing to issue certificate of independence on ground that association dependent on employers for its existence—Whether refusal justified—Trade Union and Labour Protection Act 1974, s 30(1)—Employment Protection Act 1975, s 8(1). **Blue Circle Staff Association v Certification Officer** [1977] **2** 145, EAT.
Freedom from interference of employer—Liable to interference—Association of employer's administrative staff only—Association having limited financial resorces but being provided with facilities to operate by employer—Good relationship existing between association and employer and employer recognising association as sole negotiating body for administrative staff—Whether association independent trade union—Whether 'liable to interference' from employer as a result of provision of facilities—Trade Union and Labour Relations Act 1974, s 30(1)(b). **Squibb UK Staff Association v Certification Officer** [1979] **2** 452, CA.
Jurisdiction of employment tribunal. *See* **Employment tribunal** (Jurisdiction—Detriment on grounds related to union membership or activities—Independent trade union).
Collective agreement—
Inducements relating to collective bargaining—
Recognised trade union entering negotiations with employer on pay offer—Union members voting to reject offer—Employer writing to employees direct—Letter providing bonus not to be paid if offer not accepted—Whether acceptance of offer having 'prohibited result' that terms of agreement not determined by collective agreement negotiated by union—Trade Union and Labour Relations (Consolidation) Act 1992, ss 145B, 145D. **Kostal UK Ltd v Dunkley** [2022] **2** 607, SC.

TRADE UNION (cont)—
  Collective agreement (cont)—
    Joint negotiating committee of employer and unions—
      Agreements over period of years on procedure, wages and conditions of work—New agreement negotiated by committee on majority decision of participating unions—Strike action by dissenting minority—Intention to create legally enforceable contracts not expressed in agreements—Surrounding circumstances showing climate of opinion adverse to such intention—Wording of agreements largely aspirational—Whether agreements enforceable at law. **Ford Motor Co Ltd v Amalgamated Union of Engineering and Foundry Workers** [1969] **2** 481, QBD.
    Proper law of contract. *See* **Conflict of laws** (Contract—Proper law of contract—Collective agreement).
  Committee meeting—
    Presence of non-member. *See* **Meeting** (Committee meeting—Presence of non-member).
  Condition of employment—
    Employment by public authority—
      Employee given right to be represented by official of one union—Employee joining another union—Whether entitled to be represented by official of that union—Whether employee placed under disability or disadvantage by 'condition' of employment—Whether restriction as to representation a 'condition'—Trade Disputes and Trade Unions Act 1927, s 6. **London Passenger Transport Board v Moscrop** [1942] **1** 97, HL.
  Conspiracy—
    Position at common law—
      Acts causing loss—Real purpose of combiners—Embargo. **Crofter Hand Woven Harris Tweed Co Ltd v Veitch** [1942] **1** 142, HL.
  Definition of trade union—
    Combination for regulating relations between masters and masters—
      Combination for imposing restrictive conditions on trade or business—Whether Co-operative Union Ltd registered as an industrial and provident society a trade union—Trade Union Act Amendment Act 1876, s 16—Trade Union Act 1913, s 2(1). **Birtley District Co-op Society Ltd v Windy Nook and District Industrial Co-op Society Ltd** [1959] **1** 623, QBD.
  Dismissal—
    Dismissal for refusal to join union—
      Refusal to join in accordance with union membership agreement—Unfair dismissal. *See* **Unfair dismissal** (Determination whether dismissal fair or unfair—Dismissal for refusing to join trade union in accordance with union membership agreement).
    Official—
      Elected officer. *See* Official—Dismissal—Elected officer, *below*.
  Dissolution—
    Registered trade union—
      Jurisdiction of court to order dissolution—Absence of statutory machinery to secure proper winding-up. **Keys v Boulter (No 2)** [1972] **2** 303, Ch D.
  Domestic tribunal—
    Recommendation—
      Trade union representing certain exhibitors represented on tribunal of film renters' association—Tribunal's recommendation to ban films to exhibitor, member of another trade union—Validity of recommendation. **Byrne v Kinematograph Renters Society Ltd** [1958] **2** 579, Ch D.
  Review of decision—
    Jurisdiction of court—Adjudication by executive council on member's complaint—Provision for appeal to general council—Whether court having jurisdiction to review decision of executive council and general council. **Hamlet v General Municipal Boilermakers and Allied Trades Union** [1987] **1** 631, Ch D.
    Jurisdiction of court—Adjudication by tribunal on member's conduct—Provision for appeal to executive of federation—Action begun by member without proceeding to appeal—Jurisdiction of court. **White v Kuzych** [1951] **2** 435, PC.
    Jurisdiction of court—Disciplinary action against member. **Lee v Showmen's Guild of GB** [1952] **1** 1175, CA.
    Whether jurisdiction of court ousted. *See* Rules—Election—Nominee member of proscribed organisation, *below*.
  Duty to consult—
    Civil service compensation scheme—
      Amendment—Consultation—Protection of property—Equality duty—Remedies for judicial review—Whether inadequate consultation with 'persons likely to be affected'—Whether entitlements under scheme constituting possessions—Whether amendment to scheme constituting unlawful interference with possessions—Whether breach of public sector equality duty—Whether relief to be refused as 'highly likely that the outcome … would not have been substantially different'—Superannuation Act 1972, ss 1(3), 2(3D)—Senior Courts Act 1981, s 31(2A)—Human Rights Act 1998, Sch 1, Pt II, art 1—Equality Act 2010, s 149. **R (on the application of Public and Commercial Services Union) v Minister for the Cabinet Office** [2018] **1** 142, DC.
  Expulsion of member—
    Appeal—
      Appeal allowed against finding that charge not proved—Decision on appeal in absence of member charged—Contrary to natural justice—Union's rule empowering executive council or management committee to expel member—Decision of management committee that charge against member not proven—Appeal by member of management committee to executive council—Decision by executive council, in absence of member charged, to expel him—Whether executive council empowered under rules to hear appeal against acquittal—Interlocutory injunction at suit of expelled member. **Hiles v Amalgamated Society of Woodworkers** [1967] **3** 70, Ch D.

TRADE UNION (cont)—
  Expulsion of member (cont)—
    Appeal by member to appeal committee—
      Date of hearing of appeals fixed by rules—Amalgamation of union with another union prior to date of hearing-New rules containing no provision for pending appeals—Validity of expulsion. **Braithwaite v Electrical Electronic and Telecommunication Union-Plumbing Trades Union** [1969] **2** 859, CA.
    Application of rules of natural justice—
      Opinion of council—Rule empowering executive council to expel any member in its opinion unfit for membership—Right of appeal to annual conference—No requirement that right of appeal be exhausted before application to court—Decision to expel member made without notice of charge or opportunity for him to be heard—Whether opinion of executive council was one to be formed after inquiry, so that rules of natural justice would apply to the making of the decision—Whether resort to court could be had before exhaustion of right of appeal. **Lawlor v Union of Post Office Workers** [1965] **1** 353, Ch D.
      Rule under which expulsion awarded not mentioned in charges—Member expelled not present at hearing—Power of court to grant relief against expulsion. **Annamunthodo v Oilfields Workers' Trade Union** [1961] **3** 621, PC.
    Damages—
      Action by member against union for breach of contract—Right to damages for breach of contract. **Bonsor v Musicians' Union** [1955] **3** 518, HL.
      Trade union member expelled from membership and employer induced to terminate contract of service—Factors relevant to assessment of damages—On appeal, undertaking by union to reinstate as member—Effect on damages. **Edwards v Society of Graphical and Allied Trades** [1970] **3** 689, CA.
    Deficiency in natural justice—
      Whether curable. *See* **Natural justice** (Trade union—Deficiency of natural justice before trial tribunal—Curability).
    Power to expel member—
      Member leaving employment without notice—Rule providing for suspension for such conduct—Rule providing for expulsion upon conduct detrimental to interests of the union—Expulsion of member—Validity. **Evans v National Union of Printing, Bookbinding and Paper Workers** [1938] **4** 51, KBD.
      Plaintiff members employed as full-time fire fighters—Union opposing full-time fire fighters undertaking additional retained duties—Members subsequently expelled for undertaking additional duties contrary to union policy—Whether members unjustifiably disciplined—Whether union policy constituting 'other industrial action'—Trade Union and Labour Relations (Consolidation) Act 1992, s 65(2)(a). **Knowles v Fire Brigades Union** [1996] **4** 653, CA.
    Right of union to expel member—
      Implied term of contract of membership—Expulsion by union, affiliated to Trades Union Congress, pursuant to award of disputes committee—All members recruited in certain areas after a certain time to be excluded—Recruitment in disregard of principles of Bridlington Agreement—Whether term implied in contract of membership that union entitled to do everything necessary to conform with Bridlington Agreement. **Spring v National Amalgamated Stevedores and Dockers Society** [1956] **2** 221, Ch Ct.
    Rules giving unfettered power. *See* Rules—Validity, *below.*
  Foss v Harbottle—
    Application of rule. *See* Legal proceedings—Action for wrong done to union, *below.*
  Funds—
    Disposition of funds—
      Disposition on secession from union—Union seceding from federation of merged unions—No provision in rules for seceding union to take proportion of funds with it—Whether seceding union entitled to share of funds—Trade Union and Labour Relations Act 1974, s 2(1)(b). **Burnley Nelson Rossendale and District Textile Workers' Union v Amalgamated Textile Workers' Union** [1986] **1** 885, QBD.
    Investment—
      Held by trustees. *See* Rules—Alteration of rules—Property of union, *below.*
    Political. *See* Political fund, *below.*
  Income tax—
    Exemption. *See* **Income tax** (Exemption—Trade union).
  Inter-union relations—
    Bridlington principles—
      Breach—Termination of membership of union. *See* Membership—Termination of membership—No-poaching agreement between unions—Bridlington principles, *below.*
  Jurisdiction of court. *See* Domestic tribunal—Review of decision—Jurisdiction of court, *above.*
  Legal assistance—
    Advice not tendered before limitation period expired—
      Extension of time. *See* **Limitation of action** (Extension of time limit—Material fact of decisive character outside knowledge of plaintiff—Ignorance of claim against employer).
    Implied power to support servant's litigation to vindicate reputation. *See* **Maintenance of action** (Common interest—Trade union employing salaried officials).
    Members, to. *See* Legal assistance to members, *below.*
  Legal assistance to members—
    Duty of union—
      Alleged failure of union to pursue a claim on behalf of a member against her employers for damages for personal injuries—Cause of action becoming statute barred—Action by member against union, and against union's officer, for alleged breach of contract and for alleged negligence—Union's rules provided for legal assistance to members—Whether this created a contractual obligation and extent of such obligation—Whether any loss or damage where member's alleged claim had no prospect of success at law. **Buckley v National Union of General and Municipal Workers** [1967] **3** 767, Assizes.

TRADE UNION (cont)—

Legal assistance to members (cont)—

Duty of union (cont)—

Alleged negligence of union in relation to member's claim for damages—Member's claim investigated and reported to central office by branch secretary in accordance with union's rules—Union's solicitor advised no cause of action—Advice communicated to member—Some two years later member apparently again raised the matter with branch secretary—No warning that any claim would become statute-barred on expiration of three-year period—Whether union in breach of duty. **Cross v British Iron, Steel and Kindred Trades Association** [1968] **1** 250, CA.

Legal proceedings—

Action for wrong done to union—

Proper plaintiff—Remedy within power of union itself—Application of rule in Foss v Harbottle—Applicability of rule in cases of urgency—Right of action by individual members—Executive council of union acting contrary to union policy—Power of union conference to approve or disapprove actions of executive council—Urgency precluding union from taking effective action in time—Individual members entitled to injunction requiring executive council to act in accordance with union policy. **Hodgson v National and Local Government Officers Association** [1972] **1** 15, Ch D.

Proper plaintiff—Unregistered trade union not entitled to sue in own name—Executive council of union acting contrary to policy declared by union conference—Action by individual members of union—Rule in Foss v Harbottle not applicable to unregistered trade union—Individual members entitled to injunction requiring executive council to act in accordance with union policy. **Hodgson v National and Local Government Officers Association** [1972] **1** 15, Ch D.

Right of audience in High Court and Court of Appeal—

Appearance by trade union official—Union an unincorporated body—General rule that unions to be legally represented—Discretion of court to dispense with rule—Dispute between two unions as to recognition by employers—Small union with limited means added as party to proceedings—Application by small union to be represented by deputy general secretary in those proceedings—Only minor matter involved—Whether application should be granted. **Engineers' and Managers' Association v Advisory, Conciliation and Arbitration Service (No 1)** [1979] **3** 223, CA.

Right of union to sue—

Defamatory statements relating to reputation of trade union—Trade union not a body corporate because not a special register body—Trade union which not a special register body suing in its own name for damages for libel—Whether union able to sue in its own name for damages for defamation in relation to its reputation as a legal entity—Whether union able to bring action for damages for defamation in its own name on behalf of all the members of the union—Trade Union and Labour Relations Act 1974, s 2(1). **Electrical Electronic Telecommunication and Plumbing Union v Times Newspapers Ltd** [1980] **1** 1097, QBD.

Defamatory statements relating to reputation of trade union—Trade union suing in registered name for damages for libel—Right to sue—Issue raised as preliminary point of law under RSC Ord 25, r 2. **National Union of General and Municipal Workers v Gillian** [1945] **2** 593, CA.

Defamatory statements relating to reputation of trade union—Trade union which not a special register body not a body corporate—Trade union which not a special register body suing in its own name for damages for libel—Whether union able to sue in its own name for damages for defamation in relation to its reputation as a legal entity—Whether union able to bring action for damages for defamation in its own name on behalf of all members of union—Trade Union and Labour Relations Act 1974, s 2(1). **Electrical Electronic Telecommunication and Plumbing Union v Times Newspapers Ltd** [1980] **1** 1097, QBD.

Libel against union—Allegation of 'rigging' a ballot. **Willis v Brooks** [1947] **1** 191, KBD.

Right to sue for procurement of breach of contract. **British Motor Trade Association v Salvadori** [1949] **1** 208, Ch D.

Libel—

Right to sue. See Legal proceedings—Right of union to sue, above.

Member—

Action by member against union. See Action by member against union, above.

Action by member for wrong done to union—

Application of rule in Foss v Harbottle. See Legal proceedings—Action for wrong done to union—Proper plaintiff, above.

Contracting out of political fund. See Political fund—Member contracting out, below.

Expulsion. See Expulsion of member, above.

Membership of union—

Generally. See Membership, below.

Membership—

Eligibility—

Director of film production company—Union rule stating that the union shall consist of all employees on the technical side of film production including film directors, employee producers and script-writers—Managing directors of film production company engaged on technical side as producers, directors and script-writers—Conflict of interest—Whether managing directors were 'employees' within the rule—Validity of rule—Whether there was jurisdiction to grant an injunction against apprehended tort by a trade union—Trade Disputes Act 1906, s 4. **Boulting v Association of Cinematograph Television and Allied Technicians** [1963] **1** 716, CA.

Person convicted of criminal offence—Rule that no person convicted of criminal offence be eligible for or retain membership—Non-disclosure in 1950 of criminal convictions in Channel Islands in 1938 and 1940—Appellant became de facto member in 1950—Whether membership void—Whether rule validated by Trade Union Act 1871, s 3. **Faramus v Film Artistes Association** [1964] **1** 25, HL.

Rules—

Amendment—Whether union entitled to amend its rules to include persons deemed to be employees—Industrial Arbitration Act 1940-1964, (NSW) ss 5, 88E—Trade Union Act 1881-1959, (NSW), s 14(7). **Green Cab Service Pty Ltd v Whitfield** [1965] **3** 695, PC.

TRADE UNION (cont)—
 Membership (cont)—
  Temporary membership for duration of the war—
   No provision for temporary membership in union's rules—Admission otherwise than in accordance with rules void. **Martin v Scottish Transport and General Workers Union** [1952] **1** 691, HL.
  Termination of membership—
   No-poaching agreement between unions—Bridlington principles—Admission by union to membership of person recently belonging to another union—Failure of new union to inquire of former union if it objected to member joining new union—TUC disputes committee holding new union to be in breach of Bridlington principles and requiring new union to expel new member—Member concerned not allowed to make personal representations to disputes committee—Union's executive committee purporting to terminate membership without giving member opportunity to be heard—Committee terminating membership under union rule giving it discretion to terminate membership where necessary to comply with decision of TUC disputes committee—Whether termination of membership valid—Whether disputes committee and union's executive committee acting in breach of rules of natural justice. **Cheall v Association of Professional, Executive, Clerical and Computer Staff** [1983] **1** 1130, HL.
  Union membership agreement—
   Dismissal from employment for refusing to join union in accordance with agreement—Unfair dismissal. *See* **Unfair dismissal** (Determination whether dismissal fair or unfair—Dismissal for refusing to join trade union in accordance with union membership agreement).
 Membership and activities—
  Activities of an independent trade union. *See* **Unfair dismissal** (Trade union membership and activities—Activities of an independent trade union).
  Dismissal for exercising right to take part in union activities—
   Unfair dismissal. *See* **Unfair dismissal** (Trade union membership and activities).
  Membership. *See* Membership, *above.*
  Rights of workers. *See* **Industrial relations** (Trade union membership and activities).
 Natural justice—
  Dismissal of union official. *See* **Natural justice** (Trade union—Dismissal of union official from office).
  Expulsion of member. *See* Expulsion of member, *above.*
  Generally. *See* **Natural justice** (Trade union).
  Termination of membership. *See* Membership—Termination of membership, *above.*
 Official—
  Dismissal—
   Elected officer—Restoration of officer pending trial—Interlocutory injunction. **Leary v National Union of Vehicle Builders** [1970] **2** 713, Ch D.
   Natural justice—Dismissal from office. *See* **Natural justice** (Trade union—Dismissal of union official from office).
 Wrongful acts—
  Liability of union—Shop stewards—Scope of authority as agents of union—Test of liability—Whether shop stewards acting on behalf of and within scope of authority—Shop stewards guilty of unfair industrial practice—Shop stewards persisting in activities in disobedience of court orders—Union an unregistered organisation of workers—Authority of shop stewards derived from custom and practice as well as from rules of union—Shop stewards having authority to negotiate with employers and to take industrial action—Shop stewards initiating unfair industrial practice—Whether union liable—Union advising shop stewards to comply with court order to refrain from practice—Shop stewards ignoring advice—Whether union having effectively terminated shop stewards' authority so as to avoid liability for contempt—Industrial Relations Act 1971, s 96(1). **Heatons Transport (St Helens) Ltd v Transport and General Workers Union** [1972] **3** 101, HL.
 Picketing—
  Generally. *See* **Trade dispute** (Picketing).
  Whether ultra vires trade union. *See* Ultra vires—Picketing, *below.*
 Political fund—
  Member contracting out—
   Rules approved by Registrar of Friendly Societies—Effect of approval—Rule resulting in exclusion of exempted member from office—Validity—Trade Union Act 1913, s 3(1)(b). **Birch v National Union of Railwaymen** [1950] **2** 253, Ch D.
 Recognition—
  Central Arbitration Committee—
   Territorial jurisdiction—Employer retaining flight crew operating flights from various countries in Europe—Employment contracts making explicit reference to office in Great Britain and application of law of Great Britain—Employer having offices in Portugal—Union seeking right to represent flight crew as collective bargaining unit—Whether Central Arbitration Committee having territorial jurisdiction—Nature of appropriate test for territorial jurisdiction of employment tribunals—Trade Union and Labour Relations (Consolidation) Act 1992, Sch A1. **Netjets Management Ltd v Central Arbitration Committee** [2013] **1** 288, QBD.
  Claim for—
   Trade dispute. *See* **Trade dispute** (Dispute between employers and workmen or workmen and workmen—Claim by union for recognition).
  Redundancy—
   Duty of employer to consult trade union recognised by him. *See* **Redundancy** (Employer's duty to consult appropriate trade union—Recognition of trade union—Duty to consult trade union recognised by employer).
  Reference of recognition issue to Advisory, Conciliation and Arbitration Service—
   Duty of Service to ascertain opinions of workers to whom issue relates—Scope of duty—Not reasonably practicable to ascertain views of all groups forming part of employer's work force—Employer withholding names and addresses of workers on payroll—Whether duty only to ascertain opinions of workers only where reasonably practicable to do so—Whether mandatory duty to ascertain opinions of all workers or of work force as a whole—Employment Protection Act 1975, s 14(1). **Grunwick Processing Laboratories Ltd v Advisory, Conciliation and Arbitration Service** [1978] **1** 338, CA and HL.

TRADE UNION (cont)—
　Recognition (cont)—
　　Reference of recognition issue to Advisory, Conciliation and Arbitration Service (cont)—
　　　Duty of Service to ascertain opinions of workers to whom issue relates—Whether Service has a discretion to defer making enquiries—Employment Protection Act 1975, ss 12, 14. **Engineers' and Managers' Association v Advisory, Conciliation and Arbitration Service (No 2)** [1980] 1 896, HL.
　　　Duty of Service to ascertain opinions of workers to whom issue relates—Workers to whom issue relates—Dismissed workers—Part of employer's work force going on strike—Strikers subsequently joining union—Strikers dismissed by employer—Union seeking recognition for purpose of collective bargaining on behalf of whole work force—Dismissed workers seeking re-engagement—Recognition issue referred to Service—Whether dismissed workers 'workers to whom the [recognition] issue relates'—Whether Service under duty to ascertain opinions of dismissed workers—Trade Union and Labour Relations Act 1974, s 30(1)—Employment Protection Act 1975, s 14(1). **Grunwick Processing Laboratories Ltd v Advisory, Conciliation and Arbitration Service** [1978] 1 338, CA and HL.
　　　Duty of Service to improve industrial relations and encourage extension of collective bargaining—Duty of Service to prepare report setting out findings and recommendations—Scope of duties—Recognition sought by small union—Opposition by larger employees' unions and by employers' federation—Report by Service recommending non-recognition—Whether Service performing statutory duties properly in making report—Employment Protection Act 1975, ss 1(2), 12(4). **UK Association of Professional Engineers v Advisory, Conciliation and Arbitration Service** [1980] 1 612, HL.
　　Sole bargaining agent. *See* **Industrial relations** (Collective bargaining—Sole bargaining agent—Recognition—Application to Industrial Court—Organisation of workers seeking negotiating rights—Trade union).
　　Statutory duty—
　　　Withdrawal of recognition by Post Office—Whether breach of statutory duty—Post Office Act 1969, Sch 1, para 11(1). **R v Post Office, ex p Association of Scientific, Technical and Managerial Staffs** [1981] 1 139, CA.
　　Withdrawal of recognition of employee's trade union—
　　　Whether breach of statutory duty. *See* Recognition—Statutory duty—Withdrawal of recognition by Post Office, *above*.
　　　Whether in breach of contract of service. *See* **Employment** (Contract of service—Breach of contract—Withdrawal of recognition from employees' trade union).
　Redundancy—
　　Employer's duty to consult appropriate trade union. *See* **Redundancy** (Employer's duty to consult appropriate trade union).
　Right to form and to join trade unions—
　　Delivery drivers/riders. *See* **Employment** ('Worker'—Contract to perform work or services personally—Delivery drivers/riders—Right to form and to join trade unions).
　Right to sue. *See* Legal proceedings—Right of union to sue, *above*.
　Rules—
　　Alteration of rules—
　　　Property of union—Investment of union's funds to be held by trustees of union, of whom there were to be three—Alteration of rules with a view to establishing nominee company controlled by trustees to hold investments—Separation of functions—Alterations of rules invalid as contravening Trade Union Act 1871, s 8. **National Union of Railwaymen's Rules, Re** [1968] 1 5, Ch D.
　　　Validity—Requirement that 40 per cent of affected members vote in favour of change of rules—Union's rules revision committee passing resolution to abolish 40 per cent vote requirement—Whether committee's resolution effective—Whether 40 per cent requirement could be abolished without 40 per cent vote. **Jacques v Amalgamated Union of Engineering Workers (Engineering Section)** [1987] 1 621, Ch D.
　　Breach of rules—
　　　Complaint to industrial tribunal. *See* **Industrial relations** (Organisation of workers—Breach of rules—Complaint by member against organisation).
　　Election—
　　　Construction—Rules for election of executive council—Condition for nomination—Nominee to have worked at industry or signed vacant book and resided in division for 12 months immediately preceding nomination—Nominee absent for eight out of 12 months—Whether nominee complied with conditions. **Watson v Smith** [1941] 2 725, Ch D.
　　　Nominee member of proscribed organisation—Whether ineligible for election—Whether court's jurisdiction can be ousted by rules. **Leigh v National Union of Railwaymen** [1969] 3 1249, Ch D.
　　Membership. *See* Membership—Rules, *above*.
　　Validity—
　　　Rules giving unfettered power of expulsion from membership—Infringement of right to work—Restraint of trade—Trade Union Act 1871, ss 3, 4. **Edwards v Society of Graphical and Allied Trades** [1970] 3 689, CA.
　Shop steward. *See* Official, *above*.
　Solicitor—
　　Power of trustees to authorise. *See* Trustees, *below*.
　Trade dispute—
　　Generally. *See* **Trade dispute**.
　　Non-recognition of union—
　　　Trinidad and Tobago. *See* **Trinidad and Tobago** (Master and servant—Trade dispute).
　　Recognition of union—
　　　Claim for recognition. *See* **Trade dispute** (Dispute between employers and workmen or workmen and workmen—Claim by union for recognition).
　Tribunal. *See* Domestic tribunal, *above*.

1379

TRADE UNION (cont)—
  Trustees—
    Powers—
      Action touching or concerning property of union—Executive council of union not functioning—Power to authorise solicitors to defend action—Trade Union Act 1871, s 9. **Keys v Boulter** [1971] **1** 289, CA.
  Ultra vires—
    Picketing—
      Picketing by union in course of trade dispute—Tortious picketing—Resolution by union to pay any fines incurred by any members arrested for picket offences—Whether acts done in course of picketing bound to be tortious ultra vires union—Whether acts done in course of picketing involving risk that tort might be committed ultra vires—Whether resolution ultra vires and void for public policy—Whether union entitled to consider individual cases and pay costs of fines if in the interests of union and its members. **Thomas v National Union of Mineworkers (South Wales Area)** [1985] **2** 1, Ch D.
    Suspension of member—
      Declaration sought that suspension void—Period of suspension almost expired. *See* **Declaration** (Discretion to grant—Principles governing exercise of discretion—Declaration sought that trade union's decision to expel member, and subsequent decision on appeal to suspend him were ultra vires and void).
  Unfair dismissal—
    Dismissal for refusing to join trade union in accordance with union membership agreement. *See* **Unfair dismissal** (Determination whether dismissal fair or unfair—Dismissal for refusing to join trade union in accordance with union membership agreement).
  Unregistered trade union—
    Legal proceedings. *See* Legal proceedings—Action for wrong done to union—Proper plaintiff, *above*.

TRADE USAGE
  False trade description. *See* **Trade description** (False trade description—Falsity of description).

TRADING
  Fraudulent trading—
    Company—
      Winding up. *See* **Company** (Winding up—Fraudulent trading).
    Insolvency. *See* **Insolvency** (Fraudulent trading).
  Sunday—
    Prohibition. *See* **Sunday observance** (Prohibition on transaction of business by tradesmen etc on Sunday).

TRADING ASSOCIATION
  Club. *See* **Club** (Trading association).

TRADING RECEIPTS
  Income tax. *See* **Income tax** (Profits—Trading receipts).

TRADING WITH THE ENEMY
  Custody of enemy property—
    Vesting of property in custodian of enemy property—
      Effect of vesting—Restriction of former owner's rights to participate in any arrangements made on conclusion of peace—Meaning of property—RSC Ord 25, r 4—Trading with the Enemy (Custodian) Order 1951 (SI 1951 No 153), art 1(a). **Maerkle v British & Continental Fur Co Ltd** [1954] **3** 50, CA.
      Liability of custodian for income tax on proceeds of property vested in him. **Bank Voor Handel en Scheepvaart NV v Administrator of Hungarian Property** [1954] **1** 969, HL.
      Power of Board of Trade to prescribe power of sale. **Vamvakas v Custodian of Enemy Property** [1952] **1** 629, QBD.
      Trade marks—Trade marks vested in custodian by Board of Trade—Assignment by custodian—Extent of powers of board and of custodian—'With a view to preventing the payment of money to enemies and of preserving enemy property...'—Trading with the Enemy Act 1939, s 7(1)—Distribution of German Enemy Property Act 1949, s 1(1)—Distribution of German Enemy Property (No 1) Order 1950 (SI 1950 No 1642), para 18(1)(3). **Reuter (R J) Co Ltd v Mulhens (Ferd)** [1953] **2** 1160, CA.
  Discretionary trust—
    Principal beneficiary an enemy. *See* **Trust and trustee** (Discretionary trust—Statutory discretionary trust—Principal beneficiary an enemy).
  Enemy—
    Body of persons controlled by person who enemy—
      English company having enemy character—Validity of acts performed on behalf of company in Germany during the war of 1939—45—Executory contract—Intercourse with enemy involved—Severance of contractual provisions. **Kuenigl v Donnersmarck** [1955] **1** 46, QBD.
    Individual resident in enemy territory—
      Resident—Non-enemy alien resident in enemy territory—Residence not voluntary—Vesting of property by Board of Trade in Custodian of Enemy Property—Right to confer power of sale—Trading with the Enemy Act 1939, ss 2(1)(b), 7(1)(b), (c), (d). **Vamvakas v Custodian of Enemy Property** [1952] **1** 629, QBD.
  Having commercial, financial etc intercourse for the benefit of enemy—
    Sum deposited by British subject for help of refugees—
      Right to bring proceedings for recovery of deposit—Trading with the Enemy Act 1939, s 1. **Weiner v Central Fund for German Jewry** [1941] **2** 29, KBD.

TRADING WITH THE ENEMY (cont)—
  Performing obligation to or discharging obligation of enemy—
    Guarantee by English company of debt due to neutral by German company—
      Payment under guarantee—Whether payment for benefit or in discharge of obligation of enemy—Trading with the Enemy Act 1939, s 1(2)(a). **Stockholms Enskilda Bank Aktiebolag v Schering Ltd** [1941] **1** 257, CA.
    Guarantee by English company to another English company of debt of enemy—
      Action on guarantee—Performing or discharging obligation of enemy—Transaction under which all obligations performed by plaintiff before commencement of war—Trading with the Enemy Act 1939, s 1(2)(a)(iii). **Kohnstamm (R & A) Ltd v Krumm (Ludwig) (London) Ltd** [1940] **3** 84, KBD.
  Transfer of chose in action by enemy—
    English copyright owned by enemy—
      Contract for sale of business executed in Germany on 22nd July 1939 subject to consent of German government—Consent given on 25th September 1939—Whether effective to pass English copyright—Trading with the Enemy Act 1939, s 4(1). **Novello & Co Ltd v Hinrichsen Edition Ltd** [1951] **1** 779, Ch D.

TRAFFIC
  Air traffic—
    Carriage by air—
      Generally. *See* **Carriage by air**.
    Generally. *See* **Air traffic**.
  Road traffic. *See* **Road traffic**.

TRAFFIC LIGHTS
  Collision—
    Contributory negligence. *See* **Negligence** (Contributory negligence—Collision between vehicles on road—Traffic lights).
  Negligence—
    Duty of driver to take care. *See* **Negligence** (Duty to take care—Driver of motor vehicle—Traffic lights).
    Police—
      Malfunctioning of traffic lights. *See* **Police** (Negligence—Duty to take care—Malfunctioning of traffic lights).
    Vehicles. *See* **Negligence** (Vehicles—Traffic lights).

TRAFFIC SIGN
  Generally. *See* **Road traffic** (Traffic sign).
  Siting—
    Duty of Ministry. *See* **Highway** (Traffic sign—Siting—Duty of Ministry).

TRAFFIC SIGNAL
  Duty to take care. *See* **Negligence** (Duty to take care—Traffic signal).

TRAFFICKING
  Drugs. *See* **Drugs** (Drug trafficking).
  Human trafficking—
    Criminal law. *See* **Criminal law** (Trafficking people for exploitation).

TRAILER
  Road traffic. *See* **Road traffic** (Trailer).

TRAINER
  Horse-racing—
    Trainer's Licence. *See* **Licence** (Horse-racing—Trainer's licence).

TRAINING
  Detention and training order. *See* **Sentence** (Detention and training order).
  Industrial training. *See* **Industrial training**.
  Industrial training board—
    Generally. *See* **Industrial training** (Training board).
    Registration as a charity—
      Control by court. *See* **Charity** (Registration—Control by the court—Control by court in exercise of its charitable jurisdiction—Statutory corporation—Industrial training board).
  Minor—
    Maintenance. *See* **Minor** (Maintenance—Education or training).

TRAMCAR
  Duty of conductor to take care. *See* **Negligence** (Duty to take care—Conductor of tramcar).
  Stage carriage. *See* **Road traffic**.

TRAMWAY
  Purchase by local authority—
    Purchase price—
      Method of ascertaining purchase price—Total capital of company actually invested in undertaking at time of purchase—Sale by purchasers from original company—Tramways Act 1870, s 44—Great Orme Tramways Act 1898, s 57(1). **Llandudno UDC v Great Orme Ry Ltd** [1948] **2** 782, Ch D.
  Repair of road—
    Liability for repair—
      Extent of liability—Tramway abandoned by London Passenger Transport Board—Notice by highway authority of intention to remove tramway equipment—Fatal accident—Liability of highway authority for non-feasance—Tramways Act 1870, ss 25, 28—London Passenger Transport Act 1933, s 23(2), (5), (7). **Simon v Islington BC** [1943] **1** 41, CA.

TRAMWAY (cont)—
  Repair of road (cont)—
    Liability for repair (cont)—
      Tramway operated by local authority—Tramway discontinued and lines filled in but rails not removed—Liability for repair of road as tramway authority—Tramways Act 1870, s 28. **Browne v De Luxe Car Service and Birkenhead Corp** [1941] **1** 383, CA.

TRANSACTION AT UNDERVALUE
  Insolvency. *See* **Insolvency** (Transaction at undervalue).
  Limitation. *See* **Limitation of action** (When time begins to run—Transaction at undervalue).
  Limitation of action—
    Concealment of right of action. *See* **Limitation of action** (Concealment of right of action—Breach of duty—Transactions defrauding creditors—Transactions entered into at an undervalue).

TRANSACTION IN SECURITIES
  Tax advantage—
    Counteracting. *See* **Income tax** (Tax advantage—Counteracting—Transaction in securities).
    Generally. *See* **Income tax** (Tax advantage—Transaction in securities).

TRANSCRIPT
  Admissibility in evidence—
    Transcript of evidence given at earlier trial—
      Admissibility in subsequent civil proceedings. *See* **Document** (Admissibility in evidence—Record as evidence of facts stated therein—Transcript of criminal proceedings).
    Transcript of summing up in criminal proceedings—
      Whether transcript admissible in subsequent civil proceedings. *See* **Document** (Admissibility in evidence—Transcript of criminal proceedings).
  Cost of—
    Appeal to Court of Appeal. *See* **Costs** (Appeal to Court of Appeal—Shorthand transcript of evidence at trial—Cost of transcript).
    Legal aid. *See* **Legal aid** (Costs—Transcript).
  Court of Appeal—
    Civil proceedings. *See* **Court of Appeal** (Practice—Transcript).
    Criminal appeal—
      Practice. *See* **Criminal law** (Court of Appeal—Practice—Transcript).
  Court proceedings in relation to children—
    Proceedings in private—
      Practice. *See* **Child** (Practice—Court proceedings in relation to children—Proceedings in private—Publication of information—Transcripts).
  Examination by company liquidators—
    Disclosure of transcript. *See* **Disclosure and inspection of documents** (Disclosure against persons not parties to proceedings—Witness—Witness at trial of action for recovery of assets transferred to defendant—Plaintiff seeking to obtain transcript of private examination of witness by liquidators of company closely associated with defendant).
  Revision—
    Summing-up. *See* **Criminal law** (Trial—Shorthand note—Summing up—Transcript—Revision of transcript by judge).

TRANSFER OF TRADE, BUSINESS OR UNDERTAKING
  Court sanction—
    Transfer of long-term insurance business. *See* **Insurance** (Transfer of long-term insurance business—Sanction by court of scheme for transfer of long-term insurance business).
  Employment—
    Continuity. *See* **Employment** (Continuity—Transfer of trade, business or undertaking).
  Pension annuities. *See* **Pension** (Annuities—Transfers).
  Sanction of court for business transfer schemes—
    Insurance. *See* **Insurance** (Transfer of long-term insurance business—Sanction by court of scheme for transfer of long-term insurance business).

TRANSLATION
  Evidence in criminal proceedings—
    Translation of tape recordings. *See* **Criminal evidence** (Best evidence—Tape recording—Translations).

TRANSMISSION MACHINERY
  Fencing of—
    Factory, in. *See* **Factory** (Dangerous parts of machinery—Duty to fence—Fencing to be kept in position while machinery in motion or use—Transmission machinery).

TRANSPORT
  Air—
    Air traffic. *See* **Air traffic**.
    Carriage. *See* **Carriage by air**.
  Australia. *See* **Australia** (Transport).
  British Transport Commission. *See* **British Transport Commission**.
  Carriers—
    Generally. *See* **Carriers**.
  Local authority. *See* **Local authority** (Transport).
  London Passenger Transport Board. *See* **London Passenger Transport Board**.
  London Transport Executive. *See* **London Transport Executive**.

TRANSPORT (cont)—
    Maritime transport—
        International maritime transport—
            EC rules on competition—Abuse of dominant position. *See* **European Union** (Rules on competition—Abuse of dominant position—Collective dominant position—International maritime transport).
    Private air and boat transport—
        Taxation—
            European Union. *See* **European Union** (Freedom of movement—Services—Private air and boat transport).
    Public transport. *See* **Road traffic** (Public transport).
    Railway. *See* **Railway**.
    Road transport—
        Carriage by road. *See* **Carriers**.
        European Community. *See* **European Union** (Road transport).
        Nationalisation—
            Compensation to employees of transferred undertaking. *See* **British Transport Commission** (Transferred undertaking—Compensation to employee).
        Tachograph charts. *See* **Road traffic** (Carriage of goods and passengers—Tachograph charts).
    Schoolchildren, for—
        Provision by local education authority. *See* **Education** (Local education authority—Provision of transport for pupils).
    Sea transport—
        Generally. *See* **Shipping**.
    Tramway. *See* **Tramway**.
    Value added tax—
        Transport of passengers—
            Zero-rating. *See* **Value added tax** (Zero-rating—Transport of passengers).

TRANSPORT TRIBUNAL
    Appeal from order of tribunal—
        Jurisdiction to entertain appeal—
            Court of Appeal—Transport Act 1947, Sch X, para 5—Railway and Canal Commission (Abolition) Act 1949, s 8(2). **British Transport Commission v London CC** [1953] **1** 801, CA.
    Appellate jurisdiction—
        Public carrier's licence. *See* **Road traffic** (Goods vehicle—Public carrier's licence—Transport tribunal—Appellate jurisdiction).
    British Transport Commission Charges Scheme—
        Jurisdiction of tribunal. *See* **British Transport Commission** (Charges scheme—Jurisdiction of Transport Tribunal).

TRAP
    Danger or trap to child—
        Occupier's liability. *See* **Occupier's liability** (Children—Danger or trap to child).
    Man trap—
        Setting man trap or other engine calculated to inflict grievous bodily harm. *See* **Criminal law** (Trap—Setting man trap with intent).
    Police—
        Admission obtained by trap. *See* **Criminal evidence** (Admissions and confessions—Trap—Police).
    Setting engine calculated to inflict grievous bodily harm. *See* **Criminal law** (Trap).

TRAPEZE ARTISTE
    Industrial injury benefit—
        Right to—
            Whether trapeze artiste employed under contract of service. *See* **Industrial injury** (Insurable employment—Employment under contract of service—Trapeze artiste in circus).

TRAVAUX PRÉPARATOIRES
    Statute—
        Construction—
            International convention given effect by legislation—Reference to travaux préparatoires. *See* **Statute** (Construction—Convention given effect by legislation—References to travaux préparatoires).

TRAVEL
    Carriage by air—
        Passengers. *See* **Carriage by air** (Carriage of passengers).

TRAVEL CONCESSIONS
    Public transport—
        Local authority. *See* **Local authority** (Transport—Travel concessions).
    Voucher—
        Value added tax—
            Zero-rating. *See* **Value added tax** (Zero-rating—Transport of passengers—Supply of travel concession voucher).

TRAVEL EXPENSES
    Deduction from emoluments for income tax. *See* **Income tax** (Emoluments from office or employment—Expenses wholly, exclusively and necessarily incurred—Travelling expenses).
    Deduction in computing profits for income tax purposes. *See* **Income tax** (Deduction in computing profits—Travelling expenses).

TRAVEL INSURANCE
  Construction of policy. *See* **Insurance** (Policy—Construction—Travel insurance).

TRAVEL SERVICES
  Value added tax—
    Place of supply—
      European Community. *See* **European Union** (Value added tax—Supply of goods or services—Place of supply—Travel services).
    Tour operator's margin scheme. *See* **Value added tax** (Assessment—Tour operator's margin scheme).

TRAVELLER
  Inn—
    Refreshment and lodging—
      Duty of innkeeper to provide. *See* **Inn** (Duty to supply refreshment and lodging to traveller).
  Traveller's cheque—
    Bank's position. *See* **Bank** (Cheque—Traveller's cheque).

TRAVELLING SHOWMEN
  Caravan site licence—
    Land used as caravan site by travelling showmen—
      Exemption from licensing requirements. *See* **Caravan site** (Licence—Exemption from licensing requirements—Travelling showmen).

TREASON
  See **Criminal law** (Treason).

TREASURE TROVE
  Crown's right to treasure trove—
    Coins—
      Silver coins—Whether Crown's right to treasure trove limited to articles of gold and silver. **A-G of the Duchy of Lancaster v G E Overton (Farms) Ltd** [1982] **1** 524, CA.
  Theft. *See* **Criminal law** (Theft—Treasure trove).

TREASURY
  Control of borrowing. *See* **Money** (Borrowing—Treasury control).
  Currency control. *See* **Currency control.**

TREASURY SOLICITOR
  Local authority—
    Representation. *See* **Local authority** (Representation by Treasury Solicitor).

TREATY
  Accession to treaty—
    Lesotho. *See* **Lesotho** (Treaty—Accession to treaty).
  Construction of statute giving effect to treaty. *See* **Statute** (Construction—Convention given effect by legislation—Effect to be given to plain words notwithstanding international treaty).
  Crown—
    Prerogative—
      Power to make treaties. *See* **Crown** (Prerogative—Treaty-making power).
  European Union—
    International treaty. *See* **European Union** (International treaties).
    Treaty provisions. *See* **European Union** (Treaty provisions).
  Extradition. *See* **Extradition** (Treaty).
  International convention. *See* **International law** (Convention).
  Treaty relevant to dispute between private persons—
    Relevance of government's attitude to treaty—
      Whether government's attitude should be taken into consideration by court when deciding dispute. **British Airways Board v Laker Airways Ltd** [1983] **3** 375, QBD and CA.
  Treaty-making power. *See* **Constitutional law** (Treaty-making power).
  Waitangi—
    New Zealand. *See* **New Zealand** (Treaty of Waitangi).

TREE
  Fall of tree on road—
    Speeding vehicle—
      Collision. *See* **Negligence** (Vehicles—Speed—Sudden and unexpected danger—Fall of tree).
  Highway—
    Generally. *See* **Highway** (Trees).
    Tree adjacent to highway—
      Negligence. *See* **Negligence** (Duty to take care—Tree adjacent to highway).
  Negligence—
    Tree adjacent to highway. *See* **Negligence** (Duty to take care—Tree adjacent to highway).
  Nuisance—
    Continuing nuisance—
      Right to sue—Occupier of land—Damage occurring while land occupied by plaintiff's predecessor in title. *See* **Nuisance** (Right to sue—Continuing nuisance—Roots of defendant's tree desiccating ground beneath property and causing structural cracking).
    Injunction—
      Roots causing damage. *See* **Injunction** (Nuisance—Continuing damage—Roots of trees causing damage to adjoining premises).

TREE (cont)—
Overhanging highway—
Negligence—
Duty of highway authority. *See* **Negligence** (Highway—Duty of highway authority—Tree overhanging highway).
Preservation order. *See* **Town and country planning** (Trees—Preservation order).
Roots causing damage—
Nuisance. *See* **Nuisance** (Tree—Roots causing damage).

TREE PRESERVATION
Local authority—
Duty to protect areas of natural beauty. *See* **Practice** (Parties—Local authority—Promotion or protection of interests of inhabitants of their area—Local authority obtaining injunction to restrain breaches by defendant of tree preservation order).
Preservation order. *See* **Town and country planning** (Trees—Preservation order).

TRESPASS
Aggravated trespass—
Criminal proceedings. *See* **Criminal law** (Trespass—Aggravated trespass).
Air space. *See* **Trespass to land** (Air space).
Conspiracy—
Indictable offence. *See* **Criminal law** (Conspiracy—Unlawful act—Tort—Agreement to do unlawful act—Trespass).
Trespass to goods. *See* **Trespass to goods**.
Trespass to land. *See* **Trespass to land**.
Trespass to the person. *See* **Trespass to the person**.

TRESPASS TO GOODS
Conversion. *See* **Conversion**.
Defence—
Involuntary accident—
Accidental damages to underground electric cable—Cable laid by plaintiff's predecessors without knowledge of owner of land—Excavation by contractors employed by owner of land—Damage caused during excavation. **National Coal Board v Evans (JE) & Co (Cardiff) Ltd** [1951] **2** 310, CA.
Foreign chattels—
Conversion of foreign chattels. *See* **Conflict of laws** (Foreign chattels—Conversion of chattels in foreign currency).
Right to bring action—
Jus tertii—
No title to goods (a motor car) in either plaintiff or defendants but both purchasers of car—Car left by plaintiff for repair at garage where plaintiff had monthly credit terms—Car taken from garage by defendants—Car subsequently delivered by defendants to true owner—Whether plaintiff entitled to recover in trespass against defendants. **Wilson v Lombank Ltd** [1963] **1** 740, Assizes.

TRESPASS TO LAND
Air space—
Aircraft—
Statutory defence—Flight of aircraft over property—Aerial photography—Whether statutory defence limited to bare passage over property—Whether defence applicable to flight over property for purpose of aerial photography—Civil Aviation Act 1949, s 40(1). **Bernstein (Lord) of Leigh v Skyviews & General Ltd** [1977] **2** 902, QBD.
Invasion of air space of another—
Advertisement sign on adjoining building projecting some eight inches into air space above one-storey shop—Right of occupier of shop to injunction requiring sign to be removed. **Kelsen v Imperial Tobacco Co (of GB and Ireland) Ltd** [1957] **2** 343, QBD.
Injunction—Interlocutory injunction—Behaviour of the parties. **Woollerton & Wilson Ltd v Richard Costain Ltd** [1970] **1** 483, Ch D.
Rights of owner of land in air space above land—Rights in air space restricted to such height above the land as is necessary for ordinary use and enjoyment of land—Flight by aircraft over land for purpose of taking one photograph of the land—Aircraft flying at several hundred feet above the land—Whether flight for purpose of taking one photograph constituted trespass in owner's air space. **Bernstein (Lord) of Leigh v Skyviews & General Ltd** [1977] **2** 902, QBD.
Animal—
Distress damage feasant. *See* **Animal** (Distress damage feasant).
Generally. *See* **Animal** (Trespass).
Breach of the peace—
Whether civil trespass capable of amounting to breach of the peace. *See* **Breach of the peace** (Civil trespass).
Burglary. *See* **Criminal law** (Burglary—Entering a building as a trespasser).
Child trespasser—
Negligence—
Allurement. *See* **Negligence** (Child—Allurement—Child trespasser).
Conspiracy to trespass—
Indictable offence. *See* **Criminal law** (Conspiracy—Unlawful act—Tort—Agreement to do unlawful act—Trespass).
Constable—
Arrest by constable who had become a trespasser—
Arrest for failure to provide specimen of breath—Accident owing to presence of motor vehicle on road. *See* **Road traffic** (Breath test—Arrest—Arrest for failure to provide specimen of breath—Validity—Constable a trespasser at time of request for specimen of breath).
Criminal law. *See* **Criminal law** (Trespass).

TRESPASS TO LAND (cont)—
Damages—
    Consequential losses—
        Expropriation of property by defendant involving destruction of fire escape attaching to claimant's property—Destruction of fire escape preventing use of claimant's premises as function room—Whether permissible to award cost of reinstating fire escape as well as diminution in value of land—Whether consequential losses including loss of profits from use of function room. **Ramzan v Brookwide Ltd** [2011] **2** 38, Ch D; [2012] **1** 903, CA; [2012] **1 Comm** 979, CA.
    Damages in lieu of injunction—
        Breach of restrictive covenant affecting land. *See* **Injunction** (Damages in lieu of injunction—Breach of restrictive covenant affecting land).
    Exemplary damages. *See* **Damages** (Exemplary damages—Trespass to land).
    Extinction of title—
        Adverse possession—Whether true owner entitled to damages for trespass once title extinguished by adverse possession. **Mount Carmel Investments Ltd v Peter Thurlow Ltd** [1988] **3** 129, CA.
    Generally. *See* **Damages** (Trespass to land).
    Mesne profits—
        Measure of damages—Defendant expropriating claimant's store room to create new flat—Whether measure of damages for mesne profits being loss in tort or in restitution for the value of benefit received by occupier—Whether loss to be calculated on basis of property's previous use as store room or as part of new flat. **Ramzan v Brookwide Ltd** [2011] **2** 38, Ch D; [2012] **1** 903, CA; [2012] **1 Comm** 979, CA.
Defence—
    Lawful possession—
        Burden of proof—Defendant in possession—Owner proving title to land and intention to recover possession—Burden on defendant to set up title or right consistent with fact of ownership vested in plaintiff. **Portland Managements Ltd v Harte** [1976] **1** 225, CA.
    Leave and licence—
        Adjoining buildings—Leave to underpin wall—Extension of concrete foundation beyond wall—Permission to underpin wall not authorising extension of foundations. **Willcox v Kettell** [1937] **1** 222, Ch D.
        Deserted wife in occupation of dwelling-house—Undertaking by husband, on summons for maintenance, to allow wife and children to remain in house rent free—Conveyance by husband to plaintiff—Action by plaintiff for possession—Whether wife trespasser. **Thompson v Earthy** [1951] **2** 235, KBD.
        Husband and wife living apart—Husband occupying home not the matrimonial home—Whether wife entitled to give permission to third party to enter husband's home. **Jolliffe v Willmett & Co** [1971] **1** 478, QBD.
        Scope of permission—Entry into building in excess of permission—Intention to steal. *See* **Criminal law** (Burglary—Entering a building as a trespasser—Permission to enter building—Entry in excess of permission).
    Necessity—
        Local authority—Homeless family—Duty of local authority to provide accommodation for homeless—Homeless family unable to obtain accommodation—Unoccupied property owned by local authority—Homeless family entering into occupation of property—Whether defence of necessity available in proceedings for possession. **Southwark London Borough v Williams** [1971] **2** 175, CA.
        Negligence by defendant—Defendant's negligence creating necessity—Police firing CS gas canister into building to flush out armed intruder under seige—Building catching fire—Building owner alleging trespass to land by police—Whether police negligent—Whether negligence by police creating necessity—Whether defence of necessity available. **Rigby v Chief Constable of Northamptonshire** [1985] **2** 985, QBD.
    Statutory defence—
        Flight of aircraft over property of another. *See* Air space—Aircraft—Statutory defence—Flight of aircraft over property, *above*.
Distress damage feasant—
    Cattle straying. *See* **Animal** (Distress damage feasant—Lien of distrainor—Cattle straying).
Duty of care to trespasser. *See* **Negligence** (Duty to take care—Trespasser).
Exclusion of owner by trespassers—
    Rates—
        Owner having legal possession—Presumption of occupation. *See* **Rates** (Rateable occupation—Owner having legal possession—Presumption of occupation—Rebuttal—Occupation by another—Exclusion of owner from hereditament by trespassers in occupation).
Forcible entry and detainer. *See* **Criminal law** (Forcible entry and detainer).
Foreign land—
    Conflict of laws. *See* **Conflict of laws** (Foreign land—Trespass to foreign land).
Interlocutory injunction. *See* **Injunction** (Interlocutory—Trespass).
Ladders and planks placed against wall of adjoining owner—
    Damage—
        Technical trespass. **Westripp v Baldock** [1939] **1** 279, CA.
Mandatory injunction. *See* **Injunction** (Mandatory injunction—Trespass).
Occupier—
    Duty to trespasser. *See* **Occupier's liability** (Trespasser).
Oil—
    Discharge of oil into public navigable waters—
        Damage to adjoining land—Discharge of oil to lighten vessel stranded in estuary—Damage to adjoining foreshore—Necessity—Need to prove negligence. **Esso Petroleum Co Ltd v Southport Corp** [1954] **2** 561, CA.
Police powers to remove trespassers. *See* **Police** (Powers—Power to remove trespassers on land).
Possession sufficient to support trespass—
    Evidence—
        Inference of possession where land not used—Title temporarily vested in state—Continuance of former possession. **Wuta-Ofei v Danquah** [1961] **3** 596, PC.

TRESPASS TO LAND (cont)—
Possession sufficient to support trespass (cont)—
  Sea-bed—
    Title shown by documents vested in plaintiff company which had purported to act as owner of tidal creek—Acts done by plaintiff company having accordingly the quality of assertions of ownership—Sufficient possession to maintain an action for trespass established. **Fowley Marine (Emsworth) Ltd v Gafford** [1968] **1** 979, CA.
  Tenancy agreement—
    Agreement subsequently cancelled—Occupation of premises without consent of owner—Forcible ejectment by owner—Action by occupier against owner for damages for trespass—Possession not sufficient to support action against lawful owner—Law of Property Act 1925, s 40. **Delaney v Smith (TP) Ltd** [1946] **2** 23, CA.
Rateable occupation. *See* **Rates** (Rateable occupation—Occupation by trespassers).
Remedy—
  Self-redress—
    Circumstances in which common law right of self-redress available—Wall of building encroaching on adjoining property—Plaintiff's claim for mandatory injunction refused—Whether right of self-redress available. **Burton v Winters** [1993] **3** 847, CA.
Residential property—
  Acquisition of title by possession. *See* **Land registration** (Acquisition of title by possession—Registration of adverse possession—Offence of squatting in a residential building).
  Damages. *See* **Damages** (Trespass to land—Residential property).
Right to maintain action—
  Premises subject to Rent Restrictions Acts—
    Non-occupying tenant—Licence to defendant to occupy—Defendant's occupation not such as to preserve premises for tenant's return—Tenant no longer statutory tenant—Tenant not entitled to maintain trespass against defendant—Increase of Rent and Mortgage Interest (Restrictions) Act 1920, s 15(1). **Thompson v Ward** [1953] **1** 1169, CA.
Sewer—
  Construction of sewer on plaintiff's land—
    Oral permission by plaintiff while ignorant of his proprietary right—Permission revoked after sewer constructed—Defendants continuing to discharge effluent through plaintiff's land—Injunction—Damages. **Armstrong v Sheppard & Short Ltd** [1959] **2** 651, CA.
Statutory defence—
  Flight of aircraft over property of another. *See* Air space—Aircraft—Statutory defence—Flight of aircraft over property, *above.*
Summary proceedings for possession of land—
  Generally. *See* **Land** (Summary proceedings for possession).
Trespassory assembly. *See* **Criminal law** (Trespassory assembly).

TRESPASS TO THE PERSON
Assault—
  Damages—
    Contributory negligence. *See* **Tort** (Assault and battery—Contributory negligence—Damages).
    Exemplary damages. *See* **Damages** (Exemplary damages—Trespass to the person).
    Generally. *See* Damages, *below.*
  Defence—
    Conduct of plaintiff provoking assault by defendant—Severe blow struck, out of proportion to occasion—Plaintiff old and defendant young—Defendant convicted of unlawful wounding—Subsequent civil action—Defences of ex turpi causa non oritur actio, and of volenti non fit injuria, not sustainable. **Lane v Holloway** [1967] **3** 129, CA.
    Use of force in prevention of crime—Suspected terrorists shot dead in Northern Ireland by army patrol protecting bank—Whether circumstances in which operation to protect bank planned relevant in determining whether use of force by soldiers reasonable 'in the circumstances' to prevent crime—Criminal Law Act (Northern Ireland) 1967, s 3(1). **Farrell v Secretary of State for Defence** [1980] **1** 166, HL.
  Picketing—
    Trade dispute. *See* **Trade dispute** (Picketing—Assault).
Battery—
  Defence —
    Self-defence—Mistaken belief that self-defence necessary—Whether mistaken belief must be reasonable. **Ashley v Chief Constable of Sussex Police** [2008] **3** 573, HL.
  Ingredients of tort—
    Intention—Hostility—Schoolboy injured in horseplay—Whether intention to injure essential ingredient of battery—Whether intentional act has to be hostile—What must be proved. **Wilson v Pringle** [1986] **2** 440, CA.
Civil proceedings for trespass to the person brought by offender—
  Permission to bring proceedings—
    Person convicted of obstructing police officers in execution of their duty bringing proceedings against police for trespass to the person without securing permission—Whether proceedings a nullity—Criminal Justice Act 2003, s 329. **Adorian v Metropolitan Police Comr** [2009] **4** 227, CA.
Damages—
  Exemplary damages. *See* **Damages** (Exemplary damages—Trespass to the person).
  General damages—
    Damages for rape and sexual assault—Damages to be related to awards in conventional personal injury cases. **W v Meah** [1986] **1** 935, QBD.
  Liability of person of unsound mind—
    Knowledge of nature and quality of act—No knowledge that act wrongful. **Morriss v Marsden** [1952] **1** 925, QBD.
  Mitigation—
    Conduct of person assaulted provoking assault—Whether plaintiff's behaviour a ground for mitigation of damages for physical injury. **Lane v Holloway** [1967] **3** 129, CA.
False imprisonment. *See* **False imprisonment.**

TRESPASS TO THE PERSON (cont)—
Intention or negligence—
    Burden of proof—
        Whether necessary to prove that act intentional or negligent. **Fowler v Lanning** [1959] **1** 290, QBD.
Intentional trespass—
    Limitation period—
        Whether action for breach of duty within proviso to Limitation Act 1939, s 2(1) as amended. *See*
            Limitation of action (Trespass to the person).
Limitation of action. *See* **Limitation of action** (Trespass to the person).
Medical practitioner. *See* **Medical practitioner** (Trespass to the person).
Permission to bring proceedings. *See* Civil proceedings for trespass to the person brought by
    offender—Permission to bring proceedings, *above*.
Police search—
    Arrested person. *See* **Police** (Right of search—Arrested person—Good reason for search—Trespass to
    person).

TRESPASSER
Occupier's duty to trespasser—
    Child trespasser. *See* **Occupier's liability** (Child trespasser).
    Generally. *See* **Occupier's liability** (Trespasser).

TRESPASSORY ASSEMBLY
See **Criminal law** (Trespassory assembly).

TRIAL
Admiralty practice. *See* **Admiralty** (Practice).
Civil action—
    Function of judge. *See* **Judge** (Function of judge—Civil action).
    Practice. *See* **Practice** (Trial).
Clergyman—
    Ecclesiastical offence. *See* **Ecclesiastical law** (Clergyman—Offence—Trial).
Committal for trial at Crown Court. *See* **Crown Court** (Committal to Crown Court for trial).
County court—
    Notice of trial date. *See* **County court** (Practice—Notice of trial date).
Court-martial. *See* **Court-martial** (Trial).
Criminal—
    Children and young persons. *See* **Criminal law** (Trial of children and young persons).
    Evidence. *See* **Criminal evidence**.
    Generally. *See* **Criminal law** (Trial).
    Indictment. *See* **Indictment**.
    Jamaica. *See* **Jamaica** (Criminal law—Trial).
    Jury. *See* **Jury**.
    Sentence. *See* **Sentence**.
    Stay of proceedings. *See* **Criminal law** (Trial—Stay of proceedings).
    Trinidad and Tobago. *See* **Trinidad and Tobago** (Criminal law—Trial).
    Verdict. *See* **Criminal law** (Verdict).
    Witnesses—
        Identity. *See* **Criminal law** (Trial—Witnesses—Identity).
Date—
    Commercial Court. *See* **Commercial Court** (Practice—Date for hearing).
Direction to jury—
    Generally. *See* **Criminal law** (Trial—Direction to jury).
Early trial—
    Practice. *See* **Practice** (Trial—Order for early trial).
Fair trial—
    Hearsay evidence. *See* **Criminal evidence** (Hearsay—Right to a fair trial).
    Human rights legislation. *See* **Human rights** (Right to a fair hearing).
    Prosecution not disclosing material evidence to defence—
        Prosecution not disclosing to defence names of witnesses not proposed to be called at
            trial—Certiorari. *See* **Certiorari** (Justices—Natural justice—Prosecution not disclosing material
            evidence to defence—Prosecution not disclosing to defence before trial names of witnesses not
            proposed to be called at trial—Defendant convicted—Whether defendant denied fair trial).
High Court. *See* **Practice** (Trial).
Inaccurate report of—
    Contempt of court. *See* **Contempt of court** (Publications concerning legal proceedings—Inaccurate
    report of trial).
Indictment. *See* **Indictment**.
Information—
    Magistrates' jurisdiction. *See* **Magistrates** (Jurisdiction—Trial of information).
Judge—
    Reference to European Court—
        Factors to be considered by judge. *See* **European Union** (Reference to European Court—Request for
            preliminary ruling concerning interpretation of treaty—Power of national court to refer question it
            considers necessary to enable it to give judgment—Discretionary power of trial judge).
Jury—
    Right to trial by jury—
        Fraud in issue—Transfer of proceedings from Chancery Division to Queen's Bench Division. *See*
            Practice (Transfer of proceedings between Divisions of High Court—Jury trial available as of right
            in action begun in Queen's Bench Division where fraud in issue—Action begun in Chancery
            Division including allegation of fraud).
        Summary offence—Right of accused to claim trial by jury. *See* **Magistrates** (Right of accused to
            claim trial by jury for summary offence).

TRIAL (cont)—
  Jury (cont)—
    Trial by jury—
      County court. *See* **County court** (Trial by jury).
      Generally. *See* **Jury**.
      Jamaica. *See* **Jamaica** (Constitutional law—Entrenched provisions of Constitution—Trial by jury).
      Libel action—Practice. *See* **Practice** (Trial—Trial by jury—Libel).
  Language—
    Ceylon. *See* **Ceylon** (Criminal law—Trial—Language).
  Matrimonial causes. *See* **Divorce** (Practice—Trial).
  Mode of trial—
    Magistrates' jurisdiction. *See* **Magistrates** (Jurisdiction—Mode of trial).
  New trial—
    County court. *See* **County court** (New trial).
    Defamation case. *See* **Libel and slander** (New trial).
    Order—
      Court of Appeal—Generally. *See* **Court of Appeal** (New trial).
      Court of Appeal—Jurisdiction. *See* **Court of Appeal** (Jurisdiction—Order for new trial).
    Relief not claimed at trial—
      Appeal—Order for new trial. *See* **Court of Appeal** (Order for new trial—Relief not claimed at trial).
    Unreasonable verdict—Appeal. *See* **Criminal law** (Appeal—Unreasonable verdict—New trial).
  No case to answer—
    Submission—
      Practice. *See* **Practice** (No case to answer).
  Official referee, before. *See* **Practice** (Reference to referee).
  Patent action—
    Preparation for trial. *See* **Patent** (Practice—Preparation for trial).
  Pre-trial review—
    Criminal cases. *See* **Criminal law** (Trial—Pre-trial review).
    Matrimonial causes—
      Applications for property adjustment and lump sums. *See* **Practice** (Matrimonial causes—Trial—Directions for trial—Applications for property adjustment and lump sums).
  Retrial. *See* **Criminal law** (Trial—Retrial).
  Separate trials—
    Civil proceedings. *See* **Practice** (Trial—Separate trials).
  Setting down action. *See* **Practice** (Trial—Setting down action).
  Solicitor—
    Error in estimate of length of trial—
      Personal liability for costs. *See* **Solicitor** (Payment of costs by solicitor personally—Error in estimate of length of trial).
  Speedy trial—
    Practice. *See* **Practice** (Trial—Order for early trial).
  Submission of no case to answer. *See* **Practice** (No case to answer).
  Subpoena—
    Subpoena ad testificandum. *See* **Practice** (Subpoena ad testificandum).
    Subpoena duces tecum. *See* **Practice** (Subpoena duces tecum).
  Summary trial—
    Arson. *See* **Criminal law** (Damage to property—Arson—Trial—Summary trial).
    Generally. *See* **Magistrates** (Summary trial).
  Trinidad and Tobago, in. *See* **Trinidad and Tobago** (Criminal law—Trial).
  Verdict—
    Generally. *See* **Criminal law** (Verdict).
    Jury—
      Generally. *See* **Jury** (Verdict).
      Majority verdict. *See* **Jury** (Majority verdict).
      Unanimity. *See* **Jury** (Direction to jury—Requirement of unanimity in decision).
  Witness—
    Evidence in criminal proceedings. *See* **Criminal evidence** (Trial—Witness).

TRIBUNAL
  Administrative tribunal—
    Review of decision of. *See* Review of decision—Administrative tribunal, *below*.
  Agricultural land tribunal. *See* **Agricultural Land Tribunal**.
  Appeal on point of law—
    Bias—
      Whether appeal on ground of bias appeal on point of law. **Gillies v Secretary of State for Work and Pensions** [2006] **1** 731, HL.
    Divisional Court, to. *See* Appeal to Divisional Court on point of law, *below*.
    Interpretation of word in statute—
      Tribunal giving incomplete or unsatisfactory definition of ordinary English word in applying statute—Value added tax tribunal basing decision on inadequate definition of word 'maintenance' in relation to assessing building works to value added tax—Whether misinterpretation an error of law—Whether appeal lying to High Court. **ACT Construction Ltd v Customs and Excise Comrs** [1979] **2** 691, QBD.
  Appeal to Divisional Court on point of law—
    Jurisdiction of Divisional Court—
      Decision on point of law—Jurisdiction restricted to cases when tribunal has made a decision on a point of law—Need to establish that point decided by tribunal—Tribunals and Inquiries Act 1958, s 9. **Esso Petroleum Co Ltd v Minister of Labour** [1968] **3** 425, CA.

TRIBUNAL (cont)—
Appeal to Divisional Court on point of law (cont)—
    Point of law—
        Exercise of a judicial discretion—Adjournment—Party absent and unrepresented—Message to tribunal explaining absence but not requesting adjournment—Determination in absence of party—Wrongful exercise of discretion—Whether point of law—RSC Ord 55, r 7(7)—Tribunal and Inquiries Act 1958, s 9(1). **Priddle v Fisher & Sons** [1968] 3 506, QBD.
        Finding of implied term in contract—Whether point of law. **O'Brien v Associated Fire Alarms Ltd** [1969] 1 93, CA.
Application for new tenancy—
    Business premises. *See* **Landlord and tenant** (Business premises—Application for new tenancy—Tribunal).
Arbitration. *See* **Arbitration**.
Bias—
    Appeal on point of law. *See* Appeal on point of law—Bias, *above*.
    Membership. *See* Membership—Bias, *below*.
Closed material procedure—
    First-tier tribunal. *See* First-tier Tribunal—Hearing—Closed material procedure, *below*.
Competition Appeal Tribunal. *See* **Competition** (Competition Appeal Tribunal).
Competition Commission Appeal Tribunal. *See* **Competition** (Competition Commission Appeal Tribunal).
Copyright Tribunal—
    Costs. *See* **Costs** (Copyright Tribunal).
Decision—
    Amendment of decision—
        Power of statutory tribunal to amend own decision. **Corchester, The** [1956] 3 878, Admin Ct; **R v Agricultural Land Tribunal (South Eastern Area), ex p Hooker** [1951] 2 801, KBD.
        Slip rule—Upper Tribunal—Scope of tribunal's jurisdiction to correct errors in its decision—Decision containing error as to calculation of percentage of risk—Whether tribunal could be asked to resolve question whether error was substantive or only an error of expression—Whether appropriate to correct error—Tribunal Procedure (Upper Tribunal) Rules 2008, SI 2008/2698, r 42.
    Majority decision—
        Validity—Rent assessment committee—Determination of fair rent—Whether unanimous decision necessary. **Picea Holdings Ltd v London Rent Assessment Panel** [1971] 2 805, QBD.
    Review of. *See* Review of decision, *below*.
Disability Appeal Tribunal—
    Bias. *See* Membership—Bias—Disability appeal tribunal, *below*.
Domestic tribunal—
    Disciplinary committee of professional society—
        Impartiality—Whether disciplinary committee of professional society capable of considering fairly a charge of misconduct brought against fellow member of society. **S (a barrister), Re** [1981] 2 952, Visitors of Inner Temple.
        Non-statutory tribunal—Two complaints about discreditable conduct of accountant brought before disciplinary committee—Nemo debet bis vexari pro una et eadem causa—Whether cause of action estoppel arising—Whether principle of res judicata applicable to proceedings of non-statutory disciplinary tribunal. **R (on the application of Coke-Wallis) v Institute of Chartered Accountants in England and Wales** [2011] 2 1, SC.
    Exceeding jurisdiction. *See* Domestic tribunal exceeding jurisdiction, *below*.
    Natural justice. *See* **Natural justice** (Domestic tribunal).
    Trade union. *See* **Trade union** (Domestic tribunal).
Domestic tribunal exceeding jurisdiction—
    Remedy of person aggrieved—
        Absence of malice—Liability for damage caused by ultra vires acts. **Abbott v Sullivan** [1952] 1 226, CA.
        Declaration for reinstatement of person aggrieved—Whether contractual relationship necessary. **Davis v Carew-Pole** [1956] 2 524, QBD.
EC Commission—
    Complaint to commission containing defamatory remarks—
        Whether protected by absolute privilege. *See* **Libel and slander** (Privilege—Absolute privilege—Tribunal recognised by law—EC Commission).
Employment Appeal Tribunal. *See* **Employment Appeal Tribunal**.
Employment tribunal—
    Costs. *See* **Costs** (Employment tribunal).
    Generally. *See* **Employment tribunal**.
    Tribunal. *See* **Employment tribunal**.
Evidence—
    Foreign tribunal. *See* **Evidence** (Foreign tribunal).
    Fresh evidence discovered after hearing—
        Whether certiorari lies to quash decision of tribunal. *See* **Certiorari** (Evidence—Fresh evidence—Quarter sessions).
    Legal rules of evidence inapplicable. *See* **Evidence** (Tribunal—Rules of evidence governing admissibility in court of law not applicable).
First-tier Tribunal—
    Costs-sharing order. *See* **Costs** (Order for costs—Costs-sharing order—First-tier Tribunal).
    Hearing—
        Closed material procedure—Exclusion of legal representative—Whether tribunal rules permitting exclusion of legal representative willing to give undertaking as to confidentiality—Whether fundamental principles of open justice and natural justice demanding restrictive interpretation of rules—Freedom of Information Act 2000, ss 41(1), 43(2) — Tribunals, Courts and Enforcement Act 2007, s 22, Sch 5, paras 7(g), 11(1), 16—Tribunal Procedure (First-tier Tribunal) (General Regulatory Chamber) Rules 2009, SI 2009/1976, rr 5(3)(g), 35. **Browning v Information Comr** [2015] 3 797, CA.

TRIBUNAL (cont)—
  First-tier Tribunal (cont)—
    Procedure—
      Costs—Award of costs—Party acting unreasonably in bringing, defending or conducting proceedings—HMRC issuing information notice where it was not entitled to—Taxpayer appealing—HMRC withdrawing notice after being notified of appeal—Whether decision to issue information notice amounting to bringing or conducting proceedings—Whether omission to withdraw decision HMRC knew to be wrong unreasonable behaviour—Whether taxpayer entitled to costs—Whether costs incurred before start of proceedings incidental to proceedings—Tribunals, Courts and Enforcement Act 2007, s 29—Tribunal Procedure (First-tier Tribunal) (Tax Chamber) Rules 2009, SI 2009/273, r 10(1)(b). **Distinctive Care Ltd v Revenue and Customs Comrs** [2019] **4** 111, CA.
      Striking out—Barring order—FTT barring HMRC from further participation—Upper Tribunal allowing HMRC's appeal—Whether FTT wrong in law—Whether barring order should be implemented—Whether case dealt with fairly and justly in accordance with overriding objective—Tribunal Procedure (First-tier Tribunal) (Tax Chamber) Rules 2009, SI 2009/273, r 8. **Revenue and Customs Comrs v BPP Holdings Ltd** [2016] 3 245, CA; [2017] **4** 756, SC.
  Foreign tribunal—
    Evidence. *See* **Evidence** (Foreign tribunal).
  Human rights—
    Right to a fair hearing. *See* **Human rights** (Right to a fair hearing—Impartial and independent tribunal).
  Immigration appeal tribunal—
    Generally. *See* **Immigration** (Appeal—Tribunal).
    Time limit for appealing. *See* **Immigration** (Appeal—Time limit for appealing—Appeal to tribunal from adjudicator).
  Income tax—
    Income tax tribunal—
      Duty to hear parties etc. *See* **Natural justice** (Income tax tribunal—Duty to hear parties etc).
    Tax advantage—
      Tribunal to consider transactions in securities. *See* **Income tax** (Tax advantage—Counteracting—Tribunal).
  Industrial Disputes Tribunal—
    Certiorari to quash decision of. *See* **Certiorari** (Jurisdiction—Industrial Disputes Tribunal).
  Industrial injuries tribunal—
    Evidence. *See* **Natural justice** (Industrial injuries tribunal—Evidence).
  Industrial tribunal—
    Generally. *See* **Employment tribunal**.
  Inferior tribunal—
    Procedure. *See* Procedure—Procedure of inferior tribunal, *below*.
  Investigatory powers tribunal—
    Scrutiny of investigatory powers and functions of intelligence services. *See* **Intelligence services** (Scrutiny of investigatory powers and functions of intelligence services).
  Issue estoppel—
    Inferior tribunal. *See* **Estoppel** (Issue estoppel—Inferior tribunal).
  Judicial discretion—
    Review of exercise of discretion—
      Duty of appellate court. *See* **Appeal** (Review of exercise of discretion—Duty of appellate court).
  Judicial review—
    Superior court of record—
      Upper Tribunal. *See* **Judicial review** (Upper Tribunal—Amenability of Upper Tribunal to judicial review).
    Upper tribunal. *See* **Judicial review** (Availability of remedy—Upper Tribunal).
  Jurisdiction—
    Error going to jurisdiction—
      Certiorari. *See* **Certiorari** (Jurisdiction—Statutory tribunal's decision).
    Jurisdiction of court—
      Declaration on originating summons. *See* **Originating summons** (Declaration on originating summons—Jurisdiction—Statutory tribunal's decision final by statute).
  Lands Tribunal. *See* **Lands Tribunal**.
  Medical appeal tribunal—
    Duty to make due enquiry—
      Extent of duty. *See* **Natural justice** (Medical appeal tribunal—Duty to make due enquiry—Extent of duty).
    Industrial injury. *See* **Industrial injury** (Medical appeal tribunal).
  Membership—
    Bias—
      Disability appeal tribunal—Tribunal members including doctor engaged to provide reports for benefits agency—Whether fair-minded and informed observer would conclude existence of unconscious bias on part of doctor. **Gillies v Secretary of State for Work and Pensions** [2006] **1** 731, HL.
      Inquiry into dismissal—Tribunal members also members of dismissing body—Tribunal members not present at meeting of dismissing body effecting dismissal—Local education authority staff sub-committee—Inquiry into dismissal of teacher by governing body of aided voluntary school. **Hannam v Bradford City Council** [1970] **2** 690, CA.
  Mental health review tribunal—
    Appeal against decision of tribunal—
      Procedure—Dissatisfaction with reasons for tribunal's decision—Whether application for judicial review an appropriate alternative to statement of special case—Mental Health Act 1983, s 78(8). **Bone v Mental Health Review Tribunal** [1985] **3** 330, QBD.
    Contempt of court—
      Whether mental health review tribunal a 'court'. *See* **Contempt of court** (Publications concerning legal proceedings—Court—Inferior court—Mental health review tribunal).
    Generally. *See* **Mental health** (Mental health review tribunal).

TRIBUNAL (cont)—
Natural justice—
    Domestic tribunal. *See* **Natural justice** (Domestic tribunal).
Pensions appeal tribunal. *See* **Pensions Appeal Tribunal**.
Precedent—
    Previous decisions of statutory tribunal as precedent—
        Not to inhibit examining into merits of each case in which called on to exercise statutory discretion. **Merchandise Transport Ltd v British Transport Commission** [1961] **3** 495, CA.
Procedure—
    Determination whether prima facie case—
        No obligation to hear evidence or argument at that stage—Tribunal to consider tax advantages. *See* **Income tax** (Tax advantage—Counteracting—Tribunal—Determination whether there is a prima facie case—Procedure).
First-tier Tribunal. *See* First-tier Tribunal, *above*.
Natural justice—
    Domestic tribunal. *See* **Natural justice** (Domestic tribunal).
No rules prescribed—
    Comparable rules applied by analogy—Tribunal acting in accord with natural justice and bearing objectives in mind—Tribunal not disabled from performing functions. **Qureshi v Qureshi** [1971] **1** 325, Div.
Procedure of inferior tribunal—
    Method of challenge—Certiorari. **Wiseman v Borneman** [1967] **3** 1045, CA.
Rent tribunal. *See* **Rent tribunal**.
Review of decision—
    Administrative tribunal—
        Jurisdiction of court—Defence Council—Council refusing to issue certificate that deceased died from wound sustained on active service—Council applying wrong construction of statutory provision in making determination—Whether court having jurisdiction to grant declaration that on material before it council should have issued certificate. **Barty-King v Ministry of Defence** [1979] **2** 80, QBD.
    Domestic tribunal—
        Jurisdiction of court—Extent of jurisdiction. **Lee v Showmen's Guild of GB** [1952] **1** 1175, CA.
Royal Commission—
    Natural justice. *See* **Natural justice** (Royal Commission).
Solicitors' Disciplinary Tribunal. *See* **Solicitor** (Disciplinary proceedings—Disciplinary tribunal).
Special Immigration Appeals Commission—
    Admissibility of evidence. *See* **Evidence** (Admissibility—Special Immigration Appeals Commission).
Statutory tribunal—
    Certiorari. *See* **Certiorari** (Statutory tribunal).
    Delegation of judicial duty—
        Power to delegate. **Barnard v National Dock Labour Board** [1953] **1** 1113, CA; **Vine v National Dock Labour Board** [1956] **3** 939, HL.
    Disciplinary committee of professional society—
        Misconduct rendering convicted person unfit to be on register of society—Effect of conditional discharge on conviction—Whether disciplinary committee prohibited from hearing evidence of facts leading to conviction in support of complaint of misconduct—Whether maxim that person not to be punished twice for same offence applicable to disciplinary committee proceedings—Powers of Criminal Courts Act 1973, s 13(3). **R v Statutory Committee of Pharmaceutical Society of GB, ex p Pharmaceutical Society of GB** [1981] **2** 805, QBD.
Supplementary Benefits Appeal Tribunal. *See* **Social security** (Supplementary benefit—Appeal tribunal).
Trade union—
    Domestic tribunal. *See* **Trade union** (Domestic tribunal).
Transport tribunal—
    Appeal from—
        Jurisdiction of Court of Appeal. *See* **Court of Appeal** (Jurisdiction—Appeal from order of transport tribunal).
    Generally. *See* **Transport tribunal**.
Tribunal of inquiry—
    Evidence—
        Newspaper reporter—Refusal to disclose source of information of newspaper report—Whether a question which tribunal may legally require him to answer—Relevance—Privilege—Discretion of court—Tribunals of Inquiry (Evidence) Act 1921, s 1. **A-G v Clough** [1963] **1** 420, QBD; **A-G v Mulholland** [1963] **1** 767, CA.
    Witness—
        Immunity from civil action. *See* **Action** (Immunity from suit—Witness—Tribunal).
        Right to life—Common law duty of fairness to witnesses—Tribunal investigating murder in Northern Ireland—Police witnesses fearing reprisals and asking for anonymity—Whether real and immediate risk to life—Whether risk materially increased—Whether subjective fear sufficient—Whether test under common law differing from test under human rights convention—Human Rights Act 1988, Sch 1, Pt I, art 2. **Officer L, Re** [2007] **4** 965, HL.
        Tribunal investigating 'Bloody Sunday' shootings in Northern Ireland—Military witnesses fearing reprisals and asking to be identified by letters only—Tribunal refusing soldiers' request—Whether tribunal's decision unreasonable or unfair. **R v Lord Saville of Newdigate, ex p A** [1999] **4** 860, CA.
Upper Tribunal—
    Costs—
        Jurisdiction to award costs—Protective costs order—Whether Upper Tribunal having jurisdiction to make protective costs order—Approach to be taken—Tribunals, Courts and Enforcement Act 2007, s 29—Tribunal Procedure (Upper Tribunal) Rules 2008, SI 2008/2698, r 10. **Drummond v Revenue and Customs Comrs** [2016] **4** 884, UT.
    Judicial review. *See* **Judicial review** (Availability of remedy—Upper Tribunal).
    Judicial review. *See* **Judicial review** (Upper Tribunal—Amenability of Upper Tribunal to judicial review).

TRIBUNAL (cont)—
 Value Added Tax and Duties Tribunal—
  Jurisdiction—
   Review officer dismissing respondent's appeal against refusal to restore forfeited vehicle—Tribunal allowing respondent's appeal and ordering restoration of vehicle or payment of compensation in lieu—Whether tribunal having jurisdiction to make such an order—Finance Act 1994, s 16(4). **Lindsay v Customs and Excise Comrs** [2002] **3** 118, CA.
 Value added tax tribunal. *See* **Value added tax** (Tribunal).
 Witness—
  Attendance—
   Power of High Court to aid tribunal by issuing subpoena ad testificandum. *See* **Witness** (Attendance—Tribunal—Power of High Court to aid tribunal by issuing subpoena ad testificandum).
  Immunity from civil action. *See* **Action** (Immunity from suit—Witness—Tribunal).

TRICK
 Larceny by a trick. *See* **Criminal law** (Larceny—Trick).

TRINIDAD AND TOBAGO
 Colonial courts—
  Judges—
   Appointment as acting judge of Supreme Court—Whether puisne judge and as such entitled to sit in Court of Criminal Appeal—Judicature Ordinance 1880, s 7(1), (3)—Judicature (Amendment) Ordinance 1936 (No 24 of 1936), s 4(1)—Criminal Appeal Ordinance 1931 (No 31 of 1931), s 3(1)—Interpretation Ordinance 1933 (No 19 of 1933), ss 17, 20. **Butler v R** [1939] **3** 121, PC.
 Constitutional law—
  Entrenched provisions of constitution—
   Effect of entrenched provisions—Entrenchment by infection—Whether entrenching of specific provisions having effect of impliedly entrenching other provisions—Constitution of the Republic of Trinidad and Tobago 1976, ss 49, 54. **A-G of Trinidad and Tobago v McLeod** [1984] **1** 694, PC.
  Freedom of association—
   Abridgment of right to free collective bargaining—Abridgment of freedom to strike—Freedom of association not violated—Industrial Stabilisation Act 1965 (No 8 of 1965)—Trinidad and Tobago (Constitution) Order in Council 1962 (SI 1962 No 1875), Sch 2, s 1(j). **Collymore v A-G of Trinidad and Tobago** [1969] **2** 1207, PC.
  Human rights and freedoms—
   Constitution prohibiting cruel and unusual punishment or deprivation of life except by due process of law—Death penalty—Delay in carrying out death penalty—Delay caused by problems in judicial system—Whether excessive delay in appellate procedure a cruel and unusual punishment—Constitution of Trinidad and Tobago, ss 4(a), 5(2)(b). **Guerra v Baptiste** [1995] **4** 583, PC.
   Constitution prohibiting cruel and unusual punishment or deprivation of life except by due process of law—Mandatory death sentence—Whether mandatory death sentence a cruel and unusual punishment—Constitution of the Republic of Trinidad and Tobago, ss 4(a) and 5(2)(b). **Daniel v State of Trinidad and Tobago** [2014] **2** 461, PC.
   Right not to be deprived of liberty otherwise than by due process of law—Redress—Committal for contempt of court—Appellant admitting contempt of court and being sentenced to imprisonment—Appellant not appealing—Appellant later claiming that he had been imprisoned otherwise than by due process of law because judge had wrongly interpreted law—Whether appellant committed according to due process of law—Whether appellant entitled to exercise parallel remedies—Constitution of Trinidad and Tobago 1962 (SI 1962 No 1875) ss 1(a), 6(1). **Chokolingo v A-G of Trinidad and Tobago** [1981] **1** 244, PC.
   Right not to be deprived of liberty otherwise than by due process of law—Redress—Committal for contempt of court—Judge failing to specify nature of contempt charged—Contemnor applying by motion to another High Court judge for redress by award of damages against the Attorney General as representing the state—Whether judge having jurisdiction to entertain motion—Whether committal contravention of constitutional right—Whether 'redress' including damages—Whether award of damages contrary to rule of public policy that a judge is not liable for anything done in his judicial capacity—Constitution of Trinidad and Tobago 1962 (SI 1962 No 1875), ss 1(a), 6(1), (2)(a). **Maharaj v A-G of Trinidad and Tobago (No 2)** [1978] **2** 670, PC.
   Right to equal treatment by public authority—Employment—Respondent employing appellant as permanent worker—Appellant convicted of criminal offence and imprisoned—Respondent later re-employing appellant as temporary worker—Appellant bringing claim for breach of constitutional rights—Whether abuse of process—Whether breach of right to equal treatment—Constitution of the Republic of Trinidad and Tobago 1976, s 4(d). **Port Authority of Trinidad and Tobago v Daban** [2020] **1** 373, PC.
   Right to protection of the law—Whether non-compliance with entrenching provisions in constitution amounting to infringement of 'right to protection of the law'—Whether access to courts to challenge validity of statute sufficient 'protection of the law'—Constitution of the Republic of Trinidad and Tobago 1976, ss 4(b), 54(3). **A-G of Trinidad and Tobago v McLeod** [1984] **1** 694, PC.
  Prohibition on imposing penalty on public officer except as a result of disciplinary proceedings—
   Police—Compulsory retirement—Whether compulsory retirement constituting 'penalty'—Constitution of the Republic of Trinidad and Tobago, s 129—Police Service Commission Regulations 1966 (Trinidad and Tobago), reg 50. **Long v Police Service Commission (Trinidad and Tobago)** [2019] **2** 35, PC.
 Criminal law—
  Corruption—
   Ingredients of offence—Corruptly soliciting or receiving gift on account of agent doing anything in respect of any matter in which State or public body concerned—Apparent purpose of transaction to affect conduct of public body corruptly—Whether necessary that public body aware of improper transaction—Prevention of Corruption Act 1987 (Trinidad and Tobago), s 3(1). **Singh v The State** [2005] **4** 781, PC.

TRINIDAD AND TOBAGO (cont)—

Criminal law (cont)—

Execution of death penalty—

Notice of execution—Amount of notice condemned man required to be given before execution—Constitution of Trinidad and Tobago, ss 4(a), 5(2)(b), (h). **Guerra v Baptiste** [1995] **4** 583, PC.

Murder—

Killing in the course or furtherance of an arrestable offence involving violence—Felony/murder rule of 'constructive malice'—Whether defence of provocation available on felony/murder charge—Criminal Law Act 1979, ss 2A, 4A—Homicide Act 1957, s 3. **Daniel v State of Trinidad and Tobago** [2014] **2** 461, PC.

Trial—

Counsel—Duty to client—Duty to explain options open to defendant—Counsel placed in embarrassing position because of defendant's instructions—Counsel unilaterally deciding not to put forward defence and merely putting prosecution to proof—Whether counsel's conduct depriving defendant of opportunity of considering whether to give evidence or make unsworn statement—Whether counsel under duty to explain options open to defendant before withdrawing from case. **Sankar v The State of Trinidad and Tobago** [1995] **1** 236, PC.

Fatal accident—

Action—

Provision that dependant of deceased may sue if no action commenced by executor within six months of death—Executors appointed by will—Action commenced by dependants three months after death—Whether claim commenced prematurely—Whether action a nullity—Trinidad and Tobago Compensation for Injuries Ordinance, s 8. **Austin v Hart** [1983] **2** 341, PC.

Income tax—

Dividend paid by cancellation of credit due to company from foreign company—

Liability of company to tax as statutory agent of foreign company—'Transmission' of revenue—Income Tax Ordinance 1940, ss 5, 30. **Trinidad Lake Asphalt Operating Co Ltd v Trinidad and Tobago Income Tax Comrs** [1945] **1** 9, PC.

Emoluments from office or employment—

Basis of assessment. *See* **Income tax** (Emoluments from office or employment—Basis of assessment).

Judge—

Removal from office—

Suspension from judicial duties—Natural justice—Chief Justice deciding that judge should not be rostered to sit—Chief Justice making complaint about judge to Judicial and Legal Service Commission—Commission not giving judge opportunity to rebut complaint before making representation to President that his removal be investigated—Whether Chief Justice having power to bar judge from sitting as part of administrative arrangements—Whether Chief Justice acted outside his administrative powers—Whether Commission required to give judge opportunity to rebut complaint before making representation to President that his removal be investigated—Constitution of the Republic of Trinidad and Tobago (Trinidad and Tobago), s 137. **Rees v Crane** [1994] **1** 833, PC.

Jury—

Verdict—

Verdict announced as unanimous—Four jurors subsequently stating they had disagreed with verdict—Verdict returned in sight and hearing of all jurors without protest—Whether evidence of jurors that they had disagreed with verdict admissible on appeal—Whether trial judge required to direct jury that verdict must be unanimous. **Nanan v The State** [1986] **3** 248, PC.

Legal profession—

Attorney at Law—

Professional misconduct—Disciplinary proceedings—Standard of proof. **Campbell v Hamlet** [2005] **3** 1116, PC.

Master and servant—

Trade dispute—

Board of inquiry—Jurisdiction—Dismissal of workmen by employers—Non-recognition of union by employers—Power of governor to appoint board of inquiry—Trade Disputes (Arbitration and Inquiry) Ordinance (Laws of Trinidad and Tobago 1950 (c 22 No 10)), ss 2(1), 8(1). **Beetham v Trinidad Cement Co Ltd** [1960] **1** 274, PC.

Pardon—

Pardon granted subject to 'lawful conditions'—

Power to pardon—Future offences—Pardon granted to participants in insurrection in Trinidad—Respondents participating in insurrection—Pardon granted by acting president in return for surrender and release of hostages—Respondents not surrendering and releasing hostages immediately—Respondents subsequently arrested, detained and charged with offences encompassed by pardon—Whether pardon valid—Whether pardon can expunge offences not yet committed—Whether pardon obtained by duress—Whether abuse of process to proceed against respondents—Constitution of the Republic of Trinidad and Tobago 1976, s 87(1). **A-G of Trinidad and Tobago v Phillip** [1995] **1** 93, PC.

Statute—

Construction—

Power to arrest without warrant a person having in his possession 'in any place' articles reasonably suspected of being stolen—Search warrant obtained on suspicion of certain articles being in respondent's possession at his home—Those articles not found there, but other articles seized—Whether words 'in any place' meant in any public place—Whether Judicial Committee should remit case to appellate court, magistrate having found no reasonable cause for suspicion but appellate court having decided appeal on another ground—Summary Offences Ordinance s 36(1). **Felix v Thomas** [1966] **3** 21, PC.

TROUT

See **Fish** (Salmon and trout).

TROVER
Limitation of action—
  Date of accrual of cause of action—
    Car stolen by unknown person—Discovery in hands of innocent purchaser for value—Action for recovery brought seven years after theft. **R B Policies at Lloyd's v Butler** [1949] **2** 226, KBD.
  Postponement of limitation period—
    Action based on fraud—Whether 'right of action concealed by fraud'. **Beaman v ARTS Ltd** [1949] **1** 465, CA.
Right of possession—
  Finder—
    Bracelet found in airport lounge by passenger—Occupier of lounge not manifesting intention to exercise exclusive control over lounge and chattels on or in it—Whether finder entitled to bracelet. **Parker v British Airways Board** [1982] **1** 834, CA.
    Brooch found in public park by member of public using metal detector—Owner of park bound to allow public to use park for pleasure and recreation—Whether finder entitled to brooch. **Waverley BC v Fletcher** [1995] **4** 756, CA.
    Brooch found in requisitioned house—Freeholder never in physical occupation of house—True owner of brooch not known—Finder entitled to retain brooch. **Hannah v Peel** [1945] **2** 288, KBD.

TRUCK ACTS
Wages—
  Generally. See **Employment** (Remuneration).

TRUNK ROADS
See **Highway** (Trunk roads).

TRUST AND TRUSTEE
Accounting for benefit. See Profit from trust—Account of profits—Agents for trust, *below.*
Accounts—
  Audit—
    Judicial trustee. See Judicial trustee—Power of compromise—Audit of accounts, *below.*
  Limitation of action—
    Charitable trust. See **Limitation of action** (Trust property—Charitable trust—Action by Attorney General for accounts to be taken of trust property).
  Profits. See Profit from trust—Account of profits, *below.*
Accumulation of income. See **Accumulation**.
Additional trustee—
  Appointment—
    Appointment by appointor of himself—Trustee Act 1925, s 36(6). **Power's Settlement Trusts, Re** [1951] **2** 513, CA.
Administration of trust—
  Annuity fund—
    Annuity never payable—Capital of fund payable to legatee—Appropriation of investments to satisfy legacy—Discretion of trustees. **Nicholson's Will Trusts, Re** [1936] **3** 832, Ch D.
  Chancery Division practice. See **Practice** (Chancery Division—Trusts).
  Child-bearing—
    Leave to administer trusts on footing that married woman past child-bearing—Married woman entitled to protected life interest—Thrice married and having had two children by first marriage but none for 27 years—Medical evidence of incapacity to have further children. **Westminster Bank Ltd's Declaration of Trust, Re** [1963] **2** 400, Ch D.
    Woman over 70. See **Variation of trusts** (Child-bearing—Arrangement proposed to meet contingency of a woman over 70 having a further child).
  Disposal of surplus on closure of fund—
    Fund raised by employees of company—Fund to provide grants for ex-employees in the Forces and for contributors in respect of air-raid damage—Non-charitable purposes—Fund to be distributed amongst contributors in proportion to amount contributed—Amounts received by way of grant to be brought into hotchpot. **Hobourn Aero Components Ltd's Air-Raid Distress Fund's Trusts, Re** [1945] **2** 711, Ch D.
  Jurisdiction—
    Joint venture agreement—Property held by company for benefit of various family trusts pursuant to joint venture agreement—Agreement preventing assignment, pledging or encumberment of shares in company without prior approval of other parties except where new trustees appointed or shares transferred to trustees for benefit of family members—Restructuring of company leading to transfer of shares to trustees and subsequent trustees—Whether under joint venture agreement consent of all parties needed on transfer to new trustees. **Walbrook Trustees (Jersey) Ltd v Fattal** [2010] **1 Comm** 526, Ch D.
    Joint venture agreement—Property held by company for benefit of various family trusts pursuant to joint venture agreement—Two members of company holding shares as nominees for four interests—Restructuring of company leading to transfer of shares to new trustees and subsequent trustees so that each interest represented by one member—Whether under terms of trust deed unanimity required. **Walbrook Trustees (Jersey) Ltd v Fattal** [2011] **1 Comm** 647, CA.
  Rule in Howe v Dartmouth—
    Leaseholds—Beneficial interests in undivided shares—Statutory trust for sale—Law of Property Act 1925, ss 25, 28(2), 34, 35. **Berton, Re** [1938] **4** 286, Ch D.
Advancement—
  Power of advancement. See Powers of trustee—Advancement, *below.*
Agent—
  Accountability of solicitor as agent for trust. See Profit from trust—Account of profits—Agents for trust, *below.*
  Authority. See **Agent** (Authority—Ostensible authority—Trust deed vesting management of company pension plan in trustees).
Allhusen v Whittell—
  Rule in. See Rule in Allhusen v Whittell, *below.*

TRUST AND TRUSTEE (cont)—
  Alteration of beneficial interests—
    Charitable trust. *See* **Charity** (Charitable trust—Alteration of beneficial interests).
  Annuity—
    Annuity to trustee conditional on his acting as such—
      Assessment to special contribution. **Dale v IRC** [1953] **2** 671, HL.
  Appointing person to convey property—
    Infant beneficially interested—
      Disentailing deed—Trustee Act 1925, s 53. **Bristol's Settled Estates, Re** [1964] **3** 939, Ch D;
        Lansdowne's Will Trusts, Re [1967] **1** 888, Ch D.
  Appointment of new trustee—
    By administrators with the will annexed—
      Administration completed. **Cockburn (decd), Re** [1957] **2** 522, Ch D.
    By court—
      Appointment in place of trustee of unsound mind. *See* **Mental health** (Court of
        Protection—Practice—Appointment of new trustee in place of trustee of unsound mind).
      Former trustee wishing to continue in office—Friction between trustees—Appointment of Public
        Trustee—Jurisdiction—Trustee Act 1925, s 41(1). **Henderson, Re** [1940] **3** 295, Ch D.
    By infant—
      Appointment of mother of infant as sole trustee—Mother also interested in fund—Validity of
        appointment. **Parsons' Settlement, Re** [1940] **4** 65, Ch D.
    By personal representative of last surviving trustee—
      Need for grant of representation—Executor not having obtained probate—New trustee bringing
        proceedings in court—Whether executor having power to appoint trustee in absence of grant of
        probate—Whether title of executor to make appointment may be proved otherwise than by a
        proper grant of representation—Trustee Act 1925, s 36(1). **Crowhurst Park, Re** [1974] **1** 991, Ch D.
    Concurrence of continuing trustee—
      Refusal to concur—Enforcement by beneficiaries of concurrence—Trustee Act 1925, s 36(1)(b).
        Brockbank (decd), Re [1948] **1** 287, Ch D.
      Retiring trustee—Trustee compulsorily retired for remaining out of the United Kingdom for more
        than twelve months—Trustee Act 1925, s 36(1) (8). **Stoneham's Settlement Trusts, Re**
        [1952] **2** 694, Ch D.
    Objection—
      Costs—Liability of present trustees for possible future claim to estate duty—Whether right to order
        for impounding beneficiary's interest lost by ceasing to be trustee—Trustee Act 1925, s 62.
        Pauling's Settlement, Re (No 2) [1963] **1** 857, Ch D.
    Self appointment. *See* Additional trustee—Appointment—Appointment by appointor of himself, *above*.
    Settlement—
      Power of appointment. *See* **Settlement** (Trustees—Power to appoint new trustees).
    Settlement created by will—
      Executors by representation—Executors becoming trustees of settlement for purposes of Settled
        Land Act under provisions of the Act—Settled Land Act 1925, s 30(3)—Trustee Act 1925, ss 36(1),
        64(1), 68(5). **Dark's Will Trusts, Re** [1954] **1** 681, Ch D.
    Trustee not to be discharged on appointment of new trustee unless there would be either a trust
      corporation or at least two individuals to act as trustees—
      Whether 'individual' including body corporate—Trustee Act 1925, s 37(1)(c). **Jasmine Trustees Ltd v**
        Wells & Hind (a firm) [2007] **1** 1142, Ch D.
    Trustee of unsound mind—
      Appointment in place of person of unsound mind. **Practice Direction** [1957] **1** 581, Ct of Protection.
    Vesting order in some of several trustees without removal of other trustee. *See* Vesting
      order—Continuing trustees—Necessity for removal of remaining trustee, *below*.
  Appointment of trustees—
    Additional trustee. *See* Additional trustee—Appointment, *above*.
    Appointment by attorney administrators—
      Trustees' powers to maintain infant. **Kehr (decd), Re** [1951] **2** 812, Ch D.
    Appointment of bank—
      Beneficiaries customers of bank—Overdraft—Power of advancement—Protected life interest—
        Discretionary trust of income. **Northcliffe's Settlements, Re** [1937] **3** 804, CA.
    Completion of administration. *See* **Administration of estates** (Completion of administration—New
      trustees).
    Judicial trustee. *See* Judicial trustee—Power to appoint, *below*.
    New trustee. *See* Appointment of new trustee, *above*.
  Bank—
    Account—
      Fiduciary duty owed by bank. *See* **Bank** (Account—Trust account—Fiduciary duty).
      Money credited to separate account. *See* **Bank** (Account—Separate accounts—Trust).
      Remuneration as trustee. *See* Remuneration of trustee—Bank, *below*.
  Bankruptcy—
    Bankrupt's estate—
      Vesting in trustee. *See* **Insolvency** (Bankrupt's estate—Vesting in trustee).
    Trustee in bankruptcy. *See* **Bankruptcy** (Trustee in bankruptcy).
  Bare trust—
    Company shares—
      Voting power. *See* **Company** (Shares—Voting power —Bare trust).
    Variation of trust. *See* **Variation of trusts** (Bare trust).
  Beneficiaries' rights. *See* Duty of trustee, *below*.
  Beneficiary also trustee—
    Liability of trustee. *See* Liability of trustee—Defaulting trustee also beneficiary under trust fund, *below*.
  Body corporate, capacity to act as trustee. *See* Appointment of new trustee—Trustee not to be discharged
    on appointment of new trustee unless there would be either a trust corporation or at least two individuals
    to act as trustees—Whether 'individual' including body corporate, *above*.
  Borrowing money for investments. *See* Investments—Borrowing money for, *below*.

Breach of trust—
Account of profits—
Damages—Plaintiff's right to elect between remedies—Alternative and inconsistent remedies—Whether plaintiff electing to take remedy of an account of profits—Whether plaintiff precluded from pursuing claim for damages. **Tang Man Sit (decd) (personal representative) v Capacious Investments Ltd** [1996] **1** 193, PC.

Action by beneficiary—
Constructive trustee—Solicitor acting for trustees—Solicitor drawing trust deed—Solicitor acting honestly on instructions of trustees. **Williams-Ashman v Price and Williams** [1942] **1** 310, Ch D.

Compensation—
Date at which compensation for breach of trust is to be assessed—Trustee mortgaging trust property in breach of trust—Property sold by mortgagee resulting in total loss of trust funds—Value of property falling between issue of writ and judgment—Whether compensation to be assessed as at date of issue of writ or judgment. **Jaffray v Marshall** [1994] **1** 143, Ch D.

Compensation for breach—
Trustee's duty to compensate beneficiary for losses—Re-mortgage—Solicitors holding mortgage moneys on trust for lender until completion—Solicitors in breach of trust discharging only part of existing mortgage debt and releasing balance of moneys to borrowers—Lender not obtaining first charge—Lender suffering loss on borrowers' default—Whether trust fund to be reconstituted by solicitors—Method of equitable compensation—Principles to be applied. **AIB Group (UK) plc v Mark Redler & Co Solicitors** [2015] **1** 747, SC; [2015] **2 Comm** 189, SC.

Concealment of right of action by fraud—
Limitation of action. See **Limitation of action** (Concealment of right of action by fraud—Fraud—Action against trustee for breach of trust).

Consent to breach—
Requisites to disentitle beneficiary from suing for breach—Invalid exercise of power of advancement—Undue influence of father—Consents of young beneficiaries to payment to parent of money advanced to them—Extent of trustee's right to relief—Application of Limitation Act—Laches and Acquiescence—Trustee Act 1925, s 61—Limitation Act 1939 s 19(2), proviso. **Pauling's Settlement Trusts, Re** [1963] **3** 1, CA.

Conversion of trust securities—
Forgery—Restoration of name to register—Costs. **Welch v Bank of England (Francis & Praed, third parties)** [1955] **1** 811, Ch D.

Dishonest assistance—
Company director. See **Company** (Director—Duty—Fiduciary duty—Breach of fiduciary duty—Dishonest assistance).

Fraud or dishonesty—
Pleading constructive trust. See **Pleading** (Particulars—Constructive trust—Knowledge of fraudulent or dishonest breach of trust—Pleading of fraud or dishonesty).
Trust's assets consisting of shares in holding company—Trustee charging shares as security for guarantee of loan given to subsidiary—Charge and guarantee forming part of transaction to ease financial plight of third party—Trustee genuinely believing transaction to be in interests of beneficiaries—Beneficiaries bringing action for dishonest breach of trust—Whether test for honesty entirely subjective. **Walker v Stones** [2000] **4** 412, CA.

Guernsey—
Exclusion of liability—Liability for loss arising from gross negligence—Trusts (Guernsey) Law 1989, s 34(7). **Spread Trustee Co Ltd v Hutcheson** [2012] **1** 251, SC.

Impounding interest of beneficiary—
Equitable or statutory right to impound—Right not limited to trustee who was in possession of trust fund—Appointment of new trustees would not, therefore, prejudice right to impound—Trustee Act 1925, s 62. **Pauling's Settlement, Re (No 2)** [1963] **1** 857, Ch D.

Interest chargeable against trustee—
Rate of interest. **Bartlett v Barclays Bank Trust Co Ltd (No 2)** [1980] **2** 92, Ch D.

Investments—
Majority shareholding in private company—Duty of trustees in regard to management of the company's affairs—Family business—Trustee, himself a substantial shareholder and a director, failing to supervise adequately the drawings of a director and manager from the company's confidential account—Cheques in blank signed by trustee—Co-trustee unaware of excess drawings by manager and not himself a director—Manager unable to repay indebtedness to company—Whether trustees liable to beneficiary for loss due to manager's acts. **Lucking's Will Trusts, Re** [1967] **3** 726, Ch D.

Majority shareholding in private company—Duty of trustees in regard to management of the company's affairs—Trust corporation—Bank trustee of settlement—Trust fund consisting of majority of shares in private property company—Bank not represented at board meetings and not insisting on regular flow of information from board—Bank content to receive information dispensed at annual general meetings—Company suffering substantial loss through hazardous investment in property development—Bank unaware of nature of investment—Whether bank in breach of trust—Whether bank under duty to obtain regular flow of information from board—Whether bank entitled to set off profit from one speculative investment against loss in another—Trustee Act 1925, s 61. **Debtor (No 37 of 1976, Liverpool), Re a, ex p Taylor v The Debtor** [1980] **1** 129, Ch D.

Majority shareholding in private company—Trust's assets consisting of all shares in company having controlling interest in another company—Subsidiary having controlling interests in other companies—Trustee allegedly acquiescing in wrongful diversion of funds from subsidiaries—Whether rule precluding shareholders from recovering company's loss barring action for breach of trust in respect of alleged diversions. **Walker v Stones** [2000] **4** 412, CA.

TRUST AND TRUSTEE (cont)—
Breach of trust (cont)—
Letting of trust property—
House consisting of two flats held by defendant on trust for himself and plaintiff in equal shares—Defendant and plaintiff contributing in equal shares to mortgage on house—One flat becoming vacant—Plaintiff wishing to sell house with vacant possession and not wishing to relet flat because new tenancy would be protected—Plaintiff withholding payments for house until dispute over sale of house resolved—Defendant reletting flat to provide money for mortgage instalments—Whether breach of trust—Whether reletting reasonable and prudent conduct. **Peffer v Rigg** [1978] **3** 745, Ch D.

Misappropriation of trust money—
Investment scheme—Funds in solicitor's client account—Whether funds to be distributed on basis of 'first in, first out' rule—Whether 'North American' method to be applied to the account—Whether fund to be distributed pari passu rateably in proportion to investments. **Russell-Cooke Trust Co v Prentis** [2003] **2** 478, Ch D.

Trustee using misappropriated trust funds to pay last two of five premiums on life assurance policy—Trustee dying and insurers paying death benefit—Death benefit payable without payment of last two premiums—Whether beneficiaries of trust entitled to pro rata share in proceeds of life assurance policy. **Foskett v McKeown** [1997] **3** 392, CA; [2000] **3** 97, HL.

Mixing trust moneys with trustee's own money—
Rights of beneficiaries—Trust moneys forming part of deceased's estate paid into trustee's (his widow's) own bank account—Overdraft facilities accorded by bank to widow for property dealings—Liabilities of deceased's estate met by widow out of her own moneys—Whether beneficiary in deceased's estate entitled to a share of the profit from widow's property dealings. **Tilley's Will Trusts, Re** [1967] **2** 303, Ch D.

Partnership. *See* **Partnership** (Breach of trust).

Payment of trust moneys to stranger—
Compensation for breach—Trustee's duty to compensate beneficiary for losses—Principles to be applied—Solicitor acting for mortgagor and mortgagee releasing mortgage moneys to strangers without authority before mortgage security executed—Mortgage security executed some days later—Solicitor in breach of trust—Whether solicitor under immediate duty to make restitution of mortgage moneys subject to mortgagee giving credit for moneys recovered from sale of property—Whether trustee liable to compensate beneficiary for losses which beneficiary would have suffered if there had been no breach. **Target Holdings Ltd v Redferns (a firm)** [1995] **3** 785, HL.

Power of court to relieve trustee from liability—
Liability for anticipated breach—Trustee of deceased's estate—Deceased having specifically devised house to B—Trustee having transferred house to B without having taken security for estate duty in respect of house—Amount of duty irrecoverable from B—Proposal to pay duty out of residue of estate—Payment in breach of trust—Whether trustee entitled to seek relief in respect of anticipated breach—Trustee Act 1925, s 61. **Rosenthal (decd), Re** [1972] **3** 552, Ch D.

Procedure by originating summons inappropriate. *See* Procedure—Originating summons or writ, *below.*

Sale by trustee of trust property to own nominee—
Declaration of trust by nominee in favour of trustee—Specific devise of property by will of trustee—Avoidance of sale—Right of specific devisee to repaid purchase money. **Sherman (decd), Re** [1954] **1** 893, Ch D.

Sale of trust property in breach of trust and wrongful distribution of proceeds—
Measure of liability to replace trust fund—Constructive trustee—Solicitor liable as constructive trustee to replace money—Farm sold in breach of trust in 1947 and proceeds wrongfully distributed—Farm resold by purchasers for proper price in 1949—Action by beneficiaries commenced by writ in 1970—Plaintiffs conceding farm would have been sold in 1949 in course of proper administration of trust for price in fact sold in 1949—Judgment in action given in 1979—Estate Duty Office deciding not to charge estate duty on money replaced—Whether measure of liability the value of farm at date of writ or judgment or price at which farm in fact sold in 1949—Whether there should be a deduction from the liability for estate duty that which would have been payable if trust fund had remained intact. **Bell's Indenture, Re** [1980] **3** 425, Ch D.

Set-off—
Separate transactions resulting in loss to trust—Transactions stemming from policy of trustee to make speculative investments—Whether trustee able to set off profit resulting from one transaction against loss resulting from another. **Bartlett v Barclays Bank Trust Co Ltd** [1980] **1** 139, Ch D.

Severing defences—
Separate representation. *See* Trustee's costs—Reimbursement of trustee—Contractual right, *below.*

Solicitor—
Duty. *See* **Solicitor** (Duty—Breach of trust).

Trustee exemption clause—
Clause excluding liability of trustees for loss or damage to trust property unless caused by actual fraud—Beneficiary commencing action for breach of trust—Whether trustees absolved from liability—Meaning of 'actual fraud'—Whether exemption clause void for repugnancy or on grounds of public policy. **Armitage v Nurse** [1997] **2** 705, CA.

Wilful default by trustee—
Compensation payable for default—Settled trust fund consisting of shares in company—Some beneficiaries becoming absolutely entitled to their shareholdings before default made good but shareholding retained in settlement until total shareholding subsequently sold—Whether loss suffered by beneficiaries to be assessed at date they become absolutely entitled—Whether tax payable by beneficiaries to be taken into account in assessing compensation—Whether if instances of wilful default are pleaded and proved plaintiff entitled to an account on the footing of all wilful default that has occurred. **Bartlett v Barclays Bank Trust Co Ltd (No 2)** [1980] **2** 92, Ch D.

TRUST AND TRUSTEE (cont)—
Burden of proof—
  Life tenant—
    Continuance of life. *See* Life interest—Continuance of life of life tenant—Burden of proof, *below.*
Capital gains tax—
  Settlement. *See* **Capital gains tax** (Settlement).
Capital transfer tax. *See* **Capital transfer tax**.
Charging clause. *See* Remuneration of trustee—Professional trustee—Charging clause, *below.*
Charitable trust. *See* **Charity** (Charitable trust).
Charity. *See* **Charity**.
Chesterfield's Trusts—
  Rule in. *See* Tenant for life—Reversionary interest—Rule in Re Chesterfield's Trusts, *below.*
Company—
  Fiduciary duty of director. *See* **Company** (Director—Duty—Fiduciary duty).
Company documents—
  Right of beneficiaries to inspect. *See* Shares in company—Trustees shareholders and directors—Rights of beneficiaries to inspect company's documents, *below.*
Compensation—
  Breach of trust. *See* Breach of trust—Compensation, *above.*
  Compensation under statute received by trustees—
    Subjection to trusts—Whether compensation subjected to trusts of property from which it arose. **Meux's Will Trusts, Re** [1957] **2** 630, Ch D.
Compromise—
  Trustees surrendering their discretion to the court. *See* Powers of trustee—Compromise—Trustees surrendering their discretion to the court, *below.*
Conflict of laws—
  Jurisdiction. *See* **Conflict of laws** (Jurisdiction—Challenge to jurisdiction—Civil and commercial matters—Trusts).
  Trustee's liability to third parties. *See* **Conflict of laws** (Trust and trustee—Trustee's liability to third parties).
Constitution of trust—
  Exercise of special power of appointment—
    When trusts so appointed became constituted. **Batty (decd), Re** [1952] **1** 425, Ch D; **Bransbury's Will Trusts, Re** [1954] **1** 605, Ch D.
Constructive trust—
  Breach of fiduciary duty—
    Agent—Secret commission—Purchasers' agent in negotiations for sale of shares receiving secret commission from vendor—Whether purchasers having proprietary interest in secret commission. **FHR European Ventures LLP v Mankarious** [2013] **2 Comm** 257, CA; [2013] **3** 29, CA; [2014] **2 Comm** 425, SC; [2014] **4** 79, SC.
    Knowing receipt of trust property—Sale of company assets at undervalue—Directors of vendor company in breach of fiduciary duty in respect of sale of company assets—Whether purchaser company liable as constructive trustee—Whether purchaser company having knowledge of directors' breach of duty—Proper test to be applied. **Cowan de Groot Properties Ltd v Eagle Trust plc** [1992] **4** 700, Ch D.
    Plaintiff acquiring option to purchase site with development potential—Plaintiff's surveyors disclosing confidential information about site to rival developers—Site owners exercising right to terminate option and selling site to plaintiff 's rivals—Whether rival developers held site on constructive trust for plaintiff. **Satnam Investments Ltd v Dunlop Heywood & Co Ltd** [1999] **3** 652, CA.
  Breach of trust—
    Fraud or dishonesty—Pleading. *See* **Pleading** (Particulars—Constructive trust—Knowledge of fraudulent or dishonest breach of trust).
  Bribe—
    Equitable duty of fiduciary who receives bribe—Property purchased with proceeds of bribe—Increase in value of property purchased with proceeds of bribe—Whether recipient of bribe entitled to keep increase in value of property purchased with proceeds of bribe—Whether fiduciary who receives bribe under equitable duty to account for profits from bribe. **A-G for Hong Kong v Reid** [1994] **1** 1, PC.
  Business and lease bequeathed to executors beneficially—
    New lease granted to one executor—Business carried on by one executor—Form of account to be taken—Laches. **Jarvis (decd), Re** [1958] **2** 336, Ch D.
  Cheque drawn by director on company's account—
    Director appropriating company's funds to settle personal debt incurred by deceased director—Creditor knowing that payment made in breach of trust—Whether creditor a constructive trustee for company of money received. **International Sales and Agencies Ltd v Marcus** [1982] **3** 551, QBD.
  Cheque fraudulently drawn by executor on executor's account—
    Recovery from payee—Cheque taken for value and in good faith—Constructive notice of want of authority. **Nelson v Larholt** [1947] **2** 751, KBD.
  Contract to divide a company's land between shareholders—
    Memorandum—Minutes of company meeting sufficient memorandum—Law of Property Act 1925, s 53(1)(a). **Strathblaine Estates Ltd, Re** [1948] **1** 162, Ch D.
  Executor de son tort—
    Plaintiff 's mother owning family home—Mother dying intestate and the property being held on statutory trusts for plaintiff and her two siblings—Plaintiff's brother not taking out letters of administration and acting as owner of the property—Plaintiff claiming share of the property and commencing proceedings more than 12 years after mother's death—Whether executor de son tort could be constructive trustee—Whether plaintiff 's claim statute-barred—Limitation Act 1980, s 21. **James v Williams** [1999] **3** 309, CA.

TRUST AND TRUSTEE (cont)—
Constructive trust (cont)—
Expenditure on property of another—
Family arrangement—Equitable principle applicable—Imposition of trust whenever justice and good conscience require it—Improvement to property paid for by person other than legal owner—Mother-in-law coming to live at son-in-law's house—Extension to house to provide bedroom for mother-in-law—Extension paid for by mother-in-law—Mother-in-law subsequently leaving to live elsewhere—Resulting trust for mother-in-law giving her an interest in the house proportionate to money expended on extension—Resulting trust consistent with transaction being a loan to son-in-law. **Hussey v Palmer** [1972] **3** 744, CA.
Fiduciary relationship—
Debtor and creditor—Agreement between plaintiff and company whereby plaintiff providing company with funds paid into special bank account for sole purpose of paying particular debts owed by company to third parties—Company going into voluntary liquidation—Liquidator claiming money in special bank account an asset of company available for distribution to general body of creditors—Plaintiff claiming money in special bank account held by company on primary trust for third parties—Whether money a company asset or held by company on trust for particular creditors. **Carreras Rothmans Ltd v Freeman Mathews Treasure Ltd (in liq)** [1985] **1** 155, Ch D.
Fraud—
Knowing assistance in fraudulent design—Plaintiff's employee forging payment order in favour of nominee company set up and controlled by defendant accountants—Plaintiff's funds transferred to nominee company's bank account and then to account operated by defendants' firm—Funds later transferred to firm's clients' account—Defendants disposing of money on clients' instructions in disregard of plaintiff's request for its return—Defendants in receipt of legal advice as to possibility of fraud but failing to act—Whether defendants liable to account for funds as constructive trustees—Whether defendants knowingly assisting in fraudulent design. **Agip (Africa) Ltd v Jackson** [1992] **4** 451, CA.
Knowing assistance in furtherance of dishonest breach of trust—Accessory liability—Individual controlling company used for fraud—Whether individual owing victim of fraud fiduciary duty—Whether individual liable to victim on basis of unconscionable and dishonest assistance in breach of trust. **Sinclair Investment Holdings SA v Versailles Trade Finance Ltd** [2007] **2 Comm** 993, Ch D.
Knowing assistance in furtherance of dishonest breach of trust—Accessory liability—Test to be applied for determining dishonesty. **Twinsectra Ltd v Yardley** [2002] **2** 377, HL.
Knowing assistance in furtherance of dishonest breach of trust—Accessory liability—Test to be applied for determining dishonesty—Whether accessory's views about standards of honesty relevant. **Barlow Clowes International Ltd (in liq) v Eurotrust International Ltd** [2006] **1** 333, PC; [2006] **1 Comm** 478, PC.
Knowing assistance in furtherance of fraudulent and dishonest breach of trust—Accessory liability—Whether a dishonest and fraudulent breach of trust by trustee prerequisite for accessory liability. **Royal Brunei Airlines Sdn Bhd v Tan** [1995] **3** 97, PC.
Incomplete agreement for sale, purchase and development of land. *See* **Estoppel** (Proprietary estoppel—Constructive trust—Owner and developer entering into unenforceable incomplete agreement for sale, purchase and development of land after grant of planning permission).
Invalid trust—
Trust for reform of alphabet—Whether effect could be given to directions of trust as empowering trustee to act on them. **Shaw (decd), Re** [1958] **1** 245, CA.
Joint account—
Money placed in names of donor and another—Investment in joint names—Gifts not to take effect until death of donor—Whether gifts of testamentary nature not conforming with Wills Act 1837. **Young v Sealey** [1949] **1** 92, Ch D.
Joint tenants—
Extent of beneficial interests held under constructive trust—Valuation—Whether court having discretion to order valuation of interests at date earlier than date of realisation of interests—Whether discretion to order valuation at date of separation. **Turton v Turton** [1987] **2** 641, CA.
Knowing receipt—
Commercial transaction—Constructive notice—Defendant agreeing to underwrite costs of plaintiff's take-over offer and subsequently arranging to sub-underwrite its liability—Plaintiff alleging that its funds were misapplied to satisfy sub-underwriting costs—Whether third party liable as constructive trustee for trust property already passed on—Test to be applied in determining liability—Whether constructive notice sufficient for liability—Whether principle of constructive notice applicable to commercial transactions. **Eagle Trust plc v SBC Securities Ltd** [1992] **4** 488, Ch D.
Whether dishonesty essential ingredient of claim for knowing receipt—Test for determining knowledge in claim for knowing receipt. **Bank of Credit and Commerce International (Overseas) Ltd (in liq) v Akindele** [2000] **4** 221, CA.
Licence to occupy land—
Contractual licence—Sale of licensor's interest—Rights of licensee against third party. *See* **Licence** (Licence to occupy land—Contractual licence—Rights of licensee against third parties—Constructive trust).
Oral arrangements—
Exchange of shares owned by life tenant for reversionary interest in settled shares—Oral agreement to transfer reversionary interest (by exchange) to life tenant—Whether any need for writing—Law of Property Act 1925, s 53(1), (2). **Oughtred v IRC** [1959] **3** 623, HL.
Informal agreement for liquidation of family company—Agreement including division of company's equitable interest in shares of second company amongst family company shareholders in proportion to shareholding—Whether agreement creating implied or constructive trust—Whether disposition required to be in writing—Law of Property Act 1925, s 53(1)(c), (2). **Neville v Wilson** [1996] **3** 171, CA.

TRUST AND TRUSTEE (cont)—
Constructive trust (cont)—
Oral arrangements (cont)—
Parties agreeing in principle to form joint venture to acquire development site but not finalising agreement—Defendant acquiring company as joint venture vehicle but having doubts about claimant as partner—Defendant not informing claimant about doubts and acquiring site for itself through proposed joint venture company—Whether circumstances giving rise to constructive trust. **Banner Homes Group plc v Luff Developments Ltd** [2000] **2** 117, CA.

Proprietary estoppel—Parties agreeing to transfer of freehold subject to lease—Lease containing break clause—One party unaware of break clause—Whether other party could rely on break clause—Whether conduct unconscionable. **Crossco No 4 Unlimited v Jolan Ltd** [2012] **2** 754n, CA.

Prospective purchaser of property orally offering claimant part of property in return for repairing it and acting as managing agent—Property being purchased by prospective purchaser's son with knowledge of arrangement—Claimant carrying out works on property but being excluded by purchaser—Whether circumstances giving rise to constructive trust—Law of Property (Miscellaneous Provisions) Act 1989, s 2. **Yaxley v Gotts** [2000] **1** 711, CA.

Sale of cottage—Oral undertaking by purchaser to permit vendor to occupy cottage rent free. **Bannister v Bannister** [1948] **2** 133, CA.

Voluntary transfer of legal estate—Oral arrangement that transferor would remain beneficial owner—Beneficial owner not intending gift—Transfer of house by registered proprietor—Whether absence of writing precluding transferor from asserting entitlement in equity—Whether expression of intention in oral agreement negativing resulting trust—Whether transferor prevented from asserting beneficial interest as overriding interest—Law of Property Act 1925, s 53(1), (2). **Hodgson v Marks** [1971] **2** 684, CA.

Participation in dishonest design—
Knowingly assisting in fraudulent design on part of trustee—Knowingly receiving trust property—Knowingly assisting in breach of trust—Knowledge—Bank—Bank having knowledge that company was transferring substantial sums off shore—Funds transferred fraudulently—Whether bank having cause to suspect improprieties—Whether bank should have been put on inquiry as to whether there were improprieties in transfer. **Polly Peck International plc v Nadir (No 2)** [1992] **4** 769, CA.

Knowingly assisting in fraudulent design on part of trustee—Knowingly receiving trust property—Knowingly assisting in breach of trust—Knowledge—Stranger—Knowledge required of stranger to trust to make him accountable as constructive trustee—Whether carelessness or negligence in failing to make inquiries amounting to knowledge—Whether want of probity necessary to make stranger accountable as constructive trustee for assisting in fraudulent design on part of trustee. **Lipkin Gorman (a firm) v Karpnale Ltd (1986)** [1992] **4** 331, QBD.

Knowingly assisting in fraudulent design on part of trustee—Knowledge—Stranger—Bank—Knowledge required of stranger to trust to make him accountable as constructive trustee—Bank's duty of care to beneficiary—When bank will be accountable as constructive trustee for assisting in fraudulent design on part of trustee. **Baden v Société Générale pour Favoriser le Développement du Commerce et de l'Industrie en France SA (1982)** [1992] **4** 161, Ch D.

Knowingly receiving trust property—Knowledge—Trustees of settlement releasing settled property to beneficiary absolutely in breach of trust—Beneficiary's solicitor aware of terms of settlement—Whether beneficiary having knowledge of breach of trust—Whether beneficiary acting with want of probity—Whether knowledge of beneficiary's solicitor to be imputed to beneficiary—Whether beneficiary a constructive trustee of property. **Montagu's Settlement Trusts (1985), Re** [1992] **4** 308, Ch D.

Takeover transaction involving purchase by director of company's issued share capital—Director using company's assets to finance purchase of shares—Director drawing cheque on company's account in favour of third party to repay loan by third party for purchase of shares—Payment of cheque by bank—Liability of bank to company as constructive trustee—Circumstances such as to put reasonable banker on enquiry as to propriety of transaction. **Karak Rubber Co Ltd v Burden (No 2)** [1972] **1** 1210, Ch D.

Purchase of house as home—
Family enterprise—Equality is equity. **Macdonald v Macdonald** [1957] **2** 690, Ch D.

Sale of registered land—
Vendor agreeing to sell land to plaintiffs and erect house on it—Vendor going into liquidation—Vendor's bank selling land to defendant in exercise of mortgagee's power of sale—Contract between bank and defendant stipulating that sale subject to plaintiffs' contract with vendor—Whether stipulation imposing constructive trust on defendant to give effect to plaintiffs' contract—Whether registration giving defendant absolute title free from plaintiffs' unregistered interest—Land Registration Act 1925, ss 20(1), 34(4). **Lyus v Prowsa Developments Ltd** [1982] **2** 953, Ch D.

Shares in company—
Article of association providing for automatic transmission of shares to director's widow on his death—Article invalid as contrary to Companies Act 1929. **Greene (decd), Re** [1949] **1** 167, Ch D.

Plaintiff wishing to bid for company but restrained by undertaking given to Secretary of State—Plaintiff selling shareholding to defendants—Defendants mounting successful bid for company—Plaintiff not making counter-bid—Plaintiff alleging that defendants dishonestly misrepresented to plaintiff that they would not bid for company—Plaintiff seeking declaration that defendants held entire issued share capital in company in trust for plaintiff—Whether constructive trust arising in view of plaintiff's inaction when defendants mounted take-over. **Lonrho plc v Fayed (No 2)** [1991] **4** 961, Ch D.

Transfer by company in liquidation of shares in another company—Allegation that company in liquidation received shares subject to trust—No claim made that company constructive trustee—Whether liquidator having constructive knowledge of trust. **Competitive Insurance Co Ltd v Davies Investments Ltd** [1975] **3** 254, Ch D.

TRUST AND TRUSTEE (cont)—
  Constructive trust (cont)—
    Tenancy agreement—
      Contribution to rent—Informal arrangement between plaintiffs and defendant to share unfurnished flat—Flat let to defendants for a year under tenancy agreement—No premium—Draft agreement approved by plaintiffs—Plaintiffs and defendant contributing to rent, purchase of furniture and other expenses—No express agreement in relation to beneficial ownership of tenancy—Whether defendant trustee of tenancy for himself and plaintiffs. **Savage v Dunningham** [1973] **3** 429, Ch D.
    Trade mark—
      Sole United Kingdom agent of German manufacturer registered owner of mark—Whether held mark in trust for manufacturer. **Diehl KG's Application, Re** [1969] **3** 338, Ch D.
    Trustee. *See* Constructive trustee, *below.*
    Unmarried couple—
      Contributions by woman to joint home—House in name of man—Death of man intestate—Rights of woman—Joint venture—'Equity is equality'. **Diwell v Farnes** [1959] **2** 379, CA.
      Contributions to acquisition of property—Contributions to household expenses—Contribution to deposit on house—Man and mistress living in rented accommodation—Mistress paying housekeeping expenses and man paying other outgoings—House acquired on mortgage—Mistress contributing by way of loan to balance of purchase price—House conveyed to man—Mistress continuing to meet housekeeping expenses—Man paying mortgage instalments and other outgoings—Whether mistress entitled to beneficial interest in house. **Richards v Dove** [1974] **1** 888, Ch D.
      Conveyance of house into joint names of cohabiting couple without express declaration of beneficial interests—Principles applicable in determining beneficial interests in property. **Stack v Dowden** [2007] **2** 929, HL.
      House acquired by joint efforts for joint benefit—Claim for beneficial interest in house—Defence of illegality—House purchased jointly but in plaintiff's sole name to facilitate defendant's fraudulent claims for social security benefit—Plaintiff moving out leaving defendant in occupation—Plaintiff claiming possession and asserting ownership of house—Defendant counterclaiming for beneficial interest—Plaintiff raising defence of illegality to counterclaim—Whether defendant entitled to beneficial interest notwithstanding fraudulent purpose of purchase in plaintiff's sole name. **Tinsley v Milligan** [1992] **2** 391, CA.
      House acquired by joint efforts for joint benefit—Claim for beneficial interest in house—Defence of illegality—House purchased jointly but registered in plaintiff's sole name to facilitate defendant's fraudulent claims for socal security benefit—Plaintiff moving out leaving defendant in occupation—Plaintiff claiming possession and asserting ownership of house—Defendant counterclaiming for beneficial interest—Plaintiff raising defence of illegality to counterclaim—Whether defendant entitled to benefical interest notwithstanding fraudulent purpose of registration of ownership—Whether plaintiff entitled to succeed under resulting trust—Whether evidence of illegal purpose of registration in plaintiff's sole name rebutting presumption of resulting trust. **Tinsley v Milligan** [1993] **3** 65, HL.
      House acquired by joint efforts for joint benefit—Date of valuation of their respective shares—House purchased by man for purpose of family home for mistress and children—House conveyed in sole name of man—Couple separating—Mistress and children remaining in occupation—Intention that no order for sale should be made while children living in house—Mistress claiming share in property—Whether share to be valued at date of separation or date of sale. **Gordon v Douce** [1983] **2** 228, CA.
      House acquired by joint efforts for joint benefit—Principles applicable in determining beneficial interests in property—House acquired in sole name of one—Both contributing unequally to purchase price—Common intention that each should have a share in the property—Couple sharing outgoings referable to ownership approximately equally—Sale of property—Share of proceeds of sale to which each entitled. **Oxley v Hiscock** [2004] **3** 703, CA.
      House acquired by joint efforts for joint benefit—Principles governing apportionment of beneficial interests—Relevance of principles governing rights of husband and wife in matrimonial home—House acquired by engaged couple in joint names—Both going into occupation and letting rooms to meet mortgage instalments—Couple separating—Man thereafter occupying house alone—Share of proceeds of sale to which woman entitled—Whether order for sale should be made. **Bernard v Josephs** [1982] **3** 162, CA.
      House acquired by joint efforts for joint benefit—Principles governing apportionment of beneficial interests—Relevance of principles governing rights of husband and wife in matrimonial home—Land acquired by man in his name for purpose of building bungalow for himself and his mistress to set up home together—Mistress not contributing to purchase price of land—Mistress helping in physical work of building bungalow and contributing to mortgage instalments and other expenses—Couple separating before going into occupation—Man occupying bungalow alone for two years rent free paying the mortgage instalments over that period—Sale of property—Man holding proceeds as trustee for himself and mistress—Share of proceeds of sale to which mistress entitled. **Cooke v Head** [1972] **2** 38, CA.
      Principles applicable in determining beneficial interests in property—Man acquiring house in his sole name—Man telling mistress her name would not be on title deeds because of prejudice to her pending divorce proceedings—Mistress not directly contributing to purchase price or mortgage instalments—Mistress indirectly contributing to mortgage instalments by substantial contributions to housekeeping, household expenses and by bringing up children—Whether common intention that mistress was to have beneficial interest—Whether mistress acting to her detriment on basis of such common intention—Whether mistress entitled to beneficial interest in house. **Grant v Edwards** [1986] **2** 426, CA.
      Principles applicable in determining beneficial interests in property—Man acquiring house in his sole name—Mistress not directly contributing to purchase price or mortgage instalments—Couple living in house with their children for 17 years—Mistress looking after well-being of family by performing domestic duties and caring for children—Whether mistress entitled to beneficial interest—Whether common intention that mistress was to have beneficial interest. **Burns v Burns** [1984] **1** 244, CA.

TRUST AND TRUSTEE (cont)—

Constructive trust (cont)—

Unmarried couple (cont)—

Principles applicable in determining beneficial interests in property—Man acquiring house in sole name—Mistress not directly contributing to purchase price or mortgage instalments—Mistress indirectly contributing by contributions to man's business interests, housekeeping and bringing up children—Whether common intention that mistress should have beneficial interest—Whether mistress acting to her detriment on basis of such common intention—Whether mistress entitled to beneficial interest in property and other assets—Observations on conduct of proceedings between unmarried couples relating to disputed proprietary rights and ownership of chattels. **Hammond v Mitchell** [1992] **2** 109, Fam D.

Transfer of property acquired by both into name of one party—Declaration of trust by transferee—Declaration supported by agreement or estoppel—Inference of agreement from parties' conduct—Contributions to repair and restoration of house—House transferred into man's name—Mistress making no contribution to purchase price—Man telling mistress that house belonged to them both but that mistress too young to join in transfer—Couple intending to marry—Mistress helping to improve and repair house by heavy physical work—Couple subsequently separating—Whether mistress entitled to beneficial interest in house. **Eves v Eves** [1975] **3** 768, CA.

Constructive trustee—

Account of profits. See Profit from trust—Account of profits—Agents for trust—Constructive trustees, below.

Solicitor—

Liability. See **Solicitor** (Liability—Constructive trustee).

Unmarried couple—

Conveyance of house into joint names of cohabiting couple without express declaration of beneficial interests—Principles applicable in determining beneficial interests in property—Couple separating—Woman staying in occupation with children—Whether court justified in inferring or imputing change in intentions with regard to respective beneficial interests following separation. **Jones v Kernott** [2010] **1** 947, Ch D; [2010] **3** 423, CA; [2012] **1** 1265, SC.

Contingent interest—

Carrying intermediate income—

No payment to be made to beneficiary—Beneficiary entitled to payment under statute—Trustee Act 1925, s 31(1)(ii). **Ricarde-Seaver's Will Trusts, Re** [1936] **1** 580, Ch D.

No payment to be made to beneficiary until a later age than 21—

Statutory provision for payment to beneficiary—Whether subject to contrary direction in will—Trustee Act 1925, ss 31, 69(2). **Turner's Will Trusts, Re** [1936] **2** 1435, CA.

Vesting—

Share of residue to be divided, after life interests, among such of named charities as were in existence as independent charities—Three named charities became subject to National Health Service Act 1946, during the subsistence of the life interests—Whether a charity's interest was a vested remainder subject to a condition subsequent divesting it before it vested in possession or whether it was a contingent gift in remainder. **Lowry's Will Trusts, Re** [1966] **3** 955, Ch D.

Contract—

Sale of business—

Widow's annuity—Whether trust. See **Contract** (Stranger to contract—Annuitant—Widow of deceased owner of business—Sale of business by deceased on terms under which widow was to be paid weekly sum).

Corporate trustee—

Bank—

Winding up of bank—Bank appointed trustee of trust funds—Funds deposited with bank as banker—Bank becoming insolvent and going into liquidation—Whether beneficiaries under trust ranking in priority to or pari passu with unsecured creditors. **Space Investments Ltd v Canadian Imperial Bank of Commerce Trust Co (Bahamas) Ltd** [1986] **3** 75, PC.

Friendly society—

Appointment as sole trustee of pension fund—Friendly Societies Act 1896, s 25(1), (3). **Pilkington Bros Ltd Workmen's Pension Fund, Re** [1953] **2** 816, Ch D.

Production of record of administration to successor. See Duty of trustee—Production of record of administration to successor—Corporate trustee, below.

Remuneration. See Remuneration of trustee—Approval by court for increase in fees of corporate trustee, below.

Corporation sole—

Trust imposed on corporation sole—

Land conveyed to corporation sole and others as school site—Resulting trust on closure of school. **Bankes v Salisbury Diocesan Council of Education Inc** [1960] **2** 372, Ch D.

Costs—

Trustee's costs—

Generally. See Trustee's costs, below.

Counsel's opinion—

Court's power to authorise action to be taken on counsel's opinion—

Practice—Affidavits and documents required to support application to court—Consideration by judge—Service of notices—Costs—Administration of Justice Act 1985, s 48—RSC Ord 15, r 13A, Ord 93, r 21. **Practice Direction** [1987] **1** 608, Ch D.

Creation of trust—

Absence of writing. See Constructive trust—Oral arrangements, above.

Acceptance of bequest conditional on bequeathing own property on trusts of donor's will—

Trust arising on acceptance of condition. **Harmsworth (decd), Re** [1967] **2** 249, CA.

Declaration of trust—

Express oral trust—Declaration of trust over 5% of issued share capital of company—Company having only one class of shares—Majority shareholder promising employee that he would be given 5% of shares—Whether trust declared by majority shareholder void for uncertainty as to subject matter. **Hunter v Moss** [1994] **3** 215, CA.

1403

TRUST AND TRUSTEE (cont)—
  Creation of trust (cont)—
    Declaration of trust (cont)—
      Whether ineffective assignment at law capable of being effective in equity as declaration of trust. **Don King Productions Inc v Warren** [1998] **2** 608, Ch D; [1999] **2** 218, CA.
      Whether milk quotas capable of forming subject matter of trust. **Swift v Dairywise Farms Ltd** [2000] **1** 320, Ch D.
    Disposition of sum of money to individual recipient—
      Acceptance of trusts by him possibly subsequently to receipt of money—Instructions of donor communicated by letter—Gift for benefit of donor's friend during her lifetime at discretion of recipient of money—Residue applicable as to part for recipient of money and as to remainder on charitable trusts—Memorandum of recipient after donor's death recording wishes of donor—Whether memorandum admissible in evidence—Whether trust in favour of recipient of money established—Whether charitable trust of balance established—Evidence Act 1938, s 1—Law of Property Act 1925, s 53. **Tyler's Fund Trusts, Re** [1967] **3** 389, Ch D.
    Express trust—
      Declaration of trust—Words evidencing intention to create trust—Married man and mistress living together as husband and wife—Moneys received by man placed in bank deposit account in sole name—Man stating to mistress on many occasions that money as much hers as his—Joint winnings paid into account—Moneys withdrawn from account shared between them—Whether statements by man to mistress sufficient to constitute a declaration of trust. **Paul v Constance** [1977] **1** 195, CA.
    Manifestation of intention to create trust—
      Company—Moneys paid by customers in advance for goods—Oral arrangement made by company to place moneys in special bank account—Arrangement made on professional advice—Purpose to protect customers in view of possible insolvency of company—Whether sufficient manifestation of intention to create trust in favour of customers. **Kayford Ltd, Re** [1975] **1** 604, Ch D.
    Payment under guarantee—
      Applicant bank providing on demand guarantee for buyer's payment under shipbuilding contract—Buyer refusing to pay instalment—Respondent sellers demanding payment from bank—Arbitration award determining that payment not having fallen due—Bank making payment pursuant to guarantee—Whether money held by seller on trust for bank. **Wuhan Guoyu Logistics Group Co Ltd v Emporiki Bank of Greece SA (No 2)** [2014] **1 Comm** 870, CA.
    Purpose trust—
      Applicant making payment to company intending company to forward payment to third party—Company going into administration before forwarding payment—Company then going into liquidation—Whether payment to company subject to purpose trust—Whether payment traceable into liquidators' hands. **Cooper v PRG Powerhouse Ltd** [2008] **2 Comm** 964, Ch D.
      Benefit to individuals—Sports ground for employees of company—Trustees empowered to allow other persons to use sports ground—Uncertainty—Condition that if less than 75 per cent of employees were subscribing (at rate of 2d weekly per man) land should be conveyed to hospital—Women and juniors subscribing 1d weekly—Validity of trust and of gift over—Whether reference to man's subscribing rate included woman's—Law of Property Act 1925, s 61(d). **Denley's Trust Deed, Re** [1968] **3** 65, Ch D.
    Statutory creation of trust—
      Cash belonging to prisoner paid into account under prison governor's control—Whether trust imposed upon prison governor—Construction of relevant statutory instrument—Prison Rules 1999, r 43(3). **Duggan v Governor of Full Sutton Prison** [2003] **2** 678, Ch D.
  Creation of trust. *See* Creation of trust—Purpose trust, *below*.
  Custodian trustee—
    Corporation entitled to act as custodian trustee—
      Grant of probate. *See* **Probate** (Grant—Trust corporation—Corporation entitled to act as custodian trustee).
    Profit from trust. *See* Profit from trust—Custodian trustee, *below*.
  Declaration of trust—
    Creation of express trust. *See* Creation of trust—Express trust—Declaration of trust, *above*.
    Stamp duty. *See* **Stamp duty** (Voluntary disposition inter vivos—Declaration of trust).
    Transfer by way of declaration of new trust and determination of subsisting equitable interest—
      Personalty—Whether a 'disposition' for which writing needed—Law of Property Act 1925, s 53(1)(c). **Grey v IRC** [1959] **3** 603, HL.
  Defaulting trustee—
    Trustee also beneficiary under trust fund—
      Liability of trustee. *See* Liability of trustee—Defaulting trustee also beneficiary under trust fund, *below*.
  Delegation of trusts—
    Delegation by trustee during absence abroad—
      Statutory declaration to be filed with each power of attorney—Trustee Act 1925, s 25(4). **Practice Direction** [1960] **1** 716, QBD.
  Director-trustee—
    Remuneration—
      Order of court. *See* Remuneration of trustee—Order of court—Circumstances in which court will exercise jurisdiction to award remuneration—Director-trustee, *below*.
  Disclosure of trust documents—
    Duty to disclose to beneficiary on request—
      Deliberations as to exercise of discretionary power—Whether duty extends to documents relating to trustees' deliberations—What documents in that connection are not trust documents. **Londonderry's Settlement, Re** [1964] **3** 855, CA.
    Isle of Man—
      Whether dependent upon proprietary interest of beneficiary—Whether object of mere power entitled to disclosure. **Schmidt v Rosewood Trust Ltd** [2003] **3** 76, PC.

TRUST AND TRUSTEE (cont)—
Disclosure of trust documents (cont)—
Letter of wishes—
Family discretionary trusts—Wish letter substantially contemporaneous with family settlement—
Whether wish letter confidential—Whether beneficiaries entitled to disclosure of wish letter.
Breakspear v Ackland [2008] **2 Comm** 62, Ch D.
Discretionary trust—
Accumulation—
Accumulation of income as part of capital fund. *See* **Settlement** (Power of appointment—Transfer
of assets to trustees to hold on discretionary trusts—Trustees directed to accumulate income as
part of capital fund).
Exercise of trust—Trustees directed 'to pay or apply' income of trust fund during specified period to
or for 'the support or benefit of all or any one or more' of a named class of persons—Corpus to
be divided at end of specified period—Beneficiaries of discretionary trust having only contingent
interest in corpus—Allocations of income in favour of infant beneficiaries—Resolution of trustees
that sums 'shall belong' to each of the infant beneficiaries—Sums allocated to infants not being
required for their maintenance, resolution to accumulate—Trustee Act 1925, s 31(2). **Vestey's
Settlement, Re** [1950] **2** 891, CA.
Class of beneficiaries including employees and dependants—
Impracticability of ascertaining all members of class of possible beneficiaries—Whether term
'dependants' too vague—Whether trust void for uncertainty. **Saxone Shoe Co Ltd's Trust Deed,
Re** [1962] **2** 904, Ch D.
Class of beneficiaries including employees and relatives—
Power or imperative trust—Imperative direction that trustees 'shall apply' net income of
fund—Whether deed created a valid power or a trust that would be void for uncertainty. **McPhail
v Doulton** [1970] **2** 228, HL.
Test of validity—Whether test same for a trust as for a power—Whether class including 'relatives
and dependants' void for uncertainty. **Baden's Deed Trusts, Re (No 2)** [1972] **2** 1304, CA.
Class of beneficiaries including past, present or future employees of settlor—
Date of ascertainment of class—Whether trust valid. **Hain's Settlement, Re** [1961] **1** 848, CA.
Class of beneficiaries unascertainable—
Bare power of selection not coupled with trust—Settlement containing discretionary trusts in
favour of specified class of beneficiaries—Power of trustees with written consent of settlor to
include 'any other person or persons except the settlor' in the specified class—Whether power
void for uncertainty. **Blausten v IRC** [1972] **1** 41, CA.
Certain members of class ascertainable—Invalidity of trust. **IRC v Broadway Cottages Trust**
[1954] **3** 120, CA.
Individual members ascertainable—Whether sufficient to show individual fell within class—Trust to
benefit employees and ex-employees of company. **Sayer Trust, Re** [1956] **3** 600, Ch D.
Discretion as to objects—
Discretion to make payment to such children as 'shall appear to be most in need'—Discretionary
power to divide the corpus—Time when such power may be exercised—Construction against
intestacy. **Magee v Magee** [1936] **3** 15, PC.
Discretion as to quantum—
Income given on trust to apply it for education or benefit in such manner as trustee should think fit
for benefit of children of testator's four children—Subject thereto widow to have the benefit of
the income—Whether trustee had discretion as to amount of income to be applied for a
grandchild or the grandchildren—Whether gift to widow was to be rejected as repugnant. **Ward's
Will Trusts, Re** [1964] **3** 442, Ch D.
Doubts as to validity of discretionary power—
Income trust—Non-payment of income pending decision on validity—Whether postponement
reasonable—Whether discretion exercisable retrospectively. **Gulbenkian's Settlement Trusts, Re
(No 2)** [1969] **2** 1173, Ch D.
Income tax—
Generally. *See* **Income tax** (Settlement—Discretionary trust).
Non-exercise of discretion—
Settlor creating trust giving trustees discretion to appoint members of his family beneficiaries to
receive income or capital—Trustees at settlor's behest appointing all of settlor's children as
beneficiaries—Later at settlor's behest trustees revoking appointment of one son as beneficiary
and appointing other children—At settlor's behest trustees later purporting to appoint son as
beneficiary and transferring trust property to him—Whether any or all appointments an invalid
exercise of discretionary powers. **Turner v Turner** [1983] **2** 745, Ch D.
Trust in favour of beneficiaries subject to discretion to apply income for the maintenance of
A—Entitlement of beneficiaries after lapse of reasonable time for exercise of discretion—Whether
discretion could be surrendered to the court. **Allen-Meyrick's Will Trusts, Re** [1966] **1** 740, Ch D.
Payment of income to named object—
Object's release of interests under settlement for valuable consideration—Effect of release on
trustees' discretion—Whether competent to trustees to exercise discretion in favour of object.
Gulbenkian's Settlement Trusts, Re (No 2) [1969] **2** 1173, Ch D.
Payment or application of income—
Exercise of trust—Trustees directed 'to pay or apply' income of trust fund during specified period to
or for 'the support or benefit of all or any one or more' of a named class of persons—Corpus to
be divided at end of specified period—Beneficiaries of discretionary trust having only contingent
interest in corpus—Allocations of income in favour of infant beneficiaries—Resolution of trustees
that sums 'shall belong' to or be divided among each of the infant beneficiaries—Sums allocated
to infants not being required for their maintenance, resolution to accumulate—Trustee Act 1925,
s 31(2). **Vestey's Settlement, Re** [1950] **2** 891, CA.
Failure to distribute income within reasonable time of receipt—Obligatory discretionary
power—Power expressed to be absolute and uncontrolled—Whether discretion extinguished
after lapse of time—Whether court entitled to direct exercise of discretion. **Locker's Settlement
Trusts, Re** [1978] **1** 216, Ch D.

TRUST AND TRUSTEE (cont)—
  Discretionary trust (cont)—
    Payment or application of income (cont)—
      Failure to distribute income within reasonable time of receipt—Subsequent exercise of discretion by trustees on court's direction to distribute—Whether beneficiaries nominated subsequently to default of trustees entitled to benefit in distribution. **Locker's Settlement Trusts, Re** [1978] **1** 216, Ch D.
    Resort to capital—
      Power to hand over capital—Discretion to trustees to 'resort to and spend' any part of capital of trust fund 'and apply the same for the beneficiaries maintenance and general benefit during his life or until the cesser of his interest'—Protected life interest—Capital of fund to fall into residue on death of beneficiary or on forfeiture—Trustees' power to hand over capital absolutely to beneficiary. **Powles (decd), Re** [1954] **1** 516, Ch D.
    Statutory discretionary trust—
      Principal beneficiary an enemy—Forfeiture of interest of principal beneficiary—Trustee Act 1925, s 33—Trading with the Enemy Act 1939, s 7—Trading with the Enemy (Custodian) Order 1939 (SR & O 1939 No 1189). **Gourju, Re** [1942] **2** 605, Ch D.
    Uncertainty—
      Gift of residue on trust for a class of persons difficult to ascertain—Beneficiaries, and amount of their shares, in discretion of trustees—Whether trust valid. **Eden (decd), Re** [1957] **2** 430, Ch D.
      Power coupled with a trust—Class of beneficiaries including persons whom trustee should consider to have a moral claim on the deceased—Impossibility of all persons within class being known to trustee—Second trust 'failing them'—Some persons within class of objects of first trust known to be living—Second trust, therefore, not arising—Both first and second trust ineffective—Pension provision for managing director of company. **Leek (decd), Re** [1967] **2** 1160, Ch D; [1968] **1** 793, CA.
      Power of selection—Bare power not coupled with duty to select—Class of beneficiaries including persons considered to have moral claim on deceased—Impracticability of ascertaining beneficiaries—Power exercisable on several occasions and thus possibly beyond perpetuity limit—Whether void for uncertainty or perpetuity—Trust of proceeds of endowment assurance under pension scheme—Whether resulting trust for deceased. **Leek (decd), Re** [1967] **2** 1160, Ch D.
      Purposes—Specified period—Application of income of trust funds to be applied during specified period for all or any of certain public, but non-charitable, purposes—Application in discretion of trustees, subject to directions of settlors—Person entitled to fund at end of specified period not at present ascertainable. **Astor's Settlement Trusts, Re** [1952] **1** 1067, Ch D.
    Settlement. *See* **Settlement** (Power—Discretionary power—Discretion over income of trust fund).
  Disentailing deed. *See* Appointing person to convey property—Infant beneficially interested—Disentailing deed, *above*.
  Disposition of equitable interest or trust. *See* **Equity** (Disposition of equitable interest on trust).
  Distribution—
    Distribution in specie—
      Distribution regarded as distribution of property of certain cash value. **Gollin's Declaration of Trust, Re** [1969] **3** 1591, Ch D.
  Document—
    Inspection by beneficiary. *See* Disclosure of trust documents—Duty to disclose to beneficiary on request, *above*.
  Domicile of trust. *See* **Conflict of laws** (Jurisdiction—Challenge to jurisdiction—Civil and commercial matters—Trusts).
  Duty of trustee—
    Beneficiary absolutely entitled—
      Shares in private company—Persons interested in settled portion desiring retention of whole by trustees—Right of beneficiary absolutely entitled to receive transfer of his portion. **Weiner's Will Trusts, Re** [1956] **2** 482, Ch D.
      Transfer of trust estate. **Sandeman's Will Trusts, Re** [1937] **1** 368, Ch D.
    Beneficiary conditionally entitled—
      Beneficiary entitled to be paid on attaining the age of 21 years or marrying—Beneficiary marrying at the age of 18 years—Whether beneficiary can demand payment. **Somech (decd), Re** [1956] **3** 523, Ch D.
    Benefit—
      Accounting for. *See* Profit from trust—Account of profits, *below*.
    Disclosure of documents. *See* Disclosure of trust documents—Duty to disclose to beneficiary on request, *above*.
    Discretion—
      Exercise of discretion—Approval of court—Duty of trustee to court—Approach of court in exercising discretion. **Marley v Mutual Security Merchant Bank and Trust Co Ltd** [1991] **3** 198, PC.
    Duty towards beneficiary—
      Duty to inform beneficiary of his benefits under trust instrument—Duty to disclose to beneficiary on demand documents relating to the trust—Duty to pay income and capital without demand by beneficiary. **Hawksley v May** [1955] **3** 353, QBD.
      Investments—Power of investment—Bank acting as trustee—Duty of trustee to review trust investments regularly and properly—Bank failing to review trust investments regularly—Beneficiary not proving that value of trust would have increased if investments had been reviewed regularly—Whether prudent trustee would have invested better—Whether bank in breach of trust. **Nestle v National Westminster Bank plc** [1994] **1** 118, CA.
      Investments—Power of investment—Bank acting as trustee—Investment decision made on untenable grounds—Investment justifiable on other grounds—Whether bank liable for breach of trust. **Nestle v National Westminster Bank plc** [1994] **1** 118, CA.

TRUST AND TRUSTEE (cont)—
Duty of trustee (cont)—
Duty towards beneficiary (cont)—
Investments—Power of investment—Pension fund—Mineworkers' pension scheme—Scheme authorising overseas investment and investment in energy resources competing with coal—Trustees appointed by mineworkers seeking to restrict investments to investments in Britain and in industries not competing with coal—Whether trustees of pension fund subject to general law relating to trustees—Whether trustees entitled to prohibit particular investment for social or political reasons. **Cowan v Scargill** [1984] **2** 750, Ch D.
Self-dealing rule—Fair-dealing rule—Lease of trust property assigned to company—Trustee managing director and majority shareholder of company to which lease assigned—Relationship between self-dealing rule and fair-dealing rule—Whether assignment falling within self-dealing rule—Whether self-dealing rule applying to assignment to company. **Thompson's Settlement, Re** [1985] **2** 720, Ch D.
Investments—
Duty towards beneficiary. *See* Duty of trustee—Duty towards beneficiary—Investments, *above.*
Knowledge—
Trustee a director of development company—Trustees agreeing to take leases from company about to become a subsidiary of development company. **Lindgren v L & P Estates Co Ltd** [1968] **1** 917, CA.
Production of record of administration to successor—
Corporate trustee—Bank—Right to withhold documents relating to estate from successors in office. **Tiger v Barclays Bank Ltd** [1952] **1** 85, CA.
Profit. *See* Profit from trust—Account of profits, *below.*
Sale of property—
Overriding duty to obtain best price—Negotiations in advanced stage—Higher purchase price offered by third party. **Buttle v Saunders** [1950] **2** 193, Ch D.
Security agreement of assets held by structured investment vehicle—Structured investment vehicle facing insolvency—Dispute between creditors as to action to be taken by security trustee—Whether security trustee obliged to follow directions of senior creditors as to time, place and manner of sale of assets—Whether security agreement mandating specific timing for liquidation of collateral. **Bank of New York v Montana Board of Investments** [2009] **1 Comm** 1081, Ch D.
Ecclesiastical courts—
Jurisdiction—
Title to chattel—Whether ecclesiastical courts having jurisdiction to determine whether chattel mentioned in petition subject to a trust. *See* **Ecclesiastical law** (Ecclesiastical courts—Jurisdiction—Extent of jurisdiction—Chattel—Title to chattel—Trust).
Exclusion of liability—
Guernsey. *See* Breach of trust—Guernsey—Exclusion of liability, *above.*
Expenditure on property of another—
Constructive trust. *See* Constructive trust—Expenditure on property of another, *above.*
Express trust—
Creation. *See* Creation of trust—Express trust, *above.*
Trust for sale. *See* Trust for sale—Realty—Express trust, *below.*
Following trust property—
Fraudulent payment to innocent third party—
Value not given by third party—Whether beneficiary can recover from third party. **Baker (GL) Ltd v Medway Building & Supplies Ltd** [1958] **3** 540, CA.
Payment under mistake—
Money paid to charitable institutions by executors under a mistake as to the construction of a will—Directions in will void for uncertainty—Right of those entitled under an intestacy to trace. **Ministry of Health v Simpson** [1950] **2** 1137, HL.
Use of trust money to discharge mortgage—
Exchange of contracts for sale of property—Banks mortgage advance paid to vendors solicitors pending completion—Money applied before completion towards discharge of vendors prior mortgage—Mortgage discharged partly by vendors own payments—Sale falling through—Whether bank entitled to trace—Whether vendor an innocent volunteer—Whether vendor ranking pari passu. **Boscawen v Bajwa** [1995] **4** 769, CA.
Foreign trust—
Variation—
Jurisdiction. *See* **Variation of trusts** (Jurisdiction—Trust containing foreign element).
Forfeiture clause—
Attachment of earnings order made against husband—
Order bringing forfeiture clause in pension trust into operation—Discretionary trust arising for benefit of husband, wife and others—Consequences of order in relation to payments by the trustees in the exercise of their discretion—Maintenance Orders Act 1958, s 6(1)(b). **Edmonds v Edmonds** [1965] **1** 379, Div.
Fraud—
Accessory liability. *See* Constructive trust—Fraud—Knowing assistance in furtherance of dishonest breach of trust—Accessory liability, *above.*
Breach of trust—
Constructive trust—Pleading of fraud or dishonesty. *See* **Pleading** (Particulars—Constructive trust—Knowledge of fraudulent or dishonest breach of trust—Pleading of fraud or dishonesty).
Dishonest assistance in furtherance of breach of trust—
Limitation of action. *See* **Limitation of action** (Trust property—Fraud or fraudulent breach of trust to which trustee a party—Dishonest assistance).
Following trust property. *See* Following trust property—Fraudulent payment to innocent third party, *above.*
Fraudulent breach of trust—
Limitation of action. *See* **Limitation of action** (Period of limitation—Fraudulent breach of trust).
Fraudulent conversion by trustee. *See* **Criminal law** (Fraudulent conversion—Trustee).

Fraud (cont)—
Knowing assistance in furtherance of breach of trust—
Accessory liability—Claimants victims of fraud—Claimants paying moneys into bank account on instruction of fraudsters—Bank paying moneys out—Bank having suspicion that account used for money laundering but not having suspicions about particular transactions—Whether bank knowingly or dishonestly assisting in breach of trust. **Abou-Rahmah v Abacha** [2006] **1 Comm** 247, QBD; [2007] **1 Comm** 827, CA.
Friendly society. *See* Corporate trustee—Friendly society, *above*.
Gift to trustee—
In will—
Gifts to 'my trustees absolutely they well knowing my wishes concerning the same'—Gift of estate on trust and not gift conditional on discharge of testator's wishes. **Rees' Will Trusts, Re** [1949] **2** 1003, CA.
Governmental obligation—
Justiciability in court. *See* Nature of trust justiciable in court—Governmental obligation, *below*.
Howe v Dartmouth, Rule in. *See* Administration of trust—Rule in Howe v Dartmouth, *above*.
Imperfect trust—
Validation by Charitable Trusts (Validation) Act 1954. *See* **Charity** (Validation by statute—Imperfect trust provision).
Impounding beneficiary's interest. *See* Breach of trust—Impounding interest of beneficiary, *above*.
Income tax—
Annual payments. *See* **Income tax** (Annual payment—Personal debt or obligation by virtue of contract—Trust).
Foreign possessions. *See* **Income tax** (Foreign possessions—Income arising from possessions out of United Kingdom—Trustee).
Generally. *See* **Income tax** (Settlement).
Indemnity as to costs—
Trustee. *See* Trustee's costs—Indemnity as to costs, *below*.
Information of beneficiaries' rights—
Duty of trustee. *See* Duty of trustee, *above*.
Insurance—
Life insurance—
Policy moneys. *See* **Insurance** (Life insurance—Policy moneys).
Investments—
Borrowing money for—
Settlement conferring absolute discretion as to investments—Trustees wishing to borrow money for further investment on security of trust property—Power to raise money by sale or mortgage—Whether acquisition of additional investments a purpose authorised by settlement—Whether trustees having power to raise money on security of trust property for that purpose—Trustee Act 1925, s 16. **Suenson-Taylor's Settlement, Re** [1974] **3** 397, Ch D.
Charity—
Chartered corporation—Whether limited to trustee investments. *See* **Charity** (Chartered corporation—Investments).
Description—
Direction to invest in stocks, shares, and/or convertible debentures in the 'blue chip' category—Uncertainty—Whether clause valid. **Kolb's Will Trusts, Re** [1961] **3** 811, Ch D.
Direction in will to invest in specified securities—
'South African trustee securities only'—Whether investments confined to such South African securities as were trustee investments by the law of England. **Sebba (decd), Re** [1958] **3** 393, Ch D.
Statutory power—Whether statutory power available to trustee—Trustee Act 1893, s 1—Trustee Act 1925, ss 1(1), 69(2). **Warren, Re** [1939] **2** 599, Ch D.
Direction to invest in authorised securities—
No power to buy land. *See* Trust for sale—Investments—Direction in will to invest in authorised securities—No power to buy land, *below*.
Duty of trustee to beneficiary. *See* Duty of trustee—Duty towards beneficiary—Investments, *above*.
Investment clause—
Variation of trusts by the court. *See* **Variation of trusts** (Variation by the court—Investment clause).
Limitation of powers—
Best interest of beneficiary—Power to invest 'in any shares stocks property or property holding company as the trustees in their discretion shall consider to be in the best interest' of the beneficiary—Whether trustees' power of investment unlimited. **Peczenik's Settlement, Re** [1964] **2** 339, Ch D.
Guaranteed stocks—'In or upon any stocks...guaranteed by the Government of the United Kingdom or of any British Colony or Dependency...but not otherwise'—Investments in Dominion stocks and stock of local authority—Whether authorised—Trustee Act 1925, ss 1, 69(2). **Rider's Will Trusts, Re** [1958] **3** 135, Ch D.
In or upon such investments as to trustees 'may seem fit'. **Harari's Settlement Trusts, Re** [1949] **1** 430, Ch D.
Majority shareholding in private company. *See* Breach of trust—Investments—Majority shareholding in private company, *above*.
Power of beneficiary to direct investments whether authorised or not—
Purchase of shares from beneficiary himself—Whether beneficiary may direct trustees to purchase shares from himself. **Hart's Will Trusts, Re** [1943] **2** 557, Ch D.
Power to invest in freehold property—
House—Whether empowered to purchase freehold house as home for widow and children. **Power's Will Trusts, Re** [1947] **2** 282, Ch D.
Securities—
On such securities as they think fit—Power to invest in stocks and shares. **Douglas's Will Trusts, Re** [1959] **3** 785, CA.
Securities for money—Proceeds of life assurance policies. **Lilly's Will Trusts, Re** [1948] **2** 906, Ch D.
Separation of functions of holding investments and management of trust affairs—
Trade union's funds. *See* **Trade union** (Rules—Alteration of rules—Property of union).

TRUST AND TRUSTEE (cont)—
Investments (cont)—
    Shares of public company—
        Inclusion of stock. **Boys' Will Trusts, Re** [1950] **1** 624, Ch D.
    Variation of power of investment by court. See **Variation of trusts** (Variation by the court).
  Joint acquisition of property. See Resulting trust—Failure of express trust—More than one settlor, below.
  Joint tenants—
    Statutory trust for sale—
        Whole property accruing to survivor—Continuance of trust—Law of Property Act 1925, s 36(1), (2).
        Cook (decd), Re [1948] **1** 231, Ch D.
  Judicial trustee—
    Power of compromise—
        Audit of accounts—Extent of auditor's duty—Sending of copy of accounts to beneficiaries—Judicial
        Trustees Act 1896, s 1(1)—Trustee Act 1925, s 15(f)—Judicial Trustee Rules 1897, rr 12(1), 15(2).
        Ridsdel, Re [1947] **2** 312, Ch D.
    Power to appoint—
        Part of property—Whether available in respect of a part of the property of a testatrix—Factors in
        deciding whether to exercise power—Dispute in regard to part only of the estate—Conflict of duty
        and interest in position of executors—Testatrix directed extension of a lease of freehold property
        to her sons, the executors, on advantageous terms—Reversion devised to daughters—Sons were
        solicitors and had drawn the lease—Whether executors were under duty to impeach
        lease—Judicial Trustees Act 1896, s 1(2). **Wells (decd), Re** [1967] **3** 908, Ch D.
        Power of court to appoint judicial trustee for purposes of Settled Land Act—Judicial Trustees Act
        1896, s 1(1)—Settled Land Act 1925, ss 23, 30. **Marshall's Will Trusts, Re** [1945] **1** 550, Ch D.
    Remuneration—
        Common form of order—Judicial Trustees Act 1896, s 1(5)—Judicial Trustees Rules 1983, r 11.
        Practice Note [2003] **3** 974, Ch D.
  Land—
    No power to buy—
        Directions to invest in authorised securities. See Trust for sale—Investments—Direction in will to
        invest in authorised securities—No power to buy land, below.
  Lease—
    Renewal of lease by trustee. See Profit from trust—Renewal of lease by trustee, below.
  Legacy to hospital—
    Diversion of gift—
        Discretion of trustees. See **National Health Service** (Legacy to hospital—Diversion of
        gift—Discretion to trustees to divert gift if impracticable or inequitable in consequence of
        amalgamation).
  Liability of trustee—
    Defaulting trustee also beneficiary under trust fund—
        Principle that trustee should not to be ordered to pay what would come to him as
        beneficiary—Costs falling on fund—Whether principle applied before or after deduction of costs.
        Selangor United Rubber Estates Ltd v Cradock (a bankrupt) (No 4) [1969] **3** 965, Ch D.
  Liability to account for rents and profits—
    Occupation of trust property by trustee—Acquiescence by beneficiary—Application of Limitation
    Act 1939, s 19(1)(b). **Howlett (decd), Re** [1949] **2** 490, Ch D.
  Liability to make good loss and to account—
    Discretion of court—Trustee charitable corporation—Trustee acting honestly but mistakenly—
    Beneficiaries entitled to receive moiety of income of whole assets—Trustee dividing assets into
    moieties—Trustee appropriating each moiety to satisfy by its income entitlement of each
    beneficiary under trust—One moiety yielding larger income than other—Disparity in income not
    suppressed by trustee—Beneficiary delaying in pursuing claim—Whether accounts to be carried
    back to time of invalid appropriation or commencement of proceedings. **Freeston's Charity, Re**
    [1978] **1** 481, Ch D.
  Liability to third parties—
    Conflict of laws. See **Conflict of laws** (Trust and trustee—Trustee's liability to third parties).
  Life interest—
    Continuance of life of life tenant—
        Burden of proof—Discretion of Public Trustee to decline to make payment in the absence of
        evidence—Public Trustee Rules 1912 (SR & O 1912 No 348), r 27. **Wilson (decd), Re** [1964] **1** 196,
        Ch D.
    Income resulting from release—
        Resulting trust. See Resulting trust—Income resulting from release of life interest, below.
    Merger of beneficial interests. See Merger of beneficial interests, below.
    Terminable on re-marriage—
        Nullity decree in respect of re-marriage. See **Will** (Gift—Gift during widowhood—Decree of nullity
        in respect of second marriage).
  Limitation of action—
    Trust property. See **Limitation of action** (Trust property).
  Maintenance—
    Debt owing to estate by beneficiary taking protected life interest—
        Primary trust determined—Right of trustees to apply income for his maintenance before debt
        repaid. **Eiser's Will Trusts, Re** [1937] **1** 244, Ch D.
    Maintenance of children—
        Power of court to create trust. See **Minor** (Maintenance—Trust in favour of children).
    Statutory power—
        Direction to accumulate intermediate income—Intermediate income not available for maintenance
        during minority—Trustee Act 1925, ss 31(1), (3), 69(2). **Stapleton, Re** [1946] **1** 323, Ch D.
        Exclusion of power by contrary direction—Direction to accumulate—Accumulation for excessive
        period—Settlement—Accumulation after settlor's death and until beneficiary aged 22—Clause
        directing that statutory power not exercisable during settlor's life—Whether direction to
        accumulate excluding statutory power after settlor's death—Trustee Act 1925, ss 31, 69(2).
        Erskine's Settlement Trusts, Re [1971] **1** 572, Ch D.

TRUST AND TRUSTEE (cont)—
Maintenance (cont)—
  Statutory power (cont)—
    Exclusion of power by direction to accumulate—Trustee Act 1925, ss 31(1)(ii), 69(2). **Ransome's Will Trusts, Re** [1957] **1** 690, Ch D.
    Intermediate income—Trustee Act 1925, s 31. **Leng, Re** [1938] **3** 181, Ch D.
  Trustees' power to maintain—
    Trustees appointed by attorney administrators—Intestate domiciled abroad. **Kehr (decd), Re** [1951] **2** 812, Ch D.
Married woman past child-bearing. See Administration of trust—Child-bearing—Leave to administer trusts on footing that married woman past child-bearing, *above.*
Mental patient—
  Patient's property—
    Settlement. See **Mental health** (Patient's property—Settlement).
Merger of beneficial interests—
  Absolute entitlement—
    Assignment of life interest to beneficiary contingently entitled to absolute reversionary interest in trust property—Life interest not determined—Whether reversioner absolutely entitled to trust property. **Bellville's Settlement, Re** [1963] **3** 270, Ch D.
Misappropriation of trust money—
  Breach of trust. See Breach of trust—Misappropriation of trust money, *above.*
Mistake—
  Following trust property. See Following trust property—Payment under mistake, *above.*
Mistress—
  Contribution to joint home. See Constructive trust—Unmarried couple, *above.*
Mixing trust moneys with trustee's own money. See Breach of trust—Mixing trust moneys with trustee's own money, *above.*
Nature of trust justiciable in court—
  Governmental obligation—
    Enforcement of obligation—Criteria on which distinction drawn between trust and governmental obligation—Crown colony—Lease by colonial official to mining commissioners—Royalties to be held 'in trust' for islanders—Absence of intention to create a true trust or fiduciary obligation—Whether 'trust' justiciable in courts. **Tito v Waddell (No 2)** [1977] **3** 129, Ch D.
New trustee—
  Appointment. See Appointment of new trustee, *above.*
Option—
  Resulting trust. See Resulting trust—Option, *below.*
Power of attorney. See **Power of attorney.**
Powers of trustee—
  Advancement—
    Application of capital money for advancement of beneficiary—Advancement creating no interest in capital—Validity—Funds advanced to trustees of sub-settlement—Life interest with certain trusts and powers over—Trusts and powers over void for perpetuity—Whether capital money 'applied'—Whether advancement within powers of trustees—Trustee Act 1925, s 32(1). **Hastings-Bass (decd), Re** [1974] **2** 193, CA.
    Application of moneys advanced—Duty of beneficiary to apply money advanced for a particular purpose—Duty of trustee not to pay money advanced for particular purpose to a beneficiary believed or shown to be irresponsible. **Pauling's Settlement Trusts, Re** [1963] **3** 1, CA.
    Charitable donation—Benefit of beneficiary—Discharge by wealthy person of moral obligation to make donation to charity. **Clore's Settlement Trusts, Re** [1966] **2** 272, Ch D; **X v A** [2006] **1** 952, Ch D.
    Estate duty—Advancement determining discretionary trust in sums advanced—Whether estate duty leviable on sums advanced. See **Estate duty** (Determination of life interest—Discretionary trust—Accumulation of surplus income—Advancement determining discretionary trust in sums advanced).
    Exclusion of power of advancement. See Powers of trustee—Exclusion of power of advancement, *below.*
    Exercise in favour of infant by way of settlement—Statutory power. **Pilkington v IRC** [1962] **3** 622, HL.
    Payment to beneficiary—Money not required for specific purpose—Trustee Act 1925, s 32(1). **Moxon's Will Trusts, Re** [1958] **1** 386, Ch D.
    Power to 'raise' any part and to pay or 'apply' the same for the benefit of any child—Exercise of power by creating new settlement for children—Validity. **Wills' Will Trusts, Re** [1958] **2** 472, Ch D.
    Proposed advancement by conveyance of land—Avoidance of incidence of estate duty—Whether trustees could convey land to beneficiary in exercise of power conferred by Trustee Act 1925, s 32. **Collard's Will Trusts, Re** [1961] **1** 821, Ch D.
    Proposed exercise partly with a view to lessening the incidence of death duty on the death of the life tenant—Whether new voluntary settlements to be approved by trustees a valid exercise of power of advancement—Trustee Act 1925, s 32. **Ropner's Settlement Trusts, Re** [1956] **3** 332, Ch D.
    Special power—Trustee Act 1925, s 32(1). **Pilkington v IRC** [1962] **3** 622, HL.
    Trusts arising on exercise of special power of appointment—Power conferred by testamentary instrument—Death of testator before 1st January 1926—Power exercised after 1st January 1926—Whether statutory power of advancement applicable—Trustee Act 1925, s 32(3). **Batty (decd), Re** [1952] **1** 425, Ch D; **Bransbury's Will Trusts, Re** [1954] **1** 605, Ch D.
  Appointment of additional trustee—
    Appointment by appointer of himself. See Additional trustee—Appointment—Appointment by appointor of himself, *above.*
  Compromise—
    Exercise of power—Consideration for compromise—Consideration including surrender by adverse claimant of life interest under trust—Continuing interests under trust thereby accelerated—Whether compromise within power of trustee—Whether surrender effecting variation of trust—Trustee Act 1925, s 15(f). **Earl of Strafford (decd), Re** [1978] **3** 18, Ch D; [1979] **1** 513, CA.

TRUST AND TRUSTEE (cont)—
  Powers of trustee (cont)—
    Compromise (cont)—
      Trustees surrendering their discretion to the court—Compromise of claim for £15,000 for £7,500—Trustee Act 1925, s 15. **National Provincial Bank Ltd v Hyam** [1942] **2** 224, Ch D and CA.
    Delegation of powers—
      Delegation during absence abroad. *See* Delegation of trusts—Delegation by trustee during absence abroad, *above.*
      Delegation to two jointly and each of them severally—Power of one to execute conveyance—Interpretation Act 1889, s 1(1)—Execution of Trusts (Emergency Provisions) Act 1939. **Feversham's Contract, Re** [1941] **3** 100, Ch D.
    Duration of powers—
      Power of sale—Reversionary interests—Sale must be effected within reasonable time after interests fall into possession. **Holmes (W & R) and Cosmopolitan Press Ltd's Contract, Re** [1943] **2** 716, Ch D.
    Exclusion of power of advancement—
      Exclusion by contrary intention implied on construction of settlement—Express power to raise a sum not exceeding £5,000—Moiety of trust fund, which could be advanced if statutory power applied, exceeded that sum—Trustee Act 1925, s 32(1), s 69(2). **Evans' Settlement, Re** [1967] **3** 343, Ch D.
      Exclusion by trust for accumulation—Trust after settlor's death as to one-third for children and as to two-thirds for widow—Children's interests not prior interests—Trustee Act 1925, ss 32(1), s 69(2). **IRC v Bernstein** [1961] **1** 320, CA.
      Exclusion by trust for accumulation—Trustee Act 1925, ss 32(1), 69(2). **IRC v Bernstein** [1961] **1** 320, CA.
    Exercise of powers—
      Rule of equity requiring trustee to take into account all relevant considerations and not take into account any irrelevant considerations when exercising power—Scope of rule. **Sieff v Fox** [2005] **3** 693, Ch D.
      Rule of equity requiring trustee to take into account all relevant considerations and not take into account any irrelevant considerations when exercising power—Whether rule only applying to fundamental mistake—Whether rule applying to mistake even in absence of breach of fiduciary duty by trustee—Whether breach of rule rendering decision void or merely voidable. **Barr's Settlement Trusts, Re** [2003] **1** 763, Ch D.
    Intermediate power—
      Settlement. *See* **Settlement** (Power—Intermediate power).
    Investment. *See* Investments, *above.*
    Isle of Man—
      Discretionary trust. *See* **Powers of trustee** (Discretionary trusts—Isle of Man).
    Maintenance—
      Accumulation of surplus income—Destination. *See* **Accumulation** (Surplus income—Accumulation during minority—Destination of accumulations—Income of fund held on trust for grandchildren at 21—Statutory power of maintenance).
      Generally. *See* Maintenance, *above.*
    Mental health—
      Patient's property. *See* **Mental health** (Patient's property—Settlement—Receiver).
    Power of appointment. *See* **Power of appointment.**
    Power to appoint to himself—
      Power of disposition over trust property—Whether given as an individual or virtute office. **Edwards' Will Trusts, Re** [1947] **2** 521, Ch D.
    Power to form blended fund—
      Similar residuary bequests in will of two testatrices—Power of court—Trustee Act 1925, s 57. **Harvey, Re** [1941] **3** 284, Ch D.
    Power to provide for beneficiary's maintenance and education—
      Father creating accumulation and maintenance trusts for children—Trustees having power to provide for children's maintenance and education—Settlement prohibiting trustees from exercising powers in such manner that father might become entitled to a benefit—Consent order on father's divorce requiring him to pay for children's maintenance and school fees—Whether settlement prohibiting trustees from exercising power if it relieved father from obligations under consent order. **Fuller v Evans** [2000] **1** 636, Ch D.
    Statutory power—
      Maintenance. *See* Maintenance—Statutory power, *above.*
    Will—
      Power given to 'my trustees'—Capacity of trustees. *See* Will (Power of sale—Power given to 'my Trustees'—Capacity of 'trustees').
  Practice—
    Parties—
      Trustees refusing to sue—Action by benficiary under will—Adding personal representatives as defendants. *See* **Practice** (Parties—Adding defendant—Personal representatives).
    Service—
      Persons not served—Approval on behalf of respondents not served withheld. **Clarke's Will Trusts, Re** [1961] **3** 1133, Ch D.
  Precatory trust—
    Request—
      Request to leave property to certain persons—Home-made will. **Johnson, Re** [1939] **2** 458, Ch D.
  Probate judge—
    Vesting of estate of intestate—
      Whether probate judge a trustee—Administration of Estates Act 1925, s 9—Trustee Act 1925, s 51(1)(v). **Deans (decd), Re** [1954] **1** 496, Ch D.

TRUST AND TRUSTEE (cont)—
Procedure—
    Originating summons or writ—
        Contentious proceedings by beneficiaries against trustees—Proceedings involving allegation of breach of trust or default by the trustees—Whether proceedings should be begun by writ—RSC Ord 5, r 4(1). **Parkinson (Sir Lindsay) & Co Ltd's Trusts Deed, Re** [1965] **1** 609, Ch D.
Professional trustee—
    Remuneration. *See* Remuneration of trustee—Professional trustee, *below*.
Profit from trust—
    Account of profits—
        Agents for trust—Constructive trustees—Shareholding of trust used to gain knowledge of affairs of company—Solicitor to trustees and a beneficiary acquiring shares of company, realising assets and distributing profits from the realisation of assets—No sufficient disclosure of personal interest to beneficiary—Remuneration allowable for work and skill in acquiring shares and making profit. **Boardman v Phipps** [1966] **3** 721, HL.
        Commission allowed to executors under American law. **Northcote's Will Trusts, Re** [1949] **1** 442, Ch D.
        Commission—Professional indemnity insurance—Solicitors—Law Society's group scheme—Law Society arranging master policy with specified insurers through brokers—Law Society and brokers agreeing to share commission—Whether Law Society accountable to individual solicitors for commission received—Whether Law Society in fiduciary relationship with solicitors when making commission agreement with brokers. **Swain v Law Society** [1982] **2** 827, HL.
        Director allegedly holding shares in company on trust for claimant—Claimant bringing action against director as trustee for account of profit allegedly arising from sale of company subsidiaries—Company possibly having cause of action against director as director in respect of whole sum but also possible that director had extracted part of sum lawfully from company—Whether rule precluding shareholder from recovering company's loss barring claim by beneficiary against director trustee even though it could not be excluded that claim might extend to lawfully-extracted moneys in respect of which company had no claim. **Shaker v Al-Bedrawi** [2002] **4** 835, CA.
        Estate holding shares in company—Trustee appointed managing director—Appointment and remuneration recommended by all shareholders—Trust estate without majority interest in company. **Gee, Re** [1948] **1** 498, Ch D.
        Property purchased from trust estate while testatrix a trustee—Conveyance avoided by beneficiaries after death of testatrix—Right of specific devisee to repaid purchase money. **Sherman (decd), Re** [1954] **1** 893, Ch D.
        Take-over transaction involving use of company's moneys for the acquisition of its shares on the take-over—Elements requisite to establish liability as if participant were a trustee—Liability as constructive trustee based on reasonable inference from known facts and on alleged failure to make enquiry—Novation of debt created by loan of company's moneys—Whether extending to liability of borrower as constructive trustee. **Selangor United Rubber Estates Ltd v Cradock (a bankrupt) (No 3)** [1968] **2** 1073, Ch D.
    Contract entered into before creation of fiduciary relationship—
        Sale to trustee of trust property—Lease to bank with option to purchase—Appointment of bank as lessor's executor and trustee—Option exercised by bank after death of lessor. **Mulholland's Will Trusts, Re** [1949] **1** 460, Ch D.
    Custodian trustee—
        Pension fund of company—Insurance company custodian trustee of fund—Proposal by managing trustees to effect group policy with custodian trustee to secure payment of pension—Custodian trustee a subsidiary of company—Whether rule that trustee should not make a profit out of his trust applied to a custodian trustee—Whether managing trustees should be authorised to effect policy with custodian trustee—Public Trustee Act 1906, s 4. **Brooke Bond & Co Ltd's Trust Deed, Re** [1963] **1** 454, Ch D.
    Directors of charitable corporation—
        Directors empowered to make bye-laws—Validity of bye-law permitting directors to be paid for professional services. **French Protestant Hospital, Re** [1951] **1** 938, Ch D.
    Duty to account to estate—
        Trustee in occupation of trust property. *See* Liability of trustee—Liability to account for rents and profits—Occupation of trust property by trustee, *above*.
    Matrimonial home—
        Leasehold premises—Husband held leasehold interest on trust for himself and wife—After wife had presented petition for divorce husband bought freehold reversion—Freehold reversion held on same trust as leasehold premises. **Protheroe v Protheroe** [1968] **1** 1111, CA.
    Remuneration as director of company—
        Appointment of trustee as director permitted by will. **Llewellin's Will Trusts, Re** [1949] **1** 487, Ch D.
        Trust estate including shares in company—Trustees appointed directors of company—Liability of trustees to account to trust estate for remuneration. **Macadam, Re** [1945] **2** 664, Ch D.
    Renewal of lease by trustee—
        Obligation to hold on trusts of will. **Knowles' Will Trusts, Re** [1948] **1** 866, CA.
Protective trust—
    All beneficiaries resident in enemy territory—
        Forfeiture—Whether residuary gift accelerated. **Wittke (decd), Re** [1944] **1** 383, Ch D.
    Protected life interest—
        Fofeiture—Election against will—Liability to compensate disappointed beneficiaries. *See* **Equity** (Election—Election against will—Effect—Protected life interest—Liability to compensate disappointed beneficiaries).
Public Trustee—
    Generally. *See* **Public Trustee**.
    Remuneration. *See* Remuneration of trustee—Public Trustee, *below*.
Purchase of trust property by trustee. *See* **Executor and administrator** (Duty to beneficiaries—Purchase by executor of asset of estate).

TRUST AND TRUSTEE (cont)—
Purpose—
  Enforceability—
    Trust for benefit of unincorporated non-charitable association—Trust funds to be used 'solely in the work of constructing new buildings'—Whether trust unenforceable—Whether void for perpetuity—Whether trust to be construed as an absolute gift to members of association for time being who were entitled to enforce the purpose or to vary it. **Lipinski's Will Trusts, Re** [1977] **1** 33, Ch D.
  Memorial to testator—
    Public non-charitable trust—Gift to parish council 'for purpose of some useful memorial' to testator—Validity. **Endacott (decd), Re** [1959] **3** 562, CA.
Purpose trust—
  Creation of trust. *See* Creation of trust—Purpose trust, *above.*
Referential trusts—
  Will. *See* **Will** (Referential trusts).
Relief—
  Breach of trust. *See* Breach of trust—Consent to breach, *above.*
Removal of trustee—
  Continuing trustee—
    Necessity for removal of remaining trustee. *See* Vesting order—Continuing trustees—Necessity for removal of remaining trustee, *below.*
  Jurisdiction—
    Settlement—Settlement made abroad—Trust property situated abroad—Removal of trustees and appointment of new trustees—Settlements made by Indian settlors—Trust property consisting of shares in Bermudian companies—Beneficiaries domiciled in India—Trust deeds kept in London and trust administered in London—Whether English court having jurisdiction to administer settlements—Whether English courts having jurisdiction to remove and replace trustees—Whether English court forum non conveniens. **Chellaram v Chellaram** [1985] **1** 1043, Ch D.
  Trustee remaining out of the United Kingdom for more than 12 months—
    Removal against his will—Trustee Act 1925, s 36(1). **Stoneham's Settlement Trusts, Re** [1952] **2** 694, Ch D.
Remuneration as director of company. *See* Profit from trust—Remuneration as director of company, *above.*
Remuneration of trustee—
  Approval by court for increase in fees of corporate trustee—
    Application by trustee by summons—Remuneration inadequate for work done—Whether increase permissible. **Codd (decd), Re** [1975] **2** 1051, Ch D.
    Procedure—Evidence—Approval to be plainly sought in writ or summons—Application to be supported by proper evidence. **Barbour's Settlement, Re** [1974] **1** 1188, Ch D.
    Provision in settlement for remuneration to be in accordance with trustee's usual scale of fees at date of settlement—Remuneration inadequate for work being done 20 years later—No fundamental change in nature or assets of trust—Whether court having inherent jurisdiction to alter general level of scale of fees. **Norfolk's (Duke) Settlement Trusts, Re** [1981] **3** 220, CA.
  Bank—
    Annuity of £12,000 after tax—Income fee—Incidence. **Hulton, Re** [1936] **2** 207, Ch D.
    Appointment as administrator of intestate's estate—Power of court to authorise remuneration—Trustee Act 1925, s 42. **Masters, Re** [1953] **1** 19, Ch D.
    Appointment under codicil in substitution for executors appointed by will—Will making provision for remuneration of executors—Right of substituted trustee to charge for services. **Campbell (decd), In the Estate of** [1954] **1** 448, Prob.
    Deposit by bank of trust moneys with itself—Liability to account for profit. **Waterman's Will Trusts, Re** [1952] **2** 1054, Ch D.
    Direction to set aside sum to produce an annuity of stated amount—Income fee—Withdrawal fee—Incidence. **Godwin, Re** [1938] **1** 287, Ch D.
    Settled legacy—Income fee—Withdrawal fee—Incidence. **Roberts' Will Trusts, Re** [1937] **1** 518, Ch D.
  Corporate trustee—
    Investment company—Director trustees. **Cooper's Settlement, Re** [1961] **3** 636, Ch D.
  Income tax—
    Annual payment. *See* **Income tax** (Annual payment—Payment out of profits etc already taxed—Remuneration—Trustees).
    Earned income relief. *See* **Income tax** (Earned income relief—Remuneration in respect of office of profit—Trustee).
  Income tax. *See* **Income tax** (Earnings from employment—Remuneration trusts).
  Order of court—
    Circumstances in which court will exercise jurisdiction to award remuneration—Director-trustee—Settlement comprising shares in companies—Trustees of settlement appointed directors of companies—Whether trustee directors entitled to retain director's fees—Whether court having jurisdiction to authorise future retention of director's fees. **Keeler's Settlement Trusts, Re** [1981] **1** 888, Ch D.
    Circumstances in which court will exercise jurisdiction to award remuneration—Settlement making provision for remuneration of trustees—Trustees performing services outside scope of ordinary duties of trustees—Value of trust property enhanced as result of trustees' services—Application by trustees for additional remuneration—Whether court having jurisdiction to award additional remuneration. **Norfolk's (Duke) Settlement Trusts, Re** [1978] **3** 907, Ch D.
    Circumstances in which court will exercise jurisdiction to award remuneration—Trustees making unremitting efforts over 20-year period to sell trust land—Whether trustees entitled to expenses with interest thereon—Whether trustees entitled to remuneration for past and future services. **Foster v Spencer** [1996] **2** 672, Ch D.
  Professional trustee—
    Charging clause—Inquiry—Particulars of what would be reasonable remuneration sought in action for inquiry as to alleged excessive remuneration of accountant and of solicitor trustees—Beneficiary's right to have amount of charges investigated—Action in substance one for account—Particulars refused. **Wells (decd), Re** [1962] **2** 826, CA.

TRUST AND TRUSTEE (cont)—
Remuneration of trustee (cont)—
Professional trustee (cont)—
Charging clause—Will—Testator having property in England and Canada—Trust company with
separate English and Canadian scales of charges—Scale intended by testator. **Sandys' Will Trust,
Re** [1947] **2** 302, CA.
Profits made from trust. See Profit from trust—Account of profits—Agents for trust, *above*.
Public Trustee—
Income fee—Incidence. **Riddell, Re** [1936] **2** 1600, Ch D.
Remuneration trust—
Income tax. See **Income tax** (Earnings from employment—Remuneration trusts).
Resulting trust—
Donations made to fund—
Failure of objects of fund—Many donors unascertainable—Bona vacantia. **Gillingham Bus Disaster
Fund, Re** [1958] **2** 749, CA; **West Sussex Constabulary's Widows, Children and Benevolent (1930)
Fund Trusts, Re** [1970] **1** 544, Ch D.
Equitable interest in premises compulsorily purchased—
Compensation. See **Compulsory purchase** (Compensation—Disturbance—Interest in premises—
Equitable interest under resulting trust).
Failure of express trust—
Gift over on failure of charitable trust—Gift over void. **Cooper's Conveyance Trusts, Re** [1956] **3** 28,
Ch D.
More than one settlor—Common purpose of settlors—Need for common purpose to give rise to
resulting trust where purpose fails—Joint acquisition of property—Property acquired by man and
woman to be held for themselves jointly and beneficially—Both parties contributing to
purchase—Man intending property to be matrimonial home—Woman having no knowledge of
intention—Woman not contemplating marriage and not willing to marry—Whether property held
on resulting trust for both parties in equal shares. **Burgess v Rawnsley** [1975] **3** 142, CA.
Income resulting from release of life interest—
Life interest subject to trust as to part for children during joint lives of them and life tenant—Capital
or income of settlor's estate. **Guinness's Settlement, Re** [1966] **2** 497, Ch D.
Insurer providing company with guarantee on basis of director and wife depositing moneys with
insurer—
Moneys buying annuity for director's wife—Annuity assigned to creditor of company—Insurer
becoming insolvent and defaulting on guarantee—Whether moneys held on Quistclose trust.
Prickly Bay Waterside Ltd v British American Insurance Co Ltd [2022] **2 Comm** 189, PC.
Option—
Settlor granting option on trust—No effective trusts declared—Settlor giving shares in private
company to college—Purpose of gift to provide college by way of dividends with sum promised
to college by settlor—College at settlor's request granting option over shares to trustees of
settlor's family settlement—Trustees exercising option—Whether option granted to trustees by
settlor or by college—Whether option and shares held by trustees beneficially or on
trust—Whether held on trusts of family settlement or on resulting trust for settlor—Distinction
between presumed resulting trusts and automatic resulting trusts. **Vandervell's Trusts, Re (No 2)**
[1974] **1** 47, Ch D.
Option held on resulting trust for settlor—
Circumstances in which settlor may be estopped from claiming that assets over which option
exercised held on resulting trust—Settlor ignorant that he had any beneficial interest in
option—Exercise of option by trustees—Price payable on exercise of option—Use by trustees of
funds from family settlement to pay price—Whether settlor estopped from denying that assets
held on trusts of family settlement. **Vandervell's Trusts, Re (No 2)** [1974] **1** 47, Ch D.
Option to purchase shares—
Option held by trustees of settlor's family settlement—Exercise of option by trustees—Intention of
settlor and trustees that shares should be held on trusts of settlement—Funds of settlement used
for purchase of shares—Substantial dividends declared on shares added by trustees to
settlement funds—Whether settlor retaining beneficial interest in shares and dividends declared
thereon—Whether shares held on resulting trust for settlor. **Vandervell's Trusts, Re (No 2)**
[1974] **1** 47, Ch D; [1974] **3** 205, CA.
Reversionary interest—Tenant for life. See Tenant for life—Reversionary interest, *below*.
Rule against perpetuities. See **Rule against perpetuities**.
Rule in Allhusen v Whittell—
Exclusion of rule—
Gift of residuary estate charged with payment of annuity—Settlement by will of property including
that estate—No personal covenant to pay annual sums. **Darby, Re** [1939] **3** 6, CA.
Rule in Howe v Dartmouth. See Administration of trust—Rule in Howe v Dartmouth, *above*.
Sale of land—
Trustee for purchaser—
Vendor. See **Sale of land** (Vendor—Fiduciary duty to purchaser).
Sale, trust for. See Trust for sale, *below*.
Secret trust—
Expressed in writing—
Prior to date of will—Will referring to future notification to trustees—Validity. **Keen's Estate, Re**
[1937] **1** 452, Ch D.
Subsequent to date of will—Will referring to future letter to trustees—Validity. **Brierley v Perry**
[1970] **3** 817, Ch D.
Expressed orally—
Expression of trust prior to date of will—Standard of proof required—Trust to devise property by
will—Real property devised to primary donee with intention that it should be devised to
secondary donee—Intention communicated to and accepted by primary donee—Will of primary
donee devising property to third party—Whether effective secret trust. **Ottaway v Norman**
[1971] **3** 1325, Ch D.

TRUST AND TRUSTEE (cont)—
  Secret trust (cont)—
    Expressed orally (cont)—
      Purposes communicated to one executor—Trusts to take effect after death of that executor by means of will of executor—Establishment of terms of trust by affidavit evidence. **Young (decd), Re** [1950] **2** 1245, Ch D.
      Standard of proof required—Gift of residue by will—Residue devised by testatrix to brother absolutely—Testatrix stating that brother would divide residue 'as he thought best' and 'would know what to do'—Brother dying six days after testatrix and before making any division of residue—Whether secret trust or merely moral obligation imposed on brother—Whether residue passing to brother's beneficiary absolutely and free of any trust. **Snowden (decd), Re** [1979] **2** 172, Ch D.
    Revocation of will—
      Secret trust excepted from revocation—Sum subject to secret trust increased by later will—Increase not communicated to trustees—Failure of increased gift. **Cooper, Re** [1939] **3** 586, CA.
  Security trust deed—
    Construction—
      Company receiver. See **Company** (Receiver—Construction of security trust deed).
  Security trustee—
    Duty of trustee. See Duty of trustee—Sale of property—Security agreement of assets held by structured investment vehicle, *above*.
  Separate trusts—
    Fund raised by public appeal—
      Separate donations—Whether donations created more than one interest in the same property—Charitable Trusts (Validation) Act 1954, s 2(3). **Gillingham Bus Disaster Fund, Re** [1958] **2** 749, CA.
  Settlement—
    Capital gains tax. See **Capital gains tax** (Settlement).
    Generally. See **Settlement**.
    Income tax. See **Income tax** (Settlement).
  Shares in company—
    Control by beneficiaries—
      Exercise of voting rights—All beneficiaries not before court—Absence of presumption that females past child-bearing age. **Whichelow (decd), Re** [1953] **2** 1558, Ch D.
    Duty of trustee to sell securities received 'in respect of' shares—
      Government stock substituted for shares by statute—Securities—Effect of Electricity Act 1947, Sch III, Part I, para 5—Power to sell shares if 'fundamental change' made in rights attaching thereto—Ordinary stock awaiting conversion into Government stock—Gas Act 1948, Sch II, Part II, para 2—Jurisdiction of court to confer power of sale—Trustee Act 1925, s 57(1). **Municipal and General Securities Co Ltd v Lloyds Bank Ltd** [1949] **2** 937, Ch D.
    Trust to hold shares and pay income to life tenant and vest shares in remainderman on life tenant's death—
      Company reconstruction—Demerger of company—Company dividing undertaking into two parts—Shares in new company allotted to existing shareholders—Testatrix leaving shareholding in company on trust to husband for life and thereafter to son absolutely—Whether allotment of shares in new company to be treated as capital or income—Whether husband entitled to shares as income—Whether shares to be held by trustees as capital on trust for son as remainderman. **Lee (decd), Re** [1993] **3** 926, Ch D.
    Trustees shareholders and directors—
      Rights of beneficiaries to inspect company's documents. **Butt, Re** [1952] **1** 167, CA.
  Solicitor—
    Inspection of trust documents. See **Solicitor** (Trust—Trust documents—Inspection).
  Solicitor trustee. See **Solicitor** (Duty—Conflict of duty and interest—Solicitor trustee).
  Statutory trusts—
    Intestacy. See **Intestacy** (Statutory trusts).
  Tenant for life—
    Reversionary interest—
      Rule in Re Chesterfield's Trusts—Applicable only to personalty. **Woodhouse, Re** [1941] **2** 265, Ch D.
  Tracing assets—
    Purpose trust. See Creation of trust—Purpose trust—Applicant making payment to company intending company to forward payment to third party, *above*.
  Trade union—
    Property of union. See **Trade union** (Trustees—Powers—Action touching or concerning property of union).
  Transfer of equitable interest or trust. See **Equity** (Disposition of equitable interest on trust).
  Trust company—
    Duty of directors—
      Dog leg claim—Shares in family business constituting trust property—Claimant being beneficiary of trust—Family business becoming insolvent and shares becoming worthless—Beneficiary bringing claim based on directors' breach of duty to trust company—Whether trust company's claims against directors for breach of duty forming part of trust property. **Gregson v HAE Trustees Ltd** [2009] **1 Comm** 457, Ch D.
  Trust corporation—
    Reregistration as public company—
      Practice—Probate. See **Probate** (Practice—Trust corporation—Public company).
    Share capital of trust corporation acquired by another company on amalgamation—
      Transfer of business of acting as personal representative—Whether corporation continues to be a trust corporation within the definition in Supreme Court of Judicature (Consolidation) Act 1925, s 175(1)—Public Trustee Rules 1912 (SR & O 1912 No 348), r 30(1), as substituted by SR & O 1926 No 1423. **Skinner (decd), Re** [1958] **3** 273, Prob.

TRUST AND TRUSTEE (cont)—

Trust deed—
  Construction—
    Extrinsic evidence—Admissibility. *See* **Document** (Admissibility in evidence—Extrinsic evidence—Trust deed—Construction).

Trust deed and deed of charge—
  Construction—
    Securitisation of debt—Restructuring of debt—Cash option—Note controlling party requiring trustee of security to exercise cash option—Whether trustee having power to cause exercise of cash option—Whether trustee obliged to exercise option at direction of note controlling party. **Citibank NA v MBIA Assurance SA** [2007] **1 Comm** 475, CA.

Trust dispute—
  Hostile litigation—
    Trustee's costs—Trustees seeking (i) directions whether to defend action challenging validity of settlements and (ii) pre-emptive costs order—Whether trustees having duty to defend action—Whether trustees entitled to pre-emptive costs order. **Alsop Wilkinson (a firm) v Neary** [1995] **1** 431, Ch D.

Trust for sale—
  Bankruptcy—
    Matrimonial home. *See* **Bankruptcy** (Property available for distribution—Matrimonial home—Sale under trust for sale).
    Property available for distribution—Property held by bankrupt and another on trust for sale. *See* **Bankruptcy** (Property available for distribution—Trust for sale).
  Class gift—
    Date of distribution—Effect of power to postpone sale. *See* **Settlement** (Class gift—Distribution date—Settlement of land—Trust for sale—Power of trustees to postpone sale).
  'Completion'—
    Meaning. *See* Trust for sale—Realty—Direction to divide proceeds of sale amongst beneficiaries, *below.*
  Investments—
    Direction in will to invest in authorised securities—No power to buy land—Land sold before administration completed—Beneficiary desiring application of proceeds of sale to purchase of land for own use—Whether trustees 'trustees for sale'—Law of Property Act 1925, ss 28, 205. **Wakeman, Re** [1945] **1** 421, Ch D.
  Matrimonial home. *See* **Husband and wife** (Matrimonial home—Sale under trust for sale).
  Postponement—
    Trust to sell 'as soon as possible'—Law of Property Act 1925, s 25(1). **Rooke's Will Trusts, Re** [1953] **2** 110, Ch D.
  Property available for distribution on bankruptcy. *See* **Bankruptcy** (Property available for distribution—Trust for sale).
  Realty—
    Direction to divide proceeds of sale amongst beneficiaries—Such beneficiaries 'as shall be living at the date of the completion of the...sale'—Meaning of 'completion'. **Atkin's Will Trusts, Re** [1974] **2** 1, Ch D.
    Express trust—Trust in will to sell and divide proceeds among beneficiaries—Nature of beneficiaries' interests—Tenants in common of proceeds of sale—No interest in realty. **Barclay v Barclay** [1970] **2** 676, CA.
    Interest of joint tenants legally and beneficially entitled—Whether 'interest in land' within Administration of Justice Act 1956, s 35(1). *See* **Execution** (Charging order—Land—Interest in land—Property held legally and beneficially by joint tenants).
    Permission to reside in house—Permission for tenant for life of residue, given on trust for sale with power to postpone sale, to reside in testatrix' house—Option for plaintiff to take house after life tenant's death in part settlement of his reversionary share of residue—Whether immediate binding trust for sale created or whether house settled land—Whether trustees of will might sell house without prior consent of plaintiff—Law of Property Act 1925, s 205(1)(xxix). **Herklots' Will Trusts, Re** [1964] **2** 66, Ch D.
    Severance of joint tenancy. *See* **Joint tenancy** (Severance—Land held on trust for sale).
    Tenancy in common—Occupation of property by one tenant in common—Whether other tenant in common entitled to claim rent from tenant in occupation. **Jones (A E) v Jones (F W)** [1977] **2** 231, CA.
    Tenancy in common—Order for sale—Refusal of order where one tenant in possession—Estoppel—Proprietary estoppel—Representation on purchase of property that tenant entitled to possession for life rent free—Other tenant in common estopped from dispossessing tenant in possession—Refusal of order for sale when sale would defeat purpose of purchase contemplated by parties to the trust. **Jones (A E) v Jones (F W)** [1977] **2** 231, CA.
    Valuation. **Turton v Turton** [1987] **2** 641, CA.
  Refusal of trustees to concur in sale—
    How discretion of court to order sale exercised—Law of Property Act 1925, s 30. **Mayo, Re** [1943] **2** 440, Ch D.
    Husband and wife—Matrimonial home purchased jointly out of money provided equally by them—Husband and wife divorced—Law of Property Act 1925, s 30—Distinction of position on application under Married Women's Property Act 1882, s 17. **Jones v Challenger** [1960] **1** 785, CA.
    Unmarried parties living as man and wife—Home purchased jointly out of money provided by both parties—Purpose of trust to provide family home for parties and children—How discretion of court to order sale to be exercised—Whether discretion same as that under Matrimonial Causes Act 1973, s 24—Matters to be considered—Law of Property Act 1925, s 30—Matrimonial Causes Act 1973, s 24. **Evers's Trust, Re** [1980] **3** 399, CA.
  Repairs and improvements to agricultural land—
    Cost paid out of income—Whether recouped to life tenants out of capital—Law of Property Act 1925, s 28—Settled Land Act 1925, ss 73, 84—Agricultural Holdings Act 1948, s 81(1). **Wynn, Re** [1955] **2** 865, Ch D.

Trust for sale (cont)—
Repairs and improvements to agricultural land (cont)—
Incidence of cost—Discretion of trustee—Principles on which discretion should be exercised—Law of Property Act 1925, s 28—Settled Land Act 1925, ss 73(1)(iv), 75(2)—Agricultural Holdings Act 1948, ss 81(1), 96(1), Sch III, para 23. **Boston's (Lord) Will Trusts, Re** [1956] **1** 593, Ch D.
Sale of realty—
Power to apply proceeds in purchase of realty—Law of Property Act 1925, s 28(1) (as amended by Law of Property (Amendment) Act 1926, s 7, Sch)—Settled Land Act 1925, s 73(1). **Wellsted's Will Trusts, Re** [1949] **1** 577, CA.
Trust property including land—
Power to effect, under order of court, transaction not authorised by settlement or by law—Settled Land Act 1925, s 64—Law of Property Act 1925, s 28(1). **Simmons' Trust, Re** [1955] **3** 818, Ch D.
Trustee's refusal to sell—
Vesting order—Person interested—Receiver of trustee's interest appointed by way of equitable execution—Equitable interest in land—Law of Property Act 1925, ss 30, 195(1), 205(x). **Carr Lane (No 39), Acomb, Re** [1953] **1** 699, Ch D.
Trust of land—
Conveyance of legal estate in land to minor. *See* **Landlord and tenant** (Validity of notice to quit—Conveyance of legal estate in land to minor—Imposition of trusts).
Order for sale—
Application for order for sale by chargee of co-owner's interest in property—Matters to which court required to have regard in exercise of discretion to order sale—Recompense of creditor for being kept out of money—Trusts of Land and Appointment of Trustees Act 1996, ss 14, 15. **Bank of Ireland Home Mortgages Ltd v Bell** [2001] **2 Comm** 920, CA.
Application for order for sale by chargee of co-owner's interest in property—Whether new statutory provision changing law on exercise of court's discretion on such an application—Trusts of Land and Appointment of Trustees Act 1996, s 15. **Mortgage Corp v Shaire** [2001] **4** 364, Ch D.
Trust property—
Accumulation of income. *See* **Accumulation**.
Fraud or fraudulent breach of trust to which trustee a party—
Limitation of action. *See* **Limitation of action** (Trust property—Fraud or fraudulent breach of trust to which trustee a party).
Limitation of action. *See* **Limitation of action** (Trust property).
Occupied by trustee—
Liability to account for rents and profits. *See* Liability of trustee—Liability to account for rents and profits—Occupation of trust property by trustee, *above*.
Purchase of trust property by trustee—
Self-dealing rule. *See* Duty of trustee—Duty towards beneficiary—Self-dealing rule, *above*.
Tracing. *See* **Equity** (Tracing—Knowing receipt of trust property).
Trust to hold shares. *See* Shares in company, *above*.
Trust to provide village hall—
Will—
Condition—Impossibility of performance. *See* **Will** (Condition—Impossibility of performance—Trust to provide village hall).
Trustee also beneficiary. *See* Liability of trustee—Defaulting trustee also beneficiary under trust fund, *above*.
Trustee in bankruptcy. *See* **Bankruptcy** (Trustee in bankruptcy).
Trustee of unsound mind—
Appointment of new trustee. *See* **Mental health** (Court of Protection—Practice—Appointment of new trustee in place of trustee of unsound mind).
Trustee's costs—
Amount to be allowed—
Allowance in full—RSC Ord 65, r 27(29). **Grimthorpe's (Baron) Will Trusts, Re** [1958] **1** 765, Ch D.
Counsel's fees—Supreme Court Costs Rules 1959, r 31. **Whitley (decd), Re** [1962] **3** 45, Ch D.
Hostile litigation. *See* Trust dispute—Hostile litigation—Trustee's costs, *above*.
Indemnity as to costs—
Amount to be allowed. **Practice Direction** [1953] **2** 1159, Ch D.
Form of order—Trustee Act 1925, s 60. **Practice Direction** [1953] **2** 1408, Ch D.
Security—Retention of trust fund by way of security for indemnity thereout of costs awardable on pending appeal as ground for postponing appointment of new trustees. **Pauling's Settlement, Re (No 2)** [1963] **1** 857, Ch D.
Legal aid. *See* **Legal aid** (Costs—Trustee's costs).
Liability for future claim—
Contaminated land—Trustee's application for directions—Whether trustee having a lien over trust fund for liabilities to which it might be subject in respect of land held by testator—Environmental Protection Act 1990, Pt IIA. **X v A** [2000] **1** 490, Ch D.
Liability for future claim to estate duty. *See* Appointment of new trustee—Objection—Costs—Liability of present trustees for possible future claim to estate duty, *above*.
Reimbursement of trustee—
Action by beneficiaries against trustee—Taxation as between solicitor and client—Disbursements from trust fund in excess of amount of taxed costs—Right of trustee to recoup himself out of trust fund. **Dargie (decd), Re** [1953] **2** 577, Ch D.
Contractual right—Breach of trust—Action dismissed—Severance of defence by trustees—Whether entitled to two sets of costs—Legally aided plaintiffs—Trust fund insufficient. **Spurling's Will Trusts, Re** [1966] **1** 745, Ch D.
Settlement set aside for undue influence. **Bullock v Lloyds Bank Ltd** [1954] **3** 726, Ch D.
Trustee acting as landlord's agent in management of block of flats—Maintenance fund provided by tenants' contributions—Trustee's proposed scheme of building works defeated by tenants in compromised litigation—Whether trustee acting as trustee in litigation—Whether trustee entitled to costs out of maintenance fund—Trustee Act 1925, s 30(2)—RSC Ord 62, r 6(2). **Holding and Management Ltd v Property Holding and Investment Trust plc** [1990] **1** 938, CA.
Trustee's duty. *See* Duty of trustee, *above*.

TRUST AND TRUSTEE (cont)—

Trustee's liability to third parties—
Conflict of laws. *See* **Conflict of laws** (Trust and trustee—Trustee's liability to third parties).
Trustees of company pension scheme—
Liability to members—
Winding up. *See* **Pension** (Pension scheme—Winding up—Pension trustee posting statutory advertisement for former members of scheme to notify it of claims before final distribution of assets).
Mistake in rules of scheme—
Whether mistaken rule void—Whether trustees having failed to take into account considerations which they ought to have taken into account or having taken into account considerations which they ought not to have taken into account. **Smithson v Hamilton** [2008] **1** 1216, Ch D.
Trustee's powers. *See* Powers of trustee, *above*.
Uncertainty—
Condition precedent. *See* **Settlement** (Trust—Uncertainty—Condition precedent).
Settlement—
Discretionary power—Power over income of trust fund. *See* **Settlement** (Power—Discretionary power—Discretion over income of trust fund).
Generally. *See* **Settlement** (Uncertainty).
Will—
Disposition by will. *See* **Will** (Trust—Determination of matters of doubt).
University. *See* **University** (Trust).
Unmarried couple—
Joint contributions to property. *See* Constructive trust—Unmarried couple, *above*.
Variation of trusts. *See* **Variation of trusts**.
Vesting order—
Continuing trustees—
Necessity for removal of remaining trustee—Application by two of four trustees for an order vesting the trust assets in themselves and the third trustee—Fourth trustee incapable of managing her affairs—Action pending in which applicant trustees sought removal of third trustee from the trusts—Disputes between applicant trustees and third trustee as to administration of trusts—Application for vesting order made without applicant trustees first communicating with other two trustees—Jurisdiction to make an order vesting trust assets in the three continuing trustees without removing the fourth trustee from office—Whether order should be made—Whether applicant should pay costs personally—Trustee Act 1925, s 44, s 51. **Harrison's Settlement Trusts, Re** [1965] **3** 795, Ch D.
Trust for sale—
Trustee's refusal to sell. *See* Trust for sale—Trustee's refusal to sell—Vesting order, *above*.
Will—
Absolute gift—
Trust for specified purpose. *See* **Will** (Gift—Absolute gift—Trust for specified purpose).
Beneficial entitlement. *See* **Will** (Trustee—Beneficial entitlement).
Gift to trustees. *See* **Will** (Gift—Specific donees—My trustees absolutely they well knowing my wishes concerning the same).
Protective trusts—
Forfeiture clause—Deprived of right to capital or interest. *See* **Will** (Forfeiture clause—Deprived of right to capital or interest—Protective trusts).
Writing. *See* Constructive trust—Oral arrangements—Exchange of shares owned by life tenant for reversionary interest in settled shares, *above*.

TRUST CORPORATION

Grant of administration—
Intestacy. *See* **Intestacy** (Grant of administration—Grant to trust corporation).
Grant of probate. *See* **Probate** (Grant—Trust corporation).
Reregistration as public company—
Practice—
Probate. *See* **Probate** (Practice—Trust corporation—Public company).

TRUST FOR SALE

Generally. *See* **Trust and trustee** (Trust for sale).
Land held on trust for sale—
Joint tenancy—
Severance of joint tenancy. *See* **Joint tenancy** (Severance—Land held on trust for sale).
Land settled on trust for sale—
Compensation—
Town and country planning. *See* **Town and country planning** (Compensation—Land settled on trust for sale).
Matrimonial home—
Sale under trust for sale—
Bankruptcy. *See* **Bankruptcy** (Property available for distribution—Matrimonial home—Sale under trust for sale).
Generally. *See* **Husband and wife** (Matrimonial home—Sale under trust for sale).
Post-nuptial settlement—
Variation of settlement—
House purchased by spouses on trust for sale. *See* **Variation of Settlement (Matrimonial Causes)** (Post-nuptial settlement—House purchased by spouses on trust for sale).

TRUSTEE

Generally. *See* **Trust and trustee**.
Variation of settlement—
Wife a trustee with special power of appointment. *See* **Variation of Settlement (Matrimonial Causes)** (Post-nuptial settlement—Wife a trustee with special power of appointment).

TRUSTEE IN BANKRUPTCY
    See **Bankruptcy** (Trustee in bankruptcy).

TRUSTEE SAVINGS BANK
    Action—
        Tort—
            Party—Action against trustees and against bank eo nomine—Whether bank could be sued in own name—Trustee Savings Banks Act 1954, ss 9(8), 24(2), 59—Trustee Savings Banks Act 1958, s 5(9). **Knight and Searle v Dove** [1964] **2** 307, QBD.
    Closure—
        Assets—
            Transfer of bank to private ownership—Effect of transfer—Whether depositors having proprietory interest in assets over and above their contractual rights to principal and interest—Trustee Savings Banks Act 1981, ss 1(3)(a), (4), 32—Trustee Savings Banks Act 1985. **Ross v Lord Advocate** [1986] **3** 79, HL.
    Deposit—
        Transfer on death of holder—
            Right of transferee to hold in addition to sum already held by him. **Note** [1954] **1** 519, .

TUMULT
    See **Riot** (Damage—Compensation).

TURF
    Sale—
        Consideration for sale of turf from land—
            Income tax—Capital or income. *See* **Income tax** (Capital or income receipts—Sale of property—Land—Turf).

TURQUAND'S CASE
    Rule in. *See* **Company** (Director—Authority).

TYRE
    Motor vehicle. *See* **Road traffic** (Tyres).

U

UGANDA
Constitutional law—
 Legislative Council—
  Procedure for representation of Buganda in legislative council—Alleged fundamental changes invalidating a term of Buganda Agreement 1955—Buganda Agreement 1955 (Laws of Uganda 1955, p 383), art 7(2), Sch 2, reg 5—Royal Instruction dated June 5 1920 (Laws of Uganda 1951, Vol VI, p 104), cll XVA, XXV, XXVI (as amended by Royal Instructions dated 17th December 1957 (Laws of Uganda 1957, p 435)). **Katikiro of Buganda v A-G** [1960] 3 849, PC.

UMPIRE
Arbitration. *See* **Arbitration** (Umpire).

UNASSISTED PERSON
Legal aid—
 Unassisted person's costs out of legal aid fund. *See* **Legal aid** (Unassisted person's costs out of legal aid fund).

UNBORN CHILD
Change of surname. *See* **Minor** (Change of surname—Unborn child).
Trust—
 Variation of trust by the court. *See* **Variation of trusts** (Unborn persons).
Ward of court—
 Jurisdiction to make an unborn child a ward of court. *See* **Ward of court** (Jurisdiction—Unborn child).

UNCLE AND NEPHEW
Joint bank account. *See* **Bank** (Account—Joint account—Uncle and nephew).

UNCONSCIONABLE BARGAIN
Equitable relief. *See* **Equity** (Unconscionable bargain).

UNCONSCIOUS ACT
Crime—
 Commission of crime. *See* **Criminal law** (Automatism—Unconscious act).

UNCONSECRATED CHURCHYARD
Sale. *See* **Ecclesiastical law** (Incumbent—Freehold—Unconsecrated churchyard—Power to convey).

UNCONSUMMATED MARRIAGE
Approbation. *See* **Nullity** (Bar to relief—Approbation of unconsummated marriage).

UNCONTROLLABLE IMPULSE
Murder. *See* **Criminal law** (Murder—Uncontrollable impulse).

UNDEFENDED CAUSE
Divorce—
 Practice. *See* **Divorce** (Practice—Undefended causes).

UNDERGROUND WATER
See **Water and watercourses** (Underground water).

UNDERLEASE
Contract to grant underlease—
 Failure to register as estate contract. *See* **Land charge** (Failure to register—Estate contract—Contract to grant underlease).
Covenant—
 Repair—
  Nature of covenant. *See* **Landlord and tenant** (Repair—Construction of covenant).
Forfeiture of lease—
 Relief against forfeiture. *See* **Landlord and tenant** (Relief against forfeiture—Underlessee).
Rent—
 Generally. *See* **Landlord and tenant** (Rent—Underlease).
Specific performance. *See* **Specific performance** (Lease—Agreement for lease—Underlease).
Unusual covenants—
 Negotiation of grant of underlease. *See* **Solicitor** (Client—Negotiation of grant of underlease to architects—Unusual convenants in underlease restricting user).

UNDERLETTING WITHOUT CONSENT
Covenant against. *See* **Landlord and tenant** (Covenant against underletting without consent).

UNDERTAKING
Breach—
 Aiding and abetting breach—
  Injunction. *See* **Injunction** (Breach of undertaking given to court—Aiding and abetting breach).
 Contempt of court—
  Committal for contempt—County court. *See* **Contempt of court** (Committal—County court—Breach of undertaking).
  Committal for contempt—Generally. *See* **Contempt of court** (Committal—Breach of undertaking).
  Restrictive Practices Court. *See* **Restrictive trade practices** (Contempt of court—Breach of undertaking given to court).

UNDERTAKING (cont)—
  Competition—
    European Community. *See* **European Union** (Rules on competition—Abuse of dominant position—Undertaking).
  Contract of service—
    Breach of undertaking—
      Injunction. *See* **Injunction** (Breach of covenant—Breach of undertaking—Contract of service).
  Director of Public Prosecutions, by—
    Undertaking not to prosecute—
      Power to give undertaking. *See* **Criminal law** (Proceedings—Director of Public Prosecutions).
  Disclosure of documents—
    Collateral use of information obtained—
      Undertaking not to use disclosed documents for collateral or ulterior purpose. *See* **Disclosure and inspection of documents** (Collateral use of information obtained—Undertaking not to use disclosed documents for collateral or ulterior purpose).
    Confidence—
      Undertaking not to make improper use of disclosed documents. *See* **Disclosure and inspection of documents** (Production of documents—Confidence—Undertaking not to make improper use of disclosed documents).
  Disqualification undertaking—
    Company director. *See* **Company** (Director—Disqualification—Disqualification undertaking).
  Divorce—
    Alimony—
      Undertaking before decree nisi to pay wife '£3 per week alimony as from the date of the decree nisi'—Effect. *See* **Divorce** (Alimony—Undertaking before decree nisi to pay wife '£3 per week alimony as from the date of the decree nisi'—Effect of undertaking).
  Fair trading legislation. *See* **Fair trading** (Undertakings).
  Injunction—
    Breach of undertaking. *See* **Injunction** (Breach of undertaking given to court).
    Construction. *See* **Injunction** (Undertaking—Construction).
    Defence to application for injunction. *See* **Injunction** (Defence—Undertaking).
    Generally. *See* **Injunction** (Undertaking).
    Interlocutory injunction—
      Mareva injunction—Cross-undertaking as to damages. *See* **Practice** (Pre-trial or post-judgment relief—Freezing order—Cross-undertaking in damages).
      Undertaking as to damages. *See* **Injunction** (Interlocutory—Undertaking as to damages).
    Undertaking in lieu of injunction. *See* **Injunction** (Undertaking).
  Justices' off-licence—
    Grant subject to undertaking. *See* **Licensing** (Licence—Grant—Off-licence—Grant subject to undertaking).
  Payment of money—
    Undertaking given to court—
      Garnishee proceedings. *See* **Execution** (Garnishee order—Debt due to creditor pursuant to undertaking by debtor to court).
  Solicitor—
    Generally. *See* **Solicitor** (Undertaking).
    Negligence. *See* **Solicitor** (Negligence—Undertaking).

UNDERWRITER
  Income tax—
    Damages—
      Underwriting losses. *See* **Damages** (Underwriting losses—Income tax).
  Insurance—
    Liability of underwriter—
      Amendments to slip. *See* **Insurance** (Broker—Slip tendered to underwriters by broker—Underwriters' liability).
      Generally. *See* **Insurance** (Underwriter—Liability).
    Negligence—
      Lloyd's underwriting agent. *See* **Negligence** (Duty to take care—Insurance—Lloyd's underwriting agent).
  Negligence—
    Duty to take care. *See* **Negligence** (Duty to take care—Insurance—Lloyd's underwriting agent).

UNDISCHARGED BANKRUPT
  Obtaining credit—
    Offence. *See* **Bankruptcy** (Offences—Undischarged bankrupt obtaining credit).

UNDISCLOSED PRINCIPAL
  Contract. *See* **Agent** (Contract—Undisclosed principal).
  Liability of agent. *See* **Agent** (Liability as principal—Undisclosed principal).

UNDISTRIBUTED INCOME
  Income tax. *See* **Income tax** (Undistributed income).

UNDUE INFLUENCE
  Contract. *See* **Contract** (Undue influence).
  Duress—
    Contract. *See* **Contract** (Duress).
  Elections—
    Corrupt practice. *See* **Elections** (Corrupt practice—Undue influence).
  Equity. *See* **Equity** (Undue influence).
  Voluntary settlement. *See* **Settlement** (Voluntary settlement—Validity—Undue influence).

UNEMPLOYMENT BENEFIT
Damages for personal injuries—
Loss of earnings—
Whether unemployment benefit to be taken into account. *See* **Damages** (Personal injury—Loss of earnings—Deduction of unemployment benefit).
Loss of future earnings—
Whether unemployment benefit to be taken into account. *See* **Damages** (Personal injury—Loss of future earnings—Unemployment benefit).
Generally. *See* **Social security** (Unemployment benefit).

UNEMPLOYMENT INSURANCE
Equality of treatment of men and women—
European Community. *See* **European Union** (Equality of treatment of men and women—Social security—Pension and unemployment insurance).
Insured person—
Employment in agriculture—
Employee on fur farm—Whether employed in 'agriculture'—Unemployment Insurance (Agriculture) Act 1936. **Stephens (KT) and RH Branthwaite (t/a Moresdale Fur Farm) and E Otway, Re** [1938] **3** 311, KBD.
Employment otherwise than by way of manual labour—
Modeller—Production of ornament precisely defined and not creation of employee's artistic taste—Whether employment otherwise than by 'manual labour'—Unemployment Insurance Act 1935, Sch I, Part II, para 9. **Gardner, Appeal of, Re Maschek, Re Tyrell** [1938] **1** 20, KBD.
Retention of unemployment book by former employer—
Refusal of trade union to nominate employee for job until production of unemployment book—
Loss of wages—Whether any right of action against former employer—Undertakings (Restriction on Engagement) Order 1940 (SR & O 1940 No 877), arts 2, 3. **Fayers v J Jarvis & Sons Ltd** [1944] **1** 289, CA.

UNEXPLAINED WEALTH ORDER
Generally. *See* **Proceeds of crime** (Investigations—Unexplained wealth orders).

UNFAIR CONTRACT TERMS
Consumer contract—
Generally. *See* **Contract** (Consumer contract—Unfair terms).
European Community—
Consumer protection. *See* **European Union** (Consumer protection—Unfair contract terms).
Generally. *See* **Contract** (Unfair terms).

UNFAIR DISMISSAL
Burden of proof—
Decision of industrial tribunal—
Procedure. *See* **Employment tribunal** (Procedure—Decision—Complaint of unfair dismissal—Burden of proof).
Compensation—
Amount which is just and equitable having regard to the loss sustained by employee—
Constructive dismissal—Employee entitled to notice period—Compensation for loss suffered during notice period—Whether principle as to compensation derived from good industrial relations practice in direct termination by employers applicable to termination by constructive dismissal—Employment Rights Act 1996, ss 95(1), 123. **Bell v Stuart Peters Ltd** [2010] **1** 775, CA.
Constructive dismissal—Loss of earnings flowing from dismissal—Whether loss of earnings recoverable as loss flowing from dismissal where employee only accepting employer's repudiatory breach of contract after suffering medical incapacity caused by repudiatory conduct—Employment Rights Act 1996, s 123(1). **Triggs v GAB Robins (UK) Ltd** [2007] **3** 590, EAT.
Dismissal without notice—Payment of wages in lieu of notice—Loss of future redundancy payment—Employee dismissed without notice and paid wages in lieu of notice—Employee finding other employment at lower wage—Remainder of workforce subsequently made redundant and paid wages in lieu of notice—Whether wages paid to employee in lieu of notice to be deducted from award of compensation for unfair dismissal—Whether employee entitled to wages in lieu of those he would have received if subsequently made redundant—Whether earnings from new employment to be taken into account in assessing compensation—Employment Protection (Consolidation) Act 1978, s 74(1)(4). **Addison v Babcock FATA Ltd** [1987] **2** 784, CA.
Dismissal without notice—Whether loss sustained by employee including loss sustained by employer's failure to respect good industrial relations practice—Employment Rights Act 1996, s 123. **Burlo v Langley** [2006] **2** 1104, EAT; [2007] **2** 462, CA.
Incapacity benefit—Unfairly dismissed employee claiming incapacity benefit while unfit to work by reason of psychological difficulties attributable to his loss of employment—Whether amount of incapacity benefit deductible from compensation payable by employer—Employment Rights Act 1996, s 123. **Morgans v Alpha Plus Security Ltd** [2005] **4** 655, EAT.
Whether compensation recoverable for non-economic loss brought about by manner of unfair dismissal—Employment Rights Act 1996, s 123. **Dunnachie v Kingston-upon-Hull City Council** [2004] **2** 501, CA; [2004] **3** 1011, HL.
Amount which is just and equitable having regard to the loss sustained by the aggrieved party—
Discretion of court or tribunal—Discretion to be exercised judicially and on basis of principle—Duty of court or tribunal to indicate in sufficient detail principles on which assessment made—Industrial Relations Act 1971, s 116. **Norton Tool Co Ltd v Tewson** [1973] **1** 183, NIRC.
Misconduct of employee justifying dismissal—Misconduct of employee justifying dismissal—Evidence of misconduct discovered subsequent to unfair dismissal—Whether evidence may be taken into account in assessing compensation—Whether permissible for tribunal to make a nominal or nil award in light of evidence of subsequent misconduct—Trade Union and Labour Relations Act 1974, Sch 1, para 19(1). **Devis (W) & Sons Ltd v Atkins** [1977] **3** 40, HL.

UNFAIR DISMISSAL (cont)—
  Compensation (cont)—
    Calculation of award—

      Reduction where dismissal caused or contributed to by action of complainant—Tribunal finding that pressure exercised on employer to dismiss employee unfairly and that dismissal unfair—Whether open to tribunal to find that employee contributed to dismissal—Employment Protection Act 1975, s 76(6). **Ford Motor Co Ltd v Hudson** [1978] **3** 23, EAT.

      Reduction where employee's conduct or action contributed to dismissal—Dismissal in connection with strike or other industrial action—Re-engagement of some employees—Compensation for failure to re-engage dismissed employees—Whether participation in strike or other industrial action amounting to 'conduct' or 'action' capable of reducing compensation award—Employment Protection (Consolidation) Act 1978, ss 57, 62, 73(7B), 74(6). **Tracey v Crosville Wales Ltd** [1997] **4** 449, HL.

    Common law principles relating to wrongful dismissal irrelevant—

      Heads of loss—Immediate loss of wages—Manner of dismissal—Future loss of wages—Loss of future statutory protection in respect of unfair dismissal or dismissal by reason of redundancy—Industrial Relations Act 1971, s 116. **Norton Tool Co Ltd v Tewson** [1973] **1** 183, NIRC.

    Dismissal in consequence of pressure exercised on employer—

      Principles to be applied in assessing compensation—Industrial Relations Act 1971, ss 33(1), 116(5). **Morris v Gestetner Ltd** [1973] **3** 1168, NIRC.

    Entitlement to compensation. *See* Entitlement to compensation, *below*.

    Future loss of wages—

      Age limit—Normal retiring age or specified birthday—Right to compensation for prospective loss of wages after specified birthday—Woman employee dismissed when aged 59—Award made and compensation assessed to cover loss of wages after age of 60—Whether compensation should be limited to loss of pay up to age of 60—Trade Union and Labour Relations Act 1974, Sch 1, para 10(b). **Barrel Plating & Phosphating Co Ltd v Danks** [1976] **3** 652, EAT.

      Evidence of future loss—Duty of employee to provide evidence of future loss of wages. **Adda International Ltd v Curcio** [1976] **3** 620, EAT.

    Heads of loss—

      Duty of tribunal—Reasons for award—Duty to specify in detail amounts awarded under each head and matters considered. **Adda International Ltd v Curcio** [1976] **3** 620, EAT.

    Immediate loss of wages—

      Unemployment benefit—Benefit received by employee following dismissal—Whether unemployment benefit one of the circumstances which the tribunal is entitled to take into account in assessing compensation. **Adda International Ltd v Curcio** [1976] **3** 620, EAT.

    Loss attributable to action of employers—

      Personal characteristics of employee as a factor in assessing compensation—Prospective period of unemployment in consequence of dismissal—Ill-health of employee making it likely that it would take him longer to find new employment than would otherwise have been the case—Whether tribunal limited to awarding compensation for period which a person in normal health would have taken to find new employment—Trade Union and Labour Relations Act 1974, Sch 1, para 19(1). **Fougère v Phoenix Motor Co Ltd** [1977] **1** 237, EAT.

    Loss of accrued right to redundancy payment—

      Employer rebutting presumption of redundancy for purposes of redundancy payment—Employer failing to show that reason for dismissal justified—Award of compensation to reflect loss of accrued rights to redundancy payment. **Midland Foot Comfort Centre Ltd v Richmond** [1973] **2** 294, NIRC.

    Loss of earnings—

      Medical incapacity. *See* Compensation—Amount which is just and equitable having regard to the loss sustained by employee—Constructive dismissal—Loss of earnings flowing from dismissal, *above*.

    Loss sustained by aggrieved party—

      Earnings from new employment—Dismissal without notice—Payment of salary for due period of notice in lieu of notice—Employee obtaining other employment during due period of notice—Whether earnings from new employer during due period of notice to be taken into account in assessing compensation—Industrial Relations Act 1971, s 116(1). **Everwear Candlewick Ltd v Isaac** [1974] **3** 24, NIRC.

    Matters to which complaint relates caused or contributed to by aggrieved party—

      Matters to which complaint relates—Conduct of employee having caused dismissal—Conduct of employee not having contributed to unfair character of dismissal—'Matters to which complaint relates' not restricted to unfair character of dismissal—All circumstances surrounding dismissal to be taken into account—Whether employers entitled to reduction in award in consequence of employee's conduct—Industrial Relations Act 1971, s 116(3). **Maris v Rotherham Corp** [1974] **2** 776, NIRC.

      No award of compensation on ground that employee's act was sole cause of dismissal—Employee refusing to pay union arrears—Threat of strike action by employee's fellow workers if arrears not paid—Employee dismissed because of threat—Whether employee's failure to pay union arrears sole cause of dismissal—Industrial Relations Act 1971, s 116(3). **Morris v Gestetner Ltd** [1973] **3** 1168, NIRC.

      Reduction of award on ground that employee 'caused or contributed to' his dismissal—Employee dismissed for refusing to be a party to the falsification of employers' records—Employee refusing to accept reassurance by employers' manager—Whether just and equitable for tribunal to reduce assessment—Whether dismissal caused or contributed to by employee—Whether words 'caused or contributed' implying blameworthiness—Industrial Relations Act 1971, s 116(3). **Morrish v Henlys (Folkestone) Ltd** [1973] **2** 137, NIRC.

1423

UNFAIR DISMISSAL (cont)—
Compensation (cont)—
Redundancy payment—
Award of compensation in addition to redundancy payment—Redundancy a reason justifying dismissal—Presumption of redundancy for purposes of redundancy payment—Onus of employer to show redundancy as a reason justifying dismissal—Circumstances in which tribunal competent to award both compensation for unfair dismissal and redundancy payment—Redundancy Payments Act 1965, s 9(2)(b)—Industrial Relations Act 1971, s 24(1), (2), (6). **Midland Foot Comfort Centre Ltd v Richmond** [1973] **2** 294, NIRC.

Employee receiving redundancy payment from employers—Employee subsequently claiming compensation for unfair dismissal—Tribunal awarding employee compensation without making appropriate deduction for redundancy payment—Whether tribunal bound to make deduction for redundancy payment when assessing employee's loss—Industrial Relations Act 1971, s 116. **Yorkshire Engineering and Welding Co Ltd v Burnham** [1973] **3** 1176, NIRC.
Summary dismissal during period of notice—
Employee giving employer one month's notice—Employer accepting notice—Employer summarily dismissing employee before expiry of notice—Employee having no right to withdraw notice unilaterally—Tribunal not entitled to assess compensation on assumption employee might have withdrawn notice and remained in employer's service. **Harris & Russell Ltd v Slingsby** [1973] **3** 31, NIRC.
Complaint—
Employment tribunal—
Procedure. See **Employment tribunal** (Procedure—Complaint of unfair dismissal).
Constructive dismissal—
Compensation. See Compensation—Amount which is just and equitable having regard to the loss sustained by employee—Constructive dismissal, *above.*
Test to be applied in determining whether employee constructively dismissed—
Breach of contract entitling employee to treat contract as terminated—Reasonableness of employer's conduct not appropriate test—Proper test to ask whether employer's conduct such as in law to entitle employee to treat himself as discharged from contractual obligations—Trade Union and Labour Relations Act 1974, Sch 1, para 5(2)(c). **Western Excavating (ECC) Ltd v Sharp** [1978] **1** 713, CA.

Employee resigning and complaining of series of actions by employer—Whether finding of constructive dismissal precluded where final act of employer precipitating resignation was reasonable conduct by employer. **Omilaju v Waltham Forest London BC** [2004] **3** 129, EAT; [2005] **1** 75, CA.

'Final straw'—Series of acts alleged to be breach of implied term of trust and confidence—Whether employee entitled to rely on totality of acts despite previous affirmation in respect of earlier acts. **Kaur v Leeds Teaching Hospitals NHS Trust** [2018] **4** 238, CA.

Reasonableness of employee's resignation—Proper approach to ask whether employee had acted reasonably in deciding that he could not work for employer—Trade Union and Labour Relations Act 1974, Sch 1, para 6 (8). **Gilbert v Goldstone Ltd** [1977] **1** 423, EAT.

Whether fundamental breach of contract by employer curable while employee considering whether to treat it as dismissal. **Buckland v Bournemouth University Higher Education Corp** [2010] **4** 186, CA.

Whether in 'final straw' case range of reasonable responses test applying to employer's conduct of grievance procedure where that conduct was final straw relied upon. **Triggs v GAB Robins (UK) Ltd** [2007] **3** 590, EAT.
Continuity of employment. See **Employment** (Continuity).
Crown servant—
Appeal to Civil Service Appeal Board—
Duty of board to give reasons for its decision. See **Judicial review** (Duty to give reasons—Civil Service Appeal Board).
Date of dismissal—
Notice by employer terminating contract—
Employer and employee subsequently agreeing during period of notice to shorten period of notice—Whether date of dismissal date of expiry of original or of shortened notice—Industrial Relations Act 1971, s 23(2). **Lees v Arthur Greaves (Lees) Ltd** [1973] **2** 21, NIRC.

Period of notice—Whether employee dismissed when notice given or when period of notice expires—Industrial Relations Act 1971, s 23(2). **Brindle v HW Smith (Cabinets) Ltd** [1973] **1** 230, CA.
Summary dismissal—
Effective date of termination—Employer summarily dismissing employee by letter—Whether termination of employment taking effect on delivery of letter—Whether termination of employment taking effect when employee had reasonably opportunity of learning contents of letter—Whether 'reasonable opportunity' to be assessed objectively—Employment Rights Act 1996, s 97(1)(b). **Gisda Cyf v Barratt** [2010] **4** 851, SC.

Internal appeal procedure—Employee to be treated as being suspended without pay pending determination of appeal—Effective date of dismissal. **West Midlands Co-op Society Ltd v Tipton** [1986] **1** 513, HL.
Determination whether dismissal fair or unfair—
Appeal—
Domestic appeal—Refusal by employer to entertain domestic appeal—Dismissal inevitable on facts—Whether employer entitled to refuse to entertain domestic appeal. **West Midlands Co-op Society Ltd v Tipton** [1986] **1** 513, HL.
Code of Practice—
Failure of employer to follow procedure prescribed by Code of Practice—Whether failure to follow procedure rendering dismissal unfair. **Devis (W) & Sons Ltd v Atkins** [1977] **3** 40, HL.

UNFAIR DISMISSAL (cont)—
Determination whether dismissal fair or unfair (cont)—
Dismissal for an inadmissible reason—

Dismissal for trade union membership—Union applying to employer for recognition—Employer reacting by instructing chargehands to dismiss 20 employees—Dismissed employees claiming their dismissal due to union membership or activities—Whether employees dismissed for an 'inadmissible reason'—Whether necessary for each employee to show that his dismissal was due to his particular union membership or activity—Employment Protection (Consolidation) Act 1978, s 58. **Carrington v Therm-A-Stor Ltd** [1983] **1** 796, CA.

Dismissal of two employees who urged recognition of union—Other employees striking in protest at dismissals—Striking employees dismissed—Whether striking employees dismissed for an inadmissible reason—Trade Union and Labour Relations Act 1974, Sch 1, paras 6(4), 8(2). **Stock v Frank Jones (Tipton) Ltd** [1976] **3** 218, QBD.

Dismissal for misconduct—

Claimant head teacher not disclosing close friend's conviction for sexual offences towards children—Whether non-disclosure amounting to misconduct—Whether dismissal within range of reasonable responses open to employer—Employment Rights Act 1996, s 98(4). **Reilly v Sandwell Metropolitan BC** [2018] **3** 477, SC.

Correct approach to determining fairness of dismissal—Employment Rights Act 1996, s 98. **Post Office v Foley** [2001] **1** 550, CA.

Tests for determining whether employer showing substantial reason for dismissal and whether dismissal fair response—Employment Rights Act 1996, s 98. **HSBC Bank plc (formerly Midland Bank plc) v Madden** [2000] **2** 741, EAT.

Tribunal's finding of fact of direct race discrimination mitigating claimant's misconduct—Fact of discrimination known to dismissed employee's manager but not to dismissing officer—Whether mitigating circumstances known to dismissed employee's manager at time of dismissal taken to be known to employer—Whether fact of discrimination sufficient to make dismissal unfair—Employment Rights Act 1996, s 98(4). **Orr v Milton Keynes Council** [2011] **4** 1256, CA.

Dismissal for refusing to join trade union in accordance with union membership agreement—

Company employing 42 employees—Employees told that they were free to join union of their choice—33 employees joining one union and nine employees joining another—Union membership agreement concluded with first union—Employees who joined other union dismissed for refusing to join first union in accordance with agreement—Whether 'it [was] the practice' to join first union in accordance with agreement—Whether dismissals fair—Trade Union and Labour Relations Act 1974, Sch 1, para 6(5). **Himpfen v Allied Records Ltd** [1978] **3** 891, EAT.

Refusal to join on grounds of religious belief—Conscientious objection based on moral belief—Whether conscientious objection based on moral belief justifying refusal to join union—Trade Union and Labour Relations Act 1974, Sch 1, para 6(5) (as amended by the Trade Union and Labour Relations (Amendment) Act 1976, ss 1(e), 3(5)). **Saggers v British Railways Board** [1978] **2** 20, EAT.

Refusal to join on grounds of religious belief—Personal religious belief—Personal belief as opposed to belief of religious sect to which employee belongs—Sect not proscribing trade union membership—Employee's conscience based on religious convictions not permitting him to join union—Whether employee's refusal to join union based 'on grounds of religious belief'—Trade Union and Labour Relations Act 1974, Sch 1, para 6(5) (as amended by the Trade Union and Labour Relations (Amendment) Act 1976, ss 1(e), 3(5)). **Saggers v British Railways Board** [1978] **2** 20, EAT.

Union membership agreement concluded by employers and union after representation that employees were free to join union of their choice—Copy of agreement posted on employees' notice board without comment—Between date of representation and date of conclusion of agreement 33 employees joining union with which agreement concluded and nine employees joining another union—Three months after agreement concluded employees who joined other union dismissed—Whether agreement sufficiently brought to attention of employees—Whether employers estopped from contending dismissals fair because employees had refused to join union in accordance with union membership agreement—Whether dismissals fair—Trade Union and Labour Relations Act 1974, Sch 1, para 6(5). **Himpfen v Allied Records Ltd** [1978] **3** 891, EAT.

Union membership agreement—Agreement between employer and union which requires terms and conditions of employment to include condition that employee should join that union or another appropriate independent trade union—Agreement between employer and union containing provision that employees should join that union—Whether a 'union membership agreement'—Whether such an agreement must confer on employee option to join 'another appropriate independent trade union'—Trade Union and Labour Relations Act 1974, s 30(1), Sch 1, para 6(5). **Home Counties Dairies Ltd v Woods** [1977] **1** 869, EAT.

Procedure relating to dismissal—

Unfair procedure—'Band of reasonable responses' test—Right to respect for private and family life—Claimant dismissed by employer for alleged theft by—Whether right to respect for private and family life engaged by stigma attached to dismissal for alleged criminal conduct—Whether band of reasonable responses test providing adequate protection for right to respect for private and family life—Whether engagement of right requiring application of test based on proportionality—Employment Rights Act 1996, s 98- Human Rights Act 1998, Sch 1, Pt I, art 8. **Turner v East Midlands Trains Ltd** [2013] **3** 375, CA.

Unfair procedure—Res judicata—Abuse of process—Employees given final warning under simplified disciplinary procedure—Employees subsequently summarily dismissed after second disciplinary procedure arising from same facts as first disciplinary procedure—Whether doctrine of res judicata applying to bar second disciplinary procedure—Whether second disciplinary procedure barred as abuse of process—Whether fair to institute second disciplinary procedure. **Christou v Haringey London BC** [2014] **1** 135, CA.

UNFAIR DISMISSAL (cont)—
Determination whether dismissal fair or unfair (cont)—
Procedure relating to dismissal (cont)—
Unfair procedure—Right of employee to put his case before or at time of dismissal—Employee summarily dismissed with no opportunity of putting his case before or at time of dismissal—Employee having no valid answer to employers' complaints regarding his work—Employers not knowing whether employee had explanation of conduct—Whether tribunal entitled to make finding of unfair dismissal where unfair procedure leads to no injustice to employee—Whether employee entitled to compensation where unfair procedure the only matter rendering dismissal unfair—Industrial Relations Act 1971, s 24. **Earl v Slater & Wheeler (Airlyne) Ltd** [1973] **1** 145, NIRC.
Question to be determined in accordance with equity and the substantial merits of the case—
Meaning—Industrial Relations Act 1971, s 24(6). **Earl v Slater & Wheeler (Airlyne) Ltd** [1973] **1** 145, NIRC.
Reason for dismissal shown by employer—
Matters known to employer at date of dismissal—Circumstances existing which would justify dismissal—Circumstances only coming to knowledge of employers after dismissal—Discovery of facts indicating employee had been guilty of gross misconduct—Whether employers entitled to rely on those matters as constituting a reason justifying dismissal—Trade Union and Labour Relation Act 1974, Sch 1, para 6(8). **Devis (W) & Sons Ltd v Atkins** [1976] **2** 822, QBD; [1977] **3** 40, HL.
Reasons justifying dismissal—
Burden on employer to show that he acted reasonably in treating reason as sufficient reason justifying dismissal—Redundancy—Burden where common ground that dismissal for redundancy of some employees necessary—Employer required to establish how, by whom and on what basis selection for redundancy made—No evidence before tribunal as to who took decision to dismiss employees and on what information decision reached—Evidence adduced that employers gave thought to decision and obtained objective information on employees' characteristics—Whether tribunal entitled to hold that employers had not discharged burden of proof—Trade Union and Labour Relations Act 1974, Sch 1, para 6(1), (8). **Bristol Channel Ship Repairers Ltd v O'Keefe** [1977] **2** 258, EAT.
Determination of whether employer acted reasonably—Employer refusing to entertain employee's appeal—Whether employer acting 'reasonably or unreasonably'—Whether employer's unreasonableness after dismissal relevant—Whether dismissal unfair—Employment Protection (Consolidation) Act 1978, s 57(3). **West Midlands Co-op Society Ltd v Tipton** [1986] **1** 513, HL.
Determination of whether employer acted reasonably—Employer terminating employee's employment at instance of third party—Employee refusing employer's offer of alternative lower-paid work—Dismissal to be determined in accordance with equity and substantial merits of the case—Whether tribunal to have regard to any injustice suffered by the employee—Employment Protection (Consolidation) Act 1978, s 57. **Dobie v Burns International Security Services (UK) Ltd** [1984] **3** 333, CA.
Determination of whether employer acted reasonably—Redundancy—Employer failing to consult employee prior to dismissal—Industrial tribunal concluding that failure to consult not making any difference to decision to dismiss employee—Whether any distinction between reason for dismissal and manner in which dismissal effected—Whether industrial tribunal bound to consider whether failure to consult made any difference to result—Whether dismissal unfair—Employment Protection (Consolidation) Act 1978, s 57(3). **Polkey v A E Dayton Services Ltd** [1987] **3** 974, HL.
Gross misconduct—Unauthorised entry into employer's computer—Whether gross misconduct justifying summary dismissal. **Denco Ltd v Joinson** [1992] **1** 463, EAT.
Specified reasons justifying dismissal—
Disobedience—Employee refusing to be party to falsification of employers' records to cover general deficiency despite reassurance by employers' manager—Employee dismissed because of refusal—Whether employee unfairly dismissed. **Morrish v Henlys (Folkestone) Ltd** [1973] **2** 137, NIRC.
Some other substantial reason justifying dismissal—Employer wishing to employ his own son in place of dismissed employee—Employer a farmer owning his own farm—Employee a farm worker—Employer's son just completed his agricultural training—Employee dismissed so that employer's son could take his place—Whether employee's dismissal justified—Whether reason for dismissal a 'substantial reason of a kind such as to justify the dismissal'—Trade Union and Labour Relations Act 1974, Sch 1, para 6(1)(b). **Priddle v Dibble** [1978] **1** 1058, EAT.
Some other substantial reason justifying dismissal—Employers wishing to vary employee's contract by introducing restrictive covenant—Restrictive covenant necessary to protect employers' business—Employee refusing to sign new contract—Employers terminating employee's existing contract—Whether substantial reason justifying dismissal—Whether words 'some other substantial reason' to be construed ejusdem generis with reasons specified in statute—Industrial Relations Act 1971, s 24(1), (2). **RS Components Ltd v Irwin** [1974] **1** 41, NIRC.
Substantial reason justifying dismissal—
Expiry of fixed term contract—Deemed dismissal—Circumstances in which temporary nature of engagement capable of constituting substantial reason justifying dismissal—Duty of tribunal to consider whether there was a genuine reason for the contract being for a fixed term—Trade Union and Labour Relations Act 1974, Sch 1, paras 5(2)(b), 6(1)(b). **Terry v East Sussex CC** [1977] **1** 567, EAT.
Discrimination against a woman. See **Employment** (Discrimination against a woman—Unfair dismissal and redundancy payments).
Dismissal—
Dismissal in connection with strike or other industrial action. See Dismissal in connection with strike or other industrial action, *below*.
Expiry of contract for fixed term without renewal of term—
Contract liable to be determined by notice—Contract for a term which is to expire on a fixed date subject to earlier determination on either party giving notice—Whether a 'contract...for a fixed term'—Trade Union and Labour Relations Act 1974, Sch 1, para 5(2)(b). **Dixon v BBC** [1979] **2** 112, CA.
Frustration of contract of employment. See **Employment** (Contract of service—Frustration).

UNFAIR DISMISSAL (cont)—
  Dismissal (cont)—
    Notice to employee to terminate contract of employment—
      Agreement to terminate employment during period of notice negativing dismissal—Evidence of termination by mutual consent—Need to prove employee had full knowledge of implications of agreement—Employers brings pressure on employee to stop working for them before expiry of notice—Employee submitting to pressure—Whether employment terminated by agreement—Whether employee dismissed—Industrial Relations Act 1971, s 23. **Lees v Arthur Greaves (Lees) Ltd** [1974] **2** 393, CA.
      Employee verbally requesting termination of contract on date prior to expiry of notice—Employers agreeing to request—Employee leaving before expiry date—Whether employee 'dismissed' or whether consensual termination of contract—Industrial Relations Act 1971, s 23(3). **McAlwane v Boughton Estates Ltd** [1973] **2** 299, NIRC.
      Notice by employee within obligatory period of employers' notice to terminate employment on earlier date—Notice in writing—Employee to be taken to have been dismissed—Need for notice in writing—Oral request by employee to terminate employment on earlier date—Employers consenting to request—Whether employee dismissed by employers—Industrial Relations Act 1971, s 23(3). **Glacier Metal Co Ltd v Dyer** [1974] **3** 21, MIRC.
    Pregnancy—
      Reason connected with pregnancy—Redundancy—Employee selected for redundancy because she would require maternity leave—Whether employee unfairly dismissed—Employment Protection (Consolidation) Act 1978, ss 57(3), 60(1). **Stockton-on-Tees BC v Brown** [1988] **2** 129, HL.
    Procedure. *See* Determination whether dismissal fair or unfair—Procedure relating to dismissal, *above*.
  Dismissal in connection with strike or other industrial action—
    Dismissal not unfair unless one or more employees of same employer who also took part in the action were not dismissed—
      Relevance of dates when other employees took part in action—Relevant employee not dismissed at same time as strikers but later dismissed for redundancy—Whether for applicant's claim to be barred relevant employee required to be dismissed while on strike—Whether applicant's claim barred if relevant employee dismissed by the time claim heard—Employment Protection (Consolidation) Act 1978, s 62(2)(a). **McCormick v Horsepower Ltd** [1981] **2** 746, CA.
      Relevance of dates when other employees took part in action—Two of the employees on strike returning to work before end of strike—All other employees dismissed—Whether employees who returned to work before others were dismissed to be treated as 'employees...who also took part in that action'—Whether dismissal of other employees unfair—Trade Union and Labour Relations Act 1974, Sch 1, para 8(2) (a). **Stock v Frank Jones (Tipton) Ltd** [1978] **1** 948, HL.
    Dismissal not unfair unless relevant employee not dismissed—
      Relevant employee—Applicant's union going on strike—Another employee belonging to different union voluntarily refusing to cross picket line—Other employee not dismissed—Whether other employee a 'relevant employee' for purposes of determining whether applicant's claim for unfair dismissal barred—Employment Protection (Consolidation) Act 1978, s 62(4)(b). **McCormick v Horsepower Ltd** [1981] **2** 746, CA.
      Relevant employee—Relevant employee meaning employee who took part in strike—Employee who refused to go into factory to work during strike for fear of abuse from strikers not dismissed—Whether that employee a 'relevant employee'—Employment Protection (Consolidation) Act 1978, s 62(2)(a), (4)(b). **Coates v Modern Methods and Materials Ltd** [1982] **3** 946, CA.
    Employee taking part in strike on date of dismissal—
      Date of dismissal—Time of dismissal—Dismissal on date of termination of strike—Dismissal after termination of strike—Whether employee taking part in strike 'on the date of dismissal'—Industrial Relations Act 1971, s 26(1). **Heath v JF Longman (Meat Salesmen) Ltd** [1973] **2** 1228, NIRC.
    Other industrial action—
      Meaning—Refusal to work overtime because of dispute over wage increase—Refusal to work overtime not constituting breach of contract—Whether refusal to work overtime amounting to taking part in 'other industrial action'—Whether industrial tribunal having jurisdiction to hear complaint of unfair dismissal—Employment Protection (Consolidation) Act 1978, s 62(1)(b). **Power Packing Casemakers Ltd v Faust** [1983] **2** 166, CA.
    Strike or other industrial action—
      Coercive element—Action by employees to resist coercive action by employers—Employers installing new machines and proposing to prove them before securing co-operation of employees—Employees leaving places of work and surrounding machines to prevent proving operation taking place—Employers threatening to invoke disciplinary procedure—Whether action of employees constituting a 'strike or other industrial action'—Trade Union and Labour Relations Act 1974, Sch 1, para 8(1), (2). **Thompson v Eaton Ltd** [1976] **3** 384, EAT.
  Employment Appeal Tribunal—
    Generally. *See* **Employment Appeal Tribunal**.
    Jurisdiction. *See* **Employment Appeal Tribunal** (Jurisdiction—Unfair dismissal).
  Employment tribunal jurisdiction. *See* **Employment tribunal** (Jurisdiction).
  Employment tribunal proceedings—
    Complaint—
      Procedure. *See* **Employment tribunal** (Procedure—Complaint of unfair dismissal).
    Decision of tribunal. *See* **Employment tribunal** (Procedure—Decision).
    Postponement of hearing—
      Postponement pending outcome of High Court proceedings. *See* **Employment tribunal** (Procedure—Hearing—Postponement—Discretion—Proceedings for unfair dismissal).
  Entitlement to compensation—
    Period of continuous employment. *See* **Employment** (Continuity—Period of continuous employment).

Entitlement to compensation (cont)—
Qualifying period of employment—
Concurrent but separate contracts of employment—Number of hours worked each week—Employee employed under concurrent but separate contracts to teach three part-time courses—Employee not working more than six hours per week under any one contract—Aggregate of hours worked under all three contracts exceeding eight hours per week—Whether employee permitted to aggregate hours worked under separate contracts—Whether employee qualifying to claim compensation for unfair dismissal—Employment Protection (Consolidation) Act 1978, Sch 13, paras 4, 6. **Surrey CC v Lewis** [1987] **3** 641, HL.
Excluded classes of employment—
Employee who ordinarily works outside Great Britain—
Employee working as flight attendant for Saudi Arabian airline—Employment contract providing that employee might be based at any location where airline operated—Employee transferred to London—Employee resigning and bringing claim for unfair constructive dismissal—Tribunal dismissing claim because employee did not ordinarily work in Great Britain—Whether contract test or function test should be applied in determining where employee ordinarily works—Employment Rights Act 1996, s 196(2). **Carver (née Mascarenhas) v Saudi Arabian Airlines** [1999] **3** 61, CA.
Work partly inside and partly outside Great Britain—Method to be applied in determining whether employee ordinarily works outside Great Britain—Whether employee who ordinarily works in Great Britain can also ordinarily work outside Great Britain during same period of employment—Whether proper to look at terms of contract or at what had happened during period of employment to determine whether employee 'ordinarily works outside Great Britain'—Trade Union and Labour Relations Act 1974, Sch 1, para 9(2). **Wilson v Maynard Shipbuilding Consultants AB** [1978] **2** 78, CA.
Work party inside and partly outside Great Britain—Whilst in Great Britain employee ordinarily working in Great Britain—Whether also 'ordinarily working outside Great Britain'—Whether employee's right to claim compensation for unfair dismissal excluded—Trade Union and Labour Relations Act 1974, Sch 1, para 9(2). **Portec (UK) Ltd v Mogensen** [1976] **3** 565, EAT.
Employment in undertaking where less than four employees employed for prescribed period—
Employed—Identity of employer—Relevance—Employees in undertaking employed by different employers—Whether identity of employer relevant—Industrial Relations Act 1971, s 27(1)(a). **Kapur v Shields** [1976] **1** 873, QBD.
Four employees continuously employed—Total of four employees in employment during thirteen week period—One of employees in employment immediately before termination having less than thirteen weeks' service—Whether exclusion applicable—Industrial Relations Act 1971, s 27(1)(a). **Mayhew v Richard Alexander & Son** [1973] **3** 39, NIRC.
Onus of proof—Onus on employer to establish that employment within excluded class—Evidence that separate activities of employer constitute single 'undertaking'—Onus on employer to show that activity in which employee employed a separate undertaking—Industrial Relations Act 1971, s 27(1)(a). **Kapur v Shields** [1976] **1** 873, QBD.
Employment under contract for services—
Employer and manager agreeing for tax purposes that manager to be self-employed in the future—Inland Revenue accepting arrangement—Manager operating under firm name rather than own name—Manager continuing to perform same duties as before—Manager dismissed and bringing claim for unfair dismissal—Whether manager an individual who has entered into or worked under a contract of employment—Whether manager an 'employee'—Trade Union and Labour Relations Act 1974, s 30(1), Sch 1, para 4(1). **Massey v Crown Life Insurance Co** [1978] **2** 576, CA.
Employment under contract normally involving employment for less than 21 hours weekly—
Employment—Consultant available to advise employer when occasion arose—Whether consultant 'employed' at time when available to advise employer but not actually advising—Trade Union and Labour Relations Act 1974, Sch 1, para 9(1)(f). **Bromsgrove Casting & Machining Ltd v Martin** [1977] **3** 487, EAT.
Hospital staff. See **National Health Service** (Hospital—Staff—Terms and conditions of service—Dismissal).
Jurisdiction—
Employment tribunal. See **Employment tribunal** (Jurisdiction—Unfair dismissal).
Pensions appeal tribunal. See **Pensions Appeal Tribunal**.
Loss of future wages—
Age limit. See Compensation—Future loss of wages—Age limit, *above*.
Minister of religion—
Complaint of unfair dismissal—
Whether agreement between Minister and Church a contract of service. See **Employment** (Contract of service—Incidents of contract—Minister of religion).
Pressure on employer to dismiss unfairly—
Test to be applied in determining whether there was 'pressure to dismiss'—
Factors to be considered—Trade Union and Labour Relations Act 1974, Sch 1, para 15. **Ford Motor Co Ltd v Hudson** [1978] **3** 23, EAT.
Protected disclosure—
Generally. See **Employment** (Unfair dismissal—Protected disclosure).
Qualifying disclosure—
Disclosure made in good faith—Meaning of 'good faith'—Employment Rights Act 1996, ss 43C(1), 43G(1)(a). **Street v Derbyshire Unemployed Workers' Centre** [2004] **4** 839, CA.
Redundancy—
Doubt as to which claim appropriate. See **Industrial relations** (Practice—Claim for redundancy payment or compensation for unfair dismissal).

UNFAIR DISMISSAL (cont)—
  Remedies—
    Order for reinstatement—
      Terms of reinstatement—Appellant being placed on restricted duties as fingerprint expert but subsequently dismissed from role—Tribunal upholding appellant's complaint of unfair dismissal and ordering reinstatement on restricted duties—Whether reinstatement ordered on altered contractual terms—Employment Rights Act 1996, ss 114, 116. **McBride v Scottish Police Authority** [2017] **2** 875, SC.
    Orders for reinstatement and re-engagement—
      Enforcement of order and compensation—Employment Tribunal making order for re-engagement—Whether employer obliged to re-engage employee—Whether correlative right of employee to be re-engaged—Employment Rights Act 1996, ss 115, 117. **R (on the application of MacKenzie) v Chancellor, Masters and Scholars of the University of Cambridge** [2019] **4** 289, CA.
  Right not to be unfairly dismissed—
    Excluded classes of employment. *See* Excluded classes of employment, *above.*
    Exclusion of right by agreement—
      Agreement by person employed under contract for fixed term of two years or more—Meaning of 'fixed term'—Contract for a definite term—Contract terminable before expiry of term by notice on either side—Whether a contract for a 'fixed term'—Industrial Relations Act 1971, s 30(b). **BBC v Ioannou** [1975] **2** 999, CA.
    Restriction of right when employee not continuously employed for period of two years—
      Dismissal in connection with transfer of undertaking—Employees continuously employed for period of less than two years—Whether employees entitled to claim compensation for unfair dismissal—Employment Protection (Consolidation) Act 1978, ss 54, 64—Transfer of Undertakings (Protection of Employment) Regulations 1981, reg 8(1)—Council Directive (EEC) 77/187, art 4(1). **MRS Environmental Services Ltd v Marsh** [1997] **1** 92, CA.
    Restriction on right where employee not continuously employed for period of two years—
      Dismissal in course of transfer of undertaking—Transferee re-engaging employee but subsequently dismissing him—Whether employee continuously employed for period of two years by transferee—Whether employee employed by transferor 'at the time of the transfer'—Employment Protection (Consolidation) Act 1978, s 64, Sch 13, para 17(2). **Clark & Tokeley Ltd (t/a Spellbrook) v Oakes** [1998] **4** 353, CA.
    Restriction on right where employee reaches normal retiring age of 65—
      Normal retiring age—Employee in undertaking where 60 regarded as pensionable age—Employees retained in undertaking after age of 60 at discretion of employers—Employee dismissed when aged 61—Whether employee having right to present complaint of unfair dismissal—Industrial Relations Act 1971, s 28(b). **Ord v Maidstone and District Hospital Management Committee** [1974] **2** 343, NIRC.
    Restriction on right where employee reaches normal retiring age or specified age—
      Conjunctive or disjunctive requirement—Employee over specified age but under normal retiring age—Whether employee entitled to remedy only if under normal retiring age and under specified age—Whether employee over specified age but under normal retiring age entitled to remedy—Trade Union and Labour Relations Act 1974, Sch 1, para 10(b). **Nothman v Barnet London Borough** [1979] **1** 142, HL.
      Normal retiring age—Contractual provision for retirement at certain age—Employees in practice retiring at all ages—Whether 'normal retiring age' age at which employee required by contract to retire—Trade Union and Labour Relations Act 1974, Sch 1, para 10(b). **Nothman v Barnet London Borough** [1979] **1** 142, HL.
      Normal retiring age—Determination—Employee's contract providing for compulsory retirement at 60 unless conditions relating to efficiency and health complied with—Evidence that majority of employees retained beyond age of 60—Whether normal retiring age 60—Whether employee unfairly dismissed because compulsorily retired at 60 on ground of health—Trade Union and Labour Relations Act 1974, Sch 1, para 10(b). **Post Office v Wallser** [1981] **1** 668, CA.
      Normal retiring age—Determination—Employee's contract providing for compulsory retirement at minimum age of 60 unless employer decided to keep him on until he was 65—Employee compulsorily retired six months after sixtieth birthday—Employee alleging unfair dismissal—Whether contractual retiring age conclusively fixing normal retiring age—Whether tribunal having jurisdiction to entertain claim—Trade Union and Labour Relations Act 1974, Sch 1, para 10(b). **Waite v Government Communications Headquarters** [1983] **2** 1013, HL.
      Normal retiring age—Determination—Employer promulgating normal retiring age of 60 but permitting certain employees as an exception to apply for limited extension in service beyond that age—Significant number of employees retiring at different ages—Employment of employees aged between 60 and 64 terminated—Employees alleging unfair dismissal—Whether tribunal having jurisdiction to entertain claims—Whether employees having reached 'normal retiring age' before their employment was terminated—Employment Protection (Consolidation) Act 1978, s 64(1)(b). **O'Brien v Barclays Bank plc** [1995] **1** 438, CA.
      Normal retiring age—Determination—Normal retiring age depending on express or implied conditions of service—Conditions of service specifying minimum retirement age but permitting discretionary extension—Retirement age extended in many cases—Whether minimum retirement age the normal retiring age—Trade Union and Labour Relations Act 1974, Sch 1, para 10(b). **Howard v Dept of National Savings** [1981] **1** 674, CA.
  Right to claim for unfair dismissal—
    Entitlement to compensation. *See* Entitlement to compensation, *above.*
    Exclusion of right by agreement—
      Agreement by person employed under contract for fixed term of one year or more—Extension of period of contract by variation of contract—Whether fixed term being whole of period covered by contract as varied or period added to contract by variation—Employment Rights Act 1996, ss 95(1), 197(1). **BBC v Kelly-Phillips** [1998] **2** 845, CA.
  Right to respect for private and family life—
    Procedure relating to dismissal. *See* Determination whether dismissal fair or unfair—Procedure relating to dismissal—Unfair procedure—'Band of reasonable responses' test—Right to respect for private and family life, *above.*

UNFAIR DISMISSAL (cont)—
    Sex discrimination—
        Discrimination against women. *See* **Employment** (Discrimination against a woman—Unfair dismissal and redundancy payments).
    Trade union membership and activities—
        Activities before commencement of employment—
            Employee dismissed because of activities before commencement of employment—Whether a ground for claim of unfair dismissal—Trade Union and Labour Relations Act 1974, Sch 1, para 6(4)(b). **City of Birmingham DC v Beyer** [1978] **1** 910, EAT.
        Activities of an independent trade union—
            Employee dismissed for organising petition to employers regarding safety of machinery—Employee receiving union's advice but not acting as union representative or on behalf of union—Whether employee acting as an individual or taking part 'in the activities of an independent trade union'—Whether a ground for claim of unfair dismissal—Trade Union and Labour Relations Act 1974, Sch 1, para 6(4)(b). **Chant v Aquaboats Ltd** [1978] **3** 102, EAT.
        Exercise of rights by worker. *See* **Industrial relations** (Trade union membership and activities—Rights of worker as against employer—Dismissal for exercising rights—Unfair dismissal).

UNFAIR EVIDENCE
    Criminal proceedings—
        Exclusion. *See* **Criminal evidence** (Exclusion of evidence).

UNFAIR INDUSTRIAL PRACTICE
    See **Industrial relations** (Unfair industrial practice).

UNFAIR TERMS
    Contract—
        Generally. *See* **Contract** (Unfair terms).

UNFIT HOUSING
    Unfitness for human habitation. *See* **Housing** (House unfit for human habitation).

UNFORMED COMPANY
    Party to contract. *See* **Contract** (Parties—Unformed company).

UNIFORMS
    Uniforms in connection with political objects. *See* **Public order** (Uniforms in connection with political objects).

UNILATERAL CONTRACT
    Acceptance. *See* **Contract** (Offer and acceptance—Acceptance—Unilateral contract).

UNILATERAL MISTAKE
    See **Mistake** (Rectification—Unilateral mistake).

UNINCORPORATED ASSOCIATION
    Charity. *See* **Charity** (Unincorporated association).
    Contract. *See* **Contract** (Unincorporated society).
    Dissolution—
        Application of funds on dissolution—
            Literary and scientific institution—Application of funds after purported dissolution many years earlier—Dissolution to which less than three-fifths of members consented—Literary and Scientific Institutions Act 1854, s 29. **Harrow Literary Institution, Re** [1953] **1** 838, Ch D.
            Whether sole surviving member of unincorporated association entitled to its assets—Human Rights Act 1998, Sch 1, Pt II, art 1. **Hanchett-Stamford v A-G** [2008] **4** 323, Ch D.
        Distribution of surplus assets among members—
            Allotment association—Association formed with so-called capital of 210 £1 shares—Land held by trustees for use and benefit of members—Rules provided members to include shareholders and allotment holders—Association inactive after 1961—Sale of association's land in 1967—Distribution of assets—Categories of members entitled to participate—Method of distribution. **St Andrew's Allotment Association's Trusts, Re** [1969] **1** 147, Ch D.
            Body having statutory powers to own property—Territorial army unit—Declaration of trust—Premises to be held on trust for commanding officer of unit and successors 'to be held and disposed of as property belonging to' the unit—Land held by volunteer corps on disbandment vesting by statute in Secretary of State—Premises used as unit's headquarters and drill hall—Whether members of unit at time of disbandment beneficially entitled to proceeds of sale of premises—Whether premises held by trustees on purpose trust—Whether proceeds of sale vesting in Secretary of State on basis that premises were property belonging to the unit—Military Lands Act 1892, s 8(1). **Edis's Trusts, Re** [1972] **2** 769, Ch D.
            Determination of shares—Distribution per capita or in proportion to amount of subscriptions—Shares of different classes of members—Society established for provision of sickness and death benefits for teachers and scholars of Sunday school—Class of child members subscribing at half adult rate and entitled to half amount of adult members' benefits—Distribution on per capita basis—Child members entitled to half shares only. **Sick and Funeral Society of St John's Sunday School, Golcar, Re** [1972] **2** 439, Ch D.
        Loss of substratum—
            Sick and benevolent fund—Acquiescence of members—Contributory sickness fund for firm's employees—Large reduction in membership following industrial dispute—Cessation of fund's activities—Arrangement between fund's officers to cease benefit payments and collection of contributions—Fund totally inactive for period of years—Membership remaining substantial—Fund fully viable—Whether substratum of fund lost—Whether members having acquiesced in dissolution. **Denby (William) & Sons Ltd Sick and Benevolent Fund, Re** [1971] **2** 1196, Ch D.

UNINCORPORATED ASSOCIATION (cont)—

Estoppel by representation by members. *See* **Estoppel** (Representation—Existing fact—Representation by members of unincorporated association).

Funds—

Application of funds—

Payment of personal legal costs incurred by members—Interpretation of rules—Review of decision—Jurisdiction of court. **Baker v Jones** [1954] 2 553, QBD.

Gift to association—

Rule against perpetuities. *See* **Rule against perpetuities** (Unincorporated association—Gift to association).

Injunction in case of dispute as to membership. *See* **Injunction** (Interlocutory—Injunction having effect of granting sole relief claimed in action—Unincorporated association).

Litigation—

Description of parties. *See* **Practice** (Parties—Description of parties—Unincorporated body).

Meeting—

Constituency Labour Party—

Disorder—Powers of chairman to adjourn—Grounds for and length of adjournment. **John v Rees** [1969] 2 274, Ch D.

Disorder—

Constituency Labour Party—Powers of chairman to adjourn—Grounds for and length of adjournment. **John v Rees** [1969] 2 274, Ch D.

Membership in dispute—

Injunction. *See* **Injunction** (Interlocutory—Injunction having effect of granting sole relief claimed in action—Unincorporated association—Membership in dispute).

Rateable occupation of premises. *See* **Rates** (Rateable occupation—Occupation by unincorporated association).

Requirements of unincorporated association—

Political party constituted by members of local constituency associations and both Houses of Parliament—

Funds raised by party treasurers held by party's central office which provided administrative services to party—Expenditure of funds under control of party leader—Party leader providing link between members of party—Rules for selection of party leader not subject to amendment—Whether rules for selection of party leader constituting contract between members of party—Whether party an unincorporated association—Whether central office holding income from funds on behalf of an unincorporated association—Whether central office liable to corporation tax on income from funds—Income and Corporation Taxes Act 1970, s 526(5). **Conservative and Unionist Central Office v Burrell (Inspector of Taxes)** [1982] 2 1, CA.

Resignation of member—

Resignation by conduct—

Failure to pay subscription over number of years—No provision in rules for resignation—Provision for formal exclusion on failure to pay subscriptions—Member not formally excluded under rules—Member's right to resign not dependent on acceptance by society—Whether conduct of member amounting to tacit resignation. **Sick and Funeral Society of St John's Sunday School, Golcar, Re** [1972] 2 439, Ch D.

Rules—

Amendment—

Power to make alterations where no power to alter contained in rules. **Tobacco Trade Benevolent Association, Re** [1958] 3 353, Ch D.

Construction—

International athletics association—Members consisting of national associations controlling athletics in their 'countries'—Rules providing that jurisdiction of member limited to political boundaries of 'country' it represented—Association controlling athletics in mainland China elected—Subsequently association controlling athletics on island of Taiwan elected—Taiwan not recognised as separate state under international law and treated as province of Republic of China—Taiwan remaining member of international association for 22 years—International association resolving to recognise mainland association as sole body controlling athletics on mainland and in Taiwan—Resolution in effect expelling Taiwan association from international association—Taiwan association claiming declarations that decision invalid and that it remained a member of the international association—Whether 'country' in rules meaning a nation recognised in international law—Whether resolution purporting to expel Taiwan association ultra vires. **Reel v Holder** [1981] 3 321, CA.

Exclusion of jurisdiction of court—

Public policy. *See* **Contract** (Illegality—Public policy—Jurisdiction of court—Exclusion—Unincorporated body—Interpretation of rules).

National Executive Committee of Labour Party—

Power to suspend constituency officers and committees—Rules conferring on committee duty to keep in active operation constituency party—Rules also conferring on committee power to take such action as necessary to enforce rules by way of expulsion of individual or otherwise—Committee suspending constituency officers and committees pending enquiry and appointing national agent in their place—Whether ultra vires. **Lewis v Heffer** [1978] 3 354, CA.

Status—

Separate entity—

Landlord's opposition to grant of new tenancy—Landlord and Tenant Act 1954, s 30(1)(g). **Willis v Association of Universities of the British Commonwealth** [1964] 2 39, CA.

Tenants' association—

Applications for determination of fair rents on behalf of members. *See* **Rent restriction** (Fair rent—Application for determination—Application by unincorporated tenants' association).

Trade name—

Passing off. *See* **Passing off** (Trade name—Unincorporated association).

Trust for benefit of association—

Non-charitable association—

Enforceability of trust. *See* **Trust and trustee** (Purpose—Enforceability—Trust for benefit of unincorporated non-charitable association).

UNINCORPORATED ASSOCIATION (cont)—
Undue influence—
Whether claim based on presumption of undue influence can be raised against unincorporated association. See **Equity** (Undue influence—Presumption of undue influence—Unincorporated association).
Value added tax. See **Value added tax** (Club or association).
Vicarious liability—
Sexual abuse. See **Vicarious liability** (Non-employment relationship—Unincorporated association—Vicarious liability for sexual abuse).

UNION
Students'—
Educational purposes—
Generally. See **Charity** (Education—Educational purposes—Students' union).
Trade union. See **Trade union**.

UNIT TRUST
Accumulation—
Excessive period. See **Accumulation** (Excessive period—Unit trust).

UNITED KINGDOM
Admission to—
Commonwealth immigrant. See **Commonwealth immigrant** (Admission).
Citizenship. See **Citizenship** (United Kingdom citizenship).
Right of entry into—
Non-patrial. See **Immigration** (Leave to enter—Non-patrial—Right of entry).
Supreme Court. See **Supreme court** (Supreme Court of the United Kingdom).

UNITED KINGDOM PASSPORT
Meaning in Commonwealth Immigrants Act 1962. See **Commonwealth immigrant** (Commonwealth citizen other than person holding United Kingdom passport—United Kingdom passport).

UNITED NATIONS
Immigration—
Illegal entry or presence of refugee. See **Immigration** (Refugee—Illegal entry or presence—Provision of international convention protecting refugees from penalties for illegal entry or presence).
Peace-keeping force established pursuant to resolution of Security Council—
British contingents of United Nations Force—
Whether acting on behalf of Crown. **Nissan v A-G** [1969] **1** 629, HL.
Resolution—
Order in Council, to give effect to—
Criminal offence. See **Criminal law** (Offence created under power to make Order in Council giving effect to United Nations Resolution).
Sanctions—
Restriction of supply of arms without licence—
Criminal law. See **Criminal law** (Restricted goods—Arms trade—Supply of restricted goods without licence).
State obligations under United Nations Security Council Resolutions—
Human rights—
Right to liberty and security. See **Human rights** (Right to liberty and security).
Terrorism—
Sanctions. See **Terrorism** (Sanctions—Freezing of funds and economic resources—United Nations Resolutions requiring freezing of funds and economic resources of terrorists).

UNIVERSITY
Academic staff—
Dismissal—
Action for wrongful dismissal—Jurisdiction—Jurisdiction of court—Contract of service providing that dismissal only to be in accordance with university's charter, statutes, ordinances and regulations—Lecturer bringing action for wrongful dismissal—Lecturer alleging that dismissal wrongful because of failure to follow procedure set out in charter etc—Whether court having jurisdiction to hear action—Whether court entitled to construe charter etc—Whether construction of charter etc within exclusive jurisdiction of visitor of university. **Thomas v University of Bradford** [1987] **1** 834, HL.
Jurisdiction—Jurisdiction of court to grant judicial review of decision to dismiss member of academic staff—Lecturer appointed on terms that employment could be terminated by either party on three months' notice—Appointment subject to university statutes—Statutes providing that academic staff could be removed for good cause—Lecturer dismissed on ground of redundancy by three months' notice—Visitor deciding that dismissal within powers of university and refusing to intervene—Lecturer challenging visitor's decision by application for judicial review—Whether court having power to review visitor's decision as to construction of university's statutes—Whether lecturer's employment properly terminated. **Page v Hull University Visitor** [1993] **1** 97, HL.
Jurisdiction—Jurisdiction of court—Dispute between university and members of academic staff concerning proposals to dismiss staff for redundancy—Statutes of university making no provision for dismissal for redundancy—Lecturers seeking to restrain university from proceeding with proposals—Whether court having jurisdiction to hear internal university dispute—Whether jurisdiction of visitor of university over internal disputes ousted in respect of employment disputes—Education Reform Act 1988, s 206(1), (2). **Pearce v University of Aston in Birmingham (No 1)** [1991] **2** 461, CA.

UNIVERSITY (cont)—
  Academic staff (cont)—
    Dismissal (cont)—
      Jurisdiction—Jurisdiction of visitor—College initiating disciplinary procedure to dismiss professor—University initiating procedure to deprive professor of title and status—Professor claiming declaration of wrongful dismissal based on general law of contract or tort—Whether court having jurisdiction to deal with dispute—Whether dispute entirely domestic—Whether dispute subject to exclusive jurisdiction of college and university visitors. **Hines v Birkbeck College** [1985] **3** 156, Ch D.
      Jurisdiction—Jurisdiction of visitor—Contract of service providing that dismissal only to be in accordance with university's statutes, ordinances and regulations for good cause—Complainant alleging wrongful dismissal because no good cause shown for dismissal and procedural requirements not followed—Complainant having acquiesced in departure from correct procedure—Whether good cause shown for dismissal—Whether complainant having waived right to insist on correct procedure—Whether procedural irregularities vitiating decision to remove complainant from academic staff. **Thomas v University of Bradford (No 2)** [1992] **1** 964, Visitor.
      Jurisdiction—Jurisdiction of visitor—Member of college—Professor dismissed from college teaching duties—Whether jurisdiction of college visitor extending beyond corporators—Whether professor a member of college—Whether professor subject to jurisdiction of visitor. **Hines v Birkbeck College** [1985] **3** 156, Ch D.
      Jurisdiction—Withdrawal of title and status—Whether college and university entitled to refer to visitor disputes relating to termination of appointment or employment of academic staff—Education Reform Act 1988, s 206. **Hines v Birkbeck College (No 2)** [1991] **4** 450, CA.
      Redundancy—University proposing to dismiss members of academic staff for redundancy—Statutes of university providing for dismissal of academic staff for good cause—Statutes making no provision for dismissal for redundancy—Academic staff appointed under contracts incorporating provision allowing dismissal for good cause only—University's redundancy proposals in breach of contracts of employment—Whether university having power to breach contract of employment without terminating academic staff member's rights as member and office-holder of university. **Pearce v University of Aston in Birmingham (No 2)** [1991] **2** 469, Visitor.
  Buildings and land—
    Value added tax. *See* **Value added tax** (Exemptions—Buildings and land—Election to waive exemption—College building library).
  Characteristics. *See* What constitutes a university, *below.*
  Charity—
    Educational purposes. *See* **Charity** (Education—Educational purposes—Students' union).
    Exemption from death duty—
      New South Wales. *See* **New South Wales** (Death duty—Dutiable estate—Exemption—Gift of residuary estate to educational institution).
  Examination—
    Conferring of degrees—
      Complaint by member of university—Jurisdiction of High Court to hear complaint—Matter one for visitor of university. **Thorne v University of London** [1966] **2** 338, CA.
  Fees—
    Non-EEC Nationals—
      Racial discrimination. *See* **Race relations** (Unlawful discrimination—Racial group—Non-EEC nationals—University fees).
    Rate of fees—
      Fees for overseas students higher than fees for home students—Cypriot national resident in United Kingdom solely for educational purposes—Enrolment at college as overseas student not 'ordinarily resident' in EEC and fees paid at overseas students rate—'Ordinarily resident' subsequently shown to include residence for educational purposes only—Whether student liable to pay fees to college at overseas students rate or home students rate—Whether student entitled to refund. **Orphanos v Queen Mary College** [1985] **2** 233, HL.
  Freedom of speech—
    Duty to ensure freedom of speech—
      Student meeting on university premises—Permission to hold meeting withheld because of risk of public disorder in neighbourhood of university—Whether university authorities entitled to take into account possibility of unrest outside university precincts when refusing permission to hold meeting within university—Education (No 2) Act 1986, s 43. **R v University of Liverpool, ex p Caesar-Gordon** [1990] **3** 821, QBD.
  Grant for study—
    European Community—
      Citizenship. *See* **European Union** (Citizenship—Person holding nationality of a member state—Freedom to reside and move freely within territory of member states—German nationals applying for grants for studies at universities outside Germany).
    Local authority grant—
      Eligibility—Student entitled to grant from local authority for university study if ordinarily resident in United Kingdom for three years—Ordinarily resident—Education Act 1962, s 1—Local Education Authority Awards Regulations 1979 (SI 1979 No 889), reg 13(a). **Cicutti v Suffolk CC** [1980] **3** 689, Ch D; **Shah v Barnet London BC** [1983] **1** 226, HL.
      Eligibility—Student entitled to grant from local authority for university study if ordinarily resident in United Kingdom for three years—Student to be treated as ordinarily resident if absence from United Kingdom solely due to parent's temporary employment overseas—Applicant living in Hong Kong for 13 years because her father was employed there for that period—Whether exclusive employment overseas for 13 years constituting temporary employment—Whether applicant to be treated as ordinarily resident in United Kingdom—Education Act 1962, s 1(1)—Education (Mandatory Awards) Regulations 1983, reg 5(4). **R v Lancashire CC, ex p Huddleston** [1986] **2** 941, CA.

UNIVERSITY (cont)—

Membership of university—

Dispute as to membership—

Visitor's jurisdiction. *See* **Corporation** (Visitor—Jurisdiction—Dispute as to membership of corporation—University).

Modern university—

Visitor. *See* Visitor—Modern university, *below*.

Officer—

Refusal to perform duty imposed by university statutes—

Mandamus—Application for order directed to chairman of convocation—Alleged refusal to perform duty imposed by university statutes—Matter for visitor of university—Refusal to re-employ teacher in school. **R v Dunsheath, ex p Meredith** [1950] **2** 741, KBD.

Residence—

Voting at Parliamentary elections. *See* **Elections** (Parliamentary—Qualification to vote—Residence—Residence on qualifying date—University students in halls of residence or colleges on qualifying date).

Sport—

Charity—

Promotion and encouragement of sport—Trust to promote association football in schools and universities. *See* **Charity** (Education—Educational purposes—Sport—Promotion and encouragement of sport—Trust to promote, encourage and provide facilities for pupils of schools and universities to play association football and other games).

Student—

Grant for study. *See* Grant for study, *above*.

Higher education corporation—

Claimant studying at new university created by statute—University being a higher education corporation and amenable to judicial review—Claimant disputing examination mark and bringing action for breach of contract outside period for bringing judicial review proceedings—Whether contractual dispute between student and higher education corporation justiciable—Whether contractual claim an abuse of process. **Clark v University of Lincolnshire and Humberside** [2000] **3** 752, CA.

Loan. *See* **Education** (Higher education—Student loans).

Natural justice—

Student sent down for failing examination. *See* **Natural justice** (Educational establishment—Dismissal of student—Duty to hear parties etc—University—Student sent down for failing examination).

Residence—

Voting at Parliamentary elections. *See* **Elections** (Parliamentary—Qualification to vote—Residence—Residence on qualifying date—University students in halls of residence or colleges on qualifying date).

Students' union—

Charity—

Educational purposes. *See* **Charity** (Education—Educational purposes—Students' union—University).

Trust—

Scheme for administering university or college trusts—

Alteration of beneficial interests—Fund held on trust to pay moiety of income for benefit of each of two beneficiaries—College trustee of fund and one of beneficiaries—College making statutory scheme to amalgamate for purpose of investment and administration trusts of which it was trustee—College dividing trust fund into two moieties—One moiety included in scheme and one excluded—College receiving income of included moiety and other beneficiary income of excluded moiety—Whether college having power to make division—Whether division of trust fund into moieties constituting alteration of beneficial interests—Whether college entitled to divide fund into a number of distinct trusts having separate endowments—Universities and Colleges (Trusts) Act 1943, s 2(1)(a), (b). **Freeston's Charity, Re** [1978] **1** 481, Ch D; [1979] **1** 51, CA.

Power to provide for incidental, consequential and supplementary matters—Alteration of beneficial interests—Fund held on trust to pay moiety of income for benefit of each of two beneficiaries—College trustee of fund and one of beneficiaries—College making statutory scheme to amalgamate for purposes of investment and administration trusts of which it was trustee—College dividing trust fund into two moieties—One moiety included in scheme and one excluded—College receiving income of included moiety and other beneficiary income of excluded moiety—Appropriation of trust fund into moieties constituting alteration of beneficial interests—Whether appropriation a matter which was 'incidental, consequential [or] supplementary' to scheme—Whether college having power to make appropriation—Universities and Colleges (Trusts) Act 1943, s 2(1)(k). **Freeston's Charity, Re** [1978] **1** 481, Ch D.

Vice-Chancellor—

Power to suspend students—

Duty to act judicially. *See* **Natural justice** (Educational establishment—Suspension of student—Duty to hear parties etc).

Visitor—

Jurisdiction—

Domestic disputes—Dismissal of academic staff. *See* Academic staff—Dismissal—Jurisdiction—Jurisdiction of visitor, *above*.

Domestic disputes—Undergraduate sent down for failing examinations—Undergraduate bringing action for breach of contract and natural justice—Whether undergraduate a member of college—Whether visitor a general or special visitor—Whether dispute subject to exclusive jurisdiction of visitor. **Oakes v Sidney Sussex College, Cambridge** [1988] **1** 1004, Ch D.

Modern university. *See* Visitor—Modern university—Jurisdiction of visitor, *below*.

UNIVERSITY (cont)—
 Visitor (cont)—
  Jurisdiction (cont)—
   Refusal by university to award degree—Academic staff appointing examiners to assess thesis—Applicant claiming examiners not qualified to assess thesis—Applicant petitioning visitor—Visitor refusing to intervene—Visitor concluding that prescribed procedures for appointing examiners had been followed and that choice of examiners involving exercise of expert academic judgment with which visitor should not interfere—Whether visitor's decision wrong in law—Whether court's jurisdiction over visitor supervisory or appellate—Whether court can interfere with visitor's exercise of discretion or judgment or confined to correcting errors of law. **R v University of London Visitor, ex p Vijayatunga** [1989] **2** 843, CA.
  Modern university—
   Charter establishing university providing for appointment of visitor by crown—No appointment made—Whether university having a visitor—Whether visitatorial powers exercisable by Lord Chancellor on behalf of Crown in absence of appointment. **Patel v University of Bradford Senate** [1979] **2** 582, CA.
   Jurisdiction of visitor—Contract—Petitioner applying for and offered place to study particular course—Petitioner accepting offer—University unable to mount course and offering petitioner place in alternative course—Petitioner accepting new offer and admitted to university to study alternative course—Petitioner seeking damages for breach of contract—Petitioner alleging university withdrew original offer in breach of contract—Whether visitor having jurisdiction to hear petition alleging breach of contract by university—Whether visitor having jurisdiction to hear petition from stranger to university—Whether petition misconceived. **Casson v University of Aston in Birmingham** [1983] **1** 88, Visitor.
 What constitutes a university—
  College incorporated by royal charter—
   College at outset theological college—Further degree subjects added—Whether college a 'university'. **St David's College, Lampeter v Ministry of Education** [1951] **1** 559, Ch D.
  Qualities and attributes—
   College incorporated by royal charter with limited right to confer degrees—Whether a 'university'. **St David's College, Lampeter v Ministry of Education** [1951] **1** 559, Ch D.

UNJUST ENRICHMENT
 Breach of contract. *See* **Contract** (Breach—Causation—Breach of duty—Unjust enrichment).
 Company—
  Winding up—
   Distribution of assets. *See* **Company** (Winding up—Power to exclude creditors not proving in time—Exclusion of creditor from benefit of distribution of assets—Unjust enrichment).
 Restitution. *See* **Restitution** (Unjust enrichment).
 Subrogation—
  Circumstances in which doctrine applicable. *See* **Subrogation** (Circumstances in which doctrine applicable—Unjust enrichment).
 Unpaid vendor's lien. *See* **Restitution** (Unjust enrichment—Subrogation—Unpaid vendor's lien).

UNLADEN WEIGHT
 Motor vehicle. *See* **Road traffic** (Motor vehicle—Unladen weight).

UNLAWFUL ARREST
 See **Arrest** (Unlawful arrest).

UNLAWFUL ASSEMBLY
 See **Criminal law** (Unlawful assembly).

UNLAWFUL DISCRIMINATION
 Race relations. *See* **Race relations** (Unlawful discrimination).

UNLAWFUL EVICTION OF TENANT
 See **Landlord and tenant** (Eviction—Unlawful eviction of tenant).

UNLAWFUL FIGHTING
 Affray. *See* **Criminal law** (Affray—Unlawful fighting).

UNLAWFUL KILLING
 Standard of proof—
  Coroner's inquest. *See* **Coroner** (Inquest—Verdict—Unlawful killing—Standard of proof).

UNLAWFUL POSSESSION
 Cannabinol derivative. *See* **Drugs** (Dangerous drugs—Cannabinol derivative—Unlawful possession).
 Dangerous drugs. *See* **Drugs** (Dangerous drugs—Unlawful possession).

UNLICENSED VEHICLES
 See **Road traffic** (Excise licence—Unlicensed vehicle).

UNLIGHTED VEHICLE
 Highway—
  Negligence. *See* **Negligence** (Highway—Unlighted vehicle).

UNLIMITED COMPANY
 Stamp duty—
  Relief—
   Reconstruction or amalgamation of companies—Acquisition of shares in unlimited company. *See* **Stamp duty** (Reconstruction or amalgamation of companies—Acquisition of shares in existing company—Particular existing company—Existing company an unlimited company).

UNLIQUIDATED DAMAGES
Interest. *See* **Interest** (Damages—Unliquidated damages).

UNLOADING
Dock, in—
> Statutory regulation. *See* **Dock** (Loading and unloading).

Vehicle—
> Restrictions. *See* **Road traffic** (Waiting and loading restrictions).

UNMARRIED COUPLE
Child of unmarried couple—
> Financial relief. *See* **Minor** (Child of unmarried parents—Financial relief).

Constructive trust. *See* **Trust and trustee** (Constructive trust—Unmarried couple).

Injunction—
> Domestic violence—
>> Exclusion of party from home—County court—Man and woman living with each other. *See* **Injunction** (Exclusion of party from matrimonial home—County court—Man and woman who are living with each other in the same household as husband and wife).

Joint acquisition of property. *See* **Trust and trustee** (Constructive trust—Unmarried couple).

Licence to occupy premises. *See* **Licence** (Licence to occupy premises—Contractual licence—Unmarried couple).

Trust for sale—
> Family home—
>> Refusal of trustees to concur in sale. *See* **Trust and trustee** (Trust for sale—Refusal of trustees to concur in sale—Unmarried parties living as man and wife).

UNMARRIED GIRL
Abduction. *See* **Criminal law** (Abduction—Unmarried girl under 18).

UNNATURAL DEATH
Inquest. *See* **Coroner** (Inquest).

UNOCCUPIED PROPERTY
Rates. *See* **Rates** (Unoccupied property).

UNQUALIFIED PERSON
Costs—
> Recovery. *See* **Solicitor** (Costs—Recovery—Unqualified person).

Drafting of documents. *See* **Solicitor** (Unqualified person—Preparation of documents etc).

UNREGISTERED COMPANY
Administrative receiver. *See* **Company** (Receiver—Administrative receiver—Unregistered company).

Winding up by court. *See* **Company** (Compulsory winding up—Unregistered company).

UNSOLICITED PUBLICATIONS
Offences. *See* **Criminal law** (Unsolicited publications).

UNSWORN EVIDENCE
Child—
> Criminal proceedings. *See* **Criminal evidence** (Child—Unsworn evidence of child).

UNWANTED PREGNANCY
Negligence—
> Damages. *See* **Damages** (Unwanted pregnancy—Negligence).
> Hospital performing sterilisation operation on woman negligently—
>> Woman becoming pregnant and giving birth to child with behavioural difficulties—Whether damages recoverable for cost of rearing disabled child conceived as a result of negligently-performed sterilisation—Whether damages limited to costs of special needs and care attributable to child's disabilities. **Parkinson v St James and Seacroft University Hospital NHS Trust** [2001] 3 97, CA.

Personal injury—
> Damages. *See* **Damages** (Personal injury—Unwanted pregnancy).

URINE
Specimen—
> Determination of driver's blood-alcohol proportion. *See* **Road traffic** (Specimen for laboratory test to determine driver's blood-alcohol proportion—Specimen of blood or urine).
> Driving while unfit to drive through drink or drugs. *See* **Road traffic** (Driving while unfit to drive through drink or drugs).

USER OF PREMISES
Covenant in lease. *See* **Landlord and tenant** (Covenant—User of premises).

UTTERING FORGED DOCUMENT
See **Criminal law** (Forgery—Uttering a forged document).

VACANT POSSESSION

Condition of contract for sale of land. *See* **Sale of land** (Condition—Condition to which effect not given by conveyance but capable of taking effect after completion—Condition requiring vacant possession on completion).

Sale of land. *See* **Sale of land** (Vacant possession).

Specific performance—
Sale of land with vacant possession. *See* **Specific performance** (Sale of land—Sale with vacant possession).

VACATION COURT

Application for hearing by. *See* **Practice** (Long Vacation—Hearing during vacation).

VAGRANCY

See **Criminal law** (Vagrancy).

VALIDATION

Charitable trust. *See* **Charity** (Validation by statute).

VALUABLE SECURITY

Forgery. *See* **Criminal law** (Forgery—Valuable security).

Procuring execution of valuable security by deception. *See* **Criminal law** (Procuring execution of valuable security by deception).

VALUATION

Administration of estates—
Valuation of estate. *See* **Administration of estates** (Completion of administration—Valuation).

Annuity—
Estate insufficient. *See* **Administration of estates** (Annuity—Estate insufficient—Valuation of annuity).

Appeal—
Income tax—
Valuation of land. *See* **Income tax** (Appeal—Valuation of land).

Capital gains tax. *See* **Capital gains tax** (Assets—Valuation).

Compulsory purchase of land—
Compensation—
Assessment. *See* **Compulsory purchase** (Compensation—Assessment).

Purchase notice—Assumptions on valuation. *See* **Compulsory purchase** (Compensation—Purchase notice—Assumptions on valuation).

Customs—
Valuation of imported goods for purposes of duty. *See* **Customs and excise** (Duties—Valuation of goods for purposes of duty).

Damages—
Mortgagee—
Power of sale—Failure to realise full market price—Evidence of full market value—Enquiry as to damages. *See* **Damages** (Assessment—Enquiry as to damages—Property valuation—Negligence—Exercise of power of sale by mortgagee—Mortgagee negligent in failing to realise market value of property).

Estate duty. *See* **Estate duty** (Valuation).

Hereditament—
Annual value—
Drainage rates. *See* **Land drainage** (Drainage rates—Annual value of hereditament—Valuation).

Improvement—
Leasehold enfranchisement. *See* **Landlord and tenant** (Leasehold enfranchisement—Valuation—Improvement).

Income tax—
Stock-in-trade—
Computation of profits. *See* **Income tax** (Computation of profits—Stock-in-trade—Valuation).

Valuation of property—
Additional assessment. *See* **Income tax** (Additional assessment—Valuation of property).

Land—
Annual value for income tax. *See* **Income tax** (Land—Annual value—Valuation of property).

Compulsory purchase—
Compensation. *See* **Compulsory purchase** (Compensation—Assessment).

Measure of damages for injury to land—
Cost of reinstatement or diminution in market value. *See* **Damages** (Land—Measure of damages for injury to land—Cost of reinstatement of diminution in market value).

Leasehold enfranchisement. *See* **Landlord and tenant** (Leasehold enfranchisement—Valuation).

Matrimonial home—
Intestacy—
Right of surviving spouse to acquire home—Valuation of home. *See* **Intestacy** (Appropriation by personal representatives—Surviving spouse—Matrimonial home—Valuation).

Negligence—
Damages—
Measure of damages. *See* **Damages** (Measure of damages—Negligence—Valuer).

Opening stock—
Income tax—
Computation of profits. *See* **Income tax** (Computation of profits—Opening stock—Valuation).

Option—
Purchase—
Option to purchase realty at reasonable valuation. *See* **Will** (Option—Option to purchase realty—Option to purchase at reasonable valuation).

VALUATION (cont)—
Painting—
  Negligence—
    Auctioneer. *See* **Negligence** (Duty to take care—Auctioneer—Valuation of painting).
Partnership property. *See* **Partnership** (Partnership property—Valuation).
Probate valuation—
  Will—
    'Valuation agreed for probate'. *See* **Will** (Valuation of effects—Probate valuation).
Rates—
  Valuation list. *See* **Rates** (Valuation list).
Rating—
  Agricultural worker's cottage. *See* **Agriculture** (Rating—Valuation).
  Generally. *See* **Rates** (Valuation).
  Valuation list. *See* **Rates** (Valuation list).
Reversion—
  Landlord and tenant—
    Option to purchase reversion. *See* **Landlord and tenant** (Lease—Reversion—Option granted to tenant to purchase freehold reversion—Purchase price—Valuation).
Shares—
  Capital gains tax. *See* **Capital gains tax** (Assets—Valuation—Market value—Shares).
  Generally. *See* **Company** (Shares—Valuation).
Stock—
  Income tax—
    Computation of profits—Accountancy principles. *See* **Income tax** (Computation of profits—Accountancy principles—Stock).
Stock-in-trade—
  Income tax—
    Computation of profits. *See* **Income tax** (Computation of profits—Stock-in-trade—Valuation).
Trade debts—
  Income tax—
    Computation of profits. *See* **Income tax** (Computation of profits—Trade debts—Valuation).
Trust—
  Constructive trust—
    Joint tenants—Valuation of beneficial interests held under constructive trust. *See* **Trust and trustee** (Constructive trust—Joint tenants—Extent of beneficial interests held under constructive trust—Valuation).
  Trust for sale—
    Realty. *See* **Trust and trustee** (Trust for sale—Realty—Valuation).
Valuer. *See* **Valuer.**
Will—
  Valuation of effects. *See* **Will** (Valuation of effects).

VALUATION LIST
Proposal for alteration of current valuation list—
  Rates. *See* **Rates** (Proposal for alteration of current valuation list).
Rates. *See* **Rates** (Valuation list).

VALUE ADDED TAX
Appeal—
  Abuse of process—
    HMRC refusing input tax claims on basis taxpayer knew or ought to have known that transactions connected with fraud—Taxpayer's appeal struck out following repeated failure to comply with directions—HMRC subsequently imposing penalties on taxpayer—Taxpayer appealing—Whether grounds of appeal including issues raised on earlier appeal—Whether abuse of process—Human Rights Act 1998, Sch 1, Pt I, art 6. **Revenue and Customs Comrs v Kishore** [2022] 2 90, CA.
  Appeal against assessment in default of proper returns by taxpayer. *See* Assessment in default of proper returns by taxpayer—Sum assessed deemed to be amount of tax due from him—Appeal against assessment, *below.*
  Decision depending on prior decision—
    Taxpayer raising legitimate expectation issue before tribunal—Whether relevant 'prior decision'—Whether tribunal having jurisdiction to determine issue—Value Added Tax Act 1994, s 84(10). **Metropolitan International Schools Ltd v Revenue and Customs Comrs** [2019] 2 907, CA.
Assessment—
  Tour operator's margin scheme—
    Output tax—Taxable person supplying hotel and other holiday accommodation to travel agents and holiday makers—Transactions carried out by travel agents—Special scheme applying to transactions carried out by travel agents dealing with customers in their own name—Special scheme not applying to travel agents acting solely as intermediaries—Value Added Tax (Tour Operators) Order 1987, SI 1987/1806—Council Directive (EC) 2006/112, art 306. **Secret Hotels2 Ltd (formerly Med Hotels Ltd) v Revenue and Customs Comrs** [2014] 2 685, SC.
Assessment in default of proper returns by taxpayer—
  Assessment of tax for period of 21 months in a single amount—
    Whether assessment required to be restricted to 'a prescribed accounting period' of three months—Whether assessment valid—Finance Act 1972, s 31. **Grange (S J) Ltd v Customs and Excise Comrs** [1979] 2 91, QBD and CA.
  Sum assessed deemed to be amount of tax due from him—
    Appeal against assessment—Taxpayer a licensee of a public house—Assessment for period of three years based on material made available by taxpayer and on takings for a test period of five weeks—Commissioners not taking account of pilferage—Whether commissioners' assessment 'to the best of their judgment'—Finance Act 1972, s 31(1). **Van Boeckel v Customs and Excise Comrs** [1981] 2 505, QBD.

VALUE ADDED TAX (cont)—
Assessment in default of proper returns by taxpayer (cont)—
Sum assessed deemed to be amount of tax due from him (cont)—
Sum recoverable as debt due to Crown—Defence to action by Crown—Right of taxpayer to raise defence that sum not in fact due—Taxpayer failing to make any returns—Crown assessing amount of tax due to best of their judgment—Crown bringing action to recover amount assessed as debt due—Taxpayer raising defence that sum not in fact due—Whether taxpayer could challenge assessment when sued for tax assessed—Finance Act 1972, ss 31(1), (6), 33(1). **Customs and Excise Comrs v Holvey** [1978] **1** 1249, QBD.
Bad debt relief—
Creditor obtaining bad debt relief by way of refund of value added tax—
Liquidation of company producing surplus—Whether Customs and Excise Commissioners entitled to recoup out of surplus amount of value added tax refunded to creditor—Whether commissioners subrogated to rights of creditor—Finance Act 1978, s 12. **T H Knitwear (Wholesale) Ltd, Re** [1988] **1** 860, CA.
Charity—
Zero-rating for building works. *See* Zero-rating—Building works, *below*.
Club or association—
Supply of services for consideration—
Subscription from members constituting consideration—Services supplied by association—Members entitled under rules to individual benefits and advantages provided by association—Whether subscription consideration for bare right of membership or for individual benefits provided to members—Whether association entitled to claim exemption or zero-rating in respect of part of subscription attributable to services ranking as exempt or zero-rated—Finance Act 1972, ss 2(2), 5(2), (8), 45(1). **Barton v Customs and Excise Comrs** [1974] **3** 337, QBD; **Customs and Excise Comrs v Automobile Association** [1974] **1** 1257, QBD.
Test for determining whether unincorporated body making taxable supplies to members—Value Added Tax Act 1994, s 94(2)(a). **Eastbourne Town Radio Cars Association v Customs and Excise Comrs** [2001] **2** 597, HL.
Company—
Winding up—
Preferential payment. *See* **Company** (Winding up—Preferential payments—Taxes—Value added tax).
Costs—
Taxation. *See* **Costs** (Taxation—Value added tax).
European Union. *See* **European Union** (Value added tax).
European Union law—
State liability. *See* **European Union** (State liability—Infringement of European Union law attributable to state—Damage caused to individuals by infringements of European Union law—Breach of European Union law and state constitution—Rectification of self-assessment of value added tax).
Exemptions—
Betting, gaming and lotteries—
Games of chance—'Spot the Ball'—Whether rule or presumption existing about inter-player participation in 'game'—Whether Spot the Ball a game of chance—Whether exempt—Gaming Act 1968, s 52—Value Added Tax Act 1994, Sch 9, Group 4, item 1. **IFX Investment Co Ltd v Revenue and Customs Comrs** [2017] **1** 45, CA.
Games of chance—Taxpayer operating slot machines—Machines computerised with results generated by a random number generator embedded within software—Single random number generator connected to and serving number of playing terminals—Whether machines falling within games of chance exemption—Whether gaming machines—Whether element of chance provided by means of the machine—Value Added Tax Act 1994, Sch 9, Group 4, item 1, note (3)—Gaming Act 1968, s 26. **Revenue and Customs Comrs v Rank Group plc** [2015] **4** 77, SC.
Buildings and land—
Election to waive exemption—Agricultural tenancy—Rent—Landlord opting to add value added tax to rent—Tenant failing to pay rent due—Landlord serving notice to pay full amount outstanding—Sum on notice to pay including value added tax as part of rent due—Landlord subsequently issuing notice to quit—Whether notice to pay valid notice—Whether value added tax element part of rent—Agricultural Holdings Act 1986, Sch 3, Case D—Value Added Tax Act 1994, Sch 10, para 2. **Mason v Boscawen** [2009] **1** 1006, Ch D.
Election to waive exemption—College building library—College granting lease of library to company controlled by college—College selling assets of library to company and hiring assets back, seconding library staff to company and transferring management of library to company—Whether college entitled to elect to waive exemption—Whether college remaining in occupation after grant of lease to company—Value Added Tax Act 1994, Sch 10, paras 2(3AA), 3A(7). **Revenue and Customs Comrs v Newnham College, Cambridge** [2008] **2** 863, HL.
Education—
College providing courses by distance learning through printed materials and personal tuition—Whether supply of printed materials separate from supply of educational services—Value Added Tax Act 1994, Sch 9, Group 6, item 4. **College of Estate Management v Customs and Excise Comrs** [2005] **4** 933, HL.
Eligible body—Taxpayer institution providing certain educational services in relation to courses in accordance with arrangements made by taxpayer with University of Wales—Taxpayer claiming such educational services exempt from VAT—Whether provider of university courses entitled under EU law to VAT exemption even if not so entitled under domestic law—Value Added Tax Act 1994, Sch 9, Group 6, note (1)(b)—Council Directive 2006/112/EC, arts 131, 132. **Finance and Business Training Ltd v Revenue and Customs Comrs** [2017] **1** 758, CA.
Provision of education otherwise than for profit—Charitable company providing educational courses—Company charging such fees as would achieve surplus income in order to maintain and improve facilities offered—Company required to apply income and property solely to its objects and prohibited from paying profits to its members—Whether company providing education 'otherwise than for profit'—Value Added Tax Act 1983, Sch 6, Group 6, item 2(a)—Council Directive (EEC) 77/388, art 13(A)(1)(i), (2)(a). **Customs and Excise Comrs v Bell Concord Educational Trust Ltd** [1989] **2** 217, CA.

1439

VALUE ADDED TAX (cont)—
Exemptions (cont)—
Education (cont)—
Taxpayer making supplies of educational courses in partnership with university—Whether taxpayer a 'college ... of ... a university'—Whether supplies exempt—Value Added Tax Act 1994, Sch 9, Group 6, item 1, note (1)(b). **SAE Education Ltd v Revenue and Customs Comrs** [2019] **3** 934, SC.

Financial services—
Making arrangements for certain transactions—Arrangements for making of advance—Arrangements involving issue, transfer or receipt of a security not exempt—Money brokers making arrangements for an advance on behalf of bank—Second bank agreeing to advance money on condition first bank issued certificate of deposit—Brokers acting on behalf of both banks and receiving commission from both banks—Separate services to each bank—Whether services to two banks to be treated as a whole as relating to single transaction—Whether services exempt in whole or in part as consisting of making arrangements for the 'making of any advance'—Whether services taxable as consisting of making arrangements for the 'issue, transfer or receipt of any security'—Finance Act 1972, s 13(1), Sch 5, Group 5, items 2, 3, 4. **Customs and Excise Comrs v Guy Butler (International) Ltd** [1976] **2** 700, CA.

Grant of right over or licence to occupy land—
Agreement between airport authority and concessionaires—Concessionaires granted right to display and sell goods from shop premises in airport—Whether agreement conferring on concessionaires separate rights to occupy land and to sell and display merchandise—Whether whole consideration exempt for grant of right over or licence to occupy land—Finance Act 1972, Sch 5, Group 1, item 1. **British Airports Authority v Customs and Excise Comrs** [1977] **1** 497, CA.

Exclusion for provision in an hotel or similar establishment of sleeping accommodation—Taxpayer selling fractional interests in residences in property—Purchasers granted access to certain occupancy rights and various programmes in exchange for purchase price—Whether supply exempt—Whether provision of accommodation in similar establishment to hotel—Value Added Tax Act 1994, Sch 9, Group 1, item 1. **Fortyseven Park Street Ltd v Revenue and Customs Comrs** [2019] **4** 1119, CA.

Members' club—Subscriptions—Club owning land and providing facilities for sport and recreation—Right of members to share in proceeds on dissolution of club—Members paying annual subscriptions for facilities—Whether subscriptions paid for the grant of an interest in or right over land—Whether members having a licence to occupy land—Whether subscriptions exempt—Finance Act 1972, ss 13(1), 45(1)(b), Sch 5, Group I, item 1 (as substituted by the Value Added Tax (Consolidation) Order 1974 (SI 1974 No 1146)). **Trewby (on behalf of himself and the members of Hurlingham Club) v Customs and Excise Comrs** [1976] **2** 199, QBD.

Insurance—
Provision of insurance of any description—Meaning of 'provision of insurance'—Whether limited to the provision of insurance cover—Whether including the settling of claims—Finance Act 1972, Sch 5, Group 2, item 1. **National Transit Insurance Co Ltd v Customs and Excise Comrs** [1975] **1** 303, QBD.

Statutory provision requiring preparation of document setting out every 'amount' to be paid by customer in connection with transaction combining non-exempt services and exempt insurance-related services—Whether 'amount' meaning specific monetary figure rather than calculation from which amount could be ascertained—Valued Added Tax Act 1994, Sch 9, Group 2, Note (5)—Sixth Council Directive (EEC) 77/388, art 13B. **CR Smith Glaziers (Dunfermline) Ltd v Customs and Excise Comrs** [2003] **1** 801, HL.

Medical care—
European Community. *See* **European Union** (Value added tax—Exemptions—Medical care).

Medical practitioners providing pharmaceutical services to certain patients—Medical practitioners personally administering drugs to patients to whom they provided pharmaceutical services—Whether supply of drugs separate from supply of medical care—Value Added Tax Act 1994, Sch 9, Group 7, item 1(a)—National Health Service (Pharmaceutical Services) Regulations 1992, SI 1992/662, reg 20. **Beynon (Dr) and Partners v Customs and Excise Comrs** [2004] **4** 1091, HL.

Fraudulent trading—
Trading in European emissions trading scheme allowances—
Company buying allowances from companies outside European Union and selling them to United Kingdom companies—Purchases zero-rated but sales subject to value added tax at standard rate—Consideration for sales net of value added tax less than purchase prices—Purchase price paid directly or indirectly to non-European sellers—Non-European sellers alleged to have conspired with company's directors and United Kingdom purchasers to defraud company so that company unable to meet value added tax liability arising from trades in allowances—Company becoming insolvent—Non-European sellers applying to strike out claim—Whether company and liquidators prevented from bringing claim by application of maxim ex turpi causa non oritur actio—Whether insolvency proceedings to recover sum from knowing parties to fraudulent business having extra-territorial scope—Whether actions amounting to enforcement of revenue debt without jurisdiction of court—Whether claim should be struck out—Insolvency Act 1986, s 213. **Bilta (UK) Ltd (in liq) v Nazir** [2013] **1** 375, Ch D.

Higher rate—
Boats and aircraft—
Goods suitable for use as parts of boats or boat accessories—Suitable for—Items capable of being used as parts of boats or boat accessories—Items equally capable of being used for other purposes—Items not designed or adapted for use as parts of boats or boat accessories—Trailer couplings and winches—Whether couplings and winches 'goods of a kind suitable for use as parts of' trailers for carrying boats—Whether subject to tax at higher rate—Finance (No 2) Act 1975, Sch 7, Group 3, item 6. **Customs and Excise Comrs v Mechanical Services (Trailer Engineers) Ltd** [1979] **1** 501, CA.

VALUE ADDED TAX (cont)—
  Information—
    Commissioners' power to require information relating to supply of goods or services—
      Goods and documents seized under authority of Anton Piller orders—Solicitors undertaking to retain custody of seized goods and documents until further order—Commissioners' application to inspect seized goods and documents—Whether solicitors entitled to make goods and documents available to commissioners without court order—Finance Act 1972, s 35(2). **Customs and Excise Comrs v A E Hamlin & Co (a firm)** [1983] **3** 654, Ch D.
      Person in possession of another person's documents—Goods and documents seized under authority of Anton Piller orders—Solicitors undertaking to court not to use documents for collateral purpose—Whether commissioners having power to require production of documents—Whether solicitors could be required to make documents available to commissioners—Whether relevant that documents may be self-incriminating—Value Added Tax Act 1983, Sch 7, para 8(2)(3). **EMI Records Ltd v Spillane** [1986] **2** 1016, Ch D.
  Input tax—
    Adjustment of attribution of input tax—
      Intended taxable supplies—United Kingdom subsidiary of foreign bank providing services to bank's London branch—Subsidiary recovering input tax on inward supplies attributable to intended taxable supplies to branch—Branch becoming part of same value added tax group as subsidiary—Subsidiary issuing invoice for management services—Branch making exempt supplies—Whether supplies used to provide services to branch appropriated for use in making exempt supplies—Value Added Tax Act 1983, s 29—Value Added Tax (General) Regulations 1985, regs 23, 34. **Svenska International plc v Customs and Excise Comrs** [1999] **2** 906, HL.
    Claim for deduction of input tax—
      Abuse of rights—University entering into lease and leaseback agreement in respect of land—University opting to exercise statutory waiver in relation to VAT exemption for land leasing transactions and deducting input tax in relation to transactions—HMRC refusing University's right to deduct—Whether arrangements abusive. **University of Huddersfield Higher Education Corporation v Revenue and Customs Comrs** [2016] **4** 652, CA.
      Late claim for repayment of under-claimed input tax—Time limit—Transitional provisions—Principle of effectiveness—Time limit for claim for repayment of under-claimed input tax introduced without transitional provisions—After time limit introduced taxable person making claim for repayment for period earlier than time limit—Whether time limit to be disapplied for transitional period—Value Added Tax Regulations 1995, SI 1995/2518, reg 29(1A). **Fleming (t/a Bodycraft) v Revenue and Customs Comrs** [2008] **1** 1061, HL.
      Tax on supply to a taxable person of goods or services for purpose of business carried on by him—Taxpayer purchasing single farm payment entitlement units—Taxpayer claiming entitlement to repayment of VAT charged on those units—Whether taxpayer able to deduct as input tax VAT incurred in purchasing single farm payment entitlement units. **Frank A Smart & Son Ltd v Revenue and Customs Comrs** [2020] **1** 97, SC.
    Claim for repayment of input tax—
      Taxpayer using postal services on which VAT not charged—Subsequent ruling of European Court of Justice establishing that postal services should have been subject to VAT—Taxpayer making claim for input tax—Whether VAT due or paid—Whether in absence of VAT invoice HMRC should have exercised discretion to allow input tax claim—Value Added Tax Regulations 1995, SI 1995/2518, reg 29—Council Directive 2006/112/EC, arts 168(a), 226. **Zipvit Ltd v Revenue and Customs Comrs** [2020] **3** 1017n, SC.
      Taxpayer using postal services on which VAT not charged—Subsequent ruling of European Court of Justice establishing that postal services should have been subject to VAT—Taxpayer making claim for input tax—Whether VAT 'due or paid' and therefore deductible—Council Directive 2006/112/EC, art 168(a). **Zipvit Ltd v Revenue and Customs Comrs** [2022] **4** 607, SC.
    Disallowance of input tax—
      Motor vehicles—Delivery charges on supply of new cars—Whether 'consideration' for supply of car included incidental expenses such as transport costs—Value Added Tax Act 1994, s 19(2)—Council Directive (EEC) 77/388, art 11A(2)(b). **Customs and Excise Comrs v British Telecommunications plc** [1999] **3** 961, HL.
      Professional costs—Accountants' fees—Company's creditors instructing accountants to prepare report on company's financial position—Company paying costs of preparation of report—Whether accountants' services supplied to company—Whether input tax on services deductible. **Revenue and Customs Comrs v Airtours Holidays Transport Ltd** [2016] **4** 1, SC.
    Tax on supply to a taxable person of goods or services for purpose of business carried on by him—
      Supply for purpose of business—Administration of pension funds for benefit of employees—Professional services supplied for purpose of administering funds—Tax paid on supply of professional services—Whether management of pension funds part of taxpayer's business—Whether professional services supplied for purpose of business—Finance Act 1972, s 3(1). **Customs and Excise Comrs v British Railways Board** [1976] **3** 100, .
      Supply for purpose of business—Taxpayer selling homes as its business—Taxpayer paying estate agents' fees of vendors who purchased their houses—Whether taxpayer could deduct input tax paid on estate agents' fees—Value Added Tax Act 1983, s 14(3)(a). **Customs and Excise Comrs v Redrow Group plc** [1999] **2** 1, HL.
  Limitation—
    Input tax, claim for deduction of. *See* Input tax—Claim for deduction of input tax—Late claim for repayment of under-claimed input tax, *above*.
  Overpayment of tax—
    Deduction of overpayment—
      Deduction of overpayment from subsequent payment of tax—Overpayment occurring because of taxpayer's compliance with directions issued by commissioners subsequently ruled to be invalid—Taxpayer deducting overpayment from subsequent payment of tax—Whether taxpayer entitled to deduct overpayment—Value Added Tax Act 1983, s 14—Value Added Tax (General) Regulations 1985, reg 58(1), Sch, Form 4. **Customs and Excise Comrs v Fine Art Developments plc** [1989] **1** 502, HL.

VALUE ADDED TAX (cont)—
  Overpayment of tax (cont)—
    Interest on repayment of overpaid tax—
      Compound interest—Disputed decision—Traders claiming interest in respect of overpaid tax—Revenue and Customs paying simple interest—Traders making claims for compound interest—Revenue and Customs refusing claim—Traders appealing—Whether appeals brought in time—Whether traders entitled to make successive claims for interest due in a single period—Value Added Tax Act 1994, s 78. **John Wilkins (Motor Engineers) Ltd v Revenue and Customs Comrs** [2011] **1** 339, CA.

      Compound interest—Tax overpaid in breach of claimants' directly effective Community law rights—Commissioners repaying tax overpaid with simple interest—Whether claimants entitled to compound interest—High Court ruling common law restitutionary claims excluded by statutory scheme—High Court referring questions of liability to ECJ—ECJ holding principle of effectiveness requiring national law for calculation of interest should not deprive taxpayer of adequate indemnity for loss occasioned through undue payment of tax—High Court and Court of Appeal ruling common law restitutionary claims excluded by statutory scheme—High Court and Court of Appeal ruling statutory scheme depriving taxpayer of adequate indemnity—Whether statutory scheme excluding common law claims—Whether exclusion contrary to EU law—Value Added Tax Act 1994, ss 78, 80. **Littlewoods Ltd v Revenue and Customs Comrs** [2018] **1** 83, SC.

    Repayment—
      Claim by end consumers of VAT on services subsequently held to be exempt—Whether claimants having right to restitution against HMRC of amounts wrongly paid—Whether any restitutionary claim barred by statute—Whether lack of claim contrary to EU law—Value Added Tax Act 1994, s 80. **Investment Trust Companies (in liq) v Revenue and Customs Comrs** [2017] **3** 113, SC.

      Person entitled to receive repayment—Representative member of VAT group transferring business to subsidiary—Subsidiary leaving group and later making claims for repayment of VAT overpaid by representative member—HMRC incorrectly paying representative member overpaid VAT claimed by former subsidiary—HMRC issuing assessments against representative member to recover sums wrongly paid—Application of statutory time bar—Whether timeous claim by former subsidiary entitling representative member to repayment—Value Added Tax Act 1994, ss 43, 80. **Taylor Clark Leisure plc v Revenue and Customs Comrs** [2018] **4** 817, SC.

      Person entitled to repayment—Group registration of companies—Representative member—Company making supply moving out of VAT group—Whether UK VAT group regime permissible under EU law—Whether UK regime applying San Giorgio principle in manner consistent with its purpose—Who having claim where relevant VAT group dissolved—Value Added Tax Act 1994, ss 43, 80, 80A—Council Directive 2006/112/EC, art 11. **Lloyds Banking Group plc v Revenue and Customs Comrs** [2020] **1** 1045, CA.

      Person paying amount by way of value added tax which was not tax due to commissioners—Requirements for claiming overpaid value added tax—Taxpayer making claim for repayment of value added tax but omitting to quantify claims in relation to specific accounting periods—Whether valid claim for repayment—Value Added Tax Act 1994, s 80—Value Added Tax Regulations 1995, SI 1995/2518, reg 37. **Bratt Autoservices Co Ltd v Revenue and Customs Comrs** [2019] **1** 729, CA.

    Unjust enrichment by refund. *See* **European Union** (Value added tax—Refund of tax).
  Penalty—
    Continuing penalty—
      Information laid before justices in respect of taxpayer's failure to make a return—Whether for calculating daily penalty taxpayer's failure continued to the date on which the information was laid or on which it was heard—Finance Act 1972, s 38(7)—Value Added Tax (General) Regulations 1975 (SI 1975 No 2204), reg 51. **Grice v Needs** [1979] **3** 501, QBD.
    Dishonest evasion of value added tax—
      Whether imposition of penalty for dishonest evasion of value added tax or duty giving rise to criminal charge for purposes of fair trial provisions of human rights convention—Value Added Tax Act 1994, s 60(1)—Finance Act 1994, s 8(1)—Human Rights Act 1998, Sch 1, Pt I, art 6. **Han v Comrs of Customs and Excise** [2001] **4** 687, CA.
  Rate—
    Higher rate. *See* Higher rate, *above*.
  Recovery of overpaid value added tax—
    Person paying amount by way of value added tax which was not tax due to Commissioners—
      Taxpayer operating pay and display car parks—Taxpayer claiming repayment of overpaid VAT in respect of overpayments of car park tariffs by customers—Whether overpayments consideration for taxable supply of services—Whether sufficient link between consideration given and service received—Whether overpayments subject to VAT. **National Car Parks Ltd v Revenue and Customs Comrs** [2019] **3** 590, CA.
  Recovery of tax—
    Person liable—
      Person issuing invoice—Person issuing invoices in name of non-existent company and under wrong company name—Whether person liable for payment of tax due—Finance Act 1972, s 33(2). **Customs and Excise Comrs v Wells** [1982] **1** 920, QBD.
  Registration—
    Partnership—
      Registration in name of firm—Separate partnerships having same partners—Partnerships carrying on separate business—Whether partnerships separate taxable persons—Whether commissioners required to register each partnership in firm name—Finance Act 1972, s 22(1). **Customs and Excise Comrs v Glassborow** [1974] **1** 1041, QBD.
  Relief—
    Bad debt relief. *See* Bad debt relief, *above*.

VALUE ADDED TAX (cont)—
Relief (cont)—
Goods held at commencement of April 1973—
Goods on which purchase tax or other duty paid—Deduction as input tax of purchase tax or duty paid—Goods deemed to be held on material date by taxpayer—Goods supplied to taxpayer before that date and not by then supplied by him—Goods supplied to taxpayer before material date—Goods subsequently destroyed before material date—Whether goods deemed to be held by taxpayer on material date—Finance Act 1973, s 4(1)(6). **Revell Fuels Ltd v Customs and Excise Comrs** [1975] **1** 312, QBD.

Rent—
Agricultural holding. *See* Exemptions—Buildings and land—Election to waive exemption—Agricultural tenancy, *above.*

Repayment. *See* Overpayment of tax—Repayment, *above.*

Return—
Assessment in default of proper return. *See* Assessment in default of proper returns by taxpayer, *above.*

Responsibility for making return—
Taxpayer registered for value added tax—Taxpayer ceasing to trade but remaining registered—Taxpayer failing to make return—Return if submitted would have shown nil liability—Whether taxpayer required to make return—Value Added Tax (General) Regulations 1975 (SI 1975 No 2204), reg 51(4). **Keogh v Gordon** [1979] **1** 89, QBD.

Supply of goods or services—
European Community. *See* **European Union** (Value added tax—Supply of goods or services).

Repayment of expenditure incurred in the name and on behalf of customer—
Appellant denying liability for VAT in invoices from medical reporting organisation to solicitor—Judge holding VAT properly chargeable on totality of third party's invoices and not merely third party's administration fees—Whether VAT amounts 'repayment of expenditure incurred in the name and on behalf of the customer'—Whether medical reporting organisation right to charge VAT on full amounts, rather than just administration fees—Council Directive 2006/112/EC, arts 73, 79. **British Airways plc v Prosser** [2019] **4** 1104, CA.

Single supply or separate supplies—
Delivery service on sale of new car—Car delivered to buyer by manufacturer—Whether separate supply of delivery service. **Customs and Excise Comrs v British Telecommunications plc** [1999] **3** 961, HL.

Supply—
Credit card scheme—Taxpayers operating credit card schemes—Contractual agreements between taxpayers and cardholders and between taxpayers and retailers—Cardholders agreeing to pay taxpayers cost of goods and services received from retailers on presenting credit card—Taxpayers agreeing to purchase from retailers cost of providing cardholders with goods and services less discount or commission—Whether taxpayers supplying retailers with financial service for a consideration—Value Added Tax Act 1983, s 3(2)(b), Sch 6, Group 5, item 1. **Customs and Excise Comrs v Diners Club Ltd** [1989] **2** 385, CA.

Furnishing or serving goods etc—Club—Unincorporated members' social club—Club licensed to serve intoxicating liquor to members on club premises—Drinks served to members on payment of sum of money—Drink already property of members and serving of drinks not constituting sale to members—Whether serving of drinks constituting 'supply of goods or services' to members—Finance Act 1972, s 1(1). **Carlton Lodge Club v Customs and Excise Comrs** [1974] **3** 798, QBD.

Lease of land—Landlords electing to waive exemption to value added tax on leases of properties held by taxpayer—Taxpayer leaving properties vacant while seeking to find subtenants and not electing to waive exemption—Taxpayer eventually electing to make subleases taxable and seeking repayment of input tax paid during vacant unelected period—Whether taxpayer entitled to repayment—Value Added Tax Regulations 1995, regs 85, 90, 109. **Royal and Sun Alliance Insurance Group plc v Customs and Excise Comrs** [2003] **2** 1073, HL.

Motor vehicle finance—Taxpayer entering into finance agreements with customers—Customer given option at end of lease period to purchase, return, or purchase and part-exchange vehicle—Whether supply of goods or services—Whether matter to be referred to European Court of Justice for preliminary ruling—Council Directive 2006/112/EC, art 14(2)(b). **Mercedes-Benz Financial Services UK Ltd v Revenue and Customs Comrs** [2016] **2** 163n, CA.

Second-hand car dealer selling stolen cars at public auction—Whether sales a 'supply' of goods—Finance Act 1972, ss 1, 2, 5. **Customs and Excise Comrs v Oliver** [1980] **1** 353, QBD.

Supply for purpose of business—Insurance company reinsuring car breakdown insurance risks with associated non-European Union resident company—Non-European Union company delegating claims handling to associated United Kingdom company—United Kingdom company setting up arrangements with garages under which repair work under insurance policies would be authorised and paid for by it—Whether supply by garages to United Kingdom company taxable supply of services—Whether supply to taxable person for the purpose of business carried on or to be carried on by him. **WHA Ltd v Revenue and Customs Comrs** [2013] **2** 907, SC.

Supply for a consideration—
Consideration—Direct link between supply and consideration—Company selling goods through hostesses at parties—Hostess entitled to discount on purchases or cash commission calculated by reference to volume of sales at party—Whether direct link between holding of party and sale of blouse to hostess at discount—Value Added Tax Act 1983, s 10—Council Directive (EEC) 77/388, art 11A(1)(a). **Rosgill Group Ltd v Customs and Excise Comrs** [1997] **3** 1012, CA.

Consideration—Direct link between supply and consideration—Employment bureaux supplying non-employed temporary staff to clients—Clients paying fees to bureaux out of which bureaux paying temps—Whether VAT chargeable on totality of fees paid to bureaux or merely on element attributable to introduction and ancillary services. **Adecco UK Ltd v Revenue and Customs Comrs** [2019] **1** 615, CA.

VALUE ADDED TAX (cont)—
Supply of goods or services (cont)—
Supply in the course of a business—
Assignment of lease—Trust set up to advance public education by promoting the arts of drama, ballet etc—Trust fund raised by appeals to the public not involving taxable supplies—Trustees obtaining lease of land on which to build a theatre and then assigning the lease to charitable company incorporated by them—Whether assignment of lease a supply in the course of business carried on by trustees—Finance Act 1972, s 2(2). **Customs and Excise Comrs v Royal Exchange Theatre Trust** [1979] **3** 797, QBD.
Business—Body incorporated to propagate religion or religious philosophy—Courses provided to further that aim—Sale of books and other merchandise relating to the religious philosophy—Whether goods and services supplied in the course of a business carried on by the taxpayer—Finance Act 1972, s 2(2). **Church of Scientology of California v Customs and Excise Comrs** [1981] **1** 1035, CA.
Business—Pheasant shoot—Invited guests making contributions to cost of shoot—Whether taxpayer carrying on a business—Finance Act 1972, s 2(2)(b). **Customs and Excise Comrs v Lord Fisher** [1981] **2** 147, QBD.
Business—Professional body carrying out regulatory functions of granting licences, certificates and registration—Fees charged to applicants to cover costs—Whether activities carried out in course or furtherance of business—Whether activities economic activities—Whether value added tax chargeable for supply of services—Value Added Tax Act 1994, s 4—Council Directive (EEC) 77/388, art 4(1)(2). **Institute of Chartered Accountants in England and Wales v Customs and Excise Comrs** [1998] **4** 115, CA; [1999] **2** 449, HL.
Society campaigning to oppose legislation against field sports—Subscriptions paid by members—Whether campaigning activities facilities or advantages available to members— Whether society to be treated as carrying on a business—Value Added Tax Act 1983, s 47(2)(a), (3). **Customs and Excise Comrs v British Field Sports Society** [1998] **2** 1003, CA.
Supply to a government department—NHS trust—Car leasing scheme under salary sacrifice arrangements—Trust claiming refund for VAT incurred in acquiring leased cars—Whether scheme a business activity—Value Added Tax Act 1994, s 41(3)—Value Added Tax (Treatment of Transactions) Order 1992, SI 1992/630, art 2. **R (on the application of Northumbria Healthcare NHS Foundation Trust) v Revenue and Customs Comrs** [2021] **1** 85, CA.
Supply of services for a consideration—
Direct link—Society campaigning to oppose legislation against field sports—Society funded by members' subscriptions—Whether direct link between subscriptions and benefit to members of campaigning activities. **Customs and Excise Comrs v British Field Sports Society** [1998] **2** 1003, CA.
Expenses—Reimbursement—Principal and agent—Sum paid by principal to agent towards cost of agent's expenses incurred on behalf of principal—Whether sum paid a consideration for services supplied by agent—Finance Act 1972, s 5(2). **National Transit Insurance Co Ltd v Customs and Excise Comrs** [1975] **1** 303, QBD.
Expenses—Reimbursement—Solicitor—Expenditure on behalf of client—Disbursements— Travelling expenses incurred by solicitor whilst acting on behalf of client—Separate charge to client in solicitor's bill—Whether payment of sum for travelling expenses by client reimbursement of expenses or part of consideration for supply of legal services—Finance Act 1972, s 5(2). **Rowe & Maw (a firm) v Customs and Excise Comrs** [1975] **2** 444, QBD.
Loyalty reward programme—Taxpayer contracting with companies issuing points to customers redeemable for goods and services at participating suppliers—Taxpayer paying service charge including VAT to suppliers for 'redemption services'—Whether supplier providing service to taxpayer—Whether VAT deductible by taxpayer as input tax. **Revenue and Customs Comrs v Aimia Coalition Loyalty UK Ltd (No 2)** [2013] **4** 94n, SC.
Loyalty reward programme—Taxpayer contracting with companies issuing points to customers redeemable for goods and services at participating suppliers—Taxpayer paying service charge including VAT to suppliers for 'redemption services'—Whether supplier providing service to taxpayer -Whether VAT deductible by taxpayer as input tax. **Revenue and Customs Comrs v Aimia Coalition Loyalty UK Ltd** [2013] **2** 719, SC.
Maintenance services—Firm of solicitors appointed maintenance trustee of block of flats— Maintenance trustee providing staff and paying them out of maintenance fund—Lessor and tenants contributing to maintenance fund—Whether provision of services of maintenance staff by maintenance trustee a supply of services for consideration—Whether staff employed by maintenance trustee—Whether maintenance trustee merely being reimbursed expenses 'paid out in the name and for the account of' lessor and tenants as purchasers or customers—Whether supply of staff's services exempt—Value Added Tax Act 1983, s 5, Sch 6, Group 1, item 1—Council Directive (EEC) 77/388, art 11A(1). **Nell Gwynn House Maintenance Fund Trustees v Customs and Excise Comrs** [1999] **1** 385, HL.
Time of supply—
Payment in advance—Agreement to supply goods by member of group to another member—Payment in respect of supply made before delivery of goods—Supplier leaving group after payment made but before goods delivered—Whether extent of supply covered by payment to be treated as taking place at time advance payment received—Value Added Tax Act 1983, ss 4, 5, 10, 29—Council Directive (EEC) 77/388, art 4(4). **Customs and Excise Comrs v Thorn Materials Supply Ltd** [1998] **3** 342, HL.
Supply of goods on hire—Retrospective effect of statute introducing value added tax—Agreement for hire made and goods delivered under agreement before statute enacted—Agreement providing for periodic payments—Power of commissioners to make regulations providing for time of supply where goods 'are supplied' for consideration payable periodically— Commissioners making regulations—Regulations providing for goods supplied under hire agreement to be treated as being supplied on each occasion payment of hire received—Regulation applying to goods supplied under hire agreement made before statute enacted—Whether regulation ultra vires—Finance Act 1972, ss 5(2), 7(2)(8)—Value Added Tax (General) Regulations 1972 (SI 1972 No 1147), reg 14(1). **Customs and Excise Comrs v Thorn Electrical Industries Ltd** [1975] **3** 881, HL.
Value of supply. *See* Value of supply of goods or services, *below*.

1444

VALUE ADDED TAX (cont)—
Tax avoidance scheme—
Zero-rating—
Building work—Supply in the course of construction, alteration or demolition of building—
Standard-rating of alteration work as from 1 June 1984—Transitional rules for zero-rating of
alteration work if paid for before 1 June 1984—Taxpayer companies entering into arrangement
with owners of properties for payment in advance for work to be done on properties—Taxpayer
companies then making loans to or depositing equivalent amount with owners before 1 June
1984—Owners repaying loans or releasing deposits in stages against architects' certificates after
1 June 1984—Transactions discharging owners' liabilities to taxpayer companies—Whether
payment received by taxpayer companies before 1 June 1984 or on presentation of architects'
certificates—Whether works zero-rated or liable to tax at standard rate—Value Added Tax Act
1983, s 5(1). **Customs and Excise Comrs v Faith Construction Ltd** [1989] **2** 938, CA.
Civil conspiracy—Carousel fraud—Spanish company selling goods to United Kingdom company
and subsequently buying them back as part of carousel fraud—United Kingdom conspirator
claiming and receiving from commissioners input tax on acquisition of goods—Commissioners
claiming damages at common law from Spanish company for unlawful means conspiracy—
Whether commissioners entitled to maintain action at common law against person not made
accountable or otherwise liable for value added tax by Parliament—Whether levying money for
use of the Crown without grant of Parliament—Whether unlawful means conspiracy requiring
conduct giving rise to unlawful means to be separately actionable against at least one of
conspirators—Bill of Rights (1688), art 4. **Revenue and Customs Comrs v Total Network SL**
[2008] **2** 413, HL.
Tour operators—
Margin scheme. *See* Assessment—Tour operator's margin scheme, *above*.
Tribunal—
Appeal—
Prepayment rule—Taxpayer required to pay tax at issue before making appeal—Whether
prepayment rule contrary to EU principle of equivalence. **Totel Ltd v Revenue and Customs
Comrs** [2018] **4** 949, SC.
Costs—
Award of costs—Litigant in person—Appeal to tribunal against assessment—Extent of tribunal's
power to award costs—RSC Ord 62, r 18—Value Added Tax Tribunals Rules 1986, r 29. **Customs
and Excise Comrs v Ross** [1990] **2** 65, QBD.
Jurisdiction—
Review of commissioners' decision—Commissioners' discretion as to the sufficiency of records
kept by taxable person—Whether discretion subject to review by tribunal—Finance Act 1972,
s 40(1)—Value Added Tax (Works of Art, Antiques and Scientific Collections) Order 1972 (SI 1972
No 1971), art 3(5). **Customs and Excise Comrs v J H Corbitt (Numismatists) Ltd** [1980] **2** 72, HL.
Value of supply of goods or services—
Consideration not wholly consisting of money—
Company selling cars accepting customers' cars in part-exchange—Part-exchange allowance
agreed between company and customers exceeding trade value of part-exchange cars—Value to
be attributed to part-exchange cars—Council Directive (EC) 77/388, art 11A(1)(a). **Lex Services plc
v Customs and Excise Comrs** [2004] **1** 434, HL.
Company selling goods through hostesses at parties—Goods sold at discount to hostesses as
reward for holding party—Value of supply of such goods—Value of holding of party to
supplier—Value Added Tax Act 1983, s 10(3). **Rosgill Group Ltd v Customs and Excise Comrs**
[1997] **3** 1012, CA.
Decrease in consideration—
Adjustments to VAT account—Bingo—Method of calculation of VAT—Guidance changing basis of
calculation from game-by-game basis to session-by-session basis—Session-by-session basis
more advantageous to taxpayer—Taxpayer making successful repayment claim on basis of
session-by-session basis—Taxpayer making adjustment claim for period prior to time limit for
repayment claim—Whether adjustment valid—Value Added Tax Act 1994, s 80—HMRC Brief
07/07. **Revenue and Customs Comrs v KE Entertainments Ltd** [2020] **4** 441, SC.
Determination of value—
Company selling goods through non-taxable agents—Goods supplied either sold on to customers
or retained by agents—No distinction made between goods to be resold and goods to be
retained—Goods sold to agents at less than catalogue price—Direction by commissioners that
value of any supply to be sold by retail should be taken as its open market value on a sale by
retail—Validity of direction—Whether direction applicable to any individual supply of goods to
agent—Whether requirement that value of supplies to be taken at market value inconsistent with
requirements of Community law—Value Added Tax Act 1983, Sch 4, para 3. **Fine Art
Developments plc v Customs and Excise Comrs** [1996] **1** 888, HL.
Second-hand goods—Taxpayer entering into scheme whereby value added tax calculated on basis
of profit margin in relation to sale of cars—Whether scheme abusive. **Pendragon plc v Revenue
and Customs Comrs** [2015] **3** 919, SC.
Supply for consideration in money—
Payment for goods by means of cash vouchers—Vouchers issued by company—Taxpayer
accepting vouchers from customers in exchange for goods—Taxpayer entitled to reimbursement
from company of cash value of vouchers less an agreed commission due to company—Whether
goods supplied in exchange for vouchers supplied for a consideration in money—Whether tax to
be charged by reference to the value of the goods supplied less amount of commission due to
company—Finance Act 1972, ss 9(1), 10(2). **Davies v Customs and Excise Comrs** [1975] **1** 309,
QBD.
Zero-rating—
Building works—
Alteration of building—What amounts to 'alteration'—Whether any limitation on what work to
fabric of building may amount to 'alteration'—Finance Act 1972, Sch 4, Group 8, item 2. **Customs
and Excise Comrs v Viva Gas Appliances Ltd** [1984] **1** 112, HL.

VALUE ADDED TAX (cont)—
  Zero-rating (cont)—
    Building works (cont)—
      Alteration of building—Work of repair or maintenance—Underpinning of defective foundations—Existing foundations damaged by subsidence—Building company constructing additional foundations and leaving original foundations unaltered—Whether work carried out by company 'maintenance'—Finance Act 1972, Sch 4, Group 8, item 2, note 2. **ACT Construction Ltd v Customs and Excise Comrs** [1982] **1** 84, HL.
      Supply of services in the course of construction, alteration or demolition of a building—Building intended for use solely for relevant charitable purpose—Construction of cricket pavilion for village cricket club—Club registered as a community amateur sports club—Whether club established solely for charitable purposes—Whether breach of principles of equal treatment and/or fiscal neutrality—Whether supply zero-rated—Value Added Tax Act 1994, Sch 8, Group 5, item 2—Finance Act 2010, Sch 6, para 1—Charities Act 2011, s 6. **Eynsham Cricket Club v Revenue and Customs Comrs** [2021] **3** 369, CA.
      Taxpayer entering into sale and lease back of a care home—Whether sale and lease back amounting to disposal of an 'entire interest'—Whether transaction liable to value added tax—Value Added Tax Act 1994, Sch 8, Group 5, item 1, Sch 10, para 36(2). **Balhousie Holdings Ltd v Revenue and Customs Comrs** [2021] **3** 599, SC.
    Exported goods—
      Proof of export—Conditions imposed by commissioners—Validity—Conditions stating that exported goods to be zero-rated only if specified method of proof complied with—Whether conditions unreasonable—Finance Act 1972, s 12(7)—Value Added Tax (General) Regulations 1975 (SL 1975 No 2204), reg 44(1)—Customs and Excise Notice 703, para 10(b), (c). **Moss (Henry) of London v Customs and Excise Comrs** [1981] **2** 86, CA.
    Newspapers, journals and periodicals—
      Newspapers—Digital editions—Whether digital editions zero-rated—Value Added Tax Act 1994, s 30, Sch 8, Group 3, item 2—Council Directive 2006/112/EC, art 110. **News Corp UK & Ireland Ltd v Revenue and Customs Comrs** [2021] **2** 1276, CA.
    Protected building—
      Supply of services in the course of alterations to outbuilding within curtilage of protected main building—Protected main building a dwelling—Whether supply of services zero-rated—Value Added Tax Act 1994, Sch 8, Group 6, item 2, note (1). **Customs & Excise Comrs v Zielinski Baker & Partners Ltd** [2004] **2** 141, HL.
    Services to overseas traders or for overseas purposes—
      Supply to overseas resident of services not used in United Kingdom—Club or association—Overseas members—Association issuing publications and providing other facilities to members—Whether subscriptions from overseas members consideration for supply of services not used in United Kingdom—Finance Act 1972, Sch 4, Group 9, item 6. **Barton v Customs and Excise Comrs** [1974] **3** 337, QBD.
    Transport of passengers—
      Carriage of passengers from one point to another—Amusement device—Big dipper—Passengers carried by vehicle on specially constructed track consisting of corners and inclines—Movement of passengers in effect confined to one spot—Whether provision of rides constituting 'transport of passengers'—Finance Act 1972, s 12(2), Sch 4, Group 10, item 4. **Customs and Excise Comrs v Blackpool Pleasure Beach Co** [1974] **1** 1011, QBD.
      Supply of travel concession voucher—Student travel scheme—Sale of identity card for purpose of scheme—British Railways Board—Identity card entitling student to travel by rail at reduced prices—Whether sale of identity card zero-rated as a supply of transport—Finance Act 1972, s 12(2), Sch 4, Group 10, item 4. **British Railways Board v Customs and Excise Comrs** [1977] **2** 873, CA.

VALUER
  Expert evidence—
    Hearsay—
      Admissibility—Evidence of comparables—Expression of opinion on values—Opinion formed in part by matters of which valuer having no first-hand knowledge—Evidence of transactions of which valuer having no first-hand knowledge—Extent to which evidence admissible. **English Exporters (London) Ltd v Eldonwall Ltd** [1973] **1** 726, Ch D.
  Immunity from suit—
    Negligent valuation. *See* **Negligence** (Immunity from suit—Valuer).
  Negligence—
    Accrual of cause of action. *See* **Limitation of action** (Accrual of cause of action—Negligence—Valuer).
    Damages—
      Interest. *See* **Interest** (Damages—Negligence—Valuer).
      Measure of damages. *See* **Damages** (Measure of damages—Negligence—Valuer).
    Duty to exercise reasonable skill and care. *See* **Negligence** (Professional person—Duty to exercise reasonable skill and care—Estate agent—Valuation of property).
    Immunity from suit. *See* **Negligence** (Immunity from suit—Valuer).
    Information or advice—
      Damage giving rise to liability. *See* **Negligence** (Information or advice—Damage giving rise to liability—Danger to life, limb or health—Valuation of property).
      Reliance on skill and judgment. *See* **Negligence** (Information or advice—Reliance on skill and judgment—Valuer).
    Real property valuation. *See* **Negligence** (Professional person—Real property—Valuation).

VALUER (cont)—
  Valuation—
    Conclusiveness—
      Valuation made as expert rather than arbitrator—Agreement for sale of company—Dispute over
      calculation of company turnover—Parties referring dispute to independent accountants for
      determination in accordance with contract—Contract providing that experts' determination to be
      conclusive and binding for all purposes—Experts complying fully with terms of letter of
      instruction—Plaintiffs seeking to set aside experts' determination on ground of mistake—
      Whether determination open to challenge on ground of mistake—Whether plaintiffs bound by
      determination. **Jones v Sherwood Computer Services plc** [1992] **2** 170, CA.
    Contractual obligation. *See* **Contract** (Construction—Contractual term—Valuation report).
    Erroneous principle—
      Validity—Evidence of result of valuation on correct principle—Prosperous family company—
      Agreement for disposal of assets at a valuation—Valuation to be of business 'as a going
      concern'—Valuation of machinery to be by expert valuer—Valuer appointed under terms of
      agreement—Valuation of premises made on 'break-up' basis—Failure to employ expert to value
      machinery—Valuation erroneous in principle—Whether valuation binding on parties—Whether
      necessary to show that valuation on correct principle would show materially different result.
      Jones (M) v Jones (R R) [1971] **2** 676, Ch D.
    Identifcation of property. *See* **Contract** (Construction—Contractual term—Valuation report).
    Mistake—
      Speaking valuation—Shares—Private company—Valuation for purposes of sale—Price to be fixed
      by valuer—Valuer's decision final, binding and conclusive—Basis of valuation stated on face of
      valuation—Transfer of shares effected on basis of valuation—Transferor seeking declaration that
      valuation fundamentally erroneous—Whether statement of claim disclosing reasonable cause of
      action—Whether party to a contract can impugn contract if speaking valuation shows valuation to
      be erroneous—Whether completion of transaction before proceedings are commenced a bar to
      declaratory relief. **Burgess v Purchase & Sons (Farms) Ltd** [1983] **2** 4, Ch D.
      Validity—Contractual purchase price—Valuation to determine price under contract—Determination
      giving no reasons for figure determined—Evidence that figure determined by valuer
      excessive—No fraud or collusion—Whether open to purchaser to obtain order setting aside
      valuer's determination on ground of mistake. **Campbell v Edwards** [1976] **1** 785, CA.
    Setting aside valuation—
      Purchase price to be ascertained on balancing assets and liabilities—Independent accountants
      acting as experts not arbitrators—Liabilities including loans alleged to be unenforceable as made
      by unlicensed moneylenders—Whether accountants bound to consider whether Moneylenders
      Acts, 1900 to 1927, applied to loans—Accountants' report giving their reasons—Whether
      accountants' certificate of nil purchase price was open to challenge and should be set aside.
      Wright (Frank H) (Constructions) Ltd v Frodoor Ltd [1967] **1** 433, QBD.
      Shares of private company—Sale to directors at price certified by auditor as fair value—Grounds
      for setting aside valuation. **Dean v Prince** [1954] **1** 749, CA.
    Shares—
      Setting aside valuation. *See* Valuation—Setting aside valuation—Shares of private company,
      above.
      Valuation for purposes of sale—Price to be fixed by valuer—Action against valuer—Alleged breach
      of warranty—Alleged failure of consideration—No liability in absence of mala fides. **Finnegan v
      Allen** [1943] **1** 493, CA.
    Valuation of expert—
      Mandatory order—Review—Council trespassing on plaintiff's land—Council cutting down trees in
      process of laying sewage pipe on plaintiff's land—Order requiring council to carry out tree, hedge
      and shrub replacement 'so far as reasonably practicable'—Plaintiff's expert drawing up plans
      without regard to cost of reinstatement work—Estimated cost vastly exceeding cost
      contemplated when order made—Whether court having jurisdiction to review order—Whether
      phrase 'reasonably practicable' including cost. **Jordan v Norfolk CC** [1994] **4** 218, Ch D.
  Valuation report—
    Obligation to inspect. *See* **Contract** (Construction—Contractual term—Valuation report).

VAN
  Mobile—
    Equipped as shop. *See* **Shop** (Sunday closing—Retail trading elsewhere than in shop—Mobile van
    equipped as shop).

VARIATION OF LEASE
  Generally. *See* **Landlord and tenant** (Lease—Variation).

VARIATION OF SETTLEMENT (MATRIMONIAL CAUSES)
  Adopted child—
    Jurisdiction to admit adopted child to benefit under settlement—
      Compensation for natural children—Matrimonial Causes Act 1950, s 25. **Purnell v Purnell**
      [1961] **1** 369, Div.
  Ante-nuptial and post-nuptial settlement—
    Transfers of money before and after marriage—
      No element of periodicity—Transactions completed—Whether they constituted settlements for the
      purpose of anticipatory protection by injunction—Matrimonial Causes Act 1950, s 25. **Hindley v
      Hindley** [1957] **2** 653, Div.
  Ante-nuptial settlement—
    Adoption of child after marriage—
      Subsequent birth of child of marriage—Whether settlement ought to be varied to include adopted
      child—Adoption Act 1950, s 13(2)—Matrimonial Causes Act 1950, s 25. **Best v Best** [1955] **2** 839,
      Div.

VARIATION OF SETTLEMENT (MATRIMONIAL CAUSES) (cont)—
  Ante-nuptial settlement (cont)—
    Deed made in consideration of marriage—
      Deed containing covenant to transfer securities as absolute gift immediately after marriage—
      Transfer of securities to husband accordingly—Whether ante-nuptial settlement—Matrimonial
      Causes Act 1950, s 25. **Prescott (orse Fellowes) v Fellowes** [1958] **3** 55, CA.
    House purchased before marriage to provide matrimonial home—
      Contribution by wife towards purchase price—Conveyance into the name of the husband
      alone—Divorce on ground of wife's adultery—One child of marriage—Variations of wife's
      beneficial interest in half share, so as to make provision for child—Variation not
      punitive—Matrimonial Causes Act 1965, s 17(1). **Ulrich v Ulrich and Felton** [1968] **1** 67, CA.
    Income of trust fund to be paid to wife if marriage undissolved—
      Power to husband to appoint by will in favour of second wife—Supreme Court of Judicature
      (Consolidation) Act 1925, s 192. **Egerton v Egerton** [1949] **2** 238, CA.
  Application by wife for maintenance—
    Desirability of both applications being heard together—
      New circumstances arising after hearing in court below—Consideration by Court of Appeal. **Jeffrey**
      v Jeffrey [1952] **1** 790, CA.
  Application for variation—
    Application by guilty wife—
      Consents of persons interested—Interests of unborn persons. **Bowles v Bowles** [1937] **2** 263, Div.
    Application out of time—
      Consideration of facts as known at date of hearing of application—Separation deed—Covenant by
      husband to pay wife weekly sum during her life—Marriage dissolved—Re-marriage of both
      parties—Insertion in deed of dum sola clause—Supreme Court of Judicature (Consolidation) Act
      1925, s 192. **Johnson v Johnson** [1949] **2** 247, CA.
    Death of applicant—
      Survival of application for benefit of estate. *See* **Divorce** (Financial provision—Application—Practice
      and procedure—Death of applicant).
    Practice—
      Made to registrar on affidavit—Matrimonial Causes Rules 1950 (SI 1950 No 1940), r 44(1). **Practice**
      Direction [1955] **2** 465, Div.
  Covenant to pay annual sum—
    Liability to pay annual sum no longer binding owing to error in drafting—
      Order for maintenance made on assumption that covenant still binding. **Jacobs v Jacobs**
      [1942] 2 471, CA.
  Extinction of party's interests as if dead—
    Effect—
      Discretionary trust—Whether discretionary trust on forfeiture capable of operation. **Allsopp's**
      Marriage Settlement Trusts, Re [1958] **2** 393, Ch D.
      Joint power and power to survivor of spouses—Powers and interests of wife extinguished as if
      dead—Whether husband could exercise power during life of wife. **Poole's Settlements' Trusts, Re**
      [1959] **2** 340, Ch D.
  Freehold house purchased after marriage—
    Fee simple conveyed to husband and wife on trust for sale—
      Upon trust for themselves as joint tenants—Purchase money provided by mortgage and loan and
      by parties—Substantial contribution by wife—Conveyance a settlement—Matrimonial Causes Act
      1950, s 25. **Brown v Brown** [1959] **2** 266, CA.
    Purchase money provided solely by husband—
      Covenants entered into jointly and severally with vendor restricting use of house—House conveyed
      to husband and wife 'in fee simple as joint tenants'—Whether conveyance a post-nuptial
      settlement or a gift of half share of house to wife—Supreme Court of Judicature (Consolidation)
      Act 1925, s 192. **Smith v Smith** [1945] **1** 584, Div.
  Immediate annuity to husband—
    Purchased after marriage—
      Gift—Supreme Court of Judicature (Consolidation) Act 1925, s 192. **Brown v Brown** [1936] **2** 1616,
      Div.
  Insurance policy—
    Sum payable on death of husband—
      Policy expressed to be effected under Married Women's Property Act 1882, for benefit of wife
      absolutely—Payment of periodical premiums—Married Women's Property Act 1882, s 11—
      Supreme Court of Judicature (Consolidation) Act 1925, s 192. **Gunner v Gunner and Stirling**
      [1948] **2** 771, Div.
    Wife specified as beneficiary—
      Wife's rights dependent on her surviving husband—Policy obtained on payment of single
      premium—Supreme Court of Judicature (Consolidation) Act 1925, s 192. **Bown v Bown and**
      Weston [1948] **2** 778, Div.
  Jurisdiction—
    Consent order providing that wife to remain living in matrimonial home with children—
      Wife undertaking to sell home by certain date if unable to secure husband's release from mortgage
      covenants—Wife seeking to vary that undertaking—Whether court having jurisdiction to release
      wife from undertaking—Matrimonial Causes Act 1973, ss 24A, 31. **Birch v Birch** [2018] **1** 108, SC.
    Divorce Division—
      Result of variation reduction in tax payable—Matrimonial Causes Act 1950, s 25. **Thomson v**
      Thomson and Whitmee [1954] **2** 462, Div.
  Meaning of 'settlement'—
    Part of house conveyed by wife to husband for no consideration—
      Provision for husband, and in view of continuance of matrimonial relations—Supreme Court of
      Judicature (Consolidation) Act 1925, s 192. **Halpern v Halpern** [1951] **1** 315, Div.
  Post-nuptial settlement—
    Divorce—
      Financial provision. *See* **Divorce** (Financial provision).

VARIATION OF SETTLEMENT (MATRIMONIAL CAUSES) (cont)—

Post-nuptial settlement (cont)—

Gift of house to husband and wife—

Sale of house after decree absolute of divorce—Division of part of proceeds of sale before application for variation of settlement—Matrimonial Causes Act 1950, s 25. **Sievwright v Sievwright** [1956] 3 616, Div.

House purchased by spouses on trust for sale—

Decree nisi of nullity to wife—Notice of severance to husband transforming equitable joint tenancy in proceeds of sale into tenancy in common—Right of wife to apply for variation of settlement to extinguish husband's rights in property—Matrimonial Causes Act 1965, ss 17, 19. **Radziej v Radziej** [1967] 1 944, PDA.

Divorce on ground of husband's desertion—Husband paying nothing towards house from date of desertion—No prospect of wife receiving maintenance—Variation of settlement to extinguish husband's interest in house—Matrimonial Causes Act 1965, s 17. **Smith v Smith** [1970] 1 244, CA.

Divorce on ground of wife's adultery—Variation of settlement to extinguish wife's interest from date she left husband, but, in compensation, house to be charged with payment to wife of £3,360 by monthly instalments—Matrimonial Causes Act 1965, s 17. **Spizewski v Spizewski and Krywanski** [1970] 1 794, CA.

House purchased to provide matrimonial home—

Contribution by wife towards purchase money—Conveyance into the name of the husband alone—Matrimonial Causes Act 1950, s 25. **Cook v Cook** [1962] 2 811, CA.

House mortgaged, both parties undertaking liability for interest on loan—Husband taking out insurance on own life—Insurance policy assigned by husband to mortgagee—Whether, after sale of house, redemption value of insurance policy part of settled funds—Matrimonial Causes Act 1965, s 17. **Meldrum v Meldrum** [1970] 3 1084, Div.

Husband registered owner of freehold property—

Husband holding the property in trust as to one half part for himself and the remainder for his wife absolutely—Variation of settlement to extinguish husband's interest in the property—Form of order—Vesting orders under the Trustee Act 1925—Jurisdiction of the Family Division of the High Court to make vesting orders—Trustee Act 1925, s 44—Matrimonial Proceedings and Property Act 1970, s 4(1)(c)—RSC Ord 93, r 4. **Jones v Jones** [1972] 3 289, Fam D.

Life assurance policy—

Policy effected for benefit of 'widow or children'—Whether post-nuptial settlement—Matrimonial Causes Act 1950, s 25. **Lort-Williams v Lort-Williams** [1951] 2 241, CA.

Maintenance agreement—

Agreement made between decree nisi and decree absolute of divorce—Agreement including annuities for wife and children—Agreement by wife not to sue for permanent maintenance—Whether agreement was a post-nuptial settlement—Matrimonial Causes Act 1950, s 25. **Young v Young** [1961] 3 695, CA.

Pension scheme—

Variation of husband's pension scheme on divorce—Pension scheme containing option allowing husband to surrender part of pension entitlement for benefit of spouse—Pension fund varied to make limited pension provision for wife—Whether pension scheme a post-nuptial settlement—Whether court having jurisdiction to vary husband's pension fund arrangements—Whether court should exercise its jurisdiction to vary scheme—Matrimonial Causes Act 1973, s 24(1)(c). **Brooks v Brooks** [1995] 3 257, HL.

Transfer to wife of joint property—

Bond by her to pay by instalments—Relevant circumstances to be taken into account—Matrimonial Causes Act 1950, s 25. **Parrington v Parrington** [1951] 2 916, Div.

Wife a trustee with special power of appointment—

Jurisdiction of court to order removal of trustee—No evidence that wife likely to abuse position as trustee or misuse power of appointment—Matrimonial Causes Act 1950, s 25. **Compton (Marquis of Northampton) v Compton (Marchioness of Northampton) and Hussey** [1960] 2 70, Div.

Power of appointment upon petitioner's second marriage—

Children's reversionary interests affected—

Principle of quid pro quo—Acceleration of respondent's power to appoint upon second marriage refused—Costs—Supreme Court of Judicature (Consolidation) Act 1925, s 192. **Wadham v Wadham** [1938] 1 206, Div.

Proportion between amount secured and amount ordered to be paid—

Deductions allowable in assessing maintenance—

Covenant for benefit of children of former marriage—Supreme Court of Judicature (Consolidation) Act 1925, s 190(1),(2). **Chichester v Chichester** [1936] 1 271, Div.

Separation deed—

Wife's covenant to pay husband £5 per week—

Husband's adultery—Decree absolute—Variation of deed—Discretion of court. **Tomkins v Tomkins** [1948] 1 237, CA.

Variation inimical to interests of children—

Compensation of children—

Protection of children's interests provided by guilty party—Supreme Court of Judicature (Consolidation) Act 1925, ss 191(1), 192. **Maxwell v Maxwell** [1950] 2 979, Div.

Withdrawal of funds from settlement by husband—

Husband guilty party—Facts to be considered. **Garforth-Bles v Garforth-Bles** [1951] 1 308, Div.

VARIATION OF TRUSTS

Acceleration—

Accrual of son's share to daughter's settled share on his death under thirty—

Arrangement to (1) expunge trust for accumulation and (2) confer interest in son's share on his children if he died under thirty—Arrangement (2) to avoid need for proceedings for rectification—Approval of (1) granted and (2) withheld—Variation of Trusts Act 1958, s 1. **Tinker's Settlement, Re** [1960] 3 85, Ch D.

Bare trust—

Variation of statutory power of advancement—

Trustee Act 1925, s 32—Variation of Trusts Act 1958, s 1. **D (a child) v O** [2004] 3 780, Ch D.

VARIATION OF TRUSTS (cont)—
  Benefit—
    Benefit not restricted to financial, educational and social benefit—
      Forfeiture clause—Forfeiture on practising Roman Catholic faith—Variation of Trusts Act 1958, s 1(1). **Remnant's Settlement Trusts, Re** [1970] **2** 554, Ch D.
    Discretionary powers to be eliminated—
      Arrangement substituting absolute beneficial interest for discretionary interest—Whether court had jurisdiction to sanction an arrangement that would eliminate discretionary powers that trustees wished to exercise—Variation of Trusts Act 1958, s 1. **Steed's Will Trusts, Re** [1960] **1** 487, CA.
    Discretionary trusts to be established—
      Approximation of beneficial interests under arrangement to those in settlement dependent on manner of exercise of discretionary powers—Arrangement approved—Variation of Trusts Act 1958, s 1(1). **Druce's Settlement Trusts, Re** [1962] **1** 563, Ch D.
    Discretionary trusts to come into operation at future date—
      Benefit to discretionary class—Whether benefit to discretionary class must be shown. **Bristol's Settled Estates, Re** [1964] **3** 939, Ch D.
    Exercise of special power of appointment as a preliminary step to proposed arrangement—
      Genuine intention to benefit objects of power—Possible advantage to appointor if scheme approved—Whether fraud on power—Whether proposed arrangement should be approved—Variation of Trusts Act 1958, s 1. **Robertson's Will Trusts, Re** [1960] **3** 146, Ch D.
    Infant beneficially interested—
      Relative advantages between infant and adult beneficiaries—Bargaining strength of infants' position should be reflected in the figures—Benefits to infants exceeding actuarial valuation of their existing beneficial interests—Variation of Trusts Act 1958, s 1. **Van Gruisen's Will Trusts, Re** [1964] **1** 843, Ch D.
    Risk to beneficiary from proposed arrangement—
      Approval of variation—Whether court will approve variation with possible risk to beneficiary—Variation of Trusts Act 1958, s 1. **Cohen's Will Trusts, Re** [1959] **3** 523, Ch D.
    Settled estates—
      Appointing person to execute disentailing deed—Arrangement varying trusts—Plaintiff tenant in tail male of settlement subject to interests and trusts limited to take effect during his life and six months after his death—Son infant tenant in tail in remainder—Two tenants in tail capable between them of disposing of fee simple but neither capable of disposing of fee simple by himself—Scheme providing that plaintiff should execute disentailing deed barring his postponed entailed interest and that a person to be appointed by order of the court should execute, with consent of plaintiff as protector of settlement, deed disentailing son's entailed interest—Temporary discretionary trust arising on death of life tenant or forfeiture of his life interest—Whether benefit to discretionary class to be shown—Trustee Act 1925, s 53—Variation of Trusts Act 1958, s 1(1)(d), proviso. **Bristol's Settled Estates, Re** [1964] **3** 939, Ch D.
  Capital gains tax—
    Arrangement in view of prospective incidence of capital gains tax—
      Shares in private company forming trust fund—Acceleration of entitlement—Insurance policies to be effected—Variation of Trusts Act 1958, s 1(1). **Sainsbury's Settlement, Re** [1967] **1** 878, Ch D.
  Child-bearing—
    Arrangement proposed to meet contingency of a woman over 70 having a further child—
      Administration of trust fund on that basis proper without sanction of court—Variation of Trusts Act 1958, s 1. **Pettifor's Will Trusts, Re** [1966] **1** 913, Ch D.
  Costs. *See* Practice—Costs, *below.*
  Damages—
    Damages recovered by infant. *See* Jurisdiction—Damages recovered by infant, *below.*
  Discretion of court. *See* Jurisdiction—Discretion, *below.*
  Discretionary trust—
    Extension of period of discretionary trust—
      Estate duty. *See* **Estate duty** (Determination of life interest—Discretionary trust—Variation—Discretionary trust for class limited to cease on death of widow).
  Effect of arrangement—
    Variation taking effect by virtue of consents of beneficiaries—
      Court order conferring consent on behalf of beneficiaries unable to consent on own behalf—Variation of Trusts Act 1958, s 1(1). **Holmden's Settlement Trusts, Re** [1968] **1** 148, HL.
  Effect of order of court approving arrangement—
    Attempt to set up estoppel. *See* **Estoppel** (Issue estoppel—Scheme for variation of trusts).
  Entail. *See* Benefit—Settled estates, *above.*
  Estoppel. *See* **Estoppel** (Issue estoppel—Scheme for variation of trusts).
  Evidence—
    Investment—
      Evidence of stockbroker or expert. **Allen's Settlement, Re** [1959] **3** 673, Ch D.
  Extension of powers of investment—
    Discretion—
      Removal of quantitative limitations—Variation of Trusts Act 1958, s 1—Trustee Investments Act 1961, Sch 1, Part 4, para 3. **Clarke's Will Trusts, Re** [1961] **3** 1133, Ch D.
      Special circumstances to be shown to justify departure from scope prescribed by statute—Two-thirds of trust fund invested in investment trust company and one-third in authorised trustee investments—Approval sought for proposed arrangement giving trustees power to invest the whole trust fund in industrial equities—Remuneration of director trustees—Whether special circumstances established—Trustee Investments Act 1961, s 15—Variation of Trusts Act 1958, s 1. **Cooper's Settlement, Re** [1961] **3** 636, Ch D.
  Jurisdiction of court. *See* Variation by the court—Investment clause—Extension of powers of investment, *below.*

VARIATION OF TRUSTS (cont)—
Extinction of power of appointment—
Power to appoint life interest to surviving wife—
Donee of power applied to court to approve arrangement on footing that it extinguished power—Whether court satisfied arrangement had effect of extinguishing power without any express release—Fact that donee of power himself propounded it evidence of conduct inconsistent with continued exercise of power after arrangement approved—Order approving arrangement made—Variation of Trusts Act 1958, s 1. **Courtauld's Settlement, Re** [1965] 2 544, Ch D.
Fair and proper—
Defeat of testator's intentions—
Defeat not conclusive that arrangement not fair and proper. **Remnant's Settlement Trusts, Re** [1970] 2 554, Ch D.
Foreign trust. See Jurisdiction—Trust containing foreign element, *below*.
Forfeiture clause. See Benefit—Benefit not restricted to financial, educational and social benefit—Forfeiture clause, *above*.
Infant—
Guardian ad litem—
Infant beneficiary—Party to summons—Duty to guardian—Failure to perform duty—Effect—Jurisdiction of court to approve arrangement affecting infant beneficiary—Whether consent of guardian prerequisite of court's approval on behalf of infant—Variation of Trusts Act 1958, s 1. **Whittall, Re** [1973] 3 35, Ch D.
Tenant in tail—
Settlement of shares in company on trust for sale and conversion into land—Proceeds settled as in a settlement of land—Second son an infant and tenant in tail—Arrangement involving execution of disentailing deed—Person appointed to execute disentailing deed—Proposed arrangement for benefit of infant, of those with interests subsequent to his and of future male issue of eldest son—Trustee Act 1925, s 53—Variation of Trusts Act 1958, s 1. **Lansdowne's Will Trusts, Re** [1967] 1 888, Ch D.
Investment clause—
Practice. See Practice—Investment clause to be varied, *below*.
Variation by the court. See Variation by the court—Investment clause, *below*.
Joinder of parties—
Practice. See Practice—Joinder of parties, *below*.
Jurisdiction—
Arrangement introducing power of advancement—
Application to include statutory power in trusts of will—Will of testatrix who died in 1923—Interests of issue and widow of life tenants affected—Variation approved by the court—Trustee Act 1925, s 32(1)—Variation of Trusts Act 1958, s 1. **Lister's Will Trusts, Re** [1962] 3 737, Ch D.
Damages recovered by infant—
Payment to trustees to hold for benefit of infant until attaining maturity—Variation of trust by adding term postponing infant's entitlement until date after attainment of majority—Whether court having jurisdiction to add term—Variation of Trusts Act 1958, s 1(1). **Allen v Distillers Co (Biochemicals) Ltd** [1974] 2 365, QBD.
Discretion—
Principle on which discretion to be exercised. **Weston's Settlements, Re** [1968] 3 338, CA.
Proposed variation for benefit of persons unborn—Judge refusing to approve proposed variation—Proposed variation contrary to testatrix's intentions—Whether wishes of testatrix to be taken into account—Variation of Trusts Act 1958, s 1(1)(c). **Goulding v James** [1997] 2 239, CA.
Infant's resettlement—
Proposal for resettlement of trust property to which infant prospectively entitled on attaining 21 in a few months time—Infant immature and irresponsible with money—Whether court should approve proposal—Variation of Trusts Act 1958, s 1. **Towler's Settlement Trusts, Re** [1963] 3 759, Ch D.
Lancaster Chancery Court—
Approval of arrangements on behalf of unborn persons—Chancery of Lancaster Act 1890, s 3—Variation of Trusts Act 1958, s 1(1)(c),(3). **Drage's Settlements, Re** [1967] 3 978, Ch D.
Northern Ireland marriage settlement—
Trustees and trust property in England—Court's jurisdiction to vary trusts of such a settlement—Variation of Trusts Act 1958, s 1. **Ker's Settlement Trusts, Re** [1963] 1 801, Ch D.
Persons on whose behalf court may approve variation—
Person who may become entitled to interest—May become—Remote interest—Whether person with remote interest a person who 'may become' entitled to interest—Whether member of specified class with contingent interest at date of application excluded from categories of persons on whose behalf court may approve variation—Variation of Trusts Act 1958, s 1(1)(b). **Knocker v Youle** [1986] 2 914, Ch D.
Persons lacking capacity—Infant—Incapacity caused by impairment of, or disturbance in, functioning of the mind or brain—One beneficiary a minor who was severely autistic—Whether High Court or Court of Protection having jurisdiction to approve variation in respect of that beneficiary—Variation of Trusts Act 1958, s 1(3)—Mental Capacity Act 2005, s 2(1). **T v P** [2018] 3 469, Ch D.
Trust containing foreign element—
English marriage settlement to be replaced by trust abroad—Husband and wife emigrated to Canada and became domiciled there—Approval sought for proposed arrangement involving appointment of Canadian trustee in place of English trustee and resettlement of trust funds on trusts of new Canadian settlement—Variation of Trusts Act 1958, s 1. **Seale's Marriage Settlement, Re** [1961] 3 136, Ch D.
English settlements to be so varied that they could be superseded ultimately by trusts established in Jersey—Fiscal advantages only—Beneficial trusts not substantially to be varied—New trustees of English settlements to be appointed resident in Jersey and out of the jurisdiction—Settlor and family having moved to Jersey only recently—Whether court should approve variation and should appoint new trustees resident in Jersey—Trustee Act 1925, s 41—Variation of Trusts Act 1958, s 1. **Weston's Settlements, Re** [1968] 3 338, CA.

VARIATION OF TRUSTS (cont)—
    Jurisdiction (cont)—
        Trust containing foreign element (cont)—
            English trusts to be replaced by trusts established in Jersey—New trustees to be appointed in Jersey—Beneficial trusts not varied—Beneficiaries resident and domiciled in Jersey for 19 years—Whether court should approve variation—Variation of Trusts Act 1958, s 1. **Windeatt's Will Trusts, Re** [1969] **2** 324, Ch D.
            Trustees and most of trust fund in America—New York court prepared to act on proposed arrangement if approved by English court—Variation of Trusts Act 1958, s 1. **Paget's Settlement, Re** [1965] **1** 58, Ch D.
    Life tenant—
        Agreement releasing part of fund in favour of life tenant in excess of value of life interest—
            Consent of adult children to arrangement although element of gift to life tenant—Court's approval of arrangement on behalf of infants, etc—Variation of Trusts Act 1958, s 1. **Berry's Settlement, Re** [1966] **3** 431, Ch D.
    Mentally disordered patient—
        Variation of patient's beneficial interest. *See* **Mental health** (Patient's property—Variation of trusts).
    Order. *See* Practice—Order, *below.*
    Parties—
        Joinder. *See* Practice—Joinder of parties, *below.*
    Power of appointment—
        Extinguishment of power—
            Generally. *See* Extinction of power of appointment, *above.*
            Release before court's approval given. **Ball's Settlement, Re** [1968] **2** 438, Ch D.
        Fraud on power—
            Arrangement for proposed division of trust fund between life tenant and beneficiaries in remainder—Appointment to tenant for life's existing children, made in exercise of special power—Whether receipt by appointor of less than market value of life interest precludes appointment being a fraud on power—Arrangement not providing for after-born children excluded by appointment—Variation of Trusts Act 1958, s 1(1). **Brook's Settlement, Re** [1968] **3** 416, Ch D.
            Principle governing court's approach to question of approving proposed arrangement—Fair case for investigation whether fraud on power—Question to be resolved before arrangement approved—Factors of possible benefit to appointors, being life tenants of funds—Variation of Trusts Act 1958, s 1(1). **Wallace's Settlements, Re** [1968] **2** 209, Ch D.
    Practice—
        Alteration of trusts effected by court's approving the proposed arrangement—
            Written instrument not needed—Variation of Trusts Act 1958, s 1. **Hambleden's (Viscount) Will Trusts, Re** [1960] **1** 353, Ch D.
        Applicants—
            Beneficiaries not trustees should in general be applicants—Variation of Trusts Act 1958, s 1. **Druce's Settlement Trusts, Re** [1962] **1** 563, Ch D.
        Arrangement—
            Copy for use of Registrar—Variation of Trusts Act 1958, s 1. **Practice Direction** [1964] **2** 186, Ch D.
            Evidence—Arrangement affecting interests of infants or unborn beneficiaries—Counsel's opinion—Evidence showing that guardians ad litem or trustees support arrangement as being in interests of infants or unborn beneficiaries and exhibiting case to counsel and counsel's written opinion to that effect—No case or written opinion required in respect of persons having discretionary interests under protective trusts—Power of master or judge to dispense with case and written opinion—Variation of Trusts Act 1958, s 1(1). **Practice Direction** [1976] **3** 160, Ch D.
        Costs of application—
            Beneficiary under disability and receiver of income appointed—Application by receiver to master of Court of Protection to determine whether arrangement for her benefit—Costs of application paid out of settled funds—Variation of Trusts Act 1958, s 1(3). **Sanderson's Settlement Trusts, Re** [1961] **1** 25, Ch D.
        Form of order—
            Attorney General respondent to summons—Variation of Trusts Act 1958, s 1(1). **Longman's Settlement Trusts, Re** [1962] **2** 193, Ch D.
            Order made 'under the powers conferred by' the Variation of Trusts Act 1958. **Chapman's Settlement Trusts (No 2), Re** [1959] **2** 47, Ch D.
        Hearing—
            Hearing in open court—Order to be indorsed on probate—Variation of Trusts Act 1958, s 1. **Rouse's Will Trusts, Re** [1959] **2** 50, Ch D.
            Setting down in non-witness list—Certificate—Variation of Trusts Act 1958. **Practice Direction** [1988] **1** 162, Ch D.
        Investment clause to be varied—
            Amendment to or substitution of former clause—Note to be appended showing new powers of investment—Variation of Trusts Act 1958, s 1. **Blanket Manufacturers' Association's Agreement, Re** [1959] **2** 1, RPC.
            Enlargement to include power to invest in equities—Form of clause—Variation of Trusts Act 1958, s 1. **Thompson's Will Trusts, Re** [1960] **3** 378, Ch D.
        Joinder of parties—
            Objects of power of appointment in whose favour appointment might be made in future—Partial release of power of appointment so far as necessary to make variation binding—Whether prospective appointees necessary parties—Variation of Trusts Act 1958, s 1(1). **Christie-Miller's Settlement Trusts, Re** [1961] **1** 855, Ch D.
            Possible objects of discretionary trust arising on forfeiture under protective trust not made parties to application—Trustees of settlement sufficient guardians of interests of discretionary beneficiaries—Whether necessary to make discretionary beneficiaries respondents—Variation of Trusts Act 1958, s 1(1)(d), proviso. **Munro's Settlement Trusts, Re** [1963] **1** 209, Ch D.

Practice (cont)—
    Joinder of parties (cont)—
        Trust for persons who would be entitled if settlor died a widow intestate—Person so entitled at date of hearing a party—Whether necessary to join also as respondents persons who might, but only in certain events, become settlor's next of kin. **Moncrieff's Settlement Trusts, Re** [1962] 3 838, Ch D.
    Order—
        Direction that variation should be carried into effect—Inclusion in order—Direction not to be included—Alteration of trusts affected by court's approving arrangement—Variation of Trusts Act 1958, s 1. **Hambleden's (Viscount) Will Trusts, Re** [1960] 1 353, Ch D.
        Direction that variation should be carried into effect—New trusts operating subject to subsisting life interest—Variation of Trusts Act 1958, s 1. **Joseph's Will Trusts, Re** [1959] 3 474, Ch D.
        Form of order. See Practice—Form of order, *above*.
    Persons of unsound mind—
        Approval on behalf of person of unsound mind—Variation of Trusts Act 1958, s 1(3). **Practice Note** [1959] 3 897, Ct of Protection.
    Procedure—
        Alternative procedure—Procedure under Variation of Trusts Act 1958 preferable to that under Trustee Act 1925, s 57. **Blanket Manufacturers' Association's Agreement, Re** [1959] 2 1, RPC.
    Reasons for variation—
        Reasons to be stated in affidavit—Variation of Trusts Act 1958, s 1. **Oakes' Settlement Trusts, Re** [1959] 2 58, Ch D.
    Representation—
        Counsel—Separate representation—Application under, s 1 of Variation of Trusts Act 1958—Separate counsel for parties sui juris and for parties not sui juris. **Whigham's Settlement Trusts, Re** [1971] 2 568, Ch D.
        Counsel—Where leading counsel for applicant warranted, leading counsel should also represent parties on whose behalf the court's approval is sought, unless the advantage to them of the proposals is clear. **Breeden's Settlement Trusts, Re** [1964] 2 516, Ch D.
        Separate representation for trustees and next-of-kin—Practice under the Variation of Trusts Act 1958, s 1. **Chapman's Settlement Trusts (No 2), Re** [1959] 2 47, Ch D.
    Resettlement—
        Application nevertheless to 'vary' trusts. **Ball's Settlement, Re** [1968] 2 438, Ch D.
    Stamp duty—
        Submission of orders for adjudication—Orders made under the Variation of Trusts Act 1958, to be submitted to Commissioners of Inland Revenue for adjudication—Solicitor required to give undertaking to submit, within thirty days of entry of original order, duplicate order to commissioners for adjudication. **Practice Note** [1966] 1 672, Ch D.
        Undertaking with regard to stamp duty no longer required—Stamp duty position of duplicate orders—Variation of Trusts Act 1958—Stamp Duty (Exempt Instruments) Regulations 1987, Sch, category L. **Practice Direction** [1989] 3 96, Ch D.
    Summons—
        Title—Summons to be entitled 'In the matter of' the Variation of Trusts Act 1958. **Chapman's Settlement Trusts (No 2), Re** [1959] 2 47, Ch D.
Protection against possible shortfall in consequence of capital transfer tax—
    Insurance—
        Division of trust fund between tenant for life and remaindermen—Remaindermen children of life tenant one of whom an infant—Infant's share liable to be reduced by capital transfer tax—Prospect that in normal course of events shortfall would be made good by acceleration—Possibility of premature death of life tenant—Insurance policy to protect infant against shortfall in event of premature death—Policy kept up by life tenant subject to capital transfer tax—Arrangement approved subject to a with profits insurance policy to be kept up out of infant's income. **Robinson's Settlement Trusts, Re** [1976] 3 61, Ch D.
Protective trust—
    Conversion to absolute life interest—
        Discretion of court—Matters to be considered—Variation of Trusts Act 1958, s 1. **Burney's Settlement Trusts, Re** [1961] 1 856, Ch D.
    Evidence—
        Financial position of applicant life beneficiary and of applicant's husband—Evidence of that position needed in order to show to what extent protective trust continues to serve any useful purpose—Variation of Trusts Act 1958, s 1. **Baker's Settlement Trusts, Re** [1964] 1 482, Ch D.
    Like trusts to protective trusts—
        Determinable life interests—Variation of Trusts Act 1958, s 1(2). **Wallace's Settlements, Re** [1968] 2 209, Ch D.
    No forfeiture suffered—
        Provision proposed for one member of discretionary class—Variation of Trusts Act 1958, s 1(1). **Poole's Settlements' Trusts, Re** [1959] 2 340, Ch D.
Settled estates. See Benefit—Settled estates, *above*.
Settlement—
    Generally. See **Settlement** (Variation of trusts).
    Matrimonial causes. See **Variation of Settlement (Matrimonial Causes)**.
Settlor's application—
    Extension of trust for accumulation—
        Extension in view of possibility of settlor's death terminating trust for accumulation—Deletion of power to provide fund which might be available for meeting liability of settlor for surtax—Variation of Trusts Act 1958, s 1. **Lloyd's Settlement, Re** [1967] 2 314, Ch D.
    Specified description or specified class—
    Discretionary trust for specified class—
        Class included any future wife of married settlor—Subsequent alteration of tax legislation under which liability of settlor to tax might arise from inclusion of future wife within specified class—Variation of Trusts Act 1958. **Clitheroe's Settlement Trusts, Re** [1959] 3 789, Ch D.

VARIATION OF TRUSTS (cont)—
Specified description or specified class (cont)—
Next-of-kin entitled on death of applicant—
Order of court—Whether binding on existing potential next-of-kin—Variation of Trusts Act 1958, s 1(1)(b). **Suffert's Settlement, Re** [1960] **3** 561, Ch D.
Stamp duty—
Generally. See **Stamp duty** (Voluntary disposition inter vivos—Value of property conveyed or transferred—Variation of trust).
Practice. See Practice—Stamp duty, above.
Summons. See Practice—Summons, above.
Tenant for life. See Life tenant, above.
Unborn persons—
Approval sought on behalf of infants and unborn persons—
Benefit of individuals not class as a whole to be considered—Proposal to vary trusts by substituting fixed date as date of end of trust period in place of death of plaintiff—Possibility that plaintiff might survive fixed date in which case persons born after fixed date who could have benefited under unvaried trust would not benefit—Court would not give approval to variation on behalf of unborn persons—Variation of Trusts Act 1958, s 1. **Cohen's Settlement Trusts, Re** [1965] **3** 139, Ch D.
Arrangement deriving force from consent of adults and approval of court—
Arrangement thus effecting variation—Arrangement, when approved, an instrument to which Perpetuities etc Act 1964 would apply—Life tenant proposing to surrender half of income of trust fund—Trust for accumulation of that income and deferment of vesting of children's interest until age thirty—Whether court will approve arrangement involving element of risk in its application to unborn persons—Variation of Trusts Act 1958, s 1—Perpetuities and Accumulations Act 1964, s 15(5). **Holt's Settlement, Re** [1968] **1** 470, Ch D.
Release of life interest—
Application to approve transaction on behalf of tenant for life's future children—Special power of appointment exercisable by deed or will vested in tenant for life—Provision in proposed arrangement to extinguish testamentary element in power of appointment—Power to appoint by deed left untouched—Clause to be included in arrangement precluding power from being exercised until estate duty implications have been the subject of proper professional advice—Variation of Trusts Act 1958, s 1. **Drewe's Settlement, Re** [1966] **2** 844, Ch D.
Unborn issue and future husband objects of discretionary trust—
Person—Whether any 'person' includes an unborn or unascertained person in Variation of Trusts Act 1958, s 1(1)(d). **Turner's Will Trusts, Re** [1959] **2** 689, Ch D.
Validity of proposed arrangement—
Restraint of marriage—
Arrangement involving Swiss contracts that might operate in restraint of marriage—Whether arrangement should be approved—Variation of Trusts Act 1958, s 1. **Michelham's Will Trusts, Re** [1963] **2** 188, Ch D.
Variation—
Arrangement leaving substratum unchanged—
Revocation of beneficial trusts and resettlement—Rescission of clauses declaring beneficial interests and substitution of new clauses—Settlor's life interest—Testamentary power of appointment and interests in default of appointment removed—Whether arrangement leaving a substratum but effecting the purpose of the original trusts by other means was an arrangement 'varying' the original trusts—Variation of Trusts Act 1958, s 1(1). **Ball's Settlement, Re** [1968] **2** 438, Ch D.
Court, by. See Variation by the court, below.
Variation by the court—
Administrative power—
Sale of reversionary interest by trustees—No power of sale by trustees until interest in possession—Expediency—Sale for benefit of estate—Whether court will sanction sale—Trustee Act 1925, s 57(1). **Cockerell's Settlement Trusts, Re** [1956] **2** 172, Ch D.
Administrative purpose—
Special circumstances—Trustee Act 1925, s 57(1). **Forster's Settlement, Re** [1954] **3** 714, Ch D.
Charitable trust—
Consolidation of several trust funds—Extension of powers of investment—Jurisdiction by scheme—Trustee Act 1925, s 57(1). **Royal Society's Charitable Trusts, Re** [1955] **3** 14, Ch D.
Infant's interests—
Ambiguity in investments clause—Substitution of a new clause—Jurisdiction—Compromise—Trustee Act 1925, s 57(1). **Powell-Cotton's Re-Settlement, Re** [1956] **1** 60, CA.
Compromise. **Hylton's (Lord) Settlement, Re** [1954] **2** 647, CA.
Contingent interest in cpaital on surviving tenant for life—Proposed sale of reversionary interest to tenant for life—Whether court could sanction sale—Inherent jurisdiction—Trustee Act 1925, s 53. **Heyworth's Settlements, Re** [1956] **2** 21, Ch D.
Scheme for avoidance of income tax failing—Parents having always shown due regard for infants' benefit—Trustee Act 1925, s 57(1). **Basden's Settlement Trusts, Re** [1943] **2** 11, Ch D.
Tenant in tail in remainder—Proposed sale of infant's entailed interest to tenant for life, the purchase price to be paid to trustees of a new settlement for benefit of infant—Trustee Act 1925, s 53. **Meux's Will Trusts, Re** [1957] **2** 630, Ch D.
Investment clause—
Bequest of specific shares on successive trusts—Trustee Act 1925, ss 1(1), 57(1), 69(1). **Pratt (decd), Re, Barrow & McCarthy** [1943] **2** 375, Ch D.
Extension of powers of investment—Discretion—Special circumstances to be shown to justify departure from scope enacted by Trustee Investments Act 1961—Invalid clause in will sharing testator's wish that his trustees should invest only in 'blue chip' equities—Whether special circumstances established—Trustee Act 1925, s 57—Trustee Investments Act 1961, s 15. **Kolb's Will Trusts, Re** [1961] **3** 811, Ch D.

VARIATION OF TRUSTS (cont)—
    Variation by the court (cont)—
        Investment clause (cont)—
            Extension of powers of investment—Extension of powers beyond those permitted under Trustee Investments Act 1961—Factors to be taken into consideration—Whether changes in investment market and practice entitling court to vary investment powers by giving trustees wider powers of investment than those permitted under Trustee Investments Act 1961—Trustee Investments Act 1961. **British Museum (Trustees) v A-G** [1984] **1** 337, Ch D.
            Extension of powers of investment—Pension fund—Enlargement of fund due to inflation—Co-operative Society's employees' pension fund—Different views existing as to proper construction of investment clause but parties not in dispute—Whether court having power under inherent jurisdiction to confer on trustees wide modern power of investment—Whether court having statutory jurisdiction to vary trust and give trustees wider investment powers—Whether range of investments sanctioned must be limited to those permitted under Trustee Investments Act 1961—Trustee Act 1925, s 57(1)—Trustee Investments Act 1961, s 1. **Mason v Farbrother** [1983] **2** 1078, Ch D.
            Extension of range of investments—Whether court has jurisdiction to confer wider power of investment—Trustee Act 1925, s 57(1). **Shipwrecked Fishermen and Mariners' Royal Benevolent Society Charity, Re** [1958] **3** 465, Ch D.
            Investment in shares of banking companies in Dominions—Trustee Act 1925, s 57. **Brassey's Settlement, Re** [1955] **1** 577, Ch D.
        Jurisdiction of court—
            No administrative problem—Trustee Act 1925, s 57(1). **Chapman v Chapman** [1954] **1** 798, HL.
        Sale of reversionary interest by trustees—
            No power to sell until interest in possession—Whether court will sanction sale—Trustee Act 1925, s 57(1). **Cockerell's Settlement Trusts, Re** [1956] **2** 172, Ch D.

VASECTOMY OPERATION
    Contract regarding operation—
        Collateral warranty—
            Breach. *See* **Contract** (Warranty—Collateral warranty—Breach—Surgery—Vasectomy).
            Nature of contract. *See* **Contract** (Surgery—Nature of contract—Vasectomy).
    Negligence—
        Information or advice—
            Knowledge third party might rely on information. *See* **Negligence** (Information or advice—Knowledge third party might rely on information—Vasectomy operation).

VEHICLE
    Articulated. *See* **Road traffic** (Articulated vehicle).
    Capital allowances. *See* **Capital allowances** (Vehicles).
    Forfeiture—
        Vehicle used for carriage of thing liable to forfeiture under customs legislation. *See* **Customs and excise** (Forfeiture—Vehicle used for carriage of thing liable to forfeiture).
    Goods vehicle. *See* **Road traffic** (Goods vehicle).
    Hire-purchase. *See* **Hire-purchase** (Motor vehicle).
    Insurance. *See* **Motor insurance.**
    Motor vehicle—
        Generally. *See* **Road traffic** (Motor vehicle).
        Registration mark—
            Assignment. *See* **Chose in action** (Assignment—Vehicle registration mark).
    Negligence—
        Contributory negligence—
            Collision. *See* **Negligence** (Contributory negligence—Collision between vehicles on road).
        Generally. *See* **Negligence** (Vehicles).
    Owner—
        Vicarious liability for driver's negligence. *See* **Vicarious liability** (Vehicle owner's liability for driver's negligence).
    Plant—
        Investment grant. *See* **Investment grant** (Machinery and plant—Vehicle).
    Road traffic. *See* **Road traffic** (Motor vehicle).
    Vehicular access—
        Right to park. *See* **Easement** (Right to park cars).
    Waiting and loading restrictions. *See* **Road traffic** (Waiting and loading restrictions).

VENDOR AND PURCHASER
    Deposit prior to contract—
        Receipt by estate agent. *See* **Estate agent** (Deposit—Deposit prior to contract).
    Registered land. *See* **Land registration** (Transfer).
    Restrictive covenant. *See* **Restrictive covenant affecting land.**
    Rule against perpetuities. *See* **Rule against perpetuities** (Vendor and purchaser—Option to purchase land).
    Sale of goods. *See* **Sale of goods.**
    Sale of land—
        Generally. *See* **Sale of land.**
        Solicitor—
            Acting for vendor and purchaser—Danger of so acting. *See* **Solicitor** (Sale of land—Acting for vendor and purchaser—Danger of so acting).

VENDOR'S LIEN
    Generally. *See* **Lien** (Vendor's lien).
    Sale of land—
        Generally. *See* **Sale of land** (Vendor's lien).

VENDOR'S LIEN (cont)—
  Sale of land (cont)—
    Sale to company—
      Whether lien registrable as charge. *See* **Company** (Charge—Registration—Unpaid vendor's lien—Property sold to company).
    Unpaid vendor's lien—
      Registered land—Overriding interest. *See* **Land registration** (Overriding interest—Rights of person in actual occupation of land—Unpaid vendor's lien).

VENEREAL DISEASE
  Matrimonial proceedings—
    Nullity suit. *See* **Nullity** (Venereal disease).

VENIRE DE NOVO
  Criminal appeal—
    Power to order new trial—
      Jamaica. *See* **Jamaica** (Criminal law—Appeal—Allowing appeal—New trial—Venire de novo).

VENTILATION
  Coal mine—
    Statutory duty. *See* **Coal mining** (Statutory duty—Provision of ventilation).
  Easement. *See* **Easement** (Ventilation).
  Factory. *See* **Factory** (Ventilation).

VERDICT
  Alternative offence—
    Appeal—
      Substitution of verdict. *See* **Criminal law** (Appeal—Substitution of verdict—Alternative offence).
  Alternative offence. *See* **Criminal law** (Trial—Alternative verdicts).
  Defamation action. *See* **Libel and slander** (Verdict).
  Direction to jury. *See* **Criminal law** (Trial—Direction to jury—Verdict).
  Generally. *See* **Criminal law** (Verdict).
  Inquest—
    Generally. *See* **Coroner** (Inquest—Verdict).
  Jury—
    Generally. *See* **Jury** (Verdict).
    Majority verdict. *See* **Jury** (Majority verdict).
    Unanimity. *See* **Jury** (Direction to jury—Requirement of unanimity in decision).
  Unreasonable verdict—
    Appeal. *See* **Criminal law** (Appeal—Unreasonable verdict).

VERMIN
  Rats and mice. *See* **Pests** (Rats and mice).

VERTICAL SPINDLE MOULDING MACHINE
  Factory—
    Safety provisions. *See* **Factory** (Woodworking machinery—Cutter of vertical spindle moulding machine).

VESSEL
  Arrest. *See* **Admiralty** (Arrest of vessel).
  Collision at sea—
    Contributory negligence. *See* **Negligence** (Contributory negligence—Collision at sea).
  Navigation—
    Land covered by water. *See* **Water and watercourses** (Navigation).
  Overtaking—
    Collision regulations. *See* **Shipping** (Collision regulations—Overtaking vessel).
  Stranding—
    Negligence—
      Pleading. *See* **Negligence** (Pleading—Stranding of vessel).
    Salvage—
      Cargo—Storage expenses. *See* **Shipping** (Salvage—Cargo—Storage expenses—Agreement—Vessel stranding).
  Withdrawal from charterparty—
    Time charter—
      Non-payment of hire. *See* **Shipping** (Time charterparty—Withdrawal of vessel for non-payment of hire).

VESTED INTEREST
  Liable to be divested—
    Contingent interest distinguished. *See* **Settlement** (Contingent interest—Contingent interest distinguished from vested interest liable to be divested).

VETERINARY SURGEON
  Discipline—
    Professional misconduct—
      Conduct disgraceful in a professional respect—Whether conduct must be in pursuit of profession—Veterinary surgeon also a farmer—Carcases of cattle that died in severe winter lying on farm—Veterinary Surgeons Act 1881, s 6. **Marten v Disciplinary Committee of the Royal College of Veterinary Surgeons** [1965] **1** 949, QBD.

VETERINARY SURGEON (cont)—
  Refusal to register on supplementary register—
    Appeal to High Court—
      Procedure—Rehearing—Veterinary Surgeons Act 1948, s 6(5). **Allender v Royal College of Veterinary Surgeons Council** [1951] **2** 859, KBD.

VEXATIOUS PROCEEDINGS
  Civil proceedings order—
    Application by Attorney General—
      Whether Attorney General required to lead evidence that he had authorised application for civil proceedings order—Supreme Court Act 1981, s 42. **A-G v Foley** [2000] **2** 609, CA.
  Employment tribunal—
    Complaint—
      Complaint withdrawn by complainant—Industrial tribunal formally dismissing complaint—Complainant making fresh complaint on same matter within time limit for making complaint—Whether fresh complaint vexatious—Industrial Tribunals (Labour Relations) Regulations 1974 (SI 1974 No 1386), Sch, r 11(2)(e). **Acrow (Engineers) Ltd v Hathaway** [1981] **2** 161, QBD.
  Factors to be considered in determining whether proceedings vexatious—
    Actions each disclosing a cause of action—
      Regard to be had to history of the matter—Whether proceedings were vexatious—Supreme Court of Judicature (Consolidation) Act 1925, s 51(1). **A-G v Vernazza** [1960] **1** 183, CA.
  Instituting proceedings—
    Action instituted after Court of Appeal stated that there was no reason therefor—
      Subsequent proceedings by summonses in winding-up and by way of appeal, and further action—What may constitute 'institution' of legal proceedings—Supreme Court of Judicature (Consolidation) Act 1925, s 51(1). **A-G v Vernazza** [1960] **1** 183, CA.
    Appeal from county court judgment in proceedings brought against vexatious litigant—
      Plaintiffs bringing proceedings against vexatious litigant in county court and obtaining judgment against him—Whether vexatious litigant requiring leave of High Court to appeal from judgment—Whether Court of Appeal having jurisdiction to cause or allow appeal to be set down or adjudicated upon before leave given by High Court—Supreme Court Act 1981, s 42(1), (1A). **Garratt (Henry J) & Co v Ewing** [1991] **4** 891, CA.
    Appeal from final order—
      High Court giving vexatious litigant leave to bring county court action—Judge dismissing proceedings and claimant applying to Court of Appeal for permission to appeal—Whether vexatious litigant requiring High Court's permission to bring substantive appeal to Court of Appeal—Supreme Court Act 1981, s 42. **Johnson v Valks** [2000] **1** 450, CA.
    Institute—
      Appeal to High Court against decision of tribunal—Whether appeal by vexatious litigant constituting the institution of proceedings—Whether leave to appeal required—Supreme Court of Judicature (Consolidation) Act 1925, s 51(1) (as amended by the Supreme Court of Judicature (Amendment) Act 1959 s 1 (1))—Tribunals and Inquiries Act 1971, s 13(1). **Becker, Re** [1975] **2** 587, QBD.
      Application for leave to apply for judicial review—Whether application for leave constituting institution of proceedings—Whether leave to make application required—Supreme Court Act 1981, s 42(1A)(a)—RSC Ord 53, r 3. **R v Highbury Corner Magistrates' Court, ex p Ewing** [1991] **3** 192, CA.
      Bankruptcy proceedings—Proof of debt in pending proceedings by non-petitioning creditor—Order in force requiring creditor to obtain leave of High Court before instituting legal proceedings—Whether creditor required to obtain leave before proving debt or appealing against rejection of proof—Supreme Court of Judicature (Consolidation) Act 1925, s 51(1) (as amended by the Supreme Court of Judicature (Amendment) Act 1959, s 1(1)). **Wilson (ID) (a bankrupt), Re, ex p Bebbington Easton** [1973] **1** 849, Ch D.
      Counterclaim—Whether litigant 'instituting' vexatious proceedings if he makes a counterclaim—Supreme Court Act 1981, s 42(1). **A-G v Jones** [1990] **2** 636, CA.
    Proceedings—
      Actions as personal representatives of deceased person—Other actions in litigant's own right—Whether court entitled to consider all proceedings by litigant—Supreme Court of Judicature (Consolidation) Act 1925, s 51(1) (as amended by Supreme Court of Judicature (Amendment) Act 1959, s 1(1)). **Langton, Re** [1966] **3** 576, QBD CA.
      Appeal—Civil proceedings—Proceedings in Court of Appeal from High Court or inferior court—Whether 'civil proceedings' including proceedings in Court of Appeal on appeal from High Court or inferior court—Supreme Court Act 1981, s 42(1)(b). **A-G v Jones** [1990] **2** 636, CA.
  Leave to institute or continue vexatious proceedings—
    Discretion—
      Exercise of discretion—Supreme Court of Judicature (Consolidation) Act 1925, s 51(1) (as amended by the Supreme Court of Judicature (Amendment) Act 1959, s 1(1)). **Becker v Teale** [1971] **3** 715, CA.
      Permission to institute proceedings—Practice direction providing for order dismissing application for permission without hearing—Whether ultra vires enabling statute—Whether contrary to rules of natural justice—Whether breach of right of access to court—Supreme Court Act 1981, s 42(3)—Civil Procedure Act 1997, ss 1(1), 5(3), Sch 1, para 3—Human Rights Act 1998, Sch 1, Pt I, art 6—CPR PD 3, para 7.6(3). **R (on the application of Ewing) v Dept for Constitutional Affairs** [2006] **2** 993, QBD.
  Leave to apply to Court of Appeal for permission to appeal—
    Refusal of leave—Whether High Court judge's refusal to grant vexatious litigant leave to apply to Court of Appeal for permission to appeal infringing right of access to court under human rights convention—Supreme Court Act 1981, s 42—Human Rights Act 1998, Sch 1, Pt I, art 6. **Ebert v Official Receiver** [2001] **3** 942, CA.

VEXATIOUS PROCEEDINGS (cont)—
Leave to institute or continue vexatious proceedings (cont)—
Setting aside leave—
Defendant to proposed proceedings applying to set aside leave—Court setting aside leave—Whether court having power to do so—Whether proposed defendant having locus standi to apply to set aside leave—Whether proposed defendant party to proceedings—Supreme Court Act 1981, s 42(3)—RSC Ord 32, r 6. **Jones v Vans Colina** [1997] **1** 768, CA.
Litigant in person—
Persistent unmeritorious litigation—
Restriction on oral application to Court of Appeal. **Perotti v Collyer-Bristow (a firm)** [2004] **4** 53, CA.
Striking out statement of claim. *See* **Statement of case** (Striking out).

VIBRATION WHITE FINGER
Coal mining hand arm vibration syndrome action—
Practice. *See* **Practice** (Coal mining hand arm vibration syndrome (vibration white finger) actions).

VICARIOUS LIABILITY
Actual or ostensible authority. *See* Employer and employee—Act outside scope of employment—Act outside scope of actual or ostensible authority, *below.*
Authorised act done in improper manner. *See* Employer and employee—Authorised act done in improper manner, *below.*
Common employment—
Amalgamation of undertakings—
Transport vehicles—Whether doctrine applies to transport vehicles en route. **Metcalfe v London Passenger Transport Board** [1939] **2** 542, CA.
Coach-driver driving one of six coaches returning to garage—
Death caused by another coach belonging to same company. **Radcliffe v Ribble Motor Services Ltd** [1939] **1** 637, HL.
Coal mine—
Delegation of duty—Master prohibited by statute from taking part in technical management of mine—Coal Mines Act 1911, s 2(4). **Wilsons and Clyde Coal Co Ltd v English** [1937] **3** 628, HL.
Common work—
Electric trams in collision on highway—Injury to conductress. **Graham (or Miller) v Glasgow Corp** [1947] **1** 1, HL.
Special risk—Omnibus collision on highway—Injury to conductress. **Glasgow Corp v Neilson** [1947] **2** 346, HL.
Director acting as foreman—
Workman temporarily relieving fellow worker—Negligence—Volenti non fit injuria—Heart disease—Novus actus interveniens—Stay of execution—Irrecoverable payment to plaintiff. **Bloor v Liverpool Derricking and Carrying Co Ltd** [1936] **3** 399, CA.
Dissimilar tasks—
Employees engaged in different departments of duty—Plaintiff not in course of employment at time of accident. **McGovern v London, Midland and Scottish Rly Co** [1944] **1** 730, Assizes.
Plaintiff and negligent workmen in different departments of employers' organisation—Factory—Building not ready for use as factory—Preparation for performance of work when building equipped as factory—Factories Act 1937, ss 25(3), 151(1)(b). **Barrington v Kent Rivers Catchment Board** [1947] **2** 782, KBD.
Doctrine—
Modification—Whether modified by Essential Work Order—Essential Work (General Provisions) (No 2) Order 1942 (SR & O 1942 No 1594). **Alexander v Tredegar Iron & Coal Co Ltd** [1945] **2** 275, HL.
Employee voluntarily undertaking work outside scope of employment—
Necessity for contract covering work actually done when injuries sustained. **Colman v Croft (Isaac) & Sons** [1946] **2** 401, KBD.
Loading ship—
Use of married gear—Guy-rope not securely fastened—Negligence of fellow-workman. **Colfar v Coggins & Griffith (Liverpool) Ltd** [1945] **1** 326, HL.
Manager of company riding in company's car—
Injury suffered through negligence of driver employed by company—No term in manager's contract of service obliging him to travel by car. **Pollock v Burt (Charles) Ltd** [1940] **4** 264, CA.
Plaintiff one of a gang of workmen of equal status—
Injury to plaintiff due to joint negligence of members of gang. **Williams v Port of Liverpool Stevedoring Co Ltd** [1956] **2** 69, Assizes.
Provision excluding employer's liability—
Agreement collateral to contract of service—Compulsory pension scheme—Law Reform (Personal Injuries) Act 1948, s 1(3). **Smith v British European Airways Corp** [1951] **2** 737, KBD.
Servant temporarily off duty—
Injured by negligence of fellow servant—Liability of employer. **Dorrington v London Passenger Transport Board** [1947] **2** 84, KBD.
Special risk arising out of relationship—
Linesman repairing overhead wires spanning highway—Linesman injured by trolley bus—Whether carelessness of trolley bus driver a special risk to linesman or a general risk of highway. **Lancaster v London Passenger Transport Board** [1948] **2** 796, HL.
Unloading ship—
Crate of cheese rolling over side of ship through insufficient barrier—Delegation of duty. **Grantham v New Zealand Shipping Co Ltd** [1940] **4** 258, KBD.
Voluntary assistance of servant by stranger—
Servant inviting stranger to assist in shifting lorry trailer—Stranger injured in course of moving load—Vicarious liability of master to stranger—Whether doctrine of common employment precluding stranger from recovering damages from master. **Bromiley v Collins** [1936] **2** 1061, Assizes.
Contribution—
Dishonesty. *See* **Contribution** (Dishonesty—Vicarious liability).

VICARIOUS LIABILITY (cont)—
Contributory negligence—
Breach of statutory duty—
Workman and fellow employee. *See* **Negligence** (Contributory negligence—Workman and fellow employee—Breach of statutory duty—Vicarious liability of employer).
Criminal act of servant. *See* Employer and employee—Criminal act of servant, *below.*
Crown—
Salvage—
Liability for negligence when acting as salvor. *See* **Statute** (Crown—Crown entitled by statute to claim for salvage services—Vicarious liability for negligence).
Employer and employee—
Act of a class servant authorised to do—
Act done negligently—Real estate valuations—Servant doing valuations for group of companies during period when ordered not to do business with them—Ultimate client not knowing of servant's existence or authority as a valuer—Liability of master for negligence of servant in making the valuations—Whether servant had actual authority—Whether actual authority could be inferred from fact that valuations were a class of act which servant was authorised to do. **Kooragang Investments Pty Ltd v Richardson & Wrench Ltd** [1981] **3** 65, PC.
Act outside scope of employment—
Act outside scope of actual or ostensible authority—Deceit—Car salesman practising deceit on customer—Salesman acting outside scope of authority—Judge finding customer should have been put on inquiry as to salesman's lack of authority—Whether salesman's employer vicariously liable for his deceit—Whether judge erring in importing inquiry test. **Quinn v CC Automotive Group Ltd (t/a Carcraft)** [2011] **2 Comm** 584, CA.
Employee carrying fellow employee back to place of work—Vehicle owned by employee's father—Employee under no obligation to employer to carry fellow employee—Employee entitled to passenger allowance from employer—Fellow employee injured owing to negligent driving of employee—Journey in course of employment—Employee not acting as servant of employer at relevant time. **Nottingham v Aldridge (The Prudential Assurance Co Ltd, third party)** [1971] **2** 751, QBD.
Wilful misbehaviour—Employers engaged in business of breaking down scrap metal—Employees discovering live shell amongst scrap—Employees inviting plaintiff to hit shell—Plaintiff seriously injured in consequence of hitting shell—Liability of employers. **O'Reilly v National Rail and Tramway Appliances Ltd** [1966] **1** 499, Assizes.
Wilful misbehaviour—Servant injured through isolated act of wilful misbehaviour—Negligence of fellow servant outside scope of employment. **O'Reilly v National Rail and Tramway Appliances Ltd** [1966] **1** 499, Assizes.
Act within course of employment—
Act authorised but not an act in discharge of duty to master—Lorry driver permitted to stop for refreshment during long journeys—Collision with motor cyclist while lorry driver walking across road to reach café. **Crook v Derbyshire Stone Ltd** [1956] **2** 447, Assizes.
Act done on way to collect wages but after day's work completed—Servant bicycling on master's premises to collect wages at required time—Collision with fellow-servant while servant making detour across bus park—Fellow-servant killed—Servant acting in the course of his employment. **Staton v National Coal Board** [1957] **2** 667, QBD.
Authorised act done in improper manner. *See* Employer and employee—Authorised act done in improper manner, *below.*
Joint tortfeasors—Defendant's employee assisting third party in fraud on bank—Assistance including non-tortious acts carried out in course of employment—Whether employer could be vicariously liable for acts of employee which only constituted a tort when combined with acts not in the course of employment. **Credit Lyonnais Bank Nederland NV (now known as Generale Bank Nederland NV) v Export Credits Guarantee Dept** [1999] **1** 929, HL.
Journey to temporary job—Employee paid wages while travelling to and from temporary job—Time and mode of travel left to employee's discretion—Whether employee acting within course of employment when travelling to and from temporary job—Whether employer vicariously liable for employee's negligence while travelling to and from temporary job in his own car. **Smith v Stages** [1989] **1** 833, HL.
Liability of master when servant cannot be sued—Injury to servant's wife due to servant's negligence. **Broom v Morgan** [1953] **1** 849, CA.
Prohibited act—Limitation on scope of employment—Act prohibited by master—Effect of prohibition—Prohibition affecting mode of conduct within scope of employment rather than limiting scope of employment—Milkman—Employers expressly prohibiting milkmen from carrying children on milk floats—Milkman carrying child on float for purpose of assisting in delivery of milk—Child injured in consequence of milkman's negligent driving—Whether employers liable for milkman's negligence. **Rose v Plenty** [1976] **1** 97, CA.
Servant authorised to drive master's van and permitted to use van in order to obtain refreshment—Accident while returning in van to site of work after journey to café—Fellow-servant, riding in van, killed. **Hilton v Thomas Burton (Rhodes) Ltd** [1961] **1** 74, Assizes.
Servant authorised to use private motor cycle combination—Accident while returning to work after buying tools and obtaining meal—Injury to fellow servant riding in sidecar. **Harvey v R G O'Dell Ltd (Galway, third party)** [1958] **1** 657, QBD.
Servant using private car—No instructions not to use a private car—Private car previously used with knowledge of master. **McKean v Raynor Bros Ltd (Nottingham)** [1942] **2** 650, KBD.
Test to be applied in determining whether act done 'in course of employment'—Employee playing practical joke on fellow employee at work—Fellow employee injured—Whether employer vicariously liable. **Harrison v Michelin Tyre Co Ltd** [1985] **1** 918, QBD.
Threat by garage customer to report employee—Assault on customer by employee. **Warren v Henlys Ltd** [1948] **2** 935, KBD.
Volunteer—Consignee injured while assisting master's servant—Duty of carriers to avoid injury to person properly upon premises where goods are delivered apart from any implied contract of employment. **Lomas v Jones (M) & Son** [1943] **2** 548, CA.

VICARIOUS LIABILITY (cont)—
　Employer and employee (cont)—
　　Indemnity of master for servant's negligence (cont)—
　　　Injury to fellow workman—Implied terms of contract of service—Servant employed as
　　　　storekeeper—Authorised to use his own motor cycle in travelling to and from outside job—Injury
　　　　to fellow-servant in sidecar—Whether implied term of contract of service as storekeeper to use
　　　　care while driving. **Harvey v R G O'Dell Ltd (Galway, third party)** [1958] **1** 657, QBD.
　　Liability for act of sub-contractor—
　　　Workman employed by building contractor injured by fall from dangerous scaffold
　　　　platform—Platform created or altered by sub-contractor—Contractor responsible for
　　　　scaffolding—Failure to warn workman—Contributory negligence. **Simmons v Bovis Ltd**
　　　　[1956] **1** 736, Assizes.
　　Loan of servant. *See* Loan of servant, *below*.
　　Prohibited act by employee—
　　　Act within course of employment. *See* Employer and employee—Act within course of
　　　　employment—Prohibited act, *above*.
　　　Injured person's knowledge of prohibition—Prohibition likely to be known to injured
　　　　person—Opportunity to avoid danger of injury from prohibited acts—Whether prohibitions
　　　　conclusive as against injured persons of scope of servant's employment—Whether master liable
　　　　for injuries caused by prohibited acts of servant. **Stone v Taffe** [1974] **3** 1016, CA.
　　　Statutory prohibition—Harassment—Whether employer vicariously liable for harassment
　　　　committed by employee in course of employment in breach of statutory prohibition—Protection
　　　　from Harassment Act 1997, ss 3, 10. **Majrowski v Guy's and St Thomas's NHS Trust** [2006] **4** 395,
　　　　HL.
　　　Unauthorised passenger on employer's vehicle—Negligent driving of vehicle by employee—
　　　　Accident to unauthorised passenger in lorry—Passenger a trespasser on vehicle—Extent of duty
　　　　to take care. **Conway v Wimpey (George) & Co Ltd** [1951] **1** 363, CA.
　　　Unauthorised passenger on employer's vehicle—Negligent driving of vehicle by employee—Fatal
　　　　accident to unauthorised passenger—Passenger a trespasser on vehicle—Whether employer
　　　　liable for negligent driving of employee. **Twine v Bean's Express Ltd** [1946] **1** 202, KBD.
　　　Use by servant of his own uninsured car contrary to prohibition. **Canadian Pacific Rly Co v Lockhart**
　　　　[1942] **2** 464, PC.
　　Supervision or control—
　　　Producer of variety programme—Producer engaging dancers to appear in programme—Producer
　　　　exercising certain degree of supervision and control over dancers—Heel of dancer's shoe
　　　　becoming detached and hitting member of audience—Liability of producer—Whether dancer
　　　　servant or independent contractor. **Fraser-Wallas v Waters (Elsie and Doris)** [1939] **4** 609, KBD.
　Employment—
　　Common employment. *See* Common employment, *above*.
　　Generally. *See* Employer and employee, *above*.
　Exclusion. *See* Common employment—Provision excluding employer's liability, *above*.
　Fire—
　　Accidental fire. *See* Fire (Accidental fire—Vicarious liability).
　Home Office—
　　Misfeasance by prison officer. *See* **Public office** (Abuse of—Misfeasance by a public officer—Prison
　　　officer—Vicarious liability of Home Office).
　Independent contractor—
　　Fire—
　　　Escape to adjoining premises. *See* **Negligence** (Fire—Escape to adjoining premises—Independent
　　　　contractor).
　　Liability of employer—
　　　Bailment—Warehouseman—Security patrols for guarding warehouse provided by independent
　　　　contractor—Negligence by patrolman employed by independent contractor—Whether ware-
　　　　houseman liable for such negligence. **British Road Services Ltd v Crutchley (Arthur V) & Co Ltd**
　　　　[1968] **1** 811, CA.
　　　Duty of employer to see that reasonable care taken by contractor—Tort of strict liability—Explosion
　　　　on oil tanker—Exclusion of defence of independent contractor. **Pass of Ballater SS Owners v
　　　　Cardiff Channel Dry Docks & Pontoon Co Ltd** [1942] **2** 79, Admin Ct.
　　　Solicitor employing enquiry agent in divorce proceedings—Solicitor acting in divorce proceedings
　　　　on behalf of one spouse—Trespass by enquiry agent in home of other spouse. **Jolliffe v Willmett
　　　　& Co** [1971] **1** 478, QBD.
　　　Work done near highway—Work not dangerous if competently done—Tree felled so incompetently
　　　　that it brought telephone wires down on to highway, causing collision with car and consequent
　　　　injury to pedestrian. **Salsbury v Woodland** [1969] **3** 863, CA.
　　Supervision or control—
　　　Music-hall artists—Control by manager over artists—Some degree of supervision and
　　　　control—Sufficiency—Dancer—Shoe kicked off and hitting member of audience—Liability of
　　　　manager. **Fraser-Wallas v Waters (Elsie and Doris)** [1939] **4** 609, KBD.
　　　Porters at landing stage—Bogies for carrying passengers' luggage provided by shipowners and
　　　　others—Bogies used indiscriminately by porters for all business at landing stage—No
　　　　supervision or control by shipowners. **Norton v Canadian Pacific Steamships Ltd** [1961] **2** 785,
　　　　CA.
　　　Salesman driving own car—Samples provided by company who paid commission and petrol
　　　　allowance—Very little control over saleman's work—Company not liable for negligent driving.
　　　　Egginton v Reader [1936] **1** 7, KBD.
　Loan of servant—
　　Contract of service—
　　　Unskilled labourer—No consent to transfer—Duty to comply with new employers' directions as to
　　　　way of doing work—Old employers' liability for wages and insurance and right of
　　　　dismissal—Whether servant under 'contract of service' with new employer. **Denham v Midland
　　　　Employers' Mutual Assurance Ltd** [1955] **2** 561, CA.

VICARIOUS LIABILITY (cont)—
  Loan of servant (cont)—
    Dock labourer—
      General servant of harbour board—Working regularly for company acting as master stevedores at docks—Dock labourer injured through unsafe system of work—Whether harbour board or company liable. **Gibb v United Steel Companies Ltd** [1957] **2** 110, Assizes.
    Employee of sub-sub-contractor working under supervision of other employee of sub-sub-contractor and of self-employed worker contracted to sub-contractor—
      Negligent act of employee causing damage—Whether sub-sub-contractor and sub-contractor both capable of vicarious liability. **Viasystems (Tyneside) Ltd v Thermal Transfer (Northern) Ltd** [2005] **4** 1181, CA.
    Hire of crane and driver—
      Contract subject to dock regulations—Provision that 'the drivers so provided shall be the servants of the applicants'—Accident due to negligent driving of driver—Driver not subject to control of hirer in regard to manner of driving—General employer responsible for negligent driving of driver. **Mersey Docks and Harbour Board v Coggins & Griffiths (Liverpool) Ltd and McFarlane** [1946] **2** 345, HL.
      Hirer to be responsible for driver's acts as though driver were in hirer's direct employ—Accident due to negligence of driver—Whether owner entitled to be indemnified. **Herdman v Walker (Tooting) Ltd (City Plant Hirers Ltd, third party)** [1956] **1** 429, QBD.
      Injury to driver of crane hired to stevedores—Responsibility of stevedores in respect of particular operation. **Holt v Rhodes (W H) & Son Ltd** [1949] **1** 478, CA.
    Hire of crane-excavator and driver—
      Accident while excavator on site—Apportionment of responsibility as between owners and hirers—Hiring contract provided that driver should be regarded as servant of hirers for all purposes in connection with working of plant and that hirers should be responsible for claims in connection with working of plant—Maintenance of plant left as responsibility of owners—Accident caused by negligence of driver partly in connection with the working of the plant and partly in maintenance of the plant—Responsibility apportioned as to forty per cent to owners. **White (Arthur) (Contractors) Ltd v Tarmac Civil Engineering Ltd** [1967] **3** 586, HL.
    Hire of driver—
      Long-standing arrangement—Hirer's duty to servant—Whether that of invitor or employer—Driver working for hirer full time—Driver injured through unsafe method of unloading adopted by hirer—Employer liable. **O'Reilly v Imperial Chemical Industries Ltd** [1955] **3** 382, CA.
    Hire of vehicle and driver—
      Accident due to negligence of driver—Whether hirer or regular employer responsible for negligence of driver. **Mersey Docks and Harbour Board v Coggins & Griffiths (Liverpool) Ltd and McFarlane** [1945] **1** 605, CA.
      Accident to lorry while so hired—Responsibility for negligence of driver on owner. **Willard v Whiteley Ltd** [1938] **3** 779, CA.
      Contract for carriage and delivery of hirer's goods—Driver to obey all orders of hirer and wear prescribed uniform—Employer liable for driver's negligence. **Century Insurance Co Ltd v Northern Ireland Road Transport Board** [1942] **1** 491, HL.
      Hirer having no control over driver other than directing him where deliveries to be made—Owner liable for driver's negligence. **Williams v IRC** [1944] **1** 381, HL.
    Servant 'lent' by employers to occupiers of factory—
      Materials, tools and equipment provided by occupiers—Work controlled by factory foreman—Temporary employer liable for servant's negligence. **Garrard v Southey (A E) & Co** [1952] **1** 597, QBD.
    Skilled shotfirer, servant of sub-contractor, blasting rock for building contractor—
      Building contractor failing to provide flagman or ladder to assist shotfirer to get up and down slippery bank when acting as flagman—Shotfirer injured through slipping on bank—Whether shotfirer the servant for the time being of the building contractor. **Savory v Holland, Hannen and Cubitts (Southern) Ltd** [1964] **3** 18, CA.
    Transfer of entire and absolute control of servant—
      Port authority rendering stevedoring services by hiring out stevedores in its regular employment—Hire of stevedores to load ship—Harbour byelaw providing that stevedores to be under superintendence of ship's officers and port authority not to be responsible as stevedores—Member of stevedoring gang injured in loading operation due to negligence of another member of the gang—Accident occurring when cargo being transferred from wharfside to ship by ship's winch—Whether liability for negligence of stevedore transferred from port authority to ship—Whether effect of byelaw to transfer entire and absolute control of stevedores to ship—Singapore Harbour Board Byelaws, byelaw 26. **Bhoomidas v Port of Singapore Authority** [1978] **1** 956, PC.
    Tug and crew under towage contract—
      Collision between tug and another vessel—Negligence of officer-in-charge of tug—Whether tug-owners or tow-owners liable. **Panther, The, and The Ericbank** [1957] **1** 641, Admin Ct.
    What amounts to loan—
      No request for services—Liability of master. **Clelland v Edward Lloyd Ltd** [1937] **2** 605, KBD.
  Local authority—
    Foster care—
      Liability of local authority for acts of foster parents. See **Child** (Care—Local authority—Liability for acts of foster carers).
  Master and servant—
    Generally. See Employer and employee, *above*.
  Medical practitioner—
    Locum. See **Medical practitioner** (Negligence—Vicarious liability—Locum GP).
  Non-employment relationship—
    Acts of Roman Catholic priest—
      Whether diocesan bishop vicariously liable for tortious acts of priest—Appropriate test. **E v English Province of Our Lady of Charity** [2012] **1** 723, QBD; [2012] **4** 1152, CA.

Non-employment relationship (cont)—
Independent contractor—
Bank paying doctor per-report fee to perform medical examinations on prospective bank employees—Group action alleging sexual assault by doctor in course of examinations—Whether bank vicariously liable—Whether recent case law eroding distinction between relationship akin to employment and relationship with independent contractor—Whether doctor carrying on business on own account. **Various Claimants v Barclays Bank plc** [2020] **4** 19, SC.
Public authority performing statutory functions for public benefit—
Prisoner and prison service—Prisoner working in prison kitchen—Negligence of prisoner causing personal injury to prison catering manager—Whether Ministry vicariously liable for act of prisoner. **Cox v Ministry of Justice** [2017] **1** 1, SC.
Religious organisation—
Vicarious liability for sexual offences—Rape of adult member of congregation—Claimant forming friendship with 'elder' in organisation—Elder behaving inappropriately to claimant—Claimant taking issue to another elder who advised her the elder was in need of her support—Elder subsequently raping claimant—Whether religious organisation vicariously liable. **BXB v Watch Tower Bible and Tract Society of Pennsylvania** [2021] **4** 518, CA.
Unincorporated association—
Vicarious liability for sexual abuse—Institute composed of Roman Catholic lay brothers—Lay brothers teaching in residential school for vulnerable boys—Former pupils alleging abuse by lay brothers while living at residential school—Managers of school found potentially vicariously liable for acts of abuse by teachers—Whether institute having dual vicarious liability—Whether relationship between lay brothers and institute akin to employment—Whether relationship between abuse and relationship between lay brothers and institute sufficiently close. **Various claimants v Catholic Child Welfare Society** [2013] **1** 670, SC.
Partnership—
Firm. See **Partnership** (Liability of firm—Vicarious liability of firm to third parties in respect of 'wrongful act or omission' of partner 'acting in the ordinary course' of firm's business).
Principal and agent—
Act outside scope of authority—
Act outside scope of actual or ostensible authority—Employer and employee—Act outside scope of employment—Deceit—Agent/employee's deceit—Agent deceiving third party to enter into contract with principal—Whether principal liable for agent's deception—Whether third party entitled to rescind contract. **Armagas Ltd v Mundogas SA** [1986] **2** 385, HL.
Deceit—
Test to be applied—Judge finding appellant vicariously liable as principal for fraudulent misrepresentations made by his agent—Whether judge applying wrong test. **Hockley Mint Ltd v Ramsden** [2019] **2** 1054, CA.
Driving of motor vehicle—
Liability of passenger—Driver unknown—Driver driving as agent of passengers—Accident due to dangerous or careless driving and third persons injured. **Scarsbrook v Mason** [1961] **3** 767, QBD.
Supervision and control—
Ship—Defendants' employee in control of ship as captain—Negligence of third party on board ship—Defendants shipbuilders—Ship's trial—Servants of purchasers on board during trial to observe performance of ship—Injury to employee of independent contractor in consequence of negligence of purchasers' servants on board—Whether defendants vicariously liable. **Hobson v Bartram and Sons Ltd** [1950] **1** 412, CA.
Surgeon—
Operation at hospital—Negligence of resident hospital staff in course of post-operative care—Liability of surgeon for acts of hospital staff. **Morris v Winsbury-White** [1937] **4** 494, KBD.
Trade union—
Liability for acts of officials. See **Trade union** (Official—Wrongful acts—Liability of union).
Prohibited act by servant. See Employer and employee—Prohibited act by employee, *above*.
Religious organisation—
Unincorporated association. See Non-employment relationship—Unincorporated association, *above*.
Roman Catholic priest, for. See Non-employment relationship—Acts of Roman Catholic priest, *above*.
Scope of employment—
Act outside scope of employment. See Employer and employee—Act outside scope of employment, *above*.
Sub-contractor. See Employer and employee—Liability for act of sub-contractor, *above*.
Supervision or control of independent contractor. See Independent contractor—Supervision or control, *above*.
Vehicle owner's liability for driver's negligence—
Bailment of vehicle—
Motor car left with garage for repairs—Employee of garage instructed to drive owner to railway station in owner's car—Owner injured in accident due to negligence of driver—Liability of garage. **Chowdhary v Gillot** [1947] **2** 541, KBD.
Driver using car as owner's agent—
Evidence—Inference from ownership of car—Rebuttal—Prima facie inference from ownership rebutted on facts. **Rambarran v Gurrucharran** [1970] **1** 749, PC.
Driving for purposes of owner—
Car driven by friend of owner partly for owner's purposes. **Ormrod v Crosville Motor Services Ltd** [1953] **2** 753, CA.
Car driven for purposes of car owner's son—Car driven at request of car owner—Request to drive car for son's purposes as distinct from permission by car owner for use by son. **Carberry v Davies** [1968] **2** 817, CA.
Driver taking car without owner's knowledge or consent—Owner instructing driver to return car—Accident whilst driver returning car in accordance with instruction—Whether car being driven for purposes of owner—Whether driver agent of owner. **Klein v Caluori** [1971] **2** 701, QBD.
Loan of car by employers to employee on condition that fellow employee be given lifts to work—Car driven for employers' purposes—Driver employers' agent. **Vandyke v Fender (Sun Insurance Office Ltd, third party)** [1970] **2** 335, CA.

VICARIOUS LIABILITY (cont)—
Vehicle owner's liability for driver's negligence (cont)—
Husband and wife—
Husband using wife's car to travel to work—Car regarded by husband and wife as belonging to them both—Promise by husband to wife that if unfit to drive through drink he would ask friend to drive—Husband using car to visit public house after work—Husband unfit to drive—Husband asking third party to drive car—Third party offering friends lift in car—Accident caused by negligent driving of third party—Passengers injured—Whether third party driving car as wife's agent—Whether wife liable to passenger as owner of car. **Morgans v Launchbury** [1972] **2** 606, HL.
Voluntary assistance of servant by stranger. *See* Common employment—Voluntary assistance of servant by stranger, *above.*

VICTIM
Crime of violence—
Compensation. *See* **Compensation** (Criminal injuries).
Loss or damage resulting from offence—
Compensation order—
Proof of sum claimed by victim. *See* **Sentence** (Compensation—Order—Principles applicable in making order—Compensation order not to be made unless the sum claimed by the victim for the damage is agreed or proved).
Personal statement—
Criminal proceedings. *See* **Practice** (Criminal proceedings—Victim personal statements).
Victim's right to review decision not to prosecute. *See* **Criminal law** (Prosecution—Decision to prosecute—Victim's right to review).

VICTIMISATION
Burden of proof. *See* **Race relations** (Discrimination—Victimisation—Burden of proof).
Discrimination—
Race relations. *See* **Race relations** (Discrimination—Victimisation).
Employment. *See* **Employment** (Victimisation).
Sex discrimination. *See* **Sex discrimination** (Discrimination—Victimisation).

VICTORIA
Income tax—
Deduction in computing profits—
Capitalisation of profits—Allotment of bonus shares—Amount due on shares satisfied out of accumulated profits—Unemployment Relief Tax (Assessment) Act 1933 (No 4171)(Vic) s 4—Income Tax Act (Victoria) (No 4309 of 1935), s 2. **Nicholas v Taxes Comr (Victoria)** [1940] **3** 91, PC.
Worker's compensation—
Increase in statutory benefits—
Personal injury—Heart disease aggravated by nature of employment—Contributory factor leading to death—Claim by dependants under Workers Compensation Act 1958—Act amended after deceased taken ill before death—Amendment increased rates of benefit—Whether dependants entitled to increased benefit—Workers Compensation Act 1958 (No 6419)(Vic), ss 5(1), 9(1). **Ogden Industries Pty Ltd v Lucas** [1969] **1** 121, PC.

VIDEO CASSETTE
Obscene publication—
Video cassette used to show pornographic film—
Whether video cassette an article capable of being published. *See* **Criminal law** (Obscene publications—Article—Film or other record of a picture or pictures—Video cassette used to show pornographic film).

VIDEO CONFERENCING
Family Division—
Practice. *See* **Practice** (Family Division—Video conferencing).

VIDEO FILM
Evidence—
Civil proceedings—
Leave to produce video film as evidence without giving the other party opportunity to inspect it. *See* **Practice** (Document—Production in evidence—Leave to produce video film as evidence without giving the other party opportunity to inspect it).

VIDEO GAMES
Premises used for playing video games—
Whether premises need to be licensed under Cinematograph Act. *See* **Cinema** (Cinematograph exhibition—Licensing of premises—Video games).

VIDEO LINK
Evidence—
Child—
Criminal proceedings. *See* **Criminal evidence** (Child—Video recording of testimony).
Civil proceedings. *See* **Evidence** (Mode of giving evidence—Video link).

VIDEO RECORDING
Evidence—
Criminal proceedings—
Generally. *See* **Criminal evidence** (Video recording).
Testimony of child. *See* **Criminal evidence** (Child—Video recording of testimony).

VIDEO RECORDING (cont)—
  Evidence (cont)—
    Personal injury action—
      Cross-examination. *See* **Practice** (Cross-examination—Personal injury action—Video evidence).
  Offence—
    Supply in breach of classification—
      Supply to person under age—Defence—Video having '18' classification certificate—Supply of video having '18' classification certificate to person under 18—Defence—Cashier employed by company supplying video to person under 18—Cashier having reasonable grounds to believe purchaser under 18—Company charged with offence—Management of company unaware of prohibited sale—Whether company liable when employee having reasonable grounds to believe purchaser under 18—Video Recordings Act 1984, s 11. **Tesco Stores Ltd v Brent London BC** [1993] **2** 718, QBD.

VIEW
  Judge—
    Civil action. *See* **Practice** (Inspection by judge).

VILLAGE GREEN
  Registration. *See* **Commons** (Registration—Town or village green).

VIOLENCE
  Crime—
    Compensation for victims of crimes of violence. *See* **Compensation** (Criminal injuries).
    Provoking unlawful violence—
      Threatening, abusive or insulting writing. *See* **Criminal law** (Threatening, abusive or insulting writing—Provoking unlawful violence).
    Violent disorder. *See* **Criminal law** (Violent disorder).
  Domestic violence—
    Exclusion of party from matrimonial home—
      Injunction. *See* **Injunction** (Exclusion of party from matrimonial home).
    Injunction—
      Generally. *See* **Injunction** (Husband and wife—Domestic violence).
    Molestation—
      Injunction. *See* **Injunction** (Molestation—Domestic violence).
    Protection order. *See* **Husband and wife** (Summary proceedings—Order for protection of party to marriage or child of the family).
  Personal injury—
    Injury directly attributable to crime of violence—
      Entitlement to compensation. *See* **Compensation** (Criminal injuries—Entitlement to compensation—Personal injury directly attributable to crime of violence).

VIRUS
  Escape—
    Infection of cattle—
      Duty of care—Persons to whom duty owed. *See* **Negligence** (Duty to take care—Person to whom duty owed—Duty owed only to those whose persons or property may be foreseeably injured—Escape of virus from research premises leading to infection of cattle in the vicinity).

VISITING FORCES
  Defamation action—
    Privilege. *See* **Libel and slander** (Privilege—Visiting forces).
  Deserter from armed forces of foreign state. *See* **Constitutional law** (Foreign sovereign state—Armed forces of foreign state—Deserter or absentee without leave from forces of designated country).
  Learner driver—
    Permit. *See* **Road traffic** (Driving licence—Supervision of learner driver—Visiting force permit).
  Negligence—
    Personal injuries claim by member of visiting force—
      United Kingdom and United States of America parties to treaty agreement regulating status of visiting US forces—Agreement imposing obligation on United Kingdom to compensate for injuries caused to third parties—Third parties—Member of US Air Force sustaining injuries through treatment at US military hospital while stationed in England—Serviceman claiming damages for personal injuries and loss against United States government and United Kingdom Ministry of Defence—Whether agreement giving serviceman right of action against United Kingdom government—Whether serviceman a third party for purposes of agreement—Agreement regarding the Status of Forces of Parties to the North Atlantic Treaty, art VIII, para 5. **Littrell v USA** [1992] **3** 218, QBD.

VISITOR
  Corporation—
    Dispute as to membership—
      Visitor's jurisdiction. *See* **Corporation** (Visitor—Jurisdiction—Dispute as to membership of corporation).
  Educational establishment—
    Visitor's jurisdiction. *See* **Education** (College—Visitor—Jurisdiction).
  Inns of Court—
    Judges—
      Disciplinary jurisdiction. *See* **Counsel** (Disciplinary jurisdiction—Judges as visitors of Inns of Court).
  Journalist—
    Visit to prison. *See* **Prison** (Visits—Visits by journalists).
  Occupier's duty of care to visitor. *See* **Occupier's liability** (Visitor).

VISITOR (cont)—
  Prison board of visitors—
    Certiorari—
      Jurisdiction. *See* **Certiorari** (Jurisdiction—Prison board of visitors).
    Exercise of disciplinary powers—
      Generally. *See* **Prison** (Discipline—Board of visitors—Exercise of disciplinary powers).
      Nature justice. *See* **Natural justice** (Prison board of visitors—Exercise of disciplinary powers).
  University—
    Generally. *See* **University** (Visitor).

VOCATION
  Income tax—
    Profits of vocation. *See* **Income tax** (Profits—Profession or vocation).

VOICE
  Simulation of voice—
    Passing off. *See* **Passing off** (Voice).

VOIRE DIRE
  Examination on voire dire—
    Cross-examination as to truth of contents of extra-judicial statement—
      Admissibility. *See* **Criminal evidence** (Admissions and confessions—Answers and statements to
        police—Issue as to admissibility—Whether on voire dire prosecution entitled to cross-examine
        accused as to truth of confession).

VOLENTI NON FIT INJURIA
  Negligence—
    Defence. *See* **Negligence** (Volenti non fit injuria).

VOLUNTARY ADOPTION AGENCY
  See **Adoption** (Adoption agency—Voluntary adoption agency).

VOLUNTARY AIDED SCHOOL
  See **Education** (School—Voluntary aided school).

VOLUNTARY ARRANGEMENT
  Insolvency. *See* **Insolvency** (Voluntary arrangement).

VOLUNTARY BILL
  Application for grant of. *See* **Criminal law** (Bill of indictment—Preferment).

VOLUNTARY DISPOSITION
  Stamp duty. *See* **Stamp duty** (Voluntary disposition inter vivos).

VOLUNTARY HOSPITAL
  Gift by will. *See* **Will** (Gift—Specific donees—Voluntary hospitals).

VOLUNTARY PAYMENT
  Income tax—
    Payment to employee. *See* **Income tax** (Emoluments from office or employment—Voluntary payment).
    Trading receipt. *See* **Income tax** (Profits—Trading receipts—Voluntary payment).

VOLUNTARY SCHOOL
  Governor—
    Removal by local education authority. *See* **Education** (Local education authority—Removal of
      governor).

VOLUNTARY SETTLEMENT
  Generally. *See* **Settlement** (Voluntary settlement).
  Rectification. *See* **Deed** (Rectification—Voluntary settlement).

VOLUNTARY WINDING UP
  Company. *See* **Company** (Voluntary winding up).
  Industrial and provident societies. *See* **Industrial and provident societies** (Winding up—Voluntary winding
    up).

VOTING POWER
  Company shares. *See* **Company** (Shares—Voting power).

VOYAGE
  Will—
    Soldier's and mariner's privileged will—
      Seaman at sea—Nuncupative will made in contemplation of voyage. *See* **Will** (Soldier's or
        mariner's privileged will—Seaman at sea—Nuncupative will made in contemplation of voyage).

W

WAGERING
See **Gaming**.

WAGES
Admiralty action in rem. See **Admiralty** (Practice—Action in rem—Wages).
Agricultural worker. See **Agriculture** (Agricultural worker—Wages).
Bank advances to pay wages—
    Priority in winding up. See **Company** (Winding up—Preferential payments—Wages—Advances for payment of wages—Bank).
Child—
    Income tax relief—
        Income of child. See **Income tax** (Child relief—Income of child—Wages).
Crew. See **Shipping** (Crew—Wages).
Employee—
    Generally. See **Employment** (Remuneration).
Equality of treatment between men and women—
    European Community. See **European Union** (Equality of treatment of men and women).
    Generally. See **Employment** (Equality of treatment of men and women).
Generally. See **Employment** (Remuneration).
Income tax. See **Income tax** (Emoluments from office or employment).
Loss of—
    Personal injury—
        Damages—Generally. See **Damages** (Personal injury—Loss of earnings).
        Special damages. See **Damages** (Personal injury—Amount of damages—Special damages—Relevance of future contingency in assessment of special damages—Loss of wages as result of injury culminating in operation).
Minimum wage—
    Coal mining. See **Coal mining** (Workman—Minimum wage).
    Generally. See **Employment** (Remuneration—National minimum wage).
Preferential payment—
    Company's winding up. See **Company** (Winding up—Preferential payments—Wages).
Rise and fall clause—
    Building contract. See **Building contract** (Wages—Rise and fall clause).
Seaman—
    Claim for wages—
        Admiralty jurisdiction. See **Admiralty** (Jurisdiction—Action in rem—Claim for wages).
        Claim by master. See **Shipping** (Crew—Master—Wages—Claim for wages).
        Maritime lien. See **Shipping** (Maritime lien—Wages—Seaman).
Supplementary benefit—
    Calculation of benefit—
        Deduction of resources from requirements—Wages paid in arrear. See **Social security** (Supplementary benefit—Calculation of benefit—Deduction of resources from requirements—Income resources—Wages paid in arrear at termination of employment).

WAITER
Conditions of employment—
    Hotel—
        Statutory half holiday. See **Shop** (Conditions of employment—Statutory half-holiday for shop assistants—Hotel—Dining-room open to non-residents—Waiter).
Tips—
    Statutory minimum remuneration—
        Exclusion of tips. See **Employment** (Remuneration—Statutory minimum—Exclusion of waiters' tips).

WAITING AND LOADING RESTRICTIONS
Road traffic. See **Road traffic** (Waiting and loading restrictions).

WAIVER
Company—
    Compulsory winding up—
        Error in advertisement of petition. See **Company** (Compulsory winding up—Advertisement of petition—Error in advertisement—Waiver).
Contract—
    Breach of contract. See **Contract** (Breach—Waiver).
    Condition precedent. See **Contract** (Condition precedent—Waiver).
Diplomatic privilege. See **Constitutional law** (Diplomatic privilege—Immunity from legal process—Criminal proceedings—Purported waiver on behalf of accused).
Forfeiture of lease. See **Landlord and tenant** (Forfeiture of lease—Waiver of forfeiture).
Immunity from suit—
    Foreign sovereign state. See **Constitutional law** (Foreign sovereign state—Immunity from suit—Waiver).
Insurance—
    Motor insurance—
        Condition of policy. See **Motor insurance** (Conditions—Breach of condition—Waiver of breach).
Legal professional privilege—
    Disclosure and inspection of documents. See **Disclosure and inspection of documents** (Legal professional privilege—Waiver).
Notice to quit. See **Landlord and tenant** (Notice to quit—Waiver).
Obligation to repair—
    Waiver of obligation by landlord. See **Landlord and tenant** (Repair—Cost of repairs—Waiver).

1467

WAIVER (cont)—
    Privilege—
        Disclosure of documents. *See* **Disclosure and inspection of documents** (Privilege—Waiver of privilege).
        Evidence. *See* **Evidence** (Privilege—Waiver).
    Sale of land—
        Notice to complete. *See* **Sale of land** (Notice to complete—Waiver).
        Waiver of condition. *See* **Sale of land** (Condition—Waiver of condition).
        Waiver of right of rescission. *See* **Sale of land** (Rescission of contract—Waiver of right of rescission).
    Ship—
        Readiness, notice of. *See* **Shipping** (Commencement of lay days—Notice of readiness to load—Congestion at load port).
        Right of withdrawal—
            Non-payment of hire—Time charterparty. *See* **Shipping** (Time charterparty—Withdrawal of vessel for non-payment of hire—Waiver of right to withdraw).
    Tort. *See* **Tort** (Waiver).

WALES
    Cardiff—
        Recorder—
            Mode of address. *See* **Judge** (Mode of address—Recorder).
    Devolution issues—
        Constitutional law. *See* **Constitutional law** (Devolution—National Assembly for Wales).
        Practice. *See* **Practice** (Devolution issues—Wales).
    Legislature—
        Devolution. *See* **Constitutional law** (Devolution—National Assembly for Wales—Legislative power).
    Welsh language—
        Use in Crown Court. *See* **Crown Court** (Practice—Wales—Use of Welsh language).
        Use in Welsh court. *See* **Practice** (Conduct of proceedings—Language—Welsh language).

WALKING POSSESSION
    Agreement—
        Distress. *See* **Distress** (Distress for rent).
        Execution. *See* **Execution** (Writ of fi fa—Seizure of goods—Walking possession agreement).

WALSH V LONSDALE
    Doctrine that equity looks on that as done which ought to be done—
        Agreement for lease. *See* **Equity** (Agreement for lease—Doctrine that equity looks on that as done which ought to be done).

WANT OF PROSECUTION
    Arbitration—
        Practice. *See* **Arbitration** (Practice—Want of prosecution).
    Crown Office list—
        Striking out for want of prosecution. *See* **Practice** (Crown Office list—Striking out for want of prosecution).
    Dismissal of action for—
        Arbitration. *See* **Arbitration** (Practice—Want of prosecution—Dismissal of claim).
        Generally. *See* **Practice** (Dismissal of action for want of prosecution).
    Dismissal of counterclaim for. *See* **Practice** (Dismissal of counterclaim for want of prosecution).

WAR
    Aviation insurance—
        War risks. *See* **Insurance** (Aviation insurance—War risks).
    Charterparty—
        Assessment of damages. *See* **Contract** (Repudiation—Charterparty—Assessment of damages).
    Civil and commercial matters—
        Conflict of laws—
            Jurisdiction. *See* **Conflict of laws** (Jurisdiction—Civil and commercial matters).
    Conflict of laws—
        Generally. *See* **Conflict of laws**.
    Death on war service—
        Exemption from estate duty. *See* **Estate duty** (Exemption—Death on war service).
    Emergency legislation. *See* **Emergency legislation**.
    Essential work. *See* **Essential work**.
    Frustration of contract. *See* **Contract** (Frustration—War).
    Lease—
        War time lease. *See* **Landlord and tenant** (War time lease).
    Liabilities adjustment. *See* **Liabilities adjustment**.
    Marine insurance—
        Perils insured against. *See* **Marine insurance** (Perils insured against—War).
        War risks policy. *See* **Marine insurance** (War risks policy).
    Prisoners of war—
        Habeas corpus—
            Jurisdiction. *See* **Habeas corpus** (Jurisdiction—Prisoner of war).
        Privileges of prisoners protected by Geneva Convention—
            Nationals of detaining power not entitled to privileges of Geneva Convention as prisoners of war—Persons owing allegiance to detaining power, though not such nationals, also not so entitled—Geneva Conventions Act 1962 (No 5 of 1962), s 4(1). **Public Prosecutor v Koi** [1968] **1** 419, PC.
    Rule against perpetuities—
        Duration of war. *See* **Rule against perpetuities** (Gift over after uncertain period—Duration of war).

WAR (cont)—
State's obligation to investigate death—
  Human rights—
    Right to life. *See* **Human rights** (Right to life—State's obligation to investigate death).
Termination of agency—
  Duty to account. *See* **Agent** (Account—Duty to account—Agency terminated by war).
War damage. *See* **War damage**.
War injury—
  Generally. *See* **War injury**.
  War pension. *See* **War pension** (War service injury).
War memorial—
  Charitable purpose. *See* **Charity** (Benefit to community—War memorial).
Will—
  Soldier's or mariner's privileged will—
    Actual military service—Will made before mobilisation and before declaration of war. *See* **Will** (Soldier's or mariner's privileged will—Actual military service—Will made before mobilisation and before declaration of war).

WAR BONDS
Will—
  Gift—
    Specific bequests. *See* **Will** (Gift—Specific bequests—My War Bonds).

WAR DAMAGE
Compensation—
  Compulsory acquisition of interest in war-damaged hereditament. *See* **Compulsory purchase** (Compensation—Assessment—Interest in war-damaged hereditament).
Contribution—
  Sale of land—
    Outgoings—Condition. *See* **Sale of land** (Condition—Apportionment of outgoings—War damage contribution).
    Outgoings—Rights of parties. *See* **Sale of land** (Outgoings—Rights of parties pending completion—War damage contribution).
Defence to statutory nuisance. *See* **Nuisance** (Statutory nuisance—Defence—War damage).
Disclaimer of lease—
  Apportionment of rent—
    Retrospective operation of statute—Landlord and Tenant (War Damage) (Amendment) Act 1941, s 13. **London Fan & Motor Co Ltd v Silverman** [1942] **1** 307, KBD.
  Block of property let by three separate leases but used as a whole—
    Need to consider leases separately—Whether landlord liable to replace tenants' fixtures—Landlord and Tenant (War Damage) Act 1939, s 6(1)—Landlord and Tenant (War Damage) (Amendment) Act 1941. **Wallis & Co (Costumiers) Ltd v Oppenheim** [1943] **1** 114, CA.
  Ground lease—
    Order of court necessary—Transfer of proceedings from county court to High Court—Circumstances in which appropriate—County Courts Act 1934, s 111—Landlord and Tenant (War Damage) Act 1939, ss 13, 23. **Clavering v Conduit Mead Co** [1941] **1** 30, Ch D.
    Order of court necessary—Transfer of proceedings from county court to High Court—Ex parte application—County Courts Act 1934, s 111—Landlord and Tenant (War Damage) Act 1939, s 13, 23. **Metropolitan Leather Co Ltd v Herrmann** [1941] **1** 29, Ch D.
  Multiple lease. *See* Landlord and tenant—Multiple lease, *below*.
  Notice of disclaimer—
    Effect on liability to pay rent—Rent payable in advance—Notice of disclaimer followed by notice to avoid disclaimer—Liability for rent after notice of disclaimer—Landlord and Tenant (War Damage) Act 1939, s 11. **Turner v Stella Bond Ltd** [1941] **1** 449, CA.
    Effect on liability to pay rent—Rent payable in advance—Notice of disclaimer served after rent due—No valid notice to avoid disclaimer—Landlord and Tenant (War Damage) Act 1939, ss 8, 11, 24. **Hildebrand v Lewis** [1941] **2** 584, CA.
    Form of notice—Sufficiency—Landlord and Tenant (War Damage) Act 1939, ss 4, 8. **Black and Black v Mileham** [1941] **3** 269, CA.
    Notice served one year after damage but ante-dated for purposes of repayment of rent—Validity—Landlord and Tenant (War Damage) Act 1939, ss 4, 5, 8—Landlord and Tenant (War Damage) (Amendment) Act 1941, s 13. **A-G v Daimler Co Ltd** [1944] **2** 214, CA.
  Notice to avoid disclaimer—
    Application by landlord for declaration that premises capable of beneficial occupation—No basis for application—Landlord and Tenant (War Damage) Act 1939, ss 6, 11(1)(c). **Cooper v Jax Stores Ltd** [1941] **1** 502, CA.
    Form of notice—Multiple lease—Landlord and Tenant (War Damage) Act 1939, s 15—Landlord and Tenant (War Damage) (Amendment) Act 1941, Sch. **Goodman v Elkington** [1946] **2** 756, CA.
    Form of notice—Reference to wrong section—Validity of notice—Landlord and Tenant (War Damage) Act 1939, s 4. **Price v Mann** [1942] **1** 453, CA.
    Landlord's obligation to render land fit as soon as reasonably practicable—Extent of repairs required to make premises 'reasonably fit'—Factors to be considered—Use of premises in particular neighbourhood—Landlord and Tenant (War Damage) Act 1939, s 11. **Littman v Goorwitch Ltd** [1945] **1** 24, KBD.
Insurance of goods against war damage—
  Goods—
    Business scheme—Loss of account-books through enemy action—Documents owned for purpose of business excluded from definition of 'goods'—Whether account-books 'documents'—War Risk Insurance Act 1939, s 7(1)—War Damage Act 1943, ss 2(1), 83, 84(1), (4), 95, 104. **Hill v R** [1945] **1** 414, KBD.

WAR DAMAGE (cont)—
Insurance of goods against war damage (cont)—
  Goods (cont)—
    Business scheme—Loss of working drawings used in the process of manufacture through enemy action—Documents owned for purposes of business excluded from definition of 'goods'—Whether working drawings 'documents'—War Damage Act 1943, ss 84(1)(a), 104. **Tucker (JH) & Co Ltd v Board of Trade** [1955] **2** 522, Ch D.
Landlord and tenant—
  Disclaimer of lease. *See* Disclaimer of lease, *above.*
  Multiple lease—
    Disclaimer and retention of lease—Lease comprising two separate buildings—One building rendered unfit for occupation—Whether tenant entitled to disclaim as to one building and retain as to other—'Allow'—Jurisdiction of the court—Landlord and Tenant (War Damage) Act 1939, s 15(3), (4), (5)—Landlord and Tenant (War Damage) (Amendment) Act 1941, Sch. **Fitzhardinge's Lease, Re** [1944] **2** 535, CA.
    Disclaimer of part of premises—Reduction in rent—Landlord and Tenant (War Damage) Act 1939, ss 5(4), 6, 9, 10, 11, 15, 24. **Westminster Bank Ltd v Edwards** [1942] **1** 470, HL.
    Lease comprising buildings adapted for use as two or more separate tenements—Adapted for use—Disclaimer for demised premises as a whole—Landlord and Tenant (War Damage) Act 1939, s 15(3)—Landlord and Tenant (War Damage) (Amendment) Act 1941. **Herrmann v Metropolitan Leather Co Ltd** [1942] **1** 294, Ch D.
    Notice to avoid disclaimer—Form of notice—Landlord and Tenant (War Damage) Act 1939, s 15—Landlord and Tenant (War Damage) (Amendment) Act 1941, Sch. **Goodman v Elkington** [1946] **2** 756, CA.
  Power to disclaim lease—
    Power where land comprised in lease unfit by reason of war damage—Unfit—Landlord and Tenant (War Damage) Act 1939, ss 1, 4, 6, 11, 24. **Boudou v Thornton-Smith** [1941] **1** 454, CA.
  Relief from obligation to repair—
    Nuisance—Damage to roofs caused by enemy action—Abatement notice served on landlord—Liability to repair in case of war damage—Public Health Act 1936, s 92(1), s 93—Landlord and Tenant (War Damage) Act 1939, s 1(1). **Turley v King** [1944] **2** 489, KBD.
  Retention of lease—
    Conditional notice of retention—Reduction of rent under ground lease—Landlord and Tenant (War Damage) Act 1939, ss 13, 14—Landlord and Tenant (War Damage) (Amendment) Act 1941, s 10. **Orbit Trust Ltd's Lease, Re** [1943] **1** 373, Ch D.
    Notice of retention—Effect—Rent—Reduction of rent—Part of premises capable of beneficial enjoyment—Whether tenant entitled to reduction of rent as from date of damage or from date of service of notice—Landlord and Tenant (War Damage) Act 1939, ss 10(1)(b), (c), 15(5)—Landlord and Tenant (War Damage) (Amendment) Act 1941, s 2(5), Sch. **Reville Ltd v Prudential Assurance Co Ltd** [1944] **1** 458, HL.
  Short tenancy—
    Determination—Destruction of premises by enemy action—No rent paid by tenant—House rebuilt by owner—Tenant's right to possession—Landlord and Tenant (War Damage) (Amendment) Act 1941, s 1(2). **Simper v Coombs** [1948] **1** 306, KBD.
    Relief from obligation to pay rent where land unfit by reason of war damage—Whether act retrospective—Landlord and Tenant (War Damage) (Amendment) Act 1941, s 1. **Langford Property Co Ltd v Pajzs** [1943] **2** 687, KBD.
Payments—
  Capital or income. *See* **Administration of estates** (Capital or income—Settled leaseholds—War damage).
  Damage to land, for. *See* Payments in respect of damage to land, *below.*
Payments in respect of damage to land—
  Administration of estate—
    Capital or income. *See* **Administration of estates** (Capital or income—Settled leaseholds—War damage).
  Contributions towards expenses of making payments—
    Incidence of liability as between mortgagor and mortgagees—Separate mortgages of a number of properties—Whether mortgagee liable for share of contribution—Mortgage created 'in connection with...more than one contributory property'—War Damage Act 1941, s 25(4), (5). **Ideal Life Assurance Co Ltd v Hirschfield** [1943] **1** 563, CA.
    Persons liable to pay instalments—Proprietary interest in contributory property subject to mortgage—No receiver at relevant date—Liability for instalment—War Damage Act 1941, s 27. **Ridley, Re** [1943] **1** 603, Ch D.
    Proportion appropriate to a tenancy—Method of determining proportion—Proportion which rent reserved for period bears to contributory value of land—Annual payment of premium for term of lease—Premium in addition to rent reserved by the lease—Whether part of 'rent reserved'—War Damage Act 1943, s 50. **War Damages Act 1943, Re, Samuel v Salmon and Gluckstein Ltd** [1945] **2** 520, Ch D.
    Proportion appropriate to a tenancy—Method of determining proportion—Proportion which rent reserved for period bears to contributory value of land—Payment in consideration of licence—Whether part of 'rent'—War Damage Act 1943, s 50. **Westminster (Duke) v Store Properties Ltd** [1944] **1** 118, Ch D.
  Cost of works payment—
    Damage occurring as direct result of enemy action—Structural damage to defective walls—Reinstatement of building in pre-existing form—War Damage Act 1943, ss 2(1)(a), 6, 8(2), 10(1), Sch III, para 3(1). **Jamaica Street, Stepney (36, 38, 40 & 42), Re** [1947] **1** 754, CA.
    Determination to pay cost of works instead of value payment—Right to make determination before repair work done—War Damage Act 1943, s 20(3)(b). **Paddington BC v War Damage Commission** [1956] **3** 753, CA.
    Making good war damage—Front wall of house damaged by enemy action—Party walls reinstated as part of work of reinstating front wall—Work executed to conform with London Building Acts—Whether cost of reinstating party walls to be included in cost of works payment—War Damage Act 1943, s 8(2). **Bruton Street (34), Westminster, Re** [1957] **2** 539, CA.

WAR INJURY (cont)—
    Compensation (cont)—
        Physical injury (cont)—
            Organic disease and aggravation thereof—Artificial menopause resulting in highly nervous and hysterical condition—Nervous and hysterical condition aggravated by sight of bombed home—Hysteria functional disorder but not organic disease—Personal Injuries (Emergency Provisions) Act 1939, ss 1, 2, 8(1)(b)—Pensions (Mercantile Marine) Act 1942, s 5—Personal Injuries (Civilians) Scheme 1944 (SR & O 1944 No 369), Part IV, art 12(2). **Young v Minister of Pensions** [1944] 2 308, KBD.
    Death from war injury—
        Exemption from estate duty. *See* **Estate duty** (Exemption—Death on war service).
    Exclusion of right of action for damages—
        Exclusion of right where injury war injury—
            Engine-driver killed by reason of bomb crater on track—Whether direct and substantial connection between enemy act and injury—Whether action barred—Personal Injuries (Emergency Provisions) Act 1939, ss 3(1), 8. **Greenfield v London and North Eastern Rly Co** [1944] 2 438, CA.
            Fatal injury by aeroplane—Case unprovided for by scheme—Partial dependency—Funeral expenses—Claim in trespass—Whether 'war injury'—Whether claim barred—Personal Injuries (Emergency Provisions) Act 1939, ss 3, 8—Personal Injuries (Civilians) Scheme 1944 (SR & O 1944 No 369), arts 1(8), 29. **Billings v Reed** [1944] 2 415, CA.
            Injuries sustained entering air-raid shelter after air-raid warning—Air raid shelter steps uneven, inadequately lighted and no centre hand rail—Whether injuries 'war injuries' or due to nonfeasance by local authority—Whether right of action against local authority barred—Personal Injuries (Emergency Provisions) Act 1939, s 8. **Baker v Bethnal Green Corp** [1945] 1 135, CA.
            Minefield on foreshore—Injuries to children by exploded mines—Whether injury 'caused by the use of explosive in combating enemy'—Personal Injuries (Emergency Provisions) Act 1939, ss 3, 8—Personal Injuries (Civilians) Scheme 1941 (SR & O 1941 No 226). **Adams v Naylor** [1946] 2 241, HL.
    Injurious act. *See* Physical injury caused by injurious act in combating enemy—Injurious act, *below.*
    Injury sustained abroad. *See* Physical injury caused by impact on person or property of aircraft—Injury sustained by passenger in aircraft—Injury sustained abroad, *below.*
    Minefield on foreshore—
        Injuries to children. *See* Exclusion of right of action for damages—Exclusion of right where injury war injury—Minefield on foreshore—Injuries to children, *above.*
    Physical injury caused by discharge of missile—
        Approach of flying bomb when workers en route to shelter—
            Rush for cover—Injury to worker—Whether 'war injury'—Personal Injuries (Civilians) Scheme 1944 (SR & O 1944 No 369), art 1(25). **Evans v Minister of Pensions** [1947] 2 436, KBD.
    Physical injury caused by impact on person or property of aircraft—
        Causal nexus—
            Shell from enemy aeroplane passing through various hands—Injury to worker by fellow-workman sawing it about three weeks after shell found—Whether 'war injury'—Personal Injuries (Emergency Provisions) Act 1939, s 8(1)(b). **Smith v Davey Paxman & Co (Colchester) Ltd** [1943] 1 286, CA.
        Damage to building causing injury—
            Injury to workman by reason of damage to building by blast—Whether 'war injury'—Personal Injuries (Emergency Provisions) Act 1939, ss 3(1), 8. **Taylor v Sims & Sims** [1942] 2 375, KBD.
        Injury sustained by passenger in aircraft—
            Injury sustained abroad—Whether 'war injury'—Personal Injuries (Emergency Provisions) Act 1939, s 8(1). **Howgate v A-G** [1950] 2 1104, KBD.
    Physical injury caused by injurious act in combating enemy—
        Injurious act—
            Factory worker injured on way to shelter during alarm—Reduction of lights—Enforcement of blackout—Whether injury caused by 'injurious act'—Personal Injuries (Emergency Provisions) Act 1939, s 8(1). **Minister of Pensions v Ffrench** [1946] 1 272, KBD.
            Merchant seaman fatally injured by army vehicle travelling in convoy—In combating the enemy—Restricted interpretation—Actual or imagined engagements with enemy—Fatal injury not due to 'any other injurious act ... in combating the enemy'—Personal Injuries (Emergency Provisions) Act 1939, s 3—Pensions (Navy, Army, Air Force and Mercantile Marine) Act 1939, s 10. **Kemp, Re** [1945] 1 571, KBD.

WAR MEMORIAL
    Charitable purpose. *See* **Charity** (Benefit to community—War memorial).

WAR PENSION
    Aggravation of injury by war service—
        Aggravation of pre-war disability—
            Power of tribunal finding aggravation to determine duration thereof. **Ansell v Minister of Pensions** [1948] 2 789, KBD.
        Disability existing before or arising during war service aggravated by and remaining aggravated by war service—
            Jurisdiction to consider past disablement and aggravation in addition to existing disablement and aggravation—Pensions Appeal Tribunals Act 1943, ss 1, 5—Royal Warrant concerning Retired Pay, Pensions, etc, 1943 (Cmd 1943, No 6049), arts 2(3), 4. **Shipp v Minister of Pensions** [1946] 1 417, KBD.
    Anxiety state resulting from fear of overseas service. *See* Attributability of injury to war service, *below.*
    Appeal—
        Appeal against assessment of extent of disablement—
            Right to appeal to High Court—Pensions Appeal Tribunals Act 1943, ss 5(2), 6(3). **Morris v Minister of Pensions** [1948] 1 748, KBD.

WAR PENSION (cont)—
  Appeal (cont)—
    Appeal to High Court—
      Notification of leave—Retraction—Chairman of tribunal unable to state case—Reasons of tribunal in lieu—Pensions Appeal Tribunals (England and Wales) Rules 1943 (S R & O 1943 No 1757), r 23. **Heald v Minister of Pensions** [1947] **1** 748, KBD.
    Conflicting decisions of courts of co-ordinate jurisdiction—
      Later decision preferred. **Minister of Pensions v Higham** [1948] **1** 863, KBD.
    Leave to appeal—
      Leave to appeal out of time—Application made to tribunal out of time—Refusal of extension of time by tribunal—Power of judge to grant leave and extend time for appeal—RSC, Ord 55E, r 2(1)—Pensions Appeal Tribunals Act 1943, s 6(2). **James v Minister of Pensions** [1947] **2** 432, KBD.
      Refusal by High Court judge—Appeal to Court of Appeal—Competency—Pensions Appeal Tribunals Act 1943, s 6(2). **Aronsohn, Ex p** [1946] **2** 544, CA.
    Pensions appeal tribunal. *See* Pensions appeal tribunal, *below*.
    Time limits. *See* Pensions appeal tribunal—Appeal from decision of Minister—Time limits for bringing appeal, *below*.
  Attributability of death of member of forces to war service—
    Disease arising during and aggravated by war service—
      Death hastened by aggravation—Failure to report sick—Test whether course taken direct consequence of war service—Royal Warrant concerning Retired Pay, Pensions, etc, 1943 (Cmd 1943 No 6489), art 4(1)(b)(ii). **Jones v Minister of Pensions** [1946] **1** 312, KBD.
    Suicide—
      Service conditions having played a part in producing conditions that led to suicide—Causation—Widow entitled to award. **Freeman v Minister of Pensions and National Insurance** [1966] **2** 40, QBD.
      Suicide by serving soldier after receiving letter from fiancee breaking off engagement—Evidence—Statements of witnesses at, and findings of, military court of inquiry. **XY v Minister of Pensions** [1947] **1** 38, KBD.
  Attributability of injury to war service—
    Accident to soldier while billeted in own home—
      Causation. **Ridley v Minister of Pensions** [1947] **2** 437, KBD.
    Compelling presumption—
      Enlistment of appellant and medical examination five months before war—No further examination when embodied for war service—Inherent weakness—Precipitating cause. **Jewitt v Minister of Pensions** [1946] **2** 545, KBD.
      Medical examination and attestation before outbreak of war—No further examination when embodied for war service—Royal Warrant concerning Retired Pay, Pensions etc 1943 (Cmd 1943 No 6489), art 4(3). **Edwards v Minister of Pensions** [1947] **1** 379, KBD.
    Injury suffered in December 1939—
      Claim admitted by War Office—Minister of Pensions not consulted—Assurance given by War Office binding on Minister of Pensions. **Robertson v Minister of Pensions** [1948] **2** 767, KBD.
    Injury sustained while on leave—
      Command Paper disclaiming liability—Legal force—Pensions Appeal Tribunals Act 1943, ss 1(1)(a), 6(2). **Williams v Minister of Pensions** [1947] **2** 564, KBD.
    Proximate or effective cause of disability—
      Anxiety state resulting from fear of overseas service. **Hollorn v Minister of Pensions** [1947] **1** 124, KBD.
      Anxiety state resulting from matrimonial troubles caused by separation due to war service—Injury not attributable to war service. **W v Minister of Pensions** [1946] **2** 501, KBD.
    Service patient in emergency services hospital—
      Negligence in treatment—Entitlement to award—Royal Warrant 1946, (Cmd 1943 No 6489), arts 4, 56. **Minister of Pensions v Horsey** [1949] **2** 314, KBD.
    Test—
      War service a cause of disease—Hernia—Conditions of service producing cough leading to rupture. **Marshall v Minister of Pensions** [1947] **2** 706, KBD.
  Award of entitlement—
    Disablement necessary condition of award of entitlement—
      Meaning of disablement—Arthritis caused by accident while in army—Whether 'disablement'—Royal Warrant concerning Retired Pay, Pensions, etc 1943, (Cmd 1943 No 6489), art 1(4). **Harris v Minister of Pensions** [1948] **1** 191, KBD.
  Burden of proof—
    Claim. *See* Claim—Burden of proof, *below*.
  Civilians scheme. *See* Claim—Burden of proof—Civilians scheme, *below*.
  Claim—
    Burden of proof—
      Aggravation of disability by war service—Proper method of approach to consider matter—Royal Warrant concerning Retired Pay, Pensions, etc 1943, (Cmd 1943 No 6489), art 4(2)—Pensions Appeal Tribunals (England and Wales) Rules 1943, (S R & O 1943 No 1757), r 12(6). **Rowing v Minister of Pensions** [1946] **1** 664, KBD.
      Attributability of injury to war service or aggravation thereby—Benefit of any reasonable doubt to be given to claimant—Whether criminal standard of proof requisite—Royal Warrant Concerning Retired Pay, Pensions, etc 1949, (Cmd 7699), art 4(2). **Judd v Minister of Pensions and National Insurance** [1965] **3** 642, QBD.
      Attributability of injury to war service or aggravation thereby—Disease of unknown aetiology—Principles which should guide tribunals when considering a claim based on such a disease—Royal Warrant Concerning Retired Pay, Pensions etc 1949, (Cmd 7699), art 4(2), (3). **Coe v Minister of Pensions and National Insurance** [1966] **3** 172, QBD.
      Attributability of injury to war service or aggravation thereby—Royal Warrant concerning Retired Pay, Pensions, etc 1943, (Cmd 1943 No 6489), art 4(2), (3), (4). **Miller v Minister of Pensions** [1947] **2** 372, KBD.

WAR PENSION (cont)—
 Claim (cont)—
  Burden of proof (cont)—
   Civilians scheme—Causation of disablement—Claim made more than seven years after the date on
   which the war injury was sustained—Onus of proof on claimant—Benefit of reasonable doubt
   whether disablement was caused by war injury to be given to claimant—Personal Injuries
   (Civilians) Scheme 1964, (SI 1964 No 2077), art 5(3). **Cadney v Minister of Pensions and National
   Insurance** [1965] **3** 809, QBD.
   Death due to or substantially hastened by injury attributable to war service—Death more than
   seven years after termination of war service—Royal Warrant concerning Retired Pay, Pensions,
   etc 1949, (Cmd 1949 No 7699), art 5(2). **Dickinson v Minister of Pensions** [1952] **2** 1031, QBD.
   Disablement—Royal Warrant concerning Retired Pay, Pensions, etc 1943, (Cmd 1943 No 6489),
   art 1(4). **Royston v Minister of Pensions** [1948] **1** 778, KBD.
   Test of causation—Personal Injuries (Civilians) Scheme 1944, (S R & O 1944 No 369), arts 2(2), 6.
   Minister of Pensions v Williams [1947] **2** 93, KBD.
 Disablement—
  Claim—
   Burden of proof. *See* Claim—Burden of proof—Disablement, *above.*
 High Court—
  Appeal. *See* Appeal—Appeal to High Court, *above.*
 Mercantile marine—
  War risk injury—
   Injury attributable to conditions abnormal in time of peace—Aggravation of organic disease by
   service at sea—Exceptional wartime conditions aboard ship—Disablement not a war
   injury—Injury attributable to abnormal conditions—Substantial increase of 'risk of peril'—
   Whether abnormal conditions as such sufficient to qualify injury as a war risk injury—Pensions
   (Navy, Army, Air Force and Mercantile Marine) Act 1939, ss 3, 10—Pensions (Mercantile Marine)
   Act 1942, ss 1(2)(d)(3), 5. **Saffell, Re** [1945] **1** 321, KBD.
   Injury attributable to conditions abnormal in time of peace—Construction—Ejusdem generis
   rule—Pensions (Mercantile Marine) Act 1942, s 1(2)(d)—War Pensions (Naval Auxiliary Personnel)
   Scheme 1944, (S R & O 1944 No 499), Sch I(2)(d). **Minister of Pensions v Higham** [1948] **1** 863,
   KBD.
   Injury attributable to conditions abnormal in time of peace—Service in cable ship on Iceland
   station—Complaint of tinned food and bad living conditions—Pensions (Mercantile Marine) Act
   1942, s 1(2)(d). **Staynings v Minister of Pensions** [1947] **1** 347, KBD.
   Injury sustained at sea or in any other tidal water or in waters of any harbour—Coastguard
   employed at look-out hut on sea point—Whether propinquity to sea, tidal water or harbour
   sufficient for pension entitlement—Pensions (Mercantile Marine) Act 1942, s 1(2)—War Pensions
   (Coastguards) Scheme 1944, (SR & O 1944 No 500). **Ministry of Pensions v Nugent** [1946] **1** 273,
   KBD.
 Pensions appeal tribunal—
  Appeal from decision of Minister—
   Burden of proof—Attributability of injury to war service—Discharge from army on account of
   schizophrenia—Disability not noted on medical examination on enlistment—Onus of
   proof—Claim rejected by Minister—'Statement of the case'—Tribunal accepting Minister's
   findings as evidence—Advice of medical member of tribunal accepted as evidence during
   deliberations—Minister's findings insufficient—Necessity of supporting evidence—Advice of
   medical member no evidence—Onus of proof not discharged—Pensions Appeal Tribunals Act
   1943, s 6(4)—Pensions Appeal Tribunals (England and Wales) Rules 1943, (SR & O 1943 No 1757),
   rr 5, 12, 15(3)—Royal Warrant concerning Retired Pay, Pensions, etc 1943, (Cmd 1943 No 6489),
   art 4. **Moxon, Re** [1945] **2** 124, KBD.
   Burden of proof—Minister's reasons embodying medical opinion—Medical opinion conclusive only
   if authenticated by medical man—'Evidence'—Pensions Appeal Tribunals Act 1943, s 1, Schedule,
   para 5(2), (3)—Pensions appeal Tribunals (England and Wales) Rules 1943, (S R & O 1943
   No 1757), rr 12(6), 13, 14, 15, 16—Royal Warrant concerning Retired Pay, Pensions, etc 1943, (Cmd
   1943 No 6489), art 4(1), (2), (3). **Starr v Minister of Pensions** [1946] **1** 400, KBD.
   Time limits for bringing appeal—Primary time limit—Secondary time limit—Requirements for
   notice of decision—Effect of non-compliance with requirements—Amending statute introducing
   time limits—Whether Secretary of State required to give notification of introduction of time
   limits—Whether tribunal entitled to determine appeal brought after expiry of secondary time
   limit—Whether requirements for notice of decision complied with—Pensions Appeal
   Tribunals Act 1943, ss 8(1), (3), (5), 9—Pensions Appeal Tribunals (Late Appeals)
   Regulations 2001, SI 2001/1032, reg 4(a)(iii). **R (on the application of the Secretary of State for
   Defence) v Pensions Appeal Tribunal (Lockyer-Evis and others, interested parties)** [2008] **1** 287,
   QBD.
 Determination—
   Majority decision of tribunal—Validity—Pensions Appeal Tribunals Act 1943, s 6, Sch, para 3.
   Minister of Pensions v Horsey [1949] **2** 314, KBD.
   Need of unanimity—Pensions Appeal Tribunals Act 1943, Sch, para 3(1). **Brain v Minister of
   Pensions** [1947] **1** 892, KBD.
 Procedure—
   Request for opinion of medical specialist—Medical history sent by tribunal to specialist—Matters
   included unconnected with disease on which claim based—Propriety. **Jackson v Minister of
   Pensions** [1946] **2** 500, KBD.
   Request for opinion of medical specialist—Report favourable to claimant—Minister obtaining
   report of independent medical expert—Tribunal's rejection of claim based on report to
   Minister—Validity of procedure—Pensions Appeal Tribunals (England and Wales) Rules 1946, (S R
   & O 1946 No 1708), r 15(2)(3)—Royal Warrant concerning Retired Pay, Pensions, etc 1949, (Cmd
   1949 No 7699), art 4(2). **Sharp v Minister of Pensions** [1950] **2** 1012, KBD.
 Suicide. *See* Attributability of death of member of forces to war service—Suicide, *above.*
 War risk injury. *See* Mercantile marine—War risk injury, *above.*

WAR PENSION (cont)—
War service injury—
Injury arising out of and in course of performance of duties—
War reserve constable—Injury while proceeding to place of duty—Personal Injuries (Emergency Provisions) Act 1939, s 8(1). **Davis v Minister of Pensions** [1951] **2** 318, KBD.

WAR RISKS
Aviation insurance. *See* **Insurance** (Aviation insurance—War risks).
Marine insurance—
Arbitration clause, incorporation of. *See* **Marine insurance** (War risks policy—Arbitration clause—Incorporation of arbitration clause contained in rules of association).
Material non-disclosure. *See* **Insurance** (Disclosure—Non-disclosure—Material non-disclosure—Marine insurance—War risks policy).
Marine insurance. *See* **Marine insurance** (War risks policy).

WAR TIME LEASE
Commencement and termination. *See* **Landlord and tenant** (War time lease—Uncertainty—Term—Termination defined with reference to termination of war).

WAR WOUND
See **War injury**.

WARD OF COURT
Access—
Generally. *See* Care and control—Interim care and control—Access, *below*.
Termination of access—
Welfare of ward. *See* **Child** (Welfare—Access—Wardship proceedings—Access of parent—Termination of access).
Adoption—
Freeing child for adoption—
Practice. *See* **Adoption** (Practice—Freeing child for adoption—Ward of court).
Generally. *See* **Adoption** (Ward of court).
Leave of court. *See* **Adoption** (Consent—Ward of court).
Wardship proceedings pending adoption. *See* **Adoption** (Wardship proceedings pending adoption).
Adoption society—
Production of records and giving of evidence. *See* Practice—Production of records and giving of evidence by adoption society or local authority, *below*.
Affidavit—
Evidence. *See* Evidence—Affidavit, *below*.
Alien—
Jurisdiction. *See* Jurisdiction—Alien, *below*.
Appeal—
Appeal against order determining or continuing wardship—
Jurisdiction of Court of Appeal to substitute own view of right order for that of judge—Law Reform (Miscellaneous Provisions) Act 1949, s 9(2). **G (an infant), Re** [1956] **2** 876, CA.
Practice. *See* Practice—Appeal, *below*.
Review of exercise of discretion. *See* **Appeal** (Review of exercise of discretion—Duty of appellate court—Infant).
Application to make minor ward of court—
Application to Chancery Division—
Necessity for application—Divorce proceedings previously instituted between parents in Divorce Division—Custody of minors given to wife in divorce proceedings—Husband's application in Chancery Division asked also for care and control of minors and directions as to education—Relief obtainable in divorce proceedings—Unnecessary in circumstances to apply to Chancery Division. **A H (infants), Re** [1962] **3** 853, Ch D.
Appointment to hear summons—
Return date. **Practice Direction** [1966] **3** 144, Ch D.
Commonwealth immigrant refused admission to United Kingdom—
Wardship jurisdiction. *See* **Commonwealth immigrant** (Admission—Refusal of admission—Application to make infant seeking admission ward of court).
Order made on motion declaring minor to be ward of court—
Delivery of originating summons to registrar—Law Reform (Miscellaneous Provisions) Act 1949, s 9—RSC, Ord 54P. **Practice Direction** [1961] **2** 55, Ch D.
Originating summons—
Contents—Notice to defendant—Form of notice—RSC, Ord 90, r 3(4)-(7). **Practice Direction** [1973] **1** 144, Fam D.
Parties—
Need for minor to be made respondent to originating summons—Law Reform (Miscellaneous Provisions) Act 1949, s 9. **S (an infant), Re** [1950] **2** 159, Ch D.
Respondent where minor in care of local authority. **L (an infant), Re** [1963] **1** 176, Ch D.
Respondents. **Practice Note** [1962] **1** 156, Ch D.
Passport removal—
Ex parte applications—Local authorities bringing proceedings due to concern that minors would leave UK to travel to ISIS countries—Court making minors wards of court and making orders relating to retrieval of passports—Practice—Level of candour required by court in ex parte applications. **Tower Hamlets London BC v M** [2016] **1** 182, Fam D.
Production of summons at office of the chief master—
Practice—Relationship of applicant to ward to be stated—RSC Ord 91, r 1(3). **Practice Direction** [1967] **1** 828, Ch D.
Proof of date of birth of the minor—
Procedure. **Practice Direction** [1972] **1** 797, Fam D.

WARD OF COURT (cont)—
  Care and control—
    Appeal—
      Review of exercise of discretion—Duty of appellate court. *See* **Appeal** (Review of exercise of discretion—Duty of appellate court—Infant—Care and control order).
    Application—
      Applications which may be made to registrar. *See* **Minor** (Custody—Application—Applications which may be made to registrar—Wardship and guardianship proceedings).
      Jurisdiction of registrar. *See* Jurisdiction—Registrar—Application for care and control of minor, *below.*
    Contest between natural parent and foster parents—
      Test to be applied—Displacement of natural parent's normal role in care and upbringing of child—Who would provide better home irrelevant. **K (a minor) (ward: care and control),** Re [1990] 3 795, CA.
    Factors to be considered—
      Adopted child—Application to counter effect of adoption order—Dismissal of application in limine—Welfare of child first and paramount consideration—Circumstances justifying investigation by court—Application by child's natural mother—Mother and father having consented to adoption—Adoption of child by man—Intention that mother should continue to care for child after adoption—Mother living with adoptive father and caring for child—Adoptive father subsequently preventing mother from having contact with child—Mother starting wardship proceedings and seeking care and control—Whether proceedings should be dismissed in limine. **O (a minor) (wardship: adopted child),** Re [1978] 2 27, CA.
      Application made to stultify adoption proceedings brought by another party—Extent to which court will consider pending adoption proceedings in determining care and control. **F (an infant),** Re [1970] 1 344, CA.
      Child taken into voluntary care by local authority—Application by local authority to make child a ward of court and for order committing care and control to local authority—Effect of making child in voluntary care ward of court and committing care to local authority—Local authority placing child with suitable long term foster parents after period with foster mother—Natural mother a defendant to wardship proceedings—Natural mother wishing child to be transferred back to foster mother—Whether local authority required to establish that exceptional circumstances existed making it impracticable or undesirable for child to be under natural mother's care or whether sole criterion the child's best interests—Family Law Reform Act 1969, s 7(2). **C B (a minor),** Re [1981] 1 16, CA.
      Contest between natural parent and remoter relative—Father and maternal grandmother—Application of grandmother for care and control of deceased daughter's child—Application opposed by father—Child's parents divorced before mother's death—Mother given custody of child—Mother and child living with grandparents before mother's death—Father having illegitimate child by another woman—Father and other woman marrying—Grandmother hostile to father—Whether in circumstances care and control of child should be awarded to grandmother. **F (a minor) (wardship: appeal),** Re [1976] 1 417, CA.
      Religion—Illegitimate infant, baptised in Roman Catholic faith, placed for adoption with non-Roman Catholic family—Mother then decided infant should be placed for adoption by a Roman Catholic family and withdrew consent to proposed adoption—Adoption order refused—Application by former proposing adopters to make infant ward of court and for care and custody—Motion by mother to de-ward infant and dismiss application—Wardship continued, in the circumstances, and custody given to former proposing adopters on their undertaking that infant should be brought up in Roman Catholic faith. **E (an infant),** Re [1963] 3 874, Ch D.
      Welfare of minor first and paramount consideration—Wishes of unimpeachable parent—Justice of case—Factors to be balanced against minor's welfare—Father's application for care and control—Father minister of religion holding strong convictions against adultery—Very young children—Mother committing adultery—Mother intending to set up home with other man taking children with her—Excellent mother to children—Whether care and control should be given to mother. **K (minors) (wardship: care and control),** Re [1977] 1 647, CA.
      Wishes of unimpeachable parent—Child of tender years—Mother committed adultery, and left home on account of another man—Father's conduct unimpeachable—Father able to provide suitable surroundings for child—Whether father entitled to care and control. **L (infants),** Re [1962] 3 1, CA.
  Interim care and control—
    Access—Official Solicitor as guardian ad litem, seeking control of question of access by parents—Order made that parents should have access at such times as they should agree or as, in default of agreement, the Official Solicitor should direct. **R (PM) (an infant),** Re [1968] 1 691, Ch D.
    Application adjourned by master for mother to consider whether she wished matter adjourned to judge—Mother submitted ward to psychiatrist for examination without consent of court or of Official Solicitor as guardian ad litem of ward—Impropriety. **R (PM) (an infant),** Re [1968] 1 691, Ch D.
  Power to commit ward of court to care of local authority—
    Local authority initiating wardship proceedings—Local authority applying for care and control in wardship proceedings—Undesirable for mother to have care of children—Foster parent with whom local authority placed children unable to afford to maintain children—Foster parent not a party to wardship proceedings—Whether statutory power to commit ward to care of local authority where wardship initiated by local authority—Whether conditions for exercise of statutory power fulfilled—Family Law Reform Act 1969, s 7(2). **Lewisham London Borough v M** [1981] 3 307, Fam D.
  Protection of ward—
    Child sex abuse—Application in wardship proceedings for care order—Guidelines on investigative interviews, drafting of local authority affidavits and disclosure of documents. **A and ors (minors) (wardship: child abuse: guidelines),** Re [1992] 1 153, Fam D.
  Chancery Division—
    Necessity for application. *See* Application to make minor ward of court—Application to Chancery Division—Necessity for application, *above.*

WARD OF COURT (cont)—
    Child abuse—
        Protection of ward—
            Care order. *See* Care and control—Protection of ward—Child sex abuse, *above*.
    Child in care of local authority. *See* **Child** (Care—Local authority—Wardship proceedings).
    Committal—
        Contempt of court in wardship proceedings. *See* Contempt of court in wardship proceedings—
            Committal, *below*.
    Commonwealth immigrant—
        Refusal of admission to United Kingdom—
            Application to make infant seeking admission ward of court—Wardship jurisdiction excluded. *See*
                Commonwealth immigrant (Admission—Refusal of admission—Application to make infant
                seeking admission ward of court).
    Contempt of court in wardship proceedings—
        Committal—
            Form of application for committal—Interference with witness in wardship proceedings—Motion in
                wardship proceedings to commit contemnor—Whether application should be by originating
                notice of motion. **B (JA) (an infant), Re** [1965] **2** 168, Ch D.
        Publication concerning proceedings of court sitting in private. *See* **Contempt of court** (Publications
        concerning legal proceedings—Court sitting in private—Wardship or adoption proceedings).
        Removal of ward from jurisdiction without leave—
            Proceedings for punishment of contempt—Proceedings for punishment of contempt—Whether
                taking ward out of jurisdiction without consent constituting criminal contempt—Whether triable
                on indictment. **R v D** [1984] **1** 574, CA.
            Proceedings to locate parent and ward—Judge ordering ward's 16-year-old half-brother to lodge
                passport at court, give evidence and produce records of telephone and electronic
                communications—Penal notice attached to orders—Whether court having power to remove
                passports as coercive measure—Whether judge erring in ordering 16-year-old to provide
                evidence and disclose communications—Whether judge erring in attaching penal notice to
                orders. **B (a child) (removal from jurisdiction: removal of family's passports as coercive measure),**
                Re [2015] **1** 230, CA.
    Court of Appeal—
        Jurisdiction to substitute own view of right order for that of judge. *See* Appeal—Appeal against order
        determining or continuing wardship—Jurisdiction of Court of Appeal to substitute own view of right
        order for that of judge, *above*.
    Criminal proceedings—
        Caution in lieu of criminal proceedings—
            Parental consent—Consent of wardship court required. **A (a minor) (wardship: criminal**
                proceedings), Re [1989] **3** 610, Fam D.
        Interview by police, security service or other similar agencies—
            Whether judicial consent required—Guidance. **A (a child) (ward of court: security service**
                interview), Re [2017] **4** 331, Fam D.
        Ward required as witness at criminal trial—
            Whether leave of wardship court required for ward to be called as witness at trial. **K and ors**
                (minors) (wardship: criminal proceedings), Re [1988] **1** 214, Fam D.
            Witness for defence—Interviewing ward—Father of ward charged with serious sexual offences
                against three female children of family and wishing to interview ward and call him as witness at
                trial—Whether leave of wardship court required to call ward as witness at trial—Whether leave of
                wardship court required to interview ward with view to taking proof of evidence. **R and ors**
                (minors) (wardship: criminal proceedings), Re [1991] **2** 193, CA.
    Custody—
        Application—
            Applications which may be made to registrar. *See* **Minor** (Custody—Application—Applications
                which may be made to registrar—Wardship and guardianship proceedings).
        Care and control. *See* Care and control, *above*.
        Care and control and access—
            Practice. *See* **Minor** (Practice—Wardship and guardianship proceedings—Custody and access—
                Care and control and access).
        Character of parties seeking access to child—
            Evidence—Assessment of character by appeal court—Appeal court not having opportunity to
                observe parties in witness box—Duty of court in expressing its assessment of character of
                parties. **B v W (wardship: appeal)** [1979] **3** 83, HL.
        Interests of ward—
            Ward approaching age of majority—Previous arrangements for custody very old—Interests of ward
                relative to interests of comity of nations and forum conveniens. **T (an infant), Re** [1969] **3** 998,
                Vacation Ct.
        Joinder of child as party to proceedings. *See* **Minor** (Practice—Wardship and custody
        proceedings—Joinder of child as party).
        Prior custody order made by magistrates in favour of wife on her application for relief in matrimonial
        proceedings—
            Application dismissed by magistrates save as to custody of infant and maintenance for
                infant—Reasonable access by father ordered—Access in fact afforded by mother unsatisfactory—
                Application by father by originating summons to make ward of court and for directions as to care
                and control of infant—Father's application was misconceived—Proper course was to apply to
                magistrates for more specific order relating to access. **K (KJS) (an infant), Re** [1966] **3** 154, Ch D.
        Rights of custody. *See* **Minor** (Custody—Rights of custody—Ward of court).
        Wardship and guardianship proceedings—
            Practice. *See* **Minor** (Practice—Wardship and guardianship proceedings—Custody and access).
    Diplomat's child. *See* Jurisdiction—Diplomatic privilege—Diplomat's child, *below*.
    Disclosure to parties of information before court. *See* **Natural justice** (Disclosure to parties of information
    before court—Wardship proceedings).

WARD OF COURT (cont)—
Education—
Ward with special educational needs—
Jurisdiction of court over ward with special educational needs. *See* **Education** (Special educational needs—Wardship).
Evidence—
Affidavit—
Exhibited statements of fact. **B (JA) (an infant), Re** [1965] **2** 168, Ch D.
Exhibited statements to affidavits. **Practice Direction** [1967] **2** 299, Ch D.
Character of parties seeking access. *See* Custody—Character of parties seeking access to child—Evidence, *above*.
Criminal proceedings. *See* **Criminal evidence** (Child—Ward of court).
Disclosure—
Practice. *See* Practice—Proceedings in private—Disclosure of evidence, *below*.
Family Proceedings Department of Family Division—
Responsibilities of Department. *See* **Family Division** (Family Proceedings Department).
Forum conveniens—
Jurisdiction. *See* Jurisdiction—Forum conveniens, *below*.
Freedom of publication—
Protection of ward. *See* Jurisdiction—Protection of ward—Freedom of publication, *below*.
Guardian ad litem—
Official Solicitor. *See* **Official Solicitor** (Guardian ad litem—Wardship proceedings).
Two parties requiring appointment of guardians ad litem—
Appointment of Official Solicitor and of near relative or divorce court welfare officer. **Practice Direction** [1984] **1** 69, Fam D.
Guardianship order—
Removal of child outside Great Britain for purposes of adoption—
Jurisdiction of court to make guardianship order in respect of ward of court. *See* **Adoption** (Ward of court—Guardianship order—Removal of child outside Great Britain).
Injunction—
Jurisdiction. *See* Jurisdiction—Injunction, *below*.
Joinder as party to proceedings. *See* **Minor** (Practice—Wardship and custody proceedings—Joinder of child as party).
Jurisdiction—
Alien—
Alien children of American parents—Dissolution of marriage in Mexico—Custody of children given to mother with liberal access by father—Consent order for children to remain in and under control of the State of New York—Wife's removal of children to England—Consent of court and father not sought—Order by New York State court to return children there—Children made wards of court in England by mother—Whether children should be returned to State of New York in custody of father—Whether judge bound to make full inquiry into merits. **H (infants), Re** [1966] **1** 886, CA.
Ordinary residence giving jurisdiction—Parents stateless persons ordinarily resident in England—Parents living apart—Child lived with mother—Father took child to Israel without consent of mother—Child remained ordinarily resident in England—Whether wardship jurisdiction extended to child. **P (GE) (an infant), Re** [1964] **3** 977, CA.
Boy soldier—
Boy soldier subject to military law—Whether appropriate to make boy soldier ward of court. **JS (a minor) (wardship: boy soldier), Re** [1990] **2** 861, Fam D.
Child in care of voluntary adoption agency—
Whether court will exercise wardship jurisdiction to review decision of adoption agency. *See* **Adoption** (Adoption agency—Voluntary adoption agency—Wardship proceedings).
Child subject to immigration legislation—
Child brought to United Kingdom and placed with foster parents—Child overstaying leave to enter—Child liable to removal under immigration legislation—Foster parents applying to make child ward of court—Whether wardship jurisdiction exercisable if it would fetter immigration authorities' discretion—Whether court having jurisdiction to make child ward of court. **F (a minor), Re** [1989] **1** 1155, CA.
Custody—
Previous order of magistrates under guardianship jurisdiction. *See* Previous custody order of magistrates made under jurisdiction conferred by guardianship legislation, *below*.
Declaration of paternity—
Whether jurisdiction in wardship proceedings to grant bare declaration of paternity—Whether if jurisdiction discretion to grant declaration should be exercised—Whether court should order blood tests in wardship proceedings—Family Law Reform Act 1969, s 20(1). **J S (a minor), Re** [1980] **1** 1061, CA.
Diplomatic privilege—
Diplomat's child—Extent of immunity from legal process—Whether child of diplomat can be made ward of court. **C (an infant), Re** [1958] **2** 656, Ch D.
Forum conveniens—
Custody—England or Scotland—Father domiciled Scotsman—Divorce proceedings pending in Scotland—Father's application for leave to apply to Scottish court for custody of children—No conflict of jurisdiction—Orders complementary. **X's Settlement, Re** [1945] **1** 100, Ch D.
Factors relevant to determination of forum—Avoidance of possibility of conflicting orders from different jurisdictions. **S (M) (an infant), Re** [1971] **1** 459, Ch D.
Factors relevant to determination of forum—Italian mother and English father of minor—Separation order made by consent by Italian court giving father custody of minor—Father brought minor to England—Application by mother for care and control of minor and liberty to take him to Italy—Duty of English court to consider best interests of minor. **Kernot (an infant), Re** [1964] **3** 339, Ch D.
Interim care and control—Divorce proceedings commenced in Scotland—Interim order in Scotland awarding custody—Wardship proceedings commenced in England—Whether investigation should take place in England or Scotland. **G (an infant), Re** [1969] **2** 1135, Ch D.

WARD OF COURT (cont)—
  Jurisdiction (cont)—
    Forum conveniens (cont)—
      Interim care and control—Family resident in Jersey—Visit by minors to England by agreement for agreed time—Decision by father during that time not to return minors to mother in Jersey—No fraud—Father returning to reside in England—Application by father to make minors wards of court and keep them in England—Whether English court should order return of minors to Jersey. **A (infants), Re** [1970] 3 184, CA.

      Preliminary issue as to forum—Discretion as to determination as preliminary issue—Normal exercise of discretion. **S (M) (an infant), Re** [1971] 1 459, Ch D.

  Inherent jurisdiction—
    Circumstances in which exercisable. **E (an infant), Re** [1955] 3 174, Ch D.

    Circumstances in which exercisable—Discretion—Juvenile court making care order committing child to care of local authority—Application by parents for child to be made ward of court—Application opposed by local authority on merits—Objection to jurisdiction taken by local authority after conclusion of evidence—Whether objection taken too late. **H (a minor) (wardship: jurisdiction), Re** [1978] 2 903, CA.

    Circumstances in which exercisable—Factors to be considered—Juvenile court making care order committing child to care of local authority—Parents wishing to return to their own country with child—Application by parents for child to be made ward of court—Whether High Court should assume jurisdiction. **H (a minor) (wardship: jurisdiction), Re** [1978] 2 903, CA.

    Circumstances in which exercisable—Factors to be considered—Juvenile court making interim care order committing child to care of local authority—Application by father for child to be made ward of court and placed in his custody—Application opposed by local authority and mother—Whether High Court should assume jurisdiction. **M v Humberside CC** [1979] 2 744, Fam D.

    Interlocking of court's inherent jurisdiction with statutory jurisdiction of local authority having child in care—Child remaining in care of local authority and also a ward of court—Access—Form of order—Children Act 1948, s 1(3). **G (infants), Re** [1963] 3 370, Ch D.

    Jurisdiction to make order for protection of minor before commencement of wardship proceedings—Need of application to make infant a ward of court—Law Reform (Miscellaneous Provisions) Act 1949, s 9(1)—RSC Ord 54P, r 1. **E (an infant), Re** [1955] 3 174, Ch D.

    Protection of children—Court's inherent jurisdiction to protect children—Children at risk of sexual abuse from relative—Local authority applying for leave to invoke court's inherent jurisdiction for children's protection—Whether protection of children could be achieved by alternative procedure—Whether leave should be granted—Children Act 1989, s 100. **Devon CC v S** [1995] 1 243, Fam D.

    Restriction by statute. **Baker (infants), Re** [1961] 3 276, CA; **M (an infant), Re** [1961] 1 788, CA.

  Injunction—
    Interim injunction—Originating process not yet issued—Whether inherent jurisdiction to grant injunction before issue of originating process restricted by Law Reform (Miscellaneous Provisions) Act 1949, s 9. **N (infants), Re** [1967] 1 161, Ch D.

  Interlocking of court's inherent jurisdiction with statutory jurisdiction of local authority under fit person order. *See* **Children and young persons** (Fit person order—Subsequent wardship proceedings).

  Kidnapping—
    Foreign children—Canadian children of marriage of English mother to Canadian—No foreign court proceedings—Children brought to England by mother without father's consent—Application by mother to make children wards of English court—Whether English court should order return of children to Canada, leaving mother to take proceedings there if she wished. **T (infants), Re** [1968] 3 411, CA.

    Foreign children—Removal of children from foreign jurisdiction by one parent—Order to return children to custody of parent in foreign jurisdiction—Summary order without investigating merits—Circumstances in which summary order will be made—Welfare of child—Interest of child in being returned to natural environment without delay—Conduct of parent in removing child from foreign jurisdiction a factor to be considered—Expectation that dispute over custody would be satisfactorily resolved by foreign court. **L (minors) (wardship: jurisdiction), Re** [1974] 1 913, CA.

    Peremptory order for return of wards to foreign jurisdiction—Refusal to make order—Welfare of children first and paramount consideration—Circumstances rendering it proper for English court to assume jurisdiction—Likelihood of foreign court ordering return of children to custody of natural parent in England—Children living with mother and stepfather in California—Death of mother—Natural father having remarried and living in England—Application by stepfather to Californian court for custody—Father removing children to England and making them wards of court—Application by stepfather for peremptory order for return of children to California—Whether court should make order. **C (minors) (wardship: jurisdiction), Re** [1978] 2 230, CA.

  Magistrates—
    Order forbidding removal—Order a nullity. **T v T** [1968] 3 321, Div.

  Medical treatment—
    Child born with Down's syndrome and having intestinal blockage—Child requiring operation to remove blockage in order to live—Parents refusing consent to operation—Local authority making child ward of court and applying to court for authority to direct that operation be carried out—Whether court required to determine whether operation in child's best interest or whether parents' wishes should be respected. **B (a minor) (wardship: medical treatment) (1981), Re** [1990] 3 927, CA.

    Grossly handicapped baby—Baby neither on point of death nor dying—Nature of medical treatment to be administered to ward—Reventilation likely to be fatal if baby collapsed—Whether deliberate steps should be taken artificially to prolong life whatever pain and suffering caused to child—Whether court should withhold consent to reventilation—Test to be applied in assessing course to be adopted in best interests of child—Whether relevant that child a ward of court—Whether court required to exercise a higher or different standard from that of reasonable and responsible parents. **J (a minor) (wardship: medical treatment), Re** [1990] 3 930, CA.

Jurisdiction (cont)—
Protection of ward (cont)—
Fundamental rights of ward—Right of woman to reproduce—Sterilisation operation—Non-therapeutic reasons for operations—Ward a mentally retarded girl—Proposal to perform operation to sterilise girl—Operation irreversible—Fear that girl might be seduced and give birth to mentally abnormal child—Operation advised by consulting paediatrician in charge of girl's case—Girl's parent consenting to operation—Girl incapable of giving informed consent to operation—Girl having sufficient intellectual capacity to enable her to marry in due course and to make her own choice whether to be sterilised—Whether court should exercise wardship jurisdiction to prevent operation. **D (a minor) (wardship: sterilisation), Re** [1976] **1** 326, Fam D.
Registrar—
Application for care and control of minor—Order made by district registrar without referring matter to appropriate county court judge—Proper practice to refer matter to appropriate judge. **L (a minor) (wardship proceedings), Re** [1978] **2** 318, CA.
Relationship of jurisdiction over minors of Chancery Division and Probate, Divorce and Admiralty Division—
Comity between judges. **Andrews (Infants), Re** [1958] **2** 308, Ch D.
Conflict of jurisdiction—Whether jurisdiction of Chancery Division supersedes jurisdiction of Divorce Division in relation to infant made a ward of court. **Andrews v Andrews and Sullivan** [1958] **2** 305, Div; **Hall v Hall** [1963] **2** 140, CA.
Sterilisation—
Welfare and best interests of ward—Ward mentally handicapped and not able to understand connection between sexual intercourse and pregnancy—Ward not able to cope with birth and bringing up child—Ward's welfare and best interests requiring that she be sterilised—Whether court having jurisdiction to authorise sterilisation. **B (a minor) (wardship: sterilisation), Re** [1987] **2** 206, Fam D, CA & HL.
Unborn child—
Whether court has jurisdiction to make an unborn child a ward of court. **F (in utero), Re** [1988] **2** 193, CA.
Ward with special educational needs—
Conflict between wardship jurisdiction and education authority's duty. See **Education** (Special educational needs—Wardship).
Leave to take ward out of jurisdiction. See Removal of ward from jurisdiction—Leave, below.
Local authority—
Child in care. See **Child** (Care—Local authority—Wardship proceedings).
Respondent where minor in care of local authority. See Application to make minor ward of court—Parties—Respondent where minor in care of local authority, above.
Magistrates—
Jurisdiction. See Jurisdiction—Magistrates, above.
Prior custody order made by magistrates. See Custody—Prior custody order made by magistrates, above.
Medical treatment—
Jurisdiction. See Jurisdiction—Medical treatment, above.
Missing ward—
Address of ward or of person with whom ward believed to be—
Disclosure by government departments at request of registrar—Particulars to be certified in request—Information to be supplied by solictors prior to request. **Practice Direction** [1973] **1** 61, Fam D; [1979] **2** 1106, Fam D.
Disclosure by government departments—Disclosure at request of registrar—Particulars to be certified in request—Information to be supplied to registrar by applicant or solicitors prior to request—Child Abduction and Custody Act 1985—Family Law Act 1986, Pt I. **Practice Direction** [1988] **2** 573, Fam D; [1989] **1** 765, Fam D.
Official Solicitor—
Practice. See Practice—Official Solicitor, below.
Order—
Extension after expiration of wardship. See **Family proceedings** (Orders in family proceedings—Ward of court).
Originating summons—
Contents. See Application to make minor ward of court—Originating summons—Contents, above.
Parties to application. See Application to make minor ward of court—Parties, above.
Paternity—
Declaration of paternity—
Jurisdiction to grant declaration in wardship proceedings. See Jurisdiction—Declaration of paternity, above.
Place of safety order. See Protection of ward—Place of safety order, below.
Practice—
Appeal—
Cases involving transfer of child—Hearing of appeal—Listing—Appeal to be heard within 28 days where order for transfer stayed—Duty of counsel who conducted case at trial—Duty of counsel's clerks and solicitors. **W (minors), Re** [1984] **3** 58, CA.
Application in wardship proceedings—
Ex parte application—Applications for routine leave or directions where court has authorised placement of ward with view to adoption—Notice to other parties not normally necessary—Consultation with Official Solicitor when acting as guardian ad litem. **Practice Direction** [1989] **1** 169, Fam D.
Ex parte application—Circumstances in which ex parte application may be made—Necessity to inform Official Solicitor of application. **H (a minor), Re** [1985] **3** 1, CA.
Appointment of Official Solicitor as guardian ad litem—
When Official Solicitor should be appointed. **F (a minor) (adoption: parental consent), Re** [1982] **1** 321, CA.
Chancery Division—
Adjournment to judge within stated time. **Practice Direction** [1966] **3** 84, Ch D.

WARD OF COURT (cont)—
  Practice (cont)—
    Criminal injuries compensation claim—
      Application for leave to claim compensation to be made by guardian ad litem—Disclosure of documents on wardship proceedings file—Application to be made by local authority director of social services or by person having care and control of child where no guardian appointed—Award of compensation to be paid into court—Application to be made to court as to management and administration of award. **Practice Direction** [1988] **1** 182, Fam D.

      Application for leave to claim compensation—Application made by Official Solicitor acting as guardian ad litem of ward—Ward a victim of sexual abuse by father—Test to be applied by judge in deciding whether to allow application to proceed. **G (a minor) (ward: criminal injuries compensation), Re** [1990] **3** 102, CA.

    Hearing—
      Application for committal for contempt of court in relation to wardship proceedings. *See* **Contempt of court** (Committal—Application—Hearing—Contempt in relation to wardship proceedings).

      Notice of hearing—Notice sent to mother of minor and not to solicitors on record—Whether desirable. **L (a minor) (wardship proceedings), Re** [1978] **2** 318, CA.

    Judicial review—
      Concurrent wardship and judicial review proceedings—Importance of hearing wardship and judicial review proceedings at same time. **D (a minor), Re** [1987] **3** 717, CA.

    Official Solicitor—
      Appointment as guardian ad litem. *See* Practice—Appointment of Official Solicitor as guardian ad litem, *above*.

      Official Solicitor appointed as guardian ad litem—Application by ward of court to continue proceedings without guardian ad litem—Whether ward having 'sufficient understanding' to participate in proceedings as a party without guardian ad litem—Whether appropriate for Official Solicitor to act as amicus curiae—Family Proceedings Rules 1991, r 9.2A. **H (a minor) (guardian ad litem: requirement), Re** [1994] **4** 762, Fam D.

      Official Solicitor' report—Disclosure—Confidential report of Official Solicitor acting as guardian ad litem to wards of court—Whether interested parties entitled as of right to see report. **Official Solicitor v K** [1963] **3** 191, HL.

      Official Solicitor's costs—Appointment of Official Solicitor as guardian ad litem—Payment of Official Solicitor's costs—Supreme Court Act 1981, s 51(1). **G (a minor) (wardship: costs), Re** [1982] **2** 32, CA.

    Parties to proceedings—
      Application to make minor ward of court. *See* Application to make minor ward of court—Parties, *above*.

      Minor—Minor proceeding without next friend or guardian ad litem—Child applying in family proceedings for residence order authorising her to live with aunt—Child's adoptive parents opposing application—Child instructing solicitor to act for her—Solicitor considering child able, having regard to her understanding, to instruct him and accepting her instructions—Application by adoptive parents for leave to make child ward of court—Judge making child ward of court as means of appointing guardian ad litem—Whether child entitled to proceed without next friend or guardian ad litem—Whether wardship jurisdiction should be invoked to protect child—Whether guardian ad litem can be imposed against child's will—Family Proceedings Rules 1991, r 9.2A(1)(b)(i). **T (a minor) (child: representation), Re** [1993] **4** 518, CA.

      Ward seeking to make undesirable association with another person—Other person not to be party to originating summons but defendant in summons for injunction or committal—Other person to be given time to obtain representation—Title to proceedings. **Practice Direction** [1983] **2** 672, Fam D.

    Proceedings in private—
      Disclosure of evidence—Disclosure to persons not parties—Disclosure without prior leave may be contempt of court. **Practice Direction** [1987] **3** 640, Fam D.

      Publication of information—Contempt of court. *See* **Contempt of court** (Publications concerning legal proceedings—Court sitting in private—Wardship or adoption proceedings).

      Transcripts. *See* **Child** (Practice—Court proceedings in relation to children—Proceedings in private—Publication of information—Transcripts).

    Production of records and giving of evidence by adoption society or local authority—
      Contested applications—Application to court for directions. **Practice Direction** [1968] **1** 762, Ch D.

    Secure accommodation—
      Application for secure accommodation. *See* **Child** (Care—Local authority—Wardship proceedings—Secure accommodation).

    Two parties requiring appointment of guardians ad litem. *See* Guardian ad litem—Two parties requiring appointment of guardians ad litem, *above*.

    Welfare report. *See* **Child** (Welfare—Welfare report).

  Previous custody order of magistrates made under jurisdiction conferred by guardianship legislation—
    Circumstances in which High Court will make different order under wardship jurisdiction—
      Exceptional circumstances—Magistrates' court unable to give relief sought—Difficulty of enforcing order where parent having custody living outside jurisdiction of magistrates' court—Refusal of legal aid to parent to prosecute appeal against magistrates' order—Doubts as to validity of order made by magistrates' court. **D (minors) (wardship: jurisdiction), Re** [1973] **2** 993, Fam D.

      Minors in charge of local authority under fit person order—Father having custody—Summons by mother to make minors wards of court—Forum conveniens—Magistrates' order to be reconsidered in magistrates' court unless relief sought which magistrates unable to give. **P (infants), Re** [1967] **2** 229, Ch D.

      Removal of minors from jurisdiction—Mother having custody under magistrates' order—Motion by mother to restrain father from removing minor from jurisdiction—Order of High Court in exercise of prerogative jurisdiction not inconsistent with order of magistrates. **H (GJ) (an infant), Re** [1966] **1** 952, Ch D.

WARD OF COURT (cont)—
Protection of ward—
  Confidential papers in wardship proceedings—
    Disclosure of documents—Application for leave to disclose documents used in wardship proceedings—Disclosure to ward for purposes of litigation—Matters to be considered—Ward attaining majority before hearing of appeal—Interests of minor—Public interest in due administration of justice—Prospects of success in litigation for which disclosure sought—Inhibition of frankness on part of witnesses in wardship proceedings—Whether court should order disclosure of documents. **Manda, Re** [1993] **1** 733, CA.
    Release of confidential papers for use in collateral civil proceedings—Release of confidential papers for use in libel action—Matters to be considered—Effect on children and public interest in due administration of wardship jurisdiction to be weighed against public interest in due administration of justice in collateral civil proceedings—Whether court will permit inspection of wardship court's files for purpose of defending libel action if inspection would adversely affect confidential nature of wardship jurisdiction—Administration of Justice Act 1960, s 12(1). **X and ors (minors) (wardship: disclosure of documents), Re** [1992] **2** 595, Fam D.
  Jurisdiction. *See* Jurisdiction—Protection of ward, *above*.
  Place of safety order—
    Application for order—Urgent cases—Procedure. **Practice Direction** [1988] **2** 63, Fam D.
  Psychiatric examination—
    Practice. *See* **Minor** (Psychiatric examination—Wardship and matrimonial causes).
  Publication of information about ward—
    Jurisdiction to restrain—
      Generally. *See* Jurisdiction—Protection of ward—Freedom of publication, *above*.
  Publication of proceedings—
    Chambers proceedings—
      Publication of report of order made in chambers—Whether contempt of court. **De Beaujeu, Re** [1949] **1** 439, Ch D.
    Contempt of court. *See* **Contempt of court** (Publications concerning legal proceedings—Court sitting in private—Wardship or adoption proceedings).
Religion. *See* Care and control—Factors to be considered—Religion, *above*.
Removal of ward from jurisdiction—
  Generally. *See* **Minor** (Removal outside jurisdiction).
  Leave—
    Application for leave to take ward out of jurisdiction—Whether an interlocutory proceeding RSC Ord 38, r 3, proviso. **J (an infant), Re** [1960] **1** 603, Ch D.
    Leave for temporary visits abroad—Power to give general leave for such visits—Order giving general leave—Conditions attached to it—Certificate of compliance with conditions. **Practice Direction** [1973] **2** 512, Fam D.
    Leave to take ward out of jurisdiction—Factors to be considered—Bi-racial marriage—Infant son and infant daughter of Sudanese father and English mother—Matrimonial home intended at time of marriage to be in Sudan—Children subsequently brought to England by mother—Whether father should have liberty to take them or either back to the Sudan—Guardianship of Infants Act 1925, s 1. **O (infants), Re** [1962] **2** 10, CA.
  Removal without leave of court—
    Contempt of court—Sequestration. *See* **Contempt of court** (Sequestration—Removal of ward from jurisdiction without leave).
    Indorsement on originating summons applying to make child a ward—Indorsement required to contain statement that removal of child without court's leave contempt of court punishable by imprisonment—Procedure for requesting Home Office to take steps to prevent removal of ward from jurisdiction. **Practice Direction** [1977] **3** 122, Fam D.
    Rights of custody. *See* **Minor** (Custody—Rights of custody—Ward of court—Abduction of ward of court).
    Temporary visits abroad—Holidays and educational journeys—Ward of court in local authority care and control—Conditions on which ward may proceed out of England and Wales without specific authority of court. **Practice Direction** [1989] **3** 89, Fam D.
Secure accommodation—
  Application for secure accommodation—
    Practice. *See* **Child** (Care—Local authority—Wardship proceedings—Secure accommodation).
Unborn child—
  Jurisdiction to make an unborn child a ward of court. *See* Jurisdiction—Unborn child, *above*.
Welfare. *See* **Child** (Welfare—Ward of court).
Witness in criminal proceedings—
  Evidence. *See* **Criminal evidence** (Child—Ward of court—Witness in criminal proceedings).
  Whether leave of wardship court required for ward to be called as witness. *See* Criminal proceedings—Ward required as witness at criminal trial, *above*.

WAREHOUSE
Application of Factories Act. *See* **Factory** (Warehouse—Application of Factories Act to warehouses).
Excise warehousing regulations. *See* **Customs and excise** (Warehousing—Regulations).
Sunday closing. *See* **Shop** (Sunday closing—Retail trading elsewhere than in shop—Warehouse).
Wholesale—
  Development—
    Use classes. *See* **Town and country planning** (Development—Use classes—Warehouse).

WARNED LIST
Chancery Division. *See* **Practice** (Chancery Division—Warned List).

WARRANT
Arrest—
  Arrest without warrant. *See* **Arrest** (Arrest without warrant).

WARRANT (cont)—
  Arrest (cont)—
    European arrest warrant—
      Extradition offence—Hearing. *See* **Extradition** (Hearing—Extradition offence—European arrest warrant).
      Extradition proceedings. *See* **Extradition** (Extradition hearing—European arrest warrant).
    Generally. *See* **Arrest** (Warrant).
    Provisional warrant—
      Fugitive offender. *See* **Extradition** (Arrest—Provisional warrant).
    Vessel, of. *See* **Admiralty** (Arrest of vessel).
  Committal—
    Enforcement of affiliation order. *See* **Affiliation** (Affiliation order—Enforcement—Warrant of commitment).
    Jurisdiction—
      Magistrates. *See* **Magistrates** (Jurisdiction—Warrant of commitment).
    Non-payment of fine—
      Issue of warrant without hearing. *See* **Magistrates** (Fine—Committal to prison in default of payment—Issue of committal warrant without a hearing).
  Distress—
    Arrears of general rates—
      Application to issue warrant more than six years after demand. *See* **Limitation of action** (Action—Proceeding in a court of law—Application to issue distress warrant in respect of arrears of general rates).
    Non-payment of rates—
      Jurisdiction of magistrates. *See* **Magistrates** (Jurisdiction—Warrant for distress for non-payment of rates).
  Execution. *See* **Magistrates** (Warrant—Execution).
  Income tax offence—
    Suspected fraud. *See* **Income tax** (Offence—Fraud—Suspected offence—Warrant to enter and seize documents).
  Indorsement—
    Generally. *See* **Magistrates** (Warrant—Indorsement).
    Irish warrant. *See* **Magistrates** (Indorsement of Irish warrant).
  Interception of telephone calls—
    Warrant to intercept telephone calls issued by Secretary of State—
      Judicial review of decision to issue warrant—Availability of remedy—National security. *See* **Judicial review** (Availability of remedy—National security—Warrant to intercept telephone calls issued by Secretary of State).
  Irish warrant—
    Indorsement. *See* **Magistrates** (Indorsement of Irish warrant).
  Possession, for—
    Landlord and tenant—
      Procedure before magistrates. *See* **Landlord and tenant** (Recovery of possession—Procedure before magistrates—Warrant for possession).
    Leave to issue warrant—
      Whether application for leave to issue warrant an 'action'—Whether time-barred. *See* **Limitation of action** (Action—Action on judgment—Warrant for possession).
    Stay of execution—
      Jurisdiction of county court. *See* **County court** (Execution—Warrant for possession of premises—Suspension of execution—Jurisdiction).
  Search warrant—
    Competition investigation. *See* **Competition** (Investigation and enforcement—Search warrant).
    Generally. *See* **Police** (Search warrant).
    Income tax—
      Suspected offence. *See* **Income tax** (Offence—Fraud—Suspected offence—Warrant to enter and seize documents).
    Obscene publications—
      Validity of warrant. *See* **Criminal law** (Obscene publications—Power of search and seizure—Validity of warrant).

WARRANTY
  Auction—
    Exclusion clause—
      Effect. *See* **Auction** (Conditions of sale—Exclusion of liability—Conditions in catalogue excluding warranty unless specially mentioned and appearing on account).
  Authority—
    Measure of damages. *See* **Damages** (Measure of damages—Warranty of authority).
    Solicitor—
      Sale of land. *See* **Solicitor** (Sale of land—Warranty of authority).
  Breach—
    Damages—
      Loss directly and naturally resulting from breach. *See* **Contract** (Damages for breach—Sale of goods—Loss directly and naturally resulting from breach of warranty).
      Measure of damages. *See* **Damages** (Measure of damages—Warranty of authority).
      Mitigation of loss. *See* **Damages** (Mitigation of loss—Breach of warranty).
  Charterparty—
    Generally. *See* **Shipping** (Charterparty—Conditions and warranties).
  Collateral warranty. *See* **Contract** (Warranty—Collateral warranty).
  Construction—
    Contract. *See* **Contract** (Construction—Warranty).
  Feeding stuffs. *See* **Agriculture** (Feeding stuffs—Sale for use as food for cattle or poultry—Implied warranty suitable for use as such).

WARRANTY (cont)—
    Fitness—
        Implied term. *See* **Contract** (Implied term—Warranty of fitness).
        Premises. *See* **Landlord and tenant** (Fitness of premises—Legal or physical fitness—Warranty).
    Food—
        Warranty by supplier—
            Statutory defence—Prosecution for sale of food not of quality demanded. *See* **Food and drugs**
                (Sale—Not of quality demanded—Defence—Warranty by supplier).
            Statutory defence—Prosecution for sale of food not of substance demanded. *See* **Food and drugs**
                (Sale—Not of substance demanded—Defence—Warranty by supplier).
            Statutory defence—Prosecution for sale of food unfit for human consumption. *See* **Food and drugs**
                (Sale—Food unfit for human consumption—Defence—Warranty by supplier).
    Generally. *See* **Contract** (Warranty).
    Hire-purchase agreement. *See* **Hire-purchase** (Warranty).
    Legality of contract. *See* **Contract** (Implied term—Warranty that contract not illegal).
    Marine insurance. *See* **Marine insurance** (Warranty).
    Members' club—
        Safety of premises. *See* **Club** (Members' club—Safety of premises—Implied warranty).
    Reinsurance warranty—
        Breach of warranty. *See* **Insurance** (Reinsurance—Risks insured—Breach of warranty).
    Safety of premises—
        Members' club. *See* **Club** (Members' club—Safety of premises—Implied warranty).
    Sale of goods—
        Generally. *See* **Sale of goods** (Warranty).
        Implied warranty. *See* **Sale of goods** (Implied warranty).
        Reconditioned goods—
            Certificate by third party. *See* **Sale of goods** (Condition—Reconditioned goods—Certificate by third
                party).
    Sale of land—
        Damages for breach of warranty. *See* **Sale of land** (Damages for breach of contract—Warranty).
        House completed at date of sale—
            Implied warranty. *See* **Sale of land** (House completed at date of sale—Implied warranty).
        House in course of erection—
            Implied warranty as to workmanship etc. *See* **Sale of land** (House in course of erection—Implied
                warranty as to workmanship etc).
        Solicitor—
            Warranty of authority. *See* **Solicitor** (Sale of land—Warranty of authority).
    Sale of vessel. *See* **Shipping** (Sale of ship—Seller's warranty and indemnity).
    Speed warranty—
        Time charterparty. *See* **Shipping** (Time charterparty—Speed warranty).
    Statutory warranty—
        Sale of feeding stuffs for use of cattle or poultry. *See* **Agriculture** (Feeding stuffs—Sale for use as food
        for cattle or poultry—Implied warranty suitable for use as such).

WASHING FACILITIES
    House in multiple occupation. *See* **Housing** (House in multiple occupation—Personal washing facilities).

WASTE
    Criminal law. *See* **Criminal law** (Waste).
    European Community provisions. *See* **European Union** (Environment—Waste).
    Transport of waste—
        Criminal offence. *See* **Criminal law** (Waste—Transporting waste—Offence).

WASTE DISPOSAL
    See **Public health** (Waste disposal).

WASTE LAND
    Manor—
        Common land—
            Registration. *See* **Commons** (Registration—Common land and rights of common—Waste land of a
                manor).

WASTE MANAGEMENT
    Environmental protection—
        Pollution. *See* **Environment** (Protection—Pollution—Waste management).
    Waste management licence—
        Disclaimer—
            Voluntary winding up of company. *See* **Company** (Voluntary winding up—Disclaimer of onerous
                property—Waste management licence).

WASTED COSTS
    Criminal cases. *See* **Criminal law** (Costs—Wasted costs).
    Generally. *See* **Costs** (Wasted costs).
    Quasi-contract—
        Restitution. *See* **Restitution** (Quasi-contract—Wasted costs).

WATCHING AND BESETTING PREMISES
    Picketing on highway—
        Whether offence of watching and besetting also constituting nuisance. *See* **Nuisance** (Watching and
        besetting premises).

WATER AND WATERCOURSES

Banks—

Right to deposit spoil on banks of watercourse. *See* **Land drainage** (Drainage board—Right to deposit spoil on banks of watercourse).

Canal—

Canal company—

Supply of water to railway company—Statute restricting supply to mills and works on adjoining land—Whether supply ultra vires—Rochdale Canal Act 1899, s 37. **A-G v Rochdale Canal Co** [1939] **3** 57, CA.

Cleansing of watercourse—

Right to deposit soil on banks of watercourse. *See* **Land drainage** (Drainage board—Right to deposit spoil on banks of watercourse—Banks—Meaning—River board cleansing watercourse).

Coast protection. *See* **Coast protection**.

Controlled water—

Pollution. *See* Pollution of controlled water, *below*.

Depth of water—

Right to particular depth of water—

Plaintiffs owners of jetties in river—Jetties used for loading and unloading vessels—Jetties used and maintained under licences granted by river authority—Local authority building ferry terminals on river with river authority's approval—Terminals causing siltation of river bed and preventing plaintiffs from using jetties—Whether plaintiffs having right under contract, negligence or private nuisance to particular depth of water in river—Port of London Act 1968, s 66(1)(b). **Tate & Lyle Industries Ltd v Greater London Council** [1983] **1** 1159, HL.

Domestic water supply—

Duty of statutory water undertakers. *See* **Water supply**.

Easement. *See* **Easement** (Water).

Escape of water from mains—

Property insurance—

Scope of policy. *See* **Insurance** (Property insurance—Perils insured against—Escape of water from mains).

Fishing rights—

European Community. *See* **European Union** (Fishing rights).

Flooding—

Nuisance—

Generally. *See* **Nuisance** (Natural processes—Flooding).

Protection of land from flooding—

Wall erected by riparian owner to protect own land—Wall removed and re-erected leaving gaps—Land of adjoining owners damaged by flood—Whether riparian owner liable. **Thomas and Evans Ltd v Mid-Rhondda Co-op Society Ltd** [1940] **4** 357, CA.

Flow of water—

Mill deriving water power from river—

Interference with flow of water by local authority executing works under statutory powers—Whether reasonable steps to avoid interference—Onus of proof. **Provender Millers (Winchester) Ltd v Southampton CC** [1939] **4** 157, CA.

Natural watercourse—

Sewer—Watercourse piped, covered and channelled—Increased flow of surface water into watercourse—Whether watercourse becoming a sewer. **Raglan Housing Association Ltd v Southampton City Council** [2008] **2** 44, CA.

Foreshore—

Rights over foreshore. *See* **Foreshore** (Rights over foreshore).

Inland waterways—

Navigation authority—

Statutory power—Removal of vessels—Navigation authority having statutory power for removal of vessels left or moored without lawful authority—Meaning of 'lawful authority'—British Waterways Act 1983, s 8. **Moore v British Waterways Board** [2013] **3** 142, CA.

Mill deriving water power from river—

Interference with flow of water by local authority. *See* Flow of water—Mill deriving water power from river, *above*.

Navigation—

Ordinary incidents of navigation—

Laying and maintenance of permanent moorings—Whether an ordinary incident of navigation—Whether common law right exists to lay such mooring in the land of another person. **Fowley Marine (Emsworth) Ltd v Gafford** [1968] **1** 979, CA.

Public right of navigation (PRN)—

Public nuisance—Interference with public right of navigation causing particular damage to plaintiffs—Whether interference with public right of navigation giving right of action in public nuisance. **Tate & Lyle Industries Ltd v Greater London Council** [1983] **1** 1159, HL.

Public nuisance—Port authority responsible for maintenance of public right of navigation—Interference with public right of navigation by silt negligently deposited by claimant on land not owned by port authority—Port authority removing silt—Whether port authority suffering special damage so as to be entitled to sue in public nuisance. **Jan de Nul (UK) Ltd v AXA Royale Belge SA (formerly NV Royale Belge)** [2002] **1 Comm** 767, CA.

Quay on foreshore—Quay within port—Right of public to use quay for purposes incidental to navigation on payment of reasonable charge—Whether defendant, as member of public, entitled to use quay for repairing boats on payment of reasonable charge. **Iveagh (Earl) v Martin** [1960] **2** 668, QBD.

Whether PRN over Thames subsisting in 1885 capable of being extinguished by proof of exclusion of public for 20 years before 1885—Whether such PRN capable of being subject to rights of riparian owners to obstruct their exercise—Thames Preservation Act 1885, ss 2, 4, 5. **Rowland v Environment Agency** [2003] **1** 625, Ch D.

Reservoir used by sailing dinghies for pleasure purposes—Personal injuries—Person on board one dinghy suffering personal injuries as result of fault of another dinghy—Whether reservoir used for 'navigation'—Whether dinghy used on reservoir for pleasure purposes a 'vessel used in navigation'—Whether time limit for bringing personal injuries claim two years or three—Merchant Shipping Act 1894, s 742—Maritime Conventions Act 1911, s 8. **Curtis v Wild** [1991] **4** 172, QBD.
Nitrates—
European Community directive. See **European Union** (Environment—Water—Nitrates).
Nuisance—
Obstruction to flow of water in natural watercourse. See **Nuisance** (Statutory nuisance—Watercourse—Natural watercourse—Obstruction impeding flow of water and causing flooding).
Public nuisance—
Interference with public right of navigation causing particular damage. See Navigation—Public right of navigation (PRN)—Public nuisance, *above.*
Pollution of brook—
Causing poisonous, noxious or polluting matter to enter controlled waters—
Absolute offence—Engineering company having oil tank on site—Vandals damaging sight gauge on oil tank—Oil leaking into nearby brook—Whether company having 'caused' polluting matter to enter brook—Whether act of vandals reasonably foreseeable in view of earlier minor incidents of vandalism—Whether justices entitled to dismiss information against company—Water Act 1989, s 107(1)(a). **National Rivers Authority v Wright Engineering Co Ltd** [1994] **4** 281, QBD.
Pollution of controlled water—
Causing polluting matter to enter controlled water—
Defence where entry caused in an emergency in order to avoid danger to life or health—Circumstances in which defence available—Water Resources Act 1991, s 89(1). **Express Ltd (t/a Express Dairies Distribution) v Environment Agency** [2003] **2** 778, QBD.
Unincorporated association—Heating oil from land occupied by unincorporated association polluting controlled water—Prosecution brought against chairman and treasurer of association—Whether association having criminal liability for offence—Whether individual members having criminal liability for offence—Interpretation Act 1978, s 5, Sch 1—Water Resources Act 1991, ss 85(1), 217(1). **R v L** [2009] **1** 786, CA.
Pollution offences—
Sentence. See **Sentence** (Pollution offences—Polluting controlled waters).
Pollution of river—
Causing poisonous, noxious or polluting matter or solid waste to enter controlled waters—
Car company maintaining diesel tank on premises—Unknown third party opening tap on tank—Tap having no lock—Oil escaping from tank through outlet controlled by tap into drum, overflowing into yard and passing down storm drain into river—Whether 'causing' requiring some positive act by company—Whether company having 'caused' polluting matter to enter river—Water Resources Act 1991, s 85(1). **Empress Car Co (Abertillery) Ltd v National Rivers Authority** [1998] **1** 481, HL.
Causing poisonous, noxious or polluting matter to enter river—
Company discharging industrial waste into sewerage system owned by sewerage company—Day-to-day maintenance of system delegated to local authority—Failure to maintain pumping system—Sewerage system breaking down and polluting matter overflowing into stream—Whether offence of causing polluting matter to enter controlled waters capable of being committed by more than one person executing different and separate acts—Whether sewerage undertaker and local authority 'causing' waste to enter controlled waters—Water Act 1989, s 107(1)(a). **A-G's Reference (No 1 of 1994)** [1995] **2** 1007, CA.
Intervening act of third party—Escape of polluting matter caused by act of unauthorised person for purposes unconnected with accused's business—Rivers (Prevention of Pollution) Act 1951, s 2(1). **Impress (Worcester) Ltd v Rees** [1971] **2** 357, QBD.
Overflow of polluted water from tanks by side of river—Tanks and equipment under control of accused—Reasonable care by accused to prevent overflow—No intervening act of third party—Whether escape of polluting matter caused by accused—Rivers (Prevention of Pollution) Act 1951, s 2(1). **Alphacell Ltd v Woodward** [1972] **2** 475, HL.
Positive act required—Landowner allowing polluting matter to accumulate on his land—Polluting matter collected in lagoons on land—Crack in walls of lagoon—Polluting matter escaping through crack into nearby river—Whether landowner having caused polluting matter to enter river—Rivers (Prevention of Pollution) Act 1951, s 2(1). **Price v Cromack** [1975] **2** 113, QBD.
Sewage works operating by gravity—Act of unknown third party causing discharge of chemical dangerous to river life into sewer—Chemical flowing through outlet pipe into river—Whether water authority having 'caused' polluting matter to enter river—Whether water authority entitled to rely on statutory defence that contravention attributable to discharge made by another person—Water Act 1989, ss 107(1)(a), 108(7). **National Rivers Authority v Yorkshire Water Services Ltd** [1995] **1** 225, HL.
Causing polluting matter to enter river—
Cement washed into river during building operations carried out by company—Employees admitting liability—Employees not exercising controlling mind of company—Whether company liable for acts of junior employees—Water Resources Act 1991, s 85. **National Rivers Authority v Alfred McAlpine Homes East Ltd** [1994] **4** 286, QBD.
Causing sewage effluent to be discharged into controlled waters—
Causing—Sewage effluent discharging into river because of blocked sewer—Council responsible for maintenance of sewers—Failure by council to clear blockage promptly—Whether positive act required for offence to be committed—Whether council 'causing' sewage effluent to enter river by failing to discover source of pollution and clear it promptly—Water Act 1989, s 107(1)(c). **Wychavon DC v National Rivers Authority** [1993] **2** 440, QBD.

WATER AND WATERCOURSES (cont)—

Pollution of river (cont)—
- Discharge of trade effluent—
  - Consent of river authority—Application for consent granted subject to conditions—Less stringent conditions for initial period—Whether variation of conditions to consent possible—Rivers (Prevention of Pollution) Act 1961, ss 1(4), 5(2), Sch 1. **Trent River Authority v FH Drabble & Sons Ltd** [1970] **1** 22, QBD.
- Discharge of untreated sewage matter—
  - Action by riparian owner and fishery owner against local authority—Right of action against local authority—Rivers Pollution Prevention Act 1876, s 3—Derby Corporation Act 1901, ss 109(1), 113. **Pride of Derby and Derbyshire Angling Association Ltd v British Celanese Ltd** [1953] **1** 179, CA.
  - Admissibility of effluent samples—Authority taking effluent samples—Whether statutory procedure followed—Whether occupier to be notified before sample taken—Meaning of 'there and then' in relation to division of sample—Water Act 1989, s 148(1). **A-G's Reference (No 2 of 1994)** [1995] **2** 1000, CA.

Recreational craft—
- European Community. *See* **European Union** (Environment—Water—Recreational craft).

Reservoir—
- Surface water collected in reservoir on owner's land—
  - Water not taken from natural watercourse—Water taken from reservoir for spray irrigation of land—Owner's right to use water in reservoir. **Rugby Joint Water Board v Walters** [1966] **3** 497, Ch D.

Riparian rights—
- Extent—
  - Maintenance of depth of water—Obstruction of right of navigation—Plaintiffs owners of jetties on bank of river—Local authority building ferry terminals on river—Terminals causing siltation of river bed—Whether siltation interfering with plaintiffs' riparian rights—Whether jetties capable of attracting riparian rights. **Tate & Lyle Industries Ltd v Greater London Council** [1983] **1** 1159, HL.
- User—
  - Extraordinary purpose—Spray-irrigation—No right to take water for extraordinary purpose without returning it substantially undiminished—Spray-irrigation not an ordinary use of water from a river—Only very small quantity of water taken from the river would return to it—Use for spray-irrigation not justifiable in exercise of riparian rights. **Rugby Joint Water Board v Walters** [1966] **3** 497, Ch D.

River bank—
- Maintenance—
  - River bank erected and maintained under statute—Wall substituted by private owner—Liability for maintenance of wall. **Greenwood Tileries Ltd v Clapson** [1937] **1** 765, KBD.

Seashore—
- Boundary—
  - Accretion of land by gradual and imperceptible recession of sea. *See* **Boundary** (Seashore—Conveyance of land—Natural feature or right line boundary).

Sewerage—
- Public health. *See* **Public health** (Sewerage).

Supply of water. *See* **Water supply**.

Trade effluent—
- Discharge. *See* Pollution of river—Discharge of trade effluent, *above*.

Underground water—
- Abstraction—
  - Negligence—Abstraction causing subsidence of neighbouring land—Whether landowner having unrestricted right to abstract underground water from his land—Whether landowner owing duty of care not to cause subsidence of neighbouring land by abstraction of water. **Stephens v Anglian Water Authority** [1987] **3** 379, CA.

Works—
- Vesting of works in local authority. *See* **Water supply** (Local authority—Works used for gratuitous supply of water to inhabitants of district vested in local authority).

WATER AUTHORITY

Charges. *See* **Water supply** (Charges).

WATER CLOSET

Construction of water closet—
- Byelaw—
  - Validity. *See* **Byelaw** (Validity—Uncertainty—Bye-law requiring a builder constructing a closet to secure that it should not be entered from a room used for human habitation).

WATER INDUSTRY

Sewerage—
- Public health. *See* **Public health** (Sewerage).

Transfer of water authorities' functions to water and sewerage undertakers—
- Power to discharge water. *See* **Public health** (Sewerage—Drainage—Surface water—Whether sewerage undertakers having implied power to discharge water onto another's land or watercourse).

WATER RATES

Recovery—
- Dispute—
  - Jurisdiction of county court. *See* **County court** (Jurisdiction—Rates—Recovery of water rates—Dispute).

Acquisition of land for purposes of water supply—
    Joint board—
        Agreement to acquire land by constituent authority before board constituted—Whether enforceable under Bucks Water Act 1937, s 38. **Bedford (Duke) v Bucks Water Board** [1938] **1** 199, Ch D.
Buildings over mains. See Water mains—Buildings over mains, *below.*
Charges—
    Power of water authority to make charges—
        Charges for services performed—Liability of person who has not received services—Power of water authority to make such charges for services performed, facilities provided or rights made available by them as they think fit—Sewerage services—Occupier of house—House not connected to public sewers—Occupier not receiving sewerage services—Whether water authority having power to impose charge on occupier for sewerage services provided by the authority in their area—Water Act 1973, s 30(1). **Daymond v South West Water Authority** [1976] **1** 39, HL.
        Charges for services performed—Liability of person who has not received services—Power of water authority to make such charges for services performed, facilities provided or rights made available by them as they think fit—Sewerage services—Roof drainage—Occupier of shop—Shop not connected to public sewers—Occupier not receiving sewerage services—Surface water from roof on hereditament above occupier's shop draining into water authority's sewer—Whether water authority having power to impose charge on occupier for sewerage and drainage services provided by authority—Water Act 1973, s 30(1), (1A). **South West Water Authority v Rumble's** [1985] **1** 513, HL.
    Power to levy charge for supply of water for non-domestic purposes—
        Washing motor cars—Charge levied on registered owners of all cars in supply area—Burden on owner to show that no water supplied by undertakers used in respect of his car—Validity of procedure for levying charge—Whether ultra vires the undertakers—Leeds Corporation (Consolidation) Act 1905, s 24. **A-G v Leeds Corp** [1952] **1** 7, Ch D.
Domestic purposes. See Supply of water for domestic purposes, *below.*
Duty of statutory water undertakers—
    Supply of water for domestic purposes. See Supply of water for domestic purposes, *below.*
    Upkeep of fittings—
        Valve-box in roadway—Cover-plate left open by person unknown—No danger when cover closed—Liability of undertakers for injury to pedestrian. **Wells v Metropolitan Water Board** [1937] **4** 639, KBD.
Waterworks. See Waterworks, *below.*
Grant of water rights—
    Grant of water rights 'as now enjoyed'—
        Extent of grant—Right to make additional connections. **Beauchamp v Frome RDC** [1938] **1** 595, CA.
Infected water. See Supply of water for domestic purposes, *below.*
Local authority—
    Works used for gratuitous supply of water to inhabitants of district vested in local authority—
        Nature of interest vested in local authority—Fee simple absolute or determinable estate—Liability to maintain works—Supply ceasing to be a public supply—Whether local authority's liability to maintain works having determined—Public Heath Act 1936, s 124(1). **Gilson v Kerrier RDC** [1976] **3** 343, CA.
        Purpose of supply—Supply for purpose other than for human consumption—Whether works used for supply of water for any purpose vested in local authority—Whether limited to works used for supply of drinking water—Public Health Act 1936, s 124(1). **Gilson v Kerrier RDC** [1976] **3** 343, CA.
Medical practitioner. See Supply of water for domestic purposes—Domestic purposes—Water supplied to medical practitioner, *below.*
Power to obtain water outside water district of corporation—
    Pumping station situated outside water district—
        Station drawing water from within district—Whether breach of contract. **Bilston Corp v Wolverhampton Corp** [1942] **2** 447, Ch D.
Powers of statutory water undertakers—
    Power to pay interest from revenue on money borrowed—
        Power to borrow for payment of interest on money borrowed out of capital—Whether power to borrow interest already paid out of revenue—West Cheshire Water Board Act 1925, s 83—West Cheshire Water Board Act 1927, ss 41(1)(c), 46(1)(d). **West Cheshire Water Board v Crowe** [1940] **2** 351, KBD.
Sale of land—
    Contemporaneous agreement for supply of water—
        Vendor owner of adjacent land—Covenants by vendor to supply water from pump on vendor's land for use of purchaser in connection with house on conveyed land and to keep pump in repair—Whether benefit of agreement assignable to subsequent purchaser—Effect of arbitration clause—Arbitration Act 1889, s 4—Law of Property Act 1925, s 78. **Shayler v Woolf** [1946] **2** 54, CA.
Stand-pipes—
    Charges. See Water rates—Right to charge—Water board's main in village street—Ancient right to water from stand-pipes free of charge, *below.*
Supply of water for domestic purposes—
    Domestic purposes—
        Water supplied to medical practitioner—Water used in mixing medicines supplied to patients—Whether used for 'domestic' purposes—Kingston-upon-Hull Corporation Act 1897, s 82—Kingston-upon-Hull Corporation Act 1911, s 39. **Kingston-upon-Hull Corp v Yuille** [1939] **2** 48, CA.
    Duty of undertakers as respects sufficiency and purity—
        Infected water—Remedies available to person injured thereby—Water infected by typhoid bacillus—Infant plaintiff contracting typhoid—Negligence—Breach of contract—Sale of goods—Breach of warranty—Breach of statutory duty—Nuisance—Sale of Goods Act 1893, s 14—Waterworks Clauses Act 1847, s 35—Public Health Act 1936, ss 111, 115. **Read v Croydon Corp** [1938] **4** 631, KBD.

WATER SUPPLY (cont)—
  Supply of water for domestic purposes (cont)—
    Duty of undertakers as respects sufficiency and purity (cont)—
      Water pure while in mains—Water dissolving lead—Whether breach of statutory duty—Common
      law duty to warn persons supplied. **Barnes v Irwell Valley Water Board** [1938] **2** 650, CA.
    Duty of undertakers to provide domestic supply to new buildings—
      Duty on requisition by owner of land on which buildings to be erected—Power of undertakers to
      require owner to make contribution to cost of laying necessary mains—'Necessary
      mains'—Meaning—Request by landowner for supply of water to new houses—Construction of
      trunk main necessary to bring water to houses—Trunk main required for purpose of supplying
      water to existing consumers in addition to proposed new houses—Right of undertakers to require
      council to make contribution to cost of laying trunk main—Water Act 1945, s 37 (as amended by
      the Water Act 1948, s 14(4), and the Housing Act 1949, s 46). **Cherwell DC v Thames Water
      Authority** [1975] **1** 763, HL.
      Duty on requisition by owner of land on which buildings to be erected—Power of water authority to
      require owner to make contribution to cost of laying necessary mains—Necessary mains—Point
      from which necessary mains to start—Request by landowner for supply of water to new
      houses—No existing mains on site—Nearest distribution main to site too small to convey
      quantity of water required—Wider main capable of supplying water further away from
      site—Request to landowner by water authority for contribution to cost of laying new main from
      wider main to site—Whether proposed new main a 'necessary main'—Whether 'necessary main'
      must start from nearest existing main—Water Act 1945, s 37. **Royco Homes Ltd v Southern Water
      Authority** [1979] **3** 803, HL.
  Premises never previously connected to supply of water for domestic purposes—
    Two buildings connected to supply of water converted into 109 flats—Whether flats premises never
    previously connected to supply of water for domestic purposes—Water Industry Act 1991,
    s 146(2). **Thames Water Utilities Ltd v Hampstead Homes (London) Ltd** [2003] **3** 1304, CA.
  Right of owner or occupier of premises to demand supply—
    Premises—House-boat—Water Act 1945, Sch III, s 30(1). **West Mersea UDC v Fraser** [1950] **1** 990,
    KBD.
  Right to add fluoride—
    New Zealand. *See* **New Zealand** (Water supply—Domestic purposes—Pure water—Addition of
    fluoride).
  Turning off supply—
    Damage—
      Liability of water company—Request to water company to turn off water—Company assenting to
      request and turning off tap in street outside premises—Tap turned on by third person and house
      flooded—Whether water company liable. **Watson v Sutton District Water Co** [1940] **3** 502, CA.
  Upkeep of fittings. *See* Duty of statutory water undertakers—Upkeep of fittings, *above*.
  Water authority—
    Transfer of local authorities' water functions to regional water authorities—Vesting of property. *See*
    Local authority (Property—Reorganisation of local government—Vesting of property in newly
    constituted authorities—Water and sewerage functions transferred from local authorities to regional
    water authorities).
  Water company—
    Liability for turning off supply. *See* Turning off supply—Damage—Liability of water company, *above*.
  Water mains—
    Buildings over mains—
      Buildings purchased by defendants without knowledge of existence of mains—Right of local
      authority to order for demolition—Waterworks Clauses Act 1847, ss 20, 21—Public Health Act
      1875, s 26—Public Health Act 1875 (Support of Sewers) Amendment Act 1883, s 3—Public Health
      Act 1936, s 25. **Abingdon BC v James** [1940] **1** 446, Ch D.
    Necessary mains. *See* Supply of water for domestic purposes—Duty of undertakers to provide
    domestic supply to new buildings, *above*.
  Water rates—
    Payment by owner of small tenements under provisions of local Act—
      Allowance for early payment—Right to allowance—Waterworks Clauses Act 1847, s 72—Public
      Health Act 1936, s 129(1), (2), s 328. **Sowerby Bridge UDC v Stott** [1956] **2** 264, CA.
    Recovery of water rates—
      Dispute as to amount due—Jurisdiction of county court and Lands Tribunal—Water Act 1945,
      s 38(3)—Local Government Act 1948, s 62(1)—Lands Tribunal Act 1949, s 1(3)(e). **Sowerby Bridge
      UDC v Stott** [1956] **2** 264, CA.
      Summary recovery—Order by court of summary jurisdiction for payment—Direction to levy
      distress in default of payment—'Final order' against debtor—Whether precluding issue of
      bankruptcy notice. **Debtor (No 48 of 1952), Re a, ex p Ampthill RDC v The Debtor** [1953] **1** 545, CA.
    Reduction of rates—
      Special expense charged on ratepayers in contributory place—Cost of supply to that place
      thereafter small—Right of ratepayers in that place to have rate reduced to reflect cost—Public
      Health Act 1936, s 126(1). **Border RDC v Roberts** [1950] **1** 370, CA.
    Right to charge—
      Water board's main in village street—Ancient right to water from stand-pipes free of
      charge—Houses connected to main by pipes—Whether board entitled to charge—Public Health
      Act 1936, s 124(1)—Water Act 1945, Sch III, s 46(1). **South Devon Water Board v Gibson**
      [1955] **2** 813, CA.
  Waterworks—
    Duty of undertakers to reinstate streets etc after execution of work—
      Degree of reinstatement required—Defective apparatus in street—Injury to plaintiff—Liability of
      undertakers—Waterworks Clauses Act 1847, s 32. **Withington v Bolton BC** [1937] **3** 108, .
      Extent of obligation—Damage due to defective water-pipe—Duty to reinstate and repair road
      confined to portion taken up—Waterworks Clauses Act 1847, s 32. **Longhurst v Metropolitan
      Water Board** [1948] **2** 834, HL.

WATER SUPPLY (cont)—
    Waterworks (cont)—
        Duty of undertakers to reinstate streets etc after execution of work (cont)—
            Work of reinstatement taken over by highway authority—Damage due to negligent reinstatement—Liability of undertaker—Waterworks Clauses Act 1847, s 32—Metropolis Management Act 1855, s 114. **Rider v Metropolitan Water Board** [1949] **2** 97, KBD.

WATERWORKS
    See **Water supply** (Waterworks).

WAYLEAVE
    Electricity—
        Generally. See **Electricity** (Wayleave).
        Power of undertakers to place lines over land. See **Electricity** (Overhead lines—Power of undertakers to place lines over land).

WEAPON
    Dangerous weapon. See **Criminal law** (Dangerous weapons).
    Firearm. See **Firearms**.
    Offensive weapons—
        Generally. See **Criminal law** (Offensive weapons).
        Possession in public place. See **Sentence** (Possession of an offensive weapon in a public place).
        Smuggling—
            Armed with offensive weapon. See **Customs and excise** (Armed with offensive weapon).

WEAR AND TEAR
    Income tax—
        Balancing charge. See **Income tax** (Balancing charge—Wear and tear).
    Machinery or plant—
        Deduction in computing profits for income tax. See **Income tax** (Deduction in computing profits—Wear and tear of machinery or plant).

WEDDING PRESENTS
    Whether joint property of husband and wife. See **Husband and wife** (Property—Wedding presents).

WEIGHT
    Heavy motor car—
        Weight transmitted to road surface. See **Road traffic** (Heavy motor car—Weight transmitted to road surface).
    Lifting excessive weight—
        Factory. See **Factory** (Lifting excessive weights).
    Motor vehicle—
        Unladen weight. See **Road traffic** (Motor vehicle—Unladen weight).
    Weights and measures. See **Weights and measures**.

WEIGHTS AND MEASURES
    Bread—
        Deficiency in weight—
            Ascertainment of deficiency—Inconsiderable variation—Wrapped sliced loaf—Bread Order 1953 (SI 1953 No 1283), art 2, art 3(1), (2)(a), (b). **Trickers (Confectioners) Ltd v Barnes** [1955] **1** 803, QBD.
            Possession for sale of bread which is under weight—Loaves in despatch area of bakery deficient in weight—Stale bread not for sale also in dispatch area—Notice displayed that no bread was for sale until passed by bread dispatch supervisor—Whether bread in dispatch area that had not been so passed was in 'possession for sale'—Weights and Measures Act 1963, s 22(2)(a). **Worsley (Ben) Ltd v Harvey** [1967] **2** 507, QBD.
            Precautions to ensure correct weight—Whether every precaution taken to ensure that loaves of bread of correct weight—Whether deficiency of weight due to bona fide mistake or accident—Sale of Food (Weights and Measures) Act 1926, s 6(2). **Marshall v Matthews** [1939] **1** 156, KBD.
    Coal—
        Short weight—
            Ingredients of offence—Necessity for mens rea—Carman delivering sacks of less weight than that represented—Delivery delegated by coal merchants to agents—Whether agents under control of coal merchants—Whether coal merchants guilty of offence—Weights and Measures Act 1889, s 29(2)—Sale of Food (Weights and Measures) Act 1926, s 12(2). **Brentnall & Cleland Ltd v London CC** [1944] **2** 552, KBD.
            Ingredients of offence—Necessity for mens rea—Exposure of coal in sacks for sale—Representation by seller as to weight—Deficiency in weight owing to theft by servant—Whether seller guilty of offence—Weights and Measures Act 1889, s 29(2)—Sale of Food (Weights and Measures) Act 1926, s 12(5). **Winter v Hinckley & District Industrial Co-op Society Ltd** [1959] **1** 403, QBD.
        Special provisions—
            Bye-law—Provision of stamped weighing instrument on delivery vans—Validity of bye-law—Weights and Measures Act 1889, s 28. **Bridge (William) Ltd v Harrison** [1941] **3** 236, KBD.
    Defence to proceedings—
        Mistake, accident or some other cause beyond defendant's control—
            'Cause beyond his control'—Machine—Short weight—Short weight caused by unanticipated fault in operation of machine owned by defendant—Bag of potato crisps—Bag under weight—Liability of manufacturers—Bags filled by machine—Manufacturers' machines best available for purpose—No machine sufficiently accurate to produce no underweight bags—Economically impossible to weigh each bag manually—Machine for no anticipated reason failing to be accurate—Whether short weight due to cause beyond control of manufacturers—Weights and Measures Act 1963, s 26(1). **Bibby-Cheshire v Golden Wonder Ltd** [1972] **3** 738, QBD.

WEIGHTS AND MEASURES (cont)—

Defence to proceedings (cont)—
  Mistake, accident or some other cause beyond defendant's control (cont)—
    Offence committed by servant or agent—Availability of defence to principal—Weights and Measures Act 1963, s 26(1)(a). **Hall v Farmer** [1970] **1** 729, QBD.
Evidence—
  Short weight—
    Prepacked goods. *See* Prepacked goods—Short weight—Evidence, *below*.
Misrepresentation as to quantity of goods—
  Misrepresentation by word of mouth or otherwise—
    Ingredients of offence—Weight of bacon less than weight entered in customer's book—Whether a 'misrepresentation'—Sale of Food (Weights and Measures) Act 1926, s 3. **Preston v Coventry and District Co-op Society Ltd** [1946] **1** 694, KBD.
  Misrepresentation in connection with sale of goods—
    Sale of milk by farmer to marketing board—Resale by board to dairy—Milk delivered by farmer direct to dairy—No contract between farmer and dairy—Misrepresentation by dairy to farmer as to quantity received—Whether misrepresentation must be to contractual party—Weights and Measures Act 1963, s 24(2). **Collett v Co-op Wholesale Society Ltd** [1970] **1** 274, QBD.
Mistake as a defence to proceedings. *See* Defence to proceedings—Mistake, accident or some other cause beyond defendant's control, *above*.
Prepacked goods—
  Prepacked—
    Meat exposed for sale on bit of paper slightly larger than piece of meat—Whether the bit of paper was 'packaging'—Whether the meat was prepacked goods—Weights and Measures Act 1963, ss 22(1), 58(1), Sch 4, Part 1, para 2(a). **Lucas v Rushby** [1966] **2** 302, QBD.
  Short weight—
    Deficiency occurring after making up or making of goods for sale—Availability of defence to retailer—Weights and Measures Act 1963, s 26(2). **Woolworth (F W) & Co Ltd v Gray** [1970] **1** 953, QBD.
    Evidence—Admission by agent—Admissibility—Prima facie evidence that agent authorised to speak on behalf of company. **Edwards v Brookes (Milk) Ltd** [1963] **3** 62, QBD.
    Other articles of same kind available for testing but not tested—Time and place of testing—Single articles brought in by purchaser for testing—No other articles tested—Similar goods available elsewhere in locality—Whether other articles of same kind available for testing within the meaning of Weights and Measures Act 1963, s 26(7). **Sears v Smiths Food Group Ltd** [1968] **2** 721, QBD.
    Person charged not actual offender—Manager of shop responsible that articles of correct weight—Liability of owners of shop—Liability of manager of shop—'Actual offender'—Sale of Food (Weights and Measures) Act 1926, s 12(5). **Melias Ltd v Preston** [1957] **2** 449, QBD.
Sale by measurement—
  Causing to be delivered to buyer lesser quantity than that purported to be sold—
    Sale of one pint (20 fl oz) of beer in pint brim measure glass in Leeds area—Glass containing 18.25 fl oz of liquid beer with rest of contents consisting of froth—Whether proper delivery of full quantity purported to be sold—Weights and Measures Act 1963, s 24(1). **Bennett v Markham** [1982] **3** 641, QBD.
    Short measure of whisky sold by barmaid without licensee's knowledge and in his absence—Whether licensee 'caused' short measure to be delivered—Weights and Measures Act 1963, s 24(1). **Sopp v Long** [1969] **1** 855, QBD.
Servant or agent—
  Offence. *See* Defence to proceedings, *above*.
Short weight—
  Coal. *See* Coal—Short weight, *above*.
  Prepacked goods. *See* Prepacked goods—Short weight, *above*.
Weighing or measuring equipment for use for trade—
  Measures—
    Measuring instrument—Liquid fuel—Road tank wagon and dip rod—Whether separately or together a 'measure' or 'measuring instrument'—Weights and Measures Act 1878, ss 25, 29—Weights and Measures Act 1889, s 35. **Gnapp (Eric) Ltd v Petroleum Board** [1949] **1** 980, CA.
  Offences—
    Having possession for use for trade any false or unjust measuring equipment—Measuring equipment used for sale of intoxicating liquor—Measuring equipment not under control of licensee and supplied and maintained by another—Licensee forbidden to interfere with or adjust measuring equipment—Measuring equipment defective—Licensee not knowing or suspecting that measuring equipment defective—Whether licensee having 'in his possession' defective measuring equipment—Weights and Measures Act 1963, s 16(1). **Bellerby v Carle** [1983] **1** 1031, HL.
    Using article for trade not passed by inspector and not stamped as passed—Using article for trade as cubic measure for ballast when not in form prescribed—Accused suppliers of heavy building materials—Accused arranging for independent contractor to carry load of ballast—Load taken by independent contractor from third party's premises to customer of accused—Load carried in independent contractor's tipper lorry—Lorry not conforming with statutory requirements—Whether accused 'using' lorry—Weights and Measures Act 1963, s 11(2), Sch 5, para 4. **Charman (FE) Ltd v Clow** [1974] **3** 371, QBD.
  Price marking—
    Metrication—Whether subordinate legislation providing for metrication valid—European Communities Act 1972, s 2—Weights and Measures Act 1985, s 1—Units of Measurement Regulations 1994. **Thoburn v Sunderland City Council** [2002] **4** 156, QBD.

WELFARE OFFICER

Report of court welfare officer—
  Divorce proceedings—
    Practice. *See* **Divorce** (Practice—Children—Report of court welfare officer).
Supervision of access to minor. *See* **Minor** (Custody—Access—Supervised access).

WELFARE REPORT
Child—
    Practice—
        Family Division. *See* **Child** (Welfare—Welfare report).

WELFARE WORKER
Affiliation proceedings—
    Admissibility of evidence. *See* **Affiliation** (Evidence—Admissibility—Evidence of welfare worker).

WELL
Safe system of working. *See* **Safe system of working** (Safe place of work—Well).

WEST AFRICA
Appeal from high native tribunal. *See* Practice—Appeal from high native tribunal, *below.*
Appeal to Privy Council—
    Appeal as of right—
        Value of matter in dispute—Right of appeal where 'matter in dispute' amounts to or is of the value
            of £500 sterling or upwards—Costs amounting to over £500—West African (Appeal to Privy
            Council) Order in Council 1949, art 3(a). **Nana Atta Karikari v Nana Oware Agyekum II**
            [1955] **2** 654, PC.
    Leave to appeal—
        Application to be made to court within 21 days from date of judgment to be appealed from—Notice
            to be given to opposite party of intended application—Time for giving notice—West African
            (Appeal to Privy Council) Order in Council 1949, s 5. **A-G of the Gambia v N'Jie** [1961] **2** 504, PC.
        Person aggrieved—Attorney General. *See* **Privy Council** (Leave to appeal—Person aggrieved—
            Attorney General in colony).
Concession of timber rights. *See* Gold Coast—Concession of timber rights, *below.*
Courts—
    Native courts—
        Jurisdiction—Ownership of land—Public Lands Ordinance 1876, s 7. **Jackson v Cooke** [1936] **3** 680,
            PC.
Estoppel—
    Estoppel by conduct—
        Dispute as to title to lands—Previous proceedings in respect of same lands—Whether party knew
            of, but took no part in previous proceedings bound by decision in those proceedings. **Nana Ofori
            Atta II v Nana Abu Bonsra II** [1957] **3** 559, PC.
Gold Coast—
    Concession of timber rights—
        Failure to comply with statutory requirements—Whether concession invalid—Concessions
            Ordinance (Laws of the Gold Coast (1951), (as amended) ss 12(2), (3), (4), 13(11). **Ramia (Edward)
            Ltd v African Woods Ltd** [1960] **1** 627, PC.
Judgment—
    Judgment without jurisdiction—
        Inherent power of court to set aside. **Kofi Forfie (Chief) v Barima Kwabena Seifah** [1958] **1** 289, PC.
Moneylender—
    No memorandum of loan—
        Right to return of security for loan—Whether borrower put on terms—Nigerian Money Lenders
            Ordinance (Consolidated Ordinances of Nigeria), s 19(2), (3), (4). **Kasumu v Baba-Egbe**
            [1956] **3** 266, PC.
Practice—
    Appeal from high native tribunal—
        Leave to appeal—Jurisdiction of Court of Appeal to hear appeal although leave to appeal not
            given—Native Administration Ordinance 1927 (No 18 of 1927), s 77—Native Administration
            Amendment Ordinance 1935 (No 18 of 1935) s 13. **Adabla v Gbevlo Agama** [1939] **3** 381, PC.
Statute—
    Construction of colonial statute—
        Criminal law—Seditious writing concerning government—Words themselves not likely to incite to
            violence—No extrinsic evidence of seditious intention—Effect of English decisions on
            construction—Criminal Code of Gold Coast Colony, s 330. **Wallace-Johnson v R** [1940] **1** 241, PC.
Succession—
    Native tribunal—
        Jurisdiction—Native Administration Ordinance 1928, s 43. **Hagan v Effuah Adum** [1939] **4** 97, PC.

WEST INDIES ASSOCIATED STATES
Court of Appeal—
    Binding effect of previous decisions of court. *See* **Precedent** (West Indies Associated States Court of
        Appeal—Binding effect of previous decisions of court).

WESTERN AUSTRALIA
Land—
    Petroleum rights—
        Crown grants of land without reservation of petroleum rights—Effect of Western Australia
            Petroleum Act 1936, on grants—Western Australia Petroleum Act 1936 (No 36 of 1936), s 9,
            s 10—Western Australia Constitution Act 1890, s 4(2). **Midland Rly Co of Western Australia Ltd v
            State of Western Australia** [1956] **3** 272, PC.

WESTMINSTER ABBEY
Divine service—
    Right of member of public to attend. *See* **Ecclesiastical law** (Divine service—Attendance—Westminster
        Abbey—Right of member of public to attend).

WHARF
See **Shipping** (Wharves).

WHEAT
  Quota payments. *See* **Agriculture** (Wheat—Quota payments).

WHEAT COMMISSION
  Powers. *See* **Agriculture** (Wheat—Wheat Commission).

WHEELCLAMPING
  Wrongful interference with goods. *See* **Tort** (Wrongful interference with goods—Cause of action—Plaintiff parking vehicle on private property without authority).

WHITE PAPER
  Admissibility for construction of statute. *See* **Statute** (Construction—White Paper—Admissibility).

WHOLESALER
  Dangerous things—
    Liability to ultimate customer. *See* **Negligence** (Dangerous things—Wholesaler's liability to ultimate customer).

WIDOW
  Agriculture worker, of—
    Licence to occupy premises. *See* **Licence** (Licence to occupy premises—Agricultural worker—Protection of widow's occupancy).
  Annuity—
    Sale of husband's business—
      Whether enforceable against purchaser of business when widow not party to contract. *See* **Contract** (Stranger to contract—Annuitant—Widow of deceased owner of business—Sale of business by deceased on terms under which widow was to be paid weekly sum).
  Bereavement allowance—
    Income tax. *See* **Income tax** (Allowances—Widow's bereavement allowance).
  Damages under Fatal Accidents Acts—
    Death of widow before trial of action—
      Relevance in assessing damages. *See* **Fatal accident** (Damages—Widow—Death of widow before trial of action).
    Extent of dependency. *See* **Fatal accident** (Damages—Dependency—Widow).
    Lost opportunity of widow's post-retirement pension. *See* **Fatal accident** (Damages—Lost opportunity of widow's post-retirement pension).
    Remarriage—
      Effect. *See* **Fatal accident** (Damages—Remarriage of widow).
      Possibility of deceased's widow remarrying. *See* **Fatal accident** (Damages—Marriage prospects).
    Widow's earning capacity—
      Deduction from damages. *See* **Fatal accident** (Damages—Deduction from damages—Earning capacity of widow).
      Possibility of widow resuming employment—Whether to be taken into account. *See* **Fatal accident** (Damages—Deduction from damages—Earning capacity of widow).
  Domicile. *See* **Domicile** (Husband and wife—Widow).
  Financial provision. *See* **Family provision** (Widow—Reasonable financial provision).
  Intestacy—
    Distribution of estate. *See* **Intestacy** (Distribution of intestate's estate—Right of widow).
    Grant of administration. *See* **Intestacy** (Grant of administration—Grant to widow).
  Provision for widow out of husband's estate. *See* **Family provision** (Widow).
  Social security—
    Widows' benefits. *See* **Social security** (Benefit—Widows' benefits).
  Statutory tenancy—
    Succession to statutory tenancy on death. *See* **Rent restriction** (Death of tenant—Claim by widow to remain in possession).

WIDOWER
  Family provision. *See* **Family provision** (Widower).

WIDOWHOOD
  Will—
    Gift during widowhood. *See* **Will** (Gift—Gift during widowhood).

WIFE
  Alimony—
    Divorce. *See* **Divorce** (Alimony).
  Burial of—
    Expenses—
      Common law liability of husband. *See* **Burial** (Expenses—Burial of wife—Common law liability of husband).
  Costs—
    Divorce. *See* **Divorce** (Costs—Wife).
  Damages—
    Loss of husband's consortium. *See* **Husband and wife** (Consortium—Damages—Wife's loss of consortium).
  Death—
    Fatal accident—
      Damages. *See* **Fatal accident** (Damages—Death of wife).
  Domicile. *See* **Domicile** (Husband and wife—Wife's domicile).
  Family provision. *See* **Family provision** (Widow).
  Financial provision—
    Divorce. *See* **Divorce** (Financial provision).
    Summary proceedings. *See* **Husband and wife** (Summary proceedings—Financial provision).

1494

WIFE (cont)—

Former wife—
Provision from estate of deceased former husband. *See* **Divorce** (Financial provision—Deceased former spouse—Maintenance for surviving spouse out of deceased's estate).

Income tax—
Collection from wife of tax assessed on husband and attributable to wife's income. *See* **Income tax** (Husband and wife—Collection from wife of tax assessed on husband and attributable to wife's income).

Inheritance—
Family provision. *See* **Family provision** (Widow).

Injunction—
Exclusion of husband from matrimonial home. *See* **Injunction** (Exclusion of party from matrimonial home—Wife's application to exclude husband).

Kidnapping by husband. *See* **Criminal law** (Kidnapping—Husband and wife).

Maintenance—
Divorce. *See* **Divorce** (Maintenance).
Family provision. *See* **Family provision** (Widow).
Former wife—
Provision from estate of deceased husband. *See* **Divorce** (Financial provision—Deceased former spouse—Maintenance for surviving spouse out of deceased's estate).
Generally. *See* **Husband and wife** (Maintenance).
Husband's whereabouts unknown—
Disclosure of husband's address by government departments. *See* **Husband and wife** (Maintenance—Address—Husband's address for service—Disclosure by government department).
Separation. *See* **Husband and wife** (Separation—Consensual separation—Implication of agreement by husband partly to maintain wife).

Matrimonial home—
Deserted wife's rights. *See* **Husband and wife** (Deserted wife's right to remain in matrimonial home).
Interests of husband and wife. *See* **Husband and wife** (Matrimonial home).

Rateable occupier—
Husband divorced from wife—Wife in occupation. *See* **Rates** (Rateable occupation—Occupation by relatives—Husband and wife—Former matrimonial home—Wife in occupation by agreement).
Occupation by wife after separation—Liability for rates. *See* **Rates** (Rateable occupation—Joint rateable occupation—Husband separated from wife).

Pregnancy at date of marriage—
Whether constructive desertion. *See* **Divorce** (Desertion—Constructive desertion—Conduct equivalent to expulsion of other spouse—Pregnancy of wife by another man at time of marriage).

Property—
Separate property—
Savings from housekeeping allowance—Right to allowance. *See* **Husband and wife** (Property—Separate property of wife—Savings from housekeeping allowance while parties living together).
Settlement—
Divorce. *See* **Divorce** (Settlement of wife's property).

Rape—
Husband and wife. *See* **Criminal law** (Rape—Husband and wife).

Separate property—
Savings from housekeeping allowance—
Right to allowance. *See* **Husband and wife** (Property—Separate property of wife—Savings from housekeeping allowance while parties living together).

Services—
Joint efforts of husband and wife in business—
Beneficial interest in matrimonial home. *See* **Husband and wife** (Matrimonial home—Husband sole owner at law—Joint efforts of husband and wife in business).
Loss of wife's services—
Damages. *See* **Husband and wife** (Consortium—Damages—Total loss of wife's services).

Variation of settlement—
Application for variation—
Application by guilty wife. *See* **Variation of Settlement (Matrimonial Causes)** (Application for variation—Application by guilty wife).

Wilful neglect to maintain. *See* **Husband and wife** (Wilful neglect to maintain).

Witness for prosecution—
Compellability. *See* **Criminal evidence** (Compellability as witness—Spouse as witness for prosecution).
Competence. *See* **Criminal evidence** (Competence as witness—Spouse as witness for prosecution).

Young person—
Under sixteen—
Potentially polygamous foreign marriage—Protection of young person. *See* **Children and young persons** (Protection—Recognition of foreign marriage—Potentially polygamous marriage—Fit person order).

WILFUL DEFAULT

Account on footing of wilful default—
Personal representatives. *See* **Executor and administrator** (Account—Account on footing of wilful default).

Income tax—
Additional assessment. *See* **Income tax** (Additional assessment—Fraud or wilful default).
Adjournment of appeal—
Crown alleging fraud, wilful default or neglect by taxpayer. *See* **Income tax** (Appeal—Commissioners—Adjournment of appeal—Taxpayer appealing to commissioners against assessments—Crown alleging fraud, wilful default or neglect by taxpayer).

WILFUL NEGLECT
Child—
    Criminal offence. *See* **Criminal law** (Child—Wilful neglect of child).
Maintenance—
    Children. *See* **Minor** (Wilful neglect to maintain).
    Wife. *See* **Husband and wife** (Wilful neglect to maintain).

WILFUL REFUSAL TO CONSUMMATE MARRIAGE
See **Nullity** (Wilful refusal to consummate marriage).

WILL
Abatement—
    Legacy. *See* **Administration of estates** (Legacy—Abatement).
    Absolute gift. *See* Gift—Absolute gift, *below.*
Absolute interest—
    Effect of subsequent words on gift—
        Anything that is left—Ambiguity—Cutting down of absolute gift to life interest. **Last (decd), Re** [1958] **1** 316, Prob.
    Life gift initially expressed—
        Gift to testator's widow for her lifetime and anything left over after her death given in part to charity and in part for a memorial—Whether widow took an absolute interest. **Minchell's Will Trusts, Re** [1964] **2** 47, Durham Ch Ct.
Acceleration—
    Settlement—
        Beneficial interests under. *See* **Settlement** (Acceleration).
Accruer—
    Devolution of accrued share—
        Primary provision for accretion. **Lybbe's Will Trusts, Re** [1954] **1** 487, Ch D.
    Failure of trusts—
        Failure of trusts hereinbefore declared—Whether failure covered avoidance under rule against perpetuities. **Buckton's Declaration of Trust, Re** [1964] **2** 487, Ch D.
        Failure or determination of prior trusts—Whether clause in will providing for accrual on failure or determination of prior trusts under will covered trust void for perpetuity. **Robinson's Will Trusts, Re** [1963] **1** 777, Ch D.
    Implication of requirement of survival—
        Accruer 'to the shares of the daughters of mine who shall at the time of the death of such daughter not have been married'. **Walter's Will Trusts, Re** [1948] **2** 955, Ch D.
    Rule in Lassence v Tierney—
        Life interests with remainder to issue and accruer clause on failure of issue—Last survivor dying without issue—Rule in Lassence v Tierney applied to accrued shares—Last survivor absolutely entitled. **Litt's Will Trusts, Re, Parry v Cooper** [1946] **1** 314, CA.
        Life interests with remainder to issue and accruer clause on failure of issue—Last survivor dying without issue—Whether original share of last survivor absolutely vested. **Fyfe v Irwin** [1939] **2** 271, HL.
        Prior absolute gift with trusts engrafted thereon by subsequent clause—Whether accruer clause applied to an accruing share only the engrafted trusts. **Atkinson's Will Trusts, Re** [1956] **3** 738, Ch D.
        Trust after life interest for L followed by proviso revoking it and substituting a life interest with subsequent trusts for L's children—Subsequent provision for accruer—L died childless—Whether rule in Lassence v Tierney applied to entitle L to absolute interest or whether proviso for accruer applied. **Goold's Will Trusts, Re** [1967] **3** 652, Ch D.
Accumulation of surplus income—
    Destination. *See* **Accumulation** (Surplus income—Destination).
Acknowledgment of signature—
    Attestation. *See* Attestation—Acknowledgment of signature, *below.*
Ademption—
    Bank account—
        Gift of moneys in numbered account at bank—Person having power of attorney transferring moneys to account bearing higher interest—Transfer made in ignorance of terms of will—Whether moneys in second account at date of testatrix's death passing as specific legacy or to residuary legatees. **Dorman (decd), Re** [1994] **1** 804, Ch D.
    Double portions. *See* Double portions—Ademption, *below.*
    Gift of realty—
        Conditional contract for sale of property—Conditions fulfilled and contract completed after testator's death—Whether doctrine of ademption applying to conditional contracts—Whether fulfilment of conditions and completion of contract after testator's death adeeming specific gift of property in testator's will. **Sweeting (decd), Re** [1988] **1** 1016, Ch D.
        House devised as part of residue given on trusts for several beneficiaries—Subsequent agreement by testarix for valuable consideration to devise house to one beneficiary—Specific performance of agreement ordered after death of testatrix—Whether gift adeemed—Wills Act 1837, s 24. **Edwards (decd), Re** [1957] **2** 495, CA.
        Land 'including mines and minerals thereunder'—Vesting of coal and coal mines in Coal Commission—Re-publication—Confirmation of devise by codicil—Inclusion in gift of compensation moneys. **Galway's (Viscount) Will Trusts, Re** [1949] **2** 419, Ch D.
        Undivided share in land—Will made in 1912—Statutory trusts imposed in 1926—Conversion of undivided shares into personalty—Codicil made in 1927 containing reference to will but not to gift—Law of Property Act 1925, s 35, Sch I, Pt IV, para 1. **Harvey, Re** [1947] **1** 349, Ch D.
    Gift of shares etc—
        Compulsory acquisition of stock by Treasury at stated price—Value of stock at end of executor's year—Securities (Restrictions and Returns) (No 3) Order 1941 (SR & O 1941 No 1574), paras 1, 2—Acquisition of Securities (No 5) Order 1941 (SR & O 1941 No 1575), para 1. **Borne, Re** [1944] **1** 382, Ch D.

WILL (cont)—
  Ademption (cont)—
    Gift of shares etc (cont)—
      Option to purchase granted by testator after date of will—Exercise of option after testator's death—Gift inter vivos—Gift of shares in private company if such shares not transferred to legatee 'previously to my death'—Transfer executed by testator during his lifetime—Refusal of directors to register transfer until after testator's death. **Rose, Re** [1948] **2** 971, Ch D.
      Securities or investments representing the same if they have been converted into other holdings—Redeemable stock—Redeemed—Redemption moneys placed on deposit. **Lewis's Will Trusts, Re** [1937] **1** 227, Ch D.
      Shares in company to be formed by will trustees to acquire testator's business—Company formed by testator in his lifetime. **Quibell's Will Trusts, Re** [1956] **3** 679, Ch D.
  Adopted child. *See* Children, *below*.
  Advancement clause—
    Advancement in 'business'—
      Medical practice—Purchase of dwelling-house. **Williams' Will Trusts, Re** [1953] **1** 536, Ch D.
  Advances—
    Hotchpot clauses. *See* Hotchpot clauses—Advances, *below*.
  Alienation of interest—
    Forfeiture clause. *See* Forfeiture clause—Alienation of interest, *below*.
  Alteration—
    Alteration after execution—
      Alterations made by hand on original at testator's direction—Alterations witnessed but not signed by testator—Whether will in amended form could be admitted to probate as an altered will—Whether will in amended form could be admitted to probate as an original will—Wills Act 1837, ss 9, 21. **White (decd), Re** [1990] **3** 1, Ch D.
      Evidence of original contents—'Apparent'—Original words photographed by use of infra-red rays—Not visible on document itself unless slips removed—Wills Act 1837, s 21. **Itter (decd), Re** [1950] **1** 68, Prob.
    Apparent in will—
      Interlineation—Whether made before execution of will—Evidence—Onus of proof—Testator's intention—Statements by testator before execution of will—Draft will. **Oates, In the Estate of, Callow v Sutton** [1946] **2** 735, Prob.
    Evidence of original contents—
      Dependent relative revocation—Infra-red photography to reveal words hidden by slips of paper—Words 'apparent' before the alteration—Wills Act 1837, s 21. **Itter (decd), Re** [1948] **2** 1052, Prob.
  Annuity—
    Direction to set aside fund—
      To produce annuity without deduction of tax. **Williams, Re** [1936] **1** 175, CA.
    Duration—
      Gift of £50 a year—Sum 'to be applied [for donee's] maintenance and schooling until she attains the age of 21'—'To be derived from interest of my shares in War Loan 1917'. **Jackson, Re** [1946] **1** 327, Ch D.
    Estate insufficient. *See* **Administration of estates** (Annuity—Estate insufficient).
    Forfeiture clause—
      Forfeiture on annuitant, in opinion of trustee, having 'social or other relationship' with named person. **Jones (decd), Re** [1953] **1** 357, Ch D.
  Appointment of beneficiaries. *See* Gift—Appointment of beneficiaries, *below*.
  Appointment of property by will. *See* **Power of appointment** (Exercise by will).
  Apportionment—
    Clause negativing apportionment—
      Exclusion of rule in Howe v Dartmouth—Whether provisions of Apportionment Act 1870 also excluded—Apportionment Act 1870, s 7. **Bate, Re** [1938] **4** 218, Ch D.
      Profits from underwriting syndicate—Profits for year ascertainable only after passing of two further years. **Lynch-White, Re** [1937] **3** 551, Ch D.
    Income of unconverted property in residuary estate given to tenant for life—
      Discretion whether to convert not exercised by trustees—Apportionment under rule in Re Earl of Chesterfield's Trusts not excluded while discretion not exercised. **Guinness's Settlement, Re** [1966] **2** 497, Ch D.
    Interest accruing after death of tenant for life—
      Interest payable in respect of period before death of tenant for life—Residuary estate—Apportionment without sale—Right of legal personal representative of tenant for life—Apportionment Act 1870, ss 2, 3, 4, 5. **Henderson, Re** [1940] **1** 623, Ch D.
  Attestation—
    Acknowledgment of signature—
      Doubt whether signature acknowledged by testator in presence of witnesses present at same time—Whether witnesses validly acknowledging their own respective signatures—Validity of will—Wills Act 1837, s 9. **Couser v Couser** [1996] **3** 256, Ch D.
      Doubt whether signature acknowledged by testatrix in presence of witnesses present at same time—Wills Act 1837, s 9. **Weatherhill v Pearce** [1995] **2** 492, Ch D.
      Partial signature—Testator starting to sign in presence of two witnesses—One witness called away before signature finished—Testator and second witness acknowledging their signatures on first witness's return—Whether partial signature sufficient—Whether first witness's attestation valid—Wills Act 1837, s 9. **Colling (decd), Re** [1972] **3** 729, Ch D.
      Subscription by one witness before acknowledgment of signature by testatrix to second witness—Wills Act 1837, s 9. **Davies, In the Estate of** [1951] **1** 920, Assizes.
      Testator's signature on will before asking attesting witnesses to act—Attesting witnesses signing in testator's presence but not in each other's presence—Wills Act 1837, s 9. **Groffman (decd), Re** [1969] **2** 108, Prob.
    Attestation clause—
      Omission of statement that witness 'subscribed their names as witnesses'—Wills Act 1837, s 9. **Selby-Bigge (decd), Re** [1950] **1** 1009, Prob.

WILL (cont)—
  Attestation (cont)—
    Attestation clause (cont)—
      Superfluous signature—Intention with which signature affixed—Will signed by four persons below word 'witnessed'—First two signatures those of testator's daughters who were his sole residuary legatees—Presumption of signing as witnesses—Daughters signed at testator's request 'to make it stronger' after independent witnesses had signed—Application for probate excluding signatures of daughters—Whether inference that daughters signed as witnesses was rebutted—Wills Act 1837, s 15. **Bravda (decd), In the Estate of** [1968] **2** 217, CA.
    Evidence—
      Adverse evidence of attesting witnesses—Admissibility of further evidence—Wills Act 1837, s 9. **Vere-Wardale (decd), Re** [1949] **2** 250, Prob.
    Holograph will on single sheet of paper—
      Names of two unidentified persons on reverse side of paper—No attestation clause—Presumption of due execution. **Denning (decd), Re** [1958] **2** 1, Prob.
    Witness—
      Beneficiary under secret trust—Beneficiary taking under secret trust not under will—Wills Act 1837, s 15. **Young (decd), Re** [1950] **2** 1245, Ch D.
      Blind man—Codicil—Wills Act 1837, s 9. **Gibson (decd), Re** [1949] **2** 90, Prob.
      Members of convent community—Gift to abbess of convent at the time of the death of testatrix—Wills Act 1837, s 15. **Ray's Will Trusts, Re** [1936] **2** 93, Ch D.
      Solicitor—Provision for trustees' remuneration—Provision for solicitor's professional charges—Solicitor appointed trustee subsequent to death of testator—Whether entitled to remuneration or professional charges—Wills Act 1837, s 15. **Royce's Will Trusts, Re** [1959] **3** 278, CA.
  Beneficiary—
    Beneficiary pre-deceasing testator—Lapse. *See* Lapse—Beneficiary pre-deceasing testator, *below*.
    Beneficiary under secret trust—
      Witness—Attestation. *See* Attestation—Witness—Beneficiary under secret trust, *above*.
    Enemy beneficiary—
      Forfeiture. *See* Forfeiture clause—Income vesting in another—Beneficiary an enemy, *below*.
    Exclusion from benefit. *See* Benefit—Exclusion from benefit, *below*.
  Benefit—
    Exclusion from benefit—
      Public policy—Manslaughter—Beneficiary convicted of manslaughter of testator—Forfeiture rule—Modification of rule—Forfeiture Act coming into effect after death of testator but before personal representative completing administration of estate—Whether beneficiary precluded by forfeiture rule from benefiting under will and from interests accruing on survivorship—Whether court having jurisdiction to modify effect of forfeiture rule—Whether residuary beneficiaries 'acquiring' interest in estate before Act coming into effect—Forfeiture Act 1982, ss 2(7), 7(4). **K (decd), Re** [1985] **2** 833, CA.
      Public policy—Manslaughter—Beneficiary convicted of manslaughter of testator—Forfeiture rule—Modification of rule—Whether beneficiary precluded by forfeiture rule from benefiting under will and from interests accruing on survivorship—Whether application of forfeiture rule should be modified—Whether court's discretion limited to restricting offender to amount she would have obtained on divorce or by applying under Inheritance (Provision for Family and Dependants) Act 1975—Forfeiture Act 1982, s 2. **K (decd), Re** [1985] **2** 833, CA.
      Public policy—Manslaughter—Beneficiary convicted of manslaughter of testator—Manslaughter by reason of diminished responsibility—Whether relevant that beneficiary not morally blameworthy nor deserving punishment. **Giles (decd), Re** [1971] **3** 1141, Ch D.
      Public policy—Manslaughter—Beneficiary convicted of manslaughter of testator—Whether beneficiary entitled to claim reasonable financial provision out of estate of deceased—Effect of statute coming into effect after proceedings commenced giving court discretion to make financial provision for persons convicted of unlawful killing—Inheritance (Provision for Family and Dependants) Act 1975, s 2—Forfeiture Act 1982, s 2. **Royse (decd), Re** [1984] **3** 339, CA.
      Public policy—Manslaughter—Beneficiary convicted of manslaughter of testatrix—Whether beneficiary entitled to claim reasonable financial provision out of estate of deceased—Inheritance (Provision for Family and Dependants) Act 1975, s 2—Forfeiture Act 1982, ss 2(3), 3(1). **Land (decd), Re** [2007] **1** 324, Ch D.
      Public policy—Manslaughter—Relief from forfeiture rule—Claimant killing husband—Husband dying intestate—Claimant convicted of murder—Murder conviction quashed on appeal—Claimant pleading guilty to manslaughter by reason of diminished responsibility—Claimant applying for relief from forfeiture rule—Whether application in time—Test to be applied—Whether relief from forfeiture to be given—Forfeiture Act 1982, ss 2, 5. **Challen (decd), Re** [2021] **2** 738, Ch D.
      Wife general legatee under husband's will—Whether wife feloniously killed husband and thus was disentitled to benefit under his will—Law of Property Act 1925, s 184—Administration of Estates Act 1925, s 46(3) (added by Intestates' Estates Act 1952, s 1(4), Sch I). **Dellow's Will Trusts, Re** [1964] **1** 771, Ch D.
  Blind man—
    Witness—
      Attestation. *See* Attestation—Witness—Blind man, *above*.
  Business—
    Gift. *See* Gift—Business, *below*.
  Business premises—
    Option to purchase. *See* Option—Option to purchase realty—Business premises, *below*.
  Charging clause—
    Literary executor. *See* **Executor and administrator** (Executor—Literary executor—Charging clause).
  Charitable bequest—
    Condition—
      Impossibility of performance. *See* Condition—Impossibility of performance—Charitable bequest, *below*.

WILL (cont)—
  Children—
    Adopted child—
      Adoptive mother incapable of bearing children—Adoption of Children Act 1926, s 5(2). **Fletcher, Re** [1949] **1** 732, Ch D.
      Child adopted in British Columbia—Child and adoptive parent domiciled in British Columbia—Testator domiciled in England—Adoption of Children Act 1926, s 5(2). **Marshall (decd), Re** [1957] **3** 172, CA.
      Contrary intention sufficient to include adopted child—Will made before 1950—At date of will testator's daughter aged forty-seven and, as testator knew, adoptive mother of small boy—Residuary gift to 'child or children' of daughter—Adoption of Children Act 1926, s 5(2). **Jebb (decd), Re** [1965] **3** 358, CA.
      Disposition made before 1950—Adoptive mother incapable of bearing children—Whether disposition made at date of will or date of testator's death—Adoption Act 1950, s 13(2), Sch V, para 4. **Gilpin (decd), Re** [1953] **2** 1218, Ch D.
      Residuary gift to named nephews and nieces, with proviso for children to take a deceased parent's share—Niece predeceased testator leaving son and daughter—Son adopted by stranger—Successive similar testamentary gifts before and after niece's death and her son's adoption—Adoption before dates of last two wills—Whether son of niece could benefit—Court entitled to look at surrounding circumstances to ascertain whether there was a contrary intention for the purposes of Adoption Act 1958, s 16(2)(b). **Jones' Will Trusts, Re** [1965] **2** 828, Ch D.
    Child attaining the age of 21 years or marrying—
      Direction to pay on beneficiary's attaining that age or marrying—Whether married infant beneficiary entitled to call for payment. **Somech (decd), Re** [1956] **3** 523, Ch D.
    Illegitimate child—
      Effect of surrounding circumstances. **Wohlgemuth's Will Trusts, Re** [1948] **2** 882, Ch D.
      Referred to by name as specific legatee—Whether included in class of children. **Dicker (decd), Re** [1947] **1** 317, Ch D.
    Legitimated person—
      Disposition—Legitimacy Act 1926, ss 3(1), 11. **Hepworth, Re** [1936] **2** 1159, Ch D.
    Ultimate gift of daughter's settled fund—
      Issue—If daughter should die without leaving any child, fund to be divided between the other daughters of testator living at her death and 'the issue then living of any who shall have previously died leaving issue such issue to take their parent's share'—'Parent's share'—Rule in Sibley v Perry displaced by context of will—'Issue' intended to include grandchildren. **Hipwell, Re** [1945] **2** 476, CA.
    Ungrammatical use of tense and inaccurate references to time—
      Children living at the death of J, of nephews and nieces who shall have died in the lifetime of J—Nephew dying before J born leaving issue living at death of J—Intention of testator. **Donald, Re** [1947] **1** 764, CA.
  Class gift—
    Accumulation of surplus income—
      Destination. *See* **Accumulation** (Excessive period—Destination of income accruing after statutory period—Accumulation directed for the benefit of a class).
    Date of distribution. *See* **Settlement** (Class gift—Distribution date).
    Period of distribution. *See* **Settlement** (Class gift—Distribution date).
  Codicil—
    Cumulative or repetitive bequests—
      Legacy given by will—Second legacy given by codicil—Whether legacies were cumulative. **Davies (decd), Re** [1957] **3** 52, Ch D.
      Presumption that legacies given by different instruments cumulative—Annuity given by second codicil to S, who was then very young—Similar gift to S in third codicil, which was entitled as being first codicil—Whether provisions of first and second codicils revoked—Will and second codicil showed consistent scheme of benefit for children of B, of whom S was one—Rebuttal of presumption—Bequests of annuities to S not cumulative. **Le Cras v Perpetual Trustee Co Ltd** [1967] **3** 915, PC.
    Reviving revoked will. *See* Revival—Codicil reviving revoked will, *below*.
    Revocation of bequest in will—
      Bequest of annuity of specific sum out of income of estate—Gift over of 'the remainder of the income'—Revocation of annuity by codicil—Codicil directing that will to be construed as if bequest had not been made—No provision as to destination of income which was subject of annuity—Effect of revocation on gift over of remainder of income. **Lawrence's Will Trusts, Re** [1971] **3** 433, Ch D.
    Revocation of codicil. *See* Revocation—Codicil, *below*.
    Revocatory clause in codicil—
      Construction. *See* Construction—Revocatory clause in codicil, *below*.
  Coincident deaths—
    Gift over. *See* Gift—Gift over—Coincident deaths, *below*.
  Concurrent gifts. *See* Gift—Concurrent gifts, *below*.
  Condition—
    Conditional bequest—
      Annuitant to bequeath half her own property on trusts of testator's will—Acceptance of conditional annuity—Date when trust of annuitant's own property arose. **Harmsworth (decd), Re** [1967] **2** 249, CA.
      Bequest to charity—Charity to be chosen within twelve months after probate—Revocation of gift at expiration of time limit if charity not chosen—Whether time of essence. **Selinger's Will Trusts, Re** [1959] **1** 407, Ch D.
      Evidence that will subject to condition and that condition fulfilled—Testatrix intending that will only effective on completion of inter vivos gifts—Whether extrinsic evidence admissible to determine whether will subject to condition and whether condition fulfilled. **Corbett v Newey** [1996] **2** 914, CA.

WILL (cont)—
    Condition (cont)—
        Conditional bequest (cont)—
            Gift of freehold property after death of testator's widow—Gift subject to payment of £800 to
                testator's estate within 6 months of testator's death—Whether time specified of the essence of
                the matter. **Goldsmith's Will Trusts, Re** [1947] **1** 451, Ch D.
            Option to purchase freehold property—Option to be exercised within 3 months after death of
                testatrix's sister—Time of performance—Time specified of essence of matter. **Avard, Re**
                [1947] **2** 548, Ch D.
            Option to purchase land—Option to be exercised within three months of executors giving notice of
                such right—Whether option granted by will lapsing if option not exercised within time limit.
                Bowles (decd), Re [2003] **2** 387, Ch D.
            Vesting—Direction as to time of payment—Payment at future date—Contingent or vested
                gift—Postponement of payment derived from necessity of letting in prior interest—Vested gift
                subject to postponement of enjoyment—Gift to be construed as vested unless something in will
                to preclude construction. **Cohn (decd), Re** [1974] **3** 928, CA.
        Continuance in employment—
            Condition that legatee still employed at testator's death and not under notice—Military
                service—Continuation of employment—Gift of residue to 'legatee hereinbefore named'—
                Whether legatee subject to unfulfilled condition entitled to participate—Whether annuitant
                included in direction as to distribution of residue. **Feather, Re** [1945] **1** 552, Ch D.
            Gift to housekeeper if she continued in service of testatrix's husband—Marriage between husband
                and housekeeper. **Kendrew (decd), Re** [1953] **1** 551, CA.
        Divesting—
            Divesting 'if the trusts of cl 6(i) shall come into operation'. **Doughty v IRC** [1963] **3** 848, CA.
        Family matters—
            Adoption of testator's daughter—Failure to obtain adoption order—Whether failure of gift for
                non-compliance with condition—Trust for maintenance. **Frame, Re** [1939] **2** 865, Ch D.
            Condition encouraging separation of parent and child—Public policy—Malum prohibitum. **Piper, Re**
                [1946] **2** 503, Ch D.
            Condition encouraging violation of the sanctity of marriage—Absolute gift cut down during lifetime
                of donee's wife with gift over if wife survives donee—Donee separated from wife by agreement
                before death of testatrix—Whether condition or limitation. **Caborne, Re** [1943] **2** 7, Ch D.
            Condition encouraging violation of the sanctity of marriage—Small annual sum to be paid to
                daughter during her life out of income of residuary estate—Whole income of residuary estate
                payable to her if her husband died or they should be divorced or live separately—Whether
                condition or limitation and whether condition void. **Johnson's Will Trusts, Re** [1967] **1** 553, Ch D.
            Condition inducing future separation of spouses—Public policy—Construction of condition.
                Thompson, Re [1939] **1** 681, Ch D.
        Illegal condition—
            Condition precedent—Gift of personalty subject thereto—Malum prohibitum and not malum in
                se—Validity of gift. **Elliott (decd), Re** [1952] **1** 145, Ch D.
        Impossibility of performance—
            Charitable bequest—Gift over on failure of trustees to carry out trust—Subsequent impossibility for
                trustees to perform trusts—Operation of gift over. **Hanbey's Will Trusts, Re** [1955] **3** 874, Ch D.
            Trust to provide village hall—Site to be purchased by will trustees and conveyed to institute
                trustees—Institute trustees responsible for building hall—If hall not completed within specified
                time, site to be sold and gift to lapse—Gift over—Inability of will trustees to purchase site. **Jones,**
                Re [1947] **2** 716, Ch D.
        Name and arms clause—
            Clause extending to husband of married woman—'Actual receipt of rents and profits'—Specific
                devisee—Administration not yet completed. **Neeld (decd), Re** [1962] **2** 335, CA.
            Clause extending to married women and their husbands—Public policy—Severance of
                condition—Commencement of period from which time began to run—Acceleration of life
                interests by release of previous life interest. **Howard's Will Trusts, Re** [1961] **2** 413, Ch D.
            Determination of interest on 'neglect' for 12 months to take name and arms of
                testator—Non-compliance with condition owing to ignorance of terms of will—Whether breach of
                condition. **Hughes, Re** [1943] **2** 269, Ch D.
            Discontinue to bear and use. **Wood's Will Trusts, Re** [1952] **1** 740, Ch D.
            Disuse. **Bouverie, Re** [1952] **1** 408, Ch D.
            Female beneficiary required to bear testator's surname—Beneficiary not directly related to
                testator—No gift over on breach of condition—Rule against perpetuities—Public policy. **Fry, Re**
                [1945] **2** 205, Ch D.
            Forfeiture—Use and bear the surname and arms—Provision for forfeiture—Whether obligation to
                take surname separate from obligation to bear arms. **Howard v Howard-Lawson** [2012] **3** 60, CA.
            Gift on condition that donee should 'by deed poll assume' a different Christian name—Gift over if
                condition not fulfilled—Condition void for impossibility—Donee absolutely entitled to gift.
                Parrott's Will Trusts, Re [1946] **1** 321, Ch D.
            Quarter with own family arms—Devisee to quarter testator's arms with 'his or her own family
                arms'—Whether 'family arms' includes arms acquired by direct grant and after clause in will has
                taken effect—Whether devisee with no arms must get them so as to have arms with which
                quarter testator's. **Neeld (decd), Re** [1969] **2** 1025, Ch D.
            Severance. **Howard's Will Trusts, Re** [1961] **2** 413, Ch D.
            Tenant for life to 'assume' testator's surname—Assumption 'either alone or in substitution of his...
                usual surname'—Tenant for life to 'apply for proper authority to bear and use' testator's family
                arms—Interest to be determined on refusal or neglect to assume surname or arms within one
                year of becoming entitled. **Murray (decd), Re** [1954] **3** 129, CA.
            Use and bear the surname and arms. **Howard's Will Trusts, Re** [1961] **2** 413, Ch D.
        Provision of home—
            Devise and bequest to one daughter 'on condition that she will always provide a home' for another
                daughter. **Brace (decd), Re** [1954] **2** 354, Ch D.

WILL (cont)—
    Condition (cont)—
        Religion—
            Condition excluding beneficiaries who married 'out of the Jewish faith'—Whether condition void
                for uncertainty. **Selby's Will Trusts, Re** [1965] 3 386, Ch D.
            Condition in terrorem—'Conform to the Established Church of England'—'Go to or be sent to any
                Roman Catholic school'—Validity. **Tegg, Re** [1936] 2 878, Ch D.
            Devise to person 'who shall be a member of the Church of England and an adherent to the doctrine
                of that church'. **Allen (decd), Re** [1953] 2 898, CA.
            Devise to person 'who shall be a member of the Church of England and an adherent to the doctrine
                of that church'—Date at which qualification must be satisfied. **Allen (decd), Re** [1954] 1 526, Ch D.
            Endowment of medical studentship—Students not to be of the Jewish or Roman Catholic
                faith—Not contrary to public policy—Not void for uncertainty. **Lysaght (decd), Re** [1965] 2 888,
                Ch D.
            Forsaking Jewish faith—Event to be proved to satisfaction of trustees—Perpetuity. **Spitzel's Will
                Trusts, Re** [1939] 2 266, Ch D.
            Gift on marriage to person of 'Jewish race'—Validity. **Tarnpolsk (decd), Re** [1958] 3 479, Ch D.
            Gift over if daughter should marry a person who did not 'practise the Jewish religion'. **Krawitz's
                Will Trusts, Re** [1959] 3 793, Ch D.
            Impossibility of condition—Gift of fund 'on marriage to a person of the Jewish faith and the child of
                Jewish parents'—Failure of gift. **Wolffe's Will Trusts, Re** [1953] 2 697, Ch D.
            Intermarry with any person not a member of the Jewish faith—Uncertainty. **Moss's Trusts, Re**
                [1945] 1 207, Ch D.
            Jewish faith—Marriage outside Jewish faith—Whether condition void for uncertainty—Whether
                extrinsic evidence admissible to establish meaning of 'jewish faith' as practised by testator and
                his family. **Tepper's Will Trusts, Re** [1987] 1 970, Ch D.
            Jewish faith—Uncertainty. **Donn's Will Trusts, Re** [1943] 2 564, Ch D.
            Marriage with a person who is not of Jewish parentage and of the Jewish faith—Uncertainty.
                Clayton v Ramsden [1943] 1 16, HL.
            Marry person not of Jewish faith—Uncertainty. **Blaiberg, Re** [1940] 1 632, Ch D.
            Power of appointment exercisable by trustees in event of testator's son 'becoming engaged to be
                married to a person professing the Jewish faith'—Son married lady whom trustees considered to
                profess Jewish faith—Exercise of power of appointment so as to settle whole of son's share in
                testator's residuary estate. **Abrahams' Will Trusts, Re** [1967] 2 1175, Ch D.
            Proviso for forfeiture of share of testator's residuary estate if not 'member of the Church of England
                or some Church abroad professing the same tenets'—Proviso not void for uncertainty—
                Methodist Church of Australia not a church abroad professing same tenets as Church of England.
                Mills' Will Trusts, Re [1967] 2 193, Ch D.
        Residence—
            Devisee to make estate his home—Not to allow a named person to set foot on property.
                Talbot-Ponsonby's Estate, Re [1937] 4 309, Ch D.
            Direction by the testator that payments be made to his daughter 'only so long as she shall continue
                to reside in Canada'—Impossibility of determining what future conduct would fall within the
                terms of the will—Void for uncertainty. **Sifton v Sifton** [1938] 3 435, PC.
            Gift of dwelling-house—'if in the opinion of my trustees she shall have ceased permanently to
                reside therein'—Meaning of 'reside'. **Coxen, Re** [1948] 2 492, Ch D.
            Gift of house for life subject to residence—Sum settled for outgoings during life of tenant—Gift
                over—Prohibition against exercise of power of sale—Settled Land Act 1925, s 106(1). **Burden
                (decd), Re** [1948] 1 31, Ch D.
            Gift of house on trust for sister for life—Gift over to testator's housekeeper 'provided she is living
                with my sister at the time of my sister's death'—Housekeeper living in the same house, but
                entirely apart from sister, at time of sister's death. **Paskins' Will Trusts, Re** [1948] 2 156, Ch D.
            Take up permanent residence in England. **Gape's Will Trusts, Re** [1952] 2 579, CA.
            To J 'if he shall occupy my freehold property'. **Field's Will Trusts, Re** [1950] 2 188, Ch D.
        Restraint of marriage—
            Motive—Construction of words of futurity. **Fentem (decd), Re** [1950] 2 1073, Ch D.
            Partial restraint—Gift of personalty to widow provided she remain a widow—No gift over on
                remarriage. **Leong v Lim Beng Chye** [1955] 2 903, PC.
            Remarriage—Bequest of protected life interest in testatrix' residuary estate to deceased daughter's
                husband for so long as he should remain daughter's widower—Nullity decree obtained by
                second wife—Residuary estate and income retained by trustees of will—Whether deceased
                daughter's husband entitled to life interest until marrying again. **d'Altroy's Will Trusts, Re**
                [1968] 1 181, Ch D.
        Specific conditions—
            'Entitled to interest'—Whether meaning entitled to vested interest. **Macandrew's Will Trusts, Re**
                [1963] 2 919, Ch D.
            Executors to be satisfied that hospital not taken over by state—Validity of executors' decision.
                Dundee General Hospitals Board of Management v Walker [1952] 1 896, HL.
            Forfeiture upon acceptance of public office—Commission in Territorial Forces—Public policy. **Edgar,
                Re** [1939] 1 635, Ch D.
            Gift 'in the event of an armistice having been concluded between Great Britain and Germany in the
                present war before the date of my death'. **Orchard (decd), Re** [1948] 1 203, Ch D.
            Gift taking effect when the present 'war with Germany shall terminate' and 'peace be
                declared'—Coincidence of termination of war and declaration of peace—Rule against
                perpetuities. **Grotrian (decd), Re** [1955] 1 788, Ch D.
            Shall not leave a child or widow—Whether 'leave' meaning 'have'. **Macandrew's Will Trusts, Re**
                [1963] 2 919, Ch D.
            'Such period as my trustees shall think reasonable'. **Burton's Settlement, Re** [1954] 3 193, Ch D.
    Conditional revocation. *See* Revocation—Conditional revocation, *below*.
    Construction—
        Adding words or re-modelling clause—
            Unjustified for purpose of assisting forfeiture. **Murray (decd), Re** [1954] 3 129, CA.

WILL (cont)—
　Construction (cont)—
　　Ambiguity—
　　　Extrinsic evidence—Admissibility of extrinsic evidence to assist construction—Will ambiguous—
　　　　Will listing 25 names in three separate groups with no indication as to purpose of
　　　　grouping—Letter written by testatrix to solicitors asking them to 'organise' contents of
　　　　will—Whether letter admissible to assist in construing will—Whether letter of assistance in
　　　　construction—Administration of Justice Act 1982, s 21(1)(b). **Williams (decd), Re** [1985] **1** 964,
　　　　Ch D.
　　Double gift. *See* Residue—Double gift—Construction, *below.*
　　Evidence of sense in which testator used term—
　　　Special sense for particular occasion distinguished from habitual sense—Gift to 'worthy
　　　　causes'—Charitable intent—Contemporary document indicating that by worthy causes testatrix
　　　　meant charities—Whether document admissible as evidence of sense in which testatrix used
　　　　term. **Atkinson's Will Trusts, Re** [1978] **1** 1275, Ch D.
　　Foreign will. *See* **Conflict of laws** (Will—Construction).
　　Intention of testator—
　　　Ambiguity—Language of will ambiguous in light of surrounding circumstances—Amount of
　　　　residuary gift defined in relation to amount of inheritance tax nil-rate band—Change in
　　　　inheritance tax legislation changing amount of applicable nil-rate band—Whether extrinsic
　　　　evidence admissible—Whether language of will ambiguous—Administration of Justice Act 1982,
　　　　s 21(1)(c). **Loring v Woodland Trust** [2014] **2** 836, Ch D.
　　　Ambiguity—Language of will ambiguous in light of surrounding circumstances—Will executed in
　　　　relation to testator's 'UK assets'—Testator holding assets in Jersey—Whether Jersey assets
　　　　included in will—Administration of Justice Act 1982, s 21. **Rossiter (decd), Re** [2022] **4** 1021, CA.
　　　Gift of 25% of estate to (a) four cousins and (b) ex-spouse—Whether each beneficiary taking 5% of
　　　　estate. **Sammut v Manzi** [2009] **2** 234, PC.
　　　Gift to corporation described by its correct corporate title—Context showing that despite continued
　　　　existence of corporation payment not intended to be made to it. **Meyers (decd), Re** [1951] **1** 538,
　　　　Ch D.
　　　Holograph will excluding testatrix's husband from sharing in estate—Whether husband validly
　　　　excluded from taking under will and also on resulting intestacy—Whether exclusion of husband
　　　　operating as gift by implication of husband's share to persons entitled to the estate on the
　　　　intestacy. **Wynn (decd), Re** [1983] **3** 310, Ch D.
　　　Intention of making a will—Clerical error—Spouses making 'mirror' wills—Spouses each by
　　　　mistake executing each other's will—Mistake in wife's will passing unnoticed on death of
　　　　wife—Whether rectification of husband's will available after death of husband—Whether clerical
　　　　error—Whether husband intending by his signature to give effect to will signed—Wills Act 1837,
　　　　s 9(b)—Administration of Justice Act 1982, s 20(1). **Marley v Rawlings** [2011] **2** 103,
　　　　Ch D; [2012] **4** 630, CA; [2014] **1** 807, SC.
　　　Provision for disposition 'in event of husband predeceasing me or surviving for less than one
　　　　month'—No disposition in event of husband's survival for more than one month—Declaration
　　　　that surviving husband entitled absolutely. **Smith, Re** [1947] **2** 708, Ch D.
　　　Signed but undated will—Testatrix intending that will should take effect on completion of inter
　　　　vivos gifts—Whether testatrix having necessary animus testandi to make valid will. **Corbett v
　　　　Newey** [1996] **2** 914, CA.
　　　Statutory presumption—Gift made in terms which in themselves would give absolute interest to
　　　　spouse but testator by same instrument purporting to give issue an interest in same property
　　　　giving gift of absolute interest—Whether intention of testator relevant where doubt existing
　　　　whether testator intending to give spouse absolute interest although words used capable of so
　　　　meaning—Administration of Justice Act 1982, s 22. **Harrison (decd), Re** [2006] **1** 858, Ch D.
　　　Words of will showing accidental omission or mistake—Literal construction possible—Supplying of
　　　　words by the court. **Follett (decd), Re** [1955] **2** 22, CA; **Whitrick, Re** [1957] **2** 467, CA.
　　　Words of will showing omission of few words of power of appointment—Gift in default of
　　　　appointment—Supplying of words by the court. **Cory, Re** [1955] **2** 630, Ch D.
　　　Words of will showing omission of words of power of appointment and gift in default of
　　　　appointment—Supplying of words by the court. **Riley's Will Trusts, Re** [1962] **1** 513, Ch D.
　　Intestacy—
　　　Desirability of avoiding contruction leading to intestacy. **Geering (decd), Re** [1962] **3** 1043, Ch D;
　　　　Magee v Magee [1936] **3** 15, PC.
　　　Partial intestacy—Whether court should lean against construing will so that there is a partial
　　　　intestacy. **Wragg (decd), Re** [1959] **2** 717, CA.
　　Meaning of lapse—
　　　Effect of divorce on testamentary gift—Testator bequeathing entire estate to wife and in the event
　　　　the wife predeceasing him or failing to survive him for one month estate to pass to research
　　　　fund—Marriage dissolved before testator's death and wife surviving him by one
　　　　month—Whether divorce causing gift to lapse in same way as death of legatee would
　　　　have—Wills Act 1837, s 18A. **Sinclair (decd), Re** [1985] **1** 1066, CA.
　　Revocatory clause—
　　　Entailed interest—Clause revoking entailed interest and substituting life interest where tenant of
　　　　settled property born in testator's lifetime—Limitation to daughters of C as tenants in common in
　　　　tail—Whether revocatory clause applicable to interests held by tenants in common. **Caldwell's
　　　　Will Trusts, Re** [1971] **1** 780, Ch D.
　　Revocatory clause in codicil—
　　　Principles of construction of revocatory clause—Partial revocation by codicil. **Wray, Re** [1951] **1** 375,
　　　　CA.
　　　Will 'to be read as if the name of [M B] did not occur therein'—Gift to children of M B—Effect on
　　　　special power of appointment given to M B. **Spensley's Will Trusts, Re** [1952] **2** 49, Ch D.
　　Transposition of words—
　　　Income to be divided between testator's children and his wife—Subsequent trusts logically relating
　　　　to children's shares—Difficulty of construction resolved by transposition of initial gifts to children
　　　　and wife. **Bacharach's Will Trusts, Re** [1958] **3** 618, Ch D.

WILL (cont)—
  Construction (cont)—
    Two wills admitted to probate—
      Principles of construction. **Plant (decd), Re** [1952] **1** 78, Ch D.
    Will speaks from death—
      Articles 'now' deposited at stated place—Contrary intention—Wills Act 1837, s 24. **Whitby, Re**
        [1944] **1** 299, CA.
  Contingent interest—
    Vested subject to being divested. *See* **Settlement** (Contingent interest—Contingent interest
      distinguished from vested interest liable to be divested).
  Contract to make disposition by will—
    Family provision. *See* **Family provision** (Will—Contract to make disposition by will).
  Contrary intention—
    Settlement and will made before, and testatrix's death after, 1st January 1926—
      Distribution of property as on intestacy. *See* Distribution of property as on intestacy—Settlement
        and will made before, and testatrix's death after, 1st January 1926—Contrary intention, *below*.
  Creditors—
    Direction to pay debts. *See* Debts—Direction to pay debts—Creditors, *below*.
  Death duties—
    New South Wales. *See* **New South Wales** (Death duty—Dutiable estate).
    Payment of death duties. *See* Payment of death duties, *below*.
  Debts—
    Direction to pay debts—
      Creditors—Secured and unsecured creditors—Direction enuring for benefit of joint mortgagor and
        surety—Legacy—Lapse—Bequest to creditor of deceased son—Creditor predeceasing testatrix.
        Leach's Will Trusts, Re [1948] **1** 383, Ch D.
    Exoneration—
      Clause exonerating 'all people from the repayment of moneys owing to me at the time of my
        death'—Secured and unsecured debts owing to testatrix. **Coghill, Re** [1948] **1** 254, Ch D.
      Clause forgiving and rehearsing 'all sums owing to me'—Loan to company—Release. **Midland
        Bank Exor and Trustee Co Ltd v Yarners Coffee Ltd** [1937] **2** 54, Ch D.
      Will forgiving and releasing executor's debt. *See* **Executor and administrator** (Executor—
        Appointment—Appointment of debtor as executor—Release of debt in law—Equitable obligation
        to account for debt—Intention to forgive debt—Will forgiving and releasing executor from debt).
    Satisfaction—
      Annuity under deed—Bequest of sum for purchase of annuity of same amount. **Manners (decd), Re**
        [1949] **2** 201, CA.
  Deficiency of estate. *See* **Administration of estates** (Deficiency).
  Delegation of will-making power. *See* Testamentary disposition—Delegation of will-making power, *below*.
  Dependants—
    Gift. *See* Gift—Specific donees—Dependants, *below*.
  Dependent relative revocation—
    Alteration—
      Evidence of original contents. *See* Alteration—Evidence of original contents—Dependent relative
        revocation, *above*.
    Generally. *See* Revocation—Conditional revocation, *below*.
  Descendants—
    Gift. *See* Gift—Specific donees—Descendants, *below*.
  Destruction of object—
    Gift. *See* Gift—Destruction of object, *below*.
  Destruction of will. *See* Revocation—Destruction, *below*.
  Devise—
    Administration of estate. *See* **Administration of estates** (Devise).
  Direction to destroy. *See* Revocation—Revocation by written instrument—Direction to destroy, *below*.
  Disclaimer. *See* Gift—Disclaimer, *below*.
  Discovery—
    Revocation of grant of administration. *See* **Intestacy** (Grant of administration—Revocation of
      grant—Discovery of will).
  Discretion as to disposition of residue. *See* Residue—Discretion as to disposition, *below*.
  Discretion as to recipients. *See* Trustee—Discretion as to recipients, *below*.
  Distribution date—
    Class gift. *See* **Settlement** (Class gift—Distribution date).
  Distribution of property as on intestacy—
    Income from residuary estate—
      Income bequeathed to person who on death of present Earl should succeed to the earldom—Heir
        presumptive had no interest in property so given. **Midleton's (Earl) Will Trusts, Re** [1967] **2** 834,
        Ch D.
    Life estate followed by gift in remainder—
      Death of tenant for life in testator's lifetime—Whether gift lapsed. **Harward, Re** [1938] **2** 804, Ch D.
    Settlement and will made before, and testatrix's death after, 1st January 1926—
      Contrary intention—Administration of Estates Act 1925, s 50(2). **Walsh, Re** [1936] **1** 327, CA.
  Divesting—
    Condition. *See* Condition—Divesting, *above*.
  Division of residue. *See* Residue—Division, *below*.
  Domicile of testator. *See* Testator—Domicile, *below*.
  Donees—
    Specific donees. *See* Gift—Specific donees, *below*.
  Double gift—
    Residue—
      Construction. *See* Residue—Double gift—Construction, *below*.

WILL (cont)—
  Double portions—
    Ademption—
      First defendant left equal share of residuary estate under his mother's will—Testatrix subsequently executing enduring power of attorney—Attorneys making payment towards education of first defendant's son—Whether gift by mother capable of constituting a portion—Whether payment conferring benefit on first defendant—Whether payment adeeming pro tanto first defendant's share of residuary estate. **Cameron (decd), Re** [1999] **2** 924, Ch D.
      Pecuniary legacy and interest under discretionary trust in will—Settlement of share in private company—Nature of portion. **Vaux, Re, Nicholson v Vaux (No 2)** [1938] **4** 703, CA.
    Bringing portion into account against testamentary portion—
      Estate duty deductible in valuing testamentary portion. See **Administration of estates** (Ademption—Double portions).
    Rebuttal of presumption—
      Difference in character of gifts—Liabilities undertaken by donee at time of gift inter vivos—Quid pro quo for liabilities—Donor compelled to make gift. **George's Will Trusts, Re** [1948] **2** 1004, Ch D.
    Satisfaction—
      Gift of shares in private company by settlement—Pecuniary legacy under will—Partial intestacy—Perpetuities—Trusts clearly void—Dealings to be within limits prescribed by law. **Vaux, Re, Nicholson v Vaux** [1938] **4** 297, CA.
  Election—
    Application of doctrine of election to will. See **Equity** (Election—Application of doctrine of election to will).
    Election against will. See **Equity** (Election—Election against will).
  Employee—
    Gift to employee. See Gift—Specific donees—Employee 'if in my service at the time of my death', below.
  Entailed interest—
    Revocatory clause—
      Construction. See Construction—Revocatory clause—Entailed interest, above.
  Envelope—
    Signature on separate document—
      Execution. See Execution—Signature on separate document—Envelope, below.
  Estate—
    Survivorship—
      Joint account—Testator transferring accounts into joint names of self and daughter—Testator and daughter holding accounts on trust for testator—Testator subsequently stating that accounts were to be or become sole property of daughter—Testator dying—Whether account moneys passing under will—Whether disposition of equitable interest requiring writing—Law of Property Act 1925, s 53(1)(c). **Drakeford v Cotton** [2012] **3** 1138, Ch D.
  Estate duty—
    Direction for payment. See **Administration of estates** (Estate duty).
    Incidence. See **Estate duty** (Incidence).
  Evidence—
    Adverse evidence of attesting witnesses. See Attestation—Evidence—Adverse evidence of attesting witnesses, above.
    Evidence of original contents—
      Alteration after execution. See Alteration—Alteration after execution—Evidence of original contents, above.
    Executor dying without taking out probate—
      Admissibility of evidence to prove that testator had not died intestate—Administration of Estates Act 1925, s 5. **Whitmore v Lambert** [1955] **2** 147, CA.
    Revocation, of. See Revocation—Evidence of revocation, below.
    Trust of income as directed—
      Written statement by trustee as to directions—Death of trustee—Admissibility of statement. **Gardner's Will Trusts, Re** [1936] **3** 938, Ch D.
  Exclusion from benefit. See Benefit—Exclusion from benefit, above.
  Exclusion of rule in Howe v Dartmouth. See Apportionment—Clause negativing apportionment—Exclusion of rule in Howe v Dartmouth, above.
  Execution—
    Place of testator's signature—
      Above dispositive provisions—Whether signature so placed as to make it apparent testator intended to give effect to document as his will—Wills Act Amendment Act 1852, s 1. **Harris (decd), Re** [1952] **2** 409, Prob.
      Foot or end of will—Intention of testator—Wills Act 1837, s 9—Wills Act Amendment Act 1852, s 1. **Hornby (decd), Re** [1946] **2** 150, Prob.
      Signature at top of will attested—Second signature of testator below disposition and at foot of will not attested—Whether will validly executed—Force of maxim omnia praesumuntur rite esse acta—Wills Act 1837, s 9. **Bercovitz (decd), In the Estate of** [1962] **1** 552, CA.
      Signature on same page as ordinary commencement—Evidence that signature written last—Wills Act Amendment Act 1852. **Long, In the Estate of** [1936] **1** 435, Prob.
      Will consisting of several sheets—Nexus between sheets—Signing and attesting below space on last page—Inference concerning testamentary intention—Holograph additions inserted above signature—Wills Act 1837, s 9—Wills Act Amendment Act 1852, s 1. **Little (decd), Re** [1960] **1** 387, Prob.
    Signature—
      Holograph will attested properly but signed 'your loving mother'—Whether a signature within the meaning of Wills Act 1837, s 9. **Cook (decd), In the Estate of** [1960] **1** 689, Prob.
      Holograph will—Will commencing with statement 'My Will by Percy Winterbone'—Whether valid signature—Wills Act 1837, s 9(a). **Wood v Smith** [1992] **3** 556, CA.
      Partial signature—Surname incomplete—Testatrix becoming unconscious while writing name—Never regaining consciousness—Whether a 'signature'—Wills Act 1837, s 9. **Chalcraft (decd), Re** [1948] **1** 700, Prob.

WILL (cont)—
  Execution (cont)—
    Signature (cont)—
      Separate document, on. *See* Execution—Signature on separate document, *below*.
      Signature within attestation clause—Testatrix writing name within attestation clause—No separate signature appearing on document—Whether presence of name in attestation clause sufficient signature—Whether by signing attestation clause testatrix intended to give effect to document as her will—Wills Act 1837, s 9. **Weatherhill v Pearce** [1995] **2** 492, Ch D.
      Signing and attestation of wills—Will signed by some other person in testator's presence and by his direction—Requirements of 'direction'—Wills Act 1837, s 9(a). **Barrett v Bem** [2012] **2** 920, CA.
      Time of testator's signature—Testator signing will before setting out dispositive provisions—Whether will validly executed—Wills Act 1837, s 9(b). **Wood v Smith** [1992] **3** 556, CA.
    Signature on separate document—
      Dispositive document attested but not signed—Document enclosed in envelope signed by intending testator—Wills Act 1837, s 9—Wills Act Amendment Act 1852, s 1. **Bean, In the Estate of** [1944] **2** 348, Prob.
      Envelope—Dispositive document enclosed in envelope—Envelope signed by testatrix—Document and envelope sufficiently connected—Evidence that signature on envelope intended to be signature of will—Document already signed by testatrix—Signature at top of document and therefore ineffective—Whether signature on envelope intended as signature of will. **Beadle (decd), Re** [1974] **1** 493, Ch D.
  Executor—
    Appointment—
      Generally. *See* **Executor and administrator** (Executor—Appointment).
      Incomplete will. *See* Incomplete will—Appointment of executor, *below*.
    Generally. *See* **Executor and administrator** (Executor).
    Removal. *See* **Executor and administrator** (Executor—Removal).
  Failure of trusts. *See* Accruer—Failure of trusts, *above*.
  Family provision. *See* **Family provision**.
  Foreign adoption—
    Devolution of property. *See* **Adoption** (Foreign adoption—Death—Devolution of property—English will).
  Foreign and English wills—
    Gift—
      Ineffective gift. *See* Gift—Ineffective gift—Foreign and English wills, *below*.
  Foreign will—
    Power of appointment—
      Exercise by foreign will. *See* **Conflict of laws** (Power of appointment—General power—Exercise of power—Foreign will).
  Forfeiture—
    Forfeiture clause—
      Annuity. *See* Annuity—Forfeiture clause, *above*.
      Generally. *See* Forfeiture clause, *below*.
    Settled property. *See* **Settlement** (Forfeiture).
  Forfeiture clause—
    Alienation of interest—
      Absolute gift of property to four sons as tenants in common—Forfeiture in event of assurance or mortgage by a son to person 'other than a brother or brothers of such son'. **Brown (decd), Re** [1953] **2** 1342, Ch D.
      Assignment for benefit of creditors of 'whole means and estate'—Subsequent death of prior life tenant. **Pilkington's Will Trusts, Re** [1937] **3** 213, Ch D.
      Gift to son of share in residuary estate subject to forfeiture on alienation—Provision in son's marriage settlement for transfer to settlement trustees of part of son's share in testator's residue after payment thereof to him. **Haynes' Will Trusts, Re** [1948] **2** 423, Ch D.
    Annuity. *See* Annuity—Forfeiture clause, *above*.
    Clause leaving entire estate to two beneficiaries in event any other beneficiary contested will—Whether condition valid. **Nathan v Leonard** [2003] **4** 198, Ch D.
    Consent by life tenant to advancement—
      No advancement clause—Application of statutory power of advancement—Trustee Act 1925, s 32(1), s 69(2). **Rees' Will Trusts, Re** [1954] **1** 7, Ch D.
    Deprived of right to capital or interest—
      Protective trusts—Court order that principal beneficiary should charge his interest to secure maintenace—No charge executed—Whether court order caused forfeiture—Trustee Act 1925, s 33(1)(ii). **Richardson's Will Trusts, Re** [1958] **1** 538, Ch D.
    Income vesting in another—
      Annuity payable to Custodian of Enemy Property by operation of law—Whether annuity forfeited. **Hall, Re** [1943] **2** 753, Ch D.
      Authority to pay dividend from trust shares to creditors—No dividend declared. **Longman (decd), Re** [1955] **1** 455, Ch D.
      Beneficiary an enemy—Payment of income to Custodian of Enemy Property—Trading with the Enemy Act 1939, s 7(1)—Trading with the Enemy (Custodian) Order 1939 (SR & O 1939 No 1198), art 1(i), (ii). **Pozot's Settlement Trusts, Re** [1952] **1** 1107, CA.
      If the annuitant shall commit, permit or suffer any act, default or process whereby the annuity would become payable to another person—Annuity payable to Custodian of Enemy Property by operation of law—Whether annuity forfeited—'Process'—Trading with the Enemy Act 1939—Trading with the Enemy (Custodian) Order 1939 (SR & O 1939 No 1198). **Harris, Re** [1945] **1** 702, Ch D.
    Personal discharge for income—
      Income payable to beneficiary 'so long as he shall be able to give a personal discharge'—Appointment of receiver in lunacy of beneficiary's estate. **Oppenheim's Will Trusts, Re** [1950] **2** 86, Ch D.

WILL (cont)—
    Forfeiture clause (cont)—
        Severability—
            Life interest forfeited—Interest of issue—Rule against perpetuities. **Morrison's Will Trusts, Re** [1939] **4** 332, Ch D.
    Forgery—
        Evidence—
            Conviction—Admissibility. *See* **Evidence** (Conviction—Admission as evidence in civil proceedings—Subsisting conviction—Conviction subject to appeal—Adjournment of civil proceedings pending appeal—Probate—Will—Validity—Allegation that will a forgery).
    Formalities—
        Signature. *See* Execution—Signature, *above.*
    Gift—
        Absolute gift—
            Failure to dispose of whole interest devised to the beneficiary. **Cohen's Will Trusts, Re** [1936] **1** 103, Ch D.
            Gift to person and the descendants of his branch of the family—Whether construed as entailed interest—Indefinite gift of income—Law of Property Act 1925, s 130(2). **Brownlie, Re** [1938] **4** 54, Ch D.
            Gift to sister of legacy 'for life use, to revert to estate if she does not remarry'—Absolute gift to be implied on sister's remarriage. **Lane's Estate, Re** [1946] **1** 735, Ch D.
            Gift until specified age—Whether absolute gift to be implied. **Arnould (decd), Re** [1955] **2** 316, Ch D.
            Gift with request to leave property to certain persons—Precatory trust. **Johnson, Re** [1939] **2** 458, Ch D.
            Trust for specified purpose—Expression of purpose construed as mere indication of motive for gift—Overriding intention to benefit donee—Bequest of residue to wife on trust to be used for maintenance of wife and mother and education of daughter up to university grade—Whether absolute gift of residue to donees—Whether residue remaining when daughter's education finished passing as on intestacy—Whether if absolute gift donees taking as joint tenants or tenants in common. **Osoba (decd), Re** [1979] **2** 393, CA.
        Ademption. *See* Ademption, *above.*
        Amount equal to unused-nil rate band—
            Transfer of unused nil-rate band between spouses and civil partners—Gift out of residue of 'such sum as is at the date of my death the amount of my unused nil-rate band' to family beneficiaries—Gift over to charity -Sum at the date of death equal to amount of unused nil-rate band—Executors making election after death to claim pre-deceasing spouse's unused nil-rate band—Whether sum equal to amount of unused nil-rate band including spouse's unused nil-rate band—Inheritance Tax Act 1984, s 8A. **Loring v Woodland Trust** [2014] **2** 836, Ch D; [2015] **2** 32, CA.
        Amount of pecuniary legacy—
            Inconsistency between words and figures. **Hammond, Re** [1938] **3** 308, Ch D.
            Legacy of such a sum as with moneys given inter vivos will amount to stated sum—Moneys given inter vivos liable to estate duty on death of testator. **Dawson's Will Trusts, Re** [1957] **1** 177, Ch D.
        Appointment of beneficiaries—
            Born in the lifetime of the testator—Special power of appointment—Life interest appointed to a nephew's widow during widowhood if 'born in the lifetime' of the testator—En ventre sa mère at death of testator—Whether 'born in the lifetime' of the testator. **Stern's Will Trusts, Re** [1961] **3** 1129, Ch D.
        Business—
            Solicitor's practice—Whether confined to goodwill or including all assets of business. **Rhagg, Re** [1938] **3** 314, Ch D.
            What assets included in gift of testator's business of house furnisher—Whether gift subject to payment of trade liabilities. **White (decd), Re** [1958] **1** 379, Ch D.
        Charitable organisation unregistered at date of will. *See* **Charity** (Charitable trust—Will—Gift to body not registered as charity).
        Charitable purpose. *See* **Charity** (Will).
        Concurrent gifts—
            Joint tenancy or tenancy in common—Words of severance in original gift—Application to substitutional gift. **Froy, Re** [1938] **2** 316, Ch D.
        Conditional bequest. *See* **Administration of estates** (Legacy—Conditional bequest).
        Destruction of object—
            Gift to ear, nose and throat hospital at a particular address—Work of hospital at that address closed down after date of will and before testator's death—Patients transferred to special wing of general hospital—Assets transferred to general hospital exclusively for benefit of special wing. **Hutchinson's Will Trusts, Re** [1953] **1** 996, Ch D.
            Gift to non-charitable unincorporated association—Money held by members as accretion to funds subject to contract between them—Association named in will amalgamated with similar association before date of will—Whether gift could be taken by amalgamated society. **Recher's Will Trusts, Re** [1971] **3** 401, Ch D.
            Gift to teaching hospital—Institution taken over by State between death of testatrix and grant of probate. **Kellner's Will Trusts, Re** [1949] **2** 774, CA.
            Vesting of hospital in Minister of Health after date of will but before death of testatrix—National Health Service Act 1946, ss 6, 7. **Glass' Will Trusts, Re** [1950] **2** 953, Ch D; **Morgan's Will Trusts, Re** [1950] **1** 1097, Ch D.
            Vesting of hospital in Minister of Health after death of testator, but before legacy paid over—National Health Service Act 1946, s 6(1). **Hunter (decd), Re** [1951] **1** 58, Ch D.
        Disclaimer—
            Deceased's son executing voluntary deed before her death disclaiming all benefit arising on her death—Deceased leaving estate by will to son and his brother—Whether voluntary disclaimer before death of estate owner effective. **Smith (decd), Re** [2001] **3** 552, Ch D.
            Payment of estate duty on disclaimed gift. **Parsons, Re** [1942] **2** 496, CA.
            Purported disclaimer by one joint tenant operating as a release. **Schar (decd), Re** [1950] **2** 1069, Ch D.

WILL (cont)—
  Gift (cont)—
    Disclaimer (cont)—
      Right to retract—Voluntary disclaimer owing to misunderstanding—Position not altered to anyone's detriment. **Cranstoun's Will Trusts, Re** [1949] **1** 871, Ch D.
    Double gift—
      Residue. *See* Residue—Double gift, *below.*
    Effect of divorce on testamentary gift. *See* Construction—Meaning of lapse—Effect of divorce on testamentary gift, *above.*
    Fund for payment of pecuniary legacies—
      Undisposed of share of residue. **Midgley, Re** [1955] **2** 625, Ch D.
      Whether payable out of residue or primarily out of lapsed share of residue. **Beaumont's Will Trusts, Re** [1950] **1** 802, Ch D.
    Future specific devise—
      Vesting in possession deferred—'Shall not take effect'. **McGeorge (decd), Re** [1963] **1** 519, Ch D.
    Gift cum onere. *See* **Administration of estates** (Gift—Gift cum onere).
    Gift dependent on one of two events—
      Express mention of only one event—Effect given to testator's intention. **Main (decd), Re** [1947] **1** 255, Ch D.
    Gift during widowhood—
      Beneficiary a spinster known by repute as testator's wife—Testator's will providing his own dictionary—'Remarriage'. **Lynch, Re** [1943] **1** 168, Ch D.
      Beneficiary a spinster—Gift for period which cannot exist. **Gale, Re** [1941] **1** 329, Ch D.
      Decree of nullity in respect of second marriage—Whether gift restored. **Eaves, Re** [1939] **4** 260, CA.
      Gift of income of residue to wife during widowhood—Remarriage of wife—Second 'marriage' annulled—Wife's right to income, as testator's widow, since date of annulment. **Dewhirst, Re** [1948] **1** 147, Ch D.
    Gift over—
      After prior limitation—Particular condition not satisfied—Ultimate gift over on death of prior donee during lifetime of testator's mother—Death of prior donee after death of testator's mother, but during lifetime of testator. **Bowen (decd), Re** [1948] **2** 979, Ch D.
      After the 'termination of the present war'—Perpetuities—Validity. **Engels, Re** [1943] **1** 506, Ch D.
      Coincident deaths—Proviso if wife's death preceding or 'coinciding' with death of testator—Testator and wife died when ship lost at sea—No evidence of how loss occurred—No survivor—Whether wife's death coincided with testator's death. **Rowland (decd), Re** [1962] **2** 837, CA.
      Condition precedent for gift over to take effect—Exact event on which gift over to take effect not occurring—Rule that gift over to take effect if it must have been intended to take effect in event that happened—Application of rule contradicting express terms of condition precedent for gift over—Whether rule applying—Whether gift over taking effect. **Koeppler's Will Trusts, Re** [1984] **2** 111, Ch D.
      Construction of words of contingency—Whether words should be construed otherwise than literally—Share of residuary estate to testator's son, 'but if my said son shall not leave a child or widow who shall become entitled to an interest in his share', ultimate gift over—Son had no children but survived by widow—Gift over subject to interest given to widow. **Macandrew's Will Trusts, Re** [1963] **2** 919, Ch D.
      Gift to tenants in common for life—Gift over on death of all tenants in common—Implication of cross-remainders. **Riall, Re** [1939] **3** 657, Ch D.
      Impracticability of gift—Whether applicable to initial as well as future impracticability. *See* **Charity** (Failure of object—Impracticability).
      Legacy settled on daughter and her issue—Gift over if no child of daughter should attain 21—Codicil excluding issue of daughter by W from any benefit under will—Daughter having no issue other than children by W—Death of daughter leaving children who had attained 21—Effect of gift over. **Crawshay, Re** [1948] **1** 107, CA.
      Of fund to be appropriated to provide for annuity—Death of annuitant in lifetime of testatrix—Codicil confirming will after death of annuitant—Effect on gift over. **Clarke, Re** [1942] **2** 294, Ch D.
      On particular event—Attainment of 21 years—Confirmation by two codicils—Testator predeceased by sole member of class dying over 21 and after the will but before the two codicils. **May's Will Trusts, Re** [1943] **2** 604, Ch D.
    Gift subject to charge—
      Freehold property purchased during last illness of testator—Balance of purchase money advanced by solicitor—Deeds handed to solicitor—Charge—Gift cum onere—Administration of Estates Act 1925, s 35. **Riddell, Re** [1936] **2** 1600, Ch D.
      Gift subject to payment of annuities—Whether both personal obligation and charge on the subject-matter of the gift. **Lester, Re** [1942] **1** 646, Ch D.
      Motor cars which shall be ordered for any dwelling-house—Motor car ordered, but not delivered or paid for—Whether charged with payment of purchase price—Administration of Estates Act 1925, s 35. **Coxen, Re** [1948] **2** 492, Ch D.
    Gift to unincorporated association—
      Rule against perpetuities. *See* **Rule against perpetuities** (Unincorporated association—Gift to association).
    Implication—
      Moiety remaining 'after my wife shall have received her jus relictae' bequeathed by testator domiciled in England—Whether implied gift of other moiety—Meaning of 'moiety'. **Angus's Will Trusts, Re** [1960] **3** 835, Ch D.
    Impracticable charitable gift—
      Cy-près doctrine. *See* **Charity** (Cy-près doctrine—General charitable intention—Method of determining general charitable intention—Will).
    Income—
      Future defeasible gift—Inclusion of intermediate income. **Gillett's Will Trusts, Re** [1949] **2** 893, Ch D.
      Gift of income until marriage—Thereafter disposition of corpus—Death of legatee unmarried—Devolution of corpus. **Henry's Will Trust, Re** [1953] **1** 531, Ch D.

WILL (cont)—
    Gift (cont)—
        Income (cont)—
            Income free of all taxes (including income tax) and duties—Kenya income tax—Incidence of foreign income tax. **Frazer, Re** [1941] **2** 155, Ch D.
            Reasonable income—Direction to executors to let T enjoy one of testator's flats during her lifetime and to receive a reasonable income from his other properties—Whether bequest of 'reasonable income' void for uncertainty. **Golay (decd), Re** [1965] **2** 660, Ch D.
            To pay the income of the residuary trust fund up to the sum of £1,000 per annum to L for her life—Whether deficiency of income may be supplied out of surplus of subsequent years. **Carey (decd), Re** [1950] **1** 726, Ch D.
        Ineffective gift—
            Bequest of business to trustees—Half share only owned by testator—Direction to trustees to offer whole business at half value to person actually an equal partner with the testator. **Mulder, Re** [1943] **2** 150, CA.
            Bequest of 'my freehold farm'—Farm in fact owned by company in which testator held three-quarters of issued shares—Effect of bequest—Whether words 'freehold farm' could cover testator's shares in company. **Lewis's Will Trusts, Re** [1984] **3** 930, Ch D.
            Foreign and English wills—Gift under foreign will ineffective—Whether passing under residuary bequest in English will. **Wellington (Duke), Re** [1947] **2** 854, Ch D and CA.
            Trust in favour of persons named in a certain deed to be the trustees of such deed upon the trusts therein declared—Deed never operative. **Hurdle, Re** [1936] **3** 810, Ch D.
        Interest payable on—
            Legacy payable at 21—Trustees empowered to use legacy or any part thereof for education of legatee until he shall attain the age of 21—Payment of interest from date of testator's death. **Selby-Walker (decd), Re** [1949] **2** 178, Ch D.
            Legacy to be paid immediately after testator's death—Legacy to trustees on trust for son contingently—Dates from which legacies carried interest. **Pollock (decd), Re** [1943] **2** 443, Ch D.
        Latent ambiguity—
            One article available to answer two bequests—Article divisible—Moiety to each beneficiary. **Alexander's Will Trust, Re** [1948] **2** 111, Ch D.
        Misdescription—
            Bequest of 'my 750 ordinary shares' in named company—Testatrix possessed of 7,500 ordinary shares in company at date of will and date of death—Testratix' original holding consisted of 750 shares—Bonus issue of 6,750 received before date of will—Whether gift passed all testatrix' shares in the company—Whether earlier wills admissible as evidence of intention—Whether gift failed for uncertainty. **Tetsall (decd), Re** [1961] **2** 801, Ch D.
            False description of beneficiary—Validity of gift—Need to prove fraud. **Posner (decd), Re** [1953] **1** 1123, Prob.
            Identity of legatee—Falsa demonstratio non nocet. **Nesbitt's Will Trusts, Re** [1953] **1** 936, Ch D.
            Legatee—Descrjptive title—Charitable purpose rather than gift to individual indicated—Inaccuracy in description owing to change before date of will—Other bequests to charitable organisations benefing animals—Bequest to London Animal Hospital—Veterinary surgeon formerly carrying on his practice under that style—Whether gift to surgeon—Whether general charitable intention shown. **Satterthwaite's Will Trusts, Re** [1966] **1** 919, CA.
        Personal chattels—
            Articles of personal use—Furniture—Clocks—Collection of clocks—Collection inherited by testator—Collection stored in locked rooms by testator but not added to—Whether clocks 'personal chattels'—Administration of Estates Act 1925, s 55(1)(x). **Crispin's Will Trusts, Re** [1974] **3** 772, CA.
            Beneficiaries to select from personal chattels—Storage and insurance of chattels—Whether costs to be borne by beneficiaries or residue—Whether costs to be borne by income or capital of residue. **Collins's Settlement Trusts, Re** [1971] **1** 283, Ch D.
            Stamp and coin collections—Whether 'personal effects' included collections—Whether prima facie meaning of phrase displaced. **Collins's Settlement Trusts, Re** [1971] **1** 283, Ch D.
            Stamp collection—Whether 'article of personal use' within definition of personal chattels—Administration of Estates Act1925, s 55(1)(x). **Reynolds' Will Trusts, Re** [1965] **3** 686, Ch D.
        Property capable of disposition—
            Debt—Shares—Testatrix entitled to money owing to deceased husband—Testatrix entitled to have shares registered in her name—Whether capable of disposing of debt and shares. **Leigh's Will Trusts, Re** [1969] **3** 432, Ch D.
        Selection—
            Similar properties devised to several persons—No express provision as to selection—Some devisees described as a class—Right of selection—Selection by lot. **Knapton, Re** [1941] **2** 573, Ch D.
        Shares in company—
            Ademption. *See* Ademption—Gift of shares, *above*.
            Bequest to a company of shares in the company—Validity. **Castiglione's Will Trusts, Re** [1958] **1** 480, Ch D.
            Business—Bequest of shares in company to be incorporated by will trustees and to acquire testator's business—Company incorporated by testator after date of will—Whether bequest carried the shares held by the testator at his death. **Quibell's Will Trusts, Re** [1956] **3** 679, Ch D.
            Number of shares bequeathed amounting to exact number held by testator—No words indicating testator's ownership of shares bequeathed. **Rose, Re** [1948] **2** 971, Ch D.
            Shares forming part of testator's estate—Right of legatee to dividends declared before satisfaction of legacy. **Hall (decd), Re** [1951] **1** 1073, Ch D.
        Specific bequests—
            All his worldly goods and chattels both real and personal—Inclusion of real property. **Young (decd), Re** [1950] **2** 1245, Ch D.
            All moneys of which I die possessed—Absence of context—Home-made will. **Perrin v Morgan** [1943] **1** 187, HL.
            All my belongings—Exclusion of real property. **Price (decd), Re** [1950] **1** 338, Ch D.

WILL (cont)—
   Gift (cont)—
      Specific bequests (cont)—

All my bloodstock—Inclusion of half share in horse and interest as member of syndicate owning stallion. **Gillson (decd), Re** [1948] 2 990, CA.

All my furniture and movables not consisting of mortgages shares bonds or securities—Movables—Exclusion of sums of money. **Walsh (decd), Re** [1953] 1 982, Ch D.

All my home and personal belongings. **Mills' Will Trusts, Re** [1937] 1 142, Ch D.

All my horses to wife—Only horses those owned as tenant in common with wife—Admission of extrinsic evidence—No specific thing disposed of. **Sykes, Re** [1940] 4 10, Ch D.

All my plate—Whether Sheffield plate and electro-plate included. **Grimwood, Re** [1945] 2 686, Ch D.

All my real estate. **Ridley (decd), Re** [1950] 2 1, Ch D.

All my stocks and shares—Inclusion of interests in loan capital or funded indebtedness of foreign governments, municipalities and railway companies. **Purnchard's Will Trusts, Re** [1948] 1 790, Ch D.

All my stocks and shares—Whether bequest included investments other than stocks and shares of limited companies. **Everett, Re** [1944] 2 19, Ch D.

All other contents of my home or at the bank—Whether choses in action included—To be sold—Whether cash included. **Abbott, Re** [1944] 2 457, CA.

All other money invested or in the London and County Bank—Residuary gift. **Recknell, Re** [1936] 2 36, Ch D.

All stocks, shares and moneys in the care, custody or possession of bank—Bank holding only dividend mandates for stocks inscribed at the Bank of England—Testatrix afterwards of unsound mind—Order in lunancy for transfer of stocks to the name of Accountant-General—Effect of order on dividend mandates—Lunacy Act 1890, s 116—Lunacy Act 1922, s 2(8). **Palmer, Re** [1944] 2 406, CA.

Any money I may leave—Sums on deposit account—Sum on share account with building society—National development bonds—Premium savings bonds—Whether included in gift. **Barnes's Will Trusts, Re** [1972] 2 639, Ch D.

Any moneys that I have in the bank—National Savings Certificates, share certificate, post-war credit certificates and diamond ring deposited at bank—Travellers' cheques held by deceased—Extent of gift. **Trundle (decd), Re** [1961] 1 103, Ch D.

Any possessions I may have. **Brace (decd), Re** [1954] 2 354, Ch D.

Articles of vertu—Gold chain presented on election as sheriff. **Coxen, Re** [1948] 2 492, Ch D.

Cash in Lloyds Bank—Home-made will—Testatrix died leaving current and deposit accounts in Lloyds Bank—Testatrix aware of both accounts—Bequest carried credit balances on both accounts. **Stonham (decd), Re** [1963] 1 377, Ch D.

Community house—Residuary bequest to a community house—Whether a gift for the furtherance of the work of the community. **Banfield (decd), Re** [1968] 2 276, Ch D.

Entailed interest—Devise referring specifically to the property—Law of Property Act 1925, s 176(1). **Manor Farm, Kytes Hardwick, Re** [1950] 2 572, Ch D.

Everything I die possessed of—Testator's share in father's residuary estate—Death of testator before father—Testator's children surviving father—Wills Act 1837, s 33. **Hayter, Re** [1937] 2 110, Ch D.

Gift of £200 out of half of trust fund 'in the event of the death of either of my ... daughters ... without leaving issue'—Remainder of that half of fund to accrue to other daughter and her issue—Successive deaths of both daughters without either leaving issue—£200 payable on each death. **Clanchy's Will Trusts, Re** [1970] 2 489, CA.

Goodwill of my business and stock and plant—Inclusion of freehold premises—Debts due to me in respect of said business—Sum standing to credit of banking account. **Betts (decd), Re** [1949] 1 568, Ch D.

Jewellery—Unmounted cut diamonds. **Whitby, Re** [1944] 1 299, CA.

Land—Inclusion of incorporeal hereditaments—Tithe rentcharge. **Lory's Will Trusts, Re** [1950] 1 349, Ch D.

Leasehold house together with contents—Whether joint gift or two independent gifts. **Joel, Re** [1943] 2 263, CA.

Life interest in all property—Sums in consideration of past services payable after testator's death—Whether capital or income. **Payne (decd), Re** [1943] 2 675, Ch D.

My War Bonds—Testatrix possessed of Consolidated Inscribed Stock, National Savings Certificates and Defence Bonds—Falsa demonstratio non nocet. **Gifford (decd), Re** [1944] 1 268, Ch D.

My bank deposit at M bank—Current account, but no deposit account at bank—Certificates of title to investments deposited at bank—Current account closed shortly before testator's death, as testator too ill to sign cheques—Balance of account transferred to relative to pay testator's expenses—Sum in hand at testator's death. **Heilbronner (decd), Re** [1953] 2 1016, Ch D.

My cameras projectors films and other photographic appliances and my watches (other than my calendar watch) chain studs and other personal jewellery—Testator possessing certain personal jewellery of his own and having inherited jewellery from his deceased wife before making the will—Whether 'other personal jewellery' included wife's jewellery—Ejusdem generis rule. **Le Cras v Perpetual Trustee Co Ltd** [1967] 3 915, PC.

My leasehold house—Testator at date of will holding house under long lease—Testator subsequently acquiring freehold—No merger of leasehold and freehold interests—Whether gift passing freehold interest in house—Wills Act 1837, s 23. **Fleming's Will Trusts, Re** [1974] 3 323, Ch D.

My securities—Remainder of the money. **Smithers, Re** [1939] 3 689, Ch D.

Net income of residuary trust funds—Trust funds including shares in company—Capital distribution by company, in respect of shares, out of realised capital profits—Whether sum distributed capital or income. **Doughty, Re** [1947] 1 207, CA.

On condition that the beneficiaries agree to pay in equal shares to testator's widow 'for the remainder of her life ...10s per week'—Tenancy in common. **North (decd), Re** [1952] 1 609, Ch D.

Pay the income arising to my children in equal shares and after the death of all my children to grandchildren then living—Tenancy in common. **Davies (decd), Re** [1950] 1 120, Ch D.

WILL (cont)—
   Gift (cont)—
      Specific bequests (cont)—
         Personal and household goods and effects—Whether, in the particular context of the bequest, library books, etchings and mountain photographs passed thereunder. **Mengel's Will Trusts, Re** [1962] **2** 490, Ch D.
         Personal belongings. **Hynes (decd), Re** [1950] **2** 879, CA.
         Personal chattels as defined by Administration of Estates Act 1925—Article of personal use—Motor yacht bought and used entirely for pleasure cruises—Administration of Estates Act 1925, s 55(1)(x). **Chaplin (decd), Re** [1950] **2** 155, Ch D.
         Personal estate. **Cook (decd), Re** [1948] **1** 231, Ch D.
         Property—In the phrase 'income of property actually producing income' meant 'property forming part' of the testator's estate. **Hey's Settlement Trusts and Will Trusts, Re, Hey v Nickel-Lean** [1945] **1** 618, Ch D.
         Stamps of 'Great Britain and ... the British Colonies'—British Colonials—Meaning attributed by philatelists—What stamps included in gift. **Van Lessen (decd), Re** [1955] **3** 691, Ch D.
         Ten thousand preference shares in private company—Testator holding only 9,000 shares—No words indicating testator's ownership of shares bequeathed—Legacy not included in pecuniary legacies to be satisfied out of residue. **O'Connor's Will Trusts, Re** [1948] **2** 270, Ch D.
         To found a cot in a hospital—Found. **Ginger (decd), Re** [1951] **1** 422, Ch D.
         Whole estate to C—Codicil providing that 'in the event of the simultaneous death' of C and the testatrix 'the interests of my moneys to be divided between' Mrs M and E 'after the deaths of these two named the capital to go to my nephew'—Testatrix C and E killed instantaneously by the same bomb—Whether gift in will revoked by codicil—Simultaneous death—After the deaths of these two named—Gift of capital to take effect only after death of survivor of Mrs M and E—E's half share payable to Mrs M during the remainder of Mrs M's life—Law of Property Act 1925, s 184. **Pringle, Re** [1946] **1** 88, Ch D.
      Specific donees—
         All my relations—Rule of convenience—Variation of rule due to the enactment of Administration of Estates Act 1925, s 46. **Bridgen, Re** [1937] **4** 342, Ch D.
         All nephews and nieces of my late sister L—Intention of gift to children of L. **Birkin (decd), Re** [1949] **1** 1045, Ch D.
         Any national appeal to the public which may exist at the time when the residue of my estate is realised—Time of ascertainment of legatee—When residue of testatrix' estate was realised—No trust for conversion—Whether time referred to was end of executors' year. **Petrie (decd), Re** [1961] **3** 1067, CA.
         Charitable institutions referred to by me in this my will—Unitarian church. **Nesbitt's Will Trusts, Re** [1953] **1** 936, Ch D.
         Children of E J and M J—Whether child of E J alone included. **Lewis's Will Trusts, Re** [1937] **1** 556, Ch D.
         Children of child who shall die in lifetime of testatrix—Child already dead at date of will. **Valentine, Re, Re Birchall** [1940] **1** 545, CA.
         Dependants. **Ball, Re** [1947] **1** 458, Ch D.
         Descendants—Whether 'descendants' apt to include collateral relations. **Thurlow (decd), Re** [1972] **1** 10, Ch D.
         Employee 'if in my service at the time of my death'—Receiver in lunacy of testator appointed—Employment of servant continued by receiver—Release from performing any service for testator. **Silverston (decd), Re** [1949] **1** 641, Ch D.
         Employee in testator's service at date of his death—Business carried on in partnership. **Howell's Trusts, Re** [1937] **3** 647, Ch D.
         Employees 'who shall have been in the service of' a limited company 'for a period of five years and upwards'—Employment at the date of testator's death—Inclusion of service with testator before formation of company—Need for period to be continuous—Inclusion of war service—Inclusion of apprentice in term 'employee'. **Marryat, Re** [1948] **1** 796, Ch D.
         Employees who shall have 'had not less than five years' service'—Need for period to be continuous—Inclusion of way service. **Bedford (decd), Re** [1951] **1** 1093, Ch D.
         Equally between daughters of S and to E—Per stirpes or per capita. **Jeeves (decd), Re** [1948] **2** 961, Ch D.
         Equally between the children of my deceased sister T and the said F H—Children of different generation from that of testatrix, T and F H. **Birkett (decd), Re** [1950] **1** 316, Ch D.
         Grandchildren—Application of term to named persons not grandchildren. **Davidson (decd), Re** [1949] **2** 551, Ch D.
         Heir-at-law of survivor of two beneficiaries—Whether heir at common law or successors to real estate of an intestate dying in New Zealand subsequent to 1874—Real Estate Descent Act (No 84 of 1874), ss 3, 18—Administration Act (No 49 of 1879), ss 6, 10—Administration of Estates Act (No 3 of 1908), ss 4, 11. **Macleay v Treadwell** [1937] **2** 38, PC.
         Heir-at-law—Construction in popular sense. **Hooper, Re** [1936] **1** 277, CA.
         Heirs and successors—Ascertainment of class comprising 'heirs and successors'—Shares in which persons within the class are entitled—Relevance of intestate succession. **Kilvert (decd), Re** [1957] **2** 196, Ch D.
         Heirs and surviving issue—Ascertainment of class comprising heirs and surviving issue—'Heirs' of deceased person—Law of Property Act 1925, s 132. **Bourke's Will Trusts, Re** [1980] **1** 219, Ch D.
         If any daughter of mine shall die without lawful issue her surviving her share to devolve on other children—Whether death at any time would cause divesting. **Williams' Will Trusts, Re** [1949] **2** 11, Ch D.
         Individuals born after date of will—Exclusion of those born after death of testator—Rule of convenience. **Bellville, Re** [1941] **2** 629, CA.
         Issue of our marriage—Exclusion of grandchildren. **Noad (decd), Re** [1951] **1** 467, Ch D.
         M and/or J M and J being a married woman and her husband. **Lewis, Re** [1942] **2** 364, Ch D.
         Male descendants—Whether including males descended through females. **Drake's Will Trusts, Re** [1970] **3** 32, CA.
         Masonic lodge—Gift applicable as members shall direct—Fund to build masonic temple—Validity. **Turkington, Re** [1937] **4** 501, Ch D.

WILL (cont)—

Gift (cont)—

Specific donees (cont)—

'My brothers A and B, also C and D—Equally'—C and D children of a deceased brother of testatrix. **Jeffrey (decd), Re** [1948] **2** 131, Ch D.

My trustees absolutely they well knowing my wishes concerning the same—Gift of estate on trust and not gift conditional on discharge of testator's wishes. **Rees' Will Trusts, Re** [1949] **2** 1003, CA.

Nephews and nieces—Whether persons related by affinity included. **Daoust, Re** [1944] **1** 443, Ch D.

Next-of-kin—Such of testator's 'next-of-kin' according to the statutes of distribution as should be living in the United Kingdom at the decease of his daughter—Whether brothers and nieces of testator entitled to take with widow—Administration of Estates Act 1925, s 50(1). **Krawitz's Will Trusts, Re** [1959] **3** 793, Ch D.

Per stirpes and not per capita—Stirpital distribution by necessary implication from proviso. **Cockle's Will Trusts, Re** [1967] **1** 391, Ch D.

Relatives—Testatrix's daughter empowered by will to divide estate 'among her own relatives at her discretion'—Daughter appointing cousin's three daughters to take—Whether appointment limited to next of kin—Whether appointment to cousin's three daughters valid. **Poulton's Will Trusts, Re** [1987] **1** 1068, Ch D.

Such persons who would have been entitled under Part IV of the Administration of Estates Act 1925—Right of Crown to suceed as a 'person' or by prerogative right—Administration of Estates Act 1925, s 46(1)(vi). **Mitchell (decd), Re** [1954] **2** 246, Ch D.

Surviving descendants on death of last survivor of testator's children—Gift divisible per stirpes—Whether children or grandchildren to be the stirpes. **Sidey v Perpetual Trustees Estate and Agency Co of New Zealand Ltd** [1944] **2** 225, PC.

To the wife of my grandson A E H subject to prior life interest of M W H—Gift over 'in the event of my grandson not marrying'—Grandson unmarried at date of will and at death of testatrix—Subsequently married twice—First marriage dissolved—Second marriage during lifetime of M W H—Gift to first person answering description of being wife of grandson. **Hickman's Will Trusts, Re** [1948] **2** 303, Ch D.

Voluntary hospitals—Whether a 'dispensary' is a hospital—Voluntary Hospitals (Paying Patients) Act 1936, s 1. **Ford, Re** [1945] **1** 288, Ch D.

Substitutional gift—

Gift of testator's residuary estate to his sons in the event of testator and his wife dying 'during the present war'—Substitutionary dispositions if sons should also die 'during the present war'—'The present war'—Strict legal meaning displaced by context. **Cooper's Estate, Re** [1946] **1** 28, Ch D.

Gift over failing—Whether original gift divested if gift over fails. **Rooke's Will Trusts, Re** [1953] **2** 110, Ch D.

Gift over of deceased daughter's share to other sons and daughters—Any of them being then dead leaving issue who attain 21, such issue to take their deceased parents' share—Whether 'issue' construed as children of deceased son or daughter—Whether taking as tenants in common or joint tenants. **Manly's Will Trusts, Re** [1969] **3** 1011, Ch D.

Gift to children living at death of life tenant and issue of any then dead—Whether issue must survive life tenant. **Mousley v Rigby** [1954] **3** 553, Ch D.

Gift to issue attaining 21—Whether issue must survive parent. **Manly's Will Trusts, Re** [1969] **3** 1011, Ch D.

Uncertainty of object—

Broadcast appeal—Direction to set aside fund to provide £2 per week to be paid to the cause for which appeal broadcast on Sunday. **Wood (decd), Re** [1949] **1** 1100, Ch D.

Unincorporated association—

Rule against perpetuities. See **Rule against perpetuities** (Unincorporated association—Gift to association).

Vesting—

Bequest of residue and remainder—Gift over in certain events—Interests to vest at date due and payable. **Parkes (or Keswick) v Parkes (or Keswick)** [1936] **3** 653, HL.

Gift contained only in direction to divide—Postponement of gift to let in life interest—Substitution clause. **Browne v Moody** [1936] **2** 1695, PC.

Gift of fund to child on attaining the age of 21 years—Direction to executors to pay income during infancy and after death of life tenant to mother of child to be applied for advancement and education of child. **Rogers, Re** [1944] **2** 1, CA.

Real estate—Vested and contingent interests—'Upon my son attaining the age of twenty-five years'—'Shall take effect'. **Bickersteth v Shanu** [1936] **1** 227, PC.

Voluntary undertaking to pay money—

Will directing undertaking to be fulfilled—Money payable in foreign country and in foreign currency. **Schnapper, Re** [1936] **1** 322, Ch D.

Grandchildren—

Gift. See Gift—Specific donees—Grandchildren, *above*.

Heirloom—

Descent—

Rule in Shelley v Shelley—Gift to wife and heirs—Rule not applicable—Law of Property Act 1925, s 131. **McElligott, Re** [1944] **1** 441, Ch D.

Rule in Shelley v Shelley—Heirloom to be held by him and by his eldest son on his decease and to descend to the eldest son of such eldest son and so on to the eldest son of his descendants and I request my son to do all in his power by his will or otherwise to give effect to this my wish. **Steele's Will Trusts, Re** [1948] **2** 193, Ch D.

To be enjoyed by person for time being 'actually' entitled to mansion house—

Proviso against absolute ownership by tenant in tail unless attaining 21 or dying under that age leaving lawful issue—Death over 21 by first tenant in tail by purchase when prior life interests still existing—Whether actual possession condition of ownership. **Coote, Re** [1940] **2** 363, Ch D.

Holograph will—

Attestation. See Attestation—Holograph will on single sheet of paper, *above*.

Construction—

Intention of testator. See Construction—Intention of testator—Holograph will excluding testatrix's husband from sharing in estate, *above*.

WILL (cont)—
  Holograph will (cont)—
    Signature. *See* Execution—Signature—Holograph will, *above*.
  Home guard—
    Soldier's or mariner's privileged will—
      Actual military service. *See* Soldier's or mariner's privileged will—Actual military service—Home Guard, *below*.
  Hotchpot—
    Hotchpot clauses. *See* Hotchpot clauses, *below*.
    Partial intestacy. *See* **Administration of estates** (Partial intestacy—Hotchpot).
  Hotchpot clauses—
    Advances—
      Ascertainment of interest of beneficiaries—Charge of interest on advance as from death of testator. **Wills, Re** [1939] **2** 775, Ch D.
      Money lent 'to be taken in or towards satisfaction' and 'brought into hotchpot'—Estate insufficient to provide for all legacies—Whether clause operating as discharge of debt. **Horn (decd), Re** [1946] **2** 118, CA.
    Extent of interest to be brought into hotchpot—
      Life interest followed by gift to children of life tenant with general power of appointment by will in default of children. **Gordon, Re** [1942] **1** 59, Ch D.
  Husband and wife—
    Mutual wills—
      Identical terms. *See* Mutual wills—Identical terms—Husband and wife, *below*.
  Identical terms. *See* Mutual wills—Identical terms, *below*.
  Illegal condition. *See* Condition—Illegal condition, *above*.
  Illegitimate child. *See* Children—Illegitimate child, *above*.
  Implication—
    Gift. *See* Gift—Implication, *above*.
  Impossibility of performance—
    Condition. *See* Condition—Impossibility of performance, *above*.
  Income—
    Gift. *See* Gift—Income, *above*.
    Income vesting in another—
      Forfeiture clause. *See* Forfeiture clause—Income vesting in another, *above*.
  Incomplete will—
    Appointment of executor—
      No disposition of beneficial interest in estate—Executors Act 1830—Administration of Estates Act 1925, ss 46, 49. **Skeats, Re** [1936] **2** 298, Ch D.
    No appointment of executor—
      No reference to property or extent of interest—'I give devise and bequeath unto' three named persons. **Stevens (decd), Re** [1952] **1** 674, Ch D.
    Printed form of will—
      Beneficiary's name inserted—Bequest left blank. **Messenger's Estate, Re** [1937] **1** 355, Ch D.
  Intention of testator. *See* Construction—Intention of testator, *above*.
  Interest accruing after death of tenant for life—
    Apportionment. *See* Apportionment—Interest accruing after death of tenant for life, *above*.
  Interlineation—
    Alteration apparent in will. *See* Alteration—Apparent in will—Interlineation, *above*.
  Intermediate income—
    Residue. *See* Residue—Intermediate income, *below*.
  Intestacy. *See* **Intestacy**.
  Intestacy, avoidance of. *See* Construction—Intestacy, *above*.
  Investments—
    Direction in will to invest in authorised securities—
      No power to buy land. *See* **Trust and trustee** (Trust for sale—Investments—Direction in will to invest in authorised securities).
  Issue—
    Children—
      Ultimate gift of daughter's settled fund. *See* Children—Ultimate gift of daughter's settled fund—Issue, *above*.
    Descendants—
      Use of term in group life assurance scheme—Whether confined to legitimate relations. *See* **Document** (Construction—Words descriptive of family relationship—Group life assurance scheme—Descendant).
    Gift. *See* Gift—Specific donees—Issue of our marriage, *above*.
    Substitutional or original gift—
      Marriage settlement. *See* **Settlement** (Marriage settlement—Gift to issue—Substitutional or original gift).
  Lapse—
    Beneficiary pre-deceasing testator—
      Gift contingent on attaining age of 25—Death of legatee in lifetime of testator under 25—Legatee would have attained 25 had she died immediately after testator—Wills Act 1837, s 33. **Wolson, Re** [1939] **3** 852, Ch D.
      Gift of £20,000 to be held on trusts of daughter's marriage settlement—Covenant by testator in settlement to bring £10,000 into the settlement—£20,000 declared to be 'in addition' to the £10,000—Settlement trust fund vested in daughter's son—Death of son before death of testator—Destination of £20,000 on daughter's death. **Hickman's Will Trusts, Re** [1950] **2** 285, Ch D.
      Gift over on death of B in A's lifetime—B surviving A but predeceasing testatrix. **Bailey (decd), Re** [1951] **1** 391, CA.
      Ultimate gift over upon lapse by death—Gift failing by reason of donee never having had any children—Rule in Jones v Westcomb. **Fox's Estate, Re** [1937] **4** 664, CA.

WILL (cont)—
  Lapse (cont)—
    Gift of residue equally to six persons by name—
      Revocation by codicil of gift to one. **Midgley, Re** [1955] **2** 625, Ch D.
    Gift to hospitals 'to be added to the invested funds' of the hospital—
      Hospital possessing no invested funds—Receipt of proper officer to be a discharge—Corporation having no officers. **Meyers (decd), Re** [1951] **1** 538, Ch D.
    Statutory exception from lapse—
      Beneficiary dying before 1926—Testatrix dying after 1925—Distribution of interest saved from lapse—Wills Act 1837, s 33. **Hurd, Re** [1941] **1** 238, .
      Death of beneficiary intestate—Distribution of interests saved from lapse—Time of ascertainment of persons entitled to interests on beneficiary's intestacy—Wills Act 1837, s 33. **Basioli (decd), Re** [1953] **1** 301, Ch D.
      Residuary bequest to illegitimate child—Legitimation and death of child leaving issue before death of testatrix—Whether estate of legitimated child entitled to take gift—Wills Act 1837, s 33—Legitimacy Act 1926, s 3. **Brodie (decd), Re** [1967] **2** 97, Ch D.
    Substituted gifts—
      Legacy to personal representatives of deceased legatee. **Cousen's Will Trusts, Re** [1937] **2** 276, Ch D.
  Latent ambiguity—
    Gift. *See* Gift—Latent ambiguity, *above.*
  Legacy—
    Fund for payment. *See* **Administration of estates** (Fund for payment of legacies).
    Interest. *See* **Interest** (Legacy).
    Legacy to hospital. *See* **National Health Service** (Legacy to hospital).
    Legacy to personal representatives of deceased legatee—
      Lapse—Substitutional gifts. *See* Lapse—Substituted gifts, *above.*
    Payment. *See* **Administration of estates** (Legacy).
  Legitimacy—
    Succession to personal property in England—
      Child illegitimate by law of England but legitimate by law of domicile of origin. **Bischoffsheim, Re** [1947] **2** 830, Ch D.
  Legitimated person—
    Disposition. *See* Children—Legitimated person—Disposition, *above.*
    Right to take interests in property. *See* **Legitimation** (Right of legitimated persons to take interests in property).
  Life interest—
    Protective trust—
      Forfeiture—Election against will—Liability to compensate disappointed beneficiaries. *See* **Equity** (Election—Election against will—Effect—Protected life interest).
  Lost will—
    Probate—
      Soldier's or mariner's privileged will. *See* Soldier's or mariner's privileged will—Lost will, *below.*
  Male descendants—
    Gift. *See* Gift—Specific donees—Male descendants, *above.*
  Marriage—
    Condition—
      Restraint of marriage. *See* Condition—Restraint of marriage, *above.*
    Revocation by marriage. *See* Revocation—Marriage, *below.*
  Masonic lodge—
    Gift. *See* Gift—Specific donees—Masonic lodge, *above.*
  Medical practice—
    Advancement clause—
      Advancement in 'business'. *See* Advancement clause—Advancement in 'business'—Medical practice, *above.*
  Mental capacity—
    Property and affairs. *See* **Mental health** (Patient's property—Will).
    Statutory will. *See* **Mental health** (Persons who lack capacity—Principles —Best interests—Powers to make decisions and appoint deputies—Property and affairs—Statutory will).
  Mental patient—
    Execution of will. *See* **Mental health** (Patient's property—Execution of will).
    Will by patient. *See* **Mental health** (Patient's property—Will).
  Misdescription—
    False description of beneficiary. *See* Gift—Misdescription—False description of beneficiary, *above.*
  Mutual wills—
    Identical terms—
      Husband and wife—Husband and wife making wills on same date in similar terms leaving property to adult son—Wife dying and husband remarrying—Husband making new will in favour of second wife—Whether arrangements entered into between husband and first wife intended to be mutually binding—Whether evidence of agreement that wills were to be mutually binding—Whether failure to make reasonable provision for adult son—Inheritance (Provision for Family and Dependants) Act 1975, s 2. **Goodchild (decd), Re** [1997] **3** 63, CA.
      Husband and wife—Recital of agreement to make mutual wills—Each given absolute interest—In case of lapse, residuary estate divided into moieties, one moiety to be regarded as testator's personal moiety and the other as deceased spouse's moiety—Fresh will by husband after accepting benefit under wife's will—Implied trust in regard to wife's moiety of husband's residuary estate—Whether pecuniary legatees entitled to take as beneficiaries under trusts of wife's moiety and as legatees of similar legacies under second will. **Green (decd), Re** [1950] **2** 913, Ch D.

WILL (cont)—
  Mutual wills (cont)—
    Identical terms (cont)—
      Husband and wife—Wills leaving property to same beneficiary—Testators not leaving property to each other—Each will making bequests to children in equal shares—Husband dying—Wife making new will revoking former will and making different bequests—Whether wife in breach of binding contract between testators as to disposition of estates—Whether wife's new will a fraud on husband—Whether doctrine of mutual wills only applying where second testator benefiting under will of first testator. **Dale (decd), Re** [1993] **4** 129, Ch D.
    Personal representative—
      Removal—Appointment of judicial trustee—Whether person beneficially entitled under doctrine of mutual wills entitled to apply for appointment of substituted personal representative—Whether person beneficially entitled under doctrine of mutual wills entitled to apply for appointment of judicial trustee—Judicial Trustees Act 1896, s 1—Administration of Justice Act 1985, s 50. **Thomas and Agnes Carvel Foundation v Carvel** [2007] **4** 81, Ch D.
    Requirements for enforceable mutual wills—
      Implied trust—Evidence required to establish enforceable agreement to dispose of property pursuant to mutual wills—Husband and wife making wills on same date in similar terms—Wife taking benefit under husband's will in accordance with his will—Wife making new will differing from terms of mutual wills—Whether wife under legal obligations to dispose of her estate in accordance with terms of mutual wills—Whether mere fact of simultaneity of wills in similar terms sufficient to establish enforceable agreement—Whether constructive trust arising out of enforceable agreement for mutual wills. **Cleaver (decd), Re** [1981] **2** 1018, Ch D.
  Name and arms clauses—
    Condition. *See* Condition—Name and arms clause, *above*.
    Revocation. *See* Revocation—Conditional revocation—Name and arms clauses, *below*.
  Negligence—
    Solicitor—
      Damages. *See* **Solicitor** (Negligence—Damages—Will).
      Duty of care. *See* **Solicitor** (Negligence—Will—Duty of care).
  Next of kin—
    Gift. *See* Gift—Specific donees—Next-of-kin, *above*.
  Nomination—
    Exercise of power. *See* Testamentary disposition—Exercise of power—Nomination, *below*.
  Nuncupative will made in contemplation of voyage. *See* Soldier's or mariner's privileged will—Seaman at sea—Nuncupative will made in contemplation of voyage, *below*.
  Option—
    Option to purchase freehold property—
      Conditional bequest. *See* Condition—Conditional bequest—Option to purchase freehold property, *above*.
    Option to purchase realty—
      Business premises—Business carried on by tenant company in which testator and son had shares—Testator had sold business to company, but had retained freehold properties where business carried on—Son worked with testator in business—Testator bequeathed his share to son and gave him a right of pre-emption, after widow's death, over the freehold premises at a price that was realistic at the date of the will—Son died in widow's lifetime—Whether option personal to son or passed to son's personal representatives. **Zerny's Will Trusts, Re** [1968] **1** 686, CA.
      Option expressed to be exercisable on death of testator's wife or in her lifetime with her consent—Wife predeceased testator—Whether option exercisable after testator's death. **Hammersley (decd), Re** [1965] **2** 24, Ch D.
      Option to purchase at agricultural value determined for probate purposes—Machinery under will for determining value defective—Court's power to remedy defect—Will directing executor to offer property to testator's son for purchase at agricultural value determined for probate purposes 'as agreed with District Valuer'—District Valuer declining to take part in valuation—Whether court could provide alternative machinery for ascertaining value. **Malpass (decd), Re** [1984] **2** 313, Ch D.
      Option to purchase at reasonable valuation—No express reference in will to trustees fixing what the price should be—Whether option valid—Inquiry to be held to fix reasonable price. **Talbot v Talbot** [1967] **2** 920, CA.
      Option to purchase dwelling-house at value for estate duty purposes—'Chancellor's concession'—Purchase at concession value. **Dowse (decd), Re** [1951] **1** 558, Ch D.
      Subject-matter of option—Agreement by testator to purchase additional property, but sale not completed until after his death—Right of grantee to take property free from incumbrances—Purchaser or devisee—Real Estate Charges Act 1854, s 1. **Fison's Will Trusts, Re** [1950] **1** 501, Ch D.
      Will providing for testator's house to be offered for purchase to claimant—Will specifying periods for acceptance and completion—Claimant accepting offer within prescribed acceptance period but not completing within prescribed completion period—Whether principle requiring option to be accepted in strict compliance with terms also requiring strict compliance with conditions for completion. **Gray (decd), Re** [2004] **3** 754, Ch D.
    Option to purchase shares—
      Donee assigning benefit of option and dying without exercising it—Whether option exercisable by donee's executors or by assignees. **Skelton v Younghouse** [1942] **1** 650, HL.
      Option to purchase under market value—Whether specific bequest. **Eve (decd), Re** [1956] **2** 321, Ch D.
      Options to sons to purchase after death of tenant for life—'At par value'—Changes in regard to shares during tenancy of tenant for life—Amalgamation of company and substitution of increased number of shares in new company for those of old company—Substantial increase in value of holding—Liquidation of another company—Large sum paid by liquidator in respect of shares—Right of sons to exercise options. **Fison's Will Trusts, Re** [1950] **1** 501, Ch D.
    Oral statement—
      Seaman at sea. *See* Soldier's or mariner's privileged will—Seaman at sea—Oral statement, *below*.

WILL (cont)—
  Order of application of assets—
    Variation of statutory order. *See* **Administration of estates** (Order of application of assets—Statutory order).
  Partial intestacy—
    Grant of administration. *See* **Intestacy** (Grant of administration—Partial intestacy).
  Partial signature—
    Attestation—
      Acknowledgement. *See* Attestation—Acknowledgment of signature—Partial signature, *above*.
    Execution. *See* Execution—Signature—Partial signature, *above*.
  Payment of death duties—
    Payment out of residue—
      Gifts or settlements 'made in my lifetime'—Whether annuities payable by third parties under contracts with testator included—Testator 'economic source' of benefits—Prima facie meaning of 'gifts or settlements', unless restricted by context, sufficient to cover any benefaction. **Noad, Re** [1944] **2** 470, CA.
  Pecuniary legacies—
    Amount of pecuniary legacy. *See* Gift—Amount of pecuniary legacy, *above*.
    Fund for payment of pecuniary legacies. *See* Gift—Fund for payment of pecuniary legacies, *above*.
  Personal representative—
    Executor. *See* **Executor and administrator** (Executor).
    Mutual wills. *See* Mutual wills—Personal representative, *above*.
  Power of appointment—
    Exercise by will. *See* **Power of appointment** (Exercise by will).
  Power of sale—
    Power given to 'my Trustees'—
      Capacity of 'trustees'—Named persons executors and trustees—Exercise of power as executors in course of administration—Intention of testator—Power exercisable from testator's death—Whether expression 'my Trustees' indicating four named persons without limitation to their capacity as trustees—Whether exercise of power valid. **Hayes's Will Trusts, Re** [1971] **2** 341, Ch D.
  Privacy—
    Senior royalty—
      Application for will to be sealed—Direction sought to exclude value of estate from grant of probate—Whether public inspection 'undesirable or otherwise inappropriate'—Proper procedure—Senior Courts Act 1981, s 124—Non-Contentious Probate Rules 1987, SI 1987/2024, r 58. **Will of His Late Royal Highness The Prince Philip, Duke of Edinburgh, Re** [2022] **3** 187, Fam D.
  Privileged will. *See* Soldier's or mariner's privileged will, *below*.
  Probate. *See* **Probate**.
  Professional charging clause—
    Literary executor. *See* **Executor and administrator** (Executor—Literary executor—Charging clause—Professional charging clause).
  Protective trusts—
    Deprived of right to capital or interest—
      Forfeiture clause. *See* Forfeiture clause—Deprived of right to capital or interest—Protective trusts, *above*.
  Realty—
    Option to purchase. *See* Option—Option to purchase realty, *above*.
  Rebuttal of presumption of double portions. *See* Double portions—Rebuttal of presumption, *above*.
  Rectification—
    Clerical error—
      Inadvertence—Testatrix instructing solicitor to alter will—Solicitor failing to include clause from previous will exercising power of appointment in favour of husband—Husband seeking rectification of wife's will—Whether solicitor's failure constituting a 'clerical error'—Whether inadvertence constituting a ground for rectification—Whether rectification of will should be ordered—Administration of Justice Act 1982, s 20(1)(a). **Wordingham v Royal Exchange Trust Co Ltd** [1992] **3** 204, Ch D.
      Signature. *See* Construction—Intention of testator—Intention of making a will—Clerical error, *above*.
      Testator instructing solicitor in terms inconsistent with draft will—Solicitor failing to delete proviso to disposition—Class of beneficiaries restricted—Beneficiaries seeking rectification of will to delete proviso—Whether solicitor's failure consitituting a 'clerical error'—Whether rectification of will should be ordered—Administration of Justice Act 1982, s 20(1). **Segelman (decd), Re** [1995] **3** 676, Ch D.
  Referential trusts—
    Gift to daughter of income of half residuary estate subject to proviso—
      £500 after deduction of income tax to be maximum annual income payable to daughter—Surplus income to be paid under other trusts—Statutory variation of tax burden—Sum of £500 'a stated amount'—Finance Act 1941, s 25. **Lyons, Re** [1945] **2** 438, Ch D.
    Incorporation of declaration of trust—
      Existing declaration 'or any substitution therefor or modification thereof or addition thereto which I may hereafter execute'—Validity of disposition. **Jones' Will Trusts, Re** [1942] **1** 642, Ch D.
    Incorporation of trusts of earlier settlement—
      Limited power of revocation and appointment reserved to testator by settlement—Reference in will to 'deed or deeds' executed thereafter under power. **Schintz's Will Trusts, Re** [1951] **1** 1095, Ch D.
      Property devised to trustees to be held subject to prior life interest—Property to be held on same trusts as created by earlier settlement of another property, the S estates, 'or as nearly corresponding thereto as the circumstances will admit'—S estates settled on testator for life with remainder to sons successively in tail male—Creation of base fee before testator's death—Enlargement to fee simple during prior life interest in property devised. **Shelton's Settled Estates, Re** [1945] **1** 283, Ch D.

WILL (cont)—
  Referential trusts (cont)—
    Incorporation of trusts of even date—
      Disposal of residue by reference to settlement of even date—Incorporation of settlement in will—Effect of failure of one clause in settlement on another clause. **Edwards' Will Trusts, Re** [1948] **1** 821, CA.
  Religion—
    Condition. See Condition—Religion, above.
  Remarriage—
    Condition—
      Restraint of marriage. See Condition—Restraint of marriage—Remarriage, above.
    Revocation by remarriage. See Revocation—Covenant not to revoke—Revocation by remarriage, below.
  Removal of personal representative—
    Mutual wills. See Mutual wills—Personal representative—Removal, above.
  Residence—
    Condition of residence. See Condition—Residence, above.
  Residue—
    Any other personal property—
      Gift of money to brother—Gift of other personal property to nephews and nieces—Brother predeceasing testatrix—Whether lapsed gift falling into gift of other personal property. **Barnes's Will Trusts, Re** [1972] **2** 639, Ch D.
    Bank account not known to executor—
      Money deposited in her own bank by wife—Husband absolutely entitled to interest thereon after wife's death—Necessity for money to be in testator's bank. **Lowe's Estate, Re** [1938] **2** 774, Ch D.
    Discretion as to disposition—
      Direction to dispose of residuary estate in such manner as sole executor and trustee may in his absolute discretion think fit—Interposition of prior trust to dispose of it in accordance with memoranda—No memorandum left by testator—Trustee was solicitor who drafted will—Whether intestacy as to residuary estate. **Pugh's Will Trusts, Re** [1967] **3** 337, Ch D.
    Distribution of property as on intestacy. See Distribution of property as on intestacy—Income from residuary estate, above.
    Division—
      Direction to divide equally between nephew and children of cousin absolutely—Whether division referred to distribution per capita or per stirpes—Meaning of word 'between'. **Alcock, Re** [1945] **1** 613, Ch D.
      Direction to divide equally—Whether division referred to distribution per capita or per stirpes. **Daniel, Re** [1945] **2** 101, Ch D.
      Gift of residue in many and small percentages—Proviso for gift over of all gifts on failure of one—Failure of one gift—Testator's intention—Whether whole residuary gift should fail—Circumstances in which court should add words to give effect to intention. **Doland (decd), Re** [1969] **3** 713, Ch D.
      Joint tenancy or tenancy in common—Bequest of residue to wife on trust to be used for her maintenance, education of daughter and maintenance of mother 'provided my wife is resident in Nigeria'—Whether proviso qualifying whole bequest—Whether proviso indicating testator's wish to sever bequest into three parts—Whether donees taking as joint tenants or tenants in common. **Osoba (decd), Re** [1979] **2** 393, CA.
      Legacies of between £25 and £250 given to number of beneficiaries—Any residue to be divided 'between those beneficiaries who have only received small amounts'—Whether words 'who have only received small amounts' words of qualification or explanation—Whether residue to be divided among beneficiaries equally or in proportion to amount of each legacy. **Steel (decd), Re** [1978] **2** 1026, Ch D.
      Trust for sale of residue subject to 'any members of my family and friends of mine who may wish to do so' being allowed to purchase testatrix's paintings at less than current market value—Whether 'friends' too vague to be given legal effect—Whether 'family' confined to next-of-kin or extending to all blood relatives. **Barlow's Will Trusts, Re** [1979] **1** 296, Ch D.
    Double gift—
      Construction. **Gare (decd), Re** [1951] **2** 863, Ch D.
    Income from residue—
      Income tax—Total income. See **Income tax** (Total income—Income from residue under will).
    Intermediate income—
      Surplus income after gift of annuity—Capital of residue to be divided in unequal shares after death of annuitant—No express disposition of surplus income during annuitant's life—Intermediate income prima facie not carried by deferred residuary gift—Context indicating that gift should carry income—Preference for construction avoiding intestacy—Whether surplus income should be accumulated—Contrary intention within, s 69(2) of Trustee Act 1925, excluding, s 31(1)(ii). **Geering (decd), Re** [1962] **3** 1043, Ch D.
      Surplus income after gift of two annuities—Capital of residue to be divided after death of first annuitant—No express disposition of surplus income—Gift of capital 'after the death of' person having a limited interest during her life. **Wragg (decd), Re** [1959] **2** 717, CA.
      Surplus income after payment of annuities—Estate to be divided on death of survivor of annuitants and on trust established for them being wound up—Gift to residuary legatees not vested in possession but a future vested interest subject to defeasance—No express disposition of surplus income during annuitants' lives—All annuitants survived testator and still living—Trust fund as to capital and income to provide for annuitants—Surplus income to be accumulated until death of last survivor of the annuitants or earlier expiration of twenty-one years from testator's death and thereafter as on intestacy. **Nash (decd), Re** [1965] **1** 51, Ch D.
    Residuary legatee—
      Real estate not specifically disposed of—Comparative value of real and personal estate—Context—General words passing undisposed real estate. **Bailey, Re** [1945] **1** 616, Ch D.
    Secret trust—
      Standard of proof. See **Trust and trustee** (Secret trust—Expressed orally—Standard of proof required—Gift of residue by will).

WILL (cont)—
  Residue (cont)—
    Specific bequests—
      Gift of residue to A and 'thereafter to her issue'—Whether A takes absolutely. **Gouk (decd), Re** [1957] **1** 469, Ch D.
      I 'give and bequeath unto' eleven named persons followed by specific gift to one of them. **Turner, Re** [1949] **2** 935, Ch D.
      Residue of my estate 'to be divided equally' between testator's brother and sisters 'during their lifetime'—'After their death to be evenly distributed' between testator's nephew and nieces—Implied gift to survivors or survivor of first takers—Second takers to take per capita on death of last survivor of first takers. **Foster, Re** [1946] **1** 333, Ch D.
      Residue to be disposed of as my executors think fit—Executors hold on trust for persons entitled on partial intestacy and do not take beneficially. **Carville, Re** [1937] **4** 464, Ch D.
  Restraint of marriage—
    Condition. *See* Condition—Restraint of marriage, *above*.
  Revival—
    Codicil reviving revoked will—
      Codicil to and confirming revoked will but not mentioning second intermediate will which revoked the earlier will—Revoked will revived. **Pearson (decd), Re** [1963] **3** 763, Ch D.
      Earlier will and codicils—Later will revoking earlier—Final codicil expressly confirming earlier will—Absence of appropriate words of revival—Wills Act 1837, s 22. **Taylor, In the Estate of** [1938] **1** 586, Prob.
      Intention appearing on face of codicil—Evidence of surrounding circumstances—Wills Act 1837, s 22. **Davis (decd), In the Estate of** [1952] **2** 509, Prob.
      Three wills—Later will revoking earlier—Subsequent codicil altering main portions of first will—Absence of express confirmation of first will—Intention to revive first will—Wills Act 1837, s 22. **Mardon, In the Estate of** [1944] **2** 397, Prob.
  Revocation—
    Civil partnership—
      Expectation of formation of civil partnership with particular person—Deceased making will containing direction that will not be revoked by subsequent civil partnership—Subsequent civil partner of deceased sole beneficiary under will—Whether will revoked by formation of civil partnership—Wills Act 1837, s 18B(1), (3). **Court v Despallieres** [2010] **2** 451, Ch D.
    Codicil—
      Third codicil expressed as first codicil—Whether revoking prior codicils. **Le Cras v Perpetual Trustee Co Ltd** [1967] **3** 915, PC.
    Conditional revocation—
      Condition unfulfilled—Intention of testator—Revocation with intention of making new will—Mutilation or destruction of existing will—Mutilation or destruction effected with a view to making new will—No new will made—Effectiveness of revocation—Test to be applied—Act of revocation ineffective only if testator's intention that revocation should not be effective until new will made—Inference as to testator's intention to be drawn from surrounding circumstances. **Jones (decd), Re** [1976] **1** 593, CA.
      Expressed intention to alter will—Delay in carrying out intention. **Bromham, In the Estate of** [1952] **1** 110, Prob.
      Letter of testator admissible as evidence of facts stated—Evidence Act 1938, s 1. **Bridgewater (decd), In the Estate of** [1965] **1** 717, Prob.
      Name and arms clauses—Codicil expressly revoking clauses in will—New clauses in codicil invalid and ineffective—Whether clauses in will revived. **Murray (decd), Re** [1956] **2** 353, Ch D.
      Need of evidence of physical destruction of will. **Botting, In the Estate of** [1951] **2** 997, Prob.
      Revocation by codicil of testamentary disposition of German estate—Codicil stating that testatrix had made separate arrangements as to disposal of her German estate—Separate arrangements not effective—Whether foreign estate undisposed of or revocation conditional on effectiveness of such separate arrangements. **Feis (decd), Re** [1963] **3** 303, Ch D.
      Revocation clause in later will—Destruction of earlier will after execution of later will—Destruction in belief later will valid—Later will invalid. **Davies, In the Estate of** [1951] **1** 920, Assizes.
      Revocation clause in later will—Distributive reading of revocation clause—Gift in later will failing because will witnessed by devisee's husband—Gift to devisee identical in earlier and later wills but other gifts varied—Whether revocation clause in later will could be read distributively—Whether testator intending to revoke gift to devisee—Whether testator intended later will to be confirmatory of gift to devisee but revocatory in respect of other bequests—Wills Act 1837, s 15. **Finnemore (decd), Re** [1992] **1** 800, Ch D.
      Revocation clause in later will—Later will though executed left incomplete—Admission of later and earlier wills to probate. **Brown, In the Estate of** [1942] **2** 176, Prob; **Cocke (decd), Re** [1960] **2** 289, Prob.
    Covenant not to revoke—
      Revocation by remarriage—Construction of covenant—Wills Act 1837, ss 18, 20. **Marsland, Re** [1939] **3** 148, CA.
    Destruction—
      Burning, tearing or otherwise destroying will—Otherwise destroying—Obliteration of material part of will—Testatrix's signature obliterated—Whether will 'otherwise destroyed' if testatrix's signature no longer apparent—Whether will revoked—Wills Act 1837, s 20. **Adams (decd), Re** [1990] **2** 97, .
      Lower half of first page of will cut away by testator—Effect to excise clause setting out trusts on which residue to be held—Will otherwise complete and properly executed—Whether partial destruction indicating intention to revoke will—Whether will should be admitted to probate in mutilated state. **Everest (decd), Re** [1975] **1** 672, Fam D.
      Strip cut out and ends joined—Presumption of revocation of part cut out—Wills Act 1837, s 20. **Nunn, In the Estate of** [1936] **1** 555, Prob.
    Evidence of revocation—
      Oral evidence—Standard of proof required. **Wyatt (decd), Re** [1952] **1** 1030, Prob.
    Foreign will, by—
      Conflict of laws. *See* **Conflict of laws** (Will—Revocation).

WILL (cont)—
Revocation (cont)—
Marriage—
Voidable marriage—Will made prior to testator entering into voidable marriage—Marriage voidable by reason of testator's unsoundness of mind but never avoided—Whether will revoked by marriage—Wills Act 1837, s 18—Matrimonial Causes Act 1973, s 12(c). **Roberts (decd), Re** [1978] **3** 225, Ch D and CA.
Will expressed to be made in contemplation of a marriage not subject to revocation. *See* Revocation—Will expressed to be made in contemplation of a marriage, *below*.
Will made in exercise of power of appointment granted by settlement—Settlement providing that in default of appointment property to pass to those entitled on intestacy had the testator died without being married—'Person entitled as...next of kin under Statute of Distributions'—Testator's widow—Wills Act 1837, s 18. **Gilligan (decd), Re** [1949] **2** 401, Prob.
Revocation by written instrument—
Direction to destroy—Wills Act 1837, s 20. **Spracklan's Estate, Re** [1938] **2** 345, CA.
Revocation by foreign will—First will disposing of real estate in England—Foreign will not executed in accordance with English law. **Alberti (decd), In the Estate of** [1955] **3** 730, Prob.
Revocation of foreign will—English will containing revocation clause—Will expressed to apply only to estate in England—Revocation of earlier will made in Belgium and disposing only of property in Belgium. **Wayland, In the Estate of** [1951] **2** 1041, Prob.
Will expressed to be made in contemplation of a marriage—
Gift in will expressed to be made in contemplation of a marriage—Other gifts containing no such expression—No explicit statement that will itself made in contemption of a marriage—Whether sufficient expression that will made in contemplation of a marriage—Law of Property Act 1925, s 177. **Coleman (decd), Re** [1975] **1** 675, Ch D.
Gift to named person described as 'my fiancée'—Whether gift expressed to be made in contemplation of a marriage—Law of Property Act 1925, s 177. **Coleman (decd), Re** [1975] **1** 675, Ch D.
Gift 'unto my fiancée'—Whether gift expressed to be made in contemplation of a marriage—Law of Property Act 1925, s 177(1). **Langston (decd), Re** [1953] **1** 928, Prob.
Revocation of bequest in will—
Codicil. *See* Codicil—Revocation of bequest in will, *above*.
Revocatory clause—
Construction. *See* Construction—Revocatory clause, *above*.
Rule against perpetuities. *See* **Rule against perpetuities**.
Rule in Lassence v Tierney. *See* Accruer—Rule in Lassence v Tierney, *above*.
Satisfaction—
Debts. *See* Debts—Satisfaction, *above*.
Double portions. *See* Double portions—Satisfaction, *above*.
Secret trust. *See* **Trust and trustee** (Secret trust).
Selection of gift. *See* Gift—Selection, *above*.
Settled land—
Proceeds of sale. *See* Will made abroad—Proceeds of sale of settled land—Whether personalty, *below*.
Severability—
Forfeiture clause. *See* Forfeiture clause—Severability, *above*.
Shares—
Gift of shares in company. *See* Gift—Shares in company, *above*.
Option to purchase. *See* Option—Option to purchase shares, *above*.
Shelley v Shelley—
Rule. *See* Heirloom—Descent—Rule in Shelley v Shelley, *above*.
Shifting clause—
Validity—
Uncertainty. **Bromley v Tryon** [1951] **2** 1058, HL.
Signature of will—
Acknowledgment of signature. *See* Attestation—Acknowledgment of signature, *above*.
Execution. *See* Execution—Signature, *above*.
Place of testator's signature. *See* Execution—Place of testator's signature, *above*.
Time of testator's signature. *See* Execution—Signature—Time of testator's signature, *above*.
Soldier's or mariner's privileged will—
Actual military service—
Airmen training in Canada for operational duties—Wills Act 1837, s 11—Wills (Soldiers and Sailors) Act 1918, s 5(2). **Wingham, Re** [1948] **2** 908, CA.
Death in air raid—Officer living in own house near barracks—Wills Act 1837, s 11. **Gibson, In the Goods of** [1941] **2** 91, Prob.
Home Guard—Instructions to solicitor as civilian—Killed on Home Guard duties—Wills Act 1837, s 11—Army Act s 189(1)—Defence (Home Guard) Regulations 1940, reg 2(1), (2), (3). **Anderson, In the Estate of** [1943] **2** 609, Prob.
Soldier on leave in England from British army of occupation in Germany—Wills Act 1837, s 11. **Colman (decd), In the Estate of** [1958] **2** 35, Prob.
Soldier on patrol during armed and clandestine insurrection—Terrorist activities in Northern Ireland—Wills Act 1837, s 11. **Jones (decd), Re** [1981] **1** 1, Fam D.
Soldier stationed in camp in England—Death in air raid—Wills Act 1837, s 11. **Spark, In the Estate of** [1941] **2** 782, Prob.
Will made before mobilisation and before declaration of war—Soldier called out for service to ensure preparedness for the defence of the realm against external danger—Wills Act 1837, s 11. **Rippon, In the Estate of** [1943] **1** 676, Prob.
Women's Auxiliary Air Force—Wills Act 1837, s 11. **Rowson, In the Estate of** [1944] **2** 36, Prob.
Lost will—
Probate—Admissibility of secondary evidence—Statements by testator after execution of will—Cogency of evidence—Letter written after execution of will not a testamentary document. **MacGillivray, In the Estate of** [1946] **2** 301, CA.

WILL (cont)—
    Soldier's or mariner's privileged will (cont)—
        Oral declaration—
            Testamentary intention—Reference to previous disposition—Evidence—Wills Act 1837, s 11. **Spicer (decd), Re** [1949] **2** 659, Prob.
        Oral evidence of intention—
            Note of oral instructions for will admitted to probate—Whether capable of exercising special power over personalty—Wills Act 1837, ss 9, 10, 11, 27—Wills (Soldiers and Sailors) Act 1918, s 3(1). **Chichester's (Earl) Will Trusts, Re** [1946] **1** 722, Ch D.
        Seaman at sea—
            Document made in contemplation of voyage—Alteration—Presumption of alteration while 'at sea'—Wills Act 1837, s 11. **Newland, In the Estate of** [1952] **1** 841, Prob.
            Document made in contemplation of voyage—Seaman ashore on leave not under orders to sail—Seaman executing document while a minor and without attestation—Whether seaman in contemplation of voyage when orders merely expected—Whether seaman 'mariner or seaman at sea'—Wills Act 1837, s 11. **Rapley's Estate, Re** [1983] **3** 248, Ch D.
            Nuncupative will made in contemplation of voyage—Wills Act 1837, s 11. **Wilson, In the Estate of** [1952] **1** 852, Prob.
            Oral statement—Testamentary act—Casual conversation—No intention that statement to be acted on by person to whom statement made—Will Act 1837, s 11. **Knibbs, In the Estate of** [1962] **2** 829, Prob.
            Whether privilege accorded to 'mariner or seaman' restricted to persons serving or engaged to serve on British-registered ships—Wills Act 1837, s 11—Wills (Soldiers and Sailors) Act 1918, s 2. **Servoz-Gavin (decd), Re** [2010] **1** 410, Ch D.
    Solicitor—
        Attestation—
            Witness. *See* Attestation—Witness—Solicitor, *above.*
        Negligence—
            Damages. *See* **Solicitor** (Negligence—Damages—Will).
            Duty of care. *See* **Solicitor** (Negligence—Will—Duty of care).
        Residuary bequest to solicitor. *See* **Solicitor** (Gift by client to solicitor).
        Trustee. *See* **Solicitor** (Will—Trustee).
    Solicitor's practice—
        Gift. *See* Gift—Business—Solicitor's practice, *above.*
    Soundness of mind—
        Testator. *See* Testator—Soundness of mind, *below.*
    Specific bequests—
        Generally. *See* Gift—Specific bequests, *above.*
        Residue. *See* Residue—Specific bequests, *above.*
    Specific conditions. *See* Condition, *above.*
    Specific donees. *See* Gift—Specific donees, *above.*
    Statutory will—
        Execution of will in respect of mental patient. *See* **Mental health** (Patient's property—Execution of will).
    Substitutional gift. *See* Gift—Substitutional gift, *above.*
    Superfluous signature—
        Attestation. *See* Attestation—Attestation clause—Superfluous signature, *above.*
    Surviving—
        Joint account. *See* Estate—Survivorship—Joint account, *above.*
        My surviving children—
            Gift to testator's surviving children if any child should die without leaving issue—Interpretation of 'survive' or 'survivor'. **James' Will Trusts, Re** [1960] **3** 744, Ch D.
        Survive—
            Gift to such children of son as shall survive testator—Son unmarried at date of will and date of death of testator. **Hodgson (decd), Re** [1952] **1** 769, Ch D.
            Gift to such of children of granddaughter as shall survive testator—Testator eighty years old at date of will—Granddaughter married for five years at that time—One child born in his lifetime and living after his death, others born after his death. **Alsopp (decd), Re** [1967] **2** 1056, CA.
        Surviving two events—
            Satisfaction of requirement by persons living at date of second event only. **Castle's Will Trusts, Re** [1948] **2** 927, Ch D.
        Survivor—
            Gift subject to life interest to three persons 'or the survivors or survivor of them'. **Douglas's Will Trusts, Re** [1959] **3** 785, CA.
    Testamentary disposition—
        Delegation of will-making power—
            Whether will-making power may be delegated. **Beatty's Will Trusts, Re** [1990] **3** 844, Ch D.
        Exercise of power—
             Nomination—Pension scheme—Power to appoint nominee to receive contributions in event of employee's death before entitlement to pension—Power testamentary in character—Whether exercise of power a testamentary disposition—Whether need to comply with statutory requirements as to testamentary papers—Wills Act 1837. **Danish Bacon Co Ltd Staff Pension Fund, Re** [1971] **1** 486, Ch D.
    Testator—
        Domicile—
            Domiciled in England—Attested holograph will made in Scotland not requiring attestation—Legatee wife of attesting witness—Wills Act 1837, ss 15, 35—Wills Act 1861, s 2. **Priest, Re** [1944] **1** 51, Ch D.
        Soundness of mind—
            Testator a paranoid psychopath—Insane delusion affecting one clause of last codicil—Pronouncement for all dispositions deleting the one clause. **Bohrmann, In the Estate of, Cæsar and Watmough v Bohrmann** [1938] **1** 271, Prob.
            Testator enfeebled by disease—Delusion concerning relatives. **Battan Singh v Amirchand** [1948] **1** 152, PC.

WILL (cont)—
    Testator (cont)—
        Testamentary capacity—
            Testator having capacity at date of instructions but not at later date of execution—Rule in Parker v Felgate—Whether should be followed—Whether testator knew and approved contents of will at date of execution—Whether instructions 'settled'. **Perrins v Holland** [2011] **2** 174, CA.
    Transposition of words—
        Construction. *See* Construction—Transposition of words, *above*.
    Trust—
        Determination of matters of doubt—
            Determination to be binding on all persons interested under the will—Validity of Provision. **Wynn's Will Trusts, Re** [1952] **1** 341, Ch D.
        Trust for relatives 'in special need'—
            Whether charitable trust for poor relations. *See* **Charity** (Relief of poverty—Poor relations—Relatives in special need).
        Trustee. *See* Trustee, *below*.
    Trust for sale—
        Completion—
            Proceeds of sale to be divided amongst beneficiaries living at completion of sale—Meaning of 'completion'. *See* **Trust and trustee** (Trust for sale—Realty—Direction to divide proceeds of sale amongst beneficiaries).
        Realty—
            Express trust—Trust in will to sell and divide proceeds among beneficiaries. *See* **Trust and trustee** (Trust for sale—Realty—Express trust).
    Trustee—
        Beneficial entitlement—
            Gift to bank 'with the request that it will dispose of it in accordance with any memorandum signed by me'—No communication of wishes to bank during testator's lifetime—Whether bank beneficially entitled. **Stirling (decd), Re** [1954] **2** 113, Ch D.
        Determination of matters of doubt—
            Beneficiary—Beneficiary presumed to have predeceased testatrix—Testatrix leaving residue of estate to trustees to hold capital and accumulated income on trust for son—Son presumed to have predeceased testatrix—Testatrix directing that if son not coming forward to claim by specified date residue to pass to charity—Trustees seeking order giving liberty to administer trusts on footing that son predeceased testatrix—Whether residuary gift accelerated so as to take effect from testatrix's death. **Green's Will Trusts, Re** [1985] **3** 455, Ch D.
        Discretion as to recipients—
            Discretion to make payment to such children as 'shall appear to be most in need'—Discretionary power to divide the corpus—Time when such power may be exercised. **Magee v Magee** [1936] **3** 15, PC.
        Trustees' power of sale—
            Capacity of trustees. *See* Power of sale—Power given to 'my Trustees'—Capacity of 'trustees', *above*.
    Two wills admitted to probate—
        Construction. *See* Construction—Two wills admitted to probate, *above*.
    Uncertainty—
        Dispositive intention—
            Intention to create charitable trust. *See* **Charity** (Uncertainty—Intention to create charitable trust).
        Shifting clause. *See* Shifting clause—Validity—Uncertainty, *above*.
        Uncertainty of object—
            Gift. *See* Gift—Uncertainty of object, *above*.
    Validity—
        Shifting clause. *See* Shifting clause—Validity, *above*.
    Valuation of effects—
        Probate valuation—
            Contents of house up to certain value taken at probation valuation—Probate valuation—Contents. **Eumorfopoulos** [1943] **2** 719, Ch D.
            Direction to executors to transfer land at 'valuation agreed for probate'—Whether this meant valuation initially made of property to lead to grant of probate or value ultimately agreed with estate duty office for estate duty purposes. **De Lisle's Will Trusts, Re** [1968] **1** 492, Ch D.
    Vesting—
        Condition—
            Conditional bequest. *See* Condition—Conditional bequest—Vesting, *above*.
        Gift. *See* Gift—Vesting, *above*.
    Widowhood—
        Gift during widowhood. *See* Gift—Gift during widowhood, *above*.
    Will made abroad—
        Proceeds of sale of settled land—
            Whether personalty—Wills Act 1861, s 1. **Cartwright, Re** [1938] **4** 209, CA.
    Witness—
        Attestation. *See* Attestation—Witness, *above*.

WINDING UP
    Building society. *See* **Building society** (Winding up).
    Company—
        Compulsory winding up. *See* **Company** (Compulsory winding up).
        Generally. *See* **Company** (Winding up).
        Insurance company—
            Generally. *See* **Company** (Insurance company—Winding up).
        Voluntary winding up. *See* **Company** (Voluntary winding up).
    Industrial and provident societies. *See* **Industrial and provident societies** (Winding up).

WINDING UP (cont)—
    Limited partnership—
        Assignment—
            Investment fund—Unregulated collective investment scheme set up as limited partnership—Fund managed by defendants until its insolvent liquidation—Claim brought by liquidators based on assignments of investors' claims to fund—Whether claim complied with procedural rules for partnership claims—Whether assignments invalid as device to circumvent statutory limitations on investors' claims—Whether fund's liquidators acted outside statutory powers—CPR Practice Direction 7A, para 5A—The Financial Services and Markets Act 2000 (Rights of Action) Regulations 2001, SI 2001/2256, reg 6—Financial Services and Markets Act 2000, ss 138D, 150—Insolvency Act 1986, Sch 4, paras 4, 7, 13. **Connaught Income Fund, Series 1 (in liquidation) v Capita Financial Managers Ltd** [2015] **1 Comm** 751, QBD.
    Partnership. *See* **Partnership** (Dissolution).
    Pension scheme. *See* **Pension** (Pension scheme—Company pension scheme—Winding up).
    Registered trade union. *See* **Trade union** (Dissolution—Registered trade union).
    Unincorporated association. *See* **Unincorporated association** (Dissolution).

WINDOW CLEANER
    Safe system of working. *See* **Safe system of working** (Reasonable care not to expose employee to unnecessary risk—Window cleaner).

WINDWARD AND LEEWARD ISLANDS
    Conflict of laws—
        Succession—
            Immovable property in British Virgin Islands—Testator domiciled in Danish Virgin Islands leaving joint will in accordance with Danish law of community of property—Whether will effective in regard to land in British territory or whether land passed on intestacy—Effect of absence of evidence of extra-territoriality of Danish law of community. **Callwood v Callwood** [1960] **2** 1, PC.

WINE
    Importation—
        European Community restrictions. *See* **European Union** (Imports—Prohibition on imports—Quantitative restrictions on imports from another member state—Measures having equivalent effect—Importation of wine).

WINE BAR
    Sex discrimination—
        Provision of goods, facilities or services. *See* **Sex discrimination** (Provision of goods, facilities or services—Serving drinks at wine bar).

WINNINGS
    Recovery. *See* **Gaming** (Winnings—Recovery).

WIRELESS
    Broadcasting—
        Broadcasting without licence—
            Using wireless telegraphy apparatus without licence—Use—Wireless Telegraphy Act 1949, s 1(1). **Rudd v Secretary of State for Trade and Industry** [1987] **2** 553, HL.
            Using wireless telegraphy station without licence—Defendant unaware he was transmitting—Whether offence of strict liability—Whether presumption that mens rea required displaced—Wireless Telegraphy Act 1949, s 1(1). **R v Blake** [1997] **1** 963, CA.
            Wireless telegraphy apparatus—Whether records and cassettes used for broadcasting constituting wireless telegraphy apparatus—Whether records and cassettes liable to forfeiture if offence of using wireless telegraphy apparatus without licence committed—Wireless Telegraphy Act 1949, s 14(3). **Rudd v Secretary of State for Trade and Industry** [1987] **2** 553, HL.
        Government control. *See* **Broadcasting** (Government control over broadcasting).
        Political advertising—
            Radio Authority ban on political advertising—Judicial review of Radio Authority decision. *See* **Judicial review** (Radio Authority—Ban on political advertising).
        Territorial waters—
            Jurisdiction of magistrates. *See* **Magistrates** (Jurisdiction—Implied jurisdiction from enactment creating offence—Territorial waters).
    Licence—
        Generally. *See* **Telegraphs etc** (Wireless—Licence).
        Revocation—
            Statutory power to revoke licence—Misuse of power. *See* **Public authority** (Statutory powers—Misuse of powers—Exercise of power for unlawful purpose—Validity—Licence—Power to revoke licence—Threat to exercise power for unlawful purpose—Wireless telegraphy—Broadcast receiving licence).

WITCHCRAFT
    See **Criminal law** (Witchcraft).

WITHOUT NOTICE ORDER
    Family Division—
        Practice. *See* **Practice** (Family Division—Without notice order).

WITHOUT PREJUDICE
    Correspondence—
        Admissibility in evidence. *See* **Evidence** (Without prejudice correspondence).
        Judge—
            Natural justice. *See* **Natural justice** (Judge—'Without prejudice' correspondence).

WITHOUT PREJUDICE (cont)—
Offer to submit to injunction—
Effect of offer on court's discretion as to costs. *See* **Compromise** (Offer made before hearing—Injunction).
Without prejudice negotiations—
Admissibility in evidence. *See* **Evidence** (Without prejudice negotiations).
Disclosure of documents—
Privilege. *See* **Disclosure and inspection of documents** (Legal professional privilege—Negotiations without prejudice—Document obtained as result of negotiations).
Evidence. *See* **Evidence** (Without prejudice negotiations).
Land—
Acknowledgment of title. *See* **Limitation of action** (Land—Adverse possession—Acknowledgment of title).

WITNESS
Affirmation by. *See* **Evidence** (Witness—Affirmation).
Attendance—
Attendance fee. *See* **Evidence** (Witness—Fee for attendance).
Illness—
Adjournment of proceedings. *See* **Practice** (Adjournment of proceedings—Dealing with cases justly).
Local government audit—
Power to compel attendance. *See* **Local government** (Audit—Production of and declarations as to documents—Statutory power of district auditor to compel witness to attend audit).
Tribunal—
Power of High Court to aid tribunal by issuing subpoena ad testificandum—Exercise of power—Police disciplinary hearing—Subpoenas ad testificandum issued by High Court to compel attendance of non-police witnesses at hearing—Whether High Court power exercisable—Whether disciplinary hearing quasi-judicial or merely administrative—Whether disciplinary hearing having insufficient power to compel attendance of non-police witness—Whether absence of power to administer oath to witness altering character of tribunal or making it inappropriate for High Court to issue a subpoena ad testificandum—Police (Discipline) Regulations 1977 (1977 No 580), reg 12(2), (3). **Currie v Chief Constable of Surrey** [1982] **1** 89, QBD.
Bribery—
Conspiracy to bribe witness. *See* **Criminal law** (Conspiracy—Obstruction of course of justice—Bribery of witness).
Calling at criminal trial—
Authority of counsel. *See* **Criminal law** (Trial—Witnesses—Calling of witnesses—Authority of counsel).
Calling by court—
Committal proceedings for civil contempt, in. *See* **Contempt of court** (Committal—Evidence—Witness).
Calling witnesses at trial of civil suit—
Sequence—
Right of counsel to call witnesses in sequence chosen by him. *See* **Counsel** (Authority—Authority in respect of witnesses—Right to call witnesses in sequence chosen by him).
Character—
Imputation on character. *See* **Criminal evidence** (Character of accused—Imputation on character of prosecutor or witness).
Child—
Civil proceedings—
Hearsay evidence. *See* **Evidence** (Hearsay—Child).
Criminal proceedings. *See* **Criminal evidence** (Child).
Committal proceedings. *See* **Criminal law** (Committal—Preliminary hearing before justices—Prima facie case—Evidence—Witnesses).
Compellability—
Criminal proceedings. *See* **Criminal evidence** (Compellability as witness).
Expert witness. *See* **Evidence** (Expert witness—Compellability).
Competence—
Civil proceedings. *See* **Evidence** (Witness—Competency).
Criminal proceedings. *See* **Criminal evidence** (Competence as witness).
Conviction—
Admission as evidence in civil proceedings. *See* **Evidence** (Conviction—Admission as evidence in civil proceedings—Witness—Evidence of conviction of witness).
Costs—
Criminal cases—
Award of costs out of central funds. *See* **Criminal law** (Costs—Power to award costs—Award out of central funds).
Court of Appeal—
Criminal appeal—
Examination of witnesses. *See* **Criminal law** (Court of Appeal—Examination of witnesses).
Witness speaking to juror. *See* **Contempt of court** (Criminal contempt—Jurisdiction—Summary committal—Witness speaking during trial to juror about defendant).
Criminal evidence. *See* **Criminal evidence** (Witness).
Criminal trial—
Generally. *See* **Criminal law** (Trial—Witnesses).
Cross-examination—
Criminal proceedings—
Co-accused. *See* **Criminal evidence** (Co-accused—Cross-examination).
Generally. *See* **Practice** (Cross-examination).
Deceased witness—
Admissibility of statement made by witness who subsequently died—Criminal proceedings. *See* **Criminal evidence** (Evidence of deceased witness).

WITNESS (cont)—
    Overseas—
        Admission of documentary statement by person beyond the seas. *See* **Document** (Admissibility in evidence—Admission of documentary statement without calling maker—Person beyond the seas).
    Perjury—
        Criminal liability. *See* **Criminal law** (Perjury).
        Lawfully sworn as a witness. *See* **Criminal law** (Perjury—Lawfully sworn as a witness).
    Presence in court during examination of earlier witnesses—
        Discretion of court to allow—
            Exercise of discretion—Judge allowing presence of witnesses—Not contrary to natural justice. **Moore v Registrar of Lambeth County Court** [1969] **1** 782, CA.
            Exercise of discretion—Magistrates' court—Matrimonial proceedings—Magistrates' Courts Act 1952, s 57. **Tomlinson v Tomlinson** [1980] **1** 593, Fam D.
            Exercise of discretion—Whether presence of witness contrary to natural justice. **Moore v Registrar of Lambeth County Court** [1969] **1** 782, CA.
    Privilege—
        Immunity from civil action. *See* **Action** (Immunity from suit—Witness).
        Self-incrimination. *See* **Evidence** (Privilege—Incrimination of witness or spouse).
    Probate proceedings. *See* **Probate** (Action—Witness).
    Prosecution witnesses—
        Generally. *See* **Criminal law** (Trial—Prosecution—Witnesses).
        Palestine. *See* **Palestine** (Criminal law—Prosecution witnesses).
    Refreshing memory—
        Criminal proceedings. *See* **Criminal evidence** (Witness—Refreshing memory).
    Sequence in which witnesses called—
        Right of counsel to call witnesses in sequence chosen by him. *See* **Counsel** (Authority—Authority in respect of witnesses—Right to call witnesses in sequence chosen by him).
    Spouse—
        Compellability as witness for prosecution. *See* **Criminal evidence** (Compellability as witness—Spouse as witness for prosecution).
        Divorced spouse—
            Competence as witness for prosecution. *See* **Criminal evidence** (Competence as witness—Divorced spouse as witness for prosecution).
    Subpoena ad testificandum. *See* **Practice** (Subpoena ad testificandum).
    Subpoena duces tecum. *See* **Practice** (Subpoena duces tecum).
    Summoning of witnesses—
        General Commissioners of Income Tax. *See* **Income tax** (General Commissioners—Power to summon witnesses).
    Summons—
        County court. *See* **County court** (Witness summons).
        Criminal cases—
            Appeal against summons—Whether summons an order in a 'criminal cause or matter'. *See* **Criminal law** (Appeal—Criminal cause or matter—Order of Crown Court or High Court—Witness summons in criminal trial).
            Documents, production of. *See* **Criminal evidence** (Witness—Witness summons—Production of documents).
            Generally. *See* **Criminal evidence** (Witness—Witness summons).
        Generally. *See* **Practice** (Witness summons).
        Magistrates' court. *See* **Magistrates** (Witness summons).
    Tribunal—
        Privilege of witness at tribunal inquiry—
            Immunity from civil action. *See* **Action** (Immunity from suit—Witness—Tribunal).
        Right to life. *See* **Tribunal** (Tribunal of inquiry—Witness—Right to life).
        Tribunal of inquiry. *See* **Tribunal** (Tribunal of inquiry—Witness).
    Ward of court—
        Witness in criminal proceedings—
            Evidence. *See* **Criminal evidence** (Child—Ward of court—Witness in criminal proceedings).
            Generally. *See* **Ward of court** (Criminal proceedings—Ward required as witness at criminal trial).
            Whether leave of wardship court required for ward to be called as witness. *See* **Ward of court** (Criminal proceedings—Ward required as witness at criminal trial).
    Will, to. *See* **Will** (Attestation).
    Witness statement—
        Contempt of court. *See* **Contempt of court** (Contempt of court for making false statement in document verified by statement of truth without honest belief in its truth).
    Written statement by—
        Admissibility. *See* **Document** (Admissibility in evidence—Written statement made by witness).
        Generally. *See* **Criminal evidence** (Written statement).

WITNESS LIST
    Chancery Division. *See* **Practice** (Chancery Division—Witness list).

WOMAN
    Discrimination against a woman—
        Employment. *See* **Employment** (Discrimination against a woman).
        Generally. *See* **Sex discrimination**.
    Domestic violence—
        Injunction—
            Exclusion of party from matrimonial home. *See* **Injunction** (Exclusion of party from matrimonial home—County court).
            Molestation. *See* **Injunction** (Molestation—Domestic violence).
    Equality of treatment—
        Employment—
            European Community. *See* **European Union** (Equality of treatment of men and women).

WOMAN (cont)—
Equality of treatment (cont)—
Employment (cont)—
Generally. *See* **Employment** (Equality of treatment of men and women).
Human fertilisation. *See* **Medical treatment** (Human fertilisation).

WOMEN'S AUXILIARY AIR FORCE
Will—
Soldier's or mariner's privileged will—
Actual military service. *See* **Will** (Soldier's or mariner's privileged will—Actual military service—Women's Auxiliary Air Force).

WOODLANDS
Income tax. *See* **Income tax** (Woodlands).

WOODWORKING MACHINERY
Factory, in. *See* **Factory** (Woodworking machinery).

WORK AND LABOUR
Contract of service. *See* **Employment** (Contract of service).
Dock labour scheme. *See* **Employment** (Dock labour scheme).
Duty of employee. *See* **Employment** (Duty of servant).
Essential work. *See* **Essential work**.
European Union. *See* **European Union** (Workers).
Generally. *See* **Employment**.
Immigration detention. *See* **Immigration** (Detention—Work done whilst in detention).
Industrial relations. *See* **Industrial relations**.
Industrial training. *See* **Industrial training**.
Redundancy. *See* **Redundancy**.
Right to work—
Monopoly control. *See* **Restraint of trade by agreement** (Right to work).
Trade union—
Restraint of trade. *See* **Trade union** (Rules—Validity).
Social security—
Generally. *See* **Social security**.
Trade dispute. *See* **Trade dispute**.
Trade union membership and activities—
Generally. *See* **Trade union**.
Rights of worker as against employer. *See* **Industrial relations** (Trade union membership and activities—Rights of worker as against employer).
Unfair dismissal. *See* **Unfair dismissal**.
'Worker'. *See* **Employment** ('Worker').

WORK IN PROGRESS
Computation of profits—
Income tax—
Accountancy principles. *See* **Income tax** (Computation of profits—Accountancy principles—Work in progress).
Change in method of valuation—Change showing surplus representing anticipated profits of earlier years—Year in which profit arising. *See* **Income tax** (Computation of profits—Year in which profit arising—Change in method of valuation of work in progress showing surplus representing anticipated profits of earlier years).

WORK PERMIT
Racial discrimination—
Employment. *See* **Race relations** (Discrimination—Employment—Work permit).

WORKING CLASSES
Housing—
Back-to-back houses—
Fitness for human habitation. *See* **Housing** (Fitness of property for human habitation—Back-to-back houses intended for working classes).
Generally. *See* **Housing** (Accommodation of working classes).

WORKING CONDITIONS
Equality of treatment of men and women—
European Community. *See* **European Union** (Equality of treatment of men and women—Working conditions).

WORKING DAY
Goods vehicle driver—
Limitation of time on duty—
Length of working day. *See* **Road traffic** (Goods vehicle—Limitation of driver's time on duty—Length of working day).

WORKING FACILITIES
Mines. *See* **Mine** (Grant of working facilities).

WORKING PLACES
Safety of—
Building. *See* **Building** (Working places).
Coal mine, in. *See* **Coal mining** (Statutory duty—Security of road and working place).

WORKING PLACES (cont)—
Safety of (cont)—
Dock. *See* **Dock** (Working place and approach—Statutory duty to maintain with due regard to safety of persons employed).
Generally. *See* **Safe system of working** (Safe place of work).

WORKING TIME
Generally. *See* **Employment** (Working time).
Organisation. *See* **Health and safety at work** (Organisation of working time).
Worker. *See* **Employment** ('Worker'—Working time).

WORKMEN'S COMPENSATION
Alternative remedies—
Election of remedy. *See* Election of remedy, *below*.
Employer's defence to claim for negligence—
Workman's acceptance of compensation—Onus of proof. **Olsen v Magnesium Castings and Products Ltd** [1947] **1** 333, CA.
Remedies both against employer and stranger—
Proceedings against third party—Workman in receipt of full wages—Receipts signed for compensation but no compensation actually paid—Whether action barred—Workmen's Compensation Act 1925, s 30. **Lind v Johnson** [1937] **4** 201, KBD.
Recovery of compensation—Conditional payments by employer—Workman's right of action against third party not to be prejudiced—Repayment if action successful—Payments to be treated as compensation if action failed—Workmen's Compensation Act 1925, s 30(1). **Elligott v Nebbett** [1948] **1** 514, KBD.
Substitution of liability under scheme for liability under statute—
Acceptance by workman of certified scheme—Effect on right to sue independently of Act—Whether workman and dependants precluded from maintaining action by terms of separate contract—Fatal Accidents Act 1846,—Workmen's Compensation Act 1925, ss 29, 31. **Coe v London and North Eastern Rly Co** [1943] **2** 61, CA.
Amount of compensation—
Calculation of weekly payments—
Change in rates of remuneration—Alteration in working hours—Same wage paid for 44 hour week as previously paid for 48 hour week, with same rates of overtime as before—Workmen's Compensation Act 1943, s 6(1). **Railway Executive v Culkin** [1950] **2** 637, HL; **Shaw v Rootes Securities Ltd** [1948] **2** 168, CA.
Change in rates of remuneration—Miner paid a rate per shift—Normal working week reduced from six shifts, paid at rate of 25s per shift, to five consecutive shifts, paid at rate of 25s per shift, with a bonus of 25s if full qualifying five shifts worked—Workmen's Compensation Act 1943, s 6(1). **Dyde v National Coal Board (Stafford Colliery Unit)** [1948] **2** 172, CA.
Computation of workman's average weekly earnings—
Change of grade—Adoption of classification of employees by employers—Workmen's Compensation Act 1925, s 10(i). **Cocker v Sheffield Corp** [1941] **2** 34, CA.
Concurrent contracts of service—Collier acting as sub-check-weighman and collector of union subscriptions—Workmen's Compensation Act 1925, s 10(ii). **Unsworth v Pease & Partners Ltd** [1937] **2** 817, CA.
Concurrent contracts of service—One contract of service where workman is not a 'workman' within the Act—Workmen's Compensation Act 1925, ss 3(2)(e), 10(ii). **McMahon v David Lawson Ltd** [1944] **1** 36, HL.
Shortage of work—Voluntary spreadover agreement—Senior man—Custom for junior workman to be withdrawn first—Rate of remuneration—Workmen's Compensation Act 1925, s 10(i). **Morgan v Tareni Colliery Co Ltd** [1937] **4** 505, CA.
Fatal accident—
Calculation of lump sum—Deduction of weekly payments—Outdoor relief given to deceased workman—Amount not repaid by employers—Claim to deduct amount owing from sum payable to dependant—Weekly payments—Workmen's Compensation Act 1925, ss 8(2)(iii), 41. **Boswell v Partridge, Jones and John Paton Ltd** [1941] **2** 740, CA.
Employment by local authority under scheme for relief of unemployment—Employment for nine weeks—Whether employment casual—Workmen's Compensation Act 1925, ss 8(2), 10. **Summers v Rhondda UDC** [1938] **3** 585, CA.
Partial incapacity—
Calculation of amount workman is earning or is able to earn—Workman voluntarily joining Army—Inclusion of allowances and of family allowance paid direct to wife—Workmen's Compensation Act 1925, s 9(3). **Doncaster Amalgamated Collieries Ltd v Leech** [1941] **2** 7, CA.
Calculation of average weekly earnings before accident—Basis of calculation—Change from full time to half-time during period of 12 months prior to accident—Rate of pay per hour unchanged—No change of grade of employment—Workmen's Compensation Act 1925, ss 9(3), 10(iii). **Wyatt v John Knight Ltd** [1945] **1** 602, CA.
Declaration of liability—Earnings not diminished by injury—Illness causing workman's return to employment in which earnings diminished by injury—Workmen's Compensation Act 1925, ss 1, 9(3)(i). **Everett v Associated Equipment Co Ltd** [1947] **2** 132, CA.
Difference between average pre-accident earnings and amount workman able to earn in suitable employment after accident—Changes in economic position of labour market—Workmen's Compensation Act 1925, s 9(3)(i). **Sharplin v WB Bawn & Co Ltd** [1947] **1** 436, CA.
Difference between average pre-accident earnings and amount workman able to earn in suitable employment after accident—Down-grading of war-time 'dilutee'—Workmen's Compensation Act 1925, s 9(3)(i). **Plater v Consett Iron Co Ltd** [1947] **2** 460, CA.
Difference between average pre-accident earnings and amount workman able to earn in suitable employment after accident—Economic changes arising since accident—Workmen's Compensation Act 1925, s 9(3)(i). **Illston and Robson Ltd v Smith** [1948] **1** 834, HL.

WORKMEN'S COMPENSATION (cont)—
  Dependants entitled to compensation—
    Members of workman's family dependent on the earnings of the workman at the time of his death—
      Fatal accident to workman while temporarily employed as lorry driver—Usual earnings not from
      contracts of employment but from own business of radio engineer—Whether dependants entitled
      to compensation—Dependent upon the earnings of the workman at the time of his
      death—Earnings—Workmen's Compensation Act 1925, ss 1, 3 4(1), 8, 10(i)—Workmen's
      Compensation (Temporary Increases) Act 1943, s 2(2). **Rogers v Henlys Ltd** [1945] **1** 423, CA.
  Election of remedy—
    Claim by workman's solicitor for compensation under Workmen's Compensation Acts—
      Workman not informed of common law remedy—Right to recover damages at common
      law—Workmen's Compensation Act 1925, s 29(1). **Griffiths v Evans** [1953] **2** 1364, CA.
    Claim for damages at common law—
      Failure of claim—Workmen's compensation assessed but no certificate issued—Whether election
      made—Workmen's Compensation Act 1925, s 29(2). **Kennedy v Walker** [1944] **1** 177, CA.
  Receipt of compensation—
    Father acting as son's agent—Request for payments of compensation to son—Workmen's
      Compensation Act 1925, s 29(1). **Deane v H F Edwards & Co Ltd** [1941] **3** 331, CA.
    Infant—Whether contract for infant's benefit—Workmen's Compensation Act 1925, s 29. **Stimson v**
      Standard Telephones & Cables Ltd [1939] **4** 225, CA.
    Knowledge of workman—Receipt signed 'without prejudice'—Onus of proof where unequivocal act
      proved—Workmen's Compensation Act 1925, s 29(1). **Unsworth v Elder Dempster Lines Ltd**
      [1940] **1** 362, CA.
    Knowledge of workman—Workmen's Compensation Act 1925, s 29(1). **Leathley v John Fowler & Co**
      Ltd [1946] **2** 326, CA; **Selwood v Towneley Coal and Fireclay Co Ltd** [1939] **4** 34, CA; **Young v**
      Bristol Aeroplane Co Ltd [1946] **1** 98, HL.
    Notice to employer that payments being received without prejudice—Workmen's Compensation
      Act 1925, s 29(1),(2). **Perkins v Stevenson (Hugh) & Sons Ltd** [1939] **3** 697, CA.
    Recorded agreement for compensation—Benefit of infant—Estoppel by record—Workmen's
      Compensation Act 1925, ss 23, 25(4), 29(1). **Arabian v Tuffnall and Taylor Ltd** [1944] **2** 317, KBD.
  Widow and child dependants—
    Claim by widow under Fatal Accidents Acts and Law Reform (Miscellaneous Provisions) Act
      1934—Claim by child to lump sum and children's allowance under Workmen's Compensation Act
      1925—Workmen's Compensation Act 1925, s 8(1). **London Brick Co Ltd v Robinson** [1943] **1** 23,
      HL.
    Infant dependants claiming compensation—Widow proceeding under Fatal Accidents Act—
      Workmen's Compensation Act 1925, ss 8(3)(ii), 29. **Taylor v Arrol (Sir William) & Co Ltd**
      [1937] **1** 658, KBD.
    Proceedings by children but not by widow of deceased—Amount recoverable by children—
      Workmen's Compensation Act 1925, ss 8, 10, 29(1). **Avery v London and North Eastern Rly Co**
      [1938] **2** 592, HL.
  Employments excluded by statute—
    Fishing crew remunerated mainly by share in profits—
      Mainly—Workmen's Compensation Act 1925, s 35(2). **Miller v Ottilie (owners)** [1944] **1** 277, CA.
  Evidence—
    Injury by accident arising out of and in the course of employment. *See* Injury by accident arising out of
    and in the course of employment—Evidence, *below.*
  Fatal accident—
    Amount of compensation. *See* Amount of compensation—Fatal accident, *above.*
  Form of order—
    Condition to be incorporated in order. *See* Partial incapacity treated as total incapacity—Form of
    order—Condition to be incorporated in order, *below.*
  Indemnity—
    Contractor and sub-contractor—
      Negligence of contractor—Whether negligence of contractor answer to claim for indemnity—
      Workmen's Compensation Act 1925, s 6. **Heywood and Bryett Ltd v A Heywood & Son**
      [1940] **2** 483, CA.
    Employer's claim to indemnity—
      Claim paid—Further claim—Whether res judicata—Workmen's Compensation Act 1925, s 30. **A-G v**
      Arthur Ryan Automobiles Ltd [1938] **1** 361, CA.
      Loan of workman—Employer—Person other than the employer—Workmen's Compensation Act
      1925, ss 5, 30. **A-G v Arthur Ryan Automobiles Ltd** [1938] **1** 361, CA.
    Indemnity to employer by third party causing injury—
      Death of third party—Claim against estate—Workmen's Compensation Act 1925, s 30(2)—Law
      Reform (Miscellaneous Provisions) Act 1934, s 1(3), (4). **Post Office v Official Solicitor**
      [1951] **1** 522, KBD.
  Industrial disease—
    Appeal to medical referee—
      Appeal out of time—Extension of time by registrar—Good cause—Necessity for existence of facts
      showing good cause—Workmen's Compensation Act 1925, s 43—Medical Referees Regulations
      1932 (S R & O 1932 No 960), reg 25. **Conroy v Wilkinson (Thomas) & Sons Ltd** [1938] **1** 668, .
    Cataract—
      Compensation only payable for four months from date of disablement unless workman has
      undergone operation—Proviso enabling arbitrator to continue payments if satisfied on advice of
      medical referee that operation within four months of disablement inadvisable—Power to
      continue payments only exercisable on advice of medical referee—Workmen's Compensation Act
      1925, s 43, Sch I, para 11—Workmen's Compensation (Industrial Diseases) Consolidation Order
      1929, (SR & O 1929 No 2)—Workmen's Compensation (Cataract) Order 1932, (SR & O 1932
      No 424). **Green v Samuel Woodhouse & Sons** [1945] **1** 683, CA.

WORKMEN'S COMPENSATION (cont)—
Industrial disease (cont)—
Cataract (cont)—
Compensation only payable for four months from date of disablement unless workman has undergone operation—Proviso enabling arbitrator to continue payments if 'satisfied on the advice of the medical referee that an operation could not for medical reasons be performed within four months'—Could not for medical reasons—Workmen's Compensation Act 1925, s 43, Sch III—Workmen's Compensation (Industrial Diseases) Consolidation Order 1929 (SR & O 1929 No 2), para (3), proviso (a)—Workmen's Compensation (Cataract) Order 1932, (SR & O 1932 No 424). **Skelding v Perrins** [1947] **1** 490, CA.
Certifying surgeon's certificate—
Certificate given after 5th July 1948 in respect of disablement suffered before that date—Workmen's Compensation Act 1925, s 43(1), (2)—National Insurance (Industrial Injuries) Act 1946, s 89(1)(a). **Harris v Rotol Ltd** [1950] **1** 867, CA.
Certificate of disablement given after 5th July 1948—Workman not insured against disease—National Insurance (Industrial Injuries) Act 1946, s 89(1), proviso (a). **Mobberley and Perry Ltd v Holloway** [1951] **2** 627, HL.
Limit to conclusiveness—Whether disease such as could reasonably be attributed to nature of employment—Onus of proof—Workmen's Compensation Act 1925, s 43. **Hopwood v Textile Paper Tube Co Ltd** [1946] **1** 618, CA.
Date of disablement—
Finality of medical referee's certificate on certified matters. **Savage v Nightingale** [1937] **3** 30, CA.
Recovery not complete—Return to former work—Second certificate of disablement but no date of commencement stated—Whether date of second certificate conclusive evidence as to the commencement of the second disablement—Workmen's Compensation Act 1925, s 43. **Walder v Mono Concrete Co Ltd** [1943] **2** 306, CA.
Dermatitis—
Attack before 5th July 1948—Recurrence after that date—Workman insured under National Insurance (Industrial Injuries) Act 1946—Right of workman to workmen's compensation. **Hales v Bolton Leathers Ltd** [1951] **1** 643, HL.
Disease contracted after two months' exposure to liquids capable of producing dermatitis—Workman disabled only for employment in particular process in which disease contracted—Long continued exposure—Right to declaration of liability—Workmen's Compensation (Industrial Diseases) Consolidation Order 1929, (SR & O 1929 No 2), para (2). **Sloman v Harris Lebus (a firm)** [1948] **1** 133, CA.
Disease contracted whilst workman in employment of other employer—
Recovery of contribution from other employer—Meaning of 'other employer'—Coal industry—Nationalisation—Miner suffering from gradual disease—Compensation paid by National Coal Board—Right of board to contribution from miner's employers before nationalisation. **National Coal Board v Amalgamated Anthracite Collieries Ltd** [1951] **1** 844, CA.
Employer from whom compensation recoverable—
Incomplete recovery from disease contracted more than 12 months before date of disablement—Liability of employers within the 12 months—Employment to the nature of which the disease was due—Workmen's Compensation Act 1925, s 43. **Eaton v Wimpey (George) & Co Ltd** [1937] **4** 583, CA.
Injury by accident—
Date of accident—Death of workman without obtaining certificate and while not in receipt of compensation—Whether date of accident date of death—Workmen's Compensation Act 1925, ss 1(1), 43(1)(iii)(a), (2)(b). **Mayer & Sherratt v Co-op Insurance Society Ltd** [1939] **3** 158, CA.
Jurisdiction to award compensation—
False statement in writing by workman that he had not suffered from miner's nystagmus—Payment of compensation with notice that workman had previously suffered—Statutory agreement—Jurisdiction to make award in spite of misrepresentation—Workmen's Compensation Act 1925, ss 21, 23, 43(1)(b). **Pease & Partners Ltd v Birch** [1941] **1** 343, CA.
Likelihood of recurrence of disease—
Workman recovered but liable to a relapse—Whether still incapacitated. **Rees v Powell Duffryn Associated Collieries Ltd** [1938] **1** 743, CA.
Medical referee's certificate—
Variation of certifying surgeon's certificate—Form—'Therefore' used instead of 'thereby'. **Homer v Donisthorpe Colliery Co Ltd** [1936] **3** 534, CA.
Miner's nystagmus—
Disablement—Recovery from disease not complete—Return to former work at higher wages—Cessation of disablement—Workmen's Compensation Act 1925, s 43(1)(a). **Richards v Goskar** [1936] **3** 839, HL.
Order of registrar for reference to medical referee—
Order of judge dismissing appeal therefrom—Whether orders of registrar and judge final or interlocutory—Workmen's Compensation Act 1906, Sch 1 para 15—Workmen's Compensation Act 1923, s 11—Workmen's Compensation Act 1925, ss 17-19—Workmen's Compensation Rules 1913–1924 rr 57, 76—Workmen's Compensation Rules 1926 (SR & O 1926 No 448) r 1(2)—County Court Rules 1903-1922 Ord 12, r 11. **Brown v Sherwood Colliery Co Ltd** [1940] **2** 25, CA.
Pneumoconiosis—
Compensation—Agreement for lump sum in redemption of weekly payments—Registration of memorandum of agreement—Objection by approved society with which workman insured—Duty of registrar—Workmen's Compensation Act 1925, ss 13, 23, 25—Coal Mining Industry (Pneumoconiosis) Compensation Scheme 1943, (SR & O 1943 No 885), paras 4, 14(1). **R v Pontypridd County Court Registrar, ex p National Amalgamated Approved Society** [1948] **1** 218, KBD.
Suspension due to pneumoconiosis—Compensation—Contribution by previous employer to compensation payable by last employer—Recorded agreement by last employer to pay lump sum in lieu of weekly payment payable under Scheme—Liability of previous employer to contribute to lump sum payment—'Compensation'—Coal Mining Industry (Pneumoconiosis) Compensation Scheme 1943, (SR & O 1943 No 885), paras 8, 9(2)(a). **Amalgamated Anthracite Collieries Ltd v Cory Bros Ltd** [1946] **1** 232, CA.

WORKMEN'S COMPENSATION (cont)—
Industrial disease (cont)—
Pneumoconiosis (cont)—
Suspension due to pneumoconiosis—Workman not totally disabled—Rate of compensation payable while workman unable to obtain employment—Workmen's Compensation Act 1925, ss 9, 47—Workmen's Compensation Act 1943, s 1—Coal Mining Industry (Pneumoconiosis) Compensation Scheme 1943, (SR & O 1943 No 885), paras 4, 9. **Poxon v Woolaton Collieries Ltd** [1945] **1** 6, CA.
Proceedings for recovery of compensation—
Time limit—Disability stated to have commenced more than six months before date of certificate—Notice of claim—Whether reasonable cause for failure to make claim within specified period—Workmen's Compensation Act 1925, ss 14(1), 43(1). **Easterling v Peek Frean & Co Ltd** [1938] **1** 674, CA.
Right to compensation—
Notional accident—Total incapacity—Further 'notional accident' during incapacity caused by first 'accident'—Nystagmus followed by pneumoconiosis or silicosis—Partial capacity recovered— Right to compensation in respect of second 'notional accident'—Workmen's Compensation Act 1925, ss 1, 9, 43, 47—Various Industries (Silicosis) Scheme 1931, (SR & O 1931 No 342), para 9(2)(a)—Coal Mining Industry (Pneumoconiosis) Compensation Scheme 1943, (SR & O 1943 No 885), para 9(3). **Amalgamated Anthracite Collieries Ltd v Wilds** [1948] **2** 252, HL.
Widow's claim on workman's death—Certificate by medical referee negativing scheduled disease—Conclusiveness against dependants—Workmen's Compensation Act 1925, s 43(1)(f). **Huxley v Wharncliffe Woodmoor Colliery Co Ltd** [1948] **1** 572, HL.
Silicosis—
Amount of compensation—Partial incapacity from first accident at time of certification of silicosis—Amount of compensation for silicosis—Workmen's Compensation Act 1925, ss 9, 43, 47—Various Industries (Silicosis) Scheme 1931, (SR & O 1931 No 342), paras 5, 8, 9. **Evans v Oakdale Navigation Collieries Ltd (No 2)** [1940] **2** 201, CA.
Application of scheme—Matters for consideration—Authorisation by employers of process employed—Whether workman employed in the process—Various Industries (Silicosis) Scheme 1931, (SR & O 1931 No 342), para 2(viii)(c). **Brownsword v Ley's Malleable Casting Co Ltd** [1948] **1** 119, CA.
Certificate of medical board—Conclusiveness—'Conditions not associated with disease'—Silicosis and Asbestosis (Medical Arrangements) Scheme 1931, arts 3, 5. **Williams v Tredegar Iron and Coal Co Ltd** [1948] **1** 236, CA.
Crushing bricks—Breaking down furnace lining of silica bricks—Various Industries (Silicosis) Scheme 1931, (SR & O 1931 No 342), para 2(viii)(a). **Forster v Llanelly Steel Co (1907) Ltd** [1941] **1** 1, HL.
Process—Any operation underground in any coal-mine—Workman not exposed to dust from silica rock—Various Industries (Silicosis) Scheme 1931, (SR & O 1931 No 342), para 2—Various Industries (Silicosis) Amendment Scheme 1934, (SR & O 1934 No 1155). **Wragg v Samuel Fox & Co Ltd** [1937] **2** 157, HL.
Stonemason—Workman exposed to silica dust from time to time—Whether employed in scheduled process—Successive employers—Whether workman should be directly engaged in a type of work specified in the Scheme—Workmen's Compensation Act 1925, s 47—Various Industries (Silicosis) Scheme 1931, (SR & O 1931 No 342). **Reece v Ministry of Supply and Ministry of Works and Planning** [1945] **1** 239, CA.
Infant—
Election of remedy—
Receipt of compensation. *See* Election of remedy—Receipt of compensation—Infant, *above*.
Review of compensation. *See* Review of compensation—Infant workman, *below*.
Injury by accident arising out of and in the course of employment—
Acceleration of disease by accident—
Evidence—Heart disease—Acceleration due to employment. **Whittle v Ebbw Vale Steel, Iron and Coal Co Ltd** [1936] **2** 1221, CA.
Evidence—Heart disease—Contributing to death of workman—Temporary recovery. **Hilton v Billington and Newton Ltd** [1936] **3** 292, CA.
Evidence—Heart disease—Whether death accelerated by work—Evidence of physiological injury or change due to work. **Oates v Earl Fitzwilliam's Collieries Co** [1939] **2** 498, CA.
Accident happening between spells of duty—
Time between spells except for 45 minutes meal time paid for by employers—Workman proceeding from one point to another—Time and route at workman's discretion—Workman proceeding for purposes of his own—Whether accident arose out of and in the course of the employment. **Edwards v London Passenger Transport Board** [1943] **2** 241, CA.
Act contrary to statutory provision and employers' regulations—
Mineworker riding on tub—Workmen's Compensation Act 1925, s 1(2). **Seviour v Somerset Collieries Ltd** [1940] **1** 649, .
Act deemed to arise out of and in the course of employment—
Act done for the purposes of and in connection with the employer's trade or business—Van-driver leaving van to get intoxicating liquor—Prohibition against consuming intoxicating liquor while on duty—Driver killed while remounting van—Workmen's Compensation Act 1925, s 1(1), (2). **Knowles v Southern Rly Co** [1937] **2** 403, HL.
Permitted act done in manner contrary to regulations—Mineworker riding on limber of tubs—Workmen's Compensation Act 1925, s 1(2). **Riley v Wearmouth Coal Co Ltd** [1940] **4** 342, CA.
Railway employee killed while walking along line—Forbidden route—Whether act done for purposes of employers' business—Workmen's Compensation Act 1925, s 1(2). **Noble v Southern Rly Co** [1940] **2** 383, HL.
Act done in emergency—
No great danger—Stoppage of employers' work. **Dermody v Higgs and Hill Ltd** [1937] **4** 379, CA.
Boy employed to repair telephone apparatus—
Condition of employment that he should attend gymnasium class—Accident while attending class. **Lucas v Postmaster-General** [1939] **3** 660, CA.

Injury by accident arising out of and in the course of employment (cont)—
   Canteen on same premises as factory—
      Workmen permitted but not compelled to use canteen—Workman injured by dart while in canteen—Whether accident arising out of and in the course of his employment. **Knight v Howard Wall Ltd** [1938] **4** 667, CA.
   Coal mine—
      Hauling coal—Hauling divided into four operations—One operation allotted to each of four boys—Allocation of operations altered from time to time—Applicant injured while performing operation not allotted to him—Whether applicant acting within the scope of his employment—Workmen's Compensation Act 1925, s 1(2). **Hawker v Doncaster Amalgamated Collieries Ltd** [1938] **4** 577, CA.
   Commencement of employment—
      Accident on way to work—Contractual obligation to proceed by most expeditious route—Workmen's Compensation Act 1925, s 1(1). **Dunn v Lockwood (AG) & Co** [1947] **1** 446, CA.
      Accident on way to work—Emergency work—Payment commencing from time of leaving home—Workmen's Compensation Act 1925, s 1(1). **Blee v London and North Eastern Rly Co** [1937] **4** 270, HL.
      Accident on way to work—Private halt owned by railway but completely enclosed by colliery premises—Collier injured while boarding train—No duty or obligation to use train—Workmen's Compensation Act 1925, s 1(1). **Weaver v Tredegar Iron and Coal Co Ltd** [1940] **3** 157, HL.
      Accident within company's premises—Workman on way to 'clock in' before starting work—Accident where public allowed to cross company's premises, although no right of way—Workmen's Compensation Act 1925, s 1(1). **Hill v Butterley Co Ltd** [1948] **1** 233, CA.
   Death due to burns—
      Bottle of petrol accidentally dropped near fire—Act not prohibited—Whether act arising out of employment—Workmen's Compensation Act 1925, s 1(1). **Blanning v Bailey (CH) Ltd** [1942] **2** 562, CA.
   Disease as injury caused by accident—
      Succession of accidental injuries—Cumulative effect—Vibrations caused by rapidly rotating instrument—Raynaud's disease. **Fitzsimons v Ford Motor Co Ltd (Aero Engines)** [1946] **1** 429, CA.
   Domestic servant taking master's tea to field—
      Riding horse back to farm—Injuries received when horse bolted—Whether accident arose out of employment—Workmen's Compensation Act 1925, s 1(1). **Scott v Seymour** [1941] **2** 717, CA.
   Driver of tractor to which scraper was attached—
      Injury arising from adjusting a defect in the scraper—No prohibition or instruction from employers as to workman's duty regarding adjustment—Dangerous act for purposes of employer's trade or business—Whether risk incidental to employment—Workmen's Compensation Act 1925, s 1(1), (2). **Slavin v AM Carmichael & Co Ltd** [1945] **1** 292, HL.
   Epileptic riding bicycle on employer's business—
      Accident resulting from epileptic fit—Injuries sustained from falling off bicycle—Whether accident arising out of employment. **Martin v Finch** [1937] **2** 631, CA.
   Evidence—
      No evidence of cause of accident—Compensation paid after notice of accident—Whether payments evidence that accident happened in course of employment. **Way v Penrikyber Navigation Colliery Co Ltd** [1940] **1** 164, CA.
      No evidence of cause of injury—Reasonable inference—Delay in notice of accident—Reasonable cause—Workmen's Compensation Act 1925, ss 1(1), 14. **Ellison v Calvert and Heald** [1936] **3** 467, HL.
   External event—
      Need for—Death of worker on way to work due to auricular fibrillation—Whether need for external event—Workers' Compensation Act 1928 (Victoria) (No 3806 of 1928), s 5(1), as amended by Workers' Compensation Act 1946, (Victoria) (No 5128 of 1946), s 3. **Patrick (James) & Co Pty Ltd v Sharpe** [1954] **3** 216, PC.
   Interruption of employment—
      Railwayman in lodgings away from home—Accident between lodgings and railway station—Workmen's Compensation Act 1925, s 1. **Alderman v Great Western Rly Co** [1937] **2** 408, HL.
   Meaning of accident—
      Continuous process—Diseased hip caused by working pneumatic drill—Process extending over 20 years—Workmen's Compensation Act 1925, s 1(1). **Roberts v Lord Penrhyn** [1949] **1** 891, CA.
      Disease existing before date of incapacity—Workman incapacitated while working as packer—Dropped foot—Loss of power of dorsiflexion—Workmen's Compensation Act 1925, s 1(1). **Fife Coal Co Ltd v Young** [1940] **2** 85, HL.
      Disease of gradual onset—No specific event to which injury referable. **Ormond v Holmes (C D) & Co Ltd** [1937] **2** 795, CA.
      Epileptic drowned—No danger to normal healthy person—Disease not sole cause of death—Workmen's Compensation Act 1925, s 1(1). **Wilson v Chatterton** [1946] **1** 431, CA.
      Incapacity due to hernia—Existing condition aggravated by use of pneumatic drill—Cumulative effect. **Hughes v Lancaster Steam Coal Collieries Ltd** [1947] **2** 556, CA.
      Tuberculosis—Hospital nurse subjected to repeated attacks of tuberculosis germs—Whether 'injury by accident'—Workmen's Compensation Act 1925, s 1(1). **Pyrah v Doncaster Corp** [1949] **1** 883, CA.
   Novus actus interveniens—
      Defective medical treatment—Injury not discovered until too late for successful treatment—Incapacity due to defective medical treatment—Workman not entitled to compensation—Workmen's Compensation Act 1925, ss 9(1), 12(3), 19(4). **Rothwell v Caverswall Stone Co Ltd** [1944] **2** 350, CA.
   Onus of proof—
      Disease due to silica dust—Workers' Compensation Act 1926-1929, ss 5-7 (New South Wales). **Metropolitan Coal Co Ltd v Pye** [1936] **1** 919, PC.
      Explosion of firedamp in mine—Cause of ignition of firedamp inexplicable—Workmen's Compensation Act 1925, s 1. **Cadzow Coal Co Ltd v Price** [1944] **1** 54, HL.

WORKMEN'S COMPENSATION (cont)—
Injury by accident arising out of and in the course of employment (cont)—
Proof of accident—
Unexplained death—Night watchman found gassed—Workmen's Compensation Act 1925, s 1(1). **Alexander v Dickinson (J) & Son Ltd** [1939] **3** 204, CA.
Risk attaching to particular locality—
Engine fireman hit by pellet from airgun aimed at engine. **Powell v Great Western Rly Co** [1940] **1** 87, CA.
Sailor—
Return to ship after shore leave—Fall from mole—Police stationed at entrance to mole, but public allowed entry—Workmen's Compensation Act 1925, s 1(1). **Jenkins v Elder Dempster Lines Ltd** [1953] **2** 1133, CA.
Ship sent to mosquito-infested area—Death from yellow-fever and/or malaria—Dangerous locality—Whether death due to injury arising out of his employment—Workmen's Compensation Act 1925, s 1(1). **Dover Navigation Co v Craig** [1939] **4** 558, HL.
Servant delivering petrol at garage—
Servant throwing away lighted match after lighting cigarette—Whether act done in the course of his employment. **Century Insurance Co Ltd v Northern Ireland Road Transport Board** [1942] **1** 491, HL.
Silicosis—
Slate worker—Injury to lungs by inhalation of dust—Continuous process extending over a period of time—Workmen's Compensation Act 1925, s 1(1). **Roberts v Dorothea Slate Quarries Co Ltd** [1948] **2** 201, HL.
Worker developing silicosis long after she left employment—Compensation not payable for silicosis at date of worker leaving employment—Later Act providing that compensation to be payable in respect of silicosis due to nature of employment 'at any time' prior to disablement—Victoria Workers Compensation Act 1951 (No 5601), s 12(1). **Sunshine Porcelain Potteries Pty Ltd v Nash** [1961] **3** 203, PC.
Termination of employment—
Accident occurring after termination of employment—Custom for workmen arriving late to be replaced by others—Whether accident arising out of and in the course of employment—Workmen's Compensation Act 1925, s 1(1). **M'Garvey v Caledonia Stevedoring Co Ltd** [1943] **1** 611, HL.
Painter employed by contractor on outlying work—Place of work 11 miles from workman's home—Travelling allowance paid in addition to remuneration—Workman fatally injured while riding home after finishing work—Journeys of workman not forming part of his service—Accident not arising out of and in the course of employment. **Netherton v Coles** [1945] **1** 227, CA.
Workman adjusting defective machinery in motion in contravention of regulation—
Dangerous act for purposes of employers' trade or business—Whether accident arising out of and in course of employment—Workmen's Compensation Act 1925, s 1(1)(2). **Victoria Spinning Co (Rochdale) Ltd v Matthews** [1936] **2** 1359, HL.
Workman at place of employment in time of danger—
Fellow employee tampering with shell from enemy aeroplane—Employees forbidden to do anything but clearing away—Workmen's Compensation Act 1925, s 1(1). **Smith v Davey Paxman & Co (Colchester) Ltd** [1943] **1** 286, CA.
Workman drying leggings—
Permitted act—Act done rashly—Added peril—Whether act arising out of the employment—Workmen's Compensation Act 1925, s 1(1). **Harris v Associated Portland Cement Manufacturers Ltd** [1938] **4** 831, HL.
Workman going to employers' pay office to draw pay—
Jumping on passing lorry—Collision between lorry and trucks—Workmen's Compensation Act 1925, s 1(1). **Campbell v Proud's Engineering Co Ltd** [1947] **2** 97, CA.
Insolvency of employer—
Liability of insurers to workman—
Mutual indemnity society—Non-payment of calls—Workmen's Compensation Act 1925, s 7. **Wooding v Monmouthshire and South Wales Mutual Indemnity Society Ltd** [1939] **4** 570, HL.
Notional accident—
Right to compensation. *See* Industrial disease—Right to compensation—Notional accident, *above*.
Novus actus interveniens—
Defective medical treatment. *See* Injury by accident arising out of and in the course of employment—Novus actus interveniens—Defective medical treatment, *above*.
Partial incapacity—
Amount of compensation. *See* Amount of compensation—Partial incapacity, *above*.
Partial incapacity treated as total incapacity. *See* Partial incapacity treated as total incapacity, *below*.
Partial incapacity treated as total incapacity—
Circumstances in which permissible—
Fitness of workman for light work only—Workmen's Compensation Act 1925, s 9(4)—Workmen's Compensation Act 1931, s 1(1). **Addie (Robert) & Sons Collieries Ltd v McCracken** [1936] **3** 1039, HL.
Where probable workman would but for continuing effects of injury be able to obtain 'work in the same grade in the same class of employment as before the accident'—Whether employment other than employment at time of accident included—Workmen's Compensation Act 1925, s 9(4)—Workmen's Compensation Act 1931, s 1(1). **Palmer v Watts, Watts & Co Ltd** [1937] **3** 241, CA.
Workman never unfit for any kind of work—Necessity for previous total incapacity—Workmen's Compensation Act 1925, s 9(4)—Workmen's Compensation Act 1931, s 1—Coal Mining Industry (Pneumoconiosis) Compensation Scheme 1943 (SR & O 1943 No 885), para 9(2). **James v Amalgamated Anthracite Collieries Ltd** [1945] **2** 584, CA.
Form of order—
Condition to be incorporated in order—Wording of condition—Workmen's Compensation Act 1925, s 9(4)—Workmen's Compensation Act 1931, s 1. **Dan and Stone Ltd v Lennard** [1941] **1** 101, CA.

WORKMEN'S COMPENSATION (cont)—
Partial incapacity treated as total incapacity (cont)—
Inability to obtain employment—
Complete recovery from injury—Refusal of employers to employ man previously injured—Inability to obtain employment due to accident—Workmen's Compensation Act 1925, s 9. **White v Pickersgill (William) & Sons Ltd** [1941] 2 656, CA.
Contract of employment terminated—Probability of obtaining same class of work as before—Workmen's Compensation Act 1925, s 9(4)—Workmen's Compensation Act 1931, s 1. **Ebbw Vale Steel, Iron and Coal Co Ltd v Williams** [1936] 1 835, CA.
Steps taken to obtain employment—Whether all reasonable steps taken—Whether onus of proof on employer or on workman—Workmen's Compensation Act 1925, s 9(4)—Workmen's Compensation Act 1931, s 1(1). **McLaughlin v Caledonia Stevedoring Co Ltd** [1938] 3 72, HL.
Redemption of weekly payment—
Agreement both to provide work and to pay compensation—
Basis of redemption. **Pick v Paling** [1936] 2 1291, CA.
Payment continued for six months—
Amount of payment varied within the six months—Whether redemption available—Workmen's Compensation Act 1925, s 13. **Davis v Cambrian Wagon Works Ltd** [1941] 1 460, CA.
Reference to medical referee—
Application for reference—
Consideration by registrar of medical reports not submitted to other side—Whether registrar can consider such reports—Workmen's Compensation Act 1925, ss 12(3), 19(2)—Workmen's Compensation Rules 1926 (S R & O 1926 No 448), r 57(2)—County Court Rules 1936, Ord 13, r 1. **Llay Main Collieries Ltd v Jones** [1939] 1 8, CA.
Previous medical referee no longer available—Exceptional difficulty—Medical certificate signed in firm name of a partnership of doctors—Report—Certificate—Workmen's Compensation Act 1925, ss 12(3), 19(2). **Cartwright v Lilleshall Co Ltd** [1937] 4 242, CA.
Medical referee's certificate—
Certificate ambiguous—Whether any unambiguous part conclusive—Whether judge bound to send certificate back for explanation—Workmen's Compensation Act 1925, s 19. **Morgan & Co v Thomas** [1938] 1 696, CA.
Conclusiveness—Certificate of employer's doctor failing to comply with statutory requirements—Imperfect copy—Compliance with statute essential—Effect on conclusiveness of medical referee's certificate—Workmen's Compensation Act 1925, s 12(3). **Hill v Ladyshore Coal Co (1930) Ltd** [1936] 3 299, CA.
Remitted by registrar without consulting parties—Jurisdiction of registrar—Workmen's Compensation Act 1925, s 19(2)—Workmen's Compensation Rules 1926 (SR & O 1926 No 448), r 57. **Burgoyne v Rose Bridge Colliery Co Ltd** [1936] 1 743, CA.
Workman wholly recovered from injury by accident but unfit for ordinary work—Further reference to referee as to whether condition attributable to accident—Report that condition not attributable to accident—Whether arbitrator justified in ending compensation—Workmen's Compensation Act 1925, s 19(2), (3), (4). **Addie (Robert) & Sons Collieries Ltd v McAllister** [1937] 1 676, HL.
Review of compensation—
Applicability of Limitation Act 1939—
Claim made under the Workmen's Compensation Act 1906—Workmen's Compensation Act 1906, Sch I, para 16—Limitation Act 1939, s 2(2)(d), (3). **Leivers v Barber Walker & Co Ltd** [1943] 1 386, CA.
Application for review—
Admission that incapacity due to accident—Declaration of liability—Evidence that incapacity would have been the same even if there had been no accident—Whether right to review barred. **London Power Co Ltd v Lamb** [1936] 3 392, CA.
Voluntary payment of compensation—Notice to reduce—No counter-notice—Reduced payments accepted for six months without complaint—Implied agreement—Application for review treated as original application for arbitration—Workmen's Compensation Act 1925, ss 11, 12, 21. **Harding v Waters (H & E) Ltd** [1936] 3 891, CA.
Change of circumstances—
What constitutes a 'change of circumstances'—Workmen's Compensation Act 1925, s 11. **Ramsay v Gramophone Co Ltd** [1936] 2 752, CA.
Fluctuation in rates of remuneration—
Claims based on rises of more than 20 per cent in rates of remuneration during the 12 months immediately preceding the review—Whether the date at which 'review' takes place is date of right accruing or date of application for variation—Workmen's Compensation Act 1925, s 11(2), (3). **Willis v New Hucknall Colliery Co Ltd** [1944] 1 209, HL.
Increase in basic rate of wages—Increase of more than 20 per cent—Poundage—Increase in total amount of poundage but not in rate of poundage—Workmen's Compensation Act 1925, s 11(3). **Trawlers (Grimsby) Ltd v Crouchen** [1943] 1 253, CA.
Increase in basic rate of wages—Increase of more than 20 per cent—Whether fact that less work available should be considered—Workmen's Compensation Act 1925, s 11(3). **Hill v Wolverhampton Corrugated Iron Co Ltd** [1939] 3 72, CA.
Increase in basic rate of wages—Increase of more than 20 per cent—Whether 'risk rate' should be considered—Workmen's Compensation Act 1925, s 11(3). **Shirley v Fisher Renwick Ltd** [1943] 1 262, CA.
Workman entitled to compensation under 1897 Act—Review on fluctuation in wage rates—Workmen's Compensation Act 1925, ss 11(3), 50(2). **Mullet v Powell Duffryn Associated Collieries Ltd** [1943] 2 281, CA.
Infant workman—
Fluctuation in rates of remuneration—Fluctuation of more than 20 per cent since 12 months previous to review—Whether review includes review upon infant attaining full age—Workmen's Compensation Act 1925, s 11(2), (3). **Potts v Pope and Pearson Ltd** [1940] 2 263, CA.
Time within which application must be made—Meaning of 'review'—Change in probable earnings at a date later than application but prior to hearing—Workmen's Compensation Act 1925, s 11(2)—Workmen's Compensation Act 1926, s 1. **Dobson Ship Repairing Co v Burton** [1939] 3 431, HL.

WORKMEN'S COMPENSATION (cont)—
Review of compensation (cont)—
Partial incapacity treated as total incapacity—
Failure to take reasonable steps to find employment—Change of circumstances—Workmen's Compensation Act 1931, s 1. **United Dairies (London) Ltd v Stirling** [1936] **3** 272, CA.
Right to compensation—
Incapacity for work resulting from injury—
Injured workman called up for military service—Pay and allowances in army less than pre-accident wages—Whether inability to earn pre-accident wages due to injury—Whether entitled to compensation—Workmen's Compensation Act 1925, s 9(3)(i)—National Service (Armed Forces) Act 1939. **Jones v Amalgamated Anthracite Collieries Ltd** [1944] **1** 1, HL.
Loss of finger—Workman employed after accident at former work for 13 years at former rate of wages—Illness not due to employment preventing workman from working—No evidence of seeking to obtain work—Workmen's Compensation Act 1925, s 9(1). **Parr v Haworth (Richard) & Co Ltd** [1940] **3** 43, CA.
Novus actus interveniens—Improper medical treatment—Ill-advised operation on injured thumb—Incapacity due to tender stump—Workmen's Compensation Act 1925, s 9(1). **Hogan v Bentinck West Hartley Collieries (owners) Ltd** [1949] **1** 588, HL.
Injury by accident arising out of and in the course of employment. *See* Injury by accident arising out of and in the course of employment, *above*.
Statute abolishing right to compensation. *See* **Industrial injury** (Workmen's compensation—Right to compensation—Statute abolishing right).
Two accidents—
Total incapacity from first accident—Second accident supervening—Right to compensation for second accident. **Wheatley v Lambton, Hetton & Joicey Collieries Ltd** [1937] **2** 756, CA.
Termination of compensation—
Incapacity for work resulting from refusal of workman to undergo operation—
Reasonableness of refusal—Operation necessitating provision of artificial limb. **Redpath, Brown & Co Ltd v Hayes** [1942] **1** 298, CA.
Reasonableness of refusal—Question of fact. **Steele v George (Robert) & Co Ltd** [1942] **1** 447, HL.
Reasonableness of refusal—Question of fact—Private examination and report by medical assessor—Functions of medical assessor sitting with arbitrator. **Richardson v Redpath, Brown & Co Ltd** [1944] **1** 110, HL.
Whether incapacity due to accident or to refusal to undergo surgical operation—Absence of request by employers—Unreasonable conduct. **Purvis v Goole Steam Shipping (London, Midland and Scottish Rly)** [1937] **4** 345, CA.
Objection by workman—
Reference to medical referee—Medical referee's certificate—Interpretation by registrar—Arbitration proceedings started by workman—Jurisdiction of judge to entertain pending decision by registrar—Workmen's Compensation Act 1925, ss 12(3), 19(2). **Starkey v Whitwich Colliery Co Ltd** [1947] **1** 464, CA.
Two accidents—
Amount of compensation. *See* Amount of compensation—Two accidents, *above*.
Right to compensation. *See* Right to compensation—Two accidents, *above*.
Victoria. *See* **Victoria** (Worker's compensation).
Voluntary payment of compensation—
Application for review. *See* Review of compensation—Application for review—Voluntary payment of compensation, *above*.
Workman—
Person who enters into or works under contract of service with employer—
Farmer—Deed of assignment for benefit of creditors—Trustee appointed by creditors—Farmer continuing to manage farm—Accident—Whether contract of service with trustee—Workmen's Compensation Act 1925, s 3(1). **Easdown v Cobb** [1940] **1** 49, HL.
Governing director of company—Director exercising full and unrestricted control of company's affairs but also working for company as pilot and being paid wages—Death of governing director while acting as pilot on company's business—Whether contract of service with company—New Zealand Workers' Compensation Act 1922, (1922, No 39), s 2. **Lee v Lee's Air Farming Ltd** [1960] **3** 420, PC.
Hospital nurse—Injury while preparing a poultice—Whether working under a contract of service—Workmen's Compensation Act 1925, s 3. **Wardell v Kent CC** [1938] **3** 473, CA.
Salvation Army officer—Whether a 'workman'—Workmen's Compensation Act 1925, s 3. **Rogers v Booth** [1937] **2** 751, CA.

WORKROOM
Factory—
Ventilation. *See* **Factory** (Ventilation—Workroom).

WORKSHOP
Hospital—
Application of Factories Act 1961 to hospital workshop. *See* **Factory** (Definition—Premises included in definition—Hospital workshop used for repair of hospital equipment).

WORLD TRADE ORGANISATION
European Community—
Enforcement of agreement by. *See* **European Union** (International treaties—World Trade Organisation agreements).

WORLDWIDE MAREVA INJUNCTION
See **Practice** (Pre-trial or post-judgment relief—Freezing order—Worldwide freezing order).

WOUNDING
Generally. *See* **Criminal law** (Wounding).

WOUNDING (cont)—
Intent to cause grievous bodily harm. *See* **Criminal law** (Grievous bodily harm—Wounding with intent to cause grievous bodily harm).

WRECK
Droits of Admiralty. *See* **Admiralty** (Droits of Admiralty—Wreck).
Expenses of raising wreck—
Removal of wreck—
Limitation of liability. *See* **Shipping** (Limitation of liability—Wreck removal—Wreck-raising expenses).
Removal of wreck—
Limitation of liability. *See* **Shipping** (Limitation of liability—Wreck removal).

WRECK COMMISSIONER
Discretion—
Costs—
Collision cases. *See* **Shipping** (Collision—Costs—Discretion of wreck commissioner).

WRIT
Action statute-barred—
Extension of validity. *See* Extension of validity—Action statute-barred, *below.*
Action under Fatal Accidents Acts—
Extension of validity of writ. *See* Extension of validity—Action under Fatal Accidents Acts, *below.*
Additional relief—
Amendment—
Indorsement. *See* Indorsement—Amendment—Additional relief, *below.*
Admiralty—
Action in personam. *See* **Admiralty** (Practice—Action in personam—Writ).
Action in rem. *See* **Admiralty** (Practice—Action in rem—Writ).
Generally. *See* **Admiralty** (Practice—Writ).
Relief sought in rem and in personam. *See* **Admiralty** (Practice—Writ—Relief sought in rem and in personam).
Amendment—
Admiralty action in rem. *See* **Admiralty** (Practice—Action in rem—Writ—Amendment).
Amendment after expiry of limitation period—
Amendment to be allowed if just—RSC Ord 20 r 5(1). **Sterman v EW & WJ Moore Ltd (a firm)** [1970] **1** 581, CA.
Application to disapply limitation period—Application to add additional plaintiff—Whether leave to amend may be given after application to disapply limitation period granted. *See* **Practice** (Parties—Adding plaintiff—Amendment of writ—Application to disapply limitation period).
Bringing in second defendant—Leave to amend within limitation period—Failure to amend within 14 days allowed—Application for extension of time to amend writ after limitation period expired—Refusal of leave for late service—Whether second defendant a party—RSC Ord 15, r 8(4). **Braniff v Holland and Hannen and Cubitts (Southern) Ltd** [1969] **3** 959, CA.
Claim under Fatal Accidents Acts—Widow claiming as administratrix—Writ issued before grant of letters of administration—Decision in Ingall v Moran—Application to amend writ by suing as dependant—Application made after statutory period—Amendment not allowed—Fatal Accidents Act 1846—Fatal Accidents Act 1864—RSC Ord 3, r 4. **Hilton v Sutton Steam Laundry** [1945] **2** 425, CA.
Defendant substituted—Son R S P substituted for father R J P—Limitation period expired—Action for personal injuries in road accident—Genuine mistake and intended defendant not misled—Whether rule of court permitting amendment ultra vires—Whether leave to amend just in the circumstances—Supreme Court of Judicature (Consolidation) Act 1925, s 99(1), Sch 1—RSC Ord 20, r 5. **Rodriguez v Parker** [1966] **2** 349, QBD.
Name of party—Amendment of writ to change defendant 'W J D & Co (a firm)' to 'W J D & Co Ltd'—Whether a correction of a mere misnomer—Whether omission of 'Limited' meant that no person was sued—Amendment sought after limitation period expired. **Whittam v WJ Daniel & Co Ltd** [1961] **3** 796, CA.
Amendment to correct party's name—
Amendment after judgment—Whether court having jurisdiction to allow amendment of writ after final judgment in proceedings—RSC Ord 2, r 1(2), Ord 20, r 5. **Singh v Atombrook Ltd** [1989] **1** 385, CA.
Defect in title—
Failure to indicate Division of High Court—Whether capable of being rectified by amendment—Supreme Court of Judicature (Consolidation) Act 1925, s 58—RSC Ord 2, r 1, Ord 20, rr 1(1), 5. **Brady v Barrow Steelworks Ltd** [1965] **2** 639, QBD.
Indorsement. *See* Indorsement—Amendment, *below.*
New cause of action in statement of claim—
New action statute-barred—New cause of action arising out of substantially the same facts as action in writ—Architect employed on contruction of building—Writ alleging negligence in superintending work—Statement of claim alleging negligence in design and superintendence—Power to amend writ—Exercise of discretion—RSC Ord 18, r 15(2), Ord 20 r 5(1), (5). **Brickfield Properties Ltd v Newton** [1971] **3** 328, CA.
Parties. *See* **Practice** (Parties—Adding defendant—Amendment of writ).
Appearance to—
Admiralty—
Writ in rem. *See* **Admiralty** (Practice—Appearance).
Cause of action—
Statement on indorsement. *See* Indorsement—Cause of action—Statement on indorsement, *below.*
Claim under Fatal Accidents Acts—
Amendment after expiry of limitation period. *See* Amendment—Amendment after expiry of limitation period—Claim under Fatal Accidents Acts, *above.*

WRIT (cont)—

Commercial Court—

Practice. *See* **Commercial Court** (Practice—Writ).

Defect in indorsement. *See* Indorsement—Defect in indorsement, *below.*

Extension of validity—

Action statute-barred—

Discretion to renew writ—Exceptional circumstances justifying exercise of discretion. **Austin Rover Group Ltd v Crouch Butler Savage Associates (a firm)** [1986] **3** 50, CA.

Discretion to renew writ—Good reason for extension—Balance of hardship between parties—Writ issued before action statute-barred but not served—Plaintiff attempting to save costs by not proceeding with action until similar action decided—Whether good reason for extending validity of writ—RSC Ord 6, r 8. **Kleinwort Benson Ltd v Barbrak Ltd** [1987] **2** 289, HL.

Discretion to renew writ—Good reason for extension—Collateral proceedings—Beddoe application—Plaintiff trustees failing to serve writ within period of validity because of need to make Beddoe application to protect their costs—Whether plaintiffs showing good reason for failure to serve writ within period of validity—RSC Ord 6, r 8(2). **Dagnell v J L Freedman & Co (a firm)** [1993] **2** 161, HL.

Discretion to renew writ—Good reason for extension—Writ issued before action statute-barred but not served—Plaintiff relying on obtaining ex parte order for renewal—Plaintiff having sufficient time in which to serve writ during its original validity—Whether sufficient reason shown for failure to serve writ in time—Whether delays caused by operation of legal aid system relevant—Whether balance of hardship relevant in deciding whether to extend validity of writ—RSC Ord 6, r 8. **Waddon v Whitecroft-Scovill Ltd** [1988] **1** 996, HL.

Part of claim statute-barred—Discretion to renew writ—Good reason for extension—Good reason for failure to serve writ within original time-limit—Whether good reason needing to be shown in cases where limitation period not expired—Whether saving costs and serving writ with statement of claim constituting good reason—RSC Ord 6, r 8. **Binning Bros Ltd (in liq) v Thomas Eggar Verrall Bowles (a firm)** [1998] **1** 409, CA.

Writ issued before action statute-barred but not served—Action statute-barred when application for extension made—Whether principle on which renewal of writ granted affected by court's discretion to override primary limitation period—Whether extension of validity can be granted where equitable to do so even though primary limitation period expired—Limitation Act 1939, s 2D (as inserted by the Limitation Act 1975, s 1(1))—RSC Ord 6, r 8(2). **Chappell v Cooper** [1980] **2** 463, CA.

Writ issued before action statute-barred but not served—Application for extension made within 12 months of issue of writ—Burden on applicant to show good cause for extension—Defendants registered company—Service by post at very end of 12 months attempted—Address of registered office of company given by local director of defendants and not completely correct—Copy writ returned undelivered—Legal aid needs not a factor in exercise of discretion to extend validity of writ—RSC Ord 6, r 8(1), (2)—Legal Aid and Advice Act 1949, s 1(7)(b). **Baker v Bowketts Cakes Ltd** [1966] **2** 290, .

Writ issued before action statute-barred but not served—Extension granted within 12 months of issue of writ—Writ served after limitation period had expired—Conditional appearance entered by defendants—Application to set aside service of writ—Burden on applicant to show good cause for renewal of writ—RSC Ord 6, r 8(2). **Stevens v Services Window & General Cleaning Co Ltd** [1967] **1** 984, QBD.

Writ not served—Application for extension made after 12 months' validity had expired and after three years' statutory limitation period on action—Extension not granted in the absence of exceptional circumstances—RSC Ord 6, r 8(1), (2). **Heaven v Road and Rail Wagons Ltd** [1965] **2** 409, QBD.

Writ not served—Application for extension made after 12 months' validity had expired—Whether defendant having arguable case that he would be deprived of limitation defence if writ renewed—Whether special circumstances justifying renewal—RSC Ord 6, r 8(1), (2). **Wilkinson v Ancliff (BLT) Ltd** [1986] **3** 427, CA.

Action time-barred—

Validity of writ for service—Writ served on foreign defendant's London representative outside four-month period—Whether writ valid for service for four or six months—RSC Ord 6, r 8. **Payabi v Armstel Shipping Corp** [1992] **3** 329, QBD.

Action under Fatal Accidents Acts—

Writ issued within 12 months limited by Act—Not served within 12 months of date of issue—Discretion of court to extend time for service—RSC Ord 64, r 7. **Holman v George Elliot & Co Ltd** [1944] **1** 639, CA.

Writ issued within the 12 months limited by Act—Not served within 12 months of date of issue—Discretion of court to extend time for service—RSC Ord 8, rr 1, 2, Ord 64, r 7. **Battersby v Anglo-American Oil Co Ltd** [1944] **2** 387, CA.

Application—

Order for renewal made in absence of application—Validity of order—Application for leave to serve concurrent writ out of jurisdiction—Good and sufficient cause for renewal but no application made—Whether master having power to make order for renewal—RSC Ord 6, r 8(2). **Bugden v Ministry of Defence** [1972] **1** 1, CA.

Discretion—

Failure to serve writ—Exercise of discretion to extend validity of writ—Principles on which discretion to be exercised—RSC Ord 6, r 8(2), (2A). **Singh v Duport Harper Foundries Ltd** [1994] **2** 889, CA.

Failure to renew writ—

Order for substituted service of writ by serving notice of writ made after expiry of validity of writ—Impossibility of extending validity of writ to date of order for substituted service—Whether jurisdiction to cure irregularity—Whether order for substituted service invalid—RSC Ord 2, r 1, Ord 6, r 8. **Bernstein v Jackson** [1982] **2** 806, CA.

WRIT (cont)—
  Extension of validity (cont)—
    Good and sufficient reason for extension—
      Discretion—Balance of hardship between parties—Writ not served within time on one of two defendants—Failure due to reasonable mistake of law by plaintiff's solicitor—Plaintiff clearly entitled to remedy against one or other of defendants—No remedy available on facts against plaintiff's solicitor. **Jones v Jones** [1970] 3 47, CA.
      Negotiations for settlement—Negotiations proceeding when application made to extend validity of writ—Whether negotiations affording sufficient reason for not serving writ within time or for renewal of writ—RSC Ord 6, r 8(2). **Easy v Universal Anchorage Co Ltd** [1974] 2 1105, CA.
      Negotiations for settlement—RSC Ord 8, r 1. **Prins Bernhard, The** [1963] 3 735, Admin Ct.
    Jurisdiction—
      Principles on which renewal granted—Writ issued to prevent Statute of Limitations running—Writ not served on defendants—Application for renewal after expiry of writ—RSC Ord 8, rr 1, Ord 64, 7. **E Ltd v C** [1959] 2 468, Ch D.
    Order for renewal—
      Amendment of order—Action against public authority—Writ issued within time limit—Order for renewal of writ made before writ expired—Seal bearing date of renewal not affixed to writ before writ expired—Jurisdiction of master to amend renewal order—RSC Ord 8, rr 1, 2. **Duchin v Swanage UDC** [1954] 2 817, QBD.
    Overriding time limit—
      Personal injury or fatal accident claim. *See* **Limitation of action** (Court's power to override time limit in personal injury or fatal accident claim—Practice—Application to extend validity of writ).
      Writ issued before action statute-barred but not served. *See* Extension of validity—Action statute-barred, *above*.
  Fatal accident—
    Amendment of writ after expiry of limitation period. *See* Amendment—Amendment after expiry of limitation period—Claim under Fatal Accidents Acts, *above*.
    Extension of validity of writ. *See* Extension of validity—Action under Fatal Accidents Acts, *above*.
    Liability admitted—
      Writ issued more than 12 months after death. *See* **Limitation of action** (Fatal accident).
  Fax—
    Issue of writ by fax—
      Admiralty Court. *See* **Admiralty** (Practice—Writ—Issue—Issue by fax).
      Commercial Court. *See* **Commercial Court** (Practice—Writ—Issue—Issue by fax).
  Fi fa. *See* **Execution** (Writ of fi fa).
  Foreign company—
    Service on company. *See* Service on company—Foreign company, *below*.
  Foreign currency—
    Claim for sum expressed in foreign currency—
      Statement in writ. *See* **Judgment** (Foreign currency—Pleading claims in foreign currency—Statement in writ).
  Foreign defendant—
    Service on defendant when on visit to England—
      Stay of proceedings. *See* **Practice** (Stay of proceedings—Foreign defendant—Writ served on defendant whilst on short visit to England).
  Form of writ—
    Admiralty practice. *See* **Admiralty** (Practice—Form of writs and acknowledgments of service).
  Habeas corpus. *See* **Habeas corpus.**
  Indorsement—
    Amendment—
      Additional relief—Leave given to serve notice out of jurisdiction—Subsequent application to amend writ by claiming additional relief—Additional relief such that leave to serve out of jurisdiction permissible—Additional relief such that leave to serve out of jurisdiction would not have been granted—Whether court having jurisdiction to refuse leave to amend on that ground—RSC Ord 11, r 1(1), Ord 20, r 5(1). **Beck v Value Capital Ltd (No 2)** [1974] 3 442, Ch D.
    Cause of action—
      Statement on indorsement—Whether cause of action should be stated on indorsement—RSC Ord 6, r 2(1). **Sterman v EW & WJ Moore Ltd (a firm)** [1970] 1 581, CA.
    Defect in indorsement—
      Cause of action not disclosed—Irregularity curable by statement of claim—Writ not a nullity—Delay of four months in applying to set aside writ—Whether writ should be set aside—Whether service of writ should be set aside—RSC Ord 70, rr 1, 2. **Pontin v Wood** [1962] 1 294, CA.
      Cure by statement of claim—Effectiveness of writ—Issue of writ within limitation period—Service with statement of claim after expiration of period—Defect in writ cured by statement of claim—Competency of action—Limitation Act 1939, s 21(1). **Hill v Luton Corp** [1951] 1 1028, KBD.
      Cure by statement of claim—Summons to set aside service—Statement of claim delivered after service but before hearing of summons. **Grounsell v Cuthell and Linley** [1952] 2 135, QBD.
      Plaintiff company issuing writ indorsed with name of solicitor—Writ not in fact issued by solicitor or with solicitor's authority or privity—Solicitor making written declaration to that effect—Whether issue and service of writ should be set aside—RSC Ord 5, r 6(2), Ord 6, r 5(4). **Crescent Oil and Shipping Services Ltd v Importang UEE** [1997] 3 428, QBD.
    Personal injuries action. *See* **Practice** (Personal injuries action—Writ—Indorsement).
    Signature—
      Specially indorsed writ—Signed by solicitor—Served copy bearing no signature—Appearance entered—Waiver of defective service by defendant—RSC Ord 3, r 6(1), Ord 14, r 1(a), Ord 19, r 4. **Fick and Fick Ltd v Assimakis** [1958] 3 182, CA.
  Issue—
    Defendant dead at date of issue—
      Effect on proceedings. *See* **Practice** (Parties—Substitution—Action against deceased person—Defendant dead at date of issue of writ—Substitution of executors).

WRIT (cont)—
Issue (cont)—
Delay before issue of writ—
Prejudice to defendant—Dismissal of action for want of prosecution. *See* **Practice** (Dismissal of action for want of prosecution—Delay—Prejudice to defendant—Delay before issue of writ).
Fee—
Order increasing fee payable to court for issue of writ—Order repealing earlier provision under which impecunious plaintiffs entitled to exemption from fee—Applicant on income support and unable to afford fee—Order infringing citizens' right of access to courts—Whether order ultra vires legislation conferring power on Lord Chancellor to prescribe court fees—Whether legislation conferring power to abrogate right to access to courts—Supreme Court Act 1981, s 130—Supreme Court Fees (Amendment) Order 1996, art 3. **R v Lord Chancellor, ex p Witham** [1997] **2** 779, QBD.
Issue against member of Parliament. *See* **Parliament** (Privilege—Action against member of Parliament).
Issue out of Central Office—
Application—Application by post—RSC Ord 6. **Practice Direction** [1971] **1** 510, Central Office.
New practice and procedure. *See* **Practice** (Queen's Bench Division and Chancery Division—New practice and procedure).
Time—
Limitation period prescribed by agreement—Contract incorporating Hague Rules—Agreement extending time prescribed by Hague Rules—Agreed period expiring on day court offices closed—Writ issued on first day thereafter that court offices open—Whether writ issued in time—Carriage of Goods by Sea Act 1971, Sch, art 3, r 6. **Clifford Maersk, The** [1982] **3** 905, QBD.
Limitation period prescribed by statute—Period expiring on day court offices closed—Writ issued on first day thereafter that court offices open—Effect—Fatal Accidents Act 1846, s 3, as amended by the Law Reform (Limitation of Actions, etc) Act 1954, s 3—Limitation Act 1939, s 2(1), as amended by the Law Reform (Limitation of Actions, etc) Act 1954, s 2(1). **Pritam Kaur (administratrix of Bikar Singh (decd)) v Russell (S) & Sons Ltd** [1973] **1** 617, CA.
Libel action—
Issue—
Republication of alleged libel—Effect. *See* **Contempt of court** (Republication of alleged libel—Pending proceedings).
Mortgage—
Action commenced by writ—
Judgment in default of appearance. *See* **Mortgage** (Action by mortgagee for possession—Action commenced by writ).
Ne exeat regno. *See* **Equity** (Ne exeat regno).
Negotiations for settlement—
Extension of validity. *See* Extension of validity—Good and sufficient reason for extension—Negotiations for settlement, *above.*
New cause of action in statement of claim. *See* Amendment—New cause of action in statement of claim, *above.*
New form of writ of summons—
Consequential changes in Central office practice—
RSC App A—RSC (Writ and Appearance) 1979 (SI 1979 No 1716), r 49(1). **Practice Direction** [1980] **3** 822, QBD.
Order for renewal—
Amendment of order. *See* Extension of validity—Order for renewal—Amendment of order, *above.*
Originating summons—
Continuation of proceedings as if begun by writ. *See* **Originating summons** (Continuation of proceedings as if begun by writ).
Parties—
Action in name of company incorporated in foreign state—
Liquidation of company by de facto government recognised by British Government—Effect of existence of de jure monarch—Validity of action by person not having authority of liquidator. **Bank of Ethiopia v National Bank of Egypt and Liguori** [1937] **3** 8, Ch D.
Personal injuries action—
Practice. *See* **Practice** (Personal injuries action—Writ).
Possession—
Execution of writ of possession. *See* **Execution** (Possession—Writ of possession).
Leave to issue writ. *See* **Execution** (Possession—Leave to issue writ).
Wrongful and irregular execution. *See* **Execution** (Wrongful and irregular execution—Writ of possession).
Probate—
Issue by registrar. *See* **Probate** (Practice—Writ—Issue of writ).
Renewal—
Admiralty action in personam. *See* **Admiralty** (Practice—Action in personam—Writ—Renewal).
Admiralty action in rem. *See* **Admiralty** (Practice—Action in rem—Writ—Renewal).
Generally. *See* Extension of validity, *above.*
Restitution, of—
Land—
Execution of possession order. *See* **Land** (Summary proceedings for possession—Execution of possession order—Writ of restitution).
Sequestration—
Generally. *See* **Bankruptcy** (Execution—Writ of sequestration).
Position of third parties in relation to writ of sequestration. *See* **Contempt of court** (Sequestration—Position of third parties in relation to writ of sequestration).
Service—
Acknowledgment of service. *See* **Practice** (Acknowledgment of service).
Admiralty action in personam. *See* **Admiralty** (Practice—Action in personam—Writ—Service).
Admiralty action in rem. *See* **Admiralty** (Practice—Action in rem—Writ—Service).

WRIT (cont)—
  Service (cont)—
    Bankruptcy proceedings—
      Service out of the jurisdiction. *See* **Bankruptcy** (Service—Service out of jurisdiction—Writ and motion).
    Foreign defendant—
      Service on defendant when on visit to England—Stay of proceedings. *See* **Practice** (Stay of proceedings—Foreign defendant—Writ served on defendant whilst on short visit to England).
    Generally. *See* **Practice** (Service).
    Oversea company. *See* **Company** (Oversea company—Service on oversea company).
    Partnership. *See* Service on partnership, *below.*
    Service on company. *See* Service on company, *below.*
    Service on foreign company. *See* Service on company—Foreign company, *below.*
    Service out of the jurisdiction—
      Generally. *See* **Practice** (Service out of the jurisdiction).
  Service on company—
    Foreign company—
      Action by Commissioners of Customs and Excise for condemnation of seized goods—Notice of claim by solicitors in London acting on behalf of foreign company—Writ served on solicitors more than a year later—Customs and Excise Act 1952, Sch 7, para 4—RSC Ord 13, r 2. **Customs and Excise Comrs v I F S Irish Fully Fashioned Stockings Ltd** [1957] 1 108, QBD.
      Company having no place of business in Great Britain—Service at address alleged to be former place of business—Validity of service—Companies Act 1948, s 412. **Deverall v Grant Advertising Inc** [1954] 3 389, CA.
      'Oversea company'. *See* **Company** (Oversea company—Service on oversea company).
    Registered office—
      Service at registered office—RSC Ord 67, r 3. **Addis Ltd v Berkeley Supplies Ltd** [1964] 2 753, Ch D.
    Service at company's registered office—
      Failure to serve writ on company at its registered office—Whether failure nullifying proceedings—Whether failure a mere irregularity capable of remedy—Companies Act 1985, s 725(1)—RSC Ord 2, r 1. **Singh v Atombrook Ltd** [1989] 1 385, CA.
    Service by post—
      Date of service—Writ endorsed with claim for liquidated demand—Judgment in default of appearance—Copy of writ not received by company 14 days prior to judgment—Application to set aside judgment—Service deemed to have been effected on date when letter would have been received in ordinary course of post—Date of deemed service 14 days prior to date of judgment—Proof to the contrary—Proof that writ never delivered at company's registered office—Interpretation Act 1889, s 26. **Bishop (Thomas) Ltd v Helmville Ltd** [1972] 1 365, CA.
      Writ not received by company—Judgment in default of appearance—Company having changed address four weeks before issue of writ—Company having failed to notify registrar of companies of new address—Writ sent to address of company's registered office given in companies register—Company not aware of writ until after judgment entered—Whether judgment obtained regularly—Whether company entitled to have judgment set aside ex debito justitiae—Interpretation Act 1889, s 26—Companies Act 1948, s 437(1)—RSC Ord 13, r 9. **Cathrineholm (A/S) v Norequipment Trading Ltd** [1972] 2 538, CA.
      Writ not received by company—Judgment in default of appearance—Writ sent to company's registered office—Envelope containing writ returned through dead letter office marked 'not known' six days after judgment—Whether service of writ bad—Whether company entitled to have judgment set aside without regard to the merits—Interpretation Act 1889, s 26—Companies Act 1948, s 437(1). **Saga of Bond Street Ltd v Avalon Promotions Ltd** [1972] 2 545, CA.
    Service on 'secretary, treasurer or other similar officer'. *See* **Practice** (Service—Service of document on company—Service on 'secretary, treasurer or other similar officer').
  Service on partnership—
    Personal service—
      Service of writ on duly authorised agent of partner—Service on personal assistant of partner—No contract between parties providing for service on personal assistant of partner—Whether effective service on partnership—RSC Ord 10, rr 1(1), 3, Ord 81, r 3(1)(a). **Allison (Kenneth) Ltd (in liq) v A E Limehouse & Co (a firm)** [1991] 4 500, HL.
    Service by post—
      Writ posted to old address but redirected by Post Office to new address—Whether writ 'sent' to partnership's 'principal place of business'—Whether writ validly served on partnership—RSC Ord 10, r 1(2), Ord 81, r 3(1). **Austin Rover Group Ltd v Crouch Butler Savage Associates (a firm)** [1986] 3 50, CA.
    Service of writ on partner—
      Service by insertion of writ through letter box at 'usual or last known address' of partner—Whether service may be effected by insertion of writ through letter box at firm's address—Whether good service only constituted by insertion through letter box at partner's place of residence—RSC Ord 10, r 1(2)(b), Ord 81, r 3(1)(a). **Robertson v Banham & Co (a firm)** [1997] 1 79, CA.
      Service through letter box—Whether service may be effected by insertion of writ addressed to partner through letter box at firm's address—Whether good service only constituted by insertion through letter box at place where partner lives or is last known to have lived—RSC Ord 10, r 1(2)(a)(b), Ord 81, r 3(1), (a). **Marsden v Kingswell Watts (a firm)** [1992] 2 239, CA.
  Service out of the jurisdiction—
    Action for account. *See* **Account** (Action for—Service—Jurisdiction—Service of writ out of jurisdiction).
    Bankruptcy proceedings. *See* **Bankruptcy** (Service—Service out of jurisdiction—Writ and motion).
    Generally. *See* **Practice** (Service out of the jurisdiction).
  Signature—
    Indorsement. *See* Indorsement—Signature, *above.*
  Solicitor—
    Delay in issuing and serving writ. *See* **Solicitor** (Litigation—Delay in issuing and serving writ).
  Specially indorsed writ. *See* Indorsement—Signature—Specially indorsed writ, *above.*
  Subpoena ad testificandum. *See* **Practice** (Subpoena ad testificandum).
  Subpoena duces tecum. *See* **Practice** (Subpoena duces tecum).

WRIT (cont)—
   Substituted service. *See* **Practice** (Service—Substituted service).
   Time for service of writ. *See* **Practice** (Service—Time for service of writ).
   Title. *See* **Practice** (Parties—Description of parties).
   Validity—
      Extension of validity. *See* Extension of validity—Action statute-barred, *above*.

WRITING
   Absence of writing—
      Defence—
         Misrepresentation as to person's credit. *See* **Misrepresentation** (Misrepresentation as to person's
            credit—Defence of absence of writing).
   Constructive trust—
      Whether necessary. *See* **Trust and trustee** (Constructive trust—Oral arrangements).
   Contract of employment—
      Written particulars of terms of employment. *See* **Employment** (Contract of service—Written particulars
         of employment).
   Equitable interest—
      Disposition. *See* **Equity** (Disposition of equitable interest on trust—Writing).
   Guarantee—
      Note or memorandum in writing. *See* **Guarantee** (Note or memorandum of agreement in writing).
   Printed form—
      Inconsistency with writing. *See* **Printed form** (Modification—Writing).
   Sale of goods—
      Memorandum in writing. *See* **Sale of goods** (Note or memorandum in writing).
   Sale of land—
      Memorandum of contract. *See* **Sale of land** (Memorandum of contract).
   Threatening, abusive or insulting writing. *See* **Criminal law** (Threatening, abusive or insulting writing).
   Trust—
      Creation of trust—
         Transfer of house—Absence of writing. *See* **Trust and trustee** (Constructive trust—Oral
            arrangements—Voluntary transfer of legal estate).

WRITTEN CONTRACT
   Incorporation of oral terms. *See* **Contract** (Incorporation of terms—Express oral terms—Incorporation in
      written contract).

WRITTEN STATEMENT
   Evidence in criminal proceedings. *See* **Criminal evidence** (Written statement).

WRONGFUL DISMISSAL
   Academic staff—
      University. *See* **University** (Academic staff—Dismissal—Action for wrongful dismissal).
   Cause of action—
      Merger. *See* **Employment tribunal** (Decision of tribunal—Merger—Wrongful dismissal).
   Damage—
      Pleading. *See* **Pleading** (Damage—Wrongful dismissal).
   Damages—
      Contract. *See* **Contract** (Damages for breach—Wrongful dismissal).
   Generally. *See* **Employment** (Wrongful dismissal).
   Managing director—
      Breach of contract. *See* **Company** (Director—Managing director—Wrongful dismissal—Measure of
         damages).
   Master and servant. *See* **Employment** (Wrongful dismissal).
   Pleading—
      Damage. *See* **Pleading** (Damage—Wrongful dismissal).
      Particulars. *See* **Pleading** (Particulars—Wrongful dismissal).

WRONGFUL INTERFERENCE WITH GOODS
   Conversion. *See* **Conversion**.
   Generally. *See* **Tort** (Wrongful interference with goods).
   Trespass to goods. *See* **Trespass to goods**.
   Trover. *See* **Trover**.

Y

YACHT
Sale of—
Contract—
Construction. *See* **Contract** (Construction—Sale of yacht).

YARD
Vagrancy—
Enclosed yard. *See* **Criminal law** (Vagrancy—Found in enclosed premises for an unlawful purpose—Enclosed yard).

YEARLY HIRING
See **Employment** (Contract of service—Presumption of yearly hiring).

YORK PROBATE SUB-REGISTRY
Copies of wills and grants—
Practice. *See* **Probate** (Practice—Copies of wills and grants).

YOUNG OFFENDER
Detention. *See* **Children and young persons** (Detention).
Driving while disqualified—
Imprisonment. *See* **Road traffic** (Driving while disqualified for holding licence—Imprisonment—Young offender).
Generally. *See* **Criminal law** (Young offender).
Sentence—
Generally. *See* **Sentence** (Young offender).

YOUNG PERSON
Binding over—
Refusal to enter into recognisance. *See* **Magistrates** (Binding over—Refusal to enter into recognisance—Young person under 17).
Care proceedings in juvenile court. *See* **Children and young persons** (Care proceedings in juvenile court).
Compensation order—
Parent or guardian's liability. *See* **Sentence** (Compensation—Parent or guardian's liability).
Contempt of court—
Committal—
Period of committal. *See* **Contempt of court** (Committal—Period of committal—Contemnor under 21).
Court proceedings in respect of—
Generally. *See* **Children and young persons.**
Youth court—
Magistrates' jurisdiction. *See* **Magistrates** (Jurisdiction—Youth court).
Criminal offence—
Sentence. *See* **Sentence** (Youthful offender).
Factory—
Cleaning machinery. *See* **Factory** (Cleaning machinery—Women and young persons).
Sentence. *See* **Sentence** (Young person).
Trial—
Crown Court procedure. *See* **Criminal law** (Trial of children and young persons).
Ward of court. *See* **Ward of court.**

YOUTH COURT
Fair trial, right to—
Criminal proceedings—
Stay of proceedings. *See* **Criminal law** (Trial—Stay of proceedings—Abuse of process—Right to a fair trial—Youth court).
Magistrates' jurisdiction. *See* **Magistrates** (Jurisdiction—Youth court).

YOUTHFUL OFFENDER
Detention. *See* **Children and young persons** (Detention).
Imprisonment. *See* **Sentence** (Youthful offender—Imprisonment).
Sentence—
Detention—
Generally. *See* **Children and young persons** (Detention).

Z

ZEBRA CROSSING
See **Road traffic** (Pedestrian crossing—Zebra crossing).

ZERO-RATING
Value added tax. See **Value added tax** (Zero-rating).

ZIMBABWE
Probate—
Resealing of grants made in Zimbabwe. See **Probate** (Grant—Resealing—Grants made in Southern Rhodesia).

ZOOLOGICAL GARDENS
Charitable purpose—
Education. See **Charity** (Education—Zoo—Zoological gardens).